WEST'S
TEXAS DIGEST 2d

Volume 59

TABLE OF CASES
Fi — H

Mat # 40525239

CLOSING WITH CASES REPORTED IN

227 S.W.3d 894
127 S.Ct.
491 F.3d 428
227 Fed.Appx.
492 F.Supp.2d
242 F.R.D. 109
369 B.R. 49

PREFACE

West's Texas Key Number Digest 2d covers State and Federal cases decided since 1935.

The original Texas Digest should be consulted for cases prior to 1935.

This Digest is compiled and arranged under the West Key Number plan. All topics of the American Digest System are represented and each Topic carries a complete analysis of the scope of all its Key Numbers.

New and revised topics and greatly expanded key numbers have been provided for many areas of law, including those covered by the topics ABORTION AND BIRTH CONTROL, ALIENS, IMMIGRATION, AND CITIZENSHIP, ALTERNATIVE DISPUTE RESOLUTION, ANNUITIES, ANTITRUST AND TRADE REGULATION, ASYLUMS AND ASSISTED LIVING FACILITIES, CHILD CUSTODY, CHILD SUPPORT, CIVIL RIGHTS, CONSTITUTIONAL LAW, CONTROLLED SUBSTANCES, ENVIRONMENTAL LAW, HEALTH, HOMICIDE, INDEMNITY, INDIANS, INSURANCE, KIDNAPPING, LABOR AND EMPLOYMENT, LIMITED LIABILITY COMPANIES, NEGLIGENCE, PROSTITUTION, PUBLIC AMUSEMENT AND ENTERTAINMENT, SENTENCING AND PUNISHMENT, TAXATION, TELECOMMUNICATIONS, TORTS, TRADEMARKS, and UNEMPLOYMENT COMPENSATION. Refer to the Outline of the Law to assist in locating specific areas of interest.

LIBRARY REFERENCES to Corpus Juris Secundum and other publications, as well as references to Law Reviews, are included throughout this edition, providing access to a broad field of text research.

The TABLE OF CASES lists alphabetically the title of each case, by both the Plaintiff's and Defendant's names, the volume and page of the Reports in which each is published, the subsequent case history, and the digest Topic and Key Number under which each point of law is digested. A guide to title arrangement is also included in this volume.

The WORDS AND PHRASES section lists alphabetically words or phrases that have been judicially defined in the cases indexed by the Digest, and sets out the headnotes, titles and citations of the cases in which such definitions appear.

A comprehensive DESCRIPTIVE–WORD INDEX has been specially prepared, providing immediate and convenient access to the case law within the scope of the Digest.

UPDATING WITH WESTLAW

WESTLAW provides easy and quick access to those cases reported after the latest available digest supplementation.

The WESTLAW query is entered in any appropriate case law data base of interest. The query format used substitutes a numerical equivalent for the digest topic name and adds the key number through the use of "K" as illustrated in the search for later Contracts ⚯ 155 cases published after December 31, 2006.

ad(after 12-31-06) & 95K155.

A list of topics and their numerical equivalents may be found in the DIGEST TOPICS section of this volume, in the WESTLAW Reference Manual or in the WESTLAW Directory.

THE PUBLISHER

October, 2007

ABBREVIATIONS OF COURTS

Texas Courts

Supreme Court .... Tex.

Commission of Appeals .... Com.App.

Court of Criminal Appeals .... Crim.App.

Court of Appeals .... App.

Court of Civil Appeals .... Civ.App.

Commission Court .... Com.Ct.

Special Court of Review .... Spec.Ct.Rev.

Federal Courts

United States Supreme Court .... U.S.Tex.

United States Court of Appeals .... C.A.Fed. (Tex.)

C.A.5 (Tex.)

United States Circuit Court of Appeals .... C.C.A.5 (Tex.)

United States Circuit Court .... C.C.E.D.Tex.

C.C.N.D.Tex.

C.C.S.D.Tex.

C.C.W.D.Tex.

United States District Court .... E.D.Tex.

N.D.Tex.

S.D.Tex.

W.D.Tex.

United States Bankruptcy Court .... Bkrtcy.E.D.Tex.

Bkrtcy.N.D.Tex.

Bkrtcy.S.D.Tex.

Bkrtcy.W.D.Tex.

Other

Law Reviews and Journals .... Law Rev.

ABBREVIATIONS
of
PUBLICATIONS CITED

Abbreviation	Publication
A.L.R.	American Law Reports
A.L.R.2d	American Law Reports, Second Series
A.L.R.3d	American Law Reports, Third Series
A.L.R.4th	American Law Reports, Fourth Series
B.R.	Bankruptcy Reporter
Black	Black's United States Supreme Court Reports
C.J.S.	Corpus Juris Secundum
Dallam Dig.	Dallam Digest of Texas Laws and Dallam's Decisions
F.	Federal Reporter
F.2d	Federal Reporter, Second Series
F.3d	Federal Reporter, Third Series
Fed.Appx.	Federal Appendix
Fed.Cas.No.	Federal Cases
F.R.D.	Federal Rules Decisions
F.Supp.	Federal Supplement
F.Supp.2d	Federal Supplement, Second Series
How.	Howard's United States Supreme Court Reports
L.Ed.	United States Supreme Court Reports, Lawyers' Edition
L.Ed.2d	United States Supreme Court Reports, Lawyers' Edition, Second Series
L.R.A.	Lawyers' Reports Annotated
L.R.A.,N.S.	Lawyers' Reports Annotated, New Series
Pet.	Peters' United States Supreme Court Reports
Posey Unrep.Cas.	Posey's Texas Unreported Cases
S.W.	South Western Reporter
S.W.2d	South Western Reporter, Second Series
S.W.3d	South Western Reporter, Third Series
S.Ct.	Supreme Court Reporter
Tex.	Texas Reports
Tex.Civ.App.	Texas Civil Appeal Reports
Tex.Cr.R.	Texas Criminal Reports
U.S.	United States Supreme Court Reports
U.S.C.A.	United States Code Annotated
Wall.	Wallace's United States Supreme Court Reports
White & W.Civ.Cas.Ct. App.	White and Wilson's Decisions in Civil Causes in the Texas Court of Appeals
Wilson, Civ.Cas.Ct.App.	Wilson's Decisions in Civil Causes in the Texas Court of Appeals

OUTLINE OF THE LAW

Digest Topics are arranged for your convenience by Seven Main Divisions of Law. Complete alphabetical list of Digest Topics with topic numbers follows this section.

———

1. **PERSONS**
2. **PROPERTY**
3. **CONTRACTS**
4. **TORTS**
5. **CRIMES**
6. **REMEDIES**
7. **GOVERNMENT**

1. PERSONS

RELATING TO NATURAL PERSONS IN GENERAL

Civil Rights
Dead Bodies
Death
Domicile
Food
Health
Holidays
Intoxicating Liquors
Names
Seals
Signatures
Sunday
Time
Weapons

PARTICULAR CLASSES OF NATURAL PERSONS

Absentees
Aliens, Immigration, and Citizenship
Chemical Dependents
Children Out-of Wedlock
Convicts
Indians
Infants
Mental Health
Slaves
Spendthrifts

PERSONAL RELATIONS

Adoption
Attorney and Client

Child Custody
Child Support
Executors and Administrators
Guardian and Ward
Husband and Wife
Labor and Employment
Marriage
Parent and Child
Principal and Agent
Workers' Compensation

ASSOCIATED AND ARTIFICIAL PERSONS

Associations
Beneficial Associations
Building and Loan Associations
Clubs
Colleges and Universities
Corporations
Exchanges
Joint-Stock Companies and Business Trusts
Limited Liability Companies
Partnership
Religious Societies

PARTICULAR OCCUPATIONS

Accountants
Agriculture
Antitrust and Trade Regulation
Auctions and Auctioneers
Aviation
Banks and Banking
Bridges
Brokers
Canals
Carriers

3. CONTRACTS

NATURE, REQUISITES, AND INCIDENTS OF AGREEMENTS IN GENERAL

Contracts
Customs and Usages
Frauds, Statute of
Interest
Usury

PARTICULAR CLASSES OF AGREEMENTS

Bailment
Bills and Notes
Bonds
Breach of Marriage Promise
Champerty and Maintenance
Compromise and Settlement
Covenants
Deposits and Escrows
Exchange of Property
Gaming
Guaranty
Implied and Constructive Contracts
Indemnity
Joint Adventures
Lotteries
Principal and Surety
Public Contracts
Rewards
Sales
Subscriptions
Vendor and Purchaser

PARTICULAR CLASSES OF IMPLIED OR CONSTRUCTIVE CONTRACTS OR QUASI CONTRACTS

Account Stated
Contribution
Implied and Constructive Contracts

PARTICULAR MODES OF DISCHARGING CONTRACTS

Novation
Payment
Release
Subrogation
Tender

4. TORTS

Assault and Battery
Collision
Conspiracy
False Imprisonment
Forcible Entry and Detainer
Fraud
Libel and Slander
Malicious Prosecution
Negligence
Nuisance
Products Liability
Seduction
Torts
Trespass
Trover and Conversion
Waste

5. CRIMES

Abortion and Birth Control
Adulteration
Adultery
Arson
Bigamy
Breach of the Peace
Bribery
Burglary
Compounding Offenses
Controlled Substances
Counterfeiting
Criminal Law
Disorderly Conduct
Disorderly House
Disturbance of Public Assemblage
Embezzlement
Escape
Extortion and Threats
False Personation
False Pretenses
Fires
Forgery
Homicide
Incest
Insurrection and Sedition
Kidnapping
Larceny
Lewdness
Malicious Mischief
Mayhem
Neutrality Laws
Obscenity
Obstructing Justice
Perjury
Prostitution
Racketeer Influenced and Corrupt
   Organizations
Rape
Receiving Stolen Goods
Rescue
Riot

5. CRIMES—Cont'd

Robbery
Sodomy
Suicide
Treason
Unlawful Assembly
Vagrancy

6. REMEDIES

REMEDIES BY ACT OR AGREEMENT OF PARTIES

Accord and Satisfaction
Alternative Dispute Resolution
Submission of Controversy

REMEDIES BY POSSESSION OR NOTICE

Liens
Lis Pendens
Maritime Liens
Mechanics' Liens
Notice
Salvage

MEANS AND METHODS OF PROOF

Acknowledgment
Affidavits
Estoppel
Evidence
Oath
Records
Witnesses

CIVIL ACTIONS IN GENERAL

Action
Declaratory Judgment
Election of Remedies
Limitation of Actions
Parties
Set-Off and Counterclaim
Venue

PARTICULAR PROCEEDINGS IN CIVIL ACTIONS

Abatement and Revival
Appearance
Costs
Damages
Execution
Exemptions
Homestead
Judgment

Jury
Motions
Pleading
Pretrial Procedure
Process
Reference
Stipulations
Trial

PARTICULAR REMEDIES INCIDENT TO CIVIL ACTIONS

Arrest
Assistance, Writ of
Attachment
Bail
Deposits in Court
Garnishment
Injunction
Judicial Sales
Ne Exeat
Receivers
Recognizances
Sequestration
Undertakings

PARTICULAR MODES OF REVIEW IN CIVIL ACTIONS

Appeal and Error
Audita Querela
Certiorari
Exceptions, Bill of
New Trial
Review

ACTIONS TO ESTABLISH OWNERSHIP OR RECOVER POSSESSION OF SPECIFIC PROPERTY

Detinue
Ejectment
Entry, Writ of
Interpleader
Possessory Warrant
Quieting Title
Real Actions
Replevin
Trespass to Try Title

FORMS OF ACTIONS FOR DEBTS OR DAMAGES

Account, Action on
Action on the Case
Assumpsit, Action of
Covenant, Action of
Debt, Action of

X

6. REMEDIES—Cont'd

ACTIONS FOR PARTICULAR FORMS OR SPECIAL RELIEF

Account
Cancellation of Instruments
Debtor and Creditor
Divorce
Partition
Reformation of Instruments
Specific Performance

CIVIL PROCEEDINGS OTHER THAN ACTIONS

Habeas Corpus
Mandamus
Prohibition
Quo Warranto
Scire Facias
Supersedeas

SPECIAL CIVIL JURISDICTIONS AND PROCEDURE THEREIN

Admiralty
Bankruptcy
Equity
Federal Civil Procedure

PROCEEDINGS PECULIAR TO CRIMINAL CASES

Double Jeopardy
Extradition and Detainers
Fines
Forfeitures
Grand Jury
Indictment and Information
Pardon and Parole
Penalties
Searches and Seizures
Sentencing and Punishment

7. GOVERNMENT

POLITICAL BODIES AND DIVISIONS

Counties
District of Columbia
Municipal Corporations
States
Territories
Towns
United States

SYSTEMS AND SOURCES OF LAW

Administrative Law and Procedure
Common Law
Constitutional Law
International Law
Parliamentary Law
Statutes
Treaties

LEGISLATIVE AND EXECUTIVE POWERS AND FUNCTIONS

Bounties
Census
Commodity Futures Trading Regulation
Customs Duties
Drains
Eminent Domain
Environmental Law
Highways
Inspection
Internal Revenue
Levees and Flood Control
Pensions
Postal Service
Private Roads
Public Contracts
Public Utilities
Schools
Securities Regulation
Social Security and Public Welfare
Taxation
Unemployment Compensation
Weights and Measures
Zoning and Planning

JUDICIAL POWERS AND FUNCTIONS, AND COURTS AND THEIR OFFICERS

Amicus Curiae
Clerks of Courts
Contempt
Court Commissioners
Courts
Federal Courts
Judges
Justices of the Peace
Removal of Cases
Reports
United States Magistrates

CIVIL SERVICE, OFFICERS, AND INSTITUTIONS

Ambassadors and Consuls
Asylums and Assisted Living Facilities

DIGEST TOPICS AND ABBREVIATIONS

*See, also, Outline of the Law by Seven Main Divisions of Law
preceding this section.*

*The topic numbers shown below may be used in WESTLAW searches for cases
within the topic and within specified key numbers.*

DIGEST TOPICS AND ABBREVIATIONS

DIGEST TOPICS AND ABBREVIATIONS

DIGEST TOPICS AND ABBREVIATIONS

DIGEST TOPICS AND ABBREVIATIONS

GUIDELINES FOR ARRANGEMENT

The Digest Table of Cases lists alphabetically the title of each case, by both the Plaintiff's and Defendant's names. Both entries contain pertinent information such as court, cite, case history and the most current classifications for each case.

Listed below are Guidelines for arrangement that will further assist in using this product.

The following lists and all other verbiage contained in Table of Cases titles are arranged as though no spacing or punctuation exists within or between words. The lists below display the spacing only for visual aid in reference.

Mc/Mac

Are arranged as Mac.

STATE NAMES

Abbreviations of State Names are arranged as if spelled out.

NUMBERS

Numerical characters will always follow letter characters. Numbers will be arranged character by character, without consideration of the whole number:

Z
Zebco Fishing Gear...

0
0.10 Acres of Land

1
1 Hour Martinizing
111 Concord Ave...
$1,117 in U.S. Currency...
1997 Ford Ranger, VIN...

2
21st Century...
2101 Wisconsin Associates...

3
3M Corp....
3011 Corp...
318 North Market Street

GUIDELINES FOR ARRANGEMENT

When used in a title the following abbreviations are sorted as if spelled out:

ACRONYMS

AFSCME	American Federation of State County and Municipal Employees
C.I.A.	Central Intelligence Agency
C.A.B.	Civil Aeronautics Board
C.I.R.	Commissioner of Internal Revenue
C.I.R.S.	Commissioner of Internal Revenue Service
DHHR	Department of Health and Human Resources
DHHS	Department of Health and Human Services
DHSS	Department of Health and Social Services
DILHR	Department of Industry, Labor and Human Relations
DNR	Department of Natural Resources
E.P.A.	Environmental Protection Agency
E.E.O.C.	Equal Employment Opportunity Commission
F.A.A.	Federal Aviation Administration
F.B.I.	Federal Bureau of Investigation
F.C.C.	Federal Communications Commission
F.D.I.C.	Federal Deposit Insurance Corporation
F.E.R.C.	Federal Energy Regulatory Commission
F.T.C.	Federal Trade Commission
H.H.S.	Health and Human Services
H&SS	Health and Social Services
HEW	Health Education and Welfare
HUD	Housing and Urban Development
I.N.S.	Immigration and Naturalization Service
ILHR	Industry Labor and Human Relations
I.R.S.	Internal Revenue Service
I.B.M.	International Business Machines
I.C.C.	Interstate Commerce Commission
LIRC	Labor and Industry Review Commission
N.A.S.A.	National Aeronautics and Space Administration
N.A.A.C.P.	National Association for Advancement of Colored People
N.L.R.B.	National Labor Relations Board
OSHRC	Occupational Safety and Health Review Commission
OSP	Oregon State Penitentiary
Sec. H.H.S.	Secretary of Health and Human Services
Sec. of H.H.S.	Secretary of Health and Human Services
S.E.C.	Securities and Exchange Commission
SAIF	State Accident Insurance Fund
U.S.C.I.R.	United States Commissioner of Internal Revenue
U.S.E.P.A.	United States Environmental Protection Agency
U.S.E.E.O.C.	United States Equal Employment Opportunity Commission
U.S.F.A.A.	United States Federal Aviation Administration
U.S.I.N.S.	United States Immigration and Naturalization Service
U.S. Mag.	United States Magistrate
U.S.A.	United States of America
U.S.S.E.C.	United States Securities and Exchange Commission
WERC	Wisconsin Energy Regulatory Commission
W.C.A.B.	Workmen's Compensation Appeal Board

ARRANGEMENT OF OTHER ABBREVIATED WORDS

Acc.	Accident	Co. Atty.	County Attorney	Mr.	Mister
Adjt.	Adjutant			Mortg.	Mortgage
Admin	Administration	Dept.	Department	Mt.	Mount
Adm'n	Administration	Dist.	District	Mun.	Municipal
Adm'r	Administrator	Div.	Division	Mut.	Mutual
Adm'x	Administratrix	Dr.	Doctor	M.V.	MV
Agr.	Agricultural	Drs.	Doctors	Nat.	National
&	and	Ed.	Education	Nat'l	National
Asst.	Assistant	Educ.	Education	Nav.	Navigation
Ass'n	Association	Elec.	Electric	#	Number
Assur.	Assurance	Ex'r	Executor	No.	Number
Atty.	Attorney	Exp.	Express	Nos.	Numbers
Attys.	Attorneys	Ft.	Fort	Org.	Organization
Aud.	Auditor	Gen.	General	Pac.	Pacific
Auth.	Authority	Guar.	Guaranty	Pass.	Passenger
Auto.	Automobile	Hwy.	Highway	Pub.	Publishing
Ave.	Avenue	Hosp.	Hospital	R.R.	RR
Ben.	Benefit	Imp.	Improvement	Ry.	R
Benev.	Benevolent	Inc.	Incorporated	R. Co.	R Company
Bd.	Board	Indem.	Indemnity	St.	Saint
Blvd.	Boulevard	Indus.	Industrial	Ste.	Saint
Bro.	Brother	Inst.	Institution	Sav.	Savings
Broth.	Brotherhood	Ins.	Insurance	Sec.	Security
Bros.	Brothers	Intern.	International	Sr.	Senior
Bldg.	Building	Inv.	Investment	Serv.	Service
Bldgs.	Buildings	Invest.	Investment	Soc.	Society
Cas.	Casualty	Irr.	Irrigation	Sol.	Solicitor
Cent.	Central	Jr.	Junior	S.S.	SS
Comm.	Commission	Liab.	Liability	St. Ry.	Street R
Com'n	Commission	Ltd.	Limited	Sup'rs	Supervisors
Com'r	Commissioner	Mach.	Machine	Sur.	Surety
Com'rs	Commissioners	Mgr.	Manager	Tel. & Tel.	Telephone and Telegraph
Com'ns	Commissions	Mgt.	Management		
Com.	Commonwealth	Mfr.	Manufacturer	Tp.	Township
Co.	Company	Mfrs.	Manufacturers	Transp.	Transportation
Consol.	Consolidated	Mfg.	Manufacturing	Unemp.	Unemployment
Const.	Construction	Metro.	Metropolitan	U.S.	United States
Co-op.	Cooperative	Mill.	Milling	Val.	Valley
Corp.	Corporation	Min.	Mining	Wm.	William

GUIDELINES FOR ARRANGEMENT

TITLES WITHOUT VERSUS

Titles that contain the following phrases will appear in arrangement under the party's name:

Administrator of
Admission of
Adoption of
Appeal(s) of
Appeal on Behalf of
Appealed by
Application(s) for
Application(s) of
Arbitration between
Care and Protection of
Case of
Claim(s) of
Commitment of
Compensation of
Complaint Against
Complaint Concerning
Conduct of
Conservatorship of
Contempt of
Custody and Guardianship of
Custody and Support of
Custody of Death of
Deed of
Dependency of
Dependent of
Disbarment of
Disciplinary Action of
Disciplinary Action Against
Disciplinary Matter Involving
Disciplinary Proceedings Against
Discipline of
Dissolution of
Domestic Partnership of
Estate(s) of
Ex parte
Extradition of
Grand Jury Appearance of
Grand Jury Subpoena(s) Served Upon
Grievance of
Guardianship and Conservatorship of
Guardianship and Custody of

Heirs of
Heirship of
In re
In the Interest of
In Interest of
In Matter of
Injury to
Inquiry Concerning
Interdiction of
Interest of
Investigation of
Judicial Commitment of
Last Will and Testament of
Marriage of
Matter of
Matter of Heirship of
Mental Health of
Nomination Petitions of
Paternity of
Petition by
Petition for Visitation of
Petition(s) of
Proceeding(s) by
Protest of
Recall of
Receivership of
Reinstatement of
Resignation of
Succession(s) of
Support of
Suspension of
Trust of
Trust Under Will of
Trusteeship of
Tutorship of
Visitation of
Wardship of
Welfare of
Will and Estate of
Will of

TABLE OF CASES

References are to Digest Topics and Key Numbers

F

Fiallos v. Pagan-Lewis Motors, Inc., TexApp–Corpus Christi, 147 SW3d 578, reh overr, and review den (2 pets), and reh of petition for review den (2 pets).—App & E 863; Autos 192(11); Frds St of 119(1); Judgm 181(33), 518, 522, 540, 582, 584, 619, 634, 665, 675(1), 677, 678(1), 678(2), 681, 712, 713(1), 720, 724, 725(1).

Fiatallis Const. Machinery, Inc.; Brown-McKee, Inc. v., NDTex, 587 FSupp 38.—Alt Disp Res 155, 182(2).

Fiberex, Inc.; U.S. Steel Corp. v., TexApp–Dallas, 751 SW2d 628, writ gr, aff in part, mod in part and rev in part Plas-Tex, Inc v. US Steel Corp, 772 SW2d 442.—Antitrust 286, 367; App & E 989; Prod Liab 76; Sales 267, 439, 441(1), 441(3).

Fiberglass Insulators; Missouri-Kansas-Texas R. Co. v., TexApp–Houston (1 Dist), 707 SW2d 943, ref nre.—Interest 31, 38(1); Usury 11, 12, 72.

Fiberglass Specialties, Inc.; U.S. Steel Corp. v., TexApp–Tyler, 638 SW2d 950.—Antitrust 142; App & E 846(5), 852; Corp 503(1); Venue 2, 3.

Fiber Glass Systems, Inc. v. N.L.R.B., CA5 (Tex), 807 F2d 461, on remand 1990 WL 123341.—Admin Law 507, 819; Labor & Emp 1468, 1889.

Fibergrate Corp. v. Research-Cottrell, Inc., NDTex, 481 FSupp 570.—Usury 6, 48, 137.

Fiberlok, Inc. v. LMS Enterprises, Inc., CA5 (Tex), 976 F2d 958, reh den.—Damag 40(3), 190; Sales 383, 384(1).

Fiber Systems Intern., Inc. v. Roehrs, CA5 (Tex), 470 F3d 1150.—Fed Civ Proc 2338.1, 2515; Fed Cts 611, 628, 630.1, 776, 801, 822, 825.1, 893, 896.1, 937.1; Inj 9; Libel 1, 7(1), 7(13), 7(16), 8, 9(1), 10(0.5), 21, 33, 55, 103, 104(5), 112(1), 123(3), 123(5), 125; Tel 1342, 1345, 1346.

Fibreboard Corp., In re, CA5 (Tex), 893 F2d 706.—Fed Civ Proc 181; Prod Liab 23.1.

Fibreboard Corp.; Ahearn v., EDTex, 162 FRD 505, aff In re Asbestos Litigation, 90 F3d 963, reh en banc den 101 F3d 368, reh den, cert gr, vac Flanagan v. Ahearn, 117 SCt 2503, 521 US 1114, 138 LEd2d 1008, on remand 134 F3d 668, cert gr Ortiz v Fibreboard Corp, 118 SCt 2339, 524 US 936, 141 LEd2d 711, rev 119 SCt 2295, 527 US 815, 144 LEd2d 715, cert gr, cause remanded 119 SCt 2387, 527 US 1031, 144 LEd2d 789, on remand 182 F3d 1013, cert gr, vac 117 SCt 2503, 521 US 1114, 138 LEd2d 1008, on remand 134 F3d 668, cert gr 118 SCt 2339, 524 US 936, 141 LEd2d 711, rev 119 SCt 2295, 527 US 815, 144 LEd2d 715, cert gr, cause remanded 119 SCt 2387, 527 US 1031, 144 LEd2d 789, on remand 182 F3d 1013.—Compromise 51, 56.1, 61, 70; Fed Civ Proc 161.1, 181; Fed Cts 14.1, 337, 347, 358.

Fibreboard Corp.; Barron v., CA5 (Tex), 994 F2d 253. See Watkins v. Fibreboard Corp.

Fibreboard Corp.; Belton v., CA5 (Tex), 724 F2d 500.—Evid 213(1), 219(3); Fed Civ Proc 1969, 1975; Fed Cts 823.

Fibreboard Corp.; Brannen v., CA5 (Tex), 994 F2d 253. See Watkins v. Fibreboard Corp.

Fibreboard Corp. v. Caldwell, Tex, 856 SW2d 409.—Pretrial Proc 357.

Fibreboard Corp.; Dartez v., CA5 (Tex), 765 F2d 456.—Compromise 15(1); Damag 32, 52, 62(2), 185(3); Evid 146, 314(1), 363, 372(4), 571(9), 576, 578; Fed Civ Proc 1969; Fed Cts 843, 844, 846, 896.1; Prod Liab 10, 13, 14, 62, 75.1, 81.1, 83.

Fibreboard Corp.; Graffagnino v., CA5 (Tex), 781 F2d 1111.—Assign 24(2), 31, 32, 110.

Fibreboard Corp.; Graffagnino v., CA5 (Tex), 776 F2d 1307, reh den 781 F2d 1111.—Release 34.

Fibreboard Corp.; Hargrave v., CA5 (Tex), 710 F2d 1154.—Corp 1.4(1), 1.4(5), 1.7(2); Fed Civ Proc 2559; Fed Cts 34, 82, 96, 617.

Fibreboard Corp.; Migues v., CA5 (Tex), 662 F2d 1182.—Fed Cts 716; Prod Liab 83, 88.

Fibreboard Corp.; Mooney v., EDTex, 485 FSupp 242.—Const Law 4012; Fed Civ Proc 2515; Fed Cts 381, 388.1, 420; Judgm 632, 668(1), 707, 724; Prod Liab 62, 81.1.

Fibreboard Corp.; Ortiz v., USTex, 119 SCt 2295, 527 US 815, 144 LEd2d 715.—Bankr 3032.1; Compromise 67; Const Law 3981, 4008; Ex & Ad 415; Fed Civ Proc 103.2, 103.7, 161, 161.1, 176, 177.1, 180, 181, 201; Fed Cts 30, 441, 460.1; Jury 13(3), 31.2(1).

Fibreboard Corp. v. Pool, TexApp–Texarkana, 813 SW2d 658, writ gr, and writ den, and writ withdrawn, cert den Garlock Inc v. Pool, 113 SCt 2339, 508 US 909, 124 LEd2d 250, cert den Celotex Corp v Pool, 113 SCt 3037, 509 US 923, 125 LEd2d 724, cert den 113 SCt 3037, 509 US 923, 125 LEd2d 724, cert den Owens-Illinois, Inc v Pool, 113 SCt 3064, 509 US 933, 125 LEd2d 746.—App & E 204(4), 207, 232(2), 1024.4, 1026, 1048(6), 1051.1(2), 1056.1(10); Const Law 4427; Damag 15, 43, 91(1), 91(3), 94, 185(1), 191, 215(1), 216(1), 216(7), 216(10); Death 77, 86(1), 87, 101; Evid 15, 99, 146, 309, 333(1), 351, 359(1), 372(3), 372(6); Fines 1.3; Lim of Act 95(1), 95(4.1), 95(5), 197(2), 199(1); Mand 187.4; Pretrial Proc 151, 483, 486; Prod Liab 10, 14, 23.1, 27, 62, 75.1, 77, 81.1, 83, 97; Trial 56, 109, 182, 219, 260(10), 349(2), 352.1(6), 352.10.

Fibreboard Corp.; Price v., CA5 (Tex), 994 F2d 253. See Watkins v. Fibreboard Corp.

Fibreboard Corp.; Ratcliff v., WDTex, 819 FSupp 584.—Rem of C 39, 82, 94.

Fibreboard Corp.; Thibodeaux v., CA5 (Tex), 706 F2d 728.—Judgm 878(1).

Fibreboard Corp.; Watkins v., CA5 (Tex), 994 F2d 253.—Damag 49.10, 208(6), 221(7), 222; Fed Civ Proc 2216.1, 2217; Fed Cts 907; Prod Liab 71.

Fibreboard Corp. v. Williams, TexApp–Texarkana, 813 SW2d 658. See Fibreboard Corp. v. Pool.

Fibreboard Paper Products Corp.; Borel v., CA5 (Tex), 493 F2d 1076, cert den 95 SCt 127, 419 US 869, 42 LEd2d 107.—Damag 226; Evid 261; Fed Civ Proc 2142.1, 2176.1, 2182.1, 2185, 2192.1, 2214; Fed Cts 372, 844, 845, 912; Lim of Act 95(5), 105(2); Neglig 553, 554(1); Prod Liab 7, 8, 9, 13, 14, 27, 42, 75.1, 83, 87.1, 88, 96.1; Sales 427; Torts 135; Witn 257, 272.

Fibrogen, Inc. v. Cellex-C Intern., Inc., CA5 (Tex), 122 FedAppx 121.—Fed Cts 616.

FIBSA Forwarding, Inc., In re, SDTex, 244 BR 94.—Bankr 2607, 2609.

For Later Case History Information, see KeyCite on WESTLAW

FIBSA

FIBSA Forwarding, Inc., In re, BkrtcySDTex, 230 BR 334, aff 244 BR 94.—Bankr 2022, 2607, 2609, 2650(4).

Fichtner v. Richardson, TexApp–Dallas, 708 SW2d 479, ref nre.—Antitrust 368, 397, 398; Evid 588.

Fichtner v. Richardson Coach Ltd., TexApp–Dallas, 708 SW2d 479. See Fichtner v. Richardson.

Fick v. Mills, TexCivApp–Waco, 347 SW2d 381.—App & E 1135; Estop 75; Princ & A 190(3).

Fick v. Wilson, TexCivApp–Texarkana, 349 SW2d 622, ref nre.—Mines 75, 78.1(8), 78.2.

Fickas; Bowles v., TexComApp, 167 SW2d 741, 140 Tex 312.—Plead 380; Ven & Pur 16(1).

Fickas v. Bowles, TexCivApp–Amarillo, 158 SW2d 118, rev 167 SW2d 741, 140 Tex 312.—Banks 90; Dep & Escr 13; Evid 242(1); Trial 33; Ven & Pur 16(1), 44, 351(1); Witn 331.5.

Ficker v. State, TexApp–San Antonio, 762 SW2d 334, petition for discretionary review refused.—Crim Law 1169.2(1), 1169.2(3), 1169.5(1).

Fickes; Groom v., SDTex, 966 FSupp 1466, aff 129 F3d 606.—Arrest 68(4); Civil R 1037, 1088(5), 1376(1), 1376(2), 1376(9); Consp 18; Const Law 4043, 4527(1); Crim Law 393(1); Dist & Pros Attys 10; Int Rev 4457; Mal Pros 15, 18(2); Offic 114; Searches 76, 182; U S 50.5(4), 50.20; Witn 16, 298.

Fickes v. Jefferson County, EDTex, 900 FSupp 84.—Civil R 1088(4), 1335, 1345, 1351(1), 1355; Const Law 4544, 4545(3); Fed Civ Proc 2491.5; Prisons 13(4), 17(1), 17(2), 17(4); Sent & Pun 1433.

Fickes v. Talley, SDTex, 87 FSupp 136.—Autos 235(3); Plead 246(3).

Fickey; A. and M. Consol. Independent School Dist. v., TexCivApp–Waco, 542 SW2d 735, ref nre.—Schools 99, 106.12(8), 106.25(9); Tax 2403.

Fidel; Vermillion v., TexCivApp–Amarillo, 256 SW2d 969.—Mines 80.

Fideler; U.S. v., CA5 (Tex), 457 F2d 921.—Crim Law 633(1), 641.13(8), 1132.

Fidelity & Cas. Co. v. First City Bank of Dallas, TexApp–Dallas, 675 SW2d 316, ref nre.—Banks 148(2), 174; Bills & N 279.

Fidelity & Cas. Co.; Maryland Cas. Co. v., TexCivApp–San Antonio, 147 SW2d 1097, writ dism, correct.—Lim of Act 47(3); Princ & S 117; U S 67(12), 74.2.

Fidelity & Cas. Co. of New York v. Amos, TexCivApp–Waco, 390 SW2d 414.—Work Comp 1438.

Fidelity & Casualty Co. of New York v. Branton, TexCivApp–Beaumont, 70 SW2d 780, writ dism.—Trial 352.17.

Fidelity & Cas. Co. of New York v. Burrows, TexCivApp–San Antonio, 404 SW2d 353, ref nre.—Work Comp 853, 1532, 1543, 1653, 1654, 1964.

Fidelity & Cas. Co. of New York v. Burts Bros., Inc., TexApp–Houston (1 Dist), 744 SW2d 219, writ den.—Evid 405(1), 434(13); Insurance 2332, 3111(1); Judgm 181(23), 185.1(1), 185.1(3).

Fidelity & Cas. Co. of New York; Cavazos v., TexCivApp–Corpus Christi, 590 SW2d 173.—Work Comp 1719.

Fidelity & Cas. Co. of New York v. Central Bank of Houston, TexApp–Houston (14 Dist), 672 SW2d 641, ref nre.—App & E 761, 934(2), 1175(6); Corp 180; Evid 11; Insurance 1894, 1922, 2402, 2406(2), 2412, 3571; Interest 31; Plead 34(2), 427; Trial 350.4(3).

Fidelity & Cas. Co. of New York v. Cogdill, TexCivApp–San Antonio, 164 SW2d 217, writ refused wom.—Work Comp 1363, 1566, 1753, 1949.

Fidelity & Cas. Co. of New York; Creighton v., TexCivApp–Fort Worth, 581 SW2d 815.—Insurance 2673, 2839, 2840.

Fidelity & Cas. Co. of New York; Cunningham v., TexCivApp–San Antonio, 102 SW2d 1106, writ dism.—Work Comp 1283, 1572, 1683, 1927.

Fidelity & Cas. Co. of New York; Dresser Industries, Inc. v., CA5 (Tex), 580 F2d 806.—Fed Cts 850.1, 852; Insurance 2282, 2367.

Fidelity & Cas. Co. of New York; Duncan v., CA5 (Tex), 371 F2d 646.—Fed Cts 261; Work Comp 949, 1826, 1872, 1912, 1927, 2084.

Fidelity & Cas. Co. of New York; Duncan v., SDTex, 250 FSupp 907, aff 371 F2d 646.—Mand 73(1); Work Comp 2, 949, 952, 1164, 1725, 1872, 1969.

Fidelity & Cas. Co. of New York v. Ener, TexCivApp–Beaumont, 97 SW2d 267.—Damag 221(3); Trial 350.8; Work Comp 1014, 1292, 1926, 1929, 1968(8).

Fidelity and Cas. Co. of New York; First Nat. Bank of Bowie v., CA5 (Tex), 634 F2d 1000.—Insurance 2402, 2408, 3164, 3198(1).

Fidelity & Cas. Co. of New York v. Gaedcke Equipment Co., TexApp–Houston (1 Dist), 716 SW2d 542, ref nre.—Work Comp 1072.

Fidelity & Cas. Co. of New York v. Gatlin, TexCivApp–Dallas, 470 SW2d 924.—Insurance 2795, 2800, 2802.

Fidelity & Cas. Co. of New York; Gordon Yates Bldg. Supplies, Inc. v., TexCivApp–Fort Worth, 543 SW2d 709, ref nre.—Const Law 2600; Insurance 2278(21); Judgm 181(11), 181(23), 185(2), 185(6), 189.

Fidelity & Cas. Co. of N.Y.; Griffin v., CA5 (Tex), 273 F2d 45.—Insurance 3207, 3212.

Fidelity & Cas. Co. of New York v. Hailes, TexApp–El Paso, 969 SW2d 123, review den.—App & E 842(2); Work Comp 2142.15.

Fidelity & Cas. Co. of New York; Hicksbaugh Lumber Co. v., TexCivApp–Galveston, 177 SW2d 802.—Autos 19; Insurance 2677, 3066.

Fidelity & Cas. Co. of New York v. Horton & Horton Custom Works, Inc., TexCivApp–Fort Worth, 462 SW2d 613, ref nre.—Contracts 297; Insurance 2941.

Fidelity & Cas. Co. of N.Y.; Hubbard v., TexCivApp–Dallas, 285 SW2d 890, ref nre.—Judgm 139, 143(2), 143(3), 145(2), 153(1).

Fidelity & Cas. Co. of New York v. Indiana Lumbermen's Mut. Ins. Co., CA5 (Tex), 382 F2d 839.—Insurance 1633, 1634(1), 1659, 1702, 1885, 1944, 1952, 1963; Ref of Inst 1.

Fidelity & Cas. Co. of New York v. Jefferies, TexCivApp–Tyler, 545 SW2d 881, ref nre.—App & E 931(3); Estop 52.10(2), 52.15; Insurance 2132, 2187, 3070; Interest 31; Trial 350.2, 355(3), 365.1(4).

Fidelity & Cas. Co. of New York; J.E.M. v., TexApp–Houston (1 Dist), 928 SW2d 668.—App & E 837(1), 966(1); Decl Judgm 61, 165, 301; Insurance 2268, 2356, 2914, 3081, 3111(2), 3120; Judgm 185(1), 186.

Fidelity & Cas. Co. of New York v. Johnson, Tex, 419 SW2d 352.—App & E 569(3); Trial 125(1).

Fidelity & Cas. Co. of New York v. Johnson, TexCivApp–Texarkana, 413 SW2d 401, writ gr, rev 419 SW2d 352.—App & E 569(2), 569(3), 655(2), 655(3).

Fidelity & Cas. Co. of New York; Kemp v., Tex, 512 SW2d 688.—Insurance 2772, 2786.

Fidelity & Cas. Co. of New York; Kemp v., TexCivApp–Eastland, 504 SW2d 633, ref nre.—Insurance 2786, 2787.

Fidelity & Cas. Co. of New York v. Lakeside Veterinary Clinic, TexApp–Dallas, 791 SW2d 635. See Fidelity & Cas. Co. of New York v. Underwood.

Fidelity & Cas. Co. of N.Y. v. Landry, TexCivApp–Beaumont, 345 SW2d 778, writ dism woj, and order set aside, and ref nre.—Work Comp 1257, 1382, 1683, 1964.

Fidelity & Cas. Co. of N.Y. v. Lott, CA5 (Tex), 273 F2d 500.—Contracts 152; Insurance 1832(1), 2678.

Fidelity & Cas. Co. of New York; M. v., TexApp–Houston (1 Dist), 928 SW2d 668. See J.E.M. v. Fidelity & Cas. Co. of New York.

Fidelity & Cas. Co. of New York; McAdams v., TexCivApp–Houston, 406 SW2d 518, ref nre.—Work Comp 876, 1538, 2026.

Fidelity & Cas. Co. of New York v. McCollum, TexApp–Dallas, 656 SW2d 527, ref nre, appeal after remand McCollum v. Baylor University Medical Center, 697 SW2d 22.—Work Comp 1950.

Fidelity & Cas. Co. of New York v. McLaughlin, Tex, 135 SW2d 955, 134 Tex 613.—Trial 358; Work Comp 11, 80, 1424, 1930, 1968(8), 1969.

Fidelity & Cas. Co. of New York v. McLaughlin, TexCivApp–Galveston, 106 SW2d 815, aff 135 SW2d 955, 134 Tex 613.—App & E 1062.2; Trial 352.9; Work Comp 79, 820, 1961, 1968(8).

Fidelity & Cas. Co. of New York v. McMahon, TexCivApp–Beaumont, 487 SW2d 371, ref nre.—Insurance 2807.

Fidelity & Cas. Co. of New York; McVearry v., CCA5 (Tex), 87 F2d 963.—Trial 139.1(17); Work Comp 1340, 1542.

Fidelity & Cas. Co. of New York v. Manley, CCA5 (Tex), 132 F2d 127.—Trial 243, 261; Work Comp 552, 1724.

Fidelity & Cas. Co. of New York v. Maryland Cas. Co., TexCivApp–San Antonio, 151 SW2d 230.—App & E 218.2(2), 758.3(1), 1140(1); Trial 366; U S 67(4).

Fidelity and Cas. Co. of N.Y.; Merchants and Farmers State Bank of Weatherford, Tex. v., CA5 (Tex), 791 F2d 1141.—Insurance 2402, 2406(3), 2412, 2413.

Fidelity & Cas. Co. of New York v. Millican, TexCivApp–San Antonio, 115 SW2d 464, writ refused.—Courts 24, 37(3); Time 10(9).

Fidelity & Cas. Co. of New York; Mitchell v., SDTex, 43 FSupp 900, aff 134 F2d 537.—Fed Civ Proc 821, 839.1, 2236; Work Comp 877, 892, 1578.

Fidelity & Cas. Co. of N.Y. v. Moore, TexCivApp–Fort Worth, 333 SW2d 956.—App & E 1002; Judgm 253(1); Work Comp 1392, 1418, 1653, 1776, 1958.

Fidelity & Cas. Co. of New York; Moss v., TexCivApp–Fort Worth, 439 SW2d 734.—App & E 968; Jury 126, 133; Work Comp 1630, 1638, 1968(4).

Fidelity & Cas. Co. of New York v. Musick, TexCivApp–Tyler, 562 SW2d 38, ref nre.—Work Comp 664, 666.

Fidelity & Cas. Co. of New York; Mustang Beach Development Corp. v., SDTex, 348 FSupp 1270, aff 463 F2d 1136.—Insurance 1085, 1930.

Fidelity & Cas. Co. of New York v. Neas, CCA5 (Tex), 93 F2d 137.—Work Comp 515, 556, 570, 1535.

Fidelity & Cas. Co. of New York; Petty Ray Geophysical, Div. of Geosource, Inc. v., CA5 (Tex), 783 F2d 577. See Coastal Iron Works, Inc. v. Petty Ray Geophysical, Div. of Geosource, Inc.

Fidelity & Cas. Co. of New York v. Read, TexCivApp–Waco, 433 SW2d 797, ref nre.—Trial 344; Work Comp 1624.

Fidelity & Cas. Co. of New York v. Reynolds, TexCivApp–El Paso, 101 SW2d 623.—App & E 773(2), 792.

Fidelity & Cas. Co. of New York; Rhymes v., TexCivApp–Texarkana, 533 SW2d 379.—Insurance 1929(7).

Fidelity & Cas. Co. of N.Y. v. Robb, CA5 (Tex), 267 F2d 473.—Insurance 3350.

Fidelity & Cas. Co. of N.Y. v. Shores, TexCivApp–Fort Worth, 329 SW2d 911, writ refused.—Work Comp 48, 860, 862.

Fidelity & Cas. Co. of New York v. Shubert, TexApp–Tyler, 646 SW2d 270, ref nre.—Trial 350.3(8); Work Comp 548, 946, 1255, 1280, 1647, 1678, 1682, 2084, 2093, 2094, 2161.

Fidelity & Cas. Co. of New York; Shubert v., TexCivApp–Hous (1 Dist), 467 SW2d 662, ref nre.—App & E 866(3); Work Comp 51, 643, 707, 710, 718, 750, 1704.

Fidelity & Cas. Co. of N.Y.; Smith v., CA5 (Tex), 261 F2d 460.—Evid 54; Work Comp 1682.

Fidelity and Cas. Co. of New York v. Stephens, TexApp–Beaumont, 832 SW2d 68.—App & E 901; Work Comp 604, 838.

Fidelity & Cas. Co. of New York; Stone v., TexCivApp–Texarkana, 443 SW2d 783.—Judgm 199(5); Work Comp 1269, 1283, 1297, 1382.

Fidelity and Cas. Co. of New York v. Swayzer, TexCivApp–Hous (1 Dist), 583 SW2d 850, ref nre.—Insurance 2656, 2660.

Fidelity & Cas. Co. of New York; Trinity Universal Ins. Co. v., TexApp–Dallas, 837 SW2d 202, reh den.—App & E 756, 758.1, 761, 845(2), 984(5), 1078(1); Costs 194.40; Insurance 1900, 2128; Statut 174, 176, 188, 206, 214; Stip 17(1), 17(3).

Fidelity & Cas. Co. of New York v. Underwood, TexApp–Dallas, 791 SW2d 635.—Antitrust 147, 363; App & E 216(1), 761, 930(3), 931(1), 989, 1062.1; Costs 194.32; Damag 218; Evid 474(16), 543(4); Insurance 2732, 2733, 3345, 3374, 3382; Trial 349(1), 350.4(3), 352.1(1), 352.1(2), 352.15.

Fidelity & Cas. Co. of New York; U.S. for Use and Benefit of Audley Moore & Sons, Inc. v., CA5 (Tex), 438 F2d 1225.—Courts 104.

Fidelity & Cas. Co. of New York; Utica Nat. Ins. Co. of Texas v., TexApp–Dallas, 812 SW2d 656, writ den.—App & E 870(2), 1175(1); Insurance 1808, 1813, 1863, 2112, 2285(2), 2395; Judgm 185(2).

Fidelity & Cas. Co. of New York v. Van Arsdale, TexCivApp–Amarillo, 108 SW2d 550, writ dism.—App & E 1048(1); Evid 553(2), 554; Trial 237(1), 352.4(9), 352.9; Work Comp 1535.

Fidelity & Cas. Co. of New York; Van Pendley v., CA5 (Tex), 459 F2d 251.—Fed Civ Proc 2142.1; Insurance 3169, 3198(1); Witn 128, 178(1).

Fidelity & Cas. Co. of New York v. Villarreal, TexCivApp–Corpus Christi, 618 SW2d 103, ref nre.—Work Comp 1383, 1937.

Fidelity & Cas. Co. of New York; Walters v., TexCivApp–Eastland, 611 SW2d 934, ref nre.—App & E 931(1), 989; Work Comp 1005, 1262, 1548, 1981.

Fidelity & Cas. Co. of New York; Whisenant v., TexCivApp–Dallas, 354 SW2d 683, ref nre.—App & E 997(3); Judgm 199(1), 297, 340; Work Comp 726.

Fidelity & Cas. Co. of N.Y.; Willingham v., TexCivApp–Galveston, 288 SW2d 884.—Insurance 2652, 2694; Sales 202(1).

Fidelity & Cas. Co. of N. Y. v. Davis, TexCivApp–Eastland, 354 SW2d 228.—App & E 882(8); Evid 558(11).

Fidelity & Cas. Co. of N. Y. v. Griffin, SDTex, 178 FSupp 678, rev 273 F2d 45.—Insurance 3147, 3168, 3183, 3191(1), 3205, 3206, 3207, 3214.

Fidelity & Cas. Co. of N. Y. v. Mitchell, CCA5 (Tex), 134 F2d 537.—Fed Civ Proc 835.1; Work Comp 752, 877.

Fidelity & Cas. Co. of N. Y.; Rourke v., SDTex, 64 FSupp 844.—Work Comp 322, 1342.

Fidelity & Cas. Co. of N. Y. v. Stephenson, TexCivApp–Beaumont, 325 SW2d 461.—Trial 356(1); Work Comp 1930.

Fidelity & Cas. Co. of N. Y.; Weeks v., CA5 (Tex), 218 F2d 503.—Rem of C 79(1), 81, 103, 108, 111.

Fidelity & Cas. Co. of N. Y. v. Williams, CA5 (Tex), 198 F2d 128.—Fed Civ Proc 1970.1; Fed Cts 905; Work Comp 1968(3).

Fidelity and Cas. Co. of New York; Stroman v., TexApp–Austin, 792 SW2d 257, writ den.—App & E 843(2), 1177(6); Decl Judgm 390; Insurance 3350, 3543; Judgm 185(2), 203, 524.

Fidelity & Deposit Co.; McCullough v., CA5 (Tex), 2 F3d 110.—Insurance 2266, 3145, 3163, 3197.

Fidelity and Deposit Co.; U.S. v., CA5 (Tex), 10 F3d 1150, reh den, cert den 115 SCt 58, 513 US 809, 130 LEd2d 17.—Contracts 143(2), 176(2); Fed Civ Proc 2514; Fed Cts 776; Int Rev 4417, 4433.

Fidelity and Deposit Co.; Warfield v., CA5 (Tex), 904 F2d 322.—Fed Cts 18, 660.10, 666, 668, 742; Insurance 3365, 3417.

Fidelity & Deposit Co. of Md. v. Big Three Welding Equipment Co., Tex, 249 SW2d 183, 151 Tex 278.—Mun Corp 348, 374(2); Pub Contr 66.

Fidelity & Deposit Co. of Md. v. Big Three Welding Equipment Co., TexCivApp–Galveston, 244 SW2d 543, rev 249 SW2d 183, 151 Tex 278.—Judgm 18(1); Mun Corp 347(1), 348, 374(2); Pub Contr 45, 58.

Fidelity & Deposit Co. of Md. v. Browder, CA5 (Tex), 291 F2d 34.—Bankr 3282.1, 3315(2), 3317(7), 3318.1, 3353(3.1).

Fidelity and Deposit Co. of Maryland v. Caldwell Livestock Com'n Co., Inc., TexApp–Houston (14 Dist), 698 SW2d 375, ref nre.—Princ & S 66(1), 129(2), 139.

Fidelity & Deposit Co. of Maryland; Carroll v., TexCivApp–Eastland, 107 SW2d 771, writ refused.—App & E 1010.1(8.1); Des & Dist 75, 153, 157.

Fidelity & Deposit Co. of Maryland v. Citizens Nat. Bank, TexCivApp–Amarillo, 120 SW2d 113, writ dism.—Judgm 18(1), 526; Subrog 41(6).

Fidelity & Deposit Co. of Maryland v. Citizens Nat. Bank of Waco, CCA5 (Tex), 101 F2d 974.—Dep & Escr 5, 33, 34; Subrog 7(3); Tax 2761, 2814.

Fidelity & Deposit Co. of Maryland v. Citizens Nat. Bank of Waco, CCA5 (Tex), 100 F2d 807, reh den 101 F2d 974, cert den 59 SCt 827, 307 US 626, 83 LEd 1509.—Dep & Escr 34, 35; Subrog 7(3), 41(6).

Fidelity & Deposit Co. of Maryland; Citizens Nat. Bank of Waco, Tex. v., CCA5 (Tex), 117 F2d 852, cert den 61 SCt 947, 313 US 570, 85 LEd 1528.—Counties 194; Dep & Escr 35; Fed Cts 917; Subrog 7(3), 32, 38.

Fidelity & Deposit Co. of Md.; City of Orange v., CA5 (Tex), 180 F2d 369.—Contracts 167, 308; Fed Cts 611, 865; Mun Corp 374(1).

Fidelity & Deposit Co. of Maryland v. Commercial Cas. Consultants, Inc., CA5 (Tex), 976 F2d 272.—Corp 1.4(1), 1.4(2), 1.4(3), 1.7(2), 269(3), 277; Insurance 1644; Torts 113(2).

Fidelity and Deposit Co. of Maryland v. Concerned Taxpayers of Lee County, Inc., TexApp–Austin, 829 SW2d 923.—Insurance 2348, 2408, 3585.

Fidelity & Deposit Co. of Maryland v. Conner, CA5 (Tex), 973 F2d 1236, reh den 980 F2d 1442.—Contracts 108(1); Insurance 2097, 2380(2), 2380(3), 3436.

Fidelity & Deposit Co. of Maryland; Dickson Const., Inc. v., TexApp–Texarkana, 5 SW3d 353, review den.—Fraud 3, 20, 25; Judgm 181(11), 181(33), 186.

Fidelity and Deposit Co. of Maryland; Dickson Const., Inc. v., TexApp–Texarkana, 960 SW2d 845, reh overr, appeal after remand 5 SW3d 353, review den.—App & E 856(1); Judgm 185.3(5), 186; Libel 133, 139; Lim of Act 55(1), 55(6), 95(6), 187.

Fidelity & Deposit Co. of Maryland v. Farmers & Merchants Nat. Bank of Nocona, TexCivApp–Fort Worth, 121 SW2d 503, writ dism.—App & E 882(3); Dep & Escr 33; Judgm 678(1); Lim of Act 28(1); Subrog 7(3), 28.

Fidelity & Deposit Co. of Md. v. Felker, Tex, 469 SW2d 389.—Princ & S 66(1).

Fidelity & Deposit Co. of Maryland v. Fidelity Finance Co., TexCivApp–Dallas, 111 SW2d 809, writ dism.—Insurance 2407, 2412, 3198(1); Plead 290(3).

Fidelity & Deposit Co. of Maryland v. First Nat. Bank, TexCivApp–Waco, 113 SW2d 622, writ dism.—App & E 989; Courts 104; Domicile 2, 5; Evid 471(2), 472(1); Trial 140(2).

Fidelity & Deposit Co. of Md. v. First Nat. Bank, TexCivApp–Waco, 88 SW2d 605, writ refused.—Attach 201; Sheriffs 161, 169, 170.

Fidelity & Deposit Co. of Maryland; Holland v., TexApp–Corpus Christi, 623 SW2d 469.—App & E 181, 226(2); Indem 42; Lim of Act 56(3).

Fidelity & Deposit Co. of Md. v. Industrial Handling Engineers, Inc., TexCivApp–Hous (14 Dist), 474 SW2d 584.—Princ & S 59, 86.

Fidelity & Deposit Co. of Maryland; Kaphan v., TexCivApp–Hous (1 Dist), 564 SW2d 459, ref nre.—App & E 499(1); Guard & W 159; Judgm 489, 497(1), 509, 518; Princ & S 190(7).

Fidelity & Deposit Co. of Md. v. Koehler, CA5 (Tex), 424 F2d 1296.—Elect of Rem 1, 7(1).

Fidelity & Deposit Co. of Md.; Morris v., TexCivApp–Waco, 217 SW2d 678, 10 ALR2d 432, writ refused.—App & E 1073(1); Bankr 3414; Judgm 943, 946.

Fidelity & Deposit Co. of Md.; Oscar Abbott Contractors, Inc. v., TexCivApp–San Antonio, 416 SW2d 516, ref nre.—App & E 934(1), 1024.4; Judgm 199(3.14); Trial 350.4(1).

Fidelity & Deposit Co. of Md.; Piper, Stiles & Ladd v., TexCivApp–Hous (1 Dist), 435 SW2d 934, ref nre.—Contracts 143(1), 143(2), 143(3), 143.5, 152; Costs 42(6); Cust & U 15(2); Evid 384, 445(1); Insurance 1645(1); Interest 39(1).

Fidelity & Deposit Co. of Md.; Piper, Stiles & Ladd v., TexCivApp–Houston, 408 SW2d 800, writ dism.—Venue 7.5(3).

Fidelity & Deposit Co. of Maryland v. Quaid, TexCivApp–El Paso, 94 SW2d 1209, writ dism.—Assign 58.

Fidelity & Deposit Co. of Maryland v. Quaid, TexCivApp–El Paso, 88 SW2d 595.—App & E 58.

Fidelity & Deposit Co. of Maryland; Quatre C. Corp. v., SDTex, 197 BR 965. See Quatre C Corp., In re.

Fidelity & Deposit Co. of Md. v. Reed, TexCivApp–San Antonio, 150 SW2d 836.—Bankr 2133; Indem 92; Insurance 3396, 3567; Lim of Act 127(4).

Fidelity & Deposit Co. of Maryland v. Reed, TexCivApp–San Antonio, 108 SW2d 939.—Indem 92; Insurance 3433, 3441, 3457.

Fidelity & Deposit Co. of Md.; Risinger v., TexCivApp–Dallas, 437 SW2d 294.—Evid 258(1), 317(1), 596(1); Judgm 185(2), 185.1(1), 185.1(3), 185.3(12); Plead 87, 290(3).

Fidelity & Deposit Co. of Maryland; Southern States Steel Corp. v., CCA5 (Tex), 80 F2d 466.—High 113(5).

Fidelity and Deposit Co. of Maryland; State v., Tex, 223 SW3d 309.—Admin Law 229; High 2, 113(5); States 199; Statut 188, 194, 278.17, 278.30.

Fidelity and Deposit Co. of Maryland; State v., TexApp–Austin, 127 SW3d 339, review gr, vac 223 SW3d 309.—Admin Law 229; App & E 863, 893(1), 919; Courts 4; High 113(5); Plead 104(1); States 191.1, 191.4(1), 191.6(1), 191.6(2), 191.9(1), 199.

Fidelity and Deposit Co. of Maryland v. Stool, TexCivApp–Tyler, 607 SW2d 17.—Contracts 315; Damag 62(1), 62(4), 76, 78(4), 118, 123, 175.

Fidelity & Deposit Co. of Maryland; Texas Nat. Bank of Dallas v., TexCivApp–Waco, 526 SW2d 770.—Insurance 1829, 2405.

Fidelity and Deposit Co. of Maryland; U.S. v., CA5 (Tex), 813 F2d 697.—Lim of Act 13; U S 67(12).

Fidelity & Deposit Co. of Maryland; U.S. ex rel. Wright v., BkrtcyWDTex, 130 BR 482. See North American Oil & Gas Co., In re.

Fidelity & Deposit Co. of Maryland; Vermillion Const. Co. v., TexCivApp–Corpus Christi, 526 SW2d 744.—Contracts 175(3), 176(2), 176(11); Trial 420.

Fidelity & Deposit Co. of Maryland v. Walker, CCA5 (Tex), 75 F2d 115.—Damag 165; Evid 413.

Fidelity & Deposit Co. of Maryland v. Wellington Trade, Inc., TexApp–Houston (14 Dist), 640 SW2d 698.—Judgm 181(19), 185(6), 185.2(4), 185.2(9); Princ & S 66(1).

Fidelity and Deposit Ins. v. Swan Roofing, L.L.C., TexApp–Dallas, 167 SW3d 633.—App & E 856(1), 1136; Neglig 1240.

Fidelity and Guar. Ins. Co. v. Drewery Const. Co., Inc., Tex, 186 SW3d 571.—App & E 5; Judgm 138(3), 143(2), 143(3), 146, 157.1, 158, 159, 162(0.5), 335(2), 335(3); Princ & S 153; Proc 6.

FIDELITY

Fidelity & Guar. Ins. Co. v. Drewery Const. Co., Inc., TexApp–Tyler, 188 SW3d 672, review gr, rev 186 SW3d 571.—App & E 865, 893(1), 931(1), 957(1), 989, 1010.1(1), 1012.1(1), 1013; Damag 193.1; Judgm 17(9), 112, 118, 143(2), 146, 162(2), 162(4); New Tr 6; Plead 252(2); Princ & S 153; Proc 6, 48.

Fidelity & Guaranty Ins. Corp.; Jones v., TexCivApp–Waco, 250 SW2d 281, writ refused.—Hus & W 272(1); Insurance 2166(3).

Fidelity & Guaranty Ins. Corp.; Southwestern Graphite Co. v., CA5 (Tex), 201 F2d 553.—Equity 57; Insurance 1790(7), 1790(9), 3051.

Fidelity & Guaranty Ins. Corp. v. Super-Cold Southwest Co., TexCivApp–Amarillo, 225 SW2d 924, ref nre.—Insurance 3093, 3149, 3158, 3188, 3191(1), 3191(5), 3453, 3454.

Fidelity & Guar. Ins. Underwriters; Saenz v., Tex, 925 SW2d 607.—App & E 830(2); Courts 102(1); Damag 102; Work Comp 998, 1042, 1087, 1116, 1148, 1410, 1502, 2088.

Fidelity & Guaranty Ins. Underwriters, Inc. v. Gardner, TexCivApp–Amarillo, 471 SW2d 449, ref nre.—Insurance 2136(1).

Fidelity & Guaranty Ins. Underwriters, Inc.; Jacaman v., Tex, 422 SW2d 154.—Insurance 3164.

Fidelity & Guaranty Ins. Underwriters, Inc.; Jacaman v., TexCivApp–San Antonio, 410 SW2d 189, writ gr, aff 422 SW2d 154.—App & E 843(2); Evid 262; Insurance 1627, 1635, 3084; Trial 178.

Fidelity & Guaranty Ins. Underwriters, Inc. v. La Rochelle, TexCivApp–Dallas, 587 SW2d 493, ref nre, and writ withdrawn, and writ dism.—Trial 352.1(9); Work Comp 1417, 1560.

Fidelity & Guar. Ins. Underwriters, Inc. v. McManus, Tex, 633 SW2d 787.—Autos 242(1); Insurance 2278(13), 2914.

Fidelity & Guaranty Ins. Underwriters, Inc.; McManus v., TexCivApp–Hous (1 Dist), 615 SW2d 877, rev 633 SW2d 787.—Insurance 2278(13), 2278(19).

Fidelity and Guaranty Ins. Underwriters, Inc.; Mendoza v., Tex, 606 SW2d 692.—Evid 201, 211, 265(10); Work Comp 2030.

Fidelity & Guaranty Ins. Underwriters, Inc. v. Mendoza, TexCivApp–Austin, 588 SW2d 612, rev 606 SW2d 692.—Evid 313; Work Comp 2005, 2006, 2030, 2039, 2040, 2041.

Fidelity & Guar. Ins. Underwriters, Inc. v. Saenz, TexApp–Corpus Christi, 865 SW2d 103, reh den, and writ gr, reh overr 878 SW2d 605, rev 925 SW2d 607.—App & E 930(3), 989, 1001(1), 1003(7), 1004(7), 1004(11), 1050.1(12), 1062.1; Corp 398(1), 519(3); Damag 48, 91(1), 94, 192, 208(6); Fraud 3, 10, 11(1), 18, 38, 58(1), 58(2), 59(1), 62; Labor & Emp 3100(1); Lim of Act 99(1); Trial 139.1(3), 140(1), 365.2; Work Comp 984, 1162, 1937.

Fidelity and Guar. Life Ins. Co. v. Pina, TexApp–Corpus Christi, 165 SW3d 416, reh overr.—Antitrust 138, 161; App & E 913, 949; Judges 32; Parties 35.17, 35.35, 35.71, 35.85.

Fidelity Bank v. Federal Deposit Ins. Corp., NDTex, 749 FSupp 147. See Old Stone Bank v. Fidelity Bank.

Fidelity Bank v. Mortgage Funding Corp. of America, NDTex, 855 FSupp 901, aff 91 F3d 138.—Decl Judgm 5.1, 45; Fed Cts 1145.

Fidelity Bank; Old Stone Bank v., NDTex, 749 FSupp 147.—Contracts 187(1); Fed Civ Proc 2492; Land & Ten 76(1), 182.

Fidelity Bank & Trust Co.; Salmon v., TexCivApp–Fort Worth, 258 SW2d 837.—App & E 395, 907(3); Chat Mtg 162, 169; Judgm 181(25), 186; Plead 228.14.

Fidelity Bank Nat. Ass'n v. Aldrich, NDTex, 998 FSupp 717.—Admin Law 763; Banks 67, 233, 235.

Fidelity Bank of Fort Worth; Brink v., TexApp–Fort Worth, 966 SW2d 684.—Bills & N 442; Equity 72(1), 84, 87(2).

Fidelity Bond & Mortgage Co. v. Fidelity Bond & Mortgage Co. of Texas, CCA5 (Tex), 37 F2d 99.—Trademarks 1425.

Fidelity Bond & Mortgage Co. v. Fidelity Bond & Mortgage Co. of Texas, SDTex, 33 F2d 580, aff 37 F2d 99.—Antitrust 16.

Fidelity Bond & Mortgage Co. of Texas; Fidelity Bond & Mortgage Co. v., CCA5 (Tex), 37 F2d 99.—Trademarks 1425.

Fidelity Bond & Mortgage Co. of Texas; Fidelity Bond & Mortgage Co. v., SDTex, 33 F2d 580, aff 37 F2d 99.—Antitrust 16.

Fidelity Cas. Co. of N.Y. v. Braley, TexCivApp–Texarkana, 343 SW2d 559.—Work Comp 1926, 1968(6).

Fidelity Development Co.; Bockel v., TexCivApp–Galveston, 101 SW2d 628.—Cem 16, 17; Perp 8(7).

Fidelity Finance Co.; Fidelity & Deposit Co. of Maryland v., TexCivApp–Dallas, 111 SW2d 809, writ dism.—Insurance 2407, 2412, 3198(1); Plead 290(3).

Fidelity Funding, Inc.; Mims v., NDTex, 307 BR 849.—Bankr 3109, 3782; Contracts 194; Usury 11, 13, 16, 42, 50, 53, 88.

Fidelity Group Ins. Co. v. Le Bow, TexCivApp–Dallas, 107 SW2d 755, writ dism.—Bankr 2951; Insurance 1137, 1363, 1364, 1368.

Fidelity Holding Co., Ltd., Matter of, CA5 (Tex), 837 F2d 696.—Bankr 2926, 2927, 2928.

Fidelity Interstate Life Ins. Co.; Huse v., TexCivApp–Eastland, 605 SW2d 351.—Insurance 2586.

Fidelity Inv. Co.; Meinecke v., TexCivApp–Fort Worth, 62 SW2d 623, writ refused.—Trial 317.

Fidelity Investments; Cook v., NDTex, 908 FSupp 438.—Civil R 1704; Damag 50.10; Fed Civ Proc 1722, 1771, 1773, 1829, 1832, 1835, 2470, 2470.4; Work Comp 2084, 2093, 2094.

Fidelity Land & Trust Co. of Texas v. City of West University Place, TexCivApp–Hous (14 Dist), 496 SW2d 116, ref nre.—App & E 173(9); Mun Corp 62, 226, 244(1), 733(2).

Fidelity Lease Limited; Delaney v., Tex, 526 SW2d 543.—Corp 1.6(4); Partners 371.

Fidelity Lease Ltd.; Delaney v., TexCivApp–El Paso, 517 SW2d 420, writ gr, aff in part, rev in part 526 SW2d 543.—Action 60; App & E 78(1), 199, 758.3(4), 761; Corp 215, 306, 379; Partners 353, 371.

Fidelity Management Co. v. Herod, TexCivApp–Corpus Christi, 600 SW2d 380.—Land & Ten 108(1).

Fidelity Mut. Life Ins. Co. v. Robert P. Kaminsky, M.D., P.A., TexApp–Texarkana, 820 SW2d 878, writ den.—App & E 870(2); Costs 194.34; Estop 52.10(1), 52.10(2); Judgm 185(2), 540, 585(4), 713(2), 720; Set-Off 60.

Fidelity Mut. Life Ins. Co. v. Robert P. Kaminsky, M.D., P.A., TexApp–Houston (14 Dist), 768 SW2d 818.—App & E 1001(3), 1003(1); Land & Ten 172(1), 172(2), 173, 190(1), 231(8).

Fidelity Nat. Bank of Dallas; Westbrook Const. Co., Inc. v., TexApp–Fort Worth, 813 SW2d 752, writ den.—Interpl 29; Judgm 183, 185(2).

Fidelity-Phenix Fire Ins. Co. v. Farm Air Service, Inc., CA5 (Tex), 255 F2d 658.—Evid 450(5); Insurance 1813, 1831, 1844, 2201, 2202.

Fidelity Sav. & Loan Ass'n v. Morrison & Miller, Inc., TexApp–Beaumont, 764 SW2d 385.—Contracts 175(3), 187(1); Impl & C C 30, 31.

Fidelity Sav. & Loan Ass'n of Port Arthur v. Baldwin, TexCivApp–Beaumont, 416 SW2d 482, ref nre.—Costs 194.25; Home 90; Mech Liens 93, 204, 254(1), 303(1).

Fidelity Southern Fire Ins. Co. v. Crow, TexCivApp–Waco, 390 SW2d 788, ref nre.—App & E 930(1), 1062.1,

1062.2; Evid 588; Insurance 2140, 2145, 2165(2), 2199, 2201; Trial 351.5(4).

Fidelity-Southern Fire Ins. Co. v. White, TexCivApp–Fort Worth, 414 SW2d 188.—Evid 450(12); Insurance 3390; Release 30.

Fidelity-Southern Fire Ins. Co. v. Whitman, TexCivApp–Hous (14 Dist), 422 SW2d 552, ref nre.—Accord 11(2); Compromise 2; Evid 409; Insurance 3388; Release 35.

Fidelity Title Co.; Kutner-Jones Development Corp. v., TexCivApp–Dallas, 567 SW2d 81.—Elect of Rem 9; Judgm 181(19).

Fidelity Trust Co. of Houston; Highland Farms Corp. v., TexComApp, 82 SW2d 627, 125 Tex 474.—Contracts 170(1); Judgm 504(1); Mand 15; New Tr 155.

Fidelity Trust Co. of Houston v. Highland Farms Corp., TexCivApp–Galveston, 109 SW2d 1014, writ dism.—Const Law 2503(1), 3998; Courts 100(1); Judgm 237(4), 335(4), 414, 460(1), 720.

Fidelity Union Cas. Co. v. Hanson, TexCivApp–Galveston, 26 SW2d 395, writ gr, aff 44 SW2d 985, cert den 53 SCt 12, 287 US 599, 77 LEd 522.—Bankr 143(11), 421(1), 433(1).

Fidelity Union Cas. Co. v. Wilkinson, Tex, 114 SW2d 530, 131 Tex 302.—Insurance 2635.

Fidelity Union Cas. Co. v. Wilkinson, TexCivApp–Dallas, 94 SW2d 763, aff 114 SW2d 530, 131 Tex 302.—Insurance 2635; Princ & A 14(3).

Fidelity Union Fire Ins. Co. v. Mullinax, Tex, 123 SW2d 288, 132 Tex 485.—Judgm 585(2).

Fidelity Union Fire Ins. Co.; Mullinax v., TexCivApp–El Paso, 114 SW2d 323, rev 123 SW2d 288, 132 Tex 485.—Action 53(1); Judgm 585(1), 585(3), 713(2), 739.

Fidelity Union Ins. Co.; Commercial Standard Ins. Co. v., TexCivApp–Fort Worth, 111 SW2d 1167, dism.—Insurance 3590, 3592, 3616.

Fidelity Union Ins. Co.; Commercial Standard Ins. Co. v., TexCivApp–Dallas, 157 SW2d 663, writ refused wom.—Insurance 1211(4).

Fidelity Union Ins. Co. v. Hutchins, Tex, 133 SW2d 105, 134 Tex 268, reh den 135 SW2d 695, 134 Tex 268.—Hus & W 276(1), 276(4), 276(7), 276(9); Trusts 179, 233.

Fidelity Union Ins. Co. v. Hutchins, TexCivApp–Eastland, 111 SW2d 292, rev 133 SW2d 105, 134 Tex 268, reh den 135 SW2d 695, 134 Tex 268.—App & E 1008.1(8.1); Hus & W 276(1), 276(7), 276(9).

Fidelity Union Life Ins. Co.; Dillard Dept. Stores, Inc. v., CA5 (Tex), 508 F2d 331.—Fed Cts 560, 596.

Fidelity Union Life Ins. Co. v. Evans, Tex, 477 SW2d 535.—Contracts 127(4); Venue 1 1/2, 3, 7.5(1).

Fidelity Union Life Ins. Co. v. Evans, TexCivApp–Dallas, 468 SW2d 869, writ gr, aff 477 SW2d 535.—Contracts 127(4); Plead 111.39(4); Venue 7.5(2), 7.5(8), 21.

Fidelity Union Life Ins. Co. v. Fine, TexCivApp–Waco, 120 SW2d 138, writ dism.—Land & Ten 166(5).

Fidelity Union Life Ins. Co. v. Gilbert, TexCivApp–El Paso, 85 SW2d 998, writ refused.—Usury 82.

Fidelity Union Life Ins. Co.; Huff v., Tex, 312 SW2d 493, 158 Tex 433.—Costs 194.25, 194.32; Insurance 1652(3); Lim of Act 127(4); Plead 228.

Fidelity Union Life Ins. Co. v. Huff, TexCivApp–Waco, 305 SW2d 209, rev 312 SW2d 493, 158 Tex 433.—Damag 71.5; Insurance 1652(3).

Fidelity Union Life Ins. Co.; Lucky v., TexCivApp–Dallas, 339 SW2d 956.—Judgm 181(2), 181(24), 185(2); Land & Ten 172(2), 190(1), 195(1).

Fidelity Union Life Ins. Co.; McCullough v., TexCivApp–Waco, 470 SW2d 209, ref nre.—Contracts 127(4); Inj 111, 157; Venue 7.5(8).

Fidelity Union Life Ins. Co.; McGinn v., TexCivApp–Texarkana, 474 SW2d 320, ref nre.—Contracts 127(4); Inj 135; Plead 111.

Fidelity Union Life Ins. Co. v. Methven, Tex, 346 SW2d 797, 162 Tex 323.—Insurance 1874, 3471, 3475(2), 3475(3), 3475(8).

Fidelity Union Life Ins. Co.; Methven v., TexCivApp–San Antonio, 335 SW2d 875.—App & E 389(3).

Fidelity Union Life Ins. Co. v. Methven, TexCivApp–Texarkana, 341 SW2d 698, writ gr, rev 346 SW2d 797, 162 Tex 323.—Insurance 3475(5).

Fidelity Union Life Ins. Co.; Nealy v., TexCivApp–Dallas, 376 SW2d 401.—Judgm 114, 199(1); Labor & Emp 904, 3090; Trial 350.3(5), 350.5(1), 350.6(2).

Fidelity Union Life Ins. Co.; Neese v., TexCivApp–Dallas, 587 SW2d 498, ref nre.—App & E 1177(6), 1177(9); Bills & N 474, 517; Courts 12(2.30).

Fidelity Union Life Ins. Co. v. Orr, TexApp–Dallas, 648 SW2d 36.—Courts 2, 12(2.30).

Fidelity Union Life Ins. Co. v. Protective Life Ins. Co., NDTex, 356 FSupp 1199, aff 477 F2d 594.—Contracts 116(1), 116(2), 117(2), 117(4), 138(1); Torts 212, 265.

Fidelity Union Life Ins. Co.; Worsham v., TexCivApp–Tyler, 483 SW2d 44, ref nre.—Rem of C 97.

Fidinam Resources, Inc.; Nova Gulf Corp. v., TexApp–Houston (14 Dist), 821 SW2d 729, writ den.—Contracts 322(2), 322(3); Lim of Act 48(1), 184.

Fiduciary Mortg. Co. v. City Nat. Bank of Irving, TexApp–Dallas, 762 SW2d 196, writ den.—App & E 635(1), 758.3(2), 758.3(4), 766, 946, 961, 1071.1(1); Costs 194.10; Damag 189; Plead 78, 427; Pretrial Proc 44.1, 225; Trial 395(7), 396(4), 398.

Fiedler, Ex parte, TexCivApp–San Antonio, 446 SW2d 698.—Child S 445, 458, 496; Contempt 24, 70, 72; Hab Corp 201, 528.1, 613, 894.1.

Fiedler v. Denton, TexCivApp–San Antonio, 367 SW2d 362.—Des & Dist 90(1), 90(3); Venue 16 1/2.

Fiedler v. State, TexApp–San Antonio, 991 SW2d 70, reh overr.—Arrest 63.4(15), 68(3); Crim Law 412.1(2), 412.2(2), 517.2(2), 538(3), 1130(0.5), 1139, 1159.6; Homic 1184, 1186.

Field, Ex parte, TexApp–Amarillo, 921 SW2d 430.—Courts 475(1); Hab Corp 679, 892.1; Motions 54.

Field v. AIM Management Group, Inc., TexApp–Houston (14 Dist), 845 SW2d 469.—App & E 232(2), 291; Damag 208(1); Plead 36(1), 36(2); Trial 105(2), 139.1(7), 168.

Field v. Charter Oak Fire Ins. Co., TexCivApp–Eastland, 537 SW2d 130.—Evid 590; Work Comp 1410, 1490.

Field; Davis v., TexCivApp–Fort Worth, 222 SW2d 697, ref nre.—Deeds 38(1), 90, 93, 95, 111; Estop 21, 45, 47; Mines 55(1), 55(4); Pub Lands 178(1); Ven & Pur 231(16).

Field; Rudes v., Tex, 204 SW2d 5, 146 Tex 133.—Contracts 164; Deeds 99; Hus & W 279(1).

Field v. Rudes, TexCivApp–El Paso, 204 SW2d 1, rev 204 SW2d 5, 146 Tex 133.—App & E 1175(1), 1178(6); Deeds 99, 124(1), 124(3); Estates 5; Guard & W 4, 44; Perp 6(1).

Field v. Shaw, TexCivApp–Amarillo, 535 SW2d 3.—Deeds 134, 144(1), 155, 166, 168; Lim of Act 95(8).

Field v. Sosby, TexCivApp–Waco, 226 SW2d 484, writ refused.—Adv Poss 1, 31; App & E 215(1), 216(2), 499(3), 722(1); Ten in C 15(10).

Field v. State, TexCrimApp, 257 SW2d 440.—Crim Law 1090.1(1).

Field v. State, TexCrimApp, 232 SW2d 717, 155 TexCrim 137.—Crim Law 662.80, 1091(2), 1091(14), 1109(3); Homic 1470, 1472, 1473.

Field; Urban v., TexCivApp–San Antonio, 137 SW2d 137.—App & E 493, 800, 1091(1); Hus & W 262.1(3), 270(5), 270(7); Parties 75(7), 97(2).

Fieldcrest Cannon, Inc.; First Floors v., CA5 (Tex), 55 F3d 181. See Floors Unlimited, Inc. v. Fieldcrest Cannon, Inc.

Fieldcrest Cannon, Inc.; Floors Unlimited, Inc. v., CA5 (Tex), 55 F3d 181.—Fed Civ Proc 2544; Fed Cts 776; Fraud 7; Frds St of 49, 84.

Fielden; Hart v., TexCivApp–Texarkana, 295 SW2d 911, ref nre.—App & E 750(4); Health 823(11).

Fielden v. State, TexCrimApp, 216 SW2d 198, 152 Tex-Crim 597.—Burg 42(3); Crim Law 957(3), 959, 1158(3).

Fielder v. Abel, TexApp–Austin, 680 SW2d 655.—Antitrust 143(2), 256, 290; Trial 392(1).

Fielder v. Bosshard, CA5 (Tex), 590 F2d 105.—Civil R 1090, 1091, 1376(7), 1420, 1440, 1464; Const Law 3910; Evid 14; Searches 23.

Fielder; Conroy Mortgage Corp. v., TexCivApp–Fort Worth, 375 SW2d 344, ref nre.—Tax 2769.

Fielder v. Haynes, TexCivApp–Fort Worth, 97 SW2d 328, writ dism.—Frds St of 63(1); Ven & Pur 257.

Fielder v. King, CA5 (Tex), 103 F3d 17. See King, Matter of.

Fielder v. Parker, TexCivApp–Eastland, 119 SW2d 1089. —Courts 27, 478, 480(1), 480(3); Evid 1; Plead 106(1), 110, 111, 111.1, 111.8, 111.9, 111.46; Venue 15.

Fielder; Rhamey v., TexApp–San Antonio, 203 SW3d 24. —Child C 534; Courts 91(1); Divorce 159.1, 161; Judgm 135, 138(1), 139, 143(2), 145(4), 146, 153(1), 162(2), 335(2).

Fielder; Rogers v., TexCivApp–Fort Worth, 392 SW2d 797, ref nre.—Mtg 346, 376, 378, 591(2).

Fielder; Setliff v., TexCivApp–Corpus Christi, 422 SW2d 527.—Wills 441, 470(1), 470(3), 564(3).

Fielder v. State, TexCrimApp, 811 SW2d 131.—Sent & Pun 1963, 1977(2).

Fielder v. State, TexCrimApp, 756 SW2d 309, appeal after remand 834 SW2d 509, petition for discretionary review refused.—Crim Law 474.4(3), 485(2), 1170(1), 1170(2); Homic 975, 986, 999, 1015, 1058, 1193.

Fielder v. State, TexCrimApp, 198 SW2d 576, 150 Tex-Crim 17.—Const Law 1066; Health 358, 989; Nuis 91(1).

Fielder v. State, TexApp–Houston (1 Dist), 787 SW2d 453, petition for discretionary review gr, aff as reformed 811 SW2d 131.—Autos 144.1(1); Crim Law 273.4(1), 1026.10(2.1); Sent & Pun 1977(2).

Fielder v. State, TexApp–Houston (1 Dist), 673 SW2d 387. —Hab Corp 537.1, 613; Mental H 43.

Fielder v. State, TexApp–Fort Worth, 834 SW2d 509, petition for discretionary review refused.—Crim Law 273.1(2), 273.1(4), 274(3.1), 275; Sent & Pun 1976(2).

Fielder v. State, TexApp–Fort Worth, 683 SW2d 565, petition for discretionary review gr, rev 756 SW2d 309, appeal after remand 834 SW2d 509, petition for discretionary review refused.—Crim Law 369.1, 369.2(1), 369.2(4), 374, 474.4(3), 478(1), 683(1), 778(5), 822(1), 893, 925(1), 925.5(1), 925.5(3), 1116, 1170(1), 1174(5); Double J 97; Homic 795, 799, 800; Witn 9, 389.

Fielder v. Swan, TexCivApp–Beaumont, 175 SW2d 279, writ refused.—Action 70; Pretrial Proc 581, 680, 699.

Fielder Road Baptist Church; GuideOne Elite Ins. Co. v., Tex, 197 SW3d 305, reh den.—Insurance 2268, 2276, 2914, 2915.

Fielder Road Baptist Church v. Guideone Elite Ins. Co., TexApp–Fort Worth, 139 SW3d 384, reh overr, and review gr, aff 197 SW3d 305, reh den.—App & E 1175(1); Insurance 1822, 2276, 2914, 2915, 2942.

Fielding v. Anderson, TexApp–Eastland, 911 SW2d 858, reh overr, and writ den.—Admin Law 124; App & E 223, 854(1); Judgm 181(11), 185.3(1); Mun Corp 85, 89, 92, 1040.

Fielding v. Hubert Burda Media, Inc., CA5 (Tex), 415 F3d 419.—Const Law 3964, 3965(8); Corp 1.5(1); Courts 12(2.1); Fed Civ Proc 1269.1; Fed Cts 76.25, 82, 86, 94, 96, 417, 776, 820, 895.

Fielding; Mountain States Mut. Cas. Co. v., CA5 (Tex), 353 F2d 195.—Fed Cts 340.1.

Fielding v. State, TexApp–Dallas, 719 SW2d 361, petition for discretionary review refused.—Crim Law 959, 1023(1), 1156(1), 1177; Judges 53; Sent & Pun 34, 1490, 2051, 2073, 2086, 2087, 2089, 2093.

Fielding; White Stores, Inc. v., TexCivApp–Corpus Christi, 533 SW2d 431.—Plead 111.16, 111.19, 111.39(4), 111.42(4), 111.42(6), 111.42(7); Prod Liab 75.1, 86; Sales 437(3); Venue 21.

Fielding Reinsurance, Inc.; Garrison v., TexApp–Dallas, 765 SW2d 536, writ den.—Insurance 1822, 2278(5).

Field Measurement Service, Inc. v. Ives, TexCivApp–Corpus Christi, 609 SW2d 615, ref nre.—Adv Poss 68, 71(2); App & E 852; Corp 187; Fraud 22(1), 23; Lim of Act 100(1), 100(11); Princ & A 48; Trusts 365(5).

Fields, In re, BkrtcyWDTex, 127 BR 150.—Bankr 2429(1), 2429(3); Statut 189, 206.

Fields, Matter of, CA5 (Tex), 926 F2d 501, cert den Fields v. Hartford Cas Ins Co, 112 SCt 371, 502 US 938, 116 LEd2d 323.—Bankr 3352, 3385, 3420(1).

Fields; Airline Motor Coaches v., TexComApp, 166 SW2d 917, 140 Tex 221.—Carr 320(30); Courts 85(2); Neglig 440(1), 1538, 1713, 1741; Trial 232(5), 277, 283, 350.5(5), 352.5(7).

Fields; Airline Motor Coaches v., TexCivApp–Amarillo, 180 SW2d 216, writ refused wom.—Autos 245(15), 245(60); Trial 107, 110, 304; Witn 266, 282.

Fields; Airline Motor Coaches v., TexCivApp–Beaumont, 159 SW2d 187, rev 166 SW2d 917, 140 Tex 221.—App & E 882(14), 1046.1; Damag 132(3), 221(5.1); Trial 132, 194(2), 232(5).

Fields; Arrington's Estate v., TexCivApp–Tyler, 578 SW2d 173, ref nre.—App & E 179(1), 215(1), 302(1), 497(1), 714(5); Damag 94; Labor & Emp 3040, 3042, 3095, 3100(1), 3102, 3105(2); New Tr 40(4), 140(1), 150(1); Trial 350.6(2).

Fields; Asberry v., TexCivApp–Eastland, 242 SW2d 241, writ refused.—Hus & W 249(5), 254, 274(4); Trial 350.3(2.1).

Fields; Atlantic Pipe Line Co. v., TexCivApp–San Antonio, 256 SW2d 940, ref nre.—Em Dom 141(1), 149(6), 185, 204, 219, 259, 262(2); Evid 142(1), 142(4), 215(1), 215(3), 215(5), 474(18); Trial 47(2).

Fields; Austin Bros. v., TexCivApp–El Paso, 84 SW2d 311.—Action 2.

Fields; Bishop v., TexCivApp–Texarkana, 335 SW2d 878. —Wills 288(3).

Fields v. Burlison Packing Co., TexCivApp–Fort Worth, 405 SW2d 105, ref nre.—Judgm 199(3.10); Labor & Emp 2840, 2870, 2881.

Fields; Campbell v., CA5 (Tex), 229 F2d 197.—Int Rev 3319, 3349.1, 3360; Mines 47, 73.1(4), 79.1(5), 101.

Fields v. City of South Houston, Tex., CA5 (Tex), 922 F2d 1183, reh den.—Arrest 63.3; Civil R 1088(4); Const Law 4545(2); Fed Civ Proc 2470.1, 2491.5, 2543, 2544, 2642, 2659; Fed Cts 557, 775, 776, 813.

Fields v. City of Texas City, TexApp–Houston (14 Dist), 864 SW2d 66, reh den, and writ den.—App & E 733, 1078(1); Evid 51; Judgm 185(2); Lim of Act 43, 95(1), 95(7), 195(3), 199(1).

Fields v. Cotten, TexCivApp–Beaumont, 383 SW2d 84.—App & E 609, 931(1), 989; Elections 83, 126(5), 126(6), 126(7), 154(6), 154(10); Evid 387(1).

Fields v. Fields, TexCivApp–Waco, 399 SW2d 958.—Divorce 36, 54.

Fields; Fields v., TexCivApp–Waco, 399 SW2d 958.—Divorce 36, 54.

Fields; First State Bank of Childress v., TexCivApp–Amarillo, 551 SW2d 476, dism.—Plead 111.18, 111.30, 111.38, 111.42(4), 111.42(10); Princ & A 136(1); Venue 22(7).

Fields v. Ford, TexCivApp–Tyler, 383 SW2d 239, writ dism.—Plead 111.42(7).

Fields; Gillespie v., TexApp–Tyler, 958 SW2d 228, reh overr, and review den.—Damag 103; Decl Judgm 361.1;

FIELDS;

Judgm 185(2); Lim of Act 95(1), 95(7); Neglig 1507.1; Pretrial Proc 508.

Fields; Gourley v., TexCivApp–Eastland, 348 SW2d 787.—Plead 111.7, 111.8, 111.34, 111.38, 111.39(4), 111.45.

Fields; Gulf Cas. Co. v., TexCivApp–El Paso, 107 SW2d 661, writ dism.—App & E 664(4); Evid 474(3), 563; Plead 304; Trial 121(3), 125(4), 133.1, 133.6(7), 350.3(8), 351.2(4); Work Comp 76.

Fields v. Hallsville Independent School Dist., CA5 (Tex), 906 F2d 1017, reh den, cert den 111 SCt 676, 498 US 1026, 112 LEd2d 668.—Civil R 1110, 1121, 1527, 1545; Schools 130.

Fields; Hartford Cas. Ins. Co. v., CA5 (Tex), 926 F2d 501. See Fields, Matter of.

Fields; Houston Ice & Brewing Co. v., TexCivApp–Amarillo, 81 SW2d 234.—App & E 737, 742(1), 742(2), 742(3), 743(1), 758.1; Plead 293.

Fields; Interfirst Bank of Fort Worth, N.A. v., TexApp–El Paso, 706 SW2d 157.—Mand 4(3).

Fields v. J.C. Penney Co., Inc., CA5 (Tex), 968 F2d 533, reh den.—Civil R 1539, 1551; Fed Civ Proc 2142.1, 2608.1; Fed Cts 764, 765.

Fields v. Johnson, CA5 (Tex), 159 F3d 914.—Crim Law 1586; Hab Corp 603.

Fields v. Keith, NDTex, 174 FSupp2d 464, opinion am, aff 273 F3d 1099.—Fed Civ Proc 2539, 2552; Labor & Emp 818, 821, 1995; Libel 1, 6(1), 25, 44(3), 45(2), 51(1), 51(4), 54, 78; Proc 83; Rem of C 111; Torts 332, 340, 341, 351; Trover 1, 5, 9(3.1), 9(4), 12, 40(1), 60.

Fields; Lott v., TexCivApp–San Antonio, 236 SW2d 878, mandamus overr.—Fraud 37; Venue 5.3(1), 5.4, 5.5.

Fields; Minchen v., Tex, 345 SW2d 282, 162 Tex 73.—Frds St of 58(1); Mines 79.1(5), 79.2.

Fields; Minchen v., TexCivApp–Houston, 330 SW2d 683, writ gr, aff in part, rev in part 345 SW2d 282, 162 Tex 73.—Mines 55(2), 70(1), 79.1(2), 79.1(5); Ten in C 3.

Fields; Mini-Tape, Inc. v., TexCivApp–Hous (14 Dist), 566 SW2d 119.—App & E 954(1); Inj 132, 135, 138.21; Pat 212(1).

Fields v. Moore, TexApp–Texarkana, 953 SW2d 523.—Judgm 185(2); Land & Ten 164(1).

Fields; Mossler Acceptance Co. v., TexCivApp–Fort Worth, 241 SW2d 255.—Usury 142(3), 142(4).

Fields v. Pace, CA5 (Tex), 128 FedAppx 384.—Civil R 1092; Fed Civ Proc 1837.1.

Fields v. Payne, TexCivApp–Austin, 342 SW2d 363.—Venue 7.5(7), 72.

Fields v. Phillips School of Business and Technology, WDTex, 870 FSupp 149, aff 59 F3d 1242.—Civil R 1243, 1245, 1252, 1523, 1530, 1541, 1553.

Fields; Philpot v., TexApp–Texarkana, 633 SW2d 546.—Contracts 1; Land & Ten 30, 118(2), 120(1).

Fields; R. E. Huntley Cotton Co. v., TexCivApp–Amarillo, 551 SW2d 472, ref nre.—Inj 16, 135, 138.31; Wareh 15(1).

Fields v. Stanolind Oil & Gas Co., CA5 (Tex), 233 F2d 625.—Mines 73.5; Trusts 262.

Fields v. Stapler, TexCivApp–Eastland, 292 SW2d 862.—Acct Action on 12; J P 174(8).

Fields v. State, TexCrimApp, 1 SW3d 687, on remand 135 SW3d 686.—Crim Law 824(12); Sent & Pun 322.

Fields v. State, TexCrimApp, 627 SW2d 714, cert den 103 SCt 91, 459 US 841, 74 LEd2d 84, reh den 103 SCt 479, 459 US 1059, 74 LEd2d 625.—Crim Law 134(1), 134(3), 137, 145, 412.2(3), 577.14, 1120(8), 1158(4), 1166(4); Double J 59, 97.

Fields v. State, TexCrimApp, 544 SW2d 153.—Crim Law 1038.1(7), 1038.3; Obst Just 16.

Fields v. State, TexCrimApp, 500 SW2d 500.—Crim Law 438(5.1), 1134(2), 1153(2); Witn 40(1), 40(2), 45(2), 79(1).

Fields v. State, TexCrimApp, 495 SW2d 926.—Crim Law 598(7), 603.3(7), 956(5).

Fields v. State, TexCrimApp, 468 SW2d 71.—Crim Law 517.2(3), 518(1), 531(3), 534(2), 535(2).

Fields v. State, TexCrimApp, 449 SW2d 260.—Crim Law 1147, 1184(2); Sent & Pun 2003.

Fields v. State, TexCrimApp, 426 SW2d 863.—Crim Law 763(1), 780(5).

Fields v. State, TexCrimApp, 402 SW2d 740, writ dism.—Crim Law 364(1), 444; Homic 1154.

Fields v. State, TexCrimApp, 395 SW2d 36.—Burg 2, 41(1); Crim Law 863(2).

Fields v. State, TexCrimApp, 353 SW2d 470.—Crim Law 995(2), 1097(5).

Fields v. State, TexCrimApp, 352 SW2d 729, 171 TexCrim 636.—Crim Law 829(4); Homic 1154.

Fields v. State, TexCrimApp, 323 SW2d 439, 168 TexCrim 76.—Controlled Subs 111, 112; Crim Law 814(17), 814(19); Searches 165.

Fields v. State, TexCrimApp, 272 SW2d 520, 160 TexCrim 545.—Assault 92(5); Crim Law 438(5.1); Judgm 751.

Fields v. State, TexCrimApp, 272 SW2d 120, 160 TexCrim 498.—Assault 96(7); Crim Law 814(20), 1134(6); Ind & Inf 191(9); Rob 23(2).

Fields v. State, TexCrimApp, 219 SW2d 80, 153 TexCrim 212.—Crim Law 1133.

Fields v. State, TexCrimApp, 218 SW2d 462, 153 TexCrim 139, reh den 219 SW2d 80, 153 TexCrim 212.—Ind & Inf 122(1).

Fields v. State, TexCrimApp, 198 SW2d 583, 150 TexCrim 20.—Crim Law 1158(1), 1167(5).

Fields v. State, TexCrimApp, 197 SW2d 576, 149 TexCrim 590.—Crim Law 1090.14.

Fields v. State, TexCrimApp, 182 SW2d 815, 147 TexCrim 540.—Crim Law 507(2); Rape 54(1); Witn 40(1), 379(2).

Fields v. State, TexCrimApp, 182 SW2d 490, 147 TexCrim 504.—Crim Law 1120(8), 1169.6.

Fields v. State, TexCrimApp, 174 SW2d 733, 146 TexCrim 313.—Int Liq 138, 236(20).

Fields v. State, TexCrimApp, 98 SW2d 209, 131 TexCrim 281.—Crim Law 511.1(9), 511.2.

Fields v. State, TexApp–San Antonio, 966 SW2d 736, petition for discretionary review gr, remanded 1 SW3d 687, on remand 135 SW3d 686.—Crim Law 789(1), 822(1), 1036.1(9), 1038.1(1), 1038.2, 1134(2), 1172.1(1), 1173.2(2), 1173.2(5); Rob 27(1); Witn 388(2.1), 388(10), 389.

Fields v. State, TexApp–Dallas, 690 SW2d 37.—Evid 333(1).

Fields v. State, TexApp–Tyler, 932 SW2d 97, petition for discretionary review refused.—Arrest 63.5(4), 63.5(5), 68(3); Controlled Subs 26, 27, 28, 80, 115; Crim Law 394.4(3), 394.6(5), 474.5, 713, 734, 777, 814(3), 1037.1(1), 1043(3), 1134(6), 1144.12, 1144.13(2.1), 1153(1), 1158(4), 1159.2(7), 1159.6, 1171.1(2.1), 1171.1(5), 1171.1(6), 1171.3, 1224(1); Searches 49, 63, 186.

Fields; Sterling Projects, Inc. v., TexCivApp–Waco, 530 SW2d 602.—Contracts 232(3), 321(1); Damag 5, 22.

Fields v. Teamsters Local Union No. 988, TexApp–Houston (1 Dist), 23 SW3d 517, reh overr, and review den.—Civil R 1109, 1112, 1740; Damag 50.10, 54; Judgm 181(21); Labor & Emp 38, 1085(4); Statut 176, 181(1), 183, 188, 190, 212.7, 214.

Fields v. Texas Cent. Educ. Agency, EDTex, 754 FSupp 530, aff 906 F2d 1017, reh den, cert den 111 SCt 676, 498 US 1026, 112 LEd2d 668.—Civil R 1200, 1546.

Fields v. Texas Emp. Ins. Ass'n, TexCivApp–Amarillo, 565 SW2d 327, ref nre.—App & E 846(5), 975, 1032(1); Interest 50; New Tr 140(3); Trial 66, 71, 304, 315; Work Comp 840, 857, 1628, 1629, 1642, 1724.

Fields; Tiller v., TexCivApp–Texarkana, 301 SW2d 185.—Frds St of 110(1); Mines 79.1(5).

Fields; U.S. v., CA5 (Tex), 483 F3d 313.—Const Law 4708; Crim Law 338(7), 369.1, 438(6), 438(7), 486(2), 637, 641.1, 641.4(1), 641.4(2), 641.4(5), 641.5(0.5), 641.5(7), 641.7(1), 641.10(1), 641.10(2), 662.1, 662.3, 675,

700(1), 706(5), 722.3, 723(1), 730(7), 730(12), 865(1.5), 1030(1), 1035(7), 1038.1(5), 1139, 1141(2), 1144.15, 1152(1), 1152(2), 1153(1), 1155, 1162, 1166.8, 1166.10(3), 1171.1(1), 1171.1(2.1), 1186.1; Jury 34(6), 34(9), 108; Sent & Pun 302, 317, 322, 331, 348, 1621, 1652, 1656, 1658, 1756, 1766, 1769, 1771, 1780(2), 1789(3), 1789(7).

Fields; U.S. v., CA5 (Tex), 456 F3d 519, cert den 127 SCt 614, 166 LEd2d 455.—Arrest 71.1(5); Controlled Subs 114; Crim Law 1031(1); Searches 40.1, 60.1, 62, 113.1.

Fields; U.S. v., CA5 (Tex), 72 F3d 1200, cert den 117 SCt 48, 519 U.S. 807, 136 LEd2d 13, cert den Richardson v. US, 117 SCt 48, 519 US 807, 136 LEd2d 13.—Consp 24(2), 44.2, 48.1(1), 51; Const Law 2817; Controlled Subs 146; Crim Law 394.4(6), 412.2(5), 622.1(1), 622.2(11), 673(4), 723(3), 1036.1(4), 1139, 1144.13(3), 1148, 1158(1), 1158(3), 1158(4), 1159.2(7), 1166(6), 1171.1(2.1), 1171.1(6), 1181.5(8); Double J 25, 164; Jury 33(5.15); Searches 23, 111, 117, 118; Sent & Pun 658, 664(4), 664(5), 686; U S 34; Weap 4, 17(4).

Fields; U.S. v., CA5 (Tex), 923 F2d 358, cert den 111 SCt 2066, 500 US 937, 114 LEd2d 470.—Crim Law 369.2(3.1), 369.15; Sent & Pun 300, 841.

Fields; U.S. v., CA5 (Tex), 906 F2d 139, cert den 111 SCt 200, 498 US 874, 112 LEd2d 162.—Crim Law 274(3.1); Sent & Pun 764, 765, 976.

Fields; U.S. v., CA5 (Tex), 138 FedAppx 622, cert den Leatch v. US, 126 SCt 245, 546 US 902, 163 LEd2d 224, cert den Banks v US, 126 SCt 506, 546 US 971, 163 LEd2d 383, cert den 126 SCt 669, 546 US 1023, 163 LEd2d 540, post-conviction relief den 2007 WL 655763.—Consp 47(12); Crim Law 444, 935(1), 1035(1); Sent & Pun 300, 683, 726(3), 765.

Fields; U.S. v., CA5 (Tex), 131 FedAppx 42.—Searches 71, 186.

Fields; U.S. v., EDTex, 182 FSupp2d 575.—Crim Law 394.4(1), 394.4(6); Searches 113.1, 118, 191.

Fields; Universal Life & Acc. Ins. Co. v., Tex, 422 SW2d 722, on remand 424 SW2d 704, writ dism.—Courts 169(4).

Fields v. Universal Life & Acc. Ins. Co., TexCivApp–Hous (1 Dist), 424 SW2d 704, writ dism.—Insurance 3125(5).

Fields v. Universal Life & Acc. Ins. Co., TexCivApp–Houston, 418 SW2d 708, cause remanded 422 SW2d 722, on remand 424 SW2d 704, writ dism.—Courts 168, 170, 472.3; Insurance 3343.

Fields v. Worsham, TexCivApp–Dallas, 476 SW2d 421, ref nre.—App & E 1024.1, 1170.10; Contracts 175(3); Damag 221(5.1), 221(7); Libel 6(1), 6(3), 12, 112(1); Trial 255(13), 344, 352.5(3), 352.12.

Fieldsmith; Supperstein v., TexCivApp–Fort Worth, 269 SW2d 542.—Fraud 62.

Fieldsmith; Texas State Bd. of Dental Examiners v., TexCivApp–Dallas, 386 SW2d 305, ref nre, cert den 86 SCt 545, 382 US 977, 15 LEd2d 468, reh den 86 SCt 1453, 384 US 947, 16 LEd2d 545.—Const Law 4286; Health 194, 203, 204, 218, 220, 223(2).

Fieldsmith; Texas State Bd. of Dental Examiners v., TexCivApp–Dallas, 242 SW2d 213, 26 ALR2d 990, ref nre.—Admin Law 328; Courts 1; Health 219, 223(1), 223(2); Sunday 30(1), 30(7).

Fields-Shepherd, Inc., v. Armitage, TexCivApp–Galveston, 159 SW2d 985.—Plead 111.15; Sales 28; Venue 7.5(7), 22(6).

Fieldton Co-op. Gin v. Wright, TexCivApp–Amarillo, 259 SW2d 603.—Parties 1; Trial 33; Venue 8.5(3), 21.

Fiengo v. General Motors Corp., TexApp–Dallas, 225 SW3d 858.—Const Law 2315; Estop 52(2), 52.15, 87; Judgm 181(6), 183; Lim of Act 13; Prod Liab 71.5.

Fierce v. State, TexCrimApp, 287 SW2d 477.—Crim Law 1090.1(1).

Fiero Production, Inc., In re, BkrtcyWDTex, 102 BR 581.—Antitrust 161; Bankr 2671; Fraud 20; Set-Off 6.

Fiero Production, Inc. v. Conoco, Inc., BkrtcyWDTex, 102 BR 581. See Fiero Production, Inc., In re.

Fierro, Ex parte, TexCrimApp, 79 SW3d 54.—Double J 88.1, 99; Jury 90.

Fierro, Ex parte, TexCrimApp, 934 SW2d 370, reh den, cert den Fierro v. Texas, 117 SCt 2517, 521 US 1122, 138 LEd2d 1019.—Const Law 4632; Crim Law 1162, 1169.1(1), 1171.8(1); Hab Corp 490(3), 491, 719.

Fierro, In re, TexCivApp–El Paso, 476 SW2d 870.—Hab Corp 721(1), 731.

Fierro v. Cockrell, CA5 (Tex), 294 F3d 674, cert den 123 SCt 1621, 538 US 947, 155 LEd2d 489.—Hab Corp 603, 842, 843; Lim of Act 104.5.

Fierro v. Johnson, CA5 (Tex), 197 F3d 147, reh den, cert den 120 SCt 2204, 530 US 1206, 147 LEd2d 237.—Hab Corp 461, 802, 841.

Fierro v. Lynaugh, CA5 (Tex), 879 F2d 1276, cert den 110 SCt 1537, 494 US 1060, 108 LEd2d 776, reh den 110 SCt 2198, 495 US 941, 109 LEd2d 525.—Const Law 268(10), 4742, 4745; Crim Law 449.1; Hab Corp 340, 453, 775(1); Homic 1166; Sent & Pun 1681, 1720, 1774.

Fierro v. State, TexCrimApp, 706 SW2d 310, denial of habeas corpus aff 879 F2d 1276, cert den 110 SCt 1537, 494 US 1060, 108 LEd2d 776, reh den 110 SCt 2198, 495 US 941, 109 LEd2d 525, denial of habeas corpus aff Ex parte Fierro, 934 SW2d 370, reh den, cert den 117 SCt 2517, 521 US 1122, 138 LEd2d 1019, denial of habeas corpus aff 197 F3d 147, reh den, cert den 120 SCt 2204, 530 US 1206, 147 LEd2d 237, dism of habeas corpus aff 294 F3d 674, cert den 123 SCt 1621, 538 US 947, 155 LEd2d 489.—Crim Law 412.1(3), 453, 519(8), 531(3), 1043(2); Homic 1165; Sent & Pun 1626, 1757, 1772.

Fierro v. State, TexCrimApp, 437 SW2d 833.—Crim Law 273.2(1), 275, 980(1).

Fierro v. State, TexCrimApp, 121 SW2d 597, 135 TexCrim 483.—Courts 66.1; Mun Corp 700.

Fierro v. State, TexApp–Austin, 969 SW2d 51.—Crim Law 393(1), 412(3), 412.2(1), 412.2(4), 493, 553, 899, 1036.1(4), 1044.2(1), 1045, 1120(4), 1137(1), 1152(2), 1153(1), 1158(3); Jury 97(1), 107.

Fierro v. State, TexApp–El Paso, 626 SW2d 597, petition for discretionary review refused.—Double J 109, 164; Rob 24.15(1).

Fierro; U.S. v., CA5 (Tex), 38 F3d 761, cert den Grajales v. US, 115 SCt 1388, 514 US 1030, 131 LEd2d 240, cert den 115 SCt 1431, 514 US 1051, 131 LEd2d 312, appeal after remand 70 F3d 1268.—Consp 28(3), 44.2, 46, 47(2), 47(3.1), 47(12); Controlled Subs 81; Crim Law 59(5), 428, 444, 721(1), 721(6), 721.5(1), 730(5), 772(5), 1036.1(6), 1042, 1043(3), 1139, 1144.13(3), 1147, 1154, 1158(1), 1158(4), 1159.2(7), 1171.1(2.1), 1171.1(3), 1171.5; Searches 180, 197; Sent & Pun 672, 673, 675, 686, 752, 865, 866.

Fierro-Reyna; U.S. v., CA5 (Tex), 466 F3d 324.—Crim Law 1139; Sent & Pun 793.

Fierros v. Texas Dept. of Health, CA5 (Tex), 274 F3d 187.—Civil R 1245, 1249(1), 1541, 1544, 1553; Fed Civ Proc 2497.1, 2543; Fed Cts 776; States 53.

Fierros v. Texas Dept. of Health, CA5 (Tex), 213 FedAppx 321, cert den 127 SCt 2976.—Civil R 1570; Fed Cts 628.

Fiesel v. Cherry, CA5 (Tex), 294 F3d 664, cert den 123 SCt 1262, 537 US 1191, 154 LEd2d 1024.—Const Law 1928, 1929, 1941, 1947, 1957; Prisons 7.

Fiess v. State Farm Lloyds, CA5 (Tex), 392 F3d 802, certified question accepted, certified question answered 202 SW3d 744, answer to certified question conformed to 472 F3d 383.—Fed Civ Proc 2501; Fed Cts 392, 915; Insurance 2103(2), 2117.

Fiess v. State Farm Lloyds, Tex, 202 SW3d 744, answer to certified question conformed to 472 F3d 383.—Admin Law 413; Courts 89; Evid 448; Insurance 1808, 1810, 1813, 1835(2), 1863, 2142(1), 2146, 2165(2).

Fiesta Cab Co.; Smith v., TexApp–Houston (1 Dist), 933 SW2d 544, appeal after remand 1996 WL 475877.—App & E 1106(0.5).

Fiesta Homes v. White, TexApp–Corpus Christi, 697 SW2d 739. See Cocke v. White.

Fiesta Mart, Inc.; Azubuike v., TexApp–Houston (14 Dist), 970 SW2d 60.—App & E 852, 854(1); Civil R 1118, 1122, 1218(2), 1218(3), 1244, 1252, 1744; Costs 260(1), 260(5); Labor & Emp 857, 2778, 2784, 2881; Neglig 202.

Fiesta Mart, Inc.; Columbia Mut. Ins. Co. v., CA5 (Tex), 987 F2d 1124, reh den 992 F2d 326.—Insurance 2396, 3371, 3556, 3557.

Fiesta Mart, Inc. v. Hall, TexApp–Houston (1 Dist), 886 SW2d 440.—App & E 497(1), 907(3); Costs 2, 177, 208; Infants 83, 115.

Fiesta Mart, Inc.; Jackson v., TexApp–Austin, 979 SW2d 68.—App & E 863, 934(1); Judgm 181(33), 185(2), 185(5); Labor & Emp 2777; Neglig 1001.

Fiesta Mart, Inc.; Jaimes v., TexApp–Houston (1 Dist), 21 SW3d 301, review den.—Judgm 186; Neglig 202, 1692; Prod Liab 8, 11, 14, 62.

Fiesta Mart, Inc.; Lonon v., TexApp–Houston (14 Dist), 999 SW2d 458.—App & E 852; Judgm 185(5); Mal Pros 0.5, 18(2), 18(4), 20, 31, 71(2).

Fiesta Mart, Inc.; Macias v., TexApp–Houston (1 Dist), 988 SW2d 316.—Judgm 181(33); Neglig 1001.

Fiesta Texas Show Park, Inc.; Howard v., TexApp–San Antonio, 980 SW2d 716, reh overr, and review den, and reh of petition for review overr.—Antitrust 353; Hus & W 209(3), 209(4), 220; Judgm 185(2); Lim of Act 31, 43, 55(4), 84(2), 87(3), 95(1), 95(1.5), 95(4.1), 199(1); Neglig 1507.1; Parent & C 7(0.5), 7.5.

Fiew v. Qualtrough, TexApp–Corpus Christi, 624 SW2d 335, ref nre.—Home 1, 15, 58; Wills 63, 634(3), 713.

Fife, Ex parte, TexApp–Fort Worth, 49 SW3d 35, petition for discretionary review refused.—Crim Law 1174(1); Double J 1, 7, 59, 95.1, 96, 97, 99.

Fife v. Dretke, CA5 (Tex), 99 FedAppx 555.—Hab Corp 816.

Fifer v. State, TexCrimApp, 451 SW2d 757.—Crim Law 444; Forg 17, 44(0.5).

Fifley; City of Dallas v., TexCivApp–Dallas, 359 SW2d 177, ref nre.—Const Law 947; Zoning 236.1, 323, 327, 336.1, 355, 358.1, 605, 610, 613, 618, 641, 644.1, 676, 677, 680.1.

Fifteen Cartons, More or Less, of Sekov Reducer; U.S. v., SDTex, 45 FSupp 52, aff Sekov Corp v. U S, 139 F2d 197.—Health 333.

Fifth Club, Inc. v. Ramirez, Tex, 196 SW3d 788.— Damag 140.7; Labor & Emp 3040, 3042, 3043, 3125, 3127, 3141, 3143, 3159; Neglig 210.

Fifth Club, Inc.; Ramirez v., TexApp–Austin, 144 SW3d 574, review gr, aff in part, rev in part 196 SW3d 788.— App & E 930(1), 999(3), 1001(1), 1003(7), 1004(8); Assault 40; Colleges 6(5); Corp 498; Damag 32, 57.1, 94.1, 94.6, 94.7, 94.10(1), 97, 102, 127.13, 127.15; Evid 571(10); Labor & Emp 3055, 3096(1), 3100(2), 3125, 3141, 3143; Mun Corp 747(3); New Tr 74; Statut 223.4.

Fifth Court of Appeals; Dallas Morning News v., Tex, 842 SW2d 655.—Courts 112; Evid 51; Mand 57(1), 168(4), 172, 173; Records 32.

Fifth Court of Appeals; Doctors Hosp. v., Tex, 750 SW2d 177. See Doctors Hosp. Facilities v. Fifth Court of Appeals.

Fifth Court of Appeals; Doctors Hosp. Facilities v., Tex, 750 SW2d 177.—App & E 297, 438, 832(1); Mand 12, 14(1), 14(3).

Fifth Court of Appeals; Ginsberg v., Tex, 686 SW2d 105. —App & E 1092; Courts 209(2); Pretrial Proc 27.1, 382; Trial 43; Witn 214.5.

Fifth Court of Appeals; Hoffman v., Tex, 756 SW2d 723. —Pretrial Proc 411.

Fifth Court of Appeals; Holloway v., Tex, 767 SW2d 680.—Mand 4(4); Prohib 3(2), 3(3), 5(1), 16.

Fifth Court of Appeals; Howell v., Tex, 689 SW2d 396.— Courts 209(2).

Fifth Court of Appeals; Mantas v., Tex, 925 SW2d 656. —App & E 13, 804; Compromise 20(2), 21; Judgm 71.1; Mand 4(1).

Fifth Court of Appeals; Mays v., Tex, 755 SW2d 78.— Courts 57(2); Mand 157, 173.

Fifth Court of Appeals; Packer v., Tex, 764 SW2d 775.— Mand 4(4), 53.

Fifth Judicial Dist. Court of Appeals at Dallas; Schultz v., Tex, 810 SW2d 738.—App & E 82(5); Mand 4(4).

Fifth Third Bank; Nicholson v., TexApp–Houston (1 Dist), 226 SW3d 581.—App & E 497(1), 907(2).

Fifty-Six Thousand Seven Hundred Dollars in U.S. Currency v. State, Tex, 730 SW2d 659.—Controlled Subs 162, 169, 184; Crim Law 552(1), 1144.13(6); Forfeit 3, 5.

Fifty-Six Thousand, Seven Hundred Dollars in U.S. Currency v. State, TexApp–El Paso, 710 SW2d 65, writ gr, rev 730 SW2d 659.—App & E 242(1), 846(5), 931(1), 989; Controlled Subs 148(3), 184, 186; Forfeit 2, 5; Searches 111, 117, 127.

Fifty-Two Members of Schoppa Family; Cornyn v., TexApp–Amarillo, 70 SW3d 895.—Action 13; App & E 17, 70(3); Inj 114(2); Parties 48; Trusts 9, 65.

Figari & Davenport, L.L.P. v. Continental Cas. Co., NDTex, 846 FSupp 513, vac pursuant to settlement by 864 FSupp 11.—Fed Civ Proc 2470.1, 2544, 2546; Fed Cts 390; Insurance 1808, 1835(2), 1863, 2271, 2278(3), 2278(7), 2391(2), 2914, 2915.

Figaro Chemical Co. v. Stokely-Van Camp, Inc., TexCivApp–Dallas, 271 SW2d 838.—Commerce 60(2); Food 5, 15, 24(1); Prod Liab 8; Sales 274, 391(7); Trial 350.4(2), 350.6(1).

Figgins v. State, TexCrimApp, 528 SW2d 261.—Sent & Pun 2011, 2021.

Figgs v. Quick Fill Corp., CA5 (Tex), 766 F2d 901.—Civil R 1573; Fed Cts 897.

Figgs v. Vrazel, CA5 (Tex), 106 FedAppx 260.—Civil R 1037, 1092, 1445.

Figueroa v. Figueroa, TexCivApp–El Paso, 580 SW2d 621.—Child C 610.

Figueroa; Figueroa v., TexCivApp–El Paso, 580 SW2d 621.—Child C 610.

Figueroa v. Healthmark Partners, L.L.C., SDTex, 125 FSupp2d 209.—Fed Cts 417; Rem of C 3, 107(7).

Figueroa v. Santos, TexCivApp–San Antonio, 606 SW2d 350, ref nre.—Autos 181(1).

Figueroa v. State, TexCrimApp, 473 SW2d 202.—Crim Law 414, 419(12), 1169.1(10).

Figueroa v. State, TexCrimApp, 375 SW2d 907.—Assault 92(4); Crim Law 639.3.

Figueroa v. State, TexCrimApp, 234 SW2d 58.—Crim Law 1090.1(1).

Figueroa v. State, TexApp–Houston (1 Dist), 740 SW2d 537, petition for discretionary review refused.—Crim Law 412.2(5), 422(1), 507(3), 660, 662.11, 1036.1(5); Homic 1050, 1165, 1478.

Figueroa; State of Tex. v., CA5 (Tex), 389 F2d 251.—Em Dom 85, 157; Fed Cts 383.

Figueroa v. Treece, TexCivApp–San Antonio, 337 SW2d 400, ref nre.—App & E 231(5), 1050.1(12); Autos 171(13), 244(11).

Figueroa v. Treece, TexCivApp–San Antonio, 331 SW2d 250.—App & E 624.

Figueroa; U.S. v., CA5 (Tex), 215 FedAppx 343.—Sent & Pun 1175.

Figueroa v. West, TexApp–El Paso, 902 SW2d 701.— Antitrust 141, 252, 363; App & E 236(1), 866(3), 927(7), 997(3), 1056.1(3); Fraud 10, 12, 58(2); Labor & Emp 40(2), 40(3), 50, 51, 57, 758, 835; Trial 143.

Figueroa-Gomez, In re Estate of, TexApp–Corpus Christi, 76 SW3d 533.—Ex & Ad 31, 495(0.5), 499, 501.

Figueroa-Hernandez; U.S. v., CA5 (Tex), 212 FedAppx 326, cert den Fermin v. US, 127 SCt 1844, 167 LEd2d 339.—Sent & Pun 793.

Figula v. Fort Worth & D. C. Ry. Co., TexCivApp–Fort Worth, 131 SW2d 998, writ refused.—App & E 1069.1; Trial 306.

Figures; Rizzo v., TexApp–Hous (1 Dist), 512 SW2d 396, ref nre.—App & E 927(7); Autos 168(2), 242(1), 245(40.1); Neglig 259; Trial 139.1(6), 139.1(15), 139.1(17), 143.

Figure World, Inc. v. Farley, TexApp–Austin, 680 SW2d 33, ref nre.—App & E 930(3), 989, 1177(7); Clubs 12; Neglig 230, 232, 1550, 1599; Tel 1448.

Fihaley v. U.S., CA5 (Tex), 208 F2d 793.—Crim Law 1618(2), 1618(10), 1618(12).

Fike v. Riddle, TexApp–Tyler, 677 SW2d 722.—Execution 262, 319; Fixt 14; Mines 74(3), 78.1(4), 78.1(8), 78.1(9), 78.1(10), 80.

Fike; U.S. v., CA5 (Tex), 82 F3d 1315, reh and sug for reh den U.S. v. Douglas, 100 F3d 955, cert den 117 SCt 241, 519 US 896, 136 LEd2d 170, cert den 117 SCt 242, 519 US 896, 136 LEd2d 170, cert den King v US, 117 SCt 242, 519 US 896, 136 LEd2d 170, cert den 117 SCt 1280, 520 US 1131, 137 LEd2d 356.—Const Law 3308(1), 3831; Crim Law 412.2(2), 414, 422(1), 423(1), 427(5), 444, 622.1(2), 1134(3), 1139, 1144.13(3), 1144.13(5), 1148, 1153(1), 1158(1), 1158(3), 1158(4), 1172.1(3); Jury 33(1.1), 33(1.15), 33(4), 33(5.15); Searches 54, 143.1, 192.1; Sent & Pun 299, 300, 686, 850, 973; Weap 17(4), 17(6).

Fikes v. Bogle, TexCivApp–Amarillo, 376 SW2d 392, writ dism.—Chat Mtg 82, 150(2); Venue 8.5(7), 22(6), 22(8).

Fikes; Harper v., TexCivApp–Austin, 336 SW2d 631, ref nre.—Bankr 2532, 2554; Judgm 185(6); Mines 59; Spec Perf 61, 87, 94.

Fikes; King Land & Cattle Corp. v., TexCivApp–Fort Worth, 414 SW2d 521, ref nre.—App & E 874(3); Courts 483, 488(1); Equity 56, 57; Judgm 518; Mtg 535(1), 536; Receivers 1, 42, 58, 59, 138.

Fikes v. Moseley, TexComApp, 151 SW2d 202, 136 Tex 386.—Mines 55(2), 55(8).

Fikes; Moseley v., TexCivApp–Fort Worth, 126 SW2d 589, aff 151 SW2d 202, 136 Tex 386.—App & E 173(9), 837(10), 1040(4); Damag 221(2.1); Deeds 193; Estop 25; Evid 142(3), 208(3), 505; Judgm 651, 707, 743(2); Mines 55(2); Plead 304; Trusts 21(2), 352, 362, 371(2), 372(2), 374.

Fikes; Newsom v., TexCivApp–Fort Worth, 153 SW2d 962, writ refused wom.—App & E 882(7); Lim of Act 103(4); Plead 291(1), 291(2), 291(4), 376; Release 22, 55, 57(1); Witn 139(1), 164(1).

Fikes v. Ports, TexCivApp–Fort Worth, 373 SW2d 806, ref nre.—Action 20, 66; Const Law 2310; Courts 87; Receivers 1, 65, 72.

Fikes v. Sharp, TexCivApp–Austin, 112 SW2d 774, writ refused.—Evid 23(1); Schools 79, 133, 138; Statut 212.1, 220.

Fikes; Smith v., TexCivApp–Fort Worth, 153 SW2d 977, writ refused wom.—Trusts 372(2).

Fikes v. Tull, TexCivApp–Amarillo, 580 SW2d 911.—Evid 87; Land & Ten 184(2).

Fikes and Associates v. Evans, TexCivApp–Fort Worth, 610 SW2d 245.—Bills & N 491, 496(1), 519; Plead 236(2).

Fikes Estate v. King Land & Cattle Corp., TexCivApp–Fort Worth, 438 SW2d 665, writ dism.—Corp 511, 557(0.5); Evid 43(3); Judgm 715(2).

File; Burnett v., TexCivApp–Waco, 552 SW2d 955, ref nre.—App & E 959(3); Damag 185(1); Plead 236(3), 245(4); Trial 219, 352.20.

Filemyr, Ex parte, TexCivApp–Austin, 509 SW2d 731.—Divorce 269(1), 269(13); Hab Corp 445.

Files v. Buie, TexComApp, 112 SW2d 714, 131 Tex 19.—App & E 322, 327(2); Ex & Ad 122(1); Guard & W 22, 145, 161.

Files v. Buie, TexCivApp–Waco, 113 SW2d 698, certified question answered 112 SW2d 714, 131 Tex 19.—App & E 322, 327(2).

Files v. Thomasson, TexCivApp–Hous (14 Dist), 578 SW2d 883.—App & E 930(3), 989; Child C 577.

File–Steele Erectors Co. Inc.; St. Paul Fire and Marine Ins. Co. v., CA5 (Tex), 161 F3d 915. See U.S. for Varco Pruden Bldgs. v. Reid & Gary Strickland Co.

Filgo; Ellis v., TexCivApp–Dallas, 185 SW2d 739.—App & E 920(5), 955; Receivers 13, 32, 35(1).

Filgo v. U.S., NDTex, 387 FSupp 1300.—Int Rev 3009, 3071, 3133.1, 3230.1, 3232, 3254.

Filho v. Pozos Intern. Drilling Services, Inc., SDTex, 662 FSupp 94.—Courts 489(1); Rem of C 25(1), 82, 102.

Filidei; Easterly v., TexCivApp–Galveston, 287 SW2d 749, ref nre.—Child C 555, 601; Divorce 177.

Filip; Cox Enterprises, Inc. v., TexCivApp–Austin, 538 SW2d 836.—Partners 37, 56.

Filip; M/T Shinoussa v., CA5 (Tex), 980 F2d 349. See Golnoy Barge Co. v. M/T SHINOUSSA.

Filipp v. Ochoa, TexCivApp–Waco, 340 SW2d 847.—Insurance 3523(4); Plead 354; Pretrial Proc 641.

Filippone; Resolution Trust Corp. v., EDTex, 745 FSupp 404.—Rem of C 79(1).

Filley v. Ohio Cas. Ins. Co., TexApp–Corpus Christi, 805 SW2d 844, writ den.—Contracts 278(1); Insurance 3155, 3168, 3170, 3212, 3458(1).

Filley Enterprises, Inc. v. Youngstown Sheet & Tube Co., Tex, 441 SW2d 509.—Assign 41, 45, 46, 71; Const Law 2489; Garn 108.

Filley Enterprises, Inc. v. Youngstown Sheet & Tube Co., TexCivApp–Texarkana, 435 SW2d 602, writ gr, rev 441 SW2d 509.—Garn 108.

Fillinger v. Fuller, TexApp–Texarkana, 746 SW2d 506.—App & E 977(5); Costs 260(5); Trial 304, 344.

Fillion v. David Silvers Co., TexApp–Houston (14 Dist), 709 SW2d 240, ref nre.—App & E 78(1), 837(1), 870(2), 1024.4; Judgm 181(14), 181(25); Mtg 302, 529(8); Paymt 10, 16(1), 21; Tender 13(1).

Fillion v. Osborne, TexCivApp–Hous (1 Dist), 585 SW2d 842.—App & E 766, 1048(6); Ex & Ad 35(15), 35(18), 120(2), 529, 537(2), 537(11), 537(13).

Fillion v. Troy, TexApp–Houston (1 Dist), 656 SW2d 912, ref nre.—Action 38(4); App & E 1050.1(3.1); Atty & C 129(2), 129(3), 129(4); Deeds 196(3), 211(4); Evid 377; Trial 350.4(1); Witn 257.

Fillip; Genzer v., TexCivApp–Austin, 134 SW2d 730, writ dism, correct.—Const Law 193, 2340; Estop 58; Judges 37; Judgm 1; Jury 19(1); Mental H 137.1, 165; Statut 63.

Fillmon; City of Abilene v., TexCivApp–Eastland, 342 SW2d 227, ref nre.—Mun Corp 741.15, 755(1), 764(1), 812(6.1), 816(11), 819(1), 819(4); Neglig 387.

Fillmon; Texas State Highway Dept. v., Tex, 242 SW2d 172, 150 Tex 460.—Evid 555.10; Work Comp 556, 1283, 1385, 1571, 1683, 1916, 1958, 1969.

Fillmon; Texas State Highway Dept. v., TexCivApp–Eastland, 236 SW2d 635, aff 242 SW2d 172, 150 Tex 460.—App & E 1050.1(10); Evid 553(3); Work Comp 1202, 1571, 1682, 1703, 1726, 1834, 1917, 1922, 1937, 1939.1.

Fillmore; Coca-Cola Bottling Co. of Lubbock, Tex. v., TexCivApp–Amarillo, 453 SW2d 239.—App & E 1062.1; Food 25; Prod Liab 8, 75.1; Trial 352.5(1), 352.5(5).

Fillmore v. State, TexApp–Corpus Christi, 647 SW2d 300.—Larc 51(2), 64(6); Rec S Goods 3, 8(1), 8(4).

Fillmore; Tex-Wash Enterprises, Inc. v., TexCivApp–Fort Worth, 478 SW2d 623.—App & E 1, 390, 773(2); Corp 215; Estop 52(1); Guar 36(1), 48, 53(1), 85(1); Judgm 185.3(10); Land & Ten 74, 79(2); Princ & A 136(1).

Fills; U.S. v., CA5 (Tex), 408 F2d 1074.—Crim Law 1465, 1498, 1618(5).

Fillyaw v. City of Beaumont, TexCivApp–Beaumont, 564 SW2d 139.—Evid 568(1); Work Comp 1043, 1927.

Film Advertising Corp.; Bell v., TexCivApp–Dallas, 164 SW2d 578.—Contracts 204.

Film Advertising Corp.; Camp v., TexCivApp–Dallas, 159 SW2d 939, writ dism.—Contracts 42; Evid 77(5), 589.

Film Advertising Corp. v. Camp, TexCivApp–Dallas, 137 SW2d 1068.—App & E 1214; Mand 58; Plead 111.37; Prohib 5(2); Venue 7.5(3).

Filmstrips and Slides, Inc. v. Dallas Cent. Appraisal Dist., TexApp–Dallas, 806 SW2d 289.—Const Law 2314, 2324; Tax 2111, 2697.

Filsinger v. Filsinger, TexApp–El Paso, 225 SW3d 29.—App & E 185(1), 893(1); Child C 748; Courts 35, 37(1).

Filsinger; Filsinger v., TexApp–El Paso, 225 SW3d 29.—App & E 185(1), 893(1); Child C 748; Courts 35, 37(1).

Filter-Aid Co.; Gano v., TexCivApp–Austin, 414 SW2d 480.—Const Law 2647; Corp 592.5, 629.

Filter Fab, Inc. v. Delauder, TexApp–Houston (14 Dist), 2 SW3d 614.—Contrib 6; Subrog 27.

Filters, Inc. (Louisiana); Brunswick Corp. v., SDTex, 569 FSupp 1368.—Pat 16.13, 16.14, 72(1), 112.1, 168(2.1), 237, 238, 312(4), 317, 319(2), 325.11(3).

Filtronics, Inc.; El Paso Environmental Systems, Inc. v., TexCivApp–El Paso, 609 SW2d 810, ref nre.—App & E 170(1), 171(1); Interest 31, 39(1); New Tr 7; Usury 111(5).

Fimberg v. F.D.I.C., TexApp–Texarkana, 880 SW2d 83, reh overr, and writ den.—App & E 170(1); Bankr 3568(1), 3568(2); Judgm 185(3), 185.1(3), 185.3(16); Partners 353.

Fimberg v. State, TexApp–Houston (1 Dist), 922 SW2d 205, reh overr, and petition for discretionary review refused.—Crim Law 273.1(1), 273.1(4), 273.1(5), 274(3.1), 641.13(1), 1134(2), 1158(1).

FIMSA, Inc. v. Marina Bay Drive Corp., SDTex, 123 BR 222. See Marina Bay Drive Corp., In re.

FIMSA, Inc.; Marina Bay Drive Corp. v., SDTex, 123 BR 222. See Marina Bay Drive Corp., In re.

Fina, Inc. v. ARCO, CA5 (Tex), 200 F3d 266, reh and sug for reh den 210 F3d 365.—Contracts 129(1), 176(1); Environ Law 447; Fed Cts 776; Indem 27, 30(1), 31(6).

Fina, Inc. v. ARCO, EDTex, 16 FSupp2d 716, rev 200 F3d 266, reh and sug for reh den 210 F3d 365.—Action 17; Contracts 129(1), 143(2), 143.5, 152; Environ Law 447; Evid 397(1), 448, 461(1); Fed Cts 390, 391, 409.1, 412.1; Indem 30(1); Lim of Act 44(3); Sales 55.

Fina, Inc. v. Travelers Indem. Co, NDTex, 184 FSupp2d 547.—Fed Civ Proc 2501; Insurance 1806, 2104, 2120, 2281(2), 2913, 2930, 2939, 3571.

Finance Acceptance Corp.; Securities Inv. Co. of St. Louis v., TexCivApp–Hous (1 Dist), 474 SW2d 261, ref nre.—Contracts 144, 194, 280(1); Damag 87(2), 210(1), 221(5.1); Evid 417(9); Plead 127(1); Plgs 36; Trial 252(20), 350.4(1), 352.12; Usury 2(1), 102(3).

Finance America Corp.; Dale v., TexApp–Fort Worth, 929 SW2d 495, reh overr, and writ den, and writ den.—App & E 151(6), 662(4), 846(5), 852, 946, 955, 983(3), 1008.1(1); Execution 402(1), 402(5).

Finance America Private Brands, Inc.; Lawson v., TexCivApp–El Paso, 537 SW2d 483.—Bills & N 209, 489(6), 496(1), 496(2), 523; Pretrial Proc 306.1.

Finance Com'n of State of Texas; Texas Coastal Bank v., TexApp–Austin, 895 SW2d 882.—Admin Law 791; Banks 176.

Finance Com'n of Texas; Equitable Trust Co. v., TexApp–Austin, 99 SW3d 384.—Banks 310; Statut 181(1), 219(1), 219(4).

Finance Plus, Inc.; Milliorn v., TexApp–Eastland, 973 SW2d 690, reh overr, and review den.—Bills & N 451(1); Sec Tran 230, 231, 240.

Financial Acquisition Partners LP v. Blackwell, CA5 (Tex), 440 F3d 278.—Fed Civ Proc 636, 827, 833, 849, 1832, 2533.1; Fed Cts 776, 823, 894; Judgm 634, 651, 654, 715(2); Sec Reg 60.18, 60.40, 60.45(1), 60.51, 60.53, 60.54, 60.56, 60.63(1).

Financial & Real Estate Consulting Co.; Regional Properties, Inc. v., CA5 (Tex), 752 F2d 178.—Contracts 262, 270(1); Equity 54, 65(1), 65(2), 72(1); Estop 52.10(3), 90(1); Fed Civ Proc 2658; Sec Reg 11.17, 40.12.

Financial and Real Estate Consulting Co.; Regional Properties, Inc. v., CA5 (Tex), 678 F2d 552, appeal after remand 752 F2d 178.—Contracts 138(1); Courts 508(1), 508(2.1); Decl Judgm 5.1; Fed Cts 922; Sec Reg 35.24, 35.26, 131, 156.

Financial Center, Inc.; TRST Corpus, Inc. v., TexApp–Houston (14 Dist),9 SW3d 316, review den, and reh of petition for review den, appeal after remand Financial Center, Inc v. State, 2002 WL 31126788, rule 537(f) motion gr.—App & E 70(3), 893(1); Courts 35; Em Dom 2(1), 2(1.1), 285, 293(4); Mun Corp 723; Plead 104(1); Pretrial Proc 554, 695; States 78, 112.2(1), 191.1, 191.4(1), 191.4(4), 191.6(1), 191.6(2), 191.6(3), 191.8(3), 191.9(1), 191.9(2), 191.9(3), 191.10.

Financial Guardian Ins. Agency, Inc.; Rizk v., Tex, 584 SW2d 860.—Acct Action on 12, 13, 14.

Financial Guardian Ins. Agency, Inc.; Rizk v., TexCivApp–Hous (1 Dist), 576 SW2d 110, rev 584 SW2d 860.—Acct Action on 12, 13, 14; Costs 194.38; Judgm 185.3(3); Plead 36(2), 53(1).

Financial Ins. Co. v. Ragsdale, TexApp–El Paso, 166 SW3d 922.—App & E 893(1), 930(1), 989, 1001(1), 1001(3), 1003(7), 1024.1, 1182; Costs 194.18; Evid 597; Trial 219; Work Comp 1167, 1687, 1804, 1834, 1914, 1922, 1929, 1958, 1961, 1983.

Financial Review Services, Inc.; Prudential Ins. Co. of America v., Tex, 29 SW3d 74, reh overr, on remand 2002 WL 34102664, appeal dism 2003 WL 21026820.—Libel 133; Torts 212, 217, 218, 220, 245, 271, 272, 275.

Financial Review Services, Inc. v. Prudential Ins. Co. of America, TexApp–Houston (14 Dist), 50 SW3d 495, aff 29 SW3d 74, reh overr, on remand 2002 WL 34102664, appeal dism 2003 WL 21026820.—Acents 8; App & E 758.1, 866(3), 927(7); Contracts 9(1), 14; Evid 595; Insurance 3337, 3353, 3357, 3361, 3364, 3365, 3382; Judgm 185(2); Torts 119, 147, 212, 213, 220, 245, 258, 271, 275.

Financial Security Services, Inc. v. Phase I Electronics of West Texas, Inc., TexApp–Amarillo, 998 SW2d 674, reh overr, and review den.—App & E 937(1); Costs 194.32; Interest 10; Usury 11, 22, 52, 113.

Financial Universal Corp. v. Mercantile Nat. Bank at Dallas, TexApp–Dallas, 683 SW2d 815, ref nre.—Banks 140(3), 154(8); Bills & N 129(1); Judgm 181(17); Statut 226.

Fina Oil & Chemical Co. v. Alonso, TexApp–Corpus Christi, 941 SW2d 287, reh overr.—App & E 954(1), 954(2); Courts 475(1), 480(1), 483, 488(1), 488(4); Inj 132, 135, 138.27.

Fina Oil and Chemical Co.; Collazo v., EDTex, 835 FSupp 330. See E.E.O.C. v. Fina Oil and Chemical Co.

Fina Oil and Chemical Co.; Collazo v., EDTex, 145 FRD 74. See E.E.O.C. v. Fina Oil and Chemical Co.

Fina Oil & Chemical Co.; Continental Cas. Co. v., TexApp–Houston (1 Dist), 126 SW3d 163, reh overr, review gr, rev ATOFINA Petrochemicals, Inc v. Continental Cas Co, 185 SW3d 440, reh den.—Contracts 9(1), 15, 143(2), 147(2), 152, 176(2); Decl Judgm 323, 393; Evid 210; Insurance 1702, 1774, 1800, 1832(1), 2361, 2914, 3522; Work Comp 2189.

Fina Oil & Chemical Co.; Dalworth Oil Co., Inc. v., NDTex, 758 FSupp 410.—Assoc 20(1); Fed Civ Proc 103.2.

Fina Oil & Chemical Co.; Dancy v., EDTex, 3 FSupp2d 737.—Damag 50.10, 192; Torts 350, 351, 370.

Fina Oil & Chemical Co.; Dancy v., EDTex, 921 FSupp 1532.—Damag 50.10; Labor & Emp 1967; Rem of C 2, 25(1), 107(7); States 18.15, 18.46; Torts 328, 340.

Fina Oil and Chemical Co.; E.E.O.C. v., EDTex, 835 FSupp 330.—Civil R 1106, 1242, 1243, 1244, 1246; Damag 49.10, 50.10; Fed Civ Proc 2497.1, 2515, 2544; Labor & Emp 843.

Fina Oil and Chemical Co.; E.E.O.C. v., EDTex, 145 FRD 74.—Fed Civ Proc 1593, 1600(3); Records 57; Witn 198(1), 204(2), 205.

Fina Oil and Chemical Co. v. Ewen, CAFed (Tex), 123 F3d 1466.—Decl Judgm 61, 65, 231.1, 232; Fed Civ Proc 2508, 2546; Fed Cts 776; Pat 90(1), 90(5), 92, 112.1, 126, 314(5), 324.5.

Fina Oil & Chemical Co.; Fontenot v., EDTex, 772 FSupp 950.—Rem of C 54.

Fina Oil and Chemical Co.; Forman v., Tex, 858 SW2d 373.—Pretrial Proc 42.

Fina Oil and Chemical Co.; Forman v., TexApp–Eastland, 858 SW2d 498, reh den, and writ gr, rev 858 SW2d 373.—App & E 946, 961, 966(1); Pretrial Proc 42, 45, 713, 717.1, 718.

Fina Oil & Chemical Co.; Natural Resources Defense Council, Inc. v., EDTex, 806 FSupp 145.—Environ Law 226.

Fina Oil and Chemical Co. v. Port Neches I.S.D., TexApp–Beaumont, 861 SW2d 3, reh den, and writ den.—Schools 111.

Fina Oil & Chemical Co.; Reed v., EDTex, 995 FSupp 705.—Fed Cts 44, 104, 105, 113, 141, 819; Rem of C 21, 25(1).

Fina Oil and Chemical Co. v. Salinas, TexApp–Corpus Christi, 750 SW2d 32.—Pretrial Proc 403.

Fina Oil & Chemical Co.; Umphrey v., EDTex, 921 FSupp 434.—Labor & Emp 757, 809, 861, 1967; Rem of C 2, 25(1), 107(7); States 18.46, 18.49.

Fina Oil and Chemical Co.; Umphrey v., EDTex, 882 FSupp 585.—Labor & Emp 757, 1321; Rem of C 25(1), 107(7); States 18.49.

Fina Oil & Chemical Co.; West v., EDTex, 128 FSupp2d 396.—Labor & Emp 757, 968; Rem of C 25(1); States 18.46, 18.49.

Fina One Stop; Pena v., TexApp–San Antonio, 901 SW2d 663. See Pena v. Neal, Inc.

Fina Research, S.A. v. Baroid Ltd., CAFed (Tex), 141 F3d 1479.—Decl Judgm 5.1, 231.1, 232, 233, 234, 341.1, 393; Fed Cts 13; Pat 259(1), 259(2).

Fina Supply, Inc. v. Abilene Nat. Bank, CA5 (Tex), 800 F2d 469. See Brio Petroleum, Inc., Matter of.

Fina Supply, Inc. v. Abilene Nat. Bank, Tex, 726 SW2d 537.—Banks 191.20; Elect of Rem 1, 7(1), 11; Fraud 10, 11(1), 16; Ref of Inst 11, 16, 17(1), 19(1).

Fina Supply, Inc.; Abilene Nat. Bank v., TexApp–Eastland, 706 SW2d 737, writ gr, aff in part, disapproved in part 726 SW2d 537.—Fraud 10; Ref of Inst 16.

Fina Technology, Inc. v. Ewen, CAFed (Tex), 265 F3d 1325.—Fed Cts 776; Pat 126.

Fina Technology, Inc. v. Ewen, NDTex, 857 FSupp 1151, appeal dism Fina Oil and Chemical Co v. Ewen, 41 F3d 1519, dism 45 F3d 442.—Fed Civ Proc 2470.1, 2544, 2546; Pat 90(1), 97, 112.1, 129(2), 203.

Finberg; Preston State Bank v., TexCivApp–Dallas, 305 SW2d 654, dism.—App & E 265(1); Banks 126; Hus & W 87(1), 152; Interest 46(1).

Finberg Trading Co. v. Republic of China, CA5 (Tex), 220 F2d 844.—Damag 163(2); Sales 2, 407, 417, 418(7).

Fincannon; Clift by Clift v., EDTex, 657 FSupp 1535.—Civil R 1376(3), 1376(6), 1395(1); Const Law 3020, 3073(1), 3251; Death 14(1), 31(1), 31(3.1), 31(5), 32; Fed Cts 265, 266.1, 267, 268.1, 269, 411; Mental H 51.5; Offic 114; Social S 174.

Fincannon; Savidge v., CA5 (Tex), 836 F2d 898, reh den 843 F2d 499.—Civil R 1376(5), 1395(2), 1482, 1484, 1490; Fed Cts 13.10; Judgm 660.5, 664, 677.

Fincannon; Savidge by Savidge v., CA5 (Tex), 784 F2d 186.—Fed Cts 1144.

Fincannon; Savidge by Savidge v., CA5 (Tex), 768 F2d 639, opinion recalled in part 784 F2d 186.—Fed Cts 1145.

Fincannon v. State, TexCrimApp, 215 SW2d 177.—Crim Law 1094(3).

Finch, In re, SDTex, 130 BR 753.—Bankr 2786; Divorce 252.3(2), 252.3(5), 321 1/2, 322; Liens 7.

Finch v. Big Chief Drilling Co., EDTex, 56 FRD 456.—Fed Civ Proc 2416, 2417, 2441, 2443, 2451.1.

Finch; Brown v., CA5 (Tex), 429 F2d 80.—Admin Law 459; Social S 140.45, 143.35, 143.65, 143.85, 147, 148.15, 149.5.

Finch; Burchfield v., TexApp–Texarkana, 968 SW2d 422, review den.—Hus & W 249(3), 272(4).

Finch; City of Grand Prairie v., TexCivApp–Dallas, 294 SW2d 851.—App & E 174, 1071.5; Mun Corp 120; Zoning 232, 306, 789.

Finch; Craig v., CA5 (Tex), 425 F2d 1005, 10 ALR Fed 894.—Social S 137.5; Statut 181(1).

Finch; Crook v., TexCivApp–Waco, 347 SW2d 335.—App & E 846(2), 846(5); Libel 100(7); Venue 22(8).

Finch; Dawson v., CA5 (Tex), 425 F2d 1192, cert den 91 SCt 60, 400 US 830, 27 LEd2d 60, reh den 91 SCt 233, 400 US 953, 27 LEd2d 261.—Social S 142.30.

Finch v. Finch, SDTex, 130 BR 753. See Finch, In re.

Finch; Finch v., SDTex, 130 BR 753. See Finch, In re.

Finch v. Finch, TexApp–Houston (1 Dist), 825 SW2d 218.—App & E 931(1), 989, 1010.2, 1012.1(4), 1079; Costs 260(4), 260(5); Divorce 252.3(1), 252.3(2), 252.3(5), 253(1), 253(2), 253(3), 253(4), 286(2); Trial 401.

Finch; Finch v., TexApp–Houston (1 Dist), 825 SW2d 218.—App & E 931(1), 989, 1010.2, 1012.1(4), 1079; Costs 260(4), 260(5); Divorce 252.3(1), 252.3(2), 252.3(5), 253(1), 253(2), 253(3), 253(4), 286(2); Trial 401.

Finch v. Fort Bend Independent School Dist., CA5 (Tex), 333 F3d 555, reh and reh den 75 FedAppx 982.—Civil R 1376(2); Const Law 1447, 1928, 1929, 2001, 3893, 4199, 4202; Fed Civ Proc 2491.5; Fed Cts 714, 753, 766, 768.1, 770, 776, 802; Labor & Emp 826; Schools 147.28, 147.34(1), 147.38.

Finch; Fulton v., Tex, 346 SW2d 823, 162 Tex 351.—App & E 112; Judgm 485; Mand 3(1), 4(1); New Tr 165.

Finch; Fulton v., TexCivApp–San Antonio, 338 SW2d 478, dism, mandamus gr 346 SW2d 823, 162 Tex 351.—Judgm 341; New Tr 165.

Finch; Guardian Life Ins. Co. of America v., CA5 (Tex), 395 F3d 238, cert den Finch v. Galaway, 125 SCt 2305, 544 US 1056, 161 LEd2d 1102.—Fed Cts 419.

Finch; Johnson v., NDTex, 350 FSupp 945.—Child 1; Const Law 3185, 4120; Marriage 50(1); Social S 122.10, 137, 143.4.

Finch; King v., CA5 (Tex), 428 F2d 709.—Const Law 52, 2330, 2340, 2350, 3907, 4123; Fed Cts 743; Social S 140.60, 143.45, 143.70, 143.80, 148.25.

Finch; Knox v., CA5 (Tex), 427 F2d 919.—Social S 140.35, 143.75, 149.5.

Finch; McCleery v., SDTex, 332 FSupp 1116.—Social S 140.85, 143.3.

Finch v. McVea, TexCivApp–Corpus Christi, 543 SW2d 449, ref nre.—App & E 960(1), 1151(3); Can of Inst 1, 23, 24(1); Contracts 96, 98, 99(3); Deeds 211(3); Fraud 1, 12; Plead 228.23.

Finch; Norwood v., EDTex, 318 FSupp 739.—Social S 143.75.

Finch v. State, TexCrimApp, 643 SW2d 415.—Crim Law 1181(1).

Finch v. State, TexCrimApp, 643 SW2d 414, on remand 638 SW2d 215, petition for discretionary review dism 643 SW2d 415.—Crim Law 1180.

FINCH

Finch v. State, TexCrimApp, 399 SW2d 544.—Burg 41(1); Const Law 4810.

Finch v. State, TexCrimApp, 225 SW2d 861, 154 TexCrim 158.—Crim Law 665(4), 866; Jury 83(3); Rape 6, 51(1), 59(14).

Finch v. State, TexApp–Fort Worth, 66 SW3d 323.—Crim Law 1081(2).

Finch v. State, TexApp–Fort Worth, 638 SW2d 215, petition for discretionary review dism 643 SW2d 415.— Crim Law 577.11(6), 577.16(1), 625.15, 625.20, 1128(1); Jury 131(4).

Finch v. State, TexApp–Fort Worth, 629 SW2d 876, review gr, cause remanded 643 SW2d 414, on remand 638 SW2d 215, petition for discretionary review dism 643 SW2d 415.—Crim Law 438(4), 438(5.1), 494, 577.10(9), 624, 717, 789(4), 1118, 1129(3), 1171.1(3).

Finch; State v., TexCivApp–San Antonio, 349 SW2d 780. —Mand 53; Trial 315, 321, 325(1).

Finch v. State, TexCivApp–Waco, 506 SW2d 749.—Burg 29; Infants 225.

Finch v. State of Tex., CA5 (Tex), 387 F2d 366.—Hab Corp 721(2).

Finch; Terrell v., SDTex, 302 FSupp 1063.—Estop 62.2(4).

Finch v. Texas Emp. Ins. Ass'n, TexCivApp–Dallas, 564 SW2d 807, ref nre.—App & E 1070(2); Pretrial Proc 371; Trial 355(1); Work Comp 998, 999.

Finch v. Texas Emp. Ins. Ass'n, TexCivApp–Texarkana, 535 SW2d 201, ref nre.—Judgm 185.3(13); Work Comp 58, 1105, 2251.

Finch; Texas Emp. Ins. Ass'n v., TexCivApp–Tyler, 512 SW2d 51.—Assoc 20(1); Insurance 3559; Plead 111.16, 111.36, 111.40; Venue 17.

Finch; Thaxton v., NDTex, 301 FSupp 1155.—U S 39(15).

Finch; Wagner v., CA5 (Tex), 413 F2d 267.—Social S 124.20, 137.

Finch Alternator & Starter, In re, SDTex, 130 BR 753. See Finch, In re.

Fincher v. B & D Air Conditioning and Heating Co., TexApp–Houston (1 Dist), 816 SW2d 509, writ den, cert den 113 SCt 77, 506 US 823, 121 LEd2d 41.—App & E 959(3); Parties 95(7); Partners 1, 165, 200, 204, 375; Plead 234, 286(1).

Fincher v. Board of Adjustment of City of Hunters Creek Village, TexApp–Houston (1 Dist), 56 SW3d 815, reh overr.—Zoning 440.1.

Fincher; Campbell v., TexApp–Waco, 72 SW3d 723.— App & E 5.

Fincher; City of De Leon v., TexCivApp–Eastland, 344 SW2d 743, ref nre.—Mand 23(1), 74(2); Mun Corp 46, 108.1.

Fincher; City of Texarkana v., TexApp–Texarkana, 657 SW2d 842, ref nre.—Mun Corp 185(11), 185(15).

Fincher v. City of Texarkana, TexApp–Texarkana, 598 SW2d 22, ref nre.—App & E 185(1); Mun Corp 185(12).

Fincher; Eggleston v., TexCivApp–Fort Worth, 179 SW2d 427, writ refused.—Waters 154(1).

Fincher; Gibbs v., CA5 (Tex), 804 F2d 318. See Association of Professional Flight Attendants v. Gibbs.

Fincher; Gough v., TexCivApp–Waco, 228 SW2d 541.— Autos 181(1), 244(20); Evid 265(7); Plead 111.18, 111.19; Venue 21.

Fincher; Joaquin Independent School Dist. v., TexCivApp–Tyler, 510 SW2d 98, ref nre.—Schools 33.

Fincher; Simons Land Co. v., TexCivApp–Waco, 474 SW2d 503.—App & E 302(1); Trial 273, 352.9, 352.10.

Fincher v. State, TexCrimApp, 95 SW2d 131, 130 TexCrim 470.—Rob 4.

Fincher v. State, TexApp–Fort Worth, 980 SW2d 886, reh overr, and petition for discretionary review refused.— Crim Law 59(1), 586, 590(2), 629.5(2), 629.5(4), 829(1), 829(20), 1148.

Fincher; Washington Nat. Ins. Co. v., TexCivApp–Fort Worth, 157 SW2d 164.—Insurance 2522, 2525(1), 2530, 3375.

Fincher v. Wright, TexApp–Fort Worth, 141 SW3d 255. —App & E 70(6); Atty & C 148(1); Courts 99(3); Judgm 649, 668(1), 675(1), 677, 678(1), 678(2), 681, 707, 714(1); Mand 4(1), 4(4), 28, 44; Parties 53; Venue 16.5, 78.

Fincher & Son Real Estate, Inc.; Greenberg v., TexApp–Houston (1 Dist), 753 SW2d 506.—App & E 819; Bankr 2395, 2396.

Fincher, Greenberg & Baca Investments; Greenberg v., TexApp–Houston (1 Dist), 753 SW2d 506. See Greenberg v. Fincher & Son Real Estate, Inc.

Finck; International Sec. Life Ins. Co. v., Tex, 496 SW2d 544.—Insurance 1634(3), 1640, 3084, 3585; Princ & A 159(1).

Finck; International Sec. Life Ins. Co. v., TexCivApp–Amarillo, 475 SW2d 363, writ gr, rev 496 SW2d 544.— App & E 231(7), 999(1); Costs 252; Damag 87(2); Evid 152, 318(1); Fraud 1, 17, 31, 58(2), 62, 64(1); Insurance 1633, 1640, 1641, 1654, 2065, 3359, 3381(4), 3424(1), 3426, 3578, 3585; Plead 228; Trial 350.4(3), 366.

Finck Cigar Co. v. Campbell, TexComApp, 133 SW2d 759, 134 Tex 250.—App & E 930(2), 1064.1(10); Trial 127, 232(2).

Finck Cigar Co. v. Campbell, TexApp–Fort Worth, 114 SW2d 348, aff 133 SW2d 759, 134 Tex 250.—App & E 932(1), 1060.6; Death 69, 99(4); Trial 295(1), 352.17, 357.

Findeisen v. North East Independent School Dist., CA5 (Tex), 749 F2d 234, cert den North East Independent School District v. Findeisen, 105 SCt 2657, 471 US 1125, 86 LEd2d 274.—Civil R 1315; Const Law 3867, 3874(2), 4201, 4202; Fed Civ Proc 2464, 2497.1.

Finder v. E. L. Cheeney Co., TexCivApp–Beaumont, 368 SW2d 62.—App & E 80(6), 110, 281(1), 840(1), 1129.

Finder v. Jenka Corp., TexCivApp–San Antonio, 348 SW2d 236.—Action 60.

Finder; Littlejohn v., TexCivApp–San Antonio, 348 SW2d 237.—Decl Judgm 258; Inj 157; Motions 11.

Finder v. Nyegaard, TexCivApp–Waco, 367 SW2d 217, ref nre.—Mines 79.3.

Finder v. O'Connor, TexCivApp–Dallas, 615 SW2d 283, dism.—Plead 111.36; Venue 5.3(8).

Finder v. Stanford, TexCivApp–Houston, 351 SW2d 289. —App & E 846(5); Contracts 187(1); Mines 122, 125.

Findlay v. Cave, Tex, 611 SW2d 57.—Costs 194.25.

Findlay v. Cave, TexCivApp–Fort Worth, 597 SW2d 37, aff 611 SW2d 57.—Atty & C 129(4).

Findlay; City of Austin v., TexCivApp–Austin, 538 SW2d 9.—Mun Corp 85.

Findlay v. State, TexApp–Houston (14 Dist), 9 SW3d 397. —Autos 332; Statut 223.2(1.1), 223.2(35), 223.4.

Findley v. Calvert, TexCivApp–Beaumont, 509 SW2d 393. —Deeds 113; Statut 197, 226; Tax 3333(1); Wills 466.

Findley v. Decker, TexCivApp–Waco, 499 SW2d 350.— App & E 171(1), 931(6), 1170.7.

Findley v. McWhorter, TexCivApp–Waco, 526 SW2d 720. —Trial 29(1); Wills 21, 400.

Findley v. Robert C. Herd & Co., CA5 (Tex), 250 F2d 77. —Mar Liens 65.

Findley v. Southern Sales Co., TexCivApp–Texarkana, 229 SW2d 421.—App & E 846(2), 846(5), 1011.1(1); Sales 359(1), 365.

Findley v. State, TexCrimApp, 378 SW2d 850.—Burg 41(1); Crim Law 75, 507(1), 736(2), 755.5; Sent & Pun 1389.

Fine v. American Solar King Corp., CA5 (Tex), 919 F2d 290, cert dism Main Hurdman v. Fine, 112 SCt 576, 502 US 976, 116 LEd2d 601.—Crim Law 449.2; Fed Civ Proc 2511, 2543, 2546; Fed Cts 938; Sec Reg 60.18, 60.30, 60.41, 60.45(1), 60.45(3), 60.48(3).

Fine; Atkins v., TexCivApp–Austin, 508 SW2d 131.—Covenants 49, 103(2); Evid 518; Inj 62(3).

Fine; Fidelity Union Life Ins. Co. v., TexCivApp–Waco, 120 SW2d 138, writ dism.—Land & Ten 166(5).

Fine v. GAF Chemical Corp., CA5 (Tex), 995 F2d 576, reh den.—Civil R 1516, 1549; Fed Civ Proc 2497.1.

Fine; Gillette Motor Transport v., TexCivApp–Fort Worth, 131 SW2d 817, writ dism, correct.—App & E 1062.2; Autos 209, 242(8), 245(81); Neglig 1571, 1683, 1745; Trial 192, 350.5(3), 350.8, 351.2(10), 352.10.

Fine; Gillette Motor Transport v., TexCivApp–Fort Worth, 103 SW2d 196.—Trial 253(4).

Fine v. Lutz, TexCivApp–Fort Worth, 278 SW2d 889, ref nre.—Hus & W 90; Judgm 181(29), 185(2).

Fine v. Page, TexCivApp–Eastland, 572 SW2d 577, dism.—App & E 371, 382, 387(2), 387(6), 395, 607(1).

Fine v. Pratt, TexCivApp–Eastland, 150 SW2d 308.—Civil R 1027; Decl Judgm 3, 142; Estop 98(1); Inj 113; Judgm 18(1), 18(2), 19; Labor & Emp 101, 1030; Plead 8(9).

Fine v. Scott, TexCivApp–Eastland, 592 SW2d 56, ref nre.—Lim of Act 127(1); Quiet T 30(2), 42; Trial 388(1).

Fine; W. U. Tel. Co. v., TexCivApp–Beaumont, 97 SW2d 748.—App & E 770(2), 773(4).

Finehout; Epps v., TexCivApp–San Antonio, 189 SW2d 631, writ refused wom.—Adv Poss 13, 63(2), 78, 85(1), 114(1); App & E 1012.1(12); Evid 589; Trial 140(2).

Fineron v. State, TexApp–El Paso, 201 SW3d 361.—Const Law 4664(1); Crim Law 394.6(5), 519(1), 519(9), 777, 781(5), 1147, 1158(4); Searches 60.1, 61, 62, 66.

Finesilver Mfg. Co.; N.L.R.B. v., CA5 (Tex), 400 F2d 644.—Labor & Emp 766, 1455(5), 1734, 1879, 1881, 1916.

Finesod; Westheimer v., SDTex, 733 FSupp 1127. See Terra-Drill Partnerships Securities Litigation, In re.

Finesod; Westheimer v., SDTex, 726 FSupp 655. See Terra-Drill Partnerships Securities Litigation, In re.

Finger v. Garza, CA5 (Tex), 98 FedAppx 326.—Const Law 3476, 4055; Fed Civ Proc 2491.5; Mun Corp 92.

Finger v. Home Ins. Co. of New York, TexCivApp–Houston, 379 SW2d 950.—Insurance 3048, 3070; Judgm 181(5.1), 185(2), 185.3(12).

Finger v. Morris, TexCivApp–Hous (14 Dist), 468 SW2d 572, ref nre.—App & E 1151(2); Fraud 11(1), 20, 38; Lim of Act 24(4), 40(1), 40(2), 43, 46(9), 100(13); Mtg 209; Ven & Pur 130(2).

Finger; Motor Mortg. Co. v., TexCivApp–Waco, 200 SW2d 228.—Courts 155, 183; Judgm 495(1), 497(1), 503, 518; J P 31; Venue 22(9).

Finger v. St. Paul Fire & Marine Ins. Co., TexCivApp–Hous (1 Dist), 423 SW2d 460, ref nre.—Insurance 1885, 3054(2), 3081; Judgm 185.1(4); Ref of Inst 36(3).

Finger v. School Sisters of Third Order of St. Francis, TexCivApp–Austin, 585 SW2d 357.—Char 11, 12, 50.

Finger v. Southern Refrigeration Services, Inc., TexApp–Houston (1 Dist), 881 SW2d 890, supplemented on reh, and writ den.—App & E 877(1); Const Law 4012; Damag 59, 208(1); Insurance 3510, 3512; Judgm 540, 634, 668(1), 678(1), 678(2), 707, 713(1), 720, 725(1); Subrog 32; Trial 139.1(14), 139.1(17), 168, 178.

Finger Contract Supply Co. v. Republic Nat. Bank of Dallas, TexCivApp–Fort Worth, 412 SW2d 79, ref nre.—Corp 565(1), 566(1), 566(2), 566(3); Receivers 162; Schools 104; Tax 2241, 2736, 2750.

Finger Contract Supply Co.; Webb v., Tex, 447 SW2d 906.—Guar 62.

Finger Contract Supply Co. v. Webb, TexCivApp–Hous (14 Dist), 438 SW2d 112, writ gr, rev 447 SW2d 906.—Guar 27, 62; Princ & S 114, 115(1).

Finger Furniture Co. v. Chase Manhattan Bank, TexCivApp–San Antonio, 413 SW2d 131, ref nre.—Chat Mtg 17, 47, 109, 144; Corp 476(1); Mech Liens 198, 249, 281(1); Mtg 48(2).

Finger Furniture Co. Inc. v. Commonwealth Ins. Co., CA5 (Tex), 404 F3d 312.—Fed Cts 776, 830; Insurance 1809, 2163(1), 3585.

Fingold v. Cook, TexApp–Houston (1 Dist), 902 SW2d 579, reh overr, and writ den.—App & E 927(7), 997(3); Ven & Pur 317.

Finholt; Hoagland v., TexApp–Dallas, 773 SW2d 740.—Contracts 54(1), 88; Joint Adv 1.11; Partners 70, 353.

Finholt; Moore v., TexApp–Tyler, 638 SW2d 169.—Mal Pros 10, 14.

Finigan; Owen v., TexCivApp–Eastland, 381 SW2d 578, ref nre.—App & E 554(1); Judgm 72.

Finisar Corp. v. DirecTV Group, Inc., EDTex, 424 FSupp2d 896.—Fed Civ Proc 25, 1935.1; Pat 292.4, 310.7(4), 328(2).

Finisar Corp. v. The DirecTV Group, Inc., EDTex, 416 FSupp2d 512.—Pat 101(2), 101(3), 101(6), 101(8), 159, 161, 162, 165(1), 165(3), 167(1), 168(2.1), 314(5), 328(2).

Finish Line, Inc.; Dominguez v., WDTex, 439 FSupp2d 688.—Alt Disp Res 134(5), 140.

Fink v. Grevsgard, TexCivApp–Galveston, 123 SW2d 383, writ refused.—Jud S 3; Tax 3072(5), 3176.

Fink v. State, TexApp–Houston (1 Dist), 866 SW2d 333.—Autos 349(9); Searches 23.

Fink v. State, TexApp–Austin, 97 SW3d 739, petition for discretionary review refused.—Crim Law 1144.14, 1480; Homic 1195, 1347, 1480.

Fink v. White, TexCivApp–Galveston, 133 SW2d 137, writ refused.—Jud S 47; Tax 2962.

Finke; Morrell v., TexApp–Fort Worth, 184 SW3d 257, reh overr, and petition for review abated, and review den.—App & E 1008.1(1); Damag 57.27, 57.28, 226; Evid 528(1), 570, 571(10), 574; Health 611, 631, 684, 786, 822(3), 823(9), 826, 830, 832; Infants 72(2); Judgm 199(3.5); Lim of Act 55(3), 72(1); Neglig 371, 379, 380, 387, 422, 423, 1675; Parent & C 7(1).

Finke v. Wheatfall, Tex, 581 SW2d 152.—Hus & W 274(1).

Finke v. Wheatfall, TexCivApp–Hous (14 Dist), 565 SW2d 386, reformed 581 SW2d 152.—Evid 215(1), 241(1), 246; Judgm 94; Partit 107; Tresp to T T 6.1, 41(2); Trusts 89(2), 90.

Finkel, In re, BkrtcyWDTex, 151 BR 779.—Home 17, 18, 36, 57(1), 162(1), 163.

Finkel v. Docutel/Olivetti Corp., CA5 (Tex), 817 F2d 356, cert den 108 SCt 1220, 485 US 959, 99 LEd2d 421, cert den 108 SCt 1220, 485 US 959, 99 LEd2d 421.—Sec Reg 60.25, 60.28(2.1), 60.48(1), 60.53, 60.54, 60.62.

Finkelstein v. Carpenter, TexApp–Beaumont, 795 SW2d 897, writ den.—Bound 40(1); Deeds 117.

Finkelstein; Horwitz v., TexCivApp–Amarillo, 196 SW2d 951, ref nre.—App & E 1078(1); Judgm 335(1), 335(2), 335(3); New Tr 155; Plead 214(1).

Finkelstein; Horwitz v., TexCivApp–Amarillo, 189 SW2d 895, writ refused wom.—App & E 907(3), 954(1), 954(2), 954(4); Inj 135, 147, 161.

Finkelstein; Horwitz v., TexCivApp–Amarillo, 182 SW2d 751, writ refused.—App & E 564(2), 622; New Tr 155; Stip 6.

Finkelstein; Morris v., TexCivApp–Hous (14 Dist), 442 SW2d 452, ref nre.—Wills 448, 449, 470(1), 587(1), 638.

Finkelstein v. Southampton Civic Club, TexApp–Houston (1 Dist), 675 SW2d 271, ref nre.—Covenants 49, 51(2), 72.1, 103(1), 103(3), 122, 132(2); Estop 52.15; Judgm 185(3), 185.2(4), 186.

Finkelstein v. TransAmerican Natural Gas Corp., SDTex, 127 BR 800. See TransAmerican Natural Gas Corp., In re.

Finkelstein; TransAmerican Natural Gas Corp. v., TexApp–San Antonio, 933 SW2d 591, reh den, and reh overr, and writ den.—Accord 1; App & E 893(1); Bankr 3568(3); Courts 97(1); Gas 14.1(3); Impl & C C 3, 55, 58; Mines 73, 74(1), 74(8), 78.1(8), 79.1(1), 79.7.

Finkelstein; TransAmerican Natural Gas Corp. v., Tex-App–San Antonio, 911 SW2d 153.—App & E 176, 460(1), 464.

Finkelstein; TransAmerican Natural Gas Corp. v., Tex-App–San Antonio, 905 SW2d 412, petition for review dism, enforcement gr in part 911 SW2d 153.—App & E 464, 986.

Finklea; City of Brady, Tex. v., CA5 (Tex), 400 F2d 352. —Courts 37(3); Death 91; Electricity 16(1), 16(4), 16(7), 19(4), 19(5); Fed Cts 848; Judgm 828.5(5); Neglig 236, 552(1).

Finklea v. Dorn, TexCivApp–El Paso, 111 SW2d 748, writ refused.—App & E 1177(6); Wills 602(1), 602(5).

Finklea v. Estelle, CA5 (Tex), 506 F2d 438.—Hab Corp 746.

Finklea v. Jacksonville Daily Progress, TexApp–Tyler, 742 SW2d 512, writ dism woj.—App & E 204(2), 223; Evid 593; Judgm 185(1), 185(4); Libel 1, 32, 49, 61; Plead 36(1).

Finklea v. State, TexCrimApp, 579 SW2d 497.—Forg 32.

Finklea v. State, TexCrimApp, 481 SW2d 889.—Arrest 63.4(16), 71.1(3); Const Law 3781; Controlled Subs 6; Crim Law 404.60, 641.13(2.1), 1036.1(4); Ind & Inf 142.

Finkner; LeFors v., TexCivApp–Tyler, 448 SW2d 574.— Venue 7.5(2), 7.5(3).

Finks; Haskins v., TexCivApp–Eastland, 470 SW2d 717, ref nre.—Judgm 162(4).

Finlan v. City of Dallas, NDTex, 888 FSupp 779.— Admin Law 124; Inj 135, 138.1, 138.3, 138.6, 138.12, 138.15, 138.18, 138.46, 142, 147; Mun Corp 8, 92; Records 59, 65.

Finlan; Dallas Independent School Dist. v., TexApp–Dallas, 27 SW3d 220,reh overr, and review den, and reh of petition for review den, cert den Finlan v. Dallas Independent School District, 122 SCt 342, 534 US 949, 151 LEd2d 258, appeal after remand 2002 WL 31656117, review den, and reh of petition for review den.—App & E 758.1, 760(1), 761, 852, 863, 870(2), 946, 966(1), 1008.1(1); Civil R 1346, 1376(2), 1376(5); Consp 1.1, 13; Fraud 3; Judgm 178, 181(1), 181(2), 181(27), 181(33), 183, 185(2), 185(6), 185.1(4), 185.3(21), 186; Libel 7(1), 38(1), 38(5), 50.5, 123(8); Mal Pros 38; Mand 4(1), 12, 14(1), 14(3), 28; Offic 114; Pretrial Proc 713; Records 1, 30; Statut 181(1), 188, 205, 209, 212.7.

Finlan v. Dallas Independent School Dist., TexApp–Eastland, 90 SW3d 395, reh overr, and review den, and reh of petition for review den.—Action 60; App & E 196, 863, 934(1), 960(1), 966(1), 1097(1), 1195(1); Civil R 1027, 1376(1), 1376(2), 1376(5); Consp 7.5(1); Const Law 1435, 1441, 1442, 2314, 4190; Courts 99(1), 99(7); Damag 50.10; Indem 50, 65; Judgm 181(27), 185(2), 185(5), 186; Mal Pros 0.5, 11, 14; Schools 89.3; Torts 212, 213, 241, 242.

Finlan; Keever v., TexApp–Dallas, 988 SW2d 300, reh overr, and review dism.—App & E 863, 870(2), 893(1), 933(1), 946, 977(3), 984(1), 984(5), 1079; Atty & C 24; Costs 2, 208, 260(4), 260(5); Judgm 181(11); New Tr 6, 99, 102(3), 103, 108(2); Records 51, 63, 68; Trial 388(1).

Finlan v. Peavy, TexApp–Waco, 205 SW2d 647.—Abate & R 17, 81; Action 60; Courts 1, 78, 475(1); Judgm 525; Pretrial Proc 535, 583, 587, 676, 699.

Finlay; Bank of Austin v., TexCivApp–San Antonio, 588 SW2d 809, ref nre.—Banks 181; Sequest 21; Trover 24.

Finlay; F.D.I.C. v., TexApp–Houston (1 Dist), 832 SW2d 158, reh den, and writ den, and writ withdrawn, and writ gr, and writ withdrawn, writ den 849 SW2d 344.— New Tr 155; Pretrial Proc 699, 747.1, 749.1.

Finlay; Hickman v., TexCivApp–Austin, 392 SW2d 147, writ refused.—Autos 181(2), 244(6).

Finlay v. I.N.S., CA5 (Tex), 210 F3d 556.—Aliens 216; Hab Corp 521.

Finlay v. Jones, Tex, 435 SW2d 136.—App & E 842(1); Judgm 123(1), 304, 306.

Finlay v. Olive, TexApp–Houston (1 Dist), 77 SW3d 520. —App & E 840(4), 936(1), 984(1); Atty & C 24; Costs 2, 208; Pretrial Proc 44.1.

Finlayson v. McDowell, TexCivApp–El Paso, 94 SW2d 1234, writ dism.—Judgm 425, 460(3); Partners 165, 195, 206.

Finlayson v. Roberts, TexCivApp–Fort Worth, 82 SW2d 1020.—App & E 236(2); Mtg 372(2); Plead 1, 36(3), 245(3), 353, 369(6); Powers 28.

Finley, In re, BkrtcyEDTex, 138 BR 181.—Bankr 3105.1.

Finley, In re Guardianship of, TexApp–Texarkana, 220 SW3d 608.—App & E 854(2), 946; Mental H 159, 175, 176, 177; Statut 181(1), 188, 190, 214.

Finley; Brickley v., TexCivApp–El Paso, 143 SW2d 433. —Lim of Act 127(13), 145(5), 148(2), 149(6), 151(2); Plead 162, 412.

Finley; Burleson v., TexCivApp–Austin, 581 SW2d 304, ref nre.—Action 60; App & E 231(5), 964, 1170.7; Assault 27, 33; Damag 178; Evid 110, 129(5), 268; Jury 131(3); Parties 93(1); Trial 3(2), 83(1); Witn 380(5.1).

Finley v. Carr, TexCivApp–Waco, 273 SW2d 439, writ refused.—Contracts 143.5; Covenants 77.1, 79(3), 84; Deeds 93; Evid 461(2).

Finley v. Finley, Tex, 324 SW2d 551, 159 Tex 582.— Estates 8; Wills 506(1), 608(2), 608(3.1).

Finley; Finley v., Tex, 324 SW2d 551, 159 Tex 582.— Estates 8; Wills 506(1), 608(2), 608(3.1).

Finley v. Finley, TexCivApp–Eastland, 318 SW2d 478, ref nre 324 SW2d 551, 159 Tex 582.—Wills 506(1), 608(2), 608(3.1).

Finley; Finley v., TexCivApp–Eastland, 318 SW2d 478, ref nre 324 SW2d 551, 159 Tex 582.—Wills 506(1), 608(2), 608(3.1).

Finley v. Finley, TexCivApp–Tyler, 410 SW2d 818, ref nre.—App & E 876, 907(3), 927(2), 931(1), 948, 962; Judgm 217; Pretrial Proc 582, 583.

Finley; Finley v., TexCivApp–Tyler, 410 SW2d 818, ref nre.—App & E 876, 907(3), 927(2), 931(1), 948, 962; Judgm 217; Pretrial Proc 582, 583.

Finley v. Hartsook, CCA5 (Tex), 158 F2d 618.—Courts 202(1); Evid 80(1); Fed Cts 752; Judgm 501; Mental H 172, 195, 196, 251, 256.

Finley v. Hartsook, NDTex, 63 FSupp 97, aff 158 F2d 618.—Jud S 50(1); Mental H 172, 195, 251, 256, 268.

Finley; Howell v., TexCivApp–Texarkana, 489 SW2d 953, ref nre.—Evid 424, 441(8).

Finley v. Howell, TexCivApp–Texarkana, 320 SW2d 25.— App & E 758.1; Em Dom 9, 237(7), 242, 273; Judgm 16, 470.

Finley v. Hundley, TexCivApp–Dallas, 252 SW2d 958.— Contracts 10(1), 15, 39, 350(2).

Finley; Industrial Life Ins. Co. v., Tex, 382 SW2d 100.— Accord 4, 10(1), 11(2).

Finley; Industrial Life Ins. Co. v., TexCivApp–Tyler, 374 SW2d 947, writ gr, rev 382 SW2d 100.—Judgm 185.3(12); Paymt 1(1).

Finley v. J.C. Pace Ltd., TexApp–Houston (1 Dist), 4 SW3d 319, appeal decided 1999 WL 997788.—App & E 345.1, 345.2; Motions 12.1, 15.

Finley v. Johnson, CA5 (Tex), 243 F3d 215.—Hab Corp 364, 378, 380.1, 382, 401, 403, 407, 422, 431, 453.

Finley; McDonald v., TexCivApp–Waco, 328 SW2d 919, writ dism.—Venue 74.

Finley v. May, TexApp–Austin, 154 SW3d 196.—App & E 230, 242(1), 497(1), 760(1); Child C 904; Child S 539, 616.

Finley v. Pafford, TexCivApp–Amarillo, 104 SW2d 163, writ dism.—App & E 758.2, 758.3(6); Des & Dist 90(4); Evid 317(18); Hus & W 249(6), 262.1(4), 274(4); Trial 48; Witn 139(9), 140(9).

Finley; Skidmore v., TexCivApp–Dallas, 396 SW2d 952.— App & E 912, 989, 1010.1(3); Plead 111.12, 111.42(8); Venue 72.

Finley; Spradley v., Tex, 302 SW2d 409, 157 Tex 260.—Mines 55(7), 79.1(5).

Finley v. Spradley, TexCivApp–Texarkana, 294 SW2d 750, aff 302 SW2d 409, 157 Tex 260.—Decl Judgm 296; Mines 55(7), 79.1(5).

Finley v. State, TexCrimApp, 573 SW2d 238.—Crim Law 369.1, 369.2(1), 369.7, 1169.11.

Finley v. State, TexCrimApp, 528 SW2d 854.—Controlled Subs 65.

Finley v. State, TexCrimApp, 527 SW2d 553.—Const Law 3417; Crim Law 813, 956(10), 1158(1); Rape 2, 3.

Finley v. State, TexCrimApp, 440 SW2d 849.—False Pret 12, 52; Larc 13.

Finley v. State, TexCrimApp, 414 SW2d 662.—Crim Law 1182.

Finley v. State, TexCrimApp, 312 SW2d 956, 166 TexCrim 278.—Autos 355(6); Crim Law 338(7), 364(3.1), 369.6, 564(1).

Finley v. State, TexCrimApp, 278 SW2d 864, 161 TexCrim 458.—Burg 41(1); Crim Law 633(2).

Finley v. State, TexCrimApp, 169 SW2d 975, 145 TexCrim 507.—Crim Law 719(1), 1171.1(2.1), 1171.1(6); Int Liq 238(2), 239(10); Witn 337(22).

Finley v. State, TexCrimApp, 138 SW2d 1089, 139 TexCrim 40.—Crim Law 1184(5).

Finley v. State, TexApp–Austin, 917 SW2d 122, petition for discretionary review refused.—Crim Law 396(2), 662.10, 1038.1(6), 1169.12, 1172.1(1); Rob 11.

Finley v. State, TexApp–Houston (14 Dist), 809 SW2d 909, petition for discretionary review refused.—Arrest 66(2); Autos 332, 413, 415; Crim Law 394.2(1), 457, 700(9), 726, 1171.1(1).

Finley v. Steenkamp, TexApp–Fort Worth, 19 SW3d 533. —App & E 173(10); Health 804, 809, 811; Judgm 185(2), 185(5), 189; Lim of Act 55(3), 55(4), 105(1); Statut 181(1), 181(2), 184, 188.

Finley; Texas Tech University v., TexApp–Amarillo, 223 SW3d 510.—Admin Law 723; App & E 837(1), 893(1); Civil R 1505(2), 1505(3), 1505(4), 1708, 1715; Courts 39; Inj 148(1), 157; Plead 104(1), 111.36.

Finley; U.S. v., CA5 (Tex), 477 F3d 250, cert den 127 SCt 2065, 167 LEd2d 790.—Arrest 71.1(4.1), 71.1(6), 71.1(8); Crim Law 29(8), 369.2(1), 371(1), 371(12), 673(3), 795(1), 795(1.5), 795(1.10), 795(2.1), 795(2.5), 1139, 1152(1), 1153(1), 1169.11; Ind & Inf 189(1); Searches 162, 165.

Finley; U.S. v., CA5 (Tex), 434 F2d 596.—Fed Cts 743; Int Rev 3018, 4501.

Finley; Williams v., TexCivApp–Texarkana, 152 SW2d 468, dism.—Paymt 5; Sales 64; Trial 351.2(4).

Finley; Williams v., TexCivApp–Amarillo, 567 SW2d 611, ref nre.—App & E 719(8); Autos 244(60); Trial 359(1), 359(2).

Finley, Inc. v. Longview Bank & Trust Co., TexApp–Texarkana, 705 SW2d 206. See Jack M. Finley, Inc. v. Longview Bank & Trust Co.

Finn, Ex parte, TexCivApp–Dallas, 615 SW2d 293.—Contempt 20, 23; Divorce 269(1), 269(8), 269(12).

Finn v. Alexander, TexComApp, 163 SW2d 714, 139 Tex 461.—Usury 76, 104, 106.

Finn v. Alexander, TexCivApp–El Paso, 165 SW2d 500, certified question answered 163 SW2d 714, 139 Tex 461. —Attach 25; Bills & N 92(1); Usury 15, 20, 45, 104.

Finn; American Fire & Cas. Co. v., USTex, 71 SCt 534, 341 US 6, 95 LEd 702, 19 ALR2d 738.—Action 1; Courts 23; Fed Cts 3.1, 452, 543.1; Judgm 197; Rem of C 2, 11, 17, 29, 48.1, 48.2, 49, 49.7(4), 58, 61(2), 81, 107(11).

Finn v. American Fire & Cas. Co., CA5 (Tex), 207 F2d 113, cert den 74 SCt 476, 347 US 912, 98 LEd 1069.—Evid 43(2); Fed Cts 825.1; Rem of C 1, 31, 39, 48.1, 48.2.

Finn; American Fire & Cas. Co. v., CA5 (Tex), 181 F2d 845, cert gr 71 SCt 79, 340 US 849, 95 LEd 622, rev 71 SCt 534, 341 US 6, 95 LEd 702, 19 ALR2d 738.—Fed

Civ Proc 2153.1; Fraud 64(1); Insurance 2171, 3015; Rem of C 58, 105.

Finn v. Bond, Tex, 197 SW2d 108, 145 Tex 244.—Divorce 127(3).

Finn; City of Houston v., Tex, 161 SW2d 776, 139 Tex 111.—Estop 62.6; Lim of Act 49(1), 49(2); Mun Corp 243, 249.

Finn; City of Houston v., TexCivApp–Galveston, 149 SW2d 1000, rev 161 SW2d 776, 139 Tex 111.—Estop 62.6, 62.8; Lim of Act 43, 49(2); Mun Corp 247, 249.

Finn v. Finn, TexApp–Dallas, 658 SW2d 735, ref nre.—Child C 942; Divorce 85, 184(12), 221, 249.2, 252.2, 252.3(1), 252.3(2), 252.4, 253(1), 253(3), 286(1), 287; Evid 314(1), 351, 370(1), 382, 555.6(1); Hus & W 249(2.1); Infants 77, 78(7), 83, 115; Pretrial Proc 372, 411.

Finn; Finn v., TexApp–Dallas, 658 SW2d 735, ref nre.—Child C 942; Divorce 85, 184(12), 221, 249.2, 252.2, 252.3(1), 252.3(2), 252.4, 253(1), 253(3), 286(1), 287; Evid 314(1), 351, 370(1), 382, 555.6(1); Hus & W 249(2.1); Infants 77, 78(7), 83, 115; Pretrial Proc 372, 411.

Finn v. Finn, TexCivApp–Dallas, 195 SW2d 679.—Divorce 127(3), 130, 184(6.1); Evid 43(2); Witn 388(3).

Finn; Finn v., TexCivApp–Dallas, 195 SW2d 679.—Divorce 127(3), 130, 184(6.1); Evid 43(2); Witn 388(3).

Finn v. Finn, TexCivApp–Dallas, 185 SW2d 579.—App & E 1175(5); Divorce 12, 13, 27(1), 27(3), 53, 93(1), 93(3), 103, 108, 130, 186.

Finn; Finn v., TexCivApp–Dallas, 185 SW2d 579.—App & E 1175(5); Divorce 12, 13, 27(1), 27(3), 53, 93(1), 93(3), 103, 108, 130, 186.

Finn; First Nat. Bank v., TexCivApp–Galveston, 132 SW2d 151, writ dism.—App & E 179(1); Hus & W 268(9); Insurance 3445.

Finnell; Enterprise Concepts, Inc. v., TexApp–Beaumont, 964 SW2d 348.—Labor & Emp 2375, 2377, 2387(2), 2387(4).

Finnell; Team Mates v., TexApp–Beaumont, 964 SW2d 348. See Enterprise Concepts, Inc. v. Finnell.

Finney; Aetna Cas. & Sur. Co. v., TexCivApp–Texarkana, 346 SW2d 917, ref nre.—Work Comp 1334, 1670, 1696.

Finney v. Baylor Medical Center Grapevine, TexApp–Fort Worth, 792 SW2d 859, writ den.—Judgm 185(4), 185(6), 185.3(13).

Finney; Daniels v., TexCivApp–Galveston, 262 SW2d 431, ref nre.—Evid 571(2), 571(3); Health 696, 800; Mal Pros 25(1), 38, 56, 71(2).

Finney v. Finney, TexCivApp–Fort Worth, 164 SW2d 263, writ refused wom.—App & E 500(1), 500(3), 758.1; Lim of Act 39(7), 178; Mtg 294; Trial 352.12, 355(1).

Finney; Finney v., TexCivApp–Fort Worth, 164 SW2d 263, writ refused wom.—App & E 500(1), 500(3), 758.1; Lim of Act 39(7), 178; Mtg 294; Trial 352.12, 355(1).

Finney v. State, TexApp–Austin, 672 SW2d 559.—Arrest 63.4(1), 63.4(3), 63.5(9), 71.1(5), 71.1(6); Crim Law 99, 394.4(9), 531(3), 777, 867, 1036.1(4), 1158(1), 1169.1(8); Searches 44, 82, 164; Sent & Pun 1379(2).

Finney v. State, TexCivApp–Austin, 308 SW2d 142, ref nre.—Hus & W 151(5).

Finney; Stovall v., TexCivApp–Amarillo, 152 SW2d 887. —App & E 672; Frds St of 110(1), 129(5), 129(11); Judgm 18(2); Tresp to T T 32, 47(1).

Finney; U.S. v., CA5 (Tex), 714 F2d 420.—Crim Law 1159.2(1), 1159.2(7); Postal 35(2), 35(5), 35(6), 35(20), 49(11).

Finnigan v. Blanco County, TexApp–Austin, 670 SW2d 313.—App & E 714(5); Autos 187(1), 187(3); Judgm 185.3(21).

Fino v. McCollum Min. Co., NDTex, 93 FRD 455.—Fed Civ Proc 2738.

Fino v. State, TexCrimApp, 129 SW2d 652, 137 TexCrim 340.—Crim Law 369.2(1), 371(6), 598(6), 1169.3.

Finstad; Rafferty v., TexApp–Houston (1 Dist), 903 SW2d 374, reh overr, and writ den.—Divorce 206, 252.1, 252.2, 253(2), 253(4), 286(5); Trial 388(1), 401.

Finstad; Shearson, Inc. v., TexApp–Houston (1 Dist), 888 SW2d 111. SeeSmith Barney Shearson, Inc. v. Finstad.

Finstad; Smith Barney Shearson, Inc. v., TexApp–Houston (1 Dist), 888 SW2d 111, reh overr.—Alt Disp Res 112, 113, 139, 143, 199, 200, 213(3), 419; App & E 68; Mand 53; Trial 388(1), 388(2).

Finstad; State v., TexApp–Waco, 866 SW2d 815, petition for discretionary review refused.—Crim Law 273.1(4), 275.

Finster v. Metropolitan Life Ins. Co., NDTex, 927 FSupp 201.—Labor & Emp 616, 629(2), 688, 691.

Finster v. State, TexApp–Dallas, 152 SW3d 215.—Crim Law 798(0.5), 814(1), 872.5, 881(1); Ind & Inf 72; Obst Just 16.

Finto v. Texas & N. O. R. Co., TexCivApp–San Antonio, 265 SW2d 606.—App & E 302(3); New Tr 140(3), 157; Trial 351.2(2), 352.4(7).

Fiore; Appell v., CA5 (Tex), 244 F2d 706.—Fed Cts 625; Impl & C C 22, 24.

Fiore v. Fiore, TexApp–Fort Worth, 946 SW2d 436, reh overr, and writ den.—App & E 946, 969, 1035; Jury 32(3), 149.

Fiore; Fiore v., TexApp–Fort Worth, 946 SW2d 436, reh overr, and writ den.—App & E 946, 969, 1035; Jury 32(3), 149.

Fiore v. HCA Health Services of Texas, Inc., TexApp–Fort Worth, 915 SW2d 233, reh overr, and writ den.—App & E 863, 901, 934(1); Const Law 328, 990, 2312, 2314, 2315; Lim of Act 4(2), 55(3), 95(12).

Fiore v. North Hills Medical Center, TexApp–Fort Worth, 915 SW2d 233. See Fiore v. HCA Health Services of Texas, Inc.

Fiorenza v. First City Bank-Central, EDTex, 710 FSupp 1104.—Action 69(5); Civil R 1572, 1575(1); Damag 49.10; Fed Civ Proc 217.

Fiorenza; Tran v., TexApp–Houston (1 Dist), 934 SW2d 740, reh overr, and extension of time to file for writ of error overr.—App & E 169; Const Law 1329, 1340(1); Evid 1, 22(1); Libel 36; Relig Soc 1.

Fiori v. State, TexApp–Dallas, 918 SW2d 532.—Larc 88.

Fire Ass'n of Philadelphia v. Ballard, TexCivApp–Waco, 112 SW2d 532.—Insurance 3256.

Fire Ass'n of Philadelphia v. Coomer, TexCivApp–Waco, 158 SW2d 355.—App & E 1003(6); Estop 110; Insurance 2201, 2202; Judgm 648; Trial 253(5); Witn 336.

Fire Ass'n of Philadelphia v. Da Camara, TexCivApp–San Antonio, 85 SW2d 338.—Evid 185(1), 370(4); Insurance 2165(2), 3571; Trial 81.

Fire Ass'n of Philadelphia; McClendon v., TexCivApp–Amarillo, 278 SW2d 447.—Evid 182, 183(13); Witn 16.

Firebaugh; Granite State Ins. Co. v., TexCivApp–Eastland, 558 SW2d 550, ref nre.—Work Comp 1105.

Fire Dept. of City of Fort Worth v. City of Fort Worth, Tex, 217 SW2d 664, 147 Tex 505.—Admin Law 8, 324, 656, 763, 791; Const Law 2541, 2563, 2564; Mun Corp 176(3.1).

Fire Dept. of City of Fort Worth; City of Fort Worth v., TexCivApp–Fort Worth, 213 SW2d 347, aff in part, rev in part 217 SW2d 664, 147 Tex 505.—Admin Law 8, 656, 754.1, 812; Const Law 2445, 2564; Costs 233; Mun Corp 44, 75, 79, 176(3.1).

Firefighters' and Police Officers' Civil Service Com'n of City of Houston v. Ceazer, TexApp–Houston (14 Dist), 725 SW2d 431, ref nre.—Admin Law 470; Mand 10, 12; Mun Corp 185(4), 198(5).

Firefighters' and Police Officers' Civil Service Com'n of City of Houston; Goode v., TexApp–Houston (1 Dist), 976 SW2d 822, review den, and reh of petition for review overr.—Mun Corp 185(5).

Firefighters' & Police Officers' Civil Service Com'n of City of Houston v. Herrera, TexApp–Houston (1 Dist), 981 SW2d 728, reh overr, and review den.—Admin Law 229; App & E 1008.1(1); Interest 31, 66; Mun Corp 184(1), 197, 199, 216(1), 217.3(5), 1040; Offic 72.70.

Firefighters' and Police Officers' Civil Service Com'n of Mesquite; Moore v., TexApp–Dallas, 809 SW2d 527, writ den.—Admin Law 704; Mun Corp 197, 198(4); Offic 11.7.

Fire Ins. Exchange; Allison v., TexApp–Austin, 98 SW3d 227, reh overr, and reh overr, and petition for review withdrawn (1 pet), and petition for review abated (2 pets), and review gr, judgment vac, and remanded by agreement.—Antitrust 221, 392, 398; App & E 70(6), 930(1), 1024.3, 1043(8); Damag 56.10, 178; Evid 146, 213(1), 508, 535, 555.2, 555.10, 557; Insurance 2103(2), 3256, 3261, 3262, 3263, 3335, 3336, 3337, 3360, 3362, 3375, 3376, 3381(4), 3382, 3571; Neglig 404, 1599, 1661; Statut 227; Venue 5.5, 7(2), 45.

Fire Ins. Exchange; Gallagher v., Tex, 950 SW2d 370, on remand 980 SW2d 833, review den.—App & E 654.

Fire Ins. Exchange; Gallagher v., TexApp–San Antonio, 980 SW2d 833, review den.—App & E 163, 230, 231(9), 232(3); 946, 969, 1067; Insurance 3579; Trial 350.4(3).

Fire Ins. Exchange; Gallagher v., TexApp–San Antonio, 950 SW2d 379, writ gr, rev 950 SW2d 370, on remand 980 SW2d 833, review den.—App & E 557, 638.

Fire Ins. Exchange; Insurance Co. of North America v., TexCivApp–Waco, 525 SW2d 44, ref nre.—Insurance 2193, 3530.

Fire Ins. Exchange; Insurance Co. of North America v., TexCivApp–Waco, 508 SW2d 703.—Plead 111.5; Pretrial Proc 480.

Fire Ins. Exchange; Insurance Co. of North America v., TexCivApp–Eastland, 590 SW2d 642, ref nre.—Insurance 3523(3).

Fire Ins. Exchange; Maida v., TexApp–Fort Worth, 990 SW2d 836.—App & E 235, 758.3(1), 758.3(3), 852, 962; Pretrial Proc 583, 584, 587, 593, 594.1.

Fire Ins. Exchange; Murrah v., CA5 (Tex), 480 F2d 613. —Fed Civ Proc 1759.

Fire Ins. Exchange; Paulson v., Tex, 393 SW2d 316.—Insurance 2199, 2201.

Fire Ins. Exchange v. Paulson, TexCivApp–San Antonio, 381 SW2d 199, aff as reformed 393 SW2d 316.—Insurance 2142(5), 2199, 2201.

Fire Ins. Exchange v. Sullivan, TexApp–Houston (14 Dist), 192 SW3d 99, review den.—Antitrust 221, 389(2), 397; Insurance 2199, 3337, 3360, 3374, 3585; Judgm 199(1), 199(3.13), 199(5), 256(1), 256(2); Stip 14(12); Trial 350.1, 350.4(3), 351.2(2), 352.3.

Fire Ins. Exchange; Trahan v., TexApp–Beaumont, 179 SW3d 669.—Contracts 221(2), 326; Insurance 1808, 1822, 1863, 3171, 3335, 3336, 3342, 3360; Judgm 185.3(12).

Fire Ins. Exchange; Wessinger v., TexApp–Dallas, 949 SW2d 834.—Insurance 2115, 2275.

Fireman's and Policeman's Civil Service Com'n of City of Houston; Lindsey v., TexApp–Houston (14 Dist), 980 SW2d 233, reh overr, and review den.—Mun Corp 185(12), 216(2).

Fireman's Fund Agribusiness, Inc.; Tucker v., SDTex, 365 FSupp2d 821.—Alt Disp Res 181, 201; Insurance 3140, 3268, 3293, 3324(3).

Fireman's Fund Am. Ins. Co. v. Patterson & Lamberty, Inc., TexCivApp–Tyler, 528 SW2d 67, ref nre.—App & E 204(4), 863; Atty & C 107, 129(2), 129(4); Judgm 181(2); Plead 307.

Fireman's Fund Am. Ins. Co.; Vickers v., TexCivApp–Waco, 445 SW2d 530, writ dism.—Venue 7.5(4).

Fireman's Fund County Mut. Ins. Co. v. Hidi, Tex, 13 SW3d 767.—Insurance 1203, 2688; Statut 181(1), 195.

Fireman's Fund Indem. Co. v. Boyle General Tire Co., Tex, 392 SW2d 352.—Insurance 1635, 1640, 1766, 1883, 1892; Princ & A 178(1), 179(0.5), 179(2).

Fireman's Fund Indem. Co. v. Boyle General Tire Co., TexCivApp–Waco, 381 SW2d 937, aff as reformed 392 SW2d 352.—App & E 882(8); Insurance 1606; Lim of Act 100(12); Princ & A 23(2), 123(1); Ref of Inst 20, 45(14).

Fireman's Fund Indem. Co. v. Hopkins, TexCivApp–San Antonio, 119 SW2d 394.—Work Comp 877, 1930.

Fireman's Fund Ins. Co. v. Abilene Livestock Auction Co., TexCivApp–Dallas, 391 SW2d 147, ref nre.—Bonds 50; Contracts 346(2); Fact 2.5.

Fireman's Fund Ins. Co.; Bybee v., Tex, 331 SW2d 910, 160 Tex 429.—App & E 23; Courts 121(2), 247(1), 247(7); Insurance 3360.

Fireman's Fund Ins. Co. v. Bybee, TexCivApp–Eastland, 322 SW2d 657, writ gr, and order set aside, writ dism 331 SW2d 910, 160 Tex 429.—Judgm 544, 724.

Fireman's Fund Ins. Co. v. Commercial Standard Ins. Co., Tex, 490 SW2d 818.—App & E 926(3), 1043(6); Compromise 15(1), 17(2); Indem 30(1), 30(5), 42, 100, 102; Pretrial Proc 471, 472, 473, 483.

Fireman's Fund Ins. Co. v. Commercial Standard Ins. Co., TexCivApp–Eastland, 478 SW2d 811, writ gr, aff 490 SW2d 818.—Indem 33(5), 111; Pretrial Proc 479.

Fireman's Fund Ins. Co.; Damron v., TexCivApp–Amarillo, 430 SW2d 956.—Action 56, 57(4), 60; App & E 837(4), 927(7), 949; Insurance 3054(1).

Fireman's Fund Ins. Co.; Fourticq v., TexApp–Dallas, 679 SW2d 562.—App & E 1178(6); Contracts 47, 82; Guar 1, 16(1), 16(2), 16(3); Indem 27; Stip 1, 14(1).

Fireman's Fund Ins. Co.; Gundle Lining Const. Corp. v., SDTex, 844 FSupp 1163.—Fed Cts 101, 103, 104, 105, 106, 144.

Fireman's Fund Ins. Co. v. Harris, TexCivApp–Waco, 475 SW2d 325, writ gr.—Insurance 3559; Venue 22(7).

Fireman's Fund Ins. Co.; Hofland v., TexApp–Corpus Christi, 907 SW2d 597, reh overr.—App & E 842(2), 852; Contracts 143(2), 143.5, 147(3), 152, 176(1), 176(2); Insurance 1808, 2278(11), 2278(13).

Fireman's Fund Ins. Co.; Insurance Co. of North America v., TexCivApp–Hous (1 Dist), 471 SW2d 878, ref nre.—Insurance 2168, 2247(1).

Fireman's Fund Ins. Co.; Jekel v., CA5 (Tex), 318 F2d 321.—Fed Cts 354.

Fireman's Fund Ins. Co. v. Jekel, WDTex, 214 FSupp 27, rev 318 F2d 321.—Fed Cts 354, 356.

Fireman's Fund Ins. Co. v. Leopold, TexCivApp–Galveston, 84 SW2d 840, writ dism.—Evid 448; Insurance 1796, 1812.

Fireman's Fund Ins. Co. v. McDaniel, TexCivApp, 327 SW2d 358.—Abate & R 9; Action 60; App & E 833(5); Const Law 655, 1033, 3453; Corp 637, 666; Courts 89, 92; Evid 65; Parties 51(2), 51(4); Plead 110, 409(1); Venue 2, 16 1/2, 22(4), 22(7), 22(10).

Fireman's Fund Ins. Co. v. Martinez, TexCivApp–Austin, 387 SW2d 443, ref nre.—App & E 281(1), 300, 345.1, 863; Judgm 199(3.2); New Tr 118; Trial 178; Work Comp 1492, 1639, 1653, 1969.

Fireman's Fund Ins. Co. v. Murchison, CA5 (Tex), 937 F2d 204.—Antitrust 143(2), 367; Contracts 143(2), 153, 168, 176(2); Fed Civ Proc 2264.1, 2470, 2492; Fed Cts 776; Indem 31(1), 33(1); Prine & S 175; Torts 433.

Fireman's Fund Ins. Co. v. Reynolds, TexCivApp–Waco, 85 SW2d 826, writ refused.—App & E 544(1); Insurance 2959, 3072, 3084, 3182, 3184.

Fireman's Fund Ins. Co.; Weeks Marine, Inc. v., CA5 (Tex), 340 F3d 233, reh den.—Princ & S 59, 81, 162(2).

Fireman's Fund Ins. Co.; Wilburn Boat Co. v., USTex, 75 SCt 368, 348 US 310, 99 LEd 337, reh den 75 SCt 575, 349 US 907, 99 LEd 1243.—Adm 1.6, 1.20(1), 1.20(2), 10(4); Fed Cts 504.1; Insurance 2996, 3057.

Fireman's Fund Ins. Co. v. Wilburn Boat Co., CA5 (Tex), 300 F2d 631, cert den 82 SCt 1562, 370 US 925, 8 LEd2d 505, reh den 83 SCt 17, 371 US 854, 9 LEd2d 92.—Insurance 2952, 2956, 2958, 2964, 2985, 2996, 3013, 3052, 3059, 3554.

Fireman's Fund Ins. Co. v. Wilburn Boat Co., CA5 (Tex), 259 F2d 662, cert den 79 SCt 607, 359 US 925, 3 LEd2d 628, reh den 79 SCt 873, 359 US 976, 3 LEd2d 843.—Evid 48; Fed Cts 944; Insurance 1091(1), 2991, 3052, 3057; Trial 39.

Fireman's Fund Ins. Co.; Wilburn Boat Co. v., CA5 (Tex), 201 F2d 833, cert gr 74 SCt 674, 347 US 950, 98 LEd 1097, rev 75 SCt 368, 348 US 310, 99 LEd 337, reh den 75 SCt 575, 349 US 907, 99 LEd 1243.—Adm 1.5, 1.11, 1.20(1), 1.20(2), 2, 4; Insurance 1809, 3052, 3059, 3085, 3104, 3120.

Fireman's Fund Ins. Co.; Wilburn Boat Co. v., EDTex, 199 FSupp 784, rev 300 F2d 631, cert den 82 SCt 1562, 370 US 925, 8 LEd2d 505, reh den 83 SCt 17, 371 US 854, 9 LEd2d 92.—Insurance 1091(1), 1606, 2996, 3052, 3057, 3059.

Fireman's Fund Ins. Co. of Cal.; First Prize v., TexCivApp–Galveston, 269 SW2d 939, ref nre.—Bills & N 134; Sales 21, 197.

Fireman's Fund Ins. Co. of San Francisco, Cal. v. Honnoll, TexCivApp–Waco, 128 SW2d 96.—App & E 1003(5), 1003(9.1); Evid 588.

Fireman's Fund Ins. Co. of San Francisco, Cal. v. Joseph, TexCivApp–Amarillo, 92 SW2d 518.—Insurance 1744, 1766.

Fireman's Fund Ins. Co. of Texas v. Jackson Hill Marina, Inc., TexApp–Tyler, 704 SW2d 131, ref nre.—Insurance 3072, 3089; Mtg 532; Sec Tran 230.

Fireman's Fun McGee v. Landstar Ranger, Inc., SDTex, 250 FSupp2d 684.—Carr 134, 159(2).

Fireman's Ins. Co. of Newark, N.J.; Smith v., TexCivApp–Houston, 398 SW2d 435.—Labor & Emp 30; Work Comp 351.

Fireman's Ins. Co. of Newark, N. J. v. Weatherman, TexCivApp–Eastland, 193 SW2d 247, ref nre.—Evid 8; Insurance 2732, 2733, 3579; Trial 351.2(1.1).

Firemen's Relief and Retirement Fund Trustees of City of Austin; Stewartv., TexCivApp–Austin, 489 SW2d 743.—App & E 353, 428(2).

Firemen and Policemen's Pension Fund, Bd. of Trustees of San Antonio v. Cruz, TexCivApp–San Antonio, 458 SW2d 700, ref nre.—Mun Corp 187(2).

Firemen and Policemen's Pension Fund Bd. of Trustees of San Antonio v. Guerrero, TexCivApp–San Antonio, 395 SW2d 397, ref nre.—Mun Corp 187(9), 187(10).

Firemen and Policemen's Pension Fund Bd. of Trustees of San Antonio v. Villareal, TexCivApp–San Antonio, 438 SW2d 387, ref nre.—Mun Corp 200(5), 200(9); Work Comp 949.

Firemen and Policemen's Pension Fund Bd. of Trustees of San Antonio, Tex. v. Lott, TexApp–San Antonio, 742 SW2d 730, writ den, cert den 109 SCt 312, 488 US 927, 102 LEd2d 331.—Courts 489(1).

Firemen's and Policemen's Civil Service Com'n v. Brinkmeyer, Tex, 662 SW2d 953.—Admin Law 758, 760, 786, 791; Mun Corp 185(10), 185(12); Offic 72.51.

Firemen's and Policemen's Civil Service Commission; International Ass'n of Firefighters, Local 883 v., TexCivApp–Tyler, 554 SW2d 814.—Inj 9, 118(2), 126; Judgm 181(2).

Firemen's and Policemen's Civil Service Com'n v. Kennedy, TexCivApp–Fort Worth, 502 SW2d 559, ref nre, and writ gr, rev Firemen's and Policemen's Civil Service Commission of City of Fort Worth v. Kennedy, 514 SW2d 237.—Inj 132; Mun Corp 182, 185(12), 198(4).

Firemen's and Policemen's Civil Service Commission; Scholl v., TexCivApp–Corpus Christi, 520 SW2d 470.—Action 6; Const Law 2600; Decl Judgm 392.1, 395.

Firemen's and Policemen's Civil Service Commission v. Wells, Tex, 306 SW2d 895, 157 Tex 644.—Courts 107; Mun Corp 187(2), 187(9), 200(2), 200(9).

Firemen's and Policemen's Civil Service Com'n, City of Austin v. Burnham, TexApp–Austin, 715 SW2d 809, writ den, cert den 109 SCt 112, 488 US 842, 102 LEd2d 86.—Crim Law 394.1(2); Mun Corp 185(1), 189(1); Offic 65, 66.

Firemen's and Policemen's Civil Service Commission for City of Corpus Christi v. Campbell, TexCivApp–Hous (1 Dist), 616 SW2d 424.—Judgm 544; Mun Corp 197.

Firemen's and Policemen's Civil Service Commission of City of Beaumont; Stafford v., TexCivApp–Beaumont, 355 SW2d 555.—Mun Corp 185(1), 185(10), 185(12).

Firemen's and Policemen's Civil Service Commission of City of Denton; Matheson v., TexCivApp–Fort Worth, 587 SW2d 795.—Const Law 4169; Mun Corp 184.1.

Firemen's and Policemen's Civil Service Commission of City of Fort Worth v. Blanchard, Tex, 582 SW2d 778.—Admin Law 651; Mun Corp 185(12), 216(1).

Firemen's and Policemen's Civil Service Commission of City of Fort Worth; Blanchard v., TexCivApp–Fort Worth, 577 SW2d 337, rev 582 SW2d 778.—Const Law 4172(3); Mun Corp 185(12), 185(14).

Firemen's and Policemen's Civil Service Commission of City of Fort Worth; Crain v., TexCivApp–Fort Worth, 495 SW2d 20, ref nre.—Equity 39(1), 65(1); Inj 34, 57, 114(1), 135, 138.69, 142; Mun Corp 104, 197.

Firemen's and Policemen's Civil Service Commission of City of Fort Worth v. Kennedy, Tex, 514 SW2d 237. —Admin Law 656; Mun Corp 184(2), 216(1), 217.3(1).

Firemen's and Policemen's Civil Service Commission of City of Ft. Worth v. Lockhart, Tex, 626 SW2d 492. —Mun Corp 185(7), 185(9), 185(10).

Firemen's and Policemen's Civil Service Commission of City of Fort Worth; Lockhart v., TexCivApp–Fort Worth, 616 SW2d 426, writ gr, rev 626 SW2d 492.— Const Law 2488, 2490; Mun Corp 185(14); Statut 190.

Firemen's and Policemen's Civil Service Commission of City of Ft. Worth v. Williams, Tex, 531 SW2d 327. —Mun Corp 217.3(1).

Firemen's and Policemen's Civil Service Commission of City of Ft. Worth v. Williams, TexCivApp–Fort Worth, 518 SW2d 615, writ gr, rev 531 SW2d 327.— Mun Corp 217.3(5); Offic 11.4.

Firemen's and Policemen's Civil Service Com'n of City of Galveston v. Bonds, TexApp–Houston (14 Dist), 666 SW2d 242, dism.—Admin Law 744.1, 791; Const Law 4172(3); Mun Corp 185(10).

Firemen's & Policemen's Civil Service Com'n of City of Laredo v. Martinez, Tex, 645 SW2d 431.—Mun Corp 185(6).

Firemen's & Policemen's Civil Service Com'n of City of Laredo v. Martinez, TexCivApp–San Antonio, 643 SW2d 770, rev 645 SW2d 431.—Mun Corp 185(11).

Firemen's and Policemen's Civil Service Commission of City of Lubbock; Taylor v., Tex, 616 SW2d 187.— Mun Corp 184.1, 197; Statut 188, 206, 215.

Firemen's and Policemen's Civil Service Commission of City of Lubbock v. Taylor, TexCivApp–Eastland, 607 SW2d 631, rev 616 SW2d 187.—Mun Corp 184.1, 197; Statut 181(1).

Firemen's and Policemen's Civil Service Commission of City of Port Arthur v. Hamman, Tex, 404 SW2d 308.—Const Law 4172(3); Mun Corp 185(7), 185(12), 216(1).

Firemen's and Policemen's Civil Service Commission of City of Port Arthur v. Hamman, TexCivApp–Beaumont, 393 SW2d 406, writ gr, aff in part, rev in part 404 SW2d 308.—Const Law 2450; Jury 19(12); Mun Corp 185(7), 185(8), 185(10), 185(12).

Firemen's and Policemen's Civil Service Commission of City of San Antonio; Bolieu v., TexCivApp–San Antonio, 330 SW2d 234, ref nre.—Evid 150; Mun Corp 198(2), 198(3).

Firemen's and Policemen's Civil Service Commission of City of San Antonio; Lombardino v., TexCivApp–San Antonio, 310 SW2d 651, ref nre.—Evid 82, 272, 313; Judges 49(2); Mun Corp 185(3), 185(10).

Firemen's and Policemen's Civil Service Commission of City of San Antonio v. Rodriguez, TexCivApp–San Antonio, 326 SW2d 624.—Mun Corp 197.

Firemen's and Policemen's Civil Service Commission of City of San Antonio v. Shaw, TexCivApp–San Antonio, 306 SW2d 160, ref nre.—Admin Law 791; Mun Corp 185(10), 185(12).

Firemen's and Policemen's Civil Service Commission of City of San Antonio v. Wells, TexCivApp–San Antonio, 300 SW2d 676, rev 306 SW2d 895, 157 Tex 644. —Mun Corp 184(1), 187(1), 187(8.1); Statut 223.2(21).

Firemen's and Policemen's Civil Service Commission of Galveston; Jacksonv., TexCivApp–Hous (1 Dist), 466 SW2d 412, ref nre.—Mun Corp 197, 198(2); Offic 27.

Firemen's and Policemen's Civil Service Commission of Houston v. Tinsley, TexCivApp–Texarkana, 304 SW2d 435, ref nre.—Mun Corp 185(2), 185(9), 185(10).

Firemen's and Policemen's Civil Service Commission of San Antonio; Cusson v., TexCivApp–San Antonio, 524 SW2d 88.—Admin Law 749, 750, 788; Mun Corp 185(10), 218(9); Witn 397.

Firemen's and Policemen's Civil Service Commission of San Antonio; Lee v., TexCivApp–San Antonio, 526 SW2d 553, ref nre.—Admin Law 654.1, 655, 656; Const Law 2406; Mun Corp 197.

Firemen's and Policemen's Civil Service Commission of Temple; Bartek v., TexCivApp–Tyler, 584 SW2d 358.—Admin Law 651, 656; Mun Corp 185(12), 198(4), 218(9).

Firemen's and Policemen's Civil Service Com'n of Wichita Falls; Collier v., TexApp–Fort Worth, 817 SW2d 404, writ den.—Const Law 3594; Mun Corp 67(1), 197.

Firemen's Fund Indem. Co.; Stahl v., TexCivApp–Waco, 295 SW2d 473.—Work Comp 8, 876, 893, 1492.

Firemen's Ins. Co. v. Alexander, TexCivApp–Waco, 328 SW2d 350, 74 ALR2d 750, ref nre.—App & E 173(2), 269, 596, 1097(1); Insurance 2201.

Firemen's Ins. Co.; Alexander v., TexCivApp–Waco, 317 SW2d 752.—Evid 9; Insurance 2155(1), 2199, 2202.

Firemen's Ins. Co.; Marine Supply Corp. v., SDTex, 227 FSupp 635.—Frds St of 131(1); Insurance 2136(4); Interest 31, 44; Land & Ten 101, 112.5; Tender 15(1).

Firemen's Ins. Co. of Newark, N.J. v. Board of Regents of University of Texas System, TexApp–Austin, 909 SW2d 540, reh overr, and writ den.—App & E 842(2), 863; Colleges 5; Const Law 2312; Em Dom 2(1), 2(9), 285; Plead 104(1); States 191.9(1).

Firemen's Ins. Co. of Newark, N.J. v. Burch, TexApp–Austin, 426 SW2d 306, writ gr, aff in part, rev in part 442 SW2d 331.—Debtor & C 12; Hus & W 268(9); Insurance 2661, 2740, 2755.

Firemen's Ins. Co. of Newark, N.J.; F.D.I.C. v., CA5 (Tex), 109 F3d 1084.—Fed Cts 412.1, 766, 776; Insurance 1806, 1822, 1832(1), 1832(2), 2103(1), 2406(3).

Firemen's Ins. Co. of Newark, N.J. v. Universal Credit Co., TexCivApp–Eastland, 85 SW2d 1061.—Evid 314(1), 593; Insurance 2706(1), 2730, 3013.

Firemen's Ins. Co. of Newark, N. J. v. Burch, Tex, 442 SW2d 331.—Const Law 2600, 2604; Decl Judgm 65, 66, 68, 169.

Firemen's Ins. Co. of Newark, N. J.; Johnson v., TexCivApp–Eastland, 398 SW2d 318.—Work Comp 1069, 1075, 1079, 1094, 1114.

Firemen's Pension Com'n v. Jones, TexApp–Austin, 939 SW2d 730, reh overr.—Admin Law 651, 796; App & E

185(1); Const Law 2351, 2623; Mun Corp 200(7), 200(10); States 191.5; Statut 219(1), 219(4), 223.4, 270, 276(1), 277.

Firemen's Pension Com'r; Board of Trustees of Big Spring Firemen's Relief and Retirement Fund v., TexApp–Austin, 808 SW2d 608.—Admin Law 5, 513, 744.1; Mun Corp 200(10).

Firemen's Relief and Retirement Fund Trustees of Houston; Cline v., TexCivApp–Beaumont, 545 SW2d 895, ref nre.—Admin Law 476, 741, 793; Interest 39(2.20); Mun Corp 200(9), 200(10).

Firemen's Relief and Retirement Fund Trustees of Houston v. Fontenot, TexCivApp–Austin, 446 SW2d 365, ref nre.—Mun Corp 200(9), 200(10); Pretrial Proc 474, 479.

Firence Footwear Co. v. Campbell, TexCivApp–Houston, 411 SW2d 636, ref nre.—App & E 493, 865; Appear 8(8); Judgm 101(2), 162(2), 518.

Firence Footwear Co. v. Campbell, TexCivApp–Houston, 406 SW2d 516, opinion adhered to on reh 411 SW2d 636, ref nre.—App & E 361(3); Hus & W 260, 270(1), 270(5).

Fireplaceman, Inc.; Vanguard Investments v., TexApp–Houston (14 Dist), 641 SW2d 655, ref nre.—Partners 204, 375.

Fireside Enterprises, Inc.; Gilbert v., TexCivApp–Dallas, 611 SW2d 869.—Judgm 585(3), 634, 713(2), 720, 724.

Fires Out, Inc.; Emerson v., TexApp–Austin, 735 SW2d 492.—App & E 302(1), 954(1), 954(2); Decl Judgm 258; Inj 138.21, 147.

Firestone v. Claycombe & King, TexApp–Dallas, 875 SW2d 727, reh den, and writ den, appeal after remand 1996 WL 479641, writ den.—Pretrial Proc 44.1.

Firestone v. Firestone, TexCivApp–Dallas, 567 SW2d 889.—Divorce 255; Hus & W 278(2).

Firestone; Firestone v., TexCivApp–Dallas, 567 SW2d 889.—Divorce 255; Hus & W 278(2).

Firestone v. Hall, TexCivApp–Fort Worth, 143 SW2d 797.—App & E 78(1), 704.1; Mand 4(1), 53; Trial 356(1).

Firestone; Runnells v., TexApp–Houston (14 Dist), 746 SW2d 845, writ den with per curiam opinion 760 SW2d 240.—Action 6; App & E 758.3(9); Child S 114; Contracts 176(1); Courts 12(2.1), 12(2.25), 12(2.30).

Firestone v. Sims, TexCivApp–Fort Worth, 174 SW2d 279, writ refused.—App & E 758.3(11), 931(1); Deeds 196(3), 211(4); Evid 54, 571(2), 595; Hus & W 137(1); Trusts 89(1); Wills 163(2), 166(1), 166(8); Witn 130, 178(1).

Firestone Photographs, Inc. v. Lamaster, TexCivApp–Texarkana, 567 SW2d 273.—App & E 684(1), 961; Pretrial Proc 17.1, 24, 44.1, 221.

Firestone Service Stores v. Darden, TexCivApp–San Antonio, 96 SW2d 316.—Accession 2.

Firestone Steel Products Co. v. Barajas, Tex, 927 SW2d 608.—Consp 1.1, 6, 13; Neglig 202; Prod Liab 1, 11, 14, 23.1, 36, 37, 39, 87.1; Torts 109, 148.

Firestone Steel Products Co.; Barajas v., TexApp–Corpus Christi, 895 SW2d 789, reh overr, and writ gr, rev 927 SW2d 608.—App & E 863, 934(1); Judgm 181(33), 185(2), 185.3(21); Neglig 202; Prod Liab 5, 8, 23.1.

Firestone Stores, Division of Firestone Tire & Rubber Co.; Williams v., TexCivApp–Eastland, 438 SW2d 645. —Autos 264.

Firestone Synthetic Rubber & Latex Co. v. Marshall, EDTex, 507 FSupp 1330.—Admin Law 382.1, 413, 416.1; Civil R 1055, 1302, 1421.

Firestone Synthetic Rubber & Latex Co., Division of Firestone Tire & Rubber Co. v. Potter, CA5 (Tex), 400 F2d 897.—Labor & Emp 2026.

Firestone Tire & Rubber Co. v. Battle, TexApp–Houston (1 Dist), 745 SW2d 909, writ den.—App & E 207; Damag 130.1, 132(8), 134(3); Plead 149; Prod Liab 14, 77.5, 81.5, 83.5; Trial 216, 260(8), 314(1).

Firestone Tire & Rubber Co. v. Blacksher, TexCivApp–El Paso, 477 SW2d 338.—Autos 192(1), 244(22.1), 244(26).

Firestone Tire & Rubber Co.; Bowers v., CA5 (Tex), 832 F2d 64.—Compromise 15(1).

Firestone Tire & Rubber Co.; Bowers v., CA5 (Tex), 800 F2d 474, appeal after remand 832 F2d 64.—Fed Civ Proc 2215; Fed Cts 615; Interest 66; Prod Liab 83.5.

Firestone Tire and Rubber Co. v. Bullock, Tex, 573 SW2d 498.—Statut 219(1); Tax 3704.

Firestone Tire & Rubber Co.; Bullock v., TexCivApp–Austin, 561 SW2d 596, writ gr, rev 573 SW2d 498.—Statut 181(1), 212.4, 212.6; Tax 3627, 3645, 3677.

Firestone Tire & Rubber Co.; Burks v., CA5 (Tex), 633 F2d 1152.—Fed Cts 388.1, 621; Prod Liab 8, 96.5.

Firestone Tire & Rubber Co. v. Chipman, TexCivApp–San Antonio, 194 SW2d 609.—App & E 1177(6); Contracts 143(1); Plead 111.42(8); Stip 14(10).

Firestone Tire & Rubber Co. v. Fisk Tire Co., TexCom-App, 113 SW2d 175, 131 Tex 158.—Contracts 187(5); Evid 441(9).

Firestone Tire & Rubber Co.; Fisk Tire Co. v., TexCivApp–Amarillo, 143 SW2d 828.—App & E 1010.1(3); Contracts 28(3).

Firestone Tire & Rubber Co. v. Fisk Tire Co., TexCivApp–Amarillo, 87 SW2d 794, rev 113 SW2d 175, 131 Tex 158.—Corp 399(7), 432(12); Evid 443(2).

Firestone Tire & Rubber Co.; Gonzalez v., CA5 (Tex), 610 F2d 241, on remand 512 FSupp 1101.—Civil R 1106, 1379, 1395(8), 1505(4), 1505(7), 1513, 1523, 1530; Fed Civ Proc 1758.1, 1788.6, 1824; Fed Cts 425, 818; Lim of Act 105(2).

Firestone Tire & Rubber Co.; Gonzalez v., EDTex, 512 FSupp 1101.—Civil R 1141, 1142, 1530.

Firestone Tire & Rubber Co. v. Happy Motor Co., TexCivApp–Amarillo, 152 SW2d 778.—Lim of Act 148(2), 149(1).

Firestone Tire & Rubber Co.; Jackson v., CA5 (Tex), 788 F2d 1070.—Evid 146; Fed Civ Proc 2141, 2173.1(1), 2182.1; Fed Cts 866; Neglig 213; Prod Liab 81.1, 81.5, 96.5.

Firestone Tire & Rubber Co.; Jackson v., CA5 (Tex), 779 F2d 1047, opinion vac 788 F2d 1070.

Firestone Tire & Rubber Co.; Malinak v., TexCivApp–Hous (1 Dist), 436 SW2d 210, ref nre.—Evid 5(2); Prod Liab 77.5, 83.5, 88.5.

Firestone Tire & Rubber Co.; Moon v., TexApp–Houston (14 Dist), 742 SW2d 792, writ den.—New Tr 44(2), 56, 143(2).

Firestone Tire & Rubber Co. v. N. L. R. B., CA5 (Tex), 449 F2d 511.—Labor & Emp 1440, 1451, 1455(6), 1457(3), 1461(4), 1749.

Firestone Tire & Rubber Co.; Price v., TexApp–Dallas, 700 SW2d 730.—App & E 863, 962; Courts 78; Pretrial Proc 583, 587, 697, 699.

Firestone Tire & Rubber Co. v. Rhodes, TexCivApp–Austin, 256 SW2d 448, ref nre.—App & E 1048(5); Autos 168(4), 201(1.1), 201(2), 201(6), 244(2.1), 244(35), 244(36.1), 245(39), 245(50.1); Damag 185(1); Evid 123(11), 244(11); Neglig 213.

Firestone Tire & Rubber Co.; Thomas v., NDTex, 392 FSupp 373.—Civil R 1041, 1118, 1166, 1177, 1234.

Firestone Tire and Rubber Co.; Turner v., EDTex, 896 FSupp 651.—Atty & C 21.10, 21.15.

Firestone Tire & Rubber Co. v. White, TexCivApp–Dallas, 274 SW2d 452.—Accord 11(1), 26(3); App & E 1177(7); Compromise 23(3).

Firman Leather Goods Corp. v. McDonald & Shaw, TexCivApp–El Paso, 217 SW2d 137.—App & E 436, 440; Judgm 17(1); Proc 24.

Firo, Ex parte, TexCrimApp, 815 SW2d 568, reh den.—Sent & Pun 1350.

Firo v. State, TexCrimApp, 657 SW2d 141.—Crim Law 1170.5(1); Witn 283.

Firo v. State, TexCrimApp, 272 SW2d 370, 160 TexCrim 469.—Homic 999.

Firo v. State, TexApp–Corpus Christi, 885 SW2d 534, petition for discretionary review refused.—Crim Law 1166(12).

Firo v. State, TexApp–Corpus Christi, 878 SW2d 254, reh overr, and petition for discretionary review refused, opinion supplemented 885 SW2d 534, petition for discretionary review refused.—Crim Law 625.15, 663, 670, 1043(1), 1166(12).

Firo v. State, TexApp–Corpus Christi, 654 SW2d 503, aff 657 SW2d 141.—Crim Law 517.2(2), 535(1), 562, 680(1), 867, 1043(3), 1137(5), 1144.13(2.1), 1153(3), 1169.5(1), 1169.5(2), 1170.5(3), 1170.5(5); Homic 1186; Witn 319, 349.

Firo v. U.S., CA5 (Tex), 367 F2d 159.—Crim Law 627.10(1); Ind & Inf 130; Sent & Pun 645.

Firo v. U.S., CA5 (Tex), 340 F2d 597, cert den 85 SCt 1568, 381 US 929, 14 LEd2d 687.—Crim Law 627.10(1), 1478, 1505; Ind & Inf 201.

First v. State, TexCrimApp, 846 SW2d 836, reh den.—Const Law 4705, 4745; Sent & Pun 312, 323, 1626, 1667, 1675, 1750, 1757, 1780(3).

First Aircraft Leasing, Ltd. v. Bexar Appraisal Dist., TexApp–San Antonio, 48 SW3d 218, review den.—Statut 181(2), 189, 206, 208; Tax 2188, 2212, 2214, 2288.

First Alief Bank v. White, Tex, 682 SW2d 251.—Attach 295; Judgm 297, 340; Parties 42.

First American Bank; Volkswagen Credit, Inc. v., SDTex, 957 FSupp 103.—Costs 194.32, 194.40; Decl Judgm 1, 255.

First American Bank, Bryan, Tex.; Lester v., TexApp–Waco, 866 SW2d 361, writ den.—Const Law 2760; Courts 89, 92; Judgm 181(25); Mtg 330; States 4.1(1).

First American Title Co. of El Paso v. Prata, TexApp–El Paso, 783 SW2d 697, writ den.—Abate & R 7; Antitrust 199, 209; App & E 1175(1); Const Law 2600; Em Dom 1; Insurance 1576, 3426; Ven & Pur 129(1), 130(2).

First American Title Ins. Co. v. Adams, TexApp–Corpus Christi, 829 SW2d 356, reh overr, and writ den.—App & E 154(1), 154(4), 231(9), 232(3); Ease 61(9 1/2); Judgm 71.1, 72; Nav War 36(1), 37(2), 37(8); Pub Lands 176(1), 176(2); States 85, 89; Trial 136(3), 278, 279, 350.2.

First American Title Ins. Co. v. Strayhorn, TexApp–Austin, 169 SW3d 298, review den, and review gr, and withdrawn, and reh of petition for review gr.—App & E 70(8), 93, 854(1), 856(1), 893(1), 1175(1); Const Law 228.5, 990, 3355, 3560; Dep & Escr 13; Insurance 1171, 1625; Statut 176, 188, 206, 212.1, 219(1), 219(4), 219(5), 223.2(1.1); Tax 2033, 2243, 2705, 2762.

First American Title Ins. Co.; Zimmerman v., TexApp–Tyler, 790 SW2d 690, writ den.—Abstr of T 3; Antitrust 141, 147, 148, 150, 251, 292; App & E 901, 927(7), 989, 997(3); Dep & Escr 13; Elect of Rem 7(1); Estop 52.10(2); Lim of Act 13, 100(13), 197(2); Plead 53(1), 93(1); Ven & Pur 229(1).

First American Title Ins. Co. of Texas; Koenig v., TexApp–Houston (14 Dist), 209 SW3d 870.—Adv Poss 19, 31; Insurance 2618, 2935.

First American Title Ins. Co. of Texas; Rose v., TexApp–Corpus Christi, 907 SW2d 639.—App & E 852, 863; Damag 50.10; Judgm 185(2), 185(6); Libel 36, 38(1), 51(2); Proc 168.

First American Title Ins. Co. of Texas v. Willard, TexApp–Tyler, 949 SW2d 342, reh overr, and reh overr, and writ den.—Abstr of T 3; Antitrust 161, 221; App & E 878(4), 882(1), 1180(2); Costs 194.10, 194.40; Fraud 20; Insurance 1013, 1864, 2626, 3365, 3421, 3424(1); Plead 34(1); Tresp 46(1), 56.

First Am. Life Ins. Co. v. Slaughter, TexCivApp–Houston, 400 SW2d 590, ref nre.—App & E 281(1); Costs 241; Insurance 1652(1); Judgm 198, 199(3.11), 199(3.14).

First Assembly of God Church of Cleburne; Brooks v., TexApp–Waco, 86 SW3d 793, reh overr, and review dism.—App & E 863; Judgm 181(33), 185.3(21); Neglig 1001, 1014, 1033, 1706.

First Assembly of God, Inc. v. Texas Utilities Elec. Co., TexApp–Dallas, 52 SW3d 482.—App & E 863, 934(1); Electricity 16(1), 16(5), 19(5); Judgm 185(2), 185(5); Neglig 202, 218, 234, 273, 372, 375, 379, 380, 387, 421, 422, 1675, 1692, 1713; Pub Ut 103, 119.1, 184.

First Austin Co.; Thompson v., TexApp–Fort Worth, 572 SW2d 80, ref nre.—Bills & N 139(1), 139(2); Cons Cred 4; Contracts 242.

First Bancredit Corp.; McGary v., TexCivApp–Texarkana, 273 SW2d 905, ref nre.—App & E 173(2); Bills & N 518(1); Trial 39.

Firstbank v. Pope, EDTex, 141 BR 115, aff Matter of Pope, 979 F2d 1534.—Bankr 3779, 3782, 3786, 3787; Home 171, 181(1), 181(2).

First Bank; Progressive Cas. Ins. Co. v., SDTex, 828 FSupp 473.—Insurance 2406(3).

First Bank v. Tony's Tortilla Factory, Inc., Tex, 877 SW2d 285.—Interest 1; Usury 6, 11, 16, 119.

First Bank; Tony's Tortilla Factory, Inc. v., TexApp–Houston (1 Dist), 857 SW2d 580, reh den, and writ gr, aff in part, rev in part 877 SW2d 285.—App & E 866(3), 927(7), 949, 1026; Banks 150, 228; Interest 9, 12; Judgm 948(1); Lim of Act 193, 201; New Tr 124(1), 140(1); Parties 38, 40(2), 44; Trial 143, 178; Usury 1, 11, 42, 53, 76, 119, 134.

First Bank and F.D.I.C. v. Shiflett, TexApp–Houston (14 Dist), 843 SW2d 610, reh den, and writ den.—App & E 1128.1, 1157.5, 1178(1); Pretrial Proc 44.1, 46, 304, 314, 315.

First Bank and Trust v. Goss, TexCivApp–Hous (1 Dist), 533 SW2d 93.—Trusts 12, 28, 152, 280; Wills 674.

First Bank and Trust v. Gross, EDTex, 179 BR 504. See Reid, In re.

First Bank & Trust v. Knachel, CA5 (Tex), 999 F2d 107.—Interest 39(2.25); Mar Liens 3, 66.

First Bank and Trust, Bryan; Norman v., TexCivApp–Hous (1 Dist), 557 SW2d 797, ref nre.—App & E 232(3), 846(5), 1069.1; Home 115(1), 117, 141(1), 164, 181(1), 181(3), 213, 214; Judgm 193; New Tr 44(1), 56, 159; Trial 194(1), 194(10), 304, 344, 349(1).

First Bank & Trust Co.; Scarth v., TexApp–Amarillo, 711 SW2d 140.—Decl Judgm 271; Venue 5.3(1), 5.3(2.1).

First Bank & Trust Co., Booker v. Dumas Independent School Dist., Dumas, TexCivApp–Waco, 527 SW2d 499, ref nre.—Bills & N 151; Estop 52(1), 62.4; Schools 95(3), 95(5).

First Bank & Trust East Texas; U.S. v., EDTex, 477 FSupp2d 777.—Int Rev 4857; Labor & Emp 593; U S 75.5, 147(1), 147(5).

First Bank and Trust of Bryan; Inwood Nat. Bank of Dallas v., TexCivApp–Waco, 485 SW2d 842.—Corp 503(2); Plead 111.42(10); Venue 22(10).

First Bank and Trust of Cleveland; Campbell v., TexApp–Beaumont, 714 SW2d 363, ref nre.—Usury 117.

First Bank & Trust of Cleveland; Denson v., TexApp–Beaumont, 728 SW2d 876.—Mtg 59, 90; Ven & Pur 228(3).

First Bank and Trust of Groves v. Kraehnke, TexApp–Beaumont, 732 SW2d 69, writ gr, aff in part, rev in part Southern County Mut Ins Co v. First Bank and Trust of Groves, 750 SW2d 170.—Insurance 1340, 1571, 1611, 1669, 1671, 1929(12), 1944, 2100.

First Bank and Trust of Groves; Southern County Mut. Ins. Co. v., Tex, 750 SW2d 170.—Insurance 1656, 1748, 3571; Judgm 204.

First Bank and Trust of Groves v. Southern County Mut. Ins. Co., TexApp–Beaumont, 732 SW2d 69. See First Bank and Trust of Groves v. Kraehnke.

First Bank and Trust of Groves, Texas; First Nat. Indem. Co. v., TexApp–Beaumont, 753 SW2d 405.—App

FIRST

& E 218.2(1), 239, 240, 269, 500(2), 1178(6); Judgm 199(3.13), 199(5).

First Bank and Trust of Richardson; Stephens v., TexCivApp–Waco, 540 SW2d 572, ref nre.—Guar 78(1); Judgm 185(1); Princ & S 143; Usury 63.

First Bankers Ins. Co. v. Howell, TexCivApp–Amarillo, 446 SW2d 711.—App & E 1170.6; Insurance 2532, 3545, 3585, 3586; Judgm 28; Trial 9(1), 350.4(4).

First Bankers Ins. Co. v. Lockwood, TexCivApp–Amarillo, 417 SW2d 738.—Jury 25(1), 25(2), 25(6), 26.

First Bankers Ins. Co. v. Newell, Tex, 471 SW2d 795.—App & E 758.2.

First Bankers Ins. Co. v. Newell, TexCivApp–Amarillo, 463 SW2d 745, writ gr, aff 471 SW2d 795.—Insurance 2018, 3579; Trial 350.4(3).

First Bankers Ins. Co. v. O'Hair, TexCivApp–Amarillo, 417 SW2d 654.—Judgm 183, 185(2), 185.2(9), 185.3(12).

First Bank in Groveton; Balas v., TexCivApp–Hous (1 Dist), 623 SW2d 666.—Antitrust 357; Bills & N 315; Venue 5.2.

First Bank N.A.; Heimlich v., CA5 (Tex), 80 FedAppx 947.—Fed Cts 630.1; Mal Pros 72(2).

First Bank of Chico; First Nat. Bank of Wichita Falls v., Tex, 290 SW2d 506, 155 Tex 601.—Chat Mtg 49(1), 139.

First Bank of Chico; First Nat. Bank of Wichita Falls v., TexCivApp–Fort Worth, 285 SW2d 286, rev 290 SW2d 506, 155 Tex 601.—Chat Mtg 140, 152, 197(1), 227; Mtg 116, 131, 134.

First Bank of Deer Park v. Deer Park Independent School Dist., TexApp–Texarkana, 770 SW2d 849, writ den.—App & E 837(10); Courts 100(1); Tax 2477, 2556, 2756, 2773.

First Bank of Deer Park v. Harris County, TexApp–Houston (1 Dist), 804 SW2d 588.—Admin Law 229; Fraud 47; Judgm 185.2(4); Tax 2556, 2696, 2698, 2777, 2780, 2790, 2791.

First Bank of Houston v. Bradley, TexApp–Houston (14 Dist), 702 SW2d 683.—App & E 223, 863; Guar 24(1), 36(3), 72; Judgm 185(2), 185.2(4), 185.3(16).

First Bank of Houston; Horn v., TexCivApp–Hous (14 Dist), 530 SW2d 864.—Evid 314(1), 373(1); Judgm 185(2), 185.1(8), 185.3(5).

First Bank of Houston, Tex.; Logan v., TexApp–Beaumont, 736 SW2d 927, ref nre.—Judgm 585(1), 590(1), 654, 717, 735, 739; Tresp to T T 11.

First Bank of Muleshoe; Pitcock v., BkrtcyNDTex, 208 BR 862. See Pitcock, In re.

First Bank of Rowlett v. Paris Sav. and Loan Ass'n, TexApp–Dallas, 756 SW2d 329, writ den.—App & E 863, 1175(1); Banks 191.10, 191.20.

First Baptist/Amarillo Foundation v. Potter County Appraisal Dist., TexApp–Amarillo, 813 SW2d 192.— App & E 996, 1008.1(1); Tax 2289, 2339, 2343, 2389, 2392, 2395.

First Baptist Church; Bexar County Appraisal Review Bd. v., TexApp–San Antonio, 846 SW2d 554, reh den, and writ den, cert den 114 SCt 1221, 510 US 1178, 127 LEd2d 567.—App & E 1060.1(6); Const Law 1386(2); Costs 194.40, 260(5); Evid 106(1); Tax 2288, 2355, 2388, 2389, 2393; Trial 122.

First Baptist Church; Bexar County Appraisal Review Bd. v., TexApp–San Antonio, 800 SW2d 892, writ gr, rev 833 SW2d 108, on remand 846 SW2d 554, reh den, and writ den, cert den 114 SCt 1221, 510 US 1178, 127 LEd2d 567.—Tax 2355.

First Baptist Church of Corsicana; Super-Cold Southwest Co. v., TexCivApp–Waco, 219 SW2d 569, ref nre. —Alt Disp Res 137; Contracts 275, 284(4), 291, 292, 322(3).

First Baptist Church of Fort Worth v. Baptist Bible Seminary, Tex, 347 SW2d 587, 162 Tex 441.—Deeds 144(1); Mtg 1, 32(1), 32(2).

First Baptist Church of Fort Worth; Bible Baptist Seminary v., TexCivApp–Fort Worth, 339 SW2d 710, writ gr, rev 347 SW2d 587, 162 Tex 441.—Mtg 38(2), 39, 608.5.

First Baptist Church of Haltom City; Birdville Independent School Dist. v., TexApp–Fort Worth, 788 SW2d 26, writ den.—Admin Law 229; App & E 216(7), 242(1), 499(4), 500(4), 989, 1010.1(1), 1012.1(1); Const Law 945, 975; Tax 2355, 2698.

First Baptist Church of Houston; Marshall v., TexApp–Houston (14 Dist), 949 SW2d 504.—Action 52; Infants 13; Lim of Act 43, 55(6), 70(1), 95(1), 95(4.1), 104(1).

First Baptist Church of Pyote; Amoco Production Co. v., Tex, 611 SW2d 610.—Mines 78.7(4), 79.3.

First Baptist Church of Pyote; Amoco Production Co. v., TexCivApp–El Paso, 579 SW2d 280, ref nre 611 SW2d 610.—Evid 142(1); Mines 78.1(8), 79.3.

First Baptist Church of San Antonio v. Bexar County Appraisal Review Bd., Tex, 833 SW2d 108, on remand 846 SW2d 554, reh den, and writ den, cert den 114 SCt 1221, 510 US 1178, 127 LEd2d 567.—App & E 930(3), 1082(2), 1163; Tax 2355, 2394.

First Baptist Church of San Marcos, Colored v. Giles, TexCivApp–Austin, 219 SW2d 498, ref nre.—App & E 930(1), 989; Relig Soc 25.

First Baptist Church of Taft v. West, TexCivApp–San Antonio, 120 SW2d 528, writ refused.—App & E 1099(7); Bills & N 485; Estop 72; Mtg 151(1); Relig Soc 10, 29, 31(5).

First Baptist Church of Trinity Heights v. Dennis, TexCivApp–Austin, 253 SW2d 695.—Relig Soc 18, 25.

First Business Inv. Corp.; House Builders, Inc. v., TexCivApp–Waco, 448 SW2d 829, ref nre.—Corp 591; Lim of Act 58(1).

First Care, Inc.; Keeper v., TexApp–Tyler, 794 SW2d 879.—Costs 207; Judgm 340.

First Care, Inc.; Law Firm of Paul Keeper v., TexApp–Tyler, 794 SW2d 879. See Keeper v. First Care, Inc.

First Century Christian Church, Inc.; Overseas Motors Corp. v., TexCivApp–Dallas, 608 SW2d 288.—Sales 441(1), 442(2).

First Choice Food Distributors, Inc.; Carney v., TexApp–Tyler, 837 SW2d206. See Carney v. Roberts Inv. Co., Inc.

First Christian Church of Beaumont; Livesay v., TexCivApp–Beaumont, 482 SW2d 403.—Estop 59; Lim of Act 13, 197(1); Trial 174.

First Christian Church of Temple v. Moore, TexCivApp–Austin, 295 SW2d 931, ref nre.—Wills 184(3), 184(4), 476.

First Church of Christ, Scientist; Moser Co. v., TexCivApp–Waco, 525 SW2d 946.—Brok 58; Contracts 134, 138(1), 138(4).

First Church of Christ, Scientist v. Snowden, TexCivApp–Beaumont, 276 SW2d 571, ref nre.—Char 22(1); Perp 4(15.1), 8(3), 8(7); Trusts 1, 154, 159; Wills 18, 473.

First Citizens Bank; Mathews v., TexCivApp–Dallas, 374 SW2d 794, ref nre.—App & E 846(5), 878(6); Corp 134; Equity 1; Trover 40(6).

First City; City of Houston v., TexApp–Houston (1 Dist), 827 SW2d 462, writ den.—Accord 1, 11(2); App & E 994(1), 1008.1(3), 1012.1(2); Contracts 3, 16, 27, 29; Corp 156; Costs 194.10, 194.12, 194.18; Mun Corp 725; Schools 89.1; Statut 263; Tax 2695, 2703, 2863, 3211, 3212, 3216, 3221.

First City v. Heard, Goggan, Blair & Williams, TexApp–Houston (1 Dist), 827 SW2d 462. See City of Houston v. First City.

First City Asset Servicing Co., In re, BkrtcyNDTex, 158 BR 78.—Admin Law 229; Bankr 2048.5; B & L Assoc 42(16); Statut 223.1.

First City Asset Servicing Co. v. F.D.I.C., BkrtcyNDTex, 158 BR 78. See First City Asset Servicing Co., In re.

First City Bancorporation of Texas Inc., In re, CA5 (Tex), 282 F3d 864.—Bankr 2187, 3782, 3784, 3786.

First City Bancorporation of Texas, Inc., In re, NDTex, 270 BR 807, aff 282 F3d 864.—Atty & C 32(6), 32(7), 32(8); Bankr 2187, 3782, 3784, 3786.

First City Bancorporation of Texas, Inc.; Castillo v., CA5 (Tex), 43 F3d 953.—Atty & C 26, 30; Corp 1.6(13); Fed Civ Proc 636, 1811, 2507; Fraud 7, 38, 43; Mtg 209; Torts 445; Tresp 1, 35.

First City Bancorporation of Texas, Inc.; Doe v., SDTex, 81 FRD 562.—Fed Civ Proc 164, 165, 172, 179, 184.10, 184.15.

First City Bank v. Exxon Corp., SDTex, 892 FSupp 914. See Burns v. Exxon Corp.

First City Bank; Exxon Corp. v., SDTex, 892 FSupp 914. See Burns v. Exxon Corp.

First City Bank; McCartney v., CA5 (Tex), 970 F2d 45.—Antitrust 212; Civil R 1326(5), 1326(9); Decl Judgm 61; Fed Cts 763.1, 794.

First City Bank-Central; Fiorenza v., EDTex, 710 FSupp 1104.—Action 69(5); Civil R 1572, 1575(1); Damag 49.10; Fed Civ Proc 217.

First City Bank-Central Park v. Powell, BkrtcyWDTex, 88 BR 114. See Powell, In re.

First City Bank-Farmers Branch v. Guex, TexApp–Dallas, 659 SW2d 734, writ gr, aff 677 SW2d 25.—App & E 169, 994(2); Damag 87(2), 89(2), 91(1); Sec Tran 229.1, 242.1, 243; Trial 261, 272.

First City Bank-Farmers Branch, Texas v. Guex, Tex, 677 SW2d 25.—App & E 177; Costs 194.16, 194.25, 194.32; Sec Tran 230, 243.

First City Bank-Northwest Hills, N.A.; Austin Area Teachers Federal Credit Union v., TexApp–Austin, 825 SW2d 795, writ den.—B & L Assoc 40; Costs 207; Estop 90(1); Evid 5(2), 471(20); Plead 427; Princ & A 99; Sec Tran 43.1, 47, 81, 113.1.

First City Bank of Alice; Adcock v., TexApp–San Antonio, 802 SW2d 305.—Bills & N 516; Guar 36(3), 91; Interest 65; Sec Tran 165.

First City Bank of Aransas Pass; Cathey v., TexApp–Corpus Christi, 758 SW2d 818, writ den.—Corp 202, 207; Judgm 185(1), 185(2); Lim of Act 55(1), 95(3).

First City Bank of Corpus Christi v. Anthony, BkrtcyS-DTex, 102 BR 600. See Anthony, In re.

First City Bank of Dallas; Fidelity & Cas. Co. v., TexApp–Dallas, 675 SW2d 316, ref nre.—Banks 148(2), 174; Bills & N 279.

First City Bank of Dallas; Moore By Moore v., Tex-App–Fort Worth, 707 SW2d 286.—Mental H 176.

First City Bank of Dallas; Pesch v., NDTex, 637 FSupp 1539.—Fed Cts 373, 388.1; Inj 138.42, 147.

First City Bank of Dallas; Pesch v., NDTex, 637 FSupp 1530.—Rem of C 30, 31, 36, 43, 47, 107(4), 107(7).

First City Bank of Dallas; Sherman v., CA5 (Tex), 893 F2d 720. See United Sciences of America, Inc., Matter of.

First City Bank of Dallas; Sherman v., NDTex, 99 BR 333, aff Matter of United Sciences of America, Inc., 893 F2d 720.—Bankr 2678; Com Law 11; Guar 78(2); Princ & S 144.

First City Bank of Dallas; Sherman v., BkrtcyNDTex, 84 BR 79. See United Sciences of America, Inc., In re.

First City Bank of Dallas; Wider v., TexApp–Dallas, 804 SW2d 160, writ den.—Banks 219.

First City Bank of Highland Village; Houston Inv. Bankers Corp. v., TexApp–Houston (14 Dist), 640 SW2d 660.—Judgm 753, 767, 772; Mtg 378; Subrog 31(4).

First City Bank of Houston v. Salinas, TexApp–Corpus Christi, 754 SW2d 497.—Judges 25(2); Mand 3(1), 3(3), 12.

First City Bank of Plano, N.A.; Stone v., TexApp–Dallas, 794 SW2d 537, writ den.—Banks 38, 148(2);

Bills & N 308; Compromise 5(3); Impl & C C 10; Judgm 181(17); Lim of Act 95(7); Release 10, 27, 29(1).

First City Bank of Richardson v. Global Auctioneers, Inc., TexApp–Texarkana, 708 SW2d 12, ref nre.—App & E 302(6); Banks 100; Bills & N 529, 534; Fraud 22(1), 64(1); Pretrial Proc 42, 45, 431.

First City Bank-Westheimer Plaza, N.A.; Toro v., Tex-App–Houston (1 Dist), 821 SW2d 633, writ den.—Banks 219; Lim of Act 125, 193.

First City Beaumont v. Durkay, CA5 (Tex), 967 F2d 1047. See Ford, Matter of.

First City Capital Corp.; ITT Diversified Credit Corp. v., Tex, 737 SW2d 803.—Sec Tran 147.

First City Capital Corp.; ITT Diversified Credit Corp. v., TexApp–Houston (14 Dist), 717 SW2d 419, writ gr, rev 737 SW2d 803.—Contracts 186(1); Liens 13; Sec Tran 147.

First City Capital Corp.; U.S. v., CA5 (Tex), 53 F3d 112.—Guar 27, 81.

First City Capital Corp.; U.S. v., SDTex, 840 FSupp 69, rev 53 F3d 112.—Lim of Act 46(10).

First City Center Associates, II; PRC Kentron, Inc. v., TexApp–Dallas, 762 SW2d 279, writ den.—Land & Ten 110(1), 112(1), 112.5, 124(1), 172(1), 195(1).

First City Energy Finance Co.; Endrex Exploration Co. v., NDTex, 101 BR 474. See Endrex Exploration Co., In re.

First City Energy Finance Co.; Halliburton Services v., NDTex, 101 BR 474. See Endrex Exploration Co., In re.

First City Mortg. Co., In re, BkrtcyNDTex, 69 BR 765.—Bankr 2576.5(2); Sec Tran 10, 82.1, 84, 181.

First City Mortgage Co. v. Gatling, TexCivApp–Corpus Christi, 530 SW2d 636, dism.—App & E 186; Plead 45, 111.15, 111.30, 111.39(4), 111.42(4), 111.42(6); Venue 7.5(2), 7.5(3), 22(1), 22(4).

First City Mortg. Co. v. Gillis, TexApp–Houston (14 Dist), 694 SW2d 144, ref nre.—Antitrust 134, 162, 209; Brok 19, 34; Contracts 93(2).

First City Nat. Bank; Ellis v., TexApp–Tyler, 864 SW2d 555, reh den.—App & E 80(6), 870(3), 1011.1(2); Partit 73, 91, 94(2), 94(3), 95, 112, 114(3).

First City Nat. Bank; Jensen v., Tex, 623 SW2d 924.—Mech Liens 115(1).

First City Nat. Bank; Jensen v., TexCivApp–Hous (14 Dist), 616 SW2d 452, ref nre 623 SW2d 924.—Mech Liens 115(1).

First City Nat. Bank v. Rhode, TexCivApp–San Antonio, 129 SW2d 323.—Banks 119; Venue 22(8).

First City Nat. Bank in Grand Prairie; Golden v., TexApp–Dallas, 751 SW2d 639.—App & E 217, 230; Trial 314(1), 344.

First City Nat. Bank of Beaumont v. Durkay, EDTex, 125 BR 735. See Ford, In re.

First City Nat. Bank of Beaumont; Owens v., EDTex, 714 FSupp 227.—Fed Cts 231, 241, 246; Rem of C 11, 18, 19(1), 25(1).

First City Nat. Bank of Beaumont v. Phelan, TexApp–Beaumont, 718 SW2d 402, ref nre.—Child S 440, 442, 459; Execution 31.1.

First City Nat. Bank of Binghamton, N. Y.; Kirkegaard v., TexCivApp–Beaumont, 486 SW2d 893.—Judgm 17(1), 17(2); Proc 74, 135.

First City Nat. Bank of El Paso v. U.S., WDTex, 602 FSupp 146.—Fed Cts 23; Int Rev 4549, 4551, 4638.

First City Nat. Bank of Fort Worth v. Cook, NDTex, 117 FRD 390.—Fed Civ Proc 463.1, 2415.

First City Nat. Bank of Houston v. Brazosport Towing Co., Inc., SDTex, 585 FSupp 115.—Adm 99.

First City Nat. Bank of Houston v. Cardiovascular Associates, BkrtcySDTex, 88 BR 788. See Cooley, In re.

First City Nat. Bank of Houston v. Cooley, BkrtcyS-DTex, 88 BR 788. See Cooley, In re.

First City Nat. Bank of Houston; Day v., TexApp–Houston (14 Dist), 654 SW2d 794.—App & E 781(2); Trusts 270.

First City Nat. Bank of Houston v. Hardy, TexCivApp–Corpus Christi, 620 SW2d 732, dism.—App & E 1, 634, 1177(9); Venue 22(4).

First City Nat. Bank of Houston v. Japhet, TexCivApp–Houston, 390 SW2d 70, writ dism.—Autos 155, 245(66); Tresp 12; Trial 351.5(2).

First City Nat. Bank of Houston; Keck v., TexApp–Houston (14 Dist), 731 SW2d 699.—App & E 837(9); Inj 157.

First City Nat. Bank of Houston v. Toombs, TexCivApp–San Antonio, 431 SW2d 404, ref nre.—Wills 717, 778, 781.

First City Nat. Bank of Houston; U.S. v., USPa, 87 SCt 1088, 386 US 361, 18 LEd2d 151.—Antitrust 900, 960, 972(3); 976, 979, 996; Banks 283; Statut 228.

First City Nat. Bank of Lufkin; Haskins v., TexApp–Beaumont, 698 SW2d 754.—Deeds 145, 165.

First City Nat. Bank of Midland v. Concord Oil Co., TexApp–El Paso, 808 SW2d 133.—Contracts 143(2), 143.5, 147(2), 152, 176(1); Costs 194.40; Estop 83(1); Mines 74(8).

First City Nat. Bank of Midland v. F.D.I.C., CA5 (Tex), 782 F2d 1344.—Banks 148(3), 149, 174, 175(2), 175(5).

First City Nat. Bank of Midland v. Honda of Midland, BkrtcyNDTex, 82 BR 439. See Mid-West Motors, Inc., In re.

First City Nat. Bank of Midland v. Mid–West Motors, Inc., BkrtcyNDTex, 82 BR 439. See Mid-West Motors, Inc., In re.

First City Nat. Bank of Midland; Puckett v., TexApp–Eastland, 702 SW2d 232, ref nre.—App & E 273(10), 428(2); Contrib 6, 8; Mines 79.3, 79.7.

First City Nat. Bank of Paris v. Haynes, TexCivApp–Texarkana, 614 SW2d 605.—Damag 91(1), 91(3), 221(5.1); Interest 31, 47(1); Trial 366; Trusts 262.

First City Nat. Bank of San Angelo, N.A.; Alpha, Inc. v., NDTex, 100 BR 831. See B.W. Alpha, Inc., In re.

First City Nat. Bank of San Angelo, N.A.; B.W. Alpha, Inc. v., NDTex, 100 BR 831. See B.W. Alpha, Inc., In re.

First City Realty & Financial Corp.; Maykus v., TexCivApp–Dallas, 518 SW2d 887.—Contracts 176(1); Joint Adv 1.11, 1.14, 4(1); Partners 21, 70, 92, 93, 94, 295; Trusts 91, 92.5, 99, 110, 171, 179, 237, 343, 375(1).

First City, Texas-Beaumont, N.A. v. Treece, EDTex, 848 FSupp 727.—Banks 502, 505, 508; Bills & N 148.1, 327, 337, 365(1); Fed Civ Proc 2117, 2461, 2470.3, 2488, 2544; Guar 36(9), 62, 91; Judgm 128, 187, 217; Rem of C 95, 114.

First City, Texas-Bryan, N.A.; Central Texas Hardware, Inc. v., TexApp–Houston (14 Dist), 810 SW2d 234, writ den.—Antitrust 143(2), 397, 575, 972(3); Atty & C 21.5(1); Banks 505; Evid 146.

First City, Texas-Houston N.A. v. Gnat Robot Corp., TexApp–Houston (1 Dist), 813 SW2d 230.—App & E 954(1); Banks 191.10, 191.15, 191.30.

First City, Texas/Houston, N.A.; Prince v., TexApp–Houston (1 Dist), 853 SW2d 691, reh den.—App & E 389(2), 607(1), 797(1); Banks 219.

First City Texas, Houston, N.A.; Putnam High Yield Mun. Trust v., SDTex, 862 FSupp 146.—Mun Corp 937; Trusts 58, 173, 270, 282, 286.

First City, Texas-Northeast; Wheelis v., TexApp–Houston (14 Dist), 853 SW2d 81, reh den, and writ den.—App & E 946, 948, 961.

First City, Texas—Tyler, N.A.; Phillips v., CA5 (Tex), 966 F2d 926. See Phillips, Matter of.

First Coleman Nat. Bank; Shield v., TexCivApp–Waco, 175 SW2d 267.—Plead 110.

First Coleman Nat. Bank of Coleman v. Childs, TexCivApp–Eastland, 113 SW2d 602, writ refused.—Home 35, 38, 154, 177(1), 177(2).

First Coleman Nat. Bank of Coleman v. Shield, TexComApp, 166 SW2d 688, 140 Tex 117.—App & E 179(1); Mtg 375.

First Coleman Nat. Bank of Coleman; Shield v., TexCivApp–Austin, 160 SW2d 277, aff 166 SW2d 688, 140 Tex 117.—App & E 21, 22, 387(3), 389(3), 392; Contrib 6; Mtg 249(1), 295(5), 561.5, 561.6; Release 28(1); Trial 139.1(5.1), 141, 168, 177.

First Coleman Nat. Bank of Coleman v. Vaughan, TexCivApp–Austin, 139 SW2d 870, writ dism, correct.—Home 142(1).

FirstCollect, Inc. v. Armstrong, TexApp–Corpus Christi, 976 SW2d 294, review dism woj, and reh of petition for review overr.—App & E 66, 70(1), 913, 946, 949; Judgm 707, 713(1), 724; Parties 35.1, 35.11, 35.13, 35.17, 35.31, 35.33, 35.71.

First Colony Community Services Ass'n, Inc.; Roman Catholic Diocese of Galveston-Houston v., TexApp–Houston (1 Dist), 881 SW2d 161, reh den, and writ den. —Contracts 143(2), 176(1), 176(2); Covenants 70; Judgm 181(15.1).

First Colony Life Ins. Co. v. LFC Resolution Payment Fund, Ltd., NDTex, 83 FSupp2d 767.—Fed Cts 12.1, 13.

First Comanche Bank v. Boyd, BkrtcyNDTex, 96 BR 694. See Boyd, In re.

First Comanche Bank v. Boyd Carpets, BkrtcyNDTex, 96 BR 694. See Boyd, In re.

First Commerce Bank v. J.V.3, Inc., TexApp–Corpus Christi, 165 SW3d 366, reh overr, and review gr, rev 226 SW3d 396.—App & E 842(2), 866(3), 893(1), 1071.2; Guar 16(3).

First Commerce Bank v. Palmer, Tex, 226 SW3d 396.—App & E 1175(2); Guar 16(2), 16(3), 16(4), 72.

First Commerce Realty Investors v. K-F Land Co., TexCivApp–Hous (14 Dist), 617 SW2d 806, ref nre.—Contracts 2, 129(1), 144; Deeds 91; Mtg 561.1.

First Community Bank, N.A.; Young v., TexApp–Houston (1 Dist), 222 SW3d 454.—App & E 66; Ex & Ad 35(19).

First Continental Inv. Corp.; Dennett v., TexCivApp–Dallas, 559 SW2d 384.—Appear 9(1), 9(2), 9(5); Const Law 3964, 3965(3).

First Continental Life & Acc. Co. v. Bolton, TexCivApp–Hous (14 Dist), 524 SW2d 727, ref nre.—Insurance 1733, 1801, 2955, 2979, 3128; Trial 350.4(3).

First Continental Life & Acc. Ins. Co. v. Hankins, TexCivApp–Amarillo, 480 SW2d 244, ref nre.—Insurance 1808, 1809, 1822, 2588(2).

First Continental Life and Acc. Ins. Co. v. Hanner, TexApp–Beaumont, 658 SW2d 798.—App & E 994(2), 995, 1057(1); Evid 59; Insurance 2445.

First Continental Real Estate Inv. Trust v. Continental Steel Co., TexCivApp–Fort Worth, 569 SW2d 42.—App & E 218.2(6), 1048(3); Mech Liens 170, 281(1), 281(5); Mtg 151(3), 186(5); Subrog 41(5).

First Continental Real Estate Inv. Trust; Dawson v., TexCivApp–Hous (1 Dist), 590 SW2d 560.—App & E 347(1), 352.1, 353, 387(2), 387(3), 387(6), 833(3); Judgm 293, 335(2); Motions 57.

First Court of Appeals; Carter v., Tex, 795 SW2d 704. See Correa v. First Court of Appeals.

First Court of Appeals; Correa v., Tex, 795 SW2d 704.—Const Law 977.

First Court of Appeals; Houston Health Clubs, Inc. v., Tex, 722 SW2d 692.—Judgm 128, 140, 217.

First Court of Appeals; McGough By and Through Wonzer v., Tex, 842 SW2d 637.—Infants 21, 82; Mand 4(4), 53.

First Court of Appeals; O'Connor v., Tex, 837 SW2d 94. —App & E 830(1); Courts 90(2), 104; Mand 12, 14(1), 14(3), 57(1).

First Credit Corp.; Cruz v., TexCivApp–San Antonio, 380 SW2d 749.—App & E 544(1), 931(1), 1046.1; Trial 350.1.

First Credit Corp.; Norris v., TexCivApp–San Antonio, 366 SW2d 659, writ dism.—App & E 218.2(2), 842(1), 933(1), 989; Contracts 350(1), 350(2), 354; New Tr 144, 157; Trial 358.

First Dallas Petroleum, Inc. v. Hawkins, TexApp–Dallas, 727 SW2d 640.—App & E 5, 176, 181, 859, 865, 934(1); Fraud 49, 58(1); Judgm 112, 126(1); Pretrial Proc 44.1, 46.

First Dallas Petroleum, Inc. v. Hawkins, TexApp–Dallas, 715 SW2d 168.—App & E 79(1); Parties 65(1); Proc 63.

First Data Corp.; DataTreasury Corp. v., NDTex, 243 FSupp2d 591.—Fed Cts 101, 104, 105, 110, 144.

First Deposit Credit Services Corp. v. Preece, BkrtcyWDTex, 125 BR 474. See Preece, In re.

First Deposit Nat. Bank; Bird v., TexApp–El Paso, 994 SW2d 280, reh overr, and review den.—Acct Action on 10; App & E 5.

First Divine Ass'n in America; State v., TexCivApp–Fort Worth, 248 SW2d 291, ref nre.—Corp 374, 596; Evid 22(1); Quo W 29, 48; Relig Soc 35.

First Employees Ins. Co. v. Skinner, Tex, 646 SW2d 170. —App & E 1170.1; Statut 212.1, 212.7; Trial 307(1); Work Comp 1727, 1937.

First Employees Ins. Co. v. Skinner, TexApp–Texarkana, 636 SW2d 258, writ gr, aff 646 SW2d 170.—Trial 307(1).

First Equipment Leasing Corp.; L & L Intern. v., CA5 (Tex), 960 F2d 1277. See Luce, Matter of.

First Equipment Leasing Corp. v. L & L Intern., BkrtcyNDTex, 109 BR 202. See Luce, In re.

First Equipment Leasing Corp.; Luce v., CA5 (Tex), 960 F2d 1277. See Luce, Matter of.

First Equipment Leasing Corp. v. Luce, BkrtcyNDTex, 109 BR 202. See Luce, In re.

First Equitable Title Co., Inc. v. Products Diversified, Inc., TexApp–Houston (14 Dist), 678 SW2d 524, ref nre. —Costs 260(5); Evid 71, 174.1, 174.4, 177, 181, 182.

First Extended Service Corp.; Extended Services Program, Inc. v., TexCivApp–Dallas, 601 SW2d 469, ref nre.—Judgm 185(1), 186; Trial 162.

First Federal Sav. and Loan Ass'n; Aetna Finance Co. v., TexCivApp–Austin, 607 SW2d 312, ref nre.—Garn 49.

First Federal Sav. & Loan Ass'n; Brett v., CA5 (Tex), 461 F2d 1155.—Antitrust 560, 972(3), 972(4), 977(1); Commerce 62.10(1), 62.14; Fed Civ Proc 1773; Fed Cts 743, 797.

First Federal Sav. and Loan Ass'n; Roberd v., TexCivApp–Austin, 490 SW2d 243, ref nre.—B & L Assoc 38(6); Contracts 93(3), 266(2); Fraud 18; Mtg 1, 78, 114, 316; Plead 236(7).

First Federal Sav. and Loan Ass'n v. Sharp, TexCivApp–Dallas, 347 SW2d 337, ref nre, and writ gr, aff 359 SW2d 902.—Mtg 209, 329, 333, 364; Trial 350.1; Ven & Pur 76.

First Federal Sav. and Loan Ass'n v. Vandygriff, TexApp–Austin, 639 SW2d 492, dism.—Admin Law 416.1; B & L Assoc 3.5(2), 3.5(3); Statut 174.

First Federal Sav. and Loan Ass'n of Beaumont v. Stewart Title Co., TexApp–Beaumont, 732 SW2d 98, writ gr, and writ withdrawn, writ den 756 SW2d 295.— Damag 62(3); Judgm 181(15.1); Mech Liens 166, 168, 170; Mtg 151(3); Princ & A 56.

First Federal Sav. and Loan Ass'n of Breckenridge, Tex.; Vandergriff v., Tex, 586 SW2d 841.—App & E 1177(5); B & L Assoc 3.5(3).

First Federal Sav. and Loan Ass'n of Breckenridge, Tex. v. Vandygriff, TexCivApp–Austin, 576 SW2d 904,

rev Vandergriff v. First Federal Sav and Loan Ass'n of Breckenridge, Tex, 586 SW2d 841.—Admin Law 816; B & L Assoc 3.5(3); Judgm 335(1).

First Federal Sav. and Loan Ass'n of Conroe, Inc.; Bruce v., CA5 (Tex), 837 F2d 712.—Antitrust 571, 575, 972(3); Statut 197.

First Federal Sav. and Loan Ass'n of Dallas; Crowder v., TexCivApp–Tyler, 567 SW2d 550, ref nre.—Cons Cred 2, 11, 14; Statut 181(1), 184.

First Federal Sav. and Loan Ass'n of Dallas; Lewis v., TexCivApp–Austin, 524 SW2d 783.—B & L Assoc 4; Corp 49(0.5); Trademarks 1419.

First Federal Sav. & Loan Ass'n of Dallas v. Sharp, Tex, 359 SW2d 902.—Mtg 209, 364; Trial 365.1(1).

First Federal Sav. & Loan Ass'n of Esterville & Emmettsburg, Iowa; Hart v., TexApp–Austin, 727 SW2d 723.—Guar 78(2), 97.

First Federal Sav. and Loan Ass'n of Lubbock v. Lewis, TexCivApp–Austin, 509 SW2d 941.—B & L Assoc 3.5(2), 3.5(3).

First Federal Sav. and Loan Ass'n of Nacogdoches, Tex.; Najarro v., CA5 (Tex), 918 F2d 513.—Fed Cts 712; Princ & A 29.5, 109(4), 123(9), 137(1); Sec Tran 89, 242.1.

First Federal Sav. and Loan Ass'n of Navasota v. Community Sav. and Loan Ass'n of College Station, TexCivApp–Waco, 592 SW2d 418, ref nre.—B & L Assoc 3.1(3), 3.5(2), 3.5(3).

First Federal Sav. & Loan Ass'n of New Braunfels; Howell v., TexCivApp–San Antonio, 383 SW2d 484, ref nre.—App & E 907(3), 1170.6; Evid 384; Jury 25(11); Plead 291(2).

First Federal Sav. and Loan Ass'n of New Braunfels v. Lewis, TexCivApp–Austin, 561 SW2d 38, ref nre.—App & E 839(1); B & L Assoc 3.5(2), 3.5(3).

First Federal Sav. & Loan Ass'n of Paragould; Wolfe v., NDTex, 67 BR 260. See M & E Contractors, Inc. v. Kugler-Morris General Contractors, Inc.

First Federal Sav. & Loan Ass'n of Paragould; Wolfe v., BkrtcyNDTex, 68 BR 80. See Wolfe, In re.

First Federal Sav. & Loan Ass'n of San Antonio; Bustamante v., CA5 (Tex), 619 F2d 360.—Cons Cred 36, 60, 67; Fed Cts 941.

First Federal Sav. & Loan Ass'n of San Antonio v. Bustamante, TexCivApp–San Antonio, 609 SW2d 845. —Cons Cred 2, 15, 16, 17, 18; Judgm 829(3).

First Federal Sav. & Loan Ass'n of San Antonio v. Northside State Bank, TexCivApp–San Antonio, 436 SW2d 393.—App & E 863, 934(1), 989; Banks 147.2; Judgm 199(3.10), 199(3.14); Trial 352.5(5), 352.7, 352.12.

First Federal Sav. and Loan Ass'n of San Antonio v. Ritenour, TexApp–Corpus Christi, 704 SW2d 895, ref nre.—Antitrust 141, 290, 363; App & E 927(1), 984(5); Banks 189; Costs 207, 208; Joint Ten 1, 14; Judgm 185(2), 185.2(4).

First Federal Sav. and Loan Ass'n of San Antonio; Vannetter v., TexCivApp–Waco, 614 SW2d 920.—Lim of Act 58(1).

First Federal Sav. & Loan Ass'n of San Marcos; Savings and Loan Commissioner of Tex. v., TexCivApp–Austin, 434 SW2d 883, ref nre.—B & L Assoc 2.1, 3.5(1), 3.5(2).

First Federal Sav. and Loan Ass'n of Temple v. U.S., CA5 (Tex), 887 F2d 593, reh den 894 F2d 1335, cert den US v. Resolution Trust Corp, 111 SCt 1618, 499 US 974, 113 LEd2d 716.—Int Rev 3184.

First Federal Sav. & Loan Ass'n of Temple v. U.S., WDTex, 694 FSupp 230, aff 887 F2d 593, reh den 894 F2d 1335, cert den US v. Resolution Trust Corp, 111 SCt 1618, 499 US 974, 113 LEd2d 716.—Int Rev 3095, 3175, 3178, 3184, 3389.

First Federal Sav. and Loan Ass'n of Tyler; Pack v., TexApp–Tyler, 828 SW2d 60.—Contracts 168; Dep & Escr 13.

First Federal Sav. & Loan Ass'n of Wilmette, Ill. v. Pardue, NDTex, 545 FSupp 433, aff 1st Fed Sav/Loan-Wilmette v. Pardue, 703 F2d 555.—Brok 60; Fed Civ Proc 2729, 2743.1; Ven & Pur 185, 330.

First Federal Sav. and Loan of Lubbock, Tex.; Swinburn v., CA5 (Tex), 487 F2d 338.—Fed Cts 716.

First Financial Development Corp., Matter of, CA5 (Tex), 960 F2d 23.—Bankr 3767, 3768, 3772.

First Financial Development Corp.; Adams v., CA5 (Tex), 960 F2d 23. See First Financial Development Corp., Matter of.

First Financial Development Corp. v. Hughston, TexApp–Corpus Christi, 797 SW2d 286, writ gr, and writ withdrawn, and writ den.—App & E 205, 662(4), 762, 907(4), 931(1), 989, 1008.1(1), 1008.1(13), 1010.1(1), 1010.1(3), 1010.1(16), 1010.2, 1042(1); Condo 14; Labor & Emp 3050; Neglig 1110(3), 1263, 1680, 1708, 1713, 1750; Pretrial Proc 304, 313; Princ & A 177(1), 181; Trial 398.

First Financial Enterprises, Inc., In re, BkrtcyWDTex, 99 BR 751.—Bankr 3502.10, 3502.15; Fed Cts 47.1.

First Financial Group of Texas; Securities and Exchange Commission v., CA5 (Tex), 645 F2d 429.—Bankr 2402(1); Fed Cts 558, 815; Inj 158; Sec Reg 171, 178.1, 179.

First Financial Group of Texas, Inc., In re, BkrtcyS-DTex, 11 BR 67.—Jury 14(5), 19(9).

First Financial Group of Texas, Inc.; Federal Life Ins. Co. (Mut.) v., SDTex, 3 BR 375.—Bankr 2159.1, 2396; Fed Civ Proc 1957.1.

First Financial Group of Texas, Inc.; Securities and Exchange Commission v., CA5 (Tex), 659 F2d 660.—Abate & R 5; Action 69(5); Contempt 20, 28(2), 70; Fed Civ Proc 1278, 1558.1, 1636.1, 1640, 2419; Fed Cts 625, 640, 792, 816, 820; Sec Reg 85, 177; Witn 307, 308.

First Financial Resolution Enterprises, Inc.; Moore v., TexApp–Dallas, 165 SW3d 456.—App & E 852; Execution 172(2).

First Financial Sav. & Loan Ass'n; Gavey Properties/762 v., CA5 (Tex), 845 F2d 519.—B & L Assoc 32.

First Financial Sav. Assoc. v. Kipp, BkrtcyWDTex, 86 BR 490. See Kipp, In re.

First Floors v. Fieldcrest Cannon, Inc., CA5 (Tex), 55 F3d 181. See Floors Unlimited, Inc. v. Fieldcrest Cannon, Inc.

First Foods Co., Inc.; Trapnell v., TexApp–Corpus Christi, 809 SW2d 606. See Trapnell v. John Hogan Interests, Inc.

First Freeport Nat. Bank v. Brazoswood Nat. Bank, TexApp–Houston (14 Dist), 712 SW2d 168.—App & E 346.2, 395.

First General Realty Corp. v. Maryland Cas. Co., TexApp–Austin, 981 SW2d 495, review den.—App & E 842(2); Compromise 2; Insurance 2926, 2927, 3111(1), 3367, 3556; Lim of Act 43, 55(1), 55(6), 173.

First Georgia Bank, Inc.; MJCM, LLC. v., SDTex, 392 FSupp2d 901, aff MJCM, LLC v. United Community Banks, Inc, 212 FedAppx 323.—Banks 96; Contracts 143.5, 147(1), 152, 169.

First Gibraltar Bank; Simms v., CA5 (Tex), 83 F3d 1546, reh and sug for reh den 95 F3d 56, cert den 117 SCt 610, 519 US 1041, 136 LEd2d 535, reh den 117 SCt 1021, 519 US 1143, 136 LEd2d 897.—Civil R 1075, 1079, 1403, 1419.

First Gibraltar Bank, FSB v. Farley, TexApp–San Antonio, 895 SW2d 425, reh overr, and writ den.—App & E 854(1); Judgm 181(1), 181(25), 181(26), 185(6), 185.3(16); New Tr 100, 140(1).

First Gibraltar Bank, F.S.B.; Jon Luce Builder, Inc. v., TexApp–Austin, 849 SW2d 451, reh overr, and writ den. —App & E 863; Assign 128; Fed Cts 423; Judgm 186.

First Gibraltar Bank, F.S.B.; Luce Builder, Inc. v., TexApp–Austin, 849SW2d 451. See Jon Luce Builder, Inc. v. First Gibraltar Bank, F.S.B.

First Gibraltar Bank, F.S.B.; McClennahan v., Tex-App–Dallas, 791 SW2d 607.—App & E 66, 76(1), 80(6), 782; Courts 39.

First Gibraltar Bank, FSB v. Morales, CA5 (Tex), 42 F3d 895.—B & L Assoc 2; Const Law 2383, 2390; Decl Judgm 392.1; Fed Cts 776, 924.1, 949.1; Home 4, 90; States 18.19, 18.69; Statut 219(1).

First Gibraltar Bank, FSB v. Morales, CA5 (Tex), 19 F3d 1032, cert den 115 SCt 204, 513 US 876, 130 LEd2d 134, opinion vac and superseded 42 F3d 895.

First Gibraltar Bank, FSB v. Morales, WDTex, 815 FSupp 1008, rev 19 F3d 1032, cert den 115 SCt 204, 513 US 876, 130 LEd2d 134, opinion vac and superseded 42 F3d 895, aff 42 F3d 895.—B & L Assoc 42(1); Home 4; States 18.3, 18.9, 18.19.

First Gibraltar Bank, FSB; Rubarts v., CA5 (Tex), 896 F2d 107. See Rubarts, Matter of.

First Gibraltar Bank, FSB v. Smith, CA5 (Tex), 62 F3d 133, reh den.—Antitrust 212; Fed Civ Proc 1824; Fed Cts 776; Guar 36(2), 41; Rem of C 114.

First Gibraltar Bank, FSB; Stowell v., CA5 (Tex), 956 F2d 96. See Stowell v. Macandrews & Forbes.

First Gibraltar Bank FSB; Vail v., TexApp–Dallas, 859 SW2d 425, reconsideration den.—App & E 395, 839(2).

First Gibraltar Bank, FSB; Village Homes v., CA5 (Tex), 947 F2d 1282. See Village Mobile Homes, Inc., Matter of.

First Gibraltar Bank, FSB; Village Mobile Homes, Inc. v., CA5 (Tex), 947 F2d 1282. See Village Mobile Homes, Inc., Matter of.

First Gibraltar Bank, FSB San Antonio; Soto v., Tex-App–San Antonio, 868 SW2d 400, writ refused.—Banks 134(1), 134(7); Gifts 4, 18(2); Trusts 59(2), 136.5, 140(1).

First Gibraltar Mortg. Corp. v. Gibraltar Sav. Ass'n, TexApp–Dallas, 658 SW2d 709, dism.—Corp 503(1); Decl Judgm 26, 237.

First Greenville Nat. Bank; Pickering v., TexCivApp–Dallas, 495 SW2d 16, ref nre.—Accord 1, 5, 8(1), 25(2), 26(3); App & E 1073(1); Bills & N 519; Evid 434(8); Judgm 185(1), 185.1(3).

First Greenville Nat. Bank; Pickering v., TexCivApp–Dallas, 479 SW2d 76.—Bills & N 485; Plead 111.3, 111.15, 291(2); Trial 39.

First Guar. Ltd.; Charwell Development v., NDTex, 578 FSupp 331. See Couch v. First Guar. Ltd.

First Guar. Ltd.; Couch v., NDTex, 578 FSupp 331.—Contracts 127(4).

First Health Strategies (TPA), Inc. v. Security Life of Denver Ins. Co., NDTex, 998 FSupp 712.—Action 69(6); Decl Judgm 5.1, 45, 361.1; Fed Cts 419, 421; Labor & Emp 600.

First Heights Bank, FSB v. Gutierrez, TexApp–Corpus Christi, 852 SW2d 596, reh overr, and writ den.—App & E 543, 930(2), 1050.1(3.1), 1053(6); Banks 505; Bills & N 452(1), 534; B & L Assoc 42(1), 42(16), 48; Courts 70; Equity 3, 46, 54, 56, 57; Estates 10(1); Evid 188, 235, 373(2); Impl & C C 3; Judges 56; Liens 12; Lim of Act 66(1); Paymt 1(1), 50, 65, 78; Trial 3(4), 18; Venue 45, 50.

First Heights Bank, FSB v. Marom, TexApp–Houston (14 Dist), 934 SW2d 843.—App & E 981; Judgm 72, 80, 88, 90, 91, 191, 340, 345; New Tr 6, 99.

First Heights Bank, fsb v. Piperi, BkrtcySDTex, 137 BR 644. See Piperi, In re.

First Heights, F.S.A.; Halligan v., TexApp–Houston (14 Dist), 850 SW2d 801.—App & E 852; Appear 8(1); Judgm 143(3), 145(2), 146, 162(4); Proc 44.

First Houston Capital Resources Fund, Inc.; S.E.C. v., CA5 (Tex), 979 F2d 380.—Fed Civ Proc 1921.

First Houston Inv. Corp.; Wilson v., CA5 (Tex), 566 F2d 1235, reh den 569 F2d 1155, vac 100 SCt 442, 444 US 959, 62 LEd2d 371, on remand 612 F2d 232.—Fed Civ Proc 852.1; Fed Cts 207, 544, 614; Sec Reg 60.16, 223.

First Huntsville Properties Co.; Laster v., Tex, 826 SW2d 125.—Divorce 252.5(1), 321 1/2; Home 1, 55, 78, 81, 90, 118(3), 118(5), 154; Mtg 11, 12; Partit 13; Propty 11; Ten in C 3.

First Huntsville Properties Co. v. Laster, TexApp–Houston (14 Dist), 797 SW2d 151, writ gr, aff 826 SW2d 125.—Divorce 252.5(1); Home 84, 90, 126; Partit 14; Ten in C 3.

First Hutchings-Sealy Nat. Bank of Galveston v. Aetna Cas. & Sur. Co., TexCivApp–Hous (1 Dist), 532 SW2d 114, ref nre.—Assign 94; Pub Contr 16, 23; Subrog 6.

First Indem. of America Ins. Co.; Davis v., TexApp–Amarillo, 56 SW3d 106, reh overr.—App & E 856(1), 863; Judgm 183, 185(2), 185.3(6); Princ & S 66(1), 145(1).

First Indiana Federal Sav. Bank v. F.D.I.C., CA5 (Tex), 964 F2d 503.—B & L Assoc 42(6), 42(17); Fed Cts 12.1.

First Intern. Bank; Morris, Estate of v., TexApp–San Antonio, 664 SW2d 132.—App & E 931(1), 994(3), 1010.1(3); Mental H 116.1, 135, 148.1; Trial 396(4).

First Intern. Bank in San Antonio v. Roper Corp., Tex, 686 SW2d 602.—App & E 1066(6); Courts 100(1); Prod Liab 1, 75.1, 96.1, 98; Trial 350.3(5), 350.5(2).

First Interstate Bank of Arizona, N.A. v. Interfund Corp., CA5 (Tex), 924 F2d 588, reh den.—Damag 91(1); Estop 52.10(2), 52.10(3); Fed Cts 765, 801, 825.1; Sec Tran 89, 92.1, 145.1, 171, 224.

First Interstate Bank of Bedford v. Bland, TexApp–Fort Worth, 810 SW2d 277.—Antitrust 141; App & E 946, 961, 1062.1; Home 29, 31, 33, 177(1), 177(2), 181(1); Pretrial Proc 45, 434; Trial 122, 133.6(6).

First Interstate Bank of Texas, N.A. v. Burns, TexApp–Austin, 951 SW2d 237.—Alt Disp Res 251, 263; Pretrial Proc 716, 724.

First Interstate Bank of Texas, N.A.; Highlands Management Co., Inc. v., TexApp–Houston (14 Dist), 956 SW2d 749, review den.—App & E 392, 242(2), 500(1); Covenants 49, 52, 134; Estop 85; Evid 448, 450(3).

First Interstate Bank of Texas, N.A. v. S.B.F.I., Inc., TexApp–Dallas, 830 SW2d 239.—App & E 930(3), 999(3), 1001(1), 1024.4; Banks 100, 131; Consp 1.1, 19; Fraud 13(3); Judgm 199(1); Neglig 234, 1713.

First Interstate Bank of Texas, N.A.; State v., TexApp–Austin, 880 SW2d 427, reh overr, and writ den, and motion withdrawn.—Em Dom 152(1), 154, 177, 188, 243(3); Mtg 188.

First Interstate Bank of Texas, N.A. v. Turner, TexApp–Texarkana, 791 SW2d 179, writ den.—Guar 27, 36(2), 53(1); Judgm 181(22), 185(2).

First Interstate Credit Alliance, Inc.; Coastal Cement Sand Inc. v., TexApp–Houston (14 Dist), 956 SW2d 562, reh overr, and review den, and reh of petition for review overr.—Afft 11, 17; App & E 242(2), 863, 934(1), 1175(1), 1178(1), 1178(6); Judgm 183, 185(4), 185.1(1), 185.1(3); Usury 6, 16, 22, 88, 113.

First Investors Corp.; Hanley v., EDTex, 793 FSupp 719. —Fed Civ Proc 2511; Fraud 38; Lim of Act 100(12); Neglig 1507.1; Sec Reg 134, 149, 154.1, 305, 309.

First Investors Corp.; Hanley v., EDTex, 761 FSupp 40. —Rem of C 107(1).

First Investors Corp.; Hanley v., EDTex, 151 FRD 76.— Fed Civ Proc 241, 776, 786, 1956.

First Liberty Nat. Bank; Pearl Assur. Co. v., CCA5 (Tex), 140 F2d 200.—Fed Civ Proc 759, 835.1, 882; Fed Cts 855.1, 874; Insurance 3100(1), 3146.

First M. E. Church South v. Anderson, TexCivApp–Dallas, 110 SW2d 1177, dism.—Hus & W 49.3(4); Lim of Act 45; Wills 439, 441, 446, 450, 470(1), 565(1), 651, 665.

First Medical Associates; Flynn Bros., Inc. v., TexApp–Dallas, 715 SW2d 782, ref nre.—App & E 173(6); Contracts 138(1); Health 108, 164.

FirstMerit Bank, N.A., In re, Tex, 52 SW3d 749.—Alt Disp Res 134(3), 134(6), 139, 141, 143, 145, 193, 199, 205,

210; Commerce 80.5; Contracts 1; Fraud 3; Mand 1, 3(2.1), 12, 60.

First Methodist Church v. Jinkins, TexCivApp–Beaumont, 219 SW2d 577.—Inj 34, 123, 128(3.1); Ven & Pur 201.

First Methodist Church of Shiner v. Wright, TexApp–Corpus Christi, 706 SW2d 720, ref nre.—Ex & Ad 314(11); Wills 455, 858(5).

First Mortg. Atrium Bldg., Ltd., Matter of, EDTex, 92 BR 202.—Bankr 3781.

First Mortg. Atrium Bldg., Ltd. v. Mutual Life Ins. Co. of New York, EDTex, 92 BR 202. See First Mortg. Atrium Bldg., Ltd., Matter of.

First Mortg. Co. of Texas, Inc.; Priest v., TexApp–San Antonio, 659 SW2d 869, ref nre.—App & E 934(1); Bills & N 123(1), 140; Contracts 242; Evid 459(1); Judgm 185(2); Usury 11, 83.

First Mortg. Loan Co. of San Angelo; Johnson v., TexCivApp–Austin, 135 SW2d 806.—Courts 475(2); Ex & Ad 314(6), 431(2), 438(5), 438(7), 443(1), 443(7); Mental H 478; Princ & S 140, 152.

First Mortg. of Texas, R. E. I. T.; Wilder v., TexCivApp–Waco, 577 SW2d 760.—Adv Poss 114(1); App & E 768.

First Mun. Leasing Corp. v. Blankenship, Potts, Aikman, Hagin and Stewart, TexApp–Dallas, 648 SW2d 410, ref nre.—Antitrust 142, 145, 256; Atty & C 26; Courts 97(6); Sec Reg 249.1, 252.

First Nat Bank of Forth Worth v. C I R, CCA5 (Tex), 140 F2d 938.—Int Rev 3425, 3441.

First Nat Bank of Houston, Houston, Tex. v. Scofield, SDTex, 62 FSupp 297, rev Scofield v. First Nat Bank in Houston, 158 F2d 268, cert den 67 SCt 1188, 331 US 806, 91 LEd 1827.—Int Rev 3436.

First Nat. Acceptance Co. v. Bishop, TexApp–Corpus Christi, 187 SW3d 710.—Bills & N 340; Costs 194.18, 194.40, 207; Evid 18; Princ & A 1, 3(2), 19, 24, 138, 143(2), 145(2), 166(3).

First Nat. Acceptance Co. v. Dixon, TexApp–Beaumont, 154 SW3d 218, review den.—Bills & N 330.

First Nat. Bank; Alexander Co. v., TexCivApp–Austin, 123 SW2d 908.—Evid 590; Partit 70; Ten in C 15(2), 15(10), 55(9); Witn 92.

First Nat. Bank; Alexander Co. v., TexCivApp–Austin, 119 SW2d 718, dism.—App & E 927(7), 997(3); Estop 58, 76; Execution 272(1), 283; Trial 177; Trusts 72.

First Nat. Bank v. Gamble, TexComApp, 132 SW2d 100, 134 Tex 112, 125 ALR 265.—Corp 1.4(3); Lim of Act 148(1), 164.

First Nat. Bank; American Indemnity Co. v., TexCivApp–Austin, 94 SW2d 1258.—Acct St 8; Banks 147.2, 147.3, 148(1), 149; Bills & N 359; Mental H 187.1, 190, 217.

First Nat. Bank; Anderson v., TexCivApp–El Paso, 118 SW2d 1006.—Plead 111.42(1).

First Nat. Bank v. Arnold, TexComApp, 128 SW2d 1151, 133 Tex 462.—Lim of Act 143(6), 164.

First Nat. Bank v. Arnold, TexCivApp–Beaumont, 107 SW2d 737, rev 128 SW2d 1151, 133 Tex 462.—App & E 500(2), 544(1); Fraud Conv 226, 237(1); Hus & W 171(10), 171(11), 229.6, 266.4; Lim of Act 39(7); Plead 8(11).

First Nat. Bank; Bass v., TexCivApp–Dallas, 130 SW2d 901.—App & E 917(1); Frds St of 139(5).

First Nat. Bank v. Bell, TexCivApp–Fort Worth, 88 SW2d 119, writ dism.—App & E 553(1); Bills & N 48.1, 94(1), 183, 226; Plgs 1, 40.

First Nat. Bank; Bewley Mills v., TexCivApp–Fort Worth, 110 SW2d 201, writ dism.—App & E 216(6), 740(1), 742(1), 1033(7), 1041(2); Chat Mtg 138(1); Debtor & C 17, 19; Exceptions Bill of24; Home 124; Trial 128, 351.2(4), 351.2(8), 352.5(1), 359(2); Wareh 32.

First Nat. Bank v. Blades, CCA5 (Tex), 93 F2d 154.— Fed Cts 430; Mines 97; Princ & A 97, 100(3).

See Guidelines for Arrangement at the beginning of this Volume

First Nat. Bank v. Blewett, TexCivApp–Fort Worth, 89 SW2d 487, writ dism woj.—Banks 154(8); Trial 404(2).

First Nat. Bank; Bohannan v., TexCivApp–Eastland, 85 SW2d 989, writ refused.—New Tr 97, 102(1); Usury 34, 47, 72.

First Nat. Bank; Brainerd v., TexCivApp–Galveston, 169 SW2d 802, mod Ward v. First Nat Bank, 174 SW2d 953, 141 Tex 558.—App & E 907(3); Ex & Ad 56, 326; Judgm 668(1); Trusts 59(1), 124; Wills 91, 732(1), 775, 820(1), 822.

First Nat. Bank; Brinker v., TexComApp, 37 SW2d 136. —Bills & N 338.5.

First Nat. Bank; Brod v., TexCivApp–Austin, 91 SW2d 772, writ dism.—Fraud Conv 49(1), 118(3), 310; Trusts 72, 84, 89(2).

First Nat. Bank v. Brown, TexComApp, 131 SW2d 958, 134 Tex 38.—Bills & N 140, 371.

First Nat. Bank v. Brown, TexCivApp–Austin, 111 SW2d 806, rev 131 SW2d 958, 134 Tex 38.—App & E 1060.1(8); Bills & N 518(2); Compromise 23(2); Evid 423(6), 464, 465; New Tr 29.

First Nat. Bank v. Brownson, TexCivApp–San Antonio, 106 SW2d 1076.—Bills & N 98.

First Nat. Bank; Bryan v., TexCivApp–El Paso, 103 SW2d 395, writ dism.—App & E 500(2); Mech Liens 73(2); Mun Corp 568(2), 586.

First Nat. Bank; Camden Fire Ins. Ass'n v., TexCiv-App–Fort Worth, 84 SW2d 889, writ dism.—Evid 43(3); Garn 87, 88, 93, 148.

First Nat. Bank; Campbell v., TexComApp, 82 SW2d 954, 125 Tex 303.—App & E 622, 624.

First Nat. Bank; Campbell v., TexCivApp–Amarillo, 88 SW2d 1084, writ refused.—Home 38, 146, 214.

First Nat. Bank; Century Ins. Co. v., CCA5 (Tex), 102 F2d 726, cert den 60 SCt 84, 308 US 570, 84 LEd 478.— Bankr 2549; Fed Civ Proc 6, 44; Fed Cts 419, 799; Insurance 1870, 3443; Interpl 11, 17, 31, 32, 35; Wareh 22, 30.

First Nat. Bank; Chain Inv. Co. v., TexCivApp–Austin, 135 SW2d 192.—Statut 207; Venue 19, 27.

First Nat. Bank; Chambers v., TexCivApp–Beaumont, 104 SW2d 58.—App & E 595; Courts 247(5); Plead 111.15, 111.39(5).

First Nat. Bank v. Continental Cas. Co., CCA5 (Tex), 100 F2d 308, cert den 59 SCt 833, 307 US 630, 83 LEd 1513.—Fed Cts 764; Insurance 2405, 2412, 2413; Trial 177.

First Nat. Bank v. Coyle, TexCivApp–Beaumont, 95 SW2d 1337.—App & E 781(4); Inj 118(4).

First Nat. Bank; Currie v., TexCivApp–Eastland, 96 SW2d 731, writ refused.—App & E 1040(13); Const Law 2650; Garn 2; Hus & W 133(8), 133.5.

First Nat. Bank; Davis v., TexCivApp–El Paso, 106 SW2d 760.—App & E 773(2).

First Nat. Bank v. Davis v., TexCivApp–Waco, 135 SW2d 259.—App & E 1175(1); Garn 109, 162, 201; Plgs 30(2).

First Nat. Bank v. Donald, TexCivApp–Fort Worth, 84 SW2d 325, writ dism.—Bills & N 60; Wareh 15(1), 15(3), 25(4), 25(5).

First Nat. Bank v. Dorbandt, CCA5 (Tex), 92 F2d 948.— Bankr 3274, 3317(2.1); Banks 116(1).

First Nat. Bank v. Dupuy, TexCivApp–Waco, 133 SW2d 238, writ dism, correct.—App & E 931(4); Assign 90; Estop 62.5; Lim of Act 104(1); Mun Corp 230, 248(3), 978(1); Schools 80(1), 106.4(2).

First Nat. Bank; Eaton v., TexCivApp–Amarillo, 85 SW2d 268.—App & E 219(2); J P 129(4).

First Nat. Bank; Evans v., TexCivApp–Waco, 101 SW2d 1080, writ refused.—Bills & N 516, 518(2); Princ & S 129(1).

First Nat. Bank v. Farrier, TexCivApp–Beaumont, 113 SW2d 285.—Bills & N 49; Home 115(2), 116, 122; Mtg 38(1); Ven & Pur 15.

First Nat. Bank; Fidelity & Deposit Co. of Maryland v., TexCivApp–Waco, 113 SW2d 622, writ dism.—App & E 989; Courts 104; Domicile 2, 5; Evid 471(2), 472(1); Trial 140(2).

First Nat. Bank; Fidelity & Deposit Co. of Md. v., TexCivApp–Waco, 88 SW2d 605, writ refused.—Attach 201; Sheriffs 161, 169, 170.

First Nat. Bank v. Finn, TexCivApp–Galveston, 132 SW2d 151, writ dism.—App & E 179(1); Hus & W 268(9); Insurance 3445.

First Nat. Bank; Fisher v., TexCivApp–Beaumont, 112 SW2d 1085.—Mtg 468(1), 468(2); Receivers 1, 6, 14.

First Nat. Bank v. Fite, TexComApp, 115 SW2d 1105, 131 Tex 523.—App & E 837(12); Princ & A 143(2), 145(2); Wareh 45, 47.

First Nat. Bank; Gill v., TexCivApp–San Antonio, 114 SW2d 428.—App & E 843(2); Home 129(1).

First Nat. Bank v. Graham, TexCtApp, 22 SW 1102.— Garn 175.

First Nat. Bank v. Graham, TexCtApp, 22 SW 1101.— Afft 11.

First Nat. Bank; Grigsby v., TexCivApp–Amarillo, 125 SW2d 368, rev 144 SW2d 244, 136 Tex 54, opinion corrected on denial of reh 146 SW2d 174, 136 Tex 54.— Banks 130(1), 154(8); Evid 263(1), 265(1), 425.

First Nat. Bank v. Hancock, TexCivApp–Amarillo, 60 SW2d 871.—Banks 285.

First Nat. Bank; Harrison v., TexComApp, 238 SW 209. —Judgm 784.

First Nat. Bank; Hartman v., TexCivApp–El Paso, 97 SW2d 969.—App & E 1050.1(10); Chat Mtg 49(1).

First Nat. Bank v. Hickman, TexCivApp–Austin, 89 SW2d 838, writ refused.—Hus & W 265, 266.3, 269.

First Nat. Bank; Jenkins v., CCA5 (Tex), 107 F2d 764.— Child S 24; Trusts 46, 280; Wills 81.

First Nat. Bank; Jenkins v., NDTex, 26 FSupp 312, aff 107 F2d 764.—Child S 24, 108; Const Law 1066; Fed Cts 409.1; Trusts 51; Wills 18.

First Nat. Bank; Jenkins v., TexCivApp–Austin, 101 SW2d 845.—Chat Mtg 32; Ex & Ad 7, 151, 169, 263.

First Nat. Bank v. John Hancock Mut. Life Ins. Co., TexCivApp–Fort Worth, 101 SW2d 1062, rev John Hancock Mut Life Ins Co v. Morse, 124 SW2d 330, 132 Tex 534.—Ex & Ad 57, 426, 431(3), 453(2); Fraud Conv 74(1), 95(1), 95(2), 96(1), 96(2), 261, 277(1); Mtg 342.

First Nat. Bank; Joyce v., TexCivApp–Eastland, 99 SW2d 1092.—App & E 846(6); Banks 260(1), 261(3), 281; Corp 398(1), 429.

First Nat. Bank; Kane v., CCA5 (Tex), 56 F2d 534, 85 ALR 362, cert den 53 SCt 8, 287 US 603, 77 LEd 524.— Bankr 166(1), 188(1); Banks 130(1), 134(2), 136, 156, 159; Schools 85.

First Nat. Bank v. Mabry, TexCivApp–Fort Worth, 126 SW2d 59, writ dism, correct.—Home 103; Wills 638, 692(4).

First Nat. Bank v. McCamey, TexComApp, 105 SW2d 879, 130 Tex 148.—App & E 1177(6); Mines 79.1(4); Plgs 1.

First Nat. Bank v. McClellan, TexCivApp–Amarillo, 117 SW2d 807.—App & E 172(3), 176, 223.

First Nat. Bank v. McClellan, TexCivApp–Amarillo, 105 SW2d 394.—App & E 274(7), 766, 770(2); Mtg 295(4); Ven & Pur 228(7), 265(4).

First Nat. Bank; McFarlane v., TexCivApp–Beaumont, 97 SW2d 754, writ refused.—App & E 187(3), 193(5), 882(5), 1039(2.1); Bills & N 469, 516; Home 33, 57(3).

First Nat. Bank; Maryland Cas. Co. v., CCA5 (Tex), 82 F2d 465, cert den 57 SCt 12, 299 US 549, 81 LEd 405.— Insurance 1875.

First Nat. Bank; Maryland Cas. Co. v., CCA5 (Tex), 80 F2d 274.—Fed Cts 641, 691.

First Nat. Bank v. Morris, TexCivApp–Beaumont, 94 SW2d 867.—Chat Mtg 235, 272.

FIRST

59 Tex D 2d—30

First Nat. Bank v. Murchison Independent School Dist., TexCivApp–Dallas, 114 SW2d 382.—Estop 62.4; Schools 92(1), 95(1), 95(2), 95(3), 114.

First Nat. Bank; Nesbitt v., TexCivApp–Austin, 108 SW2d 318.—Ex & Ad 444(2); Hus & W 276(1); Lost Inst 23(2), 24; Trusts 156; Witn 133, 149(2), 150(3), 150(4), 159(5).

First Nat. Bank; New Amsterdam Cas. Co. v., TexCivApp–El Paso, 134 SW2d 470, writ dism, correct.—Counties 80(1); Dep & Escr 35; Evid 245, 265(18); Interest 46(1); Subrog 7(3); Tax 2814.

First Nat. Bank; Ocean Acc. & Guarantee Corp. v., TexCivApp–Galveston, 84 SW2d 1111, writ dism.—Contracts 147(1); Insurance 1805, 1834(1), 1836, 1837, 2136(1), 2201, 3072.

First Nat. Bank v. Osborne, TexCivApp–Beaumont, 113 SW2d 695.—Banks 175(3); Evid 12.

First Nat. Bank; Peavy-Moore Lumber Co. v., TexComApp, 128 SW2d 1158, 133 Tex 467, 125 ALR 1185.—App & E 861; Banks 156, 162, 169; Bills & N 133, 134.

First Nat. Bank; Peter v., TexCivApp–Austin, 92 SW2d 1079.—Bills & N 98, 452(1); Corp 218, 306, 327, 361, 363.

First Nat. Bank v. Phillips, TexCivApp–Fort Worth, 101 SW2d 319, writ dism.—App & E 725(2), 727, 742(1), 742(6), 1039(4), 1062.1; Banks 105(2); Ex & Ad 213; Frds St of 35; Hus & W 273(1), 274(1), 274(4); Lim of Act 143(1); Trial 350.4(1).

First Nat. Bank; Powers v., TexCivApp–Waco, 137 SW2d 839, aff 161 SW2d 273, 138 Tex 604.—Char 1, 4, 8, 21(1), 21(2), 23, 31, 37(3); Perp 8(1); Wills 446.

First Nat. Bank; Reid v., TexCivApp–El Paso, 97 SW2d 970.—Lim of Act 119(1).

First Nat. Bank v. San Jacinto Trust Co., TexCivApp–Beaumont, 82 SW2d 706.—App & E 931(3), 1024.2.

First Nat. Bank; Schaer v., TexComApp, 124 SW2d 108, 132 Tex 499.—Banks 126, 154(4).

First Nat. Bank v. Schaer, TexCivApp–Beaumont, 94 SW2d 272, rev 124 SW2d 108, 132 Tex 499.—Banks 154(5).

First Nat. Bank; Simons v., CCA5 (Tex), 107 F2d 979.—Mines 109.

First Nat. Bank; Smith v., TexCivApp–Fort Worth, 114 SW2d 317.—App & E 680(1), 1062.2; Chat Mtg 275, 279; Plead 8(20).

First Nat. Bank v. Solis, TexCivApp–Waco, 137 SW2d 142, writ refused.—Home 74, 115(2), 162(1), 177(1), 177(2), 181(3), 181.5.

First Nat. Bank v. State Life Ins. Co. of Indianapolis, Ind., CCA5 (Tex), 80 F2d 499.—Fed Cts 374; Insurance 1868, 2028.

First Nat. Bank; Stetson v., TexCivApp–Beaumont, 44 SW2d 792, writ refused.—Bills & N 338.5.

First Nat. Bank v. Texas Pacific Coal & Oil Co., TexCivApp–Austin, 82 SW2d 706.—App & E 930(3); Sales 52(6).

First Nat. Bank; Tom v., TexCivApp–El Paso, 104 SW2d 130, writ dism.—App & E 846(5); Banks 130(1); Bills & N 59; Estop 68(2); Lim of Act 49(1); Mtg 155; Names 10; Partners 142(2), 146(2), 157(3), 183(6), 258(8); Trusts 89(1); Ven & Pur 237.

First Nat. Bank; Tucker v., TexCivApp–El Paso, 110 SW2d 926.—Costs 272.

First Nat. Bank; U.S. v., NDTex, 10 FSupp 494.—Agric 3.5(1).

First Nat. Bank; U.S. Fidelity & Guaranty Co. v., TexCivApp–Fort Worth, 81 SW2d 213, writ dism.—Banks 130(1), 130(3), 154(6); Trusts 352.

First Nat. Bank; U.S. Fidelity & Guaranty Co. v., TexCivApp–El Paso, 93 SW2d 562, writ gr, and writ dism by agreement.—Banks 174, 175(1); Insurance 2408; Lim of Act 28(1), 96(2), 100(2), 102(6), 102(8), 103(2), 110.

First Nat. Bank v. Upper, TexCivApp–Austin, 122 SW2d 340.—Trial 25(4).

First Nat. Bank v. Virginia Oil & Refining Co., CCA5 (Tex), 86 F2d 770, cert den 57 SCt 669, 300 US 676, 81 LEd 881.—Bankr 2900(1).

First Nat. Bank; Ward v., Tex, 174 SW2d 953, 141 Tex 558.—Estates 1; Wills 630(5), 683.

First Nat. Bank; Whitaker v., TexCivApp–Galveston, 125 SW2d 1066, rev 147 SW2d 1074, 136 Tex 117.—Banks 148(2); Evid 20(2).

First Nat. Bank; White v., TexCivApp–El Paso, 112 SW2d 1062.—Banks 130(1).

First Nat. Bank v. White, TexCivApp–Waco, 91 SW2d 1120, writ dism.—App & E 218.2(1); Insurance 1995; Judgm 627, 720, 740, 949(5).

First Nat. Bank; Williams v., TexCivApp–El Paso, 115 SW2d 1209, dism.—Plead 111.39(4); Venue 22(6).

First Nat. Bank; Winkler v., TexCivApp–El Paso, 134 SW2d 341.—Princ & S 45, 188.

First Nat. Bank; Womack v., TexCivApp–Eastland, 81 SW2d 99.—App & E 500(1); Hus & W 229.3, 232.1.

First Nat. Bank & Trust Co. of Oklahoma City v. Port Lavaca Vending Machines, Inc., SDTex, 334 FSupp 375.—Rem of C 56.

First Nat. Bank at Brownsville; Gerdes v., TexCivApp–Corpus Christi, 557 SW2d 840.—App & E 765, 773(2).

First Nat. Bank at Brownsville; Hopkins v., Tex, 551 SW2d 343.—Courts 247(7); Guar 34, 36(3), 77(2), 78(1); Venue 7.5(3).

First Nat. Bank at Brownsville; Hopkins v., TexCivApp–Corpus Christi, 546 SW2d 84, ref nre 551 SW2d 343.—Venue 7.5(3).

First Nat. Bank at Brownsville, Tex.; Banco Nacional De Comercio Exterior, S. A. v., CA5 (Tex), 211 F2d 409.—Alt of Inst 18.

First Nat. Bank at Lubbock; Consolidated Bearing and Supply Co., Inc. v., TexApp–Amarillo, 720 SW2d 647.—Corp 113, 115.1, 123(1); Fraud 50; Trusts 94.5, 102(1), 103(1), 376.

First Nat. Bank at Lubbock v. John E. Mitchell Co., TexApp–Amarillo, 727 SW2d 360, writ dism.—Costs 194.40; Fraud Conv 309(8); Quiet T 47(2); Trial 358.

First Nat. Bank at Lubbock v. U.S., CA5 (Tex), 463 F2d 716, cert den 93 SCt 939, 409 US 1125, 35 LEd2d 257.—Fed Civ Proc 2126.1, 2127, 2146, 2148.1, 2151, 2152, 2608.1, 2609; Int Rev 4159(2), 4185.

First Nat. Bank, Bridgeport; Metroplex Factors, Inc. v., TexCivApp–Fort Worth, 610 SW2d 862, ref nre.—Afft 3; App & E 1043(3); Garn 1, 86.1, 87, 88, 93, 97, 194, 243.

First Nat. Bank, Franklin; Sturm Jewelry, Inc. v., TexCivApp–Waco, 593 SW2d 813.—App & E 714(1); Judgm 185(4), 185.1(3), 189.

First Nat. Bank, Giddings v. Helwig, TexCivApp–Austin, 464 SW2d 953.—App & E 1177(2); Princ & S 115(1).

First Nat. Bank, Grapevine v. State Banking Bd., TexCivApp–Austin, 419 SW2d 878, ref nre.—Banks 4, 6.

First Nat. Bank, Henrietta v. Small Business Administration, CA5 (Tex), 429 F2d 280.—Banks 100; Fed Civ Proc 25, 2171, 2177.1, 2182.1; Fed Cts 413, 629, 638, 774, 799; Fraud 13(3); Guar 20, 92(1); Neglig 210, 321.

First Nat. Bank in Big Spring v. Conner, TexCivApp–Amarillo, 320 SW2d 391, ref nre.—Autos 19, 54; Liens 7; Propty 9.

First Nat. Bank in Brownwood v. First Nat. Bank of Coleman, TexCivApp–Austin, 264 SW 1020, rev First Nat Bank of Coleman v. First Nat Bank of Brownwood, 278 SW 188.—Bills & N 338.5.

First Nat. Bank in Canyon; Happy Cattle Feeders, Inc. v., TexCivApp–Amarillo, 618 SW2d 424, ref nre.—Banks 138, 153, 154(8); Judgm 178, 185(2).

First Nat. Bank in Canyon; Northrup v., TexCivApp–Amarillo, 467 SW2d 666, ref nre.—Bills & N 517.

See Guidelines for Arrangement at the beginning of this Volume

First Nat. Bank in Center; Talbert v., TexApp–Tyler, 664 SW2d 126, ref nre.—Usury 42, 61, 72.

First Nat. Bank in Center, Texas; Sherman v., Tex, 760 SW2d 240.—App & E 989, 1024.4; Mtg 463.

First Nat. Bank in Clarksville v. Moore, TexApp–Texarkana, 628 SW2d 488, ref nre.—Estop 85; Frds St of 23(1).

First Nat. Bank in Cleburne; Wilson v., TexApp–Waco, 635 SW2d 887.—Judgm 256(2); Sec Tran 242.1, 243; Trial 365.1(1), 365.3.

First Nat. Bank in Conroe; Associates Inv. Co. v., TexCivApp–Texarkana, 381 SW2d 717, writ dism by agreement.—App & E 912; Venue 22(6).

First Nat. Bank in Conroe; C. & G. Coin Meter Supply Corp. v., TexCivApp–Eastland, 413 SW2d 151, ref nre. —Bills & N 137(1), 138, 140, 301; Guar 56; Princ & S 161.

First Nat. Bank in Dalhart v. Flack, TexCivApp–Amarillo, 222 SW2d 455, rev Flack v. First Nat Bank of Dalhart, 226 SW2d 628, 148 Tex 495.—App & E 989; Chat Mtg 153, 157(2), 157(3); Evid 590; Notice 6, 15; Sales 450.

First Nat. Bank in Dalhart; Hicks v., TexApp–Amarillo, 778 SW2d 98, writ den.—Action 70; Const Law 3953; Garn 7; Judgm 153(1), 335(1); Pretrial Proc 583.

First Nat. Bank in Dallas; Aberg v., TexCivApp–Dallas, 450 SW2d 403, ref nre.—Evid 58; Remaind 5; Trusts 39, 112, 140(3); Wills 439, 470(1).

First Nat. Bank in Dallas; Alford v., TexCivApp–Dallas, 349 SW2d 650, ref nre.—App & E 70(8), 78(1).

First Nat. Bank in Dallas; Asch v., TexCivApp–Dallas, 304 SW2d 179, ref nre.—Assign 137; Garn 164.

First Nat. Bank in Dallas v. Banco Longoria, S. A., TexCivApp–San Antonio, 356 SW2d 192, ref nre.—App & E 1170.12; Garn 56, 77, 105, 110, 134, 141, 145, 158, 195, 244.

First Nat. Bank in Dallas; Bell v., TexCivApp–Dallas, 597 SW2d 521.—Release 27.

First Nat. Bank in Dallas; Bohart v., TexCivApp–Eastland, 536 SW2d 234, ref nre.—Action 60.

First Nat. Bank in Dallas; Bridges v., TexCivApp–Dallas, 430 SW2d 376, ref nre.—Atty & C 123(2); Wills 6, 439, 440, 472, 476, 600(1), 614(4), 616(1), 692(5), 706, 707(1), 858(1).

First Nat. Bank in Dallas; Coke Lumber & Mfg. Co. v., TexCivApp–Dallas, 529 SW2d 612, writ refused.—Contracts 186(2); Mech Liens 159, 198; Mtg 15, 163(3), 167, 335; Trusts 30.5(1).

First Nat. Bank in Dallas v. Dyes, TexApp–Eastland, 638 SW2d 957.—App & E 395; Divorce 261.

First Nat. Bank in Dallas; Ellis v., TexCivApp–Dallas, 311 SW2d 916, ref nre.—App & E 839(1), 1172(5); Decl Judgm 345.1; Statut 195; Wills 455, 458, 692(5).

First Nat. Bank in Dallas; Grey v., CA5 (Tex), 393 F2d 371, cert den 89 SCt 398, 393 US 961, 21 LEd2d 374.— Appear 8(3); Atty & C 70, 72; Damag 91(1); Evid 370(1), 374(8); Fed Civ Proc 1971, 1975, 2117, 2142.1, 2151, 2152, 2173.1(1), 2182.1, 2183, 2215, 2237.1, 2742.5; Fed Cts 372, 631, 822, 841; Judgm 29, 373, 497(1); Princ & A 19; Trusts 227, 262, 263, 377.

First Nat. Bank in Dallas; Haas Drilling Co. v., Tex, 456 SW2d 886.—Frds St of 23(1), 33(2), 160; Guar 92(2); Trial 350.4(1).

First Nat. Bank in Dallas v. Haas Drilling Co., TexCivApp–Dallas, 446 SW2d 29, rev 456 SW2d 886.—App & E 1062.1; Frds St of 160; Trial 350.4(1), 352.5(3).

First Nat. Bank in Dallas v. Hawn, TexApp–Dallas, 392 SW2d 377, ref nre.—Abate & R 64; Parties 59(3), 60.

First Nat. Bank in Dallas; Holland v., TexCivApp–Dallas, 597 SW2d 406, dism.—App & E 1041(4); Bills & N 139(3); Guar 35, 36(3), 53(1), 86, 87, 89; Lim of Act 46(10), 48(1); Plead 233, 261, 280; Pretrial Proc 713, 723.1.

First Nat. Bank in Dallas v. Kinabrew, TexCivApp–Tyler, 589 SW2d 137, ref nre.—App & E 170(1), 768, 842(2), 842(8), 931(1), 1010.1(3); Contracts 147(1), 147(2), 170(1), 176(2); Decl Judgm 329; Evid 207(1); Hus & W 273(9); Mines 55(1), 55(2), 55(5), 74(1), 74(5); Princ & A 10(1), 93, 97, 99, 103(7), 163(1); Stip 1, 3, 14(1), 14(4).

First Nat. Bank in Dallas; Lampman v., TexCivApp–Waco, 463 SW2d 28, ref nre.—App & E 273(2), 1201(1), 1201(6); Trial 350.3(1).

First Nat. Bank in Dallas v. Lampman, TexCivApp–Eastland, 442 SW2d 858, ref nre, appeal after remand 463 SW2d 28, ref nre.—Bills & N 209, 524; Garn 40, 56, 110.

First Nat. Bank in Dallas; Liberty Mut. Ins. Co. v., Tex, 245 SW2d 237, 151 Tex 12.—Banks 148(4); Bills & N 6; Damag 64; Elect of Rem 1; Lim of Act 25(9).

First Nat. Bank in Dallas; Liberty Mut. Ins. Co. v., TexCivApp–Fort Worth, 239 SW2d 738, aff in part, rev in part 245 SW2d 237, 151 Tex 12.—Banks 148(2); Elect of Rem 3(1).

First Nat. Bank in Dallas v. Love, TexCivApp–Eastland, 584 SW2d 345, dism.—Evid 419(11), 419(17), 441(12); Interest 67.

First Nat. Bank in Dallas; Minzer v., TexCivApp–Dallas, 390 SW2d 784, ref nre.—Contracts 143.5; Evid 450(4); Judgm 185.3(14); Land & Ten 55(2), 157(1).

First Nat. Bank in Dallas; Nuclear-Medical Laboratories, Inc. v., TexApp–Dallas, 629 SW2d 74, ref nre.— Contracts 143(2); Evid 448; Land & Ten 91(2).

First Nat. Bank in Dallas; Paul Revere Life Ins. Co. v., CA5 (Tex), 359 F2d 641.—Insurance 1808, 1812, 1816, 2432(2).

First Nat. Bank in Dallas; Pope v., TexApp–Dallas, 658 SW2d 764.—Adop 7.1.

First Nat. Bank in Dallas; Reed v., TexApp–Dallas, 645 SW2d 843.—Fraud 39; Guar 16(1), 17; Judgm 185.3(10).

First Nat. Bank in Dallas; Richardson Co. v., TexCivApp–Tyler, 504 SW2d 812, ref nre.—Bills & N 333, 337, 352.1, 359; Evid 60.

First Nat. Bank in Dallas; Rozelle v., TexCivApp–Waco, 535 SW2d 768, ref nre.—Guar 86; Interest 50; Tender 28.

First Nat. Bank in Dallas; Sanderson v., TexCivApp–Dallas, 446 SW2d 720, ref nre.—App & E 1036(1); Parties 35.7; Wills 77, 435, 439, 449, 462, 463, 523.

First Nat. Bank in Dallas v. Smith, TexCivApp–Dallas, 141 SW2d 735, writ dism, correct.—Brok 53, 55(1), 81, 82(4), 86(8), 88(3).

First Nat. Bank in Dallas v. Steves Sash & Door Co., TexCivApp–San Antonio, 468 SW2d 133, ref nre.—Garn 158.

First Nat. Bank in Dallas v. Texas Federal Sav. & Loan Ass'n, TexApp–Texarkana, 628 SW2d 497, ref nre.—App & E 931(3); Partit 16.

First Nat. Bank in Dallas; Texas Utilities Fuel Co. v., TexCivApp–Dallas, 615 SW2d 309.—App & E 241; Evid 384, 458; Gas 13(1); Judgm 181(30).

First Nat. Bank in Dallas v. Trinity Patrick Lodge No. 7, K. of P., TexCivApp–Fort Worth, 238 SW2d 576, ref nre.—Ben Assoc 20(7); Frds St of 49, 63(5), 108(1), 125(1), 129(1), 131(1), 158(4); Trusts 243.

First Nat. Bank in Dallas v. U.S., CA5 (Tex), 635 F2d 391, stay den Yeoham v. US, 101 SCt 2043, 451 US 966, 68 LEd2d 346, cert den 101 SCt 3051, 452 US 916, 69 LEd2d 420.—Int Rev 4490, 4500.

First Nat. Bank in Dallas; U.S. v., NDTex, 468 FSupp 415, rev 635 F2d 391, stay den Yeoham v. US, 101 SCt 2043, 451 US 966, 68 LEd2d 346, cert den 101 SCt 3051, 452 US 916, 69 LEd2d 420.—Int Rev 4493.

First Nat. Bank in Dallas v. U.S., NDTex, 418 FSupp 955, aff 592 F2d 1188.—Hus & W 249(3), 265, 267(0.5),

FIRST

272(5); Insurance 3470, 3490; Int Rev 3016, 4177.10(4), 5024.

First Nat. Bank in Dallas v. Walker, TexCivApp–Dallas, 544 SW2d 778.—Alt of Inst 7; Contracts 42, 221(1); Evid 420(3); Guar 91; Judgm 199(3.7), 297, 300, 329; Trial 139.1(6).

First Nat. Bank in Dallas v. Whirlpool Corp., Tex, 517 SW2d 262.—Const Law 642; Corp 1.6(7); Mech Liens 5, 10, 23, 30, 31, 35, 45, 132(13), 161(1), 239, 272, 279; Mtg 163(3).

First Nat. Bank in Dallas v. Whirlpool Corp., TexCivApp–Waco, 502 SW2d 185, writ gr, rev 517 SW2d 262.—Corp 1.6(7); Mech Liens 5, 132(10), 132(13), 281(1); Mtg 163(3); Plead 404.

First Nat. Bank in Dallas v. Zimmerman, Tex, 442 SW2d 674.—Frds St of 110(1), 152(1), 152(2); Judgm 256(2).

First Nat. Bank in Dallas; Zimmerman v., TexCivApp–Waco, 436 SW2d 401, writ gr, rev 442 SW2d 674.—Evid 80(1); Frds St of 74(1), 110(1), 152(1); Plead 110; Spec Perf 12.

First Nat. Bank in Dallas, Tex.; U.S. Fidelity & Guaranty Co. v., CA5 (Tex), 172 F2d 258.—Banks 119, 127, 129, 148(2), 148(3), 148(4); Elect of Rem 1, 3(4), 14; Insurance 3517, 3523(1), 3525; Subrog 1, 6, 7(1).

First National Bank In Durant v. Lane & Douglass, NDTex, 961 FSupp 153, rev First Nat Bank of Durant v. Trans Terra Corp Intern, 142 F3d 802, reh den.—Atty & C 63, 64, 105; Contracts 15.

First Nat. Bank in Edinburg; Reyna v., TexApp–Corpus Christi, 55 SW3d 58, reh overr, and reh overr.—App & E 242(4), 843(3), 854(5), 927(7), 930(1), 946, 970(2), 984(1), 1001(1), 1003(5); Contracts 322(3); Corp 327, 397; Costs 32(2), 60; Damag 49.10, 50.10; Estop 85; Fraud 3, 4; Frds St of 44(3), 49; Labor & Emp 40(2), 40(3), 55; Torts 212, 242; Trial 43, 139.1(7), 139.1(12), 139.1(14), 139.1(17), 141, 142.

First Nat. Bank in Garland v. Murphy, TexCivApp–Dallas, 441 SW2d 661.—App & E 78(1); Bills & N 537(1); Evid 461(1).

First Nat. Bank in George West v. Frost Nat. Bank of San Antonio, TexCivApp–San Antonio, 142 SW2d 555, writ dism, correct.—App & E 644(1); Evid 43(1); Garn 1, 88, 193; Paymt 42.

First Nat. Bank in George West; Landry v., TexApp–Corpus Christi, 814 SW2d 86, writ den.—App & E 863; Banks 100; Judgm 178, 181(2), 181(3), 185(2), 185(6).

First Nat. Bank in Glen Rose; Brooks Supply Co. v., TexCivApp–Waco, 242 SW2d 956.—Evid 10(2); Plead 111.3, 111.42(5).

First Nat. Bank in Graham v. Corbin, TexCivApp–Fort Worth, 153 SW2d 979, writ refused wom.—App & E 267(1), 291, 662(1), 900, 909(1); Courts 99(1); Mines 54.5; Trial 356(6).

First Nat. Bank in Graham v. Corbin, TexCivApp–Fort Worth, 148 SW2d 439.—App & E 640, 655(1), 659(1), 669, 1126; Courts 155.

First Nat. Bank in Graham; Fultz v., Tex, 388 SW2d 405.—Banks 121, 126, 151.

First Nat. Bank in Graham v. Fultz, TexCivApp–Fort Worth, 380 SW2d 894, rev 388 SW2d 405.—Banks 148(3); Judgm 185.3(5), 186.

First Nat. Bank in Graham v. Sledge, Tex, 653 SW2d 283.—Mech Liens 5, 115(1), 115(4), 116, 122, 172, 196, 310(3).

First Nat. Bank in Graham v. Sledge, TexCivApp–Fort Worth, 616 SW2d 954, writ gr, rev 653 SW2d 283.—App & E 1194(2); Mech Liens 113(1), 113(2), 115(1), 310(3).

First Nat. Bank in Grand Prairie v. H. Hentz & Co., Inc., TexCivApp–Waco, 498 SW2d 478.—App & E 1146; Brok 72; Corp 120; Interest 46(1); Princ & A 85, 171(1), 171(7).

First Nat. Bank in Grand Prairie v. Lone Star Life Ins. Co., TexCivApp–Dallas, 524 SW2d 525, ref nre First

Nat Bank of Grand Prairie v. Lone Star Life Ins, 529 SW2d 67.—App & E 854(1); Assign 18; Banks 134(7), 152; Bills & N 147; Sec Tran 26, 88, 89, 138, 161, 228.

First Nat. Bank in Grand Prairie, Tex.; U.S. v., NDTex, 240 FSupp 347, aff Lawrence v. US, 378 F2d 452.—Bankr 2580.1, 3061; Decl Judgm 113; U S 76(4).

First Nat. Bank in Groveton; Smith v., TexCivApp–Galveston, 147 SW2d 856.—App & E 449.

First Nat. Bank in Groveton; Smith v., TexCivApp–Galveston, 146 SW2d 270.—Venue 22(2).

First Nat. Bank in Houston v. Scofield, CA5 (Tex), 201 F2d 219.—Int Rev 3830.1.

First Nat. Bank in Houston v. Scofield, SDTex, 106 FSupp 300, aff 201 F2d 219.—Int Rev 3668.

First Nat. Bank in Houston v. Whitaker, TexComApp, 147 SW2d 1074, 136 Tex 117.—Banks 174.

First Nat. Bank in Lockney; National Empire Life Ins. Co. v., TexCivApp–Amarillo, 371 SW2d 592, ref nre.—App & E 846(2), 846(5); Insurance 1634(1), 3098.

First Nat. Bank in Luling; Norris v., CA5 (Tex), 70 F3d 27. See Norris, Matter of.

First Nat. Bank in McAllen v. Martinez De Villagomez, TexApp–Corpus Christi, 54 SW3d 345, review den, and reh of petition for review den.—App & E 66, 76(1), 78(1), 79(1), 80(1), 80(6); Judgm 217.

First Nat. Bank in Mount Pleasant, Tex.; Union Bank of Benton, Ark. v., CA5 (Tex), 677 F2d 1074.—Fed Cts 939; Interest 39(1), 39(2.15), 39(2.20).

First Nat. Bank in Mt. Pleasant, Tex.; Union Bank of Benton, Ark. v., CA5 (Tex), 621 F2d 790, appeal after remand 677 F2d 1074.—Banks 119, 140(3), 140(5), 156, 174; Bills & N 15.

First Nat. Bank in Munday v. Lubbock Feeders, L.P., TexApp–Eastland, 183 SW3d 875, review den.—Judgm 185.1(2), 185.1(3), 185.1(4), 185.2(8); Sec Tran 89, 146.

First Nat. Bank in Orange v. MacFarlane, TexCivApp–Beaumont, 160 SW2d 969, writ refused wom.—Ex & Ad 176, 177, 194(7), 244, 252, 256(7), 256(8).

First Nat. Bank in Pleasanton v. Southwestern Inv. Co., TexCivApp–Amarillo, 301 SW2d 192, writ dism.—Bills & N 485; Chat Mtg 275; Venue 22(6).

First Nat. Bank in Port Lavaca; Hargus v., SDTex, 666 FSupp 111, aff 835 F2d 286.—Banks 521.1.

First Nat. Bank in Port Lavaca; Nautical Landings Marina, Inc. v., TexApp–Corpus Christi, 791 SW2d 293, writ den.—App & E 907(2), 946; Bankr 2394.1, 2462; Consp 1.1; Contracts 93(2), 99(1); Guar 18, 20, 30, 62, 78(1); Judgm 185(2), 185(4), 186; Mtg 369(2); New Tr 100, 101, 102(1); Pretrial Proc 724; Torts 432; Usury 82.

First Nat. Bank in Quanah; Grigsby v., TexComApp, 146 SW2d 174, 136 Tex 54.—Banks 154(8).

First Nat. Bank in Quanah; Grigsby v., TexComApp, 144 SW2d 244, 136 Tex 54, opinion corrected on denial of reh 146 SW2d 174, 136 Tex 54.—Banks 130(1), 154(8).

First Nat. Bank in Weatherford v. Exxon Corp., TexCivApp–El Paso, 597 SW2d 783, aff 622 SW2d 80.—Evid 142(1); Mines 79.5, 79.7.

First Nat. Bank in Weatherford, Tex. v. Exxon Corp., Tex, 622 SW2d 80.—Evid 142(1).

First Nat. Bank LaGrange v. Martin, CA5 (Tex), 963 F2d 809. See Martin, Matter of.

First Nat. Bank, Lubbock, Tex.; Wilson v., CA5 (Tex), 796 F2d 752. See Missionary Baptist Foundation of America, Inc., Matter of.

First Nat. Bank, Lubbock, Tex.; Wilson v., BkrtcyND-Tex, 69 BR 540. See Missionary Baptist Foundation of America, Inc., In re.

First Nat. Bank, Lubbock, Tex.; Wilson v., BkrtcyND-Tex, 69 BR 536. See Missionary Baptist Foundation of America, Inc., In re.

First Nat. Bank Mansfield v. Nelson, BkrtcyNDTex, 134 BR 838. See Nelson, In re.

First Nat. Bank, Mercedes; Drake v., TexCivApp–San Antonio, 254 SW2d 230.—Judgm 178, 181(2), 185.3(1), 335(1).

First Nat. Bank, Mesquite; Smith v., TexCivApp–Dallas, 326 SW2d 301.—Accord 26(1); App & E 761; Trial 352.1(3).

First Nat. Bank of Abilene; Moore v., CA5 (Tex), 345 F2d 638.—Bankr 2851, 2852, 2894, 3061; Plgs 19.

First Nat. Bank of Abilene; Palmer & Ray Dental Supply of Abilene, Inc. v., TexCivApp–Eastland, 477 SW2d 954.—Bills & N 183.

First Nat. Bank of Alpine; Minchen v., TexCivApp–El Paso, 263 SW2d 601, ref nre.—App & E 732; Evid 213(2), 543(3); Notice 6; Refer 29, 61, 89, 100(7); Trial 81, 82, 194(14), 350.3(1), 350.3(2.1), 351.5(1), 351.5(3), 352.1(3), 352.9, 352.10, 412, 426.

First Nat. Bank of Alvin; Pierce v., TexApp–Houston (14 Dist), 899 SW2d 365.—Const Law 45, 2500; Decl Judgm 271; Judgm 181(25), 185(2); Sec Tran 87, 141; Ship 17.5, 19, 24; Statut 206.

First Nat. Bank of Amarillo v. Amarillo Nat. Bank, TexCivApp–Amarillo, 531 SW2d 905.—Deeds 93; Ease 3(1), 15.1, 16; Life Est 5, 23.

First Nat. Bank of Amarillo v. Arrow Oil & Gas, Inc., TexApp–Amarillo, 818 SW2d 159.—App & E 170(1); Banks 134(7); Judgm 181(2).

First Nat. Bank of Amarillo v. Bauert, TexApp–Amarillo, 622 SW2d 464.—Evid 596(1); Pretrial Proc 718; Trial 350.1, 350.3(1); Trusts 91, 103(5), 108, 374.

First Nat. Bank of Amarillo; Fuqua v., TexCivApp–Amarillo, 332 SW2d 357.—Wills 439, 453, 471, 488, 684.8.

First Nat. Bank of Amarillo v. Holmes, BkrtcyNDTex, 121 BR 505. See Holmes, In re.

First Nat. Bank of Amarillo v. Jarnigan, TexApp–Amarillo, 794 SW2d 54, writ den.—App & E 927(7), 997(3); Bills & N 537(1); Cons Cred 60; Contracts 164; Evid 5(1); Trial 186, 295(10).

First Nat. Bank of Amarillo; Kritser v., TexCivApp–Beaumont, 463 SW2d 751, ref nre 467 SW2d 408.—Deeds 105; Evid 461(2).

First Nat. Bank of Amarillo v. Lyco Acquisition 1984 Ltd. Partnership v., TexApp–Amarillo, 860 SW2d 117, reh overr, and writ den.—App & E 854(1); Costs 194.12, 194.18, 194.40, 194.48; Lim of Act 95(3), 95(7); Trusts 30.5(1).

First Nat. Bank of Amarillo v. Martin, NDTex, 48 BR 317.—Fed Civ Proc 2486, 2531, 2549; Sec Tran 168; Trusts 358(1).

First Nat. Bank of Amarillo; Seals v., BkrtcyNDTex, 122 BR 958. See Church and Institutional Facilities Development Corp., In re.

First Nat. Bank of Amarillo; Weaver v., TexCivApp–Waco, 532 SW2d 416.—Ref of Inst 19(2), 44, 45(1).

First Nat. Bank of Andrews v. F.D.I.C., WDTex, 707 FSupp 265.—Banks 505.

First Nat. Bank of Andrews v. Jones, TexApp–Eastland, 635 SW2d 950, ref nre.—Bills & N 453; Ref of Inst 6, 44.

First Nat. Bank of Angleton; Pelton v., TexCivApp–Houston, 400 SW2d 398.—Receivers 3, 9, 12.

First Nat. Bank of Angleton; Tigner v., Tex, 264 SW2d 85, 153 Tex 69.—Courts 247(5); Judgm 181(1), 185(2); Land & Ten 246(2); Liens 8.

First Nat. Bank of Angleton v. Tigner, TexCivApp–Fort Worth, 258 SW2d 153, rev 264 SW2d 85, 153 Tex 69.—Contracts 141(1); Land & Ten 246(2), 254(3), 328(2); Statut 212.1, 223.2(1.1), 230.

First Nat. Bank of Anson; Jones v., TexApp–Eastland, 846 SW2d 107, reh den.—Hus & W 270(10); Judgm 693; Set-Off 60.

First Nat. Bank of Athens; Dean v., TexCivApp–Tyler, 494 SW2d 222, ref nre.—Divorce 255; Hus & W 265.5; Judgm 507, 707, 948(1), 951(2).

First Nat. Bank of Atlanta v. Hargrove, TexCivApp–Texarkana, 503 SW2d 856.—App & E 624; Banks 153; Bills & N 183, 237, 245; Courts 107; Guar 71; Princ & A 177(1).

First Nat. Bank of Azle; Longview Bank & Trust Co. v., TexApp–Fort Worth, 750 SW2d 297.—Banks 148(2), 149, 174; Bills & N 196, 296, 437, 443(2).

First Nat. Bank of Baird; King v., TexApp–Eastland, 161 SW3d 661.—App & E 984(1); Costs 2; Jury 16(1); Mtg 216.

First Nat. Bank of Bastrop; Dennis and Art Stein Real Estate Joint Venture v., TexApp–Austin, 950 SW2d 172. See Stein v. First Nat. Bank of Bastrop.

First Nat. Bank of Bastrop; Stein v., TexApp–Austin, 950 SW2d 172.—Decl Judgm 8, 61, 65, 83.

First Nat. Bank of Bastrop; Stein Real Estate Joint Venture v., TexApp–Austin, 950 SW2d 172. See Stein v. First Nat. Bank of Bastrop.

First Nat. Bank of Bay City; Le Blanc, Inc. v., TexCivApp–Houston, 320 SW2d 886, writ dism.—Contracts 186(1); Plead 45, 111.18, 111.39(3); Venue 27.

First Nat. Bank of Beaumont v. Howard, Tex, 229 SW2d 781, 149 Tex 130.—Wills 684.10(4), 684.10(5).

First Nat. Bank of Beaumont v. Howard, TexCivApp–Beaumont, 223 SW2d 694, aff in part, rev in part 229 SW2d 781, 149 Tex 130.—Atty & C 140; Evid 314(1); Wills 684.2(5), 684.10(3.1), 684.10(4), 684.10(5).

First Nat. Bank of Beaumont; McDougald v., TexCivApp–Beaumont, 239 SW2d 145, ref nre.—Plead 106(1), 110, 111.32, 111.39(1), 304.

First Nat. Bank of Beaumont; O'Fiel v., TexCivApp–Beaumont, 152 SW2d 475, writ dism, correct.—App & E 907(2), 1122(3); Judgm 685; Mtg 459(2), 463, 478.

First Nat. Bank of Beaumont; Pylman v., TexCivApp–Beaumont, 247 SW2d 580, ref nre.—Adop 18, 21; Statut 126; Wills 506(5).

First Nat. Bank of Beeville v. Fojtik, Tex, 775 SW2d 632.—App & E 882(18).

First Nat. Bank of Beeville; Fojtik v., TexApp–Corpus Christi, 752 SW2d 669, writ den with per curiam opinion 775 SW2d 632.—App & E 209.1, 218.1, 882(18), 1056.1(10); Consp 1.1, 2, 21; Evid 244(4).

First Nat. Bank of Beeville v. Fojtik Auction & Equipment Co., Tex, 775 SW2d 632. See First Nat. Bank of Beeville v. Fojtik.

First Nat. Bank of Beeville; Fojtik Auction & Equipment Co. v., TexApp–Corpus Christi, 752 SW2d 669. See Fojtik v. First Nat. Bank of Beeville.

First Nat. Bank of Beeville; State Bank and Trust Co. of Beeville v., TexApp–Corpus Christi, 635 SW2d 807, ref nre.—Sec Tran 91.

First Nat. Bank of Bellaire v. Hubbs, TexCivApp–Hous (1 Dist), 566 SW2d 375.—App & E 1177(2); Banks 119, 133, 134(1), 143(7), 154(1), 154(5); Trover 2.

First Nat. Bank of Bellaire v. Huffman Independent School Dist., TexApp–Houston (14 Dist), 770 SW2d 571, writ den, cert den 110 SCt 1838, 494 US 1091, 108 LEd2d 967.—Const Law 4138(2); Liens 1; Tax 2105, 2106, 2672.

First Nat. Bank of Bellaire; Lakeland Pipe & Supply, Inc. v., TexApp–Houston (14 Dist), 899 SW2d 230, reh overr, and writ den.—App & E 758.3(9); Banks 148(2), 174, 175(5); Bills & N 279.

First Nat. Bank of Bellaire v. Prudential Ins. Co. of America, TexCivApp–Hous (14 Dist), 551 SW2d 112, ref nre.—Mun Corp 987; States 168.5.

First Nat. Bank of Bells/Savoy; Adams v., TexApp–Dallas, 154 SW3d 859.—App & E 169, 758.3(11), 852, 856(1), 870(2), 960(1), 1073(1), 1079, 1175(1); Bills & N 129(2), 422(1); Decl Judgm 8, 41, 43, 45, 61; Deeds 26, 43, 45, 54, 56(2), 56(3), 66, 67, 82, 194(5); Equity 65(1); Estop 32(3), 52(1), 116; Judgm 181(6), 185(2); Mtg 97, 99, 101, 105, 113, 335; Plead 228.14.

First Nat. Bank of Bellville; Eubank v., TexApp–Corpus Christi, 814 SW2d 130.—Contracts 93(2), 99(1); Guar 1, 18, 30, 86; Judgm 178, 181(2), 181(3), 183, 185(2), 185.3(2), 185.3(10).

First Nat. Bank of Bellville; Evans v., TexApp–Houston (14 Dist), 946 SW2d 367, reh overr, and writ den.—App & E 93, 151(1), 151(2), 169, 500(1), 719(1), 852, 854(1), 863; Contracts 143(2); Evid 426, 450(1), 452, 461(4); Ex & Ad 35(13.5), 35(16), 35(18), 35(19), 91, 111(8); Fraud 7; Joint Ten 3, 6; Judgm 12, 181(19), 185(1), 185.3(1), 186; Jury 32(2); Parties 95(6).

First Nat. Bank of Bellville; Farrington v., TexApp–Houston (1 Dist), 753 SW2d 248, writ den.—Home 13, 31, 32, 58, 161; Judgm 181(15.1).

First Nat. Bank of Bellville; Reese v., TexCivApp–Galveston, 196 SW2d 48, 171 ALR 516, ref nre.—App & E 882(3); Banks 152; Bills & N 153, 162, 363; Evid 121(1), 317(18), 318(8), 450(10); Ex & Ad 43.

First Nat. Bank of Bogata; Carico v., EDTex, 734 FSupp 768.—Banks 502, 505.

First Nat. Bank of Borger v. Phillips Petroleum Co., CA5 (Tex), 513 F2d 371, reh den 515 F2d 1183, reh den Phillips Petroleum Company v. Alstar Production Corporation, 515 F2d 1183, reh den Alstar Production Corporation v First National Bank of Borger, 515 F2d 1183, cert den 96 SCt 281, 423 US 930, 46 LEd2d 259.—Interest 9; Mines 74(3), 74(6).

First Nat. Bank of Boston v. Champlin Petroleum Co., TexApp–Corpus Christi, 709 SW2d 4, ref nre.—App & E 852, 1001(1), 1003(5); Lim of Act 1, 95(8), 195(3), 195(5), 197(2).

First Nat. Bank of Boston v. Silberstein, Tex, 398 SW2d 914.—Corp 349.

First Nat. Bank of Boston; Silberstein v., TexCivApp–Austin, 391 SW2d 573, writ gr, rev 398 SW2d 914.—Corp 340(2); Statut 241(1).

First Nat. Bank of Bowie v. Cone, TexCivApp–Fort Worth, 170 SW2d 782, writ refused.—App & E 854(1); Execution 118, 247, 258, 275(1); Ex & Ad 224, 261; Judgm 768(1).

First Nat. Bank of Bowie v. Elam, TexCivApp–Fort Worth, 432 SW2d 186.—Contracts 143(4), 229(3).

First Nat. Bank of Bowie v. Fidelity and Cas. Co. of New York, CA5 (Tex), 634 F2d 1000.—Insurance 2402, 2408, 3164, 3198(1).

First Nat. Bank of Bowie; Lambert v., TexApp–Fort Worth, 993 SW2d 833, review den.—Mtg 335, 369(2).

First Nat. Bank of Bowie; Warner v., TexCivApp–Fort Worth, 142 SW2d 897.—Mines 79.1(4); Plead 111.3, 111.8; Venue 22(6).

First Nat. Bank of Bowie; Zimmerman v., TexCivApp–Fort Worth, 235 SW2d 720, ref nre.—App & E 865; Garn 64, 91, 93, 97, 139; Judgm 17(1); Names 16(1).

First Nat. Bank of Brownfield; Giles v., TexCivApp–Amarillo, 257 SW2d 945.—Hus & W 152, 229.3, 238.1, 268(5).

First Nat. Bank of Brownsville, Tex. v. U.S., SDTex, 172 FSupp 757.—Fed Cts 229, 263, 288; U S 131.

First Nat. Bank of Brownwood v. Chambers, TexCivApp–Eastland, 398 SW2d 313.—App & E 931(3); Partners 1, 5, 15, 17, 22, 44, 55, 349; Plgs 36; Princ & A 23(3), 23(5); Trial 351.2(2).

First Nat. Bank of Bryan; Brunson v., CA5 (Tex), 405 F2d 1193.—Bankr 2727(2); Fed Civ Proc 2152.

First Nat. Bank of Bryan; Ferrell v., TexCivApp–Waco, 576 SW2d 677.—App & E 920(4); Garn 88, 148.

First Nat. Bank of Bryan v. Peterson, TexApp–Houston (14 Dist), 709 SW2d 276, ref nre.—Evid 265(7); New Tr 6, 157.

First Nat. Bank of Bryan v. Roberts, TexCivApp–Austin, 286 SW2d 462.—App & E 1235.

First Nat. Bank of Bryan v. Roberts, TexCivApp–Austin, 280 SW2d 788, ref nre.—App & E 281(1), 345.1, 356, 624; New Tr 117(1), 119.

First Nat. Bank of Bryan; Weihausen v., TexCivApp–Waco, 501 SW2d 477.—App & E 282, 1177(2); Garn 9.

First Nat. Bank of Canadian; Garver v., TexCivApp–Amarillo, 432 SW2d 745, ref nre.—App & E 854(1); Estop 90(3), 119; Partners 120, 138, 216(2), 217(1); Plead 290(3).

First Nat. Bank of Canadian; Garver v., TexCivApp–Amarillo, 406 SW2d 797, ref nre, appeal after remand 432 SW2d 745, ref nre.—App & E 78(1), 837(4); Plead 228.23, 354, 360; Pretrial Proc 674, 692, 695.

First Nat. Bank of Chicago; Foster v., TexCivApp–Tyler, 604 SW2d 508.—App & E 173(2); Judgm 181(17), 185(1), 185.3(5).

First Nat. Bank of Chicago; Klein v., TexCivApp–Amarillo, 266 SW2d 448.—Adv Poss 114(1); Estop 32(1); Wills 722.

First Nat. Bank of Chicago v. Pendell, CA5 (Tex), 651 F2d 419.—Fed Civ Proc 2492, 2510.

First Nat. Bank of Chicago; Santa Ana Citrus Groves v., TexCivApp–San Antonio, 149 SW2d 310, writ refused.—Fraud 35; Lim of Act 24(1), 32(1), 100(1); Tresp to T T 38(2).

First Nat. Bank of Claude v. Chaparral Elec. Supply Corp., TexApp–Amarillo, 727 SW2d 353.—Liens 5; Mech Liens 99, 115(4), 116.

First Nat. Bank of Claude, Tex. v. Forrest Williams, Contractor, BkrtcyNDTex, 62 BR 590. See Williams, In re.

First Nat. Bank of Claude, Tex. v. Williams, BkrtcyNDTex, 62 BR 590. See Williams, In re.

First Nat. Bank of Cleveland v. Smith Motor Co., Inc., EDTex, 633 FSupp 621, rev 1st Nat'l Bk/Cleveland v. Smith, 822 F2d 57.—RICO 79.

First Nat. Bank of Coleman; First Nat. Bank in Brownwood v., TexCivApp–Austin, 264 SW 1020, rev First Nat Bank of Coleman v. First Nat Bank of Brownwood, 278 SW 188.—Bills & N 338.5.

First Nat. Bank of Commerce v. Anderson Ford-Lincoln-Mercury, Inc., TexApp–Dallas, 704 SW2d 83, ref nre.—Banks 189; Costs 194.32, 194.40.

First Nat. Bank of Coolidge; Ross Bros. Horse & Mule Co. v., TexCivApp–Waco, 158 SW2d 819.—App & E 1177(7); Evid 10(2); Plead 111.18, 111.32.

First Nat. Bank of Corsicana v. DeFoe, TexCivApp–Waco, 384 SW2d 926, writ refused.—Wills 6, 601(2).

First Nat. Bank of Corsicana; Powers v., TexComApp, 161 SW2d 273, 138 Tex 604.—Char 4, 8, 10, 11, 12, 13, 21(1), 21(2), 22(2), 23, 27, 31, 43, 47, 49; Const Law 1310; Perp 6(1), 8(1), 8(7); Wills 450, 463.

First Nat. Bank of Corsicana; Rentz v., TexCivApp–Waco, 325 SW2d 958, writ refused.—Wills 671.

First Nat. Bank of Corsicana v. Wm. Cameron & Co., TexCivApp–Waco, 149 SW2d 132, writ dism.—App & E 1175(6); Banks 162, 166(4).

First Nat. Bank of Dalhart; Flack v., Tex, 226 SW2d 628, 148 Tex 495.—App & E 842(7); Chat Mtg 139, 157(3); Evid 590, 594; Notice 1, 2, 3, 5, 6; Trial 141.

First Nat. Bank of Dalhart, Tex.; Weisbart & Co. v., CA5 (Tex), 568 F2d 391.—Estop 52.10(3); Sales 3.1, 201(1); Sec Tran 164.1, 166, 171; Statut 194.

First Nat. Bank of Denver City v. Brewer, TexApp–Amarillo, 775 SW2d 51.—Guar 59; Sec Tran 98, 231, 237.

First Nat. Bank of Dona Ana County; Moody v., TexCivApp–Hous (1 Dist), 530 SW2d 879, ref nre.—Judgm 185(2), 818(2), 818(4), 818(5).

First Nat. Bank of Dona Ana County, N.M.; Restrepo v., TexApp–El Paso, 892 SW2d 237.—App & E 389(1), 389(2), 390, 411, 784.

First Nat. Bank of Dona Ana County, N.M.; Restrepo v., TexApp–El Paso, 888 SW2d 606, reh overr.—App & E 781(1).

First Nat. Bank of Dumas; General Elec. Credit Corp. v., TexCivApp–Amarillo, 432 SW2d 737.—App & E

173(6), 556; Chat Mtg 144, 169; Contracts 1, 6; Judgm 185(1), 186; Sales 201(1).

First Nat. Bank of Duncanville v. U.S., NDTex, 481 FSupp 633.—Forfeit 1; Int Rev 3270, 3420, 3422, 3441, 3442.

First Nat. Bank of Durant v. Douglass, CA5 (Tex), 142 F3d 802. See First Nat. Bank of Durant v. Trans Terra Corp. Intern.

First Nat. Bank of Durant v. Trans Terra Corp. Intern., CA5 (Tex), 142 F3d 802, reh den.—Atty & C 26, 63, 64, 105, 129(1); Evid 546; Fed Civ Proc 2142.1, 2152, 2334; Fed Cts 372, 382.1, 383, 823; Fraud 59(1); Interest 10, 39(2.50), 39(3).

First Nat. Bank of Eagle Lake; Engstrom v., CA5 (Tex), 47 F3d 1459, cert den 116 SCt 75, 516 US 818, 133 LEd2d 35.—Armed S 34.2(3), 34.2(6), 34.12; Fed Civ Proc 833, 841, 2546; Fed Cts 18, 817; Rem of C 101.1, 107(9).

First Nat. Bank of Eagle Lake; Engstrom v., TexApp–Houston (14 Dist), 936 SW2d 438, reh overr, and writ den.—Antitrust 138; App & E 843(2); Consp 1.1, 19; Fraud 17; Judgm 183, 185(2), 713(2), 715(1), 720, 724, 829(3).

First Nat. Bank of Eagle Pass v. Levine, Tex, 721 SW2d 287.—Lim of Act 39(13).

First Nat. Bank of Eagle Pass; Levine v., TexApp–San Antonio, 706 SW2d 749, ref nre, and writ gr, and writ withdrawn, rev 721 SW2d 287.—Torts 210, 211, 213, 253, 255.

First Nat. Bank of Edinburg v. Cameron County, Tex-App–Corpus Christi, 159 SW3d 109, reh overr, and review den.—App & E 1175(2); Banks 152; Contracts 1, 326; Impl & C C 30; Judgm 181(11), 183, 185(2); Plead 205(1).

First Nat. Bank of El Campo v. Gann, TexCivApp–Galveston, 150 SW2d 290, writ refused.—Hus & W 273(1), 273(2), 274(1).

First Nat. Bank of El Campo, TX v. Buss, TexApp–Corpus Christi, 143 SW3d 915, review den.—App & E 852, 893(1), 1175(1); Autos 19; Judgm 185(2), 185(5); Sales 10, 200(1); Sec Tran 141.

First Nat. Bank of Euless; Cantrell v., TexCivApp–Fort Worth, 560 SW2d 721, ref nre.—Antitrust 209, 220, 389(2), 393, 397; App & E 76(1), 293, 1178(6); Banks 134(1); Cons Cred 19, 33.1, 67; Costs 194.18; Judgm 199(3.14); Stip 14(12).

First Nat. Bank of Euless v. Schauss, CA5 (Tex), 757 F2d 649. See Schauss v. Metals Depository Corp.

First Nat. Bank of Evant; Medford v., TexCivApp–Waco, 212 SW2d 485.—App & E 1024.3; Plead 111.38, 111.42(2); Venue 7.5(4), 22(6).

First Nat. Bank of Fabens v. Pacific Cotton Agency, TexCivApp–San Antonio, 329 SW2d 504.—Garn 88, 178.

First Nat. Bank of Floresville; Looney v., TexCivApp–San Antonio, 322 SW2d 53, ref nre.—Judgm 17(2), 185(4), 335(1), 478, 681; Tresp to T T 40(7); Wills 614(4).

First Nat. Bank of Flour Bluff; Williams v., TexCiv-App–Corpus Christi, 524 SW2d 795.—Insurance 1701; Judgm 185(2), 185.1(5).

First Nat. Bank of Fort Smith, Ark. v. Phillips, CA5 (Tex), 261 F2d 588.—Bankr 2576; Sales 450.

First Nat. Bank of Fort Worth v. Brown, TexCivApp–Fort Worth, 172 SW2d 151, writ refused wom.—Bills & N 49; Evid 423(8); Princ & S 99, 115(2), 126(3); Proc 4.

First Nat. Bank of Fort Worth v. Bullock, TexCivApp–Austin, 584 SW2d 548, ref nre.—Princ & A 3(2); Statut 245; Tax 3646, 3650, 3653.

First Nat. Bank of Fort Worth; Carruth v., TexCivApp–Eastland, 544 SW2d 678, ref nre.—App & E 930(3), 989; Consp 1.1, 4, 21; Corp 1.4(1); Evid 589; Judgm 199(3.7); Mtg 308; Trial 351.2(2).

First Nat. Bank of Fort Worth; Central Sur. & Ins. Corp. v., TexCivApp–Fort Worth, 367 SW2d 377.—App

& E 1175(5), 1177(2), 1177(7); Mtg 217; Venue 15, 22(1), 22(2).

First Nat. Bank of Fort Worth; Dauley v., TexCivApp–Fort Worth, 565 SW2d 346, ref nre.—Brok 43(1); Evid 441(6); Judgm 185.3(5).

First Nat. Bank of Fort Worth; Eckel v., TexCivApp–Fort Worth, 165 SW2d 776, writ refused.—App & E 1173(1), 1173(2); Evid 424; Release 29(1), 57(1).

First Nat. Bank of Ft. Worth; Farah v., TexApp–Fort Worth, 624 SW2d 341, ref nre.—Estates 1; Stip 14(10); Wills 435, 470(2), 487(4), 703, 706, 862.

First Nat. Bank of Fort Worth; Harrold v., NDTex, 93 FSupp 882.—Char 12; Courts 472.4(6), 489(13), 509; Fed Cts 9; Wills 421.

First Nat. Bank of Fort Worth; Joe Moody Machinery Co. v., TexApp–Fort Worth, 660 SW2d 584.—Plead 111.6, 111.38, 111.39(8), 111.42(10).

First Nat. Bank of Fort Worth; Johnson v., TexCivApp–Fort Worth, 306 SW2d 927.—App & E 1010.1(1); Hus & W 257, 262.1(3), 262.2, 264(3), 266.1, 266.4.

First Nat. Bank of Fort Worth v. Kelley, TexCivApp–Eastland, 278 SW2d 350.—Judgm 335(1); Prohib 11.

First Nat. Bank of Fort Worth; Kelley v., TexCivApp–Eastland, 270 SW2d 644.—Judgm 101(1), 101(2), 112, 113; Parties 59(3), 61.

First Nat. Bank of Fort Worth; Life Ins. Co. of North America v., Tex, 464 SW2d 362.—App & E 1094(2).

First Nat. Bank of Fort Worth; Life Ins. Co. of North America v., TexCivApp–Fort Worth, 453 SW2d 310, writ gr, aff 464 SW2d 362.—Insurance 1735, 2600(1), 3541.

First Nat. Bank of Fort Worth; Lusher v., TexCivApp–Fort Worth, 260 SW2d 621, ref nre.—App & E 22, 609; Mtg 1, 6, 27, 32(1), 33(3); Ven & Pur 1, 3(4), 18, 18(3), 57.

First Nat. Bank of Fort Worth; McLain v., TexCivApp–Texarkana, 263 SW2d 324, ref nre.—Mines 74.5.

First Nat. Bank of Fort Worth; Moody Machinery Co. v., TexApp–Fort Worth, 660 SW2d 584. See Joe Moody Machinery Co. v. First Nat. Bank of Fort Worth.

First Nat. Bank of Ft. Worth; O'Hara v., TexCivApp–Fort Worth, 613 SW2d 306.—Sec Tran 240.

First Nat. Bank of Ft. Worth; Petroleum Equipment Financial Corp. v., TexApp–Fort Worth, 622 SW2d 152, ref nre.—Judgm 304, 306, 324, 326.

First Nat. Bank of Ft. Worth v. U.S., CA5 (Tex), 633 F2d 1168.—Int Rev 4957; Interpl 1; U S 111(10).

First Nat. Bank of Fort Worth v. U.S., NDTex, 301 FSupp 667.—Atty & C 140; Int Rev 3377, 4177; Judgm 828.21(3).

First Nat. Bank of Fort Worth; U.S. Cold Storage Corp. v., TexCivApp–Fort Worth, 350 SW2d 856, ref nre.—Banks 139; Bills & N 356, 434.

First Nat. Bank of Franklin, Tex. v. Associated Attorneys Title Agency, Inc., TexApp–Waco, 759 SW2d 481. —Insurance 2639.

First Nat. Bank of Frisco; Irrigation Ass'n v., TexApp–Dallas, 773 SW2d 346, writ den.—Assign 125.

First Nat. Bank of Galveston; Morse v., TexCivApp–Galveston, 194 SW2d 578, ref nre.—Char 47; Wills 464.

First Nat. Bank of Galveston v. Trinity Protestant Episcopal Church of Galveston, TexCivApp–Galveston, 219 SW2d 828.—Wills 440, 487(3), 601(6).

First Nat. Bank of Gatlinburg v. RepublicBank Dallas, N.A., NDTex, 676 FSupp 128.—Banks 356.

First Nat. Bank of Giddings; Fajkus v., TexApp–Austin, 735 SW2d 882, writ den.—App & E 218.2(5.1), 238(2), 989, 1177(7); Bills & N 28; Evid 43(3); Home 32, 33, 35, 62, 63, 175, 213, 214; Hus & W 232.1; Mtg 497(1); Pretrial Proc 45.

First Nat. Bank of Giddings; Fajkus v., TexApp–Austin, 654 SW2d 42, dism.—Banks 275; Venue 5.3(1), 5.3(5).

FIRST

See Guidelines for Arrangement at the beginning of this Volume

First Nat. Bank of Giddings, Tex. v. Birnbaum, Tex-App–Austin, 826 SW2d 189, reh den.—App & E 82(4), 654.

First Nat. Bank of Gilmer v. First State Bank of Hawkins, TexCivApp–Texarkana, 456 SW2d 173, writ dism.—App & E 101(1).

First Nat. Bank of Glen Rose v. Johnson, TexCivApp–Waco, 608 SW2d 834.—App & E 219(2), 907(3).

First Nat. Bank of Goliad; Hosey v., TexCivApp–Corpus Christi, 595 SW2d 629, dism.—App & E 154(4); Costs 260(5).

First Nat. Bank of Gonzales; Rost v., TexCivApp–Corpus Christi, 472 SW2d 579.—Venue 7.5(3).

First Nat. Bank of Granbury; Fauth v., TexCivApp–Eastland, 214 SW2d 168.—App & E 662(3); Lim of Act 199(1); Tresp to T T 41(1); Trial 121(2), 133.6(4), 133.6(5).

First Nat. Bank of Grand Prairie v. Lone Star Life Ins., Tex, 529 SW2d 67.—Sec Tran 8.1.

First Nat. Bank of Grapevine v. Nu-Way Transports, Inc., TexCivApp–Fort Worth, 585 SW2d 813, ref nre.—Lim of Act 32(2), 55(1), 55(5), 105(1).

First Nat. Bank of Hallettsville; Heldenfels Bros., Inc. v., TexApp–Corpus Christi, 657 SW2d 883, ref nre.—Banks 134(7).

First Nat. Bank of Hallettsville; San Antonio Livestock Market Institutev., TexCivApp–Corpus Christi, 431 SW2d 408.—Banks 155, 175(3).

First Nat. Bank of Harlingen; Meadows v., TexCivApp–San Antonio, 149 SW2d 591, writ dism, correct.—Banks 143(7); Damag 87(2); Mal Pros 48.

First Nat. Bank of Hereford; B & W Cattle Co. v., TexApp–Amarillo, 692 SW2d 946.—App & E 758.3(6), 846(5); Receivers 1, 8, 16, 30, 36, 38, 57.

First Nat. Bank of Hereford; Bellah v., Tex, 484 SW2d 558.—Mtg 572.

First Nat. Bank of Hereford; Bellah v., TexCivApp–Amarillo, 478 SW2d 636, ref nre 484 SW2d 558.—Mtg 11, 12, 369(2), 369(3); Trusts 10.

First Nat. Bank of Hereford; Bellah v., TexCivApp–Eastland, 474 SW2d 785, ref nre.—Hus & W 156; Judgm 181(26), 189; Mtg 355, 358.

First Nat. Bank of Hereford; Gulf Oil Co. U.S. v., TexCivApp–Amarillo, 503 SW2d 300.—Attach 140, 143; Sec Tran 82.1, 98, 140.

First Nat. Bank of Hereford; Howard Gault & Son, Inc. v., TexCivApp–Amarillo, 541 SW2d 235.—Banks 140(1), 154(8); Partners 17, 32, 44.

First Nat. Bank of Hereford; Howard Gault & Son, Inc. v., TexCivApp–Amarillo, 523 SW2d 496.—App & E 79(1), 792; Judgm 217.

First Nat. Bank of Hereford, Tex.; Bellah v., CA5 (Tex), 495 F2d 1109.—Fed Cts 931; Sec Reg 5.13, 5.16, 35.10.

First Nat. Bank of Hico v. English, TexCivApp–Waco, 240 SW2d 503.—Armed S 34.11(1); Banks 154(1), 154(2), 154(5); Damag 5, 23; Plead 34(1).

First Nat. Bank of Highlands; Clark v., TexApp–Houston (1 Dist), 794 SW2d 953.—Judgm 181(25), 185(2), 185.3(15).

First Nat. Bank of Hobbs; Vahlsing Christina Corp. Inc. v., TexCivApp–El Paso, 491 SW2d 954, ref nre.—Liens 12, 13.

First Nat. Bank of Houston; Lang v., CA5 (Tex), 215 F2d 118.—Bankr 2608(2); Fed Cts 854.

First Nat. Bank of Hughes Springs, Tex.; Century Ins. Co. v., CCA5 (Tex), 133 F2d 789.—Fed Cts 921; Insurance 1721, 2140, 2161, 2193, 3043, 3442, 3446; Interest 50; Interpl 35; Judgm 713(1).

First Nat. Bank of Ingleside; St. Clair v., TexCivApp–Corpus Christi, 422 SW2d 558.—Libel 89(1).

First Nat. Bank of Irving v. Shockley, TexApp–Corpus Christi, 663 SW2d 685.—Antitrust 358, 393; App & E 865; Damag 193.1, 194, 199; Interest 39(2.20), 39(3); Judgm 101(1), 116.

First Nat. Bank of Jacksonville; Bundrick v., TexCivApp–Tyler, 570 SW2d 12, ref nre.—Bills & N 530; Cons Cred 12, 13, 14, 15, 18; Sec Tran 242.1; Usury 48.

First Nat. Bank of Jacksonville; Guarantee Ins. Co. v., TexCivApp–Tyler, 552 SW2d 855, dism.—App & E 907(3), 912; Insurance 3450; Liens 7; Plead 111.9; Venue 22(3), 22(4).

First Nat. Bank of Jefferson v. Joseph T. Ryerson & Son, Inc., TexCivApp–Texarkana, 487 SW2d 377, ref nre.—Sales 1(1), 53(1).

First Nat. Bank of Jefferson v. Laco Const. Co., TexCivApp–Tyler, 568 SW2d 195, dism.—Banks 275; Plead 111.42(4); Venue 7.5(3).

First Nat. Bank of Jefferson; McLaughlin v., TexApp–Texarkana, 858 SW2d 511, reh overr, and writ den.—Banks 55(6); Parties 65(1), 65(3).

First Nat. Bank of Jefferson v. Tri-State General Agency, Inc., TexCivApp–Texarkana, 578 SW2d 456, ref nre.—Estop 102, 103; Insurance 1654, 1703, 1734, 1740, 2094.

First Nat. Bank of Kerrville v. Hackworth, TexApp–San Antonio, 673 SW2d 218.—Abate & R 52, 57; Antitrust 141; App & E 931(3), 994(2), 995, 999(1); Banks 148(2), 148(3), 148(4), 154(8); Damag 87(1), 221(2.1); Interest 39(2.6), 39(2.30); Statut 212.1, 215; Trial 133.6.

First Nat. Bank of Kerrville v. O'Dell, Tex, 856 SW2d 410.—Subrog 7(7), 38.

First Nat. Bank of Kerrville; O'Dell v., TexApp–San Antonio, 855 SW2d 1, writ gr, rev 856 SW2d 410.—Mtg 298(4), 378.

First Nat. Bank of Killeen; Roberts v., TexCivApp–Austin, 395 SW2d 420, ref nre.—App & E 623, 624.

First Nat. Bank of Killeen, Tex.; Davis v., CA5 (Tex), 976 F2d 944, reh den 983 F2d 234, cert den 113 SCt 2341, 508 US 910, 124 LEd2d 251.—Civil R 1551; Fed Cts 638.

First Nat. Bank of La Grange; Pentad Joint Venture v., TexApp–Austin, 797 SW2d 92, writ den.—Judgm 181(11), 181(25), 185(2), 185(6), 185.3(15); Mtg 360, 369(2), 369(3), 377, 379; Plead 36(2); Sec Tran 240.

First Nat. Bank of Lake Jackson; Patterson v., TexApp–Houston (14 Dist), 921 SW2d 240, reh overr.—App & E 173(1), 870(2), 960(3); Home 18, 23, 96, 97, 105, 115(1), 116, 154, 158, 181(1), 187, 192; Judgm 181(6), 181(11), 185(2), 185(5); Partit 12(3), 60; Plead 234, 420(2).

First Nat. Bank of Lamarque v. Smith, CA5 (Tex), 610 F2d 1258.—Banks 235, 253; Fed Cts 724, 757.

First Nat. Bank of La Marque v. Smith, SDTex, 436 FSupp 824, aff in part, vac in part 610 F2d 1258.—Banks 253, 258; Corp 307; Insurance 1604, 1611, 1613.

First Nat. Bank of Lancaster v. Glens Falls Ins. Co., TexCivApp–Waco, 329 SW2d 115, ref nre.—Insurance 2403.

First Nat. Bank of Las Vegas, N. M. v. Russell's Estate, CA5 (Tex), 657 F2d 668.—Fed Civ Proc 2511; Sec Reg 5.29.

First Nat. Bank of Levelland v. Jaggers, TexCivApp–Amarillo, 86 SW2d 812.—Plead 111.39(5), 111.42(5).

First Nat. Bank of Levelland v. McDonald, BkrtcyND-Tex, 41 BR 285. See Lane, In re.

First Nat. Bank of Libby, Montana v. Rector, TexApp–Austin, 710 SW2d 100, ref nre.—Const Law 3965(7); Courts 12(2.5), 12(2.10); Judgm 178, 818(1), 928, 942, 944, 945; Proc 145, 149, 153.

First Nat. Bank of Littlefield; American Tank & Mfg. Co. v., TexCivApp–Amarillo, 370 SW2d 948, ref nre.—Banks 173; Fraud 7; Princ & A 48.

First Nat. Bank of Littlefield; Maberry v., TexCivApp–Amarillo, 351 SW2d 96.—App & E 1170.10; Chat Mtg 17, 89, 278; Land & Ten 247, 248(1), 252(3); Plead 310; Propty 9.

First Nat. Bank of Livingston, Texas; Lacy v., TexApp–Beaumont, 809 SW2d 362.—App & E 907(1), 1008.1(5),

1008.1(7), 1010.1(3); Evid 1, 18, 51; Plead 403(1); Sec Tran 231, 240.

First Nat. Bank of Longview; Century Indem. Co. v., TexCivApp–Texarkana, 272 SW2d 150.—App & E 219(2), 931(4); Bills & N 149; Corp 432(12), 433(1).

First Nat. Bank of Longview; Judson Bldg. Co., Inc. v., EDTex, 587 FSupp 852.—Civil R 1071, 1401; Fed Civ Proc 2470, 2470.4, 2547.1; Land & Ten 120(1); Mtg 191; Trover 9(1).

First Nat. Bank of Longview, Tex.; City of Longview, Tex. v., CCA5 (Tex), 152 F2d 97, cert den First National Bank of Longview, Texas v. City of Longview, Texas, 66 SCt 684, 327 US 784, 90 LEd 1011.—Mun Corp 54, 966(6).

First Nat. Bank of Louisville; Great-Ness Professional Services, Inc. v., TexApp–Houston (14 Dist), 704 SW2d 916.—Acct Action on 10; Judgm 181(5.1), 186.

First Nat. Bank of Lubbock; Biggs v., TexApp–El Paso, 808 SW2d 232, writ den.—Interest 39(2.20); Partners 67, 68(1), 108, 249, 258(7), 258(13); Trial 352.1(1).

First Nat. Bank of Lubbock; Great Plains Life Ins. Co. v., TexCivApp–Amarillo, 316 SW2d 98, ref nre.—Banks 133; Contracts 278(1), 318; Corp 425(5), 426(2), 432(12); Land & Ten 111, 112.5; Tender 16(2), 16(3), 28.

First Nat. Bank of Lubbock v. Jenkins, TexCivApp–Amarillo, 350 SW2d 52.—Int Rev 4785; Mech Liens 115(1).

First Nat. Bank of Lubbock, Tex.; McClure v., CA5 (Tex), 497 F2d 490, reh den 502 F2d 1167, cert den 95 SCt 1132, 420 US 930, 43 LEd2d 402.—Courts 90(2); Fed Cts 797; Sec Reg 5.10, 5.13, 60.16.

First Nat. Bank of Lubbock, Tex.; McClure v., NDTex, 352 FSupp 454, aff 497 F2d 490, reh den 502 F2d 1167, cert den 95 SCt 1132, 420 US 930, 43 LEd2d 402.—Sec Reg 5.13, 60.10, 60.16.

First Nat. Bank of Luling v. Nugent, TexCivApp–San Antonio, 384 SW2d 224, ref nre.—Contracts 152; Mtg 309(1); Release 33.

First Nat. Bank of McAllen v. Brown, TexApp–Corpus Christi, 644 SW2d 808, ref nre.—App & E 930(3), 989; Courts 169(1); Damag 221(2.1); Evid 474(16); Sec Tran 242.1, 243; Trover 3, 35.

First Nat. Bank of McGregor v. Collins, TexCivApp–Austin, 266 SW2d 506, ref nre.—Accord 11(1); Contracts 354; Fraud 58(4); Trial 350.4(1).

First Nat. Bank of Marshall v. Beavers, TexCivApp–Texarkana, 619 SW2d 288, ref nre.—Tresp 45(1).

First Nat. Bank of Marshall v. Beavers, TexCivApp–Texarkana, 602 SW2d 327.—Adv Poss 43(2), 43(3), 60(3), 85(2); Ease 24; Waters 164.

First Nat. Bank of Marshall v. Kilgore First Nat. Bank, TexApp–Texarkana, 626 SW2d 546.—Banks 275; Venue 8.5(7).

First Nat. Bank of Marshall, Tex.; Ender v., TexCivApp–Texarkana, 494 SW2d 606.—Action 60; App & E 183; Bills & N 502.

First Nat. Bank of Marshall, Texas v. Texas Foundries, Inc., TexCivApp–Beaumont, 512 SW2d 690.—Banks 275; Plead 85(1), 110, 290(3), 292; Venue 32(2).

First Nat. Bank of Memphis; Fisher v., TexCivApp–Amarillo, 584 SW2d 515.—Estop 52.10(3); Sec Tran 12, 141, 171; Trial 3(2).

First Nat. Bank of Mercedes; La Sara Grain Co. v., Tex, 673 SW2d 558, on remand 676 SW2d 183.—Antitrust 130, 143(2), 145, 147, 205, 208, 209; App & E 1078(1), 1106(4), 1114; Banks 138, 148(2), 148(3), 148(4); Bills & N 337; Contracts 205.10, 205.15(1); Costs 207; Interest 39(2.30); Princ & A 177(1); Statut 223.1, 273.

First Nat. Bank of Mercedes v. La Sara Grain Co., TexApp–Corpus Christi, 676 SW2d 183.—App & E 1178(6); Costs 194.18; Stip 14(1).

First Nat. Bank of Mercedes v. La Sara Grain Co., TexApp–Corpus Christi, 646 SW2d 246, writ gr, aff in part, rev in part 673 SW2d 558, on remand 676 SW2d

183.—Antitrust 130, 145; App & E 1008.1(1); Banks 148(2), 148(4), 154(8); Estop 95.

First Nat. Bank of Mesquite; Knox v., TexCivApp–Waco, 422 SW2d 832.—Bills & N 139(3), 140, 518(1).

First Nat. Bank of Mexia v. Anderson, TexCivApp–Waco, 352 SW2d 851, ref nre.—App & E 1029; Bills & N 334.

First Nat. Bank of Mexia; Naylor Automotive Service v., TexCivApp–Waco, 284 SW2d 759, writ dism.—Venue 8.5(7), 16 1/2.

First Nat. Bank of Midland; Clay Bldg. Material Co. v., TexCivApp–Eastland, 161 SW2d 799.—App & E 99, 1043(1); Garn 77, 83, 194.

First Nat. Bank of Midland; Exxon Corp. v., TexCivApp–El Paso, 529 SW2d 110, ref nre.—Mines 92.79; States 203.

First Nat. Bank of Midland; Lewis v., TexCivApp–El Paso, 445 SW2d 629.—Des & Dist 36.

First Nat. Bank of Midland; National Sur. Corp. v., Tex, 431 SW2d 353.—Insurance 2408.

First Nat. Bank of Midland; National Sur. Corp. v., TexCivApp–El Paso, 424 SW2d 27, rev 431 SW2d 353.—Insurance 2408.

First Nat. Bank of Midland; New v., TexCivApp–El Paso, 476 SW2d 121, ref nre.—App & E 692(1), 846(5); Corp 432(12); Plead 427; Stip 1, 12, 13, 14(12), 17(1), 17(3).

First Nat. Bank of Midland v. Protective Life Ins. Co., CA5 (Tex), 511 F2d 731.—Insurance 1810, 1816, 1827, 1831, 2037.

First Nat. Bank of Midland; Rogers v., TexCivApp–El Paso, 448 SW2d 149, ref nre.—Des & Dist 39, 41; Statut 181(1), 205.

First Nat. Bank of Midland v. Stoutco, Inc., TexCivApp–San Antonio, 530 SW2d 619, dism.—Banks 275; Estop 52.10(2).

First Nat. Bank of Midland, Tex. v. U.S., CA5 (Tex), 423 F2d 1286.—Int Rev 4155, 4159(2).

First Nat. Bank of Midlothian v. Harrell, BkrtcyWD-Tex, 94 BR 86. See Harrell, In re.

First Nat. Bank of Midlothian v. Lometa Com'n Co., BkrtcyWDTex, 94 BR 86. See Harrell, In re.

First Nat. Bank of Mineola; Mineola State Bank v., TexCivApp–Austin, 574 SW2d 246, ref nre.—Banks 6, 17.

First Nat. Bank of Mineola, Tex. v. Farmers and Merchants State Bank of Athens, Tex., TexCivApp–Tyler, 417 SW2d 317, ref nre.—Banks 174, 175(1), 189, 190; Bills & N 6, 151, 296; Princ & A 1; Statut 212.6.

First Nat. Bank of Mission; Morriss v., TexCivApp–San Antonio, 249 SW2d 269, ref nre.—Contracts 147(2); Mines 78.1(3), 78.2, 79.1, 79.1(1), 79.1(2), 79.4, 79.6.

First Nat. Bank of Mission; Teton Intern. v., TexApp–Corpus Christi, 718 SW2d 838.—App & E 173(12); Const Law 3965(4); Sec Tran 12, 90, 139.1.

First Nat. Bank of Mission v. Thomas, Tex, 402 SW2d 890.—App & E 1083(6), 1095; Chat Mtg 136, 170(1); Crops 2.

First Nat. Bank of Mission; Thomas v., TexCivApp–San Antonio, 384 SW2d 219, writ gr, rev 402 SW2d 890.—Chat Mtg 136, 177(1), 177(2), 177(3); Crops 2; Trial 351.2(3.1).

First Nat. Bank of Missouri City v. Gittelman, TexApp–Houston (14 Dist), 788 SW2d 165, writ den.—Costs 194.32; Damag 15, 94; Evid 474(19), 501(7), 568(4); Interest 22(1); Sec Tran 230, 237, 242.1, 243; Trover 44, 46, 60, 61, 72.

First Nat. Bank of Mt. Pleasant, Tex.; Hayden v., CA5 (Tex), 595 F2d 994.—Fed Civ Proc 2497.1.

First Nat. Bank of New Boston, Texas; Ketcham v., TexApp–Texarkana, 875 SW2d 753.—Banks 100; Home 90, 96, 105, 128, 179; Judgm 181(17), 185(2).

FIRST

See Guidelines for Arrangement at the beginning of this Volume

First Nat. Bank of Odessa; Lone Star Beer, Inc. v., TexCivApp–El Paso, 468 SW2d 930, ref nre.—Bills & N 356; Judgm 185.3(21); Trover 4, 16.

First Nat. Bank of O'Donnell; Hamilton v., TexCivApp–Amarillo, 155 SW2d 626, writ refused wom.—Judgm 715(3); Lim of Act 103(4); Trial 29(1), 114; Trusts 69.

First National Bank of Olney; Berry v., TexApp–Fort Worth, 894 SW2d 558.—App & E 863, 934(1); Banks 100; Fraud 7, 64(1); Judgm 185(2).

First Nat. Bank of Paducah; Havins v., TexApp–Amarillo, 919 SW2d 177.—Evid 5(1), 20(1); Sec Tran 230, 231, 240.

First Nat. Bank of Panhandle; Hankins v., TexCivApp–Amarillo, 287 SW2d 493, ref nre.—Contracts 25.

First Nat. Bank of Panhandle; Hood v., TexCivApp–Amarillo, 410 SW2d 449, ref nre.—App & E 1008.1(7), 1010.1(1); Bills & N 250, 517; Evid 420(7), 441(1).

First Nat. Bank of Paris; Furgerson v., TexCivApp–Texarkana, 218 SW2d 1019.—Chat Mtg 281; Sales 315.

First Nat. Bank of Paris; Penix v., TexCivApp–Texarkana, 260 SW2d 63, writ refused.—App & E 946, 994(3), 1010.1(5), 1012.1(2); Evid 14; Trusts 112, 167, 270; Wills 102, 439, 470(1), 684.6.

First Nat. Bank of Perryton; Industrial Life Ins. Co. v., TexCivApp–Tyler, 449 SW2d 129.—Insurance 1758, 2983, 3003(8), 3571.

First Nat. Bank of Plainview, Texas; Springer v., TexApp–Amarillo, 866 SW2d 626, reh den, and writ gr, rev 866 SW2d 592.—App & E 78(1), 79(1), 80(6), 782, 934(1), 1078(2); Courts 39; Judgm 183, 187; Plead 234, 238(3).

First Nat. Bank of Plano v. Fairfield, TexCivApp–Waco, 446 SW2d 353, ref nre.—Frds St of 28.

First Nat. Bank of Plano v. State, TexCivApp–Dallas, 555 SW2d 200.—App & E 19; Receivers 71, 72.

First Nat. Bank of Port Arthur; Duke v., TexApp–Beaumont, 698 SW2d 230.—Bills & N 49, 96, 97(1); Sec Tran 226, 228, 240.

First Nat. Bank of Port Arthur v. Sassine, TexCivApp, 556 SW2d 116.—Trusts 61(1), 61(3), 182.

First Nat. Bank of Post v. Republic Supply Co., TexCivApp–Eastland, 166 SW2d 373, writ refused wom.—App & E 1075; Banks 105(3), 227(3); Estop 52.10(2), 70(2); Plead 111.42(3).

First Nat. Bank of Quitaque; Cogdill v., TexCivApp–Amarillo, 193 SW2d 701.—Gifts 15, 18(1), 49(5).

First Nat. Bank of Quitman v. Moore, TexCivApp–Texarkana, 220 SW2d 694, writ dism.—Bills & N 356; Evid 25(1).

First Nat. Bank of Quitman; Petty v., TexCivApp–Texarkana, 278 SW2d 361.—App & E 192.2; Evid 591; Partners 55, 213(1), 213(2); Plead 362(4).

First Nat. Bank of Richardson; Genico Distributors, Inc. v., TexCivApp–Texarkana, 616 SW2d 418, ref nre.—Antitrust 143(2); App & E 216(1); Costs 194.44.

First Nat. Bank of Rotan; Lawson v., TexCivApp–Amarillo, 150 SW2d 279, writ dism, correct.—Chat Mtg 136, 150(1), 229(1), 229(3); Estop 83(6); Trial 350.1, 351.5(1), 352.4(3).

First Nat. Bank of Round Rock; National Bank of Texas v., TexApp–Tyler, 682 SW2d 366.—Judgm 335(2), 335(3).

First Nat. Bank of San Angelo; Cornelison v., TexCivApp–Austin, 218 SW2d 888, ref nre.—App & E 1033(1); Receivers 137.

First Nat. Bank of San Angelo; Greig v., TexCivApp–Beaumont, 511 SW2d 86, ref nre.—Corp 617(2); Guar 37; Lim of Act 50(1); Usury 16, 52.

First Nat. Bank of San Angelo v. Sheffield, TexCivApp–Austin, 475 SW2d 820.—Assign 31, 34, 121, 134; Plead 292.

First Nat. Bank of San Angelo, Tex.; Hill & Combs v., CCA5 (Tex), 139 F2d 740.—Contracts 166, 176(1); Evid 448, 450(7); U S 74.2.

First Nat. Bank of San Angelo, Tex. v. Hill & Combs, TexCivApp–Austin, 177 SW2d 75.—Plead 111.43.

First Nat. Bank of San Antonio; Abercia v., TexCivApp–San Antonio, 500 SW2d 573.—Evid 459(2); Judgm 143(1), 143(2), 145(4), 153(1), 158, 162(2), 162(4).

First Nat. Bank of San Antonio; Heusinger Hardware Co. v., TexCivApp–Eastland, 367 SW2d 710, ref nre.—App & E 916(1); Banks 174; Contracts 150; Judgm 185.3(16), 186; Lim of Act 24(2).

First Nat. Bank of San Augustine; Womack v., TexCivApp–Tyler, 613 SW2d 548.—App & E 768, 837(8), 1050.1(11); Bills & N 59, 537(2); Evid 459(2); Jury 83(1), 97(1); New Tr 44(2), 56; Partners 146(1), 217(3), 218(3); Witn 178(1).

First Nat. Bank of Schulenburg v. Winkler, TexComApp, 161 SW2d 1053, 139 Tex 131.—Banks 119, 134(1), 134(6).

First Nat. Bank of Schulenburg v. Winkler, TexCivApp–Austin, 146 SW2d 201, aff 161 SW2d 1053, 139 Tex 131.—Banks 130(3), 134(4), 134(6), 134(7), 154(5); Evid 77(5), 590; Trial 356(1).

First Nat. Bank of Seguin; Magnum Machine & Tool Corp. v., TexCivApp–Eastland, 545 SW2d 549.—Mtg 338.

First Nat. Bank of Seminole v. Hooper, Tex, 104 SW3d 83.—Fraud Conv 88.

First Nat. Bank of Seminole, Texas v. Hooper, TexApp–El Paso, 48 SW3d 802, reh overr, and review den, and reh of petition for review gr, and withdrawn, and review gr, rev 104 SW3d 83.—App & E 842(1), 969, 989, 1001(1), 1002, 1003(2), 1003(3), 1003(7); Fraud Conv 77, 186, 272, 273, 277(1), 283, 297, 300(1), 309(1), 314; Jury 13(5.1); Trial 202.

First Nat. Bank of Snyder v. Evans, TexCivApp–Eastland, 169 SW2d 754, writ refused.—Deeds 109; Mines 55(2), 55(4).

First Nat. Bank of Stanton; Eberley v., TexCivApp–Eastland, 272 SW2d 532, ref nre.—Bills & N 426; Fraud 49, 50, 64(1); Mtg 319(3).

First Nat. Bank of Sudan; Bradley v., TexCivApp–Amarillo, 470 SW2d 273, ref nre.—App & E 223; Judgm 185.3(16).

First Nat. Bank of Temple v. Continental Cas. Co., CCA5 (Tex), 133 F2d 197.—Insurance 2412.

First Nat. Bank of Temple; Continental Cas. Co. v., CCA5 (Tex), 116 F2d 885, 135 ALR 1141, cert den 61 SCt 1087, 313 US 575, 85 LEd 1533.—Evid 506; Fraud 50, 58(1); Insurance 2406(5), 2412; Trial 235(7).

First Nat. Bank of Temple; Narrell v., TexCivApp–Austin, 241 SW2d 361.—Banks 119, 129, 138, 153.

First Nat. Bank of Temple; Nettles v., TexCivApp–Austin, 168 SW2d 920, writ refused wom.—Evid 442(1); Release 58(2); Trusts 13, 17(3), 343, 352.

First Nat. Bank of Temple; Pruett v., TexCivApp–Austin, 175 SW2d 658.—App & E 877(3), 1054(1); Banks 305; Costs 42(1); Evid 397(2); Gifts 30(4); Joint Ten 12; Release 29(1); Witn 141, 142, 178(1), 178(4).

First Nat. Bank of Throckmorton; Fisher v., TexCivApp–Eastland, 171 SW2d 223.—Des & Dist 80; Home 96.

First Nat. Bank of Trenton, Trenton, Tex.; Walton v., TexApp–Texarkana, 956 SW2d 647, reh overr, and review den, and reh of petition for review overr.—Courts 202(4); Elect of Rem 15; Ex & Ad 202.15, 222(1), 224, 251, 261; Judgm 501; Mtg 212.1; Notice 5; Ven & Pur 92, 246, 251, 257, 260(1), 266(4), 296, 299(1), 301, 302.

First Nat. Bank of Trinity; Thompson v., BkrtcyEDTex, 111 BR 582. See Franklin, In re.

First Nat. Bank of Trinity, Texas v. McKay, TexCivApp–Hous (1 Dist), 521 SW2d 661.—Banks 139; Bills & N 149, 342, 365(1), 452(1); Equity 72(1); Evid 65.

First Nat. Bank of Troup; Dawson v., TexCivApp–Tyler, 420 SW2d 249.—App & E 954(1); Mines 52.

First Nat. Bank of Troup; Dawson v., TexCivApp–Tyler, 417 SW2d 652.—Courts 207.1, 207.3; Mtg 338.

First Nat. Bank of Tulia; Herndon v., TexApp–Amarillo, 802 SW2d 396, writ den.—Antitrust 141, 358; App & E 1136; Banks 226; Contracts 95(1), 168.

First Nat. Bank of Waco; Bates v., TexCivApp–Waco, 502 SW2d 181.—Action 60; App & E 1106(1), 1173(2); Contracts 94(1), 100; Judgm 181(22), 185(2).

First Nat. Bank of Waco; Burnett v., TexCivApp–Eastland, 536 SW2d 600, ref nre.—App & E 286, 291, 927(7); Plgs 19; Trial 139.1(7); Trusts 231(1), 237.

First Nat. Bank of Waco; Burnett v., TexCivApp–Tyler, 567 SW2d 873, ref nre.—App & E 863; Judgm 185(2); Trusts 171, 231(1).

First Nat. Bank of Waco; Davis v., TexComApp, 161 SW2d 467, 139 Tex 36, 144 ALR 1.—App & E 540, 714(1); Des & Dist 68; Judgm 665, 666, 670, 713(2), 717, 719, 720, 725(1), 739, 958(1); Wills 608(5).

First Nat. Bank of Waco; Davis v., TexCivApp–Waco, 145 SW2d 707, aff 161 SW2d 467, 139 Tex 36, 144 ALR 1.—Action 6; Costs 238(2); Courts 93(1); Deeds 38(1); Estates 8; Judgm 524, 665; Partit 34, 116(1); Tax 2768; Wills 608(3.1), 608(5), 695(4).

First Nat. Bank of Waco; Prewitt v., TexCivApp–Waco, 491 SW2d 950.—Evid 222(1), 222(10), 265(17); Venue 7.5(2), 7.5(3).

First Nat. Bank of Waco v. U.S., WDTex, 327 FSupp 1119.—Int Rev 3514, 4045.

First Nat. Bank of Waco; Warner v., TexCivApp–San Antonio, 369 SW2d 651.—Guar 61.

First Nat. Bank of Waco, Texas; Denton v., CA5 (Tex), 765 F2d 1295, reh den 772 F2d 904.—Labor & Emp 563(3), 610, 635, 682, 683, 686.

First Nat. Bank of Weatherford; Christian v., TexCivApp–Fort Worth, 531 SW2d 832, ref nre.—App & E 866(3), 927(7), 989; Lim of Act 40(1), 41, 187; Plead 78; Sec Tran 231, 240; Trover 16.

First Nat. Bank of Weatherford; Phillips ex rel. Estate of Fullingim v., NDTex, 258 FSupp2d 501.—Atty & C 77; Fed Civ Proc 2757, 2771(15).

First Nat. Bank of Wellington; Chapman v., TexCivApp–Amarillo, 221 SW2d 318.—App & E 1177(2); Plead 111.3, 111.4, 111.5, 111.6, 111.15, 255.

First Nat. Bank of West University Place; Turk v., TexApp–Houston (1 Dist), 802 SW2d 264, writ den.—App & E 977(1); Courts 70; Judges 51(2); Judgm 135, 145(2); Jury 25(6).

First Nat. Bank of Whitewright; Henslee v., TexCivApp–Dallas, 314 SW2d 881.—App & E 707(2); Bills & N 245, 250; Evid 403; Judgm 181(25); Plead 258(3); Princ & S 190(6).

First Nat. Bank of Wichita Falls; Avis v., Tex, 174 SW2d 255, 141 Tex 489.—Mines 5.2(2.1), 73.1(3); Trusts 205; Wills 439, 440, 441, 455.

First Nat. Bank of Wichita Falls; Avis v., TexCivApp–Fort Worth, 162 SW2d 1072, writ gr, aff 174 SW2d 255, 141 Tex 489.—Evid 20(1); Ex & Ad 138(1); Trusts 172, 191(1), 205; Wills 439, 440, 441, 470(1).

First Nat. Bank of Wichita Falls v. First Bank of Chico, Tex, 290 SW2d 506, 155 Tex 601.—Chat Mtg 49(1), 139.

First Nat. Bank of Wichita Falls v. First Bank of Chico, TexCivApp–Fort Worth, 285 SW2d 286, rev 290 SW2d 506, 155 Tex 601.—Chat Mtg 140, 152, 197(1), 227; Mtg 116, 131, 134.

First Nat. Bank of Wichita Falls; King v., Tex, 192 SW2d 260, 144 Tex 583, 163 ALR 1128.—Deeds 138; Evid 5(2); Mines 55(5).

First Nat. Bank of Wichita Falls; King v., TexCivApp–Fort Worth, 189 SW2d 347, aff 192 SW2d 260, 144 Tex 583, 163 ALR 1128.—Deeds 90, 93, 100; Evid 461(5); Mines 55(1), 55(5).

First Nat. Bank of Wichita Falls; Taylor v., TexCivApp–Fort Worth, 207 SW2d 428.—Wills 435, 439, 453,

470(1), 471, 472, 486, 488, 590, 597(2), 629, 634(8), 634(14).

First Nat. Bank of Yorktown v. Pickett, TexCivApp–Corpus Christi, 555 SW2d 547.—Fraud 58(1); Plead 111.18, 111.38, 111.39(4), 111.42(1), 111.42(4); Venue 5.3(1), 5.3(2), 5.5.

First Nat. Bank, Perryton, Tex. v. McClung, TexCivApp–Amarillo, 483 SW2d 935, ref nre.—Home 99.

First Nat. Bank, Port Lavaca; Bures v., TexApp–Corpus Christi, 806 SW2d 935.—Sec Tran 170, 171; Trial 168; Trover 1, 4, 9(3.1), 54.

First Nat. Bank, Tulia; Langston v., TexCivApp–Amarillo, 449 SW2d 855.—Wills 435, 440, 462, 463, 488, 519, 704, 706.

First Nat. Development Corp.; Federal Sav. and Loan Ins. Corp. v., SDTex, 497 FSupp 724.—Admin Law 464; B & L Assoc 48; Const Law 4027; Fed Civ Proc 1269.1; Inj 147; U S 53(13.1); Witn 21.

First Nat. Gun Banque Corp.; Nagy v., TexApp–Dallas, 684 SW2d 114, ref nre.—Antitrust 161, 162, 193, 367, 369; App & E 931(1), 989; Evid 85.1; Trial 395(1).

First Nat. Indem. Co. v. Conway, TexCivApp–Hous (1 Dist), 495 SW2d 11, ref nre.—Ref of Inst 17(1), 43, 45(14).

First Nat. Indem. Co. v. First Bank and Trust of Groves, Texas, TexApp–Beaumont, 753 SW2d 405.—App & E 218.2(1), 239, 240, 269, 500(2), 1178(6); Judgm 199(3.13), 199(5).

First Nat. Indem. Co. v. Mercado, TexCivApp–Austin, 511 SW2d 354.—App & E 931(1), 989, 1010.1(1); Insurance 2770, 3191(1), 3198(1), 3198(2), 3371, 3549(4).

First Nat. Ins. Co. of America; National Credit Control, Inc. v., EDTex, 749 FSupp 154.—Fed Cts 318; Rem of C 107(7).

First Nat. Ins. Co. of America; Round Rock Independent School Dist. v., CA5 (Tex), 324 F2d 280.—Fed Civ Proc 2127, 2152; Insurance 2199, 3154, 3188, 3198(2).

First Nat. Life Ins. Co. v. Herring, TexCivApp–Waco, 318 SW2d 119.—App & E 196, 201(1), 256, 285, 554(3), 907(3), 918(3), 959(3); Const Law 4426; Judgm 284; Plead 236(2), 365(3).

First Nat. Life Ins. Co.; Richardson v., Tex, 419 SW2d 836.—Courts 32, 122, 155, 472.1, 472.3; Plead 34(2).

First Nat. Life Ins. Co.; Richardson v., TexCivApp–San Antonio, 408 SW2d 524, writ gr, aff 419 SW2d 836.—Courts 120, 122.

First Nat. Life Ins. Co. v. Vititow, TexCivApp–Texarkana, 323 SW2d 313, writ dism.—Abate & R 3; App & E 185(2); Courts 121(5); Evid 320; Hus & W 208, 270(1); Insurance 3335, 3336, 3379, 3381(5); Plead 311.

First Nat. Mobile Home Sales, Inc.; Mid-Texas Tel. Co. v., TexCivApp–Austin, 506 SW2d 728.—App & E 223; Judgm 183, 185.2(9), 185.3(5), 186.

First Nat. Petroleum Corp. v. Lloyd, TexApp–Houston (1 Dist), 908 SW2d 23, reh overr.—Lis Pen 20.

First Nat. Sec. Corp.; Wrigley v., TexApp–Beaumont, 104 SW3d 259.—App & E 437, 781(1), 781(7); Garn 7, 105, 108, 110, 167; Interpl 11.

First Nat. Sec. Corp.; Wrigley v., TexApp–Beaumont, 104 SW3d 252.—App & E 460(1), 781(1), 781(7); Execution 402(1); Garn 112, 123, 167, 174.1.

First Nat. Title Ins. Co.; Hanson Business Park, L.P. v., TexApp–Dallas, 209 SW3d 867, review den.—App & E 870(2), 1175(1); Insurance 1013, 1716, 2610, 2616.

First Nationwide Bank; Commonwealth Mortg. Corp. v., CA5 (Tex), 873 F2d 859, reh den 881 F2d 1071.—Antitrust 393; Contracts 97(2), 99(3), 227, 312(1), 353(2), 353(8); Fraud 58(2), 65(4).

First Nationwide Bank v. Summer House Joint Venture, CA5 (Tex), 902 F2d 1197, reh den 909 F2d 1479.—Fed Civ Proc 2341, 2366.1, 2579; Fed Cts 595, 657, 668, 829.

First Nationwide Mortg. Corp.; Blanche v., TexApp–Dallas, 74 SW3d 444.—Antitrust 213; App & E 223,

863; Damag 49.10, 50.10; Evid 370(1), 373(1); Judgm 181(33), 185(4), 185.3(15), 185.3(21), 189; Libel 4, 6(1), 51(1), 68; Mtg 211, 216; Neglig 463; Torts 340, 341, 350, 351.

First Newport Realty Investors; Schubiger v., TexCiv-App–Dallas, 601 SW2d 218, ref nre.—Contracts 169; Guar 36(3), 56, 62, 89.

First of Denver Mortg. Investors; Fandel, Inc. v., Tex-CivApp–Dallas, 522 SW2d 721.—Mtg 159.

First Office Management, a Div. of Equity Property Management Corp.; McReynolds v., TexApp–Dallas, 948 SW2d 342.—App & E 843(2), 969; Carr 280(4), 286; Trial 202, 219, 238, 242, 251(1), 251(8), 252(1), 352.1(1).

First Pasadena State Bank v. Marquette, TexCivApp–Hous (1 Dist), 425 SW2d 450, ref nre.—Contracts 28(3), 332(2); Frds St of 17; Impl & C C 1.

First Pasadena State Bank; Smith v., TexCivApp–Houston, 401 SW2d 123.—App & E 1170.10; Bills & N 49, 137(1), 140, 437, 499, 517, 534; Lim of Act 127(4); Nova 12; Paymt 39(4), 43.

First Paving Corp.; Moran v., TexCivApp–Fort Worth, 469 SW2d 30.—Plead 111.3, 111.4, 111.26, 111.42(11).

First Permian, L.L.C. v. Graham, TexApp–Amarillo, 212 SW3d 368, review den.—Covenants 30, 53, 71, 77.1; Mines 74(3).

Firstplus Financial, Inc., In re, BkrtcyNDTex, 254 BR 888.—Bankr 2021.1, 2182.1, 2877, 3181, 3182; Statut 181(1), 181(2), 188, 189.

FIRSTPLUS Financial, Inc., In re, BkrtcyNDTex, 248 BR 60.—Bankr 2021.1, 2129, 2159.1, 2163, 2892.1, 2895.1, 2900(1), 2901.1, 2928, 3784; Const Law 4478; Fed Civ Proc 161.1, 163, 164, 165, 175; Princ & A 1, 4, 5, 92(1), 163(1).

First Preferred Ins. Co. v. Bell, TexCivApp–Amarillo, 587 SW2d 798, ref nre.—App & E 218.2(5.1), 237(5), 758.3(9), 930(3), 989, 1003(5); Costs 194.22; Insurance 1743, 1790(1), 1790(5), 2175, 2183, 2201, 3163, 3585; Judgm 199(3.13).

First Preferred Ins. Co.; Nicholson v., TexCivApp–Amarillo, 618 SW2d 560.—Insurance 2131, 2136(5), 3055(1).

First Preferred Ins. Co. v. Robertson, TexCivApp–Texarkana, 614 SW2d 851, dism.—App & E 846(5); Plead 111.42(1).

First Presbyterian Church of Paris, Inc.; Presbytery of the Covenant v., TexCivApp–Texarkana, 552 SW2d 865.—Const Law 1329, 1338; Relig Soc 11, 14, 23(3), 24, 25, 35.

First Print, Inc.; Hobson & Associates, Inc. v., TexApp–Amarillo, 798 SW2d 617.—Garn 64, 248; Judgm 181(14).

First Prize v. Fireman's Fund Ins. Co. of Cal., TexCiv-App–Galveston, 269 SW2d 939, ref nre.—Bills & N 134; Sales 21, 197.

First Professionals Ins. Co., Inc. v. Heart & Vascular Institute of Texas, TexApp–San Antonio, 182 SW3d 6, reh overr, and review den.—Contracts 143(2), 143.5, 169, 176(2); Insurance 1808, 1836, 2266.

First Pyramid Life Ins. Co. of America; Pickering v., TexCivApp–Beaumont, 491 SW2d 184, ref nre.—App & E 845(2); Contracts 346(6); Courts 91(1); Insurance 1806, 1809, 2586.

First Realty Bank v. Ehrle, TexCivApp–Dallas, 521 SW2d 295.—Interpl 4, 11.

First Realty Bank and Trust v. Youngkin, TexCivApp–Eastland, 568 SW2d 428.—App & E 931(3); Home 11.

First RepublicBank Corp., In re, BkrtcyNDTex, 113 BR 277.—Bankr 2467.

First RepublicBank Corp., In re, BkrtcyNDTex, 95 BR 58.—Bankr 2126, 3024.

First RepublicBank Corp. v. NCNB Texas Nat. Bank, BkrtcyNDTex, 113 BR 277. See First RepublicBank Corp., In re.

First RepublicBank Corp.; Official Committee of Sr. Unsecured Creditors of First RepublicBank Corp. v., NDTex, 106 BR 938.—Bankr 2164.1, 3070, 3766.1, 3770, 3776.5(5), 3781, 3789.1.

First RepublicBank Corp.; Pacific Mut. Life Ins. Co. v., CA5 (Tex), 997F2d 39, reh den (#92-3375), cert gr Morgan Stanley & Co, Inc v. Pacific Mut Life Ins Co, 114 SCt 680, 510 US 1039, 126 LEd2d 648, aff 114 SCt 1827, 511 US 658, 128 LEd2d 654, reh den 114 SCt 2774, 512 US 1248, 129 LEd2d 887, cert gr, vac BDO Seidman v Simmons, 115 SCt 1789, 514 US 1079, 131 LEd2d 718, on remand 53 F3d 1409, on remand TGX Corp v Simmons, 62 F3d 666, cert gr, vac Continental Ins Co v Simmons, 115 SCt 1789, 514 US 1079, 131 LEd2d 718, on remand 53 F3d 1409, opinion vac 53 F3d 1409.—Const Law 186, 2350, 2384, 3907, 4295; Fed Cts 616; Judgm 1; Lim of Act 6(1), 6(9); Sec Reg 2.10; Statut 261.

First Republicbank Corp.; Pacific Mut. Life Ins. Co. v., NDTex, 806 FSupp 108, rev 997 F2d 39, reh den (#92-3375), cert gr Morgan Stanley & Co, Inc v. Pacific Mut Life Ins Co, 114 SCt 680, 510 US 1039, 126 LEd2d 648, aff 114 SCt 1827, 511 US 658, 128 LEd2d 654, reh den 114 SCt 2774, 512 US 1248, 129 LEd2d 887, cert gr, vac BDO Seidman v Simmons, 115 SCt 1789, 514 US 1079, 131 LEd2d 718, on remand 53 F3d 1409, on remand TGX Corp v Simmons, 62 F3d 666, cert gr, vac Continental Ins Co v Simmons, 115 SCt 1789, 514 US 1079, 131 LEd2d 718, on remand 53 F3d 1409, opinion vac F3d 1409, aff 53 F3d 1409.—Const Law 1025, 2357, 2648, 2653; Lim of Act 6(9); Sec Reg 2.10.

First Republicbank Dallas v. Argyle Apartments, NDTex, 91 BR 398. See First Republicbank Dallas v. Gargyle Corp.

First Republicbank Dallas v. Gargyle Corp., NDTex, 91 BR 398.—Bankr 2151, 2440; Fed Civ Proc 2011.

First RepublicBank Fort Worth v. Norglass, Inc., CA5 (Tex), 958 F2d 117.—Fed Civ Proc 2642, 2658, 2771(18); Fed Cts 551, 571, 584, 825.1; Rem of C 95.

First RepublicBank Ft. Worth, N.A. v. Norglass, Inc., CA5 (Tex), 958 F2d 117. See First RepublicBank Fort Worth v. Norglass, Inc.

First RepublicBank Fort Worth, N.A. v. Norglass, Inc., NDTex, 751 FSupp 1224, aff 958 F2d 117.—Banks 505.

First RepublicBank Fort Worth, N.A.; Ortega v., Tex, 792 SW2d 452.—Adop 16; Judgm 335(1), 335(3), 550.

First Republic Bank, Fort Worth, N.S.; Martin v., TexApp–Fort Worth, 799 SW2d 482, writ den.—Action 60; Bills & N 134; Evid 404; Guar 77(1); Joint Adv 1, 7; Judgm 185.3(10), 185.3(16), 190; Partners 165, 200; Set-Off 60.

First RepublicBank San Antonio, N.A.; Osherow v., BkrtcyWDTex, 100 BR 856. See Linen Warehouse, Inc., In re.

First Republic Bank Waco, N.A.; United Bank of Waco, N.A. v., WDTex, 758 FSupp 1166.—Banks 508.

First Republic Life Ins. Co. v. Republic of Texas Sav. Ass'n, CA5 (Tex), 776 F2d 520.—Trover 40(1).

First Sav. & Loan Ass'n; American Ins. Co. v., TexCiv-App–Fort Worth, 434 SW2d 170, ref nre.—Action 22; App & E 169, 301, 302(5), 1026, 1062.1; Estop 52(1), 52.15, 95, 96, 118; Evid 54, 111; Insurance 3040, 3073, 3450; Trial 350.4(3).

First Sav. & Loan Ass'n; Rosch v., TexCivApp–El Paso, 203 SW2d 1006.—B & L Assoc 12(1); Decl Judgm 201, 209, 303; Tax 2126, 2313, 2314, 2403, 2556, 2578, 2625, 2656, 2657, 2755.

First Sav. & Loan Ass'n; Vanlandingham v., TexCiv-App–El Paso, 410 SW2d 218, ref nre.—Judgm 185.3(21), 186; Neglig 1286(1), 1313.

First Sav. and Loan Ass'n of Borger; Vandygriff v., Tex, 617 SW2d 669.—App & E 1031(1); B & L Assoc 2.1, 3.1(2).

First Sav. & Loan Ass'n of Borger v. Vandygriff, TexCivApp–Austin, 605 SW2d 740, rev 617 SW2d 669.—Admin Law 490, 750; B & L Assoc 3.1(2).

First Sav. & Loan Ass'n of Burkburnett; Breathless Associates v., NDTex, 654 FSupp 832.—Banks 191.15, 191.20, 191.30.

First Sav. and Loan Ass'n of Del Rio, Texas v. Lewis, TexCivApp–Austin, 512 SW2d 62, ref nre.—Admin Law 817.1; B & L Assoc 3.1(2), 3.1(3).

First Sav. and Loan Ass'n of El Paso v. Avila, TexCiv-App–El Paso, 538 SW2d 846, ref nre.—Mtg 415(1); Records 19.

First Sav. & Loan of Burkburnett, Tex.; Buckner Development Group v., CA5 (Tex), 873 F2d 858.—Fed Cts 24.

First Sav. of Louisiana; Allen v., BkrtcyWDTex, 89 BR 13. See Liberty Trust Co., In re.

First Sec. Bank & Trust Co. v. Roach, TexCivApp–Dallas, 493 SW2d 612, ref nre.—App & E 930(3), 989, 1001(1), 1004(11); Autos 20; Bills & N 497(1); Damag 91(1), 94; Evid 597; Sec Tran 184, 242.1, 243; Sequest 21.

First Sec. Nat. Bank; Meador v., EDTex, 100 FSupp2d 433, appeal dism 237 F3d 630.—Courts 93(1); Evid 43(3); Judgm 681.

First Sec. Nat. Bank of Beaumont; Schepps v., TexCiv-App–Beaumont, 462 SW2d 341, ref nre.—Guar 16(1), 18, 27, 36(9), 37.

First Sec. State Bank of Cranfills Gap, Tex.; Fisher v., TexCivApp–Waco, 576 SW2d 886.—App & E 544(1), 569(4), 1177(9).

First Small Business Inv. Co. of California v. Butler, Binion, Rice and Knapp, CA5 (Tex), 914 F2d 61. See Sioux, Ltd., Securities Litigation v. Coopers & Lybrand.

First Small Business Inv. Co. of California v. Butler, Binion, Rice & Knapp, CA5 (Tex), 901 F2d 51. See Sioux, Ltd., Securities Litigation v. Coopers & Lybrand.

First Southern Partners, II, Ltd.; First South Sav. Ass'n v., CA5 (Tex), 957 F2d 174.—B & L Assoc 42(6); Usury 16, 88.

First Southern Properties, Inc. v. Gregory, TexCivApp–Hous (1 Dist), 538 SW2d 454.—App & E 931(3); Fraud Conv 159(1), 300(1); Hus & W 6(3).

First Southern Properties, Inc.; Henke v., TexCivApp–Waco, 586 SW2d 617, ref nre.—Interest 17; Judgm 18(1); Mtg 372(3); Subrog 23(6).

First Southern Properties, Inc.; Johnson v., TexApp–Houston (14 Dist), 687 SW2d 399, ref nre.—Condo 12; Home 31, 93, 169.

First Southern Properties, Inc. v. Vallone, Tex, 533 SW2d 339.—Divorce 207; Mtg 372(1); Receivers 73, 77(1), 77(2), 77(3).

First Southern Properties, Inc. v. Vallone, TexCivApp–Hous (1 Dist), 523 SW2d 92, writ gr, aff 533 SW2d 339. —Divorce 207; Mtg 369(1).

First Southern Trust Co.; Szczepanik v., Tex, 883 SW2d 648, on remand 1995 WL 634138.—App & E 927(7), 997(3); Damag 190.

First Southern Trust Co. v. Szczepanik, TexApp–Dallas, 880 SW2d 10, writ gr, rev 883 SW2d 648, on remand 1995 WL 634138.—App & E 704.1, 714(5), 866(3), 907(5), 927(7), 930(3), 1062.2; Damag 117, 176, 190, 208(1); Trial 143, 350.1, 352.1(3).

Firstsouth, F.A.; Coit Independence Joint Venture v., CA5 (Tex), 829 F2d 563, cert gr 108 SCt 1105, 485 US 933, 99 LEd2d 267, rev 109 SCt 1361, 489 US 561, 103 LEd2d 602, on remand 874 F2d 249.—B & L Assoc 2, 48; Const Law 978, 4477.

First South Sav. Ass'n, In re, CA5 (Tex), 820 F2d 700.—Bankr 2966, 2972, 3776.5(2), 3776.5(4), 3784; Fed Cts 529; Mand 57(1).

First South Sav. Ass'n v. Burnap, SDTex, 833 FSupp 607, aff 41 F3d 664.—Compromise 7.1, 100.

First South Sav. Ass'n v. First Southern Partners, II, Ltd., CA5 (Tex), 957 F2d 174.—B & L Assoc 42(6); Usury 16, 88.

First Southwest Lloyds Ins. Co. v. Armstrong McCall Beauty Supply, TexApp–Texarkana, 769 SW2d 954. See First Southwest Lloyds Ins. Co. v. MacDowell.

First Southwest Lloyds Ins. Co. v. MacDowell, TexApp–Texarkana, 769 SW2d 954, writ den.—Evid 106(5), 121(1), 123(1), 123(12), 129(5), 146, 333(1), 555.3; Insurance 3147, 3580.

First Southwest Sav. & Loan Ass'n; Crum Co. v., TexApp–Tyler, 704 SW2d 925. See M.P. Crum Co. v. First Southwest Sav. & Loan Ass'n.

First Southwest Sav. & Loan Ass'n; M.P. Crum Co. v., TexApp–Tyler, 704 SW2d 925.—Judgm 199(3.7), 199(3.14); Sec Tran 240.

First State Bank v. Asay, BkrtcyNDTex, 184 BR 265. See Asay, In re.

First State Bank; Box v., SDTex, 340 BR 782.—Bankr 3779, 3782, 3786; Const Law 591, 592; Cons Cred 4; Contracts 194; Home 90, 99, 115(2).

First State Bank v. Dorst, TexApp–Austin, 843 SW2d 790, reh overr, and writ den.—Usury 6, 36.1, 88.

First State Bank; Katy Personal Storage, Inc. v., Tex-App–Houston (14 Dist), 968 SW2d 579, reh overr, and review withdrawn.—Mtg 570.

First State Bank v. Keilman, TexApp–Austin, 851 SW2d 914, reh overr, and writ den.—Alt of Inst 2, 20, 27.1(2), 29; Antitrust 141, 290, 369; App & E 758.1, 758.3(1), 758.3(7), 836, 1001(1), 1003(7), 1177(7), 1177(8); Consp 1.1, 19; Contracts 147(1), 176(1), 176(2); Damag 221(7); Judgm 199(3.14); Mtg 209, 354, 360, 369(2), 369(3), 379, 514, 529(6); Usury 34, 117, 121.

First State Bank; Matthews v., TexCivApp–Beaumont, 312 SW2d 571, ref nre.—Bills & N 459, 520, 525; Estop 118; Evid 442(5); Hus & W 238.3; Liens 22; Parties 80(1), 84(1).

First State Bank; Miller v., TexCivApp–Fort Worth, 551 SW2d 89, writ gr, aff as mod 563 SW2d 572.—App & E 761; Dep in Court 10; Estop 52(2); Evid 244(4), 265(10); Usury 12, 16, 45, 52, 103, 113, 134, 137, 138, 140, 142(1), 142(3), 142(4), 142(5), 143, 144, 146.

First State Bank v. National Bank of Commerce, Tex-CivApp–Amarillo, 99 SW2d 406, writ refused.—App & E 931(3); Lim of Act 100(7), 127(2.1); Trusts 1, 265.

First State Bank; Trinity Universal Ins. Co. v., Tex, 183 SW2d 422, 143 Tex 164.—Banks 129, 134(1).

First State Bank; Vescovo v., BkrtcyWDTex, 125 BR 468. See Vescovo, In re.

First State Bank; Ward v., TexCivApp–Amarillo, 605 SW2d 404, ref nre 1980 WL 98415.—App & E 218.2(1); Sec Tran 240.

First State Bank; Worthey v., TexCivApp–Waco, 549 SW2d 450, ref nre.—App & E 78(1).

First State Bank; Yoakum County Water Control and Imp. Dist. No. 2 v., Tex, 449 SW2d 775.—Const Law 4064; Mun Corp 72, 918(1), 931; Waters 183.5, 230(8).

First State Bank; Yoakum County Water Control and Imp. Dist. No. 2 v., TexCivApp–Tyler, 433 SW2d 200, writ gr, aff 449 SW2d 775.—Bills & N 339; Const Law 4057, 4061; Mun Corp 943(1), 944; Waters 216, 225, 230(2), 230(5), 231.

First State Bank, Abilene; Stim-O-Stam Enterprises, Inc. v., TexCivApp–Eastland, 385 SW2d 622.—Corp 630(1).

First State Bank & Trust Co.; McCarty v., TexApp–Texarkana, 723 SW2d 792, rev 730 SW2d 656.—Afft 18; Banks 129; Evid 318(7); Joint Ten 6.

First State Bank & Trust Co.; Manges v., TexCivApp–Corpus Christi, 572 SW2d 104.—App & E 624, 765, 770(1); Judgm 185(2), 185.1(4), 185.3(2).

First State Bank & Trust Co.; Pena v., TexCivApp–Corpus Christi, 404 SW2d 56.—Banks 154(2); Judgm 181(7), 185(2); Lim of Act 99(1), 100(11), 199(2).

First State Bank and Trust Co., Carthage, Tex. v. McCarty, Tex, 730 SW2d 656.—App & E 840(1).

First State Bank & Trust Co. of Edinburg v. George, TexCivApp–Corpus Christi, 519 SW2d 198, ref nre.— App & E 216(2), 614, 648, 653(3), 688(2), 1003(9.1); Banks 21, 126; Bills & N 327, 335, 337, 365(1), 452(1), 452(3); Trial 215, 219, 349(2).

First State Bank & Trust Co. of Houston v. Tanner, TexCivApp–Hous (1 Dist), 509 SW2d 375, ref nre.— Banks 102; Bills & N 340, 437.

First State Bank & Trust Co. of Port Lavaca; Texas Land Drilling Co. v., TexCivApp–Corpus Christi, 445 SW2d 571, ref nre.—Action 50(1), 50(3); App & E 870(2), 949; Chat Mtg 258, 286.

First State Bank & Trust Co. of Port Lavaca; Vector Corp. v., TexCivApp–Waco, 430 SW2d 536, ref nre.— App & E 758.1; Estop 99; Evid 384, 418, 423(6), 450(5), 450(10); Indem 97; Mtg 111; Princ & A 163(1); Trusts 43(1).

First State Bank & Trust Co. of Port Lavaca v. Vector Corp., TexCivApp–Waco, 427 SW2d 958, ref nre.—App & E 440, 456; Judgm 306.

First State Bank & Trust Co. of Rio Grande City v. Colpaugh, TexCivApp–San Antonio, 489 SW2d 675.— Bills & N 23, 281, 444, 468; Evid 25(1); Partners 173, 217(1); Plead 110; Venue 7.5(4), 8.5(2), 22(4).

First State Bank & Trust Co. of Rio Grande City; Laborde v., TexCivApp–San Antonio, 101 SW2d 389.— Des & Dist 47(1); Wills 184(1), 184(2), 184(3), 184(4), 199, 215, 421, 475, 476, 598, 692(5).

First State Bank & Trust Co. of Rio Grande City v. Ramirez, TexComApp, 126 SW2d 16, 133 Tex 178.—Ex & Ad 99; Lim of Act 118(2), 124, 127(2.1), 127(4).

First State Bank & Trust Co. of Rio Grande City; Ramirez v., TexCivApp–San Antonio, 92 SW2d 523, rev 126 SW2d 16, 133 Tex 178.—Ex & Ad 99; Lim of Act 127(13); Pretrial Proc 501.

First State Bank & Trust Co. of Rio Grande City v. Raymond, TexCivApp–Austin, 275 SW2d 191, ref nre. —Counties 57, 125, 204(1), 206(1); Dep & Escr 34; Inj 211, 212; Mun Corp 249.

First State Bank & Trust Co. of Rio Grande City v. Starr County, TexCivApp–San Antonio, 306 SW2d 246. —Inj 5, 138.31, 147.

First State Bank, Bandera, Texas; Basse Truck Line, Inc. v., TexApp–San Antonio, 949 SW2d 17, reh overr, and writ den.—Antitrust 208, 209; App & E 758.3(11), 854(1), 870(2); Banks 148(4); Bills & N 279.

First State Bank, Bishop v. Chappell & Handy, P.C., TexApp–Corpus Christi, 729 SW2d 917, ref nre.—Pretrial Proc 44.1, 222, 225, 314, 718; Trial 122, 133.2.

First State Bank, Hearne; Citizens Bank of Bryan v., Tex, 580 SW2d 344.—Admin Law 489.1; Banks 32; Statut 181(2), 184, 205, 206.

First State Bank, Hearne v. Citizens Bank of Bryan, TexCivApp–Austin, 569 SW2d 604, rev 580 SW2d 344.— Banks 5, 17, 31, 32; Const Law 77, 2502(2), 2621; Statut 234.5, 261.

First State Bank, Hubbard, Texas v. Lewis, TexCivApp–Waco, 560 SW2d 191, ref nre.—B & L Assoc 3.5(2), 24; Const Law 667, 885; Statut 219(2).

First State Bank In Archer City v. Schwarz Co., TexApp–Dallas, 687 SW2d 453, ref nre.—Estop 85, 118.

First State Bank in Caldwell; Bates v., TexCivApp–Galveston, 105 SW2d 784, writ dism.—App & E 1179; Assign 10, 15; Offic 96; Tax 2438.

First State Bank in Caldwell; Clanton v., TexCivApp–Galveston, 143 SW2d 981.—App & E 475, 792.

First State Bank-Keene v. Metroplex Petroleum Inc., CA5 (Tex), 155 F3d 732.—Banks 505; Lim of Act 48(1), 173; Tax 2929, 2936, 3067.

First State Bank, Memphis; Martin v., TexCivApp–Amarillo, 490 SW2d 208.—App & E 1024.4; Banks 119, 134(4); Judgm 181(2), 181(4), 181(17), 185(2).

First State Bank, Milford; Worthey v., TexCivApp–Waco, 573 SW2d 279.—Bills & N 126, 363; Judgm 181(17).

First State Bank, Monahans; Adams v., TexCivApp–El Paso, 383 SW2d 223, ref nre.—Fraud Conv 47, 170, 299(13).

First State Bank, Monahans; Pogue v., TexApp–El Paso, 750 SW2d 826.—Estop 116; Guar 78(1).

First State Bank, Morton v. Chesshir, TexApp–Amarillo, 634 SW2d 742, ref nre.—Antitrust 141; App & E 832(4), 931(3), 931(4); Costs 241; Trial 284, 350.1, 351.2(3.1), 351.2(4), 366; Trover 1, 5, 35, 66.

First State Bank, Morton v. Chesshir, TexCivApp–Amarillo, 613 SW2d 61, rev 620 SW2d 101, on remand 634 SW2d 742, ref nre.—Antitrust 130, 141, 145; Courts 91(1).

First State Bank, Morton; McCoy v., TexCivApp–Amarillo, 424 SW2d 451.—Evid 10(2); Plead 111.15, 111.36, 111.37; Venue 7.5(4).

First State Bank, N.A. v. Morse, TexApp–Amarillo, 227 SW3d 820.—App & E 930(1), 1001(1), 1003(5); Banks 100, 227(3), 228; Costs 194.16; Damag 15; Joint Adv 1.2(1), 1.2(8); Larc 3(2); Neglig 371, 379, 380, 387, 433, 1675; Princ & A 1; Trial 350.6(1); Trover 4, 9(3.1), 9(6), 54; Trusts 356(1).

First State Bank, Odessa, N.A.; Manning v., WDTex, 735 FSupp 708. See Successor Trust Committee of Permian Distributing, Inc. Employees' Profit Sharing Plan and Trust v. First State Bank, Odessa, N.A.

First State Bank, Odessa, N.A.; Permian Tank & Mfg., Inc. v., WDTex, 735 FSupp 708. See Successor Trust Committee of Permian Distributing, Inc. Employees' Profit Sharing Plan and Trust v. First State Bank, Odessa, N.A.

First State Bank, Odessa, N.A.; Successor Trust Committee of Permian Distributing, Inc. Employees' Profit Sharing Plan and Trust v., WDTex, 735 FSupp 708.—Banks 505; Indem 33(1); Labor & Emp 461, 464, 477, 488, 496, 630, 659; U S 50.1, 78(12).

First State Bank of Abernathy; Donaldson v., TexCivApp–Amarillo, 352 SW2d 302, ref nre.—Judgm 17(9), 486(1), 497(3), 501; Proc 96(4).

First State Bank of Abilene; Earp v., TexCivApp–Eastland, 356 SW2d 178, ref nre.—Contracts 93(5); Evid 397(1), 404; Guar 19; Judgm 185.1(1).

First State Bank of Abilene; Federal Deposit Ins. Corp. v., CA5 (Tex), 779 F2d 242.—Banks 505; Fed Civ Proc 2737.1, 2737.6.

First State Bank of Abilene; McCook v., TexCivApp–Eastland, 367 SW2d 66, ref nre.—Banks 148(2); Bills & N 54.

First State Bank of Amarillo; Braswell v., TexCivApp–Amarillo, 367 SW2d 944, ref nre.—Bills & N 334, 356.

First State Bank of Amarillo; Preston v., TexCivApp–Amarillo, 344 SW2d 724, ref nre.—Banks 139, 189; Gaming 19(3).

First State Bank of Andrews; Davidson v., TexCivApp–El Paso, 310 SW2d 678.—App & E 934(1); Mal Pros 16, 35(1), 64(1).

First State Bank of Arlington; Bardin v., TexCivApp–Fort Worth, 129 SW2d 1147, writ refused.—Banks 80(7).

First State Bank of Athens; Douglas v., TexCivApp–Dallas, 538 SW2d 179.—Judgm 185(2), 185.3(2).

First State Bank of Athens Mabank Branch v. Purina Ag Capitol Corp., TexApp–Tyler, 113 SW3d 1.—Corp 1.4(1), 1.4(2), 1.4(3), 1.7(2); Judgm 181(15.1).

First State Bank of Avinger; Brimberry v., TexCivApp–Texarkana, 500 SW2d 675, ref nre.—Execution 226, 230, 249, 250, 251(2).

First State Bank of Bedford v. Miller, Tex, 563 SW2d 572.—Contracts 318; Judgm 18(1); Statut 241(1); Usury 12, 52, 111(1), 138, 146.

First State Bank of Bedford, Tex.; British Caledonian Airways Ltd. v., CA5 (Tex), 819 F2d 593.—Banks 148(2), 174; Bills & N 279, 292; Contracts 176(1); Fed Civ Proc 2533.1, 2651.1; Fed Cts 802, 829.

First State Bank of Bedias v. Bishop, TexApp–Houston (1 Dist), 685 SW2d 732, ref nre.—Courts 475(2); Judgm 7.

First State Bank of Bellaire v. Citizens Nat. Bank & Trust Co., TexCivApp–Houston, 407 SW2d 365.—Banks 148(1), 149.

First State Bank of Bellaire v. Olde Colony House, Inc., TexCivApp–Waco, 414 SW2d 221, ref nre.—Bills & N 239, 489(3), 520; Contracts 94(5); Set-Off 28(1).

First State Bank of Bellaire v. Standard Bank, Tex-App–Houston (14 Dist), 666 SW2d 198.—Judgm 185.3(5).

First State Bank of Bishop v. Frost Nat. Bank of San Antonio, TexApp–San Antonio, 665 SW2d 198.—App & E 395.

First State Bank of Bishop; Grebe v., Tex, 150 SW2d 64, 136 Tex 226.—Banks 119, 130(1), 133; Guard & W 35; Hus & W 273(1), 273(2), 273(8.1), 273(9), 274(1), 276(2).

First State Bank of Bishop v. Grebe, TexCivApp–San Antonio, 162 SW2d 165, writ refused wom.—App & E 1097(5), 1122(2), 1198, 1202.

First State Bank of Bishop; Grebe v., TexCivApp–San Antonio, 106 SW2d 382, rev 150 SW2d 64, 136 Tex 226.—Banks 130(1); Hus & W 273(1), 273(2), 274(1).

First State Bank of Bishop; Gregg v., TexCivApp–Amarillo, 125 SW2d 319, writ dism, correct.—Arrest 70(2); Const Law 4534, 4544; False Imp 2, 39; Sheriffs 171; Torts 135.

First State Bank of Bishop; Maryland Am. General Ins. Co. v., TexCivApp–Corpus Christi, 515 SW2d 57, ref nre.—App & E 934(1); Judgm 185.3(12).

First State Bank of Bishop, Tex. v. Norris, TexCivApp–Tyler, 611 SW2d 680, ref nre.—Abate & R 7, 8(7), 9; Set-Off 60.

First State Bank of Bremond v. Brannon, TexCivApp–Waco, 486 SW2d 179.—Judgm 18(2).

First State Bank of Bryson; Broaddus v., TexApp–Fort Worth, 681 SW2d 879, ref nre.—App & E 1073(1); Bills & N 92(1).

First State Bank of Bryson; Broaddus v., TexCivApp–Fort Worth, 605 SW2d 735, ref nre.—App & E 1177(9).

First State Bank of Bryson v. Johnson, TexCivApp–Fort Worth, 585 SW2d 917, ref nre.—Bills & N 516, 527(1), 537(8); Evid 241(1), 244(4).

First State Bank of Canadian, Texas v. McMordie, TexApp–Amarillo, 861 SW2d 284.—Antitrust 141, 145, 363.

First State Bank of Chico; Donald v., TexCivApp–Fort Worth, 448 SW2d 196.—App & E 231(1), 302(4), 302(5).

First State Bank of Chico v. Smith, TexCivApp–Fort Worth, 488 SW2d 837.—Bills & N 537(5).

First State Bank of Childress v. Fields, TexCivApp–Amarillo, 551 SW2d 476, dism.—Plead 111.18, 111.30, 111.38, 111.42(4), 111.42(10); Princ & A 136(1); Venue 22(7).

First State Bank of Chilton; Cooper v., TexCivApp–Waco, 121 SW2d 399.—Mtg 48(1), 178, 295(4), 319(3).

First State Bank of Clute; U.S. v., CA5 (Tex), 626 F2d 1227, reh den 632 F2d 894, cert den Jarvis v. US, 101 SCt 3037, 452 US 908, 69 LEd2d 410.—Fed Cts 13; Int Rev 4490, 4491.

First State Bank of Clute, Tex. v. Board of Governors of Federal Reserve System, CA5 (Tex), 553 F2d 950.—Banks 522, 525, 526.

First State Bank of Corpus Christi v. Ake, TexCivApp–Corpus Christi, 606 SW2d 696, ref nre.—App & E 1058(1), 1062.1; Damag 94; Evid 471(2); Libel 6(2), 23.1, 33, 113, 120(1), 121(1), 123(2), 123(9), 124(1), 124(4), 124(7), 125.

First State Bank of Corpus Christi v. Austin, TexCivApp–San Antonio, 315 SW2d 390, writ refused.—Autos 20.

First State Bank of Corpus Christi; A. Wolfson's, Inc. v., TexApp–Corpus Christi, 752 SW2d 614, writ den.—Garn 158, 165, 199.

First State Bank of Corpus Christi; A. Wolfson's Sons, Inc. v., TexApp–Corpus Christi, 697 SW2d 753, appeal after remand 752 SW2d 614, writ den.—Corp 509.1(1); Garn 9, 194; Sec Tran 115.1, 116, 145.1, 168, 221.

First State Bank of Corpus Christi v. James, TexApp–Corpus Christi, 471 SW2d 868.—App & E 842(7), 931(1), 931(3), 989, 994(2), 1001(1), 1003(3), 1064.4, 1068(2); Covenants 72.1, 77.1, 103(3), 108(2), 118, 135; Inj 128(6), 130; Trial 225(1), 350.3(2.1).

First State Bank of Corpus Christi; Nixon v., TexCivApp–Corpus Christi, 540 SW2d 817, ref nre 544 SW2d 378.—App & E 843(3); Contracts 143(2), 143.5, 147(1), 176(1), 176(2); Judgm 181(19), 181(21), 185(2), 185(6); Labor & Emp 177.

First State Bank of Corpus Christi v. Shuford Mills, Inc., TexApp–Corpus Christi, 716 SW2d 649, ref nre.—Banks 191.20; Bills & N 129(3).

First State Bank of Corpus Christi v. Von Boeckmann-Jones Co., TexCivApp–Austin, 365 SW2d 700, ref nre.—Fraud 58(1), 58(4).

First State Bank of Corpus Christi v. Von Boeckmann-Jones Co., TexCivApp–Austin, 359 SW2d 171.—Corp 503(2); Fraud 3; Venue 8.5(3).

First State Bank of Corpus Christi; Wolfson's, Inc. v., TexApp–Corpus Christi, 752 SW2d 614. See A. Wolfson's, Inc. v. First State Bank of Corpus Christi.

First State Bank of Corpus Christi; Wolfson's Sons, Inc. v., TexApp–Corpus Christi, 697 SW2d 753. See A. Wolfson's Sons, Inc. v. First State Bank of Corpus Christi.

First State Bank of Deanville; Hruska v., Tex, 747 SW2d 783.—Bills & N 534; Estop 52(7), 52.10(1); Home 177(2); Liens 7.

First State Bank of Deanville; Hruska v., TexApp–Houston (1 Dist), 727 SW2d 732, writ gr, aff in part, rev in part 747 SW2d 783.—App & E 232(2); Bills & N 534; Fraud 7, 50; Home 97, 177(2); Hus & W 212; Liens 7.

First State Bank of Dell City; Hays v., TexCivApp–El Paso, 377 SW2d 210, ref nre.—Bills & N 140, 537(8); Princ & A 36, 50; Princ & S 128(2).

First State Bank of Denton v. Maryland Cas. Co., CA5 (Tex), 918 F2d 38.—Evid 121(1), 148, 314(1); Fed Cts 433; Insurance 2199, 2201, 2202.

First State Bank of Denton; Reece v., Tex, 566 SW2d 296.—Guar 5, 22, 27.

First State Bank of Denton; Reece v., TexCivApp–Fort Worth, 555 SW2d 929, writ gr, aff 566 SW2d 296.—Guar 5, 38(1).

First State Bank of Denton v. Smoot-Curtis Co., TexCivApp–Fort Worth, 121 SW2d 667, writ dism by agreement.—App & E 882(14); Bills & N 493(2), 504, 537(1); Evid 459(2); Trial 350.4(1), 350.8.

First State Bank of Dumas; Jones v., TexCivApp–Amarillo, 145 SW2d 681.—Banks 86, 96, 101, 228; Evid 413, 450(10), 461(1); Trial 139.1(14).

First State Bank of Dumas v. Sharp, TexApp–Austin, 863 SW2d 81, reh overr.—Decl Judgm 213.1, 216; States 191.10.

First State Bank of El Paso; U.S. Fire Ins. Co. v., TexCivApp–El Paso, 538 SW2d 209, 85 ALR3d 1097, ref nre.—Insurance 2153(1).

First State Bank of Euless v. Bolinger, TexCivApp–Fort Worth, 431 SW2d 782, ref nre.—Corp 202.

First State Bank of Euless v. Fair, TexCivApp–Fort Worth, 468 SW2d 600.—Chat Mtg 90, 124, 127, 138(2), 157(3); Evid 455.

First State Bank of Frankston v. Hughes, TexApp–Tyler, 654 SW2d 31.—Banks 189; Judgm 181(26).

First State Bank of Gainesville; Clayton v., TexApp–Fort Worth, 777 SW2d 577, writ den.—App & E 1043(1); Pretrial Proc 282, 313.

First State Bank of Gainesville; State Banking Bd. v., TexCivApp–Austin, 618 SW2d 905.—Banks 6.

First State Bank of Gainesville v. Thomas, NDTex, 38 FSupp 849.—Int Rev 3054, 4370.

First State Bank of Grandview; Grandview Farm Center, Inc. v., TexCivApp–Waco, 596 SW2d 190, ref nre.—App & E 1170.7; Damag 140, 184; Trover 40(4), 66; Usury 125.

First State Bank of Granger; Urban v., TexCivApp–Austin, 609 SW2d 857.—Bills & N 517; Corp 414(2).

First State Bank of Grapeland v. Brown, TexCivApp–Tyler, 490 SW2d 248.—App & E 846(5); Bankr 2784.1; Home 214, 216.

First State Bank of Greens Bayou; Kimberly Development Corp. v., TexCivApp–Houston, 404 SW2d 631, ref nre.—App & E 390, 395, 417(2), 692(1), 934(1); Evid 5(2); Judgm 181(14); Mtg 97, 341.

First State Bank of Green's Bayou v. Tanner, TexCivApp–Hous (1 Dist), 495 SW2d 267.—Banks 226; Hus & W 17; Lim of Act 24(2), 127(4), 199(1).

First State Bank of Gustine v. New Amsterdam Cas. Co. of New York, CCA5 (Tex), 83 F2d 992.—Insurance 2963, 2999, 3026.

First State Bank of Hawkins; First Nat. Bank of Gilmer v., TexCivApp–Texarkana, 456 SW2d 173, writ dism.—App & E 101(1).

First State Bank of Honey Grove; Hackney v., TexApp–Texarkana, 866 SW2d 59, reh den.—App & E 543, 559, 573; Damag 188(2), 221(7).

First State Bank of Hubbard v. Zeanon, TexCivApp–Waco, 169 SW2d 735, writ refused.—Home 32, 122, 129(1), 157.

First State Bank of Jacksonville, Tex. v. Pure Van Pipe Line Co., CCA5 (Tex), 77 F2d 820.—Assign 41, 93, 101.

First State Bank of Keene; Hynum v., TexCivApp–Waco, 575 SW2d 431.—App & E 907(4).

First State Bank of Keene v. Northrop, TexCivApp–Waco, 519 SW2d 161.—Sec Tran 240.

First State Bank of Liberty; Farmers State Bank v., TexCivApp–Waco, 317 SW2d 768.—Guar 9; Judgm 185.1(4), 185.2(5).

First State Bank of Liberty; Trinity Universal Ins. Co. v., TexCivApp–Amarillo, 179 SW2d 391, rev 183 SW2d 422, 143 Tex 164.—Banks 119, 129, 134(1).

First State Bank of Livingston; Moore v., TexCivApp–Beaumont, 127 SW2d 536.—Chat Mtg 87, 138(3), 277; Courts 170; Venue 22(6).

First State Bank of McKinney v. American Bank of Sherman, N.A., TexApp–Dallas, 732 SW2d 404.—Banks 140(3).

First State Bank of McKinney; Texoma Nat. Bank of Sherman v., TexApp–Dallas, 653 SW2d 91.—Action 60; App & E 912; Banks 275.

First State Bank of Marquez; Southern Sur. Co. of New York v., TexCivApp–Waco, 54 SW2d 888, writ refused.—App & E 846(5); High 113(4); Lim of Act 1, 118(1), 127(2); Pub Contr 61.

First State Bank of Mathis; Edmondson v., TexApp–Corpus Christi, 819 SW2d 605.—App & E 1003(6); Bills & N 520, 539; Usury 42, 88.

First State Bank of Memphis v. Seago, TexCivApp–Amarillo, 120 SW2d 951, writ refused.—Home 36, 168, 181(3).

First State Bank of Memphis; Strickland Transp. Co. v., Tex, 214 SW2d 934, 147 Tex 193.—Banks 138, 140(2), 148(2), 155.

First State Bank of Memphis; Strickland Transp. Co. v., TexCivApp–Amarillo, 207 SW2d 941, aff 214 SW2d 934, 147 Tex 193.—Banks 148(2).

First State Bank of Miami v. Fatheree, TexApp–Amarillo, 847 SW2d 391, reh overr, and writ den.—Bills & N 103(1), 520, 538(8); Pretrial Proc 45; Trial 25(1).

First State Bank of Miami; Walls v., TexApp–Amarillo, 900 SW2d 117, reh overr, and writ den.—Banks 100; Com Law 11; Const Law 190, 191, 2648; Judgm 181(33), 185(2); Statut 265, 267(1), 267(2); U S 34.

First State Bank of Mobeetie v. Goodner, TexCivApp–Amarillo, 168 SW2d 941.—Fraud Conv 64(1), 96(1), 206(2); Judgm 767, 769; Trial 145.

First State Bank of Monahans v. Henderson, TexCivApp–El Paso, 377 SW2d 96.—Judgm 181(17), 185.1(3), 185.1(4), 185.2(3).

First State Bank of Monahans, Tex. v. Holt, BkrtcyWDTex, 41 BR 132. See McDaniel, In re.

First State Bank of Morton, Tex.; Chesshir v., Tex, 620 SW2d 101, on remand 634 SW2d 742, ref nre.—App & E 835(2).

First State Bank of Morton, Tex.; Gillie v., BkrtcyND–Tex, 96 BR 689. See Gillie, In re.

First State Bank of Odessa, N.A. v. Arsiaga, TexApp–Eastland, 804 SW2d 343, writ den.—Autos 384; Sec Tran 144, 170.

First State Bank of Odessa, N.A. v. Trini's Paint and Body Works, TexApp–Eastland, 804 SW2d 343. See First State Bank of Odessa, N.A. v. Arsiaga.

First State Bank of Pittsburg, Texas; Copher v., TexApp–Fort Worth, 852 SW2d 738.—App & E 1074(2); Execution 402(5).

First State Bank of Riesel v. Dyer, Tex, 254 SW2d 92, 151 Tex 650.—Evid 418; Partners 128, 136, 139, 145, 157(1).

First State Bank of Riesel v. Dyer, TexCivApp–Waco, 248 SW2d 785, aff 254 SW2d 92, 151 Tex 650.—Bills & N 59; Estop 52(7); Evid 418; Partners 146(2), 155.

First State Bank of Rio Vista; West Am. Ins. Co. v., TexCivApp–Waco, 213 SW2d 298.—Evid 18; Insurance 1892, 1893(1), 3147, 3191(7), 3571; Judgm 5, 18(1); Trial 351.2(2).

First State Bank of Rocksprings v. Standard Acc. Ins. Co. of Detroit, Mich., CCA5 (Tex), 94 F2d 726.—Insurance 2402, 2406(5).

First State Bank of Rogers v. Wallace, TexApp–Houston (1 Dist), 788 SW2d 41.—App & E 93; Interest 39(3).

First State Bank of San Diego; Amaya v., TexCivApp–San Antonio, 570 SW2d 95.—Bills & N 493(3); Usury 113.

First State Bank of San Diego v. Duval County, TexCivApp–Waco, 567 SW2d 271, ref nre.—Judgm 185.1(3); Jury 16(9).

First State Bank of San Diego; Parr v., TexCivApp–San Antonio, 507 SW2d 579.—App & E 237(1); Appear 24(1); Divorce 73, 207; Inj 115, 157; Plead 110; Receivers 6, 9, 16, 39, 51.

First State Bank of San Diego; Parr v., TexCivApp–Eastland, 307 SW2d 309.—Action 65; App & E 781(4); Counties 196(1).

First State Bank of San Diego; Republic Nat. Life Ins. Co. v., TexCivApp–Eastland, 384 SW2d 429, writ refused.—Insurance 2422.

First State Bank of San Diego, Tex.; Clower v., CA5 (Tex), 343 F2d 808.—Bankr 2608(2).

First State Bank of San Diego, Tex.; Clower v., SDTex, 227 FSupp 653, rev 343 F2d 808.—Bankr 2608(2), 2727(2).

First State Bank of Seagraves; Bozeman v., TexCivApp–El Paso, 468 SW2d 538.—App & E 1178(8); Plead 45, 111.3; Venue 22(6).

First State Bank of Shallowater; General Steel Warehouse, Inc. v., BkrtcyNDTex, 49 BR 25. See Stone, In re.

First State Bank of Shallowater v. Onley, BkrtcyND–Tex, 48 BR 891. See Onley, In re.

First State Bank of Smithville; Catherman v., TexApp–Austin, 796 SW2d 299.—Antitrust 212; App & E 302(1), 760(1), 1003(3), 1079; Bills & N 59; Evid 207(1), 246, 265(3), 265(7); Judgm 185(1).

First State Bank of Smithville; Ebner v., TexApp–Austin, 27 SW3d 287, reh overr, and review den, and reh of petition for review den.—App & E 1175(1); Atty & C 101(1); Compromise 5(3), 20(1); Equity 72(1), 84; Estop 52.10(2), 68(2); Judgm 178, 181(6), 181(19), 183, 185(5), 185(6), 713(2), 855(1); Princ & A 96, 99, 166(1), 171(1).

First State Bank of Smithville; Ford Motor Credit Co. v., Tex, 679 SW2d 486.—Sec Tran 146.

First State Bank of Smithville; Ford Motor Credit Co. v., TexApp–Tyler, 674 SW2d 437, rev 679 SW2d 486.—Sec Tran 146.

First State Bank of Stratford; C.I.R. v., CCA5 (Tex), 168 F2d 1004, 7 ALR2d 738, cert den 69 SCt 137, 335 US 867, 93 LEd 412.—Corp 152; Int Rev 3089, 3114, 3115, 3138, 3419.1, 3620, 3626, 3695, 3698, 3749, 4731.

First State Bank of Stratford; Roberts v., TexApp–Amarillo, 774 SW2d 415, writ gr, and writ withdrawn, and writ den.—Wills 547.

First State Bank of Stratford, Tex. v. Roach, CCA5 (Tex), 124 F2d 325.—Bankr 2229, 2264(1); Ex & Ad 7, 33.

First State Bank of Tenaha v. Collinsworth, TexCiv-App–Beaumont, 111 SW2d 309, writ dism.—App & E 20, 79(1), 219(2), 877(3); Contracts 284(4); Dep & Escr 20.

First State Bank of Texas; Dennis v., TexApp–Fort Worth, 989 SW2d 22.—Action 13; App & E 760(1), 863, 1078(5); Judgm 585(2), 586(1), 678(1), 678(2), 713(2); Sequest 21; Set-Off 60.

First State Bank of Tulia; Ranchers & Farmers Livestock Auction Co. of Clovis, New Mexico v., TexCiv-App–Amarillo, 531 SW2d 167, ref nre.—Garn 2; Judgm 185(2); Sales 290; Sec Tran 10, 140.

First State Bank of Vernon; Commercial Standard Ins. Co. v., TexCivApp–Amarillo, 142 SW2d 621, writ dism. —Damag 113; Evid 568(1), 570, 588, 590; Insurance 2720, 2733, 3023, 3450; Trial 136(1).

First State Bank of Vernon; Persky v., TexCivApp–Amarillo, 117 SW2d 861.—Evid 18, 23(1); Mines 73.5.

First State Bank of Weimar; Brown v., TexCivApp–Galveston, 199 SW 895, writ dism woj.—App & E 931(3), 994(3); Bankr 303(1).

First State Bank of Wichita Falls v. Oak Cliff Sav. & Loan Ass'n, Tex, 387 SW2d 369.—Banks 133, 138, 148(2), 148(3); Bills & N 6, 119; Judgm 185.3(1).

First State Bank of Wichita Falls v. Oak Cliff Sav. & Loan Ass'n, TexCivApp–Eastland, 379 SW2d 952, aff 387 SW2d 369.—Banks 148(2), 148(3).

First State Bank of Willis; Fulton Fire Ins. Co. v., TexCivApp–Waco, 353 SW2d 937, ref nre.—App & E 1170.7; Evid 544; Witn 345(2).

First State Bank, Overton, Tex.; Bandy v., Tex, 835 SW2d 609.—App & E 671(4); Banks 119, 133, 134(1), 134(2), 152, 154(8); Ex & Ad 26(2), 122(1); Judgm 518, 957; Set-Off 8(2); Trover 4.

First State Bank, Spearman; Riley v., TexCivApp–Amarillo, 469 SW2d 812, ref nre.—Bills & N 120, 337, 338, 342, 422(1), 489(1), 497(1); Judgm 185(1), 185(4).

First State Bank, Stratford; Tri-State Chemicals, Inc. v., TexApp–Amarillo, 185 SW3d 519, reh overr.—Fact 65; Judgm 181(17); Sec Tran 82.1; Trover 11.

First State Bank, Tulia, Tex.; Ruthart v., TexCivApp–Amarillo, 431 SW2d 366, writ refused.—Action 56; App & E 964; Bills & N 460; Corp 99(1); Parties 51(2); Trial 2.

First State Bank-Wylie; Hannigan v., TexApp–Dallas, 700 SW2d 7, ref nre.—Sec Tran 113.1.

First State Bldg. and Loan Ass'n v. B.L. Nelson and Associates, TexApp–Dallas, 735 SW2d 287.—Judgm 143(3), 145(1), 146, 161, 163.

First States Life Co.; Castel v., TexCivApp–Fort Worth, 122 SW2d 1113.—Insurance 2420, 2439, 2445, 3611(1), 3611(2).

First States Life Co. v. Mote, TexCivApp–Waco, 110 SW2d 591.—App & E 204(2), 843(1); Can of Inst 45, 46; Insurance 1635, 3015; Trial 132, 133.6(4).

First States Life Co. v. Ransom, TexCivApp–Waco, 110 SW2d 143.—App & E 909(5); Insurance 2445.

First States Life Co. v. Stroud, TexCivApp–El Paso, 120 SW2d 491.—Fraud 21; Insurance 3618; Plead 111.39(8); Venue 8.5(3).

First Strawn Nat. Bank v. Glidewell, TexCivApp–Eastland, 307 SW2d 297, ref nre.—Banks 121, 155, 156.

First Tape, Inc.; Alliance Ins. Co., Inc. v., TexApp–Houston (14 Dist), 713 SW2d 718, ref nre.—Insurance 3523(4).

First Tape, Inc.; Interstate Fire Ins. Co. v., TexApp–Houston (1 Dist), 817 SW2d 142, writ den.—App & E 863; Contracts 1, 114; Insurance 3512, 3523(4), 3526(11); Judgm 181(1), 185(2); Land & Ten 55(1), 79(1), 79(3), 80(1), 80(3); Subrog 32.

First Tennessee Nat. Corp.; Williams v., TexApp–Dallas, 97 SW3d 798.—Contracts 326; Damag 50.10, 208(6); Labor & Emp 40(1), 40(2), 50, 51, 55, 217, 861.

First Tex. Chemical Mfg. Co.; Webb v., TexCivApp–Eastland, 86 SW2d 818.—Bankr 2297, 2584; Sheriffs 106, 154, 169.

First Texas Homes, Inc., In re, Tex, 120 SW3d 868.—Alt Disp Res 137, 139, 144; States 18.15.

First Texas Joint Stock Land Bank v. Holloway, Tex-CivApp–Amarillo, 77 SW2d 301.—Banks 405.

First Texas Joint Stock Land Bank v. Kaufman County Levee Imp. Dist. No. 13, TexCivApp–Amarillo, 130 SW2d 463, writ refused.—Judgm 17(10).

First Texas Joint Stock Land Bank of Houston; Corn v., TexCivApp–Fort Worth, 131 SW2d 752, writ refused. —App & E 930(1), 1011.1(4), 1073(7); Deeds 136; Joint Ten 1, 8; Mtg 372(1); Ten in C 9, 19(2); Trial 382; Trusts 102(1), 177; Ven & Pur 215.

First Texas Joint Stock Land Bank of Houston; Fawver v., TexCivApp–Amarillo, 115 SW2d 1217.—App & E 78(4); Deeds 124(1); Inj 129(1), 163(1).

First Texas Joint Stock Land Bank of Houston v. Webb, TexCivApp–Fort Worth, 82 SW2d 159, writ dism.—Hus & W 85(3); Infants 110; Judgm 456(1); Trusts 359(2).

First Texas Petroleum, Inc., In re, BkrtcyNDTex, 52 BR 322.—Bankr 2369, 2370; Courts 508(1).

First Tex. Prudential Ins. Co.; Martinez v., TexCivApp–Eastland, 90 SW2d 645, writ dism.—App & E 1097(1); Insurance 3084, 3091.

First Texas Prudential Ins. Co. v. Ryan, TexComApp, 82 SW2d 635, 125 Tex 377.—App & E 172(1), 1094(2); Contracts 346(1); Insurance 1713, 1835(1), 1938, 1950, 1953, 2035, 2050, 2054; Spec Perf 78.

First Texas Sav. Ass'n; Farmer v., TexApp–Fort Worth, 665 SW2d 612. See Farmer v. First Texas Service Corp.

First Texas Sav. Ass'n v. Jergins, TexApp–Fort Worth, 705 SW2d 390.—Contracts 16, 22(1), 244.

First Texas Sav. Ass'n v. Reliance Ins. Co., CA5 (Tex), 950 F2d 1171, reh den.—Fed Civ Proc 1952, 1954.1; Insurance 2405, 3349, 3360, 3417.

First Texas Sav. Ass'n v. Stiff Properties, TexApp–Corpus Christi, 685 SW2d 703.—Antitrust 134, 135(1), 143(2), 145, 209, 369.

First Texas Sav. Ass'n of Dallas v. Dicker Center, Inc., TexApp–Tyler, 631 SW2d 179.—B & L Assoc 28; Contracts 95(1), 99(3), 103, 105, 322(3); Costs 207; Damag 40(3), 89(2); Release 21, 25.

FIRST

59 Tex D 2d—46

See Guidelines for Arrangement at the beginning of this Volume

First Texas Sav. Ass'n of Dallas; Packer v., TexCivApp–Eastland, 567 SW2d 574, ref nre.—Bills & N 474; Judgm 183; Mtg 561.3; Parties 51(4); Pretrial Proc 483.

First Texas Service Corp.; Farmer v., TexApp–Fort Worth, 665 SW2d 612.—Pretrial Proc 698.

First Texas Service Corp. v. McDonald, TexApp–Fort Worth, 762 SW2d 935, writ den.—App & E 216(7), 230, 232(0.5); Frds St of 78; Mtg 364, 369(8).

FirstTier Bank, N.A. v. Rush, BkrtcyWDTex, 136 BR 999. See Rush, In re.

First Title Co. of Corpus Christi, Inc. v. Cook, TexApp–Fort Worth, 625 SW2d 814, dism.—Antitrust 128, 141, 147, 290, 292, 357, 358; App & E 846(5), 1010.1(1); Plead 111.16; Venue 3, 17.

First Title Co. of Waco v. Garrett, Tex, 860 SW2d 74.—Antitrust 130, 221, 297; Contrib 1, 5(1), 9(6); Insurance 2610, 2637(1); Neglig 549(5); Prod Liab 2; Sales 260, 425.

First Title Co. of Waco v. Garrett, TexApp–Waco, 802 SW2d 254, writ gr, rev 860 SW2d 74.—Antitrust 162, 221, 297, 369; App & E 1056.1(3); Damag 49.10, 63, 130.1, 190; Insurance 2610, 2616, 2639; Pretrial Proc 42, 45; Trial 351.2(4).

First Trade Union Sav. Bank; City of Dallas v., TexApp–Dallas, 133 SW3d 680, reh overr, and review den, and reh of petition for review den.—Action 13; App & E 173(1), 840(4), 874(4), 893(1), 916(1); Courts 4, 35; Mun Corp 723, 724, 742(5); Plead 104(1), 111.37, 111.46, 111.48; States 191.1, 191.4(1), 191.10.

First Trust Co. v. Good Land Lumber Co., TexCivApp–Waco, 297 SW2d 312.—Corp 503(2), 619; Liens 22; Venue 6, 22(7), 22(8).

First Trust Corporation TTEE FBO v. Edwards, TexApp–Dallas, 172 SW3d 230, reh overr, and review den, and reh of petition for review den.—App & E 846(5), 852, 866(1), 893(1), 1010.1(1), 1010.2; Compromise 17(2); Corp 417, 619; Release 25, 27.

First Trust Joint Stock Land Bank of Chicago v. Bates, TexCivApp–Dallas, 164 SW2d 734.—Plead 111.16, 111.46.

First Trust Joint Stock Land Bank of Chicago v. City of Dallas, TexCivApp–Dallas, 167 SW2d 783, writ refused.—Mun Corp 966(1), 966(6), 972(3); Tax 2063, 2064, 2212.

First-Trust Joint Stock Land Bank of Chicago; Gossett v., TexCivApp–Dallas, 138 SW2d 904, writ dism.—Banks 63.5; Courts 478; Receivers 35(1).

First Trust Joint Stock Land Bank of Chicago; Hayes v., TexCivApp–Fort Worth, 111 SW2d 1172, writ dism.—Home 5, 33, 55, 70, 73, 81, 90, 95, 96.

First Trust Joint Stock Land Bank of Chicago v. Hayes, TexCivApp–Waco, 90 SW2d 331.—App & E 863; Inj 135; Mtg 335, 338.

First Trust Joint Stock Land Bank of Chicago; Jones v., TexCivApp–San Antonio, 119 SW2d 98, dism.—Judgm 713(1), 720.

First-Trust Joint Stock Land Bank of Chicago; Kennedy v., TexCivApp–San Antonio, 103 SW2d 192, writ dism.—App & E 909(3); Mtg 341, 378.

First Trust Joint Stock Land Bank of Chicago v. Morrison, TexCivApp–Fort Worth, 92 SW2d 503.—Brok 84(1); Corp 666.

First Union Nat. Bank v. Richmont Capital Partners I, L.P., TexApp–Dallas, 168 SW3d 917.—App & E 852; Contracts 143.5, 147(3), 152, 156, 164, 175(1), 176(2), 187(1); Evid 584(1); Guar 27, 34; Impl & C C 3, 55; Sec Tran 115.1, 147.

First Union Real Estate Investments v. Taylor County Appraisal Dist., TexApp–Eastland, 758 SW2d 380, writ den.—Tax 2573(4), 2694.

First Unitarian Church of Austin; Kermacy v., TexCivApp–Austin, 361 SW2d 734, ref nre.—Alt Disp Res 379, 380, 392, 405; Interest 37(1), 39(1).

First United Bank v. Panhandle Packing and Gasket, Inc., TexApp–Amarillo, 190 SW3d 10, reh overr.—App & E 171(1), 843(2), 1062.1; Banks 148(2), 154(8); Const Law 2600.

First United Methodist Church of Huntington; Stradt v., Tex, 573 SW2d 186.—App & E 930(3); Joint Ten 1; Partit 3, 4, 5.

First United Methodist Church of Huntington; Stradt v., TexCivApp, 567 SW2d 810, writ gr, rev 573 SW2d 186.—Partit 4, 8; Tresp to T T 41(1).

First United Methodist Church of Marlin v. Allen, TexCivApp–Waco, 557 SW2d 175, ref nre.—Wills 439, 442, 450, 456, 467, 470(1), 476.

First USA Bank, N.A.; Marsh v., NDTex, 103 FSupp2d 909.—Alt Disp Res 113, 121, 132, 134(6), 139, 141, 143, 147, 178, 210, 211, 235, 276, 335, 342; Contracts 1, 93(2); Estop 52.10(4); Evid 71, 89; Fed Civ Proc 182.5; Jury 28(7).

First USA Management, Inc. v. Esmond, Tex, 960 SW2d 625.—Usury 11, 16, 18, 36.1.

First USA Management, Inc. v. Esmond, TexApp–Dallas, 911 SW2d 100, writ gr, aff in part, rev in part 960 SW2d 625.—App & E 863, 934(1); Fraud 11(1), 12, 64(1); Interest 1; Judgm 185(2), 185.3(1), 185.3(21); Usury 1, 11, 36.1, 53, 119.

First USA Merchant Services, Inc.; United Marketing Technology, Inc. v., TexApp–Dallas, 812 SW2d 608, writ den.—Plead 236(2), 236(3), 245(3), 258(3).

First Valley Bank of Los Fresnos v. Martin, Tex, 144 SW3d 466, reh den.—Corp 398(2), 399(6); Mal Pros 3, 16, 18(1), 18(2), 27; Princ & A 99; Sec Tran 111, 224.

First Valley Bank of Los Fresnos v. Martin, TexApp–Corpus Christi, 55 SW3d 172, review gr, review gr, rev 144 SW3d 466, reh den.—Antitrust 392; App & E 535.1, 930(1), 996, 1001(1), 1004(1); Banks 100; Corp 397; Damag 50.10, 100, 187, 192, 208(6); Evid 427; Fraud 3, 12, 17; Mal Pros 0.5, 3, 20, 31, 64(1), 64(2), 67, 69, 71(2); Princ & A 1, 8, 14(1), 14(2), 99; Sec Tran 224; Trial 351.2(1.1), 366.

First Victoria Nat. Bank; Barnes v., TexApp–Corpus Christi, 878 SW2d 666.—Records 32.

First Victoria Nat. Bank v. Briones, TexApp–Corpus Christi, 788 SW2d 632, writ den.—Contracts 143.5, 147(1), 147(3), 152, 176(9); Evid 417(1), 417(9), 448; Indem 33(5).

First Victoria Nat. Bank; Chilcoat v., TexCivApp–Corpus Christi, 421 SW2d 122, ref nre.—Judgm 185.3(8).

First Victoria Nat. Bank; Hodgson v., CA5 (Tex), 446 F2d 47, 20 Wage & Hour Cas (BNA) 132.—Fed Cts 858.

First Victoria Nat. Bank; Mumphord v., TexCivApp–Corpus Christi, 605 SW2d 701.—Fraud 3, 12, 25, 49, 66; Mtg 369(3); Trial 168.

First Victoria Nat. Bank; Shultz v., CA5 (Tex), 420 F2d 648, 19 Wage & Hour Cas (BNA) 275, 19 Wage & Hour Cas (BNA) 343, 7 ALR Fed 691, on remand Wirtz v. First Victoria Nat Bank, 19 Wage & Hour Cas (BNA) 684, aff Hodgson v First Victoria Nat Bank, 446 F2d 47, 20 Wage & Hour Cas (BNA) 132, on remand 19 Wage & Hour Cas (BNA) 774, appeal after remand 446 F2d 47, 20 Wage & Hour Cas (BNA) 132, appeal after remand 447 F2d 416, 20 Wage & Hour Cas (BNA) 148, 20 Wage & Hour Cas (BNA) 185.—Fed Cts 792, 850.1; Labor & Emp 2453, 2466, 2481(2).

First Victoria Nat. Bank; Tumlinson v., TexApp–Corpus Christi, 865 SW2d 176.—Banks 148(3); Judgm 181(17).

First Victoria Nat. Bank v. U.S., CA5 (Tex), 620 F2d 1096.—Int Rev 4149.10.

First Victoria Nat. Bank v. U.S., SDTex, 443 FSupp 865, rev 620 F2d 1096.—Int Rev 4149.10, 5008.

First Wichita Nat. Bank v. Manuel, CA5 (Tex), 896 F2d 1435. See Transco Leasing Corp. v. U.S.

For Later Case History Information, see KeyCite on WESTLAW

First-Wichita Nat. Bank v. Steed, TexCivApp–Fort Worth, 374 SW2d 932.—Banks 142.

First-Wichita Nat. Bank v. Wood, TexApp–Fort Worth, 632 SW2d 210.—Contracts 322(4); Costs 194.32, 207; Trial 350.4(1).

First Wichita Nat. Bank of Wichita Falls; Birk v., TexCivApp–Fort Worth, 352 SW2d 781, ref nre.—Deeds 8, 28, 109, 120; Trusts 13, 119, 125.

First-Wichita Nat. Bank of Wichita Falls; Blandin v., TexCivApp–Fort Worth, 398 SW2d 663.—App & E 19, 781(1), 781(4), 781(6).

First-Wichita Nat. Bank of Wichita Falls; Chapman v., TexCivApp–Fort Worth, 392 SW2d 772, ref nre.—Acct 1; App & E 758.1; Mtg 131; Princ & A 79(4); Receivers 154(1), 183, 199; Trover 35.

First-Wichita Nat. Bank of Wichita Falls; Republic Heater Co. v., TexCivApp–Fort Worth, 465 SW2d 395, ref nre.—Judgm 185.3(21).

First-Wichita Nat. Bank of Wichita Falls; Ward v., TexCivApp–Fort Worth, 387 SW2d 913, ref nre.—App & E 1170.7; Wills 87, 133, 302(6).

First Wichita Nat. Bank of Wichita Falls, Tex.; Kausch v., CA5 (Tex), 470 F2d 1068.—Decl Judgm 241; Fed Cts 9.

First Wisconsin Mortg. Trust; American Nat. Bank & Trust Co. v., TexCivApp–Beaumont, 577 SW2d 312, 7 ALR4th 1206, ref nre.—App & E 766; Costs 194.30; Evid 317(4), 506, 597; Labor & Emp 3057, 3066, 3100(2); Land & Ten 75(2), 80(1), 81(2); Libel 130, 131, 139; Quiet T 54; Trial 136(3), 382.

Firth v. State, TexCrimApp, 276 SW2d 268.—Crim Law 1090.1(1).

Firth; Texarkana Memorial Hosp., Inc. v., TexApp–Texarkana, 746 SW2d 494.—Damag 94; Health 703(2), 823(14), 832; Neglig 273, 1584, 1659.

Firth; Wadley Regional Medical Center v., TexApp–Texarkana, 746 SW2d 494. See Texarkana Memorial Hosp., Inc. v. Firth.

Fisbeck v. State, TexCrimApp, 311 SW2d 865, 166 TexCrim 105.—Crim Law 829(20); Int Liq 236(20), 239(4); Witn 330(3), 383.

Fisch, In re, TexApp–Houston (1 Dist), 95 SW3d 732.—Contempt 20.

Fisch; Levin v., TexCivApp–Eastland, 404 SW2d 889, ref nre.—Wills 467.

Fisch v. Transcontinental Ins. Co., TexApp–Houston, 356 SW2d 186, ref nre.—App & E 927(7), 997(3); Evid 380; Insurance 2200, 3261, 3262, 3263, 3314, 3395, 3396; Interest 44; Plead 93(1); Trial 136(1).

Fischbach & Moore, Inc.; Daniel Intern. Corp. v., CA5 (Tex), 916 F2d 1061, reh den 921 F2d 273.—Damag 78(1), 163(3); Fed Civ Proc 422; Jury 25(6), 28(17).

Fischbach & Moore, Inc.; Weakley v., CA5 (Tex), 515 F2d 1260.—Damag 165; Electricity 19(5), 19(9), 19(12), 19(13); Fed Cts 415, 909; Neglig 554(1), 554(2), 1533, 1719; Prod Liab 11.

Fischel; Smock v., Tex, 207 SW2d 891, 146 Tex 397.—App & E 301; Judgm 97; New Tr 34; Pretrial Proc 583, 587; Set-Off 1.

Fischel; Smock v., TexCivApp–San Antonio, 207 SW2d 888, aff in part, rev in part 207 SW2d 891, 146 Tex 397.—App & E 301, 945; Judgm 344, 366.

Fischel; U.S. v., CA5 (Tex), 686 F2d 1082.—Controlled Subs 46, 81; Crim Law 37(1), 59(4), 59(5), 330, 627.10(6), 629(3.1), 666.5, 772(6), 829(1), 1166(10.10); Ind & Inf 144.2.

Fischer, Ex parte, TexApp–Fort Worth, 950 SW2d 140. See Dharmagunaratne, Ex parte.

Fischer; A & S Elec. Contractors, Inc. v., TexApp–Tyler, 622 SW2d 601.—App & E 170(1); Judgm 178, 185(5), 185.1(2), 185.1(3), 185.2(4); Princ & A 8, 23(1), 123(2).

Fischer; Ancira Enterprises, Inc. v., TexApp–Austin, 178 SW3d 82.—App & E 171(1), 179(3), 213, 215(1), 237(5), 238(2), 1001(1); Civil R 1109, 1110, 1111, 1112, 1740,

1744, 1769; Courts 155; Fed Cts 5; Labor & Emp 870; Parties 96(2).

Fischer; Board of Regents of University of Texas System v., TexCivApp–Austin, 498 SW2d 230, ref nre.—Em Dom 124, 133, 155, 222(4).

Fischer v. Britton, Tex, 83 SW2d 305, 125 Tex 505.—Ex & Ad 7; Mtg 334, 375.

Fischer v. Coastal Towing Inc., EDTex, 168 FRD 199.—Fed Civ Proc 1651, 1654.

Fischer; Correa v., CA5 (Tex), 982 F2d 931.—Const Law 1475(9); Counties 67.

Fischer v. Dallas Federal Sav. and Loan Ass'n, CA5 (Tex), 835 F2d 567.—Fed Civ Proc 2178; Fed Cts 628, 630.1, 635.

Fischer v. Dallas Federal Sav. and Loan Ass'n, NDTex, 106 FRD 465, aff 835 F2d 567.—Fed Civ Proc 103.7, 182.5.

Fischer; Dowden v., TexCivApp–Waco, 338 SW2d 534.—Child C 76, 722, 726, 749, 766, 788; Divorce 409; Evid 80(1), 89.

Fischer; English v., Tex, 660 SW2d 521.—Antitrust 130, 145; Contracts 168; Estop 85, 87; Mtg 201.

Fischer; English v., TexApp–Corpus Christi, 649 SW2d 83, writ gr, rev 660 SW2d 521.—Antitrust 143(2), 290, 397, 398; Contracts 164; Damag 23; Interest 39(1), 39(2.30); Mtg 137, 201, 205, 216, 403; Princ & S 157.

Fischer; English v., TexApp–Corpus Christi, 632 SW2d 163.—Motions 1; New Tr 124(1).

Fischer; Horizon/CMS Healthcare Corp., Inc. v., Tex, 111 SW3d 67.—Health 804.

Fischer v. Huffman, TexCivApp–Amarillo, 254 SW2d 878.—App & E 1078(5); Judgm 304, 306, 326.

Fischer; Leach v., TexApp–Fort Worth, 669 SW2d 844.—Courts 207.4(3); Elections 10, 120, 126(4); Estop 62.2(2); Mand 71, 168(2), 187.9(6); Offic 1.

Fischer; Lydick v., CCA5 (Tex), 135 F2d 983.—Courts 490; Fed Civ Proc 2575; Fed Cts 589; Insurance 1405; Rem of C 49.1(1).

Fischer v. Reissig, TexCivApp–Austin, 143 SW2d 130, writ refused.—Covenants 49, 51(2).

Fischer v. Richard Gill Co., TexCivApp–San Antonio, 253 SW2d 915, writ refused.—App & E 1175(5); Consp 19; Const Law 1119; Contracts 303(5); Extort 34; Paymt 87(2); Torts 436.

Fischer v. Rosenthal & Co., NDTex, 481 FSupp 53.—Com Fut 52, 72; Fed Cts 18; Sec Reg 5.20.

Fischer v. State, TexCrimApp, 361 SW2d 395, 172 TexCrim 592.—Crim Law 406(3), 531(3), 721(3); Extort 26, 30, 31, 32.

Fischer; State v., TexApp–Corpus Christi, 769 SW2d 619, writ dism woj.—Dist & Pros Attys 2(3), 3(1); Elections 152; Offic 22; Quo W 29, 43.

Fischer v. State, TexApp–Houston (14 Dist), 207 SW3d 846, petition for discretionary review gr.—Crim Law 419(1), 419(1.5), 419(1.10), 419(2.15), 429(1), 1036.1(6), 1043(2), 1169.1(9).

Fischer; Stenzel v., TexCivApp–Austin, 195 SW2d 254.—Wills 52(1), 229, 290.

Fischer v. Tenet Hospitals, Ltd., TexApp–Dallas, 106 SW3d 110, review gr, rev Horizon/CMS Healthcare Corp, Inc v. Fischer, 111 SW3d 67.—Health 804; New Tr 163(1).

Fischer; Tenngasco Gas Gathering Co. v., TexApp–Corpus Christi, 653 SW2d 469, ref nre.—App & E 181, 554(1), 994(2), 999(1), 1177(9); Em Dom 3, 8, 13, 34, 55, 58, 67, 198(2), 205, 255, 259, 262(2); Evid 555.6(10), 571(7).

Fischer; Tenngasco Gas Gathering Co. v., TexApp–Corpus Christi, 624 SW2d 301, ref nre.—App & E 961, 1024.1; Em Dom 202(1); Evid 555.1, 555.6(10), 588; Pretrial Proc 44.1, 313; Trial 317, 344.

Fischer v. Williams, Tex, 331 SW2d 210, 160 Tex 342.—App & E 77(2); Wills 307, 358.

Fischer v. Williams, TexCivApp–Amarillo, 322 SW2d 667, rev 331 SW2d 210, 160 Tex 342.—Judgm 553; Wills 229, 358.

Fischer v. Wood, TexCivApp–San Antonio, 119 SW2d 114, writ dism.—Bills & N 129(2), 139(1); Chat Mtg 279.

Fischer; Wynne v., TexApp–Dallas, 809 SW2d 264, writ den.—Equity 65(1), 65(2); Judgm 185(1), 185(2), 186.

Fischer-Stoker, In Re, TexApp–Houston (1 Dist), 174 SW3d 268, review den.—Contempt 63(1), 66(1); Divorce 284; Mand 4(1), 12.

Fischer-Stoker v. Stoker, TexApp–Houston (1 Dist), 174 SW3d 272, reh overr, and review den.—App & E 842(2), 893(1), 946, 1008.1(1), 1010.2, 1071.2; Contracts 143.5, 152; Divorce 249.1, 252.3(2), 285, 286(5), 287; Hus & W 31(2), 31(3), 31(7), 248.5, 257, 266.2(1), 266.2(2), 266.3.

Fiserv Solutions, Inc.; Horelica v., TexApp–San Antonio, 123 SW3d 492.—Labor & Emp 355, 365, 389(2).

Fish; American Bankers Ins. Co. v., TexCivApp–Amarillo, 412 SW2d 723.—App & E 966(1), 1140(4); Evid 320; Insurance 1822, 2494(1), 2524; Jury 25(2); Pretrial Proc 713, 724; Witn 271(1).

Fish; Ameritec Realty v., TexApp–Houston (14 Dist), 864 SW2d 745. See LA & N Interests, Inc. v. Fish.

Fish v. Bannister, TexApp–San Antonio, 759 SW2d 714. —Adv Poss 11, 13, 19, 22, 27, 29, 36, 38, 43(3), 57, 65(1), 89, 113; App & E 302(1), 768, 1003(5), 1062.1, 1182; New Tr 99, 102(3), 124(1).

Fish; Bollinger Ins. Co. v., TexApp–Austin, 699 SW2d 645. See C.W. Bollinger Ins. Co. v. Fish.

Fish v. Bush, TexCivApp–Amarillo, 143 SW2d 834.—Bills & N 140, 537(3), 537(4), 537(6).

Fish; C.W. Bollinger Ins. Co. v., TexApp–Austin, 699 SW2d 645.—Courts 21; Insurance 3570(2); Judgm 17(3), 951(1); Proc 73, 77, 80.

Fish v. Dallas Independent School Dist., TexApp–Dallas, 170 SW3d 226, review den.—App & E 930(1), 989; Records 31; Trial 273, 277.

Fish v. Dallas Independent School Dist., TexApp–Eastland, 31 SW3d 678, review den, on remand Russell FISH and Dallas Naacp Branch, Plaintiffs, v. DALLAS INDEPENDENT SCHOOL DISTRICT, Defendant, 2004 WL 5031784, appeal dism 2004 WL 1983456, aff 170 SW3d 226, review den.—Judgm 181(15.1); Records 50, 62.

Fish; LA & N Interests, Inc. v., TexApp–Houston (14 Dist), 864 SW2d 745.—App & E 854(1), 934(1); Brok 1, 35, 39, 40, 43(2), 73, 82(1), 86(1), 100; Contracts 143(2), 176(1), 176(2); Evid 398; Judgm 185(2); Torts 242.

Fish v. Ovalle, TexCivApp–Hous (1 Dist), 512 SW2d 718, ref nre.—App & E 930(3), 989, 1060.4, 1067; Autos 227(2), 245(72), 245(91); Damag 162; Neglig 530(1), 554(1); Trial 186.

Fish v. State, TexApp–Dallas, 734 SW2d 741, petition for discretionary review refused.—Bail 97(1), 97(3).

Fish v. Tandy Corp., TexApp–Fort Worth, 948 SW2d 886, reh overr, and writ den.—App & E 230, 231(1), 854(1), 863, 931(3), 1010.1(8.1), 1012.1(7.1), 1024.3; Appear 9(2); Const Law 3964; Contracts 245(1), 247; Corp 30(1), 30(5), 397; Courts 12(2.1), 12(2.5), 12(2.10), 35; Evid 397(2); Judgm 181(19), 181(33).

Fish; Texas Emp. Ins. Ass'n v., TexCivApp–Fort Worth, 276 SW2d 907, ref nre.—Work Comp 1042, 1105.

Fish; Texas Emp. Ins. Ass'n v., TexCivApp–Fort Worth, 266 SW2d 435, ref nre.—App & E 715(2); Evid 314(1); Work Comp 1105, 1968(3).

Fishback; Smith v., TexCivApp–Texarkana, 123 SW2d 771, writ refused.—App & E 719(6), 846(5); Const Law 4295; Sec Reg 244, 246, 263, 293.

Fishbeck v. State, TexCrimApp, 225 SW2d 854, 154 TexCrim 186.—Crim Law 398(1), 400(2), 448(3), 476.1, 552(3), 650, 720(9), 1091(10), 1137(8); Homic 1114, 1174, 1301, 1330; Jury 127.

Fishbein; Brinkley v., CCA5 (Tex), 110 F2d 62, cert den 61 SCt 34, 311 US 672, 85 LEd 432.—Fed Cts 757; Libel 25, 34, 48(1), 54, 112(3).

Fishbein; Hoxsey v., NDTex, 83 FSupp 282.—Libel 48(1), 54, 112(1).

Fishbein v. Thornton, TexCivApp–Dallas, 247 SW2d 404. —App & E 78(3); Appear 9(2), 9(4); Courts 79, 207.4(2), 207.5; Plead 104(1).

Fishburn v. W. B. Fishburn Cleaners, NDTex, 19 FSupp 676.—Trademarks 1425, 1526, 1800.

Fishel; U.S. v., CA5 (Tex), 747 F2d 271.—Hab Corp 465.1, 670(6), 745.1.

Fishel's Fine Furniture v. Rice Food Market, TexCivApp–Hous (14 Dist), 474 SW2d 539, writ dism.—Action 50(4.1); Lim of Act 55(2), 56(1); Parties 51(4); Subrog 1, 33(2).

Fisher, Ex parte, Tex, 206 SW2d 1000, 146 Tex 328, cert gr Fisher v. Pace, 68 SCt 1339, 334 US 827, 92 LEd 1755, aff 69 SCt 425, 336 US 155, 93 LEd 569, reh den 69 SCt 653, 336 US 928, 93 LEd 1089.—Atty & C 32(4); Contempt 6; Hab Corp 447, 528.1; Trial 349(1); Work Comp 1926.

Fisher, Ex parte, TexCrimApp, 492 SW2d 528.—Bail 53; Hab Corp 469.

Fisher, Ex parte, TexCrimApp, 327 SW2d 579, 168 TexCrim 336.—Extrad 32.

Fisher, In re, BkrtcyEDTex, 242 BR 908.—Bankr 2045, 2057, 2164.1.

Fisher, In re, BkrtcyEDTex, 186 BR 70.—Bankr 2045, 2060.1, 3384, 3388.

Fisher, In re, TexCivApp–Amarillo, 184 SW2d 519.—Infants 196, 197, 198, 221, 223.1, 230.1, 253.

Fisher, In re Commitment of, Tex, 164 SW3d 637, cert den Fisher v. Texas, 126 SCt 428, 546 US 938, 163 LEd2d 326.—Action 18; Const Law 990, 1034, 4335, 4344; Mental H 433(2), 455, 467; Statut 47; Witn 297(13.1).

Fisher v. Agios Nicolaos V, CA5 (Tex), 628 F2d 308, 68 ALR Fed 342, reh den 636 F2d 1107, cert den Valmas Brothers Shipping, SA v. Fisher, 102 SCt 92, 454 US 816, 70 LEd2d 84, reh den 102 SCt 982, 454 US 1129, 71 LEd2d 117.—Adm 1.15, 118.7(5); Courts 28; Fed Cts 63, 65, 813, 818, 868, 914; Interest 31; Seamen 3, 29(5.14).

Fisher; American Oil Co. v., TexApp–Houston (14 Dist), 659 SW2d 80.—App & E 867(1), 931(5), 989, 1057(1), 1067, 1140(2), 1169(1); Damag 228; Labor & Emp 3045, 3096(9); New Tr 162(1).

Fisher; Angelina Cas. Co. v., TexCivApp–Beaumont, 319 SW2d 387.—App & E 110; Judgm 297, 316, 340, 381; Mand 50, 51; New Tr 4; Work Comp 1932.

Fisher; Appraisal Review Bd. of El Paso County Central Appraisal Dist. v., TexApp–El Paso, 88 SW3d 807, reh overr, and review den.—App & E 842(2), 893(1), 931(1), 946, 1008.1(2), 1010.2; Const Law 3912, 4138(1), 4138(2); Courts 4, 37(1), 39; Damag 95, 103, 117, 208(1); Judgm 7, 15, 16; Tax 2105, 2693, 2776, 2777, 2783, 2791.

Fisher v. Beach, TexApp–Dallas, 671 SW2d 63.—App & E 863; Judgm 181(33), 185(2), 185(6), 185.3(21); Libel 76; Mal Pros 16, 18(1), 22, 24(2), 42, 64(2).

Fisher; Bland Lake Fishing and Hunting Club v., TexCivApp–Beaumont, 311 SW2d 710.—Des & Dist 8; Ease 42, 44(1), 50; Fish 5(2); Game 3; Licens 43, 46, 53.

Fisher; Boyle v., TexCivApp–El Paso, 103 SW2d 866, writ dism.—App & E 1175(5); Judgm 198.

Fisher v. Burkburnett Independent School Dist., NDTex, 419 FSupp 1200.—Const Law 4209(3), 4212(2); Schools 55, 172, 175, 177.

Fisher; Calvert v., TexCivApp–Austin, 259 SW2d 944, writ refused.—Statut 188, 219(3); Tax 3341.

Fisher v. Capp, TexCivApp–Amarillo, 597 SW2d 393, ref nre.—App & E 241, 863; Courts 85(3); Judgm 185.2(3), 185.2(9); Wills 58(2), 62.

Fisher v. Carrousel Motor Hotel, Inc., Tex, 424 SW2d 627.—Assault 2, 38; Damag 50.10; Labor & Emp 3100(1), 3100(2); Princ & A 159(1).

Fisher v. Carrousel Motor Hotel, Inc., TexCivApp–Waco, 414 SW2d 774, rev 424 SW2d 627.—Assault 2; Damag 50, 57.12; Torts 424.

Fisher; Celotex Corp. v., TexCivApp–Fort Worth, 288 SW2d 319.—Sales 439, 441(3), 441(4), 442(1), 442(2).

Fisher; Citibank (South Dakota), N.A. v., BkrtcyEDTex, 186 BR 70. See Fisher, In re.

Fisher v. City of Bartlett, TexCivApp–Austin, 88 SW2d 1068, writ dism.—App & E 803.

Fisher; City of Houston v., TexCivApp–Texarkana, 322 SW2d 297, writ dism.—Em Dom 262(5); Evid 142(1), 501(7).

Fisher v. City of Irving, TexCivApp–Dallas, 345 SW2d 547.—Mun Corp 655; Zoning 64, 134.1, 384.1, 385, 417.

Fisher; City of Port Lavaca v., TexCivApp–San Antonio, 355 SW2d 785.—Dedi 39, 44; Evid 555.3; Judgm 199(5); Mun Corp 654, 697(1).

Fisher v. Clayton, CA5 (Tex), 168 FedAppx 620.—Mand 187.8.

Fisher; Clem Lumber Co. v., TexCivApp–Waco, 84 SW2d 282, writ dism.—Autos 149, 193(13), 201(1.1), 245(28).

Fisher v. Coastal Transport Co., Tex, 230 SW2d 522, 149 Tex 224.—App & E 1178(6); Damag 166(2), 172(1), 216(7), 216(8), 221(5.1).

Fisher; Coastal Transport Co. v., TexCivApp–San Antonio, 225 SW2d 995, rev 230 SW2d 522, 149 Tex 224.—App & E 1064.1(7), 1178(6); Costs 237; Damag 20, 216(7), 221(5.1).

Fisher; Community Sav. & Loan Ass'n v., Tex, 409 SW2d 546.—B & L Assoc 38(3); Evid 441(5); Interest 31, 36(1), 56, 59(1); Paymt 42.

Fisher; Community Sav. and Loan Ass'n v., TexCivApp–Austin, 400 SW2d 927, writ gr, rev 409 SW2d 546.—Interest 56; Usury 82.

Fisher v. Continental Illinois Nat. Bank & Trust Co. of Chicago, TexCivApp–Hous (14 Dist), 424 SW2d 664, ref nre.—App & E 961; Appear 19(4); Pretrial Proc 14.1, 20, 27.1, 37, 41, 44.1, 63, 92, 183.1, 221, 226, 309; Wills 314; Witn 217.

Fisher v. Dallas County Democratic Executive Committee, TexCivApp–Dallas, 333 SW2d 604.—Elections 126(1); Mand 172.

Fisher; Davis v., CA5 (Tex), 546 F2d 66.—Civil R 1395(7); Const Law 1105; Hab Corp 338, 482.1.

Fisher; D. C. Edwards & Co. v., TexCivApp–Hous (1 Dist), 610 SW2d 546, ref nre.—Contracts 143(2), 176(2), 229(2), 294, 320, 350(1).

Fisher v. Elkins, TexCivApp–Texarkana, 411 SW2d 799. —Plead 111.42(10); Venue 8.5(3), 22(6).

Fisher v. Evans, TexApp–Waco, 853 SW2d 839, reh den, and writ den.—App & E 557, 907(4), 930(1), 1001(1), 1024.4.

Fisher v. First Nat. Bank, TexCivApp–Beaumont, 112 SW2d 1085.—Mtg 468(1), 468(2); Receivers 1, 6, 14.

Fisher v. First Nat. Bank of Memphis, TexCivApp–Amarillo, 584 SW2d 515.—Estop 52.10(3); Sec Tran 12, 141, 171; Trial 3(2).

Fisher v. First Nat. Bank of Throckmorton, TexCivApp–Eastland, 171 SW2d 223.—Des & Dist 80; Home 96.

Fisher v. First Sec. State Bank of Cranfills Gap, Tex., TexCivApp–Waco, 576 SW2d 886.—App & E 544(1), 569(4), 1177(9).

Fisher; Fort Worth Primitive Baptist Church v., TexCivApp–Fort Worth, 237 SW2d 377, ref nre.—Relig Soc 23(3), 25.

Fisher v. Franke, TexCivApp–Texarkana, 321 SW2d 903. —App & E 989, 1177(7); Autos 244(12), 244(34), 244(35); Trial 356(3).

Fisher v. Frito Co., TexCivApp–Dallas, 81 SW2d 282.— App & E 492, 954(1), 954(4); Inj 135, 161, 163(1).

Fisher; Gatlin v., TexCivApp–Texarkana, 178 SW2d 870. —App & E 688(2), 1053(2); Land & Ten 331(1); Witn 236(1), 387.

Fisher v. Gulf Coast Mach. & Supply Co., TexCivApp–Beaumont, 400 SW2d 941.—Em Dom 2(1.1).

Fisher v. Halliburton, SDTex, 390 FSupp2d 610, reconsideration den 2005 WL 2001351.—U S 78(1), 78(11), 125(3); Work Comp 262, 2085, 2093.

Fisher v. Halliburton, Inc., SDTex, 454 FSupp2d 637.—Const Law 2580.

Fisher; Hardy v., EDTex, 901 FSupp 228.—Insurance 1117(3), 1654; Labor & Emp 407, 426, 428; States 18.15, 18.41, 18.51.

Fisher v. Harris County Republican Executive Committee, TexApp–Houston (1 Dist), 744 SW2d 339.—Mand 154(3), 154(5).

Fisher; Hawthorne v., NDTex, 33 FSupp 891.—Agric 3.3(4); Const Law 2438, 2488; Inj 46, 76, 114(3), 118(3); Offic 1; Tresp 25.

Fisher v. Henderson, NDTex, 105 FRD 515.—Fed Civ Proc 1278, 1366, 1451, 1636.1, 1758.1.

Fisher; Houston Lighting & Power Co. v., TexCivApp–Hous (14 Dist), 559 SW2d 682, ref nre.—App & E 1060.1(1); Em Dom 169, 262(5); Evid 113(19), 314(2); Trial 114, 121(2), 133.6(3.1).

Fisher v. Howard, TexCivApp–Dallas, 389 SW2d 482.—Action 60; Attach 248, 322; Bills & N 103(1), 129(3), 395, 489(6), 534; Evid 413, 416, 423(6), 441(11), 444(6); Fraud 49; Judgm 185.2(4), 185.3(16).

Fisher; Humble Oil & Refining Co. v., Tex, 253 SW2d 656, 152 Tex 29.—App & E 1194(2), 1203(1), 1206; Const Law 321, 2311; Courts 207.5; Judgm 497(1), 660; Jury 31.2(1).

Fisher; Humphrys v., CA5 (Tex), 178 F2d 846.—Contracts 123(1).

Fisher v. Indiana Lumbermens Mut. Ins. Co., CA5 (Tex), 456 F2d 1396.—Fed Civ Proc 831, 836, 2142.1, 2178; Fed Cts 631, 743, 912; Insurance 1807, 2090, 2183, 3049(5), 3085, 3091, 3092, 3579.

Fisher v. Johnson, CA5 (Tex), 174 F3d 710, reh and sug for reh den 189 F3d 471, cert den 121 SCt 1124, 531 US 1164, 148 LEd2d 991.—Hab Corp 603.

Fisher v. Jordan, CCA5 (Tex), 116 F2d 183, cert den 61 SCt 734, 312 US 697, 85 LEd 1132.—Attach 209(1), 209(3); Divorce 168, 252.1, 255; Judgm 17(9), 828.5(4); Proc 70.

Fisher v. Jordan, NDTex, 32 FSupp 608, rev 116 F2d 183, cert den 61 SCt 734, 312 US 697, 85 LEd 1132.—Adv Poss 52; Divorce 254(1); Evid 386(1); Judgm 17(1), 17(9), 101(2), 489, 497(1), 807; Life Est 8; Proc 85, 96(4); Ten in C 15(2); Ven & Pur 337.

Fisher; Kansas City Life Ins. Co. v., TexCivApp–Amarillo, 83 SW2d 1063, writ dism.—App & E 218.2(7); Death 2(1); Evid 159; Insurance 2445; Trial 351.5(4), 352.5(1), 352.10.

Fisher v. Kerlin, TexCivApp–San Antonio, 279 SW2d 637, ref nre.—Compromise 11; Trusts 91, 104.

Fisher v. Kerr County, TexApp–San Antonio, 739 SW2d 434.—App & E 970(4); Tax 2106, 2128, 2473, 2571; Trial 66.

Fisher; King v., TexApp–Fort Worth, 918 SW2d 108, reh overr, and writ den.—App & E 927(7); Evid 571(3); Health 615, 629, 823(1), 825; Neglig 202; Trial 143.

Fisher; Kirkland Corrosion Control, Inc. v., TexApp–Austin, 632 SW2d 231.—App & E 765, 771.

Fisher; Klayman v., TexCivApp–Tyler, 396 SW2d 157.—Venue 8.5(3).

Fisher v. Lake Jackson Inn, TexApp–Houston (14 Dist, 935 SW2d 222. See Fisher v. Westmont Hospitality.

Fisher v. Leach, TexCivApp–San Antonio, 221 SW2d 384, ref nre.—App & E 215(1), 499(1), 692(1), 758.3(6), 867(1), 930(1), 1015(2), 1047(1), 1056.1(5), 1056.1(7), 1062.1; Autos 245(90), 246(58); Damag 132(3); Evid

207(4), 471(3), 474(8), 477(2), 558(1); Neglig 1713, 1741; New Tr 77(1), 140(3); Trial 232(2), 304, 350.6(3), 352.21.

Fisher v. Lee and Chang Partnership, TexApp–Houston (1 Dist), 16 SW3d 198, petition for review den.—Judgm 185(2); Neglig 1020, 1204(5), 1205(1); Statut 181(1), 181(2), 184, 188, 205.

Fisher; McGarry v., TexCivApp–Galveston, 183 SW2d 1010, writ refused.—Child S 58; Des & Dist 26.

Fisher v. Montgomery, TexCivApp–Austin, 274 SW2d 858, ref nre.—Adop 7.8(5), 13; Child C 578, 637.

Fisher; Morse v., TexCivApp–Hous (1 Dist), 493 SW2d 550, dism.—Venue 22(4), 22(7).

Fisher; Nash v., TexCivApp–Beaumont, 325 SW2d 187.—Courts 65, 66.1; New Tr 0.5, 117(3), 121; Trial 18.

Fisher; North River Ins. Co., New York, N. Y. v., TexCivApp–Amarillo, 481 SW2d 443, ref nre.—Insurance 1782, 1791(1), 1791(2), 1791(3).

Fisher v. Pace, USTex, 69 SCt 425, 336 US 155, 93 LEd 569, reh den 69 SCt 653, 336 US 928, 93 LEd 1089.—Atty & C 32(8); Const Law 4494; Contempt 6, 30; Hab Corp 528.1; Jury 24.5; Work Comp 1926.

Fisher; Perkins v., TexCivApp–Amarillo, 395 SW2d 657.—Autos 150, 151, 172(6), 204, 244(14), 244(36.1); Trial 350.6(3), 351.2(5).

Fisher v. P.M. Clinton Intern. Investigations, TexApp–Houston (1 Dist), 81 SW3d 484.—App & E 66, 80(3), 80(6), 82(1); Judgm 217.

Fisher v. Procter & Gamble Mfg. Co., CA5 (Tex), 613 F2d 527, reh den 618 F2d 1389, cert den 101 SCt 929, 449 US 1115, 66 LEd2d 845.—Civil R 1141, 1142, 1511, 1529, 1535, 1536, 1542, 1545, 1548, 1554, 1560, 1564, 1565, 1587, 1589; Fed Civ Proc 164, 176; Fed Cts 823, 891.

Fisher v. Railroad Commission, TexCivApp–Austin, 138 SW2d 829.—Autos 78, 104.

Fisher; Railroad Commission of Texas v., TexCivApp–Waco, 127 SW2d 925.—App & E 71(3); Autos 107(2).

Fisher v. Roper, TexApp–San Antonio, 727 SW2d 78, ref nre.—App & E 758.1, 761, 1177(8); Fraud 7; Judgm 199(3.7).

Fisher v. Shipp, TexCivApp–Texarkana, 411 SW2d 638, ref nre.—Damag 167.

Fisher v. Southland Royalty Co., TexCivApp–Eastland, 270 SW2d 677, ref nre.—Deeds 13; Lim of Act 174(2); Trusts 59(1), 134, 140(3).

Fisher v. State, TexCrimApp, 887 SW2d 49.—Const Law 4770; Controlled Subs 65, 67; Crim Law 770(3), 772(3), 789(3), 1032(5), 1134(2), 1188; Ind & Inf 166.

Fisher v. State, TexCrimApp, 851 SW2d 298, dism of habeas corpus aff 174 F3d 710, reh and sug for reh den 189 F3d 471, cert den 121 SCt 1124, 531 US 1164, 148 LEd2d 991.—Const Law 4694; Crim Law 26, 535(1), 535(2), 1144.13(6), 1159.2(7); Homic 511, 1129, 1184, 1186.

Fisher v. State, TexCrimApp, 538 SW2d 623.—Crim Law 1032(5); Rob 17(1), 17(7).

Fisher v. State, TexCrimApp, 511 SW2d 506.—Const Law 271, 4766; Crim Law 721.5(1), 721.5(2).

Fisher v. State, TexCrimApp, 493 SW2d 841.—Arrest 63.3; Controlled Subs 151; Crim Law 369.1, 369.2(7), 814(3), 1169.5(3).

Fisher v. State, TexCrimApp, 487 SW2d 335.—False Pret 7(5), 49(1).

Fisher v. State, TexCrimApp, 379 SW2d 900.—Crim Law 520(1), 520(2), 520(5), 781(5), 1036.1(5).

Fisher v. State, TexCrimApp, 378 SW2d 680.—Autos 355(6).

Fisher v. State, TexCrimApp, 274 SW2d 397, 160 Tex-Crim 634.—Infants 20.

Fisher v. State, TexCrimApp, 185 SW2d 567, 148 Tex-Crim 133.—Crim Law 338(1), 364(3.1), 413(2), 419(11), 456, 680(1), 683(1), 808.5, 829(5), 1169.2(4), 1169.5(2); Homic 1031, 1484.

Fisher v. State, TexCrimApp, 170 SW2d 773, 146 Tex-Crim 16.—Crim Law 1038.1(1); Homic 1193, 1478, 1479, 1480.

Fisher v. State, TexCrimApp, 138 SW2d 1071, 139 Tex-Crim 41.—Crim Law 1182.

Fisher v. State, TexApp–Fort Worth, 829 SW2d 403, petition for discretionary review refused.—Autos 339, 355(10), 357; Crim Law 808.5, 1172.1(1), 1172.1(3).

Fisher; State v., TexApp–Austin, 212 SW3d 378, reh overr, and petition for discretionary review refused.—Crim Law 303.15, 1024(2); Double J 1, 56.1, 59, 103; Jury 29(3).

Fisher v. State, TexApp–San Antonio, 121 SW3d 38, petition for discretionary review refused, habeas corpus den 2006 WL 2129062.—Crim Law 449.1, 1036.6, 1153(1), 1169.9.

Fisher v. State, TexApp–San Antonio, 830 SW2d 831, petition for discretionary review gr, aff 851 SW2d 298, dism of habeas corpus aff 174 F3d 710, reh and sug for reh den 189 F3d 471, cert den 121 SCt 1124, 531 US 1164, 148 LEd2d 991.—Crim Law 535(2); Homic 1128; Statut 157.

Fisher v. State, TexApp–San Antonio, 827 SW2d 597, on reconsideration 830 SW2d 831, petition for discretionary review gr, aff 851 SW2d 298, dism of habeas corpus aff 174 F3d 710, reh and sug for reh den 189 F3d 471, cert den 121 SCt 1124, 531 US 1164, 148 LEd2d 991.—Crim Law 1038.2, 1038.3, 1159.6; Homic 1128, 1129.

Fisher v. State, TexApp–Dallas, 839 SW2d 463, reh den 1992 WL 224559, petition for discretionary review refused.—Controlled Subs 40, 87; Crim Law 394.1(3), 394.5(4), 552(3), 742(1), 757(1), 1114.1(1), 1134(2), 1144.13(2.1), 1159.2(7), 1159.6, 1224(1); Double J 201.

Fisher v. State, TexApp–Dallas, 803 SW2d 828, petition for discretionary review refused.—Atty & C 33; Crim Law 721.5(2), 1167(1); Ind & Inf 65, 110(3), 110(4); Lim of Act 118(2); Statut 223.1, 223.2(35), 223.4.

Fisher v. State, TexApp–Texarkana, 220 SW3d 599.—Crim Law 702.1, 703, 1144.13(2.1), 1147, 1159.2(1), 1159.2(2), 1159.2(7), 1171.2; Infants 13.

Fisher; State v., TexApp–Texarkana, 198 SW3d 343, petition for discretionary review refused.—Crim Law 577.12(1), 577.15(3), 577.16(4).

Fisher; State v., TexApp–Texarkana, 198 SW3d 332, petition for discretionary review refused.—Crim Law 577.2, 577.4, 577.8(2), 577.10(1), 577.10(7), 577.10(10), 577.12(1), 577.12(2), 577.15(1), 577.15(3), 577.16(4), 1024(2), 1139, 1158(1); Hab Corp 271.

Fisher, Commitment of v. State, TexApp–Corpus Christi, 123 SW3d 828, review gr, rev In re Commitment of Fisher, 164 SW3d 637, cert den Fisher v. Texas, 126 SCt 428, 546 US 938, 163 LEd2d 326.—Const Law 3879, 3893, 3894, 4041, 4342, 4344, 4500, 4504, 4555, 4784; Mental H 37.1, 331, 433(2), 454, 455, 456, 462.

Fisher v. State, TexApp–Corpus Christi, 832 SW2d 641, reh overr.—Bail 59, 74(1), 75.2(3), 77(1); Judgm 185(2), 185(4), 185.3(2).

Fisher v. State, TexApp–Houston (14 Dist), 104 SW3d 923.—Crim Law 274(1), 274(8).

Fisher v. State, TexApp–Houston (14 Dist), 921 SW2d 814, petition for discretionary review refused.—Crim Law 273.1(4), 1167(5).

Fisher v. State, TexApp–Houston (14 Dist), 681 SW2d 202, petition for discretionary review refused.—Crim Law 622.2(1), 622.3, 723(3), 730(3), 730(14), 1044.2(1), 1128(2); Ind & Inf 133(2); Judgm 487; Sent & Pun 329, 372.

Fisher v. State, TexApp–Houston (14 Dist), 642 SW2d 257.—Ind & Inf 110(6); Rape 29; Witn 414(2).

Fisher v. State Farm Mut. Auto. Ins. Co., EDTex, 999 FSupp 866, aff 176 F3d 479.—Damag 50.10; Fed Civ Proc 2535; Labor & Emp 351(2), 351(3), 372.

Fisher v. Temco Aircraft Corp., TexCivApp–Texarkana, 324 SW2d 571.—App & E 1203(4); Land & Ten 37, 55(3), 152(3), 152(4), 160(1), 160(2); Neglig 1672; Trial 3(4).

Fisher v. Texas, CA5 (Tex), 169 F3d 295.—Hab Corp 380.1, 408, 421, 422, 424, 461, 496, 770, 816, 841.

Fisher; Texas Dept. of Public Safety v., TexApp–Dallas, 56 SW3d 159.—Admin Law 786, 791, 793; Arrest 63.4(2), 63.4(3), 63.5(4); Autos 144.2(3), 144.2(10), 144.2(10.5), 349(2.1), 349(6); Crim Law 394.5(4).

Fisher; Texas Employers Ins. Ass'n v., TexApp–Beaumont, 667 SW2d 589.—Work Comp 546, 872, 876, 1396, 1553, 1639, 1668, 1723, 1907, 1939.11(9).

Fisher v. Trees, Inc., TexApp–Texarkana, 713 SW2d 162, ref nre.—App & E 219(1), 901; Fraud 64(1); Insurance 3408; Jury 28(6).

Fisher v. U.S., USTex, 96 SCt 1569, 425 US 391, 48 LEd2d 39.—Crim Law 393(1), 412(1); Witn 201(1), 217, 297(1), 298.

Fisher; U.S. v., CA5 (Tex), 106 F3d 622.—Banks 509.25; Consp 45; Crim Law 338(7), 372(6), 372(14), 622.1(1), 622.2(8), 673(4), 700(2.1), 700(4), 1137(5), 1166(6), 1170.5(1); Double J 151(4); Fraud 69(5); Ind & Inf 125(5.5), 125(43.1); Witn 345(11).

Fisher; U.S. v., CA5 (Tex), 22 F3d 574, reh den, cert den Dunkins v. US, 115 SCt 529, 513 US 1008, 130 LEd2d 433, cert den 115 SCt 529, 513 US 1008, 130 LEd2d 433.—Consp 51; Controlled Subs 6, 151; Crim Law 394.4(5.1), 394.4(6), 870, 881(1), 1168(2); Jury 33(5.15); Searches 117; Sent & Pun 995, 1490; Weap 17(4).

Fisher; U.S. v., CA5 (Tex), 7 F3d 69.—Crim Law 1158(1); Sent & Pun 758.

Fisher; U.S. v., CA5 (Tex), 895 F2d 208, cert den 110 SCt 2192, 495 US 940, 109 LEd2d 520.—Const Law 4733(2); Sent & Pun 2010, 2012, 2025, 2033.

Fisher; U.S. v., CA5 (Tex), 868 F2d 128, reh den, cert den 110 SCt 111, 493 US 834, 107 LEd2d 73.—Sent & Pun 841.

Fisher v. U.S., CA5 (Tex), 382 F2d 31.—Crim Law 423(3), 532(0.5), 671, 741(3), 1189.

Fisher v. U.S., CA5 (Tex), 359 F2d 59, cert den 87 SCt 231, 385 US 920, 17 LEd2d 143.—U S 140, 143.

Fisher; U.S. v., NDTex, 264 FSupp2d 468, appeal dism 202 FedAppx 834.—Crim Law 1668(9); Sent & Pun 2250.

Fisher; Vass v., TexCivApp–Houston, 405 SW2d 866.—App & E 548(3), 609; Contracts 82, 90.

Fisher; Vidor Walgreen Pharmacy v., TexApp–Beaumont, 722 SW2d 744, rev 728 SW2d 353.—Interest 39(2.50), 66.

Fisher v. Walker, TexApp–El Paso, 683 SW2d 885, ref nre.—Contracts 143.5, 162; Mines 78.1(7), 78.2.

Fisher; Way v., TexCivApp–Hous (14 Dist), 425 SW2d 704.—Child S 508(4).

Fisher v. Westinghouse Credit Corp., TexApp–Dallas, 760 SW2d 802.—Evid 47; Judgm 181(15.1); Usury 11, 22, 61.

Fisher v. Westmont Hospitality, TexApp–Houston (14 Dist), 935 SW2d 222.—Lim of Act 55(4); Time 9(2).

Fisher; Wilson v., Tex, 188 SW2d 150, 144 Tex 53.—Evid 417(12), 450(8), 460(3), 461(1); Frds St of 110(1), 113(3); Spec Perf 29(2); Ven & Pur 22.

Fisher; Wilson v., TexCivApp–Austin, 105 SW2d 304, writ refused, cert den 58 SCt 264, 302 US 746, 82 LEd 577.—Armed S 77(19), 78; Cert 65; Ex & Ad 471, 510(8); Infants 77, 81, 84, 105.

Fisher v. Wilson, TexCivApp–Dallas, 185 SW2d 186, aff 188 SW2d 150, 144 Tex 53.—Evid 458, 460(3), 460(7), 460(8), 461(3); Frds St of 125(3); Judgm 217; Spec Perf 3, 8, 16, 28(2), 29(2), 106(1), 121(3), 126(2); Ven & Pur 22.

Fisher; Woods v., TexCivApp–Texarkana, 106 SW2d 774.—Contracts 97(2); Fraud 31; Sales 51, 121.

Fisher; Xenos Yuen v., TexApp–Houston (1 Dist), 227 SW3d 193.—App & E 846(5), 893(1), 977(5); Appear 10; Const Law 3964; Courts 12(2.1), 12(2.5), 12(2.10), 12(2.25), 12(2.30), 15, 37(3), 39; Judgm 144; New Tr 99, 101, 124(1).

Fisher; Yates v., Tex, 988 SW2d 730, reh overr.—Judgm 185.3(21); Pretrial Proc 306.1.

Fisher v. Yates, TexApp–Texarkana, 953 SW2d 370, reh overr, review den with per curiam opinion 988 SW2d 730, reh overr.—App & E 66, 70(8), 76(1), 78(1), 79(1), 934(1); Consp 1.1, 2, 19; Corp 310(1); Evid 113(4); Fraud 1, 3, 12, 17, 18, 20, 31, 41; Judgm 181(17), 183, 185(1), 185(4), 185(5), 185.1(1), 185.1(3), 185.2(5); Lim of Act 95(3), 100(1); Plead 48, 87; Pretrial Proc 308.

Fisher Const. Co. v. Riggs, Tex, 325 SW2d 126, 160 Tex 23, on remand 326 SW2d 915.—App & E 930(1), 989, 1094(1).

Fisher Const. Co. v. Riggs, TexCivApp–Houston, 326 SW2d 915.—Labor & Emp 3003; Neglig 1683.

Fisher Const. Co. v. Riggs, TexCivApp–Houston, 320 SW2d 200, rev 325 SW2d 126, 160 Tex 23, on remand 326 SW2d 915.—App & E 379, 380, 392, 464, 465(2), 930(1), 989; Evid 219.55(1); Indem 31(2), 33(5), 36, 37, 75, 76; Labor & Emp 2890, 3006; Neglig 213, 1037(1), 1040(3), 1205(7), 1205(9), 1635, 1710, 1717; Trial 86.

Fisher Controls; Redd v., WDTex, 814 FSupp 547, aff 35 F3d 561.—Civil R 1122, 1505(3), 1505(7); Fed Civ Proc 2539, 2546.

Fisher Controls; Redd v., WDTex, 147 FRD 128.—Civil R 1484; Fed Civ Proc 2753, 2769, 2774(1), 2774(5), 2783(1), 2810, 2812, 2814.

Fisher Controls Intern., Inc. v. Gibbons, TexApp–Houston (1 Dist), 911 SW2d 135, writ den.—Antitrust 141, 145, 272, 363; App & E 930(3), 989, 1003(6); Contracts 148; Fraud 3, 16, 17, 23, 38.

Fisher Controls Intern., Inc.; Rylander v., TexApp–Austin, 45 SW3d 291, reh overr, and rule 537(f) motion gr.—Const Law 2488; Statut 189, 205, 219(1), 219(3), 219(10); Tax 2233, 2540.

Fisher County Pipe Line Co. v. Snowden & McSweeney Co., TexCivApp–Eastland, 143 SW2d 675.—App & E 917(2); Contracts 245(2); Plead 34(6); Sales 89, 90, 353(1), 359(1).

Fisher Governor Co.; Dover Corp. v., SDTex, 221 FSupp 716.—Fed Cts 110; Pat 288(1), 288(3), 288(4), 288(6), 288(7).

Fisher Ins. Agency, Inc.; Memorial Hosp. System v., TexApp–Houston (14 Dist), 835 SW2d 645, reh den.—Const Law 3964; Courts 12(2.1), 12(2.5), 12(2.10), 12(2.25); Judgm 143(2), 143(3), 146, 162(2).

Fisherman's Harvest, Inc. v. PBS & J, CAFed (Tex), 490 F3d 1371.—Fed Cts 101, 574, 763.1, 776, 1134, 1139, 1158.

Fisherman's Harvest, Inc. v. Weeks Marine, Inc., SDTex, 401 FSupp2d 745, motion den 2005 WL 3479635, rev and remanded 490 F3d 1371.—Fed Cts 1139.

Fisherman's Reef v. Golden West Wholesale Meats, Inc., EDTex, 18 FSupp2d 656. See Farmer Boys' Catfish Kitchens Intern., Inc. v. Golden West Wholesale Meats, Inc.

Fisher's Estate; Rose v., TexCivApp–Galveston, 91 SW2d 476, writ dism.—Courts 472.4(4); Marriage 51.

Fisher's Truck World v. Yates, TexApp–Texarkana, 953 SW2d 370. See Fisher v. Yates.

Fishing Fleet, Inc. v. Trident Ins. Co., Ltd., CA5 (Tex), 598 F2d 925.—Fed Civ Proc 759; Fed Cts 611, 612.1, 800, 897; Insurance 2225, 2226, 2236, 2242, 2253, 3183.

Fishing Publications, Inc. v. Williams, TexApp–Corpus Christi, 661 SW2d 323.—Jury 28(6); Trial 6(1).

Fishing Vessel Mary Ann; U.S. v., CA5 (Tex), 466 F2d 63, cert den Walter v. US, 93 SCt 1365, 410 US 929, 35 LEd2d 590.—Adm 30; Courts 37(3); Insurance 3450; Ship 32.

Fishing Vessel Mary Ann; U.S. v., SDTex, 330 FSupp 1102, aff 466 F2d 63, cert den Walter v. US, 93 SCt 1365, 410 US 929, 35 LEd2d 590.—Fed Civ Proc 1751; Insurance 3449; Ship 32; Subrog 1, 2.

Fishman v. State, TexApp–Corpus Christi, 771 SW2d 573, petition for discretionary review refused, cert den 110 SCt 1924, 495 US 905, 109 LEd2d 287.—Atty & C 130, 152; Crim Law 1077.2(1), 1077.2(3).

Fish Oil Well Servicing Co., Inc.; Augusta Development Co. v., TexApp–Corpus Christi, 761 SW2d 538.—Contracts 35, 234; Impl & C C 30, 102; Labor & Emp 34(2); Mines 109; Plead 427; Princ & A 1, 14(1), 99, 101(1), 101(4), 119(1); Trial 105(1), 392(1), 401; Usury 11, 42.

Fisk; Dial v., TexCivApp–Amarillo, 197 SW2d 598, ref nre.—Courts 8; Insurance 1791(3), 3464.

Fisk v. State, TexCrimApp, 432 SW2d 912.—Crim Law 363, 364(1), 364(3.1).

Fisk v. State, TexApp–Texarkana, 958 SW2d 506, petition for discretionary review refused.—Ind & Inf 144.

Fisk; Stevenson v., CCA5 (Tex), 151 F2d 1010.—Bankr 2295.1; Fed Cts 793.

Fisk v. Stevenson, TexCivApp–Eastland, 179 SW2d 432, writ refused wom.—Corp 271; Judgm 627, 713(2).

Fisk-Allied v. Manhattan Const. Co., Inc., EDTex, 835 FSupp 334.—Inj 86, 138.63.

Fiske; Austin State Hosp. v., Tex, 106 SW3d 703, judgment withdrawn.—Health 768.

Fiske v. City Of Dallas, TexApp–Texarkana, 220 SW3d 547.—Action 6; Admin Law 124; App & E 781(1); Decl Judgm 61, 292; Judges 3, 7, 9; Judgm 185(5).

Fisk Elec. Co. v. Constructors & Associates, Inc., Tex, 888 SW2d 813.—Contracts 176(1); Indem 30(1), 31(6), 104.

Fisk Elec. Co.; Constructors and Associates, Inc. v., TexApp–Houston (14 Dist), 880 SW2d 424, writ gr, rev 888 SW2d 813.—Indem 30(5); Judgm 185.3(8).

Fisk Elec. Co.; Davis v., TexApp–Houston (14 Dist), 187 SW3d 570, review gr.—App & E 199, 200, 206.2, 223, 230, 232(2), 516, 961, 968, 1024.3; Civil R 1744, 1765, 1769; Courts 89; Evid 146; Jury 33(5.15), 131(6); Labor & Emp 868(4); Pretrial Proc 19, 44.1, 309.

Fisk Tire Co.; Aero-Gas Refining Co. v., TexCivApp–El Paso, 137 SW2d 191, writ refused.—Corp 374, 410, 414(6), 487(1); Evid 397(1), 441(9).

Fisk Tire Co.; Firestone Tire & Rubber Co. v., TexComApp, 113 SW2d 175, 131 Tex 158.—Contracts 187(5); Evid 441(9).

Fisk Tire Co. v. Firestone Tire & Rubber Co., TexCivApp–Amarillo, 143 SW2d 828.—App & E 1010.1(3); Contracts 28(3).

Fisk Tire Co.; Firestone Tire & Rubber Co. v., TexCivApp–Amarillo, 87 SW2d 794, rev 113 SW2d 175, 131 Tex 158.—Corp 399(7), 432(12); Evid 443(2).

Fismer v. Ray, TexCivApp–Fort Worth, 206 SW2d 287, ref nre.—Courts 202(5).

Fisons Corp.; Hunter v., CA5 (Tex), 776 F2d 1.—Antitrust 432; Fed Civ Proc 2743.1.

Fisons Corp.; Hunter's Calculators v., CA5 (Tex), 776 F2d 1. See Hunter v. Fisons Corp.

Fister v. Jackson, TexCivApp–San Antonio, 276 SW2d 910.—App & E 1010.1(17); Autos 244(10), 244(36.1), 245(66); Evid 589.

Fit-All Pricing Corp.; Sanders v., TexCivApp–Texarkana, 417 SW2d 886.—Plead 238(2), 262.

Fitch, Ex parte, TexCrimApp, 580 SW2d 372.—Crim Law 29(11).

Fitch, In re, BkrtcyNDTex, 349 BR 133.—Bankr 2060.1, 2157, 2162, 3375, 3395, 3397; Judgm 632, 636, 652, 665, 666, 675(1), 678(1), 681, 713(1), 724, 725(1), 828.21(2); Larc 1.

Fitch v. Estelle, CA5 (Tex), 587 F2d 773, cert den 100 SCt 170, 444 US 881, 62 LEd2d 111.—Const Law 4782;

Crim Law 625.10(1), 625.10(2.1), 1481; Hab Corp 747, 864(3), 864(7); Mental H 432, 434.

Fitch v. Fourteenth Court of Appeals, Tex, 834 SW2d 335.—Elections 158.

Fitch; Gratton v., TexCivApp–El Paso, 352 SW2d 902.—Neglig 1612, 1625, 1696.

Fitch; Hlawiczka v., TexCivApp–Galveston, 197 SW2d 135, ref nre.—Frds St of 116(5).

Fitch v. International Harvester Co., Tex, 354 SW2d 372, 163 Tex 221.—App & E 803.

Fitch v. International Harvester Co., TexCivApp–El Paso, 350 SW2d 395, ref nre 354 SW2d 372, 163 Tex 221.—App & E 638, 773(4), 1073(5); Judgm 273(2).

Fitch v. Jones, Tex, 441 SW2d 187.—Bankr 2062; Costs 194.32; Impl & C C 6.

Fitch; Jones v., TexCivApp–Hous (14 Dist), 435 SW2d 252, writ gr, rev 441 SW2d 187.—Bankr 2062; Courts 21, 30; Pretrial Proc 694.

Fitch; King v., TexCivApp–San Antonio, 181 SW2d 926.—App & E 781(4), 802; Elections 121(1), 126(5); Statut 241(1).

Fitch; Milner v., TexApp–Houston (1 Dist), 651 SW2d 809.—Plead 111.42(11), 111.43; Venue 5.1, 5.3(1).

Fitch v. Missouri-Kansas-Texas Transp. Co., CA5 (Tex), 441 F2d 1.—Fed Civ Proc 2182.1, 2336; R R 303(2), 307.3, 307.4(1).

Fitch v. Morrow, CA5 (Tex), 199 FedAppx 347, cert den 127 SCt 1814, 167 LEd2d 317.—Civil R 1375, 1376(6).

Fitch; Prudential-Bache Securities, Inc. v., CA5 (Tex), 966 F2d 981, reh den.—Alt Disp Res 152, 184, 414; Courts 489(1); Fed Cts 668, 670.

Fitch v. Reliant Pharmaceuticals, LLC, CA5 (Tex), 192 FedAppx 302.—Labor & Emp 786.

Fitch; Sibley v., TexCivApp–Waco, 226 SW2d 885, writ refused.—Trover 9(3.1), 9(4), 70.

Fitch v. State, TexCrimApp, 384 SW2d 719.—Crim Law 1092.12.

Fitch v. State, TexCrimApp, 378 SW2d 313.—Crim Law 996(1), 1097(1), 1110(8).

Fitch v. State, TexCrimApp, 235 SW2d 896.—Crim Law 1023(9).

Fitch v. State, TexApp–Houston (14 Dist), 812 SW2d 403, petition for discretionary review refused.—Double J 1, 148.

Fitch; Suggs v., TexApp–Texarkana, 64 SW3d 658.—App & E 217; Jury 32(4); Trial 325(1), 345.

Fitch v. U.S., CA5 (Tex), 387 F2d 146.—Autos 355(12).

Fitch; Wallace v., TexApp–Hous (1 Dist), 533 SW2d 164.—Child C 567, 637; Evid 110.

Fitch v. Wilkins Properties, TexApp–Fort Worth, 635 SW2d 661.—Damag 194; Forci E & D 16(1), 16(3); Land & Ten 291(2), 291(17).

Fitchett v. Bustamente, TexCivApp–El Paso, 329 SW2d 920, ref nre.—App & E 907(2); Hus & W 47(1), 266.3; Lim of Act 60(5).

Fite, Ex parte, TexApp–Austin, 814 SW2d 253.—Double J 151(4).

Fite; Beggs v., Tex, 106 SW2d 1039, 130 Tex 46.—Ex & Ad 96; Garn 1, 4, 13, 93, 110, 175; Trusts 210.

Fite v. Brevoort, TexCivApp–Fort Worth, 90 SW2d 913, rev First Nat Bank v. Fite, 115 SW2d 1105, 131 Tex 523.—Contracts 163; Ex & Ad 80; Wareh 43, 45.

Fite v. Cherokee Water Co., TexApp–Texarkana, 6 SW3d 337.—App & E 242(4); Labor & Emp 40(2), 758, 782, 783, 786; Mun Corp 188; Obst Just 7; Offic 1.

Fite; First Nat. Bank v., TexComApp, 115 SW2d 1105, 131 Tex 523.—App & E 837(12); Princ & A 143(2), 145(2); Wareh 45, 47.

Fite v. Johnson, TexApp–Dallas, 654 SW2d 51.—App & E 387(2), 387(3), 387(6).

Fite v. King, TexApp–Dallas, 718 SW2d 345, ref nre.—Child 68; Infants 74, 78(1); Statut 63.

Fite v. Nelson, TexApp–Houston (14 Dist), 869 SW2d 603. —App & E 989, 1010.1(1), 1012.1(5); Child S 224; Courts 486; Evid 596(1); Infants 155.

Fite; Payne v., CA5 (Tex), 184 F2d 977.—Fed Cts 724; Inj 114(3); Offic 119; Prohib 6(1); U S 125(3), 125(18).

Fite v. Payne, NDTex, 91 FSupp 896, rev 184 F2d 977.— Postal 23.

Fite v. Payne, NDTex, 91 FSupp 21, rev 184 F2d 977.— Fed Cts 192, 232; Inj 114(3), 148(1); Postal 23.

Fite; Pendley v., TexCivApp–Amarillo, 602 SW2d 560.— Adv Poss 13, 27; App & E 930(3), 989; Evid 588; Trial 139.1(3), 140(1).

Fite v. Port City State Bank, TexCivApp–Hous (1 Dist), 582 SW2d 210.—App & E 781(4).

Fite; Sosa v., CA5 (Tex), 498 F2d 114.—Cons Cred 32, 36, 67.

Fite; Sosa v., CA5 (Tex), 465 F2d 1227, appeal after remand 498 F2d 114.—Cons Cred 33.1, 64.1; Fed Cts 197.

Fite v. State, TexCrimApp, 290 SW2d 897, 163 TexCrim 279.—Crim Law 274(3.1), 365(1), 706(5), 1097(4), 1169.2(7); Rape 51(1).

Fite v. State, TexCrimApp, 259 SW2d 198, 158 TexCrim 611.—Crim Law 339.9(3), 419(12), 436(1), 436(3), 775(2); Rob 24.10.

Fite v. State, TexCrimApp, 140 SW2d 848, 139 TexCrim 392.—Crim Law 814(3), 829(12), 858(3), 1091(2), 1091(5), 1166(7); Rape 4, 40(1), 59(10), 59(14), 59(17), 59(20.1).

Fite v. State, TexApp–Houston (14 Dist), 60 SW3d 314, petition for discretionary review refused.—Crim Law 339.8(5), 409(5), 1144.13(2.1), 1144.13(3), 1144.13(6), 1159.2(2), 1159.2(7), 1159.2(9), 1162, 1177.5(1); Ind & Inf 114; Rob 24.25; Sent & Pun 1254, 1257.

Fittger Realty Co. v. U.S., CA5 (Tex), 272 F2d 761.—Em Dom 155.

Fitting Supply Co., Inc. v. Bell County Solar Control Corp., Tex, 605 SW2d 856.—Usury 108.

Fitting Supply Co., Inc.; Bell County Solar Control Corp. v., TexCivApp–Waco, 593 SW2d 118, rev 605 SW2d 856.—Usury 108.

Fitts v. Calvert, TexCivApp–Fort Worth, 374 SW2d 274, writ dism.—Plead 111.18, 111.38; Venue 22(9).

Fitts v. Carpenter, TexCivApp–Eastland, 124 SW2d 420. —Adop 7.2(1), 7.5, 7.6(3), 12, 16; App & E 901, 930(3), 931(1), 1062.1; Judgm 199(1); Trial 356(1).

Fitts v. City of Beaumont, TexApp–Beaumont, 688 SW2d 182, ref nre.—Mun Corp 723, 741.10.

Fitts; Consolidated Underwriters v., TexCivApp–Beaumont, 106 SW2d 793, writ refused.—Work Comp 1435, 1924.

Fitts v. Crain, CA5 (Tex), 108 FedAppx 865.—Const Law 4198; Decl Judgm 210; Fed Civ Proc 1825; Fed Cts 715.

Fitts; McElroy v., TexApp–El Paso, 876 SW2d 190, reh den, and writ dism by agreement.—App & E 232(0.5), 232(1), 930(3), 931(1), 946, 989, 994(2), 1001(3), 1003(6), 1004(11), 1010.2, 1043(6); Autos 249.2; Damag 43, 91(3), 135, 191, 215(1), 215(3); Interest 39(2.6); Plead 238(3); Pretrial Proc 45, 312.

Fitts; Sawyer v., TexApp–Fort Worth, 630 SW2d 872.— Damag 40(3), 105, 210(1), 221(5.1).

Fitts v. State, TexApp–Houston (1 Dist), 982 SW2d 175, corrected, and petition for discretionary review refused. —Arson 3, 11, 15, 37(1); Crim Law 388.1, 388.2, 476.2, 494, 568, 1134(2), 1181.5(1), 1184(1); Double J 150(1); Homic 1139, 1141, 1174; Ind & Inf 56, 79, 107.1, 110(7), 110(17), 125(19.1), 132(1).

Fitts; State v., TexCivApp–Austin, 405 SW2d 90, ref nre. —Decl Judgm 345.1; Tax 3683, 3696.

Fitts; Stewart v., TexCivApp–El Paso, 604 SW2d 371, ref nre.—App & E 232(0.5); Dedi 15, 31, 37; Neglig 1683.

Fitts v. Stone, Tex, 166 SW2d 897, 140 Tex 206.—Frds St of 74(1), 125(2); Hus & W 80; Joint Ten 4, 13; Mtg 32(5); Spec Perf 39; Trusts 30.5(1).

Fitts; Stone v., TexCivApp–Fort Worth, 160 SW2d 1013, rev 166 SW2d 897, 140 Tex 206.—Afft 18; App & E 1056.1(1); Contracts 108(2); Frds St of 74(1); Trial 178; Trusts 43(1), 72, 371(2).

Fitts v. U.S., CA5 (Tex), 406 F2d 518, cert den 91 SCt 84, 400 US 842, 27 LEd2d 77.—Crim Law 339.10(6.1), 339.10(11), 641.13(6).

Fitts; Young v., TexComApp, 157 SW2d 873, 138 Tex 136. —Tresp to T T 10; Ven & Pur 89, 95(1), 95(2), 101, 189, 299(1).

Fitts; Young v., TexCivApp–Fort Worth, 183 SW2d 186, writ refused wom.—App & E 927(7), 1001(1), 1002; Contracts 143(2), 170(1); Mtg 32(5), 33(5), 37(1), 37(2), 39.

Fitts; Young v., TexCivApp–Fort Worth, 138 SW2d 579, rev 157 SW2d 873, 138 Tex 136.—Estop 98(1); Trial 26; Ven & Pur 296, 299(1), 299(3).

Fitts-Smith Dry Goods Co.; Thomas v., TexCivApp– Amarillo, 151 SW2d 243.—App & E 1050.1(5), 1051(3); Estop 97; Evid 318(4); Trial 350.4(2).

Fitz v. Days Inns Worldwide, Inc., TexApp–San Antonio, 147 SW3d 467, reh overr, and review den.—App & E 173(9), 856(1), 893(1), 934(1); Autos 17; Judgm 185(2), 665, 713(1), 724, 948(1); Labor & Emp 3141; Neglig 1011, 1032, 1205(7), 1706.

Fitz v. Toungate, TexCivApp–Austin, 419 SW2d 708, ref nre.—App & E 859; Damag 71, 94; Fraud 61; Judgm 101(1), 112, 253(1); Spec Perf 114(1).

Fitze; Sakser v., TexApp–Dallas, 708 SW2d 40.—App & E 80(1), 80(6).

Fitzgerald, In re, BkrtcyWDTex, 155 BR 711.—Bankr 2254, 2264(2); Statut 188, 189.

Fitzgerald, In re, Tex, 140 SW3d 380.—Mun Corp 12(8).

Fitzgerald v. Advanced Spine Fixation Systems, Inc., Tex, 996 SW2d 864, answer to certified question conformed to 182 F3d 296.—Indem 72; Statut 176, 181(1), 188, 190, 205, 206, 214.

Fitzgerald v. Agnew, TexCivApp–Texarkana, 402 SW2d 811.—Wills 87, 99, 206, 384.

Fitzgerald v. Andrade, TexCivApp–Austin, 402 SW2d 563, ref nre.—App & E 1170.7; Damag 191; Evid 513(2); Labor & Emp 3096(9); Neglig 1204(1), 1205(1), 1205(7); Trial 350.7(2).

Fitzgerald v. Antoine Nat. Bank, TexApp–Houston (14 Dist), 980 SW2d 228.—App & E 226(2); Costs 194.40; Damag 163(1), 184; Fraud Conv 52(1), 182(1), 219.

Fitzgerald v. Beto, CA5 (Tex), 479 F2d 420, on reh 505 F2d 1334, cert den 95 SCt 2636, 422 US 1011, 45 LEd2d 675.—Const Law 3799, 4813; Hab Corp 721(1).

Fitzgerald v. Bonham, TexCivApp–Galveston, 247 SW2d 265, ref nre.—Judgm 181(15.1); Jury 25(2); Mental H 163.1.

Fitzgerald v. Caterpillar Tractor Co., TexApp–Fort Worth, 683 SW2d 162, ref nre.—Evid 568(1); Judgm 185.3(18); Lim of Act 55(4); Sales 273(2), 284(1), 284(4).

Fitzgerald; Charette v., TexApp–Houston (14 Dist), 213 SW3d 505.—App & E 430(1), 842(2), 852, 893(1), 931(1), 946, 984(1), 989, 1010.1(1), 1012.1(4); Costs 194.25, 194.34, 207; Evid 18; Land & Ten 110(1), 127.

Fitzgerald v. Estelle, CA5 (Tex), 505 F2d 1334, cert den 95 SCt 2636, 422 US 1011, 45 LEd2d 675.—Const Law 3821, 4600, 4813, 4838; Crim Law 641.13(1), 1166.10(1); Hab Corp 319.1, 486(1), 721(2), 768.

Fitz-Gerald v. Hull, Tex, 237 SW2d 256, 150 Tex 39.— App & E 927(7); Joint Adv 4(1); Sec Reg 256.1; Trusts 92.5, 99, 365(5), 372(2).

Fitz-Gerald; Hull v., TexCivApp–Amarillo, 232 SW2d 93, aff 237 SW2d 256, 150 Tex 39.—App & E 927(7), 989, 997(3); Equity 66; Sec Reg 256.1; Trusts 91, 92.5, 108, 111.

Fitzgerald; Kirby v., TexComApp, 89 SW2d 408, 126 Tex 411.—App & E 890, 1070(2), 1108; Bankr 3418; Estop 3(2); Judgm 888.

FITZGERALD;

See Guidelines for Arrangement at the beginning of this Volume

Fitzgerald; LaFreniere v., Tex, 669 SW2d 117.—Condo 12; Costs 194.14; Evid 351, 355(3).

Fitzgerald v. LaFreniere, TexApp–Corpus Christi, 658 SW2d 692, rev 669 SW2d 117.—Condo 12; Evid 370(1), 377; Judgm 199(3.10); Trial 54(1), 352.1(1).

Fitzgerald v. Lane, TexComApp, 155 SW2d 602, 137 Tex 514.—App & E 304; New Tr 119, 153, 155.

Fitzgerald v. Lane, TexCivApp–Eastland, 161 SW2d 523. —App & E 493, 782, 911.3; Guard & W 105(1).

Fitzgerald v. Lane, TexCivApp–Eastland, 126 SW2d 64, rev 155 SW2d 602, 137 Tex 514.—App & E 76(3), 78(6), 219(2), 281(1), 396, 428(2), 516, 596, 597(1), 901, 917(2); New Tr 0.5, 155; Trial 392(1).

Fitzgerald v. Le Grande, TexCivApp–El Paso, 187 SW2d 155.—App & E 717, 854(2); Execution 315; Judgm 504(1), 779(2); Mtg 174, 495, 538; Ven & Pur 228(7), 231(4), 231(16), 242, 244.

Fitzgerald; Navar, Estate of v., TexApp–El Paso, 14 SW3d 378.—Courts 202(5); Ex & Ad 26(2).

Fitzgerald v. Neutze, TexCivApp–El Paso, 348 SW2d 677. —Evid 10(2); Infants 154.1; Plead 111.36; Venue 21.

Fitzgerald v. Rogers, TexApp–Tyler, 818 SW2d 892.— Mand 1, 16(1), 32; Pretrial Proc 24.

Fitzgerald v. Russ Mitchell Constructors, Inc., TexCivApp–Hous (14 Dist), 423 SW2d 189, ref nre.—App & E 989, 1003(5); Autos 168(1), 244(43); Trial 142, 143.

Fitzgerald; St. John v., TexCivApp–Eastland, 281 SW2d 201.—Evid 265(7); Judgm 178, 181(4), 185(2), 185.3(1).

Fitzgerald v. State, TexCrimApp, 782 SW2d 876.—Crim Law 369.2(1), 369.2(3.1), 371(1); Escape 1.

Fitzgerald v. State, TexCrimApp, 271 SW2d 428, 160 TexCrim 414.—Rob 24.10.

Fitzgerald v. State, TexCrimApp, 232 SW2d 854.—Crim Law 1131(1).

Fitzgerald v. State, TexCrimApp, 145 SW2d 190, 140 TexCrim 359.—Crim Law 510, 511.2.

Fitzgerald v. State, TexCrimApp, 143 SW2d 940.—Crim Law 1182.

Fitzgerald v. State, TexApp–Tyler, 722 SW2d 817, petition for discretionary review gr, aff 782 SW2d 876.— Crim Law 369.2(8), 639.3, 1038.2; Sent & Pun 1302, 1348, 1367, 1381(5).

Fitzgerald; Thomas v., TexApp–Waco, 166 SW3d 746.— App & E 68, 70(4), 78(1).

Fitzgerald; U.S. v., CA5 (Tex), 89 F3d 218, cert den 117 SCt 446, 519 US 987, 136 LEd2d 342.—Controlled Subs 65, 74; Crim Law 388.2, 795(1.5), 795(2.1), 795(2.70), 1030(1), 1032(1), 1134(3), 1139, 1158(1); Ind & Inf 3, 21, 56, 59, 60, 71.2(2); Sent & Pun 300, 686, 963.

Fitzgerald; U.S. v., CA5 (Tex), 139 FedAppx 604.—Crim Law 1073, 1578.

Fitzgerald; Upson v., TexComApp, 103 SW2d 147, 129 Tex 211.—Const Law 2490; Frds St of 75, 106(2), 119(2), 130(1), 158(1); Wills 781.

Fitz-Gerald; Wooten v., TexCivApp–El Paso, 440 SW2d 719, ref nre.—App & E 1078(5); Char 1, 4, 11, 21(1), 21(3), 22(3), 23, 31, 34, 37(1), 37(3); Const Law 3258; Trusts 160(2).

Fitzgerald & Hawthorne; U.S. Mach. Shop v., TexCivApp–Fort Worth, 99 SW2d 676.—App & E 719(4); Plead 8(5), 34(4), 111.36; Venue 22(8).

Fitzgerald Marine Sales v. LeUnes, TexApp–Fort Worth, 659 SW2d 917, dism.—Prod Liab 8, 74, 82.1, 83.

Fitzgerald Realty Co. v. Muller, TexApp–Tyler, 846 SW2d 110. See Ben Fitzgerald Realty Co. v. Muller.

Fitz-Gibbon; Juliani v., TexCivApp–San Antonio, 234 SW2d 448.—Brok 42; Evid 397(1), 444(2); Plead 406(5).

Fitzgibbons; Clark v., CA5 (Tex), 105 F3d 1049.—Bankr 2225; Const Law 4014; Fed Cts 41, 47.1, 420, 813; Insurance 1350; Judgm 828.4(2).

Fitzharris; U.S. v., CA5 (Tex), 633 F2d 416, cert den 101 SCt 2325, 451 US 988, 68 LEd2d 847.—Consp 40.1, 47(12); Controlled Subs 145, 146; Crim Law 394.4(1), 745, 1159.2(8); Sent & Pun 115(3).

Fitzhugh v. Associated Indem. Corp., TexApp–Eastland, 746 SW2d 361.—Trial 365.1(6); Work Comp 507, 1727.

Fitzhugh; U.S. v., CA5 (Tex), 984 F2d 143, reh den, cert den 114 SCt 259, 510 US 895, 126 LEd2d 211.—Crim Law 1134(3), 1134(6), 1139, 1158(1); Sent & Pun 797, 841, 995; Statut 190; Weap 4.

Fitzhugh; U.S. v., CA5 (Tex), 954 F2d 253, appeal after remand 984 F2d 143, reh den, cert den 114 SCt 259, 510 US 895, 126 LEd2d 211.—Sent & Pun 1219, 1245, 1424.

Fitzhugh-Straus Medina Ranch; Mann v., TexApp–San Antonio, 640 SW2d 367.—Fraud 12; Plead 111.21; Venue 7(4), 7(7), 8.5(1), 8.5(2).

Fitzjarrald v. Panhandle Pub. Co., Tex, 228 SW2d 499, 149 Tex 87.—App & E 837(1); Libel 1, 5, 10(1), 10(3), 19, 48(2), 48(3), 49, 50.5, 51(5), 101(4), 123(8); Trial 350.3(4), 352.5(3).

Fitzjarrald; Panhandle Pub. Co. v., TexCivApp–Amarillo, 223 SW2d 635, rev 228 SW2d 499, 149 Tex 87.— Courts 99(6); Libel 19, 48(2), 48(3), 51(5), 86(1), 123(8); Plead 104(2), 111.37; Trial 351.2(4).

Fitzjarrald; Panhandle Pub. Co. v., TexCivApp–Amarillo, 215 SW2d 659, mandamus overr.—Libel 10(1), 10(4), 75; Plead 111.24, 111.39(3).

Fitzmaurice, In re, TexApp–Beaumont, 141 SW3d 802.— Mand 62.

Fitzmaurice v. U.S., SDTex, 81 FSupp2d 741.—Int Rev 4960, 5080; U S 125(5), 125(7).

Fitzpatrick, Ex parte, TexCrimApp, 320 SW2d 683, 167 TexCrim 376.—Hab Corp 623, 676.

Fitzpatrick; Akasike v., CA5 (Tex), 26 F3d 510.—Aliens 413; Civil R 1442; Fed Cts 1150.

Fitzpatrick; Allen v., TexCivApp–San Antonio, 487 SW2d 146.—App & E 396, 417(1).

Fitz-Patrick v. Commonwealth Oil Co., CA5 (Tex), 285 F2d 726.—Corp 1.5(3), 378; Fed Civ Proc 635, 1773; Mines 6.

Fitzpatrick v. Copeland, TexApp–Fort Worth, 80 SW3d 297, review den.—Damag 49, 49.10, 50, 51; Neglig 202, 210.

Fitzpatrick; Edmonds v., CA5 (Tex), 1 F3d 315. See Graves v. Hampton.

Fitzpatrick; Ford, Inc. v., CA5 (Tex), 892 F2d 1230. See Hamilton, Matter of.

Fitzpatrick; Howard Thornton Ford, Inc. v., CA5 (Tex), 892 F2d 1230. See Hamilton, Matter of.

Fitzpatrick; Jansen v., TexApp–Houston (14 Dist), 14 SW3d 426.—Action 13; App & E 840(1), 919; Courts 18, 19, 32, 35, 40, 472.1, 472.4(5); Des & Dist 71(1), 90(4); Evid 264, 265(7); Ex & Ad 429; Parties 59(3); Plead 104(1); Pretrial Proc 3; Wills 220.

Fitzpatrick v. Marlowe, TexCivApp–Tyler, 553 SW2d 190, ref nre.—App & E 863, 934(1); Judgm 181(2), 181(7), 185(2), 186; Lim of Act 95(12), 100(1), 100(11), 104(1), 104(2).

Fitzpatrick; Miller v., TexCivApp–Corpus Christi, 418 SW2d 884, ref nre.—Adv Poss 11, 29, 57; Hus & W 21, 25(1), 25(3), 265.

Fitzpatrick v. Procunier, CA5 (Tex), 750 F2d 473.— Const Law 4594(1); Crim Law 594(3), 627.10(1), 627.10(6), 662.5, 700(9); Hab Corp 421, 479; U S Mag 11; Witn 2(1).

Fitzpatrick v. State, TexCrimApp, 458 SW2d 924.—Crim Law 1023(9), 1081(4.1), 1106(1), 1130(4).

Fitzpatrick v. State, TexApp–Fort Worth, 632 SW2d 935, petition for discretionary review refused.—Arrest 63.4(8), 63.4(15), 71.1(3); Const Law 4594(1), 4594(8); Controlled Subs 69; Crim Law 596(1), 627.6(1), 627.6(5), 627.10(6), 700(9), 1077.3; Searches 15.

Fitzpatrick v. Texas Water Com'n, CA5 (Tex), 803 F2d 1375.—Fed Cts 542, 657, 668.

Fitzrandolph; Praylor v., CA5 (Tex), 124 FedAppx 251.— Civil R 1358, 1395(7); Prisons 13(4); Sent & Pun 1548.

Fitzsimmons v. Anthony, TexApp–Corpus Christi, 716 SW2d 719.—Contracts 212(2), 303(1); Spec Perf 133; Ven & Pur 75.

Fitzsimmons v. Brake Check, Inc., TexApp–Houston (14 Dist), 832 SW2d 446.—App & E 836, 842(1), 842(2), 931(1), 989, 994(3), 1008.1(2), 1008.1(3), 1010.1(1), 1010.1(3), 1012.1(2), 1012.1(5); Autos 368; Neglig 540, 1741.

Fitzsimmons v. State, TexCrimApp, 471 SW2d 858.— Crim Law 338(1), 768(4), 980(1), 1032(7).

Five Citizens of Corpus Christi; City of Corpus Christi v., TexApp–Corpus Christi, 103 SW3d 660, reh overr, and review den.—App & E 893(1), 946, 954(1), 954(2); Mun Corp 65, 72, 79.

Five D's Pub. Co., Inc.; Associated Telephone Directory Publishers, Inc.v., TexApp–Austin, 849 SW2d 894.— Antitrust 16, 110(1), 112; App & E 173(2), 931(1), 989, 1008.1(2), 1010.1(1); Compromise 12; Damag 190; Estop 52.10(2); Interest 39(1), 39(2.50), 60; Sec Tran 170, 183; Trademarks 1420, 1427, 1657; Trial 395(1), 401; Trover 46, 61.

Fivel, Ex parte, TexApp–Houston (1 Dist), 704 SW2d 125, petition for discretionary review refused.—Crim Law 99; Hab Corp 470.

Five Oaks Achievement Center; Columbus Independent School Dist. v., Tex, 197 SW3d 384.—Schools 86(0.5), 114.

Five Oaks Achievement Center; Columbus Independent School Dist. v., TexApp–Houston (14 Dist), 162 SW3d 812, review gr, rev 197 SW3d 384.—Admin Law 228.1; App & E 893(1); Courts 155; Mun Corp 254, 723; Schools 86(0.5), 89, 114.

Five Parcels of Land in Harris County, Tex.; U.S. v., CA5 (Tex), 180 F2d 75, cert den 71 SCt 39, 340 US 812, 95 LEd 597.—Em Dom 133.

Five Star Energy Corp. v. Sowell, Ogg & Hinton, TexApp–Houston (14 Dist), 640 SW2d 722, dism.—Acct Action on 13; Judgm 181(1); Perj 12; Plead 301(1), 301(3).

Five Star Transfer & Terminal Warehouse Corp. v. Flusche, TexCivApp–Texarkana, 339 SW2d 384, ref nre.—Corp 1.4(4), 1.6(2); Fraud 30; Judgm 199(3.14); Plead 22.

Five Unknown INS/Border Patrol Agents; Covarrubias v., CA5 (Tex), 192 FedAppx 247.—Fed Civ Proc 1686; Fed Cts 915.

Fix; U.S. v., CA5 (Tex), 264 F3d 532.—Weap 4.

Fix My PC, L.L.C. v. N.F.N. Associates, Inc., NDTex, 48 FSupp2d 640.—Const Law 3964; Fed Cts 76, 76.5, 84; Trademarks 1558.

Fixture Exchange Corp.; Bleakley v., TexCivApp–Waco, 470 SW2d 296, ref nre.—Land & Ten 55(2), 160(2).

F. Jay, a Corp.; Hibbard Office World, Inc. v., TexCivApp–Tyler, 580 SW2d 55.—App & E 79(1), 80(6).

F.J.K., In Interest of, TexCivApp–Fort Worth, 608 SW2d 301.—Child C 633, 637.

FKM, Inc., for Exoneration from or Limitation of Liability, In re Complaint of, CA5 (Tex), 122 FedAppx 783.—Ship 209(1.6).

FKM Partnership, Ltd.; Board of Regents of University of Houston System v., TexApp–Houston (14 Dist), 178 SW3d 1, reh overr, and review gr (2 pets).—Em Dom 13, 56, 58, 122, 166, 167(4), 172, 178.5, 194, 210, 238(1), 246(2), 246(4).

Flabiano; Eckert-Fair Const. Co. v., TexCivApp–Dallas, 342 SW2d 629, ref nre.—Contracts 284(4), 322(4), 346(2); New Tr 72(8); Trial 351.5(1), 351.5(4).

Flach; Bonham v., TexApp–San Antonio, 744 SW2d 690. —App & E 218.2(2), 1004(11); Counties 59; Damag 91(1), 189, 208(8); High 96(2); Labor & Emp 913, 923; Offic 114, 116; Torts 212.

Flache; Nelson v., TexCivApp–Amarillo, 487 SW2d 843, ref nre.—App & E 931(4); Covenants 1, 73, 74, 77.1, 79(3), 122; Trial 392(1).

Flack; First Nat. Bank in Dalhart v., TexCivApp–Amarillo, 222 SW2d 455,rev Flack v. First Nat Bank of Dalhart, 226 SW2d 628, 148 Tex 495.—App & E 989; Chat Mtg 153, 157(2), 157(3); Evid 590; Notice 6, 15; Sales 450.

Flack v. First Nat. Bank of Dalhart, Tex, 226 SW2d 628, 148 Tex 495.—App & E 842(7); Chat Mtg 139, 157(3); Evid 590, 594; Notice 1, 2, 3, 5, 6; Trial 141.

Flack v. Sarnosa Oil Corp., TexCivApp–San Antonio, 293 SW2d 688, ref nre.—Land & Ten 109(4), 194(2).

Flack; Smith v., TexCrimApp, 728 SW2d 784.—Atty & C 132; Counties 139, 204(1), 204(2); Mand 3(2.1), 3(3), 12, 61, 105, 172, 178.

Flack v. State, TexCrimApp, 332 SW2d 704, 169 TexCrim 201.—Crim Law 814(17).

Flagg; Caraway v., TexCivApp–Dallas, 277 SW2d 803, ref nre.—App & E 1047(5), 1050.1(5), 1057(1); Contracts 117(0.5), 117(2), 117(4), 117(8), 117(9), 141(2), 142; Sales 358(1); Trial 141, 350.4(2), 417.

Flaggman; Palmer v., CA5 (Tex), 93 F3d 196.—Labor & Emp 25, 3038(1), 3045; U S 50.5(3), 50.10(6), 50.20, 78(3), 78(14).

Flagg Realtors, Inc. v. Harvel, TexCivApp–Amarillo, 509 SW2d 885, ref nre.—Accord 1, 11(1), 26(3); App & E 747(1), 931(4), 1071.6; Cust & U 1, 19(3); Estop 52.10(2); Evid 265(10), 588; Labor & Emp 256(5), 265, 271, 2204; Trial 382, 395(5), 401.

Flag Oil Corp. of Del.; Ramirez v., TexCivApp–San Antonio, 266 SW2d 270.—Clerks of C 70; Courts 207.4(1.1); Life Est 6; Mand 159.

Flag Oil Corp. of Del.; Ramirez v., TexCivApp–San Antonio, 257 SW2d 131, ref nre.—Evid 460(9); Hus & W 249(2.1); Mines 55(1); Ten in C 44.

Flag-Redfern Oil Co. v. Humble Exploration Co., Inc., Tex, 744 SW2d 6.—Mines 55(2); Mtg 137, 151(5), 274, 295(1); Ven & Pur 257.

Flag-Redfern Oil Co.; State v., Tex, 852 SW2d 480.— Const Law 2317, 2425(3); Mines 5.2(2.1).

Flagship Hotel, Ltd.; City of Galveston v., TexApp–Houston (1 Dist), 73 SW3d 422.—Admin Law 229; Inj 138.6, 138.18; Statut 176, 181(1), 181(2), 188, 205, 208; Waters 203(13).

Flagship Hotel, Ltd. v. City of Galveston, TexApp–Texarkana, 117 SW3d 552, reh overr, and review den.— App & E 984(5), 1078(1); Contracts 143(2), 147(2), 147(3), 156, 170(1), 176(2); Costs 194.12, 194.14, 194.18, 194.32, 194.40, 198, 207, 208; Evid 448; Judgm 181(19); Mun Corp 719(4), 1040; Waters 203(12).

Flagship Intern.; Jones v., CA5 (Tex), 793 F2d 714, 27 Wage & Hour Cas (BNA) 1153, cert den 107 SCt 952, 479 US 1065, 93 LEd2d 1001.—Civil R 1184, 1185, 1243, 1244, 1248, 1535, 1549; Labor & Emp 2461, 2481(5).

Flagship Intern.; Smith v., NDTex, 609 FSupp 58.—Civil R 1505(4), 1513, 1530; Fed Civ Proc 184.10, 1754, 2546; Lim of Act 126, 126.5.

Flaherty; Lipscomb v., Tex, 264 SW2d 691, 153 Tex 151. —Courts 247(1).

Flaiz v. Moore, Tex, 359 SW2d 872.—App & E 170(1), 179(1), 792; Autos 226(3); Courts 8, 9, 28; Neglig 549(1).

Flaiz v. Moore, TexCivApp–San Antonio, 353 SW2d 74, writ gr, rev 359 SW2d 872.—Courts 9, 28.

Flake v. State, TexCrimApp, 258 SW2d 797, 158 TexCrim 582.—Crim Law 531(3); Obscen 17.

Flake Indus. Services, Inc.; NL Well Service/NL Industries, Inc. v., TexApp–Fort Worth, 656 SW2d 584, ref nre.—App & E 724(3), 843(2); Contracts 122; Damag 163(3); Estop 52.10(4); Trial 105(2), 105(4).

Flakes v. State, TexCrimApp, 440 SW2d 652.—Assault 96(1), 96(3).

Flakes v. State, TexApp–Houston (14 Dist), 802 SW2d 844, petition for discretionary review refused.—Crim Law 275, 641.10(2), 641.13(2.1).

Flake Uniform & Linen Service, Inc.; Clayton Mfg. Co. v., TexCivApp–Fort Worth, 451 SW2d 934.—App & E 66, 79(1), 337(1).

Flake Uniform & Linen Service, Inc.; Oetting v., TexCivApp–Fort Worth, 553 SW2d 793.—App & E 846(5), 931(1), 989; Damag 78(6), 79(1), 79(5), 80(1), 80(3), 157(1), 157(3).

Flameout Design & Fabrication, Inc. v. Pennzoil Caspian Corp., TexApp–Houston (1 Dist), 994 SW2d 830.— Antitrust 142, 145, 147; App & E 173(6), 396; Contracts 313(1); Corp 499, 615.5; Extort 34; Fraud 13(3), 32; Frds St of 44(4), 85, 106(1), 115.2, 119(1), 144, 158(1); Judgm 185(2), 185(4), 185.1(3); Torts 436.

Flamm v. Ball, TexCivApp–Amarillo, 476 SW2d 710.— Damag 96, 187; Evid 570; Health 821(2), 821(3), 823(11), 832.

Flamm; King v., Tex, 442 SW2d 679.—Evid 571(3); Health 618, 619, 621, 624, 641; Judgm 185.3(21).

Flamm; King v., TexCivApp–Amarillo, 434 SW2d 197, writ gr, rev 442 SW2d 679.—App & E 863; Health 637, 675, 821(2); Judgm 185(2), 186; Trial 382.

Flammia v. U.S., CA5 (Tex), 739 F2d 202, 78 ALR Fed 677.—Aliens 142, 277; U S 78(12).

Flanagan v. Ahearn, CA5 (Tex), 134 F3d 668. See Asbestos Litigation, In re.

Flanagan v. Ahearn, CA5 (Tex), 90 F3d 963. See Asbestos Litigation, In re.

Flanagan v. Beto, CA5 (Tex), 437 F2d 895.—Hab Corp 500.1, 827.

Flanagan; City of Houston v., TexCivApp–Hous (1 Dist), 446 SW2d 348, ref nre.—Mun Corp 742(5); Plead 59, 290(1); Trial 305.

Flanagan; Fuller v., TexCivApp–Fort Worth, 468 SW2d 171, ref nre.—App & E 699(4), 1004(8); Autos 198(4), 227.5, 244(61), 245(93); Infants 59; Joint Adv 1.2(3); Judgm 199(3.10); Neglig 575.

Flanagan; Giles v., TexCivApp–San Antonio, 123 SW2d 477, writ dism, correct.—App & E 1069.1; Mtg 154(3); Trial 304, 351.5(1).

Flanagan v. Havertys Furniture Cos, Inc., WDTex, 484 FSupp2d 580.—Civil R 1484, 1592; Fed Civ Proc 2737.3; Labor & Emp 2403.

Flanagan; Humble Oil & Refining Co. v., TexCivApp–Austin, 165 SW2d 508, writ refused wom.—App & E 843(2); Mines 92.39, 92.40.

Flanagan; Humphrey v., TexCivApp–Texarkana, 91 SW2d 449.—Mines 50, 74.5, 79.1(1).

Flanagan v. Johnson, CA5 (Tex), 154 F3d 196.—Hab Corp 603; Lim of Act 6(1).

Flanagan v. Martin, TexApp–Waco, 880 SW2d 863, writ dism woj.—Accord 15.1; App & E 78(1), 173(2), 758.1; Judgm 181(6), 185(2), 185(5), 185.1(1), 185.1(3), 185.1(4), 185.1(8), 185.3(2), 186; Nova 1, 4, 12; Proc 48.

Flanagan; Mayer v., TexCivApp, 34 SW 785, 12 TexCivApp 405, writ refused.—Trademarks 1198, 1201(1), 1800.

Flanagan; Rusk County Elec. Co-op., Inc. v., TexCivApp–Tyler, 538 SW2d 498, ref nre.—Contracts 212(2), 214; Costs 194.30; Electricity 11.1(1), 11.1(3); Sales 82(2), 82(3).

Flanagan v. State, TexCrimApp, 675 SW2d 734.—Crim Law 339.10(8), 641.13(1), 641.13(2.1), 641.13(6); Homic 505, 558, 908, 1135, 1177.

Flanagan v. State, TexCrimApp, 620 SW2d 591.—Burg 41(1); Crim Law 552(3), 1032(7), 1131(1); Names 16(1), 16(2); Sent & Pun 378.

Flanagan v. State, TexCrimApp, 465 SW2d 755.—Arrest 63.4(12); Crim Law 531(3), 814(16), 1119(4).

Flanagan v. State, TexCrimApp, 235 SW2d 655.—Assault 92(1); Crim Law 1091(11).

Flanagan v. State, TexCrimApp, 151 SW2d 803, 142 TexCrim 177.—Crim Law 598(6), 956(13), 957(3), 1091(11), 1092.17, 1099.14, 1104(7); Rape 52(1).

Flanagan v. State, TexCrimApp, 100 SW2d 1015, 131 TexCrim 491.—Crim Law 1086.13, 1094(2.1).

Flanagan v. State of Ariz., SDTex, 313 FSupp 664.—Hab Corp 319.1, 362.1, 374.1, 633, 637.

Flanagan; U.S. v., CA5 (Tex), 80 F3d 143.—Controlled Subs 100(8), 100(9), 100(10); Crim Law 1139, 1158(1); Sent & Pun 650, 804, 963.

Flanagan; U.S. v., CA5 (Tex), 592 F2d 252.—Crim Law 1177; Sent & Pun 325.

Flanagan; U.S. v., CA5 (Tex), 445 F2d 263, cert den 92 SCt 741, 404 US 1060, 30 LEd2d 748.—Crim Law 627.9(1), 1030(1), 1036.1(7), 1038.1(3.1), 1132; Rob 24.10, 24.15(2).

Flanagan; U.S. v., CA5 (Tex), 438 F2d 1223, cert den 92 SCt 131, 404 US 839, 30 LEd2d 72.—Crim Law 1132; Ind & Inf 121.2(6).

Flanagan; U.S. v., CA5 (Tex), 423 F2d 745.—Searches 104, 111, 115.1, 117, 119.

Flanagan v. U.S., CA5 (Tex), 308 F2d 841, cert den 83 SCt 1889, 374 US 838, 10 LEd2d 1059.—Crim Law 573, 1036.1(8); Prost 26; Witn 9.

Flanagan v. U.S., CA5 (Tex), 277 F2d 109, cert den 81 SCt 831, 365 US 862, 5 LEd2d 825, reh den 81 SCt 1049, 366 US 906, 6 LEd2d 205.—Crim Law 553, 1044.1(3), 1059(2), 1060, 1186.4(3); Prost 28; Witn 282.5.

Flanagan; U.S. Fidelity & Guaranty Co. v., TexComApp, 136 SW2d 210, 134 Tex 374.—App & E 1082(2); Statut 220; Work Comp 725, 746.

Flanagan; U.S. Fidelity & Guaranty Co. v., TexCivApp–Beaumont, 103 SW2d 446, rev 136 SW2d 210, 134 Tex 374.—Work Comp 746, 1889.

Flanagan Farms; Loewer v., TexApp–San Antonio, 661 SW2d 751.—App & E 219(2), 265(1), 957(1); Judgm 139, 143(3), 145(2), 153(1).

Flanary v. Mills, TexApp–Austin, 150 SW3d 785, reh overr, and review den.—App & E 1071.6; Corp 174, 180, 186, 187; Damag 208(1); Fraud 1, 3, 6, 7, 16, 64(1), 66; Partners 70; Trial 395(5), 401.

Flanary; Reynolds, Shannon, Miller, Blinn, White & Cook v., TexApp–Dallas, 872 SW2d 248.—App & E 71(3), 954(1); Courts 475(1); Inj 135, 138.6, 138.27; Mand 4(1).

Flanary v. State, TexCrimApp, 316 SW2d 897, 166 TexCrim 495.—Autos 355(6); Crim Law 1036.8.

Flanary v. State, TexCrimApp, 117 SW2d 71, 134 TexCrim 606.—Crim Law 394.4(8); Int Liq 249.

Flancher v. State, TexCrimApp, 102 SW2d 221.—Crim Law 1094(2.1).

Flanders; U.S. v., CA5 (Tex), 468 F3d 269.—Crim Law 394.4(6); Obscen 7.6.

Flanery v. Terry Farris Stores, Inc., TexCivApp–Corpus Christi, 438 SW2d 864.—App & E 866(3), 927(7), 989; Neglig 1708, 1714; Plead 228.23; Prod Liab 14, 88; Trial 352.4(1).

Flanigan v. Carswell, Tex, 324 SW2d 835, 159 Tex 598.— App & E 854(6), 979(5), 1004(13), 1083(5), 1151(3), 1177(2); Autos 175(2), 245(51); New Tr 162(1).

Flanigan v. Carswell, TexCivApp–Austin, 329 SW2d 902, ref nre.—Damag 130.1.

Flanigan v. Carswell, TexCivApp–Austin, 315 SW2d 295, rev 324 SW2d 835, 159 Tex 598.—Autos 6, 175(2), 201(1.1); Damag 130.3; Judgm 293; Mun Corp 111(4).

Flanigan v. Texas & P. Ry. Co., TexCivApp–El Paso, 273 SW2d 110, ref nre.—App & E 999(1), 1062.1, 1122(3); Pretrial Proc 81; R R 335(1), 338.5, 352; Trial 350.5(2), 350.7(6), 352.5(7), 352.10.

Flaniken; City of Houston v., TexApp–Houston (14 Dist), 108 SW3d 555, on remand 2004 WL 5142795.—Autos 175(4); Offic 114.

Flaniken v. State, TexCivApp–Austin, 249 SW2d 700.— Int Liq 251; Liens 1.

Flannery, Ex parte, TexCrimApp, 736 SW2d 652.—Sent & Pun 329.

Flannery v. Carroll, CA5 (Tex), 676 F2d 126.—Fed Civ Proc 839.1, 1935.1, 1942, 2584; Fed Cts 813.

Flannery; Chenoworth v., TexCivApp–Amarillo, 202 SW2d 480.—Evid 271(1), 271(16), 271(17), 272, 273(5), 317(18); Interpl 29; Propty 9.

Flannery v. Eblen, TexCivApp–Amarillo, 106 SW2d 837, writ dism.—Judgm 303; Venue 21, 36.

Flannery; Marine Production Co. v., Tex, 175 SW2d 399, 141 Tex 621.—Corp 448(1).

Flannery v. Marine Production Co., TexCivApp–Texarkana, 170 SW2d 834, rev 175 SW2d 399, 141 Tex 621.—Compromise 15(1); Contracts 147(3), 154; Corp 448(1).

Flannery v. State, TexCrimApp, 676 SW2d 369.—Crim Law 683(1), 1170.5(1); Witn 383, 405(1).

Flannery v. State, TexCrimApp, 258 SW2d 805, 158 TexCrim 584.—Autos 355(6).

Flannery v. State, TexCrimApp, 216 SW2d 980, 153 TexCrim 36.—Crim Law 1153(1), 1153(4), 1158(4), 1169.3; Witn 41, 78.

Flannery v. State, TexCrimApp, 117 SW2d 1111, 135 TexCrim 235.—Crim Law 400(2), 728(4), 822(1), 1159.2(7); Infants 65, 152; Rape 7, 43(2), 51(3), 54(3), 59(15); Witn 40(1), 40(2), 45(2), 243.

Flannery v. State, TexApp–Tyler, 673 SW2d 592, aff 676 SW2d 369.—Crim Law 577.10(8), 577.16(9), 665(2), 730(1), 730(11), 796, 1044.2(1), 1171.1(2.1); Witn 37(4), 379(1), 382.

Flannery v. State, TexCivApp–El Paso, 85 SW2d 1052, writ refused.—Const Law 4290; Evid 317(1); Mines 92.3(2), 92.50, 92.83.

Flannigan, Ex parte, TexCivApp–Hous (1 Dist), 489 SW2d 341.—Hab Corp 529, 730.

Flannigan v. State, TexCrimApp, 430 SW2d 511.—Crim Law 1130(1), 1130(2).

Flanz v. Farias, TexApp–Houston (14 Dist), 662 SW2d 685.—App & E 756, 766; Autos 244(12), 244(34), 245(15).

Flasher Co. of Texas; U.S. v., SDTex, 460 FSupp 231.—Guar 44, 62, 77(1), 77(2).

Flashtax, Inc.; Rayna Fastax v., SDTex, 162 FRD 530. See Reyna v. Flashtax, Inc.

Flashtax, Inc.; Reyna v., SDTex, 162 FRD 530.—Fed Civ Proc 392, 834; Lim of Act 121(2).

Fla-Tex Corp.; Primitive Baptist Church at Fellowship v., TexCivApp–Fort Worth, 158 SW2d 549, writ refused wom.—Abate & R 22; Adv Poss 1, 15, 28, 29, 100(2); App & E 1175(1), 1177(6), 1177(8), 1178(8); Home 118(5); Judgm 570(12); Lim of Act 105(1).

Flato; City of Corpus Christi ex rel. Harris v., TexCivApp–San Antonio, 83 SW2d 433, writ dism.—Can of Inst 37(1); Inj 118(1); Mun Corp 79, 918(1), 999, 1000(1), 1000(5); Quiet T 34(1).

Flato; Maddox v., TexCivApp–Corpus Christi, 423 SW2d 371, ref nre.—App & E 934(1); Sec Reg 298; Statut 181(1), 211.

Flato Bros., Inc. v. Builders Loan Co. of Dallas, TexCivApp–Dallas, 457 SW2d 154.—App & E 237(1); Fraud 12; Guar 27, 53(1); Judgm 185.1(3), 185.3(15); Mtg 369(3), 375.

Flato Bros., Inc. v. McKinney, TexCivApp–Corpus Christi, 399 SW2d 957.—App & E 82(3), 719(11).

Flato Bros., Inc.; McKinney v., TexCivApp–Corpus Christi, 397 SW2d 525.—App & E 79(2), 949; Chat Mtg 235; Nova 1, 11; Plead 228.23.

Flato Elec. Supply Co. v. Grant, TexCivApp–Corpus Christi, 620 SW2d 915, ref nre.—App & E 996, 1010.1(6); Usury 32, 53, 117, 145.

Flatonia Independent School Dist. v. Broesche, TexCivApp–Austin, 176 SW2d 223, writ refused.—Schools 90.

Flatonia State Bank v. Southwestern Life Ins. Co., TexComApp, 128 SW2d 790, 133 Tex 243.—App & E 833(5).

Flatonia State Bank v. Southwestern Life Ins. Co., TexComApp, 127 SW2d 188, 133 Tex 243, set aside 128

SW2d 790, 133 Tex 243.—Insurance 1945, 1991, 3374; Liens 22; Lim of Act 130(4).

Flato Realty Investments v. City of Big Spring, NDTex, 388 FSupp 131, aff 519 F2d 1087.—Decl Judgm 276; Fed Cts 27, 172, 343, 355.1.

Flatow; Lomas Bank USA v., TexApp–San Antonio, 880 SW2d 52, reh den, and writ den.—App & E 930(3); Cred R A 1; Libel 44(1), 45(1), 51(1), 51(4), 101(4).

Flatt; Cartwright v., TexCivApp–Waco, 244 SW2d 523.—Chat Mtg 219, 229(3); Trial 350.3(2.1).

Flatt v. Hill, TexCivApp–Dallas, 379 SW2d 926, ref nre.—App & E 1004(5), 1170.6; Damag 132(14); Release 12(1), 31; Trial 127, 133.3.

Flatt v. Johns Manville Sales Corp., EDTex, 488 FSupp 836.—Fed Cts 420; Judgm 632, 634, 707, 715(2); Prod Liab 15, 62, 81.1, 83.

Flatt v. State, TexCrimApp, 294 SW2d 406.—Crim Law 1094(3).

Flatt v. State, TexCrimApp, 169 SW2d 168.—Crim Law 1090.1(1).

Flatte; Collins v., TexCivApp–Texarkana, 614 SW2d 580.—Courts 481; Pretrial Proc 690.

Flatte v. Kossman Buick Co., TexCivApp–Texarkana, 265 SW2d 643, ref nre.—App & E 302(1); Liens 15; Plead 403(2); Sales 202(2), 221, 473(1), 473(2); Trover 32(1).

Flavin v. Flavin, TexCivApp–Hous (1 Dist), 523 SW2d 94.—App & E 768; Ex & Ad 194(5.5); Marriage 13, 50(1).

Flavin; Flavin v., TexCivApp–Hous (1 Dist), 523 SW2d 94.—App & E 768; Ex & Ad 194(5.5); Marriage 13, 50(1).

Flawn; Kelleher v., CA5 (Tex), 761 F2d 1079.—Civil R 1028, 1418; Colleges 8.1(6.1), 9.30(1), 9.30(7); Const Law 1490, 1989, 4158, 4161, 4162, 4223(2); Fed Cts 858; Judgm 641; Labor & Emp 826.

Flax v. McNew, TexApp–Waco, 896 SW2d 839.—App & E 223, 758.1, 934(1); Damag 101, 102; Health 686, 687(2), 687(3), 830; Judgm 181(11).

Flax v. Potts, CA5 (Tex), 915 F2d 155.—Schools 13(4), 13(19), 13(20), 13(21).

Flax v. Potts, CA5 (Tex), 864 F2d 1157.—Fed Cts 829; Schools 159.5(3).

Flax v. Potts, CA5 (Tex), 464 F2d 865, cert den 93 SCt 433, 409 US 1007, 34 LEd2d 299.—Inj 22; Schools 13(6), 13(11), 13(12), 13(19).

Flax; Potts v., CA5 (Tex), 313 F2d 284.—Fed Civ Proc 165, 181.5, 186.15, 187.5, 381; Fed Cts 914, 951.1, 1000; Inj 189; Schools 13(4), 13(7), 13(8), 13(10), 13(12), 13(18.1), 13(20).

Flax v. Potts, NDTex, 725 FSupp 322, aff and remanded 915 F2d 155.—Schools 13(19), 13(20).

Flax v. Potts, NDTex, 680 FSupp 820, aff 864 F2d 1157.—Schools 13(2), 159.5(3).

Flax v. Potts, NDTex, 567 FSupp 859.—Schools 13(6).

Flax v. Potts, NDTex, 333 FSupp 711, vac 450 F2d 1118, appeal after remand 464 F2d 865, cert den 93 SCt 433, 409 US 1007, 34 LEd2d 299.—Schools 13(12), 13(19).

Flax v. Potts, NDTex, 218 FSupp 254.—Schools 13(6), 13(11), 13(14), 13(17), 13(19).

Flax v. Potts, NDTex, 204 FSupp 458, aff 313 F2d 284.—Admin Law 303.1; Const Law 3010, 3278(1), 3278(3), 3278(4); Decl Judgm 305; Fed Civ Proc 162, 2581; Fed Cts 1000, 1002; Schools 10, 13(8), 13(18.1), 13(19); Statut 223.1, 223.2(10).

Fleck v. Baldwin, Tex, 172 SW2d 975, 141 Tex 340.—Evid 60; Gifts 5(3), 11, 30(1); Trusts 14, 34(1), 41, 63.9.

Fleck; Baldwin v., TexCivApp–Galveston, 168 SW2d 904, aff 172 SW2d 975, 141 Tex 340.—Gifts 1, 4, 11, 18(2), 29, 30(2); Trusts 34(1), 41, 44(3).

Fleck; Community Bank & Trust, S.S.B. v., Tex, 107 SW3d 541, reh of petition for review den, and reh den.—Banks 148(4), 226, 227(1).

Fleck; Community Bank & Trust, S.S.B. v., TexApp–Beaumont, 21 SW3d 923, review den with per curiam opinion 107 SW3d 541, reh of petition for review den, and reh den.—Banks 148(4).

Fleck v. State, TexCrimApp, 380 SW2d 621.—Crim Law 338(1), 404.75, 655(5), 1035(3), 1036.1(9), 1168(1); Rob 24.40.

Fleck v. State, TexApp–Houston (14 Dist), 201 SW3d 268.—Crim Law 678(1), 678(2), 1165(1), 1168(2).

Fleckenstein, Matter of Guardianship of, TexCivApp–El Paso, 589 SW2d 788.—Bills & N 442; Mental H 112.

Fleckenstein; Hooten v., TexApp–Tyler, 836 SW2d 300, writ dism woj.—App & E 934(1); Const Law 2315; Lim of Act 4(2).

Fleeger v. Clarkson Co. Ltd., NDTex, 86 FRD 388.—Const Law 3967; Corp 560(7); Courts 9, 512; Fed Civ Proc 187, 1751; Fed Cts 76.5, 305; Judgm 585(2); Receivers 168.

Fleeger; General Ins. Co. of America v., CA5 (Tex), 389 F2d 159.—Fed Civ Proc 2242, 2295; Indem 27, 111; Princ & S 190(7).

Fleener v. Williams, TexApp–Houston (1 Dist), 62 SW3d 284.—App & E 934(1); Judgm 181(2), 185(2); Lim of Act 121(1).

Fleet v. Fleet, Tex, 711 SW2d 1.—App & E 230, 233(1); Trial 356(1), 356(3), 356(5), 356(7).

Fleet; Fleet v., Tex, 711 SW2d 1.—App & E 230, 233(1); Trial 356(1), 356(3), 356(5), 356(7).

Fleet; Free v., TexCivApp–Galveston, 250 SW2d 398.—Lim of Act 197(1).

Fleet v. State, TexCrimApp, 607 SW2d 257.—Crim Law 275, 577.10(9).

Fleet Nat. Bank; CGR, Ltd. v., BkrtcySDTex, 56 BR 305. See CGR, Ltd., In re.

Fleet Nat. Bank f/k/a Summit Bank; Halliburton Energy Services, Inc. v., SDTex, 334 FSupp2d 930.—Banks 149, 174; Bills & N 201, 327; Fed Civ Proc 2487.

Fleetwood; Med Center Bank v., TexApp–Austin, 854 SW2d 278, reh overr, and writ den.—App & E 161, 1195(1); Courts 99(1); Land & Ten 95; Subrog 23(1), 23(2), 31(4); Trial 370(3).

Fleetwood v. Med Center Bank, TexApp–Austin, 786 SW2d 550, writ den, appeal after remand 854 SW2d 278, reh overr, and writ den.—Judgm 181(15.1), 181(17); Subrog 1, 31(4).

Fleetwood Community Home v. Bost, TexApp–Austin, 110 SW3d 635.—Admin Law 669.1, 676, 749, 750, 754.1, 760, 763, 788, 791, 793; Health 489, 508, 512(5).

Fleetwood Const. Co.; North Harris County Junior College Dist. v., TexCivApp–Hous (14 Dist), 604 SW2d 247, ref nre.—App & E 761; Colleges 5; Contracts 186(2), 214, 232(1), 299(2), 322(4), 353(8); Damag 68, 71; Evid 351; Pub Contr 23.

Fleetwood Const. Co., Inc.; Community Development Const. Corp. v., TexApp–Houston (1 Dist), 640 SW2d 331, ref nre.—Compromise 15(1); Contracts 342; Judgm 90, 91; Release 16, 38.

Fleetwood Const. Co., Inc. v. Western Steel Co., TexCivApp–Corpus Christi, 510 SW2d 161.—App & E 931(3), 989; Corp 406(1); Plead 34(1), 45, 111.1, 111.39(4); Princ & A 23(5); Venue 7.5(7).

Fleetwood Enterprises, Inc. v. Gaskamp, CA5 (Tex), 280 F3d 1069, opinion supplemented on denial of reh 303 F3d 570.—Action 17; Alt Disp Res 116, 119, 134(1), 134(6), 137, 139, 141, 143, 200, 213(5); Contracts 187(1); Fed Cts 403.

Fleetwood Enterprises, Inc.; McManus v., CA5 (Tex), 320 F3d 545, reh and reh den 64 FedAppx 419.—Fed Civ Proc 182.5; Fed Cts 817; Sales 262, 434.

Fleetwood Enterprises, Inc.; Richard v., EDTex, 4 FSupp2d 650.—Action 3; Antitrust 290; Consp 15; Fed Cts 15, 191, 192, 241, 243; Prod Liab 42; Rem of C 19(1), 107(7); Sales 427; States 18.1, 18.3, 18.65.

Fleetwood Enterprises, Inc. v. U.S. Dept. of Housing and Urban Development, CA5 (Tex), 818 F2d 1188.—Admin Law 470; Antitrust 331; Statut 219(6.1).

Fleischer v. Levenson, TexCivApp–San Antonio, 418 SW2d 581, ref nre.—Brok 49(1), 53, 86(1), 86(5), 86(6).

Fleischer v. U.S. Dept. of Veterans Affairs, SDTex, 955 FSupp 731.—Fed Cts 1139; U S 78(5.1), 127(2).

Fleishman v. Guadiano, Tex, 651 SW2d 730.—Plead 53(2); Trial 215.

Fleishman; Guadiano v., TexApp–San Antonio, 636 SW2d 785, rev 651 SW2d 730.—Prod Liab 10, 11, 15, 27, 96.1.

Fleishman v. State, TexCivApp–Texarkana, 91 SW2d 493.—Admin Law 12, 390.1; Mines 92.3(2), 92.67, 94; Witn 4, 293.5, 306.

Fleming, Ex parte, TexCivApp–Dallas, 532 SW2d 122.—Divorce 228; Judgm 18(1).

Fleming v. Adams, TexCivApp–Houston, 392 SW2d 491, ref nre.—Covenants 84; Ease 13, 16; Frds St of 60(1); Mtg 137, 138; Ven & Pur 231(17).

Fleming v. A. H. Belo Corp., CCA5 (Tex), 121 F2d 207, cert gr 62 SCt 137, 314 US 601, 86 LEd 484, aff Walling v. A H Belo Corp, 62 SCt 1223, 316 US 624, 86 LEd 1716, reh den 63 SCt 76, 317 US 706, 87 LEd 563.—Const Law 967; Labor & Emp 23, 34(1), 1262, 2217(2), 2301, 2307; Statut 181(1), 205, 216, 219(3), 219(8).

Fleming v. Ahumada, TexApp–Corpus Christi, 193 SW3d 704, reh overr.—Action 13; App & E 842(1), 912, 920(3), 946, 1011.1(4), 1024.3; Compromise 21; Contracts 127(4); Courts 475(1), 480(1); Decl Judgm 1, 8, 45, 65, 68, 142, 143.1, 299.1, 385, 392.1; Inj 26(1), 126, 189; Trial 382; Venue 3, 15, 21, 56.

Fleming v. Ashcroft, Tex, 175 SW2d 401, 142 Tex 41.—Hus & W 273(10); Mines 79.1(4); Ven & Pur 239(1).

Fleming; Ashcroft v., TexCivApp–Texarkana, 168 SW2d 304, aff 175 SW2d 401, 142 Tex 41.—Deeds 93, 97; Hus & W 273(10); Mines 73.5, 79.1(4); Ven & Pur 239(1).

Fleming; Baylor University Medical Center v., Tex, 561 SW2d 797.—Health 825, 826.

Fleming v. Baylor University Medical Center, TexCivApp–Waco, 554 SW2d 263, ref nre 561 SW2d 797.—Health 823(4), 825; Witn 178(4).

Fleming; Box v., TexCivApp–Eastland, 484 SW2d 617.—Child C 602; Divorce 81; Plead 110.

Fleming; Burge v., TexCivApp–Eastland, 261 SW2d 215.—Release 29(1).

Fleming v. Campbell, CA5 (Tex), 205 F2d 549.—Int Rev 3184.

Fleming v. Campbell, TexCivApp–Hous (14 Dist), 537 SW2d 118, ref nre.—Atty & C 151.

Fleming; Carter Publications v., TexComApp, 106 SW2d 672, 129 Tex 667.—Libel 21, 86(1).

Fleming v. C I R, CCA5 (Tex), 121 F2d 7.—Int Rev 3494, 4018.

Fleming; Clayton v., CA5 (Tex), 107 FedAppx 403.—Const Law 4829; Courts 100(1); Prisons 15(3).

Fleming v. Collins, CA5 (Tex), 954 F2d 1109.—Crim Law 412.1(4), 412.2(3).

Fleming v. Collins, CA5 (Tex), 917 F2d 850, reh gr 927 F2d 824, on reh 954 F2d 1109.

Fleming v. C.I.R., CA5 (Tex), 241 F2d 78, rev CIR v. P G Lake, Inc, 78 SCt 691, 356 US 260, 2 LEd2d 743, reh den Commissioner of Internal Revenue v P G Lake, Inc, 78 SCt 991, 356 US 964, 2 LEd2d 1071.—Int Rev 3085, 3184, 3498.

Fleming; C.I.R. v., CCA5 (Tex), 155 F2d 204.—Hus & W 262.1(5); Int Rev 4200, 4655.

Fleming; Commissioner of Internal Revenue v., CCA5 (Tex), 82 F2d 324.—Int Rev 3115, 3178, 3478, 3481, 3500, 3501.

Fleming v. Easton, TexApp–Dallas, 998 SW2d 252.—Child C 404; Child S 173; Ex & Ad 219.7(1), 250.

Fleming v. Entzminger, TexCivApp–Austin, 569 SW2d 54.—Const Law 2487; Schools 97(4); Statut 212.3.

Fleming v. Exline, SDTex, 74 FSupp 232.—War 154.

Fleming v. Fleming, TexCivApp–Dallas, 203 SW2d 989.
—App & E 76(1), 79(1), 80(1); Divorce 253(1); Judgm 194.

Fleming; Fleming v., TexCivApp–Dallas, 203 SW2d 989.
—App & E 76(1), 79(1), 80(1); Divorce 253(1); Judgm 194.

Fleming v. Fleming, TexCivApp–Waco, 595 SW2d 199, dism.—Child S 159; Divorce 59, 252.1, 252.2, 252.3(1), 252.3(3), 252.3(4), 252.3(5), 252.5(1), 286(5), 321 1/2; Partit 96.

Fleming; Fleming v., TexCivApp–Waco, 595 SW2d 199, dism.—Child S 159; Divorce 59, 252.1, 252.2, 252.3(1), 252.3(3), 252.3(4), 252.3(5), 252.5(1), 286(5), 321 1/2; Partit 96.

Fleming; Gabriel v., CA5 (Tex), 106 FedAppx 290.—Prisons 13(5).

Fleming; Garza v., TexCivApp–San Antonio, 323 SW2d 152, ref nre.—Child S 386, 429, 484; Hab Corp 442, 443.1, 445, 528.1, 532(2); Judgm 524.

Fleming v. Ginsberg, CCA5 (Tex), 163 F2d 965.—Fed Cts 730, 933.

Fleming v. Ginsberg, NDTex, 71 FSupp 7, rev 163 F2d 965.—War 152.

Fleming; Hammett v., TexCivApp–Austin, 324 SW2d 70, ref nre.—Autos 181(1), 245(87); Judgm 181(12), 185(2), 185.2(9), 185.3(21), 186; Neglig 1717.

Fleming; Hardy v., TexCivApp–El Paso, 553 SW2d 790, ref nre.—Judgm 185(2), 632, 713(2), 720.

Fleming v. Hernden, TexCivApp–El Paso, 564 SW2d 157, ref nre.—App & E 865; Appear 26; Judgm 17(9), 123(1), 143(2), 145(2), 162(2); Proc 105, 153, 166.

Fleming; Holland v., TexApp–Houston (1 Dist), 728 SW2d 820, ref nre.—Land & Ten 86(1), 92(1); Ven & Pur 18(1).

Fleming v. Honeycutt, TexCivApp–Texarkana, 205 SW2d 137.—Child C 42, 76, 554, 921(1); Hab Corp 731.

Fleming v. Houston Lighting & Power Co., Tex, 143 SW2d 923, 135 Tex 463.—Electricity 8.1(1).

Fleming v. Houston Lighting & Power Co., Tex, 138 SW2d 520, 135 Tex 463, reh den 143 SW2d 923, 135 Tex 463, cert den Houston Lighting & Power Co v. City of West University Place, 61 SCt 836, 313 US 560, 85 LEd 1520.—Electricity 8.1(1); Mun Corp 63.20.

Fleming; Houston Lighting & Power Co. v., TexCivApp–Galveston, 128 SW2d 487, rev 138 SW2d 520, 135 Tex 463, reh den 143 SW2d 923, 135 Tex 463, cert den 61 SCt 836, 313 US 560, 85 LEd 1520.—Const Law 134, 2341, 2715, 2888; Electricity 8.1(1); Mun Corp 111(2), 226, 244(2), 269(2), 269(3), 589, 620, 649, 673, 676, 680(1), 722, 956(1).

Fleming v. Lee and Beaulah Moor Children's Home, TexCivApp–El Paso, 470 SW2d 908.—Courts 207.4(1.1), 207.4(2).

Fleming; Leggett v., CA5 (Tex), 380 F3d 232.—Hab Corp 816, 842, 846; Sent & Pun 1155, 1169.

Fleming v. Lon Morris College, TexCivApp–El Paso, 85 SW2d 276, writ refused.—Princ & A 159(1), 159(2); Ven & Pur 266(2), 274(3).

Fleming; McCoy v., CCA5 (Tex), 160 F2d 4.—War 219, 222.

Fleming; McCoy v., TexCivApp–Fort Worth, 567 SW2d 589.—Child S 537; Contempt 40, 66(2).

Fleming; McDonald v., CA5 (Tex), 107 FedAppx 395.—Crim Law 1576, 1668(3).

Fleming; McKinzie v., CA5 (Tex), 588 F2d 165.—App & E 1004(8); Fed Cts 827, 873.

Fleming; McMahon v., CA5 (Tex), 145 FedAppx 887.—Hab Corp 277.

Fleming; Mendoza v., TexApp–Corpus Christi, 41 SW3d 781.—App & E 854(1), 934(1), 949; Atty & C 26; Judges 25(1), 29; Judgm 181(6), 185(2), 185(6); Venue 42.

Fleming; Miller v., Tex, 233 SW2d 571, 149 Tex 368.—App & E 1083(6), 1175(5); Deeds 207; Evid 53, 587; Mines 55(8); Ven & Pur 259.

Fleming v. Miller, TexCivApp–Eastland, 228 SW2d 355, rev in part 233 SW2d 571, 149 Tex 368.—Lost Inst 23(3); Mines 54.5, 55(4).

Fleming; Montoya v., CA5 (Tex), 121 FedAppx 35.—Hab Corp 282.

Fleming; New York Fire & Marine Underwriters, Inc. v., EDTex, 276 FSupp 479.—Fed Cts 390; Insurance 3066.

Fleming; Ortloff v., CA5 (Tex), 88 FedAppx 715, cert dism 124 SCt 2865, 542 US 901, 159 LEd2d 265.—Hab Corp 480, 690, 751.

Fleming; Pierce v., CA5 (Tex), 150 FedAppx 344, cert den 126 SCt 2018, 164 LEd2d 779.—Sent & Pun 635.

Fleming v. Rhodes, USTex, 67 SCt 1140, 331 US 100, 91 LEd 1368.—Const Law 3907; Courts 508(2.1); Fed Cts 491; War 202, 224.

Fleming; Richardson v., CA5 (Tex), 651 F2d 366.—Civil R 1319, 1369, 1404; Consp 18; Fed Civ Proc 657.5(1), 1788.6, 1788.10.

Fleming; Rublee v., CA5 (Tex), 160 F3d 213.—Const Law 3053, 3823, 3873, 4829; Prisons 15(3).

Fleming v. Sondock, SDTex, 43 FSupp 339, rev Walling v. Sondock, 132 F2d 77, cert den 63 SCt 769, 318 US 772, 87 LEd 1142.—Commerce 62.49; Labor & Emp 2269.

Fleming v. State, TexCrimApp, 502 SW2d 822.—Crim Law 304(16); Sent & Pun 2011, 2018, 2021.

Fleming v. State, TexCrimApp, 423 SW2d 309.—Crim Law 627.2, 739.1(3), 772(6), 1169.5(3); Int Liq 236(3), 239(10).

Fleming v. State, TexCrimApp, 419 SW2d 379.—Crim Law 1105(1), 1130(4), 1132.

Fleming v. State, TexCrimApp, 408 SW2d 510.—Int Liq 236(3).

Fleming v. State, TexCrimApp, 360 SW2d 153, 172 Tex-Crim 520.—Crim Law 706(3), 1137(5); Homic 956, 1134.

Fleming v. State, TexCrimApp, 330 SW2d 457, 168 Tex-Crim 595.—Crim Law 29(3), 29(5.5), 1086.14; Double J 139.1.

Fleming v. State, TexCrimApp, 279 SW2d 340, 161 Tex-Crim 519.—Crim Law 1097(1), 1099.2, 1099.10, 1099.13; Witn 345(2).

Fleming v. State, TexCrimApp, 279 SW2d 103, 161 Tex-Crim 517.—Assault 92(5); Crim Law 260.11(6).

Fleming v. State, TexCrimApp, 92 SW2d 252, 130 Tex-Crim 63.—Autos 356; Crim Law 936(4), 1144.18.

Fleming v. State, TexApp–Austin, 819 SW2d 237, petition for discretionary review refused.—Const Law 4671; Crim Law 367, 438(8), 662.40, 1037.1(2), 1043(3), 1162, 1169.2(6); Witn 414(2).

Fleming v. State, TexApp–Beaumont, 987 SW2d 912, petition for discretionary review gr, review dism as improvidently gr 21 SW3d 275.—Autos 355(14), 411; Crim Law 394.6(5), 1144.13(2.1), 1153(1), 1158(4), 1159.2(7); Searches 13.1.

Fleming v. State, TexApp–Beaumont, 973 SW2d 723, reh overr.—Crim Law 134(1), 730(1), 770(2), 824(1), 940; Homic 1197, 1202.

Fleming v. State, TexApp–Eastland, 958 SW2d 846.—Crim Law 29(5.5).

Fleming v. State, TexApp–Eastland, 956 SW2d 620, petition for discretionary review refused.—Const Law 4705; Crim Law 369.2(4), 1036.1(8); Sent & Pun 8, 310.

Fleming v. State, TexApp–Houston (14 Dist), 774 SW2d 751, petition for discretionary review refused.—Admin Law 419; Autos 424.

Fleming v. State, TexApp–Houston (14 Dist), 704 SW2d 530, ref nre.—App & E 373(1); Forfeit 5.

Fleming v. Taylor, NDTex, 70 FSupp 222.—Abate & R 47; Courts 99(6); Fed Civ Proc 362; Statut 190; War 152, 160.

FLEMING

See Guidelines for Arrangement at the beginning of this Volume

Fleming v. Taylor, TexApp–Corpus Christi, 814 SW2d 89. —App & E 219(2), 907(3).

Fleming v. Texas Coastal Bank of Pasadena, TexApp–Houston (14 Dist), 67 SW3d 459, reh overr, and review den.—Banks 100, 106, 119, 152; Fraud 17, 24.

Fleming; U.S. v., CA5 (Tex), 293 F2d 953.—Int Rev 4376.

Fleming v. U.S., CA5 (Tex), 162 FedAppx 383.—Atty & C 32(8); Fed Cts 576.1, 587.

Fleming; U.S. v., CA5 (Tex), 84 FedAppx 396, cert den 124 SCt 2088, 541 US 1018, 158 LEd2d 635.—Autos 349(5).

Fleming; U.S. v., TexCivApp–El Paso, 565 SW2d 87.—App & E 187(3); Const Law 4482; Exemp 3, 48(2), 49; Garn 99; Judgm 5.

Fleming v. Wich, Tex, 652 SW2d 353.—Const Law 2522(1); Judgm 181(15.1); Wills 114, 123(3), 372, 416.

Fleming v. Wich, TexApp–Houston (14 Dist), 638 SW2d 31, rev 652 SW2d 353.—Wills 114, 123(3).

Fleming; Wise v., CA5 (Tex), 89 FedAppx 877.—Hab Corp 285.1.

Fleming; Wottlin v., CA5 (Tex), 136 F3d 1032, reh den.—Const Law 2816, 3053, 3062, 3821, 3823, 3873, 4830; Hab Corp 256; Prisons 15(3).

Fleming & Sons v. Gulf, C. & S. F. Ry. Co., CA5 (Tex), 187 F2d 536.—Admin Law 759; Carr 79; Courts 89.

Fleming Companies, Inc.; Bonner v., TexApp–Fort Worth, 734 SW2d 764, writ den.—Labor & Emp 757, 1549(19), 1996; States 18.49.

Fleming Companies, Inc. v. Due, TexApp–Beaumont, 715 SW2d 855.—App & E 71(3), 190(2), 219(2), 846(5), 901, 920(1), 946, 1008.1(3); Inj 157.

Fleming Companies, Inc.; Food City, Inc. v., TexCivApp–San Antonio, 590 SW2d 754.—Mtg 151(2); Sec Tran 161, 163, 207, 223, 230, 231, 242.1, 243.

Fleming Companies, Inc.; Hicks v., CA5 (Tex), 961 F2d 537, 124 ALR Fed 777.—Labor & Emp 483(1).

Fleming Companies, Inc.; Hicks v., SDTex, 802 FSupp 39, aff 961 F2d 537, 124 ALR Fed 777.—Labor & Emp 483(1).

Fleming Companies, Inc. v. U.S. Dept. of Agriculture, EDTex, 322 FSupp2d 744, aff 164 FedAppx 528.—Admin Law 390.1, 402, 676, 760, 763, 817.1; Courts 90(2), 96(4); Fact 59, 60; Fed Civ Proc 2533.1, 2545; Statut 188, 190, 206, 217.4, 219(1), 219(4), 219(6.1).

Fleming Co., Inc.; Jackson v., TexCivApp–Hous (14 Dist), 487 SW2d 190.—App & E 1051.1(2), 1060.6; Dep in Court 9; Tender 18; Trial 105(2).

Fleming Co., Inc.; Mendenhall v., CA5 (Tex), 504 F2d 879.—Corp 207.

Fleming Foods of Texas, Inc. v. Rylander, Tex, 6 SW3d 278.—Statut 147, 170, 181(1), 188, 189, 203, 210, 217.4, 223.1, 223.5(1), 223.5(3), 231; Tax 3635, 3700.

Fleming Foods of Texas, Inc. v. Sharp, TexApp–Austin, 951 SW2d 278, reh overr, and review den, and review gr, and reh gr, order withdrawn, rev 6 SW3d 278.—Evid 506; Statut 176, 181(1), 206, 219(3), 220, 245; Tax 3638, 3704.

Fleming Foundation v. Texaco, Inc., TexCivApp–Amarillo, 337 SW2d 846, ref nre.—Contracts 156; Deeds 90, 93, 111, 120; Mines 48, 55(2), 55(5), 55(6), 55(8); Waters 156(4).

Fleming Hospital v. Williams, TexCivApp–Austin, 169 SW2d 241, writ refused wom.—Tax 3275, 3289.

Fleming, Hovenkamp & Grayson, P.C.; Dardas v., TexApp–Houston (14 Dist), 194 SW3d 603, review den.—App & E 707(1); Atty & C 32(2), 151; Contracts 143(2), 147(2), 168, 176(2); Fraud 7; Impl & C C 55; Judgm 183.

Fleming, Hovenkamp & Grayson, P.C.; Spera v., TexApp–Houston (14 Dist), 25 SW3d 863.—App & E 758.3(11), 843(2); Atty & C 105, 129(2), 134(2), 153; Contracts 326; Damag 6; Estop 68(2); Fraud 25; Judgm 181(16), 518, 634, 713(1), 715(3), 725(1), 958(2); Neglig 460; Release 33.

Fleming, Hovenkamp & Grayson, P.C.; Spera v., TexApp–Houston (14 Dist), 4 SW3d 805.—App & E 913, 949; Parties 35.1, 35.9, 35.13, 35.17, 35.33, 35.37, 35.69.

Fleming Mfg. Co., Inc.; Capitol Brick, Inc. v., Tex, 722 SW2d 399, on remand 734 SW2d 405, ref nre.—Antitrust 393; App & E 1114; Corp 668(14); Courts 12(2.1); Judgm 17(3), 112, 118.

Fleming Mfg. Co., Inc. v. Capitol Brick, Inc., TexApp–Austin, 734 SW2d 405, ref nre.—Antitrust 392; App & E 865; Damag 176, 190; Judgm 112, 865.

Fleming Mfg. Co., Inc. v. Capitol Brick, Inc., TexApp–Austin, 703 SW2d 365, writ gr, rev 722 SW2d 399, on remand 734 SW2d 405, ref nre.—Judgm 17(1), 138(3); Proc 80.

Fleming Oil Co. v. Anco Gas Corp., TexCivApp–El Paso, 217 SW2d 29, ref nre.—Contracts 147(1), 169, 170(1); Estop 90(2); Gas 13(1); Licens 32; Lim of Act 24(4); Trial 404(2).

Fleming Oil Co.; Gulf Coast Operators, Inc. v., TexCivApp–Houston, 393 SW2d 954.—App & E 758.1, 931(1), 1008.1(2), 1010.1(3); Costs 32(2), 194.22; Evid 590; Mines 110.

Fleming Oil Co. v. Watts, TexCivApp–Texarkana, 193 SW2d 979, ref nre.—App & E 1051.1(1); Damag 93; Death 10, 57, 103(4); Gas 20(2); Judgm 256(5); Plead 406(5).

Fleming-Roberts Corp., Ltd., In re, BkrtcySDTex, 60 BR 353.—Bankr 2535(3), 2547, 3063.1, 3170.

Fleming's Fraternal Undertaking Co. v. Quarrels, TexCivApp–Beaumont, 116 SW2d 1160.—App & E 1042(1); Autos 246(57); Trial 350.5(5), 350.6(3).

Fleming-Wood; Ryan Mortg. Investors v., TexApp–Fort Worth, 650 SW2d 928, ref nre.—App & E 215(1), 216(7), 218.2(3.1), 221, 1071.5; Costs 194.36; Damag 87(2), 89(2); Evid 586(1); Fraud 60; Trial 105(1), 350.2, 350.4(2), 366; Ven & Pur 130(2), 159, 343(3), 343(4), 351(1), 351(3), 351(8).

Flemister; Dysart v., TexCivApp–Dallas, 140 SW2d 350, writ refused.—Bankr 2553, 3066(1); Corp 228; Fraud 50; Plead 8(15).

Flemister; Texarkana Mack Sales, Inc. v., TexApp–Texarkana, 741 SW2d 558.—Antitrust 369, 389(2), 390; App & E 989, 1051.1(2); Evid 314(1), 320.

Flemming; Butler v., CA5 (Tex), 288 F2d 591.—Social S 140.21, 140.41, 140.50, 143.55, 146.

Flemming; Marek v., SDTex, 192 FSupp 528, vac 295 F2d 691.—Divorce 382; Fed Cts 410; Judgm 828.14(7); Marriage 3; Social S 136.

Flemming; Spears v., SDTex, 187 FSupp 740.—Social S 143.60, 148.15, 148.25.

Flemming v. State, TexApp–Houston (14 Dist), 949 SW2d 876.—Crim Law 412.1(1), 412.2(3), 412.2(5), 519(1), 523, 641.13(2.1), 641.13(6), 641.13(7), 1153(1).

Flemon v. State, TexApp–Houston (14 Dist), 629 SW2d 809.—Crim Law 641.4(1), 641.4(2), 641.4(4), 641.4(5), 641.7(1), 1168(3).

Flemons v. State, TexCrimApp, 451 SW2d 495.—Crim Law 436(5).

Flener v. City of Dallas, TexCivApp–Dallas, 272 SW2d 643, ref nre.—Gaming 58, 61; Judgm 648; Trial 356(7).

Flener; Martin v., TexCivApp–Tyler, 543 SW2d 756, ref nre.—App & E 994(3), 1011.1(1); Divorce 321 1/2; Hus & W 279(1).

Flenniken v. Longview Bank and Trust Co., Tex, 661 SW2d 705.—Antitrust 141, 147, 212, 290, 292.

Flenniken; Longview Bank & Trust Co. v., TexApp–Tyler, 642 SW2d 568, writ gr, rev 661 SW2d 705.—Antitrust 141, 290; App & E 1170.7; Trial 314(1); Witn 276.

Flenoy v. Yarbrough, TexCivApp–Austin, 318 SW2d 15, ref nre.—Labor & Emp 1109, 1112, 1376.

Flenteroy v. State, TexCrimApp, 187 SW3d 406, on remand 2005 WL 2043584.—Rob 20.

Flenteroy v. State, TexApp–Austin, 105 SW3d 702, petition for discretionary review gr, rev 187 SW3d 406, on remand 2005 WL 2043584.—Crim Law 822(1), 1038.1(1), 1042, 1177; Ind & Inf 113; Pardon 49; Sent & Pun 80, 238, 240.

Flesher; Panhandle Const. Co. v., TexCivApp–Amarillo, 87 SW2d 273, writ dism.—Ack 37(1), 55(1), 55(2); Home 58, 70; Mech Liens 281(1).

Flesher Const. Co., Inc. v. Hauerwas, TexCivApp–Dallas, 491 SW2d 202.—App & E 345.1, 758.3(3), 758.3(11), 1024.4; Contracts 322(5), 352(1); Costs 194.18, 194.32; Impl & C C 99.1; New Tr 11(1).

Fleshman on Behalf of Fleshman v. Heckler, CA5 (Tex), 709 F2d 999, cert den 104 SCt 727, 464 US 1049, 79 LEd2d 188.—Social S 8.20, 175.20, 175.30.

Fletcher, Ex parte, TexCrimApp, 442 SW2d 705.—Sent & Pun 1318.

Fletcher, Ex parte, TexCrimApp, 282 SW2d 717.—Hab Corp 224.1.

Fletcher; Adams v., TexCivApp–Austin, 81 SW2d 555, writ refused.—Usury 22.

Fletcher v. Apfel, CA5 (Tex), 210 F3d 510.—Fed Civ Proc 2659; Fed Cts 776, 829; Social S 146.

Fletcher v. Beto, CA5 (Tex), 431 F2d 575.—Hab Corp 827, 898(2).

Fletcher v. Beto, NDTex, 323 FSupp 1317.—Crim Law 273.1(2); Sent & Pun 1314, 1318.

Fletcher v. Beto, NDTex, 302 FSupp 41.—Hab Corp 746, 794.1, 895.

Fletcher; Blair v., Tex, 849 SW2d 344, on remand 874 SW2d 83, reh overr, and writ den.—App & E 1106(1), 1107, 1175(1).

Fletcher v. Blair, TexApp–Austin, 874 SW2d 83, reh overr, and writ den.—App & E 931(1), 1024.3, 1163; Const Law 3987; Pretrial Proc 44.1.

Fletcher v. Blair, TexApp–Austin, 843 SW2d 601, reh overr, and writ gr, rev 849 SW2d 344, on remand 874 SW2d 83, reh overr, and writ den.—App & E 1106(1), 1107, 1167; Judgm 336.

Fletcher v. Califano, NDTex, 471 FSupp 317.—Evid 597; Social S 140.15, 140.35, 140.41, 140.70, 143.40, 143.70, 148.5.

Fletcher; City of Big Spring v., TexCivApp–Eastland, 156 SW2d 316.—App & E 930(3); Evid 568(4), 571(7), 601(4); Mun Corp 819(4), 819(6); Neglig 1537; Trial 352.16.

Fletcher; City of Houston v., TexApp–Eastland, 166 SW3d 479, reh overr, and review den.—App & E 946, 969; Civil R 1147, 1213, 1736, 1744, 1753; Damag 57.21, 57.22, 57.23(1), 57.24, 57.51, 57.58, 208(6); Interest 30(3), 39(2.45), 66; Statut 226; Trial 182, 232(1), 250.

Fletcher; City of Houston v., TexApp–Houston (14 Dist), 63 SW3d 920.—Civil R 1715, 1724; Statut 188, 205, 206.

Fletcher; Cushman and Wakefield, Inc. v., TexApp–Dallas, 915 SW2d 538, writ den.—App & E 931(1), 989, 1012.1(5), 1023; Interest 39(2.20); Labor & Emp 837, 861, 863(1), 867, 880.

Fletcher; Edward D. Jones & Co. v., Tex, 975 SW2d 539.—App & E 215(1); Brok 34, 38(4), 38(5); Exchanges 11(4); Neglig 215; Sec Reg 40.15.

Fletcher v. Edwards, TexApp–Waco, 26 SW3d 66, review den.—Antitrust 297; App & E 171(1), 173(2), 179(1), 232(0.5), 236(1), 241, 500(1), 766, 856(1), 1078(5); Brok 102, 106; Fraud 3, 4, 13(2), 13(3), 25, 61; Judgm 181(18), 183, 185.3(7), 185.3(18), 186; Plead 234; Princ & A 186; Ven & Pur 36(2).

Fletcher v. Exxon Shipping Co., EDTex, 727 FSupp 1086.—Fed Cts 113.

Fletcher v. Fletcher, TexCivApp–San Antonio, 397 SW2d 911.—Divorce 130, 184(6.1), 184(10).

Fletcher; Fletcher v., TexCivApp–San Antonio, 397 SW2d 911.—Divorce 130, 184(6.1), 184(10).

Fletcher v. Fletcher, TexCivApp–Corpus Christi, 404 SW2d 866.—Child C 719, 922(1); Hab Corp 532(1), 863.

Fletcher; Fletcher v., TexCivApp–Corpus Christi, 404 SW2d 866.—Child C 719, 922(1); Hab Corp 532(1), 863.

Fletcher; Guerra v., TexCivApp–San Antonio, 475 SW2d 612.—App & E 110, 387(3), 395; New Tr 4.

Fletcher v. Hightower, CA5 (Tex), 381 F2d 371.—Fed Civ Proc 1832.

Fletcher v. Huffman, TexCivApp–Fort Worth, 149 SW2d 313.—Chat Mtg 250; Mal Pros 40.

Fletcher; Jones & Co. v., Tex, 975 SW2d 539. See Edward D. Jones & Co. v. Fletcher.

Fletcher; McFall v., Tex, 157 SW2d 131, 138 Tex 93.—App & E 1003(11), 1094(5), 1175(5); Autos 247; Neglig 452.

Fletcher v. McFall, TexCivApp–Fort Worth, 138 SW2d 609, rev 157 SW2d 131, 138 Tex 93.—Autos 226(2); Trial 352.4(7).

Fletcher v. Minnesota Min. and Mfg. Co., TexApp–Houston (1 Dist), 57 SW3d 602, review den.—App & E 205, 230, 260(2), 882(14), 1047(1); Trial 168, 178, 268.

Fletcher v. Minton, TexApp–Dallas, 217 SW3d 755.—App & E 931(1), 1071.2; Deeds 88; Quiet T 44(4); Ven & Pur 220, 226(1), 227, 228(1), 228(3), 229(1), 232(1), 232(2), 232(3).

Fletcher; Morgan v., CA5 (Tex), 518 F2d 236, reh den 522 F2d 1280.—Const Law 4172(6); Fed Cts 815; Inj 132, 138.21, 152; U S 36.

Fletcher v. National Bank of Commerce, TexApp–Amarillo, 825 SW2d 176.—Judgm 632.

Fletcher; National Family Care Life Ins. Co. v., TexApp–Beaumont, 57 SW3d 662, review den (2 pets), and reh of petition for review den.—App & E 840(1), 840(4), 932(1), 970(2), 1004(1), 1048(6), 1056.1(3); Damag 189; Insurance 1652(8); Venue 68; Witn 275(6).

Fletcher v. Olivas, TexCivApp–El Paso, 134 SW2d 776.—Fraud 58(1).

Fletcher; Pension Ben. Guar. Corp. v., WDTex, 750 FSupp 233.—Labor & Emp 493, 515.

Fletcher; Prairie Cattle Co. v., TexCivApp–Amarillo, 610 SW2d 849, dism.—Antitrust 135(2), 363, 365, 369; App & E 766, 846(5).

Fletcher v. Ricks Exploration, CA5 (Tex), 905 F2d 890.—Mines 83; Sales 3.1, 10.

Fletcher v. Security Ins. Co. of New Haven, TexCivApp–Dallas, 387 SW2d 743.—Judgm 335(2), 335(3).

Fletcher; Shaw's D.B. & L., Inc. v., TexCivApp–Hous (1 Dist), 580 SW2d 91.—App & E 768, 846(5), 989, 1010.1(16); Evid 587; Trover 4, 9(3.1), 10, 35, 40(2), 40(4), 44, 61.

Fletcher; Smith v., CA5 (Tex), 559 F2d 1014.—Civil R 1549, 1587, 1599; Fed Cts 757, 858.

Fletcher; Smith v., SDTex, 393 FSupp 1366, aff 559 F2d 1014.—Offic 11.7.

Fletcher v. Southern Pacific Transp. Co., EDTex, 648 FSupp 1400.—Fed Cts 141, 1153.

Fletcher v. State, Tex, 439 SW2d 656.—Const Law 967; Statut 64(1), 109.5, 114(1).

Fletcher v. State, TexCrimApp, 214 SW3d 5.—Crim Law 304(16); Sent & Pun 1378, 1381(2).

Fletcher v. State, TexCrimApp, 633 SW2d 895.—Obscen 2.5.

Fletcher v. State, TexCrimApp, 547 SW2d 634.—Sent & Pun 2003.

Fletcher v. State, TexCrimApp, 437 SW2d 849.—Controlled Subs 65, 121; Crim Law 400(2), 404.60, 706(3); Sent & Pun 8, 1490; Witn 363(1).

Fletcher v. State, TexCrimApp, 396 SW2d 393, cert den 87 SCt 871, 386 US 928, 17 LEd2d 800.—Burg 14, 28(1), 41(1); Const Law 4813; Crim Law 577, 641.13(1), 1116; Sent & Pun 1208, 1362, 1381(3).

Fletcher v. State, TexCrimApp, 382 SW2d 931.—Autos 355(6); Crim Law 394.1(1), 478(1), 1092.10, 1099.10.

Fletcher v. State, TexCrimApp, 362 SW2d 845.—Abort 11.

FLETCHER

59 Tex D 2d—62

See Guidelines for Arrangement at the beginning of this Volume

Fletcher v. State, TexCrimApp, 344 SW2d 683, 171 Tex-Crim 74.—Crim Law 218(1), 671; Ind & Inf 171; Searches 145.1.

Fletcher v. State, TexCrimApp, 335 SW2d 613, 169 Tex-Crim 506.—Sent & Pun 1257, 1260, 1389.

Fletcher v. State, TexCrimApp, 324 SW2d 2, 168 Tex-Crim 157.—Crim Law 448(8); Int Liq 236(7).

Fletcher v. State, TexCrimApp, 317 SW2d 57, 166 Tex-Crim 561.—Autos 355(13); Homic 1352.

Fletcher v. State, TexCrimApp, 298 SW2d 581, 164 Tex-Crim 321.—Arrest 63.3; Autos 355(6); Crim Law 814(17), 1044.1(5.1), 1090.14, 1169.2(2).

Fletcher v. State, TexCrimApp, 282 SW2d 230, 162 Tex-Crim 100.—Controlled Subs 65; Crim Law 1038.2, 1038.3, 1097(1), 1099.7(2), 1099.7(3).

Fletcher v. State, TexCrimApp, 255 SW2d 204.—Crim Law 1094(3).

Fletcher v. State, TexCrimApp, 242 SW2d 377, 156 Tex-Crim 335.—Bail 63.1; Crim Law 1087.1(2).

Fletcher v. State, TexCrimApp, 229 SW2d 74, 154 Tex-Crim 518.—Crim Law 1086.13, 1133.

Fletcher v. State, TexCrimApp, 181 SW2d 582.—Crim Law 1094(3).

Fletcher v. State, TexCrimApp, 147 SW2d 233, 141 Tex-Crim 26.—Crim Law 621(2), 719(4), 763(19), 814(13), 829(11), 925(1), 939(3), 1035(3), 1092.12, 1169.3, 1171.3; Rape 27, 57(1), 59(17).

Fletcher v. State, TexCrimApp, 128 SW2d 404, 137 Tex-Crim 191.—Crim Law 1137(2), 1172.7, 1172.9, 1176; Larc 55.

Fletcher v. State, TexCrimApp, 80 SW2d 321.—Crim Law 1182.

Fletcher v. State, TexApp–Houston (1 Dist), 902 SW2d 165, petition for discretionary review refused.—Crim Law 404.65, 404.80, 1036.3, 1043(3).

Fletcher v. State, TexApp–Dallas, 852 SW2d 271, petition for discretionary review refused, denial of habeas corpus aff Ex parte Fletcher, 1997 WL 277991, petition for discretionary review refused.—Crim Law 338(1), 338(7), 351(2), 369.2(1), 867, 1169.5(1); Infants 20.

Fletcher v. State, TexApp–Texarkana, 39 SW3d 274.—Controlled Subs 34, 64, 67, 82; Crim Law 459, 461, 477.1, 478(1), 481, 1043(2), 1043(3), 1144.13(3), 1144.13(6), 1159.2(4), 1159.2(7).

Fletcher v. State, TexApp–Texarkana, 993 SW2d 774.—Crim Law 787(2), 789(4), 1172.2, 1173.2(8).

Fletcher v. State, TexApp–Amarillo, 90 SW3d 419, reh overr.—Arrest 65; Crim Law 394.1(3).

Fletcher v. State, TexApp–Tyler, 960 SW2d 694.—Crim Law 407(1), 419(2), 422(1), 423(1), 427(2), 438(6), 517.1(2), 517.2(2), 517.2(3), 519(1), 519(3), 519(8), 531(1), 655(1), 656(3), 1166.22(1), 1166.22(6); Witn 37(5).

Fletcher v. State, TexApp–Corpus Christi, 848 SW2d 761.—Crim Law 339.9(1), 660, 698(1), 804(9), 822(1), 1172.1(5); Jury 33(5.15); 121.

Fletcher; Texas Emp. Ins. Ass'n v., TexCivApp–Texarkana, 356 SW2d 359, ref nre.—Work Comp 1392, 1417, 1724.

Fletcher; Texas Emp. Ins. Ass'n v., TexCivApp–Texarkana, 339 SW2d 542.—Plead 111.42(10); Venue 8.5(2); Work Comp 820, 1148, 1619.

Fletcher; Texas Emp. Ins. Ass'n v., TexCivApp–Amarillo, 214 SW2d 873, ref nre.—Evid 555.10; Trial 352.1(9); Work Comp 1642, 1724, 1929, 1930, 1935.

Fletcher v. Texas Liquor Control Bd., TexCivApp–Galveston, 280 SW2d 754.—Int Liq 108.10(8).

Fletcher; Traders & General Ins. Co. v., TexCivApp–Fort Worth, 118 SW2d 347, writ dism.—Work Comp 331, 725, 1931.

Fletcher v. Travis County Child Welfare Dept., TexCivApp–Austin, 539 SW2d 184.—App & E 931(6), 1054(1); Infants 173.1, 179, 250.

Fletcher; Triangle Supply Co. v., TexCivApp–Eastland, 408 SW2d 765, ref nre.—Execution 275(1); Mines 74(3), 74(6), 74(10); Notice 5; Ven & Pur 232(11).

Fletcher; U.S. v., CA5 (Tex), 121 F3d 187, cert den Watts v. US, 118 SCt 640, 522 US 1034, 139 LEd2d 618, cert den 118 SCt 725, 522 US 1063, 139 LEd2d 664, cert den 118 SCt 726, 522 US 1063, 139 LEd2d 664, cert den Wilson v US, 118 SCt 738, 522 US 1068, 139 LEd2d 675.—Consp 24(1), 27, 47(11); Crim Law 339.7(1), 339.7(3), 339.7(4), 339.8(1), 339.10(2), 662.10, 719(1), 730(3), 1032(1), 1038.1(2), 1139, 1144.13(2.1), 1144.13(5), 1153(1), 1158(4), 1159.2(7), 1169.1(5), 1171.1(2.1), 1171.3, 1181.5(8); Ind & Inf 159(2); Rob 1, 24.10; Sent & Pun 726(3).

Fletcher; U.S. Fire Ins. Co. v., TexCivApp–Hous (14 Dist), 423 SW2d 89, ref nre.—Insurance 1929(7), 1929(8); Work Comp 1069.

Fletcher; Valley Gin Co. v., TexCivApp–Beaumont, 109 SW2d 567.—Fraud 28, 58(1); Judgm 715(1); Release 27.

Fletcher v. White, TexCivApp–Waco, 469 SW2d 808.—Ven & Pur 341(5).

Fletcher & Co.; Nueces County v., TexCivApp–San Antonio, 181 SW2d 970, writ refused.—App & E 919; Counties 123.

Fletcher L. Yarbrough & Co. v. Texas & N. O. Ry. Co., TexCivApp–Dallas, 226 SW2d 257, writ refused, cert den 71 SCt 52, 340 US 820, 95 LEd 603.—Carr 41, 51, 52(1), 107, 108, 113, 151.1.

Fletcher Properties, Inc.; Taylor v., CA5 (Tex), 592 F2d 244.—Civil R 1419.

Flett; Bunte v., Tex, 243 SW2d 828, 150 Tex 592.—Courts 63.

Flewellen v. Brownfield State Bank & Trust Co. of Brownfield, TexCivApp–Amarillo, 517 SW2d 384.—Inj 111; Plead 4, 111.18, 111.38; Venue 7.5(4), 16.

Flewellen; Faircloth v., TexCivApp–Eastland, 130 SW2d 1098.—Ven & Pur 196.

Flewellen v. Logan, CCA5 (Tex), 106 F2d 151.—Bankr 3770, 3787; Courts 106; Fed Cts 842, 921; Mines 78.1(2).

Flewellen v. Logan, CCA5 (Tex), 105 F2d 268, reh den 106 F2d 151.—Mines 78.2.

Flewellen; Simms Oil Co. v., TexComApp, 156 SW2d 521, 138 Tex 63.—Mines 78.1(2).

Flewellen v. Simms Oil Co., TexCivApp–El Paso, 134 SW2d 687, rev 156 SW2d 521, 138 Tex 63.—Contracts 154; Mines 58, 73, 73.2, 78.1(1), 78.1(4), 78.1(11), 78.7(2); Plead 34(1), 214(2), 214(4), 214(5), 310.

Flewellen v. State, TexCrimApp, 289 SW2d 767.—Crim Law 1090.4.

Flex v. Houston Bank & Trust Co., TexCivApp–Hous (14 Dist), 489 SW2d 126.—Bankr 3422(6); Bills & N 534.

Flexonics; Ruiz v., TexCivApp–Corpus Christi, 517 SW2d 853, ref nre.—App & E 989, 1012.1(10), 1177(7); Damag 221(8); Evid 54, 584(1); Prod Liab 26, 27, 82.1; Trial 350.5(1).

Flick; State v., TexCivApp–El Paso, 180 SW2d 371, writ refused wom.—Bound 1, 3(7), 36(3), 37(3); Pub Lands 175(0.5).

Flight Engineer's Intern. Ass'n, AFL-CIO v. American Airlines, Inc., CA5 (Tex), 303 F2d 5, appeal dism 314 F2d 500.—Fed Civ Proc 2651.1; Fed Cts 767, 902, 903; Inj 132, 139; Labor & Emp 1523, 1526, 2018, 2038, 2107, 2121, 2125.

Flight Safety Intern., Inc.; Buenrostro v., WDTex, 151 FSupp2d 788.—Civil R 1185; Fed Civ Proc 642, 673.

Flightsafety Services Corp. v. Department of Labor, CA5 (Tex), 326 F3d 607.—Records 54, 59, 62, 63, 65, 66.

Flink; City of Austin v., Tex, 454 SW2d 389.—Em Dom 222(1), 262(5).

Flink; City of Austin v., TexCivApp–Austin, 443 SW2d 397, rev 454 SW2d 389.—App & E 774; Em Dom

For Later Case History Information, see KeyCite on WESTLAW

222(4), 224, 262(5); Evid 142(1), 142(3), 314(1), 317(6), 486, 568(4); Jury 131(15.1); Trial 84(1).

Flinn; Smith v., TexApp–Corpus Christi, 968 SW2d 12.— App & E 852; Judgm 185(2), 185.3(4); Lim of Act 21(1), 55(3), 95(1), 95(11), 197(2).

Flinn v. State, TexCrimApp, 288 SW2d 785.—Crim Law 1090.1(1).

Flint; Bryant v., TexApp–Houston (1 Dist), 894 SW2d 397.—App & E 846(5), 852; Contracts 143.5, 147(1), 176(1), 176(2); Hus & W 273(4); Int Rev 3566.1; Wills 740(4).

Flint v. Culbertson, Tex, 319 SW2d 690, 159 Tex 243.— Hus & W 97, 98; Partners 274.

Flint v. Culbertson, TexCivApp–Fort Worth, 309 SW2d 269, rev in part 319 SW2d 690, 159 Tex 243.—Hus & W 98; Joint-St Co 1.

Flint; Great Liberty Life Ins. Co. v., TexCivApp–Fort Worth, 336 SW2d 434.—Judgm 138(1), 162(4); Witn 68, 71.

Flint v. Knox, TexCivApp–Galveston, 173 SW2d 214, writ refused wom.—App & E 846(2), 846(5); Plead 20, 36(3).

Flint v. Mickelsen, TexApp–Houston (1 Dist), 781 SW2d 409.—Neglig 1085, 1088, 1283(3), 1286(1).

Flint; Savell v., TexCivApp–Eastland, 347 SW2d 24, ref nre.—Evid 590; Home 57(1), 57.5, 177(2).

Flint v. State, TexCrimApp, 266 SW2d 382.—Crim Law 1090.1(1).

Flint & Associates v. Intercontinental Pipe & Steel, Inc., TexApp–Dallas, 739 SW2d 622, writ den.—Costs 194.10, 194.18, 194.32, 194.36, 204, 208.

Flintco Inc.; U.S. for use of Wallace v., CA5 (Tex), 143 F3d 955, reh den.—Contracts 258, 261(1), 299(2), 318; Costs 194.18; Damag 184; Fed Civ Proc 2602, 2741; Fed Cts 611, 612.1, 626, 633, 634, 641, 642, 795; Impl & C C 65; U S 67(4), 67(9).

Flintco Inc.; U.S. for Use of Wallace Const. Co. v., CA5 (Tex), 143 F3d955. See U.S. for use of Wallace v. Flintco Inc.

Flintco Inc. v. Victore Ins. Co., CA5 (Tex), 143 F3d 955. See U.S. for use of Wallace v. Flintco Inc.

Flint Engineering and Const. Co., Inc.; Gentry v., CA5 (Tex), 76 F3d 95.—Fed Cts 776; Statut 188; Work Comp 2161, 2189, 2190.

Flintex Oil Co. v. Guillory, TexCivApp–Eastland, 337 SW2d 757.—Plead 111.36, 111.42(8).

Flintkote Co.; Douglass v., TexCivApp–Dallas, 207 SW2d 635.—App & E 179(1), 1024.3; Corp 503(1); Plead 111.3, 111.8, 111.9, 111.42(3).

Flintkote Co.; Longhorn Roofing Products v., CCA5 (Tex), 141 F2d 466.—Sales 77(1).

Flintkote Co.; MacMillan Bloedel Ltd. v., CA5 (Tex), 760 F2d 580.—Antitrust 968; Contracts 129(1); Contrib 6; Corp 445.1; Evid 43(3); Fed Civ Proc 2547.1, 2559; Fed Cts 755; Impl & C C 6; Subrog 2; Torts 135.

Flintkote Co.; Ortiz v., TexApp–Corpus Christi, 761 SW2d 531, writ den.—App & E 863, 934(1); Damag 89(2), 111; Fraud 58(1); Judgm 199(3.3); Pretrial Proc 201.1; Sales 441(1), 441(4), 442(1), 442(6), 446(9).

Flintkote Supply Co. v. Thompson, TexCivApp–Beaumont, 607 SW2d 41.—Antitrust 393; App & E 219(2); Evid 208(1), 594; Plead 36(2); Sales 442(6).

Flippen v. Flippen, TexApp–Eastland, 628 SW2d 462.— Lim of Act 197(2); Mines 55(4); Ref of Inst 19(2), 45(7).

Flippen; Flippen v., TexApp–Eastland, 628 SW2d 462.— Lim of Act 197(2); Mines 55(4); Ref of Inst 19(2), 45(7).

Flippen; James v., TexCivApp–Beaumont, 122 SW2d 1090.—Evid 589; Trial 131(3).

Flippen; Pierce v., TexCivApp–Amarillo, 197 SW2d 366, ref nre.—Evid 460(3); Frds St of 110(4).

Flippen-Prather Realty Co.; Thomason v., TexCivApp–Dallas, 93 SW2d 799.—Chat Mtg 213.

Flippin v. City of Beaumont, TexCivApp–Beaumont, 525 SW2d 285.—Courts 91(1); Mun Corp 734.

Flippin v. State, TexCrimApp, 145 SW2d 1098, 140 Tex-Crim 615.—Crim Law 401, 448(8), 452(4), 706(6), 1170.5(3); Witn 388(1).

Flippin v. State, TexCrimApp, 115 SW2d 665, 134 Tex-Crim 352.—Crim Law 401, 452(4), 1144.3; Larc 40(6).

Flippin v. State, TexCrimApp, 99 SW2d 307, 131 Tex-Crim 356.—Crim Law 595(2).

Flippin v. Wilson State Bank, TexApp–Amarillo, 780 SW2d 457, writ den.—App & E 170(1); Judgm 829(3).

Flitcraft; U.S. v., CA5 (Tex), 863 F2d 342, reh den, cert den 109 SCt 2100, 490 US 1080, 104 LEd2d 661.—Crim Law 393(1), 517.2(3), 1172.1(2); Int Rev 5317.

Flitcraft; U.S. v., CA5 (Tex), 803 F2d 184, appeal after remand 863 F2d 342, reh den, cert den 109 SCt 2100, 490 US 1080, 104 LEd2d 661.—Crim Law 675, 1030(1), 1038.1(4), 1153(1); Int Rev 5250.

Flix v. State, TexApp–Houston (14 Dist), 782 SW2d 1, petition for discretionary review refused.—Crim Law 369.2(4), 412(6), 734, 775(2), 925.5(2), 925.5(3); Homic 1387; Searches 198; Witn 46.

F. L. J. v. State, TexCivApp–Waco, 577 SW2d 532.— Infants 223.1.

Floating Decks of America, Inc.; Hill v., TexCivApp–San Antonio, 590 SW2d 723.—Acct Action on 11, 13; Afft 3, 12.

Floboots Corp. v. Teas, TexCivApp–San Antonio, 110 SW2d 180, dism.—Costs 260(4), 262; Estop 63; Evid 571(1); Mines 109; Nova 12.

Floca, In re, BkrtcyWDTex, 126 BR 274.—Sec Tran 230, 240.

Floca v. Homcare Health Services, Inc., CA5 (Tex), 845 F2d 108.—Civil R 1535, 1536, 1571, 1573.

Flock; Guthrie v., TexCivApp–Amarillo, 360 SW2d 804.— Atty & C 141.

Flock v. Kelso, TexCivApp–Amarillo, 366 SW2d 698.— App & E 758.1, 758.3(1), 758.3(10); Mal Pros 64(2); Sequest 21; Trover 40(4).

Flock v. Scripto-Tokai Corp., CA5 (Tex), 319 F3d 231.— Evid 595; Fed Civ Proc 2515; Fed Cts 776; Prod Liab 11, 15, 62, 82.1, 87.1.

Flock v. Scripto-Tokai Corp., SDTex, 183 FSupp2d 917, aff in part, vac in part 319 F3d 231.—Antitrust 235; Prod Liab 8, 11, 15, 62, 83.

Floerchinger v. Intellicall, Inc., NDTex, 802 FSupp 1480.—Fed Cts 246; Labor & Emp 407, 425, 510; Rem of C 25(1); States 18.51; Statut 219(8).

Floeter; Kaplan v., TexApp–Houston (1 Dist), 657 SW2d 1.—Evid 571(7); Land & Ten 88(2), 144.

Flood v. Shell Services Intern., Inc., SDTex, 287 FSupp2d 732.—Civil R 1246; Judgm 828.7, 828.15(1); Labor & Emp 368, 371, 795, 797.

Flood; State v., TexApp–Houston (1 Dist), 814 SW2d 548. —Const Law 2564; Double J 60.1; Sent & Pun 2236.

Flood; U.S. v., CA5 (Tex), 586 F2d 391, reh den 590 F2d 333.—Assault 75; Crim Law 589(5).

Floors, Inc. of Tex.; Glasgow v., TexCivApp–Dallas, 356 SW2d 699.—Autos 197(7); Judgm 185(2); Labor & Emp 3031(1), 3045.

Floors Unlimited, Inc. v. Fieldcrest Cannon, Inc., CA5 (Tex), 55 F3d 181.—Fed Civ Proc 2544; Fed Cts 776; Fraud 7; Frds St of 49, 84.

Flora v. Mills, TexCivApp–Waco, 417 SW2d 648, ref nre. —Partners 53.

Flora v. Scott, TexCivApp–Dallas, 398 SW2d 627, ref nre. —App & E 671(3), 704.1, 708, 1041(3), 1046.5, 1047(4), 1050.1(11), 1060.1(2.1), 1060.1(6), 1069.1; Evid 380; Exceptions Bill 45(4), 56(1); Pretrial Proc 69.1, 73, 76.1, 309; Trial 29(1), 59(1), 106, 305.

Florek v. Shaw, TexCivApp–Dallas, 357 SW2d 769.—App & E 82(4).

Florence v. Asherton Independent School Dist., TexCiv-App–San Antonio, 509 SW2d 676, ref nre.—Schools 103(1), 106.23(2); Tax 2680.

Florence v. Crawford, TexCivApp–Texarkana, 351 SW2d 77.—Hab Corp 537.1, 702; Mental H 37.1, 40, 42, 59.1.

Florence v. Crummer, CCA5 (Tex), 93 F2d 542, cert den 58 SCt 944, 304 US 563, 82 LEd 1530, reh den 58 SCt 1037, 304 US 589, 82 LEd 1549.—Fraud 59(3), 64(3).

Florence v. Florence, TexCivApp–Tyler, 388 SW2d 220, writ dism.—App & E 847(3), 954(1); Divorce 87, 179; Inj 135, 147, 151, 157.

Florence; Florence v., TexCivApp–Tyler, 388 SW2d 220, writ dism.—App & E 847(3), 954(1); Divorce 87, 179; Inj 135, 147, 151, 157.

Florence v. Frank, NDTex, 774 FSupp 1054.—Civil R 1018, 1137, 1218(4), 1225(2), 1536, 1544, 1545, 1548, 1549; Labor & Emp 1208, 1213, 1219(9), 1597.

Florence v. Frontier Airlines, Inc., CA5 (Tex), 149 FedAppx 237.—Fed Civ Proc 2539; Jury 31.2(4); Labor & Emp 819; Libel 23.1.

Florence v. J. Ray McDermott, Inc., SDTex, 999 FSupp 927.—Rem of C 79(1).

Florence v. Runyon, NDTex, 990 FSupp 485.—Civil R 1217, 1218(4), 1220, 1221, 1240, 1243, 1245, 1531, 1540; Fed Civ Proc 2497.1.

Florence; Sharber v., Tex, 115 SW2d 604, 131 Tex 341.—Const Law 48(1), 2357, 2745; Mtg 330, 381, 538; Statut 63, 64(1), 64(7).

Florence; Sharber v., TexCivApp–Texarkana, 108 SW2d 942, rev 115 SW2d 604, 131 Tex 341.—Jud S 2, 37; Mtg 381, 510(2), 529(5), 554; Statut 64(1); Trial 45(1).

Florence v. State, TexCrimApp, 273 SW2d 631, 160 TexCrim 591.—Autos 352; Crim Law 1184(1); Ind & Inf 79.

Florence v. Swails, TexCivApp–El Paso, 85 SW2d 257.—Attach 338; Judgm 17(9), 273(1).

Florentine Marble & Tile Corp.; Aetna Cas. & Sur. Co. v., TexCivApp–El Paso, 549 SW2d 24.—App & E 1015(2); Insurance 2174, 2200, 2201, 3191(7); New Tr 52, 144, 157; Trial 304, 306.

Florentino, Ex parte, TexCrimApp, 206 SW3d 124.—Crim Law 641.13(7), 1069(6).

Flores, Ex parte, TexCrimApp, 548 SW2d 31.—Extrad 32, 36.

Flores, Ex parte, TexCrimApp, 537 SW2d 458.—Crim Law 304(16), 1036.1(3.1), 1169.1(1), 1177, 1189; Sent & Pun 100, 2014.

Flores, Ex parte, TexCrimApp, 452 SW2d 443.—Searches 126.

Flores, Ex parte, TexApp–El Paso, 130 SW3d 100, petition stricken, and petition for discretionary review refused.—Action 6; App & E 170(2), 781(4); Breach of P 16, 21; Const Law 656, 657, 977, 990, 1030, 3912, 4488.

Flores, In re, BkrtcyNDTex, 363 BR 799.—Accession 2; Bankr 3708(6).

Flores, In re, BkrtcySDTex, 270 BR 203.—Bankr 2832.1, 2896, 2921.

Flores, In re, BkrtcySDTex, 208 BR 30.—Bankr 3715(7), 3716.30(10).

Flores, In re, BkrtcySDTex, 32 BR 455.—Bankr 3116, 3710(7); Ven & Pur 101, 104.

Flores, In re, TexApp–Houston (1 Dist), 135 SW3d 863.—Child C 959; Const Law 2317, 4396.

Flores, In re, TexApp–Houston (1 Dist), 111 SW3d 817.—Mand 4(1), 4(4), 12, 53.

Flores, In re, TexApp–San Antonio, 53 SW3d 428.—Judges 51(1), 56; Mand 4(4).

Flores, In re Estate of, TexApp–Corpus Christi, 76 SW3d 624.—Judgm 185(2), 185(5), 185(6); Wills 21, 50, 52(1), 55(1), 107, 111(1), 152, 288(1), 289, 292, 300.

Flores v. Allstate Texas Lloyd's Co., SDTex, 278 FSupp2d 810.—Fed Civ Proc 2501; Insurance 1806, 2117, 2127, 2146, 2165(2), 3147, 3153, 3156, 3160(2), 3167, 3168, 3200.

Flores v. Allstate Texas Lloyd's Co., SDTex, 229 FSupp2d 697.—Evid 555.2, 555.5, 555.10; Insurance 2162; Land & Ten 125(1).

Flores v. Anaya, TexCivApp–Austin, 348 SW2d 410, ref nre.—Autos 209.

Flores v. Arrieta, TexApp–San Antonio, 790 SW2d 75, writ den.—App & E 170(1), 497(1), 554(1), 907(3); Venue 64.1.

Flores v. Bailey, TexCivApp–El Paso, 341 SW2d 473, ref nre.—Bankr 3412; Hus & W 270(11).

Flores v. Banner, Tex, 932 SW2d 500.—Judges 51(1), 51(2), 51(3), 51(4), 56; Mand 29.

Flores v. Barlow, TexCivApp–Austin, 354 SW2d 173, ref nre.—Autos 172(7), 244(35), 247; Evid 545, 555.8(2); Trial 81, 350.7(3.1), 352.10.

Flores v. Beto, CA5 (Tex), 374 F2d 225, cert den 87 SCt 2087, 387 US 948, 18 LEd2d 1338.—Courts 100(1); Fed Cts 191; Hab Corp 452, 471.

Flores; Board of Adjustment of City of Corpus Christi v., TexApp–Corpus Christi, 860 SW2d 622, reh overr, and writ den.—Zoning 509, 565, 574, 612, 621, 642, 676, 680.1, 701, 703.

Flores; Borg-Warner Corp. v., TexApp–Corpus Christi, 153 SW3d 209, reh overr, and review gr.—App & E 766, 977(5), 1004(3), 1050.1(11), 1050.1(12), 1133; Damag 63, 91.5(1), 91.5(4), 184, 189.5; Evid 506, 513(1), 571(9), 571(10); Neglig 202, 549(8), 1718; Prod Liab 8, 11, 14, 62, 75.1, 83; Trial 139.1(14), 139.1(17), 141.

Flores; Borg-Warner Protective Services Corp. v., TexApp–Corpus Christi, 955 SW2d 861, reh overr.—App & E 1060.1(1); Civil R 1123, 1704, 1765, 1769, 1772, 1773; Const Law 4427; Costs 194.18, 252; Damag 215(1); Interest 39(2.50); Labor & Emp 826, 867, 3049(3); Trial 111, 125(1).

Flores v. Brimex Ltd. Partnership, TexApp–San Antonio, 5 SW3d 816.—App & E 5, 859, 931(1), 1010.2, 1175(5), 1177(7); Judgm 111, 112, 126(2); Trover 40(4).

Flores; Burlington Coat Factory Warehouse of El Paso, Inc. v., TexApp–El Paso, 951 SW2d 542.—Damag 102, 119, 130.1, 192; Labor & Emp 810, 867, 868(3), 870, 871, 873.

Flores v. Cameron County, Tex., CA5 (Tex), 92 F3d 258, reh den.—Civil R 1351(1), 1351(4), 1379, 1395(1), 1426, 1437; Evid 383(12); Fed Civ Proc 2183; Fed Cts 411, 427, 775; Lim of Act 121(2).

Flores; Casualty Underwriters v., TexCivApp–Galveston, 125 SW2d 371, writ dism, correct.—Marriage 40(6); Plead 433(2); Work Comp 515, 548, 1919, 1924, 1927, 1958.

Flores v. Center for Spinal Evaluation and Rehabilitation, TexApp–Amarillo, 865 SW2d 261.—App & E 863, 934(1); Health 611, 618, 674, 800, 821(1); Judgm 185(6); Neglig 379, 380, 1675.

Flores v. Charlie Thomas Courtesy Ford, Inc., TexApp–Corpus Christi, 669 SW2d 165.—Cons Cred 4.

Flores v. Citizens State Bank of Roma, Texas, TexApp–San Antonio, 954 SW2d 78, reh overr.—App & E 430(1).

Flores; City of Boerne v., USTex, 117 SCt 2157, 521 US 507, 138 LEd2d 624, on remand 119 F3d 341.—Civil R 1005; Const Law 2352, 4850, 4852, 4853, 4867; States 4.16(2); U S 5.

Flores v. City of Boerne, WDTex, 877 FSupp 355, rev 73 F3d 1352, reh and sug for reh den 83 F3d 421, cert gr 117 SCt 293, 519 US 926, 136 LEd2d 212, motion gr 117 SCt 762, 519 US 1088, 136 LEd2d 709, rev 117 SCt 2157, 521 US 507, 138 LEd2d 624, on remand 119 F3d 341, aff and remanded 119 F3d 341.—Const Law 1290, 1303, 2382.

Flores v. City of Boerne, Tex., CA5 (Tex), 73 F3d 1352, reh and sug for reh den 83 F3d 421, cert gr 117 SCt 293, 519 US 926, 136 LEd2d 212, motion gr 117 SCt 762, 519 US 1088, 136 LEd2d 709, rev 117 SCt 2157, 521 US 507, 138 LEd2d 624, on remand 119 F3d 341.—Civil R 1005; Const Law 1303, 1310, 2352, 4850, 4857, 4867; States 4.16(2).

Flores v. City of Palacios, CA5 (Tex), 381 F3d 391, on remand 2005 WL 3005659.—Arrest 68(2), 68(4); Civil R

1035, 1088(4), 1376(2), 1376(6); Fed Civ Proc 2491.5; Fed Cts 574; Searches 23.

Flores v. City of Palacios, SDTex, 270 FSupp2d 865, aff in part, rev in part 381 F3d 391, on remand 2005 WL 3005659.—Arrest 68(1), 68(2); Civil R 1035, 1088(4), 1088(5), 1351(1), 1376(2), 1376(6), 1395(6); Const Law 1050, 3849, 4040, 4537; Fed Civ Proc 630, 941, 943, 971, 1773, 1829, 1835, 2481, 2491.5; Mal Pros 0.5.

Flores; City of San Antonio v., TexCivApp–Hous (14 Dist), 619 SW2d 601, ref nre.—Admin Law 791; Mun Corp 198(3).

Flores; Coastal Oil & Gas Corp. v., TexApp–San Antonio, 908 SW2d 517.—Abate & R 4; App & E 1039(16); Mand 29; Plead 106(2).

Flores v. Coffield Warehouse Co., TexApp–Texarkana, 683 SW2d 31, cert den 106 SCt 89, 474 US 828, 88 LEd2d 73.—App & E 863, 934(1); Labor & Emp 2773; States 18.46.

Flores; Commercial Credit Corp. v., TexCivApp–Eastland, 345 SW2d 432, ref nre.—Chat Mtg 169, 176(4), 176(5), 176(6); Trover 46.

Flores v. Contreras, TexApp–San Antonio, 981 SW2d 246, reh overr, and review den.—App & E 893(1), 949; Child C 800, 803, 804; Statut 181(2); Treaties 8.

Flores v. County of Hardeman, Tex., CA5 (Tex), 124 F3d 736, sug for reh den 132 F3d 1458.—Civil R 1088(4), 1351(4), 1376(7); Fed Cts 18, 763.1.

Flores; Cuellar v., TexCivApp–San Antonio, 238 SW2d 991.—Adop 13, 15; App & E 931(6).

Flores v. Dairyland County Mut. Ins. Co. of Texas, TexCivApp–Eastland, 595 SW2d 893, ref nre.—Insurance 2673.

Flores; Davila v., TexApp–Corpus Christi, 6 SW3d 788.—Judgm 185(2); Offic 114, 116; States 78.

Flores v. De Galvan, TexCivApp–San Antonio, 127 SW2d 305, writ dism, correct.—App & E 930(1), 1004(3); Dead Bodies 4, 5.

Flores v. Didear Van & Storage Co., Inc., TexCivApp–Corpus Christi, 489 SW2d 406.—Interest 39(1); Wareh 33, 34(5), 34(6), 34(7).

Flores v. Dosher, Tex, 622 SW2d 573.—App & E 989, 1024.1; Health 826; New Tr 44(1), 44(2), 56.

Flores v. Dosher, TexCivApp–Corpus Christi, 608 SW2d 831, writ gr, rev 622 SW2d 573.—App & E 837(1), 842(1), 863, 989; Health 825; New Tr 44(1), 56, 140(3).

Flores v. Dretke, CA5 (Tex), 82 FedAppx 92, cert den 124 SCt 1880, 541 US 976, 158 LEd2d 472.—Hab Corp 818.

Flores; Drilex Systems, Inc. v., Tex, 1 SW3d 112.—App & E 854(4), 970(1); Damag 63; Statut 181(1), 212.7; Trial 41(1), 41(2), 41(4), 41(5).

Flores; Drilex Systems, Inc. v., TexApp–San Antonio, 961 SW2d 209, reh overr, and writ gr, aff as mod 1 SW3d 112.—App & E 216(1), 231(9), 970(1), 1048(1), 1058(1); Damag 63; Prod Liab 85; Trial 41(1), 41(2), 41(4), 352.1(6), 352.10.

Flores v. Edinburg Consol. Independent School Dist., CA5 (Tex), 741 F2d 773, reh den 747 F2d 1465.—Courts 489(1); Judgm 585(3), 653, 713(2), 715(1), 720, 828.3, 828.16(1).

Flores v. Edinburg Consol. Independent School Dist., SDTex, 554 FSupp 974, rev 741 F2d 773, reh den 747 F2d 1465.—Civil R 1070, 1351(1), 1376(2), 1376(5), 1395(2); Fed Civ Proc 2491.5; Fed Cts 265, 270; Judgm 634, 828.1, 828.15(1); Lim of Act 72(1).

Flores v. Employees Retirement System of Texas, TexApp–Austin, 74 SW3d 532, review den.—Admin Law 314, 416.1, 472, 502, 513; Const Law 3879, 4027; Neglig 379, 384; Offic 101.5(1), 101.5(2); States 64.1(1); Statut 219(1), 219(4); Work Comp 11, 597, 598, 803, 2084.

Flores v. Employers' Fire Ins. Co. of San Antonio, Tex., CA5 (Tex), 464 F2d 1276, cert den 93 SCt 545, 409 US 1046, 34 LEd2d 497, reh den 93 SCt 2275, 411 US 987, 36 LEd2d 966.—Fed Cts 743, 852; Work Comp 725, 1940.

Flores; Enron Oil & Gas Co. v., TexApp–San Antonio, 810 SW2d 408, reh of motion for mandamus overr.—App & E 961; Mand 12; Pretrial Proc 371, 411.

Flores; Esparza Rico v., SDTex, 405 FSupp2d 746, rev 481 F3d 234.—Action 4; Fed Civ Proc 751; Fed Cts 660.1; Neglig 202, 409, 451, 454, 525, 560, 1045(2), 1247, 1295, 1314; Plead 78; Rem of C 36, 45, 107(4), 107(7), 107(9).

Flores v. Estelle, CA5 (Tex), 578 F2d 80, cert den 99 SCt 1253, 440 US 923, 59 LEd2d 477.—Crim Law 273.1(1), 273.1(2); Hab Corp 475.1, 476, 717(2), 725, 747, 765.1, 766.

Flores v. Estelle, CA5 (Tex), 513 F2d 764, cert den 96 SCt 401, 423 US 989, 46 LEd2d 308.—Crim Law 419(2.35), 698(1), 1036.5; Hab Corp 816.

Flores v. Estelle, CA5 (Tex), 492 F2d 711, appeal after remand 513 F2d 764, cert den 96 SCt 401, 423 US 989, 46 LEd2d 308.—Hab Corp 864(1).

Flores v. Flores, TexApp–El Paso, 225 SW3d 651, reh overr, and rule 537(f) motion gr, and review den, and reh of petition for review den.—Adv Poss 13, 40; App & E 223; Frds St of 55; Gifts 4, 18(2), 25; Judgm 186; Trusts 72, 91, 94.5, 102(1).

Flores; Flores v., TexApp–El Paso, 225 SW3d 651, reh overr, and rule 537(f) motion gr, and review den, and reh of petition for review den.—Adv Poss 13, 40; App & E 223; Frds St of 55; Gifts 4, 18(2), 25; Judgm 186; Trusts 72, 91, 94.5, 102(1).

Flores v. Flores, TexApp–Waco, 847 SW2d 648, reh den, and writ den.—App & E 846(5), 846(6), 931(1), 999(1), 1001(1), 1001(3), 1003(1); Divorce 59; Evid 587; Marriage 13, 20(1), 50(1), 50(4); Statut 188, 214.

Flores; Flores v., TexApp–Waco, 847 SW2d 648, reh den, and writ den.—App & E 846(5), 846(6), 931(1), 999(1), 1001(1), 1001(3), 1003(1); Divorce 59; Evid 587; Marriage 13, 20(1), 50(1), 50(4); Statut 188, 214.

Flores v. Flores, TexApp–Corpus Christi, 116 SW3d 870. —App & E 1175(1); Equity 46, 54, 65(1), 65(2), 65(3); Judgm 335(1), 335(2), 335(3); Notice 14; Pretrial Proc 11, 15.

Flores; Flores v., TexApp–Corpus Christi, 116 SW3d 870. —App & E 1175(1); Equity 46, 54, 65(1), 65(2), 65(3); Judgm 335(1), 335(2), 335(3); Notice 14; Pretrial Proc 11, 15.

Flores v. Fort Bend Cent. Appraisal Dist., TexApp–Houston (14 Dist), 720 SW2d 243.—Statut 181(1), 206; Tax 2694.

Flores v. Fourth Court of Appeals, Tex, 777 SW2d 38.—Admin Law 466; Pretrial Proc 33; Work Comp 1167, 1703.5.

Flores v. George Braun Packing Co., Division of Leonard & Harral Packing Co., CA5 (Tex), 482 F2d 279, reh den 485 F2d 687.—Aliens 137.

Flores v. Great Am. Ins. Co., TexCivApp–Waco, 401 SW2d 690, ref nre.—Insurance 2320, 2914; Work Comp 1066.

Flores; Grimes v., TexApp–San Antonio, 717 SW2d 956.—Hab Corp 798.

Flores; Grimes v., TexApp–San Antonio, 717 SW2d 949.—Child C 20; Hab Corp 532(1), 532(2); Mand 51.

Flores v. Haberman, Tex, 915 SW2d 477.—Lis Pen 3(1), 15.

Flores; H.E.B. Food Stores, Inc. v., TexApp–Corpus Christi, 661 SW2d 297, dism.—Neglig 1037(4), 1076, 1077, 1088, 1579, 1595; Plead 111.12, 111.42(7).

Flores v. H.E. Butt Grocery Co., TexApp–Corpus Christi, 802 SW2d 53.—App & E 5, 859; Pretrial Proc 44.1, 46.

Flores v. H.E. Butt Stores, Inc., TexApp–Corpus Christi, 791 SW2d 160, writ den.—Judgm 185(1), 185(2), 185(6); Neglig 1104(3), 1568; Pretrial Proc 483.

Flores v. Heckler, CA5 (Tex), 755 F2d 401.—Fed Civ Proc 2464; Social S 143.60, 145, 149.5.

FLORES;

Flores; Hervey v., TexApp–El Paso, 975 SW2d 21, reh overr, and review den, and reh of petition for review overr.—App & E 78(1), 80(6), 343.1, 347(1), 842(2), 870(2), 893(1), 1010.1(3), 1010.1(8.1), 1012.1(5); Courts 30; Judgm 181(14), 297.

Flores; Hicks v., TexApp–Amarillo, 900 SW2d 504.—Judgm 143(3), 145(2), 146, 159; Plead 85(5).

Flores v. Johnson, CA5 (Tex), 210 F3d 456, cert den 121 SCt 445, 531 US 987, 148 LEd2d 449.—Hab Corp 490(3).

Flores v. Johnson, WDTex, 957 FSupp 893.—Burg 16, 42(3), 42(4); Const Law 4659(2); Crim Law 59(5), 224, 339.6, 339.8(6), 339.10(11), 552(4), 641.3(4), 641.13(1), 641.13(2.1), 641.13(5), 641.13(6), 641.13(7), 742(1), 772(6), 814(19), 1077.3, 1159.2(7); Hab Corp 319.1, 351, 352, 364, 365, 370, 374.1, 380.1, 382, 383, 402, 431, 450.1, 452, 453, 493(3), 709, 712.1, 769.

Flores; King Const. Co. v., TexCivApp–Houston, 359 SW2d 919, ref nre.—App & E 207; Evid 76; Mech Liens 310(3); Princ & A 123(3); Trial 114, 123, 131(1), 133.2.

Flores v. Law, TexApp–Houston (1 Dist), 8 SW3d 785, review den.—Const Law 2314; Health 770; Judgm 181(6), 702.

Flores; Lindley v., TexApp–Corpus Christi, 672 SW2d 612.—App & E 199, 961; Judgm 22; Motions 1, 2; Pretrial Proc 44.1.

Flores v. Lively, TexApp–Corpus Christi, 818 SW2d 460, writ den.—Lim of Act 43, 55(4), 95(5).

Flores v. Logan, TexCivApp–San Antonio, 307 SW2d 813, ref nre.—App & E 854(5); Neglig 1709.

Flores v. Lone Star Fish & Oyster Co., TexCivApp, 241 SW2d 443.—Mal Pros 33; Venue 8.5(4).

Flores; Martinez v., TexApp–Corpus Christi, 820 SW2d 937.—Child C 603; Mand 28; Venue 54, 61.

Flores v. Melo-Palacios, TexApp–Corpus Christi, 921 SW2d 399, reh overr, and writ den.—Child C 921(1); Child S 173, 507, 508(3), 525; Const Law 3965(1); Courts 21; Domicile 2; Parties 44.

Flores v. Metropolitan Transit Authority, TexApp–Houston (14 Dist), 964 SW2d 704.—App & E 1079; Labor & Emp 968, 995, 1219(4), 1243, 1322; Lim of Act 95(14); States 18.46, 18.53.

Flores v. Military Highway Water Supply Corp., TexApp–Corpus Christi, 714 SW2d 382.—Em Dom 8, 32.

Flores v. Millennium Interests, Ltd., CA5 (Tex), 464 F3d 521.—Cons Cred 16.

Flores v. Millennium Interests, Ltd., SDTex, 273 FSupp2d 899, question certified 390 F3d 374, certified question accepted, certified question answered 185 SW3d 427, reh den, aff 464 F3d 521.—Antitrust 214; Cons Cred 17; Lim of Act 58(1).

Flores v. Millennium Interests, Ltd., Tex, 185 SW3d 427, reh den.—Cons Cred 3.1, 16, 17; Damag 74; Statut 241(2).

Flores; Mission Consolidated Independent School Dist. v., TexApp–Corpus Christi, 39 SW3d 674.—Courts 32, 35; Plead 104(1), 111.36, 111.38; Schools 159.5(6).

Flores v. Missouri-Kansas-Texas R. Co., TexCivApp–Dallas, 365 SW2d 379, ref nre.—App & E 1170.1, 1170.7; Evid 318(4), 512, 527; Plead 85(1), 568(1).

Flores; Missouri Pacific R. Co. v., TexApp–San Antonio, 762 SW2d 271. See Missouri Pacific R. Co. v. Killam Oil Co.

Flores; Morrow v., TexCivApp–Fort Worth, 225 SW2d 621, ref nre.—App & E 231(9), 1053(2); Assault 2, 3, 19, 40, 43(5); Jury 97(4), 103(3).

Flores v. North American Technologies Group, Inc., TexApp–Houston (1 Dist), 176 SW3d 442, reh overr, and review den, and reh of petition for review den.—App & E 852, 934(1); Judgm 185(2); Work Comp 203, 208, 2161.

Flores v. Norton & Ramsey Lines, Inc., WDTex, 352 FSupp 150.—Fed Civ Proc 51; Fed Cts 265, 266.1;

Neglig 1040(3); States 112(2), 191.8(1), 191.9(7), 191.10, 203.

Flores; Noyola v., TexApp–Corpus Christi, 740 SW2d 493.—App & E 70(8).

Flores v. Onion, TexApp–San Antonio, 693 SW2d 756.—Compromise 18(1); Divorce 152; Judgm 215, 276; Mand 51.

Flores; Ontiveros v., Tex, 218 SW3d 70, reh den.—App & E 1082(2).

Flores v. Ontiveros, TexApp–Corpus Christi, 218 SW3d 98, reh overr, and review gr, aff in part, rev in part 218 SW3d 70, reh den.—Action 13; Equity 65(3); Fraud 3, 16, 17; Fraud Conv 221; Joint Adv 1.2(1); Judgm 181(7), 181(33), 185.3(5), 185.3(21), 668(1), 713(1), 720, 724; Lim of Act 95(7), 195(3), 199(1); Partners 1; Torts 212, 253.

Flores; Perales v., TexCivApp–San Antonio, 147 SW2d 974, writ refused.—Marriage 13, 50(1); Trusts 79, 80.

Flores v. Peschel, TexApp–Corpus Christi, 927 SW2d 209.—Abate & R 4; Courts 474, 480(1), 483, 484; Mand 3(3), 4(1), 4(4), 12, 31.

Flores v. Procunier, CA5 (Tex), 745 F2d 338, cert den 105 SCt 1851, 470 US 1086, 85 LEd2d 148.—Fed Civ Proc 2651.1, 2658; Hab Corp 818.

Flores v. Quarterman, CA5 (Tex), 467 F3d 484, cert den 127 SCt 2909, 168 LEd2d 242.—Courts 100(1); Hab Corp 603, 843.

Flores; Ramirez v., TexCivApp–San Antonio, 505 SW2d 406, ref nre.—App & E 713(1); Const Law 600, 633; Counties 42, 43, 46; Jury 12(3); Mand 3(1), 3(10), 10; Offic 30.5; Plead 4; Schools 53(5).

Flores; Rico v., CA5 (Tex), 481 F3d 234.—Action 4; Contracts 138(1); Rem of C 36, 82, 107(7), 107(9).

Flores v. Riveria, TexCivApp–Amarillo, 473 SW2d 613, ref nre.—Child C 277, 579.

Flores v. Rizik, TexApp–San Antonio, 683 SW2d 112.—App & E 931(1), 989, 1012.1(4), 1170.7; Damag 113; Evid 474(18); Land & Ten 55(1), 55(3), 94(6), 161(3); Witn 276.

Flores v. Robinson Roofing & Const. Co., Inc., TexApp–Fort Worth, 161 SW3d 750, review den.—Fraud Conv 1, 3, 8, 155, 165, 170, 282, 308(1); Judgm 181(6), 181(15.1), 185.3(5).

Flores; Rodriguez v., TexCivApp–San Antonio, 426 SW2d 285.—App & E 765, 771, 773(2).

Flores; Rodriguez v., TexCivApp–San Antonio, 403 SW2d 172.—Bound 37(3); Evid 265(5).

Flores; Salinas v., SDTex, 359 FSupp 233.—Civil R 1348, 1358, 1376(8), 1395(5); Counties 141; Fed Cts 15; Mun Corp 182, 744, 747(3).

Flores; Salinas v., TexCivApp–San Antonio, 583 SW2d 813, dism.—Interest 31, 39(1); Sales 199, 363; Trial 139.1(8), 178.

Flores v. Secretary of Navy, SDTex, 159 FRD 472, aff 51 F3d 1044.—Fed Civ Proc 44, 533, 1751.

Flores; Simmons v., TexApp–Texarkana, 838 SW2d 287, reh den, and writ den.—Autos 173(8), 201(5), 201(9), 244(14), 244(36.1); Judgm 185(5), 185.3(21).

Flores; Soltner v., TexCivApp–El Paso, 335 SW2d 771.—Gifts 47(1), 49(4); Witn 180, 183.

Flores v. Stag Sales Co., TexApp–San Antonio, 697 SW2d 493, ref nre.—Mines 55(2), 55(4).

Flores v. State, TexCrimApp, 155 SW3d 144, reh den.—Const Law 4674; Crim Law 641.12(1), 671, 1170.5(1); Witn 67, 405(1).

Flores v. State, TexCrimApp, 904 SW2d 129, cert den 116 SCt 716, 516 US 1050, 133 LEd2d 670.—Const Law 3053, 3060, 3250, 3819, 3823, 3877, 3899, 3901, 4731; Sent & Pun 1802, 1809, 1812, 1821, 1888.

Flores; State v., TexCrimApp, 896 SW2d 198.—Homic 833; Ind & Inf 71.4(7).

Flores v. State, TexCrimApp, 884 SW2d 784.—Sent & Pun 311, 313.

Flores v. State, TexCrimApp, 871 SW2d 714, reh den, cert den Angel Flores v. Texas, 115 SCt 313, 513 US 926, 130 LEd2d 276, denial of habeas corpus aff 210 F3d 456, cert den 121 SCt 445, 531 US 987, 148 LEd2d 449.—Crim Law 388.2, 531(3), 1045, 1152(2), 1172.1(1), 1172.9; Jury 42, 83(1), 85, 107; Searches 61, 102, 171; Sent & Pun 1720.

Flores v. State, TexCrimApp, 716 SW2d 505.—Weap 8.

Flores v. State, TexCrimApp, 690 SW2d 281.—Crim Law 1184(4.1); Sent & Pun 329.

Flores v. State, TexCrimApp, 650 SW2d 429.—Controlled Subs 27, 80.

Flores v. State, TexCrimApp, 606 SW2d 859.—Crim Law 577.10(9).

Flores v. State, TexCrimApp, 576 SW2d 632.—Crim Law 641.13(1), 641.13(6).

Flores v. State, TexCrimApp, 551 SW2d 364.—Crim Law 552(1), 552(3); Homic 1019, 1184.

Flores v. State, TexCrimApp, 524 SW2d 71.—Crim Law 995(8); Ind & Inf 144.2; Sent & Pun 1018.

Flores v. State, TexCrimApp, 513 SW2d 66.—Crim Law 1126, 1172.9; Sent & Pun 1916, 1960, 1965.

Flores v. State, TexCrimApp, 509 SW2d 580.—Crim Law 273.4(1), 300, 642.

Flores v. State, TexCrimApp, 493 SW2d 785.—Crim Law 134(2), 1166(4).

Flores v. State, TexCrimApp, 491 SW2d 144.—Crim Law 507(1), 1170.5(1); Homic 975, 986, 999, 1045, 1184; Witn 4, 21.

Flores v. State, TexCrimApp, 489 SW2d 901.—Controlled Subs 80; Crim Law 552(3).

Flores v. State, TexCrimApp, 487 SW2d 122.—Assault 92(1); Courts 97(1); Crim Law 100(1), 100(3), 102, 105; Homic 726, 728; Ind & Inf 144.2; Sent & Pun 1802, 1843, 1893, 1899.

Flores v. State, TexCrimApp, 486 SW2d 577.—Weap 11(0.5), 17(6).

Flores v. State, TexCrimApp, 472 SW2d 146.—Crim Law 364(3.1), 855(5); Ind & Inf 192; Sent & Pun 1238, 1513.

Flores v. State, TexCrimApp, 458 SW2d 686.—Crim Law 1184(2).

Flores v. State, TexCrimApp, 452 SW2d 918.—Crim Law 1043(2).

Flores v. State, TexCrimApp, 436 SW2d 135.—Controlled Subs 80.

Flores v. State, TexCrimApp, 419 SW2d 202.—Crim Law 1023(9), 1081(4.1); Sent & Pun 201.

Flores v. State, TexCrimApp, 372 SW2d 687.—Crim Law 404.65, 742(1), 814(17); Homic 1332.

Flores v. State, TexCrimApp, 353 SW2d 852, 172 TexCrim 73, cert den 82 SCt 1556, 370 US 918, 8 LEd2d 498.—Crim Law 1090.16, 1090.19; Homic 1134.

Flores v. State, TexCrimApp, 352 SW2d 287, 171 TexCrim 598, cert den 82 SCt 1153, 369 US 880, 8 LEd2d 282.—Crim Law 522(3), 531(4), 1099.6(2.1), 1158(4), 1169.12.

Flores v. State, TexCrimApp, 334 SW2d 813, 169 TexCrim 413.—Weap 17(4).

Flores v. State, TexCrimApp, 334 SW2d 306, 169 TexCrim 338.—Arrest 71.1(3); Crim Law 394.4(9), 478(1).

Flores v. State, TexCrimApp, 332 SW2d 715, 169 TexCrim 202.—Burg 41(1); Crim Law 511.1(9).

Flores v. State, TexCrimApp, 331 SW2d 219, 168 TexCrim 629.—Assault 92(4); Homic 908, 1154.

Flores v. State, TexCrimApp, 331 SW2d 217, 169 TexCrim 2.—Sent & Pun 2004, 2021.

Flores v. State, TexCrimApp, 319 SW2d 303, 167 TexCrim 210.—Crim Law 875(4); Weap 17(4).

Flores v. State, TexCrimApp, 318 SW2d 663, 167 TexCrim 91.—Crim Law 706(3), 1169.2(5); Ind & Inf 87(3).

Flores v. State, TexCrimApp, 301 SW2d 914.—Crim Law 1086.8, 1090.1(1).

Flores v. State, TexCrimApp, 294 SW2d 102.—Crim Law 1090.1(2).

Flores v. State, TexCrimApp, 292 SW2d 127.—Crim Law 1090.1(1).

Flores v. State, TexCrimApp, 289 SW2d 579.—Crim Law 1090.1(1).

Flores v. State, TexCrimApp, 266 SW2d 386, 159 TexCrim 608.—Crim Law 429(2), 686(2), 720(7.1); Disorderly H 16, 17.

Flores v. State, TexCrimApp, 264 SW2d 952, 159 TexCrim 458.—Crim Law 304(17); Ind & Inf 51(2).

Flores v. State, TexCrimApp, 264 SW2d 116.—Crim Law 1090.1(1).

Flores v. State, TexCrimApp, 259 SW2d 198, 159 TexCrim 1.—Int Liq 146(3).

Flores v. State, TexCrimApp, 235 SW2d 653, 155 TexCrim 391.—Ind & Inf 187.

Flores v. State, TexCrimApp, 212 SW2d 161.—Crim Law 1090.1(1).

Flores v. State, TexCrimApp, 209 SW2d 168, 151 TexCrim 478.—Crim Law 338(7), 369.1, 371(4), 371(12), 730(3), 730(16), 1168(2).

Flores v. State, TexCrimApp, 172 SW2d 506, 146 TexCrim 192.—Homic 1193, 1207.

Flores v. State, TexCrimApp, 172 SW2d 336, 146 TexCrim 232.—Crim Law 814(3), 829(4), 1091(2), 1169.2(7), 1169.9; Homic 1032, 1479.

Flores v. State, TexCrimApp, 166 SW2d 706, 145 TexCrim 134.—Larc 1; Rob 1; Sent & Pun 1250, 1260.

Flores v. State, TexCrimApp, 158 SW2d 1012, 143 TexCrim 382.—Crim Law 537, 1032(5), 1169.12; Ind & Inf 43.

Flores v. State, TexCrimApp, 155 SW2d 932, 142 TexCrim 589.—Crim Law 561(2); Larc 58.

Flores v. State, TexCrimApp, 120 SW2d 1065, 135 TexCrim 496.—Crim Law 741(1), 742(1), 814(17), 1159.3(1); Rob 26.

Flores v. State, TexApp–Houston (1 Dist), 177 SW3d 8, reh overr, and petition for discretionary review refused, cert den 126 SCt 2298, 164 LEd2d 821.—Crim Law 394.6(5), 1134(2), 1134(6), 1144.12, 1153(1), 1158(4); Searches 54, 143.1.

Flores v. State, TexApp–Houston (1 Dist), 125 SW3d 744, habeas corpus gr Ex parte Guerrero Flores, 2005 WL 774456.—Crim Law 338(7), 713, 720(6), 723(3), 726, 1043(3), 1153(1); Sent & Pun 308.

Flores v. State, TexApp–Houston (1 Dist), 84 SW3d 675, reh overr, and petition for discretionary review refused.—Crim Law 37(2.1), 37(8), 369.2(1), 369.2(7), 372(13), 407(2), 412(5), 655(2), 661, 739.1(1), 752.5, 1134(8), 1144.13(2.1), 1144.13(3), 1144.13(6), 1153(1).

Flores v. State, TexApp–Houston (1 Dist), 43 SW3d 628.—Crim Law 1023(3), 1081(1), 1081(2), 1081(5), 1134(10).

Flores v. State, TexApp–Houston (1 Dist), 888 SW2d 193, petition for discretionary review refused.—Crim Law 1081(2); Searches 40.1, 111, 112, 126.

Flores v. State, TexApp–Houston (1 Dist), 888 SW2d 187, petition for discretionary review refused.—Crim Law 258, 260.11(4), 553, 1144.13(2.1), 1159.2(7), 1159.4(2), 1159.6, 1181.5(8), 1184(3); Ind & Inf 191(0.5), 191(5); Larc 3(2), 3(4), 44.

Flores v. State, TexApp–Houston (1 Dist), 866 SW2d 682, petition for discretionary review gr, aff 884 SW2d 784.—Sent & Pun 313.

Flores v. State, TexApp–Houston (1 Dist), 789 SW2d 694.—Crim Law 586, 641.2(2), 641.2(4), 641.4(1), 641.4(2), 641.6(3), 641.7(1), 641.10(3), 1035(7), 1044.2(1), 1063(1).

Flores v. State, TexApp–Houston (1 Dist), 767 SW2d 811.—Bail 79(1).

Flores v. State, TexApp–Fort Worth, 784 SW2d 579, petition for discretionary review refused.—Atty & C 77; Crim Law 641.13(1), 641.13(5).

Flores v. State, TexApp–Fort Worth, 625 SW2d 91.—Crim Law 364(1), 671, 718, 814(17), 1043(3).

FLORES

Flores v. State, TexApp–Austin, 18 SW3d 796.—Crim Law 273.1(5), 641.13(1), 641.13(2.1), 641.13(7), 951(1), 951(6), 956(2), 956(4), 959, 1156(1).

Flores v. State, TexApp–Austin, 902 SW2d 618, reh overr, and petition for discretionary review refused.—Burg 3, 41(3); Crim Law 44, 562, 1159.2(7).

Flores v. State, TexApp–Austin, 827 SW2d 529.—Crim Law 859.

Flores v. State, TexApp–San Antonio, 150 SW3d 750.—Crim Law 1134(3), 1134(10), 1139, 1158(1), 1590.

Flores v. State, TexApp–San Antonio, 90 SW3d 875, petition for discretionary review gr, rev 155 SW3d 144, reh den.—Crim Law 641.5(0.5), 824(12), 1030(1), 1038.1(1), 1038.1(2), 1042, 1170.5(1), 1172.1(1).

Flores v. State, TexApp–San Antonio, 49 SW3d 29, reh en banc den, and petition for discretionary review refused.—Crim Law 412.2(4), 412.2(5), 414, 517.2(2), 553, 641.3(2), 1139, 1158(1), 1158(4); Homic 1474, 1483, 1484, 1487.

Flores v. State, TexApp–San Antonio, 30 SW3d 29, petition for discretionary review refused.—Autos 355(8); Crim Law 29(1), 29(14), 412.2(4), 1044.2(1), 1144.13(2.1), 1144.13(3), 1159.2(2), 1159.2(7), 1159.2(9), 1159.3(2), 1159.4(2).

Flores v. State, TexApp–San Antonio, 940 SW2d 189, appeal after remand 1999 WL 15929, petition for discretionary review refused.—Const Law 4594(1), 4594(4), 4594(9); Crim Law 627.7(3).

Flores v. State, TexApp–San Antonio, 920 SW2d 347, petition for discretionary review gr, and petition for discretionary review refused, petition for discretionary review dism per curiam opinion 940 SW2d 660, denial of post-conviction relief aff 150 SW3d 750.—Crim Law 507(1), 510, 670, 697, 780(1), 780(2), 814(15), 822(11), 829(12), 898, 1152(2), 1158(3), 1163(1), 1166.16, 1166.18, 1168(2), 1172.1(1); Jury 33(5.15), 131(4), 131(8), 131(13), 131(15.1).

Flores v. State, TexApp–San Antonio, 906 SW2d 133.—Crim Law 295, 438(1), 438(5.1), 1130(5); Double J 1, 135, 150(1); Ind & Inf 191(0.5); Judgm 724, 725(1), 751, 958(1).

Flores v. State, TexApp–San Antonio, 895 SW2d 435.—Arrest 63.4(10), 63.4(11), 63.4(17), 63.5(1), 63.5(4), 63.5(7), 63.5(8), 68(4), 71.1(5); Crim Law 394.6(4), 394.6(5), 753.2(3.1), 1134(2), 1158(4), 1159.2(7); Searches 40.1; Weap 10, 17(4).

Flores v. State, TexApp–San Antonio, 764 SW2d 37.—Crim Law 1172.9.

Flores v. State, TexApp–San Antonio, 756 SW2d 86, petition for discretionary review refused.—Controlled Subs 26, 27, 30, 80, 106.

Flores v. State, TexApp–San Antonio, 727 SW2d 691, vac 761 SW2d 7, on remand 764 SW2d 37.—Const Law 203, 2371, 2789, 2790, 2823.

Flores v. State, TexApp–San Antonio, 625 SW2d 44, petition for discretionary review refused.—Crim Law 577.8(2), 577.10(1), 577.10(10), 577.16(4), 1077.3.

Flores v. State, TexApp–Texarkana, 194 SW3d 34, petition for discretionary review gr, vac 224 SW3d 212.—Crim Law 1165(1), 1172.1(1), 1172.1(4), 1480; Homic 1347, 1480.

Flores v. State, TexApp–Texarkana, 139 SW3d 61, petition for discretionary review refused.—Crim Law 561(1), 995(1), 1141(2), 1144.13(2.1), 1159.2(2), 1159.2(7), 1162, 1165(1), 1167(1), 1167(4), 1187, 1189; Ind & Inf 113, 159(1), 171; Sent & Pun 1324, 1365, 1381(6).

Flores v. State, TexApp–Amarillo, 170 SW3d 722, reh overr, and petition for discretionary review refused, cert den 127 SCt 141, 166 LEd2d 103.—Crim Law 662.8.

Flores v. State, TexApp–Amarillo, 883 SW2d 383, petition for discretionary review refused.—Courts 91(1), 247(8).

Flores v. State, TexApp–El Paso, 840 SW2d 753, denial of habeas corpus aff 58 F3d 637.—Crim Law 369.1, 369.2(1), 369.2(5), 374, 1036.1(2), 1044.2(1), 1169.11.

Flores v. State, TexApp–El Paso, 783 SW2d 793.—Const Law 3310; Gr Jury 2.5, 19.

Flores v. State, TexApp–Beaumont, 215 SW3d 520, petition for discretionary review gr.—Const Law 656, 990, 1030, 1144, 1170, 1295, 1414, 3051, 3417, 3423, 3781, 4509(14); Crim Law 13.1(1), 338(1), 338(7), 369.2(2), 369.2(4), 795(1.5), 795(2.10), 1036.1(4), 1036.9, 1153(1), 1173.1, 1173.2(4); Homic 503, 580, 581, 1456, 1457; Ind & Inf 189(8).

Flores v. State, TexApp–Waco, 48 SW3d 397, reh overr, and petition for discretionary review refused.—Crim Law 338(7), 417(14), 553, 561(1), 737(1), 741(1), 742(1), 747, 822(1), 1030(1), 1036.5, 1038.1(2), 1038.2, 1134(3), 1144.13(3), 1147, 1153(1), 1159.2(2), 1159.2(7), 1162, 1165(1), 1169.1(9), 1172.1(1), 1172.1(3); Homic 1174; Jury 34(2); Witn 379(1), 383, 386, 388(2.1), 389.

Flores v. State, TexApp–Eastland, 164 SW3d 435, petition for discretionary review refused.—Crim Law 1144.13(1), 1144.13(2.1), 1159.2(2), 1159.2(7); Homic 1168.

Flores v. State, TexApp–Eastland, 102 SW3d 336, petition for discretionary review refused.—Sent & Pun 2004.

Flores v. State, TexApp–Eastland, 102 SW3d 328, petition stricken, and petition for discretionary review refused.—Crim Law 552(1), 1144.13(2.1), 1158(1), 1159.2(2), 1159.2(7), 1159.2(9), 1159.4(2), 1159.6, 1167(3); Homic 581, 603, 850, 1165; Ind & Inf 55, 60, 88, 108.

Flores v. State, TexApp–Eastland, 936 SW2d 478, petition for discretionary review refused.—Crim Law 1177; Rob 30.

Flores; State v., TexApp–Eastland, 856 SW2d 614, reh den, and petition for discretionary review refused.—Searches 102.

Flores v. State, TexApp–Corpus Christi, 129 SW3d 169, reh overr.—Crim Law 394.6(1), 394.6(3), 695(2), 899, 1036.1(5), 1042, 1044.2(1), 1044.2(2), 1045.

Flores v. State, TexApp–Corpus Christi, 42 SW3d 277.—Crim Law 641.13(1), 641.13(7), 795(2.1), 795(2.10), 795(2.80), 814(1), 1038.1(1), 1038.1(2), 1038.3, 1038.4, 1134(2).

Flores; State v., TexApp–Corpus Christi, 951 SW2d 134.—Courts 97(6); Crim Law 577.7, 577.10(1), 577.10(6), 577.10(7), 577.10(9), 577.10(10), 577.12(1), 577.12(2), 577.15(1), 577.15(3), 577.15(4), 577.16(4), 577.16(8), 735, 1118, 1139, 1144.7, 1151, 1158(1); Hab Corp 775(1); Ind & Inf 7.

Flores v. State, TexApp–Corpus Christi, 934 SW2d 858.—Weap 4.

Flores v. State, TexApp–Corpus Christi, 894 SW2d 803, reh overr, and petition for discretionary review refused.—Crim Law 1035(3), 1040, 1159.2(7); Homic 1181.

Flores; State v., TexApp–Corpus Christi, 878 SW2d 651, review gr, aff 896 SW2d 198.—Autos 344, 351.1; Homic 659; Ind & Inf 109, 121.1(6.1), 136.

Flores v. State, TexApp–Corpus Christi, 853 SW2d 139.—Crim Law 1077.3.

Flores v. State, TexApp–Corpus Christi, 827 SW2d 416, petition for discretionary review refused.—Crim Law 394.4(6), 394.6(4), 1044.2(1), 1158(2); Searches 113.1, 114, 121.1.

Flores v. State, TexApp–Corpus Christi, 824 SW2d 704, petition for discretionary review refused.—Crim Law 394.1(1); Searches 23, 67.1, 192.1.

Flores v. State, TexApp–Corpus Christi, 778 SW2d 526.—Crim Law 713, 718, 730(6), 1171.3, 1186.1; Ind & Inf 55, 110(2); Rape 20, 59(4).

Flores v. State, TexApp–Corpus Christi, 754 SW2d 419.—Controlled Subs 34, 82; Crim Law 1159.2(7), 1159.6.

Flores v. State, TexApp–Corpus Christi, 664 SW2d 426.—Crim Law 1033.2, 1134(6), 1158(1); Sent & Pun 2006, 2020, 2021.

Flores v. State, TexApp–Corpus Christi, 654 SW2d 14, petition for discretionary review gr, petition for discretionary review dism 676 SW2d 364.—Crim Law 438(6), 1174(2); Double J 107.1; Homic 1152.

FLORES;

Flores v. State, TexApp–Corpus Christi, 647 SW2d 363.—Crim Law 577.10(10), 577.16(8), 577.16(9).

Flores v. State, TexApp–Houston (14 Dist), 172 SW3d 742.—Arrest 63.5(4); Const Law 4460; Crim Law 394.6(5), 1134(6), 1139, 1153(1), 1158(1), 1158(4); Searches 23, 24, 171, 179.1, 180, 181, 183, 198.

Flores v. State, TexApp–Houston (14 Dist), 33 SW3d 907, petition for discretionary review refused.—Const Law 3306, 4505; Crim Law 13.1(1), 92, 99, 304(9), 304(12), 1028, 1035(5), 1134(2), 1134(3), 1144.1, 1144.13(2.1), 1144.13(3), 1144.13(5), 1147, 1149, 1159.2(1), 1159.2(2), 1159.2(7), 1159.2(8), 1159.2(9), 1159.4(2), 1167(1); Ind & Inf 11.1, 43, 55, 56, 58.1, 60, 65, 71.2(3), 75(1), 107.1, 110(3), 110(4), 136, 196(5); Jury 33(5.15); Mun Corp 122.1(2), 621; Obscen 2.5, 6, 11, 12, 17; Statut 188.

Flores v. State, TexApp–Houston (14 Dist), 967 SW2d 481.—Arrest 63.5(4), 63.5(5), 63.5(6); Crim Law 1134(3), 1139, 1158(1); Searches 23.

Flores v. State, TexApp–Houston (14 Dist), 942 SW2d 735.—Crim Law 1173.2(3); Obst Just 18.

Flores v. State, TexApp–Houston (14 Dist), 915 SW2d 651, petition for discretionary review refused.—Crim Law 438(1), 438(8), 665(4), 1134(3).

Flores v. State, TexApp–Houston (14 Dist), 681 SW2d 94, petition for discretionary review gr, aff 690 SW2d 281.—Crim Law 511.1(1), 511.1(7), 791, 899, 1137(5), 1159.2(7), 1159.6, 1165(1), 1169.1(9), 1169.7; Homic 1167, 1465, 1551.

Flores v. Sullivan, CA5 (Tex), 945 F2d 109, reh den.—Fed Civ Proc 2533.1; Social S 146.

Flores; Sullivan v., TexComApp, 132 SW2d 110, 134 Tex 55, conformed to 137 SW2d 799, writ dism woj.—App & E 1114; Autos 201(1.1), 245(55); Neglig 387.

Flores v. Sullivan, TexCivApp–San Antonio, 137 SW2d 799, writ dism woj.—App & E 231(1), 231(9), 1004(13); Trial 232(5).

Flores v. Sullivan, TexCivApp–San Antonio, 112 SW2d 321, rev 132 SW2d 110, 134 Tex 55, conformed to 137 SW2d 799, writ dism woj.—App & E 616(1); Autos 201(6); Neglig 381, 386, 387, 1713.

Flores v. Texas Dept. of Health, TexApp–Austin, 835 SW2d 807, writ den.—Admin Law 483, 484.1, 676, 817.1; Environ Law 17, 358, 387, 698; Evid 265(7), 265(15).

Flores; Texas Emp. Ins. Ass'n v., TexCivApp–Fort Worth, 564 SW2d 831, ref nre.—Work Comp 1981.

Flores; Texas Emp. Ins. Ass'n v., TexCivApp–El Paso, 603 SW2d 330.—Trial 118, 124; Work Comp 847, 1639, 1940.

Flores v. Texas Emp. Ins. Ass'n, TexCivApp–El Paso, 515 SW2d 938.—App & E 882(1), 968; Jury 131(2); Work Comp 1362, 1492, 1929, 1965, 1968(1).

Flores v. Texas Property And Cas. Ins. Guar. Ass'n ex rel. Paula Ins. Co., TexApp–San Antonio, 167 SW3d 397, reh overr, and review den, and reh of petition for review den.—Time 8.5; Work Comp 1874, 1914.

Flores; Tower Contracting Co. v., Tex, 302 SW2d 396, 157 Tex 297.—App & E 1178(6), 1201(3); Contracts 152, 164, 198(1), 232(1), 321(1).

Flores; Tower Contracting Co. v., TexCivApp–Galveston, 294 SW2d 266, mod 302 SW2d 396, 157 Tex 297.—App & E 766, 999(2), 1050.1(2), 1172(3); Contracts 75(2), 198(1), 199(1), 313(1), 324(1); Damag 124(1), 124(4), 163(4), 189; Impl & C C 65.

Flores; TransAmerican Natural Gas Corp. v., Tex, 870 SW2d 10.—Mand 3(2.1), 4(4), 12, 53; Pretrial Proc 404.1, 407; Witn 219(1).

Flores; U.S. v., CA5 (Tex), 404 F3d 320.—Aliens 772; Crim Law 1139; Ind & Inf 144.1(1), 144.2; Statut 184, 188.

Flores; U.S. v., CA5 (Tex), 135 F3d 1000, reh den, cert den 119 SCt 846, 525 US 1091, 142 LEd2d 700, reh den 119 SCt 1135, 525 US 1188, 143 LEd2d 128.—Const Law 191; Crim Law 700(6), 1134(6), 1586, 1660; Lim of Act 6(1); Statut 181(1), 263.

Flores; U.S. v., CA5 (Tex), 63 F3d 1342, reh and sug for reh den U.S. v. Garza, 77 F3d 481, cert den 117 SCt 87, 519 US 825, 136 LEd2d 43, reh den 117 SCt 542, 519 US 1022, 136 LEd2d 426, stay den In re Garza, 253 F3d 201, stay den Garza v Lappin, 253 F3d 918, cert den 121 SCt 2543, 533 US 924, 150 LEd2d 708.—Autos 349(2.1), 349.5(3); Crim Law 396(2), 406(2), 412.2(5), 423(3), 444, 451(4), 517(7), 613, 627.7(2), 627.7(3), 627.7(5), 627.8(6), 629(1), 629(3.1), 629(4), 655(1), 656(2), 656(5), 700(4), 700(9), 721(3), 730(1), 741(3), 769, 798.5, 822(1), 1036.1(5), 1038.1(2), 1038.1(3.1), 1038.2, 1134(2), 1134(5), 1139, 1151, 1152(2), 1153(1), 1158(4), 1166(7), 1167(1), 1172.1(1); Homic 581, 1562; Ind & Inf 55, 110(3); Jury 90, 97(1), 97(2), 103(14), 108, 131(4); Searches 186; Sent & Pun 8, 53, 67, 1618, 1625, 1652, 1660, 1665, 1780(2), 1780(3), 1784(2); U S 34.

Flores; U.S. v., CA5 (Tex), 985 F2d 770, reh den 1 F3d 1239, appeal after remand 40 F3d 385, denial of post-conviction relief aff 135 F3d 1000, reh den, cert den 119 SCt 846, 525 US 1091, 142 LEd2d 700, reh den 119 SCt 1135, 525 US 1188, 143 LEd2d 128.—Crim Law 622.3, 662.8, 662.9, 662.60, 1168(2).

Flores; U.S. v., CA5 (Tex), 981 F2d 231.—Crim Law 1134(3), 1147, 1602, 1668(2), 1668(5), 1668(9); Fed Civ Proc 2331, 2651.1; Fed Cts 825.1, 829; Hab Corp 441, 898(1).

Flores; U.S. v., CA5 (Tex), 887 F2d 543, reh den.—Crim Law 36.6, 1110(1); Int Rev 5128, 5264, 5290, 5295.

Flores; U.S. v., CA5 (Tex), 875 F2d 1110, denial of post-conviction relief aff 981 F2d 231.—Sent & Pun 1263, 1308, 1381(5).

Flores; U.S. v., CA5 (Tex), 616 F2d 840.—Crim Law 273.1(2), 1426(2), 1655(3); Sent & Pun 1155.

Flores; U.S. v., CA5 (Tex), 594 F2d 438.—Crim Law 394.4(12); Cust Dut 126(9.1).

Flores; U.S. v., CA5 (Tex), 564 F2d 717.—Controlled Subs 81; Crim Law 351(3).

Flores; U.S. v., CA5 (Tex), 531 F2d 222, cert den 97 SCt 484, 429 US 976, 50 LEd2d 584.—Cust Dut 126(5).

Flores; U.S. v., CA5 (Tex), 507 F2d 229.—Crim Law 1017; Sent & Pun 2285.

Flores v. U.S., CA5 (Tex), 379 F2d 905.—Crim Law 622.1(2), 622.2(3), 622.2(8), 622.2(9), 673(1), 867, 1134(8), 1169.5(1); Ind & Inf 130.

Flores v. U.S., CA5 (Tex), 234 F2d 604.—Crim Law 394.4(2); Searches 23, 40.1, 60.1, 201.

Flores; U.S. v., CA5 (Tex), 217 FedAppx 346.—Consp 51; Crim Law 371(1).

Flores; U.S. v., CA5 (Tex), 152 FedAppx 394.—Autos 349(14.1), 349(17), 349(18), 349.5(7).

Flores; U.S. v., CA5 (Tex), 149 FedAppx 262, cert den 126 SCt 1401, 546 US 1200, 164 LEd2d 102.—Crim Law 1042.

Flores; U.S. v., CA5 (Tex), 122 FedAppx 720, cert gr, vac 125 SCt 1994, 544 US 1015, 161 LEd2d 851, on remand 149 FedAppx 262, cert den 126 SCt 1401, 546 US 1200, 164 LEd2d 102.—Courts 90(2); Crim Law 1042; Jury 34(8); Sent & Pun 764, 832, 973.

Flores; U.S. v., CA5 (Tex), 102 FedAppx 400, cert den Cazares-Alvarado v. US, 125 SCt 366, 543 US 950, 160 LEd2d 268.—Controlled Subs 100(9).

Flores; U.S. v., CA5 (Tex), 95 FedAppx 528, cert den 124 SCt 2435, 541 US 1081, 158 LEd2d 998.—Sent & Pun 930.

Flores; U.S. v., CA5 (Tex), 79 FedAppx 723, cert den 124 SCt 1693, 541 US 952, 158 LEd2d 383.—Sent & Pun 686.

Flores; U.S. v., CA5 (Tex), 70 FedAppx 196, cert den 124 SCt 591, 540 US 1027, 157 LEd2d 448.—Sent & Pun 765.

Flores; U.S. v., CA5 (Tex), 70 FedAppx 172, cert den 124 SCt 933, 540 US 1079, 157 LEd2d 753.—Controlled Subs 100(9).

FLORES

See Guidelines for Arrangement at the beginning of this Volume

Flores v. Velasco, TexApp–Dallas, 68 SW3d 86.—Judges 51(2), 56.

Flores; Virgil T. Walker Const. Co., Inc. v., TexApp–Corpus Christi, 710 SW2d 159.—App & E 846(5); Trover 1, 3, 7, 10, 44, 54, 70.

Flores; Walker Const. Co., Inc. v., TexApp–Corpus Christi, 710 SW2d 159. See Virgil T. Walker Const. Co., Inc. v. Flores.

Flores; Wilhelm v., Tex, 195 SW3d 96.—Anim 66.9.

Flores; Wilhelm v., TexApp–Corpus Christi, 133 SW3d 726, reh overr, review gr, rev 195 SW3d 96.—Anim 66.9; App & E 213, 215(1), 237(5), 238(2), 294(1), 348(2), 930(3), 989, 994(2), 994(3), 999(1), 1001(1), 1001(3), 1002, 1003(3), 1003(6), 1003(7), 1004(3), 1079, 1140(1); Damag 208(6); Death 82, 89; Evid 588, 597; Neglig 202, 210, 212, 213, 214, 215, 220, 273, 371, 372, 387, 1692.

Flores; Williams v., Tex, 88 SW3d 631, on remand 2004 WL 1797574, reh overr, and petition stricken, and review den.—App & E 428(2); New Tr 116.2.

Flores; Williams v., TexApp–Corpus Christi, 90 SW3d 724, review gr, rev 88 SW3d 631, on remand 2004 WL 1797574, reh overr, and petition stricken, and review den.—App & E 428(2).

Flores-Chapa; U.S. v., CA5 (Tex), 48 F3d 156.—Consp 28(3), 47(12); Controlled Subs 31; Crim Law 719(4), 862, 1037.1(2), 1159.2(7), 1159.2(8).

Flores-Fernandez; U.S. v., SDTex, 418 FSupp2d 908.—Autos 326, 328, 349(4).

Flores-Garza v. I.N.S., CA5 (Tex), 328 F3d 797.—Aliens 385; Fed Cts 542, 611; Hab Corp 521, 842.

Flores-Garza v. Reno, SDTex, 369 FSupp2d 894.—Admin Law 753, 763, 791; Aliens 216.

Flores Gonzalez v. Viuda de Gonzalez, TexCivApp–Dallas, 466 SW2d 839, ref nre.—Judgm 185.3(13); Marriage 22, 50(5); Work Comp 998, 1471.

Flores-Guzman; U.S. v., CA5 (Tex), 121 FedAppx 557, cert den 125 SCt 2313, 544 US 1055, 161 LEd2d 1101.—Crim Law 1042.

Flores-Leal; U.S. v., CA5 (Tex), 134 FedAppx 691.—Crim Law 148.1.

Flores-Ochoa; U.S. v., CA5 (Tex), 139 F3d 1022, cert den 118 SCt 2383, 524 US 959, 141 LEd2d 749.—Crim Law 641.13(1), 641.13(7), 1042, 1139.

Flores-Peraza; U.S. v., CA5 (Tex), 58 F3d 164, cert den 116 SCt 782, 516 US 1076, 133 LEd2d 733.—Aliens 773; Crim Law 1139; Double J 131, 139.1.

Floresville Elec. Power & Light System, City of; Texas Dept. of Transp. v., TexApp–San Antonio, 53 SW3d 447.—App & E 893(1); Autos 187(4); Courts 39; Electricity 17; Joint Adv 1.2(1), 1.12; Mun Corp 723, 847; Plead 101, 104(1), 111.36, 111.37; States 112.2(2), 191.6(1), 191.10.

Florey; Holland v., TexCivApp–Texarkana, 151 SW2d 926.—Princ & S 200(7).

Florey v. Estate of McConnell, TexApp–Austin, 212 SW3d 439, reh overr, and review den.—Action 13; App & E 893(1), 984(5); Costs 194.40, 207; Home 1, 3, 5, 15, 31, 33, 90, 116, 124, 154, 161, 181(3), 181.5, 214, 216; Hus & W 276(9); Quiet T 1, 7(1), 27, 54; Tresp to T T 1, 50.

Florey Common School Dist. No. 5 of Andrews County v. Board of School Trustees of Andrews County, TexCivApp–El Paso, 126 SW2d 536, writ refused.—Schools 38.

Florez; American General Ins. Co. v., TexCivApp–Houston, 327 SW2d 643.—App & E 216(3), 671(1), 900; Evid 528(1), 528(2); Work Comp 1396, 1418, 1639, 1661, 1704, 1724, 1968(3), 1969.

Florez v. State, TexCrimApp, 479 SW2d 683.—Sent & Pun 1352.

Florez v. State, TexCrimApp, 158 SW2d 72, 143 TexCrim 160.—Crim Law 1172.6, 1173.1.

Florez v. State, TexApp–Dallas, 936 SW2d 681, petition for discretionary review refused.—Jury 149.

Florez-Florez; U.S. v., CA5 (Tex), 74 FedAppx 363.—Crim Law 1134(2), 1181.5(8); Sent & Pun 779, 787.

Florida Aircraft Exchange, Inc.; Beagles and Elliott Enterprises, LLC v., CA5 (Tex), 70 FedAppx 185.—Fed Civ Proc 1942.

Florida Dept. of Ins. v. Chase Bank of Texas Nat. Ass'n, CA5 (Tex), 274 F3d 924, reh den 31 FedAppx 837, cert den 122 SCt 2294, 535 US 1097, 152 LEd2d 1052.—Estop 54, 55, 87; Fed Civ Proc 103.2, 103.3, 103.4, 2544; Fed Cts 776; Fraud 20, 29; Insurance 1407; Trusts 181(1), 234.

Florida Gas Transmission Co.; Nicor Exploration Co. v., TexApp–Corpus Christi, 911 SW2d 479, reh overr, and writ den.—Action 60; App & E 78(1), 80(6), 782, 949, 1178(1).

Florida Power Corp.; Brown Schools, Inc. v., WDTex, 806 FSupp 146.—Fed Cts 106; Labor & Emp 407, 677; States 18.51.

Florida Power Corp.; Oaks Treatment Center v., WDTex, 806 FSupp 146. See Brown Schools, Inc. v. Florida Power Corp.

Florida Treco, Inc.; Edmundson Inv. Co. v., Tex, 640 SW2d 859.—Mtg 375.

Florida Treco, Inc.; Edmundson Inv. Co. v., TexApp–Houston (14 Dist), 633 SW2d 599, ref nre, ref nre 640 SW2d 859, cert den 103 SCt 1776, 460 US 1085, 76 LEd2d 348.—Const Law 4416; Estop 68(1); Judgm 715(1), 829(3); Mtg 529(6), 529(9).

Florio; State v., TexCrimApp, 845 SW2d 849.—Double J 81, 88.1, 89, 131, 150(1).

Florio v. State, TexCrimApp, 784 SW2d 415.—Infants 13.

Florio v. State, TexCrimApp, 568 SW2d 132.—Crim Law 1166.16; Jury 131(4), 131(8), 131(13).

Florio v. State, TexCrimApp, 532 SW2d 614.—Crim Law 338(4), 369.2(5), 641.12(1), 785(7), 1169.5(2), 1169.5(3), 1170.5(1), 1170.5(6), 1171.1(1); Rape 59(10); Witn 328, 414(2).

Florio v. State, TexApp–Fort Worth, 626 SW2d 189.—Crim Law 655(4), 1166.22(1).

Florio v. State, TexApp–Houston (14 Dist), 814 SW2d 778, petition for discretionary review gr, aff 845 SW2d 849.—Double J 55, 95.1, 99, 104, 136, 150(1), 161.

Florio v. State, TexApp–Houston (14 Dist), 758 SW2d 351, petition for discretionary review gr, rev 784 SW2d 415.—Crim Law 13.1(1); Infants 13, 20.

Florsheim Co. v. Miller, EDTex, 575 FSupp 84.—Counties 129; Pub Contr 23.

Flota Mercante Grancolombiana, S. A.; Gulf Stevedore Corp. v., CA5 (Tex), 401 F2d 537.—Ship 84(6).

Flota Mercante Grancolombiana, S.A.; Harrison v., CA5 (Tex), 577 F2d 968.—Adm 1.15, 50, 80; Fed Cts 841, 853, 868, 870.1, 875; Interest 38(1), 39(2.25); Neglig 282, 372, 378, 383, 484; Prod Liab 14, 15, 43; Ship 73, 84(3.2), 84(3.3), 84(6), 85.

Flota Mercante Grancolombiana, S. A.; Lattin v., SDTex, 290 FSupp 893.—Ship 84(6).

Flota Mercante Grancolombiana, S.A.; O'Neill v., SDTex, 589 FSupp 1028. See Medina v. O'Neill.

Flo Trend Systems, Inc. v. Allwaste, Inc., TexApp–Houston (14 Dist), 948 SW2d 4, reh overr.—Action 27(1); App & E 215(1), 216(2); Frds St of 17, 23(1), 159; Plead 245(1); Trial 29(3), 139.1(17).

Flour Bluff Independent School Dist. v. Bass, Tex, 133 SW3d 272.—Lim of Act 121(1); Work Comp 1874, 1885.

Flour Bluff Independent School District v. Katherine M. by Lesa T., CA5 (Tex), 91 F3d 689, cert den Katherine M by Lesa T v. Flour Bluff Independent School Dist, 117 SCt 948, 519 US 1111, 136 LEd2d 836.—Schools 154(2.1), 155.5(2.1).

Flour Bluff Independent School Dist.; Obersteller for Obersteller v., SDTex, 874 FSupp 146.—Civil R 1070, 1346, 1395(2); Const Law 4212(1); Schools 163.

Flour Bluff Oil Corp.; Railroad Commission of Tex. v., TexCivApp–Austin, 219 SW2d 506, writ refused.—Mines 92.44(2).

Flournoy, Ex parte, Tex, 312 SW2d 488, 158 Tex 425.—Contempt 44, 48, 52; Indians 27(2); Mental H 41.

Flournoy; Brazosport Bank of Texas v., TexApp–Tyler, 985 SW2d 281, review den, and reh of petition for review overr.—App & E 835(2).

Flournoy v. Flournoy, TexCivApp–El Paso, 315 SW2d 150.—App & E 893(1); Divorce 27(1), 252.3(2).

Flournoy; Flournoy v., TexCivApp–El Paso, 315 SW2d 150.—App & E 893(1); Divorce 27(1), 252.3(2).

Flournoy v. Gallagher, TexCivApp–Eastland, 189 SW2d 108.—Sec Reg 253, 260, 293, 298.

Flournoy v. Kilday, CA5 (Tex), 260 F2d 909.—Hab Corp 528.1.

Flournoy v. State, TexCrimApp, 668 SW2d 380, on remand 670 SW2d 773, petition for discretionary review refused, untimely filed.—Burg 41(10); Crim Law 1144.13(3).

Flournoy v. State, TexCrimApp, 589 SW2d 705.—Const Law 4733(2); Crim Law 1036.9, 1090.15, 1147; Sent & Pun 1961, 2001, 2010, 2020, 2021, 2032.

Flournoy v. State, TexCrimApp, 481 SW2d 898.—Crim Law 1042, 1127; Sent & Pun 2029, 2030.

Flournoy v. State, TexCrimApp, 356 SW2d 147, 172 TexCrim 263.—Crim Law 959; Health 186(5).

Flournoy v. State, TexCrimApp, 254 SW2d 129.—Crim Law 1094(3).

Flournoy v. State, TexApp–Fort Worth, 670 SW2d 773, petition for discretionary review refused, untimely filed.—Crim Law 641.13(1), 641.13(2.1), 1036.2, 1130(2); Witn 410.

Flournoy v. State, TexApp–Fort Worth, 650 SW2d 526, petition for discretionary review gr, rev 668 SW2d 380, on remand 670 SW2d 773, petition for discretionary review refused, untimely filed.—Burg 2, 41(1), 41(4).

Flournoy; State v., TexApp–Houston (14 Dist), 187 SW3d 621.—Crim Law 1144.2, 1149, 1167(3); Gr Jury 30; Ind & Inf 136, 137(3), 140(1), 140(2).

Flournoy v. U.S. Aviation Underwriters, Inc., WDTex, 206 FSupp 237.—Fed Cts 342.

Flournoy v. Wilz, TexApp–Waco, 201 SW3d 833, reh overr, review gr, rev 228 SW3d 674.—Evid 87; Trusts 91, 102(1), 103(1), 107, 110, 352, 358(1), 376; Witn 309.

Flournoy Drilling Co.; Greene's Pressure Testing & Rentals, Inc. v., CA5 (Tex), 113 F3d 47, reh den (#96-20856).—Fed Cts 660.1, 660.20; Indem 30(5).

Flournoy Drilling Co. v. Walker, TexApp–Corpus Christi, 750 SW2d 911, writ den.—Ex & Ad 224; Liens 8; Mines 114.

Flournoy Production Co. v. Kain, TexApp–San Antonio, 626 SW2d 850.—Plead 111.15, 111.38, 111.39(4), 111.42(5); Venue 5.1, 7.5(2).

Flow v. Friesen, TexCivApp–San Antonio, 213 SW2d 873, ref nre.—App & E 1064.1(6), 1067; Evid 334(1); Food 3; Sales 1(4).

Flowdata, Inc.; Additive Controls & Measurement Systems, Inc. v., CAFed (Tex), 154 F3d 1345, reh den, in banc sug declined.—Contempt 55, 61(1); Inj 192, 226, 228; Judgm 713(1); Pat 282, 317, 324.54, 324.55(2).

Flowdata, Inc.; Additive Controls & Measurement Systems, Inc. v., CAFed (Tex), 96 F3d 1390, appeal after remand 154 F3d 1345, reh den, in banc sug declined.—Fed Civ Proc 2771(8); Fed Cts 10.1; Inj 192, 228; Pat 302.

Flowdata, Inc.; Additive Controls & Measurement Systems, Inc. v., CAFed (Tex), 986 F2d 476, on remand 1994 WL 425107, mod 1994 WL 749595, motion den 40 F3d 1249.—Pat 305, 317; Rem of C 19(6).

Flowdata, Inc. v. Cotton, SDTex, 871 FSupp 925, rev in part 62 F3d 1430, reh den, in banc sug declined.—Judgm 650, 701; Pat 266, 323.2(2); Stip 17(1).

Flowdata, Inc. v. Trugear, Inc., CAFed (Tex), 96 F3d 1390. See Additive Controls & Measurement Systems, Inc. v. Flowdata, Inc.

Flower v. Dort, TexApp–Fort Worth, 260 SW2d 685, ref nre.—Wills 435, 439, 440, 442, 457, 470(1), 470(2), 566.

Flower v. Federal Bureau of Investigation, WDTex, 448 FSupp 567.—Const Law 1228; Records 50, 54, 63, 65, 68.

Flower v. U. S., USTex, 92 SCt 1842, 407 US 197, 32 LEd2d 653, conformed to 462 F2d 1133.—Armed S 28; Const Law 2039.

Flower; U.S. v., CA5 (Tex), 452 F2d 80, rev 92 SCt 1842, 407 US 197, 32 LEd2d 653, conformed to 462 F2d 1133.—Armed S 2, 28; Const Law 1150, 1154, 1431, 1460, 1526, 1730, 4509(1).

Flowerette v. Heartland Healthcare Center, NDTex, 903 FSupp 1042.—Fed Cts 241, 246; Labor & Emp 757; Rem of C 25(1), 79(1), 103, 107(11); States 18.46.

Flower Mound, Tex., City of; Teague v., CA5 (Tex), 179 F3d 377.—Const Law 1928, 1929, 1930, 1955; Mun Corp 185(1).

Flower Mound, Town of; Crawford, Estate of v., TexApp–Fort Worth, 933 SW2d 727, reh overr, and writ den.—App & E 5, 174; Courts 472.4(2.1); Parties 76(7); Plead 123; Tax 2836, 2854, 2927.

Flower Mound, Town of; Freeman v., TexApp–Fort Worth, 173 SW3d 839.—Mun Corp 33(3); Statut 181(2), 188, 190, 206, 214.

Flower Mound, Town of; Hanson v., CA5 (Tex), 679 F2d 497.—Const Law 2583; Courts 90(2); Fed Civ Proc 642, 1742(1), 1742(2), 1832; Fed Cts 172, 219.1, 542, 571, 584, 654, 666, 712; Searches 85; Treaties 7, 8.

Flower Mound, Town of; Hanson v., TexCivApp–Fort Worth, 539 SW2d 178.—Mun Corp 956(1); Tax 2167, 2187, 2413, 2420.

Flowers, Ex parte, TexCrimApp, 136 SW2d 611, 138 TexCrim 359.—Hab Corp 817.1, 823.

Flowers v. Bauer, TexCivApp–Corpus Christi, 394 SW2d 526.—App & E 634, 653(1), 654; Wills 370.

Flowers v. Central Power & Light Co., TexCivApp–Waco, 314 SW2d 373, ref nre.—Evid 211; Judgm 185(2), 185(3), 185.3(21); Mal Pros 16; Witn 379(8.1).

Flowers v. Collins, TexCivApp–Austin, 357 SW2d 179, writ dism.—App & E 846(2), 846(5); Evid 181, 215(3); Lim of Act 103(4); Trial 105(4); Witn 178(1).

Flowers; Dallas Ry. & Terminal Co. v., TexCivApp–Waco, 284 SW2d 160, ref nre.—Autos 244(50), 246(31); Damag 130.2, 208(1); Jury 131(2); Neglig 1717; New Tr 20; Trial 108.5, 350.7(4).

Flowers v. Dempsey-Tegeler & Co., Tex, 472 SW2d 112.—Evid 5(2); Plead 111.3, 111.9, 111.42(6); Sec Reg 246, 302; Statut 181(1), 184.

Flowers; Dempsey-Tegeler & Co. v., TexCivApp–Beaumont, 465 SW2d 208, writ gr, rev 472 SW2d 112.—Const Law 990; Courts 247(1); Plead 111.36, 111.39(7), 111.42(6); Sec Reg 246, 302, 303.1, 306, 307, 308; Statut 212.1; Venue 3.

Flowers v. Diamond Oaks Terrace Apartments, TexApp–Fort Worth, 669 SW2d 432.—Forci E & D 38(1), 43(1).

Flowers v. Diamond Shamrock Corp., CA5 (Tex), 693 F2d 1146.—Accord 4, 8(1), 10(1), 11(1), 11(2), 26(3), 27; Mines 79.3; Nova 3.

Flowers v. Flowers, TexCivApp–Dallas, 589 SW2d 746.—App & E 1180(1), 1180(2); Child S 496; Contempt 63(1).

Flowers; Flowers v., TexCivApp–Dallas, 589 SW2d 746.—App & E 1180(1), 1180(2); Child S 496; Contempt 63(1).

Flowers v. Flowers, TexCivApp–Dallas, 585 SW2d 334.—App & E 544(1), 1177(8).

Flowers; Flowers v., TexCivApp–Dallas, 585 SW2d 334.—App & E 544(1), 1177(8).

Flowers v. Flowers, TexCivApp–Amarillo, 397 SW2d 121.—App & E 1046.3; Jury 97(1); New Tr 56; Trial 25(1).

FLOWERS;

Flowers; Flowers v., TexCivApp–Amarillo, 397 SW2d 121.—App & E 1046.3; Jury 97(1); New Tr 56; Trial 25(1).

Flowers v. Flowers, TexCivApp–Eastland, 433 SW2d 31, ref nre.—App & E 931(6); Child C 404; Child S 173; Marriage 6, 60(0.5), 66.

Flowers; Flowers v., TexCivApp–Eastland, 433 SW2d 31, ref nre.—App & E 931(6); Child C 404; Child S 173; Marriage 6, 60(0.5), 66.

Flowers; Houston Chronicle Pub. Co. v., TexCivApp–Beaumont, 413 SW2d 435.—Libel 7(11), 7(19), 9(1); Plead 111.34, 111.42(4), 111.45; Pretrial Proc 581, 583.

Flowers; Kansas City Southern Ry. Co. v., TexCivApp–Texarkana, 336 SW2d 235, ref nre.—Courts 89; R R 337(1), 352; Trial 358.

Flowers v. Klump, TexCivApp–Eastland, 121 SW2d 1025.—Witn 164(6), 164(7), 171.

Flowers v. Lavaca County Appraisal Dist., TexApp–Corpus Christi, 766 SW2d 825, writ den.—Autos 48; Courts 122; Tax 2640, 2849, 2855, 2927; Trial 405(2).

Flowers; L. H. Lacy Co. v., TexCivApp–Beaumont, 169 SW2d 790, writ dism.—App & E 339(2), 782, 1126.

Flowers v. Michulka, TexCivApp–Waco, 389 SW2d 367.—Land & Ten 49(2); Plead 291(2).

Flowers v. Muse, TexCivApp–San Antonio, 427 SW2d 727, writ refused.—App & E 387(2), 387(3); New Tr 155.

Flowers; Mustang Tractor & Equipment Co. of Houston v., TexCivApp–Beaumont, 596 SW2d 586.—Plead 111.39(2), 111.47.

Flowers v. Pan American Refining Corp., TexCivApp–Austin, 154 SW2d 982, writ refused.—Stip 14(10); Tax 2545.

Flowers v. Pecos River R. Co., Tex, 156 SW2d 260, 138 Tex 18.—Corp 37; Courts 247(8); R R 14; Statut 162.

Flowers v. Pecos River R. Co., TexCivApp–Austin, 152 SW2d 502, rev 156 SW2d 260, 138 Tex 18.—Corp 37; R R 14, 19; Statut 142, 158.

Flowers; Provident Life & Acc. Ins. Co. of Chattanooga v., TexCivApp–El Paso, 91 SW2d 847, writ dism.—App & E 273(5); Evid 213(1); Insurance 3001, 3003(3), 3013, 3016, 3091, 3096(2); Trial 194(11).

Flowers; Scott v., CA5 (Tex), 910 F2d 201, 108 ALR Fed 91.—Civil R 1390, 1480; Const Law 1929, 1933, 2050, 2052, 2085; Courts 509; Fed Civ Proc 2771(3); Fed Cts 224, 265, 541; J P 10; Offic 66.

Flowers v. Shearer, TexCivApp–Amarillo, 107 SW2d 1049, writ dism.—Int Liq 25, 29, 34(5); Statut 206.

Flowers v. State, TexCrimApp, 220 SW3d 919.—Autos 359.6; Sent & Pun 313, 322.

Flowers v. State, TexCrimApp, 935 SW2d 131, on remand 951 SW2d 883.—Crim Law 1026.10(4).

Flowers v. State, TexCrimApp, 843 SW2d 38, on remand 890 SW2d 906, reh overr.—Crim Law 1180; Rec S Goods 8(4).

Flowers v. State, TexCrimApp, 815 SW2d 724, on remand 824 SW2d 801, petition for discretionary review gr, rev 843 SW2d 38, on remand 890 SW2d 906, reh overr.—Ind & Inf 57, 110(18), 159(1), 159(2), 159(4), 161(1), 161(5).

Flowers v. State, TexCrimApp, 510 SW2d 605.—Crim Law 363, 1037.1(1), 1170.5(5).

Flowers v. State, TexCrimApp, 482 SW2d 268.—Crim Law 260.11(2), 730(3), 1043(2); Sent & Pun 94; Witn 286(2).

Flowers v. State, TexCrimApp, 415 SW2d 178.—Crim Law 438(3); Larc 64(7).

Flowers v. State, TexCrimApp, 252 SW2d 191, 157 TexCrim 635.—Crim Law 1174(2).

Flowers v. State, TexCrimApp, 203 SW2d 539, 150 TexCrim 467.—Autos 359; Crim Law 1184(2).

Flowers v. State, TexCrimApp, 202 SW2d 462, 150 TexCrim 467, opinion supplemented 203 SW2d 539, 150 TexCrim 467.—Autos 346, 355(13); Crim Law 847,

1038.2, 1169.5(1), 1169.5(3); Ind & Inf 132(5); Sent & Pun 1804; Witn 379(1), 379(3).

Flowers v. State, TexCrimApp, 165 SW2d 1001.—Crim Law 1094(2.1).

Flowers v. State, TexApp–Houston (1 Dist), 124 SW3d 801, petition for discretionary review refused.—Crim Law 641.13(6).

Flowers v. State, TexApp–Houston (1 Dist), 959 SW2d 644, petition for discretionary review refused.—Crim Law 1035(6), 1166.16.

Flowers v. State, TexApp–Fort Worth, 696 SW2d 303.—Ind & Inf 5.

Flowers v. State, TexApp–San Antonio, 951 SW2d 883.—Crim Law 268, 273.1(2), 275, 1134(3).

Flowers v. State, TexApp–El Paso, 890 SW2d 906, reh overr.—Const Law 4581, 4694; Crim Law 312, 552(1), 700(2.1), 755.5, 761(1), 761(6), 1032(5), 1038.1(1), 1134(2), 1144.13(3), 1159.2(7), 1172.1(1), 1172.7; Ind & Inf 105, 110(18), 159(2); Larc 32(1), 58; Rec S Goods 8(3), 8(4); Statut 188.

Flowers v. State, TexApp–El Paso, 824 SW2d 801, petition for discretionary review gr, rev 843 SW2d 38, on remand 890 SW2d 906, reh overr.—Crim Law 1144.13(2.1), 1159.2(7), 1159.2(9), 1159.3(2); Rec S Goods 7(6).

Flowers v. State, TexApp–El Paso, 785 SW2d 890, petition for discretionary review gr, rev 815 SW2d 724, on remand 824 SW2d 801, petition for discretionary review gr, rev 843 SW2d 38, on remand 890 SW2d 906, reh overr.—Crim Law 13.1(1), 1167(4); Ind & Inf 105, 156, 159(1), 159(2), 159(4); Larc 2.

Flowers v. State, TexApp–Beaumont, 133 SW3d 853.—Crim Law 335, 564(1), 564(2), 564(4), 641.13(1), 641.13(6), 641.13(7), 713, 717, 720(2), 720(6), 720(7.1), 723(3), 726; Sent & Pun 1287.

Flowers; State v., TexCivApp–Dallas, 94 SW2d 193.—States 112.1(1), 112.2(1).

Flowers v. Steelcraft Corp., Tex, 406 SW2d 199.—Plead 111.39(1), 111.42(1).

Flowers v. Steelcraft Corp., TexCivApp–Amarillo, 398 SW2d 796, writ gr, rev 406 SW2d 199.—Parties 95(1); Plead 76, 106(1), 111.42(1), 111.47.

Flowers v. Texas Alcoholic Beverage Com'n, TexApp–Beaumont, 782 SW2d 343, writ den.—Int Liq 59(1), 59(2).

Flowers v. Texas Alcoholic Beverage Com'n, TexApp–Beaumont, 777 SW2d 781, on reh 782 SW2d 343, writ den.—Admin Law 677, 784.1, 791; Int Liq 75(6), 75(7).

Flowers; Texas & N. O. R. Co. v., TexCivApp–Beaumont, 336 SW2d 907, ref nre.—App & E 752, 1004(14), 1052(1); Damag 132(12); Evid 90; R R 348(1), 348(8), 350(13); Trial 114, 235(4).

Flowers v. Texas Dept. of Human Resources, Tarrant County Welfare Unit, TexApp–Fort Worth, 629 SW2d 891.—App & E 931(1), 931(3), 989; Evid 596(1); Infants 178, 252.

Flowers v. Texas Mexican Ry. Co., TexCivApp–Austin, 174 SW2d 70.—Statut 219(10); Tax 2295, 2781.

Flowers v. Travelers Ins. Co., CA5 (Tex), 258 F2d 220, cert den 79 SCt 591, 359 US 920, 3 LEd2d 582, reh den 79 SCt 741, 359 US 956, 3 LEd2d 764.—Work Comp 262, 2085.

Flowers v. Turbine Support Division, CA5 (Tex), 507 F2d 1242.—Fed Civ Proc 2734; Fed Cts 596, 932.1.

Flowers v. United Ins. Co. of America, TexApp–Houston (14 Dist), 807 SW2d 783.—App & E 863, 934(1), 1177(1); Insurance 3015, 3571; Judgm 181(23).

Flowers v. Warlick, TexCivApp–El Paso, 142 SW2d 274.—App & E 773(4).

Flowers v. Wiley, CA5 (Tex), 675 F2d 704.—Elections 12(10).

Flowers v. Wilson, TexCivApp–Austin, 319 SW2d 199.—Autos 244(7), 244(35); New Tr 102(2); Trial 350.5(3), 350.7(8).

Flowers; York v., TexApp–San Antonio, 872 SW2d 13, reh den, and writ den.—App & E 863; Child 3, 86; Judgm 181(15.1), 185(2), 186; Quiet T 29; Ten in C 15(2), 15(10).

Flowserve Corp.; Ryan v., NDTex, 444 FSupp2d 718.— Fed Cts 580, 660.1, 660.5.

Floyd, In re, BkrtcyNDTex, 37 BR 890.—Bankr 3312.

Floyd v. Bowen, CA5 (Tex), 833 F2d 529, reh den 838 F2d 1214.—Fed Civ Proc 173; Fed Cts 12.1; Social S 140.15, 140.30, 143.65, 149.5.

Floyd v. Chief Medical Director of UTMB, CA5 (Tex), 210 FedAppx 387.—Civil R 1091; Fed Cts 915.

Floyd; City of Paris v., TexApp–Texarkana, 150 SW3d 224.—App & E 863, 916(1); Labor & Emp 29; Mun Corp 745, 845(2); Plead 111.34, 111.43, 111.48.

Floyd v. C.I.R., CA5 (Tex), 309 F2d 95.—Int Rev 3254.

Floyd; Conner v., TexCivApp–Dallas, 95 SW2d 183, writ dism.—App & E 544(1); Wills 324(2), 386.

Floyd v. Continental State Bank, TexCivApp–Texarkana, 212 SW2d 945, writ refused.—Judgm 462.

Floyd; Continental State Bank of Big Sandy v., TexComApp, 114 SW2d 530, 131 Tex 388.—Prohib 5(3).

Floyd; Dews v., TexCivApp–Tyler, 413 SW2d 800.—Action 45(2); Can of Inst 32, 58; Equity 54; Forci E & D 6(2), 16(0.5); Judgm 16, 27, 577(1), 577(2), 660.5; J P 119.2, 130; Land & Ten 291(14); Ven & Pur 299(3).

Floyd v. Dunson, BkrtcySDTex, 209 BR 424. See Ramirez Rodriguez, In re.

Floyd v. Eggleston, TexCivApp–El Paso, 137 SW2d 182, writ refused, cert den 61 SCt 314, 311 US 708, 85 LEd 460, reh den 61 SCt 609, 312 US 713, 85 LEd 1143.—Inj 219; Judgm 403, 456(1), 590(2), 590(3).

Floyd; Ellington v., TexCivApp–Galveston, 255 SW2d 948.—Child C 602; Venue 21.

Floyd; F.D.I.C. v., NDTex, 854 FSupp 449.—Bills & N 491, 492, 499; Sec Tran 165, 231.

Floyd; F.D.I.C. v., NDTex, 827 FSupp 409.—Banks 505.

Floyd v. Floyd, TexApp–El Paso, 813 SW2d 758, writ den.—Judgm 181(15.1); Wills 440, 470(2), 471, 472, 486, 487(2), 491, 497(4).

Floyd; Floyd v., TexApp–El Paso, 813 SW2d 758, writ den.—Judgm 181(15.1); Wills 440, 470(2), 471, 472, 486, 487(2), 491, 497(4).

Floyd; Gray v., TexApp–Houston (1 Dist), 783 SW2d 214.—App & E 994(2); Damag 191; Evid 570, 588, 594.

Floyd; Harbor Perfusion, Inc. v., TexApp–Corpus Christi, 45 SW3d 713.—App & E 842(2), 893(1), 946, 954(1), 954(2); Inj 12, 26(3), 126, 138.1, 138.6, 138.39, 189.

Floyd; Hart v., TexCivApp–San Antonio, 558 SW2d 578.—Names 14, 18.

Floyd; Hayes v., TexApp–Beaumont, 881 SW2d 617.—App & E 949; Mand 3(2.1), 4(1), 4(4), 12, 26.

Floyd; Henderson v., Tex, 891 SW2d 252.—Atty & C 19, 21.15, 21.20.

Floyd; Homsy v., CA5 (Tex), 51 F3d 530. See Vitek, Inc., Matter of.

Floyd; Houston Oilers, Inc. v., TexCivApp–Hous (1 Dist), 518 SW2d 836, ref nre.—Contracts 278(1); Release 25, 38.

Floyd; King v., TexCivApp–Hous (1 Dist), 538 SW2d 166, ref nre.—Exemp 48(2).

Floyd v. MMD, BkrtcySDTex, 209 BR 424. See Ramirez Rodriguez, In re.

Floyd; Mobil Oil Corp. v., TexApp–Beaumont, 810 SW2d 321, reh of motion for mandamus overr.—Mand 32; Mental H 16, 18, 162, 165; Pretrial Proc 99, 202; Witn 39, 45(1), 78.

Floyd; Nueces County v., TexCivApp–Corpus Christi, 609 SW2d 271, ref nre.—App & E 1051.1(2), 1078(1); Em Dom 280; Indem 64; Waters 179(4); Witn 37(2).

Floyd v. Organ, TexCivApp–Austin, 359 SW2d 190, ref nre.—Damag 185(1), 208(6).

Floyd v. Park Cities People, Inc., TexApp–Dallas, 685 SW2d 96.—App & E 1024.4, 1041(2), 1073(1); Torts 340, 350, 357.

Floyd; Paul v., TexCivApp–Texarkana, 337 SW2d 632, writ refused.—Autos 181(2).

Floyd; Powers v., TexApp–Waco, 904 SW2d 713, reh overr, and writ den, cert den 116 SCt 941, 516 US 1126, 133 LEd2d 866.—App & E 852, 934(1); Health 906; Infants 2; Neglig 1692.

Floyd v. Rice, TexCivApp–Beaumont, 444 SW2d 834, ref nre.—Home 164; Mech Liens 14, 173.

Floyd v. Scofield, CA5 (Tex), 193 F2d 594.—Int Rev 3066, 3100, 3115, 3896.

Floyd v. Seward, TexCivApp–El Paso, 520 SW2d 873.—Adop 7.4(6), 15.

Floyd v. Shindler, BkrtcySDTex, 204 BR 510. See Rodriguez, In re.

Floyd v. State, TexCrimApp, 983 SW2d 273.—Crim Law 145.5.

Floyd v. State, TexCrimApp, 768 SW2d 307.—Crim Law 1072.

Floyd v. State, TexCrimApp, 575 SW2d 21, appeal dism 99 SCt 2817, 442 US 907, 61 LEd2d 272.—Const Law 4509(23); Crim Law 13.1(1); Prost 14, 17; Statut 47, 188.

Floyd v. State, TexCrimApp, 494 SW2d 828.—Controlled Subs 68, 80; Crim Law 1159.2(2), 1159.3(3.1).

Floyd v. State, TexCrimApp, 488 SW2d 830.—Judges 29; Sent & Pun 2021.

Floyd v. State, TexCrimApp, 296 SW2d 523, 164 TexCrim 50.—Crim Law 437, 448(1), 814(17), 878(2), 881(1), 1036.1(2), 1120(3), 1169.2(1); Embez 26, 29, 44(6); Ind & Inf 125(19.1), 125(27), 128, 132(4), 203; Larc 5; Witn 225.

Floyd v. State, TexCrimApp, 255 SW2d 864.—Crim Law 1090.1(1).

Floyd v. State, TexCrimApp, 249 SW2d 215.—Crim Law 1090.1(1).

Floyd v. State, TexCrimApp, 243 SW2d 171.—Crim Law 1086.13.

Floyd v. State, TexCrimApp, 176 SW2d 946, 146 TexCrim 529.—Int Liq 236(3).

Floyd v. State, TexCrimApp, 115 SW2d 948, 134 TexCrim 439.—Int Liq 233(2), 236(7), 239(1).

Floyd v. State, TexCrimApp, 113 SW2d 894, 133 TexCrim 614.—Crim Law 1097(5), 1099.7(2).

Floyd v. State, TexCrimApp, 106 SW2d 301, 132 TexCrim 541.—Crim Law 1182.

Floyd v. State, TexCrimApp, 82 SW2d 645, 128 TexCrim 592.—Crim Law 511.6; Larc 62(1).

Floyd v. State, TexApp–Fort Worth, 959 SW2d 706.—Crim Law 367, 474.4(1), 474.4(4), 479, 577.4, 577.8(2), 577.10(3), 577.10(6), 577.10(7), 577.10(10), 577.12(2), 577.14, 577.15(1), 577.15(3), 577.15(4), 577.16(8), 641.10(3), 698(1), 899, 1043(3), 1139, 1144.13(3), 1144.13(6), 1158(1), 1159.2(2), 1159.2(9), 1159.4(2); Sod 6.

Floyd v. State, TexApp–Fort Worth, 710 SW2d 807, petition for discretionary review gr, petition for discretionary review dism with per curiam opinion 768 SW2d 307.—Const Law 4666; Crim Law 393(1), 641.3(8.1).

Floyd v. State, TexApp–Texarkana, 914 SW2d 658, reh overr, and petition for discretionary review refused.—Crim Law 145.5, 273(1), 273.1(2), 275, 516, 641.13(5), 938(2), 1031(4), 1063(1), 1134(4), 1144.13(3), 1159.2(7), 1183; Evid 207(4); Sent & Pun 60.

Floyd v. State, TexApp–Texarkana, 914 SW2d 656, reh overr, and petition for discretionary review gr, rev 983 SW2d 273.—Crim Law 145.5, 147; Ind & Inf 196(1).

Floyd v. State, TexApp–Eastland, 662 SW2d 683.—Crim Law 665(1), 1171.5.

Floyd; Texas & P. Ry. Co. v., TexCivApp–Dallas, 309 SW2d 525, ref nre.—Neglig 1713; R R 337(6).

FLOYD;

Floyd; Texas Liquor Control Bd. v., TexCivApp–Fort Worth, 117 SW2d 530.—App & E 31; Int Liq 61(1), 106(4), 108.10(6), 108.10(7), 108.10(8), 108.10(10), 110.

Floyd; U.S. v., CA5 (Tex), 343 F3d 363, cert den 124 SCt 2190, 541 US 1054, 158 LEd2d 752, leave to file for reh den, leave to file for reh den 125 SCt 349, 543 US 940, 160 LEd2d 251, appeal after new sentencing hearing 122 FedAppx 98, cert den 127 SCt 141, 166 LEd2d 103. —Consp 23.1, 48.1(3); Const Law 4581, 4709; Crim Law 369.2(1), 370, 371(1), 730(3), 1139, 1144.13(2.1), 1144.13(5), 1153(1), 1158(1), 1159.2(7), 1159.2(9), 1159.4(1), 1171.1(2.1), 1171.8(1); Ind & Inf 113; Jury 34(1); Postal 35(2), 35(6), 35(8), 35(20); Sent & Pun 300, 725, 975, 976, 982.

Floyd; U.S. v., CA5 (Tex), 992 F2d 498, reh den 997 F2d 883, appeal after remand 84 F3d 433.—Crim Law 1023(3); Forfeit 3.

Floyd; U.S. v., CA5 (Tex), 681 F2d 265.—Controlled Subs 116; Crim Law 444.

Floyd; U.S. v., CA5 (Tex), 122 FedAppx 98, cert den 127 SCt 141, 166 LEd2d 103.—Crim Law 1023(11), 1023(14).

Floyd; U.S. v., NDTex, 814 FSupp 1355, rev 992 F2d 498, reh den 997 F2d 883, appeal after remand 84 F3d 433, dism 35 F3d 562.—Forfeit 3, 4, 5.

Floyd; U.S. v., SDTex, 65 FSupp2d 487.—Const Law 2815; Sent & Pun 1828.

Floyd v. U.S. Dept. of Treasury, Office of Comptroller of Currency, NDTex, 809 FSupp 24.—Banks 251; Const Law 4282.

Floyd v. Willacy County Hosp. Dist., TexApp–Corpus Christi, 706 SW2d 731, ref nre.—App & E 173(2); Civil R 1395(1); Const Law 3045, 3054; Death 15; Health 770; Judgm 181(33).

Floyd; Woodson v., TexCivApp–Waco, 195 SW2d 601, ref nre.—Trial 350.2; Ven & Pur 144(2), 148.

Floydada, City of; American La France & Foamite Industries v., NDTex, 15 FSupp 390, mod 87 F2d 820. —Mun Corp 254, 868(1).

Floydada, City of; Massie v., TexCivApp–Amarillo, 112 SW2d 243.—App & E 1060.1(2.1); Em Dom 149(2.1), 196, 219, 262(5); Evid 543(3); Mun Corp 63.15(2), 269(2); Trial 114, 139.1(3).

Floydada Housing Authority; Eliserio v., SDTex, 455 FSupp2d 648.—Assoc 20(1); Fed Civ Proc 103.2, 103.3, 1773, 1829, 1832, 1835; Fed Cts 12.1; Labor & Emp 2721, 2724; Statut 181(1), 181(2), 188, 190, 205, 208, 217.4, 219(2).

Floydada Housing Authority; Eliserio v., SDTex, 388 FSupp2d 774.—Fed Cts 101, 103, 104, 106.5, 144; Labor & Emp 2729.

Floydada Housing Authority; Eliserio v., SDTex, 388 FSupp2d 771, subsequent determination 388 FSupp2d 774.—Fed Cts 101, 104, 106.5; Labor & Emp 2729.

Floyd County v. Clements, TexCivApp–Amarillo, 150 SW2d 447, writ dism, correct.—Em Dom 136, 149(6), 202(1), 241, 262(5); Trial 351.2(5).

Floyd County; Clements v., TexCivApp–Amarillo, 107 SW2d 380, writ dism.—Em Dom 238(1), 238(4), 238(5), 252; J P 164(2).

Floyd West & Co.; Johnson v., TexCivApp–Dallas, 437 SW2d 298.—Evid 596(1); Judgm 181(21), 185(2), 185(5), 185.1(1), 186; Princ & A 78(6).

Floyd West & Co.; Yancey v., TexApp–Fort Worth, 755 SW2d 914, writ den.—App & E 170(1); Insurance 1725, 1817, 1822, 1827, 2264, 2266, 2385, 2914, 2931, 3081.

Floyd West & Co.; Yancey Agency v., TexApp–Fort Worth, 755 SW2d 914. See Yancey v. Floyd West & Co.

F L R Corp. v. Blodgett, TexCivApp–El Paso, 541 SW2d 209, ref nre, appeal dism 98 SCt 386, 434 US 915, 54 LEd2d 273.—App & E 218.2(3.1), 302(1), 499(4), 756, 758.3(3), 846(5); Courts 475(1), 475(13); Frds St of 56(2); Mtg 338, 342, 369(7), 369(8), 372(3); New Tr 150(2); Tresp to T T 6.1, 39(2), 41(2); Trial 365.1(4).

Flucas; U.S. v., CA5 (Tex), 99 F3d 177, cert den 117 SCt 1097, 519 US 1156, 137 LEd2d 229.—Crim Law 1139, 1158(1); Sent & Pun 726(3), 764, 765, 963.

Fluellen v. Board of Ed. of Dallas County, TexCivApp–Amarillo, 202 SW2d 510.—Inj 108, 123, 126.

Fluellen v. State, TexCrimApp, 194 SW2d 556, 149 TexCrim 376.—Crim Law 949(2), 1064.5; Forg 44(3); Sent & Pun 1888.

Fluellen v. State, TexApp–Texarkana, 104 SW3d 152.— Const Law 656, 4626; Controlled Subs 64, 100(1); Courts 40; Crim Law 404.15, 404.30, 444, 446, 566, 639.1, 639.4, 695(2), 695(4), 763(24), 789(4), 822(1), 1030(2), 1030(3), 1032(5), 1038.1(1), 1043(3), 1044.2(1), 1130(5), 1134(2), 1134(3), 1134(8), 1144.1, 1144.13(2.1), 1153(1), 1159.2(7), 1172.2; Ind & Inf 113, 166; Sent & Pun 323, 368, 2283; Statut 63, 64(6).

Fluellen v. State, TexApp–Texarkana, 71 SW3d 870, petition for discretionary review refused.—Crim Law 1023(3), 1042, 1134(10), 1482; Rape 30; Sent & Pun 313, 1482, 1503.

Fluellen v. Young, TexApp–Corpus Christi, 664 SW2d 776.—App & E 692(1), 719(8), 1032(2), 1032(3); Frds St of 129(3), 159; Judgm 181(29), 185(2), 185.3(18), 186.

Flugrath v. Brickstone Products Corp., TexCivApp–Austin, 411 SW2d 426.—App & E 395; Corp 513.1; Plead 111.3, 111.42(6).

Fluid Concepts, Inc. v. DA Apartments Ltd. Partnership, TexApp–Dallas, 159 SW3d 226, reh overr.—App & E 856(1); Damag 163(3); Judgm 181(15.1).

Fluitt v. Employers Mut. Liability Ins. Co. of Wis., TexCivApp–San Antonio, 242 SW2d 649, dism.—Work Comp 1937.

Fluitt; Richmond Mfg. Co., Inc. v., TexApp–San Antonio, 754 SW2d 359.—Const Law 4010; Judgm 151.

Fluitt v. State, TexCrimApp, 333 SW2d 144, 169 TexCrim 259.—Autos 355(6); Crim Law 478(1), 553, 554.

Fluitt v. Valley Stockyards Co., TexCivApp–San Antonio, 384 SW2d 917, ref nre.—App & E 882(7), 1051(1); Evid 318(1), 355(1), 474(19); Sales 215, 218.5; Trial 350.3(4).

Fluker; Gaylor v., TexApp–Houston (14 Dist), 843 SW2d 234.—Pretrial Proc 699.

Flukinger v. Lehman, TexCivApp–Hous (14 Dist), 619 SW2d 442.—Decl Judgm 300; Judgm 181(24).

Flukinger; Prince v., TexCivApp–Texarkana, 381 SW2d 75.—App & E 1170.7; Bound 37(1); Evid 358, 383(7).

Flukinger v. Straughan, TexApp–Houston (14 Dist), 795 SW2d 779, writ den.—Antitrust 397; Evid 142(1), 383(7), 574, 601(4); Fraud 35, 58(1), 58(4), 59(1); Jury 28(12); Lim of Act 41, 139; Mines 51(3), 64.

Flume v. State Bar of Texas, TexApp–San Antonio, 974 SW2d 55, reh overr, and rule 537(f) motion gr.—App & E 497(1), 760(1), 1079; Atty & C 47.1, 48, 53(1), 53(2), 54, 56, 57, 58, 59; Const Law 4273(3).

Fluor Corp. v. Carpenters Dist. Council of Houston and Vicinity and Millwrights Local No. 2232, CA5 (Tex), 424 F2d 283.—Fed Cts 743; Labor & Emp 1545.

Fluor Corp.; Dotson v., WDTex, 492 FSupp 313.—Const Law 191, 3965(3); Corp 642(4.5); Courts 100(1); Fed Cts 33, 76.15.

Fluor Corp. v. Gulf Interstate Gas Co., CA5 (Tex), 259 F2d 405.—Pat 27(1).

Fluor Corp. v. Gulf Interstate Gas Co., SDTex, 152 FSupp 448, aff 259 F2d 405.—Pat 16.17, 17(1), 66(1.19).

Fluor Corp.; Texas Gas Exploration Corp. v., TexApp–Texarkana, 828 SW2d 28, writ gr, and writ den, and writ withdrawn.—Const Law 197, 2315, 2811, 3454, 3971; Contracts 176(2); Judgm 185(2); Lim of Act 6(1), 104(2), 195(5).

Fluor Daniel, Inc. v. Boyd, TexApp–Corpus Christi, 941 SW2d 292, reh overr, and writ den.—App & E 215(4), 231(9), 930(1), 946, 1001(3); Labor & Emp 871, 874; Trial 182, 186, 203(1), 219, 228(1).

FLYNT

Fluor Daniel, Inc. v. H.B. Zachry Co., Inc., TexApp–Corpus Christi, 1 SW3d 166, reh overr, and petition for review den, and reh of petition for review overr, on remand 2001 WL 35832899, appeal dism 2001 WL 1000711, appeal after remand 2005 WL 2559773, review den.—Judgm 570(9), 713(2), 715(1), 715(3), 720, 724, 829(3).

Fluor Daniel, Inc.; Lyondell Petrochemical Co. v., Tex-App–Houston (1 Dist), 888 SW2d 547, writ den.—App & E 970(2), 1050.1(1), 1056.1(1), 1056.1(3); Contrib 9(6); Evid 506, 512, 555.2, 568(1); Trial 43, 56.

Fluor Engineering and Constructors, Inc.; Ford v., TexApp–Beaumont, 711 SW2d 327, ref nre.—Labor & Emp 3096(10); Neglig 253, 1205(7), 1672.

Fluor Engineers and Constructors, Inc. v. Southern Pacific Transp. Co., CA5 (Tex), 753 F2d 444, reh den 760 F2d 269, reh den Southern Pacific Transp Co v. Norfolk & Western Ry Co, 760 F2d 269.—Alt Disp Res 143, 154, 386; Carr 120, 132; Fed Civ Proc 422, 551; Fed Cts 422.1; Lim of Act 129; R R 222(1), 222(5).

Fluor Enterprises, Inc., In re, TexApp–Austin, 186 SW3d 639, mandamus den.—App & E 946; Courts 247(2), 483, 487(3), 488(4); Mand 1.

Fluor Enterprises, Inc. v. Solutia Inc., SDTex, 147 FSupp2d 648.—Alt Disp Res 444; Contracts 143(2), 176(2).

Fluorine On Call, Ltd. v. Fluorogas Ltd., CA5 (Tex), 380 F3d 849.—Consp 1.1; Copyr 107, 109; Corp 1.5(1), 1.6(2); Costs 194.32; Damag 89(2); Fed Civ Proc 675.1, 2491.7, 2515, 2737.4; Fed Cts 830, 878; Fraud 3, 12, 17, 24, 25; Mun Corp 247; Torts 212, 215, 242.

Fluorogas Ltd.; Fluorine On Call, Ltd. v., CA5 (Tex), 380 F3d 849.—Consp 1.1; Copyr 107, 109; Corp 1.5(1), 1.6(2); Costs 194.32; Damag 89(2); Fed Civ Proc 675.1, 2491.7, 2515, 2737.4; Fed Cts 830, 878; Fraud 3, 12, 17, 24, 25; Mun Corp 247; Torts 212, 215, 242.

Fluor Western, Inc. v. G & H Offshore Towing Co., CA5 (Tex), 447 F2d 35, cert den 92 SCt 959, 405 US 922, 30 LEd2d 793.—Contracts 1, 108(1); Fed Cts 743; Ship 104.

Flurry v. Hillcrest State Bank of University Park, TexCivApp–Texarkana, 401 SW2d 857, ref nre.—Banks 181; Bills & N 131; Usury 42, 100(1).

Flurry; Texas Workers' Compensation Com'n v., Tex-App–Houston (1 Dist), 908 SW2d 43, reh overr, and writ den.—Work Comp 1030.1(1).

Flusche; Five Star Transfer & Terminal Warehouse Corp. v., TexCivApp–Texarkana, 339 SW2d 384, ref nre. —Corp 1.4(4), 1.6(2); Fraud 30; Judgm 199(3.14); Plead 22.

Flusche v. Uselton, TexCivApp–Austin, 201 SW2d 58.—Adj Land 5; App & E 927(7); Estop 110; Fraud 31; Judgm 143(2), 143(6), 153(1); Ven & Pur 36(1), 79.

Fluty v. Simmons Co., TexApp–Dallas, 835 SW2d 664.—App & E 304; Judgm 163; New Tr 6, 155.

Fly v. Fly, TexCivApp–Corpus Christi, 590 SW2d 179.—App & E 544(1), 1177(9); Divorce 146, 160, 186, 317.

Fly; Fly v., TexCivApp–Corpus Christi, 590 SW2d 179.—App & E 544(1), 1177(9); Divorce 146, 160, 186, 317.

Fly; Hodge v., TexCivApp–San Antonio, 105 SW2d 778.—Chat Mtg 219.

Fly v. State, TexCrimApp, 550 SW2d 684.—Bail 39, 53, 74(1).

Flye v. City of Waco, TexApp–Waco, 50 SW3d 645.—App & E 893(1); Judgm 185(2); Mun Corp 851; Neglig 273, 1085, 1197.

Flying Boat, Inc., In re, BkrtcyNDTex, 245 BR 241, aff in part, rev in part US v. McConnell, 258 BR 869.—Bankr 2534, 2543.

Flying J, Inc.; Padilla v., TexApp–Dallas, 119 SW3d 911. —App & E 171(1), 842(2), 931(1), 946, 989, 1008.1(2), 1010.1(2), 1012.1(4); Civil R 1183, 1189, 1736, 1744, 1773; Trial 393(1).

Flying-P Ranch and Cycle Park v. Moore, Tex, 711 SW2d 622. See Pope v. Moore.

Flying Tiger Line, Inc.; Hewlett Knitting Mills, Inc. v., TexApp–Dallas, 669 SW2d 412.—Carr 159(2), 405(3).

Flynn v. Aetna Cas. & Sur. Co., CA5 (Tex), 698 F2d 758. —Labor & Emp 405, 552(2).

Flynn v. Atlas Life Ins. Co., TexCivApp–Austin, 81 SW2d 772.—Plead 129(1); Usury 22; Venue 22(6), 59.

Flynn; Box v., TexApp–San Antonio, 870 SW2d 585.—Antitrust 390, 392; App & E 671(1), 836, 907(1), 930(3), 932(1), 989, 1003(6), 1004(11), 1004(12), 1032(1); Contracts 322(3); Damag 87(1), 94; Fraud 3, 43, 58(1), 62; Labor & Emp 936, 950; Plead 250; Trover 61.

Flynn; Genell, Inc. v., Tex, 358 SW2d 543, 163 Tex 632.—Land & Ten 167(8); Neglig 213, 387, 1018, 1037(4), 1102, 1228, 1267.

Flynn; Genell, Inc. v., TexCivApp–Texarkana, 348 SW2d 196, writ gr, rev 358 SW2d 543, 163 Tex 632.—App & E 930(3); Neglig 506(8), 1014, 1037(4), 1286(6), 1286(7), 1670, 1679; Trial 140(1).

Flynn; Gulf Plains Grain & Elevator Co. v., TexCivApp–Waco, 430 SW2d 526.—Corp 503(2); Venue 5.3(2), 8.5(2).

Flynn v. Gulf Plains Grain & Elevator Co., TexCivApp–Waco, 430 SW2d 525.—Plead 110.

Flynn v. Houston Emergicare, Inc., TexApp–Houston (1 Dist), 869 SW2d 403, reh overr, and writ den.—Health 752, 800.

Flynn v. Moszkowicz, TexCivApp–Corpus Christi, 469 SW2d 303.—App & E 954(1); Inj 135, 147, 151; Mtg 335, 338.

Flynn v. Pan American Hotel Co., Tex, 183 SW2d 446, 143 Tex 219.—Land & Ten 164(1), 164(2), 164(3), 165(1), 165(2), 165(6), 169(5), 169(6), 169(11).

Flynn v. Pan American Hotel Co., TexCivApp–San Antonio, 179 SW2d 849, aff 183 SW2d 446, 143 Tex 219.—Land & Ten 164(1), 165(6), 169(4), 169(5).

Flynn v. Savings and Profit Sharing Plan for Employees of Republic of Texas Corp., NDTex, 558 FSupp 861, aff 698 F2d 758.—Hus & W 265; Labor & Emp 405, 552(2).

Flynn v. State, TexCrimApp, 707 SW2d 87.—Infants 68.4, 68.8.

Flynn v. State, TexCrimApp, 82 SW2d 980, 128 TexCrim 513.—Crim Law 1087.1(1), 1121(1).

Flynn v. State, TexCrimApp, 81 SW2d 525, 128 TexCrim 333.—Crim Law 369.1, 784(1); Larc 55.

Flynn v. State, TexApp–El Paso, 667 SW2d 235, petition for discretionary review gr, aff 707 SW2d 87.—Adop 6, 7.1, 9.1, 13; Crim Law 239, 241, 1166(1), 1170(1); Homic 525, 1301; Infants 68.2, 68.6, 68.7(3), 78(1); Judges 16(1).

Flynn; Stephen F. Austin State University v., TexApp–Tyler, 202 SW3d 167, rev 228 SW3d 653.—App & E 893(1), 916(1); Autos 252, 258; Colleges 5; Courts 39; Mun Corp 728, 847; Neglig 1000, 1040(3), 1045(3), 1706; Plead 34(1), 104(1), 111.36, 111.39(0.5), 111.43, 111.48; States 112.1(1), 112.1(2), 191.4(1), 191.6(2).

Flynn Bros., Inc. v. First Medical Associates, TexApp–Dallas, 715 SW2d 782, ref nre.—App & E 173(6); Contracts 138(1); Health 108, 164.

Flynn Inv. Co.; McConnell v., TexCivApp–El Paso, 480 SW2d 58.—App & E 781(4).

Flynt; Braun v., CA5 (Tex), 731 F2d 1205.—Fed Civ Proc 2174, 2336; Fed Cts 907.

Flynt; Braun v., CA5 (Tex), 726 F2d 245, reh den 731 F2d 1205, cert denChic Magazine, Inc v. Braun, 105 SCt 252, 469 US 883, 83 LEd2d 189.—Action 38(4); Const Law 1545; Damag 49.10, 94; Libel 25, 48(1), 51(5), 103, 112(1), 112(2), 117, 119, 120(2), 121(1), 123(2), 123(6); States 4.1(2); Torts 330, 355, 366, 370, 378.

Flynt v. City of Kingsville, TexComApp, 82 SW2d 934, 125 Tex 510.—App & E 635(2); Judgm 17(9).

Flynt v. Garcia, Tex, 587 SW2d 109.—Courts 30, 170.

Flynt; Garcia v., TexCivApp–Hous (14 Dist), 574 SW2d 587, rev 587 SW2d 109.—Courts 169(1), 170; Hus & W 281.

Flyr; Miller v., TexCivApp–Amarillo, 447 SW2d 195, ref nre.—Wills 50, 55(1), 158, 166(7), 401.

F.M., In re, TexApp–Houston (14 Dist), 183 SW3d 489.—App & E 1010.1(1); Const Law 4338, 4454; Mental H 36, 41, 51.15.

F.M., Matter of, TexApp–Amarillo, 792 SW2d 564.—Infants 199, 243, 253.

F. M. C. Corp. v. Burns, TexCivApp–San Antonio, 444 SW2d 315.—App & E 1050.1(7), 1062.1, 1069.1; Evid 150; Judges 46; New Tr 56; Trial 215, 350.3(6).

FMC Corp.; Herrera v., TexApp–Houston (14 Dist), 672 SW2d 5, ref nre.—App & E 230, 1012.1(3); Evid 506, 512; Prod Liab 81.1, 85, 90; Trial 56.

F.M.C. Corp.; Martinez v., TexApp–Corpus Christi, 666 SW2d 654, dism.—Venue 16.5.

FMC Corp.; Moody v., CA5 (Tex), 995 F2d 63.—Fed Civ Proc 821, 824, 828.1, 834, 837, 840, 2213; Fed Cts 817.

FMC Corp.; Stearns Airport Equipment Co., Inc. v., CA5 (Tex), 170 F3d 518.—Antitrust 620, 621, 641, 650, 832, 833, 838, 896, 905(2), 976; Fed Civ Proc 2546, 2553, 2736, 2738; Fed Cts 766, 830, 895.

FMC Corp.; Stearns Airport Equipment Co., Inc. v., NDTex, 977 FSupp 1269, aff 170 F3d 518.—Antitrust 650, 656, 832, 833, 972(3); Fed Civ Proc 2546; Torts 213.

FMC Corp.; Stearns Airport Equipment Co., Inc. v., NDTex, 977 FSupp 1263.—Action 14; Antitrust 14, 904; Aviation 101, 102; Corp 445.1, 542(1); Fed Civ Proc 2484; States 18.17; Torts 203.

FMC Corp. v. Varco Intern., Inc., CA5 (Tex), 677 F2d 500.—Inj 138.33.

FMC Corp., Fluid Control Div.; Lodge No. 12 of Dist. 37, Intern. Ass'n of Machinists and Aerospace Workers, AFL-CIO v., SDTex, 551 FSupp 83.—Contracts 143(1), 176(1); Evid 397(2), 398, 428, 441(6), 448; Labor & Emp 1113, 1245, 1275, 1279, 1321, 1691, 1855.

FMC Corp., Niagara Chemical Division; Harper v., TexCivApp–Waco, 407 SW2d 854.—Acct Action on 14; Evid 318(7); Plead 111.42(9).

FMC Technologies Inc.; Grice v., CA5 (Tex), 216 FedAppx 401.—Civil R 1135, 1246, 1252, 1505(4), 1514.

F. M. Equipment Co.; Collins v., Tex, 347 SW2d 575, 162 Tex 423.—Courts 247(7); Plead 111.9, 111.42(5); Venue 7.5(6).

F. M. Equipment Co.; Collins v., TexCivApp–Dallas, 340 SW2d 867, writ gr, rev 347 SW2d 575, 162 Tex 423.—Plead 291(2); Venue 7.5(1), 7.5(6).

FMF Associates 1990-A, Ltd.; Arkoma Basin Exploration Co., Inc. v., TexApp–Dallas, 118 SW3d 445, reh overr, and review gr.—App & E 238(1), 238(2), 294(1), 930(2), 1004(13), 1073(1), 1073(7); Fraud 3, 6, 11(1), 12, 21, 25, 58(1), 58(3), 59(2), 62, 64(1); Neglig 463, 481; New Tr 162(1); Partners 354.

FMI Contracting Corp. v. Federal Ins. Co., TexApp–Fort Worth, 829 SW2d 907, writ dism woj.—U S 67(1), 67(4), 67(12).

F.M.I. Properties Corp.; Schwartz v., TexApp–Houston (14 Dist), 714 SW2d 97, ref nre.—Courts 29; Judgm 335(3), 930, 942.

FM Properties Operating Co. v. City of Austin, CA5 (Tex), 93 F3d 167.—Civil R 1428; Const Law 3844, 3877, 3895, 4092, 4093; Fed Cts 6, 611, 617; Zoning 6, 372.6, 561, 672.

FM Properties Operating Co. v. City of Austin, Tex, 22 SW3d 868, reh overr.—App & E 852, 870(2), 1175(1); Const Law 656, 969, 990, 2340, 2400, 2407, 2442; Environ Law 166, 188; Statut 219(1).

FM Properties Operating Co.; Travis Cent. Appraisal Dist. v., TexApp–Austin, 947 SW2d 724, reh overr, and review den.—Tax 2135, 2160, 2291, 2515, 2761.

F. M. Short Co.; United Coin Meter Co. v., TexCivApp–Waco, 585 SW2d 914, ref nre.—Venue 15.

F. M. Stigler, Inc. v. H. N. C. Realty Co., TexCivApp–Dallas, 595 SW2d 158, rev Land Title Co of Dallas, Inc v. F M Stigler, Inc, 609 SW2d 754.—Contracts 143(2), 176(2), 346(3); Princ & A 96, 97, 99, 147(2), 148(4), 166(1), 171(1), 189(4).

F. M. Stigler, Inc.; Land Title Co. of Dallas, Inc. v., Tex, 609 SW2d 754.—Contracts 338(1); Plead 403(1), 403(3); Princ & A 166(1), 169(1), 171(1), 171(7), 172.

F.N. Fausing Trading ApS v. Estate of Barbouti, TexApp–Houston (1 Dist), 851 SW2d 314, reh overr, and writ den.—App & E 893(1), 946; Const Law 3954; Pretrial Proc 44.1, 46, 225, 226.

FNFS, Ltd. v. Security State Bank and Trust, TexApp–Austin, 63 SW3d 546, reh overr, and review den.—App & E 852; Banks 138, 154(8); Judgm 185(2).

Fo; U.S. v., CA5 (Tex), 226 FedAppx 346.—Controlled Subs 100(9).

Foale; Riebe v., TexCivApp–Corpus Christi, 508 SW2d 175.—Frds St of 110(1), 158(3).

Foam Rubber Products, Inc. v. Jimenez, TexCivApp–Fort Worth, 451 SW2d 801, ref nre Foam Rubber Prod, Inc v. Jimenez, 457 SW2d 276.—Inj 138.1; Trademarks 1704(1).

Fobbs v. State, TexCrimApp, 468 SW2d 392.—Crim Law 444; Sent & Pun 1419; Witn 40(2).

Focke, Wilkens & Lange v. Heffron, TexCivApp–Galveston, 197 SW 1027, writ refused.—Mun Corp 621.

Fodge v. American Motorist Ins. Co., TexApp–Dallas, 64 SW3d 43, review gr, rev 63 SW3d 801.—App & E 893(1); Insurance 3335, 3336; Plead 104(1), 111.37, 111.38, 111.39(0.5); Pretrial Proc 554; Work Comp 1042, 1072, 2093, 2215.

Fodge; American Motorists Ins. Co. v., Tex, 63 SW3d 801.—Courts 40; Pretrial Proc 554; Work Comp 999, 1001, 1042, 1087.

Fodor; Bunting v., TexCivApp–Hous (1 Dist), 586 SW2d 144.—Antitrust 205; Sales 272, 441(3).

Foerster v. Peoples, TexCivApp–Amarillo, 362 SW2d 918.—App & E 1062.4; Trial 350.1, 352.12.

Fogarty v. U.S., CA5 (Tex), 263 F2d 201, cert den 79 SCt 1437, 360 US 919, 3 LEd2d 1534.—Crim Law 412(3), 656(9), 721(1), 728(1), 728(3), 1030(1), 1038.1(5), 1038.3, 1055, 1172.1(1).

Fogel v. C. I. R., CA5 (Tex), 203 F2d 347.—Int Rev 4722; Time 5, 9(1).

Fogel v. International Paper Co., CA5 (Tex), 517 F2d 358.—Indem 65.

Fogel; Timmons v., TexCivApp–Dallas, 278 SW2d 549.—Contracts 282, 322(4), 350(3); Damag 124(2), 140; Judgm 199(1).

Fogel v. U.S., CCA5 (Tex), 167 F2d 763, cert gr 69 SCt 39, 335 US 811, 93 LEd 366, rev 69 SCt 136, 335 US 865, 93 LEd 411.—Crim Law 938(2), 938(3), 1156(3).

Fogel v. U.S., CCA5 (Tex), 162 F2d 54, cert den 68 SCt 99, 332 US 791, 92 LEd 373.—Armed S 20.11, 40(7); Crim Law 150, 398(2).

Fogel v. White, TexApp–Houston (14 Dist), 745 SW2d 444.—Garn 1, 4, 24, 42; Mand 36.

Fogel, Ltd.; Shoemake v., Tex, 826 SW2d 933.—Contrib 1, 5(4), 5(6.1), 9(5); Death 24; Parent & C 11; Plead 78.

Fogel, Ltd. A.T. v. Shoemake, TexApp–Fort Worth, 795 SW2d 903, writ gr, rev 826 SW2d 933.—Contrib 5(5).

Fogerson v. State, TexCrimApp, 269 SW2d 407.—Crim Law 1090.1(1).

Foggle v. State, TexApp–Fort Worth, 632 SW2d 402.—Crim Law 377, 577.8(1), 577.10(8), 577.12(1), 1032(4), 1043(2), 1170(1); Witn 337(3).

Fogle v. Coxsey, TexCivApp–Eastland, 295 SW2d 471, ref nre.—Mines 54.5.

Fogle v. Southwestern Bell Telephone Co., WDTex, 800 FSupp 495.—Civil R 1711; Fed Cts 433; Jury 13(1), 13(5.1), 14(1.5).

Fogle v. State, TexCrimApp, 339 SW2d 664, 170 TexCrim 168.—Crim Law 1170.5(5); Rape 52(1).

Fogle v. State, TexCrimApp, 111 SW2d 246, 133 TexCrim 312.—Crim Law 814(17); Int Liq 138, 222, 236(20); Jury 59(1).

Fogle v. State, TexApp–Fort Worth, 988 SW2d 891, petition for discretionary review refused.—Autos 332, 355(6); Crim Law 721(1), 721(3), 1171.5.

Fogle v. State, TexApp–Dallas, 667 SW2d 296.—Const Law 2574; Sent & Pun 1963, 1982(2), 1982(3).

Fogle Equipment Corp.; Bucyrus-Erie Co. v., TexApp–Houston (14 Dist), 712 SW2d 202, ref nre.—Labor & Emp 3038(2), 3096(5); Trial 260(7).

Fogleman v. ARAMCO, CA5 (Tex), 920 F2d 278. See Fogleman v. ARAMCO (Arabian American Oil Co.).

Fogleman v. ARAMCO (Arabian American Oil Co.), CA5 (Tex), 920 F2d 278.—Adm 1.11, 1.15; Fed Civ Proc 2727, 2738, 2740; Fed Cts 776; Seamen 29(5.2).

Fogo v. State, TexCrimApp, 830 SW2d 592.—Const Law 4505; Crim Law 13.1(1); Elections 311, 317.2.

Fogo v. State, TexApp–Houston (14 Dist), 786 SW2d 777, petition for discretionary review gr, rev 830 SW2d 592. —Const Law 999; Elections 311; Statut 212.4.

Foight, Ex parte, TexCrimApp, 306 SW2d 132, 165 TexCrim 153.—Rob 30.

Foix v. Jordan, TexCivApp–El Paso, 421 SW2d 481, ref nre.—Ex & Ad 17(3); Judgm 199(3.2), 199(3.10); Marriage 11, 13.

Fojtik v. Charter Medical Corp., TexApp–Corpus Christi, 985 SW2d 625, reh overr, and review den.—False Imp 2, 5; Judgm 181(33), 183, 185(4).

Fojtik; First Nat. Bank of Beeville v., Tex, 775 SW2d 632.—App & E 882(18).

Fojtik v. First Nat. Bank of Beeville, TexApp–Corpus Christi, 752 SW2d 669, writ den with per curiam opinion 775 SW2d 632.—App & E 209.1, 218.1, 882(18), 1056.1(10); Consp 1.1, 2, 21; Evid 244(4).

Fojtik Auction & Equipment Co.; First Nat. Bank of Beeville v., Tex, 775 SW2d 632. See First Nat. Bank of Beeville v. Fojtik.

Fojtik Auction & Equipment Co. v. First Nat. Bank of Beeville, TexApp–Corpus Christi, 752 SW2d 669. See Fojtik v. First Nat. Bank of Beeville.

F. O. Ketcham Mortg. Co. v. Walker, TexCivApp–Austin, 94 SW2d 806, writ refused.—Bills & N 434, 437; Estop 52(1).

Folckemer; U.S. v., CA5 (Tex), 307 F2d 171.—Int Rev 3009, 3085, 3132.1.

Foley; Burnett v., TexApp–Fort Worth, 660 SW2d 884.—Brok 4.

Foley; Citizens Hotel Co. v., TexCivApp–Fort Worth, 131 SW2d 402, writ dism, correct.—App & E 1062.1, 1178(2); Arrest 63.1; Evid 83(2); False Imp 13, 15(2), 22, 31, 39; Trial 351.2(4).

Foley v. Cockrell, NDTex, 222 FSupp2d 826.—Hab Corp 603; Prisons 13(10).

Foley v. Currie, TexCivApp–Fort Worth, 189 SW2d 349, writ refused wom.—App & E 907(3); Frds St of 21; Lim of Act 28(1); Mech Liens 281(5).

Foley v. Farm & Home Sav. & Loan Ass'n, TexCivApp–Eastland, 81 SW2d 231.—B & L Assoc 33(5); Usury 72.

Foley v. Foley, TexCivApp–El Paso, 350 SW2d 890.—App & E 216(6), 218.2(1), 930(3); Divorce 135, 144, 148, 149; Trial 274.

Foley; Foley v., TexCivApp–El Paso, 350 SW2d 890.—App & E 216(6), 218.2(1), 930(3); Divorce 135, 144, 148, 149; Trial 274.

Foley v. Hughes, CA5 (Tex), 116 FedAppx 519.—Hab Corp 847; Judges 36.

Foley; Jess Edwards, Inc. v., TexCivApp–Waco, 321 SW2d 328.—App & E 930(1), 931(1), 994(3), 1010.1(3), 1012.1(2); Plead 34(1), 111.42(8).

Foley; Kupper, Magnus, Steckler v., CA5 (Tex), 145 F3d 320, 172 ALR Fed675. See Metro Ford Truck Sales, Inc. v. Ford Motor Co.

Foley v. Parlier, TexApp–Fort Worth, 68 SW3d 870, reh overr.—App & E 760(1), 930(1), 989, 994(2), 999(1), 1001(1), 1001(3), 1003(3), 1003(7), 1004(11), 1004(13), 1182; Damag 15, 91(1), 94, 117, 184; Elect of Rem 1, 3(1), 3(2); Fraud 3, 28, 32, 58(1), 59(2), 60, 61, 62.

Foley v. Smith, CA5 (Tex), 437 F2d 115.—Fed Cts 949.1, 951.1.

Foley v. Smith, CA5 (Tex), 421 F2d 698, appeal after remand 437 F2d 115.—Pat 326(4).

Foley v. Southwest Texas HMO, Inc., EDTex, 226 FSupp2d 886.—Estop 52(1); Fraud 31; Health 556(3), 941, 942, 952; Impl & C C 3, 30, 31, 55, 60.1; Insurance 1117(3); Labor & Emp 407, 676; Rem of C 19(5), 25(1); States 18.15, 18.51.

Foley v. Southwest Texas HMO, Inc., EDTex, 193 FSupp2d 903.—Insurance 1117(3); Labor & Emp 407, 699; Rem of C 2, 25(1); States 18.41, 18.51.

Foley v. State, TexCrimApp, 514 SW2d 449.—Crim Law 641.9, 641.10(2), 1035(7), 1077.1(4), 1077.3.

Foley v. State, TexCrimApp, 356 SW2d 686, 172 TexCrim 261.—Autos 356; Crim Law 377.

Foley v. State, TexCrimApp, 294 SW2d 838.—Crim Law 1090.1(1).

Foley v. State, TexCrimApp, 294 SW2d 832.—Crim Law 1090.1(1).

Foley v. State, TexCrimApp, 242 SW2d 887.—Crim Law 1087.1(2).

Foley; State v., TexApp–Austin, 950 SW2d 781.—Admin Law 229; App & E 893(1); Autos 74, 107(2), 108, 127; States 18.3, 18.5, 18.13, 18.21; Statut 270.

Foley v. University of Houston System, CA5 (Tex), 355 F3d 333.—Civil R 1113, 1242, 1246, 1335, 1340, 1354, 1359, 1376(1), 1376(2), 1376(10), 1421; Colleges 8.1(3); Const Law 1928, 1935; Fed Cts 579, 776.

Foley v. University of Houston System, CA5 (Tex), 324 F3d 310, opinion withdrawn and superseded 355 F3d 333.

Foley and Williams; Canton Motors v., TexCivApp–Tyler, 451 SW2d 521.—Impl & C C 61.

Foley Bros. Dry Goods Co.; Holland v., TexCivApp–Texarkana, 324 SW2d 430, writ refused.—App & E 387(3), 395; New Tr 155.

Foley Bros. Dry Goods Co.; Panos v., TexCivApp–Galveston, 198 SW2d 494.—App & E 781(4), 882(18); Equity 54.

Foley Bros. Dry Goods Co. v. Settegast, TexCivApp–Galveston, 133 SW2d 228, writ refused.—App & E 971(2), 1002; Evid 113(1), 113(11), 113(21), 498.5, 546; Land & Ten 200.5; Trial 85, 96.

Foley Bros. Dry Goods Corp.; Bullock v., TexApp–Austin, 802 SW2d 835, writ den.—Tax 3661, 3686, 3705.

Foley Co. v. Cox, TexApp–Houston (14 Dist, 679 SW2d 58. See Howard P. Foley Co. v. Cox.

Foley Newsom Oil Co. v. Crawford, TexCivApp–Hous (14 Dist), 515 SW2d 750.—Damag 57.40; Labor & Emp 900; Princ & A 3(1); Torts 438.

Foley's Dept. Store v. Gardner, TexCivApp–Hous (14 Dist), 588 SW2d 627.—App & E 1001(1); Neglig 1670; Trial 352.4(6), 352.10.

Folger Coffee Co. v. Olivebank, CA5 (Tex), 201 F3d 632. —Adm 118.7(5); Fed Civ Proc 2282.1; Ship 132(3.1), 132(4), 197.

Folk; Granger v., TexApp–Beaumont, 931 SW2d 390, reh overr, and mandamus overr.—Anim 3.5(8), 3.5(9), 3.5(10); Const Law 4310, 4500; Jury 10, 13(1), 17(1), 31.1.

Folk v. State, TexApp–Austin, 797 SW2d 141, petition for discretionary review refused.—Autos 332, 355(6); Crim Law 409(7), 535(2), 538(3), 1159.2(7).

Folkes v. Del Rio Bank and Trust Co., TexApp–San Antonio, 747 SW2d 443.—App & E 173(2); Judgm 183; Sec Tran 240.

Folks v. Kirby Forest Industries Inc., CA5 (Tex), 10 F3d 1173, reh den.—Fed Cts 776, 908.1; Neglig 253, 480, 1037(7), 1724, 1734.

Folks v. State, TexCrimApp, 334 SW2d 289, 169 TexCrim 340.—Bail 64.

Follak v. Brown, TexCivApp–Beaumont, 530 SW2d 882, ref nre.—Child C 550; Evid 80(1).

Follenfant v. Rogers, CA5 (Tex), 359 F2d 30.—Fed Civ Proc 51, 621; Insurance 3493.

Follett, Petition of, SDTex, 172 FSupp 304.—Ship 208, 209(1.6), 209(3).

Follett; MacDonald v., Tex, 180 SW2d 334, 142 Tex 616.—App & E 927(7); Mines 79.1; Partners 96; Spec Perf 105(2); Ten in C 3; Trusts 103(1), 108, 110, 111, 231(1), 343.

Follett; MacDonald v., TexCivApp–Galveston, 193 SW2d 287, writ refused.—App & E 1097(1); Trial 2; Trusts 110; Venue 70.

Follett; MacDonald v., TexCivApp–Galveston, 175 SW2d 671, aff 180 SW2d 334, 142 Tex 616.—Joint Ten 3, 8; Lim of Act 103(4), 199(1); Mines 48, 97, 101; Spec Perf 105(2); Ten in C 10, 19(1), 19(2), 34; Tresp to T T 35(1).

Follett; Prunell v., TexCivApp–Hous (14 Dist), 555 SW2d 761.—Bills & N 129(1), 129(2), 394, 405, 422(1); Judgm 181(25); Mtg 335, 360, 369(3).

Follett v. Voris, CA5 (Tex), 205 F2d 542, cert den 74 SCt 136, 346 US 885, 98 LEd 390.—Work Comp 878.

Follett v. Voris, SDTex, 104 FSupp 827, aff 205 F2d 542, cert den 74 SCt 136, 346 US 885, 98 LEd 390.—Work Comp 878.

Follette v. State, TexCrimApp, 94 SW2d 454, 130 TexCrim 400.—Crim Law 1077.2(3).

Folliard; Western Produce Co. v., CCA5 (Tex), 93 F2d 588.—Damag 168(1); Fed Civ Proc 2183; Fed Cts 641, 898.

Folliott; Bozeman v., TexCivApp–Corpus Christi, 556 SW2d 608, ref nre.—Can of Inst 24(2), 27; Ex & Ad 1, 7, 35(20), 77, 120(2); Mtg 334, 369(6).

Folliott v. Bozeman, TexCivApp–Corpus Christi, 526 SW2d 577, ref nre, appeal after remand 556 SW2d 608, ref nre.—App & E 1146; Courts 472.3.

Folloder; Schwarz v., CA5 (Tex), 767 F2d 125.—Fed Civ Proc 1693, 1700, 1713.1, 1822.1, 2282.1, 2723, 2727, 2728, 2737.1, 2737.3, 2737.5, 2737.14, 2742.5; Fed Cts 572.1, 669, 754.1, 775, 818, 830, 941, 945; Sec Reg 60.62.

Folse v. Folse, TexCivApp–Waco, 357 SW2d 772.—Divorce 130, 184(6.1).

Folse; Folse v., TexCivApp–Waco, 357 SW2d 772.—Divorce 130, 184(6.1).

Folse; Kerr v., TexCivApp–Texarkana, 137 SW2d 145.—App & E 1010.1(3); Partners 328(3), 336(3).

Folse v. Monroe, TexCivApp, 190 SW2d 604, writ refused wom.—App & E 1048(1); Courts 476; Evid 341; Home 37, 217; Marriage 39, 42, 50(1); Trial 219, 351.5(1), 352.1(3).

Folsom; Britton v., CA5 (Tex), 350 F2d 1022.—Schools 13(11).

Folsom; Britton v., CA5 (Tex), 348 F2d 158.—Schools 1, 13(11).

Folsom v. Folsom, TexCivApp–Hous (14 Dist), 601 SW2d 79, ref nre.—New Tr 104(1); Wills 155.1, 166(2), 166(12), 337.

Folsom; Folsom v., TexCivApp–Hous (14 Dist), 601 SW2d 79, ref nre.—New Tr 104(1); Wills 155.1, 166(2), 166(12), 337.

Folsom; Schecter v., TexCivApp–Dallas, 417 SW2d 180.—App & E 1178(6); Evid 18; Land & Ten 94(3), 112.5, 231(1), 231(6).

Folsom; Woolridge v., TexCivApp–Dallas, 564 SW2d 471.—Mun Corp 231(1).

Folsom Investments, Inc. v. American Motorists Ins. Co., TexApp–Dallas, 26 SW3d 556.—App & E 852; Insurance 2101, 2268, 2275, 2913, 2914.

Folsom Investments, Inc. v. Troutz, TexApp–Fort Worth, 632 SW2d 872, ref nre.—App & E 1008.1(1), 1070(1); Death 77; Judgm 126(4), 143(1), 157.1, 163.

Folterman; Bee Line Coaches v., TexCivApp–Galveston, 207 SW2d 986, ref nre.—Carr 295.2, 318(7); Damag 96, 132(3), 133; Evid 474(8), 568(6).

Foltin; State v., TexApp–Houston (14 Dist), 930 SW2d 270, writ den.—App & E 205, 1056.1(3); Evid 333(4), 351, 366(1), 373(1).

Foltting v. Kaevando, SDTex, 324 FSupp 585.—Ship 11.

Fomby v. Fomby, TexCivApp–Austin, 329 SW2d 111.—Divorce 23, 27(8.1), 43, 108, 124.4.

Fomby; Fomby v., TexCivApp–Austin, 329 SW2d 111.—Divorce 23, 27(8.1), 43, 108, 124.4.

Fondren v. C I R, CCA5 (Tex), 141 F2d 419, cert gr 65 SCt 35, 323 US 685, 89 LEd 555, aff 65 SCt 499, 324 US 18, 89 LEd 668.—Int Rev 4206.20.

Fondren; City of Houston v., TexCivApp–Galveston, 198 SW2d 480, ref nre.—Damag 132(6.1); New Tr 56, 140(3), 143(2).

Fondren; Commercial Standard Ins. Co. v., TexCivApp–Beaumont, 509 SW2d 728.—App & E 704.1, 1170.10; Insurance 2636; Plead 110.

Fondren v. Commissioner of Internal Revenue, USTex, 65 SCt 499, 324 US 18, 89 LEd 668.—Int Rev 3037, 4202, 4206.20.

Fondren v. Lawson, TexCivApp–Beaumont, 470 SW2d 797.—App & E 1078(1); Ex & Ad 438(8); Partit 46.1.

Fondren; Wood v., TexCivApp–Dallas, 131 SW2d 1070.—Plead 111.4, 111.39(2); Venue 22(1), 22(4), 22(6).

Fondren Const. Co., Inc. v. Briarcliff Housing Development Associates, Inc., TexApp–Houston (1 Dist), 196 SW3d 210.—App & E 931(1), 1010.1(1), 1012.1(5); Fraud 3, 13(1), 13(3); Impl & C C 3, 30; Lim of Act 47(3); Mech Liens 226; Princ & S 66(1), 136; Trial 382.

Fondren Green Apartments; Thornton v., SDTex, 788 FSupp 928.—Environ Law 423; Prod Liab 43.5; States 18.3, 18.5, 18.7, 18.11, 18.15, 18.65.

Fondren Southwest Bank v. Marathon LeTourneau Co., TexCivApp–Hous (14 Dist), 598 SW2d 337, ref nre.—Evid 373(1); Sec Tran 133.

Fong Chun Huang; St. Paul Lloyd's Ins. Co. v., TexApp–Houston (14 Dist), 808 SW2d 524, writ den.—Contracts 175(1); Insurance 1790(1), 1887(2), 2181, 2185, 2187, 3336, 3382, 3445; Libel 120(1); Ref of Inst 19(1).

Fonke, In re, BkrtcySDTex, 321 BR 199.—Bankr 2532, 2537, 2799.1, 2801, 3517; Statut 223.1, 223.4.

Fonke, In re, BkrtcySDTex, 310 BR 809.—Bankr 2021.1, 2323, 3022, 3716.20(4.1), 3716.20(5), 3716.20(6), 3716.20(12), 3716.30(2.1), 3716.30(3), 3716.30(5).

Fonmeadow Property Owners' Ass'n, Inc. v. Franklin, TexApp–Houston (1 Dist), 817 SW2d 104.—App & E 946; Costs 194.12, 252, 264; Covenants 132(2).

Fonseca v. Hidalgo County, TexCivApp–Corpus Christi, 527 SW2d 474, ref nre.—App & E 854(2), 1008.1(2), 1011.1(12), 1170.10; Atty & C 77; Can of Inst 3, 5; Compromise 8(4), 19(2); Em Dom 241; Judgm 368; Trial 382, 394(1), 404(1).

Fonseca v. Hidalgo County Water Improvement Dist. No. 2, CA5 (Tex), 496 F2d 109.—Fed Cts 998, 1000; Time 9(1).

Fonseca v. State, TexCrimApp, 455 SW2d 244.—Crim Law 1131(5).

Fonseca v. State, TexCrimApp, 144 SW2d 280, 140 TexCrim 292.—Crim Law 939(3), 1124(4).

Fonseca v. State, TexApp–Fort Worth, 163 SW3d 98, reh den, and reh overr, and petition for discretionary review refused.—Atty & C 62, 77; Crim Law 642.

Fonseca v. State, TexApp–San Antonio, 908 SW2d 519.—Crim Law 417(15), 1134(2), 1153(1).

Fonseca v. State, TexApp–Corpus Christi, 881 SW2d 144. —Arrest 63.5(4), 63.5(6), 63.5(9); Controlled Subs 63; Crim Law 255.2, 1153(1), 1158(4), 1163(1), 1166.16, 1172.1(2), 1181.5(1); Searches 192.1, 200.

Fonseca v. State, TexCivApp–Waco, 297 SW2d 199.— Autos 187(4); States 112.1(2), 191.8(3); Stip 14(1).

Fonseca; U.S. v., CA5 (Tex), 490 F2d 464, reh den 497 F2d 1384, cert den 95 SCt 660, 419 US 1072, 42 LEd2d 668.—Controlled Subs 69, 73, 81, 86; Crim Law 370, 371(1), 661, 865(1.5), 1169.5(4); Infants 69(8).

Fonseca-Ramos; U.S. v., NDTex, 743 FSupp 487, aff 912 F2d 1466.—Cust Dut 126(2), 126(5).

Fonseca-Sanchez; U.S. v., CA5 (Tex), 136 FedAppx 703. —Crim Law 1130(5); Sent & Pun 779.

Font v. Carr, TexApp–Houston (1 Dist), 867 SW2d 873, reh den, and writ dism woj.—Bail 60; Const Law 1117(1); Dist & Pros Attys 10; Judgm 181(27); Offic 114, 119; Statut 212.4, 223.2(0.5), 223.4.

Fontaine v. Dial, WDTex, 303 FSupp 436, appeal dism 90 SCt 2235, 399 US 521, 26 LEd2d 779.—Obscen 7.6.

Fontaine v. Fontaine, TexCivApp–Dallas, 325 SW2d 428. —Child C 553, 567, 632, 637, 650.

Fontaine; Fontaine v., TexCivApp–Dallas, 325 SW2d 428. —Child C 553, 567, 632, 637, 650.

Fontaine v. Walls, CA5 (Tex), 515 F2d 884, reh den 520 F2d 943.—Civil R 1319.

Fontaine's Clinics, Inc.; Jackson v., Tex, 499 SW2d 87. —App & E 228, 877(2), 877(6), 880(3), 1173(2); Damag 221(2.1), 221(5.1); Evid 317(2), 318(1); Release 1.

Fontaine's Clinics, Inc.; Jackson v., TexCivApp–Waco, 481 SW2d 934, writ gr, rev 499 SW2d 87.—Antitrust 111, 393, 421, 437; App & E 1151(2); Evid 177; Judgm 240.

Fontana; Cain v., TexCivApp–San Antonio, 423 SW2d 134, ref nre.—App & E 882(16), 1050.1(7), 1051(1); Costs 193; Damag 40(3), 91(1), 94, 176; Propty 9; Tresp 16, 36, 46(1), 50, 56, 57; Trial 125(4), 133.6(2).

Fontanez v. Texas Farm Bureau Ins. Companies, TexApp–Tyler, 840 SW2d 647.—Insurance 2675, 2774, 2786.

Fontecha; U.S. v., CA5 (Tex), 576 F2d 601.—Arrest 63.5(1), 63.5(6); Cust Dut 126(2), 126(5); Searches 44.

Fonteno v. State, TexApp–Houston (14 Dist), 677 SW2d 80, petition for discretionary review refused.—Crim Law 1031(1), 1042, 1069(1), 1612(1); Sent & Pun 2004, 2006, 2020, 2021.

Fontenot, Ex parte, TexCrimApp, 3 SW3d 32.—Hab Corp 898(3).

Fontenot, Ex parte, TexCrimApp, 550 SW2d 87.—Hab Corp 474; Rob 17(5).

Fontenot, In re, TexApp–Fort Worth, 13 SW3d 111.— Mand 3(2.1), 4(4), 12, 28, 32; Pretrial Proc 15, 33; Witn 206.

Fontenot; A/S Glittre v., CA5 (Tex), 327 F2d 637.—Adm 118.7(2); Collision 125.

Fontenot; Casa El Sol-Acapulco, S.A. v., TexApp–Houston (14 Dist), 919 SW2d 709, reh overr, and writ dism by agreement.—App & E 1062.1; Contracts 16, 303(1); Corp 116, 118, 121(5), 121(6); Estop 52.15, 95, 120; Jury 13(1), 13(5.1); Land & Ten 108(1); Trial 388(1).

Fontenot; Chandler v., TexApp–Beaumont, 883 SW2d 764.—Extrad 36, 39.

Fontenot v. Davis, TexCivApp–Beaumont, 296 SW2d 939. —Autos 208, 226(2), 238(4), 239(2), 240(1); Plead 36(1), 376.

Fontenot v. FedEx Group Package System, Inc., CA5 (Tex), 146 FedAppx 731.—Fed Civ Proc 2515; Neglig 200, 400, 1000.

Fontenot v. Fina Oil & Chemical Co., EDTex, 772 FSupp 950.—Rem of C 54.

Fontenot; Firemen's Relief and Retirement Fund Trustees of Houston v., TexCivApp–Austin, 446 SW2d 365, ref nre.—Mun Corp 200(9), 200(10); Pretrial Proc 474, 479.

Fontenot; Houston Title Guaranty Co. v., TexCivApp–Houston, 339 SW2d 347, ref nre.—Atty & C 141; Bound 46(1), 46(3); Insurance 1831, 1834(1), 2610, 2612, 2614, 2616, 2618, 2632, 2635, 2639.

Fontenot v. McLeod, EDTex, 889 FSupp 269, dism 77 F3d 473.—Civil R 1036, 1098, 1376(7).

Fontenot; Marange v., EDTex, 879 FSupp 679.—Autos 157; Civil R 1348, 1351(1), 1376(2), 1376(6), 1417, 1461; Const Law 1205, 1435, 4827; Courts 92; Death 82, 84, 85; Evid 207(4), 265(11); Mun Corp 742(2); Offic 114; Prisons 4(10.1), 4(11), 4(13).

Fontenot; Nelson v., EDTex, 784 FSupp 1258.—Consp 2, 7.5(1); Fed Civ Proc 2481.

Fontenot v. NL Industries, Inc., CA5 (Tex), 953 F2d 960. —Labor & Emp 429.

Fontenot v. NL Industries, Inc., TexApp–Houston (1 Dist), 877 SW2d 339, reh den, and writ den.—App & E 852; Lim of Act 130(6).

Fontenot; Port Terminal R. R. Ass'n v., TexCivApp–Hous (14 Dist), 469 SW2d 299.—App & E 930(2), 1053(3); Courts 97(5); Damag 38; Labor & Emp 2824.

Fontenot v. Sears, Roebuck & Co., TexCivApp–Beaumont, 399 SW2d 394, ref nre.—Neglig 1708.

Fontenot v. State, TexCrimApp, 500 SW2d 843.—Crim Law 662.65, 1040.

Fontenot v. State, TexCrimApp, 486 SW2d 941.—Autos 349(6), 355(6).

Fontenot v. State, TexCrimApp, 426 SW2d 861.—Crim Law 954(3), 957(1), 958(1), 959.

Fontenot v. State, TexCrimApp, 379 SW2d 334.—Crim Law 1166.15; Jury 66(1).

Fontenot v. State, TexApp–Houston (1 Dist), 903 SW2d 413, petition for discretionary review refused.—Crim Law 1038.1(2), 1038.1(5), 1043(3), 1162, 1165(1), 1171.1(3).

Fontenot v. State, TexApp–Houston (1 Dist), 708 SW2d 555, dism.—Crim Law 406(5), 772(4); Infants 20.

Fontenot v. State, TexApp–Houston (1 Dist), 704 SW2d 126, habeas corpus dism by Ex parte Fontenot, 3 SW3d 32.—Sent & Pun 1379(2), 1379(3), 1381(3), 1381(6).

Fontenot v. State, TexApp–Fort Worth, 932 SW2d 185.— Courts 1, 26; Crim Law 83, 273.1(1), 641.1, 1004, 1072, 1081(2).

Fontenot v. State, TexApp–Dallas, 792 SW2d 250.—Controlled Subs 33, 79, 81; Searches 181.

Fontenot; Texas Dept. of Transp. v., TexApp–Beaumont, 151 SW3d 753, review den.—App & E 930(1), 989, 1001(1), 1001(3), 1003(6), 1050.1(11); Autos 258, 290, 306(5), 306(7); Neglig 210, 215, 282, 1037(4), 1040(3); Prod Liab 75.1; States 112.2(1); Trial 39.

Fontenot v. U.S., CA5 (Tex), 89 F3d 205.—Ship 84(1), 84(2), 84(3.2).

Fontenot v. U.S., EDTex, 73 FSupp 607.—Salv 4.

Fontenot; Young v., TexApp–El Paso, 888 SW2d 238, reh den, and writ den.—App & E 854(1); Frds St of 49; Judgm 181(34), 185(2), 185(6); Lim of Act 43, 103(4); Trusts 17(4), 62, 86, 91.

Fontenot v. Zablocki, EDTex, 598 FSupp 747. See LeBlanc v. Shirey.

Fontenot Petro-Chem & Marine Services, Inc. v. LaBono, TexApp–Corpus Christi, 993 SW2d 455, reh overr, and review den, and reh of petition for review overr.— Corp 1.7(2), 432(1), 498; Labor & Emp 3047, 3049(1), 3049(3); Libel 112(2), 121(2); Lim of Act 1, 95(1), 95(6), 187, 195(3).

Fontes, Ex parte, TexCrimApp, 475 SW2d 781.—Extrad 32, 34, 36, 39; Ind & Inf 5.

Fontnette v. State, TexApp–Beaumont, 24 SW3d 647, petition for discretionary review refused.—Crim Law 273(2), 273.1(1), 274(7), 641.13(1).

Fonts; U.S. v., CA5 (Tex), 95 F3d 372.—Const Law 2817; Crim Law 1023(11), 1139, 1158(1); Sent & Pun 664(4), 855.

Fonville; Blocher v., SDTex, 756 FSupp 306.—Armed S 15; Inj 94.

Fonville; Mansfield State Bank v., TexCivApp–Fort Worth, 496 SW2d 945, ref nre.—App & E 837(1); Garn 137, 178.

Fonville; Reeves v., TexCivApp–Texarkana, 267 SW2d 238.—Infants 115; Tresp to T T 36, 40(1); Trial 350.3(3).

Fonville v. Southern Materials Co., TexCivApp–Galveston, 239 SW2d 885, ref nre.—Afft 18; Judgm 178, 185.1(3), 185.1(4); Mun Corp 485(5), 572.

Fonville; Tweedie Footwear Corp. v., TexCivApp–Dallas, 115 SW2d 421, writ refused.—Corp 62, 374, 439, 547(4); Estop 83(2), 87; Sec Reg 291.1, 307.

Food City, Inc., In re, BkrtcyWDTex, 110 BR 808.—Bankr 3548.1, 3558, 3568(1), 3568(3); Evid 43(2); Statut 206.

Food City, Inc., In re, BkrtcyWDTex, 95 BR 451.—Bankr 3101, 3115.1.

Food City, Inc., In re, BkrtcyWDTex, 94 BR 91.—Bankr 3110.1.

Food City, Inc. v. Fleming Companies, Inc., TexCivApp–San Antonio, 590 SW2d 754.—Mtg 151(2); Sec Tran 161, 163, 207, 223, 230, 231, 242.1, 243.

Food City, Inc.; Martinez v., CA5 (Tex), 658 F2d 369, 25 Wage & Hour Cas (BNA) 170, 65 ALR Fed 823.—Fed Civ Proc 2313, 2337, 2371; Fed Cts 825.1, 873; Labor & Emp 2371, 2390(1).

Foodland; Hargraves v., TexApp–Austin, 894 SW2d 546. See Hargraves v. Armco Foods, Inc.

Food Lion, Inc.; Black v., CA5 (Tex), 171 F3d 308, on remand 1999 WL 405231, on remand 2000 WL 4259.—Damag 185(1); Evid 508, 555.2, 555.10; Fed Cts 823.

Food Machinery & Chemical Corp.; Thrift Packing Co. v., CA5 (Tex), 191 F2d 113.—Bankr 2281, 3773.

Food Machinery Corp. v. Moon, TexCivApp–Amarillo, 165 SW2d 773.—App & E 598, 1062.5; Bills & N 97(1); Contracts 85, 320, 322(3); Mech Liens 93; Trial 352.4(4).

Foodmaker, Inc.; Griffin Industries, Inc. v., TexApp–Houston (14 Dist), 22 SW3d 33, petition for review den.—Contracts 215(1); Indem 30(1), 31(1), 33(4), 104; Neglig 252.

Foodmaker, Inc.; Hayes v., CA5 (Tex), 634 F2d 802.—U S Mag 20, 26.

Foodmaker, Inc.; Smith v., TexApp–Fort Worth, 928 SW2d 683.—Contracts 129(1); Death 8; Judgm 185(2); Labor & Emp 3127; Princ & A 1, 3(2), 19, 24.

Food Mart, Inc.; Davis v., CA5 (Tex), 334 F2d 27.—Fed Civ Proc 837, 2236; Fed Cts 629, 632, 637, 644, 912; Labor & Emp 3106(1); Neglig 1538, 1708, 1717.

Food Source, Inc. v. Zurich Ins. Co., TexApp–Dallas, 751 SW2d 596, writ den.—App & E 1046.5, 1050.1(5); Insurance 2200, 2201, 2202; Plead 245(1), 258(1), 261; Trial 29.1.

Foodway, Inc. v. Aguirre, TexCivApp–San Antonio, 550 SW2d 126.—Plead 111.42(7).

Foodway, Inc. v. Camacho, TexCivApp–El Paso, 519 SW2d 499, dism.—Plead 111.16, 111.17, 111.42(6), 111.42(7).

Foodway, Inc. v. Lopez, TexCivApp–El Paso, 480 SW2d 227.—Neglig 1076, 1104(6), 1595; Plead 111.16, 111.17, 111.39(4); Venue 21.

Foodway of El Paso; N.L.R.B. v., CA5 (Tex), 496 F2d 117.—Labor & Emp 1177, 1225.

Fooladi; U.S. v., CA5 (Tex), 746 F2d 1027, cert den 105 SCt 1362, 470 US 1006, 84 LEd2d 382.—Const Law 2415(3), 4636; Controlled Subs 6, 77, 98; Courts 90(2); Crim Law 772(6), 789(3), 829(4).

Fooladi; U.S. v., CA5 (Tex), 703 F2d 180.—Controlled Subs 146; Crim Law 1158(2); Searches 105.1, 111, 117, 118.

Foose; Roberts v., TexApp–Houston (1 Dist), 7 SW3d 311.—App & E 934(1); Judgm 181(27), 185(2), 185(6), 185.3(1); Mun Corp 723; Offic 114.

Fooshee v. U.S., CA5 (Tex), 203 F2d 247.—Crim Law 1131(4); Sent & Pun 2221.

Foote v. City of Houston, TexCivApp–Houston, 361 SW2d 247, ref nre.—Pretrial Proc 554.

Foote v. De Bogory, TexCivApp–Dallas, 179 SW2d 983, writ refused wom.—Aviation 242; Bailm 30; Evid 237; Princ & A 19, 22(1), 22(2), 23(1), 99, 119(1), 122(1), 123(1), 147(2).

Foote v. Kansas City Life Ins. Co., CCA5 (Tex), 92 F2d 744.—Execution 242, 247, 251(1); Fed Cts 2, 7.

Foote; Maryland Cas. Co. v., TexCivApp–Eastland, 139 SW2d 602, writ refused.—Damag 221(5.1); Work Comp 1919, 1927, 1930, 1968(6).

Foote v. State, TexCrimApp, 463 SW2d 445.—Crim Law 368(3); Sent & Pun 2011.

Foote v. Weinberger, SDTex, 377 FSupp 1347.—Social S 143.60, 149.

Footloose, Inc. v. Stride Rite Children's Group, Inc., NDTex, 923 FSupp 114.—Antitrust 141, 266.

F--- O. P---; L--- G--- v., TexCivApp–San Antonio, 466 SW2d 41, ref nre, probable jur noted Gomez v. Perez, 92 SCt 2479, 408 US 920, 33 LEd2d 331, rev 93 SCt 872, 409 US 535, 35 LEd2d 56.—Child 21(2).

Fopay; Tucker's Beverages, Inc. v., TexApp–Texarkana, 145 SW3d 765.—App & E 946, 970(2); Evid 241(1), 244(7), 258(1), 258(2); Trial 43.

Foran v. C.I.R., CCA5 (Tex), 165 F2d 705.—Int Rev 3254, 4707, 4736.

Foran v. Smith, TexCivApp–San Antonio, 228 SW2d 251.—App & E 219(2), 242(1), 544(1), 854(1), 901, 907(3), 931(1); Evid 96(2).

Forbau v. Aetna Life Ins. Co., Tex, 876 SW2d 132.—Contracts 143(2), 147(1), 147(3), 156; Insurance 1806, 1808, 2457(1); Labor & Emp 662.

Forbau; Aetna Life Ins. Co. v., TexCivApp–Amarillo, 808 SW2d 664, writ den, and writ withdrawn, and writ gr, aff 876 SW2d 132.—Insurance 2457(1).

Forbau v. Producers Gas Co., TexCivApp–Amarillo, 601 SW2d 550.—App & E 1122(2); Damag 87(2), 112.

Forbau v. State, TexCrimApp, 492 SW2d 516.—Assault 67, 96(7).

Forbes, Ex parte, TexCrimApp, 474 SW2d 690.—Bail 43, 49(4), 51; Crim Law 1134(8).

Forbes v. City of Houston, TexCivApp–Houston, 356 SW2d 709.—Mand 16(1), 71, 72, 98(1), 187.9(5); Mun Corp 63.1, 657(1).

Forbes v. City of Houston, TexCivApp–Galveston, 304 SW2d 542, ref nre, cert den 78 SCt 1151, 357 US 905, 2 LEd2d 1156.—Mun Corp 33(2), 33(10), 34, 112(3), 871, 995(2); Statut 77(1), 135; Waters 216.

Forbes v. Cogdell, TexCivApp–Eastland, 452 SW2d 568, writ gr, and dism.—Judgm 185(2), 185.3(17).

Forbes; Colquette v., TexApp–Austin, 680 SW2d 536.—Const Law 1210, 1248; Divorce 256; Hus & W 278(2); Ven & Pur 254(4), 269.

Forbes; Driskill v., TexApp–Eastland, 566 SW2d 90, ref nre.—Can of Inst 27; Deeds 208(1); Fraud Conv 172(2).

Forbes v. Estelle, CA5 (Tex), 559 F2d 967, cert den 98 SCt 640, 434 US 998, 54 LEd2d 494.—Hab Corp 450.1, 481.

Forbes v. Forbes, TexCivApp–Amarillo, 430 SW2d 947.—App & E 1008.1(1); Estop 107, 110; Gifts 15, 18(1), 47(1), 49(1).

Forbes; Forbes v., TexCivApp–Amarillo, 430 SW2d 947.—App & E 1008.1(1); Estop 107, 110; Gifts 15, 18(1), 47(1), 49(1).

Forbes v. Hejkal, TexCivApp–Dallas, 271 SW2d 435, dism.—App & E 216(1); Evid 318(1); Witn 380(6), 388(6), 388(7.1), 396(3).

Forbes v. Lanzl, TexApp–Austin, 9 SW3d 895, reh overr, and petition for review den, and reh of petition for review overr.—App & E 836; Assault 13, 51, 67; Mal Pros 0.5, 18(4), 20, 31, 38, 56, 64(2).

Forbes; Lerma v., TexApp–El Paso, 166 SW3d 889, reh overr, and review den, and reh of petition for review den.—App & E 756, 761, 949, 1079; Parties 42, 44.

Forbes; Lerma v., TexApp–El Paso, 144 SW3d 18.—App & E 428(2), 816.

Forbes; Lerma v., TexApp–El Paso, 144 SW3d 16.—App & E 428(2).

Forbes v. State, TexCrimApp, 513 SW2d 72, cert den 95 SCt 830, 420 US 910, 42 LEd2d 840.—Crim Law 80, 369.2(1), 369.2(4), 507(1), 511.1(1), 511.2, 511.4, 541, 543(2), 544, 662.40, 693, 1137(2), 1169.2(2); Homic 850; Ind & Inf 137(4).

Forbes v. State, TexCrimApp, 307 SW2d 92.—Crim Law 1101.

Forbes v. State, TexCrimApp, 157 SW2d 900, 143 Tex-Crim 180.—Crim Law 20, 53, 1169.11; Larc 71(2); Witn 337(10).

Forbes v. State, TexApp–Houston (1 Dist), 976 SW2d 749. —Crim Law 686(1), 1043(2), 1044.2(1), 1144.13(3), 1144.13(5), 1144.13(6), 1159.2(1), 1159.2(2), 1159.2(7), 1162, 1168(2); Forg 44(0.5).

Forbes v. State Farm Fire & Cas. Co., EDTex, 323 FSupp 227.—Explos 7, 10; Neglig 1612, 1614.

Forbes v. Texas Dept. of Public Safety, TexCivApp–Waco, 335 SW2d 439.—Autos 132; Const Law 2450, 2564; Decl Judgm 43, 276, 395.

Forbes v. Wettman, Tex, 598 SW2d 231.—Child C 427; Hab Corp 731, 744; Mand 172.

Forbes Chevrolet Co.; Hernandez v., TexApp–Corpus Christi, 680 SW2d 75, writ gr, and dism as moot.—Cons Cred 16; Contracts 153, 175(1); Sec Tran 186, 222.

Forbes Inc. v. Granada Biosciences, Inc., Tex, 124 SW3d 167.—App & E 934(1); Judgm 185(5); Libel 51(5), 112(2), 133, 136.

Forbes, Inc.; Granada Biosciences, Inc. v., TexApp–Houston (14 Dist), 49 SW3d 610, review den, and reh of petition for review gr, and review gr, and withdrawn, rev 124 SW3d 167.—App & E 852, 934(1); Const Law 1622; Judgm 181(33), 185(2), 185(5), 185.3(21); Libel 9(1), 36, 41, 50.5, 130, 131, 133, 135, 136, 139.

Forbess; Stone Fort Nat. Bank of Nacogdoches v., Tex, 91 SW2d 674, 126 Tex 568.—Banks 119, 129, 143(1); Corp 503(2).

Forbich; Moreno v., TexCivApp–San Antonio, 452 SW2d 505.—Autos 244(34).

Forbis v. Trinity Universal Ins. Co. of Kansas, Inc., TexApp–Fort Worth, 833 SW2d 316, reh overr, and writ gr, and writ withdrawn, and writ dism.—App & E 842(2), 1010.1(1), 1010.1(3); Judgm 651, 665, 668(1), 678(1), 713(1), 715(1), 720, 724, 725(1).

Forbus v. City of Denton, TexCivApp–Fort Worth, 595 SW2d 621, ref nre.—Mun Corp 734, 740(1).

Forbus v. Safeway Stores, Inc., TexCivApp–Austin, 547 SW2d 725.—App & E 554(1), 846(5), 901, 1032(1).

Forbush v. J.C. Penney Co., CA5 (Tex), 98 F3d 817.—Atty & C 130, 140, 142.1, 155, 167(4); Estop 68(2); Fed Civ Proc 2742.5; Fed Cts 611, 612.1, 614, 830.

Forbush v. J.C. Penney Co., Inc., CA5 (Tex), 994 F2d 1101.—Fed Civ Proc 164.5, 165, 184.5.

Force v. E.I. Dupont De Nemours, EDTex, 770 FSupp 335.—Rem of C 27.

Force Corp.; Anheuser–Busch, Inc. v., CA5 (Tex), 987 F2d 298. See McDaniel v. Anheuser-Busch, Inc.

Forcha v. State, TexApp–Houston (1 Dist), 894 SW2d 506. —Crim Law 273.1(1), 273.1(5), 275, 641.13(7), 1072, 1081(2).

Forcheimer v. Commercial Standard Ins. Co., CA5 (Tex), 181 F2d 182.—Fed Cts 313.

Forcheimer; Reed v., CA5 (Tex), 368 F2d 982.—Contracts 182(1); Fed Cts 305; Joint Adv 1.12; Partners 20.

Forcum-Dean Co. v. Missouri Pac. R. Co., TexCivApp–San Antonio, 341 SW2d 464, writ dism.—Bankr 2012; Commerce 8(1.5), 48; Courts 28; R R 33(2).

Ford, Ex parte, TexCrimApp, 446 SW2d 13.—Sent & Pun 1258, 1318.

Ford, In re, EDTex, 125 BR 735, aff 967 F2d 1047, reh den 974 F2d 1337.—Bankr 2002, 2826, 2829; Bills & N 120.

Ford, In re, BkrtcyEDTex, 179 BR 821.—Bankr 3714.

Ford, Matter of, CA5 (Tex), 967 F2d 1047, reh den 974 F2d 1337.—Bankr 2826, 2829; Bills & N 121.

Ford; Acme Laundry Co. v., TexCivApp–El Paso, 284 SW2d 745, ref nre.—Neglig 1076, 1103, 1635.

Ford v. Aetna Ins. Co., Tex, 424 SW2d 612.—Home 70, 209; Inj 151.

Ford; Aetna Ins. Co. v., TexCivApp–Eastland, 417 SW2d 448, writ gr, rev 424 SW2d 612.—App & E 954(1), 954(2), 1024.2; Home 57.5, 64, 70, 73; Inj 135, 147, 151.

Ford v. Aetna Ins. Co., TexCivApp–Corpus Christi, 394 SW2d 693, ref nre.—App & E 1170.1; Evid 354(2), 590; Judgm 185.3(8), 592; Princ & S 175, 185; Trial 140(2).

Ford v. Allen, TexCivApp–Austin, 526 SW2d 643.—App & E 842(2), 1010.1(3); Courts 475(2); Wills 435, 440, 488, 601(4), 614(1), 649, 672(1).

Ford v. American Motors Corp., CA5 (Tex), 770 F2d 465, reh den 776 F2d 1048.—Fed Civ Proc 1828; U S 78(12).

Ford v. American Motors Corp., SDTex, 621 FSupp 685, aff 770 F2d 465, reh den 776 F2d 1048.—U S 78(12).

Ford v. Anderson, TexCivApp–Austin, 83 SW2d 443.—Deeds 136, 192; Tresp to T T 38(1).

Ford v. Bachman, TexCivApp–San Antonio, 203 SW2d 630, ref nre.—Wills 476, 560(3), 577, 784.

Ford v. Bimbo Corp., TexCivApp–Hous (14 Dist), 512 SW2d 793.—Atty & C 32(9); Corp 207, 207.1; Parties 35.13; Pretrial Proc 556.1.

Ford v. Byrd, CA5 (Tex), 544 F2d 194.—Civil R 1311, 1358, 1376(8), 1376(9).

Ford v. Carpenter, Tex, 216 SW2d 558, 147 Tex 447.—App & E 1060.6, 1082(2); New Tr 60; Trial 127, 131(1), 355(1), 358.

Ford; Carpenter v., TexCivApp–Texarkana, 212 SW2d 984, rev 216 SW2d 558, 147 Tex 447.—App & E 1050.1(2); Trial 127, 131(1).

Ford; Carruth Mortg. Corp. v., TexApp–Houston (1 Dist), 630 SW2d 897.—Bills & N 124, 484; Evid 450(10); Lim of Act 100(11); Mtg 561.5.

Ford; Case Bros. Trucking Contractors, Inc. v., TexCivApp–Eastland, 292 SW2d 660.—Plead 111.17.

Ford; Changos v., TexCivApp–Austin, 131 SW2d 1025.—App & E 781(4).

Ford v. Cimarron Ins. Co., Inc., CA5 (Tex), 230 F3d 828. —Courts 90(2); Fed Civ Proc 2601, 2608.1; Fed Cts 776; Insurance 3347, 3349, 3350, 3353, 3355; Neglig 202, 210, 1692.

Ford; City of Bowie v., TexCivApp–Fort Worth, 300 SW2d 671.—Em Dom 235, 274(4).

Ford v. City of Huntsville, CA5 (Tex), 242 F3d 235.—Fed Civ Proc 314.1, 315, 320, 331; Fed Cts 776, 817, 820; Records 32, 54.

Ford v. City State Bank of Palacios, TexApp–Corpus Christi, 44 SW3d 121.—Antitrust 141, 145, 150, 212, 290, 291, 363; App & E 66, 68, 92, 95, 854(1); Bankr 2436; Contracts 218, 221(1), 326; Courts 97(1); Estop 85, 118; Fraud 3, 9; Frds St of 119(1), 144, 158(4); Judgm 181(6), 185(1), 185(2), 185(5), 185(6), 185.3(2), 540, 582, 634, 713(2), 720, 829(3); Plead 374.

Ford v. Cockrell, WDTex, 315 FSupp2d 831, certificate of appealability gr in part, den in part 121 FedAppx 554, aff 135 FedAppx 769, cert den 126 SCt 1026, 546 US 1098, 163 LEd2d 867.—Crim Law 641.13(1), 641.13(2.1), 641.13(6), 641.13(7); Hab Corp 378, 382, 383, 405.1, 407, 409, 422, 461, 481, 818.

Ford; Collier v., TexCivApp–Galveston, 81 SW2d 821, writ dism.—App & E 927(7); Can of Inst 35(3); Evid

FORD;

383(7); Mtg 353, 362, 369(6), 369(8), 378; Tresp to T T 35(2).

Ford; Commercial Standard Ins. Co. v., TexCivApp–Amarillo, 400 SW2d 934, ref nre.—App & E 78(1), 927(7), 934(1), 1062.1, 1078(1); Insurance 1836, 2695.

Ford v. Culbertson, Tex, 308 SW2d 855, 158 Tex 124.—App & E 878(4); Estop 52.10(2), 53, 118, 119; Ex & Ad 390; Frds St of 103(2); Mines 54(3); Princ & A 123(7); Sec Reg 253.

Ford v. Culbertson, TexCivApp–Fort Worth, 300 SW2d 152, rev 308 SW2d 855, 158 Tex 124.—Estop 52.10(2), 54, 119; Ex & Ad 148; Int Rev 4771.1; Ven & Pur 144(3).

Ford v. Darwin, TexApp–Dallas, 767 SW2d 851, writ den.—App & E 1071.1; Bills & N 168; Guar 27, 34, 77(2), 82(3); Trial 401.

Ford; Dickson v., CA5 (Tex), 521 F2d 234, cert den 96 SCt 1428, 424 US 954, 47 LEd2d 360.—Const Law 2580, 2588.

Ford v. Dretke, CA5 (Tex), 135 FedAppx 769, cert den 126 SCt 1026, 546 US 1098, 163 LEd2d 867.—Crim Law 641.13(6); Hab Corp 461.

Ford v. Dretke, CA5 (Tex), 121 FedAppx 554.—Hab Corp 818.

Ford v. Durham, TexApp–Fort Worth, 624 SW2d 737, dism.—Child S 509(1); Const Law 3965(1); Courts 12(2.5).

Ford v. Emerich, TexCivApp–Houston, 343 SW2d 527, dism, and order set aside, and ref nre.—App & E 173(10), 688(2), 842(1), 1062.5; Lim of Act 19(2), 19(7); Mtg 306, 333, 334, 372(3), 378; New Tr 140(3); Powers 43; Tresp to T T 50.

Ford v. Estelle, CA5 (Tex), 740 F2d 374.—U S Mag 21.

Ford; Exxon Mobil Chemical Co. v., TexApp–Beaumont, 187 SW3d 154, reh overr.—App & E 754(1); Equity 72(1); Lim of Act 44(1), 100(1), 100(11), 100(12), 170; Plead 78.

Ford; Fields v., TexCivApp–Tyler, 383 SW2d 239, writ dism.—Plead 111.42(7).

Ford v. Fluor Engineering and Constructors, Inc., TexApp–Beaumont, 711 SW2d 327, ref nre.—Labor & Emp 3096(10); Neglig 253, 1205(7), 1672.

Ford v. Ford, CCA5 (Tex), 100 F2d 227.—Fed Cts 769; Rem of C 115, 118.

Ford; Ford v., CCA5 (Tex), 100 F2d 227.—Fed Cts 769; Rem of C 115, 118.

Ford v. Ford, TexCivApp–Texarkana, 492 SW2d 376, ref nre.—Ref of Inst 17(2).

Ford; Ford v., TexCivApp–Texarkana, 492 SW2d 376, ref nre.—Ref of Inst 17(2).

Ford; Foust v., TexCivApp–Fort Worth, 209 SW2d 941.—Bail 64; Crim Law 1020; False Imp 22; Fines 11; Venue 8.5(5).

Ford v. Guthrie, CA5 (Tex), 101 FedAppx 978.—Civil R 1091; Fed Civ Proc 1838, 2734.

Ford v. Harlow, TexCivApp–Fort Worth, 439 SW2d 682, ref nre.—Gifts 18(1), 31(1); Trover 4; Trusts 69.

Ford v. Harris County Medical Soc., CA5 (Tex), 535 F2d 321, cert den 97 SCt 492, 429 US 980, 50 LEd2d 589.—Fed Cts 223.

Ford; Houston Fire & Cas. Ins. Co. v., TexCivApp–Texarkana, 241 SW2d 158, ref nre.—App & E 207, 758.1; Trial 131(3); Witn 287(1); Work Comp 1922, 1926, 1958, 1968(5).

Ford v. Ireland, TexApp–Texarkana, 699 SW2d 587.—Health 906, 908; Judgm 181(33), 185(3), 185.2(9), 185.3(21).

Ford v. Jones, CA5 (Tex), 149 FedAppx 316, on remand 2006 WL 3488954.—Civil R 1092, 1319; Sent & Pun 1538.

Ford; Jones v., TexCivApp–Fort Worth, 118 SW2d 333.—Plead 111.4, 111.6, 111.8, 111.33, 255, 264; Venue 5.3(1), 5.4.

Ford; Jones v., TexCivApp–El Paso, 583 SW2d 821, ref nre.—Adv Poss 16(1); Mtg 151(5), 345.

Ford v. Landmark Graphics Corp., TexApp–Texarkana, 875 SW2d 33.—Inj 135, 138.6, 138.9, 138.75; Labor & Emp 776.

Ford v. Leonard's, TexCivApp–Fort Worth, 228 SW2d 192.—App & E 927(7); Carr 320(23), 320(30); Evid 20(2).

Ford; Lone Star Bldg. & Loan Ass'n v., TexCivApp–Galveston, 141 SW2d 696, writ dism, correct.—B & L Assoc 8(2).

Ford v. Long, TexApp–Tyler, 713 SW2d 798, ref nre.—Const Law 1123; Trusts 95.

Ford; Loret v., TexCivApp–El Paso, 559 SW2d 95, writ dism by agreement.—App & E 781(4); Execution 170.

Ford; McGahey v., TexCivApp–Fort Worth, 563 SW2d 857, ref nre.—App & E 768, 931(1), 989, 1010.1(3); Home 115(2), 167, 192, 214; Mtg 154(3), 155.

Ford v. McRae, TexComApp, 96 SW2d 80, 128 Tex 106.—Adv Poss 114(1); Bound 3(5), 3(7); Ven & Pur 267.

Ford v. McWilliams, TexCivApp–Amarillo, 278 SW2d 338.—Autos 372(1), 372(2).

Ford; Malleable Iron Range Co. v., TexCivApp–San Antonio, 141 SW2d 469.—Commerce 60(1); Corp 642(3).

Ford; Manzo v., TexApp–Houston (14 Dist), 731 SW2d 673.—Action 27(1), 47; Contracts 143.5, 152, 155, 162, 189.

Ford; Martin v., TexApp–Texarkana, 853 SW2d 680, reh den, and writ den.—Bills & N 404(1); Divorce 321 1/2; Evid 384, 411, 417(1), 417(13); Lim of Act 48(2), 66(2); Mtg 27.

Ford v. Moren, TexCivApp–Texarkana, 592 SW2d 385, ref nre.—Adv Poss 27; App & E 846(5); Bound 8; Dedi 1, 15, 16.1, 19(1), 41, 45; Ease 17(4), 58(1).

Ford; New York Cas. Co. v., CCA5 (Tex), 145 F2d 599.—Evid 448; Insurance 1800, 2407.

Ford v. NYLCare Health Plans of Gulf Coast, Inc., CA5 (Tex), 301 F3d 329, reh and reh den 48 FedAppx 482, cert den 123 SCt 1574, 538 US 923, 155 LEd2d 313.—Antitrust 64; Fed Civ Proc 103.2, 103.3, 2544; Fed Cts 34; Trademarks 1563.

Ford v. Nylcare Health Plans of Gulf Coast, Inc., SDTex, 190 FRD 422, aff 301 F3d 329, reh and reh den 48 FedAppx 482, cert den 123 SCt 1574, 538 US 923, 155 LEd2d 313.—Antitrust 22; Fed Civ Proc 161.2, 165, 171, 172, 181.

Ford v. Panhandle & Santa Fe Ry. Co., Tex, 252 SW2d 561, 151 Tex 538, reh and reh gr Southern Pacific Transp Co v. Luna, 707 SW2d 113, writ gr, rev 724 SW2d 383, on remand 730 SW2d 36.—App & E 927(7); Evid 590; Neglig 530(1); R R 338.3, 338.5, 350(33); Trial 139.1(3), 140(1), 143, 350.7(9).

Ford v. Panhandle & S. F. Ry. Co., TexCivApp–Amarillo, 246 SW2d 233, rev 252 SW2d 561, 151 Tex 538, reh and reh gr Southern Pacific Transp Co v. Luna, 707 SW2d 113, writ gr, rev 724 SW2d 383, on remand 730 SW2d 36.—App & E 927(7); Neglig 530(1); R R 320, 338.4, 350(33).

Ford v. Performance Aircraft Services, Inc., TexApp–Fort Worth, 178 SW3d 330, reh overr, and review den.—App & E 232(0.5), 863, 946, 960(1); Const Law 2312, 2314, 3989; Corp 360(1); Damag 153; Plead 16, 48, 228.14, 228.23; Prod Liab 73.

Ford v. Petroleum Life Ins. Co., TexCivApp–Waco, 435 SW2d 164, ref nre.—Insurance 2035.

Ford v. Phillips, TexCivApp–Beaumont, 250 SW2d 752.—Autos 150, 162(2), 197(7), 245(8).

Ford; Price v., TexApp–Dallas, 104 SW3d 331, review den.—App & E 931(1), 1010.1(1); Evid 571(9); Neglig 371, 379, 380, 387, 1000, 1001, 1675, 1679.

Ford; Redfearn v., TexCivApp–Dallas, 579 SW2d 295, ref nre.—Hus & W 265.

Ford; Reed v., TexApp–Dallas, 760 SW2d 26.—Land & Ten 184(2).

Ford; Republic Underwriters v., CCA5 (Tex), 100 F2d 511.—Bankr 2023, 2225; Insurance 1206(1), 1222(1).

Ford v. Rio Grande Val. Gas Co., Tex, 174 SW2d 479, 141 Tex 525.—Gas 14.1(2).

Ford; Rio Grande Val. Gas Co. v., TexCivApp–San Antonio, 169 SW2d 263, aff 174 SW2d 479, 141 Tex 525.—Const Law 2524; Gas 14.1(2), 14.6.

Ford v. Roberts, TexCivApp–Dallas, 478 SW2d 129, ref nre.—App & E 192.2; Ex & Ad 7; Witn 148, 149(2), 182.

Ford v. Ross, TexCivApp–Fort Worth, 150 SW2d 144.—Wills 116, 166(12), 203, 302(1), 318(1), 324(3), 335, 341, 391; Witn 131, 139(6).

Ford; Salvation Army of Tex. v., TexCivApp–San Antonio, 256 SW2d 953.—Wills 452, 506(1).

Ford; Second Nat. Bank v., TexComApp, 123 SW2d 867, 132 Tex 448.—Bills & N 123(1); Courts 475(2); Ex & Ad 114, 202.10, 261, 453(2), 453(4).

Ford v. Second Nat. Bank, TexCivApp–Galveston, 100 SW2d 1112, rev 123 SW2d 867, 132 Tex 448.—App & E 882(5); Evid 222(2); Ex & Ad 221(9).

Ford v. Shallowater Airport, TexCivApp–Amarillo, 492 SW2d 655, ref nre.—Agric 9.5; Neglig 1652, 1655.

Ford v. Shoney's Restaurants, Inc., EDTex, 900 FSupp 57.—Rem of C 79(1), 79(7).

Ford v. Simpson, TexCivApp–Waco, 568 SW2d 468.—Hus & W 264(4); Trusts 72, 81(2).

Ford; Southern States Transp. Co. v., TexCivApp–Galveston, 102 SW2d 281, writ dism.—Ferries 33; Trial 142.

Ford v. Southwestern Greyhound Lines, CA5 (Tex), 180 F2d 934.—Autos 244(10), 244(35), 245(79), 245(89), 245(91); Evid 474(8), 568(6); Fed Cts 798; Neglig 510(1); Trial 139.1(2).

Ford v. State, TexCrimApp, 158 SW3d 488.—Arrest 63.5(4); Autos 349(2.1); Crim Law 394.4(3), 394.5(4), 1139, 1144.12, 1158(2).

Ford v. State, TexCrimApp, 73 SW3d 923, habeas corpus dism by 2002 WL 31697725.—Crim Law 1162, 1165(1), 1166.16; Jury 64.

Ford v. State, TexCrimApp, 1 SW3d 691, on remand 26 SW3d 669.—Jury 33(5.15).

Ford v. State, TexCrimApp, 919 SW2d 107, reh den, habeas corpus den 315 FSupp2d 831, certificate of appealability gr in part, den in part 121 FedAppx 554, aff 135 FedAppx 769, cert den 126 SCt 1026, 546 US 1098, 163 LEd2d 867, habeas corpus dism Ex parte Ford, 2005 WL 3429243.—Crim Law 339.10(2), 661, 698(3), 1144.17, 1153(1); Jury 131(8), 131(13); Sent & Pun 1720, 1752, 1763, 1772, 1789(3).

Ford v. State, TexCrimApp, 632 SW2d 151.—Burg 2, 18, 28(1), 41(3).

Ford v. State, TexCrimApp, 615 SW2d 727.—Crim Law 1172.1(3); Rape 59(13).

Ford v. State, TexCrimApp, 571 SW2d 924.—Autos 332, 355(6); Crim Law 552(3), 1144.13(2.1).

Ford v. State, TexCrimApp, 538 SW2d 633.—Arrest 68(2); Const Law 4534; Crim Law 1130(4); Obst Just 2; Searches 52.

Ford v. State, TexCrimApp, 509 SW2d 317.—Crim Law 739(2); Homic 1181; Jury 33(1.15), 110(14).

Ford v. State, TexCrimApp, 507 SW2d 735.—Crim Law 814(17); Homic 612; Jury 149.

Ford v. State, TexCrimApp, 502 SW2d 160.—Crim Law 308, 508(1), 599; Rob 8, 24.10.

Ford v. State, TexCrimApp, 500 SW2d 827.—Crim Law 339.11(8), 369.15, 603.2, 693.

Ford v. State, TexCrimApp, 488 SW2d 793.—Crim Law 320, 1042, 1158(1), 1177; Sent & Pun 2004, 2021, 2029.

Ford v. State, TexCrimApp, 484 SW2d 727, aff 509 SW2d 317.—Crim Law 358, 369.1, 369.2(1), 369.15, 371(1), 371(12).

Ford v. State, TexCrimApp, 477 SW2d 27.—Crim Law 721(1), 1171.5.

Ford v. State, TexCrimApp, 459 SW2d 867.—Crim Law 1031(1), 1168(1); Sent & Pun 94.

Ford v. State, TexCrimApp, 384 SW2d 874.—Crim Law 1020.

Ford v. State, TexCrimApp, 335 SW2d 606, 169 TexCrim 518.—Crim Law 1081(2), 1111(1).

Ford v. State, TexCrimApp, 314 SW2d 101, 166 TexCrim 347.—Crim Law 699, 706(3), 713.

Ford v. State, TexCrimApp, 312 SW2d 954, 166 TexCrim 280.—Sent & Pun 1381(6).

Ford v. State, TexCrimApp, 285 SW2d 735, 162 TexCrim 323.—Controlled Subs 80; Crim Law 566.

Ford v. State, TexCrimApp, 272 SW2d 740, 160 TexCrim 574.—Autos 347; Ind & Inf 71.4(1).

Ford v. State, TexCrimApp, 258 SW2d 316, 158 TexCrim 547.—Crim Law 784(1).

Ford v. State, TexCrimApp, 253 SW2d 438.—Crim Law 1094(3).

Ford v. State, TexCrimApp, 252 SW2d 948, 158 TexCrim 26.—Assault 54, 78; Crim Law 1189.

Ford v. State, TexCrimApp, 171 SW2d 885, 146 TexCrim 152.—Crim Law 380, 419(10), 761(13), 829(9), 1038.1(1), 1092.14, 1169.1(9), 1169.2(1), 1169.3.

Ford v. State, TexCrimApp, 162 SW2d 719, 144 TexCrim 348.—Crim Law 594(3), 598(3).

Ford v. State, TexApp–Houston (1 Dist), 152 SW3d 752, reh overr, and petition for discretionary review refused. —Crim Law 312, 404.45, 795(2.20), 1144.13(2.1), 1144.13(3), 1159.2(1), 1159.2(2), 1159.2(7); Rob 11, 24.15(2), 27(5).

Ford v. State, TexApp–Houston (1 Dist), 845 SW2d 315.—Crim Law 273.1(5), 1144.4, 1144.17.

Ford v. State, TexApp–Houston (1 Dist), 753 SW2d 451, petition for discretionary review refused.—Const Law 2190, 2204; Crim Law 1026.10(3), 1134(3); Obscen 1.4, 2.5.

Ford v. State, TexApp–Fort Worth, 977 SW2d 824, petition for discretionary review gr, rev 73 SW3d 923, habeas corpus dism 2002 WL 31697725.—Crim Law 1162, 1166.15; Jury 33(4), 64.

Ford v. State, TexApp–Fort Worth, 908 SW2d 32, reh overr, and petition for discretionary review refused.—Crim Law 147, 577.16(8), 1030(1), 1032(2), 1044.1(1), 1045, 1101, 1144.7; Infants 20.

Ford; State v., TexApp–San Antonio, 179 SW3d 117.—Atty & C 33; Courts 89; Crim Law 1134(6), 1139; Gr Jury 1; Ind & Inf 55, 137(6), 144.1(1); Offic 121; Records 32, 54.

Ford; State v., TexApp–San Antonio, 158 SW3d 574, reh overr, and petition for discretionary review dism (5 pets).—Dist & Pros Attys 3(1).

Ford v. State, TexApp–San Antonio, 870 SW2d 155, petition for discretionary review refused.—Crim Law 641.4(1), 641.4(4), 641.7(1), 698(1), 822(1), 847, 889, 1038.1(4), 1040, 1077.3, 1086.11, 1120(9), 1130(5), 1172.1(1); Tel 1013, 1018(4).

Ford v. State, TexApp–Dallas, 129 SW3d 541, reh overr, and petition for discretionary review refused.—Autos 332, 355(6); Crim Law 741(1), 742(1), 923(2), 925.5(1), 925.5(3), 957(1), 957(3), 957(5), 959, 961, 1038.1(1), 1134(4), 1144.13(3), 1156(1), 1156(5), 1159.2(1), 1159.2(2), 1172.1(1); Jury 131(1), 131(18).

Ford v. State, TexApp–Texarkana, 106 SW3d 765.—Sent & Pun 238.

Ford v. State, TexApp–Texarkana, 668 SW2d 477.—Autos 316, 355(5); Const Law 4653; Crim Law 577.10(9).

Ford v. State, TexApp–Amarillo, 20 SW3d 777, reh overr.—Crim Law 1023.5, 1026, 1069(5), 1069(6), 1081(4.1).

Ford v. State, TexApp–El Paso, 794 SW2d 863, petition for discretionary review refused, habeas corpus dism Ex parte Ford, 1993 WL 74710.—Const Law 4659(2); Crim Law 339.7(4), 339.8(4), 339.10(1), 339.10(6.1), 339.10(9), 1077.3, 1141(2), 1166(1); Rob 24.40.

FORD

Ford v. State, TexApp–Beaumont, 860 SW2d 731.—Burg 9(2), 41(4); Crim Law 1037.1(2).

Ford v. State, TexApp–Beaumont, 676 SW2d 609.—Controlled Subs 62; Crim Law 693, 1120(4), 1169.1(1), 1177, 1178.

Ford v. State, TexApp–Corpus Christi, 26 SW3d 669.—Arrest 63.1, 63.4(15), 63.5(8); Autos 349(3), 349(4), 349.5(10); Crim Law 338(1), 338(7), 347, 404.15, 404.30, 404.60, 661, 695.5, 741(1), 742(1), 1130(5), 1139, 1144.12, 1147, 1153(1), 1158(1), 1158(4); Searches 47.1, 49.

Ford v. State, TexApp–Houston (14 Dist), 179 SW3d 203, petition for discretionary review refused, cert den 127 SCt 281, 166 LEd2d 215.—Controlled Subs 148(3), 154; Crim Law 419(1), 627.10(1), 627.10(4), 627.10(5), 627.10(7.1), 662.8, 662.40, 1144.12, 1148; Searches 47.1, 108, 113.1.

Ford v. State, TexApp–Houston (14 Dist), 112 SW3d 788.—Crim Law 369.1, 369.2(3.1), 633(2), 661, 772(6), 1043(1), 1044.2(1); Obst Just 3, 8, 11.

Ford v. State, TexApp–Houston (14 Dist), 38 SW3d 836, reh overr, and petition for discretionary review refused.—Assault 48, 58; Const Law 4582; Crim Law 20, 83, 553, 554, 742(1), 769, 772(5), 795(1.5), 795(2.1), 795(2.20), 795(2.90), 824(3), 827, 828, 1032(1), 1045, 1134(3), 1137(3), 1137(7), 1141(2), 1144.13(3), 1159.2(2), 1159.2(7), 1191; Ind & Inf 6, 171, 191(0.5).

Ford v. State, TexApp–Houston (14 Dist), 14 SW3d 382.—Const Law 4677; Crim Law 23, 865(1), 865(2), 867, 1144.13(2.1), 1144.13(3), 1144.15, 1152(2), 1155, 1159.1, 1159.2(1), 1159.2(2), 1159.2(7), 1159.2(9), 1186.1; Int Liq 159(1), 236(11), 238(5); Jury 131(1), 131(3), 131(4), 131(7), 131(10), 131(13); Witn 17.

Ford v. State, TexApp–Houston (14 Dist), 868 SW2d 875, reh den, and petition for discretionary review refused.—Crim Law 1044.2(1), 1045, 1159.2(9), 1159.4(1); Weap 1, 2, 3, 4, 17(4).

Ford v. State, TexApp–Houston (14 Dist), 852 SW2d 641.—Crim Law 345, 347, 349, 1144.13(2.1), 1159.2(7), 1159.6, 1170.5(1); Rob 24.40; Witn 246(1).

Ford v. State, TexApp–Houston (14 Dist), 848 SW2d 776.—Crim Law 1099.13, 1141(2), 1144.10.

Ford v. State, TexApp–Houston (14 Dist), 835 SW2d 784, review gr, rev 846 SW2d 850, on remand 852 SW2d 641.—Crim Law 507(1), 507.5, 704, 730(2); Rob 24.40; Witn 246(1).

Ford v. State, TexApp–Houston (14 Dist), 828 SW2d 525, petition for discretionary review refused.—Assault 56; Crim Law 1144.13(2.1); Rob 1, 11, 24.15(2).

Ford v. State, TexApp–Houston (14 Dist), 782 SW2d 911.—Crim Law 620(6), 620(7), 1166(6).

Ford v. State, TexCivApp–Amarillo, 432 SW2d 720.—Evid 142(1), 142(2), 498.5.

Ford v. State ex rel. Schultz, TexCivApp–Amarillo, 138 SW2d 1105.—App & E 907(3).

Ford v. State Farm Mut. Auto. Ins. Co., Tex, 550 SW2d 663.—Insurance 3110(1).

Ford; State Farm Mut. Auto. Ins. Co. v., TexCivApp–Hous (14 Dist), 537 SW2d 138, writ gr, rev 550 SW2d 663.—Insurance 2793(2).

Ford; Texas & N. O. R. Co. v., TexCivApp–Beaumont, 143 SW2d 647.—App & E 1101.

Ford v. Texas & P. Ry. Co., TexCivApp–Eastland, 370 SW2d 795.—App & E 554(1), 688(3); New Tr 140(3).

Ford v. Texas Dept. of Public Safety, TexCivApp–Hous (14 Dist), 590 SW2d 786, ref nre.—Autos 144.2(7); Evid 474(19), 474(20).

Ford; Texas Emp. Ins. Ass'n v., Tex, 271 SW2d 397, 153 Tex 470.—Work Comp 820, 1619, 1927.

Ford; Texas Emp. Ins. Ass'n v., TexCivApp–Fort Worth, 93 SW2d 227, writ dism.—App & E 1003(5); Work Comp 554, 1593, 1930.

Ford; Texas Emp. Ins. Ass'n v., TexCivApp–Austin, 267 SW2d 191, rev 271 SW2d 397, 153 Tex 470.—App & E

1078(1); Judgm 199(3.7); Work Comp 1615, 1619, 1922, 1926, 1927, 1928.

Ford v. Town of Coppell, TexCivApp–Dallas, 407 SW2d 304, ref nre.—Mun Corp 29(1), 29(2), 29(3).

Ford; United Hay Co. v., TexCivApp–Galveston, 81 SW2d 776, writ refused.—Agric 3.1; Trusts 219(2).

Ford; U.S. v., CA5 (Tex), 996 F2d 83, cert den 114 SCt 704, 510 US 1050, 126 LEd2d 670.—Crim Law 1139, 1158(1); Sent & Pun 651, 797, 800, 836, 841, 995; Weap 17(8).

Ford; U.S. v., CA5 (Tex), 824 F2d 1430, cert den 108 SCt 741, 484 US 1034, 98 LEd2d 776.—Crim Law 1166.16; U S Mag 21.

Ford; U.S. v., CA5 (Tex), 797 F2d 1329, cert den 107 SCt 964, 479 US 1070, 93 LEd2d 1011, reh gr, vac 811 F2d 268, on reh 824 F2d 1430, cert den 108 SCt 741, 484 US 1034, 98 LEd2d 776.

Ford v. U.S., CA5 (Tex), 618 F2d 357, reh den 625 F2d 1016.—Courts 90(2); Int Rev 4812, 4813, 4960.

Ford v. U.S., CA5 (Tex), 233 F2d 56, cert den 77 SCt 49, 352 US 833, 1 LEd2d 53.—Crim Law 338(4), 868, 1153(4), 1169.11; Ind & Inf 10.2(8); Int Rev 5263.15, 5306, 5311.1; Witn 267, 330(1), 372(1), 372(2).

Ford v. U.S., CA5 (Tex), 210 F2d 313.—Crim Law 308, 317, 338(4), 1169.1(2.1), 1170.5(5); Hus & W 21; Int Rev 5262, 5263.15, 5293, 5294, 5305, 5312; Witn 54, 268(1).

Ford; Wallace v., NDTex, 21 FSupp 624.—Const Law 4260, 4537; Equity 65(1); Fed Cts 6; Inj 75, 89(5), 128(7); Int Liq 15, 129.5; Searches 25.1.

Ford; Wells v., TexCivApp–Beaumont, 118 SW2d 420, writ dism.—App & E 259, 742(4), 1062.1; Autos 244(12), 244(36.1); Damag 30, 132(14), 140.7, 163(1), 185(1), 187, 221(2.1), 221(4); New Tr 140(3); Trial 127, 351.5(6), 352.4(1), 352.5(5), 352.5(6), 352.18; Witn 393(6).

Ford v. Whitehead, TexApp–San Antonio, 2 SW3d 304.—App & E 422.

Ford v. Wied, TexApp–Texarkana, 823 SW2d 423, writ den.—Execution 7, 99, 171(1), 171(3), 172(1), 172(2); Judgm 189.

Ford & Calhoun GMC Truck Co.; Cloer v., TexCivApp–Tyler, 553 SW2d 183, ref nre.—App & E 497(1), 907(2), 907(3); Judgm 178.

Ford, Bacon & Davis, Inc. v. Torrance, TexCivApp–Waco, 349 SW2d 113.—Corp 432(12); Princ & A 119(4).

Ford, Bacon & Davis, Texas, Inc.; Gulf Oil Corp. v., TexApp–Beaumont, 782 SW2d 28.—Indem 30(5), 42.

Ford, Bacon & Davis Texas Inc.; Tom Hicks Transfer Co. v., TexCivApp–Texarkana, 482 SW2d 364.—Carr 194.

Ford Cattle Co., Matter of, CA5 (Tex), 967 F2d 1047. See Ford, Matter of.

Ford Dealer Computer Services, Inc.; Prestige Ford v., CA5 (Tex), 324 F3d 391, cert den 124 SCt 281, 540 US 878, 157 LEd2d 141, reh den 124 SCt 866, 540 US 1070, 157 LEd2d 736.—Alt Disp Res 258, 265, 312, 326, 329, 363(6), 363(10), 374(1).

Forder v. State, TexCrimApp, 456 SW2d 378.—Crim Law 311, 331, 404.65, 414, 480, 517(1), 957(3), 1131(5); Homic 1210, 1502; Ind & Inf 180; Infants 68.4.

Forderhase, Ex parte, TexApp–Tyler, 635 SW2d 198.—Divorce 255.

Forderhause; Cherokee Water Co. v., Tex, 741 SW2d 377.—Ref of Inst 16, 19(1).

Forderhause; Cherokee Water Co. v., Tex, 641 SW2d 522.—Action 60; Deeds 93, 109, 123; Mines 55(7), 73.1(2), 73.1(4); Perp 4(1).

Forderhause; Cherokee Water Co. v., TexApp–Texarkana, 727 SW2d 605, writ gr, rev 741 SW2d 377.—Evid 241(1), 268; Mines 55(8); Princ & A 20(2), 21, 23(4), 119(1), 171(2); Ref of Inst 19(1), 19(2); Ven & Pur 229(10).

Forderhause v. Cherokee Water Co., TexCivApp–Texarkana, 623 SW2d 435, writ gr, rev 641 SW2d 522.—

Action 60; Deeds 93, 95; Judgm 181(30); Mines 73.1(2); Perp 4(1), 4(3), 6(1); Set-Off 60; Ven & Pur 57.

Forderson v. State, TexCrimApp, 467 SW2d 476.—Autos 349(2.1), 349(6), 349.5(11); Controlled Subs 116; Crim Law 404.60, 1038.2, 1038.4.

Ford-Evans v. Smith, CA5 (Tex), 206 FedAppx 332.—Fed Civ Proc 2544, 2547.1; Labor & Emp 388.

Ford ex rel. Williams v. City of Lubbock, TexApp–Amarillo, 76 SW3d 795.—App & E 428(2).

Ford Gas Co. v. Wanda Petroleum Co., CA5 (Tex), 833 F2d 1172. See Benson and Ford, Inc. v. Wanda Petroleum Co.

Fordham v. Butane Gas & Equipment Co., TexCivApp–San Antonio, 198 SW2d 607, ref nre.—App & E 237(1); Gas 20(2).

Fordice; King v., TexApp–Dallas, 776 SW2d 608, writ den.—Evid 429, 462; Sales 382, 387.

Fordice; King Air Service v., TexApp–Dallas, 776 SW2d 608. See King v. Fordice.

Ford, Inc. v. Fitzpatrick, CA5 (Tex), 892 F2d 1230. See Hamilton, Matter of.

Ford Life Ins. Co.; Roberson v., TexCivApp–Amarillo, 474 SW2d 314, ref nre.—Insurance 3091, 3131.

Ford Memorial Hosp.; Grossling v., EDTex, 614 FSupp 1051.—Antitrust 543; Consp 7.5(1), 7.5(3), 18, 19; Const Law 3027, 3941; Health 271, 273, 275.

Ford Motor Co., In re, Tex, 211 SW3d 295.—Mand 28, 32; Pretrial Proc 33, 356.1, 371, 413.1; Stip 14(1).

Ford Motor Co., In re, Tex, 165 SW3d 315.—Const Law 3993; Mand 4(1), 4(4), 28, 45; Pretrial Proc 716, 723.1.

Ford Motor Co., In re, Tex, 988 SW2d 714.—App & E 961; Mand 1, 4(1), 4(4); Pretrial Proc 35, 39, 44.1, 130, 358, 379; Witn 199(1).

Ford Motor Co., In re, TexApp–San Antonio, 220 SW3d 21.—Alt Disp Res 141, 200; Contracts 188; Mand 60.

Ford Motor Co., In re, TexApp–Houston (14 Dist), 965 SW2d 571, mandamus overr.—Courts 485, 486; Mand 3(1), 31.

Ford Motor Co.; A.C. Collins Ford, Inc. v., TexApp–El Paso, 807 SW2d 755, writ den.—App & E 230, 231(1), 241, 756, 761, 863; Judgm 185(2); Lim of Act 100(12).

Ford Motor Co. v. Aguiniga, TexApp–San Antonio, 9 SW3d 252, review den, and reh of petition for review overr.—Action 17; App & E 23, 185(1), 840(1), 842(1), 842(7), 893(1); 912, 913, 930(1), 970(2), 971(2); 989, 1001(3), 1024.1, 1024.3; Autos 229.5; Death 34.1, 58(1); Evid 539, 555.2, 555.8(1); Ex & Ad 450; Prod Liab 3, 8, 11, 83.5; Torts 103; Treaties 8; Venue 8.5(8).

Ford Motor Co.; Allied Finance Co. v., TexCivApp–Dallas, 327 SW2d 696, ref nre.—Autos 20.

Ford Motor Co.; Ames v., SDTex, 299 FSupp2d 678.—Prod Liab 23.1, 39.

Ford Motor Co.; Ash ex rel. Estate of Vargas v., SDTex, 246 FSupp2d 629.—Fed Cts 9.

Ford Motor Co.; Barnett v., TexCivApp–Waco, 463 SW2d 33.—Prod Liab 77.5.

Ford Motor Co. v. Beauchamp, USTex, 60 SCt 273, 308 US 331, 84 LEd 304, reh den 60 SCt 385, 308 US 640, 84 LEd 531.—Commerce 63.5, 69(1); Const Law 3566; Tax 2103, 2106, 2233, 2256, 2545.

Ford Motor Co. v. Benson, TexApp–Houston (14 Dist), 846 SW2d 487, reh den, and writ gr, and cause dism.—App & E 1043(6); Pretrial Proc 413.1.

Ford Motor Co. v. Bland, TexCivApp–Waco, 517 SW2d 641, ref nre.—App & E 971(2); Damag 132(3); Evid 546; Prod Liab 40, 83.5.

Ford Motor Co.; Bricker v., SDTex, 514 FSupp 1236.—Rem of C 29, 31.

Ford Motor Co.; Builders Transport, Inc. v., EDTex, 25 FSupp2d 739, revSchneider Nat Transport v. Ford Motor Co, 280 F3d 532.—Contracts 2; Fed Cts 409.1; Insurance 1091(10), 1822, 1832(1), 1835(2), 2270(1), 2923, 2934(1).

Ford Motor Co.; Butnaru v., Tex, 84 SW3d 198.—Antitrust 130, 282, 283, 285, 383(2); App & E 946, 954(1), 1008.1(3), 1010.1(5); Const Law 191, 2312; Equity 17; Inj 57, 132, 135, 138.3, 138.6, 140; Torts 220, 242.

Ford Motor Co. v. Butnaru, TexApp–Austin, 157 SW3d 142.—Action 13; Admin Law 228.1, 817.1; Antitrust 283, 290, 343; App & E 893(1); Const Law 2563.

Ford Motor Co. v. Butnaru, TexApp–San Antonio, 18 SW3d 762, reh overr, and review gr, rev 84 SW3d 198.—Action 35; Admin Law 228.1; Antitrust 129, 283, 290; App & E 863, 954(1); Const Law 2312; Inj 57, 138.1, 138.3, 138.18, 138.37.

Ford Motor Co.; Byrnes v., EDTex, 642 FSupp 309.—Antitrust 290, 389(1); Death 31(1), 31(8).

Ford Motor Co.; Calcasieu Kennel Club, Inc. v., EDTex, 800 FSupp 482. See Emrick v. Calcasieu Kennel Club, Inc.

Ford Motor Co. v. Cammack, TexApp–Houston (14 Dist), 999 SW2d 1, opinion supplemented on denial of reh, and review den, and reh of petition for review overr.—Action 13; App & E 913, 1001(3), 1024.1; Death 10, 31(3.1), 31(5), 31(7), 39, 57, 93; Des & Dist 89; Evid 571(9); Neglig 371, 372, 379, 380, 383, 387, 1676; Prod Liab 15, 83.5.

Ford Motor Co.; Carroll v., TexCivApp–Hous (14 Dist), 462 SW2d 57.—Autos 368; Evid 54; Neglig 1012; Prod Liab 76, 77.5, 83.5, 88.5.

Ford Motor Co.; Casa Ford, Inc. v., TexApp–Texarkana, 951 SW2d 865, reh overr, and review den, and reh of petition for review overr.—Antitrust 269(2); App & E 1175(1), 1178(1); Const Law 190; Contrib 1, 9(3), 9(4); Indem 72; Statut 181(1), 209, 263.

Ford Motor Co. v. Castillo, TexApp–Corpus Christi, 200 SW3d 217, reh overr.—App & E 199, 223, 242(2), 970(2), 1043(1), 1050.1(1), 1056.1(1), 1056.1(5); Compromise 21; Judgm 72, 91, 186; Trial 43.

Ford Motor Co. v. Clark, CCA5 (Tex), 100 F2d 515, cert gr 59 SCt 775, 306 US 628, 83 LEd 1031, aff 60 SCt 273, 308 US 331, 84 LEd 304, reh den 60 SCt 385, 308 US 640, 84 LEd 531.—Commerce 69(1); Const Law 4140; Evid 84; Tax 2212, 2233, 2256, 2540, 2562.

Ford Motor Co.; Collins Ford, Inc. v., TexApp–El Paso, 807 SW2d 755. See A.C. Collins Ford, Inc. v. Ford Motor Co.

Ford Motor Co. v. Cooper, TexApp–Texarkana, 125 SW3d 794.—Antitrust 369, 389(2), 390; App & E 1175(2), 1177(7), 1178(2); Damag 103, 163(4); Evid 474(16); Sales 441(4).

Ford Motor Co.; Cullum v., CCA5 (Tex), 107 F2d 945.—Sales 77(2), 397.

Ford Motor Co.; Cullum v., CCA5 (Tex), 96 F2d 1, cert den 59 SCt 89, 305 US 627, 83 LEd 401.—Fed Cts 912; Sales 267, 273(2), 390, 391(8).

Ford Motor Co. v. Dallas Power & Light Co., CA5 (Tex), 499 F2d 400.—Bailm 21; Damag 62(1); Em Dom 2(10), 90; Fed Civ Proc 2232.1, 2234.1; Fed Cts 430, 911, 943.1; Neglig 221; Nuis 61; Waters 69, 116, 118, 119(2), 126(3), 171(1), 171(2), 173, 179(5), 179(6).

Ford Motor Co.; Darryl v., Tex, 440 SW2d 630.—App & E 302(6); Prod Liab 5, 8, 19.1, 35.1, 39, 81.1, 83.5.

Ford Motor Co. v. Darryl, TexCivApp–Amarillo, 432 SW2d 569, writ gr, aff in part, rev in part 440 SW2d 630.—Prod Liab 5, 83.5; Sales 441(3).

Ford Motor Co. v. Davis Bros., Inc., TexCivApp–Eastland, 369 SW2d 664.—Contracts 9(1), 175(1), 229(1), 230; Costs 194.32; Nova 1, 12; Trial 350.4(4), 366.

Ford Motor Co.; Dion v., TexApp–Eastland, 804 SW2d 302, writ den.—App & E 989, 999(1), 1068(2), 1070(2); Neglig 202; New Tr 72(5); Prod Liab 5, 6, 8, 16, 50, 85, 98; Sales 425; Trial 350.1, 351.2(10).

Ford Motor Co.; Dresser Industries, Inc. v., NDTex, 530 FSupp 303.—Fed Civ Proc 1951; Fed Cts 1149.1; Jury 14(1.1); Pat 112.1, 139, 140, 144, 148, 314(4).

FORD

See Guidelines for Arrangement at the beginning of this Volume

Ford Motor Co.; Duff v., TexCivApp–Dallas, 91 SW2d 871.—Labor & Emp 34(2), 40(2), 40(3), 42.

Ford Motor Co. v. Durrill, TexApp–Corpus Christi, 714 SW2d 329, writ gr, vac 754 SW2d 646.—App & E 1056.1(3), 1056.1(10), 1060.1(1), 1060.1(2.1), 1060.1(4), 1140(1), 1140(2), 1171(1); Corp 494; Damag 94, 184; Death 81, 89, 93, 99(3), 106; Evid 219.65, 345(1), 359(1), 363, 571(3), 571(9); Interest 65; Neglig 273, 1659; Pretrial Proc 204; Prod Liab 5, 11, 81.5, 83.5; Sent & Pun 1602; Trial 352.1(7), 352.5(5), 352.10.

Ford Motor Co.; Foster v., CA5 (Tex), 621 F2d 715.— Evid 195; Fed Civ Proc 1431, 2173.1(1), 2174, 2182.1; Fed Cts 896.1, 911; Prod Liab 98.

Ford Motor Co.; Foster v., CA5 (Tex), 616 F2d 1304.— Contrib 5(1), 5(6.1); Fed Civ Proc 2142.1, 2608.1; Indem 58, 72; Labor & Emp 2875, 2881; Prod Liab 11, 15, 23.1, 91.

Ford Motor Co. v. Gonzalez, TexApp–San Antonio, 9 SW3d 195, reh overr.—App & E 930(1), 1001(3); Evid 570, 571(9); Prod Liab 5, 8, 75.1, 82.1, 83.5.

Ford Motor Co.; Graham v., TexApp–Tyler, 721 SW2d 554.—Const Law 2503(2); Courts 472.2; Parent & C 7.5.

Ford Motor Co. v. Grimes, TexCivApp–Eastland, 408 SW2d 313, writ dism.—Plead 111.42(4); Sales 255, 273(1).

Ford Motor Co.; Hall v., TexCivApp–Corpus Christi, 565 SW2d 592.—Plead 111.9, 111.12; Venue 21.

Ford Motor Co.; Henderson v., Tex, 519 SW2d 87.— Neglig 552(1); Prod Liab 11, 27, 36, 40, 83.5; Torts 126.

Ford Motor Co.; Henderson v., TexCivApp–Amarillo, 547 SW2d 663.—Fraud 6, 7, 18, 33, 50; Sales 255, 267, 427, 437(1), 442(1).

Ford Motor Co. v. Henderson, TexCivApp–Beaumont, 500 SW2d 709, writ gr, rev 519 SW2d 87.—Prod Liab 26, 40, 73.5.

Ford Motor Co.; Hernandez v., SDTex, 390 FSupp2d 602.—Damag 57.27, 57.29.

Ford Motor Co.; Johnny Maddox Motor Co. v., WDTex, 202 FSupp 103.—Antitrust 847, 972(3), 972(8), 977(5); Consp 2; Contracts 229(1).

Ford Motor Co.; Lambeth v., CA5 (Tex), 439 F2d 152.— Courts 104.

Ford Motor Co. v. Ledesma, TexApp–Austin, 173 SW3d 78, reh overr, and review gr.—App & E 893(1), 930(3), 946, 971(2), 1001(3), 1064.1(1), 1064.1(8); Evid 508, 535, 536, 544, 545, 546, 555.2, 555.8(1), 571(6); Neglig 379, 380; Prod Liab 8, 15, 82.1, 83.5, 96.1.

Ford Motor Co. v. Leggat, Tex, 904 SW2d 643.—Afft 11, 18; Evid 219(3); Mand 4(4); Pretrial Proc 36.1, 371; Witn 184(2), 198(1), 199(2).

Ford Motor Co.; Lemery v., SDTex, 244 FSupp2d 720.— Courts 182.1, 472.4(8); Fed Cts 9, 101, 103, 104, 105, 113, 144, 660.5, 660.30, 668, 819; Rem of C 102.

Ford Motor Co.; Lemery v., SDTex, 205 FSupp2d 710.— Courts 472.4(8); Fed Cts 9, 41, 43, 46, 47.1; Rem of C 102.

Ford Motor Co. v. Lemieux Lumber Co., TexCivApp–Beaumont, 418 SW2d 909.—Plead 111.42(4); Sales 255, 273(2); Venue 22(8).

Ford Motor Co.; Mares v., TexApp–San Antonio, 53 SW3d 416.—App & E 946, 961, 1050.1(12); Pretrial Proc 45.

Ford Motor Co.; Marrs v., TexApp–Dallas, 852 SW2d 570.—Antitrust 234; Prod Liab 35.1; States 18.3, 18.5, 18.11, 18.15, 18.65; Statut 206.

Ford Motor Co.; Marshall v., TexApp–Dallas, 878 SW2d 629.—App & E 836, 852, 931(1), 989, 1010.2, 1012.1(5); Guar 27, 36(1), 36(5), 77(1), 87.

Ford Motor Co.; Martin v., SDTex, 914 FSupp 1449.— Antitrust 132, 234; Fed Civ Proc 2466, 2470.1, 2543, 2544, 2552, 2553; Prod Liab 35.1; Sales 284(1), 427; States 18.3, 18.11, 18.15, 18.65.

Ford Motor Co. v. Mathis, CA5 (Tex), 322 F2d 267, 3 ALR3d 1002.—Evid 318(4); Fed Civ Proc 2142.1, 2231; Fed Cts 372, 842, 908.1; Neglig 210; Prod Liab 8, 10, 15, 24, 35.1, 36, 39, 83.5; Torts 425.

Ford Motor Co.; Metro Ford Truck Sales, Inc. v., CA5 (Tex), 145 F3d 320, 172 ALR Fed 675, reh and sug for reh den 154 F3d 419, cert den 119 SCt 798, 525 US 1068, 142 LEd2d 660.—Antitrust 537, 625, 839, 882, 908; Fed Civ Proc 1261; Fed Cts 18, 776, 813, 824; RICO 55; Rem of C 19(1), 25(1), 48.1, 56, 101.1.

Ford Motor Co. v. Miles, Tex, 967 SW2d 377, on subsequent appeal 2001 WL 727355, review den, and reh of petition for review den, appeal after remand 141 SW3d 309, reh overr, and review den (2 pets).—App & E 1024.3; Corp 503(1), 666; Damag 51; Parent & C 7(1); Venue 29.

Ford Motor Co.; Miles v., Tex, 914 SW2d 135.—Abate & R 6, 8(2); Courts 475(1), 483, 487(1).

Ford Motor Co. v. Miles, TexApp–Dallas, 141 SW3d 309, reh overr, and review den (2 pets).—App & E 893(1), 930(3), 1097(1), 1177(8); Damag 91.5(1); Neglig 371, 1501; Prod Liab 8, 11, 14, 15, 36, 38, 71, 75.1; Trial 250, 358.

Ford Motor Co.; Miles v., TexApp–Texarkana, 922 SW2d 572, reh overr, and writ gr, aff in part, rev in part 967 SW2d 377, on subsequent appeal 2001 WL 727355, review den, and reh of petition for review den, appeal after remand 141 SW3d 309, reh overr, and review den (2 pets).—App & E 230, 231(1), 671(4), 758.3(9), 930(2), 970(2), 971(6), 989, 994(2), 1001(1), 1003(3), 1003(5), 1003(6), 1024.3, 1047(4), 1050.1(11), 1051(1), 1057(1), 1178(6), 1182; Const Law 4016; Corp 503(1); Damag 91(1), 91(3), 184; Death 88; Evid 150, 155(1), 359(6), 370(4), 373(1); Prod Liab 8, 9, 10, 15, 26, 71, 83.5; Sales 273(1), 273(3), 284(1), 284(4); Trial 76, 295(1), 296(3); Venue 8.2, 16.5; Witn 331.5, 406.

Ford Motor Co.; Morales v., SDTex, 313 FSupp2d 672.— Fed Cts 44, 45, 417.

Ford Motor Co. v. Motor Vehicle Bd. of Texas Dept. of Transportation/Metro Ford Truck Sales, Inc., TexApp–Austin, 21 SW3d 744, reh overr, and review den.— Admin Law 305, 325, 754.1, 791; Antitrust 269(4), 269(5), 269(6), 341, 342, 343, 369, 400; Equity 65(2); Estop 54; Statut 174, 176, 181(1), 186, 188, 212.6, 212.7, 219(1), 219(2), 219(4), 230.

Ford Motor Co.; Murray v., CA5 (Tex), 770 F2d 461.— Fed Civ Proc 2646, 2651.1, 2656; Fed Cts 761; Rem of C 97.

Ford Motor Co.; Murray v., TexApp–Dallas, 97 SW3d 888.—App & E 856(1), 863, 934(1), 1169(8); Judgm 185(2); Lim of Act 47(1), 49(7); Neglig 463; Prod Liab 17.1; Sales 427.

Ford Motor Co.; Muth v., CA5 (Tex), 461 F3d 557, reh and reh den 213 FedAppx 366.—Evid 150; Fed Civ Proc 1969, 2142.1; Fed Cts 752, 776, 823, 904, 906; Prod Liab 16, 36, 88.5.

Ford Motor Co.; Nielsen v., TexCivApp–San Antonio, 612 SW2d 209, ref nre.—Judgm 73, 570(6), 878(1).

Ford Motor Co.; Norton v., CA5 (Tex), 470 F2d 992.— Prod Liab 88.5.

Ford Motor Co. v. Nowak, TexApp–Corpus Christi, 638 SW2d 582, ref nre.—App & E 216(6), 218.2(5.1), 230, 238(1), 242(2), 882(16), 989, 1001(1), 1003(4), 1051.1(1), 1067, 1170.1, 1170.6, 1170.7; Damag 91(1), 91(3); Death 99(1); Evid 150, 359(6); Jury 149; Prod Liab 11, 83.5, 87.1; Trial 31; Witn 406.

Ford Motor Co. v. Ocanas, TexApp–Corpus Christi, 138 SW3d 447, am on denial of reh.—Action 17; App & E 913, 949; Parties 35.7, 35.17, 35.33, 35.35, 35.71; Trial 18.

Ford Motor Co.; Parsons v., CA5 (Tex), 669 F2d 308, cert den 103 SCt 73, 459 US 832, 74 LEd2d 72.—Antitrust 592, 977(5); Fed Civ Proc 2484.

Ford Motor Co.; Parsons v., TexApp–Austin, 85 SW3d 323, reh overr, and review den.—App & E 863; Judgm 183, 185(2), 185(5); Neglig 1610, 1612, 1613, 1614, 1615, 1617; Prod Liab 5, 8, 15, 35.1, 75.1, 76, 77.5, 81.5, 82.1.

Ford Motor Co.; Patterson v., WDTex, 85 FRD 152.— Fed Civ Proc 1635.

Ford Motor Co.; Pierce v., TexCivApp–Eastland, 401 SW2d 355, writ dism woj.—App & E 912, 989; Plead 111.42(3); Venue 21.

Ford Motor Co.; Pool v., Tex, 715 SW2d 629, on remand 718 SW2d 910, writ gr, set aside 749 SW2d 489.—App & E 199, 237(1), 237(2), 242(1), 768, 882(16), 1056.1(7), 1056.4, 1177(7), 1182; Damag 170; Evid 150; Prod Liab 40, 81.5; Trial 352.1(6), 352.5(5).

Ford Motor Co. v. Pool, TexApp–Texarkana, 718 SW2d 910, writ gr, set aside 749 SW2d 489.—Damag 132(3), 134(1); Prod Liab 83.5.

Ford Motor Co. v. Pool, TexApp–Texarkana, 688 SW2d 879, writ gr, aff in part, rev in part and remanded 715 SW2d 629, on remand 718 SW2d 910, writ gr, set aside 749 SW2d 489.—App & E 1032(1), 1062.1, 1170.7; Damag 172(1); Evid 146, 571(1); Hus & W 232.2; Neglig 259; Prod Liab 8, 11, 40, 83.5, 88.5, 98; Trial 352.5(5).

Ford Motor Co.; Praytor v., TexApp–Houston (14 Dist), 97 SW3d 237.—App & E 223, 971(2); Evid 508, 536, 544, 545, 546, 555.2, 555.10, 568(1); Neglig 375, 404, 1675, 1676; Prod Liab 15, 82.1, 83.5.

Ford Motor Co. v. Puskar, TexCivApp–Houston, 394 SW2d 1, writ gr, mod Jack Roach-Bissonnet, Inc v. Puskar, 417 SW2d 262.—Prod Liab 35.1, 83.5; Sales 280.

Ford Motor Co.; Quebe v., WDTex, 908 FSupp 446.— Domicile 1; Fed Cts 4, 282, 286.1, 288, 297, 300, 338, 346, 357.1; Rem of C 11, 74, 107(7).

Ford Motor Co. v. Revert, TexCivApp–Amarillo, 428 SW2d 139.—Plead 45, 111.39(4), 111.42(8); Venue 21.

Ford Motor Co. v. Ridgway, Tex, 135 SW3d 598, reh den. —Judgm 185(2), 185(5), 185.3(21); Prod Liab 8, 15, 77.5, 83.5.

Ford Motor Co.; Ridgway v., TexApp–San Antonio, 82 SW3d 26, reh overr, and review gr, rev 135 SW3d 598, reh den.—Evid 587; Judgm 178, 181(33), 183, 185(2), 185(5); Prod Liab 8, 10, 11, 35.1, 36, 82.1.

Ford Motor Co.; Roquemore v., CA5 (Tex), 400 F2d 255. —Brok 43(0.5), 52, 65(5).

Ford Motor Co.; Roquemore v., NDTex, 290 FSupp 130, aff 400 F2d 255.—Brok 6, 43(1), 65(1); Contracts 172, 245(2); Frds St of 72(1); Princ & A 69(2), 69(5); Ven & Pur 18(4).

Ford Motor Co. v. Ross, TexApp–Tyler, 888 SW2d 879.— Mand 1, 4(4); Pretrial Proc 11, 41, 351.

Ford Motor Co.; Rothe v., NDTex, 531 FSupp 189.— Death 39; Fed Cts 427; Sales 431; Time 9(2), 10(4).

Ford Motor Co. v. Russell & Smith Ford Co., TexCiv-App–Hous (14 Dist), 474 SW2d 549.—Contrib 5(7); Indem 72, 97, 102; Judgm 199(3.14), 217; Prod Liab 14, 22, 27, 37; Torts 114; Trial 141.

Ford Motor Co.; Schneider Nat. Transport v., CA5 (Tex), 280 F3d 532.—Action 17; Contracts 2, 147(3); Fed Cts 776; Insurance 1091(10), 1806, 1822, 1839, 2396, 2917.

Ford Motor Co.; Senigaur v., EDTex, 222 FSupp2d 829. —Compromise 18(3); Lim of Act 100(12).

Ford Motor Co. v. Sheldon, Tex, 22 SW3d 444, appeal after remand 113 SW3d 839.—Const Law 3053, 3078, 3466, 3981; Courts 247(1); Judgm 677; Parties 35.1, 35.37, 35.41, 35.71; Statut 66, 67, 68, 77(1), 85(4), 117(7), 126.

Ford Motor Co. v. Sheldon, TexApp–Austin, 113 SW3d 839.—App & E 913, 949; Courts 97(1); Parties 35.1, 35.5, 35.7, 35.9, 35.17, 35.33, 35.35, 35.41, 35.71; Trial 3(1).

Ford Motor Co.; Speck v., TexApp–Houston (14 Dist), 709 SW2d 273.—App & E 345.1; Pretrial Proc 587, 697, 699.

Ford Motor Co. v. State, Tex, 175 SW2d 230, 142 Tex 5. —Antitrust 550, 563, 592, 823, 826, 882, 972(3), 1005; Contracts 103; Penalties 32; Plead 34(3).

Ford Motor Co.; State v., TexCivApp–Austin, 169 SW2d 504, aff 175 SW2d 230, 142 Tex 5.—Antitrust 659, 687, 960, 972(4).

Ford Motor Co. v. Stead, TexCivApp–Waco, 574 SW2d 226.—App & E 1170.7, 1177(9); Corp 666; Plead 111.42(6); Prod Liab 8; Witn 140(1), 140(19).

Ford Motor Co.; Steenbergen v., TexApp–Dallas, 814 SW2d 755, writ den, cert den 113 SCt 97, 506 US 831, 121 LEd2d 58.—App & E 78(1), 882(1), 882(8), 970(2), 1048(6), 1056.1(1); Const Law 2474; Courts 1; Evid 382; Pretrial Proc 15, 432, 433; Trial 23; Work Comp 2247.

Ford Motor Co. v. Stern, TexCivApp–Waco, 543 SW2d 200.—Plead 111.18, 111.42(9).

Ford Motor Co.; Strauss v., NDTex, 439 FSupp2d 680.— Antitrust 193; Neglig 463, 1537; Prod Liab 17.1; Sales 272, 273(3), 284(4).

Ford Motor Co.; Surles v., NDTex, 709 FSupp 732.— Prod Liab 35.1; States 18.65.

Ford Motor Co. v. Ted Arendale Ford Sales, Inc., TexCivApp–Fort Worth, 447 SW2d 774.—Corp 666; Venue 22(8).

Ford Motor Co. v. Texas Dept. of Transp., CA5 (Tex), 264 F3d 493.—Admin Law 390.1; Antitrust 129, 269(1), 336, 341; Commerce 12, 13.5, 54.1, 60(1); Const Law 1537, 1645, 3039, 3334, 3706, 3905, 4027, 4294; Fed Civ Proc 2534, 2543; Statut 47.

Ford Motor Co. v. Texas Dept. of Transp., WDTex, 106 FSupp2d 905, aff 264 F3d 493.—Antitrust 129; Commerce 63.15; Const Law 1540, 1541, 1602, 2151, 3706, 3905, 4294.

Ford Motor Co. v. Tidwell, TexCivApp–El Paso, 563 SW2d 831, ref nre.—App & E 766, 832(4), 989; Evid 419(13); Prod Liab 83.5; Sales 255, 279, 417, 439, 441(1); Trial 366.

Ford Motor Co. v. Tyson, TexApp–Dallas, 943 SW2d 527, reh overr, subsequent mandamus proceeding In re Ford Motor Co., 988 SW2d 714.—App & E 856(1), 961; Const Law 3893, 3987; Costs 2; Courts 26; Mand 1, 4(1), 4(4), 53, 168(2); Pretrial Proc 44.1.

Ford Motor Co.; Vaughn v., TexApp–Eastland, 91 SW3d 387, reh overr, and review den.—App & E 946, 1043(6); Pretrial Proc 44.1, 45, 224, 434, 486; Prod Liab 62, 83; Trial 139.1(14), 178; Work Comp 2093, 2094, 2136.

Ford Motor Co. v. Whitt, TexApp–Amarillo, 81 SW3d 1032, writ refused.—App & E 758.3(1), 760(1), 839(1), 1033(10); Autos 242(6); Evid 119(1); Neglig 1634, 1642; New Tr 144; Trial 114, 121(2), 219, 232(3), 350.6(3), 351.5(1), 352.1(9), 352.5(6), 352.11.

Ford Motor Company/Cross v. Texas Dept. of Transp., Motor Vehicle Div., TexApp–Austin, 936 SW2d 427.— Antitrust 206, 286, 343, 367, 369.

Ford Motor Co., Edsel Division v. Boatman, TexCiv-App–Beaumont, 345 SW2d 782.—App & E 770(1); Venue 22(7).

Ford Motor Co., Inc.; Johnson v., TexApp–Eastland, 690 SW2d 90, ref nre.—App & E 863; Labor & Emp 40(2), 858.

Ford Motor Co., Inc.; Natividad v., TexApp–El Paso, 897 SW2d 475.—App & E 395, 627, 627.2.

Ford Motor Co., Inc. v. Sheldon, TexApp–Austin, 965 SW2d 65, reh overr, and review gr, rev 22 SW3d 444, appeal after remand 113 SW3d 839.—App & E 946, 949; Parties 35.13, 35.17, 35.71; Trial 3(5.1).

Ford Motor Co. Ltd.; Hopper v., SDTex, 837 FSupp 840. —Fed Civ Proc 1825; Fed Cts 45, 86.

Ford Motor Credit Co. v. **Blocker**, TexCivApp–El Paso, 558 SW2d 493, ref nre.—App & E 218.2(1), 930(3), 989; Cons Cred 3.1, 4, 52; Stip 18(1).

Ford Motor Credit Co. v. **Bright**, CA5 (Tex), 34 F3d 322, reh and sug for reh den 41 F3d 666.—Fed Civ Proc 2642, 2651.1, 2658, 2659; Fed Cts 763.1, 776, 817.

Ford Motor Credit Co. v. **Brown**, TexCivApp–Eastland, 617 SW2d 271, ref nre.—Cons Cred 12, 13, 16.

Ford Motor Credit Co. v. **Brown**, TexCivApp–Corpus Christi, 613 SW2d 521, ref nre.—App & E 14(4), 758.1; Cons Cred 2, 12, 16, 19.

Ford Motor Credit Co.; **Carbajal** v., TexApp–Corpus Christi, 658 SW2d 281, dism.—Cons Cred 12, 16; Time 9(2).

Ford Motor Credit Co.; **Ciminelli** v., Tex, 624 SW2d 903. —App & E 302(2); Cons Cred 4, 19.

Ford Motor Credit Co.; **Ciminelli** v., TexCivApp–Corpus Christi, 612 SW2d 671, rev 624 SW2d 903.—Cons Cred 2, 18; Guar 1.

Ford Motor Credit Co. v. **Cole**, TexCivApp–Fort Worth, 503 SW2d 853, dism.—Larc 3(3); Sec Tran 115.1, 228; Venue 8.5(7), 15.

Ford Motor Credit Co.; **Collins** v., TexCivApp–Beaumont, 454 SW2d 469.—App & E 846(5), 931(3), 989; Plead 111.42(2), 111.42(6); Venue 7.5(7), 8.5(5), 22(6).

Ford Motor Credit Co. v. **Commonwealth County Mut. Ins. Co.**, TexCivApp–Beaumont, 420 SW2d 732.—Contracts 143(3); Insurance 1808, 1832(1), 1929(2), 1929(11); Judgm 185.3(12).

Ford Motor Credit Co. v. **Corley**, TexCivApp–Corpus Christi, 613 SW2d 519, ref nre.—Cons Cred 12, 18.

Ford Motor Credit Co.; **Dean** v., CA5 (Tex), 885 F2d 300. —Damag 50.10, 192, 208(6); Fed Civ Proc 1824, 2533.1; Fed Cts 624, 643.

Ford Motor Credit Co. v. **Draper**, TexCivApp–Texarkana, 401 SW2d 848.—Evid 207(1); Labor & Emp 55; Pretrial Proc 242, 306.1; Venue 8.5(7).

Ford Motor Credit Co. v. **First State Bank of Smithville**, Tex, 679 SW2d 486.—Sec Tran 146.

Ford Motor Credit Co. v. **First State Bank of Smithville**, TexApp–Tyler, 674 SW2d 437, rev 679 SW2d 486. —Sec Tran 146.

Ford Motor Credit Co. v. **Galbraith**, TexCivApp–Hous (1 Dist), 619 SW2d 2, ref nre.—Cons Cred 16; Judgm 185.3(2).

Ford Motor Credit Co. v. **Gamez**, TexApp–Eastland, 617 SW2d 720, ref nre.—Cons Cred 12, 16; Statut 241(2).

Ford Motor Credit Co. v. **Garcia**, TexCivApp–San Antonio, 504 SW2d 931.—App & E 846(5); Plead 34(7), 45, 111.18, 111.42(9); Trover 1.

Ford Motor Credit Co. v. **Garcia**, TexCivApp–Waco, 595 SW2d 602.—Plead 36(2); Sec Tran 242.1; Trover 46.

Ford Motor Credit Co.; **Leal** v., TexApp–Corpus Christi, 683 SW2d 719, ref nre.—Cons Cred 12, 16; Evid 351.

Ford Motor Credit Co. v. **Long**, TexCivApp–Beaumont, 608 SW2d 293, ref nre.—Usury 48, 50, 53, 72.

Ford Motor Credit Co. v. **McDaniel**, TexCivApp–Corpus Christi, 613 SW2d 513, ref nre.—Cons Cred 12, 18, 19; Contracts 153; Sec Tran 230; Usury 61.

Ford Motor Credit Co.; **Meyers** v., TexCivApp–Hous (14 Dist), 619 SW2d 572.—Tresp 30, 67; Trial 382.

Ford Motor Credit Co.; **Onoray Davis Truck Co., Inc.** v., TexApp–Houston (14 Dist), 690 SW2d 40.—App & E 1152; States 79, 112(2), 112.1(1), 112.2(3); Statut 88.

Ford Motor Credit Co.; **Ortiz** v., TexApp–Corpus Christi, 859 SW2d 73, reh overr, and writ den.—App & E 204(1), 230, 233(1), 237(2), 241, 242(4), 1002, 1003(1), 1003(7), 1048(7), 1050.1(1); Bailm 35; Jury 139, 142; New Tr 27, 48.1, 159; Trial 139.1(3), 140(1).

Ford Motor Credit Co. v. **Powers**, TexCivApp–Corpus Christi, 613 SW2d 30.—Cons Cred 2, 12, 18; Contracts 153; Sec Tran 222.

Ford Motor Credit Co.; **Register** v., TexApp–Houston (1 Dist), 744 SW2d 301, writ gr, and writ withdrawn, and writ dism by agreement.—App & E 201(1); Evid 571(7); Fed Cts 433; Guar 39, 91; Judgm 181(25); Jury 25(6).

Ford Motor Credit Co.; **Reimer** v., TexApp–Houston (1 Dist), 635 SW2d 162.—Courts 475(1); Inj 143(2); Judgm 92; Pretrial Proc 46.

Ford Motor Credit Co. v. **Soto**, TexApp–Corpus Christi, 671 SW2d 620, ref nre.—Cons Cred 15, 16, 17, 18; Evid 117.

Ford Motor Credit Co.; **Sunjet, Inc.** v., TexApp–Dallas, 703 SW2d 285.—Sec Tran 231, 240.

Ford Motor Credit Co. v. **Syler**, TexCivApp–Eastland, 615 SW2d 778, ref nre.—Cons Cred 55, 61.1, 67.

Ford Motor Credit Co. v. **Uresti**, TexCivApp–Waco, 581 SW2d 298.—App & E 1172(1), 1173(2); Sec Tran 92.1, 97.

Ford Motor Credit Co. v. **Washington**, TexCivApp–Austin, 573 SW2d 616, ref nre.—Contracts 227; Damag 91(1); Sec Tran 228, 243.

Ford Motor Credit Co.; **Whiteside** v., TexCivApp–Dallas, 220 SW3d 191.—Acct Action on 14; App & E 837(1), 1073(1); Const Law 3881, 4011; Judgm 184, 185.3(3).

Ford Motor Credit Co. v. **Zapata** v., Tex, 615 SW2d 198, appeal dism, cert den 102 SCt 623, 454 US 1074, 70 LEd2d 607.—Sec Tran 242.1; Tresp 8, 47; Trover 44.

Ford Motor Credit Co. v. **Zapata**, TexCivApp–Beaumont, 605 SW2d 362, rev 615 SW2d 198, appeal dism, cert den 102 SCt 623, 454 US 1074, 70 LEd2d 607.—Cons Cred 2, 3.1, 15.

Ford, Powell & Carson, Inc.; **Sedona Contracting, Inc.** v., TexApp–San Antonio, 995 SW2d 192, reh overr, and review den, and reh of petition for review overr.— Contracts 16; Estop 52.10(2), 119; Indem 30(1), 33(5); Judgm 181(6); Libel 47; Neglig 210, 481; Schools 80(2); Torts 126, 424.

Ford Rent Co. v. **Hughes**, Tex, 88 SW2d 85, 126 Tex 255. —Courts 207.4(2).

Ford Rent Co. v. **Hughes**, TexCivApp–Dallas, 90 SW2d 290.—Autos 247; Trial 358.

Ford Rent Co. v. **Mayfair Taxicab Co.**, TexCivApp–Dallas, 99 SW2d 1023.—Antitrust 104(2); Inj 132, 135, 138.1, 138.3; Trademarks 1704(3).

Ford, **Texas Atty. Gen. of State of Tex. on Behalf of**, v. **Daurbigny**, TexApp–Houston (1 Dist), 702 SW2d 298. See Texas Atty. Gen. of State of Tex. on Behalf of Ford v. Daurbigny.

Ford-Wehmeyer, Inc.; **Sunrise Acres, Inc.** v., TexCivApp–Waco, 598 SW2d 916.—App & E 173(9); Contracts 232(3); Costs 194.32, 252.

Fordyce; **Silvey** v., TexCivApp–Texarkana, 81 SW2d 714. —Impl & C C 60.1; Mines 112(3).

Fordyce-Crossett Sales Co. v. **Erwin**, TexCivApp–Amarillo, 121 SW2d 491.—App & E 846(2), 846(5); Judgm 752, 769.

Fore; **Bell** v., TexCivApp–Texarkana, 419 SW2d 686, writ gr, aff 434 SW2d 117.—Autos 201(1.1), 201(7), 201(8), 201(9), 244(5), 244(36.1); Neglig 379, 383, 387, 1675.

Fore; **City of Houston** v., Tex, 412 SW2d 35.—App & E 1135, 1177(1); Const Law 4061; Mun Corp 455.

Fore; **City of Houston** v., TexCivApp–Waco, 401 SW2d 921, writ gr, aff 412 SW2d 35.—Const Law 3881, 3912, 3975; Mun Corp 298.

Fore; **Kimsey** v., TexCivApp–Beaumont, 593 SW2d 107, ref nre.—App & E 1070(2); Mines 55(4), 55(8); Trial 350.3(4).

Fore; **Nacogdoches County** v., TexApp–Tyler, 655 SW2d 347.—App & E 223; Contrib 1, 5(6.1); Indem 42, 81, 85.

Fore; **Richburg** v., TexCivApp–Eastland, 190 SW2d 164, writ dism.—App & E 781(4), 912.

Fore v. **U.S.**, CA5 (Tex), 339 F2d 70, cert den 85 SCt 1532, 381 US 912, 14 LEd2d 433.—Int Rev 4784, 4788.1; Judgm 762, 785(1).

Foreca, S.A. v. GRD Development Co., Inc., Tex, 758 SW2d 744.—Sales 53(1).

Foreca, S.A.; GRD Development Co., Inc. v., TexApp–El Paso, 747 SW2d 9, writ dism woj, and writ withdrawn, and writ gr, rev 758 SW2d 744.—Contracts 150, 218, 221(1), 221(2).

Foree v. Crown Central Petroleum Corp., Tex, 431 SW2d 312.—Admin Law 228.1, 391; Interest 39(1); Judgm 185.3(2); Mines 92.69, 92.70, 92.84; Tresp 57.

Foree v. Crown Central Petroleum Corp., TexCivApp–Waco, 417 SW2d 499, rev 431 SW2d 312.—Mines 94.

Forehand v. Light, Tex, 452 SW2d 709.—Joint Ten 6.

Forehand; Light v., TexCivApp–Tyler, 446 SW2d 355, rev 452 SW2d 709.—Joint Ten 6.

Foreign Credit Ins. Ass'n; Joseph v., NDTex, 254 FSupp 903.—Insurance 2400.

Foreman; Bluebonnet Exp., Inc. v., TexCivApp–Hous (14 Dist), 431 SW2d 45.—App & E 901, 930(1), 1004(8); Damag 132(3).

Foreman; Bolton v., TexCivApp–Galveston, 263 SW2d 618, ref nre.—Judgm 181(2), 181(19).

Foreman; Brewer v., TexCivApp–Houston, 362 SW2d 350.—App & E 688(2), 930(1); Wills 52(1), 53(7), 54(1), 155.4, 164(1), 166(1), 166(5), 229, 324(2).

Foreman v. Dallas County, Tex., USTex, 117 SCt 2357, 521 US 979, 138 LEd2d 972, on remand 990 FSupp 505. —Elections 12(8).

Foreman v. Dallas County, Tex., CA5 (Tex), 193 F3d 314, cert den 120 SCt 1673, 529 US 1067, 146 LEd2d 482.—Elections 12(10); Fed Civ Proc 2737.1; Fed Cts 776, 830, 878; Statut 216.

Foreman v. Dallas County, Tex., NDTex, 990 FSupp 505.—Elections 12(9.1); Fed Civ Proc 1824.

Foreman v. Dallas Credit Corp., TexCivApp–Waco, 360 SW2d 442.—App & E 773(2).

Foreman v. Dretke, CA5 (Tex), 383 F3d 336.—Hab Corp 603.

Foreman; Forester v., TexCivApp–Galveston, 171 SW2d 190.—App & E 1024.3; Plead 111.9, 111.39(2), 111.39(7), 111.42(2).

Foreman v. Gooch, TexCivApp–Beaumont, 184 SW2d 481, writ refused wom.—Counties 153.5, 164; Offic 100(2).

Foreman v. Graham, TexApp–Fort Worth, 693 SW2d 774, ref nre.—App & E 846(5), 852; Frds St of 158(4); Interpl 33, 34, 35; Ven & Pur 315(3).

Foreman v. Graham, TexCivApp–Beaumont, 363 SW2d 371.—Lim of Act 66(2), 66(12), 66(15), 199(1).

Foreman v. Jarrett, TexApp–Austin, 796 SW2d 316.— Mand 3(2.1), 12, 14(1), 14(3), 28, 57(1).

Foreman; Kelly v., SDTex, 384 FSupp 1352.—Consp 7.5(1), 18.

Foreman; Kennedy v., TexCivApp–El Paso, 83 SW2d 1036, writ dism.—Mtg 6, 38(1).

Foreman; Mossler v., TexCivApp–Hous (14 Dist), 493 SW2d 627, ref nre.—App & E 242(1), 554(1), 624, 688(1), 758.3(9), 1170.10; Atty & C 147, 167(2); Plead 236(1), 267; Trial 358.

Foreman; Nolan v., CA5 (Tex), 665 F2d 738, reh den 671 F2d 1380.—Atty & C 63, 64, 129(1), 143, 182(3).

Foreman v. Pettit Unlimited, Inc., TexApp–Houston (1 Dist), 886 SW2d 409.—Antitrust 205, 353; App & E 934(1); Judgm 185(2); Lim of Act 95(1), 95(3); Plead 248(4).

Foreman v. Rowe, TexCivApp–Austin, 511 SW2d 544.— Plead 111.39(6), 111.42(7); Venue 8(2).

Foreman v. Security Ins. Co. of Hartford, TexApp–Texarkana, 15 SW3d 214.—Statut 179; Work Comp 409, 2189.

Foreman; Southland Beauty Shops, Inc. v., TexCivApp–Houston, 319 SW2d 737, dism.—Evid 9; Plead 111.42(4), 111.42(6), 111.42(7).

Foreman v. State, TexCrimApp, 505 SW2d 564, cert den 95 SCt 91, 419 US 851, 42 LEd2d 81.—Const Law 3804,

4619; Courts 70; Crim Law 339.11(8), 517(1), 531(3), 532(0.5), 1036.1(6), 1043(3).

Foreman v. State, TexCrimApp, 340 SW2d 46, 170 TexCrim 265.—Autos 355(6).

Foreman v. State, TexCrimApp, 265 SW2d 816.—Crim Law 1090.1(1).

Foreman v. State, TexApp–Austin, 995 SW2d 854, reh overr, and petition for discretionary review refused.— Crim Law 1153(1); Infants 20; Witn 211(2), 214.5.

Foreman v. State, TexApp–El Paso, 743 SW2d 731, denial of habeas corpus aff 979 F2d 1534.—Assault 40, 59; Rape 51(4).

Foreman v. Texas Elec. Service Co., CA5 (Tex), 319 F2d 115.—Electricity 18(1).

Foreman v. Texas Emp. Ins. Ass'n, Tex, 241 SW2d 977, 150 Tex 468, opinion conformed to 262 SW2d 248.—App & E 1069.3, 1082(1), 1177(6); Evid 553(1); Exceptions Bill of1; Trial 314(1); Work Comp 1968(3).

Foreman; Texas Emp. Ins. Ass'n v., TexCivApp–Dallas, 262 SW2d 248.—App & E 1001(1), 1003(4); Work Comp 1969.

Foreman; Texas Emp. Ins. Ass'n v., TexCivApp–Dallas, 236 SW2d 824, rev 241 SW2d 977, 150 Tex 468, opinion conformed to 262 SW2d 248.—Damag 221(4); Trial 305; Work Comp 1389, 1396, 1727, 1937.

Foreman; Texas Emp. Ins. Ass'n v., TexCivApp–Texarkana, 359 SW2d 671, ref nre.—App & E 387(3); Work Comp 1932.

Foreman v. Texas Employment Com'n, TexApp–Austin, 828 SW2d 319.—Admin Law 744.1, 786, 791; Unemp Comp 371, 444, 480, 486.

Foreman v. Thalmayer, NDTex, 393 FSupp 1396.—Civil R 1508.

Foreman v. Tomblin, CA5 (Tex), 75 FedAppx 227.—Civil R 1395(7), 1445.

Foreman; Wichita Falls & Southern Ry. Co. v., TexCivApp–Eastland, 109 SW2d 549.—App & E 1161; Corp 401; Judgm 244; Trial 345.

Foremost Corp. of America; Homestead Mobile Homes, Inc. v., NDTex, 603 FSupp 767.—Antitrust 575, 583, 972(3); Insurance 1106(1); States 18.41.

Foremost County Mutual Ins. Co., In re, TexApp–Beaumont, 172 SW3d 128, mandamus den.—Abate & R 19; Contracts 152, 221(2); Insurance 1806, 1808, 1810, 1863, 3171, 3173, 3191(5), 3353, 3361, 3546; Mand 4(1), 28, 32.

Foremost County Mut. Ins. Co.; Castano v., TexApp–San Antonio, 31 SW3d 387.—App & E 79(1).

Foremost County Mut. Ins. Co. v. Home Indem. Co., CA5 (Tex), 897 F2d 754, reh den 902 F2d 955.—Insurance 2355, 3350, 3517; Subrog 27.

Foremost County Mut. Ins. Co. v. North Star Dodge, Inc., TexCivApp–San Antonio, 542 SW2d 270, ref nre.— False Pret 5; Insurance 2117, 2703, 2732.

Foremost Dairies; McDonald v., CA5 (Tex), 192 F2d 306. —Autos 245(14), 245(80).

Foremost Dairies; Shahan-Taylor Co. v., TexCivApp–San Antonio, 233 SW2d 885, ref nre.—Corp 399(2), 410, 411, 416, 429, 433(1); Frds St of 23(1), 26(1), 33(1), 33(2), 158(1), 158(4), 159; Princ & A 99; Sales 52(5.1).

Foremost Dairies, Inc. v. McClung, TexCivApp–Dallas, 421 SW2d 178, ref nre.—Neglig 440(1); Trial 350.1, 350.5(5), 351.5(5).

Foremost Ins. Co., In re, TexApp–Corpus Christi, 966 SW2d 770.—Action 60; Mand 1, 3(2.1), 10, 12, 28, 29.

Foremost Ins. Co.; Crestview, Ltd. v., TexCivApp–Austin, 621 SW2d 816, ref nre.—App & E 954(2); Inj 132, 134, 135, 138.18; Mtg 81, 272, 403.

Foremost Ins. Co. v. Hawkins, TexCivApp–Waco, 336 SW2d 901, ref nre.—Insurance 2719(2), 2720.

Foremost Ins. Co.; Longoria v., TexApp–Houston (14 Dist), 725 SW2d 371, ref nre.—Garn 7; Princ & S 145(1).

Foremost Ins. Co.; Mays v., TexApp–San Antonio, 627 SW2d 230.—App & E 347(1), 387(3), 623, 934(1); Judgm 181(23), 181(33), 185(2), 185.2(3).

Foremost Ins. Co.; Texas State Bank v., TexCivApp–Corpus Christi, 477 SW2d 652, ref nre.—Autos 20; Princ & A 100(4); Sec Tran 21.

Foremost Ins. Co. v. Willis, TexCivApp–Dallas, 412 SW2d 697.—Accord 9; Bailm 18(1), 31(3); Estop 92(2); Release 6.

Foremost Ins. Co., Grand Rapids, Mich.; Progress Marine, Inc. v., CA5 (Tex), 642 F2d 816, cert den 102 SCt 315, 454 US 860, 70 LEd2d 158.—Insurance 2367.

Foremost-McKesson, Inc. v. Instrumentation Laboratory, Inc., CA5 (Tex), 527 F2d 417.—Antitrust 963(2), 972(5), 977(1), 977(2).

Foremost Mobile Homes Mfg. Corp. v. Steele, TexCivApp–Fort Worth, 506 SW2d 646.—Sales 255, 267, 441(4).

Foremost Paving, Inc.; Lopez v., Tex, 709 SW2d 643, appeal after remand 796 SW2d 473, writ gr, and cause remanded for settlement, and cause dism.—App & E 1026, 1045(2).

Foremost Paving, Inc.; Lopez v., TexApp–San Antonio, 796 SW2d 473, writ gr, and cause remanded for settlement, and cause dism.—App & E 1026, 1043(1), 1043(6), 1050.1(1), 1050.1(11), 1056.1(1); Courts 87; Evid 150, 359(6); Pretrial Proc 14.1, 45, 434.

Foremost Paving, Inc.; Lopez v., TexApp–San Antonio, 699 SW2d 232, rev 709 SW2d 643, appeal after remand 796 SW2d 473, writ gr, and cause remanded for settlement, and cause dism.—Autos 306(4); Jury 120, 136(3).

Foremost Paving, Inc.; Lopez v., TexApp–San Antonio, 671 SW2d 614.—App & E 347(1), 384(1), 387(6), 388, 389(3).

Foreness; Hexamer v., CA5 (Tex), 997 F2d 93.—U S 147(6), 147(7), 147(10).

Foreness; Hexamer v., CA5 (Tex), 981 F2d 821.—Fed Cts 192, 192.5; Rem of C 102.

Foreness v. Hexamer, TexApp–Dallas, 971 SW2d 525, review den, cert den 119 SCt 240, 525 US 904, 142 LEd2d 197.—App & E 1175(1); Child S 503; Courts 4; Garn 1, 18; Judgm 495(1), 497(1), 499; States 18.5, 18.9, 18.28, 18.35; U S 125(9).

Forest v. State, TexCrimApp, 989 SW2d 365, on remand 2000 WL 136783.—Crim Law 795(2.5), 795(2.10), 814(20); Ind & Inf 191(4).

Forest Cove Property Owners Ass'n, Inc. v. Lightbody, TexApp–Houston (1 Dist), 731 SW2d 170.—App & E 242(3); Judgm 181(15.1).

Forest Dale, Inc. v. Cisneros, NDTex, 818 FSupp 954. See U.S. v. Forest Dale, Inc.

Forest Dale, Inc.; U.S. v., NDTex, 818 FSupp 954.—Civil R 1006, 1083, 1302, 1332(3), 1381, 1462, 1463, 1465(1); Damag 15; Decl Judgm 45; Elect of Rem 2; Fed Civ Proc 2491.5; Judgm 828.8; Lim of Act 124.

Forester v. Foreman, TexCivApp–Galveston, 171 SW2d 190.—App & E 1024.3; Plead 111.9, 111.39(2), 111.39(7), 111.42(2).

Forester v. State, TexCrimApp, 298 SW2d 137.—Crim Law 1090.1(1).

Forester v. State, TexCrimApp, 212 SW2d 156.—Crim Law 1090.1(1).

Forester; Texaco, Inc. v., TexCivApp–Beaumont, 456 SW2d 196, ref nre.—App & E 1140(2); Contrib 5(6.1); Damag 132(8), 208(1), 216(8); Indem 33(5); Neglig 506(8), 1012, 1037(4), 1284, 1286(6), 1287; Trial 358.

Forester v. Texas & P. Ry. Co., CA5 (Tex), 338 F2d 970, cert den 85 SCt 1785, 381 US 944, 14 LEd2d 708.—Fed Civ Proc 1973, 2182.1.

Forester; U.S. v., CA5 (Tex), 874 F2d 983, cert den 110 SCt 284, 493 US 920, 107 LEd2d 264.—Const Law 4725; Crim Law 1192; Double J 107.1; Sent & Pun 115(4).

Forester; U.S. v., CA5 (Tex), 836 F2d 856, appeal after remand 874 F2d 983, cert den 110 SCt 284, 493 US 920, 107 LEd2d 264.—Crim Law 29(1), 577.8(1); Sent & Pun 524.

Forest Hill, City of; Childress v., TexCivApp–Fort Worth, 359 SW2d 112, ref nre.—Autos 308(6); Mun Corp 788; Trial 139.1(12).

Forest Hill, City of; Herbert v., TexApp–Fort Worth, 189 SW3d 369.—Civil R 1118, 1128, 1137, 1138, 1243, 1251, 1252, 1743, 1744; Courts 97(5); Mun Corp 185(1).

Forest Hill, City of; Jenicke v., TexApp–Fort Worth, 873 SW2d 776, reh overr.—App & E 842(1), 854(1), 863, 934(1); Arrest 68(4); Civil R 1027, 1029, 1039, 1329, 1351(6), 1352(6); Mun Corp 747(3).

Forest Hills Inv., Inc.; Barnes v., EDTex, 11 FSupp2d 699.—Action 17; Compromise 11, 21; Contracts 143(1), 143(2), 143.5, 147(1), 147(2), 148, 153, 155, 169; Evid 397(1), 448; Fed Cts 409.1.

Forestier; Rice v., TexCivApp–San Antonio, 415 SW2d 711, ref nre.—Atty & C 109, 129(2); Plead 427.

Forestier v. San Antonio Sav. Ass'n, TexCivApp–El Paso, 564 SW2d 160, ref nre.—Const Law 4487; Mtg 338, 355, 369(3); Tender 13(1), 14(1).

Forest Industries, Inc. v. Kirkland, TexApp–Houston (14 Dist, 772 SW2d 226. See Kirby Forest Industries, Inc. v. Kirkland.

Forest Lane Porsche-Audi Associates v. Defries, TexApp–Dallas, 730 SW2d 80.—App & E 624, 670(1), 907(3).

Forest Lane Porsche Audi Associates v. G & K Services, Inc., TexApp–Fort Worth, 717 SW2d 470.—Accord 25(1); App & E 173(9), 901, 907(3); Contracts 245(1), 338(1); Damag 140; Nova 11; Plead 234, 236(2), 236(7), 238(3), 261, 262, 356.

Forest Lane Porsche-Audi, Inc. v. Staten, TexApp–Dallas, 638 SW2d 62.—Evid 208(2).

Forest Lawn Lot Owners Ass'n; State v., Tex, 254 SW2d 87, 152 Tex 41.—Cem 13; Em Dom 284; Ven & Pur 257, 265(1), 279, 288, 289.

Forest Lawn Lot Owners Ass'n v. State, TexCivApp–Dallas, 248 SW2d 741, rev 254 SW2d 87, 152 Tex 41.—Em Dom 85, 141(1), 153, 277, 288(1), 297, 307(2); Lim of Act 69; Ven & Pur 101.

Forest Oil Corp.; Powell v., TexCivApp–Texarkana, 392 SW2d 549.—Plead 111.17, 111.42(7), 290(3); Trover 3; Venue 8.5(7).

Forest Oil Corp.; Pritchett v., TexCivApp–El Paso, 535 SW2d 708, ref nre.—Mines 79.1(5), 79.7.

Forest Oil Corp. v. Strata Energy, Inc., CA5 (Tex), 929 F2d 1039.—Compromise 5(1), 5(3), 17(2); Contracts 155, 176(2); Fed Cts 776, 859; Insurance 2272.

Forest Oil Corp.; Van Kirk & Riles Interests, Inc. v., SDTex, 206 FSupp2d 856.—Brok 9, 11, 56(3); Princ & A 1, 3(1), 31.

Forestpark Enterprises, Inc. v. Culpepper, TexApp–Fort Worth, 754 SW2d 775, writ den.—Antitrust 143(2), 208, 369; App & E 497(1), 907(5); Lim of Act 49(7), 55(2), 58(1); Princ & A 159(2).

Forest Park Lanes, Limited v. Keith, TexCivApp–Fort Worth, 441 SW2d 920.—App & E 460(1), 1042(5), 1062.1; Atty & C 104; Damag 221(5.1); Indem 76; Insurance 3443; Interpl 35; Judgm 185.3(14), 252(5), 253(2); Land & Ten 112(1), 112.5, 157(2), 193; Mtg 460, 529(6), 529(7); Tax 2760, 2768.

Forest Park Properties of Arlington, Inc. v. Padgett, TexCivApp–Fort Worth, 323 SW2d 320, ref nre.—Bound 37(4); Deeds 101; Evid 461(2); Judgm 181(5.1); Tresp to T T 47(3).

Forest Pharmaceuticals, Inc.; Schwartz v., TexApp–Houston (1 Dist), 127 SW3d 118, reh overr, and review den.—App & E 230, 231(3), 232(2); Autos 192(11); Damag 185(1); Evid 155(8), 359(1); Labor & Emp 3027, 3045; Neglig 202, 379, 380, 387; Pretrial Proc 3.

Forest Place Homeowners' Ass'n, Inc.; Stergios v., TexApp–Dallas, 651 SW2d 396, ref nre.—App & E 846(5),

931(3); Covenants 1, 51(1), 51(2), 103(3), 122, 137; Equity 71(1), 72(1), 84; Estop 55; Inj 204.

Forest Springs Hosp. v. Illinois New Car and Truck Dealers Ass'n Employees Ins. Trust, SDTex, 812 FSupp 729.—Estop 52(1); Fed Civ Proc 2497.1; Fraud 31; Labor & Emp 407, 555; States 18.15, 18.51.

Forever Blue Entertainment Group, Inc.; Bounty-Full Entertainment, Inc. v., SDTex, 923 FSupp 950.—Const Law 3964, 3965(8); Copyr 79; Courts 12(2.10); Fed Civ Proc 1825, 1835; Fed Cts 74, 76, 76.5, 76.10, 76.35, 103, 104, 105, 106, 144, 417; Torts 241; Trademarks 1558.

Forex Asset Management LLC; S.E.C. v., CA5 (Tex), 242 F3d 325.—Fed Civ Proc 2582; Fed Cts 543.1, 544, 572.1, 580, 585.1, 813; Sec Reg 185.19.

Forfeiture, Property, All Appurtenances and Improvements, Located at 1604 Oceola, Wichita Falls, Tex.; U.S. v., NDTex, 803 FSupp 1194.—Const Law 3886, 4020, 4078; Crim Law 641.3(4); Fed Civ Proc 2734; Forfeit 5.

Forfeiture, Stop Six Center, Located at 3340 Stallcup, Fort Worth, Tex.;U.S. v., NDTex, 794 FSupp 626.—Controlled Subs 165, 170, 171, 174, 177, 180, 184; Forfeit 5.

Forfeiture, Stop Six Center, Located at 3340 Stallcup, Fort Worth, Tex.;U.S. v., NDTex, 781 FSupp 1200.—Controlled Subs 170, 174, 180, 184; Fed Civ Proc 2481; Forfeit 5.

Forgason, Ex parte, TexCrimApp, 567 SW2d 517.—Rob 17(3).

Forgason v. Forgason, TexApp–Amarillo, 911 SW2d 893, reh overr, and writ den.—Divorce 286(5), 286(8); Hus & W 272(4).

Forgason; Forgason v., TexApp–Amarillo, 911 SW2d 893, reh overr, and writ den.—Divorce 286(5), 286(8); Hus & W 272(4).

Forge v. State, TexApp–Texarkana, 717 SW2d 725.—Crim Law 792(3); Searches 18, 47.1, 62, 64.

Forgeron; Grennan v., TexCivApp–El Paso, 101 SW2d 885, writ dism.—App & E 225, 750(5); Lim of Act 19(3), 103(1), 103(4); Mines 101; Tresp to T T 47(1).

Forgey; Ampro Energy, L.P. v., CA5 (Tex), 217 FedAppx 339.—Atty & C 64; Fed Civ Proc 2794, 2812.

Forgey v. State, TexCrimApp, 350 SW2d 32, 171 TexCrim 355.—Crim Law 722.3, 723(4), 949(2), 956(2), 957(1), 957(3); Rape 51(1).

Forgus v. Hodnett, Tex, 405 SW2d 337.—Autos 181(1), 181(5).

Forgus v. Hodnett, TexCivApp–Eastland, 401 SW2d 104, ref nre 405 SW2d 337.—Autos 181(1), 181(5), 244(20).

Forgy; City of San Antonio v., TexApp–San Antonio, 769 SW2d 293, writ den.—Contracts 168; Mun Corp 360(3), 374(6).

Forgy Const. Co.; City of San Antonio v., TexApp–San Antonio, 769 SW2d 293. See City of San Antonio v. Forgy.

Forister; Coleman v., Tex, 514 SW2d 899, appeal after remand 538 SW2d 14, ref nre.—App & E 1097(2); Deeds 120; Ease 17(1), 38, 42, 51, 61(8); Estop 56; Evid 411, 413, 448; Waters 155, 158.5(1).

Forister; Coleman v., Tex, 431 SW2d 2.—Waters 156(8).

Forister v. Coleman, TexCivApp–Austin, 538 SW2d 14, ref nre.—App & E 1097(1), 1195(1), 1212(3), 1214; Ease 61(9 1/2); Evid 448.

Forister; Coleman v., TexCivApp–Austin, 497 SW2d 530, writ gr, rev 514 SW2d 899, appeal after remand 538 SW2d 14, ref nre.—App & E 281(1), 1152, 1194(1); Ease 61(2); Inj 51; Tresp 16; Waters 158.5(1).

Forister v. Coleman, TexCivApp–Austin, 418 SW2d 550, ref nre 431 SW2d 2.—App & E 1173(2); Deeds 94, 101; Ease 2, 61(7); Evid 433(4), 434(3); Judgm 181(29), 183, 185.3(18); Perp 4(1); Ven & Pur 220, 245; Waters 156(8), 158.5(1).

For Ladies Only; Klorer v., TexApp–San Antonio, 717 SW2d 754. See Klorer v. Block.

Forlano v. Joyner, TexApp–Houston (1 Dist), 906 SW2d 118.—Action 60; App & E 77(2).

Forlenza, In re, Tex, 140 SW3d 373.—App & E 893(1); Child C 735; Courts 32.

Formal Specialists Ltd. v. Wilbert Lyons Inc., CA5 (Tex), 98 FedAppx 284.—Fed Civ Proc 2444.1; Fed Cts 624, 915.

Forman v. Barron, TexCivApp–El Paso, 120 SW2d 827, writ refused.—App & E 1116; Home 35; Judgm 18(2), 249, 683; Lim of Act 167(3); Mun Corp 485(5), 513(5), 519(6); Tresp to T T 47(1).

Forman v. Fina Oil and Chemical Co., Tex, 858 SW2d 373.—Pretrial Proc 42.

Forman v. Fina Oil and Chemical Co., TexApp–Eastland, 858 SW2d 498, reh den, and writ gr, rev 858 SW2d 373.—App & E 946, 961, 966(1); Pretrial Proc 42, 45, 713, 717.1, 718.

Forman v. Forman, TexCivApp–Hous (14 Dist), 496 SW2d 243.—Divorce 399(1); Judgm 634, 818(1), 822(1).

Forman; Forman v., TexCivApp–Hous (14 Dist), 496 SW2d 243.—Divorce 399(1); Judgm 634, 818(1), 822(1).

Forman; Fulford v., CA5 (Tex), 245 F2d 145.—Agric 3.3(1), 3.3(3); Statut 181(2).

Forman; Fulford v., NDTex, 144 FSupp 536, aff 245 F2d 145.—Admin Law 390.1, 391; Agric 3.3(3), 3.3(4); Statut 219(3), 223.5(1).

Forman v. Glasgow, TexCivApp–Waco, 219 SW2d 845.—Aband L P 5; App & E 1178(1); Costs 240; Hus & W 47(4), 187, 266.3; Spec Perf 134.

Forman v. Irby, TexCivApp–Waco, 115 SW2d 1229, writ refused.—Contracts 98; Corp 262(2); Estop 72; Evid 332(1); Fraud 20; Insurance 1227(3), 1374, 1379; Motions 61.

Forman v. Massoni, TexCivApp–Galveston, 176 SW2d 366, writ refused.—Judgm 638.

Forman; Prince v., TexCivApp–Dallas, 119 SW2d 102, writ dism.—App & E 78(1), 870(2); Receivers 114.

Forman v. Prince, TexCivApp–Dallas, 97 SW2d 1002.—Abate & R 6, 8(4), 17; Action 69(5); App & E 863, 1178(1); Courts 480(1); Plead 111.3, 111.6, 111.15, 111.36, 111.46; Venue 45.

Forman; Ruiz v., TexCivApp–El Paso, 514 SW2d 817, dism.—Autos 155.

Forman v. State, TexCrimApp, 366 SW2d 944.—Crim Law 1144.19.

Formation Sec., Inc. v. Gulf Union Industries, Inc., CA5 (Tex), 842 F2d 762. See Gulf Union Industries, Inc. v. Formation Sec., Inc.

Formation Sec., Inc.; Gulf Union Industries, Inc. v., CA5 (Tex), 842 F2d 762.—Const Law 4019; Dep & Escr 26; Fed Civ Proc 2737.14; Fed Cts 415, 616.

Formation Sec., Inc. v. Panhandle Bank & Trust Co., CA5 (Tex), 842 F2d 762. See Gulf Union Industries, Inc. v. Formation Sec., Inc.

Formby v. Bradley, TexApp–Tyler, 695 SW2d 782, ref nre.—App & E 192.1; Ex & Ad 14, 20(7), 20(9); Wills 193, 440, 486.

Formby; Whitaker v., TexCivApp–Texarkana, 469 SW2d 241, ref nre.—Mines 78.2, 78.5, 78.6.

Formby's KOA v. BHP Water Supply Corp., TexApp–Dallas, 730 SW2d 428.—Judgm 215.

Form Forge Co., Division of Miley Forge Co.; Industrial Instrument Corp. v., TexCivApp–Austin, 427 SW2d 955.—Judgm 139; Trial 6(1).

Formica Corp.; Superior Laminate & Supply, Inc. v., TexApp–Houston (14 Dist), 93 SW3d 445, review den.—App & E 213, 1064.1(1), 1066(3); Contracts 245(1); Estop 85; Lim of Act 100(1), 100(12); Nova 1; Trial 251(1), 252(1).

Formosa Plastics Corp.; B.F. Goodrich Co. v., SDTex, 638 FSupp 1050.—Atty & C 19, 21.5(1), 21.20.

Formosa Plastics Corp.; Goodrich Co. v., SDTex, 638 FSupp 1050. See B.F. Goodrich Co. v. Formosa Plastics Corp.

Formosa Plastics Corp.; Parcel Tankers, Inc. v., CA5 (Tex), 764 F2d 1153.—Fed Cts 660.35.

Formosa Plastics Corp.; Parcel Tankers, Inc. v., SDTex, 569 FSupp 1459.—Adm 47; Alt Disp Res 114, 182(1), 182(2), 191, 194; Const Law 3875, 4481.

Formosa Plastics Corp. of Texas v. Sharp, TexApp–Austin, 979 SW2d 410, review den.—Tax 2573(4), 2773, 2786.

Formosa Plastics Corp., U.S.A.; Chauhan v., TexApp–Houston (14 Dist), 928 SW2d 582, writ gr, rev Kunstoplast of America, Inc v. Formosa Plastics Corp, USA, 937 SW2d 455, on remand 1998 WL 304905, review den, and reh of petition for review overr.—Atty & C 11(2.1), 11(12).

Formosa Plastics Corp., USA v. Kajima Intern., Inc., TexApp–Corpus Christi, 216 SW3d 436.—App & E 971(2), 1004(1), 1050.1(1), 1051.1(1), 1056.1(1), 1062.1, 1069.2; Contracts 97(1), 338(1); Corp 1.5(1), 1.5(3), 1.6(13); Damag 62(1), 62(4), 96, 104, 119, 214; Estop 90(1); Evid 535, 545, 555.2, 555.9; Fraud 35, 52, 57, 59(2), 59(3), 62, 65(1); Interest 39(2.6), 39(2.50); Trial 43, 56, 182, 203(1), 307(1), 307(3), 349(2), 350.2, 352.1(1), 352.1(2), 352.4(1), 352.5(2); Witn 201(1), 222.

Formosa Plastics Corp., USA; Kajima Intern., Inc. v., TexApp–Corpus Christi, 15 SW3d 289, review den, and reh of petition for review den, on subsequent appeal In re Kajima Intern, Inc, 139 SW3d 107, appeal after new trial 216 SW3d 436.—App & E 916(1), 969, 1062.2, 1064.1(1); Fraud 3, 12, 24, 65(1); Trial 228(1), 295(1).

Formosa Plastics Corp., USA; Kunstoplast of America, Inc. v., Tex, 937 SW2d 455, on remand 1998 WL 304905, review den, and reh of petition for review overr.—Atty & C 62; Corp 508; Courts 85(3).

Formosa Plastics Corp., USA v. Presidio Engineers and Contractors, Inc., TexApp–Corpus Christi, 941 SW2d 138, reh overr, and writ gr, rev 960 SW2d 41.—App & E 181, 213, 218.2(3.1), 218.2(5.1), 231(8), 237(5), 237(6), 238(2), 294(1), 1004(7), 1004(13); Costs 194.32, 194.46; Damag 40(1), 91(1), 94, 190; Elect of Rem 3(1); Fraud 3, 12, 16, 17, 32, 50, 58(1), 58(2), 58(3), 59(2), 59(3), 61, 62, 64(2); Set-Off 28(1); Trial 352.1(1), 352.1(3).

Formosa Plastics Corp. USA v. Presidio Engineers and Contractors, Inc., Tex, 960 SW2d 41.—App & E 1083(5); Contracts 94(1), 168; Fraud 3, 4, 12, 32, 59(2), 59(3), 62, 64(2).

Forney v. Commercial Credit Equipment Corp., Tex-CivApp–Beaumont, 418 SW2d 904, ref nre.—Chat Mtg 209, 215.5.

Forney v. Forney, TexApp–Houston (1 Dist), 672 SW2d 490, writ dism woj.—Divorce 166, 168, 254(2), 255; Judgm 335(4), 354, 443(1), 713(2), 720.

Forney; Forney v., TexApp–Houston (1 Dist), 672 SW2d 490, writ dism woj.—Divorce 166, 168, 254(2), 255; Judgm 335(4), 354, 443(1), 713(2), 720.

Forney v. Jorrie, TexCivApp–San Antonio, 511 SW2d 379, ref nre.—App & E 172(1), 1043(5); Child S 444; Costs 61; Divorce 252.3(5), 261, 277; Judgm 335(1), 335(3), 335(4); Proc 77, 96(4); Subrog 1, 2, 26.

Forney; McCombs v., TexCivApp–Hous (1 Dist), 607 SW2d 591.—Divorce 166; Judgm 335(4); Plead 111.47.

Forney v. Memorial Hospital, TexCivApp–Beaumont, 543 SW2d 705, ref nre.—App & E 930(3), 989; Death 79; Evid 555.10; Health 707, 818, 827, 906, 908; Trial 296(1), 352.1(1).

Forney, City of; Brodhead v., TexCivApp–Waco, 538 SW2d 873, ref nre.—Counties 222; Mun Corp 374(1), 374(4), 1034.

Forney Engineering Co. v. Cannon Computer Co., Tex-CivApp–Waco, 553 SW2d 651, writ gr, and cause dism. —Damag 89(1).

Forney Engineering Co.; Green v., CA5 (Tex), 589 F2d 243.—Atty & C 76(1); Civil R 1383, 1511; Fed Civ Proc 1758.1, 1832, 1833, 2533.1.

Forney Engineering Co.; Jefferson Chemical Co. v., TexCivApp–Hous (1 Dist), 466 SW2d 361, writ dism.— Evid 553(3); Venue 22(6).

Forney Independent School Dist.; Littlefield v., CA5 (Tex), 268 F3d 275.—Const Law 702, 825, 832, 862, 1055, 1188, 1295, 1307, 1357, 1497, 1504, 1580, 1976, 1981, 3901, 4190, 4209(2), 4391; Fed Civ Proc 2470.1, 2544; Fed Cts 776, 802; Schools 171, 172.

Forney Ind. School Dist.; Littlefield v., NDTex, 108 FSupp2d 681, aff 268 F3d 275.—Civil R 1376(1); Const Law 702, 1021, 1188, 1264(2), 1265, 1290, 1295, 1303, 1308, 1357, 1497, 1966, 1973, 1976, 1981, 3041, 3051, 3057, 4209(2); Fed Civ Proc 103.2; Schools 169, 172.

Forney Messenger, Inc. v. Tennon, NDTex, 959 FSupp 389.—Inj 22; Newsp 6.1.

Forney State Bank; Allison v., TexCivApp–Dallas, 502 SW2d 826.—Judgm 185.3(16).

Forrest v. Beynon, TexCivApp–San Antonio, 179 SW2d 355.—App & E 387(3).

Forrest v. Danielson, TexApp–Tyler, 77 SW3d 842.—App & E 941, 946; Evid 536; Health 804, 809.

Forrest v. Faust, TexCivApp–San Antonio, 110 SW2d 147, writ dism.—App & E 1004(8), 1015(5), 1062.2; Assault 40; New Tr 140(3); Trial 219, 350.1, 350.3(5), 351.5(2), 352.9.

Forrest; Fryar v., TexCivApp–San Antonio, 155 SW2d 679.—Fraud 35, 50.

Forrest v. Guardian Loan & Trustee Co., TexCivApp–El Paso, 230 SW2d 273, ref nre.—Corp 123(7), 182.2, 182.4(1); Lim of Act 167(2); Mtg 187.1.

Forrest v. Hanson, Tex, 424 SW2d 899.—App & E 1082(2); Covenants 101, 130(1), 131; Estop 32(1); Mines 55(4); Trial 66.

Forrest; Hestand Kimbell Grocery Co. v., TexCivApp–El Paso, 151 SW2d 882.—App & E 1177(7); Partners 213(2).

Forrest; Laird v., TexCivApp–San Antonio, 149 SW2d 151, writ refused.—Courts 121(9), 122.

Forrest; McMahon v., TexCivApp–Waco, 474 SW2d 815, dism.—Plead 111.42(8).

Forrest; Mapco, Inc. v., Tex, 795 SW2d 700.—App & E 436, 438, 440, 833(1), 1185; Judgm 386(3).

Forrest; Michigan Mut. Ins. Co. v., BkrtcyNDTex, 212 BR 549. See Pierce Mortuary Colleges, Inc., In re.

Forrest v. Moreno, TexCivApp–San Antonio, 161 SW2d 364, writ refused.—App & E 216(1), 231(3); Hus & W 273(1), 274(1); Trial 83(2); Witn 130.

Forrest; Motors Ins. Corp. v., TexCivApp–Eastland, 422 SW2d 772.—Insurance 2733.

Forrest; National Mar-Kit, Inc. v., TexApp–Houston (14 Dist), 687 SW2d 457.—App & E 719(1); Costs 194.32, 208; Evid 427; Lim of Act 6(1), 46(4); Nova 11; Paymt 18, 59; Release 28(1).

Forrest; Schoenberg v., TexCivApp–San Antonio, 253 SW2d 331.—Damag 40(1), 184, 190; Princ & A 41(3), 41(4), 41(6).

Forrest; Schoenberg v., TexCivApp–San Antonio, 228 SW2d 556, ref nre.—App & E 262(1), 758.3(7); Damag 221(2.1); Princ & A 41(3), 41(5); Trial 350.1, 351.2(1.1), 352.5(4), 352.12, 366.

Forrest v. State, TexCrimApp, 805 SW2d 462.—Crim Law 1159.2(9); Sent & Pun 2001, 2003, 2020.

Forrest v. State, TexApp–Houston (1 Dist), 769 SW2d 298, petition for discretionary review gr, rev 805 SW2d 462.—Crim Law 562, 1147; Sent & Pun 2018.

Forrest; Stewart v., TexCivApp–San Antonio, 124 SW2d 887.—Attach 7; Garn 4.

Forrest v. Vital Earth Resources, TexApp–Texarkana, 120 SW3d 480, review den.—App & E 173(10), 758.1, 766, 768, 856(1), 863; Estop 52.10(1); Judgm 178, 181(7), 181(21), 185(2), 185(5), 185(6); Labor & Emp 2777, 2832, 2842, 2848, 2858; Lim of Act 13; Neglig 202, 371, 379, 380, 387, 1675, 1676, 1713.

Forrest & Cotton, Inc.; Hill v., TexCivApp–Eastland, 555 SW2d 145, ref nre.—Const Law 3454, 3971; Contrib 9(3); Death 38, 39; Indem 96; Lim of Act 4(2), 6(1), 30; Statut 4, 236.

Forrester; Brotherhood of Locomotive Firemen and Enginemen v., TexCivApp–Austin, 101 SW2d 860, writ dism.—Insurance 1823, 2579, 3579.

Forrester; ETL Corp. v., TexApp–Dallas, 667 SW2d 247. —Contracts 143(2), 147(3), 176(2); Ven & Pur 81, 143.

Forrester v. State, TexCrimApp, 462 SW2d 280.—Crim Law 1130(2); Embez 44(1).

Forrester v. State, TexCivApp–Corpus Christi, 459 SW2d 698, ref nre.—Atty & C 50, 54, 58; Jury 26.

Forrest Lumber Co.; Snider v., TexCivApp–Tyler, 448 SW2d 130.—App & E 170(1), 758.3(11); Judgm 181(25), 185(6), 185.2(1), 185.2(9), 185.3(15), 186; Mtg 369(7); Tresp to T T 35(2).

Forrest Williams, Contractor, In re, BkrtcyNDTex, 62 BR 590. See Williams, In re.

Forrest Williams, Contractor; First Nat. Bank of Claude, Tex. v., BkrtcyNDTex, 62 BR 590. See Williams, In re.

Forristall; Federal Ins. Co. v., TexCivApp–Beaumont, 401 SW2d 285, ref nre.—Insurance 1831, 1832(1), 2278(13), 2278(29), 2678, 2914, 3081, 3108, 3110(1).

ForScan Corp. v. Dresser Industries, Inc., TexApp–Houston (14 Dist), 789 SW2d 389, writ den.—Antitrust 432; App & E 230, 846(5), 1008.1(1), 1008.1(2), 1008.1(3); Inj 128(3.1); Jury 26; Plead 262; Pretrial Proc 251.1; Torts 424; Trial 382.

Forscan Corp.; Dresser Industries, Inc. v., TexApp–Houston (14 Dist), 641 SW2d 311.—App & E 190(2), 559, 578, 766, 907(4), 920(3); Inj 138.21, 147.

Forscan Corp. v. Touchy, TexApp–Houston (14 Dist), 743 SW2d 722.—Mand 1, 4(1), 4(3), 26, 32, 154(3), 168(4), 187.9(6); Pretrial Proc 40.

Forse v. Forse, TexCivApp–Beaumont, 220 SW2d 342.—Child C 9, 505, 924; Divorce 62(1), 124.3, 184(1); Inj 145, 147.

Forse; Forse v., TexCivApp–Beaumont, 220 SW2d 342.—Child C 9, 505, 924; Divorce 62(1), 124.3, 184(1); Inj 145, 147.

Forse; Hervey v., TexCivApp–Beaumont, 253 SW2d 701. —J P 92, 159(11), 159(12), 163, 164(3), 164(4), 169, 183(1).

Forse; Thibodeaux v., TexCivApp–Beaumont, 592 SW2d 663, ref nre.—Child C 553.

Forseille v. State, TexCrimApp, 383 SW2d 426.—Autos 355(6).

Forsgard; Texas Dept. of Public Safety v., TexApp–Tyler, 108 SW3d 344.—Const Law 2332, 2340, 2450, 2470; Statut 227; Weap 12.

Forshage; Guadalupe-Blanco River Authority v., TexCivApp–San Antonio, 401 SW2d 376, ref nre.—Bound 37(5), 46(1).

Forshagen v. Payne, TexCivApp–Fort Worth, 225 SW2d 229.—App & E 373(1), 387(4), 981; Fraud 11(1); New Tr 108(2), 108(5).

Forsman v. Forsman, TexApp–San Antonio, 694 SW2d 112, ref nre.—App & E 169; Divorce 252.3(4), 255, 282, 322; Hus & W 247, 249(3); Partit 13.

Forsman; Forsman v., TexApp–San Antonio, 694 SW2d 112, ref nre.—App & E 169; Divorce 252.3(4), 255, 282, 322; Hus & W 247, 249(3); Partit 13.

Forson v. State, TexCrimApp, 296 SW2d 770, 164 TexCrim 102.—Big 11; Crim Law 661, 663.

Forson v. State, TexCrimApp, 282 SW2d 385, 162 TexCrim 44.—Bailm 1; Embez 10.

Forson; Travelers Ins. Co. v., TexCivApp–Fort Worth, 268 SW2d 219, ref nre.—Work Comp 11, 647, 747.

Forstar Trailers v. U.S., CA5 (Tex), 67 F3d 112. See Wilkerson v. U.S.

Forstar Trailers v. U.S., EDTex, 839 FSupp 440. See Wilkerson v. U.S.

Forster; Norwood v., TexCivApp–Waco, 290 SW2d 576.—Plead 111.2.

Forster v. State, TexCrimApp, 287 SW2d 484.—Crim Law 1090.1(1).

Forsyth v. Barr, CA5 (Tex), 19 F3d 1527, cert den 115 SCt 195, 513 US 871, 130 LEd2d 127.—Atty & C 21.5(2); Crim Law 394.3; Fed Civ Proc 2481, 2544, 2546, 2737.5; Fed Cts 597, 712, 761, 766, 802, 813; Statut 181(2), 206; Tel 1434, 1436, 1437.

Forsyth v. City of Dallas, Tex., CA5 (Tex), 91 F3d 769, cert den City of Dallas v. Kirks, 118 SCt 64, 522 US 816, 139 LEd2d 26.—Civil R 1376(10), 1424, 1472, 1473, 1474(1), 1487; Const Law 1955; Labor & Emp 776, 827; Mun Corp 180(2), 1040.

Forsyth; Dallas Joint Stock Land Bank of Dallas v., TexComApp, 112 SW2d 173, 130 Tex 563.—App & E 1176(1).

Forsyth; Dallas Joint Stock Land Bank of Dallas v., TexComApp, 109 SW2d 1046, 130 Tex 563, reh den 112 SW2d 173, 130 Tex 563.—Courts 481; Ex & Ad 98, 271, 283; Judgm 475.

Forsyth v. Dallas Joint Stock Land Bank of Dallas, TexCivApp–Dallas, 81 SW2d 1103, mod 109 SW2d 1046, 130 Tex 563, reh den 112 SW2d 173, 130 Tex 563.—App & E 1151(2); Courts 198; Ex & Ad 121(1); Guard & W 45, 50, 112; Judgm 475, 518; Wills 440, 441, 802(2), 821(6).

Forsyth v. Lake LBJ Inv. Corp., TexApp–Austin, 903 SW2d 146, writ dism woj.—App & E 946, 949; Parties 35.1, 35.9, 35.13, 35.33, 35.35, 35.79.

Forsyth v. State, TexApp–Houston (1 Dist), 742 SW2d 815, petition for discretionary review refused.—Crim Law 394.6(4).

Forsythe; Hurst v., TexCivApp–Texarkana, 584 SW2d 314, ref nre.—Labor & Emp 259.

Forsythe; Hurst v., TexCivApp–Beaumont, 529 SW2d 620, ref nre.—Contracts 175(3), 282; Release 27.

Forsythe v. Porter, TexApp–Tyler, 703 SW2d 836, ref nre.—Autos 171(8), 246(9), 246(39.1).

Forsythe v. Saudi Arabian Airlines Corp., CA5 (Tex), 885 F2d 285.—Fed Civ Proc 2646, 2659; Fed Cts 29.1, 30, 33, 45, 55, 818, 829; Intern Law 10.30, 10.38.

Forsythe v. State, TexApp–Beaumont, 664 SW2d 109, petition for discretionary review refused.—Controlled Subs 67, 80, 112, 146; Crim Law 394.6(5), 419(2.40), 419(12), 736(1), 1038.1(2), 1043(3), 1137(5), 1172.1(2), 1172.6, 1186.1; Searches 109, 111, 113.1.

Forsythe Intern., S.A. v. Gibbs Oil Co. of Texas, CA5 (Tex), 915 F2d 1017.—Alt Disp Res 220, 251, 257, 265, 307, 332, 333, 368, 374(1).

Fort v. State, TexCrimApp, 615 SW2d 738.—Searches 103.1.

Fort; U.S. v., CA5 (Tex), 248 F3d 475, reh en banc den 260 F3d 624, cert den 122 SCt 405, 534 US 977, 151 LEd2d 307.—Autos 349(5), 349(9), 349.5(5.1); Controlled Subs 6, 100(1), 100(2); Crim Law 394.5(3), 1030(1), 1139, 1158(4); Searches 79; Sent & Pun 8.

Fort; U.S. v., CA5 (Tex), 206 FedAppx 364.—Sent & Pun 736.

Fort; U.S. v., NDTex, 81 FSupp2d 694, aff 248 F3d 475, reh en banc den 260 F3d 624, cert den 122 SCt 405, 534 US 977, 151 LEd2d 307.—Autos 349(2.1), 349(5), 349(18), 349.5(1), 349.5(5.1); Searches 79.

Fort Bend Cent. Appraisal Dist.; Flores v., TexApp–Houston (14 Dist), 720 SW2d 243.—Statut 181(1), 206; Tax 2694.

Fort Bend Cent. Appraisal Dist. v. Hines Wholesale Nurseries, TexApp–Texarkana, 844 SW2d 857, reh overerr, and writ den.—App & E 863, 1175(1); Pretrial Proc 483; Tax 2706.

Fort Bend Chapter; Texas Soc. v., TexCivApp–Texarkana, 590 SW2d 156, ref nre.—Corp 181(2), 181(3), 214, 308(1), 312(3), 314(1), 370(1); Costs 240; Inj 17, 138.42, 221, 223; Pretrial Proc 377.

Fort Bend County; Brady v., CA5 (Tex), 145 F3d 691, cert den 119 SCt 873, 525 US 1105, 142 LEd2d 774.—Civil R 1351(1), 1351(5), 1405, 1421, 1438, 1472, 1492; Const Law 1183, 1440, 1446, 1474(3), 1475(9), 1929, 1947, 1948, 1955; Damag 12, 48, 192; Evid 146; Fed Civ Proc 2148.1, 2339, 2742.1; Fed Cts 795, 823, 825.1, 830, 878; Sheriffs 21.

Fort Bend County; Brady v., CA5 (Tex), 58 F3d 173, reh en banc gr, and dism.—Civil R 1376(1), 1376(2), 1376(10); Fed Cts 776; Sheriffs 21.

Fort Bend County v. Heikkila, TexApp–Houston (1 Dist), 921 SW2d 395, appeal after remand 1998 WL 418045.—App & E 70(8); Counties 146; Judgm 185.3(2); Offic 114; States 112.1(1).

Fort Bend County v. Martin-Simon, TexApp–Houston (1 Dist), 177 SW3d 479.—App & E 949, 984(5); Costs 194.40, 194.46; Courts 40; Decl Judgm 2, 8, 25, 61, 65, 216, 272; Execution 22; Garn 17; Mand 111; Mun Corp 723, 1038; States 191.1, 191.2(1); Tax 2862, 2863.

Fort Bend County; Rosas v., CA5 (Tex), 145 F3d 691. See Brady v. Fort Bend County.

Fort Bend County; Scott v., CA5 (Tex), 870 F2d 164, reh den.—Fed Cts 420; Judgm 713(2), 828.14(11), 828.16(3), 828.16(4).

Fort Bend County v. Texas Parks & Wildlife Com'n, TexApp–Austin, 818 SW2d 898.—Admin Law 450.1, 499, 668; App & E 497(1); Environ Law 654, 705.

Fort Bend County v. Wilson, TexApp–Houston (14 Dist), 825 SW2d 251.—Counties 67; Plead 228.14.

Fort Bend County Drainage Dist. v. Sbrusch, Tex, 818 SW2d 392.—App & E 1078(1); Autos 270; Bridges 39(1), 41(1); Fraud 12; Judgm 199(3.9), 934(1); Mun Corp 723; Negllg 218, 234; Torts 109, 148.

Fort Bend County Drainage Dist.; Sbrusch v., TexApp–Houston (14 Dist), 788 SW2d 896, writ gr, rev 818 SW2d 392.—Autos 270, 308(4); Bridges 21(2), 46(10); Counties 144.

Fort Bend County Mun. Utility Dist. No. 30 v. Gayle, SDTex, 755 FSupp 746.—Banks 505.

Fort Bend County, Tex.; Sanders v., SDTex, 932 FSupp 894.—Civil R 1031, 1037, 1088(4), 1348, 1358, 1394; Counties 146; Dist & Pros Attys 10; Fed Civ Proc 2466, 2491.5, 2543, 2544, 2546.

Fort Bend County Wrecker Ass'n v. Wright, TexApp–Houston (1 Dist), 39 SW3d 421.—App & E 954(2); Autos 63, 109, 121; Const Law 2406, 3869, 3874(3), 4369; Inj 128(1); Sheriffs 77; Statut 185.

Fort Bend Independent School Dist.; Ariel B. ex rel. Deborah B. v., SDTex, 428 FSupp2d 640.—Civil R 1053, 1067(3), 1069, 1304, 1351(1), 1351(2), 1402; Const Law 1490, 1553; Fed Civ Proc 675.1; Judgm 540, 563(2), 584, 585(2), 715(1); Schools 148(2.1), 148(3), 154(2.1), 155.5(2.1), 155.5(4), 155.5(5).

Fort Bend Independent School Dist. v. City of Stafford, CA5 (Tex), 651 F2d 1133.—Schools 13(4), 13(20), 147.48.

Fort Bend Independent School Dist. v. City of Stafford, CA5 (Tex), 594 F2d 73, reh den Fort Bend Independent School District v. City of Stafford, 597 F2d 772, on remand 507 FSupp 211, rev 651 F2d 1133.—Schools 13(12), 13(20), 13(21).

Fort Bend Independent School Dist. v. City of Stafford, SDTex, 507 FSupp 211, rev 651 F2d 1133.—Schools 13(4), 13(17), 34, 133.1(1), 159.5(3).

Fort Bend Independent School Dist. v. City of Stafford, SDTex, 449 FSupp 375, rev 594 F2d 73, reh den Fort Bend Independent School District v. City of Stafford, 597 F2d 772, on remand 507 FSupp 211, rev 651 F2d 1133.—Schools 13(1), 13(3), 13(18.1), 34.

Fort Bend Independent School Dist.; Farris v., TexApp–Houston (1 Dist), 27 SW3d 307.—Const Law 3041, 3618(5), 4202; Schools 147.36, 147.38, 147.40(2), 147.42, 147.44.

Fort Bend Independent School Dist.; Finch v., CA5 (Tex), 333 F3d 555, reh and reh den 75 FedAppx 982.—

Civil R 1376(2); Const Law 1447, 1928, 1929, 2001, 3893, 4199, 4202; Fed Civ Proc 2491.5; Fed Cts 714, 753, 766, 768.1, 770, 776, 802; Labor & Emp 826; Schools 147.28, 147.34(1), 147.38.

Fort Bend Independent School Dist.; McDowell by McDowell v., SDTex, 737 FSupp 386.—Fed Cts 427; Lim of Act 95(15); Schools 148(2.1), 155.5(2.1), 164.

Fort Bend Independent School Dist. v. Rivera, TexApp–Houston (14 Dist), 93 SW3d 315.—App & E 833(4), 835(2), 863, 901, 916(1); Courts 35; Offic 69.2, 69.7; Plead 104(1), 111.36; Schools 163(1).

Fort Bend Independent School Dist.; Rollins v., CA5 (Tex), 89 F3d 1205.—Elections 12(2.1), 12(3), 12(9.1); Fed Cts 752, 813; Schools 53(1).

Fort Bend Independent School Dist.; Sterzing v., SDTex, 376 FSupp 657, vac 496 F2d 92.—Civil R 1424; Consp 47(3.1); Const Law 1994, 4200; Schools 147, 147.2(1), 147.38, 147.40(1), 147.44, 147.47.

Fort Bend Independent School Dist.; Washington v., TexApp–Houston (14 Dist), 892 SW2d 156, reh overr, and writ den.—Admin Law 229, 500; App & E 916(1); Plead 34(1), 34(3), 104(1), 106(1), 228.14; Pretrial Proc 562, 622, 690, 695; Schools 47.

Fort Bend Independent School Dist. v. Weiss, TexCiv-App–Hous (1 Dist), 570 SW2d 241.—Costs 246; Judgm 181(6); Pretrial Proc 308; Schools 106.23(2).

Fort Bend Independent School Dist., Fort Bend, Texas; Sterzing v., CA5 (Tex), 496 F2d 92.—Civil R 1346, 1448; Fed Cts 943.1.

Fort Crockett Hotel, Ltd.; Summers v., TexApp–Houston (1 Dist), 902 SW2d 20, reh overr, and writ den.—App & E 169, 170(1), 852, 934(1); Evid 54, 587; Inn 10.1, 10.3; Judgm 185(2); Negllg 202, 371, 387, 1020, 1037(4), 1286(7), 1676; Prod Liab 1, 23; Trial 143.

Forte, Ex parte, TexCrimApp, 296 SW2d 542.—Hab Corp 510(1).

Forte v. State, TexCrimApp, 759 SW2d 128.—Autos 421; Crim Law 393(1), 641.1, 641.3(1), 641.3(4), 641.3(8.1).

Forte v. State, TexCrimApp, 707 SW2d 89, on remand 722 SW2d 219, petition for discretionary review gr, aff 759 SW2d 128.—Autos 316, 355(6); Crim Law 641.3(3), 641.3(8.1).

Forte v. State, TexApp–Fort Worth, 935 SW2d 172, petition for discretionary review refused.—Crim Law 304(1), 338(7), 339.10(9), 469, 472, 474.3(2), 488, 671, 726.

Forte v. State, TexApp–Fort Worth, 722 SW2d 219, petition for discretionary review gr, aff 759 SW2d 128.—Crim Law 641.3(8.1).

Forte v. State, TexApp–Fort Worth, 686 SW2d 744, petition for discretionary review gr, aff in part, rev in part 707 SW2d 89, on remand 722 SW2d 219, petition for discretionary review gr, aff 759 SW2d 128.—Crim Law 1134(3).

Fortec Const. v. Bernard Lumber Co., Inc., TexApp–Corpus Christi, 710 SW2d 737. See Kaplan v. Bernard Lumber Co., Inc.

Fortenberry; Consolidated Cas. Ins. Co. v., TexCivApp–El Paso, 103 SW2d 1049, writ refused.—App & E 1062.1; Trial 215, 350.3(8), 352.5(2), 352.5(8); Work Comp 1161.

Fortenberry v. Fortenberry, TexCivApp–Beaumont, 582 SW2d 188, ref nre.—App & E 1060.1(1), 1060.1(7); Deeds 211(2); Trial 121(2), 124, 125(1), 133.1, 133.3; Wills 55(1), 400.

Fortenberry; Fortenberry v., TexCivApp–Beaumont, 582 SW2d 188, ref nre.—App & E 1060.1(1), 1060.1(7); Deeds 211(2); Trial 121(2), 124, 125(1), 133.1, 133.3; Wills 55(1), 400.

Fortenberry v. Fortenberry, TexCivApp–Waco, 545 SW2d 40.—Divorce 186, 223, 252.1, 252.2, 252.3(1), 286(5).

Fortenberry; Fortenberry v., TexCivApp–Waco, 545 SW2d 40.—Divorce 186, 223, 252.1, 252.2, 252.3(1), 286(5).

FORTUNE

Fortenberry; Geter v., CA5 (Tex), 882 F2d 167.—Civil R 1376(6); Fed Civ Proc 1272.1, 2491.5.

Fortenberry; Geter v., CA5 (Tex), 849 F2d 1550.—Civil R 1088(5), 1375, 1376(6), 1376(9), 1398; Fed Civ Proc 1825, 2491.5.

Fortenberry v. Maryland Cas. Co., CA5 (Tex), 247 F2d 702.—Fed Cts 421; Jury 19(1); Work Comp 1269, 1297.

Fortenberry v. State, TexCrimApp, 579 SW2d 482.—Crim Law 780(3), 780(4), 1173.2(6).

Fortenberry v. State, TexApp–Houston (14 Dist), 889 SW2d 634, petition for discretionary review refused.—Assault 56; Crim Law 739(1), 1144.13(2.1), 1159.2(7); Larc 3(1); Rob 11, 24.35.

Fortenberry v. Texas, CA5 (Tex), 75 FedAppx 924, cert den 124 SCt 1152, 540 US 1152, 157 LEd2d 1047.—Civil R 1126, 1135, 1138, 1147, 1249(1); Fed Civ Proc 2416; Fed Cts 915; States 53.

Forte's Estate; McEntire v., TexCivApp–Dallas, 463 SW2d 491, ref nre.—Aviation 173, 180, 181; States 18.3, 18.17.

Fort Griffin Fandangle Ass'n, Inc.; Kerney v., CA5 (Tex), 624 F2d 717.—Const Law 3981; Fed Civ Proc 186.5, 414, 1742(3); Lim of Act 121(2).

Forth; Allstate Indem. Co. v., Tex, 204 SW3d 795.—Action 13; Insurance 3365.

Forth v. Allstate Indem. Co., TexApp–Texarkana, 151 SW3d 732, review gr, rev 204 SW3d 795.—Action 6, 13; Const Law 328, 2314, 2358; Decl Judgm 1, 301, 387; Insurance 2831(1), 2845, 3365; Plead 104(1); Pretrial Proc 554.

Fort Hood Barbers Ass'n v. Herman, CA5 (Tex), 137 F3d 302.—Admin Law 390.1, 763, 797; Labor & Emp 63, 2185, 2338, 2350(2), 2357.

Fort Hood Nat. Bank; Mennor v., CA5 (Tex), 829 F2d 553.—Civil R 1507, 1593.

Forti; City of El Paso v., Tex, 181 SW2d 579, 142 Tex 658.—Tax 2849, 2973, 3002, 3030, 3031.

Forti; City of El Paso v., TexCivApp–El Paso, 181 SW2d 576, rev 181 SW2d 579, 142 Tex 658.—Const Law 2473, 2478; Statut 158, 159, 162; Tax 2856, 3002.

Fortier v. State, TexApp–Amarillo, 105 SW3d 697, reh overr, and petition for discretionary review refused.—Crim Law 1177.5(1); Sent & Pun 1256, 1260, 1291.

Fortinberry v. Fortinberry, TexCivApp–Waco, 326 SW2d 717, ref nre.—Wills 219, 255, 259, 270, 355.

Fortinberry; Fortinberry v., TexCivApp–Waco, 326 SW2d 717, ref nre.—Wills 219, 255, 259, 270, 355.

Fortinberry v. Freeway Lumber Co., TexCivApp–Hous (1 Dist), 453 SW2d 849.—Acct Action on 13; Costs 194.38.

Fortis Benefits v. Cantu, TexApp–Waco, 170 SW3d 755, reh overr, and review gr.—App & E 1078(5), 1079; Insurance 3502, 3514(2); Judgm 185.1(8), 189.

Fortis Benefits Ins. Co.; Guin v., EDTex, 256 FSupp2d 542.—Fed Civ Proc 2547.1; Labor & Emp 407, 425, 575, 616, 685, 687, 688, 690, 691; States 18.51.

Fortna; U.S. v., CA5 (Tex), 796 F2d 724, cert den 107 SCt 437, 479 U.S. 950, 93 LEd2d 386, appeal after remand US v. Harnage, 871 F2d 119, cert den 110 SCt 123, 493 US 839, 107 LEd2d 84, reh den 110 SCt 525, 493 US 985, 107 LEd2d 525, appeal after remand 976 F2d 633.—Arrest 63.4(1), 63.4(7.1); Commerce 82.10; Consp 27, 44.2, 47(1), 47(12); Const Law 257.5, 725, 4523; Crim Law 371(1), 394.1(2), 622.2(4), 622.2(8), 622.3, 662.1, 662.7, 863(2), 1044.1(7), 1144.13(3), 1144.13(5), 1159.2(7), 1166(6), 1170.5(1); Cust Dut 126(1), 126(9.1); Ind & Inf 136; Witn 4, 9.

Fortna; U.S. v., CA5 (Tex), 769 F2d 243.—Bail 42, 49(1), 49(3.1), 49(4); Crim Law 1134(10), 1166(1).

Fortner v. Fannin Bank in Windom, TexApp–Austin, 634 SW2d 74.—Antitrust 136, 145; App & E 863; Contracts 54(1); Judgm 181(17).

Fortner v. Johnson, TexCivApp–Fort Worth, 404 SW2d 892, ref nre.—App & E 627.2, 930(3); Bills & N 220,

290, 310, 313, 322, 365(2), 496(1), 497(2), 523, 525, 537(6); Contracts 147(1); Plgs 24.

Fortner v. Merrill Lynch, Pierce, Fenner & Smith, Inc., TexApp–Dallas, 687 SW2d 8, ref nre.—Accord 1, 15.1, 25(1); App & E 173(12), 931(1), 989, 1010.1(1), 1010.1(3), 1012.1(5); Bills & N 533, 534; Damag 91(1); Fraud 43, 49, 58(1), 58(2), 58(3), 58(4); Judgm 141; Plead 34(5), 48, 387, 389, 398; Torts 115; Trial 382.

Fortner v. State, TexApp–Fort Worth, 764 SW2d 934.—Crim Law 641.2(4).

Fortner Oilfield Services, Inc., In re, BkrtcyNDTex, 49 BR 9.—Bankr 2041.1, 2404, 3568(2), 3570.

Fortner Oilfield Services, Inc.; General Motors Acceptance Corp. v., BkrtcyNDTex, 49 BR 9. See Fortner Oilfield Services, Inc., In re.

Fortney; Cooper v., TexApp–Houston (14 Dist), 703 SW2d 217, ref nre.—Antitrust 597; Elect of Rem 2, 7(1), 15.

Fortney v. Olivetti Underwood Corp., TexCivApp–Houston, 398 SW2d 178.—Trial 392(2), 405(1).

Fortney; Sulphur Springs Coca-Cola Bottling Co. v., TexCivApp–Dallas, 412 SW2d 721.—Venue 8.5(8).

Fort Quitman Land Co. v. Mier, TexCivApp–Eastland, 211 SW2d 340, ref nre.—Ease 26(1); Frds St of 129(11); Waters 145, 156(8), 158.5(1), 158.5(2).

Fortson v. Burns, TexCivApp–Waco, 479 SW2d 722, ref nre.—Bills & N 125, 129(1).

Fortson; Busha v., CCA5 (Tex), 116 F2d 325.—Judgm 828.14(1); Wills 440, 590, 597(4).

Fortson v. Golden State Mut. Life Ins. Co., TexCivApp–Houston, 398 SW2d 437.—App & E 150(2).

Fortson; Parr v., TexCivApp–Dallas, 457 SW2d 137.—Judgm 185.3(4).

Fortson v. State, TexCrimApp, 474 SW2d 234.—Crim Law 396(1); Infants 133; Rape 64.

Fortson v. State, TexCrimApp, 138 SW2d 822, 139 Tex-Crim 341.—Crim Law 1133; Ind & Inf 166.

Fortson v. State, TexApp–Amarillo, 948 SW2d 511, petition for discretionary review refused.—Autos 352; Crim Law 975; Ind & Inf 161(2), 171.

Fortson v. Williams, TexApp–Waco, 128 SW2d 89.—Cust & U 10, 17, 21; Evid 460(12).

Fortson Oil Co.; Texaco Producing, Inc. v., TexApp–Austin, 798 SW2d 622.—Admin Law 763; Mines 47, 92.27, 92.51.

Fort Stockton, City of; Shupe v., TexCivApp–El Paso, 123 SW2d 408.—Evid 83(2); Inj 85(1), 105(1), 105(2).

Fortuna Broom Co. v. Wirtz, CA5 (Tex), 379 F2d 327.—Labor & Emp 2387(9).

Fortuna Corp.; Wilkerson v., CA5 (Tex), 554 F2d 745, cert den 98 SCt 430, 434 US 939, 54 LEd2d 299.—Const Law 3965(3); Corp 642(1), 665(3); Fed Cts 79, 433.

Fortune, Ex parte, TexCrimApp, 797 SW2d 929.—Double J 107.1, 108, 131, 135; Hab Corp 276.

Fortune v. Fortune, TexCivApp–Austin, 532 SW2d 411.—App & E 564(3).

Fortune; Fortune v., TexCivApp–Austin, 532 SW2d 411.—App & E 564(3).

Fortune v. McElhenney, TexApp–Austin, 645 SW2d 934.—App & E 465(1).

Fortune v. State, TexCrimApp, 745 SW2d 364, overr in later appeal Ex parte Fortune, 797 SW2d 929.—Crim Law 29(11), 619, 1032(1); Ind & Inf 127, 128, 130, 132(7), 137(1).

Fortune v. State, TexCrimApp, 245 SW2d 492.—Crim Law 1094(3).

Fortune v. State, TexApp–Beaumont, 699 SW2d 706, petition for discretionary review gr, aff 745 SW2d 364, overr in later appeal Ex parte Fortune, 797 SW2d 929.—Crim Law 29(12); Double J 163; Sent & Pun 1324.

Fortune; Swap Shop v., Tex, 365 SW2d 151.—Jury 97(1), 133; Trial 304.

Fortune v. Swap Shop, TexCivApp–Waco, 352 SW2d 148, writ gr, rev 365 SW2d 151.—Autos 244(58), 244(59), 247; Exceptions Bill of56(3); Jury 149.

See Guidelines for Arrangement at the beginning of this Volume

Fortune; U.S. v., CA5 (Tex), 513 F2d 883, reh den 518 F2d 1407, cert den 96 SCt 459, 423 US 1020, 46 LEd2d 393.—Crim Law 311, 331, 354, 369.1, 479, 494, 570(1), 625.30, 740, 741(4), 742(1), 935(1), 1144.13(3), 1159.2(5), 1159.5.

Fortune Drilling Co., Inc.; Pilgrim v., CA5 (Tex), 653 F2d 982.—Autos 197(7); Labor & Emp 3030, 3031(1), 3046(1); Neglig 232.

Fortune Lincoln Mercury, Inc.; Goates v., TexCivApp–El Paso, 446 SW2d 913, ref nre.—Autos 213, 244(47), 244(58), 245(82).

Fortune Production Co. v. Conoco, Inc., Tex, 52 SW3d 671.—App & E 173(2); Fraud 24, 32, 35, 58(1), 59(2), 59(3); Impl & C C 55, 70, 123; Sales 23(3).

Fortune Production Co.; Conoco, Inc. v., TexApp–Houston (1 Dist), 35 SW3d 23, review gr, rev 52 SW3d 671.—App & E 218.2(7); Fraud 35, 64(1); Impl & C C 3, 55, 60.1, 98; Plead 236(3), 238(3), 245(4), 245(6).

Fort Wayne Pools, Inc.; Coffey v., NDTex, 24 FSupp2d 671.—Antitrust 136, 138, 147, 162, 203, 291, 292; Contracts 168; Fraud 3, 13(2); Frds St of 38; Princ & A 1, 3(1), 3(2), 8, 14(1), 14(2), 19, 24, 99, 122(1), 147(2), 148(1), 163(1), 166(1), 171(1); Prod Liab 17.1; Torts 118.

Fort Worth & D. C. Ry. Co.; Alexander Marketing Co. v., TexCivApp–San Antonio, 266 SW2d 400, dism.—Carr 130.

Fort Worth & D. C. Ry. Co. v. Ammons, TexCivApp–Amarillo, 215 SW2d 407, ref nre.—Const Law 2437; Em Dom 1, 2(1), 20(5), 57, 65.1, 68; High 165; Mun Corp 589, 590, 592(1), 703(1); R R 5; Zoning 6, 9, 371.

Fort Worth & D. C. Ry. Co.; Brittain v., TexCivApp–Fort Worth, 128 SW2d 874, writ dism, correct.—Labor & Emp 2874, 2887, 3011; R R 377.

Fort Worth & D. C. Ry. Co. v. Capehart, TexCivApp–Waco, 210 SW2d 839, ref nre.—App & E 1033(4); Damag 168(2), 208(2); Neglig 530(1); R R 338.2, 346(5.1), 351(15); Trial 76, 215, 350.1.

Fort Worth & D. C. Ry. Co.; Deatherage v., TexCivApp–Fort Worth, 154 SW2d 918, writ refused.—Death 11, 32.

Fort Worth & D. C. Ry. Co.; Doty v., TexComApp, 95 SW2d 104, 127 Tex 521.—Labor & Emp 2927.

Fort Worth & D. C. Ry. Co.; Figula v., TexCivApp–Fort Worth, 131 SW2d 998, writ refused.—App & E 1069.1; Trial 306.

Fort Worth & D. C. Ry. Co.; Gifford v., Tex, 249 SW2d 190, 151 Tex 282.—App & E 719(6), 1094(5), 1114; R R 400(12).

Fort Worth & D. C. Ry. Co. v. Gifford, TexCivApp–Fort Worth, 252 SW2d 204.—App & E 1004(5); Damag 127, 134(1), 163(1); Evid 18.

Fort Worth & D. C. Ry. Co. v. Gifford, TexCivApp–Fort Worth, 244 SW2d 848, rev 249 SW2d 190, 151 Tex 282.—App & E 996, 1053(2); Neglig 1694; New Tr 76(1), 76(4); R R 369(3), 381(1), 383(1), 387, 398(1).

Fort Worth & D. C. Ry. Co.; Hambright, TexCivApp–Amarillo, 130 SW2d 436, writ dism, correct.—App & E 843(2); Neglig 1010, 1037(3), 1037(4), 1037(8), 1085, 1088, 1132, 1286(2), 1291(4), 1625, 1717, 1741; R R 275(2); Trial 350.6(4), 352.21.

Fort Worth & D. C. Ry. Co.; Heflin v., TexCivApp–Fort Worth, 207 SW2d 114, ref nre.—New Tr 143(5), 144.

Fort Worth & D. C. Ry. Co. v. Kiel, Tex, 187 SW2d 371, 143 Tex 601.—R R 108, 114(4).

Fort Worth & D. C. Ry. Co. v. Kiel, TexCivApp–Fort Worth, 195 SW2d 405, ref nre.—App & E 927(7), 968, 1050.1(1), 1050.1(12); Evid 42, 380, 471(19), 472(9); Jury 131(3), 131(4); R R 114(3), 114(4); Trial 115(2), 178, 349(1).

Fort Worth & D. C. Ry. Co. v. Kiel, TexCivApp–Fort Worth, 185 SW2d 144, rev 187 SW2d 371, 143 Tex 601. —Evid 6, 471(24), 472(11), 544; R R 108, 113(5), 114(0.5), 114(4); Trial 352.1(8), 358.

Fort Worth & D. C. Ry. Co. v. Kimbrow, TexComApp, 112 SW2d 712, 131 Tex 117.—Neglig 510(1); R R 282(16).

Fort Worth & D. C. R. Co.; Kimbrow v., TexCivApp–Amarillo, 86 SW2d 78, aff 112 SW2d 712, 131 Tex 117.—App & E 863, 930(1); Judgm 256(2); Trial 352.1(8), 356(1), 397(2).

Fort Worth & D. C. Ry. Co. v. Larson, TexCivApp–Fort Worth, 169 SW2d 260, writ refused wom.—Evid 397(1), 397(2), 408(4), 411, 417(9), 441(15), 442(1), 442(9), 450(5); Labor & Emp 34(2), 873; Trial 358.

Ft. Worth & D. C. Ry. Co. v. Looney, TexCivApp–Fort Worth, 241 SW2d 322, ref nre.—Damag 185(1), 210(1); R R 347(4), 347(8), 348(3), 348(6.1), 350(5), 350(32).

Fort Worth & D. C. Ry. Co. v. Mills, TexCivApp–Amarillo, 140 SW2d 513, writ dism, correct.—App & E 1175(5); Labor & Emp 2764, 2961, 2963; Land & Ten 164(1), 164(2), 165(1), 167(2); Neglig 1040(2); R R 273.5.

Fort Worth & D. C. Ry. Co.; Railroad Commission v., TexCivApp–Austin, 161 SW2d 560, writ refused wom.—Admin Law 489.1; Evid 20(2); R R 9(1), 223.

Fort Worth & D. C. Ry. Co.; Rogers v., TexCivApp–Dallas, 91 SW2d 458, writ refused.—Death 29; Labor & Emp 2753.

Fort Worth & D. C. Ry. Co.; Smith v., CA5 (Tex), 219 F2d 43.—Death 103(2); Labor & Emp 2797, 2828, 2887, 2889.

Fort Worth & D. C. Ry. Co.; Texas Emp. Ins. Ass'n v., TexCivApp–Amarillo, 181 SW2d 828.—App & E 265(1); R R 274(3); Work Comp 2203, 2233.

Fort Worth & D. C. Ry. Co.; Warren v., TexCivApp–Fort Worth, 208 SW2d 569, ref nre.—App & E 1052(8); Labor & Emp 2925; Trial 351.2(2).

Fort Worth & D. C. Ry. Co. v. Welch, TexCivApp–Amarillo, 183 SW2d 730, writ refused.—Const Law 38, 2478, 2970, 3757, 4425; R R 405; Statut 231.

Fort Worth & D. C. Ry. Co. v. Welch, TexCivApp–Amarillo, 154 SW2d 896.—Trial 358; Waters 176, 179(6).

Fort Worth & Denver City Ry. Co. v. Bozeman, TexCivApp–Amarillo, 135 SW2d 275, writ dism, correct.—App & E 216(1), 218.2(10), 1067; Death 104(4); R R 324(1), 327(1), 351(2); Trial 350.1, 351.5(6).

Fort Worth & Denver City Ry. Co. v. Burton, TexCivApp–Amarillo, 158 SW2d 601, writ dism.—Courts 97(5); Death 104(6); Evid 529; Labor & Emp 2830, 2863, 2881; Neglig 375, 1539; Plead 387; Trial 219, 352.4(5), 352.4(9), 352.9, 357.

Fort Worth & Denver City Ry. Co. v. Childress Cotton Oil Co., CCA5 (Tex), 141 F2d 558.—Carr 30.

Fort Worth & Denver City Ry. Co. v. Childress Cotton Oil Co., NDTex, 48 FSupp 937, aff 141 F2d 558.—Admin Law 103.1, 417; Carr 30, 32(1); Commerce 85(2), 132(1).

Fort Worth & Denver City Ry. Co. v. Motley, TexCivApp–Amarillo, 87 SW2d 551, writ dism.—App & E 1050.1(1), 1050.1(2), 1051(2); Carr 177(3), 217(1), 219(5), 227(1), 227(3), 228(1), 230(6); Commerce 14.10(1); Courts 97(5); Evid 539.5(1); Plead 35; Trial 352.4(1).

Fort Worth & Denver City Ry. Co. v. Reid, TexCivApp–Fort Worth, 115 SW2d 1156.—App & E 82(3), 1153; Judgm 18(2), 251(1), 335(3); Plead 212.

Fort Worth & Denver City Ry. Co. v. Smith, CA5 (Tex), 206 F2d 667.—Death 76; Labor & Emp 2784, 2832, 2863, 2879.

Fort Worth & Denver City Ry. Co.; U.S. v., NDTex, 21 FSupp 916.—R R 229(3.1), 229(4), 254(2).

Fort Worth & Denver City Ry. Co. v. Walters, TexCivApp–Fort Worth, 154 SW2d 177, writ refused wom.—App & E 1053(1); Trial 350.5(3), 362; Urb R R 1.

Fort Worth and Denver Ry. Co.; A/S Hydraulico Works v., SDTex, 483 FSupp 518.—Estop 52.15, 95, 96; Impl & C C 1; Insurance 2895, 3090; Princ & S 1.

Ft. Worth & Denver Ry. Co. v. City of Houston, Tex-App–Houston (14 Dist), 672 SW2d 299, ref nre.—Em Dom 47(1), 149(5), 196, 201, 262(4); R R 96.

Fort Worth & Denver Ry. Co.; City of Houston v., TexCivApp–Hous (1 Dist), 561 SW2d 22, ref nre.—Em Dom 172; R R 69.

Fort Worth & Denver Ry. Co. v. Ferguson, TexCivApp–Fort Worth, 261 SW2d 874, dism.—App & E 547(3), 1033(3); Assign 117, 120; Courts 169(8); Neglig 1693; Parties 79; R R 350(5), 350(7.1), 350(22.1); Subrog 1, 41(4); Trusts 104; Witn 263, 266.

Fort Worth & Denver Ry. Co. v. Goldschmidt, NDTex, 518 FSupp 121, rev Fort Worth and Denver Ry Co v. Lewis, 693 F2d 432, reh den 707 F2d 515.—Const Law 2424(1); R R 229(1), 229(3.1); Statut 184, 217.3, 219(1), 219(6.1), 220.

Fort Worth and Denver Ry. Co. v. Lewis, CA5 (Tex), 693 F2d 432, reh den 707 F2d 515.—R R 229(1).

Fort Worth & Denver Ry. Co. v. Williams, Tex, 375 SW2d 279.—App & E 1050.1(8.1); Evid 150, 596(1); R R 303(3), 304.

Fort Worth & Denver Ry. Emp. Hospital Ass'n; Pearce v., TexCivApp–Fort Worth, 488 SW2d 903.—Judgm 185(2), 185.3(8); Princ & A 101(1).

Fort Worth & D. N. Ry. Co. v. Johnson, TexComApp, 84 SW2d 232, 125 Tex 634.—Em Dom 231, 235.

Fort Worth & D. Ry. Co.; Attaway v., TexCivApp–Fort Worth, 334 SW2d 845, ref nre.—App & E 1170.10; Plead 362(2); Trial 352.1(8), 352.21.

Fort Worth & D. Ry. Co. v. Barlow, TexCivApp–Fort Worth, 263 SW2d 278, ref nre.—Neglig 200, 502(2), 1693, 1713, 1717; R R 327(8), 350(16.1); Trial 350.7(6), 352.10, 366.

Fort Worth & D. Ry. Co.; Boone v., CA5 (Tex), 223 F2d 766.—Armed S 101, 114(1), 118(2), 118(7).

Fort Worth & D. Ry. Co. v. Britton, TexCivApp–Fort Worth, 310 SW2d 654, ref nre.—App & E 1170.7; Carr 316(1.5), 318(2), 322; Neglig 1612, 1750; Trial 358, 359(1).

Ft. Worth & D. Ry. Co.; City of Houston v., TexCivApp–Hous (1 Dist), 619 SW2d 234, ref nre, appeal after remand Ft Worth & Denver Ry Co v. City of Houston, 672 SW2d 299, ref nre.—Commerce 82.20; Em Dom 47(1), 47(7), 85, 95, 147, 203(1); Poss War 1; R R 243.

Fort Worth & D. Ry. Co.; Coffey v., TexCivApp–Eastland, 285 SW2d 453.—App & E 918(3), 959(3), 1062.2, 1170.1, 1170.7, 1170.9(3); Plead 235, 236(3), 236(6), 245(3), 248(1); Trial 255(13), 279, 349(1), 350.1, 350.6(4).

Fort Worth & D. Ry. Co. v. Coffman, TexCivApp–Fort Worth, 397 SW2d 544, writ dism.—App & E 1004(5), 1170.6; Evid 548; Labor & Emp 2824, 2830, 2881; Trial 129.

Fort Worth & D. Ry. Co. v. Goodpasture, Inc., CA5 (Tex), 442 F2d 1294.—Carr 100(1), 191; Commerce 89(3), 131.

Fort Worth & D. Ry. Co. v. Harris, CA5 (Tex), 230 F2d 680.—Fed Civ Proc 1969, 1976; Fed Cts 611, 621, 628, 641, 875, 906; Labor & Emp 2881.

Fort Worth & D. Ry. Co.; Hensley v., TexCivApp–Fort Worth, 408 SW2d 761, ref nre, cert den 88 SCt 51, 389 US 823, 19 LEd2d 75.—App & E 1067; Labor & Emp 2887; Neglig 1619, 1620, 1695; Trial 199, 352.1(9).

Fort Worth & D. Ry. Co. v. Janski, CA5 (Tex), 223 F2d 704.—Damag 208(4); Evid 528(2), 553(4), 591; Fed Cts 627.1, 628, 640, 900, 903; Labor & Emp 2824.

Ft. Worth & D. Ry. Co. v. Prine, CA5 (Tex), 211 F2d 697, cert den Fort Worth and Denver Railway Company v. Prine, 75 SCt 42, 348 US 826, 99 LEd 651.—Labor & Emp 2824, 2881, 2918, 2942.

Ft. Worth & D. Ry. Co. v. Red Ball Motor Freight, Inc., TexCivApp–Fort Worth, 384 SW2d 729, ref nre.—App & E 554(1), 692(1), 761; R R 348(1), 348(2), 350(13).

Fort Worth & D. Ry. Co. v. Roach, CA5 (Tex), 219 F2d 351.—Damag 208(4); Fed Civ Proc 2345.1; Fed Cts 692, 827; Labor & Emp 2824.

Fort Worth & D. Ry. Co.; Snodgrass v., TexCivApp–Amarillo, 441 SW2d 670.—R R 327(1), 335(5).

Ft. Worth & D. Ry. Co. v. Thompson, CA5 (Tex), 216 F2d 790.—Fed Civ Proc 2191; Fed Cts 641, 774, 872, 904, 905; Labor & Emp 3006.

Fort Worth & D. Ry. Co. v. Threadgill, CA5 (Tex), 228 F2d 307.—Contrib 5(6.1); Fed Cts 405, 866; Indem 58, 70; Labor & Emp 2941; Neglig 1713; R R 307.3, 327(1).

Fort Worth & D. Ry. Co. v. U. S., CA5 (Tex), 242 F2d 702.—Carr 135, 154, 158(1); Fed Cts 752.

Fort Worth & D. Ry. Co.; U.S. v., NDTex, 141 FSupp 381, aff 242 F2d 702.—Carr 135; Fed Cts 230; Interest 39(1).

Fort Worth & D. Ry. Co. v. Williams, TexCivApp–Amarillo, 367 SW2d 925, writ gr, rev Fort Worth & Denver Ry Co v. Williams, 375 SW2d 279.—App & E 930(1), 989, 1050.1(8.1), 1060.1(1); Death 99(4); Evid 150; Neglig 1656; R R 303(3), 346(5.1), 348(1), 348(6.1); Trial 139.1(20), 142.

Fort Worth & D.-S. P. Ry. Co.; Ferguson Seed Farms v., TexCivApp–Amarillo, 100 SW2d 177, writ dism.—App & E 232(1), 544(3), 742(1), 761, 965, 1024.3; Trial 83(2), 352.5(7); Venue 50.

Fort Worth & R. G. Ry. Co.; Allcorn v., TexCivApp–Austin, 122 SW2d 341, writ refused.—App & E 1069.1; Damag 221(5.1); Neglig 1539; R R 329, 345(3), 347(11); Trial 315, 351.5(1), 351.5(6), 352.4(5).

Fort Worth & R. G. Ry. Co. v. Pickens, TexComApp, 162 SW2d 691, 139 Tex 181.—Trial 366.

Fort Worth & R. G. Ry. Co. v. Pickens, TexCivApp–Austin, 153 SW2d 252, rev 162 SW2d 691, 139 Tex 181.—Commerce 62.21; Contracts 270(2), 270(3); Courts 97(5); Labor & Emp 2774, 2877, 2897, 2950, 2975; Neglig 255, 431; Release 17(2), 58(3), 58(6); Trial 350.5(4), 350.5(5), 350.7(7).

Fort Worth & Rio Grande Ry. Co. v. Evans, TexCiv-App–Fort Worth, 150 SW2d 408, writ dism, correct.—Labor & Emp 217; Social S 169.1.

Fort Worth & Western R. Co.; PCI Transp., Inc. v., CA5 (Tex), 418 F3d 535.—Carr 102; Fed Cts 241, 776, 815; Inj 7, 138.1, 138.37, 147, 152; Rem of C 107(9); States 18.21.

Fort Worth Aviation; Federal Deposit Ins. Corp. v., CA5 (Tex), 806 F2d 575.—Banks 505.

Fort Worth Bank & Trust; Campbell v., TexApp–Fort Worth, 705 SW2d 400.—Guar 24(1); Judgm 185.1(3).

Fort Worth Bank and Trust; Watson v., USTex, 108 SCt 2777, 487 US 977, 101 LEd2d 827, on remand 856 F2d 716.—Civil R 1126, 1138, 1140, 1535, 1536, 1542, 1544, 1545.

Fort Worth Bank & Trust; Watson v., CA5 (Tex), 798 F2d 791, reh den 802 F2d 455, cert gr in part 107 SCt 3227, 483 US 1004, 97 LEd2d 734, vac 108 SCt 2777, 487 US 977, 101 LEd2d 827, on remand 856 F2d 716.—Civil R 1138, 1140, 1535, 1548; Fed Civ Proc 173, 184.10; Fed Cts 817.

Fort Worth Baseball Club; McNiel v., TexCivApp–Fort Worth, 268 SW2d 244, writ refused.—Pub Amuse 102, 109(2), 123, 128.

Fort Worth Brake, Clutch & Equipment, Inc.; Wetsel v., TexApp–Fort Worth, 780 SW2d 952.—Action 48(1); Forci E & D 43(4), 43(6).

Fort Worth Cab & Baggage Co., Inc.; Salinas v., Tex, 725 SW2d 701, on remand 735 SW2d 303.—App & E 218.2(1), 221, 232(0.5), 237(5), 238(2), 294(1); Courts 247(1); Hus & W 232.3; Parent & C 7(12).

Fort Worth Cab & Baggage Co., Inc. v. Salinas, Tex-App–Fort Worth, 735 SW2d 303.—Carr 283(3); Damag 51, 54, 94, 185(1); Rape 65.

Fort Worth Campbell & Associates, Inc., In re, BkrtcyNDTex, 182 BR 748.—Bankr 2722, 3004.1.

Fort Worth Capital Corp.; Hunter v., Tex, 620 SW2d 547, 20 ALR4th 399.—Abate & R 39; Contrib 5(5), 5(6.1); Corp 254, 264, 349, 359, 630(1); Indem 57, 67; Statut 203, 212.4.

Fort Worth Capital Corp. v. Hunter, TexCivApp–Fort Worth, 608 SW2d 352, rev 620 SW2d 547, 20 ALR4th 399.—Corp 264.

Fort Worth Capital Corp.; Moeller v., TexCivApp–Fort Worth, 610 SW2d 857, ref nre.—Carr 280(4), 306(1), 323; Judgm 180, 181(33), 185.2(1).

Fort Worth Cavalry Club v. Sheppard, Tex, 83 SW2d 660, 125 Tex 339.—Contracts 270(1); Offic 103; States 94, 102, 119, 131, 137.

Fort Worth Children's Hosp., In re, TexApp–Fort Worth, 100 SW3d 582, mandamus dism.—App & E 946, 949, 961; Const Law 1231; Infants 77, 78(1), 82, 84; Mand 3(2.1), 4(1), 4(4), 12, 28, 32; Pretrial Proc 27.1, 31, 32, 33, 40, 41, 382; Witn 217.

Fort Worth, City of; Abdeljalil v., NDTex, 55 FSupp2d 614, aff 234 F3d 28, aff 234 F3d 28.—Arrest 68(2); Civil R 1031, 1035, 1039, 1304, 1305, 1343, 1345, 1350, 1351(1), 1351(6), 1352(1), 1352(6); Consp 1.1, 7.5(2), 7.5(3), 19; Const Law 1212, 1215, 1228; Damag 49.10, 51; Mun Corp 79, 724, 747(1); Neglig 202; Sent & Pun 1435.

Fort Worth, City of; Activated Sludge v., CCA5 (Tex), 89 F2d 278, cert den 58 SCt 20, 302 US 701, 82 LEd 541.— Pat 262, 280, 314(1), 324.2.

Fort Worth, City of, v. Adams, TexApp–Fort Worth, 888 SW2d 607. See City of Fort Worth v. Adams.

Fort Worth, City of; Airport Coach Service, Inc. v., TexCivApp–Tyler, 518 SW2d 566, ref nre.—Admin Law 491; Antitrust 606, 659; App & E 187(3), 766, 768; Aviation 229; Carr 8; Courts 183, 472.1; Decl Judgm 26, 61, 302.1, 365, 366, 385, 387; Inj 85(1), 85(2); Judgm 185(2); Statut 181(1).

Fort Worth, City of; Aycock v., TexCivApp–Fort Worth, 371 SW2d 712, ref nre.—Const Law 2314; Judgm 185.3(20), 187; Tax 2140, 2623, 2853, 2859.

Fort Worth, City of; Baker v., Tex, 210 SW2d 564, 146 Tex 600, 5 ALR2d 297.—Lim of Act 43, 55(6), 55(7); Release 35.

Fort Worth, City of; Baker v., TexCivApp–Fort Worth, 380 SW2d 128, ref nre.—Judgm 185.3(1).

Fort Worth, City of; Barree v., TexApp–Fort Worth, 685 SW2d 475, ref nre.—App & E 930(3), 989, 994(2), 1001(1), 1001(3), 1003(5), 1003(7), 1175(1), 1177(7); Autos 245(60).

Fort Worth, City of; B. E. M. Homeowners Ass'n v., TexCivApp–Fort Worth, 372 SW2d 364.—Zoning 38, 167.1, 168, 620, 649, 675, 676, 681.

Fort Worth, City of; Benedict v., TexCivApp–Fort Worth, 447 SW2d 451, ref nre.—Mun Corp 741.20, 741.25; Plead 49.

Fort Worth, City of; Berry v., Tex, 124 SW2d 842, 132 Tex 599.—Cons Cred 2; Mun Corp 111(4), 592(1), 592(3).

Fort Worth, City of; Berry v., TexCivApp–Fort Worth, 110 SW2d 95, writ gr, rev 124 SW2d 842, 132 Tex 599.— Const Law 3682, 3689; Cons Cred 2; Mun Corp 121.

Fort Worth, City of; Billingsley v., TexCivApp–Fort Worth, 278 SW2d 869, ref nre.—Courts 121(1); Evid 383(3); Mun Corp 971(4), 978(9); Plead 34(3); Schools 103(1), 106.12(7), 106.12(8); Tax 2140, 2605, 2714.

Fort Worth, City of; Bliss v., TexCivApp–Fort Worth, 314 SW2d 611.—App & E 931(6); Inj 126; Zoning 645, 684, 787.1.

Fort Worth, City of; Bliss v., TexCivApp–Fort Worth, 288 SW2d 558, ref nre.—Judgm 178, 181(4), 185(2), 185(5), 185.1(3), 185.1(4), 185.3(11); Zoning 151, 161, 490, 679.

Fort Worth, City of; Bruflat v., TexCivApp–Fort Worth, 411 SW2d 387, ref nre.—App & E 218.2(2), 930(3), 989; Mun Corp 788, 816(8.1), 819(6).

Fort Worth, City of; Calstar Properties, L.L.C. v., Tex-App–Fort Worth, 139 SW3d 433.—App & E 1079; Contracts 127(4); Elect of Rem 1, 3(1), 3(4); Fraud 31; Inn 4.

Fort Worth, City of; Carter v., CA5 (Tex), 456 F2d 572, cert den 93 SCt 128, 409 US 877, 34 LEd2d 130.— Courts 493(3); Fed Cts 243; Judgm 828.14(7).

Fort Worth, City of; Carter v., NDTex, 352 FSupp 488, aff 456 F2d 572, cert den 93 SCt 128, 409 US 877, 34 LEd2d 130.—Judgm 828.9(6).

Fort Worth, City of; Carter v., TexCivApp–Fort Worth, 357 SW2d 581, ref nre.—App & E 624, 627.3.

Fort Worth, City of; City of Arlington v., TexApp–Fort Worth, 873 SW2d 765, reh overr, and writ dism woj.— Inj 1, 46, 48, 138.3, 138.6, 138.31, 140; Tresp 10, 11, 12.

Fort Worth, City of; City of Arlington v., TexApp–Fort Worth, 844 SW2d 875, reh den, and writ den.—App & E 181; Judgm 180, 185(5); Mun Corp 62, 708, 712(1), 712(2); States 1, 100, 102.

Ft. Worth, City of; Clay v., TexApp–Austin, 90 SW3d 414.—Mun Corp 847, 848.

Fort Worth, City of; Coastal Plains, Inc. v., TexCivApp–Fort Worth, 443 SW2d 414.—Acct Action on 12; App & E 1041(3); Plead 292; Sales 441(3).

Fort Worth, City of; Couch v., TexCivApp–Fort Worth, 287 SW2d 255.—App & E 931(1); Decl Judgm 273; Mun Corp 12(8), 14, 17, 18, 29(4); Quo W 5.

Fort Worth, City of; Cox v., TexCivApp–Fort Worth, 102 SW2d 504, writ dism.—App & E 207, 525(3), 930(2), 994(2); Em Dom 262(5); Trial 191(4), 351.5(2).

Fort Worth, City of; Culwell v., CA5 (Tex), 468 F3d 868, reh den.—Civil R 1513, 1520; Fed Civ Proc 2497.1, 2553, 2793, 2820; Fed Cts 813, 820.

Fort Worth, City of; Danciger v., CA5 (Tex), 354 F2d 689.—Em Dom 153; Mun Corp 225(5).

Fort Worth, City of; Downs v., TexApp–Fort Worth, 692 SW2d 209, ref nre.—Judgm 660.5; Mun Corp 185(6).

Fort Worth, City of; Empire Pictures Distributing Co. v., CA5 (Tex), 273 F2d 529.—Courts 494; Inj 105(1), 105(2).

Fort Worth, City of; Fire Dept. of City of Fort Worth v., Tex, 217 SW2d 664, 147 Tex 505.—Admin Law 8, 324, 656, 763, 791; Const Law 2541, 2563, 2564; Mun Corp 176(3.1).

Fort Worth, City of; Fort Worth Independent School Dist. v., Tex, 22 SW3d 831, reh overr.—Const Law 948, 951, 953; Contracts 9(1), 25, 51, 52, 147(3), 164; Estop 52.10(2); Judgm 181(6), 181(32); Mun Corp 244(2), 254, 724, 868(1), 873, 1018; Tax 2127, 2128, 2160.

Fort Worth, City of; Gates v., TexCivApp–Fort Worth, 567 SW2d 871, ref nre.—Mun Corp 723; Work Comp 374, 380.

Fort Worth, City of, v. Gay, TexApp–Fort Worth, 977 SW2d 814. See City of Fort Worth v. Gay.

Fort Worth, City of, v. Gene Hill Equipment Co., Inc., TexApp–Fort Worth, 761 SW2d 816. See City of Fort Worth v. Gene Hill Equipment Co., Inc.

Fort Worth, City of; George v., TexCivApp–Fort Worth, 434 SW2d 903, ref nre.—Judgm 185(6), 185.3(21); Land & Ten 164(6), 167(8); Mun Corp 848, 855, 857.

Fort Worth, City of; Gillam v., TexCivApp–Fort Worth, 287 SW2d 494, ref nre.—Const Law 2489; Decl Judgm 319, 346; Mun Corp 59, 63.10, 63.15(1), 226, 232; Waters 203(3), 203(11).

Fort Worth, City of; Gilliland v., TexCivApp–Fort Worth, 162 SW2d 1000, rev 169 SW2d 149, 140 Tex 616. —App & E 1172(5); Em Dom 50, 119(1), 274(1); Mun Corp 657(3).

Fort Worth, City of; Greenman v., TexCivApp–Fort Worth, 308 SW2d 553, ref nre.—App & E 1170.1; Const

Law 2642; Em Dom 84, 203(2), 262(5); Evid 560; Jury 131(3), 131(15.1); Waters 40.

Fort Worth, City of, v. Groves, TexApp–Fort Worth, 746 SW2d 907. See City of Fort Worth v. Groves.

Fort Worth, City of; Harris v., Tex, 180 SW2d 131, 142 Tex 600.—Const Law 593; Statut 181(1), 184, 214, 217.1; Tax 2346, 2351, 2355.

Fort Worth, City of, v. Harty, TexApp–Fort Worth, 862 SW2d 776. See City of Fort Worth v. Harty.

Ft. Worth, City of; Hernandez v., Tex, 617 SW2d 923.—App & E 758.1, 1095; Mun Corp 180(1).

Fort Worth, City of; Holcomb v., TexCivApp–Fort Worth, 175 SW2d 427, writ refused.—Courts 91(1); Em Dom 119(1).

Fort Worth, City of, v. Holland, TexApp–Fort Worth, 748 SW2d 112. See City of Fort Worth v. Holland.

Fort Worth, City of; Howerton v., TexCivApp–Fort Worth, 231 SW2d 993, aff 236 SW2d 615, 149 Tex 614.—Const Law 611, 655, 2645; Mun Corp 67(5), 176(3.1); Statut 94(1); Tax 2016.

Fort Worth, City of; Jamestown Partners, L.P. v., TexApp–Fort Worth, 83 SW3d 376, reh overr, and review den.—App & E 219(2), 931(1), 954(1), 954(2), 989, 1008.1(2), 1010.1(1), 1010.1(3), 1010.2, 1071.6, 1136; Contracts 143(1), 143(2), 147(1), 147(2), 167, 176(2); Health 392; Mun Corp 226, 628; Trial 388(1), 401.

Fort Worth, City of; Janus Films, Inc. v., Tex, 358 SW2d 589, 163 Tex 616.—App & E 954(1); Inj 132, 135, 138.46.

Fort Worth, City of; Janus Films, Inc. v., TexCivApp–Fort Worth, 354 SW2d 597, ref nre 358 SW2d 589, 163 Tex 616.—App & E 991; Mun Corp 57, 592(1), 592(2); Obscen 5.2; Pub Amuse 17, 47.

Ft. Worth, City of; Johnson v., Tex, 774 SW2d 653.—Judgm 181(5.1); Lim of Act 11(3), 165; Statut 147.

Fort Worth, City of, v. Johnson, TexApp–Fort Worth, 765 SW2d 558. See City of Fort Worth v. Johnson.

Fort Worth, City of; Legend Airlines, Inc. v., TexApp–Fort Worth, 23 SW3d 83, review den.—Action 69(7); Admin Law 228.1; App & E 863; Aviation 101, 224; Courts 97(1), 489(1); Decl Judgm 125; Judgm 181(15.1); States 18.3, 18.5, 18.7, 18.11, 18.17; Statut 219(5).

Fort Worth, City of; Lewis v., Tex, 89 SW2d 975, 126 Tex 458.—Mun Corp 63.15(5), 911, 921(3).

Fort Worth, City of; Liberty Mut. Ins. Co. v., TexCivApp–Fort Worth, 524 SW2d 743, writ dism woj.—Estop 62.4; Judgm 184; Mun Corp 812(5), 816(7); Plead 104(1), 106(1), 111.39(1).

Ft. Worth, City of; Liberty Mut. Ins. Co. v., TexCivApp–Fort Worth, 517 SW2d 646.—App & E 79(1).

Fort Worth, City of; Lone Star Gas Co. v., CCA5 (Tex), 93 F2d 584, cert den 58 SCt 943, 304 US 562, 82 LEd 1529, reh den 58 SCt 1044, 304 US 589, 82 LEd 1549.—Const Law 4290; Equity 409; Fed Civ Proc 1900; Fed Cts 862; Gas 2; Inj 85(2); Mun Corp 122.1(2), 589.

Fort Worth, City of; Lone Star Gas Co. v., NDTex, 15 FSupp 171, rev 93 F2d 584, cert den 58 SCt 943, 304 US 562, 82 LEd 1529, reh den 58 SCt 1044, 304 US 589, 82 LEd 1549.—Const Law 1066, 2486, 3902; Equity 409; Gas 2; Mun Corp 122.1(4).

Fort Worth, City of; Lone Star Gas Co. v., TexComApp, 98 SW2d 799, 128 Tex 392, 109 ALR 374.—Em Dom 47(1), 167(3), 274(1).

Fort Worth, City of; Long v., TexCivApp–Fort Worth, 333 SW2d 644.—Inj 118(4), 138.18, 151; Mun Corp 592(1); Statut 161(1); Zoning 72, 305, 306.

Fort Worth, City of; Lott v., TexApp–Fort Worth, 840 SW2d 146.—App & E 931(1), 1008.1(8.1); Courts 100(1); Jury 33(5.15), 120, 121; Trial 114.

Fort Worth, City of; Lysaght v., TexCivApp–Fort Worth, 359 SW2d 128, writ refused.—Dedi 60; Em Dom 106; Mun Corp 691.1, 696, 757(1), 775.

Fort Worth, City of; Matthews v., TexCivApp–Fort Worth, 283 SW2d 957, writ dism.—Evid 66; Judgm 185.3(20); Mun Corp 978(6), 978(9).

Fort Worth, City of; Matthews v., TexCivApp–Fort Worth, 84 SW2d 803, writ refused.—Em Dom 153.

Fort Worth, City of; Members of Park Board of Fort Worth v., TexComApp, 128 SW2d 379, 133 Tex 228.—Mand 147.

Fort Worth, City of; Miller v., TexApp–Fort Worth, 893 SW2d 27, reh overr, and writ dism by agreement.—App & E 930(3); Autos 273, 279, 306(5); Mun Corp 723, 724.

Fort Worth, City of; Morrison v., Tex, 155 SW2d 908, 138 Tex 10.—Contracts 125, 138(1), 138(2), 140; Mun Corp 199; Offic 99.

Fort Worth, City of; Most Worshipful Prince Hall Grand Lodge, F. & A. M.of Tex. v., TexCivApp–Fort Worth, 435 SW2d 274, ref nre.—Char 1; Insurance 1001; Tax 2300, 2302, 2338, 2344.

Fort Worth, City of; Mount Olivet Cemetery Co. v., TexCivApp–Fort Worth, 275 SW2d 152, ref nre.—Mun Corp 407(1), 408(1), 434(1), 434(4), 519(1), 586.

Fort Worth, City of; National Foundation v., CA5 (Tex), 415 F2d 41, cert den 90 SCt 688, 396 US 1040, 24 LEd2d 684.—Char 41.5; Fed Cts 724; Mun Corp 111(4), 122.1(2), 621.

Fort Worth, City of; New Casino v., TexCivApp–Fort Worth, 198 SW2d 602, ref nre.—Costs 260(4); Equity 57; Frds St of 129(8); Interest 66; Land & Ten 43, 80(2), 161(1), 207(1).

Fort Worth, City of; Northwestern Distributors, Inc. v., TexCivApp–Fort Worth, 377 SW2d 783.—App & E 1010.1(3); Judgm 138(2), 145(4).

Fort Worth, City of; Pack v., Tex, 557 SW2d 771.—Release 38.

Fort Worth, City of; Pack v., TexCivApp–Fort Worth, 552 SW2d 895, ref nre 557 SW2d 771.—App & E 863, 1024.4; Equity 6; Judgm 181(2), 181(3), 185(2); Release 15, 21.

Fort Worth, City of; Parker v., TexCivApp–Fort Worth, 281 SW2d 721.—Mun Corp 63.15(3), 605, 622; Nuis 1, 59, 79, 80.

Fort Worth, City of; Persons v., TexApp–Fort Worth, 790 SW2d 865.—App & E 984(5); Costs 194.40; Inj 113, 114(2), 123; Mun Corp 721(1), 1040; Zoning 245, 302, 387, 764.

Fort Worth, City of; Peterson v., TexApp–Fort Worth, 966 SW2d 773, reh overr.—High 192; Judgm 183, 185(2); Mun Corp 768(1), 847, 854; Neglig 1032, 1086, 1706.

Fort Worth, City of; Railroad Commission v., TexCivApp–Austin, 576 SW2d 899, ref nre.—Admin Law 489.1; Const Law 4363, 4371; Gas 14.3(3), 14.4(8).

Fort Worth, City of; Ray v., TexCivApp–Fort Worth, 284 SW2d 930, dism.—Abate & R 81; App & E 532; J P 141(4), 183(0.5), 183(1); Plead 34(1).

Fort Worth, City of; Riggs v., NDTex, 229 FSupp2d 572.—Civil R 1126, 1135, 1376(1), 1376(2), 1376(10); Const Law 1885, 1955, 3040, 3041, 3272, 3390, 3593, 3595; Fed Civ Proc 2470.1, 2544; Mun Corp 180(1), 180(2), 185(1); Offic 119.

Fort Worth, City of; Ritchie v., TexApp–Fort Worth, 730 SW2d 448, ref nre.—Costs 194.40; Decl Judgm 299.1, 300, 394.

Fort Worth, City of; Rogers v., TexApp–Fort Worth, 89 SW3d 265.—App & E 766, 842(2), 893(1), 931(1), 1008.1(2), 1013, 1122(2); Damag 49.10, 130.1; Evid 588; Mun Corp 183(3); Offic 66, 69.7; Statut 179; Trial 143, 382, 404(6).

Fort Worth, City of; Ronsley v., TexCivApp–Fort Worth, 140 SW2d 257, writ dism, correct.—App & E 930(3); Judgm 199(3); Mun Corp 857; Neglig 453, 1599, 1693, 1713; Trial 351.2(5).

Fort Worth, City of; Schleuter v., TexApp–Fort Worth, 947 SW2d 920, reh overr, and review den.—App & E

946, 959(3), 1010.1(1), 1050.1(1), 1050.1(8.1), 1051.1(1); Const Law 735, 1512, 1514, 1515, 2202, 2209, 2210, 2213, 2215, 2240(2), 3384, 3405; Mun Corp 594(2); Zoning 28, 70, 76, 772, 790.

Fort Worth, City of; Spinks Industries, Inc. v., TexCivApp–Fort Worth, 452 SW2d 799.—Mun Corp 33(9).

Fort Worth, City of; State ex rel. American Mfg. Co. of Tex. v., TexCivApp–Fort Worth, 339 SW2d 707, ref nre. —Judgm 715(1); Mun Corp 24, 33(2), 85.

Fort Worth, City of; State ex rel. American Mfg. Co. of Tex. v., TexCivApp–Fort Worth, 314 SW2d 335.—Const Law 2340; Mun Corp 29(4), 33(2), 63.1, 111(4); Quo W 32.

Fort Worth, City of; State ex rel. City of Everman v., TexCivApp–Fort Worth, 363 SW2d 500, ref nre.—Mun Corp 33(1), 33(2).

Fort Worth, City of; Stillwell v., TexComApp, 169 SW2d 486, 140 Tex 560.—App & E 917(1); Lim of Act 55(7).

Fort Worth, City of; Stillwell v., TexCivApp–Fort Worth, 162 SW2d 1046, aff 169 SW2d 486, 140 Tex 560. —Lim of Act 43, 55(1), 55(7).

Fort Worth, City of; Stoughton v., TexCivApp–Fort Worth, 277 SW2d 150.—Mun Corp 63.15(3), 605, 622; Nuis 1, 59, 79, 84.

Fort Worth, City of; Taylor v., TexCivApp–Fort Worth, 421 SW2d 183, rev 427 SW2d 316.—Evid 5(2); Judgm 185.3(1); Mun Corp 30.

Fort Worth, City of; Texas Turnpike Authority v., Tex, 554 SW2d 675.—App & E 843(2); Turnpikes 1, 40(2).

Fort Worth, City of; Texas Water Com'n v., TexApp–Austin, 875 SW2d 332, reh overr, and reh overr, and writ den.—Const Law 2672, 2698; Mun Corp 226, 712(8); Waters 203(3), 203(6).

Fort Worth, City of; U.S. Fleet Services v., NDTex, 141 FSupp2d 631.—Admin Law 412.1, 413; Autos 368, 395; Fed Cts 43, 56, 386, 390, 392, 433; Mun Corp 111(2), 592(1); Statut 176, 181(1), 183, 188, 190, 212.7, 214.

Fort Worth, City of; Vey v., TexCivApp–Fort Worth, 81 SW2d 228, writ dism.—App & E 966(1); Em Dom 9, 131, 171, 191(1), 196, 241, 255, 262(5).

Fort Worth, City of; Vianello v., TexCivApp–Fort Worth, 613 SW2d 543.—App & E 554(1), 846(5); Pretrial Proc 698, 699.

Fort Worth, City of; Vista Theatre Corp. v., NDTex, 322 FSupp 1147.—Courts 508(7).

Fort Worth, City of; Wedgworth v., TexCivApp–Fort Worth, 189 SW2d 40, writ dism.—App & E 917(1), 1078(1); Damag 56.20, 149; Judgm 570(4); Mun Corp 742(4), 967(2); Pretrial Proc 554; Tax 2761; Trover 2.

Fort Worth, City of; Werthmann v., TexApp–Fort Worth, 121 SW3d 803, reh overr.—Action 13; App & E 863, 893(1), 916(1); Mun Corp 29(4), 33(1), 33(9); Plead 104(1); Quo W 8.

Fort Worth, City of; Williams v., TexApp–Fort Worth, 782 SW2d 290, writ gr, and writ withdrawn, and writ den.—App & E 219(2); Const Law 1490, 2207, 2213, 2235, 3384, 3405; Evid 14; Int Liq 11; Obscen 2.5; Zoning 76, 763.

Fort Worth, City of; Willis v., Tex, 380 SW2d 814, ref nre.—Courts 247(5).

Fort Worth, City of; Willis v., TexCivApp–Fort Worth, 380 SW2d 814.—Const Law 1472, 1473, 4174; Decl Judgm 292; Mun Corp 124(3), 151; Offic 30.5; States 4.3.

Fort Worth, City of; Wright v., TexCivApp–Fort Worth, 497 SW2d 88, ref nre.—Mun Corp 216(1).

Fort Worth, City of, v. Zimlich, TexApp–Austin, 975 SW2d 399. See City of Fort Worth v. Zimlich.

Fort Worth Civil Service Commission; Ferris v., TexCivApp–Fort Worth, 269 SW2d 586.—App & E 387(2), 389(3), 396, 1125; Evid 43(1).

Fort Worth Club of Fort Worth, Tex.; U.S. v., CA5 (Tex), 348 F2d 891.—Int Rev 5117.

Fort Worth Club of Fort Worth, Tex.; U.S. v., CA5 (Tex), 345 F2d 52, adhered to on reh 348 F2d 891.—Int Rev 3055, 4058, 4068.

Fort Worth Club of Fort Worth, Tex. v. U.S., NDTex, 218 FSupp 431, rev 345 F2d 52, adhered to on reh 348 F2d 891.—Int Rev 4058, 4065.

Fort Worth Concrete Co. v. State, Tex, 400 SW2d 314.—Em Dom 158, 188, 246(2), 262(5).

Fort Worth Concrete Co. v. State, TexCivApp–Fort Worth, 416 SW2d 518, ref nre.—Em Dom 147, 155.

Fort Worth Concrete Co. v. State, TexCivApp–Fort Worth, 391 SW2d 818, writ gr, rev 400 SW2d 314.—App & E 1234(7); Em Dom 235; Evid 207(1); Fixt 14, 27(2).

Fort Worth Distributing Co., Inc.; Miller Brewing Co. v., CA5 (Tex), 781 F2d 494.—Alt Disp Res 182(1), 182(2), 210; Judgm 589(1).

Fort Worth Hilton v. Enserch Corp., TexApp–Fort Worth, 977 SW2d 746. See Fort Worth Hotel Ltd. Partnership v. Enserch Corp.

Fort Worth Hospitals Holding Corp.; Robinson v., TexCivApp–Fort Worth, 109 SW2d 1077, dism.—App & E 1052(2); Hus & W 217, 229.3, 229.6; Impl & C C 83.1; Judgm 199(2).

Fort Worth Hotel Co. v. Waggoman, TexCivApp–Fort Worth, 126 SW2d 578, writ dism, correct.—App & E 1060.1(8), 1067; Corp 498; Evid 106(1), 106(2); False Imp 15(3), 20(3), 25, 31; Trial 48, 54(2), 114, 119, 125(1), 255(4); Witn 318.

Fort Worth Hotel Ltd. Partnership v. Enserch Corp., TexApp–Fort Worth, 977 SW2d 746.—App & E 207, 230, 946, 1003(7), 1026, 1053(2); Costs 2; Damag 191, 208(5); Evid 146, 560; Gas 18, 20(2); Judgm 634, 713(1), 725(1); Negljg 273; Pretrial Proc 3, 42; Trial 109; Witn 405(1), 406.

Fort Worth Hotel Ltd. Partnership v. Lone Star Gas Co., TexApp–Fort Worth, 977 SW2d 746. See Fort Worth Hotel Ltd. Partnership v. Enserch Corp.

Fort Worth Independent School Dist.; Bynum v., NDTex, 41 FSupp2d 641.—Civil R 1153, 1157, 1162(1), 1528, 1536, 1544; Fed Civ Proc 2497.1.

Fort Worth Independent School Dist. v. City of Fort Worth, Tex, 22 SW3d 831, reh overr.—Const Law 948, 951, 953; Contracts 9(1), 25, 51, 52, 147(3), 164; Estop 52.10(2); Judgm 181(6), 181(32); Mun Corp 244(2), 254, 724, 868(1), 873, 1018; Tax 2127, 2128, 2160.

Fort Worth Independent School Dist.; Dooley v., NDTex, 686 FSupp 1194, aff 866 F2d 1418, cert den 109 SCt 3158, 490 US 1107, 104 LEd2d 1021.—Civil R 1135, 1137, 1138, 1243, 1251, 1305; Const Law 4198, 4202; Schools 147.2(2), 147.38.

Fort Worth Independent School Dist. v. Embrey Development Co., TexCivApp–Amarillo, 116 SW2d 873.—Em Dom 205.

Fort Worth Independent School Dist.; Henderson v., CA5 (Tex), 526 F2d 286, appeal after remand 574 F2d 1210, reh gr 579 F2d 376, on reh 584 F2d 115, cert den 99 SCt 1996, 441 US 906, 60 LEd2d 375.—Const Law 703, 977, 3062, 3644, 3648; Elections 18, 21; Fed Cts 13.20.

Fort Worth Independent School Dist. v. Hodge, TexCivApp–Fort Worth, 96 SW2d 1113.—Em Dom 170, 223; Evid 586(3).

Fort Worth Independent School Dist.; Moses v., TexApp–Fort Worth, 977 SW2d 851.—Schools 147.44; Statut 181(1), 212.7, 223.2(0.5).

Fort Worth Independent School Dist.; Murphy v., CA5 (Tex), 334 F3d 470.—Civil R 1482, 1492; Fed Cts 932.1, 936.

Fort Worth Independent School Dist.; Murphy v., NDTex, 258 FSupp2d 569, vac 334 F3d 470.—Const Law 4212(2); Inj 9, 78; Schools 154(1), 177.

Fort Worth Independent School Dist.; Passel v., Tex, 440 SW2d 61, appeal after remand 453 SW2d 888, ref nre, appeal dism, cert den 91 SCt 1667, 402 US 968, 29

LEd2d 133, reh den 91 SCt 2250, 403 US 941, 29 LEd2d 721.—Hab Corp 445; Inj 85(1), 94, 108, 110, 147.

Fort Worth Independent School Dist.; Passel v., TexCivApp–Fort Worth, 453 SW2d 888, ref nre, appeal dism, cert den 91 SCt 1667, 402 US 968, 29 LEd2d 133, reh den 91 SCt 2250, 403 US 941, 29 LEd2d 721.—App & E 994(3), 1010.1(1); Const Law 2980; Schools 169, 171, 172, 172.5.

Fort Worth Independent School Dist.; Passel v., TexCivApp–Fort Worth, 429 SW2d 917, writ gr, rev and remanded 440 SW2d 61, appeal after remand 453 SW2d 888, ref nre, appeal dism, cert den 91 SCt 1667, 402 US 968, 29 LEd2d 133, reh den 91 SCt 2250, 403 US 941, 29 LEd2d 721.—Const Law 990, 2508, 2546, 2970, 4208; Courts 89, 247(2), 472.1; Inj 85(1), 85(2), 108; Schools 10, 45, 46, 171, 172, 172.5; Statut 47.

Fort Worth Independent School Dist.; Service Employment Redevelopment v., TexApp–Fort Worth, 163 SW3d 142, reh overr, and reh overr.—Action 3, 13; Admin Law 229; App & E 753(1), 856(1), 913; Contracts 177; Courts 4, 39, 89; Mun Corp 254, 723, 742(4); Plead 104(1), 111.38; Schools 86(0.5), 114, 115; Statut 147, 223.5(7).

Fort Worth Independent School Dist.; Williams v., TexApp–Fort Worth, 816 SW2d 838, writ den.—Schools 159.5(6).

Fort Worth KJIM, Inc. v. Walke, TexCivApp–Fort Worth, 604 SW2d 362, ref nre.—Corp 181(8).

Fort Worth Lloyds; Biers v., TexCivApp–Galveston, 219 SW2d 493, ref nre.—App & E 1015(5); New Tr 145, 157; Trial 352.1(9); Work Comp 622, 1364, 1526, 1928.

Fort Worth Lloyds v. Essley, TexCivApp–Galveston, 235 SW2d 700, writ refused.—Work Comp 1105.

Fort Worth Lloyds v. Garza, TexCivApp–Corpus Christi, 527 SW2d 195, ref nre.—Action 6; Decl Judgm 65, 68, 385; Insurance 2278(19), 2355, 2914, 2915.

Fort Worth Lloyds v. Hale, TexCivApp–Amarillo, 405 SW2d 639, ref nre.—App & E 930(3), 998, 1050.1(5); Evid 271(18); Insurance 2201; Interest 39(1); Pretrial Proc 388, 407; Trial 219, 350.4(3), 352.9.

Fort Worth Lloyds v. Haygood, Tex, 246 SW2d 865, 151 Tex 149.—Work Comp 1072, 2191, 2247, 2251.

Fort Worth Lloyds v. Haygood, TexCivApp–Galveston, 238 SW2d 835, rev 246 SW2d 865, 151 Tex 149.—Work Comp 2213.

Fort Worth Lloyds; Humphreys v., TexCivApp–Amarillo, 617 SW2d 788.—Judgm 181(11).

Fort Worth Lloyds v. Johnson, TexCivApp–Amarillo, 129 SW2d 1157.—App & E 934(3); Insurance 3570(2); Judgm 17(9).

Fort Worth Lloyds v. Mills, TexCivApp–Galveston, 213 SW2d 565, ref nre.—Work Comp 49, 349, 1924.

Fort Worth Lloyds v. Purcell, TexCivApp–Eastland, 529 SW2d 644, ref nre.—Insurance 3571; Plead 236(3), 259; Trial 14.

Fort Worth Lloyds v. Roberts, TexCivApp–Fort Worth, 154 SW2d 882, writ refused.—Courts 91(1); Work Comp 244, 781, 1974.

Ft. Worth Lloyds Ins. Co. v. Lane, TexCivApp–Dallas, 189 SW2d 78.—Insurance 2686.

Fort Worth Lloyds Ins. Co. v. Willham, TexCivApp–Amarillo, 406 SW2d 76, ref nre.—App & E 989, 1177(7); Contracts 143.5; Insurance 1806, 1831, 1835(2), 2166(4), 2199, 2201, 2202.

Fort Worth Mortg. Corp. v. Abercrombie, TexApp–Houston (14 Dist), 835 SW2d 262.—Antitrust 221, 390; App & E 218.2(3.1); Insurance 1766; Lim of Act 95(1), 95(9), 199(1).

Fort Worth Motors, Inc.; Federal Sign Co. of Tex. v., TexCivApp–Fort Worth, 314 SW2d 878.—Contracts 211, 278(2), 346(2); Costs 241.

Fort Worth Nat. Bank; Almar-York Co. v., TexCivApp–Fort Worth, 374 SW2d 940, ref nre.—Corp 397, 409, 426(5), 426(7), 426(9), 426(10), 426(11); Princ & A 119(1).

Fort Worth Nat. Bank v. Ballanfonte, TexCivApp–Hous (14 Dist), 469 SW2d 9.—App & E 846(5), 1108; Banks 275; Venue 5.3(1), 5.5.

Fort Worth Nat. Bank; Calvert v., Tex, 356 SW2d 918, 163 Tex 405.—Statut 217.1, 223.2(1.1); Tax 3308, 3332(1).

Fort Worth Nat. Bank; Calvert v., TexCivApp–Austin, 348 SW2d 19, writ gr, aff 356 SW2d 918, 163 Tex 405.—Tax 3332(1); Wills 800.

Fort Worth Nat. Bank; Carroll v., TexCivApp–Fort Worth, 331 SW2d 356.—Mines 55(4).

Fort Worth Nat. Bank; Cogdell v., TexCivApp–Fort Worth, 537 SW2d 304, dism.—Plead 45, 111.46; Trusts 254, 257.

Fort Worth Nat. Bank; Cogdell v., TexCivApp–Eastland, 544 SW2d 825, ref nre, cert den 98 SCt 400, 434 US 923, 54 LEd2d 280.—Action 60; Judgm 185(1); Jury 7; Trusts 181(2), 282.

Fort Worth Nat. Bank; Cogdell v., TexCivApp–Eastland, 536 SW2d 257, writ dism woj, cert den 97 SCt 1114, 429 US 1096, 51 LEd2d 544.—Banks 275; Venue 5.3(2).

Fort Worth Nat. Bank; Cushing v., TexCivApp–Fort Worth, 284 SW2d 791, ref nre.—Char 37(5), 37(6); Decl Judgm 242, 253, 384, 390; Wills 683.

Fort Worth Nat. Bank; Donald v., TexCivApp–Fort Worth, 445 SW2d 598.—Bills & N 245; New Tr 108(1), 150(3); Trial 350.4(1).

Fort Worth Nat. Bank v. Harrell, TexCivApp–Fort Worth, 544 SW2d 697, ref nre.—Compromise 15(1); Evid 397(6); Trial 105(5).

Fort Worth Nat. Bank; Higginbotham v., TexCivApp–Fort Worth, 172 SW2d 402, writ refused.—App & E 758.1; Home 117, 118(3).

Fort Worth Nat. Bank; Hughes v., TexCivApp, 164 SW2d 231, writ refused.—Atty & C 11(2.1), 32(3), 166(1); Evid 208(1), 208(6), 265(8).

Fort Worth Nat. Bank; McCord v., TexCivApp–Fort Worth, 275 SW2d 717, ref nre.—Joint Adv 1.12; Lim of Act 46(7), 96(1), 195(5); Partners 5; Trusts 30.5(1).

Fort Worth Nat. Bank v. McLean, TexCivApp–Eastland, 245 SW2d 309, ref nre.—App & E 1008.1(14); Mines 78.1(2), 78.2, 78.7(1), 78.7(3.1), 78.7(4).

Fort Worth Nat. Bank; Menczer v., TexCivApp–Fort Worth, 149 SW2d 200.—Ex & Ad 443(1); Parties 76(5).

Fort Worth Nat. Bank; Pearson v., TexCivApp–Fort Worth, 564 SW2d 175, ref nre.—Covenants 1.

Fort Worth Nat. Bank; Ryan v., TexCivApp–Austin, 433 SW2d 2.—Mines 99(3).

Fort Worth Nat. Bank; Scott v., TexCivApp–Fort Worth, 170 SW2d 576.—App & E 931(3); Child C 551, 921(4); Child S 231, 242, 339(2); Courts 90(7).

Fort Worth Nat. Bank; Scott v., TexCivApp–Fort Worth, 125 SW2d 356, writ dism.—Child C 76, 550; Child S 11, 45, 47, 54, 77, 153, 173, 223, 224, 226, 232, 241, 449, 456, 458, 462; Divorce 168, 203, 249.1, 252.1, 252.2, 252.3(3); Hus & W 4, 278(2), 278(5); Judgm 518.

Fort Worth Nat. Bank v. State, TexCivApp–Austin, 158 SW2d 885, writ refused wom.—High 113(1), 113(4).

Fort Worth Nat. Bank; Stiff v., TexCivApp–Eastland, 486 SW2d 859, ref nre.—Wills 439, 470(1), 684.7, 827.

Fort Worth Nat. Bank v. Stiff, TexCivApp–Eastland, 482 SW2d 337, dism, cert den Fort Worth National Bank v. Cogdell, 93 SCt 1375, 410 US 932, 35 LEd2d 594.—Venue 17.

Fort Worth Nat. Bank; Tallal v., TexCivApp–Fort Worth, 383 SW2d 641.—Bills & N 96, 459; Judgm 185(6), 185.3(16).

Fort Worth Nat. Bank v. U.S., NDTex, 396 FSupp 337, aff 552 F2d 158.—Int Rev 3300, 4172(5); Trusts 171; Wills 440, 470(1), 488, 684.10(2).

Fort Worth Nat. Bank v. U.S., NDTex, 137 FSupp 71.—Int Rev 4020.

Fort Worth Nat. Bank of Fort Worth v. Jones, TexCiv-App–Fort Worth, 403 SW2d 861, ref nre.—App & E 1170.6; Trial 115(4), 131(1), 260(7), 352.7.

Fort Worth Nat. Co.; Schilder v., TexCivApp–Fort Worth, 81 SW2d 247, writ dism.—Bonds 84, 87; Fraud 11(1), 18; Sales 38(3).

Fort Worth Nat. Corp. v. Federal Sav. & Loan Ins. Corp., CA5 (Tex), 469 F2d 47.—Admin Law 661; Antitrust 764; Banks 283, 451, 523; B & L Assoc 44, 48; Courts 40; Fed Cts 541; Time 2; U S 125(3), 125(24).

Fort Worth Neuropsychiatric Hospital, Inc. v. Bee Jay Corp., Tex, 600 SW2d 763.—Evid 393(2), 452, 472(6); Land & Ten 53(1).

Fort Worth Neuropsychiatric Hospital, Inc. v. Bee Jay Corp., TexCivApp–Fort Worth, 587 SW2d 746, rev 600 SW2d 763.—Com Law 9; Contracts 353(2); Evid 419(2); Frds St of 44(1), 119(1), 119(2), 128; Impl & C C 75; Land & Ten 24(3); Trial 352.10; Ven & Pur 196.

Fort Worth Neuropsychiatric Hospital, Inc.; Bee Jay Corp. v., TexCivApp–Fort Worth, 557 SW2d 161, appeal after remand 587 SW2d 746, rev 600 SW2d 763.—Judgm 181(29), 190.

Fort Worth Osteopathic Hosp., Inc. v. Reese, Tex, 148 SW3d 94, reh den.—Const Law 3753; Death 9; Judgm 181(2), 181(33), 185(2), 185(5); Parent & C 7(1).

Fort Worth Osteopathic Hosp., Inc.; Reese v., TexApp–Fort Worth, 87 SW3d 203, review gr (1 pet), and review dism (1 pet), aff in part, rev in part 148 SW3d 94, reh den.—Const Law 3753; Death 9; Health 684, 750.

Fort Worth Pipe & Supply Co.; Ka-Hugh Enterprises, Inc. v., TexCivApp–Fort Worth, 524 SW2d 418, ref nre.—App & E 499(1), 671(4), 959(3), 1078(5), 1170.7; Plead 236(3); Trial 105(3), 350.4(2), 352.4(1), 352.4(4); Witn 276, 323, 324, 345(1), 345(2).

Fort Worth Pipe & Supply Co.; Richardson v., TexCiv-App–Fort Worth, 511 SW2d 542.—Garn 108; Mtg 563.

Fort Worth Pipe & Supply Co. of Abilene; Cunningham v., TexCivApp–Fort Worth, 384 SW2d 229.—App & E 907(3).

Fort Worth Planning Com'n, City of; Minton v., TexApp–Fort Worth, 786 SW2d 563.—Const Law 2442; Zoning 27, 136.

Fort Worth Police Dept.; Parker v., CA5 (Tex), 980 F2d 1023.—Civil R 1311; Fed Civ Proc 1838, 2734; Fed Cts 830; Hab Corp 252; Judgm 720.

Fort Worth Poultry & Egg Co.; Rogers v., TexCivApp–Fort Worth, 185 SW2d 165.—App & E 931(1), 989, 1024.3; Crops 1; Fixt 4; Plead 111.16, 111.36, 111.38, 111.42(4), 111.42(8), 111.44, 111.46; Propty 4; Venue 21, 22(4), 22(6), 41.

Fort Worth Poultry & Egg Co.; Taylor v., TexCivApp–Fort Worth, 112 SW2d 292, writ dism.—App & E 1024.3; Neglig 1076; Plead 111.18; Venue 22(8).

Fort Worth Press; Van Zandt v., Tex, 359 SW2d 893.—Costs 194.32, 194.38; Damag 71.5.

Fort Worth Press; Van Zandt v., TexCivApp–Fort Worth, 353 SW2d 95, writ gr, aff as reformed 359 SW2d 893.—Brok 43(0.5); Costs 194.32.

Fort Worth Press Co. v. Davis, TexCivApp–Fort Worth, 96 SW2d 416.—Libel 48(3).

Fort Worth Primitive Baptist Church v. Fisher, TexCivApp–Fort Worth, 237 SW2d 377, ref nre.—Relig Soc 23(3), 25.

Fort Worth Radiator Mfg. Co.; City of Fort Worth v., TexCivApp–Fort Worth, 278 SW2d 184, ref nre.—Lim of Act 118(2), 199(1); Mun Corp 971(4), 972(3), 978(9); Tax 2611.

Fort Worth Sand & Gravel Co.; Irons v., TexCivApp–Fort Worth, 284 SW2d 215, ref nre.—Mines 51(3); Partit 10, 16, 77(1), 77(4).

Fort Worth Sand & Gravel Co.; Irons v., TexCivApp–Fort Worth, 260 SW2d 629, ref nre.—Ex & Ad 138(1), 138(2), 150; Mines 56; Wills 439, 442, 450, 590, 689.

Fort Worth Sand & Gravel Co. v. Peters, TexCivApp–Fort Worth, 103 SW2d 407, writ dism.—App & E 1046.3; Contracts 8; Mines 70(3), 70(6); Trial 215, 219.

Fort Worth Star–Telegram v. Doe, Tex, 915 SW2d 471. See Star-Telegram, Inc. v. Doe.

Fort Worth Star Telegram; Doe v., TexApp–Fort Worth, 864 SW2d 790. SeeDoe v. Star Telegram, Inc.

Fort Worth Star Telegram; Evans v., TexCivApp–Fort Worth, 548 SW2d 819.—Evid 590; Judgm 185(2), 185.3(21); Labor & Emp 23.

Fort Worth Star-Telegram v. Street, TexApp–Fort Worth, 61 SW3d 704, reh overr, and review den.—App & E 66, 68, 856(1), 893(1), 934(1), 1175(1); Const Law 2161; Judgm 181(33), 183, 185(2), 185(5), 185(6), 185.3(21); Libel 1, 6(1), 48(2), 51(1), 51(5), 112(2), 123(2).

Fort Worth Star–Telegram v. Walker, Tex, 834 SW2d 54. See Star-Telegram, Inc. v. Walker.

Fort Worth State School v. Jones, TexApp–Fort Worth, 756 SW2d 445.—Judgm 199(3.5), 199(3.9), 199(3.10); Trial 139.1(14), 139.1(17); Work Comp 1535.

Fort Worth Steel & Machinery Co. v. Norsworthy, TexCivApp–Tyler, 570 SW2d 132, dism.—App & E 934(2); Assoc 20(1); Corp 503(2); Evid 54, 587, 595; Joint-St Co 19; Neglig 232, 1579, 1675; Plead 111.39(2), 111.42(1), 111.42(4), 111.42(6), 111.42(8); Prod Liab 1, 15; Venue 21.

Fort Worth Stockyards Co. v. Brown, TexCivApp–Fort Worth, 161 SW2d 549.—App & E 1175(5); Commerce 54.5; Const Law 4475; Dedi 20(2), 20(3); Inj 48, 123; Judgm 585(5), 600.1, 739; Licens 51, 58(1); Wareh 8.

Fort Worth Stockyards Co.; Howell v., CCA5 (Tex), 108 F2d 593.—Neglig 1288.

Fort Worth Tent & Awning Co.; Durham v., TexCivApp–Fort Worth, 271 SW2d 181, dism.—App & E 46, 47(2), 265(1), 393, 1122(2), 1177(8); Neglig 232, 1710, 1750; Trial 404(2).

Fort Worth, Tex.; Nelson v., CA5 (Tex), 101 FedAppx 956.—Civil R 1088(5); Fed Civ Proc 2734; Fed Cts 613.

Fort Worth, Texas, City of; Allison v., NDTex, 60 FSupp2d 589.—Civil R 1101, 1107, 1118, 1135, 1234, 1343, 1345, 1351(1), 1379, 1421, 1505(3), 1507, 1530, 1719, 1757; Const Law 1051.

Fort Worth, Tex., City of; Gilliam v., CA5 (Tex), 187 FedAppx 387.—Civil R 1088(5), 1348, 1445.

Fort Worth, Tex., City of; McCloud v., CA5 (Tex), 108 FedAppx 151.—Civil R 1088(4).

Fort Worth, Tex., City of; National Foundation v., NDTex, 307 FSupp 177, aff 415 F2d 41, cert den 90 SCt 688, 396 US 1040, 24 LEd2d 684.—Civil R 1395(1); Const Law 975, 994, 1066, 3521, 3526(5), 3875, 4277; Decl Judgm 272, 315; Fed Cts 172; Mun Corp 111(1), 111(4), 121, 122.1(2), 621, 703(1); Statut 64(1).

Fort Worth, Tex., City of; Simmons v., NDTex, 805 FSupp 419.—Labor & Emp 2251, 2255, 2264(1), 2264(2), 2292(2); Statut 219(8).

Fort Worth Transit Co.; American General Ins. Co. v., TexCivApp–Fort Worth, 201 SW2d 869.—App & E 1042(2); Autos 245(13), 245(60); Evid 219(3); Insurance 3515(1), 3523(4), 3526(10).

Fort Worth Transit Co.; Bradford v., TexCivApp–Fort Worth, 450 SW2d 919, ref nre.—App & E 989, 994(2), 996, 1002; Carr 283(3), 316(1), 318(1), 349; Death 21, 58(1), 75, 76, 104(1); Homic 766; Labor & Emp 3046(1), 3047; Trial 350.3(5).

Fort Worth Transit Co.; Eldridge v., TexCivApp–Fort Worth, 136 SW2d 955, writ dism, correct.—App & E 758.3(2); Autos 82, 83, 107(2); Carr 8; Evid 23(1); Mun Corp 619, 684.

Fort Worth Transit Co.; Le Master v., Tex, 160 SW2d 224, 138 Tex 512.—App & E 758.1, 934(1), 1175(5), 1202; Autos 244(12), 244(36.1), 245(81); Judgm 199(3.3); Neglig 1571; Trial 143.

Fort Worth Transit Co.; Le Master v., TexCivApp–Fort Worth, 142 SW2d 908, rev 160 SW2d 224, 138 Tex 512.

—Autos 205, 209, 226(2); Evid 586(3); Judgm 198, 199(3.9); Neglig 452, 1693, 1694, 1704, 1713.

Fort Worth Transit Co.; Renegar v., TexCivApp–Fort Worth, 143 SW2d 443.—App & E 837(4), 917(1); Evid 20(2); Labor & Emp 2878, 2955; Neglig 372, 387, 431; Plead 34(1), 192(6), 214(4), 218(1), 218(3).

Fort Worth Transit Co.; Sneed v., TexCivApp–Fort Worth, 427 SW2d 920.—App & E 927(7), 1001(1); Autos 204, 245(39), 245(53), 245(67.1), 245(80); Neglig 502(2), 503, 1656, 1676, 1693, 1717; Trial 142.

Fort Worth Transit Co.; Swanson v., TexCivApp–Fort Worth, 209 SW2d 772.—App & E 1032(1), 1048(6), 1068(4); Trial 68(1); Witn 267.

Fort Worth Transit Co.; Yanowski v., TexCivApp–Fort Worth, 204 SW2d 1001, ref nre.—App & E 1175(1); Autos 240(1), 244(50), 245(72); Judgm 199(3.17); Neglig 1539; Trial 359(1), 359(2), 365.1(7).

Fort Worth Well Machinery & Supply Co.; Callihan v., TexCivApp–Fort Worth, 88 SW2d 1057, writ dism.— Chat Mtg 170(2), 177(2), 177(3); Evid 474(19); Judgm 581; Lim of Act 127(17); Trover 32(6).

Forty-Eight Insulations, Inc.; Williams v., NDTex, 601 F'Supp 399. See Young v. Armstrong World Industries, Inc.

Forty Oaks Co. v. Westvale Corp., TexCivApp–Fort Worth, 324 SW2d 615, ref nre.—Contracts 176(2), 355; Damag 117; Inj 128(3.1).

Forty-Seven Thousand Two Hundred Dollars U.S. Currency ($47,200.00) v. State, TexApp–El Paso, 883 SW2d 302, reh den, and writ den.—App & E 758.3(9), 931(1), 931(3), 946, 989, 994(3), 1008.1(3), 1010.2, 1011.1(1), 1012.1(4), 1071.1(1); Controlled Subs 171, 184, 185; Forfeit 4, 5; Plead 1.

Forum Bank; Vandergriff Chevrolet Co., Inc. v., TexCivApp–Fort Worth, 613 SW2d 68.—Contracts 147(3), 324(1); Sales 86, 426; Trial 136(3).

Forum Ins. Co. v. Bristol-Myers Squibb Co., TexApp–Beaumont, 929 SW2d 114, reh overr, and writ den.— App & E 954(1); Courts 511; Inj 26(1), 33.

Forum Ins. Co.; Brown v., TexCivApp–Dallas, 507 SW2d 576.—App & E 499(1), 500(1); Work Comp 795.

Forward v. Housing Authority of City of Grapeland, TexApp–Tyler, 864 SW2d 167, reh den.—App & E 840(4); Pretrial Proc 41, 250, 714.

Forward Const. Corp.; Alamo Sav. Ass'n of Texas v., TexApp–Corpus Christi, 746 SW2d 897, writ dism woj. —App & E 863; Banks 191.15, 191.30; Fraud 3; Inj 138.9.

Forwood v. City of Taylor, Tex, 214 SW2d 282, 147 Tex 161.—Admin Law 102; Mun Corp 22, 65, 79, 791(1), 971(1); Statut 223.4.

Forwood v. City of Taylor, TexCivApp–Austin, 209 SW2d 434.—Admin Law 321; Mun Corp 971(1); Offic 104.

Forwood v. City of Taylor, TexCivApp–Austin, 208 SW2d 670, reh den 209 SW2d 434, aff 214 SW2d 282, 147 Tex 161.—Admin Law 132, 321; Mun Corp 79, 957(4), 958, 971(1); Offic 42, 43.

Fory; Humble Place Joint Venture v., CA5 (Tex), 936 F2d 814. See Humble Place Joint Venture, In re.

Fosha v. Barnhart, SDTex, 372 FSupp2d 948.—Social S 140.45, 140.55, 142.5, 143.45, 143.60, 148.15.

Foshee v. Republic Nat. Bank of Dallas, Tex, 617 SW2d 675.—Char 37(6); Judgm 181(15.1); Perp 4(15.1), 8(7).

Foshee v. Republic Nat. Bank of Dallas, TexCivApp–Tyler, 600 SW2d 358, rev 617 SW2d 675.—App & E 238(4), 293; Perp 4(1), 4(15.1), 8(1), 8(7); Statut 223.2(0.5), 223.2(1.1).

Foshee; Texas Co. v., TexCivApp–Texarkana, 142 SW2d 603, writ refused.—Evid 448.

Foskett, Ex parte, TexCrimApp, 390 SW2d 273.—Extrad 29, 32; Hab Corp 729.

Foss, Ex parte, TexCrimApp, 492 SW2d 552.—Extrad 32, 34, 39.

Foss; Walker v., TexApp–San Antonio, 930 SW2d 701.— Decl Judgm 300; Deeds 120, 123, 140, 143; Estates 5, 6; Mines 55(2), 55(4); Perp 4(4).

Fossati; Quitta v., TexApp–Corpus Christi, 808 SW2d 636, writ den.—Antitrust 147, 200; App & E 961; Contracts 238(2), 324(1); Evid 241(1), 267, 397(1), 445(1), 445(3); Land & Ten 172(1), 190(1), 231(8); Pretrial Proc 313; Witn 154, 183.5.

Fossati; Urban v., TexCivApp–San Antonio, 266 SW2d 397, ref nre.—Wills 439, 448, 449, 450, 470(1), 587(1).

Fossier v. Morgan, TexCivApp–Hous (1 Dist), 474 SW2d 801.—App & E 930(3); Fraud 11(1), 11(2); Trover 40(4).

Fossler; U.S. v., CA5 (Tex), 597 F2d 478.—Arrest 63.4(1), 63.4(15), 71.1(5); Autos 349(6); Crim Law 29(4), 394.4(12), 394.6(5), 865(1.5), 1174(1); Fed Civ Proc 56; Searches 63.

Fostepco Corp. v. Uniroyal, Inc., TexCivApp–Waco, 497 SW2d 314, ref nre.—Bills & N 453; Judgm 181(26).

Foster, Ex parte, Tex, 188 SW2d 382, 144 Tex 65.—Hab Corp 443.1; Inj 212, 223, 228.

Foster, Ex parte, TexCrimApp, 283 SW2d 761, 162 Tex-Crim 191.—Hab Corp 706, 723; Jury 29(6).

Foster, In re, NDTex, 121 BR 961, aff 945 F2d 400, cert den Foster v. North Texas Production Credit Ass'n, 112 SCt 972, 502 US 1074, 117 LEd2d 136.—Bankr 3673.

Foster, In re, BkrtcyEDTex, 360 BR 210.—Bankr 2766, 2802, 3710(7); Exemp 4, 37, 148.

Foster, In re, BkrtcySDTex, 9 BR 482, vac 670 F2d 478. —Bankr 3714.

Foster, In re Estate of, TexApp–Amarillo, 3 SW3d 49.— Ex & Ad 7, 20(7), 20(10); Wills 50, 222, 300, 324(1), 656.

Foster, Matter of, CA5 (Tex), 670 F2d 478.—Bankr 2281, 2324, 2395, 2531, 3011, 3152, 3703, 3705, 3714, 3718(1), 3718(5.1), 3784.

Foster v. Aircraft Inv. Corp., TexCivApp–Fort Worth, 215 SW2d 249.—App & E 846(5); Infants 94; Plead 111.8, 111.36; Venue 7.5(1), 7.5(4), 17.

Foster; American Nat. Ins. Co. v., TexComApp, 130 SW2d 287, 133 Tex 588.—Insurance 2037.

Foster; American Nat. Ins. Co. v., TexCivApp–Fort Worth, 108 SW2d 689, aff 130 SW2d 287, 133 Tex 588.— Insurance 2028.

Foster v. Atlantic Refining Co., CA5 (Tex), 329 F2d 485. —Contracts 309(1); Estop 92(2); Fed Civ Proc 2313; Lim of Act 50(1); Mines 59, 78.1(7), 78.1(11), 78.7(1), 78.7(5), 78.7(6), 79.1(1), 79.3, 81.

Foster; Bachus v., TexComApp, 122 SW2d 1058, 132 Tex 183, answer to certified question conformed to 125 SW2d 641.—Offic 138; Sheriffs 164.

Foster; Bachus v., TexCivApp–Eastland, 125 SW2d 641. —Sheriffs 164.

Foster v. Bailey, TexApp–Houston (1 Dist), 691 SW2d 801.—App & E 1048(1); Trial 45(1); Witn 275(1), 275(2.1).

Foster v. Bay, TexCivApp–Galveston, 255 SW2d 898, ref nre, appeal dism 74 SCt 241, 346 US 907, 98 LEd 405.— Const Law 3487; Courts 89, 91(1); Tax 3237.

Foster v. Beckman, TexCivApp–Amarillo, 85 SW2d 789, writ refused.—Autos 226(2), 247; Damag 174(1), 221(5.1); Evid 123(11); Neglig 409; Trial 219, 313.

Foster v. Beto, CA5 (Tex), 412 F2d 892.—Crim Law 641.7(2), 641.13(1), 641.13(2.1).

Foster; Big D Properties, Inc. v., TexApp–Fort Worth, 2 SW3d 21.—Inj 157.

Foster; Billy Baker Mobile Homes, Inc. v., TexCivApp–Austin, 390 SW2d 385.—Fraud 12, 50, 58(1), 59(3), 64(1).

Foster v. Boise-Cascade, Inc., CA5 (Tex), 577 F2d 335, reh den 581 F2d 267.—Fed Civ Proc 267.

Foster v. Boise-Cascade, Inc., SDTex, 420 FSupp 674, aff 577 F2d 335, reh den 581 F2d 267.—Civil R 1478, 1482, 1590, 1594, 1595, 1597; Compromise 56.1, 57, 59, 62, 71; Fed Civ Proc 1696, 2737.5, 2737.13.

FOSTER

See Guidelines for Arrangement at the beginning of this Volume

Foster v. Buchele, TexCivApp–Fort Worth, 213 SW2d 738, ref nre.—App & E 655(3), 758.3(2), 773(2), 837(11), 901, 931(6), 1009(3), 1054(1), 1071.2; Costs 230, 256(4); Deeds 38(1), 38(3); Des & Dist 84; Evid 460(4), 460(9); Frds St of 158(3); Trial 379; Ven & Pur 220, 226(1), 228(1), 253; Witn 198(1), 199(2), 199(4).

Foster v. Bullard, TexCivApp–Austin, 554 SW2d 66, ref nre.—Ven & Pur 72.

Foster v. Bullard, TexCivApp–Austin, 496 SW2d 724, ref nre, appeal after remand 554 SW2d 66, ref nre.—Frds St of 110(1), 112, 118(1), 158(1); Judgm 181(1); Perp 6(1); Ref of Inst 26; Spec Perf 19, 94, 121(11); Ven & Pur 18(4), 61, 70, 214(1).

Foster v. Butler Bros., TexCivApp–Dallas, 153 SW2d 623.—Evid 424; Replev 28.

Foster v. Capshaw, CA5 (Tex), 72 FedAppx 192.—Judges 45; RICO 29.

Foster v. Carle, TexCivApp–San Antonio, 160 SW2d 999, writ refused wom.—App & E 927(7), 1135; Labor & Emp 2764, 2797, 2845, 2883, 2925, 2926, 2983; Work Comp 2110.

Foster v. Centrex Capital Corp., TexApp–Austin, 80 SW3d 140, reh overr, and review den.—App & E 837(1), 893(1); Cons Cred 12; Contracts 326; Trial 388(2).

Foster v. Christensen, TexCivApp–San Antonio, 42 SW2d 460, writ gr, rev 67 SW2d 246.—App & E 760(2); Bankr 188(2); Estop 94(2); Evid 66; Hus & W 262(1), 265 1/2; Judgm 518.

Foster; City of Austin v., TexCivApp–Austin, 623 SW2d 672, ref nre.—App & E 907(3), 930(3); Const Law 249(8), 3760, 4015; Damag 67, 141; Em Dom 148, 259; Equity 1; Interest 1, 39(2.6), 60, 65.

Foster v. City of Lake Jackson, CA5 (Tex), 28 F3d 425, reh den.—Civil R 1376(1), 1376(2), 1376(4), 1407; Const Law 328, 2311, 2314, 2317; Fed Cts 574, 579.

Foster v. City of Lake Jackson, Tex., SDTex, 813 FSupp 1262, rev 28 F3d 425, reh den.—Civil R 1056, 1376(1), 1376(4); Torts 122.

Foster v. City of Lubbock, TexCivApp–Amarillo, 412 SW2d 376, ref nre.—App & E 934(1); Judgm 185.3(1); Mun Corp 249.

Foster; Commercial Union Assur. Co. v., Tex, 379 SW2d 320.—App & E 996, 1010.1(3); Insurance 2251, 2997, 3013, 3015.

Foster v. Commercial Union Assur. Co., TexCivApp–Texarkana, 373 SW2d 395, writ gr, rev 379 SW2d 320.—Insurance 2255, 2997, 3015.

Foster; Consolidated Underwriters v., TexCivApp–Tyler, 383 SW2d 829, ref nre.—App & E 969, 978(2), 1046.1; New Tr 32; Trial 18, 56; Witn 372(1), 376; Work Comp 949, 1305, 1404, 1703, 1962, 1974.

Foster; Corder v., TexCivApp–Hous (1 Dist), 505 SW2d 645, ref nre.—App & E 1050.1(3.1); Evid 372(3), 586(1); Ex & Ad 72; Hus & W 268(1), 273(8.1), 275; Names 18; Propty 10; Tresp to T T 36, 38(1), 40(7), 41(1).

Foster; Cullins v., TexApp–Houston (14 Dist), 171 SW3d 521, review den, and reh of petition for review den.—Adv Poss 71(1), 110(2); App & E 193(5), 226(2), 870(2), 934(1), 984(5), 1024.1, 1175(1); Costs 194.25, 208, 264; Evid 571(7); Judgm 181(15.1), 183, 185(2), 185(5), 185(6), 199(3.5), 199(3.7), 199(3.10), 199(3.14); Lim of Act 96(2); Tresp 19(1), 19(8), 20(1); Tresp to T T 6, 6.2, 10, 12, 33, 50; Trial 365.1(1); Trover 16.

Foster v. Cumbie, TexCivApp–Dallas, 315 SW2d 151, ref nre.—Ack 52; App & E 1175(5); Deeds 194(2), 208(1), 211(4); Evid 268, 317(18); Trial 139.1(7).

Foster v. Cunningham, TexApp–Fort Worth, 825 SW2d 806, writ den.—App & E 1043(1); Pretrial Proc 42, 45, 181.

Foster v. Daon Corp., CA5 (Tex), 713 F2d 148.—Antitrust 286; Condo 4; Contracts 176(2); Fed Civ Proc 1700; Partners 200.

Foster v. DeLaRosa, CA5 (Tex), 103 FedAppx 532.—Fed Cts 915; Prisons 13(6).

Foster v. Denton Independent School Dist., TexApp–Fort Worth, 73 SW3d 454.—Em Dom 2(1.1), 285; Judgm 185.3(2); Neglig 202, 210, 213, 215, 250, 1010, 1018, 1692; Prod Liab 42; Schools 89.3, 89.7, 147.51; States 112.2(3), 191.4(1), 191.6(2), 191.9(3).

Foster; Duval County Ranch Co. v., TexCivApp–San Antonio, 318 SW2d 25, ref nre.—Adv Poss 57, 85(1); App & E 218.2(3.1); Bound 40(3), 46(1), 46(3), 48(8); Courts 89, 91(1); Estop 54, 55, 58; Evid 318(3); Judgm 678(1); Mines 55(7).

Foster v. Duval County Ranch Co., TexCivApp–San Antonio, 260 SW2d 103, ref nre.—Adv Poss 106(3); Bound 37(5), 46(1), 46(3), 48(8); Pub Lands 175(6), 176(2); Tresp to T T 6.1.

Foster; Elkins v., TexCivApp–Amarillo, 101 SW2d 294, writ dism.—Autos 6, 181(2); Trial 83(2).

Foster v. Estrada, TexApp–San Antonio, 974 SW2d 751, review den.—Judgm 181(27), 183, 185(2), 185.3(21); Schools 147.

Foster v. Faulkner, TexCivApp–Amarillo, 380 SW2d 198.—App & E 930(1), 989; Damag 208(1); Labor & Emp 256(9), 259.

Foster v. First Nat. Bank of Chicago, TexCivApp–Tyler, 604 SW2d 508.—App & E 173(2); Judgm 181(17), 185(1), 185.3(5).

Foster v. Ford Motor Co., CA5 (Tex), 621 F2d 715.—Evid 195; Fed Civ Proc 1431, 2173.1(1), 2174, 2182.1; Fed Cts 896.1, 911; Prod Liab 98.

Foster v. Ford Motor Co., CA5 (Tex), 616 F2d 1304.—Contrib 5(1), 5(6.1); Fed Civ Proc 2142.1, 2608.1; Indem 58, 72; Labor & Emp 2875, 2881; Prod Liab 11, 15, 23.1, 91.

Foster v. Foster, TexApp–Fort Worth, 641 SW2d 693.—Adop 5, 21.

Foster; Foster v., TexApp–Fort Worth, 641 SW2d 693.—Adop 5, 21.

Foster v. Foster, TexApp–Dallas, 884 SW2d 497, reh den.—App & E 842(1); Ex & Ad 314(3), 504(3); Powers 19, 36(1); Wills 692(1).

Foster; Foster v., TexApp–Dallas, 884 SW2d 497, reh den.—App & E 842(1); Ex & Ad 314(3), 504(3); Powers 19, 36(1); Wills 692(1).

Foster v. Foster, TexApp–Amarillo, 366 SW2d 680, writ dism.—Hus & W 272(5).

Foster; Foster v., TexApp–Amarillo, 366 SW2d 680, writ dism.—Hus & W 272(5).

Foster v. Foster, TexCivApp–Tyler, 583 SW2d 868.—App & E 843(1); Divorce 252.1, 253(2), 287.

Foster; Foster v., TexCivApp–Tyler, 583 SW2d 868.—App & E 843(1); Divorce 252.1, 253(2), 287.

Foster v. Gainesville Bus Lines, TexCivApp–Fort Worth, 187 SW2d 144, dism.—App & E 1054(1); Evid 123(12), 222(2), 265(2), 320, 474(19); Plead 111.36, 111.42; Venue 8.5(5), 8.5(6).

Foster; Gex v., TexCivApp–Amarillo, 495 SW2d 370, ref nre.—App & E 846(5), 854(1); Brok 39; Contracts 143.5; Evid 450(8); Interest 67; Trial 136(3).

Foster; Gregory v., TexApp–Texarkana, 35 SW3d 255.—App & E 66, 123, 782; Judgm 215; Motions 51.

Foster v. Gulf Oil Corp., TexCivApp–Beaumont, 335 SW2d 845, ref nre.—Des & Dist 8; Escheat 4; Plead 8(11); Pub Lands 175(7), 210, 213; Tax 2996, 3168.

Foster v. Hackworth, TexCivApp–Austin, 164 SW2d 796.—App & E 1010.1(12), 1040(16); Hus & W 25(1), 146, 249(6), 262.1(2), 268(1), 268(5), 270(8); Princ & A 136(1).

Foster; Harris v., TexCivApp–Austin, 261 SW2d 860.—Venue 7.5(5), 22(4), 22(6).

Foster; Hart v., TexCivApp–Fort Worth, 109 SW2d 504, writ dism.—App & E 662(2), 907(3), 1073(1); Judgm 216.

Foster v. Harvey, TexCivApp–Amarillo, 356 SW2d 829.—App & E 1170.6, 1170.7; Covenants 72.1; Evid 543(3).

FOSTER

Foster v. Harvill, TexCivApp–Waco, 353 SW2d 84.—Autos 181(1), 242(1), 245(5), 245(14), 245(24), 245(39), 245(40.1), 245(93); Neglig 273.

Foster v. Heard, TexApp–Houston (1 Dist), 757 SW2d 464.—Mand 32; Pretrial Proc 33, 373, 410.

Foster v. H. E. Butt Grocery Co., TexCivApp–San Antonio, 548 SW2d 769, ref nre.—Assault 13, 43(2), 67, 96(3); Plead 111.42(9); Venue 22(1).

Foster; Hill v., Tex, 186 SW2d 343, 143 Tex 482.—Ack 6(3), 29, 37(1), 43.1, 46, 61; App & E 1094(2); Ven & Pur 228(4), 231(15).

Foster; Hill v., TexCivApp–Amarillo, 181 SW2d 299, aff 186 SW2d 343, 143 Tex 482.—Ack 29, 37(2), 60; App & E 934(2), 1010.1(1); Deeds 25, 45, 193; Hus & W 194; Names 16(1), 16(2); Tresp to T T 6.1.

Foster v. Home Indem. Co., TexApp–Dallas, 757 SW2d 481.—Judgm 181(21).

Foster v. Howeth, TexApp–Beaumont, 112 SW3d 773.—App & E 223, 1079; Mal Pros 0.5, 24(4), 35(1).

Foster v. H. O. Wooten Grocer Co., TexCivApp–Eastland, 273 SW2d 461.—Courts 121(5); Plead 110.

Foster v. Hubbard Independent School Dist., TexCivApp–Waco, 619 SW2d 607, ref nre.—App & E 926(1); Judgm 185(5); Schools 103(1), 106.12(8).

Foster; Hudmon v., TexCivApp–Austin, 210 SW 262, writ gr, rev 231 SW 346.—App & E 1008.1(1).

Foster v. Jasper Production Credit Ass'n, TexCivApp–Tyler, 519 SW2d 711.—App & E 627.3.

Foster; Jim Walter Homes, Inc. v., TexCivApp–Eastland, 593 SW2d 749.—Antitrust 286, 368, 369, 398; App & E 1170.7; Trial 66; Witn 198(2).

Foster v. Kimbro, TexCivApp–Beaumont, 115 SW2d 1164.—Plead 111.1.

Foster v. Langston, TexCivApp–San Antonio, 170 SW2d 250.—App & E 1060.1(2.1); Trial 50; Work Comp 2191, 2204, 2234, 2251.

Foster v. Laredo Newspapers, Inc., Tex, 541 SW2d 809, cert den 97 SCt 1160, 429 US 1123, 51 LEd2d 573.—Libel 1, 6(1), 51(5), 123(8).

Foster v. Laredo Newspapers, Inc., TexCivApp–San Antonio, 530 SW2d 611, writ gr, rev 541 SW2d 809, cert den 97 SCt 1160, 429 US 1123, 51 LEd2d 573.—App & E 185(3); Judgm 185(2); Libel 49, 51(5).

Foster v. Lessing, TexCivApp–Waco, 346 SW2d 939, ref nre.—Frds St of 125(3); Plead 34(6); Spec Perf 117; Ven & Pur 79.

Foster; Lewis v., Tex, 621 SW2d 400.—Witn 125, 175(2), 178(1), 178(3), 178(4).

Foster v. Lewis, TexCivApp–El Paso, 607 SW2d 608, ref nre, and reh of writ of error gr, rev 621 SW2d 400.—Witn 175(1), 178(4), 181.

Foster v. Lincoln Fire Ins. Co. of New York, CCA5 (Tex), 80 F2d 336.—Insurance 1653(1), 1653(2).

Foster v. L. M. S. Development Co., TexCivApp–Dallas, 346 SW2d 387, ref nre.—Banks 90; Can of Inst 3; Contracts 211, 220; Deeds 145; Estop 119; Fraud 9; Judgm 114; Land & Ten 112(1), 157(1), 159(1); Parties 29; Tresp to T T 47(1).

Foster; Lone Star State Life Ins. Co. v., TexCivApp–Fort Worth, 250 SW2d 949, ref nre.—Evid 424; Release 25, 29(1), 29(4).

Foster; Lovejoy v., NDTex, 77 FSupp 414.—Rem of C 108.

Foster v. McClain, TexCivApp–Galveston, 197 SW2d 508.—App & E 209.1, 1015(5); Mtg 214; New Tr 102(1).

Foster; McCulley v., TexCivApp–Eastland, 123 SW2d 705.—App & E 773(4).

Foster; Malone v., Tex, 977 SW2d 562.—App & E 200; Health 820; Jury 97(1), 105(1), 133.

Foster; Malone v., TexApp–Dallas, 956 SW2d 573, writ gr, aff 977 SW2d 562.—App & E 200, 203, 230, 232(2), 242(4), 500(3), 548(5), 1045(3); Const Law 2474; Courts 91(1), 97(1); Evid 78, 121(1), 123(1), 125; Torts 304.

Foster; Metropolitan Cas. Ins. Co. v., TexApp–Houston (1 Dist), 226 SW3d 597.—Courts 202(4), 202(5).

Foster; Mitchell v., TexCivApp–Eastland, 492 SW2d 632, ref nre.—App & E 863; Judgm 181(2), 181(25); Mtg 369(3).

Foster; Montanez v., SDTex, 558 FSupp 71.—Fed Cts 92.

Foster; Mooney Aircraft Corp. v., CA5 (Tex), 730 F2d 367. See Mooney Aircraft, Inc., Matter of.

Foster; Murren v., TexApp–Amarillo, 674 SW2d 406.—App & E 169, 863; Judgm 181(15.1); Libel 139; Pub Lands 178(1); Quiet T 34(5), 35(1).

Foster v. Mutual Sav. Ass'n, TexCivApp–Fort Worth, 602 SW2d 98.—Frds St of 131(1), 144.

Foster v. National Bondholders Corp., TexCivApp–Fort Worth, 123 SW2d 506, dism.—App & E 704.2, 843(2), 931(1), 1173(1), 1173(2); Judgm 199(1); Plead 162, 166, 252(2), 269; Proc 6; Usury 76.

Foster v. North Am. Acc. Ins. Co., TexCivApp–Beaumont, 86 SW2d 476.—Insurance 1801, 1807, 1832(2), 2098, 2588(2).

Foster v. North Texas Production Credit Ass'n, NDTex, 121 BR 961. See Foster, In re.

Foster; Oliver v., SDTex, 524 FSupp 927.—Civil R 1318, 1381, 1395(3), 1465(1).

Foster v. Pace Packing Co., TexCivApp–Eastland, 296 SW2d 307.—Fraud Conv 47; Partners 141, 216(2); Princ & A 14(1), 133.

Foster v. Pace Packing Co., TexCivApp–Eastland, 269 SW2d 929.—Plead 111.42(5), 377; Venue 22(6).

Foster v. Patton, TexCivApp–Austin, 104 SW2d 944, writ dism.—App & E 995; Ease 8(2), 9(1), 32, 36(1), 36(3).

Foster; Poindexter v., TexApp–Beaumont, 772 SW2d 205, writ den.—Evid 481(2), 538, 571(3), 571(9); Health 821(5); Judgm 185(2), 185(6).

Foster v. Quarterman, CA5 (Tex), 466 F3d 359, cert den 127 SCt 2099, 167 LEd2d 817.—Courts 90(2), 100(1); Hab Corp 401, 450.1, 452, 462, 818, 842, 846; Homic 571; Sent & Pun 1482, 1495, 1669, 1678.

Foster v. Railroad Commission, TexCivApp–Austin, 326 SW2d 533, ref nre.—Mines 92.27, 92.28.

Foster v. Railroad Commission, TexCivApp–Austin, 215 SW2d 267.—Admin Law 305; Autos 63; Pub Ut 147; Statut 205, 219(3).

Foster v. Reed, TexApp–Beaumont, 623 SW2d 494.—App & E 151(5), 1056.2; Contracts 94(6), 100.

Foster; St. Paul Fire & Marine Ins. Co. v., TexCivApp–El Paso, 375 SW2d 355.—Trial 108.5.

Foster v. Security Bank & Trust Co., TexComApp, 288 SW 438.—Bills & N 338.5.

Foster; Security Bank & Trust Co. v., TexCivApp–El Paso, 249 SW 227, writ gr, rev 288 SW 438.—Bills & N 338.5.

Foster; Sellers v., TexApp–Fort Worth, 199 SW3d 385, reh overr.—App & E 105, 846(5), 931(1), 962, 989, 1010.1(1), 1010.2, 1024.5, 1043(1); Evid 71; Health 804, 809; Notice 15; Pretrial Proc 583, 676, 678, 680, 684, 697.

Foster v. Smith, TexCivApp–Waco, 424 SW2d 689.—Action 18; Child S 559; Judgm 111.

Foster v. Solvay Pharmaceuticals, Inc., CA5 (Tex), 160 FedAppx 385.—Civil R 1246, 1251, 1252.

Foster v. Spice, TexCivApp–San Antonio, 441 SW2d 212, ref nre.—Neglig 400.

Foster; Stanley v., CA5 (Tex), 464 F3d 565, on remand 2007 WL 1322371.—Civil R 1379; Const Law 4821; Fed Civ Proc 1824, 1997, 2734; Fed Cts 425, 596, 818; Lim of Act 118(2).

Foster v. State, TexCrimApp, 787 SW2d 385.—Crim Law 641.3(10).

Foster v. State, TexCrimApp, 779 SW2d 845, reh den, cert den 110 SCt 1505, 494 US 1039, 108 LEd2d 639.—Crim Law 132, 134(1), 135, 137, 145, 351(3), 369.1, 369.2(1), 369.2(4), 369.2(8), 404.65, 404.80, 419(2.10), 419(12); Homic 1015, 1020, 1021, 1184; Jury 108.

Foster v. State, TexCrimApp, 693 SW2d 412.—Crim Law 641.5(0.5), 641.5(2.1).

Foster v. State, TexCrimApp, 677 SW2d 507, on remand 687 SW2d 65, petition for discretionary review refused. —Crim Law 519(8).

Foster v. State, TexCrimApp, 639 SW2d 691.—Homic 908, 1135.

Foster v. State, TexCrimApp, 635 SW2d 710.—Controlled Subs 26, 30, 63, 80; Crim Law 1134(3).

Foster v. State, TexCrimApp, 603 SW2d 879.—Crim Law 1038.1(5); Larc 55; Sent & Pun 1254, 1367, 1373; Stip 18(7).

Foster v. State, TexCrimApp, 548 SW2d 731.—Larc 34.

Foster v. State, TexCrimApp, 497 SW2d 291.—Crim Law 596(1), 598(2), 1131(5), 1166(7).

Foster v. State, TexCrimApp, 493 SW2d 812.—Crim Law 438(5.1), 1037.2; Homic 530, 1371; Witn 64(1).

Foster v. State, TexCrimApp, 455 SW2d 243.—Crim Law 768(1), 1038.1(1), 1129(3); Sent & Pun 1212.

Foster v. State, TexCrimApp, 422 SW2d 447.—Crim Law 264; Jury 24.

Foster v. State, TexCrimApp, 400 SW2d 552.—Crim Law 517(7), 517.2(1), 1166.7; Homic 1134; Infants 68.1; Statut 47, 118(6).

Foster v. State, TexCrimApp, 386 SW2d 288.—Crim Law 736(2).

Foster v. State, TexCrimApp, 338 SW2d 458, 170 TexCrim 61.—Crim Law 507(5), 577, 1038.1(1), 1038.3, 1173.2(1); Larc 65.

Foster v. State, TexCrimApp, 282 SW2d 877, 162 TexCrim 124.—Autos 355(6), 357; Ind & Inf 132(1).

Foster v. State, TexCrimApp, 263 SW2d 772.—Crim Law 1090.1(1).

Foster v. State, TexCrimApp, 262 SW2d 408, 159 TexCrim 201.—Crim Law 778(5).

Foster v. State, TexCrimApp, 187 SW2d 575, 148 TexCrim 372.—Crim Law 641.10(3), 701, 704, 1163(2).

Foster v. State, TexCrimApp, 166 SW2d 927, 145 TexCrim 189.—Crim Law 1091(4).

Foster v. State, TexCrimApp, 155 SW2d 938, 142 TexCrim 615.—Crim Law 311, 553, 698(1), 741(1), 742(1), 1169.2(1); Homic 954, 1193; Witn 75, 78, 79(1).

Foster v. State, TexApp–Houston (1 Dist), 101 SW3d 490, reh overr.—Arrest 63.5(8); Controlled Subs 122, 137; Crim Law 394.6(4), 394.6(5), 404.20, 404.30, 404.60, 412(4), 412.1(1), 519(1), 777, 1129(4), 1130(5), 1139, 1144.12, 1153(1), 1158(4); Searches 42.1, 44, 64, 65, 171.

Foster v. State, TexApp–Houston (1 Dist), 80 SW3d 639. —Crim Law 708.1, 1037.1(1), 1042; Sent & Pun 2194.

Foster v. State, TexApp–Houston (1 Dist), 713 SW2d 789, petition for discretionary review gr, aff 787 SW2d 385. —Crim Law 637, 641.1, 641.3(10), 641.4(1).

Foster v. State, TexApp–Houston (1 Dist), 661 SW2d 205, petition for discretionary review refused.—Crim Law 303.15, 460, 1111(2), 1144.9; Ind & Inf 132(1), 132(2); Jury 29(6); Larc 23, 65.

Foster v. State, TexApp–Houston (1 Dist), 652 SW2d 474, petition for discretionary review gr, aff 693 SW2d 412. —Crim Law 622.1(2), 622.4, 641.5(4), 641.13(1), 641.13(2.1), 641.13(7), 1043(3), 1148, 1166.6, 1166.10(1).

Foster v. State, TexApp–Houston (1 Dist), 647 SW2d 27, petition for discretionary review refused.—Crim Law 641.13(6), 1035(7), 1092.4; Witn 37(4).

Foster v. State, TexApp–Fort Worth, 180 SW3d 248, petition stricken, and petition for discretionary review refused.—Assault 91.10(1); Crim Law 662.7, 1147, 1153(1).

Foster v. State, TexApp–Fort Worth, 874 SW2d 286, petition for discretionary review refused.—Controlled Subs 29, 74; Crim Law 1043(3), 1129(4), 1134(3), 1159.2(1), 1159.2(7); Searches 164.

Foster v. State, TexApp–Dallas, 767 SW2d 909, petition for discretionary review refused.—Arrest 68(9); Crim Law 394.5(4), 394.6(5), 777, 814(3), 824(5), 1224(1), 1224(2); Searches 23, 26, 49, 192.1.

Foster v. State, TexApp–Dallas, 687 SW2d 65, petition for discretionary review refused.—Crim Law 1159.4(2), 1163(3), 1165(1), 1169.12.

Foster v. State, TexApp–Dallas, 648 SW2d 31, petition for discretionary review gr, cause remanded 677 SW2d 507, on remand 687 SW2d 65, petition for discretionary review refused.—Crim Law 414, 517(7), 519(8); Larc 55.

Foster v. State, TexApp–Beaumont, 817 SW2d 390.— Crim Law 412.1(4), 641.4(1), 641.10(2), 713, 719(1), 730(1), 1167(5), 1171.1(3).

Foster v. State, TexApp–Beaumont, 814 SW2d 874, petition for discretionary review refused.—Autos 349(4), 349(17), 349.5(3); Controlled Subs 26, 27, 79; Crim Law 552(3), 783.5; Searches 171, 180, 181, 186.

Foster v. State, TexApp–Beaumont, 727 SW2d 45, petition for discretionary review refused.—Crim Law 304(16).

Foster v. State, TexApp–Waco, 25 SW3d 792, petition for discretionary review refused.—Crim Law 59(5), 80, 660, 662.7, 720(2), 720(6), 720(9), 723(3), 726, 730(1), 730(8), 730(16), 770(1), 1144.13(2.1), 1144.13(6), 1159.2(2), 1159.2(7), 1159.6, 1169.4, 1171.1(2.1); Homic 1164, 1165, 1465; Witn 345(1), 345(9).

Foster v. State, TexApp–Waco, 8 SW3d 445.—Crim Law 641.7(1), 1035(7), 1063(5).

Foster v. State, TexApp–Eastland, 633 SW2d 326.—Const Law 3227, 3809; Fines 11.

Foster v. State, TexApp–Tyler, 976 SW2d 732, petition for discretionary review refused.—Crim Law 772(4), 1038.1(1), 1173.2(2), 1174(2).

Foster v. State, TexApp–Houston (14 Dist), 909 SW2d 86, petition for discretionary review refused.—Crim Law 338(1), 338(7), 469, 469.1, 469.2, 474.5, 478(1), 494, 661, 1147, 1153(1).

Foster v. State, TexApp–Houston (14 Dist), 834 SW2d 494.—Ind & Inf 171, 191(0.5), 191(2).

Foster v. Swift & Co., CA5 (Tex), 615 F2d 701.—Fed Civ Proc 2497.1.

Foster; Texas & N. O. R. Co. v., TexCivApp–Beaumont, 266 SW2d 206, ref nre.—App & E 230, 843(2), 991, 1003(10); Damag 132(3); Evid 571(1), 586(3), 590; New Tr 32; R R 338.5, 348(4), 348(6.1), 350(7.1); Trial 133.6(3.1), 350.7(9).

Foster v. Texas & P. Ry. Co., TexCivApp–Austin, 194 SW2d 618, writ refused.—Judgm 675(1).

Foster v. Texas Dept. of Public Safety, TexCivApp–San Antonio, 443 SW2d 66.—App & E 966(1); Autos 144.2(10); Evid 318(7); Judgm 185.3(1), 186; Pretrial Proc 713.

Foster v. Texas Dept. of Public Safety, TexCivApp–Amarillo, 398 SW2d 836.—Autos 144.2(5.1), 144.2(9.1); Judgm 180, 183, 185.3(1).

Foster; Thompson v., TexCivApp–Austin, 105 SW2d 343. —App & E 917(1); Autos 84, 105.

Foster v. Truck Ins. Exchange, TexApp–Dallas, 933 SW2d 207, reh overr, and writ den.—Insurance 2772, 2774, 2780, 2786, 2787; Work Comp 2251.

Foster; Twin City Fire Ins. Co. v., TexCivApp–Texarkana, 537 SW2d 760, ref nre.—Judgm 956(1); Work Comp 1789, 1805, 1874, 1939.1, 1939.2.

Foster; U.S. v., CA5 (Tex), 229 F3d 1196, cert den 121 SCt 1202, 531 US 1197, 149 LEd2d 116.—Crim Law 1165(1); Int Rev 5263.30.

Foster; U.S. v., CA5 (Tex), 929 F2d 173. See Turnbull v. U.S.

Foster; U.S. v., CA5 (Tex), 506 F2d 444, cert den 95 SCt 1683, 421 US 950, 44 LEd2d 104.—Searches 165.

Foster v. U.S., SDTex, 85 FSupp 447.—Int Rev 3496; Trial 368.

Foster v. Upchurch, Tex, 624 SW2d 564.—Libel 51(5); Plead 111.9, 111.24.

Foster v. Upchurch, TexCivApp–El Paso, 613 SW2d 22, ref nre, rev 624 SW2d 564.—Libel 112(2); Plead 111.24.

FOUNDERS

Foster; Vise v., TexCivApp–Waco, 247 SW2d 274, ref nre.—Action 70; App & E 237(4), 1040(11); Contracts 25, 32, 313(1); Damag 117; Evid 272, 323(1); Pretrial Proc 678; Sales 52(5.1), 174, 417, 418(3).

Foster; Voss v., TexCivApp–Eastland, 466 SW2d 325.—App & E 430(1).

Foster; Wagner v., Tex, 341 SW2d 887, 161 Tex 333, on remand 343 SW2d 914, ref nre.—App & E 238(2), 241, 281(1), 296, 302(1), 302(4), 302(5).

Foster v. Wagner, TexCivApp–El Paso, 343 SW2d 914, ref nre.—App & E 215(1), 237(5), 238(2), 253, 281(1); Brok 7, 11, 43(2); Contracts 1, 25; Covenants 8, 70.

Foster v. Wagner, TexCivApp–El Paso, 337 SW2d 485, rev 341 SW2d 887, 161 Tex 333, on remand 343 SW2d 914, ref nre.—App & E 837(11), 882(10); Atty & C 104; Brok 7, 43(3); Consp 19; Evid 54, 384, 416, 593.

Foster v. Williams, TexApp–Texarkana, 74 SW3d 200, reh overr, and review den.—App & E 428(2), 430(1); Atty & C 62.

Foster v. Woodward, TexCivApp–Beaumont, 134 SW2d 417, writ refused.—Autos 225, 244(36.1), 245(65); Damag 221(2.1), 221(5.1); Evid 591; Trial 352.7, 352.10.

Foster v. Zavala, TexApp–Eastland, 214 SW3d 106.—App & E 962; Health 804, 809.

Foster Bros. Mfg. Co. v. Style-Rite Mfg. Co., TexCivApp–Waco, 594 SW2d 555, ref nre.—Acct Action on 14; App & E 1178(6); Evid 318(1); Judgm 126(4), 185.3(3).

Foster Cathead Co.; Bullock v., TexApp–Corpus Christi, 631 SW2d 208.—Costs 207; Garn 105, 191; Plgs 1, 7, 11, 21, 23; Trial 39.

Foster Cathead Co. v. Hasha, CA5 (Tex), 382 F2d 761, cert den 88 SCt 819, 390 US 906, 19 LEd2d 872.—Pat 26(1.1), 118.21, 243(1), 324.5.

Foster Co. v. Glacier Energy, Inc., TexApp–San Antonio, 714 SW2d 48. See L.B. Foster Co. v. Glacier Energy, Inc.

Foster Engineering Co.; Acme Engineers, Inc. v., CA5 (Tex), 254 F2d 259.—Appear 2; Corp 668(4), 668(5).

Foster Financial Corp.; Briercroft Savings & Loan Ass'n v., TexCivApp–Eastland, 533 SW2d 898, ref nre.—App & E 624; Contracts 186(1), 187(1); Estop 85.

Foster, Henry, Henry & Thorpe, Inc. v. J.T. Const. Co., Inc., TexApp–El Paso, 808 SW2d 139, writ den.—App & E 927(7); Contracts 187(1); Indem 27, 30(5), 33(5).

Foster Iron Works, Inc., In re, SDTex, 3 BR 715.—Bankr 3171, 3202.1, 3784; Judges 40, 49(1), 51(3); Statut 223.2(7).

Foster Lumber Co.; Musgrove v., TexCivApp–Beaumont, 89 SW2d 287, writ dism.—Adv Poss 58, 100(1), 113, 114(1).

Foster Lumber Co.; Tasher v., TexCivApp–Beaumont, 205 SW2d 665.—App & E 768, 1078(1); Hus & W 249(2.1), 255, 262.1(1), 262.1(2), 274(1); Tresp to T T 38(1), 39(4), 41(3), 44; Ven & Pur 242.

Foster Mold, Inc., In re, TexApp–El Paso, 979 SW2d 665, reh overr.—Alt Disp Res 199, 205; Mand 1, 4(4), 60.

Foster Mortg. Corp., Matter of, CA5 (Tex), 68 F3d 914, reh den.—Bankr 3033, 3782, 3784, 3786.

Foster Mortg. Corp. v. Chicago Title Ins. Co., TexApp–Fort Worth, 839 SW2d 161. See Jefmor, Inc. v. Chicago Title Ins. Co.

Foster Mortg. Corp.; McDonald v., TexApp–Houston (14 Dist), 834 SW2d 573, reh den, and writ den.—App & E 934(1); B & L Assoc 42(16); Contracts 168; Judgm 181(1), 181(6), 185(2); Mtg 211, 375, 379.

Foster's Estate; Covington v., TexCivApp–Waco, 584 SW2d 726, ref nre.—Damag 51.

Foster Wheeler Corp.; R. F. C. v., SDTex, 70 FSupp 420.—Lim of Act 11(4), 55(5).

Foster Wheeler Corp. v. Western Wood Products Co., TexCivApp–Waco, 324 SW2d 45, writ dism by agreement.—Consp 19; Contracts 322(3), 350(2); Damag 190; Evid 591; Princ & A 23(1); Trial 350.4(4).

Fotios; E.E.O.C. v., WDTex, 671 FSupp 454.—Civil R 1573.

Foto Fantasy, Inc.; KIS, S.A. v., NDTex, 240 FSupp2d 608.—Antitrust 30, 64, 732.

Foto Fantasy, Inc.; KIS, S.A. v., NDTex, 204 FSupp2d 968.—Antitrust 84.

Fotovich; U.S. v., CA5 (Tex), 885 F2d 241, cert den 110 SCt 754, 493 US 1034, 107 LEd2d 770.—Crim Law 768(1), 822(1), 1134(2).

Foty v. State, TexApp–Houston (14 Dist), 755 SW2d 195.—Crim Law 438(8), 1169.1(10); Ind & Inf 159(2); Infants 20.

Fouad & Sons v. Federal Deposit Ins. Corp., CA5 (Tex), 898 F2d 482. See Abdulla Fouad & Sons v. F.D.I.C.

Fouche; Home Ins. Co. v., TexCivApp–Texarkana, 149 SW2d 977.—Insurance 2719(2), 2732; Trial 352.5(4).

Fouche; Lone Star Gas Co. v., TexCivApp–Fort Worth, 190 SW2d 501, writ refused wom.—Autos 245(62), 245(67.1), 245(83).

Fouga v. State, TexCrimApp, 351 SW2d 240, 171 TexCrim 489.—Sent & Pun 1210; Statut 107(3), 118(6).

Fought v. Solce, TexApp–Houston (1 Dist), 821 SW2d 218, writ den, opinion dissenting to overruling of reh 837 SW2d 275.—Action 5; App & E 863, 934(1); Health 576, 611, 615, 657, 810.

Fouke v. Schenewerk, CA5 (Tex), 197 F2d 234.—Estop 98(1); Fed Cts 287, 306; Judgm 678(1), 684, 686, 687, 688, 691.

Fouke v. State, TexCrimApp, 529 SW2d 772, cert den 96 SCt 2174, 425 US 974, 48 LEd2d 798.—Crim Law 87, 92, 1026.10(6).

Foulds v. Corley, CA5 (Tex), 833 F2d 52.—Civil R 1092, 1395(7); Sent & Pun 1553.

Foulds, U.S. ex rel., v. Texas Tech University, NDTex, 980 FSupp 864. See U.S. ex rel. Foulds v. Texas Tech University.

Foulks v. China Spring Independent School Dist., TexCivApp–Waco, 452 SW2d 763, writ refused.—Inj 78; Schools 37(5).

Foulston Siefkin LLP v. Wells Fargo Bank of Texas N.A., CA5 (Tex), 465 F3d 211.—Fed Cts 776; Trusts 112, 227.

Foulston Siefkin LLP; Wells Fargo Bank Texas, N.A. v., NDTex, 348 FSupp2d 772, vac 465 F3d 211.—Action 17, 66; Damag 59; Fed Civ Proc 2557; Lim of Act 2(1), 46(6), 105(1); Statut 188; Subrog 1, 2; Trusts 268.

Foundation Engineering Co.; Madison & Pennings, Inc. v., TexCivApp–Houston, 390 SW2d 48.—Judgm 838, 887.

Foundation Oil Co.; Great Plains Oil & Gas Co. v., Tex, 153 SW2d 452, 137 Tex 324.—App & E 1175(1); Bound 3(6), 5, 30, 47(1), 48(7), 48(8), 55.

Foundation Oil Co. v. Great Plains Oil & Gas Co., TexCivApp–Texarkana, 141 SW2d 969, rev 153 SW2d 452, 137 Tex 324.—Bound 3(6).

Foundation Reserve Ins. Co. v. Cody, TexCivApp–Dallas, 458 SW2d 214.—Insurance 1087, 1091(10), 2817, 3369(2), 3523(4).

Foundation Reserve Ins. Co. v. Starnes, TexCivApp–Fort Worth, 479 SW2d 330.—App & E 1170.6, 1170.7; Evid 473, 474.5, 498.5, 512; Insurance 2731, 2732, 3365; Trial 21, 352.20.

Foundation Reserve Ins. Co. v. Wesson, TexCivApp–Dallas, 447 SW2d 436, writ refused.—App & E 931(1), 989, 1010.1(3); Insurance 1571, 1607, 1609, 1631, 2065; Princ & A 23(1), 24.

Founders Bank of Arizona v. Moore, BkrtcyNDTex, 118 BR 64. See Moore, In re.

Founders Commercial, Ltd. v. Trinity Universal Ins. Co., TexApp–Houston (1 Dist), 176 SW3d 484.—Contracts 143(1), 143(2), 169; Insurance 1808, 1813, 1814, 1832(2), 1835(2), 1863, 2295, 2911, 2914.

Founders Nat. Bank of Oklahoma City, Okl.; Logan v., TexCivApp–Austin, 443 SW2d 610.—Bills & N 440.

Fountain; Continental Cas. Co. v., TexCivApp–Dallas, 257 SW2d 338, writ refused.—Evid 54, 314(2), 383(4); Insurance 2590(1), 2607; Trial 121(1), 139.1(2).

Fountain v. Ferguson, Tex, 441 SW2d 506, cert den 90 SCt 433, 396 US 959, 24 LEd2d 424.—App & E 554(1), 933(4); New Tr 56, 157.

Fountain; Ferguson v., TexCivApp–Amarillo, 437 SW2d 323, writ gr, rev 441 SW2d 506, cert den 90 SCt 433, 396 US 959, 24 LEd2d 424.—App & E 842(1), 1069.1; Trial 304.

Fountain; Jones v., EDTex, 121 FSupp2d 571.—Civil R 1376(1), 1376(2), 1376(6), 1407; Lim of Act 55(1); Mal Pros 0.5.

Fountain v. Knebel, TexApp–Dallas, 45 SW3d 736.—App & E 966(1); Divorce 150.1(3).

Fountain v. Nelson, TexCivApp–Beaumont, 546 SW2d 102.—Exceptions Bill of27, 56(1); Hab Corp 798.

Fountain; Smith v., TexCivApp–Austin, 319 SW2d 31.— Marriage 50(1).

Fountain v. State, TexCrimApp, 342 SW2d 587.—Crim Law 1097(5).

Fountain v. State, TexApp–Beaumont, 79 SW3d 72.— Autos 355(6); Crim Law 273.4(1), 275, 412.2(2).

Fountain v. State, TexApp–Houston (14 Dist), 681 SW2d 858, petition for discretionary review refused.—Crim Law 369.2(1), 369.2(4), 772(1), 814(1), 822(6), 1120(2), 1159.6; Homic 1184, 1185, 1466; Witn 37(2).

Fountain v. Walker, TexCivApp–Eastland, 260 SW2d 717, ref nre.—Autos 193(1), 244(26); Judgm 199(3.9).

Fountain Gate Ministries, Inc. v. City of Plano, TexApp–Dallas, 654 SW2d 841, ref nre.—Const Law 1371, 1401, 2005; Zoning 26, 650, 681, 790.

Fountain Parkway, Ltd. v. Tarrant Appraisal Dist., TexApp–Fort Worth, 920 SW2d 799, reh overr, and writ den.—Action 35; Courts 4; Plead 104(1), 109; Tax 2694.

Four B Lines, Inc. v. Sam Lattner Distributing Co., TexApp–Austin, 695 SW2d 706. See Railroad Com'n of Texas v. Ennis Transp. Co., Inc.

Four Bros. Boat Works, Inc. v. S & SF, Inc., TexApp– Houston (1 Dist), 55 SW3d 12, review den, and reh of petition for review overr.—App & E 93, 173(1), 870(2); Land & Ten 80(3), 93.

Four Bros. Boat Works, Inc. v. Tesoro Petroleum Companies, Inc., TexApp–Houston (14 Dist), 217 SW3d 653, reh overr, and review den.—Antitrust 205, 484; App & E 93, 1097(1), 1175(1), 1195(1); Atty & C 63; Consp 1.1, 8; Contracts 205.15(1); Courts 92, 99(1), 102(1); Fraud 3, 7, 13(3), 17, 64(1); Judgm 181(5.1), 185.3(2), 185.3(14); Land & Ten 80(4), 130(1); Lim of Act 105(1), 105(2); Neglig 218, 234; Princ & A 48; Torts 212, 222, 243.

Four B's Inc. v. State, TexApp–Austin, 902 SW2d 683, reh overr, and writ den.—Action 18; Cons Cred 7.

Fournerat v. Beaumont Independent School Dist., EDTex, 6 FSupp2d 612.—Civil R 1448, 1471, 1473; Fed Civ Proc 928; Fed Cts 813.

Fournet; Continued Care, Inc. v., TexApp–Beaumont, 979 SW2d 419, reh overr, and review den.—Labor & Emp 3043, 3096(2); Neglig 377, 379, 380, 383, 387, 1675.

Fournet; Gulf Health Care Center v., TexApp–Beaumont, 979 SW2d 419. See Continued Care, Inc. v. Fournet.

Fournier v. C.I.R., WDTex, 468 FSupp2d 931.—Fed Cts 30; Int Rev 4855.

Fournier v. U.S., CA5 (Tex), 485 F2d 130.—Crim Law 1522; Sent & Pun 2305, 2307.

Fournier; U.S. v., CA5 (Tex), 483 F2d 68.—Crim Law 1180; Sent & Pun 2285.

Four Seasons Marine & Cycle, Inc., In re, BkrtcyEDTex, 263 BR 764.—Bankr 2126, 2127.1, 2187, 3022, 3082.1; Corp 310(1), 397.

Four Seasons Nursing Centers of San Antonio; Huizar v., TexCivApp–San Antonio, 562 SW2d 264, writ refused.—Action 27(1).

Four Star Property Services, In re, BkrtcyWDTex, 215 BR 505. See Hunt, In re.

Four Stars Food Mart, Inc. v. Texas Alcoholic Beverage Com'n, TexApp–Fort Worth, 923 SW2d 266.—Admin Law 480.1, 669.1, 749, 750, 790, 791; Int Liq 57.1, 58, 61(1), 68(3), 75(7), 102, 130.5.

Four States Grocery Co. v. Gray, TexCivApp–Fort Worth, 97 SW2d 355, writ dism.—App & E 1001(1); Evid 542; Sales 273(1), 273(3), 445(1).

Fourteenth Court of Appeals; Brady v., Tex, 795 SW2d 712.—Const Law 82(8), 990, 1465, 4231; Mand 74(3), 172.

Fourteenth Court of Appeals; Carter v., Tex, 789 SW2d 260.—Mand 3(4).

Fourteenth Court of Appeals; Deloitte & Touche, LLP v., Tex, 951 SW2d 394, reh overr.—App & E 84(1); Courts 247(1), 247(7), 247(8), 247(9); Elections 305(2); Mand 1, 4(1), 4(4), 28, 32, 141.

Fourteenth Court of Appeals; Fitch v., Tex, 834 SW2d 335.—Elections 158.

Fourteenth Court of Appeals; Hill v., Tex, 695 SW2d 554.—Elections 305(4).

Fourteenth Court of Appeals; Klein Independent School Dist. v., Tex, 720 SW2d 87.—Em Dom 258.

Fourteenth Court of Appeals; Lanford v., TexCrimApp, 847 SW2d 581, on remand State ex rel Holmes v. Lanford, 1993 WL 55907.—Courts 209(2); Judges 16(1), 51(1); Mand 3(1), 3(2.1), 4(4), 10, 53, 61; Statut 181(1), 188.

Fourteen (14) Handguns; U.S. v., SDTex, 524 FSupp 395. —Fed Civ Proc 2470.2, 2552; Forfeit 5, 9.

Fourtek, Inc.; Metallurgical Industries Inc. v., CA5 (Tex), 790 F2d 1195.—Alt of Inst 16; Antitrust 423, 433; Evid 441(9), 442(1); Fed Civ Proc 2743.1; Fed Cts 762, 798.

Fourtek, Inc.; Metallurgical Industries, Inc. v., CA5 (Tex), 771 F2d 915.—Fed Cts 665.1.

Fourth Court of Appeals; City of San Antonio v., Tex, 820 SW2d 762.—Admin Law 124; Mand 23(1), 172, 187.9(5); Mun Corp 89.

Fourth Court of Appeals; Cowan v., Tex, 722 SW2d 140. —App & E 830(1).

Fourth Court of Appeals; Flores v., Tex, 777 SW2d 38.— Admin Law 466; Pretrial Proc 33; Work Comp 1167, 1703.5.

Fourth Court of Appeals; Hooks v., Tex, 808 SW2d 56.— Courts 207.4(2); Em Dom 187, 246(2), 265(5); Mand 4(4), 43; Pretrial Proc 501.

Fourth Court of Appeals; Johnson v., Tex, 700 SW2d 916.—Mand 1, 28, 42, 172.

Fourth Court of Appeals; Montalvo v., Tex, 917 SW2d 1, motion withdrawn.—Mand 1, 3(1), 4(3), 32, 44.

Fourth Court of Appeals; Spears v., Tex, 797 SW2d 654. —Atty & C 19, 21.5(2), 21.20, 22.

Fourth Court of Appeals; Uptmore v., Tex, 878 SW2d 601.—App & E 620.1.

Fourth Nat. Bank v. Gainesville Nat. Bank in Gainesville, CCA5 (Tex), 80 F2d 490, cert den 56 SCt 598, 297 US 720, 80 LEd 1004.—Lim of Act 13, 46(10).

Four Thousand One Hundred Eighty-Two Dollars in United States Currency v. State, TexApp–Texarkana, 944 SW2d 24, reh overr.—App & E 931(1), 1010.2, 1012.1(3); Controlled Subs 184, 186; Forfeit 1, 4, 5.

Fourticq v. Fannin Bank, TexCivApp–Hous (14 Dist), 461 SW2d 251, ref nre.—Pretrial Proc 698.

Fourticq v. Fireman's Fund Ins. Co., TexApp–Dallas, 679 SW2d 562.—App & E 1178(6); Contracts 47, 82; Guar 1, 16(1), 16(2), 16(3); Indem 27; Stip 1, 14(1).

Four Wheel Center; Sibert v., TexApp–El Paso, 774 SW2d 812. See Sibert v. Enriquez.

Fouse v. Gulf, C. & S. F. Ry. Co., TexCivApp–Fort Worth, 193 SW2d 241.—Plead 104(2), 110, 111.47; Venue 21, 24, 74.

Fouse v. State, TexCrimApp, 394 SW2d 808.—Burg 41(1).

Foust v. Bibb, TexCivApp–Waco, 258 SW 921, writ gr, rev American Surety Co of New York v. Foust, 272 SW 445.—Abate & R 3, 17; App & E 916(1); Courts 169(1); High 113(5); Pub Contr 55, 62.

Foust v. City Ins. Co., WDTex, 704 FSupp 752.—Work Comp 5.

Foust v. Coyne, TexCivApp–Amarillo, 331 SW2d 386, ref nre.—Hus & W 47(3); Wills 88(1), 742.

Foust; Dungan v., TexCivApp–Fort Worth, 404 SW2d 685.—Ref of Inst 11, 13(1), 44.

Foust v. Ford, TexCivApp–Fort Worth, 209 SW2d 941.— Bail 64; Crim Law 1020; False Imp 22; Fines 11; Venue 8.5(5).

Foust v. Hanson, TexCivApp–Beaumont, 612 SW2d 251. —App & E 847(1); Damag 163(4); Equity 65(2); Spec Perf 28(1), 128(1), 129; Ven & Pur 129.

Foust v. Jones, TexCivApp–Eastland, 90 SW2d 665.— App & E 718, 719(1), 719(8), 724(1), 724(3); Judgm 114; Tresp to T T 35(1).

Foust v. Old American County Mut. Fire Ins. Co., TexApp–Fort Worth, 977 SW2d 783.—App & E 1175(1); Insurance 1779, 2652, 2655(2); Partners 67; Sales 202(4), 202(7).

Foust v. Ranger Ins. Co., TexApp–San Antonio, 975 SW2d 329, reh overr, and review den.—Decl Judgm 45, 65, 66, 142, 165; Insurance 2281(2).

Foust v. Walters ex rel. Walters, Estate of, TexApp–San Antonio, 21 SW3d 495, review den.—Agric 9.5; App & E 497(1), 671(1), 907(4), 930(1), 971(2), 1001(3); Damag 63, 112, 163(2), 188(1), 190; Evid 474(16), 508, 544, 555.2, 555.5, 555.9; Interest 49, 67; Labor & Emp 3125, 3159, 3162; Lim of Act 121(2), 125; Pretrial Proc 39, 224, 379; Prod Liab 43.5; States 18.65.

Fouts; Bass v., TexCivApp–Texarkana, 400 SW2d 15, ref nre.—Evid 597; Frds St of 20; Joint Adv 1.15.

Foux v. State, TexApp–Beaumont, 886 SW2d 561.—Crim Law 412.2(5), 414, 641.3(6).

Fowco Const. Co.; Lanphier Const. Co. v., TexCivApp– Corpus Christi, 523 SW2d 29, ref nre.—App & E 171(1), 768, 1015(1), 1170.10; Contracts 176(9); Damag 189; New Tr 143(2), 163(2); Prod Liab 81.1, 83; Sales 267, 273(1), 273(3), 441(2), 441(3), 442(1); Trial 352.12, 365.1(1), 366.

Fowkes; KTRK Television, Inc. v., TexApp–Houston (1 Dist), 981 SW2d 779, reh overr, and review den.—App & E 66, 70(8); Const Law 2314, 2317, 3057, 3078, 3450, 3466; Labor & Emp 905, 918(3); Libel 54; Statut 67, 68, 77(1), 85(4); Torts 424.

Fowle v. State, TexCrimApp, 243 SW2d 165.—Crim Law 1094(2.1).

Fowler, Ex parte, TexCrimApp, 683 SW2d 438.—Sent & Pun 145, 1352.

Fowler, Ex parte, TexCrimApp, 372 SW2d 344.—Hab Corp 296, 450.1, 713.

Fowler, In re, BkrtcyEDTex, 259 BR 856.—Bankr 2422.5(1), 2422.5(4.1), 2439(2), 2441.

Fowler; Allied Finance Co. v., TexCivApp–Austin, 358 SW2d 239.—Contracts 9(3); Plead 111.3; Venue 7.5(3), 8.5(2).

Fowler; Brown v., TexCivApp–Fort Worth, 316 SW2d 111, ref nre.—Antitrust 423; Inj 56; Pat 17(2), 182.

Fowler v. Brown, TexCivApp–Waco, 535 SW2d 46.—App & E 954(1); Covenants 49, 52, 103(3), 122; Inj 135, 138.37.

Fowler v. Carrollton Public Library, CA5 (Tex), 799 F2d 976, reh den 803 F2d 717.—Civil R 1123, 1434, 1438, 1462, 1463, 1551, 1555; Evid 351; Fed Civ Proc 2215; Mun Corp 218(1).

Fowler; City of Wichita Falls v., TexCivApp–Fort Worth, 555 SW2d 920.—Const Law 4172(3); Mun Corp 198(4).

Fowler; Dallas County Flood Control Dist. v., TexCiv-App–Waco, 280 SW2d 336, ref nre.—Admin Law 117; Offic 114; Plead 111.17, 111.42(7); Venue 8.5(6), 22(9).

Fowler; Edwards v., TexCivApp–Beaumont, 374 SW2d 302.—App & E 1062.2; Autos 201(1.1); Trial 349(1), 350.5(3), 350.6(3), 351.5(6), 351.5(7).

Fowler v. Fowler, TexCivApp–Austin, 187 SW2d 713.— Divorce 161.

Fowler; Fowler v., TexCivApp–Austin, 187 SW2d 713.— Divorce 161.

Fowler v. Fowler, TexCivApp–Amarillo, 209 SW2d 432.— Abate & R 82, 84; Divorce 98.

Fowler; Fowler v., TexCivApp–Amarillo, 209 SW2d 432. —Abate & R 82, 84; Divorce 98.

Fowler v. Fowler, TexCivApp–Eastland, 292 SW2d 800. —Abate & R 14; App & E 77(1); Child C 7, 564, 579, 602, 609; Courts 475(15).

Fowler; Fowler v., TexCivApp–Eastland, 292 SW2d 800. —Abate & R 14; App & E 77(1); Child C 7, 564, 579, 602, 609; Courts 475(15).

Fowler v. Garcia, TexApp–San Antonio, 687 SW2d 517.— App & E 758.3(9); Autos 244(35), 244(56); Neglig 371, 387, 1746; Trial 131(2), 133.6(4), 366.

Fowler; Guckian v., TexCivApp–Corpus Christi, 453 SW2d 323, writ dism.—App & E 699(4), 882(9), 1061.4; Autos 244(14); Damag 130.4; Judgm 199(1), 199(3.17); Trial 340(5).

Fowler; Hall v., TexCivApp–Dallas, 389 SW2d 730.—App & E 223, 934(1); Atty & C 124; Bills & N 92(4), 104; Judgm 185.3(16), 189.

Fowler v. Hooey, TexCrimApp, 573 SW2d 241.—Crim Law 1068.5, 1081(1); Hab Corp 814, 817.1; Mand 60; Prisons 13.3.

Fowler v. Hults, TexComApp, 161 SW2d 478, 138 Tex 636.—App & E 999(1); Sec Reg 245, 260; Trial 350.1.

Fowler; Hults v., TexCivApp–Fort Worth, 148 SW2d 249, rev 161 SW2d 478, 138 Tex 636.—Sec Reg 292.

Fowler; Jones v., Tex, 969 SW2d 429.—Parent & C 15; Statut 205, 206.

Fowler v. Jones, TexApp–Austin, 949 SW2d 442, reh overr, review gr, rev 969 SW2d 429.—Child C 919; Parent & C 15; Statut 212.5.

Fowler; Lewis v., TexCivApp–Austin, 128 SW2d 107.— Courts 169(4).

Fowler; Ludwick v., TexCivApp–Dallas, 193 SW2d 692, ref nre.—Wills 117, 118, 119, 120, 123(5), 289, 302(1), 303(4), 324(3).

Fowler v. Matthews, TexCivApp–Austin, 204 SW2d 80.— Adv Poss 13; Ease 8(4), 36(1); Estop 93(1); High 6(1), 7(1), 17, 68, 73.

Fowler v. Maytag Southwestern Co., TexCivApp–Austin, 82 SW2d 699, writ dism.—App & E 846(2), 931(1), 1054(1); Autos 244(29).

Fowler; Millers Cas. Ins. Co. of Tex. v., TexCivApp– Beaumont, 472 SW2d 863.—App & E 1050.1(12); Damag 208(3); Evid 545, 546; Trial 365.1(7).

Fowler; Missouri-Kansas-Texas R. Co. of Tex. v., Tex-CivApp–Austin, 290 SW2d 922, ref nre.—Action 60; Evid 17; R R 214, 223, 225.

Fowler v. One Seguin Art Center, TexCivApp–Hous (14 Dist), 617 SW2d 763, ref nre.—Bailm 11; Costs 194.30.

Fowler v. Pedlar, TexCivApp–Hous (1 Dist), 497 SW2d 399.—Damag 132(6.1); Judgm 199(3.2), 199(3.10), 199(3.17).

Fowler v. Pennsylvania Tire Co., CA5 (Tex), 326 F2d 526.—Bankr 2511, 2543; Contracts 147(2), 170(1); Courts 90(1); Evid 80(1); Fed Cts 406; Sales 8, 450, 465.

Fowler; Phillips v., TexCivApp–Fort Worth, 348 SW2d 224, writ dism woj.—App & E 933(5); New Tr 56, 140(3).

Fowler; Pure Oil Co. v., TexCivApp–Dallas, 302 SW2d 461, ref nre.—Action 60; App & E 501(1), 1039(4); Corp 130, 134; Judgm 18(2); Plead 264; Pretrial Proc 483.

Fowler v. Quinlan Independent School Dist., TexApp–Texarkana, 963 SW2d 941.—App & E 859, 865, 934(3); Proc 133, 141, 153.

Fowler; Ray v., TexCivApp–El Paso, 144 SW2d 665, writ dism, correct.—App & E 77(2), 1048(6); Ex & Ad 73, 473(4), 473(6); Judgm 18(2); Trusts 21(1); Wills 439, 441, 486, 487(4), 671.

Fowler v. Resolution Trust Corp., TexApp–El Paso, 855 SW2d 31.—App & E 842(2), 852, 989, 994(3), 1008.1(1), 1010.1(4), 1011.1(2), 1012.1(2), 1012.1(5), 1071.2; B & L Assoc 42(6); Contracts 97(1), 97(2), 313(2); Costs 194.40; Land & Ten 291(14).

Fowler v. Roden, TexComApp, 105 SW2d 187, 129 Tex 599.—App & E 931(4); Infants 105; Judgm 335(2), 335(3), 668(1); Partit 9(2); Tresp to T T 32, 40(1); Witn 397.

Fowler; Shannon v., TexApp–Fort Worth, 693 SW2d 54, dism.—App & E 961; Bankr 3347.1; Child S 239, 451, 456, 468; Divorce 85; Pretrial Proc 221.

Fowler; Sharp v., Tex, 252 SW2d 153, 151 Tex 490.—Deeds 120; Mines 55(1).

Fowler; Sharp v., TexCivApp–Texarkana, 248 SW2d 322, aff 252 SW2d 153, 151 Tex 490.—Deeds 90, 120; Mines 55(4).

Fowler v. Sheppeard, SDTex, 61 FSupp 817.—Work Comp 1172.

Fowler v. Smith, CA5 (Tex), 68 F3d 124.—Const Law 90.1(7.2), 1947, 1994, 3893, 4172(1), 4172(6), 4202; Fed Civ Proc 2543, 2545; Fed Cts 776; Schools 63(1).

Fowler v. State, TexCrimApp, 991 SW2d 258.—Crim Law 1181(2).

Fowler v. State, TexCrimApp, 509 SW2d 871.—Sent & Pun 2011.

Fowler v. State, TexCrimApp, 500 SW2d 643.—Crim Law 719(3), 730(1), 1171.3.

Fowler v. State, TexCrimApp, 458 SW2d 930.—Crim Law 590(2), 641.10(2).

Fowler v. State, TexCrimApp, 379 SW2d 345.—Autos 355(8); Crim Law 363, 364(1), 1144.12; Ind & Inf 119, 202(6); Names 16(1).

Fowler v. State, TexCrimApp, 352 SW2d 838, 171 Tex-Crim 600.—Crim Law 350, 695(2), 1043(2), 1090.13, 1092.7, 1169.1(3).

Fowler v. State, TexCrimApp, 333 SW2d 123, 169 Tex-Crim 172.—Assault 54, 78, 92(1), 96(7); Crim Law 1173.2(2); Ind & Inf 203.

Fowler v. State, TexCrimApp, 301 SW2d 132.—Crim Law 1087.1(2).

Fowler v. State, TexCrimApp, 292 SW2d 104.—Crim Law 1087.1(2).

Fowler v. State, TexCrimApp, 290 SW2d 905.—Crim Law 1090.1(1).

Fowler v. State, TexCrimApp, 289 SW2d 931.—Crim Law 1090.1(1).

Fowler v. State, TexCrimApp, 287 SW2d 665, 162 Tex-Crim 513.—Autos 355(6); Crim Law 364(4), 364(5), 1169.12.

Fowler v. State, TexCrimApp, 274 SW2d 705, 161 Tex-Crim 30.—Crim Law 721(1), 1091(8).

Fowler v. State, TexCrimApp, 274 SW2d 689.—Crim Law 1090.1(1).

Fowler v. State, TexCrimApp, 269 SW2d 384.—Crim Law 1087.1(2).

Fowler v. State, TexCrimApp, 253 SW2d 436, 158 Tex-Crim 56.—Crim Law 365(1), 1171.1(2.1); Int Liq 236(20); Sent & Pun 1417.

Fowler v. State, TexCrimApp, 247 SW2d 393, 157 Tex-Crim 147.—Crim Law 720(6), 721(3), 1091(2), 1091(8).

Fowler v. State, TexCrimApp, 240 SW2d 780, 156 Tex-Crim 267.—Crim Law 763(1), 1038.2, 1038.3, 1056.1(4), 1133, 1172.1(1); Ind & Inf 41(3); Int Liq 236(7).

Fowler v. State, TexCrimApp, 240 SW2d 313, 156 Tex-Crim 270.—Crim Law 814(3); Int Liq 236(4), 238(1); Searches 109.

Fowler v. State, TexCrimApp, 235 SW2d 183, 155 Tex-Crim 342.—Searches 68.

Fowler v. State, TexCrimApp, 230 SW2d 810, 155 Tex-Crim 35.—Crim Law 261(1), 1031(4); Ind & Inf 161(8).

Fowler v. State, TexCrimApp, 228 SW2d 512, 154 Tex-Crim 450.—Bail 64.

Fowler v. State, TexCrimApp, 195 SW2d 366, 149 Tex-Crim 436.—Crim Law 1090.1(1), 1099.6(1), 1133.

Fowler v. State, TexCrimApp, 162 SW2d 969, 144 Tex-Crim 382.—Crim Law 387, 594(3), 990.1, 995(3).

Fowler v. State, TexCrimApp, 136 SW2d 222.—Crim Law 1182.

Fowler v. State, TexCrimApp, 121 SW2d 990, 135 Tex-Crim 562.—Crim Law 598(2), 722.4, 1171.6.

Fowler v. State, TexCrimApp, 120 SW2d 1054, 135 Tex-Crim 399.—Crim Law 291, 292(1), 1048; Larc 55.

Fowler v. State, TexCrimApp, 39 SW2d 621, 118 TexCrim 424, reh den 41 SW2d 91.—Crim Law 720.5.

Fowler v. State, TexApp–Austin, 874 SW2d 112, reh overr, and petition for discretionary review refused, and petition for discretionary review refused.—Crim Law 1077.3, 1081(2).

Fowler v. State, TexApp–Austin, 674 SW2d 923. See Anderson, In re.

Fowler v. State, TexApp–Amarillo, 65 SW3d 116.—Autos 332; Crim Law 1144.13(3), 1159.2(1), 1159.2(4), 1159.2(7), 1159.2(9), 1159.4(2).

Fowler v. State, TexApp–Beaumont, 126 SW3d 307.—Crim Law 814(5), 822(1), 1030(1), 1045; Sent & Pun 313.

Fowler; State v., TexApp–Waco, 97 SW3d 721.—Hab Corp 815.

Fowler v. State, TexApp–Waco, 16 SW3d 426, reh overr, and petition for discretionary review refused.—Crim Law 1081(4.1), 1081(5).

Fowler v. State, TexApp–Waco, 958 SW2d 853, petition for discretionary review gr, aff 991 SW2d 258.—Crim Law 338(7), 388.1, 388.2, 469, 469.1, 472, 671, 814(20), 1038.1(4), 1043(1), 1043(3), 1134(2), 1158(1), 1162, 1163(1), 1165(1), 1169.1(1), 1169.9, 1172.6; Ind & Inf 60, 113; Kidnap 32, 41; Sent & Pun 373.

Fowler v. State, TexApp–Waco, 752 SW2d 737. See Pike v. State.

Fowler v. State, TexApp–Corpus Christi, 803 SW2d 848.—Crim Law 951(1), 1083.

Fowler v. State, TexApp–Houston (14 Dist), 863 SW2d 187, petition for discretionary review refused.—Crim Law 1035(5), 1044.1(1); Jury 120.

Fowler v. Stone, TexCivApp–Hous (14 Dist), 600 SW2d 351.—App & E 984(5); Atty & C 172; Child S 468, 479, 498; Divorce 226.

Fowler; Sumerlin v., TexCivApp–Amarillo, 229 SW2d 75.—App & E 1039(1), 1039(5.1); Counties 126, 149, 165; Mand 15, 109; Mun Corp 898.

Fowler v. Szostek, TexApp–Houston (1 Dist), 905 SW2d 336.—App & E 934(1); Judgm 181(2), 185(2), 185(6); Offic 114, 116, 119; Schools 63(3).

Fowler; Tarrant County Water Control and Imp. Dist. No. 1 v., Tex, 179 SW2d 250, 142 Tex 375.—Statut 119(1).

Fowler; Tarrant County Water Control and Imp. Dist. No. 1 v., TexCivApp–Dallas, 175 SW2d 694, writ refused 179 SW2d 250, 142 Tex 375.—Damag 228; Em Dom 2(10), 98, 124, 288(1), 300, 303; Pub Lands 176(1); Statut 119(1).

Fowler v. Texas Emp. Ins. Ass'n, TexCivApp–Fort Worth, 237 SW2d 373, writ refused.—App & E 223; Evid 589; Judgm 186; Work Comp 667, 1410, 1942.

Fowler; Texas Emp. Ins. Ass'n v., TexCivApp–Amarillo, 140 SW2d 545, writ refused.—Trial 215, 219, 352.12, 365.2; Work Comp 1297, 1683, 1969.

Fowler; U.S. v., CA5 (Tex), 216 F3d 459, cert den 121 SCt 387, 531 US 960, 148 LEd2d 298.—Courts 90(2); Crim Law 1158(1); Sent & Pun 698.

Fowler; U.S. v., CA5 (Tex), 136 FedAppx 620.—Crim Law 1042.

Fowler; White v., TexCivApp–El Paso, 149 SW2d 1022.—Alt of Inst 27.1(1); App & E 1046.3.

Fowler; Wright v., TexApp–Fort Worth, 991 SW2d 343.—Antitrust 257, 358; App & E 719(8), 863; Const Law 2314, 2315; Health 800, 811; Judgm 181(2), 185(2); Lim of Act 4(2), 43, 55(3), 95(12); Plead 16, 48.

Fowler Furniture Co., Inc.; City of Tyler v., TexApp–Tyler, 831 SW2d 399, writ den.—Damag 69; Dedi 20(2); Evid 571(10); Interest 60; Mun Corp 763(1), 776, 798, 830, 832, 845(4).

Fowler Homes, Inc. v. Welch Associates, Inc., Tex, 793 SW2d 660. See Juliette Fowler Homes, Inc. v. Welch Associates, Inc.

Fowler Homes, Inc. v. Welch Associates, Inc., TexApp–Eastland, 797 SW2d 936. See Juliette Fowler Homes, Inc. v. Welch Associates, Inc.

Fowler's Estate, In re, TexCivApp–Austin, 87 SW2d 896, writ dism.—App & E 931(1), 989, 994(3), 1010.1(3); Ex & Ad 32(2); Wills 52(1), 55(1), 203, 302(6).

Fowlerton Consol. School Dist. No. 1; Frost v., TexCivApp–Beaumont, 111 SW2d 754.—Lim of Act 124, 143(1); Schools 21, 90, 95(1), 95(4), 95(5), 107; Tax 2777.

Fowlkes v. Fowlkes, TexCivApp–Galveston, 133 SW2d 241.—App & E 294(1), 719(6), 755, 846(5), 931(3), 954(1); Dead Bodies 5.

Fowlkes; Fowlkes v., TexCivApp–Galveston, 133 SW2d 241.—App & E 294(1), 719(6), 755, 846(5), 931(3), 954(1); Dead Bodies 5.

Fowzer v. Huey & Philp Hardware Co., TexCivApp–Dallas, 99 SW2d 1100, writ dism.—Appear 8(7); Inj 106; Judgm 16, 447(1), 447(2), 447(3); Receivers 151.

Fox, In re, BkrtcyNDTex, 5 BR 317.—Bankr 2543, 3348, 3348.5, 3349, 3387.1, 3420(2).

Fox, In re, TexApp–Amarillo, 141 SW3d 795.—Atty & C 62; Mand 12, 14(1), 14(3), 26, 31, 172; Motions 40; Plead 1.

Fox v. Amarillo Nat. Bank, TexCivApp–Amarillo, 552 SW2d 547, ref nre.—App & E 204(2), 758.3(9); Parties 14, 25; Trial 105(2); Wills 55(1), 123(1), 206, 268, 302(1), 302(5), 360, 370, 384.

Fox; American Nat. Ins. Co. v., TexCivApp–Fort Worth, 184 SW2d 937, writ refused wom.—App & E 173(11), 1062.1; Evid 59; Insurance 2024, 2035, 2589(1), 2590(2), 2604, 2608, 3374, 3375, 3578; Plead 430(2); Trial 350.4(3).

Fox v. American Propane, Inc., TexCivApp–Austin, 508 SW2d 426, ref nre.—App & E 1135; Trover 10, 60, 69.

Fox v. Anonymous, TexApp–San Antonio, 869 SW2d 499, writ den.—App & E 143, 422; Const Law 1228, 1231; Records 30, 32.

Fox; Benson v., TexCivApp–Tyler, 589 SW2d 823.—App & E 80(6), 931(3); Partit 22, 73, 77(1), 91, 95.

Fox v. Boese, TexCivApp–Hous (1 Dist), 566 SW2d 682, ref nre.—App & E 768, 930(3), 989, 1170.9(2.1); Atty & C 166(3), 167(3); Evid 570.

Fox v. Burgess, Tex, 302 SW2d 405, 157 Tex 292.—Int Liq 31(1), 34(5); Statut 190, 212.6.

Fox; Burgess v., TexCivApp–Amarillo, 298 SW2d 653, rev 302 SW2d 405, 157 Tex 292.—Const Law 2474; Int Liq 31(1); Statut 181(1), 181(2), 184, 188, 194, 206, 217.1.

Fox v. Carr, TexCivApp–Texarkana, 552 SW2d 885.—Admin Law 651; App & E 185(1); Const Law 4028, 4168, 4172(1); Mun Corp 185(12), 198(4); Offic 72.40.

Fox; City of Houston v., Tex, 444 SW2d 591.—Em Dom 106, 107; Mun Corp 669.

Fox; City of Houston v., Tex, 419 SW2d 819, on remand 429 SW2d 201, writ gr, rev 444 SW2d 591.—App & E 1177(6).

Fox; City of Houston v., TexCivApp–Hous (1 Dist), 429 SW2d 201, writ gr, rev 444 SW2d 591.—Dedi 47; Em Dom 85, 102, 124, 140, 203(2), 221, 295; Mun Corp 658, 663(1).

Fox; City of Houston v., TexCivApp–Houston, 412 SW2d 745, rev 419 SW2d 819, on remand 429 SW2d 201, writ gr, rev 444 SW2d 591.—Em Dom 106, 305, 307(2).

Fox; Comanche Nation v., TexApp–Austin, 128 SW3d 745.—App & E 946, 977(1); Child C 512, 526; Indians 27(7); Judgm 143(2), 143(3), 143(10), 145(1), 146, 159, 162(2).

Fox; Cunningham v., TexApp–Houston (14 Dist), 879 SW2d 210, reh den, and writ den.—Courts 202(5); Lim of Act 127(12), 130(5), 180(7).

Fox; Daniel v., TexApp–San Antonio, 917 SW2d 106, writ den.—App & E 1010.1(1); Ease 1, 3(1), 15.1, 16, 18(1), 18(3), 26(3), 61(12).

Fox v. Doe, TexApp–San Antonio, 869 SW2d 507, writ den.—App & E 931(1), 989, 1010.1(3), 1012.1(4); Const Law 1211; Records 32; Witn 219(1).

Fox; E. F. Hutton & Co., Inc. v., TexCivApp–Dallas, 518 SW2d 849, ref nre.—App & E 837(1), 852, 931(3), 931(4); Brok 38(1), 38(3), 38(4), 38(9); Estop 52(1), 85, 99; Stip 14(10); Trial 351.2(4).

Fox v. Fox, TexApp–Beaumont, 720 SW2d 880.—Divorce 254(1); Judgm 524.

Fox; Fox v., TexApp–Beaumont, 720 SW2d 880.—Divorce 254(1); Judgm 524.

Fox v. Fox, TexCivApp–Fort Worth, 210 SW2d 622.—Child C 7, 22, 42, 63, 467, 510.

Fox; Fox v., TexCivApp–Fort Worth, 210 SW2d 622.—Child C 7, 22, 42, 63, 467, 510.

Fox v. Fox, TexCivApp–Austin, 559 SW2d 407.—Child C 742, 816; Courts 21; Divorce 62(2), 62(6), 65, 179, 201.

Fox; Fox v., TexCivApp–Austin, 559 SW2d 407.—Child C 742, 816; Courts 21; Divorce 62(2), 62(6), 65, 179, 201.

Fox v. Fox, TexCivApp–Dallas, 526 SW2d 180.—Child S 506(5); Const Law 945; Divorce 286(1), 362, 367, 389, 393(1), 394(2), 395(2); Set-Off 60.

Fox; Fox v., TexCivApp–Dallas, 526 SW2d 180.—Child S 506(5); Const Law 945; Divorce 286(1), 362, 367, 389, 393(1), 394(2), 395(2); Set-Off 60.

Fox v. Fox, TexCivApp–Galveston, 281 SW2d 122.—Venue 21.

Fox; Fox v., TexCivApp–Galveston, 281 SW2d 122.—Venue 21.

Fox v. Gallo, TexCivApp–Amarillo, 428 SW2d 127, ref nre.—Anim 25; Cust & U 15(1), 16; Evid 458.

Fox v. Grand Union Tea Co., TexCivApp–Austin, 236 SW2d 561, mandamus overr.—App & E 1177(7); Evid 20(1), 53; Names 18.

Fox v. Gulf, C. & S.F. Ry. Co., TexCivApp–Galveston, 80 SW2d 1072, writ dism.—Labor & Emp 2814.

Fox v. Hinderliter, TexApp–San Antonio, 222 SW3d 154.—Health 804, 805, 809; Pretrial Proc 508, 512, 516, 517.1.

Fox v. Holley, TexCivApp–Eastland, 155 SW2d 395.—App & E 387(2); New Tr 155.

Fox; Houghton v., TexCivApp–El Paso, 93 SW2d 781.—Gaming 58.

Fox; Johnson v., TexApp–Fort Worth, 683 SW2d 214.—App & E 770(2); Mines 47, 55(2), 55(4), 55(5).

Fox; Kimbrough v., TexApp–Fort Worth, 631 SW2d 606.—App & E 758.3(3); Contracts 141(1); Costs 194.32; Gaming 9.

Fox v. Lewis, TexApp–Austin, 344 SW2d 731, ref nre.—App & E 78(1), 170(1), 884, 1062.2, 1170.9(2.1); Contracts 100; Deeds 78, 90, 97, 125, 194(2), 194(4), 208(1); Evid 461(1), 501(3); Mand 1, 51, 143(2); Trial 122, 234(8), 350.1; Wills 88(6), 324(2).

Fox; Long v., TexApp–San Antonio, 625 SW2d 376, ref nre.—Antitrust 397; App & E 185(1); Courts 121(1), 121(5), 121(9), 122, 169(1), 169(4), 169(6), 170.

Fox v. Maguire, TexApp–El Paso, 224 SW3d 304, review den.—App & E 242(2), 856(1), 893(1), 1135; Civil R 1376(1); Courts 32, 483, 489(1); Plead 104(1).

FOX

Fox v. **Medina**, TexApp–Corpus Christi, 848 SW2d 866.—Admin Law 481, 722.1, 750, 791; Int Liq 108.5, 108.9, 108.10(4).

Fox v. **Miller**, TexCivApp–San Antonio, 198 SW2d 776, ref nre.—Contracts 97(1); Fraud 12, 35, 58(1).

Fox; **Morgan** v., TexCivApp–Corpus Christi, 536 SW2d 644, ref nre.—Aband L P 2, 3, 5; App & E 719(8), 733; Judgm 181(24), 185.3(14); Mines 78.1(8), 78.1(9), 78.5, 78.7(3.1), 78.7(4), 78.7(5), 80; Sales 226(1), 228.

Fox v. **Nail**, TexCivApp–El Paso, 294 SW2d 407.—Elections 227(8), 285(4), 295(1), 298(1), 299(2).

Fox; **Normand** v., TexApp–Waco, 940 SW2d 401.—App & E 76(1); Breach of P 21; Courts 39, 247(2); Mand 4(3), 53.

Fox v. **Parker**, TexApp–Waco, 98 SW3d 713, reh overr, and petition stricken, and review den, and reh of petition for review den.—App & E 893(1), 1079; Atty & C 24; Colleges 8(2), 8.1(4.1), 8.1(5); Contracts 143(1), 143(2), 143.5, 147(1), 152, 169, 175(1), 176(2); Cust & U 15(1); Evid 448; Libel 7(16), 33, 89(1), 112(1), 116, 118, 119, 123(2); Pretrial Proc 434; Records 30.

Fox; **Rhone** v., TexCivApp–Austin, 142 SW2d 542, writ dism.—App & E 1002; Autos 170(13), 244(12), 244(44); Trial 352.10, 352.17.

Fox v. **Roman Inn Lounge**, TexApp–Corpus Christi, 848 SW2d 866. See Fox v. Medina.

Fox v. **San Antonio Sav. Ass'n**, TexApp–San Antonio, 751 SW2d 257.—Forci E & D 44.

Fox; **Sandoval** v., CA5 (Tex), 135 FedAppx 691.—Prisons 4(9), 4(12). ·

Fox; **S.E.C.** v., CA5 (Tex), 855 F2d 247.—Fed Cts 830; Sec Reg 60.28(11), 60.28(13); U S 147(10), 147(11.1).

Fox; **S.E.C.** v., NDTex, 654 FSupp 781.—Sec Reg 60.28(1), 60.28(4), 60.28(11), 60.28(13), 60.45(1), 60.63(1).

Fox v. **Smith**, TexCivApp–Waco, 531 SW2d 654.—Hus & W 249(3), 272(1); Interpl 24, 35.

Fox v. **State**, TexCrimApp, 930 SW2d 607.—Crim Law 1179.

Fox v. **State**, TexCrimApp, 561 SW2d 495.—Int Liq 132, 214.

Fox v. **State**, TexCrimApp, 224 SW2d 480, 153 TexCrim 633.—Crim Law 560; Int Liq 236(5).

Fox v. **State**, TexCrimApp, 165 SW2d 733, 145 TexCrim 71.—Autos 343, 346, 355(13), 357; Courts 104; Crim Law 35, 800(4), 814(17).

Fox v. **State**, TexCrimApp, 99 SW2d 925, 131 TexCrim 410.—Int Liq 205(1).

Fox v. **State**, TexApp–Fort Worth, 900 SW2d 345, petition for discretionary review gr, petition for discretionary review dism with per curiam opinion 930 SW2d 607.—Arrest 63.5(4); Autos 349(2.1); Crim Law 1153(1).

Fox v. **State**, TexApp–San Antonio, 693 SW2d 593.—Crim Law 29(1), 29(12), 339.11(6), 795(2.20), 1134(2), 1172.6; Double J 148; Judgm 713(1), 715(1); Rape 1, 45, 51(1), 59(20.1).

Fox v. **State**, TexApp–Texarkana, 175 SW3d 475, petition for discretionary review refused.—Const Law 4594(1); Crim Law 469.1, 474.3(1), 474.3(3), 474.4(4), 641.13(2.1), 641.13(6), 700(2.1), 700(4), 905, 911, 938(1), 938(3), 941(1), 1043(2), 1045, 1134(2), 1147, 1153(2); Witn 40(2), 41, 45(2), 77, 79(1).

Fox; **State** v., TexApp–Beaumont, 772 SW2d 455.—Autos 355(6); Crim Law 303.15, 448(2), 451(1), 641.3(8.1); Ind & Inf 144.

Fox v. **State**, TexApp–Houston (14 Dist), 115 SW3d 550, petition for discretionary review refused.—Crim Law 338(1), 338(7), 371(1), 371(9), 469, 478(1), 661, 662.7, 1036.1(9), 1147, 1153(1), 1153(2), 1162, 1165(1), 1169.1(1), 1170(1), 1170.5(5); Witn 268(1), 363(1), 372(1), 372(3), 374(1).

Fox v. **State**, TexApp–Houston (14 Dist), 801 SW2d 173, petition for discretionary review refused.—Const Law 1807; Crim Law 38; Obst Just 2, 16.

Fox v. **State**, TexApp–Houston (14 Dist), 657 SW2d 449.—Crim Law 273(4.1), 538(3).

Fox; **State** v., TexCivApp–Austin, 133 SW2d 987, writ refused.—Banks 285; Offic 110; Statut 227; Tax 2802, 2816, 2828, 2830.

Fox v. **Texas Emp. Ins. Ass'n**, TexCivApp–Eastland, 94 SW2d 569.—Work Comp 1269, 1335, 1726.

Fox v. **Thoreson**, Tex, 398 SW2d 88.—Contracts 147(1), 152; Land & Ten 37; Mines 73, 73.5, 78.1(1), 78.1(2), 78.1(3), 78.1(9).

Fox; **Thoreson** v., TexCivApp–Amarillo, 390 SW2d 308, writ gr, rev 398 SW2d 88.—Contracts 278(2); Estates 6; Estop 118; Mines 73.1(4), 73.5, 78.1(9), 78.5, 80.

Fox; **Travelers Ins. Co.** v., TexCivApp–Fort Worth, 364 SW2d 859, ref nre.—Work Comp 1824, 1828, 1872, 1893, 1934.

Fox v. **Tropical Warehouses, Inc.**, TexApp–Fort Worth, 121 SW3d 853, reh overr.—Antitrust 413, 417, 418, 420; App & E 837(3), 920(3), 946, 954(1), 954(2); Inj 12, 14, 135, 138.3, 138.6, 138.18, 138.33, 140, 147, 151; Labor & Emp 305.

Fox; **U.S.** v., CA5 (Tex), 248 F3d 394, reh den, cert gr, vac 122 SCt 1602, 535 US 1014, 152 LEd2d 617, on remand 293 F3d 237.—Const Law 1163, 1518, 2246; Crim Law 338(7), 471, 1139, 1158(1); Obscen 2.5, 5.2, 8, 15, 17; Sent & Pun 760, 765; Statut 47.

Fox; **U.S.** v., CA5 (Tex), 69 F3d 15.—Crim Law 371(1), 1036.1(8), 1144.13(2.1), 1144.13(5), 1153(1), 1159.2(7); Fraud 68.10(2), 69(5); Postal 49(1), 49(11).

Fox v. **U.S.**, CA5 (Tex), 296 F2d 217, cert den 82 SCt 1160, 369 US 888, 8 LEd2d 287.—Crim Law 1166.16; Embez 44(1); Jury 131(13).

Fox v. **U.S.**, CA5 (Tex), 201 F2d 883.—Armed S 65, 68.

Fox; **U.S.** v., EDTex, 74 FSupp2d 696, aff 248 F3d 394, reh den, cert gr, vac 122 SCt 1602, 535 US 1014, 152 LEd2d 617, on remand 293 F3d 237.—Obscen 2.5.

Fox v. **U.S.**, EDTex, 104 FSupp 678, aff 201 F2d 883.—Armed S 60, 68.

Fox; **U.S.** v., NDTex, 766 FSupp 569.—Aliens 781.

Fox v. **Wardy**, TexApp–El Paso, 225 SW3d 198, review den.—App & E 856(4), 948, 962; Pretrial Proc 581, 583, 590.1, 594.1.

Fox v. **Wardy**, TexApp–El Paso, 224 SW3d 307, review den.—App & E 70(6), 78(1).

Fox v. **Wardy**, TexApp–El Paso, 224 SW3d 300, review den.—App & E 242(2), 856(1), 893(1); Civil R 1376(1); Courts 32, 487(1), 489(1); Plead 104(1).

Fox v. **Young**, TexCivApp–El Paso, 91 SW2d 857.—Chat Mtg 203; Proc 141; Sales 156, 162; Sheriffs 114, 140.

Foxall; **Powell** v., TexApp–Beaumont, 65 SW3d 756.—App & E 863, 901; Judgm 185(2); Offic 114, 116; States 79, 191.4(1).

Fox and Co.; **Bachynski** v., TexApp–Houston (14 Dist), 662 SW2d 771.—App & E 1062.2; Plead 427; Trial 350.4(4).

Fox & Holland, Ltd.; **Longhorn Oil and Gas Co.** v., BkrtcySDTex, 64 BR 263. See Longhorn Oil and Gas Co., In re.

Fox & Jacobs Const. Co.; **Barnwell** v., TexCivApp–Dallas, 469 SW2d 199.—App & E 1008.1(1); Evid 258(1); Plead 111.3, 111.30, 111.42(4), 111.42(5), 291(2); Pretrial Proc 306.1; Venue 7.5(2), 21.

Fox & Jacobs, Inc.; **Citizens of Texas Sav. & Loan Ass'n** v., TexApp–Dallas, 718 SW2d 2, dism.—Banks 191.30.

Fox & Jacobs, Inc.; **McCulloch** v., TexApp–Dallas, 696 SW2d 918, ref nre.—Const Law 48(1), 321, 2311, 2312, 2314, 2315, 2340, 2630, 3454, 3957, 3971; Lim of Act 4(2), 30; Prod Liab 71.5; Statut 181(1), 181(2), 188, 189, 190, 206.

Foxboro Co.; **Industrial Instrument Corp.** v., CA5 (Tex), 335 F2d 123, cert den 85 SCt 720, 379 US 1000, 13 LEd2d 702, reh den 85 SCt 887, 380 US 927, 13 LEd2d 815.—Pat 324.60, 325.10.

Foxboro Co.; Industrial Instrument Corp. v., CA5 (Tex), 307 F2d 783, reh den 310 F2d 686.—Pat 174, 178, 234, 314(6), 324.55(2).

Fox Development Co. v. City of San Antonio, Tex, 468 SW2d 338.—Mun Corp 29(4).

Fox Development Co. v. City of San Antonio, TexCiv-App–San Antonio, 459 SW2d 670, aff 468 SW2d 338.— Mun Corp 29(4), 33(10).

Fox Elec. Co., Inc. v. Tone Guard Sec., Inc., TexApp–Fort Worth, 861 SW2d 79, reh overr.—App & E 242(1); Contracts 114; Damag 78(1); Tel 1406.

Foxhall; Calaway v., TexCivApp–Hous (14 Dist), 603 SW2d 363.—Decl Judgm 124.1; Parties 35.63.

Foxmeyer Corp., In re, BkrtcyNDTex, 230 BR 791.— Bankr 2090, 2091, 2534.

FoxMeyer Corp., In re, BkrtcyNDTex, 217 BR 511.— Bankr 2082, 2083, 2160; Fed Cts 30.

Foxmeyer Drug Co.; Procter v., TexApp–Dallas, 884 SW2d 853.—Contracts 147(2), 159; Corp 445.1, 590(1); Decl Judgm 271; Judgm 178, 181(19), 185(2), 185(6); Perp 6(1); Torts 242; Ven & Pur 18(0.5), 57, 59.

Foxmeyer Health Corp.; Lusk v., CA5 (Tex), 129 F3d 773.—Civil R 1109, 1112, 1539; Corp 399(1); Fed Civ Proc 2470; Fed Cts 802.

Foxmeyer Health Corp. v. McKesson Corp., BkrtcyND-Tex, 217 BR 511. See FoxMeyer Corp., In re.

Foxmeyer Health Corp.; Zuckerman v., NDTex, 4 FSupp2d 618.—Fed Civ Proc 636; Sec Reg 60.18, 60.27(1), 60.27(5), 60.28(2.1), 60.45(1), 60.51, 60.53, 60.54, 60.62, 278.

Fox Television Station, Inc.; Hickman v., CA5 (Tex), 177 FedAppx 427.—Fed Civ Proc 1451, 1758.1.

Fox Television Station, Inc.; Hickman v., SDTex, 231 FRD 248, aff 177 FedAppx 427.—Fed Civ Proc 1278, 1741, 1758.1, 1759, 1837.1, 1991.

Fox Television Stations, Inc.; Boone R. Enterprises, Inc. v., TexApp–Dallas, 189 SW3d 795.—App & E 856(1).

Fox Television Stations, Inc.; Keane v., CA5 (Tex), 129 FedAppx 874, cert den 126 SCt 426, 546 US 938, 163 LEd2d 324.—Antitrust 417, 419; Copyr 107; Trade-marks 1025, 1136(2), 1800.

Fox Television Stations, Inc.; Keane v., SDTex, 297 FSupp2d 921, aff 129 FedAppx 874, cert den 126 SCt 426, 546 US 938, 163 LEd2d 324.—Antitrust 16, 34, 38, 135(1), 413, 414, 419, 423; Contracts 27; Copyr 107, 108, 109; Fed Civ Proc 642, 1772, 1835; Impl & C C 30, 34; States 18.87; Trademarks 1025, 1131, 1136(1), 1136(2), 1137(1), 1421, 1583.

Fox Vacuum, Inc.; Parker v., TexApp–Beaumont, 732 SW2d 722, ref nre.—Autos 243(3).

Fox Vliet Drug Co. v. Arnold, TexCivApp–Beaumont, 84 SW2d 1012, writ dism.—Judgm 815, 818(4).

Foxwood Homeowners Ass'n v. Ricles, TexApp–Houston (1 Dist), 673 SW2d 376, ref nre.—App & E 1071.1(5.1); Covenants 51(2), 103(3), 122; Equity 65(1); Inj 1, 62(1), 112, 128(6).

Foxworth; Consolidated Underwriters v., TexCivApp–Beaumont, 196 SW2d 87, writ gr.—Trial 350.3(8), 351.5(1), 351.5(8), 352.1(4); Witn 208(1); Work Comp 1926, 1962, 1968(5), 1968(7), 1969.

Foxworth; Lewis v., TexApp–Dallas, 170 SW3d 900.— Contracts 155; Ven & Pur 79, 186.

Foxworth; Murph v., TexCivApp–Galveston, 93 SW2d 817.—App & E 724(2), 742(1); Sales 38(3), 123.

Foxworth; Rogers v., TexApp–Tyler, 214 SW3d 196.— App & E 846(5), 852, 989, 1008.1(1), 1010.1(1), 1010.2; Ex & Ad 56; Hus & W 258, 265, 273(1), 276(5).

Foxworth; Southampton Civic Club v., TexCivApp–Hous (14 Dist), 550 SW2d 152, ref nre.—Covenants 103(2); Inj 62(1).

Foxworth; Superior Lloyds of America v., TexCivApp–Amarillo, 178 SW2d 724, writ refused wom.—App & E

1062.1; Damag 221(5.1); Trial 133.6(1), 237(1), 351.5(8); Work Comp 1922, 1968(3).

Foxworth-Galbraith Lumber Co.; Canfield v., TexCiv-App–Tyler, 545 SW2d 583, ref nre.—App & E 1062.1; Estop 90(1), 98(2); Trial 352.1(3).

Foxworth-Galbraith Lumber Co. v. Realty Trust Co., TexCivApp–Amarillo, 110 SW2d 1164, dism.—Const Law 4060, 4066; High 132; Mun Corp 406(1), 455, 488(5.1), 488(8), 513(5).

Foxworth-Galbraith Lumber Co. v. Southwestern Con-tracting Corp., TexCivApp–Fort Worth, 165 SW2d 221, writ refused wom.—Judgm 253(1); Mtg 116, 169; Paymt 46(1); Plead 427.

Foxworth-Galbraith Lumber Co. v. Thorp, TexCivApp–Amarillo, 86 SW2d 644.—Hus & W 137(3); Improv 3.

Foxx v. DeRobbio, TexApp–El Paso, 224 SW3d 263, reh overr.—App & E 213, 233(2), 237(5), 238(2), 294(1), 946, 971(2); Damag 174(1), 188(2); Evid 474(19), 474(20).

Foxx v. State, TexCrimApp, 424 SW2d 432.—Burg 36, 41(1).

Fox 29 v. Channel 12 of Beaumont, Inc., EDTex, 874 FSupp 756. See KVHP TV Partners, Ltd. v. Channel 12 of Beaumont, Inc.

Foy; Abbott v., TexApp–Houston (14 Dist), 662 SW2d 629, ref nre.—Lim of Act 127(10); Wills 179, 229.

Foy v. Clemmons, TexCivApp–Dallas, 365 SW2d 384, ref nre.—Wills 439, 440, 470(3), 566.

Foy; Employees Retirement System of Texas v., Tex-App–Austin, 896 SW2d 314, reh overr, and writ den.— Admin Law 383, 651, 701; Offic 101.5(2).

Foy v. Foy, TexCivApp–Waco, 387 SW2d 946, ref nre.— Child S 270, 362, 555.

Foy; Foy v., TexCivApp–Waco, 387 SW2d 946, ref nre.— Child S 270, 362, 555.

Foy v. State, TexCrimApp, 593 SW2d 707.—Crim Law 369.1, 371(12).

Foy v. State, TexApp–Waco, 726 SW2d 263.—Const Law 2564; Crim Law 393(1), 412.2(5), 438(8), 625.10(4), 625.20, 790.

Foy; U.S. v., CA5 (Tex), 28 F3d 464, cert den 115 SCt 610, 513 US 1031, 130 LEd2d 520, appeal after new sentenc-ing hearing 117 F3d 1417.—Consp 28(3), 47(12); Con-trolled Subs 148(3); Crim Law 273(4.1), 273.1(2), 274(3.1), 412.2(5), 1134(3), 1144.12, 1144.13(2.1), 1149, 1158(4), 1159.1, 1159.2(7), 1181.5(3.1); Sent & Pun 670, 675; Weap 4, 17(4).

Foye v. Montes, TexApp–Houston (14 Dist), 9 SW3d 436, reh overr, and petition for review den, and reh of petition for review overr.—App & E 931(1), 1010.2; Assault 2, 35, 48; Damag 50.10.

Foyt v. Championship Auto Racing Teams, Inc., SDTex, 947 FSupp 290.—Courts 508(1); Fed Cts 96; Inj 32, 110, 211, 212.

Foyt v. State, TexCrimApp, 126 SW2d 990, 136 TexCrim 571.—Crim Law 1168(3); Larc 55.

Foyt v. State, TexCrimApp, 122 SW2d 641, 135 TexCrim 664.—Burg 46(3); Crim Law 784(1).

Foyt v. U.S., CA5 (Tex), 561 F2d 599.—Int Rev 3071, 3314.1, 3362, 3377, 5007, 5115; U S 125(7).

Fraben Oil Corp. v. Potter, TexCivApp–Texarkana, 350 SW2d 584.—App & E 499(1), 989, 1008.1(2); Land & Ten 231(8), 233(2); Trial 142.

Fracmaster, Ltd., In re, BkrtcyEDTex, 237 BR 627.— Bankr 2341; Fed Cts 13; Statut 217.3.

Fradelis Frozen Food Corp. v. Gamble, TexCivApp–San Antonio, 326 SW2d 293.—Receivers 38, 40.

Frady v. May, TexApp–Fort Worth, 23 SW3d 558, reh overr, and review den.—App & E 1010.1(1), 1010.1(2); Brok 39, 40, 43(2), 43(3), 48, 49(1), 54, 57(2); Contracts 143(2), 147(3), 152, 176(2), 218; Ven & Pur 1.

Fraga v. Bowen, CA5 (Tex), 810 F2d 1296.—Admin Law 459, 791; Social S 140.21, 140.30, 140.41, 140.45, 140.55, 140.70, 142.5, 142.16, 143.55, 143.60, 143.75, 148.5.

Fraga v. State, TexApp–San Antonio, 940 SW2d 736, petition for discretionary review refused.—Crim Law 795(1.5), 795(2.10), 795(2.90), 814(20), 1043(3), 1177.

Fraga-Buendia, Ex parte, TexCrimApp, 433 SW2d 695.—Extrad 39.

Fragoso v. Cisneros, TexCivApp–El Paso, 154 SW2d 991, writ refused wom.—Intern Law 6; States 12.1, 13, 14; Treaties 7; U S 2.

Fragoso; U.S. v., CA5 (Tex), 978 F2d 896, cert den 113 SCt 1664, 507 US 1012, 123 LEd2d 282.—Consp 47(12); Crim Law 427(5), 428, 627.6(5), 627.8(4), 814(5), 1042.5, 1168(2), 1169.5(3), 1177.5(1); Sent & Pun 1355, 1513.

Fragozo; Castellano v., CA5 (Tex), 352 F3d 939, cert den 125 SCt 31, 543 US 808, 160 LEd2d 10, cert den 125 SCt 33, 543 US 808, 160 LEd2d 10.—Civil R 1028, 1037, 1088(5), 1319, 1395(1), 1437; Const Law 3876, 4632; Crim Law 706(2); Dist & Pros Attys 10; Fed Cts 544, 630.1, 951.1; Lim of Act 58(1); Mal Pros 0.5, 15; Mun Corp 747(3); Searches 12; Torts 122.

Fragozo; Castellano v., CA5 (Tex), 311 F3d 689, reh gr, opinion vac 321 F3d 1203, opinion after grant of reh 352 F3d 939, cert den 125 SCt 31, 543 US 808, 160 LEd2d 10, cert den 125 SCt 33, 543 US 808, 160 LEd2d 10.—Civil R 1037, 1376(6), 1432, 1437, 1486; Consp 7.5(1), 19; Damag 190; Fed Civ Proc 1938.1, 2142.1; Fed Cts 13, 629, 630.1, 763.1; Mal Pros 0.5, 64(1), 64(2), 67, 69.

Fragrance Impressions Ltd.; Robbins v., SDTex, 952 FSupp 427.—Civil R 1123, 1549; Damag 50.10; Fed Civ Proc 2497.1; Lim of Act 95(6).

Fragumar Corp., N.V. v. Dunlap, CA5 (Tex), 925 F2d 836.—Atty & C 26; Costs 194.44; Fed Civ Proc 1557, 2192.1; Fed Cts 896.1; Fraud 58(1); Sec Reg 60.63(1), 60.70.

Fragumar Corp., N.V. v. Dunlap, CA5 (Tex), 685 F2d 127.—Fed Cts 241, 243.

Frailey, Ex parte, TexCrimApp, 177 SW2d 72, 146 TexCrim 557.—Bail 3; Crim Law 624; Mental H 37.1, 41, 438.

Fraiman; Standard Fire Ins. Co. v., TexCivApp–Hous (14 Dist), 588 SW2d 681, ref nre.—App & E 907(3); Insurance 3249, 3265, 3374, 3396, 3564(7); Interest 44; Spec Perf 80.

Fraiman; Standard Fire Ins. Co. v., TexCivApp–Hous (14 Dist), 514 SW2d 343.—Decl Judgm 7, 41, 161; Insurance 3249; Judgm 181(14); Spec Perf 78.

Fraire v. City of Arlington, CA5 (Tex), 957 F2d 1268, reh den, cert den 113 SCt 462, 506 US 973, 121 LEd2d 371.—Civil R 1088(2), 1351(1), 1351(4), 1352(4), 1376(2), 1394, 1395(5); Fed Civ Proc 2544; Fed Cts 766; Offic 114.

Fraire v. State, TexCrimApp, 588 SW2d 789.—Crim Law 577.5, 1035(1), 1144.7.

Fraiser; Son v., CA5 (Tex), 71 FedAppx 304.—Civil R 1395(6).

Fraley v. City of Borger, TexCivApp–Amarillo, 257 SW2d 883.—Tax 2859, 2861, 2863, 2864, 2932, 2935, 2938.

Fraley v. Hutchinson County, TexCivApp–Amarillo, 278 SW2d 462.—App & E 20; Em Dom 172.

Fraley v. Martin, TexCivApp–Dallas, 168 SW2d 536.—Child C 606, 719, 722, 766; Evid 80(1); Hab Corp 532(1), 744, 814; Judgm 818(1), 818(5).

Fraley; U.S. v., CA5 (Tex), 858 F2d 230, cert den 109 SCt 847, 488 US 1033, 102 LEd2d 978.—Crim Law 778(5), 792(3); Postal 27, 49(8.1).

Fraley v. Zales Jewelry Co., TexCivApp–Amarillo, 289 SW2d 416.—Action 4; Contracts 138(1); Sunday 12, 15, 23.

Fram Corp. v. Boyd, CA5 (Tex), 230 F2d 931.—Antitrust 17; Trademarks 1056, 1057(1), 1057(2), 1058, 1629(3), 1630, 1715(2), 1800.

Fram Corp.; Mooring v., TexCivApp–Eastland, 420 SW2d 462.—Neglig 401; Prod Liab 15, 21, 88.5.

Frame, In re, CA5 (Tex), 6 F3d 307. See James v. Frame.

Frame; James v., CA5 (Tex), 6 F3d 307.—Fed Civ Proc 2418.1, 2422; Fed Cts 816; Usury 125, 138.

Frame v. S-H, Inc., CA5 (Tex), 967 F2d 194, appeal after remand James v. Frame, 6 F3d 307.—Bankr 2442, 3836; Const Law 3987, 4478; Fed Civ Proc 1278, 1639, 2264.1; Fed Cts 776, 820, 850.1, 893, 945.

Frame v. State, TexCrimApp, 615 SW2d 766.—Crim Law 980(1), 1144.1, 1166(6); Jury 45, 109.

Frames v. Barnhart, CA5 (Tex), 156 FedAppx 688.—Social S 143.65, 143.80.

France v. American Indem. Co., Tex, 648 SW2d 283.—Elect of Rem 16; Plead 123; Work Comp 1002, 1729.

France; Siegler v., TexApp–Houston (1 Dist), 704 SW2d 429, ref nre.—Lim of Act 48(1).

France v. State, TexCrimApp, 187 SW2d 80, 148 TexCrim 341.—Crim Law 338(4), 339, 366(3), 404.70, 448(2), 448(11), 448(12), 454, 485(1), 594(1), 603.3(8), 683(1), 730(6), 1091(8), 1169.2(1); Ind & Inf 125(37), 132(1); Rape 51(1); Witn 274(2).

Franchise Stores Realty Corp. v. Dakri, TexApp–Houston (1 Dist), 721 SW2d 397.—Land & Ten 33, 37, 208(1).

Franchise Stores Realty Corp. v. Richill Plaza, TexApp–Houston (1 Dist), 721 SW2d 397. See Franchise Stores Realty Corp. v. Dakri.

Francies; U.S. v., CA5 (Tex), 945 F2d 851.—Crim Law 1028, 1030(1), 1042, 1177; Sent & Pun 1561.

Francis, Ex parte, TexCrimApp, 510 SW2d 345.—Sent & Pun 1166.

Francis, In re, Tex, 186 SW3d 534.—App & E 941; Elections 126(1); Mand 4(1), 16(1), 172.

Francis v. Allied Service Co. of Texas, Inc., CA5 (Tex), 486 F2d 597.—Fed Civ Proc 184.5; Fed Cts 858, 938.

Francis v. Beaudry, TexApp–Dallas, 733 SW2d 331, ref nre.—Corp 1.4(1), 1.6(10), 1.7(1), 1.7(2); Ex & Ad 85(4); Insurance 3471; Plead 374.

Francis; Best Inv. Co. v., TexCivApp–Eastland, 453 SW2d 893, ref nre.—Deeds 38(6); Judgm 185(2), 185.3(15); Mtg 260, 529(10).

Francis v. Brown, CA5 (Tex), 58 F3d 191.—Admin Law 229; Civil R 1513, 1515, 1518; Fed Cts 776.

Francis; Citizens Nat. Bank of Beaumont v., TexCivApp–Beaumont, 427 SW2d 645, ref nre.—Banks 153.

Francis v. Coastal Oil & Gas Corp., TexApp–Houston (1 Dist), 130 SW3d 76.—App & E 843(2), 930(1), 959(3); Const Law 2314; Improv 1; Judgm 199(3.2); Mines 73.1(3), 118; Neglig 238, 259, 1204(5); Plead 236(3), 236(5), 245(3), 248(1), 258(3).

Francis v. Cogdell, TexApp–Houston (1 Dist), 803 SW2d 868.—App & E 292, 866(3), 927(7); Autos 245(15), 246(21), 246(57); Neglig 1698, 1713, 1726, 1741; Trial 139.1(3), 143.

Francis v. Davis, TexCivApp–Beaumont, 517 SW2d 558.—Release 38; Trial 3(3).

Francis v. Denenberg, TexApp–Houston (1 Dist), 742 SW2d 789.—App & E 5.

Francis; Dow Chemical Co. v., Tex, 46 SW3d 237, on remand 2003 WL 2002542, decision clarified on denial of reh 2003 WL 21982515, review den.—App & E 207, 216(1), 852, 856(1), 930(1), 989, 1001(1), 1003(5), 1003(6), 1182; Fraud 3; Labor & Emp 861; Trial 18, 29(1).

Francis v. Dow Chemical Co., TexApp–Houston (1 Dist), 46 SW3d 264, review gr, rev 46 SW3d 237, on remand 2003 WL 2002542, decision clarified on denial of reh 2003 WL 21982515, review den.—App & E 216(1), 230, 232(0.5), 232(2), 237(1), 934(1), 1026, 1046.5, 1050.1(1), 1056.1(1), 1058(2); Civil R 1104, 1168, 1175, 1203, 1744, 1765; Courts 97(5); Damag 186; Evid 207(1), 264, 265(7), 314(1), 317(2), 555.9; Fraud 3, 12; Judgm 185(2), 185(5), 185.3(13); Pretrial Proc 434; Trial 18, 29(1), 43.

Francis v. Francis, Tex, 412 SW2d 29.—Divorce 209, 231, 234, 249.2; Hus & W 278(1), 278(2).

Francis; Francis v., Tex, 412 SW2d 29.—Divorce 209, 231, 234, 249.2; Hus & W 278(1), 278(2).

Francis v. Francis, TexCivApp–El Paso, 407 SW2d 295, writ gr, rev 412 SW2d 29.—App & E 931(1), 989; Divorce 231, 249.2, 252.3(4), 254(1), 255; Hus & W 264(3), 278(1).

Francis; Francis v., TexCivApp–El Paso, 407 SW2d 295, writ gr, rev 412 SW2d 29.—App & E 931(1), 989; Divorce 231, 249.2, 252.3(4), 254(1), 255; Hus & W 264(3), 278(1).

Francis; Gaylord Broadcasting Co., L.P. v., TexApp–Dallas, 7 SW3d 279, reh of petition for review den, review den 35 SW3d 599, reh overr.—Const Law 2170; Judgm 181(33), 185(2); Libel 10(4), 19, 51(5), 112(2), 123(2), 129.

Francis v. Herrin Transp. Co., Tex, 432 SW2d 710, appeal after remand 473 SW2d 664.—Courts 95(2), 97(6); Death 8, 39, 51; Lim of Act 120, 126, 165.

Francis v. Herrin Transp. Co., TexCivApp–Hous (1 Dist), 473 SW2d 664.—App & E 758.3(9), 1070(2); Autos 193(1), 242(1), 244(36.1), 245(50.1); Plead 20, 127(1); Trial 350.5(3), 352.5(6).

Francis v. Herrin Transp. Co., TexCivApp–Hous (14 Dist), 423 SW2d 610, writ gr, rev 432 SW2d 710, appeal after remand 473 SW2d 664.—Death 8, 11, 38, 39; Lim of Act 1, 2(1), 104.5, 165, 166; Neglig 204.

Francis v. International Service Ins. Co., Tex, 546 SW2d 57.—Insurance 1722, 1774, 2772, 2786.

Francis v. International Service Ins. Co., TexCivApp–Texarkana, 533 SW2d 408, writ gr, aff 546 SW2d 57.—Insurance 2772, 2786; Statut 190, 206.

Francis v. Johnny Johnson Backhoe Service, TexApp–El Paso, 777 SW2d 462. See Francis v. Johnson.

Francis v. Johnson, TexApp–El Paso, 777 SW2d 462, writ den.—Judgm 185(2); Work Comp 203, 2165.

Francis v. Kane, TexCivApp–Amarillo, 246 SW2d 279.—App & E 288, 1078(6); Assault 18.

Francis; Magnolia Petroleum Co. v., TexCivApp–Beaumont, 169 SW2d 286, writ refused.—Labor & Emp 26; Ship 84(1), 86(3).

Francis v. Marshall, TexApp–Houston (14 Dist), 841 SW2d 51, reh den.—Costs 260(1), 260(4), 260(5); Evid 332(1); Insurance 3484, 3557; Judgm 181(23), 720, 724.

Francis; Parks v., TexCivApp–Fort Worth, 202 SW2d 683.—Action 6; App & E 768, 781(1), 1138; Decl Judgm 61, 62; Inj 22; Plead 339.

Francis v. Pritchett, TexCivApp–El Paso, 278 SW2d 288, writ refused.—Mines 75, 78.1(8).

Francis v. Reed, TexCivApp–Amarillo, 428 SW2d 356.—Chat Mtg 150(1).

Francis; Sonnier v., CA5 (Tex), 217 FedAppx 410.—Const Law 2816, 3823; Hab Corp 816; Prisons 15(2), 15(3).

Francis v. Stanley, TexCivApp–Fort Worth, 574 SW2d 629.—Adv Poss 114(1), 115(1); App & E 241, 499(1), 500(1), 671(4), 719(1), 1170.6; Infants 24; Tresp to T T 37.1, 38(1), 41(1); Trial 25(4), 307(1).

Francis v. State, TexCrimApp, 36 SW3d 121, on remand 53 SW3d 685, reh overr, and petition for discretionary review refused.—Assault 96(5); Crim Law 1038.1(3.1).

Francis v. State, TexCrimApp, 109 SW2d 481.—Crim Law 1133.

Francis v. State, TexCrimApp, 106 SW2d 279, 132 TexCrim 591, reh den 109 SW2d 481.—Crim Law 1077.2(3).

Francis v. State, TexApp–Houston (1 Dist), 896 SW2d 406, petition for discretionary review gr, and petition for discretionary review refused, petition for discretionary review dism 922 SW2d 176.—Arrest 63.4(1), 63.5(4), 63.5(7); Crim Law 394.6(5), 1153(1), 1158(4), 1224(1).

Francis v. State, TexApp–Fort Worth, 53 SW3d 685, reh overr, and petition for discretionary review refused.—Crim Law 1162, 1163(4), 1172.1(1), 1172.1(5).

Francis v. State, TexApp–Austin, 877 SW2d 441, petition for discretionary review refused.—Controlled Subs 29,

30, 80; Crim Law 625.10(2.1); Mental H 434; Sent & Pun 1490.

Francis v. State, TexApp–San Antonio, 636 SW2d 591.—Crim Law 507(1), 535(1), 535(2), 552(3), 780(1), 792(2), 938(1), 956(4), 1130(4), 1172.2, 1173.2(6); Gr Jury 2.5, 19; Homic 1136, 1177; Witn 37(4).

Francis v. State, TexApp–Amarillo, 890 SW2d 510, reh overr, and petition for discretionary review refused.—Controlled Subs 6, 34, 82; Crim Law 13.1(1), 1159.2(1), 1159.2(2), 1159.2(4), 1159.2(7); Mun Corp 120; Statut 188.

Francis v. State, TexApp–Corpus Christi, 774 SW2d 768.—Crim Law 273.4(1), 275, 594(1), 594(3), 1026.10(2.1), 1026.10(5), 1081(1), 1151.

Francis v. State, TexApp–Houston (14 Dist), 909 SW2d 158.—Const Law 3309; Controlled Subs 45, 82; Crim Law 232, 264, 641.3(2), 641.3(3), 641.3(4), 878(2), 1035(5), 1144.13(3), 1158(1), 1158(3), 1159.2(7); Jury 33(5.15), 33(5.20).

Francis v. State, TexApp–Houston (14 Dist), 801 SW2d 548, petition for discretionary review refused by 805 SW2d 474.—Const Law 268(5), 4594(3); Crim Law 698(1), 814(1), 825(4), 829(18), 970(7), 1035(5), 1130(2), 1130(5); Homic 1458; Time 10(11).

Francis v. State, TexApp–Houston (14 Dist), 792 SW2d 783, petition for discretionary review refused.—Crim Law 641.13(6); Sent & Pun 1139, 1381(3).

Francis v. State, TexApp–Houston (14 Dist), 746 SW2d 276, petition for discretionary review refused.—Crim Law 1130(3); Rob 11, 24.15(2), 27(5).

Francis; State Farm Mut. Auto. Ins. Co. v., TexApp–Houston (1 Dist), 669 SW2d 424, ref nre.—Insurance 2677, 2687.

Francis v. Sterling, TexApp–Tyler, 45 SW3d 194.—Lis Pen 1, 11(1), 22(1).

Francis v. TDCJ-CID, TexApp–Fort Worth, 188 SW3d 799.—App & E 946; Prisons 13(7.1), 13(10).

Francis v. Thomas, TexComApp, 106 SW2d 257, 129 Tex 579.—Courts 89; Frds St of 110(1), 129(12); Spec Perf 28(2), 39, 41, 44.

Francis v. Tover, TexCivApp–Hous (1 Dist), 516 SW2d 492.—App & E 931(3), 1008.3(4); Autos 181(2).

Francis; U.S. v., CA5 (Tex), 487 F2d 968, cert den 94 SCt 1615, 416 US 908, 40 LEd2d 113.—Arrest 63.4(16); Controlled Subs 86, 94; Crim Law 339.6, 404.60, 1036.8; Postal 47; Sent & Pun 300.

Francis v. U.S. Home Imp. Co., TexApp–Houston (1 Dist), 742 SW2d 789. See Francis v. Denenberg.

Francis v. Wakefield, TexApp–Dallas, 646 SW2d 325.—Plead 111.3.

Francisco v. Barnhart, SDTex, 366 FSupp2d 461.—Const Law 4120; Social S 145.5.

Francisco v. Board of Dental Examiners, TexCivApp–Austin, 149 SW2d 619, writ refused.—Admin Law 470, 674; Const Law 2425(3), 3879, 3935, 4027, 4028, 4286; Health 105, 111, 141, 194, 207, 215.

Francisco, Inc. v. Texas Employment Com'n, TexApp–San Antonio, 803 SW2d 884. See Elena E. Francisco, Inc. v. Texas Employment Com'n.

Francis I. duPont & Co.; Ferguson v., NDTex, 369 FSupp 1099.—Brok 38(1).

Francitas Gas Co. v. Calvert, TexCivApp–Austin, 332 SW2d 389, ref nre.—Licens 29.

Franck; IG-LO Products Corp. v., CA5 (Tex), 812 F2d 222. See TechnicalChemical Co. v. IG-LO Products Corp.

Franco v. Allstate Ins. Co., Tex, 505 SW2d 789.—Death 38; Lim of Act 24(2), 182(5).

Franco v. Allstate Ins. Co., TexCivApp–San Antonio, 496 SW2d 150, writ gr, rev 505 SW2d 789.—Death 38, 39; Lim of Act 2(1), 24(2).

Franco v. Burtex Constructors, Inc., TexCivApp–Corpus Christi, 586 SW2d 590, ref nre.—App & E 1062.2; Autos 169, 172(5.1); Neglig 1560, 1591; Trial 351.5(6).

Franco v. Franco, TexApp–El Paso, 81 SW3d 319.—App & E 930(1), 946, 970(2), 1001(3), 1008.1(2), 1010.1(3), 1010.1(4), 1050.1(1), 1056.1(1); Child C 7, 509, 576, 904, 921(2), 921(4), 923(1); Pretrial Proc 41.

Franco; Franco v., TexApp–El Paso, 81 SW3d 319.—App & E 930(1), 946, 970(2), 1001(3), 1008.1(2), 1010.1(3), 1010.1(4), 1050.1(1), 1056.1(1); Child C 7, 509, 576, 904, 921(2), 921(4), 923(1); Pretrial Proc 41.

Franco; Gomez v., TexApp–Corpus Christi, 677 SW2d 231.—App & E 999(1), 1001(1), 1008.1(3); Evid 588, 589; Impl & C C 98; Sales 1.5, 3.1, 10; Trial 350.1, 350.2, 350.4(1).

Franco; Graham v., Tex, 488 SW2d 390.—Autos 227.5; Hus & W 247, 260; Neglig 575.

Franco v. Graham, TexCivApp–Corpus Christi, 470 SW2d 429, writ gr, aff as reformed 488 SW2d 390.—App & E 882(8), 1170.7, 1170.10; Autos 227.5, 243(5), 244(45), 244(58); Damag 185(1); Evid 188, 194, 215(1), 272; Hus & W 260, 270(3); Trial 139.1(3), 140(1), 142, 143; Witn 275(3), 405(2).

Franco; Johnson v., TexApp–Houston (1 Dist), 893 SW2d 302, writ dism woj.—Pretrial Proc 678; Prisons 10.

Franco v. Slavonic Mut. Fire Ins. Ass'n, TexApp–Houston (14 Dist), 154 SW3d 777.—App & E 223, 230, 242(1), 274(7), 275, 856(1); Insurance 3251, 3256, 3262, 3263; Judgm 183, 185.3(2), 185.3(12), 189; Lim of Act 43, 58(1), 95(1), 99(1).

Franco; Southwestern Bell Mobile Systems, Inc. v., Tex, 971 SW2d 52.—App & E 930(1), 1001(3), 1172(5); Civil R 1757, 1773; Damag 50.10.

Franco; Southwestern Bell Mobile Systems, Inc. v., TexApp–Corpus Christi, 951 SW2d 218, reh overr, and review gr, aff in part, rev in part 971 SW2d 52.—App & E 204(4), 216(6), 758.3(3), 1001(1); Civil R 1744, 1757, 1773; Costs 207; Damag 50.10, 192, 221(5.1); Evid 18, 43(2), 265(18); Plead 236(1), 236(6), 238(3); Trial 182.

Franco v. State, TexCrimApp, 552 SW2d 142.—Crim Law 516; Sent & Pun 2021; Stip 13.

Franco v. State, TexCrimApp, 492 SW2d 534.—Crim Law 864, 889; Rape 52(1); Witn 77.

Franco v. State, TexCrimApp, 491 SW2d 890.—Crim Law 1170.5(1); Witn 297(13.1).

Franco v. State, TexCrimApp, 491 SW2d 876.—Crim Law 372(13), 1030(1), 1184(2).

Franco v. State, TexCrimApp, 400 SW2d 548.—Crim Law 339.6, 1169.5(3).

Franco v. State, TexCrimApp, 312 SW2d 638.—Larc 40(2), 59.

Franco v. State, TexCrimApp, 147 SW2d 1089, 141 TexCrim 246.—Crim Law 917(1), 923(1), 923(2), 925(1), 938(1), 957(1), 1038.1(5), 1147, 1152(2), 1155, 1156(3), 1156(4), 1156(5); Homic 1326; Jury 83(1); New Tr 143(1).

Franco v. State, TexCrimApp, 103 SW2d 380, 132 TexCrim 164.—Witn 337(20).

Franco v. State, TexApp–Austin, 82 SW3d 425, petition for discretionary review refused.—Autos 421; Crim Law 1169.1(7).

Franco; State v., TexApp–San Antonio, 180 SW3d 219, reh overr, and petition for discretionary review refused (2 pets).—Crim Law 338(7), 388.2, 474.2, 1153(1).

Franco v. State, TexApp–El Paso, 25 SW3d 26, petition for discretionary review refused, untimely filed, and petition for discretionary review refused.—Crim Law 469.1, 472, 476.6, 695.5, 1169.9; Homic 1009; Searches 173.1, 174.

Franco v. State, TexApp–El Paso, 737 SW2d 40, petition for discretionary review refused.—Const Law 266(3.1), 4658(4); Crim Law 784(1), 824(8); Larc 59.

Franco; Tidelands Life Ins. Co. v., TexApp–Corpus Christi, 711 SW2d 728, ref nre.—Antitrust 221, 393; Insurance 1631, 3426.

Franco; Transportation Ins. Co. v., TexApp–Amarillo, 821 SW2d 751, writ den.—Costs 194.46; Decl Judgm 61, 172, 390, 393; Lim of Act 127(1), 127(4).

Franco; WesTex Abilene Associates, L.P. v., TexApp–Eastland, 3 SW3d 45.—Brok 86(1); Courts 12(2.30); Torts 222, 242.

Franco-American Securities; State v., TexCivApp–Galveston, 172 SW2d 731, writ refused wom.—Bound 3(6), 3(7), 10, 11, 37(3); Courts 90(1); Deeds 100, 114(1); Pub Lands 176(1); States 209.

Francois v. State, TexCrimApp, 488 SW2d 454.—Sent & Pun 2021.

Francone v. Southern Pac. Co., CCA5 (Tex), 145 F2d 732.—Fed Cts 405, 893, 904; Jury 92; R R 350(13).

Franco-Torres; U.S. v., CA5 (Tex), 869 F2d 797.—Crim Law 1134(3), 1158(1); Sent & Pun 761, 976, 980, 981.

Franecke v. Dolenz, TexApp–Austin, 668 SW2d 481, dism.—App & E 859, 914.3; Proc 74, 77, 145.

Frank, Ex parte, TexCrimApp, 453 SW2d 477.—Pardon 23.1, 24.

Frank, In re, BkrtcySDTex, 254 BR 368.—Bankr 2404, 2443, 2467, 2468, 3716.30(8); Sec Tran 230.

Frank; Abell v., CA5 (Tex), 625 F2d 653.—Fed Cts 50, 53.

Frank; Alexander v., NDTex, 777 FSupp 516.—Admin Law 701; Civil R 1138, 1140, 1225(2), 1545, 1549, 1551, 1571; Fed Cts 12.1, 192; Work Comp 1833, 2085.

Frank v. Barnhart, EDTex, 455 FSupp2d 554.—Social S 140.30, 143.40, 143.65, 147, 148.15.

Frank v. Bear Stearns & Co., CA5 (Tex), 128 F3d 919, am on denial of reh.—Fed Cts 161, 191, 241, 374; Rem of C 2, 19(8), 25(1), 107(7), 107(9).

Frank v. Bear, Stearns & Co., TexApp–Houston (14 Dist), 11 SW3d 380, review den.—App & E 863, 934(1); Contracts 187(1); Judgm 185(6); Neglig 210, 215, 1692; Sec Reg 260, 302.

Frank v. Bradshaw, TexApp–Houston (1 Dist), 920 SW2d 699, reh overr.—Insurance 3234; Judgm 181(2), 181(7), 185(2); Lim of Act 13, 175.

Frank v. Canavati, TexCivApp–San Antonio, 612 SW2d 221, ref nre.—App & E 962; Pretrial Proc 699.

Frank; Castillo v., CA5 (Tex), 70 F3d 382.—U S Mag 24.1, 29, 31.

Frank v. Corbett, TexApp–Waco, 682 SW2d 587.—Const Law 3974; Judgm 106(1); Plead 287, 288.

Frank v. Delta Airlines Inc., CA5 (Tex), 314 F3d 195.—Fed Civ Proc 1773, 1829, 1835; Fed Cts 776; Libel 1.7; Mast & S 325; States 18.3, 18.15.

Frank; Delta Bail Bonds v., TexApp–Dallas, 936 SW2d 654. See Monroe v. Frank.

Frank; Florence v., NDTex, 774 FSupp 1054.—Civil R 1018, 1137, 1218(4), 1225(2), 1536, 1544, 1545, 1549; Labor & Emp 1208, 1213, 1219(9), 1597.

Frank v. Harris County, CA5 (Tex), 118 FedAppx 799, cert den 125 SCt 2530, 544 US 1062, 161 LEd2d 1112.—Civil R 1189, 1244, 1252, 1351(5); Sheriffs 21.

Frank; Jones v., WDTex, 622 FSupp 1119.—Civil R 1088(4); Crim Law 1174(1); Evid 152; Fed Civ Proc 1278, 2197; Fed Cts 631, 663; Witn 327.

Frank v. Kuhnreich, TexCivApp–San Antonio, 546 SW2d 844, ref nre.—Contracts 143.5, 318; Judgm 187; Land & Ten 37, 48(2), 103(1), 154(3), 154(4); Spec Perf 64.

Frank; Minton v., Tex, 545 SW2d 442.—Atty & C 17; Bail 60; Statut 181(1), 214.

Frank v. Minton, TexCivApp–Waco, 531 SW2d 413, writ gr, rev 545 SW2d 442.—Atty & C 17; Bail 60; Inj 89(5).

Frank; Monroe v., TexApp–Dallas, 936 SW2d 654, writ dism woj.—Antitrust 212, 397; App & E 219(2), 852, 931(1), 989, 1010.1(1), 1010.2, 1012.1(5), 1175(2), 1182; Damag 57.40; Statut 174, 176, 181(1), 181(2), 184, 188, 212.4.

Frank; Odom v., CA5 (Tex), 3 F3d 839.—Civil R 1137, 1209, 1535, 1539, 1542, 1548, 1551; Fed Cts 776, 850.1.

Frank; Odom v., NDTex, 782 FSupp 50.—Civil R 1584, 1593, 1595; Interest 31, 39(2.45).

Frank; Odom v., NDTex, 781 FSupp 1191, rev 3 F3d 839.
—Civil R 1121, 1137, 1548, 1551.

Frank v. Reese, TexCivApp–Hous (1 Dist), 594 SW2d 119.
—Const Law 1106; Divorce 261, 269(4), 269(9), 269(14).

Frank; Shaw v., TexCivApp–El Paso, 334 SW2d 476.—
Execution 20, 21, 51, 264; Judgm 181(2), 181(11),
185.2(4); Mines 74(3).

Frank v. Starnes Corp., TexCivApp–Dallas, 449 SW2d
538.—Judgm 181(24), 185(5), 186.

Frank v. State, TexCrimApp, 688 SW2d 863.—Assault
96(3); Crim Law 835, 1043(1), 1134(2), 1173.2(3); Homic
807, 1484.

Frank v. State, TexCrimApp, 558 SW2d 12.—Crim Law
913(1), 1038.1(6), 1171.1(1); Rob 17(1), 27(1).

Frank v. State, TexCrimApp, 103 SW2d 154.—Crim Law
1182.

Frank v. State, TexApp–Houston (1 Dist), 190 SW3d 136,
petition for discretionary review refused.—Crim Law
1139, 1590.

Frank v. State, TexApp–Houston (1 Dist), 992 SW2d 756,
reh overr, and petition for discretionary review refused.
—Crim Law 338(1), 632(4), 1153(1); Sent & Pun 313,
537.

Frank v. State, TexApp–Fort Worth, 183 SW3d 63, petition for discretionary review refused.—Crim Law 59(3),
59(4), 59(5), 80, 338(7), 394.6(5), 412.1(1), 412.2(3),
417(15), 438(1), 438(5.1), 438(6), 438(7), 519(1), 522(1),
789(4), 938(1), 942(2), 1134(8), 1144(1), 1144.13(2.1),
1144.13(6), 1153(1), 1156(3), 1159.2(7), 1159.2(9),
1159.4(1); Homic 569, 581, 612, 1207; Ind & Inf 83.

Frank; Stein v., TexCivApp–Dallas, 575 SW2d 399.—App
& E 373(1), 389(1), 389(3), 436, 452; Atty & C 62;
Courts 207.4(2), 209(2); Judges 47(2); Mand 68.

Frank v. Terrell, CA5 (Tex), 858 F2d 1090.—Prisons
4(14).

Frank; Texas Unemployment Compensation Commission v., TexCivApp–Austin, 229 SW2d 399.—Unemp
Comp 462.

Frank v. Walton, TexCivApp–Texarkana, 326 SW2d 295,
ref nre.—App & E 1062.1.

Frank v. Weiner, TexCivApp–Galveston, 229 SW2d 186.
—App & E 846(2), 846(5), 934(2), 1024.2; Inj 132,
138.31.

Frank; White v., CA5 (Tex), 895 F2d 243, cert den 111
SCt 232, 498 US 890, 112 LEd2d 192.—Admin Law 229;
Civil R 1513.

Frank; White v., WDTex, 718 FSupp 592, aff 895 F2d
243, cert den 111 SCt 232, 498 US 890, 112 LEd2d 192.
—Admin Law 229; Armed S 115(2), 115(7); Civil R
1502, 1513, 1514, 1518, 1524, 1530; Fed Civ Proc 2533.1,
2543.

Frank v. Xerox Corp., CA5 (Tex), 347 F3d 130, reh den.
—Civil R 1122, 1139, 1140, 1147, 1238, 1505(7), 1542,
1544; Fed Civ Proc 2497.1; Lim of Act 58(1).

Franka v. Velasquez, TexApp–San Antonio, 216 SW3d
409, reh overr, and reh overr.—Health 770; Mun Corp
745; Plead 111.43.

Frank A. Smith Sales, Inc., In re, TexApp–Corpus
Christi, 32 SW3d 871.—App & E 516; Damag 15;
Mand 4(1), 4(4), 12; Pretrial Proc 36.1, 41.

Frank A. Smith Sales, Inc. v. Atlantic Aero, Inc., Tex-
App–Corpus Christi, 31 SW3d 742.—App & E 893(1),
1010.1(8.1); Const Law 3964; Courts 12(2.1), 12(2.5),
12(2.10), 12(2.15), 15, 35, 39.

Frank B. Hall & Co.; Bard v., TexApp–San Antonio, 767
SW2d 839, writ den.—App & E 714(5), 837(4); Pretrial
Proc 582, 583, 587, 591, 684.

Frank B. Hall & Co. v. Beach, Inc., TexApp–Corpus
Christi, 733 SW2d 251, ref nre.—App & E 215(1),
1078(1), 1078(5); Damag 73, 190, 221(5.1); Evid 474(20);
Insurance 1673, 2681, 2895, 3417; Jury 136(2), 136(3);
Trial 352.10.

Frank B. Hall & Co., Inc. v. Buck, TexApp–Houston (14
Dist), 678 SW2d 612, ref nre, cert den 105 SCt 2704, 472

US 1009, 86 LEd2d 720.—App & E 1004(7), 1070(2),
1170.7; Contracts 9(1), 28(3), 29; Corp 423; Damag 94,
140, 184; Evid 130, 588; Fraud 58(1), 62; Libel 1, 23.1,
33, 38(1), 38(4), 41, 51(1), 51(4), 71, 94(1), 101(5), 112(1),
112(2), 112(3), 113, 120(2), 121(0.5), 123(2), 125; Trial
350.3(4); Witn 363(1), 368, 372(1).

Franke v. Cheatham, Tex, 303 SW2d 355, 157 Tex 397.—
App & E 1071.5, 1135, 1177(1); Wills 219.

Franke; Cheatham v., TexCivApp–Austin, 298 SW2d 202,
rev 303 SW2d 355, 157 Tex 397.—Atty & C 22; Courts
472.4(6), 480(1).

Franke; Fisher v., TexCivApp–Texarkana, 321 SW2d 903.
—App & E 989, 1177(7); Autos 244(12), 244(34),
244(35); Trial 356(3).

Franke v. Franke, TexCivApp–Eastland, 545 SW2d 545,
ref nre.—Partit 14; Perp 4(1), 4(15.1); Trusts 61(1).

Franke; Franke v., TexCivApp–Eastland, 545 SW2d 545,
ref nre.—Partit 14; Perp 4(1), 4(15.1); Trusts 61(1).

Franke v. Franke, TexCivApp–Corpus Christi, 373 SW2d
891.—App & E 554(2), 554(3), 624, 627, 765, 770(1),
773(2), 907(3).

Franke; Franke v., TexCivApp–Corpus Christi, 373
SW2d 891.—App & E 554(2), 554(3), 624, 627, 765,
770(1), 773(2), 907(3).

Franke v. Jones, TexCivApp–Amarillo, 170 SW2d 795,
writ refused.—Brok 54, 63(1); Princ & A 175(3).

Franke v. Zimmerman, TexCivApp–Austin, 526 SW2d
257.—App & E 1010.1(3); Atty & C 129(2).

Frankel; Lone Star Machinery Corp. v., TexCivApp–
Beaumont, 564 SW2d 135.—App & E 927(7); Fraud
58(4).

Frankel's Estate v. U. S., CA5 (Tex), 512 F2d 1007.—Int
Rev 4147, 4183.10; Mines 79.1(2).

Frankenburg Import–Export Ltd.; Nissho-Iwai American Corp. v., CA5 (Tex), 845 F2d 1300. See Nissho-
Iwai American Corp. v. Kline.

Frankenstein v. Acme Inv. Co., TexCivApp–Eastland, 87
SW2d 744, writ dism.—Plead 406(3).

Frankfort Distilleries v. Burgess, TexCivApp–Beaumont, 105 SW2d 410.—Venue 70.

Frankfort Distillers Corp.; Rosenthal v., CA5 (Tex), 193
F2d 137.—Corp 673; Fed Civ Proc 607; Fed Cts 417;
Rem of C 111.

Frankfurt v. City of Dallas, TexCivApp–Dallas, 299
SW2d 722.—Em Dom 205, 255; Evid 142(1), 142(3), 380.

Frankfurt v. Decker, TexCivApp–Dallas, 180 SW2d 985.
—App & E 219(2); Fraud 22(1); Frds St of 58(2);
Land & Ten 80(2), 80(4); Witn 258.

Frankfurt; Parks v., TexCivApp–Beaumont, 476 SW2d
717, ref nre.—App & E 758.3(2), 927(7), 1172(3); Contracts 150, 154, 164, 176(2); Sec Tran 88.

Frankfurt; Parks v., TexCivApp–Waco, 465 SW2d 846.—
Inj 150, 157.

Frankfurt v. Texas Turnpike Authority, TexCivApp–
Texarkana, 311 SW2d 261.—Em Dom 131, 158, 195,
202(1), 222(4); Evid 498.5, 555.6(2).

Frankfurt v. Wilson, TexCivApp–Dallas, 353 SW2d 490.
—App & E 1170.12; Consp 19; Fraud 11(1), 11(2), 50,
58(1); Lis Pen 20; Princ & A 23(5), 145(1).

Frankfurt Finance Co. v. Treadaway, TexCivApp–Dallas, 159 SW2d 514, writ refused wom.—Contracts
171(1), 318; Land & Ten 95.

Frankfurt Finance Corp. v. Cox, TexCivApp–Dallas, 142
SW2d 553.—App & E 846(5); Usury 16, 32.

Frankfurt's Texas Inv. Corp. v. Trinity Sav. & Loan
Ass'n, TexCivApp–Dallas, 414 SW2d 190, ref nre.—
Evid 43(3); Garn 32, 108, 203; Impl & C C 5; Judgm
181(11), 185(2), 185(6), 185.1(1), 185.3(1); Plead 404,
426(1).

Frank Gillman Pontiac; Hawkins v., CA5 (Tex), 102
FedAppx 394, motion gr Yang v. Yu, 130 P3d 729.—
Damag 57.58; Fed Civ Proc 2497.1.

Frank G. Love Envelopes, Inc.; Germany v., TexCiv-App–Texarkana, 582 SW2d 889, ref nre.—Judgm 181(33); Trover 22.

Frank Hrubetz & Co., Inc.; Garza v., TexCivApp–San Antonio, 496 SW2d 143.—Corp 665(1), 673.

Frankiewicz v. National Comp Associates, Tex, 633 SW2d 505.—Contracts 116(1), 117(3), 117(7).

Frankiewicz v. National Comp Associates, TexCivApp–Dallas, 620 SW2d 762, rev 633 SW2d 505.—Contracts 117(7).

Frank Inv. Co.; Borrett v., TexCivApp–El Paso, 483 SW2d 376.—Bills & N 92(1).

Frank Jester Development Co.; Commissioners' Court v., TexCivApp–Dallas, 199 SW2d 1004, ref nre.—Dedi 31, 35(1); Mand 10, 82; Mun Corp 651.

Frank Jones Ins. Agency, Inc.; MMP, Ltd. v., Tex, 710 SW2d 59. See MMP, Ltd. v. Jones.

Frank Jones Ins. Agency, Inc.; MMP, Ltd. v., TexApp–San Antonio, 695 SW2d 208. See MMP, Ltd. v. Jones.

Frank Kasmir Associates; Rockland Industries, Inc. v., NDTex, 470 FSupp 1176.—Fed Civ Proc 1600(5); Frds St of 106(1), 127, 139(1), 144; Sales 1(4).

Frank Kasmir Associates, Inc.; Houston Drapery Mfrs., Inc. v., TexCivApp–Waco, 538 SW2d 161.—App & E 907(1); Plead 111.42(5), 111.42(10).

Frankland; Murray v., TexCivApp–Houston, 347 SW2d 374.—Fraud 4; Plead 111.42(2), 111.42(10); Venue 5.3(8), 8.5(2).

Franklin, Ex parte, TexCrimApp, 72 SW3d 671.—Hab Corp 401, 462, 508, 715.1, 845.

Franklin, Ex parte, TexCrimApp, 757 SW2d 778.—Ind & Inf 113; Sent & Pun 78, 80, 373; Weap 4.

Franklin, Ex parte, TexApp–Tyler, 683 SW2d 33.—Child S 459, 497.

Franklin, Ex parte, TexCivApp–Amarillo, 393 SW2d 632, dism.—Infants 254; Jury 19.5.

Franklin, In re, BkrtcyEDTex, 111 BR 582.—Bankr 2436.

Franklin, Matter of, TexApp–Texarkana, 699 SW2d 689. —Infants 68.7(1), 68.7(3), 68.8.

Franklin; Cain v., TexCivApp–Austin, 476 SW2d 952, ref nre.—Contracts 138(1); Judges 54; Judgm 9.

Franklin v. Cherco Equipment Co., TexCivApp–Eastland, 461 SW2d 188.—Venue 8.5(7).

Franklin v. City of Galveston, TexCivApp–Galveston, 256 SW2d 997, ref nre.—Mun Corp 855; Neglig 1037(4).

Franklin v. Crosby Typesetting Co., CA5 (Tex), 568 F2d 1098, reh den 570 F2d 1391, cert den 99 SCt 147, 439 US 847, 58 LEd2d 149.—Labor & Emp 1208, 1219(12).

Franklin v. Crosby Typesetting Co., NDTex, 411 FSupp 1167, aff 568 F2d 1098, reh den 570 F2d 1391, cert den 99 SCt 147, 439 US 847, 58 LEd2d 149.—Civil R 1536, 1544, 1545, 1555; Fed Cts 425; Labor & Emp 1215, 1219(12).

Franklin v. Delgado, CA5 (Tex), 262 F2d 439.—Evid 555.5; Fed Cts 900, 911; Labor & Emp 2829, 2893, 2897, 2901, 3005, 3012.

Franklin; Doe v., TexApp–El Paso, 930 SW2d 921, reh overr.—App & E 852, 863; Judgm 181(33), 185(2), 185(6); Labor & Emp 3062; Neglig 210, 216, 220, 258, 433, 1161, 1662; Parent & C 13(1).

Franklin v. Donoho, TexApp–Austin, 774 SW2d 308.—App & E 846(5); Parties 35.39, 35.75.

Franklin v. Enserch, Inc., TexApp–Amarillo, 961 SW2d 704.—App & E 756, 1079; Civil R 1166, 1179, 1744; Damag 50.10, 208(6); Judgm 183, 184, 185.3(13).

Franklin; Fonmeadow Property Owners' Ass'n, Inc. v., TexApp–Houston (1 Dist), 817 SW2d 104.—App & E 946; Costs 194.12, 252, 264; Covenants 132(2).

Franklin v. Fugro-McClelland (Southwest), Inc., SDTex, 16 FSupp2d 732.—Insurance 2101, 2261.

Franklin v. Geotechnical Services, Inc., TexApp–Fort Worth, 819 SW2d 219, writ den.—Const Law 3965(3); Courts 12(2.1), 12(2.30); Pretrial Proc 201.1.

Franklin v. Go Services, Inc., TexCivApp–Eastland, 461 SW2d 186.—Judgm 185.3(16).

Franklin; Haug v., TexApp–Austin, 690 SW2d 646.—Action 6; Admin Law 701; Colleges 6(5), 9.30(5); Const Law 947, 3866, 3875, 3879.

Franklin; Hawkins v., TexCivApp–Eastland, 567 SW2d 596.—App & E 863; Corp 121(4).

Franklin; Ireland v., TexApp–San Antonio, 950 SW2d 155, reh overr.—App & E 846(5), 920(3); Contracts 65.5, 116(1), 142; Inj 138.18, 147; Labor & Emp 40(1), 40(2), 40(3).

Franklin v. Jackson, TexApp–El Paso, 847 SW2d 306, reh overr, and writ den.—Agric 3.3(2); Bailm 1, 2; Contracts 103, 136, 141(1), 143(2), 153, 176(2); Judgm 181(2), 181(3), 181(19), 185(2); Land & Ten 20; Sales 1(1), 4(1), 5.

Franklin; Jonco Aircraft Corp. v., NDTex, 114 FSupp 392, rev 74 SCt 126, 346 US 868, 98 LEd 378, reh den 74 SCt 272, 346 US 917, 98 LEd 412.—Admin Law 741, 908.1; Labor & Emp 1866, 1910; U S 125(28.1); War 405.

Franklin v. Kyle, TexApp–Waco, 899 SW2d 405, reh overr.—Crim Law 1023(3), 1023(10); Decl Judgm 84; Inj 74.

Franklin; Lamb v., TexApp–Amarillo, 976 SW2d 339.—Autos 245(78); Damag 185(1), 186, 208(5), 221(7); Judgm 199(5); Trial 356(1).

Franklin v. Lone Star Gas Co., TexApp–Amarillo, 961 SW2d 704. See Franklin v. Enserch, Inc.

Franklin v. Love, TexCivApp–Amarillo, 276 SW2d 927, ref nre.—Trial 365.1(7).

Franklin v. Lynaugh, USTex, 108 SCt 2320, 487 US 164, 101 LEd2d 155, reh den 109 SCt 25, 487 US 1263, 101 LEd2d 976.—Crim Law 796, 870; Sent & Pun 1685, 1780(3), 1784(4).

Franklin v. Lynaugh, CA5 (Tex), 860 F2d 165, cert den 109 SCt 332, 488 US 935, 102 LEd2d 349.—Fed Civ Proc 2792; Hab Corp 896.

Franklin v. Lynaugh, CA5 (Tex), 823 F2d 98, cert gr in part 108 SCt 221, 484 US 891, 98 LEd2d 180, aff 108 SCt 2320, 487 US 164, 101 LEd2d 155, reh den 109 SCt 25, 487 US 1263, 101 LEd2d 976.—Hab Corp 497, 498, 508.

Franklin v. M. K. & T. Ry. Co. of Tex., TexCivApp–Dallas, 221 SW2d 918, writ refused.—R R 358(1), 396(1), 396(2), 400(5).

Franklin; National Life & Acc. Ins. Co. v., TexCivApp–Hous (14 Dist), 506 SW2d 765, ref nre.—Insurance 2589(1), 2590(1), 2590(2), 2607.

Franklin; Old Republic Ins. Co. v., TexApp–Fort Worth, 727 SW2d 701, ref nre.—Compromise 21; Judgm 72; Mtg 572; Stip 6.

Franklin; Pat H. Stanford, Inc. v., TexCivApp–El Paso, 312 SW2d 703.—Bills & N 488; Plead 343, 345(1.3).

Franklin v. Pietzsch, TexCivApp–Dallas, 334 SW2d 214, ref nre.—Cem 3, 4; Const Law 2486; Statut 184, 203, 223.4.

Franklin v. Pietzsch, TexCivApp–Dallas, 325 SW2d 450. —Inj 138.31.

Franklin v. Rainey, TexCivApp–Dallas, 556 SW2d 583.—Judgm 585(5), 586(2), 634, 720, 739.

Franklin; Restivo v., TexCivApp–Waco, 177 SW2d 811, writ refused.—Tax 2900, 2936, 2962; Tresp to T T 6.1.

Franklin v. Safeway Stores, Inc., TexCivApp–Dallas, 504 SW2d 514, ref nre.—App & E 758.3(11); Neglig 1076, 1229, 1594, 1595, 1625, 1670, 1708.

Franklin; Shabazz v., NDTex, 380 FSupp2d 793.—Civil R 1448; Const Law 4826; Convicts 6; Fed Civ Proc 417, 851, 2734; Judgm 585(5); Lim of Act 58(1).

Franklin v. Sherman Independent School Dist., TexApp–Dallas, 53 SW3d 398, review den, and review den, and review den, and review den.—App & E 907(4), 962, 1061.2; Const Law 3879; Pretrial Proc 581, 583, 587, 676, 678.

Franklin v. Smalldridge, TexCivApp–Corpus Christi, 616 SW2d 655.—App & E 171(1); Evid 37, 81, 571(1); Marriage 4.1, 11, 13, 40(5), 40.1(2).

Franklin; Stanolind Oil & Gas Co. v., CA5 (Tex), 193 F2d 561.—Neglig 402, 1045(3), 1067, 1101, 1717.

Franklin v. State, TexCrimApp, 138 SW3d 351.—Crim Law 1166.16; Jury 33(4), 131(18).

Franklin v. State, TexCrimApp, 12 SW3d 473, on remand 23 SW3d 81, petition for discretionary review gr, and petition for discretionary review gr, aff 138 SW3d 351.—Crim Law 1042, 1043(1); Jury 131(1), 131(3), 131(18).

Franklin v. State, TexCrimApp, 693 SW2d 420, cert den 106 SCt 1238, 475 US 1031, 89 LEd2d 346.—Crim Law 139, 142, 359, 713, 723(1), 726, 796, 867, 1128(2), 1169.5(1), 1171.1(6); Double J 107.1, 108; Ind & Inf 32(3); Jury 107, 137(1); Witn 347.

Franklin v. State, TexCrimApp, 659 SW2d 831.—Double J 109; Ind & Inf 119, 167, 171; Rec S Goods 1, 7(6).

Franklin v. State, TexCrimApp, 640 SW2d 878.—Rob 27(1).

Franklin v. State, TexCrimApp, 607 SW2d 574.—Crim Law 1044.1(2), 1177.5(3); Rob 17(3).

Franklin v. State, TexCrimApp, 606 SW2d 818, appeal after remand 693 SW2d 420, cert den 106 SCt 1238, 475 US 1031, 89 LEd2d 346.—Crim Law 721(1); Witn 307, 347.

Franklin v. State, TexCrimApp, 576 SW2d 621.—Const Law 3856; Crim Law 884; Jury 22(1).

Franklin v. State, TexCrimApp, 523 SW2d 947.—Crim Law 1083.

Franklin v. State, TexCrimApp, 494 SW2d 825.—Controlled Subs 30, 69, 80; Crim Law 363, 478(1), 695(2), 1043(1), 1043(2).

Franklin v. State, TexCrimApp, 488 SW2d 826.—Crim Law 369.1, 369.2(1), 1169.11.

Franklin v. State, TexCrimApp, 478 SW2d 932.—Crim Law 531(3), 1038.1(7).

Franklin v. State, TexCrimApp, 457 SW2d 53.—Burg 42(4); Crim Law 393(1), 553, 661, 789(4).

Franklin v. State, TexCrimApp, 409 SW2d 422.—Burg 41(1); Crim Law 867, 1086.14.

Franklin v. State, TexCrimApp, 383 SW2d 931.—Autos 335.

Franklin v. State, TexCrimApp, 363 SW2d 137.—Crim Law 863(2), 1174(1), 1174(5).

Franklin v. State, TexCrimApp, 331 SW2d 751, 169 TexCrim 79.—Assault 92(4); Crim Law 863(2), 884.

Franklin v. State, TexCrimApp, 301 SW2d 140, 164 TexCrim 480.—Crim Law 878(3).

Franklin v. State, TexCrimApp, 291 SW2d 322, 163 TexCrim 330.—Crim Law 369.6, 374; Int Liq 249.

Franklin v. State, TexCrimApp, 261 SW2d 324, 159 TexCrim 50.—Crim Law 1087.1(2).

Franklin v. State, TexCrimApp, 247 SW2d 562, 157 TexCrim 177.—Int Liq 223(1), 236(3).

Franklin v. State, TexCrimApp, 227 SW2d 814, 154 TexCrim 375.—Sent & Pun 1381(2); Stip 18(7).

Franklin v. State, TexCrimApp, 183 SW2d 573, 147 TexCrim 636.—Crim Law 741(1), 742(1), 824(1), 1119(5), 1128(1), 1159.2(3), 1159.2(7); Weap 11(1), 17(4).

Franklin v. State, TexCrimApp, 149 SW2d 962, 141 TexCrim 479.—Crim Law 730(1), 1091(3), 1091(5), 1091(11), 1144.18.

Franklin v. State, TexCrimApp, 144 SW2d 581, 140 TexCrim 251.—Crim Law 273.2(2), 535(0.5), 535(1), 535(2).

Franklin v. State, TexCrimApp, 128 SW2d 389, 137 TexCrim 136.—Assault 96(7); Crim Law 814(1), 1038.3, 1056.1(4), 1170.5(1); Homic 507, 1136, 1388, 1400, 1486.

Franklin v. State, TexCrimApp, 109 SW2d 482, 133 TexCrim 179.—Bail 94.

Franklin v. State, TexApp–Houston (1 Dist), 219 SW3d 92.—Crim Law 795(2.5); Ind & Inf 191(5); Larc 79; Sent & Pun 1260, 1286.

Franklin v. State, TexApp–Houston (1 Dist), 976 SW2d 780, petition for discretionary review refused.—Arrest 63.1, 63.4(8); Controlled Subs 113; Crim Law 1134(6), 1158(2); Searches 24, 62.

Franklin v. State, TexApp–Houston (1 Dist), 702 SW2d 241.—Crim Law 627.5(6), 627.6(2), 627.6(5), 627.7(3), 1035(2), 1038.1(1), 1166(10.10), 1172.1(2), 1172.1(3); Rob 7, 27(2).

Franklin v. State, TexApp–Houston (1 Dist), 682 SW2d 426.—Crim Law 552(2); Fish 15; Ind & Inf 167.

Franklin v. State, TexApp–Fort Worth, 193 SW3d 616, reh overr.—Crim Law 1144.13(2.1), 1144.13(6), 1159.2(1), 1159.2(7), 1159.2(8), 1159.3(2), 1159.4(2); Ind & Inf 179; Infants 20.

Franklin v. State, TexApp–Fort Worth, 733 SW2d 715.—Crim Law 800(2), 1181(1).

Franklin v. State, TexApp–Dallas, 774 SW2d 794, petition for discretionary review refused, untimely filed.—Crim Law 412(3), 412.1(1), 517(7), 530, 713, 730(1), 730(5).

Franklin v. State, TexApp–Dallas, 658 SW2d 671.—Crim Law 1044.1(2); Ind & Inf 71.4(8).

Franklin v. State, TexApp–Texarkana, 23 SW3d 81, petition for discretionary review gr, and petition for discretionary review gr, aff 138 SW3d 351.—Crim Law 1166.16; Jury 33(4), 131(1), 131(3).

Franklin v. State, TexApp–Texarkana, 992 SW2d 698, petition for discretionary review refused.—Crim Law 273.1(2), 274(3.1), 419(1.10), 419(2.10), 662.8, 795(1.5), 795(2.10), 795(2.30), 814(5); Double J 107.1, 132.1, 166.1, 167; Ind & Inf 191(0.5); Sent & Pun 317.

Franklin v. State, TexApp–Texarkana, 986 SW2d 349, petition for discretionary review gr, rev 12 SW3d 473, on remand 23 SW3d 81, petition for discretionary review gr, and petition for discretionary review gr, aff 138 SW3d 351.—Crim Law 338(7), 369.2(5), 417(15), 419(2.20), 627.5(6), 641.3(4), 662.8, 670, 721(3), 721(4), 749, 796, 1038.3, 1090.12, 1153(1), 1166(10.10), 1166.16; Infants 20; Jury 149; Sent & Pun 238.

Franklin v. State, TexApp–El Paso, 631 SW2d 519, ref nre.—Antitrust 128, 193.

Franklin v. State, TexApp–Beaumont, 913 SW2d 234, petition for discretionary review refused.—Arrest 63.4(4); Controlled Subs 125; Crim Law 394.5(2), 394.5(4), 394.6(5), 1134(6), 1144.12, 1158(2), 1158(4); Searches 15, 24, 26, 36.1, 40.1, 162, 163, 171, 173.1, 180.

Franklin v. State, TexApp–Beaumont, 858 SW2d 537, petition for discretionary review refused.—Crim Law 419(2.15), 552(3), 594(1), 1063(1), 1064(1), 1159.2(2); Homic 1184.

Franklin v. State, TexApp–Tyler, 733 SW2d 537.—Autos 339, 355(10); Crim Law 665(4), 878(3), 1144.12; Witn 2(1), 2(2).

Franklin v. State, TexApp–Houston (14 Dist), 928 SW2d 707.—Crim Law 511.1(3), 511.1(7), 511.2, 1144.13(2.1), 1159.2(2), 1159.2(9).

Franklin v. State, TexApp–Houston (14 Dist), 855 SW2d 114.—Autos 349.5(10); Crim Law 394.6(5), 1153(1), 1158(4); Searches 47.1, 49.

Franklin v. State, TexApp–Houston (14 Dist), 742 SW2d 66, petition for discretionary review refused.—Courts 70; Crim Law 713, 720(1), 720(9), 728(2), 1035(1), 1171.1(2.1).

Franklin v. State, TexApp–Houston (14 Dist), 632 SW2d 839.—Const Law 4733(1); Homic 554, 557, 1168; Sent & Pun 1918, 2020.

Franklin; Tarka v., CA5 (Tex), 891 F2d 102, cert den 110 SCt 1809, 494 US 1080, 108 LEd2d 940, reh den 110 SCt 2605, 496 US 913, 110 LEd2d 285.—Colleges 9.40.

Franklin v. Texas Dept. of Public Safety, TexCivApp–Eastland, 462 SW2d 350.—Judgm 181(15.1).

Franklin; Trinity Const. Co. v., TexCivApp–Beaumont, 323 SW2d 668.—Autos 244(12), 244(34), 244(35); Jury 26, 28(6).

Franklin v. Wilcox, TexApp–Fort Worth, 53 SW3d 739.
—App & E 5, 859; Breach of P 21.

Franklin; Williams Distributing Co. v., Tex, 898 SW2d 816.—App & E 1056.1(1).

Franklin; Williams Distributing Co. v., TexApp–Dallas, 884 SW2d 503, writ gr, aff in part, rev in part 898 SW2d 816.—App & E 758.3(9), 970(2), 1043(1), 1043(6), 1050.1(1), 1052(8), 1056.1(1); Damag 91(1), 91(3), 191; Evid 543.5.

Franklin v. Wilson, TexCivApp–Eastland, 242 SW2d 820, mandamus overr.—Mun Corp 10, 51.

Franklin v. Wolfe, TexCivApp–Hous (14 Dist), 483 SW2d 17.—Child C 724, 788; Child S 210; Hab Corp 532(1); Proc 118.

Franklin v. Woods, TexCivApp–Corpus Christi, 598 SW2d 946.—Ex & Ad 53, 271, 450; Home 17, 90, 131, 141(1), 161, 162(1), 167, 175, 181(1), 181(3); Hus & W 248.5, 249(5), 273(8.1); Partit 12(3).

Franklin County v. Tittle, TexCivApp–Texarkana, 189 SW2d 773, writ refused.—Lim of Act 24(2), 43, 57(5), 100(7), 100(11), 104(1).

Franklin County; Wilkinson v., TexCivApp–Texarkana, 94 SW2d 1190, writ refused.—Counties 150(2), 168(3).

Franklin County Distilling Co.; East Tex. Motor Freight Lines v., TexCivApp–El Paso, 184 SW2d 505.—Carr 194, 195.

Franklin County Water Dist.; Aikin v., Tex, 432 SW2d 520.—Waters 183.5.

Franklin County Water Dist.; Gilbert v., TexCivApp–Texarkana, 520 SW2d 503.—Dedi 53, 63(1), 65; Em Dom 31, 64, 242, 319, 323, 325; Judgm 91, 217, 335(1), 335(3), 373, 443(1), 511.

Franklin County Water Dist. v. Majors, TexCivApp–Texarkana, 476 SW2d 371, ref nre.—Em Dom 196; Waters 183.5.

Franklin County Water Dist.; Postel v., CA5 (Tex), 470 F2d 189.—Consp 19.

Franklin Dress Co.; Green v., TexCivApp–El Paso, 137 SW2d 131.—App & E 758.3(1); Contracts 313(1); Sales 181(3), 181(11.1), 340.

Franklin Federal Bancorp; Mann v., TexApp–Austin, 796 SW2d 318.—App & E 377, 385(1), 390.

Franklin Federal Bancorp; Pruitt v., TexApp–Austin, 824 SW2d 798.—Judgm 185(2), 185.3(16).

Franklin Fire Ins. Co. v. Clark, TexCivApp–Texarkana, 100 SW2d 150.—Insurance 2019, 2035.

Franklin Fire Ins. Co. v. Coleman, TexCivApp–Waco, 87 SW2d 537.—Evid 116; Insurance 3396.

Franklin Fire Ins. Co.; Lindley v., TexComApp, 152 SW2d 1109, 137 Tex 196.—Insurance 1633, 2202, 2992(2), 3084, 3571; Trial 140(2), 351.2(5).

Franklin Fire Ins. Co. v. Lindley, TexCivApp–Fort Worth, 128 SW2d 869, rev 152 SW2d 1109, 137 Tex 196.—App & E 909(5); Hus & W 273(1); Insurance 2202, 3096(1), 3100(1), 3567; Judgm 194; Trial 350.4(3); Trusts 80.

Franklin Fire Ins. Co. of Philadelphia v. Fullen, TexCivApp–El Paso, 139 SW2d 370.—Contracts 94(1); Insurance 3007(1), 3131, 3191(7), 3571; Plead 354, 380.

Franklin Fire Ins. Co. of Philadelphia v. Smith, TexCivApp–Galveston, 103 SW2d 470.—Insurance 2142(5), 2145.

Franklin Intern., Inc.; Fredericksburg Industries, Inc. v., TexApp–San Antonio, 911 SW2d 518, reh den, and writ den.—App & E 1050.1(1), 1056.1(1), 1056.1(6); Corp 202; Evid 141, 146; Trial 43.

Franklin Life Ins. Co.; Chambers v., CCA5 (Tex), 80 F2d 339.—Insurance 1091(7), 2035.

Franklin Life Ins. Co.; Cole v., CCA5 (Tex), 108 F2d 130.—Abate & R 12; Courts 493(3); Fed Cts 415; Usury 34, 117.

Franklin Life Ins. Co.; Cole v., CCA5 (Tex), 93 F2d 620.—Courts 475(2); Des & Dist 89; Ex & Ad 224; Mtg 334.

Franklin Life Ins. Co. v. Durham, TexCivApp–Waco, 351 SW2d 104, ref nre.—App & E 1140(4); Costs 233; Insurance 1952, 3345.

Franklin Life Ins. Co.; Emerson v., TexCivApp–Dallas, 107 SW2d 1029, writ dism.—Bills & N 125; Usury 22, 60, 113.

Franklin Life Ins. Co. v. Faggard, TexCivApp–San Antonio, 296 SW2d 335, ref nre.—App & E 1175(5); Contracts 97(1); Equity 64; Fraud 11(1); Insurance 1800, 1952, 1969, 2439.

Franklin Life Ins. Co.; Greer v., Tex, 221 SW2d 857, 148 Tex 166.—Const Law 1123; Insurance 2593, 3374, 3375, 3484; Interpl 35.

Franklin Life Ins. Co.; Greer v., TexCivApp–Dallas, 109 SW2d 305, writ dism by agreement.—Corp 428(12); Estop 52(1), 52.15; Home 122, 133, 177(1); Mtg 138; Usury 34, 72.

Franklin Life Ins. Co. v. Greer, TexCivApp–Texarkana, 219 SW2d 137, aff in part, rev in part 221 SW2d 857, 148 Tex 166.—App & E 931(4); Insurance 2593, 3360, 3484, 3496; Interpl 1, 35.

Franklin Life Ins. Co. v. Heitchew, CCA5 (Tex), 146 F2d 71, cert den 65 SCt 914, 324 US 865, 89 LEd 1421.—Evid 59, 89; Fed Cts 774; Insurance 2445, 2605, 2608; Trial 234(7), 237(4).

Franklin Life Ins. Co.; Lasater v., TexCivApp–El Paso, 471 SW2d 99.—Mtg 122, 125.

Franklin Life Ins. Co.; Lasater v., TexCivApp–El Paso, 471 SW2d 95.—Action 60; Evid 582(3); Judgm 181(25).

Franklin Life Ins. Co.; McFarland v., Tex, 416 SW2d 378.—Insurance 3335, 3336, 3343, 3360, 3438, 3490.

Franklin Life Ins. Co.; McFarland v., TexCivApp–El Paso, 409 SW2d 467, writ gr, rev 416 SW2d 378.—Insurance 3336, 3360; Statut 241(1).

Franklin Life Ins. Co.; Mercantile Nat. Bank at Dallas v., CA5 (Tex), 248 F2d 57.—Fed Civ Proc 2533.1, 2539; Insurance 1955.

Franklin Life Ins. Co. v. Rogers, TexCivApp–Eastland, 316 SW2d 116, ref nre.—Judgm 185(2), 185.1(4), 735.

Franklin Life Ins. Co.; Stuart v., CCA5 (Tex), 165 F2d 965, cert den 68 SCt 1072, 334 US 816, 92 LEd 1746.—Pub Lands 17; Ven & Pur 17, 334(1).

Franklin Life Ins. Co. v. Winney, TexCivApp–San Antonio, 469 SW2d 21, ref nre.—Contracts 22(1), 22(3), 26; Insurance 1952, 1955.

Franklin Life Ins. Co. v. Woodyard, TexCivApp–Galveston, 206 SW2d 93.—Evid 18; Insurance 1832(1), 2558(2), 3191(7).

Franklin Life Ins. Co. of Springfield, Ill., v. Staats, CCA5 (Tex), 94 F2d 481, cert den 58 SCt 942, 304 US 560, 82 LEd 1527.—Insurance 1764(1), 1767, 3343.

Franklin Nat. Bank v. Boser, TexApp–Texarkana, 972 SW2d 98, review den.—App & E 934(1); Judgm 199(3.9), 199(3.10); Sec Tran 10, 17, 90, 116, 133, 134, 138, 139.1, 146; Trial 139.1(7).

Franklin Nat. Bank of Long Island; Bohannon v., TexCivApp–Dallas, 387 SW2d 699.—Bills & N 489(1); Evid 314(1); Judgm 185.3(16).

Franklin Nat. Bank of Long Island; Snowden v., CA5 (Tex), 338 F2d 995.—Bills & N 477; Evid 423(6).

Franklin Offices, Inc. v. Harding, TexCivApp–Dallas, 579 SW2d 254.—App & E 846(5); Inj 147; Usury 117.

Franklin Sav. Ass'n; Gibraltar Sav. Ass'n v., TexCivApp–Austin, 617 SW2d 322, ref nre.—Admin Law 454, 468; B & L Assoc 3.5(2); Const Law 3879.

Franklin Sav. Ass'n v. Kotrla, TexApp–Houston (14 Dist), 751 SW2d 218. See Benjamin Franklin Sav. Ass'n v. Kotrla.

Franklin Sav. Ass'n v. Reese, TexApp–Austin, 756 SW2d 14.—App & E 954(1); Inj 135, 138.18; Mtg 413.

Franklin Signal Corp. v. Chas. P. Davis Hardware, Inc., TexApp–Waco, 624 SW2d 328.—Judgm 497(2).

Frank L. Thomas, Inc.; Western Transport Corp. v., TexCivApp–Dallas, 270 SW2d 226, ref nre.—Bailm 20.

Franklyn v. State, TexApp–El Paso, 762 SW2d 228, petition for discretionary review refused.—Ind & Inf 144.1(1), 162.

Frank Mohn A/S; Sang Young Kim v., SDTex, 925 FSupp 491.—Const Law 3964, 3965(5); Fed Civ Proc 1825, 1831, 1835; Fed Cts 76, 76.5, 76.10, 82, 86, 96.

Frank Mohn A/S; Sang Young Kim v., SDTex, 909 FSupp 474.—Adm 5(1), 5(6), 18, 20; Const Law 3964; Fed Civ Proc 470.1, 1751, 1828; Fed Cts 76; Lim of Act 118(2); Proc 82; States 18.15; Treaties 8, 11.

Frank Mohn A/S; Kim v., SDTex, 925 FSupp 491. See Sang Young Kim v. Frank Mohn A/S.

Frank Mohn A/S; Young Kim v., SDTex, 925 FSupp 491. See Sang Young Kim v. Frank Mohn A/S.

Frankoff v. Mutual Life Ins. Co. of New York, TexApp–Houston (14 Dist), 792 SW2d 764, writ den.—Judgm 181(23).

Frank Parra Chevrolet, Inc.; Williams v., TexCivApp–Waco, 552 SW2d 635.—App & E 927(7), 997(3); Mal Pros 16, 71(1), 71(2), 71(3).

Frank Paxton Lumber Co.; Black v., TexCivApp–Dallas, 405 SW2d 412, ref nre.—App & E 1140(6); Bills & N 92(5), 123(1), 129(2), 537(1); Evid 320; Judgm 185(2), 185.1(3); Pretrial Proc 306.1.

Franks, Ex parte, TexCrimApp, 71 SW3d 327.—Pardon 44.

Franks v. Associated Air Center, Inc., CA5 (Tex), 663 F2d 583.—Antitrust 369; Aviation 238; Damag 163(1); Fed Civ Proc 2313, 2339; Fed Cts 825.1, 827; Labor & Emp 26, 58, 3094(2), 3096(5).

Franks v. Brookshire Bros., Inc., TexApp–Beaumont, 986 SW2d 375.—Judgm 181(21), 185.1(3); Release 30, 34, 38.

Franks; Chapman Air Conditioning, Inc. v., TexApp–Dallas, 732 SW2d 737.—Antitrust 989; App & E 326.1, 387(2), 747(1); Contracts 322(3); Costs 194.32, 252; Equity 65(1), 65(2).

Franks; Crowder v., TexApp–Houston (1 Dist), 870 SW2d 568.—App & E 227; J P 73(1), 73(4); Mand 44, 187.9(0.5), 187.9(6).

Franks; Easton v., TexApp–Houston (1 Dist), 842 SW2d 772.—Mand 24.

Franks v. Estelle, CA5 (Tex), 543 F2d 567, reh den 545 F2d 1298, cert den 97 SCt 1561, 430 US 935, 51 LEd2d 781.—Const Law 3824; Prisons 15(3); Sent & Pun 1175.

Franks; General Motors Corp. v., TexCivApp–Beaumont, 509 SW2d 945, dism.—Plead 111.42(4); Prod Liab 77.5.

Franks; Hallmark Personnel of Texas, Inc. v., TexCivApp–Hous (1 Dist), 562 SW2d 933.—Action 6; Antitrust 413, 417, 432; App & E 781(1), 781(6), 954(1), 954(2); Inj 12, 56, 147; Labor & Emp 121.

Franks; Harris County v., TexApp–Houston (1 Dist), 875 SW2d 1, reh den.—Work Comp 1038, 1822, 1829, 1981.

Franks v. Krohn, TexCivApp–Beaumont, 164 SW2d 529, writ refused.—App & E 863, 917(1); Mines 5.2(4); States 203.

Franks v. Mahon, TexCivApp–Waco, 460 SW2d 177, ref nre.—App & E 907(3).

Franks; Missouri-Kansas-Texas R. Co. v., TexCivApp–Dallas, 399 SW2d 905, writ dism by agreement.—App & E 1048(1), 1057(2); Evid 128; Labor & Emp 2824, 2832, 2874, 2886, 2897; Trial 260(10), 350.8, 352.21.

Franks; Missouri-Kansas-Texas R. Co. v., TexCivApp–Eastland, 379 SW2d 415, ref nre, appeal after remand 399 SW2d 905, writ dism by agreement.—App & E 1032(1), 1062.1; Plead 8(3), 18, 427; Trial 350.6(4), 366.

Franks v. Montandon, TexCivApp–Austin, 465 SW2d 800.—Judgm 17(2); Proc 74.

Franks v. National Dairy Products Corp., CA5 (Tex), 414 F2d 682.—Evid 267, 571(9); Explos 8; Fed Cts 776, 846, 848, 852; Prod Liab 76.

Franks v. National Dairy Products Corp., WDTex, 282 FSupp 528, aff 414 F2d 682.—Damag 132(1); Evid 571(1); Explos 8; Prod Liab 76.

Franks v. National Dairy Products Corp., WDTex, 41 FRD 234.—Fed Civ Proc 1600(1), 1616, 1617.

Franks v. Prudential Health Care Plan, Inc., WDTex, 164 FSupp2d 865.—Acct 1; Action 3; Fed Civ Proc 1832; Impl & C C 3; Insurance 1117(3), 3503(1), 3519(2); Labor & Emp 407, 438, 554, 602(1); RICO 58; States 18.15, 18.41, 18.51; Trover 13.

Franks; Rancher v., TexCivApp–Fort Worth, 269 SW2d 926.—App & E 768, 934(1), 1175(1); Estop 85; Judgm 199(3.14); Ven & Pur 353.

Franks v. Sematech, Inc., Tex, 936 SW2d 959.—Work Comp 2190, 2195, 2225.

Franks v. Sematech, Inc., TexApp–Austin, 938 SW2d 462, writ gr, rev 936 SW2d 959.—App & E 852, 949; Work Comp 2158, 2191, 2216, 2220, 2242.

Franks v. Semiconductor Mfg. Technology Initiative, Tex, 936 SW2d 959. See Franks v. Sematech, Inc.

Franks; Southern Underwriters v., TexCivApp–El Paso, 149 SW2d 1020.—App & E 2, 455.

Franks v. State, TexCrimApp, 688 SW2d 502.—Ind & Inf 71.4(8), 102.

Franks v. State, TexCrimApp, 574 SW2d 124.—Crim Law 721(1), 726.

Franks v. State, TexCrimApp, 532 SW2d 631.—Rob 17(5).

Franks v. State, TexCrimApp, 516 SW2d 185.—Crim Law 1184(2); Ind & Inf 191(2); Sent & Pun 2011, 2021.

Franks v. State, TexCrimApp, 513 SW2d 584.—Crim Law 273.1(4); Ind & Inf 32(3).

Franks v. State, TexCrimApp, 462 SW2d 287.—Crim Law 739(2), 753.2(2), 1169.5(1); Double J 30.

Franks v. State, TexCrimApp, 314 SW2d 586, 166 Tex-Crim 455.—Crim Law 366(3), 507(7); Witn 45(2).

Franks v. State, TexCrimApp, 244 SW2d 820, 156 Tex-Crim 556.—Crim Law 1092.9.

Franks v. State, TexCrimApp, 138 SW2d 109, 139 Tex-Crim 42.—Crim Law 134(4), 338(1), 338(2), 366(3), 394.4(9), 589(2), 594(1), 687(1), 778(2), 778(7), 938(1), 1036.1(3.1), 1111(3); Jury 51, 80, 103(14); Sent & Pun 1777.

Franks v. State, TexCrimApp, 95 SW2d 128, 130 Tex-Crim 577.—Crim Law 780(2); Homic 1352.

Franks v. State, TexCrimApp, 83 SW2d 980, 129 Tex-Crim 91.—Burg 2, 7, 22, 23.

Franks v. State, TexApp–Houston (1 Dist), 961 SW2d 253, petition for discretionary review refused.—Crim Law 1137(2), 1137(8).

Franks v. State, TexApp–Houston (1 Dist), 712 SW2d 858, petition for discretionary review refused.—Crim Law 412.2(3); Homic 1152.

Franks v. State, TexApp–Houston (1 Dist), 661 SW2d 166, petition for discretionary review gr, aff 688 SW2d 502. —Crim Law 829(3); Ind & Inf 86(3).

Franks v. State, TexApp–Fort Worth, 90 SW3d 771, reh overr, and reh overr.—Arrest 70(2); Autos 349(19); Const Law 4594(1); Crim Law 412.2(4), 412.2(5), 469.1, 474.3(1), 517.2(2), 519(1), 525, 535(1), 594(1), 629.5(1), 641.3(2), 641.3(3), 641.3(4), 641.13(1), 700(2.1), 700(3), 700(4), 753.2(3.1), 777, 781(1), 857(1), 862, 865(1), 865(1.5), 867, 868, 1036.6, 1039, 1063(5), 1086.11, 1130(5), 1137(2), 1137(5), 1166(7), 1169.2(8), 1172.1(1); Kidnap 36; Witn 68.

Franks v. State, TexApp–Fort Worth, 625 SW2d 820, petition for discretionary review refused.—Crim Law 366(6), 1036.1(3.1); Homic 1080(4); Sent & Pun 1513.

Franks v. State, TexApp–Austin, 219 SW3d 494, petition for discretionary review refused.—Crim Law 1068.5, 1081(1); Hab Corp 792.1, 900.1.

Franks v. State, TexApp–San Antonio, 724 SW2d 918.—Crim Law 788, 808.5, 1170(1).

Franks; State v., TexCivApp–Austin, 113 SW2d 589, writ refused.—Bound 25, 40(1); Judgm 743(2).

Franks v. State, TexCivApp–Texarkana, 498 SW2d 516.—Const Law 4468; Infants 78(1), 225, 241.

Franks v. State of Fla., SDTex, 211 FSupp 374.—Crim Law 243; Hab Corp 207.

Franks; U.S. v., CA5 (Tex), 46 F3d 402.—Crim Law 1028, 1030(1), 1042, 1141(2), 1147, 1158(1), 1181.5(8); Sent & Pun 653(11), 765, 771, 861, 944.

Franks v. Welch, TexCivApp–Houston, 389 SW2d 142, ref nre.—Decl Judgm 292; Judgm 181(2).

Franks v. Woodville Independent School Dist., TexApp–Beaumont, 132 SW3d 167.—Tax 2979.

Frank's Casing Crew & Rental Tools, Inc.; Excess Underwriters At Lloyd'sv., TexApp–Houston (14 Dist), 93 SW3d 178, review gr.—Insurance 1091(4), 3506(1).

Franks Estate; Eagle Life Ins. Co. v., TexCivApp–Beaumont, 588 SW2d 631, writ gr, and dism.—Judgm 162(4).

Frank's King Size Clothes, Inc.; King-Size, Inc. v., SDTex, 547 FSupp 1138.—Antitrust 17, 18, 29; Trademarks 1032, 1034, 1036, 1037, 1038, 1080, 1081, 1086, 1092, 1096(2), 1110, 1112, 1257, 1299, 1360, 1363, 1382, 1387, 1419, 1428(1), 1523(2), 1612, 1619, 1628(2), 1628(3), 1800.

Frank Smith & Sons Co. v. Lloyd, TexCivApp–Eastland, 378 SW2d 735.—Plead 111.42(8).

Frank Smith Llano Trucking; Vanderwiele v., TexApp–Austin, 885 SW2d 843. See Vanderwiele v. Llano Trucks, Inc.

Frankson; American Cyanamid Co. v., TexApp–Corpus Christi, 732 SW2d 648, ref nre.—App & E 1048(6); Evid 219(3), 219.65, 571(10); Interest 39(2.50); Jury 90, 136(3); Neglig 273, 372; Pretrial Proc 36.1, 45; Prod Liab 1, 81.1, 83; Trial 108, 352.1(6); Witn 282.5.

Frankum; Texas Emp. Ins. Ass'n v., Tex, 220 SW2d 449, 148 Tex 95.—Trial 352.4(9).

Frankum; Texas Emp. Ins. Ass'n v., Tex, 201 SW2d 800, 145 Tex 658.—App & E 837(7); Const Law 2528; Damag 221(7); Trial 355(1), 357; Work Comp 1683, 1724.

Frankum; Texas Emp. Ins. Ass'n v., TexCivApp–Galveston, 215 SW2d 899, rev 220 SW2d 449, 148 Tex 95.—App & E 1062.1, 1170.1; Work Comp 598, 1930, 1971.

Frankum; Texas Emp. Ins. Ass'n v., TexCivApp–Galveston, 198 SW2d 484, rev 201 SW2d 800, 145 Tex 658.—Work Comp 1639, 1683, 1761.

Frank Winther Investments, Inc.; Winkins v., TexApp–Houston (1 Dist), 881 SW2d 557.—App & E 387(3), 387(6); Judgm 276.

Frank W. Neal & Associates, Inc.; Dean v., TexApp–Fort Worth, 166 SW3d 352.—Estop 52.15; Judgm 185.1(4); Lim of Act 13, 43, 95(1), 95(1.5), 95(3), 95(7), 95(9), 95(16), 100(12), 175.

Franner v. Joske Bros. Co., TexCivApp–El Paso, 227 SW2d 392, writ refused.—Carr 318(3).

Frans; Performance Ins. Co. v., TexApp–Houston (1 Dist), 902 SW2d 582, reh overr, and writ den.—Work Comp 1105, 1108, 2158, 2190, 2191, 2251.

Fransaw v. Lynaugh, CA5 (Tex), 810 F2d 518, cert den 107 SCt 3237, 483 US 1008, 97 LEd2d 742.—Const Law 3855; Crim Law 795(1); Double J 51, 57, 88.1, 109, 163; Hab Corp 366, 474, 816; Homic 873.

Fransaw v. State, TexApp–Houston (14 Dist), 671 SW2d 539.—Jury 33(2.10), 126, 131(10); Witn 345(10).

Fransen; Benritto v., TexCivApp–Galveston, 274 SW2d 758.—App & E 215(1), 216(1), 882(12); Trial 284.

Frantom v. Neal, TexCivApp–Fort Worth, 426 SW2d 268, ref nre.—App & E 1070(2); Autos 201(1.1), 244(26), 247; Contrib 8; Indem 59, 66; Judgm 16, 878(1); Neglig 387.

Frantz, In re, BkrtcySDTex, 82 BR 835.—Bankr 2043(2); Jury 19(9).

Frantz, In re, TexCivApp–Amarillo, 397 SW2d 125, ref nre.—App & E 854(1); Guard & W 10, 25; Mental H 176.

Frantz; Clement v., TexCivApp–Amarillo, 333 SW2d 190.—App & E 770(1); Contracts 25; Land & Ten 285(4).

Frantz v. Frantz, TexCivApp–Amarillo, 406 SW2d 745.—App & E 937(1); Courts 202(5).

Frantz; Frantz v., TexCivApp–Amarillo, 406 SW2d 745.—App & E 937(1); Courts 202(5).

Frantz v. Frantz, TexCivApp–Eastland, 389 SW2d 149, ref nre, appeal after remand 406 SW2d 745.—Ex & Ad 6; Guard & W 33; Judgm 181(2), 181(15.1); Wills 288(1).

Frantz; Frantz v., TexCivApp–Eastland, 389 SW2d 149, ref nre, appeal after remand 406 SW2d 745.—Ex & Ad 6; Guard & W 33; Judgm 181(2), 181(15.1); Wills 288(1).

Frantz; Mutual Fire, Marine & Inland Ins. Co. of Philadelphia, Pennsylvania v., BkrtcySDTex, 82 BR 835. See Frantz, In re.

Frantz v. U.S., CA5 (Tex), 29 F3d 222.—U S 127(2).

Frantzen v. Frantzen, TexCivApp–San Antonio, 349 SW2d 765.—Child C 46; Divorce 12.

Frantzen; Frantzen v., TexCivApp–San Antonio, 349 SW2d 765.—Child C 46; Divorce 12.

Franyutti v. Hidden Valley Moving and Storage, Inc., WDTex, 325 FSupp2d 108.—Antitrust 132; Carr 108; Fed Cts 241, 246; Fraud 31; Rem of C 25(1); States 18.15.

Franz; Goss v., TexCivApp–Amarillo, 287 SW2d 289, writ refused.—Const Law 2489; Death 31(8).

Franz v. Katy Independent School Dist., TexApp–Houston (1 Dist), 35 SW3d 749.—App & E 852, 1175(1); Deeds 120; Estates 10(1); Land & Ten 157(2); Tax 2187, 2730, 2740.

Franz v. Lusk, TexCivApp–San Antonio, 107 SW2d 479, writ dism.—App & E 215(1), 1062.1; Trial 350.8; Ven & Pur 240, 244.

Franz; Maxon v., TexCivApp–Hous (14 Dist), 525 SW2d 714, ref nre.—Const Law 38; Sheriffs 10, 12.

Franz v. State, TexCrimApp, 117 SW2d 97, 135 TexCrim 47.—Autos 355.1, 355(14); Crim Law 1169.2(6).

Franz; Syn-Labs, Inc. v., TexApp–Houston (1 Dist), 778 SW2d 202.—Divorce 181.

Franz; Wilson v., TexCivApp–El Paso, 359 SW2d 630, writ refused.—Char 18, 21(2), 21(3), 47.

Franz v. Wyeth, SDTex, 431 FSupp2d 688.—Fed Cts 113; Rem of C 36, 79(1).

Franz Chemical Corp. v. Philadelphia Quartz Co., CA5 (Tex), 594 F2d 146.—Evid 397(2); Fed Civ Proc 2557; Fed Cts 543.1; Pat 211(1), 219(5).

Franzen v. Dale, TexCivApp–Hous (14 Dist), 462 SW2d 94.—App & E 931(4); Compromise 15(1); Deeds 193, 194(1); Evid 178(4), 370(8), 370(12), 590; Lost Inst 23(3); Trial 350.3(3); Ven & Pur 224.

Franzen v. Jason, TexCivApp–Galveston, 166 SW2d 727, writ refused.—App & E 1175(1), 1175(3); Autos 181(1), 181(2).

Franzen v. Universal Credit Co., TexCivApp–Galveston, 132 SW2d 148, writ dism, correct.—Corp 417; Costs 194.34; Guar 78(2); Judgm 883(13).

Franzen Motor Co. v. Wentz, TexCivApp–Galveston, 122 SW2d 236.—Action 45(4); Chat Mtg 235; Contracts 346(12); Evid 474(17).

Franzetti v. Franzetti, TexCivApp–Austin, 174 SW2d 65.—App & E 1048(7); Gifts 25, 48; New Tr 44(1), 44(2); Trial 352.10; Witn 338, 344(2), 406.

Franzetti; Franzetti v., TexCivApp–Austin, 174 SW2d 65.—App & E 1048(7); Gifts 25, 48; New Tr 44(1), 44(2); Trial 352.10; Witn 338, 344(2), 406.

Franzetti v. Franzetti, TexCivApp–Austin, 124 SW2d 195, writ refused.—App & E 877(2); Frds St of 143(1); Gifts 25, 49(4); Hus & W 49.2(7); Tresp to T T 35(1), 39(1).

Franzetti; Franzetti v., TexCivApp–Austin, 124 SW2d 195, writ refused.—App & E 877(2); Frds St of 143(1);

Gifts 25, 49(4); Hus & W 49.2(7); Tresp to T T 35(1), 39(1).

Franzetti v. Franzetti, TexCivApp–Austin, 120 SW2d 123.—App & E 218.2(10), 974(1); Courts 95(2); Divorce 54, 149, 186; Equity 87(1); Jury 13(1); Lim of Act 39(1); Trial 350.1, 352.7.

Franzetti; Franzetti v., TexCivApp–Austin, 120 SW2d 123.—App & E 218.2(10), 974(1); Courts 95(2); Divorce 54, 149, 186; Equity 87(1); Jury 13(1); Lim of Act 39(1); Trial 350.1, 352.7.

Franzheim; Reese v., TexCivApp–Houston, 381 SW2d 329, ref nre.—Wills 289, 293(1), 302(5), 324(4), 400.

Franzheim; Zimmerman v., TexCivApp–Hous (1 Dist), 483 SW2d 380.—Judgm 185.3(16).

Franzina v. Franzina's Estate, TexCivApp–Corpus Christi, 618 SW2d 570, ref nre.—Hus & W 249(1), 266.2(1).

Franzina's Estate; Franzina v., TexCivApp–Corpus Christi, 618 SW2d 570, ref nre.—Hus & W 249(1), 266.2(1).

Frappier v. Texas Commerce Bank, N.A., SDTex, 879 FSupp 715, aff 71 F3d 878.—Home 76; Int Rev 4772, 4790; Interpl 35.

Frascone; U.S. v., CA5 (Tex), 747 F2d 953.—Crim Law 569, 603.1, 627.5(5), 662.5, 700(1), 730(1), 730(16), 772(6), 1119(4).

Frasco Restaurant & Catering; Quanaim v., TexApp–Houston (14 Dist), 17 SW3d 30, reh overr, and review den, on subsequent appeal 2005 WL 856911.—App & E 76(1), 78(1), 80(6), 346.1, 346.2, 347(1), 428(2), 934(1); Civil R 1204; Corp 488; Evid 265(8); Judgm 178, 181(21), 181(33), 183, 185(1), 185(2), 185(5), 185(6), 185.3(21), 634, 713(1), 715(2), 725(1), 829(3), 958(1); Labor & Emp 810; Neglig 1001, 1692; Parties 1.

Fraser, In re, EDTex, 98 FSupp2d 788.—Fed Cts 12.1, 13, 681.1, 683.

Fraser, In re, EDTex, 75 FSupp2d 572.—Fed Cts 5, 10.1, 25, 266.1; Rem of C 1, 19(1), 25(1), 107(7).

Fraser v. City of San Antonio, Tex., CA5 (Tex), 430 F2d 1218.—Pat 324.55(5).

Fraser; Davis v., TexCivApp–Texarkana, 319 SW2d 799, ref nre.—Joint-St Co 7.

Fraser v. Fraser, EDTex, 196 BR 371.—Bankr 3341, 3347.1, 3349, 3420(2), 3422(11), 3786, 3787.

Fraser; Fraser v., EDTex, 196 BR 371.—Bankr 3341, 3347.1, 3349, 3420(2), 3422(11), 3786, 3787.

Fraser v. Goldberg, TexCivApp–Beaumont, 552 SW2d 592, ref nre.—App & E 1071.1(2); Corp 116.

Fraser v. Houston Belt & Terminal Ry. Co., CA5 (Tex), 430 F2d 934.—Courts 104; Fed Cts 743.

Fraser v. Kay, TexCivApp–San Antonio, 251 SW2d 754.—Mtg 401(1), 401(5), 414.

Fraser; Pipe Line Park Properties, Inc. v., TexCivApp–Dallas, 398 SW2d 154.—App & E 715(1), 715(2); Corp 507(13).

Fraser; Raley v., CA5 (Tex), 747 F2d 287.—Arrest 63.4(18); Civil R 1088(2), 1420, 1423, 1465(1), 1482; Damag 208(8).

Fraser; Roberts v., TexCivApp–Beaumont, 399 SW2d 211, writ dism.—Tresp to T T 6.1, 7, 11, 38(1).

Fraser; San Antonio Public Service Co. v., TexCivApp–San Antonio, 91 SW2d 948.—Carr 347, 348; Neglig 535(14); Trial 253(4).

Fraser v. State, TexCrimApp, 147 SW2d 780, 141 TexCrim 152.—Crim Law 552(3); Embez 44(1).

Fraser; State v., TexCivApp–El Paso, 276 SW2d 559, ref nre.—App & E 846(5); Pub Lands 175(0.5).

Fraser Brick & Tile Co.; Schneider Const. Co. v., TexCivApp–San Antonio, 297 SW2d 298.—Contracts 170(1); Sales 32; Venue 7.5(7).

Frasier v. Pierce, TexCivApp–Amarillo, 398 SW2d 955, ref nre.—App & E 1068(3); Autos 227(3); Stip 14(10); Trial 142, 350.5(3), 350.7(4), 350.7(9).

Frasier; Pluet v., CA5 (Tex), 355 F3d 381.—Civil R 1332(4); Death 31(1), 31(8); Fed Civ Proc 103.2, 2331, 2655; Fed Cts 611, 768.1.

Frasier v. Schauweker, TexApp–Houston (14 Dist), 915 SW2d 601.—App & E 854(1); Damag 150; Judgm 181(1), 185(2), 185(5), 185(6), 185.3(18); Ven & Pur 81, 328.

Frasier; Williams v., CA5 (Tex), 96 FedAppx 217.—Fed Civ Proc 1758.1.

Frasier v. Yanes, TexApp–Austin, 9 SW3d 422.—Admin Law 229; Civil R 1764; Const Law 502, 640, 655, 658; Counties 69.1, 212; Decl Judgm 121, 122.1, 209, 272; Mun Corp 723; Sheriffs 74.

Fraternal Bank & Trust Co. v. Cotton Belt State Bank of Timpson, TexCivApp–Fort Worth, 85 SW2d 783.—Plead 111.37.

Frates Communities, Inc.; Amistad, Inc. v., TexCivApp–Waco, 611 SW2d 121, ref nre.—Contracts 176(2); Evid 448, 460(6); Mtg 110, 298(1), 310, 319(1); Trial 350.3(2.1), 350.4(2).

Fraud Busters v. Park Nat. Bank, SDTex, 881 FSupp 276. See Kaminetzky v. Frost Nat. Bank of Houston.

Fraud-Tech, Inc. v. Choicepoint, Inc., TexApp–Fort Worth, 102 SW3d 366, reh overr, and review den, on remand 2004 WL 5025278, entered 2004 WL 5025277, aff in part, rev in part 2006 WL 1030189, aff in part, rev in part 2006 WL 1030189.—Action 17; App & E 230, 231(1), 241, 242(1), 242(2), 293, 852, 856(2), 863, 866(3), 927(7), 934(1), 946, 970(2); Contracts 27, 206; Damag 190; Evid 546, 555.9; Impl & C C 1, 55; Judgm 181(12), 183, 185(2), 185(5), 185(6), 185.3(8), 185.3(19), 185.3(21); Plead 252(1), 252(2).

Frausto v. Frausto, TexCivApp–San Antonio, 611 SW2d 656, dism.—Divorce 240(2), 252.1, 252.3(1), 252.3(3), 252.3(5).

Frausto; Frausto v., TexCivApp–San Antonio, 611 SW2d 656, dism.—Divorce 240(2), 252.1, 252.3(1), 252.3(3), 252.3(5).

Frausto v. State, TexCrimApp, 642 SW2d 506.—Crim Law 577.16(5.1), 633(2), 1166.16, 1166.20; Jury 131(4).

Frawley; Gaines v., TexApp–Fort Worth, 739 SW2d 950.—Wills 155.1, 166(12), 322, 400, 410.

Frazar v. Gilbert, CA5 (Tex), 300 F3d 530, cert gr in part Frew ex rel Frew v. Hawkins, 123 SCt 1481, 538 US 905, 155 LEd2d 223, rev 124 SCt 899, 540 US 431, 157 LEd2d 855, on remand 376 F3d 444, on remand 401 FSupp2d 619, aff 457 F3d 432, cert den 127 SCt 1039, 166 LEd2d 714.—Civil R 1027, 1052; Fed Civ Proc 2397.1; Fed Cts 265, 266.1, 270, 576.1; U S 82(2).

Frazar v. Hawkins, CA5 (Tex), 376 F3d 444, on remand Frew v. Hawkins, 401 FSupp2d 619, aff 457 F3d 432, cert den 127 SCt 1039, 166 LEd2d 714.—Fed Cts 573, 576.1, 769.

Frazar v. Ladd, CA5 (Tex), 457 F3d 432, cert den Hawkins v. Frew, 127 SCt 1039, 166 LEd2d 714.—Fed Civ Proc 2397.4; Fed Cts 776, 829.

Fraze; Nix v., TexApp–Dallas, 752 SW2d 118.—App & E 497(1), 619, 621(3), 624, 627.2; Judgm 185(2).

Frazee v. State, TexCrimApp, 252 SW2d 706.—Crim Law 1094(3).

Frazer; Glasco v., TexCivApp–Dallas, 225 SW2d 633, dism.—Acct Action on 12, 14; Acct St 1, 8; Corp 1.6(9), 590(3).

Frazer v. State, TexCrimApp, 508 SW2d 362.—Controlled Subs 80, 106, 112.

Frazer v. Texas Farm Bureau Mut. Ins. Co., TexApp–Houston (1 Dist), 4 SW3d 819, reh overr.—Antitrust 221; App & E 173(1); Evid 207(1), 265(7); Insurance 3383, 3384; Judgm 181(23); Release 12(1), 27.

Frazer v. Wallis, TexApp–Houston (14 Dist), 979 SW2d 782.—Insurance 2654.

Frazier, Ex parte, TexCrimApp, 301 SW2d 655, 164 TexCrim 572.—Hab Corp 701.1; Sent & Pun 1125.

Frazier v. **Chater**, NDTex, 903 FSupp 1030.—Admin Law 791; Social S 8.20, 140.21, 140.60, 142.5, 142.10, 142.16, 143.80.

Frazier; **Cook v.**, TexApp–Fort Worth, 765 SW2d 546.— App & E 1050.1(11); Contracts 129(1), 144; Judgm 185.1(1), 185.1(8); Lim of Act 59(2); Usury 2(1), 12, 98, 103, 113; Ven & Pur 2.

Frazier v. **Cowart**, TexCivApp–El Paso, 191 SW2d 94.— Child C 276, 279, 510; Hab Corp 532(1), 711, 731.

Frazier v. **Dikovitsky**, TexApp–Texarkana, 144 SW3d 146.—App & E 5; Appear 26; Judgm 17(2), 17(9), 17(10), 162(2); Proc 133, 153, 166.

Frazier v. **Dretke**, CA5 (Tex), 145 FedAppx 866, cert den 126 SCt 1791, 547 US 1079, 164 LEd2d 532.—Crim Law 641.13(7); Hab Corp 382, 401, 403, 405.1.

Frazier v. **Ellis**, CA5 (Tex), 196 F2d 231.—Hab Corp 341, 894.1.

Frazier v. **Employers Mut. Cas. Co.**, TexCivApp–Austin, 368 SW2d 955, ref nre.—Work Comp 512, 514, 547, 548, 550.

Frazier; **Ephran v.**, TexApp–Corpus Christi, 840 SW2d 81.—Costs 194.40; Ex & Ad 111(1); Joint Ten 6.

Frazier v. **Frazier**, TexCivApp–Beaumont, 437 SW2d 877, writ dism.—App & E 151(1).

Frazier; **Frazier v.**, TexCivApp–Beaumont, 437 SW2d 877, writ dism.—App & E 151(5), 171(1).

Frazier v. **Frazier**, TexCivApp–Waco, 394 SW2d 853, writ dism.—Hus & W 289; Judgm 815, 822(1).

Frazier; **Frazier v.**, TexCivApp–Waco, 394 SW2d 853, writ dism.—Hus & W 289; Judgm 815, 822(1).

Frazier v. **Frontier State Bank**, TexApp–San Antonio, 837 SW2d 392, appeal after new trial 1996 WL 543273, appeal after new trial 1999 WL 125441, review den.— App & E 544(1), 1043(6); Pretrial Proc 313.

Frazier v. **Garrison I.S.D.**, CA5 (Tex), 980 F2d 1514.— Civil R 1138, 1140, 1142, 1536, 1544, 1545, 1546; Const Law 3867, 3869, 3894, 4156, 4198; Fed Civ Proc 8.1, 2461; Fed Cts 714, 776, 813; Lim of Act 95(15).

Frazier v. **Glens Falls Indem. Co.**, TexCivApp–Fort Worth, 278 SW2d 388, ref nre.—App & E 837(1), 837(10), 909(1), 934(1); Insurance 3207, 3209, 3221; Judgm 181(2), 185(2), 185.3(12), 190.

Frazier; **Hartford Acc. & Indem. Co. v.**, TexCivApp– Waco, 362 SW2d 417, ref nre.—Evid 177, 506.

Frazier v. **Havens**, TexApp–Houston (14 Dist), 102 SW3d 406, reh overr.—Afft 17; App & E 1050.1(1), 1056.1(1), 1056.1(3); Corp 1.6(9); Estop 52.10(2), 52.10(3), 119; Impl & C C 30; Lim of Act 129; Plead 427; Trial 43.

Frazier; **Hearn v.**, TexCivApp–Eastland, 241 SW2d 171. —App & E 218.2(3.1), 218.2(7); Evid 351; Ten in C 3, 4, 38(7).

Frazier; **Hearn v.**, TexCivApp–Eastland, 228 SW2d 582, writ dism.—Abate & R 82; Mines 113; Partners 89; Plead 111.36, 111.37; Venue 5.2, 6.

Frazier v. **Jones**, CA5 (Tex), 466 F2d 505.—Hab Corp 373.

Frazier v. **Levi**, TexCivApp–Hous (1 Dist), 440 SW2d 393. —Const Law 4703; Mental H 57.

Frazier v. **Manson**, CA5 (Tex), 651 F2d 1078.—Partners 370; Sec Reg 5.10, 5.26, 60.36.

Frazier v. **Manson**, NDTex, 484 FSupp 449, aff 651 F2d 1078.—Atty & C 20.1; Fed Civ Proc 187; Partners 368; Sec Reg 5.10, 5.26, 60.36, 60.37.

Frazier v. **Moeller**, TexApp–Eastland, 665 SW2d 155, dism.—App & E 852, 912; Venue 8.5(6).

Frazier; **National Chemsearch Acc. v.**, TexCivApp– Waco, 488 SW2d 545.—Antitrust 83; Contracts 117(2); Equity 65(2); Inj 135; Labor & Emp 47.

Frazier v. **Phinney**, SDTex, 24 FRD 406.—Fed Civ Proc 1603, 1616, 1617, 1619.

Frazier v. **Progressive Companies**, TexApp–Dallas, 27 SW3d 592, review dism by agreement.—Pretrial Proc 690, 693.1.

Frazier v. **State**, TexCrimApp, 600 SW2d 271, 11 ALR4th 990.—Sent & Pun 2019, 2021.

Frazier v. **State**, TexCrimApp, 576 SW2d 617.—Crim Law 552(1), 784(1), 814(17), 1043(1), 1173.2(10).

Frazier v. **State**, TexCrimApp, 481 SW2d 857.—Const Law 4658(4); Crim Law 99, 101(4), 339.10(9), 723(1), 1171.1(6).

Frazier v. **State**, TexCrimApp, 480 SW2d 375.—Arrest 71.1(3); Controlled Subs 25, 29, 74, 80; Crim Law 29(1), 29(8), 720(6), 737(1), 1130(2), 1130(5); Double J 146; Searches 111, 113.1, 117, 119; Sent & Pun 313.

Frazier v. **State**, TexCrimApp, 347 SW2d 620, 171 Tex-Crim 242.—Assault 54, 92(5); Crim Law 1165(3).

Frazier v. **State**, TexCrimApp, 342 SW2d 115, 170 Tex-Crim 432.—Crim Law 800(2), 808.5, 1137(2); Rob 14, 26, 27(6).

Frazier v. **State**, TexCrimApp, 340 SW2d 303, 170 Tex-Crim 247.—Autos 355(6).

Frazier v. **State**, TexCrimApp, 289 SW2d 604.—Crim Law 1090.1(1).

Frazier v. **State**, TexCrimApp, 262 SW2d 501, 159 Tex-Crim 263.—Autos 355(6), 359.

Frazier v. **State**, TexCrimApp, 192 SW2d 159.—Crim Law 1090.1(1).

Frazier v. **State**, TexCrimApp, 158 SW2d 809, 143 Tex-Crim 334.—Crim Law 1173.2(10).

Frazier v. **State**, TexApp–Texarkana, 760 SW2d 334, petition for discretionary review refused.—Burg 6; Crim Law 693, 722.5; Sent & Pun 313.

Frazier v. **State**, TexApp–Beaumont, 115 SW3d 743.— Crim Law 507(1), 511.1(7), 511.2, 1134(2), 1184(4.1); Homic 1178, 1186; Sent & Pun 370, 373.

Frazier v. **State**, TexApp–Waco, 15 SW3d 263.—Crim Law 641.10(2), 1042, 1152(1), 1173.2(4), 1177.

Frazier v. **State**, TexApp–Houston (14 Dist), 909 SW2d 255.—Const Law 3309; Crim Law 1158(3); Jury 33(1.15), 33(5.15).

Frazier v. **Stennett**, TexCivApp–Waco, 370 SW2d 97.— Autos 170(1).

Frazier; **Stewart v.**, TexCivApp–Dallas, 461 SW2d 484.— App & E 1043(6), 1169(8); Evid 474(19); Pretrial Proc 473.

Frazier; **Tarter v.**, TexCivApp–Eastland, 159 SW2d 168, writ refused wom.—App & E 499(3), 1047(5); Evid 340(1); Judgm 564(1); Lim of Act 143(6); Trial 39; Ven & Pur 230(1).

Frazier; **Texas Emp. Ins. Ass'n v.**, TexCivApp–Eastland, 259 SW2d 242, ref nre.—Work Comp 1703, 1927, 1966.

Frazier; **United Sav. Bank of Detroit v.**, TexCivApp– Dallas, 116 SW2d 933, dism.—Ack 5, 20(3), 55(1), 55(2); App & E 722(1), 1002, 1011.1(1), 1122(2); Banks 116(1); Mech Liens 76, 296.

Frazier; **U.S. v.**, CA5 (Tex), 547 F2d 272.—Weap 17(4).

Frazier v. **U.S.**, CA5 (Tex), 322 F2d 221.—Int Rev 4151; Wills 858(4).

Frazier v. **U.S.**, CA5 (Tex), 304 F2d 528.—Int Rev 5219.25, 5219.30.

Frazier; **U.S. v.**, CA5 (Tex), 220 FedAppx 294.—Const Law 4703; Crim Law 1134(3); Ind & Inf 144.1(1); Sent & Pun 56, 793; Weap 4.

Frazier v. **Williams**, TexCivApp–Eastland, 359 SW2d 213.—App & E 931(1), 1010.1(3); Plead 111.18, 111.42(9); Trover 4; Venue 2.

Frazier; **Winston v.**, TexCivApp–Corpus Christi, 493 SW2d 600.—App & E 434, 770(1), 1170.12; Judgm 181(19), 186.

Frazier; **Worthey Motor Co. v.**, TexCivApp–Fort Worth, 443 SW2d 762.—App & E 1177(8); Damag 221(2.1).

Frazier v. **Wynn**, Tex, 472 SW2d 750, appeal after remand 492 SW2d 54, ref nre.—Des & Dist 89; Estop 92(1), 118; Ex & Ad 86(2); Hus & W 272(2), 274(4), 276(3); Land & Ten 94.5.

Frazier v. **Wynn**, TexCivApp–Amarillo, 492 SW2d 54, ref nre.—Action 57(2), 57(7); App & E 232(3), 241, 302(4),

758.3(1), 1062.1, 1078(1), 1195(4), 1215; Interpl 8(1); Land & Ten 130(4); Parties 14, 25, 44; Trial 352.14, 352.16.

Frazier v. Wynn, TexCivApp–Amarillo, 459 SW2d 895, writ gr, rev 472 SW2d 750, appeal after remand 492 SW2d 54, ref nre.—Ex & Ad 92; Land & Ten 48(1), 48(2), 94.5, 130(1), 130(2), 132(2), 132(3); Trial 350.4(1).

Frazier v. Yu, TexApp–Fort Worth, 987 SW2d 607, reh overr, and review den.—App & E 242(1), 516, 837(1), 837(12); Judgm 185(5), 185.3(21).

Frazier Jelke & Co. v. Chapman Minerals Corp., TexCivApp–Galveston, 149 SW2d 1101, writ dism, correct. —App & E 204(1), 260(1), 301, 1050.1(3.1), 1062.1; Corp 509.1(1); Garn 46, 164; Hus & W 255.

Frazier Jelke & Co.; Western Gulf Petroleum Corporation v., TexCivApp–Galveston, 163 SW2d 860, writ refused wom.—App & E 930(1); Garn 173, 191; Trial 350.3(2.1).

Frazin v. Hanley, TexApp–Dallas, 130 SW3d 373.—App & E 766, 836, 931(1), 961, 1010.1(2); Contracts 326; Mtg 216; Pretrial Proc 45.

F/R Cattle Co., Inc. v. State, Tex, 866 SW2d 200, reh dism, on remand 875 SW2d 736.—Environ Law 274, 683.

F/R Cattle Co., Inc.; State v., TexApp–Eastland, 875 SW2d 736.—App & E 989, 1012.1(5); Environ Law 286.

F/R Cattle Co., Inc.; State v., TexApp–Eastland, 828 SW2d 303, writ den, and writ gr, and writ withdrawn, rev 866 SW2d 200, reh dism, on remand 875 SW2d 736. —Environ Law 286.

Fream v. Geller, TexCivApp–Galveston, 263 SW2d 329, ref nre.—Inn 10.4, 10.12.

Freberg; Thomason v., TexCivApp–Corpus Christi, 588 SW2d 821.—App & E 934(2), 989; Impl & C C 1, 33.1, 34, 40, 110; Judgm 276, 335(3), 335(4); Lim of Act 43, 49(2), 50(1).

Frech; Allard v., Tex, 754 SW2d 111, cert den 109 SCt 788, 488 US 1006, 102 LEd2d 779.—Hus & W 249(3), 249(4), 266.1.

Frech; Allard v., TexApp–Fort Worth, 735 SW2d 311, writ gr, aff 754 SW2d 111, cert den 109 SCt 788, 488 US 1006, 102 LEd2d 779.—Ex & Ad 72, 86(3); Hus & W 249(3), 266.1, 273(1), 276(3); Trusts 91.

Fred v. Ledlow, TexCivApp–San Antonio, 309 SW2d 490. —Land & Ten 74.

Freda v. State, TexCrimApp, 704 SW2d 41.—Sent & Pun 1371.

Fred Astaire Dance Studios Corp.; Vess v., CA5 (Tex), 229 F2d 892.—Antitrust 579; Jury 14(3); Trademarks 1205(2).

Fred Bandas & Sons, Inc.; Jack Ritter Inc. Oil Co. v., TexCivApp–Austin, 387 SW2d 70.—App & E 770(1), 1146; Trial 397(1).

Fred C. v. Texas Health and Human Services Com'n, WDTex, 988 FSupp 1032, aff 167 F3d 537.—Health 478.

Fred C. v. Texas Health and Human Services Com'n, WDTex, 924 FSupp 788, vac 117 F3d 1416, on remand 988 FSupp 1032, aff 167 F3d 537.—Health 467, 478.

Fred C. Kroeger and Sons; Crowe v., TexCivApp–Beaumont, 468 SW2d 507.—App & E 901, 1032(2), 1048(2); Trial 48.

Fred Clark Felt Co.; Taylor v., TexCivApp–Hous (14 Dist), 567 SW2d 863, ref nre.—App & E 204(4), 223; Bills & N 443(1); Contracts 88; Judgm 181(2), 181(3), 181(6), 181(11), 181(26), 185(2), 185.1(3), 185.2(1), 185.3(16), 189.

Freddie Fuddruckers, Inc. v. Purdy's Hamburger Market and Bakery, NDTex, 589 FSupp 72. See Freddie Fuddruckers, Inc. v. Ridgeline, Inc.

Freddie Fuddruckers, Inc. v. Ridgeline, Inc., NDTex, 589 FSupp 72, aff 783 F2d 1062.—Evid 268, 357; Trademarks 1062, 1063, 1064, 1065(2), 1118, 1436, 1611, 1631, 1714(6).

Frede v. Lauderdale, TexCivApp–San Antonio, 322 SW2d 379, ref nre.—Ack 5; Evid 333(11); Judgm 681; Mines 54.5; Stip 14(7).

Fredeman; U.S. v., EDTex, 641 FSupp 655.—Jury 136(4).

Fredeman Litigation, In re, CA5 (Tex), 843 F2d 821, reh den Dixie Carriers, Inc v. Channel Fueling Service, Inc, 847 F2d 840, reh den 847 F2d 840.—Antitrust 383(2), 995; Fed Cts 755, 815; Fraud Conv 304; Inj 39, 138.3, 138.31; Sequest 1.

Frederick v. American Export Isbrantsen, SDTex, 164 FRD 444.—Fed Civ Proc 1693, 1700.

Frederick; Brazoria County Children's Protective Services v., TexApp–Houston (1 Dist), 176 SW3d 277.— Infants 157, 209; Trial 139.1(14).

Frederick v. Chaney, TexCivApp–Fort Worth, 589 SW2d 856.—Adv Poss 115(1); Evid 589; Judgm 199(3.6), 199(3.14).

Frederick v. Hullum, TexCivApp–Hous (1 Dist), 570 SW2d 87.—Contracts 116(1), 171(1); Inj 128(5.1).

Frederick; Kansas City Southern Ry. Co. v., TexCivApp–Beaumont, 276 SW2d 332, ref nre.—App & E 1170.7; Courts 92; Damag 39; Evid 501(7).

Frederick; Mobil Oil Corp. v., Tex, 621 SW2d 595.—App & E 1175(5).

Frederick; Mobil Oil Corp. v., TexCivApp–Fort Worth, 615 SW2d 323, aff in part, rev in part 621 SW2d 595.— Assault 39; Corp 498; Estop 52(3); Plead 396; Princ & A 99, 120(3).

Frederick v. Servicemaster, Ltd. Partnership, EDTex, 739 FSupp 1095.—Fed Cts 302.

Frederick v. State, TexCrimApp, 92 SW2d 254, 130 TexCrim 65.—Bail 93.

Frederick v. Travelers Ins. Co., TexCivApp–Beaumont, 425 SW2d 61, ref nre.—Work Comp 590, 1552.

Frederick v. U.S., CA5 (Tex), 386 F2d 481.—Fed Civ Proc 1272.1, 2488; Fed Cts 701.1; Guar 60.5, 62, 89; Mtg 360; Princ & S 145(2); U S 125(5), 130(6.1), 130(10).

Frederick v. U.S., CCA5 (Tex), 146 F2d 488, cert den 65 SCt 866, 324 US 861, 89 LEd 1418.—Aliens 795(4).

Frederick; U.S. v., SDTex, 50 FSupp 769, aff 146 F2d 488, cert den 65 SCt 866, 324 US 861, 89 LEd 1418.—Aliens 101, 211, 770, 780, 795(4).

Fredericks; Hicks v., TexCivApp–Beaumont, 286 SW2d 315.—App & E 688(1), 704.1; New Tr 40(4); Trial 273, 278.

Fredericks; Jennings v., TexCivApp–Galveston, 190 SW2d 707, writ refused.—App & E 544(1), 554(2), 564(3).

Fredericks; Republic Nat. Bank of Dallas v., Tex, 283 SW2d 39, 155 Tex 79.—Powers 19, 33(1); Trusts 172; Wills 439, 440, 450, 455, 486, 487(1), 589(1), 589(3), 589(6), 684.2(1), 684.10(3.1), 692(1).

Fredericks; Republic Nat. Bank of Dallas v., TexCivApp–Dallas, 274 SW2d 431, rev 283 SW2d 39, 155 Tex 79.—App & E 609; Decl Judgm 365, 393; Powers 10, 19, 32, 33(1), 36(1); Trusts 172, 276, 280; Wills 440, 475, 523, 589(3), 589(4), 634(9), 684.6, 705.

Fredericks v. U.S., CA5 (Tex), 208 F2d 712, cert den 74 SCt 875, 347 US 1019, 98 LEd 1140.—Consp 47(12); Controlled Subs 86; Crim Law 394.2(2); Int Rev 5295; Searches 31.1.

Fredericksburg, City of; Hallmark v., TexApp–San Antonio, 94 SW3d 703, reh overr, and review den, on remand 2004 WL 5049538, appeal after remand 2005 WL 763264.—Civil R 1345, 1351(1), 1351(4), 1352(1), 1376(6); Mun Corp 745.

Fredericksburg Hospital and Clinic; Springall v., TexCivApp–San Antonio, 225 SW2d 232.—App & E 930(1), 989; Neglig 377, 387, 1104(8), 1708, 1713; Trial 142.

Fredericksburg Hospital & Clinic v. Springall, TexCivApp–San Antonio, 220 SW2d 692.—Health 835; Neglig 387; Trial 358.

Fredericksburg Industries, Inc. v. Franklin Intern., Inc., TexApp–San Antonio, 911 SW2d 518, reh den, and writ den.—App & E 1050.1(1), 1056.1(1), 1056.1(6); Corp 202; Evid 141, 146; Trial 43.

Fredericksen v. State, TexCrimApp, 234 SW2d 872, 155 TexCrim 287.—Crim Law 917(2), 1111(3), 1165(1), 1166.14; Rob 24.15(1).

Frederickson v. Cochran, TexCivApp–Beaumont, 449 SW2d 329, ref nre.—App & E 758.3(2), 846(5), 907(3), 932(1); Damag 117; Land & Ten 136.

Frederickson v. State, TexCrimApp, 97 SW2d 206, 131 TexCrim 82.—Crim Law 938(1), 941(1), 942(1).

Fred Haas Toyota; Collins v., TexApp–Houston (1 Dist), 21 SW3d 606.—Cons Cred 10.1; Judgm 185.3(1).

Fred Hall & Son v. New, TexCivApp–Waco, 279 SW2d 174.—App & E 339(2), 395, 624, 627.

Fred Jones of Texas, Inc.; Howard v., TexCivApp–Amarillo, 295 SW2d 545, writ dism.—Damag 117; Evid 441(9); Sales 114, 422, 481.

Fred M. Manning, Inc.; O'Connor v., TexCivApp–Eastland, 255 SW2d 277, writ refused.—Sales 209; Trover 34(2), 40(3), 66.

Fred Oakley Chrysler-Dodge; Ingram v., TexApp–El Paso, 663 SW2d 561.—App & E 934(2); Labor & Emp 40(1), 40(2).

Fred Oakley Motors, Inc.; Raye v., TexApp–Dallas, 646 SW2d 288, ref nre.—Antitrust 389(1), 389(2), 390; Damag 123; Fraud 59(3), 65(1); Sales 418(1), 418(3), 442(6), 446(1).

F. Redondo & Co.; New Amsterdam Cas. Co. v., TexCivApp–San Antonio, 158 SW2d 334, writ refused.—Estop 88(3); Princ & S 115(1); Release 17(1); Schools 81(2).

Fredonia Broadcasting Corp., Inc. v. RCA Corp., CA5 (Tex), 569 F2d 251, reh den 572 F2d 320, cert den 99 SCt 177, 439 US 859, 58 LEd2d 167.—Atty & C 21.15, 30; Fraud 3, 12, 58(3), 59(3), 60, 61; Interest 26; Judges 46.

Fredonia Broadcasting Corp., Inc. v. RCA Corp., CA5 (Tex), 481 F2d 781, appeal after remand 569 F2d 251, reh den 572 F2d 320, cert den 99 SCt 177, 439 US 859, 58 LEd2d 167.—Contracts 46, 313(1); Damag 6, 40(2), 89(2); Evid 486; Fed Civ Proc 675.1, 2171, 2183, 2292; Fed Cts 374, 633, 641, 799; Fraud 12, 20, 31, 66; Judgm 589(2); Prod Liab 17.1; Ref of Inst 21; Sales 48, 51, 52(5.1), 393, 404, 418(2), 418(3), 421, 422, 441(4), 442(2), 442(5); Statut 230.

Fredonia State Bank v. General American Life Ins. Co., Tex, 881 SW2d 279, on remand 906 SW2d 88, reh overr.—App & E 294(1), 344, 766, 1079, 1182; Insurance 2983.

Fredonia State Bank v. General American Life Ins. Co., TexApp–Tyler, 906 SW2d 88, reh overr.—Insurance 3013, 3015.

Fredonia State Bank v. General American Life Ins. Co., TexApp–Tyler, 884 SW2d 167, writ gr, rev 881 SW2d 279, on remand 906 SW2d 88, reh overr.—App & E 76(1), 82(2), 346.2, 930(3), 989, 994(2), 1001(1), 1002, 1003(7); Evid 383(4), 584(1), 598(1); Insurance 2445, 3015, 3099.

Fredonia State Bank; Insurance Co. of North America v., TexCivApp–Tyler, 469 SW2d 248, ref nre.—Banks 102, 109(1), 113, 133; Cust & U 10; Judgm 181(2), 185(5), 186; Princ & A 137(1), 147(2); Subrog 33(2).

Fred Regalado Bail Bonds v. State, TexApp–Corpus Christi, 934 SW2d 852. See Regalado v. State.

Frederickson; City of Galveston v., TexCivApp–Galveston, 174 SW2d 994.—Mun Corp 186(1), 199; Statut 210, 211.

Fredrickson, Faloona by, v. Hustler Magazine, Inc., CA5 (Tex), 799 F2d 1000. See Faloona by Fredrickson v. Hustler Magazine, Inc.

Fredrickson, Faloona by, v. Hustler Magazine, Inc., NDTex, 607 FSupp 1341. See Faloona by Fredrickson v. Hustler Magazine, Inc.

Fred Rizk Const. Co. v. Cousins Mortg. & Equity Investments, TexApp–Houston (1 Dist), 627 SW2d 753, ref nre.—Judgm 768(1); Trusts 21(2), 25(1), 44(1).

Fred Roberts Memorial Hospital; City of Corpus Christi v., TexCivApp–El Paso, 195 SW2d 429, ref nre.—Tax 2343.

Fred S. James & Co. of Oklahoma, Inc. v. West Texas Compresses, Inc., TexApp–Eastland, 741 SW2d 571.—App & E 989, 1010.1(3), 1012.1(5); Evid 48, 51; Insurance 3585; Work Comp 1063.

Fredwell; Rhoades v., TexCivApp–Austin, 192 SW2d 295, ref nre.—Armed S 34.9(2); Child C 609; Child S 332; Hus & W 221, 230.

Free v. American Home Assur. Co., TexApp–Houston (1 Dist), 902 SW2d 51.—App & E 852, 934(1); Damag 50.10; Judgm 181(11), 181(33), 185(2); Libel 6(1), 9(1), 44(1), 45(1), 47, 50, 51(1), 101(4), 123(2).

Free v. Bland, USTex, 82 SCt 1089, 369 US 663, 8 LEd2d 180, opinion conformed to 359 SW2d 297, 163 Tex 594.—Fed Cts 407.1; Hus & W 248, 249(1), 254, 265; Judgm 181(2), 181(11); States 18.5, 18.19, 18.29; U S 91.

Free; Bland v., Tex, 359 SW2d 297, 163 Tex 594.—U S 91.

Free; Bland v., Tex, 344 SW2d 435, 162 Tex 72, cert gr 82 SCt 50, 368 US 811, 7 LEd2d 21, rev 82 SCt 1089, 369 US 663, 8 LEd2d 180, opinion conformed to 359 SW2d 297, 163 Tex 594.—App & E 1107.

Free v. Bland, TexCivApp–Texarkana, 337 SW2d 805, rev 344 SW2d 435, 162 Tex 72, cert gr 82 SCt 50, 368 US 811, 7 LEd2d 21, rev 82 SCt 1089, 369 US 663, 8 LEd2d 180, opinion conformed to 359 SW2d 297, 163 Tex 594, ref nre 359 SW2d 297, 163 Tex 594.—Courts 91(1); U S 91.

Free; Burleson Burial Ass'n v., TexCivApp–Waco, 176 SW2d 1021, dism.—Insurance 3398.

Free; County School Trustees of Upshur County v., TexCivApp–Texarkana, 154 SW2d 935, writ refused wom.—Em Dom 9, 40, 177, 317(1), 317(2); Estates 5; Mines 47, 48, 55(1).

Free v. Fleet, TexCivApp–Galveston, 250 SW2d 398.—Lim of Act 197(1).

Free v. Miles, CA5 (Tex), 333 F3d 550, reh den.—Hab Corp 816, 818, 842, 846; Sent & Pun 1132, 1157, 1175.

Free v. Owen, TexComApp, 113 SW2d 1221, 131 Tex 281.—Adv Poss 1, 43(3), 43(4), 106(5); Lim of Act 19(1), 60(5); Mental H 382.1; Ven & Pur 130(2).

Free; Owen v., TexCivApp–Waco, 85 SW2d 1090, rev 113 SW2d 1221, 131 Tex 281.—Adv Poss 43(1); App & E 1177(6); Des & Dist 90(1); Lim of Act 44(1); Mental H 383.

Free; Smith v., TexComApp, 107 SW2d 588, 130 Tex 23.—App & E 66, 84(1), 84(2), 776, 1082(1), 1236.

Free v. State, TexCrimApp, 307 SW2d 808, 165 TexCrim 374.—Autos 355(6); Crim Law 1111(4).

Free v. State, TexApp–Beaumont, 692 SW2d 542.—Crim Law 1177; Sent & Pun 1919.

Free v. Tidwell, TexCivApp–Eastland, 84 SW2d 512.—Labor & Emp 3096(4).

Free; Turnbow v., TexCivApp–Fort Worth, 149 SW2d 617, writ dism, correct.—App & E 877(2).

Free; Turnbow v., TexCivApp–Fort Worth, 149 SW2d 615, writ dism, correct.—App & E 1135.

Free; U.S. v., CA5 (Tex), 574 F2d 1221, cert den 99 SCt 209, 439 US 873, 58 LEd2d 187.—Crim Law 1167(2); Homic 546, 986, 1002, 1146; Ind & Inf 127.

Free & Accepted Masons of Texas v. Taylor, TexCivApp–Waco, 96 SW2d 126, writ dism.—Insurance 2082, 2086.

Freeberg v. Securities Inv. Co. of St. Louis, TexCivApp–San Antonio, 331 SW2d 825, writ refused.—Autos 20; Judgm 185(2), 185.2(9); Lim of Act 95(7).

Freeborn v. Davis, TexCivApp–Amarillo, 122 SW2d 645.—Plead 111.9, 111.39(5); Princ & A 21, 22(1), 121; Venue 70.

FREEMAN;

Freeby v. North Denver Bank, CA5 (Tex), 394 F2d 149.—Fed Civ Proc 2488.

Freeby; North Denver Bank v., NDTex, 285 FSupp 74, aff 394 F2d 149.—Fed Civ Proc 2488; Fed Cts 407.1; Hus & W 85(3); Paymt 39(1).

Freece v. Truskett, TexComApp, 106 SW2d 675, 130 Tex 90.—Mtg 334, 356.

Freed, Ex parte, TexCrimApp, 254 SW2d 792.—Hab Corp 823.

Freed v. Bozman, TexCivApp–Texarkana, 304 SW2d 235, ref nre.—App & E 238(2), 281(1), 1062.1; Evid 591; Mech Liens 247, 251; Ven & Pur 228(7).

Freed v. Dicker, TexCivApp–Dallas, 539 SW2d 211.—Judgm 181(19), 185(2).

Freedman v. Briarcroft Property Owners, Inc., TexApp–Houston (14 Dist), 776 SW2d 212, writ den.—App & E 93, 233(2), 684(1), 707(1), 854(1), 907(5), 1043(1), 1064.4; Assoc 20(1); Costs 194.16, 194.30; Judgm 256(1); Nuis 1, 23(1), 26, 29, 33, 34; Parties 76(2); Trial 199.

Freedman v. Cigna Ins. Co. of Texas, TexApp–Houston (1 Dist), 976 SW2d 776.—App & E 1079; Insurance 2101, 2275, 2914.

Freedman; City of Houston v., TexCivApp–Galveston, 293 SW2d 515, ref nre.—Evid 32; Judgm 181(15.1); Mand 87, 180; Mun Corp 591.

Freedman; Hull v., TexCivApp–Fort Worth, 383 SW2d 236, ref nre.—Contracts 326; Interest 39(2.15), 39(2.20), 66; Lim of Act 28(1); Mines 51(2), 79.7; Paymt 85(1), 85(7); Trover 1, 2, 9(5).

Freedman v. Texaco Marine Services, Inc., EDTex, 882 FSupp 580.—Labor & Emp 407, 563(1), 688, 709, 711, 717; States 18.51.

Freedman v. U.S., CA5 (Tex), 382 F2d 742.—Hus & W 249(3), 254, 262.1(5), 266.4; Int Rev 4153(1), 4155, 4185.

Freedman v. University of Houston, TexApp–Houston (1 Dist), 110 SW3d 504.—Abate & R 1; App & E 863; Colleges 2, 5; Const Law 2314; Courts 40; Em Dom 2.33; Mun Corp 254, 723; Plead 104(1); Pretrial Proc 554; States 191.1, 191.4(1), 191.6(2), 191.6(3), 191.9(1), 191.9(2), 191.9(3).

Freedman Packing Co. v. Harris, TexCivApp–Galveston, 160 SW2d 130, writ refused wom.—App & E 758.3(1), 1072; Const Law 2653; Courts 247(7); New Tr 109, 128(4), 140(1), 143(1), 152; Plead 13.

Freedom Bail Bonds v. Groff, TexApp–Dallas, 936 SW2d 661. See Perkins v. Groff.

Freedom Communications, Inc. v. Brand, TexApp–Corpus Christi, 907 SW2d 614.—App & E 66, 169, 173(2), 863; Judgm 181(1), 181(33), 183, 185(2), 185(5), 185(6), 185.3(21); Libel 22, 51(5), 112(2).

Freedom Homes of Texas, Inc. v. Dickinson, TexCivApp–Corpus Christi, 598 SW2d 714, ref nre.—Antitrust 397; App & E 216(7), 218.2(10), 499(1), 883, 930(3); Damag 48, 49.10, 192; Trial 365.1(1).

Freedom, Inc. v. State, TexCivApp–Austin, 569 SW2d 48.—Bail 60; Princ & S 52.

Freedom Newspapers, Inc.; McNamara v., TexApp–Corpus Christi, 802 SW2d 901, writ den.—Const Law 1490, 1627, 2070; Damag 49.10, 50.10, 57.49; Judgm 181(3); Torts 350, 351, 357, 377.

Freedom Newspapers of Texas v. Cantu, Tex, 168 SW3d 847, reh den.—Evid 571(1); Libel 51(5).

Freedom Newspapers of Texas v. Cantu, TexApp–Corpus Christi, 126 SW3d 185, on reh, and review gr, rev 168 SW3d 847, reh den.—App & E 863; Costs 226; Judgm 181(33), 185.3(21); Libel 1, 19, 48(1), 48(2), 49, 51(1), 51(5), 54, 55, 101(5), 112(2), 116, 123(2), 123(7), 129.

Freedson v. C. I. R., CA5 (Tex), 565 F2d 954.—Fed Cts 818; Int Rev 4654.

Freedson v. State, TexCivApp–Hous (1 Dist), 600 SW2d 349, ref nre.—Atty & C 58; Consp 33(1); Const Law 4273(3).

Free-Flow Muffler Co. v. Kliewer, TexCivApp–Texarkana, 283 SW2d 778, ref nre.—Antitrust 972(4); Pat 214, 218(5), 219(2), 219(5), 222.

Freeland; Dillard v., TexApp–Corpus Christi, 714 SW2d 378.—App & E 607(1), 1062.2; Bills & N 129(2); Mtg 335, 379; Trial 255(10).

Freeland v. Freeland, TexCivApp–Dallas, 313 SW2d 943.—Child S 444, 502; Const Law 1106; Courts 475(15).

Freeland; Freeland v., TexCivApp–Dallas, 313 SW2d 943.—Child S 444, 502; Const Law 1106; Courts 475(15).

Freeland v. State, TexCrimApp, 106 SW2d 679, 132 TexCrim 594.—Crim Law 27, 511.1(9); Sent & Pun 201.

Freelove v. Atlas Roofing Co., TexCivApp–Fort Worth, 239 SW2d 399, mandamus den Atlas Roofing Co v. Hall, 245 SW2d 477, 150 Tex 611, opinion conformed to 245 SW2d 973.—Venue 22(1), 22(6).

Freelove; San Augustine Independent School Dist. v., TexCivApp–Beaumont, 195 SW2d 175, ref nre.—App & E 1056.4; Impl & C C 63; Trial 350.4(4), 352.4(2).

Freelove; Waller County v., TexCivApp–Galveston, 210 SW2d 602, ref nre.—Counties 47, 113(1), 124(1), 125, 204(1); Impl & C C 34; Mun Corp 249.

Freels v. State, TexCrimApp, 301 SW2d 136.—Crim Law 1090.1(1).

Freels v. State, TexCrimApp, 210 SW2d 582, 151 TexCrim 589.—Crim Law 552(3), 560; Homic 1154.

Freeman, Ex parte, Tex, 191 SW2d 6, 144 Tex 392.—Child S 470, 479; Contempt 54(2); Hab Corp 529.

Freeman, Ex parte, TexCrimApp, 486 SW2d 556.—Pardon 28; Prisons 15(1); Sent & Pun 1157, 1158, 1161, 1171.

Freeman, Ex parte, TexApp–Houston (1 Dist), 778 SW2d 874.—Hab Corp 485, 816; Sent & Pun 2009.

Freeman; American Bank & Trust Co. v., TexCivApp–Beaumont, 560 SW2d 444, ref nre.—App & E 770(1); Banks 105(1), 111; Corp 297, 298(1), 398(2), 406(2), 432(5); Fraud 30.

Freeman v. American Motorists Ins. Co., TexApp–Houston (1 Dist), 53 SW3d 710.—App & E 934(2); Evid 357; Judgm 185(2); Lim of Act 74(1); Work Comp 1151.

Freeman v. Anderson, TexCivApp–Waco, 119 SW2d 1081.—App & E 714(5), 714(6); Covenants 100(1), 101, 102(1); Judgm 249; Ven & Pur 334(5).

Freeman v. Banks, TexCivApp–Fort Worth, 91 SW2d 1078, writ refused.—Courts 475(2); Ex & Ad 130(1), 154, 271, 272, 288, 336, 404.

Freeman v. B. F. Goodrich Rubber Co., TexCivApp–Dallas, 127 SW2d 476, writ dism by agreement.—Evid 66; Judgm 17(1); Lim of Act 60(1), 95(2), 95(3); Neglig 202.

Freeman v. Bianchi, TexApp–Houston (1 Dist), 820 SW2d 853, subsequent mandamus proceeding Granada Corp v. Honorable First Court of Appeals, 844 SW2d 223.—App & E 946; Mand 1, 4(4); Pretrial Proc 356.1, 401, 406, 411; Stip 6, 7; Witn 201(2), 219(1), 219(3), 222, 223.

Freeman v. Board of Adjustment of City of San Antonio, TexCivApp–San Antonio, 230 SW2d 387.—Admin Law 781; Zoning 504, 605.

Freeman; Bradley v., TexCivApp–Amarillo, 163 SW2d 693.—Plead 236(4); Subrog 41(5), 41(6).

Freeman v. Burrows, Tex, 171 SW2d 863, 141 Tex 318.—App & E 781(1).

Freeman v. Canterbury, TexCivApp–Waco, 346 SW2d 955.—App & E 1048(6), 1070(2); Autos 245(66).

Freeman v. Carroll, TexCivApp–Tyler, 499 SW2d 668, ref nre.—App & E 1069.3; Contracts 346(12); Costs 194.32; Impl & C C 55; Trial 194(20), 229, 312(3), 351.2(2), 365.1(5).

Freeman; Central Power & Light Co. v., TexCivApp–Corpus Christi, 431 SW2d 897, ref nre.—App & E 842(1), 1069.1; Em Dom 224; Jury 31.2(1); New Tr 44(1); Trial 217, 304, 306.

FREEMAN;

See Guidelines for Arrangement at the beginning of this Volume

Freeman; Chapparral Coach Mfg. Inc. v., TexCivApp–Beaumont, 440 SW2d 404.—App & E 1177(6).

Freeman; Cherokee Water Co. v., TexApp–Texarkana, 145 SW3d 809, reh overr, and review den.—Adv Poss 13, 58, 60(2), 96, 112, 114(1), 114(2), 117; App & E 863, 927(1), 930(1), 934(1), 989, 1001(3), 1003(6), 1062.2; Bound 3(1), 3(7), 40(1); Estop 15; Judgm 199(3.5), 199(3.7), 199(3.9), 199(3.10), 540, 584, 585(4), 586(0.5), 586(2), 634, 747(0.5), 948(1), 951(1), 956(1); Trial 143, 350.1.

Freeman; Cherokee Water Co. v., TexApp–Texarkana, 33 SW3d 349, reh overr.—App & E 893(1); Deeds 90, 93, 95, 143; Evid 448, 452, 458, 461(1); Trial 136(3).

Freeman v. Cherokee Water Co., TexApp–Texarkana, 11 SW3d 480, review den.—Em Dom 243(3), 323; Judgm 567, 591.1, 678(2), 713(2), 720; Lim of Act 63.

Freeman; Cheswick v., Tex, 287 SW2d 171, 155 Tex 372.—Home 31, 32, 143.

Freeman; Cheswick v., TexCivApp–Waco, 282 SW2d 315, rev 287 SW2d 171, 155 Tex 372.—Home 84, 162(1), 185; Judgm 303.

Freeman v. Chick, TexCivApp–Austin, 252 SW2d 763, dism.—Evid 597; Wills 302(4).

Freeman v. City of Dallas, CA5 (Tex), 242 F3d 642, cert den 122 SCt 47, 534 US 817, 151 LEd2d 18.—Const Law 4092; Mun Corp 589, 628; Searches 11, 13.1, 23, 24, 26, 40.1, 113.1.

Freeman v. City of Dallas, CA5 (Tex), 186 F3d 601, reh en banc gr 200 F3d 884, on reh 242 F3d 642, cert den 122 SCt 47, 534 US 817, 151 LEd2d 18.—Const Law 3879, 3882, 4097, 4416; Mun Corp 628; Searches 24, 39, 53.1, 79.

Freeman v. City of Pasadena, Tex, 767 SW2d 700. See Tice v. City of Pasadena.

Freeman v. City of Pasadena, Tex, 744 SW2d 923, reh den.—Damag 51.

Freeman; City of Pasadena v., TexApp–Houston (14 Dist), 731 SW2d 590, writ gr, aff 744 SW2d 923, reh den.—Autos 253, 277.1, 278, 279, 308(6), 313; Damag 51, 135.

Freeman v. City of San Antonio, CA5 (Tex), 142 F3d 848. See Freeman v. County of Bexar.

Freeman; Commercial Standard Ins. Co. v., TexCivApp–Beaumont, 100 SW2d 145, writ dism.—Action 48(1), 50(1), 50(5); Insurance 3515(1), 3571, 3576.

Freeman v. Commercial Union Assur. Co., TexCivApp–Texarkana, 317 SW2d 563, ref nre.—App & E 1070(2); Evid 171, 383(7); Insurance 2989.

Freeman v. County of Bexar, CA5 (Tex), 210 F3d 550, cert den 121 SCt 318, 531 US 933, 148 LEd2d 255.—Arrest 63.4(10); Civil R 1088(4), 1376(6); Crim Law 211(1); Fed Civ Proc 2491.5, 2552.

Freeman v. County of Bexar, CA5 (Tex), 142 F3d 848, appeal after remand 210 F3d 550, cert den 121 SCt 318, 531 US 933, 148 LEd2d 255.—Fed Civ Proc 2470, 2470.4; Fed Cts 776; U S Mag 14, 27.

Freeman; Cresthaven Nursing Residence v., TexApp–Amarillo, 134 SW3d 214, on reh in part, and rule 537(f) motion gr.—App & E 971(2), 984(1), 989, 1004(3); Damag 127.3, 127.5, 140.7, 184; Death 89, 99(2), 99(4), 105; Evid 78, 89, 536, 538, 544, 545; Health 611, 821(1), 834(1), 834(2); Interest 39(2.6), 39(2.50), 49, 57, 67; Partners 353; Pretrial Proc 434; Statut 188, 212.6; Trial 211, 219, 232(1), 251(1), 252(1), 252(1), 252(22), 352.4(1).

Freeman v. Crown Life Ins. Co., TexCivApp–Texarkana, 580 SW2d 897, ref nre.—Insurance 1822, 1831, 2594(3), 2594(4), 2604.

Freeman; Davis v., TexCivApp–Dallas, 347 SW2d 650.—App & E 934(1); Brok 43(1), 43(3); Frds St of 131(2); Judgm 181(18); Torts 212.

Freeman v. Davis, TexCivApp–Amarillo, 363 SW2d 952, ref nre.—Sales 179(4).

Freeman v. Del Mar College, TexApp–Corpus Christi, 716 SW2d 729.—Holidays 1; Schools 21, 89.2; States 112.2(4), 191.10; Time 10(9).

Freeman v. Dies, NDTex, 307 FSupp 1028.—Const Law 3657, 3658(6); Inj 80, 189.

Freeman; Duross v., TexApp–San Antonio, 831 SW2d 354, reh den, and writ gr, and writ withdrawn, and writ den.—Schools 63(3), 147.

Freeman v. Eastman-Whipstock, Inc., SDTex, 390 FSupp 685.—Antitrust 900, 958, 963(1), 963(3), 972(4).

Freeman; Extraction Resources, Inc. v., TexCivApp–El Paso, 555 SW2d 156, ref nre.—Deeds 120; Mines 48, 55(2), 55(4).

Freeman v. Federal Underwriters Exchange, TexCivApp–Beaumont, 155 SW2d 674.—App & E 170(2), 761; Work Comp 19, 1105.

Freeman v. Ferguson, Tex, 292 SW2d 632, 155 Tex 650.—Contempt 28(1).

Freeman v. Freeman, Tex, 327 SW2d 428, 160 Tex 148.—App & E 434; Courts 85(1); Judgm 95, 119, 470, 486(1); Trial 9(1); Wills 361, 373.1, 388.

Freeman; Freeman v., Tex, 327 SW2d 428, 160 Tex 148.—App & E 434; Courts 85(1); Judgm 95, 119, 470, 486(1); Trial 9(1); Wills 361, 373.1, 388.

Freeman v. Freeman, TexApp–San Antonio, 133 SW3d 277, reh overr.—Divorce 252.3(4); States 18.28.

Freeman; Freeman v., TexApp–San Antonio, 133 SW3d 277, reh overr.—Divorce 252.3(4); States 18.28.

Freeman v. Freeman, TexApp–Texarkana, 320 SW2d 700, aff 327 SW2d 428, 160 Tex 148.—Wills 363.

Freeman; Freeman v., TexApp–Texarkana, 320 SW2d 700, aff 327 SW2d 428, 160 Tex 148.—Wills 363.

Freeman v. Freeman, TexCivApp–Eastland, 569 SW2d 626.—Frds St of 44(1), 129(2); Wills 58(2), 66.

Freeman; Freeman v., TexCivApp–Eastland, 569 SW2d 626.—Frds St of 44(1), 129(2); Wills 58(2), 66.

Freeman v. Freeman, TexCivApp–Hous (14 Dist), 497 SW2d 97.—Divorce 252.3(4), 253(3), 286(5), 287; Hus & W 272(5).

Freeman; Freeman v., TexCivApp–Hous (14 Dist), 497 SW2d 97.—Divorce 252.3(4), 253(3), 286(5), 287; Hus & W 272(5).

Freeman; Gonzales County Sav. and Loan Ass'n v., Tex, 534 SW2d 903.—B & L Assoc 33(16), 33(22); Judgm 181(2), 181(3), 181(15.1), 185(2); Usury 16, 53, 119.

Freeman v. Gonzales County Sav. & Loan Ass'n, TexCivApp–Corpus Christi, 526 SW2d 774, writ gr, aff 534 SW2d 903.—B & L Assoc 1, 26, 33(1), 33(4), 33(5), 34(8); Judgm 181(3), 185(2), 185.3(5); Statut 181(1); Usury 53.

Freeman v. Gore, CA5 (Tex), 483 F3d 404.—Arrest 63.4(2), 63.4(4), 63.4(15), 68(2), 68(3); Civil R 1035, 1088(4), 1376(2), 1376(6); Fed Cts 574, 766, 776, 802.

Freeman v. Great Atlantic & Pacific Tea Co., TexCivApp–Austin, 135 SW2d 267, writ refused.—App & E 1002, 1003(4), 1070(2); Neglig 1679, 1691.

Freeman v. Greenbriar Homes, Inc., TexApp–Dallas, 715 SW2d 394, ref nre.—Antitrust 199, 363, 369; Ven & Pur 1, 17.

Freeman; Groendyke Transport Co. v., TexCivApp–Amarillo, 255 SW2d 393.—Plead 111.3, 111.42(8).

Freeman v. Ham, TexCivApp–Austin, 283 SW2d 438, ref nre.—Autos 181(2).

Freeman v. Harkrider, TexCivApp–Amarillo, 320 SW2d 238.—Autos 168(1), 172(5.1), 201(2); Evid 474(15).

Freeman v. Harris County, TexApp–Houston (1 Dist), 183 SW3d 885, review den.—App & E 893(1), 916(1); Counties 146; Damag 57.1, 57.14, 57.42; Dead Bodies 9; Mun Corp 745, 852; Plead 104(1), 111.37, 111.38.

Freeman v. Hernandez, TexCivApp–Dallas, 521 SW2d 108.—App & E 854(1), 1175(1), 1177(1), 1177(2), 1177(7); Ref of Inst 19(2); Usury 117.

Freeman v. Hill, TexCivApp–Hous (1 Dist), 419 SW2d 923, ref nre.—Estop 118; Sales 238; Trover 40(3).

Freeman v. Hillman, TexCivApp–Amarillo, 173 SW2d 657.—App & E 1069.1; Trial 313.

Freeman v. Hiram Walker Inc., TexApp–Beaumont, 790 SW2d 842. See McGuire v. Joseph E. Seagram & Sons, Inc.

Freeman v. Hygeia Dairy Co., CA5 (Tex), 326 F2d 271.—Food 4.5(1), 4.5(5), 4.5(6).

Freeman; Hygeia Dairy Co. v., SDTex, 197 FSupp 876, rev 326 F2d 271.—Food 4.5(4), 4.5(5).

Freeman; Kemper v., TexCivApp–Fort Worth, 254 SW2d 837.—Home 115(2), 116.

Freeman; Kirby Lumber Corp. v., TexCivApp–Eastland, 336 SW2d 838, ref nre.—Adv Poss 42, 50, 96, 114(1), 115(4); Evid 265(10).

Freeman v. Leasing Associates, Inc., TexCivApp–Hous (14 Dist), 503 SW2d 406.—Damag 194, 199.

Freeman v. Magnolia Petroleum Co., Tex, 171 SW2d 339, 141 Tex 274.—App & E 1062.1; Mines 73.1(5), 73.5, 75, 78.1(1), 78.2.

Freeman v. Magnolia Petroleum Co., TexCivApp–Amarillo, 165 SW2d 111, rev 171 SW2d 339, 141 Tex 274.—Mines 73.1(4), 77, 78.1(4), 78.1(8), 78.2, 79.2, 79.6.

Freeman; Modern Mut. Health & Acc. Ins. Co. v., TexCivApp–San Antonio, 151 SW2d 240, writ dism, correct.—App & E 909(6), 931(3); Ben Assoc 16; Plead 36(2).

Freeman; Morgan v., CA5 (Tex), 715 F2d 185.—Autos 244(26); Fed Cts 841, 844; Labor & Emp 23, 3031(1), 3031(2), 3094(2).

Freeman; Motors Ins. Corp. v., TexCivApp–Dallas, 304 SW2d 580.—Insurance 3389, 3559; Plead 111.9, 111.38; Ref of Inst 36(3).

Freeman; Motors Ins. Corp. v., TexCivApp–Texarkana, 314 SW2d 453.—App & E 20, 1187.

Freeman; Murchison v., TexCivApp–El Paso, 127 SW2d 369, writ refused.—Mtg 97, 310.

Freeman v. Nash, TexCivApp–Beaumont, 431 SW2d 794.—Contracts 306(0.5).

Freeman; National Bankers Life Ins. Co. v., TexCivApp–Fort Worth, 319 SW2d 139.—App & E 1170.10; Insurance 1652(7); Princ & A 88; Trial 352.9.

Freeman v. Northwest Acceptance Corp., CA5 (Tex), 754 F2d 553.—Fed Civ Proc 215; Fed Cts 31, 282, 286.1, 297, 622, 623, 944.

Freeman; Nugent v., TexCivApp–Eastland, 306 SW2d 167, ref nre.—Estop 98(1); Mines 79.1(5), 79.7, 92.16.

Freeman v. Parks, TexCivApp–El Paso, 102 SW2d 291.—Deeds 17(2); Mines 55(1), 55(8).

Freeman; Perkins v., Tex, 518 SW2d 532.—Child C 923(5); Jury 136(3).

Freeman; Perkins v., TexCivApp–Beaumont, 501 SW2d 424, writ gr, rev and remanded 518 SW2d 532.—Child C 7, 76, 400, 605, 923(5), 943; Child S 26; Costs 194.16; Jury 136(3).

Freeman v. Pevehouse, TexApp–Waco, 79 SW3d 637.—App & E 977(1); Evid 587; Judgm 135, 139, 143(3), 162(0.5), 162(2), 162(4), 163; New Tr 6.

Freeman v. Samedan Oil Corp., TexApp–Tyler, 78 SW3d 1, reh overr, and appeal abated, and review reinstated, and review gr, and remanded pursuant to settlement.—App & E 863, 934(1), 1175(1); Judgm 181(2), 183; Mines 73, 73.5, 78.1(7), 78.1(9), 78.2, 78.5, 92.16.

Freeman; Sample v., TexApp–Beaumont, 873 SW2d 470, reh overr, and writ den.—Antitrust 256; App & E 843(2), 1004(1), 1004(3); Atty & C 105, 129(2), 129(3), 129(4); Courts 100(1); Damag 208(1); Evid 571(3); Interest 39(2.6), 39(2.50); Lim of Act 95(11); Plead 34(1).

Freeman v. Shannon Const., Inc., TexCivApp–Amarillo, 560 SW2d 732, ref nre.—App & E 205, 218.2(3.1), 218.2(9), 548(5), 719(8); Damag 79(1), 80(1), 121, 140, 177; Evid 588; Sales 1.5; Trial 142.

Freeman; Shropshire v., TexCivApp–Austin, 510 SW2d 405, ref nre.—Atty & C 129(2).

Freeman v. Southern Nat. Bank, SDTex, 531 FSupp 94.—Cred R A 1, 3.

Freeman; Southern Underwriters v., TexCivApp–Beaumont, 118 SW2d 367, writ refused.—Work Comp 1461.

Freeman v. Southland Paper Mills, Inc., TexCivApp–Beaumont, 573 SW2d 822, ref nre.—Ten in C 3, 49, 55(1), 55(2), 55(6); Tresp to T T 38(1).

Freeman v. State, TexCrimApp, 125 SW3d 505, reh den.—Crim Law 1119(1).

Freeman v. State, TexCrimApp, 723 SW2d 727.—Crim Law 412.1(1), 412.2(4), 414, 520(2).

Freeman v. State, TexCrimApp, 707 SW2d 597.—Larc 1, 3(3), 7, 12, 14(1), 15(1), 32(2), 40(2), 60, 73.

Freeman v. State, TexCrimApp, 654 SW2d 450.—Const Law 3937, 4500; Crim Law 59(1), 552(1), 552(3), 1159.6; Larc 55.

Freeman v. State, TexCrimApp, 618 SW2d 52.—Crim Law 412.2(3), 438(4), 1038.1(4).

Freeman v. State, TexCrimApp, 556 SW2d 287, cert den 98 SCt 1284, 434 US 1088, 55 LEd2d 794.—Costs 302.3; Crim Law 121, 126(1), 365(1), 369.2(4), 531(3), 586, 594(1), 614(1), 637, 790, 854(2), 867, 932, 1033.2, 1134(2), 1166.6, 1166.10(1), 1166.17; Jury 103(6), 105(2), 108, 131(7), 131(10); Sent & Pun 1624, 1731.

Freeman v. State, TexCrimApp, 491 SW2d 408.—Crim Law 1042; Sent & Pun 2026.

Freeman v. State, TexCrimApp, 464 SW2d 151.—Assault 78; Crim Law 1043(1).

Freeman v. State, TexCrimApp, 417 SW2d 412.—Larc 60.

Freeman v. State, TexCrimApp, 357 SW2d 757, 172 TexCrim 389.—Crim Law 673(4), 1036.1(1), 1038.2, 1038.3; Larc 65.

Freeman v. State, TexCrimApp, 354 SW2d 141, 172 TexCrim 144.—Crim Law 364(3.1); Witn 390.

Freeman v. State, TexCrimApp, 352 SW2d 833, 171 TexCrim 606.—Crim Law 1097(5).

Freeman v. State, TexCrimApp, 317 SW2d 726, 166 TexCrim 626.—Crim Law 48, 50, 627.6(1), 683(1), 1169.1(3); Homic 1210, 1502, 1551.

Freeman v. State, TexCrimApp, 290 SW2d 513.—Crim Law 1090.1(1).

Freeman v. State, TexCrimApp, 266 SW2d 377.—Crim Law 1090.1(1).

Freeman v. State, TexCrimApp, 266 SW2d 152.—Crim Law 1090.1(1).

Freeman v. State, TexCrimApp, 263 SW2d 252.—Crim Law 1090.1(1).

Freeman v. State, TexCrimApp, 250 SW2d 223, 157 TexCrim 478.—Larc 34.

Freeman v. State, TexCrimApp, 188 SW2d 579.—Crim Law 1090.1(1).

Freeman v. State, TexCrimApp, 186 SW2d 683, 148 TexCrim 265.—Crim Law 1166(1); Jury 22(4), 24.

Freeman v. State, TexCrimApp, 172 SW2d 309, 146 TexCrim 236.—Burg 9(0.5), 11, 26; Ind & Inf 63.

Freeman v. State, TexCrimApp, 147 SW2d 1095, 141 TexCrim 158.—Crim Law 419(12), 1110(1); False Pret 39, 42.

Freeman v. State, TexCrimApp, 117 SW2d 93, 135 TexCrim 50.—Crim Law 1099.7(1), 1099.7(4).

Freeman v. State, TexCrimApp, 117 SW2d 75, 134 TexCrim 607.—Crim Law 1097(3).

Freeman v. State, TexCrimApp, 92 SW2d 1039, 130 TexCrim 148.—Crim Law 954(1), 1182.

Freeman v. State, TexApp–Houston (1 Dist), 864 SW2d 757, petition for discretionary review refused.—Crim Law 1036.1(4), 1036.1(5), 1144.13(2.1), 1159.2(7), 1159.6; Weap 17(4).

Freeman v. State, TexApp–Houston (1 Dist), 786 SW2d 56.—Const Law 2812; Weap 17(4); Witn 64(1), 188.1, 191, 195.

Freeman v. State, TexApp–Houston (1 Dist), 630 SW2d 868, petition for discretionary review refused.—Crim Law 517.3(4), 535(2), 1184(1); Homic 908.

FREEMAN

59 Tex D 2d—130

Freeman v. State, TexApp–Fort Worth, 917 SW2d 512.— Crim Law 907, 909, 947, 1042, 1083, 1130(5), 1134(2), 1134(10), 1144.13(6), 1144.17, 1147, 1159.2(9), 1159.4(2); Sent & Pun 2009, 2019, 2020, 2021, 2026.

Freeman v. State, TexApp–Dallas, 69 SW3d 374.—Autos 332, 355(6); Crim Law 1134(2), 1144.13(2.1), 1159.2(2), 1159.2(7).

Freeman v. State, TexApp–Dallas, 733 SW2d 662, petition for discretionary review refused.—Autos 332, 351.1; Sent & Pun 1367.

Freeman v. State, TexApp–Texarkana, 115 SW3d 183, petition for discretionary review refused.—Crim Law 865(1), 865(1.5), 867, 1038.1(3.1), 1155.

Freeman v. State, TexApp–Texarkana, 94 SW3d 827.— Crim Law 641.13(1), 641.13(5), 1134(3).

Freeman v. State, TexApp–Texarkana, 62 SW3d 883, petition for discretionary review refused.—Arrest 63.5(4), 63.5(9); Crim Law 394.6(5), 1130(5), 1134(6), 1139, 1144.12, 1153(1), 1158(4); Searches 26, 161, 162, 165.

Freeman v. State, TexApp–Texarkana, 998 SW2d 379, petition for discretionary review gr, and dism.—Crim Law 37(1), 37(2.1), 37(3), 700(2.1), 700(4), 814(8), 911, 1134(2), 1159.2(1).

Freeman v. State, TexApp–Amarillo, 74 SW3d 913, petition for discretionary review refused, habeas corpus dism 2005 WL 178220.—Crim Law 1032(5), 1042, 1166.16; Ind & Inf 58.1, 81(1), 87(1); Jury 103(1).

Freeman v. State, TexApp–Amarillo, 913 SW2d 714, petition for discretionary review refused.—Crim Law 273.1(2), 275, 1026.10(1), 1026.10(2.1).

Freeman v. State, TexApp–Beaumont, 985 SW2d 588, reh overr, and petition for discretionary review refused.— Crim Law 718, 1171.1(6).

Freeman v. State, TexApp–Waco, 167 SW3d 114.—Crim Law 641.13(6), 641.13(7), 905, 1156(1), 1166.10(1).

Freeman v. State, TexApp–Eastland, 168 SW3d 888, petition stricken, and petition for discretionary review refused, cert den 126 SCt 2892, 165 LEd2d 921, habeas corpus dism 2007 WL 2120378.—Crim Law 641.13(2.1), 1035(5), 1152(2), 1158(3), 1166.18; Jury 94, 95, 97(1), 107, 131(1), 131(3), 131(6).

Freeman v. State, TexApp–Eastland, 691 SW2d 739, petition for discretionary review gr, aff 723 SW2d 727.— Crim Law 517.2(2), 520(2), 532(0.5).

Freeman v. State, TexApp–Tyler, 970 SW2d 55.—Crim Law 641.4(1), 641.4(2), 641.4(4), 641.7(1), 1042; Sent & Pun 1351.

Freeman v. State, TexApp–Corpus Christi, 838 SW2d 772, petition for discretionary review refused.—Crim Law 872.5, 928, 932, 938(1), 957(5), 1155, 1156(3), 1163(6); Homic 1184; Jury 149.

Freeman v. State, TexApp–Houston (14 Dist), 45 SW3d 655, petition for discretionary review refused.—Const Law 4693; Crim Law 1134(2), 1144.13(2.1), 1159.2(7); Obst Just 7, 16; Statut 181(2).

Freeman v. State, TexApp–Houston (14 Dist), 828 SW2d 179, petition for discretionary review refused by 874 SW2d 685.—Crim Law 264, 641.6(3), 641.10(2), 1114.1(1), 1134(10), 1166(3).

Freeman v. State, TexApp–Houston (14 Dist), 736 SW2d 154.—Crim Law 59(1), 59(5), 594(1), 720(5), 792(2), 796, 867, 1151, 1159.2(9), 1159.4(2), 1159.6; Larc 55; Witn 318.

Freeman v. State, TexCivApp–Eastland, 199 SW2d 301. —Afft 18; Const Law 4138(1); Tax 2932, 2937.

Freeman v. Stephens Production Co., TexApp–Corpus Christi, 171 SW3d 651, reh overr, and review den (3 pets), and reh of petition for review den.—Contracts 143(2), 176(2); Deeds 95; Estop 12, 25, 26; Judgm 181(15.1), 181(24), 185.3(1); Mines 49.

Freeman v. Texas Bread Co., TexCivApp–Galveston, 111 SW2d 307.—App & E 1061.1; Autos 242(5), 242(6),

244(26), 244(32), 245(13), 245(42); Plead 110, 228.15; Princ & A 189(4).

Freeman v. Texas Compensation Ins. Co., Tex, 603 SW2d 186.—App & E 930(3), 989, 1001(1), 1001(3); Work Comp 409, 502, 718, 1005, 1394, 1578, 1937.

Freeman v. Texas Compensation Ins. Co., TexCivApp– Fort Worth, 586 SW2d 172, aff and mod 603 SW2d 186. —App & E 597(1), 613(1), 930(1), 934(1), 989, 1003(5); Evid 587; Work Comp 912, 1394, 1581, 1981.

Freeman v. Texas Dept. of Criminal Justice, CA5 (Tex), 369 F3d 854.—Civil R 1031, 1376(1), 1376(2); Const Law 1194, 1422, 1427, 2270, 2273, 2274, 3341(2), 3823; Fed Civ Proc 2546; Prisons 4(1), 4(14).

Freeman; Texas Emp. Ins. Ass'n v., TexCivApp–Texarkana, 266 SW2d 177.—Work Comp 582, 1502.

Freeman v. Town of Flower Mound, TexApp–Fort Worth, 173 SW3d 839.—Mun Corp 33(3); Statut 181(2), 188, 190, 206, 214.

Freeman; U.S. v., CA5 (Tex), 482 F3d 829.—Arrest 63.5(4); Crim Law 1139, 1158(2); Searches 171, 173.1, 180, 183, 184, 186, 194.

Freeman; U.S. v., CA5 (Tex), 164 F3d 243, reh and sug for reh den 172 F3d 871, cert den 119 SCt 1590, 526 US 1105, 143 LEd2d 683, cert den Jackson v. US, 119 SCt 1590, 526 US 1105, 143 LEd2d 683, cert den Williams v US, 119 SCt 2353, 527 US 1011, 144 LEd2d 249, cert den Franklin v US, 120 SCt 132, 528 US 852, 145 LEd2d 112, post-conviction relief den 2001 WL 492401, dism of habeas corpus vac US v Wynn, 292 F3d 226, appeal after remand 100 FedAppx 325, cert den 125 SCt 511, 543 US 993, 160 LEd2d 382.—Consp 47(12); Crim Law 700(2.1), 700(4), 1035(7), 1139, 1144.13(2.1), 1144.13(5), 1153(4), 1158(1), 1159.2(7), 1166(10.10), 1170.5(5); Sent & Pun 300, 1302; Witn 267, 387.

Freeman; U.S. v., CA5 (Tex), 77 F3d 812, reh and sug for reh den 84 F3d 435.—Consp 47(3.1); Crim Law 553, 938(1), 938(2), 945(1), 1139, 1156(1), 1156(3); Environ Law 756.

Freeman v. U.S., CA5 (Tex), 704 F2d 154.—Health 389; Neglig 387; U S 78(14).

Freeman; U.S. v., CA5 (Tex), 685 F2d 942, reh den 689 F2d 190.—Controlled Subs 129, 154; Crim Law 1139, 1158(2), 1169.1(8); Searches 48, 105.1, 113.1, 114, 120, 121.1, 123.1, 126, 148, 202.

Freeman; U.S. v., CA5 (Tex), 619 F2d 1112, cert den 101 SCt 1348, 450 US 910, 67 LEd2d 334.—Crim Law 419(12), 422(1), 427(3), 434, 444, 451(1), 641.5(3), 656(5), 778(6), 872.5, 1032(5), 1137(1), 1163(1), 1167(1), 1170(1), 1170(2), 1171.1(3), 1186.4(8); Ind & Inf 119, 121.1(4), 171, 198; Postal 35(2), 48(4), 48(4 3/4), 48(8), 49(5); Rec S Goods 1, 7(1), 8(2); Witn 198(1), 271(1).

Freeman; Upjohn Co. v., TexApp–Dallas, 906 SW2d 92.— App & E 941, 994(3), 1012.1(2); Judgm 634, 713(1), 720, 724; Records 32.

Freeman; Upjohn Co. v., TexApp–Dallas, 885 SW2d 538, reh den, and writ den, appeal after remand 906 SW2d 92.—Damag 15, 36, 87(2), 91(1), 133, 163(1), 186, 220, 221(8); Death 86(2); Hus & W 209(3), 209(4); Lim of Act 35(6), 43, 55(4), 55(6), 95(1), 170, 174(1), 178, 197(2); Neglig 370, 372; Parent & C 7(1); Plead 34(1), 34(3); Prod Liab 14.

Freeman; Upjohn Co. v., TexApp–Dallas, 847 SW2d 589. —App & E 949, 983(1); Evid 596(1), 598(1); Records 32.

Freeman v. Williams, TexCivApp–Fort Worth, 596 SW2d 652, ref nre.—Child S 242.

Freeman v. Wirecut E.D.M., Inc., TexApp–Dallas, 159 SW3d 721.—App & E 874(4), 893(1); Courts 1, 21, 35, 39, 155; Judges 36; Judgm 181(27); Offic 114, 116; Plead 104(1); Searches 84; Sheriffs 119.

Freeman; Workman v., Tex, 289 SW2d 910, 155 Tex 474. —False Imp 7(1); Sheriffs 137(1).

Freeman; Workman v., TexCivApp–Amarillo, 279 SW2d 486, aff 289 SW2d 910, 155 Tex 474.—Princ & A 159(1); Sheriffs 100, 137(1).

Freeman & Freeman Oil Co. v. Lyman, TexCivApp–Dallas, 121 SW2d 644.—App & E 766, 1140(1), 1140(8); Bailm 32.

Freeman Financial Inv. Co. v. Toyota Motor Corp., TexApp–Dallas, 109 SW3d 29, review den.—App & E 223, 837(10); Indem 72, 75, 76; Judgm 183, 185(1); Prod Liab 1, 6.

Freeman Oldsmobile Mazda Co. v. Pinson, TexCivApp–Eastland, 580 SW2d 112, ref nre.—Sales 119, 130(2).

Freeman-Park v. Barnhart, EDTex, 435 FSupp2d 597.—Social S 142.5, 145, 149.

Freemyer Industrial Pressure, Inc., In re, BkrtcyND–Tex, 281 BR 262.—Bankr 2126, 2393, 2394.1, 2461, 2462, 2467.

Freeport Chemical Co.; Jon-T Chemicals, Inc. v., CA5 (Tex), 704 F2d 1412.—Contracts 164, 176(2); Evid 146; Fed Civ Proc 2011; Fed Cts 823; Sales 54.5, 59, 83, 92, 172.

Freeport McMoran, Inc.; Bertram v., CA5 (Tex), 35 F3d 1008.—Adm 118.7(2); Contrib 5(6.1), 7; Fed Cts 754.1, 850.1, 853, 868; Indem 69, 74, 95, 102; Seamen 11(1), 11(5), 11(6), 29(5.14).

Freeport Offshore, Inc.; Bracht v., CA5 (Tex), 414 F2d 768.—Fed Cts 743, 865.

Freeport Oil Co.; Craft v., TexCivApp–Amarillo, 563 SW2d 866.—App & E 954(1); Inj 17, 138.31; Mines 55(6), 73.1(6).

Freeport Operators, Inc. v. Home Ins. Co., TexApp–Houston (14 Dist), 666 SW2d 566.—Action 6; Const Law 2600, 3989; Decl Judgm 45, 161; Judgm 570(12).

Freeport Sulphur Co.; Corrosion Rectifying Co. v., SDTex, 197 FSupp 291.—Contracts 144; Damag 2, 71; Fed Cts 373, 409.1, 415; Interest 39(3).

Freeport, Tex., City of; McDonald v., SDTex, 834 FSupp 921.—Civil R 1351(1), 1351(5), 1376(10), 1394, 1395(8), 1426; Const Law 1183, 1184(1), 1925, 1935, 1941, 1947, 4036, 4166(2), 4171, 4172(6); Fed Civ Proc 1795, 2465.1, 2470.1, 2491.5, 2543, 2544, 2546; Offic 66, 114, 119.

Freeport, Texas, City of; Stockton v., SDTex, 147 FSupp2d 642, aff 37 FedAppx 712, cert den Hill v. City of Freeport, Texas, 123 SCt 559, 537 US 1030, 154 LEd2d 445.—Schools 169.5; Searches 23, 53.1.

Freeport, Texas, City of; Western Seafood Co. v., SDTex, 346 FSupp2d 892, aff in part, vac in part, remanded 202 FedAppx 670, on remand 2007 WL 2351198.—Em Dom 8, 25, 274(1); Mun Corp 3, 18.

Freer; Texas Co. v., TexCivApp–Waco, 151 SW2d 907, writ dism, correct.—App & E 927(7); Labor & Emp 3094(2), 3181(4); Land & Ten 167(2), 167(8); Neglig 213, 1702; Trial 351.2(5).

Freer Independent School Dist. v. Manges, TexApp–San Antonio, 775 SW2d 774.—Tax 2936.

Freer Independent School Dist.; Manges v., TexApp–San Antonio, 728 SW2d 842, ref nre, on subsequent appeal 775 SW2d 774.—Schools 126; Tax 2935.

Freer Independent School Dist.; Manges v., TexApp–San Antonio, 653 SW2d 553, rev 677 SW2d 488, appeal after remand 728 SW2d 842, ref nre, on subsequent appeal 775 SW2d 774.—Const Law 591, 592, 603; Costs 194.25; Quo W 5; Schools 99, 102, 103(2); Statut 52; Tax 2003, 2481, 2736, 2918.

Freer Mun. Independent School Dist. v. Manges, Tex, 677 SW2d 488, appeal after remand 728 SW2d 842, ref nre, on subsequent appeal 775 SW2d 774.—Mun Corp 964; Schools 99, 103(2).

Freese & Nichols, Inc.; Graham v., TexApp–Eastland, 927 SW2d 294, reh overr, and writ den.—App & E 863, 934(1); Judgm 185(2); Neglig 1011, 1205(5), 1692.

Freestone Cent. Appraisal Dist.; Destec Properties Ltd. Partnership v., TexApp–Waco, 6 SW3d 601, reh overr,

and review den, and reh of petition for review den.—App & E 1097(1); Mines 47; Tax 2515, 2517, 2519, 2525.

Freestone Consol. Common School Dist. No. 13; Donie Independent School Dist. v., TexCivApp–Waco, 127 SW2d 205.—Inj 118(1); Schools 45, 48(6), 48(7).

Freestone County; Texlan, Inc. v., TexCivApp–Waco, 282 SW2d 283.—High 1, 16; Plead 34(1); Trial 139.1(3), 140(1).

Freestone County Title & Abstract Co. v. Johnson, TexCivApp–Dallas, 594 SW2d 817.—App & E 1107; Evid 222(10); Plead 111.42(9).

Freeway Lumber Co.; Fortinberry v., TexCivApp–Hous (1 Dist), 453 SW2d 849.—Acct Action on 13; Costs 194.38.

Freeway Manor Minimax; Rumsey v., TexCivApp–Hous (1 Dist), 423 SW2d 387.—Evid 5(2); Neglig 306; Prod Liab 14, 43.5; Sales 427.

Freeway Park Development Co.; Briggs v., TexCivApp–Fort Worth, 366 SW2d 270, ref nre.—App & E 655(1); Judgm 185(2); Pretrial Proc 518; Tresp to T T 16; Trusts 366(3).

Freeze v. State, TexCrimApp, 113 SW2d 539, 133 Tex-Crim 595.—Crim Law 376, 722.3, 1171.6.

Freeze; U.S. v., CA5 (Tex), 707 F2d 132.—Controlled Subs 27, 31, 68, 81, 93; Crim Law 59(5), 80, 1035(7), 1044.1(7), 1144.13(3), 1159.2(7), 1182.

Fregia; Platt v., TexCivApp–Beaumont, 597 SW2d 495, ref nre.—Autos 244(47); Damag 32.

Fregia v. State, TexApp–Beaumont, 903 SW2d 94, reh overr, and petition for discretionary review refused.—Crim Law 273.1(4), 1023(16); Sent & Pun 2009.

Freightcor Services, Inc. v. Vitro Packaging, Inc., CA5 (Tex), 969 F2d 1563, cert den 113 SCt 979, 506 US 1053, 122 LEd2d 133.—Admin Law 413; Carr 189; Commerce 85.25; Fed Cts 776; Statut 219(1).

Freightliner Corp.; Bradshaw v., CA5 (Tex), 937 F2d 197, reh den.—Fed Civ Proc 2171, 2173.1(1), 2182.1; Fed Cts 899, 912; Neglig 1617; Prod Liab 38, 40, 96.5; Work Comp 2234.

Freightliner Corp.; Jackson v., CA5 (Tex), 938 F2d 40, reh den.—Contrib 6; Indem 72, 102.

Freightliner Corp.; Maxey v., CA5 (Tex), 727 F2d 350.—Fed Civ Proc 2377.

Freightliner Corp.; Maxey v., CA5 (Tex), 722 F2d 1238, mod on denial of reh 727 F2d 350.—Damag 91(1); Fed Civ Proc 2377.

Freightliner Corp.; Maxey v., CA5 (Tex), 665 F2d 1367, appeal after remand 722 F2d 1238, mod on denial of reh 727 F2d 350.—Damag 87(1), 91(3), 94; Death 99(1); Fed Civ Proc 2126.1, 2142.1, 2146, 2148.1, 2151, 2152, 2608.1, 2609, 2610; Fed Cts 940; Neglig 554(1), 1631; Prod Liab 85, 90.

Freightliner Corp.; Maxey v., CA5 (Tex), 623 F2d 395, reh gr 634 F2d 1008, on reh 665 F2d 1367, appeal after remand 722 F2d 1238, mod on denial of reh 727 F2d 350.—Death 77; Fed Civ Proc 2608.1, 2609; Prod Liab 27, 83.5, 96.5.

Freightliner Corp.; Maxey v., NDTex, 450 FSupp 955, aff 623 F2d 395, reh gr 634 F2d 1008, on reh 665 F2d 1367, appeal after remand 722 F2d 1238, mod on denial of reh 727 F2d 350.—Damag 87(1), 87(2), 94, 184; Death 93; Neglig 553, 1604; Prod Liab 27, 36, 40.

Freightliner Corp. v. Ruan Leasing Co., TexApp–Austin, 6 SW3d 726, review gr (2 pets), aff Meritor Automotive, Inc v. Ruan Leasing Co, 44 SW3d 86.—Indem 72, 75, 82; Judgm 178; Statut 183, 188.

Freightliner Corp.; Soden v., CA5 (Tex), 714 F2d 498.—Evid 356, 472(1), 501(1), 501(9), 555.4(1), 555.4(3), 555.8(1); Fed Cts 823, 896.1; Prod Liab 81.1.

Freightliner, LLC; Irving v., CA5 (Tex), 202 FedAppx 756.—Evid 555.8(1); Pretrial Proc 434.

Freight Terminals, Inc. v. Ryder System, Inc., CA5 (Tex), 461 F2d 1046.—Corp 118, 121(7); Courts 15;

Evid 568(7); Fed Civ Proc 1974.1; Indem 33(3), 37; Land & Ten 80(3), 152(8), 154(3); Rem of C 118.

Freight Terminals, Inc. v. Ryder System, Inc., SDTex, 326 FSupp 881, aff 461 F2d 1046.—Contracts 147(3), 154; Corp 1.6(6), 118; Evid 448, 450(5), 452; Guar 36(9); Indem 31(2), 31(5), 35, 37; Land & Ten 37, 80(3), 152(3), 160(2).

Freiley; Wynne v., TexCivApp–Dallas, 349 SW2d 734.—App & E 878(4); Damag 39; Venue 5.5.

Freis v. Canales, Tex, 877 SW2d 283.—Alt Disp Res 112; Insurance 3277; Mand 4(4).

Freitas v. Twin City Fisherman's Co-Op. Ass'n, TexCivApp–Corpus Christi, 452 SW2d 931, ref nre.—Prod Liab 24; Trial 349(1), 365.1(1), 365.1(6).

Freitas v. Twin City Fisherman's Co-op. Ass'n, TexCivApp–Waco, 430 SW2d 579, ref nre, appeal after remand 452 SW2d 931, ref nre.—App & E 927(7), 989, 997(3); Damag 208(1); Neglig 1010, 1020, 1037(3), 1037(4), 1037(8), 1706, 1714; Prod Liab 62.

Frels v. Consolidated Theatres, TexCivApp–San Antonio, 153 SW2d 275.—Courts 104.

Frels v. Consolidated Theatres, TexCivApp–San Antonio, 134 SW2d 369, writ dism, correct.—Antitrust 958, 996; Inj 16, 128(3.1), 134, 135.

Frels v. Schuette, TexCivApp–Galveston, 222 SW2d 1006, ref nre.—Estop 43, 47.

French; Alamo Products Co. v., TexCivApp–San Antonio, 316 SW2d 765.—Corp 503(2).

French v. Bank of Southwest Nat. Ass'n, Houston, TexCivApp–Hous (1 Dist), 422 SW2d 1, ref nre.—App & E 1170.1, 1170.12; Covenants 102(1), 130(5); Judgm 199(3.9), 199(3.10), 199(5); Lim of Act 24(1); Mines 55(7), 55(8).

French v. Brodsky, TexCivApp–Hous (1 Dist), 521 SW2d 670, ref nre.—App & E 302(1), 768, 1170.3, 1170.7, 1170.9(3), 1175(1), 1177(1); Evid 545, 558(8), 560, 571(10); Health 820; Plead 251; Trial 29(1), 29.1, 219; Witn 16, 220, 267, 268(1), 405(1).

French v. Brown, Tex, 424 SW2d 893.—Judgm 183, 189, 335(1), 335(2), 335(3).

French; Brown v., TexCivApp–Amarillo, 413 SW2d 924, writ gr, rev 424 SW2d 893.—Courts 17; Judgm 181(11), 184.

French; Chemical Exp. Carriers, Inc. v., TexApp–Corpus Christi, 759 SW2d 683, writ den.—Carr 93; Damag 39, 63, 113, 139, 155; Evid 574.

French v. Chevron U.S.A. Inc., Tex, 896 SW2d 795.—Deeds 93; Mines 47, 55(0.5), 55(2), 55(4), 55(5).

French v. Chevron USA, Inc., TexApp–El Paso, 871 SW2d 276, reh overr, and writ gr, aff 896 SW2d 795.—Deeds 90, 93, 110; Mines 48, 55(0.5), 55(2), 55(4).

French v. Community Broadcasting of Coastal Bend, Inc., TexApp–Corpus Christi, 766 SW2d 330, writ dism woj.—Contracts 117(2), 202(2); Equity 65(1); Inj 189; Tel 1128, 1135.

French v. De Moss, TexCivApp–Dallas, 180 SW 1105, writ refused.—Health 706.

French v. Diamond Hill-Jarvis Civic League, TexApp–Fort Worth, 724 SW2d 921, ref nre.—App & E 989, 1008.1(2), 1010.1(1); Covenants 73; Deeds 192.

French v. Estelle, CA5 (Tex), 696 F2d 318.—Fed Cts 611; Hab Corp 841.

French v. Estelle, CA5 (Tex), 692 F2d 1021, reh den 696 F2d 318, reh den 698 F2d 1216, cert den 103 SCt 2108, 461 US 937, 77 LEd2d 313.—Double J 115; Hab Corp 466, 725, 767, 845; Sent & Pun 1301.

French v. French, TexCivApp–Hous (1 Dist), 454 SW2d 839, writ dism.—Child C 51; Divorce 50, 130, 184(4), 184(12).

French; French v., TexCivApp–Hous (1 Dist), 454 SW2d 839, writ dism.—Child C 51; Divorce 50, 130, 184(4), 184(12).

French v. French, TexCivApp–Amarillo, 188 SW2d 586, writ refused wom.—Des & Dist 8; Home 134, 143; Partit 4, 8, 9(1).

French; French v., TexCivApp–Amarillo, 188 SW2d 586, writ refused wom.—Des & Dist 8; Home 134, 143; Partit 4, 8, 9(1).

French v. French, TexCivApp–El Paso, 148 SW2d 930, writ dism, correct.—Des & Dist 90(1), 92; Ex & Ad 439; Wills 62, 67, 208.

French; French v., TexCivApp–El Paso, 148 SW2d 930, writ dism, correct.—Des & Dist 90(1), 92; Ex & Ad 439; Wills 62, 67, 208.

French v. George, TexCivApp–Amarillo, 159 SW2d 566, writ refused.—Mines 79.1(5).

French v. Gill, TexApp–Texarkana, 206 SW3d 737.—App & E 173(9), 173(10), 824, 856(1), 1078(1); Judgm 185(4), 665, 713(1), 724, 725(1), 815,·829(1), 829(3).

French; Globe Indem. Co. v., TexCivApp–Amarillo, 382 SW2d 771, ref nre.—Insurance 2664.

French v. Glorioso, TexApp–San Antonio, 94 SW3d 739.—App & E 846(5), 893(1), 1010.1(1), 1010.2, 1012.1(5); Appear 9(2); Const Law 3964; Courts 12(2.1), 12(2.5), 12(2.10), 12(2.15), 12(2.25), 12(5), 15, 35, 39, 97(1); Trial 404(5).

French v. Grigsby, Tex, 571 SW2d 867.—Autos 246(38); Neglig 530(2), 1745.

French v. Grigsby, TexCivApp–Beaumont, 567 SW2d 604, ref nre 571 SW2d 867.—Damag 48, 100, 216(1), 221(2.1), 221(5.1); Neglig 530(2); New Tr 44(3), 140(3), 157.

French v. Harris, TexApp–Dallas, 658 SW2d 690.—Child S 471; Mand 44; Venue 78.

French v. Insurance Co. of North America, TexCivApp–Austin, 591 SW2d 620.—Const Law 190, 2758; Insurance 1810, 1814, 1845(1), 1878, 2780; Statut 263.

French v. Johnson County, TexApp–Waco, 929 SW2d 614.—Autos 270, 306(1); Bridges 37, 46(6); Counties 141; Judgm 185.3(2), 189.

French v. Joseph E. Seagram & Sons, Inc., TexCivApp–El Paso, 439 SW2d 448, ref nre.—Damag 71; Mines 109.

French v. Kopecky, TexApp–Houston (1 Dist), 931 SW2d 34, reh overr, and writ den.—App & E 623, 627.2.

French; Law Offices of Windle Turley, P.C. v., TexApp–Fort Worth, 140 SW3d 407.—Atty & C 134(1), 134(2), 167(2); Contracts 256; Judgm 181(16), 199(5), 316, 323, 325.

French; Law Offices of Windle Turley, P.C. v., TexApp–Dallas, 164 SW3d 487.—App & E 984(1), 1024.1, 1079; Atty & C 24; Costs 2, 262, 264; Interest 39(3).

French; Law Offices of Windle Turley, P.C. v., TexApp–Dallas, 109 SW3d 599, reh overr.—App & E 80(3), 80(6); Judgm 217.

French v. May, TexApp–Corpus Christi, 484 SW2d 420, ref nre.—Bills & N 534; Mtg 218.4, 298(3), 354, 364, 372(4); Subrog 23(1); Tender 12(1), 12(2); Tresp to T T 38(1), 38(2).

French v. Moore, TexApp–Houston (1 Dist), 169 SW3d 1.—App & E 901, 911.3; Contracts 350(1); Costs 194.18, 194.32, 198, 207; Courts 4, 23, 169(1), 169(3), 169(5), 170; Impl & C C 3, 55, 98; Land & Ten 291(14), 292; Plead 111.33, 111.36; Sales 324(3); Trover 1, 9(3.1), 40(1).

French; Mutual Ben. Health & Acc. Ass'n v., TexApp–Dallas, 91 SW2d 915, writ dism.—Insurance 2054, 2056, 3015.

French; National Life & Acc. Ins. Co. v., TexCivApp–Amarillo, 144 SW2d 653.—Insurance 1786, 1791(1), 3360, 3464, 3477, 3483, 3543.

French; Oliver Farm Equipment Sales Co. v., TexCivApp–Waco, 91 SW2d 887, writ dism.—Bills & N 139(1); Plead 291(1).

French; Pacific Emp. Ins. Co. v., CA5 (Tex), 224 F2d 739.—Work Comp 1929, 1958, 1968(4), 1968(7).

French; Redburn v., TexCivApp–San Antonio, 216 SW2d 284.—Brok 73.

French v. State, TexCrimApp, 830 SW2d 607.—Const Law 2789, 2790, 2810, 2815, 2823, 4723; Crim Law 790, 796, 1184(1), 1184(2).

French v. State, TexCrimApp, 572 SW2d 934.—Judges 5, 6; Offic 40; Searches 103.1.

French v. State, TexCrimApp, 546 SW2d 612, reh overr 572 SW2d 934.—Mun Corp 592(1); Searches 103.1.

French v. State, TexCrimApp, 531 SW2d 613.—Rob 17(5).

French v. State, TexCrimApp, 484 SW2d 716.—Autos 422.1, 423.

French v. State, TexCrimApp, 415 SW2d 203.—Crim Law 1184(5); Witn 277(4).

French v. State, TexCrimApp, 284 SW2d 359, 162 TexCrim 48, cert den 76 SCt 1045, 351 US 988, 100 LEd 1501.—Arrest 63.4(9); Crim Law 394.4(9), 721(5).

French v. State, TexCrimApp, 132 SW2d 407, 137 TexCrim 500.—Int Liq 236(6.5).

French v. State, TexCrimApp, 124 SW2d 157, 136 TexCrim 86.—Crim Law 855(7).

French v. State, TexCrimApp, 112 SW2d 719, 133 TexCrim 524.—Int Liq 205(1).

French v. State, TexApp–Houston (1 Dist), 666 SW2d 369. —Crim Law 641.13(1), 641.13(5), 662.7, 662.40, 1172.6.

French v. State, TexApp–Fort Worth, 629 SW2d 279, petition for discretionary review refused.—Arrest 71.1(4.1); Crim Law 394.4(9), 577.10(7), 577.16(9); Forg 34(7); Ind & Inf 171.

French; State v., TexApp–Austin, 770 SW2d 600.—Double J 5.1, 150(1).

French v. State, TexApp–San Antonio, 699 SW2d 672.— Autos 355(10); Crim Law 339.6, 339.8(5), 339.10(11), 339.11(6), 632(4), 1137(6).

French v. State, TexApp–Corpus Christi, 636 SW2d 749. —Searches 162.

French v. State Farm Ins. Co., SDTex, 156 FRD 159.— Fed Cts 303; Insurance 1655, 1867, 3350, 3419; Princ & A 136(2), 159(2); Rem of C 36; Torts 114.

French; Vargas v., TexApp–Corpus Christi, 716 SW2d 625, ref nre.—App & E 1045(1); Jury 136(3).

French; Von Briesen, Purtell & Roper, S.C. v., TexApp–Amarillo, 78 SW3d 570, review dism woj, and reh of petition for review den.—App & E 1012.1(5); Appear 8(1), 8(3); Const Law 3964, 3965(3); Courts 4, 11, 12(2.5), 12(2.10), 12(2.15), 35, 37(1), 37(3).

French; Weber v., TexApp–Houston (14 Dist), 635 SW2d 625, ref nre.—Contracts 164; Evid 450(7); Interest 66; Plead 236(1).

French & Associates, Inc.; Russell v., TexApp–Texarkana, 709 SW2d 312, ref nre.—Costs 194.32; Fraud 16, 35, 58(1), 61; Interest 31, 39(2.15), 39(2.20); Joint Adv 1.2(1), 1.11, 5(2); Mines 110; Sec Reg 265, 278, 299.

French-Brown Floors Co.; Howard v., TexCivApp–Dallas, 542 SW2d 709.—App & E 934(2), 1010.1(1); Contracts 28(3), 175(3); Costs 194.32, 194.36, 207; Trial 382.

French Drilling & Well Service v. Wilson Mfg. Co., TexCivApp–Fort Worth, 307 SW2d 624, dism.—Action 1; App & E 912; Corp 503(2); Plead 245(4).

French Gardens, Ltd., In re, BkrtcySDTex, 58 BR 959.— Bankr 2187, 3151, 3502.15, 3568(1); Judgm 518, 668(2).

Frenchies v. Orange County, Tex., EDTex, 947 FSupp 271. See 1995 Venture I, Inc. v. Orange County, Tex.

French Independent School Dist.; H. C. Burt & Co. v., TexCivApp–Beaumont, 99 SW2d 429.—Venue 22(10).

French Independent School Dist.; Howth v., TexCivApp–Beaumont, 115 SW2d 1036, aff 134 SW2d 1036, 134 Tex 211.—Mun Corp 978(6); Schools 103(1), 106.12(3); Tax 2853; Trial 398.

French Independent School Dist. of Jefferson County v. Howth, TexComApp, 134 SW2d 1036, 134 Tex 211.— Schools 106.4(1), 106.12(11); Tax 2467.

French, Limited; Hoffman v., TexCivApp–Corpus Christi, 394 SW2d 259, ref nre.—App & E 846(5), 882(16), 1015(5), 1170.6; Autos 249; Damag 87(2), 177, 185(1), 191; New Tr 52, 140(3), 145.

Frenchman's Creek Corp.; Imperial Corp. of America v., CA5 (Tex), 453 F2d 1338.—Stip 3; Usury 12, 50, 53, 61, 113.

Frenchmen's Creek Apartments, In re, BkrtcySDTex, 153 BR 455. See 7003 Bissonnet, Inc., In re.

French Oil Co.; Republic Supply Co. v., TexCivApp–El Paso, 392 SW2d 462.—App & E 173(10); Judgm 181(33), 678(2), 707; Lim of Act 55(5), 99(1), 104(1), 195(3), 197(1); Trover 28.

Frenchy's; Mitchell v., TexApp–Houston (14 Dist, 694 SW2d 61. See Mitchell v. Jones.

Frenkil v. Silver, TexCivApp–Galveston, 197 SW2d 127, ref nre.—Compromise 15(1); Release 14.

Frenship Rural High School Dist. v. Central Ed. Agency, TexCivApp–Austin, 404 SW2d 41, ref nre.—Schools 37(3).

Frenzel v. Browning-Ferris Industries, Inc., TexApp–Houston (14 Dist), 780 SW2d 844.—App & E 907(2); Const Law 3989; Pretrial Proc 581, 587, 699.

Frenzel v. State, TexApp–Waco, 963 SW2d 911, petition for discretionary review refused.—Const Law 2370; Crim Law 1134(3), 1139, 1144.1; Ind & Inf 7.

Frenzell; Beaumont Motor Co., Inc., General Motors Corp. Chevrolet Division v., TexCivApp–Beaumont, 411 SW2d 814.—Plead 111.30, 111.47.

Frerking v. Southern County Mut. Ins. Co., TexCivApp–Amarillo, 467 SW2d 672, writ dism.—Judgm 199(3.13); Trial 388(2).

Frescas v. State, TexApp–El Paso, 636 SW2d 516.—Crim Law 641.12(1), 662.1, 1184(5); Homic 1480.

Fresh America Corp. v. Wal-Mart Stores, Inc., NDTex, 393 FSupp2d 411, reconsideration den 2005 WL 1253775.—Interpl 1, 3, 6, 17, 19, 31, 35.

Fresh Approach, Inc., In re, BkrtcyNDTex, 51 BR 412.— Bankr 2050, 2052, 2103, 2543, 2602.1, 2610, 2701; Fact 31; Statut 184.

Fresh Approach, Inc., In re, BkrtcyNDTex, 49 BR 494.— Bankr 2402(1), 2402(4).

Fresh Approach, Inc., In re, BkrtcyNDTex, 48 BR 926.— Bankr 2543; Fact 59.

Fresh Approach, Inc. v. U.S., BkrtcyNDTex, 49 BR 494. See Fresh Approach, Inc., In re.

Fresh Coat, Inc. v. Life Forms, Inc., TexApp–Houston (1 Dist), 125 SW3d 765, rule 537(f) motion gr.—App & E 66, 76(1), 78(1), 428(2).

Fresh Source Produce Inc.; Golman-Hayden Co., Inc. v., CA5 (Tex), 217 F3d 348.—Atty & C 155; Fact 59.

Fresh Source Produce, Inc.; Golman-Hayden Co., Inc. v., NDTex, 27 FSupp2d 723, aff in part, rev in part 217 F3d 348.—Fact 59.

Fresne; Lewis v., CA5 (Tex), 252 F3d 352, reh den.— Const Law 3964, 3965(5); Fed Civ Proc 824, 825, 1830, 1831, 1838; Fed Cts 76.5, 76.10, 76.15, 76.25, 76.35, 79, 776, 817; Sec Reg 11.15, 18.11, 25.56.

Fresnillo Co.; Texas & P. Ry. Co. v., CCA5 (Tex), 80 F2d 144.—Commerce 161, 212, 213.

Fresno Oil Co.; Blakeley v., TexCivApp–Fort Worth, 208 SW2d 902.—App & E 930(1); Commerce 62.67; Impl & C C 33.1; Judgm 199(1), 199(3.9); Labor & Emp 2220(2), 2305, 2312, 2319, 2387(1).

Fress; American Nat. Ins. Co. v., TexCivApp–Galveston, 142 SW2d 531, writ dism, correct.—Evid 318(7); Trial 38; Witn 266.

Fress; Texas State Life Ins. Co. v., TexCivApp–Galveston, 138 SW2d 198.—Evid 314(3); Insurance 2604.

Fretwell v. State, TexCrimApp, 442 SW2d 393.—Crim Law 366(3), 366(6), 1036.2, 1036.5, 1137(5).

Fretz; Bank of Atlanta v., Tex, 226 SW2d 843, 148 Tex 551.—Autos 20; Chat Mtg 83, 89.

Fretz; Bank of Atlanta v., TexCivApp–Galveston, 221 SW2d 297, rev 226 SW2d 843, 148 Tex 551.—Autos 20; Courts 8; Sales 312.

FRETZ

59 Tex D 2d—134

Fretz Const. Co. v. Southern Nat. Bank of Houston, Tex, 626 SW2d 478.—Contracts 322(3); Estop 85, 118; Fraud 58(2); Trial 352.4(4).

Fretz Const. Co. v. Southern Nat. Bank of Houston, TexCivApp–Hous (1 Dist), 600 SW2d 878, writ gr, rev 626 SW2d 478.—Contracts 177, 187(1); Estop 85, 102, 116; Trial 352.18.

Freudenmann, In re, BkrtcySDTex, 76 BR 600.—Bankr 2023, 2043(3), 2049; Fed Cts 47.1, 268.1, 269, 270.

Freudenmann v. Clark and Associates, Inc., TexCiv-App–Corpus Christi, 599 SW2d 132.—Evid 80(1); Judgm 185(2), 185(4), 944.

Freudenmann v. Drainage Dist. No. 2, BkrtcySDTex, 76 BR 600. See Freudenmann, In re.

Freudensprung v. Offshore Technical Services, Inc., CA5 (Tex), 379 F3d 327.—Adm 1.20(4), 5(1); Alt Disp Res 117, 134(1), 188, 213(5), 513, 514; Const Law 3964, 3965(1), 3967; Courts 12(2.1); Fed Civ Proc 44, 1267.1, 1269.1, 2626; Fed Cts 76.1, 76.15, 76.25, 82, 96, 403, 417, 551, 562, 611, 668, 751, 759.1, 776, 820; States 18.15; Treaties 8.

Freudensprung v. Offshore Technical Services, Inc., SDTex, 186 FSupp2d 716.—Const Law 3964; Courts 12(2.15); Fed Cts 76.1, 76.5, 76.10, 76.30, 82, 86, 96; Seamen 6.

Freudenstein; Breedlove v., CCA5 (Tex), 89 F2d 324, 112 ALR 777, cert den 58 SCt 20, 302 US 701, 82 LEd 541. —Banks 269.

Freudenstein; Lincoln Nat. Life Ins. Co. v., TexCivApp–San Antonio, 87 SW2d 810.—Mtg 338; Receivers 14; Statut 183.

Freudiger v. Keller, TexApp–Texarkana, 104 SW3d 294, review den.—App & E 969, 1064.1(1); Autos 169, 246(7), 246(46); Neglig 222, 238, 259, 409, 1704; Trial 182, 260(7).

Freund; U.S. v., CA5 (Tex), 532 F2d 501, cert den 96 SCt 2631, 426 US 923, 49 LEd2d 377.—Crim Law 627.10(6), 627.10(7.1).

Freund; U.S. v., CA5 (Tex), 525 F2d 873, opinion after remand 532 F2d 501, cert den 96 SCt 2631, 426 US 923, 49 LEd2d 377.—Controlled Subs 113; Crim Law 627.10(1), 627.10(8); Searches 64, 73.

Frew v. Gilbert, EDTex, 109 FSupp2d 579, stay den 2000 WL 33795091, opinion vac Frazar v. Gilbert, 300 F3d 530, cert gr in part 123 SCt 1481, 538 US 905, 155 LEd2d 223, rev 124 SCt 899, 540 US 431, 157 LEd2d 855, on remand 376 F3d 444, on remand 401 FSupp2d 619, aff 457 F3d 432, cert den Hawkins v Frew, 127 SCt 1039, 166 LEd2d 714, aff in part, appeal dism in part 376 F3d 444, on remand 401 FSupp2d 619, aff 457 F3d 432, cert den 127 SCt 1039, 166 LEd2d 714.—Civil R 1027, 1052; Contracts 143(2); Evid 450(2); Fed Civ Proc 2397.2, 2397.5, 2397.6; Fed Cts 265, 269, 272; Health 467, 473.

Frew v. Hawkins, EDTex, 401 FSupp2d 619, aff Frazar v. Ladd, 457 F3d 432, cert den 127 SCt 1039, 166 LEd2d 714.—Fed Civ Proc 2397.1, 2397.4, 2397.6.

Frey; Ambusher, Inc. v., CA5 (Tex), 20 F3d 623. See Phillips v. Frey.

Frey v. DeCordova Bend Estates Owners Ass'n, Tex, 647 SW2d 246.—Covenants 90; Inj 12, 62(1).

Frey v. DeCordova Bend Estates Owners Ass'n, Tex-App–Fort Worth, 632 SW2d 877, writ gr, aff 647 SW2d 246.—Assoc 7, 12; Const Law 2604; Covenants 61, 77.1, 84; Inj 11; Judgm 178.

Frey; Hassell v., Tex, 117 SW2d 413, 131 Tex 578.—Wills 58(2), 435, 439, 440, 441, 487(1), 506(1), 506(5), 608(1), 608(3.1).

Frey v. Hassell, TexCivApp–El Paso, 97 SW2d 970, rev 117 SW2d 413, 131 Tex 578.—Wills 439, 601(2).

Frey v. Martin, TexCivApp–Dallas, 469 SW2d 316, ref nre.—Fraud 49, 58(1), 58(4), 59(2).

Frey v. Pearson, TexCivApp–Waco, 168 SW2d 886.—Frds St of 119(2), 129(2); Lim of Act 13.

Frey; Phillips v., CA5 (Tex), 20 F3d 623.—Antitrust 83, 413, 414, 417, 418, 419, 420, 421, 427, 432; Fed Cts 641, 642; Torts 454.

Frey v. Sargent's Estate, TexCivApp–Amarillo, 533 SW2d 142, ref nre.—Contracts 325; Wills 57, 63, 775.

Frey v. State, TexCrimApp, 466 SW2d 576.—Crim Law 1036.1(8), 1130(2).

Frey v. State, TexCrimApp, 345 SW2d 416, 171 TexCrim 100, cert den 82 SCt 113, 368 US 865, 7 LEd2d 62.— Autos 423; Crim Law 377, 382, 773(2), 1120(3), 1166.22(4.1), 1170(4); Judgm 751; Rob 24.15(2).

Frey v. State, TexCrimApp, 200 SW2d 194, 150 TexCrim 201.—Health 168.

Frey v. U.S., CA5 (Tex), 558 F2d 270, cert den 98 SCt 1487, 435 US 923, 55 LEd2d 517.—Int Rev 4306; Statut 181(1).

Frey v. U.S., NDTex, 395 FSupp 994, rev 558 F2d 270, cert den 98 SCt 1487, 435 US 923, 55 LEd2d 517.—Int Rev 4306; Judgm 648.

Frey v. U.S., NDTex, 159 FSupp 436.—Int Rev 3071, 3254, 3496; Mines 79.1(1), 79.1(2).

Frey v. Valley View Independent School Dist., TexCiv-App–Fort Worth, 441 SW2d 875, ref nre.—Schools 106.12(7).

Freyer v. Michels, TexCivApp–Dallas, 360 SW2d 559, writ dism.—App & E 301; Can of Inst 8; Contracts 261(1), 266(1), 270(2); Land & Ten 34(2), 231(8).

Freyer v. State, TexCrimApp, 117 SW2d 802.—Crim Law 1182.

Freyre v. State, TexCrimApp, 291 SW2d 321, 163 Tex-Crim 315.—Burg 41(10); Crim Law 938(1); Witn 48(2).

Freytag, In re, NDTex, 173 BR 330.—Bankr 2055, 2163, 3782, 3784, 3786, 3787; Fed Cts 823; Int Rev 3566.1, 4665; Judgm 634, 642; Statut 209.

Freytag, In re, BkrtcyNDTex, 155 BR 150.—Bankr 2724, 2967.5; Fed Civ Proc 392, 824, 827, 834, 851; Fed Cts 817; Home 55, 96.

Freytag v. American Federal Bank, F.S.B., BkrtcyND-Tex, 155 BR 150. See Freytag, In re.

Freytag; Johnson v., TexCivApp–Beaumont, 338 SW2d 257, ref nre.—Dep & Escr 11, 13; Mines 55(1), 58; Parent & C 12; Princ & A 23(5).

F. R. Hernandez Const. & Supply Co., Inc. v. National Bank of Commerce of Brownsville, Tex, 578 SW2d 675.—App & E 931(4); Bills & N 126, 489(6), 534; Trial 392(1), 404(1).

F. R. Hernandez Const. & Supply Co., Inc.; National Bank of Commerce of Brownsville v., TexCivApp–Corpus Christi, 564 SW2d 499, ref nre, and writ gr, rev 578 SW2d 675.—Bills & N 534; Guar 91; Trial 404(1).

Friar; A. & M. Petroleum Co. v., TexCivApp–El Paso, 152 SW2d 470.—App & E 1177(6); Land & Ten 144, 157(4).

Frias v. Atlantic Richfield Co., TexApp–Houston (14 Dist), 104 SW3d 925.—App & E 852, 854(1), 934(1), 971(2); Evid 555.2, 555.10, 557; Judgm 185(3), 185.3(13); Neglig 404; Trial 76.

Frias v. Atlantic Richfield Co., TexApp–Houston (14 Dist), 999 SW2d 97, reh overr, and review den, and reh of petition for review den, appeal after remand 104 SW3d 925.—App & E 93, 154(1), 870(2), 1079; Judgm 181(5.1), 181(21), 183, 185(5); Neglig 201, 273, 1659; Torts 115; Work Comp 2085, 2088, 2093, 2105, 2119.

Frias v. Board of Trustees of Ector County Indepen-dent School Dist., TexCivApp–El Paso, 584 SW2d 944, writ dism woj, cert den 100 SCt 531, 444 US 996, 62 LEd2d 426.—App & E 395; Elections 311, 317.2; Jury 19(1); Schools 97(4).

Frias v. State, TexCrimApp, 376 SW2d 764.—Burg 41(1); Crim Law 531(3); Ind & Inf 83.

Frias v. State, TexCrimApp, 335 SW2d 765, 169 TexCrim 549.—Crim Law 957(1), 957(2).

Frias v. State, TexApp–Fort Worth, 775 SW2d 871.— Crim Law 719(3), 720(5), 720(7.1), 721(3), 796, 1177.

Frias; U.S. v., CA5 (Tex), 143 FedAppx 601.—Consp 47(12); Crim Law 1035(1).

Frias-Rodriguez; U.S. v., CA5 (Tex), 88 FedAppx 681.—Crim Law 1081(2); Sent & Pun 764.

Friberg v. Kansas City Southern Ry. Co., CA5 (Tex), 267 F3d 439, reh den.—Fed Cts 554.1, 776; R R 222(3); States 18.3, 18.21.

Friberg-Cooper Water Supply Corp. v. Elledge, TexApp–Fort Worth, 197 SW3d 826.—Impl & C C 3, 4, 10; Judgm 181(11), 185(2), 185.3(2); Lim of Act 28(1).

Frick v. Duge, TexCivApp–Corpus Christi, 413 SW2d 750.—App & E 846(5), 1024.3; Plead 111.12, 111.42(8).

Frick Co.; Refrigeration Engineering Corp. v., WDTex, 370 FSupp 702.—Antitrust 564, 569, 570, 571, 589, 592, 847, 882, 976, 977(3), 977(5), 996; Inj 21, 138.37, 147.

Fricke; C. V. Hill & Co. v., TexCivApp–Fort Worth, 135 SW2d 582, writ dism, correct.—App & E 758.3(1), 758.3(11); Evid 75; Fraud 59(3); Princ & A 24, 156; Sales 38(1), 129, 130(2), 130(3), 130(3.5), 130(4); Trial 350.4(2), 352.5(4).

Fricke; U.S. v., CA5 (Tex), 684 F2d 1126, reh den 690 F2d 905, cert den 103 SCt 1250, 460 US 1011, 75 LEd2d 480, reh den 103 SCt 1805, 460 US 1104, 76 LEd2d 368.—Const Law 268(10), 4689, 4692; Crim Law 641.12(2), 721(3), 1170.5(1), 1172.2; Witn 2(1), 297(1), 304(1), 308.

Fricke v. Wagner, TexCivApp–Austin, 315 SW2d 584, ref nre.—Des & Dist 68; Estop 70(2), 92(3), 119; Judgm 185.3(17), 186; Lim of Act 39(7), 74(2), 80; Mental H 384.

Frick-Reid Supply Corp.; Aero Gas Refining Co. v., TexCivApp–El Paso, 147 SW2d 1101.—App & E 169, 500(2), 839(1); Courts 30.

Frick-Reid Supply Corp.; Hawkins v., CCA5 (Tex), 154 F2d 88.—Contracts 176(1), 176(2); Fed Civ Proc 680, 2552; Sales 54, 58, 88.

Frick-Reid Supply Corp.; Meers v., TexCivApp–Amarillo, 127 SW2d 493, writ dism, correct.—App & E 173(16); Fixt 27(1); Lim of Act 172; Mines 80, 117; Time 15.

Frick-Reid Supply Corp.; Richards v., TexCivApp–Fort Worth, 160 SW2d 282, writ refused wom.—App & E 688(2), 1002, 1050.1(3.1); Chat Mtg 157(1); Estop 56, 83(1), 107, 119; Plead 11; Trial 106, 129, 315, 350.1, 350.3(2.1), 352.12.

Fricks v. Hancock, TexApp–Corpus Christi, 45 SW3d 322, reh overr.—App & E 852, 863, 946; Evid 448; Judgm 185(2), 185(3), 185.1(1), 185.1(3), 185.1(4), 185.3(17); Quiet T 1, 10, 10.1, 10.2; Tresp to T T 1, 6, 6.1; Trial 43.

Friday, Ex parte, TexCrimApp, 545 SW2d 182.—Crim Law 951(1); Sent & Pun 1352.

Friday v. Grant Plaza Huntsville Associates, Tex, 610 SW2d 747.—Venue 7.5(6), 22(6).

Friday v. Grant Plaza Huntsville Associates, TexApp–Houston (1 Dist), 713 SW2d 755.—App & E 863; Evid 434(8); Judgm 185(3).

Friday v. Spears, TexApp–Texarkana, 975 SW2d 699.—App & E 969, 1064.1(1); Autos 246(48); Neglig 440(1), 1713, 1741; Trial 219, 242, 250.

Friddell v. Greathouse, TexCivApp–Dallas, 230 SW2d 579, dism.—App & E 1177(1), 1177(6); Bills & N 22, 443(2), 473, 489(6), 491.

Friddell v. Massengill, TexCivApp–Eastland, 368 SW2d 137, ref nre.—App & E 934(1), 989; Judgm 185(5), 185.3(16).

Friddell; Rose v., TexCivApp–Tyler, 423 SW2d 658, ref nre.—App & E 866(3); Evid 571(9); Health 620, 623, 631, 821(2), 822(1), 822(3), 825, 826; Neglig 384.

Fridge; City of Dallas v., TexCivApp–Austin, 410 SW2d 40.—Em Dom 149(1), 200, 205; Evid 113(8), 142(1).

Fridia; International Order of Twelve Knights and Daughters of Tabor v., TexCivApp–Waco, 91 SW2d 404.—Corp 378; Judgm 251(1); Witn 142.

Fridl v. Cook, TexApp–El Paso, 908 SW2d 507, reh overr, and writ dism woj.—Alt Disp Res 113, 139, 141, 143,

146, 186, 188, 198, 210, 213(3), 213(5); App & E 68, 893(1); Appear 9(1), 9(5), 22; Contracts 1; Courts 11; Damag 103; Jury 19(1); Torts 212, 222.

Frieda v. Kroesche, TexCivApp–San Antonio, 288 SW2d 891.—Chat Mtg 281.

Friedan v. Pan Tex Hotel Corp., TexApp–San Antonio, 653 SW2d 365.—App & E 989, 995, 999(1), 1177(7); Inn 10.12, 10.13; Neglig 1304, 1676, 1683, 1684, 1713.

Friedel v. State, TexApp–Austin, 832 SW2d 420.—Rape 51(3).

Friedel; Texas Dept. of Public Safety v., TexApp–Beaumont, 112 SW3d 768.—Admin Law 493, 683, 791; App & E 226(1), 226(2); Autos 144.2(1), 144.2(2.1); Costs 2.

Frieden v. Duart Mfg. Co., TexCivApp–Austin, 120 SW2d 637.—Contracts 332(2); Sales 354(9).

Frieden; Lewis v., TexCivApp–Austin, 135 SW2d 284.—Chat Mtg 283.

Friedheim, In re, BkrtcyNDTex, 336 BR 110.—Bankr 2801.

Friedkin Companies, Inc.; Hester v., TexApp–Houston (14 Dist), 132 SW3d 100, review den.—App & E 218.2(5.1), 863, 866(3), 934(1); Impl & C C 30, 60.1; Judgm 199(3.10).

Friedl v. State, TexApp–Houston (1 Dist), 773 SW2d 72.—Sent & Pun 2006, 2018, 2020, 2021.

Friedlander v. Christianson, TexCivApp–Houston, 320 SW2d 404.—Brok 9, 43(3), 56(3).

Friedman, Ex parte, TexApp–El Paso, 808 SW2d 166.—Child S 472, 474, 477; Const Law 4494; Hab Corp 528.1, 529.

Friedman v. American Sur. Co. of New York, Tex, 151 SW2d 570, 137 Tex 149, answer to certified question conformed to 154 SW2d 659.—Const Law 190, 591, 990, 1002, 1100(1), 2454, 2489, 2751, 2845, 2860, 2866, 2877, 4129; Em Dom 2(11); States 119, 127, 130; Statut 64(8); Tax 2001, 2003, 2119, 3260, 3263, 3293; Unemp Comp 7.

Friedman v. American Sur. Co. of New York, TexCivApp–Fort Worth, 154 SW2d 659.—Courts 247(5); Tax 3293.

Friedman v. Atlantic Funding Corp., TexApp–San Antonio, 936 SW2d 38.—App & E 169, 170(1), 1180(2); Bills & N 369; Judgm 181(1), 183, 185(2); Sec Tran 240.

Friedman; Brown v., TexCivApp–Hous (1 Dist), 451 SW2d 588.—App & E 1003(11), 1170.6; Damag 187, 208(5); New Tr 40(1); Trial 131(2).

Friedman; Cage Bros. v., TexCivApp–San Antonio, 312 SW2d 532, ref nre.—App & E 1062.1; Labor & Emp 3138; Tresp 46(3), 50, 67; Trial 127; Witn 270(2).

Friedman; Chanowsky v., TexCivApp–Fort Worth, 219 SW2d 501, ref nre.—App & E 846(2), 846(5), 1010.1(5); Hus & W 266.4, 273(1), 276(1), 276(3), 276(5), 276(9); Witn 159(7).

Friedman; Chanowsky v., TexCivApp–Fort Worth, 205 SW2d 641, ref nre.—Evid 98; Hus & W 273(2), 274(3), 276(9).

Friedman; Chanowsky v., TexCivApp–Fort Worth, 108 SW2d 752, writ dism.—Evid 208(3), 222(10); Lim of Act 46(10); Trusts 91, 371(2), 372(1), 374.

Friedman v. Cohen, TexCivApp–Hous (14 Dist), 429 SW2d 510, ref nre.—Contracts 350(1); Trial 391, 395(5).

Friedman v. Cohen, TexCivApp–Houston, 404 SW2d 372.—Pat 215; Plead 228.2, 228.13, 228.14.

Friedman; Copland v., TexCivApp–Galveston, 195 SW2d 763.—App & E 1010.1(1); Sales 52(6).

Friedman v. Friedman, TexCivApp–Dallas, 188 SW2d 909, writ refused wom.—App & E 653(1), 1015(5); New Tr 140(3), 143(2); Trial 53, 54(1), 129.

Friedman; Friedman v., TexCivApp–Dallas, 188 SW2d 909, writ refused wom.—App & E 653(1), 1015(5); New Tr 140(3), 143(2); Trial 53, 54(1), 129.

Friedman v. Friedman, TexCivApp–Hous (14 Dist), 521 SW2d 111.—Child S 26, 82, 140(2), 200, 202, 292, 555, 556(1).

Friedman; Friedman v., TexCivApp–Hous (14 Dist), 521 SW2d 111.—Child S 26, 82, 140(2), 200, 202, 292, 555, 556(1).

Friedman v. Houston Sports Ass'n, TexApp–Houston (1 Dist), 731 SW2d 572, ref nre.—App & E 232(0.5), 289; Judgm 199(3.5); Pub Amuse 109(2), 147.

Friedman; Jenevein v., TexApp–Dallas, 114 SW3d 743, rule 537(f) motion gr.—Libel 38(1), 38(3); Torts 122.

Friedman; Levit's Jewelers, Inc. v., TexCivApp–Waco, 410 SW2d 947.—App & E 293; Neglig 1625, 1695; Trial 350.6(2).

Friedman v. Martini Tile & Terrazzo Co., TexCivApp–Fort Worth, 298 SW2d 221.—Assign 22, 30, 65, 71, 73; Contrib 9(5); Indem 97; Release 37.

Friedman; Mitchell's, Inc. v., Tex, 303 SW2d 775, 157 Tex 424.—Indem 30(1), 31(1), 31(5), 33(3), 42, 45.

Friedman; Mitchell's, Inc. v., TexCivApp–Dallas, 294 SW2d 740, rev 303 SW2d 775, 157 Tex 424.—Contrib 5(6.1); Decl Judgm 112; Indem 31(5), 33(3), 111; Judgm 715(1); Land & Ten 79(3), 127.

Friedman v. New Westbury Village Associates, TexApp–Houston (1 Dist), 787 SW2d 154.—App & E 846(5); Joint Adv 1.11, 1.15, 7; Partners 139.

Friedman v. Olson, TexCivApp–Eastland, 586 SW2d 957, ref nre.—Estop 101; Joint Adv 5(1); Plead 228; Pretrial Proc 686.1; Trial 350.3(1), 352.5(3).

Friedman v. Powell Elec. Mfg. Co., TexCivApp–Hous (1 Dist), 456 SW2d 758.—App & E 1062.1, 1175(1), 1177(5); Fraud 12; Trial 350.3(2.1); Trusts 89(3), 90, 92, 102(1), 110, 111.

Friedman v. Rogers, USTex, 99 SCt 887, 440 US 1, 59 LEd2d 100, reh den 99 SCt 2018, 441 US 917, 60 LEd2d 389, reh den Texas Optometric Ass'n, Inc v. Rogers, 99 SCt 2018, 441 US 917, 60 LEd2d 389.—Const Law 1170, 1537, 1539, 1541, 1604, 1640, 2970, 3696, 3903, 4177, 4260, 4286; Fed Cts 479; Health 105; Trademarks 1032.

Friedman; Rogers v., EDTex, 438 FSupp 428, probable jur noted 98 SCt 1604, 435 US 967, 56 LEd2d 58, aff in part, rev in part 99 SCt 887, 440 US 1, 59 LEd2d 100, reh den 99 SCt 2018, 441 US 917, 60 LEd2d 389, reh den Texas Optometric Ass'n, Inc v. Rogers, 99 SCt 2018, 441 US 917, 60 LEd2d 389.—Admin Law 109; Const Law 1504, 1600, 1604, 1647, 3696; Health 105.

Friedman; Strauss v., TexCivApp–Beaumont, 109 SW2d 553, dism.—Home 122, 214, 216.

Friedman v. Texaco, Inc., Tex, 691 SW2d 586.—Courts 100(1); Mines 55(5).

Friedman; Texas State Bd. of Dental Examiners v., TexApp–Houston (14 Dist), 666 SW2d 363, ref nre.—Health 168, 212, 223(1).

Friedman v. Worthy Fabrics, TexCivApp–El Paso, 347 SW2d 639.—Lim of Act 148(3), 199(3).

Friedman and Associates, P.C. v. Beltline Road, Ltd., TexApp–Dallas, 861 SW2d 1, reh den, and writ dism by agreement.—Costs 2; Courts 85(2).

Friedman, Driegert & Hsueh, L.L.C.; Straza v., TexApp–Dallas, 124 SW3d 404, reh overr, and review den, and reh of petition for review den.—App & E 76(1), 78(1), 428(2).

Friedmann; State v., TexCivApp–Corpus Christi, 572 SW2d 373, ref nre.—App & E 846(5), 948, 954(1), 954(2); Inj 135, 138.1, 161, 174.

Friedman Steel Sales, Inc. v. Texas Utilities Co., TexCivApp–Texarkana, 574 SW2d 849, ref nre.—Mech Liens 240; Paymt 21.

Friedman Steel Sales, Inc.; Wolf v., TexApp–Texarkana, 717 SW2d 669, ref nre.—Autos 201(5), 244(22.1); Judgm 199(3.2), 199(3.10); Neglig 371, 386, 387, 421, 431, 432.

Friedrich v. Amoco Production Co., TexApp–Corpus Christi, 698 SW2d 748, ref nre.—Mines 73, 78.1(3), 78.1(7), 78.2.

Friedrich v. Local No. 780, IUE-AFL-CIO-CLC, CA5 (Tex), 515 F2d 225.—Contracts 143.5, 156; Labor & Emp 1549(2), 1549(21).

Friedrich v. Moke, TexCivApp–San Antonio, 296 SW2d 565, ref nre.—Evid 265(10); Spec Perf 28(2), 31.

Friedrich; Trail v., TexApp–Houston (1 Dist), 77 SW3d 508, review den.—App & E 852; Electricity 16(5), 18(1); Neglig 1204(5).

Friedrich v. Whittaker Corp., SDTex, 467 FSupp 1012.—Courts 489(1); Rem of C 1, 10, 79(1), 81, 82, 103.

Friedrich Air Conditioning & Refrigeration; Castro v., TexApp–San Antonio, 880 SW2d 62. See Castro v. U.S. Natural Resources, Inc.

Friedrich Air Conditioning and Refrigeration Co. v. Bexar Appraisal Dist., TexApp–San Antonio, 762 SW2d 763.—Admin Law 501; Const Law 976, 4076; Judgm 183; Statut 212.5; Tax 2106, 2571, 2680, 2722.

Friedrich Air Conditioning and Refrigeration Co.; Williams v., TexApp–Waco, 865 SW2d 203. See Williams v. U.S. Natural Resources, Inc.

Friedrichs v. Reinhardt, TexCivApp–San Antonio, 370 SW2d 739.—Wills 55(7), 288(3), 400.

Friedsam v. Rose, TexCivApp–Waco, 271 SW 417, writ dism woj.—Bankr 264, 269, 400(1); Frds St of 74(1); Trusts 35(1).

Friedsam v. State, TexCrimApp, 116 SW2d 1081, 134 TexCrim 515.—Crim Law 730(12), 923(2), 1158(3); Homic 805.

Friedsam; Texas Power & Light Co. v., TexCivApp–Waco, 105 SW2d 1118, writ dism.—App & E 1069.1.

Friedsam; Ulbricht v., Tex, 325 SW2d 669, 159 Tex 607.—Bound 13, 40(1); Deeds 90, 93; Ease 16; Evid 5(2); Waters 111.

Friedsam v. Ulbricht, TexCivApp–Austin, 315 SW2d 442, aff in part, rev in part 325 SW2d 669, 159 Tex 607.—App & E 852; Bound 8, 10, 13, 17; Trial 367; Waters 39.

Frieling v. State, TexApp–Austin, 67 SW3d 462, reh overr, and petition for discretionary review refused.—Const Law 656, 765, 1066, 1140, 1145(1), 1150, 1163, 1498, 1504, 2473; Crim Law 5, 800(1), 805(1), 881(4), 1038.1(1), 1038.1(2); Prost 14, 15, 32; Statut 61, 188, 189, 190, 220, 223.5(8).

Friemel v. Crouch, TexCivApp–Amarillo, 189 SW2d 764, writ refused wom.—Labor & Emp 24; Land & Ten 326(5); Ten in C 3, 38(1); Trover 2; Venue 8.5(7).

Friemel v. State, TexCrimApp, 188 SW2d 175, 148 TexCrim 454.—Crim Law 730(10), 1171.3; Double J 89.

Friend v. Beard, TexCivApp–Waco, 567 SW2d 79, dism.—App & E 846(5); Plead 111.42(7).

Friend v. H.K. Porter Co., Inc., NDTex, 601 FSupp 399. See Young v. Armstrong World Industries, Inc.

Friend; Lloyds America v., TexCivApp–Amarillo, 91 SW2d 766.—Contracts 164, 166; Corp 80(12), 99(1); Evid 450(1); Venue 8.5(3).

Friend v. McComb, TexCivApp–Beaumont, 87 SW2d 767, writ refused.—App & E 846(5); Atty & C 123(2); Mtg 32(1), 37(2), 38(1).

Friend; McMullan v., TexApp–El Paso, 642 SW2d 15.—App & E 218.2(1), 930(3), 1170.9(2.1); Contracts 170(1); Evid 318(2); Lim of Act 96(2), 175; Mines 55(8); Ref of Inst 16, 32; Trial 325(1).

Friend v. Maryland Cas. Co., TexCivApp–Fort Worth, 278 SW2d 872.—Autos 372(4).

Friend; Panhandle & S. F. Ry. Co. v., TexCivApp–Austin, 91 SW2d 922.—App & E 930(3), 1064.1(9), 1177(6); Courts 107; R R 346(7), 350(5); Statut 184; Trial 350.2, 352.21, 366.

Friend In Need Ben. Ass'n v. Hardin, TexCivApp–Dallas, 88 SW2d 1103.—Insurance 2035, 2079, 2082.

Friendly Chevrolet Co.; Brown Foundation Repair and Consulting, Inc. v., TexApp–Dallas, 715 SW2d 115, ref nre.—Acct Action 6(2), 7; Afft 11; Antitrust 389(2); Trial 174.

Friendly Chevrolet, Co.; Chezik Buick Co. v., TexApp–Dallas, 749 SW2d 591. See John Chezik Buick Co. v. Friendly Chevrolet Co.

Friendly Chevrolet Co.; John Chezik Buick Co. v., TexApp–Dallas, 749 SW2d 591, writ den.—Costs 194.40; Decl Judgm 45; Plead 290(3); Princ & A 14(2), 99.

Friendly Chevrolet, Ltd.; Selz v., TexApp–Dallas, 152 SW3d 833.—App & E 719(1), 733; Judgm 183, 185(4), 185(5), 185.1(4), 185.3(13), 186.

Friendly Chrysler-Plymouth, Inc.; Grant v., TexCiv-App–Corpus Christi, 612 SW2d 667, ref nre.—Cons Cred 12, 16; Contracts 153, 175(1).

Friends for American Free Enterprise Ass'n v. Wal-Mart Stores, Inc., CA5 (Tex), 284 F3d 575.—Assoc 20(1); Fed Civ Proc 2756.1; Fed Cts 597, 812, 813, 947.

Friendship Baptist Dist. Ass'n v. Johnson, TexCivApp–Fort Worth, 230 SW2d 598, ref nre.—App & E 846(7), 854(1), 931(1), 989, 994(3), 1012.1(1); Relig Soc 20.

Friendship Missionary Baptist Church; Hawkins v., TexApp–Houston (14 Dist), 69 SW3d 756.—Const Law 1328, 1329, 1330; Relig Soc 14.

Friendship Village v. State, TexApp–Texarkana, 738 SW2d 12, ref nre.—App & E 907(3); Mun Corp 12(1), 12(2.1), 12(3), 12(8), 14, 18.

Friends of Canyon Lake, Inc. v. Guadalupe-Blanco River Authority, TexApp–Austin, 96 SW3d 519, review den.—Admin Law 124, 229, 500, 663; App & E 893(1), 895(2); Courts 39; Decl Judgm 41, 96; Plead 104(1), 111.39(0.5); Waters 145, 152(2), 183.5.

Friends of Earth, Inc. v. Chevron Chemical Co., ED-Tex, 885 FSupp 934.—Fed Civ Proc 25, 2725; Statut 214, 217.4.

Friends of the Earth, Inc. v. Chevron Chemical Co., CA5 (Tex), 129 F3d 826.—Corp 202; Environ Law 653.

Friends of the Earth, Inc. v. Chevron Chemical Co., EDTex, 919 FSupp 1042, rev 129 F3d 826.—Assoc 20(1); Environ Law 652, 653.

Friends of the Earth, Inc. v. Chevron Chemical Co., EDTex, 900 FSupp 67.—Const Law 42(1), 42(2); Environ Law 223, 226, 650, 652, 659, 663; Fed Civ Proc 2481.

Friends of the Earth, Inc. v. Crown Cent. Petroleum Corp., CA5 (Tex), 95 F3d 358, reh den.—Assoc 20(1); Environ Law 650, 652, 656; Fed Civ Proc 103.2, 1741.

Friends of WCC, Inc.; McAnally v., TexApp–Dallas, 113 SW3d 875.—Cem 5, 11, 12, 17; Const Law 4284; Em Dom 2.2; Estop 32(1), 52(1); Judgm 181(15.1), 185(2); Tresp to T T 1, 47(1), 50; Trusts 1, 21(2), 25(1).

Friendswood, City of; Green v., TexApp–Houston (14 Dist), 22 SW3d 588, reh overr, and review den.—App & E 173(13), 707(1), 863, 934(1); Autos 175(1), 187(1), 187(2), 201(1.1), 201(6); Judgm 183, 185(5), 185.3(21), 186; Neglig 375, 377, 379, 380, 383, 387, 1675.

Friendswood, City of, v. Registered Nurse Care Home, TexApp–Houston (1 Dist), 965 SW2d 705. See City of Friendswood v. Registered Nurse Care Home.

Friendswood, City of; Robinson v., SDTex, 890 FSupp 616.—Action 69(6); Civil R 1017, 1020, 1073, 1075, 1081, 1083, 1318; Zoning 21.5, 27, 64.

Friendswood Development Co. v. McDade & Co., Tex, 926 SW2d 280.—App & E 934(1); Brok 46; Contracts 143(2), 176(2); Evid 448; Judgm 185(2), 185(6); Torts 212, 220, 242.

Friendswood Development Co.; Murphy v., TexApp–Houston (1 Dist), 965 SW2d 708, reh overr.—Costs 2; Courts 85(2).

Friendswood Development Co.; Roberts v., TexApp–Houston (1 Dist), 886 SW2d 363, reh den, and writ den.—App & E 242(1), 852, 934(1); Ease 1, 40, 53; Judgm 181(2), 185(3), 185(6), 189; Neglig 1011, 1037(4), 1263, 1265.

Friendswood Development Co.; Smith-Southwest Industries v., TexCivApp–Hous (1 Dist), 546 SW2d 890, writ gr, rev 576 SW2d 21, 5 ALR4th 591.—Contrib 9(5); Indem 97; Judgm 181(11); Neglig 210, 1032; Waters 101, 107(3).

Friendswood Development Co. v. Smith-Southwest Industries, Inc., Tex, 576 SW2d 21, 5 ALR4th 591.—Waters 101.

Friendswood Development Co., Inc.; Stagner v., Tex, 620 SW2d 103.—Antitrust 141, 292.

Friendswood Development Co., Inc.; Stagner v., TexCivApp–Beaumont, 613 SW2d 793, ref nre 620 SW2d 103.—Antitrust 130, 141; Parties 35.31.

Friendswood Independent School Dist.; Howard S. v., SDTex, 454 FSupp 634.—Civil R 1330(2); Inj 147; Schools 115, 148(2.1); U S 82(2).

Friendswood Independent School Dist.; National Sur. Corp. v., Tex, 433 SW2d 690.—Garn 17; Mand 111; Mun Corp 1038; Schools 80(1), 86(2), 90, 94, 123.

Friendswood Independent School Dist. v. National Sur. Corp., TexCivApp–Hous (14 Dist), 423 SW2d 95, ref nre, and writ gr, rev 433 SW2d 690.—App & E 1173(2); Inj 88; Schools 62, 81(2), 84, 112; Statut 212.1.

Frier v. Federal Crop Ins. Corp., CCA5 (Tex), 152 F2d 149, cert den 66 SCt 1343, 328 US 856, 90 LEd 1628.—Contracts 16; Insurance 1732, 1734, 1766.

Frier v. Krohn, TexCivApp–Beaumont, 104 SW2d 537, writ refused.—App & E 387(1), 387(2), 784, 797(2).

Friermood v. Friermood, TexApp–Houston (14 Dist), 25 SW3d 758.—Child S 231, 341, 354, 356, 556(1), 558(1).

Friermood; Friermood v., TexApp–Houston (14 Dist), 25 SW3d 758.—Child S 231, 341, 354, 356, 556(1), 558(1).

Frierson; Harleysville Mut. Ins. Co. v., TexCivApp–Hous (14 Dist), 455 SW2d 370.—Work Comp 52, 962, 983, 986, 993, 998, 999, 1001, 1115, 1130, 1135, 1258, 1262.

Frierson; Johnson v., TexCivApp–Waco, 133 SW2d 594, writ dism, correct.—Lim of Act 168; Mtg 345, 372(3), 372(4), 372(5); Subrog 16.

Frierson v. Modern Mut. Health & Acc. Ins. Co., Tex-CivApp–Waco, 172 SW2d 389, writ refused wom.—App & E 1062.2; Ben Assoc 5(1), 17; Eject 107; Improv 4(6); Pretrial Proc 482.1, 483, 484; Trial 350.8.

Frierson v. State, TexApp–Dallas, 839 SW2d 841, petition for discretionary review refused.—Const Law 3309; Controlled Subs 9, 26, 27, 28, 30, 100(1); Crim Law 471, 476.3, 478(1), 795(2.20), 1043(2), 1044.2(1), 1134(2), 1158(3); Jury 33(5.15), 120; Searches 178, 180; Witn 345(1), 363(1), 367(3).

Fries v. State, TexCrimApp, 495 SW2d 909.—Arrest 63.4(8), 71.1(3); Controlled Subs 143; Crim Law 590(2), 1115(1), 1130(2).

Friesel v. State, TexApp–San Antonio, 931 SW2d 587, reh overr, and petition for discretionary review refused.—Crim Law 894; Ind & Inf 159(2).

Friesen; Flow v., TexCivApp–San Antonio, 213 SW2d 873, ref nre.—App & E 1064.1(6), 1067; Evid 334(1); Food 3; Sales 1(4).

Friesenhahn, In re, BkrtcyWDTex, 169 BR 615.—Bankr 2129, 2891, 2897.1, 2900(1), 2903, 3718(9); Const Law 4478; Statut 189.

Friesenhahn, In re Estate of, TexApp–San Antonio, 185 SW3d 16, reh overr, and review den.—Judgm 185.1(8), 185.3(4); Wills 58(1), 62, 703.

Friesenhahn v. City of New Braunfels, TexCivApp–Austin, 426 SW2d 566.—Const Law 4085; Em Dom 2(1.1); Inj 135, 211; Zoning 235.

Friesenhahn v. Ryan, Tex, 960 SW2d 656.—Judgm 181(11), 181(12), 181(33), 186; Plead 228.14, 228.23.

Friesenhahn; Ryan v., TexApp–San Antonio, 911 SW2d 113, reh overr, and writ gr, aff 960 SW2d 656.—App & E 893(1), 895(1); Int Liq 299, 306; Judgm 181(11); Neglig 202, 215, 259; Plead 228.23.

Friesing v. Vandergrift, SDTex, 126 FRD 527.—Fed Civ Proc 2769, 2771(2), 2785, 2800.

Frieze v. State, TexApp–Corpus Christi, 636 SW2d 11.—Crim Law 625.10(3), 625.10(4); Mental H 4.

Friga v. State, TexCrimApp, 488 SW2d 430.—Burg 41(1); Crim Law 372(10), 755.5, 775(2), 814(15), 1037.1(3); Witn 345(7).

Frigidaire Corp.; Gable v., TexCivApp–El Paso, 121 SW2d 456, dism.—Contracts 10(1), 10(4), 143(3), 217; Princ & A 41(1).

Frigiking, Inc. v. Century Tire & Sales Co., Inc., NDTex, 452 FSupp 935.—Contracts 249, 261(2), 321(1).

Frigiking, Inc., A Div. of Smith Jones, Inc.; Dallas Bank & Trust Co. v., TexApp–Dallas, 692 SW2d 163, ref nre.—Bankr 2062; Bills & N 332, 339; Contracts 143(2), 147(2), 176(2); Sec Tran 41, 43.1, 92.1, 138.

Friley; Owens–Illinois, Inc. v., Tex, 897 SW2d 765. See Owens-Illinois, Inc. v. Burt, Estate of.

Frink v. Blackstock, TexApp–Houston (1 Dist), 813 SW2d 602.—Mand 154(4), 168(4).

Frint v. Tate, TexCivApp–Amarillo, 162 SW2d 737.—Hus & W 59, 79; Trial 352.18; Trusts 1, 44(1), 62.

Frio Canyon Tel. Co. v. City of Leakey, TexCivApp–San Antonio, 524 SW2d 812.—Tel 981.

Frio County; Henderson v., TexCivApp–San Antonio, 362 SW2d 406.—Afft 18; App & E 1047(1); Dedi 1, 15, 16.1, 17, 41, 43, 44; Trial 350.3(1).

Frio County v. Security State Bank of Pharr, TexCivApp–Waco, 207 SW2d 231.—Counties 175, 187; Mun Corp 250, 913; Pub Contr 16; States 104; Statut 223.2(6).

Frio County Board of School Trustees; Moore Common School Dist. No. 2 ofFrio County v., TexCivApp–El Paso, 90 SW2d 288.—Schools 135, 138.

Frio Foods, Inc.; Mireles v., CA5 (Tex), 899 F2d 1407, 29 Wage & Hour Cas (BNA) 1265.—Labor & Emp 2312, 2317, 2371, 2387(2), 2387(4), 2387(6), 2390(1), 2390(4), 2394.

Frio Hosp. Ass'n; Maldonado v., TexApp–San Antonio, 25 SW3d 274.—App & E 934(2); Const Law 2492; Health 780; Judgm 185(2), 185(3), 185(5), 185(6), 185.1(3); Statut 188.

Frio Investments, Inc. v. 4M-IRC/Rohde, TexApp–San Antonio, 705 SW2d 784, ref nre.—App & E 758.1; Costs 194.40; Mtg 203, 204.1, 391, 469; Waste 18.

Frio Materials Co., Inc.; Southwestern Bell Telephone Co. v., TexCivApp–Texarkana, 571 SW2d 376, writ dism by agreement.—Tel 840; Tresp 7.

Friona, City of; Strickland v., TexCivApp–Amarillo, 294 SW2d 254, ref nre.—Em Dom 127, 202(1), 204, 222(4), 222(5), 262(5); Jury 148(2).

Friona Independent School Dist. v. King, TexApp–Amarillo, 15 SW3d 653.—Admin Law 229; App & E 71(3), 946, 954(1); Inj 132, 138.3, 138.6, 138.18, 138.54, 147; Offic 119; Schools 115, 169.

Friona State Bank v. Eaves, TexCivApp–Amarillo, 117 SW2d 818.—Agric 3.5(1).

Friona State Bank; Stewart v., TexCivApp–Amarillo, 278 SW2d 425, ref nre.—Accord 7(1), 10(1); Compromise 6(2), 6(4); Contracts 90; Des & Dist 82.

Frisbie; U.S. v., CA5 (Tex), 550 F2d 335, reh den 554 F2d 1065.—Controlled Subs 116; Crim Law 394.4(12); Cust Dut 126(2), 126(9.1); Searches 73.

Frisby; Double M Petroproperties, Inc. v., TexApp–Eastland, 957 SW2d 594.—Inj 138.3; Mines 52.

Frisby v. Rockins, TexCivApp–Dallas, 105 SW2d 362, writ dism.—App & E 100(1); Inj 16, 132, 138.31, 150; Plead 214(1); Sequest 5.

Frisco, City of; City of The Colony v., TexApp–Fort Worth, 686 SW2d 379, ref nre.—Mun Corp 29(1), 33(10).

Friske v. Graham, TexCivApp–San Antonio, 128 SW2d 139.—Autos 245(91), 247; Courts 207.4(2); Judgm 199(5), 256(1); Mand 51, 172; Neglig 530(1); Trial 358.

Friske v. State, TexCrimApp, 257 SW2d 714.—Crim Law 1094(2.1).

Friske; Stevenson v., TexCivApp–San Antonio, 141 SW2d 465.—App & E 1160.

Frison v. State, TexCrimApp, 473 SW2d 479.—Crim Law 365(1), 369.15, 371(1), 371(12), 372(1), 396(1), 719(1), 1036.1(1), 1137(5), 1169.1(5), 1169.5(3), 1171.1(3); Rob 24.40; Sent & Pun 316; Witn 37(4), 414(1).

Fritch, City of; Lake Meredith Development Co. v., TexCivApp–Amarillo, 564 SW2d 427.—Ease 22; Estop 83(1), 87, 118.

Frith v. Guardian Life Ins. Co. of America, SDTex, 9 FSupp2d 744.—Insurance 1654, 1801, 3424.

Frith v. Guardian Life Ins. Co. of America, SDTex, 9 FSupp2d 734.—Evid 405(1); Fed Civ Proc 636, 1772, 1835, 1838; Insurance 3419, 3424.

Fritiofson v. Alexander, CA5 (Tex), 772 F2d 1225.—Environ Law 577, 583, 585, 589, 591, 604(2), 689, 698, 700; Fed Cts 766, 776, 848.

Fritiofson v. Alexander, SDTex, 592 FSupp 120, aff in part, vac in part 772 F2d 1225.—Environ Law 571, 587, 589, 595(2), 613, 689.

Frito Co.; Cunningham v., TexCivApp–San Antonio, 198 SW2d 772.—Antitrust 564, 575, 823; App & E 954(1).

Frito Co.; Fisher v., TexCivApp–Dallas, 81 SW2d 282.—App & E 492, 954(1), 954(4); Inj 135, 161, 163(1).

Frito Co. v. General Mills, NDTex, 103 FSupp 563, aff 202 F2d 936, cert den 74 SCt 47, 346 US 827, 98 LEd 352.—Trademarks 1096(1), 1800.

Frito Co. v. General Mills, Inc., CA5 (Tex), 202 F2d 936, cert den 74 SCt 47, 346 US 827, 98 LEd 352.—Trademarks 1310, 1800.

Frito-Lay, Inc.; American Alliance Ins. Co. v., TexApp–Dallas, 788 SW2d 152, writ dism.—Inj 33, 138.27; Insurance 2268, 2915.

Frito-Lay, Inc. v. F.T.C., CA5 (Tex), 380 F2d 8.—Admin Law 229, 660; Antitrust 285.

Frito-Lay, Inc.; Ligon v., NDTex, 82 FRD 42.—Civil R 1139, 1586; Fed Civ Proc 103.7, 163, 164, 184.10, 184.15, 184.25.

Frito-Lay, Inc.; Luna v., TexApp–Amarillo, 726 SW2d 624.—Judgm 185(2); Labor & Emp 856; Lim of Act 43, 46(6).

Frito-Lay, Inc. v. Procter & Gamble Co., NDTex, 364 FSupp 243.—Corp 1.6(9), 1.7(2), 668(14); Fed Cts 76.10, 77, 80, 82; Pat 280.

Frito-Lay, Inc. v. Queen, TexApp–San Antonio, 873 SW2d 85, reh den, and writ den.—Autos 192(11), 201(1.1); Neglig 379, 380.

Frito-Lay, Inc.; Ramos v., Tex, 784 SW2d 667.—App & E 221, 931(4); Labor & Emp 3096(1), 3096(8), 3100(1).

Frito-Lay Inc. v. Ramos, TexApp–El Paso, 770 SW2d 887, writ gr, rev 784 SW2d 667.—Labor & Emp 3096(8), 3100(1), 3100(2), 3102.

Frito-Lay, Inc.; Rogers v., CA5 (Tex), 611 F2d 1074, cert den Moon v. Roadway Exp, Inc, 101 SCt 246, 449 US 889, 66 LEd2d 115, cert den 101 SCt 246, 449 US 889, 66 LEd2d 115.—Action 3; Civil R 1240; Const Law 2503(2); Fed Cts 5, 797; Statut 195, 216, 217.1, 217.2, 217.3; U S 63.

Frito-Lay, Inc.; Rogers v., NDTex, 433 FSupp 200, aff 611 F2d 1074, cert den Moon v. Roadway Exp, Inc, 101 SCt 246, 449 US 889, 66 LEd2d 115, cert den 101 SCt 246, 449 US 889, 66 LEd2d 115.—Action 3; Civil R 1117; Decl Judgm 272, 274.1; Fed Cts 18, 192, 197, 221; U S 82(1).

Fritsch v. J. M. English Truck Line, Tex, 246 SW2d 856, 151 Tex 168.—Pretrial Proc 718, 725.

Fritsch; J. M. English Truck Line v., TexCivApp–Galveston, 243 SW2d 464, rev 246 SW2d 856, 151 Tex 168.—Pretrial Proc 717.1, 718.

Fritsch; J. M. English Truck Line, Inc. v., TexCivApp–Galveston, 255 SW2d 597, ref nre.—App & E 1001(1); Autos 245(4); Damag 134(3), 216(4), 216(8); Trial 344.

Fritsch v. Texas Real Estate Commission, TexCivApp–Beaumont, 587 SW2d 209.—Brok 4.

FROMMER

Fritz v. City of Corrigan, EDTex, 163 FSupp2d 639.—Arrest 63.5(4), 68(4); Autos 349(17), 349(18); Civil R 1088(4), 1351(4), 1407.

Fritz; Gala Homes, Inc. v., TexCivApp–Waco, 393 SW2d 409, ref nre.—Contracts 170(1); Spec Perf 66, 99; Ven & Pur 3(4), 78.

Fritz; Lane v., TexCivApp–Corpus Christi, 404 SW2d 110.—Lis Pen 3(1), 3(4).

Fritz; Natural Gas Pipeline Co. of America v., SDTex, 853 FSupp 236.—Execution 418; Witn 21.

Fritz v. Old Am. Ins. Co., SDTex, 354 FSupp 514.—Insurance 1732, 1734, 1735, 1739, 1817.

Fritz v. Skiles, TexCivApp–Eastland, 107 SW2d 768.—Princ & A 115(1), 119(1), 150(2), 173(1).

Fritz v. State, TexCrimApp, 946 SW2d 844, on remand 1999 WL 300660.—Const Law 3428; Jury 33(1.1), 33(5.15).

Fritz v. State, TexCrimApp, 176 SW2d 187, 146 TexCrim 451.—Crim Law 635.

Fritz v. Tejas Gas Corp., TexApp–Corpus Christi, 644 SW2d 786, ref nre.—App & E 93; Sales 58, 87(3).

Fritz v. Texas Compensation Ins. Co., TexCivApp–Austin, 434 SW2d 702.—Work Comp 1283.

Fritz; Toshiba Intern. Corp. v., SDTex, 993 FSupp 571.—Fed Cts 95.

Fritz; Welder v., TexApp–Corpus Christi, 750 SW2d 930.—App & E 21, 22; Courts 206(17.3); Mand 141.

Fritz Chemical Co.; Port Distributing Corp. v., TexApp–Dallas, 775 SW2d 669, writ dism by agreement.—App & E 181, 223, 226(2), 878(1); Contracts 164; Judgm 178, 181(15.1), 186, 526.

Fritz Industries, Inc.; Baehler v., TexApp–Texarkana, 993 SW2d 181, reh overr, and review den.—Civil R 1118, 1176, 1744; Courts 97(5); Judgm 185.3(13).

Fritz Kopke, Inc.; Cooper Stevedoring Co. v., USTex, 94 SCt 2174, 417 US 106, 40 LEd2d 694.—Contrib 5(5), 5(6.1); Fed Cts 461; Ship 85.

Fritz Kopke, Inc.; Sessions v., CA5 (Tex), 479 F2d 1041, cert gr CooperStevedoring Co, Inc v. Fritz Kopke, Inc, 94 SCt 864, 414 US 1127, 38 LEd2d 752, aff 94 SCt 2174, 417 US 106, 40 LEd2d 694.—Ship 84(6), 85, 86(2.5).

Fritzler Development Corp.; Jenkins v., TexCivApp–Hous (1 Dist), 580 SW2d 63, ref nre.—Neglig 1205(7).

Fritz-Mair Mfg. Co., In re, BkrtcyNDTex, 16 BR 417.—Bankr 2535(5), 2611, 3061; Fraud Conv 139; Sales 201(3); Sec Tran 141.

Fritz-Mar Garments Mfg. Co.; Duderstadt v., TexCivApp–San Antonio, 552 SW2d 859, ref nre.—App & E 1056.6; Corp 432(12), 517; Trial 54(2).

Fritzmeier; Texas Emp. Ins. Ass'n v., TexCivApp–El Paso, 85 SW2d 1079, rev Fritzmeier v. Texas Employers' Ins Ass'n, 114 SW2d 236, 131 Tex 165.—Work Comp 742.

Fritzmeier v. Texas Employers' Ins. Ass'n, TexComApp, 114 SW2d 236, 131 Tex 165.—Trial 133.6(5), 219; Work Comp 742.

Fritz W. Glitsch & Sons, Inc. v. Wyatt Metal and Boiler Workers, NDTex, 121 FSupp 746, rev 224 F2d 331.—Pat 36.2(1), 233.1.

Fritz W. Glitsch & Sons, Inc. v. Wyatt Metal & Boiler Works, CA5 (Tex), 224 F2d 331.—Pat 112.1, 324.2, 324.54.

Frix v. Green, TexCivApp–San Antonio, 95 SW2d 219.—App & E 1010.1(10); Bills & N 430, 499, 537(8); Mtg 317; Princ & A 25(1).

Frizzell; City of San Antonio v., TexComApp, 91 SW2d 1056, 127 Tex 119.—App & E 1082(2); Mun Corp 250, 868(1).

Frizzell v. Cook, TexApp–San Antonio, 790 SW2d 41, writ den.—Antitrust 141, 162, 282; Courts 107; Damag 15; Sec Reg 278; Statut 223.1.

Frizzell; Puckett v., Tex, 402 SW2d 148.—App & E 110, 281(1), 387(1), 387(3), 388, 396, 411, 428(2), 624.

Frizzell; Puckett v., TexCivApp–Tyler, 406 SW2d 265.—Evid 383(7), 419(2), 419(4); Ven & Pur 315(2).

Frizzell; Puckett v., TexCivApp–Tyler, 396 SW2d 245, writ gr, cause remanded 402 SW2d 148.—App & E 395, 627.

Frizzell; Puckett v., TexCivApp–Tyler, 377 SW2d 715.—Evid 419(2); Ref of Inst 41, 46.

Frizzell; Sharp v., TexCivApp–Waco, 153 SW2d 543.—Lim of Act 145(5), 151(1), 151(2), 179(3); Venue 21.

Frizzell v. State, TexCrimApp, 132 SW2d 406.—Crim Law 1090.1(1).

Frizzell v. Sullivan, CA5 (Tex), 937 F2d 254.—Social S 149, 149.5.

Frizzell-Jones Lumber Co. v. Granberry, TexCivApp–Texarkana, 451 SW2d 805.—App & E 232(0.5), 1050.1(11), 1062.1; Tresp 43(3), 46(2); Trial 350.3(6).

Frobese v. Anderson, TexCivApp–Texarkana, 487 SW2d 818, writ gr, and rev.—App & E 302(1); Contracts 10(5), 15; New Tr 128(1), 128(2); Ven & Pur 49.

Froehlke; Allison v., CA5 (Tex), 470 F2d 1123.—Environ Law 604(3), 701; Evid 13; Inj 138.21.

Froehlke; Sierra Club v., CA5 (Tex), 816 F2d 205.—Admin Law 394; Const Law 2478; Environ Law 577, 586, 592, 597, 599, 600, 604(3), 605, 614, 689; Statut 129, 149.

Froehlke; Sierra Club v., SDTex, 630 FSupp 1215, rev 816 F2d 205.—Environ Law 578, 592, 597, 604(3), 608, 648; U S 85.

Froehlke; Sierra Club v., SDTex, 359 FSupp 1289, rev 499 F2d 982.—Const Law 2450; Environ Law 573, 577, 585, 586, 588, 590, 591, 595(1), 595(3), 599, 600, 601, 603, 604(3), 605, 606, 609, 610, 614, 615, 656, 689, 695, 700; Fed Civ Proc 316, 331, 338; Fed Cts 218, 243; U S 56, 125(26).

Froehlke; Sofranko v., WDTex, 346 FSupp 1380.—Armed S 15; Inj 138.69, 147, 150.

Froelich v. State, TexCrimApp, 178 SW2d 523, 147 TexCrim 103.—Crim Law 698(1), 1091(3), 1158(1).

Froelich v. Trinity Universal Ins. Co., TexCivApp–Amarillo, 355 SW2d 85.—Evid 265(1), 265(10); Insurance 2706(3).

Frogge; Graham Nat. Bank v., TexCivApp–Fort Worth, 150 SW2d 429.—Banks 174, 175(3).

Frogge; U.S. v., CA5 (Tex), 476 F2d 969, cert den 94 SCt 138, 414 US 849, 38 LEd2d 97.—Crim Law 388.5(1), 633(1); Escape 11.

Frog Leap; Meissner v., CA5 (Tex), 70 FedAppx 784.—Rem of C 107(9).

Frohne v. State, TexApp–Houston (1 Dist), 928 SW2d 570, reh overr, and petition for discretionary review refused, cert den 118 SCt 57, 522 US 812, 139 LEd2d 21.—Crim Law 474.4(4), 481, 641.13(2.1), 641.13(6); Infants 20; Sod 6.

Froman; U.S. v., CA5 (Tex), 355 F3d 882.—Arrest 63.4(2); Crim Law 394.4(6), 1139, 1158(2), 1158(4); Obscen 7.6; Searches 23, 40.1, 113.1; Sent & Pun 804, 806, 820, 934, 944.

Fromberg, Inc. v. Thornhill, CA5 (Tex), 315 F2d 407.—Fed Cts 850.1; Pat 191, 216, 234, 240, 255, 259(1), 259(3), 312(1.1), 314(6), 324.5, 324.60.

Fromen v. Goose Creek Independent School Dist., TexCivApp–Galveston, 148 SW2d 460, writ dism, correct.—Schools 135(5), 145, 147.9.

Fromme; Tennessee Gas Transmission Co. v., Tex, 269 SW2d 336, 153 Tex 352.—Lim of Act 43, 55(7).

Fromme v. Tennessee Gas Transmission Co., TexCivApp–Austin, 263 SW2d 574, rev 269 SW2d 336, 153 Tex 352.—Gas 14.50; Lim of Act 55(7).

Fromme v. West, TexCivApp–San Antonio, 226 SW2d 655, ref nre.—Joint Adv 1.15, 4(1), 5(2).

Frommer v. Frommer, TexApp–Houston (1 Dist), 981 SW2d 811, review dism.—App & E 846(5), 852, 946; Divorce 253(2), 286(2), 286(5); Judgm 220.

FROMMER;

59 Tex D 2d—140

See Guidelines for Arrangement at the beginning of this Volume

Frommer; Frommer v., TexApp–Houston (1 Dist), 981 SW2d 811, review dism.—App & E 846(5), 852, 946; Divorce 253(2), 286(2), 286(5); Judgm 220.

Fronatt v. State, TexCrimApp, 543 SW2d 140.—Crim Law 1042; Disorderly C 1; Sent & Pun 2021.

Fronatt v. State, TexApp–Houston (1 Dist), 630 SW2d 703, petition for discretionary review refused.—Controlled Subs 22, 77; Crim Law 641.13(2.1).

Frontier Airlines; Wells v., NDTex, 381 FSupp 818.—Civil R 1140, 1173, 1254, 1535, 1565; Fed Civ Proc 184.10.

Frontier Airlines, Inc.; Florence v., CA5 (Tex), 149 FedAppx 237.—Fed Civ Proc 2539; Jury 31.2(4); Labor & Emp 819; Libel 23.1.

Frontier Airlines, Inc.; Great Plains Airline Shareholders Ass'n, Inc. v., CA5 (Tex), 662 F2d 394.—Aviation 107.

Frontier Airlines, Inc.; International Ass'n of Machinists and AerospaceWorkers, Airline Dist. 146 v., CA5 (Tex), 664 F2d 538.—Labor & Emp 2034.

Frontier Airlines, Inc. v. Sky Chefs, Inc., CA5 (Tex), 447 F2d 1351.—Autos 245(39), 245(50.1), 245(67.1); Fed Cts 743; Interest 39(2.50).

Frontier Enterprises, Inc.; Camunes v., TexApp–San Antonio, 61 SW3d 579, reh overr, and review den, and reh of petition for review den.—App & E 223; Labor & Emp 40(2), 782, 783, 786.

Frontier Feedlots, Inc. v. Conklin Bros., Inc., TexCivApp–Amarillo, 476 SW2d 31.—App & E 218.2(8), 989; Contracts 231(2); Evid 568(7); Trial 351.2(3.1), 351.2(4), 366.

Frontier Ins. Co. v. State, TexApp–El Paso, 64 SW3d 481.—Bail 51, 73; Crim Law 1031(1).

Frontier Ins. Co. of New York; Metropolitan Baptist Church v., SDTex, 967 FSupp 217. See Aetna Cas. and Sur. Co. v. Metropolitan Baptist Church.

Frontier Mechanical Contractors; Bacchus Industries, Inc. v., TexApp–El Paso, 36 SW3d 579, reh overr.—App & E 842(1), 893(1); Lim of Act 129; Sales 178(4), 360(2), 368.

Frontier Mobile Homes v. Meadows, TexCivApp–Waco, 531 SW2d 240.—Plead 111.42(8), 111.42(10).

Frontier Pac. Ins. Co. v. Marathon Ashland Petroleum, L.L.C., SDTex, 87 FSupp2d 719.—Decl Judgm 41; Fed Cts 51.

Frontier-Pontiac, Inc. v. Dubuque Fire & Marine Ins. Co., TexCivApp–Fort Worth, 166 SW2d 746.—Insurance 1929(1), 1929(2), 1933.

Frontier State Bank; Frazier v., TexApp–San Antonio, 837 SW2d 392, appeal after new trial 1996 WL 543273, appeal after new trial 1999 WL 125441, review den.—App & E 544(1), 1043(6); Pretrial Proc 313.

Frontier Theatre, Inc. v. Whisenant, TexCivApp–El Paso, 291 SW2d 395, writ dism by agreement.—App & E 1045(1); Autos 192(11), 193(14), 201(1.1), 245(30); Trial 304.

Frontier Theatres, Inc.; Brown v., Tex, 369 SW2d 299.—App & E 931(1); Damag 105, 139; Evid 18; Land & Ten 162, 166(3), 169(11); Neglig 506(8), 1717; Trial 404(1).

Frontier Theatres Inc. v. Brown, TexCivApp–El Paso, 362 SW2d 360, rev 369 SW2d 299.—Carr 280(1), 397; Corp 383; Labor & Emp 2761, 2764, 2777, 2778, 2784, 2875, 2905, 2992; Land & Ten 164(1), 164(7), 166(2); Neglig 202, 554(1), 1037(4), 1051, 1537; Work Comp 2088.

Frontline Search; Ferguson & Co. v., TexApp–Dallas, 776 SW2d 692. See Ferguson & Co. v. Roll.

Frosch; Vetter v., CA5 (Tex), 599 F2d 630.—Civil R 1511, 1544; Fed Civ Proc 2534; Fed Cts 763.1, 766, 800, 802, 850.1.

Frossard v. State, TexCivApp–Dallas, 497 SW2d 473, ref nre.—Evid 333(4); Tax 2467, 2588, 2863.

Frost, In Interest of, TexApp–Amarillo, 815 SW2d 890.—Child S 393; Courts 40; Statut 183, 184.

Frost, In re, TexApp–Waco, 998 SW2d 938.—Pretrial Proc 33, 41.

Frost; Baumgarten v., Tex, 186 SW2d 982, 143 Tex 533, 159 ALR 428.—Adv Poss 104; Courts 32, 117; Evid 54, 65, 82, 372(1); Ex & Ad 375; Pub Lands 175(2), 178(3); Receivers 81, 137; Tresp to T T 6.1, 41(1).

Frost v. Baumgarten, TexCivApp–Galveston, 181 SW2d 127, rev 186 SW2d 982, 143 Tex 533, 159 ALR 428.—App & E 997(3), 1175(5); Execution 9; Jud S 31(3); Pub Lands 83; Receivers 137; Tresp to T T 6.1, 41(1), 44, 47(1).

Frost; Brandon v., TexCivApp–Waco, 256 SW2d 647.—App & E 787.

Frost; Cecil v., TexApp–Houston (14 Dist), 14 SW3d 414.—App & E 171(1), 171(3), 281(1); Libel 1, 7(1), 7(2), 19, 32, 123(2).

Frost; Chambers County v., TexApp–Waco, 356 SW2d 470, ref nre.—Estop 62.3; High 7(1), 17.

Frost v. Crain, TexCivApp–Fort Worth, 480 SW2d 754, ref nre.—App & E 1170.6; Autos 244(36.1), 244(58); Trial 114, 118, 121(2).

Frost v. Crockett, TexCivApp–Galveston, 109 SW2d 529, dism.—Adv Poss 57, 68; App & E 745, 758.3(1), 758.3(11), 931(5); Deeds 38(1); Evid 317(4), 372(2); Ex & Ad 29(2), 383, 388(1); Land & Ten 66(2); Ten in C 55(6), 55(7); Tresp to T T 38(1).

Frost; Danvers v., TexCivApp–Eastland, 348 SW2d 485.—Brok 7; Hus & W 90.

Frost v. Davis, CA5 (Tex), 288 F2d 497.—Attach 165; Execution 131; Garn 95; Rem of C 115.

Frost v. De Bogory, TexCivApp–Dallas, 291 SW2d 414.—Action 60; App & E 78(3), 79(1), 80(6); Libel 38(3); Pretrial Proc 555; Set-Off 34(2), 41.

Frost v. Fowlerton Consol. School Dist. No. 1, TexCivApp–Beaumont, 111 SW2d 754.—Lim of Act 124, 143(1); Schools 21, 90, 95(1), 95(4), 95(5), 107; Tax 2777.

Frost v. Frost, TexApp–San Antonio, 695 SW2d 279.—App & E 758.1, 931(1), 984(1), 989, 1008.1(2); Hus & W 279(1), 281; Judgm 91; Refer 76(1).

Frost; Frost v., TexApp–San Antonio, 695 SW2d 279.—App & E 758.1, 931(1), 984(1), 989, 1008.1(2); Hus & W 279(1), 281; Judgm 91; Refer 76(1).

Frost v. Frost, TexCivApp–Texarkana, 467 SW2d 683.—App & E 77(1); Child C 618.

Frost; Frost v., TexCivApp–Texarkana, 467 SW2d 683.—App & E 77(1); Child C 618.

Frost; Hicks v., TexCivApp–El Paso, 195 SW2d 606, ref nre.—App & E 929, 1003(10), 1068(1); Autos 201(10), 204, 243(3), 243(17); Evid 474(4), 478(3); Judgm 199(3.7); Neglig 510(1), 530(1); Trial 41(2), 235(4), 350.7(3.1).

Frost; McKenzie v., TexCivApp–El Paso, 448 SW2d 520, ref nre.—Evid 43(1); Judgm 713(2), 743(2), 948(1), 949(1).

Frost v. Mischer, Tex, 463 SW2d 166.—Inj 189.

Frost; Mischer v., TexCivApp–Hous (1 Dist), 451 SW2d 936, rev 463 SW2d 166.—App & E 919; Inj 123; Tresp 12.

Frost v. Molina, TexCivApp–Corpus Christi, 595 SW2d 184, dism.—App & E 1008.1(1); Plead 111.18; Quiet T 6; Venue 2, 17.

Frost; Patriacca v., TexApp–Houston (1 Dist), 98 SW3d 303.—App & E 169, 934(1), 981; Judgm 183; New Tr 102(1), 102(3).

Frost v. Periodical Publishers Service Bureau, Inc., CA5 (Tex), 981 F2d 215. See Periodical Publishers Service Bureau, Inc. v. Keys.

Frost; Podgoursky v., TexCivApp–San Antonio, 394 SW2d 185, ref nre.—Courts 472.4(4); Ex & Ad 7, 31, 122(1), 244, 435; Judgm 335(1), 335(2), 335(3), 335(4).

For Later Case History Information, see KeyCite on WESTLAW

Frost v. Public Utility Com'n of Texas, TexApp–Austin, 672 SW2d 883, ref nre.—Admin Law 764.1; Electricity 9(2), 9(5).

Frost v. Socony Mobil Oil Co., Tex, 433 SW2d 387.—Bound 3(5), 3(7), 11; Pub Lands 177.

Frost; Socony Mobil Oil Co. v., TexCivApp–El Paso, 407 SW2d 248, ref nre, rev 433 SW2d 387.—Bound 3(3), 3(5), 3(7), 3(9), 8, 37(3).

Frost v. Standard Oil Co. of Kan., TexCivApp–Galveston, 107 SW2d 1037.—Mines 73.1(2), 74(1), 79.1(3); Venue 5.1, 5.5.

Frost v. Stanolind Oil & Gas Co., TexCivApp–Houston, 307 SW2d 136, writ refused.—Mines 79.7.

Frost v. State, TexCrimApp, 369 SW2d 357.—Ind & Inf 193; Int Liq 205(1), 207.

Frost v. State, TexCrimApp, 368 SW2d 948.—Int Liq 205(2).

Frost v. State, TexApp–Fort Worth, 625 SW2d 94.—Crim Law 371(6), 444, 775(2).

Frost v. State, TexApp–Austin, 25 SW3d 395.—Crim Law 772(1), 1038.1(1), 1038.1(2), 1144.13(3), 1159.2(7); Rob 7, 11, 24.15(2), 27(6).

Frost v. State, TexApp–Houston (14 Dist), 2 SW3d 625, petition for discretionary review refused.—Crim Law 80, 552(2), 1032(1), 1159.2(7), 1159.2(9), 1159.4(1); Obst Just 16.

Frost v. State, TexCivApp–Austin, 284 SW2d 232, ref nre. —Em Dom 222(4), 262(5).

Frost; State v., TexCivApp–Hous (14 Dist), 456 SW2d 245, ref nre.—App & E 750(6); Em Dom 58, 85, 106, 194, 203(1), 222(1), 246(2), 255, 262(5), 318, 319; Evid 142(1), 219(1).

Frost v. Sun Oil Co. (Delaware), TexCivApp–Hous (1 Dist), 560 SW2d 467.—App & E 218.2(1), 232(0.5); Decl Judgm 2, 311, 329, 347, 364, 387; Equity 65(2); Evid 450(5); Inj 204; Judgm 199(3.5); Mines 92.16, 92.44(1); Plead 34(1).

Frost; U.S. v., CCA5 (Tex), 80 F2d 341, appeal dism 56 SCt 679, 298 US 691, 80 LEd 1409.—Int Rev 4423.

Frost; U.S. v., SDTex, 11 FSupp 992, rev 80 F2d 341, appeal dism 56 SCt 679, 298 US 691, 80 LEd 1409.—Const Law 631; Int Rev 4420, 4423.

Frost v. Village of Hilshire Village, TexCivApp–Houston, 403 SW2d 836, ref nre.—App & E 846(5); Evid 177; Zoning 21, 30, 137, 643, 653.

Frost v. Wells, TexCivApp–Amarillo, 388 SW2d 235, writ dism.—Joint Adv 1.13; Labor & Emp 178, 207; Partit 43; Partners 20; Plead 111.36, 312.

Frost Bros., Inc.; Sigler v., TexCivApp–El Paso, 555 SW2d 813.—Acct Action on 12, 13; App & E 959(1), 966(1); Plead 236(2), 353; Pretrial Proc 713, 717.1, 723.1.

Frost Bros., Inc.; Wells v., TexCivApp–San Antonio, 295 SW2d 958.—Insurance 1701.

Frost, City of; McAllister v., TexCivApp–Waco, 131 SW2d 975, writ dism, correct.—App & E 994(2), 1001(1), 1002, 1003(3); Mun Corp 85, 220(8).

Frost Crushed Stone Co., Inc. v. Odell Geer Const. Co., Inc., TexApp–Waco, 110 SW3d 41.—App & E 230, 231(9), 242(1); Costs 207; Damag 117, 189; Estop 85, 118; Frds St of 119(1), 144; Trial 273.

Frostex Foods, Inc.; Eckerdt v., TexApp–Austin, 802 SW2d 70.—App & E 757(1); Civil R 1724, 1732; Statut 226; Trial 114.

Frostidrink, Inc. v. Supervend Corp., NDTex, 89 FSupp 550.—Fed Civ Proc 1958; Pat 66(1.7), 118.3(8), 233.1.

Frostie Co. v. Dr. Pepper Co., CA5 (Tex), 361 F2d 124.—Antitrust 103(1); Fed Civ Proc 2252; Fed Cts 758, 814.1, 893; Inj 1; Trademarks 1629(3), 1714(3), 1717(2), 1717(3), 1750, 1800.

Frostie Co. v. Dr. Pepper Co., CA5 (Tex), 341 F2d 363.—Fed Cts 947; Trademarks 1098, 1112, 1609, 1615, 1627, 1800.

Frost Lumber Industries, Inc., of Texas; Hancock v., TexCivApp–Beaumont, 182 SW2d 747.—Trial 25(9).

Frost Lumber Industries of Texas v. Brantley, TexCivApp–Beaumont, 109 SW2d 999.—Adv Poss 85(5), 96; Bound 3(5), 6, 9; Evid 390(3); Tresp to T T 35(1).

Frost Nat. Bank, In re, TexApp–Corpus Christi, 103 SW3d 647, reh overr, and mandamus den.—Action 6; App & E 347(2), 946; Mand 4(1), 12; New Tr 0.5; Pretrial Proc 508, 514, 518, 693.1; Set-Off 29(1).

Frost Nat. Bank v. Alamo Nat. Bank, TexCivApp–San Antonio, 421 SW2d 153, ref nre.—App & E 1170.10; Estop 70(2), 116, 119; Fraud Conv 47; Torts 212, 215, 263, 271, 282.

Frost Nat. Bank; Barnes v., TexApp–San Antonio, 840 SW2d 747.—App & E 5; Judgm 17(1), 17(10); Proc 83, 145, 153.

Frost Nat. Bank; Boyd v., Tex, 196 SW2d 497, 145 Tex 206, 168 ALR 1326.—Char 4, 10, 20(2), 22(1), 22(2), 31, 43, 45(1), 49; Perp 8(1); Wills 52(1), 166(1), 199, 288(3), 290, 439.

Frost Nat. Bank v. Boyd, TexCivApp–San Antonio, 188 SW2d 199, aff 196 SW2d 497, 145 Tex 206, 168 ALR 1326.—Char 1, 4, 10, 18, 21(2), 22(1), 31, 45(1), 49; Equity 21; Evid 157(2); Perp 8(5); Wills 52(1), 157, 163(2), 288(1), 302(3), 473.

Frost National Bank v. Burge, TexApp–Houston (14 Dist), 29 SW3d 580, reh overr.—Alt of Inst 2; App & E 70(8), 856(1), 1175(2); Bills & N 116, 129(3); Contracts 164, 326; Equity 43, 46; Estop 52.10(2), 52.10(3), 119; Evid 397(1), 433(9); Frds St of 17, 43, 44(1), 106(1), 139(1), 139(3), 159; Guar 27; Judgm 181(19), 185(5), 540, 653, 720; Princ & S 59, 101(2), 128(1), 159, 162(2); Trover 1.

Frost Nat. Bank; Cragin v., TexCivApp–San Antonio, 164 SW2d 24, writ refused wom.—Deeds 126; Estates 5, 6; Wills 470(3), 488, 589(4), 590, 600(4), 602(1), 616(1).

Frost Nat. Bank; Glasscock v., TexApp–San Antonio, 928 SW2d 599, reh overr, and writ den.—Judgm 183, 185.3(16).

Frost National Bank v. Heafner, TexApp–Houston (1 Dist), 12 SW3d 104, reh overr, and review den, and reh of petition for review den.—Antitrust 220; App & E 758.3(9); Banks 148(0.5), 148(2), 154(9), 227(3), 229; Damag 5, 15, 18, 89(2), 118; Evid 595; Fraud 3, 12, 50, 58(3); Trial 139.1(3).

Frost Nat. Bank v. L & F Distributors, Ltd., Tex, 165 SW3d 310.—Bailm 22; Contracts 143(2), 143(4), 143.5, 147(2), 154, 176(2).

Frost Nat. Bank v. L & F Distributors, Ltd., TexApp–Corpus Christi, 122 SW3d 922, review gr, rev 165 SW3d 310.—App & E 840(1), 912, 1024.3; Bailm 22; Contracts 143(1), 143(2), 143(3), 143.5, 147(2), 152, 154, 168, 176(2); Cust & U 15(1); Decl Judgm 271; Evid 393(1), 397(1), 448; Judgm 181(19); Venue 16, 17.

Frost Nat. Bank; Lentino v., TexApp–Houston (14 Dist), 159 SW3d 651, reh overr.—App & E 66, 76(1), 79(1), 80(1), 80(6), 347(2), 782; Plead 228.23; Pretrial Proc 517.1, 518.

Frost Nat. Bank; Marsh v., TexApp–Corpus Christi, 129 SW3d 174, reh overr, and review den.—App & E 893(1), 895(2); Char 10, 22(1), 37(3); Perp 4(15.1), 8(1); Wills 473, 685, 686(1), 706.

Frost Nat. Bank v. Matthews, TexApp–Texarkana, 713 SW2d 365, ref nre.—App & E 901, 934(1); Consp 1.1, 8; Judgm 185(2); Mines 78.1(10); Torts 212, 220, 222, 242.

Frost Nat. Bank v. Nicholas and Barrera, TexCivApp–Tyler, 534 SW2d 927, ref nre.—App & E 934(1); Banks 119, 133, 138, 154(8); Judgm 199(3.7), 199(3.10).

Frost Nat. Bank; Nowlin v., TexApp–Houston (1 Dist), 908 SW2d 283.—App & E 93, 1175(1); Evid 397(1); Judgm 181(34); Powers 1, 25; Trusts 61(4), 119, 279, 282; Wills 475, 721.

Frost Nat. Bank; Pena v., TexCivApp–San Antonio, 119 SW2d 612, writ refused.—App & E 206, 750(3), 927(7);

FROST

Deeds 38(6); Evid 372(8); Partit 4, 5, 8; Tresp to T T 6.1, 40(4), 41(3).

Frost Nat. Bank v. U.S., WDTex, 74 FSupp 749.—Int Rev 3441, 3442.

Frost Nat. Bank; Village of Creedmoor v., TexApp–Austin, 808 SW2d 617, writ den.—Mun Corp 29(4), 33(1).

Frost Nat. Bank; Watson v., TexApp–Texarkana, 139 SW3d 118.—Judgm 185(1), 185.3(16).

Frost Nat. Bank of Houston; Kaminetzky v., SDTex, 881 FSupp 276.—Inj 26(4).

Frost Nat. Bank of San Antonio; Alterman v., TexApp–San Antonio, 675 SW2d 619.—App & E 931(1), 989, 1008.1(2), 1010.1(3), 1012.1(5); Ex & Ad 7, 227(1).

Frost Nat. Bank of San Antonio; Cluck v., TexApp–San Antonio, 714 SW2d 408, ref nre.—App & E 173(2); Bills & N 129(2); Mtg 309(1).

Frost Nat. Bank of San Antonio; Deegan v., TexCivApp–San Antonio, 505 SW2d 428, writ refused.—Wills 439, 450, 470(1), 476, 614(4), 634(7).

Frost Nat. Bank of San Antonio v. Dobbs, TexCivApp–San Antonio, 423 SW2d 145, ref nre.—Banks 139, 140(3); Bills & N 22.

Frost Nat. Bank of San Antonio; First Nat. Bank in George West v., TexCivApp–San Antonio, 142 SW2d 555, writ dism, correct.—App & E 644(1); Evid 43(1); Garn 1, 88, 193; Paymt 42.

Frost Nat. Bank of San Antonio; First State Bank of Bishop v., TexApp–San Antonio, 665 SW2d 198.—App & E 395.

Frost Nat. Bank of San Antonio; Heusinger Hardware Co. v., TexCivApp–Eastland, 364 SW2d 851.—App & E 854(3); Banks 165, 169, 175(2); Judgm 181(17); Plead 228.20, 291(2), 422; Princ & A 109(0.5), 109(4).

Frost Nat. Bank of San Antonio v. Johnson, TexApp–El Paso, 729 SW2d 319, ref nre.—App & E 223; Guar 36(1), 77(1), 91.

Frost Nat. Bank of San Antonio v. Kayton, TexCivApp–San Antonio, 526 SW2d 654, ref nre.—App & E 1178(6); Damag 191; Evid 318(1); Ex & Ad 122(1), 450, 455.

Frost Nat. Bank of San Antonio; LeLaurin v., CA5 (Tex), 391 F2d 687, cert den 89 SCt 447, 393 US 979, 21 LEd2d 440.—Bankr 2164.1, 2921, 2932, 3200; Bills & N 126, 491, 534; Fed Civ Proc 2723; Fed Cts 406.

Frost Nat. Bank of San Antonio v. Mitchell, TexCivApp–Waco, 362 SW2d 198.—Bills & N 121; Contracts 138(1); Gaming 19(1); Witn 200.

Frost Nat. Bank of San Antonio; Monarch Tile Sales v., TexCivApp–San Antonio, 496 SW2d 254.—Interest 20; Interpl 35.

Frost Nat. Bank of San Antonio v. Newton, Tex, 554 SW2d 149.—Perp 4(17); Trusts 61(3), 112; Wills 439, 440, 470(2), 686(1), 686(2).

Frost Nat. Bank of San Antonio v. Newton, TexCivApp–Waco, 543 SW2d 196, writ gr, rev 554 SW2d 149.—Trusts 61(1), 61(3); Wills 686(1).

Frost Nat. Bank of San Antonio v. Nicholas and Barrera, TexCivApp–San Antonio, 500 SW2d 906, ref nre, appeal after remand 534 SW2d 927, ref nre.—Banks 138, 147.2, 148(2), 148(3); Bills & N 170; Judgm 185.3(5).

Frost Nat. Bank of San Antonio; Parker v., TexApp–Austin, 852 SW2d 741, reh overr, and writ gr, and writ withdrawn, and writ dism by agreement.—Bills & N 129(1); Mtg 335, 414; Time 9(4).

Frost Nat. Bank of San Antonio; Sabine Production Co. v., TexCivApp–Corpus Christi, 596 SW2d 271, writ dism woj.—Contracts 96; Mines 48, 70(1); Parties 29; Plead 111.16, 111.39(4), 111.42(6); Torts 212; Venue 5.3(8), 5.5, 7.5(1), 7.5(2), 7.5(3), 7.5(6), 22(6).

Frost Nat. Bank of San Antonio; Shannon v., TexCivApp–San Antonio, 533 SW2d 389, ref nre.—Trusts 217.3(8), 263, 289.

Frost Nat. Bank of San Antonio; Stauffer v., TexCivApp–San Antonio, 291 SW2d 743.—Banks 148(4); Estop 119.

Frost Nat. Bank of San Antonio v. Stool, TexCivApp–Beaumont, 575 SW2d 321, ref nre.—Trusts 44(1).

Frost Nat. Bank of San Antonio; Transamerica Ins. Co. v., TexCivApp–Beaumont, 501 SW2d 418, ref nre.—App & E 930(3), 989; Judgm 565; Pretrial Proc 509; Trial 350.4(1); Trusts 112, 247, 262, 263.

Frost Nat. Bank of San Antonio; Weems v., TexCivApp–San Antonio, 278 SW2d 318, dism.—App & E 763; Venue 17.

Frost Nat. Bank of San Antonio; Weems v., TexCivApp–San Antonio, 275 SW2d 956, writ dism, reh den 278 SW2d 318, dism.—Decl Judgm 300, 323; Venue 15.

Frost Nat. Bank of San Antonio; Weems v., TexCivApp–El Paso, 301 SW2d 714, ref nre.—Joint Ten 3, 6; Wills 439, 440, 488, 506(2), 523, 564(1), 578(1), 627(1), 705, 706, 707(1), 858(1).

Frownfelter v. Frownfelter, TexCivApp–San Antonio, 294 SW2d 745.—Divorce 254(1).

Frownfelter; Frownfelter v., TexCivApp–San Antonio, 294 SW2d 745.—Divorce 254(1).

Frownfelter v. International Shoe Co., CA5 (Tex), 273 F2d 338.—Lim of Act 100(5), 151(3).

Froyd v. State, TexCrimApp, 633 SW2d 884, on remand 654 SW2d 19.—Crim Law 1134(3).

Froyd v. State, TexApp–Corpus Christi, 654 SW2d 19.—Rob 7, 24.50.

Froyd v. State, TexApp–Corpus Christi, 628 SW2d 866, petition for discretionary review refused, remanded 633 SW2d 884, on remand 654 SW2d 19.—Crim Law 641.4(1), 641.10(3), 643, 1166.13.

Frozen Food Exp.; East Tex. Motor Freight Lines, Inc. v., USTex, 76 SCt 574, 351 US 49, 100 LEd 917.—Commerce 85.26, 161, 168.

Frozen Food Exp.; Huckeby v., CA5 (Tex), 555 F2d 542.—Civil R 1530; Fed Civ Proc 1827.1, 2575; Fed Cts 521, 526.1, 530, 599, 600, 660.1, 660.5; Mand 1, 4(1).

Frozen Food Exp.; Huckeby v., NDTex, 427 FSupp 967, 23 Wage & Hour Cas (BNA) 212.—Civil R 1168, 1549, 1553; Labor & Emp 2463, 2481(7).

Frozen Food Exp.; Thurman v., TexCivApp–Dallas, 600 SW2d 369.—App & E 172(1); Judgm 185(1), 185.2(9).

Frozen Food Exp.; Traders & Gen. Ins. Co. v., TexCivApp–Austin, 255 SW2d 378, ref nre.—App & E 843(1), 1050.1(5); Insurance 1034; Trial 352.4(9), 352.7; Work Comp 205, 304, 348, 1063.

Frozen Food Exp. v. U.S., USTex, 76 SCt 569, 351 US 40, 100 LEd 910.—Admin Law 508, 703; Commerce 152.

Frozen Food Exp. v. U.S., NDTex, 219 FSupp 131.—Commerce 85.29(4), 104, 161, 163, 174, 175.

Frozen Food Exp. v. U.S., SDTex, 148 FSupp 399, aff Akron, Canton, and Youngstown Railroad Company v. Frozen Food Express, 78 SCt 38, 355 US 6, 2 LEd2d 22, aff American Trucking Association, Inc v Frozen Food Express, 78 SCt 40, 355 US 6, 2 LEd2d 22, aff Interstate Commerce Commission v Frozen Food Express, 78 SCt 42, 355 US 6, 2 LEd2d 22.—Autos 126.

Frozen Food Exp. v. U.S., SDTex, 136 FSupp 617.—Admin Law 763, 784.1; Commerce 168, 173.

Frozen Food Exp. v. U.S., SDTex, 128 FSupp 374, rev 76 SCt 569, 351 US 40, 100 LEd 910, aff East Tex Motor Freight Lines Inc v Frozen Food Exp, 76 SCt 574, 351 US 49, 100 LEd 917.—Commerce 85.26, 103, 151, 153.1, 171, 173, 174.

Frozen Food Exp., Inc.; Cal-Tex Beef Processors, Inc. v., TexCivApp–Waco, 530 SW2d 143, ref nre.—Acct Action on 12, 14; Evid 52.

Frozen Food Exp., Inc.; Irvan v., CA5 (Tex), 809 F2d 1165.—Fed Cts 937.1; Labor & Emp 2822, 2824.

Frozen Food Exp., Inc.; Irvan v., CA5 (Tex), 780 F2d 1228, appeal after remand 809 F2d 1165.—Fed Civ Proc 1973; Fed Cts 899; Labor & Emp 2880.

Frozen Food Exp., Inc.; John Morrell & Co. v., CA5 (Tex), 700 F2d 256.—Antitrust 161; Carr 116, 117, 134; Fed Cts 857.

Frozen Food Exp., Inc.; Kemp v., EDTex, 618 FSupp 431.—Work Comp 331.

Frozen Food Exp., Inc. v. U.S., CA5 (Tex), 535 F2d 877.—Commerce 99, 118, 161.

Frozen Food Exp., Inc. v. U.S., NDTex, 328 FSupp 666.—Commerce 85.6, 153.1; Const Law 4360; Fed Civ Proc 1951.

Frozen Food Exp., Inc. v. U.S., NDTex, 301 FSupp 1322.—Commerce 85.6, 105, 117.

Frozen Food Exp. Industries, Inc. v. Goodwin, TexApp–Beaumont, 921 SW2d 547.—Mand 4(1), 28; Pretrial Proc 101.

Frozen Foods Exp. v. Odom, TexCivApp–Eastland, 229 SW2d 92, ref nre.—App & E 218.2(3.1), 232(0.5), 1140(1); Pretrial Proc 481; Trial 114, 121(5), 350.6(3), 366.

Frozen Foods Exp. v. U.S., NDTex, 280 FSupp 661.—Commerce 85.29(1), 121.

Frozen Foods Exp., Inc. v. U.S., WDTex, 346 FSupp 254.—Admin Law 791; Commerce 85.28(3), 105, 108, 115.1, 121, 163, 164, 174, 176; Const Law 4364.

Fruechte v. State, TexCrimApp, 316 SW2d 418, 166 TexCrim 496.—Crim Law 534(2).

Fruehauf Corp.; Biggs v., TexCivApp–Fort Worth, 439 SW2d 479, ref nre.—App & E 1135.

Fruehauf Corp. v. Carrillo, Tex, 848 SW2d 83.—App & E 78(6); Judgm 297, 340; Motions 59(2); New Tr 165.

Fruehauf Corp.; Carrillo v., TexApp–San Antonio, 838 SW2d 573, reh den, and writ gr, rev 848 SW2d 83.—New Tr 165.

Fruehauf Corp.; Huddy v., CA5 (Tex), 953 F2d 955, reh den, cert den 113 SCt 89, 506 US 828, 121 LEd2d 52.—Fed Cts 409.1, 776; Prod Liab 3.

Fruehauf Corp.; Mitchell v., CA5 (Tex), 568 F2d 1139, reh den 570 F2d 1391.—Evid 208(2), 539; Fed Civ Proc 2176.3; Trial 799, 896.1; Prod Liab 8, 15, 27, 38, 81.1, 81.5, 83.5, 88.5, 96.1, 98.

Fruehauf Corp.; O'Rear v., CA5 (Tex), 554 F2d 1304.—Fed Civ Proc 1951, 1973, 1974.1, 1976, 2173.1(1), 2334, 2337.

Fruehauf Corp. v. Ortega, TexApp–Corpus Christi, 687 SW2d 777.—App & E 231(1), 994(2), 1026, 1039(13), 1062.1, 1064.1(1); Compromise 15(1); Damag 63; Electricity 17, 19(13); Indem 59; Plead 428(5); Trial 278, 350.6(2).

Fruehauf Corp. v. Ortega, TexApp–Corpus Christi, 652 SW2d 566.—App & E 622, 624.

Fruehauf Trailer Co.; Barnard v., SDTex, 260 FSupp 605.—Pat 36.2(3), 112.1.

Fruehauf Trailer Division, Fruehauf Corp.; La-Tex Supply Co. v., CA5 (Tex), 444 F2d 1366, cert den 92 SCt 287, 404 US 942, 30 LEd2d 256.—Fed Civ Proc 1693, 2337; Fed Cts 347, 893.

Fruge v. James, TexCivApp–Beaumont, 115 SW2d 1175.—App & E 218.2(4), 719(8), 1070(2); Neglig 1204(1), 1750.

Fruge; Texas Farmers Ins. Co. v., TexApp–Beaumont, 13 SW3d 509, review den.—Health 545; Insurance 1109, 3400(2), 3441; States 18.9, 18.41.

Fruge; Texas Farmers Ins. Co. v., TexApp–Beaumont, 8 SW3d 464, opinion withdrawn and superseded on reh, and withdrawn from Bound Volume.

Fruge v. Vitopil, TexCivApp–Waco, 147 SW2d 519.—App & E 1177(6); Plead 111.9, 111.42(2).

Fruhman v. Nawcas Benev. Auxiliary, TexCivApp–Dallas, 436 SW2d 912, ref nre.—Insurance 1713, 1722, 1725, 1805, 1806, 1809, 1810, 1813, 1814, 1822, 2104, 2442.

Frusher; Kitchen v., TexApp–Fort Worth, 181 SW3d 467, reh overr.—App & E 230, 836, 866(3), 927(7), 930(1), 989, 1001(1), 1001(3), 1003(5), 1003(6), 1182; Impl & C C 30, 34, 91, 93.1, 112, 121; Trial 139.1(14), 139.1(17).

Fruth v. Gaston, TexCivApp–Austin, 187 SW2d 581, writ refused wom.—App & E 927(7), 989; Compromise 24; Corp 1.6(9); Equity 84; Evid 139; Frds St of 52; Labor & Emp 34(2), 205, 265; Lim of Act 166; Trial 139.1(6), 139.1(16), 140(1); Witn 406.

Fry v. Ahrens, TexCivApp–Galveston, 256 SW2d 115.—Fraud 59(1), 59(2); J P 36(1), 36(2.1).

Fry v. Alaniz, TexCivApp–San Antonio, 329 SW2d 133.—Plead 111.46; Venue 8.5(1).

Fry; Brady v., TexCivApp–Beaumont, 517 SW2d 304.—Mand 4(1), 26, 61, 187.10.

Fry; Cain v., TexCivApp–Amarillo, 86 SW2d 270.—Can of Inst 50; Contracts 94(1), 94(5), 256, 258; J P 43(1); Ven & Pur 321.

Fry v. Commission for Lawyer Discipline, TexApp–Houston (14 Dist), 979 SW2d 331, reh overr, and review den.—App & E 223, 856(1); Atty & C 44(2), 57, 117; Judgm 183, 185(5), 187.

Fry; Daniel v., TexCivApp–San Antonio, 195 SW2d 155, ref nre.—App & E 281(1).

Fry v. Dixie Motor Coach Corp., Tex, 180 SW2d 135, 142 Tex 589.—App & E 863, 1002, 1078(1), 1114; Carr 273.1.

Fry; Dixie Motor Coach Corp. v., TexCivApp–Dallas, 177 SW2d 992, rev 180 SW2d 135, 142 Tex 589.—App & E 1001(1); Carr 276; Evid 10(2), 10(6), 383(2), 571(9), 574.

Fry v. Estelle, CA5 (Tex), 527 F2d 420.—Searches 65.

Fry; GFI Computer Industries, Inc. v., CA5 (Tex), 476 F2d 1.—Fed Civ Proc 1534, 1636.1, 1741, 2415; Witn 4.

Fry; Great Am. Reserve Ins. Co. v., TexCivApp–Austin, 418 SW2d 716, ref nre.—Insurance 3125(6).

Fry v. Guillote, TexCivApp–Hous (14 Dist), 577 SW2d 346, ref nre.—App & E 959(3); Cust & U 12(1), 13, 19(3); Plead 236(3), 236(7), 427; Trial 105(4).

Fry v. Harkey, TexCivApp–San Antonio, 141 SW2d 662, writ dism, correct.—App & E 609, 846(5), 849(1), 927(7); Frds St of 129(3); Lim of Act 44(1); Quiet T 44(3), 47(1); Spec Perf 105(2); Trial 141, 177; Waters 156(1), 156(6), 156(7), 156(9).

Fry v. Henrietta Independent School Dist., TexCivApp–Fort Worth, 98 SW2d 245.—App & E 374(2).

Fry v. Hughes Tool Co., TexCivApp–Eastland, 317 SW2d 950.—Bailm 17, 21; Judgm 181(15.1), 743(3).

Fry; J. I. Case Co. v., TexCivApp–Amarillo, 125 SW2d 395.—Can of Inst 43; Chat Mtg 278; Sales 413, 415.

Fry v. John Hancock Mut. Life Ins. Co., NDTex, 355 FSupp 1151.—Antitrust 583, 972(3); Fed Cts 402, 577; Insurance 1106(1); States 18.41.

Fry; Nissan Motor Co., Ltd. v., TexApp–Corpus Christi, 27 SW3d 573, review den.—App & E 893(1), 931(1), 934(1), 946, 949, 1024.3, 1178(6); Parties 35.1, 35.7, 35.9, 35.13, 35.17, 35.33, 35.35, 35.37, 35.71; Sales 434; Trial 18.

Fry v. Shaw, TexCivApp–Dallas, 508 SW2d 142, ref nre.—Brok 42; Joint Adv 1.1, 1.2(1), 1.2(7), 1.12, 5(1); Trover 13.

Fry v. Spencer, TexCivApp–Beaumont, 141 SW2d 730.—Land & Ten 184(2).

Fry v. State, TexCrimApp, 639 SW2d 463, cert den 103 SCt 1430, 460 US 1039, 75 LEd2d 790.—Arrest 63.1.

Fry v. State, TexCrimApp, 493 SW2d 758.—Searches 40.1, 65, 82.

Fry v. State, TexCrimApp, 387 SW2d 666.—Ind & Inf 175; Rec S Goods 8(3).

Fry v. State, TexCrimApp, 170 SW2d 231.—Crim Law 1090.1(1).

Fry v. State, TexApp–Fort Worth, 112 SW3d 611, petition for discretionary review refused.—Crim Law 1004, 1023(2), 1023(3).

Fry v. State, TexApp–Houston (14 Dist), 915 SW2d 554, reh overr.—Crim Law 772(6), 795(1.5), 795(2.5), 1170(1), 1177; Homic 668, 672, 766, 776, 793, 796, 1051(1), 1051(2), 1051(3), 1051(4), 1054, 1058, 1059, 1380, 1455, 1458, 1490; Jury 131(1), 131(3), 131(18).

Fry; State v., TexApp–Houston (14 Dist), 867 SW2d 398, reh den.—Const Law 665, 667, 990, 1030, 1144, 1163, 1520; Crim Law 13.1(1); Gaming 3; Statut 188.

Fry; Texas Technological College v., TexCivApp–Amarillo, 288 SW2d 799.—App & E 763; Colleges 8.1(6.1), 10; Labor & Emp 254.

Fry; Texas Technological College v., TexCivApp–Amarillo, 278 SW2d 480.—States 191.10, 211.

Fry v. Tucker, Tex, 202 SW2d 218, 146 Tex 18.—Judges 42, 45, 51(2), 53; Judgm 9.

Fry v. Tucker, TexCivApp–Texarkana, 197 SW2d 375, aff in part, rev in part 202 SW2d 218, 146 Tex 18.—App & E 554(2); Courts 202(5); Ex & Ad 22(3), 37(1), 37(2); Judges 45; Partit 40.

Fry; U.S. v., CA5 (Tex), 51 F3d 543.—Crim Law 1119(1), 1134(3), 1139, 1158(1); Sent & Pun 704; Weap 17(8).

Fry v. U.S., CA5 (Tex), 569 F2d 303.—Crim Law 273.4(1), 1618(3), 1618(10).

Fryar, In re, BkrtcyWDTex, 99 BR 747, vac 113 BR 317.—Bankr 3105.1, 3106.

Fryar, In re, BkrtcyWDTex, 93 BR 101, vac 113 BR 317.—Bankr 2675.

Fryar; City of Abilene v., TexCivApp–Eastland, 143 SW2d 654.—App & E 909(6); Const Law 46(1), 718; Evid 65; Inj 76; Judgm 197; Records 19; Tax 2138, 2160, 2176, 2218, 2309, 2315, 2750, 2879(2).

Fryar v. Forrest, TexCivApp–San Antonio, 155 SW2d 679.—Fraud 35, 50.

Fryar; Grady v., TexCivApp–Dallas, 103 SW2d 1080.—Land & Ten 290.5.

Fryar; Wise v., TexApp–Eastland, 49 SW3d 450, review den, cert den 122 SCt 808, 534 US 1079, 151 LEd2d 694.—Child S 220; Const Law 3736, 4396; Divorce 165(2); Judgm 335(1), 335(2), 335(3).

Frydenlund; U.S. v., CA5 (Tex), 990 F2d 822, reh den, cert den Kemp v. US, 114 SCt 192, 510 US 868, 126 LEd2d 150, cert den Pressley v US, 114 SCt 192, 510 US 868, 126 LEd2d 150, cert den 114 SCt 337, 510 US 928, 126 LEd2d 281.—Banks 509.10, 509.25; Consp 23.1, 47(1), 47(4); Crim Law 1144.13(3), 1159.2(8); Sent & Pun 736.

Frye, Ex parte, TexCrimApp, 156 SW2d 531, 143 TexCrim 9.—Breach of P 1(2), 2; Const Law 990, 996, 1430, 1558, 1807, 3781, 4509(11); Crim Law 13(1), 13.1(1); Labor & Emp 1345(1); Statut 64(6), 179, 181(1).

Frye v. Appleby Water Supply Corp., TexCivApp–Tyler, 608 SW2d 798, ref nre.—App & E 1170.10; Contracts 205.10, 322(1), 322(3), 354.

Frye v. Frye, TexCivApp–Waco, 239 SW2d 406, writ refused.—Courts 122; Home 96; Ven & Pur 249, 251.

Frye; Frye v., TexCivApp–Waco, 239 SW2d 406, writ refused.—Courts 122; Home 96; Ven & Pur 249, 251.

Frye v. Janow, TexCivApp–Dallas, 212 SW2d 883.—Insurance 3526(5); Trial 127.

Frye v. Moran, CA5 (Tex), 417 F2d 315.—Hab Corp 827.

Frye v. Moran, WDTex, 302 FSupp 1291, aff 417 F2d 315.—Infants 69(3.1).

Frye v. Paine, Webber, Jackson & Curtis, Inc., CA5 (Tex), 877 F2d 396, cert den PaineWebber, Inc v. Frye, 110 SCt 1318, 494 US 1016, 108 LEd2d 493.—Alt Disp Res 182(1), 182(2), 213(5), 414.

Frye v. Ross Aviation, Inc., TexCivApp–Amarillo, 523 SW2d 500.—App & E 78(3), 854(1), 854(2), 878(3); Corp 665(1), 665(3), 669.

Frye; Sauder v., TexCivApp–Fort Worth, 613 SW2d 63.—App & E 78(1); Mines 78.1(7).

Frye v. Sinclair Oil & Gas Co., TexCivApp–Fort Worth, 249 SW2d 102.—App & E 927(7); Autos 194(3), 245(28); Labor & Emp 3125; Trial 139.1(6).

Frye; State v., TexCrimApp, 897 SW2d 324.—Crim Law 412.2(4), 641.1, 641.3(6), 641.12(1), 700(1).

Frye; State v., TexApp–Houston (14 Dist), 846 SW2d 443, reh den, and petition for discretionary review refused, and petition for discretionary review gr, aff 897 SW2d 324.—Crim Law 412.2(1), 412.2(4), 641.1, 641.3(3), 700(1); Ind & Inf 144.1(1).

Fryer; Oilwell Division, U.S. Steel Corp. v., Tex, 493 SW2d 487.—Guar 20; Trial 350.3(4).

Fryer v. State, TexCrimApp, 68 SW3d 628.—Sent & Pun 286, 300, 1466; Statut 181(2), 189, 190.

Fryer v. State, TexCrimApp, 104 SW2d 1112.—Crim Law 1090.1(1).

Fryer v. State, TexApp–Fort Worth, 993 SW2d 385, petition for discretionary review gr, aff 68 SW3d 628.—Courts 85(1); Sent & Pun 286, 289, 300; Statut 181(1), 184, 188, 190.

Fryer; Teran v., TexCivApp–Corpus Christi, 586 SW2d 699, writ refused.—App & E 627.2; New Tr 155.

Fryer; Texas Cityview Care Center, L.P. v., TexApp–Fort Worth, 227 SW3d 345.—Alt Disp Res 116, 117, 134(1), 141, 143, 199, 213(1), 213(5); Health 910, 916; Mand 4(4), 60; Princ & A 19, 96, 97, 99, 112, 147(2); States 18.15.

Fryer; Upper Valley Aviation, Inc. v., TexCivApp–Corpus Christi, 392 SW2d 737, ref nre.—App & E 930(1), 1001(1), 1069.1; Aviation 33, 247; Bailm 31(1), 31(3); Evid 205(1), 265(12); Neglig 259, 1693, 1694.

Fryer & Willis Drilling Co. v. Oilwell, Division of U.S. Steel Corp., TexCivApp–Waco, 472 SW2d 857, writ gr, rev 493 SW2d 487.—Chat Mtg 262(1), 262(3), 265; Guar 36(2); Sec Tran 240.

Fryman v. Fryman, TexApp–Fort Worth, 926 SW2d 602, reh overr, and writ den.—Child C 178; Child S 21; Hus & W 278(2).

Fryman; Fryman v., TexApp–Fort Worth, 926 SW2d 602, reh overr, and writ den.—Child C 178; Child S 21; Hus & W 278(2).

Fryman v. Wilbarger General Hosp., TexApp–Amarillo, 207 SW3d 440.—Mun Corp 847.

Frymire Engineering Co. v. City of Mesquite, TexCivApp–Waco, 331 SW2d 380, ref nre.—Judgm 181(15.1), 185(2), 185.3(1); Mun Corp 366.

Frymire Engineering Co., Inc. v. Grantham, Tex, 524 SW2d 680.—Judgm 106(1), 106(9), 109, 126(1).

Frymire Engineering Co., Inc. v. Grantham, TexCivApp–Fort Worth, 517 SW2d 820, writ gr, rev 524 SW2d 680.—App & E 758.1, 758.3(3), 837(1), 966(1), 1064.1(7), 1140(4), 1151(2); Const Law 321, 2311; Damag 113, 163(1), 188(2), 191; Evid 474(18), 474(19); Judgm 53, 103, 162(4); Pretrial Proc 713, 716, 724.

Frymire Engineering Co., Inc., ex rel. Liberty Mut. Ins. Co. v. Jomar Intern., Ltd., TexApp–Dallas, 194 SW3d 713, reh overr, and review gr.—Action 13; Insurance 3517; Subrog 1, 2, 26.

F. R. Young Co.; Dietrich v., TexCivApp–Houston, 400 SW2d 572, ref nre.—Autos 181(2).

Fry Road Associates, Ltd., In re, BkrtcyWDTex, 66 BR 602.—Bankr 2424, 2426, 2429(1), 2429(3), 2430.5(1), 2431, 3502.20, 3503.

Fry Road Associates, Ltd., In re, BkrtcyWDTex, 64 BR 808.—Bankr 3082.1; Mtg 199(2).

F.S.L.I.C. v. Desert Inn Co., WDTex, 757 FSupp 779.—Fed Cts 12.1, 13.

FSLIC for Sunbelt Sav. Ass'n of Texas v. Browning, NDTex, 732 FSupp 690.—B & L Assoc 48; Rem of C 20, 79(1).

F.S. New Products, Inc. v. Strong Industries, Inc., TexApp–Houston (1 Dist), 129 SW3d 606, review gr, rev Tesco American, Inc v. Strong Industries, Inc, 221 SW3d 550, on remand 2006 WL 3438666.—Antitrust 412, 416; App & E 216(2), 230, 232(3), 525(3), 662(2), 699(4), 760(1), 761, 954(1), 954(2), 1136; Consp 8; Contracts 324(1); Costs 194.32; Damag 15, 124(3); Fraud 3, 12, 32, 50, 58(1), 58(3), 59(2), 59(3), 64(2); Inj 1, 56, 118(1), 123, 138.6, 138.18, 144; Judgm 525; Plead 48; Trial 271, 277.

F.S. New Products, Inc. v. Strong Industries, Inc., TexApp–Houston (1 Dist), 129 SW3d 594.—Judges 39, 42, 46, 47(1), 49(1), 51(4), 53, 56; Judgm 9; Motions 46.

FTB Mortg. Services; Ronemus v., BkrtcyNDTex, 201 BR 458. See Ronemus, In re.

FTI Corp.; Thywissen v., TexCivApp–Hous (1 Dist), 518 SW2d 947, ref nre.—App & E 232(0.5), 930(3); Brok 42; Sec Reg 298, 307, 308; Trial 366.

F.T. Kincaid Estate; Uvalde County Appraisal Dist. v., TexApp–San Antonio, 720 SW2d 678, ref nre.—App & E 949; Costs 194.18; Evid 71; Stip 13, 14(4); Tax 2572, 2699(11).

Fubar, Inc. v. DLT Laboratories, TexApp–Texarkana, 944 SW2d 64. See Fubar, Inc. v. Turner.

Fubar, Inc. v. Turner, TexApp–Texarkana, 944 SW2d 64, reh overr.—Contracts 202(1), 229(1), 236; Damag 159(4).

Fuchs; Gooch v., TexCrimApp, 339 SW2d 202, 170 Tex-Crim 136.—Prohib 14.

Fuchs v. Lifetime Doors, Inc., CA5 (Tex), 939 F2d 1275. —Costs 194.25; Fed Civ Proc 841; Interest 39(2.40), 39(3), 56; Labor & Emp 867, 870.

Fuchs v. Lifetime Doors, Inc., WDTex, 717 FSupp 465. —Fed Civ Proc 2465.1, 2470, 2544; Labor & Emp 818, 866, 867.

Fuchs; Meissner v., TexCivApp–Galveston, 290 SW2d 941, writ dism.—Courts 206(17.3), 207.3, 207.5; Inj 26(5), 128(2); Prohib 27.

Fuchs; Polis v., TexCivApp–Austin, 315 SW2d 577.—Judgm 198; Mand 51.

Fuchs; U.S. v., CA5 (Tex), 467 F3d 889, reh den 214 FedAppx 494, cert den 127 SCt 1502, 167 LEd2d 241.—Consp 25, 27, 28(3), 40.1, 44.2, 47(1), 47(2), 47(3.1), 47(12); Controlled Subs 33, 40, 87, 98; Crim Law 641.13(1), 641.13(2.1), 641.13(5), 735, 772(5), 814(3), 822(1), 911, 929, 935(1), 1030(1), 1032(5), 1035(7), 1038.1(2), 1038.1(4), 1038.2, 1043(3), 1119(1), 1139, 1144.13(3), 1144.14, 1152(1), 1153(1), 1156(2), 1158(1), 1159.2(7), 1159.2(8), 1159.6, 1169.1(1), 1169.2(2); U S 34.

Fuchs; Whitney v., TexCivApp–Austin, 82 SW2d 396.—Bills & N 140; Contracts 169.

Fuddruckers, Inc. v. Purdy's Hamburger Market and Bakery, NDTex, 589 FSupp 72. See Freddie Fuddruckers, Inc. v. Ridgeline, Inc.

Fuddruckers, Inc. v. Ridgeline, Inc., NDTex, 589 FSupp 72. See Freddie Fuddruckers, Inc. v. Ridgeline, Inc.

Fudge v. Cottle County, TexCivApp–Amarillo, 467 SW2d 570.—Plead 111.3, 111.12, 111.42(8).

Fudge v. Haggar, TexCivApp–Texarkana, 621 SW2d 196, ref nre.—Mand 7; Mun Corp 185(3), 185(12).

Fudge v. Hogge, TexCivApp–Dallas, 323 SW2d 663.—Adv Poss 6; Bound 14; Covenants 79(2); Dedi 19(5), 50; Lim of Act 14, 47(2), 100(11); Waters 111.

Fudge v. State, TexCrimApp, 210 SW2d 817.—Crim Law 1094(3).

Fudge; State v., TexApp–Austin, 42 SW3d 226, reh overr. —Arrest 63.5(4); Autos 349(6); Crim Law 1139, 1158(4).

Fuel Distributors, Inc.; Boyd v., TexApp–Austin, 795 SW2d 266, writ den.—App & E 169, 170(2), 863, 934(1); Const Law 990, 1030, 2314; Int Liq 283, 285, 286, 291, 310; Judgm 185(2); Neglig 238, 371, 387, 1713.

Fuel Distributors, Inc. v. Railroad Com'n of Texas, TexApp–Austin, 727 SW2d 56, ref nre.—Admin Law 459, 466; Autos 82, 83.

Fuel Oil Supply and Terminaling v. Gulf Oil Corp., CA5 (Tex), 762 F2d 1283.—Bankr 2160, 3837.

Fuel Oil Supply and Terminaling, Inc., In re, SDTex, 72 BR 752, rev 837 F2d 224.—Afft 18; Bailm 1; Bankr 2602.1, 2613(2), 2613(5), 2616(3), 2620, 3790; Evid 450(8), 461(1); Sales 4(1).

Fuel Oil Supply and Terminaling, Inc., In re, BkrtcyNDTex, 30 BR 360.—Action 38(1); Bankr 2045, 2088, 2091, 2397(1), 2462.

Fuel Oil Supply & Terminaling, Inc., Matter of, CA5 (Tex), 837 F2d 224.—Bankr 2613(2).

Fuel Oil Supply & Terminaling, Inc.; Gulf Oil Corp. v., CA5 (Tex), 837 F2d 224. See Fuel Oil Supply & Terminaling, Inc., Matter of.

Fuentes, In re, TexApp–Corpus Christi, 960 SW2d 261.— App & E 70(9); Judgm 270, 297, 340; Mand 1, 50, 53; Motions 51, 56(1).

Fuentes v. Barnhart, CA5 (Tex), 168 FedAppx 1.—Social S 143.60.

Fuentes; Boothe v., TexCivApp–San Antonio, 262 SW2d 754.—Adv Poss 114(2); App & E 846(5); Bound 3(5), 48(2).

Fuentes v. City of Kingsville, TexCivApp–Corpus Christi, 616 SW2d 679.—App & E 863; Judgm 185(1), 185.2(4), 185.3(11); Zoning 645, 790.

Fuentes v. Continental Conveyor & Equipment Co., Inc., TexApp–Eastland, 63 SW3d 518, review den.— App & E 934(1); Judgm 181(2), 181(6), 185(2); Lim of Act 18, 24(6), 43; Prod Liab 71.5; Sales 431.

Fuentes v. Dretke, CA5 (Tex), 89 FedAppx 868, cert den 125 SCt 248, 543 US 835, 160 LEd2d 55, miscellaneous rulings 125 SCt 519, 543 US 996, 160 LEd2d 387.— Const Law 3419; Crim Law 655(4); Hab Corp 340, 508, 816; Homic 1456.

Fuentes v. Garcia, TexApp–San Antonio, 696 SW2d 482. —Adv Poss 13, 17, 106(1), 109, 112, 114(1); App & E 758.1, 1010.1(3).

Fuentes v. Gentry, TexApp–Amarillo, 628 SW2d 459.— App & E 1010.1(1); Explos 7; Neglig 213, 380, 387, 504, 1676.

Fuentes v. Hirsch, TexCivApp–El Paso, 472 SW2d 288, ref nre.—Adv Poss 80(1); Deeds 112(2), 137, 140; Stip 18(7); Ven & Pur 233.

Fuentes v. Howard, TexCivApp–El Paso, 423 SW2d 420, writ dism.—App & E 846(5), 931(1), 989; Elections 10, 216.1, 227(8), 291, 295(1), 305(6); Statut 176.

Fuentes v. McFadden, TexApp–El Paso, 825 SW2d 772. —Action 60; App & E 917(1), 930(3), 974(1), 1003(7), 1064.1(1); Damag 120(1); Judgm 735; Plead 228.14, 228.23; Sales 195; Trial 352.5(4).

Fuentes; McFadden v., TexApp–El Paso, 790 SW2d 736, appeal after remand 825 SW2d 772.—Contracts 143(2); Damag 76, 79(1), 80(1); Sales 194; Statut 188.

Fuentes v. State, TexCrimApp, 991 SW2d 267, cert den 120 SCt 541, 528 US 1026, 145 LEd2d 420.—Const Law 3419; Crim Law 396(1), 511.9, 641.13(1), 641.13(2.1), 655(4), 683(1), 717, 721(1), 726, 730(10), 741(1), 742(1), 898, 1035(8.1), 1036.1(2), 1144.13(6), 1158(3), 1159.2(2), 1159.2(9); Homic 541, 581, 1178, 1181, 1456; Ind & Inf 189(8); Jury 33(5.15), 149; Sent & Pun 1757, 1780(3), 1788(5).

Fuentes v. State, TexCrimApp, 688 SW2d 542, on remand 1986 WL 10433.—Crim Law 273.1(4), 1026.10(4), 1141(2).

Fuentes v. State, TexCrimApp, 664 SW2d 333.—Crim Law 304(1), 709, 710, 717, 723(1), 726, 728(1), 728(5), 867, 1044.1(8), 1171.1(4); Witn 268(8).

Fuentes v. State, TexCrimApp, 491 SW2d 419.—Crim Law 1184(4.1); Sent & Pun 1326.

Fuentes v. State, TexCrimApp, 292 SW2d 117, 163 Tex-Crim 410.—Crim Law 29(12), 260.11(1); Infants 12(8), 20; Statut 184.

Fuentes v. State, TexApp–Houston (1 Dist) 775 SW2d 64. —Crim Law 539(1); Witn 61(1).

Fuentes v. State, TexApp–Houston (1 Dist), 662 SW2d 19, petition for discretionary review refused.—Crim Law 921, 1043(3), 1120(3); Witn 304(1), 307.

Fuentes v. State, TexApp–Texarkana, 960 SW2d 926.— Const Law 4587; Crim Law 273.4(1), 409(5), 1004, 1017, 1026.10(1), 1026.10(2.1).

Fuentes v. State, TexApp–Amarillo, 128 SW3d 786, petition for discretionary review refused.—Rape 51(7).

Fuentes v. State, TexApp–Amarillo, 880 SW2d 857, reh den, and petition for discretionary review refused.— Assault 92(5); Crim Law 417(15), 543(1), 543(2), 552(1), 564(3), 741(6), 1159.6, 1169.2(6).

Fuentes v. State, TexApp–Beaumont, 673 SW2d 207, petition for discretionary review refused.—Crim Law 662.7, 795(2.15); 1120(9); Homic 657, 668, 1458; Witn 267.

Fuentes v. State, TexApp–Corpus Christi, 846 SW2d 527, petition for discretionary review refused.—Crim Law 338(7), 414, 438(6), 438(7), 531(1), 675, 1168(2).

Fuentes v. State, TexApp–Houston (14 Dist), 832 SW2d 635, petition for discretionary review refused.—Crim Law 374, 641.13(1), 641.13(6), 1120(3), 1170(3); Homic 1052; Witn 267, 337(1), 337(31), 359.

Fuentes v. State, TexApp–Houston (14 Dist), 681 SW2d 91, petition for discretionary review gr, rev 688 SW2d 542, on remand 1986 WL 10433.—Controlled Subs 6; Crim Law 275, 394.5(3), 516, 538(1), 1026.10(2.1); Statut 107(3), 143.

Fuentes v. Straus-Frank Co., TexCivApp–San Antonio, 423 SW2d 633.—Costs 194.38.

Fuentes; Texas Emp. Ins. Ass'n v., TexCivApp–Eastland, 597 SW2d 811, ref nre.—Work Comp 1728, 1988.

Fuentes v. Texas Employers' Ins. Ass'n, TexApp–San Antonio, 757 SW2d 31.—Action 70; Work Comp 1042, 1072.

Fuentes; Transamerican Nat. Gas Corp. v., Tex, 962 SW2d 28. See Shepherd v. Ledford.

Fuentes v. TransAmerican Natural Gas Corp., TexApp–San Antonio, 933 SW2d 624, reh overr, and writ gr, rev Shepherd v. Ledford, 962 SW2d 28.—Death 37.

Fuentes v. U.S., CA5 (Tex), 455 F2d 910.—Crim Law 1132, 1189, 1433(2).

Fuentes; U.S. v., CA5 (Tex), 432 F2d 405, cert den 91 SCt 904, 401 US 919, 27 LEd2d 822.—Crim Law 553, 578, 586, 627.9(1), 627.9(5), 698(1), 728(2), 1036.1(3.1), 1132, 1137(5); 1159.4(2); Ind & Inf 10.1(2); Witn 2(3).

Fuentes; U.S. v., CA5 (Tex), 79 FedAppx 30, cert den Martinez-Mata v. US, 124 SCt 1484, 540 US 1209, 158 LEd2d 134.—Aliens 799; Jury 34(1).

Fuentes; U.S. v., SDTex, 379 FSupp 1145, aff 517 F2d 1401.—Cust Dut 126(4), 126(5); Searches 23, 73.

Fuentes-Berlanga; U.S. v., CA5 (Tex), 149 FedAppx 258, cert den 126 SCt 1800, 547 US 1082, 164 LEd2d 538.— Crim Law 1042; Sent & Pun 793.

Fuentes-Salgado; U.S. v., CA5 (Tex), 207 FedAppx 391.— Aliens 216, 379, 799; Crim Law 1023(11), 1177; Sent & Pun 661, 793, 794, 941.

Fuentez; City of Beaumont v., TexCivApp–Beaumont, 582 SW2d 221.—App & E 1064.2; Autos 171(9), 171(13), 208; Mun Corp 725, 733(2), 741.20, 742(4); Trial 194(16).

Fuentez v. State, TexApp–Eastland, 196 SW3d 839.— Atty & C 92; Crim Law 273.1(4), 641.10(3), 662.80, 741(1), 742(1), 747, 1144.13(2.1), 1159.2(7), 1159.3(5); Double J 96; Infants 20; Jury 29(4), 29(6); Sent & Pun 1862, 1886, 1946.

Fuerst; Christopher v., TexApp–Houston (14 Dist), 709 SW2d 266, ref nre.—App & E 345.1, 962; Courts 30; New Tr 124(1); Pretrial Proc 587, 698, 699.

Fuery v. State, TexCrimApp, 464 SW2d 666.—Controlled Subs 74; Double J 115.

Fuess; General Adjustment Bureau, Inc. v., SDTex, 192 FSupp 542.—Antitrust 13, 61; Fed Cts 429; Trademarks 1032, 1084, 1095, 1097, 1714(2), 1714(3).

Fuess v. Mueller, TexApp–Houston (1 Dist), 630 SW2d 715.—Brok 54, 57(2), 60.

Fugate v. Johnston, TexCivApp–San Antonio, 251 SW2d 792.—Elections 10, 83, 158, 216, 227(8), 285(3); Plead 228.23.

Fugate v. LeBaube, NDTex, 372 FSupp 1208.—Const Law 4168, 4171; Offic 72.13, 72.55(2), 76.

Fugate v. State, TexApp–Fort Worth, 200 SW3d 781.— Const Law 4705, 4729; Sent & Pun 239.

Fugate v. State, TexApp–Corpus Christi, 709 SW2d 29.— Burg 41(1), 41(3).

Fugate v. U.S., CA5 (Tex), 386 F2d 188.—Int Rev 3377.

Fugate v. U.S., WDTex, 259 FSupp 398, aff 386 F2d 188. —Int Rev 3345.

Fugate; United States Fire Ins. Co. v., TexApp–Waco, 171 SW3d 508, reh overr, and review den.—Insurance 3557; Judgm 540, 584, 586(0.5).

Fugett v. State, TexApp–Fort Worth, 855 SW2d 227.— Crim Law 1036.1(2), 1042, 1043(2), 1043(3), 1044.2(1), 1169.1(4); Rob 24.15(1), 24.20; Sent & Pun 276.

Fugit; Darwin v., TexApp–Fort Worth, 914 SW2d 621, reh overr, and writ den.—Fraud 3; Judgm 181(19), 181(33), 185(2); Neglig 371, 384, 387, 431, 432.

Fugitt v. Jones, CA5 (Tex), 549 F2d 1001.—Civil R 1424; Fed Civ Proc 1952, 2217; Fed Cts 640, 641, 644, 944.

Fugitt v. Slay, TexCivApp–Dallas, 329 SW2d 358, writ dism.—App & E 389(3); Judgm 203.

Fugitt; Slay v., TexCivApp–Dallas, 302 SW2d 698, ref nre.—Abate & R 5; Courts 472.7, 480(1); Forci E & D 13; Judgm 472, 480, 564(1); Tresp to T T 1.

Fugitt v. State, TexApp–Corpus Christi, 623 SW2d 471, petition for discretionary review refused.—Arrest 63.4(11), 63.4(12); Crim Law 625.10(2.1), 721(1), 721(3), 730(6), 736(2), 1169.5(1).

Fugon v. State, TexApp–Houston (1 Dist), 963 SW2d 135, reh overr, and petition for discretionary review refused. —Crim Law 409(5), 622.3, 1115(1).

Fugro-McClelland (Southwest), Inc.; Franklin v., SDTex, 16 FSupp2d 732.—Insurance 2101, 2261.

Fuhrer v. Rinyu, TexApp–Corpus Christi, 647 SW2d 315. —Judgm 495(1), 497(1), 499, 815, 942, 944, 951(1).

Fuhrman v. Cockrell, CA5 (Tex), 79 FedAppx 614, appeal after remand 442 F3d 893.—Hab Corp 818.

Fuhrman v. Dretke, CA5 (Tex), 442 F3d 893.—Fed Cts 917, 950; Hab Corp 453, 861; Prisons 15(5); Searches 78; Sent & Pun 1941.

Fuhrman v. Fuhrman, TexCivApp–El Paso, 302 SW2d 205, dism.—Divorce 252.3(1), 252.3(3); Evid 22(2); Hus & W 249(5), 262.1(3), 262.2, 264(3), 264(4).

Fuhrman; Fuhrman v., TexCivApp–El Paso, 302 SW2d 205, dism.—Divorce 252.3(1), 252.3(3); Evid 22(2); Hus & W 249(5), 262.1(3), 262.2, 264(3), 264(4).

Fuhrman Petroleum Corp.; Prince Bros. Drilling Co. v., TexCivApp–El Paso, 150 SW2d 314, writ refused.— Mines 62.1, 109; Mtg 1; Tax 2172, 2175.

Fujimoto v. Rio Grande Pickle Co., CA5 (Tex), 414 F2d 648.—Contracts 22(1), 143(1), 154, 176(2); Damag 6; Fed Civ Proc 2156; Labor & Emp 34(2), 175, 178, 266.

Fuji Photo Film Co., Inc. v. Shinohara Shoji Kabushiki Kaisha, CA5 (Tex), 754 F2d 591, reh den 761 F2d 695. —Fed Cts 776; Judgm 828.9(2), 828.14(3); Trademarks 1081, 1084, 1111, 1112, 1138, 1180, 1420, 1421, 1437, 1609, 1615, 1629(3), 1691, 1800.

Fuji Photo Film U.S.A., Inc.; Government Employees Credit Union of San Antonio v., TexApp–San Antonio, 712 SW2d 208, ref nre.—Action 13; Antitrust 130; App & E 714(1), 863; B & L Assoc 41(5); Const Law 70.1(2), 2473; Judgm 181(11), 185.2(3); Statut 212.6, 212.7.

Fujitsu Network Communications, Inc.; Jones v., NDTex, 81 FSupp2d 688.—Alt Disp Res 121, 134(1), 137, 146; Labor & Emp 47.

Fulbright; Blanchard v., TexApp–Houston (14 Dist), 633 SW2d 617, dism.—Judgm 644; Mand 12, 13, 16(2), 76, 152, 155(2); Mun Corp 159(1).

Fulbright v. Culbertson, TexCivApp–Fort Worth, 429 SW2d 179, ref nre.—App & E 731(5), 931(6), 1054(3); Evid 568(4), 589; Frds St of 139(5); Mtg 32(5), 36, 608.5; Partners 53, 121.

Fulbright; Motor Securities Corp. v., TexCivApp–Beaumont, 81 SW2d 1047.—Plead 111.4.

Fulbright v. State, TexApp–Fort Worth, 41 SW3d 228, petition for discretionary review refused.—Crim Law 641.2(2), 641.4(1), 641.4(2), 641.4(4), 641.8, 641.9, 641.10(2), 641.10(3), 1165(1), 1166.10(2).

Fulbright & Jaworski; Lacy v., CA5 (Tex), 405 F3d 254. —Labor & Emp 619, 623.

Fulbright & Jaworski, L.L.P.; Greene's Pressure Treating & Rentals, Inc.v., TexApp–Houston (1 Dist), 178 SW3d 40.—Atty & C 63, 64; Corp 445, 445.1, 589, 590(1); Fraud 7.

Fulbright & Jaworski, L.L.P.; Lahr v., NDTex, 164 FRD 204.—Civil R 1183; Damag 50.10; Fed Civ Proc 1651, 1654; U S Mag 17, 26, 27, 28, 29.

Fulbright & Jaworski, L.L.P.; Lahr v., NDTex, 164 FRD 196, aff 164 FRD 204.—Damag 50.10; Fed Civ Proc 1651, 1654.

Fulbright Grazing Ass'n, Inc. v. Randolph, TexCivApp–Texarkana, 524 SW2d 798.—Agric 6.

Fulbright Independent School Dist.; Republic Ins. Co. v., TexCivApp–Texarkana, 125 SW2d 1052.—Insurance 1831, 3072.

Fulce, Ex parte, TexCrimApp, 993 SW2d 660.—Sent & Pun 1946, 2010.

Fulce; City of Denison v., TexCivApp–Texarkana, 437 SW2d 277, ref nre.—Damag 131(5); Mun Corp 58, 741.55, 742(5).

Fulcher v. Broth. Relief and Compensation Fund, TexCivApp–Waco, 178 SW2d 751.—App & E 241.

Fulcher v. Carter, TexCivApp–Amarillo, 212 SW2d 503.— Adop 2, 3, 21; Des & Dist 3, 52(2); Ten in C 15(2), 15(7), 15(10), 44.

Fulcher; City of San Antonio v., TexApp–San Antonio, 749 SW2d 217, writ den.—Admin Law 466, 764.1; Pretrial Proc 44.1, 45; Work Comp 1167, 1937.

Fulcher; College Station State Bank v., TexCivApp–Texarkana, 296 SW2d 953.—App & E 766; Bills & N 170.

Fulcher; Federal Deposit Ins. Corp. v., WDTex, 635 FSupp 27.—Banks 505; Usury 42.

Fulcher v. Hall, TexCivApp–El Paso, 170 SW2d 321.— Attach 178; Autos 19.

Fulcher v. State, TexCrimApp, 607 SW2d 581.—Sent & Pun 2006.

Fulcher v. State, TexCrimApp, 289 SW2d 588, 163 TexCrim 177.—Crim Law 404.55, 720(10), 728(2), 728(5), 763(6), 956(13), 957(1), 1036.1(3.1), 1091(7), 1091(13), 1169.1(9), 1173.2(3), 1177.5(1); Int Liq 236(6.5).

Fulcher v. Texas Bd. of Public Accountancy, SDTex, 532 FSupp 683.—Fed Cts 59; Judgm 713(2), 720, 828.3, 828.16(1).

Fulcher v. Texas State Bd. of Public Accountancy, TexCivApp–Corpus Christi, 571 SW2d 366, ref nre.— Accnts 3.1; App & E 169, 170(1), 179(1), 843(2), 1046.1; Atty & C 74; Const Law 77, 1539, 1607, 2621; Inj 130; States 111.

Fulcher; Texas State Bd. of Public Accountancy v., TexCivApp–Corpus Christi, 515 SW2d 950, ref nre.— Accnts 2, 3.1; Const Law 965, 976, 990, 1007, 1020, 1066, 1112(1), 1121(3), 2486, 2489, 3683; Evid 383(3); Licens 5, 7(1), 7(2), 20.

Fulcher v. Young, TexCivApp–Austin, 189 SW2d 28, writ refused wom.—App & E 204(1), 237(2); Deeds 211(1); Evid 63, 91, 155(9), 317(1), 474(4), 498.5, 568(2); Wills 52(1); Witn 130, 138.

Fulcrum Central v. AutoTester, Inc., TexApp–Dallas, 102 SW3d 274.—Judgm 181(24); Nova 1, 2, 4, 10, 12, 13.

Fulenwider v. City of Teague, TexApp–Waco, 680 SW2d 582.—Judgm 181(15.1), 185(2), 185(3), 185.1(4), 185.2(9).

Fulenwider v. State, TexApp–Houston (1 Dist), 176 SW3d 290, petition for discretionary review refused.—Autos 332; Crim Law 394.6(5), 475.2(4), 488, 798(0.5), 814(1), 881(1), 1038.1(1), 1166.18, 1172.1(1).

Fulfer v. State, TexCrimApp, 91 SW2d 742.—Crim Law 15.

Fulfer v. State, TexCrimApp, 91 SW2d 741.—Crim Law 15.

Fulford v. Forman, CA5 (Tex), 245 F2d 145.—Agric 3.3(1), 3.3(3); Statut 181(2).

Fulford v. Forman, NDTex, 144 FSupp 536, aff 245 F2d 145.—Admin Law 390.1, 391; Agric 3.3(3), 3.3(4); Statut 219(3), 223.5(1).

Fulford v. Heath, TexCivApp–Amarillo, 212 SW2d 649, ref nre.—Adv Poss 13, 16(1), 112, 114(1), 114(2); App & E 989, 1011.1(4), 1012.1(3); Bound 3(2), 20(1), 33, 37(3), 37(5).

Fulfs; Atlantic Ins. Co. v., TexCivApp–Fort Worth, 417 SW2d 302, 30 ALR3d 1038, ref nre.—Costs 194.18; Ex & Ad 7, 130(1), 154; Insurance 2660; Wills 205.

Fulgham; FFE Transp. Services, Inc. v., Tex, 154 SW3d 84, on remand 2005 WL 1621425, review den.—App & E 893(1); Bailm 9, 31(3); Evid 571(3); Neglig 236, 1657; Prod Liab 23.1, 39.

Fulgham v. FFE Transp. Services, Inc., TexApp–Dallas, 152 SW3d 140, reh overr, and review gr, rev 154 SW3d 84, on remand 2005 WL 1621425, review den.—Autos 244(33), 245(38); Bailm 2.

Fulgham v. Gulf, C. & S.F. Ry. Co., TexCivApp–Austin, 288 SW2d 811, ref nre.—Tax 2560, 3221.

Fulgham v. Southland Cotton Oil Co., TexCivApp–Austin, 296 SW2d 332, writ refused.—Statut 219(10); Tax 2562, 2791.

Fulgham; Weatherly v., Tex, 271 SW2d 938, 153 Tex 481. —Elections 142, 143, 156.

Fulghum v. Baxley, TexCivApp–Dallas, 219 SW2d 1014. —Courts 80(1); Time 10(4).

Fulgium, In re, TexApp–Texarkana, 150 SW3d 252.— Infants 201; Mand 1, 3(2.1), 4(4), 12, 32, 172; Pretrial Proc 19.

Fulgium v. State, TexApp–Waco, 4 SW3d 107, petition for discretionary review refused.—Autos 355(6); Crim Law 480, 553, 641.5(0.5), 641.13(1), 641.13(2.1), 641.13(6), 741(1), 742(1), 1134(2), 1144.13(1), 1144.13(2.1), 1144.13(3), 1144.13(6), 1159.1, 1159.2(1), 1159.2(2), 1159.2(7), 1159.2(9), 1159.3(5), 1159.6; Witn 247.

Fulkerson; Nelson v., Tex, 286 SW2d 129, 155 Tex 298.— Autos 226(1), 227.5.

Fulkerson; Nelson v., TexCivApp–Amarillo, 277 SW2d 286, rev 286 SW2d 129, 155 Tex 298.—App & E 1175(1); Autos 200, 224(5), 227.5, 245(93); Trial 351.2(4).

Fulkes; Round Mountain Community v., TexCivApp–Austin, 501 SW2d 474.—Inj 157.

Fulks; McNamara v., TexApp–El Paso, 855 SW2d 782.— App & E 852; Mand 175, 190; Records 68; Trial 68(1).

Fulks v. State, TexCrimApp, 138 SW2d 118, 138 TexCrim 583.—Crim Law 1172.2; Int Liq 239(5).

Fullbright; Rudolph Chevrolet Co. v., TexCivApp–El Paso, 449 SW2d 355.—Autos 368.

Fullbright v. State, TexCrimApp, 818 SW2d 808.—Crim Law 1042, 1177.5(1); Sent & Pun 1325.

Fullbright v. State, TexCrimApp, 101 SW2d 571, 131 TexCrim 640.—Crim Law 598(3), 598(6), 688, 956(5), 1087.1(2), 1144.10, 1169.2(6), 1171.6; Larc 28(1), 55.

Fullbright v. State, TexApp–Texarkana, 633 SW2d 634.— Arrest 63.4(1), 63.4(8), 63.4(11), 63.4(17), 63.5(1), 63.5(2), 71.1(4.1); Crim Law 394.4(9); Searches 44.

Fullen; Franklin Fire Ins. Co. of Philadelphia v., TexCivApp–El Paso, 139 SW2d 370.—Contracts 94(1); Insurance 3007(1), 3131, 3191(7), 3571; Plead 354, 380.

Fullen; Thomas' Estate v., TexCivApp–Beaumont, 172 SW2d 118, writ refused wom.—Ex & Ad 111(1), 122(3), 506(3), 510(1).

Fullenweider; Brown v., Tex, 52 SW3d 169.—Atty & C 130, 157.1; Divorce 4, 321.5.

Fullenweider; Brown v., TexApp–Texarkana, 135 SW3d 340, reh overr, and review den, and reh of petition for review den.—App & E 893(1); Costs 194.14, 194.16, 194.32; Lim of Act 1, 130(7).

Fullenweider; Brown v., TexApp–Beaumont, 7 SW3d 333, review gr, rev 52 SW3d 169.—Divorce 70, 226, 228; Motions 11; Parties 1, 21.

Fullenwider v. American Guarantee & Liability Ins. Co., TexApp–San Antonio, 821 SW2d 658, writ den.—App & E 1043(1); Work Comp 1686, 1703.

Fuller, Ex parte, TexCrimApp, 435 SW2d 515.—Sent & Pun 1318.

Fuller, Ex parte, TexCrimApp, 432 SW2d 537.—Extrad 32, 39.

Fuller; Abouk v., TexApp–Dallas, 738 SW2d 297.—Crim Law 106, 1018.

Fuller v. Amerijet Intern., Inc., SDTex, 273 FSupp2d 902.—Carr 156(1); Treaties 8.

Fuller; Bates v., TexApp–Tyler, 663 SW2d 512.—Consp 1.1, 3, 9, 21; Wills 765, 767.

Fuller; Blake v., TexCivApp–Dallas, 184 SW2d 148.—Ex & Ad 53; Home 38, 43, 47, 56, 62, 71, 115(2), 141(1), 142(1), 151, 187, 206, 214; Partit 12(3).

Fuller; Blessing-Giddens Mill & Lumber Co. v., TexCiv-App–Dallas, 166 SW2d 173, writ refused wom.—App & E 880(1); Corp 119; Ref of Inst 33.

Fuller v. Burran, Tex, 250 SW2d 587, 151 Tex 335.—App & E 1175(5); Courts 247(7).

Fuller; Burran v., TexCivApp–Austin, 248 SW2d 1015, rev 250 SW2d 587, 151 Tex 335.—Adop 7.8(5), 11.

Fuller; Cassidy v., Tex, 568 SW2d 845.—Child C 407; Child S 323.

Fuller; Culinary Workers' Union No. 331 v., TexCiv-App–Beaumont, 105 SW2d 295.—Labor & Emp 2081.

Fuller v. Dretke, CA5 (Tex), 161 FedAppx 413, cert den 127 SCt 28, 165 LEd2d 1008.—Crim Law 641.5(0.5), 641.13(5); Hab Corp 401, 496; Jury 33(5.15); Sent & Pun 1756, 1758(4).

Fuller; Dunbar v., TexCivApp–Austin, 253 SW2d 684, writ refused.—Judgm 181(19); Mines 74(5), 78.2, 92.21, 92.32(2).

Fuller; F.D.I.C. v., CA5 (Tex), 994 F2d 223.—Banks 508; Interest 39(2.20).

Fuller; Fillinger v., TexApp–Texarkana, 746 SW2d 506. —App & E 977(5); Costs 260(5); Trial 304, 344.

Fuller v. Flanagan, TexCivApp–Fort Worth, 468 SW2d 171, ref nre.—App & E 699(4), 1004(8); Autos 198(4), 227.5, 244(61), 245(93); Infants 59; Joint Adv 1.2(3); Judgm 199(3.10); Neglig 575.

Fuller v. Fuller, TexCivApp–San Antonio, 315 SW2d 167. —Divorce 127(1).

Fuller; Fuller v., TexCivApp–San Antonio, 315 SW2d 167. —Divorce 127(1).

Fuller v. Fuller, TexCivApp–Beaumont, 518 SW2d 250, ref nre.—App & E 996, 1010.1(8.1); Atty & C 30; Partners 17, 20.

Fuller; Fuller v., TexCivApp–Beaumont, 518 SW2d 250, ref nre.—App & E 996, 1010.1(8.1); Atty & C 30; Partners 17, 20.

Fuller v. General Cable Industries, Inc., EDTex, 81 FSupp2d 726.—Civil R 1135, 1140, 1545; Fed Civ Proc 2497.1.

Fuller; Graue-Haws, Inc. v., TexApp–El Paso, 666 SW2d 238.—Statut 228; Venue 3.

Fuller; Gulf Oil Corp. v., TexApp–El Paso, 695 SW2d 769.—App & E 1011.1(8.1); Mand 11; Pretrial Proc 24, 35, 43, 379, 406.

Fuller v. Harris County, CA5 (Tex), 137 FedAppx 677, appeal after remand 207 FedAppx 450, on remand 2007 WL 1672100.—Const Law 4823; Prisons 17(2); Sent & Pun 1546.

Fuller; Home Indem. Co. v., TexCivApp–Austin, 427 SW2d 97, ref nre.—Evid 264; Insurance 2278(29), 2369; Plead 69, 280, 283.

Fuller v. Johnson, CA5 (Tex), 158 F3d 903, cert den 119 SCt 1809, 526 US 1133, 143 LEd2d 1012.—Crim Law 641.13(1), 641.13(2.1), 641.13(7); Gr Jury 35; Hab Corp 352, 378, 403, 453, 496.

Fuller v. Johnson, CA5 (Tex), 114 F3d 491, cert den 118 SCt 399, 522 US 963, 139 LEd2d 312.—Const Law 1440, 4632; Costs 302.4; Crim Law 706(2), 1166.17; Hab Corp 452, 490(1), 508, 770, 818, 841, 847, 883.1; Jury 97(1), 108; Sent & Pun 1463, 1756.

Fuller; Jones v., TexApp–Waco, 856 SW2d 597, reh den, and writ den.—Deeds 93, 99; Ease 3(2), 12(3), 22, 26(1), 30(1), 42, 44(1), 44(2), 50, 53, 58(1); Ven & Pur 227, 229(2), 231(1).

Fuller; Landwer v., TexCivApp–Amarillo, 187 SW2d 670, writ refused wom.—App & E 931(3), 931(6), 954(2), 1009(3), 1010.1(2), 1078(1); Inj 1, 46, 113; Nuis 3(2), 19, 33, 34.

Fuller v. McDaniel, TexCivApp–Galveston, 213 SW2d 574.—App & E 954(1); Covenants 103(2); Inj 128(6).

Fuller v. Maxus Energy Corp., TexApp–Waco, 841 SW2d 881.—Const Law 990, 1030, 2312, 2314, 3041, 3105, 3957; Infants 1; Int Liq 282, 283; Judgm 185(2).

Fuller v. Middleton, TexCivApp–Fort Worth, 453 SW2d 372, ref nre.—Evid 62; Judgm 185(2), 186, 335(3), 713(2), 720, 743(2), 747(0.5), 747(4); Mental H 7, 512.1; Pretrial Proc 518.

Fuller v. Minter, TexCivApp–Galveston, 215 SW2d 207.— Evid 34, 47; War 155.

Fuller v. Mitchell, TexCivApp–Dallas, 269 SW2d 517, ref nre.—Admin Law 665.1, 744.1, 763, 791; Const Law 2541; Inj 81; Mand 10, 75, 168(4); Mun Corp 180(1), 185(10), 217.1, 218(2), 218(9).

Fuller; Monroe v., TexApp–El Paso, 701 SW2d 73.— Pretrial Proc 379.

Fuller v. Mullins, TexCivApp–Waco, 277 SW2d 815, ref nre, appeal dism 76 SCt 315, 350 US 928, 100 LEd 811. —Courts 475(11).

Fuller; Neel v., Tex, 557 SW2d 73.—Lis Pen 26(1); Receivers 137, 138, 142.

Fuller v. Neel, TexCivApp–El Paso, 535 SW2d 719, writ gr, rev 557 SW2d 73.—Estop 21; Receivers 77(2).

Fuller; Old Republic Ins. Co., Inc. v., TexApp–Texarkana, 919 SW2d 726, reh overr, and writ den.—App & E 842(2); Compromise 11; Contracts 97(1), 97(2), 100; Princ & A 163(1), 166(1); Work Comp 1120.

Fuller; Patterson v., TexCivApp–Eastland, 110 SW2d 1230, writ dism.—App & E 972; Contrib 6; Plead 93(1); Princ & S 194(7), 200(6); Subrog 9; Trial 106, 121(2); Trusts 262.

Fuller v. Phillips Petroleum Co., CA5 (Tex), 872 F2d 655.—Contracts 147(1); Mines 101.

Fuller v. Phillips Petroleum Co., NDTex, 408 FSupp 643.—Estop 52.10(2); Gas 14.1(3); Interest 13, 26, 44; Nova 1.

Fuller v. Preston State Bank, TexApp–Dallas, 667 SW2d 214, ref nre.—Antitrust 141, 369; App & E 843(3); Estop 119; Evid 78, 108; Home 96, 214, 216; Pretrial Proc 358, 433.

Fuller v. Rainbow Resources, Inc., TexApp–Texarkana, 744 SW2d 232.—Mines 73.1(2), 77, 78.1(3), 78.3.

Fuller v. Rich, CA5 (Tex), 11 F3d 61.—Hab Corp 279, 289, 401, 408, 706, 843.

Fuller v. Rich, NDTex, 925 FSupp 459, aff in part 91 F3d 138.—Const Law 3082, 3588, 4450; Convicts 7(1); Fed Civ Proc 1773, 1829, 1835, 1838; Prisons 13(5); Sent & Pun 1533, 1535, 1537; U S 50.1, 50.5(1), 125(3), 125(24).

Fuller; Rowson v., TexCivApp–Dallas, 230 SW2d 355, ref nre.—Contracts 2, 19, 22(1), 205.10, 205.40, 280(1), 320, 322(4); Evid 400(6); Labor & Emp 29; Princ & A 3(2), 23(5).

Fuller v. Sechelski, TexCivApp–Hous (1 Dist), 573 SW2d 587, ref nre.—Wills 260, 293(4), 390.

Fuller v. Southwestern Greyhound Lines, Inc., TexCiv-App–Austin, 331 SW2d 455, ref nre.—Carr 284; Judgm 181(33), 185(2), 186; Neglig 387.

Fuller; Starling v., WDTex, 146 FRD 149, aff in part 74 F3d 1236.—Fed Civ Proc 1278.

Fuller v. State, Tex, 461 SW2d 595.—Em Dom 131, 202(1).

Fuller; State v., Tex, 407 SW2d 215.—Bound 22; Decl Judgm 182; Deeds 120; High 80, 85; Mines 55(7); R R 82(5).

Fuller v. State, TexCrimApp, 73 SW3d 250, reh overr.—Assault 91; Const Law 4693; Ind & Inf 171, 180.

Fuller v. State, TexCrimApp, 829 SW2d 191, reh den, cert den 113 SCt 2418, 508 US 941, 124 LEd2d 640, denial of habeas corpus aff 114 F3d 491, cert den 118 SCt 399, 522 US 963, 139 LEd2d 312.—Action 6; Const Law 1440; Crim Law 338(1), 394.5(2), 412(4), 412(5), 438(7), 476.6, 517.2(2), 519(8), 641.3(2), 641.3(3), 641.3(4), 675, 696(3), 1036.1(1), 1036.1(2), 1043(1), 1044.1(5.1); Jury 104.1, 108; Sent & Pun 1720, 1762, 1765, 1769, 1780(3).

Fuller v. State, TexCrimApp, 827 SW2d 919, cert den 113 SCt 3035, 509 US 922, 125 LEd2d 722, reh den 114 SCt 13, 509 US 940, 125 LEd2d 765, dism of habeas corpus aff 158 F3d 903, cert den 119 SCt 1809, 526 US 1133, 143 LEd2d 1012.—Crim Law 369.1, 388.1, 388.2, 539(2), 552(3), 660, 878(2), 1036.1(9), 1043(1), 1043(3), 1044.1(1), 1044.2(1), 1045, 1134(3), 1144.13(2.1), 1144.13(3), 1144.13(6), 1152(2), 1159.2(7), 1159.5, 1162, 1165(1), 1169.5(3), 1174(1); Homic 569, 1184; Jury 108; Sent & Pun 1670, 1720, 1756, 1772, 1780(3).

Fuller v. State, TexCrimApp, 576 SW2d 856.—Crim Law 273.1(4), 1167(5).

Fuller v. State, TexCrimApp, 501 SW2d 112.—Crim Law 730(1), 730(3), 1036.9, 1104(6), 1130(2), 1169.1(9), 1170.5(3), 1170.5(6).

Fuller v. State, TexCrimApp, 423 SW2d 924.—Crim Law 48, 311, 354, 456, 465, 570(1), 570(2), 624, 641.13(2.1), 667(1), 740, 773(1), 814(10), 1038.2, 1038.3, 1173.2(3).

Fuller v. State, TexCrimApp, 409 SW2d 866.—Assault 96(7); Jury 136(5); Sent & Pun 100, 313.

Fuller v. State, TexCrimApp, 397 SW2d 434.—Homic 1134.

Fuller v. State, TexCrimApp, 380 SW2d 619.—Crim Law 369.2(8), 1038.1(7), 1120(3); Homic 1154.

Fuller v. State, TexCrimApp, 289 SW2d 763, 163 TexCrim 142.—Bail 63.1; Crim Law 1092.11(3), 1166.22(6); Int Liq 236(7); Searches 127.

Fuller v. State, TexCrimApp, 180 SW2d 361, 147 TexCrim 250.—Courts 70; Crim Law 101(2), 829(3), 938(1), 996(2), 1119(4); Rape 17.

Fuller v. State, TexCrimApp, 167 SW2d 170, 145 TexCrim 190.—Ind & Inf 101, 180; Rob 24.10.

Fuller v. State, TexApp–Fort Worth, 194 SW3d 52, petition for discretionary review refused.—Mental H 469(7).

Fuller v. State, TexApp–Austin, 819 SW2d 254, petition for discretionary review refused.—Crim Law 469.1, 469.2, 470(1), 772(2), 1172.1(1), 1172.1(3); Sent & Pun 320.

Fuller v. State, TexApp–Texarkana, 224 SW3d 823.—Crim Law 474.3(1), 474.3(3), 577.3, 577.10(1), 577.16(2), 641.13(1), 641.13(6), 1035(1), 1119(1), 1134(2), 1144.13(2.1), 1159.2(7); Double J 3; Judgm 724, 958(1); Sod 6; Witn 318.

Fuller v. State, TexApp–Texarkana, 30 SW3d 441, reh overr, and petition for discretionary review refused.—Crim Law 625.15, 625.35, 1077.3; Jury 25(11).

Fuller v. State, TexApp–Texarkana, 11 SW3d 393, on subsequent appeal 30 SW3d 441, reh overr, and petition for discretionary review refused.—Crim Law 625.20, 1181.5(4); Mental H 432.

Fuller v. State, TexApp–Texarkana, 700 SW2d 5.—Const Law 4466; Infants 68.5, 68.7(5).

Fuller v. State, TexApp–Eastland, 858 SW2d 528, reh den, and petition for discretionary review refused, denial of post-conviction relief aff 2005 WL 2585659.—Crim Law 393(1), 730(14); Rape 51(7); Searches 117, 178; Witn 222.

Fuller v. State, TexApp–Eastland, 835 SW2d 768, petition for discretionary review refused.—Witn 219(3), 222.

Fuller v. State, TexApp–Tyler, 737 SW2d 113.—Crim Law 419(1.10), 662.8, 686(1), 686(2), 795(2.35), 1153(3).

Fuller v. State, TexApp–Tyler, 653 SW2d 65.—Sent & Pun 2014.

Fuller v. State, TexApp–Corpus Christi, 716 SW2d 721, petition for discretionary review refused.—Crim Law 824(3), 841, 847, 859, 1173.2(4); Homic 558, 559, 908, 1168; Jury 142.

Fuller; State v., TexCivApp–Beaumont, 451 SW2d 573, aff 461 SW2d 595.—Em Dom 202(1); Evid 43(3); Judgm 582, 585(5).

Fuller v. State, TexCivApp–Beaumont, 394 SW2d 203, writ gr, mod 407 SW2d 215.—High 85; R R 82(5).

Fuller v. State Farm County Mut. Ins. Co., TexApp–Fort Worth, 156 SW3d 658.—App & E 840(4), 913, 946, 949; Courts 97(1); Parties 35.5, 35.9, 35.13, 35.41, 35.73.

Fuller v. State Farm Mut. Auto. Ins. Co., NDTex, 971 FSupp 1098, aff 141 F3d 1165.—Contracts 328(1); Fed Civ Proc 2501; Insurance 3147, 3337.

Fuller; Sunrizon Homes, Inc. v., TexApp–San Antonio, 747 SW2d 530, writ den.—Damag 194; Judgm 101(1), 112, 126(1), 126(4), 143(3), 162(2); Trial 114.

Fuller v. Temple–Inland Forest Products Corp., EDTex, 942 FSupp 307.—Labor & Emp 757; Rem of C 25(1), 107(7), 107(11); States 18.46, 18.49; Work Comp 93.

Fuller v. Texas Park Lot, TexCivApp–Fort Worth, 133 SW2d 605.—Autos 244(36.1), 245(4); Evid 14, 76; Labor & Emp 2922, 2961, 2962; Partners 44, 55.

Fuller v. Texas Western Financial Corp., Tex, 644 SW2d 442.—Sales 8.

Fuller v. Texas Western Financial Corp., TexApp–Tyler, 635 SW2d 787, ref nre 644 SW2d 442.—Sales 8, 199, 222.

Fuller; Travelers Indem. Co. of Illinois v., Tex, 892 SW2d 848.—Const Law 606, 990, 1030, 2312; Death 11, 93; Work Comp 29.

Fuller v. Travelers Indem. Co. of Illinois, TexApp–Beaumont, 874 SW2d 958, reh overr, and writ gr, rev 892 SW2d 848.—App & E 863, 934(1); Death 93; Work Comp 1072.

Fuller; Trinity Universal Ins. Co. v., TexCivApp–Dallas, 524 SW2d 335, ref nre.—Contracts 328(1); Damag 62(1); Insurance 1644, 1646.

Fuller; U.S. v., CA5 (Tex), 453 F3d 274.—Arrest 71.1(1); Const Law 2623; Crim Law 370, 720(2), 1166.22(2); Em Dom 2.35; Gr Jury 34; Sent & Pun 1263, 1307, 1381(7).

Fuller; U.S. v., CA5 (Tex), 974 F2d 1474, reh den U.S. v. Foster, 986 F2d 1420, cert den 114 SCt 112, 510 US 835, 126 LEd2d 78.—Commerce 82.6; Consp 43(6), 47(3.1), 48.2(2); Crim Law 476.3, 772(5), 1144.13(3), 1144.13(5), 1159.2(1), 1159.2(7); U S 34.

Fuller; U.S. v., CA5 (Tex), 769 F2d 1095.—Crim Law 273(4.1), 641.13(5), 1519(13), 1655(3); Hab Corp 486(3).

Fuller v. Upshur Rural Elec. Co-op. Corp., TexCivApp–Texarkana, 332 SW2d 762, ref nre.—Judgm 335(1).

Fuller v. Wainwright, TexCivApp–El Paso, 415 SW2d 234.—Autos 238(1), 238(7); Trial 350.3(7).

Fuller; Wallace v., TexApp–Austin, 832 SW2d 714.—Divorce 252.3(2), 252.3(4); Hus & W 272(4).

Fuller v. Walter E. Heller & Co., TexCivApp–Dallas, 483 SW2d 348.—Inj 57, 210; Judgm 203; Trial 2.

Fuller v. Wilkie, TexCivApp–Eastland, 370 SW2d 237.—Evid 265(7); Parent & C 12.

Fuller v. Wright, TexCivApp–Waco, 82 SW2d 179.—Contracts 98; Equity 39(1); Inj 144; Receivers 182; Sales 43(6), 319; Sequest 5.

Fuller Aircraft Sales, Inc. v. Republic of Philippines, CA5 (Tex), 965 F2d 1375. See Walter Fuller Aircraft Sales, Inc. v. Republic of Philippines.

Fuller-Austin Insulation Co., Inc. v. Bilder, TexApp–Beaumont, 960 SW2d 914, review gr, and case abated, and petition for review dism, and set aside.—App & E

893(1), 969, 1026, 1050.1(1), 1056.1(1), 1056.1(10), 1064.1(1), 1066(7); Damag 63; Evid 577, 581; Interest 39(2.50), 56; Neglig 202; Prod Liab 14, 19.1, 71.5, 88, 98; Trial 139.1(14), 139.1(17), 168, 219, 295(1).

Fuller Co.; Metal Arts Co. v., CA5 (Tex), 389 F2d 319.— Pat 37, 46, 112.1, 226, 312(1.2), 314(5), 324.55(4).

Fuller Co. v. Metal Arts Co., SDTex, 276 FSupp 605, aff 389 F2d 319.—Pat 62(3), 283(1), 312(5), 312(6).

Fuller Co. of Texas, Inc. v. Carpet Services, Inc., Tex, 823 SW2d 603. See George A. Fuller Co. of Texas, Inc. v. Carpet Services, Inc.

Fuller Cotton Oil Co.; Holt v., TexCivApp–Amarillo, 175 SW2d 272, writ refused wom.—Neglig 1036, 1040(3), 1051, 1066, 1076, 1090, 1175, 1176.

Fuller Nurseries & Tree Service v. Jones, TexCivApp–Austin, 253 SW2d 946.—Pretrial Proc 472, 481.

Fuller's Food Products; George H. Dentler & Sons v., TexCivApp–Galveston, 183 SW2d 768, writ refused wom.—Plead 228.21; Trademarks 1096(2), 1259, 1609, 1691, 1800.

Fuller Springs v. State ex rel. City of Lufkin, Tex, 513 SW2d 17.—Mun Corp 33(1), 33(2); Quo W 1, 32, 50(1), 57.

Fuller Springs v. State ex rel. City of Lufkin, TexCiv-App–Beaumont, 503 SW2d 351, writ gr, rev 513 SW2d 17.—Mun Corp 29(4), 33(1), 33(10), 122.1(2).

Fullerton; Commissioners Court of Harris County v., TexCivApp–Hous (1 Dist), 596 SW2d 572, ref nre.— Counties 47, 159; Inj 76.

Fullerton v. Holliman, TexApp–Eastland, 730 SW2d 168, ref nre.—App & E 747(3); Child S 343; Hus & W 279(1), 280, 281; Judgm 654.

Fullerton v. Holliman, TexApp–Eastland, 721 SW2d 478, dism.—Child S 390.

Fullerton v. State, TexCrimApp, 186 SW2d 994, 148 TexCrim 299.—Crim Law 1090.1(1).

Fullerton v. State, TexCrimApp, 155 SW2d 608.—Crim Law 1182.

Fullerton; State Farm Fire and Cas. Co. v., CA5 (Tex), 118 F3d 374.—Const Law 4012; Fed Cts 385, 391; Insurance 3549(4), 3557; Judgm 634, 644, 651, 678(1), 678(2), 713(1), 720, 725(1).

Full Gospel Assemblies in Christ v. Montgomery Ward & Co., TexCivApp–Amarillo, 237 SW2d 657, dism.— Bills & N 15, 22, 153, 338, 363, 365(1), 370, 491, 497(1).

Fullick v. City of Baytown, TexApp–Houston (1 Dist), 820 SW2d 943.—Afft 18; App & E 232(2); Evid 366(2).

Fullilove; H. B. Zachry Co. v., TexCivApp–El Paso, 177 SW2d 980, writ refused wom.—Damag 91(3); Labor & Emp 2825.

Fullingim v. Dunaway, TexCivApp–Beaumont, 267 SW2d 483.—Plead 236(6); Trial 351.5(6); Witn 275(1).

Full Line Glass Distributors, Inc.; Massoud v., TexCiv-App–Fort Worth, 617 SW2d 773.—Evid 174.1, 355(3); Trial 66.

Fullwood; Alexander v., TexCivApp–Waco, 143 SW2d 646.—App & E 440, 659(2), 660(2).

Fullwood; U.S. v., CA5 (Tex), 342 F3d 409, cert den 124 SCt 1087, 540 US 1111, 157 LEd2d 899.—Crim Law 388.1, 388.2, 398(2), 720(2), 1030(1), 1036.2, 1037.1(3), 1153(1), 1158(1); Sent & Pun 752.

Fullylove v. State, TexCrimApp, 279 SW2d 357, 161 TexCrim 629.—Crim Law 814(3); Int Liq 223(1); Sent & Pun 1379(2), 1381(3).

Fullylove v. State, TexCrimApp, 261 SW2d 711, 159 TexCrim 120.—Sent & Pun 1260.

Fullylove v. State, TexApp–Dallas, 629 SW2d 176.—Arrest 63.4(16), 63.4(17); Obst Just 16.

Fulmer v. Barfield, TexCivApp–Tyler, 480 SW2d 413, writ dism woj.—App & E 927(2), 948, 962; Pretrial Proc 583, 683.

Fulmer v. Rider, TexApp–Tyler, 635 SW2d 875, ref nre. —Elect of Rem 3(1); Witn 178(1), 178(4).

Fulmer v. State, TexCrimApp, 731 SW2d 943.—Crim Law 577.14; Double J 55.

Fulmer v. State, TexCivApp–Fort Worth, 445 SW2d 546, ref nre.—Action 69(5); Atty & C 46, 54, 57; Const Law 3954; Evid 268, 317(3); Tel 1434.

Fulmer v. Thompson, TexCivApp–Tyler, 573 SW2d 256, ref nre.—App & E 758.3(6), 930(3), 989, 1170.1, 1170.6; Assault 35; Damag 208(1), 208(4); Trial 18.

Fulton, In re, BkrtcyEDTex, 236 BR 626.—Bankr 2164.1, 2185, 3348, 3349, 3350(6), 3350(7), 3423; Fed Civ Proc 2486, 2737.1; Judgm 828.21(2).

Fulton, In re, BkrtcySDTex, 148 BR 838.—Bankr 2785, 2829, 2852, 3702; Judgm 777, 780(1), 785(1), 787, 828.21(2).

Fulton v. Abramson, TexCivApp–Dallas, 369 SW2d 815. —App & E 758.1, 1078(1); Bankr 2553, 3066(4.1); Corp 80(12), 90(6), 228, 262(1), 550(10), 560(10).

Fulton v. Associated Indem. Corp., TexApp–Austin, 46 SW3d 364, review den.—Admin Law 387, 391; Work Comp 45, 47, 52, 1092.

Fulton; City of Temple v., TexCivApp–Austin, 430 SW2d 737, ref nre.—Mun Corp 30, 33(6).

Fulton v. Duhaime, TexCivApp–Hous (1 Dist), 525 SW2d 62, ref nre.—Hus & W 264(4), 270(9); Judgm 185.2(1), 185.3(9); New Tr 150(2), 153, 155; Trial 388(2).

Fulton v. Edge, TexCivApp–Waco, 435 SW2d 263, ref nre.—Guar 100; Judgm 683; Subrog 7(1).

Fulton v. Finch, Tex, 346 SW2d 823, 162 Tex 351.—App & E 112; Judgm 485; Mand 3(1), 4(1); New Tr 165.

Fulton v. Finch, TexCivApp–San Antonio, 338 SW2d 478, dism, mandamus gr 346 SW2d 823, 162 Tex 351.— Judgm 341; New Tr 165.

Fulton v. Kaiser Steel Corp., CA5 (Tex), 397 F2d 580.— Interpl 6, 8(1), 11, 15, 16; Stip 17(3).

Fulton; Krchnak v., TexApp–Amarillo, 759 SW2d 524, writ den.—Action 1, 61; Anim 25; App & E 867(1); Judgm 183, 184, 384, 390; Proc 145; Venue 7(8).

Fulton; Page v., TexApp–Beaumont, 30 SW3d 61.—App & E 930(1), 989, 1001(1), 1001(3), 1003(2), 1003(6), 1004(1), 1004(3), 1004(8), 1182; Damag 133, 192; Death 95(1); Evid 587, 597; Homic 1188.

Fulton; Reed v., TexCivApp–Corpus Christi, 384 SW2d 173, ref nre.—App & E 1236; Contracts 103; Damag 67; Gaming 17(1), 62, 71; Insurance 1704; Interest 39(1); Sales 52(5.1), 417.

Fulton v. Shaw, CA5 (Tex), 321 F2d 545.—Neglig 440(1); Trial 350.5(3).

Fulton v. South Oak Cliff State Bank, TexCivApp–Dallas, 439 SW2d 730, ref nre.—Guar 100; Judgm 585(3); Princ & S 185; Subrog 31(1).

Fulton v. State, TexCrimApp, 103 SW2d 755, 132 Tex-Crim 192.—Crim Law 134(4), 781(6).

Fulton v. State, TexCrimApp, 101 SW2d 251, 131 Tex-Crim 542.—Crim Law 1077.2(3).

Fulton; State Bd. of Ins. Com'rs of Tex. v., TexCivApp–Waco, 229 SW2d 652, ref nre 234 SW2d 389, 149 Tex 347.—Admin Law 746; App & E 781(1), 781(4); Insurance 1127; J P 175.

Fulton v. Texas Farm Bureau Ins. Co., TexApp–Dallas, 773 SW2d 391, writ den.—Contracts 152; Insurance 2670, 2671, 2673.

Fulton v. U.S., CA5 (Tex), 250 F2d 281.—Sent & Pun 1129.

Fulton; U.S. v., CA5 (Tex), 131 FedAppx 441, as mod, cert den 126 SCt 1020, 546 US 1097, 163 LEd2d 866, reh den 126 SCt 1647, 547 US 1052, 164 LEd2d 356.—Crim Law 637, 641.7(1), 1042.

Fulton; W. C. Turnbow Petroleum Corp. v., Tex, 194 SW2d 256, 145 Tex 56.—App & E 1, 345.1; Motions 14; New Tr 152, 163(2); Plead 288.

Fulton; W. C. Turnbow Petroleum Corp. v., TexCivApp–Texarkana, 199 SW2d 263, ref nre.—App & E 1008.1(14); Atty & C 20.1, 130; Courts 97(1), 493(3); Judgm 829(3).

Fulton Bag & Cotton Mills; Thompson v., Tex, 286 SW2d 411, 155 Tex 365.—Courts 475(1); Garn 167, 206.

Fulton Bag & Cotton Mills v. Valley Products Corp., TexCivApp–Dallas, 277 SW2d 241, aff Thompson v. Fulton Bag & Cotton Mills, 286 SW2d 411, 155 Tex 365. —Corp 509.1(1); Courts 475(1); Interpl 10.

Fulton Brown Feed Store v. Roberts, TexCivApp–Waco, 388 SW2d 723.—Plead 111.42(8).

Fulton Fire Ins. Co. v. First State Bank of Willis, TexCivApp–Waco, 353 SW2d 937, ref nre.—App & E 1170.7; Evid 544; Witn 345(2).

Fulton Property Co.; Wood v., TexCivApp–San Antonio, 92 SW2d 549.—App & E 237(5), 500(1), 501(1), 843(1); Fraud Conv 57(4); Plead 180(1), 353; Pretrial Proc 723.1.

Fulton Property Co.; Wood v., TexCivApp–Eastland, 90 SW2d 617.—App & E 719(1); Corp 503(4); Plead 339; Venue 77.

Fults v. Anzac Corp., TexCivApp–Eastland, 381 SW2d 156, ref nre.—Mines 53.

Fults v. Duren, TexCivApp–Hous (1 Dist), 427 SW2d 951, ref nre.—App & E 758.3(9); Contracts 99(3); Fraud 12; Mtg 86(3), 369(3).

Fultz v. Anzac Oil Corp., CA5 (Tex), 240 F2d 21.—Corp 616.

Fultz v. Cummins Sales & Service, Inc., TexCivApp–Corpus Christi, 587 SW2d 515, ref nre.—Pretrial Proc 315.

Fultz v. First Nat. Bank in Graham, Tex, 388 SW2d 405. —Banks 121, 126, 151.

Fultz; First Nat. Bank in Graham v., TexCivApp–Fort Worth, 380 SW2d 894, rev 388 SW2d 405.—Banks 148(3); Judgm 185.3(5), 186.

Fultz v. State, TexApp–Texarkana, 940 SW2d 758, reh overr, and petition for discretionary review refused.—Crim Law 438(8), 662.40, 1030(1), 1043(1), 1043(2), 1043(3), 1153(2); Witn 227.

Fultz v. State, TexApp–Houston (14 Dist), 770 SW2d 595, petition for discretionary review refused.—Crim Law 475.2(4).

Fultz v. State, TexApp–Houston (14 Dist), 632 SW2d 787, petition for discretionary review refused.—Crim Law 374, 641.4(4), 641.10(1), 641.10(3), 641.13(6), 1045.

Fulwiler v. Fulwiler, TexCivApp–Eastland, 419 SW2d 251.—Divorce 249.1, 252.3(5), 253(2), 282, 285, 286(5), 286(9).

Fulwiler; Fulwiler v., TexCivApp–Eastland, 419 SW2d 251.—Divorce 249.1, 252.3(5), 253(2), 282, 285, 286(5), 286(9).

Fulwiler; Stegall v., TexCivApp–Amarillo, 423 SW2d 182. —Ref of Inst 11, 17(1), 20; Ven & Pur 261(1).

Funari v. State, TexApp–San Antonio, 70 SW3d 175, petition for discretionary review dism as untimely filed.— Crim Law 637, 1086.11, 1152(1).

Functional Living, Inc.; Tarver v., WDTex, 796 FSupp 246.—Civil R 1006; Statut 265, 267(1).

Functional Restoration Associates; Continental Cas. Ins. Co. v., Tex, 19 SW3d 393.—Admin Law 387, 651; Statut 181(1), 188, 206, 208; Work Comp 1001, 1164, 1822, 1848, 1948, 1964.

Functional Restoration Associates; Continental Cas. Ins. Co. v., TexApp–Austin, 964 SW2d 776, reh overr, and review gr, rev 19 SW3d 393.—Admin Law 651, 763; Const Law 3847, 3895, 4028, 4186; Statut 206; Work Comp 1001, 1163, 1822, 1914.

Funderberg; Pullin v., TexCivApp–San Antonio, 342 SW2d 63.—Tresp to T T 36, 41(2); Ven & Pur 189, 299(1).

Funderburg v. Pullin, TexCivApp–Waco, 362 SW2d 343. —Garn 162, 191; Insurance 1996, 3441.

Funderburg v. Southwestern Drug Corp., TexCivApp–Fort Worth, 210 SW2d 607.—Princ & A 99, 116(1), 119(1), 124(3); Trial 174.

Funderburg v. State, TexCrimApp, 717 SW2d 637.—Crim Law 641.4(1), 641.9, 641.10(2), 1088.1, 1109(2).

Funderburgh v. State, TexCrimApp, 160 SW2d 942, 144 TexCrim 35.—Crim Law 393(3), 1170.5(1).

Funderburk; Dallas/Fort Worth Intern. Airport Bd. v., TexApp–Fort Worth, 188 SW3d 233, review gr, and remanded by agreement, opinion after remand from Supreme Court 2006 WL 3248013.—App & E 893(1); Civil R 1116(1); Courts 39.

Funderburk v. Dofflemyer, TexCivApp–Austin, 234 SW2d 889, writ refused.—Home 57(3), 162(1); Trial 140(2), 260(1).

Funderburk; Lewis v., TexApp–Waco, 191 SW3d 756, reh overr, and review gr.—Health 804, 809.

Funderburk; Metropolitan Life Ins. Co. v., TexCivApp–Beaumont, 81 SW2d 132, writ dism.—Evid 186(6), 571(9), 574; Insurance 2590(2), 2607, 3153, 3163, 3195, 3571; Trial 350.4(3).

Funderburk v. Schulz, TexCivApp–Galveston, 293 SW2d 803.—Const Law 2508; Schools 97(4).

Funderburk v. State, TexApp–Houston (14 Dist), 659 SW2d 122.—Crim Law 369.1, 867, 1169.11, 1174(1); Ind & Inf 171; Sent & Pun 1379(2).

Funding Resource Group; Quilling v., CA5 (Tex), 227 F3d 231.—Contempt 3, 4, 66(2); Fed Cts 585.1; Sec Reg 88.

Funds Recovery, Inc.; Dallas County Appraisal Dist. v., TexApp–Dallas, 887 SW2d 465, writ den.—Admin Law 721; App & E 17, 18, 23, 185(1), 374(4), 422, 766, 911.3; Courts 32; Mand 1; Tax 2711.

Funds, Third Parties, and Reeves County, Tex.; Victims v., WDTex, 715 FSupp 178.—Char 48(1), 50; Fed Cts 13.

Funeral Directors' Life Ins. Co.; Stewart Family Funeral Home, Ltd. v., EDTex, 410 FSupp2d 514.— Antitrust 22, 105; Contracts 147(2), 175(1), 187(1); Decl Judgm 62, 64; Insurance 3436.

Funk; Blond Lighting Fixture Supply Co. v., TexCivApp–San Antonio, 392 SW2d 586.—Corp 1.7(2), 230, 243(1), 243(8), 326, 361, 560(12); Judgm 186.

Funk v. State, TexApp–Fort Worth, 188 SW3d 229.—Atty & C 76(1); Crim Law 641.3(4), 641.10(2), 641.10(3), 641.13(7), 1181.5(3.1).

Funke; Zess v., TexApp–San Antonio, 956 SW2d 92.— Judgm 185(6); Larc 60; Mal Pros 16, 18(1), 18(3), 31.

Funk Farms, Inc. v. Montoya, TexApp–Corpus Christi, 736 SW2d 803, ref nre.—App & E 959(1), 1015(4); Damag 132(3), 134(1), 228; Labor & Emp 2797, 2921, 2927, 2932, 2941; Plead 229, 237(6).

Funkhouser v. Hurricane Fence Co., TexCivApp–Hous (1 Dist), 524 SW2d 780, ref nre.—Judgm 633.

Funkhouser v. Missouri-Kansas-Texas R. Co., TexCivApp–San Antonio, 358 SW2d 246.—App & E 655(3), 1069.1.

Fun Motors of Longview, Inc. v. Gratty, Inc., TexApp–Texarkana, 51 SW3d 756, review gr, rev Latch v. Gratty, Inc, 107 SW3d 543.—App & E 219(1), 852, 893(1), 990, 1010.1(1), 1010.1(2), 1010.1(3), 1012.1(4); Contracts 10(1), 10(4), 221(1); Damag 137, 163(4); Neglig 375, 379, 380, 387; Plead 290(3), 427; Torts 212, 222, 242; Trial 140(1).

Funston; Cars & Concepts, Inc. v., TexCivApp–Fort Worth, 601 SW2d 801, ref nre.—Judgm 7, 17(3), 134.

Funston Mach. and Supply Co.; Cox Engineering, Inc. v., TexApp–Fort Worth, 749 SW2d 508.—App & E 170(1); Frds St of 127; Venue 68.

Fun Time Centers, Inc. v. Continental Nat. Bank of Ft. Worth, TexCivApp–Tyler, 517 SW2d 877, ref nre.—App & E 172(1); Consp 19; Fraud 50, 58(1), 58(4), 64(1); Impl & C C 6, 10, 83.1.

Fun Travel World, Inc.; Sher v., TexApp–Dallas, 118 SW3d 500.—Antitrust 369; App & E 179(1); Judgm 185(4).

Fuqua, Ex parte, TexCrimApp, 548 SW2d 909.—Hab Corp 474; Rob 17(5).

Fuqua, Ex parte, TexCrimApp, 283 SW2d 50, 162 TexCrim 126.—Extrad 39.

Fuqua, In re, CA5 (Tex), 53 F3d 72. See Resolution Trust Corp. v. Smith.

Fuqua; Acklin v., TexCivApp–Amarillo, 193 SW2d 297, ref nre.—App & E 878(6); Mines 55(2), 55(5), 55(8), 64, 70(1).

Fuqua v. Burrell, TexCivApp–Waco, 474 SW2d 333, ref nre.—Mtg 362, 374.

Fuqua v. Cunningham, TexCivApp–Texarkana, 576 SW2d 171.—Plead 111.42(5).

Fuqua v. First Nat. Bank of Amarillo, TexCivApp–Amarillo, 332 SW2d 357.—Wills 439, 453, 471, 488, 684.8.

Fuqua v. Fuqua, TexApp–Dallas, 750 SW2d 238, writ den.—App & E 1012.1(7.1); Costs 194.40; Decl Judgm 393; Judgm 654, 747(2); Land & Ten 182; Lim of Act 46(1), 46(5), 151(3), 197(1), 197(3); Ten in C 33.

Fuqua; Fuqua v., TexApp–Dallas, 750 SW2d 238, writ den.—App & E 1012.1(7.1); Costs 194.40; Decl Judgm 393; Judgm 654, 747(2); Land & Ten 182; Lim of Act 46(1), 46(5), 151(3), 197(1), 197(3); Ten in C 33.

Fuqua v. Fuqua, TexCivApp–Tyler, 541 SW2d 228.—App & E 846(5); Divorce 252.1, 252.2, 252.3(1), 286(5).

Fuqua; Fuqua v., TexCivApp–Tyler, 541 SW2d 228.—App & E 846(5); Divorce 252.1, 252.2, 252.3(1), 286(5).

Fuqua v. Fuqua, TexCivApp–Hous (14 Dist), 559 SW2d 440, writ refused.—Judgm 518.

Fuqua; Fuqua v., TexCivApp–Hous (14 Dist), 559 SW2d 440, writ refused.—Judgm 518.

Fuqua v. Fuqua, TexCivApp–Hous (14 Dist), 528 SW2d 896, ref nre.—Deeds 58(1), 108; Spec Perf 59.

Fuqua; Fuqua v., TexCivApp–Hous (14 Dist), 528 SW2d 896, ref nre.—Deeds 58(1), 108; Spec Perf 59.

Fuqua v. Graber, TexApp–Corpus Christi, 158 SW3d 635, review gr.—App & E 893(1), 919; Bankr 2002, 2060.1, 2062; Mal Pros 0.5, 0.7, 47; Plead 104(1), 111.37, 111.39(0.5); States 18.5, 18.7, 18.11.

Fuqua v. Horizon/CMS Healthcare Corp., NDTex, 199 FRD 200, reconsideration den.—Fed Civ Proc 1278, 1636.1, 2757, 2820.

Fuqua; Montgomery County v., TexApp–Beaumont, 22 SW3d 662, reh overr, and review den.—App & E 68, 863, 874(4), 1079; Counties 144; Mun Corp 723, 736, 742(4), 742(6); Nuis 1, 59; Plead 78; Pretrial Proc 561.1.

Fuqua v. Moody & Clary Co., TexCivApp–Hous (14 Dist), 462 SW2d 321.—Evid 383(7); Lim of Act 187; Paymt 38(1), 71.

Fuqua; Palmer v., CA5 (Tex), 641 F2d 1146.—Contracts 176(1), 256; Damag 89(2), 91(1); Estop 52.10(2), 95; Fed Civ Proc 2126.1, 2127, 2152, 2608.1, 2609; Fraud 61; Frds St of 55, 76; Mines 99(2); Partners 70, 366; Trusts 92.5, 102(1).

Fuqua; Second Nat. Bank of Houston v., TexCivApp–Waco, 262 SW2d 834, ref nre.—Judgm 457, 704.

Fuqua; Specialty Retailers, Inc. v., TexApp–Houston (14 Dist), 29 SW3d 140, reh overr, and review den.—App & E 863, 934(1), 949; Consp 1.1; Corp 1.4(1), 1.7(2); Impl & C C 30; Judgm 183, 185(5), 185.3(5), 185.3(21), 186; Trover 1.

Fuqua v. State, TexCrimApp, 457 SW2d 571.—Crim Law 939(3).

Fuqua v. Taylor, TexApp–Dallas, 683 SW2d 735, ref nre. —Fraud 7, 64(1); Joint Adv 4(1); Judgm 243; Mines 101; Trusts 102(1).

Fuquay-Mouser, Inc.; Montgomery v., TexCivApp–Amarillo, 567 SW2d 268.—Estop 52.10(2); Sec Tran 131, 148.1, 149; Trial 397(1).

Furay; King v., TexCivApp–Galveston, 130 SW2d 1029, writ refused.—App & E 907(3), 927(6); Trial 388(2).

Furey; Adkins v., TexApp–San Antonio, 2 SW3d 346.—Judgm 181(27).

Furgerson v. Dixie Motor Coach Corp., NDTex, 48 FSupp 746.—Courts 96(1); Fed Cts 80.

Furgerson v. First Nat. Bank of Paris, TexCivApp–Texarkana, 218 SW2d 1019.—Chat Mtg 281; Sales 315.

Furgeson; Gartin v., TexCivApp–Amarillo, 144 SW2d 1114.—Judgm 853(3), 866.1.

Furgison v. State, TexApp–Houston (14 Dist), 800 SW2d 587, petition for discretionary review refused.—Crim Law 59(3), 59(5), 552(3), 1162, 1170.5(5), 1175; Rob 24.20, 24.50; Witn 372(2).

Furley; State v., TexApp–Waco, 890 SW2d 538.—Crim Law 1024(1), 1081(2).

Furlow v. Harris County Child Welfare Unit, TexCivApp–Hous (1 Dist), 527 SW2d 802.—Adop 4, 13, 15; Child 3, 20.2.

Furlow; U.S. v., CA5 (Tex), 194 FedAppx 252.—Sent & Pun 2038.

Furman; Clay Drilling Co. v., TexCivApp–Fort Worth, 150 SW2d 869.—Health 935, 943; Mines 105(2); Trial 350.4(4), 352.5(1), 352.5(4), 352.21.

Furman v. Georgia, USTex, 92 SCt 2726, 408 US 238, 33 LEd2d 346, reh den 93 SCt 89, 409 US 902, 34 LEd2d 163, reh den Jackson v. Georgia, 93 SCt 89, 409 US 902, 34 LEd2d 164, reh den Branch v Texas, 93 SCt 90, 409 US 902, 34 LEd2d 164, on remand Sullivan v State, 194 SE2d 410, 229 Ga 731, on remand Stanley v State, 490 SW2d 828.—Const Law 4742, 4745, 4746; Sent & Pun 1612.

Furman v. Keith, TexCivApp–San Antonio, 226 SW2d 218, writ refused.—Brok 1, 42; Fraud 10.

Furman v. Sanchez, TexCivApp–San Antonio, 523 SW2d 253.—Ven & Pur 89, 105(1).

Furmanite Australia Pty., Ltd.; Garner v., TexApp–Houston (1 Dist), 966 SW2d 798, reh overr, and review den.—App & E 846(5), 863, 893(1); Appear 9(1); Const Law 3964; Corp 1.5(3), 665(0.5); Courts 12(2.1), 12(2.5), 12(2.10), 12(2.20), 12(2.25), 39.

Furnace v. Furnace, TexApp–Houston (14 Dist), 783 SW2d 682, writ dism woj.—App & E 218.2(5.1), 882(14), 930(3), 989, 1001(1), 1003(7), 1062.2; Contracts 266(1); Trial 358; Trusts 57, 372(3), 373.

Furnace; Furnace v., TexApp–Houston (14 Dist), 783 SW2d 682, writ dism woj.—App & E 218.2(5.1), 882(14), 930(3), 989, 1001(1), 1003(7), 1062.2; Contracts 266(1); Trial 358; Trusts 57, 372(3), 373.

Furnace v. State, TexCrimApp, 157 SW2d 893, 143 TexCrim 184.—Bail 65; Crim Law 1131(7).

Furniture Barn, Inc.; Leal v., Tex, 571 SW2d 864.—Antitrust 209.

Furniture Barn, Inc. v. Leal, TexCivApp–Austin, 560 SW2d 533, writ gr, rev 571 SW2d 864.—Antitrust 209.

Furniture Connection, In re, BkrtcySDTex, 168 BR 591. See Husain, In re.

Furniture Discount Stores, Inc., In re, BkrtcyNDTex, 11 BR 5.—Bankr 2576, 2581; Sec Tran 82.1.

Furniture Dynamics, Inc. v. Hurley's Estate, TexCivApp–Dallas, 560 SW2d 486.—Ex & Ad 225(2), 228(5), 241; Judgm 649.

Furniture Technicians of Houston, Inc.; Cruz v., TexApp–San Antonio, 949 SW2d 34, reh overr, and writ den.—App & E 153, 863, 934(1), 971(2); Electricity 19(5); Pretrial Proc 40, 313.

Furr; Allstate Ins. Co. v., TexCivApp–Amarillo, 449 SW2d 295, ref nre.—Damag 221(2.1), 221(7); Estop 95; Evid 411; Princ & A 19, 23(3); Sales 418(1), 421; Trial 397(1).

Furr v. Furr, TexApp–Amarillo, 721 SW2d 565.—App & E 389(1), 389(3).

Furr; Furr v., TexApp–Amarillo, 721 SW2d 565.—App & E 389(1), 389(3).

Furr v. Furr, TexCivApp–Fort Worth, 440 SW2d 367, ref nre.—Wills 164(1), 164(4), 166(1), 324(3); Witn 159(3).

Furr; Furr v., TexCivApp–Fort Worth, 440 SW2d 367, ref nre.—Wills 164(1), 164(4), 166(1), 324(3); Witn 159(3).

Furr v. Furr, TexCivApp–Fort Worth, 403 SW2d 866.—Wills 156, 158, 159, 164(7), 166(2), 384.

Furr; Furr v., TexCivApp–Fort Worth, 403 SW2d 866.—Wills 156, 158, 159, 164(7), 166(2), 384.

Furr v. Furr, TexCivApp–Fort Worth, 346 SW2d 491, ref nre.—App & E 100(1).

Furr; Furr v., TexCivApp–Fort Worth, 346 SW2d 491, ref nre.—App & E 100(1).

Furr; Greenwood v., TexCivApp–Fort Worth, 251 SW 332.—Mental H 141.

Furr v. Hall, TexCivApp–Amarillo, 553 SW2d 666, ref nre.—Abate & R 8(2), 9; App & E 756, 757(1), 758.3(3); Decl Judgm 45, 253, 324; Equity 65(1); Estop 52.10(2), 52.10(3); Ex & Ad 144, 163.

Furr v. Young, TexCivApp–Fort Worth, 578 SW2d 532.—Ex & Ad 225(1), 225(2), 231; Judgm 634, 715(1), 743(2).

Furrer v. Furrer, TexCivApp–Austin, 267 SW2d 226.—Child C 413, 637, 921(1).

Furrer; Furrer v., TexCivApp–Austin, 267 SW2d 226.—Child C 413, 637, 921(1).

Furrh; City of Dallas v., TexCivApp–Texarkana, 541 SW2d 271, ref nre.—Admin Law 741, 791, 796; App & E 846(5), 878(2); Const Law 4292; Evid 471(1), 568(1); Licens 22.

Furrh v. Furrh, TexCivApp–Texarkana, 251 SW2d 927, ref nre.—App & E 300; Deeds 90; Partit 55(3), 63(3), 73, 89, 91, 103; Trial 120(1); Trusts 191(1); Wills 759(3).

Furrh; Furrh v., TexCivApp–Texarkana, 251 SW2d 927, ref nre.—App & E 300; Deeds 90; Partit 55(3), 63(3), 73, 89, 91, 103; Trial 120(1); Trusts 191(1); Wills 759(3).

Furrh v. State, TexCrimApp, 582 SW2d 824.—Sent & Pun 2026.

Furrh v. State, TexCrimApp, 325 SW2d 699, 168 TexCrim 299.—Crim Law 368(1), 368(3).

Furr's/Bishop's Inc.; Loran v., CA5 (Tex), 988 F2d 554.—Fed Cts 544.

Furr's Cafeterias, Inc. v. N.L.R.B., CA5 (Tex), 566 F2d 505.—Fed Cts 730, 943.1.

Furr's Cafeterias, Inc. v. N. L. R. B., NDTex, 416 FSupp 629.—Records 54, 58, 60.

Furr's Estate, Matter of, TexCivApp–Amarillo, 553 SW2d 676, ref nre.—Ex & Ad 343; Hus & W 273(2), 276(8); Judgm 185.3(9), 186; Statut 190, 206.

Furr's, Inc.; Balandran v., TexApp–El Paso, 833 SW2d 648.—App & E 930(1), 989, 1003(5), 1003(6); Damag 192; Evid 586(3), 588.

Furr's, Inc. v. Behringer, TexCivApp–Eastland, 340 SW2d 125.—Corp 503(2); Venue 8.5(1), 21.

Furr's, Inc. v. Bernard, TexCivApp–Amarillo, 489 SW2d 345, dism.—Neglig 1037(4), 1233, 1242, 1706; Plead 111.42(6).

Furr's, Inc. v. Bolton, TexCivApp–El Paso, 333 SW2d 688.—Plead 111.42(6).

Furrs, Inc.; Carey v., TexCivApp–Amarillo, 455 SW2d 786, ref nre.—App & E 1170.7, 1170.9(3); Neglig 212, 506(5), 1679, 1683, 1745; Witn 240(1), 321.

Furr's, Inc. v. Hernandez, TexCivApp–El Paso, 579 SW2d 320, dism.—Plead 111.39(2), 111.42(6), 111.42(7).

Furr's, Inc. v. Leyva, TexCivApp–El Paso, 553 SW2d 202, ref nre.—Neglig 1104(7); Plead 111.42(7).

Furr's, Inc. v. Logan, TexApp–El Paso, 893 SW2d 187.—App & E 1003(5); Damag 96, 97, 102, 132(6.1), 135, 153, 191; Neglig 1076, 1088, 1286(8), 1288, 1571, 1669, 1679, 1684, 1707.

Furr's, Inc. v. McCaslin, TexCivApp–El Paso, 335 SW2d 284.—Neglig 1104(6), 1104(7); Plead 111.42(7).

Furr's, Inc. v. Martin, TexCivApp–Eastland, 296 SW2d 607.—Plead 111.39(6), 111.42(7).

Furr's Inc. v. Patterson, TexCivApp–Amarillo, 618 SW2d 417.—App & E 846(5); Neglig 375, 1076; Plead 111.12, 111.39(4), 111.42(8).

Furr's, Inc. v. Quijano, TexCivApp–El Paso, 571 SW2d 343.—Plead 111.16, 111.39(4), 111.42(7).

Furr's, Inc. v. Sigala, TexCivApp–El Paso, 608 SW2d 789.—Plead 111.42(7).

Furr's, Inc.; Stoker v., TexApp–El Paso, 813 SW2d 719, writ den.—App & E 863; Judgm 185(2), 185(6); Labor & Emp 23, 24, 827, 857; Statut 188, 190, 206.

Furr's Inc. v. United Specialty Advertising Co., TexCivApp–El Paso, 385 SW2d 456, ref nre, cert den 86 SCt 59, 382 US 824, 15 LEd2d 71.—Antitrust 412, 418, 419, 432; App & E 1195(1); Consp 1.1, 8; Inj 56, 128(3.1); Judgm 564(2); Pat 182.

Furr's Inc. v. United Specialty Advertising Co., TexCivApp–El Paso, 338 SW2d 762, ref nre.—Antitrust 31, 412, 413, 417, 420.

Furr's, Inc.; Whitfield v., TexCivApp–El Paso, 502 SW2d 897.—Neglig 1104(1), 1104(7), 1670; Plead 111.39(6), 111.42(2), 111.42(7).

Furr's No. 974; West Texas Water Refiners, Inc. v., TexApp–El Paso, 915SW2d 623. See West Texas Water Refiners, Inc. v. S & B Beverage Co., Inc.

Furr's Super Market v. Garrett, TexCivApp–El Paso, 615 SW2d 280, ref nre.—Neglig 1089, 1537; Plead 111.42(7).

Furr's Supermarket, Inc. v. Bethune, TexApp–El Paso, 68 SW3d 678, review gr, rev 53 SW3d 375.—App & E 984(1); Costs 12, 32(1), 208.

Furr's Super Market, Inc. v. Jernigan, TexCivApp–Amarillo, 380 SW2d 193.—Neglig 1088; Plead 111.39(6), 111.41, 111.42(7).

Furr's Supermarket, Inc. v. Williams, TexApp–Amarillo, 664 SW2d 154.—App & E 912, 1010.1(1), 1010.2, 1011.1(1); Evid 5(1), 10(2), 10(4), 10(6), 314(1); Plead 111.12, 111.42(7), 111.42(8); Trial 105(2).

Furr's Supermarket No. 939; Duran v., TexApp–El Paso, 921 SW2d 778. See Duran v. Furr's Supermarkets, Inc.

Furr's Supermarkets; Ortiz v., TexApp–El Paso, 26 SW3d 646, reh overr.—App & E 930(1), 946, 948, 971(6), 989, 1001(1), 1001(3), 1002, 1003(3), 1003(5); Damag 37, 38, 48, 186, 187, 192; Labor & Emp 26, 3038(1), 3096(5); Neglig 1684; Witn 345(1), 345(2), 345(6).

Furr's Supermarkets; Patino v., TexCivApp–El Paso, 512 SW2d 54, ref nre.—App & E 301, 930(3), 989; Neglig 452, 504, 506(6), 506(8), 1679, 1683, 1750.

Furr's Supermarkets v. Patino, TexCivApp–El Paso, 491 SW2d 449, appeal after remand 512 SW2d 54, ref nre.—App & E 1177(2); Plead 111.3, 404.

Furr's Supermarkets, Inc. v. Arellano, TexCivApp–El Paso, 492 SW2d 727, ref nre.—Neglig 1104(6), 1670.

Furr's Supermarkets, Inc. v. Bethune, Tex, 53 SW3d 375.—App & E 907(4); Costs 32(1).

Furr's Supermarkets, Inc.; De Leon v., TexApp–El Paso, 31 SW3d 297.—App & E 230, 242(1), 893(1), 969, 1026; Trial 295(1); Work Comp 2112, 2141.

Furr's Supermarkets, Inc.; Duran v., TexApp–El Paso, 921 SW2d 778, reh overr, and writ den.—App & E 854(1), 863; Arrest 63.4(2); Disorderly C 1, 11; False Imp 2; Judgm 181(6), 181(21), 181(27), 181(33), 185(2), 185(6), 185.3(21); Labor & Emp 29, 58, 3040, 3042, 3100(1), 3125, 3132, 3135; Libel 1, 22, 33, 94(1), 123(2); Lim of Act 127(2.1), 127(5), 127(7); Mun Corp 747(3), 753(1); Neglig 371, 379, 380, 383, 387, 432, 1011; Offic 114; Princ & A 150(2), 159(1).

Furr's Supermarkets, Inc.; Hernandez v., TexApp–El Paso, 924 SW2d 193, reh overr, and writ den.—Judgm 181(7), 185(2); Lim of Act 1, 121(1), 121(2).

Furr's Supermarkets, Inc. v. Mulanax, TexApp–El Paso, 897 SW2d 442, reh overr.—Mand 1, 7, 143(2).

Furr's Supermarkets, Inc.; Wyatt v., TexApp–El Paso, 908 SW2d 266, reh overr, and writ den.—App & E 863;

Judgm 185(2), 185(6), 185.3(21), 186, 189; Neglig 1001, 1032, 1086, 1104(6); Proc 145.

Furst v. Smith, TexApp–Houston (1 Dist), 176 SW3d 864.—App & E 5, 859, 893(1), 914(1); Courts 21, 39; Proc 4, 48, 64, 74, 77, 127, 133, 135, 141, 149.

Furst & Thomas; Lemmon v., TexCivApp–Dallas, 166 SW2d 755, writ refused wom.—Antitrust 537, 831, 865.

Furst & Thomas; Young v., TexCivApp–Dallas, 172 SW2d 359.—Plead 111.2; Venue 21.

Furstonberg v. Mintz, NDTex, 170 FSupp2d 695.—Fed Cts 241; Health 607; Labor & Emp 407; Rem of C 25(1), 102, 107(7); States 18.15, 18.51.

Furstonburg v. State, TexCrimApp, 190 SW2d 362, 148 TexCrim 638.—Sod 1.

Furtick v. State, TexCrimApp, 592 SW2d 616.—Crim Law 412.2(5), 1169.2(6), 1169.5(2).

Fury; State v., TexApp–Houston (1 Dist), 186 SW3d 67, petition for discretionary review refused.—Assault 91.10(1); Const Law 4594(1); Crim Law 700(5), 737(1), 742(1), 919(1), 939(1), 941(2), 947, 1134(4), 1144.13(2.1), 1147, 1156(1), 1159.2(1), 1159.2(2), 1159.2(7).

Fusbahn; Perez v., TexCivApp–Beaumont, 501 SW2d 475.—App & E 989, 1003(11); Autos 245(15).

Fusco v. Birdville Independent School Dist., TexCivApp–Eastland, 609 SW2d 648, ref nre.—Trial 350.2, 350.3(8); Work Comp 1729.

Fusco v. Johns-Manville Products Corp., CA5 (Tex), 643 F2d 1181.—Fed Cts 421; Lim of Act 55(2), 55(4), 104(1), 105(2).

Fusco; U.S. v., CA5 (Tex), 748 F2d 996.—Witn 318, 374(1).

Fuselier, In re, TexApp–Houston (1 Dist), 56 SW3d 265, reh overr.—Judgm 215, 303, 304, 306; Mand 3(2.1), 10, 53.

Fuselier; Bray v., TexApp–Texarkana, 107 SW3d 765, reh overr, and review den.—App & E 223, 242(2), 934(1), 946; Judgm 183, 185(2), 185(5), 185.1(8), 185.2(8), 185.3(21), 189.

Fuselier; Buls v., TexApp–Texarkana, 55 SW3d 204, reh overr.—Action 12; App & E 852, 922, 968, 969, 970(2), 1045(3), 1064.1(1); Evid 99, 508, 555.10, 570; Health 827; Jury 91, 97(1), 105(1), 131(6), 132, 133; Neglig 431; Plead 382(1); Trial 203(1), 219, 250, 295(2), 350.1.

Fuselier; Buzzini Drilling Co. v., TexApp–Hous (1 Dist), 562 SW2d 878.—Parties 47; Venue 15, 32(2).

Fuselier; Cortez v., TexApp–Texarkana, 876 SW2d 519, reh overr, and writ den, and.—Evid 545; Health 631; Judgm 181(33), 185(2), 185(4); Neglig 1675.

Fuselier v. Dow Chemical Co., TexApp–Hous (1 Dist), 590 SW2d 624, ref nre.—Evid 222(1), 246, 264; Witn 379(1).

Fuselier; Johnson v., TexApp–Texarkana, 83 SW3d 892.—App & E 635(1), 946; Judgm 181(12), 183, 185.1(7); Lim of Act 55(3).

Fussell, In re, CA5 (Tex), 928 F2d 712, reh den, cert den Fussell v. Price, 112 SCt 1203, 502 US 1107, 117 LEd2d 443.—Bankr 2370, 3782, 3786.

Fussell v. Price, CA5 (Tex), 928 F2d 712. See Fussell, In re.

Fussell v. Rinque, TexCivApp–Galveston, 269 SW2d 442, ref nre.—Adv Poss 114(1); App & E 204(4); Evid 372(3); Tresp to T T 26, 27, 40(1).

Fussell v. State, TexCrimApp, 274 SW2d 837.—Crim Law 1090.1(1).

Fuston; Spain v., TexCivApp–Fort Worth, 242 SW2d 892.—Contracts 93(2); Deeds 69, 94; Ven & Pur 79, 315(3).

Fuston v. Wilson, Tex, 192 SW2d 444, 144 Tex 588.—Witn 130, 159(3).

Fuston; Wilson v., TexCivApp–Amarillo, 189 SW2d 769, rev 192 SW2d 444, 144 Tex 588.—App & E 1009(2); Home 129(1), 134; Trover 69; Witn 130, 135.

Futch; Faulk v., Tex, 214 SW2d 614, 147 Tex 253, 5 ALR2d 963.—App & E 846(5); Bills & N 128, 129(2), 422(1); Corp 553(6); Receivers 81.

Futch; Faulk v., TexCivApp–San Antonio, 209 SW2d 1008, aff 214 SW2d 614, 147 Tex 253, 5 ALR2d 963.—Bills & N 128, 129(2), 394, 526; Corp 123(14), 553(6); Plgs 56(3).

Futch v. Greer, TexCivApp–Amarillo, 353 SW2d 896, ref nre, cert den 83 SCt 728, 372 US 913, 9 LEd2d 721.—App & E 1078(1); Const Law 4475; High 99.1, 105(1); Judgm 185(2), 185.2(1), 185.2(4), 185.2(9), 185.3(11).

Futch; Railroad Commission of Tex v., TexCivApp–Austin, 108 SW2d 289.—Commerce 14.10(1).

Futch v. State, TexCrimApp, 632 SW2d 743, 33 ALR4th 1056.—Crim Law 625.15; Jury 21.5.

Futch v. State, TexCrimApp, 376 SW2d 758.—Crim Law 303.50, 404.65, 444.

Futerfas; City of Garland v., TexApp–Dallas, 665 SW2d 140.—App & E 71(3), 80(6), 934(2).

Futerfas v. Park Towers, TexApp–Dallas, 707 SW2d 149, ref nre.—App & E 766; Inj 261; Judgm 181(15.1), 181(33), 185(2), 185.2(9); Mal Pros 4, 16; Proc 168, 171; Torts 212.

Futrell; Haddox v., TexCivApp–Waco, 321 SW2d 110.—App & E 218.2(2); Autos 244(6), 244(54), 244(58), 247.

Futrell v. Indiana Lumbermens Mut. Ins. Co., TexCivApp–Hous (1 Dist), 471 SW2d 926.—Insurance 1822, 2653.

Futrell; McGraw-Hill, Inc. v., TexApp–Houston (1 Dist), 823 SW2d 414, writ den.—Judgm 17(1), 133, 162(2); Proc 64, 67, 153.

F/V Tempest; Geophysical Service, Inc. v., SDTex, 293 FSupp 179.—Collision 12; Ship 81(1), 86(2.5).

FWA Drilling Co. v. Lambert, TexCivApp–El Paso, 418 SW2d 878, writ dism.—Damag 91(3); Labor & Emp 2881; Neglig 1553; Plead 111.42(7); Venue 8.5(8).

F.W. Gartner Co.; Sharp v., TexApp–Austin, 971 SW2d 707.—Tax 3638, 3682, 3692, 3701.

F. W. Heitmann Co.; Grissom v., TexCivApp–Galveston, 130 SW2d 1054, writ refused.—Execution 118, 171(1); Judgm 853(3).

F.W. Industries, Inc. v. McKeehan, TexApp–Eastland, 198 SW2d 217.—App & E 856(1), 961; Atty & C 105.5, 129(2); Judgm 185.1(1), 185.1(8).

F. W. Merrick, Inc.; Overton Refining Co. v., TexCivApp–Austin, 161 SW2d 856, writ refused wom.—App & E 1047(1); Mines 92.38.

F.W. Myers & Co., Inc.; Alpine Ocean Seismic Survey, Inc. v., CA5 (Tex), 23 F3d 946.—Carr 97, 98; Contracts 187(1).

FW/PBS, Inc. v. City of Dallas, USTex, 110 SCt 596, 493 US 215, 107 LEd2d 603, on remand 896 F2d 864.—Const Law 874, 1440, 4287; Fed Civ Proc 103.5; Fed Cts 461; Mun Corp 121.

FW/PBS, Inc. v. City of Dallas, CA5 (Tex), 837 F2d 1298, stay gr 108 SCt 1605, 485 US 1042, 99 LEd2d 919, cert gr in part 109 SCt 1309, 489 US 1051, 103 LEd2d 578, aff in part, vac in part 110 SCt 596, 493 US 215, 107 LEd2d 603, on remand 896 F2d 864.—Const Law 82(6.1), 1170, 1176, 1879, 2204, 2208, 2212, 2219; Licens 7(1); Searches 79.

F. W. Woolworth Co.; Allen v., TexCivApp–El Paso, 315 SW2d 612, ref nre.—Judgm 181(2), 185.3(21), 186; Neglig 506(3), 1286(1), 1286(7).

F. W. Woolworth Co. v. Bell, CA5 (Tex), 291 F2d 912, cert den 82 SCt 194, 368 US 915, 7 LEd2d 131.—Neglig 1104(6).

F. W. Woolworth Co.; Coffee v., Tex, 536 SW2d 539.—App & E 934(1); Neglig 1289, 1670.

F. W. Woolworth Co.; Coffee v., TexCivApp–Corpus Christi, 526 SW2d 793, writ gr, rev 536 SW2d 539.—App & E 934(1), 1024.4; Neglig 1001, 1119.

F. W. Woolworth Co. v. Ellison, TexCivApp–Eastland, 232 SW2d 857.—Neglig 1314, 1639, 1679, 1717; Trial 79, 90, 350.6(2), 352.14, 356(1).

F. W. Woolworth Co. v. Garza, TexCivApp–San Antonio, 390 SW2d 90, ref nre.—App & E 768, 930(1), 989; Sales 427, 441(3).

F. W. Woolworth Co. v. Goldston, TexCivApp–Amarillo, 155 SW2d 830, writ refused wom.—Evid 121(2), 123(11); Neglig 1088, 1670, 1708; Trial 105(1), 105(2).

F. W. Woolworth Co.; Hambrice v., CA5 (Tex), 290 F2d 557.—Damag 168(1); Evid 472(9); Fed Civ Proc 36; Fed Cts 416; Neglig 1639, 1670.

F. W. Woolworth Co.; Mackey v., TexCivApp–Amarillo, 277 SW2d 180, ref nre.—Neglig 1076, 1670.

F. W. Woolworth Co., Inc.; Parra v., TexCivApp–El Paso, 545 SW2d 596.—Mun Corp 808(1), 808(7).

Fyfe Cement & Gravel Co. v. Mathis, TexCivApp–Amarillo, 310 SW2d 770, ref nre.—App & E 930(1), 1010.1(3), 1062.1; Sales 181(12), 416(1).

Fyfe Cement & Supply Co. v. Hacker, TexCivApp–Amarillo, 372 SW2d 735, writ dism.—Plead 111.42(4); Sales 273(2).

Fyffe v. Fyffe, TexApp–Texarkana, 670 SW2d 360, dism. —Divorce 252.1, 252.3(2); Hus & W 258.

Fyffe; Fyffe v., TexApp–Texarkana, 670 SW2d 360, dism. —Divorce 252.1, 252.3(2); Hus & W 258.

Fyke v. Fyke, TexCivApp–Fort Worth, 463 SW2d 242.— Decl Judgm 182; Hus & W 264(1), 272(4).

Fyke; Fyke v., TexCivApp–Fort Worth, 463 SW2d 242.— Decl Judgm 182; Hus & W 264(1), 272(4).

Fyke v. Fyke, TexCivApp–Fort Worth, 442 SW2d 764.— App & E 281(1).

Fyke; Fyke v., TexCivApp–Fort Worth, 442 SW2d 764.— App & E 281(1).

Fyke v. Fyke, TexCivApp–Fort Worth, 442 SW2d 760.— Divorce 152, 354.

Fyke; Fyke v., TexCivApp–Fort Worth, 442 SW2d 760.— Divorce 152, 354.

Fyke v. State, TexCrimApp, 184 SW 197, 79 TexCrim 247. —Controlled Subs 10, 69, 96.

Fyke v. U. S., CCA5 (Tex), 254 F 225, 165 CCA 513.—Int Rev 5259, 5285.

Fylipoy v. Gulf Stevedore Corp., SDTex, 257 FSupp 166. —Fed Cts 270; Mun Corp 723; Nav Wat 8.5; States 191.7.

F/V Betty N, TexApp–Corpus Christi, 870 SW2d 95. See Ricardo N., Inc. v. Turcios de Argueta.

F/V Gloria B, CA5 (Tex), 38 F3d 755. See Liberty Seafood, Inc., Complaint of.

F/V Tio Mario, TexApp–Corpus Christi, 778 SW2d 529. See Tio Mario, Inc. v. Matos.

G

G., Guardianship of, TexApp–Corpus Christi, 794 SW2d 510. See B.A.G., Guardianship of.

G., In Interest of, TexApp–San Antonio, 980 SW2d 764. See N.J.G., In Interest of.

G., In re, TexApp–Houston (1 Dist), 746 SW2d 500. See V.G., In re.

G., Matter of, Tex, 866 SW2d 199. See R.A.G., Matter of.

G., Matter of, TexApp–Austin, 905 SW2d 56. See C.M.G., Matter of.

G., Matter of, TexApp–Austin, 883 SW2d 411. See C.M.G., Matter of.

G., Matter of, TexApp–Austin, 728 SW2d 939. See L.G., Matter of.

G., Matter of, TexApp–San Antonio, 940 SW2d 246. See J.D.G., Matter of.

G., Matter of, TexApp–Dallas, 860 SW2d 160. See A.G.G., Matter of.

G., Matter of, TexApp–Texarkana, 953 SW2d 483. See K.W.G., Matter of.

G., Matter of, TexApp–Texarkana, 905 SW2d 676. See J.G., Matter of.

G., Matter of, TexApp–Amarillo, 687 SW2d 774. See R.G., Matter of.

G., Matter of, TexApp–Beaumont, 942 SW2d 227. See P.S.G., Matter of.

G., Matter of, TexApp–Waco, 861 SW2d 106. See S.D.G., Matter of.

G., Matter of, TexApp–Tyler, 805 SW2d 10. See C.C.G., Matter of.

G. v. Baum, TexApp–Houston (1 Dist), 790 SW2d 839. See O.G. v. Baum.

G------ v. G------, TexCivApp–Dallas, 604 SW2d 521.— Child 53.

G------; G------ v., TexCivApp–Dallas, 604 SW2d 521.— Child 53.

G. v. Murray, TexApp–Corpus Christi, 915 SW2d 548. See J.G. v. Murray.

G. v. State, TexApp–San Antonio, 730 SW2d 182. See G.K.G. v. State.

G. v. State, TexApp–San Antonio, 727 SW2d 96. See I.G. v. State.

G. v. State, TexApp–Dallas, 870 SW2d 79. See R.A.G. v. State.

G. v. State, TexApp–El Paso, 775 SW2d 758. See L.G. v. State.

G. v. State, TexApp–Houston (14 Dist), 936 SW2d 371. See S.D.G. v. State.

G., C. & S. F. Ry. Co. v. Taylor, TexCivApp–Austin, 101 SW2d 642.—Carr 228(1).

G., Jr., Matter of, TexApp–San Antonio, 935 SW2d 919. See S.G., Jr., Matter of.

G., Jr., Matter of, TexApp–Corpus Christi, 865 SW2d 504. See R.G., Jr., Matter of.

Gaal v. BASF Wyandotte Corp., TexCivApp–Hous (14 Dist), 533 SW2d 152.—Antitrust 421; Const Law 1117(1); Inj 138.31, 138.39, 147.

Gabaldon v. General Motors Corp., TexApp–El Paso, 876 SW2d 367.—App & E 236(1), 966(1); Fraud 17; Judgm 185(2); Neglig 202, 483, 1692; Pretrial Proc 713, 714; Princ & A 3(1).

Gabbai, In re, Tex, 968 SW2d 929.—Child C 855; Child S 470; Contempt 33, 34; Divorce 269(2), 269(13), 287.

Gabbard; Gifford v., TexCivApp–El Paso, 305 SW2d 668. —Hus & W 254, 257, 264(5); Refer 8(8).

Gabbert v. Atchison, T. & S. F. Ry. Co., CCA5 (Tex), 93 F2d 562.—Carr 202; Commerce 212.

Gabbert v. City of Brownwood, TexCivApp–Eastland, 176 SW2d 344, writ refused.—Autos 254; High 198; Mun Corp 723, 759(1), 763(1), 796, 797; Statut 212.1, 219(9.1), 223.4.

Gabbert v. Miller, TexCivApp–El Paso, 258 SW2d 383.— Bailm 17, 31(3), 32; Damag 105.

GAB Business Services, Inc.; Eubanks v., TexApp–Texarkana, 909 SW2d 212.—App & E 863; Insurance 1867; Work Comp 1042.

GAB Business Services, Inc.; Hanks v., Tex, 644 SW2d 707.—Contracts 303(1).

GAB Business Services, Inc.; Hanks v., TexApp–Amarillo, 626 SW2d 564, writ gr, rev 644 SW2d 707.—Contracts 175(1), 176(1); Elect of Rem 7(1); Sales 65, 195, 368.

GAB Business Services, Inc. v. Moore, TexApp–Texarkana, 829 SW2d 345.—Antitrust 221, 369; App & E 500(4), 544(1), 989, 1003(6), 1043(6); Damag 49, 56.10, 130.1, 178, 208(6); Judges 36; Mun Corp 724, 745; Pretrial Proc 202; States 53; Trial 269; Witn 240(1), 282; Work Comp 1042, 1072.

Gabel v. Blackburn Operating Corp., TexCivApp–Amarillo, 442 SW2d 818.—Hus & W 19(1), 19(2), 235(2); Trial 350.4(2), 350.8; Witn 379(1), 392(1).

Gabel v. Blackburn Operating Corp., TexCivApp–Amarillo, 415 SW2d 726.—Plead 111.18; Venue 22(1), 22(6).

Gabel; Engra, Inc. v., CA5 (Tex), 958 F2d 643.—Fed Civ Proc 320, 331, 2844.

GABEL

Gabel v. Engra, Inc., SDTex, 86 BR 890. See Engra, Inc., In re.

Gabel; Engra, Inc. v., SDTex, 86 BR 890. See Engra, Inc., In re.

Gabel v. Estelle, SDTex, 677 FSupp 514.—Civil R 1092, 1098, 1396; Prisons 4(5), 13(2), 17(1).

Gabel v. Lynaugh, CA5 (Tex), 835 F2d 124.—Fed Civ Proc 2847; Fed Cts 611.

Gabel v. McCotter, CA5 (Tex), 803 F2d 814, reh den 806 F2d 1257, cert den 107 SCt 3215, 482 US 929, 96 LEd2d 701.—Const Law 203, 2816, 4729; Hab Corp 775(2).

Gabel v. Sandoval, TexApp–San Antonio, 648 SW2d 398, dism.—Atty & C 129(1).

Gaber; U.S. v., CA5 (Tex), 745 F2d 952.—Crim Law 273(4.1), 1158(2); Postal 44.

Gaber Co. v. Rawson, TexCivApp–Hous (14 Dist), 549 SW2d 19, ref nre.—App & E 302(6); Autos 180, 242(6), 242(8), 244(36.1), 245(23), 245(36), 245(81); Death 77, 103(4); New Tr 152; Trial 352.12.

Gabert; Eastus v., TexComApp, 93 SW2d 396, 127 Tex 290.—App & E 931(4); Autos 19; Larc 2.

Gabert, R.M.H. by, v. Messick, TexApp–Fort Worth, 828 SW2d 226. See R.M.H. by Gabert v. Messick.

Gable v. Frigidaire Corp., TexCivApp–El Paso, 121 SW2d 456, dism.—Contracts 10(1), 10(4), 143(3), 217; Princ & A 41(1).

Gable; O'Connor v., TexCivApp–Dallas, 298 SW2d 209, ref nre.—App & E 281(1), 544(3); Contracts 141(3); Partners 220(2); Ten in C 55(4).

Gable v. Spain, TexCivApp–Texarkana, 421 SW2d 756.—App & E 1015(5); Neglig 253, 1683.

Gable; Wood v., TexApp–Fort Worth, 656 SW2d 623, ref nre.—Anim 23(2).

Gable v. Wood, TexApp–Fort Worth, 622 SW2d 884, dism.—Antitrust 143(2); Venue 2.

Gable Elec. Service, Inc. v. Mims, TexCivApp–Dallas, 364 SW2d 292.—App & E 882(17); Evid 461(1); Trover 34(2), 40(4).

Gabler; Duncan v., Tex, 215 SW2d 155, 147 Tex 229.—Const Law 48(1), 599, 602, 651, 969, 990, 996, 1002, 2340; Tax 2901, 2942.

Gabler v. Minnesota Mut. Life Ins. Co., TexCivApp–Texarkana, 498 SW2d 413.—Evid 267, 269(1); Insurance 3360, 3381(5); Interpl 8(2).

Gables Realty Ltd. Partnership v. Travis Central Appraisal Dist., TexApp–Austin, 81 SW3d 869, review den.—Statut 181(1), 188, 206, 212.7, 245; Tax 2300, 2309, 2311, 2358.

Gabner v. Metropolitan Life Ins. Co., EDTex, 938 FSupp 1295.—Banks 4; Insurance 1117(1); Labor & Emp 407, 461, 465, 467, 475, 643; Rem of C 19(5), 25(1); Sec Reg 244; States 18.3, 18.51.

Gabor; Hollywood Fantasy Corp. v., CA5 (Tex), 151 F3d 203.—Contracts 22(1), 23, 24, 29, 250, 328(3); Damag 30, 45, 140, 190; Evid 540; Fed Cts 433, 612.1, 763.1, 776, 823; Judges 49(2), 51(2).

Gabor; U.S. v., CA5 (Tex), 905 F2d 76.—Crim Law 1557(2).

Gabourel; Diesel Fuel Injection Service, Inc. v., TexApp–Corpus Christi, 893 SW2d 610, reh overr.—App & E 918(1); Lim of Act 95(1), 95(3), 95(9), 193.

Gabrel; Meadows v., CA5 (Tex), 563 F2d 1231.—Civil R 1319.

Gabriel, Ex parte, TexCrimApp, 56 SW3d 595.—Pardon 67; Sent & Pun 630.

Gabriel v. Alhabbal, TexCivApp–Hous (1 Dist), 618 SW2d 894, ref nre.—Lim of Act 25(3), 43, 51(2), 66(2), 163(1).

Gabriel; Board of Law Examiners of State of Tex. v., Tex, 953 SW2d 227.—Atty & C 61.

Gabriel v. City of Plano, CA5 (Tex), 202 F3d 741, reh and reh den 211 F3d 127.—Civil R 1351(1), 1352(4), 1420; Fed Civ Proc 2251; Fed Cts 776, 813, 814.1, 823, 850.1, 896.1, 901.1.

Gabriel; Cole v., TexApp–Fort Worth, 822 SW2d 296.—Mand 22; Witn 198(1), 217.

Gabriel v. Fleming, CA5 (Tex), 106 FedAppx 290.—Prisons 13(5).

Gabriel; Groschke v., TexApp–Houston (1 Dist), 824 SW2d 607, writ den.—Action 60; App & E 768; Inj 239; Judgm 185.3(16), 252(1), 256(1); Ven & Pur 79.

Gabriel; Groves v., Tex, 874 SW2d 660.—Pretrial Proc 382.

Gabriel v. Lovewell, TexApp–Texarkana, 164 SW3d 835.—Anim 23(2); App & E 930(1), 1001(1), 1001(3), 1003(7); Contracts 326; Damag 208(1); Evid 155(1), 505, 560, 570, 571(3), 593; Neglig 371, 372, 375, 379, 380, 387, 1675, 1676, 1713; Trial 207, 255(4).

Gabriel v. Mendez, TexCivApp–San Antonio, 517 SW2d 447, ref nre.—App & E 729, 901, 927(7); Consp 19; Fraud 12, 50.

Gabriel v. Snell, TexCivApp–Hous (14 Dist), 613 SW2d 810.—App & E 762; Guard & W 15, 65, 173, 175, 177; Interest 39(1); Judgm 585(1), 634, 713(2), 720.

Gabriel v. State, TexCrimApp, 900 SW2d 721.—Controlled Subs 74.

Gabriel v. State, TexApp–Houston (1 Dist), 756 SW2d 68.—Crim Law 304(1), 790, 1038.1(1), 1172.1(2).

Gabriel v. State, TexApp–Dallas, 842 SW2d 328, reh den, and petition for discretionary review gr, aff 900 SW2d 721.—Controlled Subs 28, 81; Crim Law 486(8), 488, 494, 561(1).

Gabriel v. State, TexApp–Waco, 973 SW2d 715.—Crim Law 695.5, 1043(1), 1128(2), 1162, 1166(10.10); Infants 20.

Gabrielsen v. BancTexas Group, Inc., NDTex, 675 FSupp 367.—Corp 320(4), 320(7); Fed Civ Proc 103.2, 103.3, 103.5, 164, 1745; Sec Reg 49.21, 49.24, 49.26(3).

Gabryelski v. State, TexApp–San Antonio, 885 SW2d 203.—Autos 344, 355(13); Crim Law 1144.13(3), 1159.2(7), 1159.6.

Gabrysch; Hendrix v., TexCivApp–San Antonio, 190 SW2d 516.—App & E 499(4), 699(1); Lim of Act 197(2); Mines 81; Mtg 364, 378; Subrog 23(2).

Gaby; Ivanhoe v., SDTex, 616 FSupp 122.—Civil R 1502; U S 50.10(7).

G. A. C. Halff Foundation v. Calvert, TexCivApp–San Antonio, 281 SW2d 178, ref nre.—Powers 1, 7, 19; Tax 3328(2); Trusts 159.

G. A. C. Leasing Corp.; Armstrong v., TexCivApp–Beaumont, 512 SW2d 708.—Contracts 278(1); Evid 420(2); Judgm 199(3.2), 199(3.9), 199(3.10), 199(3.14); Land & Ten 231(8).

G. A. C. Leasing Corp.; Armstrong v., TexCivApp–Beaumont, 484 SW2d 811, appeal after remand 512 SW2d 708.—Acct Action on 12, 14.

Gadberry; Griffith v., TexCivApp–El Paso, 182 SW2d 739.—Alt of Inst 23, 27.1(1); App & E 1053(2); Usury 15, 115, 117.

Gadbois; Dartez v., TexCivApp–Hous (1 Dist), 541 SW2d 502.—App & E 172(2), 930(1), 989, 1170.10; Neglig 201, 387, 453, 504, 1677; Parent & C 7(9), 7(10); Trial 209, 278, 350.3(5), 351.2(10), 365.1(6), 366.

Gadd v. Lynch, TexCivApp–San Antonio, 258 SW2d 168, writ refused.—App & E 499(1), 499(3), 544(1); Child 11, 90.

Gaddis; Armstrong v., TexComApp, 144 SW2d 539, 135 Tex 580.—App & E 1083(5); Atty & C 80; Waters 153.

Gaddis; Armstrong v., TexCivApp–San Antonio, 214 SW2d 149.—Mand 23(1).

Gaddis; Armstrong v., TexCivApp–San Antonio, 122 SW2d 1115, aff 144 SW2d 539, 135 Tex 580.—App & E 843(2); Elect of Rem 3(1).

Gaddis v. Calgon Corp., CA5 (Tex), 506 F2d 880.—Pat 16(1), 16.17, 36.1(1), 36.2(1), 112.1, 234, 237, 238, 312(1.2), 312(4), 314(5), 325.11(5).

Gaddis v. Calgon Corp., CA5 (Tex), 449 F2d 1318.—Const Law 2473; Pat 288(3), 288(4), 324.57.

Gaddis v. Calgon Corp., NDTex, 325 FSupp 16, rev 449 F2d 1318.—Pat 288(4).

Gaddis v. Smith, Tex, 417 SW2d 577.—App & E 761; Health 819; Judgm 185(2); Lim of Act 1, 55(3), 100(1).

Gaddis v. Smith, TexCivApp–Amarillo, 407 SW2d 873, writ gr, rev 417 SW2d 577.—Lim of Act 95(13).

Gaddis v. State, TexCrimApp, 753 SW2d 396, on remand 1989 WL 28354, petition for discretionary review refused.—Crim Law 713, 720(6), 720(7.1), 1171.1(2.1).

Gaddis v. State, TexApp–Houston (1 Dist), 714 SW2d 458, petition for discretionary review gr, rev 753 SW2d 396, on remand 1989 WL 28354, petition for discretionary review refused.—Crim Law 713, 719(1), 1171.1(2.1), 1171.1(3).

Gaddis v. U.S., CA5 (Tex), 381 F3d 444.—Fed Civ Proc 2723; Fed Cts 776, 830; Infants 77, 78(1), 81, 83, 85; U S 147(13).

Gaddis v. U.S., CA5 (Tex), 70 FedAppx 190, reh gr, opinion vac 352 F3d 979, on reh 381 F3d 444.

Gaddison v. State, TexCrimApp, 90 SW2d 256.—Crim Law 1099.7(2).

Gaddy; C.I.R. v., CA5 (Tex), 344 F2d 460.—Int Rev 3118.

Gaddy; Gulf Ins. Co. v., TexComApp, 103 SW2d 141, 129 Tex 481.—Antitrust 583, 980; Insurance 1627.

Gaddy; Jefferson County Inv. & Bldg. Ass'n v., TexCivApp–Beaumont, 90 SW2d 295, writ refused.—Home 56, 112, 154.

Gaddy v. Texas Dept. of Public Safety, TexCivApp–Eastland, 380 SW2d 783.—Autos 144.2(5.1).

Gaddy; Zeek v., TexCivApp–Austin, 287 SW2d 490, ref nre.—App & E 231(3), 289, 1051(1); High 1, 6(1), 7(1).

Gadison v. Economy Mud Products Co., Inc., TexApp–Houston (14 Dist), 964 SW2d 652, reh overr, and review den, and reh of petition for review overr.—App & E 863, 919; Courts 32; Pretrial Proc 695; Work Comp 1087, 1116, 1123, 1148, 1908, 2084, 2088, 2093.

Gadison; U.S. v., CA5 (Tex), 8 F3d 186.—Consp 47(12), 48.1(4); Costs 302.3; Crim Law 371(1), 508(9), 562, 1139, 1158(1), 1159.4(1), 1159.4(6), 1169.1(1), 1169.11; Sent & Pun 672, 673, 675, 752, 764, 793, 976; Witn 41, 42.

Gadsden v. State, TexApp–El Paso, 915 SW2d 620.—Crim Law 795(1.5), 795(2.1), 795(2.5); Homic 607, 648, 1372, 1457, 1458; Ind & Inf 189(8).

Gadzooks, Inc., In re, BkrtcyNDTex, 352 BR 796.—Bankr 3024, 3030, 3154, 3160, 3171, 3183, 3622.

Gaebler v. Harris, TexCivApp–San Antonio, 625 SW2d 5, ref nre.—App & E 962; Pretrial Proc 581, 582, 583, 584.

Gaechter; City of Dallas v., TexCivApp–Dallas, 524 SW2d 400, dism.—Estop 62.1; Inj 46; Zoning 562, 779.1, 790.

Gaedcke Equipment Co.; Fidelity & Cas. Co. of New York v., TexApp–Houston (1 Dist), 716 SW2d 542, ref nre.—Work Comp 1072.

Gaede v. SK Investments, Inc., TexApp–Houston (14 Dist), 38 SW3d 753, review den.—Contracts 10(1), 29, 54(1); Judgm 181(19); Labor & Emp 35; Princ & A 9, 11, 29.5.

Gafas; Norris of Houston, Inc. v., TexCivApp–Hous (1 Dist), 562 SW2d 894, ref nre.—App & E 846(5), 954(1), 954(2), 1010.1(8.1), 1011.1(1); Contracts 116(1), 316(1); Equity 65(1), 65(2); Estop 54, 85; Evid 380; Inj 21, 138.39, 189.

GAF Bldg. Materials Corp.; Elk Corp. of Dallas v., CAFed (Tex), 168 F3d 28, reh den, in banc sug declined, cert den 120 SCt 178, 528 US 873, 145 LEd2d 150.—Pat 97, 324.54, 324.55(2).

GAF Building Materials Corp. v. Elk Corp. of Dallas, CAFed (Tex), 90 F3d 479.—Decl Judgm 62, 232, 233, 272, 324; Fed Cts 776.

GAF Chemical Corp.; Fine v., CA5 (Tex), 995 F2d 576, reh den.—Civil R 1516, 1549; Fed Civ Proc 2497.1.

GAF Corp. v. Bamber, TexApp–Beaumont, 29 SW3d 650, petition for review abated.—Alt Disp Res 151, 213(3); App & E 66; Contracts 143(2), 143.5, 156, 162, 176(2); Judgm 217.

GAF Corp. v. Caldwell, TexApp–Houston (14 Dist), 839 SW2d 149.—App & E 946; Mand 1, 4(1), 28, 32; Pretrial Proc 35; Witn 201(1).

GAF Corp. v. N. L. R. B., CA5 (Tex), 524 F2d 492.—Labor & Emp 982, 1191(1), 1195(7), 1219(13), 1660, 1866, 1871, 1880.

GAF Corp.; U.S. v., SDTex, 389 FSupp 1379.—Environ Law 165, 173, 183, 206, 634; Statut 220.

GAF Corporation-Chemical Group; Albonetti v., SDTex, 520 FSupp 825.—Rem of C 79(1), 82, 103, 107(7).

Gaffney; Bush v., TexCivApp–San Antonio, 84 SW2d 759. —App & E 1060.1(1); Corp 1.4(1), 1.6(2); Damag 87(1); Equity 65(1), 66, 423; Evid 213(4); Trial 350.2, 351.2(5), 352.1(3); Trusts 110, 374; Ven & Pur 123.

Gaffney v. State, TexCrimApp, 575 SW2d 537.—Const Law 699; Controlled Subs 2, 6, 68, 80, 97, 114; Crim Law 627.10(3), 791; Sent & Pun 1342.

Gaffney v. State, TexApp–Texarkana, 940 SW2d 682, reh overr, and petition for discretionary review refused.—Crim Law 620(7), 1036.1(1), 1137(5); Kidnap 15, 18, 36.

Gaffney v. State, TexApp–Texarkana, 937 SW2d 540, reh overr, and petition for discretionary review refused.—Crim Law 720(5), 724(1); Kidnap 27, 36; Witn 337(25).

Gaffney v. State, TexApp–Texarkana, 812 SW2d 439, petition for discretionary review refused.—App & E 842(1); Evid 35, 51; Extrad 34, 36, 39; Ind & Inf 3.

Gafford, Ex parte, TexCrimApp, 472 SW2d 118.—Extrad 36.

Gafford; Batto v., TexApp–Waco, 119 SW3d 346.—App & E 930(3), 1001(3); Evid 208(0.5), 265(7), 265(8); Fraud 12, 64(2); Plead 36(1).

Gafford; Desemo v., TexApp–Eastland, 692 SW2d 571, ref nre.—Const Law 2315; Health 811; Lim of Act 4(2), 74(1).

Gafford; Great Nat. Life Ins. Co. v., TexCivApp–Waco, 108 SW2d 917.—App & E 1062.1; Insurance 1635, 1636; Princ & A 99.

Gafney; Simms v., TexCivApp–Texarkana, 227 SW2d 848, ref nre.—Health 628, 822(3), 823(12).

Gaford v. Arnold, TexApp–Amarillo, 238 SW2d 225.—App & E 931(1), 1010.1(3), 1024.3; Evid 473, 474(15), 498.5, 503; Neglig 250; Plead 111.9, 111.42(2), 111.42(8); Tresp 1; Venue 8.5(3), 8.5(6).

Gage v. Boswell, NDTex, 717 FSupp 458. See Marriott Bros. v. Gage.

Gage; Brown v., TexCivApp–Fort Worth, 519 SW2d 190. —App & E 497(1); Pretrial Proc 724, 725, 726.

Gage; Container Port Services, Inc. v., TexApp–El Paso, 719 SW2d 662.—App & E 624, 628(1).

Gage v. Curtner, TexCivApp–Fort Worth, 215 SW2d 411, ref nre.—Courts 475(2); Life Est 12; Remaind 14, 16.

Gage v. Dallas Power & Light Co., TexCivApp–Dallas, 241 SW2d 196.—App & E 395; Courts 66.1; Em Dom 257; Judgm 341; New Tr 118.

Gage; Delta Enterprises v., TexCivApp–Fort Worth, 555 SW2d 555, ref nre.—Evid 384, 455; Trial 273; Usury 16, 32.

Gage; Green v., CA5 (Tex), 186 F2d 984.—Bankr 2051, 2058.1, 3066(1); Fed Civ Proc 1742(2); Fed Cts 247.

Gage v. Hollywood Overhead Door Co. of Fort Worth, TexCivApp–Fort Worth, 482 SW2d 406, ref nre.—Mech Liens 115(4).

Gage v. Langford, TexCivApp–Eastland, 615 SW2d 934, ref nre.—Antitrust 141; App & E 931(1), 989; Can of Inst 24(1); Contracts 98, 99(3); Mines 74(8); Plead 252(2), 267.

Gage v. Langford, TexCivApp–Eastland, 582 SW2d 203, ref nre, appeal after remand 615 SW2d 934, ref nre.—App & E 1064.1(6); Contracts 155, 176(2), 266(1); Estop 120; Mines 74(8), 74(9.1), 74(10).

GAGE;

See Guidelines for Arrangement at the beginning of this Volume

Gage; Livingston v., TexCivApp–El Paso, 581 SW2d 187, ref nre.—Abate & R 9; Courts 85(2), 85(3); Damag 91(1); Fraud 62; Plead 110; Set-Off 60; Venue 5.1.

Gage v. Lone Star Gas Co., TexCivApp–Austin, 278 SW2d 231, ref nre.—App & E 1015(5); New Tr 56, 143(2), 144, 157.

Gage; McMillan v., TexCivApp–Austin, 165 SW2d 754, writ refused wom.—Evid 222(1), 265(1), 265(2), 265(14), 265(18), 272, 313; Labor & Emp 2881; Trial 142.

Gage; Marriott Bros. v., CA5 (Tex), 911 F2d 1105, reh den.—Brib 1(1); Brok 100; Fed Civ Proc 1922, 1939; Postal 35(5); RICO 59; Tel 1014(3).

Gage; Marriott Bros. v., NDTex, 717 FSupp 458.—Banks 509.10; Brib 1(2); Fed Civ Proc 2533.1; Princ & A 14(3).

Gage; Marriott Bros. v., NDTex, 704 FSupp 731, opinion supplemented on denial of reconsideration 717 FSupp 458, aff 911 F2d 1105, reh den.—Brib 1(1), 1(2); Commerce 82.10; Fed Civ Proc 636; Fed Cts 18; Fraud 7; Postal 35(2), 35(6); RICO 10, 14, 16, 25, 35, 50, 62; Tel 1014(12).

Gage; Missouri-Kansas-Texas R. Co. v., TexCivApp–Fort Worth, 438 SW2d 879, ref nre.—App & E 959(3), 1052(5); Damag 221(2.1), 221(6); Evid 545, 546, 558(1); Plead 236(1), 240, 241, 245(3); Trial 192, 350.5(5), 350.6(4), 351.2(4).

Gage v. Owen, TexCivApp–Fort Worth, 435 SW2d 559, ref nre.—Deeds 90, 93, 95, 115, 119; Evid 390(3), 448, 460(5); Lim of Act 41.

Gage v. Owen, TexCivApp–Fort Worth, 396 SW2d 189, appeal after remand 435 SW2d 559, ref nre.—Judgm 185(2), 185.3(17), 186; Lim of Act 5(3), 195(3); Ref of Inst 41; Tresp to T T 35(2).

Gage; Pacific Emp. Ins. Co. v., TexCivApp–Fort Worth, 199 SW2d 537, ref nre.—App & E 662(3), 1002; Plead 34(1); Trial 114, 115(2), 121(3), 129, 142, 178, 350.3(8); Work Comp 52, 1339, 1382, 1683, 1920, 1926, 1927, 1968(8).

Gage v. Railroad Commission, Tex, 582 SW2d 410.—Mines 92.49, 92.50, 92.59(1); Pub Ut 168, 194.

Gage; Ray v., TexCivApp–Fort Worth, 269 SW2d 411, ref nre.—App & E 502(6), 1015(5), 1048(6), 1056.1(5), 1170.7; Autos 244(56); Costs 256(1), 257; Evid 118, 126(3); New Tr 140(3), 152, 157; Trial 46(2), 49; Witn 379(2), 388(2.1).

Gage; Saikowski v., TexCivApp–Fort Worth, 549 SW2d 781, ref nre.—Parties 51(4); Ven & Pur 330, 334(1).

Gage; Snidow v., TexCivApp–El Paso, 118 SW2d 910.—App & E 931(4), 1010.1(1); Plead 111.42(4).

Gage v. State, TexCrimApp, 387 SW2d 679.—Crim Law 393(1); False Pret 49(1); Sent & Pun 1276.

Gage v. State, TexCrimApp, 263 SW2d 553, 159 TexCrim 336.—Crim Law 366(3), 414, 730(8), 814(5), 829(3), 1137(3), 1171.3; Rape 59(14).

Gage v. State, TexCrimApp, 174 SW2d 491, 146 TexCrim 305.—Crim Law 1159.2(3); Homic 1174.

Gage v. State, TexCrimApp, 102 SW2d 216, 132 TexCrim 97.—Autos 355(6), 357; Crim Law 1156(2).

Gage v. Tom Fairey Co., TexApp–Dallas, 692 SW2d 127, ref nre.—App & E 422, 907(2); Judgm 585(2), 713(2), 720.

Gage; White v., CCA5 (Tex), 128 F2d 500.—Pat 17(2), 112.3(1), 168(2.1), 233.1.

Gage v. Wimberley, TexCivApp–Tyler, 476 SW2d 724, ref nre.—App & E 930(3), 1001(3); Contracts 253, 350(3); Release 57(1); Spec Perf 6, 73.

Gager v. Reeves, TexCivApp–Fort Worth, 235 SW2d 688, ref nre.—App & E 930(1); Consp 19.

Gage Van Horn & Associates, Inc. v. Tatom, TexApp–Eastland, 26 SW3d 730, review gr, and withdrawn, review den with per curiam opinion 87 SW3d 536.—Costs 194.12, 194.16, 194.18, 194.40, 198, 208; Statut 188, 190, 214.

Gagliardi; Tibbetts v., TexApp–Houston (14 Dist), 2 SW3d 659, reh overr, and petition for review den.—Costs 194.16, 207; Health 804.

Gagliardi v. Wood, TexCivApp–Hous (14 Dist), 556 SW2d 840, ref nre.—Evid 538; Health 821(5).

Gagliardo v. State, TexApp–Tyler, 78 SW3d 469, reh overr, and petition for discretionary review refused.—Const Law 2812; Crim Law 145.5, 146, 369.1, 374, 741(1), 742(1), 1030(2), 1038.1(3.1), 1134(2), 1144.13(2.1), 1144.13(5), 1144.13(6), 1159.2(1), 1159.2(2), 1159.2(7), 1159.2(9), 1159.3(2), 1159.4(1); Infants 20; Rape 2; Sod 6.

Gagne v. City of Galveston, CA5 (Tex), 805 F2d 558, cert den 107 SCt 3266, 483 US 1021, 97 LEd2d 764.—Civil R 1376(6).

Gagne v. City of Galveston, SDTex, 671 FSupp 1130, aff 851 F2d 359.—Civil R 1091, 1351(4), 1352(4), 1394; Fed Civ Proc 851; Fed Cts 18.

Gagne v. Sears, Roebuck and Co., TexApp–Waco, 201 SW3d 856, reh overr.—Neglig 1133.

Gagnier v. Wichelhaus, TexApp–Houston (1 Dist), 17 SW3d 739, reh overr, and review den.—Const Law 2314, 2315; Health 811; Judgm 181(7), 185(2), 185(5); Lim of Act 4(2), 55(3), 95(12), 199(1).

Gago v. Raines, TexCivApp–Galveston, 268 SW2d 724.—App & E 907(3); Divorce 168, 249.2; Hus & W 272(5).

Gahagan; Miller v., TexCivApp–Fort Worth, 316 SW2d 160.—App & E 281(1), 295; Lim of Act 46(1).

Gahagan v. Texas & P. Ry. Co., TexCivApp–Dallas, 231 SW2d 762, ref nre.—App & E 238(6), 387(5); Deeds 67, 144(1); Judgm 142; New Tr 0.5; Trusts 189, 191(2), 200(1).

Gahl v. State, TexApp–Dallas, 721 SW2d 888, petition for discretionary review refused.—Brib 1(1), 11; Crim Law 438.1; Ind & Inf 71.2(2), 71.4(10), 125(1), 125(19.1), 127, 129(1), 130.

Gahn; Jones v., SDTex, 246 FSupp2d 622.—Fed Civ Proc 1773, 1829, 1835; Fed Cts 266.1, 267, 269; Rem of C 21; U S 50.5(1), 127(2).

Gaia Technologies, Inc. v. Reconversion Technologies, Inc., CAFed (Tex), 93 F3d 774, reh and sug for reh den, am on reh in part 104 F3d 1296, appeal after remand 175 F3d 365, mandate withdrawn 104 F3d 1298.—Fed Cts 18, 776; Pat 183, 196.1, 286; Trademarks 1198, 1199, 1201(1), 1563.

Gaia Technologies Inc. v. Recycled Products Corp., CA5 (Tex), 175 F3d 365.—Antitrust 413, 414, 420; Damag 87(1); Fed Civ Proc 2117, 2219, 2242, 2342; Fed Cts 382.1, 383, 629, 759.1, 776, 937.1; Torts 213, 215, 242; Trademarks 1199, 1420.

Gailey; Headstream v., TexCivApp–Amarillo, 192 SW2d 795, ref nre.—Bound 25, 46(2).

Gailey v. State, TexApp–Houston (1 Dist), 671 SW2d 123, petition for discretionary review refused.—Crim Law 730(3), 1169.5(1).

Gailey; The State Bar v., TexApp–Houston (14 Dist), 889 SW2d 519, reh overr.—App & E 842(2), 989, 1008.1(2), 1012.1(4); Atty & C 44(2).

Gainan's Chevrolet City, Inc.; Gonzalez v., Tex, 690 SW2d 885.—Cons Cred 4, 19.

Gainan's Chevrolet City, Inc.; Gonzalez v., TexApp–Corpus Christi, 684 SW2d 740, writ gr, rev 690 SW2d 885.—Cons Cred 2, 4, 16; Sec Tran 64, 186, 221, 228.

Gainer v. Balcar, TexCivApp–Beaumont, 135 SW2d 1012.—Plead 111.40.

Gainer v. Johnson, TexCivApp–Galveston, 211 SW2d 789.—Wills 1, 118, 123(5), 155.1, 166(1).

Gainer v. State, TexCrimApp, 630 SW2d 277.—Crim Law 1069(6).

Gainer v. State, TexApp–Corpus Christi, 636 SW2d 15.—Crim Law 1068.5, 1071, 1193.

Gainer; U.S. v., CA5 (Tex), 169 FedAppx 841, cert den Flores-Serrano v. US, 127 SCt 119, 166 LEd2d 89.—

GAINES

Controlled Subs 81; Crim Law 1181.5(8); Sent & Pun 661.

Gaines, Ex parte, TexCrimApp, 455 SW2d 210.—Hab Corp 500.1.

Gaines v. Allstate Ins. Co., TexCivApp–Eastland, 353 SW2d 471, ref nre.—Work Comp 1709.

Gaines v. Bader, TexCivApp–San Antonio, 253 SW2d 1014.—Venue 8.5(6).

Gaines v. Baldwin, TexApp–Dallas, 629 SW2d 81.—Child C 512; Divorce 73; Judgm 217; New Tr 111; Parties 42.

Gaines; Beverly Enterprises, Inc. v., TexApp–Waco, 652 SW2d 600.—App & E 837(1), 999(2); Damag 134(1), 187.

Gaines; Brown v., TexCivApp–Galveston, 131 SW2d 801, writ refused.—Deeds 38(1), 38(4).

Gaines v. Copeland, TexCivApp–San Antonio, 209 SW2d 231.—App & E 1064.1(3); Autos 170(8), 246(22); Neglig 387.

Gaines v. CUNA Mut. Ins. Soc., CA5 (Tex), 681 F2d 982.—Fed Cts 915; Libel 34, 44(1), 44(3), 45(1), 45(2), 50.5, 51(4), 51(5), 101(4).

Gaines v. Davis, CA5 (Tex), 928 F2d 705, reh den.—Fed Civ Proc 1828; Fed Cts 594; Offic 114.

Gaines v. Dillard, TexCivApp–Fort Worth, 545 SW2d 845, ref nre.—Ven & Pur 130(2), 140, 141, 144(1), 334(5), 336, 341(3).

Gaines v. Frawley, TexApp–Fort Worth, 739 SW2d 950.—Wills 155.1, 166(12), 322, 400, 410.

Gaines v. Gaines, TexApp–Corpus Christi, 677 SW2d 727.—App & E 1043(1); Divorce 145; Judges 39, 51(2), 51(3), 51(4); Jury 10, 25(6).

Gaines; Gaines v., TexApp–Corpus Christi, 677 SW2d 727.—App & E 1043(1); Divorce 145; Judges 39, 51(2), 51(3), 51(4); Jury 10, 25(6).

Gaines v. Gaines, TexCivApp–Hous (1 Dist), 519 SW2d 694, ref nre.—Divorce 254(1), 261; Judgm 312, 855(1); Partners 76, 219(1).

Gaines; Gaines v., TexCivApp–Hous (1 Dist), 519 SW2d 694, ref nre.—Divorce 254(1), 261; Judgm 312, 855(1); Partners 76, 219(1).

Gaines v. Gaines, TexCivApp–Fort Worth, 119 SW2d 427.—App & E 1062.1; Contrib 6; Hus & W 80, 230, 239; Lim of Act 28(1).

Gaines; Gaines v., TexCivApp–Fort Worth, 119 SW2d 427.—App & E 1062.1; Contrib 6; Hus & W 80, 230, 239; Lim of Act 28(1).

Gaines v. Gaines, TexCivApp–San Antonio, 234 SW2d 250.—Divorce 72, 130.

Gaines; Gaines v., TexCivApp–San Antonio, 234 SW2d 250.—Divorce 72, 130.

Gaines v. Hamman, Tex, 358 SW2d 557, 163 Tex 618.—App & E 516; Judgm 178, 181(1), 185(2), 185(6), 185.2(8), 185.3(1); Trusts 103(1).

Gaines v. Hamman, TexCivApp–Fort Worth, 346 SW2d 186, writ gr, rev 358 SW2d 557, 163 Tex 618.—Frds St of 129(1); Trusts 17(3), 103(1).

Gaines; Hudson v., TexCivApp–Corpus Christi, 501 SW2d 734.—App & E 934(1), 1001(1), 1073(1); Dedi 12, 15, 31, 44; High 1, 7(1), 17; Judgm 199(3.7), 199(3.14); New Tr 72(6); Trial 139.1(6).

Gaines; Kelly v., TexApp–Waco, 181 SW3d 394, review gr.—Action 27(1); App & E 223, 241, 984(1), 1135; Contracts 34, 194; Costs 194.16; Damag 91.5(1); Fraud 3, 7, 59(2), 60, 61; Judgm 183, 185.3(5), 185.3(7), 186, 190; Mal Pros 67; Pretrial Proc 23, 44.1, 222, 406, 434, 716; Princ & A 48, 137(1); Witn 204(2).

Gaines; Klitgaard v., TexCivApp–Austin, 479 SW2d 765, ref nre.—Abate & R 40; Plead 293; Tax 2478, 2640, 2643, 2711.

Gaines v. Lee, TexCivApp–Waco, 175 SW2d 728, writ refused wom.—Equity 57; Estates 10(2); Ten in C 35, 38(1), 45; Trial 358.

Gaines; Mainline Inv. Corp. v., NDTex, 407 FSupp 423.—Contracts 190, 303(1), 322(3), 322(5); Costs 194.14, 194.32; Evid 18.

Gaines v. Martinez, NDTex, 353 FSupp 780.—Admin Law 741, 753; Evid 83(1); U S 82(4), 82(7).

Gaines; Mass Marketing, Inc. v., TexApp–San Antonio, 70 SW3d 261, review den.—App & E 930(1), 1001(1), 1001(3); Neglig 1001, 1089, 1670.

Gaines v. Shank, TexCivApp–Amarillo, 312 SW2d 268, ref nre.—Mun Corp 187(4).

Gaines v. State, TexCrimApp, 786 SW2d 295. See Arnold v. State.

Gaines v. State, TexCrimApp, 501 SW2d 315.—Crim Law 273.2(2); Ind & Inf 71.2(3), 71.2(4), 71.4(8); Larc 65.

Gaines v. State, TexCrimApp, 481 SW2d 835.—Crim Law 438(4), 633(1), 655(5), 1130(2), 1130(5); Witn 274(2), 345(1), 345(7).

Gaines v. State, TexCrimApp, 479 SW2d 678.—Crim Law 1036.1(1), 1115(2); Sent & Pun 34, 1483, 1800.

Gaines v. State, TexCrimApp, 468 SW2d 853.—Sent & Pun 2021, 2025.

Gaines v. State, TexCrimApp, 400 SW2d 925.—Crim Law 867; Homic 1154.

Gaines v. State, TexCrimApp, 361 SW2d 389, 172 TexCrim 577.—Ind & Inf 30.

Gaines v. State, TexCrimApp, 353 SW2d 34, 171 TexCrim 638.—Crim Law 1086.13.

Gaines v. State, TexCrimApp, 320 SW2d 157, 167 TexCrim 271.—Crim Law 787(1); Int Liq 236(20).

Gaines v. State, TexCrimApp, 301 SW2d 110, 164 TexCrim 516.—Bail 63.1; Crim Law 824(9), 881(3), 893, 1111(3); Ind & Inf 41(3); Int Liq 223(3), 236(20).

Gaines v. State, TexCrimApp, 281 SW2d 94, 161 TexCrim 589.—Crim Law 641.4(2).

Gaines v. State, TexCrimApp, 279 SW2d 96, 161 TexCrim 589, reh den 281 SW2d 94, 161 TexCrim 589.—Int Liq 248; Searches 126.

Gaines v. State, TexCrimApp, 274 SW2d 397.—Sent & Pun 1388.

Gaines v. State, TexCrimApp, 269 SW2d 680.—Ind & Inf 41(3).

Gaines v. State, TexCrimApp, 269 SW2d 679.—Ind & Inf 41(3).

Gaines v. State, TexCrimApp, 247 SW2d 253, 157 TexCrim 102.—Crim Law 394.4(2); Int Liq 138, 233(3).

Gaines v. State, TexCrimApp, 247 SW2d 251, 157 TexCrim 105.—Crim Law 741(2), 1169.2(1); Int Liq 138, 233(3), 247; Stip 14(10).

Gaines v. State, TexCrimApp, 244 SW2d 239.—Crim Law 1090.1(1).

Gaines v. State, TexCrimApp, 231 SW2d 429, 155 TexCrim 79.—Crim Law 369.6, 1131(1), 1184(4.1); Int Liq 224.

Gaines v. State, TexCrimApp, 176 SW2d 315, 146 TexCrim 496.—Crim Law 432, 1171.3.

Gaines v. State, TexApp–Houston (1 Dist), 874 SW2d 733.—Crim Law 366(5), 553, 742(1), 1159.2(7); Weap 17(4).

Gaines v. State, TexApp–San Antonio, 723 SW2d 302, petition for discretionary review gr, vac 761 SW2d 2, appeal after remand Arnold v. State, 786 SW2d 295, cert den 111 SCt 110, 498 US 838, 112 LEd2d 80.—Const Law 2371; Crim Law 790.

Gaines v. State, TexApp–Dallas, 811 SW2d 245, petition for discretionary review refused.—Crim Law 1090.12, 1134(5), 1158(3); Jury 33(5.15), 120, 121.

Gaines v. State, TexApp–Dallas, 789 SW2d 926.—Const Law 4659(2); Crim Law 338(4), 339.10(1), 339.10(6.1), 339.10(9), 339.10(10), 363, 365(2), 369.2(5), 369.2(6), 1030(1), 1043(2), 1045, 1169.1(5), 1169.11, 1177.

Gaines v. State, TexApp–Dallas, 710 SW2d 630, petition for discretionary review refused.—Crim Law 818, 819.

Gaines v. State, TexApp–El Paso, 888 SW2d 504.—Arrest 63.4(5), 63.4(11), 63.4(14), 63.5(3.1), 63.5(4), 63.5(6),

GAINES

59 Tex D 2d—160

See Guidelines for Arrangement at the beginning of this Volume

63.5(7), 63.5(9), 71.1(5); Autos 349.5(2); Crim Law 394.5(4), 394.6(5), 1134(6), 1134(10), 1158(4).

Gaines v. State, TexApp–Houston (14 Dist), 99 SW3d 660. —Arrest 63.4(1), 63.4(2), 63.4(16), 63.5(4), 63.5(5), 63.5(7), 63.5(8), 68(4); Crim Law 1026.10(4), 1081(2), 1224(1); Searches 70.

Gaines v. Texas Tech University, NDTex, 965 FSupp 886.—Fed Cts 265, 266.1, 269, 272; RICO 59, 64.

Gaines v. Traders & General Ins. Co., TexCivApp–Amarillo, 99 SW2d 984, writ dism.—App & E 843(1); Estop 54; Insurance 1641, 1642, 1844, 3475(8); Princ & A 166(1), 178(1); Work Comp 270, 1063, 1065, 1066.

Gaines; Universal Statuary Corp. v., CA5 (Tex), 310 F2d 647.—Copyr 87(4).

Gaines; University of Tex. v., TexCivApp–Austin, 359 SW2d 514, ref nre.—Wills 470(1), 601(5), 656.

Gaines; Weiss v., TexComApp, 81 SW2d 39, 125 Tex 106. —Brok 86(1); Lim of Act 49(2).

Gaines; Williams v., TexApp–Amarillo, 943 SW2d 185, reh overr, and writ den.—App & E 1178(6); Fraud 62; Frds St of 84.

Gaines Bros.; Polasek v., TexCivApp–San Antonio, 185 SW2d 609, writ refused.—App & E 930(1); Autos 171(5), 208, 243(17), 245(14), 245(44), 245(61), 245(80), 245(90).

Gaines Bldg., Inc.; Yeager Elec. & Plumbing Co., Inc. v., TexCivApp–Corpus Christi, 492 SW2d 921.—Mech Liens 16, 198; Mtg 151(3).

Gaines County v. Terry County, TexCivApp–El Paso, 152 SW2d 509, rev Yoakum County v. Gaines County, 163 SW2d 393, 139 Tex 442.—Counties 8, 47.

Gaines County; Yoakum County v., Tex, 163 SW2d 393, 139 Tex 442.—Counties 8, 57; Plead 214(1).

Gaines Motor Sales Co. v. Hastings Mfg. Co., TexCivApp–Fort Worth, 104 SW2d 548, writ dism.—Evid 419(1), 419(15), 432, 448; Sales 348(1), 354(9).

Gaines Towing and Transp., Inc. v. Atlantia Tanker Corp., CA5 (Tex), 191 F3d 633, appeal after remand 234 F3d 30.—Collision 133, 134; Damag 15, 18, 44; Ship 81(1), 86(3).

Gainesville Bus Lines; Foster v., TexCivApp–Fort Worth, 187 SW2d 144, dism.—App & E 1054(1); Evid 123(12), 222(2), 265(2), 320, 474(19); Plead 111.36, 111.42; Venue 8.5(5), 8.5(6).

Gainesville, City of; McKinney v., TexApp–Fort Worth, 814 SW2d 862.—Mun Corp 724, 725, 728, 742(6).

Gainesville, City of; Perry v., TexCivApp–Fort Worth, 267 SW2d 270, ref nre.—App & E 761, 846(5), 1073(1); Ease 30(1), 31; Judgm 346, 486(1); Waters 156(2), 156(9).

Gainesville Livestock Marketing; McMurtrey v., TexApp–Fort Worth, 682 SW2d 728.—Judgm 181(33).

Gainesville Memorial Hosp. v. Tomlinson, TexApp–Fort Worth, 48 SW3d 511, review den.—App & E 874(4), 893(1); Mun Corp 847, 854; States 79, 112(1).

Gainesville Nat. Bank; Brown v., TexCivApp–Fort Worth, 250 SW2d 616, writ refused.—App & E 994(3), 1008.1(4); Banks 130(1), 154(8); Carr 55; Nova 12; Sales 1(1).

Gainesville Nat. Bank in Gainesville; Fourth Nat. Bank v., CCA5 (Tex), 80 F2d 490, cert den 56 SCt 598, 297 US 720, 80 LEd 1004.—Lim of Act 13, 46(10).

Gainesville Nat. Bank in Gainesville, Tex.; Hartford Acc. & Indem. Co. v., CCA5 (Tex), 124 F2d 97.—Lim of Act 46(10); Princ & S 145(1).

Gainesville Nat. Bank of Gainesville; Etter's Welding, Inc. v., TexApp–Fort Worth, 687 SW2d 521.—App & E 66, 76(1), 79(1), 80(3).

Gainesville Oil & Gas Co., Inc. v. Farm Credit Bank of Texas, TexApp–Texarkana, 847 SW2d 655.—App & E 436, 907(3), 934(1); Judgm 181(25), 185.3(15); Mtg 379, 416, 533, 535(1).

Gainesville Oil & Gas Co., Inc. v. Farm Credit Bank of Texas, TexApp–Texarkana, 795 SW2d 826.—App & E 80(6); Judgm 183, 203, 284.

Gainesville, Tex., City of; Ratliff v., CA5 (Tex), 256 F3d 355, reh and reh den 273 F3d 1097.—Civil R 1539, 1545, 1551, 1556; Fed Civ Proc 1636.1, 2182.1; Fed Cts 823, 908.1, 909.

Gainous v. Gainous, TexApp–Houston (1 Dist), 219 SW3d 97.—App & E 846(5), 852, 893(1), 1010.1(1); Courts 24, 37(1), 37(2); Divorce 163, 169, 171, 184(5), 252.3(3), 252.3(4), 254(1), 254(2), 255, 261, 280, 286(2), 286(3.1); Estop 52(8); Judgm 7, 16, 470, 486(1), 501, 518, 524, 577(1); Marriage 65; Motions 61; Mun Corp 200(2).

Gainous; Gainous v., TexApp–Houston (1 Dist), 219 SW3d 97.—App & E 846(5), 852, 893(1), 1010.1(1); Courts 24, 37(1), 37(2); Divorce 163, 169, 171, 184(5), 252.3(3), 252.3(4), 254(1), 254(2), 255, 261, 280, 286(2), 286(3.1); Estop 52(8); Judgm 7, 16, 470, 486(1), 501, 518, 524, 577(1); Marriage 65; Motions 61; Mun Corp 200(2).

Gainous v. State, TexCrimApp, 436 SW2d 137.—Crim Law 641.13(2.1), 784(1), 1036.1(3.1), 1044.1(5.1).

Gains v. State, TexApp–Houston (14 Dist), 966 SW2d 838, petition for discretionary review refused.—Crim Law 1036.2, 1043(1), 1043(2), 1170.5(1); Witn 246(1).

Gainsco County Mutual Insurance Co. v. Martinez, TexApp–San Antonio, 27 SW3d 97, review gr, and dism by agreement.—App & E 842(11), 863, 901, 930(1), 930(3), 970(2), 994(1), 1001(1), 1002, 1003(3), 1003(5), 1003(6), 1013, 1026, 1050.1(4), 1056.1(5), 1140(8), 1169(4); Damag 134(2), 134(3), 185(1), 186, 187, 191, 221(7); Evid 532, 536, 542, 546; Trial 43, 143.

Gaiser; McKinney v., TexCivApp–Texarkana, 366 SW2d 268, ref nre.—Action 57(1); Deeds 211(1).

Gaitan; Cedillo v., TexApp–San Antonio, 981 SW2d 388. —App & E 863, 893(1), 895(1), 934(1), 1097(1), 1195(3), 1212(3); Lim of Act 44(4); Tax 2992, 3065.

Gaitan; Farias v., TexCivApp–San Antonio, 312 SW2d 273, ref nre.—App & E 1062.1, 1062.3, 1203(1); Autos 245(72); Trial 350.5(3), 354.

Gaitan; Lamb v., TexApp–Houston (14 Dist), 643 SW2d 498, rev Texas RealEstate Commission v. Lamb, 650 SW2d 66.—Brok 4.

Gaitan v. Reyes Salvatierra, TexCivApp–San Antonio, 485 SW2d 602.—App & E 989; Autos 172(7), 244(12); Judgm 199(3.7); Trial 142.

Gaitan v. State, TexApp–Houston (14 Dist), 905 SW2d 703, reh overr, and petition for discretionary review refused.—Crim Law 42, 419(1), 419(2), 429(1), 632(5), 639.3, 661, 1086.4, 1144.2, 1148, 1153(1); Dist & Pros Attys 3(1); Ind & Inf 137(1), 144.1(1), 144.2; Notaries 4.

Gaitan; U.S. v., CA5 (Tex), 171 F3d 222.—Costs 317; Crim Law 1026.10(4); Sent & Pun 934.

Gaitan; U.S. v., CA5 (Tex), 954 F2d 1005.—Crim Law 274(1), 274(7), 1134(3), 1139, 1158(1); Sent & Pun 1271.

Gaitan-Campanioni v. Thornburgh, EDTex, 777 FSupp 1355.—Hab Corp 688.

Gaither v. Davis, TexCivApp–Fort Worth, 582 SW2d 913, dism.—Libel 38(1), 38(4); Torts 122.

Gaither v. Gaither, TexCivApp–Fort Worth, 234 SW2d 135, ref nre.—Lim of Act 60(6), 199(1); Ref of Inst 19(1), 43, 45(7), 46.

Gaither; Gaither v., TexCivApp–Fort Worth, 234 SW2d 135, ref nre.—Lim of Act 60(6), 199(1); Ref of Inst 19(1), 43, 45(7), 46.

Gaither v. Moody, TexCivApp–Hous (14 Dist), 528 SW2d 875, ref nre.—Corp 307; Judgm 181(31), 185(2).

Gaither v. State, TexCrimApp, 479 SW2d 50.—Crim Law 224, 273.1(4), 1186.1; Extrad 42.

Gaither v. State, TexCrimApp, 244 SW2d 209, 156 TexCrim 503.—App & E 773(2).

Gaither v. State, TexCivApp–El Paso, 461 SW2d 245, ref nre.—Em Dom 219, 222(5); Trial 46(1), 194(20).

For Later Case History Information, see KeyCite on WESTLAW

Gaither; Whittington v., NDTex, 272 FSupp 507, rev State of Tex v. Whittington, 391 F2d 905.—Const Law 268(10), 3875, 4550, 4556, 4601, 4788, 4813, 4836; Crim Law 641.11, 641.13(1), 641.13(6); Hab Corp 253; Paupers 1.

Gaither; Yates v., TexApp–Dallas, 725 SW2d 529.—Courts 483; Mand 44.

Gaitonde; Knetsch v., TexApp–San Antonio, 898 SW2d 386.—App & E 181, 843(2), 934(1); Judgm 185.3(21).

Gaitz; Markman v., TexCivApp–Hous (1 Dist), 499 SW2d 692, ref nre.—App & E 93, 1140(6); Brok 43(2); Compromise 2, 21, 23(3); Damag 71, 91(1); Fraud 12, 61; Stip 9.

Gaitz v. Markman, TexCivApp–Hous (14 Dist), 482 SW2d 391.—App & E 79(1); Judgm 185.3(7).

Gajewski v. State, TexApp–Houston (14 Dist), 944 SW2d 450.—Arrest 63.5(4); Autos 335, 349(2.1); Crim Law 394.6(5), 1153(1).

Galacia v. Texas Emp. Ins. Ass'n, TexCivApp–Waco, 348 SW2d 417, ref nre.—Work Comp 1092, 1094, 1774, 1795, 1876, 1880.

Gala Homes, Inc. v. Board of Adjustment of City of Killeen, TexCivApp–Austin, 405 SW2d 165, ref nre.—Zoning 325, 440.1, 441.

Gala Homes, Inc. v. Fritz, TexCivApp–Waco, 393 SW2d 409, ref nre.—Contracts 170(1); Spec Perf 66, 99; Ven & Pur 3(4), 78.

Galan v. Luna, TexCivApp–San Antonio, 103 SW2d 844.—New Tr 56.

Galan v. State, TexCrimApp, 301 SW2d 141, 164 TexCrim 521.—Autos 355(6); Crim Law 787(1), 800(2), 814(1), 1043(2), 1173.2(5).

Galarza; Ochotorena v., TexCivApp–El Paso, 210 SW2d 473.—Child C 23.

Galarza; Union Bus Lines, Inc. v., CA5 (Tex), 369 F2d 402.—Fed Cts 289.

Galarza v. Union Bus Lines, Inc., SDTex, 38 FRD 401, aff 369 F2d 402.—Fed Civ Proc 131, 1951, 1970.1, 1973, 2195, 2343, 2371; Fed Cts 289; Hus & W 260, 265, 270(1), 270(5); Propty 5.5.

Galaviz v. Langdeau, TexCivApp–Austin, 352 SW2d 352.—App & E 237(1); Plead 236(3), 239(2), 356.

Galaway v. State, TexCrimApp, 354 SW2d 943, 172 TexCrim 147.—Crim Law 1094(2.1).

Galaxy Boat Mfg. Co. v. East End State Bank, TexApp–Houston (14 Dist), 641 SW2d 584.—Banks 139, 140(1), 140(3); Contracts 175(2); Cust & U 15(1).

Galaznik v. Galaznik, TexApp–San Antonio, 685 SW2d 379.—App & E 82(2), 934(1); Child S 241; Divorce 176, 179, 254(2); Fraud 12, 20, 50; Hus & W 278(1); Judgm 335(1), 335(3), 367, 375, 379(1); Plead 422; Trial 3(5.1).

Galaznik; Galaznik v., TexApp–San Antonio, 685 SW2d 379.—App & E 82(2), 934(1); Child S 241; Divorce 176, 179, 254(2); Fraud 12, 20, 50; Hus & W 278(1); Judgm 335(1), 335(3), 367, 375, 379(1); Plead 422; Trial 3(5.1).

Galberth; U.S. v., CA5 (Tex), 846 F2d 983, cert den 109 SCt 167, 488 US 865, 102 LEd2d 137.—Arrest 63.5(5); Crim Law 394.5(3), 412.2(2), 1158(2); Searches 180, 183, 198.

Galbraith; Ford Motor Credit Co. v., TexCivApp–Hous (1 Dist), 619 SW2d 2, ref nre.—Cons Cred 16; Judgm 185.3(2).

Galbraith v. Galbraith, TexCivApp–Texarkana, 619 SW2d 238.—App & E 970(4), 1071.1(5.1); Divorce 170; Evid 590; Marriage 59, 60(2), 60(7); New Tr 82; Plead 123; Trial 66, 367.

Galbraith; Galbraith v., TexCivApp–Texarkana, 619 SW2d 238.—App & E 970(4), 1071.1(5.1); Divorce 170; Evid 590; Marriage 59, 60(2), 60(7); New Tr 82; Plead 123; Trial 66, 367.

Galbreath; Allright, Inc. v., TexCivApp–Hous (14 Dist), 469 SW2d 810.—App & E 905; Judgm 17(1), 17(9), 335(3).

Galbreath; Campbell v., TexCivApp–Waco, 441 SW2d 297, writ dism.—Judgm 570(3); Venue 22(5), 32(1).

Galbreath; Lee v., TexCivApp–El Paso, 234 SW2d 91, ref nre.—App & E 1015(5), 1052(5); Autos 201(5); Damag 182; Evid 265(18); New Tr 143(1), 144; Trial 305, 321, 352.4(7), 355(1).

Galbreth; Dennis v., TexCivApp–Fort Worth, 228 SW2d 579.—App & E 833(3); Chat Mtg 282; Contracts 94(1), 97(1), 97(2), 98, 99(1); Damag 157(1); Fraud 61; Plead 396.

Galdi v. State, TexCrimApp, 141 SW2d 608, 139 TexCrim 488.—Crim Law 1182.

Gale; Davis v., Tex, 330 SW2d 610, 160 Tex 309.—App & E 1177(1); Evid 460(3); Mtg 48(1); Tresp to T T 38(2), 41(2); Trial 54(1).

Gale; Davis v., TexCivApp–Austin, 319 SW2d 144, rev 330 SW2d 610, 160 Tex 309.—Deeds 93; Mtg 48(1).

Gale; Hendes v., TexCivApp–San Antonio, 376 SW2d 922, ref nre.—Deeds 99, 110, 124(0.5); Lim of Act 60(6), 95(8); Ref of Inst 19(1).

Gale v. Spriggs, TexCivApp–Waco, 346 SW2d 620, ref nre.—App & E 230, 232(0.5), 1170.1; Damag 189; Evid 552; Pretrial Proc 19, 44.1; Princ & A 23(5); Trial 273.

Gale v. State, TexCrimApp, 998 SW2d 221.—Crim Law 1144.13(3), 1159.2(7), 1159.5; Sent & Pun 372, 373.

Gale v. State, TexCrimApp, 98 SW2d 195, 131 TexCrim 283.—Autos 355(8); Crim Law 1170.5(6); Witn 274(1).

Gale v. State, TexCrimApp, 84 SW2d 481.—Crim Law 1097(5).

Gale v. State, TexApp–Fort Worth, 747 SW2d 564.—Crim Law 31, 369.1, 369.2(1), 552(3), 556, 673(2), 784(1), 1169.11; Infants 13, 20.

Galen v. State, TexApp–Houston (14 Dist), 672 SW2d 235, petition for discretionary review refused.—Crim Law 1130(2); Obscen 17.

Galena Oaks Corp. v. Scofield, CA5 (Tex), 218 F2d 217.—Fed Cts 754.1, 848, 850.1, 853; Int Rev 3233, 3251.

Galena Oaks Corp. v. Scofield, SDTex, 116 FSupp 333, aff 218 F2d 217.—Int Rev 3143, 3231, 3251.

Galena Park Independent School Dist.; Alaniz v., TexApp–Houston (14 Dist), 833 SW2d 204.—App & E 934(1); Labor & Emp 26; Schools 63(1).

Galena Park Independent School Dist.; Cox v., TexApp–Corpus Christi, 895 SW2d 745.—App & E 852, 863, 934(1), 1010.1(2); Consp 1.1; Judgm 181(11), 185(1), 185(6); Plead 228.14, 228.23; Schools 62, 63(3), 89.2, 147.

Galena Park Independent School Dist.; Garza v., SDTex, 914 FSupp 1437.—Civil R 1067(1), 1067(3), 1376(5); Schools 89.11(1).

Galena Park Independent School Dist. v. Harris County Appraisal Dist., CA5 (Tex), 132 F3d 1095. See Deer Park Independent School Dist. v. Harris County Appraisal Dist.

Galen Hosp. Corp.; Payne v., Tex, 28 SW3d 15.—Work Comp 11, 597, 876, 946, 957, 2093, 2162.

Galen Hosp. Corp.; Payne v., TexApp–Houston (1 Dist), 4 SW3d 312, petition stricken, and review gr, aff 28 SW3d 15.—Work Comp 604, 616, 617, 957, 2084, 2093, 2094.

Galen Hosp. Corp., Inc.; Porterfield v., TexApp–San Antonio, 948 SW2d 916, writ den.—Damag 50.10; Judgm 181(21), 185.3(13), 189; Labor & Emp 810, 861, 863(2).

Gale Realtors v. Belisle, TexApp–Dallas, 694 SW2d 195. See Arthur P. Gale Realtors v. Belisle.

Galerie Barbizon, Inc. v. National Asset Placement Corp., TexApp–Houston (1 Dist), 16 SW3d 506.—App & E 428(2), 430(2).

Galerie D'Tile, Inc. v. Shinn, TexApp–Houston (14 Dist), 792 SW2d 792.—Compromise 18(1); Frds St of 144; Judgm 215.

Gale-Sobel, a Div. of Angelica Corp.; Davis Apparel v., TexApp–Eastland, 117 SW3d 15.—App & E 761,

1001(3), 1003(7); Lim of Act 46(6), 50(1), 51(2), 95(9), 182(2), 195(3), 197(1).

Galey; Boyett v., TexCivApp–Beaumont, 254 SW2d 807.—App & E 1041(2); Plead 111.3, 111.42(8).

Galiardi, In re, CA5 (Tex), 745 F2d 335.—Fed Civ Proc 2651.1, 2653; Fed Cts 145.

Galil Moving & Storage, Inc. v. McGregor, TexApp–San Antonio, 928 SW2d 172.—Cert 14; Courts 176.5, 247(2).

Galin Corp. v. MCI Telecommunications Corp., CA5 (Tex), 12 F3d 465, reh and reh den 16 F3d 1217, cert den 114 SCt 2743, 512 US 1237, 129 LEd2d 862.—Contracts 198(1), 206, 227; Evid 213(1), 448; Fed Civ Proc 2558; Release 30, 58(1).

Galindo, Ex parte, TexCrimApp, 338 SW2d 954, 170 TexCrim 64.—Hab Corp 729, 823.

Galindo v. Alexander, TexCivApp–San Antonio, 248 SW2d 171, ref nre.—Adv Poss 50, 60(2), 60(4), 85(3).

Galindo; Commercial Standard Fire & Marine Co. v., TexCivApp–El Paso, 484 SW2d 635, ref nre.—Aliens 121, 133; Const Law 3013; Contracts 103; Work Comp 256.

Galindo v. Dean, TexApp–Eastland, 69 SW3d 623.—Afft 3, 17; App & E 837(10), 856(1), 934(1); Death 39; Health 766, 804; Judgm 181(6), 183, 185(2); Statut 188.

Galindo v. Garcia, Tex, 199 SW2d 499, 145 Tex 507.—App & E 692(1); Wills 38(2), 324(2).

Galindo; Garcia v., TexCivApp–San Antonio, 336 SW2d 459, writ dism by agreement.—Estop 68(2); Inj 138.31.

Galindo; Garcia v., TexCivApp–San Antonio, 329 SW2d 95, writ refused.—Ease 61(6).

Galindo v. Garcia, TexCivApp–San Antonio, 222 SW2d 477.—Courts 247(7); Plead 111.38; Venue 5.4.

Galindo; Garcia v., TexCivApp–San Antonio, 199 SW2d 488, rev 199 SW2d 499, 145 Tex 507.—App & E 930(1), 1175(5); Evid 594; Trial 139.1(8); Wills 31, 32, 38(1), 52(1), 53(2), 55(3), 324(2).

Galindo; Garcia v., TexCivApp–San Antonio, 189 SW2d 12, writ refused wom.—Hus & W 221; Wills 21, 55(10); Witn 139(1), 140(9), 146.

Galindo v. Johnson, WDTex, 19 FSupp2d 697.—Crim Law 1426(2); Fed Civ Proc 657.5(3); Hab Corp 201, 311, 603; Statut 181(1), 188, 239.

Galindo; Luciano v., CA5 (Tex), 944 F2d 261.—Civil R 1093, 1420; Fed Civ Proc 2734; Prisons 13(1).

Galindo v. Old Republic Insurance Co., TexApp–El Paso, 146 SW3d 755, review den.—App & E 863; Judgm 178, 183, 185(5); Work Comp 891, 1688.

Galindo v. Precision American Corp., CA5 (Tex), 754 F2d 1212, reh den 762 F2d 1004.—Bailm 9; Fed Civ Proc 2470, 2470.4, 2471, 2515, 2539, 2543, 2544, 2545; Fed Cts 390, 785, 935.1; Prod Liab 23.1, 47.

Galindo v. State, TexCrimApp, 267 SW2d 552.—Crim Law 1090.1(1).

Galindo v. State, TexCrimApp, 89 SW2d 990, 129 TexCrim 532.—Perj 24, 29(2), 33(1).

Galindo v. State, TexCivApp–Corpus Christi, 535 SW2d 923.—App & E 930(3), 989; Atty & C 34, 38, 46, 48, 53(2), 58; Const Law 3879, 3881, 3912, 4273(3); Jury 31.2(4).

Galindo v. U.S. Dept. of Justice, CA5 (Tex), 153 FedAppx 333.—Lim of Act 104.5.

Galitz v. State, TexCrimApp, 617 SW2d 949.—Arrest 63.5(7); Courts 17; Crim Law 1004, 1026.10(2.1), 1026.10(4), 1072; Searches 69, 184.

Gall v. City of Vidor, Tex., EDTex, 903 FSupp 1062.—Anim 107; Civil R 1304, 1315, 1318, 1321, 1376(1), 1376(2); Const Law 3911, 4311; Fed Cts 411; Searches 79.

Gall v. U.S., CA5 (Tex), 521 F2d 878, reh den 524 F2d 1232, cert den 96 SCt 2170, 425 US 972, 48 LEd2d 796.—Int Rev 4206.20.

Gallager v. State, TexCrimApp, 97 SW2d 954, 131 TexCrim 254.—Infants 20.

Gallagher, Ex parte, TexApp–Houston (1 Dist), 814 SW2d 839. See Andrews, Ex parte.

Gallagher, In re, BkrtcySDTex, 70 BR 288.—Bankr 3009, 3312.

Gallagher; Aetna Life Ins. Co. v., TexComApp, 94 SW2d 410, 127 Tex 553.—App & E 1175(1); Courts 247(7); Mand 57(1).

Gallagher; Apel v., TexCivApp–Amarillo, 278 SW2d 527, ref nre.—Estop 78(3); Frds St of 130(2); Trusts 17(3), 44(1); Wills 421, 722, 742; Witn 144(4), 146.

Gallagher v. Balasco, TexApp–Houston (1 Dist), 789 SW2d 618, writ den.—App & E 766, 768; Evid 51.

Gallagher v. City of Brownsville, TexCivApp–Corpus Christi, 429 SW2d 663, ref nre.—Judgm 183, 185.3(17), 186; Plead 34(1).

Gallagher v. Die, TexCivApp–Waco, 260 SW2d 128.—Child C 42, 63, 468, 510, 921(1); Divorce 62(6), 124.3, 184(4), 184(10).

Gallagher v. Fire Ins. Exchange, Tex, 950 SW2d 370, on remand 980 SW2d 833, review den.—App & E 654.

Gallagher v. Fire Ins. Exchange, TexApp–San Antonio, 980 SW2d 833, review den.—App & E 163, 230, 231(9), 232(3), 946, 969, 1067; Insurance 3579; Trial 350.4(3).

Gallagher v. Fire Ins. Exchange, TexApp–San Antonio, 950 SW2d 379, writ gr, rev 950 SW2d 370, on remand 980 SW2d 833, review den.—App & E 557, 638.

Gallagher; Flournoy v., TexCivApp–Eastland, 189 SW2d 108.—Sec Reg 253, 260, 293, 298.

Gallagher v. Gallagher, TexCivApp–San Antonio, 153 SW2d 541, dism.—Plead 111.8, 111.36, 111.46; Venue 2.

Gallagher; Gallagher v., TexCivApp–San Antonio, 153 SW2d 541, dism.—Plead 111.8, 111.36, 111.46; Venue 2.

Gallagher v. Joyce, TexCivApp–Corpus Christi, 459 SW2d 221, ref nre.—Jury 26.

Gallagher; Lowry v., TexCivApp, 190 SW2d 165, writ refused wom.—Ex & Ad 7; Trusts 262; Wills 681(2), 683.

Gallagher v. McClure Bintliff, TexApp–Austin, 740 SW2d 118, writ den.—Corp 1.4(1); Lim of Act 16, 31, 55(4).

Gallagher; Mecom v., TexCivApp–El Paso, 213 SW2d 304.—Land & Ten 92(4).

Gallagher; Mecom v., TexCivApp–Waco, 192 SW2d 804, ref nre.—Plead 49; Venue 5.3(1), 5.3(6), 5.3(8).

Gallagher v. O'Brien, TexCivApp–San Antonio, 158 SW2d 345.—Courts 475(2); Partit 46.1; Wills 478, 751, 822.

Gallagher v. Schlundt, TexCivApp–San Antonio, 452 SW2d 529, writ refused.—App & E 624, 627, 627.2, 627.3; New Tr 155.

Gallagher; Scott v., TexApp–Houston (1 Dist), 209 SW3d 262, reh overr.—App & E 893(1); Convicts 6; Courts 4, 37(2); Venue 1.5, 17.

Gallagher; Southern Underwriters v., Tex, 136 SW2d 590, 135 Tex 41.—Work Comp 51, 74, 78, 80, 1341, 1424, 1971.

Gallagher; Southern Underwriters v., TexCivApp–Eastland, 116 SW2d 450, rev 136 SW2d 590, 135 Tex 41.—Trial 140(2), 350.3(8); Work Comp 52, 81, 1424, 1975.

Gallagher v. State, TexCrimApp, 690 SW2d 587.—Const Law 588, 591, 592, 593, 2355; Courts 40, 472.1; Crim Law 93, 1033.1; Judges 11(4).

Gallagher v. State, TexCrimApp, 159 SW2d 508, 143 TexCrim 545.—Crim Law 761(9), 806(2), 806(3), 1134(3), 1170.5(3), 1172.7, 1172.8; Homic 1193, 1484.

Gallagher v. State, TexCrimApp, 151 SW2d 819, 142 TexCrim 133.—Crim Law 1091(2), 1115(2); Ind & Inf 114; Int Liq 205(2), 223(1); Searches 126; Sent & Pun 1250, 1260, 1367.

Gallagher v. State, TexCrimApp, 138 SW2d 815, 139 TexCrim 2.—Crim Law 1090.16; Int Liq 238(5).

Gallagher v. State, TexApp–Houston (1 Dist), 778 SW2d 153.—Arrest 63.1, 63.3, 63.4(13), 63.4(15); Chem Dep 4.1.

Gallagher v. Unenrolled Motor Vessel River Queen (Hull No. A-681 84), CA5 (Tex), 475 F2d 117.—Adm 8; Fact 63.

Gallagher; U.S. v., NDTex, 714 FSupp 811.—Arrest 63.4(1), 63.5(4), 63.5(5), 68(4); Crim Law 394.1(3).

Gallagher Co. v. White, TexApp–Houston (14 Dist, 709 SW2d 379. See R.J. Gallagher Co. v. White.

Gallaher v. American-Amicable Life Ins. Co., TexCivApp–Waco, 462 SW2d 626, ref nre.—Interpl 11; Lim of Act 165, 167(1), 173.

Gallaher; Austin v., TexCivApp–San Antonio, 417 SW2d 363, writ dism.—App & E 846(5), 931(3), 989, 1010.1(3); Estop 52(7); Evid 265(10); New Tr 99, 102(1), 102(3); Parent & C 12; Princ & A 99; Sales 52(5.1); Trial 139.1(2), 382.

Gallaher v. City Transp. Co. of Dallas, TexCivApp–El Paso, 262 SW2d 807, writ refused.—App & E 66, 79(2); Judgm 217.

Galland's Estate v. Rosenberg, TexApp–Houston (14 Dist), 630 SW2d 294, ref nre.—Contracts 99(1); Insurance 1806; Judgm 185(2), 185.2(1), 185.2(4), 185.3(12), 189.

Gallant; Morrow v., TexCivApp–Austin, 312 SW2d 526.—Hab Corp 814.

Gallardo; Employers Mut. Liability Ins. Co. of Wis. v., TexCivApp–Waco, 359 SW2d 933, ref nre.—Work Comp 51, 840, 1639.

Gallardo; Gebhardt v., TexApp–San Antonio, 891 SW2d 327.—Abate & R 8(2); Action 60; Mand 3(3), 4(1), 4(4), 26, 28, 32; Pretrial Proc 534; Witn 293.5, 305(1), 307, 309.

Gallardo; Salazar v., TexApp–Corpus Christi, 57 SW3d 629, reh overr.—App & E 863, 920(3), 954(1); Inj 114(3), 138.1, 138.3, 138.18, 138.46, 192; Schools 57, 118.

Gallardo v. State, TexCrimApp, 321 SW2d 581, 167 TexCrim 511.—Mal Mis 5.

Gallardo v. State, TexApp–San Antonio, 809 SW2d 540, petition for discretionary review gr, vac 849 SW2d 825.—Sent & Pun 313; Statut 212.6, 230.

Gallardo v. State, TexApp–San Antonio, 768 SW2d 875, petition for discretionary review refused.—Crim Law 145.5, 146, 147.

Gallardo v. State, TexApp–San Antonio, 700 SW2d 727.—Crim Law 1099.6(2.1).

Gallardo v. Ugarte, TexApp–El Paso, 145 SW3d 272, reh overr, and review den.—App & E 2, 185(1), 945, 946, 1079; Health 804, 809.

Gallardo; U.S. v., CA5 (Tex), 915 F2d 149, reh den, cert den 111 SCt 707, 498 US 1038, 112 LEd2d 696, reh den 111 SCt 1125, 113 LEd2d 232, denial of habeas corpus aff In re Gallardo, 166 F3d 1205.—Const Law 4711; Crim Law 29(12); Double J 148.

Gallardo-Trapero; U.S. v., CA5 (Tex), 185 F3d 307, reh den, cert den Hernandez v. US, 120 SCt 961, 528 US 1127, 145 LEd2d 834.—Consp 28(3), 40.1, 43(12), 47(12), 48.1(1); Crim Law 713, 717, 719(1), 719(3), 720(5), 720(6), 726, 730(8), 753.2(3.1), 1030(1), 1037.1(1), 1037.1(2), 1130(0.5), 1139, 1144.13(3), 1144.13(5), 1144.15, 1158(1), 1159.2(7), 1159.2(8), 1159.2(10), 1171.1(2.1), 1171.1(3), 1171.3; Sent & Pun 670, 764, 996.

Gallas v. Car Biz, Inc., TexApp–Dallas, 914 SW2d 592, writ den.—App & E 901; Autos 20; Judgm 199(3.5).

Gallaspy v. Raytheon Technical Services Co., CA5 (Tex), 211 FedAppx 269.—Civil R 1137.

Gallaway v. Sheppard, TexCivApp–Austin, 89 SW2d 417, writ dism.—States 78, 140, 193, 209.

Gallaway; U.S. v., EDTex, 199 FSupp2d 605.—Const Law 4728; Jury 34(1); Sent & Pun 322.

Gallegos, Ex parte, TexCrimApp, 511 SW2d 510.—Crim Law 641.13(1), 641.13(5).

Gallegos; Arana v., TexCivApp–San Antonio, 284 SW2d 958.—App & E 213, 731(5), 761; New Tr 152.

Gallegos; Arana v., TexCivApp–San Antonio, 279 SW2d 491.—New Tr 117(2), 152, 155.

Gallegos v. Clegg, TexCivApp–Corpus Christi, 417 SW2d 347, ref nre.—Autos 226(1), 227.5; Damag 96, 104, 119, 185(1); Guard & W 10; Infants 70, 78(1), 81.

Gallegos v. Equity Title Co. of America, Inc., WDTex, 484 FSupp2d 589.—Fed Civ Proc 2498; Labor & Emp 2257, 2370, 2371, 2385(6), 2390(3), 2390(4), 2397(2); Lim of Act 121(2); U S Mag 26, 27, 29.

Gallegos v. Escalon, TexApp–Corpus Christi, 993 SW2d 422.—Libel 34, 36, 38(1), 50.

Gallegos v. Escalon, TexApp–Corpus Christi, 918 SW2d 62, reh overr.—Judgm 181(33), 185.1(2), 185.1(4), 185.2(5); Schools 63(3).

Gallegos v. Gallegos, TexApp–San Antonio, 788 SW2d 158.—Divorce 252.3(4), 253(4).

Gallegos; Gallegos v., TexApp–San Antonio, 788 SW2d 158.—Divorce 252.3(4), 253(4).

Gallegos v. Gulf Coast Inv. Corp., Tex, 491 SW2d 659.—App & E 1175(1).

Gallegos v. Gulf Coast Inv. Corp., TexCivApp–Hous (1 Dist), 483 SW2d 944, writ gr, set aside 491 SW2d 659.—App & E 927(1), 1058(1); Bills & N 146, 343, 452(3), 452(4); Contracts 86, 94(5); Evid 381; Judgm 252(5); Plead 339, 420(2).

Gallegos v. Millers Mut. Fire Ins. Co. of Texas, TexCivApp–El Paso, 550 SW2d 350.—Insurance 1952; Judgm 185(2); Plead 409(1); Work Comp 1069.

Gallegos v. State, TexCrimApp, 635 SW2d 527.—Crim Law 452(1); Ind & Inf 10.2(11); Larc 40(5).

Gallegos v. State, TexCrimApp, 548 SW2d 50.—Assault 96(1); Ind & Inf 189(2).

Gallegos v. State, TexCrimApp, 425 SW2d 648.—Crim Law 264, 273.1(5), 577.1, 641.4(2), 641.9.

Gallegos v. State, TexCrimApp, 295 SW2d 907, 164 TexCrim 23.—Autos 356; Witn 270(2).

Gallegos v. State, TexCrimApp, 252 SW2d 162.—Crim Law 1087.1(2).

Gallegos v. State, TexCrimApp, 215 SW2d 344, 152 TexCrim 508.—Crim Law 622.2(10), 683(2), 720(1), 789(1), 800(1), 800(6), 829(4); Homic 959, 1489.

Gallegos v. State, TexApp–Houston (1 Dist), 828 SW2d 577.—Bail 97(1), 97(4); Crim Law 32, 33, 36.6.

Gallegos v. State, TexApp–Houston (1 Dist), 776 SW2d 312, mandamus den 1991 WL 22346.—Controlled Subs 26, 80; Crim Law 404.20, 404.30, 404.60.

Gallegos v. State, TexApp–Houston (1 Dist), 754 SW2d 485.—Crim Law 641.1, 641.10(1), 641.10(2), 641.13(2.1), 641.13(5), 641.13(6), 641.13(7), 1086.13; Pardon 64.1.

Gallegos v. State, TexApp–San Antonio, 971 SW2d 626, petition for discretionary review refused.—Sent & Pun 2010.

Gallegos; State v., TexApp–San Antonio, 840 SW2d 775.—Child 64.

Gallegos v. State, TexApp–San Antonio, 783 SW2d 327, petition for discretionary review refused.—Crim Law 273.4(1), 1032(5), 1044.1(2).

Gallegos v. State, TexApp–San Antonio, 756 SW2d 45, petition for discretionary review refused.—Crim Law 641.13(1), 641.13(7), 1035(10); Ind & Inf 176; Sent & Pun 354.

Gallegos v. State, TexApp–San Antonio, 715 SW2d 139, petition for discretionary review refused.—Assault 96(7); Crim Law 519(1), 520(2), 795(2.10); Homic 1177; Ind & Inf 189(8).

Gallegos v. State, TexApp–Dallas, 76 SW3d 224, petition for discretionary review refused.—Const Law 4723; Crim Law 796, 959, 1130(2), 1130(5); Homic 1134, 1135, 1181.

Gallegos v. State, TexApp–Dallas, 711 SW2d 300.—Ind & Inf 110(3); Rape 20; Witn 388(10).

Gallegos v. State, TexApp–Amarillo, 625 SW2d 812, rev 635 SW2d 527.—Larc 60, 62(2).

Gallegos v. State, TexApp–Corpus Christi, 918 SW2d 50, petition for discretionary review refused.—Assault 92(5); Crim Law 713, 720(7.1), 728(1), 728(5), 730(1),

GALLEGOS

730(12), 867, 1037.1(1), 1134(2), 1144.13(2.1), 1159.2(7), 1159.6, 1171.1(2.1); Infants 20.

Gallegos; Texas Emp. Ins. Ass'n v., TexCivApp–San Antonio, 415 SW2d 708.—Trial 350.1, 352.1(1); Work Comp 618, 1504, 1548, 1927.

Gallegos v. Truck Ins. Exchange, TexCivApp–San Antonio, 546 SW2d 667, ref nre.—Work Comp 876, 1375, 1665.

Gallegos v. Truck Ins. Exchange, TexCivApp–San Antonio, 539 SW2d 353.—App & E 628(1).

Gallegos; U.S. v., CA5 (Tex), 868 F2d 711.—Crim Law 1158(1); Sent & Pun 764, 800.

Gallegos; U.S. v., CA5 (Tex), 161 FedAppx 375, cert den Caballero-Martinez v. US, 126 SCt 2289, 164 LEd2d 817.—Controlled Subs 6; Crim Law 273.1(2), 1031(4), 1134(3), 1181.5(8).

Gallegos-Garcia v. Casillas, SDTex, 771 FSupp 186.—Admin Law 669.1; Aliens 390.

Galler; Williams v., TexCivApp–San Antonio, 540 SW2d 463.—App & E 207, 290, 1004(8); Damag 191.

Gallerano; Goodman v., TexApp–Dallas, 695 SW2d 286.—Judgm 181(33), 185(6); Libel 36, 50, 51(1).

Galleria Area Ford, Inc.; Brown v., Tex, 752 SW2d 114.—Antitrust 135(1), 367, 369.

Galleria Area Ford, Inc. v. Brown, TexApp–Houston (14 Dist), 748 SW2d 239, writ gr, rev 752 SW2d 114.—Antitrust 291; App & E 930(3), 989, 1177(7).

Galleria Bank v. Southwest Properties, Inc., TexCivApp–Hous (1 Dist), 498 SW2d 5.—Corp 517; Plead 111.3, 111.42(6); Venue 2, 22(4), 22(10).

Gallery Datsun, Inc. v. Metcalf, TexApp–Houston (1 Dist), 630 SW2d 853.—Antitrust 359; App & E 554(1), 907(5).

Gallery Model Homes, Inc.; Burgess v., TexApp–Houston (1 Dist), 101 SW3d 550, reh overr, and review den.—Admin Law 228.1, 229, 417; App & E 893(1), 916(1); Courts 4, 35; Judgm 181(6); Plead 104(1), 111.36; Tax 3635, 3703, 3704.

Galley v. Apollo Associated Services, Ltd., TexApp–Houston (1 Dist), 177 SW3d 523.—App & E 23, 76(1), 79(1); Corp 308(1), 445.1, 590(1); Estop 68(2); Partners 353.

Galley v. Hedrick, TexCivApp–Amarillo, 127 SW2d 978.—App & E 846(5), 907(3); Courts 39, 163; Inj 118(2); Judgm 16; Land & Ten 127.

Gallia v. Schreiber, TexApp–Houston (1 Dist), 907 SW2d 864.—App & E 66, 70(8), 934(1); Evid 571(3), 574; Judgm 181(2), 181(6); Mun Corp 747(3), 753(1); Offic 114, 119.

Gallia v. State, TexCrimApp, 91 SW2d 737.—Crim Law 1182.

Gallien; City of Beaumont v., TexApp–Beaumont, 949 SW2d 57, review den.—App & E 173(1); Mun Corp 747(3); Offic 119.

Gallien v. State, TexCrimApp, 301 SW2d 674, 164 TexCrim 622.—Crim Law 913(1), 1090.16.

Gallien v. Washington Mut. Home Loans, Inc., TexApp–Texarkana, 209 SW3d 856.—App & E 66, 79(1), 80(1), 80(6); Courts 78; Judgm 181(11); Plead 34(1), 228.23, 356.

Galliford v. State, TexApp–Houston (1 Dist), 101 SW3d 600, petition for discretionary review refused.—Crim Law 1026.10(2.1), 1081(2), 1147, 1149, 1167(1); Ind & Inf 60, 71.2(3), 110(3); Obscen 11.

Galliher, In Interest of, TexCivApp–Beaumont, 546 SW2d 665.—App & E 907(3), 1008.1(2); Guard & W 10.

Gallimore v. Missouri Pac. R. Co., CA5 (Tex), 635 F2d 1165.—Fed Civ Proc 2214, 2217, 2372.1, 2606; Fed Cts 596, 660.35; Judges 24.

Gallini v. Whelan, TexApp–San Antonio, 625 SW2d 755.—Acct Action on 3; App & E 846(5), 912, 989; Corp 503(1); Judgm 185(2), 185(6), 185.3(3); Plead 111.42(6).

Gallman; Transport Co. of Tex. v., TexCivApp–San Antonio, 186 SW2d 1003.—App & E 1010.1(1); Evid 265(10); Venue 8.5(3).

Gallo, In re, BkrtcyNDTex, 49 BR 28.—Bankr 2766, 2769, 2780.

Gallo; Central Motor Co. v., TexCivApp–Waco, 94 SW2d 821.—App & E 1069.1; Labor & Emp 3046(1), 3049(1), 3056(2); Trial 315.

Gallo; Fox v., TexCivApp–Amarillo, 428 SW2d 127, ref nre.—Anim 25; Cust & U 15(1), 16; Evid 458.

Gallo; U.S. v., CA5 (Tex), 927 F2d 815.—Autos 349.5(3); Consp 24(1), 24.5, 47(2), 47(12); Controlled Subs 45, 81; Crim Law 59(5), 394.4(3), 1134(3), 1144.13(2.1), 1158(1); Searches 58, 66; Sent & Pun 771; U S 34.

Gallogly, Ex parte, TexCrimApp, 137 SW2d 776, 138 TexCrim 585.—Extrad 34.

Gallogly, Ex parte, TexCrimApp, 134 SW2d 666, 138 TexCrim 115.—Hab Corp 822; Judgm 815.

Gallop, Ex parte, TexCivApp–Beaumont, 486 SW2d 836, ref nre.—App & E 756; Child C 76, 400, 922(1); Infants 155, 231, 232, 246.

Gallop v. Seagoville Investments, Inc., TexCivApp–Dallas, 417 SW2d 727, ref nre.—App & E 837(11); Judgm 181(30), 185(2), 186; Princ & A 121, 123(2).

Gallow v. Autozone, Inc., SDTex, 952 FSupp 441.—Civil R 1122, 1137, 1535, 1555; Fed Civ Proc 2539.

Gallow v. State, TexApp–Houston (14 Dist), 56 SW3d 117.—Double J 134, 135, 146.

Galloway; Associates Inv. Co. v., TexCivApp–Amarillo, 403 SW2d 542.—Autos 20.

Galloway v. Beto, CA5 (Tex), 421 F2d 284, cert den 91 SCt 137, 400 US 912, 27 LEd2d 151.—Courts 100(1); Crim Law 290, 292(1), 867; Double J 96, 98; Fed Cts 404; Homic 538, 1136.

Galloway v. Beto, NDTex, 296 FSupp 230, aff 421 F2d 284, cert den 91 SCt 137, 400 US 912, 27 LEd2d 151.—Const Law 4563; Crim Law 867; Double J 6, 150(1); Hab Corp 745.1.

Galloway v. Galloway, TexCivApp–Dallas, 236 SW2d 832.—App & E 1177(7); Home 32, 70, 134; Partit 12(3).

Galloway; Galloway v., TexCivApp–Dallas, 236 SW2d 832.—App & E 1177(7); Home 32, 70, 134; Partit 12(3).

Galloway; Gomez v., SDTex, 428 FSupp 358.—Fed Cts 995.

Galloway; Hugh Wood Ford, Inc. v., TexApp–Houston (14 Dist), 830 SW2d 296, reh den, and writ den.—Antitrust 369; Costs 194.18; Evid 186(1).

Galloway; Johnson v., TexCivApp–Austin, 277 SW2d 127.—App & E 781(4); Child C 850, 902; Venue 15.

Galloway v. Matagorda County, Tex., SDTex, 35 FSupp2d 952.—Civil R 1183, 1185, 1189, 1244, 1252, 1528, 1532.

Galloway v. Moeser, TexCivApp–Eastland, 82 SW2d 1067.—Appear 19(1); Evid 185(1); Home 57(1), 57(3); Judgm 252(3); Mtg 131, 480; Partners 142(1), 213(1), 213(2); Plead 312.

Galloway v. Nichols, TexCivApp–Dallas, 269 SW2d 850.—App & E 219(2); Evid 208(1), 208(6); Plead 111.38, 111.39, 111.42(6).

Galloway; San Jacinto Ford v., TexApp–Houston (14 Dist), 830 SW2d 296. See Hugh Wood Ford, Inc. v. Galloway.

Galloway v. State, TexCrimApp, 578 SW2d 142.—Crim Law 1177.5(2); Sent & Pun 1311, 1326, 1328.

Galloway v. State, TexCrimApp, 420 SW2d 721.—Crim Law 290, 291, 295, 296, 913(6), 1128(1), 1144.18; Double J 95.1, 98; Homic 522; Ind & Inf 191(4); Searches 172.

Galloway v. State, TexCrimApp, 252 SW2d 160.—Crim Law 1090.1(1).

Galloway v. State, TexApp–Houston (1 Dist), 916 SW2d 69, petition for discretionary review refused.—Sent & Pun 2028.

Galloway v. State, TexApp–Waco, 716 SW2d 556, petition for discretionary review refused.—Assault 83, 92(5), 96(5); Crim Law 730(15); Ind & Inf 119.

Galloway v. State, TexApp–Houston (14 Dist), 778 SW2d 110.—Crim Law 364(4), 412.1(1), 412.1(4), 412.2(2), 519(9).

Galloway; U.S. v., CA5 (Tex), 951 F2d 64.—Const Law 3078, 3251, 3301, 3808, 4709; Sent & Pun 658.

Galloway; Wilburn v., TexCivApp–Beaumont, 179 SW2d 540.—Elections 269, 285(1); Schools 38.

Galloway; Wood Ford, Inc. v., TexApp–Houston (14 Dist, 830 SW2d 296. See Hugh Wood Ford, Inc. v. Galloway.

Gallup v. St. Paul Ins. Co., Tex, 515 SW2d 249.—Contracts 152; Insurance 1822, 2673.

Gallup; St. Paul Ins. Co. v., TexCivApp–Tyler, 506 SW2d 757, writ gr, aff 515 SW2d 249.—Courts 91(1); Insurance 2673.

Gallups v. State, TexCrimApp, 151 SW3d 196.—Arrest 68(13); Autos 349(12); Crim Law 1031(1).

Gallups v. State, TexApp–Dallas, 104 SW3d 361, petition for discretionary review gr, aff 151 SW3d 196.—Arrest 63.1, 63.4(1), 63.4(2), 63.4(11), 68(13); Crim Law 394.6(5), 1139, 1144.12; Searches 13.1, 24, 25.1, 171, 172, 180, 198, 201.

Galo; Gregg v., TexApp–San Antonio, 720 SW2d 116.—Judgm 181(7), 181(30), 185(2).

Galoostian; Guardian Life Ins. Co. of Texas v., TexCivApp–Eastland, 155 SW2d 396, writ refused wom.—Insurance 2439, 3001, 3003(11), 3125(2), 3125(6).

Galpin v. Zenith Ins. Co., TexApp–San Antonio, 993 SW2d 146, reh overr.—Work Comp 1887.

Galstian Family Trust; Vartanian Family Trust No. 1 v., TexApp–Dallas, 724 SW2d 126.—Action 17; Judgm 335(1), 509, 634, 713(2), 720.

Galt; Broderick v., TexCivApp–Texarkana, 81 SW2d 268.—Banks 218; Venue 7.5(5), 22(6), 22(7).

Galt; McDonald v., TexCivApp–Fort Worth, 173 SW2d 962, writ refused wom.—Estop 31; Evid 383(7); Hus & W 273(8.1), 276(6); Quiet T 46, 49; Ven & Pur 242.

Galt v. U.S., NDTex, 175 FSupp 360.—Int Rev 3624.

Galtex Property Investors, Inc. v. City of Galveston, TexApp–Houston (14 Dist), 113 SW3d 922.—App & E 85, 843(1), 893(1); Const Law 2600; Contempt 3, 4, 20, 30, 63(1), 66(2); Equity 64; Judgm 183, 186; Mand 1, 4(1), 4(4), 7, 168(4).

Galusha; Scott v., TexApp–Fort Worth, 890 SW2d 945, reh den, and writ den.—Antitrust 529, 960, 963(1), 963(3); App & E 80(6), 169, 173(2), 223, 238(4), 293, 671(4), 733, 852, 863, 1136; Pretrial Proc 501, 506.1; Torts 219.

Galutia; Christian v., TexCivApp–Waco, 236 SW2d 177, ref nre.—Evid 317(2), 593; Health 684, 817, 821(2), 821(3), 821(5), 823(9).

Galvan, Ex parte, TexCrimApp, 770 SW2d 822.—Crim Law 641.13(7); Hab Corp 603.

Galvan v. Aetna Cas. & Sur. Co., TexApp–El Paso, 831 SW2d 39, reh overr, and writ den.—Work Comp 1937.

Galvan v. America's Favorite Chicken Co., TexApp–San Antonio, 934 SW2d 409, writ den.—Judgm 570(3).

Galvan; America's Favorite Chicken Co. v., TexApp–San Antonio, 897 SW2d 874, reh overr, and writ den, on subsequent appeal 934 SW2d 409, writ den.—Judgm 197, 217, 297, 304, 325, 326; Pretrial Proc 583, 693.1, 694.

Galvan v. Bexar County, Tex., CA5 (Tex), 785 F2d 1298, reh den 790 F2d 890.—Civil R 1516, 1519, 1551; Fed Civ Proc 840, 841; Lim of Act 127(3).

Galvan; Carr v., TexApp–San Antonio, 650 SW2d 864, ref nre.—App & E 930(1), 930(3), 1024.4; Assault 33, 35, 38, 40, 45; Damag 94, 173(1); Hus & W 210(2); Judgm 199(1), 199(3.9), 199(3.10), 199(3.14).

Galvan; City of Brownsville v., TexComApp, 162 SW2d 98, 139 Tex 128.—App & E 672; Mun Corp 741.10, 741.55; Plead 360.

Galvan v. City of Brownsville, TexCivApp–El Paso, 144 SW2d 966, rev 162 SW2d 98, 139 Tex 128.—Mun Corp 742(3), 742(6); Plead 76, 87, 106(1).

Galvan v. City of Bryan, Tex, CA5 (Tex), 121 FedAppx 567.—Civil R 1218(3), 1218(4).

Galvan v. City of Bryan, Tex., SDTex, 367 FSupp2d 1081, aff 121 FedAppx 567.—Civil R 1019(1), 1019(2), 1019(3), 1218(3), 1218(4), 1516, 1552, 1590.

Galvan v. Cockrell, CA5 (Tex), 293 F3d 760.—Crim Law 641.13(1), 641.13(2.1), 1144.15; Hab Corp 447, 481, 498, 706, 746, 773, 845, 846.

Galvan; Dixie Motor Coach Corp. v., TexComApp, 86 SW2d 633, 126 Tex 109.—Trial 114, 219, 350.1, 350.5(3), 350.5(5).

Galvan v. Downey, TexApp–Houston (14 Dist), 933 SW2d 316, reh overr, and writ den.—App & E 78(1), 499(1); Health 906, 908, 911, 926; Judgm 185(2); Motions 59(2); Trial 18.

Galvan v. Fedder, TexApp–Houston (14 Dist), 678 SW2d 596.—App & E 928(1), 989, 1066(7); Damag 34, 208(1); Death 77, 98; Health 827; Neglig 432, 1741.

Galvan v. Galvan, TexCivApp–Austin, 534 SW2d 398, writ dism woj.—App & E 719(8); Divorce 286(8); Evid 383(7), 419(2), 461(2); Gifts 50; Hus & W 49.2(9).

Galvan; Galvan v., TexCivApp–Austin, 534 SW2d 398, writ dism woj.—App & E 719(8); Divorce 286(8); Evid 383(7), 419(2), 461(2); Gifts 50; Hus & W 49.2(9).

Galvan v. Garmon, CA5 (Tex), 710 F2d 214, reh den 716 F2d 901, cert den 104 SCt 2150, 466 US 949, 80 LEd2d 536.—Civil R 1376(3), 1376(8).

Galvan; Massey v., TexApp–Houston (14 Dist), 822 SW2d 309, writ den.—Alt Disp Res 113, 132, 133(2), 143, 172, 210; App & E 395; Atty & C 166(3); Death 109; Guard & W 28; Jury 28(7); Parent & C 14; Work Comp 2247.

Galvan v. Public Utilities Bd., TexApp–Corpus Christi, 778 SW2d 580.—App & E 223; Const Law 3603, 4186; Judgm 185(1), 185(2), 185(5), 185.1(3), 185.1(8), 185.2(9), 185.3(1), 189; Neglig 1620; Plead 36(1); Torts 141; Work Comp 19, 2145.

Galvan v. SBC Pension Benefit Plan, CA5 (Tex), 204 FedAppx 335.—Labor & Emp 635, 650, 682.

Galvan v. Sisk, TexCivApp–Amarillo, 526 SW2d 717.—Autos 150, 198(1), 198(2), 198(4); Judgm 185(2), 185(6); Labor & Emp 3031(1).

Galvan v. State, TexCrimApp, 598 SW2d 624.—Controlled Subs 27; Crim Law 59(1), 552(3), 784(1), 784(4), 792(1), 815(12), 1172.2; Searches 164.

Galvan v. State, TexCrimApp, 525 SW2d 24.—Crim Law 273(1), 273.1(2), 273.1(4), 274(1), 274(3.1); Sent & Pun 1802.

Galvan v. State, TexCrimApp, 461 SW2d 396.—Crim Law 543(1), 544, 603.2, 627.8(1), 814(17).

Galvan v. State, TexCrimApp, 440 SW2d 636.—Controlled Subs 80, 93.

Galvan v. State, TexCrimApp, 269 SW2d 404.—Crim Law 1090.1(1).

Galvan v. State, TexCrimApp, 190 SW2d 728.—Crim Law 1090.1(1).

Galvan v. State, TexCrimApp, 86 SW2d 768, 129 TexCrim 349.—Crim Law 1133.

Galvan v. State, TexCrimApp, 86 SW2d 228, 129 TexCrim 349, reh den 86 SW2d 768, 129 TexCrim 349.—Crim Law 614(1); Homic 1139; Witn 374(1).

Galvan v. State, TexApp–Houston (1 Dist), 846 SW2d 161.—Autos 336; Crim Law 1144.17; Sent & Pun 2001, 2022.

Galvan v. State, TexApp–Austin, 699 SW2d 663, petition for discretionary review refused.—Child S 23; Crim Law 26, 478(1), 479, 481, 485(1), 486(4), 486(5), 675, 1134(3), 1153(2); Ind & Inf 125(1), 125(19.1); Infants 20.

Galvan v. State, TexApp–San Antonio, 995 SW2d 764.—Autos 332; Crim Law 297, 798(0.5), 822(1), 865(1); Double J 135, 142; Sent & Pun 1139.

Galvan v. State, TexApp–Texarkana, 988 SW2d 291, petition for discretionary review refused.—Const Law 3880, 3882, 3885; Crim Law 37.10(1), 37.10(2), 306, 641.13(1), 641.13(7), 739(1), 913(1), 959, 1134(3), 1156(1), 1166.23, 1181.5(3.1); Ind & Inf 137(1); Judges 47(1); Witn 246(2).

Galvan v. State, TexApp–Corpus Christi, 869 SW2d 526, reh overr, and petition for discretionary review refused. —Crim Law 865(2), 867; Double J 98; Hab Corp 496, 753.

Galvan; Tagle v., TexApp–San Antonio, 155 SW3d 510.— App & E 232(2), 931(6), 1008.1(2), 1054(1); Damag 32, 96, 97, 100, 101, 127.33, 127.65, 127.71(1), 127.71(2), 140.7, 187, 191, 192, 221(4); Interest 49.

Galvan; U.S. v., CA5 (Tex), 949 F2d 777.—Const Law 4705; Crim Law 1042, 1147, 1177; Double J 134, 135, 150(1); Homic 1168; Ind & Inf 196(7); Sent & Pun 283, 306, 323, 964; Weap 4.

Galvan; U.S. v., CA5 (Tex), 693 F2d 417.—Consp 28(3), 44.2, 47(2), 47(12); Controlled Subs 28, 68, 81; Crim Law 1144.13(3), 1159.2(7), 1159.6.

Galvan; U.S. v., CA5 (Tex), 133 FedAppx 154, cert den 126 SCt 496, 546 US 967, 163 LEd2d 376, appeal after remand 177 FedAppx 462, cert den 127 SCt 699, 166 LEd2d 540.—Controlled Subs 81; Crim Law 1042, 1169.11, 1173.2(4).

Galvan v. U. S. Fire Ins. Co., TexApp–Amarillo, 629 SW2d 209, ref nre.—App & E 389(3), 775; Evid 43(2), 51; Work Comp 1490, 1960, 1969, 1971.

Galvan v. Winfrey, CA5 (Tex), 181 FedAppx 428.—Aliens 357; Const Law 4438.

Galvan-Garcia; U.S. v., CA5 (Tex), 872 F2d 638, cert den 110 SCt 164, 493 US 857, 107 LEd2d 122.—Controlled Subs 28, 81; Crim Law 700(9), 1036.1(8), 1037.1(2); Sent & Pun 761.

Galvan-Revuelta; U.S. v., CA5 (Tex), 958 F2d 66.—Crim Law 1139; Sent & Pun 653(13).

Galvan-Rodriguez; U.S. v., CA5 (Tex), 169 F3d 217, cert den 120 SCt 100, 528 US 837, 145 LEd2d 85.—Aliens 799; Crim Law 1134(3), 1139.

Galvan-Torres; U.S. v., CA5 (Tex), 350 F3d 456.—Crim Law 394.6(4), 1139, 1144.12, 1158(4); Cust Dut 126(2), 126(5).

Galveston Autoplex; Kelley v., SDTex, 196 FRD 471.— Fed Civ Proc 164, 174, 182.5; Fed Cts 817; Fraud 20; Lim of Act 104.5.

Galveston Bay Conservation and Preservation Ass'n v. Texas Air Control Bd., TexCivApp–Austin, 586 SW2d 634, ref nre.—App & E 960(1); Environ Law 265, 293, 300, 301, 657, 695, 700; Parties 38, 40(2); Plead 236(3).

Galveston Bay Conservation and Preservation Ass'n v. U.S. Army Corps of Engineers, SDTex, 55 FSupp2d 658.—Admin Law 751, 763; Environ Law 141.

Galveston By and Through Its Bd. of Trustees of Galveston Wharves, City of; Highlands Ins. Co. v., TexApp–Houston (14 Dist), 721 SW2d 469, ref nre.— Insurance 1009, 1010, 1822, 1836, 2090, 2125, 2133, 2137(1), 2260, 2277, 2349.

Galveston Central Appraisal Dist.; ABT Galveston Ltd. Partnership v., TexApp–Houston (1 Dist), 137 SW3d 146.—App & E 852; Const Law 4135, 4138(1); Tax 2640, 2698, 2791.

Galveston Cent. Appraisal Dist.; G.E. American Communication v., TexApp–Houston (14 Dist), 979 SW2d 761.—Admin Law 744.1, 746, 749, 763, 791, 811; Tax 2603, 2641, 2676, 2699(5).

Galveston Central Appraisal Dist.; TRQ Captain's Landing L.P. v., TexApp–Houston (1 Dist), 212 SW3d 726, reh en banc den.—App & E 1175(1), 1175(2); Corp 182.1(2); Ltd Liab Cos 27; Tax 2061, 2187, 2190, 2286, 2300, 2340, 2369(2), 2750.

Galveston, City of; Barker v., TexApp–Houston (1 Dist), 907 SW2d 879, reh overr, and writ den.—App & E 852, 934(1), 1107; Judgm 181(2), 185(6); Mun Corp 723,

742(6), 763(1), 847, 851, 857; Neglig 1032, 1040(3); Offic 114.

Galveston, City of; Basiardanes v., CA5 (Tex), 682 F2d 1203.—Civil R 1029, 1461, 1462, 1482; Const Law 735, 759, 795, 855, 880, 1130, 1502, 1504, 1509, 1535, 1537, 1539, 1541, 2219, 2227, 2245; Statut 47; Zoning 12, 76, 570, 571, 581, 602, 651.

Galveston, City of; Basiardanes v., SDTex, 514 FSupp 975, aff in part, rev in part 682 F2d 1203.—Const Law 228.2, 2227, 2246, 3514; Zoning 76, 571.

Galveston, City of, v. Burns, TexApp–Houston (14 Dist, 949 SW2d 881. See City of Galveston v. Burns.

Galveston, City of; Chaney v., CA5 (Tex), 368 F2d 774.— Fed Cts 792, 848, 852, 853, 868; Ship 84(3.3).

Galveston, City of; Crossman v., TexCivApp–Galveston, 204 SW 128, writ gr, rev 247 SW 810, 112 Tex 303, 26 ALR 1210.—Mun Corp 621.

Galveston, City of; Davis v., TexApp–Waco, 635 SW2d 634.—App & E 219(2); Damag 208(1).

Galveston, City of; Develo-cepts, Inc. v., TexApp–Houston (14 Dist), 668 SW2d 790.—Action 13; Courts 85(1); Mental H 481.1; Parties 75(5), 95(1), 97(1); Plead 106(1); Zoning 360, 571.

Galveston, City of; Fair v., SDTex, 915 FSupp 873, aff 100 F3d 953.—Const Law 1164, 1520, 1814, 3045, 4509(1); Mun Corp 111(2), 122.1(2), 592(1), 594(1), 594(2), 632, 703(1); Obst Just 7.

Galveston, City of; Farmer's Marine Copper Works, Inc. v., TexApp–Houston (1 Dist), 757 SW2d 148.—Ease 3(1); Em Dom 269; Estop 62.1, 62.4; R R 69, 73(4).

Galveston, City of; Flagship Hotel, Ltd. v., TexApp–Texarkana, 117 SW3d 552, reh overr, and review den.— App & E 984(5), 1078(1); Contracts 143(2), 147(2), 147(3), 156, 170(1), 176(2); Costs 194.12, 194.14, 194.18, 194.32, 194.40, 198, 207, 208; Evid 448; Judgm 181(19); Mun Corp 719(4), 1040; Waters 203(12).

Galveston, City of; Franklin v., TexCivApp–Galveston, 256 SW2d 997, ref nre.—Mun Corp 855; Neglig 1037(4).

Galveston, City of; Gagne v., CA5 (Tex), 805 F2d 558, cert den 107 SCt 3266, 483 US 1021, 97 LEd2d 764.— Civil R 1376(6).

Galveston, City of; Gagne v., SDTex, 671 FSupp 1130, aff 851 F2d 359.—Civil R 1091, 1351(4), 1352(4), 1394; Fed Civ Proc 851; Fed Cts 18.

Galveston, City of; Galtex Property Investors, Inc. v., TexApp–Houston (14 Dist), 113 SW3d 922.—App & E 85, 843(1), 893(1); Const Law 2600; Contempt 3, 4, 20, 30, 63(1), 66(2); Equity 64; Judgm 183, 186; Mand 1, 4(1), 4(4), 7, 168(4).

Galveston, City of; Galveston Racquet Club, Inc. v., TexApp–Houston (1 Dist), 178 SW3d 167.—Autos 187(1); Mun Corp 742(4); Plead 111.48; Waters 208.

Galveston, City of, v. Giles, TexApp–Houston (1 Dist), 902 SW2d 167. See City of Galveston v. Giles.

Galveston, City of; Graef v., TexCivApp–Hous (14 Dist), 538 SW2d 816, writ gr, cause dism.—App & E 1169(2); Plead 228.23.

Galveston, City of; Hatcher v., TexApp–Houston (1 Dist), 775 SW2d 37.—Judgm 181(33); Mun Corp 741.40(1).

Galveston, City of; Hill v., TexCivApp–Galveston, 241 SW2d 229, rev 246 SW2d 860, 151 Tex 139.—App & E 1039(5.1); Commerce 48; Evid 5(2); Work Comp 2142.30.

Galveston, City of; Hime v., TexCivApp–Waco, 268 SW2d 543, ref nre.—Mun Corp 186(1), 199; Statut 199.

Galveston, City of; Jackson v., TexApp–Houston (14 Dist), 837 SW2d 868, reh den, and writ gr, and writ withdrawn, and writ den.—App & E 103, 960(1); Mun Corp 723, 857; Plead 228.14; Pretrial Proc 622.

Galveston, City of; Lebohm v., Tex, 275 SW2d 951, 154 Tex 192.—Const Law 2312; Mun Corp 724, 733(2), 756; Work Comp 2.

Galveston, City of; Lulac Councils 4433 & 4436 v., SDTex, 979 FSupp 514.—Civil R 1119, 1135, 1555; Fed Civ Proc 2497.1.

Galveston, City of; Lulac Councils 4433 & 4436 v., SDTex, 942 FSupp 342.—Assoc 20(1); Fed Civ Proc 103.2, 103.3, 184.10, 841, 843, 1825.

Galveston, City of; Mabe v., TexApp–Houston (1 Dist), 687 SW2d 769, dism.—App & E 1078(1); Const Law 1253, 1527, 1870; Inj 94.

Galveston, City of; McKenna v., TexCivApp–Galveston, 113 SW2d 606, dism.—Const Law 2671; Food 1.8(3); Monop 4; Mun Corp 63.15(3), 63.20, 121.

Galveston, City of; Mikeska v., CA5 (Tex), 451 F3d 376. —Const Law 3516, 3531, 3895, 4093, 4360; Fed Civ Proc 2491.5; Fed Cts 712; Nav Wat 33; Zoning 601, 745.1.

Galveston, City of; Mikeska v., CA5 (Tex), 419 F3d 431, opinion withdrawn and superseded on denial of reh 451 F3d 376.

Galveston, City of; Mikeska v., SDTex, 328 FSupp2d 671, vac and remanded 419 F3d 431, opinion withdrawn and superseded on denial of reh 451 F3d 376.—Const Law 978, 3053, 3512, 3532, 3895, 3905, 4093, 4101, 4360; Em Dom 277; Fed Civ Proc 2491.5; Nav Wat 33, 36(1), 36(3), 41(1).

Galveston, City of; Miranda v., SDTex, 123 FSupp 889. —Work Comp 2247.

Galveston, City of; Moody v., TexCivApp–Hous (1 Dist), 524 SW2d 583, ref nre.—App & E 1062.2, 1177(6); Gas 18, 20(3), 20(4); Mun Corp 733(4), 743; Neglig 503, 1624; Prod Liab 8, 62; Sales 445(1); Trial 352.12, 352.16; Waters 201.

Galveston, City of; Morales v., CA5 (Tex), 291 F2d 97, cert gr 82 SCt 104, 368 US 816, 7 LEd2d 23, aff 82 SCt 1226, 370 US 165, 8 LEd2d 412, reh den 83 SCt 16, 371 US 853, 9 LEd2d 93.—Seamen 29(1), 29(5.16); Ship 84(3.2).

Galveston, City of; Morales v., CA5 (Tex), 275 F2d 191, vac 81 SCt 107, 364 US 295, 5 LEd2d 84, on remand 291 F2d 97, cert gr 82 SCt 104, 368 US 816, 7 LEd2d 23, aff 82 SCt 1226, 370 US 165, 8 LEd2d 412, reh den 83 SCt 16, 371 US 853, 9 LEd2d 93.—Adm 118.7(5); Mun Corp 742(5); Seamen 29(1).

Galveston, City of; Morales v., SDTex, 181 FSupp 202, aff 275 F2d 191, vac 81 SCt 107, 364 US 295, 5 LEd2d 84, on remand 291 F2d 97, cert gr 82 SCt 104, 368 US 816, 7 LEd2d 23, aff 82 SCt 1226, 370 US 165, 8 LEd2d 412, reh den 83 SCt 16, 371 US 853, 9 LEd2d 93.—Adm 1.20(1); Mun Corp 741.20, 741.25, 742(5); Ship 86(2.5); Work Comp 2225.

Galveston, City of; Parsons v., Tex, 84 SW2d 996, 125 Tex 568.—Autos 59, 121; Mun Corp 703(1).

Galveston, City of; Payne v., TexApp–Houston (14 Dist), 772 SW2d 473, writ den.—Levees 36; Mun Corp 658, 759(1), 786, 847.

Galveston, City of; Pehnke v., SDTex, 977 FSupp 827.—Action 2; Const Law 3595, 4171, 4172(6); Contracts 326; Labor & Emp 40(2); Mun Corp 218(10).

Galveston, City of; Rorie v., Tex, 471 SW2d 789, cert den Strachan Shipping Co v. City of Galveston, 92 SCt 1250, 405 US 988, 31 LEd2d 454, cert den 92 SCt 1250, 405 US 988, 31 LEd2d 454.—Carr 150; Labor & Emp 26, 3038(2); Ship 84(1), 84(6), 103.

Galveston, City of; Rorie v., TexCivApp–Hous (14 Dist), 456 SW2d 421, rev 471 SW2d 789, cert den Strachan Shipping Co v. City of Galveston, 92 SCt 1250, 405 US 988, 31 LEd2d 454, cert den 92 SCt 1250, 405 US 988, 31 LEd2d 454.—App & E 1106(2); Judgm 199(3.2), 199(3.10); Labor & Emp 26, 3096(5); Neglig 1614; Trial 350.7(2).

Galveston, City of; Seawall East Townhomes Ass'n, Inc. v., TexApp–Houston (14 Dist), 879 SW2d 363.—Mun Corp 120; Statut 181(2), 188, 219(1); Zoning 278.1.

Galveston, City of; State v., TexApp–Houston (1 Dist), 175 SW3d 1, review gr, rev 217 SW3d 466.—App & E 893(1); Atty Gen 6, 7; Const Law 2314, 2332; Mun Corp 54, 65, 723, 724, 733(4); Plead 111.36; States 1, 112(2), 190, 191.1, 191.10.

Galveston, City of; Thompson v., SDTex, 979 FSupp 504, aff 158 F3d 583.—Civil R 1088(1), 1088(2), 1351(1), 1351(4), 1376(6); Consp 2; Crim Law 275, 700(2.1); Damag 50.10, 208(6); False Imp 5, 7(5); Mal Pros 5.1, 35(1); Proc 168.

Galveston, City of; Turcuit v., TexApp–Houston (1 Dist), 658 SW2d 832.—Zoning 338, 351, 676, 681, 702, 703.

Galveston, City of, v. Whitman, TexApp–Houston (14 Dist, 919 SW2d 929. See City of Galveston v. Whitman.

Galveston, City of; Wicker v., SDTex, 944 FSupp 553.—Arrest 63.4(1), 63.4(2); Civil R 1088(2), 1376(1), 1376(2), 1376(6), 1396; Damag 91(1), 91(3); False Imp 2, 13; Fed Civ Proc 2470.1, 2515; Mun Corp 743, 747(3); Offic 119.

Galveston, City of; Woods v., SDTex, 5 FSupp2d 494.—Admin Law 501; Civil R 1041, 1121, 1126, 1127, 1137, 1312, 1405; Fed Civ Proc 2497.1, 2533.1; Judgm 540, 828.16(3), 828.16(4); Mun Corp 200(8.1).

Galveston, City of; Woomer v., TexApp–Houston (1 Dist), 765 SW2d 836, writ den.—App & E 863; Counties 141, 212; Judgm 181(33); Mun Corp 723, 741.15, 741.40(1).

Galveston County; City of Galveston v., TexCivApp–Galveston, 159 SW2d 976, writ refused.—Autos 5(3); Counties 23, 105(1); Mun Corp 63.15(4), 63.20, 661(1), 703(1).

Galveston County; Drain v., SDTex, 999 FSupp 929.—Civil R 1088(2), 1088(4), 1315, 1319, 1345, 1348, 1351(1), 1376(2), 1432; Fed Civ Proc 2491.5; Mun Corp 747(3); Offic 114.

Galveston County; Drain v., SDTex, 979 FSupp 1101.—Civil R 1031, 1319, 1351(1), 1351(4), 1395(6); Mun Corp 743.

Galveston County; Gulf View Courts v., TexCivApp–Galveston, 150 SW2d 872, writ refused.—App & E 1011.1(8.1); Deeds 109, 120; Ease 38; Inj 93; Levees 13.5.

Galveston County; Guynes v., Tex, 861 SW2d 861.—Counties 47, 113(1), 113(5); Dist & Pros Attys 9.

Galveston County; Harris v., TexApp–Houston (14 Dist), 799 SW2d 766, writ den.—Counties 143; Health 260; Judgm 181(11), 185(6); Lim of Act 127(1), 127(14); Mun Corp 847.

Galveston County v. Hartford Fire Ins. Co., TexCivApp–Galveston, 231 SW2d 684, writ refused.—Insurance 3191(7).

Galveston County; Kelly v., TexCivApp–Hous (14 Dist), 520 SW2d 507.—Consp 19; Counties 59, 122(1), 141, 142; Judgm 178, 181(27), 181(33), 185(2); Labor & Emp 904; Mun Corp 170, 724; Offic 114; Torts 215; U S 62.

Galveston County v. Lothrop, TexCivApp–Galveston, 80 SW2d 1004, writ dism.—Const Law 2839.

Galveston County; Markwell v., TexCivApp–Galveston, 186 SW2d 273, writ refused.—Judges 22(8); Offic 94, 101; Statut 210, 211, 223.2(7), 223.5(1), 230.

Galveston County; Moody House, Inc. v., TexApp–Houston (14 Dist), 687 SW2d 433, ref nre.—App & E 609, 907(3); Tax 2381, 2692.

Galveston County; Murphy v., TexApp–Houston (14 Dist), 788 SW2d 938, writ den.—Afft 9; App & E 223; Judgm 181(33), 185.2(4), 185.3(21); Offic 116.

Galveston County; Pierson v., TexCivApp–Austin, 131 SW2d 27.—Action 57(2), 69(5); App & E 1046.1; Coroners 7, 10; J P 15; Offic 100(1), 112.

Galveston County; Slocum v., TexCivApp–Tyler, 410 SW2d 487, ref nre.—Courts 91(1).

Galveston County; Soule v., TexCivApp–Galveston, 246 SW2d 491, writ refused.—App & E 524; Em Dom 98; High 120(2), 120(3).

Galveston County; T. & N. O. R. R. Co. v., TexComApp, 169 SW2d 713, 141 Tex 34.—Counties 149, 152; Mun Corp 858.

Galveston County; Texas & N. O. R. Co. v., TexCivApp–Galveston, 161 SW2d 530, aff T & N O R R Co v. Galveston County, 169 SW2d 713, 141 Tex 34.—Counties 152, 154(1); Mun Corp 871, 873.

Galveston County v. Texas Dept. of Health, TexApp–Austin, 724 SW2d 115, ref nre.—Admin Law 472, 485, 486; Environ Law 378, 381.

Galveston County; Thomas v., SDTex, 953 FSupp 163.—Civil R 1093, 1345, 1351(1), 1351(4), 1352(1).

Galveston County Appraisal Review Bd.; Tex-Air Helicopters, Inc. v., TexApp–Houston (14 Dist), 76 SW3d 575, review den (2 pets).—Adm 1.20(1); App & E 893(1); Const Law 990, 1012, 1030, 1040, 2489, 2540, 3580; Statut 181(1), 181(2), 184, 188, 206, 212.6, 214; Tax 2214, 2288, 2641, 2680, 2699(4), 2723, 2728.

Galveston County Beach Park Bd.; Johnson v., Tex, 848 SW2d 689.—Counties 110.

Galveston County Beach Park Bd. v. Johnson, TexApp–Houston (14 Dist), 822 SW2d 828, writ den with per curiam opinion 848 SW2d 689.—Counties 110, 196(1); Inj 200.

Galveston County Cent. Appraisal Dist.; Pizzitola v., TexApp–Houston (1 Dist), 808 SW2d 244.—App & E 931(1), 1010.2, 1012.1(5); Tax 2473, 2523.

Galveston County Cent. Appraisal Dist.; Wilson v., Tex, 713 SW2d 98.—Tax 2105.

Galveston County Children's Protective Services; Bates v., TexApp–Houston (1 Dist), 783 SW2d 592. See Cassey D., In Interest of.

Galveston County Com'rs Court; Lohec v., Tex, 841 SW2d 361.—Counties 1, 47; Courts 100(1); Inj 76, 88; States 45.

Galveston County Commissioners' Court v. Lohec, TexApp–Houston (14 Dist), 814 SW2d 751, writ gr, rev 841 SW2d 361.—Counties 1, 122(1), 159, 228; Decl Judgm 306; Parties 44.

Galveston County Dist. Clerk; Anderson v., CA5 (Tex), 91 FedAppx 925.—Civil R 1088(5); Fed Cts 894.

Galveston County Emp. Credit Union; Parsons v., Tex-CivApp–Hous (1 Dist), 576 SW2d 99.—App & E 447, 458(2); Courts 207.1.

Galveston County Fair & Rodeo, Inc. v. Glover, Tex, 940 SW2d 585.—App & E 1062.1; Trial 352.1(3).

Galveston County Fair & Rodeo, Inc. v. Glover, TexApp–Texarkana, 880 SW2d 112, writ den with per curiam opinion 940 SW2d 585.—Agric 5; App & E 216(1), 836, 930(3), 989, 999(1), 1001(1), 1001(3), 1140(1); Contracts 22(1), 312(1); Evid 588; Libel 1, 21, 23.1, 36, 41, 44(1), 45(1), 50, 51(1), 123(8); New Tr 162(1); Torts 220, 242; Trial 349(2), 350.2, 351.5(3), 352.1(1), 352.4(1).

Galveston County Fair and Rodeo, Inc. v. Kauffman, TexApp–El Paso, 910 SW2d 129, reh overr, and writ den.—Antitrust 128, 135(1), 138, 141, 369, 397; App & E 232(0.5), 930(3), 989, 994(2), 999(1), 1001(1), 1001(3), 1002, 1003(3), 1003(7), 1004(7), 1062.1, 1062.5; Damag 15, 49.10, 130.

Galveston County Mun. Utility Dist. No. 3 v. City of League City, Texas, TexApp–Houston (14 Dist), 960 SW2d 875, review den, and set aside, and review gr, and reh gr, order withdrawn.—Estop 62.1, 62.4; Judgm 185(2); Mun Corp 114, 589, 590, 708; States 4.4(2); Waters 183(1).

Galveston County Nav. Dist. No. 1 v. Hopson Towing Co., Inc., CA5 (Tex), 92 F3d 353.—Adm 121; Fed Civ Proc 2737.1, 2737.3, 2737.14.

Galveston County Nav. Dist. No. 1 v. Hopson Towing Co., Inc., SDTex, 877 FSupp 363, rev 92 F3d 353.—Adm 124; Fed Civ Proc 2737.5; Ship 81(1), 81(2), 86(2.3), 86(2.5).

Galveston, County of, v. Morgan, TexApp–Houston (14 Dist, 882 SW2d 485. See County of Galveston v. Morgan.

Galveston County, Tex.; Gayden v., SDTex, 178 FRD 134, aff in part 177 F3d 978.—Fed Civ Proc 1839.1, 1935.1; Fed Cts 818.

Galveston County, Texas; Martorell v., CA5 (Tex), 103 FedAppx 538.—Civil R 1252; Counties 67.

Galveston County Water Control and Imp. Dist. No. 1; Schroeder v., TexCivApp–Houston, 385 SW2d 629.—App & E 597(1), 758.3(6); Em Dom 203(2); Evid 163; Trial 194(20).

Galveston, H. & S.A. Ry. Co.; Norwood v., TexCivApp, 34 SW 180, 12 TexCivApp 560.—Civil R 1048.

Galveston, H. & S. A. Ry. Co.; Swilley v., TexCivApp–Galveston, 96 SW2d 105, writ dism.—Labor & Emp 763, 854, 863(1).

Galveston, H. & S. A. Ry. Co. v. Uvalde County, TexCivApp–San Antonio, 167 SW2d 305, writ refused wom.—Counties 47, 111(1).

Galveston Historical Foundation v. Zoning Bd. of Adjustment of City of Galveston, TexApp–Houston (1 Dist), 17 SW3d 414, review den.—Action 13; App & E 174; Zoning 571, 621.

Galveston Housing Authority; Hill v., TexCivApp–Hous (1 Dist), 593 SW2d 741.—App & E 758.1; Land & Ten 169(7).

Galveston, Houston & Henderson R. Co.; Denke v., SDTex, 353 FSupp 315.—Fed Cts 105, 1153.

Galveston-Houston Breweries v. Naylor, TexCivApp–Galveston, 249 SW2d 262, ref nre.—Autos 157, 245(71); Death 77; Evid 99; Neglig 381, 535(14); Trial 139.1(3), 350.5(3); Witn 388(7.1).

Galveston-Houston Breweries, Inc.; Laughlin v., TexCivApp–Beaumont, 360 SW2d 572, writ dism.—App & E 907(3), 934(1); Frds St of 74(1); Judgm 181(4), 185(2), 185.1(1), 186.

Galveston-Houston Co.; Three Bee Inv. Corp. v., TexCivApp–Galveston, 166 SW2d 382.—Plead 111, 111.2.

Galveston/Houston Diocese; Miller v., TexApp–Amarillo, 911 SW2d 897.—App & E 854(1); Damag 50.10, 208(6); Judgm 185(2).

Galveston Independent School Dist.; Boone v., CA5 (Tex), 126 FedAppx 660.—Civil R 1138; Fed Civ Proc 2771(5), 2814.

Galveston Independent School Dist. v. Boothe, TexCivApp–Hous (1 Dist), 590 SW2d 553.—Const Law 4212(2); Inj 189, 204; Schools 169, 177.

Galveston Independent School Dist.; Gonzales v., SDTex, 865 FSupp 1241.—Civil R 1251, 1376(2); Const Law 277(2), 1929, 1941, 1947, 1991, 1994, 3278(6), 4171, 4173(3), 4173(4), 4198, 4203; Fed Civ Proc 2497.1; Fed Cts 13.10; Offic 72.61, 114; Rem of C 101.1; Schools 63(1).

Galveston Independent School Dist. v. Heartland Federal Sav. and Loan Ass'n, SDTex, 159 BR 198.—Bankr 2582, 2852, 2853.30; Interest 31; Judgm 735; Statut 223.4; Tax 2733, 2763, 2787, 2810, 3211, 3212, 3216, 3218, 3220.

Galveston Independent School Dist.; Schwartz v., SDTex, 309 FSupp 1034.—Civil R 1315, 1317, 1387; Const Law 1053; Courts 489(1); Decl Judgm 272; Fed Civ Proc 1837.1; Fed Cts 62, 219.1; Inj 114(3), 114(5), 192; Schools 148(1), 170.1, 172.

Galveston Independent School Dist.; Williams v., CA5 (Tex), 78 FedAppx 946, cert den 124 SCt 1714, 541 US 959, 158 LEd2d 400.—Civil R 1136, 1138.

Galveston Independent School Dist.; Williams v., SDTex, 256 FSupp2d 668, aff 78 FedAppx 946, cert den 124 SCt 1714, 541 US 959, 158 LEd2d 400.—Civil R 1136, 1137, 1138, 1243, 1405, 1536.

Galveston Linehandlers, Inc. v. International Longshoremen's Ass'n, SDTex, 140 FSupp2d 741.—Fed Cts

241; Fraud 31; Labor & Emp 968, 1973; Rem of C 11; States 18.3, 18.46, 18.55; Torts 203.

Galveston Maritime Ass'n; International Longshoremen's Ass'n, Independent v., TexCivApp–Houston, 358 SW2d 607.—App & E 684(3), 907(3); Courts 489(9); Inj 139, 158; Judgm 564(1); Labor & Emp 1321, 1326, 2041, 2121, 2126, 2141, 2143; Plead 228.23.

Galveston Maritime Ass'n v. South Atlantic & Gulf Coast Dist., Intern. Longshoremen's Ass'n, SDTex, 234 FSupp 250.—Alt Disp Res 198, 201; Fed Civ Proc 217; Labor & Emp 1437, 1495, 1556(5), 1672, 1675; Spec Perf 80, 106(1).

Galveston Model Dairy; Ryan v., TexCivApp–Hous (1 Dist), 473 SW2d 536.—Sales 274, 427, 439, 441(3).

Galveston Motion Picture Operators, Local No. 305 of International Alliance of Theatrical Stage Employes and Moving Picture Machine Operators of U. S. and Canada; Texas Motion Picture and Vitaphone Operators, Union No. 56,880 v., TexCivApp–Galveston, 132 SW2d 299.—Labor & Emp 900, 2082; Torts 212.

Galveston Mun. Police Ass'n; City of Galveston v., TexApp–Houston (14 Dist), 57 SW3d 532, review den.— Alt Disp Res 113, 139, 210, 374(1), 374(6), 374(7); Contracts 143.5, 157, 164; Decl Judgm 392.1; Labor & Emp 1549(12).

Galveston Newspapers, Inc. v. Norris, TexApp–Houston (1 Dist), 981 SW2d 797, reh overr, and review den.— App & E 70(8), 863, 934(1); Judgm 185(2); Libel 48(1), 51(1), 51(5), 101(4), 112(2); Torts 242.

Galveston Park Bd. of City of Galveston, Tex., City of; Mabe v., SDTex, 635 FSupp 105.—Civil R 1326(1), 1326(5), 1326(9).

Galveston Racquet Club, Inc. v. City of Galveston, TexApp–Houston (1 Dist), 178 SW3d 167.—Autos 187(1); Mun Corp 742(4); Plead 111.48; Waters 208.

Galveston Terminals, Inc. v. Tenneco Oil Co., TexApp–Houston (1 Dist), 904 SW2d 787, reh overr, and writ gr, vac pursuant to settlement 922 SW2d 549.—App & E 854(1), 901, 934(1); Contracts 147(1); Judgm 181(2), 181(29), 185(2), 185(6); Propty 12; Ven & Pur 46.

Galveston Terminals, Inc. v. Tenneco Oil, Co., TexApp–Houston (1 Dist), 824 SW2d 331, opinion superseded on reh by 1995 WL 302151, opinion withdrawn and superseded on overruling of reh 904 SW2d 787, reh overr, and writ gr, vac pursuant to settlement 922 SW2d 549. —Judgm 181(15.1).

Galveston, Tex. By and Through Bd. of Trustees of Galveston Wharves, City of; Railway Labor Executives' Ass'n v., SDTex, 685 FSupp 158, rev Railway Labor Executives Ass'n v. City of Galveston, Tex, By and Through Bd of Trustees of the Galveston Wharves, 849 F2d 145, cert gr, vac 109 SCt 3207, 492 US 901, 106 LEd2d 559, on remand 883 F2d 16, reconsideration den 897 F2d 164, aff 898 F2d 481.—Commerce 152.

Galveston, Tex., By and Through Bd. of Trustees of the Galveston Wharves, City of; Railway Labor Executives' Ass'n v., CA5 (Tex), 898 F2d 481.—Fed Cts 682.

Galveston, Tex., By and Through Bd. of Trustees of the Galveston Wharves, City of; Railway Labor Executives' Ass'n v., CA5 (Tex), 897 F2d 164.—Labor & Emp 1310, 1558.

Galveston, Tex., By and Through Bd. of Trustees of the Galveston Wharves, City of; Railway Labor Executives Ass'n v., CA5 (Tex), 849 F2d 145, cert gr, vac City of Galveston, Tex v. Railway Labor Executives' Ass'n, 109 SCt 3207, 492 US 901, 106 LEd2d 559, on remand 883 F2d 16, reconsideration den 897 F2d 164.—Admin Law 781; Commerce 85.7, 171; Labor & Emp 1125.

Galveston, Tex., City of; Brown v., SDTex, 870 FSupp 155.—Civil R 1128; Consp 1.1, 3, 4, 7.5(1), 7.5(3), 13; Const Law 3867, 3874(1), 3874(2), 3874(3), 4171, 4173(3); Damag 50.10; Labor & Emp 40(1), 50; Mun Corp 218(3), 218(10); Offic 114.

Galveston, Tex., City of; Burns v., CA5 (Tex), 905 F2d 100.—Civil R 1088(4), 1351(1), 1351(4); Const Law 4545(2); Sent & Pun 1546.

Galveston, Tex., City of; Miranda v., SDTex, 98 FSupp 245.—Work Comp 2142.30.

Galveston, Tex., City of; Morales v., USTex, 82 SCt 1226, 370 US 165, 8 LEd2d 412, reh den 83 SCt 16, 371 US 853, 9 LEd2d 93.—Adm 118.7(5); Fed Cts 456; Mun Corp 742(5); Ship 84(3.2), 86(2.5).

Galveston, Tex., City of; Mossey v., SDTex, 94 FSupp2d 793.—Arrest 63.4(2), 63.4(13), 68(2); Civil R 1351(1), 1352(1), 1352(4), 1376(2); Fed Civ Proc 2491.5; Offic 114, 116.

Galveston, Tex., City of; Paniagua v., CA5 (Tex), 995 F2d 1310.—Contracts 176(1); Labor & Emp 40(2), 177, 2317, 2347, 2348; Mun Corp 123, 220(4), 220(8).

Galveston, Tex., City of; Texas Peace Officers Ass'n v., SDTex, 944 FSupp 562.—Assoc 20(1); Civil R 1395(8).

Galveston, Tex., City of; Youngblood v., SDTex, 920 FSupp 103.—Civil R 1128, 1395(8); Const Law 3874(2), 4156, 4165(1), 4173(4), 4175; Fed Civ Proc 1773, 1835; Fed Cts 18; Judges 7; Labor & Emp 40(2); Offic 66.

Galveston-Texas City Pilots; Edwards v., SDTex, 203 FSupp2d 759.—Civil R 1015, 1118, 1121, 1231, 1505(3), 1505(7), 1535; Consp 5; Damag 50.10, 208(6); Evid 317(2); Fraud 3; Lim of Act 58(1).

Galveston Theatres v. Larsen, TexCivApp–Galveston, 124 SW2d 936.—App & E 264; Evid 141; Trial 121(2), 122, 129, 273, 365.2.

Galveston Transit Co. v. Morgan, TexCivApp–Houston, 408 SW2d 728.—App & E 1170.1, 1170.10; Autos 171(11); Carr 305(6), 318(7), 320(21), 320(30); Evid 118, 123(10); Jury 34(3); Trial 350.5(5).

Galveston Truck Line Corp. v. Moore, TexCivApp–Waco, 107 SW2d 426, writ dism.—App & E 994(3); Autos 206, 244(58); Damag 132(1).

Galveston Truck Line Corp. v. State, TexCivApp–Dallas, 123 SW2d 797, writ refused, cert den Galveston Truck Line Corporation v. Texas, 60 SCt 85, 308 US 571, 84 LEd 479.—Commerce 14.10(2), 14.10(3), 61(1).

Galveston Wharves; Maritrend, Inc. v., SDTex, 152 FRD 543.—Admin Law 228.1; Antitrust 531; Civil R 1027, 1072, 1401; Const Law 230.3(1), 3703, 3874(1), 4267; Fed Civ Proc 1772, 1829, 1832, 2533.1; Ship 103.

Galveston Yacht Basin; Winchester v., SDTex, 943 FSupp 776, aff 119 F3d 1.—Civil R 1175, 1243, 1244, 1246, 1252, 1541.

Galveston Yacht Basin, Inc.; Pavlides v., CA5 (Tex), 727 F2d 330.—Death 14(1); Fed Cts 754.1, 844, 850.1; Neglig 291; Prod Liab 8, 14, 15, 27, 60, 75.1, 82.1.

Galvez v. State, TexApp–Austin, 962 SW2d 203, petition for discretionary review refused.—Crim Law 369.1, 369.2(1), 369.15, 372(14), 661, 1153(1), 1169.11; Sent & Pun 312.

Galvin v. Gulf Oil Corp., TexApp–Dallas, 759 SW2d 167, writ den.—App & E 907(4), 961, 1043(1); Pretrial Proc 45, 313.

Galvin v. State, TexCrimApp, 444 SW2d 938.—Crim Law 1130(3).

Galyean v. State, TexCrimApp, 243 SW2d 30, 156 TexCrim 412.—Crim Law 763(1), 1130(5), 1171.5; Int Liq 236(7).

Gama-Antuniz; U.S. v., CA5 (Tex), 95 FedAppx 542.— Aliens 794, 795(2); Crim Law 273.1(4), 1042.

G. A. Mallick, Inc.; Joe R. Starks Const. Co. v., TexCivApp–Fort Worth, 425 SW2d 409.—App & E 204(2), 1170.7, 1170.10, 1170.11; Contracts 322(3); Evid 441(7); New Tr 108(3).

Gama-Reynoso; U.S. v., CA5 (Tex), 204 FedAppx 450.— Crim Law 1042; Sent & Pun 661.

Gambel v. State, TexApp–Houston (14 Dist), 835 SW2d 788.—Jury 33(5.15).

Gambill; Chauncey v., TexCivApp–Fort Worth, 126 SW2d 775, writ dism, correct.—Fraud Conv 87(1), 96(2),

96(4), 115(1), 118(3), 159(1), 159(2), 298(2), 300(4), 301(3); Infants 47, 57(2); Trial 350.2, 355(2).

Gambill v. City of Denton, TexCivApp–Fort Worth, 215 SW2d 389, dism.—Mun Corp 126, 147, 150; Offic 104.

Gambill; Clayborn v., TexCivApp–Texarkana, 87 SW2d 508, writ refused.—Bound 9; Deeds 38(1), 90; Hus & W 273(10), 274(1), 274(4).

Gambill v. Mathes, TexCivApp–Dallas, 490 SW2d 863, dism.—App & E 186, 192.1; Ex & Ad 7, 436; Plead 111.6; Venue 16 1/2.

Gambill v. Snow, TexCivApp–Eastland, 189 SW2d 33, writ refused wom.—App & E 218.2(2), 927(7), 930(3), 1001(1), 1050.1(5); Frds St of 131(2), 152(1); Spec Perf 99, 120; Stip 14(4); Trial 139.1(5.1), 142; Ven & Pur 18(3), 18(4).

Gambill v. State, TexCrimApp, 692 SW2d 106.—Crim Law 1133.

Gambill v. Town of Ponder, Tex, 494 SW2d 808, answer to certified question conformed to 497 SW2d 454.—Venue 11, 25.

Gambill v. Town of Ponder, TexCivApp–Fort Worth, 497 SW2d 454.—Venue 40.

Gambino; Plagge v., TexCivApp–Hous (1 Dist), 570 SW2d 106.—App & E 954(1); Ease 15.1, 22, 61(6); Inj 135.

Gamble, In re, BkrtcyNDTex, 196 BR 54, appeal decided 143 F3d 223.—Bankr 2363.1, 3348.5, 3420(1).

Gamble, In re, Tex, 71 SW3d 313.—Elections 126(1), 154(1), 154(3); Equity 54; Inj 106; Mand 74(1).

Gamble, Matter of, CA5 (Tex), 143 F3d 223.—Bankr 3348.5, 3420(1), 3782, 3786.

Gamble v. Banneyer, TexComApp, 151 SW2d 586, 137 Tex 7.—App & E 80(1); Judgm 217, 518; Tax 3027.

Gamble v. Banneyer, TexCivApp–Galveston, 127 SW2d 955, aff 151 SW2d 586, 137 Tex 7.—Judgm 470; Tax 2929, 2935; Wills 672(3).

Gamble v. Beto, CA5 (Tex), 363 F2d 831.—Courts 100(1).

Gamble v. Brewster, TexCivApp–El Paso, 254 SW2d 227, mandamus overr.—Venue 7.5(6).

Gamble; Canyon Loan Co. v., TexCivApp–Amarillo, 105 SW2d 272, aff FirstNat Bank v. Gamble, 132 SW2d 100, 134 Tex 112, 125 ALR 265.—Lim of Act 141, 145(1), 164; Mtg 154(1).

Gamble; Estelle v., USTex, 97 SCt 285, 429 US 97, 50 LEd2d 251, reh den 97 SCt 798, 429 US 1066, 50 LEd2d 785, on remand 554 F2d 653, reh den 559 F2d 1217, cert den 98 SCt 530, 434 US 974, 54 LEd2d 465.—Civil R 1091, 1098, 1395(7); Fed Civ Proc 657.5(3), 1788.6; Fed Cts 460.1; Prisons 17(2); Sent & Pun 1431, 1435, 1452, 1482, 1546.

Gamble v. Estelle, CA5 (Tex), 554 F2d 653, reh den 559 F2d 1217, cert den 98 SCt 530, 434 US 974, 54 LEd2d 465.—Civil R 1091, 1395(7).

Gamble v. Estelle, CA5 (Tex), 551 F2d 654, cert den 98 SCt 298, 434 US 903, 54 LEd2d 189.—Const Law 4594(1); Double J 115.

Gamble v. Estelle, CA5 (Tex), 516 F2d 937, reh den 521 F2d 815, cert gr 96 SCt 1101, 424 US 907, 47 LEd2d 311, rev 97 SCt 285, 429 US 97, 50 LEd2d 251, reh den 97 SCt 798, 429 US 1066, 50 LEd2d 785, on remand 554 F2d 653, reh den 559 F2d 1217, cert den 98 SCt 530, 434 US 974, 54 LEd2d 465.—Civil R 1091, 1395(7); Fed Civ Proc 657.5(2).

Gamble; First Nat. Bank v., TexComApp, 132 SW2d 100, 134 Tex 112, 125 ALR 265.—Corp 1.4(3); Lim of Act 148(1), 164.

Gamble; Fradelis Frozen Food Corp. v., TexCivApp–San Antonio, 326 SW2d 293.—Receivers 38, 40.

Gamble v. Gamble, CA5 (Tex), 143 F3d 223. See Gamble, Matter of.

Gamble; Gamble v., CA5 (Tex), 143 F3d 223. See Gamble, Matter of.

Gamble v. Gamble, BkrtcyNDTex, 196 BR 54. See Gamble, In re.

Gamble; Gamble v., BkrtcyNDTex, 196 BR 54. See Gamble, In re.

Gamble v. Gregg County, TexApp–Texarkana, 932 SW2d 253.—Labor & Emp 40(1), 50, 51, 182, 216.

Gamble; Industrial Underwriters Ins. Co. v., TexCivApp–Waco, 471 SW2d 626.—App & E 842(1), 1069.1; Work Comp 1653, 1968(1).

Gamble; Lewis v., TexCivApp–Eastland, 113 SW2d 659.—App & E 1070(2); Judgm 248, 251(1); New Tr 21, 125; Sales 481; Trial 350.3(6), 352.4(1).

Gamble; Lindsey v., TexCivApp–Amarillo, 359 SW2d 520, ref nre.—Courts 65; Judgm 186; Wills 297(1), 440, 543.

Gamble v. Norton, TexApp–Houston (1 Dist), 893 SW2d 129.—App & E 989, 1012.1(5); Brok 4.

Gamble v. Peyton, TexApp–Beaumont, 182 SW3d 1.—Anim 66.7, 66.9; Neglig 1101; Pub Amuse 135.

Gamble v. State, TexCrimApp, 717 SW2d 14.—Crim Law 1177; Sent & Pun 313.

Gamble v. State, TexCrimApp, 590 SW2d 507.—Crim Law 1109(3).

Gamble v. State, TexCrimApp, 509 SW2d 355.—Crim Law 419(12), 1169.1(9).

Gamble v. State, TexCrimApp, 495 SW2d 234.—Crim Law 273.1(4).

Gamble v. State, TexCrimApp, 484 SW2d 713.—Sent & Pun 2011, 2021, 2029.

Gamble v. State, TexCrimApp, 466 SW2d 556.—Autos 359.

Gamble v. State, TexCrimApp, 207 SW2d 86, 151 Tex-Crim 269.—Crim Law 730(8), 1037.1(4), 1037.2, 1169.3.

Gamble v. State, TexCrimApp, 193 SW2d 680, 149 Tex-Crim 282.—Crim Law 377, 519(2), 530, 531(3), 726, 730(1), 1158(1), 1169.5(2), 1170.5(1); Homic 983, 1001, 1134, 1478.

Gamble v. State, TexApp–Houston (1 Dist), 8 SW3d 452.—Arrest 63.5(4), 63.5(5), 63.5(7); Crim Law 1134(2).

Gamble v. State, TexApp–Houston (1 Dist), 916 SW2d 92.—Crim Law 641.13(1), 641.13(2.1), 641.13(6).

Gamble; State v., TexApp–Fort Worth, 692 SW2d 200.—App & E 554(3), 611, 846(5), 907(3); Crim Law 1226(3.1).

Gamble v. State, TexApp–Waco, 199 SW3d 619, opinion after remand 2007 WL 2127337.—Crim Law 273.1(4), 1163(1), 1167(5).

Gamble v. State, TexApp–Houston (14 Dist), 681 SW2d 769, petition for discretionary review gr, aff 717 SW2d 14.—Burg 46(1); Crim Law 1169.2(1), 1169.3, 1169.11, 1170.5(1), 1184(1); Sent & Pun 329; Weap 17(5).

Gamble v. State, TexCivApp–Eastland, 405 SW2d 384.—App & E 907(3), 934(2); Infants 191, 250.

Gamble v. Thomas, CA5 (Tex), 655 F2d 568.—Fed Cts 545.1.

Gamble; Triantaphyllis v., TexApp–Houston (14 Dist), 93 SW3d 398, review den.—App & E 19, 237(1), 241, 242(1), 946, 954(1), 1008.1(2); Elections 22, 154(1), 179; Inj 9, 12, 14, 23, 24, 80, 114(3), 128(7); Mand 178.

Gamble; U.S. v., CA5 (Tex), 208 F3d 536.—Crim Law 1586.

Gamble; U.S. v., SDTex, 295 FSupp 1192.—Bail 53, 73.1(1).

Gamble Alden Life Ins. Co.; Tuttle v., NDTex, 385 FSupp 1352, aff 531 F2d 573.—Insurance 2586, 2588(2), 2608.

Gambles v. State, TexApp–Dallas, 645 SW2d 865.—Crim Law 366(6), 730(3), 1043(2); Rape 48(1); Witn 318.

Gamble, Simmons & Co. v. Norton, TexApp–Houston (1 Dist), 893 SW2d 129. See Gamble v. Norton.

Gamblin; Bryant v., TexApp–Eastland, 829 SW2d 228, reh den, and writ den.—Judgm 123(1).

Gamblin v. Ingram, TexCivApp–Waco, 378 SW2d 941.—Agric 9.5; Neglig 1568.

Gamblin v. State, TexCrimApp, 476 SW2d 18.—Assault 96(7); Crim Law 438(7), 444, 863(2); Homic 908, 909.

Gamblin; White v., TexCivApp–Eastland, 203 SW2d 1014.—Evid 222(2); Plead 111.18, 111.42(3); Venue 22(4), 22(6).

Gambling Device; State v., TexApp–Houston (1 Dist), 859 SW2d 519, reh den, and writ den.—Const Law 47, 48(1), 1013, 1140; Crim Law 13.1(1); Gaming 3, 58, 74(0.5); Statut 47, 181(1), 188.

Gambling Paraphernalia, Devices, Equipment, and Proceeds v. State, TexApp–Dallas, 22 SW3d 625.—Crim Law 90(1), 100(1), 1226(4); Forfeit 1, 5; Gaming 61.

Gamboa; Brownsville Independent School Dist. v., TexCivApp–Corpus Christi, 498 SW2d 448, ref nre.—Schools 153.

Gamboa; Salas v., TexApp–San Antonio, 760 SW2d 838.—Health 576, 709(1).

Gamboa v. Shaw, TexApp–San Antonio, 956 SW2d 662.—App & E 754(1); Atty & C 129(1); Corp 202.

Gamboa; Southwestern Sec. Services, Inc. v., TexApp–El Paso, 172 SW3d 90.—Corp 507(4), 507(12); Judgm 17(9), 162(2); Proc 82, 153.

Gamboa v. State, TexCrimApp, 528 SW2d 247.—Crim Law 784(1).

Gamboa v. State, TexCrimApp, 481 SW2d 423.—Autos 355(6); Crim Law 260.11(2), 407(1).

Gamboa v. State, TexApp–Fort Worth, 774 SW2d 111, petition for discretionary review refused.—Crim Law 347, 678(4), 700(2.1), 700(9).

Gamboa v. State, TexApp–Beaumont, 822 SW2d 328, petition for discretionary review refused.—Crim Law 641.13(1), 641.13(2.1), 723(1), 790, 1162, 1172.1(2).

Gamboa; U.S. v., CA5 (Tex), 543 F2d 545.—Crim Law 1126, 1147; Sent & Pun 113, 1480, 1505; Weap 17(8).

Gamboa; U.S. v., CA5 (Tex), 136 FedAppx 713, cert den Martinez v. US, 126 SCt 501, 546 US 969, 163 LEd2d 379.—Crim Law 1042, 1163(1).

Gamboa; Woods v., TexCivApp–Dallas, 229 SW2d 1021, ref nre.—Judgm 143(2), 145(2), 335(1), 335(3), 335(4).

Gamboa; Xarin Real Estate, Inc. v., TexApp–Corpus Christi, 715 SW2d 80, ref nre.—Antitrust 397; Brok 3, 42; Costs 194.25; Lim of Act 24(4); Princ & A 8.

Gamboa-Cano; U.S. v., CA5 (Tex), 510 F2d 598.—Infants 69(6).

Gambrell v. Chalk Hill Theatre Co., TexCivApp–Austin, 205 SW2d 126, ref nre, appeal dism 68 SCt 1071, 334 US 814, 92 LEd 1745.—Const Law 2642, 4105(1); Dedi 19(2), 29; Inj 12, 85(2); Mun Corp 43, 657(2), 657(4).

Gambriell v. Liberty Mut. Ins. Co., CA5 (Tex), 342 F2d 755.—Work Comp 1709.

Gambrinus Company/Spoetzl Brewery; Johnson v., CA5 (Tex), 116 F3d 1052.—Civil R 1021; Fed Cts 593, 776, 850.1, 853.

Gamer v. Winchester, TexCivApp–Fort Worth, 110 SW2d 1190, writ dism.—Anim 66.5(1), 74(2), 74(6), 74(7), 74(8); App & E 758.2, 1039(13); Damag 37, 159(2), 178, 186; Trial 115(2).

Games-Forbes; U.S. v., CA5 (Tex), 145 FedAppx 901, cert den Medina-Teniente v. US, 126 SCt 839, 546 US 1080, 163 LEd2d 714.—Aliens 799; Crim Law 1042, 1177.

Game Stop/Babbage's; Roberson v., CA5 (Tex), 152 FedAppx 356, cert den 126 SCt 2982, 165 LEd2d 986.—Civil R 1135; Fed Civ Proc 2497.1; Labor & Emp 367(2), 367(4).

Game Stop, Inc.; Roberson v., NDTex, 395 FSupp2d 463, on reconsideration in part, aff 152 FedAppx 356, cert den 126 SCt 2982, 165 LEd2d 986.—Civil R 1119, 1122, 1135, 1137, 1138, 1243, 1251, 1252, 1405, 1536; Fed Civ Proc 2470, 2543, 2544, 2653, 2655; Fed Cts 13.5; Labor & Emp 367(1), 367(4), 368, 384, 810, 827, 863(2).

Gamez, Ex parte, Tex, 228 SW2d 133, 148 Tex 562.—Hab Corp 528.1, 823.

Gamez v. Beto, CA5 (Tex), 406 F2d 1000.—Arrest 63.4(8); Hab Corp 467, 470.

Gamez; Brownsville-Valley Regional Medical Center, Inc. v., Tex, 894 SW2d 753.—Infants 77, 78(1), 82, 83, 115.

Gamez; Brownsville-Valley Regional Medical Center, Inc. v., TexApp–Corpus Christi, 871 SW2d 781, reh overr, and writ gr, rev 894 SW2d 753.—App & E 984(5); Atty & C 23, 132; Infants 83, 85, 105, 115.

Gamez; Ford Motor Credit Co. v., TexCivApp–Eastland, 617 SW2d 720, ref nre.—Cons Cred 12, 16; Statut 241(2).

Gamez; Goodyear Dunlop Tires North America, Ltd. v., TexApp–San Antonio, 151 SW3d 574.—App & E 230, 840(1), 984(1); Costs 177, 207; Infants 82, 83, 84, 85, 115; Judgm 297.

Gamez v. State, TexCrimApp, 737 SW2d 315.—Crim Law 507(1), 507(2), 511.1(1), 511.1(2.1), 511.1(3), 742(2), 780(1), 1035(2), 1144.15; Judges 47(1), 51(2), 53.

Gamez v. State, TexCrimApp, 506 SW2d 618.—Crim Law 273(4.1), 273.1(4), 273.1(5); Sent & Pun 1381(6).

Gamez v. State, TexCrimApp, 403 SW2d 418, cert den 87 SCt 877, 386 US 929, 17 LEd2d 801, reh den 87 SCt 1290, 386 US 988, 18 LEd2d 242.—Controlled Subs 80; Crim Law 661; Ind & Inf 166; Sent & Pun 1376; Stip 14(10).

Gamez v. State, TexCrimApp, 352 SW2d 732, 171 TexCrim 639.—Autos 332, 349(6), 349.5(2), 351.1, 355(6), 425; Crim Law 394.4(9), 655(4), 778(5), 824(15), 844(1), 1037.1(1), 1166.16, 1166.18.

Gamez v. State, TexCrimApp, 225 SW2d 188, 154 TexCrim 64.—Burg 8, 28(4).

Gamez v. State, TexCrimApp, 112 SW2d 196, 133 TexCrim 481.—Crim Law 598(2), 603.3(5); Homic 990, 1371, 1403, 1479, 1486; Witn 240(5).

Gamez v. State, TexCrimApp, 105 SW2d 232, 132 TexCrim 389.—Crim Law 1144.18.

Gamez v. State, TexApp–San Antonio, 665 SW2d 124, petition for discretionary review gr, aff 737 SW2d 315.—Crim Law 507(1), 510.5, 511.1(7), 742(2), 814(19); Homic 876; Judges 47(1).

Gamez v. State, TexApp–San Antonio, 644 SW2d 879, petition for discretionary review refused, appeal after remand 665 SW2d 124, petition for discretionary review gr, aff 737 SW2d 315.—Crim Law 1033.1, 1144.7, 1181.5(3.1); Judges 47(1).

Gamez v. State Bar of Texas, TexApp–San Antonio, 765 SW2d 827, writ den.—App & E 1169(6); Atty & C 38, 44(1), 48, 52, 54, 57, 58; Const Law 4273(3); Lim of Act 95(3).

Gamez v. U.S., SDTex, 95 FSupp 656.—Armed S 58(3), 60, 79(7); Statut 219(6.1).

Gamez; Valley Regional Medical Center v., Tex, 894 SW2d 753. See Brownsville-Valley Regional Medical Center, Inc. v. Gamez.

Gamez; Valley Regional Medical Center v., TexApp–Corpus Christi, 871 SW2d 781. See Brownsville-Valley Regional Medical Center, Inc. v. Gamez.

Gamez-Ale; U.S. v., CA5 (Tex), 102 FedAppx 401.—Sent & Pun 793.

Gamez-de la Cruz; U.S. v., CA5 (Tex), 78 FedAppx 925, cert den 124 SCt 1489, 540 US 1211, 158 LEd2d 137.—Aliens 794, 799.

Gamez-Gonzalez; U.S. v., CA5 (Tex), 319 F3d 695, cert den 123 SCt 2241, 538 US 1068, 155 LEd2d 1126.—Controlled Subs 31, 68, 81; Crim Law 552(1), 559, 1144.13(2.1), 1159.2(7), 1171.1(2.1), 1171.1(3).

Gamez-Mendoza; U.S. v., CA5 (Tex), 203 FedAppx 678, cert den 127 SCt 1843, 167 LEd2d 338.—Jury 34(7); Sent & Pun 796, 827.

Gammage v. Compton, Tex, 548 SW2d 1, cert den Paul v. Gammage, 97 SCt 2676, 431 US 955, 53 LEd2d 271.—U S 14.

Gammage; Litton Indus. Products, Inc. v., Tex, 668 SW2d 319.—Antitrust 130, 369; App & E 294(1), 516, 882(18); Evid 54.

Gammage; Litton Indus. Products, Inc. v., TexApp–Houston (14 Dist), 644 SW2d 170, writ gr, aff in part, rev in part 668 SW2d 319.—Antitrust 393; App & E 209.1, 884.

Gammage v. State, TexApp–San Antonio, 630 SW2d 309, petition for discretionary review refused.—Crim Law 637, 1152(1); Jury 131(3).

Gammage; U.S. v., CA5 (Tex), 790 F2d 431.—Banks 509.25; Crim Law 829(4), 1038.1(2).

Gammage v. Weinberg, TexCivApp–Houston, 355 SW2d 788, 95 ALR2d 1086, ref nre.—App & E 907(3); Contrib 5(1), 5(5), 6; Evid 208(1); Indem 24, 65, 76, 85; Judgm 704.

Gammage; Welch v., TexCivApp–Austin, 545 SW2d 223, ref nre.—Costs 198; Labor & Emp 266; Plead 427; Pretrial Proc 480.

Gammex Inc.; Dunbar Medical Systems Inc. v., CA5 (Tex), 216 F3d 441, reh den.—Compromise 2, 8(3), 8(4); Contracts 94(1), 98; Damag 91(1), 184; Evid 434(8); Fed Cts 776, 792, 850.1, 915; Fraud 3, 9, 12, 24, 50, 61; Interest 39(2.55); Release 23, 33; Sales 40.

Gammill; Allied Finance Co. v., TexCivApp–Fort Worth, 440 SW2d 897, ref nre.—App & E 930(3), 989; Autos 171(2), 244(44); Damag 208(4); Neglig 1571, 1694; Trial 350.1, 356(1).

Gammill v. Jack Williams Chevrolet, Inc., Tex, 972 SW2d 713.—App & E 971(2); Evid 508, 539, 544, 545, 546, 555.2, 555.8(1); Pretrial Proc 390.

Gammill v. Jack Williams Chevrolet, Inc., TexApp–Fort Worth, 983 SW2d 1, reh overr, aff 972 SW2d 713.—App & E 946, 961; Evid 544, 545, 546, 555.2, 555.5, 555.7; Judgm 185(2); Pretrial Proc 25, 40, 390; Prod Liab 8; Trial 43.

Gammill v. Jack Williams Chevrolet, Inc., TexApp–Fort Worth, 875 SW2d 27, reh den, and writ den, appeal after remand 983 SW2d 1, reh overr, aff 972 SW2d 713. —Judgm 185.3(21).

Gammill v. Mullins, TexCivApp–Eastland, 188 SW2d 986, dism.—Autos 244(28), 245(31); Labor & Emp 3047; Trial 140(2).

Gammill v. State, TexCrimApp, 117 SW2d 790, 135 Tex-Crim 52.—Ind & Inf 114; Sent & Pun 1309.

Gammill v. State, TexCrimApp, 112 SW2d 725, 133 Tex-Crim 489.—Crim Law 400(7); Forg 44(2).

Gammill v. State, TexCrimApp, 102 SW2d 1056, 132 TexCrim 63.—Forg 44(2).

Gammill v. State, TexCrimApp, 102 SW2d 229, 132 Tex-Crim 43.—Forg 32, 44(3).

Gamon v. State, TexCrimApp, 295 SW2d 225.—Crim Law 1070.

Gamza v. Aguirre, CA5 (Tex), 619 F2d 449, 66 ALR Fed 741, reh den 625 F2d 1016.—Const Law 242.2(3), 3039, 3613(2); Elections 10 1/2, 12, 62.

Ganda, Inc. v. All Plastics Molding, Inc., TexCivApp–Waco, 521 SW2d 940, ref nre.—Costs 194.32; Damag 40(1); Guar 16(1), 36(9); Judgm 185(6), 185.3(2); Sales 359(2).

Gandara v. Carrasco, TexApp–El Paso, 718 SW2d 64.—Elections 280.

Gandara v. Novasad, TexApp–Corpus Christi, 752 SW2d 740.—App & E 223, 837(9); Health 706; Judgm 185.1(8), 185.3(21).

Gandara v. Slade, TexApp–Austin, 832 SW2d 164.—Const Law 328, 2315; Death 7, 15, 103(3); Judgm 185(2), 185.3(2).

Gandara v. State, TexApp–El Paso, 661 SW2d 749, petition for discretionary review refused.—Autos 411, 419, 422.1.

Gandara-Nunez; U.S. v., CA5 (Tex), 564 F2d 693.—Cust Dut 126(4); Searches 49.

Gandarilla-Hernandez; U.S. v., CA5 (Tex), 157 FedAppx 772, cert den Arreola-Amaya v. US, 126 SCt 1487, 547 US 1012, 164 LEd2d 264.—Crim Law 1042.

G & C Packing Co., Inc. v. Commander, TexApp–Tyler, 932 SW2d 525, writ den.—App & E 957(1), 977(5), 1178(1); Const Law 4010; Judgm 123(1), 139, 143(3), 145(2), 146, 169.

G & E Cabinet, Inc.; Gonzalez v., TexApp–San Antonio, 694 SW2d 384. See Gonzalez v. Gutierrez.

G & G Fishing Tool Service; K & G Oil Tool & Service Co. v., Tex, 314 SW2d 782, 158 Tex 594, on reh 1958 WL 91271, cert den G & G Fishing Magnets, Inc v. K & G Oil Tool & Service Co, 79 SCt 223, 358 US 898, 3 LEd2d 149, reh den 79 SCt 578, 359 US 921, 3 LEd2d 583.—Antitrust 410, 420; App & E 1089(2); Corp 306; Equity 84, 87(2); Inj 56, 113, 208, 211; Partners 153(1); Pat 182.

G & G Fishing Tools Service v. K & G Oil Tool & Service Co., TexCivApp–Texarkana, 305 SW2d 637, rev 314 SW2d 782, 158 Tex 594, on reh K & G Oil Tool & Service Co, Inc v. G & G Fishing Tool Service, 1958 WL 91271, cert den G & G Fishing Magnets, Inc v K & G Oil Tool & Service Co, 79 SCt 223, 358 US 898, 3 LEd2d 149, reh den 79 SCt 578, 359 US 921, 3 LEd2d 583.—Antitrust 420; Courts 493(3); Equity 84; Inj 12, 56.

G & H Diversified Mfg., Inc.; Mosqueda v., TexApp–Houston (14 Dist), 223 SW3d 571, reh overr.—App & E 179(3), 863, 934(1); Contracts 176(1); Corp 1.5(1), 1.5(3); Joint Adv 7; Judgm 183, 190, 199(3.2), 199(3.4), 199(3.9); Labor & Emp 943, 2764, 2791, 2820, 3096(7); Stip 11; Work Comp 201, 206, 2084, 2161, 2237.

G. & H. Equipment Co., Inc. v. Alexander, TexCivApp–Fort Worth, 533 SW2d 872.—App & E 662(4), 715(2), 1070(1); Autos 197(7), 245(30); Damag 132(3); Evid 589, 590; Exceptions Bill of54; Witn 367(1).

Gandhi v. Gandhi, TexCivApp–Hous (1 Dist), 564 SW2d 388.—Divorce 222.

Gandhi; Gandhi v., TexCivApp–Hous (1 Dist), 564 SW2d 388.—Divorce 222.

G. & H. Motor Freight Lines v. Railroad Commission, TexCivApp–Austin, 140 SW2d 946, writ dism, correct.—Admin Law 481; Autos 82; Const Law 3998, 4027, 4364.

G & H Offshore Towing Co.; Fluor Western, Inc. v., CA5 (Tex), 447 F2d 35, cert den 92 SCt 959, 405 US 922, 30 LEd2d 793.—Contracts 1, 108(1); Fed Cts 743; Ship 104.

G & H Offshore Towing Co.; Offshore Co. v., CA5 (Tex), 403 F2d 715, cert den 89 SCt 1309, 394 US 9604, 22 LEd2d 561.—Towage 15(2).

G & H Offshore Towing Co.; Offshore Co. v., SDTex, 287 FSupp 724, aff 403 F2d 715, cert den 89 SCt 1309, 394 US 9604, 22 LEd2d 561.—Towage 6, 7, 15(2), 15(3).

G & H Offshore Towing Co.; Offshore Co. v., SDTex, 262 FSupp 282.—Action 27(2); Adm 124; Towage 4, 8, 11(1), 14, 15(1), 15(2).

G & H Partners, Ltd. v. Boer Goats Intern. Ltd., WDTex, 896 FSupp 660, aff 84 F3d 432.—Const Law 3964; Fed Civ Proc 462, 492, 1835; Fed Cts 76, 76.5, 76.10, 76.30, 86, 96.

G & H Towing Co.; Gerdes v., SDTex, 967 FSupp 943.—Damag 30.

G & H Towing Co.; Vowell v., SDTex, 870 FSupp 162.—Fed Civ Proc 1441, 2512; Seamen 2, 29(5.9), 29(5.16).

G & K Services, Inc.; Forest Lane Porsche Audi Associates v., TexApp–Fort Worth, 717 SW2d 470.—Accord 25(1); App & E 173(9), 901, 907(3); Contracts 245(1), 338(1); Damag 140; Nova 11; Plead 234, 236(2), 236(7), 238(3), 261, 262, 356.

G & L Tool Co. of Utah, Inc.; Carter v., TexCivApp–San Antonio, 428 SW2d 677.—App & E 907(3); Appear 9(4), 9(5), 12, 19(1), 19(4), 20, 22; Judgm 470, 482, 497(1), 815, 822(1); Proc 4.

G & M Bear Equipment Co.; Potomac Leasing Co. v., SDTex, 126 FRD 526. See Potomac Leasing Co. v. Uriarte.

G. & M. Products Corp. v. Clayton Specialties, Inc., TexCivApp–Houston, 386 SW2d 843.—App & E 934(1); Contracts 326; Corp 503(2); Evid 95; Plead 111.42(4); Venue 22(8).

G & R Gourmet Foods, Inc. v. Blue Corn Connection, TexApp–Houston (1 Dist), 811 SW2d 184. See G & R Gourmet Foods, Inc. v. Natural Choice, Inc.

G & R Gourmet Foods, Inc. v. Natural Choice, Inc., TexApp–Houston (1 Dist), 811 SW2d 184.—Courts 12(2.15); Judgm 818(4), 818(6).

G & R Inv. v. Nance, TexApp–Houston (14 Dist), 683 SW2d 727, ref nre.—Lim of Act 48(2), 66(12).

G & R Investments v. Nance, TexCivApp–Hous (14 Dist), 588 SW2d 804, ref nre.—App & E 488(1), 790(3); Costs 226; Inj 135.

G & W Body Works, Inc. v. Eschberger's Estate, TexCivApp–Waco, 557 SW2d 835, ref nre.—Judgm 942, 944.

G & W Marine, Inc. v. Morris, TexCivApp–Beaumont, 471 SW2d 644.—Costs 194.10; Evid 450(8), 461(1); Interest 31, 44; Labor & Emp 254, 265, 2204.

Gandy, Ex parte, TexCrimApp, 603 SW2d 860.—Hab Corp 506.

Gandy, In re, CA5 (Tex), 299 F3d 489.—Alt Disp Res 121, 191, 210; Bankr 2022, 2060.1, 2084.1, 2151, 2703, 3031, 3768, 3782, 3784; Partners 353.

Gandy, In re, BkrtcySDTex, 327 BR 807.—Bankr 2761, 2774; Home 5, 31, 32, 33; Statut 188.

Gandy, In re, BkrtcySDTex, 327 BR 796.—Bankr 2062, 2391, 2402(1), 2402(3); Judgm 828.21(2).

Gandy; Continental Pipe Line Co. v., TexCivApp–San Antonio, 142 SW2d 631.—App & E 781(4).

Gandy; Continental Pipe Line Co. v., TexCivApp–El Paso, 162 SW2d 755, writ refused wom.—Dedi 57; Em Dom 2(6); High 88; Tel 792, 838.

Gandy v. Culpepper, TexCivApp–Beaumont, 528 SW2d 333.—Adv Poss 16(1), 21, 22, 57; App & E 994(3), 1008.1(2); Ven & Pur 231(1).

Gandy; Ener v., Tex, 158 SW2d 989, 138 Tex 295.—Autos 195(5.1).

Gandy; Ener v., TexCivApp–Beaumont, 141 SW2d 772, aff 158 SW2d 989, 138 Tex 295.—Autos 195(5.1), 198(4).

Gandy v. Miller's Supermarket, TexCivApp–Waco, 348 SW2d 173.—Mun Corp 819(1).

Gandy v. Pemberton, TexCivApp–Austin, 389 SW2d 612, ref nre.—Adv Poss 114(1); Tresp to T T 41(3).

Gandy v. Pillsbury Mills, TexCivApp–Austin, 235 SW2d 470, writ refused.—Antitrust 576; Contracts 143.5, 147(3).

Gandy; Sampson v., TexCivApp–Galveston, 116 SW2d 767.—Courts 85(3); Plead 111.18; Venue 22(1), 22(6).

Gandy v. Southwestern Bell Tel. Co., TexCivApp–San Antonio, 341 SW2d 554, 85 ALR2d 833.—App & E 927(7); Neglig 1612, 1619; Tel 853, 915, 916(6).

Gandy; Sparks v., TexCivApp–Beaumont, 213 SW2d 559.—App & E 931(6), 1054(1), 1073(1); Child C 76; Judgm 512.

Gandy v. State, TexCrimApp, 384 SW2d 887.—Crim Law 706(3), 863(2), 1063(5), 1090.4, 1170(1), 1170.5(2).

Gandy v. State, TexCrimApp, 143 SW2d 392, 140 TexCrim 43.—Crim Law 1097(4), 1097(5), 1099.10; Homic 1158, 1467.

Gandy v. State, TexCrimApp, 140 SW2d 182, 139 TexCrim 343.—Crim Law 390, 721(3), 730(1), 865(1.5), 928, 956(11), 956(13); Homic 1154.

Gandy v. State, TexCrimApp, 139 SW2d 275, 139 TexCrim 140.—Crim Law 566; Jury 116; Weights 12.

Gandy v. State, TexCrimApp, 129 SW2d 661, 137 TexCrim 412.—Crim Law 675, 730(3); Homic 930.

Gandy v. State, TexApp–Houston (1 Dist), 835 SW2d 238, petition for discretionary review refused.—Crim Law 394.6(4), 507(1), 510, 511.1(1), 511.1(3), 511.1(9), 511.2, 511.5, 511.7, 1144.12, 1158(4); Searches 18, 60.1, 62, 66, 171, 183, 194, 201.

Gandy v. State, TexApp–Houston (14 Dist), 222 SW3d 525.—Crim Law 29(14), 798(0.5), 814(1), 824(4), 872.5, 1038.1(1), 1038.2, 1038.3, 1162, 1169.1(1), 1172.1(1), 1172.1(2); Environ Law 746, 754; Ind & Inf 125(19.1), 125(20).

Gandy v. State, TexCivApp–Beaumont, 319 SW2d 375.—App & E 554(1); Em Dom 157, 191(8), 195, 246(2), 263.

Gandy v. State, TexCivApp–Waco, 293 SW2d 534, ref nre.—App & E 930(1), 1010.1(1); Em Dom 221, 223, 241, 262(5); Plead 34(1).

Gandy; State Farm Fire and Cas. Co. v., Tex, 925 SW2d 696.—Compromise 2, 7.1; Courts 100(1); Insurance 3441, 3556.

Gandy; State Farm Fire & Cas. Co. v., TexApp–Texarkana, 880 SW2d 129, reh overr, and writ gr, rev 925 SW2d 696.—Antitrust 141, 291, 292, 369, 390, 398; App & E 169, 970(2), 989, 999(1), 1001(1); Costs 194.18, 208; Evid 538, 546; Insurance 2278(3), 2358, 2937, 2941, 3579; Neglig 234.

Gandy; Thompson v., TexCivApp–Eastland, 160 SW2d 113, writ refused wom.—Bills & N 92(1), 139(3), 493(3).

Gandy v. U.S., CA5 (Tex), 234 F3d 281.—Fed Cts 755, 869; Int Rev 4482; U S 133.

Gandy; Western Tank & Steel Corp. v., TexCivApp–Texarkana, 385 SW2d 406.—Contracts 28(1), 322(1); Corp 503(2); Plead 111.12; Sales 255, 262.5; Venue 8.5(8).

Gandy Nursery, Inc. v. U.S., CA5 (Tex), 412 F3d 602.—Fed Cts 776; Interest 39(3); Int Rev 4915; U S 110.

Gandy Nursery, Inc. v. U.S., CA5 (Tex), 318 F3d 631, on remand 2004 WL 838062, rev 412 F3d 602.—Fed Cts 776, 850.1; Int Rev 4665, 4915; Judgm 634, 713(1); Lim of Act 58(1); U S 125(1), 133.

Ganesan v. James, CA5 (Tex), 115 FedAppx 670.—Civil R 1036, 1094; Fed Cts 714, 915.

Ganesan v. State, TexApp–Austin, 45 SW3d 197, reh overr, and petition for discretionary review refused.—Crim Law 45, 369.2(1), 695.5, 713, 719(1), 723(3), 730(1), 730(7), 730(14), 1037.1(1), 1037.1(2), 1045, 1136, 1171.1(2.1), 1171.1(6); Homic 562, 1465; Ind & Inf 58.1.

Ganesan v. Vallabhaneni, TexApp–Austin, 96 SW3d 345, reh overr, and review den.—App & E 757(1), 840(4), 901, 907(4), 930(1), 946, 969, 989, 996, 1001(1), 1003(6), 1050.1(1), 1056.1(1); Divorce 148, 151, 179; Evid 596(1); Hus & W 264(1), 270(8); Marriage 50(1); Records 22; Trial 43, 182, 202, 219, 251(1), 252(1), 295(2).

Gani v. Gani, Tex, 495 SW2d 576, on remand 500 SW2d 254.—Child C 902; Child S 537; Courts 247(1).

Gani; Gani v., Tex, 495 SW2d 576, on remand 500 SW2d 254.—Child C 902; Child S 537; Courts 247(1).

Gani v. Gani, TexCivApp–Texarkana, 500 SW2d 254.—Child C 178, 188, 218; Child S 444.

Gani; Gani v., TexCivApp–Texarkana, 500 SW2d 254.—Child C 178, 188, 218; Child S 444.

Gani v. Gani, TexCivApp–Texarkana, 488 SW2d 901, rev 495 SW2d 576, on remand 500 SW2d 254.—App & E 77(1).

Gani; Gani v., TexCivApp–Texarkana, 488 SW2d 901, rev 495 SW2d 576, on remand 500 SW2d 254.—App & E 77(1).

Gani v. Gani, TexCivApp–Texarkana, 475 SW2d 810.—App & E 77(1); Child C 525.

Gani; Gani v., TexCivApp–Texarkana, 475 SW2d 810.—App & E 77(1); Child C 525.

Ganim v. State, TexApp–Houston (1 Dist), 638 SW2d 628.—Const Law 2604; Crim Law 1010, 1106(1).

Gann; First Nat. Bank of El Campo v., TexCivApp–Galveston, 150 SW2d 290, writ refused.—Hus & W 273(1), 273(2), 274(1).

Gann v. Hopkins, TexCivApp–San Antonio, 119 SW2d 110.—App & E 1176(1); Judgm 137; Mand 50.

Gann v. Keith, Tex, 253 SW2d 413, 151 Tex 626.—Autos 11, 316; Const Law 42(2), 695; Statut 47; Venue 8.5(4).

GANN

Gann v. Keith, TexCivApp–San Antonio, 249 SW2d 683, certified question answered 253 SW2d 413, 151 Tex 626.—Autos 316; Plead 111.42(7); Statut 47, 220; Venue 8.5(4).

Gann v. Keith, TexCivApp–San Antonio, 240 SW2d 822, certified question answered 246 SW2d 616, 151 Tex 130.—Plead 111.17; Venue 8.5(4), 8.5(8).

Gann v. Meek, CCA5 (Tex), 165 F2d 857, cert den 68 SCt 1500, 334 US 849, 92 LEd 1772.—Armed S 77(5), 77(19); Evid 23(1).

Gann; Miller v., Tex, 842 SW2d 641.—Estop 68(2).

Gann; Miller v., TexApp–Houston (1 Dist), 822 SW2d 283, writ den with per curiam opinion 842 SW2d 641.—App & E 863, 927(7), 946, 962, 984(1), 997(3); Costs 2; Evid 207(1), 265(7); Partners 115, 196; Pretrial Proc 558; Quiet T 47(1).

Gann v. Montgomery, TexCivApp–Fort Worth, 210 SW2d 255, ref nre.—Home 1, 58, 69, 73, 81; Judgm 455.

Gann v. Murray, Tex, 246 SW2d 616, 151 Tex 130.—Mand 172; Plead 111.17, 111.39(6), 111.41; Venue 8.5(4).

Gann v. Putman, TexCivApp–San Antonio, 159 SW2d 931, writ refused.—Inj 26(5); Judgm 461(1), 747(4); Lim of Act 39(1).

Gann v. Putman, TexCivApp–El Paso, 141 SW2d 758, writ dism, correct.—Judgm 497(1), 518; Plead 205(2), 209, 228.15, 228.16, 404; Tresp to T T 32.

Gann v. State, TexApp–Houston (1 Dist), 818 SW2d 69, petition for discretionary review refused by 825 SW2d 466.—Const Law 2793; Crim Law 1134(3).

Gann; U.S. v., CA5 (Tex), 142 FedAppx 826, cert den 126 SCt 839, 546 US 1080, 163 LEd2d 714.—Crim Law 1042.

Gannaway; Barrera v., TexComApp, 105 SW2d 876, 130 Tex 142.—App & E 1073(1); Des & Dist 90(1); Evid 87; Lim of Act 99(1), 197(2).

Gannaway v. Lundstrom, TexCivApp–San Antonio, 204 SW2d 999, dism.—Contracts 188; Frds St of 23(4); Impl & C C 33.1, 72; Trial 365.2.

Gannaway v. State, TexApp–Dallas, 823 SW2d 675, petition for discretionary review refused.—Crim Law 419(4), 419(12), 1169.1(9); Witn 363(1), 372(1).

Gannaway v. Trinity Universal Ins. Co., TexCivApp–San Antonio, 85 SW2d 345, writ refused.—New Tr 102(1), 108(2); Venue 42, 70.

Ganne, In re, TexApp–Austin, 643 SW2d 195.—Contempt 20.

Gannett Outdoor Co. of Texas v. Kubeczka, TexApp–Houston (14 Dist), 710 SW2d 79.—App & E 207, 213, 237(1), 930(3), 1004(5), 1004(11), 1026, 1060.1(1); Damag 71, 91(1), 94, 103, 105, 109, 110, 163(1), 165; Evid 474(19), 508, 525, 538; Neglig 232, 250, 273, 379, 380, 387, 423, 431, 1241, 1579, 1672, 1679, 1708, 1714, 1742; Pretrial Proc 40, 45; Trial 114, 131(1), 139.1(7).

Gannon v. Baker, Tex, 818 SW2d 754, on remand 830 SW2d 706, writ den.—Evid 385, 389, 410.

Gannon v. Baker, TexApp–Houston (1 Dist), 830 SW2d 706, writ den.—App & E 854(1), 934(1); Contracts 9(1), 9(2), 9(3); Corp 116; Frds St of 84, 111, 112; Gifts 4, 29; Judgm 185(2); Sec Reg 248.

Gannon v. Baker, TexApp–Houston (1 Dist), 807 SW2d 793, writ gr, rev in part 818 SW2d 754, on remand 830 SW2d 706, writ den.—App & E 293, 854(1), 1031(1); Corp 182.4(6), 320(4); Evid 441(1), 441(9); Trial 392(0.5), 395(1).

Gannon; Bywaters v., Tex, 686 SW2d 593.—Adv Poss 33, 114(1), 115(1); Trial 139.1(17).

Gannon v. Bywaters, TexApp–Dallas, 669 SW2d 756, writ gr, rev 686 SW2d 593.—Adv Poss 13, 19; App & E 770(1); Evid 594.

Gannon v. Payne, Tex, 706 SW2d 304.—Courts 480(1), 507, 511, 512, 516.

Gannon v. Payne, TexApp–Dallas, 695 SW2d 741, writ gr, rev 706 SW2d 304.—App & E 954(1); Courts 28, 512, 516; Inj 32, 151.

Gano v. City of Houston, TexApp–Houston (14 Dist), 834 SW2d 585, reh den, and writ den.—Tax 2699(11).

Gano v. Filter-Aid Co., TexCivApp–Austin, 414 SW2d 480.—Const Law 2647; Corp 592.5, 629.

Gano v. Jamail, TexApp–Houston (14 Dist), 678 SW2d 152.—Estop 92(2); Frds St of 44(2), 49, 159.

Gano v. State, TexCrimApp, 466 SW2d 730.—Autos 316, 351.1; Crim Law 419(1.5), 1130(2), 1166(1), 1168(1); Ind & Inf 54.

Gano v. State, TexApp–Amarillo, 684 SW2d 727, petition for discretionary review gr, and rev.—Crim Law 273.1(2), 1026.10(4), 1036.1(4), 1134(3).

Gano v. Villarreal, TexApp–Corpus Christi, 745 SW2d 586.—Contempt 66(5); Prohib 1, 5(1), 10(1).

Gans & Smith Ins. Agency, Inc.; Calk v., TexCivApp–Tyler, 535 SW2d 755.—App & E 300, 387(3), 387(6), 395, 428(2), 430(1), 503, 609, 640, 656(1); New Tr 117(1), 119; Time 9(6).

Gans & Smith Ins. Agency, Inc.; Huckaby v., EDTex, 293 FSupp2d 715.—Rem of C 36, 107(7).

Ganschow; Doran Chevrolet-Peugeot, Inc. v., TexApp–Dallas, 701 SW2d 260, ref nre.—Sales 255.

Gansel v. Amarillo Hardware Co., TexCivApp–Amarillo, 592 SW2d 435, dism.—Paymt 6; Venue 7.5(3).

Ganske v. Spence, TexApp–Waco, 129 SW3d 701.—App & E 856(1), 946, 970(2); Contracts 143(2), 143.5, 147(1), 147(2), 152, 169, 176(2); Evid 161.1, 165(1), 397(1), 397(3); Ex & Ad 420; Indem 31(1), 33(1); Judgm 181(19), 185(6).

Gansky v. State, TexApp–Fort Worth, 180 SW3d 240, petition for discretionary review refused.—Arrest 63.4(1), 63.5(4); Autos 349(6); Crim Law 1139, 1144.12, 1158(4).

Gansle; Strain v., TexApp–Corpus Christi, 768 SW2d 345, writ den.—Damag 189.

Gant; Bexar County v., TexApp–San Antonio, 70 SW3d 289, review den.—Admin Law 229; App & E 93, 893(1), 911.3; Civil R 1147, 1708, 1715; Counties 67.

Gant v. DeLeon, Tex, 786 SW2d 259.—Lim of Act 119(3); Pretrial Proc 560.

Gant; De Leon v., TexApp–San Antonio, 773 SW2d 396, rev Gant v. DeLeon, 786 SW2d 259.—Judgm 185.1(8), 185.3(2); Lim of Act 119(3), 199(1).

Gant v. Dumas Glass and Mirror, Inc., TexApp–Amarillo, 935 SW2d 202, reh overr.—App & E 922, 968, 1004(7); Autos 242(6); Damag 48, 135, 192; Jury 90, 97(1), 105(4), 133; Labor & Emp 3045, 3046(1).

Gant v. Garofano, CA5 (Tex), 119 FedAppx 602, cert den 126 SCt 159, 546 US 862, 163 LEd2d 145.—Lim of Act 105(2), 130(7).

Gant; General American Life Ins. Co. v., TexCivApp–Austin, 119 SW2d 693, dism.—Evid 241(1), 244(8); Insurance 2031, 3015; Trial 237(4), 352.10.

Gant; Hartford Acc. & Indem. Co. v., TexCivApp–Dallas, 346 SW2d 359.—App & E 766, 931(1), 989; Work Comp 535, 1519, 1536, 1927.

Gant; James' Estate v., TexCivApp–Waco, 469 SW2d 927.—Evid 471(14), 505, 568(2), 571(2); Mental H 13, 510.

Gant v. Lockheed Martin Corp., CA5 (Tex), 152 FedAppx 396, cert den 126 SCt 1919, 547 US 1110, 164 LEd2d 662.—Civil R 1326(1); Fed Civ Proc 2840; Tel 1298.

Gant v. Lowry, TexCivApp–Beaumont, 156 SW2d 564, writ refused wom.—Mines 92.38, 92.39.

Gant; Parker v., TexCivApp–Dallas, 568 SW2d 163, ref nre.—App & E 82(3), 873(2); Judgm 335(3), 335(4).

Gant v. Principi, CA5 (Tex), 180 FedAppx 489, appeal dism 127 SCt 289, 166 LEd2d 9.—Fed Cts 663.

Gant v. Sabine Pilots, EDTex, 204 FSupp2d 977.—Civil R 1120, 1137, 1544; Fed Civ Proc 2497.1.

Gant v. St. Louis-San Francisco Ry. Co., TexCivApp–Dallas, 474 SW2d 516.—App & E 1170.10; R R 276(3), 282(5), 282(10); Trial 366.

Gant v. State, TexCrimApp, 649 SW2d 30, cert den 104 SCt 122, 464 US 836, 78 LEd2d 120.—Crim Law 369.1, 390, 394.6(4), 519(8), 1169.1(7); Homic 963.

Gant v. State, TexCrimApp, 606 SW2d 867.—Crim Law 784(1), 1203.27; Larc 40(2); Sent & Pun 1209, 1260, 1321, 1388.

Gant v. State, TexCrimApp, 513 SW2d 52.—Crim Law 338(1), 370, 372(14), 376, 1169.11.

Gant v. State, TexCrimApp, 328 SW2d 768, 168 TexCrim 448.—Crim Law 730(1), 730(3); Homic 1481.

Gant v. State, TexCrimApp, 292 SW2d 127.—Crim Law 1090.1(1).

Gant v. State, TexCrimApp, 291 SW2d 741.—Crim Law 1090.1(1).

Gant v. State, TexCrimApp, 291 SW2d 729.—Crim Law 1090.1(1), 1094(1).

Gant v. State, TexCrimApp, 289 SW2d 771.—Crim Law 1090.1(1).

Gant v. State, TexCrimApp, 287 SW2d 483.—Crim Law 1090.1(1).

Gant v. State, TexCrimApp, 283 SW2d 942.—Crim Law 1090.1(1).

Gant v. State, TexCrimApp, 268 SW2d 169.—Crim Law 1090.1(1).

Gant v. State, TexCrimApp, 257 SW2d 113, 158 TexCrim 484.—Crim Law 1171.1(2.1).

Gant v. State, TexApp–Austin, 814 SW2d 444.—Crim Law 13.1(1), 562, 772(6), 814(5), 1144.13(3), 1159.2(7); Sec Reg 244, 245, 323, 326, 329.

Gant v. State, TexApp–Beaumont, 153 SW3d 294, petition for discretionary review dism as untimely filed, and petition for discretionary review refused, cert den 126 SCt 1574, 547 US 1023, 164 LEd2d 307.—Crim Law 406(1), 407(1), 412.1(1), 412.1(4), 412.2(2), 419(1), 419(14), 1035(5), 1036.5, 1153(1), 1169.2(6).

Gant v. State, TexApp–Tyler, 116 SW3d 124, petition stricken, and petition for discretionary review refused. —Arrest 63.5(4), 63.5(9); Autos 349(2.1), 349(4), 349(8), 349(17), 349.5(1); Const Law 4693; Controlled Subs 26, 27, 28, 30, 46, 79, 80, 97, 137; Crim Law 59(5), 394.6(4), 394.6(5), 720(2), 720(6), 720(7.1), 723(3), 726, 792(2), 1134(2), 1139, 1144.13(1), 1144.13(2.1), 1144.13(6), 1147, 1153(1), 1158(4), 1159.2(1), 1159.2(2), 1159.2(7), 1159.2(9), 1159.3(1), 1159.4(2), 1171.1(2.1), 1187; Searches 62.

Gant v. Stewart, TexCivApp–Waco, 347 SW2d 1, ref nre. —Mtg 338, 379; Subrog 29.

Gant v. Texas, CA5 (Tex), 123 FedAppx 622, cert den 126 SCt 1372, 546 US 1188, 164 LEd2d 80.—Courts 509.

Gant; U.S. v., CA5 (Tex), 759 F2d 484, reh den 765 F2d 1120, cert den 106 SCt 149, 474 US 851, 88 LEd2d 123. —Crim Law 394.4(6), 394.5(4), 1158(4); Searches 113.1.

Gant; U.S. v., CA5 (Tex), 691 F2d 1159.—Assault 69; Crim Law 38, 255.4, 260.11(2), 260.11(3.1), 569, 1144.13(7), 1158(1); Weap 4, 13, 17(5).

Gant; U.S. v., EDTex, 858 FSupp 74, aff 81 F3d 157.— Arrest 63.5(4); Autos 349(2.1), 349(17), 349.5(8); Searches 180, 181.

Gant; U.S. v., SDTex, 587 FSupp 128, rev 759 F2d 484, reh den 765 F2d 1120, cert den 106 SCt 149, 474 US 851, 88 LEd2d 123.—Action 69(5); Crim Law 394.4(6), 394.5(4); Searches 113.1, 114, 115.1, 117, 192.1, 200.

Gant Cooley Cotton Co., Inc. v. Thoms, TexCivApp–Corpus Christi, 500 SW2d 537.—Plead 111.3, 111.15; Venue 7.5(2), 7.5(7).

Ganther v. Ingle, CA5 (Tex), 75 F3d 207.—Civil R 1331(4), 1376(2), 1376(7); Fed Civ Proc 1992, 2411, 2419, 2553; Fed Cts 269, 272, 776, 815.

Ganther v. State, TexApp–Houston (14 Dist), 187 SW3d 641, petition for discretionary review refused.—Crim Law 641.4(1), 641.4(2), 641.4(4), 641.10(3), 655(4), 1030(1), 1147.

Ganther v. State, TexApp–Houston (14 Dist), 848 SW2d 881, petition for discretionary review refused.—Crim Law 1152(2); Jury 131(4).

Gant, Inc.; Texas Employment Commission v., TexCivApp–San Antonio, 604 SW2d 211.—App & E 327(2); Unemp Comp 455, 465, 470, 486, 493(10).

Gantt; Blackburn v., TexCivApp–Hous (1 Dist), 561 SW2d 269.—Mental H 114, 116.1, 135.

Gantt v. Gantt, TexApp–Houston (14 Dist), 208 SW3d 27, reh overr, and review den, and reh of petition for review den.—App & E 23, 185(1), 428(2), 430(1), 1097(1); Bankr 2157; Courts 24, 37(1), 37(2), 40, 90(1), 99(1); Divorce 165(4), 181, 186; Estop 52(8).

Gantt; Gantt v., TexApp–Houston (14 Dist), 208 SW3d 27, reh overr, and review den, and reh of petition for review den.—App & E 23, 185(1), 428(2), 430(1), 1097(1); Bankr 2157; Courts 24, 37(1), 37(2), 40, 90(1), 99(1); Divorce 165(4), 181, 186; Estop 52(8).

Gantt v. Mobil Chemical Co., CA5 (Tex), 463 F2d 691.— Damag 134(1); Fed Cts 909, 911; Indem 33(5); Neglig 1696, 1719, 1745; Prod Liab 43.

Gantt; Russ Berrie and Co., Inc. v., TexApp–El Paso, 998 SW2d 713.—Alt Disp Res 114, 116, 117, 134(1), 137, 213(1), 213(5); Commerce 80.5; Contracts 10(1), 129(1); Labor & Emp 34(2), 40(2), 79; Mand 60; States 18.15.

Gantz v. State, TexApp–San Antonio, 661 SW2d 213, petition for discretionary review refused.—Assault 96(7); Crim Law 351(3), 552(2), 673(5), 778(2), 784(1), 790, 795(1), 814(19), 1043(3), 1130(2), 1169.5(1), 1169.5(3), 1186.1; Homic 852, 854, 881, 908, 975, 1021, 1022, 1168, 1332, 1465; Ind & Inf 65, 71.2(2), 137(6), 191(4); Sent & Pun 98.

Ganz v. Lyons Partnership, L.P., NDTex, 961 FSupp 981.—Banks 191.10, 191.15; Contracts 147(1), 176(2), 176(10), 202(1), 211; Damag 40(1), 189, 190; Evid 264, 571(5), 571(10); Fed Civ Proc 1938.1, 2173.1(1), 2313, 2336, 2377; Sales 81(1), 89, 179(6), 417, 418(16.1).

Ganz v. Lyons Partnership, L.P., NDTex, 173 FRD 173. —Fed Civ Proc 2736, 2741; Partners 375.

Ganze v. Dart Industries, Inc., CA5 (Tex), 741 F2d 790. —Fed Cts 205; Labor & Emp 488, 548, 558; Trusts 231(1).

Ganzer; Combined Am. Ins. Co. v., TexCivApp–Waco, 350 SW2d 211.—Autos 1; Insurance 2445, 2588(2).

G.A.O. v. State, TexApp–San Antonio, 854 SW2d 710.— Const Law 3855; Crim Law 1028, 1030(1), 1184(3); Double J 2, 5.1, 33, 100.1, 148, 201; Estop 52.10(3); Infants 131, 203, 210, 241, 243, 253, 254.

Gaona v. Erwin, CA5 (Tex), 224 FedAppx 327.—Const Law 4822, 4824, 4838; Pardon 46; Prisons 4(7), 13(4).

Gaona v. Gaona, TexApp–San Antonio, 627 SW2d 821.— Child C 633, 637.

Gaona; Gaona v., TexApp–San Antonio, 627 SW2d 821.— Child C 633, 637.

Gaona v. Gonzales, TexApp–Austin, 997 SW2d 784, reh overr.—Judgm 181(15.1), 780(1), 780(3), 785(1), 787; Ven & Pur 54, 231(1), 231(16.1), 233.

Gaona v. Pastor, TexCivApp–Corpus Christi, 515 SW2d 337.—App & E 989; Autos 244(42), 244(58), 247; Neglig 1656, 1676, 1693.

Gaona v. State, TexApp–Corpus Christi, 733 SW2d 611, petition for discretionary review refused.—Crim Law 20, 772(6), 925.5(1), 925.5(3), 1144.13(1); Homic 663, 709, 1150, 1387; Jury 110(2).

Gaona; U.S. v., WDTex, 445 FSupp 1237.—Evid 42; Jury 33(1.1), 33(1.10), 33(1.15).

Gaona-Rodriguez; U.S. v., CA5 (Tex), 144 FedAppx 405, cert den 126 SCt 815, 546 US 1068, 163 LEd2d 641.— Crim Law 1042.

Gap Inc.; Laxton v., CA5 (Tex), 333 F3d 572, reh and reh den 75 FedAppx 982.—Civil R 1137, 1176, 1535, 1537, 1544, 1545, 1555; Fed Civ Proc 2338.1, 2339, 2373, 2377; Fed Cts 765, 801, 825.

GAP

Gap, Inc.; Soverain Software LLC v., EDTex, 340 FSupp2d 760.—Fed Cts 776, 870.1; Witn 198(1), 217, 219(3), 222, 223.

Gappelberg v. Landrum, Tex, 666 SW2d 88.—Sales 113, 153, 168.5(1), 398.

Gappelberg v. Landrum, TexApp–Dallas, 654 SW2d 549, writ gr, rev 666 SW2d 88.—Sales 166(1).

Gappelberg; McCarty v., TexCivApp–Fort Worth, 273 SW2d 943, 46 ALR2d 93, ref nre.—App & E 1170.1, 1170.7; Autos 217(5), 243(17); Damag 169; Neglig 1642; Witn 414(1).

Gappelberg v. Video Station, Tex, 666 SW2d 88. See Gappelberg v. Landrum.

Garabed Gulbenkian; Penn v., TexCivApp–Dallas, 243 SW2d 220, aff 252 SW2d 929, 151 Tex 412.—Judgm 181(4), 181(5.1), 181(19); Pat 219(2).

Garabrant v. Burns, TexComApp, 111 SW2d 1100, 130 Tex 518.—Insurance 3471, 3473, 3475(2), 3475(3), 3475(5), 3475(8).

Garabrant v. Burns, TexCivApp–Fort Worth, 85 SW2d 859, rev 111 SW2d 1100, 130 Tex 518.—App & E 1058(1), 1062.1; Insurance 3465, 3470, 3471, 3475(2), 3475(8).

Garage De Le Paix, Inc.; Catania v., TexCivApp–Tyler, 542 SW2d 239, ref nre.—App & E 171(1), 219(2); Land & Ten 161(3); Trial 396(1); Trover 1, 35.

GAR Associates III, L.P. v. State ex rel. Texas Dept. of Transp., TexApp–Houston (1 Dist), 224 SW3d 395, reh overr.—App & E 863, 893(1), 916(1); Courts 39; Dedi 18(1); Em Dom 2.1, 106, 122, 266, 293(1), 307(2); Mun Corp 663(1), 669; Plead 104(1), 111.43; States 191.4(1), 191.9(3).

Garay v. County of Bexar, TexApp–San Antonio, 810 SW2d 760, writ den.—Admin Law 701, 763, 788, 791, 793; Const Law 90.1(7.2), 1929, 1933, 1947, 1955, 1957; Health 579; Offic 69.7, 69.12, 72.51, 72.54, 72.55(2), 72.63; Prisons 7; Witn 209.

Garay v. State, TexCrimApp, 389 SW2d 952.—Sent & Pun 1381(4).

Garay v. State, TexApp–Houston (1 Dist), 940 SW2d 211, reh overr, and petition for discretionary review refused. —Const Law 967, 984, 990, 1030, 1163, 1520, 3006, 3057, 3062, 3478, 3895, 3898, 4509(25); Crim Law 13.1(1), 1130(3); Statut 47, 107(1), 107(3), 109, 188, 189; Weap 3.

Garay v. State, TexApp–San Antonio, 954 SW2d 59, reh overr, and petition for discretionary review refused.— Const Law 990, 1030, 1134; Crim Law 13.1(1), 338(7), 398(1), 438(7), 438(8), 559, 700(9), 700(10), 795(1.5), 795(2.10), 1044.2(1), 1130(3), 1156(1); Double J 2, 135, 148; Ind & Inf 110(3), 110(19), 144.1(1), 191(0.5); Infants 12, 13, 20.

Garay v. State, TexApp–San Antonio, 755 SW2d 956.— Crim Law 1172.1(2).

Garay v. State, TexApp–Waco, 683 SW2d 21, petition for discretionary review refused.—Ind & Inf 4.5.

Garay v. State, TexApp–Houston (14 Dist), 681 SW2d 190, petition for discretionary review refused.—Infants 20.

Garay; U.S. v., CA5 (Tex), 235 F3d 230, cert den 121 SCt 1633, 532 US 986, 149 LEd2d 494.—Crim Law 1023(11), 1147; Sent & Pun 860, 909.

Garay; U.S. v., CA5 (Tex), 477 F2d 1306.—Controlled Subs 64, 118; Searches 24, 192.1.

Garay v. U.S., CA5 (Tex), 399 F2d 696.—Crim Law 1036.1(5).

Garbark v. Sieber, TexCivApp–Amarillo, 344 SW2d 911. —Child S 232, 328.

Garber; Hunley v., TexCivApp–Amarillo, 254 SW2d 813. —Bills & N 64; Evid 420(3); Insurance 1766; Judgm 181(6), 185(2), 185.3(12).

Garber; Malacara v., CA5 (Tex), 353 F3d 393.—Admin Law 751; Evid 600; Fed Civ Proc 2533.1, 2544, 2552, 2554; Fed Cts 634; Fraud 3; Labor & Emp 2714; Statut 208, 219(1).

Garber v. Sir Speedy, Inc., NDTex, 930 FSupp 267, aff 91 F3d 137.—Action 69(2), 69(3); Alt Disp Res 113, 191, 198, 200; Evid 43(4); Fed Cts 41.

Garber v. State, TexCrimApp, 165 SW2d 741, 145 Tex-Crim 44.—Ind & Inf 56, 71.2(2), 125(2), 137(6).

Garber v. State, TexApp–El Paso, 671 SW2d 94.—Controlled Subs 82; Crim Law 394.5(2), 577.11(1), 637, 721(3); Searches 13.1, 15.

Garber v. State, TexApp–El Paso, 667 SW2d 611.—Crim Law 86, 105, 1167(2); Hab Corp 621.1, 651.

Garber; Turner v., TexCivApp–Dallas, 232 SW2d 173.— Evid 186(6); Plead 111.2, 111.42(5).

Garber; U.S. v., CA5 (Tex), 471 F2d 212.—Crim Law 369.1, 378, 730(8), 1030(1), 1037.1(2), 1171.3; Witn 337(27), 345(1), 362.

Garbs v. State, TexCrimApp, 240 SW2d 304, 156 TexCrim 203.—Autos 355(6); Crim Law 1134(4); Jury 24.2.

Garbs v. State, TexCrimApp, 234 SW2d 869, 155 TexCrim 290.—Crim Law 1023(9); Sent & Pun 341, 2028.

Garces v. State, TexApp–Houston (14 Dist), 727 SW2d 48, petition for discretionary review refused.—Crim Law 1137(2); Searches 164, 186, 198.

Garces; Texas Emp. Ins. Ass'n v., TexCivApp–San Antonio, 492 SW2d 723.—Work Comp 1020, 1028, 1984.

Garcia, Ex parte, Tex, 795 SW2d 740.—Child S 496.

Garcia, Ex parte, TexCrimApp, 988 SW2d 240.—Crim Law 1081(1); Hab Corp 274, 817.1; Mand 3(1), 60.

Garcia, Ex parte, TexCrimApp, 682 SW2d 581.—Crim Law 273.1(2), 274(3.1), 275; Hab Corp 791.

Garcia, Ex parte, TexCrimApp, 578 SW2d 141.—Hab Corp 509(1).

Garcia, Ex parte, TexCrimApp, 560 SW2d 948.—Courts 490; Hab Corp 474; Ind & Inf 60, 196(5); Sent & Pun 1310, 1311; Weap 4.

Garcia, Ex parte, TexCrimApp, 548 SW2d 405.—Crim Law 1077.2(1), 1077.3; Hab Corp 724, 792.1, 845.

Garcia, Ex parte, TexCrimApp, 547 SW2d 271.—Arrest 70(2); Crim Law 223, 233; Hab Corp 701.1, 715.1, 716.

Garcia, Ex parte, TexCrimApp, 544 SW2d 432.—Hab Corp 474; Weap 17(1).

Garcia, Ex parte, TexCrimApp, 491 SW2d 669, cert den Garcia v. Texas, 94 SCt 172, 414 US 833, 38 LEd2d 68. —Crim Law 1136.

Garcia, Ex parte, TexCrimApp, 319 SW2d 328, 167 Tex-Crim 159.—Extrad 36, 39.

Garcia, Ex parte, TexCrimApp, 271 SW2d 942.—Bail 53.

Garcia, Ex parte, TexApp–Austin, 927 SW2d 787.—Double J 1, 51, 55; Ind & Inf 144.2, 159(1).

Garcia, Ex parte, TexApp–San Antonio, 100 SW3d 243.— Bail 39, 51, 52; Crim Law 1134(10), 1148.

Garcia, Ex parte, TexApp–El Paso, 831 SW2d 1.—Child S 543; Contempt 63(3).

Garcia, In Interest of, TexApp–Amarillo, 944 SW2d 725. —Child C 409; Statut 212.1, 212.2, 212.7.

Garcia, In re, TexApp–Corpus Christi, 94 SW3d 832.— App & E 345.1; Mand 29; New Tr 124(1); Pretrial Proc 698, 699.

Garcia, In re, TexCivApp–El Paso, 443 SW2d 594.—Crim Law 1077.2(2), 1137(2); Infants 174, 207, 210, 241.

Garcia, Matter of, CA5 (Tex), 955 F2d 16.—Bankr 2957, 3782.

Garcia v. Aetna Cas. & Sur. Co., TexCivApp–San Antonio, 322 SW2d 415.—Work Comp 1746, 1968(4).

Garcia v. Aetna Cas. & Sur. Co., TexCivApp–Tyler, 542 SW2d 477.—Work Comp 818, 820, 1374, 1410, 1652, 1924.

Garcia; Aguilar v., TexApp–Houston (14 Dist), 880 SW2d 279.—App & E 941; Infants 27; Mand 3(2.1), 4(1), 4(4).

Garcia v. Alejos, TexCivApp–San Antonio, 311 SW2d 943. —Infants 177.

Garcia v. Allen, TexApp–San Antonio, 751 SW2d 236, writ den.—Pretrial Proc 304, 313.

Garcia v. Allen, TexApp–Corpus Christi, 28 SW3d 587, reh overr, and review den.—App & E 981; Civil R 1018,

1019(2), 1218(2), 1218(3); Judgm 181(33), 185(2), 185.3(13); Labor & Emp 40(2), 806, 832, 861, 863(2), 2778, 2935, 3040, 3043; Libel 54, 101(5); Neglig 210, 1692; New Tr 99, 102(6), 103.

Garcia; Allstate Ins. Co. v., TexApp–San Antonio, 822 SW2d 348, reh of motion for mandamus overr.—Mand 4(4), 31.

Garcia; American Indem. Co. v., TexCivApp–San Antonio, 398 SW2d 146, ref nre.—Insurance 2451, 2654, 3360.

Garcia; American Physicians Ins. Exchange v., Tex, 876 SW2d 842.—Insurance 2281(1), 2285(1), 2285(4), 2914, 2917, 3336, 3337, 3349, 3350.

Garcia v. American Physicians Ins. Exchange, TexApp–San Antonio, 812 SW2d 25, writ gr, rev 876 SW2d 842.—Antitrust 221; App & E 215(1), 218.2(1), 758.1; Compromise 16(1); Contrib 5(6.1); Evid 219(3); Insurance 1631, 1973, 2923, 2926, 2934(3), 3111(3), 3335, 3347, 3349, 3374, 3380, 3390, 3441, 3506(1), 3530; Release 37; Trial 351.2(4).

Garcia v. Amfels, Inc., CA5 (Tex), 254 F3d 585, reh den.—Rem of C 25(1), 107(9), 107(11); Ship 86(1).

Garcia v. Andrews, TexApp–Corpus Christi, 867 SW2d 409.—Damag 50.10; Pretrial Proc 201.1, 202.

Garcia v. Angelini, TexCivApp–Eastland, 412 SW2d 949.—App & E 934(2); Inj 74; Quo W 5; Schools 53(4), 53(5), 57, 61, 113.

Garcia v. Arbor Green Owners Ass'n, Inc., TexApp–Houston (1 Dist), 838 SW2d 800, reh den, and writ den.—App & E 5, 516, 714(5), 859, 901, 907(4), 1013, 1024.1; Judgm 109, 139, 163, 335(1), 336.

Garcia v. Avila, TexCivApp–San Antonio, 597 SW2d 400, dism.—Elections 216.1, 227(1), 280, 285(4), 298(1); Evid 333(1).

Garcia v. Aycock, TexCivApp–San Antonio, 203 SW2d 982, writ refused.—Tax 2984, 3011, 3117.

Garcia; Banda v., Tex, 955 SW2d 270.—Compromise 23(3); Trial 105(2); Witn 227.

Garcia v. Banda, TexApp–San Antonio, 935 SW2d 790, reh overr, and error gr, rev 955 SW2d 270.—App & E 931(1), 1010.2; Compromise 5(1), 18(1); Evid 597; Judgm 72; Trial 105(1), 105(2), 114, 384; Witn 227.

Garcia v. Barreiro, TexApp–Corpus Christi, 115 SW3d 271.—App & E 758.3(4), 946, 962, 1043(1), 1078(1); Pretrial Proc 583, 676, 678, 697.

Garcia v. Barrera, TexCivApp–Eastland, 385 SW2d 606, ref nre.—Wills 324(2), 324(3), 400; Witn 146, 178(4).

Garcia v. Bauer Dredging Co., Inc., CA5 (Tex), 506 F2d 19.—Damag 62(2), 132(3); Ship 86(3).

Garcia; Benavides v., TexApp–San Antonio, 687 SW2d 397.—Child C 328, 606; Divorce 139; Mand 71, 151(1), 157; Pretrial Proc 508, 512.

Garcia v. Beto, CA5 (Tex), 452 F2d 655.—Crim Law 633(1); Hab Corp 827.

Garcia v. Beto, CA5 (Tex), 447 F2d 151.—Courts 104; Fed Cts 743.

Garcia v. Beto, SDTex, 348 FSupp 884.—Double J 144.

Garcia; Bituminous Cas. Corp. v., NDTex, 223 FRD 308.—Decl Judgm 306, 392.1; Fed Civ Proc 311, 320, 2447; Fed Cts 686.

Garcia v. Boldin, CA5 (Tex), 691 F2d 1172.—Aliens 352, 353(1), 379, 387, 389, 391, 392, 397, 411; Decl Judgm 203; Hab Corp 257, 282, 681, 847; U S Mag 21, 26, 27.

Garcia v. Bradley, TexCivApp–San Antonio, 311 SW2d 751.—App & E 931(6); Hus & W 256, 262.1(5), 264(5); Witn 163.

Garcia v. BRK Brands, Inc., SDTex, 266 FSupp2d 566.—Death 31(7); Evid 555.2, 555.4(2), 555.7; Prod Liab 62.

Garcia v. Burlington Northern, Inc., TexApp–Tyler, 543 SW2d 425, ref nre.—App & E 930(3), 989; Neglig 530(1), 1683; R R 338.2, 338.3, 338.4, 338.5, 346(5.1), 348(6.1).

Garcia v. Burris, TexApp–San Antonio, 961 SW2d 603, reh overr, and review den, and reh of petition for review overr.—Libel 7(2), 19, 44(3), 51(1), 51(4), 123(2), 123(8).

Garcia; Byler v., TexApp–Austin, 685 SW2d 116, ref nre.—Action 35; App & E 1030; Costs 194.25; Crim Law 20; Damag 15; Land & Ten 180(3), 180(4), 184(2).

Garcia v. Caletka, TexCivApp–Corpus Christi, 486 SW2d 880, ref nre.—App & E 959(3); Plead 236(3), 236(6); Trial 127, 352.18.

Garcia v. Canales, TexCivApp–San Antonio, 456 SW2d 790.—Plead 111.12, 111.42(7); Trover 35.

Garcia v. Canales, TexCivApp–Corpus Christi, 434 SW2d 895.—Adop 7.4(6), 7.8(3.1), 11; App & E 966(1); Pretrial Proc 726.

Garcia v. Cantu, BkrtcyWDTex, 363 BR 503.—Bankr 2081, 2158, 2162, 2163, 2164.1.

Garcia v. Caremark, Inc., TexApp–Corpus Christi, 921 SW2d 417, reh overr.—App & E 174, 380, 387(2), 913; Death 39, 57; Lim of Act 80, 83(2).

Garcia v. Carpenter, Tex, 525 SW2d 160.—Elections 153, 154(10).

Garcia; CEBI Metal Sanayi Ve Ticaret A.S. v., TexApp–Houston (14 Dist), 108 SW3d 464, reh overr.—Judgm 185(4), 185.3(21); Pretrial Proc 482.1.

Garcia; Cedillo-Gonzalez v., WDTex, 55 FSupp2d 653.—Aliens 216; Const Law 48(4.1), 188; Fed Civ Proc 2333.1, 2350.1, 2653, 2655.

Garcia; Cedillo-Gonzalez v., WDTex, 38 FSupp2d 479, am in part, vac in part 55 FSupp2d 653.—Const Law 3013, 3057, 3060, 3900; Hab Corp 521.

Garcia v. Central Power & Light Co., Tex, 704 SW2d 734.—App & E 989, 1045(1); Jury 136(3).

Garcia v. Central Power & Light Co., TexApp–Corpus Christi, 703 SW2d 696, writ gr, rev 704 SW2d 734.—Jury 33(5.15), 136(3).

Garcia v. C.F. Jordan, Inc., TexApp–El Paso, 881 SW2d 155.—App & E 863; Consp 1.1; Judgm 185(2), 185(5), 185.3(21).

Garcia; Chapa v., Tex, 848 SW2d 667.—Mand 28; Pretrial Proc 15, 371.

Garcia; Chapa v., TexCivApp–San Antonio, 513 SW2d 953, ref nre.—Adv Poss 19, 22, 27, 29, 36, 68, 112, 114(1).

Garcia v. City of Abilene, CA5 (Tex), 890 F2d 773.—Civil R 1088(5); Const Law 3227; Crim Law 641.3(1).

Garcia; City of Alamo v., TexApp–Corpus Christi, 960 SW2d 221, reh overr.—Admin Law 124; Const Law 3875, 3912, 4174; Mun Corp 65, 89, 92, 104, 159(4), 159(6).

Garcia; City of Alamo v., TexApp–Corpus Christi, 878 SW2d 664.—Alt Disp Res 112, 133(2), 137, 183; App & E 854(1); Contracts 221(1), 221(2), 278(0.5).

Garcia v. City of Alice, TexCivApp–San Antonio, 505 SW2d 611.—Mun Corp 438, 439, 455, 511(1).

Garcia v. City of Houston, CA5 (Tex), 201 F3d 672.—Civil R 1137, 1171, 1536, 1544, 1548, 1560, 1587, 1590, 1594; Fed Cts 763.1, 799, 830, 847, 878.

Garcia v. City of Houston, TexApp–El Paso, 799 SW2d 496, writ den.—App & E 989; Autos 242(6), 245(30); Judgm 199(3.3).

Garcia v. City of Kingsville, TexApp–Corpus Christi, 641 SW2d 339.—Admin Law 124, 701; Judgm 181(27).

Garcia v. City of Lubbock, TexApp–Amarillo, 634 SW2d 776, ref nre.—App & E 78(1), 93, 389(2), 870(2); Work Comp 872, 1133, 1135.

Garcia; City of San Antonio v., TexApp–San Antonio, 974 SW2d 756.—Judgm 185(2), 185(6), 185.3(21); Mun Corp 747(3).

Garcia v. City of San Antonio, TexCivApp–San Antonio, 427 SW2d 947, ref nre.—Mun Corp 198(3), 198(4).

Garcia; City of San Antonio v., TexCivApp–San Antonio, 243 SW2d 252, writ refused.—Judgm 143(3), 143(6), 145(2).

GARCIA;

Garcia; Clack v., TexCivApp–San Antonio, 323 SW2d 468.
—Mines 55(5).

Garcia v. Clifford Jackson Funeral Homes, TexCivApp–
Corpus Christi, 526 SW2d 750.—Carr 320(1); Death 76.

Garcia; Coastal Bend Milk Producers Ass'n v., TexCiv-
App–San Antonio, 368 SW2d 260.—Damag 85; Food
4.5(1), 4.5(6); Inj 132, 134, 148(2).

Garcia v. Coastal Bend Production Credit Ass'n, Tex-
CivApp–Corpus Christi, 430 SW2d 385.—Evid 10(2),
458; Venue 7.5(4).

Garcia v. Commissioners Court of Cameron County,
TexApp–Corpus Christi, 101 SW3d 778.—App & E 23,
66, 68, 76(1), 80(6), 503, 893(1), 1106(2); Costs 194.40;
Courts 35; Decl Judgm 8; Judgm 218.

Garcia v. Cook, TexCivApp–Austin, 366 SW2d 873, writ
dism.—Divorce 49(2), 197, 198; Hus & W 268(1).

Garcia; County of Bexar v., TexApp–San Antonio, 974
SW2d 107, reh overr.—Abate & R 81; App & E 946;
Counties 213; States 191.6(1); Trial 386(1).

Garcia; County of El Paso v., CA5 (Tex), 79 FedAppx
667.—Civil R 1351(4), 1352(4), 1358.

Garcia; Crawford & Co. v., TexApp–El Paso, 817 SW2d
98, writ den.—Antitrust 138, 221, 257; Labor & Emp
914; Trial 213, 219, 241; Work Comp 974.

Garcia; Crisp v., TexCivApp–Waco, 542 SW2d 947.—
Judgm 199(3.17).

Garcia v. Cross, TexApp–San Antonio, 27 SW3d 152.—
Autos 146, 192(11), 197(1), 201(6), 238(3); Neglig 202,
210, 213, 215, 353, 371, 377, 379, 380, 387, 1692; Weap
20.

Garcia; Crown Cent. Petroleum Corp. v., Tex, 904 SW2d
125.—Pretrial Proc 131, 133, 135.

Garcia; Cuellar v., TexCivApp–Austin, 621 SW2d 646, ref
nre.—Autos 246(60); Neglig 1612, 1616; Plead 229,
246(3).

Garcia; Cuevas v., TexApp–San Antonio, 668 SW2d 897.
—Evid 461(2); Home 167; Hus & W 273(8.1), 276(1),
276(6).

Garcia; Curan v., TexCivApp–San Antonio, 250 SW2d
929.—Mental H 10.1, 122, 123.

Garcia v. Daggett, TexApp–Houston (1 Dist), 742 SW2d
808.—Child C 409; Divorce 83, 138.1.

Garcia; Dallas Morning News v., TexApp–San Antonio,
822 SW2d 675. See Dallas Morning News Co. v. Garcia.

Garcia; Dallas Morning News Co. v., TexApp–San Antonio, 822 SW2d 675.—Const Law 2171; Libel 112(1);
Mand 32; Pretrial Proc 40, 41, 411; Witn 196.1, 223.

Garcia; Davenport v., Tex, 834 SW2d 4.—Const Law 617,
1050, 2093, 2094; Infants 82; Records 32.

Garcia; Davidson Texas, Inc. v., TexApp–Austin, 664
SW2d 791.—App & E 1071.1(5.1); Exemp 48(1), 48(2).

Garcia; Dawson v., TexApp–Dallas, 666 SW2d 254.—App
& E 218.2(2), 946, 1153, 1175(1); Damag 51, 192; Death
1, 23; Hus & W 260, 276(9); Infants 77, 83, 115, 116;
Interest 66; Mental H 485.1; Trial 127.

Garcia v. Dean, TexApp–Austin, 795 SW2d 763. See
Dean v. Garcia.

Garcia; Dean v., TexApp–Austin, 795 SW2d 763, writ den.
—Wills 169, 170, 173, 174.

Garcia v. De Enriquez, TexCivApp–San Antonio, 313
SW2d 918, writ refused.—Adop 11, 14, 16.

Garcia v. Dependable Shell Core Machines, Inc., Tex-
App–Corpus Christi, 783 SW2d 246.—App & E 994(2);
Evid 588; Prod Liab 71, 85; Trial 358.

Garcia v. Dial, TexCrimApp, 596 SW2d 524.—Courts 1,
24, 26, 209(1); Crim Law 99, 303.10, 303.45, 577.16(1);
Mand 4(1), 61.

Garcia v. Discrobis Oil Co., Inc., TexCivApp–San Antonio, 612 SW2d 264.—Plead 111.15; Venue 7.5(1), 7.5(2),
7.5(6).

Garcia; Dominguez v., TexApp–San Antonio, 746 SW2d
865, writ den.—App & E 169; Judgm 185(4); Neglig
1040(4), 1298(2).

Garcia; Dow Chemical Co. v., Tex, 909 SW2d 503.—
Mand 29.

Garcia; Draper v., TexApp–Houston (14 Dist), 793 SW2d
296.—App & E 966(2); Atty & C 64, 129(1); Judgm
181(16); Pretrial Proc 717.1, 718.

Garcia; Draper & Associates v., TexApp–Houston (14
Dist, 793 SW2d 296. See Draper v. Garcia.

Garcia v. Dretke, CA5 (Tex), 388 F3d 496.—Const Law
3243, 3774; Double J 107.1, 109, 182; Hab Corp 205,
818, 842, 846; Judgm 751, 956(1); Rob 4; U S Mag 31.

Garcia; Duran v., TexApp–El Paso, 224 SW3d 309.—App
& E 931(1), 946, 989, 1010.1(1), 1010.1(3), 1011.1(4),
1012.1(2); Child C 921(1), 921(3); Child S 556(1), 556(5),
557(1), 557(4); Child 21(2), 53, 67; Divorce 286(5); Hus
& W 272(4).

Garcia v. Duval County, TexCivApp–San Antonio, 354
SW2d 237, ref nre.—Counties 178.

Garcia v. Elf Atochem North America, CA5 (Tex), 28
F3d 446.—Civil R 1106, 1112, 1113, 1187, 1189, 1527,
1561, 1571; Fed Civ Proc 2470.1, 2544; Fed Cts 776,
802.

Garcia v. El Paso Ltd. Partnership, TexApp–El Paso,
203 SW3d 432.—Judgm 185.3(21); Neglig 202, 220, 371,
387, 431, 433, 1019, 1070, 1242, 1567, 1692.

Garcia v. Employers Cas. Co., TexCivApp–Amarillo, 519
SW2d 685, ref nre.—App & E 327(3), 914(1); Lim of
Act 125; Parties 94(2); Work Comp 1869, 1880.

Garcia v. Employers Ins. of Wausau, TexApp–Houston
(1 Dist), 856 SW2d 507, reh den, and writ den.—Judges
51(1), 51(2), 51(4), 56.

Garcia; Escamilla v., TexApp–San Antonio, 653 SW2d 58,
ref nre.—App & E 930(3), 989; Autos 201(8), 244(2.1),
244(36.1); Judgm 199(3.10).

Garcia v. Excel Corp., CA5 (Tex), 102 F3d 758.—Fed Cts
611, 625; Jury 33(5.15), 117.

Garcia v. Fabela, TexApp–San Antonio, 673 SW2d 933.—
Frds St of 142; Judgm 181(34), 185(2), 185.2(9); Trusts
17(4), 103(1), 111.

Garcia; Flynt v., Tex, 587 SW2d 109.—Courts 30, 170.

Garcia v. Flynt, TexCivApp–Hous (14 Dist), 574 SW2d
587, rev 587 SW2d 109.—Courts 169(1), 170; Hus & W
281.

Garcia; Ford Motor Credit Co. v., TexCivApp–San Antonio, 504 SW2d 931.—App & E 846(5); Plead 34(7), 45,
111.18, 111.42(9); Trover 1.

Garcia; Ford Motor Credit Co. v., TexCivApp–Waco, 595
SW2d 602.—Plead 36(2); Sec Tran 242.1; Trover 46.

Garcia; Fowler v., TexApp–San Antonio, 687 SW2d 517.
—App & E 758.3(9); Autos 244(35), 244(56); Neglig
371, 387, 1746; Trial 131(2), 133.6(4), 366.

Garcia; Fuentes v., TexApp–San Antonio, 696 SW2d 482.
—Adv Poss 13, 17, 106(1), 109, 112, 114(1); App & E
758.1, 1010.1(3).

Garcia v. Galindo, Tex, 199 SW2d 499, 145 Tex 507.—
App & E 692(1); Wills 38(2), 324(2).

Garcia v. Galindo, TexCivApp–San Antonio, 336 SW2d
459, writ dism by agreement.—Estop 68(2); Inj 138.31.

Garcia v. Galindo, TexCivApp–San Antonio, 329 SW2d
95, writ refused.—Ease 61(6).

Garcia; Galindo v., TexCivApp–San Antonio, 222 SW2d
477.—Courts 247(7); Plead 111.38; Venue 5.4.

Garcia v. Galindo, TexCivApp–San Antonio, 199 SW2d
488, rev 199 SW2d 499, 145 Tex 507.—App & E 930(1),
1175(5); Evid 594; Trial 139.1(8); Wills 31, 32, 38(1),
52(1), 53(2), 55(3), 324(2).

Garcia v. Galindo, TexCivApp–San Antonio, 189 SW2d
12, writ refused wom.—Hus & W 221; Wills 21, 55(10);
Witn 139(1), 140(9), 146.

Garcia v. Garcia, TexApp–San Antonio, 751 SW2d 274.—
Const Law 4171; Mun Corp 185(1), 185(4), 185(5).

Garcia; Garcia v., TexApp–San Antonio, 751 SW2d 274.—
Const Law 4171; Mun Corp 185(1), 185(4), 185(5).

Garcia v. Garcia, TexApp–El Paso, 170 SW3d 644.—App
& E 852, 930(1), 931(3), 946, 1001(1), 1008.1(2); Divorce

252.2, 252.3(2), 286(5), 286(8); Evid 474(18); Hus & W 258, 265, 272(4).

Garcia; Garcia v., TexApp–El Paso, 170 SW3d 644.—App & E 852, 930(1), 931(3), 946, 1001(1), 1008.1(2); Divorce 252.2, 252.3(2), 286(5), 286(8); Evid 474(18); Hus & W 258, 265, 272(4).

Garcia v. Garcia, TexApp–Corpus Christi, 878 SW2d 678. —Ex & Ad 35(18), 506(1), 510(12).

Garcia; Garcia v., TexApp–Corpus Christi, 878 SW2d 678. —Ex & Ad 35(18), 506(1), 510(12).

Garcia v. Garcia, TexCivApp–San Antonio, 469 SW2d 920.—Child S 537; Contempt 63(1).

Garcia; Garcia v., TexCivApp–San Antonio, 469 SW2d 920.—Child S 537; Contempt 63(1).

Garcia v. Garcia, TexCivApp–San Antonio, 334 SW2d 621, ref nre.—Elections 154(1), 154(3), 154(6), 154(8).

Garcia; Garcia v., TexCivApp–San Antonio, 334 SW2d 621, ref nre.—Elections 154(1), 154(3), 154(6), 154(8).

Garcia v. Garcia, TexCivApp–San Antonio, 232 SW2d 782.—Divorce 1; Marriage 57, 60(3).

Garcia; Garcia v., TexCivApp–San Antonio, 232 SW2d 782.—Divorce 1; Marriage 57, 60(3).

Garcia v. Garcia, TexCivApp–San Antonio, 185 SW2d 227.—Divorce 130, 160, 186.

Garcia; Garcia v., TexCivApp–San Antonio, 185 SW2d 227.—Divorce 130, 160, 186.

Garcia v. Garcia, TexCivApp–San Antonio, 144 SW2d 605.—App & E 1160; Marriage 58(8), 60(6).

Garcia; Garcia v., TexCivApp–San Antonio, 144 SW2d 605.—App & E 1160; Marriage 58(8), 60(6).

Garcia v. Garcia, TexCivApp–San Antonio, 94 SW2d 864. —Divorce 186, 189, 253(4); Judgm 256(2).

Garcia; Garcia v., TexCivApp–San Antonio, 94 SW2d 864. —Divorce 186, 189, 253(4); Judgm 256(2).

Garcia v. Garcia, TexCivApp–Corpus Christi, 618 SW2d 117, writ dism woj.—App & E 5; Divorce 281.

Garcia; Garcia v., TexCivApp–Corpus Christi, 618 SW2d 117, writ dism woj.—App & E 5; Divorce 281.

Garcia v. Garcia, TexCivApp–Corpus Christi, 526 SW2d 152, ref nre.—Child C 651; Jury 25(2), 26, 28(6).

Garcia; Garcia v., TexCivApp–Corpus Christi, 526 SW2d 152, ref nre.—Child C 651; Jury 25(2), 26, 28(6).

Garcia v. Garcia, TexCivApp–Corpus Christi, 444 SW2d 207.—App & E 1165; Child C 328; Child 7.

Garcia; Garcia v., TexCivApp–Corpus Christi, 444 SW2d 207.—App & E 1165; Child C 328; Child 7.

Garcia v. Garcia De Ortiz, TexCivApp–San Antonio, 257 SW2d 804.—Afft 17; Fraud Conv 188; Judgm 178; Plead 36(2); Trusts 4, 13, 17(3), 17(5).

Garcia v. Garza, SDTex, 729 FSupp 553.—Hab Corp 332.1, 335, 362.1, 364, 479; Judgm 751.

Garcia; Garza v., Tex, 137 SW3d 36.—App & E 428(2), 912; Courts 85(3); New Tr 153.

Garcia v. Garza, TexApp–Corpus Christi, 70 SW3d 362, review gr, rev 137 SW3d 36.—App & E 106, 840(1), 931(4); Venue 17, 31, 58, 68, 72, 75.

Garcia; Garza v., TexApp–Corpus Christi, 785 SW2d 421, writ den.—Mun Corp 65, 104, 155; Offic 60.

Garcia v. Garza, TexCivApp–San Antonio, 161 SW2d 297, writ refused wom.—App & E 758.3(3), 1178(6); Bound 3(2), 3(5), 3(9), 32, 33; Propty 9; Tresp to T T 12, 34, 38(1), 41(2), 47(3); Trial 351.2(4).

Garcia; Gashaj v., WDTex, 234 FSupp2d 661.—Aliens 436, 466, 470; Const Law 978, 1063, 1089, 3875, 3921, 4439.

Garcia; Gaxiola v., TexApp–El Paso, 169 SW3d 426.— App & E 181, 219(2), 931(3); Child S 88, 195, 214, 337, 339(3), 339(5), 539, 550, 555, 556(1), 558(3).

Garcia v. General Motors Corp., TexApp–San Antonio, 786 SW2d 12, application for writ of error withdrawn.— Pretrial Proc 413.1.

Garcia; Gillett Const. Co. v., TexApp–Houston (1 Dist), 816 SW2d 131. See Kahn v. Garcia.

Garcia v. Gloor, CA5 (Tex), 618 F2d 264, reh den 625 F2d 1016, cert den 101 SCt 923, 449 US 1113, 66 LEd2d 842. —Civil R 1118, 1120, 1121, 1137, 1140, 1231; Consp 7.5(1), 7.5(2); Evid 333(7), 366(2); Fed Civ Proc 161.1, 163, 174, 184.10; Fed Cts 901.1; Statut 188.

Garcia v. Gloor, CA5 (Tex), 609 F2d 156, opinion withdrawn and superseded 618 F2d 264, reh den 625 F2d 1016, cert den 101 SCt 923, 449 US 1113, 66 LEd2d 842.

Garcia; Gonzalez v., TexCivApp–San Antonio, 352 SW2d 913.—Elections 307, 308.

Garcia; Green Tree Financial Corp. v., TexApp–San Antonio, 988 SW2d 776, reh overr.—App & E 232(3), 969, 1067, 1172(5), 1177(5); Corp 498, 521; Evid 584(1); Libel 112(1), 124(8); Trial 228(1).

Garcia v. Guerra, CA5 (Tex), 744 F2d 1159, reh den 751 F2d 383, cert den 105 SCt 2139, 471 US 1065, 85 LEd2d 497.—Civil R 1482; Elections 1, 12(4), 12(8), 12(10), 38, 40.

Garcia; Gulf Energy Pipeline Co. v., TexApp–San Antonio, 884 SW2d 821.—Em Dom 172, 225.1, 231, 235; Mand 4(4), 45, 53.

Garcia v. Gutierrez, TexApp–Corpus Christi, 697 SW2d 758.—Judgm 17(2); Proc 53, 61.

Garcia v. Haynes, TexCivApp–Beaumont, 99 SW2d 433. —Venue 22(8).

Garcia v. H. E. Butt Grocery Co., TexCivApp–Corpus Christi, 461 SW2d 439.—Judgm 185.3(21).

Garcia; Hess, Inc. v., TexCivApp–Eastland, 358 SW2d 391.—App & E 1170.7; Damag 221(2.1); Seamen 29(1), 29(2), 29(5.14), 29(5.16); Trial 18, 352.5(5), 352.10.

Garcia; Hinojosa v., TexApp–San Antonio, 260 SW2d 711.—App & E 781(4); Costs 232.

Garcia v. Home Indem. Co., TexCivApp–Amarillo, 474 SW2d 535.—Work Comp 1922, 1958, 1968(5), 1974.

Garcia; Home Ins. Co. v., TexApp–El Paso, 74 SW3d 52, reh overr.—App & E 930(1), 946, 948, 969, 984(5), 989, 999(1), 1001(1), 1001(3), 1003(3), 1003(5), 1003(7); Trial 279, 284; Work Comp 1624, 1672, 1861, 1981.

Garcia v. Insurance Co. of State of Pa., Tex, 751 SW2d 857.—Work Comp 1643, 1935.

Garcia; International Elevator Co. v., TexApp–Houston (1 Dist), 76 SW3d 778, reh overr.—App & E 931(1), 1012.1(5); Const Law 3964; Corp 665(1); Courts 12(2.1), 12(2.5), 12(2.10), 12(2.15), 35, 39; Joint Adv 1.2(1); Neglig 484.

Garcia; International Elevator Co., Inc. v., TexApp–Houston (1 Dist), 73 SW3d 420.—Subrog 1; Work Comp 2237.

Garcia v. J.J.S. Enterprises, Inc., TexApp–El Paso, 225 SW3d 57.—App & E 852; Contracts 114.

Garcia v. John Hancock Variable Life Ins. Co., TexApp–San Antonio, 859 SW2d 427, reh den, and writ den. —App & E 231(1), 863, 934(1), 1177(1); Insurance 3571; Judgm 178, 181(5.1), 181(6), 181(23), 185(2), 185(5), 185(6), 185.1(3), 185.1(8), 185.3(12).

Garcia; Jones v., CA5 (Tex), 63 F3d 411. See Jones, In re.

Garcia; Jones v., TexCivApp–San Antonio, 538 SW2d 492. —App & E 954(1), 954(2); Inj 138.21, 144, 147, 157; Mtg 338; Plead 407; Sec Tran 228, 229.1.

Garcia v. Jones, TexCivApp–San Antonio, 155 SW2d 671, writ refused wom.—Courts 85(3); Equity 67; Judgm 242, 335(1), 335(3); Lim of Act 39(1).

Garcia v. Jones, TexCivApp–El Paso, 147 SW2d 925, writ dism, correct.—Action 16; App & E 78(1), 136; Judgm 217; Plead 216(2).

Garcia; Jordan v., TexCivApp–San Antonio, 197 SW2d 873.—Courts 472.4(4).

Garcia; Kahn v., TexApp–Houston (1 Dist), 816 SW2d 131.—Mand 28, 53.

Garcia v. Karam, Tex, 276 SW2d 255, 154 Tex 240.—App & E 1178(1); Evid 445(1), 445(2); Frds St of 108(4), 131(1).

GARCIA;

59 Tex D 2d—180

See Guidelines for Arrangement at the beginning of this Volume

Garcia; Karam v., TexCivApp–El Paso, 282 SW2d 415.—Estop 68(1); New Tr 99; Trial 350.4(2); Ven & Pur 350, 352.

Garcia; Karam v., TexCivApp–El Paso, 267 SW2d 890, rev 276 SW2d 255, 154 Tex 240.—Damag 221(5.1); Frds St of 131(1), 144.

Garcia v. Kastner Farms, Inc., Tex, 774 SW2d 668, appeal after remand 789 SW2d 656.—App & E 387(6).

Garcia v. Kastner Farms, Inc., TexApp–Corpus Christi, 789 SW2d 656.—App & E 1008.1(2); Contracts 97(1), 97(2), 320; Damag 140; Estop 85; Improv 4(1); Plead 78.

Garcia v. Kastner Farms, Inc., TexApp–Corpus Christi, 761 SW2d 444, writ gr, rev and remanded 774 SW2d 668, appeal after remand 789 SW2d 656.—App & E 387(6).

Garcia v. Kelly, TexCivApp–Corpus Christi, 565 SW2d 112.—App & E 569(3), 1177(9); Trial 31.

Garcia; Kendrick v., TexApp–Eastland, 171 SW3d 698, reh overr, and review den, and reh of petition for review den.—Evid 71; Health 804, 805, 809; Notice 10; Proc 145; Statut 230.

Garcia v. King, Tex, 164 SW2d 509, 139 Tex 578.—Land & Ten 37; Mines 73.5, 78.1(8).

Garcia; King v., TexCivApp–San Antonio, 152 SW2d 918, rev 164 SW2d 509, 139 Tex 578.—Mines 73, 73.1(4), 73.5.

Garcia v. Kingsville First Sav. & Loan Ass'n, TexCivApp–San Antonio, 415 SW2d 537, writ dism.—Plead 111.9, 111.42(5); Venue 5.3(2), 7.5(4).

Garcia v. Koch Oil Co. of Texas Inc., CA5 (Tex), 351 F3d 636.—Fed Cts 317, 358; Rem of C 74, 107(7), 107(9).

Garcia v. Krausse, CA5 (Tex), 534 F2d 609.—Fed Cts 491, 998.

Garcia v. Krausse, SDTex, 380 FSupp 1254, vac 534 F2d 609.—Const Law 4484; Fed Cts 998; Sequest 2.

Garcia; Kvanvig v., TexApp–Corpus Christi, 928 SW2d 777, reh overr.—Mand 4(1), 12, 28, 50; New Tr 6, 153.

Garcia v. Lacey, TexCivApp–San Antonio, 316 SW2d 183.—App & E 692(1), 1078(1); Sales 479.4.

Garcia v. Laredo Collections, Inc., TexCivApp–San Antonio, 601 SW2d 97.—App & E 954(1), 954(2); Contracts 47, 65.5, 90; Inj 61(2).

Garcia v. Laughlin, Tex, 285 SW2d 191, 155 Tex 261.—Counties 45; Dist & Pros Attys 7(1); Offic 74.

Garcia v. Levi Strauss & Co., TexApp–El Paso, 85 SW3d 362.—App & E 863; Civil R 1541; Judgm 181(21); Labor & Emp 806, 807, 809, 810, 827, 861, 863(2).

Garcia; Lopez v., TexCivApp–San Antonio, 139 SW2d 671, dism.—App & E 624.

Garcia v. Lozano-Castaneda v., WDTex, 238 FSupp2d 853.—Aliens 436, 468, 469, 485; Const Law 978, 1067, 1089, 3875, 3921, 4439.

Garcia v. LumaCorp, Inc., CA5 (Tex), 429 F3d 549.—Compromise 6(1), 8(3); Contracts 53; Fed Civ Proc 2545; Fed Cts 776, 850.1; Labor & Emp 685, 2792; Release 13(1), 18.

Garcia; Lumbermens Mut. Cas. Co. v., TexApp–Corpus Christi, 758 SW2d 893, writ den.—Work Comp 847, 1653, 1728.

Garcia; Manges v., TexCivApp–San Antonio, 616 SW2d 380.—Const Law 3462, 3992; Courts 70.

Garcia v. Marichalar, TexApp–San Antonio, 198 SW3d 250.—Health 804, 809, 818; Neglig 1610, 1613, 1614, 1620.

Garcia v. Marichalar, TexApp–San Antonio, 185 SW3d 70.—App & E 449, 1169(10); Health 809.

Garcia; Marker v., TexApp–San Antonio, 185 SW3d 21.—Antitrust 397; Cons Cred 16, 17; Costs 194.16, 194.36; Judgm 181(29), 186.

Garcia; Marshall v., TexCivApp–Corpus Christi, 514 SW2d 513, ref nre.—App & E 79(2), 80(6); Judgm 181(2), 181(3), 181(14), 181(29), 185(2); Plead 38, 53(1); Tresp to T T 32; Ven & Pur 104.

Garcia v. Martinez, Tex, 988 SW2d 219.—App & E 226(2), 946, 984(1), 1192; Costs 60, 177, 207.

Garcia v. Martinez, TexApp–Corpus Christi, 989 SW2d 758, reh overr, rev 988 SW2d 219.—App & E 226(2), 1031(1), 1071.6; Costs 12, 207.

Garcia v. Martinez, TexApp–Corpus Christi, 894 SW2d 806, reh overr, on subsequent appeal 989 SW2d 758, reh overr, rev 988 SW2d 219.—Costs 207, 208; Courts 30; Infants 83.

Garcia; Masonite Corp. v., TexApp–San Antonio, 951 SW2d 812, mandamus gr, and review dism, subsequent mandamus proceeding In re Masonite Corp, 997 SW2d 194.—App & E 4, 70(1); Judgm 7, 15, 16; Mand 4(1), 4(4), 28, 44; Motions 62; Statut 181(1), 188, 243; Venue 1.5, 16.5, 68.

Garcia v. Maverick County, TexApp–San Antonio, 850 SW2d 626, reh den, and writ den.—App & E 704.2, 846(5), 852; Counties 59, 67, 141; Offic 114; Trial 393(1).

Garcia; Mayor v., TexApp–Texarkana, 104 SW3d 274, review dism woj.—App & E 172(3), 761; Deeds 38(1); Evid 417(12); Frds St of 110(1), 158(3), 159; Judgm 199(3.5); Spec Perf 29(2), 133, 134; Trial 139.1(17); Ven & Pur 22.

Garcia v. Memorial Hospital, TexCivApp–San Antonio, 557 SW2d 859.—Health 661, 770.

Garcia; Memorial Medical Center v., TexApp–Corpus Christi, 712 SW2d 619.—App & E 66, 76(1); Judgm 199(3.5); Spec Perf 29(2), 133, 134; Trial 139.1(17).

Garcia v. Mireles, TexApp–Amarillo, 14 SW3d 839.—Alt Disp Res 463; App & E 704.2, 760(1), 852, 900, 901, 973; Judgm 524; Motions 66; Plead 352; Pretrial Proc 24, 534, 563, 583, 681.

Garcia; Mission Consol. Independent School Dist. v., TexApp–Corpus Christi, 166 SW3d 902, reh overr, and review gr.—Schools 63(1); Statut 181(1), 181(2), 184, 188, 190, 205, 206, 212.3, 212.6.

Garcia v. Moncada, TexComApp, 94 SW2d 123, 127 Tex 453.—App & E 837(3), 854(2), 1094(2); Autos 224(1), 227.5, 245(68), 245(93); Neglig 210; Trial 350.7(5).

Garcia; Moore's, Inc. v., TexCivApp–Corpus Christi, 604 SW2d 261, ref nre.—App & E 1004(5), 1004(11); Assault 2, 35, 48; Corp 498; Damag 48, 94, 95; False Imp 2, 31, 36, 40; Labor & Emp 767, 3056(1); Princ & A 99, 159(1); Trial 260(6).

Garcia v. Mo–Vac Service Co., TexApp–Corpus Christi, 867 SW2d 409. See Garcia v. Andrews.

Garcia v. Munoz, TexCivApp–San Antonio, 309 SW2d 502, writ refused.—Estop 68(4); Forci E & D 41; J P 36(7).

Garcia v. National Eligibility Exp., Inc., TexApp–Houston (1 Dist), 4 SW3d 887.—App & E 223; Costs 207; Judgm 185(3), 185.3(13), 189.

Garcia; National Old Line Ins. Co. v., TexCivApp–Fort Worth, 517 SW2d 621, ref nre.—App & E 302(1), 837(8), 1175(5); Estop 61; Insurance 1758, 1800.

Garcia; Niemann v., TexCivApp–San Antonio, 144 SW2d 621, writ dism, correct.—Adv Poss 32, 111; App & E 692(1), 1058(1); Courts 80(4); Evid 271(17), 317(18); Hus & W 276(6); Infants 24.

Garcia; Northwestern Nat. Ins. Co. v., TexApp–El Paso, 729 SW2d 321, ref nre.—App & E 218.2(5.1), 218.2(10), 930(3); Evid 318(2), 555.10; Judgm 199(3.2), 199(3.10); Trial 349(1); Work Comp 847, 1011, 1021, 1195, 1198, 1325, 1376, 1391, 1649, 1728, 1776, 1795.

Garcia; Olivares v., TexComApp, 91 SW2d 1059, 127 Tex 112.—Attach 217, 375(1); Bills & N 445, 534; Costs 42(3); Evid 43(2); Interest 50.

Garcia v. O'Neill, CA5 (Tex), 838 F2d 800. See Medina v. O'Neill.

Garcia v. Ozark Mahoney & Co., CA5 (Tex), 28 F3d 446. See Garcia v. Elf Atochem North America.

For Later Case History Information, see KeyCite on WESTLAW

GARCIA;

Garcia; Pace v., WDTex, 631 FSupp 1417.—Corp 325; Torts 242; Ven & Pur 18(1), 330.

Garcia; Pacific Emp. Indem. Co. v., TexCivApp–Corpus Christi, 440 SW2d 335, ref nre.—Work Comp 1396, 1703, 1920, 1927, 1958.

Garcia v. Palacios, TexApp–San Antonio, 667 SW2d 225, ref nre.—Adv Poss 11, 13, 33, 38, 57, 85(3), 86, 95, 100(1); Land & Ten 56(1).

Garcia; Parrott v., Tex, 436 SW2d 897.—Autos 202.1, 226(1), 226(2); Judgm 181(2), 185(2), 186; Neglig 259, 452, 525, 549(6).

Garcia; Parrott v., TexCivApp–Beaumont, 428 SW2d 476, writ gr, aff 436 SW2d 897.—Autos 202.1, 226(1); Evid 265(7); Judgm 185.3(21).

Garcia v. Pasquarell, CA5 (Tex), 117 FedAppx 337.—Aliens 274, 322.

Garcia v. Peeples, Tex, 734 SW2d 343, 83 ALR4th 975.—Decl Judgm 345.1; Pretrial Proc 24, 41, 371, 411.

Garcia v. Pellegrin, TexCivApp–San Antonio, 411 SW2d 554.—Adv Poss 40; Evid 273(3), 273(5), 317(18); Gifts 49(1).

Garcia; Pepe Intern. Development Co. v., TexApp–Houston (1 Dist), 915 SW2d 925. See Pepe Intern. Development Co. v. Pub Brewing Co.

Garcia v. Pharr, San Juan, Alamo Independent School Dist., TexCivApp–Corpus Christi, 513 SW2d 141, ref nre.—App & E 724(1), 1079; Schools 133.6(5), 147.51.

Garcia v. Phoenix Assur. Co. of New York, TexCivApp–Corpus Christi, 376 SW2d 77, ref nre.—New Tr 56; Work Comp 1932, 1966.

Garcia; Pierce, Pace & Associates v., WDTex, 631 FSupp 1417. See Pace v. Garcia.

Garcia v. Plains Coop Oil Mill, Inc., NDTex, 396 FSupp 189.—Civil R 1544, 1547, 1548.

Garcia v. Prescott, TexCivApp–Corpus Christi, 570 SW2d 562, ref nre.—App & E 215(0.5), 930(3), 989, 1068(1); Autos 244(34), 244(35), 244(58), 246(57), 246(58); Neglig 440(1), 1741.

Garcia v. Quarterman, CA5 (Tex), 456 F3d 463.—Hab Corp 450.1, 452; Sent & Pun 1709, 1716.

Garcia v. Quarterman, CA5 (Tex), 454 F3d 441.—Hab Corp 450.1, 452, 486(2), 486(5), 498, 768.

Garcia v. Quiroz, TexCivApp–San Antonio, 228 SW2d 953, ref nre.—Adop 6, 17; Decl Judgm 294; Mental H 487; New Tr 41(1); Witn 140(4).

Garcia v. Rainbo Baking Co. of Houston, SDTex, 18 FSupp2d 683.—Labor & Emp 757, 861, 1967; Rem of C 2; States 18.46, 18.49.

Garcia; Ramirez v., TexCivApp–Corpus Christi, 437 SW2d 363.—App & E 1003(10), 1003(11); Neglig 371, 387.

Garcia; Ramos v., TexApp–Corpus Christi, 676 SW2d 214.—App & E 637, 989; Autos 244(44); Trial 351.5(6).

Garcia v. Ramos, TexCivApp–San Antonio, 208 SW2d 111, writ refused.—Judgm 335(2), 335(3), 443(1).

Garcia v. Ramos, TexCivApp–Corpus Christi, 546 SW2d 400.—App & E 758.3(4); Covenants 130(1); Trial 401.

Garcia v. Ray, TexCivApp–Corpus Christi, 556 SW2d 870, dism.—App & E 758.3(11), 901; Atty & C 23; Judgm 185(2), 186, 559, 648; Trial 21.

Garcia v. Reeves County, Tex., CA5 (Tex), 32 F3d 200.—Civil R 1376(2), 1376(10), 1421; Const Law 3874(2); Fed Civ Proc 2497.1; Labor & Emp 40(2), 50; Offic 66; Sheriffs 24.

Garcia v. Reno, CA5 (Tex), 234 F3d 257.—Aliens 385; Hab Corp 521, 842.

Garcia v. Robinson, Tex, 817 SW2d 59.—App & E 169, 758.1.

Garcia; Robinson v., TexApp–Corpus Christi, 5 SW3d 348, petition for review den.—Compromise 16(1); Estop 78(1); Judgm 585(2), 586(2), 713(2).

Garcia; Robinson v., TexApp–Corpus Christi, 804 SW2d 238, writ den with per curiam opinion 817 SW2d 59.—

Accord 11(3); Atty & C 143, 166(1); Judgm 181(16), 185.3(5).

Garcia v. Rodriguez, TexApp–El Paso, 155 SW3d 334, appeal after remand 2007 WL 1934762.—Action 13; App & E 138, 150(1); Judgm 137; New Tr 165.

Garcia; Rodriguez v., TexCivApp–San Antonio, 309 SW2d 509.—App & E 931(1), 989, 1010.1(1); Partners 55.

Garcia; Rodriguez v., TexCivApp–Corpus Christi, 519 SW2d 908, ref nre.—App & E 713(1), 930(3), 989; Deeds 68(1.5), 196(3), 211(1), 211(4); Trial 350.1.

Garcia v. Rutledge, TexApp–Amarillo, 649 SW2d 307.—Antitrust 141, 393; App & E 173(6), 1024.4; Autos 378, 381; Bailm 18(2), 18(3); Contracts 170(1), 328(1), 341; Fraud 1, 49, 50; Judgm 199(3.2), 199(3.9); Sales 1.5; Trial 351.2(4); Trover 9(5), 35, 44, 54, 57.

Garcia v. Saenz, TexCivApp–San Antonio, 242 SW2d 230.—Adop 1, 17; Evid 592.

Garcia; Safety-Kleen Corp. v., TexApp–San Antonio, 945 SW2d 268.—Mand 32, 42; Motions 40; Pretrial Proc 25.

Garcia; St. Luke's Episcopal Hosp. v., TexApp–Houston (14 Dist), 928 SW2d 307.—Mand 1, 3(1), 3(2.1), 4(1), 4(4), 28; Pretrial Proc 156.

Garcia; Salazar v., TexCivApp–San Antonio, 232 SW2d 685, writ refused.—App & E 609, 1050.1(3.1), 1152; Improv 1; Tresp to T T 34, 57, 59.

Garcia; Saldana v., Tex, 285 SW2d 197, 155 Tex 242.—App & E 757(3), 761, 835(2).

Garcia; Saldana v., TexCivApp–San Antonio, 275 SW2d 563, aff 285 SW2d 197, 155 Tex 242.—App & E 291, 761; Des & Dist 74.

Garcia v. San Antonio Housing Authority, TexApp–San Antonio, 859 SW2d 78.—Damag 51.

Garcia v. San Antonio Metropolitan Transit Authority, USTex, 105 SCt 1005, 469 US 528, 27 Wage & Hour Cas (BNA) 65, 83 LEd2d 1016, reh den 105 SCt 2041, 471 US 1049, 85 LEd2d 340, reh den Donovan v. San Antonio Metropolitan Transit Authority, 105 SCt 2041, 471 US 1049, 85 LEd2d 340, appeal after remand 838 F2d 1411, 28 Wage & Hour Cas (BNA) 857, cert den 109 SCt 221, 488 US 889, 28 Wage & Hour Cas (BNA) 1568, 102 LEd2d 212.—Labor & Emp 2213; States 18.37, 18.46.

Garcia v. San Antonio Metropolitan Transit Authority, CA5 (Tex), 838 F2d 1411, 28 Wage & Hour Cas (BNA) 857, cert den 109 SCt 221, 488 US 889, 28 Wage & Hour Cas (BNA) 1568, 102 LEd2d 212.—Courts 100(1).

Garcia; Santa Rosa Health Care Corp. v., Tex, 964 SW2d 940.—Health 196, 357, 384, 400, 750.

Garcia v. Santa Rosa Health Care Corp., TexApp–Corpus Christi, 925 SW2d 372, reh overr, and writ gr, rev 964 SW2d 940.—App & E 863, 934(1); Damag 49.10; Health 196, 400, 750, 811; Judgm 181(1), 185.3(21); Lim of Act 43, 95(1), 95(5), 95(12); Neglig 202, 210, 215, 220, 1692; Prod Liab 46.1; States 18.15, 18.65.

Garcia; Santos v., TexCivApp–San Antonio, 624 SW2d 919.—App & E 80(2).

Garcia; Schliemann v., TexApp–San Antonio, 685 SW2d 690.—App & E 1198, 1203(1), 1206; Execution 170, 402(1), 402(5); Judgm 294, 883(12); Mand 58.

Garcia; Schrader v., TexCivApp–Corpus Christi, 516 SW2d 690, ref nre.—App & E 547(2), 548(2), 758.3(9); Autos 178, 242(1), 242(7); Judgm 181(2).

Garcia; Schrader v., TexCivApp–Corpus Christi, 516 SW2d 687, ref nre.—App & E 436, 564(3), 624; Trial 5.

Garcia; Schrader v., TexCivApp–Corpus Christi, 512 SW2d 830.—App & E 454, 465(1), 478.

Garcia v. Schwab, TexApp–Corpus Christi, 967 SW2d 883.—Civil R 1184, 1185, 1740; Judgm 183.

Garcia; Second Injury Fund of Texas v., TexApp–Amarillo, 970 SW2d 706, reh overr, and review den.—Judgm 199(1); Pretrial Proc 303; Work Comp 1030.1(1), 1030.1(4.1), 1030.1(6), 1030.1(7).

GARCIA

59 Tex D 2d—182

See Guidelines for Arrangement at the beginning of this Volume

Garcia v. Secretary of Labor, CA5 (Tex), 10 F3d 276.—Admin Law 741; Aliens 788, 791; Evid 597; Labor & Emp 1866; Statut 219(4).

Garcia; Sifuentes-Barraza v., WDTex, 252 FSupp2d 354.—Aliens 385; Hab Corp 521.

Garcia v. Sky Climber, Inc., TexCivApp–Hous (1 Dist), 470 SW2d 261, ref nre.—Bailm 35; Evid 194, 258(1); Indem 97, 102; Prod Liab 8, 11, 79; Trial 214, 350.5(2), 362; Witn 389.

Garcia v. Smith, CA5 (Tex), 208 FedAppx 351.—Fed Civ Proc 2734.

Garcia v. Smith, TexCivApp–Beaumont, 612 SW2d 255.—App & E 553(1), 664(4), 1177(9).

Garcia; Solis v., TexApp–Houston (14 Dist), 702 SW2d 668.—App & E 715(2), 846(5), 931(6), 1073(7), 1151(2), 1171(1); Courts 85(3); Death 77, 106; Judges 30; Judgm 99; Time 10(2).

Garcia v. Southern Farm Bureau Cas. Ins. Co., TexCivApp–El Paso, 490 SW2d 616.—Insurance 2654.

Garcia v. South Texas Sec. and Alarm Co., TexApp–Corpus Christi, 911 SW2d 483, reh overr.—App & E 854(1), 934(1); Detectives 4; Judgm 183, 185.3(21).

Garcia; Specialized Carriers, Inc. v., TexCivApp–Fort Worth, 391 SW2d 582.—App & E 1024.3; Plead 111.42(8).

Garcia v. Spohn Health System Corp., TexApp–Corpus Christi, 19 SW3d 507, reh overr, and review den.—App & E 1031(1), 1043(6), 1045(1), 1047(4); Health 835; Judgm 186, 256(1); Jury 33(1.1), 33(2.10); Pretrial Proc 39; Trial 3(4), 18, 356(5).

Garcia v. State, TexCrimApp, 201 SW3d 695, reh den, cert den 127 SCt 1289, 167 LEd2d 106.—Courts 85(2); Crim Law 338(1), 338(7), 369.1, 369.2(1), 369.2(4), 1134(3); Homic 999; Statut 206.

Garcia v. State, TexCrimApp, 149 SW3d 135, on remand 161 SW3d 28.—Crim Law 642, 662.1, 662.65, 662.70, 1035(1).

Garcia v. State, TexCrimApp, 126 SW3d 921, habeas corpus den Ex Parte Garcia, 2007 WL 1783194.—Crim Law 436(2), 436(5), 720(1), 721(3), 1171.1(6); Sent & Pun 1612, 1760, 1762, 1766, 1767, 1789(9).

Garcia v. State, TexCrimApp, 57 SW3d 436, cert den 123 SCt 1351, 537 US 1195, 154 LEd2d 1030.—Crim Law 641.13(1), 641.13(7); Sent & Pun 1705, 1756, 1771, 1772, 1789(6), 1789(8), 1789(10).

Garcia v. State, TexCrimApp, 43 SW3d 527.—Arrest 63.5(4); Autos 349(5); Crim Law 1139, 1158(2).

Garcia v. State, TexCrimApp, 15 SW3d 533, on remand 2000 WL 991638, appeal after remand 2001 WL 32742, petition for discretionary review refused.—Courts 247(2); Crim Law 414, 736(2), 1158(1), 1179, 1192.

Garcia v. State, TexCrimApp, 981 SW2d 683.—Ind & Inf 2(0.5), 71.2(3), 71.3, 87(7).

Garcia v. State, TexCrimApp, 919 SW2d 370, reh gr, and on reh.—Afft 11; Const Law 3310, 3833, 4664(1), 4760; Crim Law 412.2(5), 517.2(2), 520(1), 520(2), 526, 531(3), 553, 1035(6), 1130(5), 1134(5), 1144.13(3), 1144.13(6), 1144.17, 1148, 1152(2), 1153(1), 1158(3), 1158(4), 1159.2(7), 1159.4(2), 1166.16, 1169.1(5), 1172.1(1), 1172.2; Gr Jury 2.5, 8, 35; Homic 1135, 1163, 1329; Jury 33(1), 33(1.1), 33(1.10), 33(1.15), 33(5.15), 62(3), 64, 70(2), 83(1), 108, 118, 131(1), 131(8), 131(13); Rob 24.10, 24.30; Sent & Pun 1720, 1772, 1780(3); Statut 181(1), 188, 189.

Garcia v. State, TexCrimApp, 887 SW2d 862, reh den, cert den Torres Garcia v. Texas, 115 SCt 1368, 514 US 1021, 131 LEd2d 223.—Crim Law 511.1(7), 511.1(9), 641.13(1), 641.13(2.1), 673(1), 673(3), 698(1), 723(1), 737(1), 824(8), 857(3), 1035(5), 1036.2, 1037.1(1), 1037.1(2), 1037.1(4), 1038.3, 1043(3), 1045, 1101, 1130(5), 1134(2), 1134(3), 1134(5), 1144.13(2.1), 1152(2), 1158(1), 1158(3), 1159.2(7); Homic 908, 1181, 1184; Jury 108, 110(14); Sent & Pun 1720, 1772, 1780(2), 1780(3), 1789(3); Witn 321.

Garcia v. State, TexCrimApp, 887 SW2d 846, reh den, cert den 115 SCt 1317, 514 US 1005, 131 LEd2d 198, habeas corpus den 2003 WL 22329007, aff 456 F3d 463.—Crim Law 800(2), 1030(2), 1035(5), 1134(2), 1152(2), 1166.18; Jury 83(1), 104.1, 105(1), 105(4), 106, 107, 108, 126; Searches 173.1, 175; Sent & Pun 1626, 1780(3), 1788(3).

Garcia v. State, TexCrimApp, 868 SW2d 337.—Crim Law 429(1).

Garcia; State v., TexCrimApp, 861 SW2d 386.—Courts 107; Tresp 87.

Garcia v. State, TexCrimApp, 840 SW2d 957.—Crim Law 1070.

Garcia v. State, TexCrimApp, 829 SW2d 796, appeal after remand 2002 WL 1164135, petition for discretionary review refused, cert den 123 SCt 2217, 538 US 1059, 155 LEd2d 1110.—Crim Law 394.1(3); Statut 188, 228.

Garcia v. State, TexCrimApp, 827 SW2d 937.—Arrest 58, 63.4(4), 63.5(1), 63.5(4); Autos 349.5(3).

Garcia v. State, TexCrimApp, 806 SW2d 835.—Double J 148, 182.

Garcia v. State, TexCrimApp, 792 SW2d 88.—Crim Law 1153(1); Infants 20.

Garcia v. State, TexCrimApp, 787 SW2d 957.—Crim Law 641.3(8.1).

Garcia v. State, TexCrimApp, 768 SW2d 726.—Double J 182; Judgm 751.

Garcia v. State, TexCrimApp, 760 SW2d 260.—Crim Law 1134(3).

Garcia v. State, TexCrimApp, 747 SW2d 379.—Autos 351.1; Ind & Inf 93, 110(3).

Garcia v. State, TexCrimApp, 661 SW2d 96.—Rape 51(1).

Garcia v. State, TexCrimApp, 641 SW2d 246.—Crim Law 1181.5(8).

Garcia v. State, TexCrimApp, 640 SW2d 939.—Crim Law 814(1), 1038.1(2); Obst Just 1, 18.

Garcia v. State, TexCrimApp, 626 SW2d 46.—Const Law 266(3.3), 4658(3), 4659(2); Crim Law 339.10(2), 486(6), 641.3(9), 641.3(10), 1166.10(2), 1166.17, 1166.18; Jury 125; Sent & Pun 311, 1772.

Garcia v. State, TexCrimApp, 605 SW2d 565.—Crim Law 772(6); Homic 1343, 1492.

Garcia v. State, TexCrimApp, 601 SW2d 369.—Sent & Pun 2021.

Garcia v. State, TexCrimApp, 595 SW2d 538, appeal reinstated 601 SW2d 369.—Crim Law 339.11(6), 625.10(2.1), 625.10(3), 625.15, 625.20, 1036.1(7), 1044.1(5.1), 1148, 1181.5(4); Sent & Pun 2292.

Garcia v. State, TexCrimApp, 595 SW2d 533.—Crim Law 1038.1(4); Rob 17(6).

Garcia v. State, TexCrimApp, 581 SW2d 168, vac 101 SCt 3133, 453 US 902, 69 LEd2d 988, on remand 641 SW2d 246.—Crim Law 393(1), 404.30, 412.2(5), 414, 589(1), 599, 847, 1038.1(3.1), 1043(3); Jury 39, 42, 108; Sent & Pun 1752, 1759, 1762; Witn 258.

Garcia v. State, TexCrimApp, 574 SW2d 133.—Crim Law 29(1), 1038.1(2), 1038.1(4), 1172.1(3); Sent & Pun 518.

Garcia v. State, TexCrimApp, 573 SW2d 12.—Crim Law 369.2(5), 370, 693, 695(2), 1153(2); Witn 52(3), 61(1), 77, 79(1).

Garcia v. State, TexCrimApp, 571 SW2d 896.—Burg 2, 3; Ind & Inf 191(2); Sent & Pun 2003, 2011, 2016, 2021.

Garcia v. State, TexCrimApp, 563 SW2d 925.—Const Law 266(3.3), 4658(1); Crim Law 339.8(4), 339.9(1), 339.9(3), 925.5(4), 1169.1(5); Rape 51(3), 51(7); Sent & Pun 316.

Garcia v. State, TexCrimApp, 541 SW2d 428.—Homic 527, 558, 559, 908, 931, 1168; Sent & Pun 1318.

Garcia v. State, TexCrimApp, 537 SW2d 930.—Crim Law 121, 134(1), 134(4), 404.36, 404.50, 621(1), 645, 822(17); Escape 1, 9, 10; Ind & Inf 125(19.1), 159(2); Sent & Pun 636.

Garcia v. State, TexCrimApp, 528 SW2d 604.—Crim Law 347.

For Later Case History Information, see KeyCite on WESTLAW

Garcia v. State, TexCrimApp, 522 SW2d 203.—Crim Law 449.1, 643, 865(1), 865(2), 1092.12, 1136, 1174(1); Gr Jury 7; Homic 909, 1136, 1301, 1347, 1480; Ind & Inf 10.1(2).

Garcia v. State, TexCrimApp, 513 SW2d 559.—Crim Law 339.11(10), 721(3), 721(6), 1044.1(8), 1119(4); Sent & Pun 1404, 1416.

Garcia v. State, TexCrimApp, 513 SW2d 82.—Crim Law 126(1), 134(4), 1042, 1090.15.

Garcia v. State, TexCrimApp, 502 SW2d 718.—Burg 29, 41(3); Sent & Pun 312.

Garcia v. State, TexCrimApp, 501 SW2d 652.—False Pret 39, 49(4).

Garcia v. State, TexCrimApp, 499 SW2d 126.—Crim Law 1192.

Garcia v. State, TexCrimApp, 498 SW2d 936.—Autos 316.

Garcia v. State, TexCrimApp, 496 SW2d 592.—Burg 41(5).

Garcia v. State, TexCrimApp, 495 SW2d 257.—Crim Law 627.5(6), 627.9(1), 730(3), 1036.1(3.1), 1119(2), 1130(2), 1134(3), 1184(4.1); Homic 564, 1177.

Garcia v. State, TexCrimApp, 492 SW2d 592.—Homic 1479.

Garcia v. State, TexCrimApp, 488 SW2d 448, appeal after remand 499 SW2d 126.—Const Law 4733(2); Sent & Pun 2029, 2030.

Garcia v. State, TexCrimApp, 475 SW2d 262.—Arrest 63.4(13), 71.1(3).

Garcia v. State, TexCrimApp, 473 SW2d 488.—Controlled Subs 45, 74, 82, 98; Crim Law 37(8), 494, 675.

Garcia v. State, TexCrimApp, 472 SW2d 784.—Arrest 63.4(16); Crim Law 339.10(11), 693, 1169.1(5); Sent & Pun 2014.

Garcia v. State, TexCrimApp, 472 SW2d 516.—Searches 114.

Garcia v. State, TexCrimApp, 459 SW2d 839.—Arrest 63.4(8), 71.1(3).

Garcia v. State, TexCrimApp, 459 SW2d 838.—Controlled Subs 148(3).

Garcia v. State, TexCrimApp, 455 SW2d 271.—Crim Law 371(4), 372(4), 438(7), 792(3).

Garcia v. State, TexCrimApp, 454 SW2d 400.—Crim Law 627.6(1), 627.6(6), 627.9(1), 627.9(2.1), 674, 822(11), 1169.1(6); Homic 1345; Ind & Inf 144.1(1); Witn 337(4), 344(1).

Garcia v. State, TexCrimApp, 453 SW2d 822.—Burg 29, 46(2); Crim Law 404.75, 774, 864, 995(3), 1166(1), 1174(5).

Garcia v. State, TexCrimApp, 443 SW2d 847.—Disorderly C 1.

Garcia v. State, TexCrimApp, 440 SW2d 295.—Autos 349.5(2); Crim Law 1158(4).

Garcia v. State, TexCrimApp, 436 SW2d 911.—Crim Law 641.13(1), 641.13(2.1), 1166.10(1).

Garcia v. State, TexCrimApp, 436 SW2d 139.—Crim Law 641.10(2), 1084, 1130(2).

Garcia v. State, TexCrimApp, 435 SW2d 533.—Crim Law 29(1), 857(1), 938(1), 957(3), 1166.8, 1166.10(1); Rob 24.20.

Garcia v. State, TexCrimApp, 429 SW2d 468.—Const Law 268(2.1), 4615, 4813; Crim Law 101(2), 740, 829(3).

Garcia v. State, TexCrimApp, 428 SW2d 334.—Crim Law 715, 720(7.1), 730(13), 1037.1(2), 1044.1(8).

Garcia v. State, TexCrimApp, 427 SW2d 897.—Crim Law 99, 650, 655(1), 656(9), 852, 1166.22(2), 1166.22(7); Rob 24.15(1); Witn 267, 328.

Garcia v. State, TexCrimApp, 396 SW2d 123.—Crim Law 627.7(3), 822(6); Homic 1134.

Garcia v. State, TexCrimApp, 394 SW2d 801.—Sent & Pun 2009.

Garcia v. State, TexCrimApp, 386 SW2d 138.—Crim Law 1086.13.

Garcia v. State, TexCrimApp, 378 SW2d 72.—Bail 68; Crim Law 1081(2).

Garcia v. State, TexCrimApp, 373 SW2d 744.—Burg 41(10).

Garcia v. State, TexCrimApp, 364 SW2d 687.—Sent & Pun 2021.

Garcia v. State, TexCrimApp, 358 SW2d 625, 172 TexCrim 467.—Crim Law 949(2).

Garcia v. State, TexCrimApp, 340 SW2d 803, 170 TexCrim 328.—Controlled Subs 69, 145, 146; Crim Law 448(4), 884.

Garcia v. State, TexCrimApp, 336 SW2d 164, 169 TexCrim 640.—Homic 1177, 1492.

Garcia v. State, TexCrimApp, 335 SW2d 381, 169 TexCrim 487.—Sent & Pun 1349.

Garcia v. State, TexCrimApp, 332 SW2d 734, 169 TexCrim 138.—Assault 96(3).

Garcia v. State, TexCrimApp, 331 SW2d 53, 169 TexCrim 30.—Crim Law 97(4), 596(1), 939(1), 1158(1); Rape 53(2); Witn 224.

Garcia v. State, TexCrimApp, 322 SW2d 536, 167 TexCrim 593.—Witn 337(21).

Garcia v. State, TexCrimApp, 319 SW2d 727, 167 TexCrim 211.—Witn 337(24).

Garcia v. State, TexCrimApp, 316 SW2d 734, 166 TexCrim 482.—Controlled Subs 100(2); Crim Law 1159.5.

Garcia v. State, TexCrimApp, 305 SW2d 605, 165 TexCrim 134.—Crim Law 369.1, 369.5, 1169.11.

Garcia v. State, TexCrimApp, 301 SW2d 118.—Crim Law 1090.1(1).

Garcia v. State, TexCrimApp, 298 SW2d 831, 164 TexCrim 273.—Controlled Subs 80, 145, 148(3); Searches 150.

Garcia v. State, TexCrimApp, 297 SW2d 824.—Crim Law 1090.1(1).

Garcia v. State, TexCrimApp, 297 SW2d 156.—Crim Law 1090.1(1).

Garcia v. State, TexCrimApp, 296 SW2d 256.—Crim Law 1090.1(1).

Garcia v. State, TexCrimApp, 289 SW2d 766, 163 TexCrim 146, ref nre.—Controlled Subs 80; Crim Law 394.4(2).

Garcia v. State, TexCrimApp, 288 SW2d 513, 162 TexCrim 594.—Crim Law 530, 720(5), 730(8), 798.5, 1171.3; Homic 1193.

Garcia v. State, TexCrimApp, 285 SW2d 738.—Crim Law 1090.1(1).

Garcia v. State, TexCrimApp, 284 SW2d 731.—Crim Law 1090.1(1).

Garcia v. State, TexCrimApp, 283 SW2d 60.—Crim Law 981(1).

Garcia v. State, TexCrimApp, 276 SW2d 527, 161 TexCrim 249.—Crim Law 594(1), 596(1), 597(1), 614(1), 1151, 1171.3; Homic 1134.

Garcia v. State, TexCrimApp, 275 SW2d 489.—Crim Law 1090.1(1).

Garcia v. State, TexCrimApp, 275 SW2d 120.—Crim Law 1090.1(1).

Garcia v. State, TexCrimApp, 275 SW2d 118.—Crim Law 1090.1(1).

Garcia v. State, TexCrimApp, 255 SW2d 197.—Crim Law 1090.1(1).

Garcia v. State, TexCrimApp, 255 SW2d 196.—Crim Law 1090.1(1).

Garcia v. State, TexCrimApp, 254 SW2d 389.—Crim Law 1094(3).

Garcia v. State, TexCrimApp, 227 SW2d 811, 154 TexCrim 451.—Crim Law 1177.5(3); Rob 27(1); Sent & Pun 1388.

Garcia v. State, TexCrimApp, 227 SW2d 569, 154 TexCrim 413.—Crim Law 1090.7; Homic 1154.

Garcia v. State, TexCrimApp, 210 SW2d 574, 151 TexCrim 593.—Aliens 136; Crim Law 633(1), 642, 662.1, 662.80, 736(2), 1158(3), 1158(4), 1165(1), 1166.13, 1169.3; Homic 612, 1466.

Garcia v. State, TexCrimApp, 207 SW2d 877, 151 TexCrim 488, reh den 208 SW2d 901, 151 TexCrim 488.—Crim Law 857(2), 858(3), 918(3), 925.5(3), 1036.2, 1054(1), 1166.16, 1170.5(2).

Garcia v. State, TexCrimApp, 207 SW2d 624, 151 TexCrim 272.—Ind & Inf 86(5); Larc 22.

Garcia v. State, TexCrimApp, 207 SW2d 389, 151 TexCrim 275.—Assault 92(1); Crim Law 829(5), 1043(3), 1170.5(6).

Garcia v. State, TexCrimApp, 183 SW2d 468.—Crim Law 1090.1(1).

Garcia v. State, TexCrimApp, 162 SW2d 714, 144 TexCrim 300.—Crim Law 857(1), 925.5(3), 1174(2).

Garcia v. State, TexCrimApp, 158 SW2d 73, 143 TexCrim 161.—Crim Law 1097(5).

Garcia v. State, TexCrimApp, 149 SW2d 113, 141 TexCrim 444.—Crim Law 1184(2); Ind & Inf 137(6); Obscen 11, 17.

Garcia v. State, TexCrimApp, 145 SW2d 180, 140 TexCrim 340.—Sent & Pun 1213, 1276, 1277, 1278; Statut 220.

Garcia v. State, TexCrimApp, 139 SW2d 790, 139 TexCrim 269.—Crim Law 1092.11(2), 1159.2(10); Homic 1193, 1202.

Garcia v. State, TexCrimApp, 135 SW2d 107, 138 TexCrim 180.—Crim Law 1177; Int Liq 242; Searches 178, 182, 194.

Garcia v. State, TexCrimApp, 122 SW2d 631, 135 TexCrim 667.—Crim Law 478(1), 1170.5(3); Sent & Pun 1257, 1379(2), 1381(6).

Garcia v. State, TexCrimApp, 122 SW2d 306, 135 TexCrim 641.—Jury 66(1), 70(2); Statut 223.2(8).

Garcia v. State, TexCrimApp, 96 SW2d 977, 131 TexCrim 84.—Autos 336, 355(8).

Garcia v. State, TexApp–Houston (1 Dist), 218 SW3d 756.—Arrest 63.4(2); Autos 349(2.1), 349.5(5.1); Controlled Subs 26, 27, 30, 68, 81; Crim Law 474.5, 778(10), 795(1.5), 795(2.10), 795(2.70), 1144.13(2.1), 1159.2(1), 1159.2(7), 1159.2(9); Ind & Inf 81(5), 191(0.5).

Garcia v. State, TexApp–Houston (1 Dist), 106 SW3d 854, petition for discretionary review refused, cert den 124 SCt 2076, 541 US 1013, 158 LEd2d 626.—Crim Law 59(1), 412.2(2), 632(4), 641.13(2.1), 641.13(6), 1028, 1036.1(9), 1044.2(1); Homic 612.

Garcia v. State, TexApp–Houston (1 Dist), 95 SW3d 522.—Autos 411; Crim Law 1026.10(4); Witn 212.

Garcia v. State, TexApp–Houston (1 Dist), 17 SW3d 1, petition for discretionary review refused.—Assault 56, 92(4), 96(1); Crim Law 369.1, 369.2(1), 369.2(2), 369.2(4), 371(12), 753.2(3.1), 795(1.5), 795(2.10), 814(20), 882, 890, 1036.1(8), 1134(2), 1144.13(2.1), 1144.13(6), 1144.14, 1159.2(2), 1159.2(7).

Garcia v. State, TexApp–Houston (1 Dist), 802 SW2d 817, petition for discretionary review refused.—Crim Law 1144.13(3), 1144.13(6), 1159.2(7), 1159.6; Homic 1184, 1188; Jury 33(5.15), 33(5.20), 120.

Garcia v. State, TexApp–Houston (1 Dist), 769 SW2d 345.—Arrest 64; Searches 15.

Garcia v. State, TexApp–Houston (1 Dist), 630 SW2d 303.—Forg 44(0.5); Fraud 68.

Garcia v. State, TexApp–Fort Worth, 6 SW3d 765, petition for discretionary review refused.—Crim Law 899, 1137(5), 1165(1), 1169.1(1), 1169.11.

Garcia v. State, TexApp–Fort Worth, 943 SW2d 215.—Crim Law 713, 723(1), 730(1), 730(14), 1134(3), 1171.1(2.1).

Garcia; State v., TexApp–Fort Worth, 859 SW2d 125, petition for discretionary review refused.—Crim Law 394.1(2), 1158(4); Searches 26.

Garcia; State v., TexApp–Fort Worth, 838 SW2d 830, petition for discretionary review gr, rev 861 SW2d 386.—Tresp 87.

Garcia v. State, TexApp–Austin, 212 SW3d 877.—Assault 96(8); Breach of P 15.1; Const Law 656, 990, 1003,

1030, 1140, 1141, 1163, 1520, 1800, 1813, 1827, 1830, 4509(11); Crim Law 13(1), 13.1(1), 662.8, 798(0.7), 814(1), 872.5, 881(1), 1134(6), 1139, 1169.2(6); Statut 188.

Garcia v. State, TexApp–Austin, 97 SW3d 343, appeal decided 2003 WL 22095778, petition stricken, and petition for discretionary review refused.—Crim Law 641.3(2), 641.3(3), 641.3(4), 641.7(1), 641.12(1), 641.12(4), 641.13(3), 641.13(7), 913(1), 920, 959, 1063(1), 1162, 1166.10(1), 1166.10(2).

Garcia v. State, TexApp–Austin, 92 SW3d 574.—Assault 56, 96(1); Autos 355(14); Crim Law 795(2.10).

Garcia v. State, TexApp–Austin, 46 SW3d 323, petition for discretionary review refused.—Consp 24(1), 27, 28(3); Crim Law 866, 881(1); RICO 104.

Garcia v. State, TexApp–Austin, 45 SW3d 740, reh overr, and petition for discretionary review refused.—Crim Law 1004, 1023(3).

Garcia v. State, TexApp–Austin, 967 SW2d 902.—Arrest 63.4(1), 63.5(4), 63.5(6), 63.5(7), 63.5(8); Controlled Subs 121; Crim Law 394.6(5), 1144.12.

Garcia v. State, TexApp–Austin, 649 SW2d 163.—Ind & Inf 144.1(1).

Garcia v. State, TexApp–San Antonio, 150 SW3d 598, reh overr, and petition for discretionary review gr, and petition for discretionary review refused, rev 201 SW3d 695, reh den, cert den 127 SCt 1289, 167 LEd2d 106.—Crim Law 342, 369.1, 369.3, 371(1), 371(4), 371(12), 374, 552(3), 1139, 1144.13(2.1), 1153(1), 1159.2(7), 1159.6, 1162, 1169.11; Homic 1184.

Garcia v. State, TexApp–San Antonio, 75 SW3d 493, petition for discretionary review refused, cert den 123 SCt 1362, 537 US 1237, 155 LEd2d 203.—Crim Law 128, 273.1(2), 273.1(4), 273.2(1), 911, 938(1), 942(2), 958(6), 1026.10(4), 1081(2), 1130(2), 1134(2), 1136, 1150, 1156(1), 1177; Ind & Inf 196(1); Jury 24.

Garcia v. State, TexApp–San Antonio, 32 SW3d 328.—Crim Law 772(2), 822(1), 1032(1), 1043(2), 1172.1(1), 1172.2; Ind & Inf 17, 60.

Garcia v. State, TexApp–San Antonio, 988 SW2d 862.—Crim Law 339.7(4), 339.10(2), 339.11(3), 438(6), 675, 1153(1); Homic 975, 984.

Garcia; State v., TexApp–San Antonio, 905 SW2d 7, petition for discretionary review refused, petition for discretionary review refused 910 SW2d 499.—Autos 359; Crim Law 977(1); Sent & Pun 1311, 1314.

Garcia; State v., TexApp–San Antonio, 823 SW2d 793, petition for discretionary review refused.—Admin Law 441; Const Law 656, 665, 667, 753, 969, 1163, 1490, 1514, 1515, 1520, 1521, 1600, 1790, 2222, 2225; Counties 55; Crim Law 13.1(1), 1014; Mun Corp 120, 594(2); Statut 47, 188, 208.

Garcia v. State, TexApp–San Antonio, 817 SW2d 741, writ den.—App & E 934(1); Autos 273; Judgm 185(2); Neglig 1040(3); States 112.2(2).

Garcia; State v., TexApp–San Antonio, 801 SW2d 137, petition for discretionary review refused.—Arrest 71.1(5); Autos 349.5(1); Searches 66.

Garcia v. State, TexApp–San Antonio, 800 SW2d 872. See State v. $50,600.00.

Garcia v. State, TexApp–San Antonio, 790 SW2d 22, petition for discretionary review gr, appeal abated 840 SW2d 957.—Controlled Subs 26, 27, 28, 30, 79; Crim Law 552(3), 562.

Garcia v. State, TexApp–San Antonio, 775 SW2d 879.—Arrest 63.4(18); Crim Law 223, 234; Hab Corp 705.1, 712.1, 715.1; Searches 191.

Garcia v. State, TexApp–San Antonio, 753 SW2d 189, petition for discretionary review refused.—Controlled Subs 30, 80; Crim Law 254.2, 260.11(6), 260.12.

Garcia v. State, TexApp–San Antonio, 753 SW2d 187, petition for discretionary review refused.—Controlled Subs 27, 30, 80; Crim Law 254.2, 260.11(6), 260.12.

GARCIA

Garcia v. State, TexApp–San Antonio, 730 SW2d 202.—Crim Law 1043(3), 1170.5(1); Witn 337(11), 337(28), 337(30).

Garcia v. State, TexApp–San Antonio, 720 SW2d 655, petition for discretionary review gr, aff 747 SW2d 379.—Autos 351.1, 354; Crim Law 734, 1044.1(2); Ind & Inf 56, 136, 138.

Garcia v. State, TexApp–San Antonio, 696 SW2d 262, petition for discretionary review gr, rev 751 SW2d 507.—Crim Law 577.11(2), 577.16(7), 577.16(8).

Garcia v. State, TexApp–San Antonio, 686 SW2d 281.—Bail 74(1), 80.

Garcia v. State, TexApp–San Antonio, 685 SW2d 420.—Assault 54; Autos 351.1, 355(14), 356; Crim Law 911, 1032(5), 1038.1(1), 1038.1(2), 1038.1(4), 1038.2, 1038.3, 1044.1(2), 1064(2), 1144.13(8), 1156(1), 1159.2(7), 1178.

Garcia v. State, TexApp–San Antonio, 649 SW2d 697.—Arrest 63.5(8).

Garcia v. State, TexApp–San Antonio, 634 SW2d 888.—Crim Law 388.2, 637, 770(3), 772(3), 814(1), 829(9); Jury 110(14); Sent & Pun 1379(2).

Garcia v. State, TexApp–San Antonio, 630 SW2d 727, petition for discretionary review refused.—Crim Law 1043(3), 1090.1(1), 1091(7); Sent & Pun 1318.

Garcia v. State, TexApp–Dallas, 153 SW3d 755.—Sent & Pun 1157, 1158.

Garcia v. State, TexApp–Dallas, 833 SW2d 564, petition for discretionary review gr, aff 868 SW2d 337.—Courts 97(1); Crim Law 429(1), 436(3), 488, 629(3.1), 629.5(1), 713, 730(1), 730(8), 1144.13(2.1), 1148, 1158(1), 1158(3), 1159.2(7), 1170.5(6); Homic 1172; Jury 33(5.15); Witn 318, 414(1).

Garcia v. State, TexApp–Dallas, 829 SW2d 830, petition for discretionary review refused.—Crim Law 519(1), 525.

Garcia v. State, TexApp–Dallas, 669 SW2d 169, petition for discretionary review refused.—False Pret 14, 26; Statut 207, 223.1.

Garcia v. State, TexApp–Texarkana, 880 SW2d 189, petition for discretionary review refused.—Crim Law 1184(4.1); Ind & Inf 10.2(2), 184; Searches 42.1; Sent & Pun 1139.

Garcia v. State, TexApp–Amarillo, 76 SW3d 33, petition for discretionary review refused.—Crim Law 1026.10(4), 1069(1), 1081(2), 1131(4).

Garcia v. State, TexApp–Amarillo, 725 SW2d 385, petition for discretionary review gr, vac 760 SW2d 260.—Const Law 2823, 4723; Crim Law 790.

Garcia v. State, TexApp–Amarillo, 630 SW2d 914.—Crim Law 772(2), 808.5, 814(8), 822(1), 938(1), 1032(1), 1038.1(2), 1130(4), 1156(3); Rape 59(5), 59(14), 59(22).

Garcia v. State, TexApp–El Paso, 172 SW3d 270, reh overr.—Child C 971; Crim Law 37.10(1), 37.10(2), 37.15(1), 627.8(3), 739(1), 1139; Statut 181(1), 188, 189.

Garcia v. State, TexApp–El Paso, 16 SW3d 401, petition for discretionary review refused.—Crim Law 1035(6), 1042, 1130(5), 1144.13(2.1), 1159.2(7), 1159.4(2), 1166.18; Double J 1, 5.1, 28, 29.1; Homic 1186; Sent & Pun 1435, 1439, 1466, 1532.

Garcia v. State, TexApp–El Paso, 911 SW2d 866.—Const Law 4723; Crim Law 770(3), 790, 1134(3), 1184(3); Ind & Inf 60, 166.

Garcia v. State, TexApp–El Paso, 874 SW2d 688.—Autos 422.1, 426; Crim Law 842, 1172.1(1), 1173.2(5).

Garcia v. State, TexApp–El Paso, 871 SW2d 279.—Controlled Subs 82, 94; Crim Law 59(1), 80, 552(2), 627.6(3), 629(1), 814(19); Witn 331.5, 379(1), 379(2).

Garcia; State v., TexApp–El Paso, 794 SW2d 472, petition for discretionary review gr, aff 827 SW2d 937.—Controlled Subs 117; Crim Law 394.4(12), 394.4(14).

Garcia v. State, TexApp–El Paso, 758 SW2d 937.—Crim Law 721(3), 1115(1), 1171.5.

Garcia v. State, TexApp–El Paso, 712 SW2d 249, petition for discretionary review refused.—Crim Law

641.13(2.1), 641.13(6), 698(3), 1036.1(2), 1036.2, 1043(1), 1044.1(8), 1159.4(2); Jury 90; Witn 406, 414(1).

Garcia v. State, TexApp–El Paso, 659 SW2d 843, rev 661 SW2d 96.—Rape 12, 13, 51(4).

Garcia v. State, TexApp–El Paso, 633 SW2d 611.—Crim Law 211(4), 720(7.1); Ind & Inf 137(1); Obscen 1.4, 2.5, 12, 13, 16.

Garcia v. State, TexApp–Beaumont, 972 SW2d 848.—Crim Law 38, 569, 772(6), 893, 1144.13(3), 1159.5.

Garcia v. State, TexApp–Beaumont, 762 SW2d 263, petition for discretionary review gr, rev 806 SW2d 835.—Double J 148.

Garcia v. State, TexApp–Beaumont, 661 SW2d 754.—Const Law 3741; Crim Law 438(6), 531(3); Infants 68.3.

Garcia v. State, TexApp–Waco, 885 SW2d 641. See Johnson v. State.

Garcia v. State, TexApp–Tyler, 930 SW2d 621.—Crim Law 304(1), 388.2, 393(1), 429(2), 444, 641.3(8.1), 1141(2), 1144.17; Sent & Pun 280, 282, 283, 284, 289, 299, 300, 311.

Garcia v. State, TexApp–Corpus Christi, 45 SW3d 733.—Courts 39, 40; Crim Law 1045, 1081(1), 1081(2).

Garcia v. State, TexApp–Corpus Christi, 960 SW2d 329.—Crim Law 394.5(2), 406(1), 410, 412(3), 949(1), 956(2), 956(4), 956(13), 959, 1035(5), 1044.1(2), 1156(1), 1166.18; Searches 164; Witn 331.5.

Garcia v. State, TexApp–Corpus Christi, 960 SW2d 151.—Crim Law 273(4.1), 273.1(4), 273.1(5), 274(2), 274(3.1), 274(9), 1031(4), 1072, 1081(2), 1130(2), 1130(5), 1134(2), 1167(5).

Garcia v. State, TexApp–Corpus Christi, 928 SW2d 666, reh overr.—Crim Law 1167(4); Ind & Inf 159(1).

Garcia v. State, TexApp–Corpus Christi, 909 SW2d 563, petition for discretionary review refused.—Crim Law 641.4(1), 641.4(2), 641.4(4), 641.7(1), 1141(2); Sent & Pun 1378, 1381(5).

Garcia v. State, TexApp–Corpus Christi, 907 SW2d 635, petition for discretionary review gr, aff 981 SW2d 683.—Crim Law 147, 388.5(1), 629(1), 1032(5), 1036.5, 1166(10.10); Ind & Inf 87(7).

Garcia v. State, TexApp–Corpus Christi, 894 SW2d 865.—Arrest 63.5(6), 68(4); Autos 349(4); Crim Law 1144.12, 1158(4).

Garcia v. State, TexApp–Corpus Christi, 893 SW2d 17.—Crim Law 369.2(1), 369.15, 371(1), 371(6), 1028, 1134(3), 1139, 1165(1), 1169.5(3), 1169.11.

Garcia v. State, TexApp–Corpus Christi, 882 SW2d 856.—Crim Law 59(3), 59(4), 80, 562, 829(20), 1144.13(2.1), 1159.2(7); Homic 1207.

Garcia v. State, TexApp–Corpus Christi, 880 SW2d 497.—Controlled Subs 67, 68, 74, 80; Crim Law 553, 562, 1036.5, 1144.13(2.1), 1159.2(7), 1159.2(9), 1159.4(2), 1171.1(2.1), 1171.3.

Garcia v. State, TexApp–Corpus Christi, 877 SW2d 809, petition for discretionary review refused.—Const Law 3804; Crim Law 273.1(4), 273.1(5), 274(8), 662.80, 1134(2), 1167(5); Judges 51(1); Jury 29(6), 31.3(1); Sent & Pun 375.

Garcia v. State, TexApp–Corpus Christi, 871 SW2d 769, reh overr, and petition for discretionary review refused.—Controlled Subs 26, 27, 79; Crim Law 369.1, 1169.11.

Garcia v. State, TexApp–Corpus Christi, 853 SW2d 157, petition for discretionary review refused.—Arrest 68(4); Autos 349(4), 349(9); Searches 23, 192.1.

Garcia v. State, TexApp–Corpus Christi, 827 SW2d 27.—Crim Law 369.2(1), 370, 1169.11; Infants 20.

Garcia v. State, TexApp–Corpus Christi, 827 SW2d 25.—Crim Law 864, 1144.13(6), 1159.2(7), 1172.1(3); Homic 845, 1179.

Garcia v. State, TexApp–Corpus Christi, 819 SW2d 667.—Assault 92(5); Crim Law 380.

Garcia v. State, TexApp–Corpus Christi, 819 SW2d 634.—Assault 56; Crim Law 304(5).

GARCIA

See Guidelines for Arrangement at the beginning of this Volume

Garcia v. State, TexApp–Corpus Christi, 801 SW2d 20.—
Crim Law 273.1(1), 273.1(2), 1026.10(2.1), 1181.5(1).

Garcia v. State, TexApp–Corpus Christi, 791 SW2d 279,
petition for discretionary review refused.—Crim Law
494, 552(3), 552(4), 770(2), 814(6), 893, 1038.1(1), 1115(1),
1172.1(1); Homic 1558; Sent & Pun 78, 323.

Garcia v. State, TexApp–Corpus Christi, 773 SW2d 694.
—Pardon 64.1; Sent & Pun 294, 2145, 2198.

Garcia v. State, TexApp–Corpus Christi, 760 SW2d 817,
petition for discretionary review gr, aff 792 SW2d 88.—
Crim Law 1038.1(1), 1042; Ind & Inf 180; Infants 20.

Garcia v. State, TexApp–Corpus Christi, 756 SW2d 880.
—Crim Law 1120(3).

Garcia v. State, TexApp–Corpus Christi, 750 SW2d 922.
—Crim Law 553, 742(1); Rape 51(4).

Garcia v. State, TexApp–Corpus Christi, 718 SW2d 785,
petition for discretionary review gr, rev 768 SW2d 726.
—Crim Law 878(3); Double J 182; Judgm 751.

Garcia v. State, TexApp–Corpus Christi, 718 SW2d 782.
—Crim Law 406(4), 899, 900, 1037.1(2), 1137(7); Ind &
Inf 101.

Garcia v. State, TexApp–Corpus Christi, 704 SW2d 495.
—Const Law 4594(1), 4594(4); Crim Law 700(2.1),
700(4), 706(2), 1144.13(6); Sent & Pun 308.

Garcia v. State, TexApp–Corpus Christi, 694 SW2d 583.
—Const Law 75, 2572, 2574; Crim Law 1147; Sent &
Pun 2160, 2188(1).

Garcia v. State, TexApp–Corpus Christi, 676 SW2d 202,
petition for discretionary review refused.—Controlled
Subs 148(2); Crim Law 1158(2); Searches 23, 114, 117,
200.

Garcia v. State, TexApp–Corpus Christi, 673 SW2d 696,
petition for discretionary review gr, petition for discretionary review dism 770 SW2d 571.—Crim Law 577.14.

Garcia v. State, TexApp–Corpus Christi, 649 SW2d 70.—
Burg 3, 41(3); Courts 97(5); Crim Law 568, 641.13(1),
671.

Garcia v. State, TexApp–Corpus Christi, 629 SW2d 196,
petition for discretionary review refused.—Crim Law
372(7), 632(4), 1031(4), 1035(3), 1038.2, 1038.3, 1064(3),
1064(6), 1137(5), 1144.6; Witn 267.

Garcia v. State, TexApp–Houston (14 Dist), 191 SW3d
870.—Arrest 70(2); Crim Law 394.4(9), 394.6(5),
412.2(1), 412.2(4), 519(8), 641.1, 641.3(3), 641.3(4),
1134(3), 1134(6), 1139, 1153(1), 1158(4).

Garcia v. State, TexApp–Houston (14 Dist), 161 SW3d 28.
—Crim Law 642, 1166.6, 1168(2).

Garcia v. State, TexApp–Houston (14 Dist), 112 SW3d
839.—Admin Law 412.1; Autos 344, 355(13), 356, 411,
422.1, 423; Crim Law 641.13(1), 641.13(6), 742(1), 745,
1134(2), 1134(3), 1139, 1144.13(2.1), 1147, 1153(1),
1158(4), 1159.2(1), 1159.2(2), 1159.2(7), 1159.2(9),
1159.4(1), 1159.6; Searches 14; Statut 51.

Garcia v. State, TexApp–Houston (14 Dist), 29 SW3d 899.
—Crim Law 1081(4.1), 1081(5); Sent & Pun 2070.

Garcia; State v., TexApp–Houston (14 Dist), 25 SW3d
908.—Arrest 63.5(4), 63.5(6), 63.5(7); Crim Law 1128(4),
1139.

Garcia v. State, TexApp–Houston (14 Dist), 3 SW3d 227,
petition for discretionary review gr, aff 43 SW3d 527.—
Arrest 63.4(4), 63.5(4), 63.5(9), 68(4); Autos 349(2.1),
349(5), 349(7), 349(17); Crim Law 394.6(4), 394.6(5),
1134(2), 1139; Searches 182, 183, 184.

Garcia v. State, TexApp–Houston (14 Dist), 979 SW2d
809, petition for discretionary review refused, and petition for discretionary review refused.—Crim Law
394.6(4), 641.5(4).

Garcia v. State, TexApp–Houston (14 Dist), 901 SW2d
731, petition for discretionary review refused.—Courts
487(1), 487(7); Crim Law 100(3), 101(4), 105.

Garcia v. State, TexApp–Houston (14 Dist), 901 SW2d
724, petition for discretionary review refused.—Crim
Law 388.2, 412.1(4), 412.2(2), 429(1), 438(1), 438(6),

438(7), 438(8), 796, 829(1), 829(5), 1120(9), 1137(5),
1169.1(1), 1169.1(7), 1169.12; Homic 1111.

Garcia v. State, TexApp–Houston (14 Dist), 726 SW2d
231, petition for discretionary review gr, aff 787 SW2d
957.—Crim Law 393(1), 438(8), 1044.2(1).

Garcia v. State, TexApp–Houston (14 Dist), 704 SW2d
512, petition for discretionary review refused.—Arrest
63.4(16), 63.5(1), 68(4), 71.1(7); Crim Law 412.2(2),
1169.1(10); Searches 28, 29; Stip 18(4).

Garcia v. State, TexApp–Houston (14 Dist), 699 SW2d
589, petition for discretionary review refused.—Crim
Law 730(1), 730(8), 1043(3); Rape 51(4), 59(18), 59(24);
Witn 37(4).

Garcia v. State, TexApp–Houston (14 Dist), 683 SW2d
715, petition for discretionary review refused.—Crim
Law 407(1), 552(3), 729, 730(3), 1169.5(1), 1169.5(2);
Homic 1181, 1184.

Garcia v. State, TexApp–Houston (14 Dist), 625 SW2d
831, petition for discretionary review refused.—Crim
Law 577.10(8), 577.10(9), 577.16(1), 1032(1); Rob 7, 11,
24.15(2), 24.50; Sent & Pun 1286, 1325, 1338.

Garcia v. State, TexApp–Houston (14 Dist), 625 SW2d
431, petition for discretionary review refused.—Const
Law 4826; Crim Law 577.8(2).

Garcia; State v., TexCivApp–San Antonio, 348 SW2d 231.
—Int Liq 250.

Garcia v. State, TexCivApp–San Antonio, 290 SW2d 555,
ref nre.—Counties 58, 113(5), 196(3); Inj 26(6), 163(1).

Garcia; Stockwell v., TexCivApp–San Antonio, 325 SW2d
405, ref nre.—Estop 64; Sheriffs 2.

Garcia; Summit Sav. Ass'n v., TexApp–San Antonio, 727
SW2d 106.—Mand 141.

Garcia v. Sunbelt Rentals, Inc., CA5 (Tex), 310 F3d 403.
—Labor & Emp 880.

Garcia v. Sun Oil Co., TexCivApp–Beaumont, 300 SW2d
724, ref nre.—App & E 837(3), 954(1); Inj 134, 135, 144,
157; Mines 52.

Garcia; Supreme Forest Woodmen Circle v., TexCiv-
App–San Antonio, 124 SW2d 951.—Evid 263(1), 265(2);
Insurance 2445, 2446.

Garcia; Supreme Forest Woodmen Circle v., TexCiv-
App–San Antonio, 103 SW2d 1108, writ refused.—App
& E 1177(6); Evid 215(1), 265(2); Insurance 2445, 3571.

Garcia v. Swift & Co., SDTex, 276 FSupp 625.—Labor &
Emp 2279.

Garcia v. Tenorio, TexApp–Fort Worth, 69 SW3d 309,
review den.—App & E 930(1); Judgm 143(3), 199(3.9),
199(3.10), 335(1), 335(2), 335(4); Trial 139.1(14),
139.1(17).

Garcia; Terrell v., TexCivApp–San Antonio, 496 SW2d
124, ref nre, cert den 94 SCt 1434, 415 US 927, 39
LEd2d 484.—Health 686.

Garcia; Terry v., TexApp–San Antonio, 800 SW2d 854,
writ den.—App & E 1004(1); Damag 54, 130.1, 184,
208(1).

Garcia; Texaco, Inc. v., Tex, 891 SW2d 255.—Atty & C
21.5(3).

Garcia v. Texas Cable Partners, L.P., TexApp–Corpus
Christi, 114 SW3d 561, reh overr.—Judgm 564(1), 567,
677; Usury 1, 6, 11, 16, 61.

Garcia v. Texas Dept. of Criminal Justice, TexApp–
Houston (14 Dist), 902 SW2d 728.—App & E 852,
934(1); Judgm 181(11), 185(2); Mun Corp 741.15,
741.40(1); States 197.

Garcia v. Texas Dept. of Human Services, TexApp–
Corpus Christi, 721 SW2d 528.—App & E 497(1), 635(3),
959(3); Infants 196; Plead 236(3), 238(1), 245(6), 258(5);
Witn 46.

Garcia v. Texas Emp. Ins. Ass'n, TexCivApp–Dallas, 620
SW2d 716.—Work Comp 1283, 1292, 1758.

Garcia v. Texas Employers' Ins. Ass'n, TexApp–Amarillo, 622 SW2d 626, ref nre.—Abate & R 81; App & E
920(2), 966(1); Const Law 3306; Evid 268, 334(1); Jury
33(1), 33(1.1), 33(1.15), 33(5.15), 120; Pretrial Proc 713,

726; Work Comp 847, 1374, 1491, 1853, 1907, 1937, 1987.

Garcia v. Texas Employers Ins. Ass'n, TexCivApp–Corpus Christi, 597 SW2d 519, ref nre.—Work Comp 1832, 1875.

Garcia v. Texas Indem. Ins. Co., Tex, 209 SW2d 333, 146 Tex 413.—Work Comp 566, 649, 1593, 1975.

Garcia v. Texas Indem. Ins. Co., TexCivApp–Galveston, 205 SW2d 803, rev 209 SW2d 333, 146 Tex 413.—Evid 122(6), 123(10), 546; Work Comp 610, 617, 1360, 1487, 1493, 1922, 1942.

Garcia v. Texas Instruments, Inc., Tex, 610 SW2d 456, 20 ALR4th 900.—Const Law 2503(2); Sales 255, 427, 431.

Garcia v. Texas Instruments, Inc., TexCivApp–Tyler, 598 SW2d 24, rev 610 SW2d 456, 20 ALR4th 900.—Prod Liab 71.5; Sales 255, 427, 431.

Garcia; Texas Osage Co-op. Royalty Pool v., TexCivApp–San Antonio, 176 SW2d 798, writ refused wom.—App & E 1010.1(1); Lim of Act 96(2); Ref of Inst 32, 45(6).

Garcia v. Texas State Bd. of Medical Examiners, CA5 (Tex), 492 F2d 131, on remand 384 FSupp 434, motion gr 95 SCt 1653, 421 US 928, 44 LEd2d 85, aff 95 SCt 2391, 421 US 995, 44 LEd2d 663.—Fed Cts 998.

Garcia v. Texas State Bd. of Medical Examiners, WDTex, 384 FSupp 434.—Const Law 1430, 2516(1), 3683, 3696, 4286, 4329; Health 105, 111.

Garcia v. Texas State Bd. of Medical Examiners, WDTex, 358 FSupp 1016, vac 492 F2d 131, on remand 384 FSupp 434, motion gr 95 SCt 1653, 421 US 928, 44 LEd2d 85, aff 95 SCt 2391, 421 US 995, 44 LEd2d 663. —Const Law 1066, 1430, 1440, 2516(1), 3696; Fed Cts 998; Health 105, 108, 111, 136, 137, 164, 212; Licens 1.

Garcia; Texas Tech Medical Center v., TexApp–El Paso, 190 SW3d 774.—App & E 837(4), 863; Neglig 1040(3); States 112(2), 112.2(1), 112.2(2), 191.1.

Garcia; Texas Workers' Compensation Com'n v., Tex, 893 SW2d 504.—App & E 23; Assoc 20(1); Const Law 328, 656, 665, 667, 712, 765, 969, 2311, 2314, 2317, 2752, 2758, 3219, 3603, 3867, 3877, 3893, 3903, 4186; Decl Judgm 61; Jury 9, 12(1), 12(1.1), 14(1.4), 16(1), 17(1), 31.2(7), 34(1), 34(3); Work Comp 17, 22, 26, 30, 34, 35, 40, 43, 1939.4(3), 1939.4(4).

Garcia; Texas Workers' Compensation Com'n v., Tex, 817 SW2d 60.—Courts 247(1).

Garcia; Texas Workers' Compensation Com'n v., TexApp–San Antonio, 862 SW2d 61, reh den, and writ gr, rev 893 SW2d 504.—Action 13; App & E 840(3), 1039(1); Assoc 20(1); Const Law 712, 951, 978, 990, 1030, 2311, 2312, 2314, 2357, 2489, 2494, 2601, 2671, 2672, 3057, 3219, 3603, 3847, 3902, 4186; Decl Judgm 61; Evid 507, 555.1; Jury 9; States 191.9(1), 191.10; Work Comp 13, 17, 26, 30, 38, 42, 1325.

Garcia; Tobin v., Tex, 316 SW2d 396, 159 Tex 58.—App & E 78(1), 1175(1); Courts 247(7); Judgm 178, 185.3(1); Offic 25.

Garcia v. Tobin, TexCivApp–San Antonio, 307 SW2d 836, writ gr, aff 316 SW2d 396, 159 Tex 58.—Elections 265; Judgm 181(27), 185(2); Offic 25, 31.

Garcia; Total Oilfield Services, Inc. v., Tex, 711 SW2d 237.—Work Comp 74.

Garcia v. Total Oilfield Services, Inc., TexApp–Amarillo, 703 SW2d 411, ref nre 711 SW2d 237.—Death 8; States 5(2).

Garcia; Transport Ins. Co. v., TexCivApp–Hous (1 Dist), 580 SW2d 96, ref nre.—App & E 930(3), 989; Work Comp 1414, 1418, 1492, 1533, 1723, 1728.

Garcia v. Travelers Indemnity Co. of Rhode Island, WDTex, 892 FSupp 153.—Fed Civ Proc 2470.1, 2547.1; Insurance 1867, 3336; Work Comp 551, 1072.

Garcia v. Travelers Ins. Co., Tex, 365 SW2d 916.—Work Comp 952.

Garcia; Travelers Ins. Co. v., TexCivApp–Austin, 360 SW2d 415, rev 365 SW2d 916.—Work Comp 880, 952, 1846, 1931.

Garcia; Travelers Ins. Co. v., TexCivApp–El Paso, 417 SW2d 630, ref nre.—Trial 360; Work Comp 998, 999, 1001, 1284, 1529, 1648, 1683.

Garcia v. Travelers Ins. Co., TexCivApp–Hous (14 Dist), 501 SW2d 754.—Insurance 2786.

Garcia; Traylor Bros., Inc. v., TexApp–San Antonio, 49 SW3d 430, reh overr, and review den, and reh of petition for review den.—Autos 290; Contracts 170(1), 170(2); Neglig 210, 1205(7), 1692.

Garcia; Traylor Bros., Inc. v., TexApp–San Antonio, 949 SW2d 368.—App & E 347(3).

Garcia; Trevino v., Tex, 627 SW2d 147.—Adop 6, 14; Child C 271; Hab Corp 532(1).

Garcia v. Tubbs, TexCivApp–Beaumont, 300 SW2d 736, ref nre.—App & E 499(1), 500(1), 1078(1); Evid 318(7); Inj 138.21, 144, 147, 157; Tresp 44.

Garcia; U.S. v., CA5 (Tex), 483 F3d 289.—Crim Law 1077.3.

Garcia; U.S. v., CA5 (Tex), 470 F3d 1143.—Crim Law 1030(1).

Garcia; U.S. v., CA5 (Tex), 416 F3d 440.—Crim Law 1042, 1181.5(8).

Garcia; U.S. v., CA5 (Tex), 322 F3d 842.—Crim Law 1139; Sent & Pun 563, 643.

Garcia; U.S. v., CA5 (Tex), 242 F3d 593, appeal after new sentencing hearing 322 F3d 842.—Consp 41; Controlled Subs 31, 46, 71; Crim Law 1139, 1178; Jury 24; Sent & Pun 764, 963.

Garcia; U.S. v., CA5 (Tex), 179 F3d 265, reh and reh den 209 F3d 721, cert den 120 SCt 2235, 530 US 1222, 147 LEd2d 264.—Arrest 63.4(1), 63.4(2), 63.4(3), 63.4(15), 66(1).

Garcia v. U.S., CA5 (Tex), 88 F3d 318.—Autos 193(10), 197(2), 242(6); Fed Cts 776; Labor & Emp 3047, 3049(3); Rem of C 101.1; Statut 181(2), 195.

Garcia; U.S. v., CA5 (Tex), 86 F3d 394, reh den, cert den 117 SCt 752, 519 US 1083, 136 LEd2d 688.—Consp 24(1), 24.5, 47(12); Controlled Subs 31, 46, 81; Crim Law 474.5, 1139, 1158(1), 1166.16; Jury 131(10); Sent & Pun 299, 995, 996; Weap 4, 17(4).

Garcia; U.S. v., CA5 (Tex), 77 F3d 857, cert den 117 SCt 147, 519 US 853, 136 LEd2d 93.—Arrest 63.5(6); Crim Law 412.2(2), 641.5(0.5), 641.5(5), 641.13(1), 641.13(2.1), 641.13(6).

Garcia v. U.S., CA5 (Tex), 62 F3d 126, on remand 88 F3d 318.—U S 50.5(1), 50.5(3), 78(14).

Garcia; U.S. v., CA5 (Tex), 27 F3d 1009, cert den Chavez v. US, 115 SCt 531, 513 US 1009, 130 LEd2d 435.—Crim Law 369.2(3.1), 394.4(6), 795(1.5), 795(2.1), 795(2.5), 795(2.26), 1134(3); Ind & Inf 125(5.5), 142, 189(1); Searches 111.

Garcia v. U.S., CA5 (Tex), 22 F3d 609, reh en banc gr, on reh 62 F3d 126, on remand 88 F3d 318.

Garcia; U.S. v., CA5 (Tex), 1 F3d 330. See U.S. v. Maseratti.

Garcia; U.S. v., CA5 (Tex), 995 F2d 556.—Crim Law 423(3), 508(9), 577.4, 577.8(1), 577.8(2), 577.10(1), 577.10(3), 577.13, 577.15(4), 577.16(8), 1036.1(2).

Garcia; U.S. v., CA5 (Tex), 963 F2d 693. See U.S. v. Ramirez.

Garcia; U.S. v., CA5 (Tex), 962 F2d 479, 128 ALR Fed 753, cert den 113 SCt 293, 506 US 902, 121 LEd2d 217. —Crim Law 1139, 1177; Sent & Pun 1308, 1309.

Garcia; U.S. v., CA5 (Tex), 954 F2d 273.—Crim Law 1177.5(1); Sent & Pun 1367, 1372.

Garcia; U.S. v., CA5 (Tex), 942 F2d 873, cert den 112 SCt 989, 502 US 1080, 117 LEd2d 151.—Arrest 63.4(4), 63.5(6); Crim Law 1139; Cust Dut 126(2), 126(10).

Garcia; U.S. v., CA5 (Tex), 931 F2d 1017.—Controlled Subs 31; Sent & Pun 653(5).

GARCIA;

See Guidelines for Arrangement at the beginning of this Volume

Garcia; U.S. v., CA5 (Tex), 918 F2d 1156. See U.S. v. Andrews.

Garcia; U.S. v., CA5 (Tex), 917 F2d 1370, reh den.— Consp 28(3), 41, 44.2, 47(2), 47(12); Controlled Subs 28, 31, 68, 79, 81; Crim Law 700(3), 1158(1), 1166(10.10); Sent & Pun 764, 765.

Garcia; U.S. v., CA5 (Tex), 903 F2d 1022, cert den 111 SCt 364, 498 US 948, 112 LEd2d 327.—Sent & Pun 548, 631, 654, 664(2).

Garcia; U.S. v., CA5 (Tex), 900 F2d 45.—Sent & Pun 800, 820, 909, 995.

Garcia; U.S. v., CA5 (Tex), 889 F2d 1454, cert den 110 SCt 1829, 494 US 1088, 108 LEd2d 958.—Sent & Pun 670, 686, 975.

Garcia; U.S. v., CA5 (Tex), 849 F2d 917, reh den 856 F2d 191.—Searches 15, 22, 164.

Garcia; U.S. v., CA5 (Tex), 821 F2d 1051.—Crim Law 1181.5(8).

Garcia v. U.S., CA5 (Tex), 776 F2d 116.—U S 78(9), 125(6).

Garcia; U.S. v., CA5 (Tex), 762 F2d 1222, cert den 106 SCt 238, 474 US 907, 88 LEd2d 239.—Crim Law 641.13(1), 641.13(6), 829(3), 1144.10, 1166.10(1); Int Rev 5263.35, 5303.

Garcia; U.S. v., CA5 (Tex), 732 F2d 1221, reh den 738 F2d 437.—Crim Law 865(1.5), 957(1); Cust Dut 126(9.1); Searches 49, 73.

Garcia; U.S. v., CA5 (Tex), 719 F2d 108.—Crim Law 1181.5(2).

Garcia; U.S. v., CA5 (Tex), 719 F2d 99.—Crim Law 1144.13(3), 1159.2(7); Elections 311, 316, 329; States 4.16(2).

Garcia; U.S. v., CA5 (Tex), 693 F2d 412.—Const Law 3798, 3809, 4706; Crim Law 1141(2), 1158(1); Sent & Pun 35, 56, 98, 299, 301, 313, 317, 366.

Garcia v. U.S., CA5 (Tex), 680 F2d 29.—Fed Cts 558; Inj 81, 138.21, 150.

Garcia; U.S. v., CA5 (Tex), 676 F2d 1086, reh den 695 F2d 806, cert gr, vac 103 SCt 3105, 462 US 1127, 77 LEd2d 1360, on remand 719 F2d 108.—Arrest 62, 63.5(6); Crim Law 394.4(9); Statut 223.2(1.1), 223.4.

Garcia; U.S. v., CA5 (Tex), 636 F2d 122.—Crim Law 273(4.1), 273.1(4).

Garcia; U.S. v., CA5 (Tex), 617 F2d 1176.—Consp 51; Crim Law 273.1(4), 1177; Sent & Pun 372.

Garcia; U.S. v., CA5 (Tex), 616 F2d 210.—Arrest 63.4(6); Cust Dut 126(4), 126(5); Searches 49.

Garcia; U.S. v., CA5 (Tex), 592 F2d 259.—Cust Dut 126(5).

Garcia; U.S. v., CA5 (Tex), 589 F2d 249, cert den Munoz v. US, 99 SCt 2821, 442 US 909, 61 LEd2d 274.—Crim Law 1023(8); Double J 57, 59, 88.1, 146, 151(2), 151(3.1), 151(5).

Garcia; U.S. v., CA5 (Tex), 553 F2d 432.—Crim Law 577.16(3); Int Rev 5294.

Garcia; U.S. v., CA5 (Tex), 546 F2d 613, cert den 97 SCt 1608, 430 US 958, 51 LEd2d 810.—Crim Law 37(1), 37(3), 37(4), 739.1(2), 772(6).

Garcia; U.S. v., CA5 (Tex), 531 F2d 1303, cert den 97 SCt 359, 429 US 941, 50 LEd2d 311.—Crim Law 822(1), 829(3), 1036.2, 1043(3); Witn 345(7).

Garcia; U.S. v., CA5 (Tex), 530 F2d 650.—Consp 47(12); Controlled Subs 81; Crim Law 1038.2; Weap 17(4); Witn 321, 331.5.

Garcia; U.S. v., CA5 (Tex), 528 F2d 580, reh den 531 F2d 575, cert den Sandoval, v. US, 96 SCt 3177, 426 US 952, 49 LEd2d 1190, cert den 97 SCt 262, 429 US 898, 50 LEd2d 182.—Crim Law 394.1(2), 555, 569, 785(4), 1038.2, 1169.1(8), 1173.2(5), 1177.

Garcia; U.S. v., CA5 (Tex), 526 F2d 958.—Crim Law 1177.5(3); Sent & Pun 1366, 1372.

Garcia; U.S. v., CA5 (Tex), 517 F2d 272.—Const Law 43(1), 947, 1067; Crim Law 641.1, 641.4(1), 641.4(2), 1023(3).

Garcia; U.S. v., CA5 (Tex), 496 F2d 670, reh den 502 F2d 1168, cert den 95 SCt 1347, 420 US 960, 43 LEd2d 436, reh den 95 SCt 1455, 420 US 1009, 43 LEd2d 768.— Crim Law 412.2(2), 1158(4); Searches 171, 183, 184, 194, 201.

Garcia; U.S. v., CA5 (Tex), 479 F2d 322.—Weap 17(4).

Garcia; U.S. v., CA5 (Tex), 474 F2d 1202.—Const Law 4149; Em Dom 2(11); Int Rev 4860.

Garcia; U.S. v., CA5 (Tex), 452 F2d 419.—Crim Law 394.4(12), 770(2), 772(6), 867; Cust Dut 126(2), 126(5).

Garcia v. U.S., CA5 (Tex), 449 F2d 1304, cert den 92 SCt 2423, 406 US 969, 32 LEd2d 668.—Courts 104; Crim Law 1132.

Garcia v. U.S., CA5 (Tex), 421 F2d 1231, cert den 91 SCt 251, 400 US 945, 27 LEd2d 251, reh den 91 SCt 1383, 402 US 925, 28 LEd2d 664.—Const Law 1102, 3562, 4149; Fed Cts 870.1; Int Rev 4778; Sent & Pun 1566; Trusts 1.

Garcia v. U.S., CA5 (Tex), 315 F2d 679.—Consp 47(12); Crim Law 622.1(2), 622.2(4), 783(1), 1148; Int Rev 5295.

Garcia v. U.S., CA5 (Tex), 315 F2d 133, cert den 84 SCt 117, 375 US 855, 11 LEd2d 82.—Crim Law 394.6(3), 394.6(5), 721(5), 1038.1(1), 1038.2, 1169.1(2.1); Int Rev 5316.

Garcia v. U.S., CA5 (Tex), 243 F2d 98.—Crim Law 1556.

Garcia; U.S. v., CA5 (Tex), 224 FedAppx 426.—Crim Law 394.4(6); Sent & Pun 585, 600, 601.

Garcia; U.S. v., CA5 (Tex), 202 FedAppx 825.—Sent & Pun 299, 300.

Garcia; U.S. v., CA5 (Tex), 196 FedAppx 285.—Sent & Pun 764.

Garcia; U.S. v., CA5 (Tex), 186 FedAppx 486.—Sent & Pun 2250.

Garcia; U.S. v., CA5 (Tex), 176 FedAppx 549, cert den 127 SCt 419, 166 LEd2d 296.—Sent & Pun 979.

Garcia; U.S. v., CA5 (Tex), 144 FedAppx 379.—Controlled Subs 81, 86; Crim Law 1169.12.

Garcia; U.S. v., CA5 (Tex), 136 FedAppx 654, post-conviction relief den 2006 WL 3827472.—Crim Law 1035(7), 1042.

Garcia; U.S. v., CA5 (Tex), 132 FedAppx 11.—Controlled Subs 81, 86.

Garcia; U.S. v., CA5 (Tex), 113 FedAppx 639.—Sent & Pun 752, 765.

Garcia; U.S. v., CA5 (Tex), 104 FedAppx 955.—Crim Law 1031(1), 1130(5).

Garcia; U.S. v., CA5 (Tex), 104 FedAppx 396, cert den 126 SCt 170, 546 US 869, 163 LEd2d 158, reh den 126 SCt 1135, 546 US 1132, 163 LEd2d 934.—Sent & Pun 683, 979.

Garcia; U.S. v., CA5 (Tex), 70 FedAppx 789, cert den 124 SCt 848, 540 US 1066, 157 LEd2d 727.—Crim Law 1167(1).

Garcia v. U.S., SDTex, 538 FSupp 814.—Civil R 1395(6); Decl Judgm 272; Fed Cts 979; Offic 116; U S 125(9), 125(17), 125(18), 127(2).

Garcia v. U.S., WDTex, 799 FSupp 674, aff 22 F3d 609, reh en banc gr, on reh 62 F3d 126, on remand 88 F3d 318, aff in part, rev in part 62 F3d 126, on remand 88 F3d 318, rev 88 F3d 318.—Autos 193(8.1); Rem of C 102; U S 50.5(3), 78(14), 127(2).

Garcia; U.S. v., WDTex, 688 FSupp 1170.—Arrest 63.4(16); Controlled Subs 137, 138; Searches 164.

Garcia; U.S. v., WDTex, 358 FSupp 1042.—Arrest 63.5(3.1), 63.5(6), 63.5(8); Crim Law 394.4(12), 394.4(13).

Garcia v. Universal Gas Corp., TexApp–San Antonio, 653 SW2d 362, ref nre.—App & E 989, 1177(7); Gas 18, 20(2).

Garcia; Urschel v., TexCivApp–San Antonio, 164 SW2d 804, writ refused wom.—Adv Poss 19, 20, 25, 38, 57, 85(1), 85(3), 109, 114(1), 115(1); App & E 1061.4, 1175(5).

Garcia v. Uvalde County, WDTex, 455 FSupp 101, aff 99 SCt 821, 439 US 1059, 59 LEd2d 26, aff US v. Uvalde

County, 99 SCt 822, 439 US 1059, 59 LEd2d 26.—
Elections 12(8), 12(9.1).

Garcia v. Vasquez, SDTex, 524 FSupp 40.—Const Law 3965(3); Fed Cts 76.15, 143; Labor & Emp 249.

Garcia v. Vasquez, TexCivApp–San Antonio, 621 SW2d 425.—App & E 338(2), 387(3), 388, 468, 472.

Garcia; Villarreal v., TexCivApp–San Antonio, 294 SW2d 754.—Plead 111.42(2), 111.42(4), 111.46.

Garcia v. Villarreal, TexCivApp–Corpus Christi, 478 SW2d 830.—App & E 1024.4; Contracts 15, 16, 22(1), 34, 42, 47, 51, 52; Judgm 185(2), 185.2(5), 185.3(2); Release 1.

Garcia; Wal-Mart Stores, Inc. v., TexApp–San Antonio, 30 SW3d 19.—App & E 930(1), 1001(3), 1002, 1003(7), 1004(1), 1079; Damag 95, 101, 135, 191, 221(8); Neglig 1001, 1076, 1077, 1104(7), 1670.

Garcia; Wal-Mart Stores, Inc. v., TexApp–San Antonio, 974 SW2d 83, reh overr.—App & E 232(2), 760(2); Evid 508, 512, 538, 555.4(1), 555.7; Trial 360.

Garcia v. Wash, CA5 (Tex), 20 F3d 608.—Fed Cts 666.

Garcia v. Webb County Dist. Atty., SDTex, 764 FSupp 457.—Civil R 1376(10), 1379, 1383; Damag 50.10; Dist & Pros Attys 10; Fed Civ Proc 2491.5; Labor & Emp 135(2); Lim of Act 31, 58(1).

Garcia; White v., CA5 (Tex), 117 FedAppx 912.—Autos 349(2.1), 349.5(2).

Garcia v. Willman, TexApp–Corpus Christi, 4 SW3d 307, reh overr.—Action 60; App & E 949; Judgm 185.3(21), 186.

Garcia v. Willmuth, TexCivApp–El Paso, 531 SW2d 397.—Autos 246(11); Trial 350.5(3), 350.7(4).

Garcia; Withrow v., CA5 (Tex), 116 FedAppx 524.—Fed Civ Proc 657.5(3); Judgm 632, 739.

Garcia v. Woman's Hosp. of Texas, CA5 (Tex), 143 F3d 227.—Civil R 1176; Fed Cts 776, 819, 916.1, 951.1; Judges 49(2).

Garcia v. Woman's Hosp. of Texas, CA5 (Tex), 97 F3d 810, reh den, appeal after remand 143 F3d 227.—Civil R 1140, 1176; Fed Civ Proc 2016; Fed Cts 764, 765, 776, 798, 801, 823.

Garcia; Wyler Indus. Works, Inc. v., TexApp–El Paso, 999 SW2d 494.—App & E 205, 221, 241, 242(4), 302(6), 758.3(9), 946, 948, 989, 1001(1), 1001(3), 1002, 1003(3), 1003(5), 1003(7), 1056.1(7); Damag 48, 102, 182, 192; Interest 39(2.6), 39(2.10), 39(2.50), 49; Labor & Emp 863(2), 871, 874; Trial 43, 139.1(7), 219, 238, 251(1), 252(1).

Garcia; "Y" Propane Service, Inc. v., TexApp–San Antonio, 61 SW3d 559.—App & E 882(1), 893(1), 930(1), 989, 1045(1); Contrib 3; Gas 20(2); Indem 41, 79; Jury 136(3); Pretrial Proc 517.1.

Garcia Abrego; U.S. v., CA5 (Tex), 141 F3d 142, cert den 119 SCt 182, 525 US 878, 142 LEd2d 148, reh den 119 SCt 582, 525 US 1035, 142 LEd2d 486.—Consp 23.5, 24.5, 47(2), 47(3.1); Const Law 268(10), 2802, 2815, 4526, 4664(1); Controlled Subs 40, 45, 71, 87; Crim Law 369.2(2), 369.2(3.1), 369.2(4), 412(4), 412.1(1), 412.1(2), 412.2(3), 412.2(5), 414, 436(3), 444, 479, 485(1), 485(2), 508(9), 629.5(2), 662.40, 700(4), 805(1), 829(16), 835, 1030(1), 1038.1(4), 1130(0.5), 1139, 1144.13(3), 1144.13(5), 1152(1), 1153(1), 1158(4), 1159.2(7), 1173.1; Double J 25; Ind & Inf 188; U S 34.

Garcia-Alvarez; U.S. v., CA5 (Tex), 105 FedAppx 596.—Crim Law 1026.10(2.1); Sent & Pun 300, 764, 973.

Garcia-Alvarez; U.S. v., CA5 (Tex), 101 FedAppx 962, opinion withdrawn and superseded 105 FedAppx 596.—Crim Law 1026.10(2.1); Sent & Pun 976.

Garcia-Avalino; U.S. v., CA5 (Tex), 444 F3d 444, cert den 127 SCt 141, 166 LEd2d 103.—Pardon 66; Sent & Pun 1961, 2012.

Garcia-Baeza; U.S. v., CA5 (Tex), 191 FedAppx 306.—Crim Law 412.2(2), 519(8).

Garcia-Bonilla; U.S. v., CA5 (Tex), 11 F3d 45.—Crim Law 273.1(2), 273.1(5), 335, 1134(3); Sent & Pun 946, 947, 989.

Garcia-Cantu; State v., TexApp–Beaumont, 225 SW3d 820.—Arrest 68(4); Crim Law 1134(3), 1134(6), 1139, 1144.12, 1153(1), 1158(1), 1159.2(9), 1159.4(2), 1224(1).

Garcia-Cardenas; U.S. v., CA5 (Tex), 129 FedAppx 96, cert den 126 SCt 239, 546 US 900, 163 LEd2d 221.—Crim Law 1042.

Garcia-Chapa, In re Estates of, TexApp–Corpus Christi, 33 SW3d 859.—Abate & R 4, 13; Action 17; Courts 514; Des & Dist 5; Intern Law 10.14; Trial 6(1).

Garcia-Contreras; U.S. v., CA5 (Tex), 170 FedAppx 312, cert den Duenas-Aleman v. US, 126 SCt 2339, 164 LEd2d 854.—Crim Law 1181.5(8).

Garcia-Coronado; U.S. v., CA5 (Tex), 132 FedAppx 547.—Crim Law 1026.10(4), 1035(1).

Garcia-Coronado; U.S. v., CA5 (Tex), 108 FedAppx 939, cert gr, vac 125 SCt 1362, 543 US 1137, 161 LEd2d 99, on remand 132 FedAppx 547.—Crim Law 273.4(1), 1026.10(4).

Garcia-Costilla; U.S. v., CA5 (Tex), 113 FedAppx 616.—Crim Law 273.1(2), 1031(4).

Garcia-Covarrubias; U.S. v., CA5 (Tex), 133 FedAppx 141, cert den 126 SCt 456, 546 US 950, 163 LEd2d 346.—Crim Law 1042.

Garcia de Bretado; Ramirez v., TexCivApp–El Paso, 547 SW2d 717.—App & E 854(1); Guard & W 10, 13(4), 13(8), 24.

Garcia De Ortiz; Garcia v., TexCivApp–San Antonio, 257 SW2d 804.—Afft 17; Fraud Conv 188; Judgm 178; Plead 36(2); Trusts 4, 13, 17(3), 17(5).

Garcia Distributing, Inc. v. Fedders Air Conditioning, U.S.A., Inc., TexApp–San Antonio, 773 SW2d 802, writ den.—App & E 442, 961; Pretrial Proc 44.1, 309, 314, 434.

Garcia Distributing, Inc. v. Fedders U.S.A., TexApp–San Antonio, 773 SW2d 802. See Garcia Distributing, Inc. v. Fedders Air Conditioning, U.S.A., Inc.

Garcia-Duarte; U.S. v., CA5 (Tex), 193 FedAppx 331.—Aliens 771; Crim Law 273(4.1), 1177; Sent & Pun 300.

Garcia-Flores; U.S. v., CA5 (Tex), 246 F3d 451.—Controlled Subs 68, 81; Crim Law 370, 721(4), 1037.1(1), 1037.1(2), 1166.16, 1169.12; Jury 131(2).

Garcia-Flores; U.S. v., CA5 (Tex), 906 F2d 147.—Crim Law 273.1(4), 1068.5, 1167(5).

Garcia-Flores; U.S. v., CA5 (Tex), 207 FedAppx 397.—Crim Law 273.1(4), 1030(3), 1042, 1167(5); Sent & Pun 724, 765, 975.

Garcia-Flores; U.S. v., CA5 (Tex), 136 FedAppx 685, cert den 126 SCt 1165, 546 US 1151, 163 LEd2d 1130.—Consp 47(3.1); Crim Law 419(1.10), 427(5), 1042, 1134(3), 1166.14, 1166.16, 1169.1(9); Sent & Pun 1980(2).

Garcia for Rodriguez v. Sullivan, CA5 (Tex), 883 F2d 18.—Social S 135.1, 137.

Garcia Garcia; State v., TexApp–El Paso, 810 SW2d 240.—Double J 142.

Garcia-Garcia; U.S. v., CA5 (Tex), 319 F3d 726, cert den 123 SCt 2264, 539 US 910, 156 LEd2d 124.—Aliens 444, 445; Crim Law 1139, 1158(4); Cust Dut 126(4), 126(5), 126(9.1).

Garcia-Garcia; U.S. v., CA5 (Tex), 939 F2d 230.—Crim Law 273.1(4), 1167(5).

Garcia-Garcia; U.S. v., CA5 (Tex), 203 FedAppx 590.—Crim Law 1023(16); Jury 34(7); Sent & Pun 793.

Garcia Garcia; U.S. v., NDTex, 727 FSupp 318.—Bail 42, 44(1), 44(3.1).

Garcia-Gil; U.S. v., CA5 (Tex), 133 FedAppx 102, cert den 126 SCt 308, 546 US 922, 163 LEd2d 266.—Controlled Subs 100(9); Crim Law 407(1), 474.5, 720(1); Sent & Pun 661, 764.

Garcia-Gonzalez; U.S. v., CA5 (Tex), 702 F2d 520.—Crim Law 304(1).

Garcia-Gonzalez; U.S. v., CA5 (Tex), 168 FedAppx 564, cert den 127 SCt 187, 166 LEd2d 132.—Crim Law 1042.

Garcia-Gregory; Edwards v., TexApp–Houston (14 Dist), 866 SW2d 780, reh den, and writ den.—App & E 934(1); Health 821(1), 906, 908; Judgm 181(1), 185(1), 185(2), 185.3(21); Neglig 210.

Garcia-Guerrero; U.S. v., CA5 (Tex), 313 F3d 892.—Crim Law 1042, 1134(3), 1139, 1158(1); Sent & Pun 665, 722, 724.

Garcia Guevara v. City of Haltom City, CA5 (Tex), 106 FedAppx 900.—Civil R 1348, 1351(4); Fed Civ Proc 1838; Prisons 4(4).

Garcia-Gutierrez; U.S. v., CA5 (Tex), 835 F2d 585.—Crim Law 1134(3); Sent & Pun 1175, 2222.

Garcia-Hernandez; U.S. v., CA5 (Tex), 169 FedAppx 230. —Crim Law 1134(3).

Garcia-Hernandez; U.S. v., CA5 (Tex), 74 FedAppx 412. —Crim Law 641.4(4).

Garcia-Jasso; U.S. v., CA5 (Tex), 472 F3d 239.—Crim Law 641.5(0.5), 641.5(7), 1119(1), 1139.

Garcia-Jordan; U.S. v., CA5 (Tex), 860 F2d 159.—Crim Law 36.6, 412.1(3).

Garcia-Leal; U.S. v., CA5 (Tex), 166 FedAppx 138, cert den 126 SCt 2370, 165 LEd2d 292.—Crim Law 1134(3), 1181.5(8); Jury 31.1; Sent & Pun 661.

Garcia-Lopez; U.S. v., CA5 (Tex), 234 F3d 217, cert den 121 SCt 1389, 532 US 935, 149 LEd2d 313.—Crim Law 830, 1139, 1152(1), 1158(1), 1173.1; Sent & Pun 653(8).

Garcia-Macias; U.S. v., CA5 (Tex), 206 FedAppx 376.— Crim Law 1170(5).

Garcia-Marroquin v. Nueces County Bail Bond Bd., TexApp–Corpus Christi, 1 SW3d 366.—Admin Law 229; App & E 23, 893(1), 901, 911.3, 920(3), 954(4); Bail 60; Const Law 2600, 2601; Counties 212; Courts 4, 35, 37(1); Decl Judgm 8, 41, 66, 201, 319; Inj 9, 14, 76, 135, 138.46, 163(1), 164; Judgm 16; Notice 9; Plead 106(1); Pretrial Proc 554.

Garcia-Mejia; U.S. v., CA5 (Tex), 394 F3d 396, miscellaneous rulings 125 SCt 1969, 544 US 1016, 161 LEd2d 855, cert gr, vac 125 SCt 2555, 545 US 1102, 162 LEd2d 273, on remand 145 FedAppx 954, cert den 126 SCt 1897, 547 US 1104, 164 LEd2d 579, post-conviction relief den 2006 WL 2524091.—Aliens 770; Crim Law 1147; Jury 31.1.

Garcia-Mejia; U.S. v., CA5 (Tex), 169 FedAppx 238, cert den Castillo-Penaloza v. US, 126 SCt 2343, 164 LEd2d 858.—Crim Law 1042.

Garcia-Mejia; U.S. v., CA5 (Tex), 145 FedAppx 954, cert den 126 SCt 1897, 547 US 1104, 164 LEd2d 579, post-conviction relief den 2006 WL 2524091.—Crim Law 1042; Fed Cts 462.

Garcia-Mendez; U.S. v., CA5 (Tex), 420 F3d 454, cert den 126 SCt 1398, 546 US 1199, 164 LEd2d 100.—Sent & Pun 793.

Garcia Mendez; U.S. v., CA5 (Tex), 437 F2d 85.— Searches 143.1.

Garcia-Nava; U.S. v., CA5 (Tex), 168 FedAppx 617, cert den Castillo-Penaloza v. US, 126 SCt 2343, 164 LEd2d 858.—Crim Law 1042.

Garcia on Behalf of Garcia v. Sullivan, CA5 (Tex), 874 F2d 1006.—Social S 143.4.

Garcia-Ortiz; U.S. v., CA5 (Tex), 310 F3d 792.—Crim Law 1023(11), 1023(16), 1181.5(8); Sent & Pun 851, 1934.

Garcia-Pillado; U.S. v., CA5 (Tex), 898 F2d 36.—Crim Law 1028, 1042.

Garcia-Ramirez; U.S. v., CA5 (Tex), 148 FedAppx 201.— Crim Law 1042.

Garcia Ramirez; U.S. v., CA5 (Tex), 116 FedAppx 480, cert gr, vac 125 SCt 1684, 544 US 917, 161 LEd2d 473, on remand 148 FedAppx 201.—Consp 47(12); Controlled Subs 81; Crim Law 1035(1).

Garcia-Ramirez; U.S. v., CA5 (Tex), 112 FedAppx 346, cert den Baez-Leon v. US, 125 SCt 1095, 543 US 1128, 160 LEd2d 1082, reh den, reh den 125 SCt 1380, 543 US 1180, 161 LEd2d 169.—Ind & Inf 113; Sent & Pun 793, 973.

Garcia-Rico; U.S. v., CA5 (Tex), 46 F3d 8, cert den 115 SCt 2596, 515 US 1150, 132 LEd2d 843.—Aliens 799; Crim Law 1139.

Garcia Rodriguez v. State, TexApp–Corpus Christi, 750 SW2d 906, petition for discretionary review refused.— Courts 85(2); Crim Law 1026.10(3), 1081(2); Double J 5.1, 109, 201; Sent & Pun 323, 370.

Garcia-Rodriguez; U.S. v., CA5 (Tex), 415 F3d 452, cert den 126 SCt 641, 546 US 1010, 163 LEd2d 519.—Crim Law 1042; Sent & Pun 665.

Garcia's Enterprises, Inc. v. Snadon, TexApp–Dallas, 751 SW2d 914. See Joe T. Garcia's Enterprises, Inc. v. Snadon.

Garcia-Tejeda; U.S. v., CA5 (Tex), 112 FedAppx 986.— Crim Law 641.10(2), 1440(2); Jury 149.

Garcia-Trevino; U.S. v., SDTex, 843 FSupp 1134.—Double J 23.

Garcia-Trigo v. U.S., CA5 (Tex), 671 F2d 147.—Crim Law 1451, 1480.

Garcia Trucking Co. v. Kastner Farms, Inc., Tex, 774 SW2d 668. See Garcia v. Kastner Farms, Inc.

Garcia Trucking Co. v. Kastner Farms, Inc., TexApp–Corpus Christi, 789 SW2d 656. See Garcia v. Kastner Farms, Inc.

Garcia Trucking Co. v. Kastner Farms, Inc., TexApp–Corpus Christi, 761 SW2d 444. See Garcia v. Kastner Farms, Inc.

Garcia-Udall v. Udall, TexApp–Dallas, 141 SW3d 323.— App & E 842(2), 946, 989; Child C 35, 106, 419, 924; Compromise 21; Contracts 143(2), 152, 176(2); Judgm 87; Statut 223.4.

Garcia-Vargas; U.S. v., CA5 (Tex), 150 FedAppx 301, cert den 126 SCt 1401, 546 US 1200, 164 LEd2d 102.—Crim Law 1181.5(8).

Garcia V State, TexCrimApp, 254 SW2d 390.—Crim Law 1090.1(1).

Garcia-Zamudio; U.S. v., CA5 (Tex), 171 FedAppx 478.— Sent & Pun 786.

Garcilazo-Martinez; U.S. v., SDTex, 881 FSupp 265.— Arrest 63.4(13); Searches 161, 162, 164, 183.

Garcini; Home Indem. Co. v., TexApp–Houston (1 Dist), 757 SW2d 77, writ den.—Work Comp 900, 1552.

Gard; Alsop v., TexCivApp–Galveston, 227 SW2d 323, ref nre.—Trusts 8.

Gard v. Gard, Tex, 241 SW2d 618, 150 Tex 347.—Child S 506(2), 506(5); Divorce 395(1).

Gard; Gard v., Tex, 241 SW2d 618, 150 Tex 347.—Child S 506(2), 506(5); Divorce 395(1).

Gard v. Gard, TexCivApp–El Paso, 244 SW2d 884.—App & E 931(6), 1050.1(8.1), 1050.3, 1054(1); Evid 51; Judgm 929, 938, 942, 943, 944; Lim of Act 175; Plead 360; Trial 98.

Gard; Gard v., TexCivApp–El Paso, 244 SW2d 884.—App & E 931(6), 1050.1(8.1), 1050.3, 1054(1); Evid 51; Judgm 929, 938, 942, 943, 944; Lim of Act 175; Plead 360; Trial 98.

Gard v. Gard, TexCivApp–El Paso, 239 SW2d 410, rev 241 SW2d 618, 150 Tex 347.—Child S 179, 425, 480, 508(1).

Gard; Gard v., TexCivApp–El Paso, 239 SW2d 410, rev 241 SW2d 618, 150 Tex 347.—Child S 179, 425, 480, 508(1).

Gar-Dal, Inc.; Life Ins. Co. of Virginia v., Tex, 570 SW2d 378.—App & E 223; Judgm 185(2), 185(4), 185.1(4), 185.3(10), 185.3(16).

Gar-Dal, Inc. v. Life Ins. Co. of Virginia, TexCivApp–Beaumont, 557 SW2d 565, writ gr, rev 570 SW2d 378.— App & E 223, 230, 1173(2); Bills & N 443(1); Judgm 185(1), 185.1(8), 185.3(16).

Gardea Carrasco; U.S. v., CA5 (Tex), 830 F2d 41.—Consp 27, 40.1, 47(12); Controlled Subs 28, 31, 81; Crim Law 510, 553.

GARDNER

Gardemal v. Westin Hotel Co., CA5 (Tex), 186 F3d 588, reh den.—Const Law 3964, 3965(5); Corp 1.4(4), 1.5(1), 1.5(3), 1.6(13); Fed Civ Proc 1825; Fed Cts 34, 86, 776, 802.

Garden City Boxing Club, Inc.; Dallas County Constable Precinct No. 5 v., TexApp–Dallas, 219 SW3d 613.—App & E 931(3), 1008.1(2), 1008.1(3); Sheriffs 124, 137(2), 138(1), 138(3); Trial 404(6).

Gardendale Volunteer Fire Dept.; Norrell v., TexApp–San Antonio, 115 SW3d 114.—Mun Corp 746, 747(3), 847; Plead 104(1); States 191.1, 191.4(1), 208.

Garden Oaks Bd. of Trustees v. Gibbs, TexCivApp–Hous (1 Dist), 489 SW2d 133, ref nre.—Covenants 51(2), 72.1, 79(1), 103(3), 108(1), 110, 122.

Garden Oaks Bd. of Trustees; Gibbs v., TexCivApp–Hous (14 Dist), 459 SW2d 478, ref nre, appeal after remand 489 SW2d 133, ref nre.—Inj 126.

Gardere & Wynne v. Turoff, NDTex, 196 BR 356. See Hunt, In re.

Gardere & Wynne, L.L.P.; Liberty Mut. Ins. Co. v., CA5 (Tex), 82 FedAppx 116.—Atty & C 129(2), 153.

Gardere Wynne Sewell LLP; Baxter v., TexApp–Dallas, 182 SW3d 460, review den.—App & E 173(10); Lim of Act 43, 95(1), 100(12), 104(1), 104.5.

Gardiner; Jetco Electronic Industries v., SDTex, 325 FSupp 80.—Damag 142; Evid 51; Fed Civ Proc 672, 1742(4), 1773, 1829, 1835; Fed Cts 76, 79, 350.1; Libel 15, 133, 139; Proc 72.

Gardiner; Jetco Electronic Industries, Inc. v., CA5 (Tex), 473 F2d 1228, reh den 474 F2d 1347.—Const Law 3964; Courts 99(3); Fed Civ Proc 461; Fed Cts 33, 75, 76, 84, 88, 96, 417, 599.

Gardiner; Marshall Field Stores, Inc. v., TexApp–Houston (1 Dist), 859 SW2d 391, decision clarified on denial of reh, and writ dism woj.—App & E 930(3), 989, 999(1), 1001(1), 1002, 1003(6); Evid 53, 54, 587; Libel 1, 23.1, 24, 112(1), 124(1); Lim of Act 55(4), 95(6), 127(7).

Gardiner v. U.S., CA5 (Tex), 341 F2d 896, cert den 86 SCt 43, 382 US 818, 15 LEd2d 65.—Crim Law 956(7), 1660.

Gardiner v. U.S., CA5 (Tex), 321 F2d 159, cert den 84 SCt 445, 375 US 953, 11 LEd2d 314.—Consp 47(12); Crim Law 577, 622, 1038.1(1), 1038.1(5), 1038.3.

Gardiner v. U.S., SDTex, 237 FSupp 692, aff 341 F2d 896, cert den 86 SCt 43, 382 US 818, 15 LEd2d 65.—Crim Law 1433(2), 1618(10).

Gardipee v. Petroleum Helicopters, Inc., EDTex, 49 FSupp2d 925.—Fed Cts 101, 103, 104, 105, 106, 144.

Gardner, Ex parte, TexCrimApp, 959 SW2d 189, reh gr, and on reh.—Crim Law 412.2(3); Hab Corp 287.1, 603.

Gardner, Ex parte, TexCrimApp, 264 SW2d 125, 159 TexCrim 365.—Crim Law 210; Evid 80(1); Extrad 32; Witn 58.2.

Gardner v. Amerada Petroleum Corp., SDTex, 91 FSupp 134.—Bound 20(1); Estop 32(2); Mines 73.1(1), 81; Ref of Inst 45(9).

Gardner v. Associates Inv. Co., TexCivApp–Amarillo, 171 SW2d 381, writ refused wom.—App & E 1152; Bills & N 534; Chat Mtg 129, 169, 176(5), 255; Usury 32.

Gardner; Bailey v., TexApp–Dallas, 154 SW3d 917.—Judgm 185.3(2); Lim of Act 72(1), 104.5, 130(5).

Gardner v. Bailey, TexCivApp–El Paso, 376 SW2d 85, ref nre.—App & E 994(1); Autos 171(5), 171(9), 244(11), 244(36.1), 244(43).

Gardner; Baker v., CA5 (Tex), 388 F2d 493.—Social S 143.60.

Gardner v. Baker & Botts, L.L.P., TexApp–Houston (1 Dist), 6 SW3d 295, reh overr, and petition for review den.—App & E 552, 635(1), 638, 907(4), 1047(1).

Gardner v. Best Western Intern., Inc., TexApp–Texarkana, 929 SW2d 474, reh overr, and writ den.—Action 3; App & E 852, 856(1), 934(1), 1078(1); Contracts 188; Courts 9; Evid 517, 571(4); Judgm 183, 185(2), 185(6), 185.3(1); Plead 420(2); Trial 136(1), 136(4).

Gardner; Bridges v., CA5 (Tex), 368 F2d 86.—Social S 140.45, 140.60, 142.10, 147.5, 148.5, 148.15, 149.5.

Gardner v. Bryan, TexCivApp–Galveston, 241 SW2d 297, ref nre.—App & E 946; Child C 511, 921(1); Evid 119(3); Hab Corp 532(1), 662.1, 752.1, 799.

Gardner; Calaway v., TexCivApp–Hous (14 Dist), 525 SW2d 262.—App & E 189(3), 419(1); Pretrial Proc 696.1, 698, 699.

Gardner v. Cato, CA5 (Tex), 841 F2d 105.—Civil R 1091; Fed Civ Proc 2734.

Gardner v. Chevron U.S. A., Inc., CA5 (Tex), 675 F2d 658.—Evid 351; Fed Cts 898, 902; Labor & Emp 2880; Neglig 1076; Prod Liab 23.1, 77.

Gardner v. City of Dallas, CCA5 (Tex), 81 F2d 425, cert den 56 SCt 834, 298 US 668, 80 LEd 1391.—Mun Corp 244(1), 244(3), 247, 252, 607.

Gardner v. City of Hamilton, TexCivApp–Waco, 536 SW2d 422, ref nre.—Em Dom 9, 27, 169.

Gardner v. City of Houston, TexCivApp–Houston, 320 SW2d 715.—Mun Corp 741.50, 816(11).

Gardner; Craig v., NDTex, 299 FSupp 247, rev 425 F2d 1005, 10 ALR Fed 894.—Social S 124.10, 137, 137.5.

Gardner; Crawford v., TexApp–Dallas, 690 SW2d 296.—Child S 479, 489.

Gardner v. Dillard, TexCivApp–Galveston, 258 SW2d 93, writ refused.—Courts 89; Deeds 128; Estates 8; Perp 4(6); Wills 506(1), 608(1), 608(6).

Gardner; Dobbins v., TexCivApp–Houston, 402 SW2d 804, ref nre.—App & E 930(3); Damag 221(7); Health 823(9).

Gardner; Dobbins v., TexCivApp–Houston, 377 SW2d 665, ref nre.—App & E 1170.7; Exceptions Bill of22; Health 825, 830; Pretrial Proc 33, 356.1; Witn 16, 196.4, 217, 219(3).

Gardner; Drake v., CA5 (Tex), 374 F2d 497.—Social S 143.75.

Gardner; Echols v., SDTex, 276 FSupp 499.—Social S 140.15, 140.21, 142.20, 143.60.

Gardner; Economy v., CA5 (Tex), 396 F2d 115.—Fed Cts 926.1.

Gardner; Economy v., WDTex, 286 FSupp 472, aff 396 F2d 115.—Social S 137.5.

Gardner; El Paso Furniture Co. v., TexCivApp–El Paso, 182 SW2d 818.—App & E 1010.1(1); Courts 170; Sales 48; War 120, 166.

Gardner; Enserch Exploration, Inc. v., TexApp–Eastland, 836 SW2d 739, reh den.—Mines 73.1(6).

Gardner; Fidelity & Guaranty Ins. Underwriters, Inc. v., TexCivApp–Amarillo, 471 SW2d 449, ref nre.—Insurance 2136(1).

Gardner; Foley's Dept. Store v., TexCivApp–Hous (14 Dist), 588 SW2d 627.—App & E 1001(1); Neglig 1670; Trial 352.4(6), 352.10.

Gardner v. Gardner, TexApp–Eastland, 622 SW2d 654, dism.—Divorce 261; Venue 7.5(3).

Gardner; Gardner v., TexApp–Eastland, 622 SW2d 654, dism.—Divorce 261; Venue 7.5(3).

Gardner v. Gardner Park Amusement Co., TexCivApp–Dallas, 119 SW2d 1064.—App & E 71(4), 389(3), 544(1), 846(5); Fraud Conv 272.

Gardner; Garrett v., NDTex, 289 FSupp 829.—Social S 140.70, 143.45, 143.60, 143.75.

Gardner; Green v., CA5 (Tex), 391 F2d 606.—Social S 143.60, 147.5, 148.15.

Gardner; Hanna v., CA5 (Tex), 352 F2d 70.—Social S 143.70.

Gardner; Harrison v., CA5 (Tex), 369 F2d 172.—Social S 140.60, 143.75.

Gardner; Hennig v., NDTex, 276 FSupp 622.—Social S 142.5, 143.50, 143.55, 143.60.

Gardner v. Herring, TexApp–Amarillo, 21 SW3d 767, reh overr.—Admin Law 124; Costs 194.44; Judgm 181(15.1); Schools 57.

Gardner v. Hill, EDTex, 195 FSupp2d 832.—Civil R 1345, 1351(1), 1352(4), 1354, 1376(2), 1376(6), 1432; False Imp 15(1); Fed Civ Proc 2491.5, 2515; Mun Corp 747(3).

Gardner v. Johnson, CA5 (Tex), 247 F3d 551, corrected on reh.—Crim Law 393(1); Hab Corp 450.1, 452, 481, 508, 768.

Gardner v. Jones, TexCivApp–Hous (1 Dist), 570 SW2d 198.—App & E 1024.4; Judgm 135, 143(3), 145(2), 153(1); Trover 16, 22, 60.

Gardner; Keene Corp. v., TexApp–Dallas, 837 SW2d 224, reh den, and writ den.—Alt Disp Res 462; App & E 170(1), 221, 635(1), 760(1), 930(3), 1001(3), 1003(1); Costs 252; Evid 80(1), 99, 143, 560; Prod Liab 1, 8, 11, 14, 74, 83; Witn 267, 268(1), 349, 372(1), 405(2).

Gardner v. Kerly, TexCivApp–Hous (14 Dist), 613 SW2d 795.—Damag 91(1); Fences 27; Trial 355(2).

Gardner; King v., CA5 (Tex), 391 F2d 401, appeal after remand 428 F2d 709.—Social S 149.

Gardner; Koen v., TexCivApp–Waco, 178 SW2d 173.—App & E 989, 1001(1); Bills & N 139(3), 518(1), 537(3).

Gardner; Lo-Vaca Gathering Co. v., TexCivApp–San Antonio, 566 SW2d 366.—Em Dom 65.1, 166, 197, 233; Inj 28.

Gardner; McAllister v., TexCivApp–Dallas, 373 SW2d 316, ref nre.—App & E 302(5), 846(5), 1062.1; Gas 20(2), 20(6); Trial 350.2, 350.7(1), 352.1(1), 365.1(6).

Gardner v. Martin, Tex, 345 SW2d 274, 162 Tex 156.—Evid 43(3); Judgm 183, 185(2), 185.1(1).

Gardner v. Martin, TexCivApp–Texarkana, 336 SW2d 263, writ gr, rev 345 SW2d 274, 162 Tex 156.—App & E 554(1), 654, 863, 1032(1); Judgm 186.

Gardner; Martinez v., CA5 (Tex), 390 F2d 874.—Social S 143.60.

Gardner; Newton v., TexCivApp–Eastland, 225 SW2d 598, ref nre.—App & E 989; Evid 597; Frds St of 56(5), 56(6); Mines 79.7; Trial 352.12; Trusts 99, 110.

Gardner v. Railroad Commission, Tex, 333 SW2d 585, 160 Tex 467.—Courts 247(1).

Gardner; Railroad Commission of Tex. v., TexCivApp–Austin, 338 SW2d 753, ref nre.—Mines 92.59(1), 92.64, 92.65.

Gardner; Ramirez v., CA5 (Tex), 368 F2d 319.—Social S 140.21.

Gardner; Ramsey v., Tex, 279 SW2d 584, 154 Tex 457.—Courts 207.3; Mand 40; Plead 352; Pretrial Proc 12, 62, 63, 64, 66, 72.

Gardner; Scott v., TexComApp, 156 SW2d 513, 137 Tex 628, 141 ALR 50.—App & E 861; Autos 181(1), 244(20), 245(24); Evid 471(14), 568(2); Neglig 239, 250, 535(14), 1634; Plead 34(6); Trial 140(2), 350.6(3), 352.5(6).

Gardner; Scott v., TexCivApp–Fort Worth, 159 SW2d 121, writ refused wom.—App & E 719(8), 1004(8), 1067, 1140(1); Damag 18, 210(1); Judgm 272; Lim of Act 55(4); Trial 295(1); Witn 397.

Gardner; Scott v., TexCivApp–Fort Worth, 106 SW2d 1109, writ dism.—Autos 181(1), 240(1), 246(2.1), 246(22); Courts 91(1); New Tr 100; Statut 223.5(6).

Gardner; Simmons v., TexComApp, 144 SW2d 538, 135 Tex 408.—App & E 1161.

Gardner; Simmons v., TexCivApp–Fort Worth, 134 SW2d 338, rev 144 SW2d 538, 135 Tex 408.—Wills 174, 376, 384, 389.

Gardner; Smalling v., TexApp–Houston (14 Dist), 203 SW3d 354, reh overr, and reh en banc den, and review den.—App & E 756, 757(1), 761(1), 893(1), 962; Const Law 2317, 4419; Estop 52.10(2), 52.10(3); Health 800, 804, 805, 808, 809, 821(5), 835; Pretrial Proc 122, 132, 537; Statut 66, 85(1).

Gardner v. Smith, CA5 (Tex), 368 F2d 77.—Social S 121, 140.10, 140.41, 140.60, 140.65, 142.10, 143.75, 147, 149.

Gardner v. Smith, TexCivApp–Beaumont, 168 SW2d 278.—Assign 73; Contracts 147(1), 160; Ref of Inst 45(15).

Gardner; Staples v., CA5 (Tex), 357 F2d 922.—Social S 143.75, 149.5.

Gardner v. State, TexCrimApp, 164 SW2d 393, reh den.—Crim Law 273.1(1), 273.1(4).

Gardner v. State, TexCrimApp, 780 SW2d 259.—Autos 339; Aviation 16; Crim Law 20, 335; Ship 17.

Gardner v. State, TexCrimApp, 777 SW2d 717.—Courts 107.

Gardner v. State, TexCrimApp, 733 SW2d 195, cert den 109 SCt 848, 488 US 1034, 102 LEd2d 979, habeas corpus den Ex parte Gardner, 959 SW2d 189, reh gr, and on reh, habeas corpus gr 247 F3d 551, corrected on reh.—Const Law 4761; Costs 302.4; Crim Law 126(1), 126(2), 412(4), 625.10(2.1), 629.5(7), 641.5(1), 641.12(1), 655(4), 1043(3), 1044.2(1), 1166.16, 1166.22(2); Jury 34(1), 131(1), 131(10); Mental H 434.

Gardner v. State, TexCrimApp, 730 SW2d 675, cert den 108 SCt 248, 484 US 905, 98 LEd2d 206.—Crim Law 511.1(1), 511.1(3), 511.2, 511.5, 698(3), 720(5), 729, 730(8), 730(10), 867, 945(2), 1166.16; Jury 29(6), 42, 107, 108, 131(13); Sent & Pun 1720, 1780(3).

Gardner v. State, TexCrimApp, 699 SW2d 831.—Crim Law 419(1), 419(2.30), 476.6, 1144.13(6), 1159.2(7); Weap 4, 17(5).

Gardner v. State, TexCrimApp, 542 SW2d 127.—Bail 44(2); Prisons 15(1), 15(3); Sent & Pun 2021, 2032.

Gardner v. State, TexCrimApp, 486 SW2d 805.—Burg 41(1), 42(1); Crim Law 451(1), 661; Sent & Pun 1378; Stip 14(10).

Gardner v. State, TexCrimApp, 352 SW2d 129, 171 TexCrim 521.—Contempt 66(1).

Gardner v. State, TexCrimApp, 263 SW2d 560, 159 TexCrim 289.—Burg 41(1).

Gardner v. State, TexCrimApp, 235 SW2d 639.—Crim Law 1090.1(1).

Gardner v. State, TexCrimApp, 209 SW2d 178, 151 TexCrim 495.—Crim Law 369.2(4), 939(1), 940, 942(2); Homic 1134; Sent & Pun 1668.

Gardner v. State, TexCrimApp, 144 SW2d 284, 140 TexCrim 227.—Crim Law 301.

Gardner v. State, TexCrimApp, 116 SW2d 403, 134 TexCrim 520.—Health 186(5).

Gardner v. State, TexCrimApp, 116 SW2d 402, 134 TexCrim 521.—Health 186(5).

Gardner v. State, TexCrimApp, 81 SW2d 98, 128 TexCrim 393.—Larc 62(1), 68(1).

Gardner v. State, TexApp–Houston (1 Dist), 782 SW2d 541, petition for discretionary review refused.—Const Law 2600; Crim Law 1128(4), 1144.8, 1158(3); Jury 33(5.15).

Gardner v. State, TexApp–Austin, 745 SW2d 955.—Crim Law 552(3), 700(9); Homic 1184, 1186.

Gardner v. State, TexApp–Dallas, 736 SW2d 179, petition for discretionary review gr, aff 780 SW2d 259.—Autos 339, 355(10); Crim Law 568, 1159.6.

Gardner v. State, TexApp–Dallas, 711 SW2d 278, petition for discretionary review gr, petition for discretionary review dism with per curiam opinion 777 SW2d 717.—Crim Law 338(7); Sent & Pun 1757, 1766.

Gardner v. State, TexApp–Houston (14 Dist), 632 SW2d 851.—Crim Law 1172.6; Larc 70(3); Sent & Pun 1973(2), 1976(2).

Gardner v. State Farm Lloyds, TexApp–Houston (1 Dist), 76 SW3d 140.—Alt Disp Res 501; Insurance 3256, 3262.

Gardner v. Stewart, TexApp–Amarillo, 223 SW3d 436, reh overr, and review den, and reh of petition for review den.—App & E 20; Atty & C 62; Courts 39; Execution 172(1).

Gardner; Svacina v., TexApp–Texarkana, 905 SW2d 780.—App & E 169, 173(2), 934(1); Bills & N 129(3); Divorce 256; Home 191; Interest 22(1); Judgm 181(1), 185(2); Liens 1.

Gardner v. Tulia Independent School Dist., CA5 (Tex), 71 FedAppx 314.—Fed Cts 724.

Gardner v. Union Bank & Trust Co., TexCivApp–Fort Worth, 159 SW2d 932, writ refused wom.—Ex & Ad 29(2), 383, 388(1); Judgm 804, 812(3).

Gardner v. Union Bank & Trust Co. of Fort Worth, TexCivApp–Fort Worth, 176 SW2d 789.—App & E 173(2); Mtg 473; Receivers 137, 139.

Gardner; U.S. v., CA5 (Tex), 18 F3d 1200, cert den 115 SCt 212, 513 US 879, 130 LEd2d 141.—Sent & Pun 1213.

Gardner v. U. S. Fidelity and Guaranty Co., TexCivApp–Amarillo, 574 SW2d 636, ref nre.—Judgm 181(21), 199(3.7); Trial 139.1(6); Work Comp 725, 734, 1940.

Gardner v. Universal Life & Acc. Ins. Co., TexCivApp–Dallas, 164 SW2d 582, dism.—Insurance 2018, 2034; Time 5.

Gardner; Uvalde Rock Asphalt Co. v., TexCivApp–Galveston, 153 SW2d 604.—Courts 163; Lim of Act 51(2); Mun Corp 370.

Gardner; Warehouse Partners v., TexApp–Dallas, 910 SW2d 19, writ den.—App & E 842(1), 842(2), 931(1), 946, 989, 1008.1(2), 1010.2, 1012.1(5); Atty & C 24; Land & Ten 25, 172(1), 179.

Gardner; Young v., TexCivApp–Hous (1 Dist), 507 SW2d 250, ref nre.—Bound 3(3); Covenants 49, 51(1); Ease 44(2); Evid 425, 429, 443(1), 450(1); Frds St of 158(2); Ref of Inst 45(5).

Gardner; Young v., TexCivApp–Hous (14 Dist), 435 SW2d 192.—Inj 135, 140, 143(1), 147, 148(1), 151, 157, 199.

Gardner–Denver Co.; Crisman v., TexApp–Dallas, 748 SW2d 273. See Crisman v. Cooper Industries.

Gardner ex rel. Gardner v. Tulia Independent School Dist., NDTex, 183 FSupp2d 854, vac 48 FedAppx 481, on remand 2002 WL 32172310, appeal dism 71 FedAppx 314.—Const Law 977; Schools 62, 164, 169.5.

Gardner Flyers, Inc.; Wideman v., TexCivApp–Eastland, 464 SW2d 160, ref nre.—Contracts 322(3); Costs 194.14; Garn 1.

Gardner Machinery Corp.; Chaq Oil Co. v., TexCivApp–Hous (14 Dist), 500 SW2d 877.—Sales 272, 279, 427, 430, 442(1), 442(2), 442(6); Statut 223.1.

Gardner Machinery Corp. v. U. C. Leasing, Inc., TexCivApp–Beaumont, 561 SW2d 897, ref nre, and writ gr, and dism.—App & E 1170.10; Corp 306, 423; Princ & A 72; Trial 366; Trover 60; Trusts 102(1), 289.

Gardner Park Amusement Co.; Gardner v., TexCivApp–Dallas, 119 SW2d 1064.—App & E 71(4), 389(3), 544(1), 846(5); Fraud Conv 272.

Gardner Zemke Co., In re, TexApp–El Paso, 978 SW2d 624.—Alt Disp Res 114, 133(2), 137, 143, 201, 205; Commerce 80.5; Mand 29.

Garduno, Ex parte, TexApp–El Paso, 956 SW2d 823, petition for discretionary review refused.—Sent & Pun 1963, 1976(3).

Garduno v. Garduno, TexApp–Corpus Christi, 760 SW2d 735.—Divorce 209, 286(1); Hus & W 248, 262.1(3), 272(1); Marriage 13, 40(1), 40(4), 51, 54.

Garduno; Garduno v., TexApp–Corpus Christi, 760 SW2d 735.—Divorce 209, 286(1); Hus & W 248, 262.1(3), 272(1); Marriage 13, 40(1), 40(4), 51, 54.

Gareau v. State, TexApp–Fort Worth, 923 SW2d 252.—Crim Law 1023(16).

Gared, Inc.; Castillo v., TexApp–Houston (1 Dist), 1 SW3d 781, reh overr, and petition for review den, and reh of petition for review overr.—App & E 863, 934(1); Judgm 199(3.10); Labor & Emp 3040, 3043, 3079, 3087, 3096(2); Neglig 202, 375, 379, 380, 383, 387.

Gareis v. Gordon, TexCivApp–Galveston, 243 SW2d 259.—Judgm 572(2), 717, 743(2); Lim of Act 39(7).

Garey Const. Co., Inc. v. Thompson, TexApp–Austin, 697 SW2d 865.—Tresp 46(3), 50, 57, 67.

Garfield; El Rancho Restaurants, Inc. v., TexCivApp–San Antonio, 440 SW2d 873, ref nre.—App & E 882(14), 1060.1(2.1); Evid 118, 121(12); Neglig 1020, 1037(4),

1530, 1562, 1656, 1670, 1676, 1679, 1708, 1713, 1742; Trial 127.

Garfield Mut. Fire and Storm Ins. Ass'n v. Calhoun, TexCivApp–Corpus Christi, 532 SW2d 663.—App & E 499(1), 927(7), 989; Insurance 2143(1), 2143(2), 2165(1), 2199, 2202, 3343.

Garfield Mut. Fire and Storm Ins. Ass'n v. Calhoun, TexCivApp–Corpus Christi, 532 SW2d 652.—App & E 396.

Garg v. Narron, SDTex, 710 FSupp 1116.—Labor & Emp 757; Rem of C 19(1), 19(5), 86(1); States 18.49.

Gargiulo; Winship v., Tex, 761 SW2d 301.—Armed S 34.5(5).

Garguillo; Winship v., TexApp–Waco, 754 SW2d 360, writ den with per curiam opinion 761 SW2d 301.—Armed S 34.5(4), 34.5(5); Judgm 335(1), 335(4).

Gargyle Corp.; First Republicbank Dallas v., NDTex, 91 BR 398.—Bankr 2151, 2440; Fed Civ Proc 2011.

Garibaldo; Becerra v., TexCivApp–Corpus Christi, 526 SW2d 780, ref nre.—Abate & R 7; Child C 510, 512, 553, 555, 556, 578, 637, 639, 920, 922(1); Judgm 742; Witn 40(1), 45(2).

Garibay v. Brand, TexCivApp–Beaumont, 98 SW2d 230. —Banks 49(8).

Garibay v. Decker, SDTex, 331 FSupp 1093.—Work Comp 2149.

Garibay; Rivas v., TexApp–San Antonio, 974 SW2d 93, reh overr, and review den.—App & E 837(1), 969, 1064.1(1), 1067; Damag 163(1), 191, 210(1); Evid 570, 571(10), 594.

Garibay; State v., TexApp–El Paso, 838 SW2d 268, reh overr.—Crim Law 393(1), 412.2(4), 517.2(1), 517.2(2), 641.3(2), 641.3(3), 641.3(6).

Garibay v. State, TexApp–Corpus Christi, 787 SW2d 128, petition for discretionary review refused.—Assault 83; Crim Law 661.

Gariepy; Southern Underwriters v., TexCivApp–Amarillo, 105 SW2d 760, writ dism.—Damag 221(5.1), 221(7); Judgm 256(1); Mines 97; Trial 295(1), 358; Work Comp 1335, 1969.

Garig v. N.L. Industries, Inc., SDTex, 671 FSupp 1460, aff 792 F2d 1120.—Civil R 1551.

Garijak, Inc.; Morales v., CA5 (Tex), 829 F2d 1355.—Fed Cts 908.1; Interest 39(2.25); Seamen 11(6), 11(9).

Garland, Ex parte, TexCrimApp, 154 SW2d 834, 142 TexCrim 414.—Autos 59, 73; Const Law 4360; Statut 47.

Garland v. Brown, NDTex, 52 FSupp 401.—Arrest 63.2; Autos 59; Equity 65(1), 65(3); Inj 75, 90; Searches 11, 79.

Garland v. Garland, TexApp–Dallas, 868 SW2d 847.—Courts 472.4(8), 475(15).

Garland; Garland v., TexApp–Dallas, 868 SW2d 847.—Courts 472.4(8), 475(15).

Garland; Home Fund, Inc. v., TexCivApp–Fort Worth, 520 SW2d 939, ref nre.—App & E 544(3), 548(5), 549(3), 549(4), 555, 624, 627; Inj 261.

Garland v. Lane-Wells Co., CA5 (Tex), 185 F2d 857.—Fed Civ Proc 2233; Fed Cts 428, 630.1; Labor & Emp 3096(11).

Garland v. Meyer, TexCivApp–San Antonio, 169 SW2d 531.—Trusts 97; Wills 62, 64, 188, 417, 421, 600(1).

Garland v. Sanders, TexCivApp–Dallas, 114 SW2d 302, dism.—High 99.1; Inj 88.

Garland v. Shepherd, TexCivApp–Dallas, 445 SW2d 602, reh den.—Attach 28; Inj 1, 9, 40, 128(1).

Garland v. State, TexCrimApp, 170 SW3d 107, reh den.—Rape 64; Sent & Pun 60.

Garland v. State, TexCrimApp, 246 SW2d 204, 157 TexCrim 4.—Autos 355(6); Crim Law 364(3.1), 364(4), 1043(1), 1169.2(1).

Garland; State v., TexApp–Austin, 963 SW2d 95, review den.—App & E 758.3(1), 761; Em Dom 235, 241, 250.1, 253(1).

Garland v. U.S., CCA5 (Tex), 164 F2d 487, cert den 68 SCt 739, 333 US 861, 92 LEd 1140, reh den 68 SCt 1015, 334 US 813, 92 LEd 1744.—Brok 5.

Garland v. U.S., CCA5 (Tex), 158 F2d 93, cert den 67 SCt 866, 330 US 827, 91 LEd 1276.—Crim Law 1182.

Garland Chrysler-Plymouth, Inc.; Day v., TexCivApp–Dallas, 460 SW2d 272.—App & E 770(1); Trial 350.3(1), 350.3(4); Usury 114, 115.

Garland, City of; Acton Const. Co., Inc. v., CA5 (Tex), 847 F2d 234. See Zurn Industries, Inc. v. Acton Const. Co., Inc.

Garland, City of; Appolo Development, Inc. v., TexCivApp–Dallas, 476 SW2d 365, ref nre.—Zoning 9, 131, 191, 236.1, 279.

Garland, City of; B & B Vending Co. v., TexApp–Tyler, 711 SW2d 132, ref nre.—Statut 110.1; Zoning 14, 76.

Garland, City of; Barrera v., TexApp–Dallas, 776 SW2d 652, writ den, and writ withdrawn, and rev, and writ gr, and writ den, and writ withdrawn.—Autos 258, 271, 277.1, 278, 279; Judgm 178, 181(6), 185(6); Mun Corp 757(1), 798.

Garland, City of, v. Booth, TexApp–Dallas, 971 SW2d 631. See City of Garland v. Booth.

Garland, City of, v. Booth, TexApp–Dallas, 895 SW2d 766. See City of Garland v. Booth.

Garland, City of; Borne v., TexApp–Dallas, 718 SW2d 22, ref nre.—Const Law 2314; Mun Corp 741.55.

Garland, City of; Breaux v., CA5 (Tex), 205 F3d 150, cert den 121 SCt 52, 531 US 816, 148 LEd2d 21.—Civil R 1355, 1359; Const Law 1184(1), 1928, 1955; Fed Cts 830; Mun Corp 185(1); Offic 72.41(2).

Garland, City of; Callejo v., TexCivApp–Dallas, 583 SW2d 925, ref nre.—Deeds 97; Ease 42; Electricity 9(1).

Garland, City of; Caudle v., TexCivApp–Dallas, 583 SW2d 826, ref nre.—Judgm 677, 713(2).

Garland, City of; Cornyn v., TexApp–Austin, 994 SW2d 258.—Const Law 2604; Decl Judgm 41; Mun Corp 1040; Records 54, 57, 63, 65.

Garland, City of; Dearmore v., NDTex, 400 FSupp2d 894, subsequent determination 2005 WL 3276384, motion den 237 FRD 573.—Civil R 1457(4); Const Law 695, 714, 1234; Fed Civ Proc 103.2, 103.3; Health 392; Inj 150; Searches 79.

Garland, City of; Dearmore v., NDTex, 237 FRD 573.—Civil R 1482; Fed Civ Proc 2646, 2653, 2655, 2658, 2727.

Garland, City of; General Tel. Co. of Southwest v., TexCivApp–Dallas, 522 SW2d 732.—App & E 462.1, 479(1); Courts 207.1.

Garland, City of; General Tel. Co. of Southwest v., TexCivApp–Dallas, 509 SW2d 927, ref nre.—Const Law 2524; Plead 111.12, 111.39(1), 111.42(1); Pub Ut 121; Tel 927, 939(1).

Garland, City of; Gregory v., TexCivApp–Dallas, 333 SW2d 869, ref nre.—App & E 758.1, 1122(1); Em Dom 271; Mun Corp 837, 845(4), 845(6); Neglig 1694; Trial 136(3), 142, 143.

Garland, City of; Howard v., CA5 (Tex), 917 F2d 898.—Const Law 3512; Zoning 86.

Garland, City of; Hughes v., CA5 (Tex), 204 F3d 223.—Const Law 4172(6), 4173(2), 4173(3), 4173(4); Mun Corp 218(10).

Garland, City of; Kopplin v., TexApp–Dallas, 869 SW2d 433, writ den.—App & E 173(2); Const Law 2314; Judgm 181(1), 183, 185(2); Mun Corp 851; Neglig 1040(3), 1045(3), 1172, 1175, 1194.

Garland, City of; Kordus v., TexCivApp–Tyler, 561 SW2d 260, ref nre.—Mun Corp 987, 994.

Garland, City of; Kuhl v., Tex, 910 SW2d 929.—Mun Corp 218(10).

Garland, City of, v. Long, TexApp–Dallas, 722 SW2d 49. See City of Garland v. Long.

Garland, City of; Moore Indus. Disposal, Inc. v., TexCivApp–Dallas, 587 SW2d 430, ref nre.—Carr 8.

Garland, City of; Norlock v., CA5 (Tex), 768 F2d 654.—Fed Civ Proc 414, 531, 1751.

Garland, City of; Swafford v., TexCivApp–Eastland, 491 SW2d 175, ref nre.—Const Law 243.2, 3747, 4420; Mun Corp 724.

Garland, City of; Texas Power & Light Co. v., Tex, 431 SW2d 511.—Electricity 1, 8.1(1); Monop 6; Mun Corp 63.15(1), 120, 595, 597, 598, 682(1), 690.

Garland, City of, v. URS Co., CA5 (Tex), 847 F2d 234. See Zurn Industries, Inc. v. Acton Const. Co., Inc.

Garland, City of; Valley Oil Co. v., TexCivApp–Dallas, 499 SW2d 333.—Decl Judgm 391, 395; Judgm 713(2), 719, 729.

Garland, City of, v. Vasquez, TexApp–Dallas, 734 SW2d 92. See City of Garland v. Vasquez.

Garland, City of; Wade v., TexApp–Dallas, 671 SW2d 657, dism.—Mun Corp 185(12), 218(9); Statut 188.

Garland, City of, v. Zurn Industries, Inc., CA5 (Tex), 870 F2d 320. See City of Garland v. Zurn Industries, Inc.

Garland, City of, By and Through Mayor and City Council v. Louton, TexApp–Dallas, 683 SW2d 725. See City of Garland By and Through Mayor and City Council v. Louton.

Garland Community Hosp. v. Rose, Tex, 156 SW3d 541, on remand 168 SW3d 352.—Health 660, 800, 804.

Garland Community Hosp.; Rose v., TexApp–Dallas, 168 SW3d 352.—App & E 945, 946; Health 804, 809, 821(5).

Garland Community Hosp.; Rose v., TexApp–Dallas, 87 SW3d 188, review gr, rev 156 SW3d 541, on remand 168 SW3d 352.—Health 660, 800, 804.

Garland Grain Co. v. Bailey, TexCivApp–Dallas, 393 SW2d 945, ref nre.—App & E 499(1), 500(1), 1170.7; Contracts 280(2), 295(1), 323(1), 350(1).

Garland Grain Co. v. D-C Home Owners Imp. Ass'n, TexCivApp–Tyler, 393 SW2d 635, ref nre.—App & E 934(2); Environ Law 162; Inj 16, 126; Nuis 23(2), 26, 33, 34, 39, 82; Waters 42, 51, 64, 73.1, 77.

Garland Independent School Dist.; Barbre v., NDTex, 474 FSupp 687.—Civil R 1009; Const Law 82(11), 90.1(7.3), 1991, 1995, 4171, 4173(3), 4173(4), 4201; Schools 147.18, 147.40(2).

Garland Independent School Dist.; City of Garland v., TexCivApp–Dallas, 468 SW2d 110, ref nre.—Mun Corp 426, 488(5.1).

Garland Independent School Dist.; Duenas v., TexApp–Dallas, 961 SW2d 19, error den.—App & E 93, 396; Compromise 19(2); Costs 194.40; Decl Judgm 205; Judgm 178; Work Comp 1120, 1144, 1154.

Garland Independent School Dist.; Kissick v., TexCivApp–Dallas, 330 SW2d 708, ref nre.—Const Law 188, 242.2(5.1), 3204, 4208; Marriage 1; Schools 61, 172.

Garland Independent School Dist.; Texas State Teachers Ass'n v., USTex, 109 SCt 1486, 489 US 782, 103 LEd2d 866, on remand 874 F2d 242.—Civil R 1482, 1486, 1491.

Garland Independent School Dist.; Texas State Teachers Ass'n v., CA5 (Tex), 837 F2d 190, cert gr 109 SCt 51, 488 US 815, 102 LEd2d 30, rev 109 SCt 1486, 489 US 782, 103 LEd2d 866, on remand 874 F2d 242.—Civil R 1482.

Garland Independent School Dist.; Texas State Teachers Ass'n v., CA5 (Tex), 777 F2d 1046, reh den 784 F2d 1113, aff 107 SCt 41, 479 US 801, 93 LEd2d 4.—Const Law 242.2(1), 1730, 1969, 1970, 1989, 2002, 3616; Schools 20.

Garland Independent School Dist.; Tutton v., NDTex, 733 FSupp 1113.—Civil R 1544, 1592; Fed Civ Proc 2470.1, 2497.1, 2544, 2758, 2768, 2771(5).

Garland Independent School Dist. v. Wilks, NDTex, 657 FSupp 1163.—Civil R 1418; Fed Civ Proc 2737.5; Inj 22; Schools 154(2.1), 154(3).

Garland Power and Light v. Huston, TexApp–Dallas, 702 SW2d 697. See City of Garland v. Huston.

Garland, Tex., City of; Gassner v., CA5 (Tex), 864 F2d 394, reh den.—Autos 349(8); Civil R 1088(4), 1376(6).

Garland, Tex., City of; News-Texan, Inc. v., CA5 (Tex), 814 F2d 216.—Fed Civ Proc 2840; Rem of C 70, 107(4), 107(9), 107(11).

Garland, Texas, City of; U.S. v., NDTex, 124 FSupp2d 442.—Mun Corp 92; U S Mag 15.1.

Garland, Tex., City of; Waggoner v., CA5 (Tex), 987 F2d 1160.—Civil R 1209, 1539, 1551; Fed Civ Proc 2497.1, 2543, 2545; Fed Cts 766; Statut 263, 267(2).

Garlington v. Boudreaux, TexApp–Beaumont, 921 SW2d 550.—App & E 662(4), 1008.1(1), 1010.1(1); Covenants 103(3).

Garlington; City of Big Spring v., TexCivApp–Eastland, 88 SW2d 1095.—Courts 207.4(1.1); Mand 27.

Garlington; Everts v., TexCivApp–El Paso, 117 SW2d 820.—App & E 878(3); Plead 264, 303; Venue 17, 32(2).

Garlington; Harper v., TexCivApp–Eastland, 85 SW2d 1098.—Mand 45, 152.

Garlington; National Union Fire Ins. Co. of Pittsburg, Pa. v., TexApp–Beaumont, 697 SW2d 778, writ refused. —Work Comp 1396, 1988.

Garlington v. Reed, TexCivApp–Eastland, 319 SW2d 367. —App & E 771, 773(2).

Garlington; Reed v., TexCivApp–Eastland, 233 SW2d 185.—App & E 106, 1043(8); Plead 110.

Garlington v. State, TexCrimApp, 150 SW2d 253, 141 TexCrim 595.—Ind & Inf 180; Larc 89; Names 16(3).

Garlington v. State, TexCrimApp, 109 SW2d 752, 133 TexCrim 218.—Records 22.

Garlington v. State, TexCrimApp, 104 SW2d 852.—Crim Law 1182.

Garlington v. Wasson, CCA5 (Tex), 164 F2d 243, cert den 68 SCt 1337, 334 US 827, 92 LEd 1755.—Bankr 2235, 3673, 3674; Fed Cts 523.

Garlington v. Wasson, CCA5 (Tex), 139 F2d 183, cert den 64 SCt 1046, 322 US 734, 88 LEd 1568, reh den 64 SCt 1259, 322 US 714, 88 LEd 1556, and 64 SCt 1260, 322 US 770, 88 LEd 1596.—Bankr 3673.

Garlington v. Wasson, TexCivApp–Eastland, 279 SW2d 668, ref nre, appeal dism 77 SCt 38, 352 US 806, 352 US 979, 1 LEd2d 38, 1 LEd2d 364, reh den 77 SCt 219, 352 US 937, 1 LEd2d 170.—App & E 714(2); Bankr 2060.1; Evid 43(2), 43(3); Judgm 335(1), 335(4), 373, 405, 435, 436, 668(1), 694, 713(2), 743(1); Mental H 7, 514.

Garlitz; Burlington-Rock Island R. Co. v., TexCivApp–Beaumont, 151 SW2d 889.—Carr 312; Evid 10(4); R R 22(3); Venue 74.

Garlitz v. Carrasco, TexCivApp–El Paso, 339 SW2d 92, ref nre.—Contracts 168, 323(1); Crops 3; Damag 124(1); Land & Ten 1.

Garlock Inc.; Arnold v., CA5 (Tex), 288 F3d 234.—Bankr 2395; Contrib 5(1), 5(6.1), 6, 9(1); Fed Cts 431, 744; Pretrial Proc 508.

Garlock, Inc.; Arnold v., CA5 (Tex), 278 F3d 426, reh en banc den 288 F3d 234.—Bankr 2043(3), 2087, 2091, 2391, 2396; Contrib 1; Fed Civ Proc 2700; Fed Cts 684.1; Indem 20; Rem of C 107(0.5), 107(8), 107(9).

Garlock, Inc.; Gilcrease v., TexApp–El Paso, 211 SW3d 448.—App & E 840(1), 912, 1024.3; Damag 63, 87(1); Death 91, 93; Judgm 658, 714(1); Torts 134; Venue 16, 45, 78.

Garlynn Common County Line School Dist.; Lynn County School Board v., TexCivApp–Amarillo, 118 SW2d 1070, writ refused.—Inj 114(4); Parties 47; Schools 24(2), 38, 39.

Garman v. Reynolds, TexCivApp–Fort Worth, 284 SW2d 262, writ refused.—Judgm 942, 944.

Garmon; Galvan v., CA5 (Tex), 710 F2d 214, reh den 716 F2d 901, cert den 104 SCt 2150, 466 US 949, 80 LEd2d 536.—Civil R 1376(3), 1376(8).

Garmong v. Montgomery County, SDTex, 668 FSupp 1000.—Civil R 1485, 1486, 1487, 1488; Fed Civ Proc 2737.4.

Garms v. State, TexCrimApp, 93 SW2d 743.—Crim Law 1090.1(1).

Garner, In re, BkrtcyWDTex, 339 BR 610.—Bankr 3312, 3398.

Garner, Matter of, CA5 (Tex), 56 F3d 677.—Bankr 3355(2.1); Judgm 92, 828.21(2).

Garner; Bartholow v., NDTex, 43 BR 463.—Exemp 50(1).

Garner v. Boyd, CA5 (Tex), 447 F2d 1373.—Fed Cts 743.

Garner v. Boyd, NDTex, 330 FSupp 22, aff 447 F2d 1373. —Bankr 2554, 2648; Contracts 32; Corp 116; Equity 21; Trusts 231(1).

Garner v. City of Houston, TexCivApp–Houston, 323 SW2d 659.—Evid 18, 25(2); Health 955, 961; Judgm 181(15.1).

Garner v. Corpus Christi Nat. Bank, TexApp–Corpus Christi, 944 SW2d 469, reh overr, and writ den, cert den 119 SCt 410, 525 US 965, 142 LEd2d 333, appeal after remand 2002 WL 34215940.—Antitrust 141, 252, 363; App & E 934(1); Banks 53.1, 54(7), 100; Contracts 143(2), 143.5, 147(1), 152, 175(1), 176(2), 326; Fraud 3, 13(3), 20, 45, 46; Frds St of 106(1); Guar 1; Judgm 183, 185(6), 185.3(13); Plead 48, 236(1), 236(7); Torts 213.

Garner v. East Texas Nat. Bank of Palestine, TexCiv-App–Tyler, 608 SW2d 939, ref nre.—Cons Cred 4, 33.1; Evid 461(1), 461(4).

Garner v. Furmanite Australia Pty., Ltd., TexApp–Houston (1 Dist), 966 SW2d 798, reh overr, and review den.—App & E 846(5), 863, 893(1); Appear 9(1); Const Law 3964; Corp 1.5(3), 665(0.5); Courts 12(2.1), 12(2.5), 12(2.10), 12(2.20), 12(2.25), 39.

Garner v. Garner, TexApp–Fort Worth, 673 SW2d 413, dism.—Child C 42, 76, 275, 417, 420, 510, 907, 917, 921(1), 943; Evid 318(1), 471(3), 536; Guard & W 13(1); Infants 8; Trial 18.

Garner; Garner v., TexApp–Fort Worth, 673 SW2d 413, dism.—Child C 42, 76, 275, 417, 420, 510, 907, 917, 921(1), 943; Evid 318(1), 471(3), 536; Guard & W 13(1); Infants 8; Trial 18.

Garner v. Garner, TexApp–Dallas, 200 SW3d 303.—App & E 1008.1(4); Child C 28, 48, 922(2); Child S 9, 82, 88, 201, 450, 458, 487, 556(1).

Garner; Garner v., TexApp–Dallas, 200 SW3d 303.—App & E 1008.1(4); Child C 28, 48, 922(2); Child S 9, 82, 88, 201, 450, 458, 487, 556(1).

Garner v. Garner, TexCivApp–Eastland, 567 SW2d 281. —App & E 161; Divorce 281.

Garner; Garner v., TexCivApp–Eastland, 567 SW2d 281. —App & E 161; Divorce 281.

Garner v. Gately, TexApp–Waco, 909 SW2d 61.—Mand 141.

Garner; Great Atlantic & Pacific Tea Co. v., TexCiv-App–Dallas, 170 SW2d 502, writ refused wom.—App & E 301, 758.1; Labor & Emp 2848, 2889, 2890; Neglig 1631, 1650; Trial 352.4(9), 352.18, 362.

Garner; Grimm v., Tex, 589 SW2d 955.—Mand 4(3).

Garner; Grimm v., TexCivApp–Waco, 577 SW2d 573, rev 589 SW2d 955.—Courts 155; Mand 1, 27, 61.

Garner v. Hair Naturally, TexApp–Austin, 771 SW2d 242. See Garner v. McGinty.

Garner; Hicks v., CA5 (Tex), 69 F3d 22.—Civil R 1098; Const Law 1422, 1424; Fed Civ Proc 2734; Fed Cts 830; Prisons 4(14).

Garner v. I.C.H. Corp., NDTex, 732 FSupp 692. See Wabash Life Ins. Co. v. Garner.

Garner v. I.R.S., SDTex, 632 FSupp 390.—Int Rev 4767, 4792, 4803.1.

Garner; Jennings v., TexApp–Tyler, 721 SW2d 445.—App & E 185(3); Courts 489(1), 493(2).

Garner v. Jones, TexCivApp–El Paso, 81 SW2d 536, writ dism.—Hus & W 90; Insurance 1203.

Garner v. Lehrer, CA5 (Tex), 56 F3d 677. See Garner, Matter of.

Garner; Lockhart v., Tex, 298 SW2d 108, 156 Tex 580.—Ack 6(3); App & E 931(4); Can of Inst 27; Hus & W 262.1(4), 267(2).

Garner v. Lockhart, TexCivApp–Texarkana, 285 SW2d 393, writ gr, aff 298 SW2d 108, 156 Tex 580.—Ack 4, 6(3); Home 57(3); Hus & W 254, 267(2); Mines 55(2); Ven & Pur 227, 231(14).

Garner v. Long, TexApp–Fort Worth, 106 SW3d 260.—Ex & Ad 72, 245, 453(4), 455, 510(2); Judgm 183, 185(2), 185(4), 185.1(2), 185.1(4), 185.3(1), 540, 584, 586(0.5), 948(1); Stip 17(1), 17(3), 18(4).

Garner v. Long, TexApp–Fort Worth, 49 SW3d 920, reh overr, and review den, and reh of petition for review den.—App & E 842(2), 852, 893(1); Wills 783.

Garner v. Lumberton Independent School Dist., TexCivApp–Austin, 430 SW2d 418.—Admin Law 797; App & E 712, 863; Const Law 2408; Schools 47, 55, 63(1); Statut 171, 212.1.

Garner v. McGinty, TexApp–Austin, 771 SW2d 242.—Neglig 1076, 1078, 1162, 1692.

Garner v. McKinney, TexCivApp–Eastland, 255 SW2d 529, ref nre.—App & E 931(3); Tax 2930, 2932, 2936; Ven & Pur 232(1).

Garner; Miro v., TexApp–Corpus Christi, 52 SW3d 407, reh overr, and review den.—App & E 930(1), 1001(3), 1003(6); Land & Ten 55(1), 55(3), 184(2).

Garner v. Morales, SDTex, 237 FRD 399.—Fed Civ Proc 802, 803.

Garner; Porter v., TexCivApp–El Paso, 386 SW2d 618, ref nre.—Insurance 3475(3).

Garner; Potter v., TexCivApp–Tyler, 407 SW2d 537, ref nre.—App & E 930(1), 989; Judgm 359; Labor & Emp 2881, 2885; Work Comp 2110, 2113, 2133, 2138.

Garner; Pouncy v., TexApp–Tyler, 626 SW2d 337, ref nre.—Adop 6, 21; App & E 200, 731(5), 882(8); Des & Dist 34, 71(7); Evid 286; Ex & Ad 221(10); New Tr 26; Pretrial Proc 79; Slaves 25; Trial 131(2).

Garner v. Prescott, TexCivApp–Eastland, 234 SW2d 704.—App & E 930(3); Autos 201(9), 240(2), 244(10), 245(13), 245(49), 245(65), 246(57); Neglig 432, 1741; Trial 350.2, 350.5(3), 350.7(5), 352.12; Witn 379(4.1).

Garner v. Redeaux, TexApp–Houston (14 Dist), 678 SW2d 124, ref nre.—App & E 1047(1); Costs 194.36; Evid 10(3), 397(2), 400(2); Frds St of 106(2), 108(1), 110(1), 113(1), 158(3); Spec Perf 31.

Garner; Rucker v., TexCivApp–Eastland, 489 SW2d 683.—Autos 244(58).

Garner v. State, TexCrimApp, 556 SW2d 332.—Game 9.

Garner v. State, TexCrimApp, 552 SW2d 809.—Sent & Pun 1381(4).

Garner v. State, TexCrimApp, 545 SW2d 178.—Const Law 4733(2); Sent & Pun 2011.

Garner v. State, TexCrimApp, 464 SW2d 111.—Crim Law 364(3.1), 406(1), 516.

Garner v. State, TexCrimApp, 446 SW2d 867.—Autos 359; Crim Law 1036.1(3.1), 1170.5(1), 1171.1(3).

Garner v. State, TexCrimApp, 286 SW2d 625.—Crim Law 1090.1(1).

Garner v. State, TexCrimApp, 286 SW2d 421.—Crim Law 1090.1(1).

Garner v. State, TexCrimApp, 243 SW2d 165.—Crim Law 1094(3).

Garner v. State, TexCrimApp, 109 SW2d 182, 133 TexCrim 86.—Crim Law 304(20), 394.4(12), 404.55, 763(1), 763(6); Int Liq 222, 226.

Garner v. State, TexApp–Houston (1 Dist), 864 SW2d 92, petition for discretionary review refused.—Assault 56; Const Law 4810; Crim Law 429(1), 429(2), 430, 444, 446, 475.5, 553, 641.5(0.5), 641.5(7), 641.10(1), 641.10(2), 641.13(1), 641.13(2.1), 641.13(5), 641.13(6), 641.13(7), 1119(1), 1144.13(3), 1144.13(6), 1159.2(3), 1159.2(7), 1159.2(9), 1159.4(2), 1166.10(2), 1184(4.1); Ind & Inf 113; Jury 29(2); Pardon 64.1; Sent & Pun 323, 1840; Weap 17(4).

Garner v. State, TexApp–Fort Worth, 939 SW2d 802, petition for discretionary review refused.—Controlled Subs 8, 82; Crim Law 374, 404.30, 404.60, 663, 728(2), 829(14), 1035(2), 1036.1(9), 1044.1(8), 1144.13(3), 1159.2(2), 1159.2(7), 1159.2(8), 1159.2(9), 1159.3(2).

Garner v. State, TexApp–Fort Worth, 858 SW2d 656, petition for discretionary review refused.—Assault 92(2); Crim Law 258, 553, 734, 1030(2), 1134(3), 1144.13(3), 1159.2(7), 1159.2(9), 1159.4(2); Double J 7, 59, 96, 99; Obst Just 8.

Garner v. State, TexApp–Fort Worth, 779 SW2d 498, petition for discretionary review refused by 785 SW2d 158.—Arrest 58, 63.5(1), 64; Autos 413; Crim Law 394.1(1), 394.1(3), 394.2(1), 407(1), 412.1(4), 412.2(4), 438(8), 777, 1169.1(10).

Garner v. State, TexApp–Fort Worth, 648 SW2d 436.—Crim Law 717, 721(3), 784(1), 1171.1(3), 1171.7; Larc 57.

Garner v. State, TexApp–Amarillo, 957 SW2d 112.—Crim Law 695(2), 854(7), 1043(3), 1166.22(4.1).

Garner v. State, TexApp–Waco, 214 SW3d 705.—Crim Law 1012, 1042.

Garner v. State, TexApp–Corpus Christi, 848 SW2d 799.—Controlled Subs 26, 27, 29, 80; Crim Law 388.3, 404.15, 404.20, 404.30, 1036.1(1), 1043(1), 1144.13(2.1), 1144.13(6), 1153(1), 1159.2(7), 1159.6, 1169.1(7).

Garner v. State, TexApp–Houston (14 Dist), 852 SW2d 687.—Double J 1, 135, 149.

Garner v. Texas State Bd. of Pharmacy, TexCivApp–Eastland, 304 SW2d 530, writ refused.—Const Law 4286; Controlled Subs 10; Health 211, 218, 223(1), 223(2); Licens 38.

Garner; Tex-Hio Partnership v., TexApp–Dallas, 106 SW3d 886.—App & E 153, 171(1), 430(1), 883; Judgm 183, 189; Parties 54; Partners 202; Plead 162, 228.14.

Garner; Triton Ins. Co. v., TexCivApp–Beaumont, 460 SW2d 262, ref nre.—App & E 1012.1(11), 1177(7); Insurance 3523(4); Trial 368.

Garner; U.S. v., NDTex, 945 FSupp 990, aff 136 F3d 138.—Arrest 63.1, 63.4(1), 63.4(2), 63.4(15); Autos 349(4), 349.5(3), 349.5(12); Crim Law 412.2(2); Searches 24, 32, 53.1, 58, 66, 186.

Garner; Wabash Life Ins. Co. v., NDTex, 732 FSupp 692.—Contracts 116(1); Fed Cts 660.25; Jury 14(1).

Garner v. Wallace, EDTex, 139 FSupp2d 801.—Civil R 1304, 1326(2), 1326(8).

Garner, Lovell & Stein, P.C. v. Burnett, TexApp–Amarillo, 911 SW2d 108, reh overr.—Mand 4(1), 4(4), 12, 28, 32; Pretrial Proc 35, 371; Witn 219(3).

Garner Motors, Inc. v. Innes, TexCivApp–Amarillo, 503 SW2d 655, ref nre.—Evid 574, 588, 591; Sales 279; Trial 140(1), 350.8, 366; Trover 40(6).

Garnett; Herring v., TexCivApp–Hous (1 Dist), 463 SW2d 52, ref nre.—Autos 201(5).

Garnett; Williams v., TexCivApp–Waco, 608 SW2d 794.—Tresp 12, 40(1), 47, 56; Trial 350.4(2).

Garnica; Mack Massey Motors, Inc. v., TexApp–El Paso, 814 SW2d 167. See Jeep Eagle Sales Corp. v. Mack Massey Motors, Inc.

Garnica; Massey Motors, Inc. v., TexApp–El Paso, 814 SW2d 167. See Jeep Eagle Sales Corp. v. Mack Massey Motors, Inc.

Garnica v. State, TexApp–Texarkana, 53 SW3d 457.—Const Law 4793; Crim Law 662.65, 662.80; Sent & Pun 2026.

Garnica-Vasquez v. Reno, CA5 (Tex), 210 F3d 558.—Aliens 216, 281(1); Hab Corp 521, 742.

Garnica-Vasquez v. Reno, WDTex, 40 FSupp2d 398, aff 210 F3d 558.—Aliens 281(2); Hab Corp 521; Statut 181(1), 188, 205, 212.6, 216, 219(2).

Garnor-Evans & Co. v. Webber, TexCivApp–Houston, 363 SW2d 383, ref nre.—Insurance 1654.

Garnsey; Reedy Co., Inc. v., TexCivApp–Dallas, 608 SW2d 755, ref nre.—Antitrust 369; Judgm 139, 160, 162(2).

Garofano; Gant v., CA5 (Tex), 119 FedAppx 602, cert den 126 SCt 159, 546 US 862, 163 LEd2d 145.—Lim of Act 105(2), 130(7).

Garonzik v. Shearson Hayden Stone, Inc., CA5 (Tex), 574 F2d 1220, reh den 581 F2d 267, cert den 99 SCt 844, 439 US 1072, 59 LEd2d 39.—Fed Civ Proc 187.

Garrard v. Henderson, TexCivApp–Dallas, 209 SW2d 225. —Home 1, 17, 18, 31, 32, 33, 154; Infants 47, 59, 62; Receivers 12.

Garrard; St. Elizabeth Hosp. v., Tex, 730 SW2d 649.—Damag 50; Dead Bodies 9.

Garrard v. St. Elizabeth Hosp., TexApp–Beaumont, 708 SW2d 571, writ gr, aff 730 SW2d 649.—App & E 103, 916(1); Dead Bodies 9.

Garrard v. State, TexCrimApp, 128 SW2d 33, 137 TexCrim 75.—Crim Law 376; Homic 1321; Sent & Pun 1870, 1900; Witn 318.

Garrard v. Texas Emp. Ins. Ass'n, TexCivApp–Amarillo, 423 SW2d 93.—Evid 219(1); Work Comp 853, 1043, 1374, 1619.

Garre; Marsalis v., TexCivApp–Amarillo, 391 SW2d 522, ref nre.—Accord 2(0.5), 24; Evid 471(1), 471(2); Guar 1; Judgm 181(2), 185.1(4); Subrog 33(2).

Garrels v. Wales Transp., Inc., TexApp–Dallas, 706 SW2d 757.—App & E 859, 937(1); Proc 69, 73, 153.

Garretson; Yancey v., TexCivApp–Eastland, 425 SW2d 832.—Autos 244(41.1), 244(58).

Garrett, In re, BkrtcyEDTex, 315 BR 431.—Child S 507; Fed Cts 30, 31, 34; Judgm 27.

Garrett v. American Airlines, Inc., CA5 (Tex), 332 F2d 939, 3 ALR3d 930.—Carr 280(1), 284, 318(1), 320(1), 320(6), 347; Evid 471(1); Fed Civ Proc 2142.1; Fed Cts 955.

Garrett v. Anderson, TexCivApp–San Antonio, 144 SW2d 971, writ dism, correct.—Courts 57(2); Evid 83(1).

Garrett v. Autozone, Inc., EDTex, 71 FSupp2d 617, aff 224 F3d 765.—Civil R 1217, 1218(2), 1218(3), 1218(6); Damag 50.10.

Garrett v. Bankers Life & Cas. Co., SDTex, 334 FSupp 368.—Rem of C 2, 82, 107(8).

Garrett; Benkendorfer v., TexCivApp–San Antonio, 143 SW2d 1020, writ dism, correct.—App & E 930(1), 994(3); Damag 130.2; Neglig 1614, 1620, 1695; Prod Liab 78, 84.

Garrett v. Bennett, TexCivApp–Waco, 242 SW2d 221.—Adv Poss 27, 46.1, 114(1); App & E 704.2.

Garrett; Biggs v., TexApp–El Paso, 651 SW2d 342.—Parties 76(1); Usury 9, 117, 138.

Garrett; Blanton v., Tex, 129 SW2d 623, 133 Tex 399.—Courts 99(5); Plead 111.24.

Garrett; Blanton v., TexCivApp–Eastland, 124 SW2d 451, certified question answered 129 SW2d 623, 133 Tex 399. —App & E 544(1), 562, 672; Libel 75; Plead 111.38.

Garrett; Blythe County Line Independent School Dist. v., TexCivApp–El Paso, 232 SW2d 248.—Trial 352.5(6).

Garrett v. Borden, TexApp–Amarillo, 202 SW3d 463.—Prisons 13(4), 17(3).

Garrett; Boys Town, Inc. v., TexCivApp–Waco, 283 SW2d 416, ref nre.—Adj Land 10(1); Inj 51.

Garrett; Breshears v., CA5 (Tex), 143 FedAppx 570.—Civil R 1097; Const Law 4838; Pardon 46, 57.1.

Garrett v. Brock, TexCivApp–Fort Worth, 144 SW2d 408, writ dism, correct.—App & E 207, 662(2), 972, 1052(5), 1060.4; Autos 227.5, 244(61); Damag 182; Trial 129.

Garrett v. Campbell, CA5 (Tex), 360 F2d 382.—Fed Civ Proc 2182.1, 2183; Fed Cts 630.1; Int Rev 5095.

Garrett; Cantrell v., TexCivApp–Houston, 342 SW2d 466. —App & E 704.1; Contracts 176(8); Impl & C C 100, 121; Trial 349(1), 365.4.

Garrett v. Celanese Corp., CA5 (Tex), 102 FedAppx 387. —Fed Civ Proc 851, 1838.

Garrett, Estate of v. Cherokee Water Co., CA5 (Tex), 109 FedAppx 674.—Lim of Act 95(7), 100(1).

Garrett; Christopher v., TexCivApp–Texarkana, 292 SW2d 926, ref nre.—Frds St of 129(9); Tresp to T T 45(2), 56, 59.

Garrett v. Circuit City Stores, Inc., CA5 (Tex), 449 F3d 672.—Alt Disp Res 121, 134(1), 141, 210, 213(5); Armed S 122(1), 122(2); Statut 212.1.

Garrett v. Circuit City Stores, Inc., NDTex, 338 FSupp2d 717, rev 449 F3d 672.—Alt Disp Res 114, 119, 121, 124, 134(1), 134(6), 135, 137, 139; Armed S 114(2); Contracts 137(2); Labor & Emp 47.

Garrett; City of Houston v., TexApp–Houston (14 Dist), 816 SW2d 800, writ den.—App & E 836; Work Comp 1283, 1286, 1297, 1382.

Garrett v. City of Houston, Tex., CA5 (Tex), 102 FedAppx 863.—Civil R 1395(8), 1514, 1523.

Garrett v. City of Wichita Falls, TexCivApp–Fort Worth, 334 SW2d 624.—Courts 207.1; Mand 111; Mun Corp 1037, 1038, 1040.

Garrett v. City of Wichita Falls, TexCivApp–Fort Worth, 329 SW2d 491.—App & E 1040(13), 1175(4); Mun Corp 819(3), 819(6); Plead 228.14, 236(4), 264, 404.

Garrett v. Coastal Financial Management Co., Inc., SDTex, 765 FSupp 351, rev 938 F2d 591.—Banks 77(4).

Garrett; Coats v., TexCivApp–Texarkana, 283 SW2d 289. —App & E 130; Judgm 210, 276; Mun Corp 374(4); Plead 238(4).

Garrett v. Collins, CA5 (Tex), 951 F2d 57, cert den 112 SCt 1072, 502 US 1083, 117 LEd2d 277.—Sent & Pun 1641.

Garrett v. C.I.R., CA5 (Tex), 411 F2d 615.—Int Rev 3537, 4679, 4731.

Garrett v. Commonwealth Mortg. Corp. of America, CA5 (Tex), 938 F2d 591.—Fed Civ Proc 1772, 1773, 1788, 1828; Fed Cts 763.1, 776; Rem of C 79(1), 107(9).

Garrett; Conklin v., TexApp–Tyler, 179 SW3d 676.—Autos 187(6); Judgm 185.1(4), 185.3(2); Mun Corp 745; Offic 114.

Garrett; Daugherty v., TexCivApp–San Antonio, 336 SW2d 642, writ dism woj.—App & E 863; Quiet T 38; Venue 5.3(5).

Garrett; Desdemona Gasoline Co. of Texas v., TexCivApp–Eastland, 90 SW2d 636, writ dism.—App & E 1050.1(6); Corp 432(2), 432(10), 433(1); Explos 7; Neglig 1571; Trial 350.1, 352.4(5), 352.9, 352.10.

Garrett v. Dils Co., Tex, 299 SW2d 904, 157 Tex 92.—Deeds 90, 93; Evid 20(1); Mines 55(5), 79.1(3).

Garrett; Dils Co. v., TexCivApp–Waco, 294 SW2d 730, aff 299 SW2d 904, 157 Tex 92.—Mines 55(5).

Garrett v. Downs, TexCivApp–Dallas, 377 SW2d 113.—Adv Poss 57, 112, 114(1); App & E 1175(5), 1177(7); Des & Dist 82; Hus & W 25(5); Ten in C 15(10); Tresp to T T 41(1).

Garrett; Duke v., TexCivApp–Waco, 276 SW2d 587, ref nre.—Costs 270; Mines 54(3); Ven & Pur 53, 142, 308(5), 308(7).

Garrett; Duke v., TexCivApp–Waco, 263 SW2d 680.—Accord 12(1); App & E 927(7); Covenants 134; Ref of Inst 46; Tender 16(1), 16(2); Trial 139.1(7); Ven & Pur 170.

Garrett v. Estelle, CA5 (Tex), 556 F2d 1274, reh den 560 F2d 1023, cert den 98 SCt 3142, 438 US 914, 57 LEd2d 1159.—Const Law 90.1(8), 242.1(1), 1150, 1194, 2070, 2078, 3811; Sent & Pun 1797.

Garrett v. Estelle, NDTex, 424 FSupp 468, rev 556 F2d 1274, reh den 560 F2d 1023, cert den 98 SCt 3142, 438 US 914, 57 LEd2d 1159.—Const Law 90.1(1.3), 1775, 2077, 2078, 2276; Prisons 4(6); Sent & Pun 1797.

Garrett v. F.D.I.C., NDTex, 142 FRD 438. See Peoples State Bank v. Garrett.

Garrett; First Title Co. of Waco v., Tex, 860 SW2d 74.—Antitrust 130, 221, 297; Contrib 1, 5(1), 9(6); Insurance 2610, 2637(1); Neglig 549(5); Prod Liab 2; Sales 260, 425.

Garrett; First Title Co. of Waco v., TexApp–Waco, 802 SW2d 254, writ gr, rev 860 SW2d 74.—Antitrust 162, 221, 297, 369; App & E 1056.1(3); Damag 49.10, 63, 130.1, 190; Insurance 2610, 2616, 2639; Pretrial Proc 42, 45; Trial 351.2(4).

Garrett; Furr's Super Market v., TexCivApp–El Paso, 615 SW2d 280, ref nre.—Neglig 1089, 1537; Plead 111.42(7).

Garrett v. Gardner, NDTex, 289 FSupp 829.—Social S 140.70, 143.45, 143.60, 143.75.

Garrett v. Garrett, TexApp–Tyler, 858 SW2d 639.—Divorce 395(1).

Garrett; Garrett v., TexApp–Tyler, 858 SW2d 639.—Divorce 395(1).

Garrett v. Garrett, TexCivApp–Hous (1 Dist), 534 SW2d 381.—Divorce 200, 252.3(2), 252.3(5), 253(2), 254(1), 286(2).

Garrett; Garrett v., TexCivApp–Hous (1 Dist), 534 SW2d 381.—Divorce 200, 252.3(2), 252.3(5), 253(2), 254(1), 286(2).

Garrett v. Giblin, TexApp–Beaumont, 940 SW2d 408.—Antitrust 256; Atty & C 112; Judgm 185(2).

Garrett; Glenn v., TexCivApp–Amarillo, 84 SW2d 515.—Time 9(5); Venue 8.5(3).

Garrett v. Great Western Distributing Co. of Amarillo, TexApp–Amarillo, 129 SW3d 797, review den.—App & E 863, 934(1); Corp 488; Labor & Emp 2927, 3029, 3036, 3043, 3045, 3056(1), 3056(2), 3079, 3096(2).

Garrett v. Hamilton Standard Controls, Inc., CA5 (Tex), 850 F2d 253.—Fed Cts 907, 911; Prod Liab 8, 15.

Garrett v. Hartford Acc. & Indem. Co., TexCivApp–Eastland, 107 SW2d 726.—Lim of Act 130(5); Work Comp 1832, 1874, 1880.

Garrett v. International Mill. Co., TexCivApp–Texarkana, 223 SW2d 67.—Contracts 16, 23, 24, 147(1), 147(2); Evid 265(2), 461(1); Sales 23(1), 23(3), 23(4), 52(5.1), 54.

Garrett v. John Deere Plow Co., TexCivApp–Dallas, 90 SW2d 861.—Nova 6; Sales 428.

Garrett; Kiser v., CA5 (Tex), 67 F3d 1166.—Civil R 1376(2); Fed Cts 730, 762, 769.

Garrett v. Koepke, TexCivApp–Dallas, 569 SW2d 568, ref nre.—Partners 354, 371.

Garrett; Kyles v., CA5 (Tex), 222 FedAppx 427.—Civil R 1097, 1395(7); Const Law 975; Fed Civ Proc 1838.

Garrett v. L.P. McCuistion Community Hosp., TexApp–Texarkana, 30 SW3d 653.—App & E 78(1); Health 782; Judgm 183.

Garrett v. Lynaugh, CA5 (Tex), 842 F2d 113.—Crim Law 700(9).

Garrett v. McCotter, CA5 (Tex), 807 F2d 482.—Brib 1(1), 6(4); Hab Corp 775(2).

Garrett v. Mathews, TexCivApp–Amarillo, 343 SW2d 289.—Judgm 597.

Garrett; Mayhew v., TexCivApp–Eastland, 90 SW2d 1104, writ refused.—Int Liq 25, 31(2); Mand 10.

Garrett v. Mercantile Nat. Bank at Dallas, Tex, 168 SW2d 636, 140 Tex 394.—Courts 85(1), 85(3); Statut 223.2(0.5), 223.3.

Garrett v. Mercantile Nat. Bank at Dallas, TexCivApp–El Paso, 170 SW2d 238, aff 168 SW2d 636, 140 Tex 394.—App & E 2, 627; Exceptions Bill of39(1).

Garrett; Mickle v., TexCivApp–Eastland, 110 SW2d 1235.—App & E 71(3), 100(1), 811; Inj 114(2), 132, 150, 157, 190; Int Liq 37.

Garrett; Nabelek v., TexApp–Houston (14 Dist), 94 SW3d 648, review dism woj, and reh of petition for review den.—Crim Law 641.8.

Garrett; Pan Am. Life Ins. Co. v., TexCivApp–El Paso, 199 SW2d 819, ref nre.—Insurance 1905, 1934, 1938, 2066, 2095, 2425, 3191(7), 3395, 3540; Interest 31.

Garrett; Peoples State Bank v., NDTex, 142 FRD 438.—Admin Law 229; Banks 508; Fed Civ Proc 1833; Fed Cts 13.

Garrett v. Phillips Petroleum Co., TexCivApp–Amarillo, 218 SW2d 238, dism.—Corp 665(3); Courts 8; Venue 7.5(1), 7.5(7), 21.

Garrett; Pope v., Tex, 211 SW2d 559, 147 Tex 18.—Trusts 91, 92.5, 97, 110.

Garrett; Pope v., TexCivApp–Galveston, 204 SW2d 867, rev 211 SW2d 559, 147 Tex 18.—Damag 114; Equity 39(1); Estates 1; Fed Cts 7; Impl & C C 12; Judgm 204; Torts 289; Trusts 348, 374.

Garrett v. Reno Oil Co., TexCivApp–Fort Worth, 271 SW2d 764, ref nre.—Hus & W 209(4), 260; Neglig 575; Propty 5.5; Work Comp 1072, 2101, 2144.

Garrett v. Rose, TexCivApp–Amarillo, 161 SW2d 893.—Courts 120, 168; Inj 77(1), 194.

Garrett; Russell v., TexCivApp–Fort Worth, 392 SW2d 375.—Wills 63, 66, 230, 634(1).

Garrett v. Sinclair Refining Co., TexCivApp–Fort Worth, 94 SW2d 1218, writ dism.—Neglig 383, 387, 404, 1679.

Garrett; Sledd v., TexApp–Houston (14 Dist), 123 SW3d 592.—App & E 854(1); Counties 59; Judges 36; Judgm 181(6); Offic 114.

Garrett; Southern Pac. Transp. Co. v., TexCivApp–Corpus Christi, 611 SW2d 670.—App & E 989, 1067; R R 327(9), 346(6), 348(6.1), 348(8), 348(9), 350(16.1), 351(16), 352; Trial 215, 260(8).

Garrett v. Standard Fire Ins. Co. of Hartford, Conn., TexCivApp–Beaumont, 541 SW2d 635, ref nre.—App & E 289, 294(1), 729, 970(2), 1051(1); Arson 37(1); Evid 546, 555.4(3), 555.5; Insurance 2201.

Garrett v. State, TexCrimApp, 220 SW3d 926.—Crim Law 324, 1130(2), 1162, 1173.2(5), 1177.

Garrett v. State, TexCrimApp, 851 SW2d 853, reh den.—Crim Law 1144.13(3), 1159.2(7), 1166.17; Homic 1141, 1143, 1164; Jury 108.

Garrett; State v., TexCrimApp, 824 SW2d 181.—Crim Law 1023(8).

Garrett v. State, TexCrimApp, 791 SW2d 137.—Pardon 90.

Garrett v. State, TexCrimApp, 749 SW2d 784.—Crim Law 1179, 1193; Homic 1135, 1389.

Garrett v. State, TexCrimApp, 682 SW2d 301, cert den 105 SCt 1876, 471 US 1009, 85 LEd2d 168, habeas corpus den Ex parte Garrett, 831 SW2d 304, cert den 112 SCt 1072, 502 US 1083, 117 LEd2d 277, stay vac 951 F2d 57, cert den 112 SCt 1072, 502 US 1083, 117 LEd2d 277.—Crim Law 412.2(3), 700(3), 772(2), 1038.1(2), 1038.1(4), 1038.3, 1120(1), 1144.13(3), 1159.2(7), 1159.6, 1173.2(1); Homic 843, 847, 1139, 1184, 1371, 1401, 1422; Ind & Inf 72; Jury 108; Witn 390.

Garrett v. State, TexCrimApp, 658 SW2d 592.—Crim Law 438.1.

Garrett v. State, TexCrimApp, 642 SW2d 779, on remand 656 SW2d 97, petition for discretionary review gr, aff in part, rev in part 749 SW2d 784.—Crim Law 1038.1(4), 1172.7.

Garrett v. State, TexCrimApp, 641 SW2d 232.—Crim Law 1169.1(9).

Garrett v. State, TexCrimApp, 632 SW2d 350.—Crim Law 719(1), 721(1), 721.5(1), 721.5(2), 1171.1(2.1), 1171.1(5).

Garrett v. State, TexCrimApp, 619 SW2d 172.—Assault 48; Crim Law 1158(1); Sent & Pun 2020, 2021, 2022.

Garrett v. State, TexCrimApp, 573 SW2d 543.—Homic 581, 597.

Garrett v. State, TexCrimApp, 566 SW2d 605.—Crim Law 549, 552(1), 1128(4); Prost 28.

Garrett v. State, TexCrimApp, 500 SW2d 531.—Larc 61.

Garrett v. State, TexCrimApp, 434 SW2d 142, cert den 89 SCt 1287, 394 US 949, 22 LEd2d 484.—Crim Law 867, 1166.13; Ind & Inf 137(1); Rob 30.

Garrett v. State, TexCrimApp, 400 SW2d 906.—Controlled Subs 80; Crim Law 698(1); Searches 197.

Garrett v. State, TexCrimApp, 391 SW2d 65.—Autos 316.

Garrett v. State, TexCrimApp, 387 SW2d 53.—Crim Law 1090.1(1); Double J 186; Perj 12, 15, 26(4), 33(8), 34(1).

Garrett v. State, TexCrimApp, 366 SW2d 584.—Crim Law 552(3), 560, 566; Int Liq 224, 236(7).

Garrett v. State, TexCrimApp, 352 SW2d 112, 171 TexCrim 543.—Autos 355(6); Crim Law 1092.7.

Garrett v. State, TexCrimApp, 307 SW2d 270, 165 TexCrim 328.—Crim Law 260.11(2); Weap 17(4).

Garrett v. State, TexCrimApp, 298 SW2d 945, 164 TexCrim 275.—Assault 56, 92(3).

Garrett v. State, TexCrimApp, 292 SW2d 133.—Crim Law 1094(3).

Garrett v. State, TexCrimApp, 279 SW2d 366, 161 TexCrim 556.—Autos 316, 351.1; Crim Law 1028; Statut 149, 152, 157, 158, 159, 161(1).

Garrett v. State, TexCrimApp, 262 SW2d 414, 159 TexCrim 203.—Crim Law 804(1), 885.

Garrett v. State, TexCrimApp, 262 SW2d 202.—Crim Law 1090.1(1).

Garrett v. State, TexCrimApp, 261 SW2d 574, 159 TexCrim 103.—Autos 351.1; Crim Law 1167(1).

Garrett v. State, TexCrimApp, 233 SW2d 498, 155 TexCrim 214.—Crim Law 977(1); Judges 47(1).

Garrett v. State, TexCrimApp, 228 SW2d 521, 154 TexCrim 482.—Sent & Pun 1014.

Garrett v. State, TexCrimApp, 143 SW2d 964.—Crim Law 1182.

Garrett v. State, TexCrimApp, 109 SW2d 487, 133 TexCrim 125.—Larc 62(2).

Garrett v. State, TexCrimApp, 91 SW2d 727, 129 TexCrim 616.—Crim Law 1181.5(9).

Garrett; State v., TexApp–Houston (1 Dist), 177 SW3d 652, petition for discretionary review refused (3 pets).—Arrest 71.1(5); Crim Law 394.5(4), 394.6(5), 1134(6), 1139, 1144.12, 1153(1), 1158(4); Searches 23, 24, 171, 180, 186.

Garrett v. State, TexApp–Houston (1 Dist), 834 SW2d 605, petition for discretionary review refused.—Const Law 4723; Crim Law 790.

Garrett v. State, TexApp–Houston (1 Dist), 815 SW2d 333, petition for discretionary review refused.—Crim Law 1144.8, 1158(3), 1169.1(4); Jury 33(5.15), 120; Rob 23(2).

Garrett; State v., TexApp–Houston (1 Dist), 798 SW2d 311, petition for discretionary review gr, aff 824 SW2d 181.—Controlled Subs 34, 64; Crim Law 1024(2); Ind & Inf 137(1), 142.

Garrett v. State, TexApp–Houston (1 Dist), 702 SW2d 724, petition for discretionary review refused.—Crim Law 772(5), 1172.1(3).

Garrett v. State, TexApp–Fort Worth, 161 SW3d 664, reh overr, and petition for discretionary review refused.—Controlled Subs 26, 27, 29, 81; Crim Law 1144.13(2.1), 1144.13(3), 1144.13(6), 1159.2(1), 1159.2(7), 1159.2(9), 1159.4(1), 1181.5(8), 1184(3), 1191; Ind & Inf 159(1), 159(3).

Garrett v. State, TexApp–Fort Worth, 159 SW3d 717, reh overr, and petition for discretionary review gr, aff 220 SW3d 926.—Crim Law 324, 778(2), 1038.1(1), 1038.1(5), 1172.1(1).

Garrett v. State, TexApp–Fort Worth, 639 SW2d 18, aff 658 SW2d 592.—Crim Law 338(4), 363, 364(0.5), 444, 717, 720(1), 720(6), 723(3), 726, 730(6), 730(8), 730(14), 806(2).

Garrett; State v., TexApp–Austin, 22 SW3d 650.—Arrest 63.4(2); Autos 349(2.1), 349(6); Crim Law 1139.

Garrett v. State, TexApp–Austin, 875 SW2d 444, petition for discretionary review refused.—Controlled Subs 26, 27, 30, 79; Crim Law 369.1, 369.2(1).

Garrett v. State, TexApp–San Antonio, 818 SW2d 227.—Sent & Pun 253, 260.

Garrett v. State, TexApp–San Antonio, 656 SW2d 97, petition for discretionary review gr, aff in part, rev in

part 749 SW2d 784.—Const Law 4582; Crim Law 1130(4), 1180; Homic 1135.

Garrett v. State, TexApp–San Antonio, 624 SW2d 953, rev 642 SW2d 779, on remand 656 SW2d 97, petition for discretionary review gr, aff in part, rev in part 749 SW2d 784.—Crim Law 755.5, 795(3), 1030(1), 1038.1(1), 1038.1(2), 1038.1(3.1); Homic 555, 1377, 1389, 1458, 1492.

Garrett v. State, TexApp–Texarkana, 998 SW2d 307, petition for discretionary review refused, untimely filed, habeas corpus dism 2001 WL 896926.—Const Law 947; Crim Law 338(1), 338(7), 369.1, 369.2(1), 369.2(5), 641.4(1), 641.4(2), 641.10(2), 641.13(6), 641.13(7), 662.4, 662.7, 662.65, 1077.3, 1128(2), 1130(2), 1153(1); Estop 52.10(4); Rape 51(1); Weap 4, 14.

Garrett v. State, TexApp–Texarkana, 847 SW2d 268.—App & E 946; Infants 69(1).

Garrett v. State, TexApp–Amarillo, 768 SW2d 943, petition for discretionary review gr, aff 791 SW2d 137.—Const Law 2625(1), 4838; Pardon 43, 81, 92.

Garrett v. State, TexApp–Beaumont, 721 SW2d 480.—Gaming 63(1); Hab Corp 276, 464.

Garrett v. State, TexApp–Houston (14 Dist), 625 SW2d 809.—Crim Law 37(1), 37(3), 37(8); Ind & Inf 5.

Garrett v. State, TexCivApp–Eastland, 365 SW2d 670.—App & E 773(2).

Garrett v. State of Tex., CA5 (Tex), 435 F2d 709.—Hab Corp 332.1, 827.

Garrett; Strong v., Tex, 224 SW2d 471, 148 Tex 265.—App & E 889(3); Deeds 114(1), 115; Des & Dist 75, 84; Evid 448; Hus & W 248.5, 249(2.1); Judgm 5, 586(1); Life Est 8, 23; Lim of Act 44(2), 44(6), 197(1); Ten in C 15(10).

Garrett; Strong v., TexCivApp–Texarkana, 218 SW2d 873, rev 224 SW2d 471, 148 Tex 265.—Adv Poss 27; Judgm 586(1), 953; Subrog 23(6).

Garrett v. Texas Emp. Ins. Ass'n, TexCivApp–San Antonio, 226 SW2d 663, writ refused.—Statut 263; Work Comp 9, 60, 409.

Garrett v. Thompson, TexCivApp–San Antonio, 152 SW2d 412.—App & E 773(2).

Garrett; U.S. v., CA5 (Tex), 238 F3d 293, reh and reh den 250 F3d 745, cert den 121 SCt 2523, 533 US 917, 150 LEd2d 695, cert den Keith v. US, 121 SCt 2570, 533 US 938, 150 LEd2d 734.—Crim Law 627.8(6), 700(1), 1148.

Garrett; U.S. v., CA5 (Tex), 716 F2d 257, reh den 720 F2d 1291, cert den 104 SCt 1910, 466 US 937, 80 LEd2d 459, cert den Moore v. US, 104 SCt 1910, 466 US 937, 80 LEd2d 459.—Brib 1(1); Commerce 82.6; Const Law 257.5, 4523; Crim Law 37(1), 37(6.1), 338(1), 396(2), 438.1, 569, 675, 739.1(3), 1169.5(3).

Garrett; U.S. v., CA5 (Tex), 479 F2d 598.—Int Rev 4309.

Garrett; U.S. v., CA5 (Tex), 396 F2d 489, cert den 89 SCt 374, 393 US 952, 21 LEd2d 364, reh den 89 SCt 615, 393 US 1046, 21 LEd2d 599.—Banks 502, 509.15, 509.25; Statut 241(1).

Garrett; U.S. v., SDTex, 495 FSupp 159.—Arrest 63.4(1), 63.4(2), 63.4(3), 63.4(7.1), 63.4(8), 63.4(9), 63.5(4), 63.5(6), 65; Crim Law 339.7(1), 394.1(3), 394.4(9), 394.5(2), 412(4), 412.1(3).

Garrett; U.S. Fidelity & Guaranty Co. v., TexComApp, 105 SW2d 868, 129 Tex 587.—App & E 654; Work Comp 1937.

Garrett v. Unity Common School Dist., TexCivApp–Eastland, 211 SW2d 238, ref nre.—Schools 38.

Garrett; Vanderburg v., TexCivApp–El Paso, 443 SW2d 68.—Autos 224(8).

Garrett; Vaughn v., TexCivApp–Fort Worth, 341 SW2d 667.—Judgm 205.

Garrett v. Waits Bus Lines, TexCivApp–Texarkana, 229 SW2d 381, writ refused.—Carr 305(1); Neglig 386.

Garrett v. Whalen, Tex, 470 SW2d 632.—App & E 1194(1).

GARRETT

Garrett v. Williams, TexCivApp–Eastland, 146 SW2d 456.—App & E 773(4).

Garrett Bros.; San Antonio River Authority v., TexCivApp–San Antonio, 528 SW2d 266, ref nre.—App & E 1043(6), 1050.1(11); Em Dom 2(1), 106, 143; Equity 72(1); Evid 359(5); Mun Corp 230, 724, 741.25, 742(3), 742(6), 743, 745, 745.5, 747(2); Trial 352.5(5).

Garrett Engineering Co.; Bell Pub. Co. v., TexComApp, 170 SW2d 197, 141 Tex 51.—App & E 1135; Corp 382; Libel 32, 33, 48(2), 50.5, 112(3), 123(2), 123(9), 124(4), 124(8); Trial 350.3(4), 355(2).

Garrett Engineering Co.; Bell Pub. Co. v., TexCivApp–Galveston, 154 SW2d 885, aff 170 SW2d 197, 141 Tex 51.—App & E 1064.1(2.1); Libel 112(3), 123(7), 124(8).

Garrett Engineering Co.; Bell Pub. Co. v., TexCivApp–Galveston, 146 SW2d 301, dism.—App & E 854(2); Libel 9(6), 42(2), 48(2), 75; Plead 111.42(4).

Garrett Oil Tools, Inc.; Bryan v., CA5 (Tex), 245 F2d 365.—Fed Cts 850.1.

Garrett Oil Tools, Inc.; Guiberson Corp. v., CA5 (Tex), 205 F2d 660, cert den 74 SCt 137, 346 US 886, 98 LEd 390, reh den 74 SCt 273, 346 US 917, 98 LEd 413.—Courts 96(1); Pat 26(1), 32, 36.2(3), 288(3), 288(4).

Garrett Place, Inc.; Texas Parks & Wildlife Dept. v., TexApp–Dallas, 972 SW2d 140.—App & E 916(1); Courts 32; Plead 104(1); States 112(2), 112.2(2), 112.2(6), 191.4(1), 191.6(2), 200, 208.

Garrett's Estate v. Gay, TexCivApp–Tyler, 392 SW2d 565, dism.—Plead 45, 111.18, 111.42(4); Stip 14(1); Venue 22(7).

Garrietty; Weaver v., TexCivApp–Dallas, 84 SW2d 878, writ refused.—Adv Poss 74, 78; App & E 150(1), 302(5); Divorce 167; Judgm 490(2), 707.

Garrigo v. U.S., NDTex, 296 FSupp 1110.—Int Rev 3194, 3249, 3255, 3396, 3397, 3403, 3418, 3430.1, 3439, 3460.

Garris v. Rowland, CA5 (Tex), 678 F2d 1264, cert den City of Fort Worth, Texas v. Garris, 103 SCt 143, 459 US 864, 74 LEd2d 121.—Civil R 1088(4), 1358, 1376(6), 1398, 1407, 1420, 1429; Crim Law 211(3); Fed Cts 14.1, 913.

Garrison, Ex parte, TexApp–Houston (1 Dist), 853 SW2d 784.—Child S 549; Contempt 81; Evid 590; Hab Corp 203, 529.

Garrison, Ex parte, TexApp–Waco, 47 SW3d 105, petition for discretionary review refused.—Hab Corp 271, 274, 275.1, 469, 812; Ind & Inf 41(3).

Garrison; American Nat. Ins. Co. v., TexCivApp–Eastland, 97 SW2d 534, writ dism.—App & E 931(7), 989; Insurance 2595(1), 2595(2), 2595(3).

Garrison; Antimony Products of America (APOA) v., TexApp–Corpus Christi, 818 SW2d 79. See Bernal v. Garrison.

Garrison; Bernal v., TexApp–Corpus Christi, 818 SW2d 79, reh overr, and writ den.—App & E 934(1), 1024.4; Contracts 83, 94(1), 303(4), 346(2); Costs 194.18, 194.32, 252; Labor & Emp 47, 112, 855; Plead 106(1); Trial 349(1), 350.4(4), 351.2(10), 352.1(1).

Garrison v. Bexar-Medina-Atascosa Counties Water Imp. Dist. No. 1, Tex, 407 SW2d 771.—Nav Wat 22(1).

Garrison v. Bexar-Medina-Atascosa Counties Water Imp. Dist. No. 1, TexCivApp–Austin, 404 SW2d 376, ref nre 407 SW2d 771.—Nav Wat 2, 22(1).

Garrison; Bostick v., TexCivApp–Galveston, 302 SW2d 945.—Autos 144.2(2.1).

Garrison; Boston v., Tex, 256 SW2d 67, 152 Tex 253.—Autos 144.2(2.1); Courts 247(1); Inj 1; Mand 1, 171.

Garrison v. City of Texarkana, Tex., EDTex, 910 FSupp 1196.—Civil R 1352(4), 1376(6); Consp 18; Fed Civ Proc 2466, 2491.5, 2515, 2543, 2544, 2546, 2552; Mun Corp 747(3); Offic 114.

Garrison; Corona v., Tex, 274 SW2d 541, 154 Tex 124.—Courts 247(8).

Garrison; David v., CA5 (Tex), 553 F2d 923, reh den 559 F2d 1217.—Const Law 1482, 3658(1), 3658(5); Elections 11, 12(7); Mun Corp 80.

Garrison v. Dunaway, TexCivApp–Texarkana, 440 SW2d 408.—Damag 140; Judgm 199(3.9); New Tr 68.1, 76(3).

Garrison; Eakens v., TexCivApp–Amarillo, 278 SW2d 510, ref nre.—Covenants 49, 72.1, 77.1; Inj 128(6), 130; Mun Corp 648, 697(4); Nuis 1, 5, 10, 11.

Garrison; Evans v., TexCivApp–Amarillo, 155 SW2d 659.—App & E 1056.1(1); Carr 135, 136; Evid 121(3), 377.

Garrison v. Fielding Reinsurance, Inc., TexApp–Dallas, 765 SW2d 536, writ den.—Insurance 1822, 2278(5).

Garrison v. Garrison, TexCivApp–Austin, 544 SW2d 797, ref nre.—Child C 610; Contempt 66(1); Divorce 252.3(1), 261, 269(14), 286(1); Hab Corp 528.1.

Garrison; Garrison v., TexCivApp–Austin, 544 SW2d 797, ref nre.—Child C 610; Contempt 66(1); Divorce 252.3(1), 261, 269(14), 286(1); Hab Corp 528.1.

Garrison v. Garrison, TexCivApp–Beaumont, 568 SW2d 709.—Divorce 83, 143(1), 192; Jury 25(1), 31, 31.2(6).

Garrison; Garrison v., TexCivApp–Beaumont, 568 SW2d 709.—Divorce 83, 143(1), 192; Jury 25(1), 31, 31.2(6).

Garrison v. Gulf Bowl, Inc., TexCivApp–Corpus Christi, 582 SW2d 603.—App & E 205, 544(1), 554(3), 569(3), 907(3).

Garrison; Hernandez v., CA5 (Tex), 916 F2d 291, reh den 928 F2d 403.—Hab Corp 231, 688, 847; Pardon 48.1; Sent & Pun 15, 17(1).

Garrison; Howze v., TexCivApp–Waco, 363 SW2d 381, writ refused.—Autos 144.1(4).

Garrison; Manville v., TexCivApp–Hous (14 Dist), 538 SW2d 819, ref nre.—App & E 164.

Garrison v. Mead, TexCivApp–Hous (1 Dist), 553 SW2d 25.—Courts 207.1, 207.4(2), 207.5; Divorce 83, 156, 249.1.

Garrison; Minnock v., TexCivApp–Waco, 144 SW2d 328.—App & E 66, 78(4); Judgm 217; Partit 51.

Garrison v. Morrow, TexCivApp–Beaumont, 300 SW2d 175, dism.—Decl Judgm 271; Land & Ten 70; Plead 8(1), 111.3, 111.38; Venue 5.3(8), 7.5(6).

Garrison; Northwest Bank v., TexApp–Houston (1 Dist), 874 SW2d 278.—App & E 946, 954(1); Inj 138.18; Mtg 413.

Garrison; Petroleum Cas. Co. v., TexCivApp–Beaumont, 174 SW2d 74, writ refused wom.—App & E 5; Work Comp 853, 1269, 1279, 1283, 1683, 1954, 1960.

Garrison; Prince v., TexCivApp–Eastland, 248 SW2d 241.—Autos 144.2(2.1).

Garrison v. Smith, TexCivApp–Fort Worth, 306 SW2d 244.—Autos 139, 144.2(3), 144.2(4); Judgm 18(1).

Garrison; Smith v., TexCivApp–Austin, 303 SW2d 506.—Decl Judgm 213.1.

Garrison v. State, TexCrimApp, 726 SW2d 134.—Arrest 63.4(11), 63.4(18); Crim Law 800(1), 1172.1(3), 1181.5(7).

Garrison v. State, TexCrimApp, 642 SW2d 168.—Crim Law 351(2), 412.1(3), 414.

Garrison v. State, TexCrimApp, 528 SW2d 837.—Crim Law 722.3, 726, 1037.1(1).

Garrison v. State, TexCrimApp, 517 SW2d 553.—Crim Law 1087.1(2).

Garrison v. State, TexCrimApp, 158 SW2d 815, 143 TexCrim 403.—Assault 96(7); Crim Law 842, 1043(2); Homic 731, 1205.

Garrison v. State, TexCrimApp, 114 SW2d 557, 134 TexCrim 159.—Autos 354, 355(6), 356; Crim Law 814(17).

Garrison v. State, TexCrimApp, 84 SW2d 477, 129 TexCrim 32.—Crim Law 404.70, 663, 723(1), 730(14), 782(1), 787(1).

Garrison v. State, TexApp–Houston (14 Dist, 744 SW2d 224. See Martinez v. State.

Garrison v. Tenneco Chemicals, Inc., TexCivApp–Hous (14 Dist), 612 SW2d 708.—Plead 111.17, 111.42(7); Venue 8.5(5).

Garrison v. Texas Commerce Bank, TexCivApp–Hous (1 Dist), 560 SW2d 451, ref nre.—Action 60; App & E 1172(3); Divorce 83, 249.1, 322; Judgm 216, 217, 345; Marriage 63; Trial 3(1); Wills 229.

Garrison; Texas Dept. of Transp. v., TexApp–Beaumont, 121 SW3d 808.—Autos 259, 277.1, 279; States 112.1(1), 191.4(1).

Garrison v. U.S., CA5 (Tex), 524 F2d 920.—Crim Law 1655(1).

Garrison Contractors, Inc.; Liberty Mut. Ins. Co. v., Tex, 966 SW2d 482.—Insurance 1560, 3415; Judgm 181(23); Statut 181(1), 188, 208, 212.4, 217.2.

Garrison Contractors, Inc. v. Liberty Mut. Ins. Co., TexApp–El Paso, 927 SW2d 296, reh overr, and writ gr, aff 966 SW2d 482.—Antitrust 161, 221; App & E 863; Contracts 97(2); Courts 97(1); Fraud 7; Insurance 1563, 1564, 1654, 1866, 1867; Judgm 185(6), 185.3(12); Statut 188, 190.

Garrison Independent School Dist. v. McDuffie, TexCivApp–Tyler, 414 SW2d 492, ref nre.—Schools 80(1), 95(1), 95(2), 100.

Garrison I.S.D.; Frazier v., CA5 (Tex), 980 F2d 1514.—Civil R 1138, 1140, 1142, 1536, 1544, 1545, 1546; Const Law 3867, 3869, 3894, 4156, 4198; Fed Civ Proc 8.1, 2461; Fed Cts 714, 776, 813; Lim of Act 95(15).

Garrison Tool & Die, Ltd.; Elk River, Inc. v., TexApp–Dallas, 222 SW3d 772, reh overr.—App & E 714(5), 893(1), 1010.1(8.1), 1071.2; Const Law 3964, 3965(4); Corp 665(1); Courts 12(2.1), 12(2.5), 12(2.10), 12(2.25), 15, 35, 39; Princ & A 1.

Garrity v. Holiday Inns, Inc., TexApp–Amarillo, 664 SW2d 854, ref nre.—App & E 621(1), 624, 627.2, 628(2).

Garrity v. Home Indem. Co. of New York, CCA5 (Tex), 84 F2d 484.—Work Comp 1335, 1683.

Garrod Investments, Inc. v. Schlegel, TexApp–Corpus Christi, 139 SW3d 759.—App & E 856(1), 863, 901, 945, 946, 984(5); Contracts 24, 29; Costs 194.18, 208; Frds St of 113(2), 113(3), 115.1, 119(1); Judgm 183, 185(5); Spec Perf 133, 134; Trial 6(1); Ven & Pur 75.

Garrow, MacClain & Garrow v. Bass, CCA5 (Tex), 88 F2d 574, cert den 58 SCt 15, 302 US 697, 82 LEd 538.—Exceptions Bill of22; Fed Cts 701.1, 722; Int Rev 4135, 4560, 4733, 4984, 5068.

Garry; Traders & General Ins. Co. v., Tex, 143 SW2d 370, 135 Tex 290.—Work Comp 1167, 1958.

Garry; Traders & General Ins. Co. v., TexCivApp–Beaumont, 118 SW2d 340, aff 143 SW2d 370, 135 Tex 290.—App & E 901, 1062.1; Damag 221(3), 221(5.1); Trial 352.19; Work Comp 1842, 1926, 1929, 1968(3), 2171.

Garson v. Barnhart, CA5 (Tex), 162 FedAppx 301.—Social S 142.5, 143.85.

Garson; Hall v., CA5 (Tex), 468 F2d 845.—Const Law 4417; Land & Ten 241.

Garson; Hall v., CA5 (Tex), 430 F2d 430, appeal after remand 468 F2d 845.—Civil R 1318, 1325, 1326(9), 1395(3); Const Law 3020; Fed Cts 47.1, 222, 223, 333, 743, 1002.

Gar-Tex Const. Co. v. Employers Cas. Co., TexApp–Dallas, 771 SW2d 639, writ den.—Insurance 2278(23).

Garth, Ex parte, TexCrimApp, 103 SW2d 759, 132 Tex-Crim 194.—Autos 316.

Garth, In re, TexApp–Beaumont, 214 SW3d 190.—App & E 907(1); Consp 18; Courts 91(1); Plead 34(3); Pretrial Proc 19, 375, 388.

Garth; Klein v., TexApp–Tyler, 677 SW2d 712, ref nre.—Mtg 369(7), 369(8).

Garth v. Staktek Corp., TexApp–Austin, 876 SW2d 545, reh overr, and writ dism woj.—Antitrust 414, 416, 420; App & E 946, 954(1); Const Law 90.1(1), 1526, 1527, 1600; Inj 7, 9, 56, 113, 138.6, 138.18, 138.33, 158; States 18.84.

Garth v. State, TexApp–Dallas, 3 SW3d 218.—Ind & Inf 101; Offic 121, 122.

Garth; U.S. v., CA5 (Tex), 773 F2d 1469, cert den 106 SCt 2246, 476 US 1140, 90 LEd2d 693.—Const Law 1117(1), 3064, 3070; Crim Law 37.10(1), 37.10(2), 409(6.1), 534(1), 1030(1), 1128(4); Judgm 648; Sec Tran 168.5.

Garth Co. v. Jefferson County, TexCivApp–Beaumont, 587 SW2d 64.—Counties 122(1); Judgm 185(2).

Gartin v. Furgeson, TexCivApp–Amarillo, 144 SW2d 1114.—Judgm 853(3), 866.1.

Gartman v. City of McAllen, TexComApp, 107 SW2d 879, 130 Tex 237.—Mun Corp 747(4).

Gartman; City of McAllen v., TexCivApp–San Antonio, 81 SW2d 147, aff 107 SW2d 879, 130 Tex 237.—Char 45(2); Mun Corp 734.

Gartman; Dezendorf Marble Co. v., Tex, 343 SW2d 441, 161 Tex 535.—Explos 8; Trial 350.5(2), 350.6(5).

Gartman; Dezendorf Marble Co. v., TexCivApp–Austin, 333 SW2d 404, writ gr, aff 343 SW2d 441, 161 Tex 535.—App & E 927(7), 989; Evid 5(2), 14; Explos 8; Neglig 1067.

Gartman; Hedgpeth v., Tex, 135 SW2d 86, 134 Tex 260.—Courts 247(5).

Gartman v. Hedgpeth, TexComApp, 157 SW2d 139, 138 Tex 73, 138 ALR 666.—Libel 15, 19, 41, 86(1), 86(4), 97; Plead 214(1).

Gartman; Hedgpeth v., TexCivApp–Waco, 136 SW2d 641, certificate dism 135 SW2d 86, 134 Tex 260, rev 157 SW2d 139, 138 Tex 73, 138 ALR 666.—Libel 19, 80, 81, 86(1); Plead 214(1).

Gartman; Worth Steel Corp. v., TexCivApp–Fort Worth, 361 SW2d 426, ref nre.—App & E 218.2(9), 302(1), 931(4), 989; Labor & Emp 2785, 2830, 2881; Neglig 1617; New Tr 155; Trial 351.2(2).

Gartner, In re, BkrtcySDTex, 326 BR 357.—Bankr 2322, 3022, 3251, 3271, 3274, 3278.1, 3279, 3282.1, 3284, 3315(2).

Gartner v. Board of Adjustment of City of San Antonio, TexCivApp–San Antonio, 324 SW2d 454, ref nre.—Zoning 212, 384.1, 507.

Garton; Big State Pawn and Bargain Center No. 1 v., TexApp–Eastland, 833 SW2d 669, reh den and writ den.—App & E 931(1); Cert 15; J P 196(1), 196(2); Land & Ten 179.

Garton; Parkem Indus. Services, Inc. v., TexCivApp–Amarillo, 619 SW2d 428.—App & E 989; Inj 11, 14, 61(2), 128(5.1), 130.

Garton v. Rockett, TexApp–Houston (1 Dist), 190 SW3d 139, reh overr.—Wills 206, 302(8), 324(1), 412.1.

Gartrell v. Gaylor, CA5 (Tex), 981 F2d 254.—Civil R 1319, 1379; Fed Civ Proc 2734; Fed Cts 425, 427; Lim of Act 58(1), 75.

Gartrell v. Gaylor, SDTex, 866 FSupp 325, aff 66 F3d 322.—Civil R 1090, 1397; Fed Cts 425, 427; Lim of Act 58(1), 104.5, 105(1); Prisons 13(7.1).

Gartrell v. Lynaugh, CA5 (Tex), 833 F2d 527.—Hab Corp 383.

Garver v. First Nat. Bank of Canadian, TexCivApp–Amarillo, 432 SW2d 745, ref nre.—App & E 854(1); Estop 90(3), 119; Partners 120, 138, 216(2), 217(1); Plead 290(3).

Garver v. First Nat. Bank of Canadian, TexCivApp–Amarillo, 406 SW2d 797, ref nre, appeal after remand 432 SW2d 745, ref nre.—App & E 78(1), 837(4); Plead 228.23, 354, 360; Pretrial Proc 674, 692, 695.

Garver v. State, TexCrimApp, 258 SW2d 812, 158 Tex-Crim 585.—Burg 41(1); Crim Law 530, 780(3), 792(1), 844(1), 925.5(3), 956(13).

Garvey, Ex parte, TexCrimApp, 112 SW2d 747, 133 Tex-Crim 560.—Bail 47; Extrad 30.

Garvey; Ham v., TexCivApp–San Antonio, 155 SW2d 976.—Counties 58, 165.

Garvey v. Vawter, Tex, 795 SW2d 741, on remand 805 SW2d 601.—Autos 238(8); Plead 48.

Garvey; Vawter v., Tex, 786 SW2d 263, on remand 790 SW2d 403, writ gr, rev 795 SW2d 741, on remand 805 SW2d 601.—App & E 169, 719(1), 758.1.

Garvey v. Vawter, TexApp–Beaumont, 805 SW2d 601.— Autos 192(1); Judgm 181(33).

Garvey v. Vawter, TexApp–Beaumont, 790 SW2d 403, writ gr, rev 795 SW2d 741, on remand 805 SW2d 601.— App & E 758.1; Judgm 181(33).

Garvey v. Vawter, TexApp–Beaumont, 774 SW2d 86, writ gr, rev 786 SW2d 263, on remand 790 SW2d 403, writ gr, rev 795 SW2d 741, on remand 805 SW2d 601.— Autos 201(9); Judgm 181(11), 181(33); Neglig 213, 387, 431; Plead 228.14.

Garvey v. Wood, TexCivApp–San Antonio, 101 SW2d 288. —App & E 712; Mand 187.4; Sheriffs 29; Statut 47, 76(4), 125(6).

Garvey Elevators, Inc.; City of Saginaw v., TexCivApp– Fort Worth, 431 SW2d 575, ref nre.—Mun Corp 972(3), 979.

Garvey Elevators, Inc. v. Eagle Mountain-Saginaw Independent School Dist., TexCivApp–Fort Worth, 423 SW2d 455.—Tax 2514, 2681, 2695, 2855.

Garvey Elevators, Inc.; St. Louis Southwestern Ry. Co. v., CA5 (Tex), 505 F2d 625.—Carr 188; Cust & U 12(1).

Garvie v. Duo-Fast Corp., CA5 (Tex), 711 F2d 47.—Lim of Act 47(1), 49(7).

Garvie; Rawdon v., TexCivApp–Dallas, 227 SW2d 261, ref nre.—Const Law 4001; Fraud 12, 28, 32, 35, 50; Ven & Pur 349.

Garvin v. Goldsmith, TexCivApp–Waco, 406 SW2d 545, ref nre.—App & E 877(4), 931(4); Fraud 13(2), 58(1), 58(4); Trial 365.1(4), 366.

Garvin; Hitchcock v., TexApp–Dallas, 738 SW2d 34.— Judgm 181(33), 185.2(4); Schools 89.13(4).

Garvin v. Hudson, TexCivApp–Texarkana, 353 SW2d 508, ref nre.—Deeds 120, 137, 141.

Garvin v. Hufft, TexCivApp–Dallas, 243 SW2d 391, ref nre.—App & E 300, 387(2), 468, 485(1); Child C 7, 42, 76, 409, 473, 904; New Tr 116.2, 155.

Garvin; Nesbitt v., TexCivApp–Texarkana, 308 SW2d 86. —Adv Poss 114(1); Tresp to T T 38(2).

Garwood v. Locke, TexCivApp–San Antonio, 552 SW2d 892, ref nre.—Health 813.

Garwood Irr. Co. v. Lower Colorado River Authority, TexCivApp–Austin, 387 SW2d 746, ref nre.—Costs 194.25; Waters 156(1), 158.5(1), 249.

Garwood Irr. Co. v. Lundquist, TexCivApp–Galveston, 252 SW2d 759, writ refused.—Decl Judgm 143.1.

Garwood Irr. Co. v. Williams, TexCivApp–Galveston, 243 SW2d 453, ref nre.—Waters 232.1, 263.

Gary, Ex parte, TexApp–Amarillo, 895 SW2d 465, reh overr, and petition for discretionary review refused.— Double J 132.1, 186; Hab Corp 466.

Gary v. Gary, TexApp–El Paso, 631 SW2d 781, writ dism woj.—App & E 846(5); Child C 555, 632, 637, 923(4); Divorce 222.

Gary; Gary v., TexApp–El Paso, 631 SW2d 781, writ dism woj.—App & E 846(5); Child C 555, 632, 637, 923(4); Divorce 222.

Gary v. Gary, TexCivApp–Tyler, 490 SW2d 929, ref nre. —App & E 930(3), 989, 1177(7); Marriage 13, 20(2), 22, 40(3), 50(1), 50(4).

Gary; Gary v., TexCivApp–Tyler, 490 SW2d 929, ref nre. —App & E 930(3), 989, 1177(7); Marriage 13, 20(2), 22, 40(3), 50(1), 50(4).

Gary; Hand v., CA5 (Tex), 838 F2d 1420.—Arrest 58; Civil R 1088(4), 1088(5), 1339; Const Law 3845, 3850, 3873, 3896, 4536; Mal Pros 24(7), 48, 56; Searches 23.

Gary; Henwood v., TexCivApp–Fort Worth, 196 SW2d 958, ref nre.—Labor & Emp 2862; Trial 350.6(6), 352.1(1).

Gary; Jefferson County Drainage Dist. No. 6 v., Tex, 362 SW2d 305.—Const Law 2474; Em Dom 76.

Gary; Louisiana & Arkansas Ry. Co. v., TexApp–Texarkana, 780 SW2d 413, writ den.—App & E 1001(1), 1001(3); Courts 97(1); Labor & Emp 2941.

Gary; Plemmons v., TexCivApp–Beaumont, 321 SW2d 625.—Neglig 372, 421, 1750.

Gary; Port Arthur Independent School Dist. v., TexCivApp–Beaumont, 364 SW2d 446, mandamus overr.—App & E 447.

Gary v. State, TexCrimApp, 647 SW2d 646.—Searches 66.

Gary v. State, TexCrimApp, 379 SW2d 661.—Crim Law 511.1(9).

Gary v. State, TexCrimApp, 201 SW2d 820, 150 TexCrim 397.—Crim Law 379; Ind & Inf 7, 125(3); Larc 30(8), 37, 61.

Gary v. State, TexApp–Austin, 880 SW2d 485, reh overr, and petition for discretionary review refused.—Crim Law 90(1), 260.7, 260.11(1), 260.11(2), 260.11(6), 1023(16), 1042; Sent & Pun 2086.

Gary v. State, TexApp–Waco, 195 SW3d 339.—Crim Law 769, 778(5), 1032(5), 1038.1(2), 1134(2); Obst Just 3.

Gary; State ex rel. Dishman v., Tex, 359 SW2d 456, 163 Tex 565.—Mand 53; Offic 74; Pretrial Proc 501, 520; Sheriffs 6.

Gary; Terrell v., CCA5 (Tex), 98 F2d 14.—Courts 493(2), 500, 508(2.1); Fed Cts 433; Mines 92.44(3).

Gary v. Vick, TexCivApp–El Paso, 203 SW2d 869.—Child C 76, 557(2); Courts 117; Hab Corp 532(1); Judgm 270.

Gary Aircraft Corp., In re, BkrtcyWDTex, 92 BR 1023.— Bankr 3776.5(1).

Gary Aircraft Corp., Matter of, CA5 (Tex), 698 F2d 775, cert den Gary Aircraft Corporation v. US, 104 SCt 82, 464 US 820, 78 LEd2d 92.—Bankr 2060.1; U S 73(9).

Gary Aircraft Corp., Matter of, CA5 (Tex), 681 F2d 365, cert den General Dynamics Corporation v. Gary Aircraft Corporation, 103 SCt 3110, 462 US 1131, 77 LEd2d 1366.—Bankr 2927; Sec Tran 141, 149; States 18.3, 18.7, 18.11, 18.17.

Gary Aircraft Corp.; N.L.R.B. v., CA5 (Tex), 468 F2d 562.—Labor & Emp 1439, 1491.

Gary Aircraft Corp.; N.L.R.B. v., CA5 (Tex), 368 F2d 223, cert den 87 SCt 2032, 387 US 918, 18 LEd2d 971.— Labor & Emp 1743(1).

Gary Aircraft Corp. v. U. S., WDTex, 342 FSupp 473.— Inj 114(2); U S 64.5, 64.60(3.1).

Gary Carlton Camp v. State, TexApp–Tyler, 925 SW2d 26, petition for discretionary review refused.—Assault 92(3); Crim Law 369.1, 369.2(1), 371(1), 371(12), 1153(1), 1169.5(3); Ind & Inf 164, 166.

Gary Greene Co.; Corporation R, Inc. v., TexCivApp– Hous (14 Dist), 476 SW2d 921.—Contracts 326; Corp 503(1); Plead 111.3, 111.42(4).

Gary-Nees Lumber Co.; Bryant v., TexCivApp–Fort Worth, 374 SW2d 336.—App & E 1056.1(4.1), 1062.2; Bound 46(1); Tresp to T T 41(2); Ven & Pur 245.

Gary Pools, Inc. v. Associated Pools, Inc., CA5 (Tex), 340 F2d 585.—Fed Civ Proc 1938.1; Pat 7.3, 311.

Gary Pools, Inc.; Salinas v., TexApp–San Antonio, 31 SW3d 333.—App & E 934(1); Judgm 181(7), 185(2); Lim of Act 43, 95(1), 95(3), 95(16), 100(1), 104(1); Notice 5.

Gary Safe Co. v. A. C. Andrews Co., Inc., TexCivApp– Dallas, 568 SW2d 166, ref nre.—Contracts 47; Princ & A 81(4); Trial 398.

Gary Safe Co. v. Transport Ins. Co., TexCivApp–Hous (14 Dist), 525 SW2d 64.—Insurance 2660, 2681.

Garza, Ex parte, TexApp–Texarkana, 115 SW3d 123.— Double J 105, 132.1, 135, 182.

Garza, Ex parte, TexApp–Corpus Christi, 192 SW3d 658, reh overr.—Crim Law 641.13(5), 1026.10(4); Hab Corp 292, 486(3), 705.1; Sent & Pun 500, 2032, 2037.

Garza, Ex parte, TexCivApp–Amarillo, 593 SW2d 114.— Child S 474; Const Law 4494, 4495; Contempt 40, 61(1).

Garza, In re, CA5 (Tex), 253 F3d 201.—Courts 100(1).

Garza, In re, CA5 (Tex), 222 FedAppx 350.—Bankr 2902, 2903.

Garza, In re, BkrtcyNDTex, 217 BR 197.—Bankr 3341, 3347.1, 3348.5, 3348.10, 3349, 3355(2.1), 3356, 3420(1); Judgm 828.21(2).

Garza, In re, TexApp–San Antonio, 153 SW3d 97, reh overr.—Child C 906, 943; Child S 541; Const Law 2314; Divorce 228, 252.2, 252.5(1), 254(1), 254(2), 284; Mand 4(1), 4(4), 12, 28.

Garza, In re, TexApp–San Antonio, 126 SW3d 268, mandamus den.—App & E 154(4); Contempt 21; Hab Corp 528.1; Inj 138.3, 148(1), 157, 219; Mand 3(1), 3(2.1), 12; Motions 62.

Garza, In re, TexApp–San Antonio, 981 SW2d 438.—Child C 601; Courts 40, 475(15); Divorce 86; Mand 4(1), 26, 28.

Garza, In re, TexApp–Amarillo, 984 SW2d 344.—Autos 355(10); Infants 250, 252.

Garza, In re, TexApp–Corpus Christi, 990 SW2d 372.—J P 166(5), 166(6), 170.1, 175; Mand 12, 28, 53.

Garza; Aetna Cas. & Sur. Co. v., TexApp–San Antonio, 906 SW2d 543, reh den, and writ dism by agreement.—Antitrust 221, 393; App & E 930(3), 1001(3); Damag 91(1); Insurance 1654, 1867, 2166(3), 3336, 3347, 3353, 3359, 3360, 3361, 3363, 3376, 3381(3), 3419; Interest 39(2.50); Statut 279.

Garza; Allan v., TexCivApp–San Antonio, 194 SW2d 814.—Venue 8.5(6).

Garza; Allied Finance Co. v., TexApp–Corpus Christi, 626 SW2d 120, ref nre.—App & E 930(3), 961, 989, 1024.1; Bills & N 534; Cons Cred 64.1, 67; Costs 194.18; Courts 30, 169(4); Pretrial Proc 313.

Garza v. Allied Finance Co., TexCivApp–Corpus Christi, 566 SW2d 57, also published at 1978 WL 388487, appeal after remand 626 SW2d 120, ref nre.—Bills & N 484; Cons Cred 16, 67; Judgm 185.1(3), 185.2(3), 185.2(4), 185.3(16), 186; Lim of Act 41, 129; Mtg 218.1; Sec Tran 221, 226, 228.

Garza v. Alviar, Tex, 395 SW2d 821.—App & E 302(5), 362(1), 768, 930(3), 989, 1001(1), 1083(6), 1094(1), 1122(2), 1175(5), 1177(7); Judgm 199(3.10); Trial 350.1.

Garza; Alviar v., TexCivApp–Eastland, 387 SW2d 905, writ gr, rev 395 SW2d 821.—Autos 244(55), 245(90); Mun Corp 120.

Garza; Amerada Hess Corp. v., TexApp–Corpus Christi, 973 SW2d 667, appeal dism Coastal Corp v. Garza, 979 SW2d 318, reh overr.—Action 13; App & E 174, 931(1), 946, 949; Nuis 3(3), 50(1), 50(2); Parties 35.1, 35.9, 35.13, 35.17, 35.31, 35.35, 35.41, 35.49, 35.79.

Garza v. American Mut. Liability Ins. Co., TexCivApp–San Antonio, 467 SW2d 488.—Work Comp 323, 350, 357.

Garza; American States Ins. Co. v., TexApp–Corpus Christi, 657 SW2d 522.—Trial 350.3(8); Work Comp 76, 77, 79, 1728.

Garza; A.M.I. Riverside Hosp. v., TexApp–Corpus Christi, 894 SW2d 850. See Riverside Hosp., Inc. v. Garza.

Garza; Anderson v., TexCivApp–Austin, 311 SW2d 910, ref nre.—App & E 761; Autos 206, 211, 244(37), 244(40), 244(58), 245(50.1), 247; Damag 130.2, 185(1); Trial 365.3.

Garza v. Anderson, TexCivApp–Corpus Christi, 417 SW2d 368.—App & E 758.3(9), 930(1), 930(3), 989, 994(2), 996, 1001(1), 1002, 1170.7; Autos 243(5), 243(7), 244(11); Evid 587; Plead 87; Trial 142, 352.4(7).

Garza; Apex Financial Corp. v., TexApp–Dallas, 155 SW3d 230, review den.—Ack 6(2); App & E 232(2), 984(5); Costs 194.40, 207; Deeds 37.1, 38(1), 82; Execution 264, 272(2), 285, 286, 303, 319; Frds St of 110(1), 118(2); Liens 12; Ven & Pur 231(17), 232(1), 232(2).

Garza; Aquaslide 'N' Dive Corp. v., CA5 (Tex), 737 F2d 1395. See National Maritime Union v. Aquaslide 'N' Dive Corp.

Garza v. Arizona Refining Co., SDTex, 634 FSupp 959.—Contrib 9(1), 9(5); Indem 81, 91, 97.

Garza v. Attorney General, TexApp–Corpus Christi, 166 SW3d 799.—App & E 842(2), 852, 893(1), 931(1), 935(1), 945, 946, 982(1), 982(2), 989, 1008.1(1), 1008.1(2), 1008.1(3), 1008.1(4), 1010.1(1), 1012.1(3), 1012.1(4), 1012.1(5), 1071.2, 1073(2); Child 39, 64, 72.1; Equity 87(2); Judgm 17(9), 138(2), 138(3), 162(2), 163, 335(1), 335(2), 335(3), 335(4); Proc 148, 149.

Garza v. Bancorp Group, Inc., SDTex, 955 FSupp 68.—Antitrust 212, 213, 291; Fed Civ Proc 621, 671, 2539.

Garza; Barrientos v., TexCivApp–Dallas, 559 SW2d 399.—Child C 101, 284.

Garza; Bazan v., TexCivApp–San Antonio, 352 SW2d 792.—Plead 111.17, 111.42(7).

Garza; Ben Griffin Tractor Co. v., TexCivApp–Fort Worth, 497 SW2d 69.—Corp 503(2).

Garza v. Berlanga, TexCivApp–San Antonio, 575 SW2d 639.—App & E 621(1), 624.

Garza v. Berlanga, TexCivApp–El Paso, 598 SW2d 377, ref nre.—App & E 231(7), 232(2), 1170.7; Evid 547, 555.9; Health 823(5), 823(11).

Garza; B-F-W Const. Co., Inc. v., TexApp–Fort Worth, 748 SW2d 611.—Indem 30(1), 30(5).

Garza v. Blanton, TexApp–Corpus Christi, 55 SW3d 708.—App & E 941, 945, 946.

Garza v. Block Distributing Co., Inc., TexApp–San Antonio, 696 SW2d 259.—Tax 2695, 2697.

Garza v. Brazos County Federal Credit Union, TexCivApp–Waco, 603 SW2d 298.—App & E 1178(6); Sec Tran 230, 243.

Garza v. Brownsville Independent School Dist., CA5 (Tex), 700 F2d 253.—Civil R 1560, 1562.

Garza; Castellano v., TexApp–San Antonio, 110 SW3d 70.—App & E 893(1), 946, 1008.1(1); Health 804, 809, 819.

Garza v. Cavazos, Tex, 221 SW2d 549, 148 Tex 138.—Judgm 668(1), 682(1), 686, 720, 747(2); Partit 95, 116(1); Remaind 17(2); Stip 18(7); Wills 430, 435, 721.

Garza v. Cavazos, TexApp–San Antonio, 213 SW2d 758, aff in part, rev in part 221 SW2d 549, 148 Tex 138.—App & E 172(3); Partit 95, 116(1); Wills 421.

Garza v. C-G-R, Inc., TexApp–San Antonio, 523 SW2d 59, ref nre.—Corp 82.

Garza v. Chavarria, TexApp–El Paso, 155 SW3d 252.—Antitrust 393; App & E 782, 1166; Courts 30, 35, 39, 169(4), 170; J P 42, 44(8), 141(2), 141(4), 183(1); Plead 104(1).

Garza; Citgo Refining and Marketing, Inc. v., TexApp–Corpus Christi, 187 SW3d 45, on reh, and petition for review abated (2 pets).—App & E 187(1), 837(1), 913, 949, 1071.2, 1097(1), 1149, 1178(6); Compromise 2, 6(2), 56.1, 61; Courts 97(1); Estop 52.10(3), 92(1); Nuis 4; Parties 35.1, 35.5, 35.7, 35.11, 35.13, 35.17, 35.33, 35.35, 35.49, 35.79.

Garza; Citgo Refining And Marketing, Inc. v., TexApp–Corpus Christi, 94 SW3d 322.—App & E 68, 70(1), 76(1); Compromise 21; Judgm 72, 217.

Garza; City of Austin v., TexApp–Austin, 124 SW3d 867.—App & E 984(5); Const Law 2442; Costs 194.12; Estop 62.4; Zoning 8, 376.

Garza v. City of La Joya, TexCivApp–Corpus Christi, 524 SW2d 818.—App & E 624, 627.2.

Garza; City of McAllen v., TexApp–Corpus Christi, 869 SW2d 558, reh overr, and writ den.—App & E 927(2); Courts 2, 32; Decl Judgm 96; Inj 80.

Garza v. City of Mission, TexApp–Corpus Christi, 684 SW2d 148, dism.—App & E 846(5), 900, 920(3), 946, 954(1); Inj 135, 138.1, 138.69, 140, 151; Offic 72.62.

Garza v. City of Robstown, TexCivApp–Corpus Christi, 483 SW2d 32.—Courts 206(17.3); Elections 269; Mun Corp 80, 918(1), 918(5), 920.

Garza; Claymex Brick and Tile, Inc. v., TexApp–San Antonio, 216 SW3d 33, reh overr.—Civil R 1204, 1209, 1744.

GARZA;

59 Tex D 2d—204

See Guidelines for Arrangement at the beginning of this Volume

Garza; Coastal Corp. v., Tex, 979 SW2d 318, reh overr.—Courts 247(7).

Garza v. Cole, TexApp–Houston (14 Dist), 753 SW2d 245, ref nre.—App & E 970(1); Evid 150, 359(6); Trial 41(5).

Garza v. Commercial Ins. Co. of Newark, N. J., TexCiv-App–Amarillo, 508 SW2d 701.—Work Comp 1410, 1637, 1638, 1927, 1969.

Garza v. Conner, CA5 (Tex), 101 FedAppx 973.—Sent & Pun 635, 1175.

Garza; Cooper v., CA5 (Tex), 431 F2d 578.—Fed Cts 743; Sec Reg 60.52.

Garza; Cotham v., SDTex, 905 FSupp 389.—Const Law 90.1(4), 1461, 1466, 1680, 1688, 1692, 1693, 1733, 1735, 3068, 4230, 4232; Elections 1, 24; Statut 47.

Garza; County of El Paso, Tex. v., WDTex, 904 FSupp 1429. See Lightbourn v. County of El Paso, Tex.

Garza; Crandell v., TexCivApp–San Antonio, 265 SW2d 846, ref nre.—Adv Poss 19, 22, 68, 115(5).

Garza v. Dare, TexCivApp–Corpus Christi, 475 SW2d 340. —App & E 863; Elections 280, 285(1); Judgm 185(2), 185(6); Mun Corp 989, 993(3), 1000(4).

Garza v. Deaf Smith County, NDTex, 604 FSupp 46.—Civil R 1138, 1535, 1536, 1544, 1545.

Garza v. De Leon, TexCivApp–Waco, 193 SW2d 844.—App & E 882(9), 1054(1); Plead 11, 228.15; Trusts 89(1), 371(6), 372(3); Witn 130.

Garza v. De Montalvo, Tex, 217 SW2d 988, 147 Tex 525.—Evid 448; Mines 48, 74(5), 79.1(3), 79.1(5); Partit 4, 8, 9(1).

Garza v. De Montalvo, TexCivApp–San Antonio, 213 SW2d 762, rev 217 SW2d 988, 147 Tex 525.—Estop 22(1); Evid 336(1); Mines 62.1, 70(1), 79.1(5), 79.3, 79.7; Partit 9(1), 116(1).

Garza; Department of Transp. v., Tex, 70 SW3d 802.—Autos 279; Courts 247(7); States 112.1(1); Statut 188, 208.

Garza; DeRuy v., TexApp–San Antonio, 995 SW2d 748, rule 537(f) motion gr.—Const Law 2314, 2315, 3957; Health 811; Judgm 181(7), 185(2); Lim of Act 4(2), 55(3), 95(12), 199(1).

Garza; DeVonish v., WDTex, 510 FSupp 658.—Am Cur 1, 3.

Garza v. Doctors on Wilcrest, P.A., TexApp–Houston (14 Dist), 976 SW2d 899, review den, and reh of petition for review overr.—Labor & Emp 40(2), 777, 786; Plead 245(3), 258(3).

Garza v. Edinburg Consolidated Independent School Dist., TexCivApp–Corpus Christi, 576 SW2d 916.—Judgm 178; Schools 89.1, 89.4; States 112.1(2).

Garza; El Tropicano, Inc. v., BkrtcyWDTex, 128 BR 153. See El Tropicano, Inc., In re.

Garza v. Excel Logistics, Inc., TexApp–Houston (1 Dist), 100 SW3d 280, reh overr, and review gr, aff in part, rev in part 161 SW3d 473.—App & E 852, 934(1); Judgm 181(2), 185(2); Labor & Emp 25, 26; Work Comp 208, 306, 2161, 2164, 2168.

Garza v. Exel Logistics, Inc., Tex, 161 SW3d 473.—Judgm 185.3(13); Work Comp 2161.

Garza; Exxon Corp. v., TexApp–San Antonio, 981 SW2d 415, reh overr, and review den.—App & E 80(1), 930(1); Electricity 17, 19(5); Judgm 203, 216, 217; Neglig 200, 1001, 1032, 1086, 1668.

Garza v. Exxon Corp., TexCivApp–San Antonio, 604 SW2d 385.—Ease 61(9); Evid 575, 577, 581.

Garza; Finger v., CA5 (Tex), 98 FedAppx 326.—Const Law 3476, 4055; Fed Civ Proc 2491.5; Mun Corp 92.

Garza v. Fleming, TexCivApp–San Antonio, 323 SW2d 152, ref nre.—Child S 386, 429, 484; Hab Corp 442, 443.1, 445, 528.1, 532(2); Judgm 524.

Garza; Fort Worth Lloyds v., TexCivApp–Corpus Christi, 527 SW2d 195, ref nre.—Action 6; Decl Judgm 65, 68, 385; Insurance 2278(19), 2355, 2914, 2915.

Garza v. Frank Hrubetz & Co., Inc., TexCivApp–San Antonio, 496 SW2d 143.—Corp 665(1), 673.

Garza; F. W. Woolworth Co. v., TexCivApp–San Antonio, 390 SW2d 90, ref nre.—App & E 768, 930(1), 989; Sales 427, 441(3).

Garza v. Galena Park Independent School Dist., SDTex, 914 FSupp 1437.—Civil R 1067(1), 1067(3), 1376(5); Schools 89.11(1).

Garza; Garcia v., SDTex, 729 FSupp 553.—Hab Corp 332.1, 335, 362.1, 364, 479; Judgm 751.

Garza v. Garcia, Tex, 137 SW3d 36.—App & E 428(2), 912; Courts 85(3); New Tr 153.

Garza; Garcia v., TexApp–Corpus Christi, 70 SW3d 362, review gr, rev 137 SW3d 36.—App & E 106, 840(1), 931(4); Venue 17, 31, 58, 68, 72, 75.

Garza v. Garcia, TexApp–Corpus Christi, 785 SW2d 421, writ den.—Mun Corp 65, 104, 155; Offic 60.

Garza; Garcia v., TexCivApp–San Antonio, 161 SW2d 297, writ refused wom.—App & E 758.3(3), 1178(6); Bound 3(2), 3(5), 3(9), 32, 33; Propty 9; Tresp to T T 12, 34, 38(1), 41(2), 47(3); Trial 351.2(4).

Garza v. Garza, BkrtcyNDTex, 217 BR 197. See Garza, In re.

Garza; Garza v., BkrtcyNDTex, 217 BR 197. See Garza, In re.

Garza v. Garza, TexApp–San Antonio, 217 SW3d 538, reh overr.—Child C 76, 105, 106, 147, 210, 451, 462, 500, 904, 921(1), 921(3), 922(2), 923(1); Child S 556(1); Courts 176.5; Hus & W 249(6), 249(6), 258, 262.1(1), 262.1(8), 264(2), 264(5), 265, 268(8), 272(4); Witn 208(1), 214.5.

Garza; Garza v., TexApp–San Antonio, 217 SW3d 538, reh overr.—Child C 76, 105, 106, 147, 210, 451, 462, 500, 904, 921(1), 921(3), 922(2), 923(1); Child S 556(1); Courts 176.5; Hus & W 249(6), 249(6), 258, 262.1(1), 262.1(8), 264(2), 264(5), 265, 268(8), 272(4); Witn 208(1), 214.5.

Garza v. Garza, TexApp–San Antonio, 182 SW3d 69.—Lim of Act 124, 127(1), 127(14); Parent & C 7(1).

Garza; Garza v., TexApp–San Antonio, 182 SW3d 69.—Lim of Act 124, 127(1), 127(14); Parent & C 7(1).

Garza v. Garza, TexApp–San Antonio, 155 SW3d 471, opinion after remand 217 SW3d 538, reh overr.—App & E 161, 162(1), 389(3), 946, 985; Costs 128; Divorce 181, 184(2), 286(1).

Garza; Garza v., TexApp–San Antonio, 155 SW3d 471, opinion after remand 217 SW3d 538, reh overr.—App & E 161, 162(1), 389(3), 946, 985; Costs 128; Divorce 181, 184(2), 286(1).

Garza v. Garza, TexApp–San Antonio, 713 SW2d 123, dism.—Divorce 186; Jury 19.10(1).

Garza; Garza v., TexApp–San Antonio, 713 SW2d 123, dism.—Divorce 186; Jury 19.10(1).

Garza v. Garza, TexApp–San Antonio, 666 SW2d 205, dism, and ref nre.—Courts 89, 207.3, 207.5; Divorce 186, 252.1, 252.3(2), 252.3(3), 254(1), 255, 286(2), 286(5); Evid 43(3); Judgm 486(1), 634, 713(2).

Garza; Garza v., TexApp–San Antonio, 666 SW2d 205, dism, and ref nre.—Courts 89, 207.3, 207.5; Divorce 186, 252.1, 252.3(2), 252.3(3), 254(1), 255, 286(2), 286(5); Evid 43(3); Judgm 486(1), 634, 713(2).

Garza v. Garza, TexApp–Corpus Christi, 718 SW2d 825. —App & E 232(1), 1032(1); Child C 7, 28, 904, 923(1); Trial 133.6(7).

Garza; Garza v., TexApp–Corpus Christi, 718 SW2d 825. —App & E 232(1), 1032(1); Child C 7, 28, 904, 923(1); Trial 133.6(7).

Garza v. Garza, TexCivApp–Austin, 371 SW2d 934.—App & E 1051(1); Evid 377, 441(8), 441(9); Ven & Pur 281(3).

Garza; Garza v., TexCivApp–Austin, 371 SW2d 934.—App & E 1051(1); Evid 377, 441(8), 441(9); Ven & Pur 281(3).

Garza v. Garza, TexCivApp–San Antonio, 608 SW2d 260, dism.—Divorce 181.

Garza; Garza v., TexCivApp–San Antonio, 608 SW2d 260, dism.—Divorce 181.

For Later Case History Information, see KeyCite on WESTLAW

Garza v. Garza, TexCivApp–San Antonio, 390 SW2d 45, ref nre.—Wills 163(1), 163(8), 164(5), 166(1), 166(12), 400.

Garza; Garza v., TexCivApp–San Antonio, 390 SW2d 45, ref nre.—Wills 163(1), 163(8), 164(5), 166(1), 166(12), 400.

Garza v. Garza, TexCivApp–San Antonio, 297 SW2d 874, dism.—Adv Poss 114(2), 115(1); Propty 9; Tresp 20(4.1); Tresp to T T 6.1, 41(1).

Garza; Garza v., TexCivApp–San Antonio, 297 SW2d 874, dism.—Adv Poss 114(2), 115(1); Propty 9; Tresp 20(4.1); Tresp to T T 6.1, 41(1).

Garza v. Garza, TexCivApp–San Antonio, 223 SW2d 964. —Judgm 17(9); Proc 33.

Garza; Garza v., TexCivApp–San Antonio, 223 SW2d 964. —Judgm 17(9); Proc 33.

Garza v. Garza, TexCivApp–San Antonio, 191 SW2d 767. —Divorce 27(14), 50, 125, 146, 184(5); Evid 265(7), 265(10), 265(13), 265(14).

Garza; Garza v., TexCivApp–San Antonio, 191 SW2d 767. —Divorce 27(14), 50, 125, 146, 184(5); Evid 265(7), 265(10), 265(13), 265(14).

Garza v. Garza, TexCivApp–San Antonio, 109 SW2d 1079, dism.—Marriage 51; Witn 338, 344(1), 344(2).

Garza; Garza v., TexCivApp–San Antonio, 109 SW2d 1079, dism.—Marriage 51; Witn 338, 344(1), 344(2).

Garza v. Garza, TexCivApp–Eastland, 209 SW2d 1012.— Child S 179; Parent & C 7.5, 11.

Garza; Garza v., TexCivApp–Eastland, 209 SW2d 1012.— Child S 179; Parent & C 7.5, 11.

Garza v. Garza, TexCivApp–Tyler, 552 SW2d 947.—Dedi 16.1, 20(5), 45; High 9.

Garza; Garza v., TexCivApp–Tyler, 552 SW2d 947.—Dedi 16.1, 20(5), 45; High 9.

Garza v. Gates, WDTex, 482 FSupp 1211.—Counties 38.

Garza; General Motors Corp. v., TexApp–San Antonio, 179 SW3d 76.—Parties 35.1, 35.5, 35.17, 35.33, 35.71; Sales 262, 284(1).

Garza v. Gonzalez, TexApp–San Antonio, 737 SW2d 588. —New Tr 165.

Garza v. Greyhound Lines, Inc., TexCivApp–San Antonio, 418 SW2d 595.—Carr 234; Courts 8, 9; Evid 362; Torts 103.

Garza; Guerra v., TexCrimApp, 987 SW2d 593.—Crim Law 90(5); Mand 1; Prohib 1.

Garza; Guerra v., TexApp–Corpus Christi, 865 SW2d 573, reh overr, and writ dism woj.—App & E 719(8), 1008.1(2); Elections 239, 289, 291, 299(1), 305(6).

Garza; Guerra v., TexCivApp–Eastland, 93 SW2d 537.— Home 57(3); Judgm 564(1); Mtg 39, 608.5; Trial 143.

Garza v. Guerrero, TexApp–San Antonio, 993 SW2d 137, reh overr.—App & E 204(4), 204(7), 232(2), 1051.1(2); Damag 130.1, 135; Evid 378(1); Pretrial Proc 139, 202.

Garza v. Guevara, TexCivApp–San Antonio, 421 SW2d 691.—App & E 994(3); Autos 244(36.1).

Garza v. Harney, TexApp–Amarillo, 726 SW2d 198.— Child C 802, 816; Mand 11.

Garza; Harris County v., TexApp–Houston (14 Dist), 971 SW2d 733.—Autos 196; Counties 146; Judgm 199(1), 199(3.10), 256(1); Offic 114; Sheriffs 140.

Garza v. Heckler, CA5 (Tex), 771 F2d 871.—Social S 149.5.

Garza v. Hibernia Nat. Bank, TexApp–Houston (1 Dist), 227 SW3d 233.—App & E 430(1).

Garza; International Paper Co. v., TexApp–Corpus Christi, 872 SW2d 18.—Mand 1, 4(3), 4(4).

Garza; JCW Electronics, Inc. v., TexApp–Corpus Christi, 176 SW3d 618, reh overr, and review gr.—Action 27(1); App & E 171(1), 193(1), 253, 673.3, 852, 882(18), 994(2), 1002, 1003(3); Costs 146, 169, 187, 190, 194.36; Fraud 36; Plead 1, 16, 34(3), 37, 48, 228.14, 427; Prod Liab 48; Sales 1.5, 273(1), 404, 425, 427, 441(3); Trial 1, 182, 351.2(5), 351.5(5), 352.1(2).

Garza; Jimenez v., SDTex, 509 FSupp 973.—Decl Judgm 65; Inj 22.

Garza; Jimenez ex rel. Little v., TexApp–El Paso, 787 SW2d 601.—Child 21(2); Infants 155, 178.

Garza; Johnson v., TexApp–Austin, 884 SW2d 831, reh overr, and writ den.—App & E 205, 241, 242(4), 544(1), 548(5), 833(5), 901, 1043(1), 1079; Fires 7; Insurance 2166(3); Pretrial Proc 3; Trial 169.

Garza v. Keillor, TexCivApp–Hous (1 Dist), 623 SW2d 669, ref nre.—Evid 528(1), 538, 547, 547.5; Health 631, 825, 826; Trial 140(1).

Garza v. King, TexCivApp–San Antonio, 233 SW2d 884, writ refused.—Judgm 217, 335(1), 518; New Tr 117(3).

Garza; Kirk v., TexApp–Houston (1 Dist), 875 SW2d 24, reh den, and writ den.—Parties 65(1).

Garza; Krishnan v., TexCivApp–Corpus Christi, 570 SW2d 578.—App & E 930(3), 989; Health 782, 823(9); Indem 58, 65; Trial 365.1(6).

Garza; La Salle Life Ins. Co. v., TexCivApp–San Antonio, 109 SW2d 1087, writ dism.—App & E 773(2).

Garza v. Levin, TexApp–Corpus Christi, 769 SW2d 644, writ den.—App & E 712; Health 611, 823(1); Judgm 185(3).

Garza; Lightbourn v., WDTex, 928 FSupp 711, vac 127 F3d 33.—Civil R 1053; Elections 1, 10, 24.

Garza; Lopez v., TexCivApp–San Antonio, 423 SW2d 935, ref nre.—Sales 359(1).

Garza; Lumbermens Mut. Cas. Co. v., TexApp–Corpus Christi, 777 SW2d 198.—Abate & R 71.

Garza v. Maddux, TexApp–Corpus Christi, 988 SW2d 280, reh overr, and review den, and reh of petition for review overr.—Adv Poss 28, 104; App & E 854(1); Bound 48(1); Contracts 143(2); Deeds 95, 97, 111, 119; Lim of Act 95(8); Mines 49.

Garza; Maldonado v., CA5 (Tex), 579 F2d 338.—Prisons 17(1).

Garza; Mapus v., TexCivApp–San Antonio, 508 SW2d 857, ref nre.—New Tr 155.

Garza v. Martinez Mercantile Co., TexCivApp–Waco, 208 SW2d 567, ref nre.—Frds St of 129(3), 129(7), 129(12), 149; Spec Perf 115.

Garza; Matlock v., TexApp–Corpus Christi, 725 SW2d 527.—App & E 389(3).

Garza v. Maverick Market, Inc., Tex, 768 SW2d 273.— Child 82; Death 7, 31(8), 60, 75, 103(1); Trial 139.1(14).

Garza v. Mitchell, TexCivApp–Tyler, 607 SW2d 593.— Crops 2; Impl & C C 3, 30, 34; Judgm 634, 650, 668(1), 724, 725(1), 743(2); Torts 200, 217, 220.

Garza; Montgomery Ward & Co. v., TexApp–Corpus Christi, 660 SW2d 619.—App & E 866(3); False Imp 2, 36, 39; Trial 420.

Garza v. Morales, TexApp–Corpus Christi, 923 SW2d 800.—App & E 66, 70(8); Judges 36; Libel 38(1); Mun Corp 723.

Garza; Murillo v., TexApp–San Antonio, 904 SW2d 688, reh overr, and writ den.—Judgm 181(27), 185(2); Offic 114, 119.

Garza; Murillo v., TexApp–San Antonio, 881 SW2d 199.— Autos 209, 290, 304(1); Judges 36; Judgm 185(2); Offic 114.

Garza; National Committee of U.S. Taxpayers Party v., WDTex, 924 FSupp 71.—Decl Judgm 387; Elections 15, 21; Inj 138.1.

Garza; Pena v., TexApp–San Antonio, 61 SW3d 529.— Courts 85(1); Crim Law 255.3, 260.11(4); Inj 132, 202.1.

Garza v. Perez, TexCivApp–Corpus Christi, 443 SW2d 855.—App & E 837(1); Autos 162(5); Judgm 181(33), 183, 186.

Garza v. Perez, TexCivApp–Corpus Christi, 403 SW2d 849.—Courts 23, 37(3).

Garza v. Pope, TexApp–San Antonio, 949 SW2d 7, reh overr.—Ease 18(1), 26(3), 44(1); Lis Pen 2, 15; Mand 62.

GARZA;

See Guidelines for Arrangement at the beginning of this Volume

Garza; Post v., TexApp–Corpus Christi, 867 SW2d 88, reh overr.—Divorce 163, 226; Mand 4(1), 12, 53.

Garza v. Prolithic Energy Co., L.P., TexApp–San Antonio, 195 SW3d 137, reh overr, and review den.—App & E 870(2), 1175(1); Deeds 90, 95, 110; Mines 55(4), 55(5).

Garza; Prudential-Bache Securities, Inc. v., TexApp–Corpus Christi, 848 SW2d 803.—Alt Disp Res 113, 114, 137, 139, 143, 178, 182(1), 192, 211, 213(3), 419, 421; Mand 4(1), 53.

Garza; Radford v., TexCivApp–Corpus Christi, 586 SW2d 656.—Adv Poss 13, 31, 33, 86, 114(1); App & E 846(5), 931(4), 1012.1(9); Land & Ten 61, 66(1), 66(2); Trial 382; Ven & Pur 244, 245.

Garza v. Resendez, TexCivApp–San Antonio, 251 SW2d 747.—Bills & N 49; Des & Dist 8; Princ & S 190(1).

Garza v. Ringold, TexCivApp–Eastland, 146 SW2d 464, writ refused.—Schools 106.25(7).

Garza; Rittmer v., TexApp–Houston (14 Dist), 65 SW3d 718.—App & E 893(1), 946, 1008.1(1); Health 804, 805.

Garza; Riverside Hosp., Inc. v., TexApp–Corpus Christi, 894 SW2d 850.—Health 270, 271; Pretrial Proc 41, 373, 382; Witn 184(1).

Garza v. Rodriguez, CA5 (Tex), 559 F2d 259, reh den 568 F2d 1367, cert den 99 SCt 215, 439 US 877, 58 LEd2d 191.—Fed Cts 336.1, 340.1; Offic 69.7.

Garza v. Rodriguez, TexApp–San Antonio, 87 SW3d 628, reh overr, and review den, on remand 2005 WL 4889996, aff 2007 WL 2116411.—App & E 843(2), 893(1); Courts 472.3; Wills 698.

Garza v. Rodriguez, TexApp–San Antonio, 18 SW3d 694, reh overr.—App & E 4, 893(1), 911.3; Courts 481; Decl Judgm 273; Ex & Ad 513(8); Judgm 336; Wills 257.

Garza; Rourke v., Tex, 530 SW2d 794.—App & E 930(1), 989; Contracts 97(1); Estop 54; Indem 30(1); Negl 547; Princ & A 99, 123(1), 124(2), 137(1), 170(1); Prod Liab 5, 8, 14, 27, 54, 83, 94, 96.1; Trial 260(8).

Garza; Rourke v., TexCivApp–Hous (1 Dist), 511 SW2d 331, writ gr, aff 530 SW2d 794.—Contracts 159; Indem 27, 30(4), 33(4); Negl 384, 422, 554(2); Prod Liab 8, 19.1, 54, 75.1, 83, 94.

Garza; Ryals v., TexCivApp–Dallas, 264 SW2d 548, ref nre.—App & E 846(5); Evid 265(18), 589; Fraud 58(1); Fraud Conv 278(2); Garn 218; Hus & W 262.1(3), 264(3).

Garza; Saldana v., CA5 (Tex), 684 F2d 1159, cert den 103 SCt 1253, 460 US 1012, 75 LEd2d 481.—Civil R 1376(1), 1376(6), 1398, 1407, 1423; Fed Civ Proc 1788.6.

Garza v. Salinas, TexCivApp–San Antonio, 434 SW2d 153.—App & E 770(1); Elections 72, 216.1, 291, 295(1).

Garza v. Salvatierra, TexApp–San Antonio, 846 SW2d 17, reh den, and writ dism woj.—App & E 934(1); Autos 196; Judges 36; Judgm 181(2), 181(3); Offic 114, 116; States 79, 112.1(1).

Garza v. San Antonio Light, TexCivApp–Corpus Christi, 531 SW2d 926, ref nre.—App & E 230, 232(3), 883, 1170.9(3); Damag 87(2); Trial 186, 355(1), 356(1), 366.

Garza v. San Antonio Transit Co., TexCivApp–San Antonio, 180 SW2d 1006, writ refused wom.—App & E 207; Carr 316(1), 322; Evid 150, 325; Trial 352.4(7), 356(5).

Garza; Sanchez v., TexCivApp–Corpus Christi, 581 SW2d 258.—False Imp 2, 7(3), 12; Judgm 185(2).

Garza v. Schilling, TexCivApp–Corpus Christi, 576 SW2d 147.—Child C 3, 407; Hab Corp 532(1), 636; Venue 1 1/2.

Garza v. Scott and White Memorial Hosp., WDTex, 234 FRD 617.—Fed Civ Proc 1591; Fed Cts 373, 416, 428; States 18.5; Witn 184(1).

Garza; Serano v., TexCivApp–San Antonio, 119 SW2d 413.—Autos 181(1); Labor & Emp 2929, 2933; Work Comp 2084.

Garza v. Serrato, TexApp–San Antonio, 699 SW2d 275, ref nre.—Notaries 4; Pretrial Proc 91, 138, 139, 156, 724.

Garza v. Serrato, TexApp–San Antonio, 671 SW2d 713.—App & E 346.2, 351(1); Interest 39(3); Judgm 321.

Garza v. Smith, CA5 (Tex), 450 F2d 790.—Fed Cts 593, 743, 922.

Garza v. Smith, WDTex, 320 FSupp 131, vac 91 SCt 1257, 401 US 1006, 28 LEd2d 542, appeal after remand 450 F2d 790.—Const Law 1021, 3162; Elections 1, 9, 11, 12(5), 15, 27; Inj 21.

Garza v. Smith, TexApp–Corpus Christi, 860 SW2d 631.—App & E 70(8), 78(1); Judges 36; Judgm 181(11), 181(27); Offic 114, 119; Pretrial Proc 622.

Garza; Smith v., TexCivApp–Hous (1 Dist), 432 SW2d 142.—Autos 193(8.1); Labor & Emp 2769; Plead 111.3, 111.18; Venue 22(4), 22(6).

Garza v. Southland Corp., TexApp–Houston (14 Dist), 836 SW2d 214.—App & E 216(7), 217, 232(0.5), 497(1), 930(3), 1001(1), 1041(2); Contracts 323(1); Evid 434(8); Plead 245(3); Trial 186, 259(1), 274, 277, 279, 312(2); Ven & Pur 80, 81.

Garza; Southwestern Bell Telephone Co. v., Tex, 164 SW3d 607, reh den.—App & E 840(3), 930(1), 999(1), 1001(1), 1064.1(2.1); Evid 597; Labor & Emp 858, 863(2), 870; Trial 139.1(4), 241.

Garza; Southwestern Bell Telephone Co. v., TexApp–Corpus Christi, 58 SW3d 214, reh overr, and review gr, aff in part, rev in part 164 SW3d 607, reh den.—App & E 901, 1004(8), 1050.1(1), 1051.1(1), 1051.1(2), 1056.1(1), 1062.1, 1151(2); Damag 49, 49.10, 50, 102, 192, 208(6); Evid 532, 587, 588; Labor & Emp 824, 862, 863(2), 867, 870, 871, 874; Plead 34(1), 48; Trial 56, 352.1(3).

Garza; State v., Tex, 783 SW2d 198.—Controlled Subs 102, 182.

Garza v. State, TexCrimApp, 213 SW3d 338.—Crim Law 27, 393(3), 394.6(5), 404.45, 414, 641.13(1), 641.13(6), 641.13(7), 1134(2), 1144.10, 1144.13(2.1), 1158(1), 1159.2(2); Double J 134, 150(1); Homic 1207; Statut 212.4, 212.7.

Garza v. State, TexCrimApp, 126 SW3d 79, on remand 137 SW3d 878, petition for discretionary review refused.—Crim Law 777, 1036.1(4), 1043(2), 1044.2(1).

Garza v. State, TexCrimApp, 7 SW3d 164, on remand 18 SW3d 813, petition for discretionary review refused.—Jury 64, 131(13).

Garza; State v., TexCrimApp, 931 SW2d 560.—Courts 82, 85(2); Crim Law 964.

Garza v. State, TexCrimApp, 896 SW2d 192, on remand 1995 WL 638483.—Crim Law 1069(1), 1071, 1072.

Garza v. State, TexCrimApp, 771 SW2d 549.—Arrest 63.5(5), 63.5(7); Autos 349(18); Crim Law 394.1(1); Searches 49.

Garza v. State, TexCrimApp, 736 SW2d 710.—Bail 49(1).

Garza v. State, TexCrimApp, 725 SW2d 256.—Crim Law 1109(2); Sent & Pun 2010.

Garza v. State, TexCrimApp, 715 SW2d 642.—Crim Law 369.2(1), 371(1), 371(9), 1134(3), 1192.

Garza v. State, TexCrimApp, 687 SW2d 325.—Crim Law 29(10), 273.2(2), 274(1), 619, 1179; Rec S Goods 7(6), 8(1); Sent & Pun 548, 585; Statut 223.4.

Garza v. State, TexCrimApp, 658 SW2d 152, cert den 104 SCt 194, 464 US 863, 78 LEd2d 171.—Double J 59, 89, 98, 99.

Garza v. State, TexCrimApp, 633 SW2d 508.—Const Law 4658(1), 4658(3), 4659(2); Crim Law 339.8(1), 339.8(6), 339.9(1), 339.9(2), 339.9(3), 641.3(10), 721.5(2), 730(5).

Garza v. State, TexCrimApp, 630 SW2d 272.—Crim Law 868, 925.5(1), 925.5(3), 928, 1174(2).

Garza v. State, TexCrimApp, 622 SW2d 85.—Controlled Subs 82; Crim Law 622.1(2), 622.2(2), 723(3), 730(1), 730(14), 814(17), 957(3), 1091(2), 1115(1), 1134(2); Jury 97(1).

Garza v. State, TexCrimApp, 573 SW2d 536.—Controlled Subs 82, 98; Crim Law 404.60; Witn 331.5.

Garza v. State, TexCrimApp, 548 SW2d 55.—Sent & Pun 1367, 1381(6).

Garza v. State, TexCrimApp, 532 SW2d 624.—Crim Law 1036.2; Witn 373.

Garza v. State, TexCrimApp, 522 SW2d 693.—Burg 18; Crim Law 273.1(4), 625.10(2.1).

Garza v. State, TexCrimApp, 502 SW2d 155.—Crim Law 273.1(2), 958(1), 958(6).

Garza v. State, TexCrimApp, 479 SW2d 294.—Crim Law 784(1), 1038.1(7), 1038.3, 1042, 1122(1), 1126, 1130(2); Homic 1371.

Garza v. State, TexCrimApp, 469 SW2d 169.—Crim Law 240, 412.2(5), 1130(2); Infants 68.7(1).

Garza v. State, TexCrimApp, 468 SW2d 440.—Controlled Subs 30, 97; Crim Law 531(3), 814(17), 1038.2, 1038.3, 1043(1); Searches 197.

Garza v. State, TexCrimApp, 442 SW2d 693.—Crim Law 457, 632(2), 992, 1169.3.

Garza v. State, TexCrimApp, 440 SW2d 860.—Crim Law 641.10(2).

Garza v. State, TexCrimApp, 433 SW2d 428.—Crim Law 1130(4).

Garza v. State, TexCrimApp, 397 SW2d 847.—Crim Law 358, 517(5), 519(8), 1137(5); Rob 24.15(1); Witn 406.

Garza v. State, TexCrimApp, 369 SW2d 36.—Const Law 4563; Infants 68.1.

Garza v. State, TexCrimApp, 368 SW2d 213.—Crim Law 925.5(3), 959, 1156(5), 1184(4.1); Larc 65.

Garza v. State, TexCrimApp, 358 SW2d 622, 172 TexCrim 468.—Controlled Subs 80; Crim Law 351(8), 698(1).

Garza v. State, TexCrimApp, 351 SW2d 248, 171 TexCrim 420.—Autos 351.1; Crim Law 1167(1).

Garza v. State, TexCrimApp, 347 SW2d 265, 171 TexCrim 267.—Burg 31; Crim Law 516; Ind & Inf 182.

Garza v. State, TexCrimApp, 300 SW2d 95.—Crim Law 1090.1(1).

Garza v. State, TexCrimApp, 296 SW2d 267, 164 TexCrim 9.—Crim Law 742(2); Larc 65.

Garza v. State, TexCrimApp, 288 SW2d 785, 162 TexCrim 655.—Crim Law 1038.1(4), 1056.1(1); Int Liq 239(5).

Garza v. State, TexCrimApp, 262 SW2d 722, 159 TexCrim 234.—Sent & Pun 1381(3).

Garza v. State, TexCrimApp, 261 SW2d 581, 159 TexCrim 134.—Crim Law 631(3), 631(4), 826; Homic 1134; Jury 70(12), 116.

Garza v. State, TexCrimApp, 261 SW2d 575, 159 TexCrim 105.—Crim Law 404.70, 730(3); Homic 1193, 1478.

Garza v. State, TexCrimApp, 249 SW2d 212, 157 TexCrim 381.—Judges 16(2).

Garza v. State, TexCrimApp, 246 SW2d 635, 157 TexCrim 6.—Crim Law 1092.14.

Garza v. State, TexCrimApp, 244 SW2d 817, 156 TexCrim 557.—Crim Law 925.5(3).

Garza v. State, TexCrimApp, 230 SW2d 819.—Crim Law 1094(3).

Garza v. State, TexCrimApp, 199 SW2d 162, 150 TexCrim 22.—Burg 28(3), 41(1); Crim Law 598(2), 736(2).

Garza v. State, TexCrimApp, 194 SW2d 406, 149 TexCrim 359.—Crim Law 919(5); Homic 570, 1207; Jury 99, 110(5).

Garza v. State, TexCrimApp, 185 SW2d 444.—Crim Law 1090.1(1).

Garza v. State, TexCrimApp, 160 SW2d 926, 143 TexCrim 624.—Crim Law 713, 719(1), 719(3); Witn 345(2).

Garza v. State, TexCrimApp, 136 SW2d 861, 138 TexCrim 403.—Crim Law 304(6), 304(13), 736(2), 1091(2); Jury 58, 65.

Garza v. State, TexCrimApp, 117 SW2d 429, 135 TexCrim 138.—Crim Law 134(4), 814(17), 1159.3(1).

Garza v. State, TexCrimApp, 94 SW2d 439, 130 TexCrim 401.—Crim Law 448(11), 656(9), 675, 730(15), 1092.16; Jury 131(13); Rape 53(2), 64.

Garza v. State, TexCrimApp, 88 SW2d 113, 129 TexCrim 443.—Crim Law 1110(8), 1124(4); Witn 274(1), 274(2).

Garza v. State, TexApp–Houston (1 Dist), 137 SW3d 878, petition for discretionary review refused.—Autos 349.5(12); Crim Law 1139, 1153(1); Searches 12, 66, 195.1.

Garza v. State, TexApp–Houston (1 Dist), 50 SW3d 559.—Crim Law 549, 1159.2(1); Ind & Inf 120, 161(1), 161(3), 161(7); Weap 15.

Garza; State v., TexApp–Houston (1 Dist), 908 SW2d 60, petition for discretionary review refused, review gr, rev Ex parte Garza, 934 SW2d 144.—Crim Law 295; Double J 1, 25; Hab Corp 843.

Garza v. State, TexApp–Houston (1 Dist), 846 SW2d 936, reh den, and petition for discretionary review refused.—Autos 332; Crim Law 1036.1(9), 1159.2(7).

Garza v. State, TexApp–Houston (1 Dist), 721 SW2d 582.—Crim Law 641.5(3), 641.5(5), 1035(7), 1132.

Garza v. State, TexApp–Fort Worth, 18 SW3d 813, petition for discretionary review refused.—Crim Law 338(1), 359, 393(1), 412.1(1), 412.1(2), 412.1(4), 412.2(1), 412.2(3), 641.3(3), 662.1, 662.7, 713, 721.5(1), 730(1), 730(16), 781(1), 814(16), 1134(2), 1152(2), 1170.5(5), 1171.1(2.1), 1173.2(7); Jury 97(1), 131(1), 131(2), 131(3), 131(4), 131(6), 131(13); Rape 51(1), 54(1); Witn 257, 267, 319, 355, 386, 388(2.1), 390.

Garza v. State, TexApp–Fort Worth, 988 SW2d 352, reh overr, and petition for discretionary review refused, and petition for discretionary review gr, rev 7 SW3d 164, on remand 18 SW3d 813, petition for discretionary review refused.—Crim Law 1134(3), 1163(1), 1166.16; Jury 64, 131(1).

Garza v. State, TexApp–Austin, 212 SW3d 503.—Crim Law 1035(3), 1166.13.

Garza v. State, TexApp–Austin, 828 SW2d 432, petition for discretionary review refused.—Crim Law 369.2(5), 1130(2), 1130(5), 1162, 1169.1(9); Infants 20.

Garza v. State, TexApp–San Antonio, 161 SW3d 636.—Arrest 63.4(1), 63.4(2), 65; Crim Law 211(3), 211(4), 213, 1139, 1153(1), 1158(4); Searches 111, 112, 113.1.

Garza; State v., TexApp–San Antonio, 143 SW3d 144, petition for discretionary review refused.—Crim Law 641.13(1), 920, 1152(2), 1156(1), 1158(3), 1166.16; Jury 97(1).

Garza v. State, TexApp–San Antonio, 100 SW3d 347, habeas corpus gr Ex Parte Garza, 2006 WL 3307092.—Crim Law 351(3), 1144.13(3), 1159.2(2), 1159.2(7), 1166(1); Rob 11, 24.15(1).

Garza; State v., TexApp–San Antonio, 88 SW3d 353.—Crim Law 1130(4).

Garza v. State, TexApp–San Antonio, 61 SW3d 585, petition for discretionary review gr, judgment vac 77 SW3d 292, on remand 100 SW3d 347, habeas corpus gr Ex Parte Garza, 2006 WL 3307092.—Crim Law 1166(1); Jury 21.1, 21.2, 29(2), 29(6).

Garza v. State, TexApp–San Antonio, 37 SW3d 130.—Crim Law 1042, 1064(1); Sent & Pun 606.

Garza v. State, TexApp–San Antonio, 34 SW3d 591, reh overr, and petition for discretionary review refused.—Crim Law 273.4(1), 275, 394.6(5), 412.2(2), 414, 517.2(2), 1139, 1158(4).

Garza v. State, TexApp–San Antonio, 2 SW3d 331, petition for discretionary review refused.—Autos 359; Crim Law 273.1(4), 347, 369.2(2), 641.13(1), 641.13(7), 796, 824(1), 1026.10(4), 1038.1(5), 1167(5); Sent & Pun 370, 372.

Garza v. State, TexApp–San Antonio, 974 SW2d 251, petition for discretionary review refused.—Const Law 3869, 3873, 4559; Courts 74; Crim Law 25, 106, 107, 108(1), 128, 133, 134(1), 134(2), 135, 142, 772(6), 808.5, 865(1), 1038.2, 1144.13(2.1), 1144.16, 1159.2(1), 1159.2(2), 1159.2(9), 1159.3(2), 1166(4); Homic 1135, 1492.

Garza v. State, TexApp–San Antonio, 963 SW2d 926.—Courts 85(1); Crim Law 338(1), 438(3), 683(1), 1153(1), 1162, 1165(1), 1169.1(1), 1169.1(10).

Garza v. State, TexApp–San Antonio, 937 SW2d 569, petition for discretionary review refused.—Rob 3, 5, 22, 24.15(1).

GARZA;

Garza; State v., TexApp–San Antonio, 824 SW2d 324, petition for discretionary review refused.—Crim Law 996(1); Sent & Pun 1382, 1399, 1400, 1838, 1872(2).

Garza v. State, TexApp–San Antonio, 822 SW2d 174.— Arrest 63.2, 63.3; Crim Law 1031(1), 1043(3).

Garza v. State, TexApp–San Antonio, 783 SW2d 796.— Crim Law 633(1), 722.4, 723(3), 1039, 1152(1).

Garza v. State, TexApp–San Antonio, 705 SW2d 818.— Crim Law 394.5(2), 1184(1); Sent & Pun 1379(2).

Garza v. State, TexApp–San Antonio, 678 SW2d 183, petition for discretionary review gr, aff 771 SW2d 549.— Arrest 63.4(4), 63.5(3.1), 63.5(4), 63.5(5), 63.5(6), 63.5(9); Burg 41(1); Courts 97(1); Crim Law 394.1(1), 394.1(2), 511.1(4), 511.1(9), 511.2, 1144.13(6); States 4.1(2).

Garza v. State, TexApp–Dallas, 996 SW2d 276, reh overr, and petition for discretionary review refused.—Crim Law 304(1), 427(2), 427(5), 642, 663, 858(3), 1134(6), 1137(2), 1168(1).

Garza v. State, TexApp–Dallas, 912 SW2d 835.—Sent & Pun 372, 373.

Garza v. State, TexApp–Dallas, 841 SW2d 19.—Burg 2, 41(4), 42(3), 42(4); Crim Law 260.11(4), 561(1), 562, 1042, 1147, 1158(1), 1159.6, 1181.5(8); Sent & Pun 1973(2), 2175.

Garza v. State, TexApp–Dallas, 829 SW2d 291, petition for discretionary review refused.—Crim Law 763(1), 772(6), 777.5, 814(3), 1130(2); Homic 1506, 1507.

Garza v. State, TexApp–Dallas, 695 SW2d 726, petition for discretionary review gr, aff 725 SW2d 256.—Assault 56, 92(3); Crim Law 105, 1033.1; Sent & Pun 2010, 2011, 2012.

Garza v. State, TexApp–Dallas, 632 SW2d 823, petition for discretionary review gr, case remanded 715 SW2d 642.—Crim Law 369.2(1), 371(9); Kidnap 36.

Garza v. State, TexApp–Amarillo, 635 SW2d 644, petition for discretionary review refused.—Crim Law 641.10(3), 641.12(1), 1134(2).

Garza v. State, TexApp–Corpus Christi, 82 SW3d 791.— Crim Law 553, 566, 572, 741(1), 742(1), 911, 925(5), 925.5(1), 925.5(3), 961, 1156(1), 1159.2(1), 1159.2(2), 1159.2(9), 1159.4(1); Rob 24.15(2).

Garza v. State, TexApp–Corpus Christi, 55 SW3d 74, reh overr, and petition for discretionary review refused.— Crim Law 863(0.5), 1038.1(1), 1039, 1134(2), 1162.

Garza v. State, TexApp–Corpus Christi, 50 SW3d 619.— Bail 55, 58, 77(2); Crim Law 1031(1), 1043(1).

Garza v. State, TexApp–Corpus Christi, 10 SW3d 765, petition for discretionary review refused.—Crim Law 372(7), 374, 637, 660, 1153(1), 1158(3), 1163(2); Ind & Inf 7; Infants 20; Jury 33(5.15); 85, 97(1), 103(1), 121.

Garza v. State, TexApp–Corpus Christi, 915 SW2d 204, reh overr, and petition for discretionary review refused. —Crim Law 412.2(2), 511.1(2.1), 511.1(7), 531(3), 532(0.5), 535(1), 1036.1(5), 1181.5(2); Homic 563, 1128.

Garza v. State, TexApp–Corpus Christi, 904 SW2d 877, reh overr, and petition for discretionary review gr, aff 931 SW2d 560.—Crim Law 964.

Garza v. State, TexApp–Corpus Christi, 878 SW2d 671.— Autos 259, 279, 282; Judgm 181(11), 181(33), 186; Plead 228.14, 228.23, 229; States 112(2).

Garza v. State, TexApp–Corpus Christi, 878 SW2d 213, reh overr, and petition for discretionary review refused. —Crim Law 273(2), 273.2(1), 273.2(2), 273.3, 407(1), 720(1), 730(8), 1144.13(1), 1144.13(3), 1144.13(6), 1159.2(7), 1159.3(2), 1159.4(2); Homic 668, 669, 672, 938, 1135, 1152.

Garza v. State, TexApp–Corpus Christi, 839 SW2d 131.— Crim Law 1023(3).

Garza v. State, TexApp–Corpus Christi, 839 SW2d 130.— Burg 45; Crim Law 1036.1(5).

Garza v. State, TexApp–Corpus Christi, 815 SW2d 832.— Crim Law 1023(3), 1023(16).

Garza v. State, TexApp–Corpus Christi, 803 SW2d 873, petition for discretionary review refused.—Hab Corp 715.1.

Garza v. State, TexApp–Corpus Christi, 794 SW2d 497, petition for discretionary review refused.—Crim Law 572, 1144.13(2.1); Rob 3, 11, 24.40.

Garza; State v., TexApp–Corpus Christi, 774 SW2d 724, petition for discretionary review refused.—Crim Law 1023(7), 1069(5), 1131(4), 1134(3); Double J 96.

Garza v. State, TexApp–Corpus Christi, 764 SW2d 843.— Crim Law 796, 1032(1), 1038.1(2), 1038.1(4).

Garza; State v., TexApp–Corpus Christi, 760 SW2d 734, rev 783 SW2d 198.—Controlled Subs 177, 182.

Garza v. State, TexApp–Corpus Christi, 739 SW2d 374.— Jury 121.

Garza v. State, TexApp–Corpus Christi, 725 SW2d 482, appeal after remand 739 SW2d 374.—Crim Law 1036.1(9); Jury 33(5.15).

Garza; State v., TexApp–Corpus Christi, 709 SW2d 18.— Mand 3(3), 3(11); Sent & Pun 1976(2).

Garza v. State, TexApp–Corpus Christi, 704 SW2d 64, petition for discretionary review refused.—Autos 349(3), 349(6); Crim Law 394.4(12).

Garza v. State, TexApp–Corpus Christi, 695 SW2d 249, petition for discretionary review refused.—Crim Law 438(5.1), 641.13(1), 641.13(2.1), 824(3), 824(4), 925(1), 956(13), 1032(5), 1038.1(3.1); Gr Jury 19; Homic 672, 1134, 1186, 1195; Witn 46.

Garza v. State, TexApp–Corpus Christi, 695 SW2d 58.— Crim Law 855(1), 868, 957(2), 957(3), 959, 1156(1).

Garza v. State, TexApp–Corpus Christi, 688 SW2d 666.— Autos 359; Crim Law 273(4.1), 273.1(4), 1031(4), 1167(5).

Garza v. State, TexApp–Corpus Christi, 676 SW2d 185, petition for discretionary review refused.—Crim Law 29(1), 29(13), 1129(1), 1134(3), 1159.2(7); Ind & Inf 127; Infants 20; Kidnap 40; Sent & Pun 500.

Garza v. State, TexApp–Corpus Christi, 653 SW2d 850.— Crim Law 556, 784(1), 1173.2(10); Ind & Inf 21, 26, 93, 110(3); Larc 28(1), 30(1), 31, 40(2), 64(6), 64(7), 68(3).

Garza v. State, TexApp–Corpus Christi, 627 SW2d 520.— Crim Law 339.11(1), 938(1), 939(1), 1045, 1130(2), 1156(3).

Garza v. State, TexApp–Houston (14 Dist), 919 SW2d 788. —Bail 75.2(3); Records 7.

Garza; State v., TexCivApp–San Antonio, 358 SW2d 749. —App & E 286; Infants 202; Pretrial Proc 501.

Garza v. State, TexCivApp–Corpus Christi, 503 SW2d 415.—App & E 624, 628(1).

Garza; State ex rel. Grievance Committee of State Bar of Tex. for Dist. No. 15-B v., TexCivApp–San Antonio, 269 SW2d 596.—Atty & C 36(1).

Garza v. State Farm Mut. Auto. Ins. Co., SDTex, 208 FSupp2d 693, aff 54 FedAppx 409.—Insurance 2645, 2657, 2772, 2786.

Garza v. State of Tex., CA5 (Tex), 474 F2d 905.—Hab Corp 342.

Garza v. Sumrall, TexCivApp–San Antonio, 267 SW2d 912, writ refused.—Lim of Act 131; Work Comp 2216.

Garza v. Sun Oil Co., TexApp–San Antonio, 727 SW2d 115.—Perp 4(2).

Garza v. Tan, TexApp–Corpus Christi, 849 SW2d 430.— App & E 923, 1045(1); Jury 85, 97(1), 105(1); Pretrial Proc 303, 403.

Garza v. Texas Alcoholic Beverage Com'n, Tex, 89 SW3d 1.—Int Liq 75(8); Judgm 215.

Garza v. Texas Alcoholic Beverage Com'n, TexApp–El Paso, 83 SW3d 161, reh overr, and review gr, aff 89 SW3d 1.—App & E 20, 516, 782, 901, 907(1), 934(1); Int Liq 75(4), 75(8); Judgm 215, 276, 287, 392(2), 470.

Garza v. Texas Alcoholic Beverage Com'n, TexApp–Houston (14 Dist), 138 SW3d 609.—Admin Law 486, 791, 793; Const Law 4025; Int Liq 75(7), 102, 129.5, 130.5.

Garza; Texas Animal Health Com'n v., TexApp–San Antonio, 27 SW3d 54, reh overr, and reh en banc den, and review den.—App & E 863, 930(1), 934(1), 1004(8); Costs 194.40; Damag 192; Decl Judgm 366; Judgm 199(3.10), 702; Labor & Emp 810, 861, 863(2), 867, 868(3), 868(4), 871, 873; Mun Corp 723; States 53, 191.4(1).

Garza; Texas Animal Health Com'n v., TexApp–San Antonio, 980 SW2d 776, opinion supplemented 27 SW3d 54, reh overr, and reh en banc den, and review den.—Judges 24.

Garza v. Texas Dept. of Family and Protective Services, TexApp–Austin, 212 SW3d 373.—App & E 893(1); Infants 202, 221; Statut 181(1), 181(2), 184, 206, 212.7, 217.4.

Garza v. Texas Dept. of Human Services, TexApp–San Antonio, 757 SW2d 44, writ den.—Courts 486, 487(3); Infants 242.

Garza v. Texas Dept. of Human Services in Interest of J.L.G., TexApp–Corpus Christi, 794 SW2d 521.—Infants 155, 157, 178, 179, 242.

Garza; Texas Dept. of Transp. v., TexApp–Corpus Christi, 72 SW3d 369, reh overr, rev 70 SW3d 802.—App & E 66, 893(1), 1099(3); Courts 4, 35, 39; Judgm 720; Mun Corp 742(4); Plead 104(1), 111.36, 111.37; States 112(2), 191.1, 191.4(1), 208.

Garza; Texas Eastern Transmission Corp. v., SDTex, 894 FSupp 1055.—Deeds 17(1), 17(3); Ease 40, 42; Fed Civ Proc 2466, 2470.1, 2543, 2544; Gas 9; Lim of Act 46(6); Ven & Pur 220, 235.

Garza v. Texas Educational Foundation, Inc., CA5 (Tex), 565 F2d 909.—Civil R 1568.

Garza; Texas Emp. Ins. Ass'n v., TexCivApp–Amarillo, 308 SW2d 521, ref nre.—Action 7; App & E 846(5), 971(3), 1015(5); Witn 267, 372(1); Work Comp 803, 1399, 1404, 1932, 1968(5).

Garza; Texas Emp. Ins. Ass'n v., TexCivApp–Corpus Christi, 557 SW2d 843, ref nre.—App & E 201(2), 205, 1170.6, 1170.7; Evid 558(1), 560; Trial 18, 29(1), 29(2), 110; Witn 267; Work Comp 1861, 1937.

Garza; Texas Employers' Ins. Ass'n v., Tex, 687 SW2d 299.—Pretrial Proc 313.

Garza v. Texas Employers' Ins. Ass'n, TexApp–Corpus Christi, 814 SW2d 96, writ den.—Pretrial Proc 45; Work Comp 984, 1937.

Garza; Texas Employers' Ins. Ass'n v., TexApp–Corpus Christi, 675 SW2d 245, ref nre 687 SW2d 299.—Pretrial Proc 304, 307, 313; Work Comp 1262, 1686, 1696.

Garza v. Texas Employment Commission, TexCivApp–San Antonio, 577 SW2d 765.—Unemp Comp 275, 371, 486.

Garza; Texas Medical Liability Trust v., TexApp–Corpus Christi, 918 SW2d 632, subsequent mandamus proceeding State v. Thirteenth Court of Appeals, 933 SW2d 43, vac 930 SW2d 940.—App & E 852; Const Law 2315; Health 511; Insurance 3517; Lim of Act 4(2), 43, 95(1), 95(12); States 111.

Garza v. Texas Real Estate Com'n, TexApp–Houston (1 Dist), 808 SW2d 212.—App & E 846(5), 907(3); Judgm 668(1), 678(1), 702, 715(1).

Garza; Thompson v., TexApp–Corpus Christi, 809 SW2d 640.—App & E 389(4).

Garza; Threadgill v., TexCivApp–San Antonio, 82 SW2d 699.—App & E 767(1).

Garza v. Traditional Kickapoo Tribe of Texas, CA5 (Tex), 79 FedAppx 10.—Assault 7; Civil R 1035; Const Law 4162, 4255; False Imp 6; Indians 27(1), 32(12).

Garza; Trans-World Bonded Warehouses and Storage, Inc. v., TexApp–San Antonio 570 SW2d 2, ref nre.—App & E 1177(6); Tresp to T T 10.

Garza v. Trevino, TexCivApp–San Antonio, 541 SW2d 524.—Domicile 5; Elections 126(4), 154(10).

Garza v. Trevino, TexCivApp–San Antonio, 91 SW2d 420. —App & E 1127; Pretrial Proc 697.

Garza; U.S. v., CA5 (Tex), 448 F3d 294.—Crim Law 406(1), 410, 465, 486(8), 627.8(6), 1153(1), 1177, 1181.5(8); Sent & Pun 661.

Garza; U.S. v., CA5 (Tex), 429 F3d 165, cert den 126 SCt 1444, 546 U.S. 1220, 164 LEd2d 143, appeal after new sentencing hearing US v. Elizondo, 475 F3d 692, cert den 127 SCt 1865, 167 LEd2d 355.—Consp 32, 47(5); Crim Law 641.5(0.5), 1030(1), 1042, 1043(1), 1139, 1152(1), 1163(1), 1177, 1181.5(8); Postal 35(2); Sent & Pun 754, 2105.

Garza; U.S. v., CA5 (Tex), 165 F3d 312, cert den 120 SCt 502, 528 US 1006, 145 LEd2d 388.—Const Law 4705; Courts 104; Crim Law 700(1), 1073, 1191; Sent & Pun 1745, 1782.

Garza; U.S. v., CA5 (Tex), 118 F3d 278, reh den, cert den Innocenio v. US, 118 SCt 699, 522 US 1051, 139 LEd2d 643, appeal after remand US v Garcia, 176 F3d 478.—Consp 47(12); Controlled Subs 28, 79; Crim Law 338(7), 369.2(1), 369.2(3.1), 1144.12, 1144.13(2.1), 1158(1), 1158(4), 1159.2(7); Searches 183, 197; Sent & Pun 675, 726(5), 764; U S 34.

Garza; U.S. v., CA5 (Tex), 63 F3d 1342. See U.S. v. Flores.

Garza; U.S. v., CA5 (Tex), 42 F3d 251, reh and sug for reh den 47 F3d 428, cert den 115 SCt 2263, 515 US 1110, 132 LEd2d 268.—Consp 47(3.1); Crim Law 369.2(3.1), 370, 673(5), 1038.1(4), 1144.13(2.1), 1144.13(5), 1159.2(7), 1159.4(6); Sent & Pun 752; U S 34.

Garza; U.S. v., CA5 (Tex), 990 F2d 171, reh den, cert den 114 SCt 332, 510 US 926, 126 LEd2d 278.—Controlled Subs 27, 68, 81; Crim Law 338(8), 369.1, 1035(7), 1036.1(8), 1134(3), 1144.13(5).

Garza; U.S. v., CA5 (Tex), 921 F2d 59, cert den 112 SCt 91, 502 US 825, 116 LEd2d 63.—Arrest 63.5(8); Sent & Pun 1381(3).

Garza; U.S. v., CA5 (Tex), 887 F2d 55, reh den, cert den 110 SCt 2561, 495 US 957, 109 LEd2d 743.—Crim Law 709, 720(1), 1171.1(2.1), 1171.3.

Garza; U.S. v., CA5 (Tex), 884 F2d 181.—Tel 1022.

Garza v. U.S., CA5 (Tex), 809 F2d 1170.—U S 78(8), 78(9), 78(14).

Garza; U.S. v., CA5 (Tex), 807 F2d 394.—Crim Law 1035(6).

Garza; U.S. v., CA5 (Tex), 754 F2d 1202.—Consp 28(2); Crim Law 419(3), 722.5, 800(4), 829(1), 829(3), 863(1), 1162, 1170(1), 1170.5(1), 1171.1(3); Judgm 713(1), 751; Witn 267, 374(1).

Garza; U.S. v., CA5 (Tex), 674 F2d 396, cert den 103 SCt 121, 459 US 854, 74 LEd2d 105.—Crim Law 1023(8); Double J 97.

Garza; U.S. v., CA5 (Tex), 608 F2d 659.—Crim Law 713, 719(1), 719(3), 720(1), 720(5), 720.5, 730(1), 1037.1(2).

Garza; U.S. v., CA5 (Tex), 603 F2d 578.—Double J 97.

Garza; U.S. v., CA5 (Tex), 574 F2d 298, appeal after remand 603 F2d 578.—Consp 47(1), 47(12); Controlled Subs 81; Crim Law 577.10(9); Jury 94, 131(1); Witn 374(1).

Garza; U.S. v., CA5 (Tex), 563 F2d 1164, cert den 98 SCt 1268, 434 US 1077, 55 LEd2d 783.—Crim Law 622.2(3), 622.2(6), 622.2(7), 641.13(1), 641.13(2.1).

Garza; U.S. v., CA5 (Tex), 554 F2d 257.—Cust Dut 126(4); Ind & Inf 7.

Garza; U.S. v., CA5 (Tex), 547 F2d 1234.—Cust Dut 126(5); Ind & Inf 7; Searches 73.

Garza; U.S. v., CA5 (Tex), 544 F2d 222.—Crim Law 394.4(12); Cust Dut 126(5); Searches 49.

Garza; U.S. v., CA5 (Tex), 539 F2d 381.—Cust Dut 126(4).

Garza; U.S. v., CA5 (Tex), 531 F2d 309, cert den 97 SCt 324, 429 US 924, 50 LEd2d 292.—Controlled Subs 30, 31, 81, 98; Crim Law 730(14).

Garza v. U.S., CA5 (Tex), 530 F2d 1208.—Crim Law 273.1(2), 641.13(5).

Garza v. U.S., CA5 (Tex), 498 F2d 1066.—Homic 1572; Ind & Inf 99, 144.2; Sent & Pun 529, 537.

Garza; U.S. v., CA5 (Tex), 484 F2d 88.—Crim Law 1147; Sent & Pun 2001, 2004, 2020, 2021.

Garza; U.S. v., CA5 (Tex), 426 F2d 949.—Consp 48.1(4); Crim Law 300, 552(3), 815(12), 823(10), 1144.13(3), 1159.2(5).

Garza v. U.S., CA5 (Tex), 385 F2d 899.—Controlled Subs 79, 86; Crim Law 1144.13(3).

Garza; U.S. v., CA5 (Tex), 222 FedAppx 433.—Controlled Subs 74, 81, 86; Crim Law 432, 1169.1(10).

Garza; U.S. v., CA5 (Tex), 214 FedAppx 470.—Sent & Pun 726(3).

Garza; U.S. v., CA5 (Tex), 187 FedAppx 397.—Controlled Subs 81, 94; Crim Law 1035(1), 1042; Sent & Pun 661, 670, 980, 995.

Garza; U.S. v., CA5 (Tex), 178 FedAppx 343, cert den 127 SCt 529, 166 LEd2d 393.—Crim Law 273.1(2); Sent & Pun 765.

Garza v. U.S., CA5 (Tex), 161 FedAppx 341.—U S 78(12).

Garza; U.S. v., CA5 (Tex), 124 FedAppx 891.—Bail 79(2).

Garza; U.S. v., CA5 (Tex), 116 FedAppx 478.—Crim Law 961, 1083, 1181.5(3.1), 1192.

Garza; U.S. v., CA5 (Tex), 103 FedAppx 528, cert gr, vac 125 SCt 1054, 543 US 1111, 160 LEd2d 1044, on remand 135 FedAppx 687, cert den 126 SCt 495, 546 US 967, 163 LEd2d 375, opinion reinstated 135 FedAppx 687, cert den 126 SCt 495, 546 US 967, 163 LEd2d 375.—Sent & Pun 686.

Garza; U.S. v., CA5 (Tex), 93 FedAppx 640.—Controlled Subs 69, 81.

Garza; U.S. v., CA5 (Tex), 78 FedAppx 351.—Crim Law 1023(12).

Garza; U.S. v., CA5 (Tex), 70 FedAppx 212, cert den 124 SCt 591, 540 US 1027, 157 LEd2d 449.—Crim Law 1044.2(1).

Garza v. U.S., CCA5 (Tex), 159 F2d 413.—Assault 74, 91; Crim Law 1167(1); Ind & Inf 110(17).

Garza v. U.S., SDTex, 881 FSupp 1103.—Action 14; Arrest 63.5(4); Assault 2, 10; Cust Dut 54; Damag 49.10, 50.10; False Imp 2, 13; Offic 114; Torts 121.

Garza; U.S. v., SDTex, 881 FSupp 1099.—Arrest 63.5(4); Civil R 1035, 1376(6); Cust Dut 126(2), 126(5), 126(9.1).

Garza; U.S. v., SDTex, 502 FSupp 537.—Crim Law 577.2, 577.5, 577.8(2), 577.15(1), 577.15(4), 577.16(4).

Garza v. U.S. Fidelity & Guaranty Co., TexCivApp–San Antonio, 251 SW2d 781, ref nre.—Work Comp 1105, 1269, 1283, 1927, 1958, 1961.

Garza; Valencia v., TexCivApp–San Antonio, 765 SW2d 893. —App & E 78(1), 170(1), 989, 1008.1(2), 1012.1(5), 1071.2; Judgm 747(6); Princ & A 23(5); Trial 382; Ven & Pur 16(3), 23.

Garza; Vela v., TexApp–Corpus Christi, 975 SW2d 801.—Autos 226(3); Contrib 6; Damag 63; Neglig 549(8).

Garza v. Waco Scaffold and Shoring Co., TexCivApp–El Paso, 576 SW2d 442, ref nre.—App & E 1056.1(10), 1069.1; Neglig 1750; Prod Liab 71, 88; Trial 358, 359(1).

Garza; Wal-Mart Stores, Inc. v., TexApp–San Antonio, 27 SW3d 64, reh overr, and review den.—App & E 396, 930(1), 1169(5); Neglig 1000, 1001, 1119, 1736.

Garza; Weber v., CA5 (Tex), 570 F2d 511.—Atty & C 11(2.1); Hab Corp 663; Judges 47(2).

Garza v. Westergren, CA5 (Tex), 908 F2d 27, reh den.—Fed Civ Proc 2840, 2844; Fed Cts 724.

Garza; Wilkins v., TexApp–San Antonio, 693 SW2d 553. —Wills 399, 435, 440, 448, 449, 470(1), 486, 587(1), 775, 858(4).

Garza v. Wilkinson, TexCivApp–San Antonio, 129 SW2d 839, writ dism, correct.—App & E 742(2); Ex & Ad 438(5); Lim of Act 179(2); Parties 87; Trial 90.

Garza v. Williams Bros. Const. Co., Inc., TexApp–Houston (14 Dist), 879 SW2d 290.—Courts 113; Judgm 185(2); Lim of Act 118(2).

Garza v. Wirsing, TexCivApp–Fort Worth, 604 SW2d 391.—Autos 244(22.1); Pretrial Proc 307.

Garza; Zamora v., TexCivApp–San Antonio, 129 SW2d 401.—Ex & Ad 17(7), 37(3), 37(4).

Garza; Zamora v., TexCivApp–San Antonio, 117 SW2d 165.—Cert 1, 5(1), 42(8); Ex & Ad 37(4).

Garza; Zamora v., TexCivApp–San Antonio, 117 SW2d 160.—App & E 1089(5); Ex & Ad 256(5).

Garza v. Zavala, TexApp–El Paso, 905 SW2d 312.—Judgm 17(1), 17(10), 99; Proc 153.

Garza Barreda v. State, TexApp–Corpus Christi, 739 SW2d 368, reh den, on reconsideration 760 SW2d 1, petition for discretionary review refused, and petition for discretionary review gr, petition for discretionary review dism with per curiam opinion 760 SW2d 1.—Crim Law 662.1, 790; Rape 40(1), 40(2); Witn 383, 405(1).

Garza County; St. Paul Fire & Marine Ins. Co. v., TexCivApp–Amarillo, 215 SW2d 644, writ refused.—Counties 187.

Garza County Warehouse & Marketing Ass'n; St. Paul Fire & Marine Ins. Co. v., CCA5 (Tex), 93 F2d 590.—Fed Cts 931; Insurance 3023, 3100(1), 3396; Plgs 18.

Garza Energy Trust; Mission Resources, Inc. v., TexApp–Corpus Christi, 166 SW3d 301, review gr.—Abate & R 4, 8(2), 9, 14; Action 13; App & E 204(2), 854(4), 930(1), 946; Const Law 4426, 4427; Damag 87(1), 87(2), 91.5(1), 94.1, 189.5; Evid 99, 146; Interest 30(3); Mines 51(1), 51(5), 78.1(2), 78.1(7), 78.6, 78.7(3.1), 78.7(5), 78.7(6); Pretrial Proc 556.1; Tresp 75; Trial 62(1), 63(1), 125(2), 129.

Garza-Fuentes v. U.S., CA5 (Tex), 400 F2d 219, cert den 89 SCt 1311, 394 US 963, 22 LEd2d 563.—Arrest 68(11), 71.1(9); Crim Law 394.4(11), 1036.1(1), 1036.1(3.1), 1158(2), 1186.4(3); Searches 23, 164.

Garza Garcia v. State, TexApp–Corpus Christi, 787 SW2d 185.—Crim Law 693, 694, 1043(3).

Garza Garcia v. State, TexApp–Corpus Christi, 732 SW2d 673, petition for discretionary review refused.—Burg 9(1), 41(1); Crim Law 1038.1(2), 1038.1(4), 1172.1(1).

Garza Garza v. State, TexApp–Corpus Christi, 788 SW2d 651.—Const Law 4711; Crim Law 507(1), 507(2), 507.5, 641.12(1), 641.13(7), 742(2), 780(1), 780(2), 1030(2), 1032(1), 1120(9), 1159.2(7), 1166.18; Homic 1174, 1181; Jury 129; Kidnap 18, 36; Rape 51(1); Sent & Pun 545, 547, 548.

Garza-Garza; U.S. v., CA5 (Tex), 79 FedAppx 635, cert den 124 SCt 2096, 541 US 1031, 158 LEd2d 713.—Aliens 377, 799.

Garza Gonzalez v. State, TexApp–Corpus Christi, 783 SW2d 774.—Controlled Subs 26, 27, 30, 68, 80; Crim Law 552(3), 1043(2), 1043(3), 1144.13(3), 1159.2(7).

Garza Investments, Inc. v. Madaria, TexApp–San Antonio, 931 SW2d 597. See Chale Garza Investments, Inc. v. Madaria.

Garza-Lopez; U.S. v., CA5 (Tex), 410 F3d 268, cert den 126 SCt 298, 546 US 919, 163 LEd2d 260.—Crim Law 1030(1), 1042, 1139, 1181.5(8); Ind & Inf 113; Jury 34(7); Sent & Pun 700, 780, 793.

Garza on Behalf of de la Rosa v. Maverick Market, Inc., TexApp–Corpus Christi, 744 SW2d 286, writ gr, rev 768 SW2d 273.—Child 6, 12, 13; Death 31(8); Evid 332(1); Trial 139.1(17).

Garza's Estate v. McAllen Independent School Dist., TexCivApp–Beaumont, 613 SW2d 526, ref nre.—Schools 89.13(1).

Garza-Vale v. Kwiecien, TexApp–San Antonio, 796 SW2d 500, writ den.—Const Law 228.3, 328, 2312, 3043, 3498, 3751, 4410; Death 21; Jury 31.2(1); Land & Ten 164(1), 167(1), 167(2), 167(3).

Gasanova; U.S. v., CA5 (Tex), 332 F3d 297, reh and reh den 75 FedAppx 982, cert den 124 SCt 550, 540 US 1011, 157 LEd2d 422.—Aliens 776; Forfeit 5.

Gasaway; Miller v., TexCivApp–Texarkana, 514 SW2d 90. —Improv 4(2); Partit 85.

Gasaway v. Nesmith, TexCivApp–Hous (1 Dist), 548 SW2d 457, ref nre.—Wills 288(1), 302(1), 324(4), 400.

Gasaway v. State, TexCrimApp, 160 SW2d 961.—Crim Law 1094(3).

Gas Butano, S. A. v. Rodriguez, TexCivApp–San Antonio, 375 SW2d 542.—Corp 465; Courts 28; Judgm 944.

Gasch v. Hartford Acc. & Indem. Co., CA5 (Tex), 491 F3d 278, reh den.—Fed Cts 30, 31, 776; Insurance 3242; Rem of C 2, 36, 107(7); Work Comp 1072.

Gas Equipment Co.; Federal Petroleum Co. v., TexApp–Corpus Christi, 105 SW3d 281.—App & E 856(1), 893(1), 1175(1); Indem 53, 72; Judgm 178.

Gasery, In re, CA5 (Tex), 116 F3d 1051.—Hab Corp 894.1.

Gasery v. State, TexCrimApp, 474 SW2d 201.—Burg 28(6).

Gasery v. State, TexCrimApp, 465 SW2d 377.—Arrest 63.4(13), 71.1(2.1); Burg 28(1); Crim Law 1119(4).

Gashaj v. Garcia, WDTex, 234 FSupp2d 661.—Aliens 436, 466, 470; Const Law 978, 1063, 1089, 3875, 3921, 4439.

Gaskamp v. Fleetwood Enterprises, Inc., CA5 (Tex), 280 F3d 1069, opinion supplemented on denial of reh 303 F3d 570.—Action 17; Alt Disp Res 116, 119, 134(1), 134(6), 137, 139, 141, 143, 200, 213(5); Contracts 187(1); Fed Cts 403.

Gaskamp; Massachusetts Mut. Life Ins. Co. v., TexCivApp–Beaumont, 420 SW2d 739.—App & E 846(5); Evid 416; Insurance 1837, 2457(1).

Gaskill v. Sneaky Enterprises, Inc., TexApp–Fort Worth, 997 SW2d 296, reh overr, and petition for review den.—Courts 176.5.

Gaskill v. U.S., NDTex, 188 FSupp 507.—Int Rev 4003.1, 4007, 4029.

Gaskin; City of Port Arthur v., TexCivApp–Beaumont, 107 SW2d 610.—Mun Corp 33(3), 33(10).

Gaskin v. Hand, SDTex, 560 FSupp 930.—Receivers 1, 29(1); Rem of C 97.

Gaskin v. Perritt, TexCivApp–Texarkana, 472 SW2d 211. —App & E 387(5), 395; Damag 216(8); Judgm 199(3.17).

Gaskin v. State, TexCrimApp, 365 SW2d 185.—Controlled Subs 80; Searches 164.

Gaskin v. State, TexCrimApp, 353 SW2d 467, 172 TexCrim 7.—Crim Law 627.6(5), 627.7(3), 1086.11, 1141(2), 1166(10.10).

Gaskin v. Titus County Hosp. Dist., TexApp–Texarkana, 978 SW2d 178, reh overr, and review den.—Judgm 181(33); Mun Corp 741.40(1).

Gaskin v. Titus County Memorial Hosp., TexApp–Texarkana, 978 SW2d 178. See Gaskin v. Titus County Hosp. Dist.

Gaskins v. Duke, TexCivApp–Hous (1 Dist), 483 SW2d 499.—Bills & N 442.

Gaskins; National Sav. Ins. Co. v., TexCivApp–Fort Worth, 572 SW2d 573.—Const Law 2600; Decl Judgm 61, 65, 68, 165; Evid 207(1), 264; Insurance 1864, 2913, 2914.

Gaskins v. State, TexCrimApp, 299 SW2d 710, 164 TexCrim 431.—Autos 355(6), 359; Crim Law 1120(3).

Gas Lift Corp.; Price-Trawick, Inc. v., CCA5 (Tex), 101 F2d 134.—Pat 1, 165(2), 233.1.

Gasmark Ltd., In re, CA5 (Tex), 193 F3d 371, reh and reh den.—Bankr 2671, 3568(2).

GasMark Ltd., Matter of, CA5 (Tex), 158 F3d 312. See Gasmark Ltd. Liquidating Trust v. Louis Dreyfus Natural Gas Corp.

Gasmark, Ltd. v. Kimball Energy Corp., TexApp–Fort Worth, 868 SW2d 925, reh overr.—Contracts 1, 20, 22(1), 24, 31; Sales 10, 22(0.5), 22(1), 23(0.5), 23(2), 23(4), 54.

Gasmark Ltd. Liquidating Trust v. Louis Dreyfus Natural Gas Corp., CA5 (Tex), 158 F3d 312.—Bankr 2164.1, 2607, 2616(1), 2725.1, 2726(2), 2727(2); Fed Civ Proc 2486.

Gaspard v. Beadle, TexApp–Houston (1 Dist), 36 SW3d 229, review den.—App & E 930(1), 984(1), 1001(3), 1003(7), 1030, 1071.6; Atty & C 24, 114; Costs 2; Damag 49.10, 50.10, 87(2), 149, 208(6); Fraud 3, 4, 12, 13(1); Motions 40; Plead 34(1), 48; Seduct 1.

Gaspard v. Cox, TexCivApp–El Paso, 583 SW2d 877, ref nre.—Labor & Emp 3125, 3157.

Gaspard v. DuPont Dow Elastomers, L.L.C., TexApp–Beaumont, 140 SW3d 415.—Judgm 185(2); Labor & Emp 3125; Neglig 1000, 1011, 1037(7), 1076, 1086, 1205(7).

Gaspard v. Gaspard, TexCivApp–Beaumont, 582 SW2d 629.—App & E 205; Courts 37(3), 472.1; Divorce 66; Judges 29.

Gaspard; Gaspard v., TexCivApp–Beaumont, 582 SW2d 629.—App & E 205; Courts 37(3), 472.1; Divorce 66; Judges 29.

Gaspard; Jim Austin Olds-Cadillac and Toyota Co. v., TexCivApp–Beaumont, 592 SW2d 364.—App & E 215(1), 758.1, 758.3(9), 1010.1(1), 1010.1(3), 1010.1(10).

Gasper; Vega v., CA5 (Tex), 36 F3d 417, reh den, on remand 886 FSupp 1335.—Bankr 2151, 2152.1, 3717; Fed Cts 724, 865, 945, 947; Labor & Emp 36, 2298, 2315, 2316, 2317, 2319, 2390(4), 2394.

Gasper; Vega v., WDTex, 886 FSupp 1335.—Labor & Emp 2317, 2320, 2390(4), 2731.

Gasperson v. Christie, Mitchell & Mitchell Co., TexCivApp–Fort Worth, 418 SW2d 345, ref nre.—App & E 1170.7; Estop 56, 99; Evid 382; Frds St of 119(1); Mines 64, 65, 68(1), 75, 78.7(2), 79.1(1); Trial 350.3(2.1), 351.2(2), 351.2(4), 366; Trusts 102(1), 103(1).

Gasperson v. Madill Nat. Bank, TexCivApp–Fort Worth, 455 SW2d 381, ref nre.—App & E 717, 931(4), 1071.5, 1073(1); Chat Mtg 49(1), 157(2), 278, 289; Compromise 5(1); Contracts 39; Costs 93; Estop 92(2); Frds St of 74(1), 106(2); Interest 39(3), 44; Judgm 5, 21, 251(1); Lim of Act 28(1), 175; Mines 54.5; Spec Perf 31; Tresp 57; Trial 393(3); Trusts 103(1).

Gasperson v. Morris, TexCivApp–Fort Worth, 362 SW2d 392, ref nre.—App & E 1170.7; Bills & N 134; Evid 139, 444(1), 445(1), 469; Lim of Act 183(1); Partners 71.

Gas Producing Enterprises, Inc. v. Guerra, TexCivApp–San Antonio, 576 SW2d 450.—Plead 111.30; Venue 22(4).

Gas Reclamation, Inc., In re, BkrtcySDTex, 51 BR 860. —Bankr 2256.

Gas Reclamation, Inc. v. Jones, SDTex, 113 FRD 1.—Fed Civ Proc 2790, 2791, 2800, 2812, 2819, 2828.

Gas Ridge v. Suburban Agr. Properties, CCA5 (Tex), 150 F2d 363, reh den 150 F2d 1020, cert den 66 SCt 487, 326 US 796, 90 LEd 485, reh den 66 SCt 679, 327 US 815, 90 LEd 1039, and 66 SCt 802, 327 US 817, 90 LEd 1040.—Evid 370(4); Fed Civ Proc 2016, 2251; Fed Cts 867; Mines 59, 73.5; Ven & Pur 239(1).

Gass v. Baggerly, TexCivApp–Dallas, 332 SW2d 426.—App & E 692(1), 748, 758.3(3), 1078(1); Judgm 198; Trial 131(3), 306; Witn 204(2).

Gass v. State, TexApp–Beaumont, 785 SW2d 834.—Const Law 258(5), 3789, 4509(23); Crim Law 29(12), 371(9), 1042, 1043(2), 1120(3), 1130(2); Witn 37(4), 376.

Gassaway v. State, TexCrimApp, 957 SW2d 48.—Autos 421; Crim Law 393(1).

Gassaway v. State, TexCrimApp, 274 SW2d 79.—Crim Law 1090.1(1).

Gasser, Estate of; Calloway v., TexCivApp–Tyler, 558 SW2d 571, ref nre.—Wills 193, 440, 448, 449, 656.

Gassett v. State, TexCrimApp, 587 SW2d 695.—Homic 1480.

Gassett v. State, TexCrimApp, 532 SW2d 328.—Crim Law 419(1.5), 429(1), 432, 436(6), 1169.1(9).

Gassner v. City of Garland, Tex., CA5 (Tex), 864 F2d 394, reh den.—Autos 349(8); Civil R 1088(4), 1376(6).

Gas Solutions, Ltd.; Vial v., TexApp–Texarkana, 187 SW3d 220.—Abate & R 52, 55(3), 58(2); Action 13; App

GAS

& E 174, 893(1), 1010.2; Fraud 17, 29; Judgm 185.3(2); Lim of Act 43, 95(1), 104(1), 104(2); Mines 55(8); Plead 104(1); Ven & Pur 218.

Gassoway v. State, TexCrimApp, 385 SW2d 386.—Autos 359; Crim Law 1177.

Gast v. Singleton, SDTex, 402 FSupp2d 794.—Civil R 1345, 1351(1), 1352(1), 1352(4), 1395(6), 1401.

Gaston, Ex parte, TexCivApp–Beaumont, 501 SW2d 447. —Hab Corp 529.

Gaston v. B. F. Walker, Inc., CA5 (Tex), 400 F2d 671.— Death 8, 38; Lim of Act 2(3), 165.

Gaston v. Bruton, TexCivApp–El Paso, 358 SW2d 207, writ dism.—App & E 842(7), 930(1), 989, 1170.1, 1177(7); Deeds 68(1.5), 203, 211(1); Des & Dist 90(4); Evid 588; Witn 409.

Gaston v. Chaney, TexApp–Eastland, 734 SW2d 735.— Child S 508(1).

Gaston; Cicero Smith Lumber Co. v., TexCivApp–Amarillo, 447 SW2d 736, ref nre.—App & E 1178(6); Evid 422, 441(1).

Gaston v. Copeland, TexCivApp–Amarillo, 335 SW2d 406, ref nre.—Contracts 97(1), 97(2), 98, 100; Deeds 75; Judgm 181(11), 185(5), 185.1(1), 185.1(2), 185.1(3), 185.3(1); Mental H 372.1.

Gaston; Fruth v., TexCivApp–Austin, 187 SW2d 581, writ refused wom.—App & E 927(7), 989; Compromise 24; Corp 1.6(9); Equity 84; Evid 139; Frds St of 52; Labor & Emp 34(2), 205, 265; Lim of Act 166; Trial 139.1(6), 139.1(16), 140(1); Witn 406.

Gaston v. Gaston, TexCivApp–Tyler, 608 SW2d 332.— Divorce 203, 252.1, 252.2, 252.3(1), 252.3(5), 253(2), 286(1), 286(2), 286(5), 322.

Gaston; Gaston v., TexCivApp–Tyler, 608 SW2d 332.— Divorce 203, 252.1, 252.2, 252.3(1), 252.3(5), 253(2), 286(1), 286(2), 286(5), 322.

Gaston v. Gaston, TexCivApp–Houston, 371 SW2d 707, ref nre.—App & E 930(1), 1001(1); Child C 271; Infants 154.1, 158.

Gaston; Gaston v., TexCivApp–Houston, 371 SW2d 707, ref nre.—App & E 930(1), 1001(1); Child C 271; Infants 154.1, 158.

Gaston v. Houston County, Texas, EDTex, 202 FSupp2d 564.—Civil R 1352(1), 1376(2); Const Law 3488, 3938, 4830; Fed Cts 15; Mun Corp 740(1).

Gaston v. Houston County, Texas, EDTex, 196 FSupp2d 445.—Civil R 1304; Const Law 4830; Counties 146.

Gaston; Kirkland v., TexCivApp–Dallas, 544 SW2d 694.— Contracts 280(1).

Gaston; Northeastern Life Ins. Co. of New York v., TexCivApp–Tyler, 470 SW2d 128, ref nre.—Insurance 3093; Nova 1, 10.

Gaston; Reynolds v., TexCivApp–Dallas, 121 SW2d 651, dism.—App & E 874(4); Plead 111.8, 111.18; Venue 22(8).

Gaston; Roadway Exp. v., TexCivApp–Texarkana, 90 SW2d 874.—Afft 18; App & E 1052(8); Evid 121(12), 332(3); Plead 111.9, 111.12, 111.36, 111.38, 111.42(6), 111.46.

Gaston; Roadway Express v., TexCivApp–El Paso, 91 SW2d 883, writ dism.—App & E 1064.1(3), 1173(2); Autos 245(28); Evid 241(1), 242(5); Trial 215, 219, 350.5(3), 350.5(5), 350.6(3), 352.20.

Gaston v. State, TexCrimApp, 574 SW2d 120.—Crim Law 337, 363, 1169.1(2.1).

Gaston v. State, TexCrimApp, 440 SW2d 297, cert den 90 SCt 452, 396 US 969, 24 LEd2d 435.—Controlled Subs 146.

Gaston v. State, TexCrimApp, 435 SW2d 858.—Crim Law 531(3), 814(16), 824(5), 1169.12.

Gaston v. State, TexCrimApp, 206 SW2d 597, 151 TexCrim 185.—Crim Law 1081(1), 1087.1(2).

Gaston v. State, TexApp–Houston (1 Dist), 136 SW3d 315, petition stricken.—Crim Law 641.5(0.5), 641.5(3), 641.5(7), 641.13(1), 641.13(6), 956(1).

Gaston v. State, TexApp–Austin, 930 SW2d 222.—Crim Law 795(1.5), 795(2.10), 1169.1(9); Double J 25; Homic 669, 672, 1150, 1458.

Gaston v. State, TexApp–Dallas, 63 SW3d 893.—Crim Law 304(1), 304(9), 304(13), 641.13(1), 641.13(7), 990.1, 1081(1), 1088.20, 1134(3), 1134(8), 1134(10), 1450; Sent & Pun 1064.

Gaston v. State, TexApp–Dallas, 672 SW2d 819.—Assault 56.

Gaston v. State, TexApp–Houston (14 Dist), 641 SW2d 261.—Controlled Subs 165, 174, 184; Evid 222(1).

Gaston v. Woodmen of World Life Ins. Soc., TexCivApp–Fort Worth, 167 SW2d 263, writ dism, and writ refused wom.—Insurance 1840, 3003(1), 3015, 3016, 3110(3).

Gasway v. State, TexCrimApp, 248 SW2d 942, 157 TexCrim 647, cert den 73 SCt 167, 344 US 874, 97 LEd 677. —Const Law 268(8), 4623; Crim Law 519(8), 736(2), 824(5), 1090.14, 1159.2(4); Rape 52(1).

G.A.T., In re, TexApp–Houston (14 Dist), 16 SW3d 818, reh overr, and petition for review den.—Const Law 4465; Crim Law 339.10(1), 339.11(1), 1030(1), 1043(2), 1043(3), 1045, 1134(2), 1144.13(2.1), 1144.13(3), 1159.2(1), 1159.2(2), 1159.2(3), 1159.2(7), 1159.4(1), 1159.6; Infants 173.1, 176, 194.1, 195, 196, 197, 243, 253.

Gateley v. Humphrey, Tex, 254 SW2d 98, 151 Tex 588, answer to certified question conformed to 254 SW2d 571.—Courts 247(5); Damag 71.5; Statut 190.

Gateley v. Humphrey, TexCivApp–Dallas, 254 SW2d 571. —Damag 71.5.

Gateley v. Humphrey, TexCivApp–Dallas, 247 SW2d 919, certified question answered 254 SW2d 98, 151 Tex 588, answer to certified question conformed to 254 SW2d 571.—Costs 32(5); Damag 71.5.

Gateley; Lesage v., TexCivApp–Waco, 287 SW2d 193, writ dism.—Courts 89; Divorce 252.1, 252.3(5); Hus & W 248.5, 249(1), 250, 251, 257.

Gately; Garner v., TexApp–Waco, 909 SW2d 61.—Mand 141.

Gately; Taylor v., TexApp–Waco, 870 SW2d 204, writ dism woj.—Crim Law 211(1); Mand 3(2.1), 12, 61.

Gates v. Asher, Tex, 280 SW2d 247, 154 Tex 538.—Deeds 38(1), 40, 196(2), 196(3); Evid 460(4); Trial 350.3(2.1).

Gates; Asher v., TexCivApp–Galveston, 272 SW2d 585, aff in part, rev in part 280 SW2d 247, 154 Tex 538.—Deeds 38(1), 42, 118, 119; Evid 460(7); Ref of Inst 2.

Gates; Bankers Commercial Life Ins. Co. v., TexCivApp–Hous (1 Dist), 448 SW2d 198.—Courts 63, 207.4(2); Mand 10; New Tr 155; Time 10(7).

Gates v. City of Dallas, CA5 (Tex), 729 F2d 343.—Const Law 1620, 1625, 3781, 4509(21); Mun Corp 185(7).

Gates v. City of Dallas, Tex, 704 SW2d 737.—Mun Corp 725, 1040.

Gates; City of Dallas v., TexApp–Eastland, 684 SW2d 792, writ gr, rev 704 SW2d 737.—Mun Corp 1.1, 1040.

Gates; City of Dayton v., TexApp–Beaumont, 126 SW3d 288.—App & E 893(1); Courts 39; Mun Corp 747(1); Plead 104(1); States 191.1.

Gates v. City of Fort Worth, TexCivApp–Fort Worth, 567 SW2d 871, ref nre.—Mun Corp 723; Work Comp 374, 380.

Gates v. Coquat, TexCivApp–San Antonio, 210 SW2d 614. —Tresp to T T 10; Trusts 91; Venue 5.1.

Gates v. Dow Chemical Co., TexApp–Houston (14 Dist), 777 SW2d 120, writ gr, vac 783 SW2d 589.—Courts 472.1; Judgm 181(1), 181(2), 185(1), 185.2(3), 186; New Tr 99, 102(7), 163(2), 165; Pretrial Proc 480; Prod Liab 43, 71; Time 10(7).

Gates; E. L. Cheeney Co. v., CA5 (Tex), 346 F2d 197.— Autos 242(6), 243(3), 244(31), 245(14), 245(30), 245(35), 245(80); Fed Civ Proc 51, 1998, 2212.1, 2233; Fed Cts 898, 941, 955; Princ & A 22(1); Witn 379(1), 379(2).

Gates; Garza v., WDTex, 482 FSupp 1211.—Counties 38.

Gates v. Hampton, TexCivApp–Amarillo, 350 SW2d 62.— Frds St of 129(11), 158(4).

Gates v. Hays, TexCivApp–San Antonio, 95 SW2d 1020, writ dism.—Elect of Rem 7(1); Elections 269; Offic 83; Quo W 11.

Gates; Kennelly v., TexCivApp–Houston, 406 SW2d 351. —Elections 154(6), 154(10), 154(12), 227(1), 293(3), 305(8); Evid 5(2), 317(13).

Gates; Loggins v., TexCivApp–Waco, 301 SW2d 525, ref nre.—App & E 1048(2); Contracts 354; Damag 123, 221(2.1); Evid 501(7).

Gates; Moreno v., TexCivApp–San Antonio, 449 SW2d 366, ref nre.—App & E 1175(3); Autos 245(15); Judgm 199(3.9), 199(3.17).

Gates v. State, TexCrimApp, 543 SW2d 360.—Crim Law 273(4.1), 273.1(4), 273.3, 1109(1), 1144.4.

Gates v. State, TexCrimApp, 471 SW2d 857.—Sent & Pun 1327.

Gates v. State, TexCrimApp, 458 SW2d 676.—Crim Law 339.10(9).

Gates v. State, TexCrimApp, 332 SW2d 333.—Crim Law 960, 1026.10(6).

Gates v. State, TexCrimApp, 285 SW2d 728, 162 TexCrim 327.—Crim Law 720(10); Int Liq 236(20).

Gates v. State, TexCrimApp, 210 SW2d 413, 151 TexCrim 504.—Crim Law 93; Ind & Inf 3.

Gates v. State, TexCrimApp, 143 SW2d 780, 140 TexCrim 228.—Crim Law 134(2), 136, 140, 145, 730(8), 1044.1(3), 1091(11), 1144.6, 1150, 1166(4).

Gates v. State, TexApp–Houston (1 Dist), 24 SW3d 439, petition for discretionary review refused.—Crim Law 419(2.20), 478(1), 1144.13(2.1), 1144.13(3), 1159.2(2), 1159.2(7), 1163(6); Homic 960, 1174, 1184, 1188.

Gates v. State, TexApp–Dallas, 696 SW2d 671.—Const Law 4725; Double J 115; Sent & Pun 1811, 2009.

Gates v. State, TexApp–Beaumont, 628 SW2d 125.—Burg 41(6); Crim Law 814(11), 1043(2).

Gates v. State, TexApp–Tyler, 643 SW2d 183.—Crim Law 339.10(7), 339.11(1), 808.5, 1038.1(2), 1128(2).

Gates v. State Farm County Mut. Ins. Co. of Texas, TexApp–Dallas, 53 SW3d 826.—Insurance 3335, 3336, 3337, 3359, 3557.

Gates; U.S. v., CA5 (Tex), 557 F2d 1086, cert den 98 SCt 737, 434 US 1017, 54 LEd2d 763.—Crim Law 593, 627.8(6), 641.4(4), 1035(5), 1130(1); Double J 59.

Gates v. U.S., CA5 (Tex), 481 F2d 850.—Armed S 84.

Gates; U.S. v., CA5 (Tex), 481 F2d 605.—Crim Law 369.15, 1134(1); Postal 49(9).

Gates v. U.S., WDTex, 351 FSupp 273, aff 481 F2d 850.— Armed S 84; U S 78(5.1).

Gates; U.S. (I.R.S.) v., SDTex, 80 FSupp2d 682.—Fed Civ Proc 2514; Int Rev 4568.

Gates ex rel. Estate of Badouh; Gorham v., TexApp–Austin, 82 SW3d 359, review den.—Ex & Ad 219.9, 402; Judgm 731.

Gates Learjet Corp.; Adams v., NDTex, 711 FSupp 1377. —Lim of Act 46(6), 55(1), 95(3).

Gates Learjet Corp.; Adams v., NDTex, 711 FSupp 1374. —Prod Liab 3.

Gates Rubber Co.; Huntsinger v., TexCivApp–Amarillo, 149 SW2d 632.—App & E 1126, 1236.

Gates Rubber Co.; Security Tire & Rubber Co. v., CA5 (Tex), 598 F2d 962, cert den 100 SCt 298, 444 US 942, 62 LEd2d 309.—Antitrust 849, 882.

Gates Rubber Co. Sales Division, Inc.; Tri-State Tire Service, Inc. v., CA5 (Tex), 339 F2d 573.—Fraud 58(1); Interest 18(2), 51; Jury 25(6); Princ & S 99.

Gates Rubber Co., Sales Division, Inc. v. Wood, TexCiv–App–Beaumont, 374 SW2d 785.—Contracts 15; Sales 260, 262.5, 279, 439, 441(2), 441(3), 441(4), 447.

Gatesville, City of; Hooten v., TexCivApp–Waco, 130 SW2d 1067.—Mun Corp 857; Neglig 1655.

Gatesville Redi-Mix, Inc. v. Jones, TexApp–Waco, 787 SW2d 443, writ den.—App & E 499(1); Ex & Ad 7.

Gateway Center Associates, Ltd.; Tarrant Appraisal Dist. v., TexApp–Fort Worth, 34 SW3d 712.—Action 35; Const Law 3847, 3865, 3879, 4138(2); Tax 2523, 2572, 2603, 2647, 2693.

Gateway East, Inc.; Larned v., TexApp–El Paso, 186 SW3d 597.—App & E 756, 761, 1078(1); Atty & C 62; Judgm 183, 185(2), 185.2(9).

Gateway Nat. Bank of Beaumont; Coward v., Tex, 525 SW2d 857.—Costs 194.18, 194.22; Evid 571(7), 584(1); Judgm 185.3(1), 185.3(4), 186.

Gateway Nat. Bank of Beaumont; Coward v., TexCiv–App–Beaumont, 515 SW2d 129, writ gr, rev 525 SW2d 857.—App & E 671(4); Evid 18; Judgm 180, 185.3(16).

Gateway Technologies, Inc. v. MCI Telecommunications Corp., CA5 (Tex), 64 F3d 993.—Alt Disp Res 229, 235, 251, 265, 342, 363(6), 374(1); Damag 87(2), 89(2); Fraud 7, 61, 64(1).

Gateway Technologies, Inc.; MCI Telecommunications Corp. v., CA5 (Tex),64 F3d 993. See Gateway Technologies, Inc. v. MCI Telecommunications Corp.

Gateway Tugs, Inc. v. American Commercial Lines, Inc., CA5 (Tex), 72 F3d 479. See Kristie Leigh Enterprises, Inc., Petition of.

Gatewood; Fechtel v., TexCivApp–Tyler, 470 SW2d 293, ref nre.—Evid 161.1, 166, 171, 181, 262, 317(4).

Gatewood; Graham v., TexCivApp–Amarillo, 166 SW2d 768, writ refused wom.—App & E 882(12), 1062.1; Neglig 1694, 1717; Trial 352.1(1), 352.4(7), 352.18, 352.19.

Gatewood; Southland Life Ins. Co. v., TexComApp, 141 SW2d 588, 135 Tex 177.—App & E 1089(5); Evid 419(15); Insurance 2035.

Gatewood; Southland Life Ins. Co. v., TexCivApp–Dallas, 115 SW2d 723, aff 141 SW2d 588, 135 Tex 177.— App & E 1060.1(1), 1071.1(6); Insurance 1940, 2027, 2035, 3156, 3191(7).

Gatewood v. State, TexApp–Amarillo, 156 SW3d 679, petition for discretionary review refused.—False Pers 6.

Gathe v. Cigna Healthplan of Texas, Inc., TexApp–Houston (14 Dist), 879 SW2d 360, writ den.—Alt Disp Res 368; App & E 66, 68.

Gathers v. Walpace Co., Inc., TexCivApp–Beaumont, 544 SW2d 169, ref nre.—Corp 672(1); Proc 145.

Gathright v. Carl Markley Motor Co., TexCivApp–Beaumont, 146 SW2d 307.—Autos 192(7), 193(3.1); Bailm 21; Princ & A 3(1).

Gathright; Hancock v., TexCivApp–Waco, 451 SW2d 591. —App & E 78(4); Judgm 335(1); New Tr 109; Pretrial Proc 698, 699.

Gathright v. Riggs, TexCivApp–Waco, 344 SW2d 757.— Judgm 570(3); Venue 21.

Gathright v. Russell, TexCivApp–Tyler, 383 SW2d 441, writ dism.—Chat Mtg 176(2), 176(3), 176(5), 176(6), 209, 213; Trover 46.

Gathright v. State, TexApp–Fort Worth, 698 SW2d 260. —Crim Law 407(1), 641.12(1), 1165(1), 1169.12.

Gathright v. U.S., WDTex, 239 FSupp 491.—Int Rev 3236, 3255, 4984.

Gathright v. Western Alliance Ins. Co., TexCivApp–Austin, 324 SW2d 894, ref nre.—Trusts 34(1), 102(1).

Gatlin; City of Richardson v., TexCivApp–Eastland, 497 SW2d 537, ref nre.—Pretrial Proc 552.

Gatlin v. Countryside Industries, Inc., NDTex, 564 FSupp 1490.—Rem of C 19(1), 82.

Gatlin; Davis v., TexCivApp–Beaumont, 462 SW2d 54, ref nre.—Autos 242(7), 247.

Gatlin; Fidelity & Cas. Co. of New York v., TexCivApp–Dallas, 470 SW2d 924.—Insurance 2795, 2800, 2802.

Gatlin v. Fisher, TexCivApp–Texarkana, 178 SW2d 870. —App & E 688(2), 1053(2); Land & Ten 331(1); Witn 236(1), 387.

Gatlin v. Mason, TexCivApp–Tyler, 459 SW2d 200.—Lim of Act 197(1), 199(1); Proc 48.

Gatlin v. Southwestern Settlement & Development Corp., TexCivApp–Beaumont, 166 SW2d 150, writ refused wom.—Evid 588; Judgm 199(3.9), 199(3.14).

Gatlin v. State, TexCrimApp, 296 SW2d 540.—Crim Law 1090.1(1).

Gatlin v. State, TexApp–Houston (14 Dist), 863 SW2d 236.—Crim Law 1081(2).

Gatling; First City Mortgage Co. v., TexCivApp–Corpus Christi, 530 SW2d 636, dism.—App & E 186; Plead 45, 111.15, 111.30, 111.39(4), 111.42(4), 111.42(6); Venue 7.5(2), 7.5(3), 22(1), 22(4).

Gatling v. Perna, TexApp–Dallas, 788 SW2d 44, writ den.—Judgm 178, 181(33); Lim of Act 95(12), 182(2), 195(3).

Gator Hawk, Inc.; Project Engineering USA Corp. v., TexApp–Houston (1 Dist), 833 SW2d 716.—Abate & R 4, 13; Action 69(2); App & E 219(2), 543, 863, 949, 1051.1(2); Corp 665(1); Courts 12(2.1), 12(2.5), 12(2.10), 12(2.15), 12(2.20), 35.

Gatpandan; Hilal v., TexApp–Corpus Christi, 71 SW3d 403, reh overr.—App & E 5, 846(5), 859; Compromise 5(3), 20(1); Judgm 109, 335(3); Trial 6(1).

Gatson v. State, TexCrimApp, 387 SW2d 65.—Homic 1134; Witn 405(1).

Gatson; Texas Emp. Ins. Ass'n v., TexCivApp–Beaumont, 367 SW2d 168.—App & E 930(1), 989; Work Comp 1342, 1386, 1446.

Gatter; HSAM Inc. v., TexApp–San Antonio, 814 SW2d 887, writ dism by agreement.—Cons Cred 13, 18; Equity 34, 65(1).

Gatter; HSA Mortg. Co. v., TexApp–San Antonio, 814 SW2d 887. See HSAM Inc. v. Gatter.

GATX Leasing Corp. v. DBM Drilling Corp., TexApp–San Antonio, 657 SW2d 178.—Banks 191.10, 191.15, 191.30; Inj 138.21; Interpl 10; Sec Tran 12, 161, 164.1.

G.A.T.X. Logistics, Inc.; Wrenn v., TexApp–Fort Worth, 73 SW3d 489, rule 537(f) motion gr.—App & E 223, 719(8), 907(1), 1136; Judgm 181(21), 185(2); Labor & Emp 2921, 3040, 3047, 3049(3), 3055, 3056(1), 3056(2), 3061(2), 3132; Neglig 375, 387; Pretrial Proc 151.

GATX Tank Erection Corp. v. Tesoro Petroleum Corp., TexApp–San Antonio, 693 SW2d 617, ref nre.—Costs 207; Damag 163(4), 191; Pretrial Proc 313.

GATX Terminals Corp. v. Rylander, TexApp–Austin, 78 SW3d 630.—App & E 895(1), 989, 1008.1(2), 1010.1(2), 1010.1(3), 1012.1(3), 1012.1(5); Tax 3642, 3693, 3704.

Gatz v. Smith, TexCivApp–Galveston, 205 SW2d 616, writ refused.—Autos 194(3); Labor & Emp 3026.

Gau v. State, TexCrimApp, 236 SW2d 126.—Crim Law 1090.1(1).

Gau; Warren v., TexCivApp–El Paso, 18 SW2d 768, writ dism woj.—Mun Corp 621.

Gaubert, In re, BkrtcyEDTex, 149 BR 819.—Bankr 3357(2.1), 3357(4).

Gaubert; F.D.I.C. v., BkrtcyEDTex, 149 BR 819. See Gaubert, In re.

Gaubert v. Hendricks, NDTex, 679 FSupp 622.—B & L Assoc 23(8), 48; Fed Civ Proc 343.

Gaubert; Safeco Ins. Co. of America v., TexApp–Dallas, 829 SW2d 274, writ den.—App & E 93, 863; Indem 31(1), 31(2), 31(5), 42, 81; Inj 242.1, 243, 251, 252(5); Judgm 185(2); Princ & S 175, 185, 190(3), 190(6).

Gaubert; U.S. v., USTex, 111 SCt 1267, 499 US 315, 113 LEd2d 335, on remand 932 F2d 376.—B & L Assoc 2.1; Fed Cts 794; U S 78(12).

Gaubert v. U.S., CA5 (Tex), 885 F2d 1284, reh den 894 F2d 406, cert gr 110 SCt 3211, 496 US 935, 110 LEd2d 659, rev 111 SCt 1267, 499 US 315, 113 LEd2d 335, on remand 932 F2d 376.—B & L Assoc 42(4), 48; U S 78(12), 127(1).

Gaudet; Junior Football Ass'n of Orange v., TexCivApp–Beaumont, 546 SW2d 70.—Const Law 3020, 3027.

Gaudette v. State, TexApp–Tyler, 713 SW2d 206, petition for discretionary review refused.—Const Law 266(3.2),

4658(4); Crim Law 531(3), 814(20), 867; Kidnap 36; Rape 51(1); Searches 178; Witn 257.10.

Gaudette v. Wendt, CA5 (Tex), 191 FedAppx 251.—U S Mag 31.

Gaudin v. State, TexApp–Waco, 703 SW2d 789, petition for discretionary review refused.—Ind & Inf 71.2(2), 71.4(2), 121.1(2), 137(6).

Gaudion, Ex parte, TexApp–Austin, 628 SW2d 500.—Courts 100(1).

Gaudion v. Gaudion, TexCivApp–Austin, 601 SW2d 805.—Exemp 49; Hus & W 249(3), 262.1(3).

Gaudion; Gaudion v., TexCivApp–Austin, 601 SW2d 805.—Exemp 49; Hus & W 249(3), 262.1(3).

Gaughan v. Spires Council of Co-Owners, TexApp–Houston (1 Dist), 870 SW2d 552.—App & E 766; Costs 260(4); Judgm 509, 585(3), 678(1), 678(2), 707, 713(2).

Gaul; Williams v., TexApp–Waco, 687 SW2d 85.—Infants 155, 156, 172, 178, 179.

Gaulden v. Johnson, TexApp–Dallas, 801 SW2d 561, writ den.—Insurance 1806, 1809, 1810, 1812, 1814, 1835(2), 1863; Judgm 181(8), 181(23), 185(2).

Gauldin; Continental Nat. American Co., Ltd. v., TexCivApp–Dallas, 594 SW2d 793.—Insurance 1836, 3053.

Gauldin v. State, TexCrimApp, 683 SW2d 411.—Arrest 71.1(1), 71.1(4.1), 71.1(5); Crim Law 412.1(4), 1036.1(5), 1043(3), 1169.1(1), 1169.1(8); Searches 64, 66.

Gauldin v. State, TexApp–Fort Worth, 632 SW2d 652, petition for discretionary review gr, aff 683 SW2d 411.—Arrest 71.1(5); Const Law 266(3.2), 4658(2); Crim Law 406(1), 406(3), 412.2(2), 641.3(10), 1043(2), 1166.22(2); Rob 20, 27(1), 27(2).

Gaulding v. Celotex Corp., Tex, 772 SW2d 66.—Neglig 1612, 1613, 1614; Prod Liab 1, 62; Torts 130.

Gaulding v. Celotex Corp., TexApp–Eastland, 748 SW2d 627, writ gr, aff 772 SW2d 66.—Plead 228.14; Prod Liab 42.

Gaulding v. Gaulding, TexCivApp–Dallas, 256 SW2d 684.—App & E 164; Divorce 252.5(3), 281; Hus & W 268(1), 272(5).

Gaulding; Gaulding v., TexCivApp–Dallas, 256 SW2d 684.—App & E 164; Divorce 252.5(3), 281; Hus & W 268(1), 272(5).

Gaulding v. Gaulding, TexCivApp–Eastland, 503 SW2d 617.—Divorce 286(9); Hus & W 246.

Gaulding; Gaulding v., TexCivApp–Eastland, 503 SW2d 617.—Divorce 286(9); Hus & W 246.

Gaulding; Mitchell v., TexCivApp–Waco, 483 SW2d 41, 75 ALR3d 1090, ref nre.—App & E 1073(1); Covenants 49, 51(1); Judgm 186.

Gaulding; Reeves v., TexCivApp–Galveston, 106 SW2d 742, writ dism.—Brok 49(1).

Gaulke; Rea v., TexCivApp–Hous (14 Dist), 442 SW2d 826, ref nre.—App & E 1070(2); Health 786, 823(5), 906, 923, 925, 926; Trial 350.6(2), 355(1).

Gault; Brazell v., TexCivApp–Amarillo, 160 SW2d 540.—App & E 719(8); Evid 83(1); Inj 105(1).

Gault Co. v. Texas Rural Legal Aid, Inc., CA5 (Tex), 848 F2d 544. See Howard Gault Co. v. Texas Rural Legal Aid, Inc.

Gaumond v. City of Melissa, Texas, EDTex, 227 FSupp2d 627.—Civil R 1304; Const Law 1254, 3865, 4156, 4164, 4165(1), 4166(2), 4167, 4171; Fed Cts 18; Labor & Emp 40(1), 40(2); Mun Corp 183(0.5).

Gaunce; Wadley v., CCA5 (Tex), 87 F2d 379.—Mines 52.

Gaunt v. Lloyds America of San Antonio, WDTex, 11 FSupp 787.—Assoc 20(1); Fed Cts 29.1, 32, 297, 302, 312.1, 314, 315, 319; Labor & Emp 1978; Partners 375.

Gauntt; Clark v., TexComApp, 161 SW2d 270, 138 Tex 558.—Assign 8; Covenants 47; Deeds 116; Des & Dist 68; Estop 38; Mtg 131.

Gauntt; Clarke v., TexCivApp–Waco, 149 SW2d 193, rev 161 SW2d 270, 138 Tex 558.—Estop 38, 45, 50; Interest 38(2); Lim of Act 124; Mtg 128, 416.

Gauntt v. State, TexCrimApp, 335 SW2d 616, 169 TexCrim 520.—Crim Law 706(3), 722.3, 730(14), 785(3), 868, 925.5(3), 956(2); Homic 1345; Witn 323, 380(5.1).

Gaus; Apcar Inv. Partners VI, Ltd. v., TexApp–Eastland, 161 SW3d 137, rule 537(f) motion gr.—App & E 80(6); Partners 314, 353.

Gause; City of Fort Worth v., TexComApp, 101 SW2d 221, 129 Tex 25.—Judgm 18(1), 145(2), 160.

Gause v. Gause, TexCivApp–Austin, 430 SW2d 409.—App & E 236(2), 253, 302(1), 934(1); Equity 71(1); Judgm 252(5); Lim of Act 95(8); Plead 67, 78, 79, 193(4); Quiet T 51; Trusts 43(1), 44(3), 103(2), 110, 374; Wills 67.

Gause; Gause v., TexCivApp–Austin, 430 SW2d 409.—App & E 236(2), 253, 302(1), 934(1); Equity 71(1); Judgm 252(5); Lim of Act 95(8); Plead 67, 78, 79, 193(4); Quiet T 51; Trusts 43(1), 44(3), 103(2), 110, 374; Wills 67.

Gause-Ware Service Ins Co v. Thomas, NDTex, 76 FSupp 626.—Int Rev 4359.

Gausman v. State, TexCrimApp, 478 SW2d 458.—Crim Law 507(2); Larc 55.

Gaut v. Amarillo Economic Development Corp., TexApp–Austin, 921 SW2d 884, reh overr.—App & E 863; Judgm 185(2); Mun Corp 247.

Gaut v. Quast, Tex, 510 SW2d 90.—Damag 221(7); Trial 350.3(5).

Gaut v. Quast, TexCivApp–Hous (14 Dist), 505 SW2d 367, ref nre 510 SW2d 90.—App & E 758.3(8), 1070(2); Damag 87(2); Fraud 3; Health 821(2), 908, 928; Trial 350.3(5).

Gauthia v. State, TexCrimApp, 352 SW2d 129, 171 TexCrim 522.—Ind & Inf 79.

Gauthier v. Aetna Cas. and Sur. Co., TexApp–Houston (14 Dist), 720 SW2d 174.—Stip 14(1); Trial 350.3(8); Work Comp 1172, 1377, 1653.

Gauthier v. Aetna Cas. & Surety Co., TexApp–Houston (14 Dist), 704 SW2d 377, opinion superseded 720 SW2d 174.

Gauthier; J. Weingarten, Inc. v., TexCivApp–Beaumont, 305 SW2d 181.—App & E 692(1), 1004(8), 1170.6; Damag 20, 130.1, 166(2), 210(1), 216(1), 221(5.1); Evid 539; Neglig 1613, 1615, 1625, 1736; Trial 122, 350.6(2).

Gauthier; Moore v., TexApp–San Antonio, 957 SW2d 169.—Neglig 1161.

Gauthier v. State, TexCrimApp, 496 SW2d 584.—Perj 29(2), 37(2).

Gauthreaux v. Baylor University Medical Center, NDTex, 879 FSupp 634.—Civil R 1217, 1218(4); Fed Civ Proc 2470, 2497.1, 2544; Labor & Emp 808, 861, 863(2), 873.

Gauthreaux v. Baylor University Medical Center, NDTex, 876 FSupp 847.—Fed Civ Proc 1961; Fed Cts 15; Jury 13(9), 14(1.5).

Gautreaux v. City of Port Arthur, TexCivApp–Beaumont, 406 SW2d 531, ref nre.—App & E 878(2); Judgm 668(1); Set-Off 60; Work Comp 2191, 2195.

Gauvey v. Johnson, TexCivApp–El Paso, 209 SW2d 978.—Commerce 62.66, 85.32(1); Labor & Emp 2290(4).

Gavagan v. U.S., CA5 (Tex), 955 F2d 1016.—Adm 118.7(5); Seamen 29(1), 29(2), 29(4), 29(5.14).

Gavenda v. Strata Energy, Inc., Tex, 705 SW2d 690, appeal after remand 753 SW2d 789.—Atty & C 102; Impl & C C 25; Mines 79.1(3), 79.7.

Gavenda; Strata Energy, Inc. v., TexApp–Houston (14 Dist), 753 SW2d 789.—App & E 1175(1), 1176(1); Interest 31, 39(2.20); Mines 79.1(3).

Gavenda v. Strata Energy, Inc., TexApp–Houston (14 Dist), 683 SW2d 859, writ gr, rev in part 705 SW2d 690, appeal after remand 753 SW2d 789.—Judgm 181(15.1); Mines 79.1(3), 79.1(4).

Gavey Properties/762 v. First Financial Sav. & Loan Ass'n, CA5 (Tex), 845 F2d 519.—B & L Assoc 32.

Gavia v. State, TexCrimApp, 488 SW2d 420.—Crim Law 772(6); Homic 1484.

Gavilan; U.S. v., CA5 (Tex), 761 F2d 226.—Crim Law 273.1(4), 641.13(5).

Gavin v. Potter County, TexCivApp–Amarillo, 187 SW2d 705, writ refused.—App & E 840(1); Counties 183(1), 183(2), 187; Mun Corp 951; Statut 223.4, 231.

Gavin v. Webb, Tex, 101 SW2d 217, 128 Tex 625.—App & E 43.

Gavin v. Webb, TexCivApp–Fort Worth, 99 SW2d 372, writ dism woj 101 SW2d 217, 128 Tex 625.—App & E 1, 722(1), 724(4), 742(1), 742(4), 742(6), 742(7), 745, 756, 759; Trial 215.

Gavin Co. v. Gibson, TexApp–Houston (14 Dist, 780 SW2d 833. See David Gavin Co. v. Gibson.

Gavrel v. Rodriguez, TexApp–Houston (14 Dist), 225 SW3d 758.—App & E 497(1), 930(1), 989, 1074(3), 1177(9).

Gavrel v. Young, TexCivApp–Houston, 407 SW2d 518, ref nre.—App & E 294(1), 302(6), 1070(2), 1079; Autos 244(44); Neglig 547.

Gawerc, In re, Tex, 165 SW3d 314.—Child S 497; Contempt 78, 79.

Gawerc; Fairfield Financial Group, Inc. v., TexApp–Houston (1 Dist), 814 SW2d 204.—App & E 920(3), 954(1), 1024.2; Contracts 305(1); Inj 138.21; Mtg 408, 465.5.

Gawerc v. Montgomery County, TexApp–Beaumont, 47 SW3d 840, review den.—Contracts 318; Em Dom 238(6), 243(2), 252; Fixt 1; Improv 1; Judgm 181(15.1); Trial 136(1), 137.

Gawlik; Ebeling v., TexApp–Hous (1 Dist), 487 SW2d 187.—App & E 153; Pretrial Proc 44.1, 45, 46, 304, 305, 309, 315.

Gawlik v. Gawlik, TexApp–Corpus Christi, 707 SW2d 256.—App & E 846(5), 984(5); Child C 609; Child S 363, 450, 537, 542; Costs 194.12.

Gawlik; Gawlik v., TexApp–Corpus Christi, 707 SW2d 256.—App & E 846(5), 984(5); Child C 609; Child S 363, 450, 537, 542; Costs 194.12.

Gawlik v. Padre Staples Auto Mart, Inc., TexApp–Corpus Christi, 666 SW2d 161, ref nre.—App & E 270(4); Cons Cred 4, 16, 17, 18.

Gawlik; Smothers v., TexApp–Waco, 214 SW2d 894, ref nre.—App & E 900; Contracts 138(1), 139, 354.

Gawlik v. State, TexCrimApp, 608 SW2d 671.—Crim Law 330, 1030(2), 1184(2); Larc 41, 55.

Gaxiola v. Garcia, TexApp–El Paso, 169 SW3d 426.—App & E 181, 219(2), 931(3); Child S 88, 195, 214, 337, 339(3), 339(5), 539, 550, 555, 556(1), 558(3).

Gay v. Board of Trustees of San Jacinto College, CA5 (Tex), 608 F2d 127, on remand 1980 WL 18663.—Civil R 1528, 1535, 1544, 1587.

Gay; Budd v., TexApp–Houston (14 Dist), 846 SW2d 521.—App & E 497(1), 554(1), 640, 1079; Costs 194.12, 207; Pretrial Proc 313; Trial 107.

Gay; Central Trailer Sales, Inc. v., TexCivApp–Eastland, 533 SW2d 476.—Bailm 31(3).

Gay v. Chambers, TexCivApp–San Antonio, 207 SW2d 940, writ refused.—App & E 766; Bankr 3415.1.

Gay; City of Fort Worth v., TexApp–Fort Worth, 977 SW2d 814.—App & E 1043(6), 1051.1(1); High 192; Mun Corp 728, 733(2), 742(6), 770, 788, 805(0.5), 847, 857; Pretrial Proc 40, 45.

Gay v. City of Hillsboro, Tex, 545 SW2d 765.—App & E 609.

Gay v. City of Hillsboro, TexCivApp–Waco, 536 SW2d 425, writ gr, rev 545 SW2d 765.—App & E 596, 926(8).

Gay v. Crow, TexCivApp–Waco, 111 SW2d 782, dism.—App & E 1032(1); Labor & Emp 256(16); Lim of Act 27, 195(3); Trial 351.2(2), 351.2(5).

Gay; Garrett's Estate v., TexCivApp–Tyler, 392 SW2d 565, dism.—Plead 45, 111.18, 111.42(4); Stip 14(1); Venue 22(7).

Gay v. Gay, TexApp–El Paso, 737 SW2d 94, writ den.—Child C 80; Divorce 203.

See Guidelines for Arrangement at the beginning of this Volume

Gay; Gay v., TexApp–El Paso, 737 SW2d 94, writ den.—Child C 80; Divorce 203.

Gay v. Grinnan, TexCivApp–Texarkana, 218 SW2d 1021, ref nre.—Mines 78.1(2), 78.7(1).

Gay; Jones v., TexCivApp–Fort Worth, 258 SW2d 403.—Child C 23, 460, 465.

Gay; Montgomery v., TexCivApp–Fort Worth, 222 SW2d 922, writ dism.—App & E 758.3(8), 1050.1(6), 1053(6), 1078(1); Evid 107; Plead 53(1), 380; Trial 139.1(15), 350.4(1); Witn 383, 390.

Gay; Montgomery v., TexCivApp–Fort Worth, 212 SW2d 941.—Trial 350.1, 352.4(2), 352.17, 352.20.

Gay v. Ocean Transport and Trading, Ltd., CA5 (Tex), 546 F2d 1233, reh den 549 F2d 203, reh den Bulk Transport Corp v. Texas Employers' Insurance Association, 549 F2d 203, reh den Guerra v Bulk Transport Corp, 549 F2d 203.—Neglig 233, 371, 405; Ship 84(1), 84(3.2), 84(4), 84(5), 86(1).

Gay v. Pennington, TexCivApp–San Antonio, 105 SW2d 375.—Assault 39.

Gay v. State, TexCrimApp, 115 SW2d 929, 134 TexCrim 356.—Crim Law 719(1), 723(3), 728(4), 1038.2, 1056.1(4), 1171.1(2.1), 1171.3, 1172.8, 1173.2(3), 1173.2(8); Homic 732, 908, 1032, 1385, 1401, 1470, 1483; Witn 274(1), 274(2).

Gay v. State, TexApp–Houston (1 Dist), 981 SW2d 864, petition for discretionary review refused.—Assault 92(5); Crim Law 366(6), 396(1), 419(1), 629(1), 1162, 1169.1(9), 1186.4(11).

Gay v. State, TexApp–Amarillo, 730 SW2d 154.—Action 60; Autos 252, 259; Civil R 1350; Const Law 4413; Fed Cts 265; Judgm 181(11), 181(14); States 191.6(1), 191.10.

Gay v. Stratton, TexCivApp–Texarkana, 559 SW2d 131, ref nre.—Contracts 147(2), 229(2).

Gay v. Texas Dept. of Corrections State Jail Div., CA5 (Tex), 117 F3d 240.—Fed Cts 661.

Gay v. Wheeler, SDTex, 363 FSupp 764.—Civil R 1130, 1132; Const Law 4172(6), 4200, 4201, 4202, 4203; Schools 55, 133, 147.2(2), 147.14.

Gay; Whitfield v., TexCivApp–Eastland, 253 SW2d 54.—App & E 931(3); Crops 2, 7; Land & Ten 139(5), 144, 200.9, 213(1), 291(4).

Gayden v. Galveston County, Tex., SDTex, 178 FRD 134, aff in part 177 F3d 978.—Fed Civ Proc 1839.1, 1935.1; Fed Cts 818.

Gay Engineering & Sales Co.; Transmation, Inc. v., SDTex, 336 FSupp 959.—Action 69(6); Fed Cts 105.

Gay Harris & Son, Inc. v. E. H. Schlather and Sons, TexCivApp–Austin, 423 SW2d 467.—Corp 306.

Gay Inv. Co. v. Texas Turnpike Authority, TexCivApp–Dallas, 510 SW2d 147, ref nre.—Em Dom 6.1; Turnpikes 15.

Gayken; Ewton v., TexApp–Beaumont, 130 SW3d 382, review den.—Judgm 335(2), 335(3).

Gayle, In re, BkrtcySDTex, 189 BR 914.—Elect of Rem 1, 7(1); Judgm 582; Mtg 218.1, 337; Sec Tran 223.

Gayle; Alpha Life Ins. Co. v., TexApp–Houston (14 Dist), 796 SW2d 834.—Mand 3(2.1), 12; Pretrial Proc 382.

Gayle; Bell v., NDTex, 384 FSupp 1022.—Civil R 1326(11), 1461, 1469, 1473, 1474(1), 1487; Const Law 3869, 4172(6); Libel 54; Mun Corp 185(1), 185(6), 185(8), 189(1).

Gayle v. Dixon, TexCivApp–Hous (1 Dist), 583 SW2d 648, ref nre.—Evid 248(7), 314(1); Trial 58; Wills 53(9), 400.

Gayle; Dunn Equipment, Inc. v., TexApp–Houston (14 Dist), 725 SW2d 372.—Pretrial Proc 373, 410.

Gayle; Farm Credit Bank of Texas v., BkrtcySDTex, 189 BR 914. See Gayle, In re.

Gayle; Fort Bend County Mun. Utility Dist. No. 30 v., SDTex, 755 FSupp 746.—Banks 505.

Gayle; General Motors Corp. v., Tex, 951 SW2d 469, reh overr.—Evid 150; Mand 4(4), 45, 176; Pretrial Proc 35, 38, 40, 390, 713, 714.

Gayle; General Motors Corp. v., Tex, 940 SW2d 598.—Motions 39.

Gayle; General Motors Corp. v., TexApp–Houston (14 Dist), 924 SW2d 222, mandamus conditionally gr, motion to file mandamus overr with per curiam opinion 940 SW2d 598, subsequent mandamus proceeding 951 SW2d 469, reh overr.—App & E 1035; Evid 150; Jury 25(2), 25(6), 25(8), 26; Mand 4(1), 4(3), 4(4), 12, 28, 32; Pretrial Proc 35, 40, 358.

Gayle; Giesecke v., TexCivApp–Galveston, 129 SW2d 334.—Mun Corp 162.

Gayle; Home Ben. Ass'n v., TexCivApp–Waco, 147 SW2d 280.—Debtor & C 10; Interest 45; Lim of Act 100(1), 197(2).

Gayle; Kirkpatrick v., TexCivApp–San Antonio, 265 SW2d 185, mandamus overr.—Damag 221(7); Fraud 66; Mand 51.

Gayle; Lloyds Ins. Co. v., TexApp–Houston (1 Dist), 717 SW2d 166. See Victoria Lloyds Ins. Co. v. Gayle.

Gayle v. Lockhart, TexCivApp–Waco, 167 SW2d 230, writ refused.—Garn 34; Insurance 1137; Statut 263.

Gayle; Maeberry v., TexApp–Corpus Christi, 955 SW2d 875.—App & E 846(6), 931(1), 989, 994(3), 1010.1(2), 1011.1(1), 1012.1(4), 1180(2); Costs 194.25; Deeds 70(6); Fraud 3, 58(1), 58(2), 61; Guard & W 20, 117, 130, 137; Judgm 250; Lim of Act 44(2); Trial 404(5); Trusts 270.

Gayle; Moody v., TexApp–Houston, 311 SW2d 419.—App & E 761; Tax 2930, 2936.

Gayle; Smith v., TexApp–Houston (1 Dist), 834 SW2d 105.—App & E 971(1); Pretrial Proc 27.1; Witn 208(1), 214.5.

Gayle; Spear v., TexApp–Houston (1 Dist), 857 SW2d 122.—App & E 842(1); Damag 206(2); Mand 3(3), 4(1), 28.

Gayle v. State, TexApp–Houston (1 Dist), 713 SW2d 425.—Burg 42(1), 42(3); Crim Law 721(3), 995(2), 1045, 1171.5.

Gayle; Tucker v., TexApp–Houston (14 Dist), 709 SW2d 247.—App & E 961; Mand 32; Pretrial Proc 15, 19, 34, 373.

Gayle; Victoria Lloyds Ins. Co. v., TexApp–Houston (1 Dist), 717 SW2d 166.—Mand 32; Pretrial Proc 373.

Gayler v. Renfro, TexCivApp–Amarillo, 576 SW2d 911.—Work Comp 473, 1130, 1179, 1184, 1262, 1266.

Gaylor v. Fluker, TexApp–Houston (14 Dist), 843 SW2d 234.—Pretrial Proc 699.

Gaylor; Gartrell v., CA5 (Tex), 981 F2d 254.—Civil R 1319, 1379; Fed Civ Proc 2734; Fed Cts 425, 427; Lim of Act 58(1), 75.

Gaylor; Gartrell v., SDTex, 866 FSupp 325, aff 66 F3d 322.—Civil R 1090, 1397; Fed Cts 425, 427; Lim of Act 58(1), 104.5, 105(1); Prisons 13(7.1).

Gaylord; Dauray v., TexCivApp–Dallas, 402 SW2d 948, ref nre.—App & E 1175(5); Contracts 152, 175(2), 212(2); Hus & W 279(1); Receivers 12.

Gaylord Broadcasting Co., L.P. v. Francis, TexApp–Dallas, 7 SW3d 279, reh of petition for review den, review den 35 SW3d 599, reh overr.—Const Law 2170; Judgm 181(33), 185(2); Libel 10(4), 19, 51(5), 112(2), 123(2), 129.

Gaylord Container Division of Crown Zellerbach Corp. v. H. Rouw Co., Tex, 392 SW2d 118.—Bills & N 98; Judgm 181(2), 181(26).

Gaylord Container Division of Crown Zellerbach Corp.; H. Rouw Co. v., TexCivApp–Corpus Christi, 385 SW2d 481, rev 392 SW2d 118.—Bills & N 140; Judgm 185(2), 185.3(16), 186.

Gaylord Entertainment Co.; Texas Life, Acc. Health & Hosp. Service Ins. Guar. Ass'n v., CA5 (Tex), 105 F3d 210, cert dism 117 SCt 2501, 521 US 1113, 138 LEd2d 1006.—Insurance 1117(1); Labor & Emp 407, 592, 643, 646; States 18.51.

Gaylor Oil Co.; Abadie v., TexCivApp–Galveston, 129 SW2d 319.—Garn 2, 88, 106, 193.

Gayne v. Dual-Air, Inc., TexCivApp–Hous (14 Dist), 600 SW2d 373.—Acct Action on 12, 13; App & E 846(5), 931(1), 931(3), 989, 1177(7).

Gaynes v. U.S., CA5 (Tex), 454 F2d 1142.—Fed Cts 743; Int Rev 4481, 5085.

Gaynier v. Ginsberg, TexApp–Dallas, 763 SW2d 461, appeal after remand 1994 WL 400989, writ den, dissenting opinion on denial of reh 1994 WL 672562.—Courts 37(2), 472.4(2.1), 472.4(7).

Gaynier v. Ginsberg, TexApp–Dallas, 715 SW2d 749, ref nre, appeal after remand 763 SW2d 461, appeal after remand 1994 WL 400989, writ den, dissenting opinion on denial of reh 1994 WL 672562.—Adv Poss 42, 60(4); Deeds 196(3); Joint Adv 7; Judgm 181(7), 181(15.1), 181(29); Lim of Act 100(2), 100(7); Pretrial Proc 474, 478.

Gaynier v. Johnson, TexApp–Dallas, 673 SW2d 899, subsequent mandamus proceeding Ginsberg v. Fifth Court of Appeals, 686 SW2d 105.—Mand 15, 27, 28, 40, 168(4); Pretrial Proc 183.1, 185, 434; Witn 208(1), 209, 211(2), 219(1), 219(5).

Gaynor v. State, TexApp–Houston (14 Dist), 788 SW2d 95, petition for discretionary review refused.—Crim Law 572, 641.13(2.1), 742(1), 1134(2), 1170.5(1), 1170.5(6); Rob 24.40; Sent & Pun 313, 318.

Gaynor Const. Co. v. Board of Trustees, Ector County Independent School Dist., TexCivApp–El Paso, 233 SW2d 472, writ refused.—Courts 87; Evid 25(2); Schools 71, 80(2), 81(2).

Gay Student Services v. Texas A & M University, CA5 (Tex), 737 F2d 1317, appeal dism, cert den 105 SCt 1860, 471 US 1001, 85 LEd2d 155, reh den 105 SCt 2369, 471 US 1120, 86 LEd2d 268.—Colleges 9.45(1), 9.45(2); Const Law 1150, 1440, 1448, 1747, 1759, 1761, 2007; Fed Cts 265, 269.

Gay Student Services v. Texas A & M University, CA5 (Tex), 612 F2d 160, reh den 620 F2d 300, cert den 101 SCt 608, 449 US 1034, 66 LEd2d 495, appeal after remand 737 F2d 1317, appeal dism, cert den 105 SCt 1860, 471 US 1001, 85 LEd2d 155, reh den 105 SCt 2369, 471 US 1120, 86 LEd2d 268.—Civil R 1346, 1351(2); Decl Judgm 272, 300; Fed Civ Proc 1773; Fed Cts 244, 268.1, 272, 762.

Gaytan v. Cassidy, WDTex, 317 FSupp 46, vac 91 SCt 2202, 403 US 902, 29 LEd2d 677.—Autos 130, 132; Const Law 3731, 4356.

Gaytan; M. Rivas Enterprises, Inc. v., TexApp–Corpus Christi, 24 SW3d 402, reh overr, and review den.—App & E 1001(3); Evid 597; Neglig 1037(4), 1076, 1088, 1095, 1104(6), 1670.

Gaytan; Sikes v., CA5 (Tex), 218 F3d 491.—Fed Civ Proc 2236.

Gaytan; U.S. v., CA5 (Tex), 74 F3d 545, cert den Gandara-Granillo v. US, 117 SCt 77, 519 US 821, 136 LEd2d 36, cert den Macias-Munoz v US, 117 SCt 506, 519 US 1006, 136 LEd2d 397.—Consp 24(1), 24(2), 24.5, 43(5), 43(6), 43(12); Const Law 4728; Crim Law 412.1(4), 412.2(5), 414, 627.8(6), 834(3), 835, 1023(11), 1035(7), 1036.1(5), 1036.2, 1038.1(5), 1119(1), 1139, 1152(1), 1158(1), 1158(2), 1159.2(7), 1159.2(10), 1166(10.10), 1167(1); Ind & Inf 60, 71.2(2), 71.2(4), 87(6), 108; Sent & Pun 299, 323, 653(6), 726(5), 756, 864, 900, 906, 962, 967, 973, 976; Tel 1430, 1470, 1473; U S 34.

Gayton; National Standard Ins. Co. v., TexApp–Amarillo, 773 SW2d 75.—Pretrial Proc 40, 45; Work Comp 1167.

Gayton v. State, TexApp–Corpus Christi, 732 SW2d 724, petition for discretionary review refused.—Ind & Inf 180.

Gayton; Union Carbide Corp. v., TexCivApp–Hous (14 Dist), 486 SW2d 865, ref nre.—Damag 6, 37, 158(2), 186, 221(1), 221(4); Seamen 29(5.18); Trial 365.1(2).

Gazda v. Pioneer Chlor Alkali Co., Inc., SDTex, 10 FSupp2d 656.—Civil R 1147, 1166, 1168, 1172, 1185,

1189, 1218(4), 1225(4), 1247, 1251, 1252, 1505(4); Damag 50.10; Fed Civ Proc 2497.1, 2539, 2542.1; Labor & Emp 345.

Gazley; Bexar County v., TexCivApp–San Antonio, 172 SW2d 702.—Courts 57(0.5).

G.B.B., In re, TexApp–Houston (1 Dist), 638 SW2d 162.—Infants 68.7(3).

G. B. B., Matter of, TexCivApp–El Paso, 572 SW2d 751, ref nre.—Courts 175; Infants 68.7(1), 68.7(3), 68.7(4), 196, 197.

GBL Holding Co., Inc. v. Blackburn/Travis/Cole, Ltd., NDTex, 331 BR 251.—Bankr 3069, 3073, 3782, 3785.1, 3786; Fed Cts 13.

G. B. Mueller, Inc.; Duerer v., TexCivApp–Austin, 516 SW2d 221.—App & E 758.1; Neglig 1247, 1288, 1670, 1750.

G.B.R., In Interest of, TexApp–El Paso, 953 SW2d 391.—App & E 1001(1), 1079; Mental H 37.1, 41, 440.

G. B. R. Smith Milling Co. v. Thomas, NDTex, 11 FSupp 833.—Courts 91(2), 96(1); Int Rev 4931.

G. B. Wilkinson Estate v. Yount-Lee Oil Co., CCA5 (Tex), 87 F2d 577, cert den 58 SCt 12, 302 US 693, 82 LEd 536.—Receivers 3.

G.C., In re, Tex, 22 SW3d 932, reh overr, appeal after remand 66 SW3d 517, rule 537(f) motion gr.—App & E 937(4).

G.C., In re, TexApp–Fort Worth, 66 SW3d 517, rule 537(f) motion gr.—App & E 213, 237(5), 237(6), 238(2), 294(1); Const Law 990, 1020, 1031, 1055, 3006, 3057, 3830, 3850, 3867, 3875, 3893, 4393, 4396; Courts 200, 202(1); Infants 209, 243; Jury 4, 32(2).

G., C. & S. F. Ry. Co.; Hogan v., TexCivApp–Beaumont, 411 SW2d 815, writ refused.—App & E 21, 22; Courts 247(2).

G.C. Bldgs., Inc. v. RGS Contractors, Inc., TexApp–Dallas, 188 SW3d 739, reh overr.—Action 13; App & E 854(1); Contracts 330(2); Estop 78(1); Judgm 181(6), 181(19), 185(5).

G. C. D. v. State, TexCivApp–Beaumont, 577 SW2d 302.—Courts 175; Infants 196.

G.C.F., In re, TexApp–Fort Worth, 42 SW3d 194.—Infants 241, 242.

GCJM, Inc., 2225 New York Ave. Ltd. by, v. Cisneros, CA5 (Tex), 38 F3d 210. See 2225 New York Ave. Ltd. by GCJM, Inc. v. Cisneros.

G.C., Jr., Matter of, TexApp–Corpus Christi, 980 SW2d 908, review den.—Courts 74.

G. C. McBride, Inc.; Herndon v., TexCivApp–Eastland, 342 SW2d 10.—Lim of Act 55(7).

G. C. Murphy Co. v. Lack, TexCivApp–Corpus Christi, 404 SW2d 853, ref nre.—App & E 934(1); Can of Inst 57; Contracts 250, 318; Judgm 185(2), 185.3(14), 186; Land & Ten 44(1), 47, 94(1), 112(1).

GC Services Ltd. Partnership; Youngblood v., WDTex, 186 FSupp2d 695.—Antitrust 214; Fed Civ Proc 2494.5.

GC Services L.P.; Peter v., CA5 (Tex), 310 F3d 344.—Antitrust 213, 214, 291, 390; Partners 165; Statut 181(2), 184, 188.

G.D., In re, TexApp–Waco, 10 SW3d 419.—Mental H 37.1, 41.

GDF Realty Investments, Ltd. v. Norton, CA5 (Tex), 326 F3d 622, reh and reh den 362 F3d 286, cert den 125 SCt 2898, 545 US 1114, 162 LEd2d 294.—Commerce 3, 7(2), 52.10; Const Law 27, 637; Environ Law 516.

GDF Realty Investments, Ltd. v. Norton, WDTex, 169 FSupp2d 648, aff 326 F3d 622, reh and reh den 362 F3d 286, cert den 125 SCt 2898, 545 US 1114, 162 LEd2d 294.—Commerce 1, 5, 7(2), 82.20, 82.40; Const Law 27, 665, 995; Environ Law 516, 530, 531.

G.D. Searle & Co.; Hackett v., WDTex, 246 FSupp2d 591.—Neglig 238, 259; Prod Liab 46.2.

G.E., In re, TexApp–El Paso, 225 SW3d 647.—Crim Law 1131(4); Infants 247.

G.E.

G.E. American Communication v. Galveston Cent. Appraisal Dist., TexApp–Houston (14 Dist), 979 SW2d 761.—Admin Law 744.1, 746, 749, 763, 791, 811; Tax 2603, 2641, 2676, 2699(5).

Geames; U.S. v., CA5 (Tex), 174 FedAppx 857, cert den 127 SCt 231, 166 LEd2d 183.—Controlled Subs 81, 86.

G.E.A. Power Cooling Systems, Inc.; Beta Supply, Inc. v., TexApp–Houston (1 Dist), 748 SW2d 541, writ den.—Judgm 181(15.1), 185.1(3); Plead 36(1).

Gearhart v. Eye Care Centers of America, Inc., SDTex, 888 FSupp 814.—Civil R 1147, 1184, 1185, 1189, 1537, 1549; Damag 50.10; Fed Civ Proc 2466, 2544.

Gearhart v. EyeMasters, SDTex, 888 FSupp 814. See Gearhart v. Eye Care Centers of America, Inc.

Gearhart; Gilligan v., TexCivApp–Corpus Christi, 415 SW2d 208, writ dism.—Alt of Inst 20; Judgm 199(3.14).

Gearhart v. State, TexApp–Corpus Christi, 122 SW3d 459, petition stricken, and petition for discretionary review refused.—Assault 91.10(1); Crim Law 552(1), 562, 627.6(3), 1037.1(2), 1042.5, 1044.1(2), 1077.3, 1134(2), 1144.13(3), 1159.2(1), 1159.2(2), 1159.2(9), 1159.3(1), 1159.4(2), 1181.5(3.1), 1184(3), 1186.7, 1191, 1440(2); Ind & Inf 179; Jury 91, 131(4); Sent & Pun 1381(2).

Gearhart Industries, Inc.; McGonigal v., CA5 (Tex), 851 F2d 774, reh den.—Evid 141, 146; Fed Civ Proc 2173.1(1); Fed Cts 823, 899, 950; Prod Liab 26, 60.5, 96.1.

Gearhart Industries, Inc.; McGonigal v., CA5 (Tex), 788 F2d 321, appeal after remand 851 F2d 774, reh den.—Compromise 16(1); Evid 571(3); Fed Cts 764; Neglig 1617, 1693; Prod Liab 60.5, 80.5, 86.5.

Gearhart Industries, Inc. v. Smith Intern., Inc., CA5 (Tex), 741 F2d 707.—Corp 306, 307, 310(1), 312(4), 314(2), 315, 317(1), 319(7), 320(4), 426(1); Fed Cts 767, 944; Inj 152; Sec Reg 52.15, 52.21, 52.40(1), 173, 174, 180.

Gearhart Industries, Inc. v. Smith Intern., Inc., NDTex, 592 FSupp 203, aff in part, mod in part 741 F2d 707.—Antitrust 759, 764, 771, 797, 976, 996; Corp 310(1), 318; Fraud 7; Pat 328(2); Sec Reg 52.18, 52.19, 52.39(3), 52.39(4), 178.1.

Gearhart-Owen Industries, Inc.; Lambert v., TexApp–Corpus Christi, 626 SW2d 845.—App & E 989, 1012.1(3); Autos 146; Evid 121(1), 123(11), 243(4), 258(1); Neglig 1614, 1617, 1624; Plead 111.42(8).

Gearing v. State, TexCrimApp, 685 SW2d 326.—Arrest 63.5(1), 63.5(2), 63.5(5), 63.5(6); Crim Law 899, 1036.1(4).

Gearing v. State, TexApp–Houston (14 Dist), 685 SW2d 339, aff 685 SW2d 326.—Arrest 63.5(1), 63.5(4), 63.5(5); Crim Law 586, 1114.1(1), 1119(1), 1130(5); Double J 1, 30; Jury 31.3(1); Searches 68; Sent & Pun 1262, 1347, 1349, 1381(3), 1381(6); Weap 3, 4.

Gearing v. U.S., CA5 (Tex), 432 F2d 1038, cert den 91 SCt 1213, 401 US 980, 28 LEd2d 331.—Crim Law 273.3, 1132, 1455, 1478; Ind & Inf 108; Rec S Goods 2, 7(2); Sent & Pun 2.

Gearner; Scott v., CA5 (Tex), 197 F2d 93.—Evid 395(1); Fed Civ Proc 315; Fed Cts 654, 845, 931; Int Rev 4911; Mtg 338; Partners 54.

Geary v. Peavy, Tex, 878 SW2d 602.—Child C 736, 748; Mand 4(1), 4(4), 53.

Geary v. Texas Commerce Bank, Tex, 967 SW2d 836.—Bankr 3568(2).

Geary; Texas Commerce Bank Nat. Ass'n v., TexApp–Dallas, 938 SW2d 205, reh overr, and writ gr, rev 967 SW2d 836.—Accord 1, 2(0.5), 15.1; App & E 170(1), 173(1), 179(1), 854(1), 882(18); Bankr 3501, 3568(2); Ex & Ad 7, 264(1); Judgm 183, 187, 540.

Geary, Hamilton, Brice & Lewis v. Coastal Transport Co., TexCivApp–Dallas, 399 SW2d 878.—Plead 110, 111.1.

GE Automotive Services, Inc.; Tarrant County Hosp. Dist. v., TexApp–Fort Worth, 156 SW3d 885, rule 537(f)

motion gr.—Action 27(1); App & E 724(4), 1079, 1136; Const Law 2486, 2488; Counties 216; Electricity 13; Judgm 185(5); Lim of Act 165; Neglig 463; Plead 76; Prod Liab 17.1; Sales 3.1, 374, 409, 431; Statut 181(1), 188, 206, 212.6, 212.7; Torts 118, 145.

Gebert v. Clifton, TexCivApp–Hous (14 Dist), 553 SW2d 230, dism.—Autos 193(8.1), 242(6), 244(26); Plead 111.42(6).

Gebhardt v. Gallardo, TexApp–San Antonio, 891 SW2d 327.—Abate & R 8(2); Action 60; Mand 3(3), 4(1), 4(4), 26, 28, 32; Pretrial Proc 534; Witn 293.5, 305(1), 307, 309.

Gebhardt v. Thomas, BkrtcyEDTex, 203 BR 64. See Thomas, In re.

Gebhart; Southland Supply Co. v., TexCivApp–Texarkana, 439 SW2d 393.—App & E 846(5), 934(2), 1010.1(1); Neglig 1656, 1676; Plead 111.36, 111.42(8), 111.44; Trial 382.

Gebr. Bellmer Kg. v. Terminal Services Houston, Inc., CA5 (Tex), 711 F2d 622, reh den 718 F2d 1096.—Ship 132(5.1), 132(5.4), 134, 140(2).

Gebr. Bellmer KG. v. Terminal Services Houston, Inc., SDTex, 523 FSupp 941, aff 711 F2d 622, reh den 718 F2d 1096.—Ship 106(3.1), 111, 122, 132(3.1), 132(5.1), 132(5.4), 134, 140(2).

Gebser v. Lago Vista Independent School Dist., USTex, 118 SCt 1989, 524 US 274, 158 ALR Fed 751, 141 LEd2d 277.—Action 34; Civil R 1055, 1067(3), 1330(2), 1346, 1352(2).

GE Capital Corp. v. Dallas Cent. Appraisal Dist., TexApp–Dallas, 971 SW2d 591.—App & E 934(1); Judgm 183; Tax 2603, 2640, 2699(7), 2699(8).

GE Capital Corp.; Richardson Independent School Dist. v., TexApp–Dallas, 58 SW3d 290.—App & E 842(2), 893(1); Statut 176; Tax 2762, 2862, 3216, 3220.

GE Capital Small Business Finance Corp.; Stramel v., EDTex, 955 FSupp 65.—Rem of C 79(1).

GECO Geophysical Co., Inc.; Newding v., TexApp–Houston (1 Dist), 817 SW2d 146.—App & E 607(1).

Geco-Prakla; Sabocuhan v., SDTex, 78 FSupp2d 603.—Compromise 8(1), 16(1); Contracts 127(4).

Geddes; Ramos v., SDTex, 137 FRD 11.—Fed Civ Proc 2536.1, 2539.

Geders v. Aircraft Engine and Accessory Co., Inc., TexCivApp–Dallas, 599 SW2d 646.—Corp 432(12); Prince & A 23(2), 159(1); Trover 7, 25, 40(1), 40(4), 60, 62, 67.

Gee, Ex parte, TexApp–Houston (1 Dist), 926 SW2d 615, petition for discretionary review refused.—Double J 24, 142; Ind & Inf 191(0.5).

Gee; Collins v., TexCivApp–San Antonio, 107 SW2d 754, writ refused.—Trusts 102(1).

Gee; Continental Transfer & Storage Co. v., TexCivApp–Eastland, 285 SW2d 892.—Corp 503(2); Plead 111.16; Venue 7.5(1), 7.5(6).

Gee v. Jernigan, TexCivApp–El Paso, 83 SW2d 1102, writ dism.—Witn 139(2), 144(6), 164(1).

Gee; Kumpe v., TexCivApp–Amarillo, 187 SW2d 932.—Afft 5; Divorce 76; Notaries 1, 4; Oath 5.

Gee v. Lewisville Memorial Hosp., Inc., TexApp–Fort Worth, 849 SW2d 458, reh overr, and writ den.—App & E 110, 846(5), 873(3); New Tr 140(1); Trial 39.

Gee v. Liberty Mut. Fire Ins. Co., Tex, 765 SW2d 394.—Admin Law 764.1; App & E 5, 1050.1(1), 1056.1(1); Pretrial Proc 313; Work Comp 1410, 1937.

Gee; Liberty Mut. Fire Ins. Co. v., TexApp–Texarkana, 749 SW2d 883, writ gr, rev 765 SW2d 394.—Pretrial Proc 45; Trial 98; Work Comp 1167, 1533, 1937, 1949.

Gee v. Principi, CA5 (Tex), 289 F3d 342.—Civil R 1243, 1252, 1541; Fed Civ Proc 2497.1; Fed Cts 776.

Gee v. Read, Tex, 606 SW2d 677.—Judgm 181(15.1); Wills 439, 470(1).

Gee; Read v., TexCivApp–Fort Worth, 580 SW2d 431, aff 606 SW2d 677.—Judgm 181(15.1); Wills 439, 441, 469, 470(1), 472, 488.

Gee; Read v., TexCivApp–Fort Worth, 551 SW2d 496, ref nre 561 SW2d 777.—App & E 151(3), 719(8); Const Law 3881, 3953, 3974; Ex & Ad 314(2).

Gee v. Smith, TexCivApp–Austin, 294 SW2d 415.—App & E 624.

Gee v. State, TexCrimApp, 253 SW2d 45, 158 TexCrim 34. —Bail 63.1.

Gee v. State, TexCrimApp, 87 SW2d 483, 129 TexCrim 312.—Crim Law 865(1.5), 1118; Weap 17(5); Witn 337(16).

Gee v. State, TexApp–Texarkana, 626 SW2d 603, petition for discretionary review refused.—Autos 351.1, 355(2).

Gee v. U.S., CA5 (Tex), 452 F2d 849, cert den 92 SCt 2432, 407 US 909, 32 LEd2d 683, on remand 56 FRD 377.—Armed S 20.8(4), 20.9(3); Crim Law 273.4(1), 1663.

Gee v. U.S., SDTex, 319 FSupp 581, vac 452 F2d 849, cert den 92 SCt 2432, 407 US 909, 32 LEd2d 683, on remand 56 FRD 377.—Armed S 20.6(3), 40.1(7); Courts 100(1); Crim Law 1434, 1663.

Gee; U.S. v., SDTex, 56 FRD 377.—Crim Law 1586, 1665; Sent & Pun 2283.

Gee Chee On v. Brownell, CA5 (Tex), 253 F2d 814.— Aliens 670(4); Evid 588; Marriage 3, 40(1).

Gee Chee On v. Brownell, SDTex, 146 FSupp 503, rev 253 F2d 814.—Aliens 670(4).

Geer v. Union Central Life Ins. Co., TexCivApp–Fort Worth, 91 SW2d 1146, writ dism.—App & E 742(1).

Geer; Walker v., TexApp–Eastland, 99 SW3d 244.— Consp 1.1, 19; Fraud Conv 301(2); Judgm 796; Lim of Act 95(8).

Geer; W. R. B. Corp. v., CA5 (Tex), 332 F2d 180, cert den 85 SCt 78, 379 US 841, 13 LEd2d 47.—Fed Civ Proc 1902.

Geer; W. R. B. Corp. v., CA5 (Tex), 313 F2d 750, appeal after remand 332 F2d 180, cert den 85 SCt 78, 379 US 841, 13 LEd2d 47.—Fed Civ Proc 1901; Fed Cts 633, 691, 712, 795, 849, 852, 932.1, 942, 951.1.

Geers; Banner Dairies v., TexCivApp–El Paso, 292 SW2d 169, dism.—App & E 218.2(1); Contracts 10(4); Plead 228.14, 419; Waters 296.

Geers v. State, TexCrimApp, 254 SW2d 383.—Int Liq 236(7), 242.

Geesa v. State, TexCrimApp, 820 SW2d 154.—Const Law 186; Courts 100(1); Crim Law 552(3), 789(1), 824(12), 1159.6, 1173.2(8); States 4.

Geesbreght v. Geesbreght, TexCivApp–Fort Worth, 570 SW2d 427, dism.—App & E 780(1); Child C 748, 923(1); Courts 37(3); Divorce 252.3(1), 253(3), 286(9); Hus & W 285.2.

Geesbreght; Geesbreght v., TexCivApp–Fort Worth, 570 SW2d 427, dism.—App & E 780(1); Child C 748, 923(1); Courts 37(3); Divorce 252.3(1), 253(3), 286(9); Hus & W 285.2.

Geeslin; Custom Rail Employer Welfare Trust Fund v., CA5 (Tex), 491 F3d 233.—Labor & Emp 425; Statut 188, 190, 212.6.

Geeslin v. McElhenney, TexApp–Austin, 788 SW2d 683. —Ex & Ad 7.

Geeslin; Stark v., TexApp–Austin, 213 SW3d 406, review den, and reh of petition for review den.—Admin Law 413, 749, 750, 763, 790, 791, 793; Const Law 3875, 4288; Insurance 1055, 1070, 1120, 3593; Statut 181(1), 219(1).

Geeslin v. State, TexCrimApp, 600 SW2d 309.—Crim Law 641.4(1), 641.4(2), 641.4(4), 641.7(1), 641.9, 1166.10(2).

Geeslin v. State, TexApp–Fort Worth, 630 SW2d 512.— Crim Law 369.2(1), 1036.1(2), 1043(3), 1044.1(5.1).

Geeslin; U.S. v., CA5 (Tex), 447 F3d 408.—Crim Law 1134(3), 1139, 1158(1); Sent & Pun 651, 736.

Geffen & Jacobsen, P.C.; Griffith v., TexApp–Dallas, 693 SW2d 724.—App & E 1079; Atty & C 32(13), 143, 156, 182(3); Contracts 95(1); Interest 39(5); Judgm 186; Usury 50.

Geffert; Jim Walter Homes, Inc. v., TexCivApp–Corpus Christi, 614 SW2d 843, ref nre.—Antitrust 286, 369, 390; Trial 352.1(3).

GE Financial Assurance Co.; Avalon Residential Care Homes, Inc. v., CA5 (Tex), 72 FedAppx 35.—Civil R 1083.

Gehan Homes, Ltd. v. Employers Mut. Cas. Co., TexApp–Dallas, 146 SW3d 833.—App & E 173(14), 766, 852, 854(1); Insurance 2264, 2271, 2275, 2276, 2277, 2278(3), 2278(8), 2913, 2914, 2915, 2922(1); Judgm 183.

Gehardt v. State, TexCrimApp, 277 SW2d 910.—Int Liq 236(11).

GE HFS Holdings, Inc.; Veldekens v., SDTex, 362 BR 762.—Bankr 2043(2), 2043(3), 2052, 2103, 3766.1, 3779; Fed Cts 29.1, 30.

Gehl v. State Farm Fire and Cas. Co., CA5 (Tex), 214 F3d 634.—Fed Cts 776; Insurance 2142(6).

Gehl Bros. Mfg. Co. v. Price's Producers, Inc., TexCivApp–El Paso, 319 SW2d 955.—Contracts 186(1), 249; Corp 503(1); Princ & A 14(1); Sales 202(4); Venue 8.5(2), 21.

Gehrels v. Denius, TexCivApp–Beaumont, 229 SW2d 885. —App & E 1177(7); Covenants 124, 134; Judgm 194; Trial 382.

Gehrig; Ennis Business Forms, Inc. v., TexCivApp–Waco, 534 SW2d 183, ref nre.—App & E 232(3); Contracts 313(2); Labor & Emp 219, 237, 611, 678, 696(2), 699.

Gehring v. Gehring, TexCivApp–Waco, 582 SW2d 901.— App & E 907(3); Child C 7, 637, 920, 921(1).

Gehring; Gehring v., TexCivApp–Waco, 582 SW2d 901.— App & E 907(3); Child C 7, 637, 920, 921(1).

Gehring; Strakos v., Tex, 360 SW2d 787.—Contrib 5(6.1); High 194, 200; Indem 67; Neglig 423, 484, 1205(8).

Gehring v. Strakos, TexCivApp–Houston, 345 SW2d 764, writ gr, rev 360 SW2d 787.—App & E 612(1), 613(1); Contracts 304(0.5); Damag 132(7); High 153, 156, 194, 200, 208(1), 208(2); Indem 67; Labor & Emp 3163; Neglig 210, 220, 221, 372, 1205(7); Nuis 42; Plead 228.14; Trial 131(1).

Gehrke v. State, TexCrimApp, 507 SW2d 550.—Double J 142.

Gehrke v. State, TexCivApp–San Antonio, 363 SW2d 490, writ refused.—Judgm 335(3); Plead 43, 228.23.

Gehrke v. State, TexCivApp–San Antonio, 315 SW2d 684. —Mines 79.1(5); Pretrial Proc 650; Tresp to T T 26.

Geib; Nelson v., TexCivApp–Austin, 314 SW2d 124, writ dism.—Hus & W 272(4).

Geib; Paschall v., TexCivApp–Dallas, 405 SW2d 385, ref nre.—Evid 348(2); Judgm 942, 944; Parties 93(1).

Geib; Uranga v., CA5 (Tex), 755 F2d 421. See Paso Del Norte Oil Co., Matter of.

Geick v. Zigler, TexApp–Houston (14 Dist), 978 SW2d 261.—Judgm 185(2), 185.1(4), 185.3(2), 185.3(21); Mun Corp 189, 189(1), 747(3), 753(1); Offic 114, 119.

Geico; Greil v., NDTex, 184 FSupp2d 541.—Evid 219(3); Insurance 3336, 3337, 3359, 3363.

GEICO General Ins. Co.; Simpson v., TexApp–Houston (1 Dist), 907 SW2d 942.—App & E 169, 852, 934(1); Insurance 1808, 1814, 1831, 1835(2), 1863, 2772, 2793(2), 3507(1), 3520; Judgm 181(8), 185(2).

Geier-Jackson, Inc. v. James, EDTex, 160 FSupp 524.— Mines 73.5, 78.1(9).

Geiger v. DeBusk, TexCivApp–Dallas, 534 SW2d 437.— Elections 10, 144, 158.

Geiger v. Jowers, CA5 (Tex), 404 F3d 371.—Civil R 1395(7), 1454, 1463; Const Law 4820, 4824; Damag 57.10; Fed Civ Proc 2734; Fed Cts 776, 818; Prisons 13(6).

Geiger v. Prior, CA5 (Tex), 112 FedAppx 949.—Fed Cts 611.

Geiger; U.S. v., CA5 (Tex), 891 F2d 512, cert den 110 SCt 1825, 494 US 1087, 108 LEd2d 954.—Sent & Pun 814, 841, 995.

Geigy Chemical Corp. v. Hall, TexCivApp–Amarillo, 449 SW2d 115.—Plead 111.3, 111.8, 111.16, 111.37, 111.42(6); Prod Liab 22; Venue 21.

Geigy Pharmaceuticals; Jordan v., TexApp–Fort Worth, 848 SW2d 176, reh overr.—App & E 863, 1024.4; Health 906; Judgm 185(2), 185(4), 185(5), 185(6), 185.1(3), 185.1(7), 185.3(21), 186.

Geiken, Ex parte, TexCrimApp, 28 SW3d 553.—Const Law 2324, 2372, 3879, 4838; Hab Corp 441, 516.1, 912; Pardon 43, 55.1, 61; Prisons 13(10).

GE Ionics, Inc.; Brazos River Authority v., CA5 (Tex), 469 F3d 416, reh den 214 FedAppx 495.—Evid 129(5), 141, 146, 219.20(1), 219.20(2), 219.20(3), 219.35, 219.40, 222(2), 317(2), 472(3), 474(1); Fed Civ Proc 1325; Fed Cts 776, 823, 901.1, 937.1; Sales 273(1); Witn 37(2), 100.

Geis; Stogner v., TexCivApp–Tyler, 397 SW2d 494, writ dism.—App & E 846(5), 863, 931(3), 989; Autos 244(10); Venue 8.5(8).

Geisel Compania Maritima, S.A.; Iwag v., SDTex, 882 FSupp 597.—Adm 2; Courts 489(9); Fed Cts 45, 275; Rem of C 3, 25(1), 36, 48.1, 49.1(1), 94, 102, 107(4), 107(7); Seamen 29(5).

Geiselman v. Cramer Financial Group, Inc., TexApp–Houston (14 Dist), 965 SW2d 532, reh overr.—App & E 223, 230; Banks 508; Bills & N 443(1), 489(6); Judgm 181(26), 183, 185(2), 185(4), 185.1(3), 185.1(4).

Geiser v. Lawson, TexCivApp–Eastland, 584 SW2d 347. —App & E 170(1), 1170.7; Execution 303; Home 213; Tresp to T T 38(1).

Geiserman v. MacDonald, CA5 (Tex), 893 F2d 787.— Atty & C 129(2); Fed Civ Proc 1531, 1536, 1925.1, 1938.1, 2466, 2470, 2542.1; Fed Cts 763.1, 820.

Geisler v. Mid-Century Ins. Co., TexApp–Houston (14 Dist), 712 SW2d 184, ref nre.—Insurance 2774, 2787.

Geisler v. Pansegrau, BkrtcyNDTex, 180 BR 468. See Pansegrau, In re.

Geisler v. State, TexCrimApp, 307 SW2d 95, 165 TexCrim 322.—Bail 64.

Geisler; Texas Health Enterprises, Inc. v., TexApp–Fort Worth, 9 SW3d 163, review gr (2 pets), and review dism, and review dism.—Damag 94; Death 9, 31(1), 32, 41, 96; Health 662, 812; Neglig 273; Parties 35.1.

Geisling, Ex parte, TexCrimApp, 243 SW2d 833.—Rob 30.

Geissler v. Coussoulis, TexCivApp–San Antonio, 424 SW2d 709, ref nre.—Const Law 38, 1430, 1504, 1917; Labor & Emp 1345(2), 1379, 2053, 2060, 2112; Statut 47.

Geist; Hoyt v., TexCivApp–Houston, 364 SW2d 461.—App & E 1170.10; Covenants 103(1), 136; Inj 62(1); Trial 395(5), 395(7).

Geistmann v. Schkade, TexCivApp–Austin, 121 SW2d 494.—App & E 232(0.5), 302(1), 302(6), 901, 1048(6), 1060.1(7); Contracts 333(5); Trial 115(2), 131(1), 350.3(6), 350.8, 351.2(8), 351.4, 351.5(3), 352.5(3), 352.11; Trover 34(7), 40(6).

Geitz; Burchfield v., TexCivApp–El Paso, 516 SW2d 229. —App & E 536, 927(7), 997(3); Health 669, 823(7); Trial 178.

G. E. Kadane & Sons; Allied Chemical Corp. v., TexCiv-App–Eastland, 373 SW2d 778.—Mines 49, 56, 78.7(4); Ten in C 15(7); Tresp to T T 38(1).

Gelabert v. Lynaugh, CA5 (Tex), 894 F2d 746.—Fed Civ Proc 2813.

Gelabert v. State, TexApp–Houston (1 Dist), 712 SW2d 813, petition for discretionary review refused.—Crim Law 632(4), 641.4(1), 641.13(2.1), 736(1), 1028, 1038.2, 1038.3, 1114.1(1), 1129(2); Homic 852.

Gelber; Courtney v., TexApp–Houston (1 Dist), 905 SW2d 33.—App & E 1073(1); Judgm 186.

Gelber Group, Inc.; Sinclair Gas Marketing, Inc. v., TexApp–Houston (14 Dist, 905 SW2d 786. See Thomas v. Gelber Group, Inc.

Gelber Group, Inc.; Thomas v., TexApp–Houston (14 Dist), 905 SW2d 786.—App & E 5; Judgm 106(1), 106(2); Plead 85(3), 335.

Geldard v. Watson, TexApp–Texarkana, 214 SW3d 202.— App & E 23; Courts 24, 37(1), 37(2); Forci E & D 6(2), 16(3), 29(0.5), 43(1); Home 1, 15, 87, 118(4), 118(5), 123, 124; J P 141(2).

Geldmeier; Kincheloe v., TexCivApp–Tyler, 619 SW2d 272.—Cust & U 19(3).

Gelfand v. Heath, TexCivApp–Texarkana, 124 SW2d 1017.—App & E 719(1), 752, 759.

Gelfond v. Levit, TexCivApp–San Antonio, 398 SW2d 659. —App & E 554(3), 907(3), 931(1).

GE Life and Annuity Assur. Co.; Moody Nat. Bank of Galveston v., CA5 (Tex), 383 F3d 249, cert den 125 SCt 918, 543 US 1055, 160 LEd2d 779.—Courts 90(2); Fed Cts 656, 669, 670; Statut 230.

GE Life and Annuity Assur. Co.; Moody Nat. Bank of Galveston v., SDTex, 423 FSupp2d 651.—Fed Civ Proc 2658, 2727; Insurance 3585.

GE Life and Annuity Assur. Co.; Moody Nat. Bank of Galveston v., SDTex, 270 FSupp2d 875, motion den 423 FSupp2d 651, appeal dism 383 F3d 249, cert den 125 SCt 918, 543 US 1055, 160 LEd2d 779.—Estop 85; Fed Civ Proc 1275, 1278; Fraud 13(3); Insurance 1984, 3424.

Geller; Fream v., TexCivApp–Galveston, 263 SW2d 329, ref nre.—Inn 10.4, 10.12.

Geller; Goodin v., TexCivApp–Waco, 521 SW2d 158, ref nre.—App & E 548(3), 557, 563, 907(3), 1177(9).

Geller; Page v., Tex, 941 SW2d 101.—App & E 78(1), 863, 1172(1).

Geller v. Page, TexApp–Fort Worth, 940 SW2d 102, writ gr, rev 941 SW2d 101.—Judgm 183.

Geller; Venuto v., TexCivApp–Eastland, 415 SW2d 544.— Evid 441(11).

Gellerman v. Jefferson Pilot Financial Ins. Co., SDTex, 376 FSupp2d 724.—Labor & Emp 449, 572, 612, 628, 629(2), 629(3), 687, 688, 690, 691.

Gelling; Davidson v., Tex, 263 SW2d 940, 153 Tex 56.— Dedi 47; Ease 61(9), 61(12); Judgm 743(2); Tresp to T T 38(2), 41(1), 41(2), 47(1).

Gelling; Davidson v., TexCivApp–Texarkana, 258 SW2d 163, rev 263 SW2d 940, 153 Tex 56.—Dedi 39; Judgm 720, 743(2).

Gelling v. State, TexCrimApp, 247 SW2d 95, 157 Tex-Crim 516, rev 72 SCt 1002, 343 US 960, 96 LEd 1359.— Const Law 274.1(3), 1892; Courts 97(1), 247(2).

Gellington, In re, BkrtcyNDTex, 363 BR 497.—Bankr 2187, 2401, 3713, 3715(10), 3715(11), 3715(14).

Gelo v. State, TexApp–El Paso, 1 SW3d 703, reh overr.— Const Law 3816, 4766; Crim Law 1023(3), 1035(7), 1069(6).

GE Marquette Medical Systems, Inc.; Wilborn v., Tex-App–El Paso, 163 SW3d 264, reh overr, and review den. —App & E 920(2), 946, 966(1), 1046.1, 1079; Atty & C 76(1); Pretrial Proc 713, 716; Trial 21.

Gemco Stores; Ramsey v., TexApp–Houston (1 Dist), 853 SW2d 623. See Ramsey v. Lucky Stores, Inc.

Gemcraft Homes, Inc. v. Pacific Coast Homes, EDTex, 688 FSupp 289. See Gemcraft Homes, Inc. v. Sumurdy.

Gemcraft Homes, Inc. v. Sumurdy, EDTex, 688 FSupp 289.—Copyr 6, 72.1; Rem of C 25(1); States 18.87.

Gemdrill Intern., Inc.; Harrison v., TexApp–Houston (1 Dist), 981 SW2d 714, reh overr, and review den.— Admin Law 501; App & E 846(5), 852, 931(1), 989; Costs 194.16, 207; Damag 124(1); Elect of Rem 1, 15; Judgm 542, 564(1), 577(2); Labor & Emp 222, 254, 256(4), 271, 272, 274, 2350(3).

Gem Homes, Inc. v. Contreras, TexApp–El Paso, 861 SW2d 449, writ den.—Antitrust 201, 202; App & E 78(1), 200, 1026; Contrib 5(5); Damag 63; Death 76; Interest 39(2.6); Neglig 259; Parent & C 11; Prod Liab 27, 42, 83.

Gemini Ambulance Services, Inc.; Ambulance Billings Systems, Inc. v., TexApp–San Antonio, 103 SW3d 507.—Alt Disp Res 112, 134(1), 139, 143, 178, 205, 210, 213(3), 213(5), 251; Commerce 80.5; Mand 60.

Gemini Equipment Partners Income Fund I v. Xerox Corp., EDTex, 150 FRD 87. See R & D Business Systems v. Xerox Corp.

Gemini Exploration Co.; Ard v., TexApp–Houston (14 Dist), 894 SW2d 11, petition for discretionary review den.—App & E 854(1); Compromise 17(2); Indem 30(4), 31(2), 33(4), 95, 111; Release 37.

Gemini Financial Co.; Southwest Land Title Co. v., TexApp–Dallas, 752 SW2d 5.—Atty & C 72, 81; Princ & A 99, 100(2), 131, 152(3), 159(2), 166(1).

Gemini Ins. Co. v. S & J Diving, Inc., SDTex, 464 FSupp2d 641.—Contracts 143.5, 147(3); Decl Judgm 272; Fed Cts 415; Insurance 1806, 1807, 1808, 1814, 1836, 1863, 2098, 2117, 2268, 2295, 2913, 2914, 2915, 2939.

Gem Jewelry Co. of Beaumont, Inc. v. Nolte, TexCiv-App–Beaumont, 335 SW2d 766, ref nre.—Accord 27; Hus & W 235(2); Parent & C 12.

Gemmy Industries Corp. v. Alliance General Ins. Co., NDTex, 190 FSupp2d 915, aff Gemmy Industries v. Alliance General Industries Co, 200 F3d 816.—Insurance 1822, 2298, 2301, 2302, 2914, 2919, 3147, 3153, 3155, 3168.

Gemoets v. State, TexApp–Houston (14 Dist), 116 SW3d 59.—Crim Law 552(1), 622.8(4), 656(7), 656(9), 721.5(1), 737(1), 741(1), 742(1), 1134(2), 1134(8), 1144.13(2.1), 1144.13(3), 1144.13(6), 1152(2), 1159.2(1), 1159.2(2), 1159.2(7), 1159.2(8), 1159.2(9), 1159.3(1), 1159.3(2), 1159.4(1), 1159.6, 1166.16, 1189, 1191; Ind & Inf 65, 110(3), 137(6); Jury 131(4); RICO 120, 121.

Gem Tire & Service Co., In re, BkrtcySDTex, 117 BR 874.—Atty & C 11(2.1), 21.5(1), 21.20, 32(4); Bankr 2159.1, 3008.1, 3030, 3179, 3190, 3201; Fraud 7.

Gem Vending, Inc. v. Walker, TexApp–Fort Worth, 918 SW2d 656.—App & E 163; Courts 23; Estop 52(8); Mand 4(4), 50; New Tr 116.2.

Gena v. Immigration and Naturalization Service, CA5 (Tex), 424 F2d 227.—Aliens 362(2), 385, 394, 401.

Genador v. Hagerla, TexCivApp–Fort Worth, 369 SW2d 70.—Bound 37(3); New Tr 102(1); Tresp to T T 47(1).

Gen-Aero, Inc.; Globe Indem. Co. v., TexCivApp–San Antonio, 459 SW2d 205, writ gr, ref nre 469 SW2d 164.—App & E 1170.6, 1170.7; Evid 177, 582(4); Insurance 3382; Trial 350.4(3), 351.5(4).

Genard; Bigfoot Independent School Dist. v., TexCiv-App–San Antonio, 116 SW2d 804, aff 129 SW2d 1213, 133 Tex 368.—App & E 917(1); Const Law 2340; Schools 103(2); Stip 18(3).

Genard v. City of San Antonio, TexCivApp–San Antonio, 307 SW2d 592, ref nre.—Dedi 58; Mun Corp 1000(4).

Gendebien v. Gendebien, TexApp–Houston (14 Dist), 668 SW2d 905.—App & E 966(1); Divorce 145, 179, 223, 252.3(2), 253(2), 286(2); Evid 350; Pretrial Proc 713, 716.

Gendebien; Gendebien v., TexApp–Houston (14 Dist), 668 SW2d 905.—App & E 966(1); Divorce 145, 179, 223, 252.3(2), 253(2), 286(2); Evid 350; Pretrial Proc 713, 716.

Gendke v. Travelers Ins. Co., TexCivApp–Waco, 368 SW2d 3.—Work Comp 1700, 1937.

Gendreau v. Medical Arts Hosp., TexApp–Eastland, 54 SW3d 877, reh overr, and review den, and reh of petition for review den.—Counties 208, 212; Mun Corp 154, 723, 742(5); States 191.1.

Gene Biddle Feed Co.; Nail v., TexCivApp–Beaumont, 347 SW2d 830.—App & E 1073(2); Judgm 17(2), 145(2), 161.

Genecov, Ex parte, Tex, 186 SW2d 225, 143 Tex 476, 160 ALR 1099, cert den Genecov v. State of Texas, 66 SCt 41, 326 US 733, 90 LEd 436, reh den 66 SCt 137, 326 US 808, 90 LEd 493.—Const Law 4579; Contempt 40; Hab Corp 289, 528.1; Nuis 80, 86.

Genecov v. Federal Petroleum Bd., CCA5 (Tex), 146 F2d 596, cert den 65 SCt 913, 324 US 865, 89 LEd 1420.—Admin Law 343.1; Commerce 56; Crim Law 393(1); Mines 92.5(3); Searches 76; Witn 4, 21, 306.

Genecov; Jackson v., TexCivApp–Tyler, 471 SW2d 589, ref nre.—Adv Poss 63(4), 85(4); Hus & W 273(9); Judgm 199(3.10); Land & Ten 18(1), 66(1).

Genecov v. Marcus, TexCivApp–Dallas, 285 SW2d 872.—Plead 111.42(7); Venue 2, 8.5(8).

Genecov v. U.S., CA5 (Tex), 412 F2d 556.—Int Rev 3234, 3259, 3393, 3394, 3428, 3441, 3460, 3707, 5095, 5112.

Genecov Group, Inc. v. Roosth Production Co., Tex-App–Tyler, 144 SW3d 546, review den, and reh overr, and reh of petition for review den.—Action 53(1); App & E 893(1), 901, 934(1); Decl Judgm 187; Judgm 185(2), 540, 584, 585(0.5), 585(2), 585(5), 586(2), 600.1, 601, 719, 739.

Gene D. Liggin, Inc.; Anzilotti v., TexApp–Houston (14 Dist), 899 SW2d 264.—Alt Disp Res 231, 235, 328, 329, 330, 332, 362(1), 362(2), 363(8), 376, 382; App & E 761, 766; Contracts 147(2), 170(1); Costs 262; Trusts 25(1), 339, 372(1).

Gene Duke Builders, Inc.; Abilene Housing Authority v., Tex, 226 SW3d 415.—Mun Corp 1016; States 108.

Gene Duke Builders, Inc. v. Abilene Housing Authority, Tex, 138 SW3d 907, on remand 168 SW3d 215, review gr, rev 226 SW3d 415.—Alt Disp Res 213(1).

Gene Duke Builders, Inc. v. Abilene Housing Authority, TexApp–Eastland, 168 SW3d 215, review gr, rev 226 SW3d 415.—Alt Disp Res 184, 210, 213(6); App & E 893(1); Mun Corp 253, 1016.

Gene F., Victor F. by, v. Pasadena Independant School Dist., CA5 (Tex), 793 F2d 633. See Victor F., by Gene F. v. Pasadena Independent School Dist.

Gene Hamon Ford, Inc. v. David McDavid Nissan, Inc., TexApp–Austin, 997 SW2d 298, reh overr, and review den, and reh of petition for review den.—Admin Law 749, 750, 790, 791, 799; Antitrust 269(3), 341, 342, 343; Const Law 3866, 3875, 4294; Statut 219(1), 219(4).

Gene Hill Equipment Co. v. Merryman, TexApp–Austin, 771 SW2d 207.—Estop 70(2); Lis Pen 17.

Gene Hill Equipment Co., Inc.; City of Fort Worth v., TexApp–Fort Worth, 761 SW2d 816.—Contracts 39; Costs 194.10; Damag 85; Impl & C C 60.1; Mun Corp 8, 327, 360(2), 360(6), 374(4); New Tr 72(5).

Genell, Inc. v. Flynn, Tex, 358 SW2d 543, 163 Tex 632.—Land & Ten 167(8); Neglig 213, 387, 1018, 1037(4), 1102, 1228, 1267.

Genell, Inc. v. Flynn, TexCivApp–Texarkana, 348 SW2d 196, writ gr, rev 358 SW2d 543, 163 Tex 632.—App & E 930(3); Neglig 506(8), 1014, 1037(4), 1286(6), 1286(7), 1670, 1679; Trial 140(1).

Gene Messer Ford, Inc.; Chandler v., TexApp–Eastland, 81 SW3d 493, reh overr, and review den.—Antitrust 162, 193, 234, 367; Judgm 185.3(21); Prod Liab 8, 11, 14, 35.1, 37, 75.1; Sales 273(1), 284(1), 439.

Gene Mohr Chevrolet Co.; Poser v., TexCivApp–Houston, 377 SW2d 732, writ gr, rev Hoke v. Poser, 384 SW2d 335.—App & E 765, 989, 1170.7, 1177(7); Autos 244(28); Damag 58, 158(5), 168(2), 185(1), 191, 213; Trial 277.

Gene Naumann Real Estate; Jamail v., TexApp–Austin, 680 SW2d 621, ref nre.—Adv Poss 19, 22, 31, 112; App & E 931(1), 989, 1012.1(5); Ease 24, 32.

General Acc. Fire & Life Assur. Corp.; Blickhan v., SDTex, 52 FSupp 135.—Work Comp 553, 566, 845, 1374.

General Acc. Fire & Life Assur. Corp. v. Callaway, TexCivApp–Hous (1 Dist), 429 SW2d 548.—Evid 213(1), 219(3), 471(20); Witn 77; Work Comp 1433, 1620, 1927, 1968(4).

General Acc. Fire & Life Assur. Corp. v. Camp, TexCivApp–Houston, 348 SW2d 782.—Evid 181, 355(6), 380, 382; Work Comp 1041, 1396, 1397, 1966, 1988.

General Acc. Fire & Life Assur. Corp.; Capps v., SDTex, 92 FSupp 227.—Work Comp 1066.

General Acc. Fire & Life Assur. Corp. v. Coffman, TexCivApp–Waco, 326 SW2d 287, ref nre.—Courts 91(1); Work Comp 951, 1922, 1932.

General Acc. Fire & Life Assur. Corp.; Davis v., TexCivApp–Beaumont, 127 SW2d 526.—Work Comp 235, 306, 308, 340, 717.

General Acc. Fire & Life Assur. Corp.; Dugan v., TexCivApp–Hous (14 Dist), 421 SW2d 717, ref nre.—Insurance 1634(3), 1635, 1659, 1766, 1883, 1887(1); Ref of Inst 19(1), 45(14).

General Acc. Fire & Life Assur. Corp. v. Hames, TexCivApp–Dallas, 416 SW2d 894.—Work Comp 51, 999, 1034, 1042, 1079, 1790, 1793, 1834, 1981, 1982, 1983.

General Acc. Fire & Life Assur. Corp. v. Hardin, CA5 (Tex), 290 F2d 862.—Fed Cts 381, 848; Work Comp 1297, 1969.

General Acc., Fire & Life Assur. Corp.; Johnson v., TexCivApp–Waco, 454 SW2d 837.—Insurance 2152.

General Acc. Fire & Life Assur. Corp. v. Marker, TexCivApp–Galveston, 298 SW2d 848, ref nre.—App & E 994(2), 1170.10; Fraud 11(1); Trial 352.15; Work Comp 1148.

General Acc. Fire & Life Assur. Corp. v. Martin, TexCivApp–San Antonio, 110 SW2d 258.—Work Comp 1292, 1688, 1831.

General Acc. Fire & Life Assur. Corp.; Matthews v., Tex, 343 SW2d 251, 161 Tex 622.—Damag 221(6); Work Comp 876, 1958.

General Acc. Fire & Life Assur. Corp. v. Matthews, TexCivApp–Fort Worth, 330 SW2d 221, writ gr, rev 343 SW2d 251, 161 Tex 622.—Damag 221(6); Plead 432; Work Comp 877, 1912, 1937.

General Acc. Fire & Life Assur. Corp. v. Mostert, CCA5 (Tex), 131 F2d 596.—Fed Cts 34, 342; Work Comp 1914.

General Acc. Fire & Life Assur. Corp. v. Murphy, TexCivApp–Houston, 339 SW2d 392, ref nre.—App & E 931(3); Damag 221(1), 221(4), 221(8); Work Comp 847, 869, 876, 1662, 1929.

General Acc., Fire & Life Assur. Corp. v. Perry, TexCivApp–Galveston, 264 SW2d 198, ref nre.—Work Comp 1396, 1927.

General Acc., Fire and Life Assur. Corp., Ltd. v. Legate, TexCivApp–Texarkana, 578 SW2d 505, ref nre.—Antitrust 393; Insurance 3359.

General Acc. Fire and Life Assur. Corp., Ltd.; Reina v., Tex, 611 SW2d 415.—App & E 1058(1); Trial 178; Work Comp 1410, 1418, 1629, 1653, 1937, 1955.

General Acc. Fire and Life Assur. Corp., Ltd. v. Reina, TexCivApp–Dallas, 597 SW2d 10, rev 611 SW2d 415.—Pretrial Proc 151, 271; Witn 266, 276; Work Comp 1639, 1697, 1703, 1937.

General Acc. Fire and Life Ins. Co.; Landon Beaver Funeral Home v., Tex, 701 SW2d 837. See Rivera v. Texas Employers' Ins. Ass'n.

General Acc. Ins. Co.; Dhillon v., TexApp–Houston (14 Dist), 789 SW2d 293, appeal after remand 1991 WL 51470, writ den.—App & E 856(1); Judgm 181(23), 185.2(4).

General Acc. Ins. Co.; Employers Nat. Ins. Co. v., SDTex, 857 FSupp 549.—Insurance 2926, 2934(4), 3352, 3517, 3528; Interest 31.

General Acc. Ins. Co. v. Unity/Waterford-Fair Oaks, Ltd., CA5 (Tex), 288 F3d 651.—Evid 448; Insurance 2142(6), 2146.

General Acc. Ins. Co. of America; Carroll v., CA5 (Tex), 891 F2d 1174, reh den.—Civil R 1570, 1575(1); Courts 100(1); Fed Cts 924.1.

General Acc. Ins. Co. of America; Essman v., TexApp–San Antonio, 961 SW2d 572.—Insurance 2782, 2790, 2803; Judgm 570(6), 713(2).

General Acc. Ins. Co. of America v. Howard, TexApp–Houston (14 Dist, 813 SW2d 557. See Potomac Ins. Co. v. Howard.

General Acc. Ins. Co. of America; Ran-Nan Inc. v., CA5 (Tex), 252 F3d 738.—Fed Cts 776; Insurance 1806, 2101, 2104, 2120, 2407.

General Adjustment Bureau, Inc.; Coke v., CA5 (Tex), 640 F2d 584.—Civil R 1106, 1524; Fed Civ Proc 2497.1, 2543, 2544; Fed Cts 714.

General Adjustment Bureau, Inc.; Coke v., CA5 (Tex), 616 F2d 785, reh gr 622 F2d 1226, on reh 640 F2d 584.—Civil R 1524, 1530; Fed Civ Proc 2497.1; Fed Cts 7.

General Adjustment Bureau, Inc. v. Fuess, SDTex, 192 FSupp 542.—Antitrust 13, 61; Fed Cts 429; Trademarks 1032, 1084, 1095, 1097, 1714(2), 1714(3).

General Agents Ins. Co. v. Arredondo, TexApp–San Antonio, 52 SW3d 762, reh overr, and review den.—App & E 854(1), 893(1), 1175(1); Contracts 143(2), 143.5, 176(2); Insurance 1806, 1808, 1832(1), 2098, 2278(1), 2278(19); Judgm 185(2).

General Agents Ins. Co. of America, Inc., In re, TexApp–Houston (14 Dist), 224 SW3d 806.—App & E 946; Assign 31; Fraud Conv 8; Mand 4(1), 4(4), 26, 28, 32; Pretrial Proc 358; Witn 198(1), 201(2), 204(2), 206, 217, 219(3), 222.

General Agents Ins. Co. of America, Inc. v. Home Ins. Co. of Illinois, TexApp–San Antonio, 21 SW3d 419, review dism by agreement.—App & E 232(3), 842(1), 946, 949, 969; Estop 68(2); Insurance 3517, 3526(10); Trial 367.

General Air Conditioning Co. v. Third Ward Church of Christ, Tex, 426 SW2d 541, ref nre.—Mech Liens 113(2).

General Air Conditioning Co. v. Third Ward Church of Christ, TexCivApp–Beaumont, 418 SW2d 839, rev 426 SW2d 541, ref nre.—App & E 1071.6; Mech Liens 113(2).

General Am. Cas. Co. v. Hill & Hill Motor Co., TexCivApp–Galveston, 269 SW2d 818.—Insurance 1832(1), 2652, 2885.

General Am. Cas. Co. v. Rosas, TexCivApp–Eastland, 275 SW2d 570, ref nre.—Work Comp 1789, 1790, 1795, 1811, 1834, 2026.

General American Communications Corp.; Nottingham v., CA5 (Tex), 811 F2d 873, cert den 108 SCt 158, 484 US 854, 98 LEd2d 113.—Antitrust 144, 364, 389(2), 390, 397; Damag 73, 221(7); Fed Civ Proc 211, 223, 229, 1748, 1970.1, 2603; Fed Cts 635, 898; Sec Reg 27.50.

General American Life Ins. Co. v. Day, TexCivApp–Fort Worth, 89 SW2d 1012, aff in part, rev in part 116 SW2d 697, 131 Tex 501.—Insurance 1832(1), 1836, 2035, 2037.

General American Life Ins. Co.; Fredonia State Bank v., Tex, 881 SW2d 279, on remand 906 SW2d 88, reh overr.—App & E 294(1), 344, 766, 1079, 1182; Insurance 2983.

General American Life Ins. Co.; Fredonia State Bank v., TexApp–Tyler, 906 SW2d 88, reh overr.—Insurance 3013, 3015.

General American Life Ins. Co.; Fredonia State Bank v., TexApp–Tyler, 884 SW2d 167, writ gr, rev 881 SW2d 279, on remand 906 SW2d 88, reh overr.—App & E 76(1), 82(2), 346.2, 930(3), 989, 994(2), 1001(1), 1002, 1003(7); Evid 383(4), 584(1), 598(1); Insurance 2445, 3015, 3099.

General American Life Ins. Co. v. Gant, TexCivApp–Austin, 119 SW2d 693, dism.—Evid 241(1), 244(8); Insurance 2031, 3015; Trial 237(4), 352.10.

General American Life Ins. Co. v. Hamor, TexCivApp–Amarillo, 95 SW2d 975, writ refused.—Usury 62, 97, 100(1).

General American Life Ins. Co.; Hufstedler v., TexCivApp–Austin, 82 SW2d 759, writ refused.—Mtg 567(1), 594(3).

General American Life Ins. Co. v. Johnson, TexCivApp–Beaumont, 88 SW2d 535, writ dism.—Insurance 2039.

General American Life Ins. Co.; Marineau v., TexApp–Fort Worth, 898 SW2d 397, reh overr, and writ den.—App & E 984(1), 984(5); Costs 2, 194.40; Insurance 3336, 3349, 3360, 3374, 3375, 3382, 3486, 3493; Interest 31, 35, 39(2.35), 39(3); Trusts 354, 358(1).

General American Life Ins. Co. v. Martin, TexCivApp–Beaumont, 137 SW2d 139.—Insurance 2037, 3335, 3395, 3611(2); Judgm 818(1).

General American Life Ins. Co.; Multicare Health Care Services, Inc. v., NDTex, 720 FSupp 581.—Fed Civ Proc 2501; Insurance 1117(1), 3567; States 18.41.

General American Life Ins. Co. v. Rodriguez, TexApp–Houston (14 Dist), 641 SW2d 264.—Insurance 1091(7), 2607, 3147, 3191(7), 3381(3), 3381(5); Interpl 35.

General American Life Ins. Co.; State v., TexCivApp–Waco, 575 SW2d 602, dism.—Courts 169(1); Tax 2736, 2863.

General American Oil Co. of Texas v. Gulf Oil Corp., TexCivApp–Austin, 139 SW2d 314, writ refused.—App & E 173(2); Mines 92.30, 92.32(1), 92.41.

General American Oil Co. of Texas v. Gulf Oil Corp., TexCivApp–El Paso, 170 SW2d 495, writ refused wom.—Mines 92.40, 92.41.

General American Oil Co. of Texas; Oram v., TexCivApp–Eastland, 503 SW2d 607, ref nre 513 SW2d 533, cert den 95 SCt 1355, 420 US 964, 43 LEd2d 441, reh den 95 SCt 1984, 421 US 981, 44 LEd2d 473.—Judgm 185.1(4); Lim of Act 130(7).

General American Transp. Corp.; Continental Oil Co. v., SDTex, 409 FSupp 288.—Action 17, 27(1), 27(2); Contracts 325; Courts 8; Fed Civ Proc 2510; Fed Cts 390, 409.1, 410; Prod Liab 3, 5, 62; Sales 55, 431; Torts 103.

General Am. Indem. Co. v. Pepper, Tex, 339 SW2d 660, 161 Tex 263.—Contracts 143(2), 143(3), 143.5, 147(1), 152; Insurance 2588(3).

General Am. Life Ins. Co. v. Day, TexComApp, 116 SW2d 697, 131 Tex 501.—Insurance 2028, 2035.

General Am. Life Ins. Co.; Gibson v., TexCivApp–El Paso, 89 SW2d 1070, writ dism.—Insurance 2070; Paymt 84(1), 85(1).

General Am. Life Ins. Co. v. Martinez, TexCivApp–El Paso, 149 SW2d 637, writ dism, correct.—App & E 1062.2; Insurance 2955, 2979, 2980, 3001; Trial 125(3), 350.8.

General Am. Life Ins. Co. v. National Bank of Commerce of San Antonio, TexCivApp–Eastland, 348 SW2d 393, ref nre.—Banks 174; Indem 104.

General Am. Life Ins. Co. v. Rios, TexComApp, 164 SW2d 521, 139 Tex 554.—Insurance 1834(2), 2031, 2566.

General Am. Life Ins. Co. v. Rios, TexCivApp–El Paso, 154 SW2d 191, rev 164 SW2d 521, 139 Tex 554.—Courts 90(7); Insurance 1712, 1805, 1832(1), 2537.

General Am. Life Ins. Co. v. Valley Feed Mills, Inc., TexCivApp–El Paso, 458 SW2d 860, ref nre.—Accord 10(1).

General Am. Life Ins. Co.; Walton v., TexCivApp–San Antonio, 383 SW2d 854, ref nre.—Mtg 201.

General Am. Life Ins. Co. v. Williams, TexCivApp–Texarkana, 433 SW2d 802, writ dism.—Insurance 3167, 3198(1).

General Am. Oil Co. of Texas; Oram v., Tex, 513 SW2d 533.—Mental H 274.

General & Excess Underwriters, Inc. v. Harrelson, TexCivApp–Waco, 327 SW2d 78, ref nre.—Insurance 1635, 1766, 3066, 3131.

General Asphalt Co.; Calvert v., TexCivApp–Austin, 409 SW2d 935.—Statut 220, 248, 255.

General Ass'n Branch Davidian Seventh Day Adventist v. McLennan County Appraisal Dist., TexApp–Waco, 715 SW2d 391.—App & E 169; Const Law 229(2), 1386(1), 3321; Tax 2355.

General Ass'n of Davidian Seventh Day Adventists; General Ass'n of Davidian Seventh Day Adventists, Inc. v., TexCivApp–Waco, 410 SW2d 256, ref nre.—Char 30, 37(1), 50; Receivers 12, 48; Relig Soc 35; Trusts 9, 349, 352.

General Ass'n of Davidian Seventh Day Adventists, Inc. v. General Ass'n of Davidian Seventh Day Adventists, TexCivApp–Waco, 410 SW2d 256, ref nre.—Char 30, 37(1), 50; Receivers 12, 48; Relig Soc 35; Trusts 9, 349, 352.

General Atlas Carbon Co. v. Sheppard, WDTex, 37 FSupp 51.—Fed Cts 433; Licens 8(1), 12; Statut 188, 190, 210, 216, 217.3, 245.

General Automotive Specialty Co., Inc.; Strattec Sec. Corp. v., CAFed (Tex), 126 F3d 1411.—Pat 101(2), 226.6, 235(2), 237, 314(5), 324.55(1), 325.11(2.1).

General Battery Corp.; Meza v., CA5 (Tex), 908 F2d 1262.—Fed Civ Proc 2497.1; Fed Cts 420, 762; Judgm 585(3), 632, 665, 675(1), 677, 681; Labor & Emp 683, 1518; Ref of Inst 44, 45(2).

General Beverage Distributors, Inc.; Martinez v., TexCivApp–Waco, 312 SW2d 284.—App & E 846(5), 1011.1(4), 1024.3; Plead 111.35, 111.42(8); Trial 382.

General Box Co. v. Southwest Subsidiary Co., TexCivApp–Hous (14 Dist), 598 SW2d 662.—App & E 68, 70(6), 71(3), 71(4); Courts 28; Plead 104(2).

General Brick Sales Co., Inc.; Brown v., TexApp–Fort Worth, 39 SW3d 291.—App & E 840(2), 893(1); Const Law 3964; Corp 1.4(4), 325; Courts 12(2.1), 12(2.10), 12(2.20), 12(2.25), 39.

General Brick Sales, Inc.; Roland v., TexApp–Fort Worth, 818 SW2d 896.—Mech Liens 310(4).

General Cable Corp.; Howard v., CA5 (Tex), 674 F2d 351.—Damag 63, 163(4); Fed Civ Proc 1975, 2182.1, 2183, 2610; Prod Liab 77.5, 83.5, 88.5.

General Cable Industries, Inc. v. Davis Fleet Maintenance, Inc., TexApp–El Paso, 966 SW2d 166. See Southwestern Bell Telephone Co. v. General Cable Industries, Inc.

General Cable Industries, Inc.; Fuller v., EDTex, 81 FSupp2d 726.—Civil R 1135, 1140, 1545; Fed Civ Proc 2497.1.

General Cable Industries, Inc.; Southwestern Bell Telephone Co. v., TexApp–El Paso, 966 SW2d 166, review den.—Compromise 4, 9; Contrib 5(2), 8.

General Cas. Co. of America v. Second Nat. Bank of Houston, CA5 (Tex), 178 F2d 679.—U S 111(1), 111(2).

General Cas. Co. of America v. U.S., CA5 (Tex), 205 F2d 753.—Counties 123; Int Rev 4849; Mun Corp 344.1, 347(1); Pub Contr 42, 48, 58; States 101; Statut 233.

General Chemical Corp. v. De La Lastra, Tex, 852 SW2d 916, cert dism 114 SCt 490, 510 US 985, 126 LEd2d 440.—Adm 1(1), 1.20(1), 1.20(4), 1.20(6), 2, 21; App & E 882(1); Death 77, 93, 96; Prod Liab 14; Statut 217.2.

General Chemical Corp. v. De La Lastra, TexApp–Corpus Christi, 815 SW2d 750, reh overr, and writ gr, and mandate stayed, aff in part, rev in part 852 SW2d 916, cert dism 114 SCt 490, 510 US 985, 126 LEd2d 440. —App & E 218.2(1), 302(5); Const Law 3759, 4427; Damag 87(1), 94; Death 76, 77, 88, 89, 93, 99(5); Evid 146; Neglig 379, 384, 385; Prod Liab 14, 15, 43, 75.1, 83, 87.1.

General Cinema Corp. of Texas; Glisson v., TexApp–Dallas, 713 SW2d 694, ref nre.—Work Comp 19, 2143.

General Cinema Corp. of Texas, Inc.; Universal Amusements Co., Inc. v., SDTex, 635 FSupp 1505.—Antitrust 535, 537, 541, 556, 563, 567, 580, 625, 644, 675, 714, 715,

977(1), 977(2), 977(3), 979, 980, 984; Evid 260, 501(1), 568(1); Torts 263.

General Coatings, Inc.; Degen v., TexApp–Houston (14 Dist), 705 SW2d 734.—Courts 81, 85(1); Pretrial Proc 587.

General Committee of Adjustment of Brotherhood of Locomotive Engineers for Missouri-Kansas-Texas R. R. v. Missouri-Kansas-Texas R. Co., USTex, 64 SCt 146, 320 US 323, 88 LEd 76.—Admin Law 228.1; Courts 1; Decl Judgm 99; Fed Cts 206; Labor & Emp 1523, 1527.

General Committee of Adjustment of Brotherhood of Locomotive Engineers for Missouri-K.-T. R. R. v. Missouri-K.-T. R. Co., CCA5 (Tex), 132 F2d 91, cert gr 63 SCt 1172, 319 US 736, 87 LEd 1696, rev General Committee of Adjustment of Brotherhood of Locomotive Engineers for Missouri-Kansas-Texas R R v. Missouri-Kansas-Texas R Co, 64 SCt 146, 320 US 323, 88 LEd 76.—Decl Judgm 126; Fed Cts 206, 623; Labor & Emp 1201, 1204, 1247, 1402.

General Computer Systems, Inc.; Christopher v., TexCivApp–Dallas, 560 SW2d 698, ref nre.—App & E 181, 230, 232(0.5), 241; Consp 1.1; Damag 221(2.1), 221(8); Pretrial Proc 721; Princ & A 64(1), 66, 78(1), 79(5), 79(6), 79(9); Trial 350.3(1), 350.3(4); Trover 60.

General Corp.; Cavaness v., Tex, 283 SW2d 33, 155 Tex 69.—Corp 30(1); Evid 397(1), 418; Princ & A 183(2); Ref of Inst 19(1).

General Corp.; Cavaness v., TexCivApp–Dallas, 272 SW2d 595, aff 283 SW2d 33, 155 Tex 69.—App & E 662(3), 671(4), 671(6); Corp 30(5), 34(3), 34(7), 448(1), 448(2).

General Corrosion Services Corp. v. K Way Equipment Co., Inc., TexApp–Tyler, 631 SW2d 578.—Bailm 11; Contracts 147(1), 155.

General Cotton Warehouse v. Thrash, TexApp–Houston (1 Dist), 832 SW2d 779. See Hughes v. Thrash.

General Council of the Assemblies of God; Eckler v., TexApp–San Antonio, 784 SW2d 935, writ den.—Antitrust 291; Judgm 183, 185.3(1); Relig Soc 11, 30.

General Crude Oil Co v. Scofield, WDTex, 39 FSupp 586.—Int Rev 4348.

General Crude Oil Co. v. Aiken, Tex, 344 SW2d 668, 162 Tex 104.—Courts 247(2); Mines 73.1(6), 121; Trial 365.1(4).

General Crude Oil Co. v. Aiken, TexCivApp–Eastland, 335 SW2d 229, writ gr, rev 344 SW2d 668, 162 Tex 104. —App & E 1050.1(7), 1056.1(10); Damag 110; Mines 73.1(6), 121, 125.

General Crude Oil Co.; Biskamp v., TexCivApp–San Antonio, 452 SW2d 515, writ refused.—Mines 92.62.

General Crude Oil Co.; Cowden v., TexCivApp–El Paso, 217 SW2d 109, ref nre.—Mines 74(4), 74(5), 78.1(8), 78.5, 78.7(3.1), 78.7(4).

General Crude Oil Co.; Crews v., TexCivApp–Beaumont, 287 SW2d 243.—App & E 833(2); Estop 95, 116; Home 12, 57(3), 122, 123, 154, 169, 175, 214, 216; Mines 73.5.

General Crude Oil Co. v. Harris, TexCivApp–Texarkana, 101 SW2d 1098, writ dism.—Abate & R 19; App & E 1039(16); Contracts 348, 352(1); Land & Ten 27; Mines 78.4, 78.7(6).

General Crude Oil Co.; Hoover v., Tex, 212 SW2d 140, 147 Tex 89.—App & E 927(7); Decl Judgm 187; Mines 78.3, 78.4; Ven & Pur 101.

General Crude Oil Co.; Hoover v., TexCivApp–Galveston, 206 SW2d 139, rev 212 SW2d 140, 147 Tex 89.— Contracts 176(1); Mines 74(3), 74.5, 78.1(9), 78.2, 78.4; Trial 136(3).

General Crude Oil Co.; Trad v., Tex, 474 SW2d 183.— App & E 151(5).

General Crude Oil Co.; Trad v., TexCivApp–San Antonio, 468 SW2d 612, application for writ of error dism 474 SW2d 183.—Judgm 181(15.1); Mines 79.4.

General Devices, Inc. v. Bacon, TexApp–Dallas, 888 SW2d 497, writ den.—Antitrust 537, 556, 575; App & E 866(3), 927(7), 934(1); Contracts 116(1), 117(0.5), 117(1), 117(2), 117(7), 137(4), 142, 143(1), 143(2), 153, 176(1); Damag 190, 208(1); Judgm 181(8), 181(15.1), 185(2); Labor & Emp 917; Torts 214, 242.

General Devices, Inc. v. Bacon, TexApp–Dallas, 836 SW2d 179, writ gr, vac 830 SW2d 106, on remand 888 SW2d 497, writ den.—Antitrust 566; App & E 927(7), 997(3); Contracts 116(1), 117(2), 117(8), 136, 137(4), 143(2), 143(3), 202(2), 317; Damag 190, 208(1); Evid 450(5); Judgm 181(8), 185(2); Labor & Emp 904; Ref of Inst 23; Torts 214, 242.

General Drivers, Warehousemen and Helpers, Local Union No. 968; Elliott v., SDTex, 123 FSupp 125.— Labor & Emp 1381, 2075.

General Drivers, Warehousemen and Helpers, Local Union 745 v. Dallas County Const. Emp. Ass'n, Tex-CivApp–Dallas, 246 SW2d 677, ref nre.—App & E 954(1), 954(3), 954(4); Inj 135; Labor & Emp 1345(2), 1411, 2075, 2121.

General Drivers, Warehousemen and Helpers Local Union 745; Joseph Schlitz Brewing Co. Container Div. v., EDTex, 486 FSupp 320, aff Jos Schlitz Brewing Co, Container Div v. General Drivers, Warehousemen & Helpers Local Union 745, 618 F2d 1184.—Labor & Emp 1549(16), 2106, 2111.

General Drivers, Warehousemen and Helpers Local Union 968 v. Sysco Food Services, Inc., CA5 (Tex), 838 F2d 794.—Labor & Emp 1275, 1549(19), 1595(10).

General Dynamics v. Torres, TexApp–El Paso, 915 SW2d 45, reh overr, and writ den.—App & E 662(4), 842(2), 893(1), 901, 931(1), 1008.1(1), 1008.1(2), 1010.2; Corp 307, 314(0.5), 315, 316(1), 317(1), 319(7), 320(11), 426(1), 426(12), 432(12); Evid 317(4).

General Dynamics, Convair Aerospace Division, Ft. Worth Operation; Cooper v., CA5 (Tex), 533 F2d 163, reh den 537 F2d 1143, reh den Gen Dynamics, Convair Aerospace Div, FT Worth Oprtn v. Intl Asso of Mach & Aerospace Workers, AFL-CIO, 537 F2d 1143, cert den International Ass'n of Machinists and Aerospace Workers, AFL-CIO v Hopkins, 97 SCt 2972, 433 US 908, 53 LEd2d 1091.—Civil R 1153, 1154, 1162(1), 1258; Const Law 1292, 1320; Labor & Emp 1264(2), 1331; Statut 223.1.

General Dynamics, Convair Aerospace Div., Fort Worth Operation; Cooper v., NDTex, 378 FSupp 1258, rev 533 F2d 163, reh den 537 F2d 1143, reh den Gen Dynamics, Convair Aerospace Div, FT Worth Oprtn v. Intl Asso of Mach & Aerospace Workers, AFL-CIO, 537 F2d 1143, cert den International Ass'n of Machinists and Aerospace Workers, AFL-CIO v Hopkins, 97 SCt 2972, 433 US 908, 53 LEd2d 1091.—Civil R 1511, 1523; Crim Law 97(4); Indem 36, 37; Labor & Emp 1264(2), 1282; U S 3.

General Dynamics, Convair Corp.; Roberts v., SDTex, 425 FSupp 688.—Lim of Act 119(1), 119(3), 122; Sales 255.

General Dynamics Corp.; Aeronautical Indus. Dist. Lodge 776, Intern. Ass'n of Machinists and Aerospace Workers, AFL-CIO v., NDTex, 738 FSupp 1038. —Labor & Emp 2016, 2034, 2042, 2049, 2086, 2106.

General Dynamics Corp.; Bareford v., CA5 (Tex), 973 F2d 1138, opinion vac in part on denial of rearg, cert den 113 SCt 1843, 507 US 1029, 123 LEd2d 468.— Action 1, 12; Fed Civ Proc 338, 1741; Fed Cts 895; Witn 216(1), 217.

General Dynamics Corp.; Board of Equalization of City and Independent School Dist. of Fort Worth v., TexCivApp–Fort Worth, 344 SW2d 489, ref nre.—Tax 2064.

General Dynamics Corp. v. Bullock, Tex, 547 SW2d 255, cert den 98 SCt 717, 434 US 1009, 54 LEd2d 751.—Tax 2233, 2540, 3406.

General Dynamics Corp.; Bullock v., TexCivApp–Austin, 533 SW2d 118, writ gr, aff 547 SW2d 255, cert den 98 SCt 717, 434 US 1009, 54 LEd2d 751.—Tax 3405, 3406.

General Dynamics Corp.; Burden v., CA5 (Tex), 60 F3d 213.—Damag 50.10; Rem of C 36, 107(4), 107(7), 107(9).

General Dynamics Corp.; Crenshaw v., CA5 (Tex), 940 F2d 125.—Estop 85; Fed Civ Proc 2737.3, 2737.5, 2742.5; Fraud 12; Frds St of 44(3).

General Dynamics Corp.; Cureington v., CA5 (Tex), 137 F3d 333. See Halkias v. General Dynamics Corp.

General Dynamics Corp.; Cureington v., CA5 (Tex), 31 F3d 224. See Halkias v. General Dynamics Corp.

General Dynamics Corp.; E.E.O.C. v., CA5 (Tex), 999 F2d 113, on remand 849 FSupp 1158.—Fed Civ Proc 1278, 1855.1; Fed Cts 820; Witn 268(1).

General Dynamics Corp.; E.E.O.C. v., NDTex, 849 FSupp 1158.—Civil R 1505(4), 1515, 1530; Fed Civ Proc 1788.6, 1855.1; Lim of Act 105(1), 195(3).

General Dynamics Corp.; Equal Employment Opportunity Commission v., NDTex, 382 FSupp 59, rev and remanded EEOC v. General Dynamics Corp, 510 F2d 382, cert den 96 SCt 43, 423 US 827, 46 LEd2d 43, cert den International Ass'n of Machinists & Aerospace Workers, AFL-CIO v EEOC, 96 SCt 43, 423 US 827, 46 LEd2d 43.—Civil R 1530.

General Dynamics Corp.; Halkias v., CA5 (Tex), 137 F3d 333, cert den Bryant v. General Dynamics Corp, 119 SCt 171, 525 US 872, 142 LEd2d 140.—Fed Cts 776; Labor & Emp 3232.

General Dynamics Corp.; Halkias v., CA5 (Tex), 31 F3d 224, reh en banc gr, vac on reh 56 F3d 27, on remand 899 FSupp 295, aff 101 F3d 698, on remand 955 FSupp 695, aff 137 F3d 333, cert den Bryant v. General Dynamics Corp, 119 SCt 171, 525 US 872, 142 LEd2d 140, on remand Staudt v Glastron, Inc, 1995 WL 701406, rev 92 F3d 312, reh and sug for reh den 99 F3d 1137.—Const Law 3971, 4182; Fed Cts 409.1, 422.1, 424; Labor & Emp 40(1), 1964, 1998; Lim of Act 6(1), 16, 39(1).

General Dynamics Corp.; Halkias v., NDTex, 955 FSupp 695, aff 137 F3d 333, cert den Bryant v. General Dynamics Corp, 119 SCt 171, 525 US 872, 142 LEd2d 140. —Fed Civ Proc 2553; Labor & Emp 3204, 3226.

General Dynamics Corp.; Halkias v., NDTex, 899 FSupp 295, aff 101 F3d 698, on remand 955 FSupp 695, aff 137 F3d 333, cert den Bryant v. General Dynamics Corp, 119 SCt 171, 525 US 872, 142 LEd2d 140.—Fed Cts 424.

General Dynamics Corp.; Halkias v., NDTex, 825 FSupp 123, aff 31 F3d 224, reh en banc gr, vac on reh 56 F3d 27, on remand 899 FSupp 295, aff 101 F3d 698, on remand 955 FSupp 695, aff 137 F3d 333, cert den Bryant v. General Dynamics Corp, 119 SCt 171, 525 US 872, 142 LEd2d 140, on remand Staudt v Glastron, Inc, 1995 WL 701406, rev 92 F3d 312, reh and sug for reh den 99 F3d 1137, vac 56 F3d 27, on remand 899 FSupp 295, aff 101 F3d 698, on remand 955 FSupp 695, aff 137 F3d 333, cert den 119 SCt 171, 525 US 872, 142 LEd2d 140, on remand 1995 WL 701406, rev 92 F3d 312, reh and sug for reh den 99 F3d 1137.—Fed Civ Proc 1041, 1044, 1049.1; Fed Cts 424; Lim of Act 58(1).

General Dynamics Corp. v. Harris, TexCivApp–Waco, 581 SW2d 300.—Courts 489(1); Divorce 273; States 18.28.

General Dynamics Corp.; Lindsey v., TexCivApp–Waco, 450 SW2d 895.—Labor & Emp 1518.

General Dynamics Corp. v. N. L. R. B., CA5 (Tex), 447 F2d 1370.—Courts 104.

General Dynamics Corp.; Radford v., CA5 (Tex), 151 F3d 396, reh and sug for reh den 159 F3d 1358, cert den 119 SCt 872, 525 US 1105, 142 LEd2d 773.—Labor & Emp 648; Lim of Act 100(7), 100(12), 104.5, 105(1), 165.

General Dynamics Corp. v. Sharp, TexApp–Austin, 919 SW2d 861, reh overr, and writ den.—Commerce 69(1), 70; Const Law 188, 190, 990, 4140, 4143; Statut 212.3, 263; Tax 2492, 2540.

General Dynamics Corp.; Trevino v., CA5 (Tex), 865 F2d 1474, reh den 876 F2d 1154, cert den 110 SCt 327, 493 US 935, 107 LEd2d 317.—Labor & Emp 26, 58, 3038(2); Prod Liab 14, 26, 48; U S 73(9), 78(8), 78(9), 78(12).

General Dynamics Corp.; Trevino v., EDTex, 626 FSupp 1330, aff in part, vac in part 865 F2d 1474, reh den 876 F2d 1154, cert den 110 SCt 327, 493 US 935, 107 LEd2d 317.—Prod Liab 26, 48, 75.1, 82.1; U S 78(4), 78(16); Work Comp 203, 2138.

General Dynamics Corp. v. U.S., CA5 (Tex), 865 F2d 1474. See Trevino v. General Dynamics Corp.

General Dynamics Corp.; U.S. v., NDTex, 755 FSupp 720.—Environ Law 258, 282, 700; Fed Civ Proc 2492; Indem 64; U S 130(6.1).

General Dynamics Corp.; Vincent v., NDTex, 427 FSupp 786.—Courts 90(1); Crim Law 16; Em Dom 5; U S 3, 55.

General Dynamics Corp., Convair Division; Aeronautical Indus. Dist. Lodge 776, IAM v., TexCivApp–Fort Worth, 300 SW2d 130.—Labor & Emp 1185(2), 1852.

General Dynamics Corp., Fort Worth Div.; Duckstein v., TexCivApp–Fort Worth, 499 SW2d 907, ref nre, cert den 95 SCt 61, 419 US 835, 42 LEd2d 61.—Judgm 181(6), 185(2); Labor & Emp 1320(14), 1542, 1996.

General Dynamics Long Term Disability Benefits Plan; Martin v., NDTex, 917 FSupp 475.—Insurance 2571.

General Elec.; American Wholesale Club v., BkrtcyND-Tex, 94 BR 428. See AMWC, Inc., In re.

General Elec.; AMWC, Inc. v., BkrtcyNDTex, 94 BR 428. See AMWC, Inc., In re.

General Elec. Capital Assur. v. Van Norman, SDTex, 209 FSupp2d 668.—Insurance 3481(2), 3483; Interpl 21, 30, 35.

General Elec. Capital Assurance Co. v. Jackson, TexApp–Houston (1 Dist), 135 SW3d 849, reh overr, and review den.—App & E 914(1); Child C 404; Guard & W 26, 37; Judgm 7, 16.

General Elec. Capital Auto Financial Leasing Services, Inc. v. Stanfield, TexApp–Tyler, 71 SW3d 351, reh overr, and review den, and reh of petition for review den.—App & E 347(1), 977(5); Judgm 92, 128, 138(1), 143(2), 145(2), 145(4), 151, 159, 162(2), 162(4), 169, 218, 538.

General Elec. Capital Auto Lease; Gulf States Petroleum Corp. v., TexApp–Eastland, 134 SW3d 504.—Bankr 2391, 2395, 2396, 2462; Judgm 118, 139, 143(2), 143(4), 143(8), 164; Pretrial Proc 506.1; Trover 4.

General Elec. Capital Business Asset Funding Corp.; CSH Restaurant Group, Inc. v., TexApp–Dallas, 145 SW3d 822.—Judgm 185.3(16).

General Elec. Capital Corp., In re, Tex, 203 SW3d 314. —Estop 52.10(2); Jury 28(5), 28(15).

General Elec. Capital Corp., In re, TexApp–El Paso, 63 SW3d 568, reh overr, and petition stricken, and mandamus den.—Judges 16(2), 19; Judgm 386(5); Mand 4(4), 12, 26, 53; Oath 5.

General Elec. Capital Corp. v. City of Corpus Christi, TexApp–Corpus Christi, 850 SW2d 596, reh overr, and writ den.—Admin Law 229; Evid 265(5); Tax 2188, 2189, 2642, 2667, 2723, 2727.

General Elec. Capital Corp.; County of Burleson v., TexApp–Houston (14 Dist), 831 SW2d 54, writ den.—App & E 836, 846(5), 930(3), 989, 994(2), 999(1), 1001(1), 1003(7); Em Dom 2(11), 69, 222(1), 262(5); Sales 234(1); Tax 2847, 3061.

General Elec. Capital Corp. v. Posey, CA5 (Tex), 415 F3d 391, on remand 2006 WL 708163.—Fed Civ Proc 751, 1752.1; Fed Cts 776; Fraud 13(3), 45.

GENERAL

59 Tex D 2d—226

See Guidelines for Arrangement at the beginning of this Volume

General Elec. Capital Corp.; Tryit Enterprises v., BkrtcySDTex, 121 BR 217. See Tryit Enterprises, In re.

General Elec. Co. v. Brown & Ross Intern. Distributors, Inc., TexApp–Houston (1 Dist), 804 SW2d 527, writ den.—Appear 10; Corp 665(1); Courts 12(2.1), 12(2.5), 12(2.10), 12(2.20), 12(2.25), 35.

General Elec. Co.; Browne v., TexCivApp–San Antonio, 402 SW2d 957, writ dism.—App & E 719(8); Judgm 138(1), 143(18).

General Elec. Co. v. California Ins. Guar. Ass'n, TexApp–Beaumont, 997 SW2d 923, reh overr, and petition stricken, and review den.—App & E 893(1); Appear 9(2); Const Law 3963, 3964, 3965(6); Courts 4, 11, 12(2.1); Insurance 1508.

General Elec. Co. v. City of Abilene, TexApp–Eastland, 795 SW2d 311.—Mun Corp 724, 742(4).

General Elec. Co. v. City of San Antonio, CA5 (Tex), 334 F2d 480.—Antitrust 976; Lim of Act 104(1).

General Elec. Co.; City Public Service Bd. v., CA5 (Tex), 947 F2d 747.—Sales 266.

General Elec. Co.; City Public Service Bd. v., CA5 (Tex), 935 F2d 78, opinion am on denial of reh 947 F2d 747.— Fed Cts 754.1, 785, 950; Sales 284(1).

General Elec. Co. v. Ducane Heating Corp., TexCivApp–Hous (14 Dist), 561 SW2d 47.—Indem 33(1); Plead 20.

General Elec. Co. v. Falcon Ridge Apartments, Joint Venture, Tex, 811 SW2d 942.—App & E 5.

General Elec. Co.; Falcon Ridge Apartments Joint Venture v., TexApp–Houston (1 Dist), 795 SW2d 21, writ gr, rev 811 SW2d 942.—App & E 5; Const Law 3989; Pretrial Proc 676.

General Elec. Co.; Giles v., CA5 (Tex), 245 F3d 474.— Civil R 1217, 1218(4), 1464, 1487, 1563, 1571, 1572, 1573, 1574, 1594, 1765; Damag 102, 192; Estop 68(2); Fed Civ Proc 751, 2497.1, 2544, 2602; Fed Cts 641, 642, 643, 776, 798, 799, 813, 830, 871, 872, 878, 929.

General Elec. Co. v. Inter-Ocean Shipping, SDTex, 862 FSupp 166.—Ship 101, 106(1), 132(1), 134, 140(1), 140(2), 141(2).

General Elec. Co.; Jones v., TexCivApp–El Paso, 543 SW2d 882, ref nre.—Judgm 181(11), 185.3(21).

General Elec. Co. v. Kunze, TexApp–Waco, 747 SW2d 826, writ den.—Evid 555.4(3); Interest 39(2.40); Labor & Emp 810, 862, 863(2), 871, 877; Work Comp 36.

General Elec. Co.; Rogers v., CA5 (Tex), 781 F2d 452.— Release 2, 15.

General Elec. Co. v. Salinas, TexApp–Corpus Christi, 861 SW2d 20.—Mand 4(1), 12, 32; Pretrial Proc 13, 24, 27.1, 41, 375, 390.

General Elec. Co. v. Schmal, TexApp–Texarkana, 623 SW2d 482, ref nre.—App & E 1060.1(1), 1062.2; Compromise 15(1); Evid 539; Prod Liab 26, 85, 90; Trial 129, 350.1, 350.3(5).

General Elec. Co.; Southwest Inns, Ltd. v., TexApp–Houston (14 Dist), 744 SW2d 258, writ den.—App & E 230, 882(16), 970(2); New Tr 101; Pretrial Proc 371, 406; Prod Liab 86; Trial 122.

General Elec. Corp.; Harris County Appraisal Review Bd. v., TexApp–Houston (14 Dist), 819 SW2d 915, writ den.—App & E 863, 870(2); Const Law 4138(2); Judgm 185(2); Tax 2667, 2670, 2674.

General Elec. Corp.; Rodrigues v., EDTex, 204 FSupp2d 975.—Neglig 210, 250; Prod Liab 1, 48.

General Elec. Credit Corp.; American Fiber Glass, Inc. v., TexCivApp–Fort Worth, 529 SW2d 298, ref nre.— App & E 1012.1(8); Evid 404; Guar 36(2), 87.

General Elec. Credit Corp.; Blakeway v., TexCivApp–Austin, 429 SW2d 925, ref nre.—Bailm 22, 25, 31(3), 32; Damag 117; Land & Ten 110(2), 195(2).

General Elec. Credit Corp.; Bryan v., TexCivApp–Hous (1 Dist), 553 SW2d 415.—App & E 801(1); Motions 1; New Tr 109; Pretrial Proc 28, 403, 434.

General Elec. Credit Corp.; Carroll v., TexApp–Houston (1 Dist), 734 SW2d 153.—Sec Tran 230, 231, 239, 240.

General Elec. Credit Corp. v. First Nat. Bank of Dumas, TexCivApp–Amarillo, 432 SW2d 737.—App & E 173(6), 556; Chat Mtg 144, 169; Contracts 1, 6; Judgm 185(1), 186; Sales 201(1).

General Elec. Credit Corp.; Grubbs v., USTex, 92 SCt 1344, 405 US 699, 31 LEd2d 612.—Fed Civ Proc 281; Fed Cts 461; Interpl 24; Rem of C 2, 10, 11, 94.

General Elec. Credit Corp. v. Grubbs, CA5 (Tex), 513 F2d 783, reh den 516 F2d 900, cert den 96 SCt 363, 423 US 947, 46 LEd2d 282.—Fed Cts 955.

General Elec. Credit Corp. v. Grubbs, CA5 (Tex), 478 F2d 53, cert den 94 SCt 153, 414 US 854, 38 LEd2d 104, appeal after remand 513 F2d 783, reh den 516 F2d 900, cert den 96 SCt 363, 423 US 947, 46 LEd2d 282.— Antitrust 983; Bills & N 94(1), 97(1), 103(1); Evid 317(12); Fed Cts 870.1, 945; Princ & A 22(1); Trial 105(2).

General Elec. Credit Corp. v. Grubbs, CA5 (Tex), 447 F2d 286, cert gr 92 SCt 446, 404 US 983, 30 LEd2d 366, rev 92 SCt 1344, 405 US 699, 31 LEd2d 612.—Interpl 8(1); Rem of C 10.

General Elec. Credit Corp. v. Gutierrez, TexApp–Corpus Christi, 668 SW2d 463.—App & E 767(1), 852, 912; Plead 111.42(1); Venue 2, 3.

General Elec. Credit Corp.; Hill v., TexCivApp–San Antonio, 434 SW2d 457.—Contracts 187(1); Lim of Act 41.

General Elec. Credit Corp. v. Midland Cent. Appraisal Dist., Tex, 826 SW2d 124.—Costs 260(5).

General Elec. Credit Corp. v. Midland Cent. Appraisal Dist., TexApp–El Paso, 808 SW2d 169, writ gr, aff in part, rev in part 826 SW2d 124.—App & E 863; Const Law 2314, 2600, 4137; Costs 260(5); Tax 2105, 2151, 2696.

General Elec. Credit Corp.; Morris Jewelers, Inc. v., CA5 (Tex), 714 F2d 32.—Evid 268.

General Elec. Credit Corp. v. Oil Screw Triton VI, CA5 (Tex), 712 F2d 991.—Controlled Subs 156, 175, 190; Fed Civ Proc 2737.5; Mtg 581(2); Ship 32; U S 147(11.1).

General Elec. Credit Corp. v. Smail, Tex, 584 SW2d 690. —Admin Law 416.1, 417; Const Law 2340; Cons Cred 16, 17, 32, 51, 55, 61.1; Statut 219(6.1).

General Elec. Credit Corp. v. Timely Secretarial Service, Inc., CA5 (Tex), 987 F2d 1167. See Timely Secretarial Service, Inc., Matter of.

General Elec. Credit Corp.; Zodiac Corp. v., TexCivApp–Tyler, 566 SW2d 341.—App & E 837(10), 846(5), 931(1); Corp 503(1); Evid 370(1), 373(1); Parties 32, 82; Plead 111.9, 111.12, 291(2); Trial 66; Venue 22(4).

General Elec. Mortg. Ins. Corp.; Kaigler v., TexApp–Houston (1 Dist), 961 SW2d 273, reh overr.—App & E 79(1), 345.1, 387(2).

General Elec. Supply Co.; Campbell Bros., Inc. v., TexCivApp–Dallas, 383 SW2d 61, ref nre.—Princ & S 123(2), 136, 139, 142, 159, 161.

General Elec. Supply Co. v. Epco Constructors, Inc., SDTex, 332 FSupp 112.—Assign 57; Colleges 5; Fed Civ Proc 3; Princ & S 139.

General Elec. Supply Co. v. Utley-James of Texas, Inc., CA5 (Tex), 857 F2d 1010.—Estop 52.10(3), 54; Evid 87.

General Elec. Supply Co.; William J. Burns Intern. Detective Agency, Inc. v., TexCivApp–Texarkana, 413 SW2d 775.—App & E 1177(1); Mech Liens 83, 166, 198, 202.

General Elec. Supply Co., a Div. of General Elec. Co. v. Gulf Electroquip, Inc., TexApp–Houston (1 Dist), 857 SW2d 591, reh den, and writ den.—Damag 117; Judgm 181(29), 185.1(1); Sales 195, 372, 384(4); War 504.

General Elec. Supply Corp. v. H. & H. Elec. Co., TexCivApp–Galveston, 259 SW2d 617.—Judgm 153(4).

For Later Case History Information, see KeyCite on WESTLAW

General Elec. Supply Corp.; McCamy v., CA5 (Tex), 185 F2d 944.—Estop 83(5); Evid 441(6), 444(2); Labor & Emp 36, 178, 249.

General Electrodynamics Corp., In re, BkrtcyNDTex, 368 BR 543.—Bankr 2872, 2877, 2926, 3548.1, 3559, 3566.1.

General Elevator Corp. v. Champion Papers, TexCivApp–Hous (14 Dist), 590 SW2d 763, ref nre.—Const Law 2312; Statut 158, 223.4; Work Comp 38, 2142.11, 2142.15.

General Engineering Corp.; Texas Unemployment Compensation Commission v., Tex, 217 SW2d 659, 147 Tex 503, appeal dism General Engineering Corp v. Texas Employment Commission, 70 SCt 72, 338 US 804, 94 LEd 487.—Tax 3291(2).

General Engineering Corp.; Texas Unemployment Compensation Commission v., TexCivApp–Austin, 213 SW2d 151, rev 217 SW2d 659, 147 Tex 503, appeal dism General Engineering Corp v. Texas Employment Commission, 70 SCt 72, 338 US 804, 94 LEd 487.—Tax 3291(2).

General Exchange Ins. Corp. v. Andrews, TexCivApp–San Antonio, 144 SW2d 550.—Venue 41.

General Exchange Ins. Corp. v. Appling, TexCivApp–El Paso, 144 SW2d 699.—App & E 680(1); Evid 158(6); Insurance 3567, 3571; Judgm 279, 524; Parties 19.

General Exchange Ins. Corp. v. Arnold, TexCivApp–San Antonio, 146 SW2d 781.—App & E 176, 1062.2; Trial 133.6(1).

General Exchange Ins. Corp. v. Bell, TexCivApp–Amarillo, 138 SW2d 129.—Insurance 3559.

General Exchange Ins. Corp. v. Bolles, TexCivApp–Amarillo, 143 SW2d 635.—App & E 1062.2; Insurance 2732, 3015, 3571.

General Exchange Ins. Corp. v. Collins, TexCivApp–Fort Worth, 110 SW2d 127.—App & E 187(3); Evid 317(1); Insurance 2725, 3450; Judgm 16, 678(1).

General Exchange Ins. Corp. v. Dudley, TexCivApp–Galveston, 128 SW2d 452.—Insurance 3559; Propty 1.

General Exchange Ins. Corp. v. Hill, TexCivApp–El Paso, 131 SW2d 287.—Infants 78(1); Plead 111.5, 228.14, 311, 409(3).

General Exchange Ins. Corp.; Taylor v., TexComApp, 96 SW2d 70, 128 Tex 118.—App & E 1069.1.

General Exchange Ins. Corp. v. Tierney, CCA5 (Tex), 152 F2d 224.—Insurance 2720; War 101, 166.

General Exchange Ins. Corp. v. Tierney v., NDTex, 60 FSupp 331, aff 152 F2d 224.—Insurance 2720; War 166.

General Exchange Ins. Corp. v. Young, TexCivApp–Amarillo, 143 SW2d 805.—Insurance 2732, 3374, 3375, 3567, 3571; Judgm 16; Trial 139.1(3), 140(1), 219.

General Exploration Co. v. David, TexCivApp–Hous (1 Dist), 596 SW2d 145, dism.—Judgm 813, 815.

General Export Iron & Metal Co.; Lefevers v., SDTex, 36 FSupp 838.—Commerce 62.63; Fed Cts 200; Labor & Emp 2220(2), 2390(4).

General Finance & Guaranty Co. v. Smith, TexCivApp–Amarillo, 309 SW2d 531, ref nre.—App & E 1002, 1070(2); Chat Mtg 210, 213; Contracts 305(1); Cust & U 14; Estop 102; Nova 4, 7, 12; Trial 350.4(2).

General Finance Co.; Duty v., Tex, 273 SW2d 64, 154 Tex 16.—Damag 50.20, 57.40; Labor & Emp 913.

General Finance Co. of Houston; N. Kost Furniture Co. v., TexCivApp–Galveston, 260 SW2d 700.—App & E 1073(1); Chat Mtg 47, 229(3); Damag 105, 113.

General Financial Services, Inc. v. Practice Place, Inc., TexApp–Fort Worth, 897 SW2d 516.—App & E 874(2), 954(1), 954(2); Assign 76; Banks 508; Contracts 147(2), 152, 157; Evid 265(17), 584(1); Plead 36(1), 36(2).

General Foods Corp.; Reeves v., CA5 (Tex), 682 F2d 515.—Civil R 1535, 1536, 1539, 1542, 1551, 1555; Evid 53; Fed Cts 763.1.

General Foods Corp.; River Brand Rice Mills, Inc. v., CA5 (Tex), 334 F2d 770, cert den 85 SCt 716, 379 US 998, 13 LEd2d 700.—Fed Cts 211.

General Foods Corp.; Struthers Scientific & Intern. Corp. v., SDTex, 290 FSupp 122, reconsideration den 1968 WL 162040.—Action 69(5); Decl Judgm 233, 276; Evid 20(1); Fed Civ Proc 1348, 1357, 1382, 1558.1; Fed Cts 101, 106, 110, 572.1, 660.35; Inj 126; Stip 14(11).

General Foods Corp.; Struthers Scientific & Intern. Corp. v., SDTex, 45 FRD 375.—Fed Civ Proc 1265, 1483, 1489, 1503, 1505, 1508, 1516, 1532.1, 1534, 1554; Pat 97, 292.4.

General Foods Corp.; Waples-Platter Companies v., NDTex, 439 FSupp 551.—Equity 65(1), 65(2); Fed Civ Proc 1961; Judgm 720, 724; Trademarks 1028, 1030, 1032, 1033, 1036, 1037, 1038, 1081, 1084, 1086, 1096(2), 1097, 1103, 1105, 1106, 1111, 1112, 1137(1), 1185, 1360, 1369, 1419, 1420, 1421, 1426, 1437, 1603, 1607, 1609, 1627, 1628(2), 1629(1), 1629(3), 1632, 1653, 1654, 1659, 1660, 1664, 1691, 1714(1), 1754(1).

General Foods Corp., Maxwell House Div.; Stanley v., CA5 (Tex), 508 F2d 274.—Labor & Emp 1213, 1218.

General Geophysical Co.; Kennedy v., TexCivApp–Galveston, 213 SW2d 707, ref nre.—App & E 1010.1(7); Evid 4, 9, 10(1), 29; Explos 12; Tresp 56.

General Geophysical Co.; U.S. v., CA5 (Tex), 296 F2d 86, cert den 82 SCt 932, 369 US 849, 8 LEd2d 8, reh den 82 SCt 1156, 369 US 891, 8 LEd2d 291.—Int Rev 4533.

General Geophysical Co. v. U.S., SDTex, 175 FSupp 208, rev 296 F2d 86, cert den 82 SCt 932, 369 US 849, 8 LEd2d 8, reh den 82 SCt 1156, 369 US 891, 8 LEd2d 291.—Ex & Ad 86(1); Int Rev 4533.

General Homes Corp., In re, SDTex, 199 BR 148.—Bankr 3029.1, 3063.1, 3106, 3622; Corp 310(1).

General Homes Corp., In re, BkrtcySDTex, 181 BR 898.—Bankr 3024, 3030, 3033; Records 32.

General Homes Corp., In re, BkrtcySDTex, 181 BR 870.—Bankr 2134, 2187, 2395, 2461, 2464, 2465.1, 2465.2, 2465.3, 3024, 3030; Crim Law 577.6.

General Homes Corp., In re, BkrtcySDTex, 134 BR 853.—Bankr 2154.1, 2970, 3539.1, 3544, 3550, 3555, 3558, 3560, 3561, 3566.1.

General Homes Corp.; City of Coppell v., TexApp–Dallas, 763 SW2d 448, writ den.—App & E 194(1); Judgm 185.2(9); Mun Corp 61, 85, 271; Waters 203(8), 203(12); Zoning 235, 382.4.

General Homes Corp.; Unsecured Creditors Committee v., SDTex, 199 BR 148. See General Homes Corp., In re.

General Homes Corp. FGMC, Inc., In re, BkrtcySDTex, 143 BR 99.—Bankr 2877, 3152, 3154, 3155, 3182.

General Homes, Inc. v. Denison, TexApp–Houston (14 Dist), 625 SW2d 794.—App & E 930(3), 989; Impl & C C 34, 60.1, 64, 100.

General Homes, Inc. v. Wingate Civic Ass'n, TexCivApp–Hous (14 Dist), 616 SW2d 351.—App & E 1043(5); Inj 157, 204.

General Hospital Leasing, Inc.; O J & C Co. v., TexCivApp–Hous (14 Dist), 578 SW2d 877.—App & E 170(1); Bailm 22; Sales 4(1).

General Ins. Co. v. Hughes, Tex, 255 SW2d 193, 152 Tex 159.—Autos 19, 20; Insurance 2694.

General Ins. Co. of America; Casper v., Tex, 431 SW2d 311.—Work Comp 1850, 1958.

General Ins. Co. of America v. Casper, TexCivApp–Tyler, 426 SW2d 606, ref nre 431 SW2d 311.—App & E 719(1); Hus & W 249(1), 260, 270(5); Judgm 16; Marriage 40(8); Parties 18, 29; Work Comp 1958.

General Ins. Co. of America; Esco Transp. Co. v., CA5 (Tex), 75 FedAppx 936.—Insurance 2269, 3110(3), 3164, 3173.

General Ins. Co. of America; Evans v., TexCivApp–Dallas, 390 SW2d 818.—Contracts 108(1); Corp 1.4(3),

1.4(4), 1.4(5), 1.6(2), 296; Insurance 2272, 2278(11), 2914, 2939, 2941.

General Ins. Co. of America v. Fleeger, CA5 (Tex), 389 F2d 159.—Fed Civ Proc 2242, 2295; Indem 27, 111; Princ & S 190(7).

General Ins. Co. of America v. Hallmark, TexCivApp–Eastland, 575 SW2d 134, ref nre.—Insurance 2144(3).

General Ins. Co. of America; Security Storage & Van Co. v., TexCivApp–Houston, 310 SW2d 729.—Accord 9; App & E 655(1), 907(3); Compromise 5(2); Insurance 3523(4).

General Ins. Co. of America v. Smith & Wardroup, Inc., TexCivApp–Amarillo, 388 SW2d 262, ref nre.—Princ & S 83.

General Ins. Co. of America v. Thielepape, CA5 (Tex), 400 F2d 852.—Fed Cts 844; Insurance 2694.

General Ins. Co. of America v. U.S. for Use of Audley Moore and Son, CA5 (Tex), 409 F2d 1326.—Fed Cts 744; U S 67(17).

General Ins. Co. of America v. U.S. for Use of Audley Moore and Son, CA5 (Tex), 406 F2d 442, 10 ALR Fed 548, reh den 409 F2d 1326, cert den 90 SCt 214, 396 US 902, 24 LEd2d 178.—Lim of Act 13; U S 67(16.1).

General Ins. Co. of America v. Western Fire & Cas. Co., CA5 (Tex), 241 F2d 289, cert den 77 SCt 1294, 354 US 909, 1 LEd2d 1427.—Decl Judgm 347; Insurance 1634(5), 1635, 2655(2), 3015, 3091, 3531; Princ & A 116(1), 122(1).

General Ins. Co. of America; Whitaker v., TexCivApp–Dallas, 461 SW2d 148, ref nre.—Work Comp 1365.

General Ins. Corp. v. Handy, TexCivApp–San Antonio, 267 SW2d 622, ref nre.—Pretrial Proc 714; Witn 336, 345(7); Work Comp 840, 1653, 1922, 1973, 1988.

General Ins. Corp. v. Harris, TexCivApp–Dallas, 327 SW2d 651.—Damag 87(1), 87(2); Insurance 2276, 2280, 2914.

General Ins. Corp. v. Hughes, TexCivApp–Dallas, 193 SW2d 230.—Damag 221(3); Mand 168(2); Work Comp 845, 1366, 1930.

General Ins. Corp. v. Hughes, TexCivApp–Galveston, 249 SW2d 231, rev 255 SW2d 193, 152 Tex 159.—Aband L P 5; App & E 218.2(1); Evid 263(4), 265(8), 265(9), 265(10); Insurance 2695.

General Ins. Corp. v. Laney, TexCivApp–Fort Worth, 224 SW2d 746.—Contracts 143.5, 147(3), 175(1); Insurance 1626, 1653(1).

General Ins. Corp.; Liberty Mut. Ins. Co. v., TexCivApp–Tyler, 517 SW2d 791, ref nre.—Insurance 2762(3), 3396, 3517, 3527, 3549(4); Interest 39(2.35), 66.

General Ins. Corp.; Pruitt v., TexCivApp–Galveston, 265 SW2d 908, ref nre.—App & E 907(3); Trial 358; Work Comp 1930.

General Ins. Corp. v. Smith, TexCivApp–Eastland, 232 SW2d 785, ref nre.—App & E 1177(1); Work Comp 1292, 1295, 1300, 1382, 1385, 1726, 1976.

General Ins. Corp. v. Wickersham, TexCivApp–Fort Worth, 235 SW2d 215, ref nre.—Admin Law 669.1; Work Comp 644, 649, 666, 667, 748, 1592, 1920, 1958, 1968(8).

General Inv. & Development Co. v. Guardian Sav. and Loan Ass'n, SDTex, 862 FSupp 153.—Contracts 322(1); Estop 52.10(3); Evid 207(1); Fraud 28; Nova 1; Ven & Pur 37(6), 75, 79, 137, 351(1).

General Land Office of State of Tex. v. OXY U.S.A., Inc., Tex, 789 SW2d 569.—App & E 449, 781(1); Const Law 2601; Pretrial Proc 506.1, 508.

General Land Office of State of Tex. v. Rutherford Oil Corp., TexApp–Austin, 802 SW2d 65, writ gr, aff State v. Flag-Redfern Oil Co, 852 SW2d 480.—Admin Law 305, 325; Const Law 1003; Mines 5.2(2.1).

General Land Office of State of Tex.; Rutherford Oil Corp. v., TexApp–Austin, 776 SW2d 232.—Civil R 1762; Decl Judgm 187; Inj 138.46; Mines 5.2(2.1).

General Leasing Co. v. Saxon Business Products, Inc., TexCivApp–Eastland, 533 SW2d 870.—App & E 1133.

General Leasing Co., Inc.; Haynie v., TexCivApp–Dallas, 538 SW2d 244.—App & E 157, 781(7); Courts 99(4); Inj 133, 138.6, 147, 148(1), 157.

General Life and Acc. Ins. Co. v. Handy, TexApp–El Paso, 766 SW2d 370.—Action 60; App & E 218.2(3.1), 231(2), 242(1), 699(2); Insurance 3381(4); Interest 31; Trial 350.4(3).

General Life and Acc. Ins. Co.; Hannum v., TexApp–Corpus Christi, 745 SW2d 500.—Evid 366(1); Insurance 2476.

General Life and Acc. Ins. Co.; Higginbotham v., Tex, 796 SW2d 695, on remand 817 SW2d 830, writ den.—Evid 17; Insurance 3569.

General Life and Acc. Ins. Co. v. Higginbotham, TexApp–Fort Worth, 817 SW2d 830, writ den.—App & E 936(2); Damag 227; Insurance 3374, 3375; Interest 31, 39(2.35); Judgm 143(3), 145(2), 146, 151, 153(1), 160.

General Life and Acc. Ins. Co. v. Higginbotham, TexApp–Fort Worth, 750 SW2d 19, writ gr, rev 796 SW2d 695, on remand 817 SW2d 830, writ den.—Judgm 17(1), 17(9).

General Life and Acc. Ins. Co. v. Lightfoot, TexApp–El Paso, 737 SW2d 953, writ den.—App & E 78(1); Insurance 2532, 2533, 3081, 3335; Judgm 181(23); Plead 236(6).

General Life Ins. Co. v. C. I. R., CCA5 (Tex), 137 F2d 185.—Corp 13; Insurance 1136; Int Rev 3969, 3975.

General Life Ins. Co. v. Mathes, TexCivApp–Eastland, 100 SW2d 1044, writ dism.—App & E 846(5); Insurance 3096(2).

General Life Ins. Co. v. Potter, TexCivApp–Eastland, 124 SW2d 409.—App & E 1050.2; Evid 318(6), 474(3), 493; Insurance 2445, 3365, 3375, 3381(4), 3571; Trial 133.6(7), 350.8, 352.9, 365.1(5).

General Lloyds Fire & Cas.; Yarbrough v., TexCivApp–Beaumont, 259 SW2d 644, ref nre.—App & E 1078(1); Work Comp 308, 328, 1342.

General Lloyds Fire & Cas. Co. v. Bailey, TexCivApp–San Antonio, 253 SW2d 1017, writ refused.—Insurance 2650.

General Lloyd's Fire & Cas. Ins. Co.; Security State Bank of McCamey v., TexCivApp–El Paso, 256 SW2d 185.—Plead 111.46.

General Lumber Co.; Ridglea Interests, Inc. v., TexCivApp–Fort Worth, 343 SW2d 490, ref nre.—Contracts 176(10), 212(1); Lim of Act 46(6).

General Manager of Scurlock's Supermarket; Newton v., TexCivApp–Corpus Christi, 546 SW2d 76.—App & E 927(7), 989; Evid 78; Neglig 1076, 1595, 1670, 1708.

General Mfg. Co. v. CNA Lloyd's of Texas, TexApp–Dallas, 806 SW2d 297, writ den.—Antitrust 221; App & E 173(9); Estop 115; Insurance 1883, 2278(21), 2361, 3349; Ref of Inst 19(1), 24; Trial 351.2(4).

General Mfg. Co.; Metal Stamping Co. of Greenville v., NDTex, 149 FSupp 508.—Pat 66(1.19), 317, 319(1).

General Merchandising Co. v. Walnut Equipment Leasing Co., TexApp–Houston (14 Dist, 909 SW2d 273. See Wu v. Walnut Equipment Leasing Co.

General Merchandising Co.; Walnut Equipment Leasing Co., Inc. v., Tex, 920 SW2d 285. See Walnut Equipment Leasing Co., Inc. v. Wu.

General Metal Fabricating Corp.; Stergiou v., TexApp–Houston (1 Dist), 123 SW3d 1, reh overr, and review den.—App & E 205, 1056.1(3), 1058(1), 1058(3); Evid 213(2), 318(2).

General Mills; Aldridge v., TexCivApp–Fort Worth, 188 SW2d 407.—App & E 218.2(1), 281(1), 291, 294(1); Judgm 342(1), 381; New Tr 152, 155, 159; Trial 352.4(9); Work Comp 2110, 2134, 2136.

General Mills; Frito Co. v., NDTex, 103 FSupp 563, aff 202 F2d 936, cert den 74 SCt 47, 346 US 827, 98 LEd 352.—Trademarks 1096(1), 1800.

General Mills; Steele v., USTex, 67 SCt 439, 329 US 433, 91 LEd 402, reh den 67 SCt 628, 329 US 834, 91 LEd 706.—Autos 109, 121; Carr 12(1); Fed Cts 405, 452; Lim of Act 28(1).

General Mills v. Steele, CCA5 (Tex), 154 F2d 367, cert gr 66 SCt 1341, 328 US 830, 90 LEd 1607, rev 67 SCt 439, 329 US 433, 91 LEd 402, reh den 67 SCt 628, 329 US 834, 91 LEd 706.—Autos 121; Contracts 138(2), 245(1), 246.

General Mills, Inc.; Frito Co. v., CA5 (Tex), 202 F2d 936, cert den 74 SCt 47, 346 US 827, 98 LEd 352.—Trademarks 1310, 1800.

General Mills, Inc.; Hathaway v., Tex, 711 SW2d 227, 69 ALR4th 1139.—Labor & Emp 47, 265.

General Mills, Inc. v. Hathaway, TexApp–Dallas, 694 SW2d 96, writ gr, rev 711 SW2d 227, 69 ALR4th 1139.—Judgm 199(3.14); Labor & Emp 40(2), 40(3), 169, 173.

General Mills, Inc. v. Livingston, TexCivApp–Eastland, 333 SW2d 215.—Corp 432(5); Plead 111.42(6); Venue 21.

General Mills, Inc.; Whiddon v., TexCivApp–Fort Worth, 347 SW2d 7.—Alt of Inst 6; App & E 1177(7); Contracts 205.5, 245(1), 245(2); Sales 246.

General Mills Restaurants, Inc. v. Clemons, TexApp–Corpus Christi, 865 SW2d 48.—App & E 901, 930(1), 989, 1001(1), 1003(7), 1004(11); Damag 91(3), 94; Neglig 273, 1670.

General Mills Restaurants, Inc. v. Texas Wings, Inc., TexApp–Dallas, 12 SW3d 827.—App & E 1172(1), 1178(6); Evid 584(1); Judgm 181(33), 183, 185(2), 185(6), 185.3(21); Nuis 3(1), 3(2), 4; Tresp 10, 14, 25, 47.

General Missionary Soc. of German Baptist Churches of North America v. Real Estate Land Title & Trust Co., TexComApp, 136 SW2d 599, 134 Tex 564.—App & E 295, 1090(2); Evid 378(2); Lim of Act 151(2), 195(6); Princ & A 119(1).

General Missionary Soc. of German Baptist Churches of North America; Real Estate Land Title & Trust Co. v., TexCivApp–Fort Worth, 115 SW2d 466, rev 136 SW2d 599, 134 Tex 564.—Lim of Act 145(1); Mun Corp 571.

General Missionary Soc. of German Baptist Churches of North America; Real Estate Land Title & Trust Co. v., TexCivApp–Fort Worth, 111 SW2d 1196.—App & E 336.1, 390, 455, 638, 653(3); Atty & C 96, 103.

General Motors Acceptance Corp.; Bishop v., TexCivApp–Austin, 229 SW2d 848.—Plead 111.9; Sequest 21.

General Motors Acceptance Corp. v. Boyd, TexCivApp–Fort Worth, 120 SW2d 484.—Chat Mtg 177(2), 177(3); Plead 9, 34(3), 111.3, 111.34, 111.45; Trial 350.1, 352.4(3); Trover 4, 53.

General Motors Acceptance Corp. v. Byrd, TexApp–Fort Worth, 707 SW2d 292.—Inj 76, 128(7).

General Motors Acceptance Corp.; Byrd v., TexCivApp–Waco, 581 SW2d 198.—Sec Tran 242.1.

General Motors Acceptance Corp. v. City of Houston, TexApp–Houston (14 Dist), 857 SW2d 731.—App & E 5; Pretrial Proc 676, 697.

General Motors Acceptance Corp. v. Cornelius, TexCivApp–Beaumont, 424 SW2d 498, ref nre.—Damag 132(1); Labor & Emp 3096(9); Trial 352.5(5).

General Motors Acceptance Corp.; Cullum v., TexCivApp–Amarillo, 115 SW2d 1196.—Corp 202.

General Motors Acceptance Corp. v. Fortner Oilfield Services, Inc., BkrtcyNDTex, 49 BR 9. See Fortner Oilfield Services, Inc., In re.

General Motors Acceptance Corp. v. Harris County Mun. Utility Dist. No. 130, TexApp–Houston (14 Dist), 899 SW2d 821.—Tax 2105, 2697, 2703.

General Motors Acceptance Corp. v. Howard, Tex, 487 SW2d 708.—Action 61; Libel 73, 75; Plead 111.24, 111.42(4).

General Motors Acceptance Corp. v. Howard, TexCivApp–Beaumont, 474 SW2d 929, writ gr, aff 487 SW2d 708.—Libel 6(3), 100(7); Plead 111.24.

General Motors Acceptance Corp. v. Johnston, TexCivApp–Amarillo, 104 SW2d 125.—Sales 479.1, 481.

General Motors Acceptance Corp.; Knight v., TexApp–Fort Worth, 728 SW2d 480.—Sec Tran 230, 240.

General Motors Acceptance Corp. v. Lee, TexCivApp–Fort Worth, 120 SW2d 622.—Corp 503(2); Plead 111, 111.1, 111.4, 111.16, 111.42(2), 376.

General Motors Acceptance Corp.; Lusk v., TexCivApp–Tyler, 395 SW2d 847.—Autos 20; Hus & W 254, 262.1(2), 262.1(5), 262.2, 264(3), 270(5); Interest 60.

General Motors Acceptance Corp.; Martens v., TexCivApp–Dallas, 584 SW2d 941.—Sales 48; Sec Tran 228.

General Motors Acceptance Corp. v. Matson, TexCivApp–Austin, 336 SW2d 628.—Sales 475.

General Motors Acceptance Corp. v. Matson, TexCivApp–Austin, 325 SW2d 909.—App & E 78(1).

General Motors Acceptance Corp.; Monroe v., TexCivApp–Waco, 573 SW2d 591.—Const Law 4484; Sec Tran 228, 242.1.

General Motors Acceptance Corp.; Monroe v., TexCivApp–Waco, 561 SW2d 12.—App & E 66, 78(1), 79(1), 80(1), 97; Sequest 1, 17.

General Motors Acceptance Corp.; Morin v., TexCivApp–Eastland, 602 SW2d 596, ref nre.—App & E 934(1), 989; Sec Tran 228.

General Motors Acceptance Corp. v. Musick, Tex, 379 SW2d 297.—Judgm 185.3(18).

General Motors Acceptance Corp.; Musick v., TexCivApp–Texarkana, 372 SW2d 767, writ gr, rev 379 SW2d 297.—Judgm 178, 181(29).

General Motors Acceptance Corp.; Payne v., TexCivApp–Amarillo, 420 SW2d 503.—Judgm 139, 145(2), 162(4); Sales 479.3.

General Motors Acceptance Corp.; Pedavoli v., TexApp–Eastland, 722 SW2d 39.—Judgm 273(6).

General Motors Acceptance Corp.; Phoenix Assur. Co. of New York v., TexCivApp–Waco, 369 SW2d 528, ref nre.—Insurance 3007(2), 3024, 3182, 3198(1), 3571.

General Motors Acceptance Corp.; Roark v., TexCivApp–Fort Worth, 114 SW2d 611, writ dism.—App & E 1177(6); Damag 40(2), 120(2); Insurance 3390.

General Motors Acceptance Corp.; Rogers v., TexCivApp–Beaumont, 567 SW2d 576.—Judgm 183.

General Motors Acceptance Corp.; Schultz v., TexApp–Dallas, 704 SW2d 797.—Judgm 185.1(4), 185.3(1).

General Motors Acceptance Corp. v. Uresti, TexCivApp–Tyler, 553 SW2d 660, ref nre.—App & E 863; Judgm 181(2), 185(2), 186; Paymt 7; Usury 32.

General Motors Acceptance Corp.; Watson v., TexCivApp–San Antonio, 509 SW2d 875.—Plead 111.1, 111.47.

General Motors Acceptance Corp. v. Wilcox, TexCivApp–Austin, 95 SW2d 1368.—Chat Mtg 157(2), 169, 177(1); Venue 8.5(7).

General Motors Acceptance Corp.; Williams v., TexCivApp–San Antonio, 428 SW2d 441.—App & E 1060.1(1), 1060.1(7); Fraud 58(2); New Tr 29, 31, 32, 100; Sales 440(3); Trial 382.

General Motors Acceptance Corp.; Wilson v., TexApp–Houston (1 Dist), 897 SW2d 818, reh and reh den.—App & E 188, 223, 232(2), 293, 758.1; Judgm 185(2), 185(6), 185.1(3), 185.1(4); Sec Tran 240.

General Motors Acceptance Corp./Crenshaw, Dupree & Milam, L.L.P. v. Crenshaw, Dupree & Milam, L.L.P./General Motors Acceptance Corp., TexApp–El Paso, 986 SW2d 632, reh overr, and review den, and reh of petition for review overr.—App & E 863, 893(1), 934(1); Atty & C 105, 109, 129(3); Judgm 185(2), 185(6); Neglig 1692; Princ & A 48.

General Motors Corp.; Acord v., Tex, 669 SW2d 111.—App & E 242(1), 928(4), 937(1), 1043(1), 1064.2, 1180(2), 1203(4); Parties 31; Trial 186, 228(1), 230.

General Motors Corp.; Acord v., TexApp–San Antonio, 657 SW2d 7, writ gr, aff in part, rev in part 669 SW2d 111.—App & E 204(1), 882(1), 1043(1), 1050.1(6), 1064.1(8); Trial 186.

General Motors Corp. v. Aetna Cas. and Sur. Co., CA5 (Tex), 999 F2d 964. See Harmon v. General Motors Corp.

General Motors Corp.; Bagby v., CA5 (Tex), 976 F2d 919.—Damag 50.10; Libel 68; States 18.15.

General Motors Corp.; Barnes v., TexApp–San Antonio, 653 SW2d 85, ref nre.—App & E 820, 930(3), 989, 1003(5), 1177(7); Neglig 232; Prod Liab 86.

General Motors Corp.; Bass v., TexCivApp–Fort Worth, 447 SW2d 443, ref nre.—Evid 546; Prod Liab 77.5, 83.5; Sales 427.

General Motors Corp.; Bass v., TexCivApp–Corpus Christi, 491 SW2d 941, ref nre.—App & E 927(7), 989; Neglig 1579; Prod Liab 35.1, 74, 75.1, 77.5; Trial 350.1.

General Motors Corp. v. Bloyed, Tex, 916 SW2d 949.— App & E 949; Compromise 56.1, 57, 59, 61, 67, 68, 69; Costs 194.26; Judgm 17(1); Trial 367.

General Motors Corp.; Bloyed v., TexApp–Texarkana, 881 SW2d 422, reh den, and reh den, and writ gr, aff 916 SW2d 949.—Afft 1, 9; App & E 497(1), 907(1), 946, 949, 1079; Atty & C 105, 112; Compromise 2, 56.1, 57, 58, 59, 60, 61, 68, 69, 70, 71; Costs 194.18, 194.26, 207; Courts 97(1); Judgm 185.1(3); Pretrial Proc 17.1, 19, 36.1, 124, 136, 713.

General Motors Corp. v. Brady, TexCivApp–Tyler, 477 SW2d 385.—Corp 666; Labor & Emp 29; Plead 111.3, 111.17, 111.19, 111.39(4), 111.42(8); Prod Liab 73, 82.1; Venue 7.5(1), 7.5(2), 7.5(7), 8.5(8), 22(4), 22(6).

General Motors Corp. v. Brewer, Tex, 966 SW2d 56.— Sales 284(1).

General Motors Corp.; Brewer v., TexApp–Texarkana, 926 SW2d 774, writ gr, mod 966 SW2d 56.—Antitrust 132; App & E 80(1), 169, 172(1), 173(1), 223, 852, 934(1); Judgm 185(1), 185(2), 185(6), 185.3(18), 187; Prod Liab 17.1, 35.1, 36; Sales 286, 434; States 18.3, 18.9, 18.11, 18.13, 18.65.

General Motors Corp. v. Bryant, TexCivApp–Hous (1 Dist), 582 SW2d 521, ref nre.—App & E 882(16), 1170.6; Evid 351, 555.10, 570; Prod Liab 83.5; Trial 108.5, 131(3), 133.6(4), 186, 215.

General Motors Corp. v. Burry, TexApp–Fort Worth, 203 SW3d 514.—App & E 206, 206.2, 215(1), 230, 854(4), 895(1), 930(1), 930(2), 946, 968, 970(2), 971(2), 987(1), 989, 992, 994(2), 1001(1), 1001(3), 1003(3), 1004(1), 1004(3), 1004(5), 1004(8), 1056.6; Damag 32, 57.1, 57.27, 97, 99, 100, 102, 127.15, 127.71(2), 127.75, 140.7, 163(1), 185(1), 186, 187, 192; Evid 141, 508, 535, 536, 542, 545, 546, 555.2, 555.4(1), 555.8(1), 571(6), 571(10), 587; Jury 97(1), 97(2); New Tr 74; Prod Liab 2, 11, 15, 75.1, 77.5, 82.1, 83.5, 97; Trial 56, 143.

General Motors Corp.; Carter v., CA5 (Tex), 983 F2d 40.—Fed Civ Proc 2579, 2731; Fed Cts 373, 415, 634, 654, 668.

General Motors Corp. v. Castaneda, TexApp–San Antonio, 980 SW2d 777, reh overr, and review den.—App & E 186, 930(1), 946, 965, 989, 999(3); Autos 244(41.1); Corp 666; Estop 52.10(2); Evid 571(3); Prod Liab 11, 36, 38, 40, 83.5, 88.5.

General Motors Corp.; Catlin, Estate of v., TexApp–Houston (14 Dist), 936 SW2d 447, extension of time gr.—Atty & C 146.1, 155; Infants 78(1), 82, 83, 84, 85; Int Liq 299, 302; Labor & Emp 3043, 3045; Neglig 202, 215, 220.

General Motors Corp.; Cloer v., EDTex, 395 FSupp 1070.—Sales 255, 425.

General Motors Corp.; Clophus v., TexApp–Houston (14 Dist), 769 SW2d 669.—App & E 1070(2); Prod Liab 83.5.

General Motors Corp.; Cooper v., CA5 (Tex), 651 F2d 249.—Fed Civ Proc 2547.1; Labor & Emp 1178(1), 1208, 1257, 1267.

General Motors Corp.; Correa v., TexApp–Corpus Christi, 948 SW2d 515.—App & E 181, 204(2), 233(2), 1003(5), 1026, 1051.1(1); Prod Liab 88.5; Trial 79.

General Motors Corp.; Cosper v., TexCivApp–Eastland, 472 SW2d 552, ref nre.—Judgm 181(33).

General Motors Corp. v. Dabney, TexCivApp–Waco, 510 SW2d 414, dism.—Plead 111.42(9).

General Motors Corp.; Dallas v., WDTex, 725 FSupp 902.—Prod Liab 36; States 18.65.

General Motors Corp.; Davis v., CA5 (Tex), 414 F2d 270.—Contracts 202(1).

General Motors Corp.; Dollar v., EDTex, 814 FSupp 538.—Antitrust 193; Fraud 28; Rem of C 30, 36, 45, 47, 74, 107(7), 107(11).

General Motors Corp.; Dunshie v., TexApp–Beaumont, 822 SW2d 345.—App & E 70(4); Records 32.

General Motors Corp.; Edwards v., CA5 (Tex), 153 F3d 242.—Fed Civ Proc 2755, 2759.1, 2766, 2768, 2769, 2771(5), 2778, 2784, 2785; Fed Cts 813.

General Motors Corp.; Ely v., TexApp–Texarkana, 927 SW2d 774, writ den.—App & E 863; Autos 197(1), 201(7); Contracts 114; Joint Adv 1.2(1); Judgm 181(11); Labor & Emp 3043; Neglig 202, 210, 220, 371, 379, 380, 387, 481, 1692, 1713; Parent & C 13(1); Prod Liab 37; Torts 113(2).

General Motors Corp. v. Evins, TexApp–Corpus Christi, 830 SW2d 355, reh overr.—Judges 51(4); Mand 27, 28, 143(1).

General Motors Corp. v. Ewing, TexCivApp–Waco, 300 SW2d 714.—Corp 503(2); Plead 111.42(2), 111.42(6).

General Motors Corp.; Fiengo v., TexApp–Dallas, 225 SW3d 858.—Const Law 2315; Estop 52(2), 52.15, 87; Judgm 181(6), 183; Lim of Act 13; Prod Liab 71.5.

General Motors Corp. v. Franks, TexCivApp–Beaumont, 509 SW2d 945, dism.—Plead 111.42(4); Prod Liab 77.5.

General Motors Corp.; Gabaldon v., TexApp–El Paso, 876 SW2d 367.—App & E 236(1), 966(1); Fraud 17; Judgm 185(2); Neglig 202, 483, 1692; Pretrial Proc 713, 714; Princ & A 3(1).

General Motors Corp.; Garcia v., TexApp–San Antonio, 786 SW2d 12, application for writ of error withdrawn.—Pretrial Proc 413.1.

General Motors Corp. v. Garza, TexApp–San Antonio, 179 SW3d 76.—Parties 35.1, 35.5, 35.17, 35.33, 35.71; Sales 262, 284(1).

General Motors Corp. v. Gayle, Tex, 951 SW2d 469, reh overr.—Evid 150; Mand 4(4), 45, 176; Pretrial Proc 35, 38, 40, 390, 713, 714.

General Motors Corp. v. Gayle, Tex, 940 SW2d 598.—Motions 39.

General Motors Corp. v. Gayle, TexApp–Houston (14 Dist), 924 SW2d 222, mandamus conditionally gr, motion to file mandamus overr with per curiam opinion 940 SW2d 598, subsequent mandamus proceeding 951 SW2d 469, reh overr.—App & E 1035; Evid 150; Jury 25(2), 25(6), 25(8), 26; Mand 4(1), 4(3), 4(4), 12, 28, 32; Pretrial Proc 35, 40, 358.

General Motors Corp.; Gibbs v., Tex, 450 SW2d 827.— App & E 863, 1024.4; Judgm 178, 181(1), 181(2), 185.3(21).

General Motors Corp.; Gibbs v., TexCivApp–Eastland, 445 SW2d 589, writ gr, rev 450 SW2d 827.—Judgm 185(3), 185.3(21); Neglig 1675, 1713; Prod Liab 8, 75.1, 77.5.

General Motors Corp. v. Grizzle, TexApp–Waco, 642 SW2d 837, dism.—App & E 232(2), 1004(1), 1060.1(1); Damag 51, 52, 63; Death 85, 86(1), 88, 95(4), 105; Evid 397(2); Judgm 615; Prod Liab 8, 83.5; Trial 284; Witn 275(2.1).

GENERAL

General Motors Corp. v. Grizzle, TexCivApp–Waco, 612 SW2d 275.—App & E 994(3), 1008.1(4); Autos 170(1), 244(10); Plead 111.12, 111.18, 111.42(8).

General Motors Corp.; Guerrero v., SDTex, 892 FSupp 165.—Prod Liab 23.1; Rem of C 36, 39, 79(1), 102, 107(7).

General Motors Corp.; Hamilton v., CA5 (Tex), 606 F2d 576, reh den 611 F2d 882, cert den 100 SCt 2990, 447 US 907, 64 LEd2d 856, reh den 101 SCt 288, 449 US 913, 66 LEd2d 141.—Civil R 1142, 1505(2), 1505(3), 1505(6), 1513, 1530, 1535, 1536, 1561, 1562; Fed Cts 425.

General Motors Corp.; Harmon v., CA5 (Tex), 999 F2d 964, reh den.—Fed Cts 776; Neglig 1037(7), 1045(2), 1045(3), 1706.

General Motors Corp. v. Harper, TexApp–Eastland, 61 SW3d 118, reh overr, and review den.—App & E 204(7), 930(1), 1001(3); Evid 222(2), 333(7), 555.2, 555.10, 571(6), 571(9); Prod Liab 11, 15, 36, 77.5, 81.5, 83.5; Trial 82, 85, 255(4).

General Motors Corp.; Harris v., TexApp–San Antonio, 924 SW2d 187, writ den.—App & E 758.1, 1070(2), 1136; Prod Liab 96.5; Trial 186, 194(1), 205.

General Motors Corp.; Hayles v., SDTex, 82 FSupp2d 650.—Judgm 185.3(21); Neglig 1610, 1613, 1614, 1619; Prod Liab 6, 8, 11, 15, 36, 76, 77.5; Sales 284(1).

General Motors Corp. v. Hebert, TexCivApp–Hous (1 Dist), 501 SW2d 950, ref nre.—App & E 933(6), 1045(1); Death 15; Fraud 58(1); Insurance 3526(5); Jury 139; Statut 181(2).

General Motors Corp.; Hoffert v., CA5 (Tex), 656 F2d 161, reh den 660 F2d 497, reh den Cochrane & Bresnahan, PA v. Smith, 660 F2d 497, cert den 102 SCt 2037, 456 US 961, 72 LEd2d 485.—Atty & C 147; Fed Civ Proc 2737.4; Fed Cts 12.1.

General Motors Corp. v. Hopkins, Tex, 548 SW2d 344.—App & E 1177(1); Evid 527, 571(9); Prod Liab 8, 15, 27, 28, 72.1, 75.1, 82.1, 83.5, 88.5.

General Motors Corp. v. Hopkins, TexCivApp–Hous (1 Dist), 535 SW2d 880, writ gr, aff 548 SW2d 344.—App & E 846(5), 930(3), 989, 1069.1; Prod Liab 8, 15, 27, 36, 83.5; Trial 140(1), 315, 358.

General Motors Corp. v. Hudiburg Chevrolet, Inc., Tex, 199 SW3d 249, reh den.—Indem 72, 81; Judgm 181(15.1); Prod Liab 23.1, 24.

General Motors Corp.; Hudiburg Chevrolet, Inc. v., TexApp–Dallas, 114 SW3d 680, reh overr, and review gr (2 pets), aff in part, rev in part 199 SW3d 249, reh den. —App & E 852, 856(1); Const Law 2604; Indem 72; Judgm 181(15.1), 183, 185.3(1); Neglig 202, 371, 379, 380, 384, 387.

General Motors Corp.; International Union, United Auto., Aerospace and Agr. Implement Workers of America-UAW v., TexApp–Fort Worth, 104 SW3d 126. —App & E 352.1, 845(2), 846(6); Trial 368, 388(1), 388(4); Unemp Comp 480, 486, 491(1).

General Motors Corp. v. Iracheta, Tex, 161 SW3d 462.— Evid 539, 555.8(1); Trial 76, 131(1), 131(2).

General Motors Corp. v. Iracheta, TexApp–San Antonio, 90 SW3d 725, reh overr, and review gr, rev 161 SW3d 462.—App & E 207, 232(3), 237(2), 635(1), 1060.1(2.1), 1060.1(4); Damag 89(1), 91(1), 184; Evid 539, 571(6), 571(9); Jury 33(5.15); Prod Liab 83.5; Trial 120(2), 133.6(5).

General Motors Corp.; Kimmey v., TexCivApp–Galveston, 262 SW2d 530, ref nre.—Neglig 1614; Prod Liab 77.5; Sales 445(1).

General Motors Corp.; Klo-Zik Co. v., EDTex, 677 FSupp 499.—Antitrust 569, 570, 571, 587(1), 592, 644, 646, 714, 715, 976, 977(3); Autos 368; Fed Civ Proc 2510; Prod Liab 17.1, 35.1; Sales 246, 267.

General Motors Corp. v. Lawrence, Tex, 651 SW2d 732. —Mand 32; Pretrial Proc 373.

General Motors Corp.; Martinez v., TexApp–San Antonio, 686 SW2d 349.—Pretrial Proc 676; Time 9(1), 9(4).

General Motors Corp.; Messick v., CA5 (Tex), 460 F2d 485.—Fed Civ Proc 2142.1; Neglig 552(1), 553, 554(1), 554(3), 1747; Prod Liab 5, 27, 73, 88.5.

General Motors Corp. v. Muncy, CA5 (Tex), 367 F2d 493, cert den 87 SCt 1476, 386 US 1037, 18 LEd2d 600, reh den 87 SCt 2105, 388 US 924, 18 LEd2d 1378.—Fed Civ Proc 51, 2141; Fed Cts 405, 847; Neglig 1550, 1579, 1617; Prod Liab 36, 88.5.

General Motors Corp.; Muncy v., TexCivApp–Dallas, 357 SW2d 430.—App & E 758.3(11), 1170.7; Prod Liab 10, 71, 77.5, 81.5; Venue 22(3), 22(6).

General Motors Corp.; O'Dell v., EDTex, 122 FSupp2d 721.—Antitrust 529, 540, 541, 544, 575, 641, 713, 714, 715, 720, 841, 963(1), 967, 970, 977(2); Fed Civ Proc 2484.

General Motors Corp. v. Paccar, Inc., EDTex, 677 FSupp 499. See Klo-Zik Co. v. General Motors Corp.

General Motors Corp. v. Perry Gas Companies, Inc., SDTex, 279 BR 824.—Bankr 2671; Set-Off 27(1), 33(1).

General Motors Corp.; Poston v., TexCivApp–Waco, 465 SW2d 841.—Evid 461(1); Judgm 615; Release 29(1), 29(4).

General Motors Corp.; Ramsey v., Tex, 685 SW2d 15.— Antitrust 359; Trial 350.4(2).

General Motors Corp. v. Ramsey, TexApp–Waco, 633 SW2d 646, dism.—App & E 343.1, 627.2, 627.3, 628(1); Plead 111.42(3), 111.42(6), 111.42(8), 111.47; Pretrial Proc 403, 433.

General Motors Corp. v. Ramsey, TexApp–Tyler, 669 SW2d 824, writ gr, aff in part, rev in part 685 SW2d 15. —Trial 350.4(2).

General Motors Corp.; Reed v., CA5 (Tex), 703 F2d 170. —Compromise 56.1, 58, 62; Fed Cts 817.

General Motors Corp.; Reed v., NDTex, 560 FSupp 60, aff 703 F2d 170.—Civil R 1140, 1560; Compromise 57, 62.

General Motors Corp.; Reid v., EDTex, 489 FSupp2d 614.—Contracts 143(2), 176(2); Evid 448, 455; Fed Civ Proc 103.2; Labor & Emp 309; Pat 183, 286, 290(1), 328(2).

General Motors Corp.; Reid v., EDTex, 240 FRD 260.— Fed Civ Proc 81, 1954.1; Fed Cts 585.1; Jury 31.2(1); Pat 314(2), 328(2).

General Motors Corp.; Reid v., EDTex, 240 FRD 257.— Fed Civ Proc 312, 313, 314.1; Pat 290(3), 328(2).

General Motors Corp. v. Saenz, TexApp–San Antonio, 966 SW2d 545, reh overr, opinion adopted on reh en banc 974 SW2d 407, review gr, rev 997 SW2d 584.—App & E 930(1), 1001(3); Damag 91(3), 184; Neglig 202, 213, 303(1); Prod Liab 6, 8, 10, 11, 14, 15, 27, 40, 88.5.

General Motors Corp. v. Saenz, TexApp–Corpus Christi, 829 SW2d 230, reh overr, and reh overr, and writ gr, rev 873 SW2d 353.—App & E 758.3(9), 930(3), 989, 1001(1), 1001(3), 1003(7), 1051.1(2), 1058(1); Const Law 4427; Damag 87(1), 91(1), 91(3), 94, 181, 184, 215(1); Death 77, 82; Evid 219(3); Neglig 273, 371, 387; Prod Liab 14, 15, 27, 28, 37, 40, 75.1, 83.5, 87.1; Witn 340(1), 390, 398(1); Work Comp 2234.

General Motors Corp. v. Saenz on Behalf of Saenz, Tex, 873 SW2d 353.—Evid 85.1; Prod Liab 14, 16, 37, 75.1, 77.5, 87.1.

General Motors Corp.; Salinas v., TexApp–Houston (1 Dist), 857 SW2d 944.—Neglig 210, 1260, 1692; Prod Liab 14, 35.1, 37, 39, 87.1.

General Motors Corp. v. Sanchez, Tex, 997 SW2d 584.— App & E 206; Autos 173(1); Corp 498; Damag 91(3), 184; Evid 555.2, 571(3); Neglig 273, 1659; Prod Liab 11, 27, 28, 40, 83.5.

General Motors Corp.; Seibert v., TexApp–Houston (14 Dist), 853 SW2d 773.—Const Law 2315; Lim of Act 4(2), 43, 95(1), 95(4.1), 104(1), 104(2), 199(1).

General Motors Corp.; Shipp v., CA5 (Tex), 750 F2d 418. —Damag 185(1); Evid 150, 571(3); Fed Civ Proc 2011;

Fed Cts 772, 799, 823, 824, 846, 866; Prod Liab 75.1, 87.1, 88.5, 96.1.

General Motors Corp. v. Simmons, Tex, 558 SW2d 855. —App & E 1048(6); Compromise 100; Contrib 5(1); Evid 108, 219(3); Indem 72; Prod Liab 38, 40; Witn 363(1).

General Motors Corp. v. Simmons, TexCivApp–Hous (1 Dist), 545 SW2d 502, writ gr, rev 558 SW2d 855.—App & E 1032(1), 1062.1; Autos 201(8), 201(9); Const Law 2632; Damag 63, 132(14); Evid 150; Indem 57, 58; Neglig 387, 421, 423; Prod Liab 35.1, 81.5, 82.1, 96.5; Release 56; Statut 181(2), 276(1); Trial 56, 232(5), 255(11), 261, 350.3(5), 350.5(3).

General Motors Corp.; Sipes v., TexApp–Texarkana, 946 SW2d 143, reh overr, and writ den.—App & E 946, 966(1); Evid 470, 555.4(1), 574; Judgm 181(15.1), 181(33), 183, 185(6), 185.3(21), 186; Pretrial Proc 713; Prod Liab 5, 10, 11, 14, 23.1, 35.1, 36, 37, 82.1; Sales 273(3), 284(1), 441(3).

General Motors Corp.; Smith v., NDTex, 382 FSupp 766, aff 526 F2d 804.—Courts 9; Death 35; Fed Civ Proc 1741, 1827.1; Fed Cts 410; Neglig 204; Prod Liab 3.

General Motors Corp. v. Smith, TexCivApp–Eastland, 474 SW2d 278.—Plead 111.3, 111.18, 111.42(4).

General Motors Corp. v. Tanner, Tex, 892 SW2d 862.— Pretrial Proc 390, 403, 410.

General Motors Corp.; Thomas v., EDTex, 174 FRD 386. —Fed Civ Proc 1588, 1600(3).

General Motors Corp.; Turner v., Tex, 584 SW2d 844.— App & E 1068(5); Damag 216(1); Evid 219.65; Prod Liab 38, 81.5, 96.1, 96.5.

General Motors Corp. v. Turner, TexCivApp–Beaumont, 567 SW2d 812, rev 584 SW2d 844.—App & E 971(2); Damag 212; Evid 99, 150, 512, 535, 546, 560; Neglig 387; Prod Liab 1, 5, 38, 40, 81.1, 83.5, 96.5; Trial 116.

General Motors Corp.; Turner v., TexCivApp–Hous (14 Dist), 514 SW2d 497, ref nre.—Neglig 431; Plead 111.18, 111.42(8), 111.42(9); Prod Liab 8, 11, 35.1, 36, 81.5.

General Motors Corp.; U.S. v., NDTex, 702 FSupp 133.— Environ Law 282; Fed Civ Proc 1055.

General Motors Corp.; Upchurch v., CA5 (Tex), 450 F2d 926.—Evid 555.4(3).

General Motors Corp.; Wallace v., SDTex, 672 FSupp 964.—Civil R 1507.

General Motors Corp. v. Washington, TexCivApp–Texarkana, 559 SW2d 425.—Plead 111.39(7), 111.42(4), 111.42(9); Princ & A 24; Venue 22(4).

General Motors Corp.; Watson v., TexCivApp–Hous (1 Dist), 479 SW2d 104.—App & E 846(5); Judgm 196; Lim of Act 195(3); Pretrial Proc 693.1.

General Motors Corp.; Williams v., TexCivApp–Hous (1 Dist), 501 SW2d 930, ref nre.—App & E 285, 918(1); Evid 539, 543.5, 555.9; Judgm 258; Prod Liab 71, 77.5, 83.5; Trial 96.

General Motors Corp. v. Williamson, TexCivApp–Fort Worth, 575 SW2d 120, dism.—Plead 111.18, 111.36, 111.38, 111.42(9); Venue 22(1).

General Motors Corp.; Woodard v., CA5 (Tex), 298 F2d 121, cert den 82 SCt 1161, 369 US 887, 8 LEd2d 288, reh den 82 SCt 1584, 370 US 965, 8 LEd2d 834.— Antitrust 269(1), 269(3), 269(4); Const Law 975; Contracts 217, 312(1); Estop 78(1), 78(6).

General Motors Corp.; Wright v., TexApp–Houston (1 Dist), 717 SW2d 153.—App & E 927(7), 997(3); Prod Liab 88.5; Trial 139.1(14), 139.1(17).

General Motors Corp.; Wyatt v., TexApp–Corpus Christi, 703 SW2d 708, dism.—App & E 170(2), 763; Lim of Act 4(2), 55(4).

General Motors Corp., Chevrolet Division v. Lane, Tex, 496 SW2d 533.—Pretrial Proc 673.

General Motors Corporation/Pontiac Div.; Bowe v., TexApp–Houston (1 Dist), 830 SW2d 775, writ den.—

Antitrust 294; Judgm 181(7), 185(2); Lim of Act 95(1), 193; Sales 267.

General Motors Corp., Pontiac Motor Division v. Courtesy Pontiac, Inc., TexCivApp–Tyler, 538 SW2d 3.— Plead 111.9, 111.42(2), 111.42(4), 111.42(10); Venue 21.

General Moving & Storage, Inc.; Whitener Transfer & Storage, Inc. v., TexCivApp–Austin, 364 SW2d 277, writ dism.—Venue 22(6).

General Office Outfitters, Inc. v. Holt, TexApp–Dallas, 670 SW2d 748.—App & E 496; Corp 507(12); Judgm 162(2).

General Office Service Co. v. Letbetter, TexCivApp–Eastland, 221 SW2d 932.—Assign 126; Evid 159; Princ & A 148(1), 148(4).

General Plywood Corp. v. Collins, TexCivApp–Amarillo, 414 SW2d 224.—App & E 837(1), 837(4); High 159(2); Judgm 183, 185(2), 185(4), 185.3(1), 186; Pretrial Proc 306.1.

General Portland Cement Co. v. L. P. Reed, Inc., CA5 (Tex), 221 F2d 317.—Estop 119; Sales 397.

General Portland Cement Co. v. U.S., CA5 (Tex), 628 F2d 321, cert den 101 SCt 1519, 450 US 983, 67 LEd2d 818.—Int Rev 3490, 3492.

General Portland Cement Co. v. U.S., NDTex, 438 FSupp 27, aff in part, rev in part 628 F2d 321, cert den 101 SCt 1519, 450 US 983, 67 LEd2d 818.—Int Rev 3490, 3492, 3505.

General Portland, Inc. v. Collins, TexCivApp–Fort Worth, 549 SW2d 757, ref nre.—Judgm 139.

General Portland, Inc.; Voss Intern., Inc. v., TexApp–Austin, 670 SW2d 771.—App & E 2; Statut 228.

General Portland, Inc. v. Witt & Son Sand & Gravel, Inc., TexCivApp–Waco, 589 SW2d 514.—Venue 7.5(7).

General Production Co., Inc. v. Americana Bldg., TexApp–Houston (14 Dist, 715 SW2d 121. See General Productions Co., Inc. v. Black Coral Investments.

General Productions Co., Inc. v. Black Coral Investments, TexApp–Houston (14 Dist), 715 SW2d 121, ref nre.—App & E 1139; Corp 410; Judgm 185.1(3); Princ & A 99.

General Products, Inc. v. Energy Management Group Ltd. Inc., TexApp–Houston (1 Dist), 734 SW2d 149. See Stacy v. Energy Management Group Ltd., Inc.

General Refractories Co. v. Martin, TexApp–Beaumont, 8 SW3d 818, reh overr, and review den, and mandamus den, and reh of petition for review den.—App & E 241, 1024.3; Appear 9(2); Const Law 3965(4); Courts 12(2.25).

General Resources Management Corp.; West Texas State Bank v., TexApp–Austin, 723 SW2d 304, ref nre. —App & E 842(1); Judgm 304, 306, 323, 326.

General Resources Management Corp.; West Texas State Bank v., TexApp–Austin, 717 SW2d 766.—App & E 819.

General Resources Organization, Inc. v. Deadman, TexApp–San Antonio, 907 SW2d 22, writ den 932 SW2d 485.—Action 60; App & E 93, 204(4), 207, 216(1), 218.2(10), 241, 242(1), 295, 758.3(3), 758.3(6), 949, 970(2), 1003(7), 1004(5), 1004(7), 1004(11), 1050.1(1), 1056.1(1), 1060.1(1); Atty & C 26; Brok 106; Contracts 206, 324(1); Damag 117, 140; Fraud 7, 31, 62, 64(1); Pretrial Proc 45; States 18.15; Trial 43, 268; Witn 217, 219(3).

General Retail Corp.; Calvert v., TexCivApp–Austin, 390 SW2d 10, ref nre.—Licens 15(8); Stip 18(7).

General Screw Products Co.; Star Craw v., TexCivApp–Hous (1 Dist), 501 SW2d 374, ref nre.—Corp 178, 189(12), 297, 398(2); Evid 177, 181, 317(4); Trial 350.4(1).

General Securities Service, Inc.; J. G. Boyd's Good Housekeeping Shops, Inc. v., TexCivApp–Waco, 483 SW2d 826.—Lim of Act 118(2), 124.

General Services Com'n v. Little-Tex Insulation Co., Inc., Tex, 39 SW3d 591.—Admin Law 651; Const Law 990, 994, 1030, 2332, 2357; Em Dom 2(1.1), 266, 307(2);

States 108, 191.1, 191.3(1), 191.4(1), 191.6(1), 191.6(2), 191.6(3), 191.9(1), 191.9(3).

General Services Com'n; Little-Tex Insulation Co., Inc. v., TexApp–Austin, 997 SW2d 358, reh overr, and review gr, rev 39 SW3d 591.—Courts 32, 35; Em Dom 2(1.1), 280, 285, 293(4); Estop 52.10(2), 62.1; Pretrial Proc 511; States 191.1, 191.4(1), 191.6(2), 191.9(1), 191.9(3).

General Shoe Corp. v. Hall, TexCivApp–Texarkana, 123 SW2d 721.—Contracts 9(3), 10(1), 10(4); Damag 23; Princ & A 41(5), 41(6); Sales 418(1).

General Southwestern Corp. v. State, TexCivApp–Houston, 333 SW2d 164, ref nre.—App & E 920(3), 954(1); Inj 138.78, 147, 157, 216, 229; Statut 223.2(35); Usury 16, 57, 114.

General Specialties, Inc. v. Charter Nat. Bank-Houston, TexApp–Houston (14 Dist), 687 SW2d 772.—Judgm 181(26), 185.3(1), 185.3(16).

General Sports Mfg. Co.; Russell v., TexCivApp–Amarillo, 110 SW2d 1253, dism.—App & E 204(4), 240, 424, 499(3), 544(1), 794.1, 1052(8); Garn 87, 167, 191.

General Star Indem. Co.; Blue Marlin Const. Co., Inc. v., SDTex, 16 FSupp2d 762.—Contracts 143(2), 143(4), 147(2), 152, 176(2); Insurance 1806, 2278(29).

General Star Indem. Co. v. Sherry Brooke Revocable Trust, WDTex, 243 FSupp2d 605.—Insurance 1805, 1809, 1812, 1814, 1827, 1832(1), 1832(2), 1835(2), 2142(1), 2142(6), 2146, 3335, 3336, 3337, 3359, 3360, 3361.

General Star Indem. Co. v. Spring Creek Village Apartments Phase V, Inc., TexApp–Houston (14 Dist), 152 SW3d 733.—App & E 934(1); Insurance 3256, 3262, 3419; Judgm 181(23).

General Star Indem. Co.; U.E. Texas One-Barrington, Ltd. v., CA5 (Tex), 332 F3d 274.—Insurance 2142(6), 2170, 2275.

General Star Indem. Co.; U.E. Texas One-Barrington, Ltd. v., WDTex, 243 FSupp2d 652, entered 2002 WL 31972178, aff 332 F3d 274.—Contracts 143(2), 143.5, 147(2), 169, 176(2), 176(3); Evid 448; Insurance 1806, 1808, 1810, 1836, 1845(1), 1845(2), 2142(6), 2165(2), 2191, 2199, 2201.

General Star Indem. Co. v. Vesta Fire Ins. Corp., CA5 (Tex), 173 F3d 946.—Fed Civ Proc 673; Fed Cts 776; Insurance 3349, 3352, 3513(3), 3526(9); Subrog 1.

General Steel Warehouse, Inc. v. First State Bank of Shallowater, BkrtcyNDTex, 49 BR 25. See Stone, In re.

General Supply & Equipment Co., Inc. v. Phillips, TexCivApp–Tyler, 490 SW2d 913, ref nre.—App & E 1177(2); Damag 40(1), 103, 190; Sales 261(5), 439, 441(1), 441(2), 441(3), 441(4), 442(2), 442(5), 442(6), 442(8), 445(1), 445(2).

General Surgical Innovations, Inc.; Williams v., EDTex, 178 FSupp2d 698.—Fed Civ Proc 2508; Pat 50.1, 51(1), 72(1), 76, 110, 226.6.

General Tank & Equipment Co.; Texas Tank, Inc. v., TexCivApp–Texarkana, 390 SW2d 409.—Corp 503(2); Torts 140; Venue 7.5(3), 22(8).

General Tel. Co. of Southwest v. Bi-Co Pavers, Inc., TexCivApp–Dallas, 514 SW2d 168, 73 ALR3d 978.—Neglig 386; Tresp 2, 10, 46(1); Trial 365.1(6).

General Tel. Co. of Southwest v. Carver, TexCivApp–Dallas, 474 SW2d 582.—App & E 465(2); Courts 207.3, 207.4(2); Mand 57(2).

General Tel. Co. of Southwest v. Cities Littlefield, TexCivApp–Amarillo, 498 SW2d 375, ref nre.—App & E 920(3), 954(1); Inj 135; Pub Ut 183; Tel 790, 926, 927, 983.

General Tel. Co. of Southwest v. City of Garland, TexCivApp–Dallas, 522 SW2d 732.—App & E 462.1, 479(1); Courts 207.1.

General Tel. Co. of Southwest v. City of Garland, TexCivApp–Dallas, 509 SW2d 927, ref nre.—Const Law

2524; Plead 111.12, 111.39(1), 111.42(1); Pub Ut 121; Tel 927, 939(1).

General Tel. Co. of Southwest v. City of Perryton, TexCivApp–Amarillo, 552 SW2d 888, ref nre.—Const Law 2426, 2437; Mun Corp 619; Pub Ut 181; Tel 734, 872, 927, 988.

General Tel. Co. of Southwest v. Fennen, TexCivApp–Hous (1 Dist), 568 SW2d 407.—Plead 111.12, 111.42(7); Venue 8.5(8), 15.

General Tel. Co. of Southwest; Ohmes v., TexCivApp–Amarillo, 384 SW2d 796, writ refused.—Mun Corp 592(1); Tel 788, 857, 862, 901(1), 949.

General Tel. Co. of Southwest v. U.S., CA5 (Tex), 449 F2d 846.—Admin Law 330, 390.1; Const Law 2489, 2494, 2540, 4370; Corp 1.6(1); Tel 614, 615, 617, 629, 632, 644, 754, 782, 1224, 1225(2), 1234.

General Tel. Co. of the Southwest; City of Baytown v., TexCivApp–Galveston, 256 SW2d 187, ref nre.—App & E 863, 931(1); Const Law 2437, 2524; Equity 55; Inj 138.1; Mun Corp 619; Pub Ut 183; Tel 926, 933, 943, 968, 982, 983.

General Tel. Co. of the Southwest v. City of Eden, Tex, 293 SW2d 753, 156 Tex 168.—Tel 939(1), 982, 983, 986.

General Tel. Co. of the Southwest v. City of Eden, TexCivApp–Austin, 281 SW2d 379, rev 293 SW2d 753, 156 Tex 168.—App & E 931(1), 954(2); Inj 126, 147, 152; Mun Corp 619.

General Tel. Co. of the Southwest v. City of Point Comfort, TexCivApp–Corpus Christi, 553 SW2d 808.—App & E 1175(1); Const Law 2632; Pretrial Proc 554; Pub Ut 102; Tel 967, 968.

General Tel. Co. of the Southwest v. City of Wellington, Tex, 294 SW2d 385, 156 Tex 238.—Const Law 4370; Inj 135; Tel 939(1), 943, 982, 983.

General Tel. Co. of the Southwest v. City of Wellington, TexCivApp–Amarillo, 279 SW2d 922, rev 294 SW2d 385, 156 Tex 238.—App & E 954(1), 954(2); Inj 132, 135, 138.3; Tel 943, 962, 983.

General Tel. Co. of the Southwest; City of Weslaco v., TexCivApp–San Antonio, 359 SW2d 260, ref nre.—App & E 758.3(4); Franch 1; Tel 788, 789, 927, 940(1), 943, 945(2), 964, 981, 982.

General Tel. Co. of the Southwest v. Public Utility Commission of Texas, TexApp–Austin, 628 SW2d 832, ref nre.—Const Law 3686, 4370; Pub Ut 194, 195; Tel 940(3), 941, 943, 944, 964.

General Telephone Co.; Falcon v., CA5 (Tex), 815 F2d 317.—Civil R 1140, 1536, 1544, 1545, 1590; Fed Cts 950.

General Telephone Co.; Falcon v., NDTex, 463 FSupp 315, aff in part, remanded in part 626 F2d 369, reh den 631 F2d 732, vac 101 SCt 1752, 450 US 1036, 68 LEd2d 234, on remand 647 F2d 633, cert gr 102 SCt 668, 454 US 1097, 70 LEd2d 637, rev 102 SCt 2364, 457 US 147, 72 LEd2d 740, on remand 686 F2d 261, on remand 611 FSupp 707, aff 815 F2d 317.—Civil R 1535, 1536, 1545, 1571, 1574, 1595.

General Telephone Co. of Southwest v. Blacksher, TexApp–Houston (1 Dist), 742 SW2d 465, writ den.—App & E 78(1), 934(2); Pub Ut 103; Tel 840, 841; Tresp 10.

General Telephone Co. of Southwest; Brittian v., TexCivApp–Fort Worth, 533 SW2d 886, dism.—App & E 95, 949, 1008.1(1); Contracts 9(3); Decl Judgm 305; Judgm 243; Parties 35.1, 35.11, 35.13, 35.19, 35.35; Tel 876.

General Telephone Co. of Southwest; Citizens Coop Gin v., TexApp–Austin, 728 SW2d 903.—Pub Ut 114; Tel 792, 855.

General Telephone Co. of Southwest v. Falcon, USTex, 102 SCt 2364, 457 US 147, 72 LEd2d 740, on remand 686 F2d 261, on remand 611 FSupp 707, aff 815 F2d 317.—Fed Civ Proc 161, 165, 172, 184.10.

General Telephone Co. of Southwest; Falcon v., CA5 (Tex), 626 F2d 369, reh den 631 F2d 732, vac 101 SCt 1752, 450 US 1036, 68 LEd2d 234, on remand 647 F2d

633, cert gr 102 SCt 668, 454 US 1097, 70 LEd2d 637, rev 102 SCt 2364, 457 US 147, 72 LEd2d 740, on remand 686 F2d 261, on remand 611 FSupp 707, aff 815 F2d 317.—Civil R 1135, 1138, 1536, 1544, 1548; Evid 357; Fed Civ Proc 161, 184.10, 184.25; Fed Cts 636, 941.

General Telephone Co. of Southwest; Falcon v., NDTex, 611 FSupp 707, aff 815 F2d 317.—Civil R 1544, 1545; Courts 99(6); Fed Civ Proc 161.1, 184.10, 337, 2314.1, 2339, 2748; Judgm 650.

General Telephone Co. of Southwest; Kelley v., CA5 (Tex), 485 F2d 1315,reh den General Telephone Company of Southwest v. Clark, 486 F2d 1403, reh den 486 F2d 1403.—Indem 30(5); Neglig 1032, 1037(7), 1085, 1088, 1706; Tel 834.

General Telephone Co. of Southwest; LaRue v., CA5 (Tex), 545 F2d 546.—Civil R 1203; Fed Civ Proc 2117.

General Telephone Co. of Southwest; Taylor v., CA5 (Tex), 759 F2d 437.—Civil R 1505(3), 1505(4), 1505(6).

General Telephone Co. of the Southwest; City of Jacksonville v., TexCivApp–Tyler, 538 SW2d 253, ref nre.—Estop 52.10(4); Franch 1, 2; Mun Corp 680(1); Tel 799.

General Telephone Co. of the Southwest; Porter v., TexApp–Corpus Christi, 736 SW2d 204.—Damag 185(1).

General Telephone Co. of the Southwest; Public Utility Com'n of Texas v., TexApp–Austin, 777 SW2d 827, writ dism.—App & E 863, 954(1); Inj 138.21, 189; Tel 983.

General Telephone Co. of the Southwest; Ruston v., SDTex, 115 FRD 330.—Fed Civ Proc 828.1, 1751, 2647.1, 2656.

General Texas Asphalt Co.; McElroy v., TexCivApp–Waco, 427 SW2d 719, ref nre.—Bailm 31(1), 31(3).

General Tire and Rubber Co.; Edwards v., WDTex, 540 FSupp 115. See Kincade v. General Tire and Rubber Co.

General Tire & Rubber Co.; Johnson v., CA5 (Tex), 652 F2d 574.—Civil R 1505(2), 1513, 1536, 1544, 1545, 1548; Fed Cts 865.

General Tire and Rubber Co.; Kincade v., CA5 (Tex), 716 F2d 319.—Compromise 61, 62.

General Tire and Rubber Co.; Kincade v., CA5 (Tex), 635 F2d 501.—Atty & C 101(1); Fed Civ Proc 161, 177.1, 180; Fed Cts 712, 771.1, 913.

General Tire and Rubber Co.; Kincade v., WDTex, 540 FSupp 115, rev 716 F2d 319.—Compromise 57; Interest 21.

General Tire & Rubber Co.; N.L.R.B. v., CA5 (Tex), 326 F2d 832.—Labor & Emp 1740, 1748, 1765.

General Tire & Rubber Co. v. Texas Pacific Coal & Oil Co., TexCivApp–Fort Worth, 102 SW2d 1086, writ refused.—Inj 9, 12, 23; Propty 1.

General Tire & Rubber Co.; Tire Distributors v., TexCivApp, 551 SW2d 125.—Atty & C 71; Judgm 134.

General Tire and Rubber Co.; Westbrook v., CA5 (Tex), 754 F2d 1233, reh den 760 F2d 269.—Damag 226; Fed Civ Proc 1973, 2311, 2313, 2314.1, 2315, 2377; Fed Cts 825.1, 872, 905, 944, 945.

General Tire, Inc. v. Kepple, Tex, 970 SW2d 520.—App & E 946; Pretrial Proc 413.1; Records 32.

General Tire, Inc. v. Kepple, TexApp–Houston (14 Dist), 917 SW2d 444, reh overr, and stay gr, and writ gr, rev 970 SW2d 520.—App & E 946, 961, 994(3), 1012.1(2), 1043(6); Const Law 3874(2), 3905, 4301; Em Dom 87; Pretrial Proc 41, 413.1; Records 32; Statut 47.

General Trailer Co., Inc.; Buddy L, Inc. v., TexApp–Dallas, 672 SW2d 541, ref nre.—App & E 179(1); 863; Contracts 28(1), 88, 176(2); Judgm 106(5), 123(1), 138(3), 181(19), 185.3(2), 335(2); New Tr 117(1); Release 12(1), 13(1), 58(4).

General Transport Systems, Inc.; Emery Air Freight Corp. v., TexApp–Houston (14 Dist), 933 SW2d 312.—App & E 883; Costs 194.14, 194.32; Indem 30(1); Insurance 1701.

General Transport Systems, Inc.; Emery Worldwide v., TexApp–Houston (14 Dist, 933 SW2d 312. See Emery Air Freight Corp. v. General Transport Systems, Inc.

General Trimming Products, Inc. v. S. C. Nelson & Co., TexCivApp–Tyler, 398 SW2d 775, ref nre.—App & E 172(1); Fraud Conv 182(2); Trusts 233.

General Universal Systems, Inc. v. Lee, CA5 (Tex), 379 F3d 131, on remand 2005 WL 1828565.—Antitrust 42, 414; Copyr 10.4, 51, 53(1), 67.3, 83(3.1), 83(7), 89(1), 90(2), 107; Damag 117; Fed Civ Proc 2182.1, 2515, 2533.1, 2654, 2655, 2723; Fed Cts 611, 763.1, 781, 822, 823, 830, 915; Joint Adv 4(1); Partners 70; Spec Perf 5, 62, 102.

General Universal Systems, Inc.; Transoceanic Shipping Co., Inc. v., TexApp–Houston (1 Dist), 961 SW2d 418.—App & E 5.

General Warehousemen and Helpers Local 767 v. Standard Brands, Inc., CA5 (Tex), 579 F2d 1282, reh den 588 F2d 829, cert dism 99 SCt 2420, 441 US 957, 60 LEd2d 1075, cert dism 99 SCt 3103, 443 US 913, 61 LEd2d 877.—Labor & Emp 1255, 1262, 1263, 1329, 1578, 1592, 1595(9), 1597, 1608, 1610(1), 1629, 1678(2).

General Warehousemen and Helpers Local 767 v. Standard Brands, Inc., CA5 (Tex), 560 F2d 700, on reh 579 F2d 1282, reh den 588 F2d 829, cert dism 99 SCt 2420, 441 US 957, 60 LEd2d 1075, cert dism 99 SCt 3103, 443 US 913, 61 LEd2d 877.—Labor & Emp 1549(1), 1595(9), 1604, 1608, 1615, 1678(1), 1678(2); Labor 477.

General Warehousemen and Helpers Union Local 767 v. Albertson's Distribution, Inc., CA5 (Tex), 331 F3d 485.—Labor & Emp 1549(5), 1549(6), 1549(19), 1556(3).

General Warehousemen and Helpers Union Local 767; Weber Aircraft Inc. v., CA5 (Tex), 253 F3d 821.—Labor & Emp 1255, 1519, 1595(10), 1595(12), 1609(2), 1619, 1623(1), 1624(1), 1630.

GeneScreen, Inc.; LaRue v., TexApp–Beaumont, 957 SW2d 958, review den.—Antitrust 141, 358; App & E 500(1), 852, 917(1), 946, 960(1); Fraud 20; Lim of Act 43, 95(1), 95(2), 95(3), 95(12); Plead 228.14.

Gene's Enterprises, Inc., In re, BkrtcySDTex, 112 BR 165. See Sherwood Enterprises, Inc., In re.

Geneva Capital, LLC; Burditt v., CA5 (Tex), 161 FedAppx 384.—Civil R 1395(1), 1396; Jury 31.2(1).

Gengler; Van Benthuysen v., TexCivApp–Galveston, 100 SW2d 116.—Costs 132(5), 132(6); Mand 3(11).

Gengnagel v. State, TexCrimApp, 748 SW2d 227.—Crim Law 1032(5); Ind & Inf 71.3, 133(7), 196(5); Obscen 11.

Gengo; Sorrell v., TexApp–Beaumont, 49 SW3d 627.—App & E 430(1), 842(2), 1008.1(1); Ease 15.1, 18(2), 26(3); Estop 83(1), 118.

Genico Distributors, Inc. v. First Nat. Bank of Richardson, TexCivApp–Texarkana, 616 SW2d 418, ref nre.—Antitrust 143(2); App & E 216(1); Costs 194.44.

Genie Toys, Inc.; Craig v., TexCivApp–Hous (1 Dist), 444 SW2d 309.—Acct Action on 14.

Genitempo v. Chardee, Inc., TexApp–Houston (14 Dist), 822 SW2d 824, writ den.—App & E 931(1), 1010.1(3); Brok 55(3), 86(8), 87.

Genitempo v. Sea Lake Yacht Sales, TexApp–Houston (14 Dist, 822 SW2d 824. See Genitempo v. Chardee, Inc.

Genmoora Corp. v. Moore Business Forms, Inc., CA5 (Tex), 939 F2d 1149, on reh, and mandate clarified and reissued.—Evid 555.6(1), 570; Fed Civ Proc 2334; Fed Cts 628, 859, 900; Sales 358(4).

Genmoora Corp.; Xerox Corp. v., CA5 (Tex), 888 F2d 345.—Corp 320(7), 320(8); Fed Civ Proc 103.2, 1744.1, 1856, 2513, 2641, 2655; Fed Cts 753, 763.1.

Gennedy; City of Pasadena v., TexApp–Houston (1 Dist), 125 SW3d 687, review den.—App & E 170(2), 177, 854(1), 893(1), 931(1), 989, 1008.1(2), 1010.1(1), 1010.2, 1180(2); Corp 402; Costs 194.40; Covenants 21, 49, 68, 69(2), 72.1, 73, 122, 134.

Geno Designs, Inc.; Bishop v., TexApp–Tyler, 631 SW2d 581.—App & E 327(4); Bankr 2062, 2154.1, 2159.1, 2391; Damag 87(2); Trover 1, 32(2), 35, 44, 46, 61.

Geno's v. City of Dallas, CA5 (Tex), 837 F2d 1298. See FW/PBS, Inc. v. City of Dallas.

Geno's v. City of Dallas, NDTex, 648 FSupp 1061. See Dumas v. City of Dallas.

Gensco, Inc.; Canal Ins. Co. v., TexCivApp–San Antonio, 404 SW2d 908.—Insurance 2686, 2761, 2893, 3100(1).

Gensco, Inc. v. Canco Equipment, Inc., TexApp–Amarillo, 737 SW2d 345.—Corp 1.4(1), 1.7(2), 34(3); Evid 471(2); Fraud 66.

Gensco, Inc.; Ralston Oil and Gas Co. v., CA5 (Tex), 706 F2d 685.—Antitrust 130, 208; Costs 198; Fed Civ Proc 633.1, 742, 745, 1976, 2173, 2737.4, 2737.5; Fed Cts 941; Mines 110; Princ & A 183(1); Sales 418(7), 442(6).

Gensco, Inc. v. Thomas, TexCivApp–San Antonio, 609 SW2d 650.—Contempt 66(2); Inj 157, 189, 210, 211; Plead 228.14.

Gensco, Inc. v. Transformaciones Metalurgicias Especiales, S.A., TexApp–Houston (14 Dist), 666 SW2d 549, dism.—App & E 173(2), 1073(1); Contracts 83, 211, 260; Interest 66; Judgm 185(2), 185.3(4), 186; Sales 21, 85(1), 186, 368.

Gensco, Inc.; Upton v., TexApp–Fort Worth, 962 SW2d 620, reh overr, and review den, and reh of petition for review overr.—Autos 197(2), 197(7); Labor & Emp 3046(1).

Gensheimer v. Kneisley, TexApp–Texarkana, 778 SW2d 138.—App & E 169; Hus & W 270(10); Judgm 185(1), 185(4), 189, 768(1), 788(1); Ven & Pur 229(2).

Genstar Bldg. Materials; Ortiz v., TexApp–Corpus Christi, 761 SW2d 531. See Ortiz v. Flintkote Co.

Gent; Combs v., TexApp–Dallas, 181 SW3d 378, reh overr, and rule 537(f) motion gr.—App & E 854(4), 989, 1003(7), 1051.1(1); Atty & C 106, 109, 117, 124, 129(4); Fraud 7; Trial 43; Trusts 169(1), 212, 217.1, 217.3(7), 222, 226, 227, 267, 268.

Gent v. Gmenier, TexCivApp–Waco, 435 SW2d 293.—Divorce 168, 231.

Gent; State v., TexApp–Beaumont, 887 SW2d 271, reh overr, and petition for discretionary review refused.—Crim Law 273.1(2), 274(3.1), 274(10), 954(1), 1156(1).

Genter v. State, TexCrimApp, 473 SW2d 35.—Arrest 63.3; Crim Law 517.2(3), 519(8), 522(1), 531(3), 1130(2).

Gentile v. State, TexApp–Austin, 848 SW2d 359.—Autos 359.

Gentle; Bilbrey v., TexCivApp–Dallas, 107 SW2d 597, writ dism.—App & E 1001(1), 1068(3); Autos 173(1), 211, 244(45); Evid 380; Trial 350.6(3).

Gentle; Dallas Railway & Terminal Co. v., TexCivApp–Austin, 264 SW2d 155, writ refused.—Statut 223.5(7); Tax 3678.

Gentle; Dallas Ry. & Terminal Co. v., TexCivApp–Austin, 218 SW2d 259, writ refused.—Urb R R 22.

Gentle; Guillott v., TexCivApp–Eastland, 467 SW2d 521, ref nre.—Child C 42, 452, 473, 921(1).

Gentle; Yamini v., TexCivApp–Dallas, 488 SW2d 839, ref nre.—Fraud 1; Tax 2469, 2569, 2680.

Gentry, Ex parte, TexCrimApp, 615 SW2d 228.—Bail 51, 53.

Gentry v. Central Motor Co., TexCivApp–Waco, 100 SW2d 215.—Judgm 199(1), 199(5).

Gentry v. Ciomperlik, TexCivApp–San Antonio, 378 SW2d 732.—Parent & C 5(3), 16.

Gentry v. Credit Plan Corp. of Houston, Tex, 528 SW2d 571.—Corp 1.5(3), 1.6(13), 1.7(2); Lim of Act 124.

Gentry; Credit Plan Corp. of Houston v., TexCivApp–Hous (14 Dist), 516 SW2d 471, writ gr, rev 528 SW2d 571.—Damag 50.10, 87(1), 94, 132(2), 135, 185(1), 192, 208(8); Lim of Act 30, 126; Torts 453; Trial 31.

Gentry; Dillard's, Inc. v., TexCivApp–Texarkana, 265 SW2d 222, ref nre.—App & E 927(7); Autos 245(28), 245(32); Labor & Emp 29.

Gentry v. Flint Engineering and Const. Co., Inc., CA5 (Tex), 76 F3d 95.—Fed Cts 776; Statut 188; Work Comp 2161, 2189, 2190.

Gentry; Fuentes v., TexApp–Amarillo, 628 SW2d 459.—App & E 1010.1(1); Explos 7; Neglig 213, 380, 387, 504, 1676.

Gentry v. Gentry, TexCivApp–Austin, 550 SW2d 167.—Divorce 160.

Gentry; Gentry v., TexCivApp–Austin, 550 SW2d 167.—Divorce 160.

Gentry v. Gentry, TexCivApp–Corpus Christi, 394 SW2d 544.—Divorce 12, 27(1), 27(3), 124.1, 184(6.1), 184(7).

Gentry; Gentry v., TexCivApp–Corpus Christi, 394 SW2d 544.—Divorce 12, 27(1), 27(3), 124.1, 184(6.1), 184(7).

Gentry; Hailes v., TexCivApp–El Paso, 520 SW2d 555.—App & E 1170.10; Autos 171(9), 244(11), 244(35), 244(36.1), 244(37); Evid 474(8); Trial 205, 352.18.

Gentry v. Highlands State Bank, TexApp–Houston (14 Dist), 633 SW2d 590, writ refused.—Judgm 181(22), 185.2(3), 185.2(9); Sec Tran 240.

Gentry; Ingram v., TexCivApp–Waco, 205 SW2d 673.—App & E 927(7), 989; Contracts 176(11), 346(2), 346(10); Trial 139.1(7), 178.

Gentry v. McKnight Const. Co., TexCivApp–Texarkana, 449 SW2d 287, ref nre.—Judgm 615, 631, 696.

Gentry v. Marburger, TexCivApp–Hous (1 Dist), 596 SW2d 201, ref nre.—Courts 200.7, 475(2); Forci E & D 6(2).

Gentry v. Montalbano, TexCivApp–Houston, 414 SW2d 753.—Tresp to T T 6.1, 41(1).

Gentry v. Northeast Management Co., Inc., NDTex, 472 FSupp 1248.—Civil R 1403, 1419, 1484.

Gentry; Oss v., WDTex, 634 FSupp 482, aff 788 F2d 759.—Damag 51.

Gentry v. Sellers, TexCivApp–Dallas, 468 SW2d 525, ref nre.—Wills 314; Witn 178(4).

Gentry v. Southern Pac. Co., Tex, 457 SW2d 889.—App & E 934(1); Judgm 199(3.18); Neglig 1745; R R 346(5.1), 351(22).

Gentry v. Southern Pac. Co., TexCivApp–Corpus Christi, 449 SW2d 527, aff 457 SW2d 889.—App & E 934(1); Evid 586(3), 588, 594; Judgm 199(3.18); Neglig 530(1).

Gentry v. Squires Const., Inc., TexApp–Dallas, 188 SW3d 396.—Action 3; Antitrust 282, 286, 351, 369, 388; App & E 219(2); Can of Inst 1, 8, 23; Contracts 265, 294, 319(1), 322(1), 324(1); Costs 32(1), 194.25, 194.32, 194.38; Damag 121, 123; Fraud 31; Impl & C C 30, 60.1, 63, 64, 65.

Gentry v. State, TexCrimApp, 770 SW2d 780, cert den 109 SCt 2458, 490 US 1102, 104 LEd2d 1013, denial of habeas corpus aff 95 F3d 1149.—Const Law 3811, 4744(2); Crim Law 394.1(2), 517.2(2), 519(1), 531(1), 532(0.5), 649(2), 1044.2(1), 1063(1), 1158(4), 1166(2), 1169.12; Gr Jury 7, 8, 20; Homic 607, 1184, 1186; Ind & Inf 137(3), 140(2); Sent & Pun 94, 1762; Witn 8, 17.

Gentry v. State, TexCrimApp, 640 SW2d 899.—Searches 102.

Gentry v. State, TexCrimApp, 608 SW2d 643.—Larc 30(1).

Gentry v. State, TexCrimApp, 494 SW2d 169.—Crim Law 419(1.5), 423(1), 627.2, 695(2), 698(1), 730(1), 829(3), 1090.4, 1115(1), 1119(4), 1169.5(5); Ind & Inf 191(5).

Gentry v. State, TexCrimApp, 464 SW2d 848.—Double J 119; Prisons 15(3).

Gentry v. State, TexCrimApp, 371 SW2d 566.—Crim Law 1131(5).

Gentry v. State, TexCrimApp, 369 SW2d 351.—Crim Law 1090.1(1).

Gentry v. State, TexCrimApp, 356 SW2d 793, 172 Tex-Crim 345.—Homic 839, 847, 1016, 1018, 1134; Ind & Inf 125(29).

Gentry v. State, TexCrimApp, 284 SW2d 725.—Crim Law 1090.1(1).

Gentry v. State, TexCrimApp, 278 SW2d 298, 161 Tex-Crim 520.—Crim Law 719(1), 723(1); Int Liq 236(20).

Gentry v. State, TexCrimApp, 273 SW2d 419.—Crim Law 1087.1(2).

Gentry v. State, TexCrimApp, 271 SW2d 820.—Crim Law 1087.1(2).

Gentry v. State, TexCrimApp, 257 SW2d 707.—Crim Law 1090.1(1).

Gentry v. State, TexCrimApp, 253 SW2d 862, 158 Tex-Crim 112.—Hus & W 107; Int Liq 236(4).

Gentry v. State, TexCrimApp, 252 SW2d 458, 158 Tex-Crim 4.—Crim Law 346, 404.15, 1166.22(2).

Gentry v. State, TexCrimApp, 150 SW2d 94, 141 TexCrim 565.—Crim Law 814(17).

Gentry v. State, TexCrimApp, 152 SW 635, 68 TexCrim 567.—Statut 241(1).

Gentry v. State, TexApp–Dallas, 881 SW2d 35, reh den, and petition for discretionary review refused.—Const Law 3855; Crim Law 633(2), 1165(1), 1166.15, 1166.16, 1166.18; Double J 1, 2, 131, 135, 150(1); Homic 558; Jury 131(4), 149.

Gentry v. State, TexApp–Dallas, 629 SW2d 77, aff 640 SW2d 899.—Burg 41(6); Crim Law 552(3), 641.13(1), 641.13(6), 1037.1(3), 1037.2, 1038.3, 1141(2), 1169.5(1), 1170.5(6); Searches 102.

Gentry v. State, TexApp–Beaumont, 745 SW2d 454.—Ind & Inf 159(1).

Gentry; Taylor v., TexCivApp–Fort Worth, 494 SW2d 243.—App & E 1056.1(10), 1067; Assault 12, 43(5); Damag 157(2); Evid 268; Plead 79; Trial 251(8), 252(8), 260(1), 350.3(5).

Gentry; Ted Lokey Real Estate Co. v., NDTex, 336 FSupp 741.—Rem of C 49.1(3), 58, 107(8).

Gentry; Texas Dept. of Public Safety v., Tex, 386 SW2d 758.—Autos 144.2(5.1); Evid 366(1); Judgm 185(4), 185.3(1).

Gentry v. Texas Dept. of Public Safety, TexCivApp–Houston, 379 SW2d 114, ref nre 386 SW2d 758.—App & E 909(1); Autos 144.1(3); Const Law 947; Crim Law 990.1, 990.3; Hab Corp 445; Judgm 181(13), 181(15.1), 183, 185(2), 185.1(3), 485.

Gentry; Texas Health Enterprises, Inc. v., TexApp–El Paso, 787 SW2d 604.—Contracts 94(1), 324(1); Insurance 1001; Labor & Emp 265.

Gentry; Traders & General Ins. Co. v., TexCivApp–Fort Worth, 267 SW2d 213.—Work Comp 1396, 1639.

Gentry v. Travelers Ins. Co., TexCivApp–Hous (14 Dist), 459 SW2d 709, ref nre.—Courts 100(1); Work Comp 1036, 1778, 1789, 1790, 1792, 1793, 1993.

Gentry v. Tucker, TexApp–Texarkana, 891 SW2d 766.—App & E 231(1), 236(1), 627; Venue 17, 72, 77.

Gentry; U.S. v., CA5 (Tex), 432 F3d 600.—Courts 100(1); Crim Law 1139, 1158(1); Jury 34(6); Sent & Pun 322.

Gentry v. Weaver Development Co., TexApp–Fort Worth, 909 SW2d 606.—App & E 946, 961; Pretrial Proc 44.1, 45, 221, 224, 225, 434.

Gentry; Willborg v., TexCivApp–Galveston, 93 SW2d 1204.—Ack 20(3); App & E 930(3); Mech Liens 73(6).

Gentry Plumbing & Heating Co.; Henry v., CA5 (Tex), 704 F2d 863.—Work Comp 1029, 1790, 1805, 1809.

Gentsch v. State, TexCrimApp, 468 SW2d 66.—Homic 1158, 1161, 1184.

Gentsch v. State, TexCrimApp, 324 SW2d 885.—Autos 355(13), 359; Crim Law 996(1).

Gentsch v. State, TexApp–Houston (14 Dist), 654 SW2d 768.—Crim Law 364(1), 695(4), 824(13), 1038.2, 1038.3, 1043(1), 1130(0.5), 1169.1(1), 1169.5(3), 1169.11.

Genusa v. State, TexCrimApp, 117 SW2d 899, 135 Tex-Crim 55.—Rob 24.50.

Genzel; Barko v., TexApp–Eastland, 123 SW3d 457.—Health 804.

Genzel v. State, TexCrimApp, 415 SW2d 919.—Atty & C 103; Crim Law 369.15, 1086.14, 1130(2).

Genzer v. City of Mission, TexApp–Corpus Christi, 666 SW2d 116, ref nre.—App & E 994(2); Damag 51; Explos 7, 11; Judgm 199(3.2), 199(3.10); Mun Corp 742(5), 747(3); States 112.1(2).

Genzer v. Fillip, TexCivApp–Austin, 134 SW2d 730, writ dism, correct.—Const Law 193, 2340; Estop 58; Judges 37; Judgm 1; Jury 19(1); Mental H 137.1, 165; Statut 63.

Geochemical Surveys v. Dietz, TexCivApp–Austin, 340 SW2d 114, ref nre.—App & E 231(6), 758.3(8); Lim of Act 95(7); Mines 125; New Tr 128(1); Partners 197.

Geochem Laboratories, Inc. v. Brown & Ruth Laboratories, Inc., TexApp–Houston (1 Dist), 689 SW2d 288, ref nre.—Costs 252; Plead 228.23.

GeoChem Tech Corp. v. Verseckes, Tex, 962 SW2d 541.—App & E 866(1); Venue 16, 28, 58, 64.1, 65, 68, 72.

GeoChem Tech Corp. v. Verseckes, TexApp–Eastland, 929 SW2d 85, writ gr, rev 962 SW2d 541.—Antitrust 414, 418; App & E 936(2), 966(1), 984(5), 1024.1; Costs 194.10, 194.40, 207; Evid 318(1), 355(2); Judgm 185(2), 186; Pretrial Proc 723.1; Venue 1.5, 16, 32(1), 32(2), 68, 72, 77.

Geodynamics Oil & Gas, Inc.; Diversified Resources Corp. v., TexCivApp–Corpus Christi, 558 SW2d 97, ref nre.—Corp 642(1), 665(3).

Geodynamics Oil & Gas, Inc. v. U. S. Silver & Mining Corp., SDTex, 358 FSupp 1345.—Const Law 3965(3); Contracts 206; Fed Cts 75, 89; Mines 109; Venue 7.5(2).

Geodyne Energy Income Production Partnership I-E v. Newton Corp., Tex, 161 SW3d 482.—Antitrust 294; Auctions 7, 8; Contracts 93(1); Deeds 25, 94, 120, 121; Mines 73.5, 74(3), 74(5); Sec Reg 253, 278.

Geodyne Energy Income Production Partnership I-E v. Newton Corp., TexApp–Dallas, 97 SW3d 779, review den, and reh of petition for review gr, and review gr, and withdrawn, rev in part 161 SW3d 482.—App & E 1178(6); Costs 194.18, 198, 208; Courts 97(5); Mines 92.56; Sec Reg 278, 299, 308, 309; Statut 176.

Geomap Co. v. Bullock, TexApp–Austin, 691 SW2d 98, ref nre.—Statut 245; Tax 3650.

Geophysical Data Processing Center, Inc. v. Cruz, Tex-CivApp–Beaumont, 576 SW2d 666.—Action 43.1, 60; Parties 14; Plead 111.8, 111.30; Venue 22(4).

Geophysical Data Processing Center, Inc.; Hamman v., TexCivApp–Corpus Christi, 430 SW2d 840.—App & E 624, 627.2, 628(1).

Geophysical Service, Inc., Complaint of, SDTex, 590 FSupp 1346.—Action 17, 66; Adm 1.11; Fed Cts 45; Seamen 29(5.2); Ship 209(1), 209(1.1), 209(1.6), 209(3).

Geophysical Service, Inc.; Duque & Duarte, Inc. v., CA5 (Tex), 401 F2d 496.—Collision 106.

Geophysical Service, Inc. v. F/V Tempest, SDTex, 293 FSupp 179.—Collision 12; Ship 81(1), 86(2.5).

Geo Pipe Co.; Saint Paul Surplus Lines Ins. Co. v., TexApp–Houston (1 Dist), 25 SW3d 900, remanded pursuant to settlement.—Insurance 2278(21), 2914, 2915.

Georg v. Animal Defense League, TexCivApp–San Antonio, 231 SW2d 807, ref nre.—Char 10; Evid 13; Inj 24; Judgm 199(1); Nuis 25(1), 34; Trial 3(1), 136(1).

Georg v. State, TexCrimApp, 95 SW2d 393, 130 TexCrim 512.—Crim Law 1020.

Georgandis; Richker v., TexCivApp–Houston, 323 SW2d 90, ref nre.—App & E 181; Damag 40(1), 40(3), 176; Evid 158(28); Land & Ten 37, 130(1), 130(2), 130(3), 130(4), 172(2); Trial 350.3(2.1).

George, Ex parte, USTex, 83 SCt 178, 371 US 72, 9 LEd2d 133, on remand 364 SW2d 189.—Inj 219; Labor & Emp 1677(5).

George, Ex parte, Tex, 364 SW2d 189.—Hab Corp 861; Inj 219.

George, Ex parte, Tex, 358 SW2d 590, 163 Tex 103, vac 83 SCt 178, 371 US 72, 9 LEd2d 133, on remand 364

SW2d 189.—Courts 489(1); Labor & Emp 1670, 1675, 1677(5), 2111.

George, Ex parte, TexCrimApp, 913 SW2d 523.—Courts 1; Crim Law 753.2(1), 753.2(2), 994(1), 996(1), 1144.17; Double J 57, 59, 103; Judges 1.

George, Ex parte, TexCrimApp, 215 SW2d 170, 152 Tex-Crim 465.—Const Law 1066, 2483, 2970, 3037, 3041, 3053, 3703; Hab Corp 464; Licens 5, 7(2), 7(5), 8(1).

George, Ex parte, TexApp–Houston (1 Dist), 874 SW2d 916, petition for discretionary review gr, rev 913 SW2d 523.—Double J 60.1, 100.1; Mand 61.

George, In Interest of, TexApp–Tyler, 794 SW2d 875.—Child 31, 33; Work Comp 452.

George, In re, Tex, 28 SW3d 511.—Atty & C 21.10, 21.20, 63.

George, In re, TexApp–Dallas, 30 SW3d 1, mandamus gr, subsequent mandamus proceeding 28 SW3d 511.—Atty & C 21.20; Mand 28, 29.

George v. Aztec Rental Center Inc., CA5 (Tex), 763 F2d 184.—Labor & Emp 851.

George v. Barnhart, SDTex, 458 FSupp2d 314.—Social S 140.30, 143.40, 143.60, 143.65, 143.75, 143.85, 148.15.

George v. Beneficial Finance Co. of Dallas, NDTex, 81 FRD 4.—Fed Civ Proc 182.5, 777.

George v. Blackwell, CA5 (Tex), 537 F2d 833.—Hab Corp 775(2).

George v. Bourgeois, EDTex, 852 FSupp 1341.—Civil R 1463; Const Law 1490, 3847, 3873, 4157, 4165(1), 4171, 4198, 4199, 4202, 4203, 4255; Damag 87(1); Fed Civ Proc 2117, 2461, 2462, 2544, 2552; Offic 66; Schools 147.2(1), 147.12, 147.34(1), 147.40(1), 147.51.

George v. Burd, TexCivApp–Waco, 380 SW2d 735.—Venue 7.5(4).

George; Cain v., CA5 (Tex), 411 F2d 572.—Evid 147, 157(3), 314(1); Fed Civ Proc 2215; Inn 10.1, 10.8.

George; Cameron County Water Control and Imp. Dist. No. 5 v., TexCivApp–Eastland, 349 SW2d 308, ref nre.—Courts 472.3; Decl Judgm 369; Deeds 140, 143; Waters 156(8).

George; Cammack v., TexCivApp–Beaumont, 377 SW2d 687, ref nre.—Decl Judgm 384; Judgm 183, 185(4); Wills 577, 616(1), 783.

George; City of Dallas v., Tex, 169 SW2d 473, 141 Tex 9.—Gaming 3; Mun Corp 721(3).

George; City of Dallas v., TexCivApp–Eastland, 157 SW2d 987, aff 169 SW2d 473, 141 Tex 9.—App & E 843(2); Gaming 17(1); Mun Corp 721(3).

George v. City of Fort Worth, TexCivApp–Fort Worth, 434 SW2d 903, ref nre.—Judgm 185(6), 185.3(21); Land & Ten 164(6), 167(8); Mun Corp 848, 855, 857.

George; City of Fort Worth v., TexCivApp–Fort Worth, 108 SW2d 929, writ refused.—App & E 1175(5); Autos 187(2); Evid 7; Mun Corp 54, 724, 725, 745.5.

George; City of Houston v., Tex, 479 SW2d 257.—Mun Corp 733(1), 851.

George v. City of Houston, TexCivApp–Hous (1 Dist), 465 SW2d 387, writ gr, rev 479 SW2d 257.—Mun Corp 736, 745.5, 849, 857; Nuis 44, 72.

George v. City of Patton Village, Officer Hauford Identification Number 4816, CA5 (Tex), 800 F2d 461.—Fed Civ Proc 2840.

George v. Cox, TexCivApp–Eastland, 261 SW2d 201.—Plead 111.42(7).

George v. Davis, CA5 (Tex), 419 F2d 1211. See Singleton v. Jackson Municipal Separate School Dist.

George; Eagle Life Ins. Co. v., TexCivApp–Beaumont, 473 SW2d 311, writ refused.—Insurance 3569.

George v. Elledge, TexCivApp–San Antonio, 261 SW2d 201.—Proc 33.

George v. El Paso County Water Control and Imp. Dist. No. 1, TexCivApp–El Paso, 332 SW2d 144, ref nre.—Contracts 143(2); Cust & U 15(1); Evid 450(5); Mun Corp 360(1).

George v. Farmers Elec. Co-op., Inc., CA5 (Tex), 715 F2d 175.—Civil R 1168, 1197, 1522, 1560, 1563, 1571; Fed Civ Proc 103.2.

George; First State Bank & Trust Co. of Edinburg v., TexCivApp–Corpus Christi, 519 SW2d 198, ref nre.—App & E 216(2), 614, 648, 653(3), 688(2), 1003(9.1); Banks 21, 126; Bills & N 327, 335, 337, 365(1), 452(1), 452(3); Trial 215, 219, 349(2).

George; French v., TexCivApp–Amarillo, 159 SW2d 566, writ refused.—Mines 79.1(5).

George v. George, TexApp–Tyler, 813 SW2d 236.—Ex & Ad 20(4), 20(5).

George; George v., TexApp–Tyler, 813 SW2d 236.—Ex & Ad 20(4), 20(5).

George v. George, TexCivApp–Tyler, 564 SW2d 172.—Divorce 139.5; Pretrial Proc 510, 520, 696.1, 697, 699.

George; George v., TexCivApp–Tyler, 564 SW2d 172.—Divorce 139.5; Pretrial Proc 510, 520, 696.1, 697, 699.

George; Gulf Collateral, Inc. v., TexCivApp–Tyler, 466 SW2d 21.—Gaming 19(3).

George; Haas v., TexApp–Texarkana, 71 SW3d 904.—App & E 66, 76(1), 78(1), 856(1), 863, 934(1), 946, 1073(1), 1079, 1135; Atty & C 109; Judgm 181(7), 183, 185(5), 190, 216; Lim of Act 43, 55(3), 95(1), 95(3), 95(11), 104(1), 104(2), 199(1); Pretrial Proc 11, 378; Trial 18.

George v. Hall, Tex, 371 SW2d 874.—App & E 1082(1), 1114, 1178(6); Contracts 186(2).

George v. Houston Boxing Club, Inc., TexCivApp–Hous (14 Dist), 423 SW2d 128, ref nre.—Contracts 218, 252, 278(1); Corp 1.4(4); Estop 78(5); Release 38.

George v. LeBlanc, NDTex, 78 FRD 281, aff 565 F2d 1213, reh den 568 F2d 206.—Atty & C 20.1; Corp 207; Fed Civ Proc 186.5, 187.

George; Leinneweber v., TexCivApp–Austin, 95 SW2d 478.—Hus & W 254, 255, 264(2), 274(4); Trial 142.

George; McCarthy v., Tex, 618 SW2d 762, on remand 623 SW2d 772, ref nre.—App & E 187(3).

George; McCarthy v., TexApp–Fort Worth, 623 SW2d 772, ref nre.—App & E 996, 1008.1(1), 1079; Atty & C 72; Evid 332(1); Ten in C 15(7); Tresp to T T 26, 41(1); Trial 66.

George; McCarthy v., TexApp–Fort Worth, 609 SW2d 630, rev 618 SW2d 762, on remand 623 SW2d 772, ref nre.—App & E 187(3); Parties 18, 29; Tresp to T T 26, 47(1).

George v. National Ass'n of Letter Carriers, CA5 (Tex), 185 F3d 380, reh en banc den 194 F3d 1310, cert den 120 SCt 1163, 528 US 1156, 145 LEd2d 1074.—Labor & Emp 40(3), 1403, 1407, 1410, 1411, 1968; Torts 212, 220.

George v. Northwest Engineering Co., TexCivApp–San Antonio, 156 SW2d 576.—Courts 85(1); Plead 111.3, 111.4, 111.26, 111.38; Venue 7.5(2), 7.5(4).

George; Perez v., TexCivApp–Austin, 367 SW2d 940, ref nre.—Judgm 181(33); J P 133; Ven & Pur 299(4).

George; Perez v., TexCivApp–Corpus Christi, 384 SW2d 900.—App & E 1126.

George v. Phillips, TexApp–Texarkana, 642 SW2d 275.—App & E 930(3), 989; Ease 15.1, 16, 17(1), 17(5), 36(3), 61(9 1/2); High 9, 17.

George v. Phillips Petroleum Co., TexApp–Houston (14 Dist), 976 SW2d 363.—App & E 20, 23; Courts 475(1), 488(1).

George; Querner v., TexCivApp–San Antonio, 336 SW2d 903, ref nre.—Acct Action on 15; App & E 1033(4); Trial 351.2(6).

George; Rollison v., TexCivApp–Texarkana, 319 SW2d 389, ref nre.—Deeds 114(1); Frds St of 158(3); Mines 55(1), 55(5).

George; Runyon v., TexCivApp–Eastland, 349 SW2d 107, writ dism.—Courts 483; Judges 44, 46; Mun Corp 46; Offic 77, 80.

George v. Senter, TexCivApp–Fort Worth, 194 SW2d 290, ref nre.—App & E 387(3), 501(2), 509, 528(1), 933(2); Contracts 140, 333(1).

GEORGE;

George; Silsbee Hosp., Inc. v., TexApp–Beaumont, 163 SW3d 284, review den (2 pets).—App & E 200, 840(4), 959(1), 1031(1), 1177(2); Contracts 114, 143(2), 176(2), 328(3); Estop 92(2); Evid 397(1), 409; Jury 33(2.10), 90, 97(1); Labor & Emp 23, 2792; Land & Ten 162; Plead 236(3), 245(3), 258(3).

George v. State, TexCrimApp, 890 SW2d 73.—Crim Law 374, 673(5).

George v. State, TexCrimApp, 681 SW2d 43.—Assault 48, 49, 54, 96(7); Crim Law 20.

George v. State, TexCrimApp, 589 SW2d 428.—App & E 1146; Bail 77(2), 94; Judges 29.

George v. State, TexCrimApp, 560 SW2d 93.—Crim Law 1167(1); Forg 28(2), 28(3).

George v. State, TexCrimApp, 557 SW2d 787.—Chem Dep 25.

George v. State, TexCrimApp, 509 SW2d 347.—Arrest 63.4(10); Controlled Subs 134; Crim Law 1224(1).

George v. State, TexCrimApp, 498 SW2d 202.—Crim Law 438(3), 577.8(2), 577.10(1), 577.10(2), 577.15(1); Rob 24.15(2).

George v. State, TexCrimApp, 454 SW2d 742.—Burg 28(6).

George v. State, TexCrimApp, 449 SW2d 472.—Crim Law 925.5(4), 1175; Rob 24.15(2).

George v. State, TexCrimApp, 162 SW2d 110, 144 Tex-Crim 183.—Int Liq 236(7).

George v. State, TexCrimApp, 145 SW2d 187, 140 Tex-Crim 362.—Autos 351.1.

George v. State, TexCrimApp, 120 SW2d 255, 135 Tex-Crim 340.—Crim Law 363, 676, 726, 730(1), 763(19), 1169.2(2), 1170.5(6).

George v. State, TexApp–Houston (1 Dist), 841 SW2d 544, petition for discretionary review gr, aff 890 SW2d 73.— Crim Law 371(1), 673(5), 822(1), 1144.12, 1153(1), 1172.1(1), 1173.2(1), 1173.2(9); Extort 25.1, 32; Ind & Inf 110(3), 110(26).

George v. State, TexApp–Texarkana, 117 SW3d 285, petition for discretionary review refused.—Crim Law 708.1, 720(2), 720(5), 720(6), 723(1), 723(3), 726, 1037.1(1), 1037.2, 1044.1(8), 1045, 1134(2); Sent & Pun 77, 78, 80.

George v. State, TexApp–Texarkana, 9 SW3d 234.—Crim Law 641.4(1), 641.7(1), 641.9.

George v. State, TexApp–El Paso, 883 SW2d 250.—Crim Law 951(1), 1081(4.1), 1081(6); Hab Corp 500.1.

George v. State, TexApp–Beaumont, 959 SW2d 378, petition for discretionary review refused, appeal after new trial 2000 WL 33147085, petition for discretionary review refused.—Crim Law 369.3, 374, 660, 673(5), 694, 1030(1), 1043(1), 1162, 1165(1), 1169.1(7).

George v. State, TexApp–Waco, 41 SW3d 241, petition for discretionary review refused.—Crim Law 1139, 1144.1, 1147; Double J 95.1, 96; Hab Corp 705.1.

George v. State, TexApp–Houston (14 Dist), 20 SW3d 130, petition for discretionary review refused.—Crim Law 273.1(1), 273.1(4), 273.1(5), 655(1), 656(1), 959, 961, 1026.10(4), 1081(1), 1081(2), 1110(1), 1110(2), 1156(1), 1158(1), 1166.22(4.1); Judges 49(1), 51(2).

George v. State, TexCivApp–Hous (1 Dist), 506 SW2d 275. —Assault 54, 67; Infants 176.

George v. State of Tex., CA5 (Tex), 788 F2d 1099, cert den 107 SCt 226, 479 US 866, 93 LEd2d 153.—Const Law 725; Fed Civ Proc 2840; Fed Cts 272; Prost 14; Sent & Pun 1453, 1532.

George v. Taylor, TexCivApp–Fort Worth, 296 SW2d 620, ref nre.—App & E 934(1); Home 134, 139, 141(1), 143, 144; Hus & W 248, 272(2), 273(1); Partit 12(3), 83.

George v. Texas & N. O. R. Co., TexCivApp–Galveston, 290 SW2d 264, ref nre.—App & E 927(7); Neglig 1717; R R 277.5, 359(1), 359(2), 396(1), 398(1), 400(1).

George; Texas & P. Ry. Co. v., TexCivApp–Fort Worth, 466 SW2d 659.—App & E 1106(4); Carr 52(2), 135, 137.

George; Texas Emp. Ins. Ass'n v., TexCivApp–Texarkana, 288 SW2d 218, ref nre.—Work Comp 1958, 1968(1), 1968(5).

George v. Union Bank & Trust Co. of Fort Worth, TexCivApp–Fort Worth, 220 SW2d 686.—App & E 931(1); Bills & N 92(5), 493(3); Contracts 54(1), 71(1).

George; U.S. v., CA5 (Tex), 201 F3d 370, cert den 120 SCt 2019, 529 US 1136, 146 LEd2d 967.—Consp 45; Crim Law 661, 675, 719(3), 1037.1(1), 1037.1(2), 1153(1), 1170(1); Witn 267, 286(2), 351.

George; U.S. v., CA5 (Tex), 911 F2d 1028.—Sent & Pun 300, 308, 354, 836, 935.

George; U.S. v., CA5 (Tex), 567 F2d 643, reh den 573 F2d 85.—Arrest 63.5(3.1), 63.5(6).

George v. U. S., SDTex, 181 FSupp 522.—Courts 489(16); Fed Cts 263; Rem of C 102; U S 125(22).

George v. U.S. Dept. of Labor, Occupational Safety & Health Admin., CA5 (Tex), 788 F2d 1115.—Fed Civ Proc 1751.

George; U.S. for Use and Benefit of Kilsby v., CA5 (Tex), 243 F2d 83.—Contracts 232(1); U S 67(15).

George v. Vick, Tex, 686 SW2d 99, on remand 696 SW2d 160, ref nre.—Antitrust 365; App & E 1172(1), 1178(6).

George; Vick v., TexApp–San Antonio, 696 SW2d 160, ref nre.—App & E 230, 231(9), 273(5), 1060.1(1); New Tr 40(4); Trial 108, 273, 274.

George; Vick v., TexApp–San Antonio, 671 SW2d 541, rev in part 686 SW2d 99, on remand 696 SW2d 160, ref nre. —Action 38(1); Antitrust 130, 134, 136, 369, 389(1), 389(2), 390, 393, 398; App & E 930(3), 1001(1), 1001(3), 1177(1); Joint Adv 1.2(1), 1.2(8); Partners 3, 12, 15, 17, 22, 44, 165; Sec Reg 260, 262.1, 265, 308; Trial 362.

George A. Fuller Co. of Texas, Inc. v. Carpet Services, Inc., Tex, 823 SW2d 603.—Usury 137.

George A. Fuller Co. of Texas, Inc.; Carpet Services, Inc. v., TexApp–Dallas, 802 SW2d 343, writ gr, aff 823 SW2d 603.—Contracts 305(1); Usury 11.

George A. Hormel & Co.; Scruggs v., TexCivApp–Dallas, 464 SW2d 730, ref nre.—App & E 907(5); Labor & Emp 40(3).

George B. Hatley Co., Inc.; Dalton v., TexApp–Austin, 634 SW2d 374.—App & E 931(1), 989, 1008.1(10), 1012.1(8); Bills & N 122, 313, 504; Contracts 28(1), 322(1), 322(3); Corp 414(2); Evid 588.

George Braun Packing Co.; Eggleston v., TexCivApp–San Antonio, 470 SW2d 69.—Bills & N 440; Princ & A 175(3); Subrog 4; Venue 7.5(4).

George Braun Packing Co., Division of Leonard & Harral Packing Co.; Flores v., CA5 (Tex), 482 F2d 279, reh den 485 F2d 687.—Aliens 137.

George Bros. Fabrication, Inc. v. Bryant, TexApp–Eastland, 865 SW2d 622, reh den, and writ den.—Elect of Rem 7(1).

George Bros. Fabrication, Inc. v. Jim Bryant Ins. Agency, TexApp–Eastland, 865 SW2d 622. See George Bros. Fabrication, Inc. v. Bryant.

George Consol., Inc.; Southwestern Materials Co. v., TexCivApp–Hous (14 Dist), 476 SW2d 454, ref nre.— App & E 78(1), 123, 1170.7; Judgm 199(3.10), 248; Princ & A 124(3), 174.

George C. Vaughan & Sons v. Dyess, TexCivApp–Texarkana, 323 SW2d 261, writ dism.—App & E 842(1), 846(5); Damag 132(3), 208(1); New Tr 56, 74, 140(3).

Geo. C. Vaughan & Sons; Harrisburg Nat. Bank v., TexCivApp–Galveston, 204 SW2d 9, dism.—App & E 659(3); Fraud Conv 3, 43(1), 229; Garn 49, 105; Judgm 29, 705.

Geo. C. Vaughan & Sons v. Harrisburg Nat. Bank, TexCivApp–Galveston, 195 SW2d 613, dism.—Evid 318(6), 324(3); Garn 171; Trial 169, 174.

Geo. C. Vaughan & Sons; Leeland Properties Co. v., TexCivApp–Galveston, 253 SW2d 77, ref nre.—App & E 1012.1(9); Frds St of 131(2); Land & Ten 82; Spec Perf 121(3).

Geo. D. Barnard Co. v. Lane, TexCivApp–Dallas, 392 SW2d 769.—Autos 201(7); Neglig 213, 387, 1713; Plead 34(3).

George Distributors, Inc.; Midnight Rodeo v., TexApp–Amarillo, 950 SW2d82. See Whitney Crowne Corp. v. George Distributors, Inc.

George Distributors, Inc.; Whitney Crowne Corp. v., TexApp–Amarillo, 950 SW2d 82, writ den.—Consp 2; Int Liq 124, 299; Joint Adv 1.2(1); Neglig 213, 215, 220, 1692.

George D. Thomas Builder Inc. v. Timmons, TexApp–El Paso, 658 SW2d 194, ref nre.—Antitrust 291, 369, 390; Trial 304, 313.

George Dullnig & Co.; Graves v., TexCivApp–San Antonio, 538 SW2d 149.—App & E 387(1), 388.

George Dullnig & Co.; Graves v., TexCivApp–Eastland, 548 SW2d 502.—Judgm 181(18), 185(2), 185.1(3), 185.3(7), 186.

George E. Darsey & Co.; Shaver v., TexCivApp–Beaumont, 87 SW2d 516, writ dism.—Mtg 33(3), 37(2).

George E. Failing Co., A Div. of Azcon; Transportation Ins. Co. v., TexApp–Austin, 691 SW2d 71, ref nre.—Insurance 2660.

George E. Gibbons & Co.; Hohenberg Bros. Co. v., Tex, 537 SW2d 1.—Contracts 218, 221(1); Sales 85(1).

George E. Gibbons & Co.; Hohenberg Brothers Co. v., TexCivApp–Corpus Christi, 526 SW2d 570, writ gr, rev 537 SW2d 1.—App & E 1170.10; Contracts 147(2), 176(2), 221(2), 245(2); Evid 397(1), 461(1); Fraud 58(2); Sales 379, 383.

George E. Light Boat Storage, Inc.; N.L.R.B. v., CA5 (Tex), 373 F2d 762.—Fed Cts 421; Labor & Emp 1659, 1661, 1663, 1676(1), 1741, 1743(1), 1814, 1822, 1824, 1828(4), 1828(5), 1828(8), 1917, 1943.

George E. Light Boat Storage, Inc.; Seafarers' Welfare Plan v., TexCivApp–Houston, 402 SW2d 231, ref nre.—App & E 833(5); Contracts 97(1), 98; Evid 264; Labor & Emp 179, 256(1).

George Grubbs Datsun, Inc.; Grammer v., TexApp–Fort Worth, 663 SW2d 67, ref nre.—Judgm 181(21).

George Grubbs Enterprises, Inc. v. Bien, Tex, 900 SW2d 337.—Corp 1.7(1), 498; Damag 87(1), 215(3).

George Grubbs Enterprises, Inc. v. Bien, TexApp–Fort Worth, 881 SW2d 843, reh overr, and reh den, and writ gr, rev 900 SW2d 337.—Antitrust 397; App & E 843(1), 882(19), 989, 999(1), 1004(1), 1004(7), 1004(8), 1004(11), 1058(1), 1064.1(7); Corp 1.4(4); Damag 15, 50.10, 91(1), 91(3), 94, 130, 134(1), 185(1), 187, 192, 208(2), 208(6), 215(1), 221(8); Evid 597.

George H. Dentler & Sons v. Fuller's Food Products, TexCivApp–Galveston, 183 SW2d 768, writ refused wom.—Plead 228.21; Trademarks 1096(2), 1259, 1609, 1691, 1800.

George J. Mellina & Co.; Lattimore v., TexCivApp–Fort Worth, 195 SW2d 250.—Brok 40, 60, 61(1), 61(2), 63(2).

George L. Ingram and Associates; Mahathy v., TexCivApp–Beaumont, 584 SW2d 521.—Lim of Act 55(3).

George Linskie Co. v. Miller-Picking Corp., Tex, 463 SW2d 170.—Accord 10(1); Compromise 5(2); Costs 194.32; Evid 139.

George Linskie Co. v. Miller-Picking Corp., TexCivApp–Waco, 456 SW2d 519, aff in part, rev in part 463 SW2d 170.—Accord 9, 26(3); Costs 194.36, 206.

Georgen-Saad v. Texas Mut. Ins. Co., WDTex, 195 FSupp2d 853.—Civil R 1123, 1136, 1166, 1175, 1701, 1715, 1744; Courts 97(5); Fed Civ Proc 755, 2497.1; Fed Cts 373, 433; Fraud 3, 4, 9, 11(1), 12, 13(1), 13(2), 24, 25; Labor & Emp 2461, 2463; Lim of Act 31, 55(4), 95(4.1), 182(1).

George P. Bane, Inc.; Darr Equipment Co. v., TexCivApp–Tyler, 394 SW2d 951.—Plead 45, 111.3, 111.38.

George P. Bane, Inc. v. P. P. Prescott & Sons, Inc., CA5 (Tex), 394 F2d 119.—Fed Cts 942; Joint Adv 4(1).

George Pharis Chevrolet, Inc. v. Polk, TexApp–Houston (1 Dist), 661 SW2d 314.—Antitrust 193; App & E 218.2(2), 221, 1069.3; Costs 207; Trial 350.8, 352.1(3), 366.

George P. Livermore, Inc.; Perry v., TexCivApp–Amarillo, 165 SW2d 782.—Commerce 62.56, 62.62; Labor & Emp 2314.

Georges v. U.S., CA5 (Tex), 262 F2d 426.—Crim Law 274(2), 274(5), 1149; Ind & Inf 108; Statut 223.4.

Georges; Washington v., TexApp–San Antonio, 837 SW2d 146, writ den.—Lim of Act 55(3).

George S. May Co. v. Stephens Lumber Co., TexCivApp–Fort Worth, 301 SW2d 294.—App & E 930(3), 1062.1; Contracts 98; Pretrial Proc 309; Trial 352.10.

George S. May Intern. Co.; Fairmont Travel, Inc. v., SDTex, 75 FSupp2d 666.—Antitrust 209; Corp 336; Fed Cts 34, 303, 317, 350.1, 360; Rem of C 36, 74, 107(7).

George Staton Co., Inc.; Cleaver v., TexApp–Tyler, 908 SW2d 468, writ den.—Action 17; App & E 1031(1); Appear 9(1); Courts 39; Hus & W 251, 270(4), 270(5), 270(10); Infants 70; Mental H 472.1; Parties 1.

George Thomas Homes, Inc. v. Southwest Tension Systems, Inc., TexApp–El Paso, 763 SW2d 797.—Copyr 109; Interest 39(2.50); Trover 24, 41, 60, 72.

Georgetown Associates, Ltd. v. Home Federal Sav. & Loan Ass'n, TexApp–Houston (14 Dist), 795 SW2d 252, writ dism woj.—App & E 78(1); Guar 75; Judgm 181(22), 183; Mtg 209, 360, 369(2), 375.

Georgetown Builders, Inc. v. Tanksley's Heirs, TexCivApp–Austin, 498 SW2d 222, ref nre.—Adv Poss 22.

Georgetown, City of; Domel v., TexApp–Austin, 6 SW3d 349, review den, and reh of petition for review overr.—App & E 173(9), 934(1); Em Dom 2(10), 266; Judgm 185(6), 185.1(4), 634, 948(1); Nav Wat 36(1); Waters 3, 49, 117.

Georgetown, City of; Holloman v., TexCivApp–Austin, 526 SW2d 682, ref nre.—App & E 301, 758.3(9); Contracts 176(2); Damag 60; Mun Corp 374(4), 375; Trial 351.2(1.1), 352.10.

Georgetown, City of; Humble Oil & Refining Co. v., TexCivApp–Austin, 428 SW2d 405.—App & E 758.3(1); Courts 90(7); Jury 12(3); Mun Corp 111(3), 120, 595, 600.

Georgetown, City of; Walker v., TexApp–Austin, 86 SW3d 249, review den.—Action 13; App & E 78(1), 79(1), 80(1); Const Law 2475; Decl Judgm 301; Evid 264; Mun Corp 721(3), 870, 871; Statut 176, 181(1), 188, 206, 212.5, 212.6, 212.7.

Georgetown Sav. and Loan Ass'n; Stedman v., Tex, 595 SW2d 486.—App & E 931(1), 989, 1010.1(3); B & L Assoc 33(5), 33(21); Usury 1, 53, 119.

Georgetown Sav. and Loan Ass'n; Stedman v., TexCivApp–Fort Worth, 575 SW2d 415, writ gr, aff 595 SW2d 486.—B & L Assoc 33(5); Contracts 153.

Georgetown Sav. and Loan Ass'n; Urban Renewal Agency of City of Austin v., TexCivApp–Austin, 509 SW2d 419, ref nre.—Em Dom 202(4); Evid 142(1), 142(2).

George West Independent School Dist. v. Bartlett, TexCivApp–Eastland, 211 SW2d 1010, dism.—Em Dom 219, 221, 223, 262(5); Evid 546.

George West Independent School Dist.; Central Educ. Agency v., Tex, 783 SW2d 200.—Schools 133.6(7), 147.2(1).

George West Independent School Dist.; Central Educ. Agency v., TexApp–Austin, 750 SW2d 900, writ gr, aff in part, rev in part 783 SW2d 200.—Schools 133.6(7).

Georgia; Furman v., USTex, 92 SCt 2726, 408 U.S. 238, 33 LEd2d 346, reh den 93 SCt 89, 409 US 902, 34 LEd2d 163, reh den Jackson v. Georgia, 93 SCt 89, 409 US 902, 34 LEd2d 164, reh den Branch v Texas, 93 SCt 90, 409 US 902, 34 LEd2d 164, on remand Sullivan v State, 194 SE2d 410, 229 Ga 731, on remand Stanley v

State, 490 SW2d 828.—Const Law 4742, 4745, 4746; Sent & Pun 1612.

Georgiades v. Di Ferrante, TexApp–Houston (14 Dist), 871 SW2d 878, reh den, and writ den.—App & E 984(5); Decl Judgm 92.1, 361.1; Divorce 139; Inj 122, 140; Lim of Act 43; Pretrial Proc 223, 501, 508.

Georgia Home Ins. Co. v. Golden, TexComApp, 91 SW2d 695, 127 Tex 93.—Insurance 3451.

Georgia Home Ins. Co. v. Means, CA5 (Tex), 186 F2d 783.—Insurance 2151, 2201, 3577.

Georgia Home Ins. Co.; Trice v., TexCivApp–Amarillo, 81 SW2d 1055.—Estop 52.10(2); Insurance 1928, 2066, 3080, 3083, 3090, 3091, 3093, 3571; Princ & A 166(1).

Georgian Oil Corp. v. Chemical Process Co., TexCivApp–Eastland, 151 SW2d 280.—App & E 449; Courts 207.3.

Georgia-Pacific Corp.; Colbert v., NDTex, 995 FSupp 697.—Assault 18; Civil R 1113, 1182, 1189; Damag 50.10, 192, 208(6); Labor & Emp 2937; Work Comp 2084.

Georgia-Pacific Corp. v. Federal Power Commission, CA5 (Tex), 512 F2d 782.—Fed Cts 1158; Gas 2.

Georgia–Pacific Corp.; Martz v., TexApp–Eastland, 965 SW2d 584. See Martz v. Weyerhaeuser Co.

Georgia-Pacific Corp.; Tisdale v., CA5 (Tex), 854 F2d 773.—Fed Civ Proc 569, 2481.

Georgia-Pacific Corp.; Tullis v., TexApp–Fort Worth, 45 SW3d 118.—App & E 230, 241, 949; Courts 28; Judgm 181(7); Lim of Act 2(1), 180(1); Statut 217.2.

Georgia-Pacific Corp.; Wente v., TexApp–Austin, 712 SW2d 253.—Judgm 677; Parties 35.1, 35.9, 35.17, 35.71.

Georgoulis, In re, BkrtcyNDTex, 224 BR 360. See Thompson, In re.

Georgoulis v. Allied Products Corp., NDTex, 796 FSupp 986.—Decl Judgm 83.

Geoscan, Inc. of Texas v. Geotrace Technologies, Inc., CA5 (Tex), 226 F3d 387.—Contracts 143(2), 176(2); Copyr 41(1), 51, 75.5, 107; Fed Civ Proc 2492; Fed Cts 776.

Geosearch, Inc. v. Howell Petroleum Corp., CA5 (Tex), 819 F2d 521.—Fed Civ Proc 2197, 2211, 2242; Fraud 20, 28, 36, 58(4), 64(5).

Geosonic Corp.; Mitchell v., TexCivApp–Hous (1 Dist), 431 SW2d 958.—Bills & N 489(1); Judgm 185.3(16).

Geosource Drilling Services, Inc.; Roberts v., TexApp–Houston (1 Dist), 757 SW2d 48.—App & E 863; Contracts 52; Judgm 181(21), 185(2).

Geosource, Inc.; Kuehne & Nagel (AG & Co) v., CA5 (Tex), 874 F2d 283.—Adm 10(2), 12, 18; Fed Civ Proc 777, 2337, 2491, 2602; Fed Cts 24, 194, 275, 542, 621, 944; Jury 14(1).

Geosource, Inc.; Kuehne & Nagel (AG & CO) v., SDTex, 625 FSupp 794, on subsequent appeal 874 F2d 283.—Adm 10(2), 10(5), 12, 18, 22; Fed Cts 275.

Geosource, Inc. v. Panalpina Welttransport G.m.b.H., CA5 (Tex), 874 F2d 283. See Kuehne & Nagel (AG & Co) v. Geosource, Inc.

Geosource, Inc.; Panalpina Welttransport GmBh v., CA5 (Tex), 764 F2d 352.—Corp 1.4(4), 1.5(3); Fed Cts 275, 286.1, 298, 303.

GeoSouthern Energy Corp. v. Chesapeake Operating Inc., CA5 (Tex), 274 F3d 1017, reh den, cert den 123 SCt 75, 537 US 814, 154 LEd2d 17.—Contracts 143(1), 147(2); Fed Civ Proc 2470.2; Mines 74(3); Ref of Inst 17(1), 19(1), 45(2).

GeoSouthern Energy Corp. v. Chesapeake Operating, Inc., CA5 (Tex), 241 F3d 388.—Decl Judgm 392.1; Fed Cts 571, 584, 598.1, 660.1.

GeoSurveys, Inc. v. State Nat. Bank, TexApp–Eastland, 143 SW3d 220.—Alt Disp Res 114, 134(3), 134(6), 182(1), 182(2), 210, 324, 338, 374(1), 374(3); Banks 100, 227(3).

Geotech Energy Corp. v. Gulf States Telecommunications and Information Systems, Inc., TexApp–Houston (14 Dist), 788 SW2d 386.—Antitrust 363; App & E 1003(7), 1062.1, 1062.2, 1064.1(1); Contracts 294; Costs 194.32; Damag 62(4), 163(2); Pretrial Proc 713, 716; Sales 3.1, 4(4), 5; Tel 913(1), 916(7); Trial 295(1).

Geotechnical Services, Inc.; Franklin v., TexApp–Fort Worth, 819 SW2d 219, writ den.—Const Law 3965(3); Courts 12(2.1), 12(2.30); Pretrial Proc 201.1.

Geotrace Technologies, Inc.; Geoscan, Inc. of Texas v., CA5 (Tex), 226 F3d 387.—Contracts 143(2), 176(2); Copyr 41(1), 51, 75.5, 107; Fed Civ Proc 2492; Fed Cts 776.

Geo Viking, Inc. v. Tex-Lee Operating Co., TexApp–Texarkana, 817 SW2d 357, writ gr, and writ withdrawn, writ den with per curiam opinion 839 SW2d 797.—Antitrust 208, 369; Damag 22, 23, 189, 208(1); Evid 571(9); Interest 39(2.6), 39(2.30), 60; Mines 47, 109.

Geo-Western Petroleum Development, Inc. v. Mitchell, TexApp–Waco, 717 SW2d 734.—Mines 78.1(8), 78.1(9), 78.7(4); Stip 14(10), 17(1), 17(3).

Gephart v. Beto, CA5 (Tex), 441 F2d 319, cert den 92 SCt 342, 404 US 966, 30 LEd2d 286.—Hab Corp 490(1), 490(6).

Gephart v. State, TexCrimApp, 249 SW2d 612, 157 TexCrim 414.—Crim Law 331, 365(1), 369.2(6), 412.2(3), 474, 570(3), 589(1), 625.15, 696(7), 720(1), 922(7), 939(2), 939(4), 1036.1(2), 1159.5; Mental H 14.1, 16, 432; Rape 51(1).

GE Plastic Pacific PTE Ltd.; Hall v., CA5 (Tex), 327 F3d 391.—Estop 68(2); Fed Cts 433, 776.

G. E. Posey Corp.; Mira-Pak, Inc. v., TexCivApp–Waco, 566 SW2d 86, ref nre.—Brok 11; Indem 64.

G E Power Systems, Inc.; Hill v., CA5 (Tex), 282 F3d 343.—Alt Disp Res 112, 182(1), 191, 193, 196, 205, 213(2), 213(3), 213(5); Fed Cts 812.

Geraci; Scarth v., NDTex, 382 FSupp 876, opinion aff 510 F2d 1363.—Armed S 3, 16; Hab Corp 638.

Geraghty; Anderson v., TexCivApp–San Antonio, 212 SW2d 972.—App & E 193(5), 527.2, 909(1), 931(8); Courts 481; J P 15.

Geraghty v. Randals, TexCivApp–Waco, 224 SW2d 327.—Des & Dist 86; Ex & Ad 138(2); Wills 714, 734(1), 734(4), 742.

Geraghty and Miller, Inc. v. Conoco Inc., CA5 (Tex), 234 F3d 917, reh den 247 F3d 243, cert den 121 SCt 2592, 533 US 950, 150 LEd2d 751.—Contracts 9(1); Contrib 9(3); Environ Law 439, 445(1), 447, 670, 692; Fed Civ Proc 755, 2481, 2492, 2533.1; Fed Cts 914; Lim of Act 49(7), 55(2), 95(7), 95(9), 100(1), 105(2).

Geraghty and Miller, Inc. v. Conoco Inc., SDTex, 27 FSupp2d 918, aff in part, rev in part and remanded 234 F3d 917, reh den 247 F3d 243, cert den 121 SCt 2592, 533 US 950, 150 LEd2d 751.—Compromise 5(1), 12; Contrib 9(3); Environ Law 447; Lim of Act 95(7), 95(9), 100(12), 130(5).

Gerald; Carter v., TexCivApp–Austin, 577 SW2d 797, ref nre.—App & E 719(1), 1024.4; Judgm 181(11), 181(29), 183, 189; Spec Perf 92(1); Ven & Pur 75.

Gerald; Liberty Mut. Ins. Co. v., CA5 (Tex), 170 F2d 917.—Contracts 94(3); Fed Civ Proc 2252; Fed Cts 841; Work Comp 1148.

Gerald D. Hines, Inc.; O'Grady v., TexApp–Houston (14 Dist), 683 SW2d 763.—Contracts 143(2), 176(1); Labor & Emp 174, 256(6).

Gerald D. Hines Interests; O'Grady v., TexApp–Houston (14 Dist), 683 SW2d 763. See O'Grady v. Gerald D. Hines, Inc.

Gerami v. Gerami, TexApp–Houston (14 Dist), 666 SW2d 241.—Divorce 252.5(1).

Gerami; Gerami v., TexApp–Houston (14 Dist), 666 SW2d 241.—Divorce 252.5(1).

Gerant Industries, Inc.; Holder v., BkrtcyNDTex, 165 BR 22. See Omni Video, Inc., In re.

Gerard v. National Bond & Mortg. Corp., TexCivApp–Galveston, 86 SW2d 74, writ refused.—App & E 931(4); Elect of Rem 3(1), 9.

Gerard; U.S. v., EDTex, 781 FSupp 479.—Const Law 4657; Crim Law 339.6, 339.8(1), 339.8(5), 339.8(6), 339.8(7), 519(1), 530, 641.3(3), 641.3(10).

Gerber v. Hoffmann-La Roche Inc., SDTex, 392 FSupp2d 907.—Evid 219.65; Fed Civ Proc 928, 2653, 2655; Health 687(3); Prod Liab 1, 8, 11, 14, 15, 46.1, 46.2, 87.1; Sales 267, 284(1).

Gerber v. Pike, TexCivApp–Texarkana, 249 SW2d 90.—Autos 20; Sales 218, 234(1), 234(8), 244(3).

Gerber v. State, TexApp–Houston (1 Dist), 845 SW2d 460, petition for discretionary review refused.—Const Law 919; Crim Law 26, 772(6), 814(8), 1134(5), 1158(1), 1158(3), 1159.4(2), 1172.8; Homic 1492; Jury 33(5.15), 33(5.20), 120.

Gerber & Co., Inc. v. M/V Inagua Tania, SDTex, 828 FSupp 458. See J. Gerber & Co., Inc. v. M/V Inagua Tania.

Gerber Life Ins. Co.; Ervin v., TexCivApp–Beaumont, 566 SW2d 45, ref nre.—Insurance 3390; Judgm 185.1(1).

Gerdes; Corpus Christi Nat. Bank v., TexCivApp–Corpus Christi, 551 SW2d 521, ref nre.—App & E 882(14), 1062.5; Damag 87(2); Trusts 112, 231(1), 237; Wills 435, 439, 462, 463.

Gerdes v. First Nat. Bank at Brownsville, TexCivApp–Corpus Christi, 557 SW2d 840.—App & E 765, 773(2).

Gerdes v. G & H Towing Co., SDTex, 967 FSupp 943.—Damag 30.

Gerdes v. Kennamer, TexApp–Corpus Christi, 155 SW3d 541, reh overr.—App & E 115, 225, 946, 983(3); Corp 191; Evid 80(1); Execution 369, 371, 402(1), 402(3), 402(5).

Gerdes v. Kennamer, TexApp–Corpus Christi, 155 SW3d 523, reh overr, and review den, and reh of petition for review den.—App & E 169, 209.2(1), 213, 216(3), 216(7), 230, 231(7), 231(8), 231(9), 232(2), 237(5), 237(6), 238(2), 242(1), 294(1), 302(3), 302(6), 766, 852, 912, 989, 1024.3; Courts 103; New Tr 0.5, 128(1); Venue 1.5, 8.2, 17, 33, 54.

Gerdes v. Marion State Bank, TexApp–San Antonio, 774 SW2d 63, writ den.—App & E 440, 493, 650, 654; Proc 46.

Gerdes v. Mustang Exploration Co., TexApp–Corpus Christi, 666 SW2d 640.—App & E 846(5), 907(4); Contracts 9(1); Costs 194.32, 194.34, 208; Damag 87(2), 89(2); Judgm 19, 199(1).

Gerdes v. Tygrett, TexCivApp–Texarkana, 584 SW2d 350.—Acct Action on 12; Alt Disp Res 115; Judgm 181(15.1), 185(1).

Gerdes By and Through Griffin Chiropractic Clinic; Texas Farmers Ins. Co. v., TexApp–Fort Worth, 880 SW2d 215, reh overr, and writ den.—App & E 854(1), 870(2); Assign 132; Contracts 187(1); Insurance 1805, 1806, 1808, 1822, 1863, 3436, 3441.

Gereb v. Smith-Jaye, TexApp–San Antonio, 70 SW3d 272.—App & E 893(1); Costs 194.14, 194.32.

Gerety; City of Alamo Heights v., TexCivApp–San Antonio, 264 SW2d 778, ref nre.—Zoning 198.

Gerfers; Walzem Development Co., Inc. v., TexCivApp–San Antonio, 487 SW2d 219, ref nre.—Contracts 9(1); Ex & Ad 420; Frds St of 113(3); Spec Perf 8, 10(1), 28(1), 28(2), 30, 31.

Gerhardt; Houston Fire & Cas. Ins. Co. v., TexCivApp–San Antonio, 281 SW2d 176.—App & E 78(1); Courts 207.4(2); Mand 25, 28, 70, 73(1); Trial 355(1).

Gerhardt v. State, TexApp–Houston (1 Dist), 965 SW2d 55, petition for discretionary review refused.—Crim Law 43, 553, 655(4), 742(1), 1144.13(2.1), 1152(2), 1159.2(7); Jury 131(1), 131(10); Larc 40(2).

Gerhardt v. State, TexApp–Beaumont, 935 SW2d 192.—Const Law 4623; Crim Law 553, 655(5), 656(9), 867, 1035(8.1), 1035(10), 1044.1(3), 1159.3(2), 1177; Infants 13, 20.

Gerhardt; Welsch v., Tex, 583 SW2d 615.—Courts 100(1); Divorce 357.1.

Gerhardt v. Welsch, TexCivApp–San Antonio, 568 SW2d 873, ref nre, and writ gr, and writ withdrawn, rev 583 SW2d 615.—Action 6; Divorce 254(1), 322; Hus & W 249(3), 279(1); Judgm 815.

Gerhardt; Western Resources Life Ins. Co. v., TexCivApp–Austin, 553 SW2d 783, ref nre.—Corp 445, 445.1, 590(4); Insurance 1159, 3611(2).

Gerhart; Great American Homebuilders, Inc. v., TexApp–Houston (1 Dist), 708 SW2d 8, ref nre.—Antitrust 161, 291, 358, 369, 389(1), 390; Corp 1.7(2); Trial 105(2).

Gerhart v. Hayes, CA5 (Tex), 217 F3d 320, reh den, cert den 121 SCt 573, 531 US 1014, 148 LEd2d 491.—Colleges 8.1(3); Const Law 1183, 1947, 2021.

Gerhart v. Hayes, CA5 (Tex), 201 F3d 646, opinion superseded in part on denial of reh 217 F3d 320, reh den, cert den 121 SCt 573, 531 US 1014, 148 LEd2d 491, cert den 121 SCt 573, 531 US 1014, 148 LEd2d 491.—Const Law 3879, 4172(6); Fed Cts 753, 766; States 53.

Geringer, Ex parte, TexApp–Houston (1 Dist), 778 SW2d 132.—Hab Corp 525.1, 526, 712.1, 729.

Gerjets v. Davila, TexApp–Corpus Christi, 116 SW3d 864.—App & E 151(6), 946, 983(3); Const Law 3978; Corp 1.6(3); Execution 402(1); Inj 130, 143(1), 150.

Gerke v. Texas Health Enterprises, Inc., SDTex, 791 FSupp 662. See Sperling v. Texas Health Enterprises, Inc.

Gerlach v. Barnes, TexCivApp–Amarillo, 333 SW2d 648.—App & E 1010.1(3); Contracts 350(2); Fraud 66; Trial 358.

Gerlach; Punch v., Tex, 263 SW2d 770, 153 Tex 39.—App & E 638; Courts 85(1).

Gerlach; Punch v., TexCivApp–Beaumont, 267 SW2d 182, ref nre.—Evid 353(9), 461(2); Mines 77; Tresp to T T 40(4); Witn 159(3).

Gerlach; Punch v., TexCivApp–Beaumont, 260 SW2d 240, rev 263 SW2d 770, 153 Tex 39.—App & E 565, 655(3).

Gerland's Food Fair, Inc. v. Hare, TexCivApp–Hous (1 Dist), 611 SW2d 113, ref nre.—App & E 1013; Corp 507(13); Damag 130.3, 133, 163(1), 185(1), 191, 192; Evid 314(2), 318(2), 373(1), 474(3); Neglig 1524(3); Proc 145.

Gerlich; Nationwide Mut. Ins. Co. v., TexApp–San Antonio, 982 SW2d 456,reh overr, and review gr, rev Mid-Century Ins Co of Texas v. Kidd, 997 SW2d 265.—Insurance 2790, 2806, 2813.

Gerloff; Tondre v., TexCivApp–San Antonio, 257 SW2d 158, ref nre.—Trial 306; Wills 166(1), 357, 400.

German v. Baker, CA5 (Tex), 124 FedAppx 257, cert den 126 SCt 170, 546 US 868, 163 LEd2d 158.—Action 69(5); Civil R 1097; Fed Civ Proc 2734.

German; Renner v., TexCivApp–Amarillo, 207 SW2d 671, writ refused.—Wills 470(1), 470(3), 472, 545(2), 601(1).

Germania Farm Mut. Aid Ass'n v. Anderson, TexCivApp–Waco, 463 SW2d 24.—Insurance 3049(5), 3072; Judgm 199(3.9).

Germania Farm Mut. Ins. Ass'n; Ehrig v., TexApp–Corpus Christi, 84 SW3d 320, reh overr, and review den.—App & E 934(1); Judgm 181(7), 185(2), 185(6); Lim of Act 43, 46(6), 95(1), 199(1).

Germania Mut. Aid Ass'n v. Schaefer, TexCivApp–Eastland, 275 SW2d 137.—Frds St of 72(1), 119(2), 129(11); Insurance 1836, 3051; Propty 10.

Germania Mut. Aid Ass'n v. Trotti, TexCivApp–Austin, 318 SW2d 918.—Evid 443(2); Insurance 1642, 3092, 3445.

Germann v. Kaufman's, Inc., TexCivApp–San Antonio, 155 SW2d 969, writ refused wom.—App & E 929, 1050.1(6), 1069.1; Courts 85(3); Evid 171; Trial 351.5(5), 352.12, 412; Witn 258.

Germany v. Estelle, CA5 (Tex), 639 F2d 1301, cert den 102 SCt 290, 454 US 850, 70 LEd2d 140.—Crim Law 412.2(3), 1169.12; Hab Corp 495, 767.

Germany v. Frank G. Love Envelopes, Inc., TexCivApp–Texarkana, 582 SW2d 889, ref nre.—Judgm 181(33); Trover 22.

Germany; Kilday v., Tex, 163 SW2d 184, 139 Tex 380.— Elections 123, 126(5), 135; Statut 183.

Germany v. Pope, TexCivApp–Fort Worth, 222 SW2d 172, ref nre.—Inj 135, 144, 145, 147; Mun Corp 22, 48(2); Offic 39, 44, 104; Quo W 5.

Germany; Raynes v., TexCivApp–Fort Worth, 144 SW2d 981.—App & E 230, 231(1), 237(2), 766, 1001(1), 1050.1(2), 1050.1(3.1), 1050.1(8.1); Evid 106(1), 155(2); Judgm 720; Mines 79.7; New Tr 73; Plead 9; Trial 351.2(4); Witn 361(1).

Germany; Simmons v., TexCivApp–Texarkana, 231 SW2d 774.—App & E 1177(4); Neglig 259; Plead 111.3, 111.31, 111.38; Venue 8.5(3), 8.5(5), 8.5(6).

Germany v. State, TexCrimApp, 227 SW2d 815, 154 TexCrim 454.—Double J 131; Ind & Inf 119, 167; Int Liq 223(1).

Germany v. Turner, TexComApp, 123 SW2d 874, 132 Tex 491.—Covenants 28; Deeds 93, 97; Estop 37; Evid 65; Ten in C 43, 45.

Germany; Turner v., TexCivApp–Texarkana, 94 SW2d 1177, rev 123 SW2d 874, 132 Tex 491.—Deeds 44, 51, 87; Estop 22(1), 25, 26, 95; Ten in C 43, 44, 45; Trial 54(1); Ven & Pur 229(1), 239(9).

Gernandt; Wright v., TexCivApp–Corpus Christi, 559 SW2d 864.—App & E 719(1), 756, 758.3(3), 761, 832(4), 835(2), 930(3), 989, 1170.9(6), 1170.10; Damag 103, 105; Evid 474(19), 501(7); Land & Ten 37, 156; Ref of Inst 19(1), 19(2), 44; Trial 140(1), 142, 194(11), 350.8.

Geron; City of Sweetwater v., Tex, 380 SW2d 550.—Mun Corp 65, 185(1), 198(2), 218(1), 592(1).

Geron v. City of Sweetwater, TexCivApp–Eastland, 368 SW2d 151, writ gr, rev 380 SW2d 550.—Mun Corp 158, 185(1), 185(11), 186(4).

Gerron v. State, TexApp–Waco, 119 SW3d 371.—Autos 349(2.1), 355(6), 357, 411, 423; Crim Law 553, 704, 742(1), 747, 772(6), 777, 1144.13(1), 1144.13(3), 1159.2(1), 1159.2(2), 1159.3(1).

Gerron v. State, TexApp–Waco, 57 SW3d 568, petition for discretionary review gr, judgment vac 97 SW3d 597, on remand 119 SW3d 371.—Crim Law 777, 1134(2), 1173.1, 1173.2(5); Mun Corp 188.

Gerry, In re, TexApp–Tyler, 173 SW3d 901.—Atty & C 21.5(1); Mand 3(2.1), 4(4), 28.

Gersbach v. State, TexApp–Austin, 648 SW2d 423.— Autos 355(6); Ind & Inf 22.

Gersh v. State, TexApp–Dallas, 714 SW2d 80, petition for discretionary review refused by 738 SW2d 287.—Gas 2.

Gershowitz v. Lane Cotton Mills, NDTex, 21 FSupp 579. —Fed Cts 312.1; Judgm 206, 812(3); Rem of C 73, 75, 114, 116.

Gerson; Brown v., TexApp–Beaumont, 782 SW2d 226.— Des & Dist 71(1), 71(6); Trial 141.

Gerst v. Adam, TexCivApp–Austin, 403 SW2d 832.—B & L Assoc 2.1, 3.1(2), 3.1(3).

Gerst v. American Sav. & Loan Ass'n of Houston, TexCivApp–Austin, 384 SW2d 352, ref nre.—App & E 1051(1); B & L Assoc 3.5(3); Mand 168(4).

Gerst v. Cain, Tex, 388 SW2d 168.—B & L Assoc 1, 3.1(1), 3.1(3); Courts 89.

Gerst v. Cain, TexCivApp–Austin, 379 SW2d 699, writ gr, aff 388 SW2d 168.—Antitrust 610; B & L Assoc 3.1(2).

Gerst; Gibraltar Sav. Ass'n v., Tex, 417 SW2d 584.—B & L Assoc 2.1, 3.5(2).

Gerst v. Gibraltar Sav. Ass'n, TexCivApp–Austin, 413 SW2d 718, ref nre 417 SW2d 584.—B & L Assoc 3.1(1), 3.1(2), 3.1(3); Estop 68(2); Judgm 739; Trial 105(2).

Gerst v. Goldsbury, Tex, 434 SW2d 665.—B & L Assoc 3.1(1), 3.1(2), 3.1(3).

Gerst v. Goldsbury, TexCivApp–Austin, 425 SW2d 14, writ gr, rev 434 SW2d 665.—B & L Assoc 3.1(1), 3.1(2).

Gerst v. Guardian Sav. & Loan Ass'n, Tex, 434 SW2d 113.—B & L Assoc 2.1, 3.1(1), 3.5(2), 3.5(3); Evid 83(1).

Gerst v. Guardian Sav. & Loan Ass'n, TexCivApp–Austin, 425 SW2d 382, writ gr, aff in part, rev in part 434 SW2d 113.—Admin Law 489.1; App & E 747(1); B & L Assoc 3.5(1), 3.5(2).

Gerst v. Houston First Sav. Ass'n, TexCivApp–Austin, 422 SW2d 514.—Banks 6; B & L Assoc 3.1(1), 3.5(2), 3.5(3).

Gerst v. Jefferson County Sav. & Loan Ass'n, TexCivApp–Austin, 390 SW2d 318, ref nre.—Admin Law 817.1; B & L Assoc 2.1, 3.5(1), 3.5(2), 3.5(3); Const Law 2400, 2600; Estop 98(1).

Gerst v. Nixon, Tex, 411 SW2d 350.—Admin Law 676, 751, 788, 791; App & E 843(1); B & L Assoc 3.1(1), 3.1(2), 3.1(3); Const Law 2356, 2564; Statut 64(2).

Gerst; Nixon v., TexCivApp–Austin, 412 SW2d 701, ref nre.—B & L Assoc 3.1(2), 3.1(3).

Gerst v. Nixon, TexCivApp–Austin, 399 SW2d 845, writ gr, aff 411 SW2d 350.—B & L Assoc 3.1(1), 3.1(2), 3.1(3).

Gerst v. Oak Cliff Sav. & Loan Ass'n, Tex, 432 SW2d 702.—Admin Law 386, 791; B & L Assoc 1, 2.1, 3.5(1), 3.5(2), 3.5(3); Statut 205.

Gerst v. Oak Cliff Sav. & Loan Ass'n, TexCivApp–Austin, 421 SW2d 449, rev 432 SW2d 702.—Admin Law 390.1; B & L Assoc 2.1, 3.5(1), 3.5(2); Statut 212.1.

Gerst; Spring Branch Sav. & Loan Ass'n v., TexCivApp–Austin, 420 SW2d 618, ref nre.—B & L Assoc 3.5(1), 3.5(2), 3.5(3); Equity 72(1).

Gerstacker v. Blum Consulting Engineers, Inc., Tex-App–Dallas, 884 SW2d 845, writ den.—Evid 208(0.5); Frds St of 43, 44(3), 46, 49, 119(1), 159; Judgm 178, 181(11), 185(2), 185.1(1), 185.1(8), 185.2(5); Labor & Emp 40(2), 40(3).

Gerstner v. Wilhelm, TexCivApp–Austin, 584 SW2d 955, writ dism.—App & E 756, 761; Damag 91(1); Ease 58(3), 61(9), 61(9 1/2), 61(11); Trial 350.3(2.1).

Gertner v. Hospital Affiliates Intern., Inc., CA5 (Tex), 602 F2d 685.—Fed Civ Proc 215, 2492.

Gertner, Aron & Ledet Investments; Turboff v., Tex-App–Corpus Christi, 840 SW2d 603, reh overr, and writ dism.—App & E 1097(1); Compromise 16(1); Contracts 218, 221(1), 221(2); Damag 63, 120(1); Indem 27, 33(1), 42; Ven & Pur 168.

Gertner, Aron & Ledet Investments; Turboff v., Tex-App–Houston (14 Dist), 763 SW2d 827, writ den, appeal after remand 840 SW2d 603, reh overr, and writ dism.— Judgm 181(19).

Gertner-Aron-Ledet Associates v. Dallas Tailor & Laundry Supply, TexApp–Dallas, 654 SW2d 579.—App & E 846(5), 931(5); Plead 111.15, 111.38.

Gervacio-Angel; U.S. v., CA5 (Tex), 145 FedAppx 78, cert den Ramirez-Garcia v. US, 126 SCt 497, 546 US 967, 163 LEd2d 376.—Crim Law 1042.

Gervin, In re, BkrtcyWDTex, 337 BR 854.—Bankr 2126, 2134, 2187, 2363.1, 2466, 2467.

Gervin v. Gervin, TexApp–San Antonio, 720 SW2d 150.— Divorce 184(1), 227(1).

Gervin; Gervin v., TexApp–San Antonio, 720 SW2d 150.— Divorce 184(1), 227(1).

Gervitz-Faram; Faram v., TexApp–Fort Worth, 895 SW2d 839, reh overr.—App & E 900, 931(1), 946, 989, 1010.1(1), 1010.1(2), 1010.1(5), 1010.2, 1012.1(1), 1182; Divorce 252.1, 252.2, 253(2), 254(1), 286(5); Evid 596(1); Hus & W 264(2), 264(4).

Gerwell v. Moran, TexApp–San Antonio, 10 SW3d 28.— Alt Disp Res 134(1), 134(3), 139, 143, 213(5).

Gerzin v. Beto, CA5 (Tex), 459 F2d 671.—Hab Corp 827, 862.1.

Gerzin v. State, TexCrimApp, 447 SW2d 925, cert den 90 SCt 1710, 398 US 912, 26 LEd2d 73.—Rob 17(3), 24.20, 24.35.

Gesek, Ex parte, TexCrimApp, 302 SW2d 417, 164 Tex-Crim 652.—Evid 80(1); Extrad 32, 36, 39.

Gessell v. Traweek, TexApp–Texarkana, 628 SW2d 479, ref nre.—Labor & Emp 3031(1), 3031(2), 3125, 3159, 3162; Land & Ten 167(1); Princ & A 150(2), 159(1).

Gessmann v. Stephens, TexApp–Tyler, 51 SW3d 329.—App & E 843(2), 852, 893(1), 914.3, 1024.3, 1135; Appear 9(1); Const Law 3964, 3965(4); Corp 665(1); Courts 12(2.1), 12(2.5), 12(2.10), 12(2.15), 12(2.25); Motions 31; Sales 201(2).

Geter, Ex parte, TexCrimApp, 383 SW2d 405.—Crim Law 641.4(2); Hab Corp 721(1).

Geter v. Fortenberry, CA5 (Tex), 882 F2d 167.—Civil R 1376(6); Fed Civ Proc 1272.1, 2491.5.

Geter v. Fortenberry, CA5 (Tex), 849 F2d 1550.—Civil R 1088(5), 1375, 1376(6), 1376(9), 1398; Fed Civ Proc 1825, 2491.5.

Geter v. State, TexCrimApp, 779 SW2d 403, on remand 790 SW2d 703.—Crim Law 1167(1), 1181.5(3.1); Ind & Inf 110(3), 110(4), 137(6); Larc 34.

Geter v. State, TexApp–Tyler, 795 SW2d 208, petition for discretionary review gr, vac 779 SW2d 403, on remand 790 SW2d 703.—Larc 12, 26, 28(2).

Geter v. State, TexApp–Tyler, 790 SW2d 703.—Crim Law 1167(1).

Geters v. Eagle Ins. Co., Tex, 834 SW2d 49.—Damag 15; Licens 26; Princ & S 66(1); Statut 188.

Geters v. Eagle Ins. Co., TexApp–Houston (14 Dist), 824 SW2d 664, writ gr, rev 834 SW2d 49.—App & E 223, 901; Costs 194.40; Insurance 2407; Princ & S 66(1).

Get N Go No. 103; Ramirez v., TexApp–Corpus Christi, 888 SW2d 29, opinion on merits not for publication, and writ den.—App & E 345.1; New Tr 109.

G. E. T. Service Co.; Ayco Development Corp. v., Tex, 616 SW2d 184.—App & E 1178(6); Joint Adv 1.2(1); Mines 101.

G. E. T. Service Co.; Energy Fund of America, Inc. v., TexCivApp–Eastland, 610 SW2d 833, aff in part, rev in part Ayco Development Corp v. G E T Service Co, 616 SW2d 184.—Mines 101, 109, 114.

Gette v. State, TexApp–Houston (1 Dist), 209 SW3d 139.—Autos 418; Colleges 6(5); Crim Law 304(12), 394.6(4), 394.6(5), 1134(3), 1139, 1144.12, 1153(1), 1158(4).

Getters v. State, TexCrimApp, 340 SW2d 806, 170 Tex-Crim 331.—Controlled Subs 68, 74.

Gettler; True v., TexCivApp–El Paso, 256 SW2d 958, writ refused.—Partners 213(2), 216(1), 217(3).

Getto v. Gray, TexApp–Houston (1 Dist), 627 SW2d 437, ref nre.—App & E 931(1), 989, 1008.1(1), 1175(1), 1177(1); Paymt 45; Ven & Pur 93, 101, 182.

Getts v. State, TexCrimApp, 155 SW3d 153.—Autos 359.6; Statut 188, 189, 214, 217.4.

Getts v. State, TexApp–Tyler, 156 SW3d 593, petition for discretionary review gr, reh overr 2003 WL 22956392, aff 155 SW3d 153.—Autos 359.6; Crim Law 1148.

Getty v. Kinzbach Tool Co., CCA5 (Tex), 119 F2d 249, cert den 62 SCt 97, 314 US 651, 86 LEd 522.—Pat 233.1, 246, 247.

Getty Oil Co. v. Blevco Energy, Inc., TexApp–Eastland, 722 SW2d 51, ref nre, and writ withdrawn, and writ gr, cause dism 770 SW2d 569.—Damag 89(2); Mines 74(8).

Getty Oil Co. v. Corbin, TexApp–San Antonio, 653 SW2d 342, writ gr, and cause dism.—App & E 846(5); Plead 111.9, 111.23, 111.38; Venue 5.3(1), 5.3(8).

Getty Oil Co. v. Insurance Co. of North America, Tex, 845 SW2d 794, motion to stay mandate den, cert den Youell & Companies v. Getty Oil Co, 114 SCt 76, 510 US 820, 126 LEd2d 45.—Indem 27, 30(1); Insurance 1702, 2272; Judgm 619, 675(1), 677, 678(1), 681, 704, 713(2), 715(1), 715(3), 720, 724, 739.

Getty Oil Co. v. Insurance Co. of North America, TexApp–Houston (14 Dist), 819 SW2d 908, writ gr, aff in part, rev in part 845 SW2d 794, motion to stay mandate den, cert den Youell & Companies v. Getty Oil

Co, 114 SCt 76, 510 US 820, 126 LEd2d 45.—Indem 30(1); Judgm 540, 585(1), 587, 590(1), 713(2), 720.

Getty Oil Co. v. Jones, Tex, 470 SW2d 618, 53 ALR3d 1.—App & E 1097(6); Mines 52, 73.1(6); Trial 352.10.

Getty Oil Co.; Jones v., TexCivApp–San Antonio, 458 SW2d 93, aff 470 SW2d 618, 53 ALR3d 1.—App & E 934(1), 989; Mines 73.1(6); Trial 352.1(4), 352.10.

Getty Oil Co. v. Occupational Safety and Health Review Com'n, CA5 (Tex), 530 F2d 1143.—Labor & Emp 2555, 2577, 2606.

Getty Oil Co. v. Royal, TexCivApp–Beaumont, 422 SW2d 591, ref nre.—App & E 1056.1(4.1); Mines 52, 62.1, 73.1(6).

Getty Oil Co.; Shown v., TexApp–San Antonio, 645 SW2d 555, writ refused.—Mines 56, 78.1(1), 78.1(3), 78.1(7), 78.1(8).

Getty Oil Co.; Volvo Petroleum, Inc. v., TexApp–Houston (14 Dist), 717 SW2d 134.—Acct Action on 10, 13; Corp 445.1, 590(1); Judgm 181(29), 183, 185(2); Pretrial Proc 483.

Getty Oil Corp. v. Duncan, TexApp–Corpus Christi, 721 SW2d 475, ref nre.—App & E 781(6); Explos 10; Indem 33(5), 81.

Getty Oil Corp., a Div. of Texaco, Inc. v. Insurance Co. of North America, CA5 (Tex), 841 F2d 1254.—Fed Cts 286.1, 302, 314, 317, 319, 939; Rem of C 79(1), 82, 94, 105, 107(0.5), 107(7).

Getty Reserve Oil, Inc.; Brown v., TexApp–Amarillo, 626 SW2d 810, dism.—Interpl 35; Mines 55(4), 79.1(5).

Gettysburg Corp.; Federal Deposit Ins. Corp. v., SDTex, 760 FSupp 115, aff Unitedbank v. Gettysburg Corp, 952 F2d 400, cert den Lively v FDIC, 113 SCt 70, 506 US 821, 121 LEd2d 36.—Banks 505, 508; Fraud 7; Sec Tran 240.

Gettysburg Homeowners Ass'n, Inc. v. Olson, TexApp–Houston (14 Dist), 768 SW2d 369.—Inj 147.

Getz, In re, BkrtcyNDTex, 224 BR 360. See Thompson, In re.

Getz v. Boston Sea Party of Houston, Inc., TexCivApp–Hous (1 Dist), 573 SW2d 836.—Ease 15.1, 17(5), 61(6); Inj 132.

Getz v. Collins, TexCivApp–Texarkana, 303 SW2d 818.—App & E 1078(5); Plead 428(7); Stip 14(12).

Getz; Dean v., TexApp–Tyler, 970 SW2d 629.—Ex & Ad 1, 15, 18, 20(7), 20(8), 20(10).

Getz v. Edinburg Consol. Independent School Dist., CCA5 (Tex), 101 F2d 734, cert dism 60 SCt 63, 308 US 628, 84 LEd 524.—Bankr 2251; Const Law 2673.

Getz; Sawyer v., TexCivApp–Eastland, 398 SW2d 376, ref nre.—Equity 84; Judgm 178, 185(2), 185.3(2), 186.

Getzwiller v. Fergeson, TexCivApp–Amarillo, 145 SW2d 913.—App & E 760(1), 1050.1(4), 1070(2); Autos 217(3), 247; Trial 358.

Geuder v. State, TexCrimApp, 115 SW3d 11, on remand 142 SW3d 372, reh overr, and petition for discretionary review refused.—Crim Law 632(4), 1044.2(1).

Geuder v. State, TexApp–Houston (14 Dist), 142 SW3d 372, reh overr, and petition for discretionary review refused.—Crim Law 1134(2), 1141(2), 1162, 1163(1), 1165(1), 1169.1(1), 1170.5(1); Witn 319.

Geuder v. State, TexApp–Houston (14 Dist), 76 SW3d 133, petition for discretionary review gr, vac 115 SW3d 11, on remand 142 SW3d 372, reh overr, and petition for discretionary review refused.—Crim Law 709, 719(1), 720(6), 722.5, 723(3), 726, 730(1), 730(7), 730(13), 814(13), 867, 1036.2, 1173.5; False Pret 22, 39.

Gevinson v. Manhattan Const. Co. of Okl., Tex, 449 SW2d 458.—App & E 291, 1152; Estop 118; Evid 80(1), 207(1), 211, 215(1), 234, 265(7), 590, 591; Mtg 391; Partners 227; Plgs 53; Trial 140(2).

Gevinson v. Manhattan Const. Co. of Okl., TexCivApp–Fort Worth, 420 SW2d 486, rev 449 SW2d 458.—App & E 1175(3), 1178(8); Partners 3, 69.

Gevinson v. Stephen-Leedom Carpet Co., TexCivApp–Dallas, 368 SW2d 700.—Mech Liens 3, 61, 144, 147, 148; Plead 373; Venue 22(6).

Gevinson v. U.S., CA5 (Tex), 358 F2d 761, cert den 87 SCt 51, 385 US 823, 17 LEd2d 60.—Crim Law 627.5(2), 627.5(4), 1144.13(3); Fraud 69(2), 69(5), 69(6), 69(7); Ind & Inf 110(15).

Gevinson Associates v. Ling Elec., Inc., TexCivApp–Dallas, 373 SW2d 564.—App & E 863; Costs 194.32; Judgm 181(19), 185(2), 185.3(13).

Gex v. Foster, TexCivApp–Amarillo, 495 SW2d 370, ref nre.—App & E 846(5), 854(1); Brok 39; Contracts 143.5; Evid 450(8); Interest 67; Trial 136(3).

Gex v. Texas Co., TexCivApp–Amarillo, 337 SW2d 820, ref nre.—Afft 9; Contracts 147(3); Deeds 90, 93, 97, 120, 154; Evid 20(1); Judgm 185(2), 185.3(17); Mines 55(2), 55(3), 55(5).

GEXA Corp.; Holland v., CA5 (Tex), 161 FedAppx 364.—Fed Cts 18; Sec Reg 25.56, 25.62(3), 60.37.

Geye; American Cyanamid Co. v., Tex, 79 SW3d 21, cert den 123 SCt 2637, 539 US 969, 156 LEd2d 674.—Environ Law 16, 411; States 18.3, 18.5, 18.7, 18.11, 18.65.

Geye v. American Cyanamid Co., TexApp–Eastland, 32 SW3d 916, review gr, aff 79 SW3d 21, cert den 123 SCt 2637, 539 US 969, 156 LEd2d 674.—Environ Law 411; Prod Liab 43.5; States 18.11, 18.65.

Geyer; Albright v., CCA5 (Tex), 108 F2d 578.—Contracts 9(2), 311.

Geyer; City of Wichita Falls v., TexCivApp–Fort Worth, 170 SW2d 615, writ refused wom.—Autos 261, 273, 293, 306(5); Damag 187; Mun Corp 794, 812(2), 819(6).

Geyer v. Jones, TexCivApp–San Antonio, 93 SW2d 1192, writ dism.—App & E 544(1); Lim of Act 66(12); Plead 111.9.

Geyer; Ortiz Oil Co. v., TexComApp, 159 SW2d 494, 138 Tex 373.—Accord 1, 10(1); Lim of Act 24(2); Mines 79.3, 79.7; Stip 14(12); Trial 351.2(4).

Geyer v. Ortiz Oil Co., TexCivApp–Texarkana, 134 SW2d 814, aff 159 SW2d 494, 138 Tex 373.—Accord 1; Mines 79.3.

Geyer v. State, TexCrimApp, 287 SW2d 948, 162 TexCrim 531.—Autos 351.1; Crim Law 995(3).

Geyser Ice Co. v. Sharp, TexCivApp–Waco, 87 SW2d 883.—Contracts 147(1), 169, 170(1); Evid 442(1), 443(2); Labor & Emp 57; Plead 382(1); Release 30, 53.

G.F.C. Corp.; Ed Hoffman Motors v., TexCivApp–San Antonio, 304 SW2d 216, ref nre.—Contracts 245(1); Sales 475.

G. F. C. Corp.; Pitts v., TexCivApp–Dallas, 228 SW2d 261.—Chat Mtg 235, 281, 289; Paymt 21; Receivers 57.

G. F. C. Corp. v. Williams, TexCivApp–Dallas, 231 SW2d 565.—Insurance 1904; Usury 32, 142(4).

GFH Financial Services Corp.; Pierson v., TexApp–Austin, 829 SW2d 311.—App & E 177, 219(2), 846(5), 852; Lim of Act 55(5), 66(14), 95(7), 197(1); Sec Tran 10, 25; Trover 1, 2, 4, 10, 72.

GFH Financial Services, Inc.; Hoelscher v., TexApp–Dallas, 814 SW2d 842, extension of time to file for writ of error overr.—Antitrust 136; App & E 878(1), 918(1); Evid 18; Plead 234, 245(1), 258(1), 262.

GFI Computer Industries, Inc. v. Fry, CA5 (Tex), 476 F2d 1.—Fed Civ Proc 1534, 1636.1, 1741, 2415; Witn 4.

G.F.O., Matter of, TexApp–Houston (1 Dist), 874 SW2d 729.—App & E 1012.1(4); Evid 369.1; Gr Jury 36.8; Infants 68.7(3), 68.8.

G.F.S. Ventures, Inc. v. Harris, TexApp–Houston (1 Dist), 934 SW2d 813.—App & E 5, 914(1); Corp 507(12), 507(14), 668(14); Proc 145, 149.

GFTA Trendanalysen B.G.A. Herrdum GMBH & Co., K.G. v. Varme, Tex, 991 SW2d 785, on remand 2000 WL 702635.—Appear 9(2).

G.F. Vaughan Tobacco Co., Inc.; Sanchez v., SDTex, 213 FRD 519.—Fed Civ Proc 414.

GGE Management Co. v. Commerce Sav. Ass'n of Brazoria County, Tex, 543 SW2d 862.—Interest 31.

GGE Management Co.; Commerce Sav. Ass'n of Brazoria County v., TexCivApp–Hous (1 Dist), 539 SW2d 71, mod 543 SW2d 862.—Bills & N 134; B & L Assoc 26; Guar 27, 34, 36(9), 41, 72; Usury 22, 50, 52, 53, 55, 109, 117, 119, 137.

GGM, P.C., In re, CA5 (Tex), 165 F3d 1026.—Bankr 3771, 3779, 3782, 3786, 3787; Contracts 175(1), 187(1); Corp 82; Estop 52.10(2); Sur Tran 239, 240.

G.H. v. State, TexApp–Houston (1 Dist), 96 SW3d 629.—App & E 931(1), 1010.1(1), 1010.1(3); Evid 596(1); Mental H 41, 45, 51.15.

G.H. v. State, TexApp–Houston (14 Dist), 94 SW3d 115.—Mental H 36.

Ghaleh-Assadi; Taherzadeh v., TexApp–Dallas, 108 SW3d 927, review den.—App & E 966(1); Breach of P 21; Pretrial Proc 723.1, 724.

Ghali; U.S. v., CA5 (Tex), 184 FedAppx 391, cert den 127 SCt 527, 166 LEd2d 391.—Crim Law 394.1(3); Sent & Pun 760, 761.

Ghali; U.S. v., NDTex, 317 FSupp2d 708, aff 184 FedAppx 391, cert den 127 SCt 527, 166 LEd2d 391.—Carr 71; Crim Law 394.1(3), 394.5(4), 394.6(4); Searches 26, 34, 161, 162, 164, 185.

Ghanem, In re, TexApp–Beaumont, 203 SW3d 896.—Alt Disp Res 113, 114, 191, 196; Mand 4(1), 28.

Ghanem v. Upchurch, CA5 (Tex), 481 F3d 222.—Aliens 207; Fed Cts 18.

Gharbi v. Blakeway, CA5 (Tex), 191 FedAppx 253.—Aliens 726.

Gharbi v. State, TexCrimApp, 131 SW3d 481.—Breach of P 15.1; Crim Law 1032(6).

Ghashim v. State, TexApp–Austin, 104 SW3d 184.—Estop 52.15, 62.2(2); Evid 318(7); Tax 3692, 3708.

Ghazali v. Southland Corp., TexApp–San Antonio, 669 SW2d 770.—Death 93; Judgm 178, 181(13); Labor & Emp 2832, 2842, 2848, 2870, 2901; Neglig 273, 1697; Plead 42; Work Comp 2145, 2149, 2152, 2153, 2155.

G.H. Bass & Co. v. Dalsan Properties-Abilene, TexApp–Dallas, 885 SW2d 572.—Contracts 147(2), 147(3), 153; Estop 52.10(2), 52.10(3); Judgm 178, 181(15.1), 183, 185(2), 185(6), 186; Princ & S 59, 66(2), 71.

Gheen v. Diamond Shamrock Corp., TexCivApp–Waco, 529 SW2d 289.—Contracts 318; Ease 61(9); Tender 13(1), 15(5).

G. Heileman Brewing Co.; Witherspoon v., TexCivApp–Texarkana, 144 SW2d 1017.—Hus & W 86, 229.3.

Ghiasinejad; Law Offices of Windle Turley, P.C. v., TexApp–Fort Worth, 109 SW3d 68.—App & E 946, 949; Parties 40(2), 40(5), 41, 44.

Ghiatas; Silvas v., TexApp–San Antonio, 954 SW2d 50, reh overr, and review den.—Evid 538; Judgm 185(2), 185.3(21).

Ghidoni, In re, CA5 (Tex), 99 FedAppx 517.—Bankr 3032.1, 3033.

Ghidoni v. Stone Oak, Inc., TexApp–San Antonio, 966 SW2d 573, reh overr, and review den, and reh of petition for review overr.—App & E 236(1), 927(7), 949, 984(5), 1002, 1061.4, 1062.2, 1178(1); Atty & C 19, 21.5(1), 21.20; Can of Inst 23, 24(2); Compromise 24; Consp 1.1, 2, 8; Contracts 236, 247; Costs 194.40; Decl Judgm 186; Evid 571(3); Inj 189; Land & Ten 112.5; Parties 44; Trial 139.1(7), 143, 351.2(4); Trover 4, 46, 66.

Ghiglieri v. Ludwig, CA5 (Tex), 125 F3d 941, cert den 118 SCt 1361, 523 US 1046, 140 LEd2d 511.—Banks 236, 239.

Ghiglieri v. Sun World Nat. Ass'n, CA5 (Tex), 117 F3d 309, cert den 118 SCt 1361, 523 US 1046, 140 LEd2d 511.—Banks 235, 236, 239; Statut 219(1), 219(2).

Ghiglieri v. Sun World, Nat. Ass'n, WDTex, 942 FSupp 1111, vac 117 F3d 309, cert den 118 SCt 1361, 523 US

1046, 140 LEd2d 511.—Banks 233, 235, 236, 239; Statut 219(5).

Ghilain; Mills v., TexApp–Corpus Christi, 68 SW3d 141. —App & E 105, 984(1), 1024.1; Atty & C 36(2), 52, 54; Const Law 4426; Costs 2.

Ghio v. Jambon, SDTex, 23 FSupp2d 724.—Const Law 3964; Fed Cts 76, 76.5, 76.10, 96; Seamen 29(1), 29(5.4), 29(5.5); Ship 41, 50.

Gholson; City of Ranger v., TexCivApp–Eastland, 141 SW2d 396, writ dism, correct.—Ex & Ad 225(1), 437(7); Lim of Act 83(2), 127(12), 130(7); Mech Liens 61, 68; Mun Corp 586.

Gholson v. Estelle, CA5 (Tex), 675 F2d 734.—Const Law 4744(2); Crim Law 393(1), 412.2(3), 641.3(11), 641.12(2), 899; Sent & Pun 1769; Witn 390.

Gholson v. Northside Chevrolet Co., TexCivApp–Fort Worth, 90 SW2d 579.—Chat Mtg 183; Judgm 16; J P 44(7).

Gholson v. Parrish, TexCivApp–Fort Worth, 92 SW2d 1113.—Autos 178; Neglig 250.

Gholson v. Peeks, TexCivApp–Eastland, 224 SW2d 778, writ refused.—Evid 17, 20(1); Mtg 342, 372(1); Tresp to T T 6.1, 6.2, 33; Usury 113, 117.

Gholson v. State, TexCrimApp, 542 SW2d 395, cert den 97 SCt 2960, 432 US 911, 53 LEd2d 1084, reh den 98 SCt 247, 434 US 882, 54 LEd2d 166.—Arrest 63.5(6), 63.5(9); Crim Law 338(7), 379, 419(1), 641.3(11), 726, 730(1), 730(14), 730(16), 1168(2); Sent & Pun 1624, 1769; Witn 274(1).

Gholson v. State, TexApp–Houston (14 Dist), 5 SW3d 266, reh overr, and petition for discretionary review refused. —Crim Law 641.13(1), 641.13(7), 749, 789(1), 795(2.10), 795(2.80), 796, 824(12), 1030(1), 1038.2; Ind & Inf 189(1).

Gholson v. State, TexApp–Houston (14 Dist), 667 SW2d 168, petition for discretionary review refused.—Const Law 769, 859, 1140, 1163, 1164, 2190, 2191, 4768; Crim Law 641.13(7), 1099.1, 1100, 1133; Ind & Inf 41(1), 41(3); Obscen 2.1, 2.5, 17.

Gholson v. Thorn, TexCivApp–Dallas, 597 SW2d 568.— App & E 344, 347(1), 621(3); Judges 32; Judgm 191, 215.

Gholson v. Wilmoth, TexCivApp–Texarkana, 225 SW2d 605, ref nre.—App & E 907(3); Child C 261, 579, 602, 852.

Ghoman v. New Hampshire Ins. Co., NDTex, 159 FSupp2d 928.—Fed Civ Proc 2501, 2534, 2545, 2554; Insurance 2172, 2181, 2182, 2185.

GHR Companies, Inc., In re, BkrtcySDTex, 79 BR 663. See TransAmerican Natural Gas Corp., In re.

GHR Energy Corp., In re, CA5 (Tex), 791 F2d 1200.— Bankr 3777; Fed Cts 707.1, 709.

GHR Energy Corp., In re, CA5 (Tex), 789 F2d 1194.— Bankr 3774.1.

GHR Energy Corp., In re, BkrtcySDTex, 66 BR 54.— Bankr 3103.2, 3104.

GHR Energy Corp., In re, BkrtcySDTex, 62 BR 226.— Bankr 3115.1; Damag 6; Estop 68(2), 85, 97; Fed Civ Proc 2470.1, 2486; Judgm 651.

GHR Energy Corp., In re, BkrtcySDTex, 60 BR 52.— Atty & C 21.5(6), 21.15, 21.20, 22; Bankr 2045, 3177.

GHR Energy Corp., Matter of, CA5 (Tex), 972 F2d 96, reh den 979 F2d 40,cert den Medallion Oil Co v. Transamerican Natural Gas Corp, 113 SCt 1879, 507 US 1042, 123 LEd2d 497.—Mines 74(5).

GHR Energy Corp., Matter of, CA5 (Tex), 792 F2d 476. —Bankr 3779.

GHR Energy Corp. v. Crispin Co. Ltd., CA5 (Tex), 791 F2d 1200. See GHR Energy Corp., In re.

GHR Energy Corp.; Kelley v., CA5 (Tex), 792 F2d 476. See GHR Energy Corp., Matter of.

GHR Energy Corp.; NL Industries, Inc. v., CA5 (Tex), 940 F2d 957, cert den 112 SCt 873, 502 US 1032, 116 LEd2d 778.—Alt Disp Res 231, 247, 382, 383; Bankr 2871; Contracts 176(2), 320; Fed Civ Proc 841, 2506,

2533.1, 2547.1; Fed Cts 766, 776; Mines 74(3), 79.2, 109; Neglig 234.

GHR Energy Corp. v. Texas Drilling Co., CA5 (Tex), 789 F2d 1194. See GHR Energy Corp., In re.

GHR Energy Corp.; Toma Steel Supply, Inc. v., CA5 (Tex), 978 F2d 1409. See TransAmerican Natural Gas Corp., Matter of.

GHR Energy Corp.; 523 North Belt Associates v., BkrtcySDTex, 66 BR 54. See GHR Energy Corp., In re.

Giacomel; U.S. v., CA5 (Tex), 153 F3d 257.—Const Law 4836; Crim Law 1618(10), 1650.

Giacomini, S.p.A.; Bryant v., NDTex, 391 FSupp2d 495. —Fed Civ Proc 2515; Prod Liab 8, 11, 14, 15, 62; Sales 260, 273(3).

Giacomino; Travelers Ins. Co. v., TexCivApp–Beaumont, 99 SW2d 632.—Trial 351.2(9), 352.9; Work Comp 1404, 1929.

Giacona, Ex parte, TexCrimApp, 518 SW2d 832.—Courts 100(1); Sent & Pun 1257.

Giacona v. Beto, CA5 (Tex), 377 F2d 280.—Const Law 4729.

Giacona v. Capricorn Shipping Co., SDTex, 394 FSupp 1189.—Adm 1.15; Rem of C 3, 19(5).

Giacona v. Marubeni Oceano (Panama) Corp., SDTex, 623 FSupp 1560.—Adm 1.20(2); Contracts 166, 229(1); Indem 30(1), 30(8), 35; Ship 84(3.2); Wharves 17.

Giacona v. State, TexCrimApp, 397 SW2d 863.—Controlled Subs 80; Searches 183; Sent & Pun 1358, 1362.

Giacona v. State, TexCrimApp, 372 SW2d 328, cert den 84 SCt 92, 375 US 843, 11 LEd2d 70.—Arrest 63.4(13), 71.1(1); Controlled Subs 80; Crim Law 394.1(1), 394.4(2), 394.4(9), 1070; Searches 23, 24, 80.1.

Giacona v. State, TexCrimApp, 335 SW2d 837, 169 TexCrim 101.—Controlled Subs 80, 148(3); Crim Law 218(1).

Giacona v. State, TexCrimApp, 298 SW2d 587, 164 TexCrim 325.—Arrest 62, 63.1, 63.4(17); Const Law 48(4.1); Crim Law 394.4(9).

Giacona v. State, TexCrimApp, 236 SW2d 134.—Crim Law 1090.1(1).

Giacona v. State, TexCrimApp, 207 SW2d 403, 151 TexCrim 279.—Sent & Pun 1388.

Giacona v. State, TexCrimApp, 135 SW2d 117, 138 TexCrim 267.—Crim Law 1144.18.

Giacona v. U.S., CA5 (Tex), 257 F2d 450, cert den 79 SCt 113, 358 US 873, 3 LEd2d 104.—Arrest 71.1(2.1); Const Law 4500; Controlled Subs 133; Crim Law 394.1(2), 394.4(11), 394.5(1), 394.5(2), 1144.9, 1148; Int Rev 5126; Searches 23, 113.1; Tresp 24.

Gianelle v. Morgan, TexCivApp–Texarkana, 514 SW2d 133.—App & E 496, 865, 914.3; Autos 232; Judgm 470.

Gianelloni; Hospital Ass'n of Southern Pac. Lines in Texas and Louisianav., TexCivApp–Beaumont, 431 SW2d 949.—Assoc 20(1); Stip 14(12); Trial 350.4(4).

Gianelloni; Zimmerman v., TexCivApp–Beaumont, 206 SW2d 843.—App & E 968; Evid 121(11); Jury 85, 131(6); Labor & Emp 918(3); Plead 111.17, 111.44.

Giangrosso v. Crosley, TexApp–Houston (1 Dist), 840 SW2d 765.—App & E 846(5), 852, 931(1), 1008.1(3), 1010.1(2), 1012.1(5); Child S 9, 231, 234, 240, 259, 339(2), 339(3), 339(4), 339(5), 556(3).

Giannatti, Ex parte, TexCivApp–San Antonio, 189 SW2d 191.—Hab Corp 538; Jury 19(6.5).

Giannoulas; Lyons Partnership v., CA5 (Tex), 179 F3d 384.—Copyr 53.2; Fed Cts 776; Trademarks 1021, 1524(2).

Giannoulas; Lyons Partnership v., NDTex, 14 FSupp2d 947, aff 179 F3d 384.—Copyr 51, 53.2; Trademarks 1028, 1081, 1082, 1181, 1419, 1463, 1464, 1466, 1467, 1524(2), 1609.

Giannukes v. Sfiris, Tex, 81 SW2d 999, 125 Tex 354.— Autos 244(20), 244(37); Evid 474(8), 588; Hus & W 260.

GIANT

Giant Foods, Inc.; Renfro v., TexCivApp–Hous (1 Dist), 501 SW2d 357.—Estop 83(2); Land & Ten 167(1).

Giant Mfg. Co. v. Davis, TexComApp, 121 SW2d 590, 132 Tex 220.—App & E 795(2); Contracts 346(10); Labor & Emp 265.

Giant Mfg. Co. v. Davis, TexCivApp–El Paso, 91 SW2d 1099, rev 121 SW2d 590, 132 Tex 220.—Labor & Emp 173, 210, 228, 265; Set-Off 41.

Giao v. Smith & Lamm, P.C., TexApp–Houston (1 Dist), 714 SW2d 144. See Nguyen Ngoc Giao v. Smith & Lamm, P.C.

Gibauitch, Ex parte, TexCrimApp, 688 SW2d 868.—Crim Law 273.1(1), 273.1(4), 273.1(5), 1181.5(8).

Gibb v. Delta Drilling Co., NDTex, 104 FRD 59.—Fed Civ Proc 161.1, 164, 165, 173, 187; Sec Reg 25.21(1), 25.50, 60.44, 60.48(3), 60.53.

Gibbens; Jim Walter Homes, Inc. v., TexCivApp–San Antonio, 608 SW2d 706, ref nre.—Cons Cred 2, 4, 17, 19; Forfeit 2; Statut 184, 270, 273, 274; Usury 88.

Gibbens; Montgomery v., TexCivApp–Eastland, 245 SW2d 311.—App & E 931(6), 1010.1(4), 1054(1); Hus & W 260, 270(5); Plead 111.3, 111.5, 111.42(8); Pretrial Proc 478, 479, 480, 481.

Gibbins v. Berlin, TexApp–Fort Worth, 162 SW3d 335.— App & E 946, 969, 1001(1), 1001(3), 1004(3), 1064.1(1), 1182; Assault 2, 13, 35, 42, 43(2), 48, 67; Damag 96, 97, 140.7, 185(1), 192; Evid 587, 595; Plead 78, 237(2), 427; Trial 350.1, 352.4(1).

Gibbons, Ex parte, TexApp–Waco, 992 SW2d 707, reh overr, and petition for discretionary review refused.— Crim Law 1081(2); Hab Corp 221, 225, 813, 814.

Gibbons; Daboub v., CA5 (Tex), 42 F3d 285.—Copyr 72.1, 82, 109; Fed Civ Proc 2553; Libel 9(1); Lim of Act 55(5), 55(6), 55(8), 95(3), 95(7); States 18.15, 18.87; Trover 13.

Gibbons; Fisher Controls Intern., Inc. v., TexApp–Houston (1 Dist), 911 SW2d 135, writ den.—Antitrust 141, 145, 272, 363; App & E 930(3), 989, 1003(6); Contracts 148; Fraud 3, 16, 17, 23, 38.

Gibbons; Harris County v., TexApp–Houston (14 Dist), 150 SW3d 877.—App & E 294(1), 930(3), 1001(1), 1001(3); Autos 187(3), 187(6); Evid 597; Judgm 199(1), 199(3.10), 199(3.17); Mun Corp 189(1), 723, 742(6), 745, 753(1); Offic 114.

Gibbons; Holden v., TexCivApp–Austin, 101 SW2d 837, writ dism.—App & E 201(2), 1046.5, 1050.1(2), 1056.4, 1062.2; Home 213, 214; Trial 350.1, 350.3(2.1), 351.5(1), 351.5(3), 352.5(3).

Gibbons; Mobil Oil Corp. v., TexCivApp–Fort Worth, 511 SW2d 600.—App & E 843(4); Plead 8(2), 45, 111.3, 111.8, 111.23, 111.46, 427.

Gibbons; Nightcaps v., CA5 (Tex), 42 F3d 285. See Daboub v. Gibbons.

Gibbons v. State, TexCrimApp, 652 SW2d 413.—Crim Law 1167(1); Ind & Inf 137(6); Kidnap 32, 36; Rape 51(1).

Gibbons v. State, TexCrimApp, 634 SW2d 700.—Crim Law 44; False Pret 49(1).

Gibbons v. State, TexApp–Dallas, 775 SW2d 790, petition for discretionary review refused by 815 SW2d 739.— Const Law 1493, 1725, 1730, 1742, 1759, 1760, 1780; Sent & Pun 1962, 1963, 1983(2); Tresp 76.

Gibbons v. State, TexApp–Tyler, 794 SW2d 887.—Crim Law 622.1(2), 622.2(3), 656(7), 715, 720(2), 721(3), 795(1.5), 795(2.20), 795(2.26), 829(3), 1044.1(2), 1159.2(7), 1159.6, 1163(1), 1166(6); Ind & Inf 191(0.5); RICO 103, 104, 121; Witn 52(1), 52(5), 52(7), 52(8), 188, 192, 193.

Gibbons v. State, TexApp–Houston (14 Dist), 874 SW2d 164, cert den 115 SCt 731, 513 US 1081, 130 LEd2d 635. —Crim Law 38, 772(6).

Gibbons; Thompson v., TexCivApp–San Antonio, 290 SW2d 396.—App & E 1068(2), 1170.6; Autos 245(66), 245(78); Trial 352.1(7).

Gibbons-Markey v. Texas Medical Liability Trust, CA5 (Tex), 163 FedAppx 342, on remand In re Gibbons-Markey, 2006 WL 3151558.—Insurance 2919, 2924, 3168.

Gibbs, In re, CA5 (Tex), 223 F3d 312.—Courts 101.

Gibbs, In re, CA5 (Tex), 223 F3d 308, reissued 223 F3d 312.—Const Law 191; Hab Corp 205, 770.

Gibbs v. Allstate Ins. Co., TexCivApp–Fort Worth, 386 SW2d 606, ref nre.—Insurance 1606, 1671; Judgm 199(3.13).

Gibbs; Association of Professional Flight Attendants v., CA5 (Tex), 804 F2d 318.—Fed Civ Proc 314.1, 320.

Gibbs v. Beto, CA5 (Tex), 332 F2d 442, cert den 85 SCt 127, 379 US 863, 13 LEd2d 66.—Hab Corp 721(2).

Gibbs; Boman v., TexCivApp–Amarillo, 443 SW2d 267, ref nre.—Consp 1.1, 8; Equity 54; Fraud 28; Inj 33; Judgm 830.1; Mal Pros 11; Wills 2, 70.

Gibbs; Bruckner Truck Sales, Inc. v., TexCivApp–Amarillo, 361 SW2d 619.—Impl & C C 20.

Gibbs; Choice v., TexApp–Houston (14 Dist), 222 SW3d 832.—App & E 242(4); Electricity 13; Evid 584(1); Judgm 181(33), 185.3(21); Neglig 371, 379, 380, 387, 1675.

Gibbs; City of Beaumont v., TexCivApp–Beaumont, 130 SW2d 872.—Inj 138.31.

Gibbs v. Crittenden, TexCivApp–Waco, 262 SW2d 804.— New Tr 93.

Gibbs; Curtis v., Tex, 511 SW2d 263.—Abate & R 4, 81, 82; Child C 550; Courts 207.4(2), 472.1, 475(1), 475(15), 483.

Gibbs; Dallas County v., Tex, 525 SW2d 500.—Costs 99.

Gibbs; Delhi Gas Pipeline Corp. v., TexApp–Tyler, 643 SW2d 492, ref nre.—App & E 1170.1; Em Dom 201, 203(2), 262(5).

Gibbs v. Fincher, CA5 (Tex), 804 F2d 318. See Association of Professional Flight Attendants v. Gibbs.

Gibbs; Garden Oaks Bd. of Trustees v., TexCivApp–Hous (1 Dist), 489 SW2d 133, ref nre.—Covenants 51(2), 72.1, 79(1), 103(3), 108(1), 110, 122.

Gibbs v. Garden Oaks Bd. of Trustees, TexCivApp–Hous (14 Dist), 459 SW2d 478, ref nre, appeal after remand 489 SW2d 133, ref nre.—Inj 126.

Gibbs v. General Motors Corp., Tex, 450 SW2d 827.— App & E 863, 1024.4; Judgm 178, 181(1), 181(2), 185.3(21).

Gibbs v. General Motors Corp., TexCivApp–Eastland, 445 SW2d 589, writ gr, rev 450 SW2d 827.—Judgm 185(3), 185.3(21); Neglig 1675, 1713; Prod Liab 8, 75.1, 77.5.

Gibbs v. Gibbs, CA5 (Tex), 210 F3d 491, 172 ALR Fed 783.—Evid 150, 546; Fed Civ Proc 2723; Fed Cts 626, 651, 830, 915; Infants 83; Labor & Emp 711, 712, 717.

Gibbs; Gibbs v., CA5 (Tex), 210 F3d 491, 172 ALR Fed 783.—Evid 150, 546; Fed Civ Proc 2723; Fed Cts 626, 651, 830, 915; Infants 83; Labor & Emp 711, 712, 717.

Gibbs v. Gibbs, CA5 (Tex), 167 F3d 949, reh gr, vac 173 F3d 946, on reh 210 F3d 491, 172 ALR Fed 783.—Fed Cts 830; Insurance 3585; Labor & Emp 711, 717.

Gibbs; Gibbs v., CA5 (Tex), 167 F3d 949, reh gr, vac 173 F3d 946, on reh 210 F3d 491, 172 ALR Fed 783.—Fed Cts 830; Insurance 3585; Labor & Emp 711, 717.

Gibbs v. Gibbs, TexCivApp–Amarillo, 443 SW2d 958.— App & E 78(1).

Gibbs; Gibbs v., TexCivApp–Amarillo, 443 SW2d 958.— App & E 78(1).

Gibbs v. Greenwood, TexApp–Austin, 651 SW2d 377.— App & E 719(8), 756, 761, 989; Child C 553, 555, 632, 637, 907; Divorce 183.

Gibbs; Gulf Ins. Co. v., TexCivApp–Hous (1 Dist), 534 SW2d 720, ref nre.—App & E 1069.1; Costs 260(4); Trial 29(2), 295(1), 296(13), 312(1), 313; Work Comp 554, 597, 849, 1649.

Gibbs; Herrera v., TexCivApp–El Paso, 499 SW2d 912.— App & E 1170.7, 1170.9(8), 1170.10; Autos 20; Estop

75; Evid 273(5); Trial 352.20; Trover 17, 40(3), 40(4), 40(6), 46, 57.

Gibbs; Holland v., TexCivApp–Austin, 388 SW2d 295, ref nre.—App & E 854(2), 931(1); Can of Inst 34(1); Deeds 211(3); Des & Dist 83; Lim of Act 39(7), 100(11).

Gibbs; Inter-City Properties, Inc. v., TexCivApp–Hous (14 Dist), 560 SW2d 503, ref nre.—App & E 842(8); Partit 26; Ten in C 35.

Gibbs v. Jackson, Tex, 990 SW2d 745.—Autos 178; Neglig 211.

Gibbs v. Jackson, TexApp–Tyler, 959 SW2d 668, reh overr, and review gr, rev 990 SW2d 745.—App & E 216(1); Autos 178; Neglig 210, 250, 1692, 1704.

Gibbs v. Johnson, CA5 (Tex), 154 F3d 253, cert den 119 SCt 1501, 526 US 1089, 143 LEd2d 654.—Crim Law 700(2.1), 700(4), 700(6); Hab Corp 453, 495, 688, 818; Sent & Pun 1762.

Gibbs; Jones v., TexComApp, 131 SW2d 957, 133 Tex 627. —App & E 374(2).

Gibbs; Jones v., TexComApp, 130 SW2d 274, 133 Tex 645, motion overr 131 SW2d 957, 133 Tex 627.—Ex & Ad 438(5); Logs 3(11), 3(15).

Gibbs; Jones v., TexComApp, 130 SW2d 265, 133 Tex 627, motion overr 131 SW2d 957, 133 Tex 627.—Contracts 172; Ex & Ad 41, 276, 278; Frds St of 131(2); Judgm 245; Logs 3(7), 3(11), 3(15).

Gibbs; Jones v., TexCivApp–El Paso, 103 SW2d 1018, rev 130 SW2d 274, 133 Tex 645, motion overr 131 SW2d 957, 133 Tex 627.—Ex & Ad 426, 438(5); Judgm 586(2); Logs 3(15).

Gibbs; Jones v., TexCivApp–El Paso, 103 SW2d 1011, aff 130 SW2d 265, 133 Tex 627, motion overr 131 SW2d 957, 133 Tex 627.—App & E 1062.2, 1152; Ex & Ad 438(5); Logs 3(11), 3(15); Plead 354; Trial 350.3(2.1).

Gibbs; Lawson v., TexCivApp–Hous (14 Dist), 591 SW2d 292, ref nre.—App & E 863; Bankr 2442; Bills & N 195, 214; Mtg 241, 341, 352.1, 360, 369(3).

Gibbs; McHone v., Tex, 469 SW2d 789.—Divorce 152; Mand 53.

Gibbs v. Main Bank of Houston, TexApp–Houston (1 Dist), 666 SW2d 554.—Antitrust 144, 145, 146(1), 162, 353, 363, 390, 391; App & E 901, 927(7), 989, 997(3), 1177(5); Insurance 3426; Lim of Act 6(1), 13, 104(1), 199(2).

Gibbs v. Melton, TexCivApp–Dallas, 354 SW2d 426.— App & E 21, 22, 23; Const Law 2355; Courts 1, 247(2).

Gibbs; Moss v., Tex, 370 SW2d 452.—Const Law 2500; Courts 107; Hus & W 257, 259, 266.4, 268(2), 270(11); Statut 220.

Gibbs; Moss v., TexCivApp–Amarillo, 364 SW2d 268, rev 370 SW2d 452.—Hus & W 257, 265, 268(2).

Gibbs; O'Brien v., TexCivApp–Dallas, 555 SW2d 199.— App & E 371; Divorce 178, 190.

Gibbs; Palmetto Lumber Co. v., TexComApp, 80 SW2d 742, 124 Tex 615, 102 ALR 474, reh overr 82 SW2d 376, 124 Tex 615.—Costs 32(3), 230; Courts 91(2); Eject 65.

Gibbs v. Paluk, CA5 (Tex), 742 F2d 181.—Fed Cts 553, 571, 572.1, 574.

Gibbs v. Randolph, CA5 (Tex), 250 F2d 41.—Action 38(3); Judgm 630; Paymt 50, 59; Stip 14(10).

Gibbs v. Service Lloyds Ins. Co., EDTex, 711 FSupp 874. —Insurance 1103; States 18.51; Work Comp 28, 1042.

Gibbs; Sexton v., NDTex, 327 FSupp 134, aff 446 F2d 904, cert den 92 SCt 733, 404 US 1062, 30 LEd2d 751.— Arrest 63.4(2), 63.4(3), 63.4(4), 63.4(5), 63.4(13), 71.1(2.1), 71.1(7), 71.1(8); Civil R 1088(3), 1088(4), 1333(1), 1376(6), 1407, 1460, 1461, 1463, 1465(1); Const Law 3854; Crim Law 322; Searches 24, 60.1, 62.

Gibbs v. ShuttleKing, Inc., TexApp–El Paso, 162 SW3d 603, reh overr, and review den.—App & E 171(1), 179(1); Carr 284; Labor & Emp 2773, 2777, 2782, 2784; Neglig 200, 202, 220, 250, 1000, 1019, 1070, 1673.

Gibbs; Spradlin v., TexCivApp–Texarkana, 159 SW2d 246.—Consp 6; Judgm 18(2), 19.

Gibbs v. State, TexCrimApp, 819 SW2d 821, reh den, cert den 112 SCt 1205, 502 US 1107, 117 LEd2d 444, denial of habeas corpus aff 154 F3d 253, cert den 119 SCt 1501, 526 US 1089, 143 LEd2d 654.—Crim Law 211(1), 211(3), 211(4), 364(3.1), 394.6(5), 419(2.20), 535(2), 795(2.1), 795(2.10), 906, 951(1), 957(3), 1043(3), 1134(2), 1166.13; Homic 511, 1127, 1129, 1451, 1456.

Gibbs v. State, TexCrimApp, 610 SW2d 489.—Larc 40(9).

Gibbs v. State, TexCrimApp, 544 SW2d 403.—Crim Law 444, 494; Sent & Pun 1313, 1381(6).

Gibbs v. State, TexCrimApp, 473 SW2d 208.—Sent & Pun 313.

Gibbs v. State, TexCrimApp, 468 SW2d 69.—Crim Law 386, 406(6), 1038.1(7), 1038.4.

Gibbs v. State, TexCrimApp, 385 SW2d 258.—Autos 355(6); Witn 344(1), 345(1), 345(2).

Gibbs v. State, TexCrimApp, 336 SW2d 625, 169 TexCrim 608.—Crim Law 429(1); Rob 24.10.

Gibbs v. State, TexCrimApp, 308 SW2d 515, 165 TexCrim 429.—Crim Law 1028.

Gibbs v. State, TexCrimApp, 291 SW2d 320, 163 TexCrim 370.—Crim Law 925.5(3).

Gibbs v. State, TexCrimApp, 253 SW2d 1002, 158 Tex-Crim 145.—Crim Law 1111(3); False Pret 20; Ind & Inf 191(5).

Gibbs v. State, TexCrimApp, 169 SW2d 721, 145 TexCrim 499.—Crim Law 1086.13, 1087.1(2).

Gibbs v. State, TexApp–Houston (1 Dist), 7 SW3d 175, reh en banc den, and petition for discretionary review refused.—Crim Law 641.13(2.1), 660, 1035(6), 1036.2, 1128(1), 1144.10.

Gibbs v. State, TexApp–Texarkana, 932 SW2d 256.— Assault 56; Autos 355(14); Crim Law 553, 562, 1144.13(3), 1144.13(6), 1159.2(2), 1159.2(7), 1159.2(9), 1159.3(2), 1159.4(2).

Gibbs v. Texas Emp. Ins. Ass'n, TexCivApp–Eastland, 378 SW2d 349, ref nre.—Work Comp 1283, 1726, 1966.

Gibbs; Texas Pipe Bending Co. v., TexCivApp–Hous (1 Dist), 580 SW2d 41, ref nre 584 SW2d 702.—App & E 204(2), 996, 1001(1); Autos 240(2), 246(60); Evid 241(1); Labor & Emp 3094(2); Neglig 1612, 1624; Princ & A 22(2), 23(1); Trial 105(2), 350.6(3).

Gibbs; Thompson v., Tex, 240 SW2d 287, 150 Tex 315.— Courts 247(7).

Gibbs; Thompson v., TexCivApp–Dallas, 504 SW2d 630, mandamus overr.—Divorce 151; Judgm 297.

Gibbs; Thompson v., TexCivApp–Galveston, 238 SW2d 213, cause remanded 240 SW2d 287, 150 Tex 315.—App & E 1151(2); Carr 177(3), 228(5); Damag 221(2.1); Plead 370; Trial 352.4(1), 352.4(8).

Gibbs; Traders & General Ins. Co. v., TexCivApp–Fort Worth, 229 SW2d 410, ref nre.—App & E 1015(5), 1062.1; Damag 221(5.1); New Tr 140(3); Trial 311, 351.5(2); Work Comp 552, 563, 1396, 1399, 1529, 1551, 1716, 1724, 1728, 1795.

Gibbs; U.S. v., CA5 (Tex), 108 FedAppx 992, habeas corpus den 2005 WL 1364817.—Crim Law 1038.1(4).

Gibbs; U.S. v., CA5 (Tex), 72 FedAppx 147, post-conviction relief den 2007 WL 1642376.—Crim Law 453; Sent & Pun 976.

Gibbs v. U.S. Guarantee Co., TexCivApp–Austin, 218 SW2d 522, writ refused.—Insurance 1541; Statut 190, 219(9.1), 223.5(3), 251.

Gibbs v. Wheeler, TexCivApp–Austin, 306 SW2d 929, ref nre.—App & E 1040(6), 1175(1), 1175(5); Bills & N 176, 269, 315, 324; Insurance 1402; Trial 382; Trusts 261.

Gibbs Bros. and Co.; Sheffield v., TexCivApp–Hous (1 Dist), 596 SW2d 227.—Judgm 181(19); Mines 55(5).

Gibbs Oil Co. of Texas; Forsythe Intern., S.A. v., CA5 (Tex), 915 F2d 1017.—Alt Disp Res 220, 251, 257, 265, 307, 332, 333, 368, 374(1).

Gibbud v. Moron, TexApp–Corpus Christi, 972 SW2d 797, reh overr, and review den, and reh of petition for review overr.—Tax 2640, 2703.

Giberson v. Hoerster, TexCivApp–Austin, 339 SW2d 730, writ dism.—Social S 140.3.

Giberson; Sorrells v., TexApp–Austin, 780 SW2d 936, writ den.—App & E 173(2); Judgm 185(1), 185(2), 185.3(16).

Gibler v. Houston Post Co., TexCivApp–Houston, 310 SW2d 377, ref nre.—App & E 934(1); Judgm 181(4), 181(33), 186; Libel 5, 25, 33, 48(1), 89(1).

Gibler; Rochelle v., TexCivApp–Fort Worth, 269 SW2d 515, ref nre.—App & E 927(7), 989; Brok 43(2), 106; Frds St of 116(5), 118(4); Ven & Pur 45, 352.

Giblin; Garrett v., TexApp–Beaumont, 940 SW2d 408.—Antitrust 256; Atty & C 112; Judgm 185(2).

Giblin; Mayfield v., TexApp–Beaumont, 795 SW2d 852.—Crim Law 273.1(2); Double J 103, 167; Mand 61.

Giblin; State ex rel. Hawthorn v., TexCrimApp, 589 SW2d 431.—Crim Law 864, 875(1).

Giblin v. Sudduth, TexCivApp–Austin, 300 SW2d 330, ref nre.—App & E 173(2), 852, 856(1); Deeds 38(1); Frds St of 110(1); Land & Ten 92(1); Spec Perf 29(2), 94, 121(4); Ven & Pur 18(3).

Gibner; Continental Assur. Co. v., TexCivApp–Amarillo, 119 SW2d 588, dism.—Execution 53; Hus & W 273(11); Usury 34, 130.

Gibraltar Life Ins. Co. of America; Jackson v., TexCivApp–Waco, 435 SW2d 618.—Insurance 1887(2); Ref of Inst 19(2).

Gibraltar Life Ins. Co. of America; Snow v., TexCivApp–Dallas, 326 SW2d 501, ref nre.—Estop 102; Insurance 1734, 1755, 3117; Paymt 39(1), 39(9).

Gibraltar Mortg. & Loan Corp. v. Lerman, TexCivApp–Waco, 346 SW2d 487.—Ex & Ad 261, 264(1).

Gibraltar Resources, Inc., In re, CA5 (Tex), 210 F3d 573.—Bankr 3767; Judgm 540, 567.

Gibraltar Resources, Inc., In re, NDTex, 211 BR 225.—Bankr 3781.

Gibraltar Resources, Inc., In re, NDTex, 202 BR 586.—Bankr 2601, 2602.1, 2619.1, 3777, 3789.1.

Gibraltar Resources, Inc., In re, BkrtcyNDTex, 211 BR 216.—Assign 31, 33, 48, 49, 50(1), 137; Bankr 2549, 2608(1); Execution 55; Garn 58.

Gibraltar Sav. v. LDBrinkman Corp., CA5 (Tex), 860 F2d 1275, reh den, cert den LDB Corp v. Gibraltar Sav, 109 SCt 2432, 490 US 1091, 104 LEd2d 988.—Corp 1.4(3), 1.4(4), 1.6(3), 1.7(1), 1.7(2); Fed Civ Proc 2238; Fed Cts 416, 614, 799, 841, 846; Fraud 58(2), 58(4); Guar 82(2); Torts 262; Usury 110, 111(1).

Gibraltar Sav.; Robinowitz v., CA5 (Tex), 23 F3d 951, cert den 115 SCt 725, 513 US 1078, 130 LEd2d 630.—Banks 505; B & L Assoc 42(6).

Gibraltar Sav. & Bldg. Ass'n v. Collier, TexCivApp–Galveston, 118 SW2d 639, writ refused.—App & E 931(1); Home 177(2), 181(3).

Gibraltar Sav. & Bldg. Ass'n v. Isbell, TexCivApp–Galveston, 101 SW2d 1029.—App & E 863, 1175(2); Inj 98(2), 138.75, 147, 157.

Gibraltar Sav. & Bldg. Ass'n; Logue v., TexCivApp–Galveston, 175 SW2d 117.—Forci E & D 43(4); J P 130; Land & Ten 291(18).

Gibraltar Sav. & Loan Ass'n v. Falkner, Tex, 371 SW2d 548.—B & L Assoc 3.5(2), 3.5(3).

Gibraltar Sav. & Loan Ass'n; Falkner v., TexCivApp–Austin, 359 SW2d 56, rev 371 SW2d 548.—B & L Assoc 3.5(2).

Gibraltar Sav. Ass'n; Bennett v., TexCivApp–Hous (1 Dist), 439 SW2d 458, ref nre.—Mtg 151(6).

Gibraltar Sav. Ass'n; Bluebonnet Farms, Inc. v., TexCivApp–Hous (1 Dist), 618 SW2d 81, ref nre.—Corp 202, 615.5, 630(1); Plead 101, 106(1).

Gibraltar Sav. Ass'n; Diversified, Inc. v., TexApp–Houston (14 Dist), 762 SW2d 620, writ den.—Antitrust 198; Fraud 28; Judgm 187; Mtg 372(1), 379; Neglig 1205(3).

Gibraltar Sav. Ass'n v. Falkner, Tex, 351 SW2d 534, 162 Tex 633.—Courts 247(1), 247(8).

Gibraltar Sav. Ass'n; Falkner v., TexCivApp–Austin, 348 SW2d 472, ref nre.—B & L Assoc 3.5(3); Witn 216(1).

Gibraltar Sav. Ass'n; Falkner v., TexCivApp–Austin, 348 SW2d 467, ref nre.—B & L Assoc 3.5(2), 3.5(3).

Gibraltar Sav. Ass'n; First Gibraltar Mortg. Corp. v., TexApp–Dallas, 658 SW2d 709, dism.—Corp 503(1); Decl Judgm 26, 237.

Gibraltar Sav. Ass'n v. Franklin Sav. Ass'n, TexCivApp–Austin, 617 SW2d 322, ref nre.—Admin Law 454, 468; B & L Assoc 3.5(2); Const Law 3879.

Gibraltar Sav. Ass'n v. Gerst, Tex, 417 SW2d 584.—B & L Assoc 2.1, 3.5(2).

Gibraltar Sav. Ass'n; Gerst v., TexCivApp–Austin, 413 SW2d 718, ref nre 417 SW2d 584.—B & L Assoc 3.1(1), 3.1(2), 3.1(3); Estop 68(2); Judgm 739; Trial 105(2).

Gibraltar Sav. Ass'n v. Hamilton Air Mart, Inc., TexApp–Dallas, 662 SW2d 632.—App & E 564(3), 564(5).

Gibraltar Sav. Ass'n; Keenan v., TexApp–Houston (14 Dist), 754 SW2d 392.—Costs 194.32, 207; Guar 36(2); Judgm 181(22), 185.1(1).

Gibraltar Sav. Ass'n v. Kilpatrick, TexApp–Texarkana, 770 SW2d 14, writ den.—App & E 5, 859; B & L Assoc 41(5); Evid 571(10); Judgm 17(10), 112, 126(1), 162(2); Proc 133.

Gibraltar Sav. Ass'n v. King, TexCivApp–Hous (14 Dist), 474 SW2d 758.—Lim of Act 119(3), 195(3).

Gibraltar Sav. Ass'n; Looney v., TexApp–Amarillo, 695 SW2d 336.—App & E 758.1, 1175(5); Pretrial Proc 698.

Gibraltar Sav. Ass'n; Ogden v., Tex, 640 SW2d 232.—Bills & N 394; Mtg 335, 379.

Gibraltar Sav. Ass'n; Pine v., TexCivApp–Hous (1 Dist), 519 SW2d 238, ref nre.—App & E 758.3(3); Contracts 9(1), 39; Mtg 126, 133.

Gibraltar Sav. Ass'n; Pine v., TexCivApp–Hous (1 Dist), 427 SW2d 714, appeal after remand 519 SW2d 238, ref nre.—Bills & N 534; Judgm 181(26), 185(2), 185.1(1), 185.3(16); Plead 377.

Gibraltar Sav. Ass'n; Stern v., TexApp–Houston (14 Dist), 785 SW2d 897.—Judgm 181(26).

Gibraltar Sav. Ass'n v. Turnbough, TexCivApp–Hous (1 Dist), 610 SW2d 515, dism.—App & E 846(5), 852, 989; Corp 503(1); Labor & Emp 3047; Venue 8.5(8), 22(4), 22(10); Work Comp 1832, 2100.

Gibraltar Sav. Ass'n v. Turnbough, TexCivApp–Hous (1 Dist), 610 SW2d 514, dism.—Work Comp 1832.

Gibraltar Sav. Ass'n v. Watson, TexApp–Houston (14 Dist), 683 SW2d 748.—Judgm 199(3.14); Trial 350.3(1), 423.

Gibraltar Sav. Ass'n v. Watson, TexApp–Houston (14 Dist), 624 SW2d 650, appeal after remand 683 SW2d 748.—App & E 927(7), 989; Bills & N 438; Lim of Act 48(1); Trial 142.

Gibraltar Sav. Ass'n; Wexler v., TexCivApp–Hous (14 Dist), 439 SW2d 378.—Bills & N 502, 517; Judgm 185.1(3).

Gibralter Colorado Life Co. v. Taylor, TexComApp, 123 SW2d 318, 132 Tex 328.—App & E 1175(5); Evid 197, 564(1); Insurance 2035, 3117.

Gibralter Colorado Life Co. v. Taylor, TexCivApp–Dallas, 99 SW2d 1084, rev 123 SW2d 318, 132 Tex 328.—App & E 748, 882(10), 1058(1); Evid 271(19), 373(1), 378(1), 564(1); Insurance 2035, 3375.

Gibralter Resources, Inc., In re, BkrtcyNDTex, 197 BR 246, aff 202 BR 586.—Attach 64; Bankr 2511, 2619.1, 2620; Execution 55; Garn 58; Judgm 306, 331, 392(2), 634, 636, 651, 668(1), 672, 720, 724.

Gibralter Sav. & Bldg. Ass'n; Miller v., TexCivApp–Beaumont, 132 SW2d 606, writ dism, correct.—Home 193; Mtg 354, 369(3), 372(4); Usury 22, 53.

Gibralter Sav. & Loan Ass'n; Johnson v., BkrtcySDTex, 70 BR 262. See McConnell, In re.

Gibralter Sav. Ass'n v. Martin, TexApp–Amarillo, 784 SW2d 555, writ den.—Judgm 185(3), 787, 788(1), 788(2); Notice 5, 14.

59 Tex D 2d—249

GIBSON;

See Guidelines for Arrangement at the beginning of this Volume

Gibralter Sav. Ass'n; Ogden v., TexCivApp–Corpus Christi, 620 SW2d 926, rev 640 SW2d 232.—App & E 927(7); Bills & N 129(2), 411.1, 419; Mtg 352.1, 369(2), 369(3); Trial 139.1(6).

Gibson, Ex parte, TexCrimApp, 811 SW2d 594.—Contempt 2, 10.

Gibson, Ex parte, TexCrimApp, 800 SW2d 548.—Hab Corp 474; Ind & Inf 87(5).

Gibson, Ex parte, TexCrimApp, 197 SW2d 544, 149 Tex-Crim 574.—Bail 43.

Gibson, Ex parte, TexCrimApp, 197 SW2d 543, 149 Tex-Crim 573.—Bail 43, 49(3.1).

Gibson, Ex parte, TexCrimApp, 197 SW2d 109, 149 Tex-Crim 543.—Extrad 39; Hab Corp 711, 729.

Gibson, Ex parte, TexCrimApp, 128 SW2d 396, 137 Tex-Crim 72.—Crim Law 992; Hab Corp 717(1); Sent & Pun 341.

Gibson, In re, BkrtcyNDTex, 308 BR 763.—Bankr 2671, 2672, 2674, 2675, 2679, 2680; U S 53(7).

Gibson, In re, BkrtcyNDTex, 69 BR 534.—Exemp 37, 44.

Gibson, In re, TexApp–El Paso, 804 SW2d 920, set aside Ex parte Gibson, 811 SW2d 594.—Contempt 2, 10, 28(1), 60(3), 66(7).

Gibson, In re, TexApp–Waco, 960 SW2d 418.—Decl Judgm 300; Offic 18.

Gibson, In re Estate of, TexApp–Texarkana, 893 SW2d 749.—App & E 842(2), 1071.2; Joint Ten 6; Wills 63, 634(4.1).

Gibson v. American Nat. Ins. Co., TexCivApp–Waco, 417 SW2d 650, writ dism.—Insurance 1153; Lim of Act 25(1).

Gibson v. American United Life Ins. Co., TexCivApp–Waco, 142 SW2d 693.—App & E 9; Interpl 33.

Gibson; Associated Emp. Lloyds v., TexCivApp–Eastland, 245 SW2d 738, dism.—App & E 930(1), 1175(5); Work Comp 237, 1348, 1435.

Gibson v. Associate Inv. Co., TexCivApp–Austin, 198 SW2d 123.—Penalties 3; Princ & A 158; War 121, 155.

Gibson v. Avery, TexApp–Fort Worth, 463 SW2d 277, ref nre.—App & E 927(7), 1056.6; Evid 527, 538, 547, 547.5; Health 675, 822(3), 825; Witn 139(10), 139(11), 139(12), 183.

Gibson; Ballan v., TexApp–Dallas, 151 SW3d 281.—App & E 846(5); Health 804, 805, 809, 835.

Gibson v. Barbe, TexApp–San Antonio, 907 SW2d 646, reh overr, and writ den.—Mun Corp 184(2), 184(3); Offic 55(1).

Gibson v. Bentley, TexCivApp–Hous (14 Dist), 605 SW2d 337, ref nre.—App & E 989, 994(1), 996, 1010.1(10); Contracts 143(2), 143.5, 176(1); Evid 397(2), 448; Trial 142.

Gibson v. Berry Cemetery Ass'n, TexCivApp–Dallas, 250 SW2d 600.—Adv Poss 10; App & E 770(1); Cem 12; Relig Soc 18; Schools 65; Tresp to T T 6.1.

Gibson; B.J. Hughes, Inc. v., TexApp–Tyler, 697 SW2d 39, ref nre.—Autos 244(10); Death 29, 77, 88, 99(1), 104(4); Interest 39(2.50).

Gibson v. Blanton, TexCivApp–Hous (1 Dist), 483 SW2d 372.—App & E 1061.3; Infants 82, 101; Mand 27, 28, 42; Pretrial Proc 501.

Gibson v. Bostick Roofing and Sheet Metal Co., Tex-App–El Paso, 148 SW3d 482.—Acct Action on 12; App & E 842(2), 931(1), 989, 994(1), 1008.1(1), 1008.1(3), 1010.1(1), 1010.2, 1011.1(1), 1012.1(2), 1012.1(4); Const Law 642; Estop 90(1); Impl & C C 30, 33.1, 65; Liens 22; Mech Liens 1, 57(1), 59, 61, 95, 99.1, 132(1), 173, 189, 190, 191; Princ & A 1, 14(2), 23(2), 23(5), 99, 101(4), 166(2.1); Trial 393(3), 404(6).

Gibson v. Burkhart, TexApp–Corpus Christi, 650 SW2d 185, ref nre.—Adv Poss 112; App & E 931(1), 989; Consp 19; Fraud 58(1); Ten in C 15(2).

Gibson v. Central Nat. Bank of McKinney, CA5 (Tex), 171 F2d 398.—Bankr 2622, 2678.

Gibson; City of Lufkin, Tex. v., CA5 (Tex), 447 F2d 492. —Fed Cts 943.1.

Gibson v. City of Orange, TexCivApp–Beaumont, 272 SW2d 789, writ refused.—Mun Corp 46.

Gibson v. Collins, CA5 (Tex), 947 F2d 780, cert den 113 SCt 102, 506 US 833, 121 LEd2d 61.—Burg 41(6); Const Law 4694; Crim Law 566; Hab Corp 493(2).

Gibson; Conley v., USTex, 78 SCt 99, 355 US 41, 2 LEd2d 80.—Fed Civ Proc 623, 1773; Fed Cts 459; Labor & Emp 1209(1), 1219(5), 1219(8), 1535.

Gibson; Conley v., SDTex, 138 FSupp 60, aff 229 F2d 436, cert gr 77 SCt 37, 352 US 818, 1 LEd2d 44, rev 78 SCt 99, 355 US 41, 2 LEd2d 80.—Labor & Emp 1089(1), 1321, 1523.

Gibson; Conley v., SDTex, 29 FRD 519.—Fed Civ Proc 164, 186.5, 2465.1.

Gibson v. Couch, TexCivApp–Eastland, 153 SW2d 288.— Mand 79; Schools 42(2), 48(6).

Gibson; David Gavin Co. v., TexApp–Houston (14 Dist), 780 SW2d 833, writ den.—Brok 42.

Gibson; Delta Air Lines, Inc. v., TexCivApp–El Paso, 550 SW2d 310, ref nre.—App & E 1140(4); Carr 280(1.1), 286, 318(8); Damag 163(4), 191; Neglig 387.

Gibson; Dempsey v., TexCivApp–Waco, 105 SW2d 423, writ dism.—Courts 475(2); Ex & Ad 431(2), 443(7); Hus & W 273(4), 274(3); Judgm 349.

Gibson; Dempsey v., TexCivApp–Waco, 100 SW2d 430.— App & E 957(1); Judgm 138(1), 138(2), 143(7).

Gibson v. Dennis, TexCivApp–Texarkana, 90 SW2d 319, writ dism.—Guard & W 8, 17.

Gibson v. Dretke, CA5 (Tex), 176 FedAppx 475.—Prisons 15(6).

Gibson v. Drew Mortg. Co., TexApp–Houston (14 Dist), 696 SW2d 211, ref nre.—App & E 845(2); Stip 14(10); Usury 1, 53, 119.

Gibson v. Dynegy Midstream Services, L.P., TexApp–Fort Worth, 138 SW3d 518.—App & E 893(1); Courts 35; Forci E & D 6(2), 8, 16(3), 25(0.5), 43(1), 43(7); Land & Ten 119(1), 291(6.5), 291(18); Plead 104(1).

Gibson v. Ellis, TexApp–Dallas, 126 SW3d 324.—Antitrust 397, 398; App & E 172(1), 237(5), 846(5), 852, 863, 931(3), 946, 966(1), 970(2), 984(1), 1047(1), 1058(2), 1058(3), 1079; Atty & C 106, 109, 113, 117, 129(2), 134(2); Evid 518; Judgm 185.3(2); Lim of Act 95(11); Pretrial Proc 713, 716; Trial 43, 45(1), 45(3).

Gibson v. Ellis, TexApp–Dallas, 58 SW3d 818, appeal after remand 126 SW3d 324.—App & E 916(1), 934(1); Judgm 185(2), 185.3(2), 185.3(4); Lim of Act 95(1), 95(3), 95(9), 100(1), 104(1), 177(2), 179(2).

Gibson v. Employers' Liability Assur. Corp., TexCiv-App–Texarkana, 131 SW2d 327, writ refused.—Work Comp 1142, 1155, 1159.

Gibson v. F.A.A., EDTex, 714 FSupp 233.—Aviation 34, 35.

Gibson v. Federal Bureau of Prisons, CA5 (Tex), 121 FedAppx 549.—Const Law 4823; Fed Civ Proc 2734; Prisons 17(2); U S 50.10(3), 125(28.1).

Gibson; F.T.C. v., CA5 (Tex), 460 F2d 605.—Admin Law 357, 358; Antitrust 307, 953; Const Law 2424(5); U S 40.

Gibson; Gavin Co. v., TexApp–Houston (14 Dist, 780 SW2d 833. See DavidGavin Co. v. Gibson.

Gibson v. General Am. Life Ins. Co., TexCivApp–El Paso, 89 SW2d 1070, writ dism.—Insurance 2070; Paymt 84(1), 85(1).

Gibson v. Gibson, TexApp–Fort Worth, 190 SW3d 821.— Divorce 252.3(5), 254(1), 286(9); Judgm 7, 16, 27.

Gibson; Gibson v., TexApp–Fort Worth, 190 SW3d 821.— Divorce 252.3(5), 254(1), 286(9); Judgm 7, 16, 27.

Gibson v. Gibson, TexApp–Waco, 653 SW2d 646.—Divorce 206; Inj 140, 147; Pretrial Proc 517.1.

Gibson; Gibson v., TexApp–Waco, 653 SW2d 646.—Divorce 206; Inj 140, 147; Pretrial Proc 517.1.

For Later Case History Information, see KeyCite on WESTLAW

GIBSON

See Guidelines for Arrangement at the beginning of this Volume

Gibson v. Gibson, TexCivApp–San Antonio, 202 SW2d 288.—Divorce 252.3(2), 286(0.5); Hus & W 249(1), 262.2.

Gibson; Gibson v., TexCivApp–San Antonio, 202 SW2d 288.—Divorce 252.3(2), 286(0.5); Hus & W 249(1), 262.2.

Gibson v. Gibson, TexCivApp–Beaumont, 286 SW2d 216. —Hus & W 299(1); Judgm 495(1), 713(1), 725(1), 819, 822(1), 822(3).

Gibson; Gibson v., TexCivApp–Beaumont, 286 SW2d 216. —Hus & W 299(1); Judgm 495(1), 713(1), 725(1), 819, 822(1), 822(3).

Gibson v. Gibson, TexCivApp–Tyler, 614 SW2d 487.— App & E 169; Divorce 253(2); Hus & W 262.1(6), 264(2), 264(7).

Gibson; Gibson v., TexCivApp–Tyler, 614 SW2d 487.— App & E 169; Divorce 253(2); Hus & W 262.1(6), 264(2), 264(7).

Gibson v. Gillette Motor Transport, TexCivApp–Eastland, 138 SW2d 293, writ refused.—Autos 193(3.1), 245(28), 245(30); Labor & Emp 3094(2); Princ & A 21.

Gibson v. Grocers Supply Co., Inc., TexApp–Houston (14 Dist), 866 SW2d 757.—App & E 714(5), 852, 856(1), 934(1); Judgm 185(2); Work Comp 55, 203, 208, 719, 750, 1045, 2165.

Gibson; Guion v., TexCivApp–Hous (14 Dist), 439 SW2d 715.—Inj 111; Plead 111.38, 111.43.

Gibson v. Henderson, TexCivApp–Galveston, 136 SW2d 634.—App & E 846(2), 846(5); Autos 193(1), 193(11).

Gibson v. Hines, TexCivApp–Waco, 511 SW2d 546.— Child C 7, 42, 76, 276, 908, 921(1).

Gibson; Hughes, Inc. v., TexApp–Tyler, 697 SW2d 39. See B.J. Hughes, Inc. v. Gibson.

Gibson; International Sec. Life Ins. Co. v., TexCivApp–Austin, 448 SW2d 204.—App & E 770(1).

Gibson v. John D. Campbell and Co., TexApp–Fort Worth, 624 SW2d 728.—App & E 863; Contracts 198(2); Estop 55, 59; Judgm 181(1), 181(6), 181(7), 185(2); Lim of Act 13, 95(9).

Gibson v. Johnson, CA5 (Tex), 118 F3d 1073. See Hallmark v. Johnson.

Gibson; Johnson v., TexCivApp–Beaumont, 457 SW2d 114.—Mand 3(8).

Gibson v. Johnson, TexCivApp–Tyler, 414 SW2d 235, ref nre, cert den 88 SCt 1032, 390 US 946, 19 LEd2d 1135. —Atty & C 129(2); Estop 2, 3(1), 10; Judgm 185(2), 185.3(2), 186; Labor & Emp 1023, 1075.

Gibson v. J.W.T., TexApp–Beaumont, 815 SW2d 863, writ gr, aff and remanded In Interest of JWT, 872 SW2d 189, appeal after remand 945 SW2d 911.—Child 3; Const Law 3935, 4391, 4392.

Gibson v. Klevenhagen, CA5 (Tex), 777 F2d 1056.—Crim Law 273.4(1); Extrad 60; Hab Corp 318, 373, 421, 526.

Gibson v. Kountze Independent School Dist., TexCivApp–Beaumont, 552 SW2d 588.—Estop 62.4; Schools 103(1); Tax 2523, 2720.

Gibson v. Lamesa Cotton Oil Co., CA5 (Tex), 178 F2d 959.—Fed Cts 798; Neglig 1090, 1247.

Gibson v. Liberty Mut. Group, CA5 (Tex), 129 FedAppx 94.—Fed Civ Proc 2501, 2539.

Gibson v. Lockheed Aircraft Service, USTex, 76 SCt 366, 350 US 356, 100 LEd 395, reh den 76 SCt 656, 350 US 1016, 100 LEd 875.—Fed Cts 462; Labor & Emp 2897, 3012.

Gibson; Lockheed Aircraft Service v., CA5 (Tex), 217 F2d 730, cert gr 75 SCt 871, 349 US 943, 99 LEd 1270, rev 76 SCt 366, 350 US 356, 100 LEd 395, reh den 76 SCt 656, 350 US 1016, 100 LEd 875.—Damag 59; Fed Cts 641; Labor & Emp 2829, 2897, 2943, 2976, 3012.

Gibson v. McCullough, TexCivApp–Austin, 294 SW2d 759.—App & E 624, 627.3.

Gibson; Macedonia Baptist Church v., TexApp–Texarkana, 833 SW2d 557, reh den, and writ den.—App & E 207; Neglig 387, 440(3), 1228, 1679; New Tr 104(3); Pretrial Proc 45; Relig Soc 31(2); Trial 120(2), 131(0.5), 133.3, 133.6(4), 133.6(6).

Gibson v. Marsh, TexApp–El Paso, 710 SW2d 107.—Atty & C 132; Const Law 1102; Crim Law 1181(1).

Gibson v. Methodist Hosp., TexApp–Houston (1 Dist), 822 SW2d 95, writ gr, and writ den, and writ withdrawn, reh gr, opinion withdrawn.—App & E 863; Health 611, 620, 656, 669, 782, 821(1), 906; Judgm 181(1), 181(33), 185(2), 185(5), 185(6); Prod Liab 46.1; Statut 181(1).

Gibson v. Missouri Pac. R. Co., CA5 (Tex), 441 F2d 784, cert den 92 SCt 102, 404 US 855, 30 LEd2d 96, reh den 92 SCt 308, 404 US 961, 30 LEd2d 280.—Labor & Emp 1599, 1614.

Gibson v. Missouri Pac. R. Co., EDTex, 314 FSupp 1211, motion gr 1970 WL 5520, rev 441 F2d 784, cert den 92 SCt 102, 404 US 855, 30 LEd2d 96, reh den 92 SCt 308, 404 US 961, 30 LEd2d 280.—Estop 52(1), 68(1); Judgm 713(2), 720, 828.16(4); Labor & Emp 1575, 1602, 1606, 1608.

Gibson; Mitchell v., TexCivApp–Eastland, 160 SW2d 79, writ refused wom.—App & E 933(1), 1015(5); Autos 244(28); Damag 185(3); Evid 76; New Tr 52.

Gibson v. Nadel, CCA5 (Tex), 164 F2d 970.—Lim of Act 85(2).

Gibson v. Nadel & Gussman, NDTex, 68 FSupp 356, rev 164 F2d 970.—Fed Cts 424; Lim of Act 35(1), 87(6).

Gibson; National Indus. Sand Ass'n v., Tex, 897 SW2d 769.—Const Law 3962, 3964, 3965(2); Courts 12(2.5), 12(2.10), 12(2.20), 12(2.25), 35; Mand 1, 3(2.1), 12, 29.

Gibson; National Indus. Sand Ass'n v., TexCivApp–El Paso, 855 SW2d 790, reh overr, subsequent mandamus proceeding 897 SW2d 769.—App & E 78(1); Mand 1, 4(1), 4(3), 4(4), 32.

Gibson v. Northeast Nat. Bank, TexCivApp–Fort Worth, 602 SW2d 337, ref nre.—App & E 151(6); Joint Adv 1, 1.1, 8; Trial 284, 350.3(2.1), 366.

Gibson; Pacific Emp. Ins. Co. v., TexCivApp–Dallas, 419 SW2d 239.—Work Comp 1396, 1403, 1965, 1974.

Gibson v. Park Cities Ford, Ltd., TexApp–Dallas, 174 SW3d 930.—Judgm 183, 185.3(18); Plead 34(1).

Gibson; Pure Foods Products v., TexCivApp–San Antonio, 118 SW2d 925, writ dism.—App & E 1002, 1052(5); Autos 245(78), 245(83); Trial 75, 90, 96.

Gibson v. Rich, CA5 (Tex), 44 F3d 274.—Arrest 63.4(15); Civil R 1376(1), 1376(2), 1376(6); False Imp 15(1); Mal Pros 42.

Gibson v. Richter, TexCivApp–San Antonio, 97 SW2d 351.—App & E 143, 148.

Gibson v. Robert Lange, Inc., TexCivApp–Houston, 310 SW2d 623.—App & E 1010.1(3), 1012.1(10); Venue 8.5(8); Work Comp 2084.

Gibson v. R. O. "Bill" Williams Ins. Co., TexCivApp–Beaumont, 398 SW2d 408, ref nre.—App & E 927(7); Insurance 1671; Neglig 210.

Gibson v. Robinson, TexCivApp–Amarillo, 299 SW2d 777, ref nre.—Bills & N 518(1), 525.

Gibson; Sabre Oil & Gas Corp. v., TexApp–Eastland, 72 SW3d 812, reh overr, and review den.—App & E 78(1), 79(1), 80(1); Contracts 143(1), 147(2); Judgm 190, 569, 729; Mines 73, 73.5, 78.1(7); Parties 50, 51(2), 51(4).

Gibson; Sessions v., TexCivApp–Galveston, 199 SW2d 303.—Venue 5.5.

Gibson v. Shaver, TexCivApp–Tyler, 434 SW2d 462.—Inj 151, 152; Judgm 210.

Gibson v. Sheldon, TexCivApp–Fort Worth, 90 SW2d 841, writ refused.—Mines 78.2.

Gibson v. Smith, TexCivApp–Tyler, 511 SW2d 327.—App & E 946; Partit 107; Receivers 134, 137.

Gibson; Southwestern Inv. Co. v., TexCivApp–Fort Worth, 372 SW2d 754.—Banks 314; Corp 506; Judgm 649, 654, 713(3).

Gibson v. Spinks, Tex, 895 SW2d 352. See Thomas v. Oldham.

Gibson v. Spinks, TexApp–Corpus Christi, 869 SW2d 529, reh overr, and writ gr, aff in part, rev in part Thomas v.

Oldham, 895 SW2d 352.—App & E 158(1), 781(7); Mun Corp 743, 744.

Gibson v. State, TexCrimApp, 144 SW3d 530.—Crim Law 1158(3); Jury 33(5.15).

Gibson v. State, TexCrimApp, 995 SW2d 693.—Autos 332, 359.

Gibson v. State, TexCrimApp, 803 SW2d 316.—Const Law 4590; Crim Law 273.1(2), 1032(5); Ind & Inf 87(5), 196(5).

Gibson v. State, TexCrimApp, 726 SW2d 129.—Autos 356; Crim Law 698(1), 1038.1(1), 1173.2(4).

Gibson v. State, TexCrimApp, 623 SW2d 324.—False Pret 9, 26, 49(1).

Gibson v. State, TexCrimApp, 549 SW2d 741.—Crim Law 749, 1042.

Gibson v. State, TexCrimApp, 532 SW2d 69, cert den 97 SCt 72, 429 US 822, 50 LEd2d 83.—Crim Law 273(1), 273.1(2), 273.1(4), 273.1(5), 1086.9; Sent & Pun 60.

Gibson v. State, TexCrimApp, 516 SW2d 406.—Crim Law 698(1), 1130(2), 1169.2(6); Witn 193.

Gibson v. State, TexCrimApp, 492 SW2d 526.—Rape 51(7).

Gibson v. State, TexCrimApp, 488 SW2d 462.—Crim Law 1184(1); Sent & Pun 2326.

Gibson v. State, TexCrimApp, 448 SW2d 481.—Crim Law 339.10(4); Double J 115; Rob 20, 24.40, 24.50.

Gibson v. State, TexCrimApp, 434 SW2d 851.—Burg 29, 41(3); Sent & Pun 1381(2).

Gibson v. State, TexCrimApp, 430 SW2d 507.—Crim Law 419(1.10), 730(1), 730(3), 730(14), 1171.1(2.1).

Gibson v. State, TexCrimApp, 424 SW2d 439.—Rape 51(4).

Gibson v. State, TexCrimApp, 423 SW2d 330.—Burg 41(1); Crim Law 394.5(3), 404.75.

Gibson v. State, TexCrimApp, 411 SW2d 735.—Rob 24.40.

Gibson v. State, TexCrimApp, 401 SW2d 822.—Bail 79(1).

Gibson v. State, TexCrimApp, 357 SW2d 569, 172 TexCrim 435.—Crim Law 911, 939(1), 945(1), 1134(4), 1156(1), 1192.

Gibson v. State, TexCrimApp, 290 SW2d 899.—Crim Law 1090.1(1).

Gibson v. State, TexCrimApp, 286 SW2d 167, 162 TexCrim 473.—Crim Law 730(1), 1169.1(10); Homic 1134.

Gibson v. State, TexCrimApp, 223 SW2d 625, 153 TexCrim 582.—Crim Law 404.70, 438(7), 863(1), 919(5), 1174(1); Sent & Pun 1789(8).

Gibson v. State, TexCrimApp, 205 SW2d 772, 151 TexCrim 105.—Crim Law 742(1), 1038.1(1), 1090.8; Rob 26.

Gibson v. State, TexCrimApp, 202 SW2d 236, 150 TexCrim 401.—Homic 766, 769, 774, 799, 1345, 1473.

Gibson v. State, TexCrimApp, 162 SW2d 703, 144 TexCrim 263.—Disorderly H 17; Prost 28.

Gibson v. State, TexCrimApp, 121 SW2d 361, 135 TexCrim 498.—Crim Law 398(2), 402(1), 854(9), 1133, 1144.12, 1158(4), 1166.16, 1169.1(10), 1171.1(2.1), 1171.7.

Gibson v. State, TexApp–Houston (1 Dist), 673 SW2d 352. —Sent & Pun 211.

Gibson v. State, TexApp–Fort Worth, 952 SW2d 569, petition for discretionary review refused.—Autos 359; Crim Law 429(1), 444, 1043(3).

Gibson v. State, TexApp–Fort Worth, 789 SW2d 421, petition for discretionary review refused.—Crim Law 686(1), 1168(2).

Gibson v. State, TexApp–Dallas, 972 SW2d 148, petition for discretionary review gr, aff 995 SW2d 693.—Autos 359.

Gibson v. State, TexApp–Texarkana, 875 SW2d 5, reh den, and petition for discretionary review refused.— Crim Law 369.1, 369.2(2), 673(5); Double J 145; Sent & Pun 1379(1).

Gibson v. State, TexApp–El Paso, 921 SW2d 747, reh overr, and writ den.—Arrest 68(3), 68(4); Const Law 617; Crim Law 304(2), 1130(5); Dist & Pros Attys 7(1);

Hab Corp 201, 202, 251, 253, 271, 613, 662.1, 705.1, 816; Searches 11, 12, 21, 23, 24, 53.1, 72, 79, 101, 197.

Gibson v. State, TexApp–El Paso, 908 SW2d 314.—Crim Law 511.1(2.1), 511.1(3), 511.2, 511.4, 511.5, 1129(3).

Gibson v. State, TexApp–Beaumont, 225 SW3d 824.— Crim Law 1144.13(2.1), 1153(1), 1159.2(7); Rape 52(2); Witn 212.

Gibson v. State, TexApp–Beaumont, 704 SW2d 151.— Burg 41(6); Witn 266.5.

Gibson v. State, TexApp–Eastland, 769 SW2d 706, petition for discretionary review gr, rev 803 SW2d 316.— Arrest 63.4(7.1), 71.1(5); Controlled Subs 26, 27; Crim Law 273(4.1), 273.1(2), 274(3.1), 338(1), 363, 369.2(8), 404.40, 404.65; Ind & Inf 87(1); Searches 40.1, 171.

Gibson v. State, TexApp–Corpus Christi, 117 SW3d 567, petition for discretionary review gr, rev 144 SW3d 530. —Const Law 3309; Crim Law 1134(5), 1158(3), 1163(1), 1166.17; Jury 33(5.15).

Gibson v. State, TexApp–Corpus Christi, 747 SW2d 68.— Crim Law 273(1), 273(4.1), 273.1(1), 273.1(4), 273.2(2).

Gibson v. State, TexApp–Houston (14 Dist), 29 SW3d 221, petition for discretionary review refused.—Crim Law 925.5(1), 1144.15, 1156(1).

Gibson v. State, TexCivApp–Waco, 288 SW2d 577, dism. —App & E 1177(6); Plead 110.

Gibson; Stewart v., TexCivApp–Texarkana, 154 SW2d 1002.—Judgm 210, 273(2); Mand 51.

Gibson v. Stiles, CCA5 (Tex), 90 F2d 998.—Courts 90(3); Hab Corp 464.

Gibson; Texas Co. v., TexComApp, 116 SW2d 686, 131 Tex 598.—App & E 1060.1(8); Trial 115(2), 125(4), 131(1).

Gibson; Texas Co. v., TexCivApp–Beaumont, 88 SW2d 757, rev 116 SW2d 686, 131 Tex 598.—Land & Ten 161(2); Trial 115(2), 129.

Gibson v. Texas Mun. Retirement System, TexApp– Austin, 683 SW2d 882.—Admin Law 485, 489.1; Mun Corp 187(5), 187(8.1).

Gibson v. Thompson, USTex, 78 SCt 2, 355 US 18, 2 LEd2d 1, reh den 78 SCt 258, 355 US 900, 2 LEd2d 197, on remand 310 SW2d 564, 158 Tex 231.—Labor & Emp 2881.

Gibson; Thompson v., Tex, 310 SW2d 564, 158 Tex 231.— Labor & Emp 3010.

Gibson; Thompson v., Tex, 298 SW2d 97, 156 Tex 593, cert gr, rev 78 SCt 2, 355 US 18, 2 LEd2d 1, reh den 78 SCt 258, 355 US 900, 2 LEd2d 197, on remand 310 SW2d 564, 158 Tex 231.—App & E 1083(4); Courts 90(1), 97(5); Labor & Emp 2778, 2828, 2832, 2855, 2887; Neglig 200, 213, 232.

Gibson; Thompson v., TexCivApp–Fort Worth, 290 SW2d 305, rev 298 SW2d 97, 156 Tex 593, cert gr, rev 78 SCt 2, 355 US 18, 2 LEd2d 1, reh den 78 SCt 258, 355 US 900, 2 LEd2d 197, on remand 310 SW2d 564, 158 Tex 231, aff 310 SW2d 564, 158 Tex 231.—App & E 930(1), 989, 1170.10; Courts 97(5); Labor & Emp 2828, 2887, 2950, 3006.

Gibson v. Tolbert, Tex, 102 SW3d 710.—Trial 21.

Gibson; Tolbert v., TexApp–Waco, 67 SW3d 368, reh overr, and review gr, rev 102 SW3d 710.—App & E 1061.2; Trial 21.

Gibson; Travelers Ins. Co. v., TexComApp, 130 SW2d 1026, 133 Tex 534.—Land & Ten 95.

Gibson; Travelers Ins. Co. v., TexCivApp–Waco, 110 SW2d 241, mod 130 SW2d 1026, 133 Tex 534.—Abate & R 41; App & E 292, 294(1); Evid 220(2); Judgm 682(1); Land & Ten 37; Princ & A 123(11); Tresp to T T 38(3), 41(1), 44.

Gibson v. Turner, Tex, 294 SW2d 781, 156 Tex 289.— Covenants 47, 102(1); Mines 73, 79.1(1), 79.3.

Gibson v. Turner, TexCivApp–Eastland, 274 SW2d 916, aff 294 SW2d 781, 156 Tex 289.—Covenants 130(4); Evid 20(1), 458; Mines 79.3.

Gibson; Twin City Fire Ins. Co. v., TexCivApp–Amarillo, 488 SW2d 565, ref nre.—App & E 930(2), 1060.1(1), 1060.1(3); Damag 59; Evid 10(4), 371, 588; Trial 115(2), 121(1), 121(2), 125(4), 127, 131(1), 131(2), 133.6(4), 133.6(8), 301, 307(1), 317, 412; Witn 361(1), 389, 390, 392(1), 394, 410; Work Comp 975, 976, 1219, 1248, 1265, 1385, 1679, 1846, 1914, 1919, 1968(4), 1974.

Gibson; Union Iron & Metal Co. v., TexCivApp–Texarkana, 374 SW2d 458, ref nre.—Autos 227(0.5); Contrib 5(7); Indem 57, 66; Neglig 530(1).

Gibson; U.S. v., CA5 (Tex), 55 F3d 173.—Consp 47(12); Controlled Subs 145; Crim Law 369.1, 369.2(1), 369.2(7), 512, 641.13(6), 1035(7), 1038.1(4), 1038.2, 1044.1(3), 1153(1), 1159.2(7), 1159.2(8); Disorderly H 2; Searches 112, 123.1.

Gibson; U.S. v., CA5 (Tex), 48 F3d 876, cert den 116 SCt 150, 516 US 852, 133 LEd2d 95.—Crim Law 1158(1); Sent & Pun 738.

Gibson; U.S. v., CA5 (Tex), 963 F2d 708.—Const Law 4594(8); Controlled Subs 31, 39, 75; Crim Law 700(9), 1158(1).

Gibson; U.S. v., CA5 (Tex), 820 F2d 692.—Const Law 2507(3); Crim Law 29(11), 1137(2), 1181.5(3.1); Double J 28; Ind & Inf 159(1), 159(2); Sent & Pun 591; Statut 223.4.

Gibson; U.S. v., CA5 (Tex), 421 F2d 662, cert den 91 SCt 76, 400 US 837, 27 LEd2d 71.—Crim Law 1132; Searches 62.

Gibson; U.S. v., CA5 (Tex), 416 F2d 326.—Crim Law 339.6, 1132, 1169.7.

Gibson v. U.S., CA5 (Tex), 360 F2d 457.—Int Rev 4339, 4528, 4623, 5076.

Gibson; U.S. v., CA5 (Tex), 204 FedAppx 388.—Crim Law 273.1(4), 273.4(1), 273.4(2), 1026.10(4), 1134(3).

Gibson; Vannoy v., TexCivApp–Dallas, 102 SW2d 492.—Ex & Ad 19.

Gibson v. Veteran's Admin., CA5 (Tex), 84 FedAppx 363.—Consp 18; Records 31; U S 127(1).

Gibson; Waco Independent School Dist. v., Tex, 22 SW3d 849, reh overr.—Action 6, 13.

Gibson v. Waco Independent School Dist., TexApp–Waco, 971 SW2d 199, review gr, vac 22 SW3d 849, reh overr.—Admin Law 229; Courts 207.3; Schools 47, 115, 163.

Gibson; Waggoner v., NDTex, 647 FSupp 1102.—Const Law 45, 2312, 2489, 3754; Health 606, 834(1).

Gibson; Walston v., TexCivApp–Galveston, 141 SW2d 997, writ refused.—Hus & W 273(4), 273(9), 273(10).

Gibson v. Watson, TexCivApp–Texarkana, 315 SW2d 48, ref nre.—Deeds 93, 95, 98, 114(1); Mines 55(2), 55(4), 55(5).

Gibson v. Whitley, TexCivApp–Galveston, 132 SW2d 291.—Lim of Act 199(3).

Gibson; Wilder v., TexCivApp–Hous (1 Dist), 440 SW2d 711.—App & E 989, 1003(5).

Gibson v. Worley Mills, Inc., CA5 (Tex), 614 F2d 464, opinion mod 620 F2d 567.—Agric 8, 16; Fed Civ Proc 2212.1; Neglig 387.

Gibson v. Wyatt Cafeterias, Inc., EDTex, 782 FSupp 331.—Labor & Emp 407; States 18.47, 18.51; Work Comp 2122.

Gibson v. Young, TexCivApp–Eastland, 208 SW2d 139, dism.—App & E 901, 931(8), 1008.1(8.1).

Gibson & Associates, Inc. v. Home Ins. Co., NDTex, 966 FSupp 468.—Insurance 2274, 2275, 2277, 2278(8), 2278(21), 2316, 2915.

Gibson Discount Center; Hill v., TexCivApp–Amarillo, 437 SW2d 289, ref nre.—App & E 954(2); Const Law 48(1), 990, 1002; Evid 594; Sunday 2, 29(1).

Gibson Discount Center, Inc. v. Cruz, TexCivApp–El Paso, 562 SW2d 511, ref nre.—App & E 768; Damag 94; False Imp 31, 34, 36, 39; Mal Pros 64(2), 69.

Gibson Distributing Co., Inc. v. Downtown Development Ass'n of El Paso, Inc., Tex, 572 SW2d 334,

appeal dism 99 SCt 606, 439 US 1000, 58 LEd2d 674.—Antitrust 902; Const Law 3334, 4263; States 18.84; Sunday 2.

Gibson Distributing Co., Inc.-Permian Basin, In re, BkrtcyWDTex, 40 BR 767.—Bankr 2742.

Gibson Distributing Co., Inc.-Permian Basin; Haynie v., BkrtcyWDTex, 40 BR 767. See Gibson Distributing Co., Inc.-Permian Basin, In re.

Gibson Drilling Co. v. B & N Petroleum Inc., TexApp–Tyler, 703 SW2d 822, ref nre.—Mines 55(2), 55(5), 78.1(7), 78.1(10), 78.3.

Gibson Drilling Co.; McCormick Operating Co. v., TexApp–Tyler, 717 SW2d 425.—App & E 68, 76(1), 80(1), 80(4).

Gibson Oil Co.; Scott v., TexCivApp–Tyler, 471 SW2d 924.—Autos 244(11), 244(34), 244(40); Evid 588; New Tr 68.3, 72(5); Trial 139.1(3), 140(1), 143.

Gibson Product Co., Inc., of Del Rio; Overstreet v., TexCivApp–San Antonio, 558 SW2d 58, ref nre.—Anim 66.1, 66.9; App & E 989; Judgm 199(3.15); Neglig 1085, 1088.

Gibson Products Co.; Casey v., TexCivApp–Dallas, 216 SW2d 266, writ dism.—Guar 24(1); Princ & A 177(1), 177(3.1).

Gibson Products Co.; Davis v., TexCivApp–San Antonio, 505 SW2d 682, ref nre 513 SW2d 4.—App & E 231(1); Evid 265(1); Neglig 1119, 1298(2), 1713, 1714; Prod Liab 5, 15, 19.1, 58, 83; Trial 350.3(5), 350.6(2), 351.5(5).

Gibson Products Co. v. U.S., CA5 (Tex), 637 F2d 1041.—Int Rev 3036, 3273, 3360, 3373, 3377.

Gibson Products Co. v. U.S., NDTex, 460 FSupp 1109, aff 637 F2d 1041.—Int Rev 3273, 3373, 3386, 3430.1, 3942.

Gibson Products Co., Inc. v. State, Tex, 545 SW2d 128, cert den Gibson Products, Inc of Richardson v. Texas, 97 SCt 2677, 431 US 955, 53 LEd2d 272.—Sunday 2.

Gibson Products Co., Inc.; State v., TexApp–Waco, 699 SW2d 640.—Action 6; App & E 781(1), 781(4).

Gibson Products Co., Inc.; U.S. v., SDTex, 426 FSupp 768.—Corp 526.

Gibson Products Co., Inc., of Odessa; Bingham v., TexCivApp–El Paso, 464 SW2d 713, ref nre.—Judgm 181(33), 185(2), 185(3), 186; Neglig 1542.

Gibson Products Co., Inc. of Sherman; Advance Imports, Inc. v., TexCivApp–Dallas, 533 SW2d 168.—J P 158(1), 161.1(1), 162(1), 164(3), 166(5).

Gibson Products Co. of San Angelo v. Alexander, TexCivApp–Austin, 466 SW2d 81, ref nre.—Land & Ten 152(11).

Gibson Products of San Antonio, Inc.; F.T.C. v., CA5 (Tex), 569 F2d 900.—Antitrust 295, 307, 953.

Gibson Refrigerator Sales Corp.; Major Appliance Co. v., CA5 (Tex), 254 F2d 497.—Bankr 2680; Fed Civ Proc 2282.1; Plgs 22, 53.

Gibson's Discount Center, Inc.; Texas State Bd. of Pharmacy v., TexCivApp–Austin, 541 SW2d 884, ref nre.—App & E 719(8); Const Law 1066, 4286; Health 105, 198, 308.

Gibson's Discount Center, Inc.; Texas State Bd. of Pharmacy v., TexCivApp–Austin, 530 SW2d 332, writ gr, rev 539 SW2d 141, on remand 541 SW2d 884, ref nre.—App & E 454; Courts 247(1), 472.2, 475(1).

Gibson's Discount Centers, Inc.; Texas State Bd. of Pharmacy v., Tex, 539 SW2d 141, on remand 541 SW2d 884, ref nre.—App & E 422.

Gibson's Distributing Company; State v., Tex, 436 SW2d 122.—App & E 339(2), 621(3), 627; Inj 158.

Gibson's Products, Inc. of Plano; Brennan v., EDTex, 407 FSupp 154, vacMarshall v. Gibson's Products, Inc of Plano, 584 F2d 668.—Fed Cts 1004.1; Labor & Emp 2554, 2556, 2600; Searches 79; Statut 210.

Gibson's Products, Inc. of Plano; Marshall v., CA5 (Tex), 584 F2d 668.—Admin Law 385.1, 387; Atty Gen 6; Fed Civ Proc 1742(1); Fed Cts 5, 30, 201.1, 232, 241,

242.1, 263, 442.1, 557; Inj 130; Labor & Emp 2571, 2600; Searches 109; Statut 181(1), 195.

Gibson, Traders & General Ins. Co., Intervenor; Phillips Petroleum Co. v., CA5 (Tex), 232 F2d 13, vac 77 SCt 16, 352 US 874, 1 LEd2d 77, reh den 77 SCt 220, 352 US 937, 1 LEd2d 169.—Evid 591; Explos 7, 8; Fed Civ Proc 2111, 2127, 2141, 2609; Neglig 506(6), 1037(4), 1088, 1286(7), 1693, 1713, 1717.

G.I.C. Ins. Co.; Eagle Life Ins. Co. v., TexApp–San Antonio, 697 SW2d 648, ref nre.—Contracts 143(2), 143(3), 143.5; Insurance 1806, 2425.

Gidcumb v. State, TexCrimApp, 81 SW2d 506, 128 TexCrim 395.—Crim Law 1091(15), 1092.7, 1092.8, 1092.11(1), 1099.7(2), 1099.7(3), 1120(8), 1144.1; Sod 6.

Gidden; Moore v., TexApp–Austin, 931 SW2d 726. See Moore v. Morris.

Giddens; Aetna Ins. Co. v., Tex, 476 SW2d 664.—Work Comp 817, 818, 1615.

Giddens; Aetna Ins. Co. v., TexCivApp–San Antonio, 474 SW2d 29, rev 476 SW2d 664.—Work Comp 1374, 1610, 1974.

Giddens v. Brooks, TexApp–Beaumont, 92 SW3d 878, review den.—Atty & C 62; Convicts 6; Health 804, 809; Prisons 4(10.1).

Giddens v. Donald Palmer Inc., TexApp–Houston (1 Dist), 679 SW2d 631.—Acct Action on 11.

Giddens; Laxson v., TexApp–Waco, 48 SW3d 408, reh overr, and review den, and reh of petition for review den.—App & E 241, 930(1); Consp 1.1, 9, 13, 19; Judgm 199(1), 199(3.10).

Giddens v. Moore, TexCivApp–Austin, 348 SW2d 404.—Plead 52(2); Ven & Pur 18(1), 18(3), 334(5).

Giddens v. State, TexApp–Corpus Christi, 818 SW2d 501.—App & E 911.3; Courts 4, 35; Forfeit 5.

Giddens v. Williams, TexCivApp–Texarkana, 265 SW2d 187, ref nre.—App & E 882(4); Judgm 710; Pub Lands 173(18), 175(5), 175(6); States 191.4(1), 203; Tresp to T T 27.

Giddens Bakery v. Donald Palmer, Inc., TexApp–Houston (1 Dist), 679 SW2d 631. See Giddens v. Donald Palmer Inc.

Giddings v. Chandler, CA5 (Tex), 979 F2d 1104.—Aliens 387; Fed Cts 776; Mand 72.

Giddings v. Giddings, TexApp–Austin, 701 SW2d 284, ref nre.—App & E 190(1); Divorce 255, 287; Estop 52.10(1); Hus & W 279(6), 281; Judgm 91.

Giddings; Giddings v., TexApp–Austin, 701 SW2d 284, ref nre.—App & E 190(1); Divorce 255, 287; Estop 52.10(1); Hus & W 279(6), 281; Judgm 91.

Giddings v. Harold V. Simpson & Co., TexCivApp–Waco, 532 SW2d 719.—Acct Action on 13; App & E 192.1, 907(3).

Giddings v. State, TexCrimApp, 438 SW2d 805.—Crim Law 339.11(9), 1174(2); Rape 51(3), 51(7).

Giddings v. State, TexCrimApp, 94 SW2d 1168, 130 TexCrim 406.—Assault 96(1); Crim Law 351(3), 366(6), 404.65, 1169.2(6); Homic 1154.

Giddings v. State, TexApp–Dallas, 816 SW2d 538, petition for discretionary review refused.—Controlled Subs 63, 65, 67, 74, 80; Crim Law 31, 312, 1144.13(3), 1159.2(7); Ind & Inf 91(1), 96, 110(3).

Giddings; U.S. v., CA5 (Tex), 37 F3d 1091, cert den 115 SCt 1323, 514 US 1008, 131 LEd2d 203.—Crim Law 1147; Sent & Pun 650, 2033, 2038.

Giddings; U.S. v., CA5 (Tex), 107 FedAppx 420, cert gr, vac Edwards v. US, 125 SCt 1409, 543 US 1181, 161 LEd2d 177, on remand 132 FedAppx 535, cert den 126 SCt 2312, 164 LEd2d 831.—Consp 40.4, 47(3.1), 47(12); Crim Law 423(1); Sent & Pun 752, 761.

Giddings Convalescent Home, Inc. v. Wilson, TexCivApp–Austin, 473 SW2d 246, ref nre.—Joint Adv 1.1, 1.14; Trusts 103(1).

Giddings Convalescent Home, Inc. v. Wilson, TexCivApp–Austin, 456 SW2d 784, ref nre.—Fraud 41.

Giddings Petroleum Corp. v. Peterson Food Mart, Inc., TexApp–Austin, 859 SW2d 89, reh overr, and reh overr, and reh overr, and writ den.—Bankr 2834, 3103(2), 3103.2, 3106, 3115.1, 3117; Judgm 181(11), 185(6); Torts 212.

Gidel; Glenn v., TexCivApp–Amarillo, 496 SW2d 692.—Contracts 147(3), 176(2), 250; Damag 184; Evid 323(3), 596(1); Libel 1, 6(2), 7(13), 24, 33, 123(1), 123(2); Torts 214, 242; Trial 48, 141; Witn 405(1).

Gidel; Glenn v., TexCivApp–Amarillo, 477 SW2d 331, appeal after remand 496 SW2d 692.—Judgm 181(33); Libel 50, 51(1).

Gideon, Ex parte, TexCrimApp, 493 SW2d 156.—Extrad 32, 36; Hab Corp 526.

Gideon v. Johns-Manville Sales Corp., CA5 (Tex), 761 F2d 1129.—Action 38(3); Contrib 5(1), 7; Damag 50, 52, 62(1), 62(3), 182, 184, 185(1), 208(1), 213; Evid 48, 146, 155(1), 536; Fed Civ Proc 1941, 2141, 2142.1, 2173.1(1), 2183, 2195; Fed Cts 416, 637; Neglig 202, 303(1); Prod Liab 11, 14, 17.1, 62, 75.1, 81.1, 82.1, 83, 96.1; Torts 117; Work Comp 1509, 2084.

Gideon; McFadden v., TexApp–El Paso, 639 SW2d 43, ref nre.—Admin Law 651; Mun Corp 180(2).

Gideon; Maryland Cas. Co. v., TexCivApp–El Paso, 213 SW2d 848.—Trial 312(3); Work Comp 1637, 1638, 1641, 1926, 1932, 1968(8).

Gideon v. Service Life & Cas. Ins. Co., TexCivApp–Corpus Christi, 510 SW2d 631, 88 ALR3d 1059.—Insurance 1808, 1816, 1822, 1832(1), 2432(2).

Gideon; Texaco Inc. v., TexCivApp–Austin, 366 SW2d 628.—Venue 5.3(1), 5.3(8).

Gidney; Sinnott v., Tex, 322 SW2d 507, 159 Tex 366, 74 ALR2d 544.—Tax 3356, 3370; Wills 453, 587(3), 587(5), 732(2), 736(2), 832, 836.

Gidney; Sinnott v., TexCivApp–Amarillo, 311 SW2d 951, rev 322 SW2d 507, 159 Tex 366, 74 ALR2d 544.—Ex & Ad 218; Tax 3370; Wills 440, 470(1), 493, 706, 736(1), 736(2).

Gidvani v. Aldrich, TexApp–Houston (1 Dist), 99 SW3d 760.—Dist & Pros Attys 10; Offic 114.

Gieb v. Goebel Brewing Co., TexCivApp–Fort Worth, 176 SW2d 975, writ refused wom.—App & E 846(5); Contracts 88; Evid 461(1); Guar 16(2), 25(3); Sales 291.

Giebel; Sheppard v., TexCivApp–Austin, 110 SW2d 166.—Const Law 990, 4294; Licens 7(1), 7(3), 11(1), 19(3); Nuis 6; Statut 64(1), 64(8), 121(1).

Gierczic v. Gierczic, TexCivApp–Houston, 382 SW2d 495.—Child S 537.

Gierczic; Gierczic v., TexCivApp–Houston, 382 SW2d 495.—Child S 537.

Giersch; McCain v., CCA5 (Tex), 112 F2d 70.—Contracts 147(1); Fed Cts 859; Frds St of 74(1), 158(1), 158(4).

Giesberg v. Cockrell, CA5 (Tex), 288 F3d 268, reh en banc den 45 FedAppx 327, cert den 123 SCt 663, 537 US 1072, 154 LEd2d 566.—Hab Corp 603, 842.

Giesberg v. State, TexCrimApp, 984 SW2d 245, cert den 119 SCt 1044, 525 US 1147, 143 LEd2d 51, reh den 119 SCt 1490, 526 US 1082, 143 LEd2d 571.—Crim Law 31, 772(6), 775(2).

Giesberg v. State, TexApp–Houston (1 Dist), 945 SW2d 120, supplemented on reh, and petition for discretionary review gr, and petition for discretionary review refused, aff 984 SW2d 245, cert den 119 SCt 1044, 525 US 1147, 143 LEd2d 51, reh den 119 SCt 1490, 526 US 1082, 143 LEd2d 571, dism of habeas corpus aff 288 F3d 268, reh en banc den 45 FedAppx 327, cert den 123 SCt 663, 537 US 1072, 154 LEd2d 566.—Crim Law 339.7(4), 720(5), 726, 730(16), 775(2), 1086.14, 1091(5), 1134(3), 1172.2; Homic 1184, 1185; Jury 97(1).

Giese v. NCNB Texas Forney Banking Center, TexApp–Dallas, 881 SW2d 776.—App & E 223, 231(1), 242(1), 1073(1); Judgm 178, 181(25), 185.1(3), 185.1(8), 186, 189; Plead 16, 34(1); Sec Tran 87, 90, 228, 242.1.

Giese; Wald Transfer & Storage Co. v., TexCivApp–Galveston, 101 SW2d 603, writ dism.—App & E 232(1), 1069.3; Hus & W 210(2); Trover 47.

Gieseck v. Ross, TexCivApp–Fort Worth, 243 SW2d 873. —Appear 12; Infants 198; Mental H 488.

Giesecke v. Gayle, TexCivApp–Galveston, 129 SW2d 334. —Mun Corp 162.

Giesecke; Schering Corp. v., TexCivApp–Eastland, 589 SW2d 516, ref nre.—App & E 930(1), 989; Damag 63, 208(7); Judgm 615; Prod Liab 46.2, 83.

Giesecke v. U.S., WDTex, 637 FSupp 309.—Fed Cts 681.1; Int Rev 3050, 3331, 5342, 5348.

Giesen v. State, TexApp–Dallas, 688 SW2d 176.—Crim Law 366(3), 388.5(1), 720(5), 730(1), 730(8), 730(12), 730(14), 1169.1(9), 1169.5(1), 1171.3; Rape 48(1).

Giesenschlag; Burleson County v., TexCivApp–Houston, 354 SW2d 418.—Counties 57, 113(5); Em Dom 19, 68, 167(1), 169, 171, 172.

Giesenschlag v. Valenta, TexCivApp–Galveston, 225 SW2d 914, ref nre.—Health 682, 821(5).

Giesler v. Giesler, TexCivApp–San Antonio, 309 SW2d 949.—Divorce 252.3(1), 253(4), 286(0.5); Hus & W 262.1(5), 264(3).

Giesler; Giesler v., TexCivApp–San Antonio, 309 SW2d 949.—Divorce 252.3(1), 253(4), 286(0.5); Hus & W 262.1(5), 264(3).

Giessel, Matter of Estate of, TexApp–Houston (1 Dist), 734 SW2d 27, ref nre.—Marriage 13, 50(1), 50(4), 50(5), 52.

Giffin v. Giffin, TexApp–Corpus Christi, 962 SW2d 649. —App & E 781(4), 803.

Giffin; Giffin v., TexApp–Corpus Christi, 962 SW2d 649. —App & E 781(4), 803.

Giffin v. Smith, Tex, 688 SW2d 112.—Atty & C 34; Pretrial Proc 33, 38, 181.

Gifford v. Bank of the Southwest, TexApp–Houston (14 Dist), 712 SW2d 182.—App & E 195; Estop 112; Judgm 185(2), 185.3(21); Lim of Act 95(1.5), 95(8).

Gifford; City of Austin v., TexApp–Austin, 824 SW2d 735.—App & E 930(3), 989, 1078(3); Civil R 1736, 1744, 1765; Courts 97(1); Interest 39(2.45); Plead 236(3), 236(7), 245(6), 258(5).

Gifford; Dougherty v., TexApp–Texarkana, 826 SW2d 668.—App & E 209.2(1), 930(3), 1001(1), 1003(5), 1003(7), 1015(4); Damag 96, 99, 186; Health 825, 829, 832; Hus & W 209(3), 209(4); Labor & Emp 23, 29, 58; Lim of Act 1, 55(3), 104(1), 104(2), 104(3), 121(2), 124, 127(1), 197(2), 199(2); Pretrial Proc 42.

Gifford; Dougherty & Associates v., TexApp–Texarkana, 826 SW2d 668. See Dougherty v. Gifford.

Gifford; Edwards v., Tex, 155 SW2d 786, 137 Tex 559.— App & E 218.2(5.1); Judgm 73, 91; Trial 350.1, 351.2(8).

Gifford; Edwards v., TexCivApp–Beaumont, 132 SW2d 155, aff 155 SW2d 786, 137 Tex 559.—Adv Poss 115(5); App & E 218.2(10), 742(6), 1122(2), 1122(3); Courts 247(5); Judgm 91; Trial 351.2(1.1), 351.2(6), 351.2(10), 351.5(3).

Gifford; Employers Mut. Cas. Co. v., TexApp–Fort Worth, 723 SW2d 811.—App & E 920(2), 966(1); Work Comp 1173.

Gifford v. Fort Worth & D. C. Ry. Co., Tex, 249 SW2d 190, 151 Tex 282.—App & E 719(6), 1094(5), 1114; R R 400(12).

Gifford; Fort Worth & D. C. Ry. Co. v., TexCivApp–Fort Worth, 252 SW2d 204.—App & E 1004(5); Damag 127, 134(1), 163(1); Evid 18.

Gifford; Fort Worth & D. C. Ry. Co. v., TexCivApp–Fort Worth, 244 SW2d 848, rev 249 SW2d 190, 151 Tex 282. —App & E 996, 1053(2); Neglig 1694; New Tr 76(1), 76(4); R R 369(3), 381(1), 383(1), 387, 398(1).

Gifford v. Gabbard, TexCivApp–El Paso, 305 SW2d 668. —Hus & W 254, 257, 264(5); Refer 8(8).

Gifford v. Howell, TexCivApp–Amarillo, 119 SW2d 578, dism.—Health 619, 625, 825.

Gifford; Kaiser, Estate of v., TexApp–Houston (1 Dist), 692 SW2d 525, ref nre.—Contracts 313(2); Costs 194.25, 252; Frds St of 139(1); Gifts 49(5).

Gifford v. Lone Star Steel Co., EDTex, 2 FSupp2d 909, aff 170 F3d 183.—Civil R 1137, 1204, 1209.

Gifford; Marshall K. Dougherty & Associates v., TexApp–Texarkana, 826 SW2d 668. See Dougherty v. Gifford.

Gifford v. National Gypsum Co., CA5 (Tex), 753 F2d 1345.—Fed Cts 844, 845; Prod Liab 83.

Gifford v. Old Republic Ins. Co., TexCivApp–Hous (14 Dist), 613 SW2d 43.—Afft 18; Judgm 181(26), 183.

Gifford; Skyline Furniture, Inc. v., TexCivApp–El Paso, 433 SW2d 950.—App & E 846(5), 1010.1(2); Bills & N 296, 326, 327, 516; Contracts 176(2), 338(1); Evid 461(1).

Gifford v. State, TexCrimApp, 253 SW2d 43.—Crim Law 1090.1(1).

Gifford v. State, TexApp–Fort Worth, 740 SW2d 76, petition for discretionary review refused.—Crim Law 37(1), 37(2.1), 37(5), 37(6.1), 569, 739.1(1).

Gifford v. State, TexApp–Austin, 630 SW2d 387.—Crim Law 394.1(3), 412(4), 517(1), 1177; Sent & Pun 115(4).

Gifford v. State, TexApp–Dallas, 793 SW2d 48, petition for discretionary review gr, petition for discretionary review dism with per curiam opinion 810 SW2d 225.— Autos 357, 422.1; Crim Law 388.2, 1173.2(5).

Gifford v. State, TexApp–Houston (14 Dist), 980 SW2d 791, reh overr, and petition for discretionary review refused.—Crim Law 641.13(7); Sent & Pun 310, 361.

Gifford v. State, TexCivApp–El Paso, 229 SW2d 949.— Usury 32, 94, 117.

Gifford v. State ex rel. Lilly, TexCivApp–Waco, 525 SW2d 250, writ dism by agreement.—Quo W 5, 26, 33, 48, 49.

Gifford v. Sullivan, TexCivApp–Dallas, 587 SW2d 475.— Judgm 143(17), 145(4).

Gifford v. U.S., CA5 (Tex), 261 F2d 825.—Crim Law 372(1), 564(1); Ind & Inf 180.

Gifford v. Wichita Falls & Southern Ry. Co., CA5 (Tex), 224 F2d 374, cert den 76 SCt 153, 350 US 895, 100 LEd 787.—Fed Civ Proc 392, 821.

Gifford v. Wichita Falls & S. Ry. Co., CA5 (Tex), 211 F2d 494.—Fed Civ Proc 2151; Labor & Emp 2793.

Gifford v. Woodruff, TexCivApp–Beaumont, 448 SW2d 804.—App & E 1170.6, 1170.10; Trial 122.

Gifford Hill American, Inc. v. Whittington, TexApp–Amarillo, 899 SW2d 760.—App & E 177, 218.2(7), 230, 242(2), 1001(1), 1001(3), 1003(7); Interest 39(2.40), 39(2.55), 56; Labor & Emp 863(2); Pretrial Proc 44.1; Trial 140(1).

Gifford-Hill & Co.; Commissioner of Internal Revenue v., CA5 (Tex), 180 F2d 655.—Int Rev 4132, 4134.

Gifford-Hill & Co. v. Hearne Sand & Gravel Co., TexCivApp–Waco, 183 SW2d 766.—Plead 34(1), 111.15; Venue 7.5(3), 8.5(7).

Gifford-Hill & Co. v. Henderson, TexCivApp–Texarkana, 81 SW2d 274, writ dism woj, and writ gr, and writ dism. —App & E 218.2(4), 218.2(5.1), 994(1), 1015(5), 1050.1(6); Autos 305(6); Damag 130.3; New Tr 143(2); Trial 131(2), 219.

Gifford-Hill & Co. v. Jones, TexCivApp–El Paso, 99 SW2d 656.—Assign 138; Contracts 245(2), 346(9); Trial 140(1), 206, 219, 350.4(1), 352.16, 397(6).

Gifford-Hill & Co. v. Midlothian Independent School Dist., TexCivApp–Waco, 459 SW2d 944, ref nre.— Schools 103(1), 103(4), 106, 107.

Gifford-Hill & Co. v. Moore, TexCivApp–Tyler, 479 SW2d 711.—App & E 912; Autos 193(10), 242(6); Labor & Emp 3030, 3045, 3047, 3094(4), 3096(7); Plead 111.19, 111.39(4), 111.42(4); Venue 21.

Gifford-Hill & Co.; Space City Const. Co. v., TexCivApp–Hous (1 Dist), 468 SW2d 897.—Costs 194.38; Damag 67; Judgm 181(15.1), 185(2), 187; Mech Liens 49.

Gifford-Hill & Co. v. State, Tex, 442 SW2d 320.—Tax 3642, 3645.

Gifford-Hill & Co.; State v., TexCivApp–Austin, 428 SW2d 451, writ gr, rev 442 SW2d 320.—Sales 201(4); Tax 3645, 3677, 3693.

Gifford-Hill & Co., Inc.; American Nat. Ins. Co. v., TexApp–Dallas, 673 SW2d 915, ref nre.—Accord 7(3); Bills & N 429; Contracts 93(5); Impl & C C 22; Judgm 181(6), 185.3(2); Tender 14(5).

Gifford-Hill & Co., Inc.; Burdett v., TexApp–Fort Worth, 739 SW2d 663.—Const Law 3998; Costs 260(5); New Tr 155.

Gifford-Hill & Co., Inc.; Peters v., TexApp–Dallas, 794 SW2d 856, writ den.—Evid 404; Guar 25(3), 26, 72.

Gifford-Hill & Co., Inc.; Revill v., TexApp–Texarkana, 836 SW2d 311.—Contracts 176(8), 187(1); Judgm 185(4).

Gifford-Hill & Co., Inc. v. Wise County Appraisal Dist., Tex, 827 SW2d 811, am on reh in part.—Judgm 181(32); Mines 48; Tax 2309, 2523, 2525.

Gifford-Hill & Co., Inc. v. Wise County Appraisal Dist., TexApp–Fort Worth, 791 SW2d 576, writ gr, rev 827 SW2d 811, am on reh in part.—App & E 1024.4; Judgm 185(5), 186; Statut 176; Tax 2172, 2196, 2525, 2587, 2674.

Gifford-Hill & Co., Inc.; Wright v., Tex, 725 SW2d 712, on remand 736 SW2d 828, ref nre.—Damag 87(2), 94; Work Comp 4, 2145, 2157.

Gifford-Hill & Co., Inc.; Wright v., TexApp–Waco, 736 SW2d 828, ref nre.—App & E 837(10), 854(2), 1062.1; Labor & Emp 2842, 2848, 2855, 2870, 2923; Lim of Act 121(2), 126, 193, 201, 202(1); Neglig 371, 379, 380, 387; Work Comp 2094, 2134, 2136, 2156, 2157.

Gifford-Hill & Co., Inc.; Wright v., TexApp–Waco, 705 SW2d 868, ref nre, and writ gr, and writ withdrawn, rev 725 SW2d 712, on remand 736 SW2d 828, ref nre.—Work Comp 2157.

Gifford-Hill Concrete Corp.; University State Bank v., TexCivApp–Fort Worth, 431 SW2d 561, ref nre.—Assign 46, 71; Bankr 2571; Contracts 238(2), 247; Evid 427, 441(1), 445(1); Impl & C C 30, 100, 121; Interpl 35; Mech Liens 113(1), 310(3); Notice 5, 6, 14; Paymt 75; Plead 20; Princ & A 177(1).

GI Forum Image De Tejas v. Texas Educ. Agency, WDTex, 87 FSupp2d 667.—Civil R 1033(1), 1055, 1070, 1330(1), 1406; Const Law 4207, 4212(1); Schools 178.

Gigliobianco v. State, TexCrimApp, 210 SW3d 637.—Autos 411; Crim Law 338(7).

Gigliobianco v. State, TexApp–San Antonio, 179 SW3d 136, reh overr, and petition for discretionary review gr, aff 210 SW3d 637.—Autos 355(6), 411; Const Law 4638; Crim Law 308, 338(7), 469.1, 778(3), 1134(2), 1147, 1153(1), 1162, 1165(1), 1169.1(1), 1169.9, 1172.1(1).

Giglio Distributing Co., Inc.; Miller v., EDTex, 899 FSupp 318.—Civil R 1113.

Gigowski v. Russell, TexApp–Tyler, 718 SW2d 16, ref nre.—Contracts 169; Covenants 49, 51(1), 108(1); Inj 11, 13, 16, 62(1).

Gihls Properties, Inc. v. Main Lafrentz & Co., TexCivApp–El Paso, 542 SW2d 203.—Inj 138.31, 163(3).

Gil v. Beto, CA5 (Tex), 440 F2d 666.—Controlled Subs 135.

Gil v. Beto, WDTex, 323 FSupp 1264, aff 440 F2d 666.—Courts 100(1); Crim Law 394.4(1); Hab Corp 765.1, 767; Searches 23.

Gil v. State, TexCrimApp, 394 SW2d 810.—Arrest 63.4(14), 71.1(9); Crim Law 394.4(11); Searches 17.

Gil v. State, TexApp–Austin, 756 SW2d 108.—Crim Law 790, 866, 1172.1(2), 1174(2).

Gil; Texas Dept. of Public Safety v., TexCivApp–Austin, 292 SW2d 832.—Autos 144.2(2.1), 144.2(10).

Gilbeaux v. University of Texas Medical Branch, EDTex, 42 FSupp2d 637.—Fed Civ Proc 657.5(1); Fed Cts 5, 30, 32, 161, 244, 247, 261, 282, 286.1, 287, 317.

Gilbert, Ex parte, TexCrimApp, 593 SW2d 685.—Crim Law 223.

Gilbert, Ex parte, TexCrimApp, 135 SW2d 718, 138 TexCrim 269.—Hab Corp 743.

Gilbert v. Akins & Pettiette, TexApp–Houston (1 Dist), 838 SW2d 890. See Gilbert v. Pettiette.

Gilbert; Anderson v., Tex, 897 SW2d 783, reh overr, on remand 1995 WL 634151, writ den.—App & E 756, 761; Mtg 579.

Gilbert; Anderson v., TexApp–Dallas, 900 SW2d 67, writ gr, rev 897 SW2d 783, reh overr, on remand 1995 WL 634151, writ den.—App & E 683, 758.3(2), 842(1), 970(2); Evid 113(11), 113(19), 555.6(2); Trial 43.

Gilbert v. Bartel, TexApp–Fort Worth, 144 SW3d 136, reh overr, and review den, and reh of petition for review den.—Const Law 328, 2312, 2314, 2315; Judgm 181(7); Lim of Act 4(2), 55(3), 104(1).

Gilbert v. Beto, SDTex, 274 FSupp 847.—Const Law 4664(1); Courts 100(1); Crim Law 517.1(1), 517.2(3), 518(1), 519(1), 519(8), 519(9), 527, 531(3).

Gilbert, Estate of v. Black, TexApp–Austin, 722 SW2d 548.—Mand 32; Pretrial Proc 381.

Gilbert; Brothers v., TexApp–Eastland, 950 SW2d 213, reh overr, and review den.—Civil R 1715; Lim of Act 55(4).

Gilbert v. Brownell Electro, TexApp–Tyler, 832 SW2d 143.—Judgm 143(3), 162(2), 163.

Gilbert v. Canter, TexCivApp–Hous (14 Dist), 500 SW2d 557, ref nre.—App & E 302(6); Autos 244(49), 244(58); Evid 597.

Gilbert; Chastain v., TexCivApp–Eastland, 145 SW2d 938.—App & E 218.2(7), 747(2), 1177(1); Evid 400(6); Judgm 251(2); Sales 38(1), 130(2), 347(2), 363.

Gilbert v. Collins, CA5 (Tex), 905 F2d 61.—Fed Civ Proc 2734; Sent & Pun 1548.

Gilbert; Dominguez v., TexApp–Austin, 48 SW3d 789.—App & E 497(1), 712; Decl Judgm 1, 300; Mand 187.10; Records 50, 62, 63, 66.

Gilbert v. El Paso County Hosp. Dist., Tex, 38 SW3d 85, on remand 64 SW3d 200, reh overr, and review den.—Statut 181(1), 188; Tax 2161, 2428.

Gilbert; El Paso County Hosp. Dist. v., TexApp–El Paso, 64 SW3d 200, reh overr, and review den.—Action 13; App & E 931(1), 945, 946, 954(1), 954(2), 1010.1(1), 1010.2; Counties 192; Courts 4; Decl Judgm 300; Mun Corp 987; Offic 110; Tax 2450.

Gilbert; El Paso County Hosp. Dist. v., TexApp–El Paso, 4 SW3d 66, review gr, rev 38 SW3d 85, on remand 64 SW3d 200, reh overr, and review den.—Statut 190, 219(1), 219(2), 219(3), 219(4), 223.5(1), 223.5(2); Tax 2572.

Gilbert; Fidelity Union Life Ins. Co. v., TexCivApp–El Paso, 85 SW2d 998, writ refused.—Usury 82.

Gilbert v. Fireside Enterprises, Inc., TexCivApp–Dallas, 611 SW2d 869.—Judgm 585(3), 634, 713(2), 720, 724.

Gilbert v. Franklin County Water Dist., TexCivApp–Texarkana, 520 SW2d 503.—Dedi 53, 63(1), 65; Em Dom 31, 64, 242, 319, 323, 325; Judgm 91, 217, 335(1), 335(3), 373, 443(1), 511.

Gilbert; Frazar v., CA5 (Tex), 300 F3d 530, cert gr in part Frew ex relFrew v. Hawkins, 123 SCt 1481, 538 US 905, 155 LEd2d 223, rev 124 SCt 899, 540 US 431, 157 LEd2d 855, on remand 376 F3d 444, on remand 401 FSupp2d 619, aff 457 F3d 432, cert den 127 SCt 1039, 166 LEd2d 714.—Civil R 1027, 1052; Fed Civ Proc 2397.1; Fed Cts 265, 266.1, 270, 576.1; U S 82(2).

Gilbert; Frew v., EDTex, 109 FSupp2d 579, stay den 2000 WL 33795091, opinion vac Frazar v. Gilbert, 300 F3d 530, cert gr in part 123 SCt 1481, 538 US 905, 155 LEd2d 223, rev 124 SCt 899, 540 US 431, 157 LEd2d 855, on remand 376 F3d 444, on remand 401 FSupp2d 619, aff 457 F3d 432, cert den Hawkins v Frew, 127 SCt 1039, 166 LEd2d 714, aff in part, appeal dism in part 376 F3d 444, on remand 401 FSupp2d 619, aff 457 F3d

432, cert den 127 SCt 1039, 166 LEd2d 714.—Civil R 1027, 1052; Contracts 143(2); Evid 450(2); Fed Civ Proc 2397.2, 2397.5, 2397.6; Fed Cts 265, 269, 272; Health 467, 473.

Gilbert v. Gilbert, Tex, 195 SW2d 936, 145 Tex 114.—Partit 43; Plead 111.38, 111.42(4).

Gilbert; Gilbert v., Tex, 195 SW2d 936, 145 Tex 114.—Partit 43; Plead 111.38, 111.42(4).

Gilbert v. Gilbert, TexCivApp–San Antonio, 195 SW2d 930, certified question answered 195 SW2d 936, 145 Tex 114.—Partit 43; Plead 111.38, 111.42(3).

Gilbert; Gilbert v., TexCivApp–San Antonio, 195 SW2d 930, certified question answered 195 SW2d 936, 145 Tex 114.—Partit 43; Plead 111.38, 111.42(3).

Gilbert; Grant ex rel. Family Eldercare v., CA5 (Tex), 324 F3d 383.—Decl Judgm 300; Fed Civ Proc 103.2, 103.3, 164.5, 181; Health 510; Inj 114(2).

Gilbert v. Green, Tex, 242 SW2d 879, 150 Tex 521.—Adv Poss 27, 57, 70, 85(1), 85(5); Evid 273(2), 313; Witn 379(2).

Gilbert; Green v., TexCivApp–Austin, 237 SW2d 1010, rev 242 SW2d 879, 150 Tex 521.—Adv Poss 19, 22, 25, 43(4), 50, 57, 85(1), 85(4), 114(1), 115(1); App & E 1001(1), 1002; Trial 143.

Gilbert v. Haigler, TexCivApp–Houston, 363 SW2d 337, ref nre.—App & E 547(3); Damag 127, 132(3), 208(1); Neglig 1656, 1676; Trial 350.1, 350.6(3), 365.1(1); Witn 347.

Gilbert; Hospitality House, Inc. v., CA5 (Tex), 298 F3d 424.—Compromise 21; Fed Cts 3.1, 25, 31, 542, 574, 770, 776.

Gilbert v. Huber, Hunt & Nichols, Inc., TexApp–San Antonio, 672 SW2d 9, ref nre 671 SW2d 869.—App & E 345.1, 395.

Gilbert v. Huber, Hunt, Nichols, Inc., Tex, 671 SW2d 869.—App & E 338(2); Pretrial Proc 698.

Gilbert v. Jackson, TexCivApp–Waco, 265 SW2d 181.—App & E 781(6).

Gilbert v. Jennings, TexApp–Texarkana, 890 SW2d 116, reh overr, and writ den.—Ex & Ad 226; Judgm 185(4).

Gilbert; Linkenhoger v., TexCivApp–San Antonio, 223 SW2d 308, ref nre.—App & E 1050.1(4); Autos 245(83); Damag 132(6.1); Evid 539.

Gilbert; Lobley v., Tex, 236 SW2d 121, 149 Tex 493.—Evid 53, 54, 56, 383(7).

Gilbert v. Lobley, TexCivApp–Fort Worth, 231 SW2d 969, aff 236 SW2d 121, 149 Tex 493.—Adv Poss 82, 104; Evid 56, 89, 372(3); Hus & W 47(1), 138(1), 193; Mines 49.

Gilbert v. Lobley, TexCivApp–Fort Worth, 214 SW2d 646.—App & E 384(1), 387(5), 455; Atty & C 90; Judgm 341; New Tr 109, 137, 138; Proc 5; Statut 218, 226.

Gilbert v. McSpadden, TexCivApp–Waco, 91 SW2d 889, writ refused.—Deeds 54, 56(2), 208(2).

Gilbert; McWilliams v., TexApp–Houston (1 Dist), 715 SW2d 761.—Action 60; Indem 27.

Gilbert v. Mayer, TexCivApp–Austin, 99 SW2d 1021.—Labor & Emp 2956, 2961.

Gilbert v. Mecom, TexCivApp–San Antonio, 247 SW2d 573.—Plead 111.42(3).

Gilbert; Millers Mut. Fire Ins. Co. of Tex. v., TexCivApp–Beaumont, 462 SW2d 112, ref nre.—Damag 221(3); Work Comp 1500, 1929, 1968(1), 1974.

Gilbert v. Mooring, TexCivApp–Eastland, 88 SW2d 537, writ dism.—Abate & R 81; Action 45(1), 47, 50(1); App & E 672, 1040(4); Insurance 3444, 3447, 3571.

Gilbert v. Pettiette, TexApp–Houston (1 Dist), 7 SW3d 895.—App & E 970(2), 1056.1(1), 1056.1(4.1); Costs 194.18, 194.32, 198, 208.

Gilbert v. Pettiette, TexApp–Houston (1 Dist), 838 SW2d 890.—App & E 1062.1, 1064.1(1), 1064.1(5); Compromise 8(1), 20(1); Contracts 16, 24, 29; Costs 32(1), 194.14; Damag 140; Estop 52.10(2); Indem 20.

Gilbert; Pool v., TexCivApp–San Antonio, 199 SW2d 798, ref nre.—App & E 207, 1060.1(2.1); Autos 244(15), 244(42); Trial 121(2).

Gilbert; Rowe v., TexCivApp–Fort Worth, 276 SW2d 583, ref nre.—Wills 449, 577.

Gilbert; Sapphire Homes, Inc. v., TexCivApp–Dallas, 426 SW2d 278, ref nre.—Corp 1.6(4); Usury 53, 55, 138, 141.

Gilbert v. Shenandoah Valley Imp. Ass'n, TexCivApp–Beaumont, 592 SW2d 28.—Covenants 49, 103(1).

Gilbert v. Shinee, TexCivApp–Waco, 461 SW2d 177.—Autos 244(44).

Gilbert v. Singleton, TexApp–Austin, 611 SW2d 163.—App & E 559, 1177(9).

Gilbert v. Smedley, TexCivApp–Fort Worth, 612 SW2d 270, ref nre.—App & E 170(1); Mines 74(3), 78.1(10).

Gilbert v. State, TexCrimApp, 808 SW2d 467.—Crim Law 369.1, 1153(1).

Gilbert v. State, TexCrimApp, 769 SW2d 535.—Crim Law 1172.1(2); Infants 20.

Gilbert v. State, TexCrimApp, 623 SW2d 349.—App & E 5; Bail 77(1); Judgm 17(9); Proc 31, 32, 80.

Gilbert v. State, TexCrimApp, 493 SW2d 783.—Controlled Subs 147; Crim Law 90(4); Mun Corp 189(1); Searches 103.1; States 69.

Gilbert v. State, TexCrimApp, 340 SW2d 808, 170 TexCrim 335.—Crim Law 698(1), 762(3), 822(8), 829(4), 829(5), 1171.3, 1172.6; Homic 1134, 1371, 1489.

Gilbert v. State, TexCrimApp, 284 SW2d 906, 162 TexCrim 290.—Arrest 70(2); Autos 355(6); Crim Law 603.2, 613.

Gilbert v. State, TexCrimApp, 265 SW2d 100, 159 TexCrim 424.—Crim Law 519(4), 519(9), 522(1), 696(1), 736(2).

Gilbert v. State, TexCrimApp, 265 SW2d 85.—Crim Law 1090.1(1).

Gilbert v. State, TexCrimApp, 254 SW2d 784.—Crim Law 1090.1(1).

Gilbert v. State, TexCrimApp, 249 SW2d 216.—Crim Law 1090.1(1).

Gilbert v. State, TexCrimApp, 223 SW2d 622.—Crim Law 1094(3).

Gilbert v. State, TexCrimApp, 212 SW2d 182, 152 TexCrim 200.—Autos 144.2(5.1), 355(6); Crim Law 814(8).

Gilbert v. State, TexCrimApp, 125 SW2d 298, 136 TexCrim 319.—Crim Law 1023(9), 1081(1), 1104(3).

Gilbert v. State, TexCrimApp, 123 SW2d 658, 136 TexCrim 20.—Sent & Pun 1309.

Gilbert v. State, TexApp–Houston (1 Dist), 196 SW3d 163, petition for discretionary review refused.—Crim Law 795(2.1), 795(2.5), 795(2.10); Homic 1457; Ind & Inf 191(4).

Gilbert v. State, TexApp–Houston (1 Dist), 874 SW2d 290, petition for discretionary review refused.—Arrest 63.4(4), 63.5(4), 63.5(6), 68(4); Controlled Subs 26, 27, 30, 80; Crim Law 361(1), 394.6(5), 763(1), 790, 1036.1(2), 1043(1); Witn 288(2).

Gilbert v. State, TexApp–Houston (1 Dist), 840 SW2d 138.—Const Law 4523, 4594(7), 4594(8); Crim Law 695(6), 700(9), 855(1), 945(2), 1043(2); Homic 956, 965, 987, 1050, 1052.

Gilbert v. State, TexApp–Fort Worth, 787 SW2d 233.—Arrest 68(3); Crim Law 552(3), 1144.13(3); Escape 1, 9, 10.

Gilbert v. State, TexApp–Fort Worth, 781 SW2d 296, petition for discretionary review gr, aff 808 SW2d 467.—Crim Law 369.1, 369.2(1), 1169.11.

Gilbert v. State, TexApp–Amarillo, 852 SW2d 623.—Const Law 4733(2), 4782; Crim Law 625.10(2.1), 625.10(4), 1023(16), 1134(3).

Gilbert v. State, TexApp–El Paso, 865 SW2d 601.—Crim Law 363, 368(3), 681(1), 1153(6).

Gilbert v. State, TexApp–Beaumont, 904 SW2d 210.—Ind & Inf 173, 180.

Gilbert v. State, TexCivApp–Hous (14 Dist), 437 SW2d 444, ref nre.—False Imp 2; Hab Corp 462, 662.1, 892.1; States 112.1(1); Statut 188, 238.

Gilbert; Stell Mfg. Co. v., CA5 (Tex), 372 F2d 113.—Bankr 2744.1, 2745, 3101; Sales 61.

Gilbert v. Sterrett, CA5 (Tex), 509 F2d 1389, reh den 515 F2d 510, cert den 96 SCt 373, 423 US 951, 46 LEd2d 288.—Counties 38; Fed Civ Proc 2296; Fed Cts 640, 855.1.

Gilbert v. Texas Co., TexCivApp–Beaumont, 218 SW2d 906, ref nre.—Brok 43(2), 82(1); Contracts 31, 35, 45; Evid 397(1), 420(3); Frds St of 131(1); Plead 8(13); Ven & Pur 28, 350.

Gilbert v. Texas Mental Health and Mental Retardation, EDTex, 919 FSupp 1031.—Civil R 1037, 1360; Evid 544, 547.5; Fed Civ Proc 1278, 2470, 2470.1, 2470.4, 2491.5, 2515, 2539, 2543, 2545, 2552; Mental H 51.1.

Gilbert v. Texas Mental Health and Mental Retardation, NDTex, 888 FSupp 775.—Fed Cts 122.

Gilbert; U.S. v., CA5 (Tex), 573 F2d 346, cert den 99 SCt 284, 439 US 913, 58 LEd2d 259.—Sent & Pun 604.

Gilbert; U.S. v., CA5 (Tex), 553 F2d 990, appeal after remand 573 F2d 346, cert den 99 SCt 284, 439 US 913, 58 LEd2d 259.—Rec S Goods 6.

Gilbert; U.S. v., CA5 (Tex), 537 F2d 118, vac 97 SCt 1169, 430 US 902, 51 LEd2d 578, on remand 553 F2d 990, appeal after remand 573 F2d 346, cert den 99 SCt 284, 439 US 913, 58 LEd2d 259.—Crim Law 1134(8); Rec S Goods 8(4).

Gilbert-Dallas Co., Inc.; Blaustein v., TexApp–Eastland, 749 SW2d 633.—Judgm 181(24); Neglig 387, 433.

Gilbert Gertner Enterprises; Taylor v., TexCivApp–Hous (1 Dist), 466 SW2d 337, ref nre.—Estop 92(2); Evid 65; Hus & W 17, 25(1), 25(5), 209(2); Judgm 185.3(14); Land & Ten 124(1), 162, 167(8).

Gilbert McClure Enterprises v. Burnett, TexApp–Dallas, 735 SW2d 309.—Atty & C 22.

Gilbertson v. State, TexCrimApp, 563 SW2d 606.—Burg 41(4), 41(6).

Gilbertson v. Texas Bd. of Pardons and Paroles, CA5 (Tex), 993 F2d 74.—Civil R 1097; Hab Corp 516.1; Pardon 46.

Gilbreath, Ex parte, TexCrimApp, 311 SW2d 851, 166 TexCrim 64.—Extrad 29, 39.

Gilbreath v. Douglas, TexCivApp–Amarillo, 388 SW2d 279, ref nre.—Evid 571(7); Judgm 18(2), 252(5); Mines 73.5; Partit 13, 30, 63(1), 77(4), 116(1).

Gilbreath; Edwards v., TexCivApp–Galveston, 201 SW2d 261.—Venue 6, 8.5(7), 22(6).

Gilbreath; Farmers Mut. Ins. Ass'n of Erath County v., TexCivApp–Eastland, 270 SW2d 696, ref nre.—App & E 1056.1(9), 1062.5, 1071.5; Insurance 1129, 1642, 1796, 2168, 3131; Trial 350.4(3).

Gilbreath v. Guadalupe Hosp. Foundation Inc., CA5 (Tex), 5 F3d 785.—Admin Law 358; Fed Cts 416; Offic 72.41(1); Records 31; Rem of C 19(1); U S Mag 13; Witn 208(1).

Gilbreath v. Hathaway, TexApp–Beaumont, 108 SW3d 365, review den.—Damag 38, 134(1); Neglig 440(1), 1741; Trial 351.5(6).

Gilbreath; Heath v., TexCivApp–El Paso, 536 SW2d 404.—Venue 7.5(1), 7.5(3).

Gilbreath v. Jones, TexCivApp–El Paso, 477 SW2d 305.—Child C 911.

Gilbreath; Leonhart v., TexCivApp–Houston, 347 SW2d 369.—App & E 882(16), 1060.5; Damag 132(1).

Gilbreath; Reuter v., TexCivApp–Beaumont, 401 SW2d 658, ref nre.—App & E 883, 930(3); Autos 242(8), 244(12), 244(34), 244(35), 244(36.1); Damag 132(1); Neglig 259, 387; Trial 139.1(3), 140(1), 143.

Gilbreath; Southwestern Inv. Co. v., TexCivApp–Amarillo, 380 SW2d 196.—App & E 1177(7); Autos 375, 383.

Gilbreath v. State, TexCrimApp, 500 SW2d 527.—Crim Law 627.6(2), 627.7(3), 1115(1).

Gilbreath v. State, TexCrimApp, 412 SW2d 60.—Arrest 63.4(6), 68(3); Crim Law 491(1), 517(7); Witn 277(4).

Gilbreath v. State, TexCrimApp, 408 SW2d 513.—Larc 51(2).

Gilbreath v. State, TexCrimApp, 259 SW2d 223, 158 TexCrim 616.—Burg 7, 28(6), 41(6), 41(8).

Gilbreath v. State, TexCrimApp, 124 SW2d 996, 136 TexCrim 299.—Crim Law 586, 1097(3), 1098.

Gilbreath; Texas Dept. of Public Safety v., TexApp–Austin, 842 SW2d 408.—Mand 1, 82; Records 54, 57, 62, 63; Statut 219(9.1), 226.

Gilbreath; U.S. v., CA5 (Tex), 452 F2d 992.—Crim Law 770(1), 770(2), 814(3), 1132; Forg 6, 48.

Gilbreath v. White, TexApp–Texarkana, 903 SW2d 851.—Antitrust 291; App & E 852, 901; Insurance 1669, 1779, 1790(7), 3405; Judgm 185(2); Lim of Act 46(6), 55(2), 58(1), 100(1), 182(5), 193.

Gilbreath v. Yarbrough, TexCivApp–Tyler, 472 SW2d 185, ref nre.—Adv Poss 33, 57; App & E 1175(7); Tresp to T T 47(1).

Gilbreth; State v., TexCivApp–Austin, 511 SW2d 556, writ refused.—App & E 767(2), 918(1); Pub Amuse 50, 61, 62; Tax 2735.

Gilchrest v. State, TexApp–Amarillo, 904 SW2d 935.—Crim Law 59(5), 561(1), 569, 695(4), 698(1), 783.5, 795(2.10), 795(2.75), 1159.2(1), 1159.2(4), 1159.2(7), 1159.4(2); Rob 15, 24.10.

Gilchrist, Matter of, CA5 (Tex), 891 F2d 559.—Bankr 3770, 3781.

Gilchrist v. Bandera Elec. Co-op., TexApp–San Antonio, 966 SW2d 716, reh overr, appeal after remand 2000 WL 31855, opinion withdrawn and superseded on reh 2000 WL 730469, review den, cert den 121 SCt 1603, 532 US 972, 149 LEd2d 469.—App & E 78(1), 223, 1172(1); Judgm 183.

Gilchrist; Bandera Elec. Co-op., Inc. v., Tex, 946 SW2d 336, on remand 966 SW2d 716, reh overr, appeal after remand 2000 WL 31855, opinion withdrawn and superseded on reh 2000 WL 730469, review den, cert den 121 SCt 1603, 532 US 972, 149 LEd2d 469.—App & E 1172(1), 1178(6); Judgm 187.

Gilchrist v. Bandera Elec. Co-op., Inc., TexApp–San Antonio, 924 SW2d 388, writ gr, rev 946 SW2d 336, on remand 966 SW2d 716, reh overr, appeal after remand 2000 WL 31855, opinion withdrawn and superseded on reh 2000 WL 730469, review den, cert den 121 SCt 1603, 532 US 972, 149 LEd2d 469.—App & E 76(1), 78(1), 80(6), 1073(1); Judgm 181(2), 183, 185(2).

Gilchrist v. Westcott, CA5 (Tex), 891 F2d 559. See Gilchrist, Matter of.

Gilcrease v. Garlock, Inc., TexApp–El Paso, 211 SW3d 448.—App & E 840(1), 912, 1024.3; Damag 63, 87(1); Death 91, 93; Judgm 658, 714(1); Torts 134; Venue 16, 45, 78.

Gilcrease v. Hartford Acc. & Indem. Co., TexApp–El Paso, 252 SW2d 715.—Pretrial Proc 78; Trial 358; Work Comp 1385, 1543, 1686, 1924, 1930, 1968(1), 1968(5).

Gilcrease; Jostens, Inc. v., TexApp–Austin, 798 SW2d 835, writ den.—Evid 458.

Gilcrease; Legal Sec. Life Ins. Co. v., TexCivApp–Waco, 351 SW2d 263.—Insurance 1809, 2475.

Gilcrease v. State, TexApp–San Antonio, 32 SW3d 277, petition for discretionary review refused, cert den 122 SCt 251, 534 US 911, 151 LEd2d 182.—Const Law 4689; Crim Law 700(10), 720(2), 720(7.1), 722.3, 723(3), 726, 1171.1(2.1), 1171.6.

Gilcrease v. Tesoro Petroleum Corp., TexApp–San Antonio, 70 SW3d 265, review den.—Lim of Act 2(3), 43, 55(4), 95(5); Statut 181(1).

Gilcrease Oil Co.; Armington v., TexCivApp–San Antonio, 190 SW2d 587.—Gifts 16, 18(2), 25; Interpl 11, 35;

Mines 74(8); Trusts 44(1), 371(2); Ven & Pur 54; Wills 6.

Gilcrease Oil Co. v. Cosby, CCA5 (Tex), 132 F2d 790, cert den 64 SCt 77, 320 US 772, 88 LEd 462, reh den 64 SCt 258, 320 US 814, 88 LEd 492.—Estop 9, 26, 98(1); Fed Cts 846; Mines 62.1; Quiet T 10.1.

Gilder v. Allstate Ins. Co., TexCivApp–San Antonio, 417 SW2d 752, ref nre.—Release 27.

Gilder v. Meno, TexApp–Austin, 926 SW2d 357, reh overr, and writ den.—Admin Law 472, 513, 744.1, 791; Const Law 4202; Schools 47, 147.38, 147.42, 147.44; Statut 219(9.1).

Gilder v. State, TexCrimApp, 474 SW2d 723.—Autos 355(6), 422.1.

Gilderbloom v. State, TexCrimApp, 272 SW2d 106, 160 TexCrim 471.—Autos 355(6), 425; Crim Law 763(6), 776(4), 859, 863(2), 1171.1(6); Pardon 22, 28; Statut 64(1), 64(6).

Giles, Ex parte, TexCrimApp, 502 SW2d 774.—Const Law 614, 2330, 2332, 2470, 2540; Controlled Subs 6, 8; Courts 207.4(2); Crim Law 913(4), 1083; Hab Corp 666; Jury 24; Pardon 21, 22, 27, 28; Statut 64(6).

Giles; Barber v., Tex, 208 SW2d 553, 146 Tex 401.—Pub Lands 173(7), 179; Statut 181(1), 205.

Giles v. Basore, Tex, 278 SW2d 830, 154 Tex 366.—Bound 13; Nav Wat 42(1), 44(3); Pub Lands 203, 213; Tresp to T T 35(1).

Giles v. Basore, TexCivApp–Austin, 266 SW2d 926, aff in part, rev in part 278 SW2d 830, 154 Tex 366.—Nav Wat 44(3), 46(2); Pub Lands 203, 213, 223(1).

Giles v. Beto, CA5 (Tex), 437 F2d 192.—Crim Law 273(2), 641.13(7), 1068.5, 1077.1(1); Hab Corp 361, 475.1, 508, 827.

Giles; Brett v., TexCivApp–San Antonio, 127 SW2d 473.—Plead 241; Spec Perf 87, 126(2), 126(3).

Giles; Callahan v., Tex, 155 SW2d 793, 137 Tex 571.—Equity 64, 67; Mand 1, 7, 143(2), 154(4); Pub Lands 173(21.1).

Giles v. Cardenas, TexApp–San Antonio, 697 SW2d 422, ref nre.—App & E 536, 548(1), 1024.1; Costs 194.18, 208; Covenants 72.1, 77.1, 103(1), 108(1), 118, 132(2); Inj 51; Trial 33, 37, 377(1); Ven & Pur 230(1), 231(3).

Giles; Citizens State Bank of Houston v., TexCivApp–Galveston, 145 SW2d 899, writ dism.—Judgm 199(2), 199(3.6), 199(5); Plead 236(4).

Giles; City of Galveston v., TexApp–Houston (1 Dist), 902 SW2d 167.—App & E 845(1), 845(2); Decl Judgm 342, 393, 395; Mun Corp 57, 111(2), 120, 122.1(2), 138, 185(12); Stip 14(10); Trial 368, 388(4).

Giles; Clark & Co. v., Tex, 639 SW2d 449.—New Tr 155, 163(1).

Giles; Elms v., TexCivApp–Texarkana, 173 SW2d 264, writ den State v. Stanolind Oil & Gas Co, 174 SW2d 588, 141 Tex 446.—Judgm 672; Pretrial Proc 582; Pub Lands 173(16.2), 173(16.4).

Giles; First Baptist Church of San Marcos, Colored v., TexApp–Austin, 219 SW2d 498, ref nre.—App & E 930(1), 989; Relig Soc 25.

Giles v. First Nat. Bank of Brownfield, TexCivApp–Amarillo, 257 SW2d 945.—Hus & W 152, 229.3, 238.1, 268(5).

Giles v. Flanagan, TexCivApp–San Antonio, 123 SW2d 477, writ dism, correct.—App & E 1069.1; Mtg 154(3); Trial 304, 351.5(1).

Giles v. General Elec. Co., CA5 (Tex), 245 F3d 474.—Civil R 1217, 1218(4), 1464, 1487, 1563, 1571, 1572, 1573, 1574, 1594, 1765; Damag 102, 192; Estop 68(2); Fed Civ Proc 751, 2497.1, 2544, 2602; Fed Cts 641, 642, 643, 776, 798, 799, 813, 830, 871, 872, 878, 929.

Giles v. Giles, TexApp–Fort Worth, 830 SW2d 232.—Compromise 18(1); Costs 260(5); Divorce 160, 222, 236, 278.1; Judgm 71.1.

Giles; Giles v., TexApp–Fort Worth, 830 SW2d 232.—Compromise 18(1); Costs 260(5); Divorce 160, 222, 236, 278.1; Judgm 71.1.

Giles v. Giles, TexCivApp–Austin, 94 SW2d 208, writ dism.—Deeds 59(1), 208(4); Evid 441(8); Gifts 4, 22, 23, 28(1), 41.

Giles; Giles v., TexCivApp–Austin, 94 SW2d 208, writ dism.—Deeds 59(1), 208(4); Evid 441(8); Gifts 4, 22, 23, 28(1), 41.

Giles; Grayburg Oil Co. v., Tex, 186 SW2d 680, 143 Tex 497.—Mines 5.2(2.1); Nav Wat 37(1), 37(6); Statut 210.

Giles; Great Atlantic & Pacific Tea Co. v., TexCivApp–Dallas, 354 SW2d 410, ref nre.—Judgm 199(3.10); Neglig 1076, 1104(6), 1595, 1670; Trial 139.1(8), 139.1(14), 139.1(17), 178.

Giles; Harlow v., TexApp–Eastland, 132 SW3d 641, review den.—Adv Poss 13, 16(1), 19, 20, 22, 24, 31, 34, 37, 57, 86, 88, 114(1), 115(1); App & E 994(3), 1008.1(2), 1010.1(1), 1012.1(3); Evid 588; Trial 382.

Giles; Holt v., Tex, 240 SW2d 991, 150 Tex 351.—Mines 5.2(3).

Giles; Home Indem. Co. v., TexCivApp–Austin, 392 SW2d 568.—App & E 854(2); Insurance 3141.

Giles; Kier v., TexCivApp–San Antonio, 240 SW2d 818, ref nre.—Mand 168(4); Pub Lands 172.9.

Giles v. Kretzmeier, TexCivApp–Waco, 239 SW2d 706, ref nre.—App & E 1002; Bound 1, 3(7), 37(3), 40(1); Evid 99, 472(6); New Tr 72(6); Pub Lands 175(5), 180.

Giles v. Lehman, TexCivApp–San Antonio, 163 SW2d 720.—Autos 19.

Giles; Lemmon v., TexCivApp–Dallas, 342 SW2d 56, writ dism.—Em Dom 166, 234(5), 235, 266; Judges 24; Mand 53, 73(1).

Giles v. McKanna, TexCivApp–Austin, 200 SW2d 709, ref nre.—Mines 5.2(2.1), 78.2.

Giles v. Missouri-Kansas-Texas R. Co., EDTex, 712 FSupp 542.—Compromise 18(1); Fed Civ Proc 2397.4; Judgm 828.9(2).

Giles; Norman v., Tex, 219 SW2d 678, 148 Tex 21.—Mines 5.2(3); Statut 64(2).

Giles v. NYLCare Health Plans, Inc., CA5 (Tex), 172 F3d 332.—Fed Cts 18, 29.1, 30, 205, 241, 542; Rem of C 25(1), 100, 107(9); States 18.51.

Giles; O'Connor v., TexCivApp–Dallas, 308 SW2d 902.—App & E 560.

Giles; Ohio Oil Co. v., Tex, 235 SW2d 630, 149 Tex 532.—Const Law 48(1); Mines 5.2(2.1); States 109; Statut 64(1).

Giles; Philips v., TexCivApp–Dallas, 620 SW2d 750.—Action 62.

Giles v. Ponder, TexCivApp–San Antonio, 275 SW2d 509, aff Rudder v. Ponder, 293 SW2d 736, 156 Tex 185.—Evid 317(10), 341; Nav Wat 37(7); Pub Lands 176(2).

Giles; Poole v., Tex, 248 SW2d 464, 151 Tex 224.—App & E 781(7); Inj 176.

Giles v. Poole, TexCivApp–Austin, 239 SW2d 665, appeal dism 248 SW2d 464, 151 Tex 224.—App & E 151(2); States 191.10.

Giles; Pridgen v., TexCivApp–Austin, 267 SW2d 187, ref nre.—Offic 114; Pub Lands 176(2).

Giles; Rayburn v., TexCivApp–San Antonio, 182 SW2d 9, writ refused.—App & E 671(6), 761, 762, 843(2), 930(1), 971(2), 1001(1), 1078(1); Evid 474(16), 498.5, 546; Partners 325(2), 329, 336(3); Witn 92.

Giles v. Rayburn, TexCivApp–San Antonio, 173 SW2d 371.—Labor & Emp 207.

Giles; Stanolind Oil & Gas Co. v., CA5 (Tex), 197 F2d 290.—Damag 138; Fed Cts 431; Mines 121, 125; Neglig 1612.

Giles; State v., Tex, 368 SW2d 943.—Em Dom 210, 238(1); Mand 53.

Giles v. State, TexCrimApp, 617 SW2d 690.—Homic 708, 709, 908, 1135, 1458.

Giles v. State, TexCrimApp, 489 SW2d 286.—Homic 1154.

Giles v. State, TexCrimApp, 112 SW2d 473, 133 TexCrim 454.—Burg 42(1); Crim Law 112(9), 394.4(10); Searches 25.1.

Giles v. State, TexCrimApp, 110 SW2d 916, 133 TexCrim 316.—Crim Law 1094(2.1).

Giles v. State, TexApp–Houston (1 Dist), 53 SW3d 718.—Crim Law 1026.10(2.1).

Giles v. State, TexApp–El Paso, 908 SW2d 303, petition for discretionary review refused by 921 SW2d 235.—Extrad 53.1.

Giles; State v., TexApp–El Paso, 867 SW2d 105, reh overr, and petition for discretionary review refused.—Crim Law 394.5(4), 394.6(5), 641.3(8.1), 1134(6), 1158(4); Searches 40.1, 62, 66.

Giles; Swearingen v., TexCivApp–Eastland, 565 SW2d 574, ref nre.—Wills 439, 449, 478, 866.

Giles; Texas Cab Co. v., TexApp–El Paso, 783 SW2d 695.—App & E 5, 859; Judgm 144; Plead 332.

Giles; Tide Water Associated Oil Co. v., TexCivApp–Austin, 277 SW2d 291, ref nre.—Judgm 73, 651; Mines 5.2(2.1); States 191.9(1), 191.10.

Giles v. TI Employees Pension Plan, TexApp–Dallas, 715 SW2d 58, ref nre.—States 18.51.

Giles; Tobin & Rooney Plastering Co. v., TexCivApp–Texarkana, 418 SW2d 598.—Indem 67.

Giles; U.S. v., USTex, 57 SCt 340, 300 US 41, 81 LEd 493, reh den 57 SCt 505, 300 US 687, 81 LEd 888.—Banks 256(1); Statut 241(1).

Giles; U.S. v., CA5 (Tex), 932 F2d 358. See U.S. v. Ainsworth.

Giles v. U.S., CCA5 (Tex), 84 F2d 943, cert gr 57 SCt 46, 299 US 531, 81 LEd 390, rev 57 SCt 340, 300 US 41, 81 LEd 493, reh den 57 SCt 505, 300 US 687, 81 LEd 888.—Banks 256(1), 257(1.2), 257(4); Statut 223.1, 241(1).

Giles; Universe Life Ins. Co. v., Tex, 950 SW2d 48.—App & E 297, 1001(3); Courts 100(1); Damag 56.10; Insurance 3337, 3360, 3374, 3376, 3381(5), 3382, 3419; Trial 141.

Giles; Universe Life Ins. Co. v., TexApp–Texarkana, 982 SW2d 488, reh overr, and review den, and reh of petition for review overr.—App & E 485(2), 1188, 1191; Const Law 4013(3); Execution 402(1), 402(5).

Giles; Universe Life Ins. Co. v., TexApp–Texarkana, 881 SW2d 44, reh den, and writ gr, aff in part, rev in part 950 SW2d 48.—Accord 11(2), 26(3); App & E 969, 1004(3), 1004(11), 1140(1), 1182; Compromise 2, 5(2), 25; Damag 192, 208(6); Insurance 1117(3), 3336, 3376, 3381(5); Labor & Emp 414; States 18.41; Tender 17; Trial 252(2).

Giles v. Wiggins, TexCivApp–Fort Worth, 442 SW2d 839, ref nre.—App & E 846(5), 854(1), 901, 931(3); Insurance 3496.

Giles Associates, Ltd., In re, BkrtcyWDTex, 92 BR 695.—Bankr 3103.2, 3114, 3115.1.

Giles Dalby Correctional Facility; Fairweather v., NDTex, 154 FSupp2d 921.—Civil R 1027; Fed Civ Proc 2734; Prisons 13(10); Sent & Pun 1546, 1548; U S 50.1, 50.20.

Giles Lowery Stockyards, Inc. v. Department of Agriculture, CA5 (Tex), 565 F2d 321, cert den 98 SCt 3070, 436 US 957, 57 LEd2d 1122.—Admin Law 324, 389, 749; Antitrust 237, 328, 331, 333, 369; Const Law 4264; Pub Ut 123, 129, 162, 194.

Gilfeather; State ex rel. Curry v., TexApp–Fort Worth, 937 SW2d 46, reh overr.—Autos 144.2(1), 144.2(2.1), 144.2(5.1); Courts 178; Mand 4(3), 28; Motions 62; Statut 223.4.

Gilfond v. Lynch, TexApp–Houston (14 Dist), 696 SW2d 195.—Courts 178.

Gilford; J. C. Penney Co. v., TexCivApp–Hous (1 Dist), 422 SW2d 25, ref nre.—Mal Pros 16, 18(1), 20, 22, 30; Proc 168.

Gilford v. State, TexCrimApp, 362 SW2d 843.—Alt of Inst 7; Bail 64.

Gilford; U.S. v., CA5 (Tex), 135 FedAppx 656, cert den 126 SCt 455, 546 US 950, 163 LEd2d 346, reh den, reh den 126 SCt 727, 546 US 1058, 163 LEd2d 623.—Crim Law 1035(1), 1192.

Gilford; U.S. v., CA5 (Tex), 95 FedAppx 549, cert gr, vac 125 SCt 1011, 543 US 1102, 160 LEd2d 1012, on remand 135 FedAppx 656, cert den 126 SCt 455, 546 US 950, 163 LEd2d 346, reh den, reh den 126 SCt 727, 546 US 1058, 163 LEd2d 623.—Sent & Pun 726(3).

Gilger; Hawkins v., TexCivApp–Houston, 399 SW2d 203, writ dism.—Courts 39; Plead 110, 111.23; Venue 5.3(1).

Gilger; Pfau v., CA5 (Tex), 211 FedAppx 271.—Civil R 1249(2), 1252; Fed Civ Proc 2544, 2554; States 53.

Gilgon, Inc. v. Hart, TexApp–Corpus Christi, 893 SW2d 562, reh overr, and writ den.—App & E 216(1), 216(7), 230, 231(9), 970(2), 977(3), 977(5), 1001(1), 1056.1(3), 1058(1), 1062.2; Autos 193(12), 193(14), 244(26), 246(15), 246(42); Evid 188; Labor & Emp 3046(1); New Tr 6; Trial 277.

Gilkerson; Alexander v., TexCivApp–Eastland, 433 SW2d 13, ref nre.—App & E 1003(9.1), 1056.2; Evid 99, 143, 474.5, 589; New Tr 31; Trial 121(1); Trusts 91, 95, 107, 366(3).

Gilkerson; Pacific Finance Corp. v., TexCivApp–Beaumont, 217 SW2d 440, ref nre.—App & E 173(9), 301; Autos 20, 52; Estop 70(1), 116; Evid 434(11), 474(19), 498.5, 543(4), 546; Fraud 28; Parent & C 8; Sales 481.

Gilkey, In re, BkrtcyNDTex, 224 BR 360. See Thompson, In re.

Gilkey v. Allen, TexCivApp–Tyler, 617 SW2d 308.—Wills 289, 297(2), 302(3), 324(4), 487(1).

Gilkey v. Chambers, Tex, 207 SW2d 70, 146 Tex 355.—Wills 455, 457, 559, 565(3).

Gilkey; Chambers v., TexCivApp–Dallas, 200 SW2d 858, rev 207 SW2d 70, 146 Tex 355.—Wills 440, 448, 487(3), 488, 490, 565(3).

Gilkey v. Southland Life Ins. Co., TexCivApp–Beaumont, 141 SW2d 1000, writ dism, correct.—Lim of Act 197(1).

Gilkie v. State, TexCrimApp, 331 SW2d 50, 168 TexCrim 635.—Crim Law 720(8), 800(2); Larc 55.

Gilkison; Shaper v., TexCivApp–Austin, 217 SW2d 878, ref nre.—Action 60; Brok 106; Ven & Pur 79, 341(4).

Gill, Ex parte, TexCrimApp, 509 SW2d 357.—Crim Law 1036.1(8); Sent & Pun 313, 2014.

Gill, In re, TexApp–Texarkana, 183 SW3d 904.—Courts 247(2); Garn 117.

Gill, In re Marriage of, TexApp–Waco, 41 SW3d 255.—App & E 1011.1(7); Divorce 252.3(1), 252.3(5), 252.4, 253(2), 287.

Gill; Abilene Hotel Corp. v., TexCivApp–Waco, 187 SW2d 708, writ refused wom.—App & E 931(1), 931(3); Interpl 29; Land & Ten 204; Trial 368; Trusts 44(1).

Gill; American Broadcasting Companies, Inc. v., TexApp–San Antonio, 6 SW3d 19, reh overr, and reh overr, and petition for review den, and reh of petition for review overr.—App & E 70(8), 837(12), 893(1), 934(1), 1175(1); Judgm 559; Labor & Emp 904; Libel 4, 6(1), 10(5), 19, 21, 30, 48(1), 51(5), 54, 101(1), 112(2), 123(1), 123(2), 123(5), 123(8); Proc 171; Torts 204, 351; Tresp 30.

Gill v. Boyd Distribution Center, TexApp–Texarkana, 64 SW3d 601, review den.—Antitrust 134, 138, 161, 162, 292; App & E 893(1), 931(1), 1122(2); Damag 49, 49.10, 50, 149, 208(6); Fraud 3, 9; Pretrial Proc 621, 622, 678; Prod Liab 62.

Gill v. Chavarria, WDTex, 657 FSupp 1394. See Gill v. Neaves.

Gill; Chicago, R. I. & P. R. Co. v., CA5 (Tex), 217 F2d 195.—Labor & Emp 2845, 2883, 2889.

Gill v. Col-Tex Refining Co., SDTex, 1 FRD 255.—Fed Civ Proc 1271, 1616.

Gill v. Com. Nat. Bank of Dallas, TexCivApp–Dallas, 504 SW2d 521, ref nre.—Bills & N 37, 129(3), 348, 370.

Gill v. Estelle, CA5 (Tex), 544 F2d 1336, cert den 97 SCt 2199, 431 US 924, 53 LEd2d 239.—Sent & Pun 2014.

Gill v. Estelle, CA5 (Tex), 530 F2d 1152, adhered to 544 F2d 1336, cert den 97 SCt 2199, 431 US 924, 53 LEd2d 239.—Const Law 947; Courts 100(1); Crim Law 1165(1); Hab Corp 492, 506; Sent & Pun 313, 2014; Witn 345(1).

Gill; Exxon Mobil Corp. v., TexApp–Corpus Christi, 221 SW3d 841.—Action 27(1); Antitrust 493; App & E 946, 949, 1024.1; Contracts 326; Courts 97(1); Lim of Act 104(1); Parties 35.5, 35.7, 35.9, 35.13, 35.17, 35.31, 35.35, 35.67; Paymt 82(4); Sales 78.

Gill v. Falls County, TexCivApp–Waco, 243 SW2d 277.—Const Law 639; Courts 480(1); Em Dom 19, 191(3), 191(5), 195.

Gill v. First Nat. Bank, TexCivApp–San Antonio, 114 SW2d 428.—App & E 843(2); Home 129(1).

Gill; French v., TexApp–Texarkana, 206 SW3d 737.—App & E 173(9), 173(10), 824, 856(1), 1078(1); Judgm 185(4), 665, 713(1), 724, 725(1), 815, 829(1), 829(3).

Gill v. Grimes, TexCivApp–Waco, 238 SW2d 989.—Bound 8, 37(3).

Gill v. Guy Chipman Co., TexApp–San Antonio, 681 SW2d 264.—App & E 931(1), 989, 1008.1(3), 1010.1(3), 1012.1(5); Contracts 65.5, 116(1), 116(2), 141(3); Damag 6, 189; Labor & Emp 34(2).

Gill v. Houston Produce Terminal, Inc., TexCivApp–Hous (14 Dist), 444 SW2d 800, ref nre.—Corp 254, 629; Damag 221(2.1), 221(7); Frds St of 64; Trial 350.3(1), 352.20.

Gill v. Hudspeth County Conservation & Reclamation Dist. No. 1, TexCivApp–El Paso, 88 SW2d 517.—App & E 837(1), 843(2); Evid 6; Inj 132, 135, 138.15; Waters 177(1).

Gill; Kuykendall v., TexCivApp–El Paso, 131 SW2d 249, writ dism, correct.—Courts 185; Wills 370.

Gill; Liberty Universal Ins. Co. v., TexCivApp–Houston, 401 SW2d 339, ref nre.—App & E 971(2); Evid 546; Work Comp 998, 999, 1396, 1397, 1639, 1653, 1724, 1929, 1968(5).

Gill; Mahaffey v., TexApp–Texarkana, 459 SW2d 919.—App & E 846(2), 846(5); Elections 10, 216.1, 229.

Gill v. Minter, TexCivApp–San Antonio, 233 SW2d 585, writ refused.—Autos 181(1), 244(20).

Gill; Mooney v., NDTex, 310 BR 543.—Bankr 2422.5(1), 2422.5(2), 2424, 2425, 2440, 2441, 3782, 3784, 3786; Equity 54.

Gill v. Neaves, WDTex, 657 FSupp 1394.—Action 6, 13; Civil R 1090, 1094, 1457(5); Fed Civ Proc 664, 851, 1741, 2734; Fed Cts 662.1.

Gill v. Oak Cliff Bank & Trust Co., TexCivApp–Amarillo, 331 SW2d 832.—Garn 148, 191, 196.

Gill; Onwuteaka v., TexApp–Houston (1 Dist), 908 SW2d 276.—App & E 931(1), 946, 957(1), 984(1), 1010.1(1); Atty & C 129(2); Const Law 3987; Evid 555.2, 555.4(2); Judgm 126(1); Neglig 321, 322, 1662, 1675; Parties 48, 56; Pretrial Proc 44.1.

Gill v. Peterson, TexComApp, 86 SW2d 629, 126 Tex 216.—Bound 1, 3(6), 5, 6, 7, 48(3); Deeds 111; Evid 390(3).

Gill v. Phillips, CA5 (Tex), 337 F2d 258, reh den 340 F2d 318, appeal after remand Tinney Produce Co v. Phillips, 415 F2d 511.—Bankr 2058.1.

Gill v. Pringle, TexCivApp–Waco, 224 SW2d 525, writ refused.—Ease 7(5), 8(4).

Gill v. Quinn, TexCivApp–Eastland, 613 SW2d 324.—Home 29, 161, 181(1); Judgm 185.2(1), 185.3(2).

Gill v. Randolph, TexCivApp–Galveston, 269 SW2d 529, ref nre.—Atty & C 143, 159, 167(4); Corp 406(1); Impl & C C 60.1.

Gill; Rodriguez v., TexApp–San Antonio, 849 SW2d 442.—App & E 80(6), 782, 1074(3); Judgm 183; Plead 34(1).

Gill v. Rosas, TexApp–El Paso, 821 SW2d 689.—Anim 66.5(2); App & E 345.1.

Gill v. Russo, TexApp–Houston (1 Dist), 39 SW3d 717, review den.—Const Law 328, 2325; Health 604.

Gill; Sheppard v., TexComApp, 90 SW2d 563, 126 Tex 603.—Plead 216(2).

Gill v. Smith, TexCivApp–Galveston, 233 SW2d 223, ref nre.—Brok 42; Contracts 141(1), 141(3); Corp 1.7(2); Joint Adv 1, 1.2(9), 1.15.

Gill v. Snow, TexApp–Fort Worth, 644 SW2d 222.—Damag 50, 192; Torts 330, 340, 341, 354, 357.

Gill v. State, Tex, 531 SW2d 322.—App & E 1114; Em Dom 133, 202(1), 205.

Gill v. State, TexCrimApp, 873 SW2d 45.—Crim Law 510, 511.1(2.1), 511.1(3), 511.2, 511.4, 511.6, 742(2).

Gill v. State, TexCrimApp, 625 SW2d 307.—Arrest 71.1(5); Controlled Subs 116; Searches 58, 60.1, 61, 62, 65, 66, 192.1.

Gill v. State, TexCrimApp, 593 SW2d 697.—Sent & Pun 2021, 2025.

Gill v. State, TexCrimApp, 556 SW2d 354, appeal after remand 593 SW2d 697.—Sent & Pun 2021.

Gill v. State, TexCrimApp, 521 SW2d 866.—Crim Law 841, 1133, 1172.1(5).

Gill v. State, TexCrimApp, 479 SW2d 289.—Crim Law 358, 369.2(6), 857(2), 1036.5, 1044.1(5.1), 1120(1); Witn 345(11), 395.

Gill v. State, TexCrimApp, 334 SW2d 181, 169 TexCrim 297.—Int Liq 236(4).

Gill v. State, TexCrimApp, 210 SW2d 170, 151 TexCrim 604.—Crim Law 1097(1), 1097(4), 1097(5), 1099.7(2), 1133, 1167(3).

Gill v. State, TexCrimApp, 188 SW2d 584, 148 TexCrim 513.—Crim Law 394.1(1), 543(1), 544, 1180.

Gill v. State, TexCrimApp, 181 SW2d 276, 147 TexCrim 392.—Homic 956, 1479, 1480; Witn 345(1).

Gill v. State, TexCrimApp, 115 SW2d 923, 134 TexCrim 363.—Arrest 63.4(3), 63.4(11), 71.1(1); Crim Law 394.4(12).

Gill v. State, TexApp–Houston (1 Dist), 646 SW2d 532.—Crim Law 564(1), 564(2), 564(3), 1037.1(1), 1144.6, 1144.17.

Gill; State v., TexApp–Austin, 967 SW2d 540, petition for discretionary review refused.—Crim Law 641.13(1), 911, 920, 1134(6), 1139, 1144.18, 1152(1).

Gill v. State, TexApp–Texarkana, 111 SW3d 211.—Crim Law 641.13(1), 641.13(2.1), 641.13(6), 641.13(7), 1041.

Gill v. State, TexApp–Beaumont, 981 SW2d 517, petition for discretionary review refused.—Autos 330, 355(14); Crim Law 1042, 1043(2), 1043(3), 1134(2).

Gill v. State, TexApp–Waco, 57 SW3d 540.—Crim Law 404.30, 404.65, 444, 1144.13(2.1), 1144.13(6), 1159.2(7); Sent & Pun 1379(3), 1381(2), 1381(6); Weap 4, 17(4).

Gill v. State, TexApp–Waco, 852 SW2d 7, am on denial of reh, and petition for discretionary review gr, rev 873 SW2d 45.—Crim Law 511.1(1), 511.1(9), 511.2, 511.5, 511.6.

Gill v. State, TexApp–Corpus Christi, 670 SW2d 758, petition for discretionary review refused.—Bills & N 60; Crim Law 835; Ind & Inf 171; Larc 13, 40(6), 62(2), 75(2).

Gill v. State, TexApp–Houston (14 Dist), 675 SW2d 549.—Crim Law 338(1), 829(1), 1153(1), 1170(3); Obscen 16, 20.

Gill; State v., TexCivApp–Texarkana, 519 SW2d 514, writ gr, rev 531 SW2d 322.—Em Dom 202(1); Evid 568(4), 571(7).

Gill v. State of Texas, CA5 (Tex), 153 FedAppx 261.—Civil R 1395(6), 1445; Fed Cts 192, 714, 752, 768.1.

Gill; Stein v., TexApp–Fort Worth, 895 SW2d 501, reh overr.—Land & Ten 162, 164(1).

Gill; Taylor v., TexCivApp–Eastland, 211 SW2d 363.—Can of Inst 63; Contracts 143(3); Frds St of 72(1), 131(1), 141, 142; Ref of Inst 1, 11; Spec Perf 25.

Gill v. Texas Dept. of Criminal Justice, Institutional Div., TexApp–Houston (1 Dist), 3 SW3d 576.—App & E

185(3), 223, 241, 854(1); Autos 187(1), 187(4); Judges 51(1); Judgm 183; Labor & Emp 3045; Mun Corp 745, 847; Neglig 273; Prisons 10.

Gill v. Transamerica Ins. Co., TexCivApp–Dallas, 417 SW2d 720.—Work Comp 11, 552, 554, 845, 1929.

Gill v. U.S., CA5 (Tex), 641 F2d 195.—U S 131; Work Comp 4, 1833, 2084.

Gill v. U.S., CA5 (Tex), 449 F2d 765.—Fed Cts 743, 863.

Gill v. U.S., CA5 (Tex), 429 F2d 1072, appeal after remand 449 F2d 765.—Aviation 237; Damag 63; Fed Cts 866, 941; U S 78(8), 78(14).

Gill v. U.S., EDTex, 285 FSupp 253, aff in part, rev in part 429 F2d 1072, appeal after remand 449 F2d 765.—Aviation 141, 232.1, 232.5, 235; Death 81, 84, 95(1), 95(3); U S 78(6), 78(14).

Gill v. Universal C. I. T. Credit Corp., TexCivApp–Texarkana, 282 SW2d 401, ref nre.—Contracts 279(2), 330(1); Corp 519(2); Estop 83(5); Evid 383(7); Guar 82(2); Princ & S 152; Usury 117.

Gill; Valdez v., TexCivApp–San Antonio, 537 SW2d 477, ref nre.—Action 56; App & E 22, 281(1); New Tr 8, 9; Pretrial Proc 511, 517.1, 518; Trial 2, 3(2).

Gill v. Willis, TexCivApp–Eastland, 282 SW2d 88.—App & E 544(1), 900, 901, 907(3), 1032(1).

Gill; Zurich American Ins. Co. v., TexApp–Fort Worth, 173 SW3d 878, review den.—Admin Law 787, 793; App & E 994(1), 1008.1(3), 1122(2); Evid 588; Statut 181(1), 188, 205, 219(1), 219(4); Work Comp 532, 549, 604, 1704, 1716.

Gillam v. Baker, TexCivApp–Galveston, 195 SW2d 826, dism.—App & E 32; Forci E & D 43(7); Land & Ten 18(3), 291(14); Trial 352.4(2).

Gillam v. Baker, TexCivApp–Galveston, 195 SW2d 824, ref nre.—Courts 480(1).

Gillam v. City of Fort Worth, TexCivApp–Fort Worth, 287 SW2d 494, ref nre.—Const Law 2489; Decl Judgm 319, 346; Mun Corp 59, 63.10, 63.15(1), 226, 232; Waters 203(3), 203(11).

Gillam v. Matthews, TexCivApp–Fort Worth, 122 SW2d 348, dism.—Judgm 855(1), 866, 866.1; Statut 159, 223.2(35).

Gillam v. State, TexCivApp–Waco, 95 SW2d 1019.—Em Dom 124, 222(4).

Gillam v. Sullivan, TexCivApp–Fort Worth, 352 SW2d 507, ref nre.—Judgm 181(29), 186; Trusts 30.5(1).

Gillam Soap Works; Keeton v., TexCivApp–Amarillo, 215 SW2d 675, ref nre.—App & E 882(3), 989, 1010.1(1), 1012.1(4); Interest 39(6), 50; Sales 397, 417, 422.

Gillard; Federal Deposit Ins. Corp. v., NDTex, 740 FSupp 427.—Banks 505.

Gillard; Republic Bankers Life Ins. Co. v., TexCivApp–Waco, 496 SW2d 231, ref nre.—Insurance 2484, 3343, 3381(5).

Gillard v. State, TexCrimApp, 82 SW2d 678, 128 TexCrim 514.—Crim Law 59(3), 1159.2(7); Rob 24.20.

Gillard v. State, TexApp–Beaumont, 662 SW2d 34.—Autos 349.5(8); Controlled Subs 114, 116; Crim Law 273.2(2), 273.4(1), 275, 1023(3).

Gillaspie v. Department of Public Safety, Tex, 259 SW2d 177, 152 Tex 459, cert den 74 SCt 625, 347 US 933, 98 LEd 1084.—Autos 130, 132, 137, 142, 144.1(4), 144.2(7), 144.2(10); Const Law 2425(2), 2430(2), 4105(1), 4357.

Gillaspie; Department of Public Safety v., TexCivApp–San Antonio, 254 SW2d 180, aff 259 SW2d 177, 152 Tex 459, cert den 74 SCt 625, 347 US 933, 98 LEd 1084.—Autos 132, 142, 144.1(4), 144.2(7); Const Law 4357; Statut 47.

Gill Co. v. Jackson's Landing Owners' Ass'n, TexApp–Corpus Christi, 758 SW2d 921. See Richard Gill Co. v. Jackson's Landing Owners' Ass'n.

Gilleland v. Meadows, TexCivApp–Dallas, 351 SW2d 656. —App & E 907(3); Costs 230, 234; Partit 86, 87.

Gilleland v. Meadows, TexCivApp–Waco, 329 SW2d 485. —Divorce 252.5(1), 252.5(2); Partit 16.

Gillen; Davis v., TexCivApp–Beaumont, 227 SW2d 834, ref nre.—App & E 931(1); Inj 132, 138.9, 138.31, 152; Propty 7; Tresp to T T 13.

Gillen v. Diadrill, Inc., TexApp–Corpus Christi, 624 SW2d 259, dism.—App & E 768, 832(4), 846(5), 954(1); Contracts 116(1), 117(3), 118; Equity 65(1); Inj 61(2), 157, 204.

Gillen; Pinnacle Data Services, Inc. v., TexApp–Texarkana, 104 SW3d 188, reh overr, and reh overr.—App & E 707(1), 863, 893(1), 907(1), 1172(1), 1178(1); Consp 1.1; Corp 40, 180, 307, 313, 314(1), 361; Fraud 7; Impl & C C 3; Judgm 178, 183, 189; Ref of Inst 19(1).

Gillen v. Stevens, TexCivApp–Waco, 330 SW2d 253, ref nre.—App & E 931(3); Brok 32, 67(1).

Gillen v. Williams Bros. Const. Co., Inc., TexApp–Houston (14 Dist), 933 SW2d 162, reh overr, and error den, opinion ordered published.—App & E 543, 907(1), 907(3).

Gillentine v. State, TexApp–Houston (1 Dist), 781 SW2d 382.—Arrest 63.4(14), 63.5(4); Autos 349(8).

Gillenwaters v. State, TexCrimApp, 205 SW3d 534, reh den.—Const Law 656; Crim Law 1030(1), 1043(2), 1063(1), 1064(1).

Giller; Shurtleff v., TexCivApp–Waco, 527 SW2d 214.—Bills & N 104; Contracts 95(3), 100.

Giller; Tajchman v., TexApp–Dallas, 938 SW2d 95, reh overr, and writ den.—Health 800, 906, 908; Judgm 178, 185(2).

Giller Industries, Inc. v. Consolidated Casting Corp., TexCivApp–Dallas, 590 SW2d 818.—Evid 471(19); Judgm 185(3), 185.3(18); Plead 93(3).

Giller Industries, Inc. v. Hartley, TexApp–Dallas, 644 SW2d 183.—App & E 846(5), 1079; Land & Ten 112(2).

Gilles v. Yarbrough, TexCivApp–Fort Worth, 224 SW2d 720.—App & E 916(2), 946; Mines 52; Receivers 60, 110.

Gillespey v. Sylvia, TexCivApp–El Paso, 496 SW2d 234.—App & E 302(6), 1177(7); Autos 244(34), 244(35), 245(39); Neglig 1578; Trial 355(1).

Gillespie, Ex parte, TexCrimApp, 124 SW2d 151, 136 TexCrim 203.—Extrad 34; Hab Corp 704, 729.

Gillespie, In re, TexApp–Houston (14 Dist), 124 SW3d 699, reh overr.—Guard & W 116(1); Judgm 297, 340; Mand 4(1), 4(4), 28, 50, 176; New Tr 155; Trial 390, 392(0.5), 404(5).

Gillespie; Barton v., TexApp–Houston (1 Dist), 178 SW3d 121.—App & E 934(1); Divorce 254(1); Judgm 215, 297, 304, 306, 324, 325, 326.

Gillespie; Bullion v., CA5 (Tex), 895 F2d 213.—Const Law 3964, 3965(4); Fed Cts 76.5, 76.10, 96, 776.

Gillespie v. Century Products Co., TexApp–San Antonio, 936 SW2d 50, reh overr.—Antitrust 234; Prod Liab 38, 75.1, 77.5, 83.5.

Gillespie; Citizens Mut. Life & Acc. Ass'n of Texas v., TexCivApp–Texarkana, 93 SW2d 200.—App & E 846(2), 846(5); Judgm 129, 407(6), 461(1).

Gillespie v. Citizens Nat. Bank of Weatherford, TexCivApp–Texarkana, 97 SW2d 310.—Garn 107; Interpl 6, 11, 22.

Gillespie; Continental Oil Co. v., TexCivApp–San Antonio, 178 SW2d 728.—App & E 219(2); Mines 74(3).

Gillespie v. Crawford, CA5 (Tex), 858 F2d 1101.—Decl Judgm 84; Fed Civ Proc 180, 186.10; Judgm 677.

Gillespie v. Crawford, CA5 (Tex), 833 F2d 47, on reh 858 F2d 1101.—Civil R 1395(7); Fed Civ Proc 2734; Sent & Pun 1533, 1546, 1548.

Gillespie v. Fields, TexApp–Tyler, 958 SW2d 228, reh overr, and review den.—Damag 103; Decl Judgm 361.1; Judgm 185(2); Lim of Act 95(1), 95(7); Neglig 1507.1; Pretrial Proc 508.

Gillespie v. Gillespie, Tex, 644 SW2d 449.—App & E 931(5), 1054(1); Child C 7, 921(1), 923(1).

Gillespie; Gillespie v., Tex, 644 SW2d 449.—App & E 931(5), 1054(1); Child C 7, 921(1), 923(1).

Gillespie v. Gillespie, TexApp–Beaumont, 631 SW2d 592, writ gr, rev 644 SW2d 449.—Witn 211(2).

Gillespie; Gillespie v., TexApp–Beaumont, 631 SW2d 592, writ gr, rev 644 SW2d 449.—Witn 211(2).

Gillespie v. Gillespie, TexCivApp–Dallas, 343 SW2d 281, ref nre.—Child C 553, 560, 637, 920, 921(1), 922(5).

Gillespie; Gillespie v., TexCivApp–Dallas, 343 SW2d 281, ref nre.—Child C 553, 560, 637, 920, 921(1), 922(5).

Gillespie v. Gillespie, TexCivApp–Eastland, 110 SW2d 89, dism.—Divorce 223, 228, 252.3(1), 252.3(3), 253(1), 253(2), 253(4); Evid 353(3); Home 81; Hus & W 255, 262.2, 264(1).

Gillespie; Gillespie v., TexCivApp–Eastland, 110 SW2d 89, dism.—Divorce 223, 228, 252.3(1), 252.3(3), 253(1), 253(2), 253(4); Evid 353(3); Home 81; Hus & W 255, 262.2, 264(1).

Gillespie v. Grimes, TexCivApp–Tyler, 577 SW2d 538.—Nuis 44, 49(1), 49(5), 50(1).

Gillespie; Heffington v., TexCivApp–Fort Worth, 176 SW2d 205.—Ex & Ad 124, 142, 438(8), 451(2).

Gillespie; Ketchum v., TexCivApp–Austin, 145 SW2d 215.—App & E 970(4); Autos 242(2), 245(17); Trial 68(1).

Gillespie v. Matney, TexCivApp–Austin, 497 SW2d 957.—Damag 185(1).

Gillespie v. Moore, TexApp–Amarillo, 635 SW2d 927, ref nre.—Hus & W 279(1); Insurance 1971, 1974, 3437, 3481(2).

Gillespie; Morton Intern. v., TexApp–Texarkana, 39 SW3d 651, review den, and reh of petition for review den.—App & E 836, 931(1), 946, 1008.1(2), 1010.1(1), 1010.2, 1011.1(1), 1011.1(2), 1012.1(5); Evid 99, 508, 535, 539, 546, 571(6), 587, 595; Neglig 375, 384, 385; Prod Liab 8, 83.5.

Gillespie; Pierce v., TexApp–Corpus Christi, 761 SW2d 390.—Adv Poss 13, 27, 70, 71(3), 86; App & E 123, 223, 241, 931(1), 946, 989, 1001(1), 1003(5); Costs 194.22, 194.30; Evid 574; Trusts 138.

Gillespie v. Rossi, TexCivApp–Waco, 238 SW2d 547, ref nre.—App & E 1053(2), 1060.6; Evid 5(2); New Tr 10, 144, 155, 157; Trial 127, 131(1).

Gillespie v. Scherr, TexApp–Houston (14 Dist), 987 SW2d 129, clarified on denial of reh, and review den.—App & E 171(1); Atty & C 26, 64; Courts 91(0.5), 97(1); Judgm 185(2); Parties 35.1, 35.31; Plead 427.

Gillespie; Seymour v., Tex, 608 SW2d 897.—App & E 1056.1(3); Evid 359(5), 380; Trial 82.

Gillespie; Seymour v., TexCivApp–Beaumont, 584 SW2d 528, rev 608 SW2d 897.—Evid 359(5).

Gillespie; Sun Oil Co. v., TexCivApp–Austin, 85 SW2d 652, writ dism.—Mines 92.26, 92.27, 92.32(1), 92.51.

Gillespie; Wesson v., Tex, 382 SW2d 921.—Neglig 1288, 1289, 1564.

Gillespie v. Wesson, TexCivApp–Fort Worth, 370 SW2d 918, writ gr, rev 382 SW2d 921.—Neglig 1037(4), 1562, 1568, 1711, 1717; Trial 350.6(2), 351.2(4), 366.

Gillespie County; Hohmann v., TexCivApp–San Antonio, 104 SW2d 573.—App & E 773(2).

Gillespie County; Meyer v., TexCivApp–San Antonio, 109 SW2d 220, writ dism.—App & E 692(1); Em Dom 150, 201, 224, 262(5).

Gillespie County, Tex.; Rothgery v., CA5 (Tex), 491 F3d 293.—Crim Law 641.3(2), 641.3(3), 641.3(4).

Gillespie County, Tex.; Rothgery v., WDTex, 413 FSupp2d 806, aff 491 F3d 293.—Const Law 3799, 4806; Crim Law 641.3(2), 641.3(3), 641.3(4).

Gillespie Drilling Co.; Intervest Energy and Development Corp. v., TexApp–Eastland, 636 SW2d 13.—Corp 666.

Gillespie, Rozen, Tanner & Watsky, P.C.; Allbritton v., TexApp–Dallas, 180 SW3d 889, reh overr, and review den.—App & E 970(2); Atty & C 105.5; Evid 535, 555.2; Judgm 185(3), 185(5), 185(6), 185.1(4), 185.1(8).

Gillett v. Achterberg, Tex, 325 SW2d 384, 159 Tex 591.—App & E 719(11).

Gillett; Achterberg v., TexCivApp–El Paso, 322 SW2d 306, ref nre 325 SW2d 384, 159 Tex 591.—Contracts 10(2), 16, 147(1), 147(3), 168; Frds St of 129(1); Judgm 181(19), 185(2); Trial 136(3).

Gillett; Rothman v., TexCivApp–Fort Worth, 315 SW2d 956, ref nre.—Adop 3, 17; Witn 158, 159(3).

Gillett v. State, TexCrimApp, 588 SW2d 361.—Crim Law 394.2(1); Larc 62(2); Searches 25.1, 26.

Gillett v. State, TexApp–Corpus Christi, 663 SW2d 480.—Crim Law 577.10(9), 859, 925(1), 956(1), 959, 1156(5), 1174(5); Double J 97.

Gillett Const. Co. v. Garcia, TexApp–Houston (1 Dist), 816 SW2d 131. See Kahn v. Garcia.

Gillette; Barrick v., TexCivApp–Eastland, 187 SW2d 683, writ refused wom.—App & E 930(1), 930(3), 989; Ease 16, 18(1), 36(3), 37; Judgm 199(3.10); Trial 351.2(3.1), 366.

Gillette v. Houston Nat. Bank, TexCivApp–Galveston, 139 SW2d 646, writ dism, correct.—Corp 123(14), 126, 149; Estop 72; Trover 70.

Gillette; Musslewhite v., TexCivApp–Amarillo, 258 SW2d 104.—App & E 1048(4), 1060.6, 1169(1), 1169(6); New Tr 77(1); Trial 127; Witn 255(4).

Gillette; Texas & P. R. Co. v., TexComApp, 83 SW2d 307, 125 Tex 563.—App & E 1015(5), 1069.1; Courts 97(1); New Tr 44(3); R R 350(6), 350(13).

Gillette; Texas & P. Ry. Co. v., TexCivApp–El Paso, 100 SW2d 170, writ dism.—App & E 1060.4, 1070(2); R R 346(5.1), 350(1), 350(16.1), 351(16); Trial 133.6(7), 232(5), 351.2(10), 352.5(7), 352.9, 352.10, 358.

Gillette; Vilbig v., TexCivApp–Amarillo, 238 SW2d 569, ref nre.—App & E 265(1); Mines 70(1).

Gillette Motor Transport v. Blair, TexCivApp–Beaumont, 136 SW2d 656, writ dism, correct.—App & E 216(2); Damag 228; Death 104(4); Trial 115(2), 118, 278.

Gillette Motor Transport v. Fine, TexCivApp–Fort Worth, 131 SW2d 817, writ dism, correct.—App & E 1062.2; Autos 209, 242(8), 245(81); Neglig 1571, 1683, 1745; Trial 192, 350.5(3), 350.8, 351.2(10), 352.10.

Gillette Motor Transport v. Fine, TexCivApp–Fort Worth, 103 SW2d 196.—Trial 253(4).

Gillette Motor Transport; Gibson v., TexCivApp–Eastland, 138 SW2d 293, writ refused.—Autos 193(3.1), 245(28), 245(30); Labor & Emp 3094(2); Princ & A 21.

Gillette Motor Transport v. Kelly, TexCivApp–Waco, 141 SW2d 959.—Autos 244(17); Evid 123(12).

Gillette Motor Transport v. Lucas, TexCivApp–Galveston, 138 SW2d 887, writ dism, correct.—Autos 216, 244(3), 244(35), 244(36.1), 244(40), 244(49); Trial 351.5(6).

Gillette Motor Transp. Co. v. Whitfield, TexCivApp–Fort Worth, 197 SW2d 157, aff Gillette Motor Transport Co v. Whitfield, 200 SW2d 624, 145 Tex 571.—App & E 837(2), 1003(1), 1047(1), 1064.1(9); Autos 245(86); Costs 241; Damag 59, 96, 104, 119; Labor & Emp 2824; New Tr 76(1); Trial 54(3), 194(16), 217, 311, 350.1, 350.5(3), 350.6(3), 351.5(1), 352.1(7), 352.5(6), 352.10.

Gillette Motor Transport Co. v. Whitfield, Tex, 200 SW2d 624, 145 Tex 571.—App & E 1064.1(9); Trial 217, 311.

Gillette Motor Transport Co. v. Whitfield, TexCivApp–Fort Worth, 186 SW2d 90, writ refused wom.—App & E 930(1), 1053(2), 1062.1; Autos 215, 245(86); Estop 3(2), 103; Evid 208(6), 265(8); Release 7, 37, 58(1); Trial 194(20), 350.6(6), 352.1(7), 352.1(8), 352.5(7), 352.9, 352.18; Witn 379(6).

Gillette Motor Transport Co. v. Whitfield, TexCivApp–Fort Worth, 160 SW2d 290.—App & E 758.1, 1069.1, 1100, 1166, 1203(3); Autos 247; Judgm 17(1); Labor & Emp 2807; New Tr 56; Parties 18, 29; Plead 111.3; Proc 31; R R 24(1); Venue 22(6), 22(10).

Gillette Motor Transport Co. v. Wichita Falls & Southern R. Co., TexCivApp–Fort Worth, 170 SW2d 629, mandamus den Wichita Falls & S R Co v. McDonald, 174 SW2d 951, 141 Tex 555.—App & E 78(3), 758.1, 766, 870(5); Courts 85(3); Judgm 217, 564(2); Plead 111.49.

Gilley v. Anthony, TexCivApp–Dallas, 404 SW2d 60.— Adop 13; App & E 846(5), 900, 931(3), 989, 1008.1(3); Com Law 9; New Tr 99.

Gilley; Citizens Standard Life Ins. Co. v., TexCivApp–Dallas, 521 SW2d 354.—Fraud 3, 49; Plead 45, 111.21, 111.39(4); Venue 8.5(2).

Gilley; City of Corpus Christi v., TexCivApp–Corpus Christi, 458 SW2d 124, ref nre.—App & E 554(1), 846(5), 907(3); Autos 62; Courts 99(4); Inj 105(1), 105(2).

Gilley; City of Corpus Christi v., TexCivApp–Corpus Christi, 379 SW2d 84, ref nre.—App & E 954(1); Autos 134; Inj 85(1), 128(7), 135.

Gilley v. Collins, CA5 (Tex), 968 F2d 465.—Controlled Subs 26, 27, 28, 30, 80; Hab Corp 493(2), 767, 770, 823.

Gilley; Dallas County Sheriff's Dept. v., TexApp–Dallas, 114 SW3d 689, reh overr.—App & E 216(7), 232(2), 232(3), 893(1), 946, 970(2), 974(0.5), 1050.1(1), 1056.1(1), 1058(1), 1064.1(1); Civil R 1539; Trial 237(3), 295(2).

Gilley v. Merchants Cold Storage Co., TexCivApp–Fort Worth, 114 SW2d 283.—Wareh 34(9).

Gilley v. Morse, TexCivApp–Dallas, 375 SW2d 569.— Plead 111.41; Stip 17(2); Venue 21.

Gilley; Talib v., CA5 (Tex), 138 F3d 211.—Convicts 1; Fed Civ Proc 2734; Fed Cts 269, 818; Prisons 4(1), 17(3); Sent & Pun 1438, 1439, 1532, 1540, 1553.

Gilley; U.S. v., CA5 (Tex), 166 FedAppx 142.—Crim Law 1042, 1192.

Gilley's Enterprises, Inc., In re, BkrtcySDTex, 112 BR 165. See Sherwood Enterprises, Inc., In re.

Gilley's Publications, In re, BkrtcySDTex, 112 BR 165. See Sherwood Enterprises, Inc., In re.

Gillham v. City of Dallas, TexCivApp–Dallas, 207 SW2d 978, ref nre.—App & E 1054(1); Judgm 713(3); Mun Corp 63.5, 299, 321(2), 911, 921(3), 995(1).

Gilliam, In re, BkrtcyNDTex, 224 BR 360. See Thompson, In re.

Gilliam; Austin Lake Estates Recreation Club, Inc. v., TexCivApp–Austin, 493 SW2d 343, ref nre.—App & E 1078(1); Clubs 8; Corp 99(1); Deeds 18, 56(2), 194(5); Ease 26(1), 48(1); Ref of Inst 19(1); Trial 66, 366; Trusts 13, 31, 59(2).

Gilliam; Brazos River Authority v., TexCivApp–Fort Worth, 429 SW2d 949, ref nre.—App & E 713(1), 846(5); Em Dom 82, 134, 155, 202(4), 205, 262(2), 262(5); Evid 142(1), 555.6(9), 555.6(10), 558(9).

Gilliam; Casas v., TexCivApp–San Antonio, 869 SW2d 671.— App & E 934(1); Judgm 185(2), 185.1(8); Mun Corp 744, 747(4); Offic 114.

Gilliam; City of Floydada v., TexCivApp–Amarillo, 111 SW2d 761.—Corp 298(1); Em Dom 317(2); Judgm 251(1), 252(1); Mun Corp 85; Plead 72.

Gilliam v. City of Fort Worth Tex., CA5 (Tex), 187 FedAppx 387.—Civil R 1088(5), 1348, 1445.

Gilliam v. Global Leak Detection U.S.A., Inc., SDTex, 141 FSupp2d 734.—Alt Disp Res 112, 113, 134(1), 134(3), 139, 141, 143, 200, 203, 210; Fed Cts 403.

Gilliam; Gonzales v., TexCivApp–Eastland, 506 SW2d 650.—Damag 221(2.1); Evid 351, 373(1).

Gilliam; Henwood v., TexCivApp–Dallas, 207 SW2d 904, writ refused.—App & E 930(1), 1001(1); Neglig 231, 503, 1717; R R 328(8), 346(5.1), 350(1), 350(26).

Gilliam; Howsley v., Tex, 517 SW2d 531.—Homic 751; Neglig 230, 238, 259, 510(6).

Gilliam; Howsley v., TexCivApp–El Paso, 503 SW2d 628, writ gr, rev 517 SW2d 531.—Const Law 2473; Crim Law 29(10); Death 21; Judgm 185(4).

Gilliam v. Kouchoucos, Tex, 340 SW2d 27, 161 Tex 299, 88 ALR2d 693.—Frds St of 50(2).

Gilliam; Kouchoucos v., TexCivApp–Fort Worth, 328 SW2d 817, writ gr, rev 340 SW2d 27, 161 Tex 299, 88 ALR2d 693.—Frds St of 50(2), 51.

Gilliam; McLain v., TexCivApp–Eastland, 389 SW2d 131, ref nre.—Gifts 34.

Gilliam; Panhandle Const. Co. v., TexCivApp–Amarillo, 84 SW2d 531, writ dism.—Lim of Act 150(1); Mech Liens 199.

Gilliam v. Riggs, TexCivApp–Beaumont, 385 SW2d 444, writ dism woj.—Divorce 62(2), 108, 168, 172.

Gilliam; Schronk v., TexCivApp–Waco, 380 SW2d 743.— Aviation 3, 4.1, 5; Tresp 10, 12.

Gilliam v. State, TexCrimApp, 177 SW2d 782, 146 TexCrim 620.—Crim Law 1131(3).

Gilliam v. State, TexCrimApp, 167 SW2d 528, 145 TexCrim 242.—Ind & Inf 71.2(4).

Gilliam v. State, TexCrimApp, 96 SW2d 86, 131 TexCrim 8.—Double J 89.

Gilliam v. State, TexApp–Houston (1 Dist), 766 SW2d 867.—Crim Law 1172.1(2).

Gilliam v. State, TexApp–Beaumont, 691 SW2d 42, petition for discretionary review refused.—Crim Law 412.1(3), 414, 736(2), 1158(4).

Gilliam v. State, TexApp–Eastland, 749 SW2d 582.— Crim Law 369.2(7), 730(14), 795(2.70), 1172.1(2).

Gilliam v. State, TexApp–Eastland, 746 SW2d 323.— Burg 4; Crim Law 796, 1167(1), 1174(1).

Gilliam; State v., TexApp–Houston (14 Dist), 832 SW2d 119.—Arrest 63.5(2), 63.5(4), 63.5(5); Crim Law 1148, 1158(4).

Gilliam; Wachovia Bank of Delaware, N.A. v., Tex, 215 SW3d 848.—App & E 865, 914(1); Mtg 440.

Gilliam; Whitehall Laboratories, Inc. v., TexCivApp–Eastland, 536 SW2d 286, ref nre.—Trial 350.7(2).

Gilliam v. Williams, TexApp–Houston (14 Dist), 683 SW2d 761.—App & E 989, 994(2), 1177(7); Autos 244(37).

Gillian v. Day, Tex, 182 SW2d 687, 143 Tex 56.—App & E 1159.

Gillian v. Day, TexCivApp–Galveston, 181 SW2d 327, rev 182 SW2d 687, 143 Tex 56.—App & E 954(1), 954(2); Inj 34, 37, 132, 135, 138.21; Land & Ten 290.5.

Gillian v. Day, TexCivApp–Galveston, 179 SW2d 575, writ refused.—Lim of Act 182(2); Trial 60(2), 142; Ven & Pur 93, 219, 232(9), 242, 244.

Gillie, In re, BkrtcyNDTex, 96 BR 689.—Nova 3; Sec Tran 146.

Gillie v. Boulas, TexApp–Dallas, 65 SW3d 219, reh overr, and review den.—App & E 1046.1; Atty & C 76(1); Evid 555.10; Pretrial Proc 716.

Gillie v. First State Bank of Morton, Tex., BkrtcyNDTex, 96 BR 689. See Gillie, In re.

Gillie v. State, TexApp–Waco, 181 SW3d 768, petition for discretionary review refused.—Autos 336, 355(8), 357(8); Crim Law 822(1), 1134(2); Ind & Inf 119.

Gillies v. State, TexCrimApp, 346 SW2d 612, 171 TexCrim 175.—Crim Law 796; Homic 1572.

Gilligan v. Gearhart, TexCivApp–Corpus Christi, 415 SW2d 208, writ dism.—Alt of Inst 20; Judgm 199(3.14).

Gilliland, In re, BkrtcyNDTex, 67 BR 410.—Bankr 2853.40.

Gilliland; Anderson v., Tex, 684 SW2d 673.—Hus & W 258, 273(1).

Gilliland; Anderson v., TexApp–Dallas, 677 SW2d 105, writ gr, aff in part, rev in part 684 SW2d 673.—Hus & W 258, 262.1(3), 273(1), 273(12).

Gilliland; Anderson v., TexCivApp–Dallas, 624 SW2d 243, ref nre, appeal after remand 677 SW2d 105, writ gr, aff in part, rev in part 684 SW2d 673.—Evid 448, 461(2); Hus & W 265, 266.3, 274(1).

Gilliland; City of Fort Worth v., TexComApp, 169 SW2d 149, 140 Tex 616.—Em Dom 274(1), 293(3).

Gilliland v. City of Fort Worth, TexCivApp–Fort Worth, 162 SW2d 1000, rev 169 SW2d 149, 140 Tex 616.—App

& E 1172(5); Em Dom 50, 119(1), 274(1); Mun Corp 657(3).

Gilliland v. Employers Liability Assur. Corp., TexCivApp–El Paso, 417 SW2d 921, ref nre.—Insurance 2356.

Gilliland v. Kimbrough, TexCivApp–Fort Worth, 146 SW2d 1101.—Frds St of 129(8), 129(11), 131(2), 150(3); Mines 57.

Gilliland v. Manhattan Laundry and Dry Cleaning Co., Inc., TexCivApp–Dallas, 583 SW2d 873.—App & E 948, 954(1), 954(2); Inj 135.

Gilliland; Miller & Miller Motor Freight Lines v., TexCivApp–Fort Worth, 232 SW2d 886, dism.—Carr 153, 181.1; Costs 194.22; Statut 263.

Gilliland; Pon Lip Chew v., Tex, 398 SW2d 98, on remand 401 SW2d 137.—App & E 213, 1083(5), 1089(2), 1094(1); Trial 362.

Gilliland v. Pon Lip Chew, TexCivApp–El Paso, 401 SW2d 137.—Assault 40.

Gilliland v. Pon Lip Chew, TexCivApp–El Paso, 381 SW2d 671, writ gr, rev 398 SW2d 98, on remand 401 SW2d 137.—App & E 1170.6, 1177(2); Assault 43(2), 44; Trial 241, 358.

Gilliland v. State, TexCrimApp, 342 SW2d 327.—Autos 359.

Gilliland v. State, TexApp–Beaumont, 786 SW2d 385.—Crim Law 407(2), 662.8; Homic 1134, 1186.

Gilliland; Travelers Ins. Co. v., TexCivApp–El Paso, 459 SW2d 500.—Work Comp 1348, 1374, 1929.

Gilliland v. Tucker, TexCivApp–Fort Worth, 89 SW2d 475.—Brok 66, 86(4).

Gilliland; U.S. v., USTex, 61 SCt 518, 312 US 86, 85 LEd 598.—Fed Cts 472; Fraud 68.10(1); Statut 194.

Gilliland; U.S. v., EDTex, 35 FSupp 181, probable jur noted 61 SCt 33, rev 61 SCt 518, 312 US 86, 85 LEd 598.—Consp 43(5), 43(6); Crim Law 313; Statut 217.3; U S 121, 123.

Gilliland; Waller v., TexCivApp–Amarillo, 231 SW2d 939, writ refused.—Wills 435, 775, 778, 800.

Gilliland Refining Co.; Eastern States Petroleum Co. v., CCA5 (Tex), 103 F2d 186.—Fed Civ Proc 1713.1; Fed Cts 541, 792, 855.1, 895; Sales 130(4).

Gilliland Refining Co.; Eastern States Petroleum Co. v., TexCivApp–Texarkana, 151 SW2d 933, writ dism, correct.—Judgm 724, 725(1), 829(3).

Gillin; U.S. v., SDTex, 345 FSupp 1145.—Bail 40, 42.5, 53.

Gillingham v. State, TexCrimApp, 318 SW2d 659, 167 TexCrim 116.—Assault 56, 92(3); Crim Law 363, 721(6).

Gillingham v. Timmins, TexCivApp–Galveston, 104 SW2d 115, writ dism.—App & E 930(1), 1062.1; Evid 99; Inj 62(3), 113, 127, 130.

Gillingwater; Jamail v., TexCivApp–Austin, 612 SW2d 279.—Inj 34; Mtg 413.

Gillis; Chandler v., TexCivApp–El Paso, 589 SW2d 552, ref nre.—App & E 1073(1); Judgm 181(6), 181(11); Libel 38(4); Plead 345(1).

Gillis; First City Mortg. Co. v., TexApp–Houston (14 Dist), 694 SW2d 144, ref nre.—Antitrust 134, 162, 209; Brok 19, 34; Contracts 93(2).

Gillis v. Gillis, TexCivApp–Fort Worth, 435 SW2d 171, writ dism.—Divorce 241; Equity 54; Hus & W 247, 249(2.1).

Gillis; Gillis v., TexCivApp–Fort Worth, 435 SW2d 171, writ dism.—Divorce 241; Equity 54; Hus & W 247, 249(2.1).

Gillis; Memorial Hosp. of Galveston County v., Tex, 741 SW2d 364.—Pretrial Proc 698; Work Comp 1174.

Gillis; Memorial Hosp. of Galveston County v., TexApp–Houston (1 Dist), 731 SW2d 692, ref nre, and writ gr, and writ withdrawn, rev 741 SW2d 364.—Plead 48; Trial 350.3(8), 352.1(9); Work Comp 1174, 1282, 1283, 1297, 1382, 1683.

Gillis v. State, TexApp–Fort Worth, 694 SW2d 245, petition for discretionary review refused.—Crim Law 349, 396(1), 566, 717, 726, 1171.1(2.1); Rape 64.

Gillis v. U.S., CA5 (Tex), 402 F2d 501.—Int Rev 3075, 3078, 3079, 3273, 3372.1, 3373, 3432.

Gillis v. U.S., SDTex, 267 FSupp 547, aff in part, rev in part 402 F2d 501.—Int Rev 3273, 3432.

Gillis, P.C. v. Wilbur, TexApp–Dallas, 700 SW2d 734. See John M. Gillis, P.C. v. Wilbur.

Gillispie v. Prudential Ins. Co. of America, TexCivApp–Dallas, 587 SW2d 452, ref nre.—Armed S 84.

Gillispie v. Reinhardt, TexCivApp–Beaumont, 596 SW2d 558, ref nre.—Wills 50, 55(1), 55(2), 206, 289, 290, 302(6).

Gillispie v. State, TexCrimApp, 95 SW2d 695, 131 TexCrim 13.—Bail 63.1, 70; Crim Law 1131(7).

Gillit; Western Cottonoil Co. v., TexCivApp–Eastland, 270 SW2d 512, ref nre.—Trial 125(4), 129.

Gillman; Accent Energy Corp. v., TexApp–Amarillo, 824 SW2d 274, writ den, appeal after remand 1997 WL 196062.—Corp 180, 307, 310(1); Venue 17, 25, 46.

Gillman v. Gillman, TexCivApp–Amarillo, 313 SW2d 931, ref nre.—Compromise 2, 8(3), 8(4), 23(3), 24; Interpl 35; Wills 6, 800.

Gillman; Gillman v., TexCivApp–Amarillo, 313 SW2d 931, ref nre.—Compromise 2, 8(3), 8(4), 23(3), 24; Interpl 35; Wills 6, 800.

Gillman v. Martin, TexCivApp–San Antonio, 366 SW2d 89, writ refused.—Deeds 26; Quiet T 7(2).

Gillman v. Phillips Petroleum Co., TexCivApp–Amarillo, 601 SW2d 513.—Contracts 170(1); Paymt 1(1).

Gillman; Phillips Petroleum Co. v., TexCivApp–Amarillo, 593 SW2d 152, ref nre.—Contracts 143(3), 152, 176(2); Gas 14.1(3).

Gillman Acura; Johnson v., SDTex, 143 FRD 656. See Johnson v. Gillman North, Inc.

Gillman Film Corp.; Boyd v., TexCivApp–Dallas, 447 SW2d 759, ref nre.—Execution 171(3), 172(5); Judgm 27, 360, 486(1); New Tr 163(1); Pretrial Proc 696.1.

Gillman Inc.; Hall v., CA5 (Tex), 81 F3d 35.—Civil R 1209; Fed Civ Proc 2470, 2497.1; Fed Cts 776.

Gillman North, Inc.; Johnson v., SDTex, 143 FRD 656.—Civil R 1006.

Gillman's Marriage, In re, TexCivApp–Amarillo, 507 SW2d 610, dism.—Divorce 152, 165(1), 165(3), 168, 176.

Gill-Massar v. Dallas County By and Through Com'rs Court of Dallas County, TexApp–Dallas, 781 SW2d 612.—Courts 42(1), 57(2); Tax 2100.

Gillmore, Ex parte, TexCrimApp, 369 SW2d 356.—Bail 52.

Gillmore v. State, TexApp–Houston (1 Dist), 707 SW2d 218.—Crim Law 687(2), 1035(10), 1184(4.1); Sent & Pun 631, 1064.

Gillock v. State, TexCrimApp, 90 SW2d 570.—Crim Law 1182.

Gillock v. Texas & P. Ry. Co., TexCivApp–Texarkana, 302 SW2d 717.—App & E 999(2), 1056.6, 1062.1; Labor & Emp 2830, 2886; Trial 142.

Gillon v. State, TexCrimApp, 492 SW2d 948.—Crim Law 369.2(6), 783(1), 796.

Gillon v. State, TexCrimApp, 491 SW2d 893, cert den 94 SCt 255, 414 US 924, 38 LEd2d 158.—Crim Law 374, 641.3(10).

Gill on Behalf of $2,583.45; Texas Workforce Com'n v., TexApp–Corpus Christi, 964 SW2d 308.—Const Law 2600, 2608; Interpl 1, 13, 21, 29.

Gillring Oil Co. v. Federal Energy Regulatory Commission, CA5 (Tex), 566 F2d 1323, cert den 99 SCt 91, 439 US 823, 58 LEd2d 115, reh den 99 SCt 599, 439 US 997, 58 LEd2d 671.—Admin Law 413; Gas 2, 14.6.

Gillring Oil Co. v. Hughes, TexCivApp–Beaumont, 618 SW2d 874.—Mines 92.79, 109.

Gill Sav. Ass'n v. Chair King, Inc., Tex, 797 SW2d 31.—Costs 194.34, 252.

Gill Sav. Ass'n v. Chair King, Inc., TexApp–Houston (14 Dist), 783 SW2d 674, writ den, and writ gr, aff in part, mod in part 797 SW2d 31.—App & E 1008.1(2), 1008.1(3), 1046.5; Costs 194.10, 194.34, 252; Damag

87(2); Estop 52.15, 85; Evid 18; Land & Ten 180(3), 180(4), 188(1); Pretrial Proc 45; Trial 382.

Gill Sav. Ass'n; Hondo Nat. Bank v., CA5 (Tex), 696 F2d 1095.—Action 3; Fed Cts 18; Inj 22.

Gill Sav. Ass'n v. International Supply Co., Inc., TexApp–Dallas, 759 SW2d 697, writ den.—App & E 931(1), 989, 1175(1); Costs 194.18; Mech Liens 5, 154(3), 157(3), 277(2), 310(3).

Gill, State for, In re, TexApp–Amarillo, 680 SW2d 41. See State for Gill, In re.

Gillum v. City of Kerrville, CA5 (Tex), 3 F3d 117, cert den 114 SCt 881, 510 US 1072, 127 LEd2d 76.—Civil R 1128, 1719; Consp 18; Const Law 1947, 1955, 4173(4); Damag 50.10; Mun Corp 180(1), 185(15), 723, 744, 747(3).

Gillum v. Gillum, TexCivApp–Austin, 236 SW2d 192.— Child C 554; Child S 350.

Gillum; Gillum v., TexCivApp–Austin, 236 SW2d 192.— Child C 554; Child S 350.

Gillum; Home Ins. Co. v., TexApp–Corpus Christi, 680 SW2d 844, ref nre.—App & E 969; Trial 232(5), 350.2, 350.3(8); Witn 388(2.1); Work Comp 957, 1369, 1383, 1389, 1687, 1696, 1703, 1728, 1904, 1937.

Gillum v. Mesquite Physicians' Hosp., TexApp–Dallas, 778 SW2d 558. See Gillum v. Republic Health Corp.

Gillum; Norkan Lodge Co. Ltd. v., NDTex, 587 FSupp 1457.—Judgm 831.

Gillum v. Republic Health Corp., TexApp–Dallas, 778 SW2d 558.—App & E 154(4); Estop 85; Fraud 6, 7, 12; Health 260, 269, 275, 656; Judgm 91; Libel 36, 44(1), 51(1), 73, 101(1); Torts 213, 214, 245.

Gillum v. Rogers, TexCivApp–Texarkana, 430 SW2d 822, ref nre.—App & E 927(1), 989; Waters 77.

Gillum v. State, TexCrimApp, 147 SW2d 778, 141 Tex-Crim 162.—Big 2, 11; Crim Law 1169.1(2.1).

Gillum v. State, TexApp–Houston (1 Dist), 959 SW2d 642, petition for discretionary review refused.—Crim Law 273.1(1), 273.4(2), 275.

Gillum v. State, TexApp–Houston (1 Dist), 788 SW2d 443, petition for discretionary review refused.—Arrest 63.4(15), 63.4(18), 63.5(4), 63.5(5); Const Law 3057, 3205; Crim Law 99, 406(2); Infants 12; Int Liq 15; Searches 52.

Gillum v. State, TexApp–El Paso, 888 SW2d 281, petition for discretionary review refused.—Assault 56; Crim Law 369.2(2), 369.2(4), 374, 798.5, 855(1), 863(2), 923(1), 923(9), 1043(1), 1166.18, 1169.2(1); Homic 977, 1174.

Gillum v. State, TexApp–Houston (14 Dist), 792 SW2d 745, petition for discretionary review refused.—Assault 96(1); Crim Law 417(14), 641.13(2.1), 641.13(5), 721(3), 721(6), 795(2.20); Sent & Pun 262.

Gillum; Stites v., TexApp–Fort Worth, 872 SW2d 786, reh overr, and writ den.—App & E 946, 984(1); Atty & C 24; Costs 2; Damag 149; Plead 34(1), 48.

Gillum v. Temple, TexApp–Corpus Christi, 546 SW2d 361, ref nre.—App & E 201(2), 205, 692(1); Evid 158(27); Exceptions Bill of54; Tresp to T T 6.1, 11, 38(1), 38(2), 41(2), 44, 47(1); Trial 31.

Gillund; Peters v., TexCivApp–Galveston, 186 SW2d 1019, writ refused wom.—Adv Poss 1, 70, 85(4), 109, 115(5); App & E 217.

Gilmartin; Greathouse v., TexCivApp–Fort Worth, 164 SW2d 757.—Mand 35, 154(4).

Gilmartin v. KVTV-Channel 13, TexApp–San Antonio, 985 SW2d 553.—Damag 50.10, 208(6); Estop 55, 85; Fraud 3, 12, 20, 32; Judgm 178, 181(2), 181(3), 185(2), 185(5); Labor & Emp 40(1), 40(2), 40(3).

Gilmer v. Ferguson, TexCivApp–El Paso, 148 SW2d 984. —Receivers 12, 14, 32.

Gilmer v. Griffin, TexCivApp–San Antonio, 265 SW2d 252, ref nre.—App & E 970(2), 1050.1(12), 1052(8), 1062.1; Autos 244(34), 244(35), 244(36.1), 244(40), 247; Damag 130.1; Evid 118, 121(1), 123(10); Trial 127, 351.5(6).

Gilmer v. Griffin, TexCivApp–San Antonio, 265 SW2d 250, ref nre.—Plead 111.2; Venue 8.5(5).

Gilmer v. Harris, TexCivApp–Fort Worth, 460 SW2d 215. —Ex & Ad 7, 15, 25.

Gilmer v. State, TexCrimApp, 246 SW2d 639, 157 Tex-Crim 109.—Assault 96(7); Crim Law 419(1.5), 1159.2(3), 1169.1(10); Homic 1032, 1154, 1483.

Gilmer v. U.S., SDTex, 91 FSupp 887.—Estop 62.2(3); Int Rev 4009.

Gilmer, City of; Ashley v., TexCivApp–Texarkana, 271 SW2d 100, writ refused.—Inj 128(7); Pub Ut 165.

Gilmer Co.; Bishop v., TexCivApp–Beaumont, 131 SW2d 173.—Adv Poss 47, 96; App & E 1028.

Gilmer Independent School Dist.; Crump v., EDTex, 797 FSupp 552.—Inj 138.54, 150.

Gilmer Independent School Dist. v. Dorfman, TexApp–Tyler, 156 SW3d 586.—App & E 893(1), 916(1); Const Law 2601; Courts 39; Parties 29, 79, 82; Plead 104(1); Schools 103(0.5).

Gilmer, Tex., City of; Southwestern Gas & Elec. Co. v., CA5 (Tex), 224 F2d 794.—Electricity 8.1(2.1).

Gilmer, Tex., City of; Southwestern Gas & Elec. Co. v., EDTex, 123 FSupp 11, aff 224 F2d 794.—Courts 385, 387(1); Courts 107; Electricity 8.1(2.1); Inj 65, 68.

Gilmore, In re, BkrtcyEDTex, 198 BR 686, reconsideration gr in part, onreconsideration in part 1996 WL 1056889, aff US v. Gilmore, 226 BR 567.—Bankr 2125, 2157, 2162, 3352, 3420(1); Equity 64.

Gilmore, In re, TexApp–Beaumont, 637 SW2d 513.—Contempt 20, 70.

Gilmore, Matter of, TexCivApp–Tyler, 559 SW2d 879.— Infants 155, 178, 230.1, 243.

Gilmore; Beckstrom v., TexApp–Eastland, 886 SW2d 845, reh den, and writ den.—Costs 194.46; Frds St of 49.

Gilmore; Brown v., TexCivApp–El Paso, 267 SW2d 908, dism.—Venue 5.3(2).

Gilmore; Combined Am. Ins. Co. v., TexCivApp–Fort Worth, 428 SW2d 857.—Evid 244(2), 318(1); Lost Inst 23(1); Plead 111.42(1).

Gilmore; Davis v., TexCivApp–San Antonio, 244 SW2d 671, writ refused.—Acct Action on 7, 14; Acct St 6(2); Partners 1, 6, 11, 44, 55.

Gilmore v. Dennison, TexComApp, 115 SW2d 902, 131 Tex 398.—App & E 1175(5); Home 29, 57(3).

Gilmore v. Dennison, TexCivApp–Beaumont, 91 SW2d 371, rev 115 SW2d 902, 131 Tex 398.—Execution 172(4).

Gilmore v. James, NDTex, 274 FSupp 75, aff 88 SCt 695, 389 US 572, 19 LEd2d 783, reh den 88 SCt 1027, 390 US 975, 19 LEd2d 1195.—Abate & R 8(2); Action 6; Const Law 42(2), 82(6.1), 274(2), 710, 1156, 1440, 1447, 1490, 4188; Crim Law 43; Fed Civ Proc 187.5, 242; Fed Cts 26.1, 48, 91, 993.1, 1002; Inj 1, 5, 11, 74, 114(2), 114(3), 114(4); Mun Corp 170; Offic 18, 19; States 44, 53.

Gilmore v. Lopez, TexApp–San Antonio, 974 SW2d 67, reh overr, and review den.—Debt Action of 7, 11; Plead 48.

Gilmore; Prestige Ford Co. Ltd. Partnership v., TexApp–Houston (14 Dist), 56 SW3d 73, reh overr, and review den.—App & E 866(3), 927(7), 977(1), 1050.1(1), 1050.1(11), 1051.1(2), 1056.1(1), 1056.1(3), 1079; Civil R 1204, 1539, 1744; Judgm 363, 364, 379(1); New Tr 6; Pretrial Proc 41, 130; Trial 39, 43, 120(1).

Gilmore; Robb v., TexCivApp–Fort Worth, 302 SW2d 739, ref nre.—App & E 1170.7; Labor & Emp 2859, 2875, 2879, 2888, 2895, 2895; Neglig 1694; New Tr 144; Pretrial Proc 390; Trial 351.5(5), 352.1(5), 420.

Gilmore; Rubin v., TexCivApp–Hous (1 Dist), 561 SW2d 231.—App & E 934(2), 954(1), 1152, 1177(2); Inj 135, 142, 152, 157, 189, 204; Partners 325(1), 325(2), 325(3); Receivers 42, 47.

Gilmore v. State, TexCrimApp, 493 SW2d 163.—Crim Law 683(1), 899, 1169.11; Witn 405(1).

Gilmore v. State, TexCrimApp, 493 SW2d 161.—Crim Law 1177.5(1); Sent & Pun 313.

Gilmore v. State, TexCrimApp, 332 SW2d 721, 169 TexCrim 141.—Larc 65.

Gilmore v. State, TexCrimApp, 261 SW2d 854, 159 TexCrim 121.—Crim Law 371(10); Int Liq 236(7).

Gilmore v. State, TexCrimApp, 257 SW2d 300, 158 TexCrim 534.—Crim Law 829(3).

Gilmore v. State, TexCrimApp, 229 SW2d 167.—Crim Law 1090.1(1).

Gilmore v. State, TexCrimApp, 109 SW2d 758, 133 TexCrim 221.—Bail 70; Crim Law 1104(2), 1131(7); Ind & Inf 69.

Gilmore v. State, TexCrimApp, 87 SW2d 722, 129 TexCrim 363.—Crim Law 1092.7; Larc 55.

Gilmore v. State, TexApp–Houston (1 Dist), 792 SW2d 553.—Crim Law 686(1); Sent & Pun 367.

Gilmore v. State, TexApp–Fort Worth, 822 SW2d 350.—Crim Law 549, 553; Rob 1, 5, 24.10.

Gilmore v. State, TexApp–Dallas, 744 SW2d 630, petition for discretionary review refused.—Crim Law 396(2), 1170(3).

Gilmore v. State, TexApp–Amarillo, 666 SW2d 136, petition for discretionary review refused.—Arrest 62, 63.1, 63.2, 63.3, 63.4(2), 63.4(5), 63.4(11), 63.4(15), 68(3); Crim Law 59(1), 59(3), 320, 338(7), 394.1(3), 394.5(3), 394.6(5), 404.45, 419(2), 419(12), 475.2(3), 488, 552(3), 736(1), 741(1), 770(2), 792(1), 814(19), 1035(10), 1036.1(2), 1134(3), 1144.13(3), 1153(1), 1159.2(9), 1159.4(2), 1159.6, 1169.1(9), 1169.1(10), 1169.5(1), 1169.5(3); Cust Dut 54; Homic 1184, 1465; Searches 13.1, 26, 180, 186, 194.

Gilmore v. State, TexApp–Beaumont, 44 SW3d 92, petition for discretionary review refused.—Assault 82, 92(6); Crim Law 772(6), 795(1.5), 795(2.10), 814(8); Ind & Inf 191(0.5).

Gilmore v. State, TexApp–Houston (14 Dist), 68 SW3d 741, petition for discretionary review refused, habeas corpus gr Ex parte Gilmore, 2005 WL 768068.—Crim Law 641.13(1), 641.13(6), 796, 1141(2).

Gilmore v. State, TexApp–Houston (14 Dist), 871 SW2d 848.—Assault 91, 96(1), 96(2), 96(3); Crim Law 795(1.5), 795(2.10), 1036.1(9), 1130(5); Witn 345(9).

Gilmore v. State, TexApp–Houston (14 Dist), 788 SW2d 866.—Controlled Subs 69, 80; Evid 121(1), 146.

Gilmore v. Transit Grain & Commission Co., TexCivApp–Fort Worth, 213 SW2d 880.—App & E 846(2), 846(5), 912, 1050.1(8.1); Sales 26; Venue 7.5(7).

Gilmore; U.S. v., CA5 (Tex), 435 F2d 170.—Armed S 20.1(2), 40.1(7).

Gilmore v. U.S., CA5 (Tex), 264 F2d 44, cert den 79 SCt 1126, 359 US 994, 3 LEd2d 982, reh den 79 SCt 1298, 360 US 914, 3 LEd2d 1264.—Consp 47(2); Crim Law 1023(2), 1023(3); Double J 98, 109; Fed Cts 598.1.

Gilmore v. U. S., CA5 (Tex), 256 F2d 565.—Crim Law 627.5(4), 627.6(2), 627.10(3); Witn 16.

Gilmore v. U.S., CA5 (Tex), 228 F2d 121.—Consp 47(12); Crim Law 1177; Int Rev 5295.

Gilmore; U.S. v., EDTex, 226 BR 567.—Bankr 2125, 2157, 2954.1, 3352.

Gilmore; Vickrey v., TexCivApp–Waco, 554 SW2d 36.—Wills 62, 63, 440, 487(1), 488.

Gilmore & Tatge Mfg. Co.; Shook v., TexApp–Waco, 851 SW2d 887, reh den, and writ den, appeal after remand 951 SW2d 294, reh overr, and review den.—App & E 863; Const Law 3954, 3989, 4494; Contempt 2, 40, 55; Courts 78; Pretrial Proc 44.1, 46, 531, 534, 551, 552, 678, 749.1.

Gilmore & Tatge Mfg. Co., Inc.; Shook v., TexApp–Waco, 951 SW2d 294, reh overr, and review den.—App & E 854(1), 863, 962; Pretrial Proc 583, 697, 699.

Gil-Perez; Southwest Key Program, Inc. v., Tex, 81 SW3d 269.—App & E 930(1); Asylums 8; Neglig 371, 379, 380, 387.

Gil-Perez; Southwest Key Program, Inc. v., TexApp–Corpus Christi, 79 SW3d 571, rev 81 SW3d 269.—App & E 930(1), 1001(1), 1003(5); Damag 61; Evid 568(1); Infants 17; Neglig 202, 210, 213, 233, 238, 331, 371, 379, 380, 387, 1579, 1692; Parent & C 7(1); Pub Amuse 82.

Gilreath v. State, TexCrimApp, 251 SW2d 540, 157 TexCrim 526.—Burg 41(1); Crim Law 590(2).

Gilson v. Central Power & Light Co., TexCivApp–San Antonio, 231 SW2d 683.—App & E 954(2); Inj 132, 138.31.

Gilson v. State, TexCrimApp, 154 SW2d 839, 142 TexCrim 422.—Crim Law 1081(1); Witn 410.

Gilson v. State, TexCrimApp, 145 SW2d 182, 140 TexCrim 345.—Assault 83; Crim Law 379, 925.5(1), 925.5(3); Witn 370(1), 372(1).

Gilson; Trice Contract Carpets & Furniture Co. v., TexCivApp–Houston, 329 SW2d 476, ref nre.—App & E 842(1), 933(5), 1069.1, 1170.6; Neglig 1664; New Tr 29; Trial 127, 304, 356(5).

Gilson v. Universal Realty Co., TexCivApp–Houston, 378 SW2d 115, ref nre.—App & E 151(5), 1056.1(4.1), 1062.5; Bound 7, 8, 10, 35(1), 37(3), 40(1); Estop 21; New Tr 99; Trial 244(3), 255(13), 260(1), 260(5), 350.3(3).

Gilstrap v. Beakley, TexApp–Corpus Christi, 636 SW2d 736.—Banks 100; Neglig 1658; Plead 111.18, 111.38, 111.42(9); Sec Tran 165; Venue 22(1), 22(6), 22(10).

Gilstrap v. Imperator Oil Corporation, TexCivApp–Galveston, 168 SW2d 300.—Bound 3(3); Trial 352.4(3).

Gilstrap; Kokernot v., Tex, 187 SW2d 368, 143 Tex 595.—Contracts 138(1); Mtg 32(3), 81; Tresp to T T 16.

Gilstrap; Kokernot v., TexCivApp–Texarkana, 180 SW2d 183, rev 187 SW2d 368, 143 Tex 595.—Contracts 140; Evid 265(10); Tresp to T T 16; Ven & Pur 220, 235, 236, 237.

Gilstrap v. Park Lane Town Home Ass'n, TexApp–Amarillo, 885 SW2d 589.—App & E 856(1); Land & Ten 167(2).

Gilstrap v. State, TexCrimApp, 158 SW2d 312, 143 TexCrim 276.—Crim Law 1131(5).

Gilstrap v. State, TexApp–Fort Worth, 945 SW2d 192, petition for discretionary review refused.—Crim Law 1036.2; Witn 331.5, 372(2).

Gilstrap v. State, TexApp–Waco, 65 SW3d 322, petition for discretionary review refused.—Const Law 4657, 4658(1), 4658(2); Crim Law 339.6, 339.8(1), 339.8(4), 339.9(1), 339.10(1), 1139, 1144.12, 1144.13(3), 1144.13(6), 1159.2(2), 1159.2(7); Homic 1168, 1181.

Gil–Tex Pipeline Const. Co.; Wasson v., TexApp–Texarkana, 786 SW2d 414. See Wasson v. Stracener.

Gilvin-Terrill, Inc.; N.L.R.B. v., CA5 (Tex), 338 F2d 971, cert-den 85 SCt 1335, 380 US 974, 14 LEd2d 270.—Labor & Emp 1182, 1185(3).

Gindratt; State v., TexCivApp–Waco, 155 SW2d 967.—New Tr 144; Trial 315.

Gingell, Ex parte, TexCrimApp, 842 SW2d 284.—Sent & Pun 1976(2), 2047.

Gini's Home Cooking & Bakery; H & C Communications, Inc. v., TexApp–San Antonio, 887 SW2d 475. See H & C Communications, Inc. v. Reed's Food Intern., Inc.

Gini's Home Cooking & Bakery; KSAT–TV v., TexApp–San Antonio, 887 SW2d 475. See H & C Communications, Inc. v. Reed's Food Intern., Inc.

Ginn v. City of Tyler, Tex, 227 SW2d 1022, 148 Tex 604.—App & E 361(5).

Ginn; City of Tyler v., TexCivApp–Texarkana, 225 SW2d 997, writ dism 227 SW2d 1022, 148 Tex 604.—Em Dom 134, 202(1), 204, 262(5).

Ginn; Matrix Network, Inc. v., TexApp–Dallas, 211 SW3d 944.—Antitrust 103(2); App & E 781(4), 954(1), 954(2); Costs 260(5); Inj 132, 135, 138.1, 138.6.

Ginn v. Southwest Bitulithic Co., TexCivApp–El Paso, 149 SW2d 201, writ dism, correct.—App & E 392, 493, 1173(1); Infants 80(2), 105, 115.

Ginn v. State, TexCrimApp, 439 SW2d 840.—Autos 355(6); Witn 255(2.1).

Ginns; H. T. Cab Co. v., TexCivApp–Galveston, 280 SW2d 360, ref nre.—App & E 1036(2); Carr 247, 283(3), 316(1), 318(1), 318(12); Hus & W 260, 273(12).

Ginsberg; Dowdell v., TexCivApp–Fort Worth, 244 SW2d 265.—Venue 7.5(1), 7.5(7).

Ginsberg v. Fifth Court of Appeals, Tex, 686 SW2d 105.—App & E 1092; Courts 209(2); Pretrial Proc 27.1, 382; Trial 43; Witn 214.5.

Ginsberg; Fleming v., CCA5 (Tex), 163 F2d 965.—Fed Cts 730, 933.

Ginsberg; Fleming v., NDTex, 71 FSupp 7, rev 163 F2d 965.—War 152.

Ginsberg; Gaynier v., TexApp–Dallas, 763 SW2d 461, appeal after remand 1994 WL 400989, writ den, dissenting opinion on denial of reh 1994 WL 672562.—Courts 37(2), 472.4(2.1), 472.4(7).

Ginsberg; Gaynier v., TexApp–Dallas, 715 SW2d 749, ref nre, appeal after remand 763 SW2d 461, appeal after remand 1994 WL 400989, writ den, dissenting opinion on denial of reh 1994 WL 672562.—Adv Poss 42, 60(4); Deeds 196(3); Joint Adv 7; Judgm 181(7), 181(15.1), 181(29); Lim of Act 100(2), 100(7); Pretrial Proc 474, 478.

Ginsberg v. Johnson, TexApp–Dallas, 673 SW2d 942, subsequent mandamus proceeding 686 SW2d 105.—Evid 351; Pretrial Proc 93.

Ginsberg v. Leal, TexCivApp–Waco, 462 SW2d 110, ref nre.—Lim of Act 148(3).

Ginsberg; Mr. Eddie, Inc. v., TexCivApp–Eastland, 430 SW2d 5, ref nre.—App & E 205, 242(4), 1073(7); Corp 407(2), 518(1); Damag 226; Evid 5(2); Interest 39(1), 66; Labor & Emp 863(1), 866, 867, 868(1), 868(4), 868(5), 871, 874; Social S 121; Trial 29(2), 350.3(4).

Ginsberg v. Royal Ins. Co., CA5 (Tex), 179 F2d 152.—Fed Cts 776, 864, 913; Insurance 2202.

Ginsberg; Sachs v., CCA5 (Tex), 87 F2d 28.—Usury 14, 16, 52.

Ginsberg v. Selbest Dress, Inc., TexCivApp–Dallas, 238 SW2d 621, ref nre.—App & E 1050.1(5); Evid 213(1), 213(2), 272; Sales 73, 119, 124, 417, 422; Trial 140(2).

Ginsberg v. U.S., CCA5 (Tex), 96 F2d 433.—Consp 48.1(4); Crim Law 423(1), 590(1), 622.1(2), 622.3, 730(1), 814(1), 919(5), 1036.1(4), 1184(4.1); Ind & Inf 121.1(3), 121.2(7), 136, 137(1), 138; Sent & Pun 1487.

Ginsberg & Foreman; Criswell v., TexApp–Dallas, 843 SW2d 304.—App & E 983(3); Com Law 11; Const Law 2312, 2314; Execution 402(1), 402(3).

Ginsberg 1985 Real Estate Partnership v. Cadle Co., CA5 (Tex), 39 F3d 528.—Banks 182; Corp 416; Fed Civ Proc 2470.1, 2487, 2544; Fed Cts 776; Interest 36(1); Usury 82, 126.

Ginsburg v. Arnold, CA5 (Tex), 185 F2d 913.—Int Rev 3910, 3914.1, 3918; Partners 1, 12.

Ginsburg v. Arnold, CA5 (Tex), 176 F2d 879.—Int Rev 3913, 3926.

Ginsburg v. Arnold, NDTex, 88 FSupp 903, rev 185 F2d 913.—Int Rev 3916.1, 3926.

Ginsburg v. Chernoff/Silver & Associates, Inc., TexApp–Houston (1 Dist), 137 SW3d 231.—App & E 267(1), 959(1); Courts 91(1); Divorce 255, 276(0.5), 276(3).

Ginsburg; Myers v., TexApp–Dallas, 735 SW2d 600.—Antitrust 161, 363; Costs 194.34; Land & Ten 109(1), 109(5), 161(1), 223(2), 233(2), 251(0.5), 262(7); Sec Tran 231, 237; Trover 10, 23.

Ginsburg; Pech v., TexCivApp–Galveston, 145 SW2d 262, writ dism.—Brok 63(1), 82(1), 88(14).

Ginther, In re, CA5 (Tex), 791 F2d 1151.—Bankr 3033; Const Law 2086; Fed Civ Proc 1623, 2774(1), 2846, 2847.

Ginther v. Bammel, TexCivApp–Waco, 336 SW2d 759.—Bound 20(1); Ease 3(1), 3(2), 14(2), 27.

Ginther v. Domino's Pizza, Inc., TexApp–Houston (14 Dist), 93 SW3d 300, review den.—App & E 852, 934(1); Autos 197(2); Judgm 181(11), 185(2); Labor & Emp 3045; Neglig 202, 210, 211, 215.

Ginther v. O'Connell, CA5 (Tex), 791 F2d 1151. See Ginther, In re.

Ginther; Siegler v., TexApp–Houston (1 Dist), 680 SW2d 886.—App & E 930(4); Assumpsit 1; Bills & N 313, 437, 439, 440, 518(2); Contracts 148.

Ginther v. Southwest Workover Co., TexCivApp–San Antonio, 286 SW2d 291.—App & E 171(1), 218.2(2), 1001(1), 1026; Const Law 990; Costs 194.46; Mines 110; Statut 199; Trial 350.1, 350.4(4), 352.1(2), 365.1(1).

Ginther v. State, TexCrimApp, 672 SW2d 475.—Autos 411; Crim Law 388.1, 1153(1).

Ginther v. State, TexCrimApp, 605 SW2d 610, appeal after remand 672 SW2d 475.—Autos 357; Crim Law 1173.2(5).

Ginther v. State, TexApp–Houston (1 Dist), 706 SW2d 115, petition for discretionary review refused.—Arrest 63.4(16); Controlled Subs 80; Crim Law 338(1), 419(1), 438(8), 650, 1153(1); Judges 49(2); Witn 2(1).

Ginther v. Taub, Tex, 675 SW2d 724.—App & E 1175(1); Trusts 92.5, 103(4), 376.

Ginther; Taub v., TexApp–Beaumont, 631 SW2d 775, writ gr, rev 675 SW2d 724.—Trusts 103(1), 103(5), 110.

Ginther v. Taub, TexCivApp–Waco, 570 SW2d 516, ref nre.—App & E 934(1), 989; Atty & C 123(2); Brok 42; Judgm 181(34), 542; Sec Reg 265, 298; Trusts 92.5, 95, 102(1), 107, 111.

Ginther v. Texas Commerce Bank, N.A., SDTex, 111 FRD 615.—Atty & C 32(11); Bankr 3033; Fed Civ Proc 2771(16), 2793, 2805.

Ginther-Davis Center, Ltd. v. Houston Nat. Bank, TexCivApp–Hous (1 Dist), 600 SW2d 856, ref nre.—Inj 14; Mtg 83, 86(3), 395, 413.

Ginther-Davis Const. Co. v. Bryant-Curington, Inc., TexCivApp–Waco, 614 SW2d 923.—Plead 111.5, 111.16, 111.42(5).

Ginther Trusts, In re, CA5 (Tex), 238 F3d 686, cert den Ginther v. Ginther Trusts, 122 SCt 39, 534 US 814, 151 LEd2d 12.—Bankr 2228, 3770, 3776.5(5), 3782.

Ginzburg v. Memorial Healthcare Systems, Inc., SDTex, 993 FSupp 998.—Antitrust 534, 535, 537, 556, 557, 558, 563, 593, 625, 631, 641, 960, 963(1), 963(2), 963(3), 964, 976, 977(1), 977(2).

Ginzel; Remund v., TexCivApp–Waco, 259 SW2d 619.—Land & Ten 92(1); Spec Perf 121(11).

Giordano v. U.S., USTex, 89 SCt 1163, 394 US 310, 22 LEd2d 297, reh den Di Pietto v. US, 89 SCt 1451, 394 US 994, 22 LEd2d 771, on remand US v Hoffa, 307 FSupp 1129, aff 437 F2d 11, cert den 91 SCt 1664, 402 US 988, 29 LEd2d 154, appeal after remand US v Clay, 430 F2d 165, cert gr in part 91 SCt 457, 400 US 990, 27 LEd2d 438, rev 91 SCt 2068, 403 US 698, 29 LEd2d 810, conformed to 446 F2d 1406, appeal after remand 436 F2d 1243, cert den 91 SCt 455, 400 US 1000, 27 LEd2d 451, cert den Dranow v US, 91 SCt 457, 400 US 1000, 27 LEd2d 451, appeal after remand US v Battaglia, 432 F2d 1115, cert den Evans v US, 91 SCt 868, 401 US 924, 27 LEd2d 828, cert den Amabile v US, 91 SCt 869, 401 US 924, 27 LEd2d 828, cert den 91 SCt 883, 401 US 924, 27 LEd2d 828, appeal after remand US v Randaccio, 440 F2d 1337, appeal after remand US v Aiuppa, 440 F2d 893, cert den 92 SCt 60, 404 US 871, 30 LEd2d 114.—Fed Cts 460.1.

Giordenello v. U.S., USTex, 78 SCt 1245, 357 US 480, 2 LEd2d 1503.—Crim Law 209, 211(1), 211(3), 217, 219, 225, 226, 1043(3), 1189.

Giordenello v. U.S., CA5 (Tex), 241 F2d 575, cert gr 78 SCt 66, 355 US 811, 2 LEd2d 30, rev 78 SCt 1245, 357

US 480, 2 LEd2d 1503.—Arrest 65; Crim Law 211(1), 211(3), 219.

Giossi v. State, TexApp–Austin, 831 SW2d 887, reh den, and petition for discretionary review refused.—Arrest 63.5(4), 63.5(5); Crim Law 394.1(3).

Gips v. Red Robin Corp., TexCivApp–Houston, 366 SW2d 853, ref nre.—App & E 170(1), 705, 846(5); Assign 58; Brok 76; Contracts 318; Ven & Pur 130(2), 141, 144(2), 341(3).

Gipson v. Aetna Ins. Co., TexCivApp–Eastland, 373 SW2d 311.—Evid 571(9); Insurance 2575, 2577; Trial 365.1(5).

Gipson; Anderson v., TexCivApp–Galveston, 144 SW2d 948.—App & E 907(3); Frds St of 56(1); Game 3; Licens 44(1); Perp 1.

Gipson v. Callahan, WDTex, 18 FSupp2d 662, appeal dism 157 F3d 903.—Civil R 1088(5), 1376(2), 1376(6), 1376(8), 1376(9); Dist & Pros Attys 10; Judges 36; Offic 119.

Gipson v. Randall, TexCivApp–Waco, 324 SW2d 436, ref nre.—App & E 171(1); Deeds 211(3); Judgm 256(2).

Gipson v. Rosenberg, CA5 (Tex), 797 F2d 224, cert den 107 SCt 1633, 481 US 1007, 95 LEd2d 206, reh den 107 SCt 2470, 481 US 1072, 95 LEd2d 879.—Civil R 1326(10), 1492.

Gipson; Safeco Ins. Co. v., TexCivApp–Texarkana, 619 SW2d 275, ref nre.—App & E 912, 931(1), 989; Plead 111.18, 111.42(9); Pretrial Proc 202.

Gipson v. Skelly Oil Co., CCA5 (Tex), 152 F2d 588.—Work Comp 207, 208, 1347.

Gipson v. Southwest Oil Co. of San Antonio, Inc., TexCivApp–Tyler, 604 SW2d 396.—Acct Action on 12, 13, 14; App & E 557, 569(2); Costs 207; New Tr 93.

Gipson v. State, TexCrimApp, 844 SW2d 738.—Crim Law 260.11(2), 260.11(6).

Gipson v. State, TexCrimApp, 619 SW2d 169.—Crim Law 369.1, 369.2(1), 369.2(5), 374.

Gipson v. State, TexCrimApp, 503 SW2d 796.—Crim Law 713, 1037.2, 1038.1(1), 1038.1(5), 1038.3, 1169.5(2), 1169.6, 1171.1(3); Rob 20.

Gipson v. State, TexCrimApp, 403 SW2d 794.—Assault 56; Homic 734, 1154, 1161.

Gipson v. State, TexCrimApp, 181 SW2d 76, 147 TexCrim 428.—Crim Law 736(2); Homic 1136, 1193, 1326.

Gipson v. State, TexCrimApp, 161 SW2d 1088, 144 Tex-Crim 216.—Crim Law 1144.15, 1159.2(4), 1183; Sent & Pun 1495.

Gipson v. State, TexApp–Fort Worth, 669 SW2d 351.—Crim Law 1128(2), 1131(4); Sent & Pun 2009.

Gipson v. State, TexApp–Dallas, 819 SW2d 890, petition for discretionary review gr, aff 844 SW2d 738.—Crim Law 312, 412.1(2), 511.1(1), 511.1(3), 511.1(5), 511.1(7), 511.2, 511.4, 511.7, 520(1), 530, 558, 1144.13(2.1), 1144.13(6), 1159.2(7), 1159.2(9), 1159.4(2), 1169.12; Homic 908, 986, 1325.

Gipson v. State, TexApp–Waco, 82 SW3d 715.—Const Law 4745; Crim Law 369.1, 369.2(4), 371(4), 371(12), 394.6(5), 414, 1152(2), 1153(1), 1158(3), 1158(4), 1166.18; Jury 107; Searches 24, 25.1, 26, 42.1, 47.1; Sent & Pun 8.

Gipson; U.S. v., CA5 (Tex), 46 F3d 472.—Const Law 2817; Crim Law 1130(5), 1139, 1167(1); Ind & Inf 59, 60, 71.2(4); Sent & Pun 664(5), 787, 1309.

Gipson; U.S. v., CA5 (Tex), 985 F2d 212, on subsequent appeal 12 F3d 1099.—Crim Law 641.13(1), 641.13(7), 1026.10(1), 1134(3), 1139, 1158(1).

Gipson v. Wood, TexCivApp–Hous (1 Dist), 506 SW2d 321.—Damag 132(3).

Giraldi; U.S. v., CA5 (Tex), 86 F3d 1368.—Bail 44(4); Banks 509.15, 509.25; Consp 47(4); Crim Law 369.2(3.1), 720(7.1), 824(1), 824(8), 829(3), 829(4), 835, 935(1), 1134(4), 1144.13(2.1), 1144.13(6), 1152(1), 1153(1), 1156(1), 1158(1), 1159.2(7), 1159.6; Sent & Pun 764; U S 34.

Giraldi; U.S. v., SDTex, 858 FSupp 85.—Jury 76.

Giraldo; U.S. v., CA5 (Tex), 111 F3d 21, cert den 118 SCt 322, 522 US 925, 139 LEd2d 249.—Sent & Pun 752.

Giraldo-Lara; U.S. v., CA5 (Tex), 919 F2d 19.—Crim Law 1158(1); Sent & Pun 677, 686, 764, 765, 790.

Girand v. Kimbell Milling Co., CCA5 (Tex), 116 F2d 999.—Bankr 2617; Evid 20(2); Fact 1, 47(2); Rem of C 100; Wareh 12, 28, 30.

Girard, In re, BkrtcyWDTex, 104 BR 817.—Home 29, 99, 99.5, 110, 112.

Girard; Curry v., TexCivApp–Fort Worth, 502 SW2d 933.—App & E 1004(8), 1070(2); Consp 19.

Girard v. Drexel Burnham Lambert, Inc., CA5 (Tex), 807 F2d 490.—Alt Disp Res 415.

Girard v. Drexel Burnham Lambert, Inc., CA5 (Tex), 805 F2d 607.—Alt Disp Res 412, 413, 414.

Girard v. Drexel Burnham Lambert, Inc., SDTex, 644 FSupp 52, appeal dism 807 F2d 490.—Alt Disp Res 413, 414.

Girard v. Girard, TexCivApp–Hous (1 Dist), 521 SW2d 714.—App & E 1033(8); Divorce 231, 252.3(5), 252.5(2), 252.5(3), 253(2); Hus & W 249(4), 265.

Girard; Girard v., TexCivApp–Hous (1 Dist), 521 SW2d 714.—App & E 1033(8); Divorce 231, 252.3(5), 252.5(2), 252.5(3), 253(2); Hus & W 249(4), 265.

Girard; Southern Underwriters v., TexCivApp–Texarkana, 107 SW2d 775.—App & E 930(1); Propty 9; Trial 139.1(3), 140(1); Work Comp 1386, 1429, 1446, 1489.

Girard v. State, TexCrimApp, 631 SW2d 162.—Crim Law 419(1), 552(3), 719(1), 726, 1159.2(7), 1171.3; Rob 24.25, 26.

Girard v. Unilife Ins. Co., BkrtcyWDTex, 104 BR 817. See Girard, In re.

Girard & Pastel Corp.; Commander's Palace Park Associates v., CA5 (Tex), 572 F2d 1084.—Sec Reg 5.19.

Girard Independent School Dist.; Jayton Rural High School Dist. v., Tex, 301 SW2d 80, 157 Tex 115.—Schools 32, 37(1), 37(5).

Girard Independent School Dist.; Jayton Rural High School Dist. v., TexCivApp–Amarillo, 295 SW2d 487, rev 301 SW2d 80, 157 Tex 115.—Schools 37(5).

Girard Life Ins. Co. of America; Givens v., TexCivApp–Dallas, 480 SW2d 421, ref nre.—Gifts 28(3); Hus & W 249(3), 265, 273(12); Insurance 3360; Interpl 6, 35; Trial 368.

Girard Properties, Inc.; Tobin v., CA5 (Tex), 206 F2d 524.—Commerce 62.40, 62.50, 62.60.

Girards; Intercontinental Hotels Corp. v., TexApp–Dallas, 217 SW3d 736.—App & E 840(4), 949; Parties 35.41, 35.67.

Girard Trust Bank; Placid Investments, Ltd. v., CA5 (Tex), 789 F2d 1191.—Sales 87(3), 89.

Girard Trust Bank; Placid Investments, Ltd. v., CA5 (Tex), 689 F2d 1218.—Fed Cts 76.

Giraud v. Crockett, TexCivApp–Austin, 142 SW2d 243, writ refused.—Wills 470(1), 545(1), 629, 634(9), 634(18).

Giraud v. Reserve Realty Co., TexCivApp–San Antonio, 94 SW2d 198, writ refused.—Judgm 91; Stip 3.

Giraud v. Winslow, Tex, 137 SW 917, 104 Tex 318.—Zoning 67.5.

Giraud; Zepeda v., TexApp–San Antonio, 880 SW2d 833, reh den, and writ den.—App & E 14(1), 627.

Girdley; American Star Ins. Co. v., CA5 (Tex), 19 F3d 966.—Indem 27; Insurance 3590.

Girdley; American Star Ins. Co. v., CA5 (Tex), 12 F3d 49, reh den, opinion withdrawn and superseded 19 F3d 966.

Girdley v. Southwestern Bell Yellow Pages, Inc., TexApp–El Paso, 869 SW2d 409, reh overr, and reh overr, and writ den.—App & E 5, 80(3); Costs 260(4).

Girdner v. Rose, TexApp–Eastland, 213 SW3d 438.—App & E 221, 226(2), 941, 946, 1008.1(2), 1012.1(5); Costs 194.12, 194.40, 198, 207; Jury 25(6); Land & Ten 92(1), 152(3), 231(8), 232; Pretrial Proc 25.

Girdner; State v., TexCivApp–Dallas, 287 SW2d 706.—App & E 1170.7; Em Dom 259, 262(3), 262(5); Witn 48(4).

Girdner; Trinity Universal Ins. Co. v., CA5 (Tex), 379 F2d 317.—U S 67(2), 67(16.1).

Girdy v. State, TexCrimApp, 213 SW3d 315, reh den.—Double J 161, 162; Ind & Inf 191(0.5).

Girdy v. State, TexApp–Amarillo, 175 SW3d 877, petition for discretionary review gr, and petition for discretionary review refused, aff 213 SW3d 315, reh den.—Crim Law 312, 1030(2); Double J 161, 162; Ind & Inf 191(0.5); Kidnap 27, 36.

Girling Health Care, Inc. v. Shalala, CA5 (Tex), 85 F3d 211.—Admin Law 704; Fed Civ Proc 2512.5; Health 535(1), 535(4), 556(1), 556(2), 557(1); Statut 219(6.1).

Girls Haven of Orange; Chambers v., TexCivApp–Beaumont, 268 SW2d 250.—Child C 409, 410, 617, 923(4); Infants 196, 230.1, 231; Plead 111.49.

Girndt v. State, TexCrimApp, 623 SW2d 930.—Crim Law 693, 730(13); Witn 390.

Girnus, Ex parte, TexCrimApp, 640 SW2d 619.—Crim Law 1177.5(2); Sent & Pun 1379(2), 1381(4), 1399.

Girnus v. State, TexCrimApp, 595 SW2d 118.—Sent & Pun 1387, 1513.

Giron v. State, TexApp–Houston (1 Dist), 695 SW2d 292.—Crim Law 374, 1043(3); Homic 975, 999; Witn 230, 247, 390.

Giron v. State, TexApp–Beaumont, 19 SW3d 572, petition for discretionary review refused.—Crim Law 627.8(6), 1035(2), 1042, 1166(10.10); Homic 947, 1210.

Girosky-Garibay; U.S. v., WDTex, 176 FSupp2d 705.—Aliens 271, 346, 376, 379, 384; Const Law 4438; Courts 100(1).

Giroux-Daniel; Bexar County v., TexApp–San Antonio, 956 SW2d 692.—App & E 93, 863; Costs 260(4); Judgm 181(27); Offic 114, 119.

Girsh v. St. John, TexApp–Beaumont, 218 SW3d 921.—Action 13; App & E 174, 893(1); Covenants 77.1, 110; Lim of Act 1, 47(2), 95(3), 179(2), 193.

Girvin; Buchanan v., Tex, 176 SW2d 729, 142 Tex 134.—Absentees 4, 5; Clerks of C 18; Judgm 17(1); Statut 219(9.1).

Gish; Blaugrund v., Tex, 179 SW2d 266, 142 Tex 379.—App & E 216(1); New Tr 144; Trial 234(9), 304, 351.5(6), 352.4(7).

Gish; Blaugrund v., TexCivApp–El Paso, 179 SW2d 257, aff 179 SW2d 266, 142 Tex 379.—App & E 930(3), 981, 1015(5), 1060.1(2.1), 1069.1; Autos 209; Evid 341; New Tr 99, 144, 151; Trial 120(2), 304, 315, 351.5(6), 358, 365.3.

Gish; Jackson v., TexCivApp–Waco, 440 SW2d 121, ref nre.—Corp 316(3), 320(14); Evid 5(2); Judgm 144, 273(3), 276; New Tr 116.2.

Gish v. State, TexCrimApp, 606 SW2d 883.—Controlled Subs 77, 155; Crim Law 1166(1); Searches 101, 111, 113.1, 119, 123.1.

Gisler; Union Gas Corp. v., TexApp–Corpus Christi, 129 SW3d 145.—Action 60; App & E 931(3), 949, 984(5); Contracts 143(2); Costs 194.18, 208; Equity 65(1), 66; Interpl 1, 6, 10, 18, 21, 35; Mines 78.1(7), 79.1(5).

Gisondi; Johnson v., TexApp–Houston (1 Dist), 627 SW2d 448.—Damag 207; Judgm 112.

Gissel; U.S. v., CA5 (Tex), 493 F2d 27, cert den 95 SCt 332, 419 US 1012, 42 LEd2d 286.—Cust Dut 86; Princ & A 50; Princ & S 35, 97, 115(2).

Gissel; U.S. v., SDTex, 353 FSupp 768, aff 493 F2d 27, cert den 95 SCt 332, 419 US 1012, 42 LEd2d 286.—Admin Law 741; Contracts 154; Cust Dut 23, 86, 130(1); Forfeit 1; Princ & A 26, 136(2); Princ & S 55.

Gist, In re, TexApp–San Antonio, 974 SW2d 843, reh overr.—Oath 1.

Gist; Eckels v., TexApp–Houston (1 Dist), 743 SW2d 330.—Counties 67; Mand 53.

Gist; Harris County, Tex. v., SDTex, 976 FSupp 620.—Fed Cts 12.1, 13; U S 82(2).

Gist; Harris County, Tex. v., SDTex, 976 FSupp 601.—Atty Gen 8; Const Law 994, 2407; Decl Judgm 8, 303; Evid 23(1); Fed Civ Proc 2533.1; Fed Cts 12.1, 13, 14.1, 269, 272; Inj 14, 132, 138.1, 138.66, 147; Statut 39, 190, 195, 196, 200, 219(2), 219(4); U S 82(2).

Gist v. Holt, TexCivApp–Beaumont, 173 SW2d 216, writ refused wom.—App & E 387(3), 395, 653(1), 662(1), 668, 670(1).

Gist; LeBlanc v., TexCrimApp, 603 SW2d 841.—Infants 68.6; Prohib 1, 5(4), 10(1), 13.

Gist v. Lugo, EDTex, 165 FRD 474.—Fed Civ Proc 1758.1, 1824, 1837.1; Fed Cts 818.

Gist v. Stamford Hospital Dist., TexCivApp–Eastland, 557 SW2d 556, ref nre, cert den 99 SCt 89, 439 US 822, 58 LEd2d 114.—Judgm 677.

Gist v. Stamford Hospital Dist., TexCivApp–Eastland, 541 SW2d 510, ref nre.—Evid 43(3); Judgm 185.3(2).

Gist v. State, TexCrimApp, 279 SW2d 100, 161 TexCrim 593.—Crim Law 1099.6(2.1), 1099.7(3).

Gist v. State, TexCrimApp, 278 SW2d 163.—Crim Law 1090.1(1).

Gist v. State, TexCrimApp, 267 SW2d 835, 160 TexCrim 169.—Sent & Pun 2013, 2025.

Gist; State v., TexCivApp–Beaumont, 374 SW2d 736, ref nre.—App & E 499(3); Em Dom 202(4), 203(2), 262(5); Evid 142(1).

Gist v. Tsesmelis, TexCivApp–San Antonio, 153 SW2d 277, writ refused wom.—App & E 187(3), 907(3); Hus & W 270(1), 270(5); Plead 212.

Gist; U.S. v., CA5 (Tex), 101 F3d 32.—Sent & Pun 775, 776.

G. I. Surplus v. Renfro, TexCivApp–Galveston, 246 SW2d 293, ref nre.—App & E 1069.1; Damag 132(13); Neglig 1076, 1228, 1670, 1679, 1683; Trial 350.5(5).

Gittelman; First Nat. Bank of Missouri City v., TexApp–Houston (14 Dist), 788 SW2d 165, writ den.—Costs 194.32; Damag 15, 94; Evid 474(19), 501(7), 568(4); Interest 22(1); Sec Tran 230, 237, 242.1, 243; Trover 44, 46, 60, 61, 72.

Gittings; Haig v., TexCivApp–Dallas, 260 SW2d 311.—App & E 954(1); Contracts 215(1); Inj 189.

Gittings, Neiman-Marcus, Inc. v. Estes, TexCivApp–Eastland, 440 SW2d 90.—App & E 846(5); Princ & A 97, 100(2), 110(1), 132(1).

Giuffre; Brown v., TexCivApp–Hous (1 Dist), 548 SW2d 102.—Relig Soc 9.

Giun; Gulf, C. & S. F. Ry. Co. v., TexComApp, 116 SW2d 693, 131 Tex 548, 116 ALR 795.—App & E 203.3, 207, 1060.1(2.1); Evid 314(4); Trial 352.10, 352.11.

Giun v. Gulf, C. & S. F. R. Co., TexCivApp–Austin, 89 SW2d 465, rev 116 SW2d 693, 131 Tex 548, 116 ALR 795.—Evid 314(2); R R 396(1); Trial 114, 120(1), 228(3).

Giunta v. Mobil Corp. Employee Severance Plan, SDTex, 205 FSupp2d 715, aff 66 FedAppx 524.—Admin Law 791; Contracts 152; Labor & Emp 576, 685, 686, 687, 688, 690, 691.

Giurintano; American Medical Intern., Inc. v., TexApp–Houston (14 Dist), 821 SW2d 331.—App & E 930(3), 1003(6); Damag 50.10, 192; Fraud 7, 12; Labor & Emp 900, 911, 918(3); Plead 250; Torts 213, 214, 222, 223, 241.

Given Bros.; Crawford v., TexCivApp–El Paso, 318 SW2d 123, ref nre.—Evid 5(2); Neglig 1102.

Givens; Castillo v., CA5 (Tex), 704 F2d 181, 26 Wage & Hour Cas (BNA) 184, cert den 104 SCt 160, 464 US 850, 26 Wage & Hour Cas (BNA) 757, 78 LEd2d 147.—Fed Cts 630.1; Labor & Emp 2232, 2233, 2313, 2333, 2371, 2397(1), 2527, 2718(2).

Givens v. Cockrell, CA5 (Tex), 265 F3d 306.—Crim Law 641.13(1), 641.13(7); Hab Corp 489.1, 490(1), 505.

Givens v. Dougherty, Tex, 671 SW2d 877.—Brok 10; Frds St of 1, 131(2).

GIVENS

Givens v. Dougherty, TexApp–Fort Worth, 663 SW2d 88, writ gr, rev 671 SW2d 877.—App & E 78(1), 870(2); Brok 88(2), 88(9); Contracts 252, 253, 254, 255; Trial 350.1.

Givens; Employers Cas. Co. v., TexCivApp–Dallas, 190 SW2d 155.—Insurance 2498.

Givens v. Girard Life Ins. Co. of America, TexCivApp–Dallas, 480 SW2d 421, ref nre.—Gifts 28(3); Hus & W 249(3), 265, 273(12); Insurance 3360; Interpl 6, 35; Trial 368.

Givens v. Givens, TexCivApp–Dallas, 304 SW2d 577.—App & E 113(1); Divorce 49(3), 62(2), 139.5, 162, 165(3).

Givens; Givens v., TexCivApp–Dallas, 304 SW2d 577.—App & E 113(1); Divorce 49(3), 62(2), 139.5, 162, 165(3).

Givens v. Givens, TexCivApp–Hous (14 Dist), 616 SW2d 450.—Courts 57(1); Divorce 151, 183; New Tr 99.

Givens; Givens v., TexCivApp–Hous (14 Dist), 616 SW2d 450.—Courts 57(1); Divorce 151, 183; New Tr 99.

Givens v. M&S Imaging Partners, L.P., TexApp–Texarkana, 200 SW3d 735.—App & E 863, 866(3); Health 684; Judgm 185(5); Neglig 379, 380, 383, 387.

Givens v. Missouri, K. & T. R. Co. of Tex., CA5 (Tex), 195 F2d 225, mandate am 196 F2d 905.—Labor & Emp 2862, 2881.

Givens v. Missouri-Kansas-Texas R. Co. of Tex., CA5 (Tex), 196 F2d 905.—Fed Cts 948; Interest 39(3).

Givens; Smith v., TexCivApp–Dallas, 97 SW2d 532.—Child S 59, 650; Divorce 172; Judgm 415.

Givens v. State, TexCrimApp, 554 SW2d 199.—Crim Law 717, 723(1), 730(14), 1171.1(3).

Givens v. State, TexCrimApp, 438 SW2d 810.—Ind & Inf 144.1(3); Rob 24.15(2).

Givens v. State, TexCrimApp, 254 SW2d 395.—Crim Law 1090.1(1).

Givens v. State, TexCrimApp, 235 SW2d 899, 155 TexCrim 409.—Ind & Inf 162.

Givens v. State, TexCrimApp, 158 SW2d 535, 143 TexCrim 277.—Larc 6, 41, 59.

Givens v. State, TexApp–Fort Worth, 949 SW2d 449, petition for discretionary review refused.—Arrest 63.1, 63.4(1), 63.4(2), 63.4(4), 63.4(18), 63.5(2); Autos 349(4); Crim Law 394.6(4).

Givens v. State, TexApp–Fort Worth, 749 SW2d 954, petition for discretionary review refused.—Consp 40.1; Const Law 4594(1); Crim Law 577.12(2), 577.15(3), 577.16(4), 627.8(6), 700(3), 700(5), 700(8), 770(2), 772(6), 790, 814(19), 1038.1(1), 1129(3), 1172.1(3); Homic 612, 1167.

Givens v. State, TexApp–Austin, 26 SW3d 739, reh overr, and petition for discretionary review refused.—Controlled Subs 80; Crim Law 327, 1036.8, 1044.1(7), 1063(4), 1144.13(2.1), 1144.13(6), 1159.2(2), 1159.2(7), 1159.2(9).

Givens v. Terrell, TexCivApp–Amarillo, 461 SW2d 201, ref nre.—Autos 227.5, 284, 306(8).

Givens; Texas Youth Com'n v., TexApp–Austin, 925 SW2d 760, reh overr, and extension of time gr.—App & E 66, 68, 863, 934(1); Judgm 185(2), 185(6), 185.3(2); Mun Corp 723, 745, 847; Offic 114.

Givens v. Woodward, Tex, 208 SW2d 363, 146 Tex 396.—App & E 345.2.

Givens v. Woodward, Tex, 196 SW2d 456, 145 Tex 150.—Courts 207.4(3).

Givens v. Woodward, TexCivApp–Austin, 207 SW2d 234, writ dism 208 SW2d 363, 146 Tex 396.—Colleges 3, 5, 7; Const Law 642; Mand 79.

Giventer; State Farm Mut. Auto. Ins. Co. v., NDTex, 212 FSupp2d 639.—Fraud 3; Insurance 3182, 3184, 3186; RICO 47, 73.

Giwa; U.S. v., CA5 (Tex), 831 F2d 538.—Crim Law 577.8(2); Ind & Inf 7, 144.1(1); Searches 148.

Gizzo v. State, TexCrimApp, 272 SW2d 898, 160 TexCrim 593.—Crim Law 394.5(3), 726; Rob 20; Searches 16.

G.J. Deasy Inv., Inc. v. Mattox, CA5 (Tex), 778 F2d 1091, cert den 106 SCt 1972, 476 US 1116, 90 LEd2d 656.—Const Law 4294; Licens 7(1).

GJR Management Holdings, L.P. v. Jack Raus, Ltd., TexApp–San Antonio, 126 SW3d 257, reh overr, and review den.—Alt Disp Res 328, 332, 350, 362(4), 363(8), 371, 374(1), 374(5), 376; New Tr 99, 150(4).

G.J.S., In Interest of, TexApp–San Antonio, 940 SW2d 289.—App & E 662(4), 1008.1(1); Child C 28; Child S 21, 82, 89, 143, 234, 256, 258, 356, 556(1), 558(3), 609; Infants 27.

G.K. v. K.A., TexApp–Austin, 936 SW2d 70, reh overr, and error den.—Child C 7, 921(1); Child 1, 20.9, 73, 75; Names 20.

G.K.G. v. State, TexApp–San Antonio, 730 SW2d 182.—Burg 41(6); Crim Law 552(3); Infants 176, 203, 253.

G. K. H., In Interest of, TexApp–Texarkana, 623 SW2d 447.—Infants 174.

GK Intelligent Systems, Inc.; Griffin v., SDTex, 87 FSupp2d 684.—Consp 2; Fraud 13(3), 20, 46; Sec Reg 35.25, 60.18, 60.27(1), 60.45(1), 60.47, 60.48(3), 60.51, 60.53, 60.62.

GK Intelligent Systems, Inc.; Griffin v., SDTex, 196 FRD 298.—Fed Civ Proc 164, 165, 172, 187.

G.L.A., In re, TexApp–Beaumont, 195 SW3d 787, review den.—Child S 506(2), 506(3), 507, 508(2), 539, 543; Courts 28; Judgm 815, 818(6), 823.

Glacier Energy, Inc.; Foster Co. v., TexApp–San Antonio, 714 SW2d 48. See L.B. Foster Co. v. Glacier Energy, Inc.

Glacier Energy, Inc.; L.B. Foster Co. v., TexApp–San Antonio, 714 SW2d 48, ref nre.—Judgm 151, 153(1).

Glacier General Assur. Co.; Woods v., TexApp–Texarkana, 717 SW2d 391. See William M. Mercer, Inc. v. Woods.

Glacier Guides, Inc.; Zimmerman v., TexApp–Waco, 151 SW3d 700.—Appear 9(2); Courts 12(2.10), 12(2.30), 32, 35, 39, 89, 91(1); Proc 157.

Glad; Lee v., TexCivApp–Galveston, 267 SW2d 230, writ dism.—App & E 1050.1(11); Autos 198(1).

Gladden; Collins v., TexCivApp–Beaumont, 466 SW2d 629, ref nre.—App & E 1170.6; Death 99(3); Evid 474.5; New Tr 20; Plead 228.14; Trial 215, 304.

Gladden; Green v., TexCivApp–Fort Worth, 369 SW2d 69.—Brok 53, 82(1); Trial 352.1(4).

Gladden v. Roach, CA5 (Tex), 864 F2d 1196, cert den 109 SCt 3192, 491 US 907, 105 LEd2d 700.—Arrest 63.4(2); Const Assue 4550; Crim Law 412.1(4), 1172.7; Damag 62(1); False Imp 8; Fed Cts 912; Inj 11, 114(2).

Gladding v. Prudential Ins. Co. of America, TexCivApp–Hous (1 Dist), 521 SW2d 736, ref nre.—Insurance 3475(2), 3475(3), 3475(5).

Glade v. Dietert, Tex, 295 SW2d 642, 156 Tex 382.—Em Dom 285; Mun Corp 400; Tresp 12.

Glade v. Dietert, TexCivApp–Fort Worth, 286 SW2d 955, rev 295 SW2d 642, 156 Tex 382.—Em Dom 293(4); Princ & A 159(2); Trial 122, 350.3(6).

Gladewater, City of; Cooks v., TexApp–Tyler, 808 SW2d 710.—Work Comp 1188, 1653, 1895.

Gladewater, City of; Gladewater Lumber & Supply Co. v., TexCivApp–Texarkana, 87 SW2d 527.—Dedi 12.

Gladewater, City of, v. Pike, Tex, 727 SW2d 514. See City of Gladewater v. Pike.

Gladewater, City of, v. Pike, TexApp–Texarkana, 708 SW2d 524. See City of Gladewater v. Pike.

Gladewater, City of; State ex rel. Armstrong v., TexCivApp–Texarkana, 242 SW2d 650, writ refused.—Mun Corp 33(2); Statut 120(1), 120(2), 181(1).

Gladewater, City of; State ex rel. Walker v., TexCivApp–Texarkana, 139 SW2d 283, rev 157 SW2d 641, 138 Tex 173.—Const Law 4056; Judgm 586(1); Mun Corp 29(3); Quo W 55; Statut 181(2).

Gladewater Independent School Dist.; Edwards v., CA5 (Tex), 572 F2d 496.—Civil R 1133, 1544; Fed Cts 844, 848.

Gladewater Laundry & Dry Cleaners v. Newman, Tex-CivApp–Texarkana, 141 SW2d 951, writ dism, correct.—Autos 242(5), 242(6), 243(12); Trial 127.

Gladewater Lumber & Supply Co. v. City of Gladewater, TexCivApp–Texarkana, 87 SW2d 527.—Dedi 12.

Gladewater Municipal Hosp. v. Daniel, TexApp–Texarkana, 694 SW2d 619.—App & E 1050.1(2); Health 782, 821(1), 823(1), 825, 830, 832; Labor & Emp 3137.

Gladewater Refining Co. Pipe Line; Railroad Commission v., TexCivApp–Austin, 179 SW2d 320.—Courts 207.3; Inj 5; Mines 92.69, 92.71.

Gladiola Biscuit Co. v. Southern Ice Co., CA5 (Tex), 267 F2d 138.—Prod Liab 62; Sales 255, 274, 441(1), 441(3), 441(4).

Gladiola Biscuit Co. v. Southern Ice Co., EDTex, 163 FSupp 570, rev 267 F2d 138.—Courts 92; Fed Cts 431; Sales 255, 441(2), 441(3), 441(4).

Gladney; Dean v., CA5 (Tex), 621 F2d 1331, cert den 101 SCt 1521, 450 US 983, 67 LEd2d 819.—Civil R 1358, 1480; Counties 146; Fed Cts 878; Mun Corp 744.

Gladney; Dean v., SDTex, 451 FSupp 1313, aff in part, rev in part 621 F2d 1331, cert den 101 SCt 1521, 450 US 983, 67 LEd2d 819.—Civil R 1479; Counties 146; Crim Law 1226(4); Fed Civ Proc 2737.6; Mun Corp 747(3); Sheriffs 100, 105, 139(4), 140.

Gladney; Hartford Acc. & Indem. Co. v., TexCivApp–Waco, 335 SW2d 792, ref nre.—App & E 933(1), 977(1); Judgm 335(1), 344; New Tr 6, 118, 152; Work Comp 1859, 1932.

Gladney; Smith v., TexComApp, 98 SW2d 351, 128 Tex 354.—Alt Disp Res 123.

Gladstrong Investments (USA) Corp.; SSP Partners v., TexApp–Corpus Christi, 169 SW3d 27, reh overr, and review gr (2 pets).—App & E 242(4), 843(2); Corp 1.5(1); Indem 72, 92, 100; Judgm 181(15.1), 183, 185(4), 185.3(1), 189; Prod Liab 1, 5, 23.1, 24.

Gladys; City of Corinth v., TexApp–Fort Worth, 916 SW2d 618, reh overr.—App & E 93, 863; Autos 252, 290; Judgm 185(2); Mun Corp 745, 847; Plead 237(2), 245(1), 258(1).

Gladys City Co. v. Amoco Production Co., EDTex, 528 FSupp 624.—Mines 62, 62.1, 68(1), 68(2); Quiet T 7(1).

Gladys City Co.; Texas Gulf Sulphur Co. v., TexCivApp–Beaumont, 506 SW2d 281, ref nre.—Accord 1, 8(1); Evid 558(9); Mines 1, 70(6); Trial 350.3(2.1), 352.12.

Gladys J. v. Pearland Independent School Dist., SDTex, 520 FSupp 869.—Schools 148(2.1), 148(3), 154(3), 155.5(4).

Glafkos, M/V, CA5 (Tex), 744 F2d 461. See Cardinal Shipping Corp. v. M/S Seisho Maru.

Glagola v. North Texas Mun. Water Dist., EDTex, 705 FSupp 1220.—Const Law 3874(3), 4171; Offic 66.

Glameyer; High v., TexCivApp–Hous (14 Dist), 428 SW2d 872, ref nre.—Deeds 90, 100, 110, 112(0.5); Hus & W 48(4).

Glanz; Medical Protective Co. v., TexApp–Corpus Christi, 721 SW2d 382, writ refused.—Costs 260(4); Pretrial Proc 44.1, 221, 403, 406, 411.

Glasco, In re, TexCivApp–San Antonio, 619 SW2d 567.—App & E 846(5), 931(3), 1010.1(1), 1011.1(1); Des & Dist 33, 34, 52(2); Marriage 20(1), 50(4), 50(5), 54.

Glasco v. Frazer, TexCivApp–Dallas, 225 SW2d 633, dism.—Acct Action on 12, 14; Acct St 1, 8; Corp 1.6(9), 590(3).

Glascock; Romo v., TexCivApp–Dallas, 620 SW2d 829.—Judgm 181(7), 185(2); Lim of Act 100(1), 100(11).

Glascow; Ellis v., TexCivApp–San Antonio, 168 SW2d 946.—Crim Law 216, 218(1), 218(5); Dist & Pros Attys 8; Evid 83(1); False Imp 8, 22; Plead 111.37; Tresp 43(3); Venue 8.5(5).

Glaser; Buckholts Independent School Dist. v., Tex, 632 SW2d 146.—App & E 151(1), 151(2), 151(6), 185(3); Const Law 4195; Judges 53, 56; Jury 31; Schools 97(4.5); Statut 47.

Glaser v. Buckholts Independent School Dist., TexApp–Austin, 625 SW2d 419, rev 632 SW2d 146.—Judges 44, 51(1), 56.

Glaser v. Texon Energy Corp., CA5 (Tex), 702 F2d 569.—Corp 109.

Glasgow v. De Lapp, TexCivApp–Galveston, 149 SW2d 128.—Bills & N 463, 464, 488; Plead 403(3).

Glasgow v. Floors, Inc. of Tex., TexCivApp–Dallas, 356 SW2d 699.—Autos 197(7); Judgm 185(2); Labor & Emp 3031(1), 3045.

Glasgow; Forman v., TexCivApp–Waco, 219 SW2d 845.—Aband L P 5; App & E 1178(1); Costs 240; Hus & W 47(4), 187, 266.3; Spec Perf 134.

Glasgow; Gunter v., TexCivApp–Eastland, 608 SW2d 273.—Abate & R 13; Child C 411, 702; Judgm 815, 822(2).

Glasgow v. Hall, TexApp–Austin, 668 SW2d 863, ref nre.—Antitrust 198, 397; App & E 930(1), 989, 1012.1(5).

Glasgow v. Hurley, TexCivApp–Dallas, 333 SW2d 658.—App & E 282, 934(2); Child C 555, 914; Divorce 145.

Glasgow; John Hancock Mut. Life Ins. Co. v., TexComApp, 141 SW2d 942, 135 Tex 470.—Home 115(2).

Glasgow v. John Hancock Mut. Life Ins. Co., TexCivApp–Dallas, 117 SW2d 888, aff 141 SW2d 942, 135 Tex 470.—App & E 909(3), 1078(1); Contracts 147(1), 147(3); Fixt 18.4; Home 1, 115(2), 129(1).

Glash; Williams v., Tex, 789 SW2d 261.—Contracts 93(5); Evid 433(1); Judgm 181(23); Release 16, 17(1), 25, 55, 57(1).

Glash; Williams v., TexApp–Houston (1 Dist), 769 SW2d 684, writ gr, rev 789 SW2d 261.—Release 1, 6, 13(1), 15, 16, 17(1), 38.

Glasheen v. City of Austin, WDTex, 840 FSupp 62.—Civil R 1351(4); Const Law 4289; Em Dom 2(1.1); Int Liq 11, 15.

Glaskox; Village of Bayou Vista v., TexApp–Houston (14 Dist), 899 SW2d 826.—App & E 70(8), 852; Judgm 185(2), 185.1(3); Libel 36, 38(1), 51(2); Mun Corp 745.

Glasper, Ex parte, TexCrimApp, 343 SW2d 712, 170 TexCrim 628.—Extrad 34.

Glasper v. State, TexCrimApp, 486 SW2d 350.—Crim Law 1171.3; Rob 11, 24.50; Witn 309.

Glasper v. State, TexApp–Beaumont, 695 SW2d 74.—Crim Law 1086.4, 1099.7(1), 1109(1).

Glaspy v. Grubbs, TexCivApp–Dallas, 110 SW2d 1188.—App & E 644(1); Receivers 3, 8, 16, 29(1), 39.

Glaspy; Snowden v., TexCivApp–Dallas, 127 SW2d 508.—App & E 1119; Execution 283; Judgm 21, 251(1), 255; Tresp to T T 38(2).

Glaspy v. State, TexCrimApp, 299 SW2d 700.—Crim Law 1090.1(1).

Glass, Ex parte, TexCrimApp, 205 SW2d 46, 151 TexCrim 23.—Breach of P 20.

Glass, Matter of Estate of, TexApp–Houston (1 Dist), 961 SW2d 461, review den.—App & E 893(1); Mental H 167.

Glass v. Anderson, Tex, 596 SW2d 507.—Spec Perf 87.

Glass v. Anderson, TexCivApp–Hous (1 Dist), 582 SW2d 479, rev 596 SW2d 507.—App & E 842(2), 989, 1010.1(1), 1010.2, 1151(1); Contracts 313(2); Spec Perf 121(3), 121(10), 121(11), 126(2); Ven & Pur 76, 168, 196.

Glass; A.T. & T. Communications v., TexApp–Tyler, 783 SW2d 305.—App & E 544(1), 554(3); Costs 260(1), 260(4); Pretrial Proc 45.

Glass v. Barnhart, CA5 (Tex), 158 FedAppx 530.—Social S 142.5, 143.65, 143.85.

Glass; Burleson v., WDTex, 268 FSupp2d 699, aff 393 F3d 577.—Civil R 1376(1), 1376(2); Evid 528(1), 555.2, 555.10; Prisons 17(1); Sent & Pun 1532, 1533, 1536.

Glass v. Carpenter, TexCivApp–San Antonio, 330 SW2d 530, ref nre.—App & E 1170.6; Assign 64, 100, 126, 129;

GLASS

59 Tex D 2d—272

See Guidelines for Arrangement at the beginning of this Volume

Can of Inst 27; Ex & Ad 439; Fraud Conv 111; Parties 1; Perp 6(2); Trusts 12, 147(1), 153.

Glass v. City of Austin, TexCivApp–Austin, 533 SW2d 411.—App & E 19, 781(1); Inj 22; Mun Corp 987.

Glass v. Glass, TexApp–Texarkana, 826 SW2d 683, writ den.—Const Law 328, 2317, 4426; Costs 2.

Glass; Glass v., TexApp–Texarkana, 826 SW2d 683, writ den.—Const Law 328, 2317, 4426; Costs 2.

Glass v. Glass, TexCivApp–Waco, 199 SW2d 678, dism.— Divorce 166; Judgm 298, 335(3), 341, 342(1).

Glass; Glass v., TexCivApp–Waco, 199 SW2d 678, dism.— Divorce 166; Judgm 298, 335(3), 341, 342(1).

Glass v. Great Southern Life Ins. Co., TexCivApp– Galveston, 170 SW2d 247, writ refused wom.—Costs 96; Courts 89, 91(1); States 215; Tax 2558.

Glass v. Hoblitzelle, TexCivApp–Dallas, 83 SW2d 796, writ dism.—Action 10; Antitrust 9, 580, 977(3); App & E 954(1); Commerce 62.7; Inj 135.

Glass v. Houston Singing Soc., TexCivApp–Galveston, 192 SW2d 300.—App & E 215(2), 301; Evid 141; Neglig 1631, 1635.

Glass v. Kottwitz, TexCivApp–Galveston, 297 SW 573, writ refused.—Trademarks 1419.

Glass; McCray v., TexApp–Beaumont, 96 SW3d 690.— App & E 224.

Glass; Martin v., NDTex, 571 FSupp 1406, aff 736 F2d 1524.—Fed Cts 430; Mines 74(4), 74(5), 78.1(8), 79.1(1), 79.3, 79.4.

Glass v. Missouri Pac. R. Co., TexCivApp–San Antonio, 343 SW2d 288, ref nre, cert den 82 SCt 383, 368 US 944, 7 LEd2d 341, reh den 82 SCt 401, 368 US 962, 7 LEd2d 393.—Labor & Emp 2881.

Glass v. O'Hearn, TexCivApp–Fort Worth, 553 SW2d 15. —App & E 569(3); Child C 467; Child S 202.

Glass v. Petro-Tex Chemical Corp., CA5 (Tex), 757 F2d 1554.—Civil R 1168, 1505(3), 1537, 1549, 1571, 1573, 1594; Fed Civ Proc 843; Fed Cts 841, 843, 844.

Glass v. Phillips, CCA5 (Tex), 139 F2d 1016.—Bankr 2954.1.

Glass v. Prcin, TexApp–Amarillo, 3 SW3d 135, petition for discretionary review den.—App & E 1010.2; Bankr 2062, 2825, 3353(1.45); Judgm 540, 713(2), 720, 829(3).

Glass; Seber v., TexCivApp–Fort Worth, 258 SW2d 122.— App & E 797(1); Child C 609.

Glass v. Skelly Oil Co., TexCivApp–El Paso, 469 SW2d 237, ref nre.—Land & Ten 70; Life Est 1, 3, 25; Mines 52; Wills 614(2), 689, 692(1), 692(5), 728.

Glass v. Smith, Tex, 244 SW2d 645, 150 Tex 632.—Mand 74(2); Mun Corp 8, 60, 65, 108.1, 108.2, 108.3, 184(2), 197.

Glass v. Smith, TexCivApp, 238 SW2d 243, aff 244 SW2d 645, 150 Tex 632.—Inj 80; Mand 74(2); Mun Corp 108.2, 108.3, 108.8; Offic 110.

Glass v. Sponsel, TexApp–Houston (1 Dist), 916 SW2d 25. —App & E 347(1), 347(2), 799.

Glass v. State, TexCrimApp, 681 SW2d 599.—Arrest 63.4(10), 63.4(12), 63.5(4), 63.5(6), 63.5(9); Searches 38, 41, 62.

Glass v. State, TexCrimApp, 450 SW2d 320.—Crim Law 1177.

Glass v. State, TexCrimApp, 411 SW2d 728.—Crim Law 721(1), 721(3).

Glass v. State, TexCrimApp, 402 SW2d 173.—Crim Law 412.1(4), 1169.2(6); Homic 1136.

Glass v. State, TexCrimApp, 288 SW2d 522, 162 TexCrim 598.—Crim Law 1182; Ind & Inf 41(3).

Glass v. State, TexCrimApp, 235 SW2d 183.—Crim Law 1090.1(1).

Glass v. State, TexCrimApp, 157 SW2d 399, 143 TexCrim 88.—Crim Law 595(1), 857(2), 925(1), 925.5(1), 1137(5), 1156(5), 1169.5(2).

Glass v. State, TexApp–Houston (1 Dist), 761 SW2d 806. —Crim Law 1159.2(6), 1159.2(7); Obscen 16, 17.

Glass; State v., TexApp–Austin, 723 SW2d 325, ref nre.— App & E 931(3); Tax 2300, 3692, 3693.

Glass; State v., TexCivApp–Galveston, 167 SW2d 296, writ refused 170 SW2d 470, 141 Tex 83.—Autos 29, 49; Counties 80(1); Interpl 11.

Glass; Texas & N. O. R. Co. v., TexCivApp–Waco, 107 SW2d 924, writ dism.—Evid 560; R R 455, 481(4), 484(3), 484(4).

Glass v. Texas Liquor Control Bd., TexCivApp–Waco, 267 SW2d 897.—Int Liq 69, 70, 75(7).

Glass v. U.S., NDTex, 335 FSupp2d 736, am in part 2004 WL 2189634.—Fed Civ Proc 2723, 2737.4, 2742.5; Int Rev 5343, 5347, 5348.

Glass v. Upton, TexCivApp–Austin, 226 SW2d 244.—Lim of Act 60(10); Trial 232(2), 234(7), 350.3(2.1); Ven & Pur 242, 244.

Glass; Vacca v., TexApp–Texarkana, 148 SW3d 207, reh overr, and reh overr, and review den.—App & E 66, 76(1), 79(1), 79(2), 80(1), 80(6).

Glass; Warner v., Tex, 135 SW3d 681.—Convicts 6; Records 7; Statut 181(1), 188, 205.

Glass; Warner v., TexApp–Texarkana, 96 SW3d 640, review gr, rev 135 SW3d 681.—App & E 984(1); Convicts 6.

Glass v. Williamson, TexApp–Houston (1 Dist), 137 SW3d 114.—App & E 1031(1); Child S 452, 506(3), 508(3), 539, 558(4); Trial 388(1), 392(1).

Glass; Winchester Oil Co. v., TexApp–Texarkana, 683 SW2d 35.—Frds St of 113(1), 139(1), 139(4); Impl & C C 24; Trusts 94.5, 102(1), 103(1), 103(5), 110.

Glass Club Lake, Inc.; Parham v., TexApp–Texarkana, 533 SW2d 96, ref nre.—Forfeit 1; Land & Ten 37, 83(4), 86(1), 157(1).

Glass Club Lake, Inc.; Parham v., TexApp–Texarkana, 485 SW2d 796.—Venue 5.3(2).

Glasscock; Alexander v., TexCivApp–Texarkana, 271 SW2d 333.—Dep & Escr 26; Frds St of 113(1); Mines 74(8).

Glasscock v. Armstrong Cork Co., CA5 (Tex), 946 F2d 1085, reh den 951 F2d 347, cert den Celotex Corp v. Glasscock, 112 SCt 1778, 503 US 1011, 118 LEd2d 435. —Compromise 15(1); Const Law 4427; Corp 590(4); Damag 38, 91(1), 91(3), 94, 100, 163(1), 179, 184, 186, 187, 208(4); Fed Cts 765; Fines 1.3; Lim of Act 95(4.1), 95(5); Neglig 549(8); New Tr 76(1).

Glasscock v. Black, TexCivApp–Austin, 272 SW2d 388, dism.—App & E 417(1), 425.

Glasscock v. Bradley, TexCivApp–Texarkana, 152 SW2d 439, writ refused wom.—Bound 48(6); Estop 52(5), 88(2).

Glasscock v. Bryant, TexCivApp–El Paso, 185 SW2d 595, writ refused wom.—Action 60; App & E 76(3), 80(6), 837(9), 1043(1); Judgm 298, 341, 526; Mines 5.2(4); New Tr 6, 27, 96; Pretrial Proc 717.1.

Glasscock v. Citizens Nat. Bank, TexCivApp–Tyler, 553 SW2d 411, ref nre.—Divorce 168, 252.4; Fraud Conv 256, 310; Judgm 678(2), 707.

Glasscock v. Console Drive Joint Venture, TexApp–San Antonio, 675 SW2d 590, ref nre.—Estop 68(2); Guar 27, 56, 59; Land & Ten 193.

Glasscock; Duncan v., TexCivApp–Dallas, 118 SW2d 658. —Abate & R 77; Venue 5.1, 26, 76.

Glasscock; Edwards v., CCA5 (Tex), 91 F2d 625.—Fed Cts 286.1, 304.1, 305, 931.

Glasscock v. Farmers Royalty Holding Co., CCA5 (Tex), 152 F2d 537.—Deeds 39, 51; Mines 55(1).

Glasscock v. Farmers Royalty Holding Co., SDTex, 63 FSupp 666, aff 152 F2d 537.—Ack 4; Deeds 39.

Glasscock v. Frost Nat. Bank, TexApp–San Antonio, 928 SW2d 599, reh overr, and writ den.—Judgm 183, 185.3(16).

Glasscock v. Income Property Services, Inc., TexApp– Houston (1 Dist), 888 SW2d 176, reh den, and writ dism

For Later Case History Information, see KeyCite on WESTLAW

by agreement.—App & E 970(2), 1032(2), 1056.1(1), 1056.1(3); Evid 506, 507, 508, 512, 536; Neglig 236.

Glasscock; Lambe v., TexCivApp–San Antonio, 360 SW2d 169, ref nre.—App & E 931(1); Deeds 8; Estop 22(2), 92(3); Mines 74(5), 79.1(1), 79.1(2), 79.7.

Glasscock; Moore v., TexCivApp–Eastland, 217 SW2d 428, ref nre.—Adv Poss 115(1); Home 132; Lim of Act 199(1); Mtg 33(2), 39, 608.5; Tresp to T T 44.

Glasscock v. Permian Oil Co., TexCivApp–El Paso, 185 SW2d 740, writ refused wom.—Courts 107; Estop 62.2(2); Mines 5.2(4).

Glasscock v. Sinclair Prairie Oil Co., CA5 (Tex), 185 F2d 910.—Mines 78.1(7).

Glasscock v. Sinclair Prairie Oil Co., SDTex, 87 FSupp 915, aff 185 F2d 910.—Lim of Act 60(6); Mines 77, 78.1(3), 78.1(7).

Glasscock v. Travelers Ins. Co., TexCivApp–Austin, 113 SW2d 1005, writ refused.—Adv Poss 31, 60(1), 86; Deeds 109; Judgm 787; Mtg 372(1); Subrog 23(1), 23(2), 36.

Glasscock Underground Water Conservation Dist. v. Pruit, TexApp–El Paso, 915 SW2d 577, reh overr.—Admin Law 229; Courts 89; Decl Judgm 185; Mines 55(4); Statut 181(2), 190, 206, 212.1, 214; Tax 2128, 2140, 2173, 2478; Waters 198.

Glass Containers Corp. v. Miller Brewing Co., CA5 (Tex), 643 F2d 308.—Costs 4, 194.16; Fed Civ Proc 751, 759, 2174, 2296; Fed Cts 691, 842; Sales 412, 417.

Glasse; Robinson v., TexCivApp–Galveston, 188 SW2d 598.—Plead 111.3, 111.4, 111.18, 111.42(9).

Glassell; Comegys v., EDTex, 839 FSupp 447.—Witn 198(2), 199(2).

Glassell v. Ellis, TexApp–Texarkana, 956 SW2d 676, reh overr, and review dism woj.—App & E 10, 946, 949, 1024.1; Atty & C 129(1), 129(2); Mines 47; Parties 35.1, 35.5, 35.9, 35.13, 35.17, 35.31, 35.33, 35.35, 35.41, 35.49, 35.79.

Glassell; MCEN 1996 Partnership v., TexApp–Corpus Christi, 42 SW3d 262, review den.—App & E 854(1); Mines 48, 78.1(7); Partit 14, 22.

Glassey v. State, TexApp–Fort Worth, 117 SW3d 424.—Crim Law 59(1), 59(4), 59(5), 552(2), 730(3), 795(2.1), 795(2.10), 795(2.20), 867, 1037.1(3), 1144.15, 1155, 1169.5(1); Homic 1207, 1460.

Glassman v. Feldman, TexCivApp–Amarillo, 106 SW2d 721.—Autos 181(1), 238(7), 240(1), 245(24); Neglig 259.

Glassman and Glassman v. Somoza, TexApp–Houston (14 Dist), 694 SW2d 174.—App & E 989, 994(3), 1008.1(3), 1012.1(5), 1170.1; Courts 485; Evid 588, 594; Garn 110, 112, 194; Trial 382.

Glass Master Corp.; Weidman Metal Masters Co., Inc. v., CA5 (Tex), 623 F2d 1024, reh den 628 F2d 1354, reh den 628 F2d 1354, cert den 101 SCt 1519, 450 US 982, 67 LEd2d 817.—Pat 157(1), 157(3), 165(2), 168(2.1), 226, 226.6, 226.8, 237, 314(5).

Glasspool; Mooney v., TexCivApp–Beaumont, 602 SW2d 364, ref nre.—App & E 846(1); Divorce 252.3(2), 254(1), 322.

Glass, Sorenson & McDavid Ins. Co.; Usher v., TexCivApp–Corpus Christi, 409 SW2d 880, ref nre.—Ex & Ad 532; Insurance 1667; Judgm 185(2), 185.3(6).

Glast, Phillips & Murray; Ingram v., CA5 (Tex), 196 FedAppx 232.—Const Law 4426; Fed Civ Proc 2828, 2830.

Glastron Boat Co.; Baxter v., TexCivApp–Austin, 379 SW2d 101, ref nre.—Judgm 181(21).

Glastron, Inc.; Staudt v., CA5 (Tex), 92 F3d 312, reh and sug for reh den 99 F3d 1137.—Fed Cts 424; Labor & Emp 240, 2191, 2197, 3225, 3235, 3236, 3245.

Glastron, Inc.; Staudt v., CA5 (Tex), 31 F3d 224. See Halkias v. General Dynamics Corp.

Glattly v. CMS Viron Corp., TexApp–Houston (1 Dist), 177 SW3d 438.—App & E 179(4), 846(5), 893(1), 1010.1(1); Appear 9(2); Const Law 3964, 3965(7); Corp

335, 336; Courts 12(2.1), 12(2.5), 12(2.10), 12(2.15), 12(2.20), 12(5), 35, 39.

Glatzmayer v. U. S., CCA5 (Tex), 84 F2d 192.—Ind & Inf 63; Int Rev 5259, 5285.

Glau-Moya Parapsychology Training Institute, Inc. v. Royal Life Ins. Co., TexCivApp–San Antonio, 507 SW2d 824.—Courts 155; Forci E & D 6(1); Judgm 720, 747(6).

Glau-Moya Parapsychology Training Institute, Inc. v. Royal Life Ins. Co., TexCivApp–San Antonio, 500 SW2d 884.—Insurance 1384.

Glauser v. State, TexApp–Houston (1 Dist), 66 SW3d 307, petition for discretionary review refused, cert den 122 SCt 1068, 534 US 1129, 151 LEd2d 971.—Autos 344, 355(13); Crim Law 713, 723(1), 728(2), 730(7), 1134(2), 1162, 1166.16, 1171.1(2.1), 1171.1(6); Jury 108, 131(10); Sent & Pun 1858.

Glavic v. Beechie, CA5 (Tex), 340 F2d 91.—Fed Cts 611.

Glavic v. Beechie, SDTex, 225 FSupp 24, aff 340 F2d 91. —Aliens 266, 341, 532; Const Law 4440.

Glaze, Matter of Marriage of, TexCivApp–Amarillo, 605 SW2d 721.—Divorce 132(6), 184(10), 249.1, 252.1, 252.3(2), 286(8).

Glaze; Beacon Nat. Ins. Co. v., TexApp–Tyler, 114 SW3d 1, review den.—Contracts 143(2), 143.5, 147(2), 169, 176(2), 221(2); Insurance 1806, 1836, 3173, 3585; Interest 39(2.6), 39(2.35), 67.

Glaze; Caughman v., TexCivApp–San Antonio, 412 SW2d 357, ref nre.—App & E 843(3), 989, 1003(5), 1003(11), 1069.1; Autos 172(7), 172(8); Neglig 232; Trial 304, 306, 315, 352.4(5), 356(4).

Glaze v. State, TexCrimApp, 675 SW2d 768.—Crim Law 274(7), 951(1), 1023(9); Sent & Pun 2009.

Glaze v. State, TexCrimApp, 310 SW2d 88, 165 TexCrim 626.—Controlled Subs 80, 112, 146; Crim Law 519(4), 678(1); Searches 142.

Glaze v. State, TexApp–Beaumont, 628 SW2d 252, petition for discretionary review gr, set aside 675 SW2d 768.—Atty & C 106; Crim Law 273(1), 273(4.1), 273.1(4), 274(7), 641.7(1), 641.7(2), 641.13(1), 641.13(2.1), 641.13(3), 641.13(6), 1134(8).

Glazener; Vaughn v., TexCivApp–Amarillo, 459 SW2d 898, ref nre.—App & E 1062.1; Autos 244(43), 244(58), 247; Neglig 291; Trial 352.5(5).

Glazener; Withrow v., TexCivApp–Waco, 120 SW2d 122. —Mand 164(4), 168(4).

Glazer v. American Ecology Environmental Services Corp., EDTex, 894 FSupp 1029.—Environ Law 297, 385, 432, 460, 642, 644, 658, 659, 670, 673; Fed Civ Proc 2481.

Glazer; Wheeler v., Tex, 153 SW2d 449, 137 Tex 341, 140 ALR 1301.—App & E 1067; Carr 280(3); Contrib 5(1), 5(2), 5(6.1); Indem 58; Neglig 1741; Trial 351.5(6).

Glazer v. Wheeler, TexCivApp–Amarillo, 130 SW2d 353, rev 153 SW2d 449, 137 Tex 341, 140 ALR 1301.—Autos 240(1), 245(22), 246(22); Carr 320(21); Contrib 5(4), 9(1), 9(5); Parties 51(4); Trial 350.6(4), 352.18.

Glazer v. Woodward, TexCivApp–Waco, 127 SW2d 938, writ dism, correct.—App & E 1069.1; Autos 245(28); Damag 186; Evid 588; New Tr 52; Trial 142, 143.

Glazer's Wholesale Distributors, Inc. v. Heineken USA, Inc., TexApp–Dallas, 95 SW3d 286, review gr, judgment vac, and remanded by agreement.—Alt Disp Res 112, 114, 117, 132, 143, 191, 205, 213(3), 213(4), 357, 380; App & E 941, 945, 946; Const Law 990, 1030, 2311, 2312, 2314, 2352, 2450, 2570; Contracts 143(3), 147(2), 152, 176(2); Int Liq 124; Judgm 540, 584; Jury 25(2), 26, 31.2(1); Mand 1, 3(2.1), 4(1), 12, 26, 28; States 18.15.

Glazer's Wholesale Drug Co.; Goldfarb v., TexCivApp–Dallas, 274 SW2d 460.—Plead 111.39(2), 111.41, 111.42(5); Venue 7.5(7).

Glazer's Wholesale Drug Co.; N.L.R.B. v., CA5 (Tex), 368 F2d 1005.—Labor & Emp 1741, 1755.

Glazier; NuGrape Co. of America v., CCA5 (Tex), 22 F2d 596.—Antitrust 34, 47.

Glazier v. Roberts, TexCivApp–Fort Worth, 114 SW2d 273.—App & E 1185.

Glazier v. Roberts, TexCivApp–Fort Worth, 108 SW2d 829.—App & E 1045(1), 1069.1; Autos 244(29); Death 44; Jury 136(3); Labor & Emp 3094(2), 3179(2); New Tr 140(3).

Glazier v. Tilton, TexCivApp–Fort Worth, 81 SW2d 145, writ dism.—Bills & N 484; Compromise 17(2); Ten in C 22, 38(7).

Glazier; Whittington v., TexCivApp–Texarkana, 81 SW2d 543, writ refused.—Plead 403(1); Ref of Inst 36(3); Tresp to T T 10; Trial 351.2(3.1).

Glazner; Haase v., Tex, 62 SW3d 795.—App & E 863, 934(1); Fraud 20, 24, 59(2); Frds St of 119(1); Judgm 181(11).

Glazner v. Haase, TexApp–Texarkana, 61 SW3d 10, review gr, aff in part, rev in part 62 SW3d 795.—Contracts 9(1), 10(1), 56, 85; Corp 1.4(4); Fraud 24, 25, 32, 36; Frds St of 106(1), 108(1), 113(2), 118(1), 118(2); Guar 17; Judgm 181(11), 185(6); Plead 228.23.

Glazner v. State, TexCrimApp, 175 SW3d 262.—Arrest 63.5(1), 63.5(4), 63.5(8), 63.5(9); Autos 349.5(5.1), 349.5(7), 349.5(10); Searches 23, 70.

Gleasman, In re, BkrtcyWDTex, 111 BR 595.—Bankr 3776.5(1), 3776.5(2), 3776.5(3); Mtg 413.

Gleasman, Matter of, CA5 (Tex), 933 F2d 1277.—Lim of Act 95(11).

Gleasman v. Jones, Day, Reavis & Pogue, CA5 (Tex), 933 F2d 1277. See Gleasman, Matter of.

Gleasman v. Jones, Day, Reavis & Pogue, BkrtcyWD-Tex, 111 BR 595. See Gleasman, In re.

Gleason v. Beesinger, SDTex, 708 FSupp 157.—Fed Cts 391; States 79.

Gleason v. Coman, TexApp–Houston (14 Dist), 693 SW2d 564, ref nre.—App & E 954(2); Atty & C 21, 21.5(1), 21.20, 32(10), 32(13); Inj 94, 138.21, 151; Mand 4(1); Pretrial Proc 674.

Gleason; Crouch v., TexApp–Amarillo, 875 SW2d 738.—Damag 206(2); Mand 28.

Gleason v. Davis, Tex, 289 SW2d 228, 155 Tex 467.—App & E 761; Evid 148; Judgm 162(4).

Gleason v. Davis, TexCivApp–San Antonio, 277 SW2d 125, rev 289 SW2d 228, 155 Tex 467.—App & E 1175(5); Judgm 143(17), 162(4); Princ & A 23(2).

Gleason; Ferguson v., TexApp–Amarillo, 197 SW2d 863.—App & E 1078(1); Hab Corp 532(2), 902; Judgm 720, 725(1).

Gleason; Kern v., TexApp–Amarillo, 840 SW2d 730.—Corp 1.4(1), 1.4(2), 1.4(4), 215, 325, 547(4); Mand 3(3), 4(4), 28, 173, 187.7, 187.9(1); Pretrial Proc 24, 27.1, 28, 32, 36.1, 44.1, 375, 377, 388.

Gleason v. Lawson, TexApp–Corpus Christi, 850 SW2d 714.—App & E 930(3), 931(1), 989, 1001(1), 1003(7), 1010.1(3); Autos 244(12), 244(60); Costs 2; Neglig 1713, 1717.

Gleason v. Southwestern Sugar & Molasses Co., TexCivApp–Waco, 214 SW2d 640.—App & E 768; Contracts 145, 326; Corp 503(2).

Gleason v. Taub, TexApp–Fort Worth, 180 SW3d 711, review den.—Action 13; App & E 893(1); Dedi 53; Mun Corp 722; Torts 440; Tresp 27, 29.

Gleason; Williams v., TexApp–Houston (14 Dist), 26 SW3d 54, reh overr, and review den, and reh of petition for review den, cert den 121 SCt 2242, 533 US 902, 150 LEd2d 231.—Const Law 1328, 1331, 1336(2), 1337, 1338, 1414; Plead 104(1); Relig Soc 14, 30.

Gleaves v. W. B. Fishburn Co., CCA5 (Tex), 82 F2d 627.—Trademarks 1425, 1800.

Gleckler v. Denton, TexCivApp–Austin, 149 SW2d 213, writ dism, correct.—Adv Poss 13, 19, 50, 65(1), 114(1); App & E 1011.1(1); Trial 395(5).

Gleffe v. State, TexCrimApp, 509 SW2d 323.—Const Law 4658(4); Crim Law 339.10(2), 339.11(2), 723(3), 726, 728(1), 730(14), 783.5, 867, 1168(2).

Gleffe v. State, TexCrimApp, 501 SW2d 672.—Const Law 3819; Crim Law 641.10(1), 641.10(2), 1170.5(1); Sent & Pun 1825, 1975(2).

Gleghorn v. City of Wichita Falls, Tex, 545 SW2d 446.—Em Dom 131, 222(1); Trial 194(10).

Gleghorn; City of Wichita Falls v., TexCivApp–Eastland, 531 SW2d 879, ref nre 545 SW2d 446.—Em Dom 219, 221, 222(4), 222(5), 262(5); Trial 194(10).

Gleghorn v. Koontz, CA5 (Tex), 178 F2d 133.—Fed Cts 827, 869; Mal Pros 21(2), 64(2), 69, 71(2), 71(3).

Gleghorn; Russell v., TexCivApp–Dallas, 96 SW2d 728.—App & E 1064.1(1), 1064.1(9), 1064.1(10).

Gleghorn v. State, TexCrimApp, 182 SW2d 920, 147 TexCrim 544.—Crim Law 394.4(6); Int Liq 248, 249.

Gleghorn; Waggoner Estate v., TexCivApp–Eastland, 370 SW2d 786, writ gr, aff 378 SW2d 47.—Const Law 47; Ease 18(2), 36(1).

Gleghorn; Waggoner's Estate v., Tex, 378 SW2d 47.—Ease 18(1), 18(4); Em Dom 2(1), 2(6), 85.

Gleghorn; Waggoner's Estate v., TexCivApp–Eastland, 199 SW2d 225.—Explos 8; Venue 8.5(5), 8.5(6).

Gleich v. Bongio, TexComApp, 99 SW2d 881, 128 Tex 606.—Hus & W 249(6), 254, 255, 258.

Gleich; Varnell v., TexCivApp–Beaumont, 274 SW2d 896.—Ex & Ad 433; Hus & W 80; Witn 178(1), 178(3).

Gleichert; Mayfield v., TexCivApp–Dallas, 437 SW2d 638.—Action 60; App & E 949; Char 45(2); Libel 45(1), 47.

Gleichert; Mayfield v., TexCivApp–Tyler, 484 SW2d 619.—App & E 927(7); Libel 5, 45(1), 51(1), 101(4), 104(1), 109, 123(8).

Gleinser; Medrano v., TexApp–Corpus Christi, 769 SW2d 687.—Elections 291, 295(1), 300.

Glenbrook Patiohome Owners Ass'n; Harris County Flood Control Dist. v., TexApp–Houston (1 Dist), 933 SW2d 570, reh overr, and writ den.—App & E 216(7); Covenants 21, 53, 68, 70, 77.1, 84; Em Dom 2(1), 63, 85, 91, 255, 263, 266, 307(2); Ven & Pur 231(3).

Glendale Const. Services, Inc. v. Accurate Air Systems, Inc., TexApp–Houston (1 Dist), 902 SW2d 536, reh overr, and writ den.—Indem 30(1), 33(5), 37, 97; Work Comp 2142.25.

Glendenning; International Harvester Co. v., TexCivApp–Dallas, 505 SW2d 320, 87 ALR3d 1.—Sec Tran 149, 150.

Glendinning v. State, TexCrimApp, 240 SW2d 768, 156 TexCrim 205.—Crim Law 603.4, 1144.7; Larc 62(2).

Glendon Investments, Inc.; Albritton Development Co. v., TexApp–Houston (1 Dist), 700 SW2d 244, ref nre.—Contracts 88; Evid 402, 419(15), 420(7), 432, 434(12).

Glendon Investments, Inc. v. Brooks, TexApp–Houston (1 Dist), 748 SW2d 465, writ den.—Brok 87, 88(9); Corp 431; Fraud 64(1); Trial 350.4(4), 351.2(2), 352.1(4).

Glen Falls Group; Harris v., TexCivApp–Corpus Christi, 478 SW2d 561, ref nre.—Insurance 2019, 2039, 3541.

Glengarry Oil Co.; White v., TexComApp, 156 SW2d 523, 137 Tex 626.—Adv Poss 114(1); App & E 719(1), 755.

Glenmore, Inc. v. Amador, TexApp–Corpus Christi, 472 SW2d 219.—Plead 111.42(5); Venue 21.

Glenn, Ex parte, TexCrimApp, 690 SW2d 578.—Pardon 86, 87.

Glenn v. Abrams/Williams Bros., TexApp–Houston (14 Dist), 836 SW2d 779, reh den, and writ den.—App & E 961, 968; Jury 97(1), 97(4); Pretrial Proc 304, 312.

Glenn v. Arkansas Best Corp., CA5 (Tex), 525 F2d 1216.—Fed Cts 585.1.

Glenn v. Armstrong, TexCivApp–Fort Worth, 284 SW2d 165.—App & E 302(1), 719(1), 719(3); Courts 24, 37(1).

Glenn v. Barnhart, CA5 (Tex), 124 FedAppx 828.—Social S 142.5, 143.60, 143.65.

Glenn; Bondies v., TexCivApp–Eastland, 119 SW2d 1095, writ dism.—Action 27(1); Attach 361, 373, 375(1), 377;

Damag 3, 87(2); Fraud 1, 9, 13(2), 13(3), 16; Mal Pros 15, 26; Plead 49; Torts 117.

Glenn v. C & G Elec., Inc., TexApp–Fort Worth, 977 SW2d 686, reh overr, and review den, and reh of petition for review overr.—App & E 946, 970(2), 1056.1(3); Evid 536; Pretrial Proc 45; Trial 39, 139.1(17).

Glenn v. City of Arlington, TexCivApp–Fort Worth, 365 SW2d 197, ref nre.—High 105(2), 113(1), 132.

Glenn v. City of Tyler, CA5 (Tex), 242 F3d 307.—Arrest 63.4(1), 63.4(2), 68(1); Civil R 1035, 1088(4), 1376(1), 1376(2), 1376(4), 1376(6); Fed Cts 557, 574, 766, 776.

Glenn; Coon v., TexCivApp–Austin, 83 SW2d 379, writ refused.—Plead 111.3; Usury 11.

Glenn; Cutler v., TexCivApp–Austin, 81 SW2d 1050.— Assign 109; Usury 140, 143.

Glenn; Dallas Ry. & Terminal Co. v., TexCivApp–Dallas, 144 SW2d 961, writ den, correct.—App & E 1001(1), 1175(5); Evid 588, 594, 597; Judgm 199(3.15); Neglig 530(1); Trial 139.1(3), 139.1(16); Urb R R 28, 30.

Glenn v. Daniel, TexCivApp–Eastland, 337 SW2d 319, ref nre.—App & E 846(5), 930(1), 1175(5); Evid 313, 317(5).

Glenn; E. v., TexApp–Fort Worth, 884 SW2d 189. See R.R.E. v. Glenn.

Glenn; Eakin v., TexCivApp–Amarillo, 141 SW2d 420.— App & E 241, 692(1), 1050.1(10); Atty & C 104; Evid 536; Execution 222(1); Home 108; Judgm 486(1); Jud S 1, 47; Lis Pen 8; Mtg 529(10), 538.

Glenn v. Garrett, TexCivApp–Amarillo, 84 SW2d 515.— Time 9(5); Venue 8.5(3).

Glenn v. Gidel, TexCivApp–Amarillo, 496 SW2d 692.— Contracts 147(3), 176(2), 250; Damag 184; Evid 323(3), 596(1); Libel 1, 6(2), 7(13), 24, 33, 123(1), 123(2); Torts 214, 242; Trial 48, 141; Witn 405(1).

Glenn v. Gidel, TexCivApp–Amarillo, 477 SW2d 331, appeal after remand 496 SW2d 692.—Judgm 181(33); Libel 50, 51(1).

Glenn v. Glenn, TexCivApp–Eastland, 183 SW2d 231.— App & E 930(1), 931(1), 994(3), 1001(1), 1002, 1010.1(1), 1011.1(1), 1012.1(1); Divorce 130.

Glenn; Glenn v., TexCivApp–Eastland, 183 SW2d 231.— App & E 930(1), 931(1), 994(3), 1001(1), 1002, 1010.1(1), 1011.1(1), 1012.1(1); Divorce 130.

Glenn; Hanover Fire Ins. Co. v., TexCivApp–Fort Worth, 153 SW2d 993.—App & E 758.3(1), 758.3(2), 758.3(3), 758.3(5), 758.3(9); Insurance 3191(7), 3546, 3571; Trial 350.4(3).

Glenn; Hicks v., TexCivApp–Amarillo, 155 SW2d 828.— Carr 408(4); Judgm 244.

Glenn v. Hollums, CCA5 (Tex), 80 F2d 555.—Bankr 2062, 2397(2); Execution 264; Fed Cts 407.1.

Glenn; Hollums v., TexCivApp–Austin, 82 SW2d 731, writ dism.—App & E 1011.1(1); Mech Liens 73(2), 76.

Glenn; Hood v., TexCivApp–Austin, 98 SW2d 1036.— Pretrial Proc 690.

Glenn; Hufstedler v., TexCivApp–Austin, 82 SW2d 733.— App & E 1140(1); Home 29, 47, 97, 213; Mech Liens 76; Mun Corp 434(5).

Glenn; Industrial Acc. Bd. v., Tex, 190 SW2d 805, 144 Tex 378.—Mand 3(2.1), 5, 72, 73(1); Work Comp 2, 1124, 1130, 1131, 1833, 1838.

Glenn v. Industrial Acc. Bd., TexCivApp–Austin, 184 SW2d 302, rev 190 SW2d 805, 144 Tex 378.—Courts 472.2; Mand 73(1), 141, 168(4); Venue 11; Work Comp 867, 893, 1142.

Glenn v. Ingram, Tex, 126 SW2d 951, 133 Tex 431.— Usury 22, 117.

Glenn v. Ingram, TexCivApp–Austin, 81 SW2d 1052.— Venue 5.4.

Glenn; Keltner v., TexCivApp–Austin, 130 SW2d 452, writ dism, correct.—App & E 930(1); Usury 16, 75, 117.

Glenn; Keltner v., TexCivApp–Austin, 81 SW2d 1051.— Deeds 136; Home 17; Usury 130.

Glenn v. Kinco Crane, Inc., TexApp–Houston (1 Dist), 836 SW2d 646.—App & E 205, 207, 230, 241, 242(2), 989, 1003(7); Prod Liab 14, 85, 87.1.

Glenn v. Lavender, TexCivApp–Austin, 130 SW2d 391.— Usury 89, 130.

Glenn; Lavender v., TexCivApp–Austin, 82 SW2d 714.— Usury 130.

Glenn v. McCarty, Tex, 110 SW2d 1148, 130 Tex 641.— App & E 361(2), 361(5); Courts 78, 80(4), 85(2).

Glenn v. McCarty, Tex, 107 SW2d 363, 130 Tex 641, reh den 110 SW2d 1148, 130 Tex 641.—App & E 361(2).

Glenn v. McCarty, TexComApp, 155 SW2d 912, 137 Tex 608.—Usury 26, 34, 130.

Glenn v. McCarty, TexCivApp–Amarillo, 130 SW2d 295, writ gr, aff 155 SW2d 912, 137 Tex 608.—Bills & N 59; Trusts 81(4); Usury 6, 15, 16, 34, 126, 127, 130; Witn 139(5), 173.

Glenn v. McCarty, TexCivApp–Amarillo, 103 SW2d 1098, writ dism 107 SW2d 363, 130 Tex 641, reh den 110 SW2d 1148, 130 Tex 641.—Usury 142(4).

Glenn v. McDonald, TexCivApp–Austin, 127 SW2d 514.— Usury 22.

Glenn; McQuerry v., TexApp–Fort Worth, 1 SW2d 339, writ dism woj.—Bankr 396(1); Mech Liens 3, 199; Mtg 151(3).

Glenn v. Miller, TexCivApp–Austin, 82 SW2d 167, writ dism.—Estop 83(1); Home 122.

Glenn v. Nelis, TexCivApp–Houston, 400 SW2d 395.— Judgm 72, 181(11).

Glenn v. Noah, TexCivApp–Austin, 130 SW2d 1069.— Home 97; Usury 42.

Glenn; Noah v., TexCivApp–Austin, 83 SW2d 382.—Plead 111.3.

Glenn; Northwestern Nat. Life Ins. Co. v., TexCivApp–Fort Worth, 568 SW2d 693, ref nre.—Insurance 2521.

Glenn v. Panhandle Const. Co., TexCivApp–Amarillo, 110 SW2d 1217.—Home 57(3), 97, 213; Mun Corp 519(6).

Glenn v. Prestegord, Tex, 456 SW2d 901.—App & E 1097(1); Health 684.

Glenn; Prestegord v., Tex, 441 SW2d 185, appeal after remand 451 SW2d 791, rev 456 SW2d 901.—Judgm 185.3(21).

Glenn; Prestegord v., TexCivApp–Amarillo, 451 SW2d 791, rev 456 SW2d 901.—Health 825.

Glenn; Prestegord v., TexCivApp–Amarillo, 436 SW2d 623, writ gr, rev 441 SW2d 185, appeal after remand 451 SW2d 791, rev 456 SW2d 901.—Judgm 185.2(9).

Glenn; Robinson v., Tex, 238 SW2d 169, 150 Tex 169.— Deeds 93, 128, 129(1), 129(3); Estates 8.

Glenn; Robinson v., TexCivApp–Amarillo, 233 SW2d 214, aff 238 SW2d 169, 150 Tex 169.—Deeds 93, 105, 124(4), 128, 130.

Glenn; R.R.E. v., TexApp–Fort Worth, 884 SW2d 189, writ den.—Const Law 580; Convicts 1; Jury 28(13), 33(2.10), 45, 142; Pardon 21; Sent & Pun 1953; Statut 181(1), 188, 208.

Glenn v. Runo, TexCivApp–Texarkana, 87 SW2d 506.— Labor & Emp 249.

Glenn; Simpson v., TexCivApp–Austin, 103 SW2d 433.— App & E 957(1); Judgm 139, 143(1), 153(3).

Glenn; Simpson v., TexCivApp–Amarillo, 537 SW2d 114, ref nre.—Evid 538, 546, 547, 547.5, 571(1).

Glenn; Skidmore v., TexApp–Dallas, 781 SW2d 672.— Child C 525; Compromise 18(1); Judgm 72, 88, 215, 284.

Glenn; Southern v., TexApp–San Antonio, 677 SW2d 576, ref nre.—Action 38(1); App & E 854(2), 1008.1(2), 1010.1(8.1); Armed S 13.5(1); Courts 12(2.5), 12(2.10), 12(2.40); Divorce 199.7(10), 252.3(4), 322; Domicile 4(2), 8; Hus & W 272(4); States 18.5.

Glenn; Spear v., TexCivApp–Austin, 83 SW2d 381.— Usury 34.

Glenn v. State, TexCrimApp, 659 SW2d 438.—Burg 46(2); Crim Law 1038.1(4).

Glenn v. State, TexCrimApp, 465 SW2d 371.—Crim Law 1169.3, 1169.5(3).

Glenn v. State, TexCrimApp, 442 SW2d 360.—Crim Law 273.4(1), 379; Sent & Pun 313, 1336.

Glenn v. State, TexCrimApp, 436 SW2d 344.—Crim Law 995(2), 1177; Ind & Inf 176.

Glenn v. State, TexCrimApp, 360 SW2d 146, 172 TexCrim 513.—Crim Law 822(7), 829(5); Homic 1134, 1492.

Glenn v. State, TexCrimApp, 327 SW2d 763, 168 TexCrim 312.—Sent & Pun 1918, 1961, 2002.

Glenn v. State, TexCrimApp, 277 SW2d 113.—Crim Law 1090.1(1).

Glenn v. State, TexCrimApp, 252 SW2d 943, 158 TexCrim 59.—Crim Law 394.4(6); Searches 112.

Glenn v. State, TexCrimApp, 236 SW2d 809, 155 TexCrim 498.—Bail 77(1), 94; Execution 161; Judgm 853(2), 853(3).

Glenn v. State, TexCrimApp, 235 SW2d 922, 155 TexCrim 411.—Larc 55.

Glenn v. State, TexCrimApp, 224 SW2d 263, 153 TexCrim 635.—Larc 55.

Glenn v. State, TexApp–Houston (1 Dist), 991 SW2d 285, petition for discretionary review refused, on reh 1998 WL 224009.—Courts 55; Crim Law 1072, 1081(2), 1081(6), 1167(5).

Glenn v. State, TexApp–Houston (1 Dist), 754 SW2d 290. —Jury 33(5.15).

Glenn v. State, TexApp–Amarillo, 967 SW2d 467, reh overr, and petition for discretionary review gr, and petition for discretionary review dism, review dism as improvidently gr 988 SW2d 769.—Arrest 63.4(6), 63.5(4), 63.5(5), 63.5(7); Crim Law 394.6(5), 1139, 1158(4).

Glenn v. State, TexApp–Tyler, 779 SW2d 466, petition for discretionary review refused.—Crim Law 564(2), 564(3); Ind & Inf 10.2(8), 86(2).

Glenn v. State, TexApp–Houston (14 Dist), 675 SW2d 568. —Arrest 63.5(2), 63.5(5), 63.5(8).

Glenn; Travelers Ins. Co. v., TexCivApp–Beaumont, 358 SW2d 136, ref nre.—Damag 221(7); Work Comp 904, 1927, 1968(5), 1968(8).

Glenn; Union Life Ins. Co. v., TexCivApp–Beaumont, 106 SW2d 1105.—Insurance 3125(2), 3125(6).

Glenn; United Sav. Life Ins. Co. v., TexCivApp–Waco, 473 SW2d 629, ref nre.—App & E 173(2), 882(17); 1170.7; Can of Inst 37(6); Insurance 3576; Judgm 198; Lim of Act 39(7).

Glenn; Walker v., TexCivApp–Austin, 82 SW2d 766, writ refused.—Usury 26.

Glenn; Watson v., TexCivApp–Austin, 82 SW2d 704.— Infants 55, 89, 95; Proc 164(1).

Glenn; White v., TexCivApp–Amarillo, 138 SW2d 914, writ dism, correct.—Atty & C 77; Deeds 38(4); Fraud 25; Home 141(1), 199, 210; Judgm 437, 634, 801; Partit 95; Ten in C 47.

Glenn; York v., TexCivApp–Fort Worth, 242 SW2d 653.— App & E 971(6), 1026, 1060.2; Witn 280, 345(1), 345(8), 351, 359.

Glenn Advertising, Inc. v. Black, TexCivApp–Hous (14 Dist), 454 SW2d 841, ref nre.—App & E 954(1), 1152; Contracts 117(2); Inj 135.

Glenney; Burkitt v., TexCivApp–Houston, 371 SW2d 412, writ dism woj, and order set aside, and ref nre.—Garn 123, 143, 180, 191.

Glenney v. Crane, TexCivApp–Houston, 352 SW2d 773, ref nre.—Deeds 17(1), 17(3), 117; Execution 47, 262; Fraud Conv 77, 87(2), 159(1), 206(1), 230, 273; Judgm 181(5.1), 185.3(17); Propty 5.5.

Glenn Heights, City of; Sheffield Development Co., Inc. v., Tex, 140 SW3d 660, reh den.—Const Law 3053; Courts 89, 91(1); Em Dom 2.1, 2.10(1), 2.10(6), 69, 300, 307(2); Mun Corp 63.10; Zoning 570.

Glenn H. McCarthy, Inc. v. Knox, TexCivApp–Galveston, 186 SW2d 832, writ refused.—Consp 1.1, 13; Corp 560(2); Evid 65; Interest 31, 39(3); Lim of Act 25(2), 60(5), 95(2), 95(3), 104(3), 179(2), 195(3); Work Comp 1063.

Glenn H. McCarthy, Inc. v. Southern Underwriters, TexCivApp–Austin, 192 SW2d 469, ref nre.—Insurance 1209(2), 1211(3), 1211(4), 1365; Work Comp 1061.

Glennie v. Petty, TexCivApp–Tyler, 591 SW2d 951.—Inj 148(1).

Glenn Justice Mortgage Co., Inc.; Skeen v., TexCivApp–Dallas, 526 SW2d 252.—Corp 1.3; Hus & W 268(6); Judgm 185.1(1), 185.1(4), 185.3(2), 185.3(10); Mtg 362, 369(3); Usury 42, 83.

Glenn McMillan Developing Co.; NEI Corp. v., TexCivApp–Hous (14 Dist), 550 SW2d 113.—App & E 300, 302(5), 347(3), 387(4); Damag 85, 189.

Glenn Martin Agency v. Lou Poliquin Enterprises, Inc., TexApp–Houston (14 Dist, 696 SW2d 180. See Martin v. Lou Poliquin Enterprises, Inc.

Glenn Thurman, Inc. v. Moore Const., Inc., TexApp–Tyler, 942 SW2d 768.—App & E 193(1), 231(9), 1064.1(6); Com Law 11; Sales 174, 178(3), 179(6), 195, 377; Stip 1, 3, 14(12).

Glenn V State, TexCrimApp, 230 SW2d 817.—Crim Law 1090.1(1).

Glenn W. Casey Const., Inc. v. Citizen's Nat. Bank, TexCivApp–Tyler, 611 SW2d 695.—App & E 4, 5, 281(1), 707(1), 859; Garn 1, 7; Judgm 27, 153(1), 335(1), 386(1), 386(3).

Glenn W. Loggins, Inc.; Cypress-Fairbanks Independent School Dist. v., TexApp–San Antonio, 115 SW3d 67, review den.—App & E 295, 977(1); Revers 1, 7; Tax 2188, 2741, 3065, 3150.

Glenn W. Turner Enterprises, Inc.; Edgar v., TexCivApp–Austin, 487 SW2d 847.—App & E 954(2); Inj 4, 22, 135.

Glen Oaks Utilities, Inc. v. City of Houston, CA5 (Tex), 280 F2d 330.—Action 69(3); Courts 493(3); Fed Cts 411, 573, 576.1; Judgm 828.10(2).

Glen Oaks Utilities, Inc. v. City of Houston, Tex, 340 SW2d 783, 161 Tex 417, on remand 360 SW2d 549, ref nre.—Admin Law 651; Const Law 4361; Inj 118(3), 138.48, 151; Mun Corp 619.

Glen Oaks Utilities, Inc. v. City of Houston, TexCivApp–Waco, 334 SW2d 469, writ gr, rev 340 SW2d 783, 161 Tex 417, on remand 360 SW2d 549, ref nre.—App & E 655(1), 927(3); Inj 85(2); Mun Corp 619.

Glen Oaks Utilities, Inc.; City of Houston v., TexCivApp–Houston, 360 SW2d 549, ref nre.—Const Law 4361; Equity 65(1); Inj 85(1), 108; Judgm 181(2), 185(2); Mun Corp 619.

Glen Ridge I Condominiums, Ltd.; Federal Sav. and Loan Ins. Corp. v., Tex, 750 SW2d 757.—App & E 361(1); B & L Assoc 48; Const Law 1003.

Glen Ridge I Condominiums, Ltd. v. Federal Sav. and Loan Ins. Corp., TexApp–Dallas, 734 SW2d 374, writ den 750 SW2d 757, cert den 109 SCt 1637, 490 US 1004, 104 LEd2d 153.—Admin Law 229, 704; B & L Assoc 2, 48; Const Law 655, 2414(1); Fed Cts 1.1, 558; U S 78(3), 125(8), 125(31).

Glen Rose Independent School Dist.; Ogletree v., TexApp–Waco, 226 SW3d 629.—Admin Law 229; App & E 230, 704.2, 893(1); Civil R 1320, 1376(5); Plead 111.36, 111.38; Schools 63(1), 115, 147.51.

Glen Rose Independent School Dist. No. 1; Pruitt v., TexComApp, 84 SW2d 1004, 126 Tex 45, 100 ALR 1158. —Offic 30.1, 55(2).

Glens Falls Indem. Co.; Baker v., TexCivApp–Dallas, 293 SW2d 118, dism.—Evid 441(12); Trial 140(2).

Glens Falls Indem. Co.; Frazier v., TexCivApp–Fort Worth, 278 SW2d 388, ref nre.—App & E 837(1), 837(10), 909(1), 934(1); Insurance 3207, 3209, 3221; Judgm 181(2), 185(2), 185.3(12), 190.

Glens Falls Indem. Co.; King v., CCA5 (Tex), 124 F2d 942.—Adm 21; Work Comp 621, 1726.

Glens Falls Indem. Co. v. Roberson, TexCivApp–El Paso, 282 SW2d 438.—Insurance 1634(1), 1747, 2016.

Glens Falls Indem. Co.; Sisk v., TexCivApp–Houston, 310 SW2d 118, 66 ALR2d 1, ref nre.—Damag 221(4), 221(7); Trial 115(2), 118, 182; Work Comp 1028, 1926.

Glens Falls Indem. Co. v. Sterling, TexCivApp–Dallas, 213 SW2d 858, mandamus overr.—Decl Judgm 271; Plead 111.9, 111.16, 111.18; Venue 15, 22(3), 22(6).

Glens Falls Indem. Co.; Williams v., SDTex, 41 FSupp 780.—Adm 20.

Glens Falls Ins. Co.; Chadwick v., TexCivApp–Waco, 340 SW2d 501.—App & E 554(1), 842(1), 907(3), 1032(1), 1060.1(1), 1060.4; New Tr 56, 157.

Glens Falls Ins. Co. v. Covert, TexCivApp–Beaumont, 526 SW2d 222, ref nre.—Insurance 2155(2).

Glens Falls Ins. Co.; Employers Cas. Co. v., Tex, 484 SW2d 570.—Insurance 3149, 3153; Trial 365.1(5).

Glens Falls Ins. Co. v. Employers Cas. Co., TexCivApp–Hous (14 Dist), 469 SW2d 829, writ gr, rev 484 SW2d 570.—App & E 241; Insurance 2681, 2762(2), 2923, 3188, 3198(1), 3198(2); Judgm 199(5).

Glens Falls Ins. Co.; First Nat. Bank of Lancaster v., TexCivApp–Waco, 329 SW2d 115, ref nre.—Insurance 2403.

Glens Falls Ins. Co.; Jay Freeman Co. v., NDTex, 486 FSupp 140.—Antitrust 145, 205, 221, 358, 393; Contracts 205.15(1); Insurance 3349, 3360, 3585.

Glens Falls Ins. Co. v. McCown, Tex, 236 SW2d 108, 149 Tex 587.—Insurance 1739, 2645, 2707.

Glens Falls Ins. Co. v. McCown, TexCivApp–Fort Worth, 228 SW2d 949, rev 236 SW2d 108, 149 Tex 587. —Insurance 1806, 1812, 1813, 1816, 1827, 1828, 1832(1), 1837, 1853, 2707, 2859.

Glens Falls Ins. Co. v. Manning, TexCivApp–Texarkana, 362 SW2d 385.—Insurance 1810, 1822, 1845(1), 2522.

Glens Falls Ins. Co.; National Auto. & Cas. Ins. Co. v., TexCivApp–Tyler, 493 SW2d 909.—Insurance 2681.

Glens Falls Ins. Co. v. Peters, Tex, 386 SW2d 529.—Abate & R 19; Insurance 2175, 2176; Trial 351.2(2), 351.2(4), 351.2(5).

Glens Falls Ins. Co. v. Peters, TexCivApp–Fort Worth, 379 SW2d 946, rev 386 SW2d 529.—Evid 318(4), 333(1); Insurance 2171, 2195.

Glens Falls Ins. Co. v. State Nat. Bank of El Paso, TexCivApp–El Paso, 475 SW2d 386, ref nre.—Accession 1; Contracts 94(1); Sales 118, 130(3.5), 135.

Glens Falls Ins. Co.; Vasquez v., CA5 (Tex), 426 F2d 297.—Fed Cts 743; Work Comp 1924.

Glens Falls Ins. Co. v. Vetrano, TexCivApp–Houston, 347 SW2d 769.—App & E 931(5); Evid 596(1); Insurance 2278(29), 2292, 3571; Plead 389, 398.

Glens Falls Ins. Co.; Watson v., Tex, 505 SW2d 793.—App & E 832(4); Work Comp 1105, 2186, 2220, 2249, 2251.

Glens Falls Ins. Co.; Watson v., TexCivApp–Hous (1 Dist), 489 SW2d 322, writ gr, aff 505 SW2d 793.—Work Comp 1105.

Glens Falls Ins. Co. v. Yarbrough, TexCivApp–Waco, 396 SW2d 200, writ dism, and order set aside, and ref nre.—App & E 662(3), 842(1); Trial 75, 412; Work Comp 1703, 1926, 1968(2), 1968(5).

Glens Falls Ins. Co. v. Yarbrough, TexCivApp–Waco, 369 SW2d 640.—Hus & W 260, 265, 270(8); Work Comp 1159.

Glenshannon Townhouse Community Ass'n, Inc.; City of Houston v., TexCivApp–Hous (1 Dist), 607 SW2d 930.—App & E 253; Civil R 1351(6); Const Law 3533; Mun Corp 122.1(2), 594(1).

Glenview Hospital, Inc.; McEachern v., TexCivApp–Fort Worth, 505 SW2d 386, ref nre.—Health 664, 823(3), 835; Neglig 387, 1741; Trial 139.1(7).

Glen Willows Apartments; Plowman v., TexApp–Corpus Christi, 978 SW2d 612, on reh in part, and review den. —App & E 852, 934(1); Judgm 185(6), 185.2(8); Land & Ten 164(1), 164(6); Neglig 210, 213, 220, 250, 1019, 1024, 1037(4), 1070, 1161, 1692.

Glen Willows, Inc.; Century Sur. Co. v., SDTex, 924 FSupp 76, aff 100 F3d 952.—Insurance 435.35, 2278(5), 2914.

GLF Const. Corp. v. LAN/STV, CA5 (Tex), 414 F3d 553. —Fed Cts 390, 612.1, 776; Judgm 540; States 112(1), 112.1(4).

G------ L------ G------, Matter of, TexCivApp–Hous (1 Dist), 550 SW2d 716.—App & E 389(1); Costs 132(6); Courts 209(2); Mand 28, 57(1).

Glick; City of Amarillo v., TexApp–Amarillo, 991 SW2d 14, reh overr, and review den.—App & E 946; Costs 194.14, 194.16; Mun Corp 218(9), 1040.

Glick; Le Manquais v., WDTex, 17 FSupp 347.—Fed Cts 417; Rem of C 3, 79(2.1), 81, 107(4).

Glickman; Gore, Inc. v., CA5 (Tex), 137 F3d 863.—Fed Cts 776; Interest 39(2.6), 39(2.10), 39(2.20); Statut 220; U S 110.

Glickman; John Doe No. 1 v., CA5 (Tex), 256 F3d 371, on remand Doe v. Veneman, 230 FSupp2d 739, rev in part 380 F3d 807.—Fed Civ Proc 314.1, 315, 320, 331; Fed Cts 776, 817.

Glickman; Neal v., NDTex, 391 FSupp 1088.—Copyr 85; Equity 65(2).

Glickman; Pure Milk v., CA5 (Tex), 137 F3d 863. See Gore, Inc. v. Glickman.

Glickman; Sierra Club v., CA5 (Tex), 156 F3d 606, reh den.—Admin Law 701, 760, 763; Environ Law 537, 547, 647, 652, 661, 688; Fed Civ Proc 103.2, 103.3, 1827.1; Fed Cts 12.1, 724.

Glickman; Sierra Club v., CA5 (Tex), 82 F3d 106.—Environ Law 652; Fed Civ Proc 314.1, 315, 316, 320, 331, 338; Fed Cts 776, 817.

Glickman; Sierra Club v., CA5 (Tex), 67 F3d 90, on remand 273 FSupp2d 764.—Admin Law 657.1, 744.1, 763; Environ Law 688; Fed Cts 573, 576.1.

Glickman; Sierra Club v., EDTex, 974 FSupp 905, aff 185 F3d 349, reh enbanc gr 204 F3d 580, on reh 228 F3d 559, reh den, cert den Texas Committee on Natural Resources v. Veneman, 121 SCt 2192, 532 US 1051, 149 LEd2d 1024, vac 228 F3d 559, reh den, and reh den, cert den 121 SCt 2192, 532 US 1051, 149 LEd2d 1024.— Admin Law 661, 792; Decl Judgm 5.1, 341.1; Environ Law 536, 700; Fed Cts 12.1; Inj 1, 14, 16, 74, 189; U S 125(9); Woods 7, 8.

Glickman; Vogel v., WDTex, 117 FSupp2d 572, aff 276 F3d 729.—Subrog 1, 27, 31(4).

Glidden Co. v. Aetna Cas. & Sur. Co., Tex, 291 SW2d 315, 155 Tex 591.—App & E 387(1), 387(2), 387(6), 799, 801(1), 1083(1).

Glidden Co.; Aetna Cas. & Sur. Co. v., TexCivApp–Eastland, 283 SW2d 440, rev 291 SW2d 315, 155 Tex 591.—App & E 878(2); Mun Corp 213, 245, 348.

Glidden Co.; Greathouse v., TexApp–Houston (14 Dist), 40 SW3d 560, reh en banc den.—App & E 946, 984(5); Atty & C 140; Bills & N 534; Fraud 31; Labor & Emp 407, 425, 429, 446, 645, 662; States 18.51.

Glidden Co.; Parks v., TexCivApp–Texarkana, 433 SW2d 445, ref nre.—Sales 420.

Glidden Co.; Ray v., CA5 (Tex), 85 F3d 227.—Civil R 1019(2), 1218(3), 1218(5), 1552.

Glidewell; First Strawn Nat. Bank v., TexCivApp–Eastland, 307 SW2d 297, ref nre.—Banks 121, 155, 156.

Glikin v. Smith, CA5 (Tex), 269 F2d 641, cert den 80 SCt 260, 361 US 915, 4 LEd2d 185.—Evid 318(1); Pat 1, 9, 26(1), 36.2(1), 37, 112.1.

Glikin; Smith v., SDTex, 163 FSupp 897, rev 269 F2d 641, cert den 80 SCt 260, 361 US 915, 4 LEd2d 185.— Estop 88(1); Evid 318(1); Pat 16(1), 26(1), 41, 54, 61, 101(5), 112.1, 168(1), 168(2.1), 233.1, 236(2).

GLIMPSE

See Guidelines for Arrangement at the beginning of this Volume

Glimpse v. Bexar County, TexCivApp–San Antonio, 160 SW2d 996, writ refused.—Atty Gen 6; Counties 54, 178.

Glinski v. State, TexApp–Houston (1 Dist), 986 SW2d 79. —Double J 5.1, 6, 23, 24.

Glisson v. General Cinema Corp. of Texas, TexApp– Dallas, 713 SW2d 694, ref nre.—Work Comp 19, 2143.

Glitsch Engineering & Sales Corp.; O'Connor v., Tex-CivApp–Dallas, 589 SW2d 808.—App & E 5; Torts 214, 242.

Glitsch, Inc.; Jones v., NDTex, 489 FSupp 990, aff 634 F2d 1353, vac 101 SCt 3044, 452 US 912, 69 LEd2d 415. —Civil R 1560, 1561, 1563, 1564, 1571, 1590; Equity 55.

Glitsch, Inc. v. Koch Engineering Co., Inc., CAFed (Tex), 216 F3d 1382.—Decl Judgm 41; Fed Cts 541; Pat 327(13).

Glitsch, Inc.; McDonald v., TexCivApp–Eastland, 589 SW2d 554, ref nre.—Judgm 181(33).

Glittenberg v. Hughes, TexCivApp–Fort Worth, 524 SW2d 954.—App & E 909(1); Judgm 143(3), 145(2), 153(1), 163.

Glivens v. State, TexApp–Houston (1 Dist), 918 SW2d 30, petition for discretionary review refused, appeal after new sentencing hearing 2001 WL 1047534, petition for discretionary review refused.—Crim Law 641.13(1), 641.13(7); Jury 149; Sent & Pun 311.

Global Aerospace v. Pinson, TexApp–Corpus Christi, 208 SW3d 687.—Insurance 1824, 1836, 2281(2).

Global Auctioneers, Inc.; First City Bank of Richard-son v., TexApp–Texarkana, 708 SW2d 12, ref nre.—App & E 302(6); Banks 100; Bills & N 529, 534; Fraud 22(1), 64(1); Pretrial Proc 42, 45, 431.

Global Const. Co., L.L.C., In re, TexApp–Houston (14 Dist), 166 SW3d 795.—Alt Disp Res 200, 201, 202, 210; Mand 3(3), 4(1), 12.

Global Corp. v. Vincent, Tex, 295 SW2d 640, 156 Tex 398.—Lim of Act 127(4).

Global Corp. v. Vincent, TexCivApp–Amarillo, 290 SW2d 270, rev 295 SW2d 640, 156 Tex 398.—Lim of Act 127(13).

Global Corp.; Vincent v., TexCivApp–Amarillo, 217 SW2d 66, mandamus overr.—Venue 7.5(7).

Global Drywall Systems, Inc.; Coronado Paint Co., Inc. v., TexApp–Corpus Christi, 47 SW3d 28, reh overr, and review gr, and withdrawn, review den as improvidently gr 104 SW3d 538.—App & E 893(1), 1175(1); Assign 22, 66, 138; Compromise 2, 9; Judgm 199(3.5); Trial 168.

Global Leak Detection U.S.A., Inc.; Gilliam v., SDTex, 141 FSupp2d 734.—Alt Disp Res 112, 113, 134(1), 134(3), 139, 141, 143, 200, 203, 210; Fed Cts 403.

Global Marine Drilling Co.; Picco v., CA5 (Tex), 900 F2d 846.—Bankr 2395, 2462; Fed Civ Proc 2646, 2651.1; Fed Cts 589, 611, 714; Judgm 713(1).

Global Marine Drilling Co.; Picco v., EDTex, 590 FSupp 891. See Munusamy v. McClelland Engineers, Inc.

Global Marine Drilling Co.; Picco v., EDTex, 579 FSupp 149. See Munusamy v. McClelland Engineers, Inc.

Global Marine Drilling Co.; Robinson v., CA5 (Tex), 101 F3d 35, cert den 117 SCt 1820, 520 US 1228, 137 LEd2d 1028.—Civil R 1019(2), 1217, 1218(3).

Global Marine, Inc., In re, SDTex, 108 BR 1009.—Bankr 3768, 3772.

Global Marine, Inc., In re, SDTex, 108 BR 1007.—Bankr 3768, 3772.

Global Marine, Inc., In re, BkrtcySDTex, 108 BR 998, appeal dism 108 BR 1007, appeal dism 108 BR 1009.— Atty & C 20.1, 21.5(6), 21.10, 21.20, 32(4); Bankr 3177, 3178.

Global Marine, Inc.; Bailey v., SDTex, 714 FSupp 235.— Seamen 2; Work Comp 130.

Global Marine, Inc.; Bunn v., CA5 (Tex), 428 F2d 40.— Adm 26; Mar Liens 1, 7; Seamen 2, 4, 6, 7, 19, 26.

Global Marine, Inc.; Lawrenson v., TexApp–Texarkana, 869 SW2d 519, reh den, and writ den.—Adm 1.20(5), 34.5; App & E 863; Bankr 2157, 2391, 2404, 2462; Evid 51; Judgm 181(2), 183, 185(1), 185(2), 185.1(8); Lim of Act 110; Seamen 29(1), 29(5.4), 29(5.5), 29(5.16); States 18.57.

Global Marine, Inc.; Ross v., CA5 (Tex), 859 F2d 336.— Fed Cts 666, 668.

Global Marine, Inc.; Sikes v., CA5 (Tex), 881 F2d 176, reh den 888 F2d 1388.—Bankr 2442, 2462.

Global Marine Intern. Services Corp.; Abacan Techni-cal Services Ltd. v., TexApp–Houston (1 Dist), 994 SW2d 839.—App & E 170(1), 840(2); Appear 9(2); Const Law 3968; Contracts 127(4); Courts 12(2.1), 25, 37(1); Judgm 16.

Global Natural Resources v. Bear, Stearns & Co., Tex-App–Dallas, 642 SW2d 852.—App & E 100(1), 604; Corp 584.

Global Natural Resources, Inc.; O'Hare v., CA5 (Tex), 898 F2d 1015.—Civil R 1263; Release 12(3), 15, 18.

Global Octanes Texas, L.P. v. BP Exploration & Oil Inc., CA5 (Tex), 154 F3d 518.—Damag 78(6), 118; Fed Civ Proc 2553; Sales 91, 384(1).

Global Petrotech, Inc. v. Engelhard Corp., CA5 (Tex), 58 F3d 198.—Antitrust 136, 368; Damag 59; Fed Cts 776, 823, 896.1, 901.1; Interest 31.

Global Petrotech, Inc. v. Engelhard Corp., SDTex, 824 FSupp 103.—Contracts 317; Damag 59, 64; Insurance 1790(4).

Global Santa Fe Corp. v. Texas Property and Cas. Ins. Guar. Ass'n, TexApp–Austin, 153 SW3d 150, petition stricken, and review den, and reh of petition for review den.—Insurance 1511, 3141.

GlobalSantaFe Corp.; Transocean Offshore Deepwater Drilling, Inc. v., SDTex, 443 FSupp2d 836.—Pat 7.11, 16(2), 16(3), 16(4), 16.5(1), 16.13, 36.1(1), 36.2(1), 51(1), 68, 70, 72(1), 90(1), 90(5), 90(7), 91(3), 91(4), 112.5, 312(1.2), 314(5), 323.2(3), 323.2(5), 328(2).

GlobalSantaFe Corp.; Transocean Offshore Deepwater Drilling, Inc. v., SDTex, 400 FSupp2d 998.—Pat 226.6, 229, 230, 235(2), 237, 312(4), 314(5), 323.2(2), 328(2).

Global Santa Fe Drilling Co.; Lockerman v., SDTex, 213 FSupp2d 778.—Adm 1.20(2); Indem 27, 33(8).

Global Services, Inc. v. Bianchi, Tex, 901 SW2d 934.— Mand 3(3), 4(4), 28; Pretrial Proc 44.1, 434.

Global Truck & Equipment, Inc.; Gonzalez v., TexCiv-App–Hous (1 Dist), 625 SW2d 348.—App & E 758.3(11), 934(1); Evid 434(11); Judgm 178, 181(33), 185(1).

Global Truck & Equipment, Inc. v. Plaschinski, Tex-App–Houston (14 Dist), 683 SW2d 766.—App & E 493; Judgm 25, 123(1), 162(2).

Globe Aircraft Corp. v. Thompson, TexCivApp–Fort Worth, 203 SW2d 865.—App & E 218.2(4), 1177(8); Assign 117, 129; Damag 6; Trial 351.5(2); Waters 77.

Globe & Rutgers Fire Ins. Co. v. U.S., CA5 (Tex), 202 F2d 696.—Insurance 2143(1), 3446.

Globe & Rutgers Fire Ins. Co.; U.S. v., NDTex, 104 FSupp 632, aff 202 F2d 696.—Insurance 1716, 1834(1), 2132, 2268.

Globe Chemical Co. v. Walla, TexCivApp–Houston, 328 SW2d 341.—App & E 846(2), 846(5), 954(2); Inj 147.

Globe Discount City v. Landry, TexCivApp–Waco, 590 SW2d 813, ref nre.—Evid 268.

Globe Discount City, Inc.; Dominguez v., TexCivApp–El Paso, 470 SW2d 919.—False Imp 6.

Globe Discount City, Inc.; Rodriguez v., TexCivApp– Hous (1 Dist), 498 SW2d 283.—App & E 79(1), 80(6); Corp 508; Parties 46.

Globe Finance & Thrift Co. v. Thompson, TexCivApp– Fort Worth, 412 SW2d 955.—Plead 111.5, 111.47, 422.

Globe Indem. Co.; Bueno v., TexCivApp–Corpus Christi, 441 SW2d 643.—Insurance 1634(1); Trial 351.2(3.1), 351.2(4); Work Comp 1340, 1704.

Globe Indem. Co. v. Calbeck, SDTex, 230 FSupp 14.— Work Comp 616, 935, 1465, 1849, 1867, 1890, 1939.4(4).

Globe Indem. Co. v. Calbeck, SDTex, 230 FSupp 9.—Fed Civ Proc 2415; Judgm 828.21(1); Work Comp 98.

Globe Indem. Co. v. French, TexCivApp–Amarillo, 382 SW2d 771, ref nre.—Insurance 2664.

Globe Indem. Co. v. Gen-Aero, Inc., TexCivApp–San Antonio, 459 SW2d 205, writ gr, ref nre 469 SW2d 164. —App & E 1170.6, 1170.7; Evid 177, 582(4); Insurance 3382; Trial 350.4(3), 351.5(4).

Globe Indem. Co.; Gulf Portland Cement Co. v., CCA5 (Tex), 149 F2d 196, cert den 66 SCt 56, 326 US 743, 90 LEd 444.—Insurance 1825, 2278(19).

Globe Indem. Co.; Hudiburg Chevrolet, Inc. v., Tex, 394 SW2d 792, on remand 396 SW2d 954.—Insurance 2153(1), 2706(1), 2733; Judgm 199(3.13); Larc 3(3), 8.

Globe Indem. Co.; Hudiburg Chevrolet, Inc. v., TexCivApp–Fort Worth, 396 SW2d 954.—Insurance 2732.

Globe Indem. Co.; Hudiburg Chevrolet, Inc. v., TexCivApp–Fort Worth, 383 SW2d 65, writ gr, aff in part, rev in part 394 SW2d 792, on remand 396 SW2d 954.—Insurance 2652, 2660, 2699.

Globe Indem. Co. v. Matthews, CCA5 (Tex), 131 F2d 433. —Work Comp 597, 600, 1543, 1717.

Globe Indem. Co. v. White, TexCivApp–San Antonio, 332 SW2d 454, ref nre.—Fact 2.5.

Globe Indem. Co., New York, N. Y. v. Jett, TexCivApp–Austin, 367 SW2d 396, ref nre.—Insurance 2684.

Globe Industries, Inc.; Hereford Land Co. v., TexCivApp–Tyler, 387 SW2d 771, ref nre.—App & E 954(1), 954(2), 1043(5); Corp 316(0.5), 523; Estates 1; Evid 419(2); Execution 172(6); Inj 132, 135, 151, 152; Trusts 1, 26, 62, 69, 129.

Globe Laboratories; Smirl v., Tex, 188 SW2d 676, 144 Tex 41.—App & E 389(3), 581(1), 609, 642, 659(1), 715(2), 801(1), 1106(2), 1114; Courts 82.

Globe Laboratories; Smirl v., TexCivApp–Dallas, 190 SW2d 574, writ refused wom.—App & E 766; Trial 351.2(8), 352.20, 366.

Globe Laboratories; Smirl v., TexCivApp–Dallas, 186 SW2d 371, rev 188 SW2d 676, 144 Tex 41.—App & E 389(3).

Globe Leasing, Inc.; Carpenter v., TexCivApp–Fort Worth, 421 SW2d 413.—App & E 934(3); Judgm 101(2); Pretrial Proc 484.

Globe Leasing, Inc. v. Engine Supply and Mach. Service, TexCivApp–Hous (1 Dist), 437 SW2d 43.—Acct Action on 13; App & E 428(2); Atty & C 11(1); Corp 508; Judgm 297, 340.

Globe Life & Acc. Ins. Co. v. Dalrymple, TexCivApp–Amarillo, 487 SW2d 858, ref nre.—Insurance 2588(2).

Globe Marble & Granite Corp.; R. P. Farnsworth & Co. v., CA5 (Tex), 250 F2d 636.—Fed Civ Proc 214, 1728, 1951; Princ & S 66(2), 151.

Globe News Pub. Co.; Conkwright v., TexCivApp–Eastland, 398 SW2d 385.—Libel 48(1); Plead 111.42(4).

Globe-News Pub. Co.; Walker v., TexCivApp–Amarillo, 395 SW2d 686, ref nre.—Libel 19, 42(1), 50.5, 105(3), 123(8).

Globe Sec.; E.E.O.C. v., WDTex, 671 FSupp 454. See E.E.O.C. v. Fotios.

Globe Shopping City v. Williams, TexCivApp–Hous (14 Dist), 535 SW2d 53.—False Imp 36; New Tr 77(2).

Globe-Texas Co.; Ferguson v., TexApp–Amarillo, 35 SW3d 688, review den.—App & E 345.2, 856(5), 933(1); Courts 85(2); New Tr 116, 165; Statut 188, 189.

Glock, Ges.m.b.H.; Spence v., CA5 (Tex), 227 F3d 308.—Action 17; Contracts 129(1); Fed Civ Proc 162, 171, 172, 182.5; Fed Cts 409.1, 817; Prod Liab 3.

Glockzin v. Leon's Truck Shop, TexApp–Houston (1 Dist), 760 SW2d 665. See Glockzin v. Rhea.

Glockzin v. Rhea, TexApp–Houston (1 Dist), 760 SW2d 665, writ den.—App & E 989, 1001(1), 1003(7); Contracts 323(1); Fraud 58(1); Replev 116.

Glockzin v. State, TexApp–Waco, 220 SW3d 140, petition for discretionary review refused.—Assault 91.9, 96(1); Crim Law 304(1), 347, 369.2(2), 553, 673(5), 742(1), 755.5, 761(1), 761(6), 796, 812, 814(1), 824(1), 824(8), 1030(1),

1038.1(2), 1159.2(1), 1159.2(2), 1172.1(1), 1172.6, 1191; Ind & Inf 159(2); Infants 20; Sent & Pun 309, 312, 313.

Glo Co. v. Murchison, CA5 (Tex), 210 F2d 372.—Corp 642(1).

Glo Co. v. Murchison, CA5 (Tex), 208 F2d 714, reh den 210 F2d 372, cert den 75 SCt 27, 348 US 817, 99 LEd 644.—Commerce 60(1); Corp 642(1); Fed Civ Proc 1827.1.

Glodfelty; Peaster Independent School Dist. v., TexApp–Fort Worth, 63 SW3d 1.—Admin Law 790, 791; Evid 314(1); Schools 147.9, 147.20, 147.34(2), 147.40(2); Trial 54(1).

Gloff; Pennsylvania Threshermen & Farmers Mut. Cas. Ins. Co. v., CA5 (Tex), 238 F2d 839.—Work Comp 1703, 1924, 1927, 1929.

Glomb; U.S. v., CA5 (Tex), 877 F2d 1.—Crim Law 1131(5); Hab Corp 602.

Gloor; Garcia v., CA5 (Tex), 618 F2d 264, reh den 625 F2d 1016, cert den 101 SCt 923, 449 US 1113, 66 LEd2d 842.—Civil R 1118, 1120, 1121, 1137, 1140, 1231; Consp 7.5(1), 7.5(2); Evid 333(7), 366(2); Fed Civ Proc 161.1, 163, 174, 184.10; Fed Cts 901.1; Statut 188.

Gloor; Garcia v., CA5 (Tex), 609 F2d 156, opinion withdrawn and superseded 618 F2d 264, reh den 625 F2d 1016, cert den 101 SCt 923, 449 US 1113, 66 LEd2d 842.

Gloor v. Richard Gill Co., TexCivApp–San Antonio, 272 SW2d 920, ref nre.—App & E 766; Impl & C C 25.

Gloor v. U.S. Fire Ins. Co., TexCivApp–Beaumont, 457 SW2d 925, ref nre.—Judgm 185(3), 185.3(13).

Gloria; McIver v., Tex, 169 SW2d 710, 140 Tex 566.—Damag 38, 95, 96, 100, 134(1), 163(1), 163(4), 173(1), 185(1).

Gloria; McIver v., TexCivApp–San Antonio, 163 SW2d 890, aff 169 SW2d 710, 140 Tex 566.—App & E 1004(8), 1005(1), 1050.1(4); Autos 245(30), 245(36); Damag 163(1), 187, 208(4), 228; Evid 222(2), 383(3).

Gloria v. State, TexApp–Corpus Christi, 676 SW2d 194.—Crim Law 695(6), 1147, 1177; Sent & Pun 2003, 2019, 2020, 2021.

Gloria; U.S. v., CA5 (Tex), 494 F2d 477, reh den 496 F2d 878, cert den 95 SCt 306, 419 US 995, 42 LEd2d 267.—Consp 47(12); Controlled Subs 81; Crim Law 59(3), 388.5(1), 419(10), 594(1), 829(3), 938(1), 959, 1168(1), 1169.5(2); Witn 2(1), 37(4), 267, 300, 305(1), 345(1), 345(2), 350, 354.

Gloria v. Valley Grain Products, Inc., CA5 (Tex), 72 F3d 497.—Accord 11(2); Civil R 1571; Fed Cts 543.1, 544, 847; Interest 39(2.45); Jury 37.

Gloria Stiles Realtors v. DeAngelo, TexApp–Fort Worth, 706 SW2d 175. See Stiles v. DeAngelo.

Glorioso; French v., TexApp–San Antonio, 94 SW3d 739. —App & E 846(5), 893(1), 1010.1(1), 1010.2, 1012.1(5); Appear 9(2); Const Law 3964; Courts 12(2.1), 12(2.5), 12(2.10), 12(2.15), 12(2.25), 12(5), 15, 35, 39, 97(1); Trial 404(5).

Glorioso v. State, TexCrimApp, 746 SW2d 483, on remand 753 SW2d 454.—Sent & Pun 1367, 1378.

Glorioso v. State, TexApp–Houston (14 Dist), 753 SW2d 454.—Sent & Pun 1381(5).

Glorioso v. State, TexApp–Houston (14 Dist), 744 SW2d 202, case remanded 746 SW2d 483, on remand 753 SW2d 454.—Crim Law 273.1(4), 379, 414, 641.13(1), 641.13(2.1), 1203.27; Sent & Pun 1378; Witn 37(4).

Glossip; Brown v., CA5 (Tex), 878 F2d 871, appeal after remand 920 F2d 322.—Civil R 1376(6), 1395(5), 1395(6); Offic 119.

Glosson, Ex parte, TexApp–Houston (14 Dist), 705 SW2d 711.—Const Law 4494, 4495; Contempt 79; Hab Corp 711, 730.

Glossup v. State, TexCrimApp, 170 SW2d 228, 145 TexCrim 510.—Crim Law 721.5(3), 1171.1(5).

Glossup v. State, TexCrimApp, 101 SW2d 251, 131 TexCrim 645.—Crim Law 609, 949(2).

Gloston, Ex parte, TexCrimApp, 579 SW2d 212.—Hab Corp 474; Ind & Inf 10.1(1).

Glover, Ex parte, Tex, 701 SW2d 639.—Contempt 20.

Glover, In re, BkrtcyNDTex, 224 BR 360. See Thompson, In re.

Glover, Matter of Estate of, Tex, 744 SW2d 939.—Wills 306.

Glover, Matter of Estate of, TexApp–Amarillo, 744 SW2d 197, 70 ALR4th 311, writ den 744 SW2d 939.— Evid 89; Wills 290, 306.

Glover v. Adams, TexCivApp–Dallas, 151 SW2d 316.— App & E 1058(1); Compromise 23(2).

Glover v. American Mortg. Corp., TexCivApp–Dallas, 94 SW2d 1235.—Venue 7.5(3).

Glover v. Barnhart, CA5 (Tex), 81 FedAppx 513.—Social S 142.5, 143.70.

Glover; Bourbon v., TexCivApp–Beaumont, 431 SW2d 650.—App & E 930(3), 989; Autos 172(5.1), 244(12).

Glover v. Brazoria County Children's Protective Services Unit, TexApp–Houston (1 Dist), 916 SW2d 19.— Infants 155; Judgm 181(15.1); Stip 14(1).

Glover v. Buchman, TexCivApp–Galveston, 104 SW2d 66, writ dism.—Usury 16, 52.

Glover; Central Nat. Ins. Co. of Omaha v., TexApp– Houston (1 Dist), 856 SW2d 490.—Alt Disp Res 115, 213(3); App & E 66, 68, 76(1).

Glover v. City of Dallas, CA5 (Tex), 221 FedAppx 311.— Civil R 1137.

Glover; City of Houston v., TexCivApp–Waco, 355 SW2d 757, ref nre.—Autos 293, 306(2), 308(11); Death 77, 99(4); Lim of Act 125; Mun Corp 733(2); Neglig 1717; Plead 252(1); Witn 276.

Glover v. City of Houston, TexCivApp–Hous (14 Dist), 590 SW2d 799.—App & E 989, 999(1), 1001(1), 1003(4), 1008.1(13), 1078(1); Autos 304(1), 304(3), 306(8), 308(10), 308(11); Neglig 1713.

Glover v. City of South Houston, TexCivApp–Hous (14 Dist), 424 SW2d 723.—Autos 5(5), 258; Mun Corp 733(2), 745.5, 755(1).

Glover v. Cobb, TexCivApp–Dallas, 123 SW2d 794, writ refused.—Civil R 1058, 1721; Const Law 580, 584, 603; Elections 62.1; Jury 3, 38, 58; Mand 23(1), 23(2).

Glover v. Compagnie Generale Transatlantique, CCA5 (Tex), 103 F2d 557, cert den 60 SCt 83, 308 US 550, 84 LEd 462.—Ship 84(3.1), 84(3.3), 86(2.3), 86(3).

Glover; Curtis Sharp Custom Homes, Inc. v., TexApp– Dallas, 701 SW2d 24, ref nre.—Home 90.

Glover v. Davis, Tex, 366 SW2d 227.—Death 5; Insurance 3485.

Glover v. Davis, TexCivApp–Amarillo, 360 SW2d 924, aff 366 SW2d 227.—App & E 846(2), 846(5), 989, 1177(7); Evid 587; Insurance 3485, 3496; Interpl 29.

Glover v. Donohoo, TexCivApp–El Paso, 197 SW2d 531. —Dep & Escr 26; Evid 208(3), 230(1), 265(17), 591; Hus & W 86, 149(1), 179, 187, 197; Judgm 632, 666; Ven & Pur 85.

Glover v. Elliston, TexCivApp–Eastland, 529 SW2d 119. —Dead Bodies 6; Ex & Ad 214.

Glover v. Estelle, CA5 (Tex), 485 F2d 250.—Hab Corp 743.

Glover; Galveston County Fair & Rodeo, Inc. v., Tex, 940 SW2d 585.—App & E 1062.1; Trial 352.1(3).

Glover; Galveston County Fair & Rodeo, Inc. v., TexApp–Texarkana, 880 SW2d 112, writ den with per curiam opinion 940 SW2d 585.—Agric 5; App & E 216(1), 836, 930(3), 989, 999(1), 1001(1), 1001(3), 1140(1); Contracts 22(1), 312(1); Evid 588; Libel 1, 21, 23.1, 36, 41, 44(1), 45(1), 50, 51(1), 123(8); New Tr 162(1); Torts 220, 242; Trial 349(2), 350.2, 351.5(3), 352.1(1), 352.4(1).

Glover v. Glover, TexCivApp–Eastland, 416 SW2d 500, ref nre.—Compromise 6(1); Home 57(3); Judgm 533; Spec Perf 12; Tender 28; Time 10(10); Ven & Pur 31.

Glover; Glover v., TexCivApp–Eastland, 416 SW2d 500, ref nre.—Compromise 6(1); Home 57(3); Judgm 533; Spec Perf 12; Tender 28; Time 10(10); Ven & Pur 31.

Glover v. Glover, TexCivApp–Eastland, 331 SW2d 804.— Wills 449, 579, 587(1), 610(1).

Glover; Glover v., TexCivApp–Eastland, 331 SW2d 804.— Wills 449, 579, 587(1), 610(1).

Glover v. Glover, TexCivApp–Eastland, 287 SW2d 287, dism.—Divorce 62(2), 66.

Glover; Glover v., TexCivApp–Eastland, 287 SW2d 287, dism.—Divorce 62(2), 66.

Glover; Hendon v., TexApp–Beaumont, 761 SW2d 120, writ den.—Damag 15; Fraud 58(3); Interest 66; Mtg 298(3).

Glover v. Henry, TexApp–Eastland, 749 SW2d 502.—App & E 1064.1(9), 1173(2); Evid 383(0.5); Hus & W 254, 256, 264(5), 270(9); Trial 205.

Glover; Hogue v., TexCivApp–Waco, 302 SW2d 757, ref nre.—Clubs 6, 11; Covenants 49, 69(1), 84; Dedi 60; Inj 89(3), 128(6); Nav Wat 1(3), 37(2), 37(4); Waters 61.

Glover v. IBP, Inc., CA5 (Tex), 334 F3d 471, reh and reh den 77 FedAppx 289.—Alt Disp Res 230, 235, 324, 374(1), 405; Fed Cts 415, 776, 850.1; Interest 39(2.20).

Glover v. Johnson, CA5 (Tex), 831 F2d 99.—Fed Cts 425; Lim of Act 75.

Glover v. Landes, TexCivApp–Hous (1 Dist), 530 SW2d 910, ref nre.—Abate & R 72(6); Ex & Ad 438(5), 438(6); Wills 68, 179, 267, 306.

Glover v. McFaddin, CA5 (Tex), 205 F2d 1, cert den 74 SCt 227, 346 US 900, 98 LEd 400, reh den 74 SCt 376, 346 US 940, 98 LEd 427.—Aliens 115; Estop 92(3); Pub Lands 223(7); Tresp to T T 6.1.

Glover v. McFaddin, EDTex, 99 FSupp 385, aff 205 F2d 1, cert den 74 SCt 227, 346 US 900, 98 LEd 400, reh den 74 SCt 376, 346 US 940, 98 LEd 427.—Fed Civ Proc 321, 341, 1703; Fed Cts 14.1, 287, 295; Judgm 680; Ten in C 38(1), 38(2), 38(6).

Glover v. McFaddin, EDTex, 81 FSupp 426.—Fed Civ Proc 39, 971, 1809; Ten in C 38(13).

Glover v. Moore, TexCivApp–Eastland, 544 SW2d 777.— App & E 965; Hus & W 49.3(7); Venue 42.

Glover v. Moore, TexCivApp–Eastland, 536 SW2d 78.— Guard & W 10; Infants 232.

Glover v. Moser, TexApp–Beaumont, 930 SW2d 940, reh overr, and reh overr, and writ den.—Venue 54, 72.

Glover v. National Ins. Underwriters, Tex, 545 SW2d 755.—Insurance 1822, 1835(2), 1836, 2274, 2332.

Glover; National Ins. Underwriters v., TexCivApp–El Paso, 535 SW2d 662, writ gr, rev 545 SW2d 755.— Insurance 2332; Trial 388(4).

Glover; Quarles v., TexCivApp–Houston, 335 SW2d 446. —App & E 1078(1); Pretrial Proc 504, 508.

Glover; Rachford v., TexCivApp–Texarkana, 123 SW2d 700, writ dism, correct.—App & E 374(3), 374(4), 395, 797(2), 846(5), 994(3); Ten in C 55(1); Tresp to T T 35(4), 41(3).

Glover; Sharp Custom Homes, Inc. v., TexApp–Dallas, 701 SW2d 24. See Curtis Sharp Custom Homes, Inc. v. Glover.

Glover; Simmonds v., TexCivApp–San Antonio, 283 SW2d 808.—Child C 261, 637, 659.

Glover v. State, TexCrimApp, 825 SW2d 127.—Crim Law 388.2.

Glover v. State, TexCrimApp, 566 SW2d 636.—Autos 355(10); Crim Law 556, 814(17); Sent & Pun 1381(5).

Glover v. State, TexCrimApp, 532 SW2d 346.—Crim Law 592, 593, 1106(3), 1166(7).

Glover v. State, TexCrimApp, 486 SW2d 783.—Crim Law 273.2(1).

Glover v. State, TexCrimApp, 470 SW2d 688.—Const Law 266(3.2), 4658(2), 4658(4), 4659(1); Crim Law 339.10(7), 603.2, 608.

Glover v. State, TexCrimApp, 453 SW2d 489.—Sent & Pun 2003.

Glover v. State, TexCrimApp, 346 SW2d 121, 171 TexCrim 156.—New Tr 26; Plead 427; Princ & S 157.

Glover v. State, TexCrimApp, 256 SW2d 107, 158 TexCrim 428.—False Pret 8, 30.

Glover v. State, TexCrimApp, 225 SW2d 195, 154 TexCrim 86.—False Pret 22, 48.

Glover v. State, TexCrimApp, 152 SW2d 747, 142 TexCrim 592, cert den 62 SCt 182, 314 US 676, 86 LEd 541. —Crim Law 448(16), 736(2), 739(2), 741(1), 742(1), 783(2), 1036.2, 1111(3), 1133, 1171.1(3), 1176; Witn 337(7), 359.

Glover v. State, TexCrimApp, 299 SW 240, 108 TexCrim 46.—Crim Law 720.5.

Glover v. State, TexApp–Houston (1 Dist), 689 SW2d 300. —Burg 41(3), 41(4).

Glover v. State, TexApp–Fort Worth, 870 SW2d 198, petition for discretionary review refused.—Autos 349(6), 349(10), 349(16).

Glover v. State, TexApp–Dallas, 787 SW2d 544, petition for discretionary review gr, aff 825 SW2d 127.—Assault 92(5); Crim Law 339.7(4), 339.8(4), 339.10(10), 388.2, 855(8), 868, 1134(2).

Glover v. State, TexApp–Dallas, 740 SW2d 94.—Crim Law 339.10(9); Ind & Inf 14.

Glover v. State, TexApp–Texarkana, 102 SW3d 754, reh overr, and petition for discretionary review refused.— Crim Law 363, 366(4), 417(15), 419(2.20), 552(1), 662.1, 662.8, 1139, 1159.3(2), 1159.4(2); Infants 20.

Glover v. State, TexApp–Beaumont, 956 SW2d 146, reh overr, and petition for discretionary review refused.— Crim Law 369.2(4), 1035(3), 1036.6, 1090(3).

Glover v. State, TexApp–Waco, 110 SW3d 549, petition for discretionary review refused.—Const Law 656, 657, 4673; Crim Law 957(1).

Glover v. Texas Bd. of Pardons & Paroles, CA5 (Tex), 88 FedAppx 720, cert den 125 SCt 159, 543 US 827, 160 LEd2d 42.—Fed Civ Proc 2734.

Glover v. Texas General Indem. Co., Tex, 619 SW2d 400. —App & E 836, 930(3), 989, 1083(6), 1177(7).

Glover; Texas General Indem. Co. v., TexCivApp–Beaumont, 612 SW2d 622, ref nre 619 SW2d 400.—Work Comp 809, 869, 893, 1663, 1728.

Glover v. Tide Equipment Co., TexCivApp–Hous (1 Dist), 506 SW2d 330.—App & E 1172(1), 1173(2); Pretrial Proc 588.

Glover v. Union Pacific R. Co., TexApp–Texarkana, 187 SW3d 201, review den.—Abate & R 52, 54, 55(1), 56; Action 13; Adv Poss 13, 60(3); App & E 192, 893(1); Deeds 117, 121; Estop 12, 15, 78(1); Fraud 17; Judgm 185.3(2); Land & Ten 66(2), 119(1); Lim of Act 43, 53(1), 95(8), 104(1), 104(2); Mines 49, 55(2), 55(4), 55(8), 73.1(2); Plead 104(1); Ten in C 10, 15(2), 15(7), 22, 49; Tresp to T T 1, 6, 6.1; Ven & Pur 218.

Glover v. U.S., CA5 (Tex), 488 F2d 318.—Int Rev 5117.

Glover v. U.S., NDTex, 349 FSupp 239, aff 488 F2d 318.— Int Rev 3560.

Glover v. W.R. Grace & Co., Inc., EDTex, 773 FSupp 964.—Rem of C 2, 81, 82, 103.

Glover, Anderson, Chandler & Uzick, L.L.P.; A.W. Wright & Associates, P.C. v., TexApp–Houston (14 Dist), 993 SW2d 466, reh overr, and review den.—App & E 758.3(11), 842(8); Atty & C 64; Contracts 143(2), 176(2), 338(1); Evid 448; Judgm 181(16), 181(19).

Glover-Dorsey v. University of Texas Medical Branch at Galveston, Texas, SDTex, 147 FSupp2d 656.—Civil R 1118, 1121, 1137, 1536, 1544, 1545, 1548, 1555; Fed Civ Proc 2497.1.

G.L.S., In re, TexApp–San Antonio, 185 SW3d 56.—App & E 946; Child S 106, 146, 450, 454, 498, 556(3), 556(5).

Gluck v. CellStar Corp., NDTex, 976 FSupp 542.—Fed Civ Proc 187.

Gluck v. Texas Animal Health Commission, TexCivApp–San Antonio, 501 SW2d 412, ref nre.—App & E 1178(1); Equity 16, 17; Inj 102, 118(1), 128(8), 190; Witn 37(2).

Gluckman; Utitz v., TexCivApp–Waco, 351 SW2d 608, writ dism.—Plead 111.3; Venue 7.5(3).

Glud v. Glud, TexApp–Waco, 641 SW2d 688.—Child C 24, 907; Divorce 252.2, 252.5(2), 285; Records 32.

Glud; Glud v., TexApp–Waco, 641 SW2d 688.—Child C 24, 907; Divorce 252.2, 252.5(2), 285; Records 32.

Glunz v. Hernandez, TexApp–San Antonio, 908 SW2d 253, reh overr, and writ den.—Judgm 17(1), 486(1), 489, 497(1), 499, 501, 518.

Glusing, Sharpe & Krueger; Yaklin v., TexApp–Corpus Christi, 875 SW2d 380.—App & E 854(1), 856(1), 863; Atty & C 63, 64, 105, 106, 129(2); Hus & W 257, 259; Judgm 181(1), 181(16), 185(2); Stip 14(4), 14(10).

Glyn-Jones; Bridgestone/Firestone, Inc. v., Tex, 878 SW2d 132.—Prod Liab 35.1, 81.5; Statut 190.

Glyn-Jones v. Bridgestone/Firestone, Inc., TexApp–Dallas, 857 SW2d 640, reh den, and writ gr, decision aff and remanded 878 SW2d 132.—Autos 243(17); Const Law 2311, 2314, 3957; Prod Liab 81.5.

Glynn Dodson, Inc.; Osteen v., TexApp–Waco, 875 SW2d 429, reh den, and writ den.—App & E 683, 907(1); Pretrial Proc 483, 506.1.

G. M., In Interest of, Tex, 596 SW2d 846.—Infants 178.

G. M., In Interest of, TexCivApp–Amarillo, 580 SW2d 65, writ gr, rev 596 SW2d 846.—Const Law 82(10), 1093; Infants 156, 173.1, 178, 179, 191, 232, 252.

G.M. v. Texas Dept. of Human Resources, TexApp–Austin, 717 SW2d 185.—Infants 132, 157, 178, 191, 248.1, 252.

GMAC Commercial Finance, L.L.C., In re, TexApp–Waco, 167 SW3d 940.—Mand 32; Records 32.

GMAC Commercial Mortg. Corp. v. East Texas Holdings, Inc., EDTex, 441 FSupp2d 801.—Fed Civ Proc 636, 1831; Fraud 3, 11(1), 12, 13(3), 17, 20, 24; Mtg 216.

GMAC Commercial Mortg. Corp.; Wentwood Woodside I, LP v., CA5 (Tex), 419 F3d 310.—Action 3; Contracts 93(1); Fed Civ Proc 840; Fed Cts 817; Insurance 2211; Mtg 201.

GMAC Mortg. Corp.; Langston v., TexApp–Eastland, 183 SW3d 479.—Subrog 1, 23(2), 26, 31(4).

GMAC Mortg. Corp. of Iowa; Wagner v., TexApp–Houston (1 Dist), 775 SW2d 71.—App & E 1074(3); Mtg 238.

GMC Superior Trucks, Inc. v. Irving Bank & Trust Co., TexCivApp–Waco, 463 SW2d 274.—Sec Tran 144; Statut 223.2(20), 223.4.

Gmenier; Gent v., TexCivApp–Waco, 435 SW2d 293.— Divorce 168, 231.

GMF Investments, Inc.; Whyte v., BkrtcyWDTex, 128 BR 974. See Fairchild Aircraft Corp., In re.

GMF Investments, Inc.; Whyte v., BkrtcyWDTex, 126 BR 717. See Fairchild Aircraft Corp., In re.

GM Gold & Diamonds LP v. Fabrege Co., Inc., SDTex, 489 FSupp2d 725.—Attach 1, 2, 73; Courts 17; Fed Cts 95.

G.M. Houser, Inc. v. Rodgers, TexApp–Dallas, 204 SW3d 836.—App & E 465(1), 465(2), 482, 937(4), 986, 989, 1024.5; Fraud Conv 16, 77, 101, 271, 295, 298(0.5).

G.M.P., Matter of, TexApp–Houston (14 Dist), 909 SW2d 198.—App & E 1026; Evid 106(1), 314(1); Infants 172, 173.1, 174, 176, 194.1, 195, 197, 207, 209, 210, 243, 252, 253; Witn 274(1), 349, 406, 414(2).

GMP, L.L.C; Potter v., TexApp–San Antonio, 141 SW3d 698, review dism.—App & E 893(1), 1004(1); Contracts 143(2), 143.5, 159, 176(2); Costs 194.32; Damag 96, 104, 119, 140; Evid 448; Ltd Liab Cos 29.

GMR Gymnastics Sales, Inc. v. Walz, TexApp–Fort Worth, 117 SW3d 57, reh overr, and petition stricken, and review den.—App & E 5, 654, 865, 907(4); Judgm 99, 124.

GMRI, Inc.; Plant v., SDTex, 10 FSupp2d 753.—Civil R 1530; Fed Civ Proc 1832, 2533.1.

G.M.S., In re, TexApp–Fort Worth, 991 SW2d 923, reh overr, and review den, and reh of petition for review overr.—Infants 246.

Gnade; Fagan v., TexApp–Waco, 61 SW3d 76.—App & E 893(1); Autos 252, 290; High 187(1); Judgm 181(27); Offic 114, 116, 119; States 112(1).

Gnade; U.S. Fire Ins. Company's v., TexApp–Waco, 134 SW3d 511, opinion after remand United States Fire Ins Co v. Gnade, 2005 WL 552473, review den, and reh of petition for review den.—App & E 347(1), 1106(0.5); Decl Judgm 392.1.

Gnadt; City of Sherman v., TexCivApp–Dallas, 337 SW2d 206.—App & E 690(4); Em Dom 141(1), 150, 172, 192, 202(1), 203(2), 259, 262(5); Evid 215(5), 502.

Gnat Robot Corp.; First City, Texas-Houston N.A. v., TexApp–Houston (1 Dist), 813 SW2d 230.—App & E 954(1); Banks 191.10, 191.15, 191.30.

G.N.B., Inc. v. Collin County Appraisal Dist., TexApp–Dallas, 862 SW2d 52, writ gr, rev 874 SW2d 659.—Const Law 3012, 3013, 3039, 3062, 3116, 3564, 4135, 4138(1), 4138(2); Statut 181(2), 212.7; Tax 2106, 2121, 2124, 2523.

GNC Pumps, Inc.; Chemlawn Services Corp. v., CAFed (Tex), 823 F2d 515, on remand 690 FSupp 1560, aff 856 F2d 202.—Pat 324.1.

GNC Pumps, Inc.; Chemlawn Services Corp. v., SDTex, 690 FSupp 1560, aff 856 F2d 202.—Trademarks 1030, 1032, 1064, 1065(2), 1119, 1426, 1436, 1704(2), 1704(3), 1704(9), 1707(6).

GNC Pumps, Inc.; Chemlawn Services Corp. v., SDTex, 652 FSupp 1382, rev 823 F2d 515, on remand 690 FSupp 1560, aff 856 F2d 202.—Commerce 62.12; Inj 138.6; Trademarks 1020, 1030, 1032, 1063, 1064, 1065(2), 1081, 1118, 1436, 1563, 1704(2), 1704(9).

Gnerer v. Johnson, TexApp–Texarkana, 227 SW3d 385.—App & E 931(3), 989, 1010.1(1), 1071.1(2); Frds St of 129(11); Lim of Act 46(9); Ven & Pur 82.

Gnesoulis, Ex parte, TexCivApp–Hous (14 Dist), 525 SW2d 205.—Const Law 4494; Contempt 40, 54(2); Divorce 269(1), 269(13); Judgm 215, 276.

GNG Gas Systems, Inc. v. Dean, TexApp–Amarillo, 921 SW2d 421, reh overr, and writ den.—App & E 852, 934(1); Contracts 108(2), 212(2); Corp 312(0.5); Estop 68(2); Frds St of 84; Judgm 181(7), 181(19).

GNK, Inc.; Costilla Energy, Inc. v., TexApp–Waco, 15 SW3d 579.—Bankr 2157.

GNLV Corp. v. Jackson, TexApp–Waco, 736 SW2d 893, writ den.—Inj 28; Judgm 815.

GNLV Corp.; Mauro v., TexApp–Texarkana, 982 SW2d 530, reh overr.—Negligl 1024, 1070.

Goad, Ex parte, Tex, 690 SW2d 894.—Divorce 199.7(10), 261, 269(9), 287; Lim of Act 127(11.1), 127(12).

Goad v. Goad, TexApp–Texarkana, 768 SW2d 356, writ den, cert den 110 SCt 722, 493 US 1021, 107 LEd2d 742.—Costs 2, 260(5); Divorce 254(2), 261; Evid 43(3).

Goad; Goad v., TexApp–Texarkana, 768 SW2d 356, writ den, cert den 110 SCt 722, 493 US 1021, 107 LEd2d 742.—Costs 2, 260(5); Divorce 254(2), 261; Evid 43(3).

Goad v. Rollins, CA5 (Tex), 921 F2d 69, cert den 111 SCt 1684, 500 US 905, 114 LEd2d 79.—Fed Civ Proc 2840; Inj 26(5).

Goad; Royal Ins. Co. of America v., TexApp–Fort Worth, 677 SW2d 795, ref nre.—App & E 930(3), 989, 1001(1), 1003(7), 1177(7); Trial 202; Work Comp 571, 1536, 1783, 1785, 1983.

Goad v. State, TexCrimApp, 464 SW2d 129.—Crim Law 304(1), 366(4), 700(1), 1037.2, 1044.1(8), 1130(2); Jury 110(1); Witn 319, 350, 405(1).

Goad v. State, TexCrimApp, 350 SW2d 548, 171 TexCrim 371.—Autos 355(6); Crim Law 1144.6.

Goad; Texas Emp. Ins. Ass'n v., TexApp–Tyler, 622 SW2d 477, ref nre.—App & E 930(1), 989; Trial 142; Work Comp 721, 723, 725, 1489, 1574, 1720.

Goad v. U.S., SDTex, 661 FSupp 1073, aff in part, vac in part 837 F2d 1096, cert den 108 SCt 1079, 485 US 906, 99 LEd2d 238.—Const Law 732, 2436, 3668, 4244; Cons Cred 38; Divorce 254(1); Exemp 49; Fed Civ Proc 2768, 2790; Fed Cts 1139, 1158.

Goad-Boles Motors, Inc. v. Victoria Paving Co., TexCivApp–Corpus Christi, 408 SW2d 943.—Damag 45, 120(1), 189.

Goans; Green v., TexCivApp–El Paso, 458 SW2d 705, ref nre 464 SW2d 104.—Wills 21, 316.2, 400.

Goans v. State, TexApp–Beaumont, 671 SW2d 904.—Sent & Pun 1801, 2009.

Goar v. State, TexApp–Houston (14 Dist), 68 SW3d 269, petition for discretionary review refused.—Autos 336, 355(8); Crim Law 361(1), 742(1), 1144.13(2.1), 1144.13(3), 1159.2(2), 1159.2(7), 1159.2(9).

G.O. Associates, Ltd.; Cole v., TexApp–Fort Worth, 847 SW2d 429, reh overr, and writ den.—Judgm 634, 666, 678(1), 720, 725(1).

Goatcher; Carrasco v., TexApp–El Paso, 623 SW2d 769.—App & E 930(1), 965, 989, 999(1), 1001(1), 1003(5); Health 823(7); Venue 42, 64, 68.

Goates v. Fortune Lincoln Mercury, Inc., TexCivApp–El Paso, 446 SW2d 913, ref nre.—Autos 213, 244(47), 244(58), 245(82).

Goates v. Ingram, TexCivApp–Eastland, 386 SW2d 654, ref nre.—App & E 842(1), 1003(11); Damag 130.3; Evid 588; New Tr 56, 140(3), 144.

Goatley; Texas Gauze Mills v., TexCivApp–Austin, 119 SW2d 887, writ dism.—Action 45(1), 48(3); Lim of Act 46(3), 178, 193; Trial 351.2(4).

Goats v. State, TexCrimApp, 366 SW2d 569.—Crim Law 1081(2), 1087.1(2).

Gobble; Bayou Properties Co. v., TexCivApp–Waco, 347 SW2d 314.—Venue 7.5(6).

Gobel v. City of Houston, TexCivApp–Hous (1 Dist), 455 SW2d 776, ref nre.—Autos 187(2), 247; Judgm 199(3.7); Mun Corp 734; Neglig 1717; Trial 139.1(3), 140(1), 350.6(3).

Gobel; State v., TexApp–Tyler, 988 SW2d 852.—Crim Law 994(4), 1081(4.1).

Gobeli Research Ltd. v. Apple Computer, Inc., EDTex, 384 FSupp2d 1016.—Pat 101(2), 101(8), 159, 161, 162, 165(1), 167(1), 167(1.1), 168(2.1), 314(5), 328(2).

Gobell v. State, TexCrimApp, 528 SW2d 223.—Crim Law 15; Larc 31; Sent & Pun 2004.

Gober, Matter of, CA5 (Tex), 100 F3d 1195.—Bankr 2045, 3342, 3360, 3766.1, 3782; Damag 91(1), 194, 202; Fed Cts 41, 47.1, 420, 813; Judgm 7, 15, 16, 106(1), 106(9), 111, 112, 126(1), 127, 129, 346, 486(1), 501, 540, 634, 650, 660.5, 713(1), 713(2), 720, 724, 725(1), 828.21(2); Lim of Act 41; Plead 430(2); Pretrial Proc 44.1; Set-Off 6, 8(1).

Gober v. LSMG, CA5 (Tex), 100 F3d 1195. See Gober, Matter of.

Gober v. State, TexCrimApp, 355 SW2d 520, 172 TexCrim 222.—Burg 41(1).

Gober v. State, TexCrimApp, 276 SW2d 310, 161 TexCrim 222.—Crim Law 942(2).

Gober v. State, TexCrimApp, 181 SW2d 279, 147 TexCrim 395.—Int Liq 36(4).

Gober v. State, TexApp–Austin, 917 SW2d 501.—Crim Law 1042, 1063(1), 1177.

Gober; Teairl v., TexCivApp–Austin, 257 SW2d 782, writ dism.—Brok 43(2), 88(14), 89; Trial 365.1(1).

Gober v. Terra + Corp., CA5 (Tex), 100 F3d 1195. See Gober, Matter of.

Gober v. Wright, TexApp–Houston (1 Dist), 838 SW2d 794, reh den, and writ den.—App & E 1001(3); Costs 207; Evid 570, 571(7); Land & Ten 125(2), 148(1), 156, 233(2).

Gobert; Sisters of Charity of Incarnate Word, Houston, Tex. v., TexApp–Houston (1 Dist), 992 SW2d 25.—App & E 760(1), 930(1), 1001(1), 1001(3), 1003(6), 1079;

Health 699, 700, 821(1), 821(5), 823(14); Neglig 232, 377, 379, 380, 387, 431, 433.

Gobert v. State, TexCrimApp, 717 SW2d 21.—Crim Law 641.12(2).

Gobert v. State, TexApp–Beaumont, 690 SW2d 107, petition for discretionary review gr, rev 717 SW2d 21.— Crim Law 641.3(4), 641.13(4), 713, 1166.10(1).

Gobert v. Texas Employers Ins. Ass'n, TexCivApp–Eastland, 491 SW2d 495, ref nre.—Judgm 199(3.15); Work Comp 1961, 1966, 1969.

Gobin v. State, TexApp–Fort Worth, 690 SW2d 702, petition for discretionary review refused.—Crim Law 37(8), 369.2(7), 1169.11.

Gobin v. State, TexApp–Fort Worth, 684 SW2d 802, opinion withdrawn 690 SW2d 702, petition for discretionary review refused.

Gochicoa v. Johnson, CA5 (Tex), 238 F3d 278, reh den.— Courts 90(2), 92; Crim Law 641.12(1), 641.13(1), 641.13(2.1), 641.13(6); Hab Corp 486(1), 709, 842, 846, 864(7).

Gochicoa v. Johnson, CA5 (Tex), 118 F3d 440, reh den, cert den 118 SCt 1063, 522 US 1121, 140 LEd2d 124, on remand 53 FSupp2d 943, aff in part, rev in part 238 F3d 278, reh den.—Crim Law 419(3), 662.8, 698(1), 720(3); Hab Corp 314, 404, 421, 422, 489.1, 490(1), 490(3), 842, 845, 846.

Gochicoa v. Johnson, WDTex, 53 FSupp2d 943, aff in part, rev in part 238 F3d 278, reh den.—Crim Law 641.13(1), 641.13(6).

Gochicoa v. Johnson, WDTex, 972 FSupp 380, rev 118 F3d 440, reh den, cert den 118 SCt 1063, 522 US 1121, 140 LEd2d 124, on remand 53 FSupp2d 943, aff in part, rev in part 238 F3d 278, reh den.—Controlled Subs 26, 27, 71; Crim Law 419(1.5), 662.7, 662.8, 713; Hab Corp 205, 313.1, 315, 422, 442, 481.

Gochman; Draper v., Tex, 400 SW2d 545, 17 ALR3d 953. —Land & Ten 92(1).

Gochman v. Draper, TexCivApp–Austin, 389 SW2d 571, writ gr, rev 400 SW2d 545, 17 ALR3d 953.—Interest 31, 39(1); Land & Ten 92(1), 92(4); Spec Perf 12, 127(1), 130; Ven & Pur 57, 228(1).

Godard; P & M Elec. Co. v., Tex, 478 SW2d 79.—Atty & C 20.1.

Godawa; Butt Grocery Co. v., TexApp–Corpus Christi, 763 SW2d 27. See H.E. Butt Grocery Co. v. Godawa.

Godawa; H.E. Butt Grocery Co. v., TexApp–Corpus Christi, 763 SW2d 27.—Neglig 1037(1), 1037(4), 1076, 1077, 1088, 1104(3), 1670.

Godbehere v. State, TexApp–Amarillo, 882 SW2d 57.— Crim Law 1081(2).

Godbey; National Medical Enterprises, Inc. v., Tex, 924 SW2d 123.—App & E 842(1); Atty & C 21.5(1), 21.15; Mand 4(4), 29.

Godbolt v. Hughes Tool Co., SDTex, 63 FRD 370.—Civil R 1009; Fed Civ Proc 36, 176, 184.10, 184.15.

Goddard v. State, TexApp–Amarillo, 154 SW3d 231.— Assault 96(3).

Goddard v. State, TexApp–Beaumont, 626 SW2d 145, petition for discretionary review refused.—Hab Corp 291.

Goddard v. Stowers, TexCivApp–Dallas, 272 SW2d 400.— Zoning 162, 168.

Goddard; Waco Federation of Women's Clubs v., TexCivApp–Waco, 275 SW2d 541.—Decl Judgm 129; Zoning 284, 435.

Goddard; Wilkinson v., TexCivApp–Waco, 278 SW2d 394. —App & E 1010.1(3); Fraud Conv 47; Sales 1(1), 332, 338, 339; Spec Perf 62; Trial 395(9).

Goddard Machinery Co. v. Industrial Equipment Repairs, Inc., TexCivApp–Waco, 351 SW2d 371.—Acct Action on 12.

Godde v. Wood, TexCivApp–Corpus Christi, 509 SW2d 435, ref nre.—App & E 201(1), 219(2), 237(6), 758.1, 761,

854(1), 930(3), 1070(2); Contracts 294; Lim of Act 43, 50(1), 66(12), 197(1).

Godeaux v. Dynamic Industries, Inc., EDTex, 864 FSupp 614.—Fed Civ Proc 2546; Seamen 2, 11(4), 29(5.4), 29(5.16); Ship 80.

Godeke, Ex parte, Tex, 355 SW2d 701, 163 Tex 387.— Abate & R 7; App & E 347(1); Child C 872; Courts 85(2), 247(1), 475(15); Judgm 386(1); New Tr 116.2.

Godeke; Hoppe v., TexApp–Austin, 774 SW2d 368, writ den.—Divorce 252.3(4); Hus & W 249(3); Offic 101.5(1).

Godell; Houchin v., TexApp–Fort Worth, 635 SW2d 427. —App & E 638, 758.3(5), 907(4); Plead 228.14; Trover 32(4).

Godfrey; Barnhouse Motors, Inc. v., TexCivApp–El Paso, 577 SW2d 378.—App & E 499(4), 758.3(10), 758.3(11), 1170.7, 1170.9(2.1), 1170.10; Evid 271(18), 318(1); Fraud 60, 64(1), 64(3), 64(4); Trial 219, 349(1); Witn 386, 388(10).

Godfrey v. Dretke, CA5 (Tex), 396 F3d 681, cert den 126 SCt 205, 546 US 880, 163 LEd2d 181, reh den 126 SCt 1162, 546 US 1146, 163 LEd2d 1015.—Const Law 2790, 2816; Courts 100(1); Hab Corp 230, 253, 603, 842, 846.

Godfrey; McCutchin v., TexCivApp–Texarkana, 361 SW2d 577, writ refused.—Mines 74(5).

Godfrey v. State, TexCrimApp, 261 SW2d 715.—Crim Law 1090.1(1).

Godfrey v. State, TexApp–Houston (14 Dist), 859 SW2d 583.—Crim Law 721(3), 1162, 1171.1(2.1), 1171.5.

Godfrey; State ex rel. Cobb v., TexCrimApp, 739 SW2d 47.—Crim Law 961; Mand 3(2.1), 4(4), 12, 61.

Godfrey; Texas Van Lines, Inc. v., TexCivApp–Dallas, 313 SW2d 922, ref nre.—App & E 846(5), 1011.1(2); Dep in Court 1; Parties 52; Wareh 22, 34(7).

Godfrey v. Travis Hardy Trucking Inc., TexApp–Houston (14 Dist), 634 SW2d 6, ref nre.—Damag 63.

Godfrey; U.S. v., CA5 (Tex), 25 F3d 263, cert den 115 SCt 429, 513 US 965, 130 LEd2d 342.—Crim Law 1139, 1158(1); Sent & Pun 906.

Godfrey L. Cabot, Inc. v. J. M. Huber Corp., CCA5 (Tex), 127 F2d 805.—Pat 165(3), 228.1.

Godfrey L. Cabot, Inc. v. J. M. Huber Corp., NDTex, 35 FSupp 373, aff 127 F2d 805.—Pat 112.1, 121, 191, 228.1, 312(1.1).

Godfrey Motor Co.; Municipal Assessment Co. v., TexCivApp–Amarillo, 404 SW2d 66, ref nre.—Mun Corp 485(1).

Godin v. State, TexCrimApp, 441 SW2d 196.—Crim Law 37(1).

Godin v. U.S., CA5 (Tex), 495 F2d 560, cert den 95 SCt 308, 419 US 995, 42 LEd2d 268.—Crim Law 1068.5.

Godine v. State, TexApp–Houston (14 Dist), 874 SW2d 197.—Const Law 3309; Crim Law 1031(3), 1043(1), 1134(5), 1144.12, 1152(2); Jury 33(5.15), 121, 131(1), 131(3), 131(4), 131(17).

Godinet v. Thomas, TexApp–Houston (14 Dist), 824 SW2d 632, writ den.—Civil R 1320; Work Comp 2084.

Godinez; Skennion v., CA5 (Tex), 159 FedAppx 598.— Civil R 1137, 1171, 1209, 1535, 1537, 1539.

Godinez; Ysleta Independent School Dist. v., TexApp–El Paso, 998 SW2d 700, reh overr.—Alt Disp Res 112, 113, 137, 141, 143, 146, 213(5); App & E 893(1), 949.

Godkins; U.S. v., CA5 (Tex), 527 F2d 1321.—Crim Law 347, 370, 1166.22(6), 1169.9, 1170(1); Witn 4.

Godley v. Duval County, TexCivApp–San Antonio, 361 SW2d 629.—App & E 846(2), 846(5), 954(1), 954(2); Counties 47, 81.1, 106, 196(3); Inj 132, 135, 147.

Godley Independent School Dist. v. Woods, TexApp–Waco, 21 SW3d 656, review den.—App & E 893(1); Courts 32; Plead 104(1), 111.48, 228.14, 228.23; Schools 115, 144(4).

Godlin; Hoffman v., TexApp–El Paso, 128 SW2d 865. —Abate & R 81, 82; Mines 99(2); Partners 108, 110.

Godoy v. State, TexApp–Houston (1 Dist), 122 SW3d 315, reh overr, and petition for discretionary review refused.

—Crim Law 273(2), 553, 554, 641.13(7), 742(1), 913(1), 956(1), 956(2), 959, 1026.10(2.1), 1026.10(4), 1042, 1134(10), 1156(1), 1158(1); Hab Corp 290.1; Sent & Pun 2009.

Godsey v. State, TexCrimApp, 719 SW2d 578.—Assault 48, 56, 96(1); Crim Law 795(2.10); Homic 561(2), 908; Ind & Inf 191(4).

Godsey v. State, TexApp–San Antonio, 640 SW2d 336, petition for discretionary review gr, rev 719 SW2d 578.—Assault 96(1), 96(7); Homic 1168.

Godsey v. State, TexApp–Waco, 989 SW2d 482, petition for discretionary review refused.—Assault 82, 91; Const Law 4527(2), 4725, 4771; Crim Law 37.15(2), 273.1(2), 304(1), 304(6), 388.1, 415(1), 435, 439, 472, 476.6, 564(1), 753.2(2), 867, 1023.5, 1043(3), 1045, 1169.1(10), 1169.2(7), 1170.5(1); Double J 60.1, 119; Witn 318.

Godsey; Tarver v., TexCivApp–Beaumont, 82 SW2d 1031, writ refused.—App & E 397, 799; Bills & N 300; Deeds 19.

Godsey; Texas Indem. Ins. Co. v., TexCivApp–El Paso, 143 SW2d 639, writ refused.—App & E 758.3(1), 760(1), 1039(13), 1040(11); Damag 221(3), 221(5.1); Plead 16; Trial 351.5(1); Work Comp 558, 1919, 1920, 1926, 1927.

Godt, In re, TexApp–Corpus Christi, 28 SW3d 732, reh overr.—Alt Disp Res 112, 114, 133(2), 134(1); Atty & C 129(1); Commerce 80.5; Contracts 143(3), 143.5, 147(2), 147(3); Mand 4(1), 12, 28, 48; Trial 404(1).

Godwin v. Aldine Independent School Dist., TexApp–Houston (1 Dist), 961 SW2d 219, reh overr, and review den, and reh of petition for review overr, opinion supplemented on reh 1997 WL 514728.—App & E 893(1); Tax 2699(1), 2699(5), 2723.

Godwin; Allstate Ins. Co. v., TexCivApp–Hous (1 Dist), 426 SW2d 652.—Evid 314(5); Work Comp 1385, 1392, 1726, 1927.

Godwin; Burgin v., TexCivApp–Amarillo, 167 SW2d 614, writ refused wom.—Atty & C 114, 123(1), 147, 166(3); Equity 57; Frds St of 119(2), 129(1), 142, 159; Home 118(5).

Godwin; Eldredge v., TexCivApp–Dallas, 263 SW2d 598, ref nre.—Deeds 38(1), 111; Frds St of 110(1), 158(3); Trial 76; Ven & Pur 22, 62, 72, 170.

Godwin v. Federal Sav. and Loan Ins. Corp., CA5 (Tex), 806 F2d 1290.—Fed Civ Proc 2651.1, 2659.

Godwin; Hanna v., TexApp–El Paso, 876 SW2d 454.—Action 13; App & E 151(2), 158(1), 781(1), 781(4), 877(1), 877(2); Const Law 2600; Work Comp 1981.

Godwin; McCullough v., TexApp–Tyler, 214 SW3d 793, reh overr.—Aband L P 1.1; App & E 863, 1079; Const Law 990, 996, 1030, 4391, 4393, 4394; Damag 91.5(1); Death 14(1); Judgm 181(6), 181(12), 183, 185(2), 185(5), 185.3(2); Neglig 210, 213, 215, 216, 233, 273, 1692; Parent & C 11, 13.5(4), 15; Ship 166(1); Statut 212.3.

Godwin v. Oliver, TexCivApp–Amarillo, 156 SW2d 992.—App & E 1176(1); Plead 111.3; Venue 5.3(1), 5.5.

Godwin v. Pate, TexApp–Dallas, 667 SW2d 201, ref nre.—App & E 981; Insurance 1791(4); New Tr 99, 108(2); Subrog 1, 28.

Godwin v. Roberts, TexCivApp–Galveston, 213 SW2d 571, ref nre.—App & E 927(7), 989; Contracts 248; Evid 448, 461(1); Trial 139.1(7), 178.

Godwin; Scott v., TexApp–Corpus Christi, 147 SW3d 609, rule 537(f) motion dism.—App & E 66, 70(8), 837(4), 863, 893(1), 916(1); Civil R 1135, 1245, 1376(1), 1376(2), 1376(10), 1430; Const Law 1928, 1929, 1934, 1943, 1947, 1955; Courts 32, 35; Judgm 181(21), 181(27); Offic 61, 69.7, 119; Plead 104(1), 111.48; States 53.

Godwin v. Stanley, TexCivApp–Amarillo, 331 SW2d 341, ref nre.—Assault 12, 15, 35; Chat Mtg 158.1.

Godwin v. State, TexApp–Houston (14 Dist), 899 SW2d 387, petition for discretionary review refused.—Crim Law 406(1), 406(5), 409(6.1), 641.13(1), 641.13(2.1), 1144.13(2.1), 1159.2(7); Homic 525, 571, 1184, 1186, 1188.

Godwin v. Texas Emp. Ins. Ass'n, Tex, 195 SW2d 347, 145 Tex 100.—App & E 361(5); Cert 69; Damag 221(8); Work Comp 1971.

Godwin; Texas Emp. Ins. Ass'n v., TexCivApp–Dallas, 194 SW2d 593, rev 195 SW2d 347, 145 Tex 100.—Jury 91; Work Comp 874, 876, 1941.

Godwin; Watson v., TexCivApp–Amarillo, 425 SW2d 424, ref nre.—App & E 286, 920(2), 1078(1); Frds St of 5; Judgm 185(4), 185.3(8); Pretrial Proc 478, 479, 714, 723.1.

Godwin v. Williams, NDTex, 293 FSupp 770.—Civil R 1376(6), 1376(8); Consp 7.5(1); Judges 36; Sheriffs 99.

Godwin and Carlton, P.C.; Solomon v., NDTex, 898 FSupp 415.—Civil R 1464, 1473; Fed Civ Proc 1137, 1145.1.

Godwin White & Gruber PC v. Deuschle, CA5 (Tex), 87 FedAppx 338.—Atty & C 151.

Goebel v. Brandley, TexApp–Houston (14 Dist), 174 SW3d 359, review den.—App & E 893(1), 901, 1175(1); Exemp 48(2); Fraud Conv 51(1), 51(2); Judgm 185(2), 185(5).

Goebel v. Brandley, TexApp–Houston (14 Dist), 76 SW3d 652.—App & E 931(1), 984(5), 1010.2, 1026, 1071.1(1), 1071.2, 1178(1); Bound 26, 45; Costs 13, 194.18, 194.25, 194.40, 207, 252; Decl Judgm 181, 345.1; Tresp to T T 1.

Goebel; State v., TexApp–Houston (14 Dist), 761 SW2d 66, petition for discretionary review refused.—Controlled Subs 9.

Goebel; Youngblood's, Inc. v., TexApp–Waco, 404 SW2d 617, ref nre.—App & E 1170.10; Lim of Act 55(6).

Goebel Brewing Co.; Gieb v., TexCivApp–Fort Worth, 176 SW2d 975, writ refused wom.—App & E 846(5); Contracts 88; Evid 461(1); Guar 16(2), 25(3); Sales 291.

Goeddertz; Queen v., TexApp–Beaumont, 48 SW3d 928, reh overr.—Infants 155, 230.1; Judgm 335(1), 335(3).

Goedeke and Cleasey; Duncan v., SDTex, 837 FSupp 846.—Civil R 1327, 1362; Const Law 1284, 4460; U S 50.5(2), 50.10(1), 50.10(3), 78(5.1), 125(3), 125(5), 127(2); War 509.

Goehring v. State, TexCrimApp, 627 SW2d 159.—Controlled Subs 134; Crim Law 1184(4.1); Searches 24, 164.

Goeke v. Baumgart, TexCivApp–Beaumont, 92 SW2d 1047.—App & E 692(1), 728(1), 742(4), 1056.1(4.1), 1056.2, 1071.5; Fraud Conv 118(3), 299(13); Insurance 3474; Trial 352.4(4).

Goeke v. Houston Lighting & Power Co., Tex, 797 SW2d 12.—Admin Law 486, 784.1; Electricity 8.1(4).

Goeke v. Houston Lighting & Power Co., TexApp–Austin, 761 SW2d 835, writ gr, rev 797 SW2d 12.—Admin Law 485, 507, 746, 784.1, 819, 820; Electricity 8.1(1), 8.1(4).

Goelz v. J. K. & Susie L. Wadley Research Institute and Blood Bank, TexCivApp–Dallas, 350 SW2d 573, ref nre.—Char 1, 45(2); Death 14(1); Sales 427.

Goelz; Turner v., TexCivApp–Waco, 296 SW2d 596, ref nre.—Adop 14, 16; Child C 76, 921(1).

Goen v. Hamilton, TexCivApp–Amarillo, 159 SW2d 231.—Brok 43(2), 82(1); Frds St of 148(1); Statut 223.5(4).

Goen; Hudgens v., TexApp–Fort Worth, 673 SW2d 420, ref nre.—Antitrust 43, 103(1); Judgm 199(1); Trademarks 1104, 1420, 1437, 1696, 1714(3).

Goen v. Trinity Universal Ins. Co. of Kansas, Inc., TexApp–Texarkana, 715 SW2d 124.—Insurance 2784; Judgm 190.

Goerig; Young v., TexCivApp–Galveston, 265 SW2d 842.—App & E 78(1).

Goerlitz; City of Midland v., Tex, 201 SW3d 689.—Mun Corp 254.

Goerlitz v. City of Midland, TexApp–El Paso, 101 SW3d 573, review gr, rev 201 SW3d 689.—App & E 863, 893(1), 911.3; Courts 35; Mun Corp 254; Plead 104(1);

Pretrial Proc 554; States 191.1, 191.4(1), 191.6(2), 191.6(3), 191.8(1), 191.9(1).

Goerlitz v. Clear Lake Dodge, CA5 (Tex), 60 F3d 1146. See E.E.O.C. v. Clear Lake Dodge.

Goerlitz v. Clear Lake Dodge, CA5 (Tex), 25 F3d 265. See E.E.O.C. v. Clear Lake Dodge.

Goerlitz; E.E.O.C. v., CA5 (Tex), 60 F3d 1146. See E.E.O.C. v. Clear Lake Dodge.

Goerlitz; E.E.O.C. v., CA5 (Tex), 25 F3d 265. See E.E.O.C. v. Clear Lake Dodge.

Goerner v. Barnes, SDTex, 730 FSupp 767.—Fed Cts 47.1, 65.

Goerner; Great Southern Life Ins. Co. v., TexCivApp–Austin, 106 SW2d 750.—Corp 666; Venue 74.

Goesl; Daniel v., Tex, 341 SW2d 892, 161 Tex 490.—App & E 954(1), 954(2); Contracts 97(1); Estop 92(2); Inj 126, 138.39.

Goesl; Daniel v., TexCivApp–Texarkana, 336 SW2d 890, writ gr, rev 341 SW2d 892, 161 Tex 490.—App & E 863, 920(3), 954(2), 1024.2; Inj 126, 147.

Goeth v. McCollum, TexCivApp–San Antonio, 94 SW2d 781.—Ex & Ad 214, 221(3), 221(4.1), 451(2).

Goeth; Walter v., TexCivApp–San Antonio, 177 SW2d 794, writ refused wom.—Wills 318(3), 473.

Goethe v. Gulf Lumber Co., TexCivApp–Galveston, 161 SW2d 514.—App & E 1070(2); Neglig 1750.

Goettee v. McConnell, TexCivApp–Beaumont, 535 SW2d 396.—Judgm 181(11).

Goettee; Vandever v., TexApp–Houston (14 Dist), 678 SW2d 630, ref nre.—App & E 232(2), 854(2), 1071.1(1), 1071.1(6); Brok 11, 39, 56(1); Costs 194.32; Impl & C C 30; Trial 46(1).

Goetz; Board of Regents of State Teachers Colleges of Tex. v., Tex, 453SW2d 290, appeal dism, cert den Goetz v. Board of Regents State Senior Colleges, 91 SCt 43, 400 US 807, 27 LEd2d 36.—Evid 397(1), 399.

Goetz v. Board of Regents of State Teachers Colleges of Tex., TexCivApp–Austin, 440 SW2d 892, rev 453 SW2d 290, appeal dism, cert den 91 SCt 43, 400 US 807, 27 LEd2d 36.—Colleges 5; Contracts 164; Interest 39(1); Stip 14(1).

Goetz v. Goetz, TexApp–Houston (14 Dist), 130 SW3d 359, review den.—Alt Disp Res 149, 221; Divorce 256; Hus & W 266.2(1).

Goetz; Goetz v., TexApp–Houston (14 Dist), 130 SW3d 359, review den.—Alt Disp Res 149, 221; Divorce 256; Hus & W 266.2(1).

Goetz v. Goetz, TexCivApp–Dallas, 567 SW2d 892.—Corp 1.4(1), 1.4(3), 1.4(5); Divorce 252.2, 252.3(1), 252.3(5), 279, 286(2), 287, 321 1/2, 322; Sec Tran 2, 141.

Goetz; Goetz v., TexCivApp–Dallas, 567 SW2d 892.—Corp 1.4(1), 1.4(3), 1.4(5); Divorce 252.2, 252.3(1), 252.3(5), 279, 286(2), 287, 321 1/2, 322; Sec Tran 2, 141.

Goetz v. Goetz, TexCivApp–Dallas, 534 SW2d 716, appeal after remand 567 SW2d 892.—App & E 597(1); Costs 256(4); Divorce 144, 160, 184(12), 252.1, 253(4), 286(9); Evid 370(1), 397(3); Jury 19.10(1); Trial 352.20.

Goetz; Goetz v., TexCivApp–Dallas, 534 SW2d 716, appeal after remand 567 SW2d 892.—App & E 597(1); Costs 256(4); Divorce 144, 160, 184(12), 252.1, 253(4), 286(9); Evid 370(1), 397(3); Jury 19.10(1); Trial 352.20.

Goetz v. Lutheran Social Service of Texas, Inc., TexCivApp–Austin, 579 SW2d 82.—Adop 13, 15.

Goetz; Maryland Cas. Co. v., TexCivApp–Amarillo, 337 SW2d 749.—App & E 758.3(4); Damag 221(3); Trial 105(2); Work Comp 840, 1172, 1404, 1648.

Goetz; Pletcher v., TexApp–Fort Worth, 9 SW3d 442, review den, and reh of petition for review overr.—Contracts 1; Costs 194.16; Divorce 221, 224, 228, 249.1, 249.2, 252.1, 252.3(1), 253(2), 286(2), 286(5), 286(8); Hus & W 278(1), 279(1), 281.

Goetz v. Synthesys Technologies, Inc., CA5 (Tex), 415 F3d 481.—Fed Cts 776; Proc 73, 81, 82.

Goetz v. Synthesys Technologies, Inc., WDTex, 329 FSupp2d 828, rev and remanded 415 F3d 481.—Fed Civ Proc 2392, 2393, 2651.1; Fed Cts 95; Proc 72, 73, 75, 81, 82.

Goetz v. Synthesys Technologies, Inc., WDTex, 286 FSupp2d 796.—Consp 1.1; Corp 306; Fed Civ Proc 751, 2491.7, 2498; Labor & Emp 788, 2227, 2397(1); Torts 220.

Goetz; U.S. v., CA5 (Tex), 153 FedAppx 918.—Arrest 63.4(5); Sent & Pun 789.

Goetzmann; Thompson v., CA5 (Tex), 337 F3d 489.—Fed Cts 766, 776; Health 541, 544, 545; Statut 188, 190, 208, 217.4, 219(6.1).

Goetzmann; Thompson v., CA5 (Tex), 315 F3d 457, opinion withdrawn and superseded on denial of reh 337 F3d 489.

Goff, In re, CA5 (Tex), 250 F3d 273.—Crim Law 1602; Hab Corp 406, 898(2).

Goff, In re, CA5 (Tex), 812 F2d 931.—Bankr 3770; Fed Cts 611, 614; Judgm 780(5); Trusts 52.

Goff, In re, BkrtcyWDTex, 57 BR 442.—Int Rev 4030.

Goff, Matter of, CA5 (Tex), 706 F2d 574.—Bankr 2363.1, 2531, 2533, 2547, 2548, 2558; Int Rev 3593; States 18.51; Trusts 152.

Goff v. Branch, TexApp–San Antonio, 821 SW2d 732, writ den.—App & E 497(1), 684(4), 962; Pretrial Proc 583, 587, 696.1, 697, 699.

Goff v. Continental Oil Co., CA5 (Tex), 678 F2d 593, on remand 1983 WL 467.—Civil R 1242, 1243, 1246, 1535, 1548; Evid 99; Fed Cts 612.1, 823, 858, 901.1.

Goff v. Jones, CA5 (Tex), 500 F2d 395.—Civil R 1395(7); Const Law 4733(2); Fed Civ Proc 1788.10; Fed Cts 817; Prisons 4(10.1).

Goff v. Lubbock Bldg. Products, TexCivApp–Amarillo, 267 SW2d 201, ref nre.—Autos 245(1), 249; Damag 92; Death 93; Judgm 199(3.7).

Goff; McGill v., CA5 (Tex), 17 F3d 729.—Fraud 38; Lim of Act 100(1), 100(12), 124, 127(12); U S Mag 26, 31.

Goff v. Nevill, TexCivApp–El Paso, 118 SW2d 1004.—Child C 579, 641.

Goff v. Robert, TexCivApp–Waco, 348 SW2d 727, ref nre.—App & E 930(4); Bound 46(2), 46(3).

Goff v. Southmost Sav. & Loan Ass'n, TexApp–Corpus Christi, 758 SW2d 822, writ den.—App & E 609, 1106(5); Contracts 93(5); Evid 450(11); Guar 36(1), 77(2), 78(2), 89; Ref of Inst 19(1), 36(1); Witn 37(2).

Goff v. State, TexCrimApp, 931 SW2d 537, reh den, cert den 117 SCt 1438, 520 US 1171, 137 LEd2d 545, stay den In re Goff, 250 F3d 273.—Crim Law 59(1), 338(1), 350, 636(1), 641.12(1), 661, 683(1), 713, 720(1), 721(1), 721(3), 792(1), 814(19), 1030(1), 1043(3), 1152(1), 1153(1), 1166.10(1), 1166.14, 1166.16, 1171.1(3); Homic 1465, 1466; Jury 33(5.15), 75(1), 83(1), 131(1), 131(3), 131(4), 131(8); Sent & Pun 1480, 1756, 1757, 1763, 1780(2), 1789(9); Witn 274(1).

Goff v. State, TexCrimApp, 777 SW2d 418.—Controlled Subs 77; Crim Law 552(3).

Goff v. State, TexCrimApp, 720 SW2d 94.—Crim Law 778(2).

Goff v. State, TexCrimApp, 446 SW2d 313.—Autos 355(6), 359; Crim Law 1171.8(1).

Goff v. State, TexApp–Austin, 794 SW2d 126, petition for discretionary review refused.—Crim Law 720(7.1).

Goff v. State, TexApp–Texarkana, 727 SW2d 603, petition for discretionary review gr, rev 777 SW2d 418.—Controlled Subs 73, 77; Crim Law 1167(1); Ind & Inf 144.

Goff v. State, TexApp–Houston (14 Dist), 681 SW2d 619, petition for discretionary review refused, and reh gr, aff 720 SW2d 94.—Crim Law 351(4), 351(9), 478(1), 479, 531(3), 577.5, 577.14, 577.16(9), 728(2), 728(4), 1158(1), 1172.7; Homic 834, 1028, 1333, 1458, 1465; Ind & Inf 91(1), 110(2); Witn 372(2).

Goff v. State Bd. of Ins., TexCivApp–Dallas, 319 SW2d 383.—App & E 66; Insurance 1070, 1622; Plead 111.46.

Goff v. Texas Emp. Ins. Ass'n, TexCivApp–Fort Worth, 278 SW2d 326, ref nre.—Work Comp 946, 1930, 1932.

Goff v. Texas Instruments Inc., NDTex, 429 FSupp 973. —Civil R 1484, 1487, 1590.

Goff v. Tuchscherer, Tex, 627 SW2d 397.—App & E 344, 347(1); Courts 85(1).

Goff v. Tuchscherer, TexCivApp–Corpus Christi, 614 SW2d 934, writ dism woj, rev 627 SW2d 397.—App & E 347(1), 356, 387(3); Plead 111.47.

Goff; U.S. v., CA5 (Tex), 847 F2d 149, opinion mod on reh, cert den Kuntze v. US, 109 SCt 324, 488 US 932, 102 LEd2d 341, appeal after remand US v Schoenhoff, 884 F2d 574, appeal after remand 919 F2d 936.—Consp 23.1, 24(1), 24(2), 24(3), 24(5), 24.15, 44.2, 45, 47(1), 47(2), 47(12); Controlled Subs 39, 81, 86, 100(1), 100(2); Crim Law 295, 371(1), 394.5(2), 404.65, 444, 636(8), 700(4), 713, 719(1), 730(1), 742(1), 785(9), 872, 1035(10), 1036.1(3.1), 1037.1(2), 1171.1(1), 1171.1(3), 1171.1(4), 1171.1(6), 1171.3, 1174(6); Double J 146, 151(5); Searches 67.1, 164; Sent & Pun 645; Witn 102, 369.

Goff; U.S. v., CA5 (Tex), 155 FedAppx 773, cert den 126 SCt 1178, 546 US 1154, 163 LEd2d 1136.—Crim Law 369.2(5), 396(1), 673(5); Obscen 17.

Goffney v. Carr, CA5 (Tex), 78 FedAppx 974.—Fed Cts 574, 576.1.

Goffney v. Lowry, Tex, 554 SW2d 157.—App & E 389(1), 389(3); Courts 209(2), 247(1); Mand 9.

Goffney v. Rabson, TexApp–Houston (14 Dist), 56 SW3d 186, reh overr, and review den, and reh of petition for review den.—Action 53(2); Atty & C 63, 106, 107, 113, 117, 129(2), 129(3); Judgm 251(3).

Goffney v. State, TexCrimApp, 843 SW2d 583.—Crim Law 641.7(1), 1086.11, 1144.10; Jury 29(6).

Goffney v. State, TexCrimApp, 489 SW2d 882.—Crim Law 275; Rape 51(1).

Goffney v. State, TexApp–Waco, 812 SW2d 351, petition for discretionary review gr, aff 843 SW2d 583.—Crim Law 641.4(4), 641.7(1), 1144.10.

Goforth, In re, CA5 (Tex), 179 F3d 390, reh den.—Bankr 2021.1, 2834.

Goforth v. Alvey, Tex, 271 SW2d 404, 153 Tex 449.—Trial 125(1).

Goforth; Alvey v., TexCivApp–Fort Worth, 263 SW2d 313, rev 271 SW2d 404, 153 Tex 449.—App & E 1029, 1122(2), 1170.6, 1177(7); Autos 245(40.1); Trial 105(1), 122, 129, 350.1, 361.

Goforth; Demo v., TexCivApp–San Antonio, 556 SW2d 128.—App & E 241, 282, 302(1), 302(5); Judgm 801.

Goforth v. Goforth, TexCivApp–Eastland, 335 SW2d 281. —App & E 907(3); Divorce 62(2), 66, 109.2, 124.3.

Goforth; Goforth v., TexCivApp–Eastland, 335 SW2d 281.—App & E 907(3); Divorce 62(2), 66, 109.2, 124.3.

Goforth; Hall v., SDTex, 224 BR 580, aff In re Goforth, 179 F3d 390, reh den.—Bankr 2834.

Goforth v. State, TexApp–Eastland, 883 SW2d 251, reh overr.—Controlled Subs 22, 67.

Goforth; Texas Emp. Ins. Ass'n v., TexCivApp–Eastland, 307 SW2d 610, ref nre.—App & E 1170.6; Damag 221(3), 221(6); Work Comp 804, 1615, 1926, 1927, 1968(5).

Goggans v. Green, TexCivApp–Texarkana, 165 SW2d 928. —Evid 333(3); Execution 140, 275(3), 283.

Goggans v. Simmons, TexCivApp–Fort Worth, 319 SW2d 442, ref nre.—Courts 89; Hus & W 273(5); Wills 449, 579, 588.

Goggin v. Grimes, TexApp–Houston (14 Dist), 969 SW2d 135.—Afft 1; App & E 852; Atty & C 76(1), 105; Judgm 185.1(3), 185.1(4), 185.3(4), 585(4); Torts 138.

Goggin; Johnston v., CA5 (Tex), 323 F2d 36.—Trusts 102(1), 374.

Goggin v. Moss, NDTex, 221 FSupp 905, aff Johnston v. Goggin, 323 F2d 36.—Brok 23; Damag 91(1); Trusts 102(1), 374.

Goggins v. Leo, TexApp–Houston (14 Dist), 849 SW2d 373.—App & E 931(1), 1010.1(3), 1031(1); Condo 15, 17; Courts 472.7; Forci E & D 4, 29(3); J P 141(2); Land & Ten 117; Plead 111.42(4.1); Tax 3075; Tresp to T T 11.

Gogolin & Stelter v. Karn's Auto Imports, Inc., CA5 (Tex), 886 F2d 100, cert den 110 SCt 1480, 494 US 1031, 108 LEd2d 617.—Fed Civ Proc 131, 751; Fed Cts 78, 92, 932.1.

Goheen v. Koester, TexApp–Dallas, 794 SW2d 830, writ den.—Child 67, 75; Const Law 3738.

Gohlke v. Davis, TexCivApp–San Antonio, 279 SW2d 369, ref nre.—Frds St of 110(1), 118(4); Spec Perf 10(1), 22; Ven & Pur 219.

Gohlke; Ward v., TexCivApp–San Antonio, 279 SW2d 422, writ refused.—Can of Inst 3; Estop 118; Evid 461(1); Mines 79.1(5); Ref of Inst 19(1), 45(9); Wills 577, 782(3).

Gohman; Plata v., TexCivApp–San Antonio, 359 SW2d 163, ref nre.—Autos 206, 218, 244(51), 245(72); Neglig 1693.

Gohman; Tippit v., TexCivApp–El Paso, 145 SW2d 908, writ dism, correct.—App & E 1125; Autos 201(8), 224(4), 226(2), 227.5, 244(56), 245(62).

Gohmert; Smith v., TexCrimApp, 962 SW2d 590, reh den 976 SW2d 212.—Hab Corp 275.1; Mand 1, 3(2.1), 3(3), 7, 12.

Gohmert; Southwestern Bell Tel. Co. v., TexCivApp–San Antonio, 222 SW2d 644.—Inj 11, 67; Mun Corp 57, 85; Tel 992.

Gohring v. State, TexApp–Beaumont, 967 SW2d 459.—Crim Law 367, 565, 627.6(4), 1043(2), 1153(1), 1169.1(9), 1169.2(6).

Goidl v. Advance Neckwear Co., Tex, 123 SW2d 865, 132 Tex 308.—Trademarks 1042, 1184, 1526.

Goidl; Advance Neckwear Co. v., TexCivApp–Dallas, 77 SW2d 598.—Trademarks 1707(1).

Goidl v. Advance Neckwear Co., TexCivApp–El Paso, 98 SW2d 364, aff 123 SW2d 865, 132 Tex 308.—App & E 1060.1(3); Trademarks 1526, 1629(3).

Goidl; Lazidis v., TexCivApp–Dallas, 564 SW2d 453.—Guar 77(3); Judgm 185.1(2), 185.1(4), 185.3(16); Mtg 218.4; Sec Tran 226, 228, 240.

Goidl v. North American Mortg. Investors, TexCivApp–Dallas, 564 SW2d 493.—Contracts 143.5, 168; Judgm 181(25); Ven & Pur 253, 260(1), 266(8), 269.

Goin; Lloyds' Cas., Insurer v., TexCivApp–Fort Worth, 212 SW2d 886.—Plead 111.8, 111.9, 111.37, 111.42(3).

GO Industries, Inc.; Lund Industries, Inc. v., CAFed (Tex), 938 F2d 1273.—Fed Cts 815; Inj 235; Pat 226.6, 226.8, 252, 298, 327(12).

Goines v. State, TexApp–Houston (1 Dist), 888 SW2d 574, petition for discretionary review refused.—Arrest 63.5(4), 63.5(7), 63.5(9); Crim Law 394.5(4), 394.6(4), 394.6(5), 1144.12, 1153(1), 1158(4); Searches 23, 171, 180, 181, 182, 183.

Goines; Texas Emp. Ins. Ass'n v., TexCivApp–Beaumont, 202 SW2d 487, ref nre.—Damag 221(5.1); Trial 115(2); Work Comp 51, 1192, 1847, 1926.

Going; Harris County v., TexApp–Houston (1 Dist), 896 SW2d 305, reh overr, and writ den.—Action 1, 3; App & E 866(3), 878(1), 927(7); Civil R 1345, 1351(1), 1376(3), 1376(4), 1719; Const Law 1493; Counties 146; Lim of Act 58(1); Mun Corp 742(2); Trial 142.

Goings; City of Houston v., TexApp–Houston (14 Dist), 795 SW2d 829, writ den.—App & E 966(1), 989, 994(2), 999(1), 1003(3), 1003(7), 1068(1); Bridges 4; Contrib 5(5), 5(6.1); Evid 427; Indem 30(1), 33(5), 67; Mun Corp 733(2), 742(4), 742(6), 751(1); Neglig 1683; Pretrial Proc 15, 313, 713, 719.

Goings v. Falcon Carriers, Inc., EDTex, 729 FSupp 1140.—Adm 1.20(2), 10(2), 14; Indem 30(8).

Goins, Ex parte, TexCrimApp, 515 SW2d 918.—Extrad 39.

Goins v. American Home Products Corp., EDTex, 955 FSupp 700. See Norplant Contraceptive Products Liability Litigation, In re.

Goins v. American Home Products Corp., EDTex, 173 FRD 185. See Norplant Contraceptive Products Liability Litigation, In re.

Goins; Anderson v., TexCivApp–Eastland, 187 SW2d 415. —Contracts 111, 137(1); Deeds 17(3), 19, 73, 186, 187, 188.

Goins v. Hitchcock Independent School Dist., SDTex, 424 FSupp2d 902.—Fed Cts 25, 241; Rem of C 1, 11, 19(1), 25(1), 89(1).

Goins v. Hitchcock I.S.D., SDTex, 191 FSupp2d 860, aff 65 FedAppx 508.—Civil R 332, 1011, 1116(2), 1170, 1305, 1330(5), 1359, 1395(8), 1502, 1527; Const Law 1553, 1928, 1929, 1932, 1990, 2000; Damag 50.10; Fed Civ Proc 1872, 1877.1; Offic 119; Schools 147.12.

Goins v. League Bank and Trust, TexApp–Houston (1 Dist), 857 SW2d 628, reh den.—Action 60; Ex & Ad 261; Set-Off 60.

Goins v. Ryan's Family Steakhouses, Inc., CA5 (Tex), 181 FedAppx 435.—Alt Disp Res 134(2).

Goins v. State, TexApp–Houston (1 Dist), 841 SW2d 527, reh den, and petition for discretionary review refused.— Crim Law 290, 295, 577.2, 577.5, 739(4), 1042; Double J 135, 143.

Goins v. State, TexApp–Beaumont, 723 SW2d 212.— Autos 355(10); Crim Law 730(8), 1043(3), 1169.5(3).

Goins v. State, TexApp–Houston (14 Dist), 826 SW2d 733. —Crim Law 1023(16).

Goins v. Wyeth–Ayerst Laboratories, EDTex, 955 FSupp 700. See Norplant Contraceptive Products Liability Litigation, In re.

Goins v. Wyeth–Ayerst Laboratories, EDTex, 173 FRD 185. See Norplant Contraceptive Products Liability Litigation, In re.

Goins Const. Co., Inc. v. S.B. McLaughlin Associates, Inc., TexApp–Tyler, 930 SW2d 124. See G. Richard Goins Const. Co., Inc. v. S.B. McLaughlin Associates, Inc.

Goins, Underkofler, Crawford & Langdon; Tate v., TexApp–Dallas, 24 SW3d 627, review den, and reh of petition for review den.—App & E 856(1), 934(1); Assign 24(1); Atty & C 105, 129(1); Damag 6; Judgm 178, 181(16), 185(2), 185(6); Lim of Act 55(1), 55(3), 95(3), 95(11), 105(2), 199(1).

Go Intern., Inc. v. Big-Tex Crude Oil Co., TexCivApp– Eastland, 531 SW2d 208.—Garn 164, 191.

Go Intern., Inc. v. Lewis, TexCivApp–El Paso, 601 SW2d 495, ref nre.—Adop 20, 21; Autos 244(31), 249; Damag 87(2), 94, 127; Death 11, 31(1), 31(6), 31(7), 31(8), 32, 93, 99(4); Labor & Emp 3100(1); Princ & A 159(1).

Go Intern., Inc.; Shahan v., TexCivApp–Eastland, 465 SW2d 959.—App & E 773(2).

Goka v. State, TexApp–Houston (1 Dist), 657 SW2d 20, petition for discretionary review refused.—Crim Law 770(1), 814(1), 1172.1(3), 1172.6; Rape 35(4).

Gol; Krueger v., TexApp–Houston (14 Dist), 787 SW2d 138, writ den.—Const Law 2315; Judgm 181(7), 185(2), 185.1(3); Lim of Act 4(2).

Golasinski v. Warren Refrigerator Co., TexCivApp–Galveston, 226 SW2d 220.—App & E 863, 931(4); Plead 111.9, 111.42(4); Stip 14(10); Trial 388(2).

Golby Bag Co.; Plains Bag & Bagging Co. v., TexApp– Amarillo, 643 SW2d 509.—Const Law 3965(4); Corp 642(1).

Gold; Alamo Lumber Co. v., Tex, 661 SW2d 926.—Usury 52.

Gold v. Alamo Lumber Co., TexApp–Beaumont, 623 SW2d 453, writ gr, aff 661 SW2d 926.—Usury 103, 137, 144, 145.

Gold v. City of College Station, TexApp–Houston (1 Dist), 40 SW3d 637, review gr, vac.—App & E 852, 856(1), 863, 934(1); Judgm 178, 181(2), 181(27), 185(2),

185(5), 185(6), 185.2(8), 185.3(13); Offic 69.7; Statut 181(1), 206, 230.

Gold v. Eastridge Terrace Development Corp., TexCivApp, 397 SW2d 325.—Ven & Pur 70, 315(1).

Gold v. Exxon Co., U.S.A., TexApp–Houston (14 Dist, 960 SW2d 378. See Gold v. Exxon Corp.

Gold v. Exxon Corp., TexApp–Houston (14 Dist), 960 SW2d 378, reh overr.—App & E 863; Civil R 1122, 1204, 1744; Courts 97(1); Judgm 185(2), 185.3(13); Witn 37(1).

Gold v. Gold, Tex, 145 SW3d 212.—Hus & W 281; Judgm 335(1), 335(3); Pretrial Proc 25.

Gold; Gold v., Tex, 145 SW3d 212.—Hus & W 281; Judgm 335(1), 335(3); Pretrial Proc 25.

Gold v. Gold, TexApp–Dallas, 111 SW3d 799, reh overr, review gr, rev 145 SW3d 212.—App & E 5, 842(2), 931(1), 946, 982(1), 982(2), 989, 1008.1(2), 1010.1(1), 1010.1(2), 1012.1(4); Divorce 254(2); Judgm 335(1), 403, 407(1), 407(3), 407(4).

Gold; Gold v., TexApp–Dallas, 111 SW3d 799, reh overr, review gr, rev 145 SW3d 212.—App & E 5, 842(2), 931(1), 946, 982(1), 982(2), 989, 1008.1(2), 1010.1(1), 1010.1(2), 1012.1(4); Divorce 254(2); Judgm 335(1), 403, 407(1), 407(3), 407(4).

Gold v. McDuff, TexCivApp–Fort Worth, 324 SW2d 229. —Plead 111.3, 111.5.

Gold v. Simon, TexCivApp–Fort Worth, 424 SW2d 32.— Plead 111.39(8), 111.40, 111.47; Venue 5.2, 5.3(7), 22(1), 22(6).

Gold v. State, TexCrimApp, 736 SW2d 685.—Const Law 4653; Crim Law 1159.5; Homic 535, 938, 1137.

Gold v. State, TexApp–El Paso, 691 SW2d 760, petition for discretionary review gr, aff 736 SW2d 685.—Crim Law 438(7), 561(1), 795(2.1), 1036.2; Homic 938, 1057, 1134, 1152, 1333, 1371, 1399.

Goldapp v. Jones Lumber Co., TexCivApp–Galveston, 163 SW2d 229, writ refused wom.—Evid 434(12); Judgm 447(1), 460(10).

Goldberg v. Amarillo General Drivers, Warehousemen and Helpers Local Union No. 577, NDTex, 214 FSupp 74.—Labor & Emp 1059.

Goldberg v. Arnold Bros. Cotton Gin Co., CA5 (Tex), 297 F2d 520.—Commerce 62.67; Evid 5(2).

Goldberg; Carter v., TexCivApp–Dallas, 598 SW2d 908.— App & E 624.

Goldberg; Federal Deposit Ins. Corp. v., CA5 (Tex), 906 F2d 1087, 109 ALR Fed 231, reh den.—Banks 286.

Goldberg; Fraser v., TexCivApp–Beaumont, 552 SW2d 592, ref nre.—App & E 1071.1(2); Corp 116.

Goldberg v. Goldberg, TexCivApp–Fort Worth, 425 SW2d 830.—Divorce 255.

Goldberg; Goldberg v., TexCivApp–Fort Worth, 425 SW2d 830.—Divorce 255.

Goldberg v. Goldberg, TexCivApp–Fort Worth, 392 SW2d 168.—Divorce 226, 227(2), 231, 252.1, 252.3(2), 256, 286(0.5).

Goldberg; Goldberg v., TexCivApp–Fort Worth, 392 SW2d 168.—Divorce 226, 227(2), 231, 252.1, 252.3(2), 256, 286(0.5).

Goldberg; Lunsford v., TexCivApp–San Antonio, 604 SW2d 409.—Elections 126(7).

Goldberg v. P. & L. Equipment Co., CA5 (Tex), 311 F2d 88.—Commerce 62.52; Fed Cts 848.

Goldberg v. R.J. Longo Const. Co., Inc., CA5 (Tex), 54 F3d 243.—Contracts 187(1); Fed Cts 420; Indem 42; Liens 1, 16; Mech Liens 214.

Goldberg v. Spense, TexCivApp–Waco, 203 SW2d 330.— App & E 1126; Time 9(8).

Goldberg v. State, TexApp–Houston (1 Dist), 95 SW3d 345, petition for discretionary review refused, cert den 124 SCt 1436, 540 US 1190, 158 LEd2d 99.—Arrest 63.4(2), 63.4(11), 63.4(12), 63.4(15), 63.4(17), 63.5(4), 63.5(5), 63.5(7), 68(3); Const Law 1228, 1800, 2102; Crim Law 338(7), 339.7(3), 339.7(4), 339.8(1), 339.10(1),

GOLDBERG

See Guidelines for Arrangement at the beginning of this Volume

339.11(5.1), 374, 393(1), 393(2), 396(2), 404.65, 412(4), 412.1(4), 412.2(4), 432, 489, 517(6), 517(7), 720(2), 720(6), 721(3), 723(3), 726, 1036.1(2), 1043(1), 1043(3), 1134(2), 1162, 1169.1(10), 1169.12, 1171.1(2.1); Homic 983, 1001; Infants 68.3; Jury 33(5.15); Schools 169.5; Searches 18, 24, 42.1, 180, 183, 184; Witn 268(9).

Goldberg v. State, TexApp–Houston (14 Dist), 701 SW2d 290.—Crim Law 414, 781(1), 1043(2); Homic 1321.

Goldberg; State by Reyna v., TexCivApp–Waco, 604 SW2d 549.—Judges 4; States 215.

Goldberg; Texas Life Ins. Co. v., TexCivApp–Waco, 184 SW2d 333.—Fraud Conv 156(1); Hus & W 16; Trial 356(1).

Goldberg; Texas Life Ins. Co. v., TexCivApp–Waco, 167 SW2d 270.—Fraud Conv 308(8); Hus & W 235(2); Lim of Act 100(10), 195(3); Trial 139.1(5.1), 141, 350.2.

Goldberg; Texas Life Ins. Co. v., TexCivApp–Waco, 165 SW2d 790, writ refused wom, dissenting opinion 167 SW2d 270.—Fraud Conv 233, 308(8); Hus & W 235(2); Trial 139.1(5.1), 141, 350.2.

Goldberg v. Thompson, CA5 (Tex), 287 F2d 421.—Fed Cts 941; Labor & Emp 2387(1), 2387(2), 2387(4), 2432(3).

Goldberg v. U.S. Shoe Corp, TexApp–Houston (1 Dist), 775 SW2d 751, writ den.—Judgm 181(11), 181(33), 185(2).

Goldberg; W.E. Stephens Mfg. Co. v., TexApp–El Paso, 225 SW3d 77, review den.—Bailm 1, 5, 18(2), 18(4), 25; Liens 18.5; Statut 190; Trover 1, 3, 4.

Goldblatt, In re, CA5 (Tex), 203 FedAppx 545.—Bankr 3778.

Goldblatt, In re, TexApp–Fort Worth, 38 SW3d 802, reh overr.—Courts 202(5); Mand 3(1), 4(1), 28, 53.

Goldblatt v. City of Dallas, CA5 (Tex), 414 F2d 774.—Const Law 3658(7); Mun Corp 80.

Goldblatt v. City of Dallas, NDTex, 279 FSupp 106, appeal dism 88 SCt 1666, 391 US 360, 20 LEd2d 646, aff 414 F2d 774.—Const Law 3658(8); Mun Corp 80.

Goldblatt v. Commissioners Court of Tarrant County, TexCivApp–Fort Worth, 391 SW2d 518.—App & E 77(1), 753(2), 755.

Gold Club; Broadcast Music, Inc. v., SDTex, 598 FSupp 415. See Broadcast Music, Inc. v. Allen-Genoa Rd. Drive-In, Inc.

Golddust Twins Realty Corp.; City of Arlington, Tex. v., CA5 (Tex), 41 F3d 960, reh den.—Const Law 4076; Em Dom 9, 13, 19, 61, 66, 191(3), 324.

Golden, Ex parte, TexCrimApp, 991 SW2d 859.—Const Law 2356; Hab Corp 673, 691.1; Sent & Pun 1157.

Golden v. Ballard Co., TexApp–Houston (14 Dist), 654 SW2d 823.—App & E 842(1), 1024.1; New Tr 44(1), 44(3), 56.

Golden v. Employers Ins. of Wausau, SDTex, 981 FSupp 467.—Admin Law 228.1, 229, 305, 325; Insurance 1654; Work Comp 1061, 1072, 1086, 1090.

Golden v. First City Nat. Bank in Grand Prairie, TexApp–Dallas, 751 SW2d 639.—App & E 217, 230; Trial 314(1), 344.

Golden; Georgia Home Ins. Co. v., TexComApp, 91 SW2d 695, 127 Tex 93.—Insurance 3451.

Golden v. Golden, TexCivApp–Waco, 238 SW2d 619.—Divorce 27(1), 130, 184(6.1).

Golden; Golden v., TexCivApp–Waco, 238 SW2d 619.—Divorce 27(1), 130, 184(6.1).

Golden; Grass v., TexApp–Tyler, 153 SW3d 659, subsequent mandamus proceeding In re Grass, 2004 WL 3021876.—App & E 837(4), 907(2), 907(3); Mand 4(1), 4(4), 32, 168(2), 172; Pretrial Proc 19, 153.1.

Golden v. Halliday, TexCivApp–Dallas, 339 SW2d 715, writ dism.—Brok 63(1), 88(1); Home 118(3).

Golden v. McNeal, TexApp–Houston (14 Dist), 78 SW3d 488, review den.—App & E 223, 843(2), 854(1), 863, 934(1); Atty & C 105, 112; Fraud 7; Judges 51(1), 53;

Judgm 185(5); Lim of Act 43, 58(1), 105(2); Plead 228.14; Trial 1, 388(2).

Golden v. Murphy, TexCivApp–Hous (14 Dist), 611 SW2d 914.—App & E 984(5); Costs 32(3), 194.36; Interest 22(5), 39(3), 66.

Golden; O'Donniley v., TexApp–Tyler, 860 SW2d 267.—Courts 472.2; Ex & Ad 3(1); Mand 1, 4(4), 28, 51, 176.

Golden v. State, TexCrimApp, 851 SW2d 291, on remand 1993 WL 378083, petition for discretionary review refused.—Crim Law 741(5), 780(4), 1181.5(3.1).

Golden v. State, TexCrimApp, 475 SW2d 273.—Crim Law 824(9), 847, 1043(3); Forg 34(8), 44(3).

Golden v. State, TexCrimApp, 434 SW2d 870.—Crim Law 1184(1).

Golden v. State, TexApp–Dallas, 672 SW2d 895.—Crim Law 577.10(3), 577.16(5.1).

Golden v. State, TexApp–Dallas, 648 SW2d 29.—Weap 8.

Golden v. State, TexApp–Texarkana, 762 SW2d 630, petition for discretionary review refused.—Assault 63, 85; Crim Law 641.13(2.1), 785(8).

Golden v. State, TexApp–Beaumont, 874 SW2d 366, petition for discretionary review refused, habeas corpus gr Ex parte Golden, 2003 WL 1710845.—Crim Law 1043(3), 1045; Sent & Pun 1381(3).

Golden v. State, TexApp–Houston (14 Dist), 833 SW2d 291, reh den, and petition for discretionary review refused.—Crim Law 273(3), 1081(4.1); Ind & Inf 191(5).

Golden v. Stevens, TexCivApp–Eastland, 138 SW2d 243, writ refused.—App & E 1067; Land & Ten 331(1).

Golden; U.S. v., CA5 (Tex), 17 F3d 735.—Sent & Pun 299, 967.

Golden v. York, Tex, 410 SW2d 181.—Des & Dist 39.

Golden v. York, TexCivApp–San Antonio, 407 SW2d 293, ref nre 410 SW2d 181.—App & E 253, 882(6); Des & Dist 39; Judgm 335(1).

Golden Age Beverage Co.; N.L.R.B. v., CA5 (Tex), 415 F2d 26.—Const Law 4185; Labor & Emp 1190(1), 1190(2), 1193(1), 1193(2), 1195(7), 1195(8), 1689, 1804, 1857.

Golden Bear Distributing Systems of Texas, Inc. v. Chase Revel, Inc., CA5 (Tex), 708 F2d 944.—Const Law 2163, 4034; Damag 40(1); Evid 146; Fed Civ Proc 2011, 2178; Fed Cts 823; Libel 1, 19, 34, 48(1), 50.5, 51(5), 54, 101(4), 112(1), 112(2), 118, 123(2); States 4.1(2).

Golden Bell Songs v. Bill Miller's Bar-B-Q Enterprises, Inc., WDTex, 688 FSupp 1172. See Merrill v. Bill Miller's Bar-B-Q Enterprises, Inc.

Goldenberg; United Merchants & Mfrs., Inc. v., NDTex, 447 FSupp 918.—Bankr 2129, 2395.

Golden Blount, Inc. v. Robert H. Peterson Co., CAFed (Tex), 365 F3d 1054, on remand 2004 WL 1960098, aff in part, vac in part 438 F3d 1354.—Fed Cts 776, 850.1; Pat 101(2), 101(4), 112.5, 259(1), 314(5), 324.1, 324.5, 324.55(4), 324.55(5), 324.60, 328(2).

Golden Bridge Technology, Inc. v. Nokia, Inc., EDTex, 416 FSupp2d 525.—Antitrust 534, 535, 537, 557, 558, 605, 968.

Golden Corral Family Steakhouse No. 348, In re, TexApp–Texarkana, 973 SW2d 766. See Perritt, In re.

Goldencrest Joint Venture; NCNB Texas Nat. Bank v., NDTex, 761 FSupp 32.—Banks 505; Bills & N 516, 530; Guar 91; Mtg 379.

Golden Crest Waters, Inc.; Roberts v., TexApp–Corpus Christi, 1 SW3d 291.—Courts 107; Pretrial Proc 746, 753.

Golden Eagle Archery, Inc. v. Jackson, Tex, 116 SW3d 757, on remand 143 SW3d 477.—App & E 930(2), 932(1), 994(2), 999(1), 1001(1), 1004(1), 1004(4), 1004(5), 1062.1, 1094(1), 1182; Damag 15, 30, 48, 96, 104, 119, 208(1), 208(6), 216(3), 216(4); New Tr 75(1), 77(4).

Golden Eagle Archery, Inc. v. Jackson, Tex, 24 SW3d 362, on remand 29 SW3d 925, review gr, rev 116 SW3d 757, on remand 143 SW3d 477.—Const Law 3992, 3994;

New Tr 20, 44(1), 56, 140(1), 142, 143(2), 143(5), 144, 157.

Golden Eagle Archery, Inc.; Jackson v., TexApp–Beaumont, 143 SW3d 477.—App & E 1004(4); Damag 96, 127.8, 127.16, 140.7.

Golden Eagle Archery, Inc.; Jackson v., TexApp–Beaumont, 29 SW3d 925, review gr, rev 116 SW3d 757, on remand 143 SW3d 477.—App & E 989, 994(2), 1003(3), 1003(6), 1004(1); Damag 32, 132(1), 134(1); Evid 588.

Golden Eagle Archery, Inc.; Jackson v., TexApp–Beaumont, 974 SW2d 952, review gr, rev 24 SW3d 362, on remand 29 SW3d 925, review gr, rev 116 SW3d 757, on remand 143 SW3d 477.—App & E 842(1), 1024.1; Jury 33(2.10), 131(18); New Tr 20, 44(1), 143(2).

Golden Gate Cemetery Corp. v. Oak Park Cemetery, TexCivApp–Beaumont, 83 SW2d 711.—Plgs 38, 40.

Golden Harvest Co., Inc. v. City of Dallas, TexApp–Tyler, 942 SW2d 682, writ den.—App & E 242(2); Em Dom 2(1), 285; Judgm 178, 181(6), 183, 184; Mun Corp 723, 728, 736, 742(4), 835; Nuis 1, 2.

Golden Imports, Inc.; F.D.I.C. v., TexApp–Houston (1 Dist), 859 SW2d 635.—App & E 218.2(1), 930(3), 989, 1003(7); Banks 100, 134(1), 134(7), 231, 508; Brok 2; Costs 194.16; Interest 39(2.20); Sec Tran 115.1; Trial 143; Trover 2, 35, 72; U S 125(1), 125(3), 125(5), 125(6), 142.

Golden Jersey Creamery; Maryland Cas. Co. v., TexCivApp–Corpus Christi, 389 SW2d 701, ref nre.—App & E 597(1); Insurance 2278(29), 2293, 2770; Stip 14(1); Trial 366.

Golden Light Coffee & Equipment Co.; Reva Corp. v., TexCivApp–Waco, 379 SW2d 133.—Estop 78(1); Parties 18, 29; Replev 22; Sales 322, 351.

Golden Light Coffee Co.; Berry v., Tex, 327 SW2d 436, 160 Tex 128.—Autos 193(1), 197(1); Consp 13.

Golden Light Coffee Co.; Berry v., TexCivApp–Amarillo, 320 SW2d 684, rev 327 SW2d 436, 160 Tex 128.—Autos 197(1); Labor & Emp 58.

Goldenrod Finance Co. v. Ware, TexCivApp–Galveston, 142 SW2d 614, writ dism, correct.—Judgm 768(1); Lis Pen 8.

Golden Rule Ins. Co. v. Harper, Tex, 925 SW2d 649.—Inj 26(1), 26(3), 33.

Golden Rule Ins. Co. v. Harper, TexApp–Houston (14 Dist), 905 SW2d 804, writ gr, rev 925 SW2d 649.—App & E 954(1); Courts 516; Inj 26(1), 33, 138.27, 147.

Golden Spread Council, Inc. No. 562 of Boy Scouts of America v. Akins, Tex, 926 SW2d 287.—App & E 934(1); Judgm 181(33); Labor & Emp 3031(2), 3032, 3041; Neglig 213, 214, 215, 220, 258, 1692.

Golden Spread Elec. Co-op., Inc.; City of Brownsville v., TexApp–Dallas, 192 SW3d 876, reh overr, and review den.—Contracts 171(1); Electricity 8.4; Ven & Pur 18(0.5), 18(3).

Golden Spread Oil, Inc. v. American Petrofina Co. of Texas, TexCivApp–Amarillo, 431 SW2d 50, ref nre.—Land & Ten 34(5), 37, 39, 95; Mtg 1, 7.

Golden State Mut. Life Ins. Co. v. Adams, TexCivApp–Fort Worth, 340 SW2d 77.—App & E 758.1, 854(1), 854(2), 1036(3); Insurance 3441, 3567; Trial 395(5).

Golden State Mut. Life Ins. Co.; Fortson v., TexCivApp–Houston, 398 SW2d 437.—App & E 150(2).

Golden State Mut. Life Ins. Co. v. Hayes, TexCivApp–Waco, 301 SW2d 147, ref nre.—App & E 930(1), 1001(1), 1177(7); Insurance 2578, 3571; Plead 34(1), 406(5).

Golden State Mut. Life Ins. Co. v. Kelley, TexCivApp–Houston, 380 SW2d 139, ref nre.—Contracts 318; Insurance 1626, 1627, 1652(3), 1653(2); Trial 351.2(4).

Golden State Mut. Life Ins. Co. v. Pruitt, TexCivApp–Waco, 357 SW2d 812.—Insurance 3015; Trial 392(1).

Golden State Mut. Life Ins. Co. v. Summers, TexCivApp–Fort Worth, 301 SW2d 491.—App & E 1046.3; Insurance 2605; Trial 351.2(2).

Golden State Mut. Life Ins. Co.; Washington v., Tex, 408 SW2d 227, cert den 87 SCt 1349, 386 US 1007, 18 LEd2d 434, reh den 87 SCt 2049, 387 US 938, 18 LEd2d 1006.—New Tr 163(1).

Golden State Mut. Life Ins. Co.; Washington v., TexCivApp–Hous (14 Dist), 436 SW2d 554, ref nre.—Judgm 184, 185(2), 185.2(1), 335(1), 335(2), 335(3).

Golden State Mut. Life Ins. Co.; Washington v., TexCivApp–Houston, 405 SW2d 856, writ refused 408 SW2d 227, cert den 87 SCt 1349, 386 US 1007, 18 LEd2d 434, reh den 87 SCt 2049, 387 US 938, 18 LEd2d 1006.—App & E 387(2), 387(6), 395; New Tr 155, 163(1).

Golden State Mut. Life Ins. Co. v. White, TexCivApp–Dallas, 374 SW2d 901, ref nre.—App & E 758.3(9), 758.3(11), 882(14); Insurance 1791(2), 1970, 2590(2), 2604, 2607, 3571; Trial 54(1), 350.4(3), 351.2(4), 366.

Golden Triangle Convalescent Center; Woods v., EDTex, 22 FSupp2d 570.—Labor & Emp 407, 414, 426, 2801; States 18.51.

Golden Triangle Corp.; Johnson v., TexCivApp–Waco, 404 SW2d 44.—Land & Ten 78(1), 94(4), 193, 208(2).

Golden Triangle Development Corp.; Uhlir v., TexApp–Fort Worth, 763 SW2d 512, writ den.—App & E 173(9), 1001(3); Contracts 176(11), 232(4), 294, 295(1), 320, 335(1), 344; Costs 194.32; Impl & C C 30, 98; Trial 62(3), 66.

Golden Triangle Energy v. Wickes Lumber, TexApp–Beaumont, 725 SW2d 439.—Judgm 183, 185(2), 252(5).

Golden Triangle Raceway; Smith v., TexApp–Beaumont, 708 SW2d 574.—Judgm 181(33); Pub Amuse 130; Release 20.

Golden Villa Nursing Home, Inc. v. Smith, TexApp–Houston (14 Dist), 674 SW2d 343, ref nre.—App & E 169, 757(3), 1043(6), 1058(1), 1079; Health 662, 756, 766, 821(5), 822(3); Neglig 236, 1684; Trial 350.2, 350.5(1), 352.21; Witn 237(1).

Golden West Free Press, Inc.; Alexander v., TexCivApp–Austin, 336 SW2d 825.—App & E 984(5), 1178(1); Land & Ten 213(4), 232; Stip 14(1).

Golden West Life Ins. Co. v. Vice, TexCivApp–Beaumont, 345 SW2d 849.—Insurance 3559.

Golden West Wholesale Meats, Inc.; Farmer Boys' Catfish Kitchens Intern., Inc. v., EDTex, 18 FSupp2d 656.—Const Law 3964, 3967; Courts 12(2.30); Fed Civ Proc 1825; Fed Cts 76, 76.5, 76.10, 76.25, 76.30, 96, 417; Fraud 25.

Golden West Wholesale Meats, Inc.; Fisherman's Reef v., EDTex, 18 FSupp2d 656. See Farmer Boys' Catfish Kitchens Intern., Inc. v. Golden West Wholesale Meats, Inc.

Goldfaden v. Reuben, TexCivApp–Tyler, 373 SW2d 759.—App & E 79(2), 80(6).

Goldfaden; U.S. v., CA5 (Tex), 987 F2d 225.—Crim Law 1192; Sent & Pun 706, 761.

Goldfaden; U.S. v., CA5 (Tex), 959 F2d 1324, appeal after remand 987 F2d 225.—Const Law 4590; Crim Law 273.1(2), 662.8, 1031(4), 1042; Double J 30; Environ Law 761; Sent & Pun 200, 317, 331, 653(1), 653(13), 668, 706, 761, 765, 800.

Goldfarb v. Glazer's Wholesale Drug Co., TexCivApp–Dallas, 274 SW2d 460.—Plead 111.39(2), 111.41, 111.42(5); Venue 7.5(7).

Goldfield v. Kassoff, TexCivApp–Hous (14 Dist), 470 SW2d 216.—Judgm 181(7); Lim of Act 51(2).

Goldin v. Bartholow, CA5 (Tex), 166 F3d 710.—Bankr 2187, 3011, 3833.1, 3836, 3837; Decl Judgm 242; Fed Civ Proc 311, 2757, 2769, 2828; Fed Cts 12.1, 13, 541, 542, 545.1, 776, 812, 932.1, 936; Trusts 61(0.5), 61(4), 112, 171.

Golding; U.S. v., CA5 (Tex), 332 F3d 838.—Crim Law 1139; Sent & Pun 781.

Golding; U.S. v., CA5 (Tex), 742 F2d 840.—Bail 49(3.1), 52, 59; Crim Law 1134(1).

Golding; U.S. v., CA5 (Tex), 739 F2d 183, appeal after remand 742 F2d 840.—Crim Law 1081(6), 1181.5(3.1).

Gold Kist, Inc. v. Carr, TexApp–Eastland, 886 SW2d 425, reh den, and writ den.—Carr 63; Contracts 143(2), 176(1); Estop 85; Evid 384, 428, 433(1), 434(1), 434(8), 450(5); Fraud 12; Frds St of 113(2), 113(3), 115, 116(0.5), 144; Trial 351.2(5).

Gold Kist, Inc. v. Massey, TexCivApp–Fort Worth, 609 SW2d 645.—Antitrust 129, 369, 391, 398; Evid 515; Sales 441(3), 442(5).

Gold Kist, Inc. v. Texas Utilities Elec. Co., Tex, 830 SW2d 91.—Damag 63.

Gold Kist, Inc.; Texas Utilities Elec. Co. Through Texas Power & Light Div. v., TexApp–Eastland, 817 SW2d 749, writ gr, rev 830 SW2d 91.—App & E 218.2(4), 930(3), 1001(1), 1001(3), 1036(1), 1064.1(8); Compromise 15(1), 103; Damag 63; Electricity 14(1), 19(5); Evid 123(1), 123(12); Neglig 387; Parties 64.

Gold Knob Outdoor Advertising Co. v. Outdoor Advertising Ass'n of Tex., TexCivApp–Texarkana, 225 SW2d 645.—Assoc 8, 20(1); Corp 173.

Goldman v. Alkek, TexApp–Corpus Christi, 850 SW2d 568, am on reh, and reh overr, and motion gr.—Antitrust 147, 369; Contracts 152, 153; Costs 252, 260(1), 264; Damag 71, 73, 165, 190; Land & Ten 37, 130(0.5), 132(1), 132(2), 200.3; Release 38.

Goldman v. Campbell, TexCivApp–Fort Worth, 249 SW2d 633, ref nre.—App & E 981; Des & Dist 71(4), 71(6); Evid 292, 295; New Tr 99, 104(3); Trial 350.3(1).

Goldman; Carrigan v., TexCivApp–Hous (1 Dist), 431 SW2d 374.—App & E 931(4), 989; R R 307.3, 348(1).

Goldman v. Gordon, TexCivApp–San Antonio, 135 SW2d 1024.—App & E 773(4).

Goldman v. Lopez, TexCivApp–Galveston, 193 SW2d 284. —App & E 1024.3; Crim Law 59(2); Venue 8.5(4), 21.

Goldman v. Pre-Fab Transit Co., TexCivApp–Hous (14 Dist), 520 SW2d 597.—Corp 665(3).

Goldman v. State, TexCrimApp, 468 SW2d 381.—Controlled Subs 97; Crim Law 1173.2(2).

Goldman v. State, TexCrimApp, 198 SW2d 895, 150 TexCrim 24.—Assault 96(7); Homic 541, 567, 1387.

Goldman v. State, TexCrimApp, 160 SW2d 523, 143 TexCrim 603.—Crim Law 369.1, 673(5), 763(1), 830; Int Liq 155(1), 200, 207.

Goldman v. State, TexCrimApp, 95 SW2d 423, 130 TexCrim 471.—Consp 43(11), 48.1(2.1); Crim Law 665(2), 721(3), 772(6), 780(3), 800(3), 1153(5), 1169.2(7); Ind & Inf 125(5.5), 140(2).

Goldman v. State, TexCivApp–Amarillo, 277 SW2d 217, ref nre.—App & E 185(1); Health 106, 211, 223(1); Judgm 185.3(1); Statut 223.2(1.1), 223.2(18).

Goldman v. Torres, Tex, 341 SW2d 154, 161 Tex 437.— Const Law 2528; Work Comp 51, 52, 808, 888.

Goldman; Torres v., TexCivApp–El Paso, 335 SW2d 675, writ gr, rev 341 SW2d 154, 161 Tex 437.—Work Comp 893.

Goldman; U.S. v., SDTex, 700 FSupp 365.—Cust Dut 126(2).

Goldman v. White Rose Distributing Co., TexApp–Fort Worth, 936 SW2d 393, reh overr, vac pursuant to settlement 949 SW2d 707.—App & E 863; Atty & C 14, 77; Estop 68(2); Judgm 185(2), 713(2), 720; Lim of Act 104(1).

Goldman, Sachs & Co.; Charley T's v., TexApp–Houston (14 Dist), 797 SW2d 326. See HTM Restaurants. v. Goldman, Sachs & Co.

Goldman, Sachs & Co.; Cook v., SDTex, 726 FSupp 151. —Exchanges 11(2); Sec Reg 35.15, 60.15, 60.18, 60.32(1), 60.40.

Goldman Sachs & Co.; Eurocapital Group, Ltd. v., TexApp–Houston (1 Dist), 17 SW3d 426.—Alt Disp Res 113, 114, 362(1), 363(4), 363(8), 412, 417; Lim of Act 5(1).

Goldman, Sachs & Co.; HTM Restaurants. v., TexApp–Houston (14 Dist), 797 SW2d 326, writ den.— Fraud 3, 16, 17, 23, 36; Land & Ten 130(1), 130(2); Pretrial Proc 481.

Goldome Credit Corp. v. University Square Apartments, TexApp–Amarillo, 828 SW2d 505.—App & E 954(1), 1024.2; Banks 191.10, 191.15, 191.20, 191.30.

Goldring v. Goldring, TexCivApp–Fort Worth, 523 SW2d 749, ref nre.—App & E 154(1), 301, 302(3), 768, 854(5); Can of Inst 17, 18, 23; Statut 194; Wills 439, 442, 467, 470(1), 675, 686(1).

Goldring; Goldring v., TexCivApp–Fort Worth, 523 SW2d 749, ref nre.—App & E 154(1), 301, 302(3), 768, 854(5); Can of Inst 17, 18, 23; Statut 194; Wills 439, 442, 467, 470(1), 675, 686(1).

Goldring; Texas Commerce Bank-Arlington v., Tex, 665 SW2d 103.—Usury 53, 119.

Goldring v. Texas Commerce Bank-Arlington, TexApp–Fort Worth, 651 SW2d 361, rev 665 SW2d 103.—Judgm 181(17); Usury 12.

Gold Rush; Letson v., TexApp–Amarillo, 979 SW2d 414. See Letson v. Barnes.

Goldsberry; State v., TexApp–Houston (1 Dist), 14 SW3d 770, reh overr, and petition for discretionary review refused.—Crim Law 1032(5), 1149; Ind & Inf 65, 71.2(3), 71.3, 110(3), 110(4), 125(19.1), 137(1); Offic 121.

Goldsbury; Gerst v., Tex, 434 SW2d 665.—B & L Assoc 3.1(1), 3.1(2), 3.1(3).

Goldsbury; Gerst v., TexCivApp–Austin, 425 SW2d 14, writ gr, rev 434 SW2d 665.—B & L Assoc 3.1(1), 3.1(2).

Goldschmidt; Fort Worth & Denver Ry. Co. v., NDTex, 518 FSupp 121, rev Fort Worth and Denver Ry Co v. Lewis, 693 F2d 432, reh den 707 F2d 515.—Const Law 2424(1); R R 229(1), 229(3.1); Statut 184, 217.3, 219(1), 219(6.1), 220.

Goldschmidt v. Hunt, NDTex, 556 FSupp 123.—Antitrust 920, 965.

Goldsmith, Ex parte, Tex, 290 SW2d 502, 155 Tex 605.— Child S 33; Courts 475(15).

Goldsmith; Baker v., Tex, 582 SW2d 404.—Judgm 162(2), 335(1), 335(3), 335(4).

Goldsmith v. Baker, TexCivApp–Austin, 567 SW2d 590, aff 582 SW2d 404.—Judgm 162(2), 162(4), 335(3).

Goldsmith v. Cathey, TexCivApp–Fort Worth, 331 SW2d 358, ref nre.—Judgm 178, 181(27), 185(2), 185(6), 185.2(8).

Goldsmith; Garvin v., TexCivApp–Waco, 406 SW2d 545, ref nre.—App & E 877(4), 931(4); Fraud 13(2), 58(1), 58(4); Trial 365.1(4), 366.

Goldsmith; Goodson v., Tex, 115 SW2d 1100, 131 Tex 418.—Death 2(2); Des & Dist 71(4); Wills 555(1), 853.

Goldsmith v. Humble Oil & Refining Co., Tex, 199 SW2d 773, 145 Tex 549.—Bound 20(1), 33; Dedi 18(1); Ease 36(3); Ex & Ad 148; Mines 92.27.

Goldsmith; Humble Oil & Refining Co. v., TexCivApp–Austin, 196 SW2d 665, rev 199 SW2d 773, 145 Tex 549. —Deeds 118; Ease 36(3); Ex & Ad 148; Judgm 747(4); Mines 92.29.

Goldsmith; Midland Nat. Bank v., TexCivApp–El Paso, 81 SW2d 120.—Attach 1, 232.

Goldsmith v. Mitchell, TexCivApp–San Antonio, 96 SW2d 313, aff Goodson v. Goldsmith, 115 SW2d 1100, 131 Tex 418.—Death 2(1); Des & Dist 19; Wills 10, 439.

Goldsmith; PHB, Inc. v., Tex, 539 SW2d 60.—Pretrial Proc 518.

Goldsmith; PHB, Inc. v., TexCivApp–Hous (14 Dist), 534 SW2d 196, ref nre 539 SW2d 60.—Judgm 181(2), 335(3), 743(1); Pretrial Proc 518.

Goldsmith; Powell v., TexCivApp–Texarkana, 164 SW2d 45, dism.—Appear 8(3); Plead 110; Venue 1 1/2, 8.5(3), 21.

Goldsmith v. Salkey, Tex, 112 SW2d 165, 131 Tex 139, 116 ALR 1293.—Child C 8, 51, 406, 553, 601, 719, 731, 733; Courts 511; Judgm 822(3).

Goldsmith v. Salkey, TexCivApp–San Antonio, 115 SW2d 778, writ refused, answer to certified question conformed to 112 SW2d 165, 131 Tex 139, 116 ALR 1293.— Child C 76, 555, 719, 722, 731, 733; Domicile 5.

Goldsmith; Star Tours, Inc. v., TexApp–Dallas, 830 SW2d 614. See Travel Masters, Inc. v. Star Tours, Inc.

Goldsmith v. State, TexCrimApp, 236 SW2d 249, 155 TexCrim 428.—Autos 351.1, 352, 355(6); Crim Law 1172.1(2).

Goldsmith v. Stephenson, TexApp–Dallas, 634 SW2d 331. —App & E 609, 624.

Goldsmith; U.S. v., CA5 (Tex), 192 FedAppx 261.—Sent & Pun 95; Weap 17(8).

Goldsmith & Powell v. State, TexCivApp–Dallas, 159 SW2d 534, writ refused.—Fish 1; Nav Wat 4; Nuis 61, 80, 84; Waters 3.

Goldsoll; Levy v., TexCivApp, 131 SW 420, 62 TexCivApp 257, writ refused.—Hus & W 1.

Goldson v. Southwestern Bell Telephone Co., TexApp–Corpus Christi, 659 SW2d 902.—App & E 927(7); Tel 916(6).

Gold Star Distributors, Inc.; Independent American Const. Co., Inc. v., TexCivApp–Texarkana, 540 SW2d 586.—Judgm 585(4).

Gold Star Distributors, Inc.; Ridout v., TexCivApp–Eastland, 532 SW2d 149.—Plead 111.35.

Goldstein; Bobbie Brooks, Inc. v., TexCivApp–Eastland, 567 SW2d 902, ref nre.—App & E 1058(3); Contracts 176(2); Costs 194.32; Evid 267, 351, 448; Interest 39(2.15); Pretrial Proc 139; Trial 56, 194(1), 304.

Goldstein; Brown v., Tex, 685 SW2d 640.—Autos 245(53), 245(67.1), 245(78), 245(89), 245(90); Trial 349(1), 352.14; Witn 202.

Goldstein; Brown v., TexApp–Houston (14 Dist), 678 SW2d 539, writ gr, rev 685 SW2d 640.—App & E 215(1), 223; Autos 246(39.1), 246(48), 246(57), 246(58); Neglig 250, 291, 440(1); Trial 143, 350.1.

Goldstein v. Commission for Lawyer Discipline, TexApp–Dallas, 109 SW3d 810, reh overr, and review den. —App & E 946; Atty & C 53(2), 54, 59; Judgm 632, 644, 713(1), 715(1), 725(1).

Goldstein v. Corrigan, TexCivApp–Waco, 405 SW2d 425. —Judgm 185(2); Land & Ten 150(1), 164(1), 168(1).

Goldstein v. KDFW, Texas Pawnbrokers' Ass'n, TexCivApp–Waco, 541 SW2d 862, ref nre.—Libel 21.

Goldstein v. Mortenson, TexApp–Austin, 113 SW3d 769. —Antitrust 231; App & E 931(1), 1004(11), 1008.1(2), 1010.1(2), 1012.1(4); Brok 38(4), 38(7); Consp 1.1, 2, 9, 13, 19; Corp 1.4(2), 1.4(4), 1.7(2); New Tr 77(2); Sec Reg 308.

Goldstein; Ross v., TexApp–Houston (14 Dist), 203 SW3d 508.—App & E 917(1), 946, 960(1), 1042(1); Ex & Ad 444(2); Marriage 17.5(1), 54(2); Plead 34(7), 228.14, 228.23; Trusts 371(2).

Goldstein v. State, TexApp–Dallas, 803 SW2d 777, petition for discretionary review refused.—Crim Law 29(10), 338(1), 369.2(1), 369.2(3.1), 371(3), 553, 742(1), 859, 925.5(3), 957(1), 957(2), 957(3), 1119(1), 1169.1(1), 1170.5(1), 1176; False Pret 5, 12, 13, 14, 15, 39, 49(2), 49(4), 49(6), 51; Statut 223.2(1.1), 223.2(35); Witn 405(1).

Goldstein; Steverson v., CA5 (Tex), 24 F3d 666, reh den, cert den Harris County Sheriff's Dept Civil Service Com'rs v. Steverson, 115 SCt 731, 513 US 1081, 130 LEd2d 634.—Civil R 1126, 1421; Fed Civ Proc 2197, 2264.1; Fed Cts 641, 766; Sheriffs 99.

Goldstein Hat Mfg. Co. v. Cowen, TexCivApp–Dallas, 136 SW2d 867, writ dism, correct.—App & E 499(3), 927(7), 1003(10), 1046.5, 1053(2), 1061.4, 1069.1, 1070(2); Carr 306(1), 347; Contrib 5(4); Land & Ten 167(1), 167(8); Neglig 423, 431, 1717; Trial 29(1), 304, 351.5(5), 352.5(5), 352.10, 352.15, 365.1(6).

Goldston; Bristol-Myers Squibb Co. v., TexApp–Fort Worth, 983 SW2d 369, review dism by agreement.—App & E 70(6), 840(1), 893(1), 949, 1024.3; Parties 51(4), 53.

Goldston; Bristol-Myers Squibb Co. v., TexApp–Fort Worth, 957 SW2d 671, reh overr, and review den, appeal after remand 983 SW2d 369, review dism by agreement.—Compromise 9, 11; Contracts 127(4); Venue 1.5.

Goldston; F. W. Woolworth Co. v., TexCivApp–Amarillo, 155 SW2d 830, writ refused wom.—Evid 121(2), 123(11); Neglig 1088, 1670, 1708; Trial 105(1), 105(2).

Goldston; Houston Transit Co. v., TexCivApp–Galveston, 217 SW2d 435.—App & E 768; Damag 221(2.1); Insurance 3406; Trial 108.5, 352.10.

Goldston v. National Resort Communities, Inc., TexCivApp–Texarkana, 613 SW2d 37, ref nre.—Ven & Pur 44, 123.

Goldston; Southwest Hide Co. v., NDTex, 127 FRD 481. —Fed Civ Proc 1265, 1272.1.

Goldston v. Wieghat, TexCivApp–Galveston, 243 SW2d 404.—App & E 912; High 163(1); Plead 111.42(7); Venue 8.5(4), 8.5(5), 22(3).

Goldston Corp.; Champlin Petroleum Co. v., TexApp–Corpus Christi, 797 SW2d 165, writ den.—App & E 169; Indem 31(6), 100.

Goldston Corp. v. Hernandez, TexApp–Corpus Christi, 714 SW2d 350, ref nre.—App & E 237(6), 901, 931(3), 931(6), 932(1); Damag 2, 32, 100, 130.1, 132(1), 132(6.1), 134(1), 185(1).

Goldsum; Marek v., TexCivApp–Galveston, 243 SW2d 461.—Lim of Act 121(1), 125; Motions 58; Plead 111.47, 111.49.

Gold Sun Aluminum, Inc., In re, NDTex, 68 BR 712. See Texas Extrusion Corp., In re.

Gold Sun Aluminum, Inc. v. Lockheed Corp., CA5 (Tex), 844 F2d 1142. See Texas Extrusion Corp., Matter of.

Goldthorn; Reynolds v., TexCivApp–El Paso, 241 SW2d 643.—Venue 8.5(3), 8.5(4).

Goldtouch Technologies Inc. v. Microsoft Corp., WDTex, 102 FSupp2d 722, aff 13 FedAppx 953.—Pat 168(2.1), 168(3).

Goldwait v. State, TexApp–Houston (1 Dist), 961 SW2d 432.—App & E 1010.1(5); Mental H 33, 36, 41.

Goldwire; Dean v., TexCivApp–Waco, 480 SW2d 494, ref nre.—App & E 934(1), 989; Hus & W 248; Judgm 181(2), 181(15.1); Marriage 54.

Go Leasing, Inc. v. Groos Nat. Bank, TexApp–San Antonio, 628 SW2d 143.—Judgm 297, 304, 321, 323, 326, 340.

Golemon v. State, TexCrimApp, 247 SW2d 119, 157 TexCrim 534, cert den 73 SCt 60, 344 US 847, 97 LEd 659, reh den 73 SCt 174, 344 US 882, 97 LEd 683.—Const Law 4664(1), 4664(2); Crim Law 126(1), 134(4), 404.85, 517.3(4), 519(2), 519(8), 519(9), 532(0.5), 1134(2), 1166(4), 1169.3; Fed Cts 511.1.

Golemon v. State, TexCrimApp, 230 SW2d 816, 155 TexCrim 81.—Gr Jury 30; Ind & Inf 10.1(1).

Golfcrest Country Club; Argue v., TexCivApp–Hous (1 Dist), 461 SW2d 248.—Clubs 9; Judgm 181(11); Plead 276.

Golforms Inc.; Resorts of Pinehurst Inc. v., CA5 (Tex), 155 F3d 526. See Pebble Beach Co. v. Tour 18 I Ltd.

Golias v. Golias, TexApp–Beaumont, 861 SW2d 401.— App & E 1010.1(3); Child S 146; Divorce 226, 252.3(2), 286(8); Hus & W 258.

Golias; Golias v., TexApp–Beaumont, 861 SW2d 401.— App & E 1010.1(3); Child S 146; Divorce 226, 252.3(2), 286(8); Hus & W 258.

Golias; TMS Mortg., Inc. v., TexApp–Beaumont, 102 SW3d 768.—Mtg 215.1; Neglig 202, 210, 215, 1692; Torts 301, 437; Ven & Pur 231(1).

Golightly v. Massachusetts Bonding & Insurance Co., NDTex, 295 F 153.—Rem of C 47.

Golleher v. Herrera, TexApp–Amarillo, 651 SW2d 329.—Autos 150, 206, 244(34), 244(35); Evid 555.4(2), 555.8(1), 570.

Gollehon v. Porter, TexCivApp–Amarillo, 161 SW2d 134, writ refused wom.—Action 5; Contracts 138(1); Gaming 75(1); Land & Ten 262(6), 263, 269(5), 270(1.5), 270(5), 270(10), 273(2).

Gollihar, In re Commitment of, TexApp–Beaumont, 224 SW3d 843.—App & E 930(1), 971(2), 992, 994(2), 1002, 1003(3), 1003(5); Crim Law 1144.13(2.1), 1159.2(7); Mental H 460(2), 467; Trial 142.

Gollihar v. State, TexCrimApp, 46 SW3d 243, on remand 56 SW2d 606, petition for discretionary review gr, petition for discretionary review dism with per curiam opinion 84 SW3d 674.—Const Law 4693; Crim Law 1134(2); Ind & Inf 171.

Gollihar v. State, TexCrimApp, 112 SW2d 1053, 133 TexCrim 491.—Crim Law 531(3), 780(3), 781(5), 1172.2, 1186.4(8).

Gollihar v. State, TexApp–Texarkana, 56 SW3d 606, petition for discretionary review gr, petition for discretionary review dism with per curiam opinion 84 SW3d 674.—Crim Law 1173.2(8); Larc 23, 60, 79.

Gollihar v. State, TexApp–Texarkana, 991 SW2d 303, petition for discretionary review gr, and petition for discretionary review refused, rev 46 SW3d 243, on remand 56 SW2d 606, petition for discretionary review gr, petition for discretionary review dism with per curiam opinion 84 SW3d 674.—Crim Law 847, 1134(2), 1144.13(3), 1159.2(7); Double J 132.1; Ind & Inf 167, 171; Larc 40(6).

Gollihar v. State, TexApp–Amarillo, 701 SW2d 85, petition for discretionary review refused, vac 741 SW2d 458.—Const Law 4768, 4769; Crim Law 1005, 1119(1).

Gollin v. State, TexCrimApp, 554 SW2d 683.—Crim Law 519(8), 531(3), 547(1), 1119(1); Larc 55; Sent & Pun 1379(2), 1381(6).

Gollinger v. State, TexApp–Houston (14 Dist), 834 SW2d 553.—Const Law 90.1(7.1), 1498, 1924; Crim Law 747, 1144.13(2.1), 1144.13(6), 1159.2(7), 1159.6; Ease 1; Tresp 78, 88.

Gollott; U.S. v., CA5 (Tex), 939 F2d 255.—Crim Law 655(1), 867, 1030(1), 1155, 1169.1(1); U S 34.

Golman v. Johnson, TexCivApp–El Paso, 97 SW2d 334.—Replev 126.

Golman; Wilson v., TexCivApp–Eastland, 563 SW2d 655.—Covenants 52.

Golman-Hayden Co., Inc. v. Fresh Source Produce Inc., CA5 (Tex), 217 F3d 348.—Atty & C 155; Fact 59.

Golman-Hayden Co., Inc. v. Fresh Source Produce, Inc., NDTex, 27 FSupp2d 723, aff in part, rev in part 217 F3d 348.—Fact 59.

Golnoy Barge Co. v. M/T SHINOUSSA, CA5 (Tex), 980 F2d 349, on remand 841 FSupp 787.—Ship 209(1.5), 209(1.7).

Golnoy Barge Co. v. M/T Shinoussa, SDTex, 841 FSupp 787.—Ship 209(1.5).

Golnoy Barge Co. v. M/T Shinoussa, SDTex, 841 FSupp 783.—Fish 6.

Golob v. Stone, TexCivApp–Texarkana, 262 SW2d 536.—Trusts 254.

Golob v. Stone, TexCivApp–Waco, 322 SW2d 560, ref nre.—App & E 930(1), 1001(1); Atty & C 21.5(1), 21.10, 166(4); Trial 139.1(3), 140(1), 141, 142, 143.

Golodetz Trading Corp. v. Curland, TexApp–Houston (1 Dist), 886 SW2d 503.—Judgm 80, 87, 215, 276; Stip 1, 9.

Golson v. Capehart, TexCivApp–Eastland, 473 SW2d 627, ref nre.—App & E 1008.1(4), 1011.1(4); Deeds 17(2); Ven & Pur 13.

Golson v. State, TexApp–Corpus Christi, 931 SW2d 705, on reh.—Extort 25.1; Statut 63.

Golston v. Bartlett, TexCivApp–Austin, 112 SW2d 1077, writ dism.—Contracts 221(1); Damag 120(3), 182; Mines 109; Trial 356(1), 365.1(5).

Golston v. City of Tyler, TexCivApp–Texarkana, 262 SW2d 518, writ refused.—Const Law 2470; Mun Corp 33(2), 65.

Golub v. Nelson, TexCivApp–Hous (14 Dist), 441 SW2d 220.—Judgm 185.3(3); Plead 301(1).

Gombert v. London Guarantee & Acc. Co., CCA5 (Tex), 100 F2d 352.—Work Comp 726.

Gomes v. State, TexApp–Houston (14 Dist), 9 SW3d 373, reh overr, and petition for discretionary review refused.—Const Law 4664(1); Crim Law 412.1(4), 412.2(2), 412.2(5), 414, 519(1), 519(9), 525, 1044.2(1), 1158(4).

Gomes v. State, TexApp–Houston (14 Dist), 9 SW3d 170, reh overr.—Crim Law 1081(2).

Gomez, Ex parte, TexCrimApp, 15 SW3d 103.—Infants 69(1); Prisons 15(3); Sent & Pun 1157.

Gomez, Ex parte, TexCrimApp, 499 SW2d 158.—Bail 51.

Gomez, Ex parte, TexCrimApp, 389 SW2d 308, cert den Gomez v. Texas, 87 SCt 958, 386 US 937, 17 LEd2d 810.—Const Law 268(7), 3299, 4729; Controlled Subs 143, 148(4); Crim Law 532(0.5); Hab Corp 294, 721(2).

Gomez, Ex parte, TexCrimApp, 241 SW2d 153.—Hab Corp 506, 814; Sent & Pun 2003.

Gomez, Ex parte, TexApp–Corpus Christi, 855 SW2d 42, petition for discretionary review refused, untimely filed.—Extrad 34.

Gomez, In re Adoption of, TexCivApp–El Paso, 424 SW2d 656.—Adop 2, 4; Const Law 3292.

Gomez, In re Estate of, TexApp–San Antonio, 161 SW3d 615, reh overr.—Wills 358, 394.

Gomez v. Adame, TexApp–San Antonio, 940 SW2d 249.—App & E 901, 977(5), 994(1), 999(1), 1003(6); Autos 171(9), 242(2), 244(11); Neglig 1692, 1713.

Gomez v. American Garment Finishers Corp., WDTex, 200 FRD 579.—Fed Civ Proc 164, 184.5.

Gomez v. Beto, CA5 (Tex), 471 F2d 774, reh den 472 F2d 1405, reh den 474 F2d 1347, cert den 94 SCt 103, 414 US 843, 38 LEd2d 81.—Arrest 63.4(7.1), 71.1(8).

Gomez v. Beto, CA5 (Tex), 462 F2d 596.—Crim Law 641.13(6); Hab Corp 827.

Gomez v. Beto, CA5 (Tex), 402 F2d 766, cert den 89 SCt 1217, 394 US 936, 22 LEd2d 469.—Hab Corp 498, 765.1.

Gomez; Browning v., TexCivApp–Austin, 332 SW2d 588, ref nre.—Libel 45(1), 45(3); Relig Soc 27(2).

Gomez; Browning v., TexCivApp–Austin, 315 SW2d 79, dism.—App & E 66, 80(1), 80(6); Judgm 217; Plead 147, 263.

Gomez v. Bryant, TexApp–El Paso, 750 SW2d 810.—Judgm 137, 244.

Gomez v. Carreras, TexApp–Corpus Christi, 904 SW2d 750.—App & E 852, 863; Const Law 328, 2315; Judgm 185(2), 185(3); Lim of Act 55(3), 95(12).

Gomez; Carson v., TexApp–Houston (1 Dist), 14 SW3d 778, reh overr, and review den, cert den 121 SCt 807, 531 US 1088, 148 LEd2d 693.—App & E 907(1); Convicts 6; Crim Law 637, 1166.8; Witn 345(1).

Gomez; Carson v., TexApp–Houston (1 Dist), 841 SW2d 491, reh den, opinion designated not for publication, subsequent mandamus proceeding 908 SW2d 228.—App & E 962; Civil R 1395(7); Judges 51(1), 51(3), 51(4); Pretrial Proc 552.

Gomez v. Chandler, CA5 (Tex), 163 F3d 921.—Fed Civ Proc 2491.5; Fed Cts 915; Sent & Pun 1548.

Gomez v. City of Brownsville, TexApp–Corpus Christi, 976 SW2d 291, reh overr, and review den.—Estop 78(1); Labor & Emp 1295(1), 1564; Offic 69.12.

Gomez; City of Corpus Christi v., TexApp–Corpus Christi, 141 SW3d 767.—App & E 845(2), 893(1); Insurance 1864, 1865, 2772; Trial 368; Work Comp 2189, 2191.

Gomez v. City of Eagle Pass, WDTex, 91 FSupp2d 1000.—Civil R 1116(3), 1169; Const Law 1475(9); Courts 96(1); Fed Civ Proc 2127; Mun Corp 156; Statut 268.

Gomez v. City Transp. Co. of Dallas, TexCivApp–Dallas, 262 SW2d 417, ref nre.—Carr 283(1), 306(1); Corp 423;

Judgm 569; Labor & Emp 3134; Mun Corp 285; Release 37.

Gomez v. Collins, CA5 (Tex), 993 F2d 96.—Crim Law 641.4(4), 1077.3; Hab Corp 846.

Gomez; Couder v., Tex, 378 SW2d 14.—App & E 1177(9); Partners 87, 248, 327(1).

Gomez; Couder v., TexCivApp–El Paso, 373 SW2d 345, writ gr, aff in part, rev in part 378 SW2d 14.—App & E 927(7), 959(1), 1170.3; Consp 6, 8, 18, 19, 21; Plead 228.23, 236(3); Trial 142, 352.4(1).

Gomez v. De Gonzales, TexCivApp–San Antonio, 248 SW2d 268.—Deeds 211(1); Ven & Pur 242, 244.

Gomez v. Department of the Air Force, CA5 (Tex), 869 F2d 852.—Civil R 1530; Fed Cts 660.20, 1139.

Gomez v. Diaz, TexApp–Corpus Christi, 57 SW3d 573.—Antitrust 135(1), 257, 369; App & E 840(1); Assault 2; Fraud 3, 9; Health 813, 906, 908; Judgm 185(5).

Gomez v. Dretke, CA5 (Tex), 422 F3d 264.—Hab Corp 818.

Gomez; Elizondo v., TexApp–San Antonio, 957 SW2d 862, reh overr, and review den.—App & E 1071.1(2); Evid 448; Frds St of 110(1), 112, 129(1), 129(3), 129(8), 129(12), 139(1); Trial 388(2).

Gomez v. Franco, TexApp–Corpus Christi, 677 SW2d 231.—App & E 999(1), 1001(1), 1008.1(3); Evid 588, 589; Impl & C C 98; Sales 1.5, 3.1, 10; Trial 350.1, 350.2, 350.4(1).

Gomez v. Galloway, SDTex, 428 FSupp 358.—Fed Cts 995.

Gomez v. Gomez, TexCivApp–El Paso, 234 SW2d 941.—Divorce 51, 127(3), 130, 135, 150, 184(6.1), 184(10).

Gomez; Gomez v., TexCivApp–El Paso, 234 SW2d 941.—Divorce 51, 127(3), 130, 135, 150, 184(6.1), 184(10).

Gomez v. Gomez, TexCivApp–Corpus Christi, 577 SW2d 327.—App & E 267(1), 281(1), 293, 499(1), 554(1), 554(3), 1169(7), 1170.10, 1175(1), 1177(2); Trial 404(1).

Gomez; Gomez v., TexCivApp–Corpus Christi, 577 SW2d 327.—App & E 267(1), 281(1), 293, 499(1), 554(1), 554(3), 1169(7), 1170.10, 1175(1), 1177(2); Trial 404(1).

Gomez; Green v., TexCivApp–Eastland, 348 SW2d 185.—Hus & W 266.3; Mtg 39, 311.

Gomez v. Hartford Co. of the Midwest, TexApp–El Paso, 803 SW2d 438, writ den.—App & E 170(1), 756; Contracts 143(2), 143.5, 162; Insurance 1808, 1853, 2120, 2278(16), 2915, 2940.

Gomez; Heard v., CA5 (Tex), 321 F2d 88.—Const Law 4810.

Gomez v. Heard, SDTex, 218 FSupp 228, aff 321 F2d 88.—Const Law 4810; Crim Law 641.10(2).

Gomez v. Housing Authority of City of El Paso, WDTex, 805 FSupp 1363, aff 20 F3d 1169, cert den 115 SCt 198, 513 US 873, 130 LEd2d 129.—U S 70(5), 82(3.2), 82(3.5).

Gomez v. Housing Authority of the City of El Paso, TexApp–El Paso, 148 SW3d 471, reh overr, and review den, cert den 126 SCt 379, 546 US 872, 163 LEd2d 166.—App & E 893(1); Civil R 1304, 1326(1), 1343, 1345, 1351(1), 1355, 1376(4), 1395(3); Const Law 4112; Courts 35, 39; Mun Corp 745; Plead 104(1), 111.48; States 191.1, 191.4(1), 191.10.

Gomez; Humble Sand & Gravel, Inc. v., Tex, 146 SW3d 170.—Labor & Emp 2782, 2797; Neglig 210, 1550, 1692; Prod Liab 14, 62, 77, 87.1; Torts 101.

Gomez; Humble Sand & Gravel, Inc. v., TexApp–Texarkana, 48 SW3d 487, review gr, rev 146 SW3d 170.—App & E 969, 1050.1(1), 1051.1(1), 1056.1(1), 1058(1), 1064.1(8); Evid 208(6), 265(8); Neglig 202, 210, 213, 215, 220, 375, 379, 380, 387, 422, 423, 431, 433, 1692, 1741; Prod Liab 14, 15, 62, 75.1, 87.1, 98; Trial 43, 182, 251(1), 252(1), 295(1).

Gomez v. Kestermeier, TexApp–Eastland, 924 SW2d 210, reh overr, and writ den.—App & E 1056.1(10); Fraud Conv 24(1); Parties 18, 29; Plead 36(2).

Gomez; Liberty Mut. Ins. Co. v., TexCivApp–Corpus Christi, 462 SW2d 338.—Work Comp 11, 840.

Gomez v. McKaskle, CA5 (Tex), 734 F2d 1107, cert den 105 SCt 524, 469 US 1041, 83 LEd2d 412.—Crim Law 641.13(2.1); Hab Corp 721(2).

Gomez v. Matey, TexApp–Corpus Christi, 55 SW3d 732.—App & E 893(1); Health 607, 800, 804; States 18.15.

Gomez v. Myers, EDTex, 627 FSupp 183.—Atty & C 132; Civil R 1442, 1445; Clerks of C 72; Fed Civ Proc 625.1, 2734.

Gomez v. Newlin, TexCivApp–San Antonio, 288 SW2d 255.—App & E 186; Pretrial Proc 504; Venue 21.

Gomez; North River Ins. Co. v., TexApp–Tyler, 632 SW2d 678.—Plead 34(1); Work Comp 1335, 1417, 1639, 1728, 1949.

Gomez; Olibas v., WDTex, 481 FSupp2d 721.—Bail 60; Civil R 1395(5), 1760, 1764; Const Law 1117(1), 1166, 1490, 1553, 1827, 3039, 3041, 3867, 3874(2), 4282; Mun Corp 170, 1027; Sheriffs 97, 99.

Gomez v. Perez, USTex, 93 SCt 872, 409 US 535, 35 LEd2d 56.—Child S 24, 32, 58, 170, 651; Child 21(2); Const Law 2970, 3194; Fed Cts 508, 509.

Gomez; Raines v., TexApp–Texarkana, 143 SW3d 867.—Judgm 109, 112, 126(1), 126(4).

Gomez; Raines v., TexApp–Texarkana, 118 SW3d 875, appeal after new trial 143 SW3d 867.—Const Law 3993; Judgm 17(0.5); Land & Ten 285(7); Trial 9(2).

Gomez v. Riddle, TexCivApp–San Antonio, 334 SW2d 197.—Ack 55(1), 56, 59, 60, 62(2); App & E 846(2), 846(5), 931(1); Contracts 141(3); Evid 83(1); Mech Liens 73(4), 281(2).

Gomez; Security Southwest Life Ins. Co. v., TexApp–El Paso, 768 SW2d 505.—App & E 758.3(9), 842(1), 1050.1(11), 1058(1); Evid 357, 591; Insurance 2439, 2980, 2985, 3003(8), 3015, 3571, 3579; Interest 31, 44; Trial 356(1).

Gomez; Sovereign Camp, W. O. W. v., TexCivApp–San Antonio, 129 SW2d 784.—Insurance 3343, 3395; Pretrial Proc 712, 717.1, 718, 724.

Gomez v. State, TexCrimApp, 962 SW2d 572.—Crim Law 1098, 1104(3), 1109(2), 1109(3), 1110(2).

Gomez v. State, TexCrimApp, 704 SW2d 770.—Crim Law 713, 719(1), 730(7), 1171.1(4).

Gomez v. State, TexCrimApp, 685 SW2d 333.—Ind & Inf 167; Rob 11, 17(1), 20, 24.15(1), 24.15(2); Sent & Pun 2021.

Gomez v. State, TexCrimApp, 492 SW2d 486.—Crim Law 570(1), 625.10(4), 625.15.

Gomez v. State, TexCrimApp, 486 SW2d 338.—Controlled Subs 138; Crim Law 404.60; Searches 15.

Gomez v. State, TexCrimApp, 471 SW2d 393.—Crim Law 1130(4), 1132.

Gomez v. State, TexCrimApp, 470 SW2d 871.—Arrest 71.1(8); Controlled Subs 112; Crim Law 478(1).

Gomez v. State, TexCrimApp, 461 SW2d 422.—Controlled Subs 154; Crim Law 37(8), 507(4), 742(2).

Gomez v. State, TexCrimApp, 365 SW2d 176.—Burg 41(1); Sent & Pun 1376, 1381(4).

Gomez v. State, TexCrimApp, 365 SW2d 165.—Controlled Subs 80; Crim Law 1031(1).

Gomez v. State, TexCrimApp, 346 SW2d 847, 171 TexCrim 252, cert den 82 SCt 386, 368 US 947, 7 LEd2d 343.—Crim Law 1034, 1128(2); Rec S Goods 8(3).

Gomez v. State, TexCrimApp, 341 SW2d 180.—Bail 64.

Gomez v. State, TexCrimApp, 293 SW2d 657, 163 TexCrim 469.—Controlled Subs 80; Crim Law 369.1; Searches 197.

Gomez v. State, TexCrimApp, 289 SW2d 269, 163 TexCrim 99, 73 ALR2d 958.—Child S 653.

Gomez v. State, TexCrimApp, 280 SW2d 278, 162 TexCrim 30.—Controlled Subs 63, 75; Ind & Inf 114, 166; Sent & Pun 1219, 1367, 1371; Witn 345(2).

Gomez v. State, TexCrimApp, 263 SW2d 161, 159 TexCrim 291.—Rob 24.10.

Gomez v. State, TexCrimApp, 187 SW2d 911.—Crim Law 1090.1(1).

Gomez v. State, TexCrimApp, 166 SW2d 699, 145 TexCrim 168.—Crim Law 338(1), 448(1), 829(5), 913(3); Homic 1326, 1345, 1400.

Gomez v. State, TexCrimApp, 162 SW2d 428, 144 TexCrim 219.—Crim Law 1111(4), 1173.1.

Gomez v. State, TexCrimApp, 137 SW2d 1027, 138 TexCrim 544.—Homic 1134.

Gomez v. State, TexCrimApp, 94 SW2d 1157, 130 TexCrim 513.—Crim Law 338(1), 683(1); Witn 406.

Gomez v. State, TexApp–Houston (1 Dist), 49 SW3d 456, petition for discretionary review refused.—Crim Law 406(2), 419(1), 1147, 1153(1).

Gomez v. State, TexApp–Houston (1 Dist), 35 SW3d 746, reh overr, and petition for discretionary review refused. —Crim Law 719(1), 726, 1106(4), 1109(3).

Gomez v. State, TexApp–Houston (1 Dist), 991 SW2d 870, petition for discretionary review refused, cert den 120 SCt 1166, 528 US 1157, 145 LEd2d 1076.—Crim Law 855(1), 855(8), 925(1), 928, 956(12), 1155, 1174(5).

Gomez v. State, TexApp–San Antonio, 9 SW3d 189.— Crim Law 374, 419(1.10), 641.13(1), 641.13(2.1), 1147, 1156(1), 1169.11; Jury 90; Rape 48(1); Witn 318.

Gomez v. State, TexApp–Tyler, 183 SW3d 86.—Assault 91.8; Const Law 984; Crim Law 553, 662.7, 662.9, 1144.13(2.1), 1153(1), 1159.2(2), 1159.2(7), 1159.2(9), 1159.3(2), 1159.4(2); Witn 283.

Gomez v. State, TexApp–Corpus Christi, 921 SW2d 329. —Chem Dep 12; Crim Law 273(4.1), 273.1(1), 273.1(2), 273.1(4), 273.1(5), 273.4(1), 641.13(1), 641.13(5), 1167(5); Sent & Pun 1373, 1381(2), 1408.

Gomez v. State, TexApp–Corpus Christi, 763 SW2d 583. —Crim Law 1081(6).

Gomez v. State, TexApp–Corpus Christi, 730 SW2d 144, petition for discretionary review refused.—Const Law 2574; Crim Law 633(2), 996(1), 1032(1), 1166.20; Ind & Inf 52(2), 196(1); Jury 29(6); Sent & Pun 1982(2).

Gomez v. State, TexApp–Corpus Christi, 698 SW2d 486. —Arrest 63.4(8), 63.4(12), 71.1(3).

Gomez v. State, TexApp–Corpus Christi, 665 SW2d 849, petition for discretionary review gr, opinion after remand 698 SW2d 486.—Crim Law 275.

Gomez v. State, TexApp–Corpus Christi, 663 SW2d 662. —Crim Law 29(1); Larc 5.

Gomez v. State, TexApp–Corpus Christi, 662 SW2d 443. —Crim Law 1114.1(1).

Gomez v. State, TexApp–Corpus Christi, 638 SW2d 133, petition for discretionary review refused.—Crim Law 556, 641.13(1), 641.13(2.1); Homic 511, 1127, 1129, 1134.

Gomez v. State, TexApp–Corpus Christi, 626 SW2d 113, petition for discretionary review refused.—Crim Law 369.1, 369.2(1), 372(4).

Gomez v. State, TexApp–Houston (14 Dist), 905 SW2d 735, reh overr, and petition for discretionary review gr, aff 962 SW2d 572.—Burg 14, 25, 41(3), 41(6), 42(3); Crim Law 562, 1034, 1088.1, 1088.20, 1109(2), 1144.13(2.1), 1159.2(7), 1166.13.

Gomez v. State, TexApp–Houston (14 Dist), 709 SW2d 351, petition for discretionary review refused.—Consp 24(1), 47(2); Crim Law 423(1), 423(9), 577.16(7), 599, 629.5(3), 721(3), 1148, 1169.2(6); Jury 132.

Gomez v. State, TexApp–Houston (14 Dist), 681 SW2d 814.—Crim Law 273.1(4), 274(2), 274(9), 956(1), 956(4), 1116.

Gomez v. State Bar of Texas, TexApp–Austin, 856 SW2d 804, writ gr, rev 891 SW2d 243.—App & E 854(1); Atty & C 32(3); Courts 155, 472.1, 472.2; Decl Judgm 8, 81, 124.1, 273, 300, 385, 387; Inj 85(1).

Gomez v. Texas Cas. Ins. Co., TexCivApp–Austin, 355 SW2d 546.—Evid 20(1); Work Comp 288.

Gomez; Texas Cities Gas Co. v., TexCivApp–Galveston, 160 SW2d 74, writ refused wom.—App & E 758.3(9), 766, 882(7), 882(16); Damag 33, 133; Evid 474(4).

Gomez v. Texas Dept. of Criminal Justice, Institutional Div., Tex, 896 SW2d 176, on remand 1995 WL 688870, extension of time gr.—App & E 345.2.

Gomez v. Texas Dept. of Mental Health and Mental Retardation, CA5 (Tex), 794 F2d 1018.—Civil R 1249(2); Const Law 90.1(7.2), 1927, 1929, 1947, 1954; Fed Civ Proc 2605.1; States 4.1(1).

Gomez; Texas Emp. Ins. Ass'n v., TexCivApp–Eastland, 313 SW2d 956, ref nre.—Marriage 40(5), 40(10); Work Comp 1353, 1474.

Gomez; Texas Employers' Ins. Ass'n v., TexApp–El Paso, 756 SW2d 80.—Work Comp 1042, 1649, 1657.

Gomez; The State Bar of Texas v., Tex, 891 SW2d 243.— Action 6, 13; Atty & C 32(3); Courts 472.2; Decl Judgm 204.

Gomez v. Tri City Community Hosp., Ltd., TexApp–San Antonio, 4 SW3d 281.—App & E 863, 866(3), 934(1); Judgm 181(33), 185(4), 185(5).

Gomez; U.S. v., CA5 (Tex), 276 F3d 694.—Crim Law 662.10, 1139, 1158(4); Searches 26, 161, 162, 164.

Gomez; U.S. v., CA5 (Tex), 129 F3d 752. See U.S. v. Castro.

Gomez; U.S. v., CA5 (Tex), 947 F2d 737, cert den 112 SCt 1504, 503 US 947, 117 LEd2d 642.—Crim Law 394.5(3), 394.6(4), 736(1), 1158(2).

Gomez; U.S. v., CA5 (Tex), 900 F2d 43, reh den, appeal after remand 947 F2d 737, cert den 112 SCt 1504, 503 US 947, 117 LEd2d 642.—Crim Law 394.6(4), 1169.1(10); Tel 1440.

Gomez; U.S. v., CA5 (Tex), 776 F2d 542, reh den 777 F2d 701.—Arrest 63.5(6); Consp 47(1), 47(12); Controlled Subs 112, 122; Crim Law 338(7), 577.8(2).

Gomez; U.S. v., CA5 (Tex), 553 F2d 958.—Gr Jury 36.3(1), 36.5(2); Sent & Pun 1, 40, 94.

Gomez; U.S. v., CA5 (Tex), 529 F2d 412, reh den 532 F2d 1376.—Consp 41, 47(2), 47(12); Controlled Subs 28, 79, 113, 117; Crim Law 338(1), 348, 419(10), 655(5), 673(4), 792(3), 822(1), 1036.1(3.1), 1036.4, 1144.13(3), 1153(1), 1166.22(2), 1169.1(9).

Gomez; U.S. v., CA5 (Tex), 165 FedAppx 353, cert den Aguirre-Jaimes v. US, 126 SCt 2339, 164 LEd2d 854.— Crim Law 1177; Jury 31.1; Sent & Pun 793.

Gomez; Vela v., TexApp–Corpus Christi, 4 SW3d 911.— Offic 114; States 79.

Gomez; Vernon v., CA5 (Tex), 198 FedAppx 372.—Civil R 1376(6); Consp 7.5(1); False Imp 15(1); Fed Civ Proc 2491.5, 2491.7; Sheriffs 100.

Gomez; Voyer v., TexCivApp–Dallas, 258 SW2d 859.— Deeds 95; Ease 24; Estop 32(1).

Gomez v. Zamora, TexApp–Corpus Christi, 814 SW2d 114.—App & E 954(1); Contracts 117(3), 138(1); Inj 135, 138.3; Ref of Inst 23.

Gomez-Cavazos v. U.S. Dept. of Justice, EDTex, 75 FSupp2d 587.—Action 3; Records 31; U S 136.

Gomez de Hernandez v. Bridgestone/Firestone North American Tire, L.L.C., TexApp–Corpus Christi, 204 SW3d 473, reh overr, and review den.—App & E 189(3), 883, 946, 949, 1079; Courts 28; Damag 91.5(4); Sales 425.

Gomez de Hernandez v. New Texas Auto Auction Services, L.P., TexApp–Corpus Christi, 193 SW3d 220, reh overr, and review gr.—App & E 248; Judgm 181(33); Prod Liab 1, 5, 6, 71, 75.1, 83.5; Sales 425.

Gomez Garza Design, Inc.; La Villa Independent School Dist. v., TexApp–Corpus Christi, 79 SW3d 217, reh overr, and review den.—App & E 863, 934(1), 946, 977(5); Contracts 326; Estop 52(7), 62.5; Judgm 199(1), 199(3.5), 199(3.7); Schools 63(3), 79, 80(1), 86(2), 122.

Gomez-Guerra; U.S. v., CA5 (Tex), 485 F3d 301.—Aliens 770; Burg 4; Const Law 4509(1); Sent & Pun 781, 793.

Gomez Leon v. State, Tex, 426 SW2d 562.—App & E 1170.1; Em Dom 262(2), 262(5); Evid 142(1), 555.6(10); Witn 275(6).

Gomez Leon v. State, TexCivApp–El Paso, 418 SW2d 544, rev 426 SW2d 562.—Em Dom 222(4), 262(5).

Gomez-Morales; U.S. v., CA5 (Tex), 174 FedAppx 831, cert den Olmedo v. US, 127 SCt 177, 166 LEd2d 125.—Crim Law 1177; Sent & Pun 661.

Gomez-Moreno; U.S. v., CA5 (Tex), 479 F3d 350.—Crim Law 394.5(4), 1134(6), 1139, 1158(1), 1158(2), 1158(4); Searches 24, 40.1, 42.1, 45, 180, 182.

Gomez-Parra; City of El Paso v., TexApp–El Paso, 198 SW3d 364.—App & E 863, 893(1); Courts 35; Mun Corp 724, 725, 729, 742(4); Plead 104(1); States 191.4(1).

Gomez-Pineda; U.S. v., CA5 (Tex), 124 FedAppx 884, cert den 126 SCt 237, 546 US 899, 163 LEd2d 219.—Sent & Pun 793.

Gomez-Rojas; U.S. v., CA5 (Tex), 507 F2d 1213, cert den 96 SCt 41, 423 US 826, 46 LEd2d 42.—Consp 47(12); Controlled Subs 31, 81; Crim Law 37(3), 37(6.1), 330, 422(1), 427(2), 569, 627.10(1), 655(1), 656(1), 739.1(1), 772(6), 822(1), 822(3), 867, 1159.2(5), 1159.6, 1166.22(1), 1189; Witn 2(1), 307, 308.

Gomez-Romero; U.S. v., CA5 (Tex), 168 FedAppx 603, cert den Arevalo-Lozano v. US, 126 SCt 2337, 164 LEd2d 852.—Crim Law 1177; Sent & Pun 661.

Gomez Sanchez Vda de Gonzales v. Naviero Neptuno S.A., EDTex, 641 FSupp 75.—Death 31(3.1), 31(7); Fed Cts 247; Seamen 29(2), 29(4).

Gomez-Trujillo; U.S. v., CA5 (Tex), 107 FedAppx 406, cert gr, vac 125 SCt 1865, 544 US 970, 161 LEd2d 716, on remand 165 FedAppx 324, cert den 127 SCt 363, 166 LEd2d 137.—Crim Law 1035(1).

Gomez-Vargas; U.S. v., CA5 (Tex), 111 FedAppx 741, cert den Elizalde-Casares v. US, 125 SCt 1098, 543 US 1129, 160 LEd2d 1083, reh den, reh den 125 SCt 1380, 543 US 1180, 161 LEd2d 170.—Crim Law 1026.10(4); Sent & Pun 793.

Gomillion v. Lingold, TexCivApp–Galveston, 209 SW2d 205.—App & E 931(4), 1010.1(13); Evid 18; Plead 111.21, 111.42(10), 246(1), 249(1).

Gomillion v. Union Bridge & Const. Co. of Kansas City, Mo., CCA5 (Tex), 100 F2d 937, cert den 59 SCt 1031, 307 US 634, 83 LEd 1516.—Work Comp 2084, 2094, 2100.

Gomperts v. Wendeborn, TexCivApp–Austin, 427 SW2d 904.—Autos 244(22.1), 244(36.1); Judgm 101(1), 106(1).

Gonannies, Inc. v. Goupair.Com, Inc., NDTex, 464 FSupp2d 603.—Inj 138.1, 138.6, 147, 150; Trademarks 1133, 1137(1), 1360, 1704(2), 1705(2), 1707(4), 1800.

Gonce; Texas Cas. Ins. Co. v., TexCivApp–Eastland, 390 SW2d 405, ref nre.—Work Comp 1460, 1581, 1929, 1974.

Gondek v. State, TexCrimApp, 491 SW2d 676.—Crim Law 641.13(6), 1043(2).

Gondron v. U.S., CA5 (Tex), 256 F2d 205, cert den 79 SCt 96, 358 US 865, 3 LEd2d 98, reh den 79 SCt 228, 358 US 902, 3 LEd2d 235.—Double J 107.1; Int Rev 5290, 5291.1, 5295.

Gondron v. U.S., CA5 (Tex), 242 F2d 149.—Crim Law 1189.

Gondron; U.S. v., SDTex, 159 FSupp 691.—Crim Law 404.60; Double J 107.1; Int Rev 5295.

Gone v. Gone, TexApp–Houston (14 Dist), 993 SW2d 845, reh overr, and review den.—App & E 842(2), 852, 893(1), 1008.1(4), 1012.1(4), 1071.2; Divorce 166; Judgm 335(1), 335(2), 335(3); Trial 404(6).

Gone; Gone v., TexApp–Houston (14 Dist), 993 SW2d 845, reh overr, and review den.—App & E 842(2), 852, 893(1), 1008.1(4), 1012.1(4), 1071.2; Divorce 166; Judgm 335(1), 335(2), 335(3); Trial 404(6).

Gone v. State, TexApp–Texarkana, 54 SW3d 27, reh overr, and petition for discretionary review refused.—Convicts 1; Crim Law 304(1), 641.13(1), 641.13(2.1), 641.13(6), 641.13(7), 673(5), 693, 721(1), 721(3), 770(1), 801, 828, 1036.1(1), 1036.1(8), 1038.2, 1167(1); Ind & Inf 42; Mental H 469(5); Perj 3.

Gongora v. State, TexApp–Houston (1 Dist), 916 SW2d 570, petition for discretionary review refused.—Crim Law 295, 1083; Double J 1, 2, 60.1, 138, 146, 201; Judgm 650.

Gongora v. State, TexApp–Fort Worth, 214 SW3d 58, petition for discretionary review refused.—Crim Law 417(15), 422(5), 662.8, 662.10, 1134(6), 1139, 1153(1).

Gongora; U.S. v., CA5 (Tex), 172 FedAppx 611.—Controlled Subs 100(9).

Gongwer, Matter of Marriage of, TexCivApp–Amarillo, 554 SW2d 49.—Divorce 252.3(4); Hus & W 249(3), 264(4).

Gonnering v. Blue Cross and Blue Shield of Texas, WDTex, 420 FSupp2d 660.—Civil R 1217, 1502, 1552, 1744; Damag 57.20, 57.57; Libel 1, 19, 23.1, 123(2); Torts 350, 351.

Gonsalez Moreno v. Milk Train, Inc., WDTex, 182 FSupp2d 590.—Const Law 3964; Contracts 127(4); Fed Civ Proc 1825, 1835; Fed Cts 76.10, 87.5, 96.

Gonzaba; Limon v., TexApp–San Antonio, 940 SW2d 236, reh overr, and writ den.—Health 755, 757.

Gonzaba v. St. Paul Fire and Marine Ins. Co., CA5 (Tex), 179 FedAppx 218.—Insurance 2275, 2278(9), 2386.

Gonzales, Ex parte, Tex, 414 SW2d 656.—Child S 458, 497.

Gonzales, Ex parte, TexCrimApp, 204 SW3d 391.—Crim Law 641.13(1), 641.13(6), 641.13(7), 700(2.1); Hab Corp 486(5), 753.

Gonzales, Ex parte, TexCrimApp, 945 SW2d 830.—Const Law 4494; Contempt 24, 40, 61(1); Crim Law 641.1, 641.2(2), 641.2(3), 641.4(1).

Gonzales, Ex parte, TexCrimApp, 790 SW2d 646.—Crim Law 641.13(7).

Gonzales, Ex parte, TexCrimApp, 707 SW2d 570.—Double J 30.

Gonzales, Ex parte, TexCrimApp, 557 SW2d 790.—Burg 19.

Gonzales, Ex parte, TexApp–Austin, 12 SW3d 913, petition for discretionary review refused.—Hab Corp 271, 814.

Gonzales, Ex parte, TexApp–Austin, 667 SW2d 932, petition for discretionary review refused.—Const Law 4563; Double J 91(1); Hab Corp 288, 466.

Gonzales, Ex parte, TexCivApp–Amarillo, 606 SW2d 5.—Const Law 4495.

Gonzales, In re, BkrtcyNDTex, 224 BR 360. See Thompson, In re.

Gonzales, In re, BkrtcyNDTex, 206 BR 133.—Bankr 2576.5(1), 2576.5(2), 2788, 2802; Sec Tran 146.

Gonzales; Abdulle v., WDTex, 422 FSupp2d 774.—Aliens 469; Hab Corp 521, 670(1).

Gonzales; Al-Mousa v., CA5 (Tex), 166 FedAppx 746.—Hab Corp 282.

Gonzales; Alvarado v., TexCivApp–Corpus Christi, 552 SW2d 539.—Child 21(2), 38; Const Law 990, 2503(4); Lim of Act 1, 3(1); Statut 181(2), 263.

Gonzales v. American General Leasing & Financing Corp., TexCivApp–Waco, 555 SW2d 197.—Bills & N 480; Judgm 185.3(1).

Gonzales v. American Postal Workers Union, AFL-CIO, TexApp–San Antonio, 948 SW2d 794, reh overr, and writ den.—App & E 1177(1), 1178(1); Assoc 1, 19, 20(2); Const Law 1440; Judgm 181(11), 185.3(1), 186; Libel 74.

Gonzales v. American States Ins. Co. of Texas, TexApp–Corpus Christi, 628 SW2d 184.—Insurance 2278(21), 2914, 2915.

Gonzales v. American Title Co. of Houston, TexApp–Houston (1 Dist), 104 SW3d 588, reh overr, and review den (2 pets), and reh of petition for review den.—Antitrust 141, 291, 398; App & E 1078(1); Bills & N 340; Brok 6, 102; Consp 1.1, 9, 13; Dep & Escr 13; Fraud 24, 30; Mtg 123, 124; Princ & A 1.

Gonzales; Betancourt-Ramirez v., CA5 (Tex), 165 FedAppx 369.—Aliens 322.

Gonzales v. Beto, CA5 (Tex), 460 F2d 314.—Const Law 4658(2); Crim Law 1132; Searches 66.

Gonzales v. Beto, CA5 (Tex), 445 F2d 1202, rev 92 SCt 1503, 405 US 1052, 31 LEd2d 787, conformed to 460 F2d 1066.—Crim Law 855(3).

Gonzales v. Beto, CA5 (Tex), 425 F2d 963, cert den 91 SCt 194, 400 US 928, 27 LEd2d 189, cert den Acosta v. Beto, 91 SCt 476, 400 US 1001, 27 LEd2d 452.— Controlled Subs 148(3); Crim Law 412.2(3), 627.10(4), 1136; Searches 107, 111, 115.1, 117.

Gonzales v. Beto, NDTex, 314 FSupp 1031.—Crim Law 321, 531(3), 532(0.5), 850.

Gonzales v. Beto, WDTex, 266 FSupp 751, aff State of Tex v. Gonzales, 388 F2d 145.—Arrest 63.3, 63.4(14), 71.1(3); Const Law 4460; Crim Law 692; Searches 17, 47.1, 164.

Gonzales v. Blake, TexCivApp–Hous (1 Dist), 605 SW2d 634.—Plead 111.30, 409(1), 409(3); Pretrial Proc 480; Venue 17, 22(1), 22(10).

Gonzales; Bristol-Myers Co. v., Tex, 561 SW2d 801.— Prod Liab 14, 46.2; Witn 374(1).

Gonzales; Bristol-Myers Co. v., TexCivApp–Corpus Christi, 548 SW2d 416, writ gr, rev 561 SW2d 801.— App & E 232(0.5), 232(2), 301, 722(1), 729, 930(3), 989, 1004(5), 1140(2), 1170.7; Contrib 5(1), 5(6.1); Damag 63, 99, 132(14); Evid 208(6), 219.55(1), 314(1), 318(1), 507, 508, 519, 538, 558(11), 560; Health 823(13); Indem 72; Prod Liab 14, 27, 46.1, 46.2, 81.1, 83; Torts 135; Trial 54(1), 86, 125(3), 129, 207.

Gonzales v. Brown, SDTex, 768 FSupp 581.—Civil R 1376(1), 1376(5), 1418; Schools 114.

Gonzales; Brown v., TexCivApp–San Antonio, 653 SW2d 854.—App & E 724(3), 843(2), 1003(5); Evid 219(3), 595; Neglig 232, 250; Ship 86(2.5).

Gonzales; Calderon v., TexCivApp–San Antonio, 158 SW2d 349.—Chat Mtg 138(1); Subrog 23(5), 33(2).

Gonzales; Cameron County Drainage Dist. No. 5 v., TexApp–Corpus Christi, 69 SW3d 820.—App & E 930(1), 989, 1001(1), 1001(3), 1003(6), 1182; Em Dom 131, 136, 150, 166, 222(4); Evid 474(19), 568(4).

Gonzales v. Cassidy, CA5 (Tex), 474 F2d 67.—Const Law 4012; Fed Civ Proc 164, 181; Judgm 677, 707.

Gonzales; Caterpillar Tractor Co., Tex, 571 SW2d 867, on remand 599 SW2d 633, ref nre.—Courts 247(2); Prod Liab 8, 10, 11, 15, 83.5, 85.

Gonzales; Caterpillar Tractor Co. v., TexCivApp–El Paso, 599 SW2d 633, ref nre.—Damag 130.1, 134(1); Evid 359(0.5), 558(9); Neglig 554(1); Prod Liab 15, 81.1, 85; Trial 260(8), 351.5(5).

Gonzales; Caterpillar Tractor Co. v., TexCivApp–El Paso, 562 SW2d 573, writ gr, rev 571 SW2d 867, on remand 599 SW2d 633, ref nre.—Evid 571(6); Prod Liab 1, 5, 8, 11, 48, 49, 77.5, 83.5, 96.1.

Gonzales; Central Adjustment Bureau, Inc. v., TexCivApp–San Antonio, 528 SW2d 314.—Antitrust 216, 369; App & E 499(1); Costs 194.32, 252; Torts 453.

Gonzales; Chapman v., TexApp–Houston (14 Dist), 824 SW2d 685, writ den.—App & E 934(1); Judges 36; Offic 114, 116; Sheriffs 99.

Gonzales v. City of Corpus Christi, TexCivApp–San Antonio, 323 SW2d 495.—Mun Corp 741.15, 741.50, 742(5), 812(7).

Gonzales v. City of El Paso, TexApp–El Paso, 978 SW2d 619.—Mun Corp 723, 742(4), 747(3), 847, 854; Offic 116.

Gonzales v. City of Lancaster, TexApp–Dallas, 675 SW2d 293.—Evid 568(1), 570; Mun Corp 628; Parties 76(1), 76(2).

Gonzales v. City of New Braunfels, Tex., CA5 (Tex), 176 F3d 834.—Civil R 1140, 1217, 1218(4), 1223, 1225(3); Fed Cts 614, 915.

Gonzales; City of San Antonio v., TexApp–San Antonio, 737 SW2d 78.—Courts 91(2).

Gonzales; City of San Antonio v., TexCivApp–San Antonio, 304 SW2d 429, ref nre.—App & E 281(1); Evid 571(7); Judgm 199(3); Trial 140(1).

Gonzales v. City of Sinton, Tex., SDTex, 319 FSupp 189. —Const Law 3645, 3649; Elections 172.

Gonzales v. Columbia Hospital at Medical City Dallas Subsidiary LP., NDTex, 207 FSupp2d 570.—Compromise 11; Contracts 143(2), 143.5, 147(3), 176(2), 326; Fed Civ Proc 824, 833, 834, 851; Labor & Emp 646, 678, 857.

Gonzales v. Concerned Citizens of Webberville, TexApp–Austin, 173 SW3d 112, reh overr, and review den. —App & E 837(1); Courts 39; Mun Corp 7, 14, 18; Plead 104(1), 111.38, 111.43, 111.48; Quo W 5, 32, 34; Statut 185, 188.

Gonzales v. Conoco, Inc., TexApp–San Antonio, 722 SW2d 247.—App & E 961; Pretrial Proc 44.1, 563.

Gonzales; Dallas County v., TexApp–Dallas, 183 SW3d 94, reh overr, and review den (2 pets), and reh of petition for review den.—Action 34, 35; App & E 70(8), 762; Civil R 1308, 1398, 1426; Const Law 1555, 1929, 1955, 3867, 3874(1), 3874(2), 3893, 4171; Courts 39; Fed Cts 265, 269, 270; Judgm 181(7), 185(5); Labor & Emp 852; Offic 69.7, 114, 119; Plead 104(1), 111.36, 111.43; Records 7; Sheriffs 21, 97; States 191.4(1).

Gonzales v. Dallas County, Tex., CA5 (Tex), 249 F3d 406.—Civil R 1376(10); Fed Cts 574.

Gonzales v. Daniel, TexApp–Corpus Christi, 854 SW2d 253.—App & E 82(5), 115; Attach 64; Execution 55, 70; Garn 58; Mand 4(1), 12, 54.

Gonzales v. Davis v., WDTex, 482 FSupp2d 796.—Aliens 469; Hab Corp 662.1.

Gonzales; Davis v., TexApp–Corpus Christi, 931 SW2d 15, reh overr, and writ den.—App & E 934(1); Judgm 181(11), 185(2); Plead 228.14, 228.23; Schools 147.

Gonzales; Davis v., TexCivApp–Fort Worth, 235 SW2d 221, dism.—Autos 19; Estop 92(3); Evid 21; Paymt 85(1), 85(7); Sales 234(6), 347(5), 390, 391(4), 391(6).

Gonzales; Delgado-Reynua v., CA5 (Tex), 450 F3d 596.— Aliens 356, 385.

Gonzales v. Department of Air Force, NDTex, 110 FRD 350.—Civil R 1530; Fed Civ Proc 853.

Gonzales v. Diaz, TexCivApp–El Paso, 424 SW2d 314.— App & E 981; New Tr 99, 104(3).

Gonzales; Dillard Department Stores, Inc. v., TexApp– El Paso, 72 SW3d 398, reh overr, and review den, and reh of petition for review den.—App & E 984(5); Civil R 1123, 1182, 1184, 1185, 1187, 1189, 1736, 1740, 1769, 1773; Damag 50.10, 208(6); Labor & Emp 826.

Gonzales; Elyakoubi v., CA5 (Tex), 155 FedAppx 807.— Hab Corp 282.

Gonzales v. Farmers Ins. Exchange, TexCivApp–Eastland, 399 SW2d 888, ref nre.—Insurance 2655(1); Trial 368.

Gonzales; Farm Services, Inc. v., TexApp–Corpus Christi, 756 SW2d 747, writ den.—Agric 9.5; App & E 230, 1043(1); Damag 134(1); Neglig 1624; Pretrial Proc 40.

Gonzales v. Galveston Independent School Dist., SDTex, 865 FSupp 1241.—Civil R 1251, 1376(2); Const Law 277(2), 1929, 1941, 1947, 1991, 1994, 3278(6), 4171, 4173(3), 4173(4), 4198, 4203; Fed Civ Proc 2497.1; Fed Cts 13.10; Offic 72.61, 114; Rem of C 101.1; Schools 63(1).

Gonzales; Gaona v., TexApp–Austin, 997 SW2d 784, reh overr.—Judgm 181(15.1), 780(1), 780(3), 785(1), 787; Ven & Pur 54, 231(1), 231(16.1), 233.

Gonzales v. Gilliam, TexCivApp–Eastland, 506 SW2d 650.—Damag 221(2.1); Evid 351, 373(1).

Gonzales v. Gonzales, TexApp–San Antonio, 728 SW2d 446.—Divorce 261; Lim of Act 6(10), 6(11), 51(2).

Gonzales; Gonzales v., TexApp–San Antonio, 728 SW2d 446.—Divorce 261; Lim of Act 6(10), 6(11), 51(2).

Gonzales v. Gonzales, TexCivApp–San Antonio, 224 SW2d 520, writ refused.—App & E 768; Hus & W 221, 270(5); Judgm 743(2).

Gonzales; Gonzales v., TexCivApp–San Antonio, 224 SW2d 520, writ refused.—App & E 768; Hus & W 221, 270(5); Judgm 743(2).

Gonzales v. Gonzales, TexCivApp–El Paso, 533 SW2d 480.—Contempt 66(1).

Gonzales; Gonzales v., TexCivApp–El Paso, 533 SW2d 480.—Contempt 66(1).

Gonzales; Grace Community Church v., TexApp–Houston (14 Dist), 853 SW2d 678.—App & E 852, 931(1), 989, 1010.1(1), 1012.1(4); Contracts 176(3); Princ & A 1, 3(2), 14(2), 23(5), 99, 123(3).

Gonzales; Guzman v., CA5 (Tex), 163 FedAppx 259, cert den 127 SCt 40, 166 LEd2d 18.—Hab Corp 521.

Gonzales v. Hearst Corp., TexApp–Houston (14 Dist), 930 SW2d 275.—App & E 866(3), 927(7); Libel 51(5), 104(1), 112(2); Trial 139.1(14), 139.1(17), 142, 143, 168.

Gonzales v. H.E. Butt Grocery Co., CA5 (Tex), 226 FedAppx 342.—Civil R 1049; Consp 7.5(1); Damag 57.25(2).

Gonzales; Highlands State Bank v., TexCivApp–Waco, 340 SW2d 828.—Garn 32.

Gonzales; Hosein v., CA5 (Tex), 452 F3d 401.—Aliens 667; Decl Judgm 62, 341.1, 345.1; Fed Civ Proc 103.2, 103.3; Fed Cts 759.1.

Gonzales v. Houston Chronicle Pub. Co., TexApp–Houston (14 Dist, 930 SW2d 275. See Gonzales v. Hearst Corp.

Gonzales; Howard v., CA5 (Tex), 658 F2d 352.—Civil R 1412, 1420, 1423, 1437; Courts 90(2); Fed Cts 637, 756.1, 761, 892, 893, 903, 908.1; Witn 337(28), 379(9).

Gonzales; Insurance Agency Managers v., TexCivApp–Hous (1 Dist), 578 SW2d 803.—Assign 100; Bills & N 148.1; Impl & C C 63, 99.1, 110.

Gonzales; Jack Cane Corp. v., TexCivApp–San Antonio, 410 SW2d 953.—Courts 89; Trial 48, 352.12.

Gonzales v. John F. Grant Lumber Co., TexCivApp–El Paso, 103 SW2d 1068.—App & E 554(2), 773(2).

Gonzales v. Johnson, NDTex, 994 FSupp 759.—Const Law 3880, 4733(2); Hab Corp 450.1, 503.1, 795(1); Judges 49(2); Sent & Pun 31, 2026.

Gonzales; Jones v., TexCivApp–Amarillo, 344 SW2d 745, ref nre.—Em Dom 147, 157, 205; Land & Ten 157(2).

Gonzales; Jones v., TexCivApp–Amarillo, 326 SW2d 634, ref nre.—Judgm 185(2), 185.3(14), 186.

Gonzales; Khan v., WDTex, 481 FSupp2d 638.—Aliens 469.

Gonzales v. Knight, TexCivApp–Corpus Christi, 458 SW2d 529.—Elections 21, 169.

Gonzales; Kurth v., EDTex, 472 FSupp2d 874.—Civil R 1019(2), 1217, 1218(2), 1218(3), 1220, 1224, 1243; Fed Civ Proc 2497.1, 2533.1.

Gonzales; Kurth v., EDTex, 469 FSupp2d 415, subsequent determination 472 FSupp2d 874.—Admin Law 229; Civil R 1123, 1216, 1220, 1249(1), 1308, 1516; Offic 69.7, 72.41(1), 72.41(2), 72.53, 72.54, 72.55(2), 72.58(2); U S 36.

Gonzales v. Lang, CA5 (Tex), 469 F2d 1075, cert den Corpus v. Estelle, 94 SCt 236, 414 US 932, 38 LEd2d 162.—Hab Corp 490(6).

Gonzales v. Laughlin, TexCivApp–San Antonio, 256 SW2d 236.—Courts 47; Mand 14(1), 14(3), 168(4).

Gonzales; Lee v., CA5 (Tex), 410 F3d 778, reh den.—Aliens 385; Hab Corp 282, 841, 842.

Gonzales v. Levy Strauss & Co., TexApp–San Antonio, 70 SW3d 278.—Judgm 185.3(21); Labor & Emp 984, 997; Libel 23.1, 41, 51(1), 51(4), 112(2).

Gonzales v. Lockwood Lumber Co., TexApp–Houston (14 Dist), 668 SW2d 813, ref nre.—App & E 882(20); Interest 66; Mtg 379.

Gonzales; Long v., TexApp–San Antonio, 650 SW2d 173. —Plead 104(2).

Gonzales v. Lubbock State School, TexCivApp–Amarillo, 487 SW2d 815.—Judgm 181(11); Labor & Emp 2832, 2921; Plead 48; States 112(2), 208.

Gonzales; McFall v., CA5 (Tex), 143 FedAppx 604.—Civil R 1135.

Gonzales; Medical Center Pharmacy v., WDTex, 451 FSupp2d 854.—Admin Law 394; Health 317, 322, 324, 327; Searches 79; Statut 64(1), 64(2), 217.4.

Gonzales v. Methodist Retirement Communities, TexApp–Houston (14 Dist), 33 SW3d 882, reh overr, and review den.—Health 276.

Gonzales; Minix v., TexApp–Houston (14 Dist), 162 SW3d 635.—App & E 893(1); Convicts 6; Costs 128; Plead 34(3.5); Prisons 10.

Gonzales v. Missouri Pac. R. Co., CA5 (Tex), 511 F2d 629.—Fed Civ Proc 2211, 2214; Fed Cts 799; Hus & W 260, 270(3), 270(9); Neglig 372; R R 335.5; Trial 350.5(1).

Gonzales; Ngole v., CA5 (Tex), 136 FedAppx 698.—Hab Corp 824.

Gonzales; Nicol v., TexApp–Dallas, 127 SW3d 390, reh overr.—App & E 842(2), 893(1); Contracts 143(1), 143(2), 147(2), 147(3), 152, 156, 176(2); Ease 26(2); Frds St of 144, 152(1), 152(2).

Gonzales v. Norris of Houston, Inc., TexCivApp–Hous (14 Dist), 575 SW2d 110, ref nre.—App & E 173(6), 954(1), 1144; Contracts 117(2); Inj 135, 138.21, 138.39, 157, 158.

Gonzales v. Orsak, TexCivApp–Galveston, 205 SW2d 793. —Autos 245(78), 245(90); Trial 251(8), 350.6(3), 351.5(1), 351.5(6), 366.

Gonzales v. O/S Vessel Brazos Pilot, SDTex, 56 FSupp2d 770, aff 229 F3d 1148.—Adm 18, 20, 78; Fed Cts 41, 43, 46, 63, 65; Pilots 2.5; Seamen 29(5.3).

Gonzales v. Outlar, TexApp–Corpus Christi, 829 SW2d 931.—Evid 512, 571(3); Health 611, 618; Judgm 181(33), 185.1(4), 185.3(21).

Gonzales v. Pan American Nat. Bank, TexApp–Dallas, 692 SW2d 111.—Bills & N 473.

Gonzales; Pierson v., CA5 (Tex), 73 FedAppx 60.—Civil R 1091.

Gonzales v. Proctor & Gamble Mfg. Co., TexApp–Corpus Christi, 655 SW2d 243.—Plead 290(3).

Gonzales v. P.T. Pelangi Niagra Mitra Int'l., SDTex, 196 FSupp2d 482.—Fed Cts 45.

Gonzales v. Quarterman, CA5 (Tex), 458 F3d 384, cert den 127 SCt 1909, 167 LEd2d 568.—Crim Law 641.13(1), 641.13(6), 700(2.1), 700(3), 700(4); Hab Corp 450.1, 452, 486(4).

Gonzales; Ramirez v., CA5 (Tex), 225 FedAppx 203.—Civil R 1128, 1137, 1138, 1244, 1252, 1544; Evid 242(5); U S 36.

Gonzales; Reyes v., TexApp–El Paso, 22 SW3d 516, review den, cert den Texas v. Reyes, 121 SCt 2550, 533 US 929, 150 LEd2d 717.—Child S 94, 233, 556(1), 556(3); Social S 139.

Gonzales v. Reyes, TexCivApp–San Antonio, 564 SW2d 100, writ dism woj.—App & E 1178(6); Autos 226(3); Damag 113.

Gonzales v. Rickman, TexApp–Austin, 762 SW2d 277.—App & E 353.

Gonzales; Rodriguez v., Tex, 227 SW2d 791, 148 Tex 537. —Courts 247(8); Statut 67, 71, 77(1), 95(1).

Gonzales; Rogers v., TexApp–Corpus Christi, 654 SW2d 509, ref nre.—App & E 840(1), 971(2), 1041(2), 1047(1), 1062.2; Autos 244(34), 244(35), 244(41.1), 245(67.1); Death 68, 72, 88, 89; Evid 536, 542, 545, 546, 555.8(1), 555.8(2); Parent & C 4; Plead 229; Trial 139.1(6).

Gonzales; Salazar v., TexApp–Corpus Christi, 931 SW2d 59.—Elections 154(6).

Gonzales v. Secretary of Air Force, CA5 (Tex), 824 F2d 392, cert den 108 SCt 1245, 485 US 969, 99 LEd2d 443. —Lim of Act 125.

GONZALES

Gonzales v. Secretary of Air Force, NDTex, 638 FSupp 1323, aff 824 F2d 392, cert den 108 SCt 1245, 485 US 969, 99 LEd2d 443.—Lim of Act 124.

Gonzales v. Shing Wai Brass and Metal Wares Factory, Ltd., TexApp–San Antonio, 190 SW3d 742.—App & E 760(1), 893(1), 895(1); Judgm 183, 185(2), 185(5), 185.1(4).

Gonzales v. Singer, TexCivApp–San Antonio, 85 SW2d 273, writ dism.—Home 96; Paymt 73(1).

Gonzales; Sotelo v., TexApp–El Paso, 170 SW3d 783.— App & E 931(1), 946, 949, 989, 1010.1(1), 1010.2, 1012.1(5); Child C 42, 76, 123, 126, 147, 460, 465, 468, 579, 921(1), 922(1); Trial 139.1(3), 143, 397(2).

Gonzales v. Southwestern Bell Tel. Co., TexCivApp–Corpus Christi, 555 SW2d 219.—App & E 1004(8), 1175(1); Damag 95, 130.1, 208(1); Torts 340, 341.

Gonzales v. State, TexCrimApp, 67 SW3d 910, on remand 125 SW3d 616, petition for discretionary review gr, aff Pham v. State, 175 SW3d 767, cert den 126 SCt 490, 546 US 961, 163 LEd2d 364.—Crim Law 394.1(1), 412(4).

Gonzales v. State, TexCrimApp, 3 SW3d 915, reh den.—Crim Law 641.13(2.1), 918(3), 1166.16; Jury 131(15.1).

Gonzales v. State, TexCrimApp, 994 SW2d 170, on remand 2 SW3d 600, petition for discretionary review refused.—Crim Law 1162, 1166.16.

Gonzales v. State, TexCrimApp, 966 SW2d 521, on remand 977 SW2d 189, reh overr, and petition for discretionary review refused, appeal from denial of habeas corpus Ex parte Gonzales, 12 SW3d 913, petition for discretionary review refused.—Crim Law 1026.10(4).

Gonzales v. State, TexCrimApp, 931 SW2d 574.—Crim Law 1134(2), 1144.13(2.1), 1159.2(7); Homic 1165.

Gonzales v. State, TexCrimApp, 818 SW2d 756, on remand 831 SW2d 345, petition for discretionary review refused, cert den 113 SCt 1334, 507 US 939, 122 LEd2d 718.—Crim Law 662.65.

Gonzales v. State, TexCrimApp, 723 SW2d 746.—Crim Law 304(7); Ind & Inf 61.

Gonzales v. State, TexCrimApp, 717 SW2d 355, on remand 730 SW2d 196.—Homic 668, 912, 1380.

Gonzales v. State, TexCrimApp, 689 SW2d 900.—Const Law 4509(14); Homic 655, 672, 1205.

Gonzales v. State, TexCrimApp, 689 SW2d 231.—Courts 107; Obscen 20.

Gonzales v. State, TexCrimApp, 685 SW2d 333. See Gomez v. State.

Gonzales v. State, TexCrimApp, 685 SW2d 47, cert den 105 SCt 2704, 472 US 1009, 86 LEd2d 720, on remand 697 SW2d 50, petition for discretionary review refused. —Crim Law 1036.1(2), 1169.5(1), 1169.5(3), 1170.5(1), 1171.6.

Gonzales v. State, TexCrimApp, 648 SW2d 684.—Arrest 63.4(15), 63.4(16), 71.1(3); Searches 49.

Gonzales v. State, TexCrimApp, 605 SW2d 278.—Crim Law 641.5(3), 641.5(4).

Gonzales v. State, TexCrimApp, 581 SW2d 690.—Crim Law 351(2), 412.2(2).

Gonzales v. State, TexCrimApp, 578 SW2d 736.—Crim Law 1038.1(2).

Gonzales v. State, TexCrimApp, 577 SW2d 226, cert den 100 SCt 109, 444 US 853, 62 LEd2d 71.—Const Law 3785; Controlled Subs 143, 151; Int Liq 249; Searches 107, 112, 117, 121.1, 125.

Gonzales v. State, TexCrimApp, 576 SW2d 406.—Bail 77(1).

Gonzales v. State, TexCrimApp, 548 SW2d 60.—Crim Law 1068.5, 1182.

Gonzales v. State, TexCrimApp, 546 SW2d 617.—Homic 1451, 1458.

Gonzales v. State, TexCrimApp, 533 SW2d 801.—Autos 353; Crim Law 1159.5.

Gonzales v. State, TexCrimApp, 532 SW2d 343.—Crim Law 438(4), 444, 641.10(1), 641.10(2), 1037.1(1), 1042; Homic 713, 1209, 1210, 1213, 1460.

Gonzales v. State, TexCrimApp, 530 SW2d 570.—Controlled Subs 65.

Gonzales v. State, TexCrimApp, 527 SW2d 540.—Crim Law 1184(2); Homic 1569; Sent & Pun 2003.

Gonzales v. State, TexCrimApp, 517 SW2d 785.—Burg 2, 19; Sent & Pun 1369.

Gonzales v. State, TexCrimApp, 515 SW2d 920.—Crim Law 636(2).

Gonzales v. State, TexCrimApp, 505 SW2d 819.—Crim Law 605; Homic 1174.

Gonzales v. State, TexCrimApp, 505 SW2d 267, cert den 95 SCt 102, 419 US 856, 42 LEd2d 89.—Controlled Subs 82, 98; Crim Law 507(4), 780(2), 823(6).

Gonzales v. State, TexCrimApp, 501 SW2d 644.—Crim Law 339.11(9), 1174(2); Sent & Pun 1483.

Gonzales v. State, TexCrimApp, 500 SW2d 154.—Crim Law 633(2), 637, 1037.1(1).

Gonzales v. State, TexCrimApp, 494 SW2d 912.—Crim Law 444, 1043(3), 1115(1), 1120(1); Larc 65.

Gonzales v. State, TexCrimApp, 492 SW2d 263.—Crim Law 351(9), 369.2(6).

Gonzales v. State, TexCrimApp, 489 SW2d 616.—Crim Law 1130(2), 1159.2(10).

Gonzales v. State, TexCrimApp, 486 SW2d 380.—Crim Law 1144.6; Embez 35, 44(2).

Gonzales v. State, TexCrimApp, 480 SW2d 663.—Crim Law 273.1(4), 274(8), 534(1), 538(3); Homic 1154.

Gonzales v. State, TexCrimApp, 478 SW2d 522.—Crim Law 421(1), 460; Larc 65.

Gonzales v. State, TexCrimApp, 470 SW2d 700.—Crim Law 393(1), 603.2, 608, 641.13(2.1).

Gonzales v. State, TexCrimApp, 467 SW2d 454.—Arrest 63.4(8); Controlled Subs 128; Crim Law 394.6(4); Searches 15, 172.

Gonzales v. State, TexCrimApp, 466 SW2d 772.—Burg 41(1), 46(2); Crim Law 379, 444, 661, 741(1), 742(1), 749, 822(1), 884, 1172.9; Witn 68.

Gonzales v. State, TexCrimApp, 461 SW2d 408.—Autos 349.5(7); Searches 18.

Gonzales v. State, TexCrimApp, 458 SW2d 926.—Crim Law 273.4(1).

Gonzales v. State, TexCrimApp, 456 SW2d 137.—Crim Law 264.

Gonzales v. State, TexCrimApp, 449 SW2d 49.—Assault 96(7); Crim Law 1036.2, 1170.5(3).

Gonzales v. State, TexCrimApp, 446 SW2d 303.—Crim Law 1077.2(3).

Gonzales v. State, TexCrimApp, 441 SW2d 539.—Crim Law 742(2), 780(1), 1168(1), 1173.2(6).

Gonzales v. State, TexCrimApp, 440 SW2d 847, appeal after remand 456 SW2d 137.—Crim Law 1023(11), 1081(4.1); Sent & Pun 377.

Gonzales v. State, TexCrimApp, 429 SW2d 882.—Crim Law 412.2(5), 414, 517.2(2), 519(3), 519(8).

Gonzales v. State, TexCrimApp, 426 SW2d 859.—Homic 1136, 1479.

Gonzales v. State, TexCrimApp, 414 SW2d 181, cert den 88 SCt 795, 389 US 1052, 19 LEd2d 846.—Const Law 3310; Crim Law 729.

Gonzales v. State, TexCrimApp, 410 SW2d 435, cert den 87 SCt 2044, 387 US 925, 18 LEd2d 982.—Controlled Subs 38, 100(2); Crim Law 364(4), 369.1, 369.2(1), 369.2(8), 419(2); Searches 113.1; Sent & Pun 1381(4).

Gonzales v. State, TexCrimApp, 402 SW2d 763.—Controlled Subs 80, 104.

Gonzales v. State, TexCrimApp, 400 SW2d 772.—Homic 1134.

Gonzales v. State, TexCrimApp, 399 SW2d 360.—Burg 41(1); Crim Law 1038.1(7), 1090.13.

Gonzales v. State, TexCrimApp, 398 SW2d 132.—Crim Law 957(2).

Gonzales v. State, TexCrimApp, 389 SW2d 306, cert den 86 SCt 570, 382 US 992, 15 LEd2d 478.—Crim Law 1137(5).

Gonzales v. State, TexCrimApp, 386 SW2d 139.—Crim Law 914, 1147.

Gonzales v. State, TexCrimApp, 379 SW2d 352, cert den Gonzalez v. Texas, 85 SCt 1346, 380 US 981, 14 LEd2d 274.—Controlled Subs 80, 124; Crim Law 394.5(3).

Gonzales v. State, TexCrimApp, 373 SW2d 249.—Crim Law 364(4); Sent & Pun 1381(3), 1381(6).

Gonzales v. State, TexCrimApp, 361 SW2d 393, 172 TexCrim 556.—Crim Law 404.65, 693, 1045, 1060, 1090.8; Homic 1193.

Gonzales v. State, TexCrimApp, 350 SW2d 553, 171 TexCrim 373.—Crim Law 59(3), 781(8); Homic 1207.

Gonzales v. State, TexCrimApp, 335 SW2d 385, 169 TexCrim 492.—Autos 355(13); Crim Law 784(1).

Gonzales v. State, TexCrimApp, 330 SW2d 447.—Crim Law 1119(4).

Gonzales v. State, TexCrimApp, 330 SW2d 198, 168 TexCrim 523.—Disorderly H 17.

Gonzales v. State, TexCrimApp, 324 SW2d 872, 168 TexCrim 169.—Int Liq 236(7).

Gonzales v. State, TexCrimApp, 320 SW2d 837, 167 TexCrim 433.—Crim Law 394.5(3), 695(5), 698(1).

Gonzales v. State, TexCrimApp, 320 SW2d 679, 167 TexCrim 377.—Crim Law 265, 577; Ind & Inf 45.

Gonzales v. State, TexCrimApp, 320 SW2d 9, 167 Tex-Crim 226.—Arrest 66(2); Weap 17(4).

Gonzales v. State, TexCrimApp, 301 SW2d 655.—Crim Law 1090.1(1).

Gonzales v. State, TexCrimApp, 293 SW2d 786, 163 TexCrim 432.—Controlled Subs 34, 65.

Gonzales v. State, TexCrimApp, 286 SW2d 173, 162 TexCrim 394.—Crim Law 531(3), 1116.

Gonzales v. State, TexCrimApp, 284 SW2d 726.—Crim Law 1090.1(1).

Gonzales v. State, TexCrimApp, 283 SW2d 239.—Crim Law 1090.1(1).

Gonzales v. State, TexCrimApp, 278 SW2d 167, 161 TexCrim 488.—Arrest 63.4(12), 71.1(2.1); Crim Law 598(7), 1091(7); Jury 33(1.15); Rob 24.10.

Gonzales v. State, TexCrimApp, 272 SW2d 524, 160 TexCrim 548.—Arrest 71.1(5); Controlled Subs 80, 113; Crim Law 531(4); Witn 277(1), 337(1).

Gonzales v. State, TexCrimApp, 261 SW2d 577, 159 TexCrim 108.—Crim Law 369.6, 722.5.

Gonzales v. State, TexCrimApp, 254 SW2d 388.—Crim Law 1094(2.1); Ind & Inf 122(1), 122(4).

Gonzales v. State, TexCrimApp, 246 SW2d 199, 157 TexCrim 8.—Controlled Subs 80; Crim Law 814(17), 844(1), 844(2).

Gonzales v. State, TexCrimApp, 200 SW2d 827, 150 TexCrim 329.—Crim Law 1090.14; Homic 1154.

Gonzales v. State, TexCrimApp, 199 SW2d 525.—Crim Law 1090.1(1).

Gonzales v. State, TexCrimApp, 187 SW2d 910, 148 TexCrim 401.—Crim Law 394.4(9), 517(6), 1169.1(8).

Gonzales v. State, TexCrimApp, 186 SW2d 242.—Crim Law 1090.1(1).

Gonzales v. State, TexCrimApp, 156 SW2d 988, 143 TexCrim 48.—Int Liq 139, 236(6.5).

Gonzales v. State, TexCrimApp, 126 SW2d 492, 136 TexCrim 469.—Larc 1; Rob 1, 24.50.

Gonzales v. State, TexCrimApp, 117 SW2d 788, 135 TexCrim 57.—Hus & W 250.

Gonzales v. State, TexCrimApp, 95 SW2d 972, 131 Tex-Crim 15.—Arrest 63.4(3); Crim Law 394.1(3), 394.4(10), 394.4(11).

Gonzales v. State, TexCrimApp, 84 SW2d 243, 129 Tex-Crim 37.—Bail 70.

Gonzales v. State, TexCrimApp, 299 SW 901, 108 Tex-Crim 253.—Controlled Subs 82.

Gonzales v. State, TexApp–Houston (1 Dist), 190 SW3d 125, petition for discretionary review refused, cert den 127 SCt 504, 166 LEd2d 377.—Courts 91(1); Crim Law 26, 419(1.10), 518(3), 531(1), 535(1), 535(2), 563, 1139,

1144.12, 1153(1), 1158(4); Homic 583, 1186; Searches 15, 26, 161, 164.

Gonzales v. State, TexApp–Houston (1 Dist), 125 SW3d 616, petition for discretionary review gr, aff Pham v. State, 175 SW3d 767, cert den 126 SCt 490, 546 US 961, 163 LEd2d 364.—Crim Law 412(4), 532(0.5).

Gonzales v. State, TexApp–Houston (1 Dist), 9 SW3d 267, petition for discretionary review gr, vac 67 SW3d 910, on remand 125 SW3d 616, petition for discretionary review gr, aff Pham v. State, 175 SW3d 767, cert den 126 SCt 490, 546 US 961, 163 LEd2d 364.—Arrest 63.4(2); Crim Law 527; Infants 68.3, 192; Searches 164.

Gonzales v. State, TexApp–Houston (1 Dist), 942 SW2d 80, petition for discretionary review refused.—Homic 668, 1152.

Gonzales v. State, TexApp–Houston (1 Dist), 863 SW2d 78, reh den.—Controlled Subs 6; Crim Law 273.1(4), 956(1), 1167(5).

Gonzales v. State, TexApp–Houston (1 Dist), 838 SW2d 848, reh den, and petition for discretionary review refused, and petition for discretionary review gr, petition for discretionary review dism with per curiam opinion 864 SW2d 522, opinion withdrawn and superseded 942 SW2d 80, petition for discretionary review refused, appeal after remand 942 SW2d 80, petition for discretionary review refused, and petition for discretionary review refused.—Crim Law 338(6), 338(7), 795(1), 801, 1038.2, 1170(1), 1173.2(3); Homic 667, 938, 1051(1), 1054, 1451, 1455, 1458, 1480, 1487, 1506; Ind & Inf 189(8).

Gonzales v. State, TexApp–Houston (1 Dist), 807 SW2d 830, petition for discretionary review refused.—Crim Law 517(7), 519(1), 531(3), 532(0.5), 713, 720(9), 722.5, 1035(6), 1037.1(1), 1171.1(2.1).

Gonzales v. State, TexApp–Houston (1 Dist), 748 SW2d 510, petition for discretionary review refused.—Crim Law 641.13(7), 698(1); Infants 20; Witn 79(2), 227.

Gonzales v. State, TexApp–Houston (1 Dist), 732 SW2d 67.—Crim Law 641.13(2.1), 641.13(6).

Gonzales v. State, TexApp–Houston (1 Dist), 704 SW2d 508.—Controlled Subs 148(1); Searches 117.

Gonzales v. State, TexApp–Houston (1 Dist), 676 SW2d 437, petition for discretionary review refused by 689 SW2d 231.—Crim Law 1144.13(3), 1172.2, 1189; Obscen 17, 20.

Gonzales v. State, TexApp–Houston (1 Dist), 638 SW2d 41, petition for discretionary review refused.—Arrest 63.4(2), 63.4(11), 63.4(18), 71.1(3), 71.1(4.1); Controlled Subs 30, 64, 68, 73, 80; Crim Law 1144.13(2.1), 1167(1); Ind & Inf 115; Searches 47.1.

Gonzales v. State, TexApp–Fort Worth, 899 SW2d 819, petition for discretionary review refused.—Crim Law 273.1(4).

Gonzales v. State, TexApp–Fort Worth, 688 SW2d 263.— Crim Law 339.7(3).

Gonzales; State v., TexApp–Austin, 26 SW3d 919.—Autos 332, 351.1, 352; Crim Law 303.15, 303.30(1); Ind & Inf 144.

Gonzales v. State, TexApp–Austin, 977 SW2d 189, reh overr, and petition for discretionary review refused, appeal from denial of habeas corpus Ex parte Gonzales, 12 SW3d 913, petition for discretionary review refused. —Crim Law 394.1(3), 394.6(1), 394.6(4); Ind & Inf 166.

Gonzales v. State, TexApp–Austin, 929 SW2d 546, reh overr, and petition for discretionary review refused.— Crim Law 662.7, 736(1), 1028, 1036.1(1), 1045, 1144.1, 1147; Witn 344(1), 363(1), 370(1), 372(1), 374(2).

Gonzales v. State, TexApp–Austin, 784 SW2d 140.—Autos 355(10); Crim Law 552(1), 552(3), 564(1), 564(2).

Gonzales v. State, TexApp–Austin, 766 SW2d 395, petition for discretionary review refused by 776 SW2d 197. —Burg 41(3); Crim Law 511.7, 1134(8).

GONZALES

Gonzales v. State, TexApp–Austin, 761 SW2d 809, petition for discretionary review refused.—Arrest 65; Controlled Subs 69, 143, 146; Crim Law 218(3), 673(5).

Gonzales v. State, TexApp–San Antonio, 2 SW3d 411.—Crim Law 1137(7), 1147; Rape 6, 51(4), 64.

Gonzales v. State, TexApp–San Antonio, 963 SW2d 844.—Crim Law 273.1(1), 273.1(4), 273.1(5), 641.13(5), 1081(2), 1181.5(3.1).

Gonzales v. State, TexApp–San Antonio, 904 SW2d 175, petition for discretionary review refused.—Crim Law 274(8), 1030(1), 1137(1), 1167(5), 1180, 1192.

Gonzales; State v., TexApp–San Antonio, 850 SW2d 672, reh den, and petition for discretionary review refused.—Autos 414, 421; Crim Law 1134(6), 1147, 1153(1).

Gonzales v. State, TexApp–San Antonio, 831 SW2d 347, reh den, and reh den, and petition for discretionary review refused.—Crim Law 338(7), 474.4(4), 673(5), 1043(2), 1169.2(1), 1169.2(8); Witn 228.

Gonzales v. State, TexApp–San Antonio, 831 SW2d 345, petition for discretionary review refused, cert den 113 SCt 1334, 507 US 939, 122 LEd2d 718.—Crim Law 1179.

Gonzales v. State, TexApp–San Antonio, 822 SW2d 189, review gr, cause remanded 831 SW2d 326.—Const Law 4675; Crim Law 627.2, 662.65, 1043(2), 1043(3); Witn 228.

Gonzales v. State, TexApp–San Antonio, 784 SW2d 723, petition for discretionary review gr, rev 818 SW2d 756, on remand 831 SW2d 345, petition for discretionary review refused, cert den 113 SCt 1334, 507 US 939, 122 LEd2d 718.—Crim Law 662.65, 1162, 1168(2); Witn 228.

Gonzales v. State, TexApp–San Antonio, 775 SW2d 776, petition for discretionary review refused.—Crim Law 371(4), 713, 1036.2, 1037.1(1), 1037.2, 1043(2), 1044.1(8), 1045, 1171.1(1), 1171.1(2.1), 1171.8(1).

Gonzales v. State, TexApp–San Antonio, 730 SW2d 196.—Crim Law 720(6), 723(3), 865(2), 867, 1044.1(8), 1155; Jury 148(2); Witn 270(2).

Gonzales v. State, TexApp–San Antonio, 706 SW2d 764, petition for discretionary review refused.—Controlled Subs 80, 97, 148(1); Crim Law 29(8), 720(1), 723(3), 730(8), 1171.1(2.1).

Gonzales v. State, TexApp–San Antonio, 700 SW2d 348, petition for discretionary review refused.—Crim Law 394.4(10); Ind & Inf 71.4(7).

Gonzales v. State, TexApp–San Antonio, 695 SW2d 81, petition for discretionary review gr, rev 723 SW2d 746.—Arson 18; Crim Law 304(1), 1032(5), 1134(8); Ind & Inf 60.

Gonzales v. State, TexApp–San Antonio, 685 SW2d 385, petition for discretionary review refused.—Crim Law 556; Forg 44(0.5), 44(1).

Gonzales v. State, TexApp–San Antonio, 681 SW2d 270.—Crim Law 507(1), 507(2), 510, 563, 814(19), 901, 1159.2(7); Homic 511, 1128, 1134, 1172, 1174, 1186; Infants 68.1.

Gonzales v. State, TexApp–San Antonio, 679 SW2d 638, petition for discretionary review gr, rev 717 SW2d 355, on remand 730 SW2d 196.—Crim Law 795(2.90); Homic 1380, 1458.

Gonzales v. State, TexApp–San Antonio, 626 SW2d 888, petition for discretionary review refused.—Crim Law 641.13(1), 641.13(2.1), 641.13(6), 1166.10(1), 1169.1(1).

Gonzales v. State, TexApp–Dallas, 868 SW2d 854, appeal after remand 904 SW2d 175, petition for discretionary review refused.—Crim Law 273.1(2), 274(3.1), 796, 1043(2); Sent & Pun 421.

Gonzales v. State, TexApp–Dallas, 800 SW2d 621.—Controlled Subs 27; Crim Law 814(5), 822(1), 1038.1(1), 1134(3), 1162, 1172.1(1), 1172.6.

Gonzales v. State, TexApp–Dallas, 632 SW2d 899, petition for discretionary review refused.—Assault 54,

96(7); Crim Law 531(3), 736(2), 795(1), 795(2.15); Homic 708, 908, 1134, 1372, 1458.

Gonzales v. State, TexApp–Texarkana, 2 SW3d 600, petition for discretionary review refused.—Assault 9; Crim Law 38, 641.3(4), 655(5), 1152(2), 1166.16, 1166.22(1), 1166.23; Jury 33(4), 131(1), 131(2), 131(3), 131(8).

Gonzales v. State, TexApp–Texarkana, 972 SW2d 877, petition for discretionary review gr, vac 994 SW2d 170, on remand 2 SW3d 600, petition for discretionary review refused.—Crim Law 38, 1152(2), 1166.16; Jury 131(1), 131(2), 131(3), 131(8), 131(13), 131(15.1).

Gonzales v. State, TexApp–Amarillo, 8 SW3d 679, appeal dism 2000 WL 21266.—Crim Law 1077.3.

Gonzales v. State, TexApp–Amarillo, 672 SW2d 618.—Courts 107; Crim Law 404.60, 673(5), 1165(1), 1172.9; Witn 344(1).

Gonzales v. State, TexApp–Amarillo, 648 SW2d 724.—Crim Law 412.1(1), 412.1(4), 414, 577.10(9), 736(2).

Gonzales v. State, TexApp–El Paso, 944 SW2d 22.—Crim Law 273.1(2), 273.4(1), 1026.10(2.1), 1026.10(5), 1129(1), 1167(5).

Gonzales v. State, TexApp–Beaumont, 697 SW2d 50, petition for discretionary review refused.—Crim Law 37(8), 577.6, 577.8(1), 577.16(8), 577.16(9), 627.10(7.1).

Gonzales v. State, TexApp–Beaumont, 692 SW2d 520, rev 685 SW2d 47, cert den 105 SCt 2704, 472 US 1009, 86 LEd2d 720, on remand 697 SW2d 50, petition for discretionary review refused.—Crim Law 706(5), 1171.8(1).

Gonzales v. State, TexApp–Beaumont, 673 SW2d 627.—Controlled Subs 80.

Gonzales v. State, TexApp–Waco, 191 SW3d 741, reh overr, and petition stricken, and petition for discretionary review refused.—Assault 91.6(2), 91.7; Crim Law 29(9), 553, 742(1), 747, 798(0.6), 798(0.7), 872.5, 992, 1030(1), 1038.1(1), 1038.1(2), 1129(1), 1144.13(2.1), 1159.2(2), 1159.2(7), 1159.3(1), 1159.3(2), 1159.4(2), 1159.6, 1172.1(3); Ind & Inf 17, 129(1).

Gonzales v. State, TexApp–Waco, 4 SW3d 406.—Crim Law 26, 394.6(5), 412.1(1), 412.1(4), 412.2(2), 469, 469.1, 472, 474.3(3), 474.4(4), 477.1, 478(1), 479, 485(1), 486(4), 518(2), 535(1), 535(2), 553, 629(4), 629.5(4), 1134(3), 1134(6), 1134(8), 1139, 1144.12, 1144.13(3), 1144.13(5), 1144.13(7), 1148, 1153(1), 1153(2), 1158(4), 1159.2(7); Infants 13.

Gonzales v. State, TexApp–Waco, 684 SW2d 768.—Crim Law 577.14, 577.15(3), 577.16(9), 1026.10(5); Ind & Inf 5, 7.

Gonzales; State v., TexApp–Eastland, 146 SW3d 760, petition for discretionary review refused.—Controlled Subs 146; Crim Law 394.6(5), 1134(6), 1158(4); Searches 191.

Gonzales v. State, TexApp–Eastland, 905 SW2d 4, petition for discretionary review gr, aff 931 SW2d 574.—Burg 15; Crim Law 1144.13(3), 1159.2(7); Homic 1165; Infants 68.7(5).

Gonzales v. State, TexApp–Corpus Christi, 746 SW2d 902.—Crim Law 273.1(4), 1163(1), 1167(5).

Gonzales v. State, TexApp–Corpus Christi, 706 SW2d 671.—Crim Law 1035(6); Jury 105(4).

Gonzales v. State, TexApp–Corpus Christi, 670 SW2d 413.—Embez 5, 18, 44(2); Fraud 68.

Gonzales v. State, TexApp–Corpus Christi, 638 SW2d 132.—Crim Law 641.3(4), 1166.16; Jury 131(3), 131(4).

Gonzales v. State, TexApp–Houston (14 Dist), 831 SW2d 491, petition for discretionary review refused.—Crim Law 713, 720(8), 726, 1083, 1137(8); Sent & Pun 1333, 1378, 1379(2).

Gonzales v. State, TexApp–Houston (14 Dist), 809 SW2d 778, petition for discretionary review refused.—Controlled Subs 26, 27, 30, 80; Crim Law 1159.6.

Gonzales v. State, TexApp–Houston (14 Dist), 743 SW2d 718, petition for discretionary review refused.—Controlled Subs 79, 151; Crim Law 899, 1036.1(4).

Gonzales v. State, TexApp–Houston (14 Dist), 712 SW2d 834.—Crim Law 273.1(4), 1166(3).

Gonzales v. State, TexApp–Houston (14 Dist), 697 SW2d 35, petition for discretionary review refused.—Crim Law 893, 1038.1(2), 1038.1(4), 1038.3, 1056.1(4), 1184(1); Rob 15, 24.15(1); Sent & Pun 373, 1840.

Gonzales v. State, TexApp–Houston (14 Dist), 666 SW2d 496, petition for discretionary review refused.—Arrest 63.4(3), 63.4(6); Crim Law 273(4.1), 275, 1036.8, 1134(8), 1169.2(5); Searches 47.1, 49, 63.

Gonzales v. State, TexApp–Houston (14 Dist), 659 SW2d 62.—Crim Law 1158(1), 1184(1); Sent & Pun 2021, 2030.

Gonzales; State v., TexCivApp–San Antonio, 459 SW2d 947.—Crim Law 1023.5; Hab Corp 815.

Gonzales v. State, TexCivApp–El Paso, 81 SW2d 180.—Tax 2709(2), 2853.

Gonzales; State of Tex. v., CA5 (Tex), 388 F2d 145.—Arrest 63.4(14); Controlled Subs 129, 148(3); Hab Corp 490(4); Searches 17, 23, 164.

Gonzales v. Stevens, TexCivApp–Corpus Christi, 427 SW2d 694, ref nre.—Elections 106; Mand 3(1), 3(8), 4(1).

Gonzales v. Surplus Ins. Services, TexApp–Beaumont, 863 SW2d 96, reh den, and writ den.—App & E 949; Const Law 3867, 4008, 4011; Judgm 184, 185(4), 365, 379(1), 386(1), 392(6), 392(8); Pretrial Proc 483.

Gonzales; Tercero-Aranda v., CA5 (Tex), 169 FedAppx 368.—Hab Corp 802.

Gonzales v. Texas Aires Medical Social Services, TexApp–Corpus Christi, 791 SW2d 258. See Gonzales v. Zamora.

Gonzales v. Texas Emp. Ins. Ass'n, TexCivApp–Austin, 419 SW2d 203.—Evid 208(0.5), 589; Jury 131(6); Plead 36(7); Trial 76, 142; Work Comp 858, 1172, 1377, 1396, 1619, 1653, 1703, 1926, 1968(1), 1969.

Gonzales v. Texas Emp. Ins. Ass'n, TexCivApp–Eastland, 408 SW2d 521, ref nre.—Judgm 181(11); Work Comp 506.

Gonzales v. Texas Employment Com'n, TexApp–San Antonio, 653 SW2d 308, ref nre.—Admin Law 312; Const Law 2488, 3880, 3881, 4129; Unemp Comp 272.

Gonzales v. Texas Workers' Compensation Fund, TexApp–Houston (14 Dist), 950 SW2d 380.—Insurance 3353, 3361; Work Comp 1042.

Gonzales v. Times Herald Printing Co., TexCivApp–Dallas, 513 SW2d 124.—Libel 7(1), 73, 123(2).

Gonzales v. Trinity Industries, Inc., TexApp–Houston (1 Dist), 7 SW3d 303, petition for review den.—Autos 269, 282, 289; Neglig 202, 213, 215, 220, 259, 1071, 1692.

Gonzales; Tyler v., TexCivApp–San Antonio, 189 SW2d 519, writ refused wom.—App & E 846(2), 846(5); Bound 6, 14; Fences 18; Waters 93.

Gonzales; U.S. v., CA5 (Tex), 484 F2d 712.—Crim Law 1030(1), 1042, 1139; Ind & Inf 125(20); Sent & Pun 300, 780, 793.

Gonzales; U.S. v., CA5 (Tex), 436 F3d 560, cert den Reyna v. US, 126 SCt 2045, 164 LEd2d 799, cert den Gomez v US, 126 SCt 2362, 165 LEd2d 280, cert den 126 SCt 2363, 165 LEd2d 280, cert den 127 SCt 157, 166 LEd2d 280.—Civil R 1808, 1809; Const Law 4545(1), 4545(2), 4632; Courts 100(1); Crim Law 645, 662.8, 720(7.1), 881(2), 1028, 1038.1(2), 1139, 1158(1); Ind & Inf 56, 71.1, 71.2(3), 71.2(4), 159(1), 159(2); Sent & Pun 706, 730, 752, 754, 761; Witn 2(1).

Gonzales; U.S. v., CA5 (Tex), 327 F3d 416, reh and reh den 332 F3d 825, cert den 124 SCt 1037, 540 US 1112, 157 LEd2d 901.—Courts 100(1); Crim Law 1139.

Gonzales; U.S. v., CA5 (Tex), 121 F3d 928, reh den, cert den 118 SCt 726, 522 US 1063, 139 LEd2d 664, cert den 118 SCt 1084, 522 US 1131, 140 LEd2d 141, postconviction relief den 159 FSupp2d 555, aff 327 F3d 416, reh and reh den 332 F3d 825, cert den 124 SCt 1037, 540 US 1112, 157 LEd2d 901.—Consp 28(3), 41, 44.2,

47(2), 47(12); Const Law 4716; Controlled Subs 31, 46, 68, 81; Crim Law 59(5), 261(1), 264, 393(1), 412.1(4), 412.2(2), 700(3), 858(3), 1134(2), 1139, 1144.12, 1153(1), 1158(4), 1163(6), 1174(2), 1174(6); Ind & Inf 60, 71.2(2), 71.2(4), 71.3, 113, 144.1(1); Searches 23, 171, 173.1, 174, 180, 194, 198; Sent & Pun 1482, 1511; Weap 3, 4, 17(2), 17(4).

Gonzales; U.S. v., CA5 (Tex), 79 F3d 413, reh den, cert den Ramiro Muniz v. US, 117 SCt 183, 519 US 869, 136 LEd2d 122.—Arrest 63.5(1), 63.5(5); Consp 28(3), 44.2, 47(2), 47(12); Controlled Subs 68, 80, 81; Crim Law 1036.1(4), 1139, 1144.12, 1148, 1158(4), 1159.2(7), 1224(1); Searches 180, 181, 183; Sent & Pun 1210, 1311, 1318, 1361, 1366; Witn 2(1), 4, 9.

Gonzales; U.S. v., CA5 (Tex), 40 F3d 735, cert den 115 SCt 1716, 514 US 1074, 131 LEd2d 575.—Crim Law 1139, 1177; Double J 134, 145; Sent & Pun 726(4).

Gonzales; U.S. v., CA5 (Tex), 19 F3d 982, cert den 115 SCt 229, 513 US 887, 130 LEd2d 154.—Crim Law 1134(3), 1139, 1158(1); Sent & Pun 765.

Gonzales; U.S. v., CA5 (Tex), 996 F2d 88.—Crim Law 1139, 1158(1); Double J 29.1; Sent & Pun 653(10), 668, 755, 900, 907.

Gonzales; U.S. v., CA5 (Tex), 988 F2d 16, cert den 114 SCt 170, 510 US 858, 126 LEd2d 129.—Aliens 773; Const Law 2791; Sent & Pun 664(1), 664(5), 664(6).

Gonzales; U.S. v., CA5 (Tex), 897 F2d 1312, reh den, cert den 111 SCt 683, 498 US 1029, 112 LEd2d 675.—Crim Law 577.10(7), 577.10(8), 577.14.

Gonzales; U.S. v., CA5 (Tex), 866 F2d 781, cert den 109 SCt 2438, 490 US 1093, 104 LEd2d 994.—Consp 28(3), 47(12); Controlled Subs 40, 82, 87; Crim Law 622.2(4), 1177; Tel 1466.

Gonzales; U.S. v., CA5 (Tex), 842 F2d 748.—Arrest 63.4(1), 63.5(5), 68(4); Searches 172, 180, 198.

Gonzales; U.S. v., CA5 (Tex), 606 F2d 70.—Arrest 63.4(17); Crim Law 37(1), 330, 338(1), 419(1.10), 569, 627.10(1), 627.10(3), 627.10(5), 627.10(7.1), 1169.1(2.1), 1169.1(9).

Gonzales; U.S. v., CA5 (Tex), 211 FedAppx 306.—Crim Law 1036.1(9), 1171.1(3).

Gonzales; U.S. v., CA5 (Tex), 197 FedAppx 360, cert den 127 SCt 1016, 166 LEd2d 765.—Crim Law 412.2(5), 1144.12, 1158(4).

Gonzales; U.S. v., CA5 (Tex), 160 FedAppx 356.—Crim Law 1177; Sent & Pun 834.

Gonzales; U.S. v., CA5 (Tex), 119 FedAppx 576.—Const Law 4527(2); Crim Law 37.10(2), 1023(11).

Gonzales; U.S. v., SDTex, 159 FSupp2d 555, aff 327 F3d 416, reh and reh den 332 F3d 825, cert den 124 SCt 1037, 540 US 1112, 157 LEd2d 901.—Courts 100(1); Crim Law 1177, 1403.

Gonzales v. U.S. Fidelity & Guaranty Co., TexCivApp–San Antonio, 266 SW2d 238, aff 274 SW2d 537, 154 Tex 118.—App & E 564(3), 564(5).

Gonzales; Valley Mechanical Contractors, Inc. v., TexApp–Corpus Christi, 894 SW2d 832.—App & E 846(5), 846(6), 852, 931(1), 989, 1008.1(1), 1010.2; Corp 1.4(2), 1.4(3), 1.4(4), 1.5(1), 1.6(3); Judgm 220; Trial 392(2), 393(1).

Gonzales v. Vowell, CA5 (Tex), 490 F2d 475.—Social S 8.5, 194.16(2).

Gonzales v. Vowell, NDTex, 361 FSupp 1230, aff 490 F2d 475.—Const Law 4117; Social S 8.5, 194.16(2).

Gonzales v. Westbrook, WDTex, 118 FSupp2d 728.—Civil R 1343, 1345, 1351(1), 1351(4), 1352(1), 1352(4); Fed Civ Proc 2491.5; Fed Cts 411.

Gonzales; Western Cas. & Sur. Co. v., Tex, 518 SW2d 524.—Work Comp 876, 1396, 1647, 1662.

Gonzales; Western Cas. & Sur. Co. v., TexCivApp–Corpus Christi, 506 SW2d 303, writ gr, aff 518 SW2d 524.—App & E 989; Damag 221(7); Trial 139.1(1.1), 140(1), 142; Work Comp 876, 957, 1641, 1662, 1966.

GONZALES;

See Guidelines for Arrangement at the beginning of this Volume

Gonzales; Wharton v., TexApp–Houston (14 Dist), 761 SW2d 72.—Judgm 80, 89.

Gonzales v. Whitsitt, TexCivApp–El Paso, 583 SW2d 468. —Autos 244(12), 244(34), 245(39); Evid 265(1), 265(17).

Gonzales v. Willis, TexApp–San Antonio, 995 SW2d 729, reh overr.—App & E 854(5), 930(1), 1003(6); Civil R 1704; Damag 48, 50.10, 192, 208(6); Labor & Emp 2937, 3040; Neglig 460.

Gonzales v. Wyatt, CA5 (Tex), 157 F3d 1016.—Civil R 1382; Fed Civ Proc 660.1, 2734; Fed Cts 427, 666, 818; Lim of Act 75, 95(15), 118(2), 119(3).

Gonzales; Yorkshire Indem. Co. v., CA5 (Tex), 210 F2d 545.—Evid 98; Work Comp 51, 725, 747, 1421, 1924.

Gonzales v. Yturria Land & Livestock Co., SDTex, 72 FSupp 280.—Adv Poss 43(1), 106(2); Deeds 196(0.5); Fed Cts 430; Pub Lands 198, 209.

Gonzales v. Zamora, TexApp–Corpus Christi, 791 SW2d 258.—Antitrust 413, 417, 419; App & E 231(9), 1146; Inj 56, 189; Labor & Emp 123, 305, 323(4).

Gonzales v. Zerda, TexApp–San Antonio, 802 SW2d 794, writ den.—App & E 930(3); Gifts 53, 60, 66(2).

Gonzales Bail Bonds v. State, TexApp–Waco, 147 SW3d 557.—Bail 77(1); Judgm 181(15.1).

Gonzales County Sav. & Loan Ass'n; Fenimore v., TexApp–San Antonio, 650 SW2d 213, ref nre.—Mtg 355.

Gonzales County Sav. and Loan Ass'n v. Freeman, Tex, 534 SW2d 903.—B & L Assoc 33(16), 33(22); Judgm 181(2), 181(3), 181(15.1), 185(2); Usury 16, 53, 119.

Gonzales County Sav. & Loan Ass'n; Freeman v., Tex-CivApp–Corpus Christi, 526 SW2d 774, writ gr, aff 534 SW2d 903.—B & L Assoc 1, 26, 33(1), 33(4), 33(5), 34(8); Judgm 181(3), 185(2), 185.3(5); Statut 181(1); Usury 53.

Gonzales County Sav. and Loan Ass'n; Independence Sav. and Loan Ass'n v., TexCivApp–Austin, 568 SW2d 463, ref nre.—B & L Assoc 3.5(2), 3.5(3).

Gonzales County Sav. & Loan Ass'n; Lewis v., Tex, 474 SW2d 453, appeal after remand 486 SW2d 176, ref nre. —B & L Assoc 2.1, 3.5(1), 3.5(2), 3.5(3).

Gonzales County Sav. & Loan Ass'n v. Lewis, TexCiv-App–Austin, 486 SW2d 176, ref nre.—B & L Assoc 3.5(2), 3.5(3).

Gonzales County Sav. & Loan Ass'n v. Lewis, TexCiv-App–Austin, 461 SW2d 215, writ gr, aff and remanded 474 SW2d 453, appeal after remand 486 SW2d 176, ref nre.—Admin Law 485; B & L Assoc 3.5(2).

Gonzales County Sheriff's Dept.; Walker v., TexApp–Corpus Christi, 35 SW3d 157, reh overr, and review den.—App & E 230, 231(1), 852, 946, 984(1); Const Law 947, 4002; Convicts 6; Judgm 189; New Tr 16.

Gonzales County Water Supply Corp. v. Jarzombek, TexApp–Corpus Christi, 918 SW2d 57.—Contracts 28(1), 143(2), 186(1); Corp 1.4(1), 1.4(4), 1.6(2), 431; Judgm 181(2), 181(19), 185(2); Princ & A 136(1), 146(1).

Gonzales ex rel. Gonzales; City of Marshall v., TexApp–Texarkana, 107 SW3d 799.—App & E 80(1), 112; Motions 62; New Tr 110, 124(1); Plead 111.49.

Gonzales Healthcare Systems; Kelso v., TexApp–Corpus Christi, 136 SW3d 377, rule 537(f) motion gr.—App & E 840(2), 890, 893(1), 916(1); Health 770; Mun Corp 742(4), 847, 854; Plead 104(1), 111.38, 111.48; States 112(2), 191.6(1), 191.6(2).

Gonzales Motor Co. v. Buhidar, TexCivApp–Eastland, 348 SW2d 376, ref nre.—App & E 931(1); Impl & C C 12; Trover 40(6).

Gonzales Motor Co. v. Cain, TexCivApp–Corpus Christi, 476 SW2d 124.—App & E 80(4).

Gonzales-Velasquez; U.S. v., CA5 (Tex), 102 FedAppx 851, cert den 125 SCt 430, 543 US 968, 160 LEd2d 338. —Sent & Pun 793.

Gonzales Warm Springs Foundation for Crippled Children v. Maddox, TexCivApp–Austin, 304 SW2d 373, ref nre.—Wills 579.

Gonzales Warm Springs Rehabilitation Hosp., Inc.; Wisenbarger v., TexApp–Corpus Christi, 789 SW2d

688, writ den.—Antitrust 257; App & E 842(7), 1068(3), 1078(5); Const Law 2314, 3754; Health 604, 625, 765, 800, 823(1), 827; Judgm 178, 181(3); Neglig 440(1), 1741; Statut 176; Trial 136(1), 215, 219.

Gonzalez, Ex parte, TexApp–San Antonio, 147 SW3d 474, reh overr, and petition for discretionary review dism as untimely filed, and petition stricken, and petition for discretionary review refused, cert den Lopez v. Texas, 126 SCt 1358, 546 US 1182, 164 LEd2d 69.—Double J 5.1, 28, 134, 140; Weap 4.

Gonzalez, In re, BkrtcyEDTex, 112 BR 10.—Bankr 2832.1.

Gonzalez, In re, TexApp–San Antonio, 115 SW3d 36.—App & E 230; Judges 15(1), 16(2), 18, 39, 51(1), 51(2), 56; Mand 4(1), 4(4), 28, 52, 53.

Gonzalez, In re, TexApp–San Antonio, 993 SW2d 147, reh overr.—App & E 863; Appear 9(2); Child S 145, 200, 223, 440, 497, 498, 541, 556(1), 558(2); Child 1, 36, 67, 69(6), 69(7), 70, 73, 75; Const Law 2450, 2570, 3965(1); Contempt 66(2); Courts 12(2.1), 12(2.5); Hab Corp 253, 528.1; Interest 39(1).

Gonzalez, In re, TexApp–San Antonio, 981 SW2d 313, review den.—Child S 496; Child 73.

Gonzalez, In re, TexCivApp–El Paso, 328 SW2d 475, ref nre.—Infants 78(1), 132, 176, 194.1, 197, 204, 207, 209, 221; Jury 31.3(1).

Gonzalez v. Ables, TexApp–San Antonio, 945 SW2d 253. —Judges 51(1).

Gonzalez v. Alianza Hispano-Americana, TexCivApp–San Antonio, 112 SW2d 802, dism.—App & E 638, 729, 733, 742(4), 863, 934(1); Insurance 3003(1), 3003(10).

Gonzalez; Alviar v., TexApp–Corpus Christi, 725 SW2d 297, ref nre.—Courts 89; Wills 63, 440, 441, 449, 614(1), 616(1).

Gonzalez v. American Home Products Corp., SDTex, 223 FSupp2d 803.—Action 69(5).

Gonzalez v. Atascocita North Community Imp. Ass'n, TexApp–Houston (1 Dist), 902 SW2d 591, reh overr.—App & E 934(1); Judgm 181(2), 181(15.1).

Gonzalez; Atlantic Ins. Co. v., TexCivApp–San Antonio, 358 SW2d 716.—Insurance 2658.

Gonzalez v. Avalos, Tex, 907 SW2d 443.—App & E 1080.

Gonzalez v. Avalos, TexApp–El Paso, 866 SW2d 346, reh den, and writ gr, and writ withdrawn, writ dism woj 907 SW2d 443.—Admin Law 101; App & E 863; Evid 208(0.5); Infants 17; Judges 36; Judgm 185(2), 185(4); Offic 114; States 79, 112(1), 112(2), 112.2(2).

Gonzalez; Barrera v., TexCivApp–San Antonio, 341 SW2d 703, ref nre, appeal after remand 358 SW2d 233, ref nre.—Ack 62(3); Evid 236(2); Mtg 32(2), 32(5), 38(1).

Gonzalez; Barrera v., TexCivApp–Eastland, 358 SW2d 233, ref nre.—Mtg 32(5), 37(2), 38(1).

Gonzalez; Beard v., TexApp–El Paso, 924 SW2d 763.—App & E 236(1); Mand 44; Venue 63.

Gonzalez v. Benavides, CA5 (Tex), 774 F2d 1295, cert den 106 SCt 1789, 475 US 1140, 90 LEd2d 335.—Civil R 1249(1), 1471, 1474(1), 1479; Const Law 1929, 1930, 1934, 1947; Fed Cts 842, 858.

Gonzalez v. Benavides, CA5 (Tex), 712 F2d 142, appeal after remand 774 F2d 1295, cert den 106 SCt 1789, 475 US 1140, 90 LEd2d 335.—Const Law 1925, 1934; Fed Cts 922.

Gonzalez; Benavides v., TexCivApp–San Antonio, 396 SW2d 512.—Waters 63, 87, 172, 179(2).

Gonzalez; Birds Const., Inc. v., TexCivApp–Corpus Christi, 595 SW2d 926.—App & E 954(1); Inj 118(5), 132; Mtg 413.

Gonzalez v. Broussard, TexCivApp–San Antonio, 274 SW2d 737, ref nre.—App & E 1069.1; Neglig 1040(2), 1040(3), 1076, 1298(2).

Gonzalez; Burns v., TexCivApp–San Antonio, 506 SW2d 661, ref nre.—Courts 1, 21; Judgm 731; Lim of Act 120; Nova 1; Tel 1159(1); Venue 1 1/2.

GONZALEZ

Gonzalez; Burns v., TexCivApp–San Antonio, 439 SW2d 128, ref nre.—Partners 125, 146(1), 216(2), 217(1); Princ & A 119(1), 123(1).

Gonzalez v. Burns, TexCivApp–San Antonio, 406 SW2d 527.—Corp 666; Judgm 654, 956(5); Plead 111.3, 111.42(6); Venue 22(4), 22(6).

Gonzalez v. Burns, TexCivApp–San Antonio, 397 SW2d 898, writ dism.—App & E 713(3); Venue 7.5(4), 75.

Gonzalez; Burris v., TexCivApp–San Antonio, 269 SW2d 696.—Ack 60, 62(1); Courts 207.4(3); Mand 154(5).

Gonzalez; Butt v., TexApp–San Antonio, 646 SW2d 584. —App & E 1178(1), 1178(6).

Gonzalez; Calvillo v., Tex, 922 SW2d 928.—Judgm 185(2); Torts 245.

Gonzalez; Cameron & Willacy Counties Community Projects, Inc. v., TexCivApp–Corpus Christi, 614 SW2d 585, ref nre.—App & E 15, 747(1); Corp 294; Labor & Emp 265.

Gonzalez; C & V Club v., TexApp–Corpus Christi, 953 SW2d 755, reh overr.—App & E 5.

Gonzalez v. Carlin, CA5 (Tex), 907 F2d 573.—Atty & C 21.5(1); Civil R 1135, 1243, 1548, 1557; Compromise 20(1); Fed Cts 893; Postal 5; U S Mag 20.

Gonzalez v. Castaneda v., TexApp–Corpus Christi, 985 SW2d 500.—App & E 954(1); Bail 54.1, 55, 59; Const Law 4282; Decl Judgm 209, 300; Inj 138.1, 138.3, 151.

Gonzalez v. Cavazos, TexCivApp–Corpus Christi, 601 SW2d 202.—App & E 846(5); Land & Ten 192(2); Trial 404(2).

Gonzalez v. Chrysler Corp., CA5 (Tex), 301 F3d 377, reh en banc den 51 FedAppx 931, cert den Machuca Gonzalez v. DaimlerChrysler Corp., 123 SCt 1928, 538 US 1012, 155 LEd2d 848.—Fed Cts 45, 818; Prod Liab 5.

Gonzalez v. CIGNA Ins. Co. of Texas, TexApp–San Antonio, 924 SW2d 183, writ den.—Statut 181(1), 188, 190, 203; Work Comp 48, 1069.

Gonzalez v. City of El Paso, TexCivApp–El Paso, 316 SW2d 176.—Judgm 181(5.1), 185(2), 185.2(9), 185.3(21); Mun Corp 724, 732, 747(3); Nuis 48.

Gonzalez v. City of Harlingen, TexApp–Corpus Christi, 814 SW2d 109, writ den.—Contracts 332(2); Judgm 185(2), 185(6), 185.3(2); Lim of Act 95(16), 179(2), 182(2); Plead 1, 34(3), 48.

Gonzalez v. City of Laredo, SDTex, 879 FSupp 701.— Civil R 1376(2); Fed Civ Proc 2491.5, 2544.

Gonzalez; City of Los Fresnos v., TexApp–Corpus Christi, 848 SW2d 910.—App & E 194(1), 242(4); Judgm 106(5), 111, 128, 137, 150, 297, 340; New Tr 155; Plead 427; Trial 383; Zoning 787.1, 790.

Gonzalez; City of Los Fresnos v., TexApp–Corpus Christi, 830 SW2d 627, decision clarified on reh, opinion after remand 848 SW2d 910.—App & E 1031(1), 1071.1(2); Mun Corp 63.20, 120; Zoning 236.1, 787.1.

Gonzalez v. City of Mission, TexCivApp–Corpus Christi, 620 SW2d 918.—App & E 863; Contracts 187(1); Fraud 58(4); Judgm 181(6); Mun Corp 723; U S 70(5).

Gonzalez; City of Roma v., TexCivApp–San Antonio, 397 SW2d 943, ref nre.—App & E 846(4), 846(6); Elections 54, 83, 227(1), 227(8); Mun Corp 918(3), 918(4).

Gonzalez; City of San Juan v., TexApp–Corpus Christi, 22 SW3d 69.—Afft 12; App & E 70(8), 223; Chem Dep 4.1; Civil R 1376(1), 1376(2); Judgm 181(27), 185(2), 185(5), 185.1(4), 185.1(6), 185.3(1); Mun Corp 745, 747(3); Offic 114; Plead 252(2).

Gonzalez, Estate of; Crown Life Ins. Co. v., Tex, 820 SW2d 121.—App & E 654, 907(5).

Gonzalez; De Bolt v., TexCivApp–San Antonio, 141 SW2d 846.—Inj 51; Land & Ten 112(1), 123, 128(1).

Gonzalez; De La Garza v., TexCivApp–San Antonio, 186 SW2d 845, writ refused wom.—App & E 380; Evid 82, 83(1); Hus & W 87(3); Wills 55(1), 396.

Gonzalez v. De La Grana, CA5 (Tex), 82 FedAppx 355.— Atty & C 129(4); Fed Cts 341.

Gonzalez v. Denning, CA5 (Tex), 394 F3d 388.—Contracts 143(2), 143.5, 147(2), 152, 176(2), 212(2), 313(1), 313(2); Fed Civ Proc 2492; Fed Cts 776; Princ & A 33, 81(4), 81(5).

Gonzalez; Diesel Injection Sales & Service, Inc. v., TexApp–Corpus Christi, 631 SW2d 193.—App & E 852, 920(3); Inj 135, 138.21, 147, 151.

Gonzalez v. Doctors Hospital--East Loop, TexApp–Houston (1 Dist), 814 SW2d 536, reh of motion for mandamus overr.—App & E 346.2, 356, 387(2), 389(1), 876; Judgm 306.

Gonzalez v. Duran, TexCivApp–San Antonio, 250 SW2d 322, writ refused.—Inj 132, 147; Schools 38, 40.

Gonzalez v. El Paso Hosp. Dist., TexApp–El Paso, 68 SW3d 712.—App & E 946, 948; Courts 26; Health 804, 805, 809.

Gonzalez v. El Paso Hosp. Dist., TexApp–El Paso, 940 SW2d 793.—App & E 1064.1(8); Judgm 702; Mun Corp 741.40(1); States 211.

Gonzalez; Entex, A Div. of Noram Energy Corp. v., TexApp–Houston (14 Dist), 94 SW3d 1, reh overr, and review den.—App & E 930(1); Electricity 16(5); Evid 54, 587, 597; Gas 17, 18, 20(2), 20(5); Judgm 199(3.10); Neglig 210, 215, 218, 238, 409, 1692.

Gonzalez; Express Pub. Co. v., TexCivApp–San Antonio, 326 SW2d 544, writ dism.—Libel 19, 42(2), 50.5, 75; Plead 111.24.

Gonzalez; Express Pub. Co. v., TexCivApp–Eastland, 350 SW2d 589, ref nre.—App & E 1004(8), 1013; Libel 50.5, 54, 55, 107(1), 111, 113, 121(1).

Gonzalez; EZ Pawn v., TexApp–Corpus Christi, 921 SW2d 320. See EZ PawnCorp. v. Gonzalez.

Gonzalez; EZ Pawn Corp. v., TexApp–Corpus Christi, 921 SW2d 320, reh overr, and writ den, mandamus conditionally gr 934 SW2d 87.—Admin Law 229; Alt Disp Res 113, 134(3), 134(6), 182(1), 182(2), 205, 210, 211; App & E 846(5), 852; Civil R 1715; Fraud 3.

Gonzalez; Felix v., TexApp–San Antonio, 87 SW3d 574, reh overr, and review den, and reh of petition for review den.—App & E 969, 970(2), 1026, 1050.1(1), 1050.1(4), 1056.1(1), 1056.1(3), 1064.1(1), 1064.1(9); Autos 243(4), 243(5); Damag 179; Evid 75, 78, 121(1), 123(1), 123(10); Trial 252(22).

Gonzalez v. Firestone Tire & Rubber Co., CA5 (Tex), 610 F2d 241, on remand 512 FSupp 1101.—Civil R 1106, 1379, 1395(8), 1505(4), 1505(7), 1513, 1523, 1530; Fed Civ Proc 1758.1, 1788.6, 1824; Fed Cts 425, 818; Lim of Act 105(2).

Gonzalez v. Firestone Tire & Rubber Co., EDTex, 512 FSupp 1101.—Civil R 1141, 1142, 1530.

Gonzalez; Ford Motor Co. v., TexApp–San Antonio, 9 SW3d 195, reh overr.—App & E 930(1), 1001(3); Evid 570, 571(9); Prod Liab 5, 8, 75.1, 82.1, 83.5.

Gonzalez v. Gainan's Chevrolet City, Inc., Tex, 690 SW2d 885.—Cons Cred 4, 19.

Gonzalez v. Gainan's Chevrolet City, Inc., TexApp–Corpus Christi, 684 SW2d 740, writ gr, rev 690 SW2d 885.—Cons Cred 2, 4, 16; Sec Tran 64, 186, 221, 228.

Gonzalez v. G & E Cabinet, Inc., TexApp–San Antonio, 694 SW2d 384. See Gonzalez v. Gutierrez.

Gonzalez v. Garcia, TexCivApp–San Antonio, 352 SW2d 913.—Elections 307, 308.

Gonzalez; Garza v., TexApp–San Antonio, 737 SW2d 588. —New Tr 165.

Gonzalez v. Global Truck & Equipment, Inc., TexCivApp–Hous (1 Dist), 625 SW2d 348.—App & E 758.3(11), 934(1); Evid 434(1); Judgm 178, 181(33), 185(1).

Gonzalez v. Gonzalez, TexApp–San Antonio, 26 SW3d 657.—App & E 949; Child S 614; Infants 78(7), 82.

Gonzalez; Gonzalez v., TexApp–San Antonio, 26 SW3d 657.—App & E 949; Child S 614; Infants 78(7), 82.

Gonzalez v. Gonzalez, TexApp–El Paso, 659 SW2d 900.— Divorce 286(2), 286(5); Judges 51(1), 51(2).

Gonzalez; Gonzalez v., TexApp–El Paso, 659 SW2d 900.
—Divorce 286(2), 286(5); Judges 51(1), 51(2).

Gonzalez v. Gonzalez, TexApp–Corpus Christi, 672 SW2d 887.—Child C 28, 142; Statut 184, 205.

Gonzalez; Gonzalez v., TexApp–Corpus Christi, 672 SW2d 887.—Child C 28, 142; Statut 184, 205.

Gonzalez v. Gonzalez, TexCivApp–Fort Worth, 309 SW2d 111.—App & E 80(6); Courts 202(5); Ex & Ad 7, 510(2).

Gonzalez; Gonzalez v., TexCivApp–Fort Worth, 309 SW2d 111.—App & E 80(6); Courts 202(5); Ex & Ad 7, 510(2).

Gonzalez v. Gonzalez, TexCivApp–San Antonio, 532 SW2d 382, dism.—Child S 446, 459, 473, 498.

Gonzalez; Gonzalez v., TexCivApp–San Antonio, 532 SW2d 382, dism.—Child S 446, 459, 473, 498.

Gonzalez v. Gonzalez, TexCivApp–San Antonio, 383 SW2d 64.—Divorce 6, 124, 184(5).

Gonzalez; Gonzalez v., TexCivApp–San Antonio, 383 SW2d 64.—Divorce 6, 124, 184(5).

Gonzalez v. Gonzalez, TexCivApp–El Paso, 494 SW2d 655.—Proc 48.

Gonzalez; Gonzalez v., TexCivApp–El Paso, 494 SW2d 655.—Proc 48.

Gonzalez v. Gonzalez, TexCivApp–El Paso, 484 SW2d 611.—Appear 12; Const Law 965, 967; Divorce 253(4); Hus & W 264(7); Plead 411.

Gonzalez; Gonzalez v., TexCivApp–El Paso, 484 SW2d 611.—Appear 12; Const Law 965, 967; Divorce 253(4); Hus & W 264(7); Plead 411.

Gonzalez v. Gonzalez, TexCivApp–El Paso, 177 SW2d 328.—Child 3, 5; Divorce 90, 115.

Gonzalez; Gonzalez v., TexCivApp–El Paso, 177 SW2d 328.—Child 3, 5; Divorce 90, 115.

Gonzalez v. Gonzalez, TexCivApp–Eastland, 614 SW2d 203, dism.—Divorce 178, 249.2; Judgm 215.

Gonzalez; Gonzalez v., TexCivApp–Eastland, 614 SW2d 203, dism.—Divorce 178, 249.2; Judgm 215.

Gonzalez v. Gonzalez, TexCivApp–Corpus Christi, 552 SW2d 175, ref nre.—Costs 12; Ex & Ad 7, 129(1); Interest 1; Partit 87, 89, 114(1); Ten in C 31, 32.

Gonzalez; Gonzalez v., TexCivApp–Corpus Christi, 552 SW2d 175, ref nre.—Costs 12; Ex & Ad 7, 129(1); Interest 1; Partit 87, 89, 114(1); Ten in C 31, 32.

Gonzalez v. Gonzalez, TexCivApp–Corpus Christi, 469 SW2d 624, ref nre.—Ex & Ad 7, 288; Partit 16, 36, 53; Trusts 61(4); Wills 686(2), 686(3).

Gonzalez; Gonzalez v., TexCivApp–Corpus Christi, 469 SW2d 624, ref nre.—Ex & Ad 7, 288; Partit 16, 36, 53; Trusts 61(4); Wills 686(2), 686(3).

Gonzalez v. Gonzalez, TexCivApp–Corpus Christi, 457 SW2d 440, ref nre.—Life Est 5, 11; Trusts 9, 25(1), 159; Wills 208, 439, 441, 450, 469, 470(1), 671, 672(1), 686(3).

Gonzalez; Gonzalez v., TexCivApp–Corpus Christi, 457 SW2d 440, ref nre.—Life Est 5, 11; Trusts 9, 25(1), 159; Wills 208, 439, 441, 450, 469, 470(1), 671, 672(1), 686(3).

Gonzalez v. Greyhound Lines, Inc., TexApp–El Paso, 181 SW3d 386, reh overr, and review den, and reh of petition for review den.—Action 13; App & E 840(2), 893(1); Corp 182.3; Courts 35; Parties 1, 94(1); Partners 375; Plead 104(1), 111.36, 111.37, 111.38, 111.48.

Gonzalez; G.T. Management, Inc. v., TexApp–Dallas, 106 SW3d 880.—App & E 232(0.5), 232(2), 846(5), 852, 1004(1), 1008.1(2), 1140(1); Labor & Emp 3049(3), 3055, 3089(2), 3096(8), 3105(8); Plead 34(1), 48.

Gonzalez v. Guajardo de Gonzalez, TexCivApp–Waco, 541 SW2d 865.—Evid 589; Ex & Ad 178, 187, 188, 190; Home 145, 168; Hus & W 262.1(2), 262.1(6), 262.2, 264(2), 264(6); Partit 12(3).

Gonzalez; Guernsey Community Federal Credit Union v., TexCivApp–El Paso, 539 SW2d 896, ref nre.—App & E 291, 758.3(11), 768, 930(3), 989; Mal Pros 64(1), 64(2); Trial 352.18.

Gonzalez; Guerra v., CA5 (Tex), 340 F2d 227.—Civil R 1391; Courts 508(2.1); Mal Pros 34.

Gonzalez v. Gutierrez, TexApp–San Antonio, 694 SW2d 384.—Appear 3; Damag 20, 40(4), 49.10, 190; Evid 351; Judgm 17(1); Mun Corp 1029; Torts 211, 212, 220, 243; Trial 325(3), 352.50, 362.

Gonzalez v. Hansen, TexCivApp–San Antonio, 505 SW2d 613.—App & E 934(1), 989; Damag 186.

Gonzalez; Hatton v., TexCivApp–Corpus Christi, 541 SW2d 197.—Judgm 143(2), 151, 153(1), 160.

Gonzalez; H.B. Zachry Co. v., Tex, 847 SW2d 246.—Pretrial Proc 312.

Gonzalez v. Heard, Goggan, Blair & Williams, TexApp–Corpus Christi, 923 SW2d 764, reh overr, and writ den.—Judgm 181(2), 181(27), 185(2); Mun Corp 723; Offic 114.

Gonzalez v. H.E. Butt Grocery, Co., TexApp–Corpus Christi, 667 SW2d 188.—App & E 1107.

Gonzalez; Helms v., TexApp–Eastland, 885 SW2d 535.—App & E 852; Health 752; Judgm 185(2).

Gonzalez; Henry v., TexApp–San Antonio, 18 SW3d 684, reh overr, and review dism by agreement.—Alt Disp Res 114, 134(1), 139, 140, 143, 178, 182(1), 191, 199, 210, 374(7); App & E 893(1), 949; Contracts 143.5, 162; Jury 31.2(1); States 18.15.

Gonzalez; Hidalgo County v., TexApp–Corpus Christi, 128 SW3d 788.—App & E 70(8); Autos 187(1); Counties 141, 146; Mun Corp 745, 747(3), 847; Offic 114, 119; Sheriffs 99, 100; States 78.

Gonzalez v. Hidalgo County, Texas, CA5 (Tex), 489 F2d 1043.—Const Law 947, 948, 4417, 4480; Contracts 1.

Gonzalez; Home Indem. Co. v., TexCivApp–San Antonio, 383 SW2d 857, ref nre.—App & E 999(1); Insurance 2412.

Gonzalez; House of Falcon, Inc. v., TexCivApp–Corpus Christi, 583 SW2d 902.—Contracts 175(1), 187(1); Indem 81, 93; Lim of Act 141, 146(1), 148(1).

Gonzalez; Hygeia Dairy Co. v., TexApp–San Antonio, 994 SW2d 220.—App & E 1067; Damag 62(1), 163(2), 208(7), 214; Fraud 17; Neglig 210, 213, 215, 1692.

Gonzalez v. Immigration and Naturalization Service, CA5 (Tex), 493 F2d 461.—Aliens 317.

Gonzalez v. International Longshoremen's Ass'n Local No. 1581, AFL-CIO, CA5 (Tex), 498 F2d 330, cert den 95 SCt 658, 419 US 1070, 42 LEd2d 666.—Labor & Emp 1219(3).

Gonzalez v. Ison-Newsome, TexApp–Dallas, 68 SW3d 2, petition for review den, and reh of petition for review gr, review dism woj Collins v. Ison-Newsome, 73 SW3d 178.—Judgm 181(27), 185(5); Labor & Emp 3045; Princ & A 159(1); Schools 63(3), 147.

Gonzalez; Jim Walter Homes, Inc. v., TexApp–San Antonio, 686 SW2d 715, petition for discretionary review dism.—Antitrust 369, 390, 393; App & E 930(1), 989, 999(1), 1001(1); Damag 123; Evid 571(1); Fraud 13(2); Trial 139.1(3), 140(1), 142, 143.

Gonzalez v. John Stevenson Aircraft Supply, TexApp–Corpus Christi, 791 SW2d 250. See Gonzalez v. Stevenson.

Gonzalez v. King, TexCivApp–Corpus Christi, 548 SW2d 66.—Courts 209(2).

Gonzalez; Labor Ready Cent. III, L.P. v., TexApp–Corpus Christi, 64 SW3d 519, reh overr.—Alt Disp Res 134(2), 137, 199, 200, 205, 210, 213(5); App & E 874(1), 893(1); Commerce 80.5; Contracts 1, 10(1), 47, 85; Courts 26; Mand 4(1), 4(4), 32.

Gonzalez v. Layton, TexCivApp–Corpus Christi, 429 SW2d 215.—App & E 1003(11), 1056.4; Autos 244(44), 244(58); Evid 587; Trial 139.1(3), 140(1), 143; Witn 405(2).

Gonzalez v. McAllen Medical Center, Inc., Tex, 195 SW3d 680.—App & E 1182.

Gonzalez; McDaniel v., TexCivApp–El Paso, 149 SW2d 617.—Plead 111.45.

Gonzalez; MacWhyte Co. v., TexApp–El Paso, 688 SW2d 205.—App & E 70(6), 1097(1), 1217; Courts 100(1); Mand 4(3).

Gonzalez; Maher v., TexCivApp–San Antonio, 380 SW2d 764.—App & E 854(2); Lim of Act 2(4), 165, 180(2), 182(2), 182(5).

Gonzalez; Mann v., Tex, 595 SW2d 102.—Courts 481.

Gonzalez v. Mann, TexCivApp–Hous (14 Dist), 584 SW2d 928, ref nre.—Judgm 335(1), 335(3), 335(4), 486(1).

Gonzalez v. Mann, TexCivApp–Hous (14 Dist), 583 SW2d 637, rev 595 SW2d 102.—Courts 475(1), 476; Judgm 335(1); Pretrial Proc 46, 531.

Gonzalez v. Markle Mfg. Co., WDTex, 487 FSupp 1088, aff 614 F2d 1083, reh den 617 F2d 295.—Civil R 1536, 1542, 1554, 1563, 1574, 1595; Fed Civ Proc 2334.

Gonzalez; Mars, Inc. v., TexApp–Waco, 71 SW3d 434, reh overr, and review den, and reh of petition for review den.—App & E 930(1), 1001(1); Corp 397; Libel 23.1, 44(3), 50.5, 74, 112(1); Princ & A 119(1).

Gonzalez; Martinez-Aguero v., CA5 (Tex), 459 F3d 618, cert den 127 SCt 837, 166 LEd2d 667.—Aliens 220, 440, 453, 463; Arrest 63.4(1), 63.4(2), 68(2); Civil R 1376(1), 1376(2); Fed Cts 770, 776, 802; U S 50.10(3).

Gonzalez v. Meek, TexCivApp–San Antonio, 350 SW2d 580.—Guard & W 81, 112; Judgm 475; Witn 139(12).

Gonzalez; Mejorada v., TexApp–San Antonio, 663 SW2d 891.—Courts 472.4(2.1).

Gonzalez v. Mendoza, TexApp–San Antonio, 739 SW2d 120.—Judgm 199(5); Trial 352.1(1), 352.1(3).

Gonzalez; Miloszar v., TexCivApp–Corpus Christi, 619 SW2d 283.—App & E 1010.1(3); Damag 112, 188(1), 188(2); Tresp 16.

Gonzalez v. Mission American Ins. Co., Tex, 795 SW2d 734.—App & E 863, 934(1); Contracts 152; Insurance 1836, 2276, 2281(1).

Gonzalez; Mission American Ins. Co. v., TexApp–San Antonio, 804 SW2d 112, writ gr, rev 795 SW2d 734.—Insurance 1835(2), 1836, 2756(1), 2756(3).

Gonzalez; Morgan v., TexCivApp–San Antonio, 368 SW2d 113.—Adop 7.4(1), 7.8(5); App & E 846(2), 846(5).

Gonzalez v. Morris, CA5 (Tex), 214 FedAppx 394.—Hab Corp 285.1, 894.1.

Gonzalez v. Naviera Neptuno A.A., CA5 (Tex), 832 F2d 876.—Adm 1.11; Fed Cts 45, 574, 893.

Gonzalez v. Nielson, TexApp–Corpus Christi, 770 SW2d 99, writ den.—App & E 236(1), 984(5); Bills & N 474, 516; Costs 194.12, 207; Plead 111.3, 290(2); Venue 58, 68.

Gonzalez v. North American College of Louisiana, Inc., SDTex, 700 FSupp 362.—RICO 31, 58.

Gonzalez; O'Farrill Avila v., TexApp–San Antonio, 974 SW2d 237, reh overr, and review den.—App & E 219(2), 295, 842(2), 931(1), 946, 1010.1(1), 1010.2, 1024.1; Contracts 10(1), 168, 215(1); Costs 207, 252, 264; Damag 36, 45, 117; Evid 397(1), 419(11); Frds St of 129(1), 139(1), 156, 158(4); Interest 39(3); Marriage 54; Plead 427, 430(1); Trial 392(1).

Gonzalez; Ortega v., TexApp–El Paso, 166 SW3d 917.—App & E 223, 230, 756, 852, 863, 1079; Judgm 183, 185.2(5); Trial 388(2).

Gonzalez v. Perry, TexCivApp–San Antonio, 390 SW2d 382, ref nre.—Autos 218, 242(8), 244(55), 244(58), 245(8).

Gonzalez v. Phoenix Frozen Foods, Inc., TexApp–Corpus Christi, 884 SW2d 587.—App & E 223; Appear 8(3), 20; Judgm 185(2), 185.1(1); Lim of Act 118(2), 119(3), 199(1).

Gonzalez v. Puente, WDTex, 705 FSupp 331, 28 Wage & Hour Cas (BNA) 1525.—Labor & Emp 2227, 2713.

Gonzalez v. Regalado, TexCivApp–Waco, 542 SW2d 689, ref nre.—App & E 192.1, 361(3), 907(3); Contracts 332(2); Judgm 101(1), 176; Plead 228.15, 404.

Gonzalez v. Reliant Energy, Inc., Tex, 159 SW3d 615.—App & E 832(6), 946, 1074(3); Courts 475(1), 480(1); Ex & Ad 436; Venue 2, 8.2, 36.

Gonzalez; Reliant Energy, Inc. v., TexApp–Houston (1 Dist), 102 SW3d 868, review gr, aff 159 SW3d 615.—App & E 71(3), 954(1); Courts 2, 475(1), 480(1); Inj 26(1), 26(3); Venue 1.5, 8.2.

Gonzalez; Reyna v., TexApp–Corpus Christi, 630 SW2d 439.—Labor & Emp 174.

Gonzalez; Rodriguez v., TexApp–Corpus Christi, 830 SW2d 799.—App & E 253; Guard & W 15, 35, 37; Infants 27.

Gonzalez v. Rodriguez, TexCivApp–San Antonio, 270 SW2d 440, writ dism woj.—Schools 38, 41(1); Witn 94.

Gonzalez v. Rodriguez, TexCivApp–San Antonio, 250 SW2d 253.—App & E 1073(1); Courts 85(3); Elections 269; Inj 157, 204; Pretrial Proc 63, 66.

Gonzalez v. Rubalcaba, TexApp–El Paso, 667 SW2d 609.—Courts 472.3.

Gonzalez; Saenz v., TexApp–San Antonio, 94 SW3d 659, reh overr, and review den, on subsequent appeal 2006 WL 622578, reh overr.—Judgm 185.2(8); Offic 114.

Gonzalez; Salas v., TexCivApp–San Antonio, 181 SW2d 823.—App & E 395, 477, 489.

Gonzalez; Salas v., TexCivApp–San Antonio, 181 SW2d 821.—App & E 863, 920(5); Courts 247(2); Partners 325(2); Receivers 35(1).

Gonzalez v. Sanchez, TexApp–El Paso, 927 SW2d 218.—Courts 23, 37(1); Judgm 137, 151, 153(1), 162(2), 162(4), 340; New Tr 116, 118.

Gonzalez v. San Jacinto Methodist Hosp., TexApp–Texarkana, 880 SW2d 436, reh overr, and writ den.—Antitrust 553, 593; Health 269, 273; Torts 212, 213, 245.

Gonzalez v. San Jacinto Methodist Hosp., TexApp–El Paso, 905 SW2d 416, reh overr, and writ gr, rev Calvillo v. Gonzalez, 922 SW2d 928.—App & E 863, 901, 934(1), 1097(1), 1097(2), 1099(3), 1195(1); Consp 1.1; Courts 99(1); Judgm 181(1), 181(33), 185(2); Torts 211, 212, 245.

Gonzalez; Sendjar v., TexCivApp–San Antonio, 520 SW2d 478.—Health 615, 656, 657, 786; Labor & Emp 23; Princ & A 1.

Gonzalez v. Sociedad Mutualista Protectora Benito Juarez, TexCivApp–San Antonio, 211 SW2d 245.—Corp 514(1), 516, 517; Inj 118(4); Judgm 18(2).

Gonzalez v. South Dallas Club, TexApp–Corpus Christi, 951 SW2d 72.—Autos 197(1); Judgm 185.3(21); Neglig 215, 220, 1692.

Gonzalez v. Southern Methodist University, CA5 (Tex), 536 F2d 1071, reh den 543 F2d 756, cert den 97 SCt 1688, 430 US 987, 52 LEd2d 383.—Civil R 1061, 1325, 1395(2), 1418; Fed Civ Proc 187.5.

Gonzalez v. Southern Pacific Transp. Co., CA5 (Tex), 773 F2d 637.—Fed Civ Proc 1742(1); Fed Cts 744, 757; Inj 60, 138.75; Labor & Emp 819, 1523, 1597, 1625.

Gonzalez v. Southern Pacific Transp. Co., CA5 (Tex), 755 F2d 1179, opinion withdrawn 773 F2d 637.—Inj 94, 99; Labor & Emp 818, 819, 820, 866, 877, 1536, 2025, 3263.

Gonzalez v. State, TexCrimApp, 222 SW3d 446.—Crim Law 126(1), 126(2), 1150.

Gonzalez v. State, TexCrimApp, 195 SW3d 114, cert den 127 SCt 564, 166 LEd2d 418.—Crim Law 662.1, 662.8, 662.80, 1134(6).

Gonzalez v. State, TexCrimApp, 117 SW3d 831, habeas corpus den 2006 WL 167442.—Crim Law 641.10(1), 641.10(2), 641.13(1), 1134(6).

Gonzalez v. State, TexCrimApp, 45 SW3d 101.—Witn 184(1), 184(2).

Gonzalez v. State, TexCrimApp, 8 SW3d 640.—Crim Law 881(1), 1030(2); Hab Corp 466.

Gonzalez; State v., TexCrimApp, 855 SW2d 692.—Crim Law 913(1), 954(1), 1130(5), 1156(1), 1176.

Gonzalez v. State, TexCrimApp, 588 SW2d 574.—Controlled Subs 82.

GONZALEZ

59 Tex D 2d—306

See Guidelines for Arrangement at the beginning of this Volume

Gonzalez v. State, TexCrimApp, 588 SW2d 355.—Courts 89; Crim Law 394.1(3), 394.5(4); Game 10; Searches 11, 27, 178, 192.1.

Gonzalez v. State, TexCrimApp, 574 SW2d 135.—Assault 95, 96(2).

Gonzalez v. State, TexCrimApp, 571 SW2d 11.—Crim Law 739.1(2), 1170(2), 1173.2(3).

Gonzalez v. State, TexCrimApp, 508 SW2d 388.—Crim Law 995(2); Jury 29(6); Sent & Pun 2021, 2022.

Gonzalez v. State, TexCrimApp, 468 SW2d 85.—Crim Law 793; Homic 1207; Ind & Inf 138, 140(2); Jury 79.2, 118, 120.

Gonzalez v. State, TexCrimApp, 456 SW2d 53.—Burg 2; Crim Law 1147; Sent & Pun 2021.

Gonzalez v. State, TexCrimApp, 398 SW2d 938.—Autos 355(6).

Gonzalez v. State, TexCrimApp, 397 SW2d 440.—Crim Law 822(7).

Gonzalez v. State, TexCrimApp, 331 SW2d 748, 169 TexCrim 49.—Crim Law 1166.18; Jury 97(4), 105(2).

Gonzalez v. State, TexCrimApp, 331 SW2d 327, 169 TexCrim 48.—Controlled Subs 74.

Gonzalez v. State, TexCrimApp, 323 SW2d 55, 168 TexCrim 49.—Controlled Subs 9, 65; Crim Law 1036.1(8); Witn 345(8).

Gonzalez v. State, TexCrimApp, 318 SW2d 658.—Crim Law 1116, 1119(1).

Gonzalez v. State, TexCrimApp, 297 SW2d 144, 164 TexCrim 64.—Crim Law 631(4), 1090.11, 1090.14, 1092.1, 1092.4, 1166.15; Homic 1136; Jury 57, 70(7), 72(3).

Gonzalez v. State, TexCrimApp, 288 SW2d 776.—Crim Law 1092.14.

Gonzalez v. State, TexCrimApp, 288 SW2d 503, 162 TexCrim 600.—Burg 41(1), 41(3).

Gonzalez v. State, TexCrimApp, 238 SW2d 768, 156 TexCrim 20.—Courts 80(1); Crim Law 656(9), 728(1), 1171.1(1).

Gonzalez v. State, TexCrimApp, 176 SW2d 195, 146 TexCrim 452.—Crim Law 304(2); Jury 132.

Gonzalez v. State, TexCrimApp, 172 SW2d 97, 146 TexCrim 108.—Assault 54, 95.

Gonzalez v. State, TexApp–Houston (1 Dist), 21 SW3d 595, petition for discretionary review gr, aff 45 SW3d 101.—Action 17; Crim Law 394.6(5), 414, 1134(3); Witn 184(2), 215.

Gonzalez v. State, TexApp–Houston (1 Dist), 768 SW2d 436.—Searches 145.1.

Gonzalez v. State, TexApp–Houston (1 Dist), 752 SW2d 695, petition for discretionary review refused.—Crim Law 339.7(4), 339.10(8), 1166.13; Homic 1181.

Gonzalez v. State, TexApp–Houston (1 Dist), 734 SW2d 178.—Crim Law 790, 878(2), 1038.1(1); Kidnap 36.

Gonzalez v. State, TexApp–Houston (1 Dist), 714 SW2d 19.—Crim Law 662.1, 662.80, 708.1, 719(1), 721.5(2), 1036.1(3.1), 1036.2, 1043(3), 1090.8; Homic 1195; Witn 2(1), 391.

Gonzalez v. State, TexApp–Fort Worth, 967 SW2d 457.— Autos 418, 421.

Gonzalez v. State, TexApp–Austin, 148 SW3d 702, reh overr, and petition for discretionary review refused.— Crim Law 1134(6), 1139, 1144.12, 1158(4); Searches 24, 25.1, 42.1, 47.1, 192.1.

Gonzalez v. State, TexApp–Austin, 973 SW2d 427, petition for discretionary review gr, aff 8 SW3d 640.—Crim Law 878(2), 1130(5); Double J 1, 28, 134, 161, 162.

Gonzalez v. State, TexApp–Austin, 852 SW2d 102, petition for discretionary review refused.—Crim Law 829(18), 1036.2; Infants 13, 20.

Gonzalez v. State, TexApp–Austin, 735 SW2d 320.—Crim Law 99.

Gonzalez v. State, TexApp–San Antonio, 155 SW3d 603, petition stricken, and petition for discretionary review gr, aff 195 SW3d 114, cert den 127 SCt 564, 166 LEd2d 418.—Crim Law 363, 366(6), 419(1.10), 662.80, 795(1.5), 795(2.10), 795(2.50), 795(2.75), 822(1), 1086.11, 1134(2), 1134(6), 1172.1(1), 1173.2(4).

Gonzalez v. State, TexApp–San Antonio, 954 SW2d 98.— Crim Law 13.1(1); Embez 1, 4, 13, 44(1); Fraud 7; Sent & Pun 1973(2), 2123, 2125, 2143, 2158; Statut 188.

Gonzalez v. State, TexApp–San Antonio, 733 SW2d 589, petition for discretionary review gr, petition for discretionary review refused 762 SW2d 583.—Assault 92(4); Crim Law 772(6), 795(2.10), 1038.3, 1045, 1173.2(3), 1173.2(4), 1173.3.

Gonzalez v. State, TexApp–San Antonio, 643 SW2d 751. —Crim Law 469.1, 475.2(3), 478(1), 486(1), 925(1), 925.5(1).

Gonzalez; State v., TexApp–Dallas, 820 SW2d 9, petition for discretionary review gr, aff 855 SW2d 692.—Crim Law 911, 913(1), 913(3), 938(1), 958(6), 1130(5).

Gonzalez v. State, TexApp–Amarillo, 966 SW2d 804, petition for discretionary review gr, aff 3 SW3d 915, reh den.—Burg 29, 41(3), 41(4); Crim Law 363, 366(3), 419(1.10), 1166(10.10), 1166.8, 1174(2); Jury 131(18); Rob 24.15(2), 24.50.

Gonzalez v. State, TexApp–Amarillo, 915 SW2d 170, reh overr.—Sent & Pun 1235.

Gonzalez v. State, TexApp–Amarillo, 888 SW2d 84.—Bail 44(2), 44(3.1); Crim Law 1026.10(2.1), 1081(2).

Gonzalez v. State, TexApp–El Paso, 225 SW3d 102, reh overr, and petition for discretionary review gr, rev 222 SW3d 446.—Const Law 4559, 4754; Crim Law 126(1), 126(2).

Gonzalez v. State, TexApp–El Paso, 990 SW2d 833, petition for discretionary review refused.—Arrest 71.1(5); Crim Law 394.6(5), 1144.1, 1158(1).

Gonzalez v. State, TexApp–El Paso, 938 SW2d 482, reh overr, and petition for discretionary review refused.— App & E 893(1), 1071.2; Judges 12, 26; Quo W 13, 32.

Gonzalez v. State, TexApp–El Paso, 768 SW2d 471, petition for discretionary review refused.—Double J 108; Judges 24.

Gonzalez v. State, TexApp–El Paso, 746 SW2d 878.— Crim Law 339.10(11), 404.60, 1037.1(1).

Gonzalez v. State, TexApp–Beaumont, 648 SW2d 740.— Crim Law 438(2), 568, 795(2.20), 795(2.80), 1036.1(6); Ind & Inf 65, 71.4(12), 110(3); Infants 20; Witn 345(2).

Gonzalez v. State, TexApp–Waco, 187 SW3d 166.—Const Law 4494; Contempt 2, 3, 20, 40, 55, 63(1), 72; Crim Law 1184(4.1); Hab Corp 528.1, 813; Sent & Pun 2254.

Gonzalez v. State, TexApp–Waco, 994 SW2d 369.—Crim Law 949(1), 959, 1035(7); Jury 149.

Gonzalez v. State, TexApp–Waco, 984 SW2d 790.—Crim Law 1077.3.

Gonzalez v. State, TexApp–Corpus Christi, 115 SW3d 278, petition for discretionary review refused, appeal after new sentencing hearing 2006 WL 488681.—Const Law 4626; Crim Law 59(1), 511.1(2.1), 511.1(4), 511.1(6.1), 511.1(7), 511.2, 511.3, 511.4, 639.1, 639.4, 713, 719(1), 723(1), 730(1), 730(14), 1134(2), 1162, 1171.1(2.1), 1171.1(6).

Gonzalez v. State, TexApp–Corpus Christi, 976 SW2d 324.—Arrest 63.4(2), 63.5(4); Autos 349(17); Crim Law 394.6(5), 1035(10), 1139, 1144.12, 1153(1).

Gonzalez; State v., TexApp–Corpus Christi, 894 SW2d 857.—Sent & Pun 2057, 2065.

Gonzalez v. State, TexApp–Corpus Christi, 869 SW2d 588.—Burg 45; Crim Law 1134(3), 1139, 1158(4); Searches 172, 186, 194.

Gonzalez v. State, TexApp–Corpus Christi, 838 SW2d 770.—Controlled Subs 34, 45, 82; Ind & Inf 83.

Gonzalez v. State, TexApp–Corpus Christi, 832 SW2d 706.—Const Law 3993, 3998; Forfeit 5; Judgm 119, 145(2); Trial 9(2).

Gonzalez v. State, TexApp–Corpus Christi, 698 SW2d 462. See Sanchez, In re.

For Later Case History Information, see KeyCite on WESTLAW

Gonzalez v. State, TexApp–Corpus Christi, 688 SW2d 185.—Crim Law 338(7), 347, 369.2(1), 369.15.

Gonzalez v. State, TexApp–Corpus Christi, 683 SW2d 791.—Sent & Pun 631.

Gonzalez v. State, TexApp–Corpus Christi, 677 SW2d 731.—Controlled Subs 131; Crim Law 412.1(3); Searches 47.1, 182.

Gonzalez v. State, TexApp–Corpus Christi, 664 SW2d 797, petition for discretionary review gr, appeal after remand 683 SW2d 791.—Chem Dep 4.1; Ind & Inf 21; Sent & Pun 2010, 2020, 2021, 2032.

Gonzalez v. State, TexApp–Corpus Christi, 659 SW2d 470, petition for discretionary review refused.—Assault 54, 75, 92(3), 96(8); Crim Law 772(1), 814(1), 814(5), 822(6), 949(2), 1083; Ind & Inf 28; Sent & Pun 630.

Gonzalez v. State, TexApp–Corpus Christi, 656 SW2d 518, petition for discretionary review refused.—Crim Law 1133.

Gonzalez v. State, TexApp–Corpus Christi, 647 SW2d 369, motion gr 656 SW2d 518, petition for discretionary review refused.—Crim Law 561(1), 627.2, 1038.1(5), 1038.3, 1043(3), 1045, 1144.13(2.1), 1159.3(1), 1169.2(6), 1169.5(1), 1169.5(5); Rape 7, 51(3), 52(2), 52(4), 54(1).

Gonzalez v. State, TexApp–Corpus Christi, 636 SW2d 14. —Burg 42(1); Crim Law 1144.13(2.1).

Gonzalez v. State, TexApp–Houston (14 Dist), 63 SW3d 865, petition for discretionary review gr, aff 117 SW3d 831, habeas corpus den 2006 WL 167442.—Crim Law 507(1), 507(4), 641.1, 641.5(0.5), 641.10(1), 641.13(1), 721.5(1), 780(1), 1120(9), 1152(1); Ind & Inf 191(5); RICO 103, 107, 121.

Gonzalez v. State, TexApp–Houston (14 Dist), 996 SW2d 350.—Bail 39, 51, 52, 53.

Gonzalez v. State, TexApp–Houston (14 Dist), 967 SW2d 503, petition for discretionary review refused.—Crim Law 627.10(1), 627.10(3), 627.10(7.1), 641.13(2.1), 1170(1).

Gonzalez v. State Bar of Texas, TexApp–San Antonio, 904 SW2d 823, reh den, and writ den.—App & E 1175(1); Atty & C 32(2), 32(9), 47.1; Const Law 1646, 2044, 4273(3); Judgm 185(2), 185(6), 186, 570(3), 720, 724.

Gonzalez; State ex rel. State Dept. of Highways and Public Transp. v., Tex, 82 SW3d 322, on remand Hilda MARTINEZ and Francis Ramirez, Plaintiffs, v. CITY OF BROWNSVILLE, Texas, Defendant, 2005 WL 5630984.—App & E 842(1), 893(1), 930(1); Autos 259, 273, 277.1, 279, 308(7); Evid 75; Mun Corp 723, 742(6); Statut 181(1), 188, 205, 206.

Gonzalez; State ex rel. State Dept. of Highways and Public Transp. v., TexApp–Corpus Christi, 24 SW3d 533, reh overr, and review gr, rev 82 SW3d 322, on remand Hilda MARTINEZ and Francis Ramirez, Plaintiffs, v. CITY OF BROWNSVILLE, Texas, Defendant, 2005 WL 5630984.—App & E 1064.1(9); Autos 273, 279; Mun Corp 728, 742(6), 832; Trial 125(1), 211.

Gonzalez v. Stevenson, TexApp–Corpus Christi, 791 SW2d 250.—App & E 1026, 1043(1), 1050.1(1), 1051.1(1); Pretrial Proc 253, 313; Proc 72, 82.

Gonzalez; Supreme Forest Woodmen Circle v., TexCiv-App–El Paso, 144 SW2d 601.—App & E 846(5); Insurance 1766, 3003(8), 3015.

Gonzalez; Tasby v., NDTex, 972 FSupp 1065.—Schools 147.2(2).

Gonzalez; Teco-Westinghouse Motor Co. v., TexApp–Corpus Christi, 54 SW3d 910.—App & E 989; Parties 51(1), 53; Venue 54.

Gonzalez v. Temple-Inland Mortg. Corp., TexApp–San Antonio, 28 SW3d 622.—App & E 863, 934(1); Damag 49.10, 192; Judgm 181(25), 185(5), 185(6).

Gonzalez v. Texaco, Inc., TexApp–Corpus Christi, 645 SW2d 324.—Inj 111; Plead 111.23, 111.36; Venue 5.3(1), 5.3(8).

Gonzalez v. Texas Dept. of Human Resources, TexCiv-App–Corpus Christi, 581 SW2d 522, ref nre, cert den

100 SCt 1079, 445 US 904, 63 LEd2d 319.—App & E 692(3), 930(3), 989, 1032(2), 1058(1); Child C 22, 510; Const Law 4393; Infants 132, 155, 173.1, 178, 197, 203, 252; Trial 215.

Gonzalez v. Texas Dept. of Public Safety, TexCivApp–El Paso, 340 SW2d 860.—Autos 55, 144.1(4), 144.2(7), 144.3; Judgm 585(5).

Gonzalez v. Texas Educ. Agency, TexApp–Austin, 882 SW2d 526.—Admin Law 481, 513, 669.1; Schools 147.42.

Gonzalez v. Texas Emp. Ins. Ass'n, TexCivApp–Dallas, 509 SW2d 423, ref nre.—App & E 1180(1); Courts 100(1); Dep in Court 9; Judgm 217, 663; Work Comp 452.

Gonzalez v. Texas Employers Ins. Ass'n, TexApp–Corpus Christi, 772 SW2d 145, writ den.—Work Comp 552, 803, 847, 998, 1391, 1399, 1624, 1638.

Gonzalez v. Texas Employment Commission, CA5 (Tex), 563 F2d 776.—Fed Cts 542, 555, 598.1, 660.25.

Gonzalez v. Texas Employment Commission, SDTex, 486 FSupp 278, appeal dism 563 F2d 776, aff 614 F2d 1295.—Action 6; Const Law 4129; Decl Judgm 204; Fed Civ Proc 184.15, 219; Fed Cts 74; Inj 22.

Gonzalez v. Texas Feed & Grain Co., TexCivApp–Fort Worth, 328 SW2d 923, ref nre.—Damag 221(6); Plead 430(2); Pretrial Proc 712, 724; Sales 379, 383.

Gonzalez; Texas Liquor Control Bd. v., TexCivApp–San Antonio, 400 SW2d 619, writ refused.—Int Liq 106(4), 108.10(3).

Gonzalez v. Texas Parks and Wildlife Dept., TexApp–San Antonio, 87 SW3d 563, review gr, and reh overr, aff Kerrville State Hosp v. Fernandez, 28 SW3d 1, reh overr.—App & E 919; States 191.9(1).

Gonzalez v. Tippit, TexApp–Austin, 167 SW3d 536.—App & E 893(1), 931(1), 949, 1010.1(3), 1010.1(4), 1012.1(5); Child S 224, 457, 484, 556(1); Child 69(3), 73; Statut 181(1), 208, 223.1.

Gonzalez; Tips v., TexCivApp–San Antonio, 362 SW2d 422.—App & E 930(1); Autos 171(9), 208, 244(11), 244(36.1).

Gonzalez; Travelers Ins. Co. v., TexCivApp–Waco, 351 SW2d 374, ref nre.—Damag 221(5.1); Work Comp 1181, 1927, 1964.

Gonzalez; Trevino v., TexApp–San Antonio, 749 SW2d 221, writ den.—App & E 201(1), 925(1), 931(1), 1046.2; Bound 37(3); Const Law 3993; Courts 489(1); Judges 39.

Gonzalez v. United Broth. of Carpenters and Joiners of America, Local 551, TexApp–Houston (14 Dist), 93 SW3d 208.—Estop 85; Evid 384, 397(1), 400(2), 420(3), 420(5), 434(8), 448.

Gonzalez; United Independent School Dist. v., TexApp–San Antonio, 911 SW2d 118, reh den, writ den with per curiam opinion 940 SW2d 593.—Admin Law 124, 651, 676, 744.1, 749, 750, 754.1, 763, 783, 791; App & E 662(4), 846(5), 931(1), 1008.1(1); Const Law 3866, 4209(3), 4212(2); Schools 61, 89, 89.8(1), 177.

Gonzalez; U.S. v., CA5 (Tex), 483 F3d 390.—Crim Law 1030(1); U S Mag 13, 14, 17.

Gonzalez; U.S. v., CA5 (Tex), 445 F3d 815.—Crim Law 1139, 1147, 1158(1); Sent & Pun 905, 1911, 1946.

Gonzalez; U.S. v., CA5 (Tex), 309 F3d 882.—Crim Law 273.1(2), 274(3.1), 1026.10(4), 1139.

Gonzalez; U.S. v., CA5 (Tex), 259 F3d 355, reh en banc gr U.S. v. Longoria, 262 F3d 455, on reh 298 F3d 367, cert den 123 SCt 573, 537 US 1038, 154 LEd2d 459.—Crim Law 273.1(4), 1026.10(2.1), 1026.10(4), 1030(1), 1042, 1134(2), 1134(3); Ind & Inf 113; Jury 24; Sent & Pun 35, 322.

Gonzalez; U.S. v., CA5 (Tex), 250 F3d 923.—Crim Law 1042, 1134(3), 1139; Sent & Pun 1938, 2030, 2032, 2033, 2036; Statut 241(1).

Gonzalez; U.S. v., CA5 (Tex), 190 F3d 668.—Arrest 63.5(4); Crim Law 1139, 1144.12, 1158(4); Cust Dut 126(2), 126(5).

Gonzalez; U.S. v., CA5 (Tex), 163 F3d 255, reh den.— Consp 47(12); Controlled Subs 81; Crim Law 113, 139, 641.12(1), 938(1), 944, 1134(4), 1139, 1144.13(3), 1144.13(5), 1150, 1156(3), 1158(1), 1159.2(7); Double J 97, 201; Sent & Pun 761, 996, 2284; Weap 17(4).

Gonzalez; U.S. v., CA5 (Tex), 76 F3d 1339.—Consp 24(1), 24.5, 47(12); Controlled Subs 100(1); Crim Law 369.2(1), 369.2(7), 371(1), 673(5), 1114.1(1), 1139, 1144.13(2.1), 1144.13(5), 1153(1), 1158(1), 1159.2(7), 1159.6; Double J 1, 21, 23, 25; Sent & Pun 300, 752.

Gonzalez; U.S. v., CA5 (Tex), 967 F2d 1032.—Arrest 68(9); Crim Law 419(3), 627.7(5), 627.8(1), 1139, 1148, 1158(4), 1166(10.10); Searches 45.

Gonzalez; U.S. v., CA5 (Tex), 703 F2d 807.—Consp 47(12); Controlled Subs 81.

Gonzalez; U.S. v., CA5 (Tex), 700 F2d 196, 78 ALR Fed 399.—Consp 47(12); Controlled Subs 27, 31, 68, 81, 97; Crim Law 419(4), 427(3), 428, 656(1), 656(2), 656(3), 1036.1(9), 1039, 1044.2(2), 1144.13(3), 1158(4), 1159.2(7), 1166.22(5), 1170(1).

Gonzalez; U.S. v., CA5 (Tex), 582 F2d 991.—Crim Law 216, 594(1), 627.10(6).

Gonzalez; U.S. v., CA5 (Tex), 559 F2d 1271.—Crim Law 417(15), 419(2.5), 419(5).

Gonzalez; U.S. v., CA5 (Tex), 548 F2d 1185.—Crim Law 414, 517.1(2), 532(0.5), 769, 1038.3; Judgm 751.

Gonzalez; U.S. v., CA5 (Tex), 227 FedAppx 348.—Sent & Pun 764.

Gonzalez; U.S. v., CA5 (Tex), 224 FedAppx 325.—Crim Law 1144.17; Sent & Pun 764.

Gonzalez; U.S. v., CA5 (Tex), 223 FedAppx 398.—Crim Law 1042, 1167(5); Sent & Pun 947.

Gonzalez; U.S. v., CA5 (Tex), 192 FedAppx 253.—Crim Law 1031(4), 1042, 1130(5), 1181.5(8); Sent & Pun 834, 995, 996.

Gonzalez; U.S. v., CA5 (Tex), 166 FedAppx 124, cert den 126 SCt 2883, 165 LEd2d 908.—Consp 47(12), 48.2(2); Crim Law 772(6), 1023(11); Jury 34(8).

Gonzalez; U.S. v., CA5 (Tex), 145 FedAppx 959.—Crim Law 1042.

Gonzalez; U.S. v., CA5 (Tex), 145 FedAppx 938, cert den Martinez v. US, 126 SCt 501, 546 US 969, 163 LEd2d 379.—Crim Law 1042.

Gonzalez; U.S. v., CA5 (Tex), 134 FedAppx 696.—Crim Law 1069(6).

Gonzalez; U.S. v., CA5 (Tex), 101 FedAppx 985, cert den Ginez-Perez v. US, 125 SCt 447, 543 US 974, 160 LEd2d 349.—Crim Law 1130(5).

Gonzalez; U.S. v., CA5 (Tex), 101 FedAppx 966, cert den 125 SCt 447, 543 US 974, 160 LEd2d 349, post-conviction relief den 2005 WL 2416626.—Crim Law 1170(1), 1170(2).

Gonzalez; U.S. v., CA5 (Tex), 73 FedAppx 666, cert den 124 SCt 938, 540 US 1080, 157 LEd2d 755.—Const Law 2574; Controlled Subs 6; Jury 31.1; Sent & Pun 1139, 1988.

Gonzalez; U.S. v., SDTex, 912 FSupp 256.—Arrest 68(4); Crim Law 394.5(2); Searches 15, 28, 64, 65, 162.

Gonzalez; U.S. v., SDTex, 912 FSupp 242.—Bail 75.2(1), 76, 77(1), 79(1), 79(2).

Gonzalez v. U.S., WDTex, 600 FSupp 1390.—Health 620, 623, 631, 657, 667, 812, 821(2), 830, 832; U S 127(2), 140.

Gonzalez v. U.S. Fidelity & Guaranty Co., Tex, 274 SW2d 537, 154 Tex 118.—App & E 564(5).

Gonzalez v. U.S. Fidelity & Guaranty Co., TexCivApp–San Antonio, 267 SW2d 587, aff 274 SW2d 537, 154 Tex 118.—App & E 555.

Gonzalez v. Vaello, TexCivApp–San Antonio, 91 SW2d 904, writ dism.—Lim of Act 118(2), 197(1).

Gonzalez; Valley Baptist Medical Center v., Tex, 33 SW3d 821.—App & E 781(4); Const Law 2600, 2604.

Gonzalez; Valley Baptist Medical Center v., TexApp–Corpus Christi, 18 SW3d 673, reh overr, and review gr, vac 33 SW3d 821.—App & E 70(4), 72, 76(1), 78(1), 81; Costs 120.1; Mand 32; Pretrial Proc 24.

Gonzalez; Villanueva v., TexApp–San Antonio, 123 SW3d 461.—App & E 852, 856(1), 863, 934(1); Bail 60; Contracts 108(1), 136, 138(1), 139; Fraud 24; Judgm 199(3.7).

Gonzalez; Volk v., CA5 (Tex), 262 F3d 528.—Civil R 1481, 1482, 1485, 1486, 1487; Fed Civ Proc 2737.4; Fed Cts 776, 830, 878, 916.1.

Gonzalez v. Wagner, SDTex, 64 FSupp 737.—Courts 508(2.1).

Gonzalez; Wal-Mart Stores, Inc. v., Tex, 968 SW2d 934.—App & E 931(1); Evid 587; Neglig 1037(3), 1076, 1095, 1226, 1656, 1669, 1670, 1679.

Gonzalez v. Wal-Mart Stores, Inc., TexApp–San Antonio, 143 SW3d 118, reh overr.—App & E 204(2), 1051.1(2); Damag 127.13, 127.33, 127.74, 185(1); Judgm 536; Neglig 1683, 1718.

Gonzalez; Wal-Mart Stores, Inc. v., TexApp–San Antonio, 954 SW2d 777, reh overr, review gr, rev 968 SW2d 934.—App & E 232(3), 1004(8); Damag 96, 132(7), 135, 191; Neglig 1001, 1670; Trial 139.1(3), 140(1).

Gonzalez; Walter Homes, Inc. v., TexApp–San Antonio, 686 SW2d 715. SeeJim Walter Homes, Inc. v. Gonzalez.

Gonzalez v. Weeks Marine, Inc., CA5 (Tex), 203 FedAppx 574.—Rem of C 106, 107(1), 107(9).

Gonzalez; Wolma v., TexApp–San Antonio, 822 SW2d 302.—App & E 82(1); Costs 2; Mand 4(4), 32.

Gonzalez v. Wright, Tex, 249 SW2d 587, 151 Tex 307.—Evid 42; Mand 31.

Gonzalez v. Ysleta Independent School Dist., CA5 (Tex), 996 F2d 745, reh and reh den 20 F3d 471.—Civil R 1066, 1351(2), 1435; Fed Cts 631, 643, 908.1.

Gonzalez; Yzaguirre v., TexApp–San Antonio, 989 SW2d 111, review den, and reh of petition for review overr.—App & E 833(3).

Gonzalez v. Zachry, TexCivApp–San Antonio, 84 SW2d 855, writ refused.—App & E 931(1); Home 115(2), 167, 181(1), 181(3); Ven & Pur 249.

Gonzalez; Zachry Co. v., Tex, 847 SW2d 246. See H.B. Zachry Co. v. Gonzalez.

Gonzalez; Zamora v., TexCivApp–San Antonio, 128 SW2d 166, writ refused.—Courts 200.7, 475(2); Des & Dist 90(1).

Gonzalez-Balderas; U.S. v., CA5 (Tex), 105 F3d 981, reh den.—Crim Law 1147; Sent & Pun 679, 752, 2262.

Gonzalez-Balderas; U.S. v., CA5 (Tex), 11 F3d 1218, sug for reh den 15 F3d 1081, cert den 114 SCt 2138, 511 US 1129, 128 LEd2d 867, denial of post-conviction relief aff 105 F3d 981, reh den.—Courts 90(2); Crim Law 422(1), 427(3), 438.1, 695.5, 789(4), 1152(2), 1166.17, 1168(2), 1177; Double J 161; Ind & Inf 191(0.5); Jury 33(2.10), 33(5.15), 45, 97(1), 108.

Gonzalez-Basulto; U.S. v., CA5 (Tex), 898 F2d 1011.—Cust Dut 126(2), 126(9.1); Searches 22, 183, 186; Sent & Pun 765.

Gonzalez-Borjas; U.S. v., CA5 (Tex), 125 FedAppx 556, cert den 126 SCt 297, 546 US 919, 163 LEd2d 259.—Crim Law 1042; Sent & Pun 793.

Gonzalez-Capetillo; U.S. v., CA5 (Tex), 150 FedAppx 383, cert den 126 SCt 1448, 546 US 1222, 164 LEd2d 146.—Crim Law 1042.

Gonzalez-Chavez; U.S. v., CA5 (Tex), 432 F3d 334.—Crim Law 1030(1), 1042; Sent & Pun 781, 793.

Gonzalez-Compean; U.S. v., CA5 (Tex), 179 FedAppx 904.—Consp 51.

Gonzalez-Cuevas v. Immigration and Naturalization Service, CA5 (Tex), 515 F2d 1222.—Aliens 207, 299, 317.

Gonzalez de Lara v. U.S., CA5 (Tex), 439 F2d 1316.—Aliens 274, 282(3), 651, 653, 662(1), 690.

Gonzalez-DeLeon; U.S. v., WDTex, 32 FSupp2d 925.—Crim Law 412.1(2), 412.1(4), 412.2(2).

Gonzalez de Moreno v. U.S. Immigration and Naturalization Service, CA5 (Tex), 492 F2d 532.—Aliens 101, 317.

Gonzalez-Esquivel; U.S. v., CA5 (Tex), 193 FedAppx 288.—Crim Law 1177; Jury 34(7).

Gonzalez-Gonzalez; U.S. v., CA5 (Tex), 205 FedAppx 225.—Aliens 799; Jury 34(7).

Gonzalez-Guerra; U.S. v., CA5 (Tex), 169 FedAppx 261, cert den Elizalde-Sanchez v. US, 126 SCt 2334, 164 LEd2d 850.—Jury 31.1; Sent & Pun 8.

Gonzalez-Lira; U.S. v., CA5 (Tex), 936 F2d 184.—Controlled Subs 28, 31, 68, 79, 81; Crim Law 369.2(1), 370, 371(1), 372(1), 374, 673(5).

Gonzalez-Lopez; U.S. v., CA5 (Tex), 140 FedAppx 578, cert den Medina-Teniente v. US, 126 SCt 839, 546 US 1080, 163 LEd2d 714.—Crim Law 1042.

Gonzalez-Martinez; U.S. v., CA5 (Tex), 168 FedAppx 569, cert den Duenas-Aleman v. US, 126 SCt 2339, 164 LEd2d 854.—Crim Law 1177; Sent & Pun 661.

Gonzalez, M.D., P.A., In re, BkrtcyEDTex, 112 BR 10. See Gonzalez, In re.

Gonzalez-Mercado; U.S. v., CA5 (Tex), 221 FedAppx 356.—Crim Law 1042, 1181.5(8); Sent & Pun 793.

Gonzalez-Patino; U.S. v., CA5 (Tex), 182 FedAppx 285, cert den 127 SCt 524, 166 LEd2d 389.—Crim Law 1042; Double J 30; Sent & Pun 793.

Gonzalez Quiroz v. State, TexApp–Houston (14 Dist), 753 SW2d 230.—Crim Law 438(8), 698(1), 706(5), 1043(3), 1045, 1115(1); Witn 277(4), 337(9), 337(11), 337(16), 345(10).

Gonzalez-Ramirez; U.S. v., CA5 (Tex), 477 F3d 310.—Sent & Pun 793.

Gonzalez-Renteria; U.S. v., CA5 (Tex), 145 FedAppx 945, cert den 126 SCt 1097, 546 US 1121, 163 LEd2d 910.—Crim Law 1042; Sent & Pun 796.

Gonzalez-Ribera; U.S. v., CA5 (Tex), 167 FedAppx 981, cert den Aguirre-Jaimes v. US, 126 SCt 2339, 164 LEd2d 854.—Crim Law 1043(1), 1163(1), 1177; Sent & Pun 661.

Gonzalez-Rodriguez; U.S. v., CA5 (Tex), 966 F2d 918.—Consp 47(12); Crim Law 737(1), 1144.13(3), 1159.6; Tel 1014(6), 1018(4); U S 34.

Gonzalez-Rojas; U.S. v., CA5 (Tex), 169 FedAppx 216, cert den Amaya-Membreno v. US, 126 SCt 2955, 165 LEd2d 971.—Jury 34(7); Sent & Pun 973.

Gonzalez-Sandoval; U.S. v., CA5 (Tex), 142 FedAppx 207, cert den 126 SCt 777, 546 US 1050, 163 LEd2d 603.—Crim Law 1035(1).

Gonzalez-Silva; U.S. v., CA5 (Tex), 166 FedAppx 150, cert gr, vac Gutierrez-Tovar v. US, 127 SCt 828, 166 LEd2d 662, on remand US v Villa-Gutierrez, 222 FedAppx 393, on remand 228 FedAppx 413, on remand US v Lozano-Mireles, 224 FedAppx 431.—Crim Law 1181.5(8).

Gonzalez Trawlers, Inc.; Cano v., TexApp–Corpus Christi, 809 SW2d 238.—App & E 218.2(1); Courts 489(1); Interest 39(2.25).

Gonzalez-Trejo; U.S. v., CA5 (Tex), 169 FedAppx 858, cert den Aviles-Jaimes v. US, 127 SCt 73, 166 LEd2d 82.—Crim Law 1042; Sent & Pun 661.

Gooch, In re, TexApp–Tyler, 153 SW3d 690, subsequent mandamus proceeding 2005 WL 332074.—Crim Law 273.1(2), 274(1), 274(3.1), 275.4(2), 275.5(2); Mand 4(1), 12, 26, 27, 28, 53, 61.

Gooch v. American Sling Co., Inc., TexApp–Fort Worth, 902 SW2d 181.—App & E 842(7), 901, 931(1), 989, 994(3), 1008.1(2), 1010.1(1), 1010.1(2), 1010.2, 1012.1(1), 1012.1(2), 1012.1(3), 1012.1(5), 1182; Contracts 88, 95(1), 99(1); Guar 1, 13.1, 16(1), 16(2), 16(4), 25(3), 89.

Gooch v. Davidson, TexCivApp–Amarillo, 245 SW2d 989.—App & E 1062.2; Damag 140, 159(6); Evid 91; Trial 350.4(1), 352.1(4), 352.9, 352.10.

Gooch; Foreman v., TexCivApp–Beaumont, 184 SW2d 481, writ refused wom.—Counties 153.5, 164; Offic 100(2).

Gooch v. Fuchs, TexCrimApp, 339 SW2d 202, 170 TexCrim 136.—Prohib 14.

Gooch; Hudson Buick, Pontiac, GMC Truck Co. v., TexApp–Tyler, 7 SW3d 191, reh overr, and review den, and reh of petition for review overr.—App & E 946, 969, 1064.1(1), 1064.1(10), 1070(1); Autos 19, 20, 186, 245(36); Evid 384, 397(1), 400(3); Judgm 256(2); Propty 7, 9; Sales 10, 54, 199.

Gooch v. Keith, TexCivApp–Amarillo, 125 SW2d 628.—App & E 1140(6); Bills & N 140; Costs 238(2), 260(5).

Gooch; Mitchell v., TexCivApp–Eastland, 210 SW2d 834.—App & E 1064.1(9); Appear 18; Autos 244(36.1), 245(24); Contrib 5(7); Indem 66; Pretrial Proc 645.

Gooch; National Sec. Life & Cas. Co. of Dallas v., TexCivApp–Amarillo, 289 SW2d 336.—Evid 158(15); Insurance 1916, 2014, 3013, 3015, 3365; Witn 379(8.1).

Gooch v. State, TexCrimApp, 665 SW2d 112.—Crim Law 780(1); Rec S Goods 8(1).

Gooch v. State, TexCrimApp, 340 SW2d 299, 170 TexCrim 249.—Crim Law 721(1), 1092.12, 1111(5), 1171.5.

Gooch v. State, TexCrimApp, 321 SW2d 85, 167 TexCrim 437.—Crim Law 814(5); Rape 51(4), 57(1).

Gooch v. State, TexCrimApp, 158 SW2d 806, 143 TexCrim 407.—Crim Law 404.70, 683(1), 1111(3), 1159.4(6), 1169.1(10).

Gooch v. U.S., SDTex, 216 FSupp 514.—Autos 223(2), 244(7), 244(35).

Goocher v. State, TexCrimApp, 633 SW2d 860, appeal dism 103 SCt 32, 459 US 807, 74 LEd2d 46.—Crim Law 13.1(1), 577.15(1), 723(3), 730(7), 1171.1(2.1), 1171.3; Obscen 2.5, 16.

Gooch Packing Co.; N.L.R.B. v., CA5 (Tex), 457 F2d 361, on remand 1972 WL 4739.—Labor & Emp 1195(5), 1195(8), 1883(7).

Good v. Aramco Services Co., SDTex, 971 FSupp 254.—Intern Law 10.31, 10.32, 10.33, 10.38.

Good v. Born, TexCivApp–San Antonio, 197 SW2d 589, ref nre.—App & E 1053(2); Autos 245(79); Neglig 1713; Trial 350.7(3.1), 352.1(7), 352.4(7).

Good v. Dow Chemical Co., TexApp–Houston (1 Dist), 945 SW2d 877.—Labor & Emp 3141; Neglig 1011, 1032, 1204(1), 1204(5), 1205(7).

Good v. Dow Chemical Co., TexCivApp–Galveston, 247 SW2d 608, ref nre, appeal dism, cert den 73 SCt 41, 344 US 805, 97 LEd 627.—Const Law 1328, 1430, 1780; Inj 48, 128(3.1).

Good; McCray v., SDTex, 384 FSupp 604.—Const Law 4112; Mun Corp 717.5(6), 717.5(8).

Good; Smith v., TexCivApp–Waco, 119 SW2d 593, writ refused.—App & E 927(7); Mtg 153; Paymt 41(4); Wills 767.

Good v. State, TexCrimApp, 723 SW2d 734.—Crim Law 562, 722.3, 1171.6.

Good v. TXO Production Corp., TexApp–Amarillo, 763 SW2d 59, writ den.—Mines 78.1(11).

Good v. U.S., CA5 (Tex), 415 F2d 771, cert den 90 SCt 1131, 397 US 1002, 25 LEd2d 413.—Const Law 4653; Controlled Subs 68; Crim Law 1132.

Good v. U.S., CA5 (Tex), 410 F2d 1217, reh den 415 F2d 771, cert den 90 SCt 1131, 397 US 1002, 25 LEd2d 413.—Crim Law 393(1), 422(1), 627.6(5), 1132, 1168(1), 1169.7, 1169.12, 1172.2; Ind & Inf 130; Sent & Pun 1372.

Goodacre v. State, TexCrimApp, 412 SW2d 649.—Crim Law 264.

Goodacre v. State, TexApp–Dallas, 639 SW2d 324, petition for discretionary review refused.—Crim Law 388.5(1), 641.13(1), 641.13(6), 655(5); Rob 24.50.

Goodale, Ex parte, TexCrimApp, 248 SW2d 157, 157 TexCrim 203.—Pardon 76.

Goodale v. Goodale, TexCivApp–Hous (1 Dist), 497 SW2d 116, ref nre.—App & E 1008.1(1); Child C 78, 532, 553, 632, 637, 920, 923(4); Evid 54.

Goodale; Goodale v., TexCivApp–Hous (1 Dist), 497 SW2d 116, ref nre.—App & E 1008.1(1); Child C 78, 532, 553, 632, 637, 920, 923(4); Evid 54.

Goodale v. State, TexCrimApp, 177 SW2d 211, 146 Tex-Crim 568.—Burg 46(3); Ind & Inf 114, 171.

Goodall, Ex parte, TexCrimApp, 632 SW2d 750.—Crim Law 641.13(7); Hab Corp 792.1.

Goodall; Bankers Life & Cas. Co. v., CA5 (Tex), 368 F2d 918.—Fed Civ Proc 2182.1; Fed Cts 847; Insurance 2608, 3579.

Goodall; Montelongo v., TexApp–Austin, 788 SW2d 717.—Evid 538; Land & Ten 164(1), 164(2), 164(6), 164(7), 381.

Goodall v. State, TexCrimApp, 501 SW2d 342.—Crim Law 854(7), 1163(6).

Goodall v. State, TexCrimApp, 268 SW2d 666, 160 Tex-Crim 311.—Crim Law 698(1), 1099.7(2); Weap 17(4).

Goodall v. State, TexApp–Fort Worth, 774 SW2d 821, petition for discretionary review refused.—Controlled Subs 30, 80.

Goodall; Tilotta v., TexApp–Houston (1 Dist), 752 SW2d 160, writ den.—App & E 173(2); Health 611, 822(3), 823(5), 823(7); Judgm 185(2), 185.3(21).

Goodbody & Co., Inc. v. McDowell, CA5 (Tex), 530 F2d 1149.—Fed Cts 422.1; Lim of Act 55(5), 66(14).

Goodbodys, Inc.; Whitson v., TexApp–Dallas, 773 SW2d 381, writ gr, and writ withdrawn, and writ den.—Indem 25, 30(4).

Goodbread, Ex parte, TexCrimApp, 967 SW2d 859.—Double J 131, 132.1, 148.

Goodbread v. State, TexApp–Houston (14 Dist), 912 SW2d 336, petition for discretionary review gr, aff Ex parte Goodbread, 967 SW2d 859.—Crim Law 295; Double J 95.1, 132.1.

Goodchild v. Bombardier-Rotax GMBH Motorenfabrik, TexApp–Houston (14 Dist), 979 SW2d 1, review den.—App & E 66, 68, 70(0.5), 70(1), 70(5), 230, 242(1), 242(2), 840(2), 893(1); Const Law 3964; Courts 12(2.1), 12(2.10), 12(2.25); Mand 43; Pretrial Proc 517.1.

Goode, In re, BkrtcyEDTex, 235 BR 584.—Bankr 3062, 3082.1, 3083, 3084, 3703.

Goode v. Avis Rent-A-Car, Inc., TexApp–Houston (1 Dist), 832 SW2d 202, reh den, and writ den.—Judgm 181(5.1), 184, 190.

Goode v. Bauer, TexApp–Corpus Christi, 109 SW3d 788, review den.—Anim 48, 50(1), 53, 55; Autos 289.5; Neglig 222, 238, 259, 409.

Goode v. City of Dallas, TexCivApp–Dallas, 554 SW2d 753.—Mun Corp 121; Statut 47, 64(6); Zoning 28, 72, 779.1, 801.

Goode; Commercial Cas. Ins. Co. v., TexCivApp–Galveston, 135 SW2d 816, dism.—Insurance 2595(2); Larc 1, 12.

Goode v. Davis, TexCivApp–Fort Worth, 135 SW2d 285, writ dism, correct.—Evid 383(7); Mtg 334, 356, 374; Tax 2944; Tresp to T T 6.1, 11, 38(1), 38(2), 39(2), 41(1); Usury 34, 72.

Goode v. ETEX Auctioneers, TexApp–Tyler, 923 SW2d 746. See Goode v. Mazy.

Goode v. Farmers Produce Co., TexCivApp–Austin, 108 SW2d 443.—App & E 1176(6); Replev 126.

Goode v. Firefighters' and Police Officers' Civil Service Com'n of City of Houston, TexApp–Houston (1 Dist), 976 SW2d 822, review den, and reh of petition for review overr.—Mun Corp 185(5).

Goode v. Estate of Hoover, TexApp–El Paso, 828 SW2d 558, writ den.—Wills 167, 174, 290.

Goode v. Mazy, TexApp–Tyler, 923 SW2d 746.—App & E 854(1), 934(1); Judgm 178, 181(33), 183, 185(2).

Goode; Poole v., TexCivApp–Hous (14 Dist), 442 SW2d 810, ref nre.—Adv Poss 46.1, 114(1); J P 162(1); Lim of Act 130(4).

Goode v. Shoukfeh, Tex, 943 SW2d 441.—App & E 200, 946, 968, 1002, 1024.3; Const Law 3309; Jury 33(5.15), 97(1); Pretrial Proc 358.

Goode v. Shoukfeh, TexApp–Amarillo, 915 SW2d 666, reh overr, and writ gr, aff 943 SW2d 441.—App & E 233(2), 653(1), 671(1), 712, 761, 893(1), 1024.3, 1045(3); Const Law 3226, 3309, 3832; Jury 33(5.15); Pretrial Proc 358, 411; Trial 114.

Goode v. Shoukfeh, TexApp–Amarillo, 863 SW2d 547.—App & E 174; Health 813; Judgm 185(2); Lim of Act 124; Statut 205.

Goode v. State, TexCrimApp, 740 SW2d 453.—Crim Law 867.

Goode v. State, TexCrimApp, 233 SW2d 583.—Crim Law 1094(2.1).

Goode v. State, TexCrimApp, 141 SW2d 358, 139 Tex-Crim 528.—Crim Law 552(3), 560, 562; Homic 1183.

Goode v. State, TexApp–Fort Worth, 685 SW2d 789.—Crim Law 1147; Sent & Pun 2003, 2004, 2018, 2020, 2021.

Goode; Thompson v., TexCivApp–San Antonio, 221 SW2d 569, ref nre.—App & E 927(7), 1015(5), 1067, 1069.1; Damag 127, 134(2); Plead 245(3); R R 350(24); Trial 305.

Goode v. Westside Developers, Inc., TexCivApp–Waco, 258 SW2d 844, ref nre.—Brok 94; Corp 429; Frds St of 72(1); Princ & A 99, 103(6), 124(3); Spec Perf 3, 25, 31, 119; Ven & Pur 42.

Goodeaux; Texas Emp. Ins. Ass'n v., TexCivApp–Beaumont, 478 SW2d 865, ref nre.—Work Comp 1492, 1552.

Gooden v. Aetna Life Ins. Co., TexCivApp–Beaumont, 84 SW2d 563.—Evid 126(2); Witn 363(2), 380(5.1), 388(4); Work Comp 1940.

Gooden v. Crain, EDTex, 405 FSupp2d 714.—Civil R 1032, 1376(7), 1401, 1417; Const Law 3040, 3041, 3341(2); Offic 114; Prisons 4(14).

Gooden v. Crain, EDTex, 389 FSupp2d 722.—Civil R 1005; Const Law 1295, 1303, 1306, 1422; States 4.16(1); U S 82(2).

Gooden; Hudson v., TexCivApp–Waco, 546 SW2d 931.—Partit 89.

Gooden v. Phillips, TexCivApp–El Paso, 118 SW2d 943, dism.—App & E 1040(10); Labor & Emp 249.

Gooden v. State, TexCrimApp, 576 SW2d 382.—Crim Law 814(1), 1038.1(2).

Gooden v. State, TexCrimApp, 425 SW2d 645.—Crim Law 224, 641.12(1); Ind & Inf 10.1(1).

Gooden v. State, TexCrimApp, 145 SW2d 179, 140 Tex-Crim 351.—Crim Law 990.1; Sent & Pun 1352.

Gooden v. State, TexCrimApp, 145 SW2d 177, 140 Tex-Crim 347.—Crim Law 1056.1(5).

Gooden v. State, TexApp–Eastland, 828 SW2d 337, petition for discretionary review refused.—Assault 92(4); Double J 107.1, 161.

Gooden v. State, TexApp–Houston (14 Dist), 692 SW2d 562.—Crim Law 814(5).

Gooden v. Tips, TexApp–Tyler, 651 SW2d 364, 43 ALR4th 139.—Health 752.

Gooden; U.S. v., CA5 (Tex), 116 F3d 721, cert den 118 SCt 350, 522 US 938, 139 LEd2d 272.—Crim Law 1139, 1158(1); Weap 17(8).

Gooden; U.S. v., CA5 (Tex), 162 FedAppx 294.—Crim Law 1177.

Gooden; U.S. v., CA5 (Tex), 111 FedAppx 297, cert gr, vac 125 SCt 1612, 544 US 902, 161 LEd2d 273, on remand 162 FedAppx 294, reinstated 162 FedAppx 294.—Sent & Pun 761, 762.

Goodenbour v. Goodenbour, TexApp–Austin, 64 SW3d 69, review den.—App & E 842(2), 846(5), 852, 854(1), 893(1), 989, 1008.1(8.1), 1010.1(8.1), 1012.1(7.1); Const

Law 3964, 3965(1), 3966; Courts 12(2.1), 12(2.5), 12(2.10), 35, 39.

Goodenbour; Goodenbour v., TexApp–Austin, 64 SW3d 69, review den.—App & E 842(2), 846(5), 852, 854(1), 893(1), 989, 1008.1(8.1), 1010.1(8.1), 1012.1(7.1); Const Law 3964, 3965(1), 3966; Courts 12(2.1), 12(2.5), 12(2.10), 35, 39.

Goodfried; Kaplan v., TexCivApp–Dallas, 497 SW2d 101. —Evid 155(10); Libel 4, 45(1), 48(1), 105(2), 106; Trial 48, 255(4).

Goodgame v. State, TexCrimApp, 86 SW2d 753, 129 TexCrim 250.—Crim Law 814(1), 1172.8; Homic 1480.

Goodgion v. State, TexCrimApp, 371 SW2d 886.—Larc 65.

Good Health Plus, Inc.; Williams v., TexApp–San Antonio, 743 SW2d 373.—App & E 171(1); Health 785.

Goodie v. Houston Independent School Dist., TexApp–Houston (14 Dist), 57 SW3d 646, review den.—Schools 47, 147.34(1), 147.40(1), 147.44.

Goodie v. State, TexApp–Houston (14 Dist), 737 SW2d 37, petition for discretionary review den 745 SW2d 379.—Crim Law 273.1(4).

Goodie v. State, TexApp–Houston (14 Dist), 735 SW2d 871, on reh 737 SW2d 37, petition for discretionary review den 745 SW2d 379.—Atty & C 88; Crim Law 273.1(1), 274(8), 641.13(1), 641.13(5), 1031(4).

Goodie; U.S. v., CA5 (Tex), 524 F2d 515, cert den 96 SCt 1497, 425 US 905, 47 LEd2d 755.—Weap 4, 17(6).

Goodie Goodie Sandwich v. State, TexCivApp–Dallas, 138 SW2d 906, writ dism, correct.—Int Liq 41.

Goodier v. Duncan, TexApp–Dallas, 651 SW2d 25, ref nre.—Judgm 634, 822(3).

Goodin v. Geller, TexCivApp–Waco, 521 SW2d 158, ref nre.—App & E 548(3), 557, 563, 907(3), 1177(9).

Goodin v. State, TexCrimApp, 750 SW2d 789.—Crim Law 770(2), 772(6), 792(1), 795(1.5).

Goodin v. State, TexApp–Fort Worth, 726 SW2d 956, aff 750 SW2d 789.—Crim Law 33, 772(6), 795(2.1), 795(2.50), 824(3), 824(4); Homic 750, 765, 1492; Ind & Inf 191(4); Suicide 3.

Goodin v. State, TexApp–Corpus Christi, 750 SW2d 857, petition for discretionary review refused.—Assault 48; Autos 355(14), 357; Crim Law 38, 772(6), 829(4), 1092.4.

Gooding v. Sulphur Springs Country Club, TexCivApp–Tyler, 422 SW2d 522, writ dism.—App & E 846(5); Dedi 15, 16.1, 20(1), 31, 39, 44; Ease 5, 6, 8(1), 8(2); High 1, 8, 17.

Goodings v. State, TexCrimApp, 500 SW2d 173.—Crim Law 1097(1), 1099.6(1), 1099.7(1).

Good Land Lumber Co.; First Trust Co. v., TexCivApp–Waco, 297 SW2d 312.—Corp 503(2), 619; Liens 22; Venue 6, 22(7), 22(8).

Goodley v. State, TexCrimApp, 457 SW2d 294.—Crim Law 728(2), 730(3), 730(8), 1115(2), 1166(10.10), 1166(11), 1166.22(4.1), 1171.3.

Goodley; U.S. v., CA5 (Tex), 183 FedAppx 419, cert den 127 SCt 318, 166 LEd2d 239.—Crim Law 641.5(4), 641.13(2.1), 641.13(6), 1044.1(3).

Goodley; U.S. v., CA5 (Tex), 156 FedAppx 647, cert den 126 SCt 1451, 546 US 1223, 164 LEd2d 148.—Controlled Subs 81.

Goodloe; Coursen v., TexCivApp–Waco, 267 SW2d 259.—Anim 22; Evid 591; Partners 306; Trial 350.4(1).

Goodloe; Reserve Life Ins. Co. v., TexCivApp–Waco, 316 SW2d 443, ref nre.—App & E 1170.6; Evid 108; Judgm 18(2); Ref of Inst 43, 45(14); Trial 25(4).

Goodloe v. Williams, TexCivApp–Texarkana, 302 SW2d 235, writ refused.—Judgm 199(3.9), 199(3.14).

Goodloe & Meredith v. Harris, TexComApp, 94 SW2d 1141, 127 Tex 583.—Mines 109; Partit 12(1), 16, 62, 63(1), 83, 87.

Goodlow v. State, TexApp–Texarkana, 766 SW2d 352, petition for discretionary review refused.—Const Law

2789, 2790, 2791, 2793, 2810; Crim Law 1005; Statut 263, 267(1), 267(2).

Goodman, Ex parte, TexCrimApp, 152 SW3d 67, reh den, cert den Goodman v. TEXAS, 125 SCt 2940, 545 US 1128, 162 LEd2d 867.—Double J 6, 59, 135, 143; Ind & Inf 87(0.5).

Goodman, Ex parte, TexCrimApp, 816 SW2d 383, reh den.—Hab Corp 275.1, 287.1, 296, 443.1, 447; Sent & Pun 1780(3).

Goodman, Ex parte, TexCrimApp, 485 SW2d 785.—Extrad 36, 39.

Goodman, Ex parte, TexApp–Fort Worth, 742 SW2d 536. —Child S 491, 497; Contempt 61(1); Sent & Pun 2014.

Goodman, In re, BkrtcyNDTex, 261 BR 415.—Bankr 2903, 2928, 3715(9.1).

Goodman, In re, TexApp–Texarkana, 210 SW3d 805, reh overr.—Atty & C 21, 21.20; Const Law 4626; Courts 89; Crim Law 639.1, 1147; Mand 1, 3(1), 3(2.1), 4(4), 12, 141.

Goodman v. Art Reproductions Corp., TexCivApp–Dallas, 502 SW2d 592, ref nre.—Acct Action on 11; App & E 253; Judgm 185.3(4).

Goodman v. Bohls, TexCivApp, 22 SW 11, 3 TexCivApp 183.—Trademarks 1419, 1590, 1695, 1800.

Goodman v. Byron, TexCivApp–Beaumont, 345 SW2d 940.—Autos 171(5), 171(9), 244(41.1), 244(58).

Goodman; Chavez v., TexCivApp–El Paso, 152 SW2d 826. —App & E 934(2); Contracts 43; Land & Ten 25.3, 230(6), 231(1).

Goodman v. City of Dallas, NDTex, 73 FRD 642.—Const Law 1498; Fed Civ Proc 1758.1.

Goodman; Dietrich v., TexApp–Houston (14 Dist), 123 SW3d 413, reh overr.—App & E 1015(5); New Tr 56, 157; Trial 304, 311; Waters 118, 119(1), 125.

Goodman v. Dretke, CA5 (Tex), 89 FedAppx 866.—Hab Corp 818.

Goodman v. Gallerano, TexApp–Dallas, 695 SW2d 286.— Judgm 181(33), 185(6); Libel 36, 50, 51(1).

Goodman v. Goodman, TexCivApp–Austin, 363 SW2d 893.—Deeds 208(1).

Goodman; Goodman v., TexCivApp–Austin, 363 SW2d 893.—Deeds 208(1).

Goodman v. Goodman, TexCivApp–San Antonio, 611 SW2d 738.—App & E 1177(9).

Goodman; Goodman v., TexCivApp–San Antonio, 611 SW2d 738.—App & E 1177(9).

Goodman v. Goodman, TexCivApp–San Antonio, 236 SW2d 641.—Child C 400, 523, 532, 556, 557(1), 602, 607, 609, 610, 618, 637, 651, 856; Evid 43(1); Motions 46.

Goodman; Goodman v., TexCivApp–San Antonio, 236 SW2d 641.—Child C 400, 523, 532, 556, 557(1), 602, 607, 609, 610, 618, 637, 651, 856; Evid 43(1); Motions 46.

Goodman v. Harris County, CA5 (Tex), 443 F3d 464.— Fed Civ Proc 1654; Fed Cts 556, 571, 572.1, 574, 579.

Goodman; Lincoln Liberty Life Ins. Co. v., TexCivApp–Amarillo, 535 SW2d 7, ref nre.—Evid 222(1), 244(13), 448; Insurance 2445.

Goodman; Lumbermen's Ins. Corp. v., TexCivApp–Beaumont, 304 SW2d 139, ref nre.—Evid 126(1); Jury 96, 97(1), 97(4); Work Comp 1392, 1396, 1724, 1926, 1968(5).

Goodman v. Mayer, TexComApp, 128 SW2d 1156, 133 Tex 319.—App & E 90; Judgm 326.

Goodman v. Mayer, TexCivApp–Beaumont, 105 SW2d 281, rev 128 SW2d 1156, 133 Tex 319.—App & E 347(3), 1072; Judgm 17(1), 379(1), 518.

Goodman; Minyard Food Stores, Inc. v., Tex, 80 SW3d 573.—App & E 930(1), 1001(1); Labor & Emp 3047, 3049(3); Libel 74.

Goodman; Minyard Food Stores, Inc. v., TexApp–Fort Worth, 50 SW3d 131, review gr, rev 80 SW3d 573.—App & E 930(1), 989, 1001(1), 1001(3), 1003(7), 1004(8), 1062.1; Corp 423; Labor & Emp 3049(3); Libel 1, 6(1),

7(1), 7(16), 8, 9(1), 10(0.5), 24, 33, 41, 44(3), 45(1), 45(2), 51(1), 51(4), 54, 74, 112(1), 112(3), 113, 121(2), 124(8).

Goodman v. Mitchell, CA5 (Tex), 251 F2d 462.—Courts 106; Fed Cts 921; Labor & Emp 2387(7), 2387(9).

Goodman v. Page, TexApp–Fort Worth, 984 SW2d 299, reh overr, and review den.—App & E 173(1), 173(2), 1004(1); Damag 48, 87(2), 130.1, 187, 192; Health 266, 276; Labor & Emp 867, 868(3), 870, 871, 880.

Goodman; Prudential Ins. Co. of America v., SDTex, 895 FSupp 137.—Armed S 77(3); Fed Civ Proc 2466; Fed Cts 387; States 18.29.

Goodman; Rood v., CCA5 (Tex), 83 F2d 28, cert den 57 SCt 13, 299 US 551, 81 LEd 405.—Fed Cts 545.1; Inj 114(3), 114(5), 128(7).

Goodman v. Seely, TexCivApp–San Antonio, 243 SW2d 858, writ refused.—Contracts 64; Usury 55.

Goodman v. State, TexCrimApp, 66 SW3d 283, appeal after remand 2002 WL 1478594.—Crim Law 549, 562, 1159.5, 1179, 1181.5(3.1); Infants 20.

Goodman v. State, TexCrimApp, 701 SW2d 850, habeas corpus gr Ex parte Goodman, 816 SW2d 383, reh den.— Crim Law 436(5), 483, 625.15, 1035(2), 1043(2), 1043(3), 1134(2), 1166(12), 1166.17, 1169.1(9); Jury 105(4), 107, 108, 109; Sent & Pun 1670, 1713, 1750, 1762, 1772.

Goodman v. State, TexCrimApp, 667 SW2d 135.—Obscen 17.

Goodman v. State, TexCrimApp, 665 SW2d 788.—Crim Law 673(3), 1170.5(1); Witn 321, 323.

Goodman v. State, TexCrimApp, 591 SW2d 498.—Crim Law 641.4(4).

Goodman v. State, TexCrimApp, 233 SW2d 848, 155 TexCrim 248.—Crim Law 814(17); Int Liq 236(5), 239(7).

Goodman v. State, TexCrimApp, 187 SW2d 224, 148 TexCrim 353.—Autos 355(6); Crim Law 594(3), 1158(2).

Goodman v. State, TexCrimApp, 172 SW2d 94, 146 TexCrim 111.—Assault 78.

Goodman v. State, TexCrimApp, 114 SW2d 885, 134 TexCrim 280.—Crim Law 723(1), 1144.18, 1171.1(2.1), 1171.1(3); Homic 1484.

Goodman; State v., TexApp–Fort Worth, 221 SW3d 116. —Crim Law 308, 734, 1139; Environ Law 752; Ind & Inf 56, 71.1, 71.2(1), 71.2(2), 71.2(3), 110(3), 137(6), 159(1).

Goodman v. State, TexApp–Fort Worth, 190 SW3d 823, petition for discretionary review refused.—Crim Law 753.2(3.1), 795(1.5), 795(2.1), 795(2.10), 795(2.20), 1134(2), 1144.13(2.1), 1159.2(1), 1159.2(2), 1159.2(7), 1159.2(9), 1159.4(1), 1159.4(2), 1191; Homic 708, 709, 877, 879, 1148, 1372, 1457; Ind & Inf 171, 179.

Goodman v. State, TexApp–Austin, 8 SW3d 362, denial of habeas corpus vac 89 FedAppx 866.—Crim Law 510, 641.13(2.1), 814(12), 814(15).

Goodman v. State, TexApp–Austin, 935 SW2d 184.— Const Law 945, 947, 2802; Weap 3.

Goodman v. State, TexApp–Houston (14 Dist), 5 SW3d 891, petition for discretionary review refused, and petition for discretionary review gr, vac 66 SW3d 283, appeal after remand 2002 WL 1478594.—Crim Law 1134(2), 1144.13(3), 1159.2(1), 1159.2(2), 1179, 1191; Infants 13, 20.

Goodman v. State, TexApp–Houston (14 Dist), 710 SW2d 169.—Assault 54.

Goodman v. Summit at West Rim, Ltd., TexApp–Austin, 952 SW2d 930.—Courts 1, 24, 30, 201, 484.

Goodman v. Travelers Ins. Co., TexApp–Corpus Christi, 703 SW2d 327.—Decl Judgm 361.1; Work Comp 1108.

Goodman; U.S. v., CA5 (Tex), 914 F2d 696.—Crim Law 1158(1); Sent & Pun 1245.

Goodman; U.S. v., CA5 (Tex), 605 F2d 870.—Controlled Subs 9, 65, 94; Crim Law 422(1), 423(1), 528, 662.1, 855(5), 867, 874, 1169.7; Ind & Inf 71.1, 71.2(2), 71.2(4), 167; Sent & Pun 604, 607; Witn 266, 372(2).

Goodman v. U.S., CA5 (Tex), 341 F2d 272.—Ind & Inf 171; Postal 49(12).

Goodman; Vincent v., TexCivApp–Eastland, 568 SW2d 907.—New Tr 44(3), 56, 159.

Goodman v. Wise, TexCivApp–Corpus Christi, 620 SW2d 857, ref nre.—App & E 843(2); Const Law 3652, 4232; Elections 291, 295(1), 298(1), 298(3), 305(7); States 4.4(3).

Goodman; Woodmen of the World, Camp No. 1772 v., TexCivApp–Dallas, 193 SW2d 739.—Aband L P 1.1; Deeds 143; Ease 26(1), 30(2), 37, 42; Evid 317(1); Inj 5, 121; Trial 45(1).

Goodman Co., L.P. v. A & H Supply, Inc., SDTex, 396 FSupp2d 766.—Const Law 3964, 3965(7); Contracts 127(4); Fed Cts 76.1, 76.5, 76.10, 76.30, 79, 95, 96, 101, 104, 105, 109, 144, 417; Guar 34.

Goodman Mfg. Co., L.P.; Dias v., TexApp–Houston (14 Dist), 214 SW3d 672, review den.—App & E 854(1), 863, 893(1); Civil R 1104, 1112, 1243, 1244, 1736, 1744; Courts 97(5); Judgm 185(2), 185(5); Statut 181(2), 188, 226.

Goodman Mfg. Co., L.P.; Machado v., SDTex, 10 FSupp2d 709.—Civil R 1123, 1147, 1149, 1189, 1542, 1544; Fed Civ Proc 2497.1; Labor & Emp 826.

Goodmark Corp.; Briscoe v., Tex, 102 SW3d 714, on remand 130 SW3d 160.—App & E 1097(1), 1097(2), 1195(1).

Goodmark Corp.; Briscoe v., TexApp–El Paso, 130 SW3d 160.—App & E 204(3), 966(1), 1050.1(1); Bills & N 441.1, 444, 523; Interest 37(1), 37(2); Lost Inst 8(2); Pretrial Proc 713, 715, 723.1; Trial 37.

Goodmark Corp.; Briscoe v., TexApp–El Paso, 101 SW3d 112, review gr, rev 102 SW3d 714, on remand 130 SW3d 160.—App & E 82(1), 153, 635(1), 803, 937(1).

Goodner; First State Bank of Mobeetie v., TexCivApp– Amarillo, 168 SW2d 941.—Fraud Conv 64(1), 96(1), 206(2); Judgm 767, 769; Trial 145.

Goodney v. State, TexCrimApp, 501 SW2d 311.—Crim Law 412.2(3), 1083; Sent & Pun 2021.

Goodnight; Mewhinney Mercantile Co. v., TexCivApp– Austin, 135 SW2d 230.—Ex & Ad 86(1); Fraud Conv 87(1), 114, 115(1).

Goodnight v. Phillips, TexCivApp–Hous (1 Dist), 458 SW2d 196, ref nre.—App & E 1062.2, 1070(2); Evid 363, 560; Health 620, 665, 823(5), 925; Pretrial Proc 372; Trial 39, 350.5(2), 350.6(2), 352.9.

Goodnight v. Phillips, TexCivApp–Texarkana, 418 SW2d 862, ref nre, appeal after remand 458 SW2d 196, ref nre.—App & E 1069.1; Health 818, 821(2); New Tr 44(3), 56; Trial 306, 350.1, 356(3); Work Comp 2171.

Goodnight v. State, TexApp–Beaumont, 820 SW2d 254.— Crim Law 37(2.1), 37(5), 37(8), 338(4); Witn 344(1).

Goodnight v. Zurich Ins. Co., TexCivApp–Dallas, 416 SW2d 626, ref nre.—Work Comp 234, 305, 306, 312, 350, 1342, 1449, 1457, 1709.

Goodnight-Donald Oil Corp.; Malone v., TexCivApp– Fort Worth, 110 SW2d 929.—Trusts 44(1), 343, 373.

Goodnough; Natural Gas Pipeline Co. of America v., Tex, 457 SW2d 276.—Em Dom 58.

Goodnough v. Natural Gas Pipeline Co. of America, TexCivApp–Amarillo, 450 SW2d 372, ref nre 457 SW2d 275.—Plead 228.2.

Goodnough v. State, TexApp–San Antonio, 627 SW2d 841, petition for discretionary review refused.—Crim Law 412.2(4), 412.2(5), 531(3); Ind & Inf 125(41).

Goodpasture v. Coastal Indus. Water Authority, Tex-CivApp–Hous (1 Dist), 490 SW2d 883, ref nre.—App & E 708; Em Dom 201, 219, 255; Exceptions Bill of56(1); Jury 92.

Goodpasture Computer Service, Inc.; Plains Cotton Co-op. Ass'n of Lubbock, Texas v., CA5 (Tex), 807 F2d 1256, reh den 813 F2d 407, cert den 108 SCt 80, 484 US 821, 98 LEd2d 42.—Antitrust 414; Copyr 51, 83(3.1), 85; Fed Cts 815; Inj 147.

GOODRUM;

Goodpasture, Inc.; Fort Worth & D. Ry. Co. v., CA5 (Tex), 442 F2d 1294.—Carr 100(1), 191; Commerce 89(3), 131.

Goodpasture, Inc. v. Hosch, TexCivApp–Hous (1 Dist), 568 SW2d 662, dism.—Neglig 306, 1613, 1614, 1617, 1621, 1625, 1664; Plead 111.12, 111.16, 111.42(7).

Goodpasture, Inc.; Jon-T Farms, Inc. v., TexCivApp–Amarillo, 554 SW2d 743, 1 ALR4th 512, ref nre.—Action 60; App & E 173(9), 1122(2); Contracts 316(1); Costs 194.36, 195; Evid 455; Sales 72(4), 77(2), 81(1), 151, 179(1), 417, 418(2), 418(7), 420; Trial 352.1(4), 366.

Goodpasture, Inc. v. M/V Pollux, CA5 (Tex), 688 F2d 1003, reh den 693 F2d 133, reh den Negocios Del Mar SA v. Empac Grain Co, 693 F2d 133, cert den 103 SCt 1775, 460 US 1084, 76 LEd2d 347, reh den 104 SCt 264, 464 US 909, 78 LEd2d 248.—Fed Cts 871, 917, 948, 950; Sales 199; Ship 131; Trover 44.

Goodpasture, Inc. v. M/V Pollux, CA5 (Tex), 602 F2d 84, reh den 606 F2d 321, reh den Empac Grain Co v. a Shipment of Wheat of 19,067949 Metric Tons Presently Onboard M/V Pollux, 606 F2d 321, reh den 606 F2d 321, aff as mod 688 F2d 1003, reh den 693 F2d 133, reh den Negocios Del Mar SA v Empac Grain Co, 693 F2d 133, reh den 693 F2d 133, cert den 103 SCt 1775, 460 US 1084, 76 LEd2d 347, reh den 104 SCt 264, 464 US 909, 78 LEd2d 248.—Ship 79, 154.

Goodpasture, Inc. v. Myers, TexCivApp–Eastland, 458 SW2d 490, ref nre.—App & E 499(1), 573, 575.

Goodpasture, Inc.; Salinas v., CA5 (Tex), 978 F2d 187. See Salinas v. Rodriguez.

Goodpasture, Inc. v. S & J Farms, Inc., TexCivApp–El Paso, 528 SW2d 99.—Agric 9.5; App & E 1003(10); Damag 221(2.1); Evid 568(1); Neglig 1683; Trial 350.5(1), 350.6(1), 352.5(5), 352.10, 365.1(1), 365.1(6).

Goodpasture, Inc. v. Skaggs, TexCivApp–Waco, 532 SW2d 384.—App & E 242(2), 291, 301, 302(3), 302(5); Frds St of 138(4); Impl & C C 99.1; Judgm 199(3.14).

Goodpasture, Inc.; Wagner v., TexCivApp–Amarillo, 468 SW2d 892.—App & E 981; Guar 91, 92(1); New Tr 99, 108(3); Trial 362.

Goodpasture, Inc.; Williams v., TexCivApp–Amarillo, 607 SW2d 52.—Plead 111.15, 111.42(5).

Goodpasture, Inc., PST; Salinas v., CA5 (Tex), 963 F2d 791, 30 Wage & Hour Cas (BNA) 1647. See Salinas v. Rodriguez.

Goodrich; Burns v., Tex, 392 SW2d 689.—Deeds 97; Estop 38.

Goodrich; Burns v., TexCivApp–Tyler, 382 SW2d 501, aff 392 SW2d 689.—App & E 1078(1); Costs 47; Estop 38; Evid 187; Lim of Act 195(3); Lost Inst 8(2); Mines 52.

Goodrich; Butler, Williams & Jones v., TexCivApp–Houston, 306 SW2d 798, ref nre.—App & E 213, 253; Contracts 305(1); Damag 189, 221(2.1); Judgm 675(2), 719, 949(2); Plead 404.

Goodrich; Butler, Williams & Jones v., TexCivApp–Galveston, 288 SW2d 887, dism.—Evid 458; Venue 7.5(1), 7.5(3).

Goodrich; Fantham v., Tex, 244 SW2d 510, 150 Tex 601.—App & E 1082(2); Evid 458.

Goodrich; Fantham v., TexCivApp–Galveston, 238 SW2d 572, rev 244 SW2d 510, 150 Tex 601.—Estop 32(1); Mines 55(2), 55(5).

Goodrich v. Jasper State Bank, TexCivApp–Beaumont, 132 SW2d 146.—Frds St of 158(2).

Goodrich; Jasper State Bank v., TexCivApp–Beaumont, 107 SW2d 600, writ dism.—Deeds 38(1), 99, 111, 118; Estop 32(3); Evid 60, 390(1), 452; Mtg 48(1), 48(2), 126, 447.

Goodrich; M. A. C. Credit Corp. v., TexCivApp–Fort Worth, 280 SW2d 755, ref nre.—App & E 846(2), 846(5); Attach 308(2); Chat Mtg 152, 157(2); Evid 318(1).

Goodrich v. Masey, TexCivApp–Austin, 227 SW2d 844.—App & E 977(3), 977(5), 1015(5); New Tr 99.

Goodrich; Producers Chemical Co. v., TexCivApp–Amarillo, 351 SW2d 362, mandamus overr.—Labor & Emp 3107(1); Mand 51.

Goodrich v. Reporter Pub. Co., TexCivApp–El Paso, 199 SW2d 228, writ refused.—Evid 34; Libel 6(1), 19, 97.

Goodrich; Rothermel v., TexCivApp–Beaumont, 292 SW2d 882.—App & E 1043(5), 1170.1, 1170.6, 1170.12; Ease 36(3), 61(6); Inj 204, 206.

Goodrich v. Second Nat. Bank of Houston, TexCivApp–Beaumont, 151 SW2d 276, writ refused.—Banks 280; Home 5, 122; Liens 12; Ven & Pur 232(1).

Goodrich v. Second Nat. Bank of Houston, TexCivApp–Beaumont, 149 SW2d 232, writ refused.—Banks 280.

Goodrich v. State, TexCrimApp, 632 SW2d 349.—Crim Law 1036.2, 1043(2), 1170.5(1).

Goodrich v. State, TexApp–Dallas, 156 SW3d 141, reh overr, and petition for discretionary review refused (2 pets).—Autos 355(13), 357(13); Crim Law 38, 641.13(1), 641.13(2.1), 641.13(6), 734, 772(6), 796, 824(4), 1032(5), 1119(1), 1139, 1144.13(2.1), 1159.2(2), 1159.2(7), 1159.2(9), 1159.4(2); Homic 1470; Ind & Inf 71.4(5); Sent & Pun 1858.

Goodrich v. State, TexApp–Houston (14 Dist), 671 SW2d 920, petition for discretionary review refused, untimely filed.—Crim Law 211(1), 211(4), 369.15, 372(7), 730(1), 1064(3), 1090.4, 1092.12, 1115(1), 1115(2), 1134(2), 1169.2(1), 1171.3; Rape 40(1); Witn 387, 410.

Goodrich v. Superior Oil Co., Tex, 245 SW2d 958, 151 Tex 46.—Venue 78.

Goodrich v. Superior Oil Co., Tex, 237 SW2d 969, 150 Tex 159.—Venue 21.

Goodrich v. Superior Oil Company, TexApp–Houston (14 Dist), 640 SW2d 680.—Torts 212; Venue 5.3(8).

Goodrich v. Swinney, TexCivApp–Fort Worth, 277 SW2d 235.—App & E 1177(6); Sales 130(3), 130(3.5), 287(2); Trial 352.20.

Goodrich v. Tinker, TexCivApp–El Paso, 437 SW2d 882, ref nre.—App & E 1050.1(6), 1178(6); Evid 548, 555.10.

Goodrich; Traywick v., Tex, 364 SW2d 190.—Autos 171(9), 247; Judgm 271; Trial 358.

Goodrich; Traywick v., TexCivApp–Amarillo, 360 SW2d 904, subsequent mandamus proceeding 364 SW2d 190.—Autos 247; Trial 358.

Goodrich Co. v. Formosa Plastics Corp., SDTex, 638 FSupp 1050. See B.F. Goodrich Co. v. Formosa Plastics Corp.

Goodrich Co. v. McCorkle, TexApp–Houston (14 Dist, 865 SW2d 618. See B.F. Goodrich Co. v. McCorkle.

Goodrich Corp.; International Ass'n of Machinists and Aerospace Workers Local Lodge 2121 AFL-CIO v., CA5 (Tex), 410 F3d 204, cert den 126 SCt 647, 546 US 1015, 163 LEd2d 526.—Alt Disp Res 213(3); Fed Civ Proc 103.2, 103.3; Labor & Emp 1554, 1556(2), 1605; Statut 188.

Goodrich Independent School Dist.; Texas Educ. Agency v., TexApp–Austin, 898 SW2d 954, reh overr, and writ den.—Admin Law 791; Schools 13(20), 32, 37(1).

Goodrich Parking, In re, BkrtcyWDTex, 85 BR 399. See Hejl, In re.

Goodridge v. Goodridge, TexCivApp–Dallas, 591 SW2d 571, dism.—Divorce 281; Hus & W 249(1), 255, 262.2, 264(5).

Goodridge; Goodridge v., TexCivApp–Dallas, 591 SW2d 571, dism.—Divorce 281; Hus & W 249(1), 255, 262.2, 264(5).

Goodroe; Shell Oil Co. v., TexCivApp–Texarkana, 197 SW2d 395, ref nre.—Mines 58, 73, 78.1(3), 78.1(10), 78.5.

Goodrum v. Beto, SDTex, 296 FSupp 710.—Const Law 4729; Crim Law 273.2(1), 641.13(1), 641.13(6); Hab Corp 287.1, 441, 474, 721(2), 775(1); Sent & Pun 1210, 1314, 1367, 1404, 1421.

Goodrum; Kelley v., TexCivApp–Houston, 378 SW2d 935.—App & E 1062.5; Evid 568(1); Trial 350.7(3.1), 352.18.

GOODRUM;

Goodrum; Kimmey v., TexCivApp–Waco, 346 SW2d 901, ref nre.—Home 57(3), 57.5.

Goodrum v. State, TexCrimApp, 358 SW2d 120, 172 TexCrim 449.—Rob 4.

Goodrum v. State, TexApp–Houston (14 Dist), 700 SW2d 630, petition for discretionary review refused.—Burg 28(7), 41(8), 42(3), 42(4); Crim Law 1184(1); Forg 44(0.5), 51.

Goodrum v. State, TexCivApp–Galveston, 158 SW2d 81, writ refused wom.—App & E 909(5), 1172(1); Contracts 95(1), 95(2), 284(4), 303(5); Damag 77, 80(1); High 95(1), 113(4); States 112.1(1), 191.9(4); Trial 350.4(1).

Goodrum; Willis v., TexCivApp–San Antonio, 360 SW2d 182, ref nre.—App & E 1032(1), 1069.1, 1069.2; Trial 305, 307(3).

Good's Estate, In re, TexCivApp–El Paso, 274 SW2d 900, ref nre.—New Tr 159; Wills 31, 38(1), 38(2), 55(1), 82; Witn 159(3).

Good Shepherd Hosp.; Albright v., CA5 (Tex), 901 F2d 438.—Civil R 1482, 1488.

Good Shepherd Hospital; Hodgson v., EDTex, 327 FSupp 143, 19 Wage & Hour Cas (BNA) 1067.—Labor & Emp 2486(2).

Good Shepherd Hosp., Inc.; Healthcare Cable Systems, Inc. v., TexApp–Tyler, 180 SW3d 787.—App & E 863, 893(1); Contracts 1, 143(1), 143(2), 143(3), 143.5, 152, 170(1), 175(1), 176(2); Evid 448; Judgm 181(19), 185(2), 185(6).

Good Shepherd Hospital, Inc.; Shivers v., TexCivApp–Tyler, 427 SW2d 104, ref nre.—Char 45(2).

Good Shepherd Medical Center; Albright v., CA5 (Tex), 901 F2d 438. SeeAlbright v. Good Shepherd Hosp.

Goodson, In re, TexApp–Houston (1 Dist), 110 SW3d 81.—Divorce 254(1), 269(13); Hab Corp 445.

Goodson; Airmatic Systems, Inc. v., TexCivApp–Beaumont, 257 SW2d 467.—Plead 111.42(8); Venue 22(7).

Goodson v. Carr, TexCivApp–Hous (14 Dist), 428 SW2d 875, ref nre.—Garn 58, 83, 148, 158, 162, 165; Stip 4.

Goodson v. Castellanos, TexApp–Austin, 214 SW3d 741, reh overr.—Adop 16; App & E 181, 900, 946, 970(2), 984(5), 1024.1; Atty & C 132; Child C 9, 310, 409, 451, 460, 904; Child S 11, 82, 87, 140(2), 539, 556(2), 557(3), 612; Courts 35, 89, 155; Evid 146; Judgm 7.

Goodson; Chicago, Rock Island & Pacific R. Co. v., CA5 (Tex), 242 F2d 203.—Explos 7; Neglig 423, 431, 440(1); R R 108, 114(1); Waters 119(2).

Goodson v. City of Corpus Christi, CA5 (Tex), 202 F3d 730, reh den.—Arrest 63.4(2), 63.5(4), 63.5(5); Civil R 1035, 1037, 1088(5), 1376(2), 1376(6), 1432; Crim Law 1139, 1144.12, 1158(4); Fed Civ Proc 2470.1, 2491.5, 2515, 2544, 2552; Fed Cts 18, 776; Rem of C 101.1, 107(9).

Goodson v. Goldsmith, Tex, 115 SW2d 1100, 131 Tex 418.—Death 2(2); Des & Dist 71(4); Wills 555(1), 853.

Goodson; Hamilton v., TexCivApp–Hous (1 Dist), 578 SW2d 448.—Lim of Act 118(1), 119(1), 119(3), 119(6), 199(1).

Goodson; Missouri Pac. R. Co. v., TexCivApp–San Antonio, 345 SW2d 569, ref nre.—App & E 1004(5), 1170.6; Damag 96, 104, 119; Evid 514(3), 539.5(1); Labor & Emp 2824; New Tr 76(1); Trial 115(2).

Goodson; Railroad Commission v., TexCivApp–Austin, 81 SW2d 279.—Inj 132; Mines 87; Pub Ut 183.

Goodson v. Southland Corp., TexCivApp–El Paso, 454 SW2d 823, ref nre.—App & E 971(2); Evid 546, 548; Judgm 199(3.15); Neglig 1037(4), 1089, 1104(7), 1670, 1683, 1706; Trial 365.1(6).

Goodson v. State, TexApp–Fort Worth, 221 SW3d 303.—Const Law 4735; Crim Law 304(16); Sent & Pun 1920, 1940.

Goodson v. State, TexApp–Tyler, 840 SW2d 469, reh den, and petition for discretionary review refused.—Consp 24(2), 47(2), 48.1(4); Crim Law 422(1), 478(1), 552(3), 721(1), 721(3), 721(6), 1043(3), 1169.7; RICO 30.

Goodson; U.S. v., CA5 (Tex), 502 F2d 1303.—Consp 24(3), 43(12), 47(2), 47(6); Crim Law 622.2(4), 1167(1), 1169.1(7), 1170.5(1); Forg 27, 44(0.5), 44(3); Witn 394.

Goodson; U.S. v., CA5 (Tex), 439 F2d 1056.—Int Rev 5265, 5291.1, 5295.

Goodson; U.S. Fidelity & Guaranty Co. v., TexCivApp–Texarkana, 568 SW2d 443, ref nre.—App & E 931(1), 989, 1010.1(3); Work Comp 203, 208, 235, 237, 244, 304, 306, 345, 351, 1348, 1461.

Goodson Steel Corp., In re, CA5 (Tex), 488 F2d 776.—Bankr 2671, 3066(6); Banks 119, 129, 134(4); Fed Cts 406; Trusts 30.5(1).

Goodspeed v. Beto, CA5 (Tex), 460 F2d 398.—Const Law 266(3.3), 4658(2); Crim Law 339.11(6); Hab Corp 340, 500.1, 509(1), 509(2), 745.1.

Goodspeed v. Beto, CA5 (Tex), 341 F2d 908, cert den 87 SCt 867, 386 US 926, 17 LEd2d 798, reh den 87 SCt 1032, 386 US 969, 18 LEd2d 126.—Crim Law 99; Hab Corp 720, 721(1); Judges 47(1).

Goodspeed v. Estelle, NDTex, 436 FSupp 1383.—Const Law 4729; Crim Law 641.10(3); Double J 30; Hab Corp 481, 690, 770, 897; Sent & Pun 1251, 1513.

Goodspeed v. Harman, NDTex, 39 FSupp2d 787.—Evid 318(7); Statut 230; Tel 1436, 1437, 1451.

Goodspeed v. State, TexCrimApp, 187 SW3d 390, on remand 167 SW3d 899, habeas corpus remanded Ex Parte Goodspeed, 2006 WL 561340, opinion after remand 2006 WL 2075654.—Crim Law 641.13(1), 641.13(2.1).

Goodspeed v. State, TexApp–Texarkana, 167 SW3d 899, habeas corpus remanded Ex Parte Goodspeed, 2006 WL 561340, opinion after remand 2006 WL 2075654.—Crim Law 641.13(2.1), 641.13(5), 641.13(6), 708.1.

Goodspeed v. State, TexApp–Texarkana, 120 SW3d 408, petition for discretionary review gr, rev 187 SW3d 390, on remand 167 SW3d 899, habeas corpus remanded Ex Parte Goodspeed, 2006 WL 561340, opinion after remand 2006 WL 2075654.—Crim Law 641.3(4), 641.13(2.1); Jury 131(1), 131(3).

Goodspeed v. Street, TexApp–Fort Worth, 747 SW2d 526.—Mand 32; Witn 220, 222.

Good Spirits, Inc.; Texas Alcoholic Beverage Commission v., TexCivApp–Waco, 616 SW2d 411.—Admin Law 754.1, 788, 791; Int Liq 70, 71.

Good Sportsman Marketing LLC v. Testa Associates, LLC, EDTex, 440 FSupp2d 570.—Pat 101(2), 101(6), 159, 161, 162, 165(1), 165(3), 165(5), 167(1), 167(1.1), 168(2.1), 328(2).

Goodstein; Advance Components, Inc. v., TexCivApp–Dallas, 608 SW2d 737, ref nre.—Contracts 323(1); Land & Ten 92(1); Spec Perf 94, 134.

Goodstein v. Huffman, TexCivApp–Dallas, 222 SW2d 259, writ refused.—Contracts 1; Covenants 1, 71.

Good Times, Inc.; Marshall v., TexCivApp–Fort Worth, 537 SW2d 536, dism.—App & E 71(1), 339(2), 346.1, 356, 948, 954(4); Inj 161.

Goodtime Stores; Gutierrez v., TexApp–El Paso, 874 SW2d 103. See Gutierrez v. Karl Perry Enterprises, Inc.

Goodwill Industries of El Paso v. U.S., CA5 (Tex), 218 F2d 270.—U S 78(3), 78(4), 78(5.1), 78(12), 125(2), 125(9).

Goodwin, Ex parte, TexCrimApp, 384 SW2d 874.—Extrad 32, 39.

Goodwin, Matter of Marriage of, TexCivApp–Texarkana, 562 SW2d 532.—App & E 692(1), 1074(3); Divorce 146, 179, 184(12); Exceptions Bill of5, 17.

Goodwin; Baughan v., TexCivApp–Galveston, 162 SW2d 732, writ refused wom.—Courts 18; Judgm 813, 818(1), 822(1), 822(2).

Goodwin; Benthall v., TexCivApp–El Paso, 498 SW2d 510.—Acct Action on 3, 15; App & E 859; Judgm 126(4).

Goodwin v. Camp, TexApp–Amarillo, 852 SW2d 698.— Evid 543(2); Health 181, 186(4).

Goodwin; Candlelight Hills Civic Ass'n, Inc. v., Tex-App–Houston (14 Dist), 763 SW2d 474, writ den.—Assoc 5, 15(3); Corp 434; Covenants 21, 49, 68; Evid 448, 450(3); Inj 62(1).

Goodwin; Cantella & Co., Inc. v., Tex, 924 SW2d 943.— Alt Disp Res 113, 139, 192, 193, 205, 210, 413; Mand 3(3).

Goodwin; Caples v., TexCivApp–Hous (14 Dist), 601 SW2d 78.—Child C 579.

Goodwin; Caples v., TexCivApp–Hous (14 Dist), 578 SW2d 529.—App & E 371, 624.

Goodwin v. City of Dallas, TexCivApp–Waco, 496 SW2d 722.—Deeds 18, 76; Lim of Act 39(7); Tresp to T T 16.

Goodwin; City of Lubbock v., TexCivApp–Amarillo, 608 SW2d 835, ref nre.—Mun Corp 200(9).

Goodwin v. Collins, CA5 (Tex), 910 F2d 185, reh den, cert den 111 SCt 2896, 501 US 1253, 115 LEd2d 1060.— Hab Corp 422.

Goodwin v. Dretke, CA5 (Tex), 150 FedAppx 295.—Hab Corp 516.1, 603.

Goodwin v. Dretke, CA5 (Tex), 118 FedAppx 817, opinion after remand 150 FedAppx 295.—Hab Corp 603.

Goodwin; Frozen Food Exp. Industries, Inc. v., Tex-App–Beaumont, 921 SW2d 547.—Mand 4(1), 28; Pretrial Proc 101.

Goodwin v. Goodwin, Tex, 456 SW2d 885.—Inj 148(1).

Goodwin; Goodwin v., Tex, 456 SW2d 885.—Inj 148(1).

Goodwin v. Goodwin, TexCivApp–Amarillo, 451 SW2d 532, rev 456 SW2d 885.—Divorce 206, 270, 275(2), 275(3); Fraud Conv 217, 237(1); Judgm 252(5), 585(3).

Goodwin; Goodwin v., TexCivApp–Amarillo, 451 SW2d 532, rev 456 SW2d 885.—Divorce 206, 270, 275(2), 275(3); Fraud Conv 217, 237(1); Judgm 252(5), 585(3).

Goodwin; Gulf Brewing Co. v., TexCivApp–Galveston, 135 SW2d 812, writ dism, correct.—App & E 989; Autos 245(78), 245(80).

Goodwin; Henderson v., TexCivApp–Beaumont, 368 SW2d 800.—Adv Poss 10, 100(4), 115(2), 115(3); Trial 219, 350.3(3).

Goodwin; Hidalgo County Bank & Trust Co. v., TexCiv-App–San Antonio, 137 SW2d 161, writ dism, correct.— App & E 927(7), 989; Banks 90, 119; Lim of Act 103(4), 199(1); Trusts 1, 41, 373.

Goodwin; Houston Pilots v., TexCivApp–Galveston, 178 SW2d 308, dism.—Commerce 56; Evid 65; Pilots 1, 2.5, 5, 14; Plead 111.7; Venue 8.5(5).

Goodwin v. Johnson, CA5 (Tex), 224 F3d 450, cert den 121 SCt 874, 531 US 1120, 148 LEd2d 785.—Crim Law 412.2(4), 517.2(1); Fed Cts 917, 950, 956.1; Hab Corp 205, 603, 712.1, 722(2), 818, 846, 849, 861, 894.1.

Goodwin v. Johnson, CA5 (Tex), 132 F3d 162, appeal after remand 224 F3d 450, cert den 121 SCt 874, 531 US 1120, 148 LEd2d 785.—Autos 349(2.1); Const Law 4515, 4594(1), 4594(4), 4632, 4633, 4789(1); Costs 302.2(2); Courts 90(2), 100(1); Crim Law 53, 394.6(5), 412.2(4), 414, 641.13(1), 641.13(7), 700(2.1), 1134(3), 1158(4), 1169.12; Fed Civ Proc 2545; Hab Corp 339, 370, 452, 480, 486(1), 491, 688, 742, 745.1, 749, 769, 816, 848; Homic 524; Searches 192.1, 195.1.

Goodwin v. Kent, TexApp–Tyler, 745 SW2d 466.—Courts 198, 472.3, 475(1), 475(2); Mand 53; Propty 8; Quiet T 45.

Goodwin; Mobil Pipe Line Co. v., TexCivApp–Hous (1 Dist), 492 SW2d 608, ref nre.—App & E 768, 930(3), 1062.1; Death 99(2), 99(4), 99(5), 101; Explos 7; Gas 20(2); Neglig 322, 1599; Trial 350.3(5), 350.6(2).

Goodwin; Northbrook Nat. Ins. Co. v., TexApp–Houston (1 Dist), 676 SW2d 451, ref nre.—App & E 931(1), 989; Work Comp 52, 571, 1257, 1337, 1536.

Goodwin; Peterson v., CA5 (Tex), 512 F2d 479, cert den 96 SCt 282, 423 US 931, 46 LEd2d 260.—Armed S 36; Mil Jus 785.

Goodwin v. Railroad Retirement Bd., CA5 (Tex), 546 F2d 1169.—Social S 167, 170.

Goodwin; Rorie v., TexApp–Tyler, 171 SW3d 579.—Const Law 3881, 4011; Judgm 178, 183, 184, 185.1(1), 186, 344, 350, 379(1); Motions 36.

Goodwin; San Jacinto Trust Co. v., TexCivApp–Beaumont, 88 SW2d 525.—App & E 1062.2; Banks 315(1); Frds St of 44(1); Guar 92(1), 94; Lim of Act 127(2.1); Trial 350.1.

Goodwin v. Smith, TexCivApp–Beaumont, 84 SW2d 827, writ dism.—Ven & Pur 254(1), 254(4).

Goodwin v. Southtex Land Sales, TexCivApp–San Antonio, 243 SW2d 721, ref nre.—Damag 62(1), 117; Evid 215(3); Ex & Ad 93(1); Frds St of 49, 52; Lim of Act 46(1), 46(9); Plead 290(3); Sales 379, 384(7); Trial 351.2(4).

Goodwin v. State, TexCrimApp, 815 SW2d 586.—Const Law 197, 2815; Crim Law 1190.

Goodwin v. State, TexCrimApp, 799 SW2d 719, reh den, motion gr Madden v. Texas, 111 SCt 902, 498 US 1301, 112 LEd2d 1026, cert den 111 SCt 2913, 501 US 1259, 115 LEd2d 1076.—Arrest 71.1(7); Autos 349(16), 349(17), 349.5(1), 349.5(3), 349.5(10), 349.5(11); Crim Law 394.4(9), 394.4(12), 412.2(5), 438(6), 438(7), 1043(3), 1152(2); Homic 1165, 1456; Jury 40, 42, 108.

Goodwin v. State, TexCrimApp, 514 SW2d 942.—Const Law 2204; Crim Law 1172.1(3); Obscen 2.5, 7, 7.6, 17, 18.1.

Goodwin v. State, TexCrimApp, 320 SW2d 852, 167 Tex-Crim 485.—False Pret 38, 49(3); Ind & Inf 166.

Goodwin v. State, TexCrimApp, 307 SW2d 264, 165 Tex-Crim 375.—Arson 29, 37(1); Crim Law 507(1), 510, 511.1(6.1), 511.10.

Goodwin v. State, TexApp–Fort Worth, 91 SW3d 912.— Assault 83(1), 91.8; Crim Law 338(1), 721(3), 721(6), 730(1), 730(10); Judgm 751; Statut 181(2), 188; Witn 328, 367(1).

Goodwin v. State, TexApp–San Antonio, 898 SW2d 380.— Crim Law 1144.8, 1158(3); Jury 33(5.15).

Goodwin v. State, TexApp–Waco, 57 SW3d 560, petition for discretionary review refused.—Crim Law 1081(2).

Goodwin v. State, TexApp–Tyler, 738 SW2d 1, petition for discretionary review refused, and petition for discretionary review gr, aff 815 SW2d 586.—Crim Law 1144.13(3), 1159.2(7); Ind & Inf 105; Larc 28(2), 55, 60, 70(1).

Goodwin v. State, TexApp–Corpus Christi, 725 SW2d 314.—Crim Law 1181.5(8), 1192.

Goodwin v. State, TexApp–Corpus Christi, 694 SW2d 19, petition for discretionary review refused, appeal after remand 725 SW2d 314.—Crim Law 713, 720(2), 770(1), 772(1), 795(2.1), 1181.5(8); Homic 876, 878, 1148, 1149, 1150, 1152, 1380, 1458; Ind & Inf 188, 189(8); Sent & Pun 1400.

Goodwin v. Texas, USTex, 111 SCt 902, 498 US 1301, 112 LEd2d 1026. See Madden v. Texas.

Goodwin v. Texas General Indem. Co., TexApp–Houston (1 Dist), 657 SW2d 156, ref nre, appeal after remand 689 SW2d 469.—App & E 863, 934(1); Judgm 181(21), 186; Work Comp 51, 1283, 1726.

Goodwin; Texas General Indem. Co. v., TexApp–Houston (14 Dist), 689 SW2d 469.—Work Comp 73, 1283, 1297.

Goodwin v. Wilhelm Steel Const. Co., TexCivApp–El Paso, 311 SW2d 510, writ refused.—Work Comp 2166, 2191.

Goodwine; Southwestern Public Service Co. v., TexCiv-App–Amarillo, 228 SW2d 925, ref nre.—Em Dom 134, 137, 150, 192, 223, 262(5), 263.

Goodwyn; Kelly v., EDTex, 239 FSupp 269.—Prisons 15(1), 15(4), 15(6).

Goodwyn v. State, TexCrimApp, 306 SW2d 357, 165 TexCrim 297.—Crim Law 412(5), 814(1), 1120(3); Homic 1134.

GOODYEAR

59 Tex D 2d—316

Goodyear Dunlop Tires North America, Ltd. v. Gamez, TexApp–San Antonio, 151 SW3d 574.—App & E 230, 840(1), 984(1); Costs 177, 207; Infants 82, 83, 84, 85, 115; Judgm 297.

Goodyear Service Stores v. Clegg, TexCivApp–San Antonio, 361 SW2d 445.—App & E 846(2), 846(5); Chat Mtg 150(1), 152, 278; Fixt 35(3).

Goodyear Service Stores; Cook v., TexApp–Houston (14 Dist), 624 SW2d 761.—App & E 1135; Judgm 126(4).

Goodyear Tire and Rubber; Hanna v., EDTex, 17 FSupp2d 647.—Civil R 1185, 1189; Damag 192; Fed Civ Proc 2142.1, 2152; Labor & Emp 2937.

Goodyear Tire & Rubber; Hanna v., EDTex, 6 FSupp2d 605.—Damag 149; Labor & Emp 866, 870; Lim of Act 55(4), 104.5.

Goodyear Tire & Rubber Co.; Anderson v., EDTex, 367 FSupp2d 1061.—Civil R 1201, 1204, 1209, 1210, 1539, 1551; Fed Civ Proc 2497.1.

Goodyear Tire & Rubber Co.; Bowerman v., NDTex, 105 FSupp 119.—Action 1; Neglig 484; Prod Liab 71; Rem of C 29, 48, 48.1, 61(1).

Goodyear Tire & Rubber Co. v. Edwards, TexCivApp–Tyler, 512 SW2d 748.—Venue 22(1), 22(10).

Goodyear Tire & Rubber Co.; Fain v., CA5 (Tex), 228 F2d 508.—Autos 368.

Goodyear Tire & Rubber Co.; Hesseltine v., EDTex, 391 FSupp2d 509.—Equity 72(1); Estop 52(1), 52.10(2), 119; Labor & Emp 2312, 2315, 2316, 2322, 2327, 2385(3).

Goodyear Tire & Rubber Co. v. Jefferson Const. Co., Tex, 565 SW2d 916.—App & E 846(5), 931(3), 934(2), 989, 1010.2, 1089(2); Indem 30(1), 33(1), 102, 104.

Goodyear Tire & Rubber Co.; Jefferson Const. Co. v., TexCivApp, 552 SW2d 596, rev 565 SW2d 916.—Indem 27.

Goodyear Tire & Rubber Co.; Johnson v., SDTex, 349 FSupp 3, issued 1972 WL 275, aff in part, rev in part 491 F2d 1364, aff in part, rev in part 491 F2d 1364.—Action 6; Civil R 1107, 1118, 1121, 1141, 1312, 1502, 1506, 1516, 1536, 1545, 1560, 1564, 1565, 1574; Fed Civ Proc 184.10, 184.25.

Goodyear Tire and Rubber Co.; Kimball v., EDTex, 504 FSupp 544, 24 Wage & Hour Cas (BNA) 1269.—Commerce 62.57, 62.66; Labor & Emp 2286, 2290(4), 2371, 2385(6), 2390(4).

Goodyear Tire & Rubber Co.; McLean v., CCA5 (Tex), 85 F2d 150, cert den 57 SCt 193, 299 US 600, 81 LEd 442.—Corp 1.5(2), 668(15); Prod Liab 39.

Goodyear Tire & Rubber Co.; Martinez v., TexApp–San Antonio, 651 SW2d 18.—App & E 846(5), 1024.3; False Imp 2, 5, 31; Plead 111.42(6); Venue 2.

Goodyear Tire and Rubber Co.; Mayes v., TexApp–Houston (1 Dist), 144 SW3d 50, reh overr.—App & E 197(5), 852, 863, 934(1); Autos 192(11), 193(8.1), 201(1.1), 242(6); Judgm 181(21), 183, 185(2); Labor & Emp 3045, 3046(1), 3046(2), 3105(7).

Goodyear Tire & Rubber Co.; Moffett v., TexApp–Austin, 652 SW2d 609, ref nre.—App & E 218.2(10), 232(3), 500(1); Corp 1.5(3), 1.7(2).

Goodyear Tire & Rubber Co.; Moseley v., CA5 (Tex), 612 F2d 187.—Civil R 1141, 1565.

Goodyear Tire & Rubber Co.; Phillips v., CA5 (Tex), 651 F2d 1051, reh den 671 F2d 860.—Fed Cts 409.1; Labor & Emp 40(2), 818.

Goodyear Tire and Rubber Co. v. Portilla, Tex, 879 SW2d 47.—Contracts 227; Labor & Emp 40(1), 51.

Goodyear Tire and Rubber Co. v. Portilla, TexApp–Corpus Christi, 836 SW2d 664, reh overr, and writ gr, aff 879 SW2d 47.—Action 27(1); Atty & C 148(1); Costs 194.14, 194.46; Frds St of 44(3), 49, 158(1); Labor & Emp 40(1), 40(2), 51, 57, 58, 873; Princ & A 99.

Goodyear Tire & Rubber Co. v. Rios, TexApp–San Antonio, 143 SW3d 107, reh overr, and reh overr, and review den, and reh of petition for review den.—App & E

893(1), 971(2); Evid 535, 536, 544, 546, 555.2, 555.4(2), 555.5, 571(6), 584(1); Prod Liab 5, 8, 14, 82.1, 83.5.

Goodyear Tire and Rubber Co.; Townsend v., NDTex, 481 FSupp2d 610.—Labor & Emp 3141, 3143, 3159; Neglig 210, 1266, 1692; Princ & A 1, 3(2), 8, 14(1), 19, 99.

Goodyear Tire & Rubber Co.; White-Sellie's Jewelry Co. v., TexCivApp–Hous (14 Dist), 477 SW2d 658.—App & E 846(5), 989, 1078(5); Sec Tran 170; Trover 3, 9(3.1), 9(7), 22.

Goodyear Tire & Rubber Co.; Wilson v., TexApp–Texarkana, 753 SW2d 442, writ den.—App & E 688(2), 846(5), 1001(1), 1003(5); Death 76; Neglig 1037(7), 1086, 1204(3), 1205(7), 1560.

Goodyear Tire & Rubber Co., Beaumont Plant; Duhon v., CA5 (Tex), 494 F2d 817.—Civil R 1562, 1571, 1590.

Goodyear Tire & Rubber Co., Houston Chemical Plant v. Sanford, TexCivApp–Hous (14 Dist), 540 SW2d 478.—Commerce 62.34; Contracts 129(1); Fed Cts 202; Labor & Emp 1541, 1609(1), 1609(2), 1619, 1623(1); States 18.5.

Goodyear Tire and Rubber Co., Inc.; Thermo Tech, Inc. v., CA5 (Tex), 643 F2d 1173.—Estop 54, 87; Mech Liens 95, 115(1), 115(4), 229; Princ & S 163, 185.

Goodyear Tire & Rubber Co., Synthetic Rubber Plant; Johnson v., CA5 (Tex), 491 F2d 1364.—Civil R 1141, 1142, 1505(2), 1505(4), 1505(6), 1529, 1536, 1542, 1546, 1560, 1564, 1565, 1570, 1571, 1574, 1577; Fed Civ Proc 184.10; Fed Cts 850.1.

Googins v. E. W. Hable & Sons, TexCivApp–Waco, 237 SW2d 705, ref nre, cert den 72 SCt 556, 342 US 944, 96 LEd 702.—App & E 1008.1(2), 1010.1(1); Sales 282, 441(2); War 155.

Goolsbee v. Heft, TexCivApp–Tyler, 549 SW2d 34.—Child C 283, 285, 923(5).

Goolsbee; Moye v., TexCivApp–Beaumont, 124 SW2d 925, writ refused.—App & E 301; Des & Dist 74; Hus & W 265; Ven & Pur 257.

Goolsbee; Mozer v., TexCivApp–Waco, 293 SW2d 91, ref nre.—App & E 1010.1(3); Damag 117; Exch of Prop 13(3), 13(5); Trover 40(4).

Goolsbee v. State, TexApp–Beaumont, 927 SW2d 198.—Controlled Subs 80; Crim Law 1134(3), 1144.13(1), 1144.13(2.1), 1144.13(3), 1144.13(5), 1144.13(6), 1158(1), 1159.1, 1159.2(2), 1159.2(7), 1159.2(9), 1191.

Goolsbee; Texas & New Orleans R. Co. v., TexCivApp–Galveston, 228 SW2d 280, cause remanded Goolsbee v. Texas & N O R Co, 234 SW2d 407, 149 Tex 445.—Neglig 200, 213, 232, 250, 272, 386, 387; R R 296.

Goolsbee v. Texas & N. O. R. Co., Tex, 243 SW2d 386, 150 Tex 528.—Neglig 291, 294, 375, 510(1), 1750; R R 297(8.5); Trial 350.7(6), 351.5(8).

Goolsbee v. Texas & N. O. R. Co., Tex, 234 SW2d 407, 149 Tex 445.—App & E 1114; Neglig 291; R R 297(6.1), 297(7).

Goolsbee; Texas & N. O. R. Co. v., TexCivApp–Galveston, 238 SW2d 250, rev 243 SW2d 386, 150 Tex 528.—App & E 1178(6); Neglig 291, 1537; New Tr 162(1).

Goolsby v. Bond, Tex, 163 SW2d 830, 138 Tex 485.—App & E 1180(2); Courts 90(7), 247(7); Venue 5.1.

Goolsby v. Bush, TexCivApp–El Paso, 172 SW2d 758.—Bound 9; Courts 202(4); Ex & Ad 9, 29(4), 32(2), 347, 349(2), 383, 388(1); Judgm 496; Jud S 31(3), 47; Wills 248, 421.

Goolsby v. Kenney, TexCivApp–Tyler, 545 SW2d 591, ref nre.—Judgm 199(3.10); Labor & Emp 3151, 3159, 3160, 3181(3); Neglig 210, 1204(5).

Goolsby; Lincoln County Mut. Fire Ins. Co. v., TexCivApp–Texarkana, 240 SW2d 402.—App & E 930(3); Trial 351.2(1.1), 351.2(2), 351.2(5).

Goolsby v. State, TexCrimApp, 312 SW2d 654, 166 TexCrim 180.—Autos 352, 355(2); Crim Law 429(1), 627(2).

Goolsby; Watkins v., TexCivApp–Eastland, 337 SW2d 363.—Autos 175(3); Plead 111.42(2), 111.42(8).

Goolsby v. Wood, TexCivApp–Dallas, 131 SW2d 1052.—Partit 43; Plead 111.39(4), 111.42(11); Venue 5.3(4).

Goolsby Bldg. Corp.; Castleberry v., Tex, 617 SW2d 665.—Death 10, 31(5); Plead 48; Work Comp 2149, 2155.

Goolsby Bldg. Corp.; Castleberry v., TexCivApp–Corpus Christi, 608 SW2d 763, aff 617 SW2d 665.—App & E 173(2), 173(9), 863, 1128.1; Judgm 185(2); Work Comp 2143.

Goonsuwan v. Ashcroft, CA5 (Tex), 252 F3d 383.—Admin Law 676; Aliens 347; Const Law 4438; Hab Corp 272, 282.

Goosby, Ex parte, TexApp–Houston (1 Dist), 685 SW2d 440.—Bail 39, 51, 52, 53.

Goose Creek Consol. Independent School Dist.; Brennan v., CA5 (Tex), 519 F2d 53, 22 Wage & Hour Cas (BNA) 489.—Fed Civ Proc 2282.1; Fed Cts 941; Labor & Emp 2240, 2481(7); Statut 219(1).

Goose Creek Consol. Independent School Dist.; Citizens for Better Educ. v., TexApp–Houston (1 Dist), 719 SW2d 350, ref nre, appeal dism 108 SCt 49, 484 US 804, 98 LEd2d 14.—Civil R 1452; Const Law 3278(2), 3278(4); Schools 13(12), 61.

Goose Creek Consol. Independent School Dist.; Closs v., TexApp–Texarkana, 874 SW2d 859.—Admin Law 309.1, 500; App & E 1030; Civil R 1037, 1346, 1351(1), 1351(5), 1376(2); Consp 1.1; Const Law 3057, 3612, 3618(4), 3865, 3876, 3877, 4194, 4202; Evid 314(1); Judges 36; Judgm 185(1), 185.1(3), 186; Mal Pros 16, 18(1), 22, 27, 31, 37, 38, 42; Mun Corp 747(3), 753(1); Offic 114, 116; Schools 62, 63(1), 63(3), 77, 79, 89; Torts 212, 330, 332, 353, 355; Trial 9(1).

Goose Creek Consol. Independent School Dist. of Chambers and Harris Counties, Texas v. Jarrar's Plumbing, Inc., TexApp–Texarkana, 74 SW3d 486, reh overr, and review den (2 pets).—Action 27(1); App & E 863, 969, 1064.1(7); Contrib 9(1); Damag 39, 63, 106, 111, 188(1), 217; Evid 423(1); Indem 20; Judgm 185(5), 185(6), 199(3.5), 199(3.11); Lim of Act 11(4), 46(6), 47(1), 49(6), 49(7), 55(2), 56(2), 63; Neglig 219, 234, 463, 481, 1205(9); Parties 51(4), 55; Schools 116; Torts 111, 118; Trial 182, 295(1).

Goose Creek Consol. I.S.D.; Beavers v., TexApp–Waco, 884 SW2d 932, writ den.—App & E 707(1), 758.3(11), 901, 934(1); Contracts 175(3), 261(2), 299(1); Judgm 185(1), 185(2); Trial 388(2).

Goose Creek Consol. I.S.D. v. Continental Cas. Co., TexApp–Houston (1 Dist), 658 SW2d 338.—Insurance 2141.

Goose Creek Independent School Dist.; Fromen v., TexCivApp–Galveston, 148 SW2d 460, writ dism, correct.—Schools 135(5), 145, 147.9.

Goose Creek Independent School Dist.; Horton v., CA5 (Tex), 693 F2d 524.—Schools 169.5.

Goose Creek Independent School Dist.; Horton v., CA5 (Tex), 690 F2d 470, reh den 693 F2d 524, cert den Goose Creek Consolidated Independent School District v. Horton, 103 SCt 3536, 463 US 1207, 77 LEd2d 1387.—Const Law 4210; Fed Civ Proc 161.1, 162, 164, 165, 171, 172, 187.5, 2515; Fed Cts 761, 817; Schools 169, 169.5; Searches 22, 23, 55, 192.1.

Goose Creek Independent School Dist.; Joe Huggins Lumber Co. v., TexCivApp–Galveston, 133 SW2d 207.—Mun Corp 373(1); Pub Contr 24.1; Schools 86(2).

Gorbet; Harford Mut. Ins. Co. v., CA5 (Tex), 241 F2d 363.—Hus & W 23.5, 266.3; Insurance 1874, 1945, 1952, 1955.

Gorbett Bros. Steel Co., Inc. v. Anderson, Clayton & Co., TexCivApp–Hous (1 Dist), 533 SW2d 413.—App & E 931(1), 989; Damag 20, 113; Prod Liab 83; Sales 60, 273(3); Trial 401.

Gorbett Bros. Welding Co.; Haws & Garrett General Contractors, Inc. v., Tex, 480 SW2d 607.—Contracts 3, 16, 27; Impl & C C 1; Indem 104.

Gorbett Bros. Welding Co.; Haws & Garrett General Contractors, Inc. v., TexCivApp–Fort Worth, 471 SW2d 595, writ gr, set aside 480 SW2d 607.—Contracts 348, 350(1); Indem 27; Labor & Emp 25.

Gorbett Bros. Welding Co. v. Malone, TexCivApp–Amarillo, 254 SW2d 848.—App & E 846(5), 1024.3; Plead 111.42(8), 111.44; Venue 8.5(5).

Gorbett Bros. Welding Co. v. Reynolds, TexCivApp–Austin, 252 SW2d 1018.—Plead 111.42(8); Venue 8.5(3).

Gorden; Moore v., TexCivApp–Waco, 221 SW2d 314, ref nre.—Wills 439, 440, 470(1), 634(4.1), 692(1), 692(5).

Gordin; Shuler v., Tex, 644 SW2d 446, appeal after remand 704 SW2d 403, ref nre.—App & E 1106(2); Contracts 15; Courts 472.2; Spec Perf 121(9), 121(11), 123.

Gordin v. Shuler, TexApp–Dallas, 704 SW2d 403, ref nre.—Contracts 28(3), 221(2), 346(2); Equity 65(1); Spec Perf 1, 53, 65, 87; Ven & Pur 44, 79, 80.

Gordin v. Shuler, TexApp–Dallas, 635 SW2d 559, rev 644 SW2d 446, appeal after remand 704 SW2d 403, ref nre.—Contracts 23; Spec Perf 64, 123.

Gordon, Ex parte, Tex, 584 SW2d 686.—Const Law 4494; Contempt 2, 6, 55, 61(1); Hab Corp 445, 528.1.

Gordon, Ex parte, TexCrimApp, 439 SW2d 354.—Hab Corp 483, 721(1), 791.

Gordon v. Aetna Cas. & Sur. Co., TexCivApp–Eastland, 351 SW2d 602, writ refused.—App & E 548(5), 837(1), 926(4), 1170.7; Work Comp 1962.

Gordon v. Aetna Oil Corp., TexCivApp–Galveston, 110 SW2d 1007, writ refused.—App & E 878(6); Mines 55(4), 55(7).

Gordon; Arlington Heights Appliance Co. v., TexCivApp–Fort Worth, 244 SW2d 337.—Judgm 185(5), 185.3(18).

Gordon; Bankers Multiple Line Ins. Co. v., TexCivApp–Hous (1 Dist), 422 SW2d 244.—App & E 1031(1); Jury 28(15); Pretrial Proc 81.

Gordon v. Blackmon, TexApp–Corpus Christi, 675 SW2d 790.—Divorce 287; Mand 4(1), 10, 12, 26, 28, 32; Pretrial Proc 15, 27.1, 31, 32, 33.

Gordon; Bobbitt v., TexCivApp–Beaumont, 108 SW2d 234.—App & E 71(3); Courts 475(8); Em Dom 191(1), 274(1); High 95(1); Inj 75, 122.

Gordon v. Busick, TexCivApp–Galveston, 203 SW2d 272.—Penalties 1, 32, 33; War 152, 155.

Gordon v. Calvert, TexCivApp–Austin, 497 SW2d 313.—Pub Amuse 54.

Gordon v. Carver, TexCivApp–Amarillo, 409 SW2d 878.—Courts 170; J P 44(1), 44(10).

Gordon v. Commissioners' Court of Jefferson County, TexCivApp–Beaumont, 310 SW2d 761, ref nre.—App & E 170(2), 843(2); Counties 178, 182, 196(7); Estop 62.3; High 103.1; Inj 11.

Gordon v. Conroe Independent School Dist., TexApp–Beaumont, 789 SW2d 395.—Em Dom 197, 200, 235.

Gordon v. Continental Airlines, CA5 (Tex), 201 FedAppx 290.—Civil R 1137.

Gordon; Curton v., TexCivApp–Austin, 510 SW2d 682, ref nre.—Adop 7.4(1), 7.4(6); Child S 24.

Gordon v. Day, CA5 (Tex), 172 FedAppx 565.—Prisons 4(10.1).

Gordon v. Dretke, CA5 (Tex), 107 FedAppx 404.—Hab Corp 603, 864(7).

Gordon; Employers Reinsurance Corp. v., TexApp–Texarkana, 209 SW3d 913.—App & E 842(8); Compromise 11; Contracts 142(2), 143.5, 169, 170(1); Evid 448, 584(1); Judgm 181(23).

Gordon; E.E.O.C. v., CA5 (Tex), 903 F2d 386. See Jurgens v. E.E.O.C.

Gordon; Gareis v., TexCivApp–Galveston, 243 SW2d 259.—Judgm 572(2), 717, 743(2); Lim of Act 39(7).

Gordon; Goldman v., TexCivApp–San Antonio, 135 SW2d 1024.—App & E 773(4).

Gordon v. Gordon, TexApp–Corpus Christi, 704 SW2d 490, dism.—App & E 1192; Divorce 186, 287; Jury 28(17).

Gordon; Gordon v., TexApp–Corpus Christi, 704 SW2d 490, dism.—App & E 1192; Divorce 186, 287; Jury 28(17).

Gordon v. Gordon, TexApp–Corpus Christi, 659 SW2d 475, appeal after remand 704 SW2d 490, dism.—App & E 900; Divorce 252.1, 252.3(4), 285, 286(2), 286(5), 322.

Gordon; Gordon v., TexApp–Corpus Christi, 659 SW2d 475, appeal after remand 704 SW2d 490, dism.—App & E 900; Divorce 252.1, 252.3(4), 285, 286(2), 286(5), 322.

Gordon v. Gordon, TexCivApp–Austin, 359 SW2d 134.—Divorce 12, 130, 184(6.1), 184(7).

Gordon; Gordon v., TexCivApp–Austin, 359 SW2d 134.—Divorce 12, 130, 184(6.1), 184(7).

Gordon; Harris County v., Tex, 616 SW2d 167.—App & E 954(1), 954(2); Em Dom 279(2).

Gordon v. Harris County, TexCivApp–Hous (14 Dist), 603 SW2d 294, rev 616 SW2d 167.—App & E 954(1), 954(2); Em Dom 273.

Gordon v. James, TexApp–Houston (1 Dist), 95 SW3d 734.—App & E 370, 389(3).

Gordon; Jewel Recovery, L.P. v., NDTex, 196 BR 348.—Bankr 2021.1, 2162, 2164.1, 2701, 3442.1; Corp 544(2), 547(1), 569; Fed Civ Proc 1721, 1771, 1773, 1829, 2486, 2537.

Gordon v. Jones, TexApp–Houston (1 Dist), 196 SW3d 376.—Atty & C 26; Courts 1, 4, 24, 37(1), 37(2), 40, 475(1), 475(2), 483; Fraud 37; Quiet T 1; Tresp to T T 1, 23; Venue 1.5, 17, 33, 58, 77.

Gordon; Kentucky Central Life Ins. Co. v., TexCivApp–Beaumont, 394 SW2d 558.—App & E 889(2), 1158; Insurance 2037.

Gordon; Kirk v., Tex, 376 SW2d 560.—Courts 207.4(3); Elections 126(4); Mand 74(3).

Gordon v. Lake, Tex, 356 SW2d 138, 163 Tex 392.—Banks 311; Mand 4(5), 16(1); Statut 152, 158, 161(1).

Gordon; Lamar-Delta County Levee Imp. Dist. No. 2 v., TexCivApp–Texarkana, 158 SW2d 607, writ refused.—App & E 846(5); Judgm 590(3).

Gordon v. Levias, TexCivApp–Beaumont, 356 SW2d 462, ref nre.—App & E 199, 218.2(4), 882(1), 1060.4, 1062.1; Trial 121(1), 352.1(7), 352.10, 352.18, 352.20.

Gordon; Lockheed Martin Corp. v., TexApp–Houston (1 Dist), 16 SW3d 127, review den.—Action 17; App & E 76(1), 78(1), 80(1), 854(1), 863; Contracts 129(1), 147(2), 147(3), 176(2); Corp 445.1.

Gordon; McBurnett v., TexCivApp–Beaumont, 534 SW2d 370, ref nre.—App & E 187(3), 554(1), 758.1, 758.2, 907(3), 962.

Gordon; McGregor v., TexCivApp–Austin, 442 SW2d 751, ref nre.—Pretrial Proc 41; Witn 16, 256, 271(1).

Gordon; McKellips v., TexApp–El Paso, 628 SW2d 457, ref nre.—Afft 18.

Gordon; Madison v., Tex, 39 SW3d 604.—Ven & Pur 220, 227, 229(1), 232(1), 232(2), 232(9), 239(1).

Gordon v. Madison, TexApp–Houston (1 Dist), 9 SW3d 476, review rev, rev 39 SW3d 604.—App & E 80(2), 901, 1175(1); Ven & Pur 220, 229(1), 232(1), 232(9).

Gordon; Miller v., TexCivApp–Dallas, 284 SW2d 806, ref nre.—Bills & N 422(1), 489(6), 526.

Gordon; Moore v., TexCivApp–Beaumont, 122 SW2d 239, writ dism.—Courts 107; Evid 25(2); Mines 79.1(4); Mun Corp 225(3), 276, 658, 721(3).

Gordon v. Mortgage Realty Co., TexCivApp–Galveston, 172 SW2d 369, writ refused wom.—Mtg 270.

Gordon v. Mortgage Realty Co., TexCivApp–Galveston, 153 SW2d 707.—Action 6; App & E 1050.1(11); Evid 348(1); Sequest 17; Stip 14(9).

Gordon; Olive-Sternenberg Lumber Co. v., TexComApp, 159 SW2d 845, 138 Tex 459.—Atty & C 124; Equity 64, 67; Judgm 675(1); Tresp to T T 25; Ven & Pur 27.

Gordon; Olive-Sternenberg Lumber Co. v., TexCivApp–Beaumont, 143 SW2d 694, rev 159 SW2d 845, 138 Tex 459.—Adv Poss 89; Atty & C 73, 124; Lim of Act 44(1); Princ & A 97; Tresp to T T 10, 25; Trial 350.3(3); Ven & Pur 54, 228(2).

Gordon v. Peters, SDTex, 489 FSupp2d 729.—Civil R 1169, 1171, 1516.

Gordon v. Pledger, TexCivApp–Galveston, 271 SW2d 344, ref nre.—App & E 846(5), 931(6); Evid 458, 461(1); Interest 39(1); Witn 159(9).

Gordon v. Procunier, SDTex, 629 FSupp 192.—Hab Corp 515, 670(8); Prisons 4(10.1).

Gordon; Ramsey v., TexCivApp–Waco, 567 SW2d 868, ref nre.—Princ & A 69(1), 69(4).

Gordon v. Roseman, TexCivApp–Fort Worth, 175 SW2d 747, writ refused wom.—Estates 10(2); Estop 17; Home 57(3).

Gordon; Salcido v., TexCivApp–El Paso, 122 SW2d 665.—Bills & N 96.

Gordon v. Scott, TexApp–Beaumont, 6 SW3d 365, reh overr, and review den.—App & E 79(1), 919; Atty & C 62; Civil R 1071, 1311, 1335, 1344, 1354, 1358, 1376(7); Offic 114; Pretrial Proc 678.

Gordon; Sinclair Oil & Gas Co. v., TexCivApp–Austin, 319 SW2d 170.—App & E 1067; Explos 12.

Gordon v. SouthTrust Bank, CA5 (Tex), 108 FedAppx 837.—Bills & N 501, 516, 537(1); Costs 194.32; Interest 39(2.30).

Gordon; Southwestern Bell Telephone Co. v., TexApp–Houston (14 Dist), 705 SW2d 767, ref nre.—Em Dom 205, 265(1), 265(5).

Gordon v. State, TexCrimApp, 801 SW2d 899.—Arrest 63.4(1), 63.5(4), 65; Const Law 617; Crim Law 211(3), 211(4), 394.4(1), 1181.5(7); Ind & Inf 17, 35; Searches 36.1, 102.

Gordon v. State, TexCrimApp, 784 SW2d 410.—Crim Law 438(8).

Gordon v. State, TexCrimApp, 707 SW2d 626.—Crim Law 749, 878(3); Sent & Pun 2143, 2147.

Gordon v. State, TexCrimApp, 651 SW2d 793.—Crim Law 1036.2.

Gordon v. State, TexCrimApp, 633 SW2d 872.—Burg 41(4); Crim Law 29(1), 369.1, 619, 673(5), 814(1), 863(2), 1174(1); Sent & Pun 329, 590, 1060.

Gordon v. State, TexCrimApp, 627 SW2d 708.—Crim Law 1081(4.1); Sent & Pun 2250.

Gordon v. State, TexCrimApp, 608 SW2d 638.—Crim Law 364(6), 1169.1(7).

Gordon v. State, TexCrimApp, 575 SW2d 529.—Crim Law 1044.1(1); Sent & Pun 2013, 2032.

Gordon v. State, TexCrimApp, 492 SW2d 262.—Burg 46(1); Crim Law 1120(3).

Gordon v. State, TexCrimApp, 461 SW2d 415.—Bail 40; Crim Law 393(1), 577.15(1).

Gordon v. State, TexCrimApp, 396 SW2d 880.—Assault 92(6).

Gordon v. State, TexCrimApp, 387 SW2d 414.—Crim Law 1184(5).

Gordon v. State, TexCrimApp, 346 SW2d 841, 171 Tex-Crim 243.—Adultery 14.

Gordon v. State, TexCrimApp, 310 SW2d 328, 166 Tex-Crim 24, probable jur noted 77 SCt 389, 352 US 987, 1 LEd2d 367, aff 78 SCt 363, 355 US 369, 2 LEd2d 352, reh den 78 SCt 530, 355 US 967, 2 LEd2d 542.—Commerce 15, 77.10(1); Int Liq 6, 90(1), 246.

Gordon v. State, TexCrimApp, 280 SW2d 267, 161 Tex-Crim 594, cert den 76 SCt 214, 350 US 924, 100 LEd 809.—Crim Law 593, 723(5), 938(3); Rape 51(1).

Gordon v. State, TexCrimApp, 268 SW2d 676.—Bail 63.1; Crim Law 1090.1(1), 1131(7).

Gordon v. State, TexCrimApp, 212 SW2d 185, 152 Tex-Crim 188.—Crim Law 273.3, 1038.3; Int Liq 226, 227, 235; Sent & Pun 414; Witn 361(1).

Gordon v. State, TexCrimApp, 194 SW2d 775, 149 Tex-Crim 378.—Crim Law 1171.1(2.1); Int Liq 238(5).

Gordon v. State, TexCrimApp, 147 SW2d 817.—Crim Law 1090.1(1).

Gordon v. State, TexCrimApp, 137 SW2d 1023, 138 Tex-Crim 637.—Crim Law 823(15), 1038.1(6); Forg 34(2), 38, 44(3), 48.

Gordon v. State, TexCrimApp, 135 SW2d 484.—Crim Law 1182.

Gordon v. State, TexCrimApp, 120 SW2d 1071, 135 Tex-Crim 438.—Const Law 2507(3); Sent & Pun 1838, 1858, 1886.

Gordon v. State, TexApp–Houston (1 Dist), 757 SW2d 496, petition for discretionary review refused.—Const Law 2225, 4292; Mun Corp 111(2), 592(1), 594(1), 594(2); Pub Amuse 9(3); Zoning 14.

Gordon v. State, TexApp–Houston (1 Dist), 735 SW2d 510, petition for discretionary review gr, aff 784 SW2d 410.—Crim Law 438(8), 552(4), 659, 660; Homic 1185.

Gordon v. State, TexApp–Fort Worth, 173 SW3d 870.—Assault 56, 91.2; Crim Law 561(1), 1144.13(2.1), 1144.13(3), 1159.2(1), 1159.2(7), 1159.2(9), 1159.4(2); Homic 700; Sent & Pun 323.

Gordon v. State, TexApp–Fort Worth, 638 SW2d 654.—Crim Law 641.13(1), 641.13(2.1), 641.13(6), 1032(5), 1038.1(4); False Pret 28; Ind & Inf 137(7); Searches 65, 66.

Gordon v. State, TexApp–Austin, 796 SW2d 319, petition for discretionary review refused.—Courts 57(0.5); Crim Law 511.2, 511.5, 511.6, 665(4), 1134(2).

Gordon v. State, TexApp–San Antonio, 714 SW2d 76.—Crim Law 792(3).

Gordon v. State, TexApp–San Antonio, 640 SW2d 743.—Crim Law 59(1), 328, 394.4(8), 438(1), 438(2), 507(1), 510.5, 511.1(1), 511.1(2.1), 511.1(3), 511.1(4), 511.1(7), 511.2, 511.5, 552(1), 552(2), 568, 795(2.1), 795(2.15), 899, 1134(2), 1169.1(10); Homic 569, 612, 908, 1135, 1458; Ind & Inf 189(8); Searches 13.1, 16, 47.1, 101, 113.1, 114, 117, 120.

Gordon v. State, TexApp–Texarkana, 161 SW3d 188.—Autos 355(6); Crim Law 1137(1).

Gordon v. State, TexApp–El Paso, 4 SW3d 32, appeal after remand 2001 WL 1383134.—Arrest 63.4(1), 63.5(4), 63.5(9), 68(3), 68(4); Controlled Subs 138; Crim Law 394.4(9), 394.6(4), 1139, 1147, 1153(1), 1158(4); Searches 26, 28; Sent & Pun 2001, 2020, 2030.

Gordon v. State, TexApp–Beaumont, 667 SW2d 544, petition for discretionary review refused.—Crim Law 412.1(2), 517(1), 535(1), 535(2), 538(3), 552(3), 720(6), 720(7.1).

Gordon v. State, TexApp–Eastland, 767 SW2d 866, petition for discretionary review gr, rev 801 SW2d 899.—Crim Law 519(8).

Gordon v. State, TexApp–Tyler, 641 SW2d 368.—Crim Law 1177; Sent & Pun 2009, 2014.

Gordon v. State, TexApp–Houston (14 Dist), 191 SW3d 721.—Crim Law 404.65, 1030(1), 1035(8.1), 1144.13(2.1), 1153(1), 1159.2(2), 1159.2(7); Rob 24.40, 27(5).

Gordon v. State, TexApp–Houston (14 Dist), 744 SW2d 224. See Martinez v. State.

Gordon v. State, TexApp–Houston (14 Dist), 686 SW2d 241, petition for discretionary review refused.—Controlled Subs 30, 80; Crim Law 755.5, 761(2), 1172.7.

Gordon v. State, TexApp–Houston (14 Dist), 681 SW2d 629, petition for discretionary review gr, appeal after remand 707 SW2d 626.—Assault 96(1); Civil R 1809; Crim Law 795(2.1), 795(2.20), 1181.5(8); Ind & Inf 191(0.5); Sent & Pun 2147.

Gordon v. State of Tex., CA5 (Tex), 153 F3d 190.—Const Law 2580; Fed Cts 13, 753.

Gordon v. State of Tex., SDTex, 965 FSupp 913, rev 153 F3d 190.—Const Law 2580.

Gordon v. Terrence, TexApp–Houston (14 Dist), 633 SW2d 649.—Guard & W 65, 136; Judgm 650.

Gordon v. Texas & Pacific Mercantile & Mfg. Co., TexCivApp–Fort Worth, 190 SW 748, writ refused.—Autos 193(8), 193(8.1).

Gordon; Thomas v., TexCivApp–Amarillo, 285 SW2d 829.—App & E 916(1); Compromise 21; Lim of Act 27; Trusts 99.

Gordon; Trans–Oceanic Capital Corp. v., TexApp–Houston (14 Dist, 881 SW2d 877. See Varme v. Gordon.

Gordon; United Services Auto. Ass'n v., TexApp–San Antonio, 103 SW3d 436, reh overr.—App & E 1050.1(2), 1050.1(11), 1051.1(1), 1051.1(2); Evid 508, 555.2, 555.3, 555.4(2), 555.5, 556, 557; Insurance 1806, 1822, 2178, 3374.

Gordon; U.S. v., CA5 (Tex), 901 F2d 48, reh den 905 F2d 1536, cert den 111 SCt 510, 498 US 981, 112 LEd2d 522.—Crim Law 394.4(6), 394.4(7), 1181.5(7).

Gordon; U.S. v., CA5 (Tex), 876 F2d 1121.—Controlled Subs 34; Crim Law 700(3), 720(1), 720(7.1), 847; Sent & Pun 764, 765, 775.

Gordon; U.S. v., CA5 (Tex), 722 F2d 112.—Arrest 63.5(6); Controlled Subs 137.

Gordon; U.S. v., CA5 (Tex), 712 F2d 110.—Consp 40, 47(12); Controlled Subs 69; Courts 96(1); Cust Dut 126(2), 126(4); Jury 29(6); Searches 49.

Gordon; U.S. v., CA5 (Tex), 700 F2d 215.—Controlled Subs 81.

Gordon; U.S. v., CA5 (Tex), 410 F2d 1121, cert dism 90 SCt 283, 396 US 938, 24 LEd2d 240.—Banks 62; Crim Law 556, 901; Embez 44(1).

Gordon; U.S. v., CA5 (Tex), 406 F2d 332.—Hus & W 267(9); Int Rev 4146, 4159(4), 4159(7).

Gordon v. U.S., CA5 (Tex), 358 F2d 112.—Postal 35(8).

Gordon v. U.S., CA5 (Tex), 353 F2d 9.—Crim Law 338(7), 742(2).

Gordon v. U.S., CA5 (Tex), 268 F2d 81.—Crim Law 519(3).

Gordon; U.S. v., WDTex, 917 FSupp 485.—Arrest 63.5(4), 63.5(9); Autos 349(10), 349(17).

Gordon; U.S. v., WDTex, 902 FSupp 127.—Controlled Subs 104, 112, 113, 117.

Gordon v. U.S., WDTex, 263 FSupp 768, aff in part, rev in part 406 F2d 332.—Int Rev 4159(4), 4159(7).

Gordon; U.S. ex rel. Kelly's Tile & Supply Co., Inc. v., CA5 (Tex), 468 F2d 617.—U S 67(2).

Gordon; Varme v., TexApp–Houston (14 Dist), 881 SW2d 877, reh den, and writ den.—App & E 327(6), 913, 930(3), 946, 949, 1062.1, 1062.2; Consp 1.1; Fraud 3; Parties 50, 51(4), 52, 54, 65(1); Torts 212; Trial 349(2), 350.1, 350.3(4), 352.20.

Gordon v. Ward, TexApp–Houston (1 Dist), 822 SW2d 90, writ den.—App & E 223; Atty & C 96; Judgm 185(2), 186; Lim of Act 95(11), 180(7).

Gordon v. Western Steel Co., TexApp–Corpus Christi, 950 SW2d 743, reh overr, and writ den.—Judgm 185.1(2), 185.1(4), 185.2(5), 185.3(2); Lim of Act 30, 55(1), 95(3); Statut 176.

Gordon; Wilkinson v., TexCivApp–Austin, 123 SW2d 961, writ dism.—App & E 1062.1; Neglig 1668; Trial 352.5(5).

Gordon v. Williams, TexCivApp–Beaumont, 164 SW2d 867.—Judgm 138(1); Pretrial Proc 483.

Gordon v. Zoes, TexCivApp–Galveston, 125 SW2d 1049.—App & E 846(5), 1091(1); J P 174(2.5).

Gordon & Associates, Inc. v. Cullen Bank/Citywest, N.A., TexApp–Corpus Christi, 880 SW2d 93, reh overr.—Judgm 181(25), 185.3(15); Sec Tran 231, 240.

Gordon & Associates, Inc. v. Cullen Bank/Citywest, N.A., TexApp–Corpus Christi, 805 SW2d 490, appeal after remand 880 SW2d 93, reh overr.—Sec Tran 240.

Gordon Jewelry Corp.; Lipschutz v., SDTex, 373 FSupp 375.—Bailm 1, 11, 31(1), 31(3), 32; Contracts 143(2), 144, 175(1), 325; Corp 1.7(2); Costs 194.10, 194.32; Cust & U 1, 13, 15(1), 17, 19(2), 19(3); Damag 89(2);

Fed Civ Proc 2470, 2542.1, 2547.1; Fed Cts 409.1; Interest 44; Sales 55.

Gordon Knox Oil & Exploration Co.; Texas Machinery & Equipment Co. v., Tex, 442 SW2d 315.—Assign 120, 121; Corp 630(6); Garn 187; Judgm 335(3), 855(1).

Gordon Knox Oil & Exploration Co.; Texas Machinery & Equipment Co. v., TexCivApp–Amarillo, 434 SW2d 182, writ gr, rev 442 SW2d 315.—Corp 630(1); Judgm 15, 16, 335(1), 486(1), 489.

Gordon's Jewelry Co. of Texas, Inc.; Ramirez v., Tex-App–Corpus Christi, 763 SW2d 34.—Judgm 185.1(3); Lim of Act 55(2), 55(5), 125; Trial 388(2).

Gordon Yates Bldg. Supplies, Inc. v. Fidelity & Cas. Co. of New York, TexCivApp–Fort Worth, 543 SW2d 709, ref nre.—Const Law 2600; Insurance 2278(21); Judgm 181(11), 181(23), 185(2), 185(6), 189.

Gords v. State, TexApp–Dallas, 824 SW2d 785, petition for discretionary review refused.—Searches 11, 66.

Gordy v. Alexander, TexCivApp–Amarillo, 550 SW2d 146, ref nre.—App & E 347(3); Courts 472.1; Infants 81; Judgm 183, 273(7); Plead 101; Trusts 91, 95, 111, 347, 363, 366(1).

Gordy v. Morton, TexApp–Houston (14 Dist), 624 SW2d 705.—App & E 900; Lis Pen 25(6); Mtg 138, 186(5); Pretrial Proc 717.1, 723.1, 724; Ven & Pur 242.

Gordy v. State, TexCrimApp, 268 SW2d 126, 160 TexCrim 201.—Crim Law 369.2(4), 438(4), 590(2), 591, 721(5); Food 21; Ind & Inf 4; Jury 120.

Gordy v. State, TexCrimApp, 264 SW2d 103, 159 TexCrim 390, cert den 74 SCt 854, 347 US 991, 98 LEd 1124.—Crim Law 369.1, 1166.16; Food 21; Jury 99.1.

Gordy; U.S. v., CA5 (Tex), 526 F2d 631.—Crim Law 1134(2); Double J 98, 201.

Gordzelik v. State, TexCrimApp, 246 SW2d 638, 157 TexCrim 68.—Crim Law 594(1), 1151; Sod 7.

Gore, Ex parte, TexCrimApp, 283 SW2d 69, 162 TexCrim 128.—Extrad 32.

Gore; American Nat. Ins. Co. v., TexCivApp–Eastland, 251 SW2d 564.—Insurance 2558(2).

Gore v. Amoco Production Co., TexCivApp–Hous (1 Dist), 616 SW2d 289.—Work Comp 2162.

Gore v. Citizens State Bank, TexCivApp–Waco, 88 SW2d 721, writ refused.—Ack 55(2); Home 110, 129(1); Lim of Act 39(7).

Gore v. Cunningham, TexCivApp–Beaumont, 297 SW2d 287, ref nre.—App & E 837(1), 1173(1); Deeds 8, 114(1); Lim of Act 197(1); Pretrial Proc 473, 481; Ten in C 14, 15(10), 43; Ven & Pur 229(1).

Gore; Dallas Joint Stock Land Bank v., TexCivApp–Texarkana, 100 SW2d 396, writ dism.—App & E 930(3); Home 122; Princ & A 23(1); Trial 351.2(4).

Gore; Freeman v., CA5 (Tex), 483 F3d 404.—Arrest 63.4(2), 63.4(4), 63.4(15), 68(2), 68(3); Civil R 1035, 1088(4), 1376(2), 1376(6); Fed Cts 574, 766, 776, 802.

Gore v. Gore, TexCivApp–Texarkana, 203 SW2d 262.—Estop 47; Home 124; Ten in C 38(12); Trusts 35(4).

Gore; Gore v., TexCivApp–Texarkana, 203 SW2d 262.—Estop 47; Home 124; Ten in C 38(12); Trusts 35(4).

Gore v. Peck, TexApp–Dallas, 191 SW3d 927.—App & E 138, 148; Parties 42, 44.

Gore v. Scotland Golf, Inc., TexApp–San Antonio, 136 SW3d 26, reh overr, and review den.—App & E 238(2), 300, 878(6), 930(1), 989, 1001(1); Corp 306; Damag 189.5; Fraud 11(1), 13(2), 22(1), 23, 24, 25, 32, 58(1), 61.

Gore v. Stenson, SDTex, 616 FSupp 895.—Fed Cts 286.1, 302; Rem of C 17.

Gore; U.S. v., CA5 (Tex), 298 F3d 322, reh den.—Crim Law 1030(1), 1042, 1147; Sent & Pun 361, 994, 996.

Gore; U.S. v., CA5 (Tex), 212 FedAppx 313.—Crim Law 273(4.1).

Gore; U.S. v., CA5 (Tex), 142 FedAppx 825, appeal after remand 212 FedAppx 313.—Crim Law 1035(1); Jury 34(8).

Goree v. Carnes, TexApp–San Antonio, 625 SW2d 380.—Judgm 199(3.2), 199(3.10), 199(3.15); Libel 6(1), 7(1), 9(1), 51(1), 101(1), 101(4), 123(8), 124(6); Trial 350.3(4).

Goree v. Hansen, TexCivApp–Fort Worth, 214 SW2d 824.—App & E 930(1), 1003(5); Autos 244(42), 244(58); Judgm 199(3.17); Trial 215, 352.9.

Goree v. State, TexCrimApp, 254 SW2d 126.—Crim Law 1090.1(1).

Gore, Inc. v. Espy, CA5 (Tex), 87 F3d 767, reh den, appeal after remand 137 F3d 863.—Admin Law 413, 668, 791; Fed Civ Proc 103.2, 103.3; Food 4.5(4), 4.5(6).

Gore, Inc. v. Glickman, CA5 (Tex), 137 F3d 863.—Fed Cts 776; Interest 39(2.6), 39(2.10), 39(2.20); Statut 220; U S 110.

Gorel; U.S. v., CA5 (Tex), 622 F2d 100, cert den 100 SCt 1340, 445 US 943, 63 LEd2d 777.—Consp 48.1(2.1); Const Law 4605; Crim Law 121, 126(1), 211(3), 264, 338(1), 342, 400(1), 438.1, 444, 519(8), 627.6(2), 753.2(8), 776(2), 1038.2, 1158(4); Ind & Inf 121.1(3), 121.2(1), 125(5.5); Tel 1440.

Gorel v. U.S., SDTex, 531 FSupp 368.—Crim Law 412.1(4), 412.2(1), 412.2(4), 412.2(5).

Gorelick v. Harrison County, TexApp–Texarkana, 720 SW2d 835.—Judgm 634, 678(2), 699(1), 713(2), 720, 829(3).

Gorelick v. State of Tex., EDTex, 572 FSupp 301.—Em Dom 300, 303; Waters 119(5), 123, 125.

Goren v. Goren, TexCivApp–Hous (1 Dist), 531 SW2d 897, dism.—Child S 159; Divorce 146, 150, 252.2, 252.3(1), 252.3(5); Trial 395(5).

Goren; Goren v., TexCivApp–Hous (1 Dist), 531 SW2d 897, dism.—Child S 159; Divorce 146, 150, 252.2, 252.3(1), 252.3(5); Trial 395(5).

Goren; Yeldell v., TexApp–Dallas, 80 SW3d 634.—App & E 931(1), 1010.1(13); Fraud 3, 12, 31, 32, 50, 58(3), 61, 64(2).

Gorena, Ex parte, Tex, 595 SW2d 841.—Const Law 1106; Contempt 20, 24, 30; Divorce 269(2); Hab Corp 528.1; Judgm 91.

Gore Oil Co. v. Roosth, TexApp–Eastland, 158 SW3d 596.—App & E 893(1); Deeds 93, 95; Estop 23; Evid 448, 461(1); Interest 39(2.20); Mines 55(5); Ref of Inst 2, 33.

Goretski, In re, BkrtcyNDTex, 224 BR 360. See Thompson, In re.

Gorges Foodservice, Inc. v. Huerta, TexApp–Corpus Christi, 964 SW2d 656, reh overr, and review withdrawn.—App & E 205, 232(0.5), 1001(3), 1003(6), 1004(8), 1004(13), 1050.1(1), 1056.1(1), 1056.1(7), 1079, 1182; Civil R 1221, 1715, 1744, 1749, 1753, 1765, 1769, 1772, 1773; Costs 197; Damag 50.10, 54, 56.20, 91(1), 94, 100, 192; Evid 213(2), 597; Interest 39(2.20), 39(2.40), 39(2.45); Labor & Emp 810, 854, 863(2), 866, 867, 868(3), 870, 871; Plead 34(3), 387; Trial 43.

Gorham, Ex parte, TexCrimApp, 242 SW2d 425.—Extrad 39.

Gorham v. Gates ex rel. Estate of Badouh, TexApp–Austin, 82 SW3d 359, review den.—Ex & Ad 219.9, 402; Judgm 731.

Gorham v. State, TexCrimApp, 235 SW2d 921.—Crim Law 1184(5).

Gorham v. State, TexApp–Fort Worth, 985 SW2d 694, petition for discretionary review refused.—Crim Law 568, 1159.6; Rob 11, 24.15(2).

Gorham v. State, TexApp–Houston (14 Dist), 981 SW2d 315, petition for discretionary review refused, cert den 120 SCt 157, 528 US 864, 145 LEd2d 133.—Const Law 4587; Crim Law 273(2), 273.1(1), 273.1(4), 275, 1162, 1163(1), 1167(5).

Gorham; State Highway Dept. v., Tex, 162 SW2d 934, 139 Tex 361.—Const Law 3603; Statut 76(1), 131, 141(1), 181(2), 190, 220, 251, 259; Work Comp 18, 50, 1058.

Gorham; State Highway Dept. of Texas v., TexCivApp–Waco, 158 SW2d 330, rev 162 SW2d 934, 139 Tex 361.—Action 35; Statut 181(1), 205, 211, 220, 239; Work Comp 1058, 1683, 1768, 1930.

Gorham; Synatzske v., TexCivApp–Austin, 211 SW2d 391.—Brok 96; Princ & A 136(2).

Gorham & Johnson, Inc. v. Chrysler Corp., CA5 (Tex), 308 F2d 462, cert den 83 SCt 725, 372 US 912, 9 LEd2d 719.—Antitrust 963(3), 977(2); Fed Cts 894, 901.1.

Gorin v. Moss, TexCivApp–Fort Worth, 138 SW2d 612.—App & E 1008.1(14); Evid 589.

Gorman, In re, TexApp–Fort Worth, 1 SW3d 894.—Mand 4(4), 53.

Gorman v. American General Ins. Co., TexCivApp–San Antonio, 179 SW2d 814, writ refused wom.—Work Comp 516, 517, 550, 1546.

Gorman v. Army and Air Force Exchange Service, CA5 (Tex), 686 F2d 263.—Fed Cts 974.1.

Gorman v. Army and Air Force Exchange Service, CA5 (Tex), 619 F2d 1141, reh den 627 F2d 239, cert gr, vac 102 SCt 2898, 457 US 1102, 73 LEd2d 1310, on remand 686 F2d 263.—Fed Cts 178, 974.1.

Gorman; Charter Oak Fire Ins. Co. v., TexApp–Houston (14 Dist), 693 SW2d 686, ref nre.—Work Comp 1789, 1874, 1880, 1908.

Gorman v. Countrywood Property Owners Ass'n, TexApp–Beaumont, 1 SW3d 915, reh overr, and petition for review den.—App & E 989, 1024.1; Costs 194.18, 208; Covenants 132(2).

Gorman v. Gorman, TexApp–Houston (1 Dist), 966 SW2d 858, reh overr, and review den.—Action 13; App & E 151(1), 151(6), 174, 854(1), 877(2), 946, 984(1), 1030, 1032(1); Costs 2, 194.40, 207; Decl Judgm 392.1; Evid 18; Judgm 181(11), 217; Pretrial Proc 302, 312; Trusts 375(1).

Gorman; Gorman v., TexApp–Houston (1 Dist), 966 SW2d 858, reh overr, and review den.—Action 13; App & E 151(1), 151(6), 174, 854(1), 877(2), 946, 984(1), 1030, 1032(1); Costs 2, 194.40, 207; Decl Judgm 392.1; Evid 18; Judgm 181(11), 217; Pretrial Proc 302, 312; Trusts 375(1).

Gorman v. Gorman, TexCivApp–Texarkana, 180 SW2d 470, dism.—Hus & W 249(6), 254, 262.1(2), 264(1).

Gorman; Gorman v., TexCivApp–Texarkana, 180 SW2d 470, dism.—Hus & W 249(6), 254, 262.1(2), 264(1).

Gorman v. Grand Casino Coushatta, EDTex, 1 FSupp2d 656. See Gorman v. Grand Casino of La., Inc.-Coushatta.

Gorman v. Grand Casino of La., Inc.-Coushatta, EDTex, 1 FSupp2d 656.—Const Law 3964, 3965(3), 3965(5); Fed Cts 74, 76.5, 76.10, 76.35, 79, 101.

Gorman; J. C. Penney Co. v., TexCivApp–Waco, 386 SW2d 207.—Plead 111.42(7).

Gorman v. Life Ins. Co. of North America, Tex, 811 SW2d 542, cert den 112 SCt 88, 502 US 824, 116 LEd2d 60, on remand 859 SW2d 382, reh den, and reh den.—App & E 173(2), 893(1); Courts 489(9); Damag 56.10; Insurance 1117(1), 2607; Interest 39(2.40); Labor & Emp 634, 677, 715; Plead 78; States 18.15, 18.41.

Gorman v. Life Ins. Co. of North America, TexApp–Houston (1 Dist), 859 SW2d 382, reh den, and reh den.—App & E 207, 237(1), 989, 1001(1), 1003(5), 1003(6), 1060.1(1); Costs 194.14; Insurance 2607, 2608, 3585; Interest 31, 38(1), 39(2.35), 39(3); Trial 120(1), 121(1), 121(2).

Gorman v. Life Ins. Co. of North America, TexApp–Houston (1 Dist), 752 SW2d 710, writ gr, aff in part, rev in part 811 SW2d 542, cert den 112 SCt 88, 502 US 824, 116 LEd2d 60, on remand 859 SW2d 382, reh den, and reh den.—Estop 52.10(4); Insurance 1117(1); Labor & Emp 407, 628; States 18.51.

Gorman v. Miller, CA5 (Tex), 415 F2d 1137.—Damag 135, 187, 191; Fed Cts 743.

Gorman v. State, TexCrimApp, 634 SW2d 681.—Ind & Inf 58.1, 71.2(2), 71.4(8).

Gorman v. State, TexCrimApp, 480 SW2d 188.—Crim Law 721(5), 726; Rape 6, 11.

Gorman v. State, TexCrimApp, 317 SW2d 744, 166 TexCrim 633.—Sent & Pun 2004, 2021.

Gorman v. State, TexCrimApp, 93 SW2d 1145, 130 TexCrim 149.—Crim Law 15; Tax 3608, 3712.

Gorman v. State, TexApp–Houston (1 Dist), 945 SW2d 275.—Hab Corp 223, 253.

Gorman v. U.S., CA5 (Tex), 323 F2d 51.—Crim Law 1159.2(5), 1159.2(9), 1159.4(1), 1177; Sent & Pun 1015, 1123; Tel 1018(4).

Gorman-Rupp Co.; Mar-Len of Louisiana, Inc. v., TexApp–Beaumont, 795 SW2d 880, writ den.—App & E 930(3), 1003(6); Contracts 218, 221(1), 227, 313(1), 313(2); Sales 52(5.1), 85(1).

Gorman-Rupp Corp. v. Kirk, TexCivApp–Hous (1 Dist), 601 SW2d 49.—Plead 111.12, 111.38, 111.39(6), 111.42(8); Venue 7(7).

Gormany v. State, TexCrimApp, 640 SW2d 303.—Rob 24.25.

Gormany v. State, TexCrimApp, 486 SW2d 324.—Sent & Pun 2021.

Gorme v. Axelrad, TexCivApp–Hous (14 Dist), 519 SW2d 139.—Judgm 181(2); Spec Perf 28(1), 39, 64, 123.

Gormley v. Stover, Tex, 907 SW2d 448.—Antitrust 257; Lim of Act 55(3).

Gormley; Stover v., TexApp–Amarillo, 883 SW2d 278, reh overr, and writ gr, rev 907 SW2d 448.—Antitrust 353, 358; App & E 173(9); Fraud 41; Health 813; Judgm 183, 185.3(2); Lim of Act 55(3), 104(2).

Gornick v. State, TexApp–Texarkana, 947 SW2d 678.—Crim Law 770(2), 772(6), 795(2.1), 822(1), 1038.1(1), 1134(3), 1172.1(1), 1173.2(1), 1173.2(3); Tresp 76, 89.

Gorrell; Loom Craft Carpet Mills, Inc. v., TexApp–Texarkana, 823 SW2d 431.—Autos 192(11), 226(3); Neglig 351.

Gorrell; Setliff v., TexApp–Amarillo, 466 SW2d 74.—Const Law 46(3); Elections 8.1, 291, 305(3); Health 105, 233, 260.

Gorrell v. State, TexCrimApp, 468 SW2d 95.—Arrest 63.4(13), 71.1(3).

Gorrell v. Texas Utilities Elec. Co., TexApp–Fort Worth, 915 SW2d 55, reh overr, and writ den.—App & E 863, 934(1), 946; Autos 265; Judgm 185(2), 185(6), 186; Neglig 202, 210, 371, 387.

Gorrell v. Tide Products, Inc., TexCivApp–Amarillo, 532 SW2d 390.—Acct Action on 12; Bills & N 452(3); Evid 13; Guar 78(1); Judgm 181(6), 185(2), 185.1(5), 185.3(2).

Gorrer v. State, TexApp–Beaumont, 739 SW2d 417.—Crim Law 361(1), 723(4), 995(1); Rob 24.40; Sent & Pun 1381(3).

Gorsalitz v. Harris, TexCivApp–Tyler, 410 SW2d 956, ref nre.—App & E 883; Health 821(2), 823(10).

Gorsalitz v. Harris, TexCivApp–Houston, 360 SW2d 574, appeal after remand 410 SW2d 956, ref nre.—Health 826.

Gorsalitz v. Olin Mathieson Chemical Corp., CA5 (Tex), 456 F2d 180, cert den 92 SCt 2463, 407 US 921, 32 LEd2d 807, reh den 93 SCt 108, 409 US 899, 34 LEd2d 159.—Damag 133; Fed Cts 543.1, 917.

Gorsalitz v. Olin Mathieson Chemical Corp., CA5 (Tex), 429 F2d 1033, appeal after remand 456 F2d 180, cert den 92 SCt 2463, 407 US 921, 32 LEd2d 807, reh den 93 SCt 108, 409 US 899, 34 LEd2d 159.—Contracts 144; Fed Civ Proc 2368.1, 2377; Fed Cts 386, 409.1, 636, 642, 825.1, 827; Indem 24, 30(1), 33(5); Interest 53; Jury 37; Work Comp 76, 355, 1429.

Gorski, Estate of v. Welch, TexApp–San Antonio, 993 SW2d 298, review den.—App & E 237(6); Child 22, 86; Des & Dist 47(1), 47(2); Evid 207(2), 265(17); Ex & Ad 219.7(2); Trial 403.

Gorthy; U.S. v., CA5 (Tex), 550 F2d 1051, cert den 98 SCt 121, 434 US 834, 54 LEd2d 95.—Crim Law 577.15(3); Cust Dut 126(5).

Gorton, Ex parte, TexCrimApp, 564 SW2d 766.—Hab Corp 724, 792.1.

Gosch v. B & D Shrimp, Inc., TexApp–Houston (1 Dist), 830 SW2d 652, writ den.—App & E 842(2), 1008.1(3), 1010.1(2), 1010.1(11), 1012.1(5); Corp 661(6).

Gosch v. State, TexCrimApp, 829 SW2d 775, reh den, cert den 113 SCt 3035, 509 US 922, 125 LEd2d 722, habeas corpus den 1993 WL 484624.—Crim Law 342, 371(12), 511.1(1), 511.1(3), 511.1(7), 511.2; Homic 1003; Sent & Pun 1625.

Gosdin v. Blue Lake Estates Properties Owners Ass'n, Inc., TexCivApp–Austin, 543 SW2d 188.—App & E 781(1), 802; Const Law 2600; Inj 129(1).

Gosdin; F. C. Crane Co. v., TexCivApp–Waco, 94 SW2d 221.—App & E 1047(4); Autos 306(2); Judgm 298, 341.

Gosdin v. Montgomery, TexCivApp–Waco, 92 SW2d 463, writ dism.—App & E 882(11); Bills & N 317.

Gose v. State, TexCrimApp, 84 SW2d 234, 129 TexCrim 39.—Larc 60.

Go Services, Inc.; Franklin v., TexCivApp–Eastland, 461 SW2d 186.—Judgm 185.3(16).

Go Services, Inc.; Santana Petroleum Corp. v., TexCivApp–El Paso, 389 SW2d 96.—App & E 765, 773(2).

Gosho Cotton Co. v. U.S., NDTex, 215 FSupp 665.—Int Rev 4831.

Goshorn v. Hattman, TexCivApp–Beaumont, 387 SW2d 422, ref nre.—App & E 230, 1003(11), 1170.6, 1170.7; Autos 168(6), 171(8), 171(11); Damag 191; Evid 351.

Goslin v. Beazley, TexCivApp–Houston, 339 SW2d 689, ref nre, appeal dism, cert den 82 SCt 16, 368 US 7, 7 LEd2d 16.—Adv Poss 41, 65(3); App & E 226(1), 934(1); Judges 47(2); Judgm 181(2), 185(2), 185.3(17), 186; Land & Ten 66(1), 66(2), 66(3); Tresp to T T 35(3), 50, 52.

Goslin's Estate; Riewe v., TexApp–Austin, 632 SW2d 223.—App & E 624.

Gosney v. Sonora Independent School Dist., CA5 (Tex), 603 F2d 522.—Const Law 242.2(4), 3618(1), 4199, 4200, 4202; Schools 147.2(1), 147.47.

Gosney v. Sonora Independent School Dist., NDTex, 430 FSupp 53, rev 603 F2d 522.—Civil R 1349; Const Law 83(1), 1079, 3618(1), 4198, 4199, 4200, 4202; Fed Civ Proc 392; Schools 133, 137, 147.40(2), 147.54.

Gospel Center Church; Beaumont Ready-Mix, Inc. v., TexApp–Beaumont, 708SW2d 581. See Beaumont Ready-Mix, Inc. v. Maddoux.

Goss, Ex parte, TexCrimApp, 262 SW2d 412, 159 TexCrim 235.—Hab Corp 510(1); Rob 30.

Goss, In re, TexApp–Texarkana, 160 SW3d 288.—Mand 53; New Tr 155.

Goss; Abington v., TexCivApp–Dallas, 408 SW2d 317, ref nre.—App & E 387(2), 388, 395; Wills 366.

Goss v. Bobby D. Associates, TexApp–Tyler, 94 SW3d 65, reh overr.—App & E 199, 856(1); Atty & C 62; Contracts 326; Corp 661(6); Evid 65; Fraud 3; Judgm 185(2), 185.2(8), 185.3(2); Partners 191.

Goss; Brookshire Grocery Co. v., TexApp–Texarkana, 208 SW3d 706, reh overr, and rule 537(f) motion gr.—App & E 930(1), 1001(1), 1004(1), 1004(5); Damag 32, 38, 96, 102, 104, 119, 127.33, 127.65, 127.71(2), 140.7, 221(7), 221(8); Evid 571(10), 574; Labor & Emp 2750, 2772, 2820, 2848, 2923, 2983; Neglig 202, 371, 379, 380, 387, 1001, 1037(4), 1734; Trial 182, 350.1, 350.2, 352.1(2), 352.4(1); Work Comp 2141.

Goss; Dallas Railway & Terminal Co. v., TexCivApp–Dallas, 144 SW2d 591.—Trial 121(1), 129, 133.6(1), 219, 350.5(5), 352.4(8).

Goss; First Bank and Trust v., TexCivApp–Hous (1 Dist), 533 SW2d 93.—Trusts 12, 28, 152, 280; Wills 674.

Goss v. Franz, TexCivApp–Amarillo, 287 SW2d 289, writ refused.—Const Law 2489; Death 31(8).

Goss; Kennesaw Life & Acc. Ins. Co. v., TexApp–Houston (14 Dist), 694 SW2d 115, ref nre.—Decl Judgm 2, 272; Evid 265(8); Plead 36(3); Tresp to T T 1, 27, 50, 52.

Goss v. Longview Hilton Hotel Co., TexCivApp–Texarkana, 183 SW2d 998.—Assault 44; Trial 358.

Goss v. Memorial Hosp. System, CA5 (Tex), 789 F2d 353.—Antitrust 593; Civil R 1326(7).

Goss v. Mid-Western Life Ins. Co., TexCivApp–Tyler, 545 SW2d 878, writ gr, rev 552 SW2d 430.—App & E 927(7), 989, 997(3); Evid 570; Insurance 2533.

Goss; Mid-Western Life Ins. Co. of Texas v., Tex, 552 SW2d 430.—Insurance 2465, 2530.

Goss v. Phillips, TexCivApp–Texarkana, 292 SW2d 700.—App & E 1039(13); Can of Inst 35(1); Des & Dist 92; Evid 591.

Goss; Pittsburg Nat. Bank v., TexCivApp–Beaumont, 113 SW2d 301.—Bills & N 516.

Goss v. Rhone, TexCivApp–Texarkana, 286 SW2d 444.—Deeds 207; Trial 382.

Goss v. San Jacinto Jr. College, CA5 (Tex), 588 F2d 96, reh gr 593 F2d 23, on reh 595 F2d 1119, opinion mod 595 F2d 1119.—Civil R 1349; Colleges 8.1(6.1); Fed Cts 268.1, 339, 340.1.

Goss v. Star Engraving Co., TexCivApp–El Paso, 377 SW2d 207.—Inj 147.

Goss v. State, TexCrimApp, 826 SW2d 162, cert den 113 SCt 3035, 509 US 922, 125 LEd2d 722.—Crim Law 671, 796, 1035(10), 1036.1(2), 1173.2(5); Sent & Pun 1780(3), 1784(4).

Goss v. State, TexCrimApp, 582 SW2d 782.—Autos 336, 351.1.

Goss v. State, TexCrimApp, 580 SW2d 587.—Crim Law 1167(3); Rape 20, 51(1).

Goss v. State, TexCrimApp, 549 SW2d 404.—Crim Law 429(1), 438(5.1), 444, 1169.1(10).

Goss v. State, TexCrimApp, 283 SW2d 231, 162 TexCrim 163.—Controlled Subs 80; Crim Law 1120(1), 1168(2).

Goss v. State, TexCrimApp, 274 SW2d 697, 161 TexCrim 37.—Crim Law 575, 706(3).

Goss v. State, TexCrimApp, 124 SW2d 381, 136 TexCrim 166.—Crim Law 394.4(9), 419(10), 424(3), 424(6), 511.6, 1169.3, 1171.1(6).

Goss v. State, TexCrimApp, 95 SW2d 692.—Crim Law 1097(5).

Goss v. State, TexApp–Corpus Christi, 944 SW2d 748.—Double J 96, 97; Hab Corp 841, 844, 846.

Goss; State Farm Lloyds v., EDTex, 109 FSupp2d 574.—Insurance 1832(2), 1835(2), 2295, 2356, 2914, 2939.

Goss; U.S. v., CA5 (Tex), 650 F2d 1336.—Crim Law 394.5(4), 400(1), 419(1.5), 772(6), 791, 829(2), 1158(4), 1173.2(3); Double J 108, 109; Ind & Inf 71.4(4), 171; Postal 35(5), 35(8), 35(9), 35(10), 49(11), 50.

Gosselink v. American Tel. & Tel., Inc., CA5 (Tex), 272 F3d 722.—Fed Cts 776; Labor & Emp 438, 440, 563(2), 611, 688.

Gossett; Aeronautical Corp. of America v., TexCivApp–Dallas, 117 SW2d 893.—App & E 672; Commerce 54.5; Corp 642(1), 661(2), 672(7), 673; Insurance 1701; Sales 90, 267, 270.

Gossett v. Barnhart, EDTex, 374 FSupp2d 505.—Social S 124.20, 140.5, 140.25, 140.50, 143.45, 143.50, 143.80, 148.15.

Gossett; Dallas Ry. & Terminal Co. v., Tex, 294 SW2d 377, 156 Tex 252.—App & E 1140(4), 1172(2); Autos 14, 244(1), 245(2.1); Damag 163(4), 177, 191; Evid 211, 265(10), 568(1); Trial 352.20.

Gossett; Dallas Ry. & Terminal Co. v., TexCivApp–Waco, 284 SW2d 749, rev 294 SW2d 377, 156 Tex 252.—App & E 218.2(4); Autos 244(1), 244(2.1), 244(34); Damag 191; Evid 32; Pretrial Proc 718; Trial 118, 139.1(3), 140(1), 350.5(3), 350.6(4); Witn 8.

Gossett; Fairbanks v., TexCivApp–San Antonio, 118 SW2d 945, writ dism.—Bills & N 104.

Gossett; Fairbanks v., TexCivApp–San Antonio, 114 SW2d 930.—App & E 267(1), 396, 624, 714(1).

Gossett v. First-Trust Joint Stock Land Bank of Chicago, TexCivApp–Dallas, 138 SW2d 904, writ dism.—Banks 63.5; Courts 478; Receivers 35(1).

Gossett v. Green, TexComApp, 152 SW2d 733, 137 Tex 50, answer to certified question conformed to 153 SW2d 500.—Banks 80(2), 80(10); Plead 216(2).

Gossett v. Green, TexComApp, 133 SW2d 762, 134 Tex 282.—Banks 48(1), 49(8); Evid 65.

Gossett v. Green, TexCivApp–Fort Worth, 153 SW2d 500. —App & E 1011.1(4).

Gossett v. Griffin & Kimbrough, TexCivApp–San Antonio, 107 SW2d 1115, writ dism.—App & E 77(1); Banks 80(3), 80(10).

Gossett; Guthrie v., TexCivApp–Eastland, 142 SW2d 410. —Fraud 12, 42, 47; Judgm 248; Mines 54.5, 74(3); Ven & Pur 224.

Gossett v. Hamilton, TexCivApp–Fort Worth, 133 SW2d 297, writ dism, correct.—Banks 47(1), 63.5; Const Law 632, 633, 1066, 2632, 2734, 2757, 2761, 4410.

Gossett v. Hensley, TexCivApp–Dallas, 94 SW2d 903.—App & E 882(1); Courts 1; Mines 100; Partners 325(2).

Gossett v. Jones, TexCivApp–Galveston, 123 SW2d 724.—Attach 357, 374, 375(3), 377, 380; Damag 221(2.1); New Tr 42(4), 54; Trial 350.3(6).

Gossett; Kaliski v., TexCivApp–San Antonio, 109 SW2d 340, writ refused.—Banks 44, 47(1), 313; Const Law 633, 642.

Gossett; L. G. Balfour Co. v., Tex, 115 SW2d 594, 131 Tex 348.—Abate & R 44; Banks 63.5, 80(10); Corp 374, 382, 484(1), 484(3), 484(4), 487(1); Courts 485; Guar 11.

Gossett v. L. G. Balfour Co., TexCivApp–Fort Worth, 111 SW2d 1119, rev 115 SW2d 594, 131 Tex 348.—App & E 374(4), 1061.4; Banks 63.5; Courts 485.

Gossett v. Local Union No. 185, TexCivApp–San Antonio, 361 SW2d 957.—App & E 554(1), 564(3).

Gossett v. Lone Star Bldg. & Loan Ass'n, TexCivApp–Galveston, 143 SW2d 219, dism.—Plead 111.46.

Gossett v. Moore, TexCivApp–Fort Worth, 140 SW2d 358, dism.—Banks 49(8), 116(1).

Gossett; Reconstruction Finance Corp. v., Tex, 111 SW2d 1066, 130 Tex 535.—Banks 47(1); Const Law 591; Contracts 143(1), 147(2); Statut 199.

Gossett; Roberts v., TexCivApp–Amarillo, 88 SW2d 507. —Courts 475(13), 511; Gaming 52, 58, 68(3); Inj 105(1), 126.

Gossett v. Scofield, TexCivApp–Waco, 141 SW2d 466.—Banks 63.5; Trial 165.

Gossett v. Seggerman, Tex, 111 SW2d 685, 130 Tex 470. —Banks 3, 17, 47(1).

Gossett v. Seggerman, TexCivApp–El Paso, 105 SW2d 421, rev 111 SW2d 685, 130 Tex 470.—App & E 1008.1(8.1); Banks 47(1).

Gossett v. State, TexCrimApp, 282 SW2d 59, 162 TexCrim 52.—Crim Law 1023(9), 1081(4.1); False Pret 49(3); Sent & Pun 2009.

Gossett v. State, TexCivApp–Eastland, 417 SW2d 730, ref nre.—Action 57(1); Corp 1.3, 182.1(1); Em Dom 137, 149(6), 164, 262(4), 262(5); Evid 570; Interest 39(3); Judges 44.

Gossett v. Stubblefield, TexCivApp–Waco, 121 SW2d 665. —Bills & N 129(3), 150(1), 338, 348, 497(1), 497(2); Trial 357.

Gossett v. Tidewater Associated Oil Co., TexCivApp–Tyler, 436 SW2d 416, ref nre.—Judgm 181(7), 185(2); Ten in C 15(1), 15(7).

Gossett; Turner v., TexCivApp–San Antonio, 267 SW2d 877.—App & E 662(3), 1060.1(1), 1060.1(6); Autos 77, 107(1); Bailm 30; Evid 177.

Gossett; Wiseman Gin Co. v., TexCivApp–Amarillo, 125 SW2d 334, writ refused.—Mtg 25(1).

Gossler v. Lipper, TexCivApp–Galveston, 93 SW2d 1175. —Adv Poss 51, 115(2), 115(4); App & E 441, 574(1), 655(1), 655(3), 656(1), 938(2); Trial 343.

Gossum; Hart v., TexApp–Fort Worth, 995 SW2d 958, reh overr.—Mand 187.2, 187.7; Records 62, 63, 65; Witn 199(1).

Goston v. Hutchison, TexApp–Houston (1 Dist), 853 SW2d 729.—App & E 854(1), 863; Judgm 183, 185(2); Mun Corp 724; Plead 78; Schools 89.13(4), 159.5(6).

Goswami v. American Collections Enterprise, Inc., CA5 (Tex), 377 F3d 488, reh and reh den 395 F3d 225, cert den 126 SCt 331, 546 US 811, 163 LEd2d 44, cert den 126 SCt 331, 546 US 811, 163 LEd2d 44.—Antitrust 214; Fed Cts 776; Statut 181(2), 188, 190, 217.4, 219(2), 219(6.1).

Goswami v. American Collections Enterprise, Inc., SDTex, 280 FSupp2d 624, aff in part, rev in part and remanded 377 F3d 488, reh and reh den 395 F3d 225, cert den 126 SCt 331, 546 US 811, 163 LEd2d 44, cert den 126 SCt 331, 546 US 811, 163 LEd2d 44.—Antitrust 214; Const Law 1490, 1505, 1506.

Goswami v. Metropolitan Sav. and Loan Ass'n, Tex, 751 SW2d 487.—Bankr 3776.5(1); Judgm 185.3(15); Mtg 369(6), 455.

Goswami v. Metropolitan Sav. and Loan Ass'n, TexApp–Dallas, 713 SW2d 127, ref nre, and writ gr, and writ withdrawn, rev 751 SW2d 487.—Bankr 2062, 3776.5(4); Judgm 186; Mtg 529(10).

Goswami v. Thetford, TexApp–El Paso, 829 SW2d 317, writ den.—App & E 181, 204(1), 207, 231(9), 237(1), 882(1), 1004(11); Civil R 1769; Damag 94, 208(8), 223; New Tr 76(1), 77(2); Trial 182, 219, 278, 279.

Goswick; Chiles v., Tex, 225 SW2d 411, 148 Tex 306.—Plead 111.39(6), 111.42(7); Venue 8.5(5).

Goswick; Chiles v., TexCivApp–El Paso, 225 SW2d 407, certified question answered 225 SW2d 411, 148 Tex 306. —Venue 8.5(6).

Goswick v. Employers' Cas. Co., Tex, 440 SW2d 287.—Insurance 1860, 2278(19), 2278(29), 2934(2).

Goswick v. Employers' Cas. Co., TexCivApp–Eastland, 429 SW2d 166, writ gr, rev 440 SW2d 287.—Insurance 1822, 2278(19), 2278(29).

Goswick v. State, TexCrimApp, 656 SW2d 68.—Autos 357; Crim Law 778(5).

Gotcher v. Barnett, TexApp–Houston (14 Dist), 757 SW2d 398.—Judgm 139, 143(3), 145(4), 146, 163.

Gotcher v. Beto, CA5 (Tex), 444 F2d 696.—Hab Corp 475.1, 721(2), 766.

Gotcher v. City of Farmersville, Tex, 151 SW2d 565, 137 Tex 12.—Mun Corp 747(2), 845(2); Neglig 1172, 1175, 1177; Nuis 4.

Gotcher v. City of Farmersville, TexCivApp–Dallas, 139 SW2d 361, aff 151 SW2d 565, 137 Tex 12.—Mun Corp 733(2), 747(2), 747(3), 747(4), 841; Neglig 1045(2), 1313.

Gotcher v. Lamar State Bank, TexApp–Beaumont, 714 SW2d 365, ref nre.—Bills & N 516; Guar 25(3), 91; Trial 384.

Gotcher; Martin Hedrick Co. v., TexApp–Waco, 656 SW2d 509, ref nre.—App & E 564(5), 846(5); Time 9(8).

Gotcher v. State, TexCivApp–Austin, 106 SW2d 1104.—Const Law 2520(5); Em Dom 2(1.1); High 96(1); States 112.1(2), 112.2(2).

Gotcher; U.S. v., CA5 (Tex), 401 F2d 118.—Int Rev 3110, 3154, 3158, 3160, 3167, 3346.

Gotcher v. U.S., EDTex, 259 FSupp 340, aff in part, rev in part 401 F2d 118.—Int Rev 3150, 3160, 3340.

Gothard v. Marr, TexCivApp–Waco, 581 SW2d 276.—Damag 182, 185(1); Trial 127; Witn 379(2).

Gothard v. Metropolitan Life Ins. Co., CA5 (Tex), 491 F3d 246.—Fed Cts 763.1, 776; Labor & Emp 629(2), 687, 688.

Gothard v. Saunders, TexCivApp–Fort Worth, 415 SW2d 718, ref nre.—Bills & N 485.

Gottesman v. Toubin, TexCivApp–Waco, 326 SW2d 586. —Garn 77.

Gottesman v. Toubin, TexCivApp–Houston, 353 SW2d 294.—App & E 1177(2); Garn 137, 164, 193; Partners 208(2), 208(3), 299.

Gottlich v. State, TexApp–Fort Worth, 822 SW2d 734, petition for discretionary review refused.—Crim Law 564(1), 565, 629(1), 641.5(0.5), 641.5(7), 795(1), 795(2.1), 795(2.80); Ind & Inf 110(48), 176, 188, 191(0.5); Infants 20; Rape 48(1).

Gottlieb v. Hofheinz, TexCivApp–Hous (1 Dist), 523 SW2d 7, dism.—Elections 212, 227(1), 270, 280, 285(1), 285(3); Judgm 178.

Gottschald v. Reaves, TexCivApp–Hous (1 Dist), 457 SW2d 307.—Evid 317(18); Trial 48; Wills 55(1), 81, 161, 166(1), 166(2), 400; Witn 269(2.1).

Gottschald v. Reaves, TexCivApp–Hous (14 Dist), 470 SW2d 149, ref nre.—Judgm 589(1), 634, 725(1).

Gottschalk v. Gottschalk, TexCivApp–Austin, 212 SW2d 223.—App & E 185(2); Courts 163.

Gottschalk; Gottschalk v., TexCivApp–Austin, 212 SW2d 223.—App & E 185(2); Courts 163.

Gottschalk; Rudes v., Tex, 324 SW2d 201, 159 Tex 552.— Autos 160(4), 217(3), 245(74); Neglig 85(1), 85(7), 213, 238, 259, 535(4), 535(5), 535(6), 1717; Trial 352.1(5), 352.1(7).

Gottschalk v. Rudes, TexCivApp–San Antonio, 315 SW2d 361, aff 324 SW2d 201, 159 Tex 552.—Autos 223(2), 245(74); Infants 61, 102; Neglig 259, 535(5), 1602, 1717, 1742.

Gottschalk v. State, TexCrimApp, 248 SW2d 476, 157 TexCrim 281.—Crim Law 507(7), 510.

Gottschalk v. State, TexCrimApp, 248 SW2d 473, 157 TexCrim 276.—Crim Law 507(1), 507(7), 510.

Gottson v. State, TexApp–San Antonio, 940 SW2d 181, reh overr, and petition for discretionary review refused. —Crim Law 273(1), 273.2(1), 274(2), 274(8), 274(9), 275, 641.13(1), 641.13(6), 1149, 1167(5).

Gottwald; Adams v., TexApp–San Antonio, 179 SW3d 101, reh overr, and review den.—App & E 179(4); Const Law 2315; Lim of Act 4(2).

Gottwald v. Warlick, TexCivApp–San Antonio, 125 SW2d 1060.—Assign 8; Remaind 14; Revers 7; Tresp to T T 6.1.

Goudchaux; Priddie v., TexCivApp–Beaumont, 112 SW2d 492, dism.—Banks 71, 114; Nova 1.

Goudeau v. Marquez, TexApp–Houston (1 Dist), 830 SW2d 681.—Costs 194.12, 198, 207; Evid 543(2).

Goudeau v. State, TexCrimApp, 478 SW2d 456.—Sent & Pun 1503.

Goudeau v. State, TexApp–Houston (1 Dist), 788 SW2d 431.—Const Law 250.2(3), 268(10), 3801, 4708; Crim Law 1144.13(3), 1144.13(6), 1159.2(7), 1159.6; Kidnap 27, 36; Sent & Pun 308, 309, 312, 1900.

Goudeau v. State, TexApp–Houston (14 Dist), 209 SW3d 713.—Arrest 63.5(4), 63.5(9); Autos 349(2.1), 349(4), 349(8), 349(14.1); Crim Law 1036.1(4), 1044.1(6), 1168(2).

Goudeau v. State, TexApp–Houston (14 Dist), 946 SW2d 494, petition for discretionary review refused.—Crim Law 273.1(4).

Goudie v. HNG Oil Co., TexApp–El Paso, 711 SW2d 716, ref nre.—App & E 934(1), 989, 1062.1; Judgm 199(3.10); Labor & Emp 561, 696(1).

Goudy v. Lewis, TexCivApp–Austin, 599 SW2d 677, dism. —Plead 111.15, 111.42(5); Venue 7.5(4).

Gouger; City of Corpus Christi v., TexCivApp–San Antonio, 236 SW2d 870, writ refused.—Mun Corp 43; Statut 158.

Gough v. Fincher, TexCivApp–Waco, 228 SW2d 541.— Autos 181(1), 244(20); Evid 265(7); Plead 111.18, 111.19; Venue 21.

Gough v. Home Owners' Loan Corporation, TexCiv-App–El Paso, 135 SW2d 771, writ dism, correct.—Hus & W 273(11); Mtg 153; Ven & Pur 220.

Gough v. Natural Gas Pipeline Co. of America, CA5 (Tex), 996 F2d 763, reh den.—Damag 50, 130.1, 221(7); Judgm 632; Ship 63.

Gough; Peters v., TexCivApp–Waco, 86 SW2d 515.—App & E 931(3); Statut 94(1); Zoning 134.1.

Goulart v. State, TexApp–Waco, 26 SW3d 5, reh overr, and petition for discretionary review refused.—Crim Law 1144.13(2.1), 1159.2(1), 1159.2(2), 1159.2(7), 1159.5; Infants 20.

Goularte, In re, BkrtcyWDTex, 20 BR 246.—Bankr 3706(2), 3715(5).

Gould, In re, CA5 (Tex), 457 F2d 393.—Bankr 2549, 2762.1; Fed Cts 743.

Gould v. Awapara, TexCivApp–Houston, 365 SW2d 671. —App & E 719(1), 1047(1); Child S 429; Divorce 258; Lim of Act 2(1), 183(2); Plead 409(1).

Gould v. Barnes Brokerage Co., NDTex, 345 FSupp 294. —Fed Cts 197, 207, 345.

Gould; Boettcher v., TexCivApp–Austin, 577 SW2d 806, ref nre.—Adv Poss 13; Evid 314(1); Trial 105(2).

Gould v. City of El Paso, TexCivApp–El Paso, 440 SW2d 696, ref nre.—App & E 671(1); Const Law 990, 999, 1020, 2489, 2494, 2970, 2976; Mun Corp 200(4), 220(9); Paymt 84(2); Statut 93(2).

Gould; Groves v., TexCivApp–Fort Worth, 102 SW2d 1114.—Mand 57(1), 151(1), 154(3), 154(9).

Gould; Houston Heavy Equipment Co., Inc. v., SDTex, 198 BR 693.—Bankr 2608(1), 2608(2), 2616(1), 2616(4), 2616(5).

Gould; Lay v., TexCivApp–Amarillo, 82 SW2d 1081.— Plead 45, 111.4; Venue 8.5(5).

Gould; Middleton v., SDTex, 952 FSupp 435.—Civil R 1530; Lim of Act 104.5.

Gould v. Schlachter, TexCivApp–Eastland, 443 SW2d 764.—Land & Ten 79(3); Mines 74(5).

Gould v. Sea Link Helicopters, Inc., TexApp–Houston (1 Dist), 982 SW2d 29.—App & E 428(2).

Gould Group; Benitz v., TexApp–San Antonio, 27 SW3d 109.—App & E 852, 866(3), 893(1), 927(7), 934(2); Health 623, 631, 633, 637; Judgm 178, 181(33), 183, 185(2), 185(5), 185(6), 185.3(21); Neglig 379, 380, 387, 421, 423, 431, 1530.

Gould, Inc.; Payne v., EDTex, 503 FSupp 1060.—Compromise 16(1); Damag 63.

Goulding; Traylor v., Tex, 497 SW2d 944.—App & E 989, 1083(3).

Goulding; Traylor v., TexCivApp–Hous (1 Dist), 497 SW2d 468, rev 497 SW2d 944.—App & E 731(5), 768; Evid 597; Health 823(1), 826; Trial 215, 351.2(2), 365.1(1).

Gouldman v. Seligman & Latz of Houston, Inc., SDTex, 82 FRD 727.—Fed Civ Proc 177.1, 184.10.

Gouldman v. Southern Stevedoring Co. of Texas, Inc., CA5 (Tex), 496 F2d 91.—Seamen 29(5.14).

Gouldsby v. State, TexApp–Texarkana, 202 SW3d 329, petition for discretionary review refused.—Arrest 63.4(15), 63.4(16), 63.5(4), 63.5(5), 68(8), 71.1(1); Crim Law 394.6(5), 1134(6), 1139, 1158(4); Searches 40.1, 42.1, 44, 164.

Gouna v. O'Neill, TexCivApp–Amarillo, 149 SW2d 138.— Autos 201(1.1), 238(8); Neglig 387.

Gounaris; Pappas v., Tex, 311 SW2d 644, 158 Tex 355.— Frds St of 56(9), 76, 129(11); Home 118(5), 128, 129(2); Mtg 76.

Gounaris; Pappas v., TexCivApp–Galveston, 301 SW2d 249, reformed 311 SW2d 644, 158 Tex 355.—App & E 193(1), 216(2), 253, 761; Frds St of 119(2), 125(3); Mtg 258; Partners 24, 70, 76; Trial 295(5), 392(1); Trusts 7.

Goupair.Com, Inc.; Gonannies, Inc. v., NDTex, 464 FSupp2d 603.—Inj 138.1, 138.6, 147, 150; Trademarks 1133, 1137(1), 1360, 1704(2), 1705(2), 1707(4), 1800.

Gourley, Ex parte, TexCrimApp, 204 SW2d 993, 151 TexCrim 25.—Extrad 30; Hab Corp 526.

Gourley v. Doughty, TexCivApp–Fort Worth, 120 SW2d 480.—App & E 1126, 1236.

Gourley v. Fields, TexCivApp–Eastland, 348 SW2d 787.—Plead 111.7, 111.8, 111.34, 111.38, 111.39(4), 111.45.

Gourley v. Iverson Tool Co., TexCivApp–Fort Worth, 186 SW2d 726, writ refused wom.—App & E 930(3); Estop 52(4); Lim of Act 53(2); Mech Liens 277(3), 290(4); Mines 97, 98, 99(3), 110, 114.5, 117; Paymt 38(1), 38(4), 39(1), 47(1), 76(6); Trial 350.3(1), 350.4(1), 352.4(2), 358.

Gourley; Reed v., TexCivApp–El Paso, 109 SW2d 242, writ dism.—Execution 224, 249.

Gourley v. State, TexCrimApp, 344 SW2d 882, 171 TexCrim 89.—Bail 74(1).

Gourley; U.S. v., CA5 (Tex), 168 F3d 165, reh den, cert den 120 SCt 72, 528 US 824, 145 LEd2d 61.—Consp 24.5, 28(3), 37, 47(2), 47(12); Controlled Subs 31, 81; Crim Law 113, 126(1), 1042, 1126, 1129(2), 1144.13(3), 1144.13(4), 1150, 1158(1), 1159.2(8), 1166(4); Sent & Pun 761, 764.

Gourley; U.S. v., SDTex, 936 FSupp 412.—Bail 42, 49(3.1), 49(4), 49(5); Estop 68(2); U S Mag 27.

Gourmet, Inc. v. Hurley, TexCivApp–Dallas, 552 SW2d 509.—Corp 672(6); Courts 12(5), 15; Judgm 112, 124, 126(1).

Gourrier v. Joe Myers Motors, Inc., TexApp–Houston (14 Dist), 115 SW3d 570.—Action 3; Antitrust 193, 196, 367; App & E 766, 949; Autos 20; Cons Cred 61.1; Fraud 7; Judgm 183, 186.

Gourrier v. Joe Myers Motors, Inc., TexApp–Houston (14 Dist), 78 SW3d 651, opinion withdrawn and superseded 115 SW3d 570.

Gouse v. State, TexCrimApp, 286 SW2d 152, 162 TexCrim 422.—Crim Law 338(1), 1169.5(3), 1169.11.

Govan v. State, TexCrimApp, 682 SW2d 567.—Crim Law 1030(1), 1172.1(2).

Govan v. State, TexApp–Houston (1 Dist), 671 SW2d 660, petition for discretionary review refused.—Crim Law 372(14), 374, 398(2), 419(1.5), 1169.2(6), 1169.11; Rob 4, 24.45.

Govant v. Houston Community College System, TexApp–Houston (14 Dist), 72 SW3d 69, reh overr.—Colleges 8(1), 8.1(4.1), 8.1(5); Const Law 3627(4), 3879, 4165(1), 4223(4); Offic 114.

Govea v. ATF, CA5 (Tex), 207 FedAppx 369.—Civil R 1326(4), 1344, 1354, 1395(1), 1451; Consp 7.5(2); Fed Cts 18, 915; Searches 22; U S 127(1).

Gover v. State, TexCrimApp, 92 SW2d 258.—Crim Law 1182.

Governing Bd. v. Pannill, TexApp–Beaumont, 659 SW2d 670, ref nre.—App & E 231(1), 232(3), 930(1), 965, 989, 1001(1), 1001(2), 1069.1, 1097(1); Assoc 17, 18, 20(5); Corp 182.4(3), 195; Courts 99(1), 99(7); Evid 571(7); Jury 149, 150; Trial 257; Venue 42, 68, 70, 72.

Governing Bd.; Pannill v., TexCivApp–Texarkana, 571 SW2d 336.—Venue 22(8).

Governing Bd. v. Pannill, TexCivApp–Texarkana, 561 SW2d 517, ref nre, appeal after remand 659 SW2d 670, ref nre.—App & E 322, 377, 387(2), 395, 715(2), 797(1), 934(1); Atty Gen 9; Char 50; Corp 182.4(1), 189(3), 189(7), 189(9), 189(11), 319(0.5), 320(4), 385; Judgm 181(29), 185(2).

Government Emp. Credit Union v. Jaquez, TexCivApp–El Paso, 318 SW2d 134, ref nre.—App & E 934(1); B & L Assoc 26; Judgm 18(1), 19.

Government Emp. Credit Union of San Antonio; Texas Bankers Ass'n v., TexCivApp–San Antonio, 625 SW2d 338.—Admin Law 416.1; Banks 2, 33; B & L Assoc 2.1, 3.5(1), 40.

Government Emp. Financial Corp.; Cullum v., TexCivApp–Beaumont, 517 SW2d 317, ref nre.—Torts 332.

Government Emp. Ins. Co. v. Edelman, TexCivApp–Beaumont, 524 SW2d 546, ref nre.—Autos 227.5; Evid 589; Infants 61; Insurance 2666, 2694; Joint Adv 1.2(2).

Government Emp. Ins. Co. v. Hanna, TexCivApp–Fort Worth, 219 SW2d 122, ref nre.—Accord 1; Compromise 2; Contracts 22(1); Evid 10(2), 242(1), 461(1); Insurance 1747, 2730, 2732; Princ & A 23(2).

Government Emp. Ins. Co.; Podlewski v., TexCivApp–Hous (14 Dist), 616 SW2d 298.—Insurance 3153.

Government Emp. Ins. Co.; Tristan v., TexCivApp–San Antonio, 489 SW2d 365, ref nre.—Insurance 2663, 2664, 2666.

Government Emp. Ins. Co.; U.S. v., CA5 (Tex), 440 F2d 1338.—Insurance 2660.

Government Emp. Ins. Co. v. Vail, TexApp–Beaumont, 623 SW2d 170, ref nre.—Insurance 2525(1).

Government Employees Credit Union; Auxier v., TexApp–San Antonio, 733 SW2d 398.—App & E 204(4).

Government Employees Credit Union v. Castillo, WDTex, 213 BR 316.—Bankr 3034, 3413.1, 3415.1.

Government Employees Credit Union of El Paso; Casillas v., TexCivApp–El Paso, 570 SW2d 57, ref nre.—Cons Cred 56, 61.1, 62.

Government Employees Credit Union of San Antonio v. Fuji Photo Film U.S.A., Inc., TexApp–San Antonio, 712 SW2d 208, ref nre.—Action 13; Antitrust 130; App & E 714(1), 863; B & L Assoc 41(5); Const Law 70.1(2), 2473; Judgm 181(11), 185.2(3); Statut 212.6, 212.7.

Government Employees Ins. Co.; Hare v., EDTex, 132 FRD 448.—Fed Civ Proc 1366, 1455.

Government Employees Ins. Co.; Lichte v., Tex, 825 SW2d 431.—App & E 1041(3); Plead 246(2).

Government Employees Ins. Co. v. McGinty, WDTex, 832 FSupp 1092, aff 37 F3d 633.—Insurance 2358.

Government Employees Ins. Co.; Monroe v., TexApp–Houston (1 Dist), 845 SW2d 394, reh den, and writ den.—Insurance 2656, 2799.

Government Employees Ins. Co.; Ruiz v., TexApp–El Paso, 4 SW3d 838.—Insurance 1713, 1801, 1808, 1810, 1832(1), 1863, 2650, 3424.

Government Employees Ins. Co. (Geico) v. Lichte, TexApp–El Paso, 792 SW2d 546, writ den with per curiam opinion 825 SW2d 431.—Insurance 2793(2), 2803, 3417, 3556, 3571.

Government Nat. Mortg. Ass'n, In re, CA5 (Tex), 986 F2d 898. See Stone, In re.

Government of Japan; Aufman v., CA5 (Tex), 200 FedAppx 364.—Covenants 72.1, 73.

Government of Kingdom of Belgium v. The Lubrafol, EDTex, 43 FSupp 403.—War 14.

Government of Republic of Indonesia v. M/V Glafkos, CA5 (Tex), 744 F2d 461. See Cardinal Shipping Corp. v. M/S Seisho Maru.

Government of Turkmenistan; Bridas S.A.P.I.C. v., CA5 (Tex), 447 F3d 411, cert den 127 SCt 664, 166 LEd2d 513.—Alt Disp Res 515; Corp 1.4(2), 1.4(3), 1.4(4), 1.5(3), 1.6(2), 1.6(3); Fed Cts 776, 870.1, 917.

Government of Turkmenistan; Bridas S.A.P.I.C. v., CA5 (Tex), 345 F3d 347, reh and reh den 84 FedAppx 472, cert den State Concern Turkmenneft v. Bridas SAPIC, 124 SCt 1660, 541 US 937, 158 LEd2d 357, appeal after remand 447 F3d 411, cert den 127 SCt 664, 166 LEd2d 513.—Alt Disp Res 133(2), 141, 182(1), 199, 210, 329, 363(6), 374(7); Contracts 175(1); Corp 1.4(4), 1.5(3), 1.6(2), 1.7(2); Damag 87(1), 226; Estop 52(1); Fed Cts 269, 813, 870.1, 915; Intern Law 10.34, 10.38; Princ & A 1, 96, 99.

Government Personnel Auto. Ass'n v. Haag, TexCivApp–San Antonio, 131 SW2d 978, writ refused.—App & E 1008.1(11); Insurance 1810, 2663, 3007(1), 3013, 3015, 3549(4).

Government Personnel Automobile Ass'n v. U.S., CCA5 (Tex), 124 F2d 99.—Tax 3281.

Government Personnel Mut. Life Ins. Co. v. Kaye, CA5 (Tex), 584 F2d 738.—Divorce 321 1/2, 357.1, 358; Judgm 828.6.

Government Personnel Mut. Life Ins. Co.; Spyra v., TexCivApp–San Antonio, 236 SW2d 218, ref nre.—Insurance 1959, 2021, 2039, 3125(6).

Government Personnel Mut. Life Ins. Co. v. Wear, Tex, 251 SW2d 525, 151 Tex 454.—Const Law 191; Costs 194.22; Insurance 1652(2); Statut 174, 181(1), 214, 263.

Government Personnel Mut. Life Ins. Co. v. Wear, TexCivApp–San Antonio, 247 SW2d 284, aff in part, rev in part 251 SW2d 525, 151 Tex 454.—Const Law 191; Contracts 164, 215(2); Costs 194.22; Cust & U 15(1); Insurance 1652(2); Trial 351.2(4).

Government Services Ins. Underwriters v. Jones, Tex, 368 SW2d 560.—Const Law 2332, 2341, 2357; Courts 209(2); Mand 45; Pretrial Proc 711.

Governor's House Apartments, In re, BkrtcySDTex, 155 BR 442. See Farb Investments Interests Ltd., In re.

Govier v. Gunnels, TexCivApp–Galveston, 246 SW2d 339. —Judgm 185.3(20); Mun Corp 63.5, 446, 568(3); Trial 139.1(2).

Gowan v. Reimers, TexCivApp–Fort Worth, 220 SW2d 331, ref nre.—App & E 525(3), 692(1), 712, 760(1), 901, 933(1), 946, 980, 1058(1); Hus & W 270(5); New Tr 99, 102(3); Trial 2, 277, 365.3, 366; Trusts 84, 373.

Gowan v. State, TexApp–Fort Worth, 927 SW2d 246, petition for discretionary review refused.—Const Law 4594(1); Crim Law 627.5(1), 627.5(2), 627.6(5), 700(2.1).

Gowan v. State, TexApp–Beaumont, 18 SW3d 305, petition for discretionary review refused.—Double J 30; Sent & Pun 1302.

Gowan v. Texas Dept. of Criminal Justice, TexApp–Texarkana, 99 SW3d 319.—App & E 170(2), 179(2); Costs 129, 132(6); Pretrial Proc 678, 685.

Gowans v. State, TexCrimApp, 522 SW2d 462.—Crim Law 1130(2), 1130(4).

Gowans v. State, TexApp–Houston (1 Dist), 995 SW2d 787, reh overr, and petition for discretionary review refused.—Autos 344, 355(6), 355(13); Crim Law 795(2.1), 795(2.10), 795(2.55), 1038.1(1), 1038.1(4), 1116, 1134(3), 1172.1(1), 1172.1(3), 1172.9; Ind & Inf 189(8).

Gowen v. Willenborg, TexCivApp–Houston, 366 SW2d 695, ref nre.—Anim 66.1; Neglig 1016, 1066, 1176.

Gower; Daugherty v., TexCivApp–Amarillo, 403 SW2d 535.—Bills & N 97(1), 104; Judgm 183, 185(2), 185.3(9).

Gower; Masten v., TexCivApp–Fort Worth, 165 SW2d 901.—App & E 1032(1); Pretrial Proc 476, 483, 745.

Gower v. State, TexCrimApp, 332 SW2d 328, 169 TexCrim 81.—Autos 355(6); Crim Law 1033.1, 1115(2), 1144.5.

Gower; U.S. v., CA5 (Tex), 447 F2d 187, cert den 92 SCt 84, 404 US 850, 30 LEd2d 88.—Consp 47(12); Const Law 268(2.1), 4567, 4601, 4623; Controlled Subs 67, 86; Crim Law 422(1), 508(1), 590(2), 627.9(5), 656(1), 656(2); Cust Dut 134; Gr Jury 33; Ind & Inf 10.2(7), 17, 144.2, 174; Jury 83(1), 149.

Gowin v. State, TexCrimApp, 272 SW2d 892.—Crim Law 1090.1(1).

Gowin v. State, TexApp–Tyler, 760 SW2d 672.—Autos 351.1; Crim Law 629(1), 790, 867, 1148, 1167(1); Ind & Inf 65, 71.3, 137(6).

Goyen; Marek v., TexCivApp–Houston, 346 SW2d 926.— App & E 935(0.5), 1170.3; Contracts 47; Estop 85, 99; Frds St of 144; Mech Liens 107, 115(1), 115(4), 149(1), 195, 309.

Goyne v. McDaniel, TexCivApp–Waco, 383 SW2d 934.— App & E 230; Estop 99; Trial 351.5(1), 356(1), 366.

Goynes v. Dretke, CA5 (Tex), 139 FedAppx 616, cert den 126 SCt 1430, 546 US 1216, 164 LEd2d 135.—Hab Corp 818.

Goynes; U.S. v., CA5 (Tex), 175 F3d 350.—Crim Law 1134(3), 1139, 1147, 1158(1); Sent & Pun 688.

GPE Controls; Lozano v., SDTex, 859 FSupp 1036.— Rem of C 2, 79(1), 107(7), 107(11).

G. P. Enterprises, Inc. v. Adkins, TexCivApp–Texarkana, 543 SW2d 913.—Contracts 145, 326; Corp 503(2); Plead 111.37, 111.42(6), 111.47.

GPM Gas Corp.; Haley v., TexApp–Amarillo, 80 SW3d 114.—App & E 215(0.5), 215(1), 231(9), 232(0.5), 882(12), 1079; Land & Ten 24(1); Mines 55(2); Pretrial Proc 45; Trial 277.

G. P. Plastics; Bowie v., TexCivApp–Eastland, 572 SW2d 42, ref nre.—Evid 268; Judgm 199(3.2), 199(3.10); Neglig 1562, 1670, 1679.

GP Plastics Corp. v. Interboro Packaging Corp., CA5 (Tex), 108 FedAppx 832.—Contracts 206; Estop 68(2); Rem of C 17.

GPR Holdings, L.L.C., In re, BkrtcyNDTex, 318 BR 384. —Bankr 2154.1, 2162, 2533, 2553; Consp 1.1, 9; Fraud 3, 30; Sec Tran 170; Trover 1, 2, 4, 9(1), 10, 22, 44.

GPR Holdings, L.L.C., In re, BkrtcyNDTex, 316 BR 477. —Bankr 2164.1, 2399, 2701.

G. Property Management, Ltd. v. Multivest Financial Services of Texas, Inc., TexApp–San Antonio, 219 SW3d 37.—App & E 846(5), 852, 931(1), 931(3), 984(1), 984(5), 989, 1010.1(1), 1010.2, 1024.1; Costs 194.40; Judgm 185.3(2); Lim of Act 95(1), 95(3), 95(7), 100(7), 100(12), 104(1), 197(2); Partners 70, 370.

G.P. Show Productions, Inc. v. Arlington Sports Facilities Development Authority, Inc., TexApp–Fort Worth, 873 SW2d 120, reh overr.—App & E 852; Em Dom 81.1, 85, 95; Statut 147, 223.2(0.5).

Grabeel; Carter v., TexCivApp–Amarillo, 341 SW2d 458. —Hus & W 86, 249(5), 254, 262.1(2).

Graber; Fuqua v., TexApp–Corpus Christi, 158 SW3d 635, review gr.—App & E 893(1), 919; Bankr 2002, 2060.1, 2062; Mal Pros 0.5, 0.7, 47; Plead 104(1), 111.37, 111.39(0.5); States 18.5, 18.7, 18.11.

Graber v. State, TexCrimApp, 356 SW2d 788, 172 TexCrim 350.—Unlawf Assemb 3.

Grabes v. Fawcett, TexCivApp–Texarkana, 307 SW2d 311.—Ten in C 27; Trover 16, 30, 40(4); Venue 8.5(5).

Grabes v. Reinhard Bohle Mach. Tools, Inc., TexCivApp–Corpus Christi, 381 SW2d 395, ref nre.—Acct Action on 14, 15; App & E 597(1), 640, 989, 1048(2); Evid 376(9); Trial 366.

Grabow, Ex parte, TexCrimApp, 705 SW2d 150.—Homic 1558.

Grabow v. State, TexCrimApp, 332 SW2d 320, 169 TexCrim 86.—Sent & Pun 2004.

Grabow v. State, TexApp–San Antonio, 646 SW2d 953, petition for discretionary review refused.—Arrest 63.4(1), 63.4(2), 63.4(7.1), 63.4(15), 63.4(18), 63.5(4), 63.5(5); Controlled Subs 148(4); Searches 29, 40.1, 112.

Grabowski; Harris County Precinct Four Constable Dept. v., Tex, 922 SW2d 954.—Mun Corp 185(1); Sheriffs 21.

Grabowski v. State, TexApp–Eastland, 27 SW3d 594.— Crim Law 273.1(1), 273.1(4), 1031(4), 1134(3), 1134(8); Judgm 486(1), 501.

Grace v. Allen, TexCivApp–Dallas, 407 SW2d 321, ref nre.—Action 66; Atty & C 11(11); Int Rev 4444.1; States 4.16(3), 18.5, 18.67.

Grace; Ansley v., TexCivApp–El Paso, 300 SW2d 312, dism.—App & E 930(3); Autos 245(14), 245(61), 245(80).

Grace v. Colorito, TexApp–Austin, 4 SW3d 765, petition for review den.—App & E 1136; Evid 555.10, 570; Health 696; Judgm 185(2); Lim of Act 1, 55(3), 74(1), 95(1), 95(12), 182(2), 195(3), 197(1).

Grace v. C. I. R., CA5 (Tex), 421 F2d 165.—Const Law 2500; Int Rev 3545.

Grace v. Duke, TexApp–Austin, 54 SW3d 338, review den. —App & E 177, 920(2), 946, 961, 966(1); Costs 194.10, 194.16, 194.18, 194.32, 207, 208; Pretrial Proc 718, 723.1.

Grace v. Keystone Shipping Co., EDTex, 805 FSupp 436. —Admin Law 501; Damag 49.10, 50, 50.10; Evid

242(5); Judgm 660, 715(1), 720, 724; Seamen 29(1); Ship 14.

Grace v. McCrary, TexCivApp–Waco, 390 SW2d 397, writ dism.—Child S 339(2); Contempt 66(1).

Grace v. Orkin Exterminating Co., TexCivApp–Beaumont, 255 SW2d 279, ref nre.—Contracts 56, 101(1), 116(1), 141(1), 141(3), 176(1); Copyr 86; Inj 56, 123, 130, 189.

Grace; Parham v., TexCivApp–Fort Worth, 341 SW2d 503.—Plead 236(7).

Grace v. Parker, TexCivApp–Austin, 337 SW2d 518, ref nre.—Contracts 189, 199(1), 315; Lim of Act 104(1), 104(2), 193; Plead 8(15); Trial 355(1).

Grace; Rabel v., TexCrimApp, 335 SW2d 227, 169 TexCrim 490.—Crim Law 1081(1).

Grace v. Rahlfs, TexCivApp–El Paso, 508 SW2d 158, ref nre.—Afft 16; Costs 194.32; Evid 450(5), 461(1); Hus & W 270(5); Insurance 1702, 2058, 3567, 3582; Subrog 41(4).

Grace; Smith v., TexApp–Dallas, 919 SW2d 673, writ den, cert den 117 SCt 964, 519 US 1118, 136 LEd2d 849.—App & E 76(1), 79(2), 80(1), 501(2), 544(1), 553(2), 620.1, 624, 627, 907(4), 1013, 1182; Damag 87(1); Plead 228.17; Pretrial Proc 560.

Grace v. Starrett, TexCivApp–Dallas, 411 SW2d 774, ref nre.—App & E 750(8), 1004(14), 1170.1; Damag 130.1, 130.2, 184, 228; Hus & W 209(2), 260, 265.

Grace v. Structural Pest Control Bd. of Texas, TexCivApp–Waco, 620 SW2d 157, ref nre.—Admin Law 473; Const Law 4027, 4279; Licens 38.

Grace; Texas & N. O. R. Co. v., Tex, 188 SW2d 378, 144 Tex 71.—App & E 1114; Evid 54, 539.5(2), 590; R R 376.1, 400(8.1); Trial 350.7(9).

Grace; Texas & N. O. R. Co. v., TexCivApp–Beaumont, 204 SW2d 857.—Evid 16; R R 376.1, 376.4; Trial 350.7(9).

Grace; Texas & N. O. R. Co. v., TexCivApp, 185 SW2d 219, rev 188 SW2d 378, 144 Tex 71.—App & E 1004(13), 1053(2), 1062.1; Death 99(1); Evid 539.5(1), 546; R R 398(4), 400(14).

Grace v. Titanium Electrode Products, Inc., TexApp–Houston (1 Dist), 227 SW3d 293.—App & E 66, 76(1), 80(6), 173(2), 856(1), 863; Judgm 181(31), 185(2).

Grace v. Zimmerman, TexApp–Houston (14 Dist), 853 SW2d 92, reh den.—App & E 760(1), 1097(1); Courts 99(1); Covenants 37; Judgm 185(5), 185.3(1), 186; Pretrial Proc 714; Sales 10; Torts 213, 242; Trover 4, 16; Trusts 94.5, 102(1), 103(1).

Grace & Co. v. Continental Cas. Co., CA5 (Tex), 896 F2d 865. See W.R. Grace & Co. v. Continental Cas. Co.

Grace & Co. v. Continental Cas. Co., EDTex, 682 FSupp 1403. See Dayton Independent School Dist. v. National Gypsum Co.

Grace & Co.-Conn., In re, CA5 (Tex), 923 F2d 42. See W.R. Grace & Co.-Conn., In re.

Grace Community Church v. Alamo Contractors, TexApp–Houston (14 Dist, 853 SW2d 678. See Grace Community Church v. Gonzales.

Grace Community Church v. Gonzales, TexApp–Houston (14 Dist), 853 SW2d 678.—App & E 852, 931(1), 989, 1010.1(1), 1012.1(4); Contracts 176(3); Princ & A 1, 3(2), 14(2), 23(5), 99, 123(3).

Grace Co. v. Scotch Corp., Inc., TexApp–Austin, 753 SW2d 743. See W.R. Grace Co. v. Scotch Corp., Inc.

Grace Oil Co.; Benson v., TexCivApp–Corpus Christi, 430 SW2d 98.—Judgm 186; Lim of Act 127(8); Plead 34(1), 228.14.

Grace Oil Co.; Moncus v., TexCivApp–Galveston, 284 SW2d 375, ref nre.—App & E 1069.1, 1069.2; Ex & Ad 383, 384; Judgm 335(1), 335(3).

Grace Petroleum Corp. v. Williamson, TexApp–Tyler, 906 SW2d 66, reh overr.—Action 27(1); App & E 930(3), 1001(1); Damag 3, 87(1), 89(2), 91(1); Mines 78.7(6); Neglig 219; Torts 117.

Grace Tabernacle United Pentecostal Church; Hutchins v., TexApp–Houston (1 Dist), 804 SW2d 598.—Assoc 1, 15(3), 16, 19, 20(1); Parties 35.79.

Grace Union Presbytery, Inc.; Schismatic and Purported Casa Linda Presbyterian Church in America v., TexApp–Dallas, 710 SW2d 700, ref nre, cert den 108 SCt 85, 484 US 823, 98 LEd2d 46, reh den 108 SCt 469, 484 US 970, 98 LEd2d 408.—App & E 1071.5, 1149; Const Law 1338, 4071; Courts 91(1), 97(1); Judgm 245; Relig Soc 8, 23(4).

Gracey; C.I.R. v., CCA5 (Tex), 159 F2d 324.—Int Rev 3068, 3259, 3260, 3493.1.

Gracey v. West, Tex, 422 SW2d 913.—Judgm 92, 185.1(3), 335(1), 335(3), 570(5); Pretrial Proc 674, 691, 694, 697.

Gracey; West v., TexCivApp–Texarkana, 413 SW2d 791, writ gr, rev 422 SW2d 913.—Abate & R 48; Judgm 181(1), 181(2), 181(15.1), 335(1); Pretrial Proc 531, 581, 600; Trial 9(1).

Gracia v. Beck, TexCivApp–Austin, 286 SW2d 234.—Plead 111.42(2), 111.42(7); Trademarks 1421, 1691, 1714(2).

Gracia; Blanco v., TexApp–Corpus Christi, 767 SW2d 896.—App & E 931(6); Child C 609, 638; Child S 233, 234, 339(3).

Gracia v. Brownsville Housing, CA5 (Tex), 105 F3d 1053, reh and sug for reh den 114 F3d 1185, cert den 118 SCt 171, 522 US 865, 139 LEd2d 114.—Civil R 1027, 1082; Mun Corp 723; Neglig 1040(3).

Gracia; Brownsville Medical Center v., TexApp–Corpus Christi, 704 SW2d 68, ref nre.—App & E 236(1), 972, 1060.1(2.1), 1067; Death 77, 88, 89, 99(3); Health 658, 823(1), 823(15), 834(1); Neglig 421, 432; Trial 111, 112.

Gracia v. RC Cola-7-Up Bottling Co., Tex, 667 SW2d 517.—Accord 11(2); Contracts 147(2); Infants 74; Judgm 84, 91, 634, 693, 713(2), 720.

Gracia v. RC Cola-7-Up Bottling Co. of Harlingen, Inc., TexApp–Corpus Christi, 659 SW2d 152, writ gr, rev 667 SW2d 517.—Compromise 16(1); Judgm 634.

Gracia; State v., TexApp–Fort Worth, 56 SW3d 196.—Em Dom 167(4), 172, 265(5); Statut 181(2), 184, 190, 206, 207, 208, 227; Venue 1.5.

Gracia; U.S. v., CA5 (Tex), 983 F2d 625.—Crim Law 273.1(4), 1158(1), 1167(5), 1181.5(1), 1184(4.1); Sent & Pun 299, 658, 686.

Gracia-Cantu; U.S. v., CA5 (Tex), 302 F3d 308, reh en banc den.—Crim Law 1030(1), 1042; Sent & Pun 781, 793.

Gracia-Gracia; U.S. v., CA5 (Tex), 86 FedAppx 709, cert den 124 SCt 2406, 541 US 1070, 158 LEd2d 975.—Crim Law 641.4(4).

Gracida v. Tagle, TexApp–Corpus Christi, 946 SW2d 504. —Decl Judgm 306; Insurance 1865, 2271, 3457; Mand 1, 3(7), 28, 187.9(1), 187.9(5); Parties 38, 40(2), 44.

Gracie's Answering Service v. Elliott Industries, Inc., TexApp–Fort Worth, 711 SW2d 435. See Holt v. Elliott Industries, Inc.

Graco Children's Products, Inc., In re, Tex, 210 SW3d 598.—Mand 32; Pretrial Proc 19, 27.1, 375.

Graco Children's Products, Inc., In re, TexApp–Corpus Christi, 173 SW3d 600.—Mand 3(2.1), 4(4), 12, 28; Pretrial Proc 403.

Graco Enterprises, Ltd.; Danning v., CA5 (Tex), 750 F2d 477. See Cobb, Matter of.

Graco, Inc. v. Binks Mfg. Co., CAFed (Tex), 60 F3d 785. —Pat 99, 314(5), 314(6), 319(3), 324.55(2), 324.60, 325.11(2.1).

Graco, Inc. v. CRC, Inc. of Texas, TexApp–Dallas, 47 SW3d 742, review den.—App & E 842(2), 930(1), 1010.1(1), 1010.2, 1012.1(4), 1071.1(5.1); Costs 194.46; Damag 64; Indem 72; Insurance 3585; Statut 181(1), 181(2), 184, 217.2.

Graco Robotics, Inc. v. Oaklawn Bank, TexApp–Texarkana, 914 SW2d 633, reh overr, and dism.—App & E 946, 961, 1178(1); Assign 22, 117, 120; Contracts 154,

173, 221(2), 278(1), 279(1), 318, 321(1); Damag 15, 63; Dep & Escr 11, 13, 16, 24.1; Elect of Rem 1, 3(4), 14; Evid 80(1); Execution 145; Interest 31, 39(2.6), 39(2.10), 39(2.20), 39(2.30), 60; Judgm 875, 883(1), 890; Pretrial Proc 483, 486; Trial 358.

Gracy Meadow Owners Ass'n, Inc.; Celotex Corp., Inc. v., TexApp–Austin, 847 SW2d 384, reh overr, and writ den.—Antitrust 138, 393; App & E 773(2); Condo 6.1, 17; Plead 236(3); Pretrial Proc 720; Princ & A 177(4).

Grad; U.S. v., CA5 (Tex), 153 FedAppx 268.—Crim Law 1026.10(5).

Graddy; Central Power & Light Co. v., TexCivApp–Houston, 318 SW2d 943.—Em Dom 126(1), 134, 148, 222(4), 223, 224; Trial 194(10), 295(5).

Graddy v. Le Bus, TexCivApp–Texarkana, 127 SW2d 332.—Courts 170.

Gradilla-Gonzalez; U.S. v., CA5 (Tex), 176 FedAppx 568, cert den Bartolo-Carbajal v. US, 127 SCt 222, 166 LEd2d 177.—Crim Law 1181.5(8).

Gradley; Mobile America Sales Corp. v., TexCivApp–Beaumont, 612 SW2d 625.—Cons Cred 2, 18; Evid 71; Plead 162; Pretrial Proc 313; Statut 267(2).

Gradney v. State, TexCrimApp, 87 SW2d 715, 129 TexCrim 445.—Crim Law 633(1); Jury 131(6).

Grady v. Dallas Ry. & Terminal Co., TexCivApp–Amarillo, 278 SW2d 282, ref nre.—App & E 1011.1(8.1), 1062.5, 1069.1, 1078(1); Carr 318(4), 320(30).

Grady; Doyle v., TexCivApp–Texarkana, 543 SW2d 893.—App & E 1024.3; Plead 111.12, 111.39(4), 111.42(4); Statut 223.4.

Grady v. El Paso Community College, CA5 (Tex), 979 F2d 1111.—Civil R 1027, 1120, 1376(10), 1395(8), 1736; Fed Civ Proc 2497.1, 2544; Offic 114; Schools 63(3), 147.12.

Grady v. Faykus, TexCivApp–Corpus Christi, 530 SW2d 151, ref nre.—Judgm 181(7); Lim of Act 95(12).

Grady v. Fryar, TexCivApp–Dallas, 103 SW2d 1080.—Land & Ten 290.5.

Grady; Intermedics, Inc. v., TexApp–Houston (1 Dist), 683 SW2d 842, ref nre.—Contracts 227, 242; Corp 432(12); Labor & Emp 256(8), 266; Lim of Act 50(1), 66(2), 66(12), 66(15), 182(2), 195(3), 201; Princ & A 14(2), 96, 99; Trial 350.4(4).

Grady; Logan v., TexCivApp–Fort Worth, 482 SW2d 313.—App & E 870(2), 934(2), 1170.6, 1170.7; Evid 118, 333(1), 351, 370(4); Trial 305, 350.7(3.1); Witn 271(3).

Grady v. State, TexCrimApp, 634 SW2d 316.—Crim Law 755.5, 761(1), 1038.1(2), 1038.1(4).

Grady v. State, TexCrimApp, 614 SW2d 830.—Crim Law 814(1), 822(6), 847.

Grady v. State, TexCrimApp, 466 SW2d 770.—Crim Law 556, 781(8); Larc 60.

Grady v. State, TexCrimApp, 252 SW2d 199, 157 TexCrim 600.—Crim Law 1184(5); Homic 1551, 1558.

Grady v. State, TexCrimApp, 200 SW2d 1017, 150 TexCrim 331.—Homic 862.

Grady v. State, TexCrimApp, 113 SW2d 913, 133 TexCrim 617.—Crim Law 364(6), 518(2); Int Liq 131, 239(4).

Grady v. State, TexCrimApp, 97 SW2d 472, 131 TexCrim 156.—Int Liq 205(1).

Grady v. State, TexCrimApp, 93 SW2d 738.—Crim Law 1090.1(1).

Grady v. State, TexApp–Houston (1 Dist), 962 SW2d 128, petition for discretionary review refused.—Autos 354, 357, 411; Bail 68; Crim Law 436(3), 469.2, 1134(3).

Grady v. State, TexApp–Dallas, 730 SW2d 191, petition for discretionary review gr, vac 761 SW2d 19.—Const Law 2545(4), 3309; Crim Law 790; Jury 94, 97(1), 97(2), 108.

Grady v. Stoever, SDTex, 968 FSupp 334.—Contracts 206; Fed Cts 284; Rem of C 17.

Graebel/Houston Movers, Inc. v. Chastain, TexApp–Houston (1 Dist), 26 SW3d 24, reh overr, and review dism woj, and reh of petition for review den.—App & E

913, 949; Parties 35.1, 35.7, 35.9, 35.11, 35.13, 35.17, 35.33, 35.37, 35.41, 35.49, 35.71.

Graebel/Houston Movers, Inc.; Yelverton v., EDTex, 121 FSupp2d 604.—Civil R 1204; Damag 50.10; Fed Civ Proc 2497.1.

Graeber; Lear v., TexCivApp–El Paso, 178 SW2d 124.—Bound 6, 54(6); Pub Lands 175(0.5).

Graef v. Chemical Leaman Corp., CA5 (Tex), 106 F3d 112.—Alt Disp Res 406; Damag 181; Evid 146, 382; Fed Civ Proc 2011; Fed Cts 823; Labor & Emp 757, 810, 862, 871, 1591; States 18.5, 18.49.

Graef v. Chemical Leaman Tank Lines, EDTex, 860 FSupp 1170.—Damag 50.10; Fed Cts 16; Labor & Emp 757, 1967; Rem of C 25(1), 106, 107(1); States 18.15, 18.46, 18.49.

Graef v. Chemical Leaman Tank Lines, Inc., EDTex, 902 FSupp 723.—Damag 50.10; Fed Civ Proc 2497.1, 2515, 2543, 2544, 2546; Labor & Emp 764, 807, 861.

Graef v. City of Galveston, TexCivApp–Hous (14 Dist), 538 SW2d 816, writ gr, cause dism.—App & E 1169(2); Plead 228.23.

Graf v. Harris County, TexApp–Houston (1 Dist), 877 SW2d 82, writ den.—App & E 934(1); Counties 143; Mun Corp 755(1), 847, 857; Statut 223.4.

Graf v. State, TexCrimApp, 190 SW2d 357, 148 TexCrim 640.—Assault 67, 68, 92(5); Crim Law 1134(1), 1144.13(3).

Graf v. State, TexApp–Austin, 925 SW2d 740, reh overr, and petition for discretionary review refused.—Arrest 66(2); States 68.

Graf v. State, TexApp–Waco, 807 SW2d 762, petition for discretionary review refused.—Crim Law 494, 772(6), 800(1), 1077.2(1), 1173.2(1); Homic 1143, 1165, 1184, 1185.

Graf; Texas Co. v., TexCivApp–Fort Worth, 221 SW2d 865, writ refused.—Ten in C 33.

Graf v. Wal-Mart Stores, Inc., SDTex, 4 FSupp2d 680.—Civil R 1018, 1217, 1218(4); Estop 68(2).

Grafa v. Morgan, TexApp–El Paso, 696 SW2d 492, dism.—Trial 330(4), 365.1(5).

Graff v. Beard, Tex, 858 SW2d 918.—Int Liq 299; Neglig 210; Torts 109.

Graff; Beard v., TexApp–San Antonio, 801 SW2d 158, writ gr, rev 858 SW2d 918.—Int Liq 299, 306; Neglig 202, 210.

Graff; Palacios Townsite Co. v., TexCivApp–Texarkana, 364 SW2d 718, ref nre.—Adv Poss 85(4).

Graff v. Parker Bros. & Co., CA5 (Tex), 204 F2d 705.—Adm 118.7(2); Collision 90, 93, 95(2), 95(4); Death 23.

Graff v. State, TexCrimApp, 275 SW2d 120.—Crim Law 1090.1(1).

Graff v. State, TexApp–Waco, 65 SW3d 730, petition for discretionary review refused.—Controlled Subs 71; Crim Law 338(7), 369.1, 369.2(1), 374, 553, 721(1), 721(3), 742(1), 1134(2), 1144.13(1), 1144.13(2.1), 1153(1), 1159.2(2), 1159.2(7), 1159.2(9), 1169.1(1), 1169.9.

Graff v. Whittle, TexApp–Texarkana, 947 SW2d 629, reh overr, and writ den.—App & E 840(1), 923, 1024.3; Dedi 1, 2, 15, 41, 44, 45, 48; Evid 12, 177, 336(1), 343(2); High 17; Jury 33(5.15), 33(5.20); Pretrial Proc 42, 224; Trial 26.

Graffagnino v. Fibreboard Corp., CA5 (Tex), 781 F2d 1111.—Assign 24(2), 31, 32, 110.

Graffagnino v. Fibreboard Corp., CA5 (Tex), 776 F2d 1307, reh den 781 F2d 1111.—Release 34.

Graff Chevrolet Co. v. Campbell, CA5 (Tex), 343 F2d 568.—Int Rev 3102, 3103; Statut 206, 217.2.

Graff Chevrolet Co., Inc. v. Texas Motor Vehicle Bd., TexApp–Austin, 60 SW3d 154, review den.—Admin Law 790, 791; Const Law 4294; Licens 22.

Grafft v. State, TexCrimApp, 113 SW2d 546, 134 TexCrim 30.—Bail 70; Crim Law 419(4), 736(2), 772(6); Homic 805, 997, 1403.

Graff Vending Co.; Hampton v., CA5 (Tex), 516 F2d 100. —Antitrust 839; Commerce 62.13; Fed Cts 916.1, 943.1.

Graff Vending Co.; Hampton v., CA5 (Tex), 478 F2d 527, cert den 94 SCt 69, 414 US 859, 38 LEd2d 109, reh den 94 SCt 609, 414 US 1087, 38 LEd2d 493, appeal after remand 516 F2d 100.—Antitrust 814, 872, 913, 976, 977(5), 980, 995; Fed Cts 860, 947.

Grafham; O'Reilly v., TexApp–Austin, 797 SW2d 399.— App & E 930(3), 989, 1003(6); Interest 39(2.6), 60; Trover 7, 40(6).

Graford Oil Corp.; Railroad Commission v., Tex, 557 SW2d 946.—Admin Law 486, 676; Const Law 4084, 4290; Mines 92.50, 92.54, 92.59(1); Pub Ut 193.

Grafton; Southern Life & Health Ins. Co. v., TexCiv-App–Tyler, 414 SW2d 214, ref nre.—Insurance 3013, 3015.

Grafton Executive Search, LLC; Long v., NDTex, 263 FSupp2d 1085.—Const Law 3964, 3965(3); Fed Cts 76.5, 76.10, 76.25, 88, 96.

Gragg, Ex parte, TexCrimApp, 191 SW2d 32, 149 Tex-Crim 10.—Bail 43, 51.

Gragg v. Allen, TexCivApp–Waco, 481 SW2d 452, dism.— Agric 9.5; Labor & Emp 3159.

Gragg; Brown & Root, Inc. v., TexCivApp–Hous (1 Dist), 444 SW2d 656, ref nre.—App & E 882(10); Evid 536; Explos 7; Jury 136(3), 139, 149; Stip 21; Trial 105(2), 131(2), 352.12.

Gragg v. Cayuga Independent School Dist., Tex, 539 SW2d 861, appeal dism 97 SCt 478, 429 US 973, 50 LEd2d 581.—Const Law 584, 591, 596; Tax 2478, 2723.

Gragg v. Cayuga Independent School Dist., TexCivApp–Tyler, 525 SW2d 32, ref nre, and writ gr, aff 539 SW2d 861, appeal dism 97 SCt 478, 429 US 973, 50 LEd2d 581. —App & E 758.1; Evid 317(1); Schools 106.12(8); Tax 2478, 2723, 2858, 2859.

Gragg; O'Connor v., Tex, 339 SW2d 878, 161 Tex 273.— App & E 215(1); Dedi 15, 16.1, 20(1), 20(2), 20(5), 38, 41, 44.

Gragg; O'Connor v., TexCivApp–Eastland, 324 SW2d 294, writ gr, aff as reformed 339 SW2d 878, 161 Tex 273.—Dedi 1, 15, 20(1), 37, 38, 41, 44, 61.

Gragg v. State, TexCrimApp, 214 SW2d 292, 152 Tex-Crim 386.—Crim Law 338(6), 556, 781(8), 1180; Homic 839, 847, 1127; Ind & Inf 184.

Gragg v. State, TexCrimApp, 186 SW2d 243, 148 Tex-Crim 267.—Homic 839, 843, 847.

Gragg; Tarrant Regional Water Dist. v., Tex, 151 SW3d 546, reh den.—App & E 930(1), 949, 1001(1); Trial 3(5.1).

Gragg; Tarrant Regional Water Dist. v., TexApp–Waco, 43 SW3d 609, review den, and review gr, and reh of petition for review gr, and withdrawn, aff 151 SW3d 546, reh den.—App & E 949, 969, 1001(1), 1001(3), 1008.1(2); Em Dom 2(1), 2(10), 266, 300, 307(2), 307(3), 315; Evid 493, 555.2, 555.5, 557; States 191.9(3); Trial 3(1), 3(2), 3(5.1).

Gragg; Tarrant Regional Water Dist. v., TexApp–Waco, 962 SW2d 717.—App & E 482, 485(1).

Gragg; Taylor v., TexCivApp–Houston, 412 SW2d 937, ref nre.—Autos 244(12), 244(40); Trial 350.5(5).

Gragg v. Williams, TexCivApp–Fort Worth, 310 SW2d 394.—App & E 564(3), 1060.2; Autos 244(44); Damag 206(1); Plead 129(2); Trial 127.

Graham, Ex parte, EDTex, 58 FSupp 576.—Consp 43(10).

Graham, Ex parte, TexCrimApp, 853 SW2d 565.—Crim Law 1035(7); Sent & Pun 1798.

Graham, Ex parte, TexApp–Houston (14 Dist), 787 SW2d 141.—Divorce 269(13); Hab Corp 529.

Graham, Ex parte, TexCivApp–San Antonio, 226 SW2d 247.—Int Liq 70, 75(7).

Graham, In re, BkrtcySDTex, 64 BR 469.—Bankr 2762.1, 2769, 2777, 2784.3, 2793, 2796; Sec Tran 64.

Graham, In re, Tex, 971 SW2d 56.—Child S 173; Courts 198, 201, 485; Divorce 57.

Graham, In re Commitment of, TexApp–Beaumont, 117 SW3d 514, review den.—Const Law 4344; Mental H 433(2), 462.

Graham, In re Estate of, TexApp–Corpus Christi, 69 SW3d 598, reh overr.—App & E 863, 934(1); Judgm 185(2); Trusts 95; Wills 47, 50, 52(1), 55(1), 69, 72, 108, 153, 155, 158, 163(1), 166(1), 170, 289, 302(1), 440.

Graham v. Abbott, TexCivApp–Amarillo, 97 SW2d 746.— Brok 8(3).

Graham v. Adesa Texas, Inc., TexApp–Dallas, 145 SW3d 769, reh overr, and review den, and reh of petition for review den (2 pets).—App & E 931(1), 959(1), 1010.1(16); Labor & Emp 2935, 2940; Neglig 273, 1659; Plead 236(1), 236(7), 238(3), 248(12), 250.

Graham; Amwest Sur. Ins. Co. v., TexApp–San Antonio, 949 SW2d 724, reh overr, and writ den.—App & E 1223, 1231, 1232, 1234(1); Princ & S 66(1).

Graham v. Atlantic Richfield Co., TexApp–Corpus Christi, 848 SW2d 747, writ den.—App & E 852, 893(1); Civil R 1735; Neglig 213, 1036, 1037(4), 1242, 1692; Trial 168.

Graham; Aycock v., TexCivApp–San Antonio, 250 SW2d 935.—Judgm 198; Stip 14(11).

Graham; Barker v., TexApp–Beaumont, 149 SW2d 316.—Courts 475(2); Des & Dist 90(4); Judgm 475.

Graham v. Barnhart, CA5 (Tex), 122 FedAppx 104.— Social S 143.60.

Graham; Bloom v., TexApp–Fort Worth, 825 SW2d 244, writ den.—Atty & C 24; Divorce 151.

Graham v. Bowen, SDTex, 648 FSupp 298.—Const Law 2487, 2790, 2823, 2845, 3041, 3050, 3053, 3236, 3540, 4120, 4121, 4820; Fed Civ Proc 189; Pardon 43; Social S 121, 122.1.

Graham; Brock v., TexCivApp–Fort Worth, 321 SW2d 593.—App & E 1170.6, 1170.7; Witn 235.

Graham v. Caballero, TexCivApp–El Paso, 243 SW2d 286, ref nre.—App & E 161; Estop 92(1); Waters 183.5.

Graham; Cherry Springs Ranch Inv., Ltd. v., TexCiv-App–Waco, 599 SW2d 355, ref nre.—Damag 188(1); Neglig 1710.

Graham; Ciccarello v., CA5 (Tex), 296 F2d 858.—Fed Cts 844, 857.

Graham v. Ciccarello, SDTex, 191 FSupp 147, aff 296 F2d 858.—Autos 244(36.1); Damag 132(1).

Graham; City of Beaumont v., Tex, 441 SW2d 829.—App & E 758.3(9), 1095, 1122(2), 1170.6; Indem 33(5); Mun Corp 742(4), 742(5), 751(1); Neglig 1037(4), 1076, 1077; Trial 62(1), 365.1(6); Work Comp 2145.

Graham; City of Beaumont v., TexCivApp–Beaumont, 423 SW2d 105, writ gr, aff 441 SW2d 829.—App & E 878(7), 930(3), 989, 1060.1(2.1); Death 9(4); Mun Corp 375, 742(5), 857; Neglig 1018, 1037(4); Trial 121(1).

Graham v. City of Lakewood Village, TexApp–Fort Worth, 796 SW2d 800, writ den.—Costs 194.40; Mun Corp 712(7); Waters 203(1).

Graham v. Cockshutt Farm Equipment, Inc., CA5 (Tex), 256 F2d 358.—Pat 243(1), 245(1), 245(2), 324.5, 327(1).

Graham v. Cole, CA5 (Tex), 483 F2d 255.—Fed Cts 660.10.

Graham v. Collins, USTex, 113 SCt 892, 506 US 461, 122 LEd2d 260, reh den 113 SCt 1406, 507 US 968, 122 LEd2d 778.—Courts 100(1); Hab Corp 461, 508; Sent & Pun 1617, 1665, 1702.

Graham v. Collins, CA5 (Tex), 950 F2d 1009, cert gr 112 SCt 2937, 504 US 972, 119 LEd2d 563, aff 113 SCt 892, 506 US 461, 122 LEd2d 260, reh den 113 SCt 1406, 507 US 968, 122 LEd2d 778.—Const Law 250.2(4), 3105, 3295, 3309, 3310, 3832, 3833, 4574, 4742, 4760; Crim Law 641.13(7); Gr Jury 2.5; Hab Corp 718, 773, 818; Jury 33(2.15); Searches 12; Sent & Pun 1624, 1625, 1643, 1670, 1714, 1716, 1717, 1720, 1784(4).

Graham v. Collins, CA5 (Tex), 896 F2d 893, reh en banc gr 903 F2d 1014, opinion superseded on reh by 950 F2d 1009, cert gr 112 SCt 2937, 504 US 972, 119 LEd2d 563, aff 113 SCt 892, 506 US 461, 122 LEd2d 260, reh den 113 SCt 1406, 507 US 968, 122 LEd2d 778.

Graham v. Collins, SDTex, 829 FSupp 204, vac 94 F3d 958.—Crim Law 641.13(1), 641.13(6); Hab Corp 462, 742, 768, 769, 897, 898(2).

Graham; Cramer v., TexCivApp–San Antonio, 264 SW2d 135, writ refused.—Domicile 1; Elections 60, 72; Schools 38.

Graham v. Dallas Railway & Terminal Co., TexCivApp–Dallas, 165 SW2d 1002, writ refused.—Carr 347, 349; Trial 352.1(6), 358.

Graham; Dallas Ry. & Terminal Co. v., TexCivApp–Dallas, 185 SW2d 180.—App & E 927(7), 996, 1097(4); Carr 344, 347; Trial 350.7(2), 351.5(2), 351.5(7).

Graham v. Darnell, TexCivApp–Fort Worth, 538 SW2d 690.—App & E 758.2, 846(5), 989; Wills 38(1), 52(1), 55(3), 361, 384, 386; Witn 181.

Graham v. Dean, Tex, 188 SW2d 372, 144 Tex 61.—App & E 861; Autos 107(1); Contracts 139.

Graham v. Dean, TexCivApp–Amarillo, 186 SW2d 692, certified question answered 188 SW2d 372, 144 Tex 61.—Autos 104, 107(1); Bailm 3, 14(1), 27, 31(3); Carr 7.

Graham; Dill v., TexCivApp–Amarillo, 530 SW2d 157, ref nre.—Land & Ten 326(1), 326(2), 326(5), 328(1), 328(3), 328(4), 330(1), 331(6), 332; Stip 14(12); Trover 4, 11.

Graham v. Fashing, TexApp–El Paso, 928 SW2d 567.—Mand 53; Motions 7; New Tr 118.

Graham; F.D.I.C. v., TexApp–Houston (14 Dist), 882 SW2d 890.—Banks 74, 505, 508; Contracts 93(1), 312(3), 322(1); Costs 194.32; Guar 47.

Graham v. Federal Deposit Ins. Corp., TexCivApp–Amarillo, 470 SW2d 453.—Bills & N 527(1); Judgm 199(3.2), 199(3.10), 199(3.14).

Graham v. Federal Tender Board No. 1, CCA5 (Tex), 118 F2d 8.—Mines 92.5(3); Witn 1.

Graham v. Fed-X, Inc., TexCivApp–Fort Worth, 384 SW2d 785, ref nre.—Neglig 1550, 1579, 1614, 1625, 1696, 1708.

Graham; First Nat. Bank v., TexCtApp, 22 SW 1102.—Garn 175.

Graham; First Nat. Bank v., TexCtApp, 22 SW 1101.—Afft 11.

Graham; First Permian, L.L.C. v., TexApp–Amarillo, 212 SW3d 368, review den.—Covenants 30, 53, 71, 77.1; Mines 74(3).

Graham v. Ford Motor Co., TexApp–Tyler, 721 SW2d 554.—Const Law 2503(2); Courts 472.2; Parent & C 7.5.

Graham; Foreman v., TexApp–Fort Worth, 693 SW2d 774, ref nre.—App & E 846(5), 852; Frds St of 158(4); Interpl 33, 34, 35; Ven & Pur 315(3).

Graham; Foreman v., TexCivApp–Beaumont, 363 SW2d 371.—Lim of Act 66(2), 66(12), 66(15), 199(1).

Graham v. Franco, Tex, 488 SW2d 390.—Autos 227.5; Hus & W 247, 260; Neglig 575.

Graham; Franco v., TexCivApp–Corpus Christi, 470 SW2d 429, writ gr, aff as reformed 488 SW2d 390.—App & E 882(8), 1170.7, 1170.10; Autos 227.5, 243(5), 244(45), 244(58); Damag 185(1); Evid 188, 194, 215(1), 272; Hus & W 260, 270(3); Trial 139.1(3), 140(1), 142, 143; Witn 275(3), 405(2).

Graham v. Freese & Nichols, Inc., TexApp–Eastland, 927 SW2d 294, reh overr, and writ den.—App & E 863, 934(1); Judgm 185(2); Neglig 1011, 1205(5), 1692.

Graham; Friske v., TexCivApp–San Antonio, 128 SW2d 139.—Autos 245(91), 247; Courts 207.4(2); Judgm 199(5), 256(1); Mand 51, 172; Neglig 530(1); Trial 358.

Graham v. Gatewood, TexCivApp–Amarillo, 166 SW2d 768, writ refused wom.—App & E 882(12), 1062.1; Neglig 1694, 1717; Trial 352.1(1), 352.4(7), 352.18, 352.19.

Graham v. Graham, TexApp–Texarkana, 836 SW2d 308.—Hus & W 250, 265, 266.4, 268(1), 270(8).

Graham; Graham v., TexApp–Texarkana, 836 SW2d 308.—Hus & W 250, 265, 266.4, 268(1), 270(8).

Graham v. Graham, TexApp–Amarillo, 733 SW2d 374, ref nre.—Const Law 3974, 4089; Courts 39, 198; Ex & Ad 513(3); Judgm 346, 349, 392(5), 475, 485, 497(1); Proc 48.

Graham; Graham v., TexApp–Amarillo, 733 SW2d 374, ref nre.—Const Law 3974, 4089; Courts 39, 198; Ex & Ad 513(3); Judgm 346, 349, 392(5), 475, 485, 497(1); Proc 48.

Graham v. Graham, TexCivApp–Amarillo, 331 SW2d 499, ref nre.—Divorce 252.3(2), 313.1; Hus & W 278(1); Judgm 181(19).

Graham; Graham v., TexCivApp–Amarillo, 331 SW2d 499, ref nre.—Divorce 252.3(2), 313.1; Hus & W 278(1); Judgm 181(19).

Graham v. Graham, TexCivApp–Waco, 584 SW2d 938.—App & E 931(6); Child C 7, 27, 76, 120, 413, 467, 921(1); Divorce 151.

Graham; Graham v., TexCivApp–Waco, 584 SW2d 938.—App & E 931(6); Child C 7, 27, 76, 120, 413, 467, 921(1); Divorce 151.

Graham; Hawkins v., TexCivApp–San Antonio, 81 SW2d 754, writ refused.—Execution 171(4).

Graham v. Henegar, CA5 (Tex), 640 F2d 732, 24 Wage & Hour Cas (BNA) 1294, reh den 646 F2d 566.—Fed Cts 974.1, 979, 1139.

Graham v. Hill, WDTex, 444 FSupp 584.—Const Law 42(1), 42.2(1), 795, 990, 1016, 1497, 1520, 2190, 2225, 2249, 2250; Courts 97(6), 508(1), 508(7); Decl Judgm 64, 124.1; Fed Cts 12.1, 31; Obscen 2.1, 2.5, 15.

Graham; Hines v., NDTex, 320 FSupp2d 511.—Civil R 1036, 1090, 1098, 1358, 1376(7), 1395(7), 1463; Const Law 1422, 3823, 3825, 4824; Fed Civ Proc 41, 1700, 2734; Prisons 4(5), 13(6).

Graham v. Hollandsworth Drilling Co., TexCivApp–Texarkana, 169 SW2d 1001, writ refused wom.—App & E 989; Evid 236(6); Home 133; Trial 140(1).

Graham v. Houston Independent School Dist., SDTex, 335 FSupp 1164.—Civil R 1395(2); Const Law 1976, 1978, 4209(3); Fed Civ Proc 1826; Schools 169.

Graham v. Howard, TexCivApp–Galveston, 249 SW2d 639.—App & E 999(1); Hus & W 21, 24; Princ & A 14(2).

Graham v. Hubbard, TexCivApp–Beaumont, 406 SW2d 747.—Tresp to T T 38(2); Ven & Pur 228(3).

Graham v. Huff, TexCivApp–Dallas, 384 SW2d 904.—Contracts 245(1), 245(2); Evid 384; Frds St of 112; Mines 79.1(5); Venue 5.3(8), 22(4), 26, 41.

Graham v. Hutchinson County Appraisal Review Bd., TexApp–Amarillo, 776 SW2d 592, writ den.—Const Law 4137; Tax 2641, 2693, 2703.

Graham; International Ass'n of Heat and Frost Insulators v., TexCivApp–Eastland, 544 SW2d 519, ref nre.—App & E 931(6), 989; Labor & Emp 543, 636.

Graham; International Longshoremen's Ass'n v., TexCivApp–Beaumont, 175 SW2d 255.—Consp 19; Labor & Emp 1006, 1050.

Graham; Jeoffroy Mfg. v., CA5 (Tex), 219 F2d 511, cert den 76 SCt 55, 350 US 826, 100 LEd 738, reh den 76 SCt 176, 350 US 905, 100 LEd 794, and 87 SCt 10, 385 US 889, 17 LEd2d 122.—Pat 32, 72(5), 112.1, 324.55(4).

Graham v. Jeoffroy Mfg., Inc., CA5 (Tex), 253 F2d 72, cert den 79 SCt 28, 358 US 817, 3 LEd2d 59, reh den 79 SCt 117, 358 US 890, 3 LEd2d 118.—Pat 318(4.1), 318(6), 319(1), 319(3), 324.54, 324.55(2), 324.60, 325.11(3).

Graham; Jeoffroy Mfg., Inc. v., CA5 (Tex), 206 F2d 772, cert den 74 SCt 515, 347 US 920, 98 LEd 1075, reh den 74 SCt 626, 347 US 940, 98 LEd 1089.—Pat 66(1.5), 118.12(2), 286, 324.55(5).

Graham v. Jeoffroy Mfg., Inc., CA5 (Tex), 206 F2d 769.—Pat 16(1), 16.14, 26(1.5), 66(1.19), 112.1.

See Guidelines for Arrangement at the beginning of this Volume

Graham v. Johnson, CA5 (Tex), 168 F3d 762, cert den 120 SCt 1830, 529 US 1097, 146 LEd2d 774.—Const Law 186, 191, 4489; Crim Law 1404; Fed Cts 542, 571, 584; Hab Corp 205, 320, 401, 679, 814, 894.1, 898(1), 900.1; Lim of Act 130(5); Sent & Pun 1468, 1520; Statut 263.

Graham v. Johnson, CA5 (Tex), 94 F3d 958.—Hab Corp 320, 351, 382, 408, 421.

Graham v. Johnson, SDTex, 45 FSupp2d 555, aff 168 F3d 762, cert den 120 SCt 1830, 529 US 1097, 146 LEd2d 774.—Hab Corp 894.1.

Graham; Joseph Thomas, Inc. v., TexApp–Tyler, 842 SW2d 343.—App & E 854(5), 927(7); Guar 1, 4, 27, 42(1), 72; Indem 25; Lim of Act 46(10), 56(2); Trial 139.1(17).

Graham; King v., Tex, 126 SW3d 75, reh den.—Mal Pros 3.

Graham; King v., TexApp–San Antonio, 47 SW3d 595, review gr, rev 126 SW3d 75, reh den.—App & E 866(3), 927(7), 930(1), 994(1), 1001(1), 1002, 1003(7), 1004(8); Corp 336; Damag 49.10, 192; Mal Pros 0.5, 3, 18(2), 18(4), 18(6), 19, 20, 27, 31, 32, 38, 56, 64(1), 64(2), 69, 71(2); Partners 217(3).

Graham v. Kuzmich, TexApp–Corpus Christi, 876 SW2d 446, reh overr.—Costs 194.40, 198, 207; Deeds 120, 140, 143; Mtg 138; Waters 156.5.

Graham; Lamar v., TexCivApp–Waco, 598 SW2d 727, writ gr, ref nre 639 SW2d 303.—Lim of Act 95(12).

Graham v. Letot, TexCivApp–Dallas, 103 SW2d 1031, writ dism.—Lim of Act 167(1); Mun Corp 519(6), 565; Tresp to T T 16, 47(3).

Graham; Liberty Mut. Ins. Co. v., CA5 (Tex), 473 F3d 596.—Courts 90(2); Fed Civ Proc 2501; Fed Cts 776; Insurance 2663, 2914, 2915.

Graham; Liberty Mut. Ins. Co. v., NDTex, 407 FSupp2d 808, rev in part 473 F3d 596.—Insurance 2667, 2914, 2915.

Graham; Longoria v., TexApp–Houston (14 Dist), 44 SW3d 671.—App & E 863, 934(1), 1010.2; Judgm 181(33).

Graham v. Lynaugh, CA5 (Tex), 854 F2d 715, cert gr, vac 109 SCt 3237, 492 US 915, 106 LEd2d 585, on remand 896 F2d 893, reh en banc gr 903 F2d 1014, opinion superseded on reh by 950 F2d 1009, cert gr 112 SCt 2937, 504 US 972, 119 LEd2d 563, aff 113 SCt 892, 506 US 461, 122 LEd2d 260, reh den 113 SCt 1406, 507 US 968, 122 LEd2d 778, opinion reinstated 950 F2d 1009, cert gr 112 SCt 2937, 504 US 972, 119 LEd2d 563, aff 113 SCt 892, 506 US 461, 122 LEd2d 260, reh den 113 SCt 1406, 507 US 968, 122 LEd2d 778.—Const Law 250.2(1), 250.2(4), 3105, 3295, 3309, 3310, 3832, 3833, 4574, 4742, 4759, 4760; Crim Law 641.13(7); Gr Jury 2.5; Hab Corp 773, 818; Jury 33(2.15); Sent & Pun 1624, 1625, 1643, 1793.

Graham v. McCord, TexCivApp–San Antonio, 384 SW2d 897.—Autos 190; Hus & W 19(13), 21, 232.1; Princ & A 159(1).

Graham v. Mary Kay Inc., TexApp–Houston (14 Dist), 25 SW3d 749, review den.—Antitrust 882, 904, 905(2); Consp 2, 3, 4; Inj 9, 14, 16, 34; Libel 33, 74; Mal Pros 15, 56; Proc 168; Torts 212, 214, 242, 262, 263; Trademarks 1032, 1420, 1429(1).

Graham v. Metropolitan Bldg. & Loan Ass'n, TexCivApp–Fort Worth, 98 SW2d 429, writ dism.—B & L Assoc 44; Const Law 2671.

Graham; Metropolitan Transit Authority Harris County, Texas v., TexApp–Houston (14 Dist), 105 SW3d 754, review den, and reh of petition for review den.—Action 13; Em Dom 45, 166, 167(4), 180, 184; Ten in C 44.

Graham; Metzler v., CA5 (Tex), 112 F3d 207, 155 ALR Fed 689.—Fed Cts 776, 843, 850.1; Labor & Emp 486, 488, 490, 654.

Graham v. Morris, TexCivApp–Amarillo, 366 SW2d 792.—App & E 1032(1), 1060.1(8), 1064.1(9), 1140(4); Autos

11, 172(2), 247; Damag 127, 131(4), 135; Neglig 293; Trial 194(15), 350.6(3), 352.10.

Graham v. New Mexico Eastern Gas Co., TexCivApp–Dallas, 141 SW2d 389.—Corp 182.4(1), 182.4(5), 439, 590(2), 591, 610(2), 665(3).

Graham v. Oak Park Mobile Homes, Inc., TexCivApp–Corpus Christi, 546 SW2d 394.—App & E 934(1), 1024.4; Evid 544, 555.5, 571(9); Neglig 1612, 1617; Prod Liab 83.

Graham v. Ozuna, TexCivApp–Galveston, 275 SW2d 735. —Courts 247(2); Venue 22(1), 46.

Graham v. Pazos De La Torre, TexApp–Corpus Christi, 821 SW2d 162, writ den.—App & E 650, 654, 854(2), 1008.1(2); Bankr 2395, 2397(2), 2421, 2462; Princ & A 131, 159(2); Ven & Pur 288, 292.

Graham; Petro Bank, N.A. v., BkrtcySDTex, 64 BR 469. See Graham, In re.

Graham v. Pirkey, TexApp–Austin, 212 SW3d 507.—Judgm 181(7); Lim of Act 32(1), 55(5), 55(7), 95(7), 199(1); Nuis 1, 46; Waters 123.

Graham; Roddy v., TexCivApp–Eastland, 390 SW2d 853, ref nre.—Wills 82, 166(7).

Graham; Roseberry v., TexCivApp–San Antonio, 134 SW2d 702.—App & E 773(4).

Graham; St. Elizabeth Hosp. v., TexApp–Beaumont, 883 SW2d 433, reh overr, writ den.—App & E 970(2), 999(1); Damag 181; Health 820, 823(4), 832; Pretrial Proc 719; Trial 3(5.1), 26, 89.

Graham; Samples v., TexApp–Corpus Christi, 76 SW2d 615.—Damag 15; Interest 3, 39(2.50), 56; Statut 181(1), 181(2), 184, 190, 217.2.

Graham v. San Antonio Mach. & Supply Corp., TexCivApp–San Antonio, 418 SW2d 303, ref nre.—Acct St 6(2); Assign 110; Contracts 227; Estop 52.10(1), 56; Evid 213(1); Insurance 3197, 3198(2); Judgm 101(1), 101(2), 153(1); Mun Corp 347(1), 348, 376; Princ & S 73, 139, 183, 190(2), 190(10); Pub Contr 24.1, 50, 58, 59, 65, 66; Sales 357(1).

Graham; Scott v., Tex, 292 SW2d 324, 156 Tex 97.—Counties 57, 69, 196(4), 196(6), 196(7), 218; Dist & Pros Attys 3(5); Inj 135; Judgm 521; Parties 18, 29.

Graham; Scott v., TexCivApp–San Antonio, 283 SW2d 443, aff 292 SW2d 324, 156 Tex 97.—App & E 954(2); Counties 204(1), 206(1); Inj 138.66.

Graham v. Seale, TexCivApp–San Antonio, 221 SW2d 353.—Divorce 139, 146, 162, 168; Judgm 524.

Graham; Smith v., TexApp–Texarkana, 705 SW2d 705, ref nre.—Deeds 90, 93; Evid 448; Mines 55(5).

Graham v. Smith, TexCivApp–El Paso, 504 SW2d 567.—Trial 350.6(1).

Graham v. State, TexCrimApp, 19 SW3d 851, on remand 2000 WL 1678038, petition for discretionary review refused.—Crim Law 620(1), 620(3.1), 620(6); Ind & Inf 128, 130.

Graham v. State, TexCrimApp, 994 SW2d 651, cert den 120 SCt 420, 528 US 974, 145 LEd2d 328.—Crim Law 42, 412.1(1).

Graham v. State, TexCrimApp, 710 SW2d 588.—Autos 422.1; Const Law 4537; Crim Law 478(1), 1036.6, 1169.1(1), 1169.9.

Graham v. State, TexCrimApp, 657 SW2d 99.—Autos 355(13); Crim Law 698(1); Homic 834; Ind & Inf 71.4(1), 133(7), 189(8).

Graham v. State, TexCrimApp, 643 SW2d 920.—Crim Law 366(6), 421(6), 511.2, 511.5, 1134(3), 1166.17, 1169.1(9); Homic 1080(4); Jury 108.

Graham v. State, TexCrimApp, 620 SW2d 133.—Obscen 20.

Graham v. State, TexCrimApp, 566 SW2d 941.—Crim Law 46, 48, 331, 351(9), 351(10), 354, 494, 570(1), 570(2), 740, 1045, 1086.10; Jury 131(1), 131(4).

Graham v. State, TexCrimApp, 546 SW2d 605.—Const Law 2816; Controlled Subs 62; Crim Law 706(4),

GRAHAM

59 Tex D 2d—332

1043(3), 1045, 1170.5(1), 1170.5(6), 1203.26; Ind & Inf 71.4(7); Sent & Pun 1218; Witn 345(7).

Graham v. State, TexCrimApp, 502 SW2d 809.—Const Law 4733(2); Sent & Pun 1918, 2011.

Graham v. State, TexCrimApp, 498 SW2d 197.—Crim Law 264, 273.1(4), 1083, 1126.

Graham v. State, TexCrimApp, 487 SW2d 359.—Burg 29, 41(1); Crim Law 1086.14, 1090.8.

Graham v. State, TexCrimApp, 486 SW2d 92.—Crim Law 363, 412(1), 412.2(2), 627.7(3), 627.9(1), 829(21), 1036.2, 1037.1(1), 1166(10.10).

Graham v. State, TexCrimApp, 466 SW2d 587.—Crim Law 273.4(2).

Graham v. State, TexCrimApp, 422 SW2d 922.—Const Law 266(3.4), 4658(2), 4669; Crim Law 304(2), 339.11(8), 369.2(8), 726, 728(4), 730(5), 857(1), 864; Sent & Pun 1379(2).

Graham v. State, TexCrimApp, 387 SW2d 385.—Homic 1154.

Graham v. State, TexCrimApp, 387 SW2d 50.—Burg 41(1).

Graham v. State, TexCrimApp, 296 SW2d 543.—Crim Law 1090.1(1).

Graham v. State, TexCrimApp, 290 SW2d 906.—Crim Law 1090.1(1).

Graham v. State, TexCrimApp, 290 SW2d 904.—Crim Law 1090.1(1).

Graham v. State, TexCrimApp, 260 SW2d 887, 159 TexCrim 52.—Sent & Pun 1260.

Graham v. State, TexCrimApp, 184 SW2d 283.—Crim Law 1094(3).

Graham v. State, TexCrimApp, 139 SW2d 269, 139 TexCrim 98.—Ind & Inf 62, 70, 73(1); Perj 25(6).

Graham v. State, TexCrimApp, 136 SW2d 830, 138 TexCrim 449.—Crim Law 912.5, 956(1), 956(4), 959; Ind & Inf 11.1; Jury 21.1.

Graham v. State, TexCrimApp, 125 SW2d 562, 136 TexCrim 409.—Crim Law 93.

Graham v. State, TexCrimApp, 113 SW2d 185.—Crim Law 1182.

Graham v. State, TexApp–Fort Worth, 3 SW3d 272, petition for discretionary review refused, habeas corpus den 2003 WL 23469336.—Crim Law 412.2(2), 417(15), 662.8, 730(8), 781(2), 1036.4, 1036.5, 1037.1(2), 1130(5), 1158(4).

Graham v. State, TexApp–Fort Worth, 631 SW2d 597.—Crim Law 1090.8, 1120(3), 1170(2), 1170.5(1); Witn 367(1).

Graham v. State, TexApp–Fort Worth, 624 SW2d 785.—Costs 302.1(1); Crim Law 641.12(1), 656(9), 1059(1).

Graham v. State, TexApp–Dallas, 893 SW2d 4.—Arrest 63.5(1), 63.5(2), 63.5(8), 63.5(9); Autos 349(2.1), 349(16), 349.5(10); Crim Law 394.4(9), 394.6(5), 1158(4), 1169.1(8); Searches 47.1.

Graham v. State, TexApp–Dallas, 665 SW2d 832, petition for discretionary review gr, rev 710 SW2d 588.—Autos 355(6), 415; Const Law 257.5, 4594(7); Crim Law 1037.1(3).

Graham v. State, TexApp–Texarkana, 96 SW3d 658, petition for discretionary review refused.—Arson 37(1); Crim Law 633(1), 1036.1(5), 1144.15, 1166.7, 1174(5).

Graham v. State, TexApp–Amarillo, 767 SW2d 271.—Crim Law 1136; Obscen 2.5.

Graham v. State, TexApp–Beaumont, 964 SW2d 738, petition for discretionary review gr, aff 994 SW2d 651, cert den 120 SCt 420, 528 US 974, 145 LEd2d 328.—Crim Law 42, 330, 394.1(3), 412.1(4), 1144.12, 1153(1).

Graham v. State, TexApp–Beaumont, 950 SW2d 724, petition for discretionary review gr, petition for discretionary review dism per curiam opinion 991 SW2d 802, opinion withdrawn 976 SW2d 913.—Assault 56, 96(7); Crim Law 553, 795(1.5), 795(2.1), 795(2.10), 795(2.50), 795(3), 800(1), 814(20), 1134(2), 1144.13(3), 1159.2(1), 1159.2(2), 1159.2(7), 1172.8; Homic 558, 908, 1168.

Graham v. State, TexApp–Waco, 649 SW2d 719.—Crim Law 1181(1).

Graham v. State, TexApp–Eastland, 873 SW2d 709.—Crim Law 273.1(4); Sent & Pun 2073.

Graham v. State, TexApp–Corpus Christi, 769 SW2d 594.—Crim Law 632(5); Jury 24, 25(3), 25(8).

Graham v. State, TexApp–Houston (14 Dist), 201 SW3d 323, petition for discretionary review refused.—Controlled Subs 9, 27, 29, 67, 80; Crim Law 394.4(1), 394.6(5), 1139, 1144.1, 1153(1), 1158(4); Searches 24, 171, 180, 183, 194, 198.

Graham v. State, TexApp–Houston (14 Dist), 693 SW2d 29.—Crim Law 1184(1), 1184(4.1); Forg 7(1), 12(1).

Graham; Terrell v., Tex, 576 SW2d 610.—Deeds 5, 93, 99, 108, 120, 129(1); Estates 1; Wills 88(2).

Graham; Terrell v., TexCivApp–Eastland, 569 SW2d 595, rev 576 SW2d 610.—Deeds 5, 120; Estates 1; Ex & Ad 55; Wills 88(2).

Graham v. Texas Bd. of Pardons and Paroles, TexApp–Austin, 913 SW2d 745, reh overr, and writ dism woj.—Const Law 251, 617, 1050, 2311, 2312, 2325, 3847, 4489, 4837; Pardon 21, 25.

Graham; Texas Bd. of Pardons and Paroles v., TexApp–Austin, 878 SW2d 684.—App & E 460(1), 811, 954(1); Courts 27, 480(1).

Graham; Texas Co. v., TexCivApp–Eastland, 107 SW2d 403.—App & E 747(2), 909(1), 1241, 1245.

Graham v. Texas Gulf Sulphur Co., CA5 (Tex), 457 F2d 418.—Contracts 108(2), 143(4), 164, 187(1); Fed Civ Proc 2744; Mines 54(2); Trusts 20, 171.

Graham v. Thomas D. Murphy Co., TexCivApp–Amarillo, 497 SW2d 639, ref nre.—App & E 460(2); Execution 75, 209.

Graham v. Thomas D. Murphy Co., TexCivApp–Eastland, 474 SW2d 251, ref nre.—App & E 846(5); Corp 523; Execution 194(3).

Graham; Thomas, Inc. v., TexApp–Tyler, 842 SW2d 343. See Joseph Thomas, Inc. v. Graham.

Graham; Thompson v., TexCivApp–Eastland, 333 SW2d 663, ref nre.—App & E 230; Cust & U 15(1), 16; Neglig 219, 221, 1141, 1631; Trial 350.6(2), 365.1(6).

Graham; Thompson v., TexCivApp–Eastland, 318 SW2d 102, ref nre.—Evid 209, 450(2); Stip 13, 14(10); Work Comp 2216.

Graham v. Three or More Members of the Six Member Army Reserve General Officer Selection Bd. of 30 November 1979, SDTex, 556 FSupp 669.—Armed S 7, 33; Atty & C 62; Const Law 4173(1), 4242, 4246; Fed Civ Proc 1685.

Graham v. Truck Equipment Co. of Amarillo, Inc., TexCivApp–Amarillo, 413 SW2d 778.—Judgm 145(2), 145(3), 145(4), 153(1).

Graham; Tucker v., TexApp–Eastland, 878 SW2d 681.—Decl Judgm 45; Waters 177(1).

Graham v. Turcotte, TexApp–Corpus Christi, 628 SW2d 182.—Atty & C 26; Bills & N 534; Contracts 185.1.

Graham v. Turner, TexCivApp–Waco, 472 SW2d 831.—App & E 719(8), 1062.1; Corp 619; Damag 89(1), 89(2), 90; Lim of Act 39(11), 58(4); Trial 352.5(1), 352.12; Trover 2; Trusts 95, 107.

Graham v. Tyler County, TexApp–Beaumont, 983 SW2d 882, appeal after new trial 2001 WL 845345, review den.—App & E 946, 969; Autos 258, 273, 279, 308(4), 309(3); Trial 295(1).

Graham; U.S. v., CA5 (Tex), 858 F2d 986, reh den, cert den 109 SCt 1140, 489 US 1020, 103 LEd2d 201.—Consp 47(12); Controlled Subs 82; Crim Law 778(6); Witn 268(8).

Graham v. U.S., NDTex, 441 FSupp 741.—U S 78(9), 78(14); Ven & Pur 37(1), 37(5).

Graham; U.S. v., SDTex, 471 FSupp 123.—Health 556(3); Lim of Act 43, 58(1).

GRAMM

Graham; Verlander Enterprises, Inc. v., TexApp–El Paso, 932 SW2d 259.—App & E 5, 914(1); Corp 507(13); Proc 1, 48, 133, 153.

Graham; Village Inn v., TexApp–El Paso, 932 SW2d 259. See Verlander Enterprises, Inc. v. Graham.

Graham v. Villareal, TexCivApp–San Antonio, 242 SW2d 258.—Elections 117, 177, 289, 295(1); Estop 83(1).

Graham; Zurich Ins. Co. v., TexCivApp–Waco, 335 SW2d 673, ref nre.—Work Comp 52, 1653.

Graham & Associates, Inc.; Zoning Bd. of Adjustment of City of Lubbock v., TexApp–Amarillo, 664 SW2d 430.—App & E 23, 79(1), 80(1), 80(6), 984(1); Const Law 2470, 2540; Costs 12, 32(2); Courts 37(1); Inj 74, 132, 157, 189, 201; Judgm 27; Mun Corp 621; Zoning 378.1, 442, 584.1, 721, 729.

Graham & Locke Investments, Inc. v. Madison, TexCivApp–Dallas, 295 SW2d 234, ref nre.—App & E 747(1); Bills & N 348, 349, 351; Mtg 8, 24, 335, 369(2), 369(3), 369(7); Usury 16, 26, 52, 57, 76, 97, 113.

Graham-Brown Shoe Co. v. Snodgrass, TexCivApp–Austin, 257 SW 632, writ dism woj.—App & E 742(6), 1056(3), 1067; Bankr 168, 303(2); Depositions 83(2), 107(1); Evid 241(1), 489, 543(4); Plead 12; Trial 260(5); Witn 392(1).

Graham, City of; Blythe v., TexCivApp–Fort Worth, 327 SW2d 800, ref nre.—Inj 89(3).

Graham, City of; Blythe v., TexCivApp–Fort Worth, 303 SW2d 881.—Action 43.1; Decl Judgm 6, 296, 389; Parties 14; Zoning 471.5.

Graham, City of; Blythe v., TexCivApp–Fort Worth, 287 SW2d 527, ref nre.—Evid 330; Mun Corp 42.

Graham, City of; Brazos River Authority v., Tex, 354 SW2d 99, 163 Tex 167.—App & E 761; Const Law 2470; Em Dom 2(10), 266, 293(4), 295, 302; Estop 62.1; Lim of Act 11(2), 11(3), 16, 32(2); Mun Corp 230, 247; Statut 217.2; Trial 194(20).

Graham, City of; Brazos River Authority v., TexCivApp–Fort Worth, 335 SW2d 247, ref nre, and writ gr, aff in part, rev in part 354 SW2d 99, 163 Tex 167.—Damag 62(3), 155, 157(2); Em Dom 2(10), 69; Lim of Act 55(7), 58(3); Mun Corp 85; Trial 186, 194(20); Waters 171(1), 178(2).

Graham Const. Co. v. Robert H. Pyle, Inc., TexCivApp–Corpus Christi, 422 SW2d 485, ref nre.—App & E 1170.1, 1170.3, 1170.10; Contracts 234, 320, 322(1); Princ & S 139, 166; Trial 395(5).

Graham Const. Co. v. Walker Process Equipment, Inc., TexCivApp–Corpus Christi, 422 SW2d 478, ref nre.—Contracts 40, 143(2), 143(3), 294, 320, 322(1); Princ & S 86, 161, 166.

Graham General Hospital; Qualls v., TexCivApp–Fort Worth, 535 SW2d 932.—App & E 975, 989, 1177(7); Evid 570; Health 674, 821(5), 823(7); New Tr 44(3); Trial 140(1), 143.

Graham Holding Co., Inc.; King v., TexApp–Houston (14 Dist), 762 SW2d 296.—Action 27(1); App & E 200, 761, 766, 1078(1); Damag 89(2); Fraud 3, 58(3), 58(4); Judgm 184.

Graham Homes, Inc. v. Bowyer Real Estate, TexCivApp–Fort Worth, 619 SW2d 25.—Venue 7.5(8).

Graham Ice Cream Co.; Quesada v., TexCivApp–Austin, 207 SW2d 120.—App & E 1048(7); Witn 345(1), 372(2), 374(1).

Graham Independent School Dist.; Kristi W. by G. Russell W. v., NDTex, 663 FSupp 86.—Admin Law 512; Schools 155.5(5).

Graham Independent School Dist.; W., Kristi, by G. Russell W. v., NDTex, 663 FSupp 86. See Kristi W. by G. Russell W. v. Graham Independent School Dist.

Graham Land and Cattle Co. v. Independent Bankers Bank, TexApp–Corpus Christi, 205 SW3d 21.—App & E 179(1), 863; Judgm 181(33), 183; Labor & Emp 3074; Libel 130, 135; Lim of Act 55(1), 95(6).

Graham Magnetics Inc. v. Region, TexCivApp–Fort Worth, 471 SW2d 600.—Ref of Inst 19(2); Ven & Pur 70.

Graham Memorial Auditorium Ass'n, Inc.; Savoy v., TexCivApp–Fort Worth, 329 SW2d 352.—Const Law 1328, 1430, 1780; Judgm 178, 183, 185(1), 185.2(9), 185.3(11).

Graham Mill & Elevator Co. v. Johnson, TexCivApp–Eastland, 130 SW2d 340.—Plead 111.6; Venue 7.5(7), 22(7).

Graham Nat. Bank v. Frogge, TexCivApp–Fort Worth, 150 SW2d 429.—Banks 174, 175(3).

Graham Production Co.; Standley v., CCA5 (Tex), 83 F2d 489, cert den 57 SCt 115, 299 US 593, 81 LEd 437.—Bankr 3067.1, 3081; Evid 71; Mines 74(3).

Graham Sav. and Loan Ass'n, F.A. v. Blair, TexApp–Eastland, 986 SW2d 727.—App & E 1192.

Graham Wholesale Floral, Inc.; Winandy Greenhouse Const., Inc. v., TexCivApp–Fort Worth, 456 SW2d 470.—App & E 1060.2; Contracts 322(4); Damag 123, 140; Evid 318(2); Interest 39(2.6), 39(3); Trial 110, 350.4(1), 350.5(1), 350.6(1).

Grain Dealers Mut. Ins. Co. v. McKee, Tex, 943 SW2d 455.—Contracts 143(2); Corp 1.3, 1.4(4); Insurance 1806, 1807, 1810, 1816, 1832(1), 2660, 2661.

Grain Dealers Mut. Ins. Co. v. McKee, TexApp–San Antonio, 911 SW2d 775, reh overr, and writ gr, rev 943 SW2d 455.—App & E 852, 854(1), 863; Contracts 143(2), 176(2); Costs 199; Courts 95(1); Evid 200, 242(8); Insurance 1806, 1808, 1831, 1832(1), 1832(2), 1835(2), 1836, 1850, 2660, 2661, 3360; Judgm 181(14), 185(2), 185(4), 186.

Grain Dealers Mut. Ins. Co.; Moore v., TexCivApp–Hous (1 Dist), 450 SW2d 954.—Guar 1; Insurance 2694; Judgm 185.3(12).

Grainger v. Western Cas. Life Ins. Co., TexApp–Houston (1 Dist), 930 SW2d 609, reh overr, and writ den.—Antitrust 132; App & E 223, 870(2), 1175(1); Insurance 1117(3), 3381(5); Judgm 181(2), 185(2), 185.3(13); Labor & Emp 403, 407, 425, 426, 475, 480, 638; States 18.41, 18.51, 18.84.

Grain Handling Corp.; B & C Const. Co. v., TexCivApp–Amarillo, 521 SW2d 98.—Contracts 175(1), 186(1), 186(2), 187(1); Neglig 210; Plead 45, 111.16, 111.42(10); Venue 7.5(3), 22(4).

Grajeda v. Charm Homes, Inc., TexCivApp–El Paso, 614 SW2d 176.—App & E 387(3), 387(6).

Gramer; U.S. by Clark v., CA5 (Tex), 418 F2d 692.—Fed Civ Proc 2397.3.

Gramercy Ins. Co. v. Arcadia Financial Ltd., TexApp–Houston (14 Dist), 32 SW3d 402, reh overr.—App & E 893(1); Autos 20; Bonds 50; Licens 26; Princ & S 142, 145(1).

Gramercy Ins. Co. v. MRD Investments, Inc., TexApp–Houston (14 Dist), 47 SW3d 721, review den.—App & E 1175(1), 1178(1); Judgm 181(2); Licens 26.

Gramercy Ins. Co. v. State, TexApp–San Antonio, 834 SW2d 379.—Bail 75.3, 77(1), 79(1), 79(2); Judgm 335(1).

Gramercy Ins. Company/Arcadia Financial Ltd. v. Arcadia Financial Ltd. Gramercy Ins. Co., TexApp–Austin, 96 SW3d 320, reh overr, and review den, and reh of petition for review den.—App & E 1071.1(6); Licens 26; Princ & S 66(1); Statut 176, 181(1), 188, 205.

Gramercy Ins. Co., Inc. v. Auction Finance Program, Inc., TexApp–Dallas, 52 SW3d 360, review den.—App & E 863, 870(2), 1175(1); Judgm 185(2); Licens 26; Princ & S 59; Statut 188.

Gramling; U.S. v., CA5 (Tex), 180 F2d 498.—Controlled Subs 189; Int Rev 5128, 5145; Judgm 648.

Gramm v. Coffield, TexCivApp–Austin, 116 SW2d 1089, writ dism.—Adv Poss 95; App & E 1051(2); Bankr 3072(1); Evid 383(7); Statut 223.2(0.5), 223.2(25); Tresp to T T 39(1), 44.

GRAMMAR

See Guidelines for Arrangement at the beginning of this Volume

Grammar v. Builders Brick & Stone Co., TexCivApp–San Antonio, 277 SW2d 185.—Frds St of 33(2).

Grammar; Case v., TexApp–San Antonio, 31 SW3d 304.—App & E 846(5), 893(1), 946, 960(1); Appear 10; Const Law 3964, 3965(7); Courts 12(2.5), 12(2.10), 12(2.30), 35.

Grammar v. Hobby, TexCivApp–San Antonio, 276 SW2d 311, ref nre.—Judgm 118, 143(2), 153(1), 162(4).

Grammar; Texas Emp. Ins. Ass'n v., TexCivApp–Dallas, 157 SW2d 701, writ refused wom.—Work Comp 604, 606, 616, 617, 643, 719, 731.

Grammas; U.S. v., CA5 (Tex), 376 F3d 433, reh den.—Crim Law 641.13(1), 641.13(2.1), 641.13(5), 1139, 1181.5(6), 1440(2), 1519(4).

Grammco Computer Sales, Inc.; Heller Financial, Inc. v., CA5 (Tex), 71 F3d 518.—Action 27(1); Damag 23; Fed Civ Proc 2194.1; Fed Cts 765, 776, 871, 896.1, 901.1; Fraud 31, 61; Judgm 540, 567, 704; RICO 26, 28, 29, 31; Sec Tran 3.1, 111, 161.

Grammer v. City Nat. Bank of Cleburne, TexCivApp–Waco, 262 SW2d 106, ref nre.—App & E 927(7); Banks 258, 262.

Grammer v. County School Trustees, Hardeman County, TexCivApp–Amarillo, 304 SW2d 149.—Plead 228.16; Schools 37(1).

Grammer; Davis v., Tex, 750 SW2d 766.—App & E 758.3(9); Ref of Inst 17(1), 25.

Grammer; Davis v., TexCivApp–San Antonio, 727 SW2d 18, writ gr, rev 750 SW2d 766.—Ref of Inst 16; Ven & Pur 44.

Grammer v. George Grubbs Datsun, Inc., TexApp–Fort Worth, 663 SW2d 67, ref nre.—Judgm 181(21).

Grammer v. Richardson, SDTex, 336 FSupp 714.—Const Law 975; Social S 142.5, 143.2, 148.1, 149.

Grammer v. State, TexCrimApp, 91 SW2d 739.—Crim Law 1131(1).

Gramza; Popkowsi v., TexApp–Houston (1 Dist), 671 SW2d 915.—App & E 493, 705, 846(5), 852, 1073(2); Damag 130.1, 163(1), 173(1), 187, 190; Evid 355(1), 377, 471(13), 568(1); Interest 66; Proc 153.

Granada Biosciences, Inc. v. Barrett, TexApp–Amarillo, 958 SW2d 215, judgment mod on reh, and review den, appeal after remand 44 SW3d 221, withdrawn from Bound Volume, opinion withdrawn and superseded on overruling of reh 49 SW3d 610, review den, and review gr, and reh of petition for review gr, and withdrawn, rev Forbes Inc v. Granada Biosciences, Inc, 124 SW3d 167.—App & E 231(1), 754(1), 760(1), 854(1), 1073(1), 1136; Damag 50.10; Judgm 183; Libel 6(1), 10(5), 19, 51(5), 55, 123(2), 133.

Granada Biosciences, Inc.; Forbes Inc. v., Tex, 124 SW3d 167.—App & E 934(1); Judgm 185(5); Libel 51(5), 112(2), 133, 136.

Granada Biosciences, Inc. v. Forbes, Inc., TexApp–Houston (14 Dist), 49 SW3d 610, review den, and reh of petition for review gr, and review gr, and withdrawn, rev 124 SW3d 167.—App & E 852, 934(1); Const Law 1622; Judgm 181(33), 185(2), 185(5), 185.3(21); Libel 9(1), 36, 41, 50.5, 130, 131, 133, 135, 136, 139.

Granada Corp. v. Honorable First Court of Appeals, Tex, 844 SW2d 223.—App & E 842(8); Mand 4(4), 32, 172; Pretrial Proc 403; Witn 201(2), 204(2), 219(3).

Granada Inn v. Southwestern Bell Media, Inc., TexApp–Corpus Christi, 784 SW2d 471. See Corro v. Southwestern Bell Media, Inc.

Granada Partnership Securities Litigations, In re, SDTex, 803 FSupp 1236.—Compromise 15(1), 57, 58, 61; Damag 63.

Granader v. McBee, CA5 (Tex), 23 F3d 120.—Banks 105(2); Fed Civ Proc 2830; Fed Cts 813; Fraud 20; Sec Reg 278.

Granado v. Madsen, TexApp–Houston (14 Dist), 729 SW2d 866, ref nre.—App & E 216(1), 946; Damag 221(8); Evid 571(3); Health 605, 707, 827, 906, 908, 923,

925; Judgm 181(33); New Tr 72(9); Pretrial Proc 531, 649.

Granado v. State, TexCrimApp, 329 SW2d 864, 168 TexCrim 525.—Sent & Pun 1367.

Granado v. State, TexCrimApp, 275 SW2d 680, 161 TexCrim 128.—Arrest 63.3; Obst Just 11, 16, 18.

Granado v. State, TexCrimApp, 228 SW2d 530, 154 TexCrim 519.—Crim Law 1091(14), 1101, 1144.12.

Granado v. State, TexApp–San Antonio, 749 SW2d 238, petition for discretionary review refused.—Autos 339, 351.1, 355(10).

Granado; U.S. v., CA5 (Tex), 302 F3d 421, reh den.—Autos 316, 326, 349(2.1), 349(4); Crim Law 394.1(3), 394.4(9), 412.1(3), 1139, 1158(4).

Granados; Reyes v., SDTex, 879 FSupp 711.—Arrest 63.4(1), 68(2); Civil R 1088(4), 1351(4), 1376(6), 1395(6); Crim Law 662.3; Fed Civ Proc 2491.5; Searches 12.

Granados v. State, TexCrimApp, 85 SW3d 217, reh den, cert den 123 SCt 1578, 538 US 927, 155 LEd2d 821, denial of habeas corpus aff 455 F3d 529, cert den 127 SCt 732, 166 LEd2d 568.—Crim Law 394.6(4), 855(1), 857(1), 864, 868, 1144.15, 1152(2), 1158(3); Jury 97(1), 104.1, 108; Searches 26, 162, 164.

Granados v. State, TexApp–Corpus Christi, 843 SW2d 736.—Controlled Subs 26, 27, 80; Crim Law 145, 304(5), 304(13), 552(3), 742(1), 1159.6.

Granados Chavez v. State, TexApp–El Paso, 727 SW2d 335.—Crim Law 273(5).

Granata; Chacon v., CA5 (Tex), 515 F2d 922, cert den 96 SCt 279, 423 US 930, 46 LEd2d 258.—Decl Judgm 209; Em Dom 2(1), 124; Evid 83(1); Inj 12, 14; Mun Corp 33(2), 33(9), 35, 63.10; Statut 212.7; U S 125(28.1).

Granatelli; Brown v., CA5 (Tex), 897 F2d 1351, cert den 111 SCt 137, 498 US 848, 112 LEd2d 104.—Insurance 2460.

Granato v. Bravo, TexCivApp–San Antonio, 498 SW2d 499.—App & E 854(5), 866(3), 1061.4; Judgm 186; Spec Perf 28(1), 29(2), 57; Trial 171, 174.

Granato v. State, TexCrimApp, 493 SW2d 822, cert den 94 SCt 372, 414 US 1009, 38 LEd2d 247.—Crim Law 371(3), 371(12), 372(9), 645, 687(1); False Pret 49(1); Witn 255(1).

Granberry v. Dallas, TexCivApp–Austin, 250 SW2d 643, ref nre.—Adv Poss 114(1); App & E 930(1); Judgm 680.

Granberry; Frizzell-Jones Lumber Co. v., TexCivApp–Texarkana, 451 SW2d 805.—App & E 232(0.5), 1050.1(11), 1062.1; Tresp 43(3), 46(2); Trial 350.3(6).

Granberry v. McBride, TexCivApp–Texarkana, 138 SW2d 283.—App & E 1078(1); Mtg 32(6), 37(2).

Granberry v. State, TexApp–Beaumont, 695 SW2d 71, petition for discretionary review refused.—Jury 107, 131(18).

Granberry v. State, TexApp–Houston (14 Dist), 745 SW2d 34, petition for discretionary review refused by 758 SW2d 284.—Crim Law 393(1), 412.1(4), 412.2(4), 641.3(3), 641.3(8.1).

Granberry v. Texas Public Service Co., TexCivApp–Amarillo, 171 SW2d 184.—App & E 931(1); Fixt 14, 15, 27(2); Neglig 273; Wareh 24(1), 25(7).

Granberry; U.S. v., CA5 (Tex), 916 F2d 1008.—Const Law 2415(3); Controlled Subs 6.

Granberry; Vissering v., TexCivApp–Texarkana, 344 SW2d 898, ref nre.—Adj Land 8, 10(1); Ease 18(3); Partit 12(1).

Granbury, City of; Abbott v., TexCivApp–Fort Worth, 252 SW2d 231, ref nre.—App & E 930(1); Autos 193(5), 193(6), 194(2), 240(1), 244(27); Labor & Emp 3038(1); Pretrial Proc 78; Trial 178.

Granbury, City of; Collerain v., TexApp–Fort Worth, 760 SW2d 364.—Costs 194.16; Damag 123; Electricity 11.5(2); Mun Corp 1040; Pretrial Proc 45; Pub Ut 123, 183.

Granbury, City of; Estes v., TexCivApp–Fort Worth, 314 SW2d 154, writ refused.—Mun Corp 1000(5).

Granbury, City of; Knowles v., TexApp–Fort Worth, 953 SW2d 19, reh overr, and review den.—Action 14; Aviation 223, 241; Bailm 1; Em Dom 2(1); Judgm 181(15.1), 185(2); Mun Corp 254, 1016; Offic 114, 119.

Granbury, City of; Nutt Shell Eatery v., TexApp–Fort Worth, 760 SW2d 364. See Collerain v. City of Granbury.

Granbury Hosp. Corp.; Reed v., TexApp–Fort Worth, 117 SW3d 404.—Evid 508, 535, 536, 538, 545, 546, 555.2; Health 628, 656, 706, 820, 821(2).

Granbury Independent School Dist. v. Andrews, TexCivApp–Fort Worth, 439 SW2d 896, ref nre.—App & E 863; Inj 147; Schools 107; Tax 2876.

Granbury I.S.D.; Doe v., NDTex, 19 FSupp2d 667.—Civil R 1066, 1067(3), 1330(2), 1336, 1351(1), 1351(2), 1352(2), 1356, 1376(2), 1395(2), 1460; Fed Civ Proc 2491.5; Offic 114.

Grancolombiana (New York), Inc.; Robinson v., CA5 (Tex), 430 F2d 645.—Fed Cts 743.

Grand; Leibman v., TexApp–El Paso, 981 SW2d 426.—Action 6; App & E 983(3), 1010.1(1), 1010.2; Const Law 2601; Exemp 37, 49, 55, 145, 148; Jury 16(5), 25(6).

Grand Am. Co., Inc. v. Stockstill, TexCivApp–Amarillo, 523 SW2d 422.—Appear 9(4); Courts 12(2.30), 35; Evid 183(1).

Grand Ave. State Bank of Dallas, Tex.; Pacific Indem. Co. v., CA5 (Tex), 223 F2d 513.—Bankr 2554, 2612; Banks 134(1); Trusts 104, 354.

Grand Brittain, Inc. v. City of Amarillo, Tex., CA5 (Tex), 27 F3d 1068, reh den.—Licens 22, 38; Zoning 76.

Grand Casino Coushatta; Gorman v., EDTex, 1 FSupp2d 656. See Gorman v. Grand Casino of La., Inc.-Coushatta.

Grand Casino of La., Inc.-Coushatta; Gorman v., EDTex, 1 FSupp2d 656.—Const Law 3964, 3965(3), 3965(5); Fed Cts 74, 76.5, 76.10, 76.35, 79, 101.

Grand Court of Order of Calanthe of Texas v. Ebeling, TexCivApp–Austin, 129 SW2d 715.—Mines 54.5; Mtg 171(6); Trusts 172, 203, 206(6).

Grande; Roberts v., TexApp–Houston (14 Dist), 868 SW2d 956, reh den.—Antitrust 393, 397, 398; App & E 155, 223, 907(1); Contrib 5(6.1); Damag 63; Interest 39(2.6), 39(2.20).

Grande, Inc.; Averyt v., Tex, 717 SW2d 891.—App & E 230, 233(1); Deeds 90, 97, 134; Mines 55(2), 55(5).

Grande, Inc.; Averyt v., TexApp–Texarkana, 686 SW2d 632, ref nre, and writ withdrawn, and writ gr, aff 717 SW2d 891.—App & E 219(2), 230; Covenants 46; Deeds 90, 93, 123; Evid 448; Mines 55(2), 55(4).

Grande Lands, Inc.; Romero v., TexCivApp–San Antonio, 288 SW2d 907.—App & E 879; Inj 138.31, 143(1), 221.

Grande Motors; Bank of America, N.T.S.A. v., TexApp–San Antonio, 770 SW2d 890. See Bank of America, N.T.S.A. v. Love.

Grande Tire Co., Inc.; Harmon v., CA5 (Tex), 821 F2d 252.—Autos 244(21), 244(36.1), 247; Damag 51, 208(7); Fed Civ Proc 1856, 2241; Interest 39(2.50).

Grandey v. Pacific Indem. Co., CA5 (Tex), 217 F2d 27.—Fed Civ Proc 553, 839.1, 1744.1, 1751.

Grand Finance Co. of Austin; Deal v., TexCivApp–Austin, 228 SW2d 984, mandamus overr.—Evid 43(2), 52; Plead 111.4; Venue 22(4), 22(6).

Grandham v. State, TexCrimApp, 528 SW2d 220, cert den 96 SCt 1434, 424 US 957, 47 LEd2d 363.—Crim Law 773(1), 796, 1043(1); Rape 51(1), 59(20.1).

Grand Homes 96, L.P. v. Loudermilk, TexApp–Fort Worth, 208 SW3d 696.—Alt Disp Res 144, 182(1), 182(2), 184, 210, 230, 329, 330, 362(1), 362(2), 371, 373, 374(1), 374(5), 379; App & E 856(1).

Grandinetti v. Grandinetti, TexCivApp–Hous (14 Dist), 600 SW2d 371.—Child S 41, 60, 62, 70, 87, 556(2); Divorce 223.

Grandinetti; Grandinetti v., TexCivApp–Hous (14 Dist), 600 SW2d 371.—Child S 41, 60, 62, 70, 87, 556(2); Divorce 223.

Grand Intern. Broth. of Locomotive Engineers; Choate v., Tex, 314 SW2d 795, 159 Tex 1.—Labor & Emp 1219(3), 1523, 1528.

Grand Intern. Broth. of Locomotive Engineers; Choate v., TexCivApp–Fort Worth, 307 SW2d 854, rev 314 SW2d 795, 159 Tex 1.—Labor & Emp 1527, 1528.

Grand Intern. Broth. of Locomotive Engineers v. Marshall, TexCivApp–Waco, 157 SW2d 676.—App & E 1206; Courts 207.1, 207.5.

Grand International Brotherhood of Locomotive Engineers v. Marshall, TexCivApp–Waco, 146 SW2d 411, writ refused.—Labor & Emp 1007, 1030, 2025.

Grand International Brotherhood of Locomotive Engineers v. Marshall, TexCivApp–Waco, 119 SW2d 908, writ refused.—App & E 1175(5); Labor & Emp 1006, 1007, 1023, 1027, 1030, 1073.

Grand Intern. Broth. of Locomotive Engineers v. Wilson, TexCivApp–Fort Worth, 341 SW2d 206, ref nre.—Alt Disp Res 324, 330; Labor & Emp 1089(1), 1219(2), 1219(12), 1527, 1528, 1625; Trial 350.4(1).

Grandison v. State, TexCrimApp, 514 SW2d 763.—Crim Law 784(1), 1173.2(10).

Grand Jury, In re, CA5 (Tex), 583 F2d 128.—Fed Cts 686; Gr Jury 41.50(3), 41.50(6).

Grand Jury, In re, NDTex, 446 FSupp 1132.—Atty & C 21.5(7), 21.10, 21.20, 32(14); Crim Law 641.5(7), 641.10(2); Gr Jury 35, 36.1, 36.2.

Grand Jury Investigation, Doe, In re, SDTex, 599 FSupp 746.—Fed Cts 13; Witn 298.

Grand Jury Proceedings, In re, CA5 (Tex), 115 F3d 1240.—Crim Law 83, 394.5(1), 1148; Fed Cts 776, 795, 870.1; Gr Jury 36.4(1), 36.8; Searches 84.

Grand Jury Proceedings, In re, CA5 (Tex), 55 F3d 1012.—Fed Cts 754.1, 851, 853, 870.1; Witn 298, 308.

Grand Jury Proceedings, In re, CA5 (Tex), 43 F3d 966.—Fed Civ Proc 1600(3), 1600(5); Fed Cts 571, 572.1, 574, 594; Gr Jury 36.3(2); Witn 201(2).

Grand Jury Proceedings, In re, CA5 (Tex), 724 F2d 1157.—Crim Law 394.6(1); Fed Cts 524, 526.1, 527, 556, 594.

Grand Jury Proceedings, In re, CA5 (Tex), 647 F2d 511.—Gr Jury 36.3(2); Witn 304(3).

Grand Jury Proceedings, In re, CA5 (Tex), 604 F2d 318.—Gr Jury 36.5(1).

Grand Jury Proceedings, In re, CA5 (Tex), 558 F2d 1177.—Crim Law 393(3); Gr Jury 26, 36.4(1); Searches 75.

Grand Jury Proceedings, In re, CA5 (Tex), 517 F2d 666, reh den 521 F2d 815, reh den US v. Jones, 521 F2d 815.—Atty & C 38; Fed Cts 416, 479; Witn 199(1), 201(1), 219(3), 222.

Grand Jury Proceedings, In re, CA5 (Tex), 479 F2d 458, reh den 478 F2d 1402, reh den Woodard, Appeal of, 478 F2d 1403.—Gr Jury 42.

Grand Jury Proceedings, In re, EDTex, 632 FSupp 374.—Gr Jury 36.4(1); Searches 78; Witn 298.5.

Grand Jury Proceedings Dated May 6, 1996, In re, SDTex, 932 FSupp 904, rev 115 F3d 1240.—Fed Cts 686; Records 32; Searches 124, 125, 141.

Grand Jury Proceedings, Miscellaneous No. 1331, In re, CA5 (Tex), 712 F2d 973.—Gr Jury 41.50(5).

Grand Jury Proceedings No. 84-4, In re, CA5 (Tex), 757 F2d 1580.—Crim Law 42; Witn 21, 304(1), 304(3).

Grand Jury Proceedings 198.GJ.20, In re, TexApp–San Antonio, 129 SW3d 140, reh overr, and review dism in part, and review den.—Crim Law 1148; Gr Jury 36.8.

Grand Jury Subpoena, In re, CA5 (Tex), 220 F3d 406, 178 ALR Fed 625.—Crim Law 627.5(6), 627.6(1), 1023(3); Gr Jury 36.3(2); Witn 201(2).

Grand Jury Subpoena, In re, CA5 (Tex), 190 F3d 375, cert den Smith v. US, 120 SCt 1573, 529 US 1062, 146 LEd2d 475.—Fed Civ Proc 1640; Fed Cts 526.1, 571, 572.1, 574; Mand 32.

Grand Jury Subpoena, In re, CA5 (Tex), 767 F2d 1130.—Witn 297(12), 298.

Grand Jury Subpoena Dated December 17, 1996, In re, CA5 (Tex), 148 F3d 487, reh and sug for reh den In re Grand Jury Proceedings, 161 F3d 10, cert den Moczygemba v. US, 119 SCt 1336, 526 US 1040, 143 LEd2d 500.—Alt Disp Res 481; Fed Cts 13, 416, 585.1, 776; Gr Jury 36.3(2), 36.9(1); Witn 184(1).

Grand Jury Subpoena Duces Tecum Addressed to Armada Petroleum Corp., Matter of, SDTex, 520 FSupp 253.—Gr Jury 36.3(1), 36.4(2), 36.8.

Grand Jury Subpoena for Attorney Representing Criminal Defendant Reyes-Requena, In re, CA5 (Tex), 926 F2d 1423, reh den 946 F2d 893.—Contempt 66(2), 66(7); Fed Cts 556, 724; Gr Jury 36.5(1); Witn 201(1).

Grand Jury Subpoena for Attorney Representing Criminal Defendant Reyes-Requena, In re, CA5 (Tex), 913 F2d 1118, on remand 752 FSupp 239, aff 926 F2d 1423, reh den 946 F2d 893, cert den DeGeurin v. US, 111 SCt 1581, 499 US 959, 113 LEd2d 646.—Crim Law 1147, 1186.1; Gr Jury 35, 36.1, 36.3(1), 36.3(2), 36.4(1); Witn 201(1).

Grand Jury Subpoena for Attorney Representing Criminal Defendant Reyes-Requena, In re, SDTex, 724 FSupp 458, rev 913 F2d 1118, on remand 752 FSupp 239, aff 926 F2d 1423, reh den 946 F2d 893, cert den DeGeurin v. US, 111 SCt 1581, 499 US 959, 113 LEd2d 646.—Admin Law 386; Gr Jury 36.3(2), 36.4(1), 36.4(2).

Grand Jury Subpoena for DeGuerin, In re, CA5 (Tex), 926 F2d 1423. See Grand Jury Subpoena for Attorney Representing Criminal Defendant Reyes-Requena, In re.

Grand Jury Subpoenas Dated June 27, 1991, In re, NDTex, 772 FSupp 326.—Witn 298, 306.

Grand Jury Subpoenas on Barrett, In re, CA5 (Tex), 818 F2d 330, cert den Barrett v. US, 108 SCt 163, 484 US 856, 98 LEd2d 117.—Fed Cts 585.1.

Grand Lake Gathering System, Inc. v. Gray, TexCivApp–Beaumont, 441 SW2d 633.—High 79.6.

Grand Leader Dry Goods Co. v. Caveness, TexCivApp–Hous (14 Dist), 424 SW2d 270.—App & E 930(3), 1170.6; Labor & Emp 2830, 2877, 2926; Neglig 387, 1550; Trial 306; Work Comp 2114.

Grand Lodge Colored Knights of Pythias v. Loller, TexCivApp–Dallas, 86 SW2d 821.—Insurance 1848, 3475(1), 3475(3), 3475(8).

Grand Lodge Colored Knights of Pythias of Texas v. Adams, Tex, 110 SW2d 1152, 130 Tex 360.—App & E 361(5).

Grand Lodge Colored Knights of Pythias of Texas v. Green, TexComApp, 101 SW2d 219, 128 Tex 593.—Courts 247(7).

Grand Lodge Colored K. P. of Texas v. Adams, Tex, 107 SW2d 355, 130 Tex 360, reh den Grand Lodge Colored Knights of Pythias of Texas v. Adams, 110 SW2d 1152, 130 Tex 360.—App & E 361(2).

Grand Lodge Colored K. P. of Texas v. Adams, TexCivApp–Waco, 105 SW2d 731, writ dism 107 SW2d 355, 130 Tex 360, reh den Grand Lodge Colored Knights of Pythias of Texas v. Adams, 110 SW2d 1152, 130 Tex 360.—Insurance 1832(1), 2082, 2558(4).

Grand Lodge Colored K. P. of Texas; Baptist Missionary and Educational Convention of Texas v., TexCivApp–Dallas, 97 SW2d 985, writ refused.—App & E 989; Corp 404(1), 405, 406(1), 410, 433(1); Lim of Act 148(4).

Grand Lodge Colored K. P. of Tex. v. Carter, TexCivApp–Waco, 100 SW2d 742.—Insurance 1634(4), 2035, 2082.

Grand Lodge Colored K. P. of Texas v. Johns, TexComApp, 91 SW2d 1049, 127 Tex 241.—App & E 64.

Grand Lodge Colored K. P. of Texas v. Preston, TexCivApp–Beaumont, 91 SW2d 496, writ refused.—Insurance 2035.

Grand Lodge Colored K. P. of Texas v. Watson, TexCivApp–Waco, 145 SW2d 601.—App & E 1177(6); Insurance 1791(2), 3336, 3360; Interpl 1, 32, 35.

Grand Lodge Free and Accepted Masons of Texas v. Walker, TexCivApp–Dallas, 110 SW2d 945.—App & E 500(2), 740(4), 748, 1002; Contracts 108(1), 108(2); Insurance 1713, 2082, 3365, 3571; Lim of Act 127(4); Princ & A 131.

Grand Lodge Free and Accepted Masons of Texas v. Walker, TexCivApp–Eastland, 86 SW2d 839.—Insurance 3571; Plead 36(3).

Grand Lodge of Order of Sons of Herman; Koenig v., TexCivApp–Fort Worth, 148 SW2d 222, writ dism, correct.—App & E 216(1), 232(3), 242(1), 688(2), 691, 695(1), 713(3); Insurance 3476(2), 3490; Trial 219, 263, 273, 277.

Grand Lodge of Order of Sons of Hermann in Texas v. Curry, TexCivApp–San Antonio, 108 SW2d 574, writ refused.—Waters 226, 228, 231.

Grandlund; U.S. v., CA5 (Tex), 77 F3d 811.—Courts 100(1); Sent & Pun 2016.

Grandlund; U.S. v., CA5 (Tex), 71 F3d 507, reh den, cert den 116 SCt 1031, 516 US 1152, 134 LEd2d 108, opinion clarified 77 F3d 811.—Const Law 4735; Crim Law 1139, 1147, 1177; Sent & Pun 2016, 2020, 2026, 2029.

Grand Prairie, City of; Akers v., TexCivApp–Dallas, 572 SW2d 22.—App & E 765, 773(2).

Grand Prairie, City of; Avmanco, Inc. v., TexApp–Fort Worth, 835 SW2d 160, reh den, and appeal dism as moot.—App & E 78(1), 80(6), 169, 223, 347(1), 863, 1073(1); Judgm 181(5.1), 183, 185(2), 185(6); Mun Corp 250, 254; Pretrial Proc 508; States 191.1, 191.9(1).

Grand Prairie, City of; Bell v., TexApp–Dallas, 221 SW3d 317.—App & E 893(1); Counties 141; Courts 39; Mun Corp 199, 723, 742(4), 1016; Plead 104(1), 111.36, 111.37, 111.38, 111.43, 111.48; Schools 89; States 191.1, 191.4(1), 191.9(2).

Grand Prairie, City of; Chemline, Inc. v., CA5 (Tex), 364 F2d 721.—Const Law 90.1(6), 1892; Health 392; Infants 13; Mun Corp 592(1); Obscen 1.4, 2.5, 5.2; Pub Amuse 47, 51.

Grand Prairie, City of; City of Arlington v., TexCivApp–Fort Worth, 451 SW2d 284, ref nre.—App & E 931(6), 1054(1); Evid 320; Mun Corp 29(1), 29(4), 33(1), 33(2), 33(9).

Grand Prairie, City of; Durden v., TexApp–Fort Worth, 626 SW2d 345, ref nre.—App & E 927(7); Em Dom 2(1), 2(10), 300, 303; Lim of Act 32(3); Nuis 46; Pretrial Proc 690.

Grand Prairie, City of; Gros v., CA5 (Tex), 209 F3d 431, on remand 2000 WL 1842421.—Civil R 1039, 1088(1), 1355, 1358; Fed Cts 557, 768.1.

Grand Prairie, City of; Horrocks v., Tex, 704 SW2d 17.—Mun Corp 185(12).

Grand Prairie, City of; Livecchi v., TexApp–Dallas, 109 SW3d 920, review dism.—Mun Corp 254; Plead 104(1), 246(1).

Grand Prairie, City of; Patton v., Tex, 686 SW2d 108.—Mun Corp 185(12), 198(4).

Grand Prairie, City of; Patton v., TexApp–Dallas, 675 SW2d 794, writ gr, rev 686 SW2d 108.—Mun Corp 185(12), 198(4).

Grand Prairie, City of, v. Sisters of Holy Family of Nazareth, TexApp–Dallas, 868 SW2d 835. See City of Grand Prairie v. Sisters of Holy Family of Nazareth.

Grand Prairie, City of; Strong v., TexApp–Fort Worth, 679 SW2d 767.—Decl Judgm 393; Zoning 2, 196, 624, 643.

Grand Prairie, City of; Taggart v., CA5 (Tex), 421 F2d 1301.—Fed Cts 244, 743.

Grand Prairie, City of; Wright v., TexApp–Fort Worth, 624 SW2d 791.—Mun Corp 454, 514(1.1), 518(1), 525.

Grand Prairie, City of; Zaragoza v., TexApp–Texarkana, 998 SW2d 395.—Judgm 702; Mun Corp 745; Offic 114.

Grand Prairie Hosp. Authority v. Dallas County Appraisal Dist., TexApp–Dallas, 730 SW2d 849, ref nre.—Tax 2315.

Grand Prairie Hosp. Authority; Elbaor v., NDTex, 599 FSupp 1111, vac 788 F2d 1563.—Const Law 3874(2), 4040, 4156, 4187, 4286; Health 273.

Grand Prairie Hosp. Authority v. Tarrant Appraisal Dist., TexApp–Fort Worth, 707 SW2d 281, ref nre.—Decl Judgm 213.1; Plead 234; Tax 2343, 2642.

Grand Prairie Independent School Dist.; Dotson v., TexApp–Dallas, 161 SW3d 289.—Schools 63(1), 115, 147.44, 147.47, 147.51.

Grand Prairie Independent School Dist. v. Missouri Pacific R. Co., TexApp–Dallas, 730 SW2d 761, ref nre. —Tax 2699(11), 2728, 2858.

Grand Prairie Independent School Dist. v. Southern Parts Imports, Inc., Tex, 813 SW2d 499, on remand 1991 WL 231822.—App & E 784.

Grand Prairie Independent School Dist. v. Southern Parts Imports, Inc., TexApp–Dallas, 803 SW2d 762, writ gr, aff in part, rev in part 813 SW2d 499, on remand 1991 WL 231822.—App & E 374(4), 760(1), 989, 1012.1(4); Corp 547(4); Fraud Conv 28, 273; Schools 104, 106.12(11), 106.25(8); Sec Tran 230; Tax 2739.

Grand Prairie Independent School Dist. v. Southern Volks, TexApp–Dallas, 803 SW2d 762. See Grand Prairie Independent School Dist. v. Southern Parts Imports, Inc.

Grand Prairie Independent School Dist. v. Southern Volks, Heller Financial, Inc., Tex, 813 SW2d 499. See Grand Prairie Independent School Dist. v. Southern Parts Imports, Inc.

Grand Prairie Independent School Dist.; Stout v., TexApp–Dallas, 733 SW2d 290, ref nre, cert den 108 SCt 1082, 485 US 907, 99 LEd2d 241.—Const Law 990, 2312, 2314, 2486, 3053, 3057, 3747, 3957, 4413, 4420; Schools 10, 89.1, 89.2, 89.4, 147.

Grand Prairie Independent School Dist. v. Vaughan, Tex, 792 SW2d 944.—Schools 147.52.

Grand Prairie Independent School Dist.; Vaughn v., TexApp–Dallas, 784 SW2d 474, rev 792 SW2d 944.— Afft 17; App & E 223, 758.3(11), 863, 934(1), 1073(1); Judgm 178, 181(1), 185(2), 185(4), 185.3(13); Pretrial Proc 472, 480, 481, 483.

Grand Prairie State Bank v. U.S., CA5 (Tex), 206 F2d 217.—Int Rev 4770, 4772, 4788.1, 4792.

Grand Prairie, Texas, City of; Bell v., TexApp–Dallas, 160 SW3d 691, opinion withdrawn and superseded on reh 221 SW3d 317.

Grand Prairie, Tex., City of; Bennett v., CA5 (Tex), 883 F2d 400.—Civil R 1088(4), 1351(4), 1407; Crim Law 211(1), 211(3), 212, 217, 1134(2); Fed Cts 612.1.

Grand Prairie, Tex., City of; County Line Joint Venture v., CA5 (Tex), 839 F2d 1142, cert den 109 SCt 223, 488 US 890, 102 LEd2d 214.—Const Law 4096, 4262; Licens 20.

Grand Prairie, Tex., City of; Gros v., CA5 (Tex), 181 F3d 613, reh en banc den 193 F3d 521, appeal after remand 209 F3d 431, on remand 2000 WL 1842421.—Civil R 1345, 1351(1), 1404, 1430; Fed Cts 411.

Grand Prairie, Tex., City of; Hazelton v., NDTex, 8 FSupp2d 570.—Arrest 63.4(2); Civil R 1031, 1088(4), 1345, 1351(1), 1376(2), 1376(6), 1382, 1395(5), 1395(6), 1432; Const Law 3936; False Imp 13; Fed Cts 18; Lim of Act 124; Offic 114.

Grand Prize Distributing Co. of San Antonio v. Gulf Brewing Co., TexCivApp–San Antonio, 267 SW2d 906, writ refused.—Antitrust 582; Courts 91(1).

Grand Saline, City of; Ballenger v., TexCivApp–Waco, 276 SW2d 874.—Nuis 1, 59, 84.

Grand Saline, City of; Olympic Waste Services v., TexApp–Tyler, 204 SW3d 496.—App & E 863, 893(1); Mun Corp 92, 254, 1016; Plead 104(1), 111.38; States 191.4(1), 191.6(2).

Grandstaff, Ex parte, TexCrimApp, 282 SW2d 711.—Hab Corp 823.

Grandstaff v. City of Borger, CA5 (Tex), 846 F2d 1016.— Interest 39(2.6), 39(2.50), 39(3).

Grandstaff v. City of Borger, Tex., CA5 (Tex), 767 F2d 161, reh den 779 F2d 1129, cert den 107 SCt 1369, 480 US 916, 94 LEd2d 686, appeal after remand 846 F2d 1016.—Civil R 1034, 1088(1), 1088(2), 1348, 1351(1), 1352(1), 1352(4), 1358, 1407, 1417, 1420, 1421; Consp 19; Const Law 4528; Damag 50, 51; Death 88, 89, 95(1); Fed Civ Proc 2197; Fed Cts 415; Mun Corp 747(3).

Grandstaff v. Mercer, TexCivApp–Fort Worth, 214 SW2d 133, ref nre.—Neglig 204; Trial 142, 350.6(3); Work Comp 108, 208, 2168, 2239.

Grandstaff v. T. E. Mercer, Teaming and Trucking Contractor, TexCivApp–Fort Worth, 227 SW2d 372, ref nre.—App & E 207, 1069.1; New Tr 157; Trial 127, 131(3).

Grand Temple and Tabernacle in State of Texas of Knights and Daughters of Tabor of International Order of Twelve v. Independent Order of Knights and Daughters of Tabor of America, TexComApp, 44 SW2d 973.—Trademarks 1425, 1660.

Grand Union Tea Co.; Fox v., TexCivApp–Austin, 236 SW2d 561, mandamus overr.—App & E 1177(7); Evid 20(1), 53; Names 18.

Grand United Order of Odd Fellows v. Jones, TexCivApp–Austin, 85 SW2d 662.—App & E 1056.1(9); Evid 343(1); Insurance 2445, 3014.

Grand United Order of Odd Fellows v. Massey, TexCivApp–Dallas, 87 SW2d 310.—App & E 912, 927(7), 1062.2, 1069.1; Insurance 1940, 2079.

Grand United Order of Odd Fellows of Texas v. White, TexComApp, 105 SW2d 886, 129 Tex 590.—Courts 247(7); Insurance 2079.

Grandview Farm Center, Inc. v. First State Bank of Grandview, TexCivApp–Waco, 596 SW2d 190, ref nre. —App & E 1170.7; Damag 140, 184; Trover 40(4), 66; Usury 125.

Grandview Independent School Dist.; Rio Vista Independent School Dist. v., TexCivApp–Waco, 379 SW2d 408.—Schools 37(3), 37(4), 37(5), 39.

Grandview Independent School Dist. v. Storey, TexCivApp–Waco, 590 SW2d 215.—Schools 103(1), 106.12(8); Tax 2523, 2571.

Grandy's; Eustice v., TexApp–Dallas, 827 SW2d 12.— App & E 962; Costs 260(4), 260(5); Pretrial Proc 697, 699.

Granek v. Texas State Bd. of Medical Examiners, TexApp–Austin, 172 SW3d 761.—Admin Law 462, 513, 676, 749, 750, 760, 764.1, 787, 788, 791; App & E 893(1); Const Law 3971, 4025, 4286, 4528, 4580; Health 215, 218, 222(1), 629.

Graneri; Catalani v., TexCivApp–El Paso, 153 SW2d 1015, writ refused wom.—App & E 1050.1(1); Wills 439, 440, 449, 452, 470(1), 540.

Granfus; Bigby v., TexCivApp–Eastland, 303 SW2d 523, ref nre.—App & E 989, 1195(3); Judgm 199(3.7), 199(3.9); Lim of Act 197(2).

Grange v. Kayser, TexCivApp–El Paso, 80 SW2d 1007.— Evid 517.

Granger, Ex parte, TexCrimApp, 850 SW2d 513.—Courts 99(1); Crim Law 1180; Double J 109, 161, 164.

Granger, In re, BkrtcyNDTex, 224 BR 360. See Thompson, In re.

Granger v. Folk, TexApp–Beaumont, 931 SW2d 390, reh overr, and mandamus overr.—Anim 3.5(8), 3.5(9), 3.5(10); Const Law 4310, 4500; Jury 10, 13(1), 17(1), 31.1.

Granger; Skeeters v., TexCivApp–Texarkana, 314 SW2d 364, ref nre.—App & E 1151(1); Contracts 221(3); Evid 16, 419(9); Frds St of 110(1), 113(3), 158(3); Lim of Act 46(2); Mines 79.1(4), 79.1(5).

Granger; Skeeters v., TexCivApp–Texarkana, 304 SW2d 188.—App & E 1039(13); Des & Dist 90(4).

Granger v. State, TexCrimApp, 3 SW3d 36, on remand 2000 WL 798072, petition for discretionary review refused.—Crim Law 739(1), 772(6); Homic 795.

Granger v. State, TexCrimApp, 683 SW2d 387, cert den 105 SCt 2713, 472 US 1012, 86 LEd2d 728.—Crim Law 511.1(2.1), 511.1(7), 543(1), 942(2), 1144.13(3), 1159.2(7), 1169.7.

Granger v. State, TexCrimApp, 605 SW2d 602.—Crim Law 510, 511.2, 511.4, 1184(3).

Granger v. State, TexApp–Beaumont, 722 SW2d 175, petition for discretionary review refused.—Assault 56, 92(3), 96(1).

Granger v. State, TexApp–Corpus Christi, 653 SW2d 868, petition for discretionary review gr, aff 683 SW2d 387, cert den 105 SCt 2713, 472 US 1012, 86 LEd2d 728.—Const Law 4594(5); Crim Law 511.1(1), 511.1(3), 511.2, 511.3, 543(1), 543(2), 544, 552(3), 706(2); Double J 164; Homic 1134; Witn 367(1).

Granger v. U.S., CA5 (Tex), 275 F2d 127.—Crim Law 1147; Sent & Pun 645, 2250.

Granger v. U.S., CA5 (Tex), 262 F2d 802, cert den 79 SCt 900, 359 US 979, 3 LEd2d 929, reh den 79 SCt 1135, 359 US 1005, 3 LEd2d 1034.—Crim Law 1430, 1618(1).

Granger; Willis v., TexCivApp–El Paso, 195 SW2d 831.—Ex & Ad 9; Mand 28, 31, 51.

Granger, City of; Piazza v., TexApp–Austin, 909 SW2d 529, reh overr.—Admin Law 124; App & E 179(1), 842(2), 854(2), 893(1); Costs 194.40; Mun Corp 89, 183(3), 185(14), 186(4), 1040.

Granieri v. Schramm, CCA5 (Tex), 149 F2d 811, cert den 66 SCt 100, 326 US 758, 90 LEd 456.—Bankr 3787.

Granite Const. Co. v. Beaty, TexApp–Beaumont, 130 SW3d 362.—Alt Disp Res 114, 137, 146, 178, 182(1), 182(2), 193, 210, 213(3); Commerce 80.5; States 18.15.

Granite Const. Co. v. Mendoza, TexApp–Dallas, 816 SW2d 756, writ den.—App & E 302(1), 836, 930(3), 989, 1001(1), 1003(6), 1175(1); Evid 574, 588; Interest 39(2.6), 39(2.55); Neglig 273, 371, 387, 1675, 1676; Trial 139.1(3), 140(1); Work Comp 2235.

Granite Const. Co., Inc. v. Bituminous Ins. Companies, TexApp–Amarillo, 832 SW2d 427, reh den.—App & E 169; Decl Judgm 165; Insurance 1806, 1810, 1814, 1836, 1839, 2361, 2914.

Granite Equipment Leasing Corp.; Lodge v., TexCivApp–Hous (14 Dist), 469 SW2d 838.—Judgm 181(11), 185(2).

Granite Equipment Leasing Corp.; Robinson v., TexCivApp–Hous (1 Dist), 553 SW2d 633, ref nre.—App & E 758.3(3), 766, 931(3), 989, 1071.1(6); Bailm 22, 31(3), 33, 34; Damag 62(4), 78(6), 150, 155, 157(3), 163(2); Sec Tran 10; Trial 392(1).

Granite Shoals, City of; S.S. S. Water Systems v., TexCivApp–Austin, 601 SW2d 191.—App & E 954(1), 954(2); Inj 132, 135, 152, 163(1); Mun Corp 619.

Granite State Fire Ins. Co. v. Roberts, TexCivApp–Beaumont, 391 SW2d 825, ref nre.—App & E 877(2); Insurance 3007(2).

Granite State Ins. Co.; Bartley v., TexApp–Eastland, 633 SW2d 694, ref nre.—App & E 1178(6); Damag 185(2).

Granite State Ins. Co. v. Firebaugh, TexCivApp–Eastland, 558 SW2d 550, ref nre.—Work Comp 1105.

Granite State Ins. Co.; Jackson v., Tex, 685 SW2d 16.—Work Comp 1418, 1703, 1937.

Granite State Ins. Co.; Penrod Drilling Corp. v., SDTex, 764 FSupp 1146.—Rem of C 107(11).

Granite State Ins. Co. v. Tandy Corp., CA5 (Tex), 986 F2d 94, cert gr 113 SCt 51, 506 US 813, 121 LEd2d 21, cert dism 113 SCt 1836, 507 US 1026, 123 LEd2d 463.—Action 69(6); Fed Cts 573, 813.

Granite State Ins. Co. v. Tandy Corp., SDTex, 762 FSupp 156, aff 986 F2d 94, cert gr 113 SCt 51, 506 US 813, 121 LEd2d 21, cert dism 113 SCt 1836, 507 US 1026, 123 LEd2d 463.—Fed Cts 51, 65.

Grant, Ex parte, TexCrimApp, 687 SW2d 6.—Crim Law 273.1(2), 1026.10(4).

Grant, Ex parte, TexCrimApp, 480 SW2d 639.—Extrad 34, 36.

Grant, Ex parte, TexCrimApp, 476 SW2d 702.—Hab Corp 827.

Grant, In re, BkrtcyNDTex, 40 BR 612.—Bankr 2779, 2783.

Grant, Matter of Marriage of, TexApp–Amarillo, 638 SW2d 254.—Courts 100(1).

Grant v. American Nat. Ins. Co., TexApp–Houston (14 Dist), 808 SW2d 181.—App & E 347(1); Courts 30.

Grant v. Ammerman, Tex, 437 SW2d 547.—Counties 58; Courts 207.4(2); Elections 257, 259; J P 2; Mand 3(5), 74(4).

Grant v. Ammerman, TexCivApp–Texarkana, 451 SW2d 777, ref nre.—J P 2, 3.

Grant; Armstrong v., TexCivApp–Texarkana, 356 SW2d 398.—Plead 111.42(8); Trial 382.

Grant v. Austin Bridge Const. Co., TexApp–Houston (14 Dist), 725 SW2d 366.—App & E 66, 70(1), 70(4), 846(5), 852, 870(2), 931(4), 949, 989; Lim of Act 126.5; Parties 35.49.

Grant; Brown v., TexCivApp–San Antonio, 119 SW2d 185.—Forci E & D 2, 43(2).

Grant; Brown v., TexCivApp–San Antonio, 2 SW2d 285.—Zoning 235.

Grant; Calhoun v., TexCivApp–Austin, 129 SW2d 752.—Autos 153, 201(1.1), 244(12), 245(15), 245(60), 247; Costs 244; Neglig 440(1); Trial 351.2(4).

Grant v. Cuellar, CA5 (Tex), 59 F3d 523.—Fed Civ Proc 1741; Fed Cts 712, 714, 715.

Grant v. Dallas County, CA5 (Tex), 103 FedAppx 527.—Fed Cts 663, 726.

Grant v. Dretke, CA5 (Tex), 151 FedAppx 344, cert den 126 SCt 2358, 165 LEd2d 284.—Hab Corp 486(4).

Grant; Dudley Hodgkins Co. v., TexCivApp–Fort Worth, 261 SW2d 229, ref nre.—App & E 932(1); Labor & Emp 264; Refer 18.

Grant; Flato Elec. Supply Co. v., TexCivApp–Corpus Christi, 620 SW2d 915, ref nre.—App & E 996, 1010.1(6); Usury 32, 53, 117, 145.

Grant v. Friendly Chrysler-Plymouth, Inc., TexCivApp–Corpus Christi, 612 SW2d 667, ref nre.—Cons Cred 12, 16; Contracts 153, 175(1).

Grant v. Grant, TexCivApp–Waco, 358 SW2d 147.—Action 6; App & E 781(4), 843(1); Divorce 278.1.

Grant; Grant v., TexCivApp–Waco, 358 SW2d 147.—Action 6; App & E 781(4), 843(1); Divorce 278.1.

Grant v. Grant, TexCivApp–Waco, 351 SW2d 897, writ dism.—Divorce 124, 249.1, 252.3(1), 252.3(3), 253(2), 253(4).

Grant; Grant v., TexCivApp–Waco, 351 SW2d 897, writ dism.—Divorce 124, 249.1, 252.3(1), 252.3(3), 253(2), 253(4).

Grant v. Griffin, Tex, 390 SW2d 746.—Const Law 2489; Witn 159(2).

Grant v. Griffin, TexCivApp–Tyler, 383 SW2d 643, aff 390 SW2d 746.—Witn 158, 159(2), 159(3).

Grant; Heil Co. v., TexCivApp–Tyler, 534 SW2d 916, ref nre.—App & E 930(3), 1170.7; Contrib 5(1), 5(2), 5(6.1); Death 10, 31(6), 31(7), 31(8), 93; Indem 58, 59; Judgm 609; Neglig 551, 554(2); Prod Liab 15, 27, 49, 75.1, 85; Witn 128, 129, 158.

Grant; Hobbs v., TexCivApp–Austin, 314 SW2d 351, ref nre.—App & E 1060.1(7); Autos 216; Damag 130.2; Neglig 554(1); Trial 9(1), 90, 191(11), 194(20), 215, 350.7(3.1).

Grant v. Hughes, TexCivApp–Eastland, 198 SW2d 630.—App & E 387(2), 392.

Grant v. **Jefferies**, TexCivApp–Amarillo, 497 SW2d 946.—App & E 1177(6); Autos 244(6); Plead 111.17, 111.42(4), 111.42(8).

Grant v. **Joe Myers Toyota, Inc.**, TexApp–Houston (14 Dist), 11 SW3d 419.—App & E 863, 934(1); Civil R 1162(1); Judgm 185(5), 185.3(13).

Grant v. **Lone Star Co.**, CA5 (Tex), 21 F3d 649, cert den 115 SCt 574, 513 US 1015, 130 LEd2d 491.—Civil R 1113; Estop 68(2).

Grant; **McDonald v.**, TexCivApp–Texarkana, 312 SW2d 694, dism.—App & E 761; Autos 244(32); Evid 591; Plead 110.

Grant; **McKenzie v.**, TexCivApp–San Antonio, 93 SW2d 1160, writ dism.—Adv Poss 46.1, 51; App & E 1069.1; Deeds 211(4); Hus & W 273(1), 273(10); Ref of Inst 46; Ten in C 15(11), 19(1); Trial 232(3), 306; Wills 166(1), 166(5).

Grant v. **Marshall**, Tex, 280 SW2d 559, 154 Tex 531.—Adop 1, 3, 5, 6, 17; Estop 32(1); Ex & Ad 154, 254; Home 15, 77, 134, 140, 146, 151; Trial 351.2(4); Wills 714.

Grant v. **Marshall**, TexCivApp–Waco, 272 SW2d 580, rev 280 SW2d 559, 154 Tex 531.—Estop 83(1), 83(5); Home 144, 145, 146, 214.

Grant; **Moore v.**, CA5 (Tex), 79 FedAppx 676, cert den 124 SCt 2082, 541 US 1016, 158 LEd2d 631.—Civil R 1088(5); Courts 99(6); Fed Civ Proc 2734.

Grant v. **Pendley**, TexCivApp–Galveston, 88 SW2d 132, writ dism.—App & E 1071.6; Trial 395(1), 395(5), 396(4).

Grant v. **Richardson**, CA5 (Tex), 445 F2d 656.—Fed Cts 743; Social S 143.65, 148.1.

Grant; **Roach v.**, TexComApp, 130 SW2d 1019, 134 Tex 10.—App & E 362(1); Trusts 35(4), 96, 99; Ven & Pur 52, 79.

Grant; **Roach v.**, TexCivApp–San Antonio, 107 SW2d 1018, aff 130 SW2d 1019, 134 Tex 10.—Ven & Pur 13, 79.

Grant v. **Sherwood Shores, Inc.**, TexCivApp–Austin, 477 SW2d 667.—App & E 854(1); Damag 81; Ven & Pur 39, 95(2), 335.

Grant; **Simmans v.**, SDTex, 370 FSupp 5.—Admin Law 416.1; Environ Law 582, 583, 585, 587, 588, 589, 590, 595(3), 596, 614, 657, 667, 689, 700.

Grant; **Smith v.**, TexCivApp–Texarkana, 483 SW2d 871.—Brok 9, 100; Contracts 22(1); Ven & Pur 18(3).

Grant; **Southwestern Elec. Power Co. v.**, Tex, 73 SW3d 211.—App & E 170(2), 179(4), 934(1); Const Law 2604; Electricity 12.1; Judgm 185(6); Pub Ut 111, 119.1, 141, 145.1, 147, 194, 195; Sales 1.5.

Grant v. **Southwestern Elec. Power Co.**, TexApp–Texarkana, 20 SW3d 764, reh overr, aff in part, rev in part 73 SW3d 211.—App & E 863, 934(1); Contracts 108(1), 114, 136; Electricity 13, 16(1), 19(2); Judgm 181(33), 183, 185(5), 185.3(21); 186; Neglig 202, 210, 250, 273, 1513(2), 1692; Pub Ut 103, 119.1, 165; Sales 3.1.

Grant v. **Southwestern Elec. Power Co.**, TexApp–Texarkana, 998 SW2d 383, opinion superseded 20 SW3d 764, reh overr, aff in part, rev in part 73 SW3d 211.

Grant v. **State**, TexCrimApp, 970 SW2d 22, on remand 1998 WL 809413, petition for discretionary review gr, and rev, opinion after remand from Court of Criminal Appeals 2000 WL 1273339.—Ind & Inf 101, 180, 196(6).

Grant v. **State**, TexCrimApp, 822 SW2d 639.—Controlled Subs 34.

Grant v. **State**, TexCrimApp, 568 SW2d 353.—Ind & Inf 173; Names 16(1).

Grant v. **State**, TexCrimApp, 566 SW2d 954.—Crim Law 1158(1); Sent & Pun 2020, 2021.

Grant v. **State**, TexCrimApp, 507 SW2d 732.—Crim Law 564(2), 1038.1(1), 1038.3, 1144.6; Ind & Inf 119; Larc 31, 64(6), 68(3).

Grant v. **State**, TexCrimApp, 505 SW2d 279, cert den 94 SCt 3172, 417 US 968, 41 LEd2d 1139.—Autos 316;

Const Law 919, 2507(3), 3781; Double J 152; Ind & Inf 189(1); Statut 158.

Grant v. **State**, TexCrimApp, 505 SW2d 259.—Crim Law 1128(4); Sent & Pun 2009.

Grant v. **State**, TexCrimApp, 473 SW2d 17.—Crim Law 1043(3), 1044.1(5.1).

Grant v. **State**, TexCrimApp, 472 SW2d 531.—Crim Law 488, 722.3, 781(1), 867, 1035(10), 1037.1(2), 1130(2), 1171.6.

Grant v. **State**, TexCrimApp, 462 SW2d 954.—Witn 318.

Grant v. **State**, TexCrimApp, 456 SW2d 122.—Crim Law 1186.1.

Grant v. **State**, TexCrimApp, 450 SW2d 642.—Crim Law 404.80, 675.

Grant v. **State**, TexCrimApp, 449 SW2d 480.—Crim Law 1035(5); Homic 909, 1136; Sent & Pun 1668.

Grant v. **State**, TexCrimApp, 296 SW2d 535.—Crim Law 1090.1(1).

Grant v. **State**, TexCrimApp, 286 SW2d 422, 162 TexCrim 444.—Autos 355(6); Crim Law 723(3), 730(1).

Grant v. **State**, TexCrimApp, 143 SW2d 383, 140 TexCrim 46.—Consp 47(2); Crim Law 372(9), 423(1), 423(2), 792(2), 1092.14, 1111(3); False Pret 43(2), 47.

Grant v. **State**, TexApp–Houston (1 Dist), 738 SW2d 309, petition for discretionary review refused.—Crim Law 394.4(9), 713, 717, 719(1), 730(1), 730(7), 753.2(2).

Grant v. **State**, TexApp–Houston (1 Dist), 696 SW2d 74, petition for discretionary review refused.—Crim Law 641.13(1), 641.13(2.1), 1166.10(1); Jury 90, 103(8).

Grant v. **State**, TexApp–Fort Worth, 802 SW2d 428, petition for discretionary review gr, rev 822 SW2d 639.—Controlled Subs 34.

Grant v. **State**, TexApp–Austin, 647 SW2d 778.—Burg 2, 29, 41(1), 42(1), 46(1); Crim Law 814(17), 814(20).

Grant v. **State**, TexApp–Dallas, 753 SW2d 185.—Escape 1.

Grant v. **State**, TexApp–Texarkana, 172 SW3d 98.—Afft 17; Crim Law 274(2), 274(9), 956(2), 956(4), 959, 1134(6), 1147.

Grant v. **State**, TexApp–Amarillo, 635 SW2d 933.—Crim Law 633(2), 660, 1166.20; Sent & Pun 1010, 1014, 1064.

Grant v. **State**, TexApp–Amarillo, 625 SW2d 787.—Arrest 63.4(8), 63.5(6); Searches 69.

Grant v. **State**, TexApp–Beaumont, 950 SW2d 450, petition for discretionary review refused.—Crim Law 1136.

Grant v. **State**, TexApp–Beaumont, 944 SW2d 499, petition for discretionary review gr, rev 970 SW2d 22, on remand 1998 WL 809413, petition for discretionary review gr, and rev, opinion after remand from Court of Criminal Appeals 2000 WL 1273339.—Ind & Inf 101, 180.

Grant v. **State**, TexApp–Corpus Christi, 860 SW2d 616, reh overr, and petition for discretionary review refused.—Crim Law 1158(3); Jury 33(5.15).

Grant v. **State**, TexApp–Houston (14 Dist), 218 SW3d 225, petition for discretionary review refused.—Crim Law 662.1, 662.3, 662.8, 730(14), 867, 1035(10), 1043(3), 1130(5), 1154, 1168(2), 1171.1(2.1), 1177.

Grant v. **State**, TexApp–Houston (14 Dist), 154 SW3d 684, reh overr, and petition for discretionary review refused.—Crim Law 13.1(1), 1030(2); Mental H 469(7).

Grant v. **State**, TexApp–Houston (14 Dist), 33 SW3d 875, petition for discretionary review refused.—Assault 56; Crim Law 106, 145, 641.13(1), 956(7), 1044.2(1), 1063(5), 1119(1), 1144.6; Double J 3, 5.1, 6, 60.1, 135; Ind & Inf 113; Judgm 751; Sent & Pun 78, 80, 329, 373, 375.

Grant v. **State**, TexApp–Houston (14 Dist), 989 SW2d 428.—Controlled Subs 26, 27, 28, 68, 79, 80; Crim Law 260.11(4), 273.1(4), 552(3), 742(1), 1144.13(3), 1144.13(5), 1144.13(6), 1159.2(1), 1159.2(2), 1159.2(7), 1159.2(9), 1159.4(1).

Grant v. **State**, TexApp–Houston (14 Dist), 858 SW2d 29.—Crim Law 713, 719(1), 720(5), 728(2), 728(3),

1144.13(2.1), 1159.2(7), 1171.1(2.1), 1171.1(3); Rape 51(1).

Grant; State v., TexApp–Houston (14 Dist), 832 SW2d 624, reh den, and petition for discretionary review refused, and petition for discretionary review refused.— Arrest 63.5(1), 63.5(4), 68(4); Controlled Subs 137; Searches 28.

Grant v. State, TexApp–Houston (14 Dist), 709 SW2d 355. —Arrest 63.5(5), 68(4); Searches 180, 183.

Grant v. Stop-N-Go Market of Texas, Inc., TexApp–Houston (1 Dist), 994 SW2d 867.—False Imp 2, 5, 10; Judgm 181(33); Libel 34, 44(1), 45(1), 50, 50.5, 51(1).

Grant v. Taylor, TexCivApp–Houston, 339 SW2d 554.— New Tr 59; Tresp to T T 6.1, 35(1), 38(1), 38(3), 41(1).

Grant v. Tenney, TexCivApp–San Antonio, 270 SW2d 634. —Adv Poss 43(4); App & E 1011.1(14); Deeds 78; Improv 4(6); Lim of Act 96(2).

Grant; Texas Co. v., Tex, 182 SW2d 996, 143 Tex 145.— Labor & Emp 24; Land & Ten 80(1), 167(5), 169(11); Mun Corp 755(1), 757(1), 788, 791(1), 808(7), 809(1).

Grant; Texas Co. v., TexCivApp–Dallas, 179 SW2d 1007, rev 182 SW2d 996, 143 Tex 145.—Land & Ten 167(5), 170(4); Mun Corp 757(1), 757(2), 808(1), 808(7), 809(1); Nuis 7.

Grant v. Thirteenth Court of Appeals, Tex, 888 SW2d 466, reh overr.—Atty & C 21.10, 21.15, 21.20; Mand 32.

Grant; Traders & General Ins. Co. v., TexCivApp–Texarkana, 137 SW2d 213.—Evid 7; Insurance 2706(1).

Grant v. United Gas Pipe Line Co., TexCivApp–Corpus Christi, 457 SW2d 315, ref nre.—App & E 927(7), 989; Courts 183; Em Dom 166, 172, 221.

Grant; U.S. v., CA5 (Tex), 488 F3d 664, opinion withdrawn and superseded on rehearing in part 493 F3d 464.— Const Law 4726; Crim Law 700(3), 1030(1), 1139, 1668(8); Sent & Pun 861, 943, 946, 986.

Grant; U.S. v., CA5 (Tex), 349 F3d 192, reh and reh den 84 FedAppx 472, cert den 124 SCt 1526, 540 US 1227, 158 LEd2d 169.—Arrest 63.5(1); Autos 349(1), 349(2.1), 349(10), 349(14.1), 349(17), 349.5(1), 349.5(7); Crim Law 1139, 1144.12, 1158(4); Searches 165.

Grant; U.S. v., CA5 (Tex), 117 F3d 788.—Const Law 1417; Crim Law 274(1), 274(8), 274(9), 1149; Sent & Pun 1983(2), 2285.

Grant v. U.S., CA5 (Tex), 424 F2d 273.—Crim Law 273.1(1), 273.1(2), 1132.

Grant v. U.S., CA5 (Tex), 406 F2d 1295.—Crim Law 245, 1618(3), 1618(10), 1655(1).

Grant; U.S. v., NDTex, 933 FSupp 610, aff 117 F3d 788.— Crim Law 274(8), 274(9).

Grant v. U.S. Dept. of Veterans' Affairs, SDTex, 827 FSupp 418, aff 35 F3d 562.—Fed Civ Proc 2544, 2546; Mtg 380, 529(6), 532, 535(1), 559(3), 559(7), 567(1).

Grant; Universal Life Ins. Co. v., TexCivApp–Dallas, 117 SW2d 813.—Insurance 2426, 2433.

Grant v. Wood, TexApp–Houston (1 Dist), 916 SW2d 42. —App & E 70(8), 947; Judgm 186.

Grant, Estate of v. ZLB Corp., TexApp–Waco, 736 SW2d 190.—App & E 80(6).

Grant Evangelistic Ass'n. Inc. v. Dallas Cent. Appraisal Dist., TexApp–Dallas, 900 SW2d 789. See W.V. Grant Evangelistic Ass'n, Inc. v. Dallas Cent. Appraisal Dist.

Grant ex rel. Family Eldercare v. Gilbert, CA5 (Tex), 324 F3d 383.—Decl Judgm 300; Fed Civ Proc 103.2, 103.3, 164.5, 181; Health 510; Inj 114(2).

Grant Geophysical, Inc.; Villarreal v., TexApp–San Antonio, 136 SW3d 265, review den.—Assumpsit 8, 26; Impl & C C 3; Mines 51(1); Tresp 12.

Grantham v. Aetna Life and Cas., NDTex, 455 FSupp 440.—Fed Cts 76, 76.15, 76.35.

Grantham v. Anderson, TexCivApp–Fort Worth, 211 SW2d 275.—Estop 58; Fraud 58(1); Frds St of 63(1), 63(5); Lim of Act 103(2); Mtg 38(1); Trial 351.2(4); Trusts 43(3).

Grantham v. Big Spring Bonded Warehouse & Storage, Inc., TexCivApp–Eastland, 378 SW2d 691.—Neglig 530(1), 1297; Trial 350.7(9).

Grantham; Frymire Engineering Co., Inc. v., Tex, 524 SW2d 680.—Judgm 106(1), 106(9), 109, 126(1).

Grantham; Frymire Engineering Co., Inc. v., TexCivApp–Fort Worth, 517 SW2d 820, writ gr, rev 524 SW2d 680.—App & E 758.1, 758.3(3), 837(1), 966(1), 1064.1(7), 1140(4), 1151(2); Const Law 321, 2311; Damag 113, 163(1), 188(2), 191; Evid 474(18), 474(19); Judgm 53, 103, 162(4); Pretrial Proc 713, 716, 724.

Grantham; Moore v., Tex, 599 SW2d 287.—App & E 1140(4); Evid 548, 555.4(3), 555.4(4), 555.9.

Grantham; Moore v., TexCivApp–Tyler, 580 SW2d 142, rev 599 SW2d 287.—App & E 204(1), 204(7), 230, 232(2), 930(3), 970(2), 989, 1003(5), 1170.9(8), 1177(7); Damag 134(1), 163(4), 208(1), 208(4); Evid 508, 532, 546, 548, 549, 550(1), 555.1, 555.3, 555.4(3), 555.9, 556; Trial 76, 82.

Grantham v. Peterson, TexCivApp–Waco, 288 SW2d 226. —App & E 777.

Grantham v. Rusk County Auction Co., Inc., TexCivApp–Tyler, 553 SW2d 645.—App & E 866(3); Fact 66.

Grantham v. Seaman, TexCivApp–Eastland, 354 SW2d 231.—Evid 318(1); Mental H 10.1.

Grantham v. State, TexCrimApp, 547 SW2d 286.—Crim Law 1042; Larc 55; Sent & Pun 2011.

Grantham v. State, TexCrimApp, 408 SW2d 235.—Bail 39, 79(1).

Grantham v. State, TexCrimApp, 361 SW2d 882, 172 TexCrim 619.—Crim Law 1097(4).

Grantham v. State, TexApp–Fort Worth, 751 SW2d 321, petition for discretionary review refused, cause remanded 760 SW2d 661.—Const Law 2545(4); Controlled Subs 148(4); Crim Law 371(12), 438(4), 627.5(1), 627.6(6), 627.7(3), 660, 673(5), 790, 795(2.1), 795(2.10), 795(2.90), 1038.1(3.1), 1166(10.10), 1172.1(2); Homic 908, 1168, 1460; Searches 105.1.

Grantham v. State, TexApp–Fort Worth, 659 SW2d 494, petition for discretionary review refused.—Crim Law 721(3), 1045; Sent & Pun 1900.

Grantham v. State, TexApp–Tyler, 116 SW3d 136, petition for discretionary review refused, habeas corpus gr Ex parte Grantham, 2007 WL 1138553.—Crim Law 553, 641.5(0.5), 641.13(1), 641.13(6), 741(1), 742(1), 745, 747, 753.2(3.1), 1144.13(2.1), 1156(1), 1159.2(1), 1159.2(2), 1159.2(7), 1159.2(9); Ind & Inf 176; Weap 4, 17(4); Witn 2(1).

Grantom v. State, TexCrimApp, 415 SW2d 664.—Crim Law 369.2(8), 730(10); Ind & Inf 176.

Grantom; Texas Emp. Ins. Ass'n v., TexCivApp–Galveston, 252 SW2d 1001, ref nre.—Work Comp 1969.

Grant Plaza Huntsville Associates; Friday v., Tex, 610 SW2d 747.—Venue 7.5(6), 22(6).

Grant Plaza Huntsville Associates; Friday v., TexApp–Houston (1 Dist), 713 SW2d 755.—App & E 863; Evid 434(8); Judgm 185(3).

Grant Plaza Huntsville Associates; Seven Elves, Inc. v., TexCivApp–Hous (14 Dist), 598 SW2d 692, rev Friday v. Grant Plaza Huntsville Associates, 610 SW2d 747.— Corp 503(1); Venue 22(4), 22(7).

Grant Prideco, Inc.; Wolfe v., TexApp–Houston (1 Dist), 53 SW3d 771, review den.—App & E 5; Judgm 181(15.1), 185.3(1), 335(1), 335(2); Pretrial Proc 676.

Grant Prideco LP; Hydril Co. LP v., CAFed (Tex), 474 F3d 1344, on remand 2007 WL 1791663.—Antitrust 587(3); Courts 96(7); Fed Cts 762; Pat 286, 328(2), 328(4).

Grant Prideco, L.P.; Hydril Co., L.P. v., SDTex, 385 FSupp2d 609, rev in part, vac in part 474 F3d 1344, on remand 2007 WL 1791663.—Decl Judgm 234; Fed Cts 18; Pat 328(2).

Grant Road Public Utility Dist. v. Coulson, TexApp–Houston (1 Dist), 638 SW2d 616.—App & E 758.3(11), 863; Mun Corp 921(3).

Grant Sheet Metal, Inc.; Tacon Mechanical Contractors, Inc. v., TexApp–Houston (14 Dist), 889 SW2d 666, reh overr, and writ den.—App & E 877(1), 901, 930(3), 946, 968, 989, 1001(1), 1004(3), 1004(5), 1004(7), 1004(11), 1079, 1151(2); Contracts 294, 314, 322(4), 328(3); Costs 260(4); Damag 127; Jury 131(1); Mech Liens 115(1); Plead 78, 427; Trial 41(1), 41(5), 109.

Grant, Sosa By and Through, v. Koshy, TexApp–Houston (1 Dist), 961 SW2d 420. See Sosa By and Through Grant v. Koshy.

Grant Thornton, LLP; Prospect High Income Fund v., TexApp–Dallas, 203 SW3d 602.—Accnts 9; Action 17; App & E 854(1), 893(1); Consp 1.1, 6; Contracts 144, 187(1); Dep & Escr 13, 21; Fraud 1.5, 3, 4, 13(3), 20, 25, 29, 30; Judgm 181(31), 183, 185.2(8); Neglig 463, 481.

Grant Thornton LLP; Rahr v., NDTex, 142 FSupp2d 793.—Fed Cts 14.1, 18; Lim of Act 99(1), 100(6), 100(11), 126.5.

Grant Thornton LLP v. Suntrust Bank, TexApp–Dallas, 133 SW3d 342, review den.—Action 17; App & E 173(1), 840(4), 893(1), 913, 949, 1097(1), 1195(1); Courts 97(1), 99(1); Fraud 1.5; Judgm 540, 584, 585(2), 586(0.5); Parties 35.1, 35.9, 35.13, 35.35, 35.85.

Granviel, Ex parte, TexCrimApp, 561 SW2d 503.—Const Law 48(1), 203, 655, 990, 996, 1002, 1030, 2400, 2406, 2407, 2415(5), 2815, 4746; Crim Law 5, 323; Sent & Pun 1435, 1628, 1668, 1709, 1796; Statut 47, 49.

Granviel v. Estelle, CA5 (Tex), 655 F2d 673, cert den 102 SCt 1636, 455 US 1003, 71 LEd2d 870, cert den 102 SCt 1644, 455 US 1007, 71 LEd2d 875.—Const Law 4745; Crim Law 641.12(3); Hab Corp 337, 490(1); Jury 108; Sent & Pun 1625; Witn 206.

Granviel v. Lynaugh, CA5 (Tex), 881 F2d 185, reh den, cert den 110 SCt 2577, 495 US 963, 109 LEd2d 758.—Const Law 4744(2), 4789(2); Costs 302.4; Crim Law 393(1), 517.2(1), 641.3(11), 641.13(2.1), 1158(3); Jury 108; Sent & Pun 1641, 1757, 1758(3), 1759, 1760, 1791; Witn 198(1), 200.

Granviel v. State, TexCrimApp, 723 SW2d 141, cert den 108 SCt 205, 484 US 872, 98 LEd2d 156.—Crim Law 412.2(3), 486(6), 517.2(1), 517.2(2), 577.8(2), 577.10(5), 577.16(7), 662.60, 829(22), 1180, 1192; Jury 108, 148(4); Sent & Pun 1758(1), 1772, 1789(9); Witn 201(1).

Granviel v. State, TexCrimApp, 552 SW2d 107, cert den 97 SCt 2642, 431 US 933, 53 LEd2d 250, habeas corpus gr 655 F2d 673, cert den 102 SCt 1636, 455 US 1003, 71 LEd2d 870, cert den Estelle v. Granviel, 102 SCt 1644, 455 US 1007, 71 LEd2d 875.—Const Law 3831; Crim Law 419(12), 436(2), 627.5(3), 627.5(5), 693, 695(2), 698(1), 700(2.1), 790, 1030(1), 1036.1(2), 1043(2), 1044.1(2), 1166(10.10), 1169.1(10), 1170(1), 1170.5(6); Homic 850; Ind & Inf 139; Jury 33(1.1), 58, 62(3), 84, 108, 142; Sent & Pun 1624, 1626, 1628, 1670, 1772; Statut 267(2); Witn 208(1), 209.

Gran Villa Townhouses Homeowners Ass'n, Inc.; Jakab v., TexApp–Dallas, 149 SW3d 863.—App & E 878(3), 893(1); Contracts 176(2); Costs 194.14, 194.16, 194.22; Covenants 68, 122, 132(2).

Granville v. Lea, TexCivApp–Austin, 336 SW2d 795.—App & E 80(1), 80(3); Judgm 359, 386(4).

Granville v. Rauch, TexCivApp–Austin, 335 SW2d 799.—App & E 274(7), 554(3), 931(3); Land & Ten 239, 248(1), 252(1).

Granville v. Sheriff of Fayette County, TexCivApp–Austin, 342 SW2d 464.—Attach 193; Sheriffs 88.

Granza; U.S. v., CA5 (Tex), 427 F2d 184.—Crim Law 951(1), 958(6), 959, 1134(4), 1156(1), 1158(1), 1192.

Granza v. U.S., CA5 (Tex), 381 F2d 190.—Consp 24.15; Crim Law 393(1), 1165(1).

Granza v. U.S., CA5 (Tex), 377 F2d 746, reh den 381 F2d 190, cert den 88 SCt 291, 389 US 939, 19 LEd2d 292.—

Const Law 665; Crim Law 394.1(2), 422(1), 1169.2(5); Ind & Inf 169; Searches 164.

Grapeland, City of; Massachusetts Bonding & Insurance Co. v., TexCivApp–Galveston, 148 SW2d 1006, mod Massachusetts Bonding & Ins Co v. Farmers & Merchants State Bank, 162 SW2d 657, 139 Tex 310.—Mun Corp 347(1), 352, 353, 373(4); Pub Contr 27, 46.

Grapeland Joint Account; Herod v., TexCivApp–Waco, 366 SW2d 623, ref nre.—Mines 78.1(7).

Grapette Bottling Co.; Lombardo v., TexCivApp–Austin, 252 SW2d 1020.—App & E 846(2), 846(5), 931(3); Sales 359(1).

Grapette Co. v. Bowden, CCA5 (Tex), 165 F2d 487.—Mtg 151(3).

Grapette Co.; Shaddock v., TexCivApp–Waco, 259 SW2d 231.—Antitrust 582, 589; App & E 1062.1; Contracts 97(1); Sales 50; States 18.84, 18.87; Trial 352.1(3).

Grapevine, City of; Davis v., TexApp–Fort Worth, 188 SW3d 748, review den, and reh of petition for review den.—App & E 173(2), 863, 934(1); Civil R 1018, 1019(2), 1021, 1053, 1123, 1204, 1207, 1217, 1218(2), 1218(3), 1218(4), 1225(1), 1225(2), 1225(3), 1529, 1540, 1743, 1744; Courts 97(1); Judgm 181(27), 185(2), 185(5), 185(6), 185.2(8), 185.3(13); Labor & Emp 826.

Grapevine, City of, v. Grapevine Pool Road Joint Venture, TexApp–Fort Worth, 804 SW2d 675. See City of Grapevine v. Grapevine Pool Road Joint Venture.

Grapevine, City of, v. Roberts, Tex, 946 SW2d 841. See City of Grapevine v. Roberts.

Grapevine, City of; Roberts v., TexApp–Fort Worth, 923 SW2d 169, reh overr, writ den with per curiam opinion 946 SW2d 841.—Judgm 181(33); Mun Corp 766, 768(1), 798, 847, 857.

Grapevine, City of; Sanders v., TexApp–Fort Worth, 218 SW3d 772, reh overr, and review den (2 pets).—App & E 66, 68, 70(3), 782, 863, 893(1), 916(1); Counties 141; Courts 39; Decl Judgm 272; Mun Corp 254, 723, 724, 735, 742(1); Plead 104(1), 111.48; Schools 89; States 191.1.

Grapevine, City of; Sipes v., TexApp–Fort Worth, 146 SW3d 273, review gr, rev in part 195 SW3d 689.—Autos 255, 277.1, 278, 279, 282, 293; Joint Adv 1.2(1); Judgm 181(33), 185.3(2); Mun Corp 728, 847, 854, 857; Neglig 1040(3); States 191.4(1).

Grapevine Excavation, Inc.; Federated Mut. Ins. Co. v., CA5 (Tex), 241 F3d 396.—Insurance 3585.

Grapevine Excavation Inc.; Federated Mut. Ins. Co. v., CA5 (Tex), 197 F3d 720.—Insurance 2275, 2278(8), 2278(21), 2914, 2922(1), 2939.

Grapevine Excavation, Inc.; Federated Mut. Ins. Co. v., NDTex, 18 FSupp2d 636, rev in part 197 F3d 720, question certified 197 F3d 730, certified question answered Grapevine Excavation, Inc v. Maryland Lloyds, 35 SW3d 1, answer to certified question conformed to 241 F3d 396.—Insurance 2265, 2275, 2290, 2914, 2939.

Grapevine Excavation, Inc. v. Maryland Lloyds, NDTex, 18 FSupp2d 636. See Federated Mut. Ins. Co. v. Grapevine Excavation, Inc.

Grapevine Excavation, Inc. v. Maryland Lloyds, Tex, 35 SW3d 1, answer to certified question conformed to Federated Mut Ins Co v. Grapevine Excavation, Inc, 241 F3d 396.—Insurance 3585.

Grapevine Pool Road Joint Venture; City of Grapevine v., TexApp–Fort Worth, 804 SW2d 675.—App & E 1008.1(2), 1010.2; Em Dom 2(6), 106, 221.

Grapevine Trucking, Inc. v. Shepherd, TexApp–Fort Worth, 366 SW2d 950, ref nre.—App & E 712, 715(1); Corp 507(6); Judgm 162(2).

Graphic Arts Employee Ben. Trust; Felts v., TexApp–Houston (1 Dist), 680 SW2d 891.—Labor & Emp 426, 567, 676, 687; States 18.51.

Graphilter Corp. v. Vinson, TexCivApp–Dallas, 518 SW2d 952, ref nre.—Antitrust 575, 597; App & E 878(4), 1135; Contracts 116(1), 137(1).

Grapotte v. Adams, Tex, 111 SW2d 690, 130 Tex 587.—Land & Ten 167(5); Mun Corp 808(1).

Grapotte; Hough v., TexComApp, 90 SW2d 1090, 127 Tex 144.—App & E 1050.1(1); Trial 350.2, 350.3(2.1).

Grappi; Home Reader Service, Inc. v., TexCivApp–Dallas, 446 SW2d 95, ref nre.—Contracts 217, 352(6); Damag 190; Trial 420.

Gras v. Beechie, SDTex, 221 FSupp 422.—Admin Law 389, 408; Aliens 317, 425; Const Law 82(6.1).

Gras; U.S. v., CA5 (Tex), 446 F2d 7.—Sent & Pun 2014.

Grasberger v. Grasberger, TexApp–Houston (1 Dist), 713 SW2d 429, dism.—Child S 451, 496.

Grasberger; Grasberger v., TexApp–Houston (1 Dist), 713 SW2d 429, dism.—Child S 451, 496.

Graser v. Graser, Tex, 215 SW2d 867, 147 Tex 404.—App & E 1082(2); Hus & W 30, 267(0.5); Partit 111(1), 114(3); Wills 62, 421, 431, 781, 788, 794.

Graser; Graser v., Tex, 215 SW2d 867, 147 Tex 404.—App & E 1082(2); Hus & W 30, 267(0.5); Partit 111(1), 114(3); Wills 62, 421, 431, 781, 788, 794.

Graser v. Graser, TexCivApp–Waco, 212 SW2d 859, rev 215 SW2d 867, 147 Tex 404.—Plead 291(2); Wills 62, 63, 439, 440, 487(2), 614(1), 634(1).

Graser; Graser v., TexCivApp–Waco, 212 SW2d 859, rev 215 SW2d 867, 147 Tex 404.—Plead 291(2); Wills 62, 63, 439, 440, 487(2), 614(1), 634(1).

Grass v. Credito Mexicano, S.A., CA5 (Tex), 797 F2d 220, cert den 107 SCt 1575, 480 US 934, 94 LEd2d 766.—Antitrust 145; Fraud 41; Intern Law 10.9, 10.10, 10.34.

Grass v. Golden, TexApp–Tyler, 153 SW3d 659, subsequent mandamus proceeding In re Grass, 2004 WL 3021876.—App & E 837(4), 907(2), 907(3); Mand 4(1), 4(4), 32, 168(2), 172; Pretrial Proc 19, 153.1.

Grass v. Straus-Frank Co., TexCivApp–Texarkana, 297 SW2d 198, ref nre.—Fixt 19.

Grassedonio; Swanson v., TexApp–Corpus Christi, 647 SW2d 716.—Inj 135, 138.21; Mtg 333, 338; Ven & Pur 220, 231(2), 231(4), 231(16), 239(1), 245.

Grassi v. Ciba-Geigy, Ltd., CA5 (Tex), 894 F2d 181, reh den 899 F2d 11.—Fed Cts 281, 293.1, 294; Rem of C 35.

Grassi v. International Paper Co., CA5 (Tex), 961 F2d 558. See International Paper Co., In re.

Grasso v. Cannon Ball Motor Freight Lines, TexComApp, 81 SW2d 482, 125 Tex 154.—Action 50(1), 50(4.1); App & E 1064.1(8); Autos 92, 95; Statut 184, 185, 217, 217.2, 223.5(0.5); Trial 232(2).

Grasso v. Ellis, TexCivApp–San Antonio, 608 SW2d 347.—Judgm 78, 80, 91; Stip 14(12).

Grasso Oilfield Services, Inc.; Magcobar North American, A Div. of Dresser Industries, Inc. v., TexApp–Corpus Christi, 736 SW2d 787, writ gr, cause dism 754 SW2d 646.—App & E 1062.1; Contracts 39, 229(1), 230; Damag 45, 94, 140, 163(1), 184, 190; Estop 85; Forci E & D 48; Frds St of 129(7), 129(11), 144, 159; New Tr 108(3); Torts 242, 243, 271, 272; Trial 139.1(3), 140(1), 142, 295(1), 352.10; Wharves 9.

Grasty v. Wood, TexCivApp–Galveston, 230 SW2d 568, ref nre.—Trusts 63.5, 72, 80, 86, 89(1), 89(5), 91, 92.5, 359(1).

Grasz v. Grasz, TexCivApp–Dallas, 608 SW2d 356.—Divorce 76; Proc 8, 12, 64, 89, 90, 95.

Grasz; Grasz v., TexCivApp–Dallas, 608 SW2d 356.—Divorce 76; Proc 8, 12, 64, 89, 90, 95.

Gratehouse v. Gratehouse, TexCivApp–Waco, 417 SW2d 592.—Courts 480(1); Plead 1, 4.

Gratehouse; Gratehouse v., TexCivApp–Waco, 417 SW2d 592.—Courts 480(1); Plead 1, 4.

Gratex Corp., In re, BkrtcyNDTex, 40 BR 880. See Compton Corp., In re.

Gratex Corp., In re, BkrtcyNDTex, 40 BR 875. See Compton Corp., In re.

Gratex Corp.; U.S. Dept. of Energy v., NDTex, 66 BR 209.—Bankr 2957, 3782, 3786; Courts 96(7).

Gratton v. Fitch, TexCivApp–El Paso, 352 SW2d 902.—Neglig 1612, 1625, 1696.

Gratty, Inc.; Fun Motors of Longview, Inc. v., TexApp–Texarkana, 51 SW3d 756, review gr, rev Latch v. Gratty, Inc, 107 SW3d 543.—App & E 219(1), 852, 893(1), 990, 1010.1(1), 1010.1(2), 1010.1(3), 1012.1(4); Contracts 10(1), 10(4), 221(1); Damag 137, 163(4); Neglig 375, 379, 380, 387; Plead 290(3), 427; Torts 212, 222, 242; Trial 140(1).

Gratty, Inc.; Latch v., Tex, 107 SW3d 543.—App & E 931(1), 1010.2; Corp 397; Judgm 250; Princ & A 138, 146(2), 150(3); Torts 223, 242.

Gratzer; Texas Dept. of Public Safety v., TexApp–Houston (1 Dist), 982 SW2d 88.—Admin Law 750, 791; Autos 144.2(9.1), 144.2(10.5).

Graubart; Cadle v., TexApp–Beaumont, 990 SW2d 469.—App & E 863, 893(1); Appear 9(2); Const Law 3964, 3965(1); Corp 1.4(4); Courts 12(2.1), 12(2.5), 12(2.10), 12(2.15), 12(2.20).

Graue; Grimes v., BkrtcySDTex, 158 BR 965. See Haws, In re.

Graue v. State, TexApp–San Antonio, 783 SW2d 322.—Crim Law 1169.1(7).

Graue & Affiliates; Grimes v., BkrtcySDTex, 158 BR 965. See Haws, In re.

Graue-Haws, Inc. v. Fuller, TexApp–El Paso, 666 SW2d 238.—Statut 228; Venue 3.

Grauer; Rittenmeyer v., TexApp–Dallas, 104 SW3d 725, reh overr.—App & E 863, 893(1), 931(4), 1024.3; Const Law 3964; Courts 12(2.1), 12(2.5), 12(2.10), 12(2.15), 12(2.20), 12(2.25), 35, 39.

Gravell; Great Am. Indem. Co. v., TexCivApp–San Antonio, 297 SW2d 371.—Work Comp 574, 880, 1403, 1651, 1941.

Gravely v. Lewisville Independent School Dist., TexApp–Fort Worth, 701 SW2d 956, ref nre.—Schools 89.1, 89.4, 89.7.

Graves, Ex parte, TexCrimApp, 70 SW3d 103, reh den.—Crim Law 641.1; Hab Corp 201, 441, 500.1, 613, 690, 898(2); Statut 188.

Graves, Ex parte, TexCrimApp, 468 SW2d 63.—Hab Corp 484, 792.1.

Graves, Ex parte, TexCrimApp, 186 SW2d 248, 148 Tex-Crim 234.—Extrad 34; Hab Corp 711.

Graves, Ex parte, TexApp–Houston (1 Dist), 853 SW2d 701, reh den, and petition for discretionary review refused.—Bail 43, 49(3.1), 49(4); Crim Law 1134(10), 1158(2); Tel 1440.

Graves, In re, CA5 (Tex), 70 FedAppx 752.—Bankr 3117; Ven & Pur 92.

Graves, In re, TexApp–Waco, 217 SW3d 744.—Const Law 617, 2112; Crim Law 304(1), 304(9), 633(1); Mand 3(2.1), 61.

Graves; Adelman on Behalf of Adelman v., CA5 (Tex), 747 F2d 986.—Fed Civ Proc 1746; Mental H 488.

Graves v. Alders, TexApp–Beaumont, 132 SW3d 12, review den, and reh of petition for review den.—Action 60; App & E 223, 242(2), 707(1), 766, 837(10), 949, 966(1); Costs 198; Judgm 185.3(19), 186; Pretrial Proc 713; Spec Perf 28(2), 65, 87, 90, 92(1).

Graves; Amis Propane, Inc. v., TexCivApp–El Paso, 305 SW2d 300.—Judgm 256(6); Lim of Act 127(8); Trial 358, 365.1(5).

Graves; Atkins v., TexCivApp–Fort Worth, 367 SW2d 372, ref nre.—App & E 2, 345.1, 1170.7; Courts 85(2); Evid 314(1), 318(1), 318(4); New Tr 155.

Graves v. Barnes, USTex, 92 SCt 752, 405 US 1201, 30 LEd2d 769.—Fed Cts 446.

Graves v. Barnes, CA5 (Tex), 700 F2d 220.—Fed Civ Proc 2737.4; Fed Cts 830.

Graves v. Barnes, WDTex, 446 FSupp 560, aff Briscoe v. Escalante, 98 SCt 1444, 435 US 901, 55 LEd2d 492, reh den 98 SCt 1479, 435 US 919, 55 LEd2d 512.—Const Law 3658(6); States 27(3), 27(5), 27(10).

Graves v. Barnes, WDTex, 408 FSupp 1050, application den Escalante v. Briscoe, 96 SCt 1404, 424 US 937, 47 LEd2d 345.—Const Law 3658(6); States 27(7), 27(10); U S 10.

Graves v. Barnes, WDTex, 378 FSupp 640, probable jur noted White v. Regester, 94 SCt 2601, 417 US 906, 41 LEd2d 210, vac 95 SCt 2670, 422 US 935, 45 LEd2d 662, on remand 408 FSupp 1050, application den Escalante v Briscoe, 96 SCt 1404, 424 US 937, 47 LEd2d 345. —Const Law 1482; States 27(4.1), 27(7), 27(10).

Graves v. Barnes, WDTex, 343 FSupp 704, stay den 92 SCt 752, 405 US 1201, 30 LEd2d 769, aff Archer v. Smith, 93 SCt 62, 409 US 808, 34 LEd2d 68, probable jur noted Bullock v Regester, 93 SCt 70, 409 US 840, 34 LEd2d 79, aff in part, rev in part White v Regester, 93 SCt 2332, 412 US 755, 37 LEd2d 314, on remand 378 FSupp 640, probable jur noted 94 SCt 2601, 417 US 906, 41 LEd2d 210, vac 95 SCt 2670, 422 US 935, 45 LEd2d 662, on remand 408 FSupp 1050, application den Escalante v Briscoe, 96 SCt 1404, 424 US 937, 47 LEd2d 345. —Const Law 1460, 1464, 1465, 1466, 1480, 2970, 3039, 3068, 3070, 3250, 3285, 3658(1), 3658(3), 3658(8), 4232; Elections 1, 10 1/2, 12(9.1), 24; Evid 586(2); Fed Civ Proc 314.1, 821; Fed Cts 997; States 27(1), 27(3), 27(4.1), 27(5), 27(7), 27(10), 28(1).

Graves v. Beto, CA5 (Tex), 424 F2d 524, cert den 91 SCt 353, 400 US 960, 27 LEd2d 269.—Crim Law 388.2; Hab Corp 384.

Graves v. Beto, EDTex, 301 FSupp 264, aff 424 F2d 524, cert den 91 SCt 353, 400 US 960, 27 LEd2d 269.—Crim Law 304(3), 388.2.

Graves; Browning v., TexCivApp–Fort Worth, 152 SW2d 515, writ refused.—App & E 231(1), 882(14), 1015(5); Evid 314(1); Neglig 1741; Prisons 10; Trial 350.6(2), 352.4(6), 352.5(5).

Graves; Burnett v., CA5 (Tex), 230 F2d 49, 56 ALR2d 1, cert den 76 SCt 1051, 351 US 984, 100 LEd 1498.— Attach 134; Atty & C 166(3), 166(4), 167(4); Bonds 3; Evid 177; Fed Civ Proc 2233, 2744; Fed Cts 630.1, 774, 847; Interest 39(3).

Graves v. City of Dallas, TexCivApp–Dallas, 532 SW2d 106, ref nre.—Mand 3(1), 3(4), 63, 75; Mun Corp 185(7), 218(8).

Graves v. Cockrell, CA5 (Tex), 351 F3d 156, appeal after remand 442 F3d 334, cert den Quarterman v. Graves, 127 SCt 374, 166 LEd2d 253.—Hab Corp 818, 864(1).

Graves v. Cockrell, CA5 (Tex), 351 F3d 143, on reh in part 351 F3d 156, appeal after remand 442 F3d 334, cert den Quarterman v. Graves, 127 SCt 374, 166 LEd2d 253, cert den 124 SCt 2160, 541 US 1057, 158 LEd2d 757, appeal after remand 442 F3d 334, cert den 127 SCt 374, 166 LEd2d 253.—Const Law 4594(1); Crim Law 641.13(6), 641.13(7), 700(2.1), 700(4); Hab Corp 332.1, 341, 401, 405.1, 407, 422, 462, 690, 818.

Graves; Commercial Inv. Co. of Uvalde v., TexCivApp– San Antonio, 132 SW2d 439, writ refused.—App & E 181, 719(1), 742(1), 742(2), 758.1; Bills & N 96, 140, 237; Trial 171.

Graves v. Connecticut General Life Ins. Co., TexCiv-App–Fort Worth, 104 SW2d 121, writ dism.—App & E 770(1), 771, 772, 773(2).

Graves v. Diehl, TexApp–Houston (14 Dist), 958 SW2d 468, on subsequent appeal 2006 WL 1699527, review den.—Action 13; Courts 89; Equity 72(1), 87(2); Nuis 26, 29; Tresp 19(1), 29; Ven & Pur 1.

Graves; Dougia v., CA5 (Tex), 181 FedAppx 438, cert den 127 SCt 582, 166 LEd2d 429.—Fed Cts 915.

Graves v. Dretke, CA5 (Tex), 442 F3d 334, cert den Quarterman v. Graves, 127 SCt 374, 166 LEd2d 253.— Crim Law 700(2.1), 700(4), 735; Hab Corp 765.1, 842, 846.

Graves v. Estelle, CA5 (Tex), 556 F2d 743.—Hab Corp 431, 775(1), 775(2).

Graves; Evans v., TexCivApp–Fort Worth, 347 SW2d 267, ref nre.—Courts 1; Ex & Ad 504(2); Judgm 185.3(17).

Graves; Evans v., TexCivApp–Dallas, 166 SW2d 955, writ refused, and writ refused wom.—App & E 832(4), 1177(6); Life Est 23; Partit 95; Remaind 17(2), 17(3).

Graves v. George Dullnig & Co., TexCivApp–San Antonio, 538 SW2d 149.—App & E 387(1), 388.

Graves v. George Dullnig & Co., TexCivApp–Eastland, 548 SW2d 502.—Judgm 181(18), 185(2), 185.1(3), 185.3(7), 186.

Graves v. Graves, TexApp–Houston (1 Dist), 916 SW2d 65.—Child C 567, 606, 743, 921(1).

Graves; Graves v., TexApp–Houston (1 Dist), 916 SW2d 65.—Child C 567, 606, 743, 921(1).

Graves v. Guaranty Bond State Bank, TexCivApp–Texarkana, 161 SW2d 118.—App & E 931(1), 989; Evid 383(7); Hus & W 267(8); Mtg 153, 186(3), 186(5), 334, 356, 360.

Graves; Halliburton Co. Benefits Committee v., CA5 (Tex), 479 F3d 360.—Labor & Emp 446.

Graves; Halliburton Co. Benefits Committee v., CA5 (Tex), 463 F3d 360, decision clarified on denial of reh 479 F3d 360.—Corp 296, 426(1), 585, 589, 590(1); Labor & Emp 445, 446, 549(1), 630, 678.

Graves; Halliburton Co. Benefits Committee v., CA5 (Tex), 191 FedAppx 248, appeal after remand 463 F3d 360, decision clarified on denial of reh 479 F3d 360.— Fed Cts 595.

Graves v. Hallmark, TexCivApp–Amarillo, 232 SW2d 130, ref nre.—App & E 598; Mech Liens 161(1); Paymt 39(1).

Graves v. Hampton, CA5 (Tex), 1 F3d 315.—Civil R 1091, 1375, 1376(8), 1376(9); Fed Civ Proc 1838; Fed Cts 791, 830; Judges 36.

Graves v. Hartford Acc. & Indem. Co., TexComApp, 161 SW2d 464, 138 Tex 589.—Fraud 13(2); Judgm 199(1); Work Comp 1159, 1162.

Graves; Hartford Acc. & Indem. Co. v., TexCivApp– Eastland, 148 SW2d 859, rev 161 SW2d 464, 138 Tex 589.—Contracts 94(3); Fraud 3; Judgm 198; Work Comp 1154, 1159, 1162.

Graves; Hillman v., TexCivApp–San Antonio, 134 SW2d 436.—Estop 22(2); Evid 419(2); Fraud 4, 12, 35, 64(2); Mtg 297.

Graves v. Johnson, SDTex, 111 FSupp2d 857.—Atty & C 132; Hab Corp 690.

Graves v. Johnson, SDTex, 101 FSupp2d 496.—Hab Corp 883.1.

Graves; Komet v., TexApp–San Antonio, 40 SW3d 596.— App & E 863, 930(1), 974(0.5), 1001(3), 1003(7); Contracts 9(1), 14, 15, 16, 24, 29, 138(1), 328(1), 342; Judgm 199(3.10); Labor & Emp 57, 58, 855, 873; Plead 78; Trial 350.1.

Graves v. Komet, TexApp–San Antonio, 982 SW2d 551.— App & E 863, 866(3), 934(1); Civil R 1244; Judgm 185(5), 185.3(13).

Graves; Liberty Mut. Ins. Co. v., TexCivApp–Corpus Christi, 573 SW2d 249, ref nre.—App & E 930(1), 989; Statut 212.6; Work Comp 73, 845, 851, 1030.1(1), 1030.1(2), 1030.1(3), 1653, 1968(3).

Graves; Luther v., TexCivApp–Fort Worth, 408 SW2d 242, ref nre.—Cert 5(1).

Graves v. McClellan, TexCivApp–Waco, 190 SW2d 154.— Adv Poss 14, 31.

Graves; Miller v., TexCivApp–Fort Worth, 185 SW2d 745, writ refused.—Divorce 322; Frds St of 74(1), 119(2), 129(6), 129(11), 138(4); Fraud Conv 299(1), 313(1), 314.

Graves v. Moon, TexCivApp–Waco, 92 SW2d 290, writ refused.—Ex & Ad 129(3); Witn 159(7).

Graves v. Morales, TexApp–Austin, 923 SW2d 754, reh overr, and writ den.—Admin Law 390.1, 408; Atty & C 28; Judgm 185(2); Mun Corp 870; Tax 2801, 2878(2).

Graves v. Nashville, Chattanooga & St. Louis Ry. Co., CCA5 (Tex), 132 F2d 128.—Carr 35, 194.

Graves; Pacific Molasses Co. v., TexCivApp–San Antonio, 451 SW2d 294, ref nre.—Costs 194.38; Guar 78(2); Paymt 85(3); Trial 365.1(4).

Graves v. Poe, TexCivApp–El Paso, 118 SW2d 969, writ dism.—Damag 59, 64.

Graves; Revel Craft Mfg. Co. v., TexCivApp–Waco, 477 SW2d 643.—App & E 627.3.

Graves; Rogers v., TexCivApp–Waco, 221 SW2d 399, writ refused.—Courts 52; Statut 8.5(1).

Graves v. Slater, TexCivApp–San Antonio, 83 SW2d 1041, writ dism.—App & E 790(3); Judgm 447(1), 461(5).

Graves v. Sommerfeld, TexCivApp–Waco, 618 SW2d 952, ref nre.—Contracts 319(0.5), 322(4); Costs 207, 208; Trial 55, 339(2).

Graves v. Southern Underwriters, TexCivApp–Austin, 130 SW2d 360, writ dism, correct.—Garn 34; Insurance 2739, 3108, 3549(4).

Graves v. State, TexCrimApp, 795 SW2d 185.—Crim Law 145.5, 147.

Graves v. State, TexCrimApp, 539 SW2d 890.—Double J 150(3).

Graves v. State, TexCrimApp, 513 SW2d 57.—Controlled Subs 69, 113; Crim Law 720(7.1), 730(14), 1036.9, 1115(2); Searches 40.1.

Graves v. State, TexCrimApp, 382 SW2d 486, cert den 85 SCt 1114, 380 US 967, 14 LEd2d 157, reh den 85 SCt 1544, 381 US 921, 14 LEd2d 442.—Crim Law 722.4, 913(1), 939(3), 1186.1.

Graves v. State, TexCrimApp, 336 SW2d 156, 169 TexCrim 595, cert den 80 SCt 1256, 363 US 819, 4 LEd2d 1516.—Crim Law 404.75, 406(2), 736(1), 1064.5, 1092.14; Searches 184.

Graves v. State, TexCrimApp, 301 SW2d 156.—Crim Law 1090.1(1).

Graves v. State, TexCrimApp, 294 SW2d 100.—Bail 63.1.

Graves v. State, TexCrimApp, 284 SW2d 351.—Crim Law 1090.1(1).

Graves v. State, TexCrimApp, 274 SW2d 555, 161 TexCrim 16.—Crim Law 814(1); Rape 4.

Graves v. State, TexCrimApp, 256 SW2d 576, 158 TexCrim 429.—Crim Law 1097(1), 1147.

Graves v. State, TexApp–Houston (1 Dist), 176 SW3d 422, petition stricken.—Crim Law 396(1), 641.13(2.1), 673(5), 708.1, 720(5), 720(6), 723(1), 726, 822(1), 824(8), 919(3), 1168(2), 1171.1(2.1), 1172.1(1); Sent & Pun 313; Witn 414(2).

Graves v. State, TexApp–Dallas, 782 SW2d 5, petition for discretionary review refused.—Crim Law 44; Homic 876, 1168.

Graves v. State, TexApp–El Paso, 779 SW2d 469.—Infants 20.

Graves v. State, TexApp–Beaumont, 712 SW2d 627.—Crim Law 264, 412.2(2); Homic 1076, 1182, 1186.

Graves v. State, TexApp–Tyler, 968 SW2d 386, petition for discretionary review refused, and reh overr.—Crim Law 770(2), 792(1), 792(2), 814(21), 829(1), 829(20); Homic 1387.

Graves v. State, TexApp–Corpus Christi, 994 SW2d 238, petition for discretionary review refused, untimely filed. —Const Law 2789, 2790, 2812; Crim Law 376, 450, 622.4, 641.13(2.1), 641.13(6), 662.65, 719(3); Ind & Inf 171; Infants 12(8); Rape 17, 35(4), 42, 51(4), 52(4), 59(11); Sod 6.

Graves v. State, TexApp–Houston (14 Dist), 803 SW2d 342, petition for discretionary review refused.—Crim Law 273.1(2), 273.4(1), 274(8), 641.13(5); Sent & Pun 373, 1853, 1911.

Graves; State v., TexApp–Houston (14 Dist), 775 SW2d 32, petition for discretionary review gr, aff 795 SW2d 185.—Crim Law 150.

Graves; State v., CA5 (Tex), 380 F2d 676.—Const Law 4667; Courts 100(1); Crim Law 414.

Graves; State of Tex. v., CA5 (Tex), 352 F2d 514.—Hab Corp 818.

Graves v. Texas Dept. of Corrections Employees, TexApp–Houston (1 Dist), 827 SW2d 47, appeal after remand 1995 WL 370294, on subsequent appeal 1997 WL 197883, review den.—App & E 1203(1); Prisons 13(3); Sent & Pun 1532, 1534, 1538, 1540, 1550.

Graves; Texas Elec. Service Co. v., TexCivApp–El Paso, 488 SW2d 135, ref nre.—Em Dom 149(4), 201, 203(2), 203(7), 262(5); Evid 142(1).

Graves v. Texas Emp. Ins. Ass'n, TexCivApp–Dallas, 197 SW2d 596.—Work Comp 617, 757.

Graves; Texas Skaggs, Inc. v., TexCivApp–Texarkana, 582 SW2d 863.—App & E 1051.1(2); Evid 314(1), 317(2); False Pret 22, 39; Mal Pros 16, 27, 29, 35(1), 35(2), 40, 56, 64(2), 69, 71(3).

Graves; Travis Builders, Inc. v., TexCivApp–Tyler, 583 SW2d 865.—App & E 859; Corp 668(13); Evid 383(4); Judgm 17(2), 951(1).

Graves; Trevino v., TexCivApp–Hous (1 Dist), 418 SW2d 529.—Debtor & C 11; Fraud Conv 243, 313(1).

Graves v. Trevino, TexCivApp–Houston, 386 SW2d 831, ref nre.—App & E 187(3), 302(1), 1003(9.1), 1170.7, 1170.10; Evid 474(19); Hus & W 114, 262.1(1); Trover 44, 45, 46.

Graves; U.S. v., CA5 (Tex), 720 F2d 821.—Crim Law 273(4.1), 1086.13, 1126.

Graves; U.S. v., CA5 (Tex), 669 F2d 964.—Autos 341; Consp 23.1, 28(3), 40.1, 43(6), 47(2), 47(11), 48.2(2); Crim Law 636(7), 805(1), 822(1), 1038.1(1), 1038.3, 1166.22(2); Ind & Inf 71.4(8); Rec S Goods 3.

Graves; Wright v., TexApp–Beaumont, 671 SW2d 586.—Const Law 556; Elections 273; Health 233, 235; Statut 223.1.

Gravett; United Am. Ins. Co. v., TexCivApp–Eastland, 339 SW2d 682, ref nre.—Insurance 1816, 1828, 1836, 1898, 2532, 3375.

Gravis; Abbott Laboratories v., Tex, 470 SW2d 639.—Judgm 185.3(21), 587, 713(2).

Gravis v. Abbott Laboratories, TexCivApp–Corpus Christi, 462 SW2d 410, aff in part, rev in part 470 SW2d 639.—Judgm 185.3(21), 585(1), 586(1), 587.

Gravis v. Duval County, TexCivApp–San Antonio, 337 SW2d 306.—Counties 159, 196(3), 196(7).

Gravis v. Parke-Davis & Co., TexCivApp–Corpus Christi, 502 SW2d 863, ref nre.—App & E 201(1), 863, 927(7), 1170.7; Health 906; Pretrial Proc 473; Prod Liab 14, 46.2, 75.1, 78, 83; Trial 56.

Gravis v. Physicians and Surgeons Hospital of Alice, Tex, 427 SW2d 310.—Assault 2; Hus & W 21, 25(1); Judgm 185.3(21).

Gravis v. Physicians and Surgeons Hospital of Alice, TexCivApp–San Antonio, 415 SW2d 674, writ gr, rev 427 SW2d 310.—App & E 766, 837(10); Assault 11, 35; Evid 558(11), 560; Health 620, 625, 656, 661, 665, 821(2), 821(3), 821(5), 822(1), 823(1), 823(5), 823(13), 908, 909; Neglig 1675, 1713.

Gravis; Red Arrow Freight Lines v., TexCivApp–San Antonio, 84 SW2d 540.—Damag 163(1); Evid 123(11), 123(12), 242(10), 243(4); Trial 252(20).

Gravis v. Rogers, TexCivApp–Austin, 214 SW2d 886, ref nre.—Assign 8; Deeds 90, 111, 194(5), 208(4); Hus & W 110, 179, 195, 275, 276(3), 276(4), 276(7), 276(8); Princ & A 70.

Gravis v. State, TexApp–Austin, 982 SW2d 933, petition for discretionary review refused.—Crim Law 633(1), 637, 641.13(1), 641.13(2.1), 723(3), 1030(2); Homic 576, 581, 612.

Gravitt; Southwestern Bell Tel. Co. v., TexCivApp–San Antonio, 551 SW2d 421, ref nre.—Contracts 111, 116(1); Inj 61(2), 189; Labor & Emp 219, 614, 2792; Perp 6(1); Plead 373.

Gravitt; Southwestern Bell Tel. Co. v., TexCivApp–San Antonio, 522 SW2d 531.—App & E 670(1), 1165; Inj 157, 204.

Gravitt v. Southwestern Bell Telephone Co., USTex, 97 SCt 1439, 430 US 723, 52 LEd2d 1, reh den 97 SCt 2941, 431 US 975, 53 LEd2d 1073, on remand In re Southwestern Bell Tel Co, 556 F2d 370.—Rem of C 107(9).

Gravitt v. Southwestern Bell Telephone Co., WDTex, 416 FSupp 830, mandamus gr, order vac In re Southwestern Bell Telephone Co, 535 F2d 859, opinion mod on reh 542 F2d 297, vac 556 F2d 370, cert gr, rev 97 SCt 1439, 430 US 723, 52 LEd2d 1, reh den 97 SCt 2941, 431 US 975, 53 LEd2d 1073, on remand 556 F2d 370, vac 556 F2d 370.—Estop 68(2); Rem of C 107(11).

Gravitt v. Southwestern Bell Telephone Co., WDTex, 396 FSupp 948, motion gr 416 FSupp 830, mandamus gr, order vac In re Southwestern Bell Telephone Co, 535 F2d 859, opinion mod on reh 542 F2d 297, vac 556 F2d 370, cert gr, rev 97 SCt 1439, 430 US 723, 52 LEd2d 1, reh den 97 SCt 2941, 431 US 975, 53 LEd2d 1073, on remand 556 F2d 370, vac 556 F2d 370.—Courts 87; Fed Cts 21; Plead 252(2), 264; Pretrial Proc 511; Rem of C 17, 43, 47, 48.2.

G.R.A.V.I.T.Y. Enterprises, Inc. v. Reece Supply Co., TexApp–Dallas, 177 SW3d 537, reh overr.—Antitrust 369; App & E 170(1), 173(10), 179(3), 195, 760(1), 766, 893(1), 959(1), 964, 1079; Costs 194.14, 194.16, 194.32; Damag 71, 73; Plead 236(2), 236(7), 356; Sales 417, 441(3).

Gravley v. Gravley, TexCivApp–Dallas, 353 SW2d 333, writ dism.—Child 1, 3, 5, 6, 11, 12; Evid 14.

Gravley; Gravley v., TexCivApp–Dallas, 353 SW2d 333, writ dism.—Child 1, 3, 5, 6, 11, 12; Evid 14.

Gray, Ex parte, TexCrimApp, 649 SW2d 640.—Contempt 20, 24, 66(1); Hab Corp 528.1; Mand 1, 4(3), 42; Prohib 1, 5(2).

Gray, Ex parte, TexCrimApp, 564 SW2d 713.—Crim Law 1081(6); Hab Corp 469, 812.

Gray, Ex parte, TexCrimApp, 437 SW2d 871.—Hab Corp 724, 792.1.

Gray, Ex parte, TexCrimApp, 426 SW2d 241.—Extrad 34, 39.

Gray, Ex parte, TexApp–Dallas, 109 SW3d 917.—Crim Law 1226(3.1), 1226(4).

Gray, Ex parte, TexApp–Texarkana, 126 SW3d 565, petition for discretionary review dism as untimely filed.—Crim Law 48, 273.1(3), 311, 331, 641.13(1), 641.13(5); Hab Corp 486(1), 813.

Gray, Ex parte, TexApp–Eastland, 654 SW2d 68.—Child S 474.

Gray, In re, BkrtcyNDTex, 285 BR 379.—Bankr 3705, 3708(2), 3708(6), 3710(6), 3715(7); Interest 35.

Gray, In re, BkrtcyNDTex, 224 BR 360. See Thompson, In re.

Gray; Adams v., TexCivApp–Hous (14 Dist), 448 SW2d 854.—Anim 55, 100(9).

Gray v. Adolph, TexCivApp–Beaumont, 117 SW2d 122, writ refused.—App & E 870(3); Autos 245(88); Damag 221(6); Plead 111.8; Trial 351.5(6), 352.6; Venue 8.5(4), 22(6).

Gray v. Allen, TexApp–Fort Worth, 41 SW3d 330, reh overr.—App & E 989, 1003(7), 1004(13), 1182; Damag 94; Libel 121(2); New Tr 76(1).

Gray; Alpha Petroleum Co. v., TexCivApp–Galveston, 103 SW2d 1047.—App & E 1178(8); Plead 111.7.

Gray v. Amalgamated Meat Cutters Local 540, CA5 (Tex), 736 F2d 1055.—Courts 100(1).

Gray v. Amerada Petroleum Corp, CCA5 (Tex), 145 F2d 730.—Fed Cts 691, 927.

Gray v. Armour & Co., TexComApp, 104 SW2d 486, 129 Tex 512.—Corp 509.1(3); Garn 145, 165, 178.

Gray v. Armstrong, TexCivApp–Dallas, 364 SW2d 485.—Evid 317(5), 593; Plead 111.42(8); Pretrial Proc 479, 481; Princ & A 22(1).

Gray; Baker v., TexCivApp–Amarillo, 290 SW2d 543, ref nre.—Atty & C 74.

Gray v. Baker & Taylor Drilling Co., TexCivApp–Amarillo, 602 SW2d 64, ref nre.—Labor & Emp 3159; Mines 118; Neglig 202.

Gray v. Bertrand, Tex, 723 SW2d 957, appeal after remand 767 SW2d 498, writ den.—Banks 152.

Gray v. Bertrand, TexApp–Beaumont, 767 SW2d 498, writ den.—Banks 100; Damag 87(2); Gifts 49(5); Wills 723.

Gray; Bertrand v., TexApp–Beaumont, 718 SW2d 908, aff in part, rev in part 723 SW2d 957, appeal after remand 767 SW2d 498, writ den.—App & E 934(1), 989; Judgm 181(17).

Gray v. Bird, TexCivApp–Tyler, 380 SW2d 908, ref nre.—App & E 690(1), 931(6); Courts 202(5); Evid 222(9), 548, 555.4(3), 555.4(4), 555.10, 570; Trial 377(1); Wills 55(1), 400.

Gray v. Blau, TexCivApp–Beaumont, 223 SW2d 53, ref nre.—App & E 241; Evid 413; Licens 22, 39.40(1), 39.40(2).

Gray v. Block, TexCivApp–Eastland, 416 SW2d 848.—Land & Ten 152(1), 152(2), 164(1), 164(2).

Gray; Boddy v., TexCivApp–Amarillo, 497 SW2d 600, ref nre.—Estop 85, 102; Frds St of 106(1), 110(1), 118(1), 118(2), 125(2), 158(3); Spec Perf 39.

Gray; Brewer v., TexCivApp–Dallas, 103 SW2d 1003, writ refused.—Mun Corp 302(1), 586.

Gray; Brite v., TexCivApp–Beaumont, 377 SW2d 223.—Covenants 49, 69(1), 84; Deeds 93, 101.

Gray; Brown v., TexCivApp–Waco, 383 SW2d 950, ref nre.—Agric 3.3(1).

Gray v. Brownlow, CA5 (Tex), 157 FedAppx 753.—Civil R 1395(7); Fed Cts 714, 726.

Gray; Burges v., TexCivApp–San Antonio, 211 SW2d 776, ref nre.—Assign 8, 131, 134, 137; Tresp to T T 4, 35(2).

Gray v. Burroughs, TexCivApp–Galveston, 298 SW2d 859.—App & E 933(4), 1015(5); New Tr 142, 143(5).

Gray; Busby v., TexCivApp–San Antonio, 616 SW2d 284, ref nre.—Wills 497(1).

Gray v. Bush, TexCivApp–Fort Worth, 430 SW2d 258, ref nre.—Action 6; App & E 936(2), 1008.1(7); Decl Judgm 61, 67; Equity 39(1); Ex & Ad 92, 219.7(2), 453(2); Impl & C C 15.1; Insurance 2062; Judgm 310; Trusts 140(2), 177, 268, 273.5.

Gray; Caddell v., TexCivApp–Waco, 544 SW2d 481.—App & E 66, 112, 1024.3; Mand 53; Pretrial Proc 698.

Gray; Carter v., TexComApp, 81 SW2d 647, 125 Tex 219.—Bills & N 463; Courts 164; Elect of Rem 4.

Gray; Carver v., TexCivApp–Amarillo, 140 SW2d 227, writ dism, correct.—Home 161, 168, 181(3), 181.5, 212; Judgm 769, 801; Plead 32, 308.

Gray v. Cauble, CA5 (Tex), 849 F2d 946. See Lewisville Properties, Inc., Matter of.

Gray; Cauble v., TexCivApp–Dallas, 604 SW2d 197.—App & E 912; Domicile 1; Plead 111.42(3); Venue 28.

Gray v. CHCA Bayshore L.P., TexApp–Houston (1 Dist), 189 SW3d 855.—App & E 945, 946; Health 623, 804, 809.

Gray; City of Amarillo v., TexCivApp–Amarillo, 304 SW2d 742, aff in part, rev in part 310 SW2d 737, 158 Tex 275.—Adj Land 4(1); App & E 1064.1(8); Em Dom 69, 307(3); Lim of Act 55(5); Mun Corp 400, 723, 733(2), 845(3).

Gray; City of Denton v., TexCivApp–Fort Worth, 501 SW2d 151, ref nre.—Waters 205, 208, 209.

Gray; City of Galveston v., TexApp–Houston (14 Dist), 93 SW3d 587, reh overr, and review den, appeal after remand 2003 WL 22908145.—App & E 68, 70(3); Counties 141; Courts 4, 35; Mand 1, 4(1), 4(4), 26, 28; Mun Corp 723; Plead 104(1), 111.33, 111.36, 111.37, 111.38, 111.45; States 191.6(2).

Gray v. City of Orange, TexCivApp–Beaumont, 601 SW2d 100, ref nre.—App & E 173(2); Mun Corp 723, 724; Torts 113(1); Work Comp 2100.

Gray v. C.I.R., CA5 (Tex), 183 F2d 329.—Int Rev 3140, 3563.

Gray; Community Public Service Co. v., TexCivApp–El Paso, 107 SW2d 495.—App & E 1050.1(10), 1062.1; Damag 40(3), 113, 147, 163(1), 176, 208(1), 217, 221(2.1), 221(5.1); Electricity 19(4), 19(6.1); Evid 536, 543(4); Witn 255(5), 255(10).

Gray; County Board of School Trustees v., TexCivApp–Eastland, 142 SW2d 697, writ refused.—Schools 37(3), 38.

Gray v. Curry, TexCivApp–Hous (14 Dist), 603 SW2d 245. —Elections 121(2), 291.

Gray; Davidson v., TexCivApp–Eastland, 97 SW2d 488.— App & E 926(7), 931(3); Wills 52(6), 55(7), 166(8), 423; Witn 139(2), 140(1), 140(19).

Gray v. Davis, TexApp–Fort Worth, 792 SW2d 856.— Anim 53, 54, 66.7.

Gray; Davis v., TexCivApp–Fort Worth, 312 SW2d 529.— App & E 846(5); Fraud 50, 58(1).

Gray; Davis v., TexCivApp–Dallas, 103 SW2d 999.—Mun Corp 302(1), 434(5), 586.

Gray; Demunbrun v., TexApp–El Paso, 986 SW2d 627, reh overr, and reh of rule 537(F) motion overr.—App & E 863; Judgm 181(21); Labor & Emp 40(2), 41(1), 55.

Gray v. Ellis, CA5 (Tex), 257 F2d 159, cert den 79 SCt 241, 358 US 912, 3 LEd2d 232.—Const Law 4801; Hab Corp 746.

Gray v. Enserch, Inc., TexApp–Fort Worth, 665 SW2d 601, ref nre.—App & E 930(1), 989, 1001(1), 1003(5); Gas 18, 19, 20(2), 20(4), 20(5); Neglig 305; Prod Liab 23.1.

Gray v. Estelle, CA5 (Tex), 616 F2d 801.—Crim Law 641.5(3), 641.5(7); Hab Corp 487, 709.

Gray v. Estelle, CA5 (Tex), 574 F2d 209, appeal after remand 616 F2d 801.—Crim Law 641.9; Hab Corp 802.

Gray v. Estelle, CA5 (Tex), 538 F2d 1190.—Const Law 268(2.1), 947, 4615; Hab Corp 340.

Gray v. F.D.I.C., TexApp–Houston (1 Dist), 841 SW2d 72, reh den, and writ gr, vac pursuant to settlement 848 SW2d 85.—App & E 173(2), 330(2), 930(3), 1001(1), 1003(7); Banks 508; Partners 165, 217(3), 247, 275, 278; Plead 78; Sec Tran 230, 240; Trial 140(1).

Gray v. Floyd, TexApp–Houston (1 Dist), 783 SW2d 214. —App & E 994(2); Damag 191; Evid 570, 588, 594.

Gray; Four States Grocery Co. v., TexCivApp–Fort Worth, 97 SW2d 355, writ dism.—App & E 1001(1); Evid 542; Sales 273(1), 273(3), 445(1).

Gray; Getto v., TexCivApp–Houston (1 Dist), 627 SW2d 437, ref nre.—App & E 931(1), 989, 1008.1(1), 1175(1), 1177(1); Paymt 45; Ven & Pur 93, 101, 182.

Gray; Grand Lake Gathering System, Inc. v., TexCivApp–Beaumont, 441 SW2d 633.—High 79.6.

Gray v. Gray, TexApp–Beaumont, 971 SW2d 212.—App & E 537; Child C 576, 660, 921(4), 923(4).

Gray; Gray v., TexApp–Beaumont, 971 SW2d 212.—App & E 537; Child C 576, 660, 921(4), 923(4).

Gray v. Gray, TexCivApp–Fort Worth, 424 SW2d 309, ref nre.—Hus & W 274(4), 276(6), 276(9); Lim of Act 83(3), 102(9).

Gray; Gray v., TexCivApp–Fort Worth, 424 SW2d 309, ref nre.—Hus & W 274(4), 276(6), 276(9); Lim of Act 83(3), 102(9).

Gray v. Gray, TexCivApp–Austin, 286 SW2d 223.—Costs 32(1); Divorce 31, 109.1, 124.5, 189, 221, 223; Marriage 13, 50(1).

Gray; Gray v., TexCivApp–Austin, 286 SW2d 223.—Costs 32(1); Divorce 31, 109.1, 124.5, 189, 221, 223; Marriage 13, 50(1).

Gray v. Gray, TexCivApp–Houston, 354 SW2d 948, writ dism.—Child S 173, 199; Divorce 124.1, 139.5.

Gray; Gray v., TexCivApp–Houston, 354 SW2d 948, writ dism.—Child S 173, 199; Divorce 124.1, 139.5.

Gray; Gregory v., TexCivApp–Hous (14 Dist), 612 SW2d 658.—Plead 409(1).

Gray v. Gulf Oil Corp., TexCivApp–Fort Worth, 416 SW2d 875.—App & E 1024.3; Evid 590; Plead 111.42(3), 111.42(9).

Gray v. HEB Food Store No. 4, TexApp–Corpus Christi, 941 SW2d 327, reh overr, and writ den.—App & E 879; Judgm 181(33), 185.3(21); Libel 33, 36, 51(1).

Gray v. Helmerich & Payne, Inc., TexApp–Amarillo, 834 SW2d 579, reh overr, and writ den.—Courts 95(1); Mines 58, 73.1(2), 78.1(9), 92.26.

Gray; Hilton v., TexCivApp–Dallas, 103 SW2d 1002.— Mun Corp 586.

Gray; Hunsley Paint Mfg. Co. v., TexCivApp–Amarillo, 165 SW2d 486, dism.—Guar 7(1), 7(4), 19; Trial 357.

Gray; Jackson v., TexCivApp–Tyler, 558 SW2d 138, ref nre.—Banks 51; Corp 433(2); Judgm 181(2), 181(3); Princ & A 166(1).

Gray; James v., TexCivApp–Dallas, 281 SW2d 114, ref nre.—Ease 17(1), 18(1), 18(3), 24, 30(1).

Gray v. Johansson, CA5 (Tex), 287 F2d 852, cert den 82 SCt 61, 368 US 835, 7 LEd2d 36, reh den 82 SCt 239, 368 US 922, 7 LEd2d 137, cert den G & H Towing Co v. Johansson, 82 SCt 61, 368 US 835, 7 LEd2d 36, reh den 82 SCt 239, 368 US 922, 7 LEd2d 137.—Pilots 16; Towage 14.

Gray v. John, TexApp–Tyler, 636 SW2d 599, dism.— Venue 7.5(3.1).

Gray v. Joyce, TexCivApp–Tyler, 485 SW2d 311, ref nre. —Judgm 710; Tresp to T T 6.1.

Gray v. King, TexCivApp–Austin, 227 SW2d 872.—Adv Poss 115(1); Bound 1, 10, 37(1); Evid 390(3), 590.

Gray v. Kirk, TexCivApp–Amarillo, 106 SW2d 839, writ refused.—Mun Corp 266, 368, 485(5).

Gray v. Kirkland, TexCivApp–Corpus Christi, 550 SW2d 410, ref nre.—Contracts 29; Impl & C C 1; Judgm 585(4); Sales 52(5.1); Set-Off 60.

Gray v. Kuykendall, TexCivApp–Fort Worth, 289 SW2d 796.—Damag 163(1), 188(3).

Gray v. Laketon Wheat Growers, TexCivApp–Amarillo, 240 SW2d 353.—Impl & C C 10, 75; Interest 10; Lim of Act 1, 123, 127(2.1), 127(4); Plead 248(1).

Gray v. Lewis, TexCivApp–Austin, 88 SW2d 603.—High 20, 23, 58.1, 64.

Gray v. Lewis, TexCivApp–Galveston, 241 SW2d 313, ref nre.—Inj 128(6).

Gray; Lexcon, Inc. v., TexApp–Dallas, 740 SW2d 83.— App & E 846(5), 878(1), 931(3); Mech Liens 48, 281(1), 310(3).

Gray; Lexington Ins. Co. v., TexApp–Austin, 775 SW2d 679, writ den.—App & E 173(9); Assign 22, 76; Bills & N 158; Contracts 18; Guar 72; Insurance 3451, 3515(2), 3525; Judgm 181(22), 829(3); Subrog 1.

Gray v. L-M Chevrolet Co., TexCivApp–El Paso, 368 SW2d 861, ref nre.—App & E 1170.7; Autos 245(49), 245(66), 247; Evid 192, 558(11).

Gray v. Local 714, Intern. Union of Operating Engineers, CA5 (Tex), 778 F2d 1087.—Courts 100(1); Labor & Emp 1007; Lim of Act 105(1); States 18.53, 18.55.

Gray v. Long John Silvers, Inc., SDTex, 876 FSupp 142. —Fed Cts 303; Rem of C 102.

Gray v. Luther, TexCivApp–Dallas, 195 SW2d 434, writ refused.—App & E 954(1), 1010.1(4); Inj 7, 135.

Gray v. Martindale Lumber Co., CA5 (Tex), 527 F2d 1352.—Fed Cts 428; Neglig 1010, 1037(7), 1090, 1287, 1311.

Gray v. Martindale Lumber Co., CA5 (Tex), 515 F2d 1218, reh den 527 F2d 1352.—Fed Civ Proc 2142.1; Neglig 575, 1745.

Gray; Maryland Cas. Co. v., CCA5 (Tex), 103 F2d 493.— Work Comp 235, 1342, 1461.

Gray; Maryland Cas. Co. v., NDTex, 25 FSupp 326.— Work Comp 243.

Gray; Mercer v., TexCivApp–Fort Worth, 109 SW2d 1107. —App & E 793; J P 174(15); Venue 28.

Gray; Miller v., Tex, 149 SW2d 582, 136 Tex 196, 141 ALR 1237.—Cust & U 15(1), 16; Land & Ten 139(2).

Gray; Miller v., TexCivApp–Austin, 108 SW2d 265, rev 149 SW2d 582, 136 Tex 196, 141 ALR 1237.—Evid 6; Land & Ten 139(2), 139(5).

Gray; Mills v., Tex, 210 SW2d 985, 147 Tex 33.—Trusts 1, 17(3), 62, 69, 91, 94, 102(1), 109.

Gray v. Mills, TexCivApp–Fort Worth, 206 SW2d 278, aff 210 SW2d 985, 147 Tex 33.—App & E 692(1), 692(3), 1056.1(8); Evid 271(1), 314(1); Exceptions Bill of17; Trusts 92.5, 94, 96, 103(1), 109.

Gray v. Moore, TexCivApp–Amarillo, 172 SW2d 746, writ refused wom.—App & E 846(2), 1008.1(8.1), 1010.1(2); Judgm 335(1), 335(3), 423, 677.

Gray; Nagorny v., TexCivApp–Galveston, 261 SW2d 741. —Land & Ten 55(1).

Gray v. Newberry, TexCivApp–Texarkana, 380 SW2d 22, ref nre.—App & E 930(1); Autos 146, 242(1), 244(34), 244(42); Damag 132(7), 216(8); Neglig 387.

Gray; North River Ins. Co. of New Jersey v., TexApp–Austin, 765 SW2d 862, writ den.—Work Comp 1536.

Gray v. Noteboom, TexApp–Fort Worth, 159 SW3d 750, review den.—Alt Disp Res 307, 308, 316; App & E 497(1); Atty & C 30.

Gray; Padget v., TexApp–Amarillo, 727 SW2d 706.—App & E 930(3), 989, 1001(1), 1003(7); Damag 49.10, 132(1), 134(1), 135; Evid 532; Trial 131(1), 133.6(4).

Gray v. PHI Resources, Ltd., Tex, 710 SW2d 566, on remand Robbins v. PHI Resources, Ltd, 717 SW2d 737, ref nre.—App & E 235; New Tr 116.2; Receivers 35(2).

Gray; Pioneer Bldg. & Loan Ass'n v., TexComApp, 125 SW2d 284, 132 Tex 509.—Venue 22(4), 22(6).

Gray; Pioneer Building & Loan Ass'n v., TexCivApp–Waco, 126 SW2d 995, certified question answered 125 SW2d 284, 132 Tex 509.—Mtg 275, 427(4); Venue 22(6).

Gray v. Port Arthur City Lines, TexCivApp–Beaumont, 149 SW2d 1030, writ dism, correct.—Time 9(1), 9(8).

Gray; Railway Exp. Agency v., TexCivApp–San Antonio, 211 SW2d 1013, ref nre.—App & E 927(7), 1024.1, 1069.1; Damag 130.3, 184, 185(1), 185(2); Labor & Emp 2941; Work Comp 2110.

Gray v. Rankin, Tex, 594 SW2d 409.—Const Law 2356; Courts 247(2); Hab Corp 814.

Gray; Rankin v., TexCivApp–Waco, 584 SW2d 539, appeal dism 594 SW2d 409.—Hab Corp 532(1), 532(2), 636, 744.

Gray; Reliable Life Ins. Co. v., TexCivApp–Texarkana, 464 SW2d 412, ref nre.—Insurance 3003(8), 3003(11).

Gray; Riley v., TexCivApp–Waco, 275 SW2d 171.—Bills & N 476(2), 478, 540; Plead 210, 228.2, 228.14, 228.23.

Gray; Roadway Transport Co. v., TexCivApp–Eastland, 135 SW2d 200.—App & E 912; Neglig 452, 502(1), 1713; Partners 191; Plead 111.42(7); Venue 8.5(4), 8.5(5), 22(1), 22(7).

Gray v. Robinson, TexCrimApp, 744 SW2d 604.—Atty & C 132; Crim Law 641.6(3), 641.7(1), 641.9; Mand 3(3).

Gray v. Sage Telecom, Inc., NDTex, 410 FSupp2d 507.—Alt Disp Res 139, 146; Fed Cts 18.

Gray v. Saint Matthews Cathedral Endowment Fund, Inc., TexCivApp–Texarkana, 544 SW2d 488, 94 ALR3d 1197, ref nre.—Char 49; Parties 40(2); Relig Soc 14, 24.

Gray v. Sears, Roebuck & Co., Inc., SDTex, 131 FSupp2d 895.—Civil R 1019(2), 1201, 1202, 1203, 1217, 1218(3), 1505(7); Damag 49, 50.10; Labor & Emp 79, 367(5); Lim of Act 58(1).

Gray v. Shaunfield, TexCivApp–Waco, 212 SW2d 873.—Contracts 147(1), 176(2); Evid 461(1); Mines 109.

Gray v. Shipley, TexApp–Houston (1 Dist), 877 SW2d 806. —Crim Law 641.10(3).

Gray; Smith v., TexApp–Amarillo, 882 SW2d 103, reh den, writ den with per curiam opinion 907 SW2d 444.—Lim of Act 95(3), 100(12).

Gray; Spencer v., TexCivApp–Fort Worth, 209 SW2d 651. —Plead 111.3, 111.4.

Gray v. Stanford Research Institute, NDTex, 108 FSupp 639.—Rem of C 110.

Gray v. Stanford Research Institute, NDTex, 108 FSupp 636.—Rem of C 47, 61(1).

Gray; State v., Tex, 175 SW2d 224, 141 Tex 604.—App & E 1091(4), 1094(1); Evid 596(2); Gaming 61.

Gray v. State, TexCrimApp, 159 SW3d 95, on remand 174 SW3d 794, reh en banc den, and petition for discretionary review gr.—Crim Law 1162, 1167(5).

Gray; State v., TexCrimApp, 158 SW3d 465.—Autos 349(2.1), 349.5(2), 349.5(9); Crim Law 1158(4).

Gray v. State, TexCrimApp, 152 SW3d 125.—Autos 332, 357(6); Const Law 4694; Crim Law 814(1).

Gray v. State, TexCrimApp, 928 SW2d 561, appeal after remand 1996 WL 732421, on remand Hickerson v. State, 1997 WL 72076.—Crim Law 1077.2(3).

Gray v. State, TexCrimApp, 707 SW2d 607.—Sent & Pun 2009.

Gray v. State, TexCrimApp, 493 SW2d 236.—Crim Law 1126; Sent & Pun 1381(3).

Gray v. State, TexCrimApp, 490 SW2d 838.—R R 255(4).

Gray v. State, TexCrimApp, 489 SW2d 622.—Rob 24.15(1).

Gray v. State, TexCrimApp, 481 SW2d 892.—Crim Law 625.10(2.1); Rape 51(1).

Gray v. State, TexCrimApp, 477 SW2d 635.—Crim Law 366(3), 590(2), 593, 730(14), 867.

Gray v. State, TexCrimApp, 475 SW2d 246.—Crim Law 369.3, 577, 641.10(1), 641.13(2.1), 1038.1(3.1), 1038.3.

Gray v. State, TexCrimApp, 468 SW2d 851.—Crim Law 1181.5(8), 1184(4.1); Larc 59, 60.

Gray v. State, TexCrimApp, 467 SW2d 474.—Crim Law 369.15.

Gray v. State, TexCrimApp, 467 SW2d 466.—Crim Law 369.15, 829(13).

Gray v. State, TexCrimApp, 388 SW2d 710.—Crim Law 700(1); Homic 1205, 1345.

Gray v. State, TexCrimApp, 382 SW2d 481.—Weap 17(4).

Gray v. State, TexCrimApp, 379 SW2d 910.—Autos 355(6); Crim Law 553.

Gray v. State, TexCrimApp, 373 SW2d 672.—Crim Law 532(0.5), 1169.2(3); Rob 24.10.

Gray v. State, TexCrimApp, 333 SW2d 854, 169 TexCrim 205.—Crim Law 1101.

Gray v. State, TexCrimApp, 277 SW2d 107, 161 TexCrim 384.—Autos 355(6); Crim Law 419(1.5), 1169.1(10), 1171.1(6).

Gray v. State, TexCrimApp, 269 SW2d 377.—Crim Law 1094(3).

Gray v. State, TexCrimApp, 254 SW2d 391, 158 TexCrim 214, ref nre.—Assault 54, 92(2).

Gray v. State, TexCrimApp, 236 SW2d 125.—Crim Law 1094(3).

Gray v. State, TexCrimApp, 158 SW2d 538.—Crim Law 1094(3).

Gray v. State, TexCrimApp, 156 SW2d 526, 143 TexCrim 22.—Larc 57.

Gray v. State, TexCrimApp, 137 SW2d 777, 138 TexCrim 587.—Crim Law 741(1), 742(1), 1091(4), 1171.3; Rape 6, 13, 45, 52(1).

Gray v. State, TexCrimApp, 132 SW2d 403.—Crim Law 1090.1(1).

Gray v. State, TexCrimApp, 104 SW2d 521, 132 TexCrim 308.—Perj 32(1).

Gray v. State, TexCrimApp, 93 SW2d 1146, 130 TexCrim 289.—Rape 54(1).

Gray v. State, TexCrimApp, 91 SW2d 732, 129 TexCrim 651.—Crim Law 1092.7, 1182.

Gray v. State, TexCrimApp, 88 SW2d 487.—Crim Law 15.

Gray v. State, TexCrimApp, 82 SW2d 958, 128 TexCrim 637.—Crim Law 741(1), 742(1); Rob 24.10, 26.

Gray v. State, TexApp–Fort Worth, 980 SW2d 772.—Crim Law 700(1), 717, 798.5, 870, 872.5, 881(1), 911, 1041; Ind & Inf 72, 132(7).

Gray v. State, TexApp–Fort Worth, 726 SW2d 640.—Assault 43(1); Crim Law 393(1), 556, 629.5(1), 629.5(2), 1043(3), 1153(1); Ind & Inf 176.

Gray; State v., TexApp–Austin, 801 SW2d 10.—Dist & Pros Attys 8; Ind & Inf 42, 144.

Gray v. State, TexApp–Texarkana, 51 SW3d 856, petition for discretionary review gr, petition for discretionary review dism with per curiam opinion 85 SW3d 300.—Crim Law 1030(1), 1038.1(6), 1165(1), 1172.1(3); Rob 27(2); Sent & Pun 370, 373.

Gray v. State, TexApp–Beaumont, 986 SW2d 814.—Crim Law 438.1, 1169.1(10).

Gray v. State, TexApp–Beaumont, 658 SW2d 786.—Crim Law 365(1), 369.2(2), 369.2(4), 673(5), 1043(2).

Gray v. State, TexApp–Waco, 134 SW3d 471, habeas corpus dism by 2007 WL 1886226.—Crim Law 1081(2), 1134(10).

Gray v. State, TexApp–Waco, 69 SW3d 835.—Crim Law 641.3(8.1), 1077.3, 1132, 1590, 1602.

Gray; State v., TexApp–Tyler, 157 SW3d 1, reh overr, and petition for discretionary review gr, aff 158 SW3d 465.—Arrest 63.5(4), 63.5(9), 68(4); Autos 349(1), 349(2.1), 349(10), 349(17), 349(18); Crim Law 1134(2), 1139, 1158(4); Searches 171.

Gray v. State, TexApp–Tyler, 712 SW2d 527, rev 707 SW2d 607.—Sent & Pun 2009.

Gray v. State, TexApp–Corpus Christi, 174 SW3d 794, reh en banc den, and petition for discretionary review gr.—Crim Law 1166.16; Jury 75(1).

Gray v. State, TexApp–Corpus Christi, 133 SW3d 281, reh overr, rev 159 SW3d 95, on remand 174 SW3d 794, reh en banc den, and petition for discretionary review gr.—Crim Law 1035(6), 1162, 1166.16; Jury 75(1).

Gray v. State, TexApp–Corpus Christi, 821 SW2d 721, petition for discretionary review refused.—Arrest 58, 63.4(6), 63.5(6); Autos 349.5(3).

Gray v. State, TexApp–Corpus Christi, 628 SW2d 228, petition for discretionary review refused.—Burg 22, 28(6), 41(8); Crim Law 577.15(1), 577.16(9), 726, 730(16), 868, 1037.1(4), 1043(3), 1203.27, 1558.

Gray v. State, TexApp–Houston (14 Dist), 853 SW2d 782, petition for discretionary review refused.—Crim Law 409(5), 1100, 1101, 1144.13(1).

Gray v. State, TexApp–Houston (14 Dist), 797 SW2d 157.—Crim Law 532(0.5), 671, 686(1), 1043(2), 1153(3), 1168(2); Rob 4, 24.45.

Gray v. State, TexCivApp–Fort Worth, 172 SW2d 722, rev 175 SW2d 224, 141 Tex 604.—Gaming 61.

Gray v. State, TexCivApp–Texarkana, 508 SW2d 454, ref nre.—App & E 181, 428(2); Const Law 1066, 4401; Infants 192, 205, 242, 248.1.

Gray v. State ex rel. Brown, TexCivApp–Fort Worth, 406 SW2d 934, writ dism.—Crim Law 32; Elections 10, 126(6), 172.

Gray; State ex rel. Curry v., TexCrimApp, 726 SW2d 125.—Mand 3(2.1), 4(4), 12, 61.

Gray; State ex rel. Curry v., TexCrimApp, 599 SW2d 630.—Sent & Pun 1872(2), 1893, 1894.

Gray v. Storey, TexCivApp–Fort Worth, 383 SW2d 487.—Brok 44; Judgm 183, 185.2(9), 186.

Gray v. Taylor, TexCivApp–Fort Worth, 138 SW2d 891, writ dism, correct.—Covenants 70; Ten in C 22, 33.

Gray; Thompson v., TexCivApp–Galveston, 219 SW2d 831, ref nre.—R R 389(4), 398(1).

Gray; TMC Worldwide, L.P. v., TexApp–Houston (1 Dist), 178 SW3d 29.—App & E 842(2), 920(3), 954(1), 954(2); Contracts 50, 65.5, 116(1), 142; Inj 132, 135, 138.1, 138.6, 138.33.

Gray; Town East Ford Sales, Inc. v., TexApp–Dallas, 730 SW2d 796.—Antitrust 193, 369, 389(1), 389(2), 390, 393, 397; App & E 836, 878(2), 1026, 1079, 1153, 1175(1); Damag 48, 49, 163(2), 192, 221(2.1), 221(4); Elect of Rem 7(1); Evid 474(16), 498.5; Plead 369(1), 369(6);

Pretrial Proc 434; Sales 262; Stip 14(12), 19; Trial 307(1), 352.10.

Gray; Traders & General Ins. Co. v., TexCivApp–Waco, 257 SW2d 327.—Pretrial Proc 716; Trial 350.3(8); Work Comp 1173, 1385, 1703, 1968(3).

Gray; Traylor v., TexCivApp–Corpus Christi, 547 SW2d 644, ref nre.—App & E 766, 1050.1(10); Contrib 1; Estop 52(7), 52.15, 54, 87, 95, 118; Evid 241(1); Fraud 3, 22(1), 48, 50, 58(1), 58(2), 58(4), 59(1), 59(3), 60, 62; Indem 60, 65; Neglig 1658; Princ & A 99, 123(7), 128, 150(2), 177(2); Trial 366.

Gray v. Turner, TexApp–Amarillo, 807 SW2d 818.—App & E 876, 1024.5; Costs 260(5); Judgm 276, 297, 304, 306, 324, 325.

Gray; U.S. v., CA5 (Tex), 105 F3d 956, cert den Luchkow-ec v. US, 117 SCt 1326, 520 US 1150, 137 LEd2d 487, cert den 117 SCt 1856, 520 US 1246, 137 LEd2d 1057, cert den Satz v US, 117 SCt 2530, 521 US 1128, 138 LEd2d 1030, habeas corpus dism by 2002 WL 22080.—Consp 47(5), 48.2(2); Const Law 4623; Crim Law 632(2), 656(1), 656(2), 662.7, 676, 699, 700(2.1), 700(3), 711, 769, 772(5), 814(2), 822(1), 1030(1), 1037.1(1), 1134(5), 1139, 1144.13(3), 1144.13(5), 1144.14, 1148, 1152(2), 1158(1), 1159.2(7), 1170.5(5), 1177; Judges 49(1); Jury 131(2), 131(10); Postal 49(11), 50; Sent & Pun 284, 300, 669, 675, 678, 752, 935, 964; Witn 225, 246(2), 267.

Gray; U.S. v., CA5 (Tex), 96 F3d 769, cert den 117 SCt 1275, 520 US 1129, 137 LEd2d 351.—Consp 23.1; Crim Law 13.1(1), 1030(1), 1038.1(2), 1038.1(4), 1144.13(2.1), 1144.13(5), 1152(1), 1159.2(7); Postal 35(1), 35(2), 35(5), 35(9), 50; Tel 730, 1014(2), 1014(7), 1014(10), 1021.

Gray; U.S. v., CA5 (Tex), 751 F2d 733, reh den 755 F2d 173.—Commerce 82.10; Crim Law 822(1), 829(4); Postal 49(11); Searches 13.1, 164.

Gray; U.S. v., CA5 (Tex), 692 F2d 352.—Weap 4.

Gray; U.S. v., CA5 (Tex), 584 F2d 96.—Crim Law 273.1(4), 1167(5), 1186.7.

Gray; U.S. v., CA5 (Tex), 71 FedAppx 300.—Sent & Pun 694.

Gray v. U.S., SDTex, 445 FSupp 337.—Prod Liab 46.2, 75.1; U S 78(12).

Gray; Ussery v., TexApp–Fort Worth, 804 SW2d 232.—Atty & C 19, 21, 21.5(1); Child 57.

Gray v. Vance, TexApp–Fort Worth, 567 SW2d 16.—Elections 126(1).

Gray v. Vandver, TexApp–Beaumont, 623 SW2d 172.—Evid 18; Perp 6(1).

Gray; Van Ooteghem v., CA5 (Tex), 774 F2d 1332.—Civil R 1249(1), 1350, 1351(5), 1359, 1488; Counties 67; Fed Cts 744; Interest 56.

Gray; Van Ooteghem v., CA5 (Tex), 654 F2d 304, cert den 102 SCt 1255, 455 US 909, 71 LEd2d 447, on remand 584 FSupp 897, aff as mod 774 F2d 1332.—Const Law 1947; Counties 67.

Gray; Van Ooteghem v., CA5 (Tex), 628 F2d 488, reh gr, vac 640 F2d 12, on reh 654 F2d 304, cert den 102 SCt 1255, 455 US 909, 71 LEd2d 447, on remand 584 FSupp 897, aff as mod 774 F2d 1332.—Civil R 1351(5), 1490; Const Law 90.1(7.2), 1181, 1490, 1501, 1506, 1933, 1947, 3972; Fed Civ Proc 2742.5; Fed Cts 830, 865, 941; Offic 66, 72.63.

Gray; Van Ooteghem v., SDTex, 584 FSupp 897, aff as mod 774 F2d 1332.—Civil R 1349, 1351(5), 1480; Fed Cts 270.

Gray; Vitopil v., TexCivApp–Fort Worth, 111 SW2d 1202.—App & E 1054(3); Plead 111.8, 111.9, 111.37, 111.40, 111.46; Venue 2.

Gray v. Waste Resources, Inc., TexApp–Houston (14 Dist), 222 SW3d 522, rule 537(f) motion gr.—App & E 930(1), 1001(1), 1003(1); Fraud 3, 20, 25; Judgm 199(3.10).

Gray; Wells v., TexCivApp–San Antonio, 241 SW2d 183, writ refused.—Courts 472.4(2.1), 475(2).

Gray v. West, TexCivApp–Amarillo, 608 SW2d 771, ref nre.—App & E 1062.2; Corp 360(2), 361; Damag 221(2.1); Joint Adv 1.2(1), 1.2(7), 7, 8; Plead 228.14; Sales 384(1), 384(7); Trial 215, 335, 350.4(1), 350.4(2), 352.1(4), 352.4(4).

Gray v. West, TexCivApp–Amarillo, 572 SW2d 829.—App & E 912; Plead 111.42(5); Venue 7.5(1).

Gray v. Woodville Health Care Center, TexApp–El Paso, 225 SW3d 613, reh overr, and review den.—App & E 762, 1079; Const Law 885; Evid 555.4(2); Health 631, 818, 821(3), 822(3); Judgm 185.1(4), 185.3(21); Neglig 371, 372, 387, 409, 1613, 1614, 1620, 1675.

Gray; Young v., CA5 (Tex), 560 F2d 201.—Sent & Pun 1546.

Gray & Co., Inc.; Dolphin Titan Intern., Inc. v., BkrtcySDTex, 93 BR 508. See Dolphin Titan Intern., Inc., In re.

Gray & Co., Inc.; Vickers v., EDTex, 761 FSupp 37, aff 977 F2d 578, aff 977 F2d 578.—Fed Civ Proc 1537.1, 1636.1, 1831; Insurance 3357, 3365; RICO 27; Rem of C 19(1), 107(4).

Graybar Elec. Co.; Coleman v., CA5 (Tex), 195 F2d 374. —Fed Civ Proc 2127; Labor & Emp 40(3), 193, 210, 835, 873.

Graybar Electric Co.; Kennedy v., TexCivApp–Fort Worth, 156 SW2d 562.—App & E 1178(6); Execution 210; Plead 110.

Graybar Elec. Co.; Rich v., TexComApp, 84 SW2d 708, 125 Tex 470, 102 ALR 171.—Sheriffs 100, 157(3), 159.

Graybar Elec. Co., Inc.; Panhandle Bank & Trust Co. v., TexCivApp–Amarillo, 492 SW2d 76, ref nre.—Evid 366(1); Garn 51, 206, 218; Mech Liens 115(1).

Graybill v. State, TexCrimApp, 601 SW2d 353.—Crim Law 784(1).

Grayburg Oil Co.; Bethke v., CCA5 (Tex), 89 F2d 536, cert den 58 SCt 54, 302 US 730, 82 LEd 564.—Corp 568; Courts 508(2.1); Judgm 672.

Grayburg Oil Co. v. Giles, Tex, 186 SW2d 680, 143 Tex 497.—Mines 5.2(2.1); Nav Wat 37(1), 37(6); Statut 210.

Grayburg Oil Co. v. State, TexComApp, 3 SW2d 427, rev 49 SCt 185, 278 US 582, 73 LEd 519.—Commerce 40(1), 64; Tax 6, 3606, 3683.

Grayburg Oil Co. v. State, TexCivApp–Austin, 286 SW 489, writ gr, aff 3 SW2d 427, rev 49 SCt 185, 278 US 582, 73 LEd 519.—Commerce 64; Tax 6, 18, 3610.

Grayce Oil Co. v. Peterson, Tex, 98 SW2d 781, 128 Tex 550.—App & E 1048(2), 1082(2); Evid 474(18), 474(20), 498.5; Trial 219.

Grayco Mobile Homes, Inc.; Lane Wood, Inc. v., TexApp–Houston (14 Dist), 668 SW2d 892.—Venue 22(10).

Gray Co. v. Spee-Flo Mfg. Corp., CA5 (Tex), 361 F2d 489.—Pat 118.3(2).

Gray Co.; Spee-Flo Mfg. Corp. v., SDTex, 255 FSupp 618.—Pat 259(1).

Gray Co.; Spee-Flo Mfg. Corp. v., SDTex, 237 FSupp 616, opinion supplemented 255 FSupp 618, aff 361 F2d 489.—Pat 34, 36.2(2), 36.2(5).

Gray Co. v. Ward, TexCivApp–Waco, 145 SW2d 650, writ dism, correct.—Corp 642(1), 642(4.5), 662, 668(4); Garn 121.5.

Gray County; Lancaster v., TexCivApp–El Paso, 127 SW2d 385.—Elect of Rem 3(2); Equity 66; Plead 53(1); Pub Lands 173(2), 173(14); Schools 18; Ven & Pur 92.

Gray County v. Shouse, TexApp–Amarillo, 201 SW3d 784.—Autos 187(6); Judgm 181(27), 185.3(1); Mun Corp 745, 747(3); Offic 114, 119.

Gray County v. Warner & Finney, TexApp–Amarillo, 727 SW2d 633.—Atty & C 132; Crim Law 641.13(1), 1133, 1181.5(1).

Gray County Gas Co. v. Oldham, TexCivApp–Amarillo, 238 SW2d 596.—App & E 1050.1(7), 1062.1; Damag 40(3), 108, 174(3), 221(2.1); Gas 20(3); Trial 352.4(5), 352.5(2), 352.5(5), 352.19.

Gray County Production Co. v. Christian, TexCivApp–Amarillo, 231 SW2d 901.—App & E 917(1); Mun Corp 7, 12(12); Quo W 58; Statut 223.2(30).

Graydon; E.C., Jr. ex rel. Gonzales v., TexApp–Corpus Christi, 28 SW3d 825.—Child C 9, 76, 101, 175, 178, 216, 283, 287, 921(3); Child S 21, 556(1); Pretrial Proc 723.1; Statut 188.

Gray Electronics; Southwest Fabricating & Welding Co. v., TexCivApp–Galveston, 248 SW2d 961.—App & E 1008.1(2), 1010.1(10); Aviation 238; Impl & C C 104.

Gray Enterprises, Inc.; Texas Processed Plastics, Inc. v., TexCivApp–Tyler, 592 SW2d 412.—Contracts 186(1), 187(1); Evid 207(1), 265(7); Princ & A 1, 8; Prod Liab 17.1, 20; Sales 255, 441(1).

Grayford Oil Corp. (Oil & Gas Energy, Inc.); Henson v., TexCivApp–Dallas, 549 SW2d 7, ref nre.—Action 70; Contracts 52, 309(1); Corp 187, 190, 404(1); Elect of Rem 11; Spec Perf 4, 117.

Gray, Inc. v. Taco Villa, Inc., TexApp–Austin, 759 SW2d 509. See Ted Gray, Inc. v. Taco Villa, Inc.

Grayless v. State, TexCrimApp, 567 SW2d 216.—Crim Law 577.8(2), 577.10(1), 577.10(4), 577.10(6), 577.10(10), 577.11(6), 577.15(1), 577.15(3), 577.16(4), 577.16(9), 1166(1), 1166(7); Infants 68.5, 68.7(1), 194.1.

Grayridge Apartment Homes, Inc.; Bluebonnet Sav. Bank, F.S.B. v., TexApp–Houston (1 Dist), 907 SW2d 904, reh overr, and writ den.—App & E 930(3), 989, 1001(3), 1003(7); Banks 100; Bills & N 452(1); Contracts 305(1); Equity 67, 87(1), 87(2); Estop 52(1), 52(2), 52.10(2), 55, 85, 87; Fraud 13(3), 32; Guar 81; Mtg 408; Neglig 273.

Gray Roofing; Lexcon, Inc. v., TexApp–Dallas, 740 SW2d 83. See Lexcon, Inc. v. Gray.

Grays v. Harrison, TexCivApp–Amarillo, 179 SW2d 1020. —App & E 931(3); New Tr 150(1); Propty 9; Tresp to T T 41(1); Ven & Pur 232(7).

Grays; Shell Petroleum Corp. v., TexComApp, 114 SW2d 869, 131 Tex 515.—App & E 362(1), 877(2).

Grays; Shell Petroleum Corp. v., TexCivApp–Waco, 87 SW2d 289, writ dism 114 SW2d 869, 131 Tex 515.—App & E 448, 460(2), 1180(2); Receivers 81, 82, 200.

Grays v. State, TexCrimApp, 487 SW2d 348.—Crim Law 1026.10(4), 1044.1(2), 1130(2); Weap 17(1).

Grays v. State, TexCrimApp, 116 SW2d 1073, 134 TexCrim 479.—Homic 1174.

Grays v. State, TexApp–Dallas, 888 SW2d 876.—Crim Law 273.1(4), 273.1(5).

Grays v. State, TexApp–Amarillo, 905 SW2d 54.—Searches 177, 178.

Gray's Container Service, Inc. v. Royal Indem. Co., TexApp–Fort Worth, 644 SW2d 918.—Acct Action on 11.

Gray's Estate, In re, TexCivApp–El Paso, 279 SW2d 936, ref nre.—Evid 357, 359(2), 471(14), 474(4), 498.5; Wills 1, 53(2), 55(1), 164(1), 164(3), 164(6), 323, 324(3), 400.

Gray's Estate; Bradley v., TexCivApp–Amarillo, 385 SW2d 681, ref nre.—Judgm 185(2), 185.3(14); Land & Ten 75(3).

Grayshon; Anglo Exploration Corp. v., TexCivApp–San Antonio, 577 SW2d 742, writ dism woj.—Plead 111.23, 111.36; Venue 5.3(1), 5.3(2), 5.3(8).

Grayshon; Anglo Exploration Corp. v., TexCivApp–Corpus Christi, 576 SW2d 151, writ dism woj.—App & E 854(4), 934(2); Plead 111.44, 228.14; Trusts 94.5, 103(1); Venue 5.3(6), 5.3(8).

Grayshon; Anglo Exploration Corp. v., TexCivApp–Hous (14 Dist), 562 SW2d 567, ref nre.—App & E 1170.1; Costs 48; Pretrial Proc 139, 510, 513.

Grayson, Ex parte, TexCrimApp, 217 SW2d 1007, 153 TexCrim 91, cert den Grayson v. Moore, 70 SCt 135, 338 US 873, 94 LEd 536.—Crim Law 641.4(4), 641.6(3), 641.7(1); Jury 110(9).

Grayson v. Cate, TexCivApp–Fort Worth, 95 SW2d 194, writ dism.—Plead 111.3, 111.8; Venue 7.5(4).

GRAYSON

59 Tex D 2d—350
See Guidelines for Arrangement at the beginning of this Volume

Grayson v. Crescendo Resources, L.P., TexApp–Amarillo, 104 SW3d 736, reh overr, and review den.—Evid 571(1); Mines 78.1(2), 78.1(4), 78.1(11), 78.7(4).

Grayson v. Dunn, TexCivApp–Waco, 581 SW2d 785, ref nre.—Adv Poss 53, 114(1), 115(1); App & E 216(7); Trial 140(2).

Grayson v. Grayson, TexApp–San Antonio, 103 SW3d 559.—App & E 5, 859; Child C 213, 921(1), 921(3); Child S 146, 156, 556(1); Divorce 252.3(2), 286(5).

Grayson; Grayson v., TexApp–San Antonio, 103 SW3d 559.—App & E 5, 859; Child C 213, 921(1), 921(3); Child S 146, 156, 556(1); Divorce 252.3(2), 286(5).

Grayson v. Johnson, TexCivApp–Waco, 181 SW2d 312.—App & E 927(3); Judgm 16, 21, 217, 405, 427, 460(3), 502.

Grayson; Lumbermens Mut. Ins. Co. v., TexCivApp–Waco, 422 SW2d 755, ref nre.—Insurance 3102, 3170.

Grayson v. Petro-Drive, Inc., SDTex, 912 FSupp 258.—Fed Civ Proc 2512, 2532; Seamen 2; Ship 1.

Grayson v. Rodermund, TexCivApp–Austin, 135 SW2d 178.—Evid 43(3); Judgm 660.5, 948(2); J P 141(4); Land & Ten 230(3), 288.

Grayson v. State, TexCrimApp, 684 SW2d 691.—Witn 2(1), 293, 297(1), 305(1).

Grayson v. State, TexCrimApp, 481 SW2d 859.—Crim Law 365(1), 369.1, 369.2(1), 369.15, 370, 371(1), 371(12), 372(1), 372(4), 1038.1(5).

Grayson v. State, TexCrimApp, 468 SW2d 420.—Crim Law 578, 1034; Rob 24.40, 30; Sent & Pun 323, 1503.

Grayson v. State, TexCrimApp, 438 SW2d 553.—Crim Law 494, 736(2); Mental H 432.

Grayson v. State, TexCrimApp, 409 SW2d 850.—Crim Law 414, 530.

Grayson v. State, TexCrimApp, 236 SW2d 792, 155 TexCrim 500.—Crim Law 396(1); Ind & Inf 176; Rape 51(1).

Grayson v. State, TexCrimApp, 211 SW2d 749, 152 TexCrim 62.—Crim Law 884.

Grayson v. State, TexApp–Houston (1 Dist), 192 SW3d 790.—Crim Law 308, 637, 1045, 1166.8.

Grayson v. State, TexApp–Austin, 82 SW3d 357.—Assault 92(4); Crim Law 753.2(3.1), 1036.8, 1159.2(2), 1159.2(9), 1159.3(1).

Grayson v. State, TexApp–Dallas, 786 SW2d 504.—Crim Law 369.1, 867, 1036.2, 1169.5(1); Witn 77.

Grayson; State Farm Mut. Auto. Ins. Co. v., TexApp–San Antonio, 983 SW2d 769, reh overr, and rule 537(f) motion overr.—Costs 32(2); Insurance 2782, 2787, 3585.

Grayson; U.S. v., CA5 (Tex), 416 F2d 1073, cert den 90 SCt 754, 396 US 1059, 24 LEd2d 753, reh den 90 SCt 1114, 397 US 1003, 25 LEd2d 415, and 90 SCt 2191, 399 US 917, 26 LEd2d 576.—Const Law 4612; Crim Law 157, 275, 577.10(8), 1132; Ind & Inf 6, 7; Int Rev 5286.

Grayson County; Porter v., TexApp–Dallas, 224 SW3d 855.—App & E 893(1); Counties 143; Courts 39; Mun Corp 742(1), 847, 854; Neglig 1037(4); Plead 104(1), 111.43, 111.46, 111.47, 111.48; Pretrial Proc 690.

Grayson County Child Welfare; Benson v., TexApp–Dallas, 666 SW2d 166.—App & E 516, 520(2), 563, 578, 610, 642, 654.

Grayson County Officials v. Dennard, TexCivApp–Eastland, 574 SW2d 179, ref nre.—App & E 758.3(1); Inj 204; Judgm 217; Tax 2176, 2712.

Grayson County State Bank v. Calvert, TexCivApp–Austin, 357 SW2d 160, ref nre.—Banks 232; Const Law 3566; Tax 2006, 2125, 2135, 2242.

Grayson County State Bank; Day v., TexCivApp–Waco, 153 SW2d 599.—App & E 987(4), 1003(5); Chat Mtg 32, 40, 150(1), 282; Evid 588, 594; Judgm 248, 256(1); Partners 236; Trial 350.2.

Grayson County State Bank v. Osborne, TexCivApp–Dallas, 531 SW2d 846, ref nre.—Assign 56, 106, 109; Contracts 147(2); Evid 448.

Grayson County State Bank; U.S. v., CA5 (Tex), 656 F2d 1070, stay den First Pentecostal Church v. US, 102 SCt 968, 454 US 1119, 71 LEd2d 108, cert den 102 SCt 1276, 455 US 920, 71 LEd2d 460.—Const Law 1303, 1304, 1385, 1386(1), 2634; Fed Cts 754.1, 843; Int Rev 4490, 4499, 4500, 4512.

Grayson Enterprises, Inc.; Brown v., TexCivApp–Dallas, 401 SW2d 653, ref nre.—Corp 306, 399(4), 425(3); Estop 54; Judgm 181(2), 185(2), 185(5), 186.

Grayson Enterprises, Inc. v. Texas Key Broadcasters, Inc., TexCivApp–Eastland, 390 SW2d 346, writ dism.—Frds St of 139(4); Plead 111.16, 111.37, 111.40, 111.42(6); Venue 7.5(1), 7.5(6), 8.5(8).

Grayson Enterprises, Inc. v. Texas Key Broadcasters, Inc., TexCivApp–Eastland, 388 SW2d 204.—App & E 907(3), 920(3); Inj 57, 59(1), 118(4), 135, 138.37.

Grayson Enterprises, Inc.; Walton v., TexCivApp–Tyler, 460 SW2d 276.—App & E 912; Sales 432; Trusts 257; Venue 22(6).

Grayson Fire Extinguisher Co., Inc. v. Jackson, TexCivApp–Dallas, 566 SW2d 321, ref nre.—App & E 5, 1073(2); Judgm 123(1), 335(1).

Gray-Taylor, Inc. v. Harris County, CA5 (Tex), 569 F2d 893, cert den 99 SCt 351, 439 US 954, 58 LEd2d 344.—Fed Cts 59.

Gray-Taylor, Inc. v. Tennessee, Tex, 587 SW2d 668.—App & E 169; Cons Cred 30, 56, 60.

Gray-Taylor, Inc. v. Tennessee, TexCivApp–Hous (1 Dist), 573 SW2d 859, writ gr, rev 587 SW2d 668.—Antitrust 369; Cons Cred 51, 56; Sec Tran 242.1.

Gray Television, Inc.; Epstein v., WDTex, 474 FSupp2d 835.—Const Law 3964; Fed Cts 76.1, 76.5, 76.10, 76.25, 96.

Gray Tool Co.; Hubbard v., TexCivApp–Waco, 307 SW2d 599, ref nre.—Neglig 251, 1696; Prod Liab 47.

Gray Tool Co. v. Humble Oil & Refining Co., CA5 (Tex), 190 F2d 779.—Pat 325.15.

Gray Tool Co. v. Humble Oil & Refining Co., CA5 (Tex), 186 F2d 365, cert den 71 SCt 854, 341 US 934, 95 LEd 1363, reh den 71 SCt 1014, 341 US 956, 95 LEd 1377, reh den 71 SCt 1014, 341 US 956, 95 LEd 1377, motion gr 190 F2d 779.—Pat 118, 209(1), 283(1), 323.2(4).

Gray Tool Co. v. Humble Oil & Refining Co., SDTex, 92 FSupp 722, rev 186 F2d 365, cert den 71 SCt 854, 341 US 934, 95 LEd 1363, reh den 71 SCt 1014, 341 US 956, 95 LEd 1377, reh den 71 SCt 1014, 341 US 956, 95 LEd 1377, motion gr 190 F2d 779.—Pat 323.2(4).

Gray Wolfe Co.; Cosand v., TexCivApp–Galveston, 262 SW2d 547.—Corp 401, 425(5), 506.

Graziadei v. D.D.R. Mach. Co., Inc., TexApp–Dallas, 740 SW2d 52, writ dism.—Prod Liab 8, 11, 88.5; Sales 3.1; Trial 351.2(4), 366.

GRD Development Co., Inc.; Foreca, S.A. v., Tex, 758 SW2d 744.—Sales 53(1).

GRD Development Co., Inc. v. Foreca, S.A., TexApp–El Paso, 747 SW2d 9, writ dism woj, and writ withdrawn, and writ gr, rev 758 SW2d 744.—Contracts 150, 218, 221(1), 221(2).

Greaber v. Coca-Cola Bottling Works of Dallas, TexCivApp–El Paso, 98 SW2d 1028, writ dism.—App & E 724(1), 1070(2); Autos 247; Trial 219, 278.

Greak; Rose v., TexCivApp–Beaumont, 143 SW2d 712.—Costs 232.

Greanias v. City of Houston, TexApp–Houston (1 Dist), 841 SW2d 411.—Mand 103, 187.6.

Greanias; Perry v., TexApp–Houston (1 Dist), 95 SW3d 683, reh overr, and review den, on remand 2003 WL 25459695, aff 2005 WL 995441.—App & E 223, 856(1); Civil R 1376(1), 1376(2), 1376(4), 1407, 1737; Corp 202; Judgm 183, 185(2), 185.1(3), 185.1(4); Libel 112(1); Mun Corp 65, 169, 170, 725; Offic 114, 119.

Grease Monkey, Inc.; Robledo v., TexApp–Corpus Christi, 758 SW2d 834.—Pretrial Proc 282, 304.

For Later Case History Information, see KeyCite on WESTLAW

Great Am. Acc. Ins. Co. v. Roggen, TexCivApp–Galveston, 144 SW2d 1115.—App & E 1091(1); Insurance 2056, 3110(3), 3120.

Great Am. County Mut. Fire Ins. Co. v. Elliott, TexCivApp–Austin, 268 SW2d 484.—App & E 609; Insurance 2723, 2732; Plead 228.14, 262.

Great Am. Development Co. v. Smith, TexCivApp–Austin, 303 SW2d 861.—Waters 42, 44.

Great American Assur. Co.; Harrison v., TexApp–Dallas, 227 SW3d 890.—Insurance 1808, 1810, 1813, 1816, 1822, 1832(1), 1863, 2160(3).

Great American Homebuilders, Inc. v. Gerhart, TexApp–Houston (1 Dist), 708 SW2d 8, ref nre.—Antitrust 161, 291, 358, 369, 389(1), 390; Corp 1.7(2); Trial 105(2).

Great American Indemnity Co. v. Blakey, TexCivApp–San Antonio, 107 SW2d 1002, writ dism.—Release 12(3), 13(3), 16, 17(2); Work Comp 223, 1062, 2124, 2133.

Great American Indem. Co. v. Dabney, TexCivApp–Amarillo, 128 SW2d 496, writ dism, correct.—App & E 1175(1); Atty & C 107, 109; Evid 174.1, 325; Judgm 199(5); Trial 412; Work Comp 1283, 1300.

Great American Indem. Co.; Russell v., Tex, 94 SW2d 409, 127 Tex 458.—Trial 352.10.

Great American Ins.; Devoe v., TexApp–Austin, 50 SW3d 567.—App & E 93, 841, 863, 1125, 1178(1); Insurance 1822, 1832(2), 2275, 2914; Judgm 181(2).

Great American Ins. Co. v. Calli Homes, Inc., SDTex, 236 FSupp2d 693.—Contracts 176(2); Insurance 1806, 1832(2), 1835(2), 2264, 2268, 2290, 2911, 2913, 2914, 2922(1), 2939.

Great American Ins. Co.; Gregg & Valby, L.L.P. v., SDTex, 316 FSupp2d 505.—Insurance 1832(1), 1863, 2117, 2278(10), 2390, 2391(2), 3337.

Great American Ins. Co.; Lennar Corp. v., TexApp–Houston (14 Dist), 200 SW3d 651, concurring and dissenting opinions 2006 WL 909937.—Action 17; Antitrust 221; Fraud 13(3); Insurance 1091(4), 1806, 1813, 1814, 1863, 2101, 2117, 2261, 2268, 2269, 2275, 2277, 2278(8), 2278(19), 2278(21), 2278(24), 2278(26), 2278(27), 2281(2), 2282, 2283, 2911, 3147, 3168, 3195, 3200, 3349, 3353, 3354, 3381(2), 3417, 3419, 3424; Judgm 181(23), 185.3(12).

Great American Ins. Co.; M & M Const. Co., Inc. v., TexApp–Corpus Christi, 749 SW2d 526, writ dism woj, appeal dism, cert den 110 SCt 36, 493 US 801, 107 LEd2d 7.—App & E 223; Judgm 183.

Great American Ins. Co.; M & M Const. Co., Inc. v., TexApp–Corpus Christi, 747 SW2d 552.—Abate & R 71; App & E 554(1); Corp 615.5, 617(2); Motions 15; Plead 106(1), 106(2), 111.48; Pretrial Proc 557, 690.

Great American Ins. Co. v. North Austin Mun. Utility Dist. No. 1, Tex, 950 SW2d 371.—Interest 31, 39(2.30).

Great American Ins. Co. v. North Austin Mun. Utility Dist. No. 1, Tex, 908 SW2d 415, appeal after remand 933 SW2d 737, reh overr, and writ gr, rev 950 SW2d 371.—Contracts 198(1); Damag 62(4), 214; Insurance 3417; Princ & S 1, 66(1), 73, 136, 162(4).

Great American Ins. Co. v. North Austin Mun. Utility Dist. No. 1, TexApp–Austin, 933 SW2d 737, reh overr, and writ gr, rev 950 SW2d 371.—App & E 1079; Interest 39(2.30).

Great American Ins. Co. v. North Austin Mun. Utility Dist. No. 1, TexApp–Austin, 902 SW2d 488, reh overr, and writ gr, aff in part, rev in part 908 SW2d 415, appeal after remand 933 SW2d 737, reh overr, and writ gr, rev 950 SW2d 371.—App & E 232(3), 969, 1056.1(6), 1062.1, 1067; Contracts 93(1), 93(5), 262; Costs 198; Damag 62(1), 62(4), 118, 208(1), 210(1), 214; Insurance 1126, 3417, 3424(1), 3426; Labor & Emp 3125; Mun Corp 352, 375; Neglig 422, 1241; Princ & A 3(2), 24; Princ & S 52, 161, 166; Trial 228(1), 352.1(3).

Great American Ins. Co.; SnyderGeneral Corp. v., NDTex, 928 FSupp 674, aff 133 F3d 373, reh den.—Action 17; Contracts 143.5, 144; Evid 405(1); Fed Civ

Proc 2470, 2470.1, 2470.4, 2501, 2535, 2543, 2544; Insurance 1091(4), 1091(15), 1774, 1806, 1813, 2117, 2278(17), 3353; Torts 103.

Great American Ins. Co.; U.S. for Use and Benefit of Kinlau Sheet MetalWorks, Inc. v., CA5 (Tex), 537 F2d 222.—U S 67(13).

Great American Ins. Co. of New York; Minter v., CA5 (Tex), 423 F3d 460, reh and reh den 166 FedAppx 161. —Fed Civ Proc 2501; Fed Cts 419; Insurance 1642, 2663, 2667, 2675, 2740, 2891, 2900, 3170, 3549(3), 3556; Princ & A 177(1).

Great American Life Ins. Co. v. Lonze, TexApp–Dallas, 803 SW2d 750, writ den.—Insurance 1652(1).

Great American Lloyd's Ins. Co.; Adams v., TexApp–Austin, 891 SW2d 769, reh overr.—Insurance 2277; Propty 1, 5.5.

Great American Lloyds Ins. Co.; Archon Investments, Inc. v., TexApp–Houston (1 Dist), 174 SW3d 334, reh overr.—App & E 1175(1); Insurance 1806, 1809, 1812, 1822, 1831, 1832(2), 1863, 2268, 2269, 2271, 2275, 2911, 2913, 2914, 2915, 2922(1); Judgm 185.3(12).

Great American Lloyds Ins. Co.; Grimes Const., Inc. v., TexApp–Fort Worth, 188 SW3d 805.—Insurance 1806, 1822, 2268, 2269, 2271, 2275, 2911, 2913, 2914, 2915, 2922(1); Labor & Emp 3130, 3141, 3144.

Great American Lloyds Ins. Co.; Hartrick v., TexApp–Houston (1 Dist), 62 SW3d 270, rule 537(f) motion gr.—App & E 854(1), 1175(1); Contracts 188.5(3); Insurance 1806, 1809, 1810, 1812, 1832(1), 1835(2), 1863, 2101, 2117, 2268, 2269, 2275.

Great American Lloyds Ins. Co. v. Mittlestadt, TexApp–Fort Worth, 109 SW3d 784.—App & E 893(1); Evid 571(1); Insurance 2268, 2269, 2277, 2292, 2293, 2914.

Great American Lloyds Ins. Co.; Summit Custom Homes, Inc. v., TexApp–Dallas, 202 SW3d 823, reh overr.—App & E 852, 854(1), 901; Insurance 2265, 2268, 2271, 2275, 2277, 2362, 2911, 2914, 2934(3), 2934(4); Judgm 181(23).

Great American Management and Inv., Inc.; Continental Nat. Bank of Ft. Worth v., TexCivApp–Fort Worth, 606 SW2d 346, ref nre.—Banks 134(7); Trusts 9.

Great American Mortg. Corp. v. Plows, TexApp–Fort Worth, 783 SW2d 3.—App & E 756.

Great American Mortg. Investors v. Louisville Title Ins. Co., TexCivApp–Fort Worth, 597 SW2d 425, ref nre.—App & E 1062.1; Fraud 21, 33; Insurance 3424(1); Joint Adv 1.2(1), 1.2(7), 7; Neglig 231; Princ & A 23(5), 177(1); Trial 284, 350.3(4), 350.8, 366.

Great American Products v. Permabond Intern., a Div. of National Starch and Chemical Co., TexApp–Austin, 94 SW3d 675, reh overr, and review den.—Action 12; App & E 179(3); Costs 194.36; Judgm 199(1); Sales 427, 447.

Great American Reserve Ins. Co.; Sanders v., TexCivApp–Waco, 516 SW2d 732, writ gr, rev 525 SW2d 956.— Divorce 320; Insurance 1791(3), 3360, 3361, 3492; Interpl 6, 35.

Great Am. Health & Life Ins. Co. v. Lothringer, TexCivApp–Corpus Christi, 422 SW2d 543, ref nre.—App & E 1173(2); Evid 574; Insurance 2539, 2545(1), 2576, 2578.

Great Am. Indem. Co.; Beal v., TexCivApp–Texarkana, 322 SW2d 399.—Judgm 198, 199(1), 199(5); Trial 362.

Great Am. Indem. Co. v. Beaupre, TexCivApp–Dallas, 191 SW2d 883, ref nre.—Work Comp 974, 1001, 1893, 1924, 1969.

Great Am. Indem. Co.; Bennett v., CCA5 (Tex), 164 F2d 386.—Work Comp 349, 1297.

Great Am. Indem. Co. v. Blakey, TexCivApp–San Antonio, 151 SW2d 318, writ dism, correct.—App & E 927(7); Trial 178; Work Comp 1067, 1716, 1719.

Great Am. Indem. Co. v. Chriceol, TexCivApp–Eastland, 337 SW2d 404, ref nre.—Work Comp 1392, 1394, 1703, 1926, 1927.

Great Am. Indem. Co. v. City of Corpus Christi, TexCiv-App–San Antonio, 192 SW2d 917, ref nre.—Insurance 2270(1), 2332, 2926, 2928.

Great Am. Indem. Co. v. Dominguez, CCA5 (Tex), 84 F2d 179.—Work Comp 1881, 1883.

Great Am. Indem. Co. v. Elledge, Tex, 320 SW2d 328, 159 Tex 288.—Work Comp 1392, 1393, 1719.

Great Am. Indem. Co.; Elledge v., TexCivApp–Houston, 312 SW2d 722, ref nre 320 SW2d 328, 159 Tex 288.—App & E 842(6); Work Comp 1392, 1394, 1927.

Great Am. Indem. Co. v. Gravell, TexCivApp–San Antonio, 297 SW2d 371.—Work Comp 574, 880, 1403, 1651, 1941.

Great Am. Indem. Co.; Hooper v., CCA5 (Tex), 102 F2d 739.—Work Comp 51, 606, 1370, 1719.

Great Am. Indem. Co. v. Jordan, TexCivApp–Texarkana, 85 SW2d 264, writ dism.—App & E 930(3); Work Comp 1776.

Great Am. Indem. Co. v. Kingsbery, TexCivApp–Amarillo, 201 SW2d 611, ref nre.—App & E 1062.1, 1062.2; Damag 221(5.1); Plead 8(20); Work Comp 616, 666, 975, 1560, 1919, 1920, 1930, 1935, 1949.

Great Am. Indem. Co. v. McCaskill, CA5 (Tex), 240 F2d 80.—Work Comp 661, 1392.

Great Am. Indem. Co. v. McMenamin, TexCivApp–San Antonio, 134 SW2d 734, writ dism, correct.—Insurance 2761, 3110(3), 3204, 3367; Judgm 875; Parties 44.

Great Am. Indem. Co.; Meyer v., Tex, 279 SW2d 575, 154 Tex 408.—App & E 1082(1); Damag 221(5.1); Work Comp 876, 1657, 1926, 1930, 1958, 1975.

Great Am. Indem. Co. v. Meyer, TexCivApp–Galveston, 285 SW2d 276.—Work Comp 892, 1657, 1958.

Great Am. Indem. Co. v. Meyer, TexCivApp–Galveston, 272 SW2d 569, rev and remanded 279 SW2d 575, 154 Tex 408.—Damag 221(5.1), 221(6); Work Comp 877, 1926, 1931.

Great Am. Indem. Co. v. Ortiz, CA5 (Tex), 193 F2d 43.—Work Comp 735, 1443, 1452, 1578, 1971, 1975.

Great Am. Indem. Co. v. Pepper, TexCivApp–Fort Worth, 334 SW2d 333, writ gr, rev General Am Indem Co v. Pepper, 339 SW2d 660, 161 Tex 263.—Insurance 1816, 1822, 1832(1), 1835(2), 2588(3).

Great Am. Indem. Co.; Rodriguez v., CA5 (Tex), 244 F2d 484.—Work Comp 659.

Great Am. Indem. Co. v. Sams, Tex, 176 SW2d 312, 142 Tex 121.—Damag 221(6); Trial 351.5(8); Work Comp 1958, 1968(7).

Great Am. Indem. Co. v. Sams, TexCivApp–Beaumont, 170 SW2d 564, aff 176 SW2d 312, 142 Tex 121.—Damag 221(3), 221(5.1); Work Comp 876, 878, 1375, 1929.

Great Am. Indem. Co. v. Segal, CA5 (Tex), 229 F2d 845. —Work Comp 74, 847, 876.

Great Am. Indem. Co.; Shaffer v., CCA5 (Tex), 147 F2d 981.—Fed Civ Proc 2240; Fed Cts 600; Work Comp 1844.

Great Am. Indem. Co. v. State, TexCivApp–Austin, 229 SW2d 850, writ refused.—Insurance 1904; Princ & S 5; States 80(1).

Great Am. Ins. Co. v. Cacciola, WDTex, 213 FSupp 303. —Damag 221(5.1); Fed Cts 340.1, 352, 354; Trial 215, 349(1).

Great Am. Ins. Co. v. Cantu, TexCivApp–San Antonio, 438 SW2d 127, ref nre.—Trial 121(1), 125(4); Work Comp 1384, 1403, 1968(5).

Great Am. Ins. Co.; Capitol Aggregates, Inc. v., Tex, 408 SW2d 922.—Work Comp 2191, 2251.

Great Am. Ins. Co.; Capitol Aggregates, Inc. v., TexCiv-App–Austin, 396 SW2d 419, writ gr, aff 408 SW2d 922. —Indem 33(4); Work Comp 2245, 2251.

Great Am. Ins. Co.; Federal Deposit Ins. Corp. v., TexCivApp–Austin, 469 SW2d 254, ref nre.—App & E 1198; Princ & S 55.

Great Am. Ins. Co.; Flores v., TexCivApp–Waco, 401 SW2d 690, ref nre.—Insurance 2320, 2914; Work Comp 1066.

Great Am. Ins. Co.; Greene v., TexCivApp–Beaumont, 516 SW2d 739, ref nre.—Insurance 2660, 2772, 2778.

Great Am. Ins. Co.; Hancock v., TexCivApp–Texarkana, 510 SW2d 687.—Judgm 181(14), 185(2).

Great Am. Ins. Co. v. Lane, TexCivApp–Dallas, 398 SW2d 592, ref nre.—Insurance 2704.

Great Am. Ins. Co. v. Lang, TexCivApp–Austin, 416 SW2d 541, ref nre.—App & E 1001(1); Insurance 3054(1), 3072.

Great Am. Ins. Co. v. Langdeau, Tex, 379 SW2d 62.—App & E 758.1, 758.3(10), 1067, 1082(2), 1083(3), 1083(6); Insurance 1132, 2400, 2405, 2406(3), 2406(4); Judgm 707; New Tr 32; Trial 232(5), 260(9), 350.4(3), 352.1(4).

Great Am. Ins. Co.; Langdeau v., TexCivApp–Austin, 369 SW2d 944, writ gr, rev 379 SW2d 62.—Bonds 50; Insurance 1132, 1407, 3153, 3567.

Great Am. Ins. Co. v. Murray, Tex, 437 SW2d 264.—Insurance 3549(4); Pretrial Proc 36.1, 37, 335; Trial 127, 140(1), 382; Witn 331.5.

Great Am. Ins. Co. v. Rendon, TexCivApp–Amarillo, 390 SW2d 299, ref nre.—Judgm 326; Work Comp 1952.

Great Am. Ins. Co. v. Sharpstown State Bank, Tex, 460 SW2d 117, on remand Federal Deposit Ins Corp v. Great Am Ins Co, 469 SW2d 254, ref nre.—App & E 1090(1); Insurance 1635.

Great Am. Ins. Co.; Sharpstown State Bank v., TexCiv-App–Austin, 441 SW2d 548, rev 460 SW2d 117, on remand Federal Deposit Ins Corp v. Great Am Ins Co, 469 SW2d 254, ref nre.—Guar 12, 54; Insurance 1096, 1126, 1624; Interest 31, 44; Parties 52; Princ & A 22(2), 110(1), 116(1), 124(2), 147(2).

Great Am. Ins. Co. v. Sharpstown State Bank, TexCiv-App–Austin, 422 SW2d 787, writ dism.—App & E 185(1), 186; Const Law 2600, 3452; Corp 641; Courts 28; Decl Judgm 146, 295.

Great Am. Ins. Co.; Weigle v., TexCivApp–Amarillo, 434 SW2d 373.—Trial 358; Work Comp 1382, 1529, 1532, 1683, 1726, 1930.

Great Am. Ins. Co. of New York; Baucum v., Tex, 370 SW2d 863.—Insurance 2741(1); Tender 1, 11, 13(1), 13(4), 15(3), 15(6).

Great Am. Ins. Co. of New York; Baucum v., TexCiv-App–San Antonio, 364 SW2d 713, writ gr, rev 370 SW2d 863.—Bills & N 20; Tender 12(4), 13(1), 14(1), 14(2), 15(3), 15(6).

Great Am. Ins. Co. of New York; Hernandez v., Tex, 464 SW2d 91.—Contrib 5(1); Indem 35, 57; Insurance 3350; Lim of Act 55(2), 56(1).

Great Am. Ins. Co. of New York; Hernandez v., TexCiv-App–Corpus Christi, 456 SW2d 729, rev 464 SW2d 91.—Action 1, 27(1); Insurance 3380; Lim of Act 55(1).

Great Am. Ins. Co. of New York; Martinez v., WDTex, 286 FSupp 141.—Insurance 1606, 1608, 1636, 1898, 2035, 3457.

Great Am. Ins. Co. of New York; Pan Am Equipment v., TexCivApp–Dallas, 403 SW2d 451, dism.—Corp 503(2).

Great Am. Ins. Co. of N. Y. v. Maxey, CA5 (Tex), 193 F2d 151.—Insurance 1743, 1748, 1841, 2255.

Great Am. Inv. Co. v. McFarling, TexCivApp–Austin, 416 SW2d 479, ref nre.—Insurance 1412, 1413.

Great Am. Life & Health Ins. Co. v. Mayer, TexCivApp–Waco, 373 SW2d 391.—App & E 931(6), 959(1), 959(3), 1170.7; Insurance 2468, 3571; Plead 236(3), 276.

Great Am. Life Ins. Co. v. Dearing, TexCivApp–Galveston, 193 SW2d 250, ref nre.—App & E 930(1); Insurance 2604, 2608, 3016.

Great Am. Mortg. Investors; Lincoln Associates, Inc. v., NDTex, 415 FSupp 351.—Const Law 2503(1); Fed Cts 3.1, 5, 281, 302, 417; Rem of C 107(7).

Great Am. Mortg. Investors v. Republic of Texas Sav. Ass'n, TexCivApp–Hous (14 Dist), 538 SW2d 146.—App & E 483, 1173(2); Guar 36(3); Inj 138.31.

Great Am. Reserve Ins. Co. v. Britton, Tex, 406 SW2d 901.—App & E 1178(6); Evid 5(2), 14; Insurance 1766, 3003(8), 3013, 3015, 3016, 3343, 3379, 3381(5).

Great Am. Reserve Ins. Co. v. Britton, TexCivApp–Texarkana, 389 SW2d 320, writ gr, aff in part, rev in part 406 SW2d 901.—App & E 232(0.5), 837(5), 930(3); Insurance 1767, 3016, 3091, 3132, 3343, 3375, 3382, 3550.

Great Am. Reserve Ins. Co. v. Fry, TexCivApp–Austin, 418 SW2d 716, ref nre.—Insurance 3125(6).

Great Am. Reserve Ins. Co. v. Laney, Tex, 498 SW2d 674.—Insurance 2555.

Great Am. Reserve Ins. Co. v. Laney, TexCivApp–Fort Worth, 488 SW2d 481, writ gr, rev 498 SW2d 674.—Contracts 167; Insurance 1850, 2578.

Great Am. Reserve Ins. Co. v. Mitchell, TexCivApp–San Antonio, 335 SW2d 707, writ refused.—Insurance 3081, 3117.

Great Am. Reserve Ins. Co. v. San Antonio Plumbing Supply Co., Tex, 391 SW2d 41.—Insurance 1732; Judgm 181(2), 185(2), 185(5), 186.

Great Am. Reserve Ins. Co. v. San Antonio Plumbing Supply Co., TexCivApp–San Antonio, 378 SW2d 141, writ gr, rev 391 SW2d 41.—Insurance 1763; Judgm 185(2), 185.3(12), 186.

Great Am. Reserve Ins. Co. v. Sanders, Tex, 525 SW2d 956.—Fraud 58(1); Insurance 3360, 3393; Interpl 8(2).

Great Am. Reserve Ins. Co.; Satery v., TexCivApp–Waco, 278 SW2d 377, ref nre.—Insurance 2018.

Great Am. Reserve Ins. Co. v. Sumner, TexCivApp–Tyler, 464 SW2d 212, 49 ALR3d 667, ref nre.—Insurance 2590(2), 2595(1), 2595(3); Trial 401.

Great Am. Reserve Ins. Co. v. White v., TexCivApp–Dallas, 342 SW2d 793.—App & E 758.1, 761; Insurance 2422, 3081, 3100(3), 3128.

Great Atlantic & Pacific Tea Co.; Eisenberg v., TexCivApp–San Antonio, 169 SW2d 221.—App & E 1042(2); Labor & Emp 2859, 2881; Neglig 1655.

Great Atlantic & Pacific Tea Co. v. Evans, Tex, 175 SW2d 249, 142 Tex 1.—App & E 1175(5); Labor & Emp 2840; Neglig 200, 213, 232, 272, 387.

Great Atlantic & Pacific Tea Co.; Freeman v., TexCivApp–Austin, 135 SW2d 267, writ refused.—App & E 1002, 1003(4), 1070(2); Neglig 1679, 1691.

Great Atlantic & Pacific Tea Co. v. Garner, TexCivApp–Dallas, 170 SW2d 502, writ refused wom.—App & E 301, 758.1; Labor & Emp 2848, 2889, 2890; Neglig 1631, 1650; Trial 352.4(9), 352.18, 362.

Great Atlantic & Pacific Tea Co. v. Giles, TexCivApp–Dallas, 354 SW2d 410, ref nre.—Judgm 199(3.10); Neglig 1076, 1104(6), 1595, 1670; Trial 139.1(8), 139.1(14), 139.1(17), 178.

Great Atlantic & Pacific Tea Co.; Greenway v., TexCivApp–Eastland, 114 SW2d 435.—App & E 1001(1); Evid 588; Food 25; Trial 140(1).

Great Atlantic & Pacific Tea Co. v. Lang, TexCivApp–Eastland, 291 SW2d 366, ref nre.—Labor & Emp 2870, 2927, 2939, 2941, 2990.

Great Atlantic & Pacific Tea Co.; Najera v., Tex, 207 SW2d 365, 146 Tex 367.—App & E 930(1), 1114, 1122(1); Labor & Emp 2942, 3010; Trial 142; Work Comp 2113, 2119.

Great Atlantic & Pacific Tea Co. v. Najera, TexCivApp–Dallas, 203 SW2d 577, rev 207 SW2d 365, 146 Tex 367.—App & E 931(1); Labor & Emp 2997; Neglig 250, 387, 431; Work Comp 2110, 2113.

Great Atlantic & Pacific Tea Co.; Smith v., TexCivApp–Eastland, 100 SW2d 1041, writ dism.—Labor & Emp 2810, 2815, 2889; New Tr 99, 104(3); Plead 228.23; Pretrial Proc 714; Work Comp 2133.

Great Atlantic & Pacific Tea Co.; Walker v., Tex, 112 SW2d 170, 131 Tex 57.—App & E 231(3), 671(6), 719(1), 1050.1(1); Evid 128; Food 25; Sales 255.

Great Atlantic & Pacific Tea Co. v. Walker, TexCivApp–Eastland, 104 SW2d 627, rev 112 SW2d 170, 131 Tex 57.—Evid 126(2), 128, 470, 508, 555.10; Food 25; Neglig 422, 453; Sales 246, 255, 273(5), 274.

Great Atlantic & Pac. Tea Co. v. Athens Lodge No. 165, A. F. & A. M., TexCivApp–Fort Worth, 207 SW2d 217, ref nre.—App & E 758.3(1), 931(1), 989, 1008.2, 1010.1(1); Autos 200; Ben Assoc 19; Contracts 261(1); Costs 241; Damag 138, 163(1); Estop 52.15, 90(1), 99, 116; Land & Ten 34(2), 55(2), 55(3), 114(2), 286; Lim of Act 197(1).

Great Atlantic & Pac. Tea Co. v. Coleman, TexCivApp–Galveston, 259 SW2d 319.—Labor & Emp 2830, 2879, 2890, 2963.

Great Atlantic & Pac. Tea Co. v. McGee, TexCivApp–Dallas, 396 SW2d 896, ref nre.—Labor & Emp 2832, 2857, 2881; Neglig 1037(4); Work Comp 2114.

Great Atlantic & Pac. Tea Co. v. N. L. R. B., CA5 (Tex), 354 F2d 707.—Labor & Emp 1741, 1743(1), 1755, 1882.

Great Atlantic & Pac. Tea Co.; Shumake v., TexCivApp–Dallas, 255 SW2d 949, ref nre.—App & E 934(1); Judgm 199(3.7), 199(3.10); Labor & Emp 2840; Work Comp 2144.

Great Atlantic & Pac. Tea Co. v. Smith, TexCivApp–Galveston, 253 SW2d 58, ref nre.—Labor & Emp 2815, 2941.

Great Atlantic Life Ins. Co. v. Harris, TexApp–Austin, 723 SW2d 329, dism.—Insurance 1363, 3606, 3631.

Great Central Ins. Co.; Amundsen v., TexCivApp–El Paso, 451 SW2d 277, ref nre.—Insurance 2278(16).

Great Central Ins. Co. v. Cook, TexCivApp–Dallas, 422 SW2d 801.—App & E 870(2), 1056.1(9); Insurance 2201, 3142, 3156, 3164.

Great Com. Life Ins. Co. v. Banco Obrero De Ahorro Y Prestamos De Puerto Rico, CA5 (Tex), 535 F2d 331.—Banks 119; Const Law 3965(7); Trover 13.

Great Com. Life Ins. Co.; Debenport v., TexCivApp–Dallas, 324 SW2d 566.—App & E 766; Contracts 22(1); Insurance 1732, 1734, 1736.

Great Commonwealth Life Ins. Co. v. Olton State Bank, TexCivApp–Amarillo, 607 SW2d 604.—App & E 832(4); Insurance 2424, 2439.

Great Commonwealth Life Ins. Co. v. U.S., CA5 (Tex), 491 F2d 109, on remand 1977 WL 1226.—Int Rev 3078, 3273, 3975.

Great Dane Trailers, Inc. v. Estate of Wells, Tex, 52 SW3d 737.—Autos 5(1), 9, 11; Prod Liab 24, 35.1, 36; States 18.3, 18.5, 18.13, 18.65.

Great Dane Trailers, Inc.; Wells, Estate of v., TexApp–Houston (14 Dist), 5 SW3d 860, reh overr, and review gr, aff 52 SW3d 737.—Prod Liab 35.1, 75.1; States 18.3, 18.5, 18.7, 18.13, 18.65.

Great Eastern Life Ins. Co. v. Jones, TexCivApp–Beaumont, 526 SW2d 268, ref nre.—App & E 878(1); Home 118(5).

Great Eastern Oil Co.; T. F. Hart Inv. Co. v., EDTex, 27 FSupp 713.—Contempt 34, 46, 53; Receivers 74.

Greater Austin Apartment Maintenance; Reintsma v., TexCivApp–Austin, 549 SW2d 434, dism.—App & E 387(4), 388, 936(2), 984(5), 1024.1, 1140(6), 1151(3), 1178(6); Costs 194.12, 194.22, 194.34; Judgm 326; Land & Ten 184(2).

Greater Beauxart Garden Municipal Utility Dist. v. Cormier, TexCivApp–Beaumont, 596 SW2d 597.—App & E 1008.1(2), 1010.1(4), 1012.1(4); Elections 41; Mun Corp 80.

Greater Dallas Home Care Alliance v. U.S., NDTex, 36 FSupp2d 765.—Fed Civ Proc 2545; Health 535(2).

Greater Dallas Home Care Alliance v. U.S., NDTex, 10 FSupp2d 638.—Const Law 188, 1566, 1624, 2486, 3053,

3060, 3551, 3877, 4127; Health 455, 535(1), 535(4), 539, 547; Inj 132, 138.1, 138.66, 147.

Greater Fort Worth v. Mims, TexCivApp–Fort Worth, 574 SW2d 870, dism.—App & E 900, 955; Receivers 1, 8, 29(1), 30, 38.

Greater Ft. Worth and Tarrant County Community Action Agency v. Mims, Tex, 627 SW2d 149.—App & E 499(1); Corp 294, 426(1); Labor & Emp 867, 868(3), 871; Plead 167.

Greater Ft. Worth & Tarrant County Community Action Agency v. Mims, TexCivApp–Fort Worth, 618 SW2d 942, rev 627 SW2d 149.—App & E 272(1), 273(2); Char 40; Inj 130, 199; Labor & Emp 251; Plead 147, 228.23; Supersed 7.

Greater Fort Worth and Tarrant County Community Action Agency; Stenseth v., CA5 (Tex), 673 F2d 842.— Civil R 1509, 1510, 1532, 1592; Const Law 4172(7).

Greater Gulf Coast Enterprises, Inc.; Herbert v., TexApp–Houston (1 Dist), 915 SW2d 866, reh overr.—App & E 859, 914(1), 931(1), 1010.1(3), 1010.2, 1178(1); Const Law 3964, 3967; Courts 15; Damag 394, 194; Impl & C C 30, 55; Judgm 112; Mech Liens 115(1); Proc 64, 134.

Greater Houston Bank; Behring Intern., Inc. v., TexApp–Houston (1 Dist), 662 SW2d 642, writ dism by agreement.—App & E 840(1), 931(1), 989, 1010.1(3), 1012.1(4); Banks 134(1), 134(2), 148(3), 154(8); Bills & N 327, 342, 525; Contracts 328(1); Contrib 5(6.1); Costs 264; Damag 91(3); Interest 39(2.30); Princ & A 96, 99, 109(4), 131, 137(1), 148(1), 151(3); Trover 22.

Greater Houston Bank v. Conte, TexApp–Houston (14 Dist), 666 SW2d 296.—Judgm 585(2), 663, 713(2), 720; Prohib 9, 10(2).

Greater Houston Bank; Conte v., TexApp–Houston (14 Dist), 641 SW2d 411, ref nre.—Bills & N 129(2), 129(3), 516, 518(1); Contracts 153; Decl Judgm 143.1; Usury 45, 52.

Greater Houston Bank v. Conte, TexApp–Houston (14 Dist), 641 SW2d 407.—App & E 78(3); Inj 16; Mtg 413.

Greater Houston Bank; Hemphill v., TexCivApp–Hous (14 Dist), 537 SW2d 124.—Judgm 185(2), 185.3(2), 185.3(16); Set-Off 29(1), 60.

Greater Houston Bank; Miller & Freeman Ford, Inc. v., Tex, 544 SW2d 925.—Judgm 185.3(16).

Greater Houston Bank v. Miller & Freeman Ford, Inc., TexCivApp–Corpus Christi, 540 SW2d 390, rev 544 SW2d 925.—App & E 232(0.5), 1175(2); Autos 375; Judgm 185.1(3), 185.3(15); Sec Tran 144.

Greater Houston Bank v. Norwegian American Line, TexApp–Houston (1 Dist), 662 SW2d 642. See Behring Intern., Inc. v. Greater Houston Bank.

Greater Houston Bank; Smith v., TexCivApp–Hous (1 Dist), 580 SW2d 165.—Cons Cred 56, 67.

Greater Houston Chapter of Am. Civil Liberties Union v. Houston Independent School Dist., CA5 (Tex), 391 F2d 599.—Fed Cts 727.

Greater Houston Chapter of American Civil Liberties Union v. Eckels, CA5 (Tex), 763 F2d 180.—Fed Cts 666.

Greater Houston Chapter of American Civil Liberties Union v. Eckels, SDTex, 589 FSupp 222, appeal dism 755 F2d 426, reh den 763 F2d 180, cert den 106 SCt 383, 474 US 980, 88 LEd2d 336.—Const Law 1290, 1295, 1375, 1376.

Greater Houston Chapter of the American Civil Liberties Union v. Eckels, CA5 (Tex), 755 F2d 426, reh den 763 F2d 180, cert den 106 SCt 383, 474 US 980, 88 LEd2d 336.—Fed Civ Proc 2366.1; Fed Cts 668.

Greater Houston Civic Council v. Mann, CA5 (Tex), 906 F2d 1068. See Leroy v. City of Houston.

Greater Houston Civic Council v. Mann, SDTex, 440 FSupp 696.—Const Law 3285; Elections 12(3), 12(7); Mun Corp 80.

Greater Houston Civil Council, Inc. v. Mann, SDTex, 648 FSupp 537. See Leroy v. City of Houston.

Greater Houston Transp. Co.; Arrow Northwest, Inc. v., CA5 (Tex), 760 F2d 607. See Independent Taxicab Drivers' Employees v. Greater Houston Transp. Co.

Greater Houston Transp. Co.; Farrell v., TexApp–Houston (1 Dist), 908 SW2d 1, reh overr, and writ den.— Autos 194(2), 197(1); Judgm 185(2); Labor & Emp 29, 57; Pretrial Proc 583, 674; Proc 158.

Greater Houston Transp. Co.; Independent Taxicab Drivers' Employees v.,CA5 (Tex), 760 F2d 607, cert den Arrow Northwest, Inc v. Greater Houston Transportation Company, 106 SCt 231, 474 US 903, 88 LEd2d 230.—Antitrust 903, 905(2), 980.

Greater Houston Transp. Co. v. Phillips, Tex, 801 SW2d 523.—Child C 102; Labor & Emp 3043, 3056(2), 3143; Neglig 202, 210, 213, 220, 1692; Parent & C 13(1).

Greater Houston Transp. Co.; Shaw v., TexApp–Houston (1 Dist), 764 SW2d 390.—App & E 382, 390.

Greater Houston Transp. Co.; Shaw v., TexApp–Corpus Christi, 791 SW2d 204.—App & E 934(1), 1024.4, 1046.5; Autos 244(26); Trial 29.1, 306, 314(1), 316, 344.

Greater Houston Transp. Co. v. Wilson, TexApp–Houston (14 Dist), 725 SW2d 427, ref nre.—App & E 200, 499(1); Autos 245(50.1), 246(2.1), 246(22); Judgm 652; Neglig 200, 370; New Tr 150(1), 150(3); Pretrial Proc 226.

Greater Houston Transp. Co., Inc. v. Zrubeck, TexApp– Corpus Christi, 850 SW2d 579, reh overr, and writ den. —App & E 218.2(2), 230, 242(1), 989, 994(2), 1003(3), 1003(5), 1004(1), 1070(1); Autos 244(4), 244(20); Damag 87(1), 94, 130.2, 135, 221(5.1), 221(7), 223; Estop 52.10(2); Neglig 273; Trial 321.5, 345, 366.

Greater Mount Olive Baptist Church; Rosen v., TexCivApp–Waco, 410 SW2d 863.—Venue 22(3), 22(7).

Greater New Canaan Missionary Baptist Church, Inc.; Standard Sav. Ass'n v., TexApp–Houston (14 Dist), 786 SW2d 774.—Interest 39(2.20); Judgm 181(15.1); Usury 6, 42, 72.

Greater Southwest Intern. Airways, Inc. v. Arlington Executive Air, Inc., TexCivApp–Fort Worth, 432 SW2d 740.—Aviation 241, 243; Bailm 12; Land & Ten 162, 168(0.5), 168(1).

Greater Southwest Office Park, Ltd. v. Texas Commerce Bank Nat. Ass'n, TexApp–Houston (1 Dist), 786 SW2d 386, writ den.—App & E 1024.4; Fraud 6, 7; Judgm 181(11), 185.3(15); Mtg 209, 369(2).

Greater Swenson Grove Baptist Church; Hanger General Contractors v., TexCivApp–Austin, 597 SW2d 32. —Contracts 164; Plead 111.3, 307; Venue 7.5(1).

Greater Texas Finishing Corp.; Reyes v., WDTex, 19 FSupp2d 717.—Labor & Emp 3217, 3218, 3226.

Greater Texas Finishing Corp.; Reyes v., WDTex, 19 FSupp2d 709.—Fed Civ Proc 2497.1, 2539; Labor & Emp 3210, 3219, 3222.

Greater Texoma Utility Authority; City of Bells v., TexApp–Dallas, 790 SW2d 6, writ den.—Decl Judgm 273; Environ Law 359; Mun Corp 29(4), 33(4), 33(9), 92; Zoning 134.1.

Greater Texoma Utility Authority; City of Bells v., TexApp–Dallas, 744 SW2d 636.—Action 13; Admin Law 124; Mun Corp 1017; Pub Ut 103.

Great Fidelity Inv. Co.; Martin v., CA5 (Tex), 450 F2d 959, cert den 92SCt 1177, 405 US 955, 31 LEd2d 232, reh den 92 SCt 1311, 405 US 1049, 31 LEd2d 592, and Garrett Freightlines, Inc v. US, 92 SCt 1311, 405 US 1035, 31 LEd2d 577.—Courts 104.

Great Global Assur. Co. v. Keltex Properties, Inc., TexApp–Corpus Christi, 904 SW2d 771.—App & E 756, 758.3(9), 765, 799, 842(2), 931(1), 931(6), 946, 989, 1003(1), 1003(7), 1008.1(2); Execution 415; Trial 18; Witn 235.

Great Global Assur. Co. v. McFarlin, TexApp–Beaumont, 728 SW2d 401, ref nre.—Courts 516; Insurance 3360.

Great Global Assur. Co. v. Texergy Corp., TexApp–Corpus Christi, 904 SW2d 771. See Great Global Assur. Co. v. Keltex Properties, Inc.

Greathouse, Ex parte, TexCrimApp, 126 SW2d 670, 136 TexCrim 491.—Hab Corp 823.

Greathouse v. Aetna Life Ins. Co., EDTex, 750 FSupp 225.—Labor & Emp 682.

Greathouse v. Alvin Independent School Dist., TexApp–Houston (1 Dist), 17 SW3d 419, reh overr.—App & E 173(1), 856(1), 934(1); Civil R 1103, 1118, 1744; Judgm 181(27), 185(2), 185(5), 185.3(13).

Greathouse v. Charter Nat. Bank-Southwest, Tex, 851 SW2d 173, on reh.—Sec Tran 240.

Greathouse v. Charter Nat. Bank-Southwest, TexApp–Houston (1 Dist), 795 SW2d 1, writ gr, aff 851 SW2d 173, on reh.—Sec Tran 240.

Greathouse; Etchison v., TexCivApp–Hous (1 Dist), 596 SW2d 233.—App & E 1170.6; Child S 191, 508(4); Child 3; Const Law 250.5, 3053, 3738; Evid 80(1).

Greathouse; Friddell v., TexCivApp–Dallas, 230 SW2d 579, dism.—App & E 1177(1), 1177(6); Bills & N 22, 443(2), 473, 489(6), 491.

Greathouse v. Gilmartin, TexCivApp–Fort Worth, 164 SW2d 757.—Mand 35, 154(4).

Greathouse v. Glidden Co., TexApp–Houston (14 Dist), 40 SW3d 560, reh en banc den.—App & E 966, 984(5); Atty & C 140; Bills & N 534; Fraud 31; Labor & Emp 407, 425, 429, 446, 645, 662; States 18.51.

Greathouse v. Greathouse, TexApp–Corpus Christi, 665 SW2d 801.—App & E 920(3), 954(1); Inj 26(9), 138.21, 151; J P 36(7); Spec Perf 108.

Greathouse; Greathouse v., TexApp–Corpus Christi, 665 SW2d 801.—App & E 920(3), 954(1); Inj 26(9), 138.21, 151; J P 36(7); Spec Perf 108.

Greathouse v. McConnell, TexApp–Houston (1 Dist), 982 SW2d 165, review den, and reh of petition for review overr.—App & E 1078(5); Atty & C 105, 129(2); Courts 4, 35, 37(1), 40, 485; Judgm 181(16), 183.

Greathouse v. State, TexCrimApp, 491 SW2d 149.—Sent & Pun 2021.

Greathouse v. State, TexCrimApp, 254 SW2d 387.—Crim Law 1090.1(1).

Greathouse v. State, TexCrimApp, 245 SW2d 267.—Crim Law 1081(2), 1087.1(2).

Greathouse v. State, TexCrimApp, 184 SW2d 144, 147 TexCrim 639.—Crim Law 1169.5(2), 1170.5(5); Homic 1154; Witn 52(7).

Greathouse v. State, TexApp–Houston (1 Dist), 33 SW3d 455, petition for discretionary review refused.—Const Law 4733(1); Crim Law 1134(3), 1144.17, 1147; Sent & Pun 1963, 1973(2), 1973(3), 2001, 2018, 2020, 2021.

Greathouse v. State, TexApp–Corpus Christi, 654 SW2d 496.—Crim Law 641.13(4), 1043(3), 1119(4), 1130(5), 1170.5(1); Ind & Inf 110(8).

Greathouse v. Texas Public Utilities Corp., TexCivApp–Eastland, 217 SW2d 190, ref nre.—App & E 934(1), 1138; Labor & Emp 3045, 3049(1), 3055, 3056(2).

Greathouse Ins. Agency, Inc. v. Tropical Investments, Inc., TexApp–Houston (14 Dist), 718 SW2d 821.—App & E 71(3); Inj 135, 138.37, 163(1).

Greathouse's Estate, In re, TexCivApp–San Antonio, 184 SW2d 317.—Courts 200.7, 202(5); Marriage 11.

Great Impressions Apparel, Inc.; John Hunter, Inc. v., NDTex, 313 FSupp2d 644.—Fed Cts 345; Rem of C 79(1).

Great Lakes Carbon Corp.; Blum v., CA5 (Tex), 418 F2d 283, 19 Wage & Hour Cas (BNA) 254, cert den 90 SCt 1361, 397 US 1040, 19 Wage & Hour Cas (BNA) 445, 25 LEd2d 651.—Fed Cts 852; Labor & Emp 2316, 2317.

Great Lakes Engineering, Inc. v. Andersen, TexApp–Houston (1 Dist), 627 SW2d 436.—Inj 152.

Great Liberty Life Ins. Co.; Allen v., TexCivApp–Eastland, 522 SW2d 247, ref nre.—App & E 1050.1(11);

Corp 316(1), 319(8); Judgm 665, 708, 709, 714(1), 822(2); Lim of Act 37(4).

Great Liberty Life Ins. Co. v. Flint, TexCivApp–Fort Worth, 336 SW2d 434.—Judgm 138(1), 162(4); Witn 68, 71.

Great Nat. Corp. v. Campbell, TexApp–Dallas, 687 SW2d 450, ref nre.—App & E 1079; Evid 450(5); Joint Adv 1.15, 4(1), 5(1), 5(2); Paymt 65.11; Trial 3(5.1).

Great Nat. Ins. Co. v. Legg, TexCivApp–El Paso, 444 SW2d 324, ref nre.—Evid 568(4); Insurance 2590(1), 2606, 3360, 3396.

Great Nat. Life Ins. Co.; Campbell v., CA5 (Tex), 219 F2d 693.—Int Rev 3139, 3140, 3973.

Great Nat. Life Ins. Co. v. Campbell, NDTex, 119 FSupp 57, aff 219 F2d 693.—Int Rev 3029, 3037, 3456.1.

Great Nat. Life Ins. Co. v. Chapa, Tex, 377 SW2d 632.—Autos 60; Consp 1.1; Evid 253(2); Insurance 1611; Venue 8.5(1).

Great Nat. Life Ins. Co. v. Chapa, TexCivApp–Waco, 373 SW2d 280, writ gr, rev 377 SW2d 632.—Autos 197(7); Venue 8.5(3).

Great Nat. Life Ins. Co.; Davidson v., Tex, 737 SW2d 312.—App & E 1047(3), 1048(6); Evid 35, 359(1), 359(2), 380; Witn 184(2), 216(1).

Great Nat. Life Ins. Co. v. Davidson, TexApp–Dallas, 708 SW2d 476, writ gr, rev 737 SW2d 312.—Witn 184(1), 222.

Great Nat. Life Ins. Co.; Elliott v., Tex, 611 SW2d 620.—App & E 930(3), 989; Corp 432(12).

Great Nat. Life Ins. Co. v. Elliott, TexCivApp–Dallas, 592 SW2d 404, rev 611 SW2d 620.—Princ & A 123(8), 137(1).

Great Nat. Life Ins. Co. v. Gafford, TexCivApp–Waco, 108 SW2d 917.—App & E 1062.1; Insurance 1635, 1636; Princ & A 99.

Great Nat. Life Ins. Co. v. Harrell, TexCivApp–Waco, 157 SW2d 427, writ dism.—App & E 1091(1); Insurance 1920, 1936, 3571; J P 174(26).

Great Nat. Life Ins. Co. v. Hulme, TexComApp, 136 SW2d 602, 134 Tex 539.—Insurance 1758, 3084, 3091, 3096(2).

Great Nat. Life Ins. Co.; Hulme v., TexCivApp–Fort Worth, 116 SW2d 459, rev 136 SW2d 602, 134 Tex 539.—Insurance 3096(2).

Great Nat. Life Ins. Co.; Johnson v., TexCivApp–Dallas, 166 SW2d 935, writ refused wom.—Commerce 62.44(1), 62.63, 62.67; Labor & Emp 2238, 2385(1).

Great Nat. Life Ins. Co.; Merbitz v., TexCivApp–Texarkana, 599 SW2d 655, ref nre.—App & E 837(1); Estop 119; Evid 429; Insurance 1608, 1798, 2445; Trial 110; Witn 100.

Great Nat. Life Ins. Co.; Phillips v., TexCivApp–El Paso, 226 SW2d 660.—Evid 413; Insurance 1869, 1879.

Great Nat. Life Ins. Co. v. Presley, TexCivApp–Amarillo, 129 SW2d 730, writ dism.—Evid 397(1), 432, 434(6), 441(4), 593.

Great Nat. Life Ins. Co.; Walters v., TexComApp, 124 SW2d 850, 132 Tex 454.—App & E 917(1); Insurance 2595(2), 3571; Plead 34(3), 192(3), 228.23.

Great Nat. Life Ins. Co.; Walters v., TexCivApp–Fort Worth, 92 SW2d 1136, rev 124 SW2d 850, 132 Tex 454.—Contracts 143(2), 147(2); Homic 908; Insurance 2595(2).

Great Nat. Lloyds; Hall v., Tex, 275 SW2d 88, 154 Tex 200.—App & E 977(5); Embez 9; Insurance 1822, 1832(1), 2706(3).

Great Nat. Lloyds v. Hall, TexCivApp–Fort Worth, 265 SW2d 875, rev 275 SW2d 88, 154 Tex 200.—Crim Law 29(10); Embez 1, 9, 13, 14; Insurance 1088, 1813, 1822, 1832(1), 1851, 2153(1), 2675, 2706(3), 2732, 3579; Larc 15(1), 15(3).

Great Nat. Lloyds; National Bond & Inv. Co. v., TexCivApp–Dallas, 271 SW2d 322, ref nre.—Autos 19; Insurance 1982, 2706(3).

GREAT–NESS

Great-Ness Professional Services, Inc. v. First Nat. Bank of Louisville, TexApp–Houston (14 Dist), 704 SW2d 916.—Acct Action on 10; Judgm 181(5.1), 186.

Great North American Companies, Inc.; Hiss v., Tex-App–Dallas, 871 SW2d 218.—App & E 863, 870(4), 954(1); Inj 138.3; Trial 5.

Great North American Industries, Inc.; Tephguard Corp. v., TexCivApp–Dallas, 571 SW2d 554.—App & E 100(1); Inj 138.21; Trademarks 1707(6).

Great North American Stationers, Inc. v. Ball, TexApp–Dallas, 770 SW2d 631, writ dism.—Labor & Emp 707, 720.

Great Northern Ins. Co.; Summit Mach. Tool Mfg. Corp. v., SDTex, 883 FSupp 1532.—Fed Civ Proc 2737.4; Rem of C 107(11).

Great Northern Ins. Co.; Summit Mach. Tool Mfg. Corp. v., SDTex, 883 FSupp 1529.—Insurance 3390; Release 25; Rem of C 82, 107(7).

Great Northern Ins. Co.; Summit Mach. Tool Mfg. Corp. v., TexApp–Austin, 997 SW2d 840.—App & E 200, 231(9), 232(3), 242(1), 968; Insurance 3182, 3183, 3184, 3186, 3191(1), 3191(7), 3191(11), 3197, 3198(1), 3200; Jury 85, 149.

Great Oil Basin Securities Corp. v. Union Nat. Bank of Little Rock, Arkansas, TexCivApp–El Paso, 579 SW2d 322, ref nre.—Judgm 217, 713(2), 829(1); Set-Off 60.

Great Olympic Tire Co. v. U.S., CA5 (Tex), 597 F2d 449. —Int Rev 4336.

Great Pines Water Co., Inc. v. Liqui-Box Corp., CA5 (Tex), 203 F3d 920, reh den.—Damag 190; Fed Cts 931, 945.

Great Pines Water Co., Inc. v. Liqui-Box Corp., SDTex, 962 FSupp 990.—Fed Civ Proc 2651.1, 2655; Fed Cts 415; Interest 39(2.30), 39(2.50), 60.

Great Plains Airline Shareholders Ass'n, Inc. v. Frontier Airlines, Inc., CA5 (Tex), 662 F2d 394.—Aviation 107.

Great Plains Equipment, Inc. v. Koch Gathering Systems, Inc., CA5 (Tex), 45 F3d 962.—Contracts 299(2); Damag 174(1), 188(2); Evid 474(19), 501(7); Fed Cts 641, 692, 700, 707.1, 870.1, 892, 899; Jury 33(5.15), 33(5.20), 120.

Great Plains Land & Cattle v. F.D.I.C., CA5 (Tex), 995 F2d 626. See Lindsey, Stephenson & Lindsey, Matter of.

Great Plains Land & Cattle v. F.D.I.C., NDTex, 158 BR 75. See Lindsey, Stephenson & Lindsey v. F.D.I.C.

Great Plains Life Ins. Co. v. First Nat. Bank of Lubbock, TexCivApp–Amarillo, 316 SW2d 98, ref nre.— Banks 133; Contracts 278(1), 318; Corp 425(5), 426(2), 432(12); Land & Ten 111, 112.5; Tender 16(2), 16(3), 28.

Great Plains Oil & Gas Co. v. Foundation Oil Co., Tex, 153 SW2d 452, 137 Tex 324.—App & E 1175(1); Bound 3(6), 5, 30, 47(1), 48(7), 48(8), 55.

Great Plains Oil & Gas Co.; Foundation Oil Co. v., TexCivApp–Texarkana, 141 SW2d 969, rev 153 SW2d 452, 137 Tex 324.—Bound 3(6).

Great Plains Pipeline Const., Inc. v. Koch Gathering Systems, Inc., CA5 (Tex), 45 F3d 962. See Great Plains Equipment, Inc. v. Koch Gathering Systems, Inc.

Great Plains Trust Co. v. Morgan Stanley Dean Witter & Co., CA5 (Tex), 313 F3d 305, reh and reh den 62 FedAppx 559.—Antitrust 141, 363; Brok 19, 22; Fed Cts 303, 763.1, 776, 915; Fraud 3, 7, 13(3), 21; Neglig 202, 273, 321; Rem of C 36, 107(7), 107(9).

Great Service, Inc.; Spicer v., TexCivApp–San Antonio, 580 SW2d 14, appeal after remand 611 SW2d 702.— Antitrust 363; Trial 139.1(6), 139.1(8), 139.1(17), 178.

Great Services, Inc.; Spicer v., TexCivApp–San Antonio, 611 SW2d 702.—App & E 1133.

Greatsinger v. State, TexApp–Houston (1 Dist), 881 SW2d 18, petition for discretionary review refused.— Crim Law 1081(2).

Great Southern Bank; Ames v., Tex, 672 SW2d 447.— Antitrust 397; Banks 148(1), 152, 174; Contracts 243, 305(1); Princ & A 99, 109(0.5), 131, 137(1).

Great Southern Bank; Ames v., TexApp–Houston (1 Dist), 672 SW2d 500, aff in part, rev in part 672 SW2d 447.—App & E 1177(8); Banks 154(1), 154(8), 154(9), 231; Contracts 227; Estop 95; Judgm 199(3.14); Princ & A 99.

Great Southern Fire and Cas. Ins. Co.; Ortiz v., Tex, 597 SW2d 342.—Insurance 3503(4), 3510.

Great Southern Fire & Cas. Ins. Co.; Ortiz v., TexCivApp–Amarillo, 587 SW2d 818, rev 597 SW2d 342.— Insurance 3503(1), 3513(1), 3513(3), 3514(3), 3515(1); Judgm 181(11), 181(23).

Great Southern Life Ins Co v. Commissioner of Internal Revenue, CCA5 (Tex), 89 F2d 54, cert den 58 SCt 16, 302 US 698, 82 LEd 539.—Int Rev 3132.1, 3970, 3975.

Great Southern Life Ins. Co. v. Akins, TexCivApp–Waco, 105 SW2d 902, writ refused.—Homic 504; Insurance 2439, 2595(2).

Great Southern Life Ins. Co. v. Benson, TexCivApp–Texarkana, 326 SW2d 5, ref nre.—App & E 934(2); Insurance 2035; Trial 350.8.

Great Southern Life Ins. Co.; Board of Ins. Com'rs v., Tex, 239 SW2d 803, 150 Tex 258.—Const Law 1020, 1033, 3035, 3036; Contracts 164; Evid 5(2); Insurance 1839, 1847, 2100; Statut 184, 205, 236, 241(1), 241(2).

Great Southern Life Ins. Co. v. Cunningham, TexComApp, 97 SW2d 692, 128 Tex 196.—Insurance 2037, 2439; Statut 208.

Great Southern Life Ins. Co.; Dimmitt v., CCA5 (Tex), 124 F2d 40.—Bankr 2229.

Great Southern Life Ins. Co. v. Dodson, TexCivApp–Amarillo, 155 SW2d 379.—Adv Poss 63(2), 63(4), 114(1).

Great Southern Life Ins. Co. v. Dorough, TexCivApp–Waco, 100 SW2d 772.—Evid 590; Insurance 2037, 3343.

Great Southern Life Ins. Co. v. Doyle, TexComApp, 151 SW2d 197, 136 Tex 377.—Insurance 2051, 2052.

Great Southern Life Ins. Co.; Doyle v., TexCivApp–Galveston, 126 SW2d 735, aff 151 SW2d 197, 136 Tex 377.—Insurance 2052, 3001.

Great Southern Life Ins. Co.; Feinberg v., TexCivApp–Beaumont, 111 SW2d 729.—Evid 471(3); Insurance 2608.

Great Southern Life Ins. Co.; Glass v., TexCivApp–Galveston, 170 SW2d 247, writ refused wom.—Costs 96; Courts 89, 91(1); States 215; Tax 2558.

Great Southern Life Ins. Co. v. Goerner, TexCivApp–Austin, 106 SW2d 750.—Corp 666; Venue 74.

Great Southern Life Ins. Co. v. Harrington, TexCivApp–San Antonio, 171 SW2d 538.—Contracts 143(3); Insurance 1739, 1758, 1766, 3580.

Great Southern Life Ins. Co.; Hassell v., TexCivApp–Galveston, 103 SW2d 442, writ dism.—Insurance 2027.

Great Southern Life Ins. Co.; Houston Bank & Trust Co. v., TexCivApp–Galveston, 232 SW2d 163, rev Board of Ins Com'rs v. Great Southern Life Ins Co, 239 SW2d 803, 150 Tex 258.—Insurance 1008, 1716, 1765.

Great Southern Life Ins. Co. v. Hukill, TexCivApp–Fort Worth, 151 SW2d 603, writ dism, correct.—Insurance 3398, 3400(1), 3475(5), 3497; Trusts 181(1).

Great Southern Life Ins. Co.; Jarrett v., TexCivApp–Beaumont, 449 SW2d 361.—Costs 262; Jury 25(6).

Great Southern Life Ins. Co.; McClelland v., TexCivApp–Beaumont, 220 SW2d 515, ref nre.—App & E 1043(6); Evid 268, 474(1), 537, 544, 552, 553(3); Insurance 2445, 2594(5).

Great Southern Life Ins. Co. v. Majors, TexCivApp–Beaumont, 82 SW2d 760, writ refused.—Insurance 2029, 2032.

Great Southern Life Ins. Co. v. Peddy, Tex, 162 SW2d 652, 139 Tex 245.—Insurance 2016, 2035, 2037.

GREAT WESTERN

Great Southern Life Ins. Co. v. Peddy, TexCivApp–Beaumont, 151 SW2d 346, rev 162 SW2d 652, 139 Tex 245.—Insurance 1518, 1723, 2019, 2037, 2039, 2445; Trial 351.2(4).

Great Southern Life Ins. Co.; Perry v., TexCivApp–Hous (1 Dist), 492 SW2d 352.—Courts 475(2); Evid 82; Ex & Ad 9, 29(2); Insurance 3482, 3490; Judgm 183, 185.2(8), 501; Lim of Act 46(1), 46(5).

Great Southern Life Ins. Co.; Sellers v., TexCivApp–San Antonio, 118 SW2d 612, writ dism.—App & E 758.3(2), 818; Insurance 3015.

Great Southern Life Ins. Co.; Texaco Inc. v., TexCivApp–Hous (1 Dist), 590 SW2d 522.—App & E 863; Land & Ten 94(1).

Great Southern Life Ins. Co. v. Watson, TexCivApp–Amarillo, 343 SW2d 921, ref nre.—Insurance 2594(5).

Great Southern Life Ins. Co. v. Wester, TexComApp, 92 SW2d 238, 127 Tex 274.—Insurance 2028.

Great Southern Life Ins. Co.; Williams v., CCA5 (Tex), 124 F2d 38, cert den 62 SCt 942, 316 US 663, 86 LEd 1739, reh den 62 SCt 1040, 316 US 709, 86 LEd 1775.—Bankr 2229.

Great Southern Life Ins. Co. v. Williams, TexCivApp–Amarillo, 135 SW2d 241, writ dism, correct.—App & E 1175(1); Contracts 175(1); Princ & A 1; Usury 56, 57, 72, 117.

Great Southern Life Ins. Co. v. Williams, TexCivApp–Amarillo, 105 SW2d 277.—Usury 77, 117.

Great Southern Life Ins. Co.; Williams v., TexCivApp–Galveston, 160 SW2d 121, writ refused wom.—App & E 1123; Bankr 2062, 2395, 2397(2).

Great Southern Life Ins. Co. v. Wilmans v., TexCivApp–Dallas, 141 SW2d 407.—Inj 144; J P 128(1), 129(3).

Great Southern Life Ins. Co. Sales Practices Litigation, In re, NDTex, 192 FRD 212.—Fed Civ Proc 163, 164, 165, 172, 174, 182.5; Fraud 7, 64(1); Impl & C C 3, 60.1; Inj 16; Insurance 1866, 3424; Ref of Inst 19(1), 20.

Great Southwest Corp.; Lewis v., TexCivApp–Fort Worth, 473 SW2d 228, ref nre.—Anim 66.2; Pub Amuse 79, 80, 109(1), 147.

Great Southwestern Acceptance Corp.; Woo v., TexCivApp–Waco, 565 SW2d 290, ref nre.—Antitrust 389(2), 390, 392, 397; Damag 91(1); Fraud 61.

Great Southwestern Corp.; Ellis v., CA5 (Tex), 646 F2d 1099.—Fed Civ Proc 2515; Fed Cts 121, 146, 410; Lim of Act 2(3), 119(1), 119(3).

Great Southwest Fire Ins.; Hensley Enterprises, Inc. v., TexCivApp–Eastland, 499 SW2d 742.—Insurance 3054(1), 3072; Trial 284, 350.4(3), 366.

Great Southwest General Hospital, Inc.; Bornmann v., CA5 (Tex), 453 F2d 616.—App & E 1032(3), 1064.1(8); Evid 106(1); Fed Civ Proc 1941; Fed Cts 743, 900, 907; Health 656, 703(2), 823(1), 825; Neglig 432, 554(1).

Great Southwest Life Ins. Co. v. Camp, TexCivApp–Fort Worth, 464 SW2d 702.—App & E 1177(2); Plead 111.3, 111.22, 111.39(2), 111.39(4), 409(1).

Great Southwest Life Ins. Co.; Childre v., TexApp–Dallas, 700 SW2d 284.—Execution 390, 402(1), 402(5), 405, 407.

Great Southwest Life Ins. Co. v. Henson, TexCivApp–El Paso, 401 SW2d 89, ref nre.—App & E 758.1; Insurance 1747.

Great Southwest Sav., F.A.; Rauscher Pierce Refsnes, Inc. v., TexApp–Houston (14 Dist), 923 SW2d 112.—App & E 662(4), 931(1), 989, 1008.1(1), 1008.1(2), 1010.1(3), 1012.1(4), 1079; Brok 6, 7, 19, 22, 34, 91; Costs 194.32, 206; Damag 157(2), 163(2); Plead 139; Princ & A 1, 13, 48.

Great Southwest Supply Co. of Texas, Inc. v. Ernest and Associates, Inc., BkrtcyWDTex, 59 BR 495. See Ernest and Associates, Inc., In re.

Great Southwest Warehouses, Inc.; Department of Public Safety of Tex. v., TexCivApp–Austin, 352 SW2d 493, ref nre.—States 191.2(1), 191.9(2), 191.10.

Great Southwest Warehouses, Inc.; N.L.R.B. v., CA5 (Tex), 443 F2d 61, cert den 92 SCt 534, 404 US 991, 30 LEd2d 542.—Courts 104; Fed Cts 743.

Great Spring Waters of America, Inc.; Fain v., TexApp–Tyler, 973 SW2d 327, writ gr, aff Sipriano v. Great Spring Waters of America, Inc, 1 SW3d 75.—App & E 767(1), 767(2); Courts 89, 91(1); Judgm 181(11), 185(2); Waters 101, 107(3).

Great Spring Waters of America, Inc.; Sipriano v., Tex, 1 SW3d 75.—Waters 101.

Great State Petroleum, Inc. v. Arrow Rig Service, Inc., TexApp–Fort Worth, 714 SW2d 429.—App & E 770(1), 837(1), 989, 1003(5), 1004(7), 1178(6).

Great State Petroleum, Inc.; Arrow Rig Service, Inc. v., TexApp–Fort Worth, 714 SW2d 429. See Great State Petroleum, Inc. v. Arrow Rig Service, Inc.

Great State Petroleum, Inc. v. Arrow Rig Service, Inc., TexApp–Fort Worth, 706 SW2d 803, on reh 714 SW2d 429.—Antitrust 389(1), 390; App & E 758.3(11), 1001(1), 1001(3); Costs 194.25, 264; Damag 221(2.1); Interest 39(2.15).

Great State Petroleum, Inc.; Arrow Rig Service, Inc. v., TexApp–Fort Worth, 706 SW2d 803. See Great State Petroleum, Inc. v. Arrow Rig Service, Inc.

Great State Petroleum, Inc. v. Arrow Trucking Co., TexApp–Fort Worth, 714 SW2d 429. See Great State Petroleum, Inc. v. Arrow Rig Service, Inc.

Great State Petroleum, Inc.; Arrow Trucking Co. v., TexApp–Fort Worth, 714 SW2d 429. See Great State Petroleum, Inc. v. Arrow Rig Service, Inc.

Great State Petroleum, Inc. v. Arrow Trucking Co., TexApp–Fort Worth, 706 SW2d 803. See Great State Petroleum, Inc. v. Arrow Rig Service, Inc.

Great State Petroleum, Inc.; Arrow Trucking Co. v., TexApp–Fort Worth, 706 SW2d 803. See Great State Petroleum, Inc. v. Arrow Rig Service, Inc.

Great Texas County Mut. Ins. Co. v. Lewis, TexApp–Austin, 979 SW2d 72.—Insurance 2185, 2719(2).

Great Western Cities, Inc. of New Mexico, In re, NDTex, 107 BR 116.—Bankr 2895.1, 2926; Fed Civ Proc 2486.

Great Western Cities, Inc. of New Mexico, In re, BkrtcyNDTex, 88 BR 109, vac 107 BR 116.—Bankr 2895.1, 2926.

Great Western Coal, Inc., In re, BkrtcySDTex, 146 BR 702.—Attach 63, 77, 128, 175, 177; Bankr 2060.1, 2129, 2158, 2531, 2551, 3064; Const Law 4478; Dep in Court 4; Fed Cts 265, 266.1, 267, 269, 272; Judges 36.

Great Western Coal, Inc. v. Brown, BkrtcySDTex, 146 BR 702. See Great Western Coal, Inc., In re.

Great Western Directories, Inc. v. Southwestern Bell Telephone Co., CA5 (Tex), 74 F3d 613, vac pursuant to settlement, cert den 117 SCt 26, 518 US 1048, 135 LEd2d 1120.—Antitrust 700, 750, 963(1), 963(3).

Great Western Directories, Inc. v. Southwestern Bell Telephone Co., CA5 (Tex), 63 F3d 1378, opinion withdrawn and superseded in part 74 F3d 613, vac pursuant to settlement, cert dism 117 SCt 26, 518 US 1048, 135 LEd2d 1120, cert dism 117 SCt 26, 518 US 1048, 135 LEd2d 1120.—Antitrust 620, 621, 641, 650, 711, 713, 714, 715, 960, 963(3), 964, 976, 980, 985, 995; Fed Civ Proc 2127, 2608.1, 2609; Fed Cts 776, 798, 814.1, 862.

Great Western Distributing Co. of Amarillo; Garrett v., TexApp–Amarillo, 129 SW3d 797, review den.—App & E 863, 934(1); Corp 488; Labor & Emp 2927, 3029, 3036, 3043, 3045, 3056(1), 3056(2), 3079, 3096(2).

Great Western Drilling Co. v. Simmons, Tex, 302 SW2d 400, 157 Tex 268.—Brok 43(2); Labor & Emp 29, 30.

Great Western Drilling Co.; Simmons v., TexCivApp–Amarillo, 294 SW2d 230, rev 302 SW2d 400, 157 Tex

268.—Brok 42, 43(1); Judgm 199(3.9); Labor & Emp 262, 274; Sec Reg 298.

Great Western Drilling, Ltd., In re, TexApp–Eastland, 211 SW3d 828.—Alt Disp Res 112, 113, 116, 134(1), 137, 138, 139, 143, 200, 205, 213(5); Joint Adv 1.2(1); Mand 60; Mines 101.

Great Western Drilling, Ltd.; Paschal v., TexApp–Eastland, 215 SW3d 437, reh overr, and petition stricken, and review den.—App & E 1079; Atty & C 106; Bailm 16; Consp 1.1, 6, 13, 19, 21; Evid 555.2, 571(1); Fraud 7, 64(1); Insurance 3433, 3438, 3496, 3498; Trial 280, 350.1, 350.8, 366; Trover 1, 2, 4, 9(3.1), 44; Trusts 95, 110, 111, 173.

Great Western Energy Corp.; MCG, Inc. v., CA5 (Tex), 896 F2d 170.—Fed Civ Proc 1825; Fed Cts 29.1, 30, 207, 542; Sec Reg 1, 14.10.

Great Western Food Co.; Amalgamated Meat Cutters and Butcher Workmen of North America AFL-CIO, Local Union 540 v., CA5 (Tex), 712 F2d 122, reh den 717 F2d 1399.—Alt Disp Res 312, 374(3), 374(7); Fed Civ Proc 2737.11; Labor & Emp 1519, 1608, 1609(1), 1609(2), 1623(1), 1631.

Great Western Garment Co. v. Malouf, TexCivApp–Amarillo, 105 SW2d 262, writ dism.—Accord 11(3), 26(2), 27; Compromise 5(2); Plead 20; Princ & A 171(1); Sales 354(7), 355(1).

Great Western Inv. Co. v. Scott, TexCivApp–San Antonio, 254 SW2d 411, ref nre.—App & E 1069.1; Neglig 1696; New Tr 56, 142, 143(5), 144; Trial 311.

Great Western Leasing, Inc.; Rodriguez v., EDTex, 882 FSupp 99.—Death 77, 99(2).

Great Western Litho & Bindery; U.S. v., CA5 (Tex), 10 F3d 263. See U.S. v. Investment Enterprises, Inc.

Great Western Loan & Trust Co. v. Bass, TexCivApp–Austin, 375 SW2d 786, writ dism.—Bills & N 454, 525.

Great Western Loan & Trust Co. v. Montgomery, TexCivApp–Austin, 376 SW2d 92, writ dism.—Venue 7.5(2), 7.5(4).

Great Western Loan & Trust Co. v. Rodriguez, TexCivApp–Waco, 290 SW2d 551.—App & E 1176(1); Damag 221(2.1).

Great Western Plywood, Ltd.; Pacific Products, Inc. v., TexCivApp–Fort Worth, 528 SW2d 286.—App & E 901, 931(1), 959(1), 989, 1010.1(1), 1010.1(3); Plead 236(2); Sales 1(4), 1.5, 52(5.1), 178(1), 178(3), 181(12), 182(4); Statut 231.

Great Western Producers Co. v. Lang, TexCivApp–Eastland, 368 SW2d 867.—Autos 244(11).

Great Western Sugar Co., Matter of, CA5 (Tex), 902 F2d 351.—Sec Tran 166.

Great Western Sugar Co. v. Lone Star Donut Co., CA5 (Tex), 721 F2d 510.—Contracts 22(1).

Great Western Sugar Co. v. Lone Star Donut Co., NDTex, 567 FSupp 340, aff 721 F2d 510.—Contracts 143(2); Frds St of 127.

Great Western United Corp. v. Kidwell, CA5 (Tex), 577 F2d 1256, probable jur noted LeRoy v. Great Western United Corp, 99 SCt 829, 439 US 1065, 59 LEd2d 30, rev 99 SCt 2710, 443 US 173, 61 LEd2d 464, on remand 602 F2d 1246.—Commerce 8(1), 12, 55, 62.4; Const Law 3964, 4446; Fed Cts 74, 76, 76.5, 207, 243, 269; Sec Reg 52.10, 244; States 18.5, 18.77.

Great Western United Corp. v. Kidwell, NDTex, 439 FSupp 420, aff 577 F2d 1256, probable jur noted LeRoy v. Great Western United Corp, 99 SCt 829, 439 US 1065, 59 LEd2d 30, rev 99 SCt 2710, 443 US 173, 61 LEd2d 464, on remand 602 F2d 1246.—Commerce 13.5, 62.4; Decl Judgm 125; Fed Civ Proc 103.2, 103.6, 470.1; Fed Cts 74, 76, 197, 207, 296.1; States 18.3, 191.10.

Great Western United Corp.; Leroy v., USTex, 99 SCt 2710, 443 US 173, 61 LEd2d 464, on remand 602 F2d 1246.—Fed Cts 29.1, 71, 74, 97, 451; Sec Reg 133.

Great West Grain & Seed Co. v. Ray, TexCivApp–El Paso, 204 SW2d 26, ref nre.—Contracts 9(1), 21, 24; Sales 1(4), 22(3).

Great-West Life & Annuity Ins. Co.; Burford v., CA5 (Tex), 95 FedAppx 539.—Insurance 2450.

Great-West Life & Annuity Insurance Co.; Crossroads of Texas, LLC v., SDTex, 467 FSupp2d 705, reconsideration den 2006 WL 305793.—Fraud 31; Health 942; Labor & Emp 407; Rem of C 25(1), 107(7), 107(11); States 18.15.

Great West Life & Annuity Ins. Co.; St. Luke's Episcopal Hosp. v., SDTex, 38 FSupp2d 497.—Fed Civ Proc 2539; Labor & Emp 407, 480; States 18.3, 18.51.

Great-West Life Assur. Co.; Brown v., TexCivApp–Waco, 482 SW2d 957, dism.—Insurance 2457(3).

Great-West Life Assur. Co.; Sims v., CA5 (Tex), 941 F2d 368.—Fed Civ Proc 2743.1, 2848; Labor & Emp 722.

Great White Marine & Recreation, Inc.; S.E.C. v., CA5 (Tex), 428 F3d 553, reh den.—Bankr 2187, 2295.1; Sec Reg 150.1.

Greaves; Billingslea v., TexCivApp–Amarillo, 196 SW2d 945.—App & E 662(3), 1078(1); Costs 47; Pretrial Proc 474, 478, 483; Trial 14.

Greaves v. Driggers, TexCivApp–El Paso, 252 SW2d 782.—Elections 83, 154(10), 291.

Grebe v. First State Bank of Bishop, Tex, 150 SW2d 64, 136 Tex 226.—Banks 119, 130(1), 133; Guard & W 35; Hus & W 273(1), 273(2), 273(8.1), 273(9), 274(1), 276(2).

Grebe; First State Bank of Bishop v., TexCivApp–San Antonio, 162 SW2d 165, writ refused wom.—App & E 1097(5), 1122(2), 1198, 1202.

Grebe v. First State Bank of Bishop, TexCivApp–San Antonio, 106 SW2d 382, rev 150 SW2d 64, 136 Tex 226.—Banks 130(1); Hus & W 273(1), 273(2), 274(1).

Grebe; K-Mart Corp. v., TexApp–Corpus Christi, 787 SW2d 122, writ den.—App & E 964, 1026, 1043(1), 1050.1(1); Neglig 1001, 1095, 1226; Pretrial Proc 282, 303, 304, 313.

Greco v. Orange Memorial Hospital Corp., CA5 (Tex), 513 F2d 873, reh den 515 F2d 1183, cert den 96 SCt 433, 423 US 1000, 46 LEd2d 376.—Civil R 1325, 1326(4), 1327, 1401; Const Law 3941; Decl Judgm 300; Fed Cts 222.

Greco v. Orange Memorial Hospital Corp., EDTex, 374 FSupp 227, aff 513 F2d 873, reh den 515 F2d 1183, cert den 96 SCt 433, 423 US 1000, 46 LEd2d 376.—Civil R 1326(4); Const Law 42.1(1); Fed Cts 222; Health 256.

Green, Ex parte, Tex, 603 SW2d 216.—Contempt 55; Nuis 86.

Green, Ex parte, TexCrimApp, 688 SW2d 555.—Bail 42; Infants 134; Sent & Pun 1157, 1160.

Green, Ex parte, TexCrimApp, 644 SW2d 9.—Hab Corp 717(1), 792.1.

Green, Ex parte, TexCrimApp, 553 SW2d 382.—Bail 51.

Green, Ex parte, TexCrimApp, 548 SW2d 914.—Courts 493(2); Crim Law 1172.7; Hab Corp 634; Homic 1371; Judgm 751.

Green, Ex parte, TexCrimApp, 437 SW2d 859.—Extrad 32, 34.

Green, Ex parte, TexCrimApp, 415 SW2d 424.—Extrad 36.

Green, Ex parte, TexCrimApp, 375 SW2d 312.—Sent & Pun 2041.

Green, Ex parte, TexCrimApp, 340 SW2d 821, 170 TexCrim 311.—Hab Corp 526, 729.

Green, Ex parte, TexCrimApp, 223 SW2d 523.—Crim Law 1131(4).

Green, Ex parte, TexCrimApp, 161 SW2d 102, 144 TexCrim 37.—Int Liq 33(3).

Green, Ex parte, TexApp–El Paso, 940 SW2d 799.—Bail 39, 51, 52, 53; Crim Law 1134(10).

Green, In re, Tex, 221 SW3d 645.—Child S 497; Const Law 4494; Contempt 63(1); Divorce 269(1), 269(13); Hus & W 279(6).

Green, Matter of, CA5 (Tex), 39 F3d 582, appeal after remand Green v. Johnson, 116 F3d 1115.—Hab Corp 633.

Green; Acme Tool, Inc. v., TexCivApp–Amarillo, 442 SW2d 813, writ dism.—Venue 21, 68.

Green; Advance Ross Electronics Corp. v., TexApp–Tyler, 624 SW2d 316, ref nre, cert den 102 SCt 3488, 458 US 1108, 73 LEd2d 1370.—App & E 554(1), 707(1); Labor & Emp 110, 835, 861; Land & Ten 200.7; Trial 365.1(5).

Green v. Aetna Ins. Co., CA5 (Tex), 397 F2d 614.—Fed Cts 419, 696, 705; Insurance 2278(21), 3128.

Green v. Aetna Ins. Co., CA5 (Tex), 349 F2d 919, appeal after remand 397 F2d 614.—Fed Civ Proc 2501; Fed Cts 419, 951.1; Insurance 1806, 2271, 2278(21), 2296, 2914, 2915; Trial 349(1).

Green; Airline Motor Coaches v., TexCivApp–Beaumont, 217 SW2d 70, ref nre.—App & E 1046.5; Damag 132(3); Evid 67(1); Trial 118, 121(2), 122, 125(1), 127.

Green v. Allied Interests, Inc., TexApp–Austin, 963 SW2d 205, reh overr, and review den, and reh of petition for review overr, and reh of petition for review overr.—App & E 215(2), 930(1), 1001(1), 1003(6); Damag 142; Fraud 4, 47, 58(3), 58(4), 59(2), 64(2).

Green v. Aluminum Co. of America, TexApp–Austin, 760 SW2d 378.—Civil R 1732; Judgm 181(21); Lim of Act 5(1).

Green v. American General Ins. Co., TexCivApp–Fort Worth, 354 SW2d 616, ref nre.—Insurance 3556, 3557; Pretrial Proc 77.

Green v. American Nat. Ins. Co., TexCivApp–San Antonio, 452 SW2d 1.—Insurance 1950, 1955, 1957, 1991; Liens 16.

Green; American Nat. Ins. Co. v., TexCivApp–Eastland, 96 SW2d 727.—Insurance 3571; Trial 142, 181.

Green v. Amoco Oil Co., SDTex, 172 FRD 217.—Fed Civ Proc 1278.

Green; Anderson Chemical Co., Inc. v., TexApp–Amarillo, 66 SW3d 434.—Antitrust 413, 418; App & E 852, 920(3), 954(2); Contracts 65.5, 116(1), 118, 142, 202(2), 312(4); Inj 138.3, 138.6, 138.18, 147; Labor & Emp 121, 305, 306.

Green; A. R. Clark Inv. Co. v., Tex, 375 SW2d 425.—Chat Mtg 250, 253; Contracts 147(2), 210; Corp 218, 269(3), 627; Estop 83(1), 87, 95; Mtg 272, 408; Ven & Pur 57.

Green v. A. R. Clark Inv. Co., TexCivApp–Fort Worth, 363 SW2d 802, writ gr, rev 375 SW2d 425.—Atty & C 104; Bills & N 129(1); Chat Mtg 253; Contracts 317; Corp 308(3), 610(1), 617(2), 620, 629; Liens 7; Mtg 408; Trusts 105; Ven & Pur 172.

Green; Arnold v., CA5 (Tex), 186 F2d 18.—Infants 54; Int Rev 3571.

Green v. Arnold, NDTex, 87 FSupp 255, aff 186 F2d 18.—Int Rev 3913, 3944.

Green v. Arnold, WDTex, 512 FSupp 650.—Fed Civ Proc 1741, 2734; Judgm 570(1), 707.

Green; Aven v., Tex, 320 SW2d 660, 159 Tex 361.—Wills 199, 220, 359.

Green; Aven v., TexCivApp–Waco, 316 SW2d 78, rev 320 SW2d 660, 159 Tex 361.—Action 70; App & E 837(11), 907(3), 1010.1(3); Evid 318(7); Statut 220, 231; Wills 203, 225.

Green; Aycock v., TexCivApp–San Antonio, 94 SW2d 894, writ dism.—Autos 181(1), 226(1), 226(3), 244(20), 244(35), 245(24), 245(50.1); Evid 265(18), 588.

Green v. Baldree, TexApp–Hous (14 Dist), 497 SW2d 342.—App & E 302(6), 882(13), 1170.10; Damag 97, 100, 135, 216(1), 216(8), 221(5.1); Neglig 1514, 1610, 1612, 1625; Trial 261, 350.6(1), 352.10.

Green v. Baldwin, TexCivApp–Texarkana, 336 SW2d 291, writ dism.—Tax 2478, 2572, 2750, 2768.

Green; Balque v., TexCivApp, 193 SW2d 705, ref nre.—App & E 241, 757(1), 766, 901, 933(1), 1015(5), 1032(1); Land & Ten 169(6); New Tr 31, 140(3); Trial 350.3(5).

Green; Batton v., TexApp–Dallas, 801 SW2d 923.—Alt Disp Res 117, 213(3); App & E 66; Courts 39, 97(1); States 18.3, 18.15.

Green v. Beto, CA5 (Tex), 476 F2d 601, cert den 94 SCt 732, 414 US 1097, 38 LEd2d 555.—Crim Law 393(1), 412.2(2), 412.2(4).

Green v. Beto, CA5 (Tex), 460 F2d 322.—Fed Cts 743; Hab Corp 319.1, 372.1.

Green v. Beto, NDTex, 324 FSupp 797.—Crim Law 577.10(8), 641.13(6); Hab Corp 479, 503.1.

Green v. Blanks, TexCivApp–Austin, 342 SW2d 141, ref nre.—Adv Poss 110(3), 116(1); Evid 317(18); Land & Ten 66(2); Trial 350.2, 351.2(4), 352.5(3), 366.

Green v. Bluff Creek Oil Co., CA5 (Tex), 287 F2d 66.—Fed Cts 96, 850.1, 870.1; Judgm 828.9(2).

Green; Bluff Creek Oil Co. v., CA5 (Tex), 257 F2d 83.—Const Law 191, 3964, 3977(1); Fed Civ Proc 2471, 2503; Fed Cts 386; Proc 70.

Green v. Board of Regents of Texas Tech University, CA5 (Tex), 474 F2d 594, reh den 475 F2d 1404.—Civil R 1549, 1554; Colleges 8.1(6.1).

Green v. Board of Regents of Texas Tech University, NDTex, 335 FSupp 249, aff 474 F2d 594, reh den 475 F2d 1404.—Civil R 1549; Colleges 8.1(6.1); Fed Cts 161.

Green v. Brantley, TexApp–Fort Worth, 11 SW3d 259, petition for review den.—App & E 901; Atty & C 129(2), 153; Damag 49.10, 192; Evid 536; Judgm 185(5), 185.1(1), 185.3(4); Pretrial Proc 45.

Green; Brotherhood of R. R. Trainmen Ins. Dept. of Cleveland, Ohio v., Tex, 182 SW2d 804, 143 Tex 86.—Insurance 1236, 3003(2), 3004.

Green; Brotherhood of R. R. Trainmen Ins. Dept. of Cleveland, Ohio v., TexCivApp–Fort Worth, 179 SW2d 337, rev 182 SW2d 804, 143 Tex 86.—Insurance 2079, 2986, 3018, 3375; New Tr 77(2).

Green v. Canon, TexApp–Houston (14 Dist), 33 SW3d 855, reh overr, and review den.—Courts 30; Deeds 28; Forci E & D 13, 38(0.5); Gifts 5(2), 15, 16, 47(1).

Green v. Carlson, CA5 (Tex), 649 F2d 285, cert den 102 SCt 646, 454 US 1087, 70 LEd2d 623.—Hab Corp 691.1; Mand 169.

Green v. CBS Inc., CA5 (Tex), 286 F3d 281, cert den 123 SCt 132, 537 US 887, 154 LEd2d 148.—Fed Cts 776; Libel 1, 49, 54; Torts 350, 357.

Green; Cities Service Oil Co. v., TexCivApp–Texarkana, 251 SW2d 906, ref nre.—Adv Poss 27, 38, 51; Judgm 17(9), 18(2), 252(1), 497(1), 503; Mental H 352.

Green v. City of Dallas, TexApp–El Paso, 665 SW2d 567.—Mun Corp 724, 747(3).

Green v. City of Friendswood, TexApp–Houston (14 Dist), 22 SW3d 588, reh overr, and review den.—App & E 173(13), 707(1), 863, 934(1); Autos 175(1), 187(2), 201(1.1), 201(6); Judgm 183, 185(5), 185.3(21), 186; Neglig 375, 377, 379, 380, 383, 387, 1675.

Green v. City of Lubbock, TexApp–Amarillo, 627 SW2d 868, ref nre.—App & E 771, 773(2); Decl Judgm 209; Mun Corp 46.

Green; City of Lubbock v., TexCivApp–Amarillo, 312 SW2d 279.—Anim 76; App & E 954(1); Courts 121(1), 168; Crim Law 87, 1018; Inj 110, 132, 135, 138.46, 144; Mand 141.

Green; City of Lubbock, Tex. v., CA5 (Tex), 201 F2d 146.—Estop 62.5; Fed Cts 428; Mun Corp 742(6), 851, 857.

Green v. City of San Antonio, TexCivApp–San Antonio, 282 SW2d 769, ref nre.—Dedi 41, 44, 45, 65; Evid 324(3), 383(2), 591; Gifts 25; Judgm 704; Tresp to T T 6.1, 12, 34, 38(1), 38(2), 41(2).

Green; Clark v., CA5 (Tex), 814 F2d 221.—Fed Civ Proc 2771(5), 2835, 2846.

Green v. Collins, CA5 (Tex), 947 F2d 1230, cert den 112 SCt 412, 502 US 954, 116 LEd2d 433.—Costs 302.4; Crim Law 641.10(2); Sent & Pun 1669, 1757.

GREEN

See Guidelines for Arrangement at the beginning of this Volume

Green v. Cotton Concentration Co., SDTex, 294 FSupp 34.—Civil R 1557; Fed Civ Proc 2734.

Green v. County Attorney of Anderson County, TexCivApp–Tyler, 592 SW2d 69.—App & E 846(5); Atty & C 60; Const Law 4172(3); Dist & Pros Attys 2(5); Statut 181(1), 227.

Green v. Crawford, TexApp–Tyler, 662 SW2d 123, ref nre.—Evid 571(7); Logs 3(12); Ten in C 24, 43.

Green; Culpepper v., TexCivApp–Eastland, 324 SW2d 257.—Home 57(3).

Green v. Davis, TexCivApp–Fort Worth, 451 SW2d 579.— App & E 555, 564(3), 704.2, 907(3); Child C 7, 553, 567.

Green; Detering Co. v., TexApp–Houston (1 Dist), 989 SW2d 479, review den.—App & E 934(1); Assign 120; Const Law 642; Judgm 181(2), 185(6); Mech Liens 116, 157(1); Notice 1.6; Records 19; Ven & Pur 229(5), 231(17).

Green v. Dickson, TexCivApp–Galveston, 208 SW2d 119, ref nre.—Evid 571(2), 574; Wills 1, 47, 50, 324(2), 324(3).

Green v. Doakes, TexCivApp–Hous (1 Dist), 593 SW2d 762.—Home 214; Judgm 585(3), 948(1); Partit 83, 114(4); Receivers 8.

Green v. Doe, CA5 (Tex), 77 FedAppx 252.—Civil R 1095, 1351(4), 1377, 1395(7).

Green v. Dretke, CA5 (Tex), 82 FedAppx 333, cert den 125 SCt 35, 543 US 823, 160 LEd2d 34, reh den, reh den 125 SCt 375, 543 US 952, 160 LEd2d 270.—Hab Corp 816, 818.

Green; Duncan v., TexCivApp–Texarkana, 113 SW2d 656, dism.—App & E 719(8); Judgm 252(1); Mtg 32(2), 38(1).

Green v. Duncan, TexCivApp–El Paso, 134 SW2d 744.— Equity 66; Hus & W 239; Judgm 16, 251(1), 719, 731; Lim of Act 165.

Green v. Earnest, TexApp–El Paso, 840 SW2d 119, reh overr, and writ den.—Wills 155.1, 163(1), 164(6), 166(1), 166(7), 166(12), 316.3, 324(3).

Green v. Edmands Co., CA5 (Tex), 639 F2d 286.—Damag 182, 212; Fed Cts 372, 614; Neglig 554(3); Prod Liab 26, 27, 96.1.

Green v. Estelle, CA5 (Tex), 712 F2d 995.—Hab Corp 505.

Green v. Estelle, CA5 (Tex), 706 F2d 148, reh den 712 F2d 995.—Hab Corp 508.

Green v. Estelle, CA5 (Tex), 649 F2d 298.—Civil R 1465(1); Fed Civ Proc 1788.10, 2734; Fed Cts 830.

Green v. Estelle, CA5 (Tex), 601 F2d 877.—Judgm 751.

Green v. Estelle, CA5 (Tex), 524 F2d 1243.—Double J 202.

Green v. Estelle, CA5 (Tex), 488 F2d 918.—Crim Law 641.13(6); Witn 2(1), 17.

Green v. Evans, TexCivApp–Dallas, 362 SW2d 377.—App & E 237(5), 1053(2), 1170.7; Autos 242(1), 245(21); Trial 139.1(6), 256(1), 366.

Green v. Farmers & Merchants State Bank, TexCivApp–Amarillo, 100 SW2d 132, writ dism.—Banks 47(1); Contracts 147(2), 161; Guar 36(2), 42(1).

Green; Federal Underwriters Exchange v., TexCivApp–Dallas, 150 SW2d 98, writ dism, correct.—App & E 232(0.5), 1062.1; Trial 215, 362; Work Comp 1922, 1924, 1929, 1930.

Green v. Forney Engineering Co., CA5 (Tex), 589 F2d 243.—Atty & C 76(1); Civil R 1383, 1511; Fed Civ Proc 1758.1, 1832, 1833, 2533.1.

Green v. Franklin Dress Co., TexCivApp–El Paso, 137 SW2d 131.—App & E 758.3(1); Contracts 313(1); Sales 181(3), 181(11.1), 340.

Green; Frix v., TexCivApp–San Antonio, 95 SW2d 219.— App & E 1010.1(10); Bills & N 430, 499, 537(8); Mtg 317; Princ & A 25(1).

Green v. Gage, CA5 (Tex), 186 F2d 984.—Bankr 2051, 2058.1, 3066(1); Fed Civ Proc 1742(2); Fed Cts 247.

Green v. Gardner, CA5 (Tex), 391 F2d 606.—Social S 143.60, 147.5, 148.15.

Green; Gilbert v., Tex, 242 SW2d 879, 150 Tex 521.—Adv Poss 27, 57, 70, 85(1), 85(5); Evid 273(2), 313; Witn 379(2).

Green v. Gilbert, TexCivApp–Austin, 237 SW2d 1010, rev 242 SW2d 879, 150 Tex 521.—Adv Poss 19, 22, 25, 43(4), 50, 57, 85(1), 85(4), 114(1), 115(1); App & E 1001(1), 1002; Trial 143.

Green v. Gladden, TexCivApp–Fort Worth, 369 SW2d 69. —Brok 53, 82(1); Trial 352.1(4).

Green v. Goans, TexCivApp–El Paso, 458 SW2d 705, ref nre 464 SW2d 104.—Wills 21, 316.2, 400.

Green; Goggans v., TexCivApp–Texarkana, 165 SW2d 928.—Evid 333(3); Execution 140, 275(3), 283.

Green v. Gomez, TexCivApp–Eastland, 348 SW2d 185.— Hus & W 266.3; Mtg 39, 311.

Green; Gossett v., TexComApp, 152 SW2d 733, 137 Tex 50, answer to certified question conformed to 153 SW2d 500.—Banks 80(2), 80(10); Plead 216(2).

Green; Gossett v., TexComApp, 133 SW2d 762, 134 Tex 282.—Banks 48(1), 49(8); Evid 65.

Green; Gossett v., TexCivApp–Fort Worth, 153 SW2d 500.—App & E 1011.1(4).

Green; Grand Lodge Colored Knights of Pythias of Texas v., TexComApp, 101 SW2d 219, 128 Tex 593.— Courts 247(7).

Green v. Green, TexApp–Houston (1 Dist), 679 SW2d 640. —App & E 934(1), 989, 1024.4; Wills 31, 155.1, 166(12).

Green; Green v., TexApp–Houston (1 Dist), 679 SW2d 640.—App & E 934(1), 989, 1024.4; Wills 31, 155.1, 166(12).

Green v. Green, TexApp–El Paso, 850 SW2d 809.—App & E 930(3), 1001(3), 1008.1(2), 1010.1(4); Child C 7, 49, 78, 182, 204, 413, 921(3).

Green; Green v., TexApp–El Paso, 850 SW2d 809.—App & E 930(3), 1001(3), 1008.1(2), 1010.1(4); Child C 7, 49, 78, 182, 204, 413, 921(3).

Green v. Green, TexCivApp–San Antonio, 282 SW2d 254. —Child C 600, 606.

Green; Green v., TexCivApp–San Antonio, 282 SW2d 254. —Child C 600, 606.

Green v. Green, TexCivApp–San Antonio, 279 SW2d 395. —Divorce 124.3, 184(7); Domicile 4(1), 10.

Green; Green v., TexCivApp–San Antonio, 279 SW2d 395. —Divorce 124.3, 184(7); Domicile 4(1), 10.

Green v. Green, TexCivApp–Dallas, 247 SW2d 583.—App & E 80(3); Child C 903, 910.

Green; Green v., TexCivApp–Dallas, 247 SW2d 583.—App & E 80(3); Child C 903, 910.

Green v. Green, TexCivApp–Waco, 268 SW2d 237.—Divorce 12, 49(2), 50, 127(1), 130, 184(10).

Green; Green v., TexCivApp–Waco, 268 SW2d 237.— Divorce 12, 49(2), 50, 127(1), 130, 184(10).

Green v. Green, TexCivApp–Eastland, 485 SW2d 941, ref nre.—Child C 510.

Green; Green v., TexCivApp–Eastland, 485 SW2d 941, ref nre.—Child C 510.

Green v. Green, TexCivApp–Tyler, 424 SW2d 479.—Appear 2, 9(7), 17, 19(1); Motions 24; Venue 1 1/2, 17.

Green; Green v., TexCivApp–Tyler, 424 SW2d 479.— Appear 2, 9(7), 17, 19(1); Motions 24; Venue 1 1/2, 17.

Green; Green Machinery Co. v., TexCivApp–Amarillo, 266 SW2d 279.—Contracts 176(1), 322(1), 323(1); Trial 351.2(2).

Green; Greenspan v., TexCivApp–Dallas, 255 SW2d 917, ref nre.—Judgm 185.3(1), 585(4), 704, 878(1).

Green v. GS Roofing Products Co., Inc., TexApp–Houston (14 Dist), 928 SW2d 265.—App & E 863; Autos 201(6), 201(7); Judgm 185(2); Neglig 202, 379, 380, 383, 387, 1675.

Green v. Guenther, TexCivApp–El Paso, 452 SW2d 512. —App & E 758.3(11), 930(3), 1001(1); Autos 171(4.1), 171(13), 244(58).

Green v. Guidry, TexApp–Waco, 34 SW3d 669.—App & E 348(1), 352.1; Motions 17.

Green; Halbert v., Tex, 293 SW2d 848, 156 Tex 223.— Estop 39; Mines 55(4), 55(8); Ref of Inst 26.

Green; Halbert v., TexCivApp–Eastland, 285 SW2d 767, writ gr, rev 293 SW2d 848, 156 Tex 223.—Mines 55(4), 55(8).

Green v. Hale, CA5 (Tex), 433 F2d 324.—Courts 100(1); Fed Civ Proc 1742(1), 1742(3); Fed Cts 34, 290.1, 291, 303, 692, 922, 942; Health 821(5), 823(1), 831; Witn 178(4).

Green v. Hale, TexCivApp–Tyler, 590 SW2d 231.—App & E 901, 930(1), 932(1), 989, 1004(3), 1004(5), 1177(7); Damag 163(1), 166(1), 208(1); Death 60, 67, 68, 69, 77, 95(4), 97, 99(2), 99(3).

Green v. Hannon, TexCivApp–Texarkana, 369 SW2d 853, ref nre.—Evid 317(1); Ex & Ad 7; Princ & A 1; Spec Perf 24, 68, 70.

Green; Hanson v., TexCivApp–Texarkana, 339 SW2d 381, writ refused.—Autos 192(2), 192(11), 193(1), 201(1.1).

Green v. Harbour, CA5 (Tex), 444 F2d 223.—Courts 104; Fed Cts 743.

Green v. Harris County, Dist. Attorney's Office, CA5 (Tex), 390 F3d 839.—Hab Corp 666, 894.1.

Green v. Hassell, TexApp–Tyler, 764 SW2d 391.—Child C 602; Mand 26.

Green v. H. E. Butt Foundation, CA5 (Tex), 217 F2d 553.—Bankr 2050, 2553; Contracts 278(1); Mech Liens 113(1); Propty 10.

Green v. Heckler, CA5 (Tex), 742 F2d 237.—Mand 1, 4(1), 72; Social S 145, 175.30.

Green v. Helmcamp Ins. Agency, TexCivApp–Hous (1 Dist), 499 SW2d 730, ref nre.—Elect of Rem 3(4); Estop 85; Lim of Act 55(1), 55(3); Torts 117; Trial 366.

Green v. Hershey, CA5 (Tex), 422 F2d 1319.—Fed Cts 724, 743.

Green v. Hershey, NDTex, 302 FSupp 43, appeal dism 422 F2d 1319.—Armed S 20.6(1).

Green v. Hodge, TexCivApp–Waco, 102 SW2d 500.—Execution 172(7), 174, 177.

Green v. Houston Belt & Terminal Ry. Co., TexCivApp–Hous (14 Dist), 558 SW2d 127.—Evid 506, 546.

Green v. Hudson Engineering Corp., TexCivApp–Fort Worth, 305 SW2d 201, ref nre.—App & E 1170.6; Trial 115(1), 115(2), 131(1).

Green v. Industrial Specialty Contractors, Inc., TexApp–Houston (1 Dist), 1 SW3d 126.—App & E 223, 242(2); Assault 2, 48; Civil R 1123, 1147, 1185, 1189; Judgm 181(21), 181(33), 185.1(3), 185.1(4); Labor & Emp 826.

Green v. Jackson, TexApp–Amarillo, 674 SW2d 395, ref nre.—App & E 1024.4; Judgm 185(2); Labor & Emp 3056(1), 3056(2), 3061(2), 3065.

Green; Jackson v., TexApp–Corpus Christi, 700 SW2d 620, ref nre.—App & E 852; Evid 93; Hus & W 272(4).

Green v. Jackson, TexCivApp–Dallas, 113 SW2d 252, writ dism.—Contracts 138(2); Corp 116, 118; Sec Reg 292.

Green v. Johnson, CA5 (Tex), 160 F3d 1029, cert den 119 SCt 1107, 525 US 1174, 143 LEd2d 106.—Const Law 3821, 4646; Crim Law 641.10(1), 641.13(1), 641.13(6), 641.13(7), 717, 721(1), 721(3), 721(6), 790, 865(2), 925(1), 1073, 1139; Hab Corp 205, 481, 490(3), 500.1, 742, 752.1, 770, 775(1), 818, 824, 842, 846; Jury 105(4), 131(8), 131(13); Pardon 46; Sent & Pun 1618, 1654, 1720, 1759, 1780(2), 1780(3).

Green v. Johnson, CA5 (Tex), 116 F3d 1115.—Const Law 4614; Crim Law 636(1), 636(3), 641.13(1), 641.13(2.1), 641.13(7), 1139, 1166.10(1); Hab Corp 205, 768, 818; Sent & Pun 1757, 1768, 1769.

Green v. Johnson, NDTex, 46 FSupp2d 614.—Hab Corp 205, 452, 486(1), 486(3).

Green v. Jones, NDTex, 369 FSupp 1130.—Civil R 1395(7); Hab Corp 224.1.

Green; Jones v., TexCivApp–Beaumont, 281 SW2d 221.— App & E 907(3), 930(3); Autos 224(8), 239(2); Judgm 256(1); Trial 350.5(3), 350.7(5).

Green v. J. Weingarten, Inc., TexCivApp–Eastland, 398 SW2d 447.—Negligg 1670.

Green v. J. W. Reynolds Lumber Co., TexCivApp–Texarkana, 323 SW2d 105.—Compromise 23(3).

Green; Kahn v., TexCivApp–Fort Worth, 234 SW2d 131. —App & E 1060.1(2.1); Auctions 11; Trial 115(2), 133.6(7).

Green v. Kansas City Southern Ry. Co., EDTex, 464 FSupp2d 610.—Fed Civ Proc 2497.1; Labor & Emp 757, 1515, 1524, 1530, 2769, 2787; States 18.46.

Green v. Kaposta, TexApp–Dallas, 152 SW3d 839.—App & E 684(2), 688(1), 707(1), 756, 758.3(3), 761, 840(4), 907(4), 948, 962; Atty & C 62; Pretrial Proc 583, 587, 697, 713; Trial 107.

Green v. Kasishke, BkrtcyNDTex, 40 BR 712. See Kasishke, In re.

Green; Kelly v., TexCivApp–Eastland, 296 SW2d 576, ref nre.—Autos 193(10), 242(6), 245(30); Evid 317(12); Labor & Emp 3096(7).

Green v. Kimbell, Inc., TexApp–Fort Worth, 647 SW2d 110, ref nre.—Negligg 1076, 1104(6), 1708.

Green; Knick v., TexCivApp–Waco, 545 SW2d 269, ref nre.—App & E 692(1); Guar 46(1), 60.5; Sec Tran 237.

Green v. Kunkel, TexCivApp–Fort Worth, 183 SW2d 585. —Dedi 53; Deeds 100, 155; Ease 1; Tresp to T T 6.1; Waters 124.

Green v. Lanny Ice Truck Supply Co., TexCivApp–El Paso, 441 SW2d 320.—App & E 773(4).

Green v. Lerner, TexApp–Houston (1 Dist), 786 SW2d 486.—Mand 3(3), 12, 28; Pretrial Proc 40, 371, 386, 413.1.

Green; Liberty Cab Co. v., TexCivApp–Beaumont, 262 SW2d 522, ref nre.—App & E 933(1), 1005(2); New Tr 20, 159; Witn 392(1).

Green; Ligon v., TexCivApp–Fort Worth, 206 SW2d 629, ref nre.—App & E 301, 1032(1), 1053(2), 1170.6, 1170.7; Autos 245(74); Evid 153; Negligg 535(8).

Green v. Ligon, TexCivApp–Fort Worth, 190 SW2d 742, ref nre.—Autos 245(74); Evid 4, 52; Judgm 199(1); Jury 87; Trial 108.5, 127, 350.6(3), 351.2(2), 352.4(1), 352.4(7).

Green v. Lowe's Home Centers, Inc., TexApp–Houston (1 Dist), 199 SW3d 514, review den.—Judgm 181(21), 183; Labor & Emp 810, 827, 861, 863(2).

Green v. Lynaugh, CA5 (Tex), 868 F2d 176, cert den 110 SCt 102, 493 US 831, 107 LEd2d 66.—Crim Law 641.13(1), 641.13(2.1).

Green v. McAdams, TexApp–Houston (1 Dist), 857 SW2d 816.—App & E 977(1); Const Law 3881, 3993, 4010; Judgm 126(1), 138(3), 143(2), 153(1); New Tr 6.

Green v. McClure, TexCivApp–Amarillo, 203 SW2d 345, ref nre.—App & E 846(2), 846(5); Can of Inst 37(1); Chat Mtg 283.

Green v. McCoy, TexApp–El Paso, 870 SW2d 616.—Child C 731, 735, 736; Hab Corp 532(2); Judgm 815.

Green v. McKaskle, CA5 (Tex), 788 F2d 1116.—Civil R 1056, 1098, 1395(7), 1448, 1461; Const Law 980, 4824; Courts 100(1); Fed Civ Proc 1828, 2734; Prisons 4(14), 13(5), 17(1), 17(2).

Green v. McKaskle, CA5 (Tex), 770 F2d 445, reh gr 772 F2d 137, on reh 788 F2d 1116.—Fed Civ Proc 316, 331.

Green; Martin v., TexCivApp–Fort Worth, 86 SW2d 270. —Assault 42.

Green v. Maxwell, TexCivApp–Hous (14 Dist), 423 SW2d 384, ref nre.—App & E 758.3(4), 761.

Green; Meadows v., Tex, 524 SW2d 509, on remand 527 SW2d 496, ref nre.—App & E 232(2), 243.1, 989.

Green v. Meadows, TexCivApp–Hous (1 Dist), 527 SW2d 496, ref nre.—App & E 1004(3); Damag 102; Mal Pros 67, 69.

Green v. Meadows, TexCivApp–Hous (1 Dist), 517 SW2d 799, writ gr, rev 524 SW2d 509, on remand 527 SW2d 496, ref nre.—App & E 930(3), 934(2), 989, 994(1), 1003(5), 1175(5); Equity 65(1); Evid 596(1); Judgm 199(3.8), 199(3.10); Mal Pros 18(1), 22, 32, 38, 59(10), 64(1), 64(2), 71(3); New Tr 72(5), 72(6); Partners 26; Trial 139.1(7), 350.1, 352.10.

Green v. Me-Tex Supply Co., SDTex, 29 FSupp 851.—Fed Civ Proc 25, 2732.1; Pat 325.1.

Green; Metropolitan Life Ins. Co. v., TexCivApp–Fort Worth, 102 SW2d 1090, writ dism.—Insurance 2561(1), 2578, 3374, 3375, 3540.

Green; Michaelson v., TexCivApp–Dallas, 85 SW2d 1116, writ dism.—App & E 930(1), 999(1); Bills & N 537(2), 537(6); Evid 97; Trial 139.1(13), 140(1), 143.

Green; Mitchell Oil & Gas Co. v., TexCivApp–Eastland, 115 SW2d 729.—App & E 1004(1), 1004(7); Evid 208(6); Mines 109; Princ & A 23(1).

Green v. Morales, Tex, 834 SW2d 47.—Work Comp 904.

Green v. Morris, TexApp–Waco, 43 SW3d 604.—App & E 934(1); Contracts 93(1), 93(5), 98, 99(1); Insurance 3388; Judgm 178, 185(2), 185(5), 185.3(2).

Green; Mutual Fire & Auto. Ins. Co. v., TexCivApp–Fort Worth, 235 SW2d 739.—Evid 460(9); Execution 8; Insurance 2687, 2730, 2741(1), 2941, 3191(7), 3381(5), 3389; Judgm 223; Release 25.

Green; National Life & Acc. Ins. Co. v., TexCivApp–Waco, 477 SW2d 689.—App & E 192.1; Insurance 2117, 2605, 2607, 3571.

Green; Navarro v., CA5 (Tex), 82 FedAppx 864.—Civil R 1395(7); Fed Civ Proc 2734; Fed Cts 663.

Green; Norton v., TexCivApp–Waco, 304 SW2d 420, ref nre.—Relig Soc 23(3).

Green v. Old Sec. Life Ins. Co., TexCivApp–Dallas, 466 SW2d 857, ref nre.—App & E 960(1); Insurance 1768; Plead 228.14, 228.23.

Green; Olympic Arms, Inc. v., TexApp–Houston (1 Dist), 176 SW3d 567.—App & E 204(7), 866(3), 970(2), 1051.1(1), 1051.1(2), 1062.2; Evid 211, 535, 539, 570, 593; Pretrial Proc 434; Prod Liab 8, 14, 15, 16, 24, 27, 60.5, 73, 75.1, 86.5, 95.5; Sales 441(3); Trial 412.

Green v. Page, TexCivApp–Beaumont, 412 SW2d 952.—Schools 38.

Green v. Parrack, TexApp–San Antonio, 974 SW2d 200.—Com Law 9; Decl Judgm 255; Equity 67, 71(4), 72(1), 84, 87(2); Fences 29; Judgm 540, 713(2), 720, 743(2), 948(0.5).

Green; Pfeiffer v., TexCivApp–Beaumont, 102 SW2d 1077.—Autos 181(1), 244(20); Statut 226.

Green v. Polunsky, CA5 (Tex), 229 F3d 486.—Civil R 1090; Const Law 1424; Fed Civ Proc 8.1; Fed Cts 776, 813; Prisons 4(1), 4(14).

Green v. Pool, TexCivApp–Tyler, 421 SW2d 439.—App & E 1024.3; Autos 176(1); Plead 111.12.

Green; Precipitair Pollution Control v., TexApp–Tyler, 626 SW2d 909, ref nre.—App & E 931(1), 989, 1008.1(1); Land & Ten 34(5), 231(8); Trial 394(1).

Green; Proctor v., TexApp–Houston (1 Dist), 673 SW2d 390.—App & E 400, 1177(9); Can of Inst 37(4), 58; Judgm 739; Plead 85(1), 85(5); Sales 130(3); Time 10(2).

Green; Quarles v., TexCivApp–Hous (1 Dist), 570 SW2d 222.—App & E 387(3), 387(6), 389(3), 395.

Green v. Quarterman, CA5 (Tex), 213 FedAppx 279.—Crim Law 641.13(2.1).

Green v. Ransor, Inc., TexApp–Fort Worth, 175 SW3d 513.—Autos 192(11), 193(8.1), 193(13), 242(6); Evid 208(0.5), 265(8); Judgm 181(21), 185.3(13); Labor & Emp 3045.

Green; R. B. Spencer & Co. v., TexCivApp–El Paso, 203 SW2d 957.—Home 13, 154, 163, 164, 181.5; Hus & W 249(6); Judgm 768(1).

Green v. Remling, Tex, 608 SW2d 905, on remand 610 SW2d 817.—Adop 13, 15; Infants 208; Witn 266.

Green; Remling v., TexCivApp–Hous (1 Dist), 610 SW2d 817.—Adop 13, 15.

Green; Remling v., TexCivApp–Hous (1 Dist), 601 SW2d 84, rev 608 SW2d 905, on remand 610 SW2d 817.—Adop 13, 15, 16.

Green v. Reyes, TexApp–Houston (14 Dist), 836 SW2d 203.—App & E 1008.1(2), 1008.1(5), 1008.1(7), 1079; Elections 154(1), 154(10), 291, 293(3), 298(1), 298(3), 305(6); Evid 272, 571(1).

Green; Richardson v., Tex, 677 SW2d 497.—App & E 931(1), 1051.1(1); Courts 247(1), 472.2; Evid 118, 121(1), 314(1); Infants 155, 178, 179, 207, 221, 253.

Green v. R.J. Reynolds Tobacco Co., CA5 (Tex), 274 F3d 263.—Prod Liab 59; Rem of C 25(1), 79(1), 107(9).

Green; Ross v., Tex, 139 SW2d 565, 135 Tex 103.—Evid 67(3); Trial 142; Waters 98.

Green; Ross v., TexCivApp–Beaumont, 128 SW2d 477, aff 139 SW2d 565, 135 Tex 103.—Des & Dist 90(4); Evid 67(3); Nav Wat 46(1).

Green; Roy Lee Lumber Co. v., TexCivApp–Beaumont, 299 SW2d 349, ref nre.—App & E 1171(2); Autos 245(17), 245(39), 245(40.1), 245(53), 245(59), 245(62), 245(83); Damag 221(2.1), 221(5.1); Trial 352.5(6), 352.10.

Green; Ruby v., TexCivApp–Corpus Christi, 535 SW2d 385, ref nre.—Interest 39(1), 44, 66; Wills 439, 441, 470(1), 470(2), 732(2).

Green v. Rudsenske, TexCivApp–San Antonio, 320 SW2d 228.—App & E 688(2), 688(3), 932(1), 1004(5), 1170.6; Damag 60, 96, 100, 127, 132(3), 134(1), 216(1); Evid 75; Plead 364(5); Trial 116, 127, 133.6(1); Witn 223.

Green v. Scott, NDTex, 863 FSupp 376.—Hab Corp 352, 421, 679, 690.

Green; Seldon v., TexCivApp–Tyler, 498 SW2d 285.—High 194, 200; Plead 111.39(6), 111.42(4), 111.42(8); Venue 21.

Green v. Shalala, NDTex, 852 FSupp 558.—Admin Law 763, 786, 791, 793; Evid 597; Social S 140.10, 140.35, 140.50, 142.10, 143.40, 143.55, 147, 148.15, 149.

Green; Shapley v., CA5 (Tex), 465 F2d 874.—Civil R 1339; Fed Civ Proc 1742(2).

Green; Shaw v., TexComApp, 99 SW2d 889, 128 Tex 596, opinion conformed to 105 SW2d 767, writ dism.—Banks 47(1), 48(1); Corp 244(1); Partners 236, 247.

Green; Shaw v., TexApp–Houston (14 Dist), 659 SW2d 150.—Guard & W 13(3).

Green; Shaw v., TexCivApp–Galveston, 105 SW2d 767, writ dism.—App & E 1198; Banks 47(1), 49(9).

Green v. Smart, TexCivApp–Dallas, 333 SW2d 880, ref nre.—App & E 946, 966(1); Ex & Ad 443(8); Judgm 181(12), 186; Pretrial Proc 713.

Green; Southern Underwriters v., TexCivApp–Austin, 132 SW2d 447, writ dism, correct.—Work Comp 1065, 1066.

Green v. South Texas Coaches, TexCivApp–Dallas, 116 SW2d 799.—App & E 1052(7).

Green; Southwestern Life Ins. Co. v., TexApp–El Paso, 768 SW2d 445, writ den.—App & E 842(1), 931(1), 989, 1001(3), 1047(4); Evid 71; Insurance 3024, 3025, 3343; Trial 215, 352.20.

Green; Southwestern Life Ins. Co. v., TexCivApp–Austin, 101 SW2d 594, writ dism.—App & E 1177(7); Insurance 2593, 2607, 3070.

Green; Spell v., Tex, 192 SW2d 260, 144 Tex 535.—App & E 84(1); Venue 21.

Green; Spell v., TexCivApp–Texarkana, 200 SW2d 713, ref nre.—App & E 931(1); Child C 26, 76, 524, 639.

Green v. Spell, TexCivApp–Beaumont, 191 SW2d 92, writ refused 192 SW2d 260, 144 Tex 535.—Child C 601, 602; Child S 232; Venue 21.

Green v. State, TexCrimApp, 951 SW2d 3.—Ind & Inf 136; Obst Just 7, 11.

Green v. State, TexCrimApp, 934 SW2d 92, reh den, cert den 117 SCt 1561, 520 US 1200, 137 LEd2d 707, habeas corpus dism Ex parte Green, 2004 WL 2413313, dissenting opinion 159 SW3d 925.—Const Law 3789, 4745, 4773; Crim Law 394.6(4), 394.6(5), 396(1), 412.2(4), 414, 519(9), 523, 641.3(3), 695(5), 695.5, 790, 1152(2), 1153(1), 1158(4), 1166.18; Jury 131(8); Sent & Pun 1625, 1654, 1714, 1748, 1756, 1757, 1772, 1779(1), 1780(3), 1785(2), 1788(5), 1789(3).

Green v. State, TexCrimApp, 912 SW2d 189, cert den 116 SCt 2556, 516 US 1021, 135 LEd2d 1074, habeas corpus dism by Ex parte Green, 2004 WL 3094652.—Crim Law 1028, 1039, 1174(1); Sent & Pun 1618, 1626, 1654, 1720, 1757, 1780(3), 1788(3).

Green v. State, TexCrimApp, 906 SW2d 937, opinion after remand 934 SW2d 92, reh den, cert den 117 SCt 1561, 520 US 1200, 137 LEd2d 707, habeas corpus dism Ex parte Green, 2004 WL 2413313, dissenting opinion 159 SW3d 925.—Crim Law 414, 1083, 1110(1), 1181.5(2).

Green v. State, TexCrimApp, 893 SW2d 536.—Crim Law 1144.13(3), 1144.13(6), 1186.1, 1187, 1189; Double J 108.

Green v. State, TexCrimApp, 872 SW2d 717.—Arrest 70(1); Crim Law 641.3(2), 641.3(3), 641.3(4), 641.4(1), 641.13(4).

Green v. State, TexCrimApp, 840 SW2d 394, reh den, cert den 113 SCt 1819, 507 US 1020, 123 LEd2d 449.—Crim Law 338(7), 412(6), 438(1), 438(5.1), 438(7), 641.10(2), 865(2), 928, 932, 1035(5), 1036.2, 1043(3), 1134(5), 1144.13(2.1), 1144.13(8), 1152(2), 1155, 1158(3), 1159.2(7), 1159.6, 1163(6); Homic 1080(7), 1080(8), 1184, 1186; Jury 85, 97(1), 108, 133; Rob 5; Sent & Pun 1669, 1670, 1720, 1772.

Green v. State, TexCrimApp, 829 SW2d 222.—Bail 80; Crim Law 32.

Green v. State, TexCrimApp, 799 SW2d 756.—Searches 121.1, 123.1, 127, 145.1, 200.

Green v. State, TexCrimApp, 764 SW2d 242, appeal after remand 840 SW2d 394, reh den, cert den 113 SCt 1819, 507 US 1020, 123 LEd2d 449.—Crim Law 1035(5), 1043(2), 1115(2), 1166.16, 1166.17; Jury 42, 45, 83(1), 105(4), 109, 110(14).

Green v. State, TexCrimApp, 754 SW2d 687, appeal decided 764 SW2d 242, appeal after remand 840 SW2d 394, reh den, cert den 113 SCt 1819, 507 US 1020, 123 LEd2d 449.—Crim Law 956(13), 959.

Green v. State, TexCrimApp, 727 SW2d 272.—Crim Law 1036.1(9).

Green v. State, TexCrimApp, 727 SW2d 263.—Arrest 63.1; Crim Law 394.4(9), 1169.1(1), 1169.1(8).

Green v. State, TexCrimApp, 706 SW2d 653.—Sent & Pun 631, 636.

Green v. State, TexCrimApp, 685 SW2d 657.—Crim Law 641.7(2).

Green v. State, TexCrimApp, 682 SW2d 271, cert den 105 SCt 1407, 470 US 1034, 84 LEd2d 794, habeas corpus den Ex parte Green, 820 SW2d 796, denial of habeas corpus aff 947 F2d 1230, cert den 112 SCt 412, 502 US 954, 116 LEd2d 433.—Costs 302.2(2), 302.3; Crim Law 412.2(3), 438(1), 531(3), 532(0.5), 614(1), 632(3.1), 665(1), 665(4), 720(9), 728(2), 814(16), 1030(1), 1037.1(1), 1043(3), 1115(1), 1130(2), 1153(5), 1159.6, 1166.6, 1169.1(10); Homic 850, 1167, 1458; Jury 66(1), 97(1), 107, 108; Mental H 434; Searches 165; Sent & Pun 311, 1669, 1750, 1771, 1772; Witn 274(2).

Green v. State, TexCrimApp, 679 SW2d 516.—Crim Law 379, 722.3, 1171.6.

Green v. State, TexCrimApp, 676 SW2d 359.—Witn 374(1).

Green v. State, TexCrimApp, 667 SW2d 528.—Atty & C 64; Crim Law 412.2(5), 419(2.25), 517.2(2), 641.13(1).

Green v. State, TexCrimApp, 617 SW2d 253.—Crim Law 398(1), 1038.1(4); Sent & Pun 275; Witn 256.

Green v. State, TexCrimApp, 615 SW2d 700, cert den 102 SCt 490, 454 US 952, 70 LEd2d 258.—Arrest 63.4(18); Crim Law 211(3), 519(8), 531(3), 1158(4).

Green v. State, TexCrimApp, 594 SW2d 72.—Arrest 63.1, 63.3, 63.4(18); Crim Law 304(12); Searches 180, 181.

Green v. State, TexCrimApp, 587 SW2d 167, cert den 101 SCt 3146, 453 US 913, 69 LEd2d 996, reh den 102 SCt 889, 453 US 927, 69 LEd2d 1022.—Crim Law 627.8(3), 699, 700(5), 721(6); Sent & Pun 313, 1752, 1762.

Green v. State, TexCrimApp, 578 SW2d 411.—Ind & Inf 55, 86(2), 119, 196(2).

Green v. State, TexCrimApp, 571 SW2d 13.—Crim Law 1032(5), 1037.1(1), 1037.1(2), 1044.1(2); Ind & Inf 60; Infants 20.

Green v. State, TexCrimApp, 567 SW2d 211.—Crim Law 1168(1); Rob 6, 7, 24.15(1).

Green v. State, TexCrimApp, 566 SW2d 578, 96 ALR3d 664.—Crim Law 763(8), 770(2); Lewd 1, 10, 11; Obscen 7.6; Searches 17, 25.1; Sod 1; Witn 331.5, 373.

Green v. State, TexCrimApp, 555 SW2d 738.—Arrest 67; False Pret 49(1), 54.

Green v. State, TexCrimApp, 542 SW2d 416.—Crim Law 1169.2(1), 1169.2(3); Sent & Pun 1381(4).

Green v. State, TexCrimApp, 533 SW2d 769.—Crim Law 784(1), 1038.1(4), 1038.3, 1044.1(2); Ind & Inf 136.

Green v. State, TexCrimApp, 528 SW2d 617.—Sent & Pun 2004, 2019.

Green v. State, TexCrimApp, 510 SW2d 919.—Crim Law 339.10(2), 369.15, 566, 629.5(5), 641.3(9), 854(7), 1141(2), 1144.1; Obscen 2.5, 18.1.

Green v. State, TexCrimApp, 505 SW2d 292.—Crim Law 323, 552(1); Rape 51(7).

Green v. State, TexCrimApp, 502 SW2d 807.—Controlled Subs 34, 67.

Green v. State, TexCrimApp, 491 SW2d 882.—Crim Law 273.1(4), 1167(5); Sent & Pun 1314, 1369.

Green v. State, TexCrimApp, 490 SW2d 826.—Arrest 66(2); Autos 349(12); Crim Law 1130(4), 1134(1).

Green v. State, TexCrimApp, 488 SW2d 805.—Crim Law 339.10(9), 404.36, 1036.2, 1043(1).

Green v. State, TexCrimApp, 474 SW2d 212.—Crim Law 394.6(4), 404.65, 1130(2), 1130(5), 1167(3); Jury 24; Sent & Pun 1318, 1369, 1392.

Green v. State, TexCrimApp, 470 SW2d 901.—Arrest 63.4(11); Crim Law 394.5(3).

Green v. State, TexCrimApp, 467 SW2d 481.—Const Law 266(3.4), 4659(2); Crim Law 1064(5).

Green v. State, TexCrimApp, 454 SW2d 750.—Crim Law 721.5(2), 1037.1(1), 1037.2, 1130(2), 1171.1(3).

Green v. State, TexCrimApp, 453 SW2d 166.—Crim Law 939(2); Witn 37(4).

Green v. State, TexCrimApp, 451 SW2d 893.—Controlled Subs 69, 143, 145; Crim Law 388.3, 641.13(6), 730(1); Searches 143.1; Witn 344(2).

Green v. State, TexCrimApp, 435 SW2d 513.—Burg 29, 41(1); Sent & Pun 1486.

Green v. State, TexCrimApp, 433 SW2d 435.—Crim Law 732; Jury 90, 110(6), 110(14).

Green v. State, TexCrimApp, 423 SW2d 922.—Burg 41(1); Crim Law 508(3).

Green v. State, TexCrimApp, 423 SW2d 308.—Crim Law 1077.3.

Green v. State, TexCrimApp, 408 SW2d 709.—Crim Law 736(2), 739(2), 1169.3; Rob 24.15(1).

Green v. State, TexCrimApp, 387 SW2d 410.—Crim Law 1172.3; Sent & Pun 1388.

Green v. State, TexCrimApp, 363 SW2d 461.—Crim Law 1045, 1056.1(2); Weap 17(4).

Green v. State, TexCrimApp, 350 SW2d 560, 171 TexCrim 401.—Assault 92(2).

Green v. State, TexCrimApp, 343 SW2d 458, 171 TexCrim 6.—Crim Law 1092.7; Int Liq 236(7).

Green v. State, TexCrimApp, 320 SW2d 818, 167 TexCrim 272.—Crim Law 392, 1134(1); Disorderly H 5, 17; Ind & Inf 127.

Green v. State, TexCrimApp, 320 SW2d 139, 167 TexCrim 330.—Crim Law 295, 739(4); Rob 24.15(2).

GREEN

59 Tex D 2d—364

See Guidelines for Arrangement at the beginning of this Volume

Green v. State, TexCrimApp, 316 SW2d 750.—Lotteries 29.

Green v. State, TexCrimApp, 305 SW2d 609, 165 TexCrim 154.—Crim Law 470(2), 479, 489, 1111(3), 1170(1); Health 175, 186(5).

Green v. State, TexCrimApp, 303 SW2d 392, 165 TexCrim 46.—Crim Law 320, 641.6(3); Sent & Pun 1292.

Green v. State, TexCrimApp, 299 SW2d 134, 164 TexCrim 330.—Crim Law 534(1).

Green v. State, TexCrimApp, 296 SW2d 266.—Crim Law 1090.1(1).

Green v. State, TexCrimApp, 294 SW2d 848.—Crim Law 1094(3).

Green v. State, TexCrimApp, 292 SW2d 128.—Crim Law 1090.1(1).

Green v. State, TexCrimApp, 288 SW2d 84, 162 TexCrim 601.—Crim Law 553, 1092.14; Rape 52(1).

Green v. State, TexCrimApp, 286 SW2d 632, 162 TexCrim 475.—Crim Law 1044.2(1); Int Liq 236(3), 236(20).

Green v. State, TexCrimApp, 275 SW2d 110, 161 TexCrim 131.—Searches 66, 126.

Green v. State, TexCrimApp, 262 SW2d 202, 159 TexCrim 171.—Crim Law 665(2); Homic 1134.

Green v. State, TexCrimApp, 256 SW2d 573, 158 TexCrim 430.—Chat Mtg 232.

Green v. State, TexCrimApp, 251 SW2d 736, 157 TexCrim 546.—Crim Law 380, 381, 776(4), 1137(3), 1172.8; Homic 908, 1135.

Green v. State, TexCrimApp, 244 SW2d 813.—Crim Law 1094(3).

Green v. State, TexCrimApp, 238 SW2d 775, 156 TexCrim 22.—Crim Law 927(5).

Green v. State, TexCrimApp, 236 SW2d 139, 155 TexCrim 441.—Crim Law 655(1), 829(5), 1091(4), 1120(3), 1170.5(1); Homic 1486.

Green v. State, TexCrimApp, 231 SW2d 433, 155 TexCrim 43.—Crim Law 780(3), 814(17).

Green v. State, TexCrimApp, 230 SW2d 232.—Crim Law 1094(3).

Green v. State, TexCrimApp, 226 SW2d 454, 154 TexCrim 197.—Crim Law 768(4), 1172.3, 1172.9.

Green v. State, TexCrimApp, 221 SW2d 612, 153 TexCrim 442.—Crim Law 33, 830, 1111(3), 1171.1(2.1); Larc 40(11), 70(1), 71(4); Witn 130.

Green v. State, TexCrimApp, 221 SW2d 611, 153 TexCrim 462.—Crim Law 763(1), 823(2); Larc 71(1).

Green v. State, TexCrimApp, 219 SW2d 687, 153 TexCrim 273.—Crim Law 1111(1); Ind & Inf 171.

Green v. State, TexCrimApp, 211 SW2d 949, 152 TexCrim 201.—Crim Law 404.55, 419(3), 1091(4); Int Liq 236(7).

Green v. State, TexCrimApp, 209 SW2d 195, 151 TexCrim 505.—Assault 96(7); Crim Law 1056.1(4), 1090.8, 1182.

Green v. State, TexCrimApp, 202 SW2d 242, 150 TexCrim 404.—Crim Law 364(3.1); Int Liq 236(7).

Green v. State, TexCrimApp, 193 SW2d 528.—Crim Law 1094(3).

Green v. State, TexCrimApp, 176 SW2d 333, 146 TexCrim 469.—Crim Law 739(2), 741(1), 742(1), 1120(9), 1159.3(1), 1159.4(1).

Green v. State, TexCrimApp, 167 SW2d 764, 145 TexCrim 271.—Int Liq 236(1), 236(5).

Green v. State, TexCrimApp, 167 SW2d 532, 145 TexCrim 294.—Crim Law 1098.

Green v. State, TexCrimApp, 167 SW2d 186, 145 TexCrim 256.—Crim Law 1094(2.1).

Green v. State, TexCrimApp, 167 SW2d 185, 145 TexCrim 252.—Crim Law 1092.8, 1094(2.1), 1099.6(3).

Green v. State, TexCrimApp, 167 SW2d 183, 145 TexCrim 249.—Crim Law 273.3, 1092.8, 1099.6(3).

Green v. State, TexCrimApp, 167 SW2d 182, 145 TexCrim 247.—Crim Law 1087.2, 1133.

Green v. State, TexCrimApp, 167 SW2d 180, 145 TexCrim 243.—Crim Law 921, 1092.8, 1094(2.1), 1099.7(1); Int Liq 36(4).

Green v. State, TexCrimApp, 161 SW2d 1074, 144 TexCrim 221.—Crim Law 814(17), 823(4); Ind & Inf 137(2); Larc 65, 75(2).

Green v. State, TexCrimApp, 161 SW2d 114, 144 TexCrim 186.—Crim Law 778(5), 844(1), 844(2), 1043(2), 1056.1(4), 1111(3); False Pret 7(5), 8, 9, 26, 49(4).

Green v. State, TexCrimApp, 161 SW2d 106, 144 TexCrim 1.—False Pret 30; Ind & Inf 103.

Green v. State, TexCrimApp, 160 SW2d 940, 144 TexCrim 40.—Assault 96(1); Crim Law 1056.1(2); Homic 1154, 1373.

Green v. State, TexCrimApp, 158 SW2d 771, 143 TexCrim 337.—Crim Law 784(1), 789(3); Int Liq 239(2); Stip 14(7).

Green v. State, TexCrimApp, 147 SW2d 260, 141 TexCrim 42.—Int Liq 236(7).

Green v. State, TexCrimApp, 147 SW2d 259, 141 TexCrim 41.—Int Liq 236(7).

Green v. State, TexCrimApp, 144 SW2d 892, 140 TexCrim 295.—Crim Law 1104(2); Int Liq 40(2), 241.

Green v. State, TexCrimApp, 117 SW2d 80, 135 TexCrim 63.—Crim Law 1110(3), 1182; Ind & Inf 41(2).

Green v. State, TexCrimApp, 116 SW2d 1075, 135 Tex-Crim 61.—Crim Law 1110(3), 1182; Ind & Inf 41(2).

Green v. State, TexCrimApp, 112 SW2d 451.—Infants 68.8.

Green v. State, TexCrimApp, 101 SW2d 241, 131 TexCrim 552.—Int Liq 236(11).

Green v. State, TexCrimApp, 99 SW2d 913.—Crim Law 1182.

Green v. State, TexCrimApp, 97 SW2d 233, 131 TexCrim 218.—Crim Law 778(12), 829(9); Homic 1479.

Green v. State, TexCrimApp, 95 SW2d 965.—Crim Law 1131(1).

Green v. State, TexCrimApp, 95 SW2d 394.—Crim Law 1094(2.1).

Green v. State, TexCrimApp, 92 SW2d 441.—Crim Law 15.

Green v. State, TexCrimApp, 91 SW2d 368, 130 TexCrim 17.—Crim Law 925(1), 956(13), 1156(5); Homic 1134.

Green v. State, TexApp–Houston (1 Dist) 219 SW3d 84.—Const Law 4344; Crim Law 13.1(1); Mental H 433(2), 465(3), 467; Statut 188.

Green v. State, TexApp–Houston (1 Dist), 891 SW2d 289, petition for discretionary review refused.—Assault 92(1), 96(3), 96(7); Crim Law 641.13(1), 641.13(2.1), 641.13(6), 782(16), 822(1), 1038.1(1), 1038.1(4), 1134(2), 1144.13(2.1), 1159.2(7), 1159.2(9), 1172.1(1), 1172.1(3).

Green v. State, TexApp–Houston (1 Dist), 880 SW2d 797.—Const Law 4737; Crim Law 29(10), 673(5), 772(6), 814(3), 829(1), 1144.13(2.1), 1159.2(7), 1159.4(2), 1159.6; Larc 31, 55; Sent & Pun 2103, 2160, 2188(4).

Green v. State, TexApp–Houston (1 Dist), 866 SW2d 701.—Arrest 63.5(2), 63.5(4); Autos 349(4), 349.5(10); Searches 48, 63.

Green v. State, TexApp–Houston (1 Dist), 813 SW2d 703, petition for discretionary review refused.—Crim Law 43, 1148.

Green v. State, TexApp–Houston (1 Dist), 663 SW2d 145, petition for discretionary review refused.—Sent & Pun 1811, 2051; Witn 345(8).

Green v. State, TexApp–Houston (1 Dist), 658 SW2d 303, petition for discretionary review refused.—Crim Law 627.2, 796, 1036.1(9), 1172.6, 1175; Homic 1044, 1333, 1380, 1385, 1451, 1458; Sent & Pun 1872(2), 1899, 1902; Witn 37(4).

Green v. State, TexApp–Houston (1 Dist), 638 SW2d 51.—Crim Law 650; Ind & Inf 71.4(1), 71.4(5).

Green v. State, TexApp–Fort Worth, 78 SW3d 604.—Arrest 65, 68(8), 68(9), 68(12); Crim Law 217, 1134(2), 1139, 1144.12, 1158(4); Searches 25.1.

Green v. State, TexApp–Fort Worth, 999 SW2d 474, reh overr, and petition for discretionary review refused.—

For Later Case History Information, see KeyCite on WESTLAW

Crim Law 632(3.1), 632(5), 1023(3), 1026.10(3), 1072, 1081(2); Hab Corp 208, 814, 819.

Green v. State, TexApp–Fort Worth, 942 SW2d 149.— Crim Law 673(5), 692.

Green v. State, TexApp–Fort Worth, 930 SW2d 655, reh overr, and petition for discretionary review refused.— Controlled Subs 22, 77, 96; Crim Law 1144.13(2.1), 1159.2(7), 1159.6.

Green v. State, TexApp–Fort Worth, 908 SW2d 615, petition for discretionary review gr, aff 951 SW2d 3.—Obst Just 11.

Green v. State, TexApp–Fort Worth, 829 SW2d 938.— Crim Law 918(1).

Green v. State, TexApp–Fort Worth, 815 SW2d 906, petition for discretionary review gr, vac in part 893 SW2d 536.—Crim Law 1184(1).

Green v. State, TexApp–Fort Worth, 785 SW2d 955, petition for discretionary review gr, aff 829 SW2d 222.— Crim Law 33, 43.5, 409(5), 1038.1(4); Homic 1387; Ind & Inf 113.

Green v. State, TexApp–Fort Worth, 705 SW2d 403.— Assault 56, 59.

Green v. State, TexApp–Fort Worth, 698 SW2d 776, petition for discretionary review refused.—Crim Law 369.2(1), 374, 698(1), 708.1, 719(3), 719(4), 720(2), 721.5(1), 722.5, 726, 729, 730(1), 899, 1126, 1128(2), 1169.5(1), 1171.1(2.1), 1171.1(3), 1171.3.

Green v. State, TexApp–Austin, 137 SW3d 356, reh overr, and petition for discretionary review refused.—Crim Law 1077.3, 1144.13(2.1), 1144.13(3), 1144.13(6), 1159.2(1), 1159.2(2), 1159.2(7), 1159.2(9); Health 164, 185, 186(5); Ind & Inf 171.

Green v. State, TexApp–San Antonio, 100 SW3d 344, petition for discretionary review refused.—Crim Law 1139, 1158(2), 1590.

Green v. State, TexApp–San Antonio, 899 SW2d 245.— Crim Law 641.13(2.1), 1144.13(6), 1159.2(7), 1169.1(1), 1189.

Green v. State, TexApp–San Antonio, 773 SW2d 816.— Autos 12, 349(2.1); Crim Law 394.4(9); Statut 241(1).

Green v. State, TexApp–San Antonio, 765 SW2d 887, petition for discretionary review gr, aff 799 SW2d 756.— Controlled Subs 148(3); Searches 145.1.

Green v. State, TexApp–Dallas, 761 SW2d 824.—Crim Law 556; Forg 5, 8, 16, 44(1).

Green v. State, TexApp–Dallas, 744 SW2d 313, petition for discretionary review refused.—Arrest 63.5(3.1); Searches 165, 184.

Green v. State, TexApp–Texarkana, 93 SW3d 541, reh overr, and petition for discretionary review refused.— Arrest 63.5(4), 63.5(9); Autos 349(2.1), 349(17); Crim Law 394.6(5), 1134(3), 1144.12, 1153(1), 1158(1), 1158(4); Searches 53.1, 180, 183, 198.

Green v. State, TexApp–Texarkana, 72 SW3d 420, petition for discretionary review refused.—Controlled Subs 77; Crim Law 59(1), 507(1), 508(9), 511.1(3), 511.2, 741(5), 742(2), 747, 780(1), 796, 824(12), 1038.3, 1173.2(6); Sent & Pun 329.

Green v. State, TexApp–Texarkana, 892 SW2d 220, petition for discretionary review refused.—Controlled Subs 30, 67, 80, 131; Crim Law 394.6(5), 742(1), 1144.13(3), 1158(4), 1159.2(1), 1159.2(7), 1159.2(9), 1159.2(10); Searches 47.1.

Green v. State, TexApp–Texarkana, 892 SW2d 217, petition for discretionary review refused.—Autos 349(2.1), 349(5); Controlled Subs 131; Crim Law 394.6(5), 742(1), 1144.13(3), 1144.13(6), 1158(4), 1159.2(1), 1159.2(7), 1159.2(9); Obst Just 3; Searches 47.1.

Green v. State, TexApp–Texarkana, 887 SW2d 230.— Crim Law 20, 23, 662.6, 795(2.1), 899, 1030(1), 1036.1(2); Homic 1457, 1458; Ind & Inf 189(8), 191(1); Witn 2(1), 5.

Green v. State, TexApp–Texarkana, 880 SW2d 198.— Controlled Subs 69; Crim Law 338(1), 369.1, 436(1),

1036.1(4), 1134(5), 1153(1), 1158(1), 1158(3), 1169.2(5); Jury 33(5.15), 33(5.20); J P 31; Searches 103.1, 109, 113.1, 126, 141.

Green v. State, TexApp–Amarillo, 209 SW3d 831, petition for discretionary review refused, petition stricken 2007 WL 1217924.—Assault 59, 91.9; Const Law 1415; Crim Law 665(1), 700(1); Rape 7, 51(3).

Green v. State, TexApp–El Paso, 760 SW2d 50.—Crim Law 577.11(2), 577.15(4), 577.16(4), 577.16(7), 577.16(8).

Green v. State, TexApp–El Paso, 641 SW2d 272, petition for discretionary review gr, rev 667 SW2d 528.—Crim Law 531(3), 814(8), 1158(4).

Green v. State, TexApp–Beaumont, 891 SW2d 340.—Crim Law 1158(3); Jury 33(5.15).

Green v. State, TexApp–Beaumont, 876 SW2d 226.—Crim Law 419(1), 419(2.15), 730(10), 1144.15; Sent & Pun 313.

Green v. State, TexApp–Beaumont, 876 SW2d 211.—Crim Law 713, 720(3), 729, 730(1), 730(7), 730(13).

Green v. State, TexApp–Beaumont, 767 SW2d 919, petition for discretionary review refused.—Crim Law 1167(1); Ind & Inf 71.1; Larc 35, 63.

Green v. State, TexApp–Beaumont, 736 SW2d 253.—Crim Law 552(3), 552(4); Infants 20.

Green v. State, TexApp–Waco, 839 SW2d 935, reh den, and on reh in part, and petition for discretionary review refused.—Arrest 63.1; Crim Law 59(1), 80, 217, 409(5), 419(2.20), 419(13), 517.1(1), 517.2(2), 519(1), 525, 532(0.5), 706(2), 736(2), 790, 792(0.5), 792(2), 1153(1), 1170.5(1); Ind & Inf 10.1(1); Jury 33(5.15); Rob 17(1); Sent & Pun 65, 311, 1780(3); Witn 379(1).

Green v. State, TexApp–Eastland, 140 SW3d 776.—Autos 359.

Green v. State, TexApp–Eastland, 670 SW2d 332.—Crim Law 414, 721(3); Witn 305(2).

Green v. State, TexApp–Tyler, 55 SW3d 633, petition for discretionary review refused, and reh den, cert den 122 SCt 1366, 535 US 958, 152 LEd2d 360.—Crim Law 469.1, 472, 480, 486(2), 487, 629(1), 671, 867, 1144.12, 1153(1), 1153(4), 1155, 1158(4), 1166(10.10), 1178; Ind & Inf 171, 180; Jury 149.

Green v. State, TexApp–Corpus Christi, 841 SW2d 926.— Const Law 4606; Crim Law 643, 1129(1), 1166.13; Rob 30; Sent & Pun 300.

Green v. State, TexApp–Corpus Christi, 835 SW2d 142.— Burg 41(6); Crim Law 339.7(3), 339.7(4), 339.8(4), 339.10(2), 339.11(6), 394.6(5), 698(1), 1044.1(5.1), 1144.13(2.1), 1159.2(7).

Green v. State, TexApp–Corpus Christi, 831 SW2d 89, reh overr.—Assault 48, 56, 92(3), 96(7); Autos 347, 355(14); Crim Law 363, 369.1, 369.2(1), 371(1), 371(12), 396(1), 683(1), 822(1), 1038.1(1), 1144.13(2.1), 1159.2(7), 1169.11; Witn 363(1), 368.

Green v. State, TexApp–Corpus Christi, 745 SW2d 477, petition for discretionary review refused.—Const Law 4594(6); Crim Law 590(1), 700(9), 1129(3).

Green v. State, TexApp–Corpus Christi, 736 SW2d 218.— Controlled Subs 97, 148(3); Crim Law 1129(1); Ind & Inf 41(3), 176; Searches 113.1.

Green v. State, TexApp–Houston (14 Dist), 191 SW3d 888, petition for discretionary review refused.—Crim Law 367, 641.13(1), 641.13(6), 1119(1), 1144.10, 1152(2), 1153(1); Jury 131(2), 131(13).

Green v. State, TexApp–Houston (14 Dist), 36 SW3d 211. —Crim Law 589(1), 1134(2), 1147, 1152(1), 1166(1); Jury 29(6), 29(7).

Green v. State, TexApp–Houston (14 Dist), 971 SW2d 639, petition for discretionary review refused.—Const Law 4653; Crim Law 338(7), 369.1, 369.2(1), 369.2(4), 369.15, 371(1), 371(4), 394.5(2), 419(2.20), 1134(3), 1139, 1153(1), 1158(4); Homic 523, 938; Searches 25.1, 162, 164.

Green v. State, TexApp–Houston (14 Dist), 771 SW2d 576. —Jury 137(1).

GREEN

59 Tex D 2d—366

Green v. State, TexApp–Houston (14 Dist), 700 SW2d 760, petition for discretionary review gr, aff 727 SW2d 272. —Crim Law 675; Stip 14(7).

Green v. State, TexApp–Houston (14 Dist), 681 SW2d 84, petition for discretionary review gr, aff 685 SW2d 657. —Crim Law 577.1; Sent & Pun 1302; Stip 14(7).

Green v. State, TexApp–Houston (14 Dist), 675 SW2d 541, petition for discretionary review refused.—Crim Law 641.13(1), 641.13(6), 1045; Homic 1197, 1477.

Green v. State, TexApp–Houston (14 Dist), 666 SW2d 291. —Controlled Subs 130; Crim Law 254.2, 1224(2); Searches 42.1, 192.1.

Green v. State, TexApp–Houston (14 Dist), 650 SW2d 464. —Sent & Pun 2003, 2021.

Green v. State, TexApp–Houston (14 Dist), 640 SW2d 645. —Autos 355(6); Crim Law 552(3), 721(1), 721(3), 721(6).

Green v. State, TexCivApp–Beaumont, 272 SW2d 133, ref nre.—Const Law 4001; Mental H 244, 245, 252; Statut 47.

Green v. State, TexCivApp–Tyler, 589 SW2d 160.—App & E 966(1); Atty & C 48, 54; Evid 591; Pretrial Proc 713, 715, 724.

Green v. State Bar of Texas, CA5 (Tex), 27 F3d 1083.— Antitrust 902, 972(4); Civil R 1009, 1033(1), 1042, 1354, 1375, 1394, 1395(1); Consp 2, 18; Fed Cts 265, 269, 759.1, 763.1, 776, 794, 915.

Green; State, in Behalf of Williams v., TexApp–Austin, 746 SW2d 940, writ den.—Atty Gen 6.

Green v. State of Tex., NDTex, 351 FSupp 143.—Elections 11, 21; Fed Cts 1000.

Green v. Steigerwald, TexCivApp–Tyler, 468 SW2d 122. —Lim of Act 119(6), 138.

Green v. Stewart, Tex, 516 SW2d 133.—Offic 11.1.

Green; Stewart v., TexCivApp–Eastland, 505 SW2d 414, writ gr, rev 516 SW2d 133.—Offic 11.1.

Green v. Stienke, TexCivApp–Texarkana, 321 SW2d 95.— Waters 183.5.

Green v. Stratoflex, Inc., TexCivApp–Fort Worth, 596 SW2d 305.—App & E 863, 954(1); Inj 135, 138.21, 147, 157.

Green; Suderman Stevedores v., CA5 (Tex), 930 F2d 424. See P & M CraneCo. v. Hayes.

Green; Taylor v., CA5 (Tex), 868 F2d 162, cert den 110 SCt 127, 493 US 841, 107 LEd2d 87, reh den 110 SCt 761, 493 US 1037, 107 LEd2d 777.—Civil R 1461; Fed Civ Proc 2344; Fed Cts 611, 931; Jury 37.

Green v. Temple-Stuart Co., TexCivApp–Fort Worth, 408 SW2d 744.—Antitrust 543, 575, 592; Commerce 60(1), 62.10(1), 62.10(2).

Green; Tennyson v., TexCivApp–Amarillo, 217 SW2d 179, ref nre.—Trial 365.3; Waters 112, 116, 126(2), 179(4).

Green v. Texas & P. Ry. Co., TexComApp, 81 SW2d 669, 125 Tex 168.—Damag 64; Evid 54, 100, 587, 595; Neglig 440(1), 1602; R R 350(13), 351(2); Trial 203(1), 208, 352.4(6).

Green; Texas Beef Cattle Co. v., Tex, 921 SW2d 203.— Action 12; Damag 46.10, 91(1); Judgm 580, 663; Mal Pros 14, 16, 36, 66; Torts 115, 212, 220, 242, 272.

Green; Texas Beef Cattle Co. v., TexApp–Amarillo, 860 SW2d 722, reh den, and writ den.—Judgm 585(2), 585(3), 592, 713(2), 720, 724, 735.

Green; Texas Beef Cattle Co. v., TexApp–Beaumont, 883 SW2d 415, reh overr, and writ gr, rev 921 SW2d 203.— Damag 71, 91(1), 94; Interest 39(2.6); Judgm 720; Mal Pros 10, 14, 69, 72(5); Trial 56, 194(14).

Green; Texas Beef Cattle Co. v., TexApp–Beaumont, 862 SW2d 812.—Evid 71.

Green; Texas Dept. of Human Services v., TexApp– Austin, 855 SW2d 136, reh overr, and writ den.—App & E 230, 236(1), 836, 883, 922, 930(3), 961, 968, 969, 970(2), 989, 999(1), 1001(1), 1003(7), 1050.1(11), 1052(2); Const Law 2503(1); Damag 163(2), 208(7); Evid 505, 515, 555.5; Jury 136(2); Labor & Emp 780, 861, 865; Offic

61, 66, 72.45(1); Pretrial Proc 45, 282, 313, 713, 714; States 53, 191.7; Statut 212.6, 212.7; Trial 59(1).

Green v. Texas Dept. of Protective and Regulatory Services, TexApp–El Paso, 25 SW3d 213.—App & E 930(1), 946, 966(1), 970(2), 1001(1), 1001(3), 1003(7), 1078(1); Infants 155, 173.1, 178; Pretrial Proc 713, 723.1.

Green v. Texas Electrical Wholesalers, Inc., TexApp– Houston (1 Dist), 651 SW2d 4, writ dism by agreement, reh den 647 SW2d 1.—App & E 709; Autos 192(11), 201(1.1), 246(16); Evid 243(2).

Green v. Texas Electrical Wholesalers, Inc., TexApp– Houston (1 Dist), 647 SW2d 1.—App & E 824.

Green v. Texas Emp. Ins. Ass'n, TexCivApp–Texarkana, 339 SW2d 368, ref nre.—App & E 863; Work Comp 1670, 1683, 1927, 1966.

Green v. Texas Emp. Ins. Ass'n, TexCivApp–Waco, 168 SW2d 694, writ refused wom.—Work Comp 1927.

Green v. Texas Employment Com'n, TexApp–El Paso, 675 SW2d 809, ref nre.—Courts 85(2); Unemp Comp 461, 463; Work Comp 1874.

Green v. Texas Gulf Sulphur Co., CA5 (Tex), 393 F2d 67, cert den 89 SCt 445, 393 US 977, 21 LEd2d 438.—Decl Judgm 395.

Green; Texas Liquor Control Bd. v., TexCivApp–San Antonio, 146 SW2d 478, dism.—Int Liq 108.10(6), 108.10(7), 108.10(10).

Green v. Texas Workers' Compensation Ins. Facility, TexApp–Austin, 993 SW2d 839, reh overr, and review den.—App & E 946, 970(2), 1056.1(1); Evid 555.2; Work Comp 1396, 1417, 1418, 1859, 1937.

Green; Tips v., TexCivApp–Hous (14 Dist), 533 SW2d 155, dism.—Evid 162(2); Judgm 524; Stip 14(12); Venue 7.5(3).

Green; Transamerica Ins. Co. of Texas v., TexApp– Corpus Christi, 797 SW2d 171.—Trial 295(10), 317, 352.10; Work Comp 813, 1374, 1404, 1619, 1853, 1949, 2084.

Green v. Unauthorized Practice of Law Committee, TexApp–Dallas, 883 SW2d 293.—App & E 170(2), 954(1); Atty & C 11(1), 11(2.1); Inj 1, 11, 12, 14, 16, 85(1), 135; Judgm 178, 185(5), 185(6), 185.1(4), 185.3(4), 186.

Green v. United Pentecostal Church Intern., TexApp– Austin, 899 SW2d 28, reh overr, and writ den, cert den 116 SCt 1419, 517 US 1134, 134 LEd2d 543, reh den 116 SCt 1891, 517 US 1240, 135 LEd2d 185.—Relig Soc 14, 24, 27(2).

Green; U.S. v., CA5 (Tex), 293 F3d 855, cert den 123 SCt 403, 537 US 966, 154 LEd2d 324.—Armed S 28; Arrest 63.5(6); Autos 349(9); Crim Law 1158(4).

Green; U.S. v., CA5 (Tex), 272 F3d 748.—Crim Law 412.2(2), 412.2(4), 727, 1134(2), 1137(2), 1137(5), 1139, 1158(4), 1162, 1165(1), 1169.12.

Green; U.S. v., CA5 (Tex), 46 F3d 461, cert den 115 SCt 2629, 515 US 1167, 132 LEd2d 869.—Crim Law 700(2.1), 700(4), 1139; Sent & Pun 787.

Green; U.S. v., CA5 (Tex), 494 F2d 820, reh den 497 F2d 1368, cert den 95 SCt 325, 419 US 1004, 42 LEd2d 280. —Cons Cred 68; Crim Law 29(5.5), 35, 622.1(2); Postal 35(2), 35(8), 35(10), 49(11).

Green; U.S. v., CA5 (Tex), 223 FedAppx 408.—Crim Law 577.16(4).

Green; U.S. v., CA5 (Tex), 162 FedAppx 283.—Jury 34(7); Sent & Pun 2036.

Green; U.S. v., CA5 (Tex), 133 FedAppx 954.—Autos 349(18); Crim Law 1035(1).

Green; U.S. v., WDTex, 879 FSupp 60.—Arrest 63.5(6).

Green; U.S. v., WDTex, 824 FSupp 657. See U.S. v. Rodriguez.

Green; U.S. v., WDTex, 429 FSupp 1036.—Sent & Pun 1947, 1951, 2025.

Green v. U.S. Chewing Gum Mfg. Co., CA5 (Tex), 224 F2d 369.—Antitrust 969.

Green v. U.S. Fidelity & Guaranty Co, NDTex, 113 FSupp 927.—Fed Cts 356.

Green; University Interscholastic League v., TexCiv-App–Corpus Christi, 583 SW2d 907.—Inj 78, 94, 138.54, 151; States 191.4(4), 191.10.

Green v. Vance, Tex, 314 SW2d 794, 158 Tex 550.—Adv Poss 51.

Green v. Vance, TexCivApp–Houston, 311 SW2d 738, ref nre 314 SW2d 794, 158 Tex 550.—Adv Poss 51, 63(2).

Green v. Vidlak, TexApp–Amarillo, 76 SW3d 117.—App & E 428(2); Lim of Act 180(7), 182(2); Pretrial Proc 649.

Green v. Walgreen Drug Co. of Tex., TexCivApp–Beaumont, 368 SW2d 688, ref nre.—Trial 350.1, 351.5(1), 352.2, 352.4(1), 352.4(6).

Green v. Watson, TexApp–Austin, 860 SW2d 238, reh overr.—App & E 918(1), 1071.1(2); Courts 28, 200, 201, 472.3, 472.4(1), 472.4(7), 475(1), 475(2); Plead 245(1), 420(2); Statut 185; Trial 388(2).

Green; Watts v., TexApp–Amarillo, 190 SW3d 44.—Antitrust 392; App & E 215(1); Damag 91.5(3); Fraud 20, 61; Insurance 1672; Joint Adv 1.2(1), 7.

Green v. W. E. Grace Mfg. Co., Tex, 422 SW2d 723.—Jury 25(6), 28(9), 28(17), 31.4.

Green; W. E. Grace Mfg. Co. v., TexCivApp–Dallas, 417 SW2d 71, rev 422 SW2d 723.—Judgm 101(1), 101(2); Jury 25(8), 26, 28(8), 28(9).

Green v. Weinberger, CA5 (Tex), 500 F2d 203.—Admin Law 501; Social S 142.20, 142.25.

Green; Welder v., TexApp–Corpus Christi, 985 SW2d 170, review den.—App & E 863, 930(1), 934(1), 984(5), 1001(3); Costs 194.40; Damag 18, 192; Fraud 3, 7; Interest 39(2.20), 39(2.50); Judgm 199(3.5); Neglig 460; Partners 70, 78, 79, 92, 224, 259.5, 296(3), 296(5); Torts 117.

Green v. Westgate Apostolic Church, TexApp–Austin, 808 SW2d 547, writ den.—App & E 219(2); Inj 94, 128(9); Relig Soc 5, 8, 9, 11, 23(3), 27(1).

Green; Wheeler v., Tex, 157 SW3d 439.—Atty & C 62; Child 20.4, 20.11; Judgm 183; Pretrial Proc 486.

Green; Wheeler v., TexApp–Dallas, 119 SW3d 887, reh overr, review gr, rev 157 SW3d 439.—Child C 400, 413, 551, 555; Child 20.10, 73.

Green v. White, TexCivApp–El Paso, 203 SW2d 960.—App & E 1054(1); Child C 7, 531(1), 553, 632, 637, 921(1), 924.

Green; Wilgus v., TexApp–Tyler, 882 SW2d 6, reh den, and writ den.—App & E 238(2), 863; Judgm 199(3.10); Usury 63.

Green v. Wilkinson, CA5 (Tex), 234 F2d 120.—Lim of Act 28(1).

Green v. Wilkinson, NDTex, 135 FSupp 309, aff 234 F2d 120.—Lim of Act 28(1).

Green; Wills v., TexApp–Waco, 632 SW2d 680.—App & E 627; Partit 74.

Green v. Wimer, TexCivApp–San Antonio, 304 SW2d 147.—Autos 244(22.1).

Green; Yellow Cab & Baggage Co. v., Tex, 277 SW2d 92, 154 Tex 330.—App & E 216(1), 216(3); Damag 221(4).

Green; Yellow Cab & Baggage Co. v., TexCivApp–Fort Worth, 268 SW2d 519, aff 277 SW2d 92, 154 Tex 330.—App & E 216(3); Damag 208(3), 216(7); Trial 129, 141, 143.

Green & Romans; Super-Cold Southwest Co. v., TexCivApp–Fort Worth, 196 SW2d 340.—Damag 6, 45, 120(3), 163(4), 190; Trial 199, 251(1).

Green & Romans; Super-Cold Southwest Co. v., TexCivApp–Fort Worth, 185 SW2d 749.—App & E 9, 345.1; Contracts 54(1); Corp 503(2); Plead 111.4, 111.6, 111.8, 111.29, 111.36, 111.40, 301(1), 406(7); Trial 350.3(1); Venue 7.5(1).

Green & Welhausen; Shaw v., TexCivApp–Galveston, 106 SW2d 344, aff Gossett v. Green, 133 SW2d 762, 134 Tex 282.—Banks 47(1).

Green Ave. Apartments v. Chambers, TexCivApp–Beaumont, 239 SW2d 675.—Contracts 143(4), 147(2), 152, 153, 154; Covenants 49, 103(1), 103(2); Inj 62(1), 128(6).

Greenawalt v. Cunningham, TexCivApp–Dallas, 107 SW2d 1099.—Home 81, 142(1), 143, 209.5.

Greenbaum v. Cortez, TexApp–Corpus Christi, 644 SW2d 510, dism.—Contracts 22(1), 24, 211, 214; Spec Perf 57.

Green Bay Packaging, Inc.; Adams Extract Co., Inc. v., CA5 (Tex), 752 F2d 137. See Corrugated Container Antitrust Litigation, In re.

Greenbelt Elec. Co-op., Inc. v. Johnson, TexCivApp–Amarillo, 608 SW2d 320.—Contracts 238(2), 246; Electricity 11(3), 11.1(1), 11.4; Plead 67, 123, 427.

Green Belt Peat Moss Co.; Vermilion Parish Peat Co. v., TexCivApp–Dallas, 465 SW2d 950, ref nre.—Corp 99(2), 182.4(3); Land & Ten 80(1).

Greenberg; Bosque Asset Corp. v., TexApp–Eastland, 19 SW3d 514, review den.—App & E 430(1), 863, 934(1); Banks 505, 508; Evid 333(1), 366(2); Judgm 178, 185(5), 185.1(3), 185.3(16); Lim of Act 124.

Greenberg v. Brookshire, Tex, 640 SW2d 870.—Pretrial Proc 501, 506.1, 508, 511, 512.

Greenberg v. Crossroads Systems, Inc., CA5 (Tex), 364 F3d 657.—Fed Cts 611; Sec Reg 60.18, 60.27(4), 60.48(3), 60.62.

Greenberg v. Fincher & Son Real Estate, Inc., TexApp–Houston (1 Dist), 753 SW2d 506.—App & E 819; Bankr 2395, 2396.

Greenberg v. Fincher, Greenberg & Baca Investments, TexApp–Houston (1 Dist), 753 SW2d 506. See Greenberg v. Fincher & Son Real Estate, Inc.

Greenberg v. Mobil Oil Corp., NDTex, 318 FSupp 1025.—Assault 13, 35; Evid 207(4), 222(10), 265(11); Labor & Emp 3096(4), 3096(8), 3107(1), 3179(4).

Greenberg; Pan Am. Fire & Cas. Co. v., TexCivApp–Amarillo, 326 SW2d 274, ref nre.—App & E 846(5).

Greenberg; Regal Properties v., TexCivApp–Dallas, 538 SW2d 190.—Plead 387.

Greenberg v. Royal Commerce Bank Nat. Ass'n, TexCivApp–Eastland, 577 SW2d 576, ref nre.—Cons Cred 4, 11, 14.

Greenberg; St. Paul Reinsurance Co., Ltd. v., CA5 (Tex), 134 F3d 1250.—Fed Cts 29.1, 34, 312.1, 336.1, 337, 338, 342, 352, 357.1, 776, 812; Insurance 3349, 3360; Rem of C 75, 107(7).

Greenberg; Wright v., TexApp–Houston (14 Dist), 2 SW3d 666, review den.—App & E 852, 856(1), 863, 1079; Estop 52.15, 84; Judgm 181(34), 185.1(4), 189; Lim of Act 13, 103(4), 192(3); Powers 19; Trusts 112, 373; Wills 435, 439, 440, 456, 470(1), 470(2), 491, 589(1), 706.

Greenberg, Benson, Fisk and Fielder, P.C. v. Howell, TexApp–Dallas, 685 SW2d 694.—Judges 51(4); Mand 28, 48, 51.

Greenberg, Fisk & Fielder v. Howell, TexApp–Dallas, 676 SW2d 431.—Judges 51(4).

Greenberg Traurig of New York, P.C. v. Moody, TexApp–Houston (14 Dist), 161 SW3d 56, reh overr.—Action 17; App & E 179(1), 204(1), 204(7), 215(1), 893(1), 970(2), 1001(3), 1048(2), 1050.1(1), 1056.1(1), 1177(6); Atty & C 26, 32(6); Consp 1.1, 2, 9, 13, 14, 19; Corp 202; Evid 506, 508, 512, 535, 555.2; Fraud 7, 16, 17; Pretrial Proc 3; Sec Reg 242, 297.

Greenblatt; Permian Bldg., Inc. v., TexCivApp–Fort Worth, 442 SW2d 831, ref nre.—App & E 1039(2.1); Contracts 189, 297; Lim of Act 46(1); Ven & Pur 345.

Greenblatt; Solomon v., TexApp–Dallas, 812 SW2d 7.—Contracts 9(2), 26, 75(1), 212(2); Corp 1.7(2), 325, 617(2); Insurance 1652(1).

Greenbriar Homes, Inc.; Freeman v., TexApp–Dallas, 715 SW2d 394, ref nre.—Antitrust 199, 363, 369; Ven & Pur 1, 17.

Greenbriar North Section II; Chase Manhattan Bank, N.A. v., TexApp–Houston (1 Dist), 835 SW2d 720, reh den.—Contracts 1, 127(4), 129(1), 147(1), 176(1), 218, 221(2), 276; Mtg 561.1.

Greenbriar, Villages of, v. Hutchison, TexApp–Houston (1 Dist), 880 SW2d 777. See Villages of Greenbriar v. Hutchison.

Greenbriar, Villages of, v. Torres, TexApp–Houston (1 Dist), 874 SW2d 259. See Villages of Greenbriar v. Torres.

Greenburg; Shell Oil Co. v., TexCivApp–San Antonio, 380 SW2d 758.—Plead 111.38; Venue 22(3), 22(6).

Green Corp.; Local Union 59, Intern. Broth. of Elec. Workers, AFL-CIO v., CA5 (Tex), 725 F2d 264, reh den 729 F2d 1459, cert den 105 SCt 124, 469 US 833, 83 LEd2d 66.—Alt Disp Res 374(1); Labor & Emp 1623(1), 1624(1), 1625.

Greene, Ex parte, TexCrimApp, 406 SW2d 465, appeal dism, cert den Greene v. Texas, 87 SCt 1707, 387 US 240, 18 LEd2d 745.—Hab Corp 290.1, 474.

Greene, Ex parte, TexApp–Houston (14 Dist), 788 SW2d 724.—Child S 497; Const Law 4495.

Greene, In re, CA5 (Tex), 213 F3d 223.—Atty & C 37.1, 42; Contempt 60(3).

Greene, In re, BkrtcyNDTex, 40 BR 807.—Equity 65(3); Home 90, 96.

Greene v. Advanced Micro Devices, Inc., WDTex, 824 FSupp 653.—Armed S 118(6), 120, 122(6).

Greene v. Anders, TexCivApp–Waco, 473 SW2d 622, ref nre.—App & E 770(1); Autos 208, 226(2); Compromise 17(2); Damag 135, 208(1); Evid 493.

Greene v. Barker, TexApp–Fort Worth, 806 SW2d 274, reh of motion for mandamus overr.—Child C 603; Divorce 66.

Greene v. Bates, TexCivApp–Hous (1 Dist), 424 SW2d 5. —App & E 231(9), 934(1), 1024.4; Judgm 199(3.9); Paymt 84(1), 89(6).

Greene v. Bearden Enterprises, Inc., TexCivApp–Fort Worth, 598 SW2d 649, ref nre.—Accord 26(3); Antitrust 145, 146(1), 364, 367, 397; Costs 194.32; Damag 123; Frds St of 139(1).

Greene; Brennan v., TexCivApp–San Antonio, 154 SW2d 523, writ refused.—Deeds 207; Evid 174.3; Judgm 91, 237(1), 273(7), 497(1); Mtg 74; Parties 27; Plead 304; Pretrial Proc 511.

Greene; Brotherhood of Locomotive Firemen and Enginemen v., TexCivApp–El Paso, 122 SW2d 656, writ dism.—Insurance 1091(8), 3540; Trial 352.21.

Greene; Calvert v., TexCivApp–San Antonio, 326 SW2d 592.—Plead 111.42(11); Venue 5.1, 5.3(1), 7.5(5).

Greene; Cates v., TexCivApp–Austin, 114 SW2d 592.— Ack 37(1), 61; Frds St of 63(2); Home 81, 119, 133; Hus & W 267(1); Lim of Act 19(1), 84(1); Mines 75, 79.1(2); Ven & Pur 196.

Greene v. C I R, CCA5 (Tex), 141 F2d 645, cert den 65 SCt 45, 323 US 717, 89 LEd 577.—Int Rev 4657, 4707, 4722, 4742.

Greene v. Condor Petroleum Co., TexComApp, 140 SW2d 844, 135 Tex 215.—Partners 108; Plead 34(3), 193(1); Ten in C 31, 33, 38(7).

Greene; Condor Petroleum Co. v., TexCivApp–Eastland, 164 SW2d 713, writ refused wom.—Action 1, 61; Atty & C 103; Lim of Act 43, 50(2), 119(3), 178, 195(3); Princ & A 172.

Greene v. Condor Petroleum Co., TexCivApp–Eastland, 121 SW2d 381, rev 140 SW2d 844, 135 Tex 215.—Mines 96, 99(2); Partners 108; Plead 18, 49, 312.

Greene; Dreyer v., Tex, 871 SW2d 697.—App & E 170(2); Divorce 172.

Greene; Dreyer v., TexApp–Houston (1 Dist), 809 SW2d 262, writ gr, aff 871 SW2d 697.—Child 30, 33, 73; Divorce 172; Infants 78(1).

Greene v. Great Am. Ins. Co., TexCivApp–Beaumont, 516 SW2d 739, ref nre.—Insurance 2660, 2772, 2778.

Greene v. Gregg, TexCivApp–Tyler, 520 SW2d 924.— Action 6; App & E 781(1), 1175(3); Const Law 2600; Costs 241.

Greene; Home Ins. Co. v., Tex, 453 SW2d 470.—App & E 1060.1(1).

Greene; Home Ins. Co. v., TexCivApp–Texarkana, 443 SW2d 326, aff 453 SW2d 470.—App & E 80(1); Insurance 3164; Judgm 313, 326, 526; Trial 131(1).

Greene; Kimbell Milling Co. v., Tex, 170 SW2d 191, 141 Tex 84.—App & E 846(5); Estop 75; Sales 4(4); Wareh 8, 10, 12, 25(7).

Greene; Kimbell Milling Co. v., TexCivApp–Fort Worth, 162 SW2d 991, aff 170 SW2d 191, 141 Tex 84.—App & E 832(1), 931(1), 989, 994(3), 1008.1(3); Bailm 3, 16; Contracts 309(1); Princ & A 147(2); Sales 234(3); Trover 11; Wareh 25(7), 34(2), 34(7), 34(8).

Greene; Metropolitan Life Ins. Co. v., TexCivApp–El Paso, 93 SW2d 1241.—App & E 1050.1(12), 1151(1); Evid 509; Insurance 1088, 1091(1), 1847, 2536, 2578, 3153; Trial 352.4(4).

Greene v. Mobil Oil Corp., EDTex, 66 FSupp2d 822.— Fed Civ Proc 381; Rem of C 79(1), 101.1.

Greene v. Mobil Oil Corp., EDTex, 188 FRD 430.—Fed Civ Proc 388; Rem of C 115.

Greene v. Moore, NDTex, 373 FSupp 1194.—Const Law 4212(2); Schools 177.

Greene; North River Ins. Co. of New Jersey v., TexApp–El Paso, 824 SW2d 697, writ den.—Courts 85(2); Pretrial Proc 472, 476; Work Comp 1686.

Greene v. Plano Independent School Dist., CA5 (Tex), 103 FedAppx 542.—Const Law 4199; Schools 89.7.

Greene v. Plano, I.S.D., EDTex, 227 FSupp2d 615, aff 103 FedAppx 542.—Civil R 1039, 1304; Consp 7.5(1); Const Law 1083, 4166(2), 4199; Schools 89.7.

Greene; Postal Mut. Indem. Co. v., TexCivApp–Amarillo, 180 SW2d 220, writ refused wom.—App & E 1010.1(1); Insurance 3381(5).

Greene; St. Louis Southwestern Ry. Co. v., TexCivApp–Texarkana, 552 SW2d 880.—App & E 996, 1004(3); Damag 212; Labor & Emp 2801, 2824, 2830, 2848, 2858, 2862, 2881, 2887, 2895.

Greene v. Schuble, Tex, 654 SW2d 436.—Child C 23; Guard & W 26; Hab Corp 532(1), 532(2).

Greene v. Smith, TexCivApp–Eastland, 148 SW2d 909.— App & E 877(4); Estop 24; Evid 95, 96(1), 96(2), 98; Plead 212, 228.15, 228.19; Quiet T 44(3).

Greene v. Southland Corp., NDTex, 83 FRD 117.—Civil R 1101; Fed Civ Proc 161, 184.10.

Greene v. State, TexCrimApp, 247 SW2d 102.—Crim Law 1090.1(1).

Greene v. State, TexCrimApp, 93 SW2d 446.—Crim Law 1182.

Greene v. State, TexApp–Houston (1 Dist), 124 SW3d 789, petition for discretionary review refused.—Crim Law 566, 586, 593, 641.10(1), 641.13(1), 641.13(6), 1151.

Greene v. State, TexApp–San Antonio, 225 SW3d 324.— Crim Law 625.10(3), 1148.

Greene v. State, TexApp–San Antonio, 928 SW2d 119.— Crim Law 31.5, 351(10), 369.2(1), 641.13(1), 641.13(2.1), 641.13(6), 772(6), 775(2), 1172.1(3); Homic 527; Witn 318, 345(5).

Greene v. State, TexApp–Dallas, 651 SW2d 948, petition for discretionary review gr, aff 676 SW2d 359.—Crim Law 720(9), 1043(2); Jury 131(4); Witn 347, 367(1), 372(2).

Greene v. State, TexCivApp–Hous (1 Dist), 537 SW2d 100. —App & E 846(5), 907(3); Const Law 4337; Crim Law 393(1); Mental H 32, 41, 42; Witn 302.

Greene v. Thiet, TexApp–San Antonio, 846 SW2d 26, as mod on denial of reh, and writ den.—Assault 2; Health 821(3), 906, 907; Judgm 181(33), 185(2), 185.3(21); Neglig 375, 379.

Greene; U.S. v., CA5 (Tex), 61 F3d 1181. See U.S. v. Leonard.

Greene; U.S. v., CA5 (Tex), 697 F2d 1229, cert den 103 SCt 3542, 463 US 1210, 77 LEd2d 1391.—Crim Law 13.1(1), 37.10(1), 37.10(2); Ind & Inf 60, 71.2(1), 71.4(1); Labor & Emp 3264, 3283.

Greene; U.S. v., CA5 (Tex), 578 F2d 648, cert den 99 SCt 1056, 439 US 1133, 59 LEd2d 96.—Const Law 4612; Crim Law 42, 369.2(3.1), 577.12(1), 577.15(3), 577.16(4), 577.16(11), 641.3(4), 713, 747, 1030(1), 1037.1(1), 1037.1(2), 1171.1(2.1), 1171.1(3); Fraud 68, 69(5).

Greene; U.S. v., CA5 (Tex), 496 F2d 1317.—Crim Law 1181.5(7).

Greene v. Watts, TexCivApp–Dallas, 332 SW2d 419.—Evid 351; Wills 53(2), 55(1), 337, 400.

Greene; Wheeler v., TexApp–Tyler, 194 SW3d 1, reh overr.—App & E 230, 231(1), 242(1), 242(2), 242(3), 552, 907(4), 981; New Tr 99, 101, 102(3); Trusts 167, 376.

Greene v. White, Tex, 153 SW2d 575, 137 Tex 361, 136 ALR 626.—Adv Poss 13, 115(1); Bound 37(1); Covenants 18; Deeds 8, 105, 143, 153; Estop 22(2), 24, 26, 29, 44; Home 81, 143; Hus & W 273(1), 274(1); Logs 3(9); Mines 49, 55(1), 55(4); Tresp to T T 41(3); Ven & Pur 59, 253.

Greene; White v., TexCivApp–Eastland, 129 SW2d 801, rev 153 SW2d 575, 137 Tex 361, 136 ALR 626.—Adv Poss 52, 60(1); Estop 15, 25; Evid 584(1); Mines 55(1); Tresp to T T 38(1), 41(1).

Greene v. Young, TexApp–Houston (1 Dist), 174 SW3d 291, reh overr, and review den.—App & E 984(1); Atty & C 24; Bankr 2011, 2060.1, 2062, 2187, 2461; Const Law 4426; Costs 2; Courts 78; Plead 48, 427.

Greene Home Owners Ass'n, Inc.; Southwest Industries Inv. Co. v., TexCivApp–Dallas, 608 SW2d 758.—Afft 18; Assoc 12; Evid 264, 351, 474.5, 508, 571(1); Judgm 181(15.1).

Greene Production Co.; O'Brien v., TexCivApp–Fort Worth, 151 SW2d 900.—Judgm 252(3); Mines 74(6), 110, 113.

Greener v. Cadle Co., NDTex, 298 BR 82.—Bankr 2157, 2163, 2924, 2925.1, 3770, 3782, 3784, 3785.1, 3786; B & L Assoc 42(16); Courts 99(1), 99(3), 99(7); Evid 351, 373(1), 382; Fed Civ Proc 103.2, 111; Plead 290(3).

Greener v. Greener, TexCivApp–Amarillo, 413 SW2d 949, ref nre.—App & E 171(1), 218.2(2); Trusts 373.

Greener; Greener v., TexCivApp–Amarillo, 413 SW2d 949, ref nre.—App & E 171(1), 218.2(2); Trusts 373.

Greener & Sumner Const., Inc.; Grissom v., TexApp–El Paso, 676 SW2d 709, ref nre.—Alt Disp Res 312, 314, 354, 363(8), 369; Damag 89(2).

Greener & Sumner Const., Inc.; Wood Butchers Trim Co. v., TexApp–El Paso, 676 SW2d 709. See Grissom v. Greener & Sumner Const., Inc.

Greene's Pressure Testing & Rentals, Inc. v. Flournoy Drilling Co., CA5 (Tex), 113 F3d 47, reh den (#96-20856).—Fed Cts 660.1, 660.20; Indem 30(5).

Greene's Pressure Treating & Rentals, Inc. v. Fulbright & Jaworski, L.L.P., TexApp–Houston (1 Dist), 178 SW3d 40.—Atty & C 63, 64; Corp 445, 445.1, 589, 590(1); Fraud 7.

Greenfeld v. San Jacinto Ins. Co., TexCivApp–Houston, 319 SW2d 134.—App & E 846(5), 931(1), 989; Evid 256; Insurance 2166(3), 2201, 3571; Plead 34(1), 34(3), 34(5).

Green-Gro Seed Co. v. Perry, TexCivApp–Amarillo, 399 SW2d 898.—Corp 503(1).

Greenhalgh v. Service Lloyds Ins. Co., Tex, 787 SW2d 938.—Plead 237(6), 245(6), 250.

Greenhalgh; Service Lloyds Ins. Co. v., TexApp–Austin, 771 SW2d 688, writ gr, rev 787 SW2d 938.—App & E 218.2(2), 760(1), 1062.2; Courts 100(1); Damag 49.10, 192; Insurance 3375; Pretrial Proc 313; Work Comp 1042, 2237.

Greenhaw v. Lubbock County Beverage Ass'n, CA5 (Tex), 721 F2d 1019, reh den 726 F2d 752.—Antitrust 560, 821, 861, 977(5), 980, 984, 985, 989, 990; Commerce

62.10(1), 62.13, 209; Evid 571(9); Fed Civ Proc 162, 172, 181.5, 843; Fed Cts 830; Lim of Act 104(1).

Greenhaw; Republic Underwriters v., TexCivApp–El Paso, 114 SW2d 362.—Evid 222(2); Work Comp 1490, 1932, 1968(8).

Greenhaw Energy, Inc., In re, BkrtcySDTex, 359 BR 636.—Bankr 2154.1, 2162, 2164.1, 2532, 2545, 2553, 2556, 2645.1, 2649, 2722; Consp 1.1, 2, 10, 18; Corp 397; Fraud Conv 9, 24(1); Mtg 379.

Greenhill; Atchley v., CA5 (Tex), 517 F2d 692, reh den 521 F2d 814, cert den 96 SCt 1115, 424 US 915, 47 LEd2d 320.—Courts 509.

Greenhill; Atchley v., SDTex, 373 FSupp 512, aff 517 F2d 692, reh den 521 F2d 814, cert den 96 SCt 1115, 424 US 915, 47 LEd2d 320.—Civil R 1376(8); Courts 509; Fed Civ Proc 1835; Fed Cts 11; Judges 36; Judgm 828.20(1).

Greenhill; Cameron v., Tex, 582 SW2d 775.—Admin Law 4.1; Const Law 4273(1); Judges 42.

Greenhill; Cameron v., TexCivApp–Austin, 577 SW2d 389, writ refused 582 SW2d 775, cert den 100 SCt 142, 444 US 868, 62 LEd2d 92.—Admin Law 4.1.

Greenhill v. Merchants Fast Motor Lines, Inc., NDTex, 886 FSupp 9.—Labor & Emp 2801; States 18.46.

Greenhouse; University of Texas Medical Branch at Galveston v., TexApp–Houston (1 Dist), 889 SW2d 427, reh overr, and writ den.—Const Law 328, 2314, 2315, 3454; Mun Corp 741.15, 741.30, 741.40(1).

Greenhouse Patio Apartments v. Aetna Life Ins. Co., CA5 (Tex), 868 F2d 153.—Judgm 724; Mtg 209, 298(1); Usury 53.

Green, Inc. v. Questor Drilling Corp., TexApp–Amarillo, 946 SW2d 907. See Melvin Green, Inc. v. Questor Drilling Corp.

Green Intern., Inc. v. Allied Steel General Contractors, Tex, 951 SW2d 384. See Green Intern., Inc. v. Solis.

Green Intern., Inc. v. Solis, Tex, 951 SW2d 384.—App & E 218.2(3.1), 1062.2; Contracts 232(0.5), 299(2); Costs 194.14, 194.32, 198, 206; Fraud 3, 64(2); Pub Contr 65; Trover 4, 60.

Green Intern., Inc. v. State, TexApp–Austin, 877 SW2d 428, reh overr, and writ den, and writ withdrawn, and writ gr, and dism.—App & E 684(4), 919, 1071.1(2); Const Law 2311, 2312; Em Dom 2(1), 2(1.1), 122, 266, 280; States 191.1, 191.4(1), 191.9(1), 191.9(3), 208; Statut 22, 26; Trial 388(2).

Greenland; Burr v., TexCivApp–El Paso, 356 SW2d 370, ref nre.—App & E 1172(2); Partners 1, 44, 53; Spec Perf 1, 6, 28(1), 121(3).

Greenland; McDowell v., TexCivApp–Austin, 259 SW2d 305, ref nre.—Contracts 312(1), 322(3); Deeds 165; Evid 461(2); Tresp to T T 4; Witn 414(1).

Greenland v. Pryor, TexCivApp–San Antonio, 360 SW2d 423.—Mtg 197, 467(1), 469; Receivers 4, 9, 42.

Greenland Vistas, Inc. v. Plantation Place Associates, Ltd., TexApp–Fort Worth, 746 SW2d 923, writ den.—Usury 34.

Greenleaf Software, Inc.; Sentry Ins. Co. v., NDTex, 91 FSupp2d 920, vac 2000 WL 33254495.—Insurance 1832(1), 2098, 2270(2), 2298, 2302, 2303(1), 2934(2), 3335.

Greenlee v. Allread, CA5 (Tex), 126 FedAppx 656.—Autos 349(2.1).

Greenlee v. State, TexApp–Dallas, 648 SW2d 783, petition for discretionary review refused.—Obscen 11, 17.

Greenlee; Williams ex rel. Williams v., NDTex, 210 FRD 577.—Fed Civ Proc 1323.1, 1345, 1355.1, 1383.

Greenlees v. Eidenmuller Enterprises, Inc., CA5 (Tex), 32 F3d 197.—Civil R 1111; Statut 219(2), 219(6.1).

Greenlees v. Express Temporary Services, Inc., CA5 (Tex), 32 F3d 197. See Greenlees v. Eidenmuller Enterprises, Inc.

Green Light Co. v. U.S., CA5 (Tex), 405 F2d 1068.—Int Rev 3632.1, 3633, 5095.

Green Light Co., Inc. v. Moore, TexCivApp–Hous (14 Dist), 485 SW2d 360.—App & E 762; Evid 587; Plead 111.42(7).

Green Machinery Co. v. Green, TexCivApp–Amarillo, 266 SW2d 279.—Contracts 176(1), 322(1), 323(1); Trial 351.2(2).

Green Machinery Co. v. Smithee, TexCivApp–Amarillo, 474 SW2d 279.—Ex & Ad 437(7).

Greenman v. City of Fort Worth, TexCivApp–Fort Worth, 308 SW2d 553, ref nre.—App & E 1170.1; Const Law 2642; Em Dom 84, 203(2), 262(5); Evid 560; Jury 131(3), 131(15.1); Waters 40.

Green Motor Co.; Southern County Mut. Ins. Co. v., TexCivApp–Austin, 248 SW2d 959, ref nre.—Damag 105, 113; Insurance 2179(2), 2730, 2732.

Greeno v. Killebrew, TexApp–San Antonio, 9 SW3d 284. —Const Law 3964, 3965(5); Courts 12(2.1), 12(2.25).

Greeno v. State, TexApp–Houston (14 Dist), 46 SW3d 409. —Const Law 4582; Crim Law 641.13(1), 641.13(2.1), 641.13(6), 656(9), 1036.2; Ind & Inf 171; Infants 20; Witn 77.

Green Oaks Apts., Ltd.; Cannan v., Tex, 758 SW2d 753. —Inj 150, 230(4).

Green Oaks Apts., Ltd. v. Cannan, TexApp–San Antonio, 696 SW2d 415, appeal after remand 749 SW2d 128, writ den with per curiam opinion 758 SW2d 753.—Abate & R 12; Action 16; Courts 493(2); Equity 16, 17; Inj 106; Judgm 644, 650.

Green Oaks, Ltd. v. Cannan, TexApp–San Antonio, 749 SW2d 128, writ den with per curiam opinion 758 SW2d 753.—Assign 80; Elect of Rem 2, 7(1); Inj 219, 232; Pretrial Proc 134.

Green Oaks Operator, Inc.; Bush v., TexApp–Dallas, 39 SW3d 669.—Health 602, 700, 800, 813; Plead 34(1).

Greenpark Surgery Center Associates, Ltd.; Miller v., TexApp–Houston (14 Dist), 974 SW2d 805, reh overr, and rule 537(f) motion overr.—App & E 387(6), 782, 911.3.

Green Pastures Water Co., Inc. v. Zent, TexCivApp–Beaumont, 575 SW2d 316.—Venue 7(4), 7(7).

Greenpeace, Inc. v. Exxon Mobil Corp., TexApp–Dallas, 133 SW3d 804, reh overr, and review den.—Action 16; App & E 946, 954(1), 1010.1(3); Const Law 1845; Courts 7, 17, 18, 19; Equity 36; Inj 1, 110, 132, 135, 138.1, 138.3, 138.31, 139, 157, 192.

GreenPoint Credit Corp. v. Perez, TexApp–San Antonio, 75 SW3d 40, reh overr, and review gr (2 pets), and vac. —Antitrust 390; App & E 207, 216(1), 230, 1004(1), 1004(3), 1004(11), 1024.1, 1151(2); Corp 498; Damag 97, 102, 140.7, 221(8); Jury 97(1), 131(18), 132; New Tr 20, 27, 44(1), 56; Trial 125(1), 317.

Greensboro News & Record, Inc.; Ouazzani-Chahdi v., CA5 (Tex), 200 FedAppx 289.—Fed Cts 79.

Greenspan; Blieden v., Tex, 751 SW2d 858.—Judgm 181(34); Plead 36(2).

Greenspan; Blieden v., TexApp–Beaumont, 742 SW2d 93, rev 751 SW2d 858.—App & E 172(1), 179(1); Judgm 185(1); Plead 36(1); Trusts 38, 112, 237.

Greenspan v. Green, TexCivApp–Dallas, 255 SW2d 917, ref nre.—Judgm 185.3(1), 585(4), 704, 878(1).

Greenspan v. Ross, TexApp–Texarkana, 949 SW2d 45, reh overr, and review den.—App & E 347(1), 782; New Tr 118.

Greenspan v. Shalala, CA5 (Tex), 38 F3d 232, reh den, cert den 115 SCt 1984, 514 US 1120, 131 LEd2d 871.— Admin Law 763, 791; Social S 140.5, 140.41, 142.16, 143.40, 143.45, 143.55, 143.60, 143.65, 143.70, 148.5, 149.5.

Greenspan v. State, TexCivApp–Fort Worth, 618 SW2d 939, ref nre.—Atty & C 48, 57.

Greenspoint Co.; Greenspoint Palms, Ltd. v., TexApp–Houston (14 Dist), 795 SW2d 219.—Bankr 2395; Const Law 3998; Judgm 138(3), 143(3), 145(2), 146, 151, 159, 162(2), 163.

Greenspoint Palms, Ltd. v. Greenspoint Co., TexApp–Houston (14 Dist), 795 SW2d 219.—Bankr 2395; Const Law 3998; Judgm 138(3), 143(3), 145(2), 146, 151, 159, 162(2), 163.

Greenspun; C.I.R. v., CCA5 (Tex), 156 F2d 917.—Int Rev 3362, 3620, 3749, 4027.

Greenspun v. Greenspun, Tex, 198 SW2d 82, 145 Tex 374.—Corp 171, 312(7), 320(11); Lim of Act 24(1), 100(1).

Greenspun; Greenspun v., Tex, 198 SW2d 82, 145 Tex 374.—Corp 171, 312(7), 320(11); Lim of Act 24(1), 100(1).

Greenspun v. Greenspun, TexCivApp–Fort Worth, 211 SW2d 977, ref nre.—App & E 930(1), 989, 1060.1(8); Corp 94, 171, 619, 625; Evid 76, 568(4), 571(7); Trial 125(4), 352.4(2).

Greenspun; Greenspun v., TexCivApp–Fort Worth, 211 SW2d 977, ref nre.—App & E 930(1), 989, 1060.1(8); Corp 94, 171, 619, 625; Evid 76, 568(4), 571(7); Trial 125(4), 352.4(2).

Greenspun v. Greenspun, TexCivApp–Fort Worth, 194 SW2d 134, aff 198 SW2d 82, 145 Tex 374.—App & E 930(1), 989, 1001(1), 1178(6); Corp 65, 94, 114, 171, 312(7); Lim of Act 29(1), 100(11), 197(2), 199(2); Trial 351.5(3).

Greenspun; Greenspun v., TexCivApp–Fort Worth, 194 SW2d 134, aff 198 SW2d 82, 145 Tex 374.—App & E 930(1), 989, 1001(1), 1178(6); Corp 65, 94, 114, 171, 312(7); Lim of Act 29(1), 100(11), 197(2), 199(2); Trial 351.5(3).

Greenstein v. Simpson, TexApp–Waco, 660 SW2d 155, ref nre.—App & E 930(1), 989; Contracts 116(1), 117(2), 318, 322(1); Evid 432; Inj 61(2); Partners 22, 230, 242(5), 242(7); Trial 355(1).

Greenstein, Logan & Co. v. Burgess Marketing, Inc., TexApp–Waco, 744 SW2d 170, writ den.—Accnts 8, 10.1, 11; App & E 205, 231(1), 236(2), 499(1), 499(3), 501(1), 501(3), 548(5), 553(1), 553(2), 683, 948, 959(3), 961, 966(1), 1062.1, 1062.2; Corp 423; Courts 489(9); Damag 184, 221(5.1); Motions 19; Neglig 371, 380, 387; Plead 4, 34(1), 104(1), 228.14; Pretrial Proc 39, 40, 45, 304, 554, 695, 713; Trial 62(2), 295(1), 351.2(8), 351.2(10).

Greenstreet v. Ederer, TexCivApp–Dallas, 567 SW2d 54. —Contracts 100; Judgm 185.3(4).

Greenstreet v. Heiskell, TexApp–Amarillo, 960 SW2d 713.—Judges 51(2).

Greenstreet v. Heiskell, TexApp–Amarillo, 940 SW2d 831, reh overr, and rule 537(f) motion overr, reh den 960 SW2d 713.—App & E 5; Courts 37(3), 41.

Greenstreet; Roberts v., TexCivApp–Waco, 593 SW2d 119.—App & E 692(1), 706(4), 907(4).

Greenstreet; U.S. v., NDTex, 912 FSupp 224.—Adm 1(1); Courts 41; Decl Judgm 203, 271; Sec Tran 92.1, 95; U S 34.

Green Tree Acceptance, Inc. v. Combs, TexApp–San Antonio, 745 SW2d 87, writ den.—Corp 116, 121(5), 121(6); Damag 184; Trial 215, 219.

Green Tree Acceptance, Inc. v. Harrison, TexCivApp–Austin, 595 SW2d 608.—App & E 842(1), 931(1), 989; Evid 10(2), 314(1); Plead 111.42(1).

Green Tree Acceptance, Inc. v. Holmes, TexApp–Fort Worth, 803 SW2d 458, writ den.—Antitrust 201, 367, 369; App & E 931(1), 1008.1(2), 1008.1(3), 1177(8); Corp 428(1).

Green Tree Acceptance, Inc. v. Pierce, TexApp–Tyler, 768 SW2d 416.—Antitrust 207, 358, 389(2), 397, 401.

Green Tree Acceptance of Texas, Inc.; Thurston v., TexApp–Tyler, 853 SW2d 806, reh den, and writ den.— Antitrust 207, 208, 286; Corp 32(11); Judgm 185(2), 186.

Greentree at the Gardens v. Hoechst Celanese Corp., BkrtcyEDTex, 173 BR 1000. See U.S. Brass Corp., In re.

Green Tree Financial Corp. v. Garcia, TexApp–San Antonio, 988 SW2d 776, reh overr.—App & E 232(3), 969, 1067, 1172(5), 1177(5); Corp 498, 521; Evid 584(1); Libel 112(1), 124(8); Trial 228(1).

Green Tree Financial Corp.-Texas; St. Paul Fire & Marine Ins. Co. v., CA5 (Tex), 249 F3d 389, reh den, and motion to certify den.—Fed Cts 776; Insurance 2312, 2911, 2913, 2914, 2915, 2922(1), 3120.

Green Tree Financial Servicing Corp. v. Smithwick, CA5 (Tex), 121 F3d 211. See Smithwick, Matter of.

Green Tree Financial Servicing Corp. v. Smithwick, SDTex, 202 BR 420, rev Matter of Smithwick, 121 F3d 211, sug for reh den 132 F3d 1458, cert den 118 SCt 1516, 523 US 1074, 140 LEd2d 669.—Bankr 3413.1, 3710(6), 3787; Interest 31, 36(1).

Greenville v. State, TexApp–Beaumont, 798 SW2d 361.—Hab Corp 613, 811, 816.

Greenville Ave. State Bank v. Lang, TexCivApp–Dallas, 421 SW2d 748.—App & E 934(2); Banks 148(2); Bills & N 138; Judgm 185(2), 185(5), 185.1(3), 185.3(16), 186; Trial 140(2).

Greenville Ave. State Bank; Leibow v., TexCivApp–Texarkana, 343 SW2d 716, ref nre.—App & E 934(1); Judgm 185.3(21).

Greenville, City of; Alexander v., TexCivApp–Dallas, 585 SW2d 333, ref nre.—Decl Judgm 300; Judgm 524; Pretrial Proc 556.1.

Greenville, City of, v. Emerson, TexApp–Dallas, 740 SW2d 10. See City of Greenville v. Emerson.

Greenville, City of; LJD Properties, Inc. v., TexApp–Dallas, 753 SW2d 204, writ den.—Health 366; Nuis 79, 84, 87.

Greenville, City of; State v., TexApp–Dallas, 726 SW2d 162, ref nre.—Environ Law 361, 384, 389; Evid 245, 359(1); Statut 181(1), 188, 212.3, 227.

Greenville Cotton Oil Co.; American Federation of Grain Processors, A. F. of L. v., TexCivApp–Dallas, 217 SW2d 861.—Courts 90(1).

Greenville Hospital Authority; Childs v., TexCivApp–Texarkana, 479 SW2d 399, ref nre.—Judgm 181(33); Mun Corp 724, 747(4).

Greenville Hospital Authority; Dillon v., TexCivApp–Dallas, 404 SW2d 956.—Char 45(2); Judgm 181(33); 185(6).

Greenville Independent School Dist. v. B & J Excavating, Inc., TexApp–Dallas, 694 SW2d 410, ref nre.—App & E 497(1), 863, 907(4), 1135; Contracts 187(1); Judgm 181(15.1); Pub Contr 24.1, 41, 43, 44; Schools 81(2); Statut 181(1), 188, 239.

Greenville Independent School Dist.; Barrow v., CA5 (Tex), 480 F3d 377.—Civil R 1160, 1346, 1351(2), 1351(5); Const Law 1344; Fed Cts 776.

Greenville Independent School Dist.; Barrow v., CA5 (Tex), 332 F3d 844,reh and reh den 75 FedAppx 982, on remand 2003 WL 21653871, cert den Smith v. Barrow, 124 SCt 547, 540 US 1005, 157 LEd2d 411.—Civil R 1376(1), 1376(2), 1376(10); Const Law 1190(1); Schools 63(1).

Greenville Independent School Dist.; Barrow v., NDTex, 202 FRD 480.—Fed Civ Proc 1345; U S Mag 17, 27, 28, 29.

Greenville Nat. Exchange Bank; Benson v., TexCiv-App–Dallas, 228 SW2d 272, mandamus overr.—App & E 640; Jud S 2; Plead 111.9, 111.39(7); Venue 6, 16 1/2, 22(6).

Greenville Nat. Exchange Bank; Benson v., TexCiv-App–Texarkana, 253 SW2d 918, ref nre.—App & E 1078(5); Banks 40; Corp 63.1; Courts 89, 475(2); Execution 7, 103; Judgm 853(3); Life Est 3, 23; Perp 6(1); Propty 11; Remaind 1, 3; Venue 6; Wills 439, 455, 523, 590, 597(1), 601(1), 612(3), 614(1), 614(4), 634(19), 649.

Greenville Nat. Exchange Bank v. Nussbaum, TexCiv-App–Waco, 154 SW2d 672, writ refused wom.—App &

E 1054(1); Banks 141, 148(1), 148(2), 148(3), 154(8); Corp 617(1); Neglig 387, 1693, 1713.

Greenville, Tex., City of; Hill v., NDTex, 696 FSupp 1123, 28 Wage & Hour Cas (BNA) 1575.—Labor & Emp 789, 790, 827, 2219, 2264(1), 2292(2).

Greenville, Tex., City of; Satterwhite v., CA5 (Tex), 578 F2d 987, cert gr, vac 100 SCt 1334, 445 US 940, 63 LEd2d 773, on remand 634 F2d 231.—Civil R 1522; Fed Civ Proc 161, 164, 164.5, 172, 173, 175, 184.10, 1744.1, 1772, 1793.1; Fed Cts 660.15; Lim of Act 121(1), 124, 126.5.

Greenville, Tex., City of; Satterwhite v., CA5 (Tex), 557 F2d 414, opinion vac on reh 578 F2d 987, cert gr, vac 100 SCt 1334, 445 US 940, 63 LEd2d 773, on remand 634 F2d 231.—Fed Civ Proc 173, 184.10, 184.15; Fed Cts 922.

Greenville, Tex., City of; Satterwhite v., CA5 (Tex), 549 F2d 347, opinion withdrawn and superseded on reh 557 F2d 414, opinion vac on reh 578 F2d 987, cert gr, vac 100 SCt 1334, 445 US 940, 63 LEd2d 773, on remand 634 F2d 231, reh gr 563 F2d 147.—Fed Civ Proc 164, 184.15.

Greenville, Texas, City of; Satterwhite v., NDTex, 395 FSupp 698, aff in part, rev in part 549 F2d 347, opinion withdrawn and superseded on reh 557 F2d 414, opinion vac on reh 578 F2d 987, cert gr, vac 100 SCt 1334, 445 US 940, 63 LEd2d 773, on remand 634 F2d 231, reh gr 563 F2d 147, aff in part, rev in part 557 F2d 414, opinion vac on reh 578 F2d 987, cert gr, vac 100 SCt 1334, 445 US 940, 63 LEd2d 773, on remand 634 F2d 231, opinion vac, appeal dism 578 F2d 987, cert gr, vac 100 SCt 1334, 445 US 940, 63 LEd2d 773, on remand 634 F2d 231, remanded 634 F2d 231.—Civil R 1169, 1535, 1537, 1549; Fed Civ Proc 184.15.

Greenwade v. Bledsoe, TexCivApp–Waco, 282 SW2d 75, ref nre.—Anim 25; App & E 842(1), 930(1), 933(1), 1015(2); Judgm 222, 883(13); New Tr 157.

Greenwade; Gunlock v., TexCivApp–Waco, 280 SW2d 610, ref nre.—Action 57(2); App & E 1064.1(10); Deeds 3, 78, 194(5), 203, 207, 208(1); Sales 53(1); Wills 53(1), 164(1), 164(3), 164(4), 164(5), 164(7), 166(1), 333, 400.

Greenwade; Schmidt v., TexCivApp–Waco, 129 SW2d 324.—App & E 931(1), 931(3), 989; Fraud Conv 95(6), 96(4), 117, 118(2), 118(3).

Greenwade; Southland Life Ins. Co. v., TexComApp, 159 SW2d 854, 138 Tex 450.—Evid 53, 71, 89, 595; Insurance 2027, 2030, 3015, 3580.

Greenwade; Southland Life Ins. Co. v., TexCivApp–Waco, 143 SW2d 648, aff 159 SW2d 854, 138 Tex 450.—App & E 254, 1032(2), 1047(4), 1054(1); Evid 71, 89, 269(2); Insurance 2030; Plead 48, 180(1), 412; Trial 377(2).

Greenwald v. Integrated Energy, Inc., SDTex, 102 FRD 65.—Fed Civ Proc 187, 636; Sec Reg 25.21(1), 25.21(2), 25.30, 25.62(1), 60.18, 60.48(1), 60.51, 60.62.

Greenway, In re, BkrtcyEDTex, 126 BR 253.—Bankr 3411.

Greenway, Matter of, CA5 (Tex), 71 F3d 1177, cert den Boyce v. Greenway, 116 SCt 2499, 517 US 1244, 135 LEd2d 191.—Bankr 2021.1, 3341, 3355(1.10), 3355(1.25), 3355(5), 3782; Const Law 2473; Fed Cts 420, 776; Judgm 634, 720, 724, 828.4(1), 828.21(2); Neglig 273; Statut 188, 190, 212.6.

Greenway, Matter of, WDTex, 180 BR 179, aff in part, rev in part 71 F3d1177, cert den Boyce v. Greenway, 116 SCt 2499, 517 US 1244, 135 LEd2d 191.—Bankr 3355(2.1), 3355(5); Judgm 828.21(2).

Greenway; Boyce v., CA5 (Tex), 71 F3d 1177. See Greenway, Matter of.

Greenway; Boyce v., WDTex, 180 BR 179. See Greenway, Matter of.

Greenway v. Great Atlantic & Pacific Tea Co., TexCiv-App–Eastland, 114 SW2d 435.—App & E 1001(1); Evid 588; Food 25; Trial 140(1).

Greenway v. Greenway, TexApp–Houston (14 Dist), 693 SW2d 600.—App & E 934(1); Hus & W 333(3); Judgm 181(15.1).

Greenway; Greenway v., TexApp–Houston (14 Dist), 693 SW2d 600.—App & E 934(1); Hus & W 333(3); Judgm 181(15.1).

Greenway v. State, TexCrimApp, 101 SW2d 569, 131 TexCrim 620.—Crim Law 394.4(1); Int Liq 249.

Greenway v. State, TexCrimApp, 98 SW2d 1000, 131 TexCrim 313.—Int Liq 205(1).

Greenway Bank & Trust of Houston; R.J. Carter Enterprises, Inc. v., TexCivApp–Hous (1 Dist), 615 SW2d 826, ref nre.—App & E 223; Banks 181; Corp 617(2); Stip 14(12); Usury 82, 83.

Greenway Bank & Trust of Houston v. Smith, TexApp–Houston (1 Dist), 679 SW2d 592, ref nre.—Action 34; Estop 83(1); Evid 590; Guar 42(1), 91; Trusts 25(1); Usury 12, 82, 119, 140.

Greenway Improvement Ass'n; Bank United v., TexApp–Houston (1 Dist), 6 SW3d 705, review den.—Covenants 49.

Greenway Parks Home Owners Ass'n v. City of Dallas, Tex, 312 SW2d 235, 159 Tex 46, reh den 316 SW2d 74, 159 Tex 46.—Adv Poss 16(1), 41, 57, 115(1); App & E 931(1); Covenants 71; Dedi 15, 20(4), 31, 45; Mun Corp 43; Zoning 764.

Greenway Parks Home Owners Ass'n; Peterson v., TexCivApp–Dallas, 408 SW2d 261, ref nre.—Covenants 72.1; Ease 30(1), 36(3); Trusts 189.

Greenway Parks Owners Ass'n v. City of Dallas, Tex, 316 SW2d 74, 159 Tex 46.—Evid 31.

Greenway Park Townhomes Condominium Ass'n, Inc. v. Brookfield Municipal Utility Dist., TexCivApp–Hous (14 Dist), 575 SW2d 90.—Contracts 143.5, 187(1), 254.

Greenwell, In re, TexApp–Texarkana, 160 SW3d 286.—Mand 3(2.1), 12, 26, 28, 42; Motions 40.

Greenwell v. Court of Appeals for Thirteenth Judicial Dist., TexCrimApp, 159 SW3d 645.—Crim Law 303.35(1), 1023(3), 1073; Hab Corp 814; Mand 3(3), 4(4), 53, 61.

Greenwell v. Davis, TexApp–Texarkana, 180 SW3d 287, review den.—Action 13, 17; App & E 66, 68, 70(8), 893(1); Const Law 3970; Courts 8, 511; Mun Corp 170, 723; Offic 114, 116; States 5(1), 5(2), 191.1, 191.2(1), 191.4(1).

Greenwich Ins. Co.; Altivia Corp. v., TexApp–Houston (14 Dist), 161 SW3d 52, rule 537(f) motion gr, on remand 2006 WL 4009594.—Insurance 1835(2), 2117, 2278(11), 2313(2), 2319, 2385, 2914.

Greenwich Ins. Co.; Simmons v., CA5 (Tex), 997 F2d 39. See Pacific Mut. Life Ins. Co. v. First RepublicBank Corp.

Greenwood, Ex parte, TexCrimApp, 307 SW2d 586, 165 TexCrim 349.—Crim Law 252; Hab Corp 474.

Greenwood, In re, NDTex, 237 BR 128.—Bankr 2679, 3351.1, 3351.10(1), 3381; Fed Cts 265, 266.1, 269.

Greenwood v. City of El Paso, TexCivApp–El Paso, 186 SW2d 1015.—App & E 781(4); Const Law 2508; Elections 31, 134, 143, 144; Statut 188, 209, 219(1).

Greenwood; Davis v., TexCivApp–Texarkana, 374 SW2d 741, ref nre.—Courts 198; Lim of Act 24(4), 32(1), 46(9), 55(5); Trusts 61(3).

Greenwood v. Furr, TexCivApp–Fort Worth, 251 SW 332.—Mental H 141.

Greenwood; Gibbs v., TexApp–Austin, 651 SW2d 377.—App & E 719(8), 756, 761, 989; Child C 553, 555, 632, 637, 907; Divorce 183.

Greenwood v. Lowe Chemical Co., TexCivApp–Hous (14 Dist), 428 SW2d 358, rev 433 SW2d 695.—Death 58(1); Judgm 185(2), 185.3(21); Neglig 554(1), 1037(4), 1037(7), 1085, 1314.

Greenwood; McMahan v., TexApp–Houston (14 Dist), 108 SW3d 467, reh overr, and review den, and reh of

petition for review den.—App & E 172(1), 179(1), 179(2), 223, 242(4), 837(10), 856(1), 946, 966(1), 1078(1), 1078(6), 1079; Atty & C 104, 105.5, 114, 129(2); Compromise 8(3), 13, 17(2); Consp 1.1; Contracts 143(2), 143.5, 147(2), 147(3), 152, 159, 160, 176(2), 221(1), 221(2), 278(1), 315; Costs 260(5), 261; Deeds 96; Equity 65(1); Extort 34; Fraud 3, 17, 21, 23; Judgm 181(7), 181(16), 183, 185(2), 185.1(2), 185.3(2), 186; Lim of Act 13, 104(1); New Tr 101, 102(1), 102(3); Pretrial Proc 713; Release 27, 38; Torts 436.

Greenwood; Mohnke v., TexApp–Houston (14 Dist), 915 SW2d 585.—Adv Poss 1, 13, 19, 22, 27, 112, 115(1); App & E 219(2), 662(4), 836, 901, 931(1), 989, 994(3), 996, 1008.1(2), 1008.1(3), 1010.1(2), 1012.1(2), 1012.1(5); Bound 3(1), 26, 37(1), 37(5); Trial 401.

Greenwood v. Societe Francaise De, CA5 (Tex), 111 F3d 1239, reh and sug for reh den 117 F3d 1419, cert den 118 SCt 558, 522 US 995, 139 LEd2d 400.—Fed Civ Proc 2146, 2152, 2602, 2608.1; Fed Cts 641, 643, 764, 798; Ship 84(1), 84(2), 84(3.1), 84(3.2), 84(3.3).

Greenwood v. State, TexCrimApp, 823 SW2d 660.—Crim Law 1100, 1144.13(1), 1144.13(3), 1159.2(7).

Greenwood v. State, TexCrimApp, 495 SW2d 930.—Controlled Subs 80.

Greenwood v. State, TexCrimApp, 246 SW2d 191, 157 TexCrim 58.—Crim Law 925.5(3), 1098.

Greenwood v. State, TexCrimApp, 109 SW2d 1052.—Crim Law 1182.

Greenwood v. State, TexCrimApp, 105 SW2d 888, 132 TexCrim 505.—Crim Law 720(5), 1171.1(2.1), 1171.1(6).

Greenwood v. State, TexApp–Fort Worth, 948 SW2d 542.—Crim Law 590(2), 1036.1(9), 1043(3), 1045, 1063(1), 1153(1), 1177; Sent & Pun 2019, 2041.

Greenwood v. State, TexApp–Dallas, 740 SW2d 857.—Crim Law 347, 721(4), 1037.1(1), 1043(3), 1171.5.

Greenwood v. State, TexApp–Houston (14 Dist), 802 SW2d 10, petition for discretionary review gr, aff 823 SW2d 660.—Crim Law 957(1), 1100, 1109(1).

Greenwood; Texas Centennial Central Exposition v., TexCivApp–Austin, 94 SW2d 813, writ dism.—Inj 143(1); States 168.5.

Greenwood v. Tillamook Country Smoker, Inc., TexApp–Houston (1 Dist), 857 SW2d 654.—App & E 235, 883; Contracts 127(4), 141(3), 206; Pretrial Proc 690.

Greenwood; Transcontinental Ins. Co. of New York v., TexCivApp–Waco, 90 SW2d 1114.—App & E 1069.2; Insurance 2992(2); Trial 140(2), 350.4(3).

Greenwood; U.S. v., CA5 (Tex), 974 F2d 1449, cert den Crain v. US, 113 SCt 2354, 508 US 915, 124 LEd2d 262.—Consp 24(1), 24(3), 24.5, 47(1), 47(2), 47(12); Controlled Subs 86; Crim Law 795(2.26), 795(2.90), 1036.1(3.1), 1036.1(8), 1081(5), 1081(6), 1083; Double J 114.1; Ind & Inf 108; Obst Just 16; Searches 121.1; Sent & Pun 979.

Greenwood v. U.S., CA5 (Tex), 858 F2d 1056.—Admin Law 701; Armed S 101, 153.

Greenwood Floral Co.; Batey v., TexCivApp–Fort Worth, 113 SW2d 647.—App & E 1015(5), 1033(7); New Tr 60; Trial 358, 365.2.

Greenwood Independent School Dist.; Knowlton v., CA5 (Tex), 957 F2d 1172, 30 Wage & Hour Cas (BNA) 1395, reh den.—Const Law 1930, 1932, 1934, 1991; Fed Civ Proc 2197, 2217, 2337, 2651.1; Fed Cts 825.1; Interest 39(2.40); Labor & Emp 40(2), 2387(6); Mun Corp 218(10); Offic 66; Schools 63(1).

Greenwood Ins. Group, Inc.; All-Tex Roofing, Inc. v., TexApp–Houston (1 Dist), 73 SW3d 412, review den, on remand 2004 WL 5142792.—App & E 856(1); Const Law 2450; Insurance 1486, 2260, 2278(11), 3557; Judgm 665, 713(1), 725(1); Lim of Act 13, 55(2), 58(1), 66(6), 199(1).

Greenwood Ins. Group, Inc. v. United States Liability Ins. Co., TexApp–Houston (1 Dist), 157 SW3d 444.—

Contracts 143(2), 147(2), 152, 176(2); Insurance 1832(1), 2268, 2271, 2386, 2911, 2914, 3111(2).

Greer, Ex parte, TexCrimApp, 505 SW2d 295.—Crim Law 641.13(2.1); Hab Corp 845.

Greer, Ex parte, TexCrimApp, 408 SW2d 711.—Sent & Pun 1318.

Greer, Ex parte, TexCrimApp, 215 SW2d 630, 152 Tex-Crim 513.—Bail 42, 43; Hab Corp 800.

Greer, In re Marriage of, TexCivApp–Amarillo, 483 SW2d 490, dism.—App & E 719(9), 756; Divorce 252.3(1), 253(2), 253(4), 278.1; Hus & W 258, 262.1(1), 264(1), 264(2).

Greer; Alexander v., CCA5 (Tex), 162 F2d 65.—Autos 20.

Greer; Armstreet v., TexCivApp–Tyler, 411 SW2d 403, ref nre.—Evid 385, 417(9), 429, 461(1); Judgm 181(11), 185(2), 185.3(2), 186; Release 1, 29(1).

Greer v. Beto, CA5 (Tex), 379 F2d 923.—Const Law 4813; Crim Law 641.13(2.1), 641.13(5), 641.13(6).

Greer v. Beto, SDTex, 259 FSupp 891, rev 379 F2d 923.—Const Law 4789(2); Crim Law 331, 641.13(5); Mental H 18.

Greer v. Beto, SDTex, 230 FSupp 985.—Hab Corp 227.

Greer v. Boykins' Estate, TexCivApp–Beaumont, 82 SW2d 698.—App & E 907(3); Ex & Ad 35(11).

Greer v. Bramhall, CA5 (Tex), 77 FedAppx 254.—Fed Civ Proc 1278.

Greer v. Brock, TexCivApp–El Paso, 91 SW2d 855.—Ack 55(2); Home 128, 216.

Greer; Bullock v., TexCivApp–Eastland, 353 SW2d 929, ref nre.—Em Dom 19.

Greer v. City of Seguin, TexCivApp–San Antonio, 458 SW2d 102.—App & E 428(2).

Greer; Clark v., TexCivApp–Dallas, 232 SW2d 876.—Mun Corp 63.5, 286, 868(1), 921(3).

Greer v. C.I.R., CA5 (Tex), 334 F2d 20.—Corp 1.6(12), 380; Int Rev 3053, 3299, 3634, 4645, 4731.

Greer v. Davis, TexApp–Corpus Christi, 921 SW2d 325, reh overr, writ den 940 SW2d 582.—Assault 9; Judgm 185.3(21); Neglig 554(1), 565; Pub Amuse 82.

Greer v. Ellis, CA5 (Tex), 306 F2d 587.—Hab Corp 674.1, 686, 767.

Greer; Epperson v., TexApp–San Antonio, 626 SW2d 884.—Costs 194.16, 194.22; Trusts 268.

Greer v. Estelle, SDTex, 378 FSupp 162.—Crim Law 1083, 1426(3); Hab Corp 821.1.

Greer v. Franklin Life Ins. Co., Tex, 221 SW2d 857, 148 Tex 166.—Const Law 1123; Insurance 2593, 3374, 3375, 3484; Interpl 35.

Greer v. Franklin Life Ins. Co., TexCivApp–Dallas, 109 SW2d 305, writ dism by agreement.—Corp 428(12); Estop 52(1), 52.15; Home 122, 133, 177(1); Mtg 138; Usury 34, 72.

Greer; Franklin Life Ins. Co. v., TexCivApp–Texarkana, 219 SW2d 137, aff in part, rev in part 221 SW2d 857, 148 Tex 166.—App & E 931(4); Insurance 2593, 3360, 3484, 3496; Interpl 1, 35.

Greer; Futch v., TexCivApp–Amarillo, 353 SW2d 896, ref nre, cert den 83 SCt 728, 372 US 913, 9 LEd2d 721.—App & E 1078(1); Const Law 4475; High 99.1, 105(1); Judgm 185(2), 185.2(1), 185.2(4), 185.2(9), 185.3(11).

Greer v. Greer, Tex, 191 SW2d 848, 144 Tex 528.—Deeds 38(1); Divorce 399(2); Frds St of 100, 110(1); Judgm 226.

Greer; Greer v., Tex, 191 SW2d 848, 144 Tex 528.—Deeds 38(1); Divorce 399(2); Frds St of 100, 110(1); Judgm 226.

Greer v. Greer, TexCivApp–Texarkana, 189 SW2d 104, rev 191 SW2d 848, 144 Tex 528.—Divorce 399(1); Judgm 822(4).

Greer; Greer v., TexCivApp–Texarkana, 189 SW2d 104, rev 191 SW2d 848, 144 Tex 528.—Divorce 399(1); Judgm 822(4).

Greer; Higginbotham & Associates, Inc. v., TexApp–Texarkana, 738 SW2d 45, writ den.—Antitrust 369; Insurance 1669, 1673.

Greer; International Sec. Life Ins. Co. v., TexCivApp–Amarillo, 461 SW2d 230, writ dism woj.—Insurance 3343; Witn 16.

Greer; J. H. Hubbard & Son v., TexCivApp–Austin, 255 SW2d 389.—Acct Action on 14; App & E 1015(5), 1048(1); Costs 194.38; Evid 20(1), 377; New Tr 157, 163(2).

Greer; J. Hiram Moore, Ltd. v., Tex, 172 SW3d 609.—Deeds 90; Judgm 181(15.1).

Greer v. J. Hiram Moore, Ltd., TexApp–Corpus Christi, 72 SW3d 436, reh overr, and review den, and review gr, and reh gr, order withdrawn, aff 172 SW3d 609.—Deeds 120; Mines 55(2).

Greer; Johnson v., CA5 (Tex), 477 F2d 101.—Civil R 1088(4), 1341, 1369, 1371, 1437, 1462; False Imp 33; Fed Cts 403, 944; Mental H 40; Neglig 283; Torts 115, 119.

Greer; Lancaster v., TexCivApp–Tyler, 572 SW2d 787, ref nre.—Assign 18, 19; Ven & Pur 214(2).

Greer v. Litscher, CA5 (Tex), 211 FedAppx 238.—Civil R 1091, 1093, 1445; Fed Civ Proc 392.

Greer; McCrary v., TexCivApp–San Antonio, 242 SW2d 652.—Pretrial Proc 79, 81; Stip 14(7).

Greer v. Newton, TexCivApp–Eastland, 245 SW2d 299.—App & E 912, 989; Plead 111.18, 111.42(3); Venue 28, 29.

Greer; Peshak v., TexApp–Corpus Christi, 13 SW3d 421.—App & E 173(2), 216(1), 843(2); Libel 1, 2, 33, 101(1), 112(1), 113, 117, 119, 120(1), 120(2), 121(0.5), 121(1), 124(8).

Greer; Placemaker, Inc. v., TexApp–Tyler, 654 SW2d 830, dism.—Brok 100, 102; Inj 132, 135, 138.18; Princ & A 147(2).

Greer v. Poulter, TexCivApp–Fort Worth, 189 SW2d 883, writ refused wom.—App & E 389(3), 628(1), 1125; Statut 223.5(6).

Greer v. Railroad Commission of Tex., TexCivApp–Austin, 117 SW2d 142, writ dism.—Admin Law 229, 453, 470; Autos 106, 109, 111; Const Law 4363; Pub Ut 162, 181.

Greer v. Robertson, TexCivApp–Fort Worth, 297 SW2d 279, ref nre.—App & E 253; Dedi 16.1, 41; Ease 7(3), 36(3), 69, 70, 71; Judgm 226, 515; Mun Corp 654, 663(1).

Greer v. Rogers, TexCivApp–Waco, 131 SW2d 782.—App & E 1069.1; Trial 304.

Greer; Scofield v., CA5 (Tex), 185 F2d 551.—Evid 397(6), 424; Int Rev 3288.1, 3377.

Greer v. Scofield, WDTex, 89 FSupp 75, aff 185 F2d 551.—Int Rev 3289.

Greer v. Services, Equipment and Engineering, Inc., EDTex, 593 FSupp 1075.—Adm 1.20(2), 1.20(5); Indem 27, 30(5), 31(1), 33(5).

Greer v. State, TexCrimApp, 544 SW2d 125.—Arrest 63.5(1), 63.5(8), 63.5(9); Autos 349(6), 351.1; Crim Law 394.6(1).

Greer v. State, TexCrimApp, 523 SW2d 687.—Crim Law 404.65, 438(5.1), 599, 700(4), 730(14), 1171.3, 1186.1.

Greer v. State, TexCrimApp, 474 SW2d 203.—Crim Law 1036.1(8), 1137(5).

Greer v. State, TexCrimApp, 468 SW2d 811.—Crim Law 371(6), 1036.1(4), 1038.1(1).

Greer v. State, TexCrimApp, 437 SW2d 558.—Burg 3, 29, 41(3), 41(6); Crim Law 552(3); Oath 2; Searches 107.

Greer v. State, TexCrimApp, 382 SW2d 481.—Bail 55.

Greer v. State, TexCrimApp, 329 SW2d 885, 168 TexCrim 485.—Rob 24.20.

Greer v. State, TexCrimApp, 306 SW2d 371, 165 TexCrim 300, cert den 81 SCt 714, 365 US 827, 5 LEd2d 706.—Crim Law 1090.1(1), 1099.7(2), 1099.10, 1099.13.

Greer v. State, TexCrimApp, 292 SW2d 122, 163 TexCrim 377.—Controlled Subs 29.

Greer v. State, TexCrimApp, 220 SW2d 649, 153 TexCrim 464.—Crim Law 130, 1134(1); Larc 23, 28(1), 55, 59.

Greer v. State, TexApp–Dallas, 783 SW2d 222.—Sent & Pun 2011, 2021.

Greer v. State, TexApp–Tyler, 882 SW2d 24.—Arson 2; Crim Law 369.1, 720(5), 726, 1171.1(2.1), 1171.1(4).

Greer v. State, TexApp–Houston (14 Dist), 999 SW2d 484, reh overr, and petition for discretionary review refused, cert den 121 SCt 185, 531 US 877, 148 LEd2d 128.— Courts 487(1); Crim Law 1147; Judges 47(1), 51(2), 54, 56; Obscen 5.2; Sent & Pun 2004, 2009, 2020, 2021.

Greer; Texas & N. O. R. Co. v., TexCivApp–Austin, 117 SW2d 148, writ dism.—Autos 84, 104, 106, 107(2); Lim of Act 12(1), 39(1), 58(1), 124, 129; Pub Ut 191.

Greer; Thayer v., TexCivApp–Amarillo, 229 SW2d 833, ref nre.—High 99.1; Inj 88.

Greer; Travelers Ins. Co. v., TexCivApp–Amarillo, 83 SW2d 1020.—Plead 111.23; Usury 22, 72; Venue 5.4.

Greer; U.S. v., CA5 (Tex), 158 F3d 228, cert den 119 SCt 1129, 525 US 1185, 143 LEd2d 122.—Const Law 4782; Crim Law 1134(3), 1139, 1158(1); Sent & Pun 665, 761, 977.

Greer; U.S. v., CA5 (Tex), 137 F3d 247, cert den 118 SCt 2305, 524 US 920, 141 LEd2d 164.—Crim Law 1032(1), 1042, 1139, 1144.13(3), 1147, 1159.2(7); Postal 49(8.1).

Greer; U.S. v., CA5 (Tex), 968 F2d 433, reh den, cert den 113 SCt 1390, 507 US 962, 122 LEd2d 764.—Jury 97(1).

Greer; U.S. v., CA5 (Tex), 939 F2d 1076, reh en banc gr 948 F2d 934, opinion reinstated in part on reh 968 F2d 433, reh den, cert den 113 SCt 1390, 507 US 962, 122 LEd2d 764.—Arrest 63.5(4), 63.5(6); Consp 24(2), 29.5(1), 29.5(2), 47(3.1), 48.2(1), 48.2(2); Crim Law 29(5.5), 338(7), 394.5(2), 422(1), 423(1), 427(2), 622, 622.2(3), 622.2(8), 627.7(3), 627.9(1), 627.9(2.1), 700(2.1), 700(3), 810, 814(5), 822(1), 1144.13(3), 1144.13(5), 1158(4), 1159.2(7), 1166(6), 1169.7, 1172.4, 1173.2(2); Searches 164; Sent & Pun 754, 2260; Weap 4; Witn 344(2), 379(1).

Greer; U.S. v., CA5 (Tex), 655 F2d 51.—Crim Law 577.8(2), 577.10(4), 577.11(4), 577.16(7), 577.16(9), 594(4), 867.

Greer v. White Oak State Bank, TexApp–Texarkana, 673 SW2d 326.—Banks 171(5); Impl & C C 4, 10, 110, 122; Paymt 80, 82(1), 82(3).

Greer; Williams v., TexCivApp–Dallas, 122 SW2d 247.— App & E 911.3; Chat Mtg 277; Courts 169(2), 170; Liens 1, 7; Sales 300, 313; Ven & Pur 254(4), 266(1).

Greer; Yaquinto v., NDTex, 81 BR 870.—Bankr 2050, 2058.1, 2134, 3064, 3066(6), 3770, 3777, 3785.1, 3786, 3787; Contempt 3, 4, 72; Fed Civ Proc 837.

Greeson v. State, TexCrimApp, 408 SW2d 515.—Burg 20; Crim Law 841, 842.

Greeson v. State, TexCrimApp, 147 SW2d 804, 141 Tex-Crim 115.—Crim Law 211(3); False Pret 26, 28.

Greeson v. Texas & Pac. Ry. Co., TexCivApp–El Paso, 310 SW2d 615, ref nre.—App & E 217, 500(1), 1060.1(2.1), 1060.1(5); New Tr 32; R R 304, 348(8), 350(2), 352; Trial 118, 125(2).

Greever v. Persky, Tex, 165 SW2d 709, 140 Tex 64.— Guard & W 17; Lim of Act 127(3); Usury 28, 52, 56, 119, 137, 142(1), 142(5).

Greever; Persky v., TexCivApp–Fort Worth, 202 SW2d 303, ref nre.—App & E 1175(1); Courts 202(5); Guard & W 18; Judgm 590(1); Mental H 147.

Greever v. Persky, TexCivApp–Fort Worth, 156 SW2d 566, aff 165 SW2d 709, 140 Tex 64.—Action 24; App & E 1062.1; Lim of Act 127(12); Mental H 141; Plead 34(2); Usury 117, 137, 142(1).

Gregerman, Ex parte, TexApp–Houston (14 Dist), 974 SW2d 800.—Admin Law 501; Autos 144.2(1); Crim Law 43; Double J 3, 5.1, 6, 24, 142; Hab Corp 274, 466; Judgm 648, 751.

Gregg, Ex parte, TexCrimApp, 427 SW2d 66.—Hab Corp 445, 721(1), 792.1.

Gregg, In re, BkrtcyEDTex, 179 BR 828.—Bankr 3550, 3707.

Gregg v. Barron, TexApp–Fort Worth, 977 SW2d 654, review den.—Des & Dist 139; Ex & Ad 420, 438(7); Judgm 183, 185(2); Lim of Act 121(1).

Gregg v. Cecil, TexApp–Beaumont, 844 SW2d 851.— Judgm 186; Pretrial Proc 713, 718, 723.1, 724.

Gregg; City of Corpus Christi v., Tex, 289 SW2d 746, 155 Tex 537.—App & E 286, 373(1), 387(1), 622; Estop 62.4, 62.6, 62.8; Mun Corp 722.

Gregg; City of Corpus Christi v., TexCivApp–San Antonio, 275 SW2d 547, rev 289 SW2d 746, 155 Tex 537.— Consp 19; Fraud 58(1), 64(1); Mun Corp 225(3), 722; Statut 181(1), 190, 212.7, 223.2(1.1), 223.4.

Gregg; City of Corpus Christi v., TexCivApp–San Antonio, 267 SW2d 478.—App & E 281(2), 438, 621(1), 622.

Gregg; Cook v., TexCivApp–Amarillo, 226 SW2d 146, writ refused.—Adop 10, 12, 13; Child C 400; Courts 475(1); Hab Corp 622(1).

Gregg; Crawford v., TexApp–Fort Worth, 815 SW2d 320. See Northeast Community Hosp. v. Gregg.

Gregg v. Delhi-Taylor Oil Corp., Tex, 344 SW2d 411, 162 Tex 26.—Admin Law 228.1; Mines 47, 52, 92.44(1); Tresp 12.

Gregg; Delhi-Taylor Oil Corp. v., TexCivApp–Austin, 337 SW2d 222, writ gr, aff 344 SW2d 419, 162 Tex 38.— Mines 52.

Gregg; Delhi-Taylor Oil Corp. v., TexCivApp–Austin, 337 SW2d 216, writ gr, aff 344 SW2d 411, 162 Tex 26.— Elect of Rem 12; Mines 48, 52, 92.16, 92.42, 92.49.

Gregg v. De Shong, TexCivApp–Fort Worth, 107 SW2d 893, writ dism.—App & E 916(1); Autos 245(30), 245(36); Plead 111.33, 111.45; Venue 8.5(3).

Gregg v. First State Bank of Bishop, TexCivApp–Amarillo, 125 SW2d 319, writ dism, correct.—Arrest 70(2); Const Law 4534, 4544; False Imp 2, 39; Sheriffs 171; Torts 135.

Gregg v. Galo, TexApp–San Antonio, 720 SW2d 116.— Judgm 181(7), 181(30), 185(2).

Gregg; Greene v., TexCivApp–Tyler, 520 SW2d 924.— Action 6; App & E 781(1), 1175(3); Const Law 2600; Costs 241.

Gregg v. Howard, TexCivApp–Houston, 365 SW2d 686, writ dism.—App & E 1050.1(10); Evid 317(2); Relig Soc 31(1), 31(5).

Gregg v. Jones, TexApp–San Antonio, 699 SW2d 378, ref nre.—Wills 862.

Gregg v. Lower Nueces River Water Supply Dist., TexCivApp–San Antonio, 303 SW2d 812, writ refused.— Courts 480(1); Em Dom 166.

Gregg; Mack Financial Corp. v., TexCivApp–Dallas, 435 SW2d 310.—Chat Mtg 273.

Gregg; Mitchell v., TexCivApp–Tyler, 394 SW2d 665.— App & E 770(1), 773(2).

Gregg; Northeast Community Hosp. v., TexApp–Fort Worth, 815 SW2d 320.—Const Law 2649, 2652; Mand 3(2.1), 12, 28, 32; Pretrial Proc 12, 406, 411.

Gregg v. North Texas Bldg. & Loan Ass'n, TexCivApp–Fort Worth, 82 SW2d 1093, writ dism.—B & L Assoc 33(18), 33(19); Usury 100(1).

Gregg v. State, TexCrimApp, 667 SW2d 125.—Arrest 68(4); Const Law 947; Crim Law 517(7), 519(8); Searches 171, 180, 194.

Gregg v. State, TexCrimApp, 376 SW2d 763.—Mun Corp 598, 640.

Gregg v. State, TexCrimApp, 339 SW2d 539, 170 TexCrim 202.—Autos 351.1, 355(2); Crim Law 364(3.1), 429(1).

Gregg v. State, TexCrimApp, 194 SW2d 776, 149 TexCrim 366.—Assault 78.

Gregg v. State, TexApp–Fort Worth, 820 SW2d 191.— Sent & Pun 78, 1840, 1902.

Gregg v. State, TexApp–Corpus Christi, 881 SW2d 946, reh overr, and petition for discretionary review refused. —Burg 2, 7; Crim Law 562, 632(3.1), 660, 854(1), 854(2), 854(7), 1030(1), 1039, 1044.1(1), 1134(8), 1144.13(3), 1144.13(6), 1147, 1152(2), 1159.2(7); Homic 598, 930, 1165; Jury 149.

Gregg; Stretcher v., TexCivApp–Texarkana, 542 SW2d 954.—App & E 931(3), 931(4); Contracts 250; Ref of Inst 13(1), 46; Spec Perf 123; Trial 397(1); Ven & Pur 84.

Gregg; Taylor v., CA5 (Tex), 36 F3d 453, reh den.—False Imp 12, 15(1); Fed Civ Proc 2544, 2546; Fed Cts 776; Mal Pros 16, 35(1), 42; Mun Corp 723; Sent & Pun 2051, 2067.

Gregg & Gregg, P.C.; J.M.K. 6, Inc. v., TexApp–Houston (14 Dist), 192 SW3d 189.—App & E 223, 1079; Contrib 1; Damag 63; Judgm 181(16), 181(19); Lim of Act 49(6), 55(3), 56(2), 95(1), 95(11), 129, 199(1); Mun Corp 111(2); Parties 51(4); Princ & A 159(1), 159(2).

Gregg & Valby, L.L.P. v. Great American Ins. Co., SDTex, 316 FSupp2d 505.—Insurance 1832(1), 1863, 2117, 2278(10), 2390, 2391(2), 3337.

Gregg County; Baker v., TexApp–Texarkana, 33 SW3d 72, appeal dism.—App & E 756, 863, 934(1), 970(2); Civil R 1204, 1207, 1744; Const Law 1106, 1929, 1932, 1947, 3867, 3874(2), 4171; Counties 67; Judgm 183, 185(2), 185(3), 185(5), 185.1(8), 185.3(13); Labor & Emp 40(2).

Gregg County v. Clifford, TexCivApp–Texarkana, 156 SW2d 1006.—Judgm 590(1).

Gregg County; East Texas Chicken Ranch v., TexApp–Texarkana, 893 SW2d 724. See Hang On III, Inc. v. Gregg County.

Gregg County v. Farrar, TexApp–Austin, 933 SW2d 769, reh overr, and writ den.—Action 34; Admin Law 229; Counties 67, 212; Offic 72.41(2); Statut 223.4.

Gregg County; Gamble v., TexApp–Texarkana, 932 SW2d 253.—Labor & Emp 40(1), 50, 51, 182, 216.

Gregg County; Hang On III, Inc. v., TexApp–Texarkana, 893 SW2d 724, reh den, and writ dism by agreement.—App & E 863, 954(1), 954(2); Const Law 4095; Inj 16, 76, 85(2), 126; Zoning 321.

Gregg County Appraisal Dist.; Cherokee Water Co. v., Tex, 801 SW2d 872.—Tax 2187, 2510, 2514, 2515, 2699(5), 2702, 2752.

Gregg County Appraisal Dist.; Cherokee Water Co. v., TexApp–Tyler, 773 SW2d 949, writ gr, aff 801 SW2d 872.—Tax 2513, 2515, 2518, 2519, 2522, 2696, 2699(11), 2720, 2721, 2728; Trial 85.

Gregg County Appraisal Dist. v. Laidlaw Waste Systems, Inc., TexApp–Tyler, 907 SW2d 12, reh overr, and writ den.—Action 35; App & E 930(3), 999(1), 1001(1), 1050.1(1), 1056.1(1); Corp 1.5(1), 1.7(2); Courts 24, 25, 37(1), 37(2); Evid 146, 508; Tax 2176, 2650, 2693, 2694, 2695, 2728; Trial 43.

Gregg County Appraisal Dist.; Melton Truck Lines, Inc. v., TexApp–Texarkana, 864 SW2d 137.—Commerce 72, 73; Tax 2089, 2403.

Gregg County Appraisal Dist.; Wildwood Development v., TexApp–Texarkana, 780 SW2d 434, writ den.—Tax 2640.

Gregg County, Tex.; Craig v., CA5 (Tex), 988 F2d 18.—Counties 228.

Gregg County, Tex.; Perkins v., EDTex, 891 FSupp 361. —Witn 198(1), 199(1), 204(1), 205, 222.

Gregg Indus. Services, Inc.; Berry v., TexApp–Tyler, 907 SW2d 4, reh overr, and writ den.—Work Comp 761, 2107.

Greggs v. Faulk, TexCivApp–Fort Worth, 343 SW2d 543. —Mand 10, 74(2).

Greggs v. Hillman Distributing Co., SDTex, 719 FSupp 552.—Civil R 1122, 1150, 1395(8); Fed Civ Proc 827, 1829.

Greggton Motor Service, Inc.; Stanford v., TexCivApp–Tyler, 579 SW2d 526.—App & E 564(3), 619, 624.

Greg Lair, Inc. v. Spring, TexApp–Amarillo, 23 SW3d 443, writ gr, and review den, and reh of petition for review den.—App & E 856(1); Autos 192(7); Judgm 183, 185(2).

Grego v. State, TexCrimApp, 456 SW2d 123.—Autos 349.5(4); Crim Law 394.4(12), 736(1), 815(12).

Gregorcyk v. Al Hogan Builder, Inc., TexApp–Corpus Christi, 884 SW2d 523, reh overr, and writ den.—App & E 863, 934(1), 1024.4; Assign 110; Evid 587; Judgm 199(3.10).

Gregorian v. Ewell, TexApp–Fort Worth, 106 SW3d 257. —App & E 136, 388, 430(2).

Gregory, In re, SDTex, 214 BR 570.—Atty & C 26; Bankr 2057, 2124.1, 2762.1, 3078(1), 3175, 3192, 3766.1, 3784, 3787, 3861.

Gregory, In re, BkrtcyEDTex, 143 BR 424.—Bankr 3712.

Gregory; Anderson v., TexCivApp–Eastland, 341 SW2d 463, writ dism.—Lim of Act 80, 118(1), 195(3).

Gregory; Baker v., CCA5 (Tex), 111 F2d 770.—Bankr 2062, 2369; Corp 126.

Gregory v. Bilsing, TexApp–Waco, 633 SW2d 356.—Judgm 181(7), 185(2).

Gregory; Brosofske v., TexCivApp–Hous (14 Dist), 463 SW2d 48.—App & E 979(5); Damag 208(8); Land & Ten 161(1), 161(3); New Tr 76(1); Trial 366; Trover 35, 60.

Gregory; Carr v., TexCivApp–Corpus Christi, 472 SW2d 819.—App & E 302(5), 499(1), 500(1), 729, 989, 994(2), 999(1), 1001(1), 1002; Autos 172(6), 244(44); Judgm 199(3.17); Trial 142.

Gregory; City of Austin v., TexCivApp–Texarkana, 616 SW2d 329.—Mand 168(4).

Gregory v. City of Garland, TexCivApp–Dallas, 333 SW2d 869, ref nre.—App & E 758.1, 1122(1); Em Dom 271; Mun Corp 837, 845(4), 845(6); Neglig 1694; Trial 136(3), 142, 143.

Gregory; Cone v., TexApp–Houston (1 Dist), 814 SW2d 413.—Courts 472.1, 472.4(7); Mand 44.

Gregory; Dallas Safety Convoy Co. v., TexCivApp–Beaumont, 374 SW2d 751.—App & E 930(1), 933(1); Autos 245(39), 245(53); Evid 594.

Gregory; Downey v., TexApp–Houston (1 Dist), 757 SW2d 524.—Alt Disp Res 100; Refer 7(1), 25, 26, 27.

Gregory v. Drury, CA5 (Tex), 809 F2d 249, cert den 108 SCt 69, 484 US 816, 98 LEd2d 33.—Fed Cts 420.

Gregory; English v., TexApp–Houston (14 Dist), 714 SW2d 443.—Courts 475(1), 485; Mand 23(1), 26, 28; Mental H 487; Parties 6(2).

Gregory; First Southern Properties, Inc. v., TexCivApp–Hous (1 Dist), 538 SW2d 454.—App & E 931(3); Fraud Conv 159(1), 300(1); Hus & W 6(3).

Gregory v. Foster, TexApp–Texarkana, 35 SW3d 255.—App & E 66, 123, 782; Judgm 215; Motions 51.

Gregory v. Gray, TexCivApp–Hous (14 Dist), 612 SW2d 658.—Plead 409(1).

Gregory v. Gregory, TexCivApp–Houston, 404 SW2d 657, writ dism, and order set aside, and ref nre.—Divorce 231, 249.1, 255.

Gregory; Gregory v., TexCivApp–Houston, 404 SW2d 657, writ dism, and order set aside, and ref nre.—Divorce 231, 249.1, 255.

Gregory; Hamilton v., TexCivApp–Hous (1 Dist), 482 SW2d 287.—Mand 4(1); Wills 229, 312, 400.

Gregory; Herrin Transp. Co. v., TexApp–Waco, 384 SW2d 787.—Autos 244(2.1), 244(41.1); Witn 414(2).

Gregory; Hoover v., TexApp–Dallas, 835 SW2d 668, reh den, and writ den.—Fraud 38; Judgm 185(2); Lim of Act 21(1), 46(6), 95(1), 99(1), 100(12), 106, 179(2), 182(2), 183(5); Plead 34(1).

Gregory v. Jacob, TexCivApp–Eastland, 94 SW2d 513.—App & E 773(4).

GREGORY

See Guidelines for Arrangement at the beginning of this Volume

Gregory v. **Laird**, TexCivApp–Galveston, 212 SW2d 193. —App & E 1010.1(7); Autos 19; Sales 219(2), 235(3).

Gregory v. **Lee**, TexCivApp–Austin, 344 SW2d 698.— Autos 150, 245(39), 245(83).

Gregory v. **Lytton**, TexCivApp–San Antonio, 422 SW2d 586, ref nre.—App & E 78(1); Judgm 217, 335(1).

Gregory v. **MBank Corpus Christi, N.A.**, TexApp–Corpus Christi, 716 SW2d 662.—Char 28; Costs 260(1), 260(5), 262; Courts 26; Decl Judgm 61; Trusts 58.

Gregory v. **Missouri Pacific R. Co.**, CA5 (Tex), 32 F3d 160, reh and sug for reh den 48 F3d 533.—Fed Cts 612.1; Labor & Emp 2830, 2846, 2889.

Gregory; **Order of Ry. Conductors of America v.**, TexCivApp–Eastland, 91 SW2d 1139, writ dism.—Insurance 1822, 1834(2), 2589(1).

Gregory v. **Otts**, TexCivApp–Fort Worth, 329 SW2d 904, ref nre.—App & E 1024.1, 1170.7; Autos 181(1), 181(2), 245(24), 245(61); Evid 333(1); Plead 258(4); Trial 304, 306, 350.3(7).

Gregory; **Pirtle v.**, Tex, 629 SW2d 919.—App & E 169, 187(3), 499(1).

Gregory v. **Pirtle**, TexApp–Eastland, 623 SW2d 955, rev 629 SW2d 919.—Spec Perf 106(1).

Gregory v. **Reynolds**, TexCivApp–Texarkana, 219 SW2d 107.—App & E 500(2); Sales 417.

Gregory; **Rice v.**, TexApp–Texarkana, 780 SW2d 384, writ den.—App & E 207, 226(2), 233(2); Decl Judgm 241; Ex & Ad 7, 430, 450; Interest 39(2.50); Trial 56; Trover 11, 40(5), 46; Wills 740(1).

Gregory v. **Rice**, TexApp–Houston (14 Dist), 678 SW2d 603, ref nre, appeal after remand 780 SW2d 384, writ den.—Action 2; App & E 931(1), 989, 1010.2, 1170.6; Estop 92(1); Evid 18; Frds St of 84; Trial 352.10; Wills 230, 740(2), 740(3), 741.

Gregory; **Road Dist. No. 2, Colorado County v.**, TexCivApp–Beaumont, 120 SW2d 859.—High 90.

Gregory v. **Roberson**, TexCivApp–Hous (1 Dist), 478 SW2d 262, ref nre.—Autos 244(44), 244(58).

Gregory; **Robertson v.**, TexApp–Houston (14 Dist), 663 SW2d 4.—Venue 36, 57.

Gregory v. **Roedenbeck**, Tex, 174 SW2d 585, 141 Tex 543. —Brok 1, 42; Const Law 1066.

Gregory; **Roedenbeck v.**, TexCivApp–Beaumont, 169 SW2d 780, rev 174 SW2d 585, 141 Tex 543.—App & E 670(1); Brok 1, 3; Const Law 1066.

Gregory; **St. Louis Southwestern Ry. Co. v.**, Tex, 387 SW2d 27.—App & E 217, 302(1), 1060.6, 1094(1); New Tr 29, 32, 56, 140(3), 145; Trial 127, 304.

Gregory v. **St. Louis Southwestern Ry. Co.**, TexCivApp–Texarkana, 377 SW2d 847, writ gr, rev 387 SW2d 27.— App & E 842(1), 1170.6; New Tr 44(4), 56; Trial 108.5, 304, 306; Witn 73.

Gregory v. **Smith**, TexCivApp–Waco, 395 SW2d 921, ref nre.—App & E 173(9); Can of Inst 60; Deeds 206.

Gregory v. **State**, TexCrimApp, 495 SW2d 891.—Crim Law 101(2), 641.13(1), 641.13(2.1); Sent & Pun 1503.

Gregory v. **State**, TexCrimApp, 449 SW2d 248.—Crim Law 371(2), 1171.8(1).

Gregory v. **State**, TexCrimApp, 401 SW2d 594.—Assault 92(1); Crim Law 673(5), 706(4), 730(3).

Gregory v. **State**, TexCrimApp, 389 SW2d 301.—Crim Law 736(2); Rob 24.10.

Gregory v. **State**, TexCrimApp, 358 SW2d 388, 172 TexCrim 441.—Crim Law 1130(4).

Gregory v. **State**, TexCrimApp, 329 SW2d 94, 168 TexCrim 452.—Crim Law 507(1).

Gregory v. **State**, TexCrimApp, 99 SW2d 921, 131 TexCrim 411.—Burg 41(1); Crim Law 1038.1(1), 1090.1(3).

Gregory v. **State**, TexCrimApp, 99 SW2d 913, 131 TexCrim 411.—Crim Law 1070, 1182.

Gregory v. **State**, TexApp–Houston (1 Dist), 175 SW3d 800, petition for discretionary review refused by 176 SW3d 826.—Arrest 63.5(4), 63.5(8); Crim Law 1139, 1153(1), 1158(4); Searches 24.

Gregory v. **State**, TexApp–Austin, 815 SW2d 805. See Miller v. State.

Gregory v. **State**, TexApp–Beaumont, 159 SW3d 254, petition for discretionary review refused.—Controlled Subs 26, 27, 28, 30, 73, 75, 77, 79; Crim Law 369.2(1), 369.2(7), 673(5), 1162, 1165(1), 1168(2), 1169.11.

Gregory v. **State**, TexApp–Houston (14 Dist), 56 SW3d 164, reh overr, and petition for discretionary review gr, and petition for discretionary review dism with per curiam opinio, cert den 123 SCt 1787, 538 US 978, 155 LEd2d 667.—Arrest 68(3); Assault 59, 82, 92(5); Crim Law 367, 369.2(2), 369.2(5), 374, 388.1, 388.5(1), 412.2(2), 412.2(3), 414, 469.2, 472, 477.1, 478(1), 479, 487, 526, 671, 695(4), 730(3), 867, 1035(10), 1036.5, 1043(1), 1043(2), 1043(3), 1134(8), 1144.13(2.1), 1144.13(3), 1144.13(5), 1144.13(6), 1147, 1153(1), 1159.2(1), 1159.2(2), 1159.2(7), 1159.2(8), 1159.2(9), 1159.3(2), 1171.8(1).

Gregory; **Suiter v.**, TexCivApp–Galveston, 279 SW2d 909. —Insurance 2610; Interpl 35; Ven & Pur 137.

Gregory v. **Sunbelt Sav., F.S.B.**, TexApp–Dallas, 835 SW2d 155, reh den, and writ den.—App & E 931(1), 989, 1008.1(2), 1010.1(1), 1010.1(2), 1012.1(5); Home 29, 31, 32, 33, 57.5, 90, 95, 96, 170, 177(1), 177(2), 214; Mtg 424.

Gregory v. **Texas Emp. Ins. Ass'n**, Tex, 530 SW2d 105, on remand Texas Employers' Ins Ass'n v. Gregory, 534 SW2d 166.—Evid 570; Pretrial Proc 481; Trial 142; Work Comp 1416, 1704, 1949.

Gregory; **Texas Employers' Ins. Ass'n v.**, TexCivApp–Hous (14 Dist), 534 SW2d 166.—Work Comp 1389, 1607, 1937.

Gregory; **Texas Employers' Ins. Ass'n v.**, TexCivApp–Hous (14 Dist), 521 SW2d 898, writ gr, rev Gregory v. Texas Emp Ins Ass'n, 530 SW2d 105, on remand 534 SW2d 166.—Evid 59, 89; Pretrial Proc 481; Work Comp 637, 697, 798, 799, 1372, 1704.

Gregory v. **Texas Nat. Guard Armory Bd.**, TexCivApp–Eastland, 490 SW2d 608, ref nre.—App & E 78(1), 93, 238(1), 863; Judgm 183.

Gregory; **Texas Textile Mills v.**, Tex, 177 SW2d 938, 142 Tex 308.—App & E 662(3), 1060.6; Autos 246(22); Trial 127.

Gregory v. **Texas Youth Com'n**, CA5 (Tex), 111 FedAppx 719.—Civil R 1126, 1252; Const Law 1181; Fed Cts 269, 272; States 53.

Gregory v. **Tyler Grain & Storage Co.**, TexCivApp–Texarkana, 341 SW2d 221.—App & E 931(1), 934(2), 989; Evid 25(1); Plead 111.36, 430(2); Venue 7.5(3).

Gregory v. **Union Pacific R. Co.**, CA5 (Tex), 32 F3d 160. See Gregory v. Missouri Pacific R. Co.

Gregory v. **U.S.**, SDTex, 111 FSupp2d 851.—Contracts 1, 9(1), 40; Int Rev 4760, 4761.1.

Gregory v. **Watson**, TexCivApp–Tyler, 470 SW2d 151.— Plead 111.17.

Gregory v. **White**, TexCivApp–San Antonio, 604 SW2d 402, ref nre, cert den 101 SCt 3081, 452 US 939, 69 LEd2d 953.—Atty & C 101(1); Judgm 72, 73, 91.

Gregory **Const. Co., Inc.; Metrocon Const. Co., Inc. v.**, TexApp–Dallas, 663 SW2d 460, ref nre.—Action 12; Contracts 303(3), 309(1), 338(2), 346(2); Trial 351.2(4).

Gregory-**Edwards, Inc.; Cedar Bayou Baptist Church v.**, TexApp–Houston (14 Dist), 987 SW2d 156.—Bankr 2154.1, 2650(2); Fraud Conv 2.1; States 18.3, 18.5, 18.7, 18.15.

Gregory **Engine & Mach. Services, Inc., In re**, Bkrtcy-EDTex, 135 BR 807.—Int Rev 4832.

Gregory **Gourmet Services, Inc. v. Antone's Import Co.**, TexApp–Houston (1 Dist), 927 SW2d 31. See J.J. Gregory Gourmet Services, Inc. v. Antone's Import Co.

Gregory-**Portland Independent School Dist. v. Texas Ed. Agency**, CA5 (Tex), 576 F2d 81, reh den Gregory-Portland Independent School District v. Texas Education Agency, 582 F2d 41, cert den 99 SCt 1423, 440 US 946, 59 LEd2d 634.—Fed Cts 1145, 1158.

Gregory-Portland Independent School Dist.; U.S. v., CA5 (Tex), 654 F2d 989.—Const Law 3278(2); Schools 13(4), 13(19), 13(20), 68, 159.5(3).

Gregson v. Zurich American Ins. Co., CA5 (Tex), 322 F3d 883, reh and reh den 75 FedAppx 982.—Admin Law 741; Work Comp 1087, 1187.

Gregston; El Paso Electric Co. v., TexCivApp–El Paso, 170 SW2d 515, writ refused wom.—App & E 1001(1), 1060.1(6); Damag 95, 132(1); Labor & Emp 2778, 2849, 2881.

Greif Bros. Corp.; Gulledge v., TexCivApp–Hous (1 Dist), 499 SW2d 745.—Contracts 205.40, 312(5); Damag 191; R R 87, 109.

Greig v. First Nat. Bank of San Angelo, TexCivApp–Beaumont, 511 SW2d 86, ref nre.—Corp 617(2); Guar 37; Lim of Act 50(1); Usury 16, 52.

Greig; U.S. v., CA5 (Tex), 967 F2d 1018.—Crim Law 641.5(0.5), 641.5(7), 829(4), 1152(1), 1166.10(3).

Greig; U.S.A. v., CA5 (Tex), 796 F2d 742. See Shankle v. U.S.

Greil v. Geico, NDTex, 184 FSupp2d 541.—Evid 219(3); Insurance 3336, 3337, 3359, 3363.

Greiner v. American Motor Sales Corp., EDTex, 645 FSupp 277.—Fed Cts 104, 113.

Greiner; Innes v., TexCivApp–Amarillo, 449 SW2d 83.—App & E 553(2), 1170.6; Insurance 1671; New Tr 140(3), 157.

Greiner v. Jameson, TexApp–Dallas, 865 SW2d 493, reh den, and writ den.—App & E 436, 842(1), 946, 1030; Attach 13; Const Law 4426; Contempt 20; Costs 2; Courts 1; Execution 5.1, 402(1); Garn 7; Interest 14, 39(3); Judgm 7, 16, 232, 297, 340, 501, 505, 855(1); Motions 62.

Greiner v. Rogers, TexCivApp–Eastland, 450 SW2d 665. —Bills & N 116, 133; Lim of Act 163(1); Usury 42, 146.

Greiner v. State, TexCrimApp, 249 SW2d 601, 157 Tex-Crim 479.—Autos 332, 355(13), 357, 418; Crim Law 304(16), 1144.13(3), 1169.2(1), 1169.2(2); Ind & Inf 73(1), 125(29).

Greiner; Thornton Homes, Inc. v., TexCivApp–Eastland, 619 SW2d 8.—Antitrust 203; Sales 262.5; Venue 17.

Greiner v. Zinker, TexCivApp–Beaumont, 573 SW2d 884. —App & E 1045(1); Jury 136(2), 136(3).

Greis; Hart v., TexCivApp–Fort Worth, 155 SW2d 997, writ refused wom.—App & E 758.3(8), 882(16), 930(1); Bound 1, 8, 33, 37(1), 37(3), 40(1), 41; Evid 155(8), 157(2); New Tr 44(2); Trial 215, 219, 248.

Grella v. Berry, TexApp–Houston (1 Dist), 647 SW2d 15. —App & E 954(2); Equity 66; Inj 138.21; Mtg 338; Ven & Pur 77, 95(2).

Grelling v. Allen, TexCivApp–Texarkana, 218 SW2d 896, ref nre.—Mines 59, 79.1(4).

Grelling; Fannin Plaza Offices v., TexApp–Eastland, 837 SW2d 255. See Vivion v. Grelling.

Grelling; Vivion v., TexApp–Eastland, 837 SW2d 255, writ den.—App & E 931(1), 994(3), 1011.1(2), 1012.1(2), 1012.1(4); Nova 1, 10, 12; Trial 405(1).

Gremillion v. State, TexCrimApp, 101 SW2d 560, 131 TexCrim 583.—Crim Law 507(4), 1169.2(5); Ind & Inf 110(31), 122(4); Int Liq 236(8).

Gremillion v. State, TexCrimApp, 100 SW2d 106, 131 TexCrim 492.—Ind & Inf 70; Int Liq 211.

Gremmel v. State, TexCrimApp, 335 SW2d 614, 169 TexCrim 508.—Crim Law 364(4), 519(3); Witn 248(2).

Grenier v. Joe Camp, Inc., TexCivApp–Corpus Christi, 900 SW2d 848.—Antitrust 175, 364, 369; App & E 100(1), 1003(6), 1023; Trial 182, 193(1), 219, 295(1).

Greninger; Jones v., CA5 (Tex), 188 F3d 322, reh and sug for reh den 203 F3d 826, on remand 2000 WL 869506, aff 253 F3d 702.—Civil R 1090, 1093, 1395(7); Const Law 2325; Fed Civ Proc 1052, 1771, 1773, 1823, 1838; Fed Cts 776, 794; Prisons 4(10.1), 4(13).

Grennan v. Forgeron, TexCivApp–El Paso, 101 SW2d 885, writ dism.—App & E 225, 750(5); Lim of Act 19(3), 103(1), 103(4); Mines 101; Tresp to T T 47(1).

Grenwelge v. Shamrock Reconstructors, Inc., Tex, 705 SW2d 693.—Trial 365.1(5).

Gresham v. Beto, CA5 (Tex), 374 F2d 884.—Hab Corp 721(3), 722(1).

Gresham; Boyles v., Tex, 309 SW2d 50, 158 Tex 158.—Ex & Ad 15.

Gresham; Boyles v., Tex, 263 SW2d 935, 153 Tex 106.—Ex & Ad 14; Wills 76, 80, 104, 206.

Gresham; Boyles v., TexCivApp–Dallas, 260 SW2d 144, rev 263 SW2d 935, 153 Tex 106.—Char 4, 10, 31; Perp 8(1); Wills 73, 470(1).

Gresham v. Boyles, TexCivApp–Waco, 301 SW2d 685, rev 309 SW2d 50, 158 Tex 158.—Courts 199; Ex & Ad 15, 26(1).

Gresham v. Califano, SDTex, 510 FSupp 1151.—Social S 124.1, 140.30, 140.45, 140.55, 142.5, 143.45, 143.55, 143.75, 148.20.

Gresham; Lind v., TexApp–Houston (14 Dist), 672 SW2d 20.—App & E 883; Costs 194.32; Damag 127; Judgm 143(5), 145(2); New Tr 17, 152, 157; Pretrial Proc 226.

Gresham; Lind and Fitzmaurice Development Co. v., TexApp–Houston (14 Dist, 672 SW2d 20. See Lind v. Gresham.

Gresham v. McElroy, TexCivApp–Houston, 309 SW2d 84. —App & E 173(4); Bills & N 446; Mtg 218.1, 218.13, 218.16; Paymt 59.

Gresham; Ryans v., EDTex, 6 FSupp2d 595.—Arrest 63.1, 63.4(2), 63.4(5), 63.4(15); Civil R 1009, 1033(1), 1088(4), 1376(1); Consp 7.5(1); Const Law 1982, 3278(1), 3299; False Imp 2, 15(1); Fed Civ Proc 851; Schools 72.

Gresham v. Turner, TexCivApp–El Paso, 382 SW2d 791. —Contracts 147(1); Mines 70(1), 73.1(4), 79.1(2), 79.3.

Gresham; U.S. v., CA5 (Tex), 118 F3d 258, cert den 118 SCt 702, 522 US 1052, 139 LEd2d 645.—Const Law 4149, 4509(25); Crim Law 486(4), 494, 938(1), 942(2), 1144.13(2.1), 1153(1), 1156(3), 1159.2(7); Explos 4; Int Rev 4311, 5265; Weap 4, 17(1).

Gresham; U.S. v., CA5 (Tex), 585 F2d 103.—Autos 341; Crim Law 510, 519(2), 532(0.5), 532(1), 534(1), 534(2), 535(1), 538(3), 1028, 1169.12.

Gress v. Gress, TexCivApp–Galveston, 209 SW2d 1003, 15 ALR2d 700, ref nre.—Contracts 138(4); Divorce 320; Estop 78(1); Marriage 1, 40(1), 50(1), 58(1), 59.

Gress; Gress v., TexCivApp–Galveston, 209 SW2d 1003, 15 ALR2d 700, ref nre.—Contracts 138(4); Divorce 320; Estop 78(1); Marriage 1, 40(1), 50(1), 58(1), 59.

Gressett v. Gressett, TexCivApp–Waco, 143 SW2d 817.—Divorce 91.

Gressett; Gressett v., TexCivApp–Waco, 143 SW2d 817.—Divorce 91.

Gressett v. State, TexCrimApp, 135 SW2d 990, 138 TexCrim 295.—Bail 66; Crim Law 1109(3).

Gressett v. State, TexApp–Dallas, 669 SW2d 748, petition for discretionary review gr, aff 723 SW2d 695.—Autos 413.

Grettenberg v. State, TexCrimApp, 790 SW2d 613.—Ind & Inf 113; Sent & Pun 238.

Greubel; Arista Records LLC v., NDTex, 453 FSupp2d 961.—Copyr 53(1), 67.2, 77, 82; Fed Civ Proc 675.1, 1835.

Greutzmacher; Haase v., TexCivApp–San Antonio, 521 SW2d 666.—App & E 387(2), 387(3), 395; Courts 23, 37(1); New Tr 155.

Greve; Berger v., TexCivApp–Beaumont, 303 SW2d 466, ref nre.—App & E 622; New Tr 12.

Greve v. Cox, TexApp–Dallas, 683 SW2d 535.—App & E 846(5), 931(1), 931(3), 1010.1(1); Damag 81; Hus & W 17; Spec Perf 66; Ven & Pur 13, 80.

Greve; Union Transfer & Storage Co. v., TexCivApp–Galveston, 131 SW2d 796.—App & E 920(3), 954(2); Inj 61(2).

Grevsgard; Fink v., TexCivApp–Galveston, 123 SW2d 383, writ refused.—Jud S 3; Tax 3072(5), 3176.

Grewing; Bentley v., TexCivApp–Fort Worth, 613 SW2d 49, ref nre.—Assign 72; Interpl 35; Mines 74(3).

Grey v. First Nat. Bank in Dallas, CA5 (Tex), 393 F2d 371, cert den 89 SCt 398, 393 US 961, 21 LEd2d 374.—Appear 8(3); Atty & C 70, 72; Damag 91(1); Evid 370(1), 374(8); Fed Civ Proc 1971, 1975, 2117, 2142.1, 2151, 2152, 2173.1(1), 2182.1, 2183, 2215, 2237.1, 2742.5; Fed Cts 372, 631, 822, 841; Judgm 29, 373, 497(1); Princ & A 19; Trusts 227, 262, 263, 377.

Grey v. Longview Nat. Bank, TexCivApp–Texarkana, 161 SW2d 166.—Home 18.

Grey; Snider v., TexApp–Corpus Christi, 688 SW2d 602, dism.—App & E 1027; Child C 553, 555, 577, 601, 637, 657, 907, 920, 923(4), 943; Child S 224; Trial 136(1), 384.

Greycas, Inc.; Ocean Transport, Inc. v., TexApp–Corpus Christi, 878 SW2d 256, reh overr, and writ den.—Adm 1.20(4); Antitrust 128, 147, 286, 359, 397; App & E 901, 925(1), 930(1), 930(3), 946, 969, 984(5), 989, 1001(1), 1003(5), 1003(5), 1177(8); Courts 489(7); Guar 77(2), 81; Interest 31, 38(2); Lim of Act 43, 46(10), 48(1), 66(2), 193, 197(1), 199(1), 201; Pretrial Proc 40, 42; Ship 32; Trial 18.

Grey Forest, City of; Sub-Surface Const. Co. v., TexCivApp–San Antonio, 470 SW2d 157.—Evid 458; Plead 111.15; Venue 7.5(3).

Greyhound Bus Lines, Inc.; Mitchell v., TexCivApp–Tyler, 409 SW2d 914, ref nre.—Trial 350.1, 350.6(4), 352.20.

Greyhound Corp.; Holeman v., TexCivApp–Houston, 396 SW2d 507, ref nre.—App & E 866(3), 927(1), 989; Carr 280(1), 302(1), 316(1.5), 387; Neglig 259, 1614; Trial 350.5(2), 350.6(4).

Greyhound Corp.; Melton v., CA5 (Tex), 354 F2d 970.—Fed Civ Proc 2141, 2142.1, 2462, 2470.4, 2491; Fed Cts 416; Neglig 1104(6), 1693.

Greyhound Corp. v. Stevens, TexCivApp–Eastland, 413 SW2d 439.—Carr 12(5), 405(3), 405(4).

Greyhound Lines, Inc., In Re, TexApp–San Antonio, 138 SW3d 19.—Mand 3(2.1), 12, 32; Pretrial Proc 19, 27.1, 28, 36.1, 41.

Greyhound Lines, Inc. v. Board of Equalization for City of Fort Worth, Tex, 419 SW2d 345.—Mun Corp 971(2), 972(1); Statut 181(1); Tax 2212, 2214, 2216, 2230, 2255, 2257, 2317, 2400, 2403, 2562.

Greyhound Lines, Inc. v. Board of Equalization for City of Fort Worth, TexCivApp–Fort Worth, 412 SW2d 76, writ gr, rev 419 SW2d 345.—Tax 2068, 2401, 2403, 2529.

Greyhound Lines, Inc. v. Craig, TexCivApp–Hous (14 Dist), 430 SW2d 573, ref nre.—App & E 932(1), 979(5), 1004(8), 1140(4), 1151(3); Damag 59, 100, 132(1), 132(2), 173(1), 173(2), 185(1), 187, 208(2), 208(6), 216(4); New Tr 162(1).

Greyhound Lines, Inc. v. Duhon, TexCivApp–Hous (1 Dist), 434 SW2d 406.—App & E 932(1), 1140(4); Damag 40(1), 132(1), 161, 176, 208(2), 208(6), 210(2), 228; Torts 437.

Greyhound Lines, Inc.; Garza v., TexCivApp–San Antonio, 418 SW2d 595.—Carr 234; Courts 8, 9; Evid 362; Torts 103.

Greyhound Lines, Inc.; Gonzalez v., TexApp–El Paso, 181 SW3d 386, reh overr, and review den, and reh of petition for review den.—Action 13; App & E 840(2), 893(1); Corp 182.3; Courts 35; Parties 1, 94(1); Partners 375; Plead 104(1), 111.36, 111.37, 111.38, 111.48.

Greyhound Lines, Inc.; Holmes v., CA5 (Tex), 757 F2d 1563.—Labor & Emp 1219(4); Lim of Act 127(1), 127(11.1), 127(12), 170.

Greyhound Lines, Inc.; Longoria v., TexApp–San Antonio, 699 SW2d 298.—App & E 846(1), 931(1), 1071.1(4), 1071.5; Evid 351; Insurance 1896, 1898, 1914, 1928, 1935, 2039, 2044(1); Trial 394(1), 400(1).

Greyhound Lines, Inc.; Marsh v., CA5 (Tex), 488 F2d 278.—Labor & Emp 189, 219, 237, 256(1).

Greyhound Lines, Inc.; N.L.R.B. v., SDTex, 158 BR 421. See Eagle Bus Mfg., Inc., In re.

Greyhound Lines, Inc.; Oklahoma, State of, ex rel. Oklahoma Tax Com'n v., CA5 (Tex), 50 F3d 317. See Eagle Bus Mfg., Inc., Matter of.

Greyhound Lines, Inc. v. Rogers, CA5 (Tex), 62 F3d 730. See Eagle Bus Mfg., Inc., In re.

Greyhound Lines, Inc.; State of Okl. ex rel. Oklahoma Tax Com'n v., CA5 (Tex), 50 F3d 317. See Eagle Bus Mfg., Inc., Matter of.

Greyhound Lines, Inc.; U.S. v., CA5 (Tex), 761 F2d 211. See State of Tex. v. U.S.

Greyhound Lines, Inc., Amalgamated Council Retirement and Disability Plan; Branson v., CA5 (Tex), 126 F3d 747, cert den 118 SCt 1362, 523 US 1047, 140 LEd2d 512.—Fed Civ Proc 2497.1; Fed Cts 776, 850.1; Labor & Emp 438, 544, 688, 696(1), 1243, 1329, 1670, 1967; States 18.46.

Greyhound Van Lines, Inc. v. Bellamy, TexCivApp–Waco, 502 SW2d 586.—Autos 197(1), 197(3); Bailm 7; Labor & Emp 3027.

Greystar Const. LP; Ellison Steel, Inc. v., CA5 (Tex), 199 FedAppx 324.—Alt Disp Res 375.

Greystone III Joint Venture, In re, BkrtcyWDTex, 102 BR 560, opinion aff 127 BR 138, rev 995 F2d 1274, on reh, cert den Greystone III Joint Venture v. Phoenix Mut Life Ins Co, 113 SCt 72, 506 US 821, 121 LEd2d 37, cert den 113 SCt 72, 506 US 822, 121 LEd2d 37.—Bankr 3550, 3561, 3564.

Greystone III Joint Venture, Matter of, CA5 (Tex), 995 F2d 1274, on reh, cert den Greystone III Joint Venture v. Phoenix Mut Life Ins Co, 113 SCt 72, 506 US 821, 121 LEd2d 37, cert den 113 SCt 72, 506 US 822, 121 LEd2d 37.—Bankr 2834, 3103.2, 3544, 3550, 3787.

Greystone III Joint Venture, Matter of, WDTex, 127 BR 138, rev 995 F2d 1274, on reh, cert den Greystone III Joint Venture v. Phoenix Mut Life Ins Co, 113 SCt 72, 506 US 821, 121 LEd2d 37, cert den 113 SCt 72, 506 US 822, 121 LEd2d 37.—Bankr 3544, 3550, 3561.

Greystone III Joint Venture; Phoenix Mut. Life Ins. Co. v., CA5 (Tex), 995 F2d 1274. See Greystone III Joint Venture, Matter of.

Greystone III Joint Venture; Phoenix Mut. Life Ins. Co. v., WDTex, 127 BR 138. See Greystone III Joint Venture, Matter of.

Grey Wolf Drilling Co.; Weber Energy Corp. v., TexApp–Houston (1 Dist),976 SW2d 766, reh overr, and review den, and withdrawn, and review gr, rev Ken Petroleum Corp v. Questor Drilling Corp, 24 SW3d 344, reh overr.—Indem 27.

Grey Wolf Drilling Co., L.P. v. Boutte, TexApp–Houston (14 Dist), 154 SW3d 725, review gr, judgment vac, and remanded by agreement.—App & E 931(4), 1003(5), 1003(7), 1060.1(10); Damag 127.65, 185(1); Jury 131(1), 131(2), 131(3), 131(13); Mines 118; Neglig 503, 1001, 1011, 1013, 1037(4), 1088, 1089, 1593; Trial 106, 121(2).

Gribbin Supply Co., Inc., In re, NDTex, 371 FSupp 664.—Bankr 2553, 2927, 3066(4.1), 3066(5); Contracts 150; Corp 306, 376, 542(3), 550(10), 562(1).

Gribble; Blackstock v., TexCivApp–Eastland, 312 SW2d 289, ref nre.—App & E 1073(1); Contracts 171(1), 322(1); Estop 118; Evid 271(19), 417(9); Partners 336(3); Spec Perf 65, 121(3); Trial 350.4(2); Trusts 110, 371(8).

Gribble v. Call, TexCivApp–Eastland, 123 SW2d 711, writ dism, correct.—Adv Poss 10, 31, 96; App & E 854(1); Assoc 15(3), 20(2); Tresp to T T 6.1.

Gribble; City of Houston v., TexCivApp–Tyler, 542 SW2d 242, ref nre.—Contracts 299(1), 305(1); Cust & U 17; Estop 62.4; Mun Corp 362(2), 374(1).

Gribble; City State Bank in Wellington v., TexCivApp–Amarillo, 256 SW2d 872.—Courts 26; Impl & C C 76.

Gribble v. Harris, CA5 (Tex), 625 F2d 1173.—Fed Civ Proc 2294, 2366.1, 2658; Fed Cts 653, 657, 658.

Gribble; Humphreys v., TexCivApp–Waco, 227 SW2d 235, ref nre.—Adv Poss 31, 33, 34, 38, 43(2), 85(1); App & E 933(4); New Tr 143(5).

Gribble v. Johnson, SDTex, 8 FSupp2d 942, aff 196 F3d 1258, cert den 120 SCt 1201, 528 US 1173, 145 LEd2d 1104.—Const Law 4693, 4745; Courts 100(1); Crim Law 394.1(3), 412.1(4), 412.2(2), 412.2(4), 412.2(5), 523, 538(3), 730(14); Fed Civ Proc 2546; Hab Corp 383, 423, 461, 497, 767, 770, 775(1); Homic 1141, 1143; Jury 108; Sent & Pun 1780(2), 1780(3).

Gribble v. State, TexCrimApp, 808 SW2d 65, reh den, cert den 111 SCt 2856, 501 US 1232, 115 LEd2d 1023.—Crim Law 535(1), 535(2), 552(3), 556, 1159.2(1); Homic 1165; Sent & Pun 1654, 1780(3).

Gribble v. State, TexCrimApp, 115 SW2d 962, 134 Tex-Crim 442.—Int Liq 236(1).

Gribble v. State, TexCrimApp, 111 SW2d 1108, 133 Tex-Crim 457.—Burg 28(6); Crim Law 1091(8).

Gribble v. State, TexCrimApp, 111 SW2d 276, 133 Tex-Crim 357.—Int Liq 198, 221, 223(1), 239(7).

Gribble v. State, TexCrimApp, 95 SW2d 711, 130 Tex-Crim 152.—Crim Law 1088.19, 1182.

Gribble v. State, TexCrimApp, 88 SW2d 490.—Crim Law 15.

Grice; Brown v., TexCivApp–Austin, 357 SW2d 620.—Trover 40(1), 60.

Grice v. FMC Technologies Inc., CA5 (Tex), 216 FedAppx 401.—Civil R 1135, 1246, 1252, 1505(4), 1514.

Grice v. Hennessy, TexCivApp–San Antonio, 327 SW2d 629.—App & E 688(3), 740(1), 929, 1070(2); Neglig 1683, 1750; Trial 355(1), 358, 426.

Grice v. State, TexCrimApp, 151 SW2d 211, 142 TexCrim 4.—Burg 41(6), 45; Crim Law 304(2), 330, 475.5, 566, 572.

Grice v. State, TexApp–Dallas, 635 SW2d 890, petition for discretionary review refused.—Crim Law 371(3), 371(12), 372(9), 619, 726, 805(3), 1038.1(4), 1203.27; False Pret 49(1); Ind & Inf 119, 137(6), 137(7); Searches 173.1; Sent & Pun 1325.

Grice v. State, TexApp–Houston (14 Dist), 162 SW3d 641, petition for discretionary review refused.—Crim Law 995(8), 1026.10(1), 1026.10(4), 1111(5), 1149; Infants 13; Sent & Pun 1139.

Grice-Smith; Builders Transport, Inc. v., TexApp–Waco, 167 SW3d 18.—App & E 1177(5).

Grice-Smith; Builders Transport, Inc. v., TexApp–Waco, 167 SW3d 1, judgment withdrawn and superseded on reh 167 SW3d 18.—App & E 216(3), 232(3), 1001(3), 1062.2, 1173(2), 1177(5); Autos 192(11), 193(1), 193(11), 193(13), 244(31); Labor & Emp 3040, 3043, 3045, 3047; Neglig 218, 234, 351, 387, 1000, 1045(3); Princ & A 96, 99; Trial 352.4(1), 352.4(7).

Grice-Smith; Builders Transport, Inc. v., TexApp–Waco, 63 SW3d 822, appeal decided 167 SW3d 18.—Insurance 1385.

G. Richard Goins Const. Co., Inc. v. S.B. McLaughlin Associates, Inc., TexApp–Tyler, 930 SW2d 124, reh overr, and writ den.—Antitrust 297, 385; App & E 854(1); Corp 630(1); Costs 194.16, 194.32; Inj 138.3, 158; Judgm 199(1); Lim of Act 88, 193, 200(1), 201.

Grider v. Boston Co., Inc., TexApp–Dallas, 773 SW2d 338, writ den.—Contracts 114; Damag 87(2), 89(2); Interest 22(1); Judges 39; Partners 366.

Grider v. Cavazos, CA5 (Tex), 911 F2d 1158.—Int Rev 4973.

Grider; Harrod v., TexApp–Beaumont, 701 SW2d 937.—Neglig 1040(4), 1161; Weap 19.

Grider; McCann v., TexCivApp–San Antonio, 83 SW2d 707, writ refused.—Labor & Emp 2877.

Grider; Monroe v., TexApp–Dallas, 884 SW2d 811, writ den.—App & E 863, 866(3), 927(7), 984(1), 989, 994(3), 999(1), 1003(3), 1003(7), 1004(7), 1004(8); Atty & C 24; Autos 192(11), 242(1), 242(6); Costs 2; Damag 185(1), 221(7); Trial 139.1(14), 139.1(17), 143, 168.

Grider; Naaman v., Tex, 126 SW3d 73, reh den.—App & E 346.2, 428(2); Judgm 214.

Grider v. Naaman, TexApp–Corpus Christi, 83 SW3d 241, review gr, rev 126 SW3d 73, reh den.—App & E 294(1), 346.2, 428(2), 1001(1), 1001(3); Evid 211, 265(10), 555.4(1), 555.10; Health 618; Neglig 202, 210, 250.

Grider v. Noonan, TexCivApp–Corpus Christi, 438 SW2d 631.—Adop 4, 7.8(5), 13, 14, 16; App & E 931(1), 989; Infants 194.1, 198, 205, 210.

Grider v. State, TexCrimApp, 468 SW2d 393.—Crim Law 1166.16; Jury 108.

Grider v. State, TexCrimApp, 398 SW2d 937.—Autos 351.1; Crim Law 1097(1), 1099.13.

Grider v. State, TexApp–Texarkana, 139 SW3d 37.—Crim Law 1030(1), 1038.1(2), 1038.2, 1038.3, 1134(3), 1162, 1173.2(3); Homic 1139.

Grider v. State, TexApp–Texarkana, 69 SW3d 681.—Crim Law 338(1), 369.1, 369.2(1), 369.2(4), 371(1), 371(12), 372(1), 372(14), 374, 695.5, 1043(3), 1148, 1153(1); Jury 21.5; Mental H 434.

Grider; Western Co. of North America v., TexApp–Fort Worth, 626 SW2d 923, ref nre.—Evid 267, 314(1).

Grider; Woodland Trails North Community Imp. Ass'n v., TexApp–Houston (1 Dist), 656 SW2d 919, ref nre.—Covenants 51(2), 103(2); Inj 62(1), 128(6).

Grieder v. Grieder, TexCivApp–Beaumont, 467 SW2d 241, ref nre.—Courts 202(5); Judgm 335(1), 335(4); Wills 302(6).

Grieder; Grieder v., TexCivApp–Beaumont, 467 SW2d 241, ref nre.—Courts 202(5); Judgm 335(1), 335(4); Wills 302(6).

Grieder v. Marsh, TexCivApp–Fort Worth, 247 SW2d 590.—Home 145; Ten in C 13, 28(1).

Griege; Jones v., TexApp–Dallas, 803 SW2d 486.—App & E 23, 80(6), 715(1), 715(2), 934(1); Courts 23, 202(5).

Grieger v. Vega, Tex, 271 SW2d 85, 153 Tex 498.—App & E 232(3); Death 58(1), 75, 104(1); Evid 94; Trial 350.3(5), 352.17.

Grieger; Vega v., TexCivApp–Austin, 264 SW2d 498, rev 271 SW2d 85, 153 Tex 498.—Death 104(1); Trial 215, 349(1), 352.17.

Griego, Ex parte, TexCrimApp, 366 SW2d 572.—Prisons 13.3.

Griego; IRA Resources, Inc. v., Tex, 221 SW3d 592.—App & E 893(1); Const Law 3964, 3965(3), 3965(7); Corp 665(1); Courts 12(2.5), 12(2.10), 12(2.15), 39; Princ & A 19.

Griego; Ira Resources, Inc. v., TexApp–Corpus Christi, 161 SW3d 248, reh overr, review gr, rev 221 SW3d 592.—App & E 893(1), 931(1), 1024.3; Banks 218; Const Law 3964, 3965(7); Corp 665(1); Courts 12(2.10), 35, 39; Princ & A 19, 99; See Reg 303.1.

Griego v. State, TexApp–Houston (1 Dist), 853 SW2d 664, reh den.—Infants 132, 191, 194.1, 223.1; Statut 181(2).

Griego v. Sullivan, CA5 (Tex), 940 F2d 942.—Social S 142.5, 143.60.

Griego; Ysleta Independent School Dist. v., TexApp–El Paso, 170 SW3d 792, review den.—Admin Law 229; App & E 893(1); Plead 104(1), 111.37; Schools 63(1), 115, 147.42, 147.44.

Grier, In re, BkrtcyWDTex, 124 BR 229.—Bankr 3341, 3355(1.10), 3355(1.25), 3355(1.35), 3355(4), 3422(10.1).

Grier; American Honda Finance Corp. v., BkrtcyWD-Tex, 124 BR 229. See Grier, In re.

Grier v. Grier, Tex, 731 SW2d 931.—Divorce 253(3); Exemp 37; Hus & W 249(3).

Grier; Grier v., Tex, 731 SW2d 931.—Divorce 253(3); Exemp 37; Hus & W 249(3).

Grier v. Grier, TexApp–El Paso, 713 SW2d 213, writ gr, aff as mod 731 SW2d 931.—Divorce 252.3(1), 252.3(4), 255, 286(9).

Grier; Grier v., TexApp–El Paso, 713 SW2d 213, writ gr, aff as mod 731 SW2d 931.—Divorce 252.3(1), 252.3(4), 255, 286(9).

Grier; Holstein v., TexCivApp–San Antonio, 262 SW2d 954.—Courts 78; Damag 208(5); Trial 41(5).

Grier v. Rumsfeld, SDTex, 466 FSupp 422, 24 Wage & Hour Cas (BNA) 21.—Civil R 1169, 1175, 1549; Labor & Emp 2481(5).

Grier v. U.S., CA5 (Tex), 472 F2d 1157.—Crim Law 273.4(1), 393(1).

Grier; Vierra v., CA5 (Tex), 471 F2d 545.—Autos 244(40); Fed Cts 894.

Grierson v. Parker Energy Partners 1984-I, TexApp–Houston (14 Dist), 737 SW2d 375.—Corp 306, 325, 335, 360(1), 361; Damag 184.

Grierson v. Sreenan, TexCivApp–Beaumont, 560 SW2d 423.—App & E 223; Judgm 185(1), 185.1(1), 185.3(17); Pretrial Proc 480.

Griese v. State, TexApp–Houston (14 Dist), 820 SW2d 389, petition for discretionary review refused, denial of habeas corpus aff Ex parte Wilhelm, 901 SW2d 956, petition for discretionary review refused.—Crim Law 1139, 1158(2); Searches 23, 105.1, 116, 117.

Griesenbeck v. Schindler, TexCivApp–Eastland, 552 SW2d 203, ref nre.—Schools 37(4).

Griesing; Liberty Mut. Ins. Co. v., TexApp–Austin, 150 SW3d 640.—Admin Law 387, 390.1; App & E 893(1), 1079, 1175(1); Insurance 1022, 1541, 1542(1), 2005, 2013; Statut 174, 181(1), 190, 194.

Grievance Committee, Fifth Congressional Dist., State Bar of Texas; Hexter Title & Abstract Co. v., Tex, 179 SW2d 946, 142 Tex 506, 157 ALR 268.—Atty & C 11(3), 11(13); Corp 377.5; Inj 114(2).

Grievance Committee for Dist. 1-A, State Bar of Texas; Hefner v., TexApp–Dallas, 708 SW2d 43.—Atty & C 36(1).

Grievance Committee for State Bar Dist. No. 3-A.; Wilson v., TexCivApp–Austin, 565 SW2d 361, ref nre.—Const Law 2600; Decl Judgm 8, 66, 201, 276.

Grievance Committee of State Bar of Tex.; Rattikin Title Co. v., TexCivApp–Fort Worth, 272 SW2d 948.—App & E 954(1); Atty & C 11(3), 32(2); Inj 89(5), 132, 138.72, 147, 151, 152, 158.

Grievance Committee of State Bar of Tex., Twenty-First Congressional Dist. v. Dean, TexCivApp–Austin, 190 SW2d 126.—Atty & C 2, 11(1), 11(2.1), 11(3), 32(1); Const Law 2374, 2459.

Grievance Committee, State Bar of Tex. for Dist. 14-A; Smith v., TexCivApp–Corpus Christi, 475 SW2d 396.—Atty & C 48; Courts 207.5, 472.2, 480(1); Mand 1, 3(2.1), 7, 68; Prohib 1, 3(2), 5(1), 10(1), 10(2).

Grievance Committee State Bar of Tex., Twenty-First Congressional Dist., v. Coryell, TexCivApp–Austin, 190 SW2d 130, writ refused wom.—Atty & C 11(1), 11(2.1), 11(3).

Griffay v. Robbins, TexCivApp–Austin, 91 SW2d 1160, writ dism.—App & E 1050.1(3.1); Bills & N 465, 489(7); Costs 238(2); Evid 230(1); Guard & W 130; Home 57(3); Judgm 199(1); Mtg 480.

Griffen v. Big Spring Independent School Dist., CA5 (Tex), 706 F2d 645, cert den 104 SCt 525, 464 US 1008, 78 LEd2d 709.—Admin Law 501; Civil R 1320; Fed Civ Proc 2280; Fed Cts 425, 427; Judgm 641; Lim of Act 58(1), 130(7); Statut 184.

Griffey; San Jacinto Trust Co. v., TexCivApp–Galveston, 87 SW2d 857, writ dism.—Bills & N 516.

Griffey v. State, TexCrimApp, 344 SW2d 883, 171 Tex-Crim 49.—Lotteries 29; Searches 111, 114.

Griffey v. State, TexCrimApp, 342 SW2d 582, 170 Tex-Crim 577.—Crim Law 112(1), 422(6); Double J 139.1; Lotteries 20, 27, 29.

Griffey v. State, TexCrimApp, 327 SW2d 585, 168 Tex-Crim 338.—Crim Law 478(1), 622.2(1); Lotteries 19, 29; Searches 112.

Griffey v. State, TexCrimApp, 265 SW2d 115, 159 Tex-Crim 141.—Autos 349.5(7).

Griffey v. Travelers Ins. Co., TexCivApp–Amarillo, 452 SW2d 725, ref nre.—Trial 351.2(10).

Griffin, Ex parte, Tex, 682 SW2d 261.—Jury 22(1), 24.5, 29(1).

Griffin, Ex parte, TexCrimApp, 679 SW2d 15.—Crim Law 273.1(2); Hab Corp 224.1, 230, 476, 714, 717(2).

Griffin, Ex parte, TexCrimApp, 258 SW2d 324, 158 Tex-Crim 570.—Pardon 42.1; Sent & Pun 1838, 2041.

Griffin, Ex parte, TexApp–San Antonio, 712 SW2d 214, dism.—Child S 459; Const Law 4494; Contempt 20.

Griffin, In re, BkrtcyWDTex, 139 BR 415.—Exemp 37.

Griffin v. Aluminum Co. of America, CA5 (Tex), 564 F2d 1171.—Fed Civ Proc 1278, 1451, 1827.1; Fed Cts 818.

Griffin v. B & W Finance Co., TexCivApp–Tyler, 389 SW2d 350.—App & E 843(2); Bills & N 467(1), 489(2); Usury 42, 119.

Griffin v. Barr, TexCivApp–Dallas, 587 SW2d 477.—Evid 571(7); Jury 19(1), 19(7); Mental H 309.

Griffin; Barr v., TexCivApp–Waco, 554 SW2d 305, appeal after remand 587 SW2d 477.—Judgm 72, 87.

Griffin v. Baylor College of Medicine, TexApp–Houston (1 Dist), 945 SW2d 158.—App & E 934(1); Judgm 185.3(1).

Griffin; Berry v., TexCivApp–Hous (14 Dist), 531 SW2d 394, ref nre.—Evid 595; Trial 141; Wills 290, 306.

Griffin; Borgerding v., TexApp–Corpus Christi, 716 SW2d 694.—Divorce 165(3), 254(1), 254(2); Judgm 106(1), 106(9), 335(1), 335(2), 335(3), 375.

Griffin v. Box, CA5 (Tex), 956 F2d 89, reh den 959 F2d 969.—Inj 138.24.

Griffin v. Box, CA5 (Tex), 910 F2d 255, on subsequent appeal 956 F2d 89, reh den 959 F2d 969.—Contracts 168; Fed Cts 754.1, 850.1; Inj 158; Partners 363, 370.

Griffin v. Browne, TexCivApp–Hous (1 Dist), 482 SW2d 716, ref nre.—Judgm 153(1), 153(2), 335(1); Plead 335.

Griffin v. Camp, TexCivApp–Eastland, 272 SW2d 129, ref nre.—App & E 930(1); Deeds 72(1), 203, 211(4); Trial 141, 142, 143.

Griffin; Christus Health Southeast Texas v., TexApp–Beaumont, 175 SW3d 548, review den, and reh of petition for review den.—Equity 55; Health 803, 809; Judgm 335(1).

Griffin v. Citizens Nat. Bank in Waxahachie, TexCivApp–Fort Worth, 557 SW2d 575, writ dism by agreement.—Judgm 185(1), 185(2), 185.3(16).

Griffin v. City of Dallas, CA5 (Tex), 26 F3d 610.—Civil R 1507.

Griffin v. Collins, TexCivApp–Amarillo, 310 SW2d 137.—Venue 5.3(8), 15.

Griffin v. Connally, SDTex, 127 FSupp 203.—Fed Cts 45, 102, 106, 133; Judges 36.

Griffin; Continental Ins. Co. v., TexCivApp–Eastland, 218 SW2d 350.—Insurance 2155(1).

Griffin v. Coryell County, TexCivApp–Waco, 334 SW2d 495, writ gr, rev 341 SW2d 151, 161 Tex 422.—App & E 78(4), 347(2); Plead 354; Pretrial Proc 650; States 191.10.

Griffin; Dayle L. Smith Oil Co. v., TexCivApp–San Antonio, 104 SW2d 167, writ dism.—App & E 151(2); Dep & Escr 20; Plead 36(1), 376; Tresp to T T 3, 32, 35(1), 44; Trial 351.5(3).

Griffin; Dillard v., TexCivApp–Fort Worth, 341 SW2d 696, ref nre.—App & E 930(1); Autos 245(39), 245(44).

Griffin; Dunagan v., TexCivApp–Fort Worth, 151 SW2d 250, dism.—App & E 1172(1); Courts 247(11); Estop 75, 110; Princ & A 103(7), 152(4); Wareh 14, 15(2).

Griffin v. Duque, TexApp–Eastland, 93 SW3d 513.—Judgm 185.3(17).

Griffin v. Duty, TexCivApp–Galveston, 286 SW2d 229.—App & E 977(5); Evid 10(6), 42; Judgm 135, 139, 145(3), 162(2), 163, 169, 379(2).

Griffin v. Eakin, TexApp–Austin, 656 SW2d 187, ref nre.—App & E 837(8), 852, 989; Contracts 322(3), 322(5), 353(8); New Tr 44(3), 52, 56; Trial 121(2), 131(1), 140(1), 143, 350.4(1), 352.1(1), 352.1(4), 365.1(1).

Griffin v. Ellinger, Tex, 538 SW2d 97, 97 ALR3d 791.—Bills & N 123(1), 492, 517.

Griffin v. Ellinger, TexCivApp–Austin, 530 SW2d 329, writ gr, aff 538 SW2d 97, 97 ALR3d 791.—Bills & N 123(1).

Griffin; Fairfield Estates L.P. v., TexApp–Eastland, 986 SW2d 719.—App & E 216(1), 300; Evid 474(16), 568(4); Inj 1, 189; Waters 123, 124, 125.

Griffin; Farmers Texas County Mut. Ins. Co. v., Tex, 955 SW2d 81.—Decl Judgm 45; Insurance 2268, 2271, 2674, 2675, 2911, 2914.

Griffin; Farmers Texas County Mut. Ins. Co. v., TexApp–Dallas, 868 SW2d 861, reh den, and writ den.—App & E 854(1), 863, 934(1), 1079, 1175(1); Costs 238(1), 238(2); Insurance 2774, 2786, 2787; Judgm 183, 185(2).

Griffin; Federal Sav. & Loan Ins. Corp. v., CA5 (Tex), 935 F2d 691, rehden, cert den Griffin v. First Gibraltar Bank, FSB, 112 SCt 1163, 502 US 1092, 117 LEd2d 410.—Banks 505; B & L Assoc 48; Em Dom 2(1.1); Fed Civ Proc 1541, 2539; Guar 78(1); Partners 17, 18, 52, 53; Rem of C 19(8), 43, 44; Usury 82.

Griffin v. Fidelity & Cas. Co. of N.Y., CA5 (Tex), 273 F2d 45.—Insurance 3207, 3212.

Griffin; Fidelity & Cas. Co. of N. Y. v., SDTex, 178 FSupp 678, rev 273 F2d 45.—Insurance 3147, 3168, 3183, 3191(1), 3205, 3206, 3207, 3214.

Griffin; Gilmer v., TexCivApp–San Antonio, 265 SW2d 252, ref nre.—App & E 970(2), 1050.1(12), 1052(8), 1062.1; Autos 244(34), 244(35), 244(36.1), 244(40), 247; Damag 130.1; Evid 118, 121(1), 123(10); Trial 127, 351.5(6).

Griffin; Gilmer v., TexCivApp–San Antonio, 265 SW2d 250, ref nre.—Plead 111.2; Venue 8.5(5).

Griffin v. GK Intelligent Systems, Inc., SDTex, 87 FSupp2d 684.—Consp 2; Fraud 13(3), 20, 46; Sec Reg 35.25, 60.18, 60.27(1), 60.45(1), 60.47, 60.48(3), 60.51, 60.53, 60.62.

Griffin v. GK Intelligent Systems, Inc., SDTex, 196 FRD 298.—Fed Civ Proc 164, 165, 172, 187.

Griffin v. Grant, Tex, 390 SW2d 746.—Const Law 2489; Witn 159(2).

Griffin; Grant v., TexCivApp–Tyler, 383 SW2d 643, aff 390 SW2d 746.—Witn 158, 159(2), 159(3).

Griffin v. Griffin, TexCivApp–Austin, 535 SW2d 42.—Child C 924; Child S 224, 332, 559; Divorce 231; Hus & W 278(1), 279(2).

Griffin; Griffin v., TexCivApp–Austin, 535 SW2d 42.—Child C 924; Child S 224, 332, 559; Divorce 231; Hus & W 278(1), 279(2).

Griffin v. Griffin, TexCivApp–Texarkana, 271 SW2d 714.—App & E 930(1), 989; Wills 155.1, 155.3, 159, 163(1), 163(8), 166(1).

Griffin; Griffin v., TexCivApp–Texarkana, 271 SW2d 714.—App & E 930(1), 989; Wills 155.1, 155.3, 159, 163(1), 163(8), 166(1).

Griffin v. Griffin, TexCivApp–Texarkana, 233 SW2d 967.—Wills 270, 366.

Griffin; Griffin v., TexCivApp–Texarkana, 233 SW2d 967.—Wills 270, 366.

Griffin v. Griffin, TexCivApp–Waco, 306 SW2d 196, writ dism.—Divorce 49(3), 50, 165(3), 167, 184(12); Judgm 199(3.14); Marriage 40(5); Witn 125, 159(2), 159(3).

Griffin; Griffin v., TexCivApp–Waco, 306 SW2d 196, writ dism.—Divorce 49(3), 50, 165(3), 167, 184(12); Judgm 199(3.14); Marriage 40(5); Witn 125, 159(2), 159(3).

Griffin v. Gulf, C. & S. F. Ry. Co., TexCivApp–San Antonio, 298 SW2d 659.—Carr 132, 134, 136; Stip 14(12); Trial 352.10.

Griffin v. Hale, TexComApp, 112 SW2d 1042, 131 Tex 152.—Evid 83(1); Wills 569.

Griffin v. Hale, TexCivApp–Texarkana, 87 SW2d 497, aff 112 SW2d 1042, 131 Tex 152.—Wills 439, 440, 487(2), 590, 608(3.1).

Griffin v. Hawn, Tex, 341 SW2d 151, 161 Tex 422.—Em Dom 75; States 191.4(6), 191.10.

Griffin v. Helfrich, TexCivApp–Waco, 312 SW2d 422.—Judgm 743(1); Mines 55(4), 55(8).

Griffin v. Hidalgo County, TexCivApp–San Antonio, 185 SW2d 232, writ refused wom.—App & E 758.1; Atty & C 151; Compromise 18(2); Counties 128.

Griffin; Hlavinka v., TexApp–Corpus Christi, 721 SW2d 521.—App & E 931(1); Pretrial Proc 223, 517.1; Trial 382.

Griffin v. H. L. Peterson Co., TexCivApp–Dallas, 427 SW2d 140.—Action 70; App & E 707(1), 1073(1); Bailm 3; Evid 168, 400(6); Judgm 181(1), 186; Sales 38(3), 90, 267.

Griffin v. Holiday Inns of America, Tex, 496 SW2d 535.—Judgm 585(4), 587, 588, 592, 713(2), 720.

Griffin v. Holiday Inns of America, TexCivApp–Austin, 480 SW2d 506, writ gr, aff 496 SW2d 535.—Judgm 588, 634, 713(2).

Griffin v. Holiday Inns of America, TexCivApp–Austin, 452 SW2d 517.—Contracts 295(1), 303(5), 322(4); Damag 123, 159(6).

Griffin; Home Ben. Ass'n v., TexCivApp–Waco, 98 SW2d 862.—App & E 1002; Insurance 2445.

Griffin; Jackson v., TexCivApp–Waco, 302 SW2d 266.—App & E 173(5); Land & Ten 63(1); Tresp to T T 6.1, 38(1), 38(3).

Griffin v. Leonard, CA5 (Tex), 821 F2d 1124.—Dist & Pros Attys 8; Sent & Pun 1988; U S 50.10(3).

Griffin; Lone Star Life Ins. Co. v., TexCivApp–Beaumont, 574 SW2d 576, ref nre.—Antitrust 221; Insurance 2560(2), 3335, 3374, 3401.

Griffin; Long Trusts v., Tex, 222 SW3d 412, reh den.—Contracts 316(6), 321(1); Frds St of 63(2), 110(1), 144, 158(3).

Griffin; Long Trusts v., TexApp–Texarkana, 144 SW3d 99, reh overr, review gr, rev 222 SW3d 412, reh den.—App & E 852, 854(2); Contracts 24, 173, 318; Costs 194.22, 194.34, 194.40, 207; Damag 184, 189; Estop 52(1); Frds St of 110(1), 144; Lim of Act 13; Mines 48, 74(8), 101; Princ & A 48; Ref of Inst 47, 48; Spec Perf 4, 5, 64; Tresp to T T 1.

Griffin v. Lynaugh, CA5 (Tex), 823 F2d 856, reh den 829 F2d 1124, cert den 108 SCt 1059, 484 US 1079, 98 LEd2d 1021.—Crim Law 393(1), 412.2(4), 517.2(1), 641.12(1), 800(6); Hab Corp 339; Jury 108.

Griffin v. McCoach, USTex, 61 SCt 1023, 313 US 498, 85 LEd 1481, 134 ALR 1462, conformed to 123 F2d 550, cert den 62 SCt 1270, 316 US 683, 86 LEd 1755, reh den 62 SCt 1307, 316 US 713, 86 LEd 1778.—Courts 8; Fed Cts 409.1, 452.

Griffin v. McCoach, CCA5 (Tex), 123 F2d 550, cert den 62 SCt 1270, 316 US 683, 86 LEd 1755, reh den 62 SCt 1307, 316 US 713, 86 LEd 1778.—Courts 8; Fed Cts 382.1, 419; Insurance 1786, 1791(1).

Griffin v. McCoach, CCA5 (Tex), 116 F2d 261, cert gr 61 SCt 807, 312 US 676, 85 LEd 1116, rev 61 SCt 1023, 313 US 498, 85 LEd 1481, 134 ALR 1462, conformed to 123 F2d 550, cert den 62 SCt 1270, 316 US 683, 86 LEd 1755, reh den 62 SCt 1307, 316 US 713, 86 LEd 1778.—Insurance 1091(7), 1718, 1786, 1787, 1790(2).

Griffin v. McCullough Tool Co., TexCivApp–Fort Worth, 265 SW2d 131, ref nre.—App & E 931(6),

GRIFFIN

1054(1); Evid 460(5); Fraud Conv 76(3), 121, 130, 182(3), 188, 297, 300(2), 300(7), 308(1); Jud S 62; Mtg 25(4), 568; Plead 236(3), 236(6), 291(4), 422.

Griffin v. McFarlane, TexCivApp–Fort Worth, 96 SW2d 1000.—Judgm 675(1), 678(1), 713(1).

Griffin; McFarlane v., TexCivApp–Fort Worth, 80 SW2d 1100.—Judgm 948(0.5), 958(1).

Griffin; Martinez v., CA5 (Tex), 840 F2d 314.—Fed Civ Proc 2734.

Griffin v. Methodist Hosp., TexApp–Houston (14 Dist), 948 SW2d 72.—App & E 223; Health 821(2); Judgm 185.1(4), 185.3(21), 189.

Griffin v. Miles, TexCivApp–Hous (14 Dist), 553 SW2d 933, writ dism by agreement.—App & E 962; Pretrial Proc 501, 520.

Griffin v. Missouri Pac. R. Co., TexCivApp–Corpus Christi, 434 SW2d 954.—R R 333(1), 348(8), 352.

Griffin v. Moon, TexCivApp–Dallas, 288 SW2d 543.—Autos 20.

Griffin v. Nehls, TexCivApp–Tyler, 576 SW2d 482, ref nre.—Judgm 185.3(17); Wills 440, 488, 852.

Griffin v. New York Underwriters Ins. Co., TexCivApp–Waco, 594 SW2d 212.—Work Comp 1532.

Griffin v. Oceanic Contractors, Inc., USTex, 102 SCt 3245, 458 US 564, 73 LEd2d 973, on remand 685 F2d 139.—Seamen 18; Statut 181(2).

Griffin v. Oceanic Contractors, Inc., CA5 (Tex), 664 F2d 36, cert gr 102 SCt 595, 454 US 1052, 70 LEd2d 587, rev 102 SCt 3245, 458 US 564, 73 LEd2d 973, on remand 685 F2d 139.—Damag 37; Seamen 11(6), 16, 18.

Griffin v. Office of Atty. Gen., TexApp–San Antonio, 919 SW2d 170, appeal decided 926 SW2d 648.—App & E 387(1), 428(1).

Griffin v. Office of the Atty. Gen., TexApp–San Antonio, 926 SW2d 648.—App & E 395.

Griffin; Oil Country Haulers, Inc. v., TexApp–Houston (14 Dist), 668 SW2d 903.—Antitrust 130, 286, 389(2); Damag 59; Evid 355(1), 543(2).

Griffin v. OPI Intern., Inc., SDTex, 878 FSupp 996, aff 79 F3d 1144.—Indem 27, 33(8); Seamen 29(1), 29(2), 29(5); Ship 50.

Griffin; Padgett v., TexCivApp–Waco, 367 SW2d 222, writ refused.—Admin Law 791; Int Liq 70, 71, 72.

Griffin v. Phillips, TexCivApp–Eastland, 542 SW2d 432, ref nre.—Fraud 13(2), 58(2), 61; Health 823(5); Judgm 199(3.14).

Griffin v. Phillips Petroleum Co., TexCivApp–El Paso, 139 SW2d 318, writ dism.—Princ & A 99, 102(1), 123(3), 123(8), 147(2), 189(4).

Griffin; Pilgrim v., TexCivApp–El Paso, 237 SW2d 448, ref nre.—Child 10, 11; Des & Dist 3, 4; Evid 37, 81.

Griffin v. Pritchett, TexCivApp–Galveston, 245 SW2d 558, ref nre.—App & E 1008.1(1); Deeds 111; Ref of Inst 45(5).

Griffin; Ragsdale v., TexCivApp–El Paso, 380 SW2d 164.—Frds St of 139(4); Judgm 815; Mines 55(4), 55(8); Tresp to T T 6.1, 38(1).

Griffin; Reese v., TexCivApp–Texarkana, 281 SW2d 353.—Fraud 60; Plead 111.6, 362(5); Venue 8.5(2), 8.5(7).

Griffin v. Reynolds, TexCivApp–Texarkana, 107 SW2d 634, writ dism.—App & E 819; Land & Ten 1, 117, 119(1); Life Est 8.

Griffin v. Robertson, TexCivApp–Texarkana, 592 SW2d 31.—Evid 397(1); Gifts 47(1); Trusts 17(2), 44(1), 44(3).

Griffin; Rogers v., TexApp–Texarkana, 774 SW2d 706.—Child S 508(2).

Griffin v. Rowden, Tex, 654 SW2d 435.—Judgm 181(19).

Griffin v. Rowden, TexApp–Dallas, 702 SW2d 692, ref nre.—App & E 302(6), 842(1), 931(1), 989; Lis Pen 15; Torts 211, 212, 242, 243, 263, 264.

Griffin; Seay v., TexCivApp–Eastland, 308 SW2d 182, ref nre.—App & E 1051(1), 1062.2; Frds St of 33(1), 33(3).

Griffin v. Semperit of America, Inc., SDTex, 414 FSupp 1384.—Alt Disp Res 111, 139, 143, 198, 199, 200; Fed Cts 198, 433; Labor & Emp 1519.

Griffin v. Sevier, TexCivApp–Galveston, 234 SW2d 272.—Acct 20(2); Refer 100(2), 100(4), 100(6), 100(7), 103(2).

Griffin v. Shearson/Lehman Bros., Inc., CA5 (Tex), 845 F2d 1296. See Rodriguez De Quijas v. Shearson/Lehman Bros., Inc.

Griffin; Smith v., TexComApp, 116 SW2d 1064, 131 Tex 509.—Frds St of 109, 110(1), 158(4); Tresp to T T 32, 41(3), 47(1), 52.

Griffin v. Smith, TexCivApp–San Antonio, 457 SW2d 127, writ refused.—App & E 125.

Griffin; Smith v., TexCivApp–Beaumont, 89 SW2d 1082, aff 116 SW2d 1064, 131 Tex 509.—Tresp to T T 12.

Griffin v. Southland Life Ins. Co., TexCivApp–Eastland, 153 SW2d 722.—Insurance 2586, 2608; Lim of Act 46(5); Trial 350.4(3).

Griffin; Southwestern Bell Tel. Co. v., TexCivApp–Texarkana, 429 SW2d 576.—Em Dom 150, 205.

Griffin; Sparks v., CA5 (Tex), 460 F2d 433.—Civil R 1133, 1316, 1320; Fed Civ Proc 1531; Fed Cts 858; Schools 147.2(2), 147.40(2), 147.47.

Griffin; Speed v., TexCivApp–Waco, 427 SW2d 917.—Wills 490, 558(1), 577.

Griffin v. Stanley, TexCivApp–Waco, 562 SW2d 920.—Hab Corp 825.1.

Griffin v. Stanolind Oil & Gas Co., TexComApp, 125 SW2d 545, 133 Tex 45.—Hus & W 273(4), 273(8.1), 273(9), 273(10); Mines 73.1(2).

Griffin v. Stanolind Oil & Gas Co., TexCivApp–Texarkana, 102 SW2d 231, aff 125 SW2d 545, 133 Tex 45.—Hus & W 273(8.1), 273(9), 273(10).

Griffin v. State, TexCrimApp, 215 SW3d 403, reh den.—Arrest 63.4(16), 63.5(5), 63.5(8), 63.5(9).

Griffin v. State, TexCrimApp, 145 SW3d 645.—Crim Law 1004, 1072.

Griffin v. State, TexCrimApp, 815 SW2d 576.—Burg 9(0.5); Crim Law 730(5), 1171.1(3).

Griffin v. State, TexCrimApp, 787 SW2d 63, on remand 811 SW2d 221.—Crim Law 730(5), 790, 1181.5(3.1); Sent & Pun 1891, 1900.

Griffin v. State, TexCrimApp, 779 SW2d 431, on remand 785 SW2d 179, petition for discretionary review gr, rev 815 SW2d 576.—Crim Law 1171.1(1), 1171.1(2.1).

Griffin v. State, TexCrimApp, 765 SW2d 422.—Crim Law 412(4), 412.2(5), 414, 531(1).

Griffin v. State, TexCrimApp, 703 SW2d 193.—Crim Law 273(4.1), 273.1(1), 274(8), 300.

Griffin v. State, TexCrimApp, 665 SW2d 762, cert den 104 SCt 1327, 465 US 1051, 79 LEd2d 722.—Crim Law 404.70, 517.2(2), 1030(1); Jury 108.

Griffin v. State, TexCrimApp, 614 SW2d 155.—Const Law 4693; Crim Law 706(3), 784(7), 1134(1); Ind & Inf 189(11), 191(5), 191(9); Larc 3(4), 12; Rob 3, 5, 14, 17(1), 24.35, 27(5); Witn 274(2).

Griffin v. State, TexCrimApp, 606 SW2d 901.—Crim Law 1032(5).

Griffin v. State, TexCrimApp, 554 SW2d 688.—Crim Law 273(5), 301, 720(6), 721(3), 1171.5.

Griffin v. State, TexCrimApp, 514 SW2d 278.—Const Law 4509(23); Rape 2, 16(1), 16(5), 53(5); Witn 40(1).

Griffin v. State, TexCrimApp, 489 SW2d 290.—Crim Law 264, 577.15(4), 1166(7); Larc 65.

Griffin v. State, TexCrimApp, 487 SW2d 81.—Crim Law 720(7.1), 726, 1036.1(5), 1169.12; Judges 49(1).

Griffin v. State, TexCrimApp, 486 SW2d 948.—Crim Law 511.9, 528, 872.5, 1169.5(2); Jury 149.

Griffin v. State, TexCrimApp, 481 SW2d 838.—Crim Law 726, 918(3), 959, 1028, 1043(3), 1166.16, 1171.7; Jury 64, 94, 133, 139.

Griffin v. State, TexCrimApp, 455 SW2d 298.—Crim Law 339.11(1), 345; Witn 393(4).

Griffin v. State, TexCrimApp, 355 SW2d 532, 172 Tex-Crim 194.—False Pret 49(3).

Griffin v. State, TexCrimApp, 298 SW2d 128, 164 Tex-Crim 250.—Crim Law 863(2), 1174(1).

Griffin v. State, TexCrimApp, 272 SW2d 526, 160 Tex-Crim 478.—Crim Law 1086.1.

Griffin v. State, TexCrimApp, 272 SW2d 523.—Bail 64.

Griffin v. State, TexCrimApp, 263 SW2d 950.—Crim Law 1090.1(1).

Griffin v. State, TexCrimApp, 261 SW2d 838, 159 Tex-Crim 142.—Crim Law 368(3), 407(1), 438(3), 507(1); Infants 20.

Griffin v. State, TexCrimApp, 252 SW2d 706, 158 Tex-Crim 13.—Autos 355(8).

Griffin v. State, TexCrimApp, 250 SW2d 223, 157 Tex-Crim 487.—Autos 355(13).

Griffin v. State, TexCrimApp, 226 SW2d 869, 154 Tex-Crim 295.—Crim Law 1159.5; Ind & Inf 79; Rape 51(1).

Griffin v. State, TexCrimApp, 206 SW2d 259, 151 Tex-Crim 185.—Crim Law 1172.6; Rape 16(1), 59(19).

Griffin v. State, TexCrimApp, 198 SW2d 587, 150 Tex-Crim 27.—Crim Law 438(6), 680(1), 738, 808.5, 822(1), 823(4), 1134(3), 1159.2(3); Homic 527, 992, 1134, 1135, 1321, 1325, 1345.

Griffin v. State, TexCrimApp, 184 SW2d 475, 148 Tex-Crim 30.—Crim Law 510, 787(1), 1111(3), 1171.7; Int Liq 236(11).

Griffin v. State, TexCrimApp, 155 SW2d 805.—Crim Law 1182.

Griffin v. State, TexCrimApp, 146 SW2d 746, 140 Tex-Crim 582.—Crim Law 1090.1(3); Rape 51(1).

Griffin v. State, TexCrimApp, 128 SW2d 1197, 137 Tex-Crim 231.—Crim Law 211(3), 304(20); Ind & Inf 61; Int Liq 30, 236(3), 242; Mal Pros 18(1); Perj 10.

Griffin v. State, TexCrimApp, 114 SW2d 905, 134 Tex-Crim 129.—Autos 144.2(8).

Griffin v. State, TexCrimApp, 98 SW2d 824, 131 TexCrim 314.—Crim Law 459, 481, 486(5); Homic 1391.

Griffin v. State, TexCrimApp, 93 SW2d 1152.—Crim Law 15.

Griffin v. State, TexCrimApp, 91 SW2d 737.—Crim Law 15.

Griffin v. State, TexCrimApp, 91 SW2d 729.—Crim Law 15.

Griffin v. State, TexCrimApp, 83 SW2d 965.—Crim Law 1070.

Griffin v. State, TexApp–Houston (1 Dist), 850 SW2d 246, reh den, and petition for discretionary review refused.—Autos 355(1); Crim Law 719(3), 730(10), 823(15), 867, 898, 1036.1(8), 1038.1(1), 1144.13(3), 1159.2(2), 1159.4(2), 1166.22(1), 1166.22(3); Obst Just 7; Sent & Pun 1976(1).

Griffin v. State, TexApp–Houston (1 Dist), 811 SW2d 221.—Crim Law 1163(4), 1172.1(2); Prisons 15(3).

Griffin v. State, TexApp–Houston (1 Dist), 764 SW2d 306.—Crim Law 720(7.1), 1171.1(2.1); Sent & Pun 1373.

Griffin v. State, TexApp–Fort Worth, 936 SW2d 706.—Crim Law 1081(2), 1134(10).

Griffin v. State, TexApp–Fort Worth, 749 SW2d 497, petition for discretionary review refused.—Const Law 4733(2); Crim Law 1129(1), 1177, 1184(2); Judges 51(4); Larc 40(4); Sent & Pun 2009.

Griffin v. State, TexApp–Fort Worth, 720 SW2d 676, opinion withdrawn and superseded 749 SW2d 497, petition for discretionary review refused.

Griffin v. State, TexApp–Fort Worth, 701 SW2d 958.—Homic 1168.

Griffin v. State, TexApp–Dallas, 785 SW2d 179, petition for discretionary review gr, rev 815 SW2d 576.—Burg 2, 9(1), 9(2).

Griffin v. State, TexApp–Dallas, 725 SW2d 773, petition for discretionary review gr, rev 779 SW2d 431, on remand 785 SW2d 179, petition for discretionary review

gr, rev 815 SW2d 576.—Burg 41(1); Crim Law 1171.1(1), 1171.1(2.1).

Griffin v. State, TexApp–Texarkana, 54 SW3d 820, petition for discretionary review refused.—Autos 335, 349(2.1), 349.5(3); Crim Law 394.6(5), 1139, 1153(1); Searches 23, 24, 62, 171, 180, 194, 198.

Griffin v. State, TexApp–Beaumont, 908 SW2d 624.—Crim Law 552(2), 1144.13(3), 1159.2(7), 1159.2(9), 1159.4(2), 1159.6; Forg 5, 35, 44(1).

Griffin v. State, TexApp–Beaumont, 692 SW2d 726, petition for discretionary review gr, rev 703 SW2d 193.—Crim Law 273(4.1), 274(8).

Griffin v. State, TexApp–Waco, 683 SW2d 16.—Arrest 63.5(2), 63.5(6); Searches 47.1, 51, 63, 68.

Griffin v. State, TexApp–Tyler, 866 SW2d 754.—Autos 355(6); Sent & Pun 1378, 1379(2), 1379(4), 1381(6).

Griffin v. State, TexApp–Houston (14 Dist), 181 SW3d 818, petition for discretionary review refused.—Crim Law 728(2), 1030(1), 1037.1(2), 1043(2), 1043(3); Sent & Pun 1381(6); Witn 198(1).

Griffin v. State, TexApp–Houston (14 Dist), 936 SW2d 353, reh overr, and petition for discretionary review refused.—Crim Law 507(1), 508(9), 511.1(3), 511.1(4), 511.1(9), 511.2, 562, 713, 719(1), 720(8), 1134(8), 1144.13(2.1), 1144.13(6), 1159.2(7), 1159.6.

Griffin; State Farm Fire & Cas. Co. v., TexApp–Houston (1 Dist), 888 SW2d 150.—App & E 93, 863, 870(2); Contracts 176(1); Courts 168; Insurance 1713, 2105, 2109, 2111(1), 2111(2), 2112, 2190, 2194, 3360.

Griffin v. Stewart, TexCivApp–Amarillo, 348 SW2d 800, writ dism by agreement.—Mtg 257; Notaries 9; Usury 4, 113, 117.

Griffin v. Superior Ins. Co., Tex, 338 SW2d 415, 161 Tex 195.—Evid 265(7), 265(10), 313; Work Comp 1612.

Griffin; Superior Ins. Co. v., TexCivApp–Eastland, 323 SW2d 607, aff 338 SW2d 415, 161 Tex 195.—Evid 589; Work Comp 1374, 1615, 1641.

Griffin v. Sylvester v., TexCivApp–Austin, 507 SW2d 649.—Fraud 58(1), 58(2); Jury 25(6), 26.

Griffin; Tejas Toyota, Inc. v., TexCivApp–Waco, 587 SW2d 775, ref nre.—Courts 168, 169(1), 169(4); Judgm 16.

Griffin v. Texas Emp. Ins. Ass'n, Tex, 450 SW2d 59.—Work Comp 1492, 1552.

Griffin v. Texas Emp. Ins. Ass'n, TexCivApp–Amarillo, 441 SW2d 664, aff 450 SW2d 59.—Work Comp 899, 1362.

Griffin; Thornton v., TexCivApp–Fort Worth, 166 SW2d 737, writ refused wom.—Wills 488, 692(1).

Griffin; Tillison v., TexCivApp–Eastland, 148 SW2d 873.—App & E 1001(1); Pretrial Proc 81, 251.1, 307, 309.

Griffin v. Travelers Indemn. Co. of Rhode Island, TexApp–Dallas, 4 SW3d 915, petition for review den.—App & E 870(2), 893(1); Contracts 143(2); Insurance 1808, 1832(1), 2659.

Griffin v. Troup Independent School Dist., TexCivApp–Texarkana, 163 SW2d 412, writ refused.—Hus & W 267(1).

Griffin; U.S. v., CA5 (Tex), 324 F3d 330, appeal after new sentencing hearing 97 FedAppx 497.—Brib 11; Crim Law 59(5), 338(7), 369.2(1), 369.2(2), 369.2(3.1), 371(1), 449.1, 622.7(3), 641.5(0.5), 641.12(1), 641.13(1), 641.13(2.1), 680(1), 728(4), 730(6), 1032(1), 1035(7), 1036.1(9), 1037.1(1), 1037.1(2), 1044.2(2), 1119(1), 1139, 1144.13(2.1), 1144.13(5), 1153(1), 1154, 1158(1), 1159.2(7), 1167(4), 1168(2), 1169.2(1), 1169.2(8), 1169.9, 1170.5(1); Ind & Inf 159(1), 159(2); Postal 35(9); Sent & Pun 699, 736, 2156, 2192; U S 34; Witn 252.

Griffin; U.S. v., CA5 (Tex), 555 F2d 1323.—Crim Law 1158(4); Searches 24, 40.1, 79, 181.

Griffin; U.S. v., CA5 (Tex), 212 FedAppx 304.—Sent & Pun 976.

Griffin; U.S. v., CA5 (Tex), 97 FedAppx 497.—Crim Law 1180, 1192.

GRIFFIN

Griffin v. U.S., WDTex, 42 FSupp2d 700.—Int Rev 3056, 3057, 3071, 4200, 4203.20.

Griffin v. Walden, TexCivApp–Waco, 410 SW2d 222, ref nre.—Can of Inst 59; Contracts 94(1).

Griffin; Washington v., TexCivApp–Hous (1 Dist), 427 SW2d 136, ref nre.—App & E 930(3), 996, 1001(1), 1003(6), 1052(8), 1062.5; Autos 244(7), 244(36.1), 245(8); New Tr 143(2), 144.

Griffin; Wichita County v., TexCivApp–Fort Worth, 284 SW2d 253, ref nre.—Const Law 2403; Counties 149, 159; Courts 57(2); Mand 3(5), 27; Mun Corp 868(1).

Griffin v. Wolfe, Tex, 610 SW2d 466, on remand 626 SW2d 895.—Partit 113.

Griffin v. Wolfe, TexApp–Fort Worth, 626 SW2d 895.—Partit 14; Pretrial Proc 742.1, 751.

Griffin v. Wolfe, TexCivApp–Fort Worth, 610 SW2d 153, rev 610 SW2d 466, on remand 626 SW2d 895.—App & E 627; Partit 113.

Griffin; Young v., TexCivApp–Texarkana, 292 SW2d 376, ref nre.—Life Est 1; Wills 450, 590, 601(1), 612(1).

Griffin & Brand of McAllen; Wood v., TexApp–Corpus Christi, 671 SW2d 125.—App & E 842(1), 842(2), 935(1); Judgm 215, 270, 273(1), 304, 306, 326.

Griffin & Brand of McAllen, Inc.; Hodgson v., CA5 (Tex), 471 F2d 235, 20 Wage & Hour Cas (BNA) 1051, reh den 472 F2d 1405, cert den Griffin & Brand of McAllen, Inc v. Brennan, 94 SCt 43, 414 US 819, 21 Wage & Hour Cas (BNA) 298, 38 LEd2d 51.—Labor & Emp 2227, 2228, 2387(7), 2418.

Griffin & Brand of McAllen, Inc.; Noel v., TexCivApp–Corpus Christi, 478 SW2d 633.—Plead 111.23, 111.42(7).

Griffin & Brand Sales Agency, Inc.; Gurrola v., SDTex, 524 FSupp 115.—Fed Cts 87, 92, 101, 106.

Griffin & Kimbrough; Gossett v., TexCivApp–San Antonio, 107 SW2d 1115, writ dism.—App & E 77(1); Banks 80(3), 80(10).

Griffin Communications and Security Systems, Inc.; Stone v., TexApp–Tyler, 53 SW3d 687.—App & E 863, 920(3), 946, 954(1), 954(2), 1146; Contracts 116(1), 116(2), 117(2), 117(3); Inj 135, 138.3, 148(2), 157; Labor & Emp 40(3), 48.

Griffing Nurseries v. Texas Nat. Bank of Beaumont, TexCivApp–Beaumont, 100 SW2d 425.—Joint-St Co 15(1).

Griffin Grocery Co.; Stringer v., TexCivApp–Dallas, 149 SW2d 158, writ refused.—Courts 489(1), 489(6); Labor & Emp 2362, 2390(2).

Griffin Industries v. State, TexApp–Corpus Christi, 171 SW3d 414, petition for discretionary review refused, and petition for discretionary review refused.—Const Law 665, 667, 4509(1); Crim Law 13.1(1), 1134(2), 1159.2(7); Environ Law 735, 743, 756, 760.

Griffin Industries; Villegas v., TexApp–Corpus Christi, 975 SW2d 745, review den.—App & E 1074(3); Death 31(3.1), 31(5), 31(6), 31(7), 31(8); False Imp 2, 5, 13, 15(2); Labor & Emp 904; Mal Pros 18(1), 20, 56, 64(2), 71(2); Marriage 4.1, 11, 40(8), 40.1(1), 50(1), 54, 55; Mun Corp 188; Plead 427; Torts 214, 242; Trial 67, 169.

Griffin Industries, Inc. v. Foodmaker, Inc., TexApp–Houston (14 Dist), 22 SW3d 33, petition for review den.—Contracts 215(1); Indem 30(1), 31(1), 33(4), 104; Neglig 252.

Griffin Industries, Inc. v. Honorable Thirteenth Court of Appeals, Tex, 934 SW2d 349.—App & E 389(1), 389(3); Const Law 2317; Costs 128; Evid 96(1), 584(1).

Griffin Oil Co., Inc., In re, BkrtcyEDTex, 149 BR 419.—Bankr 2928, 3567; Const Law 3881, 4478; Int Rev 5067; Notice 9.

Griffin's Estate v. Sumner, TexCivApp–San Antonio, 604 SW2d 221, ref nre.—Appear 9(1); Contracts 9(1), 10(5), 89, 164, 167, 214, 346(3); Courts 35; Plead 111.9, 291(1); Sales 1(4); Spec Perf 1, 64, 117; Ven & Pur 13, 44, 80.

Griffis, Ex parte, TexCrimApp, 145 SW2d 192, 140 TexCrim 364.—Autos 361; Costs 309; Crim Law 1144.17; Hab Corp 253.

Griffis; Jackson v., CA5 (Tex), 289 F2d 825.—Fed Civ Proc 2486.

Griffis; State v., TexCivApp–Waco, 300 SW2d 220, ref nre.—App & E 971(2); Em Dom 148, 150, 177, 262(5); Evid 474(18), 498.5; Wills 616(1).

Griffis; Texas Emp. Ins. Ass'n v., TexCivApp–Galveston, 141 SW2d 687.—Damag 221(3), 221(5.1); Evid 471(13), 477(2), 547, 570; Work Comp 1924.

Griffis & Griffis, P.C.; Whiteside v., TexApp–Austin, 902 SW2d 739, reh overr, and writ den.—Antitrust 575; App & E 1008.1(2); Atty & C 30; Contracts 137(1); Costs 194.12, 194.40, 208.

Griffith, Ex parte, TexCrimApp, 457 SW2d 60.—Courts 97(1); Crim Law 1001, 1192; Hab Corp 223; Sent & Pun 1160, 1161, 2282, 2334.

Griffith v. Allison, TexComApp, 96 SW2d 74, 128 Tex 86.—Dedi 55, 63(1).

Griffith; Anderson v., TexCivApp–Fort Worth, 501 SW2d 695, ref nre.—App & E 706(3), 981; Brok 19, 31, 38(4), 38(5), 75; Evid 215(1); New Tr 99; Princ & A 48.

Griffith; Archer v., Tex, 390 SW2d 735.—App & E 931(4); Atty & C 123(1), 124, 140, 147, 150; Can of Inst 59, 61; Evid 5(2); Fraud 4, 6; Hus & W 82, 162.

Griffith v. Baker, TexComApp, 107 SW2d 371, 130 Tex 17.—App & E 1178(1); Trusts 35(4).

Griffith; Burrell v., EDTex, 158 FRD 104.—Civil R 1031, 1032, 1091, 1098, 1395(1), 1395(7); Fed Civ Proc 2768; Sent & Pun 1546.

Griffith v. Casteel, TexCivApp–Houston, 313 SW2d 149, ref nre.—App & E 662(3), 668, 670(2), 1170.6; Autos 245(88); Damag 208(6), 216(10); Exceptions Bill of 54; New Tr 31; Trial 127, 131(1).

Griffith v. Christian, TexCivApp–Tyler, 564 SW2d 170.—Work Comp 450.

Griffith; City and County of Dallas Levee Imp. Dist. ex rel. Guyton v., TexCivApp–Dallas, 165 SW2d 477, writ refused wom.—Courts 507; Judgm 829(3); Levees 27.

Griffith; Collins v., TexCivApp–Amarillo, 125 SW2d 419, writ refused.—App & E 1175(3); Judgm 199(3.14); Lim of Act 73(1), 73(3), 78, 84(1), 91, 100(11), 100(12), 100(13), 102(8), 103(2), 103(4), 104(1), 199(1); Trusts 91, 102(1), 354, 365(2), 372(1).

Griffith; Collins v., TexCivApp–Amarillo, 105 SW2d 895.—Action 63; Judgm 954; Lim of Act 195(1); Plead 49, 111, 111.37, 111.40; Trusts 103(5); Venue 5.3(1), 5.3(2), 5.3(7).

Griffith v. Conard, TexCivApp–Corpus Christi, 536 SW2d 658.—Judgm 181(6), 185(2), 186, 335(1), 335(2), 335(3), 407(4); Land & Ten 228.

Griffith v. Continental Cas. Co., NDTex, 506 FSupp 1332.—Fed Cts 416; Insurance 1810, 2199, 2432(2), 2445.

Griffith; Daugherty v., TexCivApp–Beaumont, 100 SW2d 197, writ dism.—Tresp to T T 6.1.

Griffith v. Gadberry, TexCivApp–El Paso, 182 SW2d 739.—Alt of Inst 23, 27.1(1); App & E 1053(2); Usury 15, 115, 117.

Griffith v. Geffen & Jacobsen, P.C., TexApp–Dallas, 693 SW2d 724.—App & E 1079; Atty & C 32(13), 143, 156, 182(3); Contracts 95(1); Interest 39(5); Judgm 186; Usury 50.

Griffith v. Griffith, TexApp–El Paso, 698 SW2d 729.—Divorce 254(2).

Griffith; Griffith v., TexApp–El Paso, 698 SW2d 729.—Divorce 254(2).

Griffith v. Griffith, TexApp–Tyler, 860 SW2d 252.—App & E 5, 859, 1140(1), 1152; Divorce 239, 278.1.

Griffith; Griffith v., TexApp–Tyler, 860 SW2d 252.—App & E 5, 859, 1140(1), 1152; Divorce 239, 278.1.

Griffith v. Griffith, TexCivApp–Beaumont, 584 SW2d
498.—App & E 553(1), 1071.6; Divorce 150, 183; Trial
395(5).

Griffith; Griffith v., TexCivApp–Beaumont, 584 SW2d
498.—App & E 553(1), 1071.6; Divorce 150, 183; Trial
395(5).

Griffith v. Griffith, TexCivApp–Eastland, 252 SW2d 517,
ref nre.—Bills & N 394.

Griffith; Griffith v., TexCivApp–Eastland, 252 SW2d 517,
ref nre.—Bills & N 394.

Griffith v. Griffith, TexCivApp–Tyler, 462 SW2d 328.—
Child C 27, 76, 413, 508, 510, 524; Child S 21.

Griffith; Griffith v., TexCivApp–Tyler, 462 SW2d 328.—
Child C 27, 76, 413, 508, 510, 524; Child S 21.

Griffith; Gulf Oil Corp. v., CA5 (Tex), 330 F2d 729.—
Electricity 19(5); Fed Cts 847.

Griffith; Gwin v., TexCivApp–Corpus Christi, 394 SW2d
191.—Judgm 181(15.1), 185(2), 185.3(17); Mtg 154(2),
186(4), 186(5), 372(1), 378; Tresp to T T 7; Ven & Pur
242.

Griffith; Hankins v., TexApp–Corpus Christi, 773 SW2d
589, writ den.—Release 52, 57(2).

Griffith; Highway Ins. Underwriters v., TexCivApp–
Austin, 290 SW2d 950, ref nre.—Garn 164, 173; Insurance 3120, 3191(12), 3200; Pretrial Proc 387; Trial 178.

Griffith v. Hipp, BkrtcyNDTex, 71 BR 643. See Hipp,
Inc., In re.

Griffith v. Hudspeth, TexCivApp–San Antonio, 378 SW2d
153.—Autos 245(39); New Tr 140(3); Trial 304.

Griffith v. Johnston, CA5 (Tex), 899 F2d 1427, reh den
904 F2d 705, cert den 111 SCt 712, 498 US 1040, 112
LEd2d 701.—Adop 20; Civil R 1034, 1304, 1395(1);
Const Law 82(10), 3740, 3869, 4110, 4111, 4117; Fed Cts
542, 666; Infants 226.

Griffith v. Jones, TexCivApp–Austin, 91 SW2d 1144.—
App & E 151(1), 832(5); Des & Dist 146.

Griffith; Jones v., TexCivApp–Eastland, 109 SW2d 565.—
App & E 750(4); Judgm 472; Mental H 264, 515.

Griffith v. Jones, TexCivApp–Tyler, 518 SW2d 435, ref
nre.—App & E 846(5), 854(1), 931(3), 989; Corp 57, 94;
Des & Dist 9.

Griffith v. Kernaghan, TexCivApp–Austin, 121 SW2d
617.—App & E 672; Neglig 381, 384; Work Comp 2110,
2119, 2140.

Griffith v. Lawrence Systems, Inc. of Mass., BkrtcyND-
Tex, 71 BR 643. See Hipp, Inc., In re.

Griffith; Lefton v., TexApp–San Antonio, 136 SW3d 271.
—Antitrust 389(2), 390, 391, 398; App & E 837(1), 901,
907(1), 1010.2, 1136; Damag 6, 18, 102, 190, 192, 194;
Evid 474(18); Judgm 112, 126(4), 144.

Griffith v. Levi Strauss & Co., CA5 (Tex), 85 F3d 185.—
Action 3; Antitrust 260, 290; Contracts 312(4); Fraud
9.

Griffith v. Mauritz, TexCivApp–Houston, 308 SW2d 599.
—Inj 128(3.1), 138.31, 147, 157, 204.

Griffith; Mostyn v., TexCivApp–Beaumont, 130 SW2d
906, writ dism, correct.—Execution 171(4); Judgm
779(1).

Griffith; Nettles v., EDTex, 883 FSupp 136.—Civil R
1031, 1335, 1351(1), 1358, 1420, 1459, 1461, 1462, 1464,
1465(1), 1485; Const Law 3869, 3873, 4824, 4826, 4828;
Damag 87(1); Prisons 13(5), 13(8), 13.5(1), 17(1), 17(4);
Sent & Pun 1433, 1528, 1532, 1533, 1537, 1553.

Griffith; Northwestern Nat. Life Ins. Co. v., TexCiv-
App–Eastland, 97 SW2d 710.—App & E 1011.1(4);
Home 162(1), 181(3).

Griffith v. Oles, CA5 (Tex), 895 F2d 1503. See Hipp,
Inc., Matter of.

Griffith v. Oles Grain Co., BkrtcyNDTex, 71 BR 643.
See Hipp, Inc., In re.

Griffith v. Pecan Plantation Owners Ass'n, Inc., Tex-
App–Fort Worth, 667 SW2d 626.—App & E 174; Inj
62(1); Judgm 185(1), 185.1(1), 185.3(2).

Griffith v. Porter, TexApp–Tyler, 817 SW2d 131.—Anti-
trust 135(1), 136, 145, 150, 209, 369, 389(2), 390, 397;
App & E 846(5); Contracts 261(1), 261(6), 313(1); Ven
& Pur 89.

Griffith v. Quarterman, CA5 (Tex), 196 FedAppx 237,
cert den 127 SCt 957, 166 LEd2d 728.—Const Law
4744(2), 4789(2); Costs 302.2(2); Crim Law 641.13(7),
662.7; Hab Corp 382; Sent & Pun 1760, 1763.

Griffith; Redmon v., TexApp–Tyler, 202 SW3d 225, reh
overr, and review den.—Action 6, 13; App & E 863,
893(1), 913, 1079; Contracts 186(1), 186(3); Corp 174,
182.3, 190, 202, 306, 307; Fraud 7; Fraud Conv 216;
Judgm 181(31), 183, 185(2), 185(5).

Griffith; Roberts v., TexCivApp–Eastland, 207 SW2d 443,
ref nre.—Estop 52.10(2); Frds St of 44(4), 119(2),
129(11); Land & Ten 95, 150(1), 280.5, 283.

Griffith; Smith and Conklin Bros. v., Tex, 268 SW2d
124, 153 Tex 341.—Neglig 1672; Trial 351.5(2).

Griffith; Smith & Conklin Bros. v., TexCivApp–Galveston, 260 SW2d 705, aff 268 SW2d 124, 153 Tex 341.—
Damag 134(1); Neglig 1683.

Griffith; Southwestern Bell Tel. Co. v., TexCivApp–
Corpus Christi, 575 SW2d 92, ref nre.—App & E
173(13), 223, 596, 715(2), 837(10), 931(1), 966(1), 970(2),
989, 1048(2); Evid 82, 118, 121(1), 123(8), 383(10),
571(9), 588; Judgm 1, 215; Pretrial Proc 25, 151, 713,
717.1, 724; Prod Liab 6, 8, 27, 28, 62, 83, 88; Trial 382.

Griffith v. State, TexCrimApp, 166 SW3d 261.—Sent &
Pun 278; Statut 188, 206.

Griffith v. State, TexCrimApp, 116 SW3d 782.—Sent &
Pun 1236, 1258; Statut 181(1), 181(2), 184, 189, 214.

Griffith v. State, TexCrimApp, 55 SW3d 598.—Autos 354,
413, 421; Const Law 4666; Crim Law 393(1), 407(1),
412.1(4), 412.2(2), 641.3(3), 641.3(8.1).

Griffith v. State, TexCrimApp, 983 SW2d 282, cert den
120 SCt 77, 528 US 826, 145 LEd2d 65, habeas corpus
dism by 2005 WL 2372044, certificate of appealability
den 196 FedAppx 237, cert den 127 SCt 957, 166 LEd2d
728.—Arrest 71.1(4.1), 71.1(9); Const Law 4773; Costs
302, 302.2(2), 302.4; Crim Law 388.1, 429(1), 469.1, 472,
481, 486(4), 749, 1134(3), 1153(1); Sent & Pun 1758(1),
1763, 1769, 1777; Witn 335.

Griffith v. State, TexCrimApp, 450 SW2d 89.—Bail 79(1).

Griffith v. State, TexCrimApp, 430 SW2d 197.—Homic
856, 857, 997, 1154; Witn 277(4).

Griffith v. State, TexCrimApp, 391 SW2d 428.—Burg
41(1); Crim Law 662.80, 698(1); Witn 266.

Griffith v. State, TexCrimApp, 354 SW2d 942, 172 Tex-
Crim 148.—Crim Law 881(2).

Griffith v. State, TexCrimApp, 191 SW2d 740, 149 Tex-
Crim 73.—False Pret 31.

Griffith v. State, TexCrimApp, 169 SW2d 173, 145 Tex-
Crim 465.—Assault 92(5), 96(7); Crim Law 661, 1111(3),
1170(2).

Griffith v. State, TexCrimApp, 155 SW2d 612, 142 Tex-
Crim 559.—Crim Law 363, 366(6), 455, 823(4), 1170.5(5);
Rape 57(1), 59(2).

Griffith v. State, TexCrimApp, 152 SW2d 349, 142 Tex-
Crim 304.—Crim Law 1166.6; Homic 931, 1032.

Griffith v. State, TexCrimApp, 149 SW2d 586, 141 Tex-
Crim 482.—Crim Law 1097(4).

Griffith v. State, TexCrimApp, 148 SW2d 429, 141 Tex-
Crim 482, reh overr 149 SW2d 586, 141 TexCrim 482.—
Crim Law 1097(4); Hus & W 304; Ind & Inf 125(20).

Griffith v. State, TexCrimApp, 118 SW2d 603, 135 Tex-
Crim 243.—Crim Law 1086.13, 1087.1(2).

Griffith v. State, TexApp–Houston (1 Dist), 81 SW3d 510,
petition for discretionary review gr, aff 116 SW3d 782.
—Const Law 2816; Sent & Pun 1216, 1286; Statut 189,
190.

Griffith v. State, TexApp–Houston (1 Dist), 686 SW2d
331.—Crim Law 865(1.5), 1131(5), 1174(1).

Griffith v. State, TexApp–Houston (1 Dist), 635 SW2d
145.—Crim Law 867, 1036.1(1); Rape 1, 51(1).

Griffith v. State, TexApp–Amarillo, 976 SW2d 241, petition for discretionary review refused.—Crim Law 388.2, 476.6, 730(3), 1169.1(7).

Griffith v. State, TexApp–Tyler, 976 SW2d 686, reh overr, and petition for discretionary review refused.— Const Law 4580; Courts 97(5); Crim Law 553, 559, 562, 577.8(2), 577.10(1), 577.10(10), 577.12(1), 577.14, 577.15(1), 577.15(4), 577.16(4), 577.16(8), 577.16(9), 745, 862, 1139, 1144.13(3), 1159.2(2), 1159.2(4), 1159.2(7), 1159.2(9), 1159.4(2); Homic 942, 1184, 1193, 1194, 1201, 1345.

Griffith v. State, TexApp–Houston (14 Dist), 135 SW3d 337, petition for discretionary review gr, aff 166 SW3d 261.—Crim Law 273.4(1), 1026.10(1); Sent & Pun 299.

Griffith v. Taylor, Tex, 291 SW2d 673, 156 Tex 1.—Mines 55(4), 79.1(2).

Griffith v. Taylor, TexCivApp–Amarillo, 284 SW2d 768, rev 291 SW2d 673, 156 Tex 1.—Mines 55(4).

Griffith; Tew v., TexCivApp–Galveston, 187 SW2d 408, writ refused wom.—App & E 192.1, 194(1), 253.

Griffith; Texas & P. Ry. Co. v., CA5 (Tex), 265 F2d 489. —Fed Civ Proc 2173, 2212.1, 2214; Fed Cts 909; Labor & Emp 2829, 2862, 2880, 2886.

Griffith v. Thomson, TexCivApp–San Antonio, 244 SW2d 722.—App & E 1010.1(1); Contracts 175(3), 318, 322(3).

Griffith v. U. S., SDTex, 403 FSupp 705.—Contracts 103; Int Rev 3231, 3254.

Griffith v. Wels, TexCivApp–Waco, 236 SW2d 166.—Lim of Act 197(3).

Griffith; West Columbia Nat. Bank v., TexApp–Houston (1 Dist), 902 SW2d 201, reh overr, and writ den.—App & E 82(2), 387(2), 387(3), 387(6); Judgm 17(10), 143(3), 143(16), 335(1), 335(2); Proc 133, 145, 153; Trial 388(2), 392(2).

Griffith; Winston v., TexComApp, 128 SW2d 25, 133 Tex 348.—App & E 1082(1), 1091(1); Wills 63, 700.

Griffith; Winston v., TexCivApp–Fort Worth, 108 SW2d 745, aff 128 SW2d 25, 133 Tex 348.—Courts 475(2); Wills 62, 449, 470(1), 472, 486, 487(1), 695(1), 700.

Griffith Amusement Co.; City of Wink v., Tex, 100 SW2d 695, 129 Tex 40.—Const Law 1109; Equity 65(1), 65(2); Evid 5(2); Inj 85(2), 114(2); Lotteries 3; Mun Corp 111(2), 111(4), 592(3); Nuis 84.

Griffith Amusement Co. v. Morgan, TexCivApp–Austin, 98 SW2d 844.—Lotteries 3.

Griffiths, In Interest of, TexApp–Amarillo, 780 SW2d 899.—Divorce 313.1.

Griffiths v. Travis, TexApp–Dallas, 102 SW2d 445, writ refused.—App & E 959(3); Lim of Act 189, 193; Plead 236(3).

Griffith-Williams Cattle Co.; Crystal City Independent School Dist. v., TexCivApp–San Antonio, 575 SW2d 336, ref nre.—Schools 103(1), 111.

Griffitts, Ex parte, Tex, 711 SW2d 225.—Contempt 51.1, 56.

Griffitts v. State, TexApp–Dallas, 789 SW2d 699.—Crim Law 147.

Grigar; Hatton v., TexApp–Houston (14 Dist), 66 SW3d 545, rule 537(f) motion den.—App & E 173(5), 846(5), 852, 989, 994(1), 1008.1(3), 1010.1(1), 1010.2, 1012.1(4), 1122(2); Costs 194.40; Dedi 1, 15, 16.1, 17, 18(2), 20(5), 30.1, 41, 45, 55; High 1, 5.

Grigg; Holley v., TexApp–Eastland, 65 SW3d 289.—Contracts 2, 93(1), 93(5), 129(1), 143(2), 143.5, 176(2), 193; Evid 207(1), 265(7); Judgm 181(2); Ref of Inst 17(1); Wills 88(1).

Griggs v. Capitol Mach. Works, Inc., Tex, 701 SW2d 238.—App & E 169.

Griggs v. Capitol Mach. Works, Inc., TexApp–Austin, 690 SW2d 287, ref nre 701 SW2d 238.—Const Law 2503(1); Corp 1.4(4), 34(0.5), 445.1; Courts 91(2); Judgm 181(2), 181(3); Neglig 480; Torts 109.

Griggs v. Curry, TexCivApp–Waco, 336 SW2d 248, ref nre.—Mtg 39; New Tr 108(2); Trial 87.

Griggs v. Griggs, TexCivApp–Amarillo, 428 SW2d 165.— Divorce 130, 135.

Griggs; Griggs v., TexCivApp–Amarillo, 428 SW2d 165.— Divorce 130, 135.

Griggs v. Griggs, TexCivApp–Beaumont, 374 SW2d 937, ref nre.—Adop 7.6(1).

Griggs; Griggs v., TexCivApp–Beaumont, 374 SW2d 937, ref nre.—Adop 7.6(1).

Griggs; Infonova Solutions, Inc. v., TexApp–San Antonio, 82 SW3d 613.—App & E 78(7), 937(1); Costs 194.10, 208; Judgm 217; Motions 51.

Griggs v. Latham, TexApp–Corpus Christi, 98 SW3d 382, reh overr, and review den.—App & E 949; Child C 605; Parties 18, 29, 50; Pretrial Proc 506.1, 508.

Griggs v. Magnolia Petroleum Co., TexCivApp–Amarillo, 319 SW2d 818.—Fixt 7; Frds St of 72(4); Judgm 185.2(9); Spec Perf 39.

Griggs; Moray Corp. v., TexApp–Houston (1 Dist), 713 SW2d 753, writ refused.—Home 5, 97; Mech Liens 73(3); Trover 17.

Griggs v. Reed, TexCivApp–Eastland, 233 SW2d 907.— Hus & W 262.1(2), 262.2, 264(5); Partit 62, 63(1); Stip 14(1).

Griggs; Sawdust Const. Co. v., TexApp–Houston (1 Dist), 713 SW2d 753. See Moray Corp. v. Griggs.

Griggs; Standard Fire Ins. Co. v., TexCivApp–Amarillo, 567 SW2d 60, ref nre.—Insurance 1808, 1825, 1832(1), 1835(2), 1855, 2168, 2202.

Griggs v. State, TexCrimApp, 213 SW3d 923.—Crim Law 1036.1(2), 1044.2(1).

Griggs v. State, TexCrimApp, 558 SW2d 474.—Crim Law 441; Larc 40(2); Stip 18(4).

Griggs v. State, TexCrimApp, 451 SW2d 481.—Controlled Subs 73; Crim Law 274(8), 394.4(6), 789(3); Sent & Pun 1490.

Griggs v. State, TexCrimApp, 311 SW2d 418, 166 TexCrim 56.—Crim Law 721(1), 1171.5.

Griggs v. State, TexCrimApp, 292 SW2d 126, 163 TexCrim 378.—Crim Law 1083.

Griggs v. State, TexCrimApp, 235 SW2d 154, 155 TexCrim 354.—Homic 1134; Ind & Inf 87(2).

Griggs v. State, TexApp–Houston (1 Dist), 99 SW3d 718, petition for discretionary review refused.—Crim Law 662.3, 1130(5), 1134(3).

Griggs v. State, TexApp–Waco, 167 SW3d 74, petition for discretionary review gr, rev 213 SW3d 923.—Crim Law 629.5(2), 706(5), 730(3), 867, 1036.1(2), 1044.2(1), 1144.13(2.1), 1155, 1159.2(7), 1169.5(3); Rape 51(7).

Griggs v. State Farm Lloyds, CA5 (Tex), 181 F3d 694, reh den.—Antitrust 138; Fed Civ Proc 2771(15); Fed Cts 830; Insurance 3146, 3336; Rem of C 36, 107(7), 107(9).

Griggs v. Triple S Indus. Corp., TexApp–Beaumont, 197 SW3d 408.—Const Law 2488; Labor & Emp 807, 808.

Griggs & Harrison; Ecotech Intern., Inc. v., TexApp– San Antonio, 928 SW2d 644, reh overr, and writ den.— Antitrust 282; Atty & C 46, 112; Insurance 3350, 3357; Judgm 181(15.1), 183, 185(2).

Griggs and Harrison; Judwin Properties, Inc. v., TexApp–Houston (1 Dist), 911 SW2d 498, appeal after remand 981 SW2d 868, petition for discretionary review den per curiam opinion 11 SW3d 188.—App & E 934(1); Atty & C 105, 109, 123(1), 129(2), 157.1, 162; Judgm 181(16), 183, 185(2), 185(4), 185(6), 186, 189.

Griggs & Harrison, P.C.; Judwin Properties, Inc. v., TexApp–Houston (1 Dist), 981 SW2d 868, petition for discretionary review den with per curiam opinion 11 SW3d 188.—App & E 852; Atty & C 109, 129(2); Witn 201(1).

Griggs Canning Co. v. Josey, Tex, 164 SW2d 835, 139 Tex 623, 142 ALR 1424, answer to certified question conformed to 165 SW2d 201.—Sales 274.

Griggs Canning Co. v. Josey, TexCivApp–San Antonio, 165 SW2d 201.—Sales 274; Venue 22(6).

Griggs Equipment, Inc.; N.L.R.B. v., CA5 (Tex), 307 F2d 275.—Labor & Emp 982, 1746, 1755, 1760, 1799.

Griggs Furniture Co. v. Bufkin, TexCivApp–Amarillo, 348 SW2d 867, ref nre.—App & E 231(7), 1051(1); Evid 506; Gas 20(4); Trial 105(1), 127, 350.5(1), 350.6(1); Witn 372(1).

Griggs Southwest Mortuary, Inc.; City of Amarillo v., TexCivApp–Amarillo, 406 SW2d 230, ref nre.—Autos 5(1); Const Law 2642; Decl Judgm 124.1, 128; Inj 85(1), 85(2); Licens 6; Mun Corp 592(1), 703(1).

Grigsby, Ex parte, TexCrimApp, 137 SW3d 673.—Hab Corp 293, 493(1), 799.

Grigsby v. Allison, TexCivApp–Austin, 322 SW2d 57.—App & E 773(2).

Grigsby; Browning v., TexApp–Texarkana, 657 SW2d 821.—Interpl 35; Mines 55(2).

Grigsby v. Coker, Tex, 904 SW2d 619.—Const Law 82(10), 2093, 2094; Divorce 87.

Grigsby; Columbia Cas. Co. v., TexCivApp–Austin, 376 SW2d 51, ref nre.—Damag 221(3), 221(5.1); Work Comp 869, 1507, 1648, 1719.

Grigsby v. Estelle, CA5 (Tex), 500 F2d 394.—Hab Corp 765.1.

Grigsby v. First Nat. Bank, TexCivApp–Amarillo, 125 SW2d 368, rev 144 SW2d 244, 136 Tex 54, opinion corrected on denial of reh 146 SW2d 174, 136 Tex 54.—Banks 130(1), 154(8); Evid 263(1), 265(1), 425.

Grigsby v. First Nat. Bank in Quanah, TexComApp, 146 SW2d 174, 136 Tex 54.—Banks 154(8).

Grigsby v. First Nat. Bank in Quanah, TexComApp, 144 SW2d 244, 136 Tex 54, opinion corrected on denial of reh 146 SW2d 174, 136 Tex 54.—Banks 130(1), 154(8).

Grigsby; French v., Tex, 571 SW2d 867.—Autos 246(38); Neglig 530(2), 1745.

Grigsby; French v., TexCivApp–Beaumont, 567 SW2d 604, ref nre 571 SW2d 867.—Damag 48, 100, 216(1), 221(2.1), 221(5.1); Neglig 530(2); New Tr 44(3), 140(3), 157.

Grigsby v. Grigsby, TexApp–San Antonio, 757 SW2d 163.—App & E 863; Judgm 181(20), 185.2(4), 185.3(9); Marriage 40(3), 40(4).

Grigsby; Grigsby v., TexApp–San Antonio, 757 SW2d 163.—App & E 863; Judgm 181(20), 185.2(4), 185.3(9); Marriage 40(3), 40(4).

Grigsby v. Hopkins, TexCivApp–Fort Worth, 218 SW2d 275, writ refused.—Atty & C 192(1); Costs 194.10; Quiet T 54.

Grigsby v. Moses, TexApp–Austin, 31 SW3d 747.—Estop 52.10(2); Schools 61.

Grigsby v. State, TexCrimApp, 298 SW2d 595, 164 Tex-Crim 248.—Crim Law 478(1); Lotteries 29.

Grigsby v. State, TexCrimApp, 257 SW2d 110, 158 Tex-Crim 484.—Crim Law 867; Double J 99.

Grigsby v. State, TexCrimApp, 253 SW2d 871, 158 Tex-Crim 114.—Autos 326.

Grigsby v. State, TexCrimApp, 245 SW2d 254.—Crim Law 1090.1(1).

Grigsby v. State, TexApp–Dallas, 833 SW2d 573, petition for discretionary review refused.—Crim Law 713, 723(1), 790, 1172.1(2), 1173.2(1).

Grigson; Clark v., TexCivApp–Dallas, 579 SW2d 263, ref nre.—Health 642, 709(1); Libel 38(4); Mal Pros 3, 24(4).

Grigson v. Creative Artists Agency L.L.C., CA5 (Tex), 210 F3d 524, reh en banc den 218 F3d 745, cert den 121 SCt 570, 531 US 1013, 148 LEd2d 488.—Alt Disp Res 113, 119, 186; Estop 52(8), 55; Fed Cts 612.1, 812, 813.

Grigson; Milliken v., SDTex, 986 FSupp 426, aff 158 F3d 583.—Alt Disp Res 113, 363(8), 379, 382, 386; Atty & C 21.10, 21.20; Judgm 634, 650, 668(1), 678(1), 678(2), 683, 724.

Grijalva; El Paso County Water Imp. Dist. No. One v., TexApp–El Paso, 783 SW2d 736, writ den with per curiam opinion El Paso County Water Imp Dist No 1 v.

Grijalva, 795 SW2d 705.—App & E 930(3), 989, 996, 1001(1), 1003(6); Contracts 29; Damag 112; Interest 66; Waters 183.5, 263.

Grijalva v. State, TexCrimApp, 614 SW2d 420.—Crim Law 1166.17; Jury 137(1).

Grijalva v. U.S., CA5 (Tex), 781 F2d 472, cert den 107 SCt 89, 479 US 822, 93 LEd2d 42.—Work Comp 2106, 2133.

Grijalva-Lopez; U.S. v., CA5 (Tex), 430 F3d 259.—Crim Law 1042.

Grijalva-Lopez; U.S. v., CA5 (Tex), 108 FedAppx 157, cert gr, vac 125 SCt 1087, 543 US 1114, 160 LEd2d 1058, on remand 430 F3d 259.—Sent & Pun 841.

Grim v. State, TexApp–Eastland, 923 SW2d 767.—Crim Law 273.1(4), 273.1(5), 641.13(1), 641.13(7), 656(3); Jury 24.

Grim v. State, TexApp–Corpus Christi, 656 SW2d 542.—Autos 349(2.1); Crim Law 1144.17, 1177; Sent & Pun 2021, 2022.

Grimaldo v. Lewis, TexApp–Corpus Christi, 915 SW2d 222, reh overr, and reh of motion for mandamus overr.—App & E 389(1); Costs 132(5); Mand 29, 57(1).

Grimaldo v. State, TexApp–Amarillo, 223 SW3d 429.—Controlled Subs 129, 130; Crim Law 394.5(3), 1139, 1158(4); Searches 42.1, 182, 184, 192.1, 198.

Grimaldo v. State, TexApp–Corpus Christi, 130 SW3d 450.—Crim Law 577.10(1), 577.10(9), 1035(1), 1118.

Grimes, Ex parte, Tex, 443 SW2d 250.—Contempt 24; Hab Corp 804, 844.

Grimes v. Andrews, TexApp–Waco, 997 SW2d 877.—App & E 78(1), 780(1), 1175(2); Contracts 143(2), 143.5, 152, 162, 175(1), 176(2); Judgm 181(19); Release 1, 25, 30, 38; Work Comp 1130.

Grimes v. Bosque County, TexCivApp–Waco, 240 SW2d 511, ref nre.—Autos 19; Bonds 50; Const Law 1066; Counties 110, 153.5; Lim of Act 24(2), 127(4); Sheriffs 61, 158, 169; Trial 350.4(1).

Grimes v. Bowman, TexApp–Waco, 122 SW2d 361.—Labor & Emp 858; Land & Ten 322, 331(2); Trial 357.

Grimes; Bowman v., TexCivApp–Eastland, 155 SW2d 420, writ refused wom.—Contracts 346(2); Land & Ten 48(1); Trial 366.

Grimes v. Castleberry, CA5 (Tex), 381 F2d 758.—Commerce 62.40, 62.43, 62.49; Labor & Emp 2269, 2387(9).

Grimes v. Collie, TexApp–El Paso, 733 SW2d 338.—App & E 882(1), 901, 931(3), 931(4), 1010.1(8.1); Partit 63(3), 96, 114(3).

Grimes v. Corpus Christi Transmission Co., TexApp–Corpus Christi, 829 SW2d 335, reh overr, and reh overr, and writ den, and reh dism.—Costs 207; Gas 9; High 13, 67, 87, 89; Judgm 185(1), 185.1(2); Mun Corp 680(4).

Grimes; Cosgrove v., Tex, 774 SW2d 662.—App & E 231(9); Atty & C 105, 106, 107, 129(2), 129(4); Damag 49.10; Trial 351.2(4).

Grimes; Cosgrove v., TexApp–Houston (1 Dist), 757 SW2d 508, writ gr, rev 774 SW2d 662.—App & E 231(1), 883; Atty & C 105, 112; Trial 350.2, 350.3(4), 351.2(4), 352.1(3).

Grimes; Dacus v., TexApp–Tyler, 624 SW2d 298.—App & E 173(12), 756, 761, 989, 1177(2); Bills & N 516, 520; Evid 441(11).

Grimes, Estate of v. Dorchester Gas Producing Co., TexApp–Amarillo, 707 SW2d 196, ref nre.—App & E 927(7), 997(3); Contracts 103; Decl Judgm 368; Estop 92(2); Judgm 114; Mines 58, 73, 78.1(6), 92.79; Trial 139.1(5.1), 178.

Grimes v. Flores, TexApp–San Antonio, 717 SW2d 956.—Hab Corp 798.

Grimes v. Flores, TexApp–San Antonio, 717 SW2d 949.—Child C 20; Hab Corp 532(1), 532(2); Mand 51.

Grimes; Ford Motor Co. v., TexCivApp–Eastland, 408 SW2d 313, writ dism.—Plead 111.42(4); Sales 255, 273(1).

Grimes; Gill v., TexCivApp–Waco, 238 SW2d 989.—Bound 8, 37(3).

Grimes; Gillespie v., TexCivApp–Tyler, 577 SW2d 538.—Nuis 44, 49(1), 49(5), 50(1).

Grimes; Goggin v., TexApp–Houston (14 Dist), 969 SW2d 135.—Afft 1; App & E 852; Atty & C 76(1), 105; Judgm 185.1(3), 185.1(4), 185.3(4), 585(4); Torts 138.

Grimes v. Graue, BkrtcySDTex, 158 BR 965. See Haws, In re.

Grimes v. Graue & Affiliates, BkrtcySDTex, 158 BR 965. See Haws, In re.

Grimes v. Grimes, TexApp–San Antonio, 706 SW2d 340, dism.—Child C 736; Contempt 66(1).

Grimes; Grimes v., TexApp–San Antonio, 706 SW2d 340, dism.—Child C 736; Contempt 66(1).

Grimes v. Grimes, TexCivApp–Austin, 365 SW2d 228.—Divorce 27(1), 27(8.1), 51, 147, 184(4).

Grimes; Grimes v., TexCivApp–Austin, 365 SW2d 228.—Divorce 27(1), 27(8.1), 51, 147, 184(4).

Grimes v. Grimes, TexCivApp–Hous (14 Dist), 612 SW2d 714.—Costs 194.16; Divorce 269(1), 288.

Grimes; Grimes v., TexCivApp–Hous (14 Dist), 612 SW2d 714.—Costs 194.16; Divorce 269(1), 288.

Grimes v. Hall, TexCivApp–Eastland, 211 SW2d 956.—App & E 220, 1022(3); Partit 92, 94(3).

Grimes v. Harris, TexApp–Dallas, 695 SW2d 648.—Child C 404; Courts 475(1), 475(15).

Grimes v. Jalco, Inc., TexApp–Houston (1 Dist), 630 SW2d 282, ref nre.—Evid 205(1), 265(7); Judgm 181(21); Witn 379(2); Work Comp 2105.

Grimes v. Jordan, TexCivApp–Beaumont, 260 SW2d 220, writ refused.—App & E 1010.1(18); Deeds 42, 111, 118, 119; Evid 452.

Grimes; Knowles v., Tex, 437 SW2d 816.—Child C 532, 555, 574, 578; Judgm 815.

Grimes v. Knowles, TexCivApp–Tyler, 431 SW2d 602, writ gr, rev 437 SW2d 816.—Child C 26, 42, 553, 555, 574, 578; Evid 80(1); Judgm 815.

Grimes; La Fon v., CCA5 (Tex), 86 F2d 809, 109 ALR 156.—Fed Cts 901.1; Hus & W 273(1), 273(12); Ven & Pur 236, 242; Witn 143(2).

Grimes v. La Gloria Corp., TexCivApp–San Antonio, 251 SW2d 755.—Contracts 143(3); Mines 79.1(5).

Grimes v. McCrary, TexCivApp–Texarkana, 211 SW2d 1005.—App & E 1173(1); Home 83; Venue 5.5, 6, 8.5(3), 8.5(4), 8.5(5).

Grimes v. Maynard, TexCivApp–Waco, 270 SW2d 282, writ refused, cert den 75 SCt 580, 349 US 904, 99 LEd 1241.—Judgm 457, 518, 725(1), 958(1).

Grimes; Mulry v., TexCivApp–Waco, 280 SW2d 350.—Ex & Ad 22(1), 22(3), 31.

Grimes v. Mulry, TexCivApp–Waco, 280 SW2d 343.—New Tr 72(1); Trial 139.1(3); Wills 55(5), 55(10), 333, 384, 386.

Grimes; Owens v., TexCivApp–Tyler, 539 SW2d 387, ref nre.—Mtg 1, 369(6), 374, 379; Trover 2.

Grimes v. Pure Milk & Ice Cream Co., TexCivApp–Waco, 527 SW2d 508, dism.—Plead 111.42(5); Trial 105(5); Venue 7.5(1).

Grimes v. Robitaille, TexCivApp–Galveston, 288 SW2d 211, ref nre.—App & E 1097(1), 1151(3); Costs 260(4), 262, 263; Judgm 21.

Grimes v. Robitaille, TexCivApp–Galveston, 279 SW2d 132, writ refused.—Judgm 720.

Grimes v. Robitaille, TexCivApp–Galveston, 257 SW2d 359, ref nre.—App & E 719(8); Judgm 518, 720.

Grimes; Southern Underwriters v., TexCivApp–San Antonio, 146 SW2d 1058, writ dism, correct.—App & E 231(1), 1062.1; Damag 221(2.1), 221(4), 221(5.1); Work Comp 511, 564, 840, 1927, 1937, 1969.

Grimes v. Stafford, TexCivApp–Austin, 212 SW2d 192.—App & E 934(1); Courts 480(3); Execution 172(4); Forci E & D 43(1); Judgm 660.

Grimes v. State, TexCrimApp, 807 SW2d 582.—Const Law 188, 2782, 2810; Crim Law 906.

Grimes v. State, TexCrimApp, 449 SW2d 270.—Crim Law 1131(4).

Grimes v. State, TexCrimApp, 349 SW2d 598, 171 TexCrim 298.—Crim Law 919(1), 959, 1111(3); Homic 1193.

Grimes v. State, TexCrimApp, 327 SW2d 583, 168 TexCrim 341.—Crim Law 755.5, 778(5), 814(17); Gaming 97(1), 98(4).

Grimes v. State, TexCrimApp, 245 SW2d 267.—Crim Law 1090.1(1).

Grimes v. State, TexCrimApp, 230 SW2d 545.—Crim Law 1090.1(1).

Grimes v. State, TexCrimApp, 225 SW2d 978, 154 TexCrim 199.—Crim Law 364(6), 404.20, 517.3(4), 675, 941(1), 1169.1(3), 1169.1(7); Homic 962, 1136.

Grimes v. State, TexCrimApp, 94 SW2d 1153, 130 TexCrim 482.—Forg 48; Ind & Inf 184.

Grimes v. State, TexApp–Houston (1 Dist), 135 SW3d 803.—Crim Law 304(1), 304(2), 412.1(4), 412.2(2), 438(8), 489, 627.8(6), 655(1), 1044.2(1), 1128(4), 1130(2), 1134(1), 1153(1), 1159.2(2), 1169.1(4), 1169.2(2); Ind & Inf 176; Perj 12, 33(2); Rape 52(1).

Grimes v. State, TexApp–Houston (1 Dist), 779 SW2d 124, petition for discretionary review refused.—Jury 136(4), 142.

Grimes v. State, TexApp–Fort Worth, 778 SW2d 193.—Crim Law 656(7), 1030(2), 1035(9), 1043(2), 1166.22(4.1); Witn 300, 307.

Grimes v. Stringer, TexApp–Tyler, 957 SW2d 865, reh overr, and review den.—App & E 852, 863, 934(1); Judgm 185(2); Pretrial Proc 508, 518; Schools 115, 147; Set-Off 11.

Grimes v. Talbot, TexCivApp–Galveston, 233 SW2d 206, ref nre.—Deeds 155; Mines 74(2); Plead 228.19.

Grimes v. Texas Dept. of Mental Health and Mental Retardation, CA5 (Tex), 102 F3d 137.—Civil R 1137, 1243, 1244, 1535, 1544, 1548; Fed Civ Proc 2497.1, 2545; Fed Cts 766, 776.

Grimes; Texas Emp. Ins. Ass'n v., Tex, 269 SW2d 332, 153 Tex 357.—Death 31(6); Infants 107, 110, 115; Work Comp 433, 438, 2194, 2251.

Grimes; Texas Emp. Ins. Ass'n v., TexCivApp–San Antonio, 256 SW2d 234, aff 269 SW2d 332, 153 Tex 357.—Death 98; Work Comp 2251.

Grimes; Texas Emp. Ins. Ass'n v., TexCivApp–Texarkana, 268 SW2d 786, ref nre.—Work Comp 1615.

Grimes; Texas Emp. Ins. Ass'n v., TexCivApp–Waco, 186 SW2d 280, writ refused wom.—Work Comp 569, 1165, 1239, 1265, 1917, 1924.

Grimes; Time Ins. Agency, Inc. v., TexCivApp–Texarkana, 613 SW2d 40.—App & E 878(2); Evid 397(3), 419(11), 448; Frds St of 33(2); Subrog 41(6).

Grimes; Travelers Ins. Co. v., TexCivApp–Fort Worth, 358 SW2d 247.—Work Comp 550, 869, 1325, 1648.

Grimes; Twin City Fire Ins. Co. v., TexApp–Tyler, 724 SW2d 956, ref nre.—Courts 91(1); Work Comp 847, 1647.

Grimes; U.S. v., CA5 (Tex), 244 F3d 375.—Crim Law 369.2(1), 371(9), 661, 761(8); Obscen 1.2, 5.2, 7.6; Searches 33; Statut 190.

Grimes v. U.S., CA5 (Tex), 379 F2d 791, cert den 88 SCt 104, 389 US 846, 19 LEd2d 113.—Consp 41, 47(7); Crim Law 59(5), 393(1), 1144.13(3); Gaming 98(1).

Grimes v. Walsh & Watts, Inc., TexApp–El Paso, 649 SW2d 724, ref nre.—Covenants 8; Mines 74(5), 74(8); Propty 1.

Grimes Const., Inc. v. Great American Lloyds Ins. Co., TexApp–Fort Worth, 188 SW3d 805.—Insurance 1806, 1822, 2268, 2269, 2271, 2275, 2911, 2913, 2914, 2915, 2922(1); Labor & Emp 3130, 3141, 3144.

Grimes Iron & Metal; Skinner v., TexApp–Fort Worth, 766 SW2d 550.—Pretrial Proc 315.

Grim Hotel Co.; Donovan v., CA5 (Tex), 747 F2d 966, 26 Wage & Hour Cas (BNA) 1647, cert den Grim Hotel Co v. Brock, 105 SCt 2654, 471 US 1124, 27 Wage & Hour Cas (BNA) 280, 86 LEd2d 272.—Const Law 3964, 3965(3), 3965(10); Fed Cts 76, 76.35, 776; Judgm 585(1), 585(3), 665, 707; Labor & Emp 2220(2), 2227, 2230, 2397(1).

Grimland v. William Cameron & Co., TexCivApp–Fort Worth, 136 SW2d 909, writ dism, correct.—Brok 52, 55(1), 73.

Grimland, Inc., In re, CA5 (Tex), 243 F3d 228, reh den.—Bankr 2125, 2157, 2854(1), 2854(2), 2854(3.1), 2854(8), 2871, 3781, 3784; Fed Civ Proc 2646, 2656.

Grimm, In re Estate of, TexApp–Eastland, 180 SW3d 602.—App & E 863, 934(1), 1010.2; Judgm 178, 185(5), 185.1(4), 185.3(1); Wills 21, 50, 324(2).

Grimm v. Beck, TexCivApp–Fort Worth, 237 SW2d 1017, ref nre.—Inj 26(9); Partit 100, 106.

Grimm v. Cates, CA5 (Tex), 532 F2d 1034, reh den 540 F2d 1085.—Civil R 1421, 1424; Colleges 8.1(6.1); Schools 147.12.

Grimm v. Garner, Tex, 589 SW2d 955.—Mand 4(3).

Grimm v. Garner, TexCivApp–Waco, 577 SW2d 573, rev 589 SW2d 955.—Courts 155; Mand 1, 27, 61.

Grimm v. Grimm, TexApp–Houston (14 Dist), 864 SW2d 160.—Contracts 278(1), 335(0.5); Divorce 285; Hus & W 281.

Grimm; Grimm v., TexApp–Houston (14 Dist), 864 SW2d 160.—Contracts 278(1), 335(0.5); Divorce 285; Hus & W 281.

Grimm; Houston Transp. Co. v., TexCivApp–Galveston, 168 SW2d 892, writ refused wom.—App & E 1064.1(8); Damag 38, 132(14); Evid 7; Explos 7; Trial 119, 140(1), 199, 251(9).

Grimm v. Lockheed Aircraft Corp., NDTex, 3 FRD 198. —U S 135.

Grimm v. Rizk, TexApp–Houston (14 Dist), 640 SW2d 711, ref nre, cert den 104 SCt 714, 464 US 1045, 79 LEd2d 177.—App & E 937(1); Judgm 565, 668(1), 675(1), 678(1), 678(2), 691, 695, 713(2), 720; Partners 125.

Grimmet v. Washington, TexCivApp–Houston, 386 SW2d 214.—Autos 244(12).

Grimmett v. Higginbotham, TexApp–Tyler, 907 SW2d 1, reh overr, and writ den.—Partners 1, 18, 44, 53.

Grimmett v. State, TexCrimApp, 292 SW2d 633, 163 TexCrim 148.—Disorderly H 5; Sent & Pun 1381(6); Statut 158, 161(1).

Grims v. State, TexCrimApp, 253 SW2d 52, 158 TexCrim 35.—Assault 92(1); Crim Law 1054(1), 1091(3), 1120(1).

Grimsley v. Grimsley, TexApp–Corpus Christi, 632 SW2d 174.—Gifts 4, 25, 29, 30(1).

Grimsley; Grimsley v., TexApp–Corpus Christi, 632 SW2d 174.—Gifts 4, 25, 29, 30(1).

Grimsley v. Life Ins. Co. of Virginia, TexCivApp–Austin, 154 SW2d 196, writ refused wom.—Contracts 9(1); Damag 76, 77, 78(1), 79(1), 80(1), 81; Evid 433(8), 434(11), 441(1); Fraud 28; Ven & Pur 21, 37(1), 46.

Grimsley; U.S. v., CA5 (Tex), 225 FedAppx 334.—Sent & Pun 982.

Grinage v. State, TexApp–San Antonio, 634 SW2d 863, petition for discretionary review refused.—Burg 9(0.5), 41(1); Crim Law 814(17), 1115(2), 1144.13(2.1), 1159.2(6), 1159.3(3.1); Sent & Pun 1381(5).

Grindstaff v. Mather, TexCivApp–Amarillo, 186 SW2d 364, writ refused wom.—Bailm 34; Contracts 127(1), 318; Trial 356(4); Ven & Pur 102, 296, 299(3).

Grindstaff v. North Richland Hills Corp. No. 2, TexCivApp–Fort Worth, 343 SW2d 742, ref nre.—Accord 1, 5, 7(1), 10(1), 11(1); Compromise 5(2), 6(2).

Grindstaff v. Taylor, TexCivApp–Amarillo, 304 SW2d 270.—Tax 2962.

Grindstaff; Twin City Fire Ins. Co. v., TexCivApp–Eastland, 152 SW2d 845.—Insurance 2205, 3571.

Griner v. D & L Well Service, TexCivApp–Beaumont, 324 SW2d 231, ref nre.—App & E 927(7); Neglig 252, 1552, 1579, 1696.

Griner; Reinarz v., TexCivApp–Austin, 401 SW2d 274.—Courts 35, 121(2), 122.

Grinfas; White v., CA5 (Tex), 809 F2d 1157.—Compromise 8(4), 23(3); Fed Civ Proc 2238, 2840; Fed Cts 799; Release 16, 57(2).

Grinnan; Gay v., TexCivApp–Texarkana, 218 SW2d 1021, ref nre.—Mines 78.1(2), 78.7(1).

Grinnell; American Tobacco Co., Inc. v., Tex, 951 SW2d 420.—Antitrust 132; Consp 5, 7; Fraud 3, 16; Judgm 181(33); Lim of Act 49(7); Prod Liab 8, 11, 14, 15, 59, 75.1, 87.1; Sales 266, 268(1); States 18.65, 18.84.

Grinnell v. American Tobacco Co., Inc., TexApp–Beaumont, 883 SW2d 791, writ gr, aff in part, rev in part 951 SW2d 420.—App & E 934(1); Judgm 181(33); Prod Liab 59; States 18.13, 18.65.

Grinnell v. Munson, TexApp–San Antonio, 137 SW3d 706.—Action 13; App & E 174, 840(4), 961; Contracts 187(1); Corp 181(7), 307, 320(4); Decl Judgm 187, 300; Fraud 7; Judgm 181(24), 185.3(5), 186; Mines 55(2), 55(8), 73.5, 78.1(8), 78.7(5); Trusts 345.

Grinnell Corp.; Jones v., CA5 (Tex), 235 F3d 972.—Civil R 1715, 1724; Fed Cts 776.

Grinnell Corp.; Willowbrook Foods, Inc. v., TexApp–San Antonio, 147 SW3d 492, reh overr, and review den, and reh of petition for review den.—Antitrust 162; App & E 758.3(11); Bailm 9; Judgm 181(33), 185(4), 185.2(8); Neglig 218, 234; Pretrial Proc 481; Prod Liab 5, 11, 15, 24, 62; Sales 267; Trial 105(2).

Gripon v. State, TexCrimApp, 100 SW2d 355, 131 TexCrim 495.—Int Liq 205(1), 236(6.5); Statut 118(1).

Gripon's Estate v. Bostick, TexCivApp–Hous (1 Dist), 610 SW2d 541.—App & E 859; Judgm 17(1); Plead 129(2).

Grisaffi, Ex parte, TexCrimApp, 144 SW2d 547, 140 TexCrim 253.—Crim Law 217; Hab Corp 470.

Grisham, In re, BkrtcyNDTex, 245 BR 65.—Bankr 2022, 2363.1, 3274, 3278.1, 3280, 3281, 3282.1, 3284, 3285, 3286, 3341, 3353(1), 3353(13), 3355(1), 3355(1.10), 3355(1.20), 3355(1.35), 3355(4), 3357(1), 3357(2.1), 3357(3), 3422(10.1), 3422(11); Sec Tran 170.

Grisham, In re, BkrtcyNDTex, 230 BR 529, aff Grisham v. Mabank Bank, 1999 WL 261849.—Bankr 2533, 2537, 2764, 2767.1, 2793; Home 5, 58, 214, 216.

Grisham; City of Denison v., TexApp–Dallas, 716 SW2d 121.—Pretrial Proc 35, 358, 371.

Grisham v. Grisham, TexCivApp–Waco, 255 SW2d 891.—Divorce 27(1), 130, 184(6.1), 252.3(1), 253(2).

Grisham; Grisham v., TexCivApp–Waco, 255 SW2d 891.—Divorce 27(1), 130, 184(6.1), 252.3(1), 253(2).

Grisham v. U.S., CA5 (Tex), 103 F3d 24.—Const Law 2424(1); U S 36.

Grisham; Young v., TexCivApp–Eastland, 163 SW2d 842, writ refused wom.—Atty & C 148(1), 148(2).

Grisham-Hunter Corp.; Caprito v., TexCivApp–Eastland, 128 SW2d 149, writ dism, correct.—Contracts 211, 245(1); Estates 10(1); Estop 54, 90(2); Mines 74(2), 74(5), 74(8); Spec Perf 93, 95, 101; Ven & Pur 119, 120, 144(2), 301.

Grismore v. State, TexApp–El Paso, 641 SW2d 593.—Crim Law 627.8(6), 698(1), 857(1), 957(1), 959, 1106(2), 1169.5(3), 1174(2); Perj 33(8).

Grismore v. State, TexApp–Eastland, 841 SW2d 111, petition for discretionary review refused.—Courts 100(1); Crim Law 369.15, 371(12).

Grissam v. State, TexCrimApp, 403 SW2d 414.—Arrest 70(2); Burg 41(1); Crim Law 412.2(3), 519(8).

Grissett; Shead v., TexCivApp–Hous (1 Dist), 566 SW2d 318, dism.—Judgm 181(7), 185(2), 185.1(3), 185.3(2); Lim of Act 24(2), 27, 29(1), 29(2).

Grissett v. State, TexCrimApp, 571 SW2d 922.—Autos 357.

Grissom; Associated Emp. Lloyds v., TexCivApp–Dallas, 291 SW2d 756, ref nre.—Trial 304, 311; Work Comp 838, 1932.

Grissom; Crown Engineering v., TexCivApp–Waco, 343 SW2d 330, writ dism.—Can of Inst 43; Contracts 270(1); Sales 365, 396, 398.

Grissom; Davis v., TexCivApp–Texarkana, 103 SW2d 466, writ dism.—Health 677, 821(2), 821(3).

Grissom v. F. W. Heitmann Co., TexCivApp–Galveston, 130 SW2d 1054, writ refused.—Execution 118, 171(1); Judgm 853(3).

Grissom v. Greener & Sumner Const., Inc., TexApp–El Paso, 676 SW2d 709, ref nre.—Alt Disp Res 312, 314, 354, 363(8), 369; Damag 89(2).

Grissom v. Grissom, TexCivApp–El Paso, 137 SW2d 227, dism.—Divorce 130, 254(1); Trusts 43(1).

Grissom; Grissom v., TexCivApp–El Paso, 137 SW2d 227, dism.—Divorce 130, 254(1); Trusts 43(1).

Grissom v. Guetersloh, TexCivApp–Amarillo, 391 SW2d 167, ref nre.—Deeds 93; Mines 55(4), 55(7), 58.

Grissom; McGee v., TexCivApp–Fort Worth, 360 SW2d 893.—Elections 216.1, 227(8).

Grissom v. Southern Farm Bureau Cas. Ins. Co., TexCivApp–Waco, 476 SW2d 448, ref nre.—Contracts 143(3); Insurance 1832(2), 2793(2).

Grissom v. State, TexApp–Fort Worth, 625 SW2d 424, petition for discretionary review refused.—Assault 56; Crim Law 829(3); Jury 131(2), 131(4); Rob 24.15(1), 27(6).

Grissom; United Copper Industries, Inc. v., TexApp–Austin, 17 SW3d 797, reh overr, and petition for review abated, and review dism.—Atty & C 62; Const Law 3882; Environ Law 220, 293, 678, 683, 692.

Grissom v. Watson, Tex, 704 SW2d 325.—Atty & C 64, 104; Judgm 135, 139, 176.

Grissom; Watson v., TexApp–El Paso, 675 SW2d 813, writ gr, rev 704 SW2d 325.—Atty & C 64; Const Law 3992; Judgm 162(4); Trial 9(1), 9(2).

Griswold v. Carlson, Tex, 249 SW2d 58, 151 Tex 246.—Acct Action on 11; Judgm 101(1).

Griswold v. Carlson, TexCivApp–Fort Worth, 245 SW2d 278, rev 249 SW2d 58, 151 Tex 246.—Acct Action on 10, 11, 12; App & E 1032(1); Judgm 17(8); Proc 6.

Griswold v. Citizens Nat. Bank in Waxahachie, TexCivApp–Waco, 285 SW2d 791, ref nre.—Ack 62(2); App & E 1001(1); Hus & W 213; Mtg 1, 32(2), 36, 38(1), 38(2); Trial 142.

Griswold v. Tucker, TexCivApp–Fort Worth, 216 SW2d 276.—Evid 222(2), 545; Sales 3.1, 261(6), 262, 441(3), 441(4), 442(2).

Gritzman v. Hatfield, TexCivApp–Dallas, 439 SW2d 468. —Plead 111.23; Venue 5.3(5).

Grivel v. Atlantic Mut. Ins. Co., TexCivApp–Corpus Christi, 513 SW2d 297, ref nre.—App & E 422, 428(2), 430(1).

Grizzaffi; Curry v., TexCivApp–Dallas, 466 SW2d 835.— Contracts 28(3); Impl & C C 100; Plead 409(1).

Grizzaffi v. Lee, TexCivApp–Fort Worth, 517 SW2d 885, dism.—App & E 148; Const Law 3455, 3974; Elections 279, 291; Int Liq 34(3), 37; Statut 181(2).

Grizzaffi; Love v., TexCivApp–Waco, 423 SW2d 164.— Autos 244(3); Evid 222(8); Pretrial Proc 723.1.

Grizzell v. State, TexCrimApp, 298 SW2d 816, 164 TexCrim 362.—Crim Law 429(1), 730(7), 911, 925.5(3), 938(1), 1037.2, 1055, 1152(2), 1156(1), 1168(2), 1169.12, 1170.5(2), 1170.5(3), 1174(2); Jury 131(2), 131(4); Rape 43(2).

Grizzle; General Motors Corp. v., TexApp–Waco, 642 SW2d 837, dism.—App & E 232(2), 1004(1), 1060.1(1); Damag 51, 52, 63; Death 85, 86(1), 88, 95(4), 105; Evid 397(2); Judgm 615; Prod Liab 8, 83.5; Trial 284; Witn 275(2.1).

Grizzle; General Motors Corp. v., TexCivApp–Waco, 612 SW2d 275.—App & E 994(3), 1008.1(4); Autos 170(1), 244(10); Plead 111.12, 111.18, 111.42(8).

Grizzle; Texas Commerce Bank, N.A. v., Tex, 96 SW3d 240.—App & E 170(1), 766, 934(1); Judgm 181(2), 677; Parties 35.1, 40(1); Pretrial Proc 556.1; Statut 2; Trusts 1, 169(2), 179, 217.4, 225, 231(1), 237.

Grizzle v. Texas Commerce Bank, N.A., TexApp–Dallas, 38 SW3d 265, review gr (2 pets), rev in part 96 SW3d 240.—Action 6; Antitrust 286; App & E 856(1), 934(1), 1097(1), 1135; Banks 235, 283; Consp 1.1, 2, 3; Contracts 114; Evid 43(2); Fraud 32; Judgm 181(17), 185(2), 186, 677; Motions 39; New Tr 90, 99, 140(1); Parties 35.1, 35.13, 35.15, 35.31, 35.33, 35.37, 35.39, 35.71, 40(2), 42, 43, 44, 48; Torts 222, 242; Trusts 171, 217.3(9), 231(1), 232.

Grizzle v. Travelers Health Network, Inc., CA5 (Tex), 14 F3d 261.—Civil R 1243, 1541, 1553, 1555; Damag 50.10, 181; Fed Civ Proc 1938.1; Fed Cts 626, 753, 870.1, 896.1, 901.1; Witn 67.

G R J v. State, TexCivApp–Hous (14 Dist), 588 SW2d 624. —Crim Law 436(5), 1044.1(2); Infants 68.7(3).

G. R. L. v. State, TexCivApp–Dallas, 581 SW2d 536.— Const Law 4466; Infants 68.7(3).

G.R.M., In re, TexApp–Fort Worth, 45 SW3d 764.—Child C 404, 601; Courts 475(1), 485, 486; Infants 196; Statut 181(1), 184, 205.

GRM v. Equine Inv. and Management Group, SDTex, 596 FSupp 307.—Const Law 3963, 3964, 3965(3), 3965(7); Fed Cts 76.5, 101, 106, 112, 417; Sec Reg 133.

Grobe v. Ottmers, TexCivApp–San Antonio, 224 SW2d 487, ref nre.—Ease 18(2), 18(3), 21, 48(4), 48(6); Evid 417(5).

Groce; Associated Emp. Lloyds v., TexCivApp–Dallas, 194 SW2d 103, ref nre.—App & E 757(1), 1170.1, 1170.10; Trial 350.3(8), 351.5(1), 351.5(8), 352.9, 352.12; Work Comp 51, 730, 1601, 1924, 1926, 1927, 1969.

Groce; Durden v., TexCivApp–Galveston, 159 SW2d 941. —Adv Poss 43(3), 57; App & E 878(1), 907(3); Mtg 280(4), 296.

Groce v. Gulf Oil Corp., TexCivApp–Dallas, 439 SW2d 718.—Plead 111.3, 111.15, 111.16, 111.42(2), 236(3), 245(4); Venue 7.5(2).

Groce; Royal Oak Stave Co. v., TexCivApp–Galveston, 113 SW2d 315, dism.—App & E 1177(4); Assault 12; Labor & Emp 45(1), 763, 835, 873; Trial 350.4(4), 366.

Groce; Wiley-Reiter Corp. v., TexApp–Houston (14 Dist), 693 SW2d 701.—App & E 173(8); Usury 11, 16.

Groce, Locke & Hebdon; Medical Protective Co. v., TexApp–Corpus Christi, 814 SW2d 124, writ den.—Atty & C 129(1); Indem 61, 64; Judgm 181(7), 185(2), 185(6); Lim of Act 95(1), 95(11).

Groce, Locke & Hebdon; Zuniga v., TexApp–San Antonio, 878 SW2d 313, reh den, and writ refused.—Assign 24(1); Atty & C 26; Courts 92.

Groceman v. U.S. Dept. of Justice, CA5 (Tex), 354 F3d 411.—Fed Civ Proc 1773; Fed Cts 776; Prisons 4(7); Searches 26; Sent & Pun 1990.

Groce-Parrish Co. v. Yakey, TexCivApp–San Antonio, 81 SW2d 273.—App & E 1008.2; Corp 340(2).

Grocers Supply Co. v. Stuckey, TexCivApp–Galveston, 152 SW2d 911, writ refused.—App & E 758.3(6), 1050.1(6), 1050.1(12); Damag 132(3), 173(1), 221(5.1); Evid 558(1), 558(2), 558(3), 558(5), 558(8), 560; Witn 268(1), 329.

Grocers Supply Co., Inc.; Anderson v., SDTex, 483 FSupp 73.—Fed Civ Proc 2497.1; Labor & Emp 1007, 1213, 1219(1), 1219(2), 1315, 1319, 1320(14), 1518, 1598.

Grocers Supply Co., Inc.; Britt v., CA5 (Tex), 978 F2d 1441, reh den Hamilton v. Grocers Supply Co, Inc 986 F2d 97, cert den 113 SCt 2929, 508 US 960, 124 LEd2d 679, cert den 113 SCt 2929, 508 US 960, 124 LEd2d 679, cert den 114 SCt 77, 510 US 821, 126 LEd2d 45.—Civil

R 1502, 1539, 1555; Damag 50.10; Fed Cts 666; Labor & Emp 1311, 1320(14); States 18.15; Torts 423, 436.

Grocers Supply Co., Inc.; Britt v., SDTex, 760 FSupp 606, aff 978 F2d 1441, reh den Hamilton v. Grocers Supply Co, Inc, 986 F2d 97, cert den 113 SCt 2929, 508 US 960, 124 LEd2d 679, cert den 113 SCt 2929, 508 US 960, 124 LEd2d 679, cert den 114 SCt 77, 510 US 821, 126 LEd2d 45.—Civil R 1203, 1502, 1551.

Grocers Supply Co., Inc.; Gibson v., TexApp–Houston (14 Dist), 866 SW2d 757.—App & E 714(5), 852, 856(1), 934(1); Judgm 185(2); Work Comp 55, 203, 208, 719, 750, 1045, 2165.

Grocers Supply Co., Inc.; Hamilton v., CA5 (Tex), 986 F2d 97.—Civil R 1210, 1539, 1551; Fed Civ Proc 2142.1, 2608.1.

Grocers Supply Co., Inc.; Hamilton v., CA5 (Tex), 978 F2d 1441. See Britt v. Grocers Supply Co., Inc.

Grocers Supply Co., Inc.; Houston v., TexApp–Houston (14 Dist), 625 SW2d 798.—App & E 1073(1); Evid 351; Judgm 185.3(21); Libel 41, 45(1), 51(1), 123(8).

Grocers Supply Co., Inc. v. Intercity Inv. Properties, Inc., TexApp–Houston (14 Dist), 795 SW2d 225.—Sec Tran 140, 170, 171.

Grocers Supply Co., Inc. v. Powell, TexApp–Houston (14 Dist), 775 SW2d 76.—Execution 414; Mand 3(2.1), 12.

Grocers Supply Co., Inc.; Rosenthal v., TexApp–Houston (1 Dist), 981 SW2d 220.—Judgm 181(33); Labor & Emp 3141, 3143; Neglig 1037(7), 1205(7).

Grocers Supply Co., Inc. v. Sharp, TexApp–Austin, 978 SW2d 638, reh overr, and review den, and reh of petition for review overr.—Const Law 190; Statut 220, 223.5(1); Tax 3635, 3638.

Grocers Supply Co., Inc.; Shields v., SDTex, 568 FSupp 61.—Civil R 1551, 1555; Fed Civ Proc 2470, 2497.1, 2548.

Grocer Supply Co., Inc.; Eans v., TexCivApp–Hous (1 Dist), 580 SW2d 17.—App & E 932(1), 934(1), 999(2), 1004(1), 1004(3), 1024.4; Mal Pros 22, 64(1), 64(2), 67, 69, 71(1).

Groce-Wearden Co.; Reynolds v., TexCivApp–San Antonio, 250 SW2d 749, writ refused.—App & E 870(2); Fraud Conv 314; Venue 7.5(3), 22(4), 22(6).

Groco Corp.; White v., TexApp–Eastland, 783 SW2d 24, writ den.—Usury 48.

Groco Corp.; White Well Service v., TexApp–Eastland, 783 SW2d 24. See White v. Groco Corp.

Groda v. State, TexCrimApp, 155 SW2d 808.—Crim Law 1182.

Grodhaus; Dimerling v., Tex, 261 SW2d 561, 152 Tex 548.—App & E 80(3), 1176(1); Costs 241.

Grodhaus v. Dimerling, TexCivApp–Galveston, 259 SW2d 350, aff 261 SW2d 561, 152 Tex 548.—App & E 76(1), 79(1), 80(1), 80(3); Tresp to T T 47(1).

Grodis v. State, TexApp–Fort Worth, 921 SW2d 502, reh overr, and petition for discretionary review refused.— Crim Law 273.1(2), 274(3.1); Sent & Pun 60.

Groebl; Thomas v., Tex, 212 SW2d 625, 147 Tex 70.— Const Law 975, 1012; Courts 247(8); Elections 10, 18, 60, 83; Statut 121(7), 170, 219(10), 227.

Groebl; Thomas v., TexCivApp–Eastland, 208 SW2d 412, rev 212 SW2d 625, 147 Tex 70.—Courts 90(7); Elections 18; Statut 121(7), 148.

Groebl v. Walker, TexCivApp–Eastland, 567 SW2d 622, ref nre.—Interest 10.

Groendyke Transport Co. v. Dye, TexCivApp–Amarillo, 259 SW2d 747, writ gr, and writ dism by agreement.— Autos 153, 201(1.1), 201(9), 226(2), 227.5, 240(1), 240(2), 242(1), 244(5), 244(36.1), 244(42), 244(57), 244(58); Contrib 5(7); Damag 99, 127, 187; Death 58(1), 99(3), 104(5); Trial 351.2(5), 366.

Groendyke Transport Co. v. Freeman, TexCivApp–Amarillo, 255 SW2d 393.—Plead 111.3, 111.42(8).

Groendyke Transport, Inc.; Bridges v., CA5 (Tex), 553 F2d 877.—Autos 242(4); Damag 130.2; Evid 595; Fed Cts 764.

Groendyke Transport, Inc. v. Davis, CA5 (Tex), 406 F2d 1158, cert den 89 SCt 1628, 394 US 1012, 23 LEd2d 39.—Const Law 4016; Courts 90(1); Fed Cts 742, 921; Labor & Emp 1187, 1191(1), 1193(1), 1857, 2035.

Groendyke Transport, Inc.; Hylander v., TexApp–Corpus Christi, 732 SW2d 692, ref nre.—Corp 498; Damag 91(3); Neglig 273, 1584, 1659, 1697; Trial 350.1, 350.3(7).

Groendyke Transport, Inc.; N.L.R.B. v., CA5 (Tex), 493 F2d 17, cert den 95 SCt 496, 419 US 1021, 42 LEd2d 295.—Labor & Emp 1195(1), 1439, 1455(6), 1468, 1469(1), 1473(3), 1473(4), 1478, 1735, 1755, 1759, 1760, 1763, 1826(3), 1935.

Groendyke Transport, Inc. v. N. L. R. B., CA5 (Tex), 438 F2d 981, cert den 92 SCt 61, 404 US 827, 30 LEd2d 56, reh den 92 SCt 306, 404 US 960, 30 LEd2d 278.—Labor & Emp 1182.

Groendyke Transport, Inc. v. Railroad Commission, TexCivApp–Austin, 426 SW2d 645, ref nre.—App & E 345.1; Autos 82, 84.

Groesbeck, City of; Continental Oil Co. v., TexCivApp–Waco, 95 SW2d 714, writ dism.—App & E 954(1); Waters 77.

Groesbeck, City of; Jones Fine Bread Co. v., TexComApp, 148 SW2d 195, 136 Tex 123, answer to certified question conformed to 151 SW2d 234.—Courts 91(2); Licens 7(1).

Groesbeck, City of; Jones Fine Bread Co. v., TexCivApp–Waco, 151 SW2d 234.—Licens 7(1).

Groesbeck Independent School Dist.; Adams v., CA5 (Tex), 475 F3d 688.—Civil R 1121, 1243, 1249(1); Schools 147.12.

Groessel; U.S. v., CA5 (Tex), 440 F2d 602, cert den 91 SCt 2263, 403 US 933, 29 LEd2d 713.—Consp 28(3); Crim Law 37(1), 37(3), 37(4), 37(5), 37(6.1), 330, 739.1(1), 739.1(3), 772(6).

Groff; Freedom Bail Bonds v., TexApp–Dallas, 936 SW2d 661. See Perkins v. Groff.

Groff; Perkins v., TexApp–Dallas, 936 SW2d 661, writ den.—App & E 854(1), 934(1); Extort 34; Judges 51(2); Judgm 183, 185(2), 185(6), 186; Lim of Act 118(2), 119(3); Statut 181(1), 181(2), 184, 188, 190, 192, 212.3, 217.4; Torts 436; Trover 28.

Grogan; Assurity Life Ins. Co. v., CA5 (Tex), 480 F3d 743.—Insurance 1763, 3003(8), 3003(11).

Grogan; Collingsworth County v., TexCivApp–Amarillo, 361 SW2d 718.—High 6(1), 7(1), 7(2), 8.

Grogan v. Grogan, Tex, 322 SW2d 514, 159 Tex 392.— Corp 198.1(2).

Grogan; Grogan v., Tex, 322 SW2d 514, 159 Tex 392.— Corp 198.1(2).

Grogan v. Grogan, TexCivApp–Beaumont, 315 SW2d 34, ref nre 322 SW2d 514, 159 Tex 392.—Corp 198.1(2); Decl Judgm 298; Plead 228.13.

Grogan; Grogan v., TexCivApp–Beaumont, 315 SW2d 34, ref nre 322 SW2d 514, 159 Tex 392.—Corp 198.1(2); Decl Judgm 298; Plead 228.13.

Grogan v. Henderson, TexCivApp–Texarkana, 313 SW2d 315, ref nre.—App & E 197(7); Hus & W 254, 255, 274(4); Insurance 3445; Lim of Act 5(3), 102(1); Plead 427; Trial 351.2(4).

Grogan; Newsome v., TexCivApp–Tyler, 599 SW2d 881, ref nre.—App & E 171(1), 758.1, 758.3(11), 766.

Grogan v. Santos, TexCivApp–Tyler, 617 SW2d 312.— App & E 207, 959(3), 1079; Damag 130.1, 185(1), 192, 208(1); Plead 236(3), 290(3); Pretrial Proc 720; Trial 122, 131(1), 186, 193(3).

Grogan v. Savings of America, Inc., SDTex, 118 FSupp2d 741, aff 202 F3d 265.—Civil R 1137, 1204, 1213, 1744; Damag 50.10, 208(6); Fed Civ Proc 2539;

Fed Cts 411, 433; Libel 1, 6(1), 44(3), 54, 74, 76; Lim of Act 55(1), 95(1); Unemp Comp 301.

Grogan v. State, TexApp–Dallas, 713 SW2d 705.—Crim Law 429(1), 577.10(6), 577.14, 577.16(9), 824(8); Rape 2, 48(1), 54(1); Sent & Pun 1379(1); Witn 414(2).

Grogan; Sweatt v., NDTex, 25 FSupp 585.—Attach 1, 7, 8, 131, 232.

Grogan Builders Supply Co.; Allied Bldg. Credits, Inc. v., TexCivApp–Houston, 365 SW2d 692, ref nre.—Acct 18, 20(3); App & E 931(3), 931(4); Bills & N 217, 324; Interest 39(5); Trover 50.

Grogan Builders Supply Co. v. Zermeno, TexCivApp–Galveston, 274 SW2d 93.—Princ & A 123(3).

Grogan-Cochran Lumber Co.; Adams v., TexCivApp–Amarillo, 181 SW2d 582, aff McCall v. Grogan-Cochran Lumber Co, 186 SW2d 677, 143 Tex 490.—Adv Poss 66(2), 85(1), 115(5); App & E 764; Bound 1, 3(5), 40(1); Deeds 41, 42; Names 16(1); Tresp to T T 35(1).

Grogan Cochran Lumber Co.; Edens v., TexCivApp–Beaumont, 172 SW2d 730, writ refused wom.—Judgm 12, 494, 497(3); Lim of Act 39(1).

Grogan-Cochran Lumber Co.; McCall v., Tex, 186 SW2d 677, 143 Tex 490.—Adv Poss 15, 19, 31, 100(4), 115(7); Bound 40(1); Propty 7.

Grogan-Cochran Lumber Co. v. McComb, TexCivApp–Beaumont, 192 SW2d 313, writ refused.—Inj 138.31; Logs 3(2), 3(12).

Grogan-Cochran Lumber Co.; Martin v., TexCivApp–Beaumont, 176 SW2d 780.—Judgm 252(1); Life Est 13; Mtg 33(3); Trover 52.

Grogan-Cochran Lumber Co.; Peel v., TexCivApp–Beaumont, 193 SW2d 557.—Fraud 50, 58(1), 64(1).

Grogan Investment Co.; Robertson v., TexApp–Dallas, 710 SW2d 678.—Action 2; Prod Liab 60.5.

Grogan-Lamm Lumber Co.; Hughes v., TexCivApp–Dallas, 331 SW2d 799, ref nre.—App & E 302(1), 757(3), 760(2), 934(1); Contracts 322(4); Mech Liens 73(4); New Tr 102(8), 150(2).

Grogan Lord & Co.; Cameron Mfg. Co. v., Tex, 262 SW2d 939, 153 Tex 16.—Courts 169(1), 169(3); Fraud Conv 322; Mtg 420.

Grogan Lord & Co. v. Cameron Mfg. Co., TexCivApp–Austin, 256 SW2d 996, aff in part, rev in part 262 SW2d 939, 153 Tex 16.—Courts 170; Fraud Conv 235.

Grogan Lord & Co. v. State, TexCivApp–Dallas, 358 SW2d 736, ref nre.—Controlled Subs 175; Forfeit 10.

Grogan Mfg. Co.; Condra v., Tex, 233 SW2d 565, 149 Tex 380.—Adv Poss 62(1); Partit 4; Ten in C 15(5), 15(10).

Grogan Mfg. Co.; Condra v., TexCivApp, 228 SW2d 588, aff 233 SW2d 565, 149 Tex 380.—Evid 222(1), 222(3), 230(3); Guard & W 107, 108; Mental H 146.1, 259, 372.1; Partit 5, 9(1); Ten in C 7, 13, 15(7), 15(11); Trial 171; Ven & Pur 232(1), 239(1); Witn 379(6).

Grogan Mfg. Co.; Davis v., TexCivApp–Texarkana, 177 SW2d 213.—App & E 204(4), 662(1); Evid 372(10), 372(12); Tresp to T T 41(3).

Grogan Mfg. Co. v. Lane, Tex, 169 SW2d 141, 140 Tex 507.—App & E 361(5), 390, 792.

Grogan Mfg. Co. v. Lane, TexCivApp–Galveston, 173 SW2d 655, writ refused wom.—Adv Poss 31, 115(1); App & E 544(1); Parties 80(1), 84(1).

Grogan Supply Co., Lumber Division; Sutton v., TexCivApp–Texarkana, 477 SW2d 930.—Contracts 187(1); Fraud 21; Lim of Act 100(11), 100(13); Mtg 25(2); Ref of Inst 32; Ven & Pur 13, 33, 90.

Grogan's Wholesale and Retail Lumber; Polk v., TexCivApp–Waco, 325 SW2d 201, ref nre.—Acct Action on 6(1), 7; App & E 242(2), 275, 846(2), 846(5); Impl & C C 81, 98; Sales 353(1), 359(1).

Grogen v. State, TexApp–Houston (1 Dist), 745 SW2d 450.—Atty & C 42; Crim Law 409(5); Larc 40(8).

Groh v. State, TexApp–Houston (1 Dist), 725 SW2d 282, petition for discretionary review refused.—Crim Law 444, 633(1), 951(6), 1134(2), 1166.8, 1166.16.

Grohman; Colson v., CA5 (Tex), 174 F3d 498.—Const Law 1550, 1553, 1620, 1625, 1681, 1926, 2170, 3851; Fed Civ Proc 1829, 2544; Fed Cts 776; Libel 51(5); Mun Corp 170, 182.

Grohman; Colson v., TexApp–Houston (1 Dist), 24 SW3d 414, review den.—Damag 50, 50.10, 208(6); Libel 1, 6(1), 10(1), 51(5), 101(1), 123(2), 123(8).

Grohn v. Marquardt, TexApp–San Antonio, 657 SW2d 851, ref nre.—App & E 977(1), 1050.1(1), 1056.1(2), 1056.6; Deeds 70(1), 70(2), 72(1), 78, 203, 211(4); Equity 65(1), 65(3); Evid 145, 434(1); Fraud 9; Trial 349(1), 350.3(2.1), 352.1(1), 412; Wills 155.1.

Grohn v. Marquardt, TexCivApp–San Antonio, 487 SW2d 214, ref nre.—App & E 148; Ex & Ad 438(8), 439; Judgm 688; Powers 25; Remaind 4, 10; Wills 634(4.1).

Grohosky v. Russell, TexCivApp–Amarillo, 216 SW2d 1005, ref nre.—Trial 352.4(2).

Gromatzky v. Blacklands Production Credit Ass'n, TexCivApp–Waco, 597 SW2d 572.—Partit 4.

Grommes v. State, TexCrimApp, 589 SW2d 461.—Sent & Pun 2003.

Gronberg v. York, TexCivApp–Tyler, 568 SW2d 139, ref nre.—Contracts 187(1); Labor & Emp 219, 265, 643; Trial 143; Trover 2, 13, 22; Witn 406.

Grondoma v. Sutton, TexApp–Austin, 991 SW2d 90, reh overr, and review den, and reh of petition for review overr.—Judgm 131, 276.

Groneman; MacDonald v., TexCivApp–Texarkana, 163 SW2d 265, writ refused wom.—Frds St of 113(3); Mines 74(8), 74(10).

Groner; U.S. v., CA5 (Tex), 494 F2d 499, cert den 95 SCt 331, 419 US 1010, 42 LEd2d 285.—Obscen 2.5, 5.1, 7.7, 15; Searches 164.

Groner; U.S. v., CA5 (Tex), 479 F2d 577, vac 94 SCt 278, 414 US 969, 38 LEd2d 213, conformed to 494 F2d 499, cert den 95 SCt 331, 419 US 1010, 42 LEd2d 285.—Crim Law 475.5, 489, 494; Obscen 5.1, 16, 17, 19.

Groner; U.S. v., CA5 (Tex), 475 F2d 550, on reh 479 F2d 577, vac 94 SCt 278, 414 US 969, 38 LEd2d 213, conformed to 494 F2d 499, cert den 95 SCt 331, 419 US 1010, 42 LEd2d 285.—Const Law 2194; Crim Law 304(1), 1134(8), 1159.2(10); Obscen 1.1, 1.3, 17.

Groninger & King; Employers Liability Assur. Corp. v., TexCivApp–Dallas, 299 SW2d 175, ref nre.—Evid 590; Insurance 2155(1); Trial 140(2); Witn 389, 397.

Gronwaldt; McClelland v., CA5 (Tex), 155 F3d 507.—Fed Cts 12.1, 18; Inj 22; Labor & Emp 1967; Rem of C 25(1), 107(9); States 18.46.

Gronwaldt; McClelland v., EDTex, 958 FSupp 280.—Fed Cts 660.15; Rem of C 119.

Gronwaldt; McClelland v., EDTex, 942 FSupp 297.—Fed Cts 819; Judges 42, 45, 47(1), 51(2), 51(3), 51(4).

Gronwaldt; McClelland v., EDTex, 909 FSupp 457, motion to certify allowed by 958 FSupp 280, rev 155 F3d 507.—Labor & Emp 407, 429, 676, 995, 1967; Rem of C 3, 19(5), 25(1); States 18.46, 18.51.

Groom; Brown v., CA5 (Tex), 174 FedAppx 847.—Civil R 1376(7).

Groom v. Federal Underwriters Exchange, TexCivApp–San Antonio, 184 SW2d 341.—Work Comp 1065.

Groom v. Fickes, SDTex, 966 FSupp 1466, aff 129 F3d 606.—Arrest 68(4); Civil R 1037, 1088(5), 1376(1), 1376(2), 1376(9); Consp 18; Const Law 4043, 4527(1); Crim Law 393(1); Dist & Pros Attys 10; Int Rev 4457; Mal Pros 15, 18(2); Offic 114; Searches 76, 182; U S 50.5(4), 50.20; Witn 16, 298.

Groom; Hawkins v., TexApp–Eastland, 893 SW2d 123.—Tax 2445.

Groome v. State, TexApp–Texarkana, 957 SW2d 919, reh overr.—Burg 2, 41(1), 41(4), 41(6); Crim Law 552(1), 552(3), 566, 1144.13(2.1), 1159.2(7), 1186.1, 1189.

Groomer; Scott v., CA5 (Tex), 79 FedAppx 48.—Civil R 1094; Consp 18.

Groomes v. USH of Timberlawn, Inc., TexApp–Dallas, 170 SW3d 802, reh overr.—App & E 893(1); Damag 57.25(4); False Imp 16; Health 800, 805.

Grooms, Ex parte, TexCrimApp, 468 SW2d 817.—Extrad 36, 39.

Grooms; Chesser v., TexCivApp–Beaumont, 302 SW2d 488.—Mand 16(1), 171.

Grooms v. Johnson, CA5 (Tex), 208 F3d 488.—Hab Corp 842, 846, 894.1.

Grooms v. State, TexCrimApp, 278 SW2d 309, 161 TexCrim 524.—Crim Law 448(2); Larc 55; Witn 248(2).

Grooms v. State, TexCrimApp, 244 SW2d 229, 156 TexCrim 504.—Autos 357; Crim Law 814(1), 1091(4), 1169.3.

Grooms v. State, TexCrimApp, 205 SW2d 986, 151 TexCrim 106.—Crim Law 1169.3, 1177.5(2).

Groos Bank, N.A.; Beltran v., TexApp–San Antonio, 755 SW2d 944.—App & E 170(1); Costs 194.32; Guar 15, 60.5; Plead 78; Sec Tran 230, 231.

Groos Bank, N.A.; Larson v., WDTex, 204 BR 500.—Bankr 2154.1, 2162, 2321, 2553; Cred R A 4; Neglig 460.

Groos Nat. Bank v. Comptroller of Currency, CA5 (Tex), 573 F2d 889.—Banks 120, 235; Decl Judgm 272; Fed Cts 231, 232.

Groos Nat. Bank; Go Leasing, Inc. v., TexApp–San Antonio, 628 SW2d 143.—Judgm 297, 304, 321, 323, 326, 340.

Groos Nat. Bank v. Norris, TexCivApp–Eastland, 384 SW2d 401.—App & E 846(5); Joint Ten 6; Wills 565(4).

Groos Nat. Bank v. Shaw's of San Antonio, Inc., TexCivApp–San Antonio, 555 SW2d 492, ref nre.—Assign 131; Banks 119, 133, 140(5).

Groos Nat. Bank; Wooldridge v., TexCivApp–Waco, 603 SW2d 335.—App & E 863; Bills & N 487, 537(4); Evid 434(12), 444(6); Judgm 185(2), 186, 191, 210.

Groos Nat. Bank of San Antonio; U.S. v., CA5 (Tex), 661 F2d 36.—Int Rev 4499.

Groos Nat. Bank of San Antonio; Wilson v., TexCivApp–Tyler, 535 SW2d 374.—App & E 624; Plead 111.2, 111.46.

Groppenbacher; Allison v., TexCivApp–El Paso, 142 SW2d 528, writ refused.—Adv Poss 22, 57, 60(1), 112, 115(1); App & E 931(3).

Gros v. City of Grand Prairie, CA5 (Tex), 209 F3d 431, on remand 2000 WL 1842421.—Civil R 1039, 1088(1), 1355, 1358; Fed Cts 557, 768.1.

Gros v. City of Grand Prairie, Tex., CA5 (Tex), 181 F3d 613, reh en banc den 193 F3d 521, appeal after remand 209 F3d 431, on remand 2000 WL 1842421.—Civil R 1345, 1351(1), 1404, 1430; Fed Cts 411.

Gros; State Farm Fire & Cas. Co. v., TexApp–Austin, 818 SW2d 908.—Antitrust 130, 221; App & E 230, 930(3), 1001(1), 1003(6), 1067; Corp 397; Damag 192, 208(6); Insurance 1642, 1654, 3417, 3424(1), 3424(2), 3426.

Groschke v. Gabriel, TexApp–Houston (1 Dist), 824 SW2d 607, writ den.—Action 60; App & E 768; Inj 239; Judgm 185.3(16), 252(1), 256(1); Ven & Pur 79.

Groseclose v. Johnston, TexCivApp–Austin, 184 SW2d 548.—Trial 350.3(2.1); Trusts 41, 43(3), 44(2), 44(3).

Groseclose v. Rum, TexApp–Dallas, 860 SW2d 554.—App & E 901, 934(1); Bills & N 429; Interest 56; Judgm 178, 181(25), 185(2), 185(6), 186; Mtg 298(1).

Grosenheider; U.S. v., CA5 (Tex), 200 F3d 321.—Crim Law 394.1(3), 394.4(6), 1139, 1144.12, 1147, 1158(4); Obscen 18.1; Searches 33; Sent & Pun 804, 805, 807, 868, 995.

Groshart; Hughes v., TexCivApp–Amarillo, 150 SW2d 827.—Home 55, 81, 84, 94, 103, 167.

Grospian v. Pan Am. Refining Corp., SDTex, 6 FRD 453.—Fed Civ Proc 703, 994; Fed Cts 424; Lim of Act 180(3), 180(7).

Gross v. Black & Decker (U.S.), Inc., CA5 (Tex), 695 F2d 858.—Evid 146; Fed Civ Proc 2111, 2127, 2338.1; Fed Cts 799, 841, 847; Neglig 431, 1577; Prod Liab 14, 58, 81.1, 85, 95.

Gross v. Blecker, TexCivApp–Galveston, 105 SW2d 282.—Adv Poss 114(2); App & E 925(3); Trial 125(2), 129.

Gross v. Burt, TexApp–Fort Worth, 149 SW3d 213, reh overr, and review den.—App & E 204(7), 238(2), 989; Contracts 27; Evid 150, 508, 555.2, 555.4(1), 555.10, 557; Health 576, 611, 615, 619, 623, 629, 631, 633, 641, 670, 819, 822(3), 823(1), 825.

Gross v. Connecticut General Life Ins. Co., TexCivApp–El Paso, 390 SW2d 388.—Insurance 3376, 3379, 3543.

Gross v. Dallas Railway & Terminal Co., TexCivApp–Dallas, 131 SW2d 113, writ dism, correct.—App & E 1052(5), 1056.4, 1062.1; Trial 191(7), 352.10, 359(1), 365.2; Urb R R 26, 30.

Gross v. Davies, TexApp–Houston (1 Dist), 882 SW2d 452, reh den, and writ den.—App & E 854(1), 934(2), 1073(1), 1172(1); Death 15; Judgm 181(11), 181(15.1).

Gross; First Bank and Trust v., EDTex, 179 BR 504. See Reid, In re.

Gross v. Gross, TexApp–Houston (14 Dist), 808 SW2d 215.—App & E 842(2), 931(1), 1008.1(2), 1010.1(3), 1012.1(5); Child S 390, 403, 406, 442, 459, 496, 602, 603; Contempt 20; Divorce 221.

Gross; Gross v., TexApp–Houston (14 Dist), 808 SW2d 215.—App & E 842(2), 931(1), 1008.1(2), 1010.1(3), 1012.1(5); Child S 390, 403, 406, 442, 459, 496, 602, 603; Contempt 20; Divorce 221.

Gross v. Innes, Tex, 988 SW2d 727.—App & E 1080.

Gross v. Innes, TexApp–Dallas, 930 SW2d 237, reh overr, and writ gr, and withdrawn, writ dism woj 988 SW2d 727.—Courts 95(1); Judgm 185(2); Mun Corp 723, 745, 747(4); Offic 114.

Gross v. Kahanek, Tex, 3 SW3d 518.—Death 39; Judgm 185(5); Lim of Act 55(3).

Gross; Kahanek v., TexApp–San Antonio, 981 SW2d 271, reh overr, and review gr, and reh of petition for review overr, aff in part, rev in part 3 SW3d 518.—Abate & R 54; App & E 173(10), 1079; Const Law 2314; Judgm 181(7), 181(33), 185(2), 185.3(21); Lim of Act 55(3); Pretrial Proc 714.

Gross; Kell v., CA5 (Tex), 171 F2d 715, cert den 70 SCt 55, 338 US 815, 94 LEd 493.—Dep & Escr 15, 16; Fed Cts 755; R R 15.

Gross; Minor v., TexCivApp–Tyler, 478 SW2d 597, ref nre.—App & E 842(1), 1170.6, 1170.7, 1177(2); Autos 244(12), 244(36.1); Damag 163(1), 208(2), 221(2.1); Evid 556; New Tr 56.

Gross; Morris Plan Life Ins. Co. v., TexCivApp–Dallas, 429 SW2d 561, ref nre.—Judgm 567, 681; Liens 18.

Gross v. Quarterman, CA5 (Tex), 211 FedAppx 251.—Civil R 1395(7); Fed Cts 947.

Gross; Smith v., TexCivApp–Dallas, 427 SW2d 712.—App & E 758.3(5); Judgm 185(2), 185.3(14).

Gross v. State, TexCrimApp, 493 SW2d 791.—Crim Law 1031(1), 1036.1(4), 1120(2).

Gross v. State, TexCrimApp, 334 SW2d 809, 169 TexCrim 454.—Crim Law 863(2), 1169.5(3); Health 105, 187; Statut 63.

Gross v. State, TexCrimApp, 308 SW2d 54, 165 TexCrim 463.—Const Law 2340, 2362, 4693; Crim Law 12.5; Sent & Pun 1376.

Gross v. State, TexCrimApp, 298 SW2d 810.—Crim Law 1081(1).

Gross v. State, TexCrimApp, 263 SW2d 951, 159 TexCrim 394.—Crim Law 763(18).

Gross v. State, TexCrimApp, 121 SW2d 601, 135 TexCrim 504.—Crim Law 1184(5); Homic 1136.

Gross v. State, TexApp–Fort Worth, 624 SW2d 287, petition for discretionary review refused.—Crim Law 400(3), 549, 814(17), 1173.2(2); Health 168; Sent & Pun 1021.

Gross v. State, TexApp–Texarkana, 730 SW2d 104.—Const Law 72, 2545(4); Crim Law 414, 449.1, 450; Sent & Pun 319.

Gross v. Texas Emp. Ins. Ass'n, TexCivApp–Dallas, 202 SW2d 862.—Courts 122; Work Comp 1947.

Gross; Texas State Bd. of Medical Examiners v., TexApp–Austin, 712 SW2d 639.—Admin Law 701; Health 154, 158.

Gross; Turboff v., TexApp–Houston (14 Dist), 833 SW2d 235, writ den.—Fraud 12, 50, 58(3), 64(2).

Gross v. Turner, TexCivApp–Amarillo, 274 SW2d 935, ref nre.—Judgm 942.

Gross; U.S. v., CA5 (Tex), 26 F3d 552.—Crim Law 1139; Sent & Pun 664(5), 752.

Gross; U.S. v., CA5 (Tex), 979 F2d 1048.—Crim Law 1028, 1042, 1181(2); Sent & Pun 630, 635, 664(4).

Gross; U.S. v., CA5 (Tex), 105 FedAppx 560.—Contempt 55; Crim Law 1031(1); Judges 49(2).

Grossenbacher; Anderson v., TexCivApp–San Antonio, 381 SW2d 72, ref nre.—Counties 3; Mand 10, 13, 74(2); States 35.

Grossenbacher; Bell v., TexCivApp–San Antonio, 432 SW2d 575, ref nre.—Mental H 176.

Grossenbacher v. Burket, Tex, 427 SW2d 595, on remand Burket v. Delaware Drilling Corp, 435 SW2d 307, writ dism.—App & E 79(1), 80(1).

Grossenbacher; State Bar of Texas v., TexApp–San Antonio, 781 SW2d 736.—App & E 497(1), 907(3); Stip 9, 13, 19; Trial 33, 105(1).

Grosser-Samuels v. Jacquelin Designs Enterprises, Inc., NDTex, 448 FSupp2d 772.—Atty & C 19, 21, 21.5(1), 21.15, 21.20, 22; Fed Cts 433; Pat 328(2).

Grosshans; Sudderth v., TexCivApp–Austin, 581 SW2d 215.—App & E 931(1), 989; Corp 503(1); Evid 10(2); Fraud 3; Plead 111.42(10).

Grossling v. Ford Memorial Hosp., EDTex, 614 FSupp 1051.—Antitrust 543; Consp 7.5(1), 7.5(3), 18, 19; Const Law 3027, 3941; Health 271, 273, 275.

Grossman v. Campbell, CA5 (Tex), 368 F2d 206.—Int Rev 4154, 4157.10(1), 4157.10(3), 4159(7); Wills 184(0.5), 199, 440, 470(1), 560(3), 718, 740(3), 784.

Grossman; Dedier v., TexCivApp–Dallas, 454 SW2d 231, ref nre.—Contracts 1, 99(1), 143(3), 147(1), 147(2), 147(3), 152, 155, 168, 175(1), 176(1), 193; Lim of Act 66(8).

Grossman v. Grossman, TexApp–Corpus Christi, 799 SW2d 511.—App & E 173(2); Divorce 179, 253(2); Hus & W 29(9), 34; Judgm 185(4).

Grossman; Grossman v., TexApp–Corpus Christi, 799 SW2d 511.—App & E 173(2); Divorce 179, 253(2); Hus & W 29(9), 34; Judgm 185(4).

Grossman v. Jones, TexCivApp–San Antonio, 157 SW2d 448, writ refused wom.—Fixt 27(2), 27(3); Trover 16, 66; Ven & Pur 231(15), 232(9).

Grossman; Liedeker v., Tex, 206 SW2d 232, 146 Tex 308.—App & E 1010.1(2), 1010.1(3); Spec Perf 93, 94, 99; Ven & Pur 229(1), 232(9).

Grossman v. Liedeker, TexCivApp–San Antonio, 202 SW2d 267, rev 206 SW2d 232, 146 Tex 308.—Contracts 256; Land & Ten 53(2); Spec Perf 102, 110, 121(11), 129; Ven & Pur 86, 152, 170, 174, 191.

Grossman v. Tiner, TexCivApp–Waco, 347 SW2d 627, ref nre.—Autos 244(12), 244(34), 244(36.1); Neglig 1599, 1656, 1676; Trial 127.

Grossman; U.S. v., CA5 (Tex), 117 F3d 255, reh den 137 F3d 1353.—Consp 23.1, 32, 47(4), 47(5); Crim Law 1144.13(2.1), 1144.13(3), 1159.2(7), 1159.6.

Grossmann v. Barney, TexCivApp–San Antonio, 359 SW2d 475, ref nre.—Land & Ten 25, 76(3), 232.

Gross Nat. Bank of San Antonio v. Merchant, TexCivApp–San Antonio, 459 SW2d 483.—Ex & Ad 286; Home 109.

Grossnickle, In re Marriage of, TexApp–Texarkana, 115 SW3d 238.—Action 9; App & E 18, 946, 949, 954(1),

954(2), 961, 1031(1), 1145, 1186.1, 1198; Child S 6, 223, 230, 231, 261, 338, 339(5), 450, 537, 556(2), 556(3), 558(3), 616; Divorce 270, 280; Evid 588; Inj 128(1); Judgm 20, 21, 217; Trial 388(1), 395(5), 401.

Grossnickle v. Clayton, TexApp–Texarkana, 900 SW2d 404.—Mand 44.

Grossnickle v. Grossnickle, TexApp–Texarkana, 935 SW2d 830, writ den.—App & E 122, 662(4), 1008.1(1), 1008.1(2); Const Law 90.1(1), 1491, 1527, 2085, 2093; Divorce 85, 182, 219, 223, 227(1), 252.3(1), 252.3(2), 252.3(4), 252.4, 252.5(1), 252.5(3), 253(2), 253(3), 254(1), 283, 284, 286(1), 286(2), 286(3.1), 286(9), 287; Evid 555.6(1); Exceptions Bill of54; Hus & W 257, 265, 268(1), 272(5); Judgm 217, 527; Pretrial Proc 42, 45; Trial 393(2), 398, 400(1), 401.

Grossnickle; Grossnickle v., TexApp–Texarkana, 935 SW2d 830, writ den.—App & E 122, 662(4), 1008.1(1), 1008.1(2); Const Law 90.1(1), 1491, 1527, 2085, 2093; Divorce 85, 182, 219, 223, 227(1), 252.3(1), 252.3(2), 252.3(4), 252.4, 252.5(1), 252.5(3), 253(2), 253(3), 254(1), 283, 284, 286(1), 286(2), 286(3.1), 286(9), 287; Evid 555.6(1); Exceptions Bill of54; Hus & W 257, 265, 268(1), 272(5); Judgm 217, 527; Pretrial Proc 42, 45; Trial 393(2), 398, 400(1), 401.

Grossnickle v. Grossnickle, TexApp–Texarkana, 865 SW2d 211, reh den.—App & E 1035; Divorce 253(4); Jury 9, 19.10(1), 25(6), 31.

Grossnickle; Grossnickle v., TexApp–Texarkana, 865 SW2d 211, reh den.—App & E 1035; Divorce 253(4); Jury 9, 19.10(1), 25(6), 31.

Grossnickle v. Turner, TexApp–Texarkana, 903 SW2d 362, reh overr.—App & E 371, 389(1), 389(3); Mand 151(1); Motions 55, 62.

Grost v. Grost, TexCivApp–Tyler, 561 SW2d 223, dism.—Divorce 252.3(1), 252.3(2), 252.3(4), 253(2), 286(2), 286(5), 286(9); Hus & W 249(3), 249(5).

Grost; Grost v., TexCivApp–Tyler, 561 SW2d 223, dism.—Divorce 252.3(1), 252.3(2), 252.3(4), 253(2), 286(2), 286(5), 286(9); Hus & W 249(3), 249(5).

Grosz; Southmark Corp. v., CA5 (Tex), 49 F3d 1111. See Southmark Corp., Matter of.

Grosz; U.S. v., CA5 (Tex), 76 F3d 1318, reh and sug for reh den 84 F3d 435, cert den 117 SCt 167, 519 US 862, 136 LEd2d 110.—Crim Law 577.5, 577.10(7), 577.10(8), 706(2), 720(1), 721(1), 729, 1134(6), 1139, 1158(1), 1171.3, 1171.8(1), 1180, 1192.

Grota; Holcombe v., Tex, 102 SW2d 1041, 129 Tex 100, 110 ALR 234.—Clerks of C 6; Courts 55; Mand 76, 168(2); Mun Corp 126, 180(3); Offic 40.

Grota v. Holcombe, TexCivApp–Galveston, 97 SW2d 301, rev 102 SW2d 1041, 129 Tex 100, 110 ALR 234.—App & E 1040(2); Courts 55; Mand 76; Mun Corp 215; Plead 214(1).

Grote; Minus v., TexCivApp–El Paso, 154 SW2d 140.—Evid 65; Plead 111.1; Rem of C 49, 49.1(1), 58, 89(1), 95, 97.

Grote v. Price, Tex, 163 SW2d 1059, 139 Tex 472.—Courts 207.4(2), 209(2), 247(7).

Grote; Service Finance Corp. v., TexComApp, 131 SW2d 93, 133 Tex 606.—App & E 781(4); Costs 232.

Grote; Service Finance Corp. v., TexCivApp–San Antonio, 172 SW2d 996.—App & E 1166.

Grote v. Service Finance Corp., TexCivApp–San Antonio, 119 SW2d 136, vac 131 SW2d 93, 133 Tex 606.—Corp 411; Guar 3; Trusts 352, 354, 358(1), 358(2), 372(1), 372(3).

Grote; U.S. v., CA5 (Tex), 632 F2d 387, cert den 102 SCt 98, 454 US 819, 70 LEd2d 88, reh den 102 SCt 983, 454 US 1129, 71 LEd2d 118.—Crim Law 105, 273.1(4), 449.1, 450, 569, 822(1), 1170(1), 1480; Int Rev 5317.

Grothaus; Kahn v., TexCivApp–San Antonio, 104 SW2d 932, writ dism.—Evid 587; Hus & W 325, 332, 335.

Grothe, Ex parte, TexCrimApp, 687 SW2d 736, cert den In re Grothe, 106 SCt 308, 474 US 944, 88 LEd2d 286. —Const Law 2121; Crim Law 662.1; Witn 266.

Grothe, Ex parte, TexCivApp–Austin, 581 SW2d 296.— Child S 459, 497; Divorce 269(1).

Grothe, Ex parte, TexCivApp–Austin, 570 SW2d 183.— Child S 444; Contempt 20.

Grothe v. Grothe, TexCivApp–Austin, 590 SW2d 238.— Divorce 252.2, 286(2).

Grothe; Grothe v., TexCivApp–Austin, 590 SW2d 238.— Divorce 252.2, 286(2).

Grothues, In re, CA5 (Tex), 226 F3d 334, on remand Grothues v. US, 2000 WL 1930707.—Bankr 2830, 3343.5, 3403(1), 3405(14), 3777, 3782, 3786; Judgm 648.

Grothues, In re, WDTex, 245 BR 828, aff in part, rev in part and remanded 226 F3d 334, on remand Grothues v. US, 2000 WL 1930707.—Bankr 2163, 2371(2), 2830, 3352, 3362, 3568(3), 3782.

Grothues, In re, BkrtcyWDTex, 84 BR 448. See Southwest Oil Co. of Jourdanton, Inc., In re.

Grothues v. City of Helotes, TexApp–San Antonio, 928 SW2d 725.—Const Law 996, 999, 1020, 1066; Environ Law 355, 368, 384; Inj 85(2); Mun Corp 120, 122.1(2), 589, 595, 607, 633(1); States 4.4(2); Statut 174, 195.

Grotjohn, In re, BkrtcyNDTex, 356 BR 393, aff 2007 WL 2379522.—Bankr 2162, 2461, 2558, 2588, 2724, 3067.1.

Grotjohn Precise Connexiones Intern., S.A. v. JEM Financial, Inc., TexApp–Texarkana, 12 SW3d 859.— App & E 223; Judgm 181(15.1), 181(31), 183, 185.1(3), 185.1(4), 185.1(8), 185.2(5); Sec Reg 249.1, 250, 278, 309; Usury 13, 14, 15, 18, 42, 113.

Grotti v. Belo Corp., TexApp–Fort Worth, 188 SW3d 768, review den.—App & E 852; Judgm 185(5); Libel 1, 9(2), 55, 101(5).

Grotti v. State, TexApp–Fort Worth, 209 SW3d 747, petition for discretionary review gr.—Crim Law 469.1, 473, 486(2), 661, 706(4), 730(3), 741(1), 742(1), 795(1.5), 795(2.10), 867, 1037.1(1), 1037.1(2), 1037.2, 1043(2), 1044.1(8), 1130(5), 1134(1), 1134(2), 1144.13(2.1), 1153(1), 1155, 1159.2(1), 1159.2(2), 1159.2(7), 1159.2(8), 1159.2(9), 1159.3(2), 1159.4(2), 1191; Double J 1, 135, 150(1); Homic 502, 708, 1151, 1174, 1457; Ind & Inf 189(8).

Ground; Bowers v., TexCivApp–Eastland, 115 SW2d 1142, writ dism.—App & E 1175(5); Chat Mtg 162, 169, 176(1).

Ground; Retzlaff v., TexApp–Houston (14 Dist), 640 SW2d 676.—App & E 768, 930(3), 989; Damag 134(1), 186.

Grounds v. Lett, TexApp–Dallas, 718 SW2d 38.—App & E 78(1); Courts 202(5).

Grounds; Montgomery County v., TexApp–Beaumont, 862 SW2d 35, writ den.—App & E 989, 1003(5), 1003(6); Work Comp 52, 571, 1536.

Grounds v. State, TexCrimApp, 144 SW2d 276, 140 TexCrim 209.—Crim Law 273.2(1); Sent & Pun 419.

Grounds v. Tolar Independent School Dist., Tex, 856 SW2d 417, on remand 872 SW2d 823, reh overr, and writ den.—Const Law 3874(1), 4198, 4202; Schools 147.34(2).

Grounds v. Tolar Independent School Dist., Tex, 707 SW2d 889.—Admin Law 229; App & E 185(1); Courts 4; Decl Judgm 210; Schools 133.6(7), 147.34(2), 147.44.

Grounds v. Tolar Independent School Dist., TexApp–Fort Worth, 872 SW2d 823, reh overr, and writ den.— App & E 927(7), 989, 1008.1(2), 1012.1(5), 1122(2); Civil R 1482; Damag 12, 192; Schools 147.54; Trial 383.

Grounds v. Tolar Independent School Dist., TexApp–Fort Worth, 827 SW2d 10, writ den, and writ withdrawn, and writ gr, rev 856 SW2d 417, on remand 872 SW2d 823, reh overr, and writ den.—Const Law 4198.

Grounds v. Tolar Independent School Dist., TexApp–Fort Worth, 694 SW2d 241, writ gr, rev 707 SW2d 889. —Admin Law 796; Contracts 167; Decl Judgm 210; Schools 45, 47, 133.6(7), 139, 147.2(1), 147.34(2), 147.44.

Ground Technology, Inc.; Karamchandani v., TexApp–Houston (14 Dist), 678 SW2d 580, dism.—App & E 954(1); Inj 135, 138.42, 150.

Ground Water Conservation Dist. No. 2; Hawley v., Tex, 306 SW2d 352, 157 Tex 643.—Const Law 2970; Waters 216.

Ground Water Conservation Dist. No. 2 v. Hawley, TexCivApp–Amarillo, 304 SW2d 764, ref nre 306 SW2d 352, 157 Tex 643.—Const Law 639, 2970, 3057, 3470; Statut 64(2); Waters 216, 226.

Group v. Vicento, TexApp–Houston (14 Dist), 164 SW3d 724.—App & E 893(1); Evid 538; Health 809; Statut 181(1), 181(2), 184, 188, 190, 205, 206, 212.7.

Group Acc. Ins. Plan for Employees of E–Systems, Inc.; Todd v., CA5 (Tex), 47 F3d 1448. See Todd v. AIG Life Ins. Co.

Group & Pension Administrators, Inc.; Burgos v., SDTex, 286 FSupp2d 812.—Insurance 1117(1), 1117(3); Labor & Emp 407, 414, 425, 426; States 18.41, 18.51.

Group Constructors, Inc.; Shintech Inc. v., TexApp–Houston (14 Dist), 688 SW2d 144.—App & E 756, 761, 931(1), 989, 996, 1008.1(3), 1008.1(7), 1010.1(1), 1010.1(3), 1010.1(4), 1010.2, 1011.1(1), 1073(1); Contracts 28(3), 114, 162, 205.15(5), 232(4), 299(2), 312(1), 316(1), 322(1), 322(4); Damag 189, 222; Estop 52.10(1), 52.10(2), 78(1), 92(2); Impl & C C 34, 55, 60.1; Trial 382.

Group Health & Life Ins. Co.; Stewart v., TexCivApp–Waco, 555 SW2d 531.—App & E 719(6), 754(1); Costs 32(2); Insurance 3375, 3400(1), 3405.

Group Health Underwriters; Crumpton v., TexApp–Fort Worth, 936 SW2d 473. See Crumpton v. Stevens.

Group Hospital Service v. Armstrong, TexCivApp–Amarillo, 240 SW2d 418, ref nre.—Insurance 1259(1), 1259(3), 2494(1).

Group Hospital Service v. Bass, TexCivApp–Beaumont, 252 SW2d 507, dism.—Insurance 2475, 3559.

Group Hospital Service, Inc. v. Barrett, TexCivApp–Hous (14 Dist), 426 SW2d 310, ref nre.—App & E 949; Decl Judgm 161, 305, 392.1; Parties 35.13.

Group Hosp. Service, Inc. v. Dellana, TexApp–Austin, 701 SW2d 75.—Pretrial Proc 358, 373.

Group Hospital Service, Inc.; Drinkard v., TexCivApp–Dallas, 366 SW2d 637, ref nre.—Insurance 1832(1), 2467, 2531, 3365.

Group Hosp. Service, Inc.; E.E.O.C. v., NDTex, 539 FSupp 185, reconsideration den 1982 WL 383.—Civil R 1104, 1106, 1176; Statut 219(1), 219(9.1).

Group Hospital Service Inc. v. State Farm Ins. Co., TexCivApp–Eastland, 517 SW2d 897.—Insurance 3519(2), 3523(4).

Group Hospital Service, Inc.; Van Court v., TexCivApp–Houston, 345 SW2d 343.—App & E 1043(6); Insurance 1879, 2494(1); Pretrial Proc 480.

Group Hosp. Services, Inc. v. Daniel, TexApp–Corpus Christi, 704 SW2d 870.—Action 56, 60; Antitrust 363; App & E 170(1), 949, 959(1), 1032(1), 1046.1; Corp 405, 498; Damag 91(1), 130.1, 163(1); Evid 129(5); Fraud 61; Insurance 1576, 2532, 3337, 3355, 3381(5), 3418; Neglig 210; Plead 236(3), 236(6), 237(6); Trial 350.6(1), 352.5(1), 358; Witn 228.

Group Hosp. Services, Inc. v. One and Two Brookriver Center, TexApp–Dallas, 704 SW2d 886.—Antitrust 147, 200, 358, 369; App & E 1061.4; Contracts 221(1), 238(2); Frds St of 131(1); Land & Ten 33, 182, 200.7, 230(7); Plead 236(3).

Group Life & Health Ins. Co. v. Brown, TexCivApp–Tyler, 611 SW2d 476.—Estop 52.15, 116; Insurance 3093, 3422; Neglig 210.

Group Life and Health Ins. Co.; Butler v., TexApp–Austin, 962 SW2d 296.—Insurance 2590(2), 2594(2), 2604, 2605, 3360.

Group Life & Health Ins. Co.; Perkins v., TexApp–Austin, 49 SW3d 503, reh overr, and review den.—App

& E 870(2), 893(1), 1175(1); Insurance 3540, 3543; States 171.

Group Life & Health Ins. Co. v. Royal Drug Co., USTex, 99 SCt 1067, 440 US 205, 59 LEd2d 261, reh den 99 SCt 2017, 441 US 917, 60 LEd2d 389, appeal after remand 737 F2d 1433, 79 ALR Fed 857, cert den 105 SCt 912, 469 US 1160, 83 LEd2d 925.—Antitrust 520, 524, 583, 873, 939; Commerce 62.3; Insurance 1001, 1022, 1101, 1106(1), 1106(2), 1108; States 18.41.

Group Life & Health Ins. Co.; Royal Drug Co. v., WDTex, 415 FSupp 343, rev 556 F2d 1375, reh den 564 F2d 98, cert gr 98 SCt 1448, 435 US 903, 55 LEd2d 494, aff 99 SCt 1067, 440 US 205, 59 LEd2d 261, reh den 99 SCt 2017, 441 US 917, 60 LEd2d 389, appeal after remand 737 F2d 1433, 79 ALR Fed 857, cert den 105 SCt 912, 469 US 1160, 83 LEd2d 925.—Antitrust 583, 873; Fed Cts 17, 18; Insurance 1106(1), 1106(2); States 18.41.

Group Life and Health Ins. Co. v. Royal Drug Co., Inc., CA5 (Tex), 737 F2d 1433, 79 ALR Fed 857. See Royal Drug Co., Inc. v. Group Life and Health Ins. Co.

Group Life and Health Ins. Co.; Royal Drug Co., Inc. v., CA5 (Tex), 737 F2d 1433, 79 ALR Fed 857, cert den 105 SCt 912, 469 US 1160, 83 LEd2d 925.—Antitrust 535, 620, 873; Fed Civ Proc 2484, 2544.

Group Life & Health Ins. Co.; Royal Drug Co., Inc. v., CA5 (Tex), 556 F2d 1375, reh den 564 F2d 98, cert gr 98 SCt 1448, 435 US 903, 55 LEd2d 494, aff 99 SCt 1067, 440 US 205, 59 LEd2d 261, reh den 99 SCt 2017, 441 US 917, 60 LEd2d 389, appeal after remand 737 F2d 1433, 79 ALR Fed 857, cert den 105 SCt 912, 469 US 1160, 83 LEd2d 925.—Antitrust 583, 873, 900; Insurance 1101, 1106(1); States 18.41.

Group Life and Health Ins. Co. v. Turner, TexCivApp–Dallas, 620 SW2d 670.—App & E 1172(5); Contracts 313(2); Evid 148; Insurance 3374, 3393, 3417, 3585; Trial 260(9), 366.

Group Life and Health Ins. Co. v. U.S., CA5 (Tex), 660 F2d 1042, reh den 667 F2d 92, cert den 102 SCt 2958, 457 US 1132, 73 LEd2d 1349.—Int Rev 3974, 3980, 4616.1, 4965, 5003.

Group Life & Health Ins. Co. v. U. S., CA5 (Tex), 434 F2d 115, cert den 91 SCt 1618, 402 US 944, 29 LEd2d 112.—Int Rev 3967, 3975.

Group Life Ins. Proceeds of Mallory, In re, TexApp–Amarillo, 872 SW2d 800.—Insurance 3475(3), 3481(3), 3497.

Group Medical & Surgical Service; Elliott v., CA5 (Tex), 714 F2d 556, reh den 721 F2d 819, cert den 104 SCt 2658, 467 US 1215, 81 LEd2d 364.—Civil R 1551; Courts 85(1); Fed Cts 641, 858.

Group Medical and Surgical Service; Red v., TexCivApp–Galveston, 298 SW2d 623.—Insurance 1832(1), 2493(1).

Group Medical and Surgical Service, Inc. v. Leong, TexApp–El Paso, 750 SW2d 791, writ den.—Accord 26(1); App & E 930(1), 1062.1; Corp 202; Evid 318(1); Insurance 3417; Interest 39(1); Plead 106(1), 228.14; Torts 245, 266, 285; Trial 39, 139.1(4), 219, 312(1), 350.3(1), 352.21.

Group No. 1 Oil Corp. v. Sheppard, TexCivApp–Austin, 89 SW2d 1021, writ refused.—Licens 1, 11(1); Mines 87.

Group Practice Affiliates; Silva v., CA5 (Tex), 125 FedAppx 541.—Bankr 2154.1.

Group Purchases, Inc. v. Lance Investments, Inc., TexApp–Dallas, 685 SW2d 729, ref nre.—App & E 458(2), 485(2), 781(7); Evid 571(7); Execution 251(2); Judgm 181(15.1), 185(6); Lis Pen 22(1), 24(1).

Grout; Broaddus v., Tex, 258 SW2d 308, 152 Tex 398.—Deeds 38(1), 38(3); Ven & Pur 22.

Grout; Broaddus v., TexCivApp–Beaumont, 253 SW2d 74, rev 258 SW2d 308, 152 Tex 398.—Deeds 38(1), 38(3).

Grove; Abell v., TexCivApp–El Paso, 152 SW2d 885.—Mines 5.2(3), 5.3, 55(1).

Grove v. Daniel Industries, Inc., TexApp–Houston (14 Dist, 874 SW2d 150. See Grove v. Daniel Valve Co.

Grove v. Daniel Valve Co., TexApp–Houston (14 Dist), 874 SW2d 150, reh den, and writ den.—App & E 934(1); Corp 308(1), 310(1); Judgm 181(19), 185(2); Labor & Emp 3045, 3075.

Grove v. State, TexCrimApp, 51 SW2d 316, 121 TexCrim 477.—Controlled Subs 80.

Grove Mfg. Co. v. Cardinal Const. Co., TexCivApp–Hous (14 Dist), 534 SW2d 153, ref nre.—Contrib 1, 5(5); Evid 265(2); Indem 20, 57, 95; Work Comp 2094, 2142, 2142.35, 2168.

Grover v. Exxon Corp., SDTex, 894 FSupp 291.—Adm 1.20(1), 1.20(4), 1.20(5); Fed Civ Proc 2466, 2470.1, 2543, 2544; Lim of Act 2(3), 31; Propty 4.

Grover v. Gulf States Utilities Co., CA5 (Tex), 776 F2d 517.—Electricity 17, 18(1); Torts 113(2).

Groves, Ex parte, TexCrimApp, 571 SW2d 888.—Const Law 3417; Courts 97(3), 107; Hab Corp 271, 288, 291; Rape 2, 7; Statut 174.

Groves; American Guardian Ins. Co. v., TexCivApp–Fort Worth, 376 SW2d 90.—Insurance 1162.

Groves v. Business Men's Assurance Co. of America, TexApp–Tyler, 635 SW2d 872.—App & E 931(5), 1010.1(3), 1033(1); Labor & Emp 262.

Groves; Campbell v., TexApp–El Paso, 774 SW2d 717, writ den.—Wills 21, 50, 53(2), 53(5), 55(3).

Groves; City of Fort Worth v., TexApp–Fort Worth, 746 SW2d 907.—Admin Law 124; App & E 1024.1; Costs 194.18, 194.40, 207, 208; Counties 23, 52, 110, 196(1); Inj 39; Plead 290(3).

Groves; Corporate Leasing Intern., Inc. v., TexApp–Fort Worth, 925 SW2d 734, reh overr, and writ den.—App & E 854(1), 863, 934(1), 1175(1); Bailm 3; Contracts 103; Costs 194.14; Environ Law 488; Judgm 185(2); Statut 205, 207.

Groves v. Gabriel, Tex, 874 SW2d 660.—Pretrial Proc 382.

Groves v. Gould, TexCivApp–Fort Worth, 102 SW2d 1114.—Mand 57(1), 151(1), 154(3), 154(9).

Groves; Halliburton Oil Well Cementing Co. v., TexCivApp–Waco, 308 SW2d 919, ref nre.—App & E 930(1), 1070(2); Death 58(1); Evid 570; Mines 118; Neglig 1579, 1696, 1714, 1719, 1745, 1750; Plead 34(1); Trial 139.1(20), 140(2), 142, 143, 352.4(6), 358.

Groves v. Hanks, TexCivApp–Corpus Christi, 546 SW2d 638, ref nre.—App & E 758.3(2), 1175(5), 1177(1), 1178(6); Crops 5; Lim of Act 80, 127(17); Princ & A 81(2); Release 33; Trial 368; Trover 1, 10, 35, 44.

Groves; National Loan & Investment Co. of Detroit, Mich., TexCivApp–Fort Worth, 102 SW2d 508.—App & E 218.2(7); B & L Assoc 33(8); Trial 350.4(1), 351.2(5), 351.2(6), 352.16, 352.18; Usury 18, 22, 56, 100(1), 113.

Groves; Poynor v., TexCivApp–Fort Worth, 88 SW2d 657. —App & E 930(1); Labor & Emp 267; New Tr 104(3).

Groves v. Rogers, CA5 (Tex), 547 F2d 898.—Fed Cts 340.1, 343.

Groves; Rosenthal v., TexCivApp–Houston, 387 SW2d 920.—Bankr 2825, 3341, 3411, 3418; Evid 43(2); Judgm 193, 197, 570(1).

Groves v. Rosenthal, TexCivApp–Houston, 371 SW2d 792, ref nre, appeal after remand 387 SW2d 920.—App & E 1071.6; Trial 391, 397(1).

Groves v. Sawyer, TexCivApp–Eastland, 384 SW2d 193, ref nre.—Accord 11(2); Compromise 5(2).

Groves; State v., TexCrimApp, 837 SW2d 103.—Crim Law 290; Judgm 751.

Groves; State v., TexApp–Houston (14 Dist), 807 SW2d 775, petition for discretionary review gr, aff and remanded 837 SW2d 103.—Crim Law 1158(2); Judgm 648.

Groves v. Western Realty Co., TexCivApp–Dallas, 97 SW2d 1015, writ dism.—Tresp to T T 35(1), 53.

Groves v. Western Realty Co., TexCivApp–Dallas, 84 SW2d 835.—App & E 381, 383, 464, 465(1), 466.

Groves v. Whittenburg, TexCivApp–Amarillo, 120 SW2d 870.—Contracts 112, 138(1).

Groves, City of; Banker v., TexCivApp–Beaumont, 295 SW2d 548, ref nre.—Can of Inst 58; Judgm 744; Waters 194.

Groves, City of; Dengler v., TexApp–Beaumont, 997 SW2d 418, petition for review den, and reh of petition for review overr.—Admin Law 754.1, 763; Judgm 181(3), 181(11), 185.3(1); Zoning 278.1, 621, 624, 642.

Groves, City of; LaBove v., Tex, 608 SW2d 162, appeal dism 101 SCt 3043, 452 US 911, 69 LEd2d 414.—App & E 172(1).

Groves, City of; LaBove v., TexCivApp–Beaumont, 602 SW2d 395, ref nre 608 SW2d 162, appeal dism 101 SCt 3043, 452 US 911, 69 LEd2d 414.—Mun Corp 733(2), 791(1).

Groves, City of; Lawson v., TexCivApp–Beaumont, 487 SW2d 439.—Tax 2400, 2403, 2859, 2860, 2862.

Groves, City of; Port Arthur Independent School Dist. v., Tex, 376 SW2d 330.—Mun Corp 601.1, 601.3; Schools 21, 64; States 21.

Groves, City of; Varnado v., TexCivApp–Fort Worth, 329 SW2d 100, ref nre.—App & E 930(1), 931(1); Em Dom 205, 222(4), 241, 262(5); Evid 570; Trial 140(1), 143; Witn 268(1), 282.5, 330(1).

Groves, City of; Wagstaff v., TexCivApp–Beaumont, 419 SW2d 441, ref nre.—Const Law 4186; Mun Corp 65, 120, 592(1), 741.20, 741.35; Work Comp 2158.

Groves Lumber Co.; Turner v., TexCivApp–Dallas, 146 SW2d 422.—Mech Liens 283.

Grovey; Reynolds v., TexCivApp–Galveston, 99 SW2d 1115.—Guard & W 157, 161.

Growe v. State, TexApp–Houston (14 Dist), 675 SW2d 564.—Autos 144.1(1.11), 415; Crim Law 393(1), 641.3(2), 641.3(3), 641.3(8.1), 1166.10(1).

Growers Seed Ass'n, In re, BkrtcyNDTex, 49 BR 17.—Bankr 2958.1, 2959.

Growers Seed Ass'n; Dunn v., TexCivApp–Amarillo, 620 SW2d 233.—App & E 768; Corp 1.4(4), 1.6(3), 327; Guar 9.

Growers Seed Ass'n; Keim v., BkrtcyNDTex, 49 BR 17. See Growers Seed Ass'n, In re.

Grow Group, Inc.; Walters v., SDTex, 907 FSupp 1030.—Rem of C 2, 79(1), 107(7); Statut 188.

Growth Program, Inc.; Harwell v., CA5 (Tex), 459 F2d 461.—Antitrust 920.

Growth Programs, Inc.; Harwell v., CA5 (Tex), 451 F2d 240, opinion mod on denial of reh 459 F2d 461, cert den National Association of Securities Dealers, Inc, v. Harwell, 93 SCt 126, 409 US 876, 34 LEd2d 129.—Antitrust 920; Banks 315(1); Contracts 309(1); Evid 65; Exchanges 2, 14; Fed Civ Proc 2490.

Growth Programs, Inc.; Harwell v., WDTex, 315 FSupp 1184, rev and remanded 451 F2d 240, opinion mod on denial of reh 459 F2d 461, cert den National Association of Securities Dealers, Inc, v. Harwell, 93 SCt 126, 409 US 876, 34 LEd2d 129.—Antitrust 906; Banks 315(1); Const Law 2406, 4295; Exchanges 4.

Grozier v. L-B Sprinkler & Plumbing Repair, TexApp–Fort Worth, 744 SW2d 306, writ den.—App & E 242(2); Judgm 181(5.1); Venue 17, 72, 84.

Grubaugh; Lykes Bros S.S. Co v., CCA5 (Tex), 130 F2d 25.—Fed Cts 744.

Grubaugh; Lykes Bros. S.S. Co. v., CCA5 (Tex), 128 F2d 387, mod on reh 130 F2d 25.—Evid 351; Fed Civ Proc 1852, 1857; Fed Cts 795; Labor & Emp 2936; Seamen 11(9), 29(5.16); Trial 260(8).

Grubaugh v. Texas Employers' Ins. Ass'n, TexApp–Fort Worth, 677 SW2d 812, dism.—App & E 954(1); Inj 138.1, 138.33, 157, 158.

Grubb v. Grubb, TexCivApp–El Paso, 525 SW2d 38, ref nre.—App & E 302(5); Judgm 199(1); Labor & Emp 2832, 2842, 2848, 2881, 2944; Neglig 554(1), 554(2); New Tr 128(1); Trial 350.6(6), 351.2(1.1), 355(3), 365.1(1), 365.1(6).

Grubb; Grubb v., TexCivApp–El Paso, 525 SW2d 38, ref nre.—App & E 302(5); Judgm 199(1); Labor & Emp 2832, 2842, 2848, 2881, 2944; Neglig 554(1), 554(2); New Tr 128(1); Trial 350.6(6), 351.2(1.1), 355(3), 365.1(1), 365.1(6).

Grubb v. Stanolind Oil & Gas Co., TexCivApp–Beaumont, 122 SW2d 278, writ refused.—Ven & Pur 93, 239(1).

Grubb & Ellis Commercial Real Estate Services; Jauregui Partners, Ltd. v., TexApp–Corpus Christi, 960 SW2d 334, reh overr, and review den.—App & E 357(1), 516; New Tr 155, 163(1).

Grubbs v. Aldine Independent School Dist., SDTex, 709 FSupp 127.—Civil R 1351(2), 1356; Fed Civ Proc 2553.

Grubbs; Bowen v., TexCivApp–Galveston, 181 SW2d 875.—Adv Poss 104, 117.

Grubbs v. Bowers, TexCivApp–Galveston, 272 SW2d 956.—Plead 111.34.

Grubbs v. General Elec. Credit Corp., USTex, 92 SCt 1344, 405 US 699, 31 LEd2d 612.—Fed Civ Proc 281; Fed Cts 461; Interpl 24; Rem of C 2, 10, 11, 94.

Grubbs; General Elec. Credit Corp. v., CA5 (Tex), 513 F2d 783, reh den 516 F2d 900, cert den 96 SCt 363, 423 US 947, 46 LEd2d 282.—Fed Cts 955.

Grubbs; General Elec. Credit Corp. v., CA5 (Tex), 478 F2d 53, cert den 94 SCt 153, 414 US 854, 38 LEd2d 104, appeal after remand 513 F2d 783, reh den 516 F2d 900, cert den 96 SCt 363, 423 US 947, 46 LEd2d 282.—Antitrust 983; Bills & N 94(1), 97(1), 103(1); Evid 317(12); Fed Cts 870.1, 945; Princ & A 22(1); Trial 105(2).

Grubbs; General Elec. Credit Corp. v., CA5 (Tex), 447 F2d 286, cert gr 92 SCt 446, 404 US 983, 30 LEd2d 366, rev 92 SCt 1344, 405 US 699, 31 LEd2d 612.—Interpl 8(1); Rem of C 10.

Grubbs; Glaspy v., TexCivApp–Dallas, 110 SW2d 1188.—App & E 644(1); Receivers 3, 8, 16, 29(1), 39.

Grubbs v. Grubbs, TexCivApp–San Antonio, 164 SW2d 216.—Child S 446, 506(1), 506(4).

Grubbs; Grubbs v., TexCivApp–San Antonio, 164 SW2d 216.—Child S 446, 506(1), 506(4).

Grubbs v. Houston First American Sav. Ass'n, CA5 (Tex), 730 F2d 236.—Bankr 3711(3), 3711(4), 3711(5), 3711(6).

Grubbs v. Houston First American Sav. Ass'n, CA5 (Tex), 718 F2d 694, reh gr 718 F2d 699, on reh 730 F2d 236.—Bankr 3711(6).

Grubbs; King v., TexCivApp–El Paso, 275 SW 855, writ dism woj.—Bankr 363; Land & Ten 185, 208(1), 209, 231(6).

Grubbs; Mecke v., TexCivApp–Amarillo, 278 SW2d 404, ref nre.—App & E 77(1); Child C 42, 276, 473.

Grubbs v. Mercantile Texas Corp., TexApp–Eastland, 668 SW2d 429.—App & E 1107.

Grubbs; Rick v., Tex, 214 SW2d 925, 147 Tex 267.—Adv Poss 37, 38; App & E 931(1).

Grubbs v. Rick, TexCivApp–Beaumont, 212 SW2d 489, rev 214 SW2d 925, 147 Tex 267.—Adv Poss 44, 115(4).

Grubbs v. State, TexCrimApp, 137 SW2d 27, 138 TexCrim 507.—Crim Law 465, 1090.16.

Grubbs v. State, TexApp–Houston (1 Dist), 177 SW3d 313, petition for discretionary review refused.—Arrest 68(4); Colleges 9.30(3); Crim Law 394.4(1), 394.6(4), 394.6(5), 1139, 1144.12, 1153(1), 1158(4); Searches 13.1, 25.1, 161, 171, 180, 181, 183, 198, 201.

Grubbs; Ungemach v., NDTex, 566 FSupp 323.—Antitrust 161.

Grubbs; U.S. v., CA5 (Tex), 776 F2d 1281.—Consp 47(3.1); Crim Law 394.3, 569, 719(4), 739.1(1), 739.1(3), 1166.16, 1170.5(1); Ind & Inf 71.2(2), 71.2(4), 110(3), 171; Witn 389, 390.

Grubbs v. White Settlement Independent School Dist., NDTex, 390 FSupp 895, aff 531 F2d 316.—Fed Cts 223, 355.1; Schools 56, 79, 147.40(1), 147.52.

Grubbs Enterprises, Inc. v. Bien, Tex, 900 SW2d 337. See George Grubbs Enterprises, Inc. v. Bien.

Grubbs Enterprises, Inc. v. Bien, TexApp–Fort Worth, 881 SW2d 843. See George Grubbs Enterprises, Inc. v. Bien.

Grubbs Nissan Mid-Cities, Inc. v. DaimlerChrysler Motors Corp., NDTex, 85 FSupp2d 660.—Antitrust 284; Fed Cts 65; Rem of C 100; Statut 181(1), 206.

Grube v. Associated Indem. Corp., CA5 (Tex), 187 F2d 119.—Work Comp 52, 1443, 1927.

Grube v. Donnell Exploration Co., TexCivApp–El Paso, 286 SW2d 179, ref nre.—App & E 1062.5, 1070(2); Cust & U 5, 6, 18, 19(1); Mines 109.

Grube v. Nick's No. 2, TexCivApp–El Paso, 278 SW2d 252, ref nre.—Impl & C C 72; Mech Liens 63.

Gruber v. Deuschle, NDTex, 261 FSupp2d 682, motion den 2003 WL 21283186, aff 87 FedAppx 338.—Atty & C 151, 157.1; Consp 1.1; Contracts 144; Damag 15; Fed Cts 409.1; Fraud 3; Torts 212; Trusts 95, 103(1).

Gruber v. State, TexApp–Corpus Christi, 812 SW2d 368, petition for discretionary review refused.—Autos 355(6); Const Law 4594(8); Crim Law 412(4), 412(6), 412.1(1), 414, 643, 660, 700(9), 995(1), 995(8), 1134(3), 1134(8), 1144.13(2.1), 1158(4).

Gruber v. Texas State Bd. of Pharmacy, TexCivApp–San Antonio, 619 SW2d 564.—Health 223(1); Judgm 335(1), 335(4).

Grubert; Mesta v., TexCivApp–Austin, 312 SW2d 528.—App & E 82(3).

Grubert; U.S. v., SDTex, 191 FSupp 326.—Int Rev 4782.1.

Grubman, Ex parte, TexCrimApp, 176 SW2d 335, 146 TexCrim 500.—Hab Corp 823.

Grubstake Inv. Ass'n v. Worley, TexCivApp–San Antonio, 116 SW2d 472, dism.—App & E 301, 672, 742(1); Evid 471(2); Judgm 181(24); Mines 78.2, 78.7(4).

Grucholski; Humble Oil & Refining Co. v., TexCivApp–Waco, 376 SW2d 950, ref nre.—Mines 121, 125.

Grudziecki v. Starr, TexCivApp–Waco, 351 SW2d 381, writ refused.—Wills 193.

Grudzien v. State, TexCrimApp, 493 SW2d 827.—Crim Law 1172.1(3).

Gruebel, In re, TexApp–Tyler, 153 SW3d 686.—Action 6; App & E 781(1); Const Law 186, 188, 190, 191; Courts 207.3; Environ Law 68, 663, 700; Statut 264, 267(1).

Gruen; Wirt Franklin Petroleum Corp. v., CCA5 (Tex), 139 F2d 659.—Attach 73; Corp 52, 182.1(2); Fed Civ Proc 603; Fed Cts 93, 877; Garn 81(1).

Grugette; U.S. v., CA5 (Tex), 678 F2d 600.—Crim Law 1134(3); Fraud 69(2).

Gruma Corp.; El Aguila Food Products, Inc. v., CA5 (Tex), 131 FedAppx 450.—Evid 555.5, 555.9.

Gruma Corp.; El Aguila Food Products, Inc. v., SDTex, 301 FSupp2d 612, aff 131 FedAppx 450.—Antitrust 528, 535, 537, 544, 582, 677, 716, 872, 964; Evid 508, 515, 555.2, 555.9.

Gruma Corp.; El Aguila Food Products, Inc. v., SDTex, 167 FSupp2d 955.—Fed Civ Proc 81, 241, 251, 387.1; Fed Cts 101, 103, 104, 105, 144, 1158.

Gruma Corp.; James v., TexApp–Fort Worth, 129 SW3d 755, review den.—App & E 223; Appear 20, 24(8); Judgm 181(7), 185(5); Lim of Act 118(2), 119(3), 121(2), 195(3), 199(1).

Grumbles v. State, TexCrimApp, 169 SW2d 720, 145 TexCrim 500.—Crim Law 419(10), 510; Int Liq 37, 39.

Grumbles v. State, TexCrimApp, 158 SW2d 71, 143 TexCrim 162.—Crim Law 784(1), 800(2); Int Liq 249.

Grumbles v. Times Herald Printing Co., CA5 (Tex), 387 F2d 593, cert den 88 SCt 1419, 390 US 1028, 20 LEd2d 285.—Sec Reg 60.63(2).

Grundman; 360 Degree Communications Co. v., TexApp–Texarkana, 937 SW2d 574.—Inj 159.

Grundmeyer v. McFadin, TexCivApp–Tyler, 537 SW2d 764, ref nre.—App & E 215(1), 934(1), 1024.4; Atty & C 20.1; Can of Inst 8; Champ 4(1); Judgm 199(3.10); Princ & A 24, 48, 70, 120(1); Spec Perf 12, 16; Trial 350.2; Ven & Pur 36(1), 45.

Grundstrom v. Beto, NDTex, 273 FSupp 912, appeal dism State of Tex v. Grundstrom, 404 F2d 644.—Arrest 71.1(4.1), 71.1(8); Autos 349.5(2), 349.5(5.1), 349.5(6); Const Law 947; Crim Law 394.4(14), 394.5(2), 394.5(3); Fed Cts 411; Hab Corp 716, 753; Searches 24, 52, 60.1, 70, 161, 165, 192.1.

Grundstrom v. Darnell, CA5 (Tex), 531 SW2d 272.—Civil R 1319, 1376(8), 1382, 1462.

Grundstrom v. State, TexCrimApp, 456 SW2d 92.—Crim Law 662.1, 1038.1(5), 1038.1(7), 1110(1), 1169.1(5); Motions 51; Sent & Pun 1421; Witn 52(5), 191.

Grundstrom v. State, TexCrimApp, 363 SW2d 945.—Crim Law 1036.4, 1044.1(6).

Grundstrom v. State, TexApp–Dallas, 733 SW2d 920, petition for discretionary review gr, vac in part, review dism in part 773 SW2d 294.—Arrest 63.4(12), 71.1(5); Const Law 2545(4), 4723; Crim Law 369.2(1), 511.1(3), 511.1(6.1), 511.2, 511.3, 511.4, 719(1), 790, 826, 1037.1(2), 1129(4); Rob 24.25.

Grundstrom; State of Tex. v., CA5 (Tex), 404 F2d 644.—Const Law 969, 975, 976; Hab Corp 825.1.

Grundy v. Broome, TexCivApp–Amarillo, 90 SW2d 939, writ dism.—Parties 76(1); Trusts 176.

Grundy v. Grundy, TexCivApp–Dallas, 589 SW2d 776.—Child S 449, 474, 479, 487, 490.

Grundy; Grundy v., TexCivApp–Dallas, 589 SW2d 776.—Child S 449, 474, 479, 487, 490.

Grundy v. State, TexCrimApp, 83 SW2d 991, 129 TexCrim 93.—Gaming 85(1).

Grunewald v. Technibilt Corp., TexApp–Dallas, 931 SW2d 593, reh overr, and writ den.—Action 13; App & E 141, 154(4); Infants 84, 85.

Grunsfeld v. State, TexCrimApp, 843 SW2d 521, appeal after remand Hunter v. State, 896 SW2d 397.—Crim Law 1177; Sent & Pun 313; Statut 212.1.

Grunsfeld v. State, TexApp–Dallas, 813 SW2d 158, petition for discretionary review gr, and petition for discretionary review refused, aff 843 SW2d 521, appeal after remand Hunter v. State, 896 SW2d 397.—Crim Law 388.1, 396(2), 650, 749, 1042, 1144.13(2.1), 1152(1), 1159.2(1), 1159.2(7), 1159.2(9), 1159.4(2), 1162, 1169.1(10), 1177; Rape 51(1), 51(4); Sent & Pun 302, 303, 308, 312, 313, 319, 322, 329, 1762, 1771, 1900; Statut 181(1), 205, 208, 217.2, 230, 241(2).

Grunwald v. City of Castle Hills, TexApp–San Antonio, 100 SW3d 350, reh overr.—Em Dom 2(1), 2(1.2), 271.

Grunwald v. Grunwald, TexCivApp–Hous (1 Dist), 487 SW2d 240, ref nre.—Evid 390(4); Lim of Act 39(11); Trial 105(5); Trusts 103(2), 110, 111.

Grunwald; Grunwald v., TexCivApp–Hous (1 Dist), 487 SW2d 240, ref nre.—Evid 390(4); Lim of Act 39(11); Trial 105(5); Trusts 103(2), 110, 111.

Grunwald v. State, TexApp–Corpus Christi, 960 SW2d 324, reh overr, and petition for discretionary review refused.—Crim Law 700(9).

Grupa v. Grupa, TexCivApp–Amarillo, 98 SW2d 217.—Can of Inst 24(2), 37(4); Des & Dist 92.

Grupa; Grupa v., TexCivApp–Amarillo, 98 SW2d 217.—Can of Inst 24(2), 37(4); Des & Dist 92.

Grupe; Lee v., TexCivApp–Texarkana, 223 SW2d 548.—Adv Poss 114(1); Bound 37(3); Drains 1; Judgm 199(3.5); Quiet T 10.2, 44(1), 44(3), 47(2); Tresp to T T 35(1), 38(1), 38(2), 52; Trial 178; Waters 38, 89.

Grupo Dataflux; Atlas Global Group, L.P. v., CA5 (Tex), 312 F3d 168, reh and reh den 61 FedAppx 924, cert gr 124 SCt 384, 540 US 944, 157 LEd2d 273, rev 124 SCt 1920, 541 US 567, 158 LEd2d 866, on remand 375 F3d 1218.—Fed Cts 29.1, 302, 776; Rem of C 15.

Grupo TMM SA; Perforaciones Exploracio 'N Y Producio 'N v., CA5 (Tex),207 FedAppx 458, on remand Perforaciones Maritimas Mexicanas, SA de CV v. GRUPO TMM, SA de CV, 2007 WL 1428654.—Adm 103.

Gruss v. Cummins, TexCivApp–El Paso, 329 SW2d 496, ref nre.—App & E 1177(7); Evid 130, 457; Frds St of 63(2), 106(1), 115.2, 118(1), 118(2), 118(5), 158(3), 158(4); Mines 79.1(2).

G. Russell W., Kristi W. by, v. Graham Independent School Dist., NDTex, 663 FSupp 86. See Kristi W. by G. Russell W. v. Graham Independent School Dist.

Gruver; Commercial Standard Ins. Co. v., TexCivApp–Amarillo, 217 SW2d 95, dism.—App & E 989, 1001(1); Autos 92, 94, 95; Evid 590, 597; Trial 365.3.

Gruver; Dilley v., TexCivApp–Amarillo, 98 SW2d 368, writ dism.—Wareh 24(2), 34(8).

Gruver State Bank; Romer v., TexCivApp–Eastland, 474 SW2d 578.—App & E 994(3), 1011.1(4); Partners 48, 55.

Gruver State Bank of Gruver; Romer v., TexCivApp–Amarillo, 456 SW2d 788.—Venue 22(2).

Gruy; Atlantic Richfield Co. v., TexApp–San Antonio, 720 SW2d 121, ref nre.—App & E 1010.1(3); Mines 78.1(1), 78.1(4), 78.1(9).

Gruy v. Jim Hogg County Appraisal Dist., TexApp–Texarkana, 715 SW2d 170.—Tax 2571.

Gruy v. Reiter Foster Oil Corp., TexCivApp–Galveston, 150 SW2d 842.—Mines 78.7(5); Trial 358.

G.R.W., In re, TexApp–Texarkana, 191 SW3d 896.—App & E 931(1), 989, 1010.1(1); Evid 597; Guard & W 13(4); Hab Corp 532(2), 799.

Grynberg v. Christiansen, TexApp–Dallas, 727 SW2d 665.—Judgm 494.

Grynberg Production Corp. v. British Gas, P.L.C., EDTex, 867 FSupp 1278.—Alt Disp Res 133(2).

Grynberg Production Corp. v. British Gas, p.l.c., EDTex, 817 FSupp 1338.—Action 17; Corp 215, 325; Estop 52(7); Fed Civ Proc 636; Fed Cts 15, 18, 191, 192.10, 241, 242.1, 243, 246, 409.1; Fraud 20; Inj 118(1); Intern Law 7; Princ & A 159(2); Rem of C 25(1), 36, 47, 86(1), 107(7); Trover 2, 4.

Grynberg Production Corp. v. British Gas, P.L.C., EDTex, 149 FRD 135.—Fed Civ Proc 840, 1700; Rem of C 118.

Grywalski v. Grywalski, TexCivApp–Waco, 263 SW2d 684.—Divorce 124.3, 130; Domicile 4(1), 8.

Grywalski; Grywalski v., TexCivApp–Waco, 263 SW2d 684.—Divorce 124.3, 130; Domicile 4(1), 8.

GSC Enterprises, Inc.; Biggs v., TexApp–Fort Worth, 8 SW3d 765.—App & E 901, 930(3), 1003(7), 1004(8); Damag 185(1), 221(7); Trial 139.1(3), 140(1), 358.

GSC Enterprises, Inc. v. Rylander, TexApp–Austin, 85 SW3d 469.—App & E 1079; Escheat 2, 6; Statut 176, 179, 181(2), 188, 212.7.

GSE Lining Technology, Inc.; Poly-America, L.P. v., CAFed (Tex), 383 F3d 1303.—Courts 96(7); Fed Cts 825.1; Pat 16.14, 66(1.25), 76, 81, 165(4), 167(1), 168(2.1), 314(5), 318(1), 324.5, 328(2).

G.S.G., In re, TexApp–Houston (14 Dist), 145 SW3d 351.—App & E 893(1); Child 57; Courts 39.

G.S.G. Royalty Corp.; Lone Star Gas Co., A Div. of Ensearch Corp. v., TexApp–Dallas, 757 SW2d 457.—Gas 13(1); Judgm 185.3(18).

G.S.K. v. T.K.N., TexApp–El Paso, 940 SW2d 797.—Infants 210.

G.S.P., Inc.; Callaway v., SDTex, 793 FSupp 133.—Fed Cts 31; Insurance 1117(1); Labor & Emp 407; Rem of C 81, 107(1); States 18.51.

GS Roofing Products Co., Inc.; Green v., TexApp–Houston (14 Dist), 928 SW2d 265.—App & E 863; Autos 201(6), 201(7); Judgm 185(2); Neglig 202, 379, 380, 383, 387, 1675.

G.S.W. Petroleum, Inc.; Mannan v., TexCivApp–Fort Worth, 594 SW2d 222.—Antitrust 141; Judgm 181(33).

GSYS Enterprises, Inc., In re, BkrtcyNDTex, 343 BR 568.—Bankr 2125, 2970; Contracts 152; Equity 64.

GT & MC, Inc. v. Texas City Refining, Inc., TexApp–Houston (1 Dist), 822 SW2d 252, writ den.—App & E 961, 969, 977(5), 1024.3, 1050.1(1), 1056.1(1); Contracts 143(2), 147(1), 152, 176(1), 206, 303(3); Evid 351, 355(3); Judgm 199(3.7), 199(3.10); New Tr 6; Pretrial Proc 44.1, 45; Sales 284(1), 426, 442(1); Trial 182, 349(2).

GTE Communications Systems Corp. v. Curry, TexApp–San Antonio, 819 SW2d 652.—Costs 2; Courts 85(2).

GTE Communications Systems Corp. v. Tanner, Tex, 856 SW2d 725.—Costs 2; Judgm 183; Mand 4(4), 172; Pretrial Proc 44.1, 354, 434.

GTE Corp.; Miller v., SDTex, 788 FSupp 312.—Fed Civ Proc 2535, 2539, 2543, 2544, 2546, 2548; Pat 207, 212(2), 215.

G.T.E. Directories Corp.; Dallas Cent. Appraisal Dist. v., TexApp–Dallas, 905 SW2d 318, reh overr, and writ den.—Estop 52(7), 62.1, 62.3; Judgm 178; Tax 2603.

GTE Directories Corp. v. McKinnon, TexApp–Fort Worth, 734 SW2d 429.—App & E 756; Bills & N 129(1); Costs 260(4); Labor & Emp 35.

GTE Directories Service Corp.; Jackson v., NDTex, 734 FSupp 258.—Civil R 1135, 1247, 1539, 1551, 1555; Courts 96(7), 100(1); Fed Civ Proc 2497.1.

GTE Mobilnet of Houston, Inc.; Chair King, Inc. v., TexApp–Houston (14 Dist), 135 SW3d 365, review gr, and motion to stay mandate den, rev 184 SW3d 707, cert den Kosoy v. GTE Mobilnet of Houston, Inc, 126 SCt 2941, 165 LEd2d 955.—App & E 60(8), 893(1); Commerce 59; Consp 1.1, 2, 6; Const Law 1537, 1640, 1800, 3705, 4426; Courts 489(1); Judgm 181(15.1); Statut 184, 190, 205, 206, 208, 217.4, 219(1), 220, 223.1; Tel 730, 888, 916(1); Torts 330, 341, 345; Tresp 6, 7.

GTE Mobilnet of Houston, Inc.; The Chair King, Inc. v., Tex, 184 SW3d 707, cert den Kosoy v. GTE Mobilnet of Houston, Inc, 126 SCt 2941, 165 LEd2d 955.—Action 3; Courts 489(1); States 4.1(1), 18.1.

GTE Mobilnet of South Texas Ltd. Partnership, In re, TexApp–Beaumont, 123 SW3d 795.—Alt Disp Res 114, 134(2), 135, 141, 151, 182(1), 213(1); App & E 71(3); Commerce 80.5; Contracts 143(1), 147(2), 148; Evid 448; Fraud 23; Mand 3(3), 60.

GTE Mobilnet of South Texas Ltd. Partnership v. Cellular Max, Inc., TexApp–Beaumont, 123 SW3d 801, review dism.—Alt Disp Res 189; App & E 71(3); Inj 138.9, 138.37, 140, 147, 148(2).

GTE Mobilnet of South Texas Ltd. Partnership v. Pascouet, TexApp–Houston (14 Dist), 61 SW3d 599, reh overr, and reh overr, and review den, and reh of petition for review den.—App & E 230, 232(2), 836, 882(8), 930(1), 954(1), 954(2), 989, 994(2), 999(1), 1001(1), 1001(3), 1003(3), 1003(6), 1004(1), 1004(7); Compromise 15(1); Damag 26, 96, 104, 119, 127, 192; Decl Judgm 181, 300; Evid 555.2; Inj 1, 9, 128(1), 130; Nuis 1, 3(1), 3(3), 18, 33, 41, 50(1), 50(4), 50(7); States 18.5, 18.7, 18.11, 18.13, 18.15; Statut 181(1), 181(2), 184, 188, 206, 212.6, 214; Torts 328, 368, 369; Zoning 14, 764, 781.

GTE Mobilnet of South Texas Ltd. Partnership v. Telecell Cellular, Inc., TexApp–Houston (1 Dist), 955 SW2d 286, reh overr, and writ den.—Action 27(1); Antitrust 141, 224, 363, 367; App & E 1062.4; Contracts 143(2), 147(1), 155, 168, 169, 170(1), 176(2), 353(6); Evid 213(2), 596(1); Fraud 32, 60; Pretrial Proc 44.1, 45; Princ & A 9, 47, 81(4); Torts 432, 433; Trial 193(1).

GTE North Inc.; Morton v., NDTex, 922 FSupp 1169, aff 114 F3d 1182, cert den 118 SCt 205, 522 US 880, 139 LEd2d 141.—Admin Law 229; Civil R 1006, 1017, 1106, 1218(4), 1225(3), 1225(4), 1413, 1505(1), 1513, 1516, 1522, 1523, 1540, 1542; Fed Civ Proc 2466, 2470, 2470.4, 2497.1, 2543, 2544, 2546, 2547.1, 2552; Lim of Act 58(1).

GTE North Inc.; Westfall v., NDTex, 956 FSupp 707.—Civil R 1122, 1209, 1218(3); Damag 50.10; Estop 85;

Evid 317(2); Fed Civ Proc 2497.1, 2515; Labor & Emp 40(1), 40(2); Libel 1, 45(1), 50, 51(1), 54, 74, 112(2), 123(8).

GTE Southwest, Inc. v. Bruce, Tex, 998 SW2d 605.—App & E 216(1), 232(2), 1051.1(2); Corp 397, 493; Damag 50.10, 192, 208(6); Evid 506, 507, 532; Labor & Emp 3045, 3055; Work Comp 546, 2090.

GTE Southwest, Inc. v. Bruce, TexApp–Texarkana, 956 SW2d 636, reh overr, and review gr, aff 998 SW2d 605. —App & E 204(1), 215(1), 216(1), 970(2), 1050.1(12); Damag 50.10, 192, 221(8); Evid 506, 507, 531; Work Comp 2093.

GTE Southwest, Inc. v. City of Dallas, TexApp–Fort Worth, 980 SW2d 928. See City of Dallas v. GTE Southwest, Inc.

GTE Southwest, Inc.; City of Dallas v., TexApp–Fort Worth, 980 SW2d 928, reh overr, and review den.—App & E 23, 185(1), 241, 989, 1010.2; Courts 37(2), 39; Decl Judgm 392.1; Estop 52.10(3); Evid 177; Judgm 199(3.5); Plead 370; Pretrial Proc 752; Tel 799, 802, 804; Trial 139.1(17).

GTE Southwest, Inc. v. Public Utility Com'n, TexApp–Austin, 102 SW3d 282, petition for review abated, and petition for review abated, and review dism.—Admin Law 676, 751, 791; Contracts 143(2), 143.5, 147(2), 169, 176(2); Cust & U 15(1); Interest 39(3); Statut 219(1), 219(4); Tel 856, 862, 864(2).

GTE Southwest Inc. v. Public Utility Com'n, TexApp–Austin, 978 SW2d 161, review den.—Tel 940(3).

GTE-Southwest, Inc.; Public Utility Com'n of Texas v., Tex, 901 SW2d 401.—Pub Ut 119.1, 128, 147, 168, 189; Tel 940(3), 944, 973.

GTE Southwest Inc. v. Public Utility Com'n of Texas, TexApp–Austin, 37 SW3d 546, reh overr.—Tel 906.

GTE Southwest Inc. v. Public Utility Com'n of Texas, TexApp–Austin, 10 SW3d 7, reh gr in part.—Admin Law 305; Em Dom 2(1), 2(1.1); Pub Ut 147; Tel 855, 904.

GTE Southwest Inc.; Stiles v., CA5 (Tex), 128 F3d 904, reh and sug for reh den 137 F3d 1353.—Fed Cts 776; Statut 181(1), 188; Tel 900.

GTE Southwest Inc.; Wieburg v., CA5 (Tex), 272 F3d 302, on remand 2002 WL 31156431, aff 71 FedAppx 440. —Bankr 2154.1, 2323, 2553; Fed Civ Proc 131; Fed Cts 544, 817.

GTE-SW; Public Utility Com'n of Texas v., TexApp–Austin, 833 SW2d 153, writ den, and writ gr, and writ withdrawn, aff in part, rev in part 901 SW2d 401.—Admin Law 325, 814; Evid 597; Pub Ut 128, 147; Tel 940(3), 943, 964, 973, 988.

GTE Telephone Operations; Westfall v., NDTex, 956 FSupp 707. See Westfall v. GTE North Inc.

G. T. H., Matter of, TexCivApp–Eastland, 541 SW2d 527. —Hab Corp 532(1).

GT, Inc.; Teal Energy USA, Inc. v., CA5 (Tex), 369 F3d 873.—Fed Cts 300, 307, 317, 318, 915.

G.T. Management, Inc. v. Gonzalez, TexApp–Dallas, 106 SW3d 880.—App & E 232(0.5), 232(2), 846(5), 852, 1004(1), 1008.1(2), 1140(1); Labor & Emp 3049(3), 3055, 3089(2), 3096(8), 3105(8); Plead 34(1), 48.

Guadalajara, Inc.; Enrique Bernat F., S.A. v., CA5 (Tex), 210 F3d 439, reh and reh den 218 F3d 745.—Fed Cts 776, 815, 862; Inj 138.1; Trademarks 1033, 1034, 1037, 1053, 1097, 1421, 1800.

Guadalupana Funeral Home; Washington Nat. Ins. Co. v., TexCivApp–Beaumont, 109 SW2d 1002.—App & E 782; Courts 91(1); J P 44(8), 141(2).

Guadalupe Blanco River Authority v. Canyon Regional Water Authority, TexApp–San Antonio, 211 SW3d 351, reh overr, and review gr.—Ease 42; Em Dom 28, 46, 47(1), 191(3); Judgm 183, 185.3(1); Waters 191.

Guadalupe-Blanco River Authority v. City of Lytle, CA5 (Tex), 937 F2d 184.—Rem of C 21.

Guadalupe-Blanco River Authority v. City of San Antonio, Tex, 200 SW2d 989, 145 Tex 611.—Antitrust 695; App & E 1195(3); Contracts 42, 164; Electricity 1 1/2; Mun Corp 226, 722.

Guadalupe-Blanco River Authority; City of San Antonio v., TexCivApp–Galveston, 191 SW2d 118, rev 200 SW2d 989, 145 Tex 611.—Electricity 1 1/2; Estop 62.6; Judgm 725(1), 735; Mun Corp 225(3), 228, 722.

Guadalupe-Blanco River Authority v. Forshage, TexCivApp–San Antonio, 401 SW2d 376, ref nre.—Bound 37(5), 46(1).

Guadalupe-Blanco River Authority; Friends of Canyon Lake, Inc. v., TexApp–Austin, 96 SW3d 519, review den.—Admin Law 124, 229, 500, 663; App & E 893(1), 895(2); Courts 39; Decl Judgm 41, 96; Plead 104(1), 111.39(0.5); Waters 145, 152(2), 183.5.

Guadalupe-Blanco River Authority v. Kraft, Tex, 77 SW3d 805.—App & E 204(7), 230, 971(2); Em Dom 255, 262(5); Evid 142(1), 524, 555.2, 555.6(2), 555.6(10).

Guadalupe-Blanco River Authority v. Kraft, TexApp–Austin, 39 SW3d 264, review gr, rev 77 SW3d 805.—App & E 232(2), 946, 971(2); Em Dom 137, 202(1); Evid 142(1), 546, 555.2, 555.6(10).

Guadalupe-Blanco River Authority; Pape v., TexApp–Austin, 48 SW3d 908, reh overr, and review den.—App & E 920(2), 946, 961, 966(1), 970(2), 1050.1(1), 1056.1(1); Clerks of C 67; Courts 91(1); Em Dom 131, 167(4), 172, 202(2), 228, 229; Pretrial Proc 714; Trial 43.

Guadalupe-Blanco River Authority v. Pitonyak, TexApp–Corpus Christi, 84 SW3d 326, rule 537(f) motion gr.—App & E 863, 893(1), 916(1); Courts 35, 37(1), 39, 40; Mun Corp 723, 723.5, 742(4), 847, 854, 857; Nav Wat 2, 22(4); Neglig 273; Plead 104(1), 111.10, 111.36, 111.39(0.5), 111.48; Pretrial Proc 695; States 112(2), 112.1(1), 112.2(1), 112.2(2), 191.1, 191.4(1), 191.8(1), 208.

Guadalupe-Blanco River Authority; Tuttle v., Tex, 174 SW2d 589, 141 Tex 523.—App & E 1100; Mun Corp 722.

Guadalupe-Blanco River Authority v. Tuttle, TexCivApp–San Antonio, 171 SW2d 520, writ refused 174 SW2d 589, 141 Tex 523.—Contracts 147(1), 153; Inj 147; Mun Corp 722.

Guadalupe–Blanco River Authority; U.S. Departments of Army and Air Force v., CA5 (Tex), 937 F2d 184. See Guadalupe-Blanco River Authority v. City of Lytle.

Guadalupe County; Lorelei Corp. v., CA5 (Tex), 895 F2d 1070. See U.S. v. Vahlco Corp.

Guadalupe County v. Poth, TexCivApp–San Antonio, 163 SW 1050.—Acct Action on 19.

Guadalupe County; Schubert v., TexCivApp–San Antonio, 189 SW2d 514.—Em Dom 300, 303, 307(2).

Guadalupe County Appraisal Dist.; Hurst v., TexApp–San Antonio, 752 SW2d 231.—Const Law 951, 958.

Guadalupe County Groundwater Conservation Dist.; Williamson v., WDTex, 343 FSupp2d 580.—Civil R 1304, 1305, 1396; Const Law 3509, 4086; Em Dom 277; Fed Civ Proc 1831; Fed Cts 41, 43, 51, 65; U S Mag 25, 27, 31; Waters 101.

Guadalupe Economic Services Corp. v. Dehoyos, TexApp–Austin, 183 SW3d 712.—Antitrust 359; App & E 859; Appear 8(3), 11.1; Const Law 4008; Corp 508; Judgm 105.1; Plead 34(1), 96; Trial 9(2).

Guadalupe Hosp. Foundation Inc.; Gilbreath v., CA5 (Tex), 5 F3d 785.—Admin Law 358; Fed Cts 416; Offic 72.41(1); Records 31; Rem of C 19(1); U S Mag 13; Witn 208(1).

Guadalupe Sav. & Loan Ass'n; Texas Mortg. Services Corp. v., CA5 (Tex), 761 F2d 1068. See Texas Mortg. Services Corp., Matter of.

Guadalupe Val. Elec. Co-op.; Erwin v., TexCivApp–San Antonio, 505 SW2d 353, ref nre.—App & E 1056.1(10), 1056.6, 1070(2); Electricity 13, 14(1), 19(2).

GUAJARDO;

Guadalupe Valley Elec. Co-op., Inc. v. South Tex. Chamber of Commerce, TexCivApp–San Antonio, 374 SW2d 329.—Assoc 7, 20(1); Corp 173.

Guadalupe Val. Elec. Co-op., Inc. v. Towns, TexCivApp–Corpus Christi, 397 SW2d 496.—Tresp 44, 45(5), 57; Trial 85.

Guadalupe Valley Hosp.; Seiler v., TexApp–Corpus Christi, 709 SW2d 37, ref nre.—App & E 715(1); Health 770; States 112.2(1).

Guadardo; U.S. v., CA5 (Tex), 40 F3d 102.—Crim Law 1134(3), 1139, 1158(4); Sent & Pun 1285.

Guadarrama-Garcia v. Acosta, SDTex, 217 FSupp2d 802. —Aliens 390.

Guadian; Border Apparel-East, Inc. v., TexApp–El Paso, 868 SW2d 894, reh overr.—App & E 946, 977(5), 989, 994(2), 1001(1), 1002, 1003(3), 1003(7); Damag 37, 38, 100, 187.

Guadian v. State, TexCrimApp, 420 SW2d 949.—Controlled Subs 80; Crim Law 255.4; Cust Dut 126(1), 126(2), 126(4), 126(5), 126(9.1).

Guadiano; Fleishman v., Tex, 651 SW2d 730.—Plead 53(2); Trial 215.

Guadiano v. Fleishman, TexApp–San Antonio, 636 SW2d 785, rev 651 SW2d 730.—Prod Liab 10, 11, 15, 27, 96.1.

Guadian-Salazar; U.S. v., CA5 (Tex), 824 F2d 344.—Crim Law 662.30.

Guagnini v. Prudential Securities, Inc., WDTex, 872 FSupp 361.—Action 60; Fed Civ Proc 1954.1; Fed Cts 5, 584, 598.1; Rem of C 2, 36, 101.1, 107(7); Trial 3(1).

Guajardo, Ex parte, TexCrimApp, 354 SW2d 141, 172 TexCrim 149.—Bail 43.

Guajardo, Ex parte, TexCrimApp, 350 SW2d 206, 171 TexCrim 328.—Bail 43.

Guajardo, Ex parte, TexApp–San Antonio, 70 SW3d 202, appeal after remand Guajardo v. Texas Dept of Public Safety, 2002 WL 1370079.—Crim Law 1226(3.1); Prisons 4(10.1).

Guajardo v. Alamo Lumber Co., Tex, 317 SW2d 725, 159 Tex 225.—App & E 781(1), 781(4), 781(7), 802.

Guajardo; Alamo Lumber Co. v., TexCivApp–Eastland, 315 SW2d 672, vac 317 SW2d 725, 159 Tex 225.—App & E 954(1), 954(2); Fraud Conv 74(2), 76(1), 272, 276, 277(1); Inj 132, 135, 144, 147; Lim of Act 60(5), 65(2), 184; Plead 246(1).

Guajardo; Ash v., CA5 (Tex), 72 FedAppx 143.—Civil R 1548; Judgm 713(1), 715(2).

Guajardo; Beto, CA5 (Tex), 449 F2d 780.—Courts 104; Fed Cts 743.

Guajardo v. Chavana, TexApp–San Antonio, 762 SW2d 683, writ den, appeal after remand In re Estate of Chavana, 993 SW2d 311, rule 537(f) motion dism.—App & E 1173(2); Ex & Ad 1, 5, 122(2).

Guajardo v. Conwell, Tex, 46 SW3d 862.—App & E 79(1), 80(6), 712.

Guajardo v. Conwell, TexApp–Houston (14 Dist), 30 SW3d 15, reh overr, and review gr, aff 46 SW3d 862.—App & E 78(1), 352.1; Costs 260(1), 260(4), 260(5), 261.

Guajardo; Cruz v., TexCivApp–Corpus Christi, 502 SW2d 610.—App & E 964; Parties 56; Trial 2, 3(2).

Guajardo; Durban v., TexApp–Dallas, 79 SW3d 198.—App & E 230, 231(9), 989, 999(1), 1001(1), 1001(3), 1003(6), 1070(1), 1073(1), 1194(1); Assault 39; Damag 49, 49.10, 102, 130.1, 181, 192; Judgm 198.

Guajardo v. Estelle, CA5 (Tex), 580 F2d 748.—Const Law 1194, 1527, 3825; Fed Civ Proc 2737.5; Fed Cts 265, 1008; Jury 14(12.5), 14.5(2.1), 25(6), 25(8); Prisons 4(6), 4(8), 4(9), 4(12).

Guajardo v. Estelle, SDTex, 568 FSupp 1354.—Compromise 57, 61; Const Law 1194, 2289, 2291.

Guajardo v. Estelle, SDTex, 432 FSupp 1373, aff in part, rev in part 580 F2d 748.—Civil R 1006, 1476, 1485, 1486, 1487; Const Law 242.1(1), 2284, 2287, 2291, 2296, 2297, 2302, 3227, 4827; Fed Cts 269, 1008; Prisons 4(7), 4(8), 4(9), 4(12), 4(13).

Guajardo; Guerra v., SDTex, 466 FSupp 1046, aff 597 F2d 769.—Const Law 77, 2450, 2551, 2580, 2588, 2621, 3057, 3062, 3065, 3869, 3898, 4067; Fed Civ Proc 103.2, 103.4; Inj 138.21, 138.46; Records 51, 54, 59; U S 66, 68.

Guajardo; Guzman v., TexApp–Corpus Christi, 761 SW2d 506, writ den.—Autos 162(2), 162(5), 168(6), 244(55); Death 88, 89, 95(1), 95(4); Infants 61.

Guajardo; Keele v., CA5 (Tex), 71 FedAppx 369.—Civil R 1358, 1376(7).

Guajardo v. Liberty Mut. Ins. Co., TexApp–Corpus Christi, 831 SW2d 358, reh overr, and writ den.—Insurance 3336, 3337, 3381(5), 3382; Judgm 181(21); Lim of Act 127(1), 127(2.1); Work Comp 1042, 1072, 1990, 2216.

Guajardo v. Luna, CA5 (Tex), 432 F2d 1324.—Atty & C 11(1); Fed Cts 743.

Guajardo v. McAdams, SDTex, 349 FSupp 211, vac Sands v. Wainwright, 491 F2d 417, cert den 94 SCt 2403, 416 US 992, 40 LEd2d 771.—Civil R 1326(2); Const Law 3825, 4821; Prisons 4(9), 4(12), 4(13), 13(6).

Guajardo; Martinez v., TexCivApp–San Antonio, 464 SW2d 944.—Divorce 169, 254(2).

Guajardo v. Neece, TexApp–Fort Worth, 758 SW2d 696. —Covenants 69(1); Inj 138.37, 147, 189.

Guajardo; Peco Const. Co. v., TexApp–San Antonio, 919 SW2d 736, reh den, and writ den.—Action 27(1); App & E 79(1), 930(3), 999(2), 1001(3), 1003(7), 1004(11), 1182; Costs 260(5); Damag 94; Fraud 3, 12, 32, 58(1), 61, 62.

Guajardo v. State, TexCrimApp, 109 SW3d 456.—Crim Law 1114.1(1), 1134(2), 1139, 1158(1); Judgm 713(1), 956(0.5), 956(1).

Guajardo v. State, TexCrimApp, 450 SW2d 663.—Crim Law 273.1(5), 274(3.1).

Guajardo v. State, TexCrimApp, 378 SW2d 853.—Controlled Subs 69; Crim Law 351(3), 363, 394.4(9), 1031(4), 1171.8(1).

Guajardo v. State, TexCrimApp, 363 SW2d 259.—Crim Law 1171.2.

Guajardo v. State, TexCrimApp, 329 SW2d 878, 168 TexCrim 503.—Controlled Subs 80; Crim Law 364(1), 1137(5).

Guajardo v. State, TexCrimApp, 139 SW2d 85, 139 TexCrim 201.—Autos 347, 357; Crim Law 772(6), 814(2), 1111(3), 1174(5).

Guajardo v. State, TexApp–Houston (1 Dist), 176 SW3d 402, petition for discretionary review refused.—Crim Law 800(1), 800(4), 863(1), 863(2), 1038.1(1); Sod 6.

Guajardo v. State, TexApp–Houston (1 Dist), 870 SW2d 667, petition for discretionary review refused.—Crim Law 1035(10).

Guajardo v. State, TexApp–Corpus Christi, 24 SW3d 423, reh overr, and petition for discretionary review gr, rev 109 SW3d 456.—Judgm 634, 751; Sent & Pun 2001, 2003, 2009, 2020, 2021.

Guajardo v. State, TexApp–Houston (14 Dist), 999 SW2d 566, petition for discretionary review refused.—Arrest 67; Crim Law 67, 577.4, 577.5, 577.8(2), 577.10(1), 577.10(4), 577.12(1), 577.15(1), 577.16(4), 577.16(8), 577.16(9).

Guajardo v. Supreme Forest, Woodmen Circle, TexCivApp–Dallas, 114 SW2d 1192.—Insurance 3189(1), 3191(2), 3192.

Guajardo v. Texas Dept. of Criminal Justice, CA5 (Tex), 363 F3d 392, cert den 125 SCt 57, 543 US 818, 160 LEd2d 26.—Convicts 6; Fed Civ Proc 2397.5; Fed Cts 776, 870.1; Inj 75.

Guajardo v. Texas Dept. of Criminal Justice Executive Director, CA5 (Tex), 108 FedAppx 848.—Fed Civ Proc 2397.5; Fed Cts 10.1, 681.1.

Guajardo; Texas Dept. of Public Safety v., TexApp–Houston (14 Dist), 970 SW2d 602.—Admin Law 676, 790, 791; Arrest 63.5(4), 63.5(9); Autos 144.2(1), 144.2(2.1), 144.2(9.1), 349(2.1).

GUAJARDO;

See Guidelines for Arrangement at the beginning of this Volume

Guajardo; U.S. v., CA5 (Tex), 950 F2d 203, cert den 112 SCt 1773, 503 US 1009, 118 LEd2d 432.—Const Law 3809, 4709, 4710; Crim Law 1134(3); Sent & Pun 658, 792, 794, 863, 865, 996.

Guajardo; U.S. v., CA5 (Tex), 508 F2d 1093, reh den 511 F2d 1192, cert dism 96 SCt 8, 423 US 801, 46 LEd2d 244, cert den 96 SCt 86, 423 US 847, 46 LEd2d 68.— Consp 23.1, 28(1), 47(12); Controlled Subs 113; Crim Law 424(1), 878(4).

Guajardo; U.S. v., CA5 (Tex), 218 FedAppx 294.—Controlled Subs 100(2); Sent & Pun 300, 780.

Guajardo de Gonzalez; Gonzalez v., TexCivApp–Waco, 541 SW2d 865.—Evid 589; Ex & Ad 178, 187, 188, 190; Home 145, 168; Hus & W 262.1(2), 262.1(6), 262.2, 264(2), 264(6); Partit 12(3).

Guajardo-Guzman; U.S. v., CA5 (Tex), 149 FedAppx 274.—Crim Law 1031(4), 1042.

Guana v. State, TexCrimApp, 501 SW2d 116.—Sent & Pun 2021.

Guana v. State, TexApp–Beaumont, 672 SW2d 248.—Crim Law 562; Ind & Inf 71.4(1), 125(3); Kidnap 32, 36.

Guaranteed Floorcovering, Inc.; Caprock Const. Co. v., TexApp–Dallas, 950 SW2d 203.—Judgm 102; Plead 129(1), 252(2).

Guarantee Ins. Co. v. First Nat. Bank of Jacksonville, TexCivApp–Tyler, 552 SW2d 855, dism.—App & E 907(3), 912; Insurance 3450; Liens 7; Plead 111.9; Venue 22(3), 22(4).

Guarantee Ins. Co.; Oakes v., TexCivApp–Eastland, 573 SW2d 899, ref nre.—App & E 930(1), 989; Contracts 139; Insurance 1645(1), 1645(2).

Guarantee Ins. Co.; Pappas v., CA5 (Tex), 217 F2d 681.—Work Comp 1385, 1937.

Guarantee Ins. Co. of Texas v. Boggs, TexCivApp–Amarillo, 527 SW2d 265, dism.—Evid 10(4); Insurance 2772, 2775, 2778, 3559; Plead 111.16, 111.22.

Guarantee Mut. Life Co.; Kennedy v., TexCivApp–Fort Worth, 103 SW2d 809, writ dism.—Insurance 1762.

Guarantee Mut. Life Ins. Co. v. Harrison, TexCivApp–Austin, 358 SW2d 404, ref nre.—Estop 54; Statut 212.6, 219(1); Tax 2263, 2562.

Guaranty Abstract Co. v. Denman, TexCivApp–Texarkana, 209 SW2d 213, writ refused.—Abstr of T 3; Damag 62(4).

Guaranty Bank v. Lone Star Life Ins. Co., TexCivApp–Dallas, 568 SW2d 431, ref nre.—Bankr 2828.1, 3343; Contracts 194, 221(2), 278(2); Estop 85; Fraud 20; Torts 111.

Guaranty Bank v. O'Dowd, TexCivApp–Waco, 619 SW2d 221, rev 632 SW2d 338.—App & E 832(4); Interest 50; Judgm 105.1, 113, 143(3), 145(2), 153(1); Tender 19(1), 21.

Guaranty Bank; Purnell v., TexApp–Dallas, 624 SW2d 357, ref nre.—Judgm 181(29), 185(2); Sales 126(1).

Guaranty Bank; Starness v., TexApp–Dallas, 634 SW2d 325, ref nre.—Bills & N 28; Plead 381(1); Usury 50, 52, 53, 75.

Guaranty Bank v. Thompson, Tex, 632 SW2d 338.—Costs 42(8); Interest 50; Judgm 162(3), 162(4); New Tr 140(1); Tender 19(2).

Guaranty Bank v. Thompson, TexCivApp–Waco, 619 SW2d 217, rev 632 SW2d 338.—App & E 832(4); Interest 50; Judgm 105.1, 143(3), 145(2), 145(4), 153(1); Tender 19(2).

Guaranty Bank v. Thornhill, TexCivApp–Waco, 596 SW2d 264, dism.—App & E 339(2), 624, 627.

Guaranty Bank & Trust Co. v. Hamacher, TexCivApp–Galveston, 112 SW2d 343.—Bills & N 64, 537(2); Contracts 42; Trial 351.5(4).

Guaranty Bank & Trust Co.; Lubbock Hotel Co. v., CCA5 (Tex), 77 F2d 152.—Contracts 153; Courts 497, 500; Mtg 209; Usury 2(3), 6.

Guaranty Bank of Dallas v. O'Dowd, TexCivApp–Waco, 595 SW2d 634, dism.—App & E 339(2), 624, 628(2).

Guaranty Bank of Dallas v. Thompson, TexCivApp–Waco, 595 SW2d 633, dism.—App & E 624, 628(2).

Guaranty Bank (South Oak Cliff Bank) v. Nat. Surety Corp., TexCivApp–Dallas, 508 SW2d 928, ref nre.—Contracts 97(1), 98; Princ & S 136; Torts 200, 241, 242; Trusts 231(1).

Guaranty Bond & Mortg. Co.; Beesley v., TexCivApp–San Antonio, 107 SW2d 447, writ dism.—App & E 909(5); Ven & Pur 267.

Guaranty Bond State Bank; Graves v., TexCivApp–Texarkana, 161 SW2d 118.—App & E 931(1), 989; Evid 383(7); Hus & W 267(8); Mtg 153, 186(3), 186(5), 334, 356, 360.

Guaranty Bond State Bank; Jenkins Common School Dist. No. 17 v., TexCivApp–Waco, 103 SW2d 394.—Dep & Escr 35; Mun Corp 902.

Guaranty Bond State Bank v. Tucker, TexCivApp–Dallas, 462 SW2d 398, ref nre.—App & E 1170.10; Banks 54(1), 55(5); Trial 350.2, 351.5(1).

Guaranty Bond State Bank, North Zulch v. Donaho, TexCivApp–Waco, 138 SW2d 249.—App & E 1126.

Guaranty Building & Loan Co. v. Brazil, TexCivApp–Galveston, 141 SW2d 694.—Courts 207.1, 207.5, 478.

Guaranty Bldg. & Loan Co.; Breland v., TexCivApp–Fort Worth, 119 SW2d 690, writ refused.—Elect of Rem 11, 12; Estop 68(2), 68(4).

Guaranty Bldg. & Loan Co.; Breland v., TexCivApp–Galveston, 103 SW2d 474.—Lim of Act 48(1); Plead 110.

Guaranty Building & Loan Co. v. Keller, TexCivApp–Fort Worth, 104 SW2d 889, writ dism.—Fraud Conv 297.

Guaranty Bldg. & Loan Co.; West Texas Const. Co. v., TexCivApp–Galveston, 93 SW2d 774.—Venue 22(4), 22(6), 22(8).

Guaranty County Mut. Ins. Co. v. Kline, Tex, 845 SW2d 810.—Insurance 2792.

Guaranty County Mut. Ins. Co. v. Reyna, Tex, 709 SW2d 647.—App & E 854(2); Judgm 143(2), 146.

Guaranty County Mut. Ins. Co. v. Reyna, TexApp–San Antonio, 700 SW2d 325, ref nre 709 SW2d 647.—Judgm 153(2); Lim of Act 95(16), 106.

Guaranty County Mut. Ins. Co. v. Williams, TexApp–Amarillo, 732 SW2d 57.—Evid 267, 314(2), 351, 474(19), 568(4); Insurance 2181, 2719(2), 3381(5), 3585.

Guaranty Emp. Ass'n v. U.S., CA5 (Tex), 241 F2d 565.—Banks 95; Int Rev 3013.1, 3620, 3624, 4060.

Guaranty Federal Sav. & Loan Ass'n v. Horseshoe Operating Co., TexApp–Dallas, 748 SW2d 519, writ den, and writ withdrawn, and writ gr, aff in part, rev in part Guaranty Federal Sav Bank v. Horseshoe Operating Co, 793 SW2d 652.—Action 60; App & E 302(6); Banks 189; Bills & N 209, 443(2), 446; Gaming 19(1); Judgm 181(26); Stip 8.

Guaranty Federal Sav. & Loan Ass'n; Lewis v., TexCivApp–Austin, 483 SW2d 837, ref nre.—B & L Assoc 3.1(2), 3.1(3); Const Law 4282.

Guaranty Federal Sav. Bank v. Hall Nestletree II Associates, BkrtcySDTex, 112 BR 201. See Hall Nestletree II Associates, In re.

Guaranty Federal Sav. Bank v. Horseshoe Operating Co., Tex, 793 SW2d 652.—Action 60; App & E 949; Banks 139, 189; Bills & N 313; Parties 40(2), 44.

Guaranty Federal Sav. Bank, N.A.; State Farm Fire & Cas. Co. v., TexApp–Austin, 916 SW2d 635, reh overr, and writ den.—App & E 1056.1(1), 1056.1(3), 1060.3, 1064.1(9), 1073(1); Insurance 3405, 3454; Tender 19(2).

Guaranty Mortg. & Realty Co. v. L. E. Whitham & Co., TexCivApp–Amarillo, 93 SW2d 512, writ dism.—App & E 742(1), 759, 766.

Guaranty Mortg. Co.; Chandler v., TexCivApp–San Antonio, 89 SW2d 250.—Corp 432(4); Evid 413; Mtg 346, 372(4); Usury 117.

Guaranty Nat. Bank; Cox v., TexCivApp–Corpus Christi, 565 SW2d 565.—App & E 758.3(3); Mtg 97, 338.

Guaranty Nat. Bank and Trust of Corpus Christi v. May, TexCivApp–Waco, 395 SW2d 80, ref nre.—Estop 92(2); Mines 79.1(5).

Guaranty Nat. Bank and Trust of Corpus Christi v. May, TexCivApp–Corpus Christi, 513 SW2d 613.— Deeds 90, 93, 110; Mines 55(7), 79.1(5).

Guaranty Nat. Ins. Co. v. Azrock Industries Inc., CA5 (Tex), 211 F3d 239.—Fed Cts 776; Insurance 1806, 1809, 1832(1), 2264, 2265, 2268, 2275, 2276, 2913, 2914.

Guaranty Nat. Ins. Co. v. Azrock Industries Inc., CA5 (Tex), 205 F3d 253, opinion withdrawn and superseded on reh 211 F3d 239.—Fed Cts 372, 409.1, 776; Insurance 1806, 1809, 1832(1), 2265, 2275, 2276, 2292, 2913, 2914, 2915.

Guaranty Nat. Ins. Co.; Baker v., TexCivApp–Austin, 615 SW2d 303, ref nre.—Insurance 3142, 3147, 3167; Licens 26; Princ & S 145(1).

Guaranty Nat. Ins. Co.; Branch v., TexCivApp–El Paso, 131 SW2d 314.—Insurance 2439.

Guaranty Nat. Ins. Co.; Eastern Texas Soils and Material v., TexApp–Houston (1 Dist), 787 SW2d 575. See Rabe v. Guaranty Nat. Ins. Co.

Guaranty Nat. Ins. Co. v. North River Ins. Co., CA5 (Tex), 909 F2d 133, reh den.—Insurance 1863, 2274, 2278(10), 2281(2).

Guaranty Nat. Ins. Co.; Rabe v., TexApp–Houston (1 Dist), 787 SW2d 575, writ den.—App & E 854(1); Insurance 3395; Judgm 183; Pretrial Proc 716.

Guaranty Nat. Ins. Co. v. Vic Mfg. Co., CA5 (Tex), 143 F3d 192, reh den.—Insurance 2117, 2278(17), 2914, 2922(1).

Guaranty Nat. Life Ins. Co.; Pickell v., TexApp–Houston (14 Dist), 917 SW2d 439, reh overr.—App & E 123; Compromise 15(1), 22; Judgm 126(1), 158, 162(2); Trial 9(1).

Guaranty Old Line Ins. Co. v. Winstead, TexCivApp–Fort Worth, 91 SW2d 1164, writ dism.—Insurance 2028.

Guaranty Old Line Life Co. v. McCallum, TexCivApp–Dallas, 97 SW2d 966.—Corp 181(8); Mand 129, 174.

Guaranty Old Line Life Ins. Co. v. Leonard, TexCivApp–Austin, 109 SW2d 1091.—App & E 773(4).

Guaranty Petroleum Corp. v. Armstrong, Tex, 609 SW2d 529.—Mines 5.2(3).

Guaranty Securities Corporation v. Marshall, TexCivApp–Galveston, 142 SW2d 632, writ dism.—App & E 1218.

Guaranty Securities Corp. v. Marshall, TexCivApp–Galveston, 140 SW2d 262, motion to recall mandate den 142 SW2d 632, writ dism.—App & E 1177(6); Bailm 25, 30, 31(3), 32.

Guaranty State Bank of New Braunfels v. Kuehler, TexCivApp–Austin, 114 SW2d 622, writ refused.—Evid 441(11); Hus & W 80, 85(3), 87(4), 229.3, 230, 238.5; Judgm 335(1); Princ & S 1, 17.

Guaranty State Building & Loan Ass'n v. Farmer, TexCivApp–Fort Worth, 84 SW2d 277, writ refused.—Usury 45.

Guaranty Title & Trust Co.; Busby v., TexCivApp–El Paso, 93 SW2d 183, writ dism.—Evid 419(1), 419(2), 441(1); Mtg 369(8).

Guaranty Title & Trust Co.; Holyfield v., SDTex, 22 FSupp 896.—Courts 493(3), 509; Ex & Ad 519(1), 522, 524(2).

Guaranty Trust Co. of New York; Cassidy-Southwestern Commission Co. v., TexCivApp–Fort Worth, 174 SW2d 494.—Corp 129; Lim of Act 66(2), 103(2), 103(3); Trusts 104.

Guardado-Ortega; U.S. v., CA5 (Tex), 225 FedAppx 227.—Crim Law 1131(4).

Guardado-Ortega; U.S. v., CA5 (Tex), 150 FedAppx 302, cert gr, vac Mendoza-Torres v. US, 127 SCt 826, 166 LEd2d 660, on remand 225 FedAppx 227.—Fed Cts 462.

Guardia v. Kontos, TexApp–San Antonio, 961 SW2d 580, reh overr.—App & E 223; Judgm 181(7), 185(2), 185.3(2); Lim of Act 83(1), 83(2), 85(2), 85(3), 87(1).

Guardian Abstract & Title Co.; San Antonio Bar Ass'n v., Tex, 291 SW2d 697, 156 Tex 7.—Corp 377.5; Inj 208, 210, 211.

Guardian Abstract & Title Co. v. San Antonio Bar Ass'n, TexCivApp–Austin, 278 SW2d 613, rev 291 SW2d 697, 156 Tex 7.—Atty & C 20.1; Inj 89(5), 128(8), 189.

Guardian Bank v. San Jacinto Sav. Ass'n, TexCivApp–Hous (1 Dist), 593 SW2d 860, ref nre.—Banks 189; Bills & N 480, 496(3); Judgm 185.3(5).

Guardian Burial Ass'n v. Rodgers, TexCivApp–Galveston, 163 SW2d 851.—Insurance 1008, 1834(1), 3398.

Guardian Consumer Finance Corp. v. Langdeau, TexCivApp–Austin, 329 SW2d 926.—App & E 934(1), 989; Contracts 139; Corp 560(7); Insurance 1359, 1404, 1652(2); Usury 126, 140.

Guardian Development Co. v. Jones, TexCivApp–Dallas, 86 SW2d 466, writ dism.—Deeds 70(1); Fraud 25.

Guardian Financial Corp. of Beaumont v. Rollins, TexCivApp–Beaumont, 312 SW2d 553, ref nre.—Cons Cred 15; Contracts 187(1); Insurance 1008; Labor & Emp 173; Usury 127.

Guardian Foundation of Texas; State v., TexCivApp–Austin, 128 SW2d 880, writ dism, correct.—App & E 1060.1(4); Corp 596, 597; Quo W 58; Trial 119, 131(2), 133.6(7).

Guardian Foundation of Texas; State v., TexCivApp–Austin, 112 SW2d 806.—App & E 954(2); Inj 135, 138.42, 151.

Guardian Industries Corp.; Jenkins v., TexApp–Waco, 16 SW3d 431, review den.—Civil R 1104, 1736; Judgm 181(21), 185(2), 185(5), 185(6); Labor & Emp 764, 806, 810, 857, 861, 863(2).

Guardian Inv. Corp. v. Phinney, CA5 (Tex), 253 F2d 326.—Int Rev 3099, 3270, 3273, 3275, 3285, 3286.

Guardian Life Ins. Co.; Reagan v., Tex, 166 SW2d 909, 140 Tex 105.—Insurance 1618, 1619; Libel 36, 38(1), 39, 51(1), 51(2); Trial 355(1).

Guardian Life Ins. Co. of America v. Eagle, CA5 (Tex), 484 F2d 382.—Estop 52(8); Fed Cts 381, 795, 848, 864; Insurance 2955, 3001, 3015, 3091.

Guardian Life Ins. Co. of America v. Finch, CA5 (Tex), 395 F3d 238, cert den Finch v. Galaway, 125 SCt 2305, 544 US 1056, 161 LEd2d 1102.—Fed Cts 419.

Guardian Life Ins. Co. of America; Frith v., SDTex, 9 FSupp2d 744.—Insurance 1654, 1801, 3424.

Guardian Life Ins. Co. of America; Frith v., SDTex, 9 FSupp2d 734.—Evid 405(1); Fed Civ Proc 636, 1772, 1835, 1838; Insurance 3419, 3424.

Guardian Life Ins. Co. of America; Hunton v., SDTex, 243 FSupp2d 686, aff 71 FedAppx 441.—Contracts 143(2), 143.5, 152, 155, 169, 170(1), 176(2); Estop 55, 85; Evid 397(1), 405(1), 448; Fed Civ Proc 824, 828.1, 834, 840, 851; Fraud 13(3); Insurance 1801, 1806, 1807, 1813, 1839, 1869, 1870, 1873, 1885, 1886(5), 2012; Lim of Act 43, 46(6), 55(2), 58(1), 95(1), 95(3), 95(9), 95(16), 99(1), 100(1), 100(12), 104(1).

Guardian Life Ins. Co. of America v. Scott, Tex, 405 SW2d 64.—Insurance 1822, 2494(1).

Guardian Life Ins. Co. of America; Scott v., TexCivApp–Tyler, 397 SW2d 463, writ gr, rev 405 SW2d 64.—Insurance 2494(1).

Guardian Life Ins. Co. of America; Shaffer v., SDTex, 986 FSupp 1066.—Fraud 3, 7; Insurance 1651, 3542; Princ & A 47; Torts 432.

Guardian Life Ins. Co. of America v. Turquette, TexCivApp–Waco, 460 SW2d 534, ref nre.—Insurance 2035, 2037.

Guardian Life Ins. Co. of Texas; Board of Ins. Com'rs of Texas v., Tex, 180 SW2d 906, 142 Tex 630.—Const Law 2488, 2489, 2490; Contracts 159; Insurance 1034, 1139; Statut 190, 197; Wills 461.

Guardian Life Ins. Co. of Texas v. Galoostian, TexCiv-App–Eastland, 155 SW2d 396, writ refused wom.—Insurance 2439, 3001, 3003(11), 3125(2), 3125(6).

Guardian Life Ins. Co. of Tex. v. Johnson, TexCivApp–Texarkana, 172 SW2d 993, writ gr, and writ dism by agreement.—Insurance 1758, 1762, 1766, 1796, 1798.

Guardian Life Ins. Co. of Texas v. Reagan, TexCivApp–Fort Worth, 155 SW2d 950, aff 166 SW2d 909, 140 Tex 105.—Libel 15, 38(1), 39, 51(1), 51(2), 123(8).

Guardian Loan & Trustee Co.; Forrest v., TexCivApp–El Paso, 230 SW2d 273, ref nre.—Corp 123(7), 182.2, 182.4(1); Lim of Act 167(2); Mtg 187.1.

Guardian Royal Exchange Assur., Ltd. v. English China Clays, P.L.C., Tex, 815 SW2d 223.—Const Law 3964, 3965(6); Courts 12(2.1), 12(2.5), 12(2.10); Insurance 3558.

Guardian Royal Exchange Assur., Ltd.; Southern Clay Products, Inc. v., TexApp–Corpus Christi, 762 SW2d 927, writ gr, rev Guardian Royal Exchange Assur, Ltd v. English China Clays, PLC, 815 SW2d 223.—Const Law 3964, 3965(3); Corp 665(1); Courts 12(2.1), 12(2.5), 12(2.15), 35.

Guardian Sav. and Loan Ass'n; General Inv. & Development Co. v., SDTex, 862 FSupp 153.—Contracts 322(1); Estop 52.10(3); Evid 207(1); Fraud 28; Nova 1; Ven & Pur 37(6), 75, 79, 137, 351(1).

Guardian Sav. & Loan Ass'n; Gerst v., Tex, 434 SW2d 113.—B & L Assoc 2.1, 3.1(1), 3.5(2), 3.5(3); Evid 83(1).

Guardian Sav. & Loan Ass'n; Gerst v., TexCivApp–Austin, 425 SW2d 382, writ gr, aff in part, rev in part 434 SW2d 113.—Admin Law 489.1; App & E 747(1); B & L Assoc 3.5(1), 3.5(2).

Guardian Sav. & Loan Ass'n; Lamar Builders, Inc. v., TexApp–Houston (1 Dist), 789 SW2d 373.—App & E 863; Banks 191.30; Inj 151.

Guardian Sav. & Loan Ass'n; Lamar Builders, Inc. v., TexApp–Houston (1 Dist), 786 SW2d 789.—App & E 458(3); Banks 191.30; Inj 139, 140.

Guardian Sav. & Loan Ass'n; Liberty State Bank v., TexComApp, 94 SW2d 133, 127 Tex 311.—Banks 148(3); Estop 52(2).

Guardian Sav. and Loan Ass'n v. Williams, TexApp–Houston (1 Dist), 731 SW2d 107.—App & E 78(1); Mtg 413.

Guardian Title Co.; Breda v., TexCivApp–Waco, 559 SW2d 449.—App & E 958, 1170.10; Plead 236(2), 279(2); Ven & Pur 335.

Guardian Title Co.; Miteff v., TexCivApp–Fort Worth, 612 SW2d 693.—Lim of Act 65(1), 127(4).

Guardian Title Co. of Houston, Inc.; Liberty Steel Co. v., TexCivApp–Dallas, 713 SW2d 358.—Indem 31(2), 31(7), 44.

Guardian Trust Co. v. Bauereisen, Tex, 121 SW2d 579, 132 Tex 396.—Contracts 143.5; Evid 458, 461(1); Guar 27; Labor & Emp 110.

Guardian Trust Co. v. Bauereisen, TexCivApp–Galveston, 99 SW2d 357, rev 121 SW2d 579, 132 Tex 396.—Evid 442(4); Guar 27; Labor & Emp 108, 862, 863(1), 873; Plead 180(2), 216(2).

Guardian Trust Co.; Hanson v., TexCivApp–Galveston, 150 SW2d 465, dism.—App & E 839(1); Garn 1, 93, 175, 178, 194.

Guardian Trust Co.; Pearson v., TexCivApp–Galveston, 84 SW2d 256.—App & E 912; Venue 22(1), 22(9).

Guardian Trust Co.; Smith v., TexCivApp–Eastland, 113 SW2d 584.—App & E 773(4).

Guardino; U.S. v., CA5 (Tex), 560 F2d 197.—Controlled Subs 81; Crim Law 1159.2(5).

Guardiola v. State, TexApp–Houston (14 Dist), 20 SW3d 216, reh overr, and petition for discretionary review refused.—Arrest 63.4(15), 68(4); Const Law 4664(1), 4770; Crim Law 394.1(4), 394.4(9), 412.1(1), 517(7), 518(2), 519(8), 519(9), 1134(3), 1139, 1158(2), 1158(4), 1224(1); Gr Jury 36.4(1).

Guardsman Life Ins. Co. v. Andrade, TexApp–Houston (1 Dist), 745 SW2d 404, writ den.—Judgm 143(3), 145(4).

Guardwear Supply and Equipment Co. v. Brabs, Inc., TexApp–Houston (14 Dist, 880 SW2d 267. See American Apparel Products, Inc. v. Brabs, Inc.

Guarino; Allen v., TexApp–Houston (1 Dist), 635 SW2d 129.—Mand 141; Prohib 16.

Guarino; Routte v., TexCivApp–Galveston, 216 SW2d 607, ref nre.—App & E 274(4); Hus & W 273(9); Partit 12(3), 109(1); Quiet T 44(1); Tresp to T T 38(1); Trial 141, 174, 181; Ven & Pur 261(4).

Guay v. Schneider, Bernet & Hickman Inc., Tex, 344 SW2d 429, 161 Tex 560.—Courts 247(7).

Guay v. Schneider, Bernet & Hickman, Inc., TexCivApp–Waco, 341 SW2d 461, ref nre 344 SW2d 429, 161 Tex 560.—Brok 16; Costs 194.38; Judgm 180.

Gubitosi v. Buddy Schoellkopf Products, Inc., TexCivApp–Tyler, 545 SW2d 528.—App & E 719(8); Const Law 3964, 3965(7); Corp 642(1); Courts 12(2.1), 12(2.5), 12(2.10), 12(2.30); Guar 15, 16(2), 25(3), 36(3), 36(9); Proc 72.

Guckian v. Fowler, TexCivApp–Corpus Christi, 453 SW2d 323, writ dism.—App & E 699(4), 882(9), 1061.4; Autos 244(14); Damag 130.4; Judgm 199(1), 199(3.17); Trial 340(5).

Gudel, Ex parte, TexCrimApp, 368 SW2d 775.—Crim Law 641.7(2).

Guderian; Chapman Parts Warehouse, Inc. v., TexCivApp–Austin, 609 SW2d 317.—Sales 316(1); Sec Tran 133.

Gue; Idalou Co-op. Cotton Gin v., TexCivApp–Dallas, 317 SW2d 240, ref nre.—Contracts 143.5; Sales 418(1), 418(15).

Gue v. State, TexCrimApp, 351 SW2d 237, 171 TexCrim 421.—Crim Law 698(3), 1036.2, 1137(5), 1169.3.

Guehring; Menefee v., TexApp–Houston (1 Dist), 665 SW2d 811, ref nre.—Health 706, 906, 923, 926, 927; New Tr 72(9).

Guelker v. Hidalgo County Water Imp. Dist. No. 6, TexCivApp–San Antonio, 269 SW2d 551, ref nre.—App & E 679(1); Waters 144.5, 153, 154(1), 154(2), 256.

Guenther, In re, BkrtcyNDTex, 333 BR 759.—Bankr 2322, 3022, 3271, 3274, 3276.1, 3278.1, 3279, 3282.1, 3283, 3284, 3288.1, 3315(1), 3315(2), 3317(1), 3317(5).

Guenther v. Amer-Tex Const. Co., TexCivApp–Austin, 534 SW2d 396.—Frds St of 110(2); Spec Perf 39.

Guenther; Cathey v., CA5 (Tex), 47 F3d 162.—Civil R 1318, 1319.

Guenther; Green v., TexCivApp–El Paso, 452 SW2d 512.—App & E 758.3(11), 930(3), 1001(1); Autos 171(4.1), 171(13), 244(58).

Guenther; Hawthorne v., TexApp–Beaumont, 917 SW2d 924, reh overr, and writ den.—Action 57(5); App & E 221, 237(5), 238(2), 294(1), 295, 676, 854(2), 946, 966(1), 1003(7); Courts 100(1); Damag 91(1); Fraud 7, 61; Partners 70, 79, 121; Pretrial Proc 713, 715, 724; Trial 3(5.1).

Guenther v. State, TexCrimApp, 221 SW2d 780, 153 TexCrim 519.—Autos 355(6), 418; Crim Law 494.

Guenther v. Thompson, TexCivApp–San Antonio, 199 SW2d 710.—Mun Corp 663(1), 671(5.1).

Guenthner; Eastern Mortgage & Securities Co. v., TexCivApp–Austin, 112 SW2d 325, writ dism.—Bills & N 342, 376, 497(1); Usury 100(1), 110, 130.

Guentzel v. Toyota Motor Corp., TexApp–San Antonio, 768 SW2d 890, writ den.—App & E 1050.1(1), 1056.1(1), 1056.1(3); Evid 544, 546; Prod Liab 83.5.

Guercia v. Guercia, Tex, 241 SW2d 297, 150 Tex 418.—Child S 508(1).

Guercia; Guercia v., Tex, 241 SW2d 297, 150 Tex 418.—Child S 508(1).

Guercia v. Guercia, TexCivApp–Waco, 239 SW2d 169, ref nre 241 SW2d 297, 150 Tex 418.—Child S 507; Divorce 408.1.

Guercia; Guercia v., TexCivApp–Waco, 239 SW2d 169, ref nre 241 SW2d 297, 150 Tex 418.—Child S 507; Divorce 408.1.

Guereque v. Thompson, TexApp–El Paso, 953 SW2d 458, reh overr, and review den.—App & E 854(1), 907(1); Judgm 183, 185.3(21), 186; Land & Ten 164(1), 379.1, 381; Neglig 1010, 1011, 1013, 1019, 1037(4), 1085, 1523, 1526; Plead 48, 234, 236(2), 236(7), 420(1).

Gueringer; American Cas. & Life Co. v., TexCivApp–San Antonio, 205 SW2d 423.—App & E 930(1), 989; Evid 14; Insurance 1822, 1860, 2475, 2532; Trial 133.6(3.1).

Gueringer v. St. Louis, B. & M. Ry. Co., TexComApp, 82 SW2d 935, 125 Tex 418.—App & E 1094(2); Lim of Act 21(3); R R 144(2).

Guernsey Community Federal Credit Union v. Gonzalez, TexCivApp–El Paso, 539 SW2d 896, ref nre.—App & E 291, 758.3(11), 768, 930(3), 989; Mal Pros 64(1), 64(2); Trial 352.18.

Guerra; Benavides Independent School Dist. v., TexApp–San Antonio, 681 SW2d 246, ref nre.—Admin Law 229; App & E 954(1); Inj 132, 148(1), 157; Schools 60, 61, 138.

Guerra; Borden, Inc. v., TexApp–Corpus Christi, 860 SW2d 515, reh overr, and writ dism by agreement.—Action 38(1); App & E 231(1), 232(0.5), 241, 930(3), 989, 1001(1), 1002, 1003(6), 1004(11); Const Law 4427; Damag 15, 87(1), 94, 100, 187, 208(4); Fraud 58(1); Judgm 253(1); Labor & Emp 810, 861, 863(2), 866, 867, 870, 871, 873; Trial 139.1(3), 140(1).

Guerra v. Brown, TexApp–Corpus Christi, 800 SW2d 343.—App & E 1078(4); Costs 194.44, 260(4); Labor & Emp 57, 851, 880.

Guerra v. Brumlow, TexApp–San Antonio, 630 SW2d 425.—Antitrust 141, 142, 355, 364, 393, 397; App & E 173(1), 215(1), 231(9); Sales 21.

Guerra; Cage v., TexCivApp–San Antonio, 511 SW2d 397.—Autos 242(1); Plead 111.42(8), 111.42(9); Venue 22(1).

Guerra; Cervantes v., CA5 (Tex), 651 F2d 974, reh den 659 F2d 1075.—Aliens 120; Const Law 3013, 3072, 3125, 3635; Courts 96(3); States 18.43; U S 82(2).

Guerra v. Chancellor, TexCivApp–San Antonio, 103 SW2d 775, writ refused.—Frds St of 56(6), 129(9); Mines 73.5, 75.

Guerra; Chancellor v., TexCivApp–San Antonio, 85 SW2d 663.—Mines 92.84.

Guerra; Citizens Bridge Co. v., Tex, 258 SW2d 64, 152 Tex 361.—Bankr 3002; Bills & N 54, 337, 339, 342, 367, 371, 537(6); Bridges 15; Corp 429, 467.

Guerra; Citizens Bridge Co. v., TexCivApp–San Antonio, 248 SW2d 538, aff in part, rev in part 258 SW2d 64, 152 Tex 361.—Bankr 2062, 2368, 3002; Corp 399(2), 413, 414(2), 426(11), 429, 432(8); Trial 350.2.

Guerra v. Collins, SDTex, 916 FSupp 620, aff 90 F3d 1075.—Const Law 4594(3), 4600, 4629, 4632, 4657, 4658(1), 4689; Crim Law 339.8(1), 339.8(4), 339.10(1), 700(2.1), 700(3), 700(7), 700(10), 706(3), 713, 715, 723(5); Hab Corp 490(2), 705.1, 715.1.

Guerra v. Datapoint Corp., TexApp–San Antonio, 956 SW2d 653.—Labor & Emp 873; Trial 139.1(5.1), 139.1(17), 171.

Guerra v. DeLuna, TexCivApp–Austin, 526 SW2d 225.—App & E 931(1), 989; Child S 508(4); Evid 201.

Guerra v. Fletcher, TexCivApp–San Antonio, 475 SW2d 612.—App & E 110, 387(3), 395; New Tr 4.

Guerra; Garcia v., CA5 (Tex), 744 F2d 1159, reh den 751 F2d 383, cert den 105 SCt 2139, 471 US 1065, 85 LEd2d 497.—Civil R 1482; Elections 1, 12(4), 12(8), 12(10), 38, 40.

Guerra v. Garza, TexCrimApp, 987 SW2d 593.—Crim Law 90(5); Mand 1; Prohib 1.

Guerra v. Garza, TexApp–Corpus Christi, 865 SW2d 573, reh overr, and writ dism woj.—App & E 719(8), 1008.1(2); Elections 239, 289, 291, 299(1), 305(6).

Guerra v. Garza, TexCivApp–Eastland, 93 SW2d 537.—Home 57(3); Judgm 564(1); Mtg 39, 608.5; Trial 143.

Guerra; Gas Producing Enterprises, Inc. v., TexCivApp–San Antonio, 576 SW2d 450.—Plead 111.30; Venue 22(4).

Guerra v. Gonzalez, CA5 (Tex), 340 F2d 227.—Civil R 1391; Courts 508(2.1); Mal Pros 34.

Guerra v. Guajardo, SDTex, 466 FSupp 1046, aff 597 F2d 769.—Const Law 77, 2450, 2551, 2580, 2588, 2621, 3057, 3062, 3065, 3869, 3898, 4067; Fed Civ Proc 103.2, 103.4; Inj 138.21, 138.46; Records 51, 54, 59; U S 66, 68.

Guerra v. Guerra, TexCivApp–Austin, 362 SW2d 421.—App & E 554(1); Divorce 286(0.5).

Guerra; Guerra v., TexCivApp–Austin, 362 SW2d 421.—App & E 554(1); Divorce 286(0.5).

Guerra v. Guerra, TexCivApp–San Antonio, 327 SW2d 625.—Divorce 27(1), 27(3), 130, 147.

Guerra; Guerra v., TexCivApp–San Antonio, 327 SW2d 625.—Divorce 27(1), 27(3), 130, 147.

Guerra; Guerrero v., TexApp–San Antonio, 165 SW3d 778.—App & E 1010.1(3), 1012.1(5); Contracts 143(2), 143.5, 169, 176(2); Divorce 169, 184(3), 249.2, 254(1), 271, 278.1; Evid 448.

Guerra; Home Sav. Ass'n v., Tex, 733 SW2d 134.—Antitrust 291; Cons Cred 61.1.

Guerra; Home Sav. Ass'n v., TexApp–San Antonio, 720 SW2d 636, writ gr, aff in part, rev in part 733 SW2d 134.—Antitrust 223, 291, 294, 365; App & E 1062.2; Assign 138; Cons Cred 17; Evid 265(8); Pretrial Proc 313; States 18.15.

Guerra; Housing Authority of City of El Paso v., TexApp–El Paso, 963 SW2d 946, reh overr, and review den, and reh of petition for review overr.—App & E 969, 1001(3), 1004(1); Labor & Emp 753, 808, 810, 861, 863(2), 867, 871, 874; Trial 352.1(1).

Guerra v. Johnson, CA5 (Tex), 90 F3d 1075.—Const Law 4594(1); Fed Cts 844; Hab Corp 719.

Guerra v. Laughlin, TexApp–San Antonio, 362 SW2d 208.—Schools 53(1).

Guerra; Lozano v., TexCivApp–San Antonio, 140 SW2d 587.—Execution 41, 45, 171(1), 265, 278; Wills 630(5), 867.

Guerra; McClellan v., Tex, 258 SW2d 72, 152 Tex 373.—Counties 159.

Guerra v. McClellan, TexCivApp–San Antonio, 250 SW2d 241, aff 258 SW2d 72, 152 Tex 373.—Action 6; Counties 159; Courts 89.

Guerra v. McClellan, TexCivApp–San Antonio, 244 SW2d 710.—Inj 113, 230(1).

Guerra v. McClellan, TexCivApp–San Antonio, 243 SW2d 715, mandamus overr.—App & E 712, 781(1), 801(1), 836, 837(9), 1175(1), 1176(1); Counties 159, 196(1), 196(3); Evid 83(4).

Guerra v. Manchester Terminal Corp., CA5 (Tex), 498 F2d 641, reh den 503 F2d 567.—Civil R 1009, 1103, 1107, 1312, 1326(11), 1448, 1511, 1517, 1577; Fed Cts 424, 612.1; Judgm 715(3), 828.21(1); Lim of Act 58(1), 105(1).

Guerra v. Manchester Terminal Corp., SDTex, 350 FSupp 529, entered 1973 WL 11523, aff in part, rev in part 498 F2d 641, reh den 503 F2d 567.—Civil R 1009, 1107, 1135, 1325, 1502, 1504, 1511, 1530, 1562; Lim of Act 21(1), 39(1), 58(1).

Guerra; Manges v., Tex, 673 SW2d 180.—App & E 1083(6); Damag 89(2); Mines 55(4); Ten in C 22, 38(9).

Guerra; Manges v., TexCivApp–Waco, 621 SW2d 652, writ gr, aff in part, rev in part 673 SW2d 180.—Contracts 274; Ten in C 22, 38(9).

Guerra; Morris Exploration, Inc. v., TexApp–San Antonio, 751 SW2d 710, writ dism woj.—Mines 78.1(9).

Guerra; Oakes v., TexCivApp–Amarillo, 603 SW2d 371.—Antitrust 199, 367, 393; Damag 210(1); Evid 427, 434(8); Fraud 64(1); Trial 350.3(4).

GUERRA

See Guidelines for Arrangement at the beginning of this Volume

Guerra v. Pena, TexCivApp–San Antonio, 406 SW2d 769. —Domicile 1; Elections 72, 73, 216.1, 224, 291, 292, 295(1), 305(8); Pretrial Proc 66, 472, 475; Stip 14(10).

Guerra v. Perez & Associates, TexApp–El Paso, 885 SW2d 531.—Bound 45.

Guerra v. Ramirez, TexCivApp–San Antonio, 364 SW2d 720, writ dism.—Elections 289, 291, 293(2), 295(1), 300, 305(5); Evid 334(1), 351; Witn 37(1).

Guerra v. Ramirez, TexCivApp–San Antonio, 351 SW2d 272, writ dism, appeal after remand 364 SW2d 720, writ dism.—Elections 54, 216.1, 239, 291, 295(1).

Guerra; Ramos v., TexCivApp–San Antonio, 311 SW2d 869.—App & E 770(1); Inj 138.37; Schools 147.47.

Guerra v. Raymondville Bank of Texas, TexApp–Corpus Christi, 791 SW2d 212.—App & E 169; Home 96.

Guerra v. Regions Bank, TexApp–Tyler, 188 SW3d 744. —Banks 100, 151; Neglig 202, 213, 215, 1692.

Guerra; Rio Grande City Consol. Independent School Dist. v., TexCivApp–Waco, 291 SW2d 384, ref nre.—Action 13; Schools 39.

Guerra v. Rodriguez, TexCivApp–Austin, 274 SW2d 715, ref nre.—Counties 150(2), 159, 164, 165, 168(3), 190.1, 193, 196(7).

Guerra v. Rodriguez, TexCivApp–San Antonio, 263 SW2d 185.—Counties 196(8).

Guerra v. Rodriguez, TexCivApp–San Antonio, 239 SW2d 915.—Counties 49, 50; High 92, 99, 113(1).

Guerra v. Roma Independent School Dist., SDTex, 444 FSupp 812.—Civil R 1009, 1326(11), 1343, 1346, 1359, 1376(10), 1470, 1471, 1473, 1480, 1482, 1488; Consp 18; Const Law 1447, 4200, 4201; Fed Cts 247, 336.1, 338; Inj 78; Schools 147.12, 147.40(1), 147.47.

Guerra; Ross v., TexApp–Texarkana, 83 SW3d 899.—App & E 428(2), 863.

Guerra; Sam's Wholesale Club, TexApp–San Antonio, 943 SW2d 56. See Guerra v. Wal-Mart Stores, Inc.

Guerra; Santos v., TexApp–San Antonio, 570 SW2d 437, ref nre.—App & E 927(7); Contracts 294; Counties 52; Evid 83(4); Trial 139.1(17).

Guerra v. Sentry Ins., TexApp–Eastland, 927 SW2d 733, reh overr, and writ den.—Insurance 2655(2).

Guerra; Skaggs v., TexApp–Corpus Christi, 704 SW2d 51, ref nre.—Atty & C 123(2).

Guerra; South Texas Natural Gas Gathering Co. v., TexCivApp–Corpus Christi, 469 SW2d 899, ref nre.— App & E 302(5); Damag 130.2, 134(3), 208(2), 208(3); Gas 20(2); Jury 136(3); New Tr 77(4); Parties 56; Trial 112, 127.

Guerra; Starr County v., TexCivApp–San Antonio, 297 SW2d 379.—Counties 47; High 93; Offic 30.5.

Guerra; Starr County v., TexCivApp–San Antonio, 282 SW2d 304.—Abate & R 7; New Tr 117(1).

Guerra v. State, TexCrimApp, 771 SW2d 453, cert den 109 SCt 3260, 492 US 925, 106 LEd2d 606, reh den 110 SCt 25, 492 US 938, 106 LEd2d 637, habeas corpus gr 916 FSupp 620, aff 90 F3d 1075.—Crim Law 419(4), 641.3(4), 665(2), 665(4), 1166.18, 1168(2); Homic 1139; Jury 107, 108, 131(2), 131(4), 131(8), 131(15.1), 131(17); Sent & Pun 238, 1772; Witn 318, 414(2).

Guerra v. State, TexCrimApp, 668 SW2d 707.—Witn 257.

Guerra v. State, TexCrimApp, 518 SW2d 815.—Crim Law 577.10(1); Sent & Pun 2025, 2041.

Guerra v. State, TexCrimApp, 496 SW2d 92, cert den 94 SCt 1559, 415 US 975, 39 LEd2d 870.—Searches 117, 148.

Guerra v. State, TexCrimApp, 478 SW2d 483.—Const Law 4465; Crim Law 134(4), 369.2(4), 730(5); Homic 1398, 1567; Ind & Inf 140(2), 159(1); Sent & Pun 124.

Guerra v. State, TexCrimApp, 396 SW2d 130.—Crim Law 1097(4), 1097(5), 1099.6(3), 1099.7(1), 1099.10.

Guerra v. State, TexCrimApp, 331 SW2d 941, 169 TexCrim 70.—Crim Law 778(5).

Guerra v. State, TexCrimApp, 298 SW2d 574, 164 TexCrim 331.—Crim Law 552(3); Homic 1134.

Guerra v. State, TexCrimApp, 243 SW2d 170, 156 TexCrim 414.—Assault 92(5); Crim Law 566.

Guerra v. State, TexCrimApp, 234 SW2d 866, 155 TexCrim 306.—Crim Law 13.1(1); Elections 314; Time 15.

Guerra v. State, TexCrimApp, 230 SW2d 230.—Crim Law 1094(3).

Guerra v. State, TexCrimApp, 168 SW2d 247, 145 TexCrim 339.—Crim Law 726; Homic 1154, 1373, 1387.

Guerra v. State, TexCrimApp, 134 SW2d 679, 138 TexCrim 120.—Crim Law 538(3), 1167(5).

Guerra v. State, TexCrimApp, 132 SW2d 120.—Crim Law 1090.1(1).

Guerra v. State, TexApp–Fort Worth, 846 SW2d 124, reh overr.—Autos 355(6).

Guerra v. State, TexApp–San Antonio, 936 SW2d 46, petition for discretionary review refused.—Crim Law 772(6), 795(2.1), 1172.1(1); Homic 1380, 1451, 1455, 1458.

Guerra v. State, TexApp–San Antonio, 737 SW2d 61.— Crim Law 795(2.1), 1032(7), 1037.1(2), 1115(2), 1171.3; Ind & Inf 191(2); Jury 135.

Guerra v. State, TexApp–San Antonio, 712 SW2d 217, petition for discretionary review refused by 733 SW2d 217.—Searches 61, 66.

Guerra v. State, TexApp–San Antonio, 690 SW2d 901.— Crim Law 126(2), 224, 552(1), 552(3), 867, 1033.2, 1166(1); Double J 5.1, 98; Homic 870, 1165; Ind & Inf 9, 184; Jury 97(4).

Guerra v. State, TexApp–San Antonio, 643 SW2d 780, petition for discretionary review refused.—Crim Law 1032(1), 1172.6; Rape 24.

Guerra v. State, TexApp–Corpus Christi, 942 SW2d 28, petition for discretionary review refused.—Crim Law 363, 364(5), 374, 695(2), 695(5), 1036.1(8), 1158(1), 1170(1), 1170(2); Sent & Pun 322.

Guerra v. State, TexApp–Corpus Christi, 860 SW2d 609, reh overr, and petition for discretionary review refused. —Controlled Subs 149; Searches 105.1, 121.1.

Guerra v. State, TexApp–Corpus Christi, 766 SW2d 830. —Crim Law 1099.6(2.1).

Guerra v. State, TexApp–Corpus Christi, 760 SW2d 681, petition for discretionary review refused.—Consp 43(12); Controlled Subs 98; Crim Law 394.3, 394.6(5), 511.1(1), 511.1(8), 556, 700(4), 706(2), 726, 734, 790, 854(1), 1035(2), 1115(1), 1120(3), 1166.14, 1166.16, 1169.1(10), 1172.1(2); Double J 56.1, 185; Gr Jury 2.5, 29; Ind & Inf 125(19.1), 168; Tel 1466, 1467(1), 1467(3), 1473, 1479; Witn 35.

Guerra v. State, TexApp–Corpus Christi, 750 SW2d 360, petition for discretionary review refused.—Crim Law 1042; Sent & Pun 1919, 2013.

Guerra v. State, TexApp–Corpus Christi, 676 SW2d 181, petition for discretionary review refused.—Crim Law 1189; Witn 255(10).

Guerra v. State, TexApp–Corpus Christi, 664 SW2d 412. —Crim Law 1134(3), 1147; Sent & Pun 2006, 2020, 2021.

Guerra v. State, TexApp–Corpus Christi, 657 SW2d 511, petition for discretionary review refused.—Burg 2, 29, 41(3), 45; Crim Law 723(3), 778(5).

Guerra v. State, TexApp–Corpus Christi, 654 SW2d 25, case remanded 668 SW2d 707.—Homic 1150.

Guerra v. State, TexApp–Corpus Christi, 648 SW2d 715, petition for discretionary review refused.—Crim Law 438(1), 627(7), 675, 720(9), 730(1), 1043(3), 1162, 1165(1), 1165(2), 1167(1), 1171.1(6), 1181(1); Witn 337(28), 345(1).

Guerra v. Tabasco Consol. Independent School Dist., TexCivApp–San Antonio, 103 SW2d 173, writ dism.— App & E 219(2), 846(6), 931(3), 1071.1(2); Home 122.

Guerra v. Texas Dept. of Protective and Regulatory Services, TexApp–San Antonio, 940 SW2d 295.—Const Law 4393; Infants 179, 203, 243, 246.

Guerra; Texas Dept. of Public Safety v., TexApp–Austin, 970 SW2d 645, review den.—Admin Law 796; Autos 144.2(1).

Guerra; Texas Dept. of Transp. v., TexApp–Houston (14 Dist), 858 SW2d 44, reh den, and writ den.—App & E 930(3), 1001(1), 1001(3); Bridges 46(14).

Guerra v. Texas Emp. Ins. Ass'n, TexCivApp–San Antonio, 343 SW2d 306.—Trial 76; Work Comp 1641, 1653, 1968(1).

Guerra v. Texas Emp. Ins. Ass'n, TexCivApp–Corpus Christi, 480 SW2d 769.—App & E 846(5); Plead 111.21, 111.42(10).

Guerra, Heirs of v. U.S., CA5 (Tex), 207 F3d 763, reh den, cert den 121 SCt 428, 531 US 979, 148 LEd2d 436.—Const Law 3500; Em Dom 13, 55, 68, 187, 243(1), 324; Fed Civ Proc 2651.1; Judgm 686, 747(0.5).

Guerra; U.S. v., CA5 (Tex), 94 F3d 989, corrected.—Const Law 4587; Crim Law 273.1(1), 273.1(4), 274(3.1), 641.13(7), 1139, 1147, 1158(1), 1181.5(1), 1437, 1438, 1439, 1440(1), 1440(4), 1441, 1447, 1451, 1482, 1575, 1586, 1668(9).

Guerra; U.S. v., CA5 (Tex), 962 F2d 484.—Crim Law 1134(2), 1139; Sent & Pun 665, 1244, 1285.

Guerra v. U.S., CA5 (Tex), 935 F2d 69. See Persyn v. U.S.

Guerra; U.S. v., CA5 (Tex), 628 F2d 410, cert den 101 SCt 1398, 450 US 934, 67 LEd2d 369.—Const Law 268(10), 4813; Crim Law 641.1, 641.13(1), 1166.10(1).

Guerra; U.S. v., CA5 (Tex), 588 F2d 519, appeal after remand 628 F2d 410, cert den 101 SCt 1398, 450 US 934, 67 LEd2d 369.—Crim Law 641.1, 641.13(1), 1652; Hab Corp 864(7).

Guerra v. U.S., CA5 (Tex), 447 F2d 457.—Crim Law 1132, 1663.

Guerra; U.S. v., CA5 (Tex), 187 FedAppx 414, cert den 127 SCt 1009, 166 LEd2d 760.—Crim Law 1073, 1429(2), 1447, 1556.

Guerra; U.S. v., CA5 (Tex), 146 FedAppx 746, cert den 126 SCt 1097, 546 US 1121, 163 LEd2d 910.—Crim Law 1042.

Guerra; U.S. v., NDTex, 809 FSupp 480.—Sent & Pun 665, 2262.

Guerra v. Wal-Mart Stores, Inc., TexApp–San Antonio, 943 SW2d 56, reh overr, and writ den.—App & E 200, 970(2), 1003(5), 1003(7), 1050.1(6), 1051.1(1), 1052(7), 1073(7); Assault 42; Damag 59; Jury 88, 97(1); Neglig 1670; Trial 365.1(1); Witn 406; Work Comp 2234.

Guerra v. Weatherly, TexCivApp–Waco, 291 SW2d 493.—Counties 47, 58, 113(5), 126, 168(1), 208; Courts 169(1); Mand 102(2), 152, 154(4).

Guerra & Moore, L.L.P., In re, TexApp–Corpus Christi, 35 SW3d 210.—App & E 946; Courts 475(1); Estop 119; Judgm 215; Mand 4(1), 12, 31; Parties 42.

Guerra De Chapa v. Allen, SDTex, 119 FSupp 129.—Autos 235(2); Const Law 191; Statut 207, 263.

Guerra-Garza; U.S. v., CA5 (Tex), 71 FedAppx 317.—Crim Law 1037.1(2).

Guerra-Marez; U.S. v., CA5 (Tex), 928 F2d 665, reh den, cert den 112 SCt 322, 502 US 917, 116 LEd2d 263, cert den Paredes-Moya v. US, 112 SCt 443, 502 US 969, 116 LEd2d 461.—Consp 24(2), 43(12), 44.2, 47(2), 47(12), 48.1(1); Controlled Subs 67; Crim Law 622.2(3), 622.2(6), 1159.2(7), 1167(1); Jury 33(5.15); Searches 199; Tel 1018(4), 1467(1), 1468.

Guerra-Mesta; U.S. v., CA5 (Tex), 213 FedAppx 299, cert den 127 SCt 2149, 167 LEd2d 878.—Sent & Pun 761, 765.

Guerra-Moya v. Winfrey, CA5 (Tex), 170 FedAppx 358.—Aliens 314.

Guerrant; Smith v., SDTex, 290 FSupp 111.—Adm 1.20(1), 7, 19.

Guerrera v. State, TexCrimApp, 148 SW2d 421, 141 TexCrim 278.—Homic 1134.

Guerrera v. State, TexCrimApp, 125 SW2d 595, 136 TexCrim 411.—Sunday 30(1), 30(6).

Guerrero, Ex parte, TexCrimApp, 521 SW2d 613.—Crim Law 1137(2); Hab Corp 503.1; Sent & Pun 2282.

Guerrero, Ex parte, TexCrimApp, 388 SW2d 713.—Bail 49(3.1).

Guerrero, Ex parte, TexApp–Corpus Christi, 811 SW2d 726.—Const Law 699, 991; Controlled Subs 6; Crim Law 13.1(1).

Guerrero, Ex parte, TexApp–Houston (14 Dist), 99 SW3d 852.—Hab Corp 221, 826(2).

Guerrero v. Aetna Cas. & Sur. Co., TexCivApp–San Antonio, 575 SW2d 323.—Insurance 2839, 2840.

Guerrero v. American Emp. Ins. Co., TexCivApp–El Paso, 520 SW2d 560.—App & E 230, 758.3(11); Judgm 185(3), 185.3(12); Trial 105(2).

Guerrero; American Mut. Liability Ins. Co. v., TexApp–Corpus Christi, 678 SW2d 264.—App & E 554(1); Trial 139.1(8); Work Comp 1904.

Guerrero v. Barlow, CA5 (Tex), 494 F2d 1190, reh den 502 F2d 1167, cert den 96 SCt 1481, 424 US 975, 47 LEd2d 746.—Civil R 1376(9); Fed Civ Proc 1827.1.

Guerrero v. Barnhart, CA5 (Tex), 214 FedAppx 485.—Social S 143.80.

Guerrero v. Beto, CA5 (Tex), 384 F2d 886.—Const Law 4594(1), 4632; Hab Corp 745.1.

Guerrero; Century 21 Casablanca Realty v., TexApp–El Paso, 885 SW2d 487. See Sanchez v. Guerrero.

Guerrero; Chrysler-Plymouth City, Inc. v., TexCivApp–San Antonio, 620 SW2d 700.—Antitrust 136, 368, 369, 397; App & E 971(2); Evid 96(1), 474(19), 498.5; Sales 261(6); Trial 350.4(2).

Guerrero; City of Laredo v., TexApp–San Antonio, 646 SW2d 581, rev 649 SW2d 296.—Mun Corp 185(7).

Guerrero; Davis v., TexApp–Austin, 64 SW3d 685, reh overr.—App & E 893(1), 949; Child C 725, 733, 748; Courts 475(1).

Guerrero; Firemen and Policemen's Pension Fund Bd. of Trustees of San Antonio v., TexCivApp–San Antonio, 395 SW2d 397, ref nre.—Mun Corp 187(9), 187(10).

Guerrero; Garza v., TexApp–San Antonio, 993 SW2d 137, reh overr.—App & E 204(4), 204(7), 232(2), 1051.1(2); Damag 130.1, 135; Evid 378(1); Pretrial Proc 139, 202.

Guerrero v. General Motors Corp., SDTex, 892 FSupp 165.—Prod Liab 23.1; Rem of C 36, 39, 79(1), 102, 107(7).

Guerrero v. Guerra, TexApp–San Antonio, 165 SW3d 778.—App & E 1010.1(3), 1012.1(5); Contracts 143(2), 143.5, 169, 176(2); Divorce 169, 184(3), 249.2, 254(1), 271, 278.1; Evid 448.

Guerrero v. Hagco Bldg. Systems, Inc., TexApp–San Antonio, 733 SW2d 635.—App & E 766; Can of Inst 24(3); Contracts 262; Judgm 256(1); Ven & Pur 117, 123.

Guerrero v. Harmon Tank Co., Inc., TexApp–Amarillo, 55 SW3d 19, review den.—Labor & Emp 26, 936; Statut 181(1), 181(2), 184, 188, 212.6; Work Comp 195, 204, 2161, 2168.

Guerrero v. Hauck, CA5 (Tex), 502 F2d 579.—Fed Civ Proc 1773, 1827.1.

Guerrero; J.J.T.B., Inc. v., TexApp–Corpus Christi, 975 SW2d 737, reh overr, and review den.—App & E 5; Evid 20(1); Pretrial Proc 474.

Guerrero; Lewis v., TexApp–Corpus Christi, 978 SW2d 689, reh overr.—Civil R 1376(1), 1376(2), 1376(10), 1423; Const Law 1929, 1932, 1934; Courts 97(1), 99(6); Judgm 540, 569, 713(2); 720.

Guerrero v. Memorial Medical Center of East Texas, TexApp–Beaumont, 938 SW2d 789.—Labor & Emp 2778, 2782, 2784.

Guerrero v. Paredes, TexCivApp–El Paso, 470 SW2d 921.—App & E 931(1), 1008.1(2), 1010.1(2), 1010.1(3); Joint Adv 5(2).

Guerrero v. Potter, CA5 (Tex), 213 FedAppx 289.—Lim of Act 130(5).

Guerrero v. Refugio County, TexApp–Corpus Christi, 946 SW2d 558, appeal after remand Lewis v. Guerrero, 978 SW2d 689, reh overr.—App & E 856(1), 863; Civil

GUERRERO

R 143, 1110, 1116(1), 1116(2), 1304, 1324, 1326(7), 1326(11), 1376(8), 1376(10), 1528, 1736; Const Law 3912, 4172(2); Counties 65, 84, 91, 93; Courts 97(1); Judges 36; Judgm 183, 185(2); Offic 1, 4, 7, 60, 114; States 74.

Guerrero; Sanchez v., TexApp–El Paso, 885 SW2d 487.—Antitrust 369; App & E 758.3(3), 930(3), 989, 994(2), 1001(1), 1001(3), 1002, 1003(3), 1003(5); Damag 57.7, 140.7.

Guerrero v. Sanders, TexApp–Fort Worth, 846 SW2d 354, opinion withdrawn in part on reh.—App & E 267(1), 878(6), 1056.1(3); Autos 246(35), 246(51); Damag 216(1); Interest 39(2.6), 47(1).

Guerrero v. Smith, TexApp–Houston (14 Dist), 864 SW2d 797.—App & E 970(1), 971(2), 972, 1050.1(1), 1051.1(1), 1056.1(1); Evid 546; Stip 14(7), 16, 17(3); Trial 41(1), 109, 133.1.

Guerrero v. Standard Alloys Mfg. Co., TexCivApp–Beaumont, 598 SW2d 656, ref nre.—App & E 970(4), 1106(1), 1106(2); Damag 132(13); Plead 4, 245(6); Trial 66, 68(1); Work Comp 2100, 2141.

Guerrero v. Standard Alloys Mfg. Co., TexCivApp–Beaumont, 566 SW2d 100, ref nre, appeal after remand 598 SW2d 656, ref nre.—App & E 934(1); Judgm 181(21), 185(2); Labor & Emp 26, 58.

Guerrero v. State, TexCrimApp, 605 SW2d 262.—Autos 351.1, 355(13); Crim Law 412.2(2).

Guerrero v. State, TexCrimApp, 507 SW2d 765.—Crim Law 37(1), 58, 507(4), 706(2), 739.1(2), 772(6), 792(2), 1168(1), 1170.5(6).

Guerrero v. State, TexCrimApp, 487 SW2d 729.—Crim Law 37(1), 339.10(6.1), 339.10(7), 419(10), 593, 599, 641.13(8), 739.1(1), 739.1(2), 772(6), 814(3), 1115(2), 1151, 1169.1(10); Witn 297(13.1).

Guerrero v. State, TexApp–Austin, 720 SW2d 233, petition for discretionary review refused.—Crim Law 552(3); Homic 1184.

Guerrero; State v., TexApp–San Antonio, 110 SW3d 155, reh overr.—Crim Law 577.4, 577.10(1), 577.10(3), 577.10(6), 577.10(7), 577.10(9), 577.10(10), 577.12(1), 577.12(2), 577.15(1), 577.15(3), 577.15(4), 577.16(4), 577.16(8), 1139, 1147.

Guerrero v. State, TexApp–San Antonio, 964 SW2d 32, petition for discretionary review refused.—Assault 80; Crim Law 662.1, 662.7, 713, 720(6), 720(7.1), 1043(2), 1044.2(1), 1137(5), 1169.2(1), 1171.1(2.1); Ind & Inf 171; Witn 372(1), 372(2).

Guerrero v. State, TexApp–San Antonio, 626 SW2d 875.—Forg 34(8).

Guerrero v. State, TexApp–El Paso, 838 SW2d 929.—Crim Law 339.9(1), 339.10(1), 339.11(3), 339.11(5.1), 633(1), 1153(1).

Guerrero v. State, TexApp–Waco, 143 SW3d 283.—Crim Law 642.

Guerrero v. State, TexApp–Waco, 64 SW3d 436, opinion after remand 143 SW3d 283.—Crim Law 273.4(3), 1077.3.

Guerrero v. State, TexApp–Waco, 893 SW2d 260.—Double J 24.

Guerrero v. State, TexApp–Corpus Christi, 820 SW2d 378, petition for discretionary review refused.—Const Law 795, 1521, 1693; Crim Law 13.1(1), 709, 720(7.1), 723(3), 1030(1), 1036.1(3.1), 1038.1(4), 1043(3), 1134(2), 1144.13(3), 1159.2(7), 1159.6; Elections 311, 317.

Guerrero v. State, TexApp–Corpus Christi, 666 SW2d 350.—Autos 339, 351.1, 355(10); Ind & Inf 91(1); Larc 34.

Guerrero v. State, TexApp–Corpus Christi, 655 SW2d 291.—Homic 1168.

Guerrero v. State, TexApp–Houston (14 Dist), 650 SW2d 102.—Crim Law 899, 1043(2).

Guerrero v. Tarrant County Mortician Services Co., TexApp–Fort Worth, 977 SW2d 829, review den.—Action 14; App & E 756, 766; Coroners 23; Evid 538;

Judgm 185(2), 185(6), 185.3(1), 185.3(2); Offic 114, 116; States 79.

Guerrero; Texas Employers' Ins. Ass'n v., TexApp–San Antonio, 800 SW2d 859, writ den.—App & E 1026, 1060.1(8); Trial 124, 125(2), 133.1; Work Comp 1532, 1676, 1683.

Guerrero; U.S. v., CA5 (Tex), 234 F3d 259, reh den, cert den 121 SCt 2234, 532 US 1074, 150 LEd2d 224.—Crim Law 1139, 1144.13(2.1), 1159.2(7); Weap 4.

Guerrero; U.S. v., CA5 (Tex), 169 F3d 933.—Crim Law 338(7), 369.2(1), 369.15, 566, 742(1), 1030(1), 1043(3), 1139, 1144.13(2.1), 1144.13(4), 1144.13(5), 1153(1), 1158(1), 1159.2(7), 1159.2(9), 1159.5, 1159.6, 1187; Rob 1, 24.10, 24.40; Sent & Pun 723, 978; Weap 17(4).

Guerrero; U.S. v., CA5 (Tex), 5 F3d 868, cert den 114 SCt 1111, 510 US 1134, 127 LEd2d 422.—Crim Law 1030(1), 1042, 1042.5; Sent & Pun 674, 1404, 1424.

Guerrero; U.S. v., CA5 (Tex), 650 F2d 728.—Controlled Subs 68, 82; Crim Law 371(1), 372(13), 374, 419(2.30), 632(4), 1159.6, 1169.1(9), 1169.11.

Guerrero; U.S. v., CA5 (Tex), 166 FedAppx 757, cert den 126 SCt 2907, 165 LEd2d 935.—Courts 100(1).

Guerrero; U.S. v., CA5 (Tex), 111 FedAppx 294, cert den 125 SCt 1429, 543 US 1193, 161 LEd2d 200.—Controlled Subs 81.

Guerrero v. U.S. Fidelity & Guaranty Co., TexComApp, 98 SW2d 796, 128 Tex 407, conformed to 101 SW2d 592, writ refused.—Work Comp 180.

Guerrero v. U.S. Fidelity & Guaranty Co., TexCivApp–Waco, 101 SW2d 592, writ refused.—App & E 901, 927(7).

Guerrero; Weatherby v., TexCivApp–Austin, 82 SW2d 1059.—App & E 1026; Trial 360.

Guerrero v. Wright, TexCivApp–Austin, 225 SW2d 609, ref nre.—App & E 1050.1(8.1), 1070(2); Autos 244(42); Evid 118, 121(1), 123(1), 123(10).

Guerrero-Aguilar v. Ruano, CA5 (Tex), 118 FedAppx 832.—Fed Civ Proc 2734; U S 50.10(3).

Guerrero-Barajas; U.S. v., CA5 (Tex), 240 F3d 428, reh en banc den 252 F3d 437, cert den 122 SCt 919, 534 US 1113, 151 LEd2d 884.—Aliens 441; Arrest 63.4(18); Autos 349(5); Crim Law 394.6(4), 1130(5), 1139, 1158(1), 1158(4); Cust Dut 126(2).

Guerrero-Ramirez v. Texas State Bd. of Medical Examiners, TexApp–Austin, 867 SW2d 911.—Admin Law 453, 470, 474; App & E 966(1); Const Law 4027, 4286; Health 205, 209, 218, 219, 223(2); Licens 38; Pretrial Proc 713.

Guerrero-Zapata Bridge Co. v. U.S., CA5 (Tex), 252 F2d 116.—Em Dom 126(1); Treaties 11.

Guerrero-Zavala; U.S. v., CA5 (Tex), 95 FedAppx 76.—Sent & Pun 797.

Guerson; Continental Ins. Co. of New York v., TexCivApp–San Antonio, 93 SW2d 591, writ dism.—App & E 1052(8), 1067; Evid 489; Insurance 3261, 3263; Trial 351.5(1).

Guertin v. Hackerman, SDTex, 496 FSupp 593.—Action 3; Civil R 1055, 1313, 1330(1); Fed Civ Proc 2497.1; U S 82(1).

Guess, Ex parte, TexCrimApp, 508 SW2d 640.—Bail 52; Prisons 17(2).

Guess v. American Petrofina Co., TexCivApp–Texarkana, 485 SW2d 926.—App & E 1024.1; Judgm 199(3.15); Trial 307(1), 321, 325(1).

Guest; Barganier v., TexCivApp–Waco, 246 SW2d 901, writ refused.—Adv Poss 114(1); Judgm 747(2); Lim of Act 70(1); States 191.4(1).

Guest; Biodynamics, Inc. v., TexApp–Houston (14 Dist), 817 SW2d 128, writ dism by agreement.—App & E 954(1); Inj 135, 138.3, 138.42, 140, 147, 148(1), 148(2).

Guest v. Bizzell, TexCivApp–Eastland, 271 SW2d 472, writ refused.—App & E 931(3); Wills 692(2).

Guest v. Cochran, TexApp–Houston (14 Dist), 993 SW2d 397.—Antitrust 134, 141, 147, 256, 292, 363; App & E

267(1), 273(10), 1073(1); Atty & C 26; Judgm 183, 185(2).

Guest v. Dixon, Tex, 195 SW3d 687, on remand 223 SW3d 531.—App & E 343.1.

Guest v. Dixon, TexApp–Amarillo, 223 SW3d 531.—App & E 948; Pretrial Proc 583, 587, 594.1, 681; Trial 9(1), 367.

Guest v. Dixon, TexApp–Amarillo, 153 SW3d 466, review gr, rev 195 SW3d 687, on remand 223 SW3d 531.—App & E 23, 428(2); Pretrial Proc 699.

Guest; Federal Underwriters Exchange v., TexCivApp–Eastland, 129 SW2d 708, writ dism, correct.—Work Comp 822, 1265, 1461, 1836, 1935, 1937.

Guest v. Guest, TexCivApp–Fort Worth, 235 SW2d 710, ref nre.—App & E 842(1), 1060.1(4); Evid 43(1), 44; Trial 121(2); Wills 111(3), 118, 302(1), 318(1), 324(2), 400; Witn 164(1).

Guest; Guest v., TexCivApp–Fort Worth, 235 SW2d 710, ref nre.—App & E 842(1), 1060.1(4); Evid 43(1), 44; Trial 121(2); Wills 111(3), 118, 302(1), 318(1), 324(2), 400; Witn 164(1).

Guest; Kolsti v., TexCivApp–Austin, 565 SW2d 556.—Const Law 2580, 2585; Inj 80.

Guest; Kolsti v., TexCivApp–Tyler, 576 SW2d 892.—Action 6; App & E 781(1); Decl Judgm 61, 395; Pretrial Proc 552.

Guest; Old Nat. Life Ins. Co. v., TexCivApp–Texarkana, 163 SW2d 241, writ refused wom.—App & E 846(2), 846(5); Ben Assoc 17; Trusts 372(1); Ven & Pur 242.

Guest; Palmer v., TexCivApp–Tyler, 533 SW2d 484, subsequent mandamus proceeding Chapman v. Texas Democratic Executive Committee, 533 SW2d 487.—Time 10(1).

Guest v. Phillips Petroleum Co., CA5 (Tex), 981 F2d 218, reh den.—Antitrust 389(2), 390; Damag 36; Interest 60.

Guest; Tandy v., TexCivApp–Fort Worth, 539 SW2d 378.—Elections 126(7); Mand 74(4), 143(1); Notice 10.

Guest v. White, TexCivApp–Waco, 374 SW2d 775, ref nre.—Autos 244(12), 244(34); Damag 130.1, 139, 191.

Guest v. Wilson, TexComApp, 109 SW2d 468, 130 Tex 272.—Ex & Ad 261, 262.

Guest v. Wilson, TexCivApp–Texarkana, 81 SW2d 812, rev 109 SW2d 468, 130 Tex 272.—Land & Ten 248(1).

Guetersloh, Ex parte, Tex, 935 SW2d 110.—Contempt 20; Inj 232.

Guetersloh; Campbell v., CA5 (Tex), 287 F2d 878.—Int Rev 4637.

Guetersloh v. Campbell, NDTex, 184 FSupp 392, rev 287 F2d 878.—Int Rev 4930, 4930.10.

Guetersloh v. C. I. T. Corp., TexCivApp–Amarillo, 451 SW2d 759, ref nre.—Bills & N 496(2); Ref of Inst 11, 45(8); Trial 39, 76, 98; Usury 6.

Guetersloh; Grissom v., TexCivApp–Amarillo, 391 SW2d 167, ref nre.—Deeds 93; Mines 55(4), 55(7), 58.

Guetersloh; Havens v., TexCivApp–Amarillo, 255 SW2d 233, ref nre.—App & E 1033(5), 1062.2, 1068(2); Autos 244(44), 245(49); Trial 352.18.

Guetersloh v. State, TexCivApp–Austin, 930 SW2d 284, reh overr, and writ den, cert den 118 SCt 1040, 522 US 1110, 140 LEd2d 106.—Action 43.1; Courts 489(1), 489(12); Em Dom 69; Judgm 586(0.5), 713(2), 828.16(1); Trial 2.

Guetersloh v. Turner, TexCivApp–Amarillo, 423 SW2d 157, ref nre.—Bills & N 493(3), 516; Brok 42; Contracts 50.

Guetersloh Grain, Inc. v. Wright, TexCivApp–Amarillo, 618 SW2d 135.—Costs 132(6).

Guevara, In re, TexApp–San Antonio, 41 SW3d 169, reh overr.—Atty & C 32(7), 32(11).

Guevara; American Home Assur. Co. v., TexApp–San Antonio, 717 SW2d 381.—Plead 420(1); Trial 344; Work Comp 1040, 1654, 1800.

Guevara; City of Beverly Hills v., Tex, 904 SW2d 655, on remand 911 SW2d 901.—App & E 70(8).

Guevara; City of Beverly Hills v., TexApp–Waco, 911 SW2d 901.—App & E 70(8), 93; Autos 187(1), 196; Mun Corp 723, 745, 747(3); Offic 114.

Guevara; City of Beverly Hills v., TexApp–Waco, 886 SW2d 833, reh den, and writ gr, rev 904 SW2d 655, on remand 911 SW2d 901.—App & E 66, 70(8), 93, 387(2), 387(3), 387(6), 624, 765; Autos 187(1); Mun Corp 723, 747(3); States 112(2).

Guevara; Counts v., CA5 (Tex), 328 F3d 212, appeal after remand 139 FedAppx 624.—Fed Cts 776; Labor & Emp 3045; Libel 74; Rem of C 21; U S 50.5(1), 50.20, 78(14).

Guevara; Ferrer v., TexApp–El Paso, 192 SW3d 39, review gr.—Action 13, 61; Assign 5, 24(1), 24(2), 43; Compromise 101; Damag 18, 33, 57.9, 57.11, 140.5, 185(1), 191, 192, 208(1); Death 10, 31(5), 31(8); Evid 568(1), 571(9); Ex & Ad 515; Neglig 371.

Guevara; Garza v., TexCivApp–San Antonio, 421 SW2d 691.—App & E 994(3); Autos 244(36.1).

Guevara v. H.E. Butt Grocery Co., TexApp–San Antonio, 82 SW3d 550, review den.—App & E 893(1); Civil R 1004, 1708, 1717, 1732.

Guevara; McNally v., Tex, 52 SW3d 195, on remand 2001 WL 1548740.—App & E 80(6); Judgm 183.

Guevara; McNally v., TexApp–Austin, 989 SW2d 380, reh overr, and review gr, rev 52 SW3d 195, on remand 2001 WL 1548740.—App & E 76(1), 78(1), 80(1); Ease 44(1).

Guevara v. Maritime Overseas Corp., CA5 (Tex), 59 F3d 1496, cert den 116 SCt 706, 516 US 1046, 133 LEd2d 662, reh den 116 SCt 1035, 516 US 1154, 134 LEd2d 112.—Damag 30, 89(2), 127; Death 96; Fed Civ Proc 2769; Fed Cts 611, 712; Seamen 2, 11(1), 11(4), 11(6), 11(9).

Guevara v. Maritime Overseas Corp., CA5 (Tex), 34 F3d 1279, reh en banc gr, opinion reinstated in part on reh 59 F3d 1496, cert den 116 SCt 706, 516 US 1046, 133 LEd2d 662, reh den 116 SCt 1035, 516 US 1154, 134 LEd2d 112.—Fed Cts 868; Seamen 11(6), 11(9), 29(5.14).

Guevara v. Maritime Overseas Corp., EDTex, 792 FSupp 520, aff 34 F3d 1279, reh en banc gr, opinion reinstated in part on reh 59 F3d 1496, cert den 116 SCt 706, 516 US 1046, 133 LEd2d 662, reh den 116 SCt 1035, 516 US 1154, 134 LEd2d 112, aff in part, rev in part 59 F3d 1496, cert den 116 SCt 706, 516 US 1046, 133 LEd2d 662, reh den 116 SCt 1035, 516 US 1154, 134 LEd2d 112.—Labor & Emp 1263; Seamen 11(6).

Guevara; Philsec Inv. Corp. v., CA5 (Tex), 939 F2d 1281. See 1488, Inc. v. Philsec Inv. Corp.

Guevara v. State, TexCrimApp, 152 SW3d 45, reh den, on remand 191 SW3d 203, petition for discretionary review refused.—Const Law 4694, 4771; Crim Law 59(1), 59(3), 312, 552(1), 552(4), 881(1), 1144.13(2.1), 1144.13(5), 1159.2(7), 1159.6, 1169.1(1), 1172.1(1); Homic 1135.

Guevara; State v., TexCrimApp, 137 SW3d 55, on remand 172 SW3d 646.—Mun Corp 594(2).

Guevara v. State, TexCrimApp, 97 SW3d 579, habeas corpus den Ex parte Guevara, 2007 WL 1493152.—Crim Law 394.6(5), 1139, 1144.17, 1158(4), 1159.5; Searches 180, 183, 198, 201; Sent & Pun 116, 1720, 1789(3).

Guevara v. State, TexCrimApp, 585 SW2d 744.—Obst Just 3, 11.

Guevara v. State, TexApp–Houston (1 Dist), 6 SW3d 759, petition for discretionary review refused.—Arrest 63.5(4), 63.5(5), 63.5(8), 63.5(9); Crim Law 394.5(3), 1134(3), 1139, 1153(1), 1158(1), 1158(4); Searches 70.

Guevara v. State, TexApp–San Antonio, 191 SW3d 203, petition for discretionary review refused.—Crim Law 59(1), 814(1), 822(1), 1030(1), 1038.1(1), 1134(2), 1172.1(3), 1175; Homic 1465; Hus & W 3(0.5); Neglig 220.

Guevara; State v., TexApp–San Antonio, 172 SW3d 646.—Courts 23, 37(1), 37(2); Crim Law 1076(2), 1081(1), 1081(5).

Guevara; State v., TexApp–San Antonio, 110 SW3d 178, petition for discretionary review gr, rev 137 SW3d 55, on remand 172 SW3d 646.—Const Law 4509(1); Crim Law 13.1(1); Mun Corp 594(2); Statut 188.

Guevara v. State, TexApp–San Antonio, 103 SW3d 549, petition stricken, and petition for discretionary review gr, and petition for discretionary review gr, aff in part, rev in part 152 SW3d 45, reh den, on remand 191 SW3d 203, petition for discretionary review refused.—Crim Law 59(1), 80, 412(4), 700(2.1), 700(3), 1037.1(2), 1037.1(3), 1130(5), 1144.13(7), 1153(1), 1159.6, 1172.1(3); Homic 1207, 1465.

Guevara v. State, TexApp–San Antonio, 4 SW3d 771.—Crim Law 374, 553, 641.13(1), 641.13(6), 747, 925.5(1), 951(1), 956(13), 959, 1134(2), 1144.13(1), 1144.13(6), 1156(1), 1159.2(1), 1159.2(2), 1159.4(2), 1159.6, 1174(1), 1187; Rape 1, 51(1).

Guevara v. State, TexApp–Houston (14 Dist), 985 SW2d 590, petition for discretionary review refused.—Courts 97(5); Crim Law 517(5), 534(2), 577.4, 577.5, 577.10(9), 577.10(10), 1035(1), 1044.1(1).

Guevara; Travelers Ins. Co. v., TexCivApp–Amarillo, 386 SW2d 567, ref nre.—Work Comp 1500, 1647, 1966, 1969.

Guevara; U.S. v., CA5 (Tex), 408 F3d 252, reh and reh den 163 FedAppx 352, cert den 126 SCt 1080, 546 US 1115, 163 LEd2d 898.—Crim Law 847, 1030(1), 1035(1), 1134(6), 1139, 1141(2), 1152(1), 1159.2(7); Extort 25.1, 32; Jury 34(7); Sent & Pun 1245; Statut 241(1).

Guevara v. U. S., CA5 (Tex), 242 F2d 745.—Crim Law 560, 1189; Int Rev 5259, 5295.

Guevara; U.S. v., CA5 (Tex), 176 FedAppx 457.—Crim Law 1026.10(2.1), 1042.

Guevara-Betancourt; U.S. v., CA5 (Tex), 169 FedAppx 205.—Crim Law 1134(3).

Guevara-Vivanco; U.S. v., CA5 (Tex), 144 FedAppx 431, cert den Rodriguez-Mendez v. US, 126 SCt 1076, 546 US 1114, 163 LEd2d 896.—Crim Law 1042.

Guex; First City Bank-Farmers Branch v., TexApp–Dallas, 659 SW2d 734, writ gr, aff 677 SW2d 25.—App & E 169, 994(2); Damag 87(2), 89(2), 91(1); Sec Tran 229.1, 242.1, 243; Trial 261, 272.

Guex; First City Bank-Farmers Branch, Texas v., Tex, 677 SW2d 25.—App & E 177; Costs 194.16, 194.25, 194.32; Sec Tran 230, 243.

Guffee; DeBusk v., TexCivApp–Eastland, 171 SW2d 194.—App & E 758.3(2), 758.3(4), 758.3(10), 758.3(11), 930(3); Costs 238(2); Ex & Ad 130(1); Partit 73, 91; Ten in C 38(3).

Guffee; De Busk v., TexCivApp–Eastland, 132 SW2d 495, writ dism, correct.—Deeds 54; Tresp to T T 47(3).

Guffey v. Borden, Inc., CA5 (Tex), 595 F2d 1111.—Fed Cts 866; Neglig 1288, 1289, 1293, 1304, 1707.

Guffey v. Collier, TexCivApp–Eastland, 203 SW2d 812.—App & E 179(1), 1062.1; Damag 117, 140; New Tr 128(1); Trial 350.8.

Guffey; Magnolia Petroleum Co. v., TexComApp, 102 SW2d 408, 129 Tex 293.—App & E 1062.2; False Imp 15(3); Princ & A 159(1).

Guffey; Magnolia Petroleum Co. v., TexComApp, 95 SW2d 690, set aside on reh 102 SW2d 408, 129 Tex 293.—False Imp 15(3); Princ & A 99, 159(1).

Guffey v. Utex Exploration Co., TexCivApp–San Antonio, 376 SW2d 1, ref nre.—Frds St of 44(4), 51, 72(1), 73, 125(2).

Guffy; Texas State Bd. of Educ. v., TexApp–Dallas, 718 SW2d 48.—Inj 140, 147.

Gugenheim v. Anheuser-Busch, Inc., TexCivApp–Austin, 198 SW2d 950.—Plead 111.3, 111.31, 111.42(6); Venue 7.5(1), 7.5(3).

Gugenheim v. C.I.R., CA5 (Tex), 239 F2d 286, on remand 1958 WL 723.—Int Rev 4756; Judgm 604.

Gugenheim v. Hancock, TexCivApp–Amarillo, 231 SW2d 935, ref nre.—Contracts 6; Corp 116; Frds St of 56(4), 74(1); Sales 61, 340.

Gugenheim v. Trevino, TexCivApp–San Antonio, 532 SW2d 698.—Venue 22(1), 22(6).

Guggenheim v. Barnett, TexApp–Fort Worth, 728 SW2d 139.—Inj 138.31.

Guggenheim; Porter v., TexCivApp–Dallas, 107 SW2d 891, writ dism.—App & E 1046.3; Contempt 20; Inj 147, 148(2), 152, 178; Liens 10.

Guia v. State, TexApp–Dallas, 220 SW3d 197.—Controlled Subs 74, 82; Crim Law 37(2.1), 37(8), 38, 569, 1144.13(2.1), 1159.2(2), 1159.2(7), 1159.4(1), 1159.4(2), 1159.5, 1184(1); Sent & Pun 1408.

Guia v. State, TexApp–Dallas, 723 SW2d 763, petition for discretionary review refused.—Crim Law 619, 620(1), 620(3.1); Infants 13, 20.

Guiberson v. R. F. C., CA5 (Tex), 196 F2d 154.—U S 70(10), 70(11), 72.1(2), 72.1(6).

Guiberson Corp. v. Equipment Engineers, Inc., CA5 (Tex), 252 F2d 431.—Fed Cts 653, 655; Pat 112.1, 312(1.2), 324.5.

Guiberson Corp. v. Garrett Oil Tools, Inc., CA5 (Tex), 205 F2d 660, cert den 74 SCt 137, 346 US 886, 98 LEd 390, reh den 74 SCt 273, 346 US 917, 98 LEd 413.—Courts 96(1); Pat 26(1), 32, 36.2(3), 288(3), 288(4).

Guiberson Corp.; Otis Pressure Control v., CCA5 (Tex), 108 F2d 930.—Pat 16.17, 32, 66(1.19), 324.55(5).

Guiberson Corp.; Webber v., SDTex, 231 FSupp 596, aff 336 F2d 461, cert den 85 SCt 701, 379 US 989, 13 LEd2d 610.—Pat 75, 76, 81.

Guiberteau; Zarsky Lumber Co. v., TexCivApp–San Antonio, 270 SW2d 630, ref nre.—Bills & N 163; Mech Liens 205, 206, 255; Partners 55; Plead 290(3).

Guice v. State, TexApp–Texarkana, 900 SW2d 387, petition for discretionary review refused.—Crim Law 858(1), 861, 862, 911, 925.5(1), 932, 1156(1), 1156(5), 1158(3).

Guice; Texas State Bd. of Medical Examiners v., TexApp–Corpus Christi, 704 SW2d 113, ref nre.—Admin Law 473; Health 215, 218, 223(1).

Guichard v. I.N.S., SDTex, 911 FSupp 255.—Aliens 469; Hab Corp 521.

Guichard; U.S. v., CA5 (Tex), 779 F2d 1139, cert den 106 SCt 1654, 475 US 1127, 90 LEd2d 197.—Crim Law 273(4.1), 273.1(1), 273.1(4), 1167(5).

GuideOne Elite Ins. Co. v. Fielder Road Baptist Church, Tex, 197 SW3d 305, reh den.—Insurance 2268, 2276, 2914, 2915.

Guideone Elite Ins. Co.; Fielder Road Baptist Church v., TexApp–Fort Worth, 139 SW3d 384, reh overr, and review gr, aff 197 SW3d 305, reh den.—App & E 1175(1); Insurance 1822, 2276, 2914, 2915, 2942.

GuideOne Ins. Co. v. Cupps, TexApp–Fort Worth, 207 SW3d 900, review den.—Action 35; Admin Law 228.1, 229; App & E 856(1), 893(1); Statut 181(2), 188, 190, 205, 214; Work Comp 1178, 2122.

GuideOne Mut. Ins. Co.; Crawford v., NDTex, 420 FSupp2d 584.—Antitrust 141, 221, 363; Contracts 143(2), 176(2), 187(1); Evid 43(4); Fed Civ Proc 1772, 2554; Insurance 1810, 1813, 1822, 1832(1), 2090, 2272, 2914, 2915, 2922(1), 2931, 2934(2), 2939, 3335, 3349, 3357, 3365.

Guido; Fazzino v., TexApp–Houston (1 Dist), 836 SW2d 271, reh den, and writ den.—App & E 1046.5; Dedi 16.1, 17, 39, 41, 44, 63(1); Jury 104.1; Trial 41(3); Witn 246(1).

Guido; Reynolds v., TexApp–Dallas, 166 SW3d 789, reh overr, and review den.—App & E 754(1); Judgm 185.3(2); Lim of Act 43, 95(1), 95(7).

Guido & Guido, Inc. v. Culberson County, TexCivApp–El Paso, 459 SW2d 674, ref nre.—Counties 119; Damag 175.

Guido Bros. Const. Co.; City of San Antonio v., TexCiv-App–Beaumont, 460 SW2d 155, ref nre.—Accord 8(2), 23; App & E 302(5); Compromise 4, 21; Joint Adv 1.2(4), 1.15; Mun Corp 328, 330(1), 373(2), 374(1), 374(3); Trial 351.2(4).

Guidroz v. Lynaugh, CA5 (Tex), 852 F2d 832.—Crim Law 709, 717, 720(9), 1165(1), 1171.1(3); Hab Corp 668, 670(1); Mental H 439.1.

Guidroz v. State, TexApp–San Antonio, 679 SW2d 586, petition for discretionary review refused, habeas corpus gr 852 F2d 832.—Crim Law 494, 720(9), 730(1), 1172.1(2); Homic 1210; Sent & Pun 256; Stip 14(10).

Guidry, In re, BkrtcyEDTex, 366 BR 624.—Bankr 3192, 3203(1).

Guidry, In re, BkrtcySDTex, 354 BR 824.—Bankr 2081, 2124.1, 2126, 2129, 2158, 2164.1, 2264(1); Const Law 2450; Courts 82, 85(1); Int Rev 4482.

Guidry; Airline Motor Coaches v., TexCivApp–Beaumont, 241 SW2d 203, ref nre.—App & E 1064.1(7); Autos 147, 244(20), 245(15), 247; Damag 216(10); Trial 358.

Guidry; City of San Antonio v., TexApp–San Antonio, 801 SW2d 142.—Damag 55, 62(1), 163(2); Em Dom 2(1.1), 116, 266, 300, 303, 307(2), 307(3), 307(4), 315.

Guidry v. Denkins, TexCivApp–Hous (1 Dist), 460 SW2d 943.—Adop 6; Child 86.

Guidry; Diamond Offshore Management Co. v., Tex, 171 SW3d 840, reh den.—Seamen 29(4), 29(5.2), 29(5.14), 29(5.16), 29(5.17); Trial 350.2, 352.1(1).

Guidry; Diamond Offshore Management Co. v., Tex-App–Beaumont, 84 SW3d 256, review gr, rev 171 SW3d 840, reh den.—Adm 1.20(1), 1.20(4); App & E 930(1), 946, 970(2), 974(0.5), 989, 1001(1), 1001(3), 1050.1(1), 1056.1(1), 1056.1(3), 1058(1); Death 99(4); Seamen 29(1), 29(5.5), 29(5.12), 29(5.14), 29(5.16); Trial 350.2, 351.5(8), 352.5(1).

Guidry v. Dretke, CA5 (Tex), 397 F3d 306, reh and reh den 429 F3d 154, cert den 126 SCt 1587, 547 US 1035, 164 LEd2d 326.—Crim Law 412.2(4), 412.2(5), 517.2(2), 662.9, 662.11; Hab Corp 205, 380.1, 481, 722(2), 749, 767, 775(1), 775(2), 816, 841, 842, 846; Homic 563.

Guidry; Green v., TexApp–Waco, 34 SW3d 669.—App & E 348(1), 352.1; Motions 17.

Guidry; Gulf Oil Corp. v., Tex, 327 SW2d 406, 160 Tex 139.—Alt Disp Res 230, 314, 395, 396; Labor & Emp 1595(8), 1595(9), 1595(10).

Guidry v. Gulf Oil Corp., TexCivApp–Austin, 320 SW2d 691, rev in part 327 SW2d 406, 160 Tex 139.—Labor & Emp 1595(8), 1595(10), 1595(12).

Guidry v. Halliburton Geophysical Services, Inc., CA5 (Tex), 976 F2d 938.—Compromise 2, 16(1); Contracts 176(2); Evid 450(5); Fed Cts 776, 859.

Guidry v. Harris County Medical Soc., TexCivApp–Hous (1 Dist), 618 SW2d 844, ref nre.—App & E 1056.1(1), 1056.4; Fraud 52, 58(2); Health 295; Trial 260(6), 352.20; Witn 16.

Guidry; Industrial Acc. Bd. v., Tex, 345 SW2d 509, 162 Tex 160.—Work Comp 1030.1(5).

Guidry v. Jefferson County Detention Center, EDTex, 868 FSupp 189.—Civil R 1093; Fed Civ Proc 392, 2466, 2471, 2491.5, 2538, 2543, 2544; Offic 114, 119; Sent & Pun 1546.

Guidry v. Massey, TexCivApp–Hous (1 Dist), 572 SW2d 47.—App & E 865; Judgm 145(2); Pretrial Proc 723.1.

Guidry v. National Freight, Inc., TexApp–Austin, 944 SW2d 807, reh overr.—Action 60; Autos 116; Judgm 181(14); Labor & Emp 3040, 3041, 3042, 3062; Neglig 213, 215.

Guidry v. Neches Butane Products Co., Tex, 476 SW2d 666.—Judgm 181(33), 185(2).

Guidry v. Neches Butane Products Co., TexCivApp–Beaumont, 466 SW2d 389, writ gr, rev 476 SW2d 666.—App & E 863; Judgm 181(1), 181(2), 185(2); Neglig 213, 1037(4), 1037(7), 1085, 1204(1), 1240, 1579.

Guidry v. Northwestern Mut. Life Ins. Co., CA5 (Tex), 88 FedAppx 12.—Insurance 2561(1).

Guidry v. Phillips, TexCivApp–Hous (14 Dist), 580 SW2d 883, ref nre.—App & E 949, 1056.1(10); Evid 506, 538, 545, 547, 560; Health 820, 825; Trial 3(4).

Guidry; Second Injury Fund v., TexCivApp–Beaumont, 336 SW2d 785, writ gr, rev Industrial Acc Bd v. Guidry, 345 SW2d 509, 162 Tex 160.—App & E 692(1); Damag 221(3); Work Comp 846, 856, 1030.1(1), 1030.1(5), 1040, 1221, 1313, 1834, 1868, 1922, 1968(6).

Guidry; Speed v., TexApp–San Antonio, 668 SW2d 807.—Adop 14; Child 13; Infants 221.

Guidry v. State, TexCrimApp, 9 SW3d 133, reh den, cert den 121 SCt 98, 531 US 837, 148 LEd2d 57, grant of habeas corpus aff 397 F3d 306, reh and reh den 429 F3d 154, cert den Dretke v. Guidry, 126 SCt 1587, 547 US 1035, 164 LEd2d 326.—Const Law 4664(2); Crim Law 412.2(4), 414, 417(15), 419(2), 419(12), 422(5), 423(1), 427(1), 531(4), 543(1), 641.2(1), 641.3(1), 641.3(3), 641.13(1), 655(4), 662.8, 662.60, 713, 719(1), 730(7), 862, 865(2), 1036.1(9), 1090.8, 1120(1), 1120(3), 1155, 1168(2), 1171.3; Judges 25(1); Sent & Pun 238, 1745, 1786.

Guidry v. State, TexCrimApp, 896 SW2d 798, on remand 909 SW2d 584, petition for discretionary review refused.—Sent & Pun 604.

Guidry v. State, TexCrimApp, 360 SW2d 152, 172 Tex-Crim 516.—Larc 30(1), 64(7).

Guidry v. State, TexApp–Houston (1 Dist), 177 SW3d 90.—Crim Law 920, 1026.10(4).

Guidry v. State, TexApp–Houston (1 Dist), 132 SW3d 611, opinion after remand 177 SW3d 90.—Crim Law 641.13(5), 956(4), 956(7), 959, 1156(1).

Guidry v. State, TexApp–Texarkana, 896 SW2d 381, reh overr, and petition for discretionary review refused.—Crim Law 312, 369.1, 374, 568, 641.13(1), 641.13(2.1), 641.13(6), 641.13(7), 753.2(3.1), 814(1), 949(2), 956(2), 956(11), 959, 1144.13(3), 1144.13(6), 1159.2(1), 1159.2(7); Ind & Inf 125(1), 127; Infants 20.

Guidry v. State, TexApp–Beaumont, 121 SW3d 849.—Crim Law 344, 406(1), 444, 670, 938(1), 938(6).

Guidry v. State, TexApp–Corpus Christi, 909 SW2d 584, petition for discretionary review refused.—Sent & Pun 604.

Guidry v. State, TexApp–Corpus Christi, 883 SW2d 275, reh overr, and petition for discretionary review gr, vac 896 SW2d 798, on remand 909 SW2d 584, petition for discretionary review refused.—Sent & Pun 604, 606, 611.

Guidry v. Texaco, Inc., CA5 (Tex), 430 F2d 781.—Adm 118.7(5), 119; Fed Cts 941; Indem 36, 37; Ship 86(3).

Guidry; Texas Emp. Ins. Ass'n v., TexComApp, 99 SW2d 900, 128 Tex 433.—Work Comp 863, 1201.

Guidry; Texas Emp. Ins. Ass'n v., TexCivApp–Beaumont, 93 SW2d 508, rev 99 SW2d 900, 128 Tex 433.—App & E 1064.1(8), 1078(1); Lim of Act 43; Work Comp 801, 853, 866, 904, 2017.

Guidry; Travelers Ins. Co. v., TexCivApp–Beaumont, 461 SW2d 170, ref nre.—Work Comp 1580, 1975.

Guidry; U.S. v., CA5 (Tex), 456 F3d 493, reh den, cert den 127 SCt 996, 166 LEd2d 752.—Civil R 1809; Consp 47(3.1); Const Law 3896; Crim Law 369.2(5), 374, 713, 723(1), 730(1), 1139, 1144.13(3), 1153(1), 1159.2(7), 1171.1(2.1), 1171.1(3); Kidnap 15; Statut 188, 190, 205, 208, 222; Weap 6, 17(4).

Guidry; U.S. v., CA5 (Tex), 406 F3d 314, cert den 126 SCt 190, 546 US 888, 163 LEd2d 198.—Const Law 4657, 4658(3); Crim Law 339.8(6), 404.50, 735, 736(1), 822(6), 1030(1), 1035(1), 1139, 1144.13(3), 1144.13(5), 1152(1), 1153(1), 1158(4), 1159.2(7), 1159.4(1), 1167(1); Ind & Inf 159(2); Jury 34(10); Weap 4, 17(4).

Guidry, East, Barnes & Bono, Inc.; M.H. Inc. v., Tex-App–Houston (14 Dist), 834 SW2d 550.—App & E 863, 901, 934(1); Judgm 181(19), 183.

Guiff v. Strain, TexCivApp–Waco, 87 SW2d 309.—App & E 1062.1.

Guiffrida; Hanover Bldg. Materials, Inc. v., CA5 (Tex), 748 F2d 1011.—Fed Cts 419; Insurance 2210; U S 147(11.1).

Guilbeau v. Anderson, TexApp–Houston (14 Dist), 841 SW2d 517.—Antitrust 161, 291; App & E 931(1), 989, 1010.1(1), 1010.2, 1012.1(4); Corp 306, 335, 488; Damag 50, 192; Fraud 25, 58(2); Neglig 273, 1584.

Guilbeau v. State, TexApp–Houston (1 Dist), 193 SW3d 156, petition for discretionary review refused.—Crim Law 737(1), 772(6), 822(1), 1134(2), 1144.13(2.1), 1173.2(3); Homic 787, 1345, 1474, 1476, 1484, 1485.

Guilbeaux v. 3927 Foundation, Inc., EDTex, 177 FRD 387.—Fed Civ Proc 824, 828.1, 834, 851, 928, 1825, 1832; Fed Cts 817; Insurance 1117(3); Labor & Emp 407; Rem of C 118; States 18.51.

Guilder v. State, TexApp–Dallas, 794 SW2d 765.—Controlled Subs 27, 80; Crim Law 627.5(6), 627.7(3), 641.13(1), 641.13(2.1), 1043(3), 1099.14, 1104(7), 1115(2), 1171.1(2.1), 1171.7.

Guild, Hagen & Clark, Ltd.; Lawler v., NDTex, 106 BR 943. See Lawler, In re.

Guild, Hagen & Clark, Ltd.; Lawler v., BkrtcyNDTex, 75 BR 979. See Lawler, In re.

Guile v. U.S., CA5 (Tex), 422 F2d 221.—Evid 555.2, 570, 571(3), 571(9); Fed Civ Proc 2127, 2608.1, 2609; Fed Cts 776; Health 631, 821(2), 821(3), 822(3), 823(14); Neglig 379, 380, 387; U S 78(12), 125(3).

Guilford Mortg. Co.; Allen v., TexCivApp–Dallas, 118 SW2d 453.—Mtg 148; Usury 34.

Guilford Mortg. Co.; Burke v., TexCivApp–Dallas, 161 SW2d 574, writ refused wom.—App & E 909(5); Ex & Ad 35(14), 228(4), 229, 231, 275, 453(2); Home 97; Lim of Act 48(3), 166; Mtg 218.15, 318; Princ & A 122(1).

Guilford Mortg. Co.; Jones v., TexCivApp–Dallas, 120 SW2d 1081.—Can of Inst 37(6); Contracts 93(2); Usury 34.

Guillebeau; Tatom v., TexApp–Tyler, 686 SW2d 705.—Evid 538; Judgm 185.3(21).

Guillen; Carrola v., TexApp–San Antonio, 935 SW2d 949.—Judgm 181(27), 185(2); Offic 114.

Guillen v. City of San Antonio, TexApp–San Antonio, 13 SW3d 428, reh overr, and review den.—App & E 852, 934(1); Health 653; Judgm 185(2), 185(5); Mun Corp 105, 723, 723.5, 747(4); Statut 2.

Guillen v. Claybrook, TexCivApp–San Antonio, 590 SW2d 146.—App & E 389(3), 596, 623, 624.

Guillen v. DeLeon, TexApp–San Antonio, 887 SW2d 503.—App & E 497(1), 620.1, 624.

Guillen v. Kuykendall, CA5 (Tex), 470 F2d 745.—Assault 35; Damag 151, 215(2); Fed Civ Proc 630; Labor & Emp 23, 3029, 3045, 3105(8).

Guillen v. State, TexCrimApp, 442 SW2d 692.—Sent & Pun 2021.

Guillen-Alvarez; U.S. v., CA5 (Tex), 489 F3d 197.—Crim Law 1139; Jury 31.1; Sent & Pun 665, 793.

Guillett v. State, TexCrimApp, 677 SW2d 46.—Autos 349.5(12); Controlled Subs 116; Crim Law 1144.9; Jury 29(1), 29(6).

Guillett v. State, TexApp–Houston (1 Dist), 651 SW2d 902, petition for discretionary review gr, aff in part, rev in part 677 SW2d 46.—Crim Law 1144.9; Jury 29(6); Searches 58, 66.

Guilliams v. Koonsman, Tex, 279 SW2d 579, 154 Tex 401, 57 ALR2d 97.—Remand 4; Wills 439, 441, 470(1), 498, 614(1), 614(6.1), 634(8), 634(12).

Guilliams v. Koonsman, TexCivApp–Eastland, 274 SW2d 135, aff as reformed 279 SW2d 579, 154 Tex 401, 57 ALR2d 97.—App & E 170(1), 843(2); Wills 602(3).

Guilliams v. State, TexCrimApp, 261 SW2d 598, 159 TexCrim 81.—Sent & Pun 1299, 1367.

Guillory, In Interest of, TexCivApp–Hous (1 Dist), 618 SW2d 948.—Child C 510; Infants 155, 156, 178, 179, 180.

Guillory v. Aetna Life Ins. Co., TexCivApp–Beaumont, 541 SW2d 883, ref nre.—Insurance 2590(1), 2595(3); Judgm 199(3.10).

Guillory; City of Beaumont v., Tex, 751 SW2d 491.—App & E 80(6), 870(2), 934(1).

Guillory v. City of Beaumont, TexApp–Beaumont, 746 SW2d 16, rev 751 SW2d 491.—App & E 80(6); Judgm 181(33).

Guillory v. Davis, TexCivApp–Beaumont, 530 SW2d 870, dism.—App & E 66, 78(1).

Guillory v. Davis, TexCivApp–Beaumont, 527 SW2d 465.—Courts 207.5.

Guillory; Espree v., TexCivApp–Houston (1 Dist), 753 SW2d 722.—Child 3; Divorce 172.

Guillory; Flintex Oil Co. v., TexCivApp–Eastland, 337 SW2d 757.—Plead 111.36, 111.42(8).

Guillory; Kansas City Southern R. Co. v., TexCivApp–Beaumont, 376 SW2d 72, ref nre.—App & E 1177(1); Evid 5(2); Neglig 1037(4), 1076, 1088, 1089, 1313; R R 275(1), 275(2), 275(3), 282(5), 282(9); Trial 350.6(4).

Guillory v. Levingston Shipbuilding Co., TexCivApp–Beaumont, 433 SW2d 515, ref nre, cert den 89 SCt 1751, 395 US 909, 23 LEd2d 221.—Work Comp 93, 2084, 2085, 2169.

Guillory; Pacific Emp. Ins. Co. v., TexCivApp–Fort Worth, 310 SW2d 584, ref nre.—App & E 1170.6; Work Comp 817, 861, 1639, 1968(5).

Guillory v. Port of Houston Authority, Tex, 845 SW2d 812, motion to stay mandate den, cert den 114 SCt 75, 510 US 820, 126 LEd2d 43.—Adm 1.20(5); Fed Cts 270; Nav Wat 8.5.

Guillory; Port of Houston Authority v., TexApp–Houston (1 Dist), 814 SW2d 119, writ gr, aff 845 SW2d 812, motion to stay mandate den, cert den 114 SCt 75, 510 US 820, 126 LEd2d 43.—Adm 2; Contrib 5(7); Nav Wat 14(2); States 112.2(2); Work Comp 1348, 2142.30.

Guillory v. Service Life and Cas. Ins. Co., TexApp–Beaumont, 52 SW3d 922.—App & E 893(1); Insurance 2421, 3567; Judgm 185(2); Parties 1, 21.

Guillory v. State, TexCrimApp, 557 SW2d 118.—Atty & C 23; Contempt 20; Courts 57(1); Crim Law 641.10(2), 641.13(7), 1077.2(1), 1077.2(3), 1077.3, 1109(1).

Guillory v. State, TexCrimApp, 487 SW2d 327.—Crim Law 394.1(2); Estop 62.2(2); Sent & Pun 2021, 2022, 2029.

Guillory v. State, TexCrimApp, 409 SW2d 402.—Homic 1136.

Guillory v. State, TexCrimApp, 400 SW2d 751.—Crim Law 516, 927(4), 956(13), 1167(5), 1169.5(2), 1174(2); Homic 976; Witn 277(4).

Guillory v. State, TexCrimApp, 250 SW2d 218, 157 TexCrim 502.—Crim Law 1111(3); Homic 1004.

Guillory v. State, TexApp–Houston (1 Dist), 99 SW3d 735, petition for discretionary review refused (1 pet), and petition for discretionary review refused (2 pets).—Autos 349(5); Crim Law 273.1(3), 1134(10); Hab Corp 475.1; Obst Just 3, 14.

Guillory v. State, TexApp–Houston (1 Dist), 877 SW2d 71, petition for discretionary review refused.—Crim Law 59(1), 59(3), 59(4), 59(5), 552(1), 792(3), 1038.1(1), 1172.1(2); Rob 24.10.

Guillory v. State, TexApp–Houston (1 Dist), 646 SW2d 467.—Crim Law 1163(2), 1181.5(6).

Guillory v. State, TexApp–Houston (1 Dist), 639 SW2d 1, petition for discretionary review refused.—Crim Law 814(1), 1038.1(2), 1038.1(4); Homic 598, 850, 1404; Searches 165, 173.1, 177.

Guillory v. State, TexApp–Houston (1 Dist), 638 SW2d 73.—Crim Law 1181.5(6).

Guillory v. State, TexApp–Beaumont, 956 SW2d 135.—Crim Law 790, 823(1), 1144.15, 1172.1(1), 1172.1(2).

Guillory; Taylor v., TexCivApp–Hous (1 Dist), 439 SW2d 362.—App & E 846(5), 931(1), 931(6), 989; Deeds 211(1); Evid 383(7); Plead 382(1); Tresp to T T 35(2), 38(1), 46.

Guillory Farms, Inc. v. Amigos Canning Co., Inc., TexApp–Beaumont, 966 SW2d 830, review den.—Sales 38(1), 195.

Guillot; Bartley v., TexApp–Houston (14 Dist), 990 SW2d 481, review den, and reh of petition for review overr.—Com Law 11; Damag 63, 64; Insurance 2805.

Guillot; Beaumont Coca Cola Bottling Co. v., TexCivApp–Beaumont, 222 SW2d 141, ref nre.—Evid 5(2); Food 25; Trial 350.6(2).

Guillot; Campos v., CA5 (Tex), 743 F2d 1123.—Civil R 1438; Const Law 4173(3), 4173(4); Fed Cts 911.

Guillot v. Halman, TexCivApp–Fort Worth, 91 SW2d 402.—App & E 216(2), 218.2(1), 1068(4); Trial 278.

Guillot v. Hix, Tex, 838 SW2d 230.—Subrog 33(1), 38, 41(3); Work Comp 2191, 2210, 2215, 2216.

Guillot; Hix v., TexApp–Houston (14 Dist), 812 SW2d 400, writ gr, aff 838 SW2d 230.—Work Comp 2216.

Guillot; McCormack v., Tex, 597 SW2d 345, mandamus gr.—Judgm 297, 340; New Tr 155.

Guillot v. Smith, TexApp–Houston (1 Dist), 998 SW2d 630, reh overr.—Lim of Act 55(3).

Guillot v. State, TexCrimApp, 543 SW2d 650.—Crim Law 304(16); Sent & Pun 2010, 2011, 2021, 2025.

Guillote; Fry v., TexCivApp–Hous (14 Dist), 577 SW2d 346, ref nre.—App & E 959(3); Cust & U 12(1), 13, 19(3); Plead 236(3), 236(7), 427; Trial 105(4).

Guillott v. Gentle, TexCivApp–Eastland, 467 SW2d 521, ref nre.—Child C 42, 452, 473, 921(1).

Guillry v. State, TexApp–Houston (1 Dist), 856 SW2d 477, reh den, and petition for discretionary review refused.—Crim Law 635.

Guin v. Fortis Benefits Ins. Co., EDTex, 256 FSupp2d 542.—Fed Civ Proc 2547.1; Labor & Emp 407, 425, 575, 616, 685, 687, 688, 690, 691; States 18.51.

Guin; Ranger County Mut. Ins. Co. v., Tex, 723 SW2d 656.—Insurance 3349, 3376, 3381(5).

Guin; Ranger County Mut. Ins. Co. v., TexApp–Texarkana, 704 SW2d 813, writ gr, aff 723 SW2d 656.—Insurance 3335, 3349, 3350, 3355, 3381(5); Neglig 1662; Princ & A 1.

Guin v. State, TexApp–Texarkana, 209 SW3d 682.—Const Law 3880; Crim Law 641.13(1), 641.13(7), 655(1), 1035(8.1), 1063(1), 1144.10; Mal Mis 1; Schools 21; Witn 246(2).

Guinn, Ex parte, TexCrimApp, 284 SW2d 721, 162 Tex-Crim 293.—Evid 80(1); Extrad 31, 36.

Guinn; A. & M. College of Tex. v., TexCivApp–Austin, 280 SW2d 373, ref nre.—Courts 65, 198, 202(5); Estop 3(1), 52(1); Evid 29, 41, 43(1), 67(1), 67(4), 82; Judgm 341; Wills 225, 337, 355, 357, 358, 400, 421.

Guinn; ACF Industries, Inc. v., CA5 (Tex), 384 F2d 15, cert den 88 SCt 1039, 390 US 949, 19 LEd2d 1140.—Action 68, 69(2), 69(4); Fed Civ Proc 1741, 1742(5), 2646; Fed Cts 45, 121, 523, 526.1; Mand 26, 28, 53; Pat 106(1).

Guinn; Acker v., Tex, 464 SW2d 348.—Mines 55(4), 55(5), 55(6).

Guinn v. Acker, TexCivApp–Tyler, 451 SW2d 549, aff 464 SW2d 348.—Mines 48, 55(4), 55(5); Statut 194.

Guinn; Agricultural and Mechanical College v., TexCivApp–Austin, 326 SW2d 609, ref nre.—Evid 54, 222(7), 222(9); Wills 21, 400.

Guinn; Bartelt v., CA5 (Tex), 485 F2d 250.—Crim Law 1655(6).

Guinn v. Bosque County, TexApp–Waco, 58 SW3d 194, reh overr, and review den.—Counties 63; Judgm 185(4), 185(6), 185.1(1), 185.1(6), 185.2(1); Labor & Emp 40(2), 50.

Guinn v. Clay, TexCivApp–Amarillo, 324 SW2d 254, ref nre.—Contracts 318; Deeds 165; Mines 78.1(6), 78.7(1).

Guinn; Collins v., TexApp–Texarkana, 102 SW3d 825, reh overr, and review den.—Action 6; Atty & C 26; Contracts 312(3), 326; Costs 207, 208; Courts 155; Judgm 13, 181(2), 181(13), 185.1(1), 185.1(2), 185.1(3), 279, 540, 561, 678(1), 739, 956(2); Lim of Act 46(6); Princ & A 136(2).

Guinn v. County School Trustees of Hays County, TexCivApp–Austin, 261 SW2d 913.—Plead 6, 110, 111.9, 111.39(2), 111.42(4), 111.46.

Guinn v. Culver, TexCivApp–Texarkana, 81 SW2d 176.—Accord 8(1).

Guinn; Ellis v., TexCivApp–El Paso, 323 SW2d 381, ref nre.—Autos 224(1), 244(56).

Guinn v. Lokey, Tex, 249 SW2d 185, 151 Tex 260.—Autos 19, 20; Estop 75; Sales 99, 106, 108; Trover 35.

Guinn v. Lokey, TexCivApp–Galveston, 243 SW2d 246, rev 249 SW2d 185, 151 Tex 260.—Estop 75.

Guinn; Miller v., TexCivApp–El Paso, 120 SW2d 474, writ dism by agreement.—Gifts 25.

Guinn; Ranger County Mut. Ins. Co. v., TexCivApp–Tyler, 608 SW2d 730, dism.—Antitrust 358; Venue 17.

Guinn v. State, TexCrimApp, 295 SW2d 908, 164 Tex-Crim 12.—Controlled Subs 69.

Guinn v. State, TexCrimApp, 289 SW2d 583, 163 Tex-Crim 181.—Crim Law 1042, 1097(1), 1097(3), 1099.7(3); Sent & Pun 1918.

Guinn v. State, TexCrimApp, 202 SW2d 235.—Crim Law 1094(3).

Guinn v. State, TexApp–Houston (14 Dist), 696 SW2d 436, petition for discretionary review refused.—Autos 332, 359; Const Law 201, 2790, 2803; Crim Law 1030(3); Statut 195.

Guinn v. State, TexCivApp–Austin, 551 SW2d 783, ref nre.—App & E 173(2); Const Law 1004, 4144; Evid 383(3); Labor & Emp 29; Plead 250; Statut 47; Tax 2016, 2118, 2160, 2859, 3285.

Guinn v. Texas Christian University, TexApp–Fort Worth, 818 SW2d 930, writ den, cert den 113 SCt 1050, 506 US 1081, 122 LEd2d 358, reh den 113 SCt 1629, 507 US 1002, 123 LEd2d 186.—Action 57(6), 58; App & E 863; Colleges 9.35(4); Courts 483; Judgm 185(2).

Guinn v. Texas Newspapers, Inc., TexApp–Houston (14 Dist), 738 SW2d 303, writ den, cert den Cox Enterprises, Inc v. Guinn, 109 SCt 864, 488 US 1041, 102 LEd2d 988.—Judgm 181(33); Libel 48(2).

Guinn; U.S. v., CA5 (Tex), 454 F2d 29, cert den Grimes v. US, 92 SCt 2437, 407 US 911, 32 LEd2d 685, cert den 92 SCt 2437, 407 US 911, 32 LEd2d 685.—Crim Law 564(1), 691, 730(8), 753.2(8), 814(1), 1132, 1134(1), 1168(1); Gaming 60, 98(1), 102; Searches 121.1; Witn 383, 414(1).

Guinn v. Zarsky, TexApp–Corpus Christi, 893 SW2d 13.—App & E 863, 934(1), 1073(1), 1177(9); Judgm 181(5.1), 184, 186.

Guinn Flying Services; McRae v., TexApp–Houston (1 Dist), 778 SW2d 189.—Evid 51; Pretrial Proc 314, 315.

Guinn Investments, Inc. v. Ridge Oil Co., TexApp–Fort Worth, 73 SW3d 523, reh overr, and review gr, rev 148 SW3d 143, reh den.—App & E 863, 934(1), 1175(1); Judgm 185(2); Mines 73.1(2), 77, 78.1(8), 78.1(9).

Guinn Investments, Inc.; Ridge Oil Co., Inc. v., Tex, 148 SW3d 143, reh den.—App & E 984(5); Costs 194.40, 208; Mines 74(3), 74(6), 77, 78.1(7), 78.1(8), 78.1(9), 78.1(10); Torts 241; Trusts 103(1).

Guinther, Ex parte, TexApp–San Antonio, 982 SW2d 506.—Double J 3; Hab Corp 843; Judgm 634, 648, 751; Obscen 1.2.

Guinyard; U.S. v., CA5 (Tex), 149 FedAppx 279.—Controlled Subs 130; Crim Law 1026.10(4).

Guion v. Gibson, TexCivApp–Hous (14 Dist), 439 SW2d 715.—Inj 111; Plead 111.38, 111.43.

Guion v. Guion, TexCivApp–Dallas, 475 SW2d 865, ref nre.—App & E 774; Compromise 18(3), 22; Equity 65(2); Plead 53(2).

Guion; Guion v., TexCivApp–Dallas, 475 SW2d 865, ref nre.—App & E 774; Compromise 18(3), 22; Equity 65(2); Plead 53(2).

Guisinger v. Hughes, TexCivApp–Dallas, 363 SW2d 861, ref nre.—Evid 420(3), 434(1), 434(9), 444(0.5), 448; Judgm 185.3(7); Princ & A 70.

Guitar v. U.S., NDTex, 135 FSupp 509.—Adv Poss 50, 68; Hus & W 273(1), 273(2); Int Rev 4153(2).

Guitar Holding Co., L.P.; Cimarron Agr., Ltd. v., Tex-App–El Paso, 209 SW3d 197.—App & E 949; Atty & C 19, 21, 21.5(1), 21.20.

Guitar Holding Co., L.P. v. Hudspeth County Underground Water Conservation Dist. No. 1, TexApp–El Paso, 209 SW3d 172, review gr.—Admin Law 749, 750, 791, 793; App & E 984(1); Const Law 3057, 3509; Contracts 171(1); Costs 32(2), 194.14, 194.18, 198, 207; Statut 64(1), 181(1), 188, 205, 219(1), 219(4); Waters 133, 145, 152(12), 152(13), 183.5.

Guitar Holding Co., L.P. v. Hudspeth County Underground Water Conservation Dist. No. 1, TexApp–El Paso, 209 SW3d 146, review gr.—Admin Law 749, 750, 791, 793; App & E 984(1); Const Law 3057, 3509; Contracts 171(1); Costs 32(2), 194.14, 194.18, 198, 207; Statut 64(1), 181(1), 188, 205, 219(1), 219(4); Waters 133, 145, 152(12), 152(13), 183.5.

Guitar Trust Estate v. Boyd, TexCivApp–Eastland, 120 SW2d 914.—Deeds 70(3), 190, 211(3); Evid 66; Fraud 11(2), 22(2), 23.

Guiterrez v. State, TexApp–Houston (1 Dist), 176 SW3d 394, petition for discretionary review refused.—Crim Law 273(4.1), 275.2, 275.3, 538(3).

Guiterrez; U.S. v., CA5 (Tex), 556 F2d 1217.—Crim Law 313, 1181.5(3.1); Sent & Pun 2280.

Guitierrez v. State, TexCrimApp, 533 SW2d 14.—Controlled Subs 27, 80.

Guiton v. State, TexCrimApp, 742 SW2d 5.—Controlled Subs 30, 79, 81; Crim Law 552(3); Double J 109.

Guiton v. State, TexApp–Dallas, 679 SW2d 66, petition for discretionary review gr, aff 742 SW2d 5.—Controlled Subs 30, 68, 81; Crim Law 673(2).

Guity v. C.C.I. Enterprise, Co., TexApp–Houston (1 Dist), 54 SW3d 526.—Costs 194.18; Judgm 181(21), 185.3(1), 186; Labor & Emp 2405.

Gulbenkian v. Penn, Tex, 252 SW2d 929, 151 Tex 412.—Estop 52.15; Judgm 178, 181(2), 181(19), 185(2), 185(5), 186.

Gulbenkian v. Penn, TexCivApp–Amarillo, 276 SW2d 939, ref nre.—Pat 218(3); Trial 391.

Gulden; Hamra v., TexApp–Dallas, 898 SW2d 16, writ dism woj.—Antitrust 397; Compromise 15(1); Damag 63.

Gulden v. McCorkle, CA5 (Tex), 680 F2d 1070, reh den 685 F2d 157, cert den 103 SCt 1194, 459 US 1206, 75 LEd2d 439.—Crim Law 393(1); Offic 69.7, 76; Witn 304(1).

Guleke; Department of Public Safety v., TexCivApp–Amarillo, 366 SW2d 662.—Autos 144.1(3), 144.2(4), 144.2(9.1), 144.2(10); Judgm 181(2).

Guleke v. Humble Oil & Refining Co., TexCivApp–Amarillo, 126 SW2d 38.—Mines 77, 78.2, 78.7(3.1), 78.7(4).

Gulf Aerospace Corp., In re, CA5 (Tex), 449 F2d 733.—Bankr 2366, 2397(1); Fed Cts 924.1.

Gulf & Basco Co. v. Buchanan, TexApp–Houston (1 Dist), 707 SW2d 655, ref nre.—App & E 173(2); Contracts 143(2), 176(2), 338(1); Evid 459(2), 459(3); Guar 30, 91; Plead 427.

Gulf & South American S.S. Co., Inc.; Strange v., CA5 (Tex), 495 F2d 1235.—Compromise 5(3), 19(1).

Gulf & South Am. S.S. Co.; McDaniel v., CA5 (Tex), 228 F2d 189.—Adm 34.1, 34.2, 34.4, 34.7, 65.

Gulf & South Am. S.S. Co.; McDaniel v., SDTex, 136 FSupp 892.—Adm 34.4.

Gulf & South Am. S.S. Co.; Phillips v., TexCivApp–Houston, 323 SW2d 631, writ refused.—Action 60; App & E 949; Damag 33, 34; Neglig 484; Torts 135.

Gulf & South Am. S.S. Co.; Stovall v., SDTex, 30 FRD 152.—Fed Civ Proc 1477, 1489, 1581, 1616, 1620.

Gulf Atlantic Life Ins. Co. v. Disbro, TexCivApp–Beaumont, 613 SW2d 511.—App & E 845(2), 934(2); Contracts 147(2); Insurance 1805, 2525(1).

Gulf Atlantic Life Ins. Co.; Hurlbut v., Tex, 749 SW2d 762.—App & E 1083(6); Libel 36, 37, 38(1), 50, 51(1), 130, 135, 136, 139; Lim of Act 199(2); Torts 244; Trial 366.

Gulf Atlantic Life Ins. Co. v. Hurlbut, TexApp–Dallas, 749 SW2d 96.—Atty & C 104; Libel 9(1); Lim of Act 100(12), 197(2).

Gulf Atlantic Life Ins. Co. v. Hurlbut, TexApp–Dallas, 696 SW2d 83, writ gr, opinion supplemented 749 SW2d 96, rev 749 SW2d 762.—Action 38(4); App & E 170(1), 218.2(7); Consp 1.1, 8, 16; Damag 114, 190; Libel 6(1), 33, 36, 38(1), 51(2), 76, 80, 93, 112(2), 130, 136, 139; Lim of Act 13, 95(6), 100(1), 100(11), 100(13), 195(3), 197(2); Mal Pros 39; Plead 36(2); Proc 168; Torts 214, 242, 244, 265, 424; Trial 366.

Gulf Atlantic Life Ins. Co.; Price v., TexCivApp–Texarkana, 621 SW2d 185, ref nre.—App & E 1074(3), 1192, 1212(3); Evid 113(14); Mtg 572.

Gulf Atlantic Life Ins. Co. v. Price, TexCivApp–Tyler, 566 SW2d 381, ref nre, appeal after remand 621 SW2d 185, ref nre.—New Tr 60; Trial 358; Usury 119.

Gulf Atlantic Warehouse Co.; Jugoslavenska Oceanska Plovidba v., TexCivApp–Hous (1 Dist), 507 SW2d 892, ref nre.—Ship 103, 105, 110, 120, 132(5.1); Wareh 34(7).

Gulf Beneficial Soc. v. Sharp, TexCivApp–Beaumont, 87 SW2d 826.—App & E 1064.1(6); Insurance 1848, 2534, 2539; J P 87(9).

Gulf Bitulithic Co.; LeBlanc, Inc. v., TexCivApp–Tyler, 412 SW2d 86, ref nre.—App & E 218.2(7), 930(1), 930(3), 1062.1; Contracts 143.5, 147(3), 166, 303(5), 328(1); Damag 22; Neglig 371, 1614, 1615, 1625, 1675, 1713, 1714; Trial 352.12.

Gulf Bitulithic Co. v. R. T. Herrin Petroleum Transport Co., TexCivApp–Hous (1 Dist), 423 SW2d 355.—App & E 994(2), 1003(3); Neglig 1664, 1678.

Gulf Bitulithic Co. v. Scanlan, TexCivApp–Galveston, 91 SW2d 814, writ refused, cert den 57 SCt 48, 299 US 582, 81 LEd 429.—Mun Corp 514(2), 522, 530.

Gulf Bitulithic Co.; Spoor v., TexCivApp–Galveston, 172 SW2d 377, writ refused wom.—Ack 25; App & E 1001(1); Mech Liens 73(6), 303(1); Mun Corp 434(5), 586.

Gulf Bowl, Inc.; Garrison v., TexCivApp–Corpus Christi, 582 SW2d 603.—App & E 205, 544(1), 554(3), 569(3), 907(3).

Gulf Brewing Co. v. Goodwin, TexCivApp–Galveston, 135 SW2d 812, writ dism, correct.—App & E 989; Autos 245(78), 245(80).

Gulf Brewing Co.; Grand Prize Distributing Co. of San Antonio v., TexCivApp–San Antonio, 267 SW2d 906, writ refused.—Antitrust 582; Courts 91(1).

Gulf Bldg. Corp.; Collins v., TexCivApp–Galveston, 83 SW2d 1093, writ refused.—Land & Ten 169(11); Neglig 1032, 1595.

Gulf Canal Lines, Inc., In re, SDTex, 216 FSupp 434.—Damag 132(9.1); Seamen 29(1), 29(2), 29(5.12), 29(5.14).

Gulf Canal Lines, Inc. v. U.S., SDTex, 258 FSupp 864, aff 87 SCt 1161, 386 US 348, 18 LEd2d 98.—Commerce 85.34, 182.1; Statut 219(7).

Gulf, C. & S. F. Ry. Co., Ex parte, CA5 (Tex), 308 F2d 803.—Fed Cts 113.

Gulf, C. & S. F. Ry. Co. v. Abbey, TexCivApp–Fort Worth, 313 SW2d 108.—App & E 1003(5), 1177(7); Em Dom 221, 224, 255; Evid 18, 568(4), 591.

Gulf, C. & S. F. Ry. Co. v. American Sugar Refining Co., TexCivApp–Austin, 130 SW2d 1030, writ refused.—

Carr 12(1), 18(1), 18(2), 18(3), 18(6); Const Law 48(1), 4363.

Gulf, C. & S.F. Ry. Co. v. Ballinger Co-op. Gin Co., TexCivApp–Austin, 351 SW2d 306, ref nre.—App & E 930(1), 989, 1001(3); Bridges 27.

Gulf, C. & S. F. Ry. Co. v. Bell, TexCivApp–Austin, 101 SW2d 363, writ dism.—Labor & Emp 2866, 2877, 2881; Neglig 210.

Gulf, C. & S.F. Ry. Co. v. Bliss, Tex, 368 SW2d 594.—App & E 218.2(4); Contrib 9(5); Indem 59, 68; Plead 34(1), 34(3), 37, 236(3); Trial 355(1).

Gulf, C. & S.F. Ry. Co. v. Bliss, TexCivApp–Beaumont, 363 SW2d 343, aff in part, rev in part 368 SW2d 594.—Contrib 5(2), 5(4), 9(5); Indem 64; Judgm 198.

Gulf, C. & S. F. Ry. Co. v. Bouchillon, TexCivApp–Eastland, 186 SW2d 1006, writ refused wom.—App & E 216(1), 927(7), 1001(1); Neglig 1656, 1676; R R 346(5.1), 350(3), 350(7.1); Trial 68(1), 122, 133.6(6), 350.2, 366.

Gulf, C. & S. F. Ry. Co.; Boyer v., TexCivApp–Houston, 306 SW2d 215, 80 ALR2d 287, ref nre.—App & E 302(1), 653(3), 930(3); Autos 244(5); Neglig 281, 282; R R 346(7); Trial 356(3), 365.4, 426.

Gulf, C. & S. F. Ry. Co. v. Burch, TexCivApp–Beaumont, 151 SW2d 288, writ dism, correct.—App & E 1175(5); R R 324(1).

Gulf, C. & S.F. Ry. Co. v. City of Beaumont, Tex, 373 SW2d 741.—App & E 22, 1145, 1180(1), 1206, 1212(3); Courts 207.4(1.1), 207.5.

Gulf, C. & S. F. Ry. Co. v. Clark, TexCivApp–Texarkana, 337 SW2d 706.—App & E 931(1), 989, 1010.1(1), 1012.1(1); R R 417, 425, 443(1).

Gulf, C. & S. F. Ry. Co. v. Coca-Cola Bottling Co. of Cleburne, CA5 (Tex), 363 F2d 465.—Fed Cts 800; Indem 27, 31(1), 102, 104.

Gulf, C. & S. F. Ry. Co.; Couch v., TexCivApp–Dallas, 292 SW2d 901, ref nre.—Em Dom 149(4), 202(1), 235, 262(5).

Gulf, C. & S. F. Ry. Co.; Davidson v., TexCivApp–Fort Worth, 136 SW2d 923, writ dism, correct.—Neglig 1040(3), 1045(3); R R 355(1), 398(1).

Gulf, C. & S.F. Ry. Co. v. Deen v., USTex, 77 SCt 715, 353 US 925, 1 LEd2d 721, on remand 306 SW2d 171, rev and remanded 312 SW2d 933, 158 Tex 466, mandamus gr 79 SCt 1, 358 US 57, 3 LEd2d 28, cert den 79 SCt 111, 358 US 874, 3 LEd2d 105.—Labor & Emp 2881.

Gulf, C. & S. F. Ry. Co. v. Deen, Tex, 317 SW2d 913, 159 Tex 238, cert den 79 SCt 725, 359 US 945, 3 LEd2d 678.—Fed Cts 513.

Gulf, C. & S.F. Ry. Co. v. Deen, Tex, 312 SW2d 933, 158 Tex 466, mandamus gr Deen v. Hickman, 79 SCt 1, 358 US 57, 3 LEd2d 28, cert den 79 SCt 111, 358 US 874, 3 LEd2d 105.—App & E 1001(1), 1003(5), 1083(3), 1083(4), 1091(1), 1140(2), 1175(5), 1177(2), 1177(7); Fed Cts 502, 513; Judgm 199(3.5), 199(3.7); New Tr 72(6), 162(1); Trial 349(1).

Gulf, C. & S.F. Ry. Co. v. Deen, TexCivApp–Eastland, 306 SW2d 171, rev and remanded 312 SW2d 933, 158 Tex 466, mandamus gr Deen v. Hickman, 79 SCt 1, 358 US 57, 3 LEd2d 28, cert den 79 SCt 111, 358 US 874, 3 LEd2d 105.—App & E 1004(8), 1198; Labor & Emp 2824.

Gulf, C. & S. F. Ry. Co. v. Deen, TexCivApp–Eastland, 275 SW2d 529, ref nre, cert gr Deen v. Gulf, Colorado and Santa Fe Railway Company, 77 SCt 52, 352 US 820, 1 LEd2d 45, rev 77 SCt 715, 353 US 925, 1 LEd2d 721, on remand 306 SW2d 171, rev and remanded 312 SW2d 933, 158 Tex 466, mandamus gr 79 SCt 1, 358 US 57, 3 LEd2d 28, cert den 79 SCt 111, 358 US 874, 3 LEd2d 105.—App & E 1175(5); Labor & Emp 2875, 2992.

Gulf, C. & S. F. Ry. Co. v. DeLeon, TexCivApp–Eastland, 373 SW2d 886, ref nre.—App & E 1051(1), 1060.1(1); Courts 97(5); Labor & Emp 2824; Trial 350.6(6).

Gulf, C. & S. F. Ry. Co.; Dennis v., Tex, 224 SW2d 704, 148 Tex 387.—Action 53(2); Death 31(8); R R 22(3).

Gulf, C. & S. F. Ry. Co.; Ealand v., TexCivApp–Beaumont, 411 SW2d 591.—App & E 930(3); Indem 33(7), 35, 102; Work Comp 2142.25.

Gulf, C. & S. F. Ry. Co.; Fleming & Sons v., CA5 (Tex), 187 F2d 536.—Admin Law 759; Carr 79; Courts 89.

Gulf, C. & S. F. Ry. Co.; Fouse v., TexCivApp–Fort Worth, 193 SW2d 241.—Plead 104(2), 110, 111.47; Venue 21, 24, 74.

Gulf, C. & S.F. Ry. Co.; Fox v., TexCivApp–Galveston, 80 SW2d 1072, writ dism.—Labor & Emp 2814.

Gulf, C. & S.F. Ry. Co.; Fulgham v., TexCivApp–Austin, 288 SW2d 811, ref nre.—Tax 2560, 3221.

Gulf, C. & S. F. Ry. Co. v. Giun, TexComApp, 116 SW2d 693, 131 Tex 548, 116 ALR 795.—App & E 203.3, 207, 1060.1(2.1); Evid 314(4); Trial 352.10, 352.11.

Gulf, C. & S. F. R. Co.; Giun v., TexCivApp–Austin, 89 SW2d 465, rev 116 SW2d 693, 131 Tex 548, 116 ALR 795.—Evid 314(4); R R 396(1); Trial 114, 120(1), 228(3).

Gulf, C. & S. F. Ry. Co.; Griffin v., TexCivApp–San Antonio, 298 SW2d 659.—Carr 132, 134, 136; Stip 14(12); Trial 352.10.

Gulf, C. & S. F. Ry. Co. v. Hamilton, TexComApp, 89 SW2d 208, 126 Tex 542.—App & E 782; Courts 247(7), 247(8).

Gulf, C. & S. F. Ry. Co. v. Hampton, TexCivApp–Eastland, 358 SW2d 690, ref nre.—App & E 932(1); Damag 132(3), 167, 208(1); Trial 115(2), 122, 133.2, 133.6(4), 133.6(7).

Gulf, C. & S. F. Ry. Co.; Hanks v., Tex, 320 SW2d 333, 159 Tex 311.—Witn 406.

Gulf, C. & S. F. Ry. Co. v. Hanks, TexCivApp–Fort Worth, 308 SW2d 165, rev 320 SW2d 333, 159 Tex 311.—Em Dom 262(5); Evid 200, 219(1), 222(1), 265(1).

Gulf, C. & S. F. R. Co. v. Harry Newton, Inc., TexCivApp–Fort Worth, 430 SW2d 223, ref nre.—Labor & Emp 3105(5).

Gulf, C. & S. F. Ry. Co.; Hauck v., TexCivApp–Dallas, 246 SW2d 913, ref nre.—Carr 51, 177(1), 177(4).

Gulf, C. & S. F. Ry. Co. v. Hillis, TexCivApp–Waco, 320 SW2d 687.—App & E 1050.1(10); Carr 104; Evid 113(16), 333(7).

Gulf, C. & S. F. Ry. Co. v. Irick, TexCivApp–Austin, 116 SW2d 1099, writ dism.—App & E 1062.2; Neglig 440(1), 503, 506(2), 506(7), 552(1), 1538, 1717; R R 273.5, 275(1), 275(2), 278(2), 282(5), 282(9); Trial 350.5(5), 352.4(1).

Gulf, C. & S. F. Ry. Co. v. Jones, TexCivApp–Eastland, 221 SW2d 1010, ref nre.—Neglig 431; R R 327(12); Trial 350.1, 350.8, 351.2(6), 352.4(1), 352.18.

Gulf, C. & S. F. Ry. Co.; Kane v., TexCivApp–Galveston, 176 SW2d 965.—Inj 133.

Gulf, C. & S. F. R. Co.; Kimmey v., TexCivApp–Beaumont, 128 SW2d 539.—App & E 1060.1(6); R R 346(6); Trial 122.

Gulf, C. & S. F. Ry. Co. v. King, CA5 (Tex), 303 F2d 124.—Fed Cts 113; Labor & Emp 2881.

Gulf, C. & S. F. Ry. Co.; Lackey v., TexCivApp–Austin, 225 SW2d 630.—Evid 5(2); R R 327(2), 348(2), 348(8); Statut 47.

Gulf, C. & S. F. Ry. Co. v. Latham, TexCivApp–Galveston, 288 SW2d 289, ref nre.—App & E 843(2), 1003(5); Neglig 530(1), 1683, 1717; R R 348(6.1), 350(33); Trial 121(4).

Gulf, C. & S. F. Ry. Co.; Lee v., TexCivApp–Austin, 157 SW2d 424.—R R 303(1), 348(1).

Gulf, C. & S. F. Ry. Co.; Lewis v., TexCivApp–Galveston, 229 SW2d 395, writ dism.—R R 22(3); Venue 21, 46.

Gulf, C. & S. F. Ry. Co. v. McBride, Tex, 322 SW2d 492, 159 Tex 442.—App & E 1089(1), 1175(2); Equity 71(1), 72(1); Indem 42, 100; Judgm 185(2), 185(6), 185.3(2); Plead 67, 78.

GULF

Gulf, C. & S.F. Ry. Co. v. McBride, TexCivApp–Eastland, 309 SW2d 846, writ gr, rev 322 SW2d 492, 159 Tex 442.—Indem 31(4), 33(3), 42, 100; Judgm 181(15.1).

Gulf, C. & S. F. Ry. Co. v. McCandless, TexCivApp–Eastland, 190 SW2d 185.—App & E 1177(6); Carr 30, 156(1); Princ & A 101(2).

Gulf, C. & S. F. Ry. Co. v. McClelland, CA5 (Tex), 355 F2d 196.—Fed Cts 907; Labor & Emp 2806; Lim of Act 199(1).

Gulf, C. & S. F. Ry. Co.; Maddox v., TexCivApp–Fort Worth, 293 SW2d 499, ref nre.—App & E 206.2, 655(2), 1170.1, 1170.6, 1170.7; Damag 184; Em Dom 205, 247(1), 262(3), 262(5), 265(4).

Gulf, C. & S. F. R. Co. v. Matlock, TexCivApp–Austin, 244 SW2d 706.—R R 410.

Gulf, C. & S. F. Ry. Co.; Matlock v., TexCivApp–Austin, 99 SW2d 1056, writ dism.—Evid 419(20); Frds St of 129(2); Labor & Emp 835.

Gulf, C. & S. F. Ry. Co.; Menefee v., TexCivApp–Amarillo, 181 SW2d 287, writ refused wom.—App & E 837(1), 933(1), 1001(1), 1015(5); New Tr 44(3), 56, 140(3), 142, 143(5); R R 348(2), 348(6.1), 350(10), 352; Trial 358, 365.3.

Gulf, C. & S. F. Ry. Co. v. Metcalf, TexCivApp–Beaumont, 100 SW2d 389.—App & E 969, 1046.5; Evid 113(22), 271(2); Trial 18, 29(1).

Gulf, C. & S. F. Ry. Co.; Murray Co. v., NDTex, 59 FSupp 366.—Admin Law 228.1; Carr 30; Commerce 89(1), 89(3).

Gulf, C. & S. F. Ry. Co. v. Ogden, TexCivApp–Beaumont, 228 SW2d 569, ref nre.—Labor & Emp 2761, 2881, 2883, 2896.

Gulf, C. & S. F. Ry. Co.; Parker v., TexCivApp–Tyler, 401 SW2d 265.—App & E 1043(6); Pretrial Proc 480; Trial 352.4(1).

Gulf, C. & S. F. R. Co. v. Parmer, TexCivApp–Beaumont, 389 SW2d 558, ref nre.—App & E 930(1), 989, 1003(10), 1170.6; Damag 163(4), 191; Evid 383(10), 568(6); Jury 87; Neglig 1717; R R 304, 307.3, 327(1), 348(2), 348(3), 348(8), 350(1), 350(11), 350(13), 350(33); Trial 122, 131(3).

Gulf, C. & S. F. Ry. Co.; Paschall v., TexCivApp–Dallas, 100 SW2d 183, mod Campbell v. Paschall, 121 SW2d 593, 132 Tex 226.—App & E 662(1), 999(1), 1001(1), 1015(5), 1040(10), 1050.1(4), 1060.1(1); Autos 6, 181(1); Counties 122(1); Evid 5(2), 353(2), 370(1); New Tr 52; R R 99(6.1), 303(4), 350(3); Trial 115(2), 133.6(4).

Gulf, C. & S. F. Ry. Co.; Pass v., TexCivApp–Austin, 83 SW2d 729, writ dism.—R R 275(4).

Gulf, C. & S. F. Ry. Co. v. Payne, TexCivApp–Fort Worth, 308 SW2d 146.—Em Dom 112, 137, 203(2), 271; Evid 591.

Gulf, C. & S. F. Ry. Co. v. Pearce, TexCivApp–Beaumont, 105 SW2d 770, writ refused.—Carr 20(5.5).

Gulf, C. & S. F. Ry. Co. v. Picard, TexCivApp–Beaumont, 147 SW2d 303, writ dism, correct.—App & E 1062.1; Damag 130.1; Neglig 1694, 1717; R R 350(26); Trial 350.6(4), 351.5(6), 352.1(8), 352.16.

Gulf, C. & S. F. Ry. Co.; Pittman v., TexCivApp–Eastland, 338 SW2d 774,ref nre, cert den Gulf, Colorado and Sante Fe Railway Company v. Pittman, 82 SCt 49, 368 US 828, 7 LEd2d 31.—Courts 97(5); Labor & Emp 2886, 2918; Trial 139.1(5.1), 143, 178.

Gulf, C. & S. F. R. Co. v. Pratt, TexCivApp–San Antonio, 262 SW2d 775, ref nre.—Autos 244(41.1), 244(58); R R 307.3, 307.4(1), 316(2), 338.1, 338.2, 348(2), 348(5), 348(6.1), 352.

Gulf, C. & S. F. Ry. Co.; Robinson v., TexCivApp–Fort Worth, 325 SW2d 432, writ refused, cert den 80 SCt 672, 362 US 919, 4 LEd2d 739.—App & E 1170.1, 1170.6; Labor & Emp 2881; Trial 350.6(6).

Gulf, C. & S. F. Ry. Co. v. Russell, TexComApp, 82 SW2d 948, 125 Tex 443.—App & E 1001(1); R R 357, 359(1), 367, 369(3), 381(3), 387, 396(1), 396(2), 398(2).

Gulf, C. & S. F. Ry. Co.; Sandsberry v., NDTex, 114 FSupp 834.—Fed Cts 247; Labor & Emp 2043; Rem of C 19(5), 25(1).

Gulf, C. & S. F. Ry. Co.; Schavrda v., SDTex, 60 FSupp 658.—Labor & Emp 2805.

Gulf, C. & S. F. Ry. Co. v. Seydler, TexCivApp–Galveston, 132 SW2d 453.—Mand 48, 50; Plead 382(1); Trial 355(1); Waters 171(3).

Gulf, C. & S.F. Ry. Co. v. Shamburger, TexCivApp–Galveston, 231 SW2d 784.—App & E 1004(5); Damag 130.1.

Gulf, C. & S.F. Ry. Co. v. Simpson, TexCivApp–Beaumont, 331 SW2d 785, ref nre.—App & E 882(17); R R 282(7.1).

Gulf, C. & S. F. Ry. Co. v. Sklar, TexCivApp–Galveston, 134 SW2d 771, writ dism.—Carr 209, 217(1), 227(1), 228(1), 228(5); Trial 352.4(8).

Gulf, C. & S. F. Ry. Co. v. Snow, TexCivApp–Beaumont, 146 SW2d 1040, writ dism, correct.—App & E 1177(7); R R 382(6), 396(1), 398(2), 398(4), 400(6), 400(11).

Gulf, C. & S. F. Ry. Co.; Sunset Exp. v., TexCivApp–Fort Worth, 154 SW2d 860, writ refused wom.—Admin Law 413, 491; Autos 104, 107(2); Evid 20(2); Pub Ut 149, 169.1.

Gulf, C. & S. F. Ry. Co. v. Tadlock, TexCivApp–Galveston, 103 SW2d 428.—Costs 214.

Gulf, C. & S. F. Ry. Co.; Ullman Estate v., TexCivApp–Dallas, 292 SW2d 897, ref nre.—Em Dom 185, 196, 239, 262(5); Pretrial Proc 718.

Gulf, C. & S. F. Ry. Co. v. Waterhouse, TexCivApp–Beaumont, 223 SW2d 654, ref nre.—App & E 933(4); Labor & Emp 2761, 2783, 2784, 2832, 2839, 2881, 2925, 2950; New Tr 56, 140(3).

Gulf, C. & S. F. Ry. Co.; Western Transport Co. v., TexCivApp–Waco, 414 SW2d 218, ref nre.—Judgm 199(3.18); R R 307.3, 307.4(1), 348(2), 348(5); Trial 350.2.

Gulf, C. & S. F. Ry. Co. v. White, TexCivApp–Dallas, 281 SW2d 441, ref nre.—App & E 662(1); Estop 92(1); Zoning 14, 331, 435, 701.

Gulf Cas. Co. v. Archer, TexCivApp–El Paso, 118 SW2d 976, writ dism.—App & E 1060.1(8); Damag 34; Evid 359(4), 553(1), 553(2), 555.10; Trial 125(3), 350.3(8), 351.2(5); Work Comp 1908, 1929, 1968(3).

Gulf Cas. Co. v. Bostick, TexCivApp–Galveston, 116 SW2d 915, writ dism.—Damag 221(5.1); Evid 574; Work Comp 1923, 1927.

Gulf Cas. Co. v. Fields, TexCivApp–El Paso, 107 SW2d 661, writ dism.—App & E 664(4); Evid 474(3), 563; Plead 304; Trial 121(3), 125(4), 133.1, 133.6(7), 350.3(8), 351.2(4); Work Comp 76.

Gulf Cas. Co. v. Hart, Tex, 175 SW2d 73, 141 Tex 642.—Work Comp 1139.

Gulf Cas. Co.; Hart v., TexCivApp–Fort Worth, 170 SW2d 491, rev 175 SW2d 73, 141 Tex 642.—Work Comp 1123, 1139, 1178, 1971.

Gulf Cas. Co. v. Hughes, TexCivApp–Beaumont, 230 SW2d 293.—App & E 1010.1(3), 1177(7); New Tr 70, 164; Trial 352.4(9); Work Comp 1283, 1726, 1924, 1927, 1928, 1964, 1975.

Gulf Cas. Co. v. Jones, TexCivApp–Texarkana, 290 SW2d 334, ref nre.—Work Comp 905, 1831, 1916, 1968(5).

Gulf Cas. Co.; Rudd v., TexCivApp–El Paso, 257 SW2d 809.—Evid 171; Witn 372(2), 374(1); Work Comp 548, 1394, 1926.

Gulf Cas. Co. v. Tucker, TexCivApp–Beaumont, 201 SW2d 81.—Plead 236(3); Trial 351.5(8), 352.4(9); Work Comp 1917, 1919, 1940.

Gulf Chemical & Metallurgical Corp. v. Associated Metals & Minerals Corp., CA5 (Tex), 1 F3d 365.—Indem 33(4); Insurance 1806, 1812, 1822, 1823, 1832(1), 2278(3), 2913, 2914, 2915, 2923, 3336, 3585.

Gulf Chemical & Metallurgical Corp. v. Associated Metals and Minerals Corp., SDTex, 765 FSupp 375, vac 1 F3d 365.—Insurance 2275.

Gulf Coast Alloy Welding, Inc.; Best Industrial Uniform Supply Co., Inc.v., TexApp–Amarillo, 41 SW3d 145, review den, and reh of petition for review den.— App & E 946, 961; Pretrial Proc 14.1, 15, 40, 44.1, 45.

Gulf Coast Alloy Welding, Inc. v. Legal Sec. Life Ins. Co., TexApp–Houston (1 Dist), 981 SW2d 239, reh overr, and review dism.—Insurance 1117(3); Judgm 181(2), 185(2); Labor & Emp 407; States 18.51.

Gulf Coast Aluminum Supply, Inc. v. Duke, TexCivApp–Tyler, 389 SW2d 480.—Evid 25(1); Venue 7.5(3), 8.5(3).

Gulf Coast Bank & Trust Co.; Holloway-Houston, Inc. v., TexApp–Houston (1 Dist), 224 SW3d 353, reh overr. —App & E 852; Sec Tran 188, 190.

Gulf Coast Builders & Supply Co.; Gutierrez v., TexApp–Corpus Christi, 739 SW2d 371, writ den.—Cons Cred 4; States 18.19.

Gulf Coast Business Forms, Inc. v. Texas Employment Commission, Tex, 498 SW2d 154.—Decl Judgm 271.

Gulf Coast Business Forms, Inc. v. Texas Employment Commission, TexCivApp–Beaumont, 493 SW2d 260, ref nre 498 SW2d 154.—Decl Judgm 253, 271.

Gulf Coast Carriers, Inc.; Powell v., TexApp–Houston (14 Dist), 872 SW2d 22, reh den.—Alt Disp Res 329, 330, 362(1), 362(2), 363(8), 374(4), 386.

Gulf Coast Centers, Ltd.; Wadkins v., SDTex, 77 FSupp2d 794.—Asylums 7; Civil R 1027, 1345, 1351(1); Const Law 1083, 1084; Fed Civ Proc 2491.5, 2515; Health 699; Lim of Act 127(5); Mun Corp 723.

Gulf Coast Chemical Co. v. Hopkins, TexCivApp–Dallas, 145 SW2d 928.—App & E 1010.1(1), 1010.1(8.1); Autos 372(3.1), 372(4); Larc 1.

Gulf Coast Cigar Co., Inc.; Astrocard Co., Inc. v., TexCivApp–Hous (14 Dist), 588 SW2d 663.—Acct Action on 15; Judgm 183.

Gulf Coast Coalition of Cities v. Public Utility Com'n, TexApp–Austin, 161 SW3d 706.—Admin Law 387, 390.1, 391, 404.1, 412.1, 413, 763, 797; Electricity 11.3(6); Pub Ut 169.1, 194.

Gulf Coast Collection Agency Co.; Cunningham v., TexCivApp–Hous (1 Dist), 422 SW2d 233.—App & E 692(1); Evid 317(1), 317(12); Plead 291(2); Princ & A 21.

Gulf Coast Community Services; Shepherd v., CA5 (Tex), 221 FedAppx 308.—Fed Civ Proc 2533.1; Fed Cts 634.

Gulf Coast Conference; Naschke v., TexApp–Houston (14 Dist), 187 SW3d 653, review den.—Damag 71; Judgm 199(3.10).

Gulf Coast Contracting Services, Inc.; Johnson v., TexApp–Beaumont, 746 SW2d 327, writ den.—App & E 1001(3); Pretrial Proc 45; Seamen 2, 29(5.14), 29(5.16), 29(5.17).

Gulf Coast Dodge, Inc.; Bosworth v., TexApp–Houston (14 Dist), 879 SW2d 152.—App & E 205, 1056.2, 1079, 1116; Autos 370, 374, 385; Consp 1.1; Damag 91(1); Fraud 1; Trover 1, 4, 10, 35, 60.

Gulf Coast Enterprises; Herbert v., TexApp–Houston (1 Dist), 915 SW2d 866. See Herbert v. Greater Gulf Coast Enterprises, Inc.

Gulf Coast Factors, Inc. v. Hamilton Supply Corp., TexCivApp–Houston, 389 SW2d 341.—Fact 53, 66; Sales 53(1), 168.5(1).

Gulf Coast Farmers Co-op. v. Valley Co-op Oil Mill, TexCivApp–Corpus Christi, 572 SW2d 726.—Agric 6; Contracts 26, 169; Damag 126; Judgm 199(3.15); Trover 40(1), 40(4), 66.

Gulf Coast Indus. Workers v. Exxon Chemical Americas, SDTex, 863 FSupp 423, aff 53 F3d 1281, cert den 116 SCt 180, 516 US 865, 133 LEd2d 119.—Labor & Emp 1591, 1592, 1595(12), 1619, 1623(1), 1624(1).

Gulf Coast Indus. Workers Union v. Exxon Co., USA, CA5 (Tex), 70 F3d 847.—Alt Disp Res 362(2), 363(6), 374(1); Labor & Emp 1608.

Gulf Coast Indus. Workers Union v. Exxon Co., U.S.A., CA5 (Tex), 991 F2d 244, cert den 114 SCt 441, 510 US 965, 126 LEd2d 375.—Alt Disp Res 312, 363(9), 374(1); Fed Cts 766; Labor & Emp 1604, 1609(2), 1619.

Gulf Coast Indus. Workers' Union v. Exxon Co., U.S.A., CA5 (Tex), 712 F2d 161.—Fed Cts 724; Labor & Emp 2034, 2037, 2038, 2163.

Gulf Coast Inv. Corp.; Avant v., TexCivApp–Dallas, 457 SW2d 134.—Trial 304, 351.2(4), 351.2(8), 352.9; Usury 142(4).

Gulf Coast Inv. Corp. v. Brown, Tex, 821 SW2d 159.— Lim of Act 105(2), 106.

Gulf Coast Inv. Corp. v. Brown, TexApp–Houston (14 Dist), 813 SW2d 218, writ gr, rev in part 821 SW2d 159. —Atty & C 129(1), 129(4); Judgm 181(5.1), 181(12), 185(2); Lim of Act 55(3), 95(1); Plead 245(1), 258(1).

Gulf Coast Inv. Corp.; Gallegos v., Tex, 491 SW2d 659.— App & E 1175(1).

Gulf Coast Inv. Corp.; Gallegos v., TexCivApp–Hous (1 Dist), 483 SW2d 944, writ gr, set aside 491 SW2d 659.— App & E 927(1), 1058(1); Bills & N 146, 343, 452(3), 452(4); Contracts 86, 94(5); Evid 381; Judgm 252(5); Plead 339, 420(2).

Gulf Coast Inv. Corp. v. Lawyers Sur. Corp., Tex, 416 SW2d 779.—Lim of Act 22(8), 28(1).

Gulf Coast Inv. Corp.; Lawyers Sur. Corp. v., TexCivApp–Tyler, 410 SW2d 654, ref nre 416 SW2d 779.—Ack 48; Lim of Act 24(2), 28(1); Notaries 2, 11.

Gulf Coast Inv. Corp. v. Nasa 1 Business Center, Tex, 754 SW2d 152.—Motions 36; Pretrial Proc 699.

Gulf Coast Inv. Corp.; Piano v., TexCivApp–Hous (14 Dist), 429 SW2d 554, writ dism.—App & E 347(1), 624, 627, 907(3); Contracts 143(1); Plead 104(2), 111.12; Pretrial Proc 716; Venue 7.5(2), 7.5(4).

Gulf Coast Inv. Corp. v. Prichard, TexCivApp–Dallas, 438 SW2d 658, writ gr, and order set aside, ref nre 447 SW2d 676.—Plead 387; Usury 42, 64, 100(1).

Gulf Coast Inv. Corp. v. Rothman, Tex, 506 SW2d 856.— Bills & N 216.

Gulf Coast Inv. Corp.; Rothman v., TexCivApp–Beaumont, 497 SW2d 792, writ gr, rev 506 SW2d 856.—App & E 1177(5); Damag 6, 117, 163(4), 189; Estop 52.10(2), 54; Lim of Act 25(3), 95(9); Trial 194(20).

Gulf Coast Land & Development Co.; Wiberg v., TexCivApp–Beaumont, 360 SW2d 563, ref nre.—App & E 241, 301; Corp 116, 307, 316(1), 316(4), 319(7); Interest 31, 39(1).

Gulf Coast Mach. & Supply Co.; Brown v., TexCivApp–Beaumont, 551 SW2d 397, ref nre.—App & E 103; Plead 111.42(9), 111.48; Venue 7.5(3).

Gulf Coast Mach. & Supply Co.; Fisher v., TexCivApp–Beaumont, 400 SW2d 941.—Em Dom 2(1.1).

Gulf Coast Marine Inc.; Toops v., CA5 (Tex), 72 F3d 483, reh den.—Fed Civ Proc 2544; Fed Cts 560, 776; Insurance 1805, 1831, 1832(1), 1835(2), 2116, 2659; Judgm 720, 724, 828.16(1).

Gulf Coast Marine Ways v. J.R. Hardee, SDTex, 107 FSupp 379.—Int Rev 4781, 4792; Liens 12; Mar Liens 14, 37(1), 37(4); Ship 31, 32; Subrog 32(1).

Gulf Coast Masonry, Inc. v. Owens-Illinois, Inc., Tex, 739 SW2d 239.—Indem 30(1).

Gulf Coast Masonry, Inc.; Owens-Illinois, Inc. v., TexApp–Beaumont, 722 SW2d 465, rev 739 SW2d 239.— Indem 30(1), 30(5).

Gulf Coast Medical Personnel; Kanida v., CA5 (Tex), 109 FedAppx 670.—Fed Civ Proc 2656.

Gulf Coast Medical Personnel LP; Kanida v., CA5 (Tex), 363 F3d 568.—Civil R 1137, 1536, 1556; Courts 90(2); Evid 106(3), 129(1); Fed Civ Proc 2015, 2182.1, 2497.1; Fed Cts 628, 630.1, 631, 763.1, 822, 823, 896.1, 901.1, 911, 915; Labor & Emp 792, 861, 874.

Gulf Coast Minerals Management Corp.; Myers v., Tex, 361 SW2d 193.—Contracts 147(1), 147(3); Courts 107; Mines 109; Trial 136(3).

Gulf Coast Minerals Management Corp. v. Myers, TexCivApp–San Antonio, 354 SW2d 944, writ gr, rev 361 SW2d 193.—Mines 109.

Gulf Coast Motor Freight Lines v. U.S., SDTex, 35 FSupp 136.—Commerce 14.10(1), 61(1), 85.27(1).

Gulf Coast Natural Gas Co.; Haas v., TexCivApp–Corpus Christi, 484 SW2d 127.—App & E 846(5); Mines 109.

Gulf Coast Natural Gas, Inc.; Shamrock Oil Co. v., TexApp–Houston (14 Dist), 68 SW3d 737, review den.—App & E 177; Compromise 20(2); Corp 508; Judgm 17(10); Pretrial Proc 44.1, 434, 435; Proc 153.

Gulf Coast Operators, Inc. v. Fleming Oil Co., TexCivApp–Houston, 393 SW2d 954.—App & E 758.1, 931(1), 1008.1(2), 1010.1(3); Costs 32(2), 194.22; Evid 590; Mines 110.

Gulf Coast Orchards Co.; Binge v., TexCivApp–San Antonio, 93 SW2d 813, writ dism.—App & E 213; Courts 121(5); Lim of Act 120, 148(1), 199(3).

Gulf Coast Orchards Co.; Felker v., TexCivApp–San Antonio, 81 SW2d 1044, writ dism.—Acct St 1; App & E 1047(3); Set-Off 26; Trial 193(1), 233(2).

Gulf Coast Real Estate Auction Co., Inc. v. Chevron Industries, Inc., CA5 (Tex), 665 F2d 574.—Evid 142(1); Fed Cts 764; Impl & C C 91, 98.

Gulf Coast Regional Blood Center v. Houston, TexApp–Fort Worth, 745 SW2d 557.—Const Law 1231, 3986; Pretrial Proc 19, 27.1, 40, 382; Records 32.

Gulf Coast Regional Blood Center; Schaefer v., CA5 (Tex), 10 F3d 327, reh den.—Death 15, 21, 37, 39; Fed Civ Proc 2544, 2546; Fed Cts 776; Lim of Act 31.

Gulf Coast Rental Tool Service, Inc.; Simon v., NDTex, 408 FSupp 911.—Fed Cts 371; Rem of C 48, 49.1(1), 49.1(6), 61(1), 61(2).

Gulf Coast Rice Mills v. Orkin Exterminating Co., Tex, 347 SW2d 250, 162 Tex 329.—App & E 356.

Gulf Coast Rice Mills; Orkin Exterminating Co. v., TexCivApp–Waco, 343 SW2d 768, writ dism 347 SW2d 250, 162 Tex 329, appeal after remand 362 SW2d 159, ref nre, cert den 84 SCt 170, 375 US 894, 11 LEd2d 123, appeal dism 84 SCt 175, 375 US 57, 11 LEd2d 122.—Contracts 323(1); Neglig 306; Sales 445(4).

Gulf Coast Rice Mills; Orkin Exterminating Co. v., TexCivApp–Houston, 362 SW2d 159, ref nre, cert den 84 SCt 170, 375 US 894, 11 LEd2d 123, appeal dism 84 SCt 175, 375 US 57, 11 LEd2d 122.—App & E 1057(1); Contracts 95(1), 323(1); Damag 62(3); Food 13; Interest 39(2.20); Judgm 256(1); Neglig 1697.

Gulf Coast Rice Producers Ass'n v. Block, SDTex, 617 FSupp 229.—Fed Cts 1073.1, 1139, 1158.

Gulf Coast Rod, Reel and Gun Club; Hearn v., CA5 (Tex), 153 F3d 190. See Gordon v. State of Tex.

Gulf Coast Rod, Reel and Gun Club; Steinhagen v., CA5 (Tex), 153 F3d 190. See Gordon v. State of Tex.

Gulf Coast Rod, Reel & Gun Club; Westchester Fire Ins. Co. v., TexApp–Houston (1 Dist), 64 SW3d 609.—Insurance 2101, 2261, 2275, 2914, 2939.

Gulf Coast Sailboats, Inc. v. McGuire, TexCivApp–Hous (14 Dist), 616 SW2d 385, ref nre.—App & E 989; Evid 570; New Tr 44(1), 44(2), 56; Nuis 4, 46, 49(5); Trial 304.

Gulf Coast State Bank v. Emenhiser, Tex, 562 SW2d 449.—App & E 302(1), 1064.4, 1078(1); Banks 189; Trial 194(12), 215, 232(2).

Gulf Coast State Bank v. Emenhiser, TexCivApp–Tyler, 544 SW2d 722, writ gr, rev 562 SW2d 449.—Cust & U 12(1), 18; Princ & A 195; Trial 366.

Gulf Coast State Bank v. Nelms, Tex, 525 SW2d 866.—Sec Tran 144.

Gulf Coast State Bank; Nelms v., TexCivApp–Hous (1 Dist), 516 SW2d 421, writ gr, aff 525 SW2d 866.—Autos 20; Sec Tran 144; Statut 206, 220, 230.

Gulf Coast Trawlers, Inc. v. Resolute Ins. Co., SDTex, 239 FSupp 424.—Insurance 2219, 2230, 2231, 2255.

Gulf Coast Waste Disposal Authority; Satterlee v., Tex, 576 SW2d 773.—Schools 102; Tax 2315.

Gulf Coast Waste Disposal Authority; Satterlee v., TexCivApp–Beaumont, 561 SW2d 869, writ gr, rev 576 SW2d 773.—Tax 2315, 2388.

Gulf Coast Water Co. v. Cartwright, TexCivApp–Galveston, 160 SW2d 269, writ refused wom.—Agric 3.4(1), 4(1); Const Law 2412; Land & Ten 200.3; Waters 257(1).

Gulf Coast Water Co. v. Hamman Exploration Co., TexCivApp–Galveston, 160 SW2d 92, writ refused.—App & E 931(6); Deeds 101; Ease 1, 36(3).

Gulf Coast Water Co.; Lower Colorado River Authority v., TexCivApp–Galveston, 107 SW2d 1101.—Inj 143(1), 144.

Gulf Collateral, Inc. v. Cauble, TexCivApp–Fort Worth, 462 SW2d 619.—App & E 1170.6; Contracts 140; Gaming 19(3); Judgm 185(2), 185(6), 186.

Gulf Collateral, Inc. v. Edwards, TexCivApp–Hous (1 Dist), 467 SW2d 690.—App & E 293, 499(1).

Gulf Collateral, Inc. v. George, TexCivApp–Tyler, 466 SW2d 21.—Gaming 19(3).

Gulf Collateral, Inc. v. Johnston, TexCivApp–Waco, 496 SW2d 123, ref nre.—Gaming 19(1), 19(3).

Gulf, Colorado & Santa Fe Ry. Co.; Dennis v., TexCivApp–Beaumont, 221 SW2d 352, certified question answered 224 SW2d 704, 148 Tex 387.—Death 41; R R 22(3).

Gulf, Colorado & Santa Fe Ry. Co. v. Smart, TexCivApp–Fort Worth, 222 SW2d 161, ref nre.—App & E 232(0.5); Labor & Emp 2941; Neglig 1741; Trial 352.1(6).

Gulf Consolidated Intern. Inc.; Burbank Intern. Ltd. v., NDTex, 441 FSupp 819.—Fed Cts 77, 104, 105, 144, 145.

Gulf Consolidated Intern., Inc. v. Murphy, Tex, 658 SW2d 565, on remand Murphy v. Gulf Consol Services, Inc, 666 SW2d 383.—App & E 719(1), 719(8), 826; Labor & Emp 867, 868(3), 868(4).

Gulf Consol. Services, Inc., In re, BkrtcySDTex, 110 BR 267.—Bankr 2955.

Gulf Consol. Services, Inc., In re, BkrtcySDTex, 91 BR 414.—Bankr 3187(1), 3187(2), 3187(3), 3193, 3196, 3197, 3198, 3203(6), 3204, 3205.

Gulf Consol. Services, Inc. v. Corinth Pipeworks, S.A., CA5 (Tex), 898 F2d 1071, cert den 111 SCt 256, 498 US 900, 112 LEd2d 214.—Fed Cts 76, 76.5, 86, 844, 850.1; Interest 39(2.20); Lim of Act 197(1); Sales 55.

Gulf Consol. Services, Inc.; Murphy v., TexApp–Houston (14 Dist), 666 SW2d 383.—Labor & Emp 868(1), 868(3), 871.

Gulf Const. Co. v. Mott, TexCivApp–Hous (14 Dist), 442 SW2d 778.—Libel 9(6), 41, 51(1), 54, 89(1), 101(4), 112(1), 112(2), 121(2).

Gulf Const. Co. v. St. Joe Paper Co., SDTex, 24 FRD 411.—Fed Civ Proc 1555, 1571, 1581, 1600(2), 1600(3), 1602, 1617.

Gulf Const. Co., Inc. v. Industrial Elec. Co., TexApp–Corpus Christi, 676 SW2d 624. See Gulf Const. Co., Inc. v. Self.

Gulf Const. Co., Inc. v. Self, TexApp–Corpus Christi, 676 SW2d 624, ref nre.—Contracts 155, 221(1), 221(2), 221(3); Evid 177; Interest 39(2.6), 39(2.30); Stip 1, 13, 14(10), 17(1), 17(3).

Gulf Const. Co., Inc. v. Shaw Plumbing Co., TexApp–Corpus Christi, 676 SW2d 624. See Gulf Const. Co., Inc. v. Self.

Gulf Copper; Vaughn v., EDTex, 54 FSupp2d 688.—Contracts 147(3), 153, 156; U S 75(1).

Gulfcraft, Inc. v. Henderson, TexCivApp–Galveston, 300 SW2d 768.—App & E 70(6), 704.2; Autos 193(10); Labor & Emp 23, 29; Plead 111.36, 111.42(8), 111.44.

Gulf Distributing Co.; Texas & N. O. R. Co. v., TexCivApp–San Antonio, 226 SW2d 653.—Carr 159(2).

Gulf Elec. Co.; Pereira v., TexCivApp–Waco, 343 SW2d 334, ref nre.—Judgm 253(2); Mech Liens 245(3), 260(1), 263(4), 281(1); Trial 352.5(1).

Gulf Electroquip, Inc.; General Elec. Supply Co., a Div. of General Elec. Co. v., TexApp–Houston (1 Dist), 857 SW2d 591, reh den, and writ den.—Damag 117; Judgm 181(29), 185.1(1); Sales 195, 372, 384(4); War 504.

Gulf Electroquip, Inc.; Naegeli Transp. v., TexApp–Houston (14 Dist), 853 SW2d 737, reh den, and writ den.—App & E 216(1), 216(7); Bailm 31(3), 32; Damag 40(2), 141, 159(1), 190; Evid 474(20), 539, 555.4(2).

Gulf Employees Credit Union; Allison v., EDTex, 836 FSupp 395, aff 32 F3d 565.—Civil R 1545; Fed Civ Proc 2497.1, 2544.

Gulf Energy & Development Corp. v. Davis, TexApp–Eastland, 624 SW2d 394, writ dism woj.—App & E 1024.3; Plead 111.42(5); Venue 7.5(8).

Gulf Energy Pipeline Co. v. Garcia, TexApp–San Antonio, 884 SW2d 821.—Em Dom 172, 225.1, 231, 235; Mand 4(4), 45, 53.

Gulf Fleet Supply Vessels Inc. v. Houston Pipe Line Co., CA5 (Tex), 71 F3d 198. See Corpus Christi Oil & Gas Co. v. Zapata Gulf Marine Corp.

Gulf Forge Co.; Bestway Systems, Inc. v., CA5 (Tex), 100 F3d 31.—Carr 194.

Gulf Forge Co. v. Ellwood Quality Steels Co., SDTex, 202 BR 238.—Sec Tran 94.

Gulf Forge Co.; Philadelphia Mfrs. Mut. Ins. Co. v., SDTex, 555 FSupp 519.—Antitrust 145; Contracts 175(1); Decl Judgm 322; Estop 85; Evid 442(1); Fed Civ Proc 2501; Insurance 3359, 3361, 3420; Neglig 1, 210, 218, 232.

Gulf Freeway Lumber Co. v. Houston Inv. Realty Trust, TexCivApp–Hous (14 Dist), 452 SW2d 39.—App & E 1010.1(1); Evid 400(2); Joint-St Co 18; Princ & A 136(2); Ven & Pur 25, 44, 79, 331.

Gulfgate Joint Venture; Allied Stores of Texas, Inc. v., TexApp–Houston (14 Dist), 726 SW2d 194, ref nre.—Evid 571(3); Waters 126(2).

Gulf Group Lloyds; Hernandez v., Tex, 875 SW2d 691.—Contracts 318; Insurance 1713, 1806, 2793(2).

Gulf Group Lloyds v. Hernandez, TexApp–San Antonio, 876 SW2d 162, writ gr, rev 875 SW2d 691.—Insurance 2793(2).

Gulf Health Care Center v. Fournet, TexApp–Beaumont, 979 SW2d 419. See Continued Care, Inc. v. Fournet.

Gulf Health Care Center-Galveston; Bartosh v., TexApp–Houston (14 Dist), 178 SW3d 434.—App & E 843(2), 1043(6), 1050.1(1), 1056.1(1), 1056.1(7), 1058(1), 1079; Evid 359(1), 508, 535, 555.2, 555.10, 571(3); Neglig 200, 212, 321, 1662; Trial 43, 56.

Gulf Holding Corp. v. Brazoria County, TexCivApp–Hous (14 Dist), 497 SW2d 614, ref nre.—App & E 954(1); Decl Judgm 185; Nav Wat 33, 41(1); Nuis 63, 78, 80, 84.

Gulf Indus. Products, Inc.; Cappuccitti v., TexApp–Houston (1 Dist), 222 SW3d 468.—App & E 842(2), 893(1), 1024.3, 1071.2; Const Law 3964, 3965(3), 3965(4); Corp 1.4(1), 1.4(4), 1.6(9), 1.7(2), 665(0.5), 665(1); Courts 12(2.1), 12(2.10), 12(2.15), 12(2.20), 35, 39.

Gulf Ins. Co. v. Adame, TexCivApp–Amarillo, 575 SW2d 87.—App & E 78(6); New Tr 110; Time 10(7).

Gulf Ins. Co.; Atlantic Mut. Ins. Co. v., TexCivApp–Texarkana, 596 SW2d 326.—Insurance 2663.

Gulf Ins. Co. v. Ball, TexCivApp–Amarillo, 324 SW2d 605, ref nre.—Aband L P 4; App & E 218.2(5.1), 736, 930(3), 1170.1; Evid 554; Insurance 1660, 2137(3), 3015; Trial 351.2(2), 366.

Gulf Ins. Co.; Bernard v., TexCivApp–El Paso, 542 SW2d 429, ref nre.—Decl Judgm 385; Insurance 2914; Judgm 735.

Gulf Ins. Co. v. Blair, TexCivApp–Dallas, 589 SW2d 786, ref nre.—Ex & Ad 20(9), 467, 506(1), 529, 537(9); Princ & S 66(1).

Gulf Ins. Co. v. Bobo, Tex, 595 SW2d 847.—Insurance 2660, 2663; Sec Tran 117, 163.

Gulf Ins. Co. v. Bobo, TexCivApp–Fort Worth, 580 SW2d 914, rev 595 SW2d 847.—Insurance 1794, 2652, 2663.

Gulf Ins. Co.; Brady Nat'l. Bank v., CA5 (Tex), 94 FedAppx 197.—Fed Cts 643; Insurance 2405, 2408.

Gulf Ins. Co.; Brownsville Fabrics, Inc. v., TexCivApp–Corpus Christi, 550 SW2d 332, ref nre, and writ dism woj.—Estop 52.10(2); Insurance 1654, 1669, 1670, 1766, 2000, 2110, 2141, 2201, 3043, 3081, 3091, 3093.

Gulf Ins. Co. v. Burns Motors, Inc., Tex, 22 SW3d 417.—Contracts 143(2), 176(2); Evid 448; Indem 31(1), 31(2); Insurance 1651, 1654; Judgm 91.

Gulf Ins. Co.; Burns Motors, Inc. v., TexApp–Corpus Christi, 975 SW2d 810, reh overr, and review gr, and rev, rev 22 SW3d 417.—App & E 934(1); Assign 22; Contracts 143(2), 176(2); Indem 30(1); Insurance 1651; Judgm 181(8), 181(23), 183, 185(2), 185(6), 185.1(1), 186.

Gulf Ins. Co.; Carpenter v., TexCivApp–San Antonio, 515 SW2d 60.—Work Comp 1923, 1924, 1941.

Gulf Ins. Co. v. Carroll, TexCivApp–Waco, 330 SW2d 227.—App & E 1046.5; Insurance 2185, 2201, 3253; Trial 365.1(5).

Gulf Ins. Co. v. Cherry, TexApp–Dallas, 704 SW2d 459, ref nre.—Evid 89; Insurance 1929(2), 2044(1), 3571.

Gulf Ins. Co. v. City of Dallas, TexCivApp–Dallas, 451 SW2d 525, ref nre.—Const Law 3564; Tax 2128, 2535, 2558.

Gulf Ins. Co. v. Clarke, TexApp–Houston (1 Dist), 902 SW2d 156, reh overr, and writ den.—App & E 173(2), 179(1); Insurance 3549(4), 3549(5); Judgm 181(1), 183.

Gulf Ins. Co.; Cox v., TexApp–Fort Worth, 858 SW2d 615.—Contracts 22(1); Insurance 2030; Judgm 181(23); Paymt 7.

Gulf Ins. Co.; Crocker v., TexCivApp–Texarkana, 524 SW2d 566.—Insurance 1822, 1825, 2278(13), 2914.

Gulf Ins. Co. v. Dunlop Tire and Rubber Corp., TexCivApp–Dallas, 584 SW2d 886, ref nre.—App & E 949; Jury 25(6), 26; New Tr 102(1), 159, 161(1); Plead 236(2), 236(3); Pretrial Proc 713, 718, 725; Trial 26.

Gulf Ins. Co. v. Gaddy, TexComApp, 103 SW2d 141, 129 Tex 481.—Antitrust 583, 980; Insurance 1627.

Gulf Ins. Co. v. Gibbs, TexCivApp–Hous (1 Dist), 534 SW2d 720, ref nre.—App & E 1069.1; Costs 260(4); Trial 29(2), 295(1), 296(13), 312(1), 313; Work Comp 554, 597, 849, 1649.

Gulf Ins. Co. v. Hodges, TexCivApp–Amarillo, 513 SW2d 267.—Damag 221(3); Trial 215, 256(12); Work Comp 836, 1021, 1624, 1662, 1671, 1724, 1961, 1964, 1969.

Gulf Ins. Co.; Hodges Food Stores, Inc. v., TexCivApp–Dallas, 441 SW2d 309.—Insurance 3234, 3502.

Gulf Ins. Co. v. James, Tex, 185 SW2d 966, 143 Tex 424.—Autos 132; Const Law 2646; Licens 7(9), 33; States 127; Statut 107(1), 109, 109.5, 121(1), 181(2), 194.

Gulf Ins. Co.; James v., TexCivApp–Austin, 179 SW2d 397, rev 185 SW2d 966, 143 Tex 424.—App & E 170(2); Const Law 48(4.1), 2646, 2986, 3560, 3694; Evid 383(2); Insurance 1127, 1350; Licens 7(2), 7(9); States 127, 132; Statut 4, 6, 16(1), 107(6), 109.3, 121(1), 129, 141(2), 149, 283(2), 285; Tax 2121, 2136.

Gulf Ins. Co. v. Johnson, TexCivApp–Hous (1 Dist), 616 SW2d 320, writ dism by agreement, and writ gr.—Witn 244; Work Comp 1374, 1384, 1392, 1404, 1414, 1426, 1568, 1573, 1619, 1937, 1939.6.

Gulf Ins. Co. v. Jones, CA5 (Tex), 143 FedAppx 583.—Atty & C 112.

GULF

Gulf Ins. Co.; Mackey v., TexCivApp–Amarillo, 443 SW2d 911.—Evid 219(3), 589; Trial 140(2); Work Comp 1403, 1590, 1968(2), 1969.

Gulf Ins. Co. v. Olson, TexCivApp–Waco, 469 SW2d 715. —Insurance 2201.

Gulf Ins. Co. v. Parker Products, Inc., Tex, 498 SW2d 676.—Insurance 1835(2), 2278(24), 3549(4).

Gulf Ins. Co.; Parker Products, Inc. v., TexCivApp–Fort Worth, 486 SW2d 610, writ gr, aff 498 SW2d 676.— Insurance 1832(1), 2278(21), 3549(4); Judgm 181(23).

Gulf Ins. Co.; Plasky v., Tex, 335 SW2d 581, 160 Tex 612. —App & E 158(2), 170(1); Bankr 3412; Insurance 2756(4); Interest 49; Tender 12(2).

Gulf Ins. Co. v. Plasky, TexCivApp–Austin, 326 SW2d 216, rev 335 SW2d 581, 160 Tex 612.—Bankr 3412; Insurance 1091(10), 2756(4); Tender 12(2).

Gulf Ins. Co. v. Riddle, TexCivApp–Fort Worth, 199 SW2d 1000.—Insurance 1809, 1812, 1832(1), 1914, 1929(7), 1929(8), 1943.

Gulf Ins. Co. v. Snyder, TexCivApp–Amarillo, 446 SW2d 947.—Judgm 597.

Gulf Ins. Co.; Switzerland General Ins. Co. v., TexCiv-App–Dallas, 213 SW2d 161, dism.—Domicile 1, 2, 4(2); Home 32; Insurance 2137(1).

Gulf Ins. Co. v. Texas Cas. Ins. Co., TexCivApp–Fort Worth, 580 SW2d 645, ref nre.—Insurance 3131, 3369(2), 3549(3).

Gulf Ins. Co.; Two Pesos, Inc. v., TexApp–Houston (14 Dist), 901 SW2d 495, reh overr.—App & E 843(2), 852; Insurance 1867, 2094, 2097, 2261, 2264, 2302, 2914, 2915, 3336, 3337, 3549(3); Lim of Act 55(6); Trademarks 1062.

Gulf Ins. Co. v. Vantage Properties, Inc., TexApp–Houston (14 Dist), 858 SW2d 52, reh den, and writ den. —App & E 270(4), 839(1); Judgm 564(1).

Gulf Ins. Co.; Vaughn v., TexCivApp–Fort Worth, 151 SW2d 227.—Abate & R 41, 42, 47; App & E 544(1), 564(3), 679(1), 712, 714(5), 901, 970(1), 1032(1), 1046.1; Tresp to T T 46; Trial 41(2), 41(4), 41(5), 355(1).

Gulf Ins. Co. v. Vela, TexCivApp–Austin, 361 SW2d 904, ref nre.—App & E 216(1); Insurance 3549(3), 3579; Trial 191(3), 232(5).

Gulf Ins. Co.; Vest v., TexApp–Dallas, 809 SW2d 531, writ den.—Contracts 153; Insurance 1806, 1808, 1832(1), 1835(2), 1863, 2168; Judgm 185(2).

Gulf Ins. Co.; Wells v., CA5 (Tex), 484 F3d 313.—Fed Cts 776; Insurance 2396, 2900.

Gulf Ins. Co.; Western Rim Inv. Advisors, Inc. v., NDTex, 269 FSupp2d 836, aff 96 FedAppx 960.—Insurance 1832(1), 2275, 2278(4), 2300, 2914, 2915.

Gulf Ins. Co. v. White, TexCivApp–Dallas, 242 SW2d 663. —Insurance 1716, 3523(4), 3526(5).

Gulf Ins. Co. v. Winn, TexCivApp–San Antonio, 545 SW2d 526, ref nre.—Insurance 1794, 2666.

Gulf Ins. Co. of Dallas; Hall v., TexCivApp–Austin, 200 SW2d 450.—App & E 919; Insurance 1812, 1825, 1832(1), 2134(3).

Gulf Ins. Group; Martin v., TexApp–Dallas, 788 SW2d 376, writ gr, and writ den, and writ withdrawn.—App & E 930(3); Trial 358; Work Comp 1504, 1554, 1846, 1847.

Gulf Interstate Engineering Co.; Nexen Inc. v., Tex-App–Houston (1 Dist), 224 SW3d 412.—App & E 179(1), 907(1), 934(1); Contracts 1, 129(1), 147(1), 206; Judgm 183, 185.3(2); Lim of Act 1, 2(1), 43, 46(6), 47(1), 49(7), 55(5).

Gulf Interstate Engineering Co. v. Pecos Pipeline and Producing Co., TexApp–Houston (1 Dist), 680 SW2d 879, dism.—Alt Disp Res 186, 196, 205; App & E 846(5), 930(3), 989; Fraud 9.

Gulf Interstate Gas Co.; Fluor Corp. v., CA5 (Tex), 259 F2d 405.—Pat 27(1).

Gulf Interstate Gas Co.; Fluor Corp. v., SDTex, 152 FSupp 448, aff 259 F2d 405.—Pat 16.17, 17(1), 66(1.19).

Gulf Iron Works, Inc.; Chuppe v., TexCivApp–Eastland, 306 SW2d 177, ref nre.—App & E 1050.1(7); Evid 155(5), 472(11); Neglig 1642; Trial 311.

Gulf Island Fabrication, Inc.; Agip Petroleum Co. v., SDTex, 17 FSupp2d 660.—Damag 122.

Gulf Island Fabrication, Inc.; Agip Petroleum Co., Inc. v., SDTex, 56 FSupp2d 776.—Damag 118; Neglig 200, 1501.

Gulf Island Fabrication, Inc.; Agip Petroleum Co., Inc. v., SDTex, 17 FSupp2d 658.—Adm 1.11, 1.20(1), 1.20(2), 7; Contracts 129(1).

Gulf Island Fabrication, Inc.; Agip Petroleum Co., Inc. v., SDTex, 3 FSupp2d 754, aff 281 F3d 1279.—Insurance 2272, 2274, 2277, 2278(26).

Gulf Island Fabrication, Inc.; AGIP Petroleum Co., Inc. v., SDTex, 920 FSupp 1330.—Adm 1.20(1), 1.20(2), 1.20(5), 6, 10(2), 12, 17.1, 18, 22; Contracts 114, 177, 187(1), 188.5(1); Damag 118; Indem 67; Prod Liab 17.1; Torts 112, 113(2).

Gulf Island Fabrication, Inc.; AGIP Petroleum Co., Inc. v., SDTex, 920 FSupp 1318.—Adm 1.20(1), 1.20(2), 10(4); Insurance 1089, 1091(1), 1805, 1806, 1808, 1810, 1812, 2098, 2214, 2285(2), 3510, 3515(1), 3522, 3523(1).

Gulf King Shrimp Co. v. Wirtz, CA5 (Tex), 407 F2d 508, 21 ALR Fed 376.—Commerce 62.49; Fed Civ Proc 2285; Labor & Emp 2225, 2232, 2295, 2387(1), 2418, 2425, 2437, 2438, 2520.

Gulf King 35, Inc.; Zacaria v., SDTex, 31 FSupp2d 560. —Adm 1.15; Seamen 29(5.2).

Gulf King 55; Solano v., CA5 (Tex), 212 F3d 902, cert den 121 SCt 312, 531 US 930, 148 LEd2d 250.—Seamen 3.

Gulf King 55, Inc.; Solano v., SDTex, 57 FSupp2d 437, rev 212 F3d 902, cert den 121 SCt 312, 531 US 930, 148 LEd2d 250.—Adm 1.15.

Gulf King 55, Inc.; Solano v., SDTex, 30 FSupp2d 960.— Adm 1.15.

Gulf Land Co. v. Atlantic Refining Co., CCA5 (Tex), 113 F2d 902.—Admin Law 501, 791; Judgm 550, 715(2), 715(3), 725(1); Mines 92.16, 92.26, 92.32(1), 92.32(2), 92.38, 92.39, 92.40.

Gulf Land Co. v. Atlantic Refining Co., Tex, 131 SW2d 73, 134 Tex 59.—Admin Law 385.1, 483, 502; App & E 839(1), 854(2), 856(1); Courts 155; Mines 86, 92.13, 92.16, 92.21, 92.23(1), 92.23(2), 92.26, 92.28, 92.29, 92.32(1), 92.32(2), 92.35, 92.39, 92.40, 92.41; Pub Ut 167.

Gulf Land Co.; Atlantic Refining Co. v., TexCivApp–Austin, 122 SW2d 197, aff 131 SW2d 73, 134 Tex 59.— Admin Law 420, 746; Evid 379; Mines 92.29, 92.30, 92.38, 92.39.

Gulf Life Ins. Co.; Ridgway v., CA5 (Tex), 578 F2d 1026, reh den 583 F2d 541.—Autos 192(6), 197(7); Insurance 2261, 2629, 2660, 2663, 2761, 3556, 3557.

Gulf Liquid Fertilizer Co.; Allison v., TexCivApp–Fort Worth, 381 SW2d 684.—App & E 218.2(2), 237(5), 238(2); New Tr 143(2), 157; Sales 359(1), 360(1); Trial 284, 350.1, 350.2, 351.5(1), 366.

Gulf Liquid Fertilizer Co.; Allison v., TexCivApp–Fort Worth, 353 SW2d 512.—Action 60; App & E 80(6).

Gulf Liquid Fertilizer Co. v. Titus, Tex, 354 SW2d 378, 163 Tex 260.—Frds St of 23(1), 33(2), 158(4), 159; Trial 404(1).

Gulf Liquid Fertilizer Co.; Titus v., TexCivApp–El Paso, 345 SW2d 422, writ gr, rev 354 SW2d 378, 163 Tex 260. —Frds St of 23(1), 33(1), 33(2); Partners 154, 181, 183(1), 223.

Gulf Lumber Co.; Goethe v., TexCivApp–Galveston, 161 SW2d 514.—App & E 1070(2); Neglig 1750.

Gulf Marine Institute of Technology; Dewhurst v., TexApp–Corpus Christi, 55 SW3d 91, reh overr, and review den.—Contracts 147(2), 153, 169, 175(1), 318; Courts 4; Decl Judgm 342, 344, 369, 393; Estop 62.2(2); Evid 65; Mines 5.2(2.1); Plead 104(1), 111.38; States 191.4(1), 191.10.

Gulf Maritime Warehouse Co. v. Towers, TexApp–Beaumont, 858 SW2d 556, writ den.—App & E 964, 1106(4); Judges 42, 43, 49(1), 51(2), 51(4), 53, 56.

Gulf Metals Industries, Inc. v. Chicago Ins. Co., TexApp–Austin, 993 SW2d 800, petition for review den.—Contracts 143(2), 170(1); Evid 448; Insurance 1808, 2278(17).

Gulf Mississippi Marine Corp.; Edwards v., SDTex, 449 FSupp 1363.—Const Law 3965(6); Fed Civ Proc 51, 492, 500; Fed Cts 75, 76.5, 84, 411.

Gulfmont Hotel Co.; N.L.R.B. v., CA5 (Tex), 362 F2d 588.—Labor & Emp 1224, 1232, 1715(11), 1766, 1796.

Gulf Neches Marine; Kiffe v., EDTex, 709 FSupp 743. See Kiffe v. Neches-Gulf Marine, Inc.

Gulf Nuclear, Inc.; Kielwein v., TexApp–Houston (14 Dist), 783 SW2d 746.—Judgm 181(21); Work Comp 394, 396, 2101.

Gulf Nuclear, Inc.; Texas Dept. of Health v., TexApp–Austin, 664 SW2d 847.—Admin Law 229; Electricity 8.5(2); Environ Law 700; Licens 38.

Gulf Offshore Co. v. Mobil Oil Corp., USTex, 101 SCt 2870, 453 US 473, 69 LEd2d 784, on remand 628 SW2d 171, ref nre, cert den 103 SCt 259, 459 US 945, 74 LEd2d 202.—Adm 1.20(1); Courts 100(1), 489(1); Fed Cts 502, 511.1.

Gulf Offshore Co. v. Mobil Oil Corp., TexCivApp–Hous (14 Dist), 594 SW2d 496, cert gr 101 SCt 607, 449 US 1033, 66 LEd2d 494, aff in part, vac in part, remanded 101 SCt 2870, 453 US 473, 69 LEd2d 784, on remand 628 SW2d 171, ref nre, cert den 103 SCt 259, 459 US 945, 74 LEd2d 202.—App & E 205, 863, 934(1); Atty & C 32(4); Courts 489(1); Damag 99, 165, 216(8), 221(5.1); Indem 24, 27, 30(5), 102, 105; Jury 136(3); New Tr 140(1); States 12.2; Trial 252(8); U S 3.

Gulf Offshore Co., a Division of the Pool Co. v. Mobil Oil Corp., TexApp–Houston (14 Dist), 628 SW2d 171, ref nre, cert den 103 SCt 259, 459 US 945, 74 LEd2d 202.—Adm 1.20(4); Damag 216(1).

Gulf Oil Co. v. Bernard, USTex, 101 SCt 2193, 452 US 89, 68 LEd2d 693.—Civil R 1515; Const Law 976; Fed Civ Proc 162, 177.1; Fed Cts 817.

Gulf Oil Co.; Bernard v., CA5 (Tex), 619 F2d 459, cert gr 101 SCt 607, 449 US 1033, 66 LEd2d 495, aff 101 SCt 2193, 452 US 89, 68 LEd2d 693.—Civil R 1511; Const Law 1050, 1079, 1154, 1526, 1527, 2070, 2085, 2091, 2100, 2114; Crim Law 31; Fed Civ Proc 161.1, 162, 173; Inj 219.

Gulf Oil Co.; Bernard v., CA5 (Tex), 596 F2d 1249, reh gr 604 F2d 449, on reh 619 F2d 459, cert gr 101 SCt 607, 449 US 1033, 66 LEd2d 495, aff 101 SCt 2193, 452 US 89, 68 LEd2d 693.—Civil R 1370, 1383, 1384, 1470, 1502, 1530; Compromise 59; Const Law 2091, 3603; Equity 72(1), 73; Fed Civ Proc 161, 164, 177.1, 184.10, 1271, 2539, 2544; Fed Cts 817; Lim of Act 55(1), 58(1).

Gulf Oil Co.; King v., CA5 (Tex), 581 F2d 1184.—Civil R 1542, 1544, 1555; Fed Civ Proc 172, 184.10; Fed Cts 853, 891, 896.1.

Gulf Oil Co.; Munoz v., Tex, 693 SW2d 372, appeal after remand 732 SW2d 62, ref nre.—App & E 713(1); Judgm 185(2), 185(5).

Gulf Oil Co.; Munoz v., TexApp–Houston (14 Dist), 732 SW2d 62, ref nre.—App & E 837(1), 1024.4; Contracts 322(1); Gas 18; Judgm 185(2); Prod Liab 14, 87.1; Sales 282.

Gulf Oil Co. U.S. v. First Nat. Bank of Hereford, TexCivApp–Amarillo, 503 SW2d 300.—Attach 140, 143; Sec Tran 82.1, 98, 140.

Gulf Oil Corp. v. Alexander, Tex, 295 SW2d 901, 156 Tex 455.—Courts 107; Mines 125.

Gulf Oil Corp. v. Alexander, TexCivApp–Amarillo, 291 SW2d 792, ref nre 295 SW2d 901, 156 Tex 455.—Lim of Act 32(1), 95(7); Mines 92.44(1), 121, 125.

Gulf Oil Corp.; Allen v., TexCivApp–Austin, 139 SW2d 207, writ refused.—App & E 189(2), 458(2), 458(3), 758.1, 1043(1); Inj 132, 208; Mines 92.13, 92.37, 92.38, 92.40.

Gulf Oil Corp. v. Amazon Petroleum Corp., TexCivApp–Texarkana, 152 SW2d 902, writ refused.—Adv Poss 66(1); Bound 4, 7, 48(4), 48(8); Evid 157(2), 372(1), 372(10).

Gulf Oil Corp.; Andress, Lipscomb & Peticolas v., CA5 (Tex), 203 F2d 148.—Pub Lands 173(14).

Gulf Oil Corp. v. Austin Contracting Co., TexCivApp–Eastland, 326 SW2d 925, ref nre.—App & E 766; High 113(5).

Gulf Oil Corp. v. Banque de Paris et des Pays-Bas, SDTex, 72 BR 752. See Fuel Oil Supply and Terminaling, Inc., In re.

Gulf Oil Corp.; Baton v., TexCivApp–Texarkana, 235 SW2d 491, writ refused.—Judgm 714(1), 725(1), 743(2).

Gulf Oil Corp.; Bernard v., CA5 (Tex), 890 F2d 735, cert den 110 SCt 3237, 497 US 1003, 111 LEd2d 748.—Civil R 1135, 1142; Fed Civ Proc 177.1.

Gulf Oil Corp.; Bernard v., CA5 (Tex), 841 F2d 547, appeal after remand 890 F2d 735, cert den 110 SCt 3237, 497 US 1003, 111 LEd2d 748.—Civil R 1120, 1135, 1141, 1142, 1535, 1536, 1542, 1544; Fed Civ Proc 184.10, 2011; Fed Cts 941, 944.

Gulf Oil Corp.; Bernard v., EDTex, 643 FSupp 1494, aff in part, vac in part 841 F2d 547, appeal after remand 890 F2d 735, cert den 110 SCt 3237, 497 US 1003, 111 LEd2d 748.—Civil R 1120, 1135, 1140, 1141, 1142, 1529, 1548; Labor & Emp 1208, 1209(1).

Gulf Oil Corp.; Birmingham v., Tex, 516 SW2d 914.—Mines 118; Neglig 1612, 1614, 1656, 1675, 1676.

Gulf Oil Corp.; Birmingham v., TexCivApp–Corpus Christi, 494 SW2d 946, writ gr, aff 516 SW2d 914.—Mines 118; Neglig 253, 371, 386, 1579, 1625, 1675; Trial 139.1(17), 143.

Gulf Oil Corp. v. Bivins, CA5 (Tex), 276 F2d 753, cert den 81 SCt 70, 364 US 835, 5 LEd2d 61, reh den 81 SCt 231, 364 US 906, 5 LEd2d 199.—Mines 109, 118; Neglig 1037(7), 1221, 1694.

Gulf Oil Corp.; Blum v., CA5 (Tex), 597 F2d 936.—Civil R 1041, 1103, 1122, 1192; Fed Civ Proc 1267.1, 1272.1, 2148.1; Fed Cts 681.1; Judges 51(3); Jury 14(1.5).

Gulf Oil Corp.; Bodin v., CA5 (Tex), 877 F2d 438.—Fed Civ Proc 2659; Fed Cts 668, 669.

Gulf Oil Corp.; Bodin v., EDTex, 707 FSupp 875, appeal dism 877 F2d 438.—Adv Poss 27, 40, 58, 85(5), 104, 109; Deeds 71; Lim of Act 55(5); Pub Lands 207; Tax 3053; Trover 2.

Gulf Oil Corp. v. Bouygues Offshore U.S.A., Inc., CA5 (Tex), 949 F2d 826. See Hardy v. Gulf Oil Corp.

Gulf Oil Corp.; Bruner v., TexCivApp–San Antonio, 359 SW2d 210, writ refused.—Mines 78.1(7).

Gulf Oil Corp.; Bryant v., TexApp–Amarillo, 694 SW2d 443, ref nre.—App & E 169, 1024.4; Electricity 17; Judgm 185(2), 185(6); Labor & Emp 3141; Neglig 250, 1011, 1031, 1037(4), 1037(7), 1692.

Gulf Oil Corp. v. Burlington Northern R.R., Inc., CA5 (Tex), 751 F2d 746.—Indem 30(1), 31(5), 31(6), 33(7), 94.

Gulf Oil Corp. v. Cantrell, TexCivApp–Beaumont, 387 SW2d 416, writ dism.—Forg 9; Libel 100(1); Plead 111.24, 111.31, 111.40, 111.42(1), 111.42(4).

Gulf Oil Corp.; Carter v., TexCivApp–Beaumont, 699 SW2d 907, writ gr, rev Chevron Corp v. Redmon, 745 SW2d 314.—Judgm 181(21).

Gulf Oil Corporation; Cook Drilling Co. v., Tex, 161 SW2d 1035, 139 Tex 80.—App & E 1177(7); Mines 92.39, 92.40.

Gulf Oil Corp.; Cook Drilling Co. v., TexCivApp–Austin, 155 SW2d 638, rev 161 SW2d 1035, 139 Tex 80.—Admin Law 499; Mines 92.26, 92.28, 92.32(1), 92.32(2), 92.35, 92.38, 92.39, 92.62.

Gulf Oil Corp. v. Crow, TexApp–Corpus Christi, 704 SW2d 849.—App & E 213, 1062.1, 1062.2, 1175(1), 1177(1); Costs 207; Fact 15; Fraud 65(1); Labor &

GULF

Emp 2783, 2820; Neglig 219, 273, 1659, 1692; Trial 182, 349(2), 350.1, 350.3(4), 352.1(5), 352.1(6), 352.5(5); Trover 36.

Gulf Oil Corp. v. Dravo Engineers & Constructors, Inc., CA5 (Tex), 745 F2d 921. See Kemp v. Gulf Oil Corp.

Gulf Oil Corp.; Dupree v., EDTex, 328 FSupp 480.—Contracts 313(2); Costs 194.32; Labor & Emp 179, 189, 246, 258, 271; Release 38; Seamen 29(5).

Gulf Oil Corp.; Evans v., TexApp–Corpus Christi, 840 SW2d 500, reh overr, and writ den.—Decl Judgm 392.1; Judgm 183, 185(2); Mines 78.1(8), 78.7(5).

Gulf Oil Corp. v. Fannett Independent School Dist., TexCivApp–Waco, 315 SW2d 584.—App & E 781(6).

Gulf Oil Corp. v. Ford, Bacon & Davis, Texas, Inc., TexApp–Beaumont, 782 SW2d 28.—Indem 30(5), 42.

Gulf Oil Corp.; Foster v., TexCivApp–Beaumont, 335 SW2d 845, ref nre.—Des & Dist 8; Escheat 4; Plead 8(11); Pub Lands 175(7), 210, 213; Tax 2996, 3168.

Gulf Oil Corp.; Fuel Oil Supply and Terminaling v., CA5 (Tex), 762 F2d 1283.—Bankr 2160, 3837.

Gulf Oil Corp. v. Fuel Oil Supply & Terminaling, Inc., CA5 (Tex), 837 F2d 224. See Fuel Oil Supply & Terminaling, Inc., Matter of.

Gulf Oil Corp. v. Fuller, TexApp–El Paso, 695 SW2d 769.—App & E 1011.1(8.1); Mand 11; Pretrial Proc 24, 35, 43, 379, 406.

Gulf Oil Corp.; Galvin v., TexApp–Dallas, 759 SW2d 167, writ den.—App & E 907(4), 961, 1043(1); Pretrial Proc 45, 313.

Gulf Oil Corp.; General American Oil Co. of Texas v., TexCivApp–Austin, 139 SW2d 314, writ refused.—App & E 173(2); Mines 92.30, 92.32(1), 92.41.

Gulf Oil Corp.; General American Oil Co. of Texas v., TexCivApp–El Paso, 170 SW2d 495, writ refused wom.—Mines 92.40, 92.41.

Gulf Oil Corp.; Gray v., TexCivApp–Fort Worth, 416 SW2d 875.—App & E 1024.3; Evid 590; Plead 111.42(3), 111.42(9).

Gulf Oil Corp. v. Griffith, CA5 (Tex), 330 F2d 729.—Electricity 19(5); Fed Cts 847.

Gulf Oil Corp.; Groce v., TexCivApp–Dallas, 439 SW2d 718.—Plead 111.3, 111.15, 111.16, 111.42(2), 236(3), 245(4); Venue 7.5(2).

Gulf Oil Corp. v. Guidry, Tex, 327 SW2d 406, 160 Tex 139.—Alt Disp Res 230, 314, 395, 396; Labor & Emp 1595(8), 1595(9), 1595(10).

Gulf Oil Corp.; Guidry v., TexCivApp–Austin, 320 SW2d 691, rev in part 327 SW2d 406, 160 Tex 139.—Labor & Emp 1595(8), 1595(10), 1595(12).

Gulf Oil Corp.; Hardy v., CA5 (Tex), 949 F2d 826.—Adm 31; Contracts 144; Contrib 1, 6, 7, 8; Damag 63; Indem 24, 27, 33(5), 33(8), 61, 67, 69, 72, 74; Torts 135.

Gulf Oil Corp.; Hayes v., CA5 (Tex), 821 F2d 285.—Fed Cts 93; Judgm 825, 829(1).

Gulf Oil Corp.; Hopson v., Tex, 237 SW2d 352, 150 Tex 1.—App & E 878(1), 878(6), 1003(9.1); Courts 97(5); Jury 37; Neglig 371, 379, 380, 387; Seamen 29(1), 29(5.1), 29(5.16); Trial 350.6(2), 352.20.

Gulf Oil Corp.; Hopson v., TexCivApp–Beaumont, 237 SW2d 323, rev in part 237 SW2d 352, 150 Tex 1.—App & E 218.2(2), 232(0.5), 301, 882(3), 1140(1); Damag 221(2.1), 221(5.1); Jury 37; Seamen 11(1), 11(6), 11(7), 11(9), 29(2), 29(5.14), 29(5.16); Trial 140(2), 232(2), 352.20, 357.

Gulf Oil Corp. v. Horton, TexCivApp–Amarillo, 143 SW2d 132.—Contracts 147(1); Land & Ten 55(2), 157(4); Waste 1.

Gulf Oil Corp.; Hurst Employers Cas. Co., Intervener v., CA5 (Tex), 251 F2d 836, reh den 254 F2d 287, cert den 79 SCt 44, 358 US 827, 3 LEd2d 66.—Labor & Emp 3159; Mines 118; Neglig 1011.

Gulf Oil Corp.; Hurst Employers Cas. Co., Interveners v., CA5 (Tex), 254 F2d 287.—Fed Cts 744.

Gulf Oil Corp. v. International Union of Operating Engineers, Local No. 715, AFL-CIO, CA5 (Tex), 279 F2d 533, cert den 81 SCt 112, 364 US 871, 5 LEd2d 92.—Labor & Emp 1549(19), 1556(3).

Gulf Oil Corp.; Jefferson County Drainage Dist. No. 6 v., TexCivApp–Beaumont, 437 SW2d 415.—Courts 472.3, 480(1); Em Dom 172.

Gulf Oil Corp.; Kemp v., CA5 (Tex), 745 F2d 921.—Fed Cts 776; Indem 31(4), 33(5), 104; Neglig 1304, 1684.

Gulf Oil Corp.; Kincaid v., TexApp–San Antonio, 675 SW2d 250, ref nre.—App & E 219(2), 931(1), 989; Contracts 155; Mines 73, 78.1(1), 78.1(3), 78.2.

Gulf Oil Corp. v. Lastrap, SDTex, 48 FSupp 947.—Adm 1.20(2); Fed Cts 419; Insurance 1791(1); Seamen 1; War 67.

Gulf Oil Corp.; Lehrman v., CA5 (Tex), 500 F2d 659, reh den 503 F2d 1403, cert den 95 SCt 1128, 420 US 929, 43 LEd2d 400.—Antitrust 975, 981, 983, 984, 985, 987; Courts 99(1); Damag 190; Fed Civ Proc 2183; Fed Cts 869, 896.1, 899, 911, 916.1, 917, 950, 955.

Gulf Oil Corp.; Lehrman v., CA5 (Tex), 464 F2d 26, cert den 93 SCt 687, 409 US 1077, 34 LEd2d 665, appeal after remand 500 F2d 659, reh den 503 F2d 1403, cert den 95 SCt 1128, 420 US 929, 43 LEd2d 400.—Antitrust 821, 823, 852, 975, 977(5), 983, 984, 985; Commerce 1, 3, 5, 7(2), 56, 60(1), 62.10(1), 80; Evid 99; Jury 37; Stip 14(10).

Gulf Oil Corp.; Letwin v., TexCivApp–Austin, 164 SW2d 234, writ refused.—Mines 92.28, 92.35, 92.38, 92.39.

Gulf Oil Corp.; Lion Oil Co. v., CA5 (Tex), 181 F2d 731.—Contracts 143(1), 147(2), 147(3); Mines 109.

Gulf Oil Corp. v. Lone Star Producing Co., CA5 (Tex), 322 F2d 28.—Lim of Act 28(1); Paymt 82(1), 85(1), 85(7); Sales 87(3), 348(1), 391(2).

Gulf Oil Corp.; Lone Star Producing Co. v., EDTex, 208 FSupp 85, rev 322 F2d 28.—Carr 12(11); Commerce 61(1); Costs 194.36; Lim of Act 24(2), 28(1); Paymt 82(2); Sales 77(2), 391(3).

Gulf Oil Corp.; Loomis v., TexCivApp–Eastland, 123 SW2d 501, writ refused.—Mines 55(4), 55(7).

Gulf Oil Corp.; L. P. & B. Oil Corporation v., TexCivApp–Austin, 115 SW2d 1034, writ refused.—Admin Law 673; Mines 92.21, 92.35, 92.37.

Gulf Oil Corp.; McBride v., TexCivApp–Beaumont, 292 SW2d 151, ref nre.—Aliens 678; App & E 927(7); Contracts 155; Evid 383(3), 383(4); Pub Lands 200, 204, 210; Trial 174, 178.

Gulf Oil Corp.; Manges v., CA5 (Tex), 394 F2d 487.—Mines 55(7), 74(6).

Gulf Oil Corp. v. Marathon Oil Co., Tex, 152 SW2d 711, 137 Tex 59.—Bound 32, 37(5), 46(1), 46(2), 46(3), 47(1), 48(7), 48(8); Lim of Act 55(5); Mines 73.1(3), 78.1(6), 105(2).

Gulf Oil Corp.; Marathon Oil Co. v., TexCivApp–El Paso, 130 SW2d 365, mod 152 SW2d 711, 137 Tex 59.—Bound 33, 40(3), 46(1), 46(3); Lim of Act 55(5); 165; Mines 51(5).

Gulf Oil Corp. v. Martindale, TexCivApp–Beaumont, 381 SW2d 141.—Inj 261; Plead 111.9, 111.19, 111.39(3).

Gulf Oil Corp.; Martindale v., TexCivApp–Beaumont, 345 SW2d 810, ref nre.—Covenants 68; Inj 34.

Gulf Oil Corp.; Masterson v., TexCivApp–Galveston, 301 SW2d 486, ref nre.—Contracts 175(1); Mines 55(4).

Gulf Oil Corp.; Myers v., CA5 (Tex), 731 F2d 281.—Fed Civ Proc 2556; Fed Cts 937.1.

Gulf Oil Corp. v. Outlaw, TexComApp, 150 SW2d 777, 136 Tex 281.—App & E 2; Pub Lands 175(7).

Gulf Oil Corp.; Outlaw v., TexCivApp–El Paso, 137 SW2d 787, rev 150 SW2d 777, 136 Tex 281.—App & E 1, 2, 927(7); Bound 1, 3(1), 3(3), 3(6), 10, 36(3), 40(1), 53; Estop 62.2(2); Evid 205(1); Pub Lands 175(7), 176(2).

Gulf Oil Corporation; Peerless Oil & Gas Co. v., TexCivApp–San Antonio, 112 SW2d 1083.—App & E 172(1); Garn 88.

Gulf Oil Corp.; Penn Oil Co. v., TexCivApp–Austin, 167 SW2d 220, writ refused wom.—Admin Law 327; App & E 773(2); Mines 92.26; Pretrial Proc 714.

Gulf Oil Corp.; Pinchback v., TexCivApp–Beaumont, 242 SW2d 242, ref nre.—Mines 55(2), 55(4), 55(8).

Gulf Oil Corp. v. Prevost, TexCivApp–San Antonio, 538 SW2d 876.—Mines 73.1(2), 73.1(5), 78.1(3), 78.1(7).

Gulf Oil Corp.; Pryor v., CA5 (Tex), 704 F2d 1364.—Fed Civ Proc 2173.1(1), 2176.1; Fed Cts 908.1.

Gulf Oil Corp. v. Railroad Com'n of Texas, TexApp–Austin, 660 SW2d 112, ref nre.—Gas 14.4(8).

Gulf Oil Corp. v. Reid, Tex, 337 SW2d 267, 161 Tex 51.—App & E 1177(6); Mines 73.5.

Gulf Oil Corp.; Reid v., TexCivApp–Beaumont, 323 SW2d 107, aff 337 SW2d 267, 161 Tex 51.—App & E 854(1), 931(1), 931(3); Evid 66; Land & Ten 45; Mines 73.5, 75, 78.1(3), 78.1(8).

Gulf Oil Corp.; Rendon v., TexCivApp–Corpus Christi, 414 SW2d 510, ref nre.—App & E 954(1), 954(2); Inj 135, 147.

Gulf Oil Corp. v. Rice & Agr. Co-op, Inc., TexCivApp–Hous (1 Dist), 536 SW2d 236, ref nre.—Costs 32(3), 194.38; Frds St of 152(1), 157; Interest 39(3); New Tr 72(5); Sales 90, 168.5(5), 182(1), 359(1), 418(8), 420; Trial 215, 350.1.

Gulf Oil Corp.; Rogge v., TexCivApp–Waco, 351 SW2d 565, ref nre.—App & E 882(19); Courts 89, 91(1).

Gulf Oil Corp.; Roskey v., TexCivApp–Houston, 387 SW2d 915, ref nre.—App & E 927(7), 997(3); Mines 118; Neglig 305.

Gulf Oil Corp.; Rudco Oil & Gas Co. v., TexCivApp–Austin, 169 SW2d 791, writ refused wom.—Courts 52; Mines 92.35, 92.39, 92.41; Pretrial Proc 714; Trial 171.

Gulf Oil Corporation v. Rudco Oil & Gas Co., TexCiv-App–Austin, 164 SW2d 222, writ refused.—Judgm 563(3); Mines 92.41.

Gulf Oil Corp.; Runnells County v., TexCivApp–El Paso, 209 SW2d 969, writ refused.—Lim of Act 40(1); Pub Lands 173(14).

Gulf Oil Corp.; Scharlack v., TexCivApp–San Antonio, 368 SW2d 705.—Adj Land 10(1); Nuis 3(1), 7.

Gulf Oil Corp. v. Senkirik, TexCivApp–Eastland, 586 SW2d 157.—Corp 666; Plead 111.19.

Gulf Oil Corp. v. Shell Oil Co., TexCivApp–Beaumont, 410 SW2d 260, ref nre.—App & E 1010.2; Deeds 97, 99, 116; Estop 38, 70(1), 90(1), 95; Guard & W 81; Hus & W 249(2.1); Infants 55; Propty 7; Pub Lands 176(2).

Gulf Oil Corp.; Sidco Products Marketing, Inc. v., CA5 (Tex), 858 F2d 1095, reh den.—Antitrust 136, 161, 162, 163, 208; Fed Cts 759.1; Sales 246, 261(1), 284(1), 284(4).

Gulf Oil Corporation v. Smith, TexCivApp–Austin, 145 SW2d 280, writ refused.—Admin Law 327, 499; App & E 1057(1), 1177(5); Estop 93(1); Mines 92.26, 92.27, 92.32(2), 92.38, 92.39, 92.40, 92.41.

Gulf Oil Corp. v. Smithey, TexCivApp–Dallas, 426 SW2d 262, writ dism.—Corp 503(1); Land & Ten 275; Plead 111.1, 111.39(4); Sec Tran 228; Venue 8.5(7), 21.

Gulf Oil Corp. v. Southland Royalty Co., Tex, 496 SW2d 547.—Mines 73.5, 78.1(10).

Gulf Oil Corp. v. Southland Royalty Co., TexCivApp–El Paso, 478 SW2d 583, ref nre, and writ gr, aff 496 SW2d 547.—App & E 837(10); Contracts 147(2), 147(3), 152, 169; Evid 65; Mines 73, 73.5.

Gulf Oil Corp.; Spence & Howe Const. Co. v., Tex, 365 SW2d 631.—Indem 30(1), 33(5).

Gulf Oil Corp. v. Spence & Howe Const. Co., TexCiv-App–Houston, 356 SW2d 382, aff 365 SW2d 631.—Contracts 32, 93(2), 147(2), 147(3), 169, 210, 245(2); Indem 27, 30(1), 33(1), 33(5).

Gulf Oil Corp.; Stantex Petroleum Co. v., TexCivApp–Beaumont, 157 SW2d 407, writ refused wom.—Estop 90(1); Mines 92.27, 92.39.

Gulf Oil Corp. v. State, TexCivApp–El Paso, 170 SW2d 798.—Evid 60, 83(1); Plead 102, 111.42(11); Venue 5.1.

Gulf Oil Corp.; State v., TexCivApp–El Paso, 166 SW2d 197.—Mines 5.2(4); Pub Lands 173(8.1); States 191.2(2), 205, 212.

Gulf Oil Corp.; State v., TexCivApp–Waco, 264 SW2d 743, ref nre.—App & E 1001(1); Bound 1, 3(3), 3(6), 6, 35(2), 35(5), 37(3), 41; Evid 274(7), 460(6).

Gulf Oil Corp.; Sword, Houston Fire & Cas. Ins. Co., Intervener v., CA5 (Tex), 251 F2d 829, cert den 79 SCt 41, 358 US 824, 3 LEd2d 65.—Fed Cts 421, 714; Labor & Emp 3159, 3162; Mines 118; Neglig 1011; Work Comp 352.

Gulf Oil Corp.; Taylor v., TexCivApp–Beaumont, 303 SW2d 541.—Des & Dist 8; Inj 34, 138.31, 163(1); Ten in C 55(1).

Gulf Oil Corp.; Tidelands Royalty B Corp. v., CA5 (Tex), 804 F2d 1344.—Fed Civ Proc 839.1; Fed Cts 193, 660.5, 939; Mines 55(2), 74(1), 74(5), 86.

Gulf Oil Corp.; Tidelands Royalty B Corp. v., NDTex, 611 FSupp 795, rev 804 F2d 1344.—Fed Cts 193; Mines 5.1(1), 78.1(1), 78.1(2), 78.1(11).

Gulf Oil Corporation v. Timms, TexCivApp–Beaumont, 116 SW2d 940, writ refused.—Bound 46(3), 55.

Gulf Oil Corp.; Vestal v., Tex, 235 SW2d 440, 149 Tex 487.—Nuis 49(1), 50(1), 50(2), 50(4).

Gulf Oil Corp. v. Vestal, TexCivApp–Fort Worth, 231 SW2d 523, aff 235 SW2d 440, 149 Tex 487.—Nuis 1, 3(3), 4, 5, 50(1), 50(2), 53, 54, 55; Trial 352.9.

Gulf Oil Corp. v. Walker, TexCivApp–Beaumont, 288 SW2d 173.—App & E 1003(5), 1015(5); Evid 553(4); Trial 70, 143, 260(5), 304, 344; Wills 38(2), 52(5), 55(1), 302(1), 302(3), 322, 330(2).

Gulf Oil Corp. v. Walton, TexCivApp–El Paso, 317 SW2d 260.—Equity 46; Inj 14, 118(4), 204; Mines 52, 55(6), 55(7), 74(3), 78.1(5), 78.1(6), 121.

Gulf Oil Corp.; Westland Oil Development Corp. v., Tex, 637 SW2d 903.—Covenants 53, 56, 57; Frds St of 110(1), 125(1), 158(3); Judgm 185.2(4); Mines 74(6); Ven & Pur 230(1), 242.

Gulf Oil Corp. v. Westland Oil Development Corp., TexCivApp–El Paso, 620 SW2d 765, writ gr, rev 637 SW2d 903.—Frds St of 110(1); Judgm 181(24), 185(2), 185.1(1); Ven & Pur 242.

Gulf Oil Corp. v. Whitaker, CA5 (Tex), 257 F2d 157.—Mines 119.

Gulf Oil Corp. v. Williams, TexApp–Texarkana, 642 SW2d 270.—App & E 497(1), 499(1), 502(1), 549(5), 684(1), 704.2, 706(2), 758.3(9), 1078(1); Labor & Emp 3038(2), 3094(1), 3096(5), 3100(2); Trial 351.2(7).

Gulf Oil Corporation v. Wood, TexCivApp–Austin, 120 SW2d 543, writ dism.—Mines 92.37.

Gulf Oil Corp.; Wood v., TexCivApp–Beaumont, 149 SW2d 1014, writ dism, correct.—App & E 830(1).

Gulf Oil Corp.; Wood v., TexCivApp–Beaumont, 147 SW2d 818, reh den 149 SW2d 1014, writ dism, correct.—Mines 92.27, 92.41.

Gulf Oil Corp. v. Wright, CA5 (Tex), 236 F2d 46.—Fed Cts 937.1.

Gulf Oil Corp.; Yates v., CA5 (Tex), 182 F2d 286.—Fed Cts 381; Mines 48, 55(6), 73, 73.1(6), 78.1(1).

Gulf Oil Corp.; York v., TexCivApp–Austin, 165 SW2d 521, writ refused.—Mines 92.26.

Gulf Oil Corporation v. York, TexCivApp–Austin, 134 SW2d 502, writ dism, correct.—Mines 92.32(1), 92.37, 92.39.

Gulf Oil Refining and Marketing Co.; Jensen v., CA5 (Tex), 623 F2d 406.—Civil R 1106, 1206; Statut 219(1).

Gulf Operators, Inc.; LeBouef v., SDTex, 20 FSupp2d 1057.—Fed Cts 101, 104, 105, 111, 143, 144.

Gulf Packing Co.; Crowe v., TexApp–Corpus Christi, 716 SW2d 623.—Damag 185(1).

Gulf Paint & Battery, Inc.; Trimble v., TexApp–Houston (1 Dist), 728 SW2d 887.—Judgm 185(4), 189.

GULF

Gulf Paving Co. v. Lofstedt, Tex, 188 SW2d 155, 144 Tex 17.—App & E 692(1), 713(3); Attach 19, 77, 101, 117, 132, 147; Atty & C 140, 166(3), 167(2); Ex & Ad 212, 453(2); Mun Corp 445, 446, 562(1), 562(2), 567(4), 569, 586.

Gulf Paving Co.; Lofstedt v., TexCivApp–Galveston, 185 SW2d 203, aff 188 SW2d 155, 144 Tex 17.—App & E 518(6), 949; Armed S 34.4(7), 34.4(8), 34.9(1), 34.9(5); Attach 232; Ex & Ad 221(4.1); Infants 70, 88; Mun Corp 454, 562(1), 567(1.1), 567(4), 572, 582.

Gulf Pension Litigation, In re, SDTex, 764 FSupp 1149, aff Borst v. Chevron Corp, 36 F3d 1308, reh and sug for reh den 42 F3d 639, cert den 115 SCt 1699, 514 US 1066, 131 LEd2d 561.—Estop 85; Fed Cts 13.5, 419, 421; Labor & Emp 407, 435, 436, 438, 449, 452, 453, 475, 477, 486, 488, 493, 513, 515, 611, 612, 651, 656, 659, 686, 688; States 18.51.

Gulf Petro Trading Co. v. Nigerian Nat. Petroleum, EDTex, 233 FRD 492.—Fed Civ Proc 1825; Fed Cts 1.1.

Gulf Petro Trading Co., Inc. v. Nigerian Nat. Petroleum Corp., NDTex, 288 FSupp2d 783, aff 115 FedAppx 201.—Alt Disp Res 515; Fed Civ Proc 1752.1; Fed Cts 433; Intern Law 10.34, 10.43; Judgm 830.1; Lim of Act 58(1); Treaties 8.

Gulf Pipe Line Co. v. Mann, TexCivApp–Beaumont, 111 SW2d 335, rev 138 SW2d 1065, 135 Tex 50, rev 138 SW2d 1069, 135 Tex 49.—Interest 39(6); Sales 187, 345, 358(1).

Gulf Pipe Line Co. v. Nearen, TexComApp, 138 SW2d 1065, 135 Tex 50.—App & E 1082(2); Contracts 221(3), 278(1); Interest 39(2), 50.

Gulf Plains Grain & Elevator Co. v. Flynn, TexCivApp–Waco, 430 SW2d 526.—Corp 503(2); Venue 5.3(2), 8.5(2).

Gulf Plains Grain & Elevator Co.; Flynn v., TexCivApp–Waco, 430 SW2d 525.—Plead 110.

Gulf Portland Cement Co. v. Globe Indem. Co., CCA5 (Tex), 149 F2d 196, cert den 66 SCt 56, 326 US 743, 90 LEd 444.—Insurance 1825, 2278(19).

Gulf Ports Crating Co.; Houston Aviation Products Co. v., TexCivApp–Hous (1 Dist), 422 SW2d 844, ref nre.—App & E 927(7), 997(3); Bailm 11, 31(1), 31(3).

Gulf Ports Crating Co. v. Ministry of Roads and Transp. An Agency of Government of Iran, CA5 (Tex), 674 F2d 318.—Fed Cts 893; War 12, 37.

Gulfport Shipbuilding Corp.; Pleason v., CA5 (Tex), 221 F2d 621.—Mar Liens 19.

Gulfport Shipbuilding Corp. v. Vallot, CA5 (Tex), 334 F2d 358, cert den 85 SCt 1333, 380 US 974, 14 LEd2d 269.—Work Comp 1949, 1956.

Gulf Production Co.; Abbott v., TexCivApp–Beaumont, 100 SW2d 722, writ dism.—Adv Poss 101; Guard & W 49, 70; Partit 9(1); Pub Lands 175(2), 175(5), 175(7), 178(3); Tresp to T T 41(1).

Gulf Production Co. v. Baton, TexCivApp–Texarkana, 108 SW2d 960, writ refused.—Bound 46(3); Mines 50, 73.1(1); Partit 95, 116(1).

Gulf Production Co.; Beck v., TexCivApp–El Paso, 113 SW2d 258, writ refused.—Bound 1, 3(8); Evid 460(8); Partit 8.

Gulf Production Co.; Cantley v., Tex, 143 SW2d 912, 135 Tex 339.—Bound 20(1), 20(2), 22; Deeds 118.

Gulf Production Co.; Cantley v., TexCivApp–Texarkana, 118 SW2d 448, aff 143 SW2d 912, 135 Tex 339.—Bound 20(1), 20(2), 20(3), 20(5).

Gulf Production Co. v. Continental Oil Co., Tex, 164 SW2d 488, 139 Tex 183.—Ack 20(1), 55(1); App & E 1010.1(1); Estop 63; Evid 219(1); Frds St of 131(1); Home 77, 117; Mines 68(1), 77, 78.5; Names 18; Paymt 9; Trusts 357(2).

Gulf Production Co.; Kilpatrick v., TexCivApp–Beaumont, 139 SW2d 653, writ dism, correct.—Adv Poss 44, 48, 112; Mines 34, 49; Tresp to T T 6.1.

Gulf Production Co. v. Kishi, TexComApp, 103 SW2d 965, 129 Tex 487.—Contracts 147(1); Mines 73.1(2), 78.1(1), 78.1(2).

Gulf Production Co. v. Kishi, TexCivApp–Beaumont, 105 SW2d 733, writ refused, certified question answered 103 SW2d 965, 129 Tex 487.—App & E 562, 630, 655(1), 655(3), 659(1), 800, 823; Contracts 168; Mines 78.1(2).

Gulf Production Co.; Mosley v., TexCivApp–Texarkana, 111 SW2d 726, dism.—Adv Poss 11, 68, 115(1); App & E 846(2), 846(5); Bound 46(1), 48(8).

Gulf Production Co.; Norris v., TexCivApp–Galveston, 149 SW2d 681.—Plead 111.1, 111.2, 111.45; Venue 5.3(8).

Gulf Production Co.; Olsen v., TexCivApp–Texarkana, 111 SW2d 784, writ refused.—App & E 1048(2); Bound 33; Evid 506, 508.

Gulf Production Co. v. Quisenberry, TexComApp, 97 SW2d 166, 128 Tex 347.—Land & Ten 164(1), 169(11); Neglig 575, 1045(3), 1051, 1602.

Gulf Production Co.; Railroad Commission of Texas v., Tex, 132 SW2d 254, 134 Tex 122.—Mines 91, 92.26, 92.27, 92.39, 92.40.

Gulf Production Co.; Railroad Commission of Texas v., TexCivApp–Austin, 115 SW2d 505, aff 132 SW2d 254, 134 Tex 122.—Mines 92.26, 92.35, 92.40, 92.41.

Gulf Production Co. v. Railroad Commission of Texas, TexCivApp–Austin, 84 SW2d 359.—App & E 781(4); Mines 92.37, 92.40.

Gulf Production Co.; Robicheaux v., TexComApp, 99 SW2d 880, 128 Tex 441.—Judgm 572(2).

Gulf Production Co. v. Spear, TexComApp, 84 SW2d 452, 125 Tex 530.—Bound 10; Contracts 147(2); Mines 73.1(1), 74(3); Tresp to T T 6.1, 11, 44.

Gulf Production Co.; Vackar v., TexCivApp–Eastland, 113 SW2d 686.—Elect of Rem 2, 3(1), 14; Evid 318(1); Mines 50.

Gulf Production Co. v. Warren, TexCivApp–Beaumont, 99 SW2d 616, writ refused, cert den Oakwood Realty Co v. Gulf Production Co, 58 SCt 27, 302 US 707, 82 LEd 546.—App & E 1061.4; Bound 33; Courts 247(7); Evid 460(6); Mines 48, 55(3), 55(5).

Gulf Production Co.; Wood v., TexCivApp–Texarkana, 100 SW2d 412.—Judgm 28, 217, 244, 686; Tresp to T T 27, 47(1).

Gulf Reduction Corp. v. Boyles Galvanizing & Plating Co., TexCivApp–Fort Worth, 456 SW2d 476.—Corp 1.4(4); Judgm 713(2).

Gulf Refining Co. v. A. F. G. Management 34 Ltd., TexCivApp–Hous (14 Dist), 605 SW2d 346, ref nre.—Em Dom 7, 191(1), 191(2); Judgm 184.

Gulf Refining Co. v. Beane, TexComApp, 127 SW2d 169, 133 Tex 157.—Neglig 1040(1), 1040(3), 1076, 1707.

Gulf Refining Co.; Beane v., TexCivApp–Galveston, 105 SW2d 334, aff 127 SW2d 169, 133 Tex 157.—Neglig 1076.

Gulf Refining Co.; Buckley v., TexCivApp–Amarillo, 123 SW2d 970, writ dism, correct.—Autos 245(28); Labor & Emp 3094(2); Princ & A 28.

Gulf Refining Co.; City of Fort Worth v., Tex, 83 SW2d 610, 125 Tex 512.—Autos 365; Evid 5(2); Licens 1, 7(1), 7(9), 9(1); Mun Corp 122.1(2).

Gulf Refining Co. v. Delavan, CA5 (Tex), 203 F2d 769.—Mines 125; Neglig 1613, 1614, 1617, 1624, 1695.

Gulf Refining Co. v. Jackson, TexCivApp–Waco, 99 SW2d 681.—Trial 234(7).

Gulf Refining Co.; Lohmann v., TexApp–Beaumont, 682 SW2d 612.—App & E 499(1), 852, 931(1), 931(3), 989; Em Dom 106; High 88; Mun Corp 655.

Gulf Refining Co. v. Nabers, TexCivApp–Amarillo, 134 SW2d 843.—Lim of Act 32(1), 43, 55(5), 55(7), 95(1.5), 197(1); Trial 352.4(2).

Gulf Refining Co. v. Needham, TexCivApp–Eastland, 233 SW2d 919.—App & E 78(4), 106, 1175(1); Corp 666; Judgm 17(1); Plead 110, 111.34.

Gulf Refining Co.; Pryzant v., TexCivApp–Beaumont, 83 SW2d 752.—Libel 45(2).

Gulf Refining Co.; Ross v., TexCivApp–Eastland, 530 SW2d 859.—Plead 111.42(4).

Gulf Refining Co. v. Shirley, TexCivApp–Eastland, 99 SW2d 613, writ dism.—Autos 193(4); Princ & A 3(1), 54; Trial 350.6(3).

Gulf Refining Co. v. Smith, TexCivApp–Fort Worth, 81 SW2d 155.—App & E 1073(7); Judgm 251(2); Trial 350.3(2.1).

Gulf Refining Co. v. Smith, TexCivApp–Texarkana, 476 SW2d 851.—Anim 44; Plead 111.3, 111.9, 111.42(4); Tresp 46(1).

Gulf Refining Co. v. U.S., EDTex, 69 FRD 300.—Adm 34.6(2.1); Courts 1; Fed Cts 1139; Statut 181(1), 205; U S 125(9), 125(10.1), 125(12).

Gulf Regional Educ. Television Affiliates v. University of Houston, TexApp–Houston (14 Dist), 746 SW2d 803, writ den.—Atty & C 74; Colleges 1, 3, 10; Trial 400(1), 401.

Gulf Rice Arkansas, LLC v. Union Pacific Railroad Co., SDTex, 376 FSupp2d 715.—Carr 108, 147, 160; Lim of Act 66(6); States 18.21.

Gulf Shores Council of Co-Owners, Inc. v. Raul Cantu No. 3 Family Ltd. Partnership, TexApp–Corpus Christi, 985 SW2d 667, reh overr, and review den, and reh of petition for review den.—Condo 8, 12, 13, 17; Contracts 147(2), 176(2); Torts 212, 220, 243.

Gulf South Pipeline Co., L.P.; Wyble v., EDTex, 308 FSupp2d 733.—Courts 99(3); Environ Law 656; Fed Civ Proc 103.2, 103.3, 103.4, 103.5, 2544; Fed Cts 12.1; Inj 114(2).

Gulf Star Foundries, Inc. v. Condon & Co., TexApp–Houston (14 Dist, 780 SW2d 894. See Gulf Star Foundries, Inc. v. Robert S. Condon & Co., Inc.

Gulf Star Foundries, Inc. v. Robert S. Condon & Co., Inc., TexApp–Houston (14 Dist), 780 SW2d 894.—App & E 80(6).

Gulf State Pipe Line Co., Inc. v. Orange County Water Control and Improvement Dist. No. 1, TexCivApp–Beaumont, 526 SW2d 724, ref nre.—Em Dom 77, 196; Evid 314(1); Inj 147; Trial 105(2), 382.

Gulf States Abrasive Mfg., Inc. v. Oertel, TexCivApp–Hous (1 Dist), 489 SW2d 184, ref nre.—Action 57(2); App & E 205; Corp 110, 113; Judgm 948(1); Set-Off 60; Stip 14(12).

Gulf States Abrasive Mfg. Inc.; Oertel v., TexCivApp–Hous (1 Dist), 429 SW2d 322.—Inj 152; Judgm 210.

Gulf States Asphalt Co., Inc.; U.S. v., CA5 (Tex), 472 F2d 933, 20 Wage & Hour Cas (BNA) 1122.—Labor & Emp 2292(3), 2367, 2399; Lim of Act 105(2).

Gulf States Drilling Co., Inc.; Colvard v., BkrtcyWD-Tex, 63 BR 343. See Bar M Petroleum Co., Inc., In re.

Gulf States Energy Corp.; Brannon v., Tex, 562 SW2d 219.—Evid 384, 385, 397(3), 424; Mines 80; Tresp 2.

Gulf States Energy Corp.; Brannon v., TexCivApp–Eastland, 548 SW2d 790, writ gr, rev 562 SW2d 219.—App & E 218.2(7), 756, 757(3), 758.3(3), 760(2), 870(2), 1043(1); Evid 419(9); Mines 78.7(4).

Gulf States Equipment Co. v. Toombs, TexCivApp–Texarkana, 317 SW2d 554, ref nre.—App & E 301, 1097(1); Damag 221(4); Evid 264; Judgm 527.

Gulf States Equipment Co. v. Toombs, TexCivApp–Waco, 288 SW2d 203, ref nre.—App & E 1062.1; Estop 120; Labor & Emp 114(3), 238, 259, 265; Trial 304, 350.4(4).

Gulf States Finance Co.; Old American Mut. Fire Ins. Co. v., TexApp–Houston (1 Dist), 73 SW3d 394, opinion supplemented on denial of reh, and review den.—Insurance 3450.

Gulf States, Inc.; Ervin v., TexCivApp–Hous (1 Dist), 594 SW2d 134, ref nre.—Evid 508, 519; Trial 351.5(6); Witn 345(1), 345(2), 345(7).

Gulf States Ins. Co. v. Alamo Carriage Service, CA5 (Tex), 22 F3d 88, reh gr, on reh 22 F3d 1095.—Fed Cts 726; Insurance 2278(13), 2913, 2914.

Gulf States Ins. Co.; Alamo Carriage Service, Inc. v., CA5 (Tex), 22 F3d 88. See Gulf States Ins. Co. v. Alamo Carriage Service.

Gulf States Ins. Co.; Farmer Enterprises, Inc. v., Tex-App–Dallas, 940 SW2d 103.—App & E 863, 934(1); Contracts 143(2), 147(2), 176(2); Corp 397; Insurance 1634(1), 1634(3), 1638, 1713, 1806, 1808, 1810, 1822, 2865, 2867; Judgm 181(23), 185(2), 185(5); Princ & A 99, 177(1).

Gulf States Marine & Min. Co.; Kitchens v., TexCivApp–Galveston, 294 SW2d 193, ref nre.—App & E 989, 1069.1; Neglig 421; Seamen 29(5.14), 29(5.18); Trial 358, 365.1(6).

Gulf States Marine & Min. Co. v. Norwich Union Fire Ins. Soc., SDTex, 168 FSupp 863, rev US Fire Ins Co v. Gulf States Marine & Min Co, 262 F2d 565.—Insurance 2219, 2367.

Gulf States Marine & Min. Co.; U.S. Fire Ins. Co. v., CA5 (Tex), 262 F2d 565.—Insurance 2214, 2285(8); Ship 81(1); Towage 4.

Gulf States Paint Co. v. Kornblee Co., TexCivApp–Texarkana, 390 SW2d 356, ref nre.—Damag 68, 69, 153, 221(2.1); Frds St of 44(4); Judgm 253(2); Princ & A 9, 22(1), 24; Sales 442(6); Trial 349(1).

Gulf States Paint Co.; Rice v., TexCivApp–Eastland, 406 SW2d 273, ref nre.—App & E 169; Neglig 554(1), 1533, 1573; Prod Liab 43, 75.1, 83, 88.

Gulf States Petroleum Corp. v. General Elec. Capital Auto Lease, TexApp–Eastland, 134 SW3d 504.—Bankr 2391, 2395, 2396, 2462; Judgm 118, 139, 143(2), 143(4), 143(8), 164; Pretrial Proc 506.1; Trover 4.

Gulf States Security Life Ins. Co. v. Edwards, TexCivApp–Amarillo, 109 SW2d 1125, writ dism.—App & E 237(2), 1001(1), 1033(1), 1069.1; Contracts 94(1); Fraud 4, 4.5; Insurance 3388, 3389, 3580; Trial 115(2), 350.4(3), 351.5(2), 355(1); Witn 37(3).

Gulf States Tel. Co.; City of Athens v., TexCivApp–Tyler, 380 SW2d 687, ref nre.—Tel 927, 943, 964, 979, 983.

Gulf States Tel. Co.; City of Athens v., TexCivApp–Tyler, 374 SW2d 757.—App & E 456, 460(1); Equity 55.

Gulf States Tel. Co. v. Local 1692, Intern. Broth. of Elec. Workers, AFL-CIO, CA5 (Tex), 416 F2d 198.—Labor & Emp 1595(8), 1595(10), 1621, 1624(1).

Gulf States Telecommunications and Information Systems, Inc.; Geotech Energy Corp. v., TexApp–Houston (14 Dist), 788 SW2d 386.—Antitrust 363; App & E 1003(7), 1062.1, 1062.2, 1064.1(1); Contracts 294; Costs 194.32; Damag 62(4), 163(2); Pretrial Proc 713, 716; Sales 3.1, 4(4), 5; Tel 913(1), 916(7); Trial 295(1).

Gulf States Theatres of Texas v. Hayes, TexCivApp–Beaumont, 534 SW2d 406, ref nre.—App & E 931(1), 989, 1010.1(1), 1010.1(3); Land & Ten 49(3), 105, 112.5.

Gulf States Theatres of Texas, Inc. v. Hayes, TexCivApp–Beaumont, 518 SW2d 604.—App & E 846(5), 854(1), 931(3), 989; Contracts 202(2); Labor & Emp 111; Princ & A 8.

Gulf States Toyota, Inc. v. Morgan, TexApp–Houston (1 Dist), 89 SW3d 766.—App & E 930(1), 1001(1), 1001(3); Civil R 1183, 1189.

Gulf States Toyota, Inc.; Moto-Sports, Inc. v., SDTex, 324 FSupp 653.—Antitrust 383(2); Fed Civ Proc 2484, 2485.

Gulf States Trading Co.; Ferrous Products Co. v., Tex, 332 SW2d 310, 160 Tex 399.—Sales 34, 368.

Gulf States Trading Co.; Ferrous Products Co. v., Tex-CivApp–Houston, 323 SW2d 292, aff 332 SW2d 310, 160 Tex 399.—Action 28; Atty & C 140; Contracts 1, 2; Costs 194.32, 194.38; Evid 18; Sales 34, 368; Trover 4, 13, 22.

Gulf States Underwriters of Louisiana, Inc. v. Wilson, TexApp–Beaumont, 753 SW2d 422, writ den.—Antitrust 393; App & E 82(2), 373(1), 396, 747(1), 878(6), 931(1), 989, 1012.1(5); Insurance 2016, 2044(1), 2561(3), 2578, 2607, 3401; Labor & Emp 23; Work Comp 230.

Gulf States Utilities Co. v. Alabama Power Co., CA5 (Tex), 824 F2d 1465, opinion am 831 F2d 557.—Admin Law 228.1; Dep in Court 2; Electricity 11.2(2), 11.3(1), 11.3(7); Fed Civ Proc 338; States 18.73.

Gulf States Utilities Co. v. Austin, TexCivApp–Hous (14 Dist), 439 SW2d 411, ref nre.—Em Dom 205, 219; Evid 474(18), 555.6(2), 568(4).

Gulf States Utilities Co.; Bailey v., TexApp–Beaumont, 27 SW3d 713, reh overr, and review den.—Antitrust 141, 144, 145; App & E 768, 863, 934(1); Damag 50.10, 52, 54, 87(2), 192; Electricity 11.4; Judgm 181(15.1); Torts 424.

Gulf States Utilities Co.; Ball v., TexCivApp–Beaumont, 123 SW2d 937, dism.—Courts 91(1); Electricity 19(3), 19(6.1); Neglig 409; Nuis 7, 42.

Gulf States Utilities Co.; Cassity v., TexApp–Beaumont, 628 SW2d 532, ref nre.—Em Dom 235, 238(4).

Gulf States Utilities Co.; Cassity v., TexCivApp–Beaumont, 628 SW2d 86, ref nre.—Em Dom 265(5).

Gulf States Utilities Co.; City of Beaumont v., TexCivApp–Beaumont, 163 SW2d 426, writ refused wom.—Const Law 2707, 4055, 4056; Mun Corp 65, 71, 79, 658, 661(1); Plead 360; States 131; Statut 64(8), 107(1), 107(6).

Gulf States Utilities Co. v. Coalition of Cities for Affordable Utility Rates, TexApp–Austin, 883 SW2d 739, reh overr, and writ gr, rev 947 SW2d 887, on remand In re Remand of Docket No 7195, 1998 WL 971285, reh gr 1998 WL 34066283, reh den 1998 WL 34066284, subsequently aff Entergy Gulf States, Inc v. Public Utility Com'n of Texas, 112 SW3d 208, review den, and reh of petition for review den.—Admin Law 229, 481, 485, 669.1, 683, 786, 788, 790, 791, 793, 819; Const Law 4361; Electricity 11.3(2), 11.3(4), 11.3(5), 11.3(6), 11.3(7); Pub Ut 119.1, 123, 124, 128, 129, 130, 147, 165, 168, 194, 196.

Gulf States Utilities Co. v. Coalition of Cities for Affordable Utility Rates, TexApp–Austin, 776 SW2d 224. See Public Utility Com'n of Texas v. Coalition of Cities for Affordable Utility Rates.

Gulf States Utilities Co. v. Coalition of Cities for Affordable Utility Rates, TexApp–Austin, 776 SW2d 222. See Public Utility Com'n of Texas v. Coalition of Cities for Affordable Utility Rates.

Gulf States Utilities Co. v. Coalition of Cities for Affordable Utility Rates, TexApp–Austin, 776 SW2d 221. See Public Utility Com'n of Texas v. Coalition of Cities for Affordable Utility Rates.

Gulf States Utilities Co. v. County of Chambers, TexApp–Beaumont, 911 SW2d 888, reh overr, and writ den.—Counties 141; Electricity 17; States 191.6(1).

Gulf States Utilities Co.; Cutler v., TexCivApp–Beaumont, 361 SW2d 221, ref nre.—App & E 961; Damag 91(3); Death 77; Pretrial Proc 336, 354, 390.

Gulf States Utilities Co. v. Dillon, TexCivApp–Waco, 112 SW2d 752.—App & E 843(3), 1067; Death 85, 104(4), 104(6); Trial 352.5(8), 352.9, 352.10, 352.18.

Gulf States Utilities Co. v. Dryden, TexApp–Beaumont, 735 SW2d 263.—App & E 215(1), 216(1), 1140(4); Damag 132(1), 208(2), 208(6); Labor & Emp 3125, 3179(4); Neglig 213, 371, 379, 380, 387, 506(8), 1011, 1672, 1675, 1676, 1683; New Tr 162(1); Trial 351.2(5), 366.

Gulf States Utilities Co.; Grover v., CA5 (Tex), 776 F2d 517.—Electricity 17, 18(1); Torts 113(2).

Gulf States Utilities Co.; Incorporated Town of Hempstead v., Tex, 206 SW2d 227, 146 Tex 250.—Const Law 2641, 2642; Electricity 9(2); Franch 2.

Gulf States Utilities Co. v. Incorporated Town of Hempstead, TexCivApp–Galveston, 198 SW2d 620, rev 206 SW2d 227, 146 Tex 250.—Electricity 9(2).

Gulf States Utilities Co.; LeJeune v., TexCivApp–Beaumont, 410 SW2d 44, ref nre.—App & E 212, 719(8), 758.1; Labor & Emp 2825, 2879, 2883, 2927, 2939, 2942; Work Comp 1072, 1789, 1791, 1792, 2084, 2142, 2148.

Gulf States Utilities Co.; Local Union No. 2286 of Intern. Broth. of Elec. Workers, AFL-CIO v., EDTex, 749 FSupp 777.—Fed Civ Proc 2737.1, 2771(9); Labor & Emp 1272, 1273, 1281, 1597.

Gulf States Utilities Co. v. Low, Tex, 79 SW3d 561.—Antitrust 389(1), 389(2), 397; App & E 930(4), 1151(3), 1178(6); Costs 194.16, 194.25; Damag 49.10, 96, 104, 113, 119; Evid 474(16); Trial 351.2(3.1).

Gulf States Utilities Co.; Low v., TexApp–Beaumont, 75 SW3d 449, reh overr, and review gr, rev 79 SW3d 561.—Antitrust 294, 397; Costs 208; Damag 49.10, 50, 57.49, 96, 104, 119, 139, 163(1), 184, 192; Interest 31, 39(2), 39(2.20), 39(3).

Gulf States Utilities Co. v. McMillon, TexApp–Beaumont, 740 SW2d 876, writ den.—Compromise 16(1); Garn 251; Labor & Emp 968, 1273, 1319, 1996; States 18.46.

Gulf States Utilities Co.; Mann v., TexCivApp–Austin, 167 SW2d 557, writ refused.—Licens 8(0.5); Pub Ut 113; Statut 251.

Gulf States Utilities Co. v. Mitchell, TexCivApp–Beaumont, 104 SW2d 652.—Neglig 1526, 1537; Plead 34(2), 381(1); Trial 352.4(4).

Gulf States Utilities Co. v. Moore, TexComApp, 106 SW2d 256, 129 Tex 604.—App & E 1064.1(9); Trial 232(2), 252(11); Work Comp 2113.

Gulf States Utilities Co. v. Public Utility Com'n of Texas, Tex, 947 SW2d 887, on remand In re Remand of Docket No 7195, 1998 WL 971285, reh gr 1998 WL 34066283, reh den 1998 WL 34066284, subsequently aff Entergy Gulf States, Inc v. Public Utility Com'n of Texas, 112 SW3d 208, review den, and reh of petition for review den.—Electricity 11.3(7).

Gulf States Utilities Co.; Public Utility Com'n of Texas v., Tex, 809 SW2d 201.—Admin Law 413, 763, 793; Electricity 11.3(1), 11.3(2); Pub Ut 149, 194.

Gulf States Utilities Co. v. Public Utility Com'n of Texas, TexApp–Austin, 841 SW2d 459, writ den.—Admin Law 793; Commerce 62.1; Electricity 1, 11.3(4), 11.3(6); Pub Ut 123, 128, 165; States 18.3, 18.73.

Gulf States Utilities Co. v. Public Utility Com'n of Texas, TexApp–Austin, 784 SW2d 519, writ gr, aff 809 SW2d 201.—Electricity 11.3(3), 11.3(4).

Gulf States Utilities Co. v. Reed, TexApp–Houston (14 Dist), 659 SW2d 849, ref nre.—App & E 968, 1004(5), 1060.1(2.1), 1151(2), 1170.6; Death 64, 85, 88, 89, 95(1), 99(2), 104(5); Evid 146; Jury 131(15.1).

Gulf States Utilities Co.; Ringo v., TexCivApp–Beaumont, 569 SW2d 31, ref nre.—Electricity 13, 18(1), 20(5); Judgm 181(33); Statut 181(1), 181(2), 190, 239, 240.

Gulf States Utilities Co.; Riverside, Inc. v., TexCivApp–Beaumont, 289 SW2d 945, ref nre.—Interest 45; Waters 203(9), 203(15).

Gulf States Utilities Co. v. Selman, TexCivApp–Beaumont, 137 SW2d 122, writ dism, correct.—App & E 1177(8); Autos 173(4), 211, 244(45), 245(17), 245(83), 245(90); Neglig 1713.

Gulf States Utilities Co.; Smith v., TexCivApp–Hous (14 Dist), 616 SW2d 300, ref nre.—Em Dom 160, 170, 180, 187, 191(6), 231, 272.1, 274(1).

Gulf States Utilities Co.; State ex rel. City of Jasper v., Tex, 189 SW2d 693, 144 Tex 184.—Counties 47; Electricity 9(2); Estop 62.4; Evid 65; Mun Corp 683(1); Quo W 49.

Gulf States Utilities Co.; State ex rel. City of Jasper v., TexCivApp, 185 SW2d 501, rev 189 SW2d 693, 144 Tex

184.—Estop 62.4, 62.8; Mun Corp 683(1); Quo W 49, 50(1), 55.

Gulf States Utilities Co.; Texas Employment Commission v., TexCivApp–Eastland, 410 SW2d 322, ref nre.— Unemp Comp 5, 101, 428, 550.

Gulf States Utilities Co.; Tonahill v., Tex, 446 SW2d 301.—Em Dom 238(6), 274(1), 293(4).

Gulf States Utilities Co. v. Tonahill, TexCivApp–Beaumont, 445 SW2d 593, ref nre 446 SW2d 301.—Courts 480(1); Em Dom 191(1), 191(7), 194, 196, 228, 231.

Gulf States Utilities Co. v. Wooldridge, TexCivApp–Beaumont, 90 SW2d 325.—Trial 219, 352.5(1), 352.5(8), 352.10, 352.15.

Gulf States Utility Co.; Martinez v., TexApp–Houston (14 Dist), 864 SW2d 802, reh den, and writ den.—Indem 30(1), 30(4), 68; Neglig 238, 259.

Gulf State Utilities Co., Local Union Number 2286; Daigle v., CA5 (Tex), 794 F2d 974, cert den 107 SCt 648, 479 US 1008, 93 LEd2d 704, on remand 1987 WL 109112, aff 860 F2d 436, cert den 109 SCt 1749, 490 US 1022, 104 LEd2d 185.—Civil R 1041; Consp 7.5(1), 18; Fed Cts 265, 269; Labor & Emp 1219(4), 1322; Lim of Act 95(14).

Gulf Stevedore Corp. v. Flota Mercante Grancolombiana, S. A., CA5 (Tex), 401 F2d 537.—Ship 84(6).

Gulf Stevedore Corp.; Fylipoy v., SDTex, 257 FSupp 166.—Fed Cts 270; Mun Corp 723; Nav Wat 8.5; States 191.7.

Gulf Stevedore Corp. v. Hollis, CA5 (Tex), 427 F2d 160, cert den 91 SCt 63, 400 US 831, 27 LEd2d 62.—Work Comp 898.

Gulf Stevedore Corp. v. Hollis, SDTex, 298 FSupp 426, aff 427 F2d 160, cert den 91 SCt 63, 400 US 831, 27 LEd2d 62.—Work Comp 869, 898, 1042, 1665, 1893, 1939.4(4).

Gulf Stevedore Corp.; Watson v., CA5 (Tex), 400 F2d 649, reh den Young & Co v. Shea, 404 F2d 1059, cert den 89 SCt 1471, 394 US 9761, 22 LEd2d 755, cert den 89 SCt 1771, 395 US 920, 23 LEd2d 237, cert den 89 SCt 1471, 394 US 9761, 22 LEd2d 755, cert den 89 SCt 1771, 395 US 920, 23 LEd2d 237.—Admin Law 784.1, 791; Work Comp 52, 853, 863, 1491, 1633, 1656, 1910, 1939.3, 1939.7, 1939.11(9), 1964, 1969.

Gulf Stevedore Corp.; Watson v., CA5 (Tex), 374 F2d 946, cert den 88 SCt 286, 389 US 927, 19 LEd2d 277.— Ship 84(3.1), 84(6), 86(1); Work Comp 2085, 2158.

Gulf Stevedore Corp.; Watson v., SDTex, 257 FSupp 503, aff 374 F2d 946, cert den 88 SCt 286, 389 US 927, 19 LEd2d 277.—Work Comp 2085.

Gulf Stream Realty Co. v. Monte Alto Citrus Ass'n, TexCivApp–San Antonio, 253 SW2d 933, writ refused.— Crops 1, 2, 5, 7; Execution 24; Mtg 374, 378; Sales 235(2), 235(3); Trover 60.

Gulfstream Steel Corp.; CGM Valve Co., Inc. v., TexCivApp–Hous (1 Dist), 596 SW2d 161, ref nre.—App & E 241; Indem 85; Judgm 699(2).

Gulf Supply Co.; Dobson v., TexCivApp–Houston, 399 SW2d 882, ref nre.—App & E 930(1), 989, 1001(3); Autos 242(1), 244(44), 244(58).

Gulf Supply Co., Inc.; Briscoe v., TexCivApp–Fort Worth, 612 SW2d 88, ref nre.—App & E 619, 624, 627, 627.2.

Gulf Television Co.; Brown v., Tex, 306 SW2d 706, 157 Tex 607.—Courts 247(7); Inj 111; Venue 1 1/2, 5.5, 15.

Gulf Television Co. v. Brown, TexCivApp–Galveston, 301 SW2d 256, aff 306 SW2d 706, 157 Tex 607.—Inj 111; Venue 2, 5.5, 21.

Gulf-Tex Brokerage v. McDade and Associates, SDTex, 433 FSupp 1015.—Fed Cts 194; Insurance 1670, 1671.

Gulftex Drug Co. v. Schachter, TexCivApp–Galveston, 110 SW2d 1220.—Abate & R 8(1); App & E 219(2), 966(1); Int Liq 327(1); Pretrial Proc 717.1, 722, 724.

Gulftex Liquor Corp. v. Blake, TexCivApp–Beaumont, 106 SW2d 1060.—Autos 197(7); Plead 111.46.

Gulftide Gas Corp. v. Cox, TexApp–Houston (1 Dist), 699 SW2d 239, ref nre.—App & E 1033(9), 1062.4, 1070(2), 1073(1); Contracts 176(11); Damag 89(2), 184; Fraud 61; Gas 14.1(3); Judgm 199(1); States 18.85.

Gulf-Tide Stevedores; Voris v., CA5 (Tex), 211 F2d 549, cert den 75 SCt 37, 348 US 823, 99 LEd 649.—Costs 103; Statut 190; Work Comp 52, 1109, 1987, 1989.

Gulf Tide Stevedores v. Voris, SDTex, 119 FSupp 708, rev 211 F2d 549, cert den 75 SCt 37, 348 US 823, 99 LEd 649.—Const Law 2528; Statut 190; Work Comp 2251.

Gulf Trading & Transp. Co. v. Vessel Hoegh Shield, CA5 (Tex), 658 F2d 363, reh den 670 F2d 182, reh den Hoegh Shiel, Vessel, 670 F2d 182, cert den 102 SCt 2932, 457 US 1119, 73 LEd2d 1332.—Adm 1.11, 66; Const Law 3994, 4480; Mar Liens 24, 65.

Gulf Union Industries, Inc. v. Formation Sec., Inc., CA5 (Tex), 842 F2d 762.—Const Law 4019; Dep & Escr 26; Fed Civ Proc 2737.14; Fed Cts 415, 616.

Gulf Union Industries, Inc.; Formation Sec., Inc. v., CA5 (Tex), 842 F2d 762. See Gulf Union Industries, Inc. v. Formation Sec., Inc.

Gulf Union Oil Co.; Isbell v., Tex, 209 SW2d 762, 147 Tex 6.—Const Law 1012; Corp 499, 599, 615.5, 617(1); Tax 2013, 2233, 3216.

Gulf Union Oil Co. v. Isbell, TexCivApp–Austin, 205 SW2d 105, rev 209 SW2d 762, 147 Tex 6.—Corp 499, 599, 615.5; Statut 147, 200, 219(10), 223.5(1).

Gulf View Courts v. Galveston County, TexCivApp–Galveston, 150 SW2d 872, writ refused.—App & E 1011.1(8.1); Deeds 109, 120; Ease 38; Inj 93; Levees 13.5.

Gulf Water Benefaction Co., In re, BkrtcySDTex, 2 BR 357.—Bankr 2369, 2374; Inj 138.18; States 4.4(3).

Gulf Water Benefaction Co. v. Public Utility Commission of Texas, CA5 (Tex), 674 F2d 462.—Courts 489(1).

Gulf Water Benefaction Co.; State of Tex. v., CA5 (Tex), 679 F2d 85.—Rem of C 70, 86(1), 107(7), 107(9), 107(11).

Gulfway General Hospital, Inc. v. Pursley, TexCivApp–Waco, 397 SW2d 93, 16 ALR3d 1232, ref nre.—Health 750; Neglig 1037(4).

Gulfway Nat. Bank; Lindeburg v., TexApp–Corpus Christi, 624 SW2d 278, ref nre.—Banks 117; Bills & N 453; Evid 434(12); Judgm 185.2(1).

Gulfway Nat. Bank of Corpus Christi; Bailey v., TexApp–Corpus Christi, 626 SW2d 70, ref nre.—Evid 208(1), 210, 264, 434(12); Judgm 185.1(3), 185.3(16).

Gulfway Shopping Center, Inc.; Thomas v., SDTex, 320 FSupp 756.—Bankr 2023, 2581, 2601, 2602.1, 2603, 2606.1, 2612, 2725.1, 2726(3), 2967.1; Land & Ten 240.

Gulick; Asgrow Seed Co. v., TexCivApp–San Antonio, 420 SW2d 438, ref nre.—Contracts 164; Cust & U 10; Fraud 23; Sales 267.

Gulihur; Purnell v., TexCivApp–El Paso, 339 SW2d 86, ref nre.—Adv Poss 29, 95, 104; App & E 854(1), 931(1); Deeds 53, 193, 207; Lim of Act 19(1).

Gulistan Carpet Inc. v. Porter, TexApp–Dallas, 4 SW3d 891.—App & E 138, 148; Corp 445.1.

Gullatt v. State, TexCrimApp, 180 SW2d 441.—Crim Law 1094(3).

Gullatt v. State, TexApp–Waco, 74 SW3d 880.—Crim Law 474.2, 478(1), 480, 481, 1153(2).

Gulledge v. Greif Bros. Corp., TexCivApp–Hous (1 Dist), 499 SW2d 745.—Contracts 205.40, 312(5); Damag 191; R R 87, 109.

Gulledge v. State, TexCrimApp, 329 SW2d 877, 168 Tex-Crim 487.—Crim Law 1087.1(2).

Gulledge; U.S. v., CA5 (Tex), 491 F2d 679, cert den 95 SCt 89, 419 US 849, 42 LEd2d 80.—Crim Law 273.1(4).

Gulledge; U.S. v., CA5 (Tex), 469 F2d 713.—Arrest 71.1(8); Consp 47(11); Crim Law 1036.1(4), 1038.1(6); Int Liq 247; Rec S Goods 4, 8(3), 9(2); Searches 18, 28, 44, 59, 62, 66.

Gulledge v. U.S., CA5 (Tex), 405 F2d 880.—Consp 47(11); Rec S Goods 8(3).

Gullett, In re, BkrtcySDTex, 230 BR 321, rev Continental Cas Co v. Gullett, 253 BR 796, aff 220 F3d 585.—Bankr 2060.1, 2391, 2394.1, 2395, 2402(2.15), 2422.5(1), 2461, 2467, 2468, 2535(1), 2537, 2671, 3362; Estop 52(1); Work Comp 2080.

Gullett v. Chater, EDTex, 973 FSupp 614.—Fed Civ Proc 921; Social S 140.1, 140.21, 142.5, 145, 146, 149.

Gullett; Continental Cas. Co. v., SDTex, 253 BR 796, aff In re Gullett, 220 F3d 585.—Bankr 2402(2.15), 3782, 3784, 3786; Courts 509; Set-Off 6; Work Comp 904.

Gullett; Detox Industries, Inc. v., TexApp–Houston (1 Dist), 770 SW2d 954.—Corp 110.

Gulley; Perez v., TexApp–Corpus Christi, 829 SW2d 388, reh overr, and writ den.—Action 27(1).

Gulley v. State, TexCrimApp, 94 SW2d 461, 130 TexCrim 335.—Crim Law 939(3), 940.

Gulley v. Sunbelt Sav., F.S.B., CA5 (Tex), 902 F2d 348, reh den, cert den 111 SCt 673, 498 US 1025, 112 LEd2d 665.—Admin Law 683; B & L Assoc 42(18), 48; Fed Cts 612.1, 757.

Gulley v. Sunbelt Sav. FSB, NDTex, 714 FSupp 819, aff 902 F2d 348, reh den, cert den 111 SCt 673, 498 US 1025, 112 LEd2d 665.—Fraud Conv 2.1; States 18.15.

Gulliver's v. Republic of Texas Properties, Inc., Tex-App–Dallas, 773 SW2d 398. See Canteen Corp. v. Republic of Texas Properties, Inc.

Gullo; City of Stafford v., TexApp–Houston (1 Dist), 886 SW2d 524.—Zoning 382.2, 382.3.

Gullo v. City of West University Place, TexCivApp–Galveston, 214 SW2d 851, writ dism.—App & E 846(5); Const Law 4093; Decl Judgm 306; Evid 546.

Gullo-Haas Toyota, Inc. v. Davidson, Eagleson & Co., TexApp–Houston (1 Dist), 832 SW2d 418.—App & E 465(1), 472.

Gully; Downing v., TexApp–Fort Worth, 915 SW2d 181, reh overr, and writ den.—App & E 863, 934(1); Const Law 2312; Health 710; Judgm 181(33), 185(1), 185(2), 185(6), 185.3(21).

Gully; Seidel v., TexCivApp–Eastland, 242 SW2d 442.—Venue 5.2.

Gully v. Southwestern Bell Telephone Co., CA5 (Tex), 774 F2d 1287.—Contracts 108(2); Damag 45; Em Dom 10(2), 63, 82, 107, 124, 133, 187, 241, 271; Tresp 47.

Gulsby Engineering, Inc.; Ortloff Corp. v., SDTex, 706 FSupp 1295, aff 884 F2d 1399.—Antitrust 423, 587(3); Pat 16.25, 97, 231, 318(3), 319(3).

Gulsby Engineering, Inc.; Tenneco Oil Co. v., TexApp–Houston (14 Dist), 846 SW2d 599, reh den, and writ den. —App & E 863, 934(1), 1005(4); Contracts 95(3), 143(2), 143.5, 147(2), 176(1); Costs 207; Guar 1, 9, 36(1); Indem 33(1), 33(5), 37, 67, 94, 103; Judgm 199(3.10); Mtg 79.

Gulton Industries, Inc.; Wentworth v., NDTex, 578 FSupp 508, aff 722 F2d 1253.—Pat 16(1), 16(2), 16(4), 26(1), 26(1.5), 26(2), 32, 36.1(3), 36.1(4), 36.2(1), 51(1), 72(1), 75, 112.3(1), 118.21, 226.10.

Gum v. Schaefer, TexApp–Corpus Christi, 683 SW2d 803. —App & E 922, 1062.2; Atty & C 123(1); Jury 91, 97(1), 97(4), 133; Partners 70, 94, 95, 121.

Gumfory v. Hansford County Com'rs Court, TexCiv-App–Amarillo, 561 SW2d 28, ref nre.—Const Law 725; Counties 18.

Guminski; C.I.R. v., CA5 (Tex), 198 F2d 265.—Int Rev 3334.

Gum Keepsake Diamond Center; Reed v., TexApp–Corpus Christi, 657 SW2d 524.—Judgm 16, 19, 237(2).

Gumm; Banks v., TexCivApp–Waco, 360 SW2d 836, ref nre.—Frds St of 138(4); Home 98; Hus & W 23, 80; Interest 39(3).

Gumm; Chalmers v., TexComApp, 154 SW2d 640, 137 Tex 467.—App & E 14(2), 1202; Judgm 199(1); Wills 288(3).

Gumm v. Chalmers, TexCivApp–Galveston, 127 SW2d 942, mod 154 SW2d 640, 137 Tex 467.—Judgm 199(1), 199(3.9), 199(3.19); Trial 139.1(6); Wills 222, 281, 324(1), 324(2).

Gumm v. Owen, TexApp–El Paso, 815 SW2d 259.—Atty & C 129(1); Lim of Act 95(11), 197(2); Trial 139.1(11), 139.1(14), 178.

Gumm; Trickey v., TexApp–Waco, 632 SW2d 167.—App & E 954(1), 954(2); Inj 138.21; Mtg 335, 338.

Gummelt v. Southwestern Indem. Co., TexCivApp–Waco, 363 SW2d 379, ref nre.—Subrog 7(1), 7(2); Tax 3696.

Gumpert v. State, TexApp–Texarkana, 48 SW3d 450, petition for discretionary review refused, cert den 122 SCt 1933, 535 US 1064, 152 LEd2d 838.—Assault 92(2); Crim Law 641.13(1), 641.13(2.1), 641.13(6), 721(3), 728(2), 728(5), 795(1.5), 795(2.10), 795(2.30), 867, 949(1), 959, 1032(5), 1134(2), 1159.2(2), 1169.2(1); Ind & Inf 191(0.5).

Gumpp v. Philadelphia Life Ins. Co., TexCivApp–San Antonio, 562 SW2d 885.—App & E 79(1); Insurance 2422, 3349, 3360, 3374, 3375.

Gunaca; Energy Plus Savers, Inc. v., TexCivApp–El Paso, 620 SW2d 898, ref nre.—App & E 241; Judgm 183, 185.2(4).

Gunaca v. State of Tex., CA5 (Tex), 65 F3d 467.—Civil R 1116(3), 1352(5), 1376(1), 1376(10), 1544; Fed Civ Proc 2491.5.

Gunderland Marine Supply, Inc. v. Bray, TexCivApp–Corpus Christi, 570 SW2d 542, ref nre.—App & E 930(3), 989; Sales 1(1); Ship 27.

Gundersen; Wright v., TexApp–Houston (14 Dist), 956 SW2d 43.—Antitrust 134, 141, 145, 256, 363; App & E 173(2); Atty & C 26, 64, 105; Courts 91(1), 202(5); Judgm 181(16), 183, 185(2).

Gunderson v. Neiman-Marcus Group, Inc., NDTex, 982 FSupp 1231.—Civil R 1176, 1185, 1220, 1224, 1225(3), 1225(4), 1251, 1553; Labor & Emp 367(2), 368, 370, 372.

Gundle Lining Const. Corp. v. Adams County Asphalt, Inc., CA5 (Tex), 85 F3d 201.—Const Law 3964; Corp 1.4(4), 1.5(3), 1.7(2); Courts 12(2.1); Fed Cts 76, 76.10, 76.30, 79, 96, 97, 101, 417, 776, 819; Princ & S 185.

Gundle Lining Const. Corp. v. Fireman's Fund Ins. Co., SDTex, 844 FSupp 1163.—Fed Cts 101, 103, 104, 105, 106, 144.

Gundolf; Massman-Johnson v., Tex, 484 SW2d 555.—Neglig 251, 400, 1037(4), 1095, 1286(7), 1717; Trial 350.7(1).

Gundolf v. Massman-Johnson, TexCivApp–Beaumont, 473 SW2d 70, ref nre 484 SW2d 555.—Neglig 1296, 1566, 1571; Work Comp 2243.

Gundrum v. Quarterman, CA5 (Tex), 191 FedAppx 313. —Hab Corp 603.

Gunera; U.S. v., CA5 (Tex), 479 F3d 373.—Aliens 773, 793; Crim Law 149, 1139, 1158(1).

Guneratne v. St. Mary's Hosp., SDTex, 943 FSupp 771, aff 119 F3d 3, cert den 118 SCt 560, 522 US 996, 139 LEd2d 401.—Civil R 1217, 1218(4), 1225(2); Labor & Emp 861, 863(2).

Gunishaw v. State, TexCrimApp, 356 SW2d 315, 172 TexCrim 266.—Crim Law 1037.1(4); Homic 1154, 1387.

Gunlock v. Greenwade, TexCivApp–Waco, 280 SW2d 610, ref nre.—Action 57(2); App & E 1064.1(10); Deeds 3, 78, 194(5), 203, 207, 208(1); Sales 53(1); Wills 53(1), 164(1), 164(3), 164(4), 164(5), 164(7), 166(1), 333, 400.

Gunn; Aetna Life and Cas. Co. v., Tex, 628 SW2d 758.—Contracts 169; Insurance 2582.

Gunn v. Aetna Life and Cas. Co., TexCivApp–Dallas, 629 SW2d 59.—Insurance 1808, 1822, 1832(1), 1836.

Gunn v. Atchison, Topeka and Santa Fe Ry. Co., Tex-App–Amarillo, 13 SW3d 52.—R R 316(1), 348(5); States 18.21.

Gunn v. Cavanaugh, Tex, 391 SW2d 723.—Adop 7.7, 15; App & E 138, 143, 148, 859; Const Law 3974, 4001; Courts 202(5); Infants 203.

Gunn v. Cavanaugh, TexCivApp–Austin, 385 SW2d 451, aff 391 SW2d 723.—Adop 15; App & E 148.

Gunn v. Harris Methodist Affiliated Hospitals, Tex-App–Fort Worth, 887 SW2d 248, reh overr, and writ den.—App & E 863, 907(1); Judgm 185(2), 186; Neglig 213, 1001, 1032, 1036, 1037(2), 1037(4), 1086, 1670, 1692.

Gunn; ICT Ins. Co. v., TexCivApp–Waco, 294 SW2d 435, ref nre.—App & E 930(1), 1001(1); Trial 141, 142, 143, 295(1), 352.10; Work Comp 853, 1681, 1683, 1958, 1988.

Gunn v. Johns, TexCivApp–Dallas, 153 SW2d 709, writ dism.—Child S 507.

Gunn v. Manness, CA5 (Tex), 219 FedAppx 371.—Fed Cts 611.

Gunn; Meadowbriar Home for Children, Inc. v., CA5 (Tex), 81 F3d 521.—Civil R 1075, 1083, 1343, 1351(1), 1351(3), 1357, 1376(2), 1376(4), 1395(3), 1398; Fed Civ Proc 103.2, 103.3, 103.5, 1342.1, 1773, 1829, 1835, 2470, 2470.1, 2470.4, 2544, 2579, 2766, 2801, 2830; Fed Cts 29.1, 557, 562, 584, 597, 598.1, 714, 776, 812, 820; Statut 184, 188, 208.

Gunn v. Phillips, TexCivApp–Houston, 410 SW2d 202, ref nre.—Wills 52(1), 55(1), 55(9), 130, 289, 302(6), 455, 466, 554; Witn 159(1).

Gunn; Rogers v., TexCivApp–Amarillo, 545 SW2d 861.— Deeds 194(3); Hus & W 249(5).

Gunn v. Schaeffer, TexCivApp–El Paso, 567 SW2d 30.— Consp 19; Judgm 185.3(14); Princ & A 108(2), 131, 150(2).

Gunn v. State, TexCrimApp, 340 SW2d 496, 170 TexCrim 288.—Crim Law 564(1); Homic 1134.

Gunn v. State, TexCrimApp, 146 SW2d 383, 140 TexCrim 519.—Crim Law 1124(3), 1182.

Gunn v. State, TexCrimApp, 114 SW2d 904, 134 TexCrim 225.—Crim Law 1099.7(2), 1182.

Gunn v. State, TexCrimApp, 114 SW2d 903, 134 TexCrim 225.—Crim Law 1099.7(2), 1099.10, 1182.

Gunn v. State, TexCrimApp, 109 SW2d 1056, 133 Tex-Crim 226.—Int Liq 215.

Gunn v. Texas Dept. of Public Safety, TexCivApp– Amarillo, 410 SW2d 207.—Evid 332(1); Judgm 180, 185.3(1).

Gunn v. University Committee to End War in Viet Nam, USTex, 90 SCt 2013, 399 US 383, 26 LEd2d 684. —Fed Cts 477; Inj 201, 204, 229.

Gunn; University Committee to End War in Viet Nam v., WDTex, 289 FSupp 469, probable jur noted 89 SCt 119, 393 US 819, 21 LEd2d 90, appeal dism 90 SCt 2013, 399 US 383, 26 LEd2d 684.—Breach of P 1(2); Const Law 1430, 1490, 1813, 1845; Decl Judgm 84; Inj 22.

Gunn; Waters v., TexCivApp–Amarillo, 218 SW2d 235, ref nre.—Elections 227(1); Schools 97(4); Statut 147, 231.

Gunn & Briggs, Inc.; Benson v., TexCivApp–Fort Worth, 438 SW2d 896, ref nre.—Contracts 280(3); Judgm 185.3(21).

Gunn Buick, Inc. v. Rosano, TexApp–San Antonio, 907 SW2d 628.—Antitrust 364, 369; App & E 916(1), 930(3), 946, 999(1), 999(2), 1001(1), 1002, 1003(7), 1062.2, 1067; Plead 48; Trial 182, 219, 230, 251(1), 260(5), 349(2).

Gunn Chevrolet; Hinerman v., TexApp–San Antonio, 877 SW2d 806, reh den, and writ gr, rev in part 898 SW2d 817.—App & E 854(1); Judgm 181(21); Labor & Emp 810, 863(2).

Gunn Chevrolet, Inc. v. Hinerman, Tex, 898 SW2d 817. —Labor & Emp 807; Work Comp 2088.

Gunnell; Adams v., CA5 (Tex), 729 F2d 362.—Civil R 1398; Const Law 1452, 2270, 4824; Fed Cts 939; Prisons 13(7.1), 13.5(1).

Gunnell; Holloway v., CA5 (Tex), 685 F2d 150.—Admin Law 229; Fed Civ Proc 1741, 1742(5), 1773; Fed Cts 74, 95; Sent & Pun 1539, 1545, 1549, 1553.

Gunnells Sand Co. v. Wilhite, TexCivApp–Waco, 389 SW2d 596, ref nre.—Autos 247; Plead 1, 380; Princ & A 189(4).

Gunnels v. Atcheson, TexCivApp–Amarillo, 288 SW2d 878.—Judgm 181(1), 181(19), 185(2), 186.

Gunnels v. City of Brownfield, TexApp–Amarillo, 153 SW3d 452, reh overr, and review den.—App & E 179(1); Civil R 1037, 1351(1), 1351(3), 1351(4); Const Law 3041, 3298, 3340, 3516, 3789; Judgm 185.3(21); Mal Pros 0.5, 15, 18(4), 18(5), 18(6), 20, 28, 29, 30, 56, 64(2); Zoning 802.

Gunnels; Govier v., TexCivApp–Galveston, 246 SW2d 339. —Judgm 185.3(20); Mun Corp 63.5, 446, 568(3); Trial 139.1(2).

Gunnels v. North Woodland Hills Community Ass'n, TexCivApp–Hous (1 Dist), 563 SW2d 334.—Assoc 20(5); Covenants 1, 49, 51(1), 79(1), 84; Inj 62(1), 133, 138.1, 138.37, 147.

Gunnels; Palais Royal, Inc. v., TexApp–Houston (1 Dist), 976 SW2d 837, petition for review abated, and petition for review abated, and review dism by agreement.— App & E 756, 836, 927(7), 930(1), 930(3), 997(3), 1001(1), 1003(6), 1033(5); Damag 91(3), 184; Estop 52.15; Evid 571(9), 601(1); Lim of Act 13; Neglig 549(8), 1001, 1011, 1037(4), 1040(3), 1141, 1669, 1679, 1725, 1738.

Gunner v. Chevron U.S.A., Inc., EDTex, 684 FSupp 916. —Civil R 1544, 1545.

Gunner; Harris v., TexCivApp–Fort Worth, 545 SW2d 856.—Plead 34(6), 404; Sales 370, 379, 383, 384(2).

Gunnerman v. Basic Capital Management, Inc., Tex-App–Dallas, 106 SW3d 821, review den, appeal after remand 2006 WL 411805.—App & E 418; Judgm 185.3(1), 335(1), 335(2), 335(3).

Gunn Infiniti, Inc. v. O'Byrne, Tex, 996 SW2d 854, on remand 18 SW3d 715.—Antitrust 392; Compromise 2; Damag 62(1), 62(4), 127, 192, 208(7), 214.

Gunn Infiniti, Inc. v. O'Byrne, TexApp–San Antonio, 18 SW3d 715.—Antitrust 392; App & E 1151(2).

Gunn Infiniti, Inc. v. O'Byrne, TexApp–San Antonio, 963 SW2d 787, reh overr, and review gr, rev 996 SW2d 854, on remand 18 SW3d 715.—Antitrust 161, 193, 389(1), 390, 392, 393; App & E 842(9), 999(1), 1001(3), 1003(7), 1062.2; Damag 15, 62(1), 91(1), 94, 163(2), 192, 214; Fraud 3, 18, 58(2), 61; Trial 182, 349(2), 352.5(3).

Gunning; Alexander v., TexCivApp–Hous (1 Dist), 572 SW2d 34.—Child C 910.

Gunning; Casteel v., TexCivApp–El Paso, 402 SW2d 529, ref nre.—App & E 776, 927(7), 1035, 1036(6); Brok 94; Corp 113, 121(6); Evid 384, 385, 400(3), 433(6), 434(8), 441(9), 461(1); Parties 48; Trial 133.4; Trusts 107, 110.

Gunning v. San Antonio Teachers Credit Union, WDTex, 652 FSupp 697.—Civil R 1524.

Gunn-Olson-Stordahl Joint Venture v. Early Bank, TexApp–Eastland, 748 SW2d 316, writ den.—Banks 191.10, 191.20; Guar 4; Judgm 181(1), 181(22); Ven & Pur 79.

Gunn Tile Co. of San Antonio, Inc.; Alamo Clay Products, Inc. v., TexApp–San Antonio, 597 SW2d 388, ref nre.—Contracts 303(1); Sales 1(3), 172, 418(7), 418(14.1).

Gunstanson v. State, TexApp–Dallas, 666 SW2d 183, petition for discretionary review refused.—Const Law 3228.

Gun Store; Robertson v., TexApp–Dallas, 710 SW2d 678. See Robertson v. Grogan Investment Co.

Gunstream; Calverley v., TexCivApp–Dallas, 497 SW2d 110, ref nre.—Adv Poss 63(2), 63(3); Const Law 3971; Evid 383(7); Lim of Act 3(1), 5(3), 19(1), 19(7); Mtg 143, 379.

Gunstream v. Oil Well Remedial Service, TexCivApp– Dallas, 233 SW2d 897.—App & E 846(2), 846(5), 1008.1(1); Plead 111.8, 111.39(2), 111.42(2), 111.42(8); Venue 8.5(3), 21, 46.

GUNTER

59 Tex D 2d—430

See Guidelines for Arrangement at the beginning of this Volume

Gunter v. Bailey, TexApp–El Paso, 808 SW2d 163.—Atty & C 152, 166(3), 167(2); Costs 194.32, 252; Judgm 199(3.5); Trial 140(2).

Gunter v. Glasgow, TexCivApp–Eastland, 608 SW2d 273.—Abate & R 13; Child C 411, 702; Judgm 815, 822(2).

Gunter v. Gunter, TexCivApp–Eastland, 538 SW2d 428.—Child S 159.

Gunter; Gunter v., TexCivApp–Eastland, 538 SW2d 428.—Child S 159.

Gunter v. Hasty, TexCivApp–Waco, 422 SW2d 198, ref nre.—Lim of Act 122.

Gunter; Henderson v., Tex, 328 SW2d 868, 160 Tex 267.—App & E 1142, 1177(1), 1177(5), 1177(6); Bound 35(1), 35(4), 37(3); Ref of Inst 13(1).

Gunter v. Henderson, TexCivApp–Austin, 320 SW2d 221, aff 328 SW2d 868, 160 Tex 267.—App & E 1177(6); Bound 33.

Gunter; Hughes v., TexCivApp–Beaumont, 136 SW2d 253.—App & E 1161.

Gunter v. KIKK Radio Station, TexApp–Houston (1 Dist), 727 SW2d 650, ref nre.—Judgm 181(19); Tel 1163.

Gunter; Maryland Cas. Co. v., TexCivApp–Galveston, 167 SW2d 545.—Damag 221(3), 221(5.1); Work Comp 900, 1923.

Gunter v. Molk, TexApp–Beaumont, 663 SW2d 674, ref nre.—App & E 852, 1012.1(5); Cem 10.1, 14; Trial 382.

Gunter v. Morgan, TexCivApp–Texarkana, 473 SW2d 952.—Autos 157, 243(1), 243(17), 244(36.1).

Gunter; Peerless Pump-FMC Corp. v., TexCivApp–Eastland, 470 SW2d 299.—Judgm 112, 335(2), 335(3).

Gunter v. Pogue, TexApp–Corpus Christi, 672 SW2d 840, ref nre.—App & E 931(3); Trial 403; Wills 1, 656, 665, 703, 705.

Gunter; Sohio Petroleum Co. v., TexCivApp–Eastland, 205 SW2d 110.—Mines 54.5.

Gunter v. State, TexCrimApp, 858 SW2d 430, reh den, cert den 114 SCt 318, 510 US 921, 126 LEd2d 265.—Crim Law 412(1), 412(3), 412(6), 517(5), 517.3(1), 556, 1035(5), 1134(5), 1158(3); Homic 1139, 1165; Jury 97(1), 104.1, 105(4), 108, 131(11), 131(18), 132; Sent & Pun 1716, 1756, 1757, 1760, 1780(3).

Gunter v. State, TexCrimApp, 421 SW2d 657.—Crim Law 531(2).

Gunter v. State, TexCrimApp, 161 SW2d 100, 144 TexCrim 43.—Crim Law 586, 594(1), 594(3), 597(3), 1151.

Gunter v. State, TexCrimApp, 150 SW2d 1037, 142 TexCrim 87.—Crim Law 369.1, 369.5, 1091(3); Witn 337(4).

Gunter v. State, TexCrimApp, 139 SW2d 116, 139 TexCrim 145.—Crim Law 331, 419(12), 595(1), 598(2), 1035(6), 1052, 1053, 1092.14; Homic 1210.

Gunter v. State, TexCrimApp, 94 SW2d 747, 130 TexCrim 488.—Crim Law 424(6), 829(4).

Gunter v. State, TexApp–Texarkana, 914 SW2d 647.—Crim Law 1169.5(1), 1169.5(2).

Gunter; State v., TexApp–El Paso, 902 SW2d 172, reh overr, and petition for discretionary review refused.—Armed S 3; Crim Law 1134(6), 1158(1).

Gunter; Sun Oil Co. v., TexCivApp–Galveston, 125 SW2d 338.—App & E 1175(1); Stip 14(10); Tresp to T T 38(1).

Gunter; U.S. v., CA5 (Tex), 876 F2d 1113, cert den 110 SCt 198, 493 US 871, 107 LEd2d 152.—Banks 509.20, 509.25; Consp 24(2); Crim Law 829(3), 1166(7), 1168(2), 1173.2(2), 1173.2(3).

Gunter; Vaughn v., Tex, 461 SW2d 599.—Trusts 124.

Gunter; Vaughn v., TexCivApp–Dallas, 458 SW2d 523, 57 ALR3d 541, ref nre 461 SW2d 599.—App & E 238(1), 267(1), 1172(5); Atty & C 140; Deeds 105; Infants 83; Trusts 112, 124; Wills 497(5).

Gunter Hotel Associates, In re, BkrtcyWDTex, 96 BR 696.—Bankr 3103(1), 3110.1, 3115.1, 3116.

Gunter Hotel Corp.; Hopkins v., TexCivApp–San Antonio, 147 SW2d 973, writ dism, correct.—App & E 688(2), 750(1), 989, 1056.4; Damag 130.4, 140.7.

Gunter Hotel Corp.; Robinson v., TexCivApp–San Antonio, 173 SW2d 318, writ refused.—Inn 10.1, 10.2; Trial 351.5(5).

Gunter Hotel of San Antonio Inc. v. Buck, TexApp–San Antonio, 775 SW2d 689, writ den.—Contracts 175(3), 196, 215(1), 312(1), 346(1); Costs 194.32; Damag 124(4), 190, 221(2.1), 221(4); Evid 264; Interest 31.

Gunter Hotel of San Antonio Inc. v. Robert V. Buck & Associates–Architects, TexApp–San Antonio, 775 SW2d 689. See Gunter Hotel of San Antonio Inc. v. Buck.

Gunter's Unknown Heirs and Legal Representatives v. Lagow, TexCivApp–Austin, 191 SW2d 111, writ refused.—Courts 21; Decl Judgm 111, 181; Proc 63, 127, 164(1); Wills 269, 270.

Gunther, Ex parte, Tex, 758 SW2d 226.—Child S 491.

Gunther v. Dorff, TexCivApp–Amarillo, 318 SW2d 131, ref nre.—Hus & W 262.1(2), 262.2, 264(1).

Gunther v. Dorff, TexCivApp–Waco, 296 SW2d 638, writ dism.—Jury 19(1); Partit 53; Receivers 6, 12, 18.

Gunther v. Gunther, TexCivApp–Dallas, 301 SW2d 207, writ dism.—Jury 16(9), 26.

Gunther; Gunther v., TexCivApp–Dallas, 301 SW2d 207, writ dism.—Jury 16(9), 26.

Gunther v. Gunther, TexCivApp–Dallas, 283 SW2d 826, writ dism.—Divorce 207; Judgm 731; Receivers 3, 7.

Gunther; Gunther v., TexCivApp–Dallas, 283 SW2d 826, writ dism.—Divorce 207; Judgm 731; Receivers 3, 7.

Gunther v. Gunther, TexCivApp–Waco, 367 SW2d 206, writ dism.—App & E 511(3); Divorce 267.

Gunther; Gunther v., TexCivApp–Waco, 367 SW2d 206, writ dism.—App & E 511(3); Divorce 267.

Gunther v. Gunther, TexCivApp–Hous (14 Dist), 478 SW2d 821, ref nre.—Child C 47, 178, 404, 410, 413, 532, 569, 577, 606, 632, 732, 733, 737, 921(1); Evid 51, 80(1); Hab Corp 532(1); Judgm 815, 818(1), 818(2), 818(4).

Gunther; Gunther v., TexCivApp–Hous (14 Dist), 478 SW2d 821, ref nre.—Child C 47, 178, 404, 410, 413, 532, 569, 577, 606, 632, 732, 733, 737, 921(1); Evid 51, 80(1); Hab Corp 532(1); Judgm 815, 818(1), 818(2), 818(4).

Gunther v. Gunther, TexCivApp–Galveston, 297 SW2d 725, dism.—Divorce 130, 161, 184(1), 184(6.1), 184(7); Evid 17.

Gunther; Gunther v., TexCivApp–Galveston, 297 SW2d 725, dism.—Divorce 130, 161, 184(1), 184(6.1), 184(7); Evid 17.

Gunther v. State, TexApp–Corpus Christi, 764 SW2d 903.—Crim Law 1030(2); Fish 13(1).

Gunther v. Thornton, TexCivApp–Dallas, 252 SW2d 1016, mandamus overr.—Divorce 160, 162; Mand 51.

Guo; State v., TexApp–Houston (1 Dist), 64 SW3d 662.—Crim Law 394.1(3), 394.6(5), 553, 742(1), 1139, 1144.13(3), 1153(1), 1158(4).

Gupta, In re, CA5 (Tex), 394 F3d 347.—Bankr 2002, 3342, 3376(3), 3376(4), 3782, 3786; Judgm 665, 713(1), 725(1), 828.21(2).

Gupta v. Eastern Idaho Tumor Institute, Inc., TexApp–Houston (14 Dist), 140 SW3d 747, review den.—App & E 213, 237(5), 238(2), 294(1); Contracts 103, 141(1), 153, 176(2), 318, 321(1), 323(1); Health 104, 108, 294; Trial 134.

Gupta v. East Texas State University, CA5 (Tex), 654 F2d 411.—Civil R 1513, 1516, 1536; Fed Civ Proc 2262.1; Fed Cts 792, 853, 858, 941.

Gupta v. Ritter Homes, Inc., Tex, 646 SW2d 168.—Contracts 186(3), 188.5(3), 205.35(1).

Gupta v. Ritter Homes, Inc., TexApp–Houston (14 Dist), 633 SW2d 626, writ gr, aff in part, rev in part 646 SW2d 168.—App & E 907(4); Contracts 186(3); Neglig 1205(2); Sales 246.

For Later Case History Information, see KeyCite on WESTLAW

GUTHEINZ;

Gupta; U.S. v., CA5 (Tex), 77 FedAppx 256, cert den 124 SCt 1620, 541 US 904, 158 LEd2d 246.—Crim Law 273(4.1), 1026.10(4).

Gupton; Aquila Southwest Pipeline Corp. v., TexApp–Houston (1 Dist), 886 SW2d 497.—App & E 842(2), 901, 989, 1008.1(2), 1008.1(3), 1012.1(4); Em Dom 172, 191(6).

Gurecky; L. M. B. Corp. v., Tex, 501 SW2d 300.—App & E 1107, 1175(1); Autos 168(4), 244(10); Neglig 291, 1560; Trial 350.3(7).

Gurecky; L. M. B. Corp. v., TexCivApp–Corpus Christi, 489 SW2d 647, writ gr, rev 501 SW2d 300.—Autos 153, 159, 244(5), 244(37); Trial 350.6(3).

Gurecky v. Owens, TexCivApp–Waco, 271 SW2d 445.—App & E 931(1); Bills & N 525.

Gurganus v. State, TexCrimApp, 113 SW2d 1237, 134 TexCrim 34.—Crim Law 394.4(9), 763(8), 1169.2(2), 1172.7, 1173.2(1), 1186.4(8); Larc 1.

Guridi v. Waller, TexApp–Houston (1 Dist), 98 SW3d 315, reh overr.—App & E 846(5); Judgm 527.

Gurinsky's Estate; Martin v., TexCivApp–Austin, 377 SW2d 710, ref nre.—App & E 1001(1), 1070(2); Autos 244(40); Evid 588; Trial 311, 350.6(1).

Gurka v. State, TexApp–Austin, 82 SW3d 416, petition for discretionary review refused.—Crim Law 419(2), 419(4), 629.5(2), 1036.1(1), 1036.1(3.1), 1036.5, 1045, 1153(1); Infants 20.

Gurleski v. U.S., CA5 (Tex), 405 F2d 253, cert den Smith v. U S, 89 SCt 2127, 395 US 977, 23 LEd2d 765, reh den 90 SCt 37, 396 US 869, 24 LEd2d 124, cert den 89 SCt 2140, 395 US 981, 23 LEd2d 769.—Autos 353, 355(12), 359; Consp 44.2; Const Law 947; Crim Law 394.4(5.1), 394.5(3), 566, 622.1(2), 622.2(8), 673(2), 721(1), 822(1), 959, 1044.1(5.1), 1148, 1159.2(5), 1168(1), 1171.1(3), 1172.2, 1186.1; Pardon 24; Searches 23, 84, 113.1, 124, 125, 141, 148, 171, 173.1, 177; Sent & Pun 31; Witn 35, 77, 79(1), 270(2), 337(28), 345(1), 345(8).

Gurley; Harris v., CCA5 (Tex), 80 F2d 744.—Courts 493(3); Evid 357; Mines 100; Trial 11(3); Trusts 17(3), 43(1), 44(3).

Gurley v. Lindsley, CA5 (Tex), 466 F2d 498.—Interest 38(1), 39(1), 39(3).

Gurley v. Lindsley, CA5 (Tex), 459 F2d 268, mandate withdrawn 466 F2d 498.—Const Law 3964, 3965(1); Courts 12(2.1); Ex & Ad 525; Fed Cts 76.15; Interest 38(1), 60; Judgm 524; Lim of Act 195(3), 197(2); Perp 4(3), 4(15.1); Trusts 1, 21(1), 30.5(1), 246, 256, 356(1), 357(1), 363, 367, 372(3).

Gurley; Moncrief v., TexCivApp–Fort Worth, 609 SW2d 863, ref nre.—Counties 61; Offic 4; Statut 181(1).

Gurley v. State, TexCrimApp, 363 SW2d 262.—Autos 355(6); Crim Law 1048, 1099.13; Ind & Inf 137(5), 138.

Gurley v. State, TexCrimApp, 334 SW2d 824, 169 TexCrim 459.—Crim Law 1171.3; Rape 53(2).

Gurley v. State, TexCrimApp, 331 SW2d 756, 169 TexCrim 51.—Crim Law 273.2(2), 1086.14.

Gurney; North River Ins. Co. v., TexCivApp–Beaumont, 603 SW2d 280.—App & E 930(3), 989; Insurance 2664, 2761.

Gurrola v. Griffin & Brand Sales Agency, Inc., SDTex, 524 FSupp 115.—Fed Cts 87, 92, 101, 106.

Gurrola v. State, TexCrimApp, 877 SW2d 300.—Arrest 63.5(1), 63.5(4), 63.5(5); Crim Law 394.4(9).

Gurrola v. State, TexApp–Houston (14 Dist), 852 SW2d 651, petition for discretionary review gr, rev 877 SW2d 300.—Arrest 63.4(16), 63.5(1), 63.5(4), 63.5(5), 63.5(8), 68(3), 68(4), 71.1(6); Crim Law 394.6(5), 1139, 1144.12, 1158(4).

Gurrola v. U.S., CA5 (Tex), 104 FedAppx 962.—Health 196, 697.

Gurtov v. Williams, TexCivApp–Galveston, 105 SW2d 328, writ dism.—Inj 34, 55, 77(2), 102, 105(1), 118(5); Plead 214(3).

Gurule; IBEW-NECA Southwestern Health and Benefit Fund v., NDTex, 337 FSupp2d 845, reconsideration

den 2004 WL 2729798.—Contempt 20, 60(3); Decl Judgm 99; Fed Civ Proc 2497.1; Labor & Emp 407, 599, 705, 718; States 18.51.

Gurvich v. Tyree, TexApp–Corpus Christi, 694 SW2d 39.—App & E 846(5), 852, 920(3), 954(1); Courts 475(1), 480(1), 514, 516; Equity 46; Inj 135, 138.27, 144.

Gus Mayer Boston Store of Delaware; Anderson v., EDTex, 924 FSupp 763.—Admin Law 413, 416.1, 751; Civil R 1017, 1019(1), 1019(2), 1019(5), 1024, 1033(1), 1042, 1216, 1217, 1218(2), 1218(5), 1218(6), 1220, 1222, 1225(1), 1228, 1504, 1510, 1529, 1555; Fed Civ Proc 2497.1; Statut 219(6.1).

Gusnowski; Wren v., TexApp–Austin, 919 SW2d 847.—App & E 931(1); Judgm 544, 587, 713(2).

Guss v. Lastrap, CCA5 (Tex), 142 F2d 872, cert den 65 SCt 117, 323 US 764, 89 LEd 611.—Seamen 1, 32.

Guss v. State, TexApp–Amarillo, 763 SW2d 609.—Ind & Inf 113; Sent & Pun 240.

Gust, Ex parte, TexApp–Houston (1 Dist), 828 SW2d 575.—Extrad 21, 27, 32, 34, 39.

Gustafson; Baribeau v., TexApp–San Antonio, 107 SW3d 52, review den, and reh of petition for review den, cert den 125 SCt 272, 543 US 871, 160 LEd2d 118.—App & E 232(3), 893(1), 974(0.5), 989, 1001(3), 1003(6), 1004(11); Assault 2, 48; Const Law 4410, 4426, 4427; Damag 15, 87(1), 87(2), 89(1); Evid 597; Fraud 3, 58(1), 62, 64(1); Judgm 252(4); Trial 182, 219, 349(2), 350.2.

Gustafson v. Chambers, TexApp–Houston (1 Dist), 871 SW2d 938.—App & E 946; Courts 26; Mand 1, 4(4); Pretrial Proc 41, 273, 285.1, 286, 303, 371, 382, 403, 410, 411.

Gustafson v. City of Austin, TexApp–Austin, 110 SW3d 652, petition stricken, and review den.—App & E 1175(1); Libel 1, 6(1), 54, 55, 123(7).

Gustafson v. National Ins. Underwriters, TexCivApp–Eastland, 517 SW2d 414, 86 ALR3d 110, ref nre.—Insurance 1822, 2332, 2749, 2914.

Gustafson v. Provider HealthNet Services, Inc., TexApp–Dallas, 118 SW3d 479, reh overr.—App & E 893(1), 1010.1(8.1); Const Law 3964; Courts 12(2.1), 12(2.5), 12(2.10), 12(2.30), 15.

Gustafson, Inc. v. Intersystems Indus. Products, Inc., CAFed (Tex), 897 F2d 508.—Pat 324.55(5), 325.11(2.1), 325.11(5).

Gustason v. Northeast Nat. Bank, TexCivApp–Fort Worth, 486 SW2d 596.—Judgm 183, 185(2), 185.1(1), 185.3(5).

Gustavus; City Nat. Bank of Bryan v., TexComApp, 106 SW2d 262, 130 Tex 83.—Banks 101, 119, 123, 154(1); Equity 57.

Gustavus; City Nat. Bank of Bryan v., TexCivApp–Waco, 77 SW2d 565, writ gr, aff 106 SW2d 262, 130 Tex 83.—Banks 154(1).

Guste; A. Copeland Enterprises, Inc. v., WDTex, 706 FSupp 1283.—Corp 310(1), 314(2), 320(4); Inj 138.42.

Guste; Copeland Enterprises, Inc. v., WDTex, 706 FSupp 1283. See A. Copeland Enterprises, Inc. v. Guste.

Guster v. State, TexCrimApp, 580 SW2d 363.—False Pret 26.

Guster v. State, TexCrimApp, 522 SW2d 494.—Crim Law 1031(4).

Gustin v. U.S. I.R.S., CA5 (Tex), 876 F2d 485.—Int Rev 4984, 5003, 5024, 5203, 5204, 5205, 5235.

Gustus; U.S. v., CA5 (Tex), 10 F3d 1135. See U.S. v. Miles.

Gutermuth; Hamlin v., TexApp–Houston (14 Dist), 909 SW2d 114, reh overr, and writ den.—Atty & C 105, 129(3).

Guthals; Barnes v., TexCivApp–Austin, 137 SW2d 883.—App & E 1069.1; Trial 350.1.

Gutheinz; Continental Sav. Ass'n v., TexApp–Amarillo, 718 SW2d 377, ref nre.—App & E 185(1); Corp 308(1); Damag 160; Judgm 99, 145(4).

Guthery v. Taylor, TexApp–Houston (14 Dist), 112 SW3d 715.—App & E 845(1), 893(1); Mand 71, 72, 173, 187.5; Mun Corp 185(7); Statut 176, 181(1), 181(2), 184, 188, 206, 209, 212.6, 223.1.

Guthmann; Postive Feed, Inc. v., TexApp–Houston (1 Dist), 4 SW3d 879.—App & E 1172(1), 1178(6); Judgm 181(11), 183, 185(2); Plead 48; Unemp Comp 499.

Guthrie, In re, TexApp–Dallas, 45 SW3d 719, review den, and reh of petition for review den.—Action 66; App & E 946; Child C 904; Child S 456, 458, 459, 556(5); Child 1, 67, 73; Compromise 5(3); Const Law 82(10); Names 20.

Guthrie v. Buckley, CA5 (Tex), 79 FedAppx 637.—Atty & C 102; Mal Pros 42.

Guthrie v. Buckley, EDTex, 246 FSupp2d 589, aff 79 FedAppx 637.—Mal Pros 40, 42.

Guthrie; City of Canadian v., TexCivApp–Amarillo, 87 SW2d 316.—App & E 47(2), 672; Courts 170; Damag 40(3), 55, 105, 113.

Guthrie; Dallas Ry. & Terminal Co. v., Tex, 210 SW2d 550, 146 Tex 585.—App & E 1050.1(8.1); Damag 99, 100, 173(2); Evid 177; Urb R R 30.

Guthrie; Dallas Ry. & Terminal Co. v., TexCivApp–Fort Worth, 206 SW2d 638, rev 210 SW2d 550, 146 Tex 585. —App & E 1062.5, 1064.1(9); Damag 100, 134(1), 135, 163(4), 176; Evid 177; Neglig 431, 440(1), 1568, 1713; Trial 350.5(3), 351.5(6); Urb R R 30.

Guthrie; Donnelly v., CA5 (Tex), 194 F2d 164.—Mines 101.

Guthrie v. Dow Chemical Co., SDTex, 445 FSupp 311.— Courts 489(9); Fed Civ Proc 1742(1); Fed Cts 243; Rem of C 3, 10, 19(1), 108.

Guthrie v. Flock, TexCivApp–Amarillo, 360 SW2d 804.— Atty & C 141.

Guthrie; Ford v., CA5 (Tex), 101 FedAppx 978.—Civil R 1091; Fed Civ Proc 1838, 2734.

Guthrie v. Gossett, TexCivApp–Eastland, 142 SW2d 410. —Fraud 12, 42, 47; Judgm 248; Mines 54.5, 74(3); Ven & Pur 224.

Guthrie; Har-Con Engineering, Inc. v., TexCivApp–Fort Worth, 408 SW2d 159, ref nre.—Contracts 175(3); Damag 191.

Guthrie; Helms v., TexCivApp–Fort Worth, 573 SW2d 855, ref nre.—Mines 55(2), 55(4), 79.1(3).

Guthrie; McBroom v., TexCivApp–Fort Worth, 389 SW2d 366, ref nre.—Contracts 346(10), 352(2); Judgm 199(3.9).

Guthrie; Mackie v., TexApp–Tyler, 78 SW3d 462, reh overr, and reh overr, and review den.—Action 6, 13; App & E 23, 174, 223, 913; Corp 211(1); Decl Judgm 301; Judgm 185(3), 185.3(18); Parties 1, 96(2).

Guthrie v. National Homes Corp., Tex, 394 SW2d 494.— App & E 909(5); Bills & N 124, 164, 537(2); Evid 418.

Guthrie v. National Homes Corp., TexCivApp–Fort Worth, 387 SW2d 158, reformed 394 SW2d 494.—App & E 909(5); Bills & N 28, 124, 491; Evid 450(10); Princ & A 175(2).

Guthrie v. Ray, TexCivApp–Dallas, 556 SW2d 589.—App & E 931(1), 931(3), 1177(5); Child C 600, 657; Trial 383.

Guthrie v. Republic Nat. Ins. Co., TexApp–Houston (1 Dist), 682 SW2d 634, ref nre.—App & E 989; Fraud 58(1); Insurance 1608, 1631, 1633, 1634(3), 1635, 2475; Princ & A 99; Trial 350.8.

Guthrie v. Russ, TexCivApp–Galveston, 148 SW2d 253, writ dism, correct.—App & E 655(1), 933(1).

Guthrie v. Sinclair Refining Co., TexCivApp–Houston, 320 SW2d 396, ref nre, cert den 80 SCt 155, 361 US 883, 4 LEd2d 120, reh den 80 SCt 366, 361 US 941, 4 LEd2d 361.—Courts 97(5); Neglig 213, 370, 372; Seamen 29(1), 29(5.16), 29(5.17); Trial 350.2, 350.6(2), 351.2(4), 351.5(3).

Guthrie; Smith v., TexCivApp–Fort Worth, 557 SW2d 163, ref nre.—App & E 927(1), 997(1); Evid 474(6), 506, 512, 547; Health 618, 621, 675, 821(2).

Guthrie v. State, TexCrimApp, 299 SW2d 301.—Bail 64.

Guthrie v. State, TexCrimApp, 299 SW2d 294.—Crim Law 1090.1(1).

Guthrie v. State, TexCrimApp, 257 SW2d 709.—Crim Law 1094(3).

Guthrie v. State, TexCrimApp, 247 SW2d 114.—Crim Law 1090.1(1).

Guthrie v. State, TexCrimApp, 231 SW2d 428.—Crim Law 1090.1(1).

Guthrie v. State, TexCrimApp, 91 SW2d 730, 130 Tex-Crim 20.—Crim Law 1028, 1044.1(1), 1090.11; Rob 24.10.

Guthrie v. State, TexApp–Waco, 149 SW3d 829, petition for discretionary review refused.—Crim Law 45, 510, 511.1(3), 511.1(6.1), 511.2, 780(1), 822(1), 1038.1(2), 1038.2, 1038.3, 1134(2), 1144.13(8), 1172.1(1), 1173.2(6).

Guthrie v. Suiter, TexApp–Houston (1 Dist), 934 SW2d 820.—Evid 372(1), 372(3), 372(4); Judgm 181(15.1), 185(4), 185(6); Wills 21, 50, 52(1), 53(1), 53(2), 72, 153, 155.1, 155.4, 156, 159, 166(1), 166(12), 206, 289, 314, 324(3).

Guthrie; Terry v., TexCivApp–Waco, 300 SW2d 217.— Abate & R 81; Plead 336.

Guthrie v. Texas Emp. Ins. Ass'n, Tex, 203 SW2d 775, 146 Tex 89.—Work Comp 581, 1927.

Guthrie v. Texas Emp. Ins. Ass'n, TexCivApp–Amarillo, 199 SW2d 685, rev 203 SW2d 775, 146 Tex 89.—Evid 14, 553(3); Work Comp 3, 518, 522, 530, 1396, 1513, 1571.

Guthrie v. Texas Pac. Coal & Oil Co., TexComApp, 122 SW2d 1049, 132 Tex 180.—App & E 1064.1(2.1); Home 162(1), 181.5; Trial 215.

Guthrie; Texas Pac. Coal & Oil Co. v., TexCivApp–Eastland, 100 SW2d 125, mod 122 SW2d 1049, 132 Tex 180.—Home 57.5, 162(1), 163, 164; Mun Corp 455, 569.

Guthrie v. Tifco Industries, CA5 (Tex), 941 F2d 374, reh den, cert den 112 SCt 1267, 503 US 908, 117 LEd2d 495. —Civil R 1123, 1137, 1209, 1539, 1551; Damag 50.10; Fed Civ Proc 1824, 2658; Fed Cts 762; Labor & Emp 40(2), 782, 783, 786.

Guthrie; Twin City Fire Ins. Co. v., TexCivApp–Fort Worth, 427 SW2d 901.—Insurance 2117, 2201; Trial 350.4(3).

Guthrie; William P. Brooks Const. Co., Inc. v., CA5 (Tex), 614 F2d 509.—Adm 8, 80; Ship 23.1.

Guthrie Trust; Holdsworth v., TexApp–San Antonio, 712 SW2d 177, ref nre.—Adv Poss 4, 57, 117; App & E 989, 1010.1(9); Judgm 251(1).

Gutierrez, Ex parte, TexCrimApp, 600 SW2d 933.—False Imp 43, 44; Ind & Inf 189(1).

Gutierrez, Ex parte, TexApp–Austin, 987 SW2d 227, reh overr, and petition for discretionary review refused.— Crim Law 295, 1134(2); Double J 1, 2, 31, 51, 60.1, 105; Hab Corp 274, 706, 823.

Gutierrez, Ex parte, TexApp–San Antonio, 989 SW2d 55, appeal decided 1999 WL 19190.—Crim Law 1023(3); Hab Corp 274, 275.1, 465.1, 825.1, 861.

Gutierrez, Ex parte, TexApp–San Antonio, 661 SW2d 763.—Contempt 20, 61(1).

Gutierrez, In re, BkrtcyWDTex, 309 BR 488.—Atty & C 21.5(6); Bankr 3029.1, 3030, 3174, 3179, 3185, 3193, 3204, 3205.

Gutierrez, In re, BkrtcyWDTex, 160 BR 788.—Bankr 2650(2), 2650(4), 2726.1(3), 2727(3).

Gutierrez, In re, TexApp–Fort Worth, 431 SW2d 428. —Bail 44(1), 44(3.1); Crim Law 1148; Infants 134.

Gutierrez v. Academy Corp., SDTex, 967 FSupp 945.— Alt Disp Res 134(2), 134(6), 193, 199.

Gutierrez; Austin Independent School Dist. v., TexApp–Austin, 54 SW3d 860, reh overr, and review dism woj, and reh of petition for review gr, and withdrawn, and review den, and reh of petition for review den.—Mun Corp 742(4); Schools 89.13(1), 89.13(4); States 191.4(1).

Gutierrez; Averitt v., TexCrimApp, 567 SW2d 505.—Witn 2(4), 8, 10.

Gutierrez v. Casanova, TexCivApp–San Antonio, 450 SW2d 771.—App & E 624, 627.

Gutierrez v. Cayman Islands Firm of Deloitte & Touche, TexApp–San Antonio, 100 SW3d 261, reh overr, and supplemented, and review dism.—App & E 874(1), 893(1), 946; Appear 9(1), 9(2); Const Law 3964, 3965(5); Courts 12(2.1), 12(2.5), 12(2.10), 12(2.25), 12(2.30), 35, 37(3); Fraud 20; Princ & A 1, 19, 23(2).

Gutierrez v. Champion Sav. Ass'n., SDTex, 727 FSupp 1088.—Fed Civ Proc 1837.1; Rem of C 102.

Gutierrez v. City of San Antonio, CA5 (Tex), 139 F3d 441.—Arrest 63.1, 68(1); Civil R 1376(2); Const Law 4534, 4537, 4544; Fed Civ Proc 2491.5; Fed Cts 542, 776, 794; Prisons 4(7); Searches 23.

Gutierrez; Clearwater Constructors, Inc. v., TexCivApp–San Antonio, 626 SW2d 789.—Contracts 187(1); Corp 666; Plead 111.19.

Gutierrez v. Collins, Tex, 583 SW2d 312.—App & E 1107; Courts 9, 89; Death 8; Neglig 204; Torts 103.

Gutierrez v. Collins, TexCivApp–El Paso, 570 SW2d 101, rev 583 SW2d 312.—App & E 907(3); Courts 91(1); Death 9; Trial 105(4).

Gutierrez v. County of Zapata, TexApp–San Antonio, 951 SW2d 831.—App & E 216(7), 231(9), 232(0.5), 930(1), 989, 1001(1), 1003(6); Dedi 13, 15, 16.1, 17, 19(2), 20(1), 31, 35(1), 37, 41, 44; High 5, 17; Trial 253(1.1), 274.

Gutierrez v. Dallas Independent School Dist., Tex, 729 SW2d 691.—Pretrial Proc 251.1, 313; Work Comp 1167, 1173, 1696.

Gutierrez v. Dallas Independent School Dist., TexApp–Dallas, 722 SW2d 530, writ gr, rev 729 SW2d 691.—Pretrial Proc 45, 282, 304.

Gutierrez v. Deloitte & Touche, L.L.P., WDTex, 147 FSupp2d 584, appeal after remand from Federal Court 100 SW3d 261, reh overr, and supplemented, and review dism.—Rem of C 2, 19(1), 19(5), 25(1), 107(7); Sec Reg 2.20.

Gutierrez v. Dresser Industries, Inc., TexApp–Corpus Christi, 769 SW2d 704.—Neglig 384, 385; Prod Liab 58.

Gutierrez v. Dretke, WDTex, 392 FSupp2d 802, certificate of appealability den 201 FedAppx 196, cert den 127 SCt 1297, 167 LEd2d 112.—Const Law 4632, 4633, 4646; Courts 100(1); Crim Law 622.7(11), 641.13(2.1), 641.13(6), 641.13(7), 700(2.1), 700(3), 700(4), 700(7), 868, 923(2); Hab Corp 314, 319.1, 332.1, 337, 364, 366, 380.1, 382, 383, 403, 405.1, 406, 407, 422, 461, 480, 491, 496, 508, 742, 766, 767, 768, 818; Jury 33(2.10), 108; Sent & Pun 1463, 1464, 1763, 1780(1).

Gutierrez; Duarte v., TexCivApp–San Antonio, 175 SW2d 480.—Home 118(2), 133.

Gutierrez v. Elizondo, TexApp–Corpus Christi, 139 SW3d 768.—App & E 173(6), 842(1), 846(5), 852, 984(5); Assign 22, 137; Contracts 143(1), 143(2), 143.5, 152, 176(2), 322(4); Costs 194.18, 207, 208; Damag 85; Ease 12(1); Judgm 301, 305, 306, 326; Jury 25(2), 26.

Gutierrez v. El Paso Community Action Program, CA5 (Tex), 462 F2d 121.—Fed Civ Proc 1827.1, 1838; Fed Cts 743.

Gutierrez; EOG Resources, Inc. v., TexApp–San Antonio, 75 SW3d 50, reh overr.—Inj 135, 138.1, 138.3, 138.18, 157.

Gutierrez v. Estelle, CA5 (Tex), 474 F2d 899.—Sent & Pun 348, 400, 1318, 1325.

Gutierrez v. Excel Corp., CA5 (Tex), 106 F3d 683.—Evid 547.5; Fed Cts 763.1, 825.1; Labor & Emp 2783, 2881, 2883; Neglig 202, 371, 379, 380, 387, 1599, 1676, 1713; New Tr 72(9).

Gutierrez v. Exxon Corp., CA5 (Tex), 764 F2d 399.—Death 99(4); Fed Civ Proc 2214; Fed Cts 871, 873; Mines 118; Neglig 1037(7).

Gutierrez v. FDIC, SDTex, 727 FSupp 1088. See Gutierrez v. Champion Sav. Ass'n.

Gutierrez; First Heights Bank, FSB v., TexApp–Corpus Christi, 852 SW2d 596, reh overr, and writ den.—App & E 543, 930(2), 1050.1(3.1), 1053(6); Banks 505; Bills & N 452(1), 534; B & L Assoc 42(1), 42(16), 48; Courts 70; Equity 3, 46, 54, 56, 57; Estates 10(1); Evid 188, 235, 373(2); Impl & C C 3; Judges 56; Liens 12; Lim of Act 66(1); Paymt 1(1), 50, 65, 78; Trial 3(4), 18; Venue 45, 50.

Gutierrez; Garcia v., TexApp–Corpus Christi, 697 SW2d 758.—Judgm 17(2); Proc 53, 61.

Gutierrez; General Elec. Credit Corp. v., TexApp–Corpus Christi, 668 SW2d 463.—App & E 767(1), 852, 912; Plead 111.42(1); Venue 2, 3.

Gutierrez; Gonzalez v., TexApp–San Antonio, 694 SW2d 384.—Appear 3; Damag 20, 40(4), 49.10, 190; Evid 351; Judgm 17(1); Mun Corp 1029; Torts 211, 212, 220, 243; Trial 325(3), 352.50, 362.

Gutierrez v. Goodtime Stores, TexApp–El Paso, 874 SW2d 103. See Gutierrez v. Karl Perry Enterprises, Inc.

Gutierrez v. Gulf Coast Builders & Supply Co., TexApp–Corpus Christi, 739 SW2d 371, writ den.—Cons Cred 4; States 18.19.

Gutierrez v. Gutierrez, TexApp–San Antonio, 791 SW2d 659.—App & E 931(1), 989, 1012.1(5); Divorce 150, 221, 227(1), 252.3(2), 252.3(3), 253(4), 257, 287; Hus & W 249(6), 255, 257, 258, 262.1(1), 264(1), 264(2), 264(3), 264(7), 265, 270(8).

Gutierrez; Gutierrez v., TexApp–San Antonio, 791 SW2d 659.—App & E 931(1), 989, 1012.1(5); Divorce 150, 221, 227(1), 252.3(2), 252.3(3), 253(4), 257, 287; Hus & W 249(6), 255, 257, 258, 262.1(1), 264(1), 264(2), 264(3), 264(7), 265, 270(8).

Gutierrez v. Gutierrez, Estate of, TexApp–San Antonio, 786 SW2d 112.—App & E 185(1); Guard & W 22, 137.

Gutierrez, Estate of; Gutierrez v., TexApp–San Antonio, 786 SW2d 112.—App & E 185(1); Guard & W 22, 137.

Gutierrez v. Gutierrez, TexApp–San Antonio, 643 SW2d 786.—App & E 907(3); Divorce 252.1, 252.3(1), 286(5).

Gutierrez; Gutierrez v., TexApp–San Antonio, 643 SW2d 786.—App & E 907(3); Divorce 252.1, 252.3(1), 286(5).

Gutierrez v. Gutierrez, TexApp–El Paso, 86 SW3d 729.—Child C 423; Pretrial Proc 3, 312.

Gutierrez; Gutierrez v., TexApp–El Paso, 86 SW3d 729.—Child C 423; Pretrial Proc 3, 312.

Gutierrez v. Gutierrez, TexApp–El Paso, 86 SW3d 721.—App & E 428(2), 863, 888(2); Child C 661, 905; Divorce 183; Judgm 303, 304, 305, 306, 326; Plead 427.

Gutierrez; Gutierrez v., TexApp–El Paso, 86 SW3d 721.—App & E 428(2), 863, 888(2); Child C 661, 905; Divorce 183; Judgm 303, 304, 305, 306, 326; Plead 427.

Gutierrez v. Hachar's Dept. Store, TexCivApp–San Antonio, 484 SW2d 433, ref nre.—App & E 766; Judgm 185(2), 185.1(8), 185.3(13), 186; Labor & Emp 210.

Gutierrez; Home Ins. Indem. Co. v., TexCivApp–Corpus Christi, 409 SW2d 450, ref nre.—App & E 170(1); Cust & U 5, 19(3); Paymt 16(1), 21, 22; Tender 11, 13(1); Work Comp 1003, 1034, 1042, 1789, 1981.

Gutierrez; Jackson v., TexApp–Houston (14 Dist), 77 SW3d 898.—App & E 5, 859, 931(1), 934(3), 989, 1010.1(1), 1010.2, 1012.1(3), 1172(5); Costs 260(5); Damag 20, 43, 49.10, 139, 186, 194; Evid 597; Judgm 112; Plead 85(3).

Gutierrez v. Johnson, TexApp–Houston (1 Dist), 934 SW2d 809.—Costs 132(6); Mand 154(1).

Gutierrez v. Karl Perry Enterprises, Inc., TexApp–El Paso, 874 SW2d 103.—App & E 842(2), 893(1), 917(1), 960(1); Autos 197(7); Const Law 2471; Courts 91(1); Insurance 1003, 1867, 3419; Neglig 1692; Plead 228.14.

Gutierrez v. Laredo Independent School Dist., TexApp–San Antonio, 139 SW3d 363.—Admin Law 229; Const Law 983; Contracts 14, 29, 176(2); Schools 47, 63(1).

GUTIERREZ;

See Guidelines for Arrangement at the beginning of this Volume

Gutierrez; Lee v., TexApp–Austin, 876 SW2d 382, reh overr, and writ den.—Banks 119, 153, 154(6); B & L Assoc 40, 42(19).

Gutierrez v. Lee, TexApp–Austin, 812 SW2d 388, writ den, appeal after remand 876 SW2d 382, reh overr, and writ den.—B & L Assoc 42(3); Const Law 2312, 2315, 3957; Lim of Act 130(7); Statut 227.

Gutierrez v. Lomas Mortg., BkrtcyWDTex, 160 BR 788. See Gutierrez, In re.

Gutierrez v. Lone Star Nat. Bank, TexApp–Corpus Christi, 960 SW2d 211, review den.—Const Law 3989; Judgm 335(3); Notice 12; Pretrial Proc 676.

Gutierrez v. Madero, TexCivApp–Eastland, 564 SW2d 185, ref nre.—Armed S 84; Divorce 244; Insurance 3481(1); Trusts 103(2).

Gutierrez v. MBank the Woodlands, N.A., TexApp–Beaumont, 761 SW2d 853.—Contracts 93(5); Guar 72; Judgm 181(22).

Gutierrez v. Mobil Oil Corp., WDTex, 798 FSupp 1280.—Environ Law 251, 258; Neglig 205; Nuis 18, 77; States 18.15, 18.31.

Gutierrez; Northern Assur. Co. of America v., TexApp–El Paso, 729 SW2d 342.—Work Comp 869.

Gutierrez; Ortiz v., TexApp–San Antonio, 792 SW2d 118, writ dism.—Mental H 122, 128, 133.

Gutierrez; Pace v., TexCivApp–Amarillo, 492 SW2d 356, ref nre.—App & E 1062.5; Autos 242(8), 244(41.1), 244(58), 247; Neglig 371, 379, 387, 1675; Trial 352.10.

Gutierrez v. Pacific Tankers, SDTex, 81 FSupp 278.—Rem of C 13, 107(4).

Gutierrez; Pairett v., TexApp–Austin, 969 SW2d 512, review den.—Antitrust 162, 198; App & E 852; Consp 2, 3; Contracts 205.30; Fraud 36; Judgm 178, 185(2), 185.3(18).

Gutierrez; Piperi v., BkrtcySDTex, 137 BR 644. See Piperi, In re.

Gutierrez; Police Civil Service Com'n v., TexApp–Austin, 182 SW3d 430.—App & E 893(1); Mun Corp 185(12); Plead 104(1), 111.36, 111.48.

Gutierrez; Port Elevator Brownsville v., CA5 (Tex), 198 FedAppx 362.—Antitrust 161; Fed Civ Proc 2481; Wareh 8, 10, 25(5).

Gutierrez v. Quarterman, CA5 (Tex), 201 FedAppx 196, cert den 127 SCt 1297, 167 LEd2d 112.—Const Law 4597; Crim Law 700(3); Hab Corp 366, 818, 883.1.

Gutierrez v. Raymond Intern., Inc., SDTex, 484 FSupp 241.—Adm 46; Const Law 3965(3), 3977(2); Corp 1.7(2), 642(1), 665(1), 668(14); Fed Civ Proc 51; Fed Cts 77, 82.

Gutierrez v. Raymond Intern., Inc., SDTex, 86 FRD 684.—Fed Civ Proc 392.

Gutierrez v. Rodriguez, TexApp–Texarkana, 30 SW3d 558.—App & E 842(1), 946; Deeds 135, 155, 156, 165; Estates 7; Estop 32(1); Evid 370(1), 370(4); Trial 367; Wills 396, 658.

Gutierrez v. Rodriguez, TexCivApp–San Antonio, 137 SW2d 220.—Evid 460(3); Execution 140, 222(3), 258, 283, 312.

Gutierrez; Salinas v., TexCivApp–San Antonio, 341 SW2d 558, ref nre.—Decl Judgm 182; Des & Dist 8; Ten in C 4, 15(10).

Gutierrez v. Scripps-Howard, TexApp–El Paso, 823 SW2d 696, writ den.—Neglig 213, 221, 433.

Gutierrez v. State, TexCrimApp, 221 SW3d 680.—Controlled Subs 130; Crim Law 1134(2), 1144.12; Searches 24, 25.1, 26, 40.1, 42.1, 44, 45, 171, 180, 181, 192.1, 198, 201.

Gutierrez; State v., TexCrimApp, 129 SW3d 113, on remand 143 SW3d 829.—Crim Law 1023(14).

Gutierrez v. State, TexCrimApp, 108 SW3d 304, on remand 2005 WL 1805614.—Crim Law 274(3.1); Sent & Pun 2009.

Gutierrez v. State, TexCrimApp, 36 SW3d 509, on remand 2001 WL 783711, petition for discretionary review refused.—Crim Law 1045.

Gutierrez v. State, TexCrimApp, 979 SW2d 659.—Crim Law 145.

Gutierrez v. State, TexCrimApp, 764 SW2d 796.—Crim Law 662.7, 951(1), 1036.2; Homic 1051(3), 1054; Witn 405(1).

Gutierrez v. State, TexCrimApp, 741 SW2d 444.—Crim Law 1184(2); Ind & Inf 113.

Gutierrez v. State, TexCrimApp, 659 SW2d 423.—Crim Law 1129(1), 1137(3).

Gutierrez v. State, TexCrimApp, 628 SW2d 57.—Controlled Subs 68, 73, 79, 80; Crim Law 338(1), 347, 417(14), 419(1.5), 552(3), 562, 698(1), 1043(2), 1088.10, 1169.1(1), 1169.1(7); Sent & Pun 1235.

Gutierrez v. State, TexCrimApp, 555 SW2d 457.—Crim Law 1181.5(9); Sent & Pun 1381(4).

Gutierrez v. State, TexCrimApp, 502 SW2d 746.—Crim Law 517(7), 519(8), 535(2), 538(3), 829(11), 1166(10.10), 1169.2(6).

Gutierrez v. State, TexCrimApp, 456 SW2d 84.—Crim Law 995(2); Sent & Pun 1025, 1377, 1379(2).

Gutierrez v. State, TexCrimApp, 423 SW2d 593.—Crim Law 394.4(1), 698(1), 814(17); Searches 40.1, 62, 65.

Gutierrez v. State, TexCrimApp, 422 SW2d 467.—Controlled Subs 116; Crim Law 404.60, 1036.1(4).

Gutierrez v. State, TexCrimApp, 386 SW2d 286.—Crim Law 1023(9), 1081(4.1), 1087.1(2).

Gutierrez v. State, TexCrimApp, 352 SW2d 124, 171 TexCrim 493.—False Pret 38.

Gutierrez v. State, TexCrimApp, 342 SW2d 314.—Crim Law 1090.1(1).

Gutierrez v. State, TexCrimApp, 327 SW2d 758, 168 TexCrim 378.—Crim Law 554; Larc 65.

Gutierrez v. State, TexCrimApp, 309 SW2d 461.—Infants 20.

Gutierrez v. State, TexCrimApp, 301 SW2d 134.—Crim Law 1090.1(1).

Gutierrez v. State, TexCrimApp, 272 SW2d 894, 160 TexCrim 550.—Child S 663.

Gutierrez v. State, TexCrimApp, 175 SW2d 968, 146 TexCrim 411.—Crim Law 130, 134(1), 406(6), 448(9), 698(1), 1169.1(7), 1169.9; Homic 1136.

Gutierrez v. State, TexCrimApp, 134 SW2d 282, 138 TexCrim 45.—Burg 41(1); Sent & Pun 1388.

Gutierrez v. State, TexApp–Austin, 85 SW3d 446, reh overr, and petition for discretionary review refused, habeas corpus gr Ex parte Gutierrez, 2003 WL 22097232, cert den 125 SCt 2245, 544 US 1034, 161 LEd2d 1062.—Const Law 4594(1); Crim Law 363, 368(3), 369.2(1), 568, 700(8), 814(1), 867, 881(2), 919(1), 1043(2), 1043(3), 1044.2(1); Homic 528, 1567; Jury 131(13); Witn 288(2).

Gutierrez v. State, TexApp–Austin, 8 SW3d 739.—Const Law 4556, 4652; Crim Law 29(1), 29(12), 369.2(5), 371(9), 409(5), 412.2(4), 641.3(3), 641.4(1), 641.13(1), 641.13(2.1), 641.13(7), 678(1), 678(2), 678(5), 855(1), 911, 956(4), 1030(1), 1036.1(5), 1038.1(2), 1139, 1156(1), 1162, 1166.10(1), 1168(2), 1177.

Gutierrez v. State, TexApp–San Antonio, 954 SW2d 86, reh overr, and petition for discretionary review gr, rev 979 SW2d 659.—Const Law 3310; Crim Law 132, 134(3); Gr Jury 2.5.

Gutierrez v. State, TexApp–San Antonio, 945 SW2d 287.—Crim Law 394.6(5), 412.2(5), 414, 777, 829(11), 1147, 1153(1), 1166.7, 1174(1); Jury 11(5).

Gutierrez v. State, TexApp–San Antonio, 702 SW2d 745.—Burg 42(3); Crim Law 641.13(1), 641.13(6).

Gutierrez v. State, TexApp–San Antonio, 625 SW2d 58, writ gr, rev 659 SW2d 423.—Crim Law 813, 1038.1(1), 1038.1(3.1).

Gutierrez v. State, TexApp–Dallas, 666 SW2d 248, petition for discretionary review refused.—Burg 2, 29,

46(2); Crim Law 743, 770(1), 795(1), 795(2.35); Ind & Inf 191(2); Sent & Pun 1513.

Gutierrez v. State, TexApp–Amarillo, 71 SW3d 372, petition for discretionary review refused.—Controlled Subs 27, 28, 34, 82; Crim Law 414, 552(2), 1030(1), 1036.1(5), 1043(1), 1043(2), 1045, 1130(5), 1134(1), 1134(2), 1144.13(3), 1144.13(6), 1159.2(7), 1159.2(9), 1159.4(2), 1162, 1169.12, 1191.

Gutierrez v. State, TexApp–Beaumont, 952 SW2d 947.—Crim Law 258, 1184(4.1); Sent & Pun 631, 1355.

Gutierrez v. State, TexApp–Eastland, 851 SW2d 396, reh den, and petition for discretionary review refused.—Crim Law 957(3), 959.

Gutierrez; State v., TexApp–Corpus Christi, 143 SW3d 829.—Crim Law 1081(1), 1083; Sent & Pun 2285.

Gutierrez; State v., TexApp–Corpus Christi, 112 SW3d 203, reh overr, and petition for discretionary review gr, rev 129 SW3d 113, on remand 143 SW3d 829.—Courts 39; Crim Law 1017, 1024(1), 1024(9), 1131(4).

Gutierrez v. State, TexApp–Corpus Christi, 65 SW3d 362, reh overr, and petition for discretionary review gr, rev 108 SW3d 304, on remand 2005 WL 1805614.—Crim Law 273.1(2), 641.13(1), 641.13(7); Sent & Pun 2009.

Gutierrez v. State, TexApp–Corpus Christi, 46 SW3d 394, petition for discretionary review gr, aff 85 SW3d 817.—Sent & Pun 1948, 2010, 2012, 2018.

Gutierrez v. State, TexApp–Corpus Christi, 22 SW3d 75.—Aliens 441, 445; Arrest 63.5(6), 70(1); Controlled Subs 137; Courts 97(5); Crim Law 394.2(2), 1139, 1158(1); Cust Dut 126(2), 126(5), 131; Searches 12, 22, 40.1, 171.

Gutierrez v. State, TexApp–Corpus Christi, 745 SW2d 529, petition for discretionary review refused.—Crim Law 398(1), 398(2), 400(2), 444.

Gutierrez v. State, TexApp–Corpus Christi, 721 SW2d 484, appeal after remand 745 SW2d 529, petition for discretionary review refused.—Crim Law 400(2), 1169.11.

Gutierrez v. State, TexApp–Corpus Christi, 708 SW2d 937.—Crim Law 414.

Gutierrez v. State, TexApp–Corpus Christi, 672 SW2d 633, petition for discretionary review gr, aff as reformed 741 SW2d 444.—Crim Law 59(5), 312, 507(1), 507(2), 824(7), 995(3), 1144.13(3); Homic 908, 1135.

Gutierrez v. State, TexApp–Houston (14 Dist), 150 SW3d 827.—Crim Law 412.2(4), 417(15), 662.11, 781(5), 829(11), 1044.2(1), 1045, 1139, 1144.12, 1158(4), 1168(2).

Gutierrez v. State, TexApp–Houston (14 Dist), 927 SW2d 783.—Bail 42, 43.

Gutierrez v. State, TexApp–Houston (14 Dist), 728 SW2d 933.—Crim Law 577.11(4).

Gutierrez v. State, TexApp–Houston (14 Dist), 681 SW2d 698, petition for discretionary review refused.—Crim Law 230, 417(15), 419(12), 700(10), 770(2), 772(6), 792(3), 814(19), 822(1), 829(3), 829(21), 1134(2), 1172.3; Homic 870, 1180, 1380, 1412, 1458, 1465, 1470; Ind & Inf 71.4(5), 110(3), 137(6); Witn 345(5), 372(1), 374(1).

Gutierrez v. State ex rel. Wichita County, TexCivApp–Fort Worth, 433 SW2d 777.—Infants 225.

Gutierrez; Sunwest Bank of El Paso v., TexApp–El Paso, 819 SW2d 673, writ den.—App & E 169, 845(2); Usury 11, 13, 16, 42.

Gutierrez v. Texas Emp. Ins. Ass'n, TexCivApp–Waco, 530 SW2d 958.—Work Comp 1890, 1893, 1908, 1923.

Gutierrez; Texas Employers' Ins. Ass'n v., TexApp–El Paso, 795 SW2d 5, writ den.—App & E 959(3); Plead 236(3); Work Comp 1325, 1337, 1906.

Gutierrez; Top Rank, Inc. v., WDTex, 236 FSupp2d 637.—Antitrust 147, 224; Contracts 27, 187(1); Fed Civ Proc 2491.9, 2492, 2519; Sales 3.1; Tel 1248(1), 1251.

Gutierrez; Trammell Crow Cent. Texas, Ltd. v., TexApp–San Antonio, 220 SW3d 33.—App & E 994(2); Evid 54; Neglig 210, 213, 220, 371, 379, 380, 383, 387, 1019, 1024, 1070, 1238, 1692, 1711.

Gutierrez; Tumlinson v., TexApp–Corpus Christi, 55 SW3d 673.—Courts 176.5.

Gutierrez v. United Foods, Inc., CA5 (Tex), 11 F3d 556, cert den 114 SCt 2164, 511 US 1142, 128 LEd2d 887.—Labor & Emp 1167, 1319, 1320(4), 1323.

Gutierrez; U.S. v., CA5 (Tex), 343 F3d 415, cert den 124 SCt 2430, 541 US 1074, 158 LEd2d 984.—Const Law 4522; Crim Law 36.6, 37(6.1), 330, 1139, 1149.

Gutierrez; U.S. v., CA5 (Tex), 849 F2d 940, reh den U.S. v. Garcia, 856 F2d 191.—Arrest 63.5(7); Searches 15, 22, 195.1.

Gutierrez; U.S. v., CA5 (Tex), 560 F2d 195.—Aliens 445; Crim Law 1036.2; Cust Dut 126(5).

Gutierrez; U.S. v., CA5 (Tex), 559 F2d 1278.—Consp 23.1, 47(1), 47(12).

Gutierrez v. U.S., CA5 (Tex), 404 F2d 62.—Autos 245(14).

Gutierrez v. U.S., CA5 (Tex), 314 F2d 334.—Controlled Subs 82.

Gutierrez; U.S. v., CA5 (Tex), 211 FedAppx 300.—Crim Law 1042.

Gutierrez; U.S. v., CA5 (Tex), 114 FedAppx 637, post-conviction relief dism by 2006 WL 3541618.—Crim Law 369.2(3.1), 370, 371(1), 371(12).

Gutierrez; U.S. v., CA5 (Tex), 79 FedAppx 639, cert den 124 SCt 2811, 541 US 1087, 159 LEd2d 248.—Sent & Pun 979.

Gutierrez; U.S. v., SDTex, 934 FSupp 836.—Consp 40.4, 41; Crim Law 150, 739(3).

Gutierrez v. Uribe, TexCivApp–Fort Worth, 104 SW2d 569.—App & E 729, 927(7); Breach of M P 13, 22, 31, 34; Lim of Act 50(1).

Gutierrez v. Virginia Agr. Growers Ass'n, Inc., SDTex, 764 FSupp 447.—Fed Cts 122.

Gutierrez; Walker v., Tex, 111 SW3d 56.—App & E 945, 946; Const Law 990, 1030, 4422; Health 604, 804, 809.

Gutierrez v. Walker, TexApp–Corpus Christi, 50 SW3d 61, reh overr, and review gr, rev 111 SW3d 56.—Health 804.

Gutierrez v. Walsh, TexApp–Corpus Christi, 748 SW2d 27.—Pretrial Proc 46, 221, 226.

Gutierrez v. Yancey, TexApp–San Antonio, 650 SW2d 169.—App & E 1010.1(8.1); Joint Adv 1.2(2), 1.2(4), 1.2(6), 1.2(7), 1.2(8), 1.12, 1.15; Partners 5, 11, 15, 17, 44, 52.

Gutierrez-Barron; U.S. v., CA5 (Tex), 602 F2d 722, cert den 100 SCt 489, 444 US 983, 62 LEd2d 412.—Courts 90(2); Crim Law 428, 1086.9.

Gutierrez-Chavez; U.S. v., CA5 (Tex), 842 F2d 77.—Consp 47(12); Crim Law 422(8), 1166(6), 1169.7.

Gutierrez-Farias; U.S. v., CA5 (Tex), 294 F3d 657, cert den 123 SCt 869, 537 US 1114, 154 LEd2d 789.—Consp 28(3), 40.1, 47(12); Controlled Subs 31, 81; Crim Law 474.5, 1134(3), 1144.13(2.1), 1153(1), 1159.2(7), 1169.9.

Gutierrez Flores; Bustamante v., TexApp–San Antonio, 770 SW2d 934.—Adv Poss 11, 13, 17, 58, 60(3), 60(4), 85(4), 114(1); App & E 989, 1008.1(5).

Gutierrez-Gonzales; U.S. v., CA5 (Tex), 111 FedAppx 732, cert den 125 SCt 1367, 543 US 1173, 161 LEd2d 155.—Aliens 795(4); Crim Law 429(1), 662.40.

Gutierrez-Guajardo; U.S. v., SDTex, 699 FSupp 608.—Arrest 63.5(6); Crim Law 394.5(2), 412.1(3).

Gutierrez-Morales v. Homan, CA5 (Tex), 461 F3d 605.—Aliens 347, 385; Const Law 3921, 4438.

Gutierrez-Morales v. Homan, CA5 (Tex), 455 F3d 537, opinion withdrawn and superseded 461 F3d 605.—Aliens 347, 385, 388; Const Law 3921, 4438.

Gutierrez-Nieto; U.S. v., CA5 (Tex), 141 FedAppx 324, cert den Ramirez-Garcia v. US, 126 SCt 497, 546 US 967, 163 LEd2d 376.—Crim Law 1042.

Gutierrez-Ramirez; U.S. v., CA5 (Tex), 405 F3d 352, cert den 126 SCt 217, 546 US 888, 163 LEd2d 198.—Crim Law 1030(1), 1043(2); Sent & Pun 785, 793.

Gutierrez-Rocha; U.S. v., CA5 (Tex), 111 FedAppx 730.—Consp 51; Sent & Pun 752.

Gutierrez-Rubio v. Immigration and Naturalization Service, CA5 (Tex), 453 F2d 1243, cert den 92 SCt 2506, 408 US 926, 33 LEd2d 337.—Aliens 278, 282(3), 384.

Gutierrez-Tovar; U.S. v., CA5 (Tex), 169 FedAppx 214, cert gr, vac 127 SCt 828, 166 LEd2d 662, on remand US v. Villa-Gutierrez, 222 FedAppx 393, on remand US v Gonzalez-Silva, 228 FedAppx 413, on remand US v Lozano-Mireles, 224 FedAppx 431.—Ind & Inf 113; Jury 34(7); Sent & Pun 973.

Gutman; Cox v., TexCivApp–El Paso, 575 SW2d 661, ref nre.—Corp 560(4), 560(5); Deeds 8; Estop 31, 39.

Gutnick v. Immigration and Naturalization Service, CA5 (Tex), 439 F2d 1128.—Courts 104; Fed Cts 743.

Gutschke; State v., Tex, 233 SW2d 446, 149 Tex 292.—Admin Law 446, 451; App & E 1177(2); Int Liq 68(2), 75(2).

Gutschke; State v., TexCivApp–San Antonio, 233 SW2d 441, rev 233 SW2d 446, 149 Tex 292.—Int Liq 68(2), 70, 75(1), 75(2), 75(4); Judges 16(1).

Gutteridge; Naylor v., TexCivApp–Austin, 430 SW2d 726, ref nre.—App & E 994(1), 1012.1(1); Bills & N 499, 516, 527(1); Contracts 189; Evid 589, 590; Lim of Act 25(3), 46(3), 51(2), 74(1), 182(5), 195(3); Paymt 41(4), 43, 45, 75.

Guttery v. State, TexCrimApp, 397 SW2d 853.—Bail 64.

Guttierez, In re, BkrtcyWDTex, 248 BR 287.—Atty & C 11(1), 11(2.1), 11(3); Bankr 2002, 3030.6, 3030.7, 3030.8, 3165.5.

Gutzman; Arguello v., TexApp–San Antonio, 838 SW2d 583.—App & E 422; Health 818, 819, 821(2), 821(4), 821(5); Judgm 185(2), 185(5), 185.2(5); Neglig 1610, 1675.

Guy; Allright, Inc. v., TexApp–Houston (14 Dist), 696 SW2d 603.—Autos 372(1), 372(4); Costs 194.25, 194.34; Lim of Act 130(1), 130(7); Trial 105(2).

Guy; Allright, Inc. v., TexCivApp–Hous (14 Dist), 590 SW2d 734, ref nre.—Courts 121(9), 122.

Guy v. Cockrell, CA5 (Tex), 343 F3d 348, on remand 2004 WL 1462196.—Crim Law 641.13(1), 641.13(6); Hab Corp 801, 842, 846.

Guy v. Crill, TexApp–Dallas, 654 SW2d 813.—Ex & Ad 7; Wills 439, 570, 573(1), 578(3), 767, 812.

Guy v. Guy, TexCivApp–San Antonio, 119 SW2d 194, writ dism.—Bills & N 537(2); Partners 216(1).

Guy; Guy v., TexCivApp–San Antonio, 119 SW2d 194, writ dism.—Bills & N 537(2); Partners 216(1).

Guy; Jones v., Tex, 143 SW2d 906, 135 Tex 398, 142 ALR 77.—Adop 20, 21; App & E 843(4), 1172(1); Equity 62; Estop 83(1), 87, 92(1); Frds St of 75; Wills 792(1), 792(5).

Guy v. Jones, TexCivApp–Texarkana, 132 SW2d 490, aff 143 SW2d 906, 135 Tex 398, 142 ALR 77.—Adop 21; Estop 83(1), 87, 92(1).

Guy; McRae Oil Corp. v., TexCivApp–Hous (14 Dist), 495 SW2d 31, ref nre.—App & E 301, 338(1), 356, 548(2), 548(5), 564(3), 619, 628(1), 671(4), 909(5); Atty & C 112; Frds St of 152(2).

Guy; Patton v., TexCivApp–Texarkana, 108 SW2d 868.—Receivers 35(1).

Guy v. State, TexCrimApp, 455 SW2d 277.—Crim Law 1087.1(2).

Guy v. State, TexApp–Houston (1 Dist), 751 SW2d 284.—Arrest 63.4(15), 63.5(1), 63.5(2), 63.5(4), 63.5(5); Controlled Subs 121.

Guy v. State, TexApp–Fort Worth, 160 SW3d 606, reh overr, and petition stricken, and petition for discretionary review refused, habeas corpus den 2007 WL 1686517.—Controlled Subs 26, 30, 68, 69, 81, 82; Crim Law 338(1), 474.1, 719(3), 720(1), 720(7.1), 723(1), 723(3), 726, 730(1), 1043(3), 1153(1), 1165(1), 1171.1(2.1), 1171.1(4), 1191.

Guy v. Stubberfield, TexApp–Dallas, 666 SW2d 176.—Child C 554, 576, 637, 920; Child S 199, 559; Trial 139.1(7), 178, 382.

Guyana Development Corp., In re, BkrtcySDTex, 201 BR 462.—Bankr 2154.1, 2201, 3003, 3009, 3152, 3159, 3160, 3167, 3182, 3192, 3193, 3196, 3203(1); Courts 9.

Guyana Development Corp., In re, BkrtcySDTex, 189 BR 393.—Bankr 2609, 2705; Int Rev 4771.1, 4772, 4783, 4789.

Guyana Development Corp., In re, BkrtcySDTex, 168 BR 892.—Bankr 2154.1, 2374, 2535(1), 2535(3), 2704; Corp 1.4(1), 1.4(2), 1.4(4); Int Rev 4761.1, 4767, 4775.

Guy Carpenter & Co., Inc. v. Provenzale, CA5 (Tex), 334 F3d 459, reh and reh den 77 FedAppx 288.—Antitrust 414, 421, 433; Contracts 65.5, 118; Fed Cts 12.1, 724, 776, 815, 862; Inj 132, 138.1, 138.33, 147.

Guy Chipman Co.; Gill v., TexApp–San Antonio, 681 SW2d 264.—App & E 931(1), 989, 1008.1(3), 1010.1(3), 1012.1(5); Contracts 65.5, 116(1), 116(2), 141(3); Damag 6, 189; Labor & Emp 34(2).

Guye v. State, TexCrimApp, 501 SW2d 675.—Crim Law 605, 1043(2), 1169.3.

Guyer; Berry v., TexCivApp–Hous (14 Dist), 482 SW2d 719, ref nre.—Release 25, 30, 33, 34.

Guyer v. Guyer, TexCivApp–Amarillo, 141 SW2d 963, writ refused.—Judgm 720; Trover 9(5), 44.

Guyer; Guyer v., TexCivApp–Amarillo, 141 SW2d 963, writ refused.—Judgm 720; Trover 9(5), 44.

Guyer; Prince v., Tex, 103 SW2d 128, 129 Tex 90.—App & E 84(1).

Guyer v. Prince, TexCivApp–Amarillo, 106 SW2d 1091, writ dism.—App & E 406, 434, 435, 627, 1126, 1127; Contracts 129(3).

Guyer v. Rose, TexCivApp–Dallas, 601 SW2d 205, ref nre.—Inj 26(9); Ven & Pur 191.

Guyger v. Hamilton Trailer Co., TexCivApp–Eastland, 304 SW2d 377.—Autos 160(1), 240(1), 244(59), 245(6), 245(91), 246(38); Neglig 1537; Trial 244(4).

Guy James Const. Co. v. Trinity Industries, Inc., CA5 (Tex), 650 F2d 93.—Fed Cts 744; Sales 418(14.1).

Guy James Const. Co. v. Trinity Industries, Inc., CA5 (Tex), 644 F2d 525, opinion mod 650 F2d 93.—Accord 10(1); Damag 45, 184; Elect of Rem 3(1), 9; Fed Civ Proc 751, 2011, 2251; Fed Cts 616, 800, 874; Interest 31, 39(2), 39(2.6); Sales 418(3), 418(14.1), 418(16.1).

Guy James Const. Co. v. Trinity Industries, Inc., NDTex, 462 FSupp 252, aff in part, rev in part 644 F2d 525, opinion mod 650 F2d 93.—Accord 23; Contracts 308; Damag 36, 45, 122; Princ & S 138.

Guyler; Byrd v., TexCivApp–San Antonio, 310 SW2d 747, dism.—Action 60; Courts 484; Divorce 166, 167; Plead 111.39(8); Venue 5.3(2), 5.3(5).

Guynes; Aetna Cas. & Sur. Co. v., CA5 (Tex), 713 F2d 1187.—Evid 110, 129(5), 146, 560; Fed Civ Proc 1931, 2011; Fed Cts 895; Insurance 3183.

Guynes v. Galveston County, Tex, 861 SW2d 861.—Counties 47, 113(1), 113(5); Dist & Pros Attys 9.

Guynes; Holbrook v., TexApp–Houston (1 Dist), 827 SW2d 487, writ gr, aff Guynes v. Galveston County, 861 SW2d 861.—App & E 713(1); Dist & Pros Attys 9.

Guynes; Williams v., TexCivApp–El Paso, 97 SW2d 988.—Child C 9, 421, 510, 552; Hab Corp 744, 798.

Guynes Printing Co. of Texas, Inc.; DeLuna v., TexApp–El Paso, 884 SW2d 206, reh den, and writ den.—App & E 863; Int Liq 299; Judgm 185(2), 185(6); Labor & Emp 3043; Neglig 220, 1019, 1692; Parent & C 13(1).

Guynn v. Corpus Christi Bank & Trust, TexCivApp–Corpus Christi, 620 SW2d 188, ref nre.—Contracts 181.1, 184; Guar 31, 36(9), 41.

Guynn v. Corpus Christi Bank & Trust, TexCivApp–Corpus Christi, 589 SW2d 764, dism.—App & E 548(5), 600(1), 692(1), 758.3(1), 866(3), 901, 927(7), 1078(1), 1078(2), 1078(5); Consp 8, 19; Contracts 352(1); Evid 253(1), 272, 350; Joint Adv 1.2(1), 1.2(4), 1.15; Torts 214, 242; Witn 276.

Guynn v. Corpus Christi Bank & Trust, TexCivApp–Corpus Christi, 580 SW2d 902, appeal after remand 620 SW2d 188, ref nre.—App & E 1173(2); Compromise 5(1); Judgm 72, 87, 89.

Guyot v. Guyot, TexApp–Fort Worth, 3 SW3d 243, rule 537(f) motion dism.—App & E 497(1), 499(1), 500(1), 516, 837(1); Divorce 179.

Guyot; Guyot v., TexApp–Fort Worth, 3 SW3d 243, rule 537(f) motion dism.—App & E 497(1), 499(1), 500(1), 516, 837(1); Divorce 179.

Guy's Foods; Andrews & Kurth L.L.P. v., CA5 (Tex), 157 F3d 414. See Pro-Snax Distributors, Inc., Matter of.

Guy's Foods v. Andrews & Kurth, L.L.P., NDTex, 212 BR 834. See Pro-Snax Distributors, Inc., In re.

Guyton v. Pronav Ship Management, Inc., SDTex, 139 FSupp2d 815.—Const Law 3964; Fed Cts 76.1, 76.5, 76.10, 82, 96; Princ & A 1.

Guyton v. State, TexCrimApp, 472 SW2d 130.—Crim Law 1038.2, 1038.3.

Guyton v. State, TexCrimApp, 365 SW2d 6.—Prost 15, 17, 28.

Guyton v. State, TexCrimApp, 296 SW2d 547.—Crim Law 1090.1(1).

Guyton v. State, TexCrimApp, 296 SW2d 545.—Crim Law 1090.1(1).

Guzik; Henrikson v., CA5 (Tex), 249 F3d 395.—Prisons 14; Statut 188, 205, 206, 219(1).

Guzik v. State Bar of Texas, CA5 (Tex), 659 F2d 528.—Antitrust 963(1), 977(5).

Guzman, Ex parte, TexCrimApp, 589 SW2d 461.—Crim Law 321; Hab Corp 705.1, 845, 848; Ind & Inf 9.

Guzman, Ex parte, TexCrimApp, 551 SW2d 387.—Judgm 476; Sent & Pun 2014.

Guzman, In re, BkrtcyWDTex, 130 BR 489.—Bankr 3361, 3444.30(6), 3444.50(3).

Guzman, In re, TexApp–Corpus Christi, 19 SW3d 522.—Pretrial Proc 11, 354.

Guzman v. Acuna, TexApp–San Antonio, 653 SW2d 315, dism.—App & E 845(2), 1008.1(3); Contracts 9(1), 143(3), 153; Conversion 1, 21(1); Interest 5; Spec Perf 1, 5, 25, 28(1), 30, 64; Ven & Pur 54, 199.

Guzman v. Aetna Cas. & Sur. Co., TexCivApp–Beaumont, 564 SW2d 116.—App & E 927(7), 989; Evid 200, 203; Plead 290(3), 291(3); Work Comp 235, 1342, 1928.

Guzman v. Allstate Ins. Co., TexApp–Eastland, 802 SW2d 877.—Insurance 2784.

Guzman v. Barnhart, CA5 (Tex), 159 FedAppx 578.—Social S 143.85.

Guzman v. Carnevale, TexApp–Corpus Christi, 964 SW2d 311.—App & E 223, 232(0.5), 293; Judgm 183, 185(2), 185.3(8); Pretrial Proc 477.1, 483.

Guzman v. City of San Antonio, TexApp–San Antonio, 766 SW2d 858.—Autos 187(2); Judgm 181(33).

Guzman v. Cordero, WDTex, 481 FSupp2d 787.—Fed Cts 303; Neglig 234; Rem of C 36, 107(4), 107(7).

Guzman v. El Paso Natural Gas Co., WDTex, 756 FSupp 994.—Civil R 1122, 1135, 1340; Contracts 168; Damag 208(6); Fed Civ Proc 842, 2470.2, 2491.5, 2497.1, 2515, 2544; Labor & Emp 79, 429, 750; Torts 115, 432, 433.

Guzman v. Estelle, CA5 (Tex), 493 F2d 532.—Controlled Subs 122; Searches 40.1.

Guzman v. Gonzales, CA5 (Tex), 163 FedAppx 259, cert den 127 SCt 40, 166 LEd2d 18.—Hab Corp 521.

Guzman v. Guajardo, TexApp–Corpus Christi, 761 SW2d 506, writ den.—Autos 162(2), 162(5), 168(6), 244(55); Death 88, 89, 95(1), 95(4); Infants 61.

Guzman v. Guzman, TexApp–Corpus Christi, 827 SW2d 445, writ gr, and writ withdrawn, writ den 843 SW2d 486.—App & E 1071.1(2); Costs 260(5); Divorce 252.3(1), 253(1), 286(9); Trial 392(1).

Guzman; Guzman v., TexApp–Corpus Christi, 827 SW2d 445, writ gr, and writ withdrawn, writ den 843 SW2d 486.—App & E 1071.1(2); Costs 260(5); Divorce 252.3(1), 253(1), 286(9); Trial 392(1).

Guzman v. Mamaloca Concerts, TexApp–Corpus Christi, 964 SW2d 311. See Guzman v. Carnevale.

Guzman v. Maryland Cas. Co., Tex, 107 SW2d 356, 130 Tex 62.—App & E 218.2(6); Trial 350.3(8), 351.5(1); Work Comp 556, 1335, 1930.

Guzman v. Phoenix Ins. Co., TexCivApp–San Antonio, 411 SW2d 642, ref nre.—Work Comp 1663, 1930, 1964.

Guzman; Plata v., TexCivApp–Corpus Christi, 571 SW2d 408, ref nre.—App & E 846(5), 900, 948, 959(1); Bound 37(3), 43; Lim of Act 182(2), 183(4), 184; Plead 236(2); Trial 6(1).

Guzman v. Safeway Stores, Inc., WDTex, 530 FSupp 29.—Fed Civ Proc 2464; Labor & Emp 1213, 1214, 1215, 1219(1), 1219(12), 1320(1), 1327(4), 1518.

Guzman; Savage v., TexCivApp–San Antonio, 91 SW2d 1178, writ dism.—Wills 503.

Guzman v. Solis, TexApp–San Antonio, 748 SW2d 108, writ den.—App & E 181, 218.2(3.1), 226(2), 241, 242(1), 270(4); Evid 265(2); Fraud 58(1); Impl & C C 98; Lim of Act 182(5); Trover 40(4).

Guzman v. State, TexCrimApp, 188 SW3d 185.—Crim Law 795(1.5), 795(2.1), 795(2.10), 795(2.50), 1173.2(4).

Guzman v. State, TexCrimApp, 85 SW3d 242, reh den, on remand 2003 WL 1654951.—Civil R 1033(1), 1743; Const Law 3309, 3428; Courts 97(5); Crim Law 1158(1), 1181.5(3.1); Jury 33(5.15).

Guzman; State v., TexCrimApp, 959 SW2d 631, on remand 1999 WL 33756621, on remand 1999 WL 33756622.—Courts 97(1), 97(5); Searches 64.

Guzman v. State, TexCrimApp, 955 SW2d 85.—Arrest 63.4(2), 63.4(12); Crim Law 1139, 1158(1), 1179.

Guzman v. State, TexCrimApp, 567 SW2d 188.—Burg 41(1); Crim Law 59(3), 339.8(1), 339.10(11), 404.65, 444, 641.3(8.1), 784(1), 784(4), 822(16), 842, 1137(5), 1181.5(8).

Guzman v. State, TexCrimApp, 521 SW2d 267.—Arrest 63.4(12); Burg 4, 8, 31, 41(5); Crim Law 394.4(9), 577, 693, 1036.1(2), 1083, 1110(1), 1110(2), 1110(5), 1144.13(3).

Guzman v. State, TexCrimApp, 508 SW2d 375.—Controlled Subs 80, 97; Searches 127.

Guzman v. State, TexCrimApp, 471 SW2d 845.—Controlled Subs 69; Crim Law 489, 641.13(6); Searches 16.

Guzman v. State, TexCrimApp, 461 SW2d 602.—Controlled Subs 121; Searches 67.1, 123.1.

Guzman v. State, TexCrimApp, 456 SW2d 133.—Const Law 4509(25); Weap 3.

Guzman v. State, TexCrimApp, 399 SW2d 824.—Crim Law 1081(2).

Guzman v. State, TexCrimApp, 329 SW2d 872, 168 TexCrim 487.—Sent & Pun 2021.

Guzman; State v., TexApp–Austin, 182 SW3d 389.—Const Law 3855; Double J 5.1, 135, 142, 161.

Guzman v. State, TexApp–Austin, 867 SW2d 126, reh overr, and petition for discretionary review gr, rev 955 SW2d 85.—Arrest 63.4(0.5), 63.4(2), 63.4(3), 63.4(8), 63.4(9), 63.4(17).

Guzman v. State, TexApp–San Antonio, 993 SW2d 232, petition for discretionary review refused, cert den 120 SCt 1174, 528 US 1161, 145 LEd2d 1082.—Crim Law 273.1(3), 273.1(4), 273.1(5).

Guzman v. State, TexApp–Dallas, 20 SW3d 237, petition for discretionary review gr, rev 85 SW3d 242, reh den, on remand 2003 WL 1654951.—Const Law 3428; Crim Law 741(1), 742(1), 1158(3), 1159.2(2), 1159.2(8), 1159.2(9), 1159.4(2), 1166.17; Homic 527, 1141, 1184; Jury 33(5.15).

Guzman v. State, TexApp–Amarillo, 625 SW2d 15.—Crim Law 419(12), 444, 507(1), 507(2), 556, 662.1, 780(1), 781(8).

Guzman v. State, TexApp–El Paso, 841 SW2d 61, reh overr, and petition for discretionary review refused.—Autos 359; Convicts 7(2); Hab Corp 201, 271, 285.1, 443.1, 447, 705.1, 715.1, 823; Sent & Pun 2260.

Guzman v. State, TexApp–Corpus Christi, 988 SW2d 884.
—Assault 49, 96(1); Crim Law 25, 772(5), 795(2.1),
795(2.10); Ind & Inf 191(0.5).

Guzman; State v., TexApp–Corpus Christi, 942 SW2d 41,
petition for discretionary review gr, rev 959 SW2d 631,
on remand 1999 WL 33756621, on remand 1999 WL
33756622.—Autos 349.5(7); Controlled Subs 114;
Searches 53.1, 62, 64, 192.1, 200.

Guzman v. State, TexApp–Corpus Christi, 923 SW2d 792.
—Crim Law 625.10(2.1), 641.13(1), 641.13(7), 655(1), 713,
981(1), 1023(16), 1086.4, 1114.1(1), 1144.17, 1147,
1166.22(1), 1166.22(2); Sent & Pun 278, 2024, 2026,
2034.

Guzman v. State, TexApp–Corpus Christi, 760 SW2d 776.
—Autos 355(7), 355(13); Crim Law 562.

Guzman v. State, TexApp–Corpus Christi, 739 SW2d 381,
petition for discretionary review refused.—Crim Law
552(1), 1038.1(4); Forg 44(0.5).

Guzman v. State, TexApp–Corpus Christi, 732 SW2d 683.
—Burg 41(1), 41(6); Crim Law 273.1(4), 295, 1030(3),
1116, 1128(1), 1128(2), 1134(2), 1166(1); Double J 51, 59,
201; Hab Corp 291; Ind & Inf 130; Sent & Pun 1934.

Guzman v. State, TexApp–Corpus Christi, 649 SW2d 77.
—Crim Law 438(1), 438(6), 438(7), 730(1), 730(14),
857(1), 925(1), 956(13), 1172.8, 1174(2); Homic 1051(1),
1051(2), 1051(3); Jury 43, 110(1).

Guzman v. Stoudt, CA5 (Tex), 208 FedAppx 362.—Fed
Cts 770.

Guzman v. Synthes (USA), TexApp–San Antonio, 20
SW3d 717, reh overr, and petition for review den, and
reh of petition for review overr.—App & E 863, 901;
Evid 571(6); Neglig 379, 380; Prod Liab 11, 14, 15, 46.1,
75.1, 77, 83.

Guzman; Texas Osage Co-op. Royalty Pool v., TexCiv-
App–San Antonio, 153 SW2d 239.—Ack 25; Exch of
Prop 8(1); Mines 55(1), 55(8).

Guzman; Tyson Foods, Inc. v., TexApp–Tyler, 116 SW3d
233.—Aliens 133; App & E 174, 854(4), 930(1), 946,
971(2), 989, 994(1), 999(1), 1001(1), 1001(3), 1003(5),
1003(7), 1050.1(1), 1056.1(1), 1122(2); Evid 219.50, 508,
535, 555.2, 555.9; Neglig 210, 371, 379, 380, 387, 1011,
1205(7), 1676, 1679, 1714; Trial 43.

Guzman v. Ugly Duckling Car Sales of Texas, L.L.P.,
TexApp–San Antonio, 63 SW3d 522, review den.—Antitrust 390, 397; App & E 843(3), 866(3), 927(7), 989,
1003(5), 1003(6); Contracts 176(1), 227, 326; Costs
194.32; Estop 52.10(2); Sec Tran 242.1; Trial 139.1(14).

Guzman; U.S. v., CA5 (Tex), 781 F2d 428, cert den 106
SCt 1798, 475 US 1143, 90 LEd2d 343.—Crim Law
29(1), 29(5.5), 721(3), 1030(1), 1036.1(6), 1171.5; Fraud
68.10(1), 68.10(2), 69(5); Ind & Inf 130.

Guzman; U.S. v., CA5 (Tex), 114 FedAppx 617.—Consp
47(12); Crim Law 772(6), 867.

Guzman-Guzman; U.S. v., CA5 (Tex), 488 F2d 965.—
Crim Law 412.2(5), 414.

Guzman-Guzman; U.S. v., CA5 (Tex), 203 FedAppx 630.
—Sent & Pun 56.

Guzman-Ocampo; U.S. v., CA5 (Tex), 236 F3d 233, cert
den 121 SCt 2600, 533 US 953, 150 LEd2d 757.—Aliens
333, 376, 773, 794, 795(2), 795(3); Const Law 4438;
Crim Law 11, 1032(5), 1167(1); Ind & Inf 60, 71.2(2),
71.2(4), 196(5).

Guzman-Reyes; U.S. v., CA5 (Tex), 162 FedAppx 281.—
Crim Law 1042.

Guzman-Reyes; U.S. v., CA5 (Tex), 113 FedAppx 607,
cert gr, vac 125 SCt 1407, 543 US 1181, 161 LEd2d 177,
on remand 162 FedAppx 281.—Consp 51; Jury 34(8).

Guzman-Ruiz v. U.S., CA5 (Tex), 831 F2d 84. See U.S.
v. $400,000.00 in U.S. Currency.

Guzman-Salinas; U.S. v., CA5 (Tex), 155 FedAppx 809,
cert den 126 SCt 1802, 547 US 1083, 164 LEd2d 539.—
Crim Law 1042; Sent & Pun 752.

Guzmon, Ex parte, TexCrimApp, 730 SW2d 724.—Hab
Corp 223.

Guzmon v. State, TexCrimApp, 697 SW2d 404, cert den
106 SCt 1479, 475 US 1090, 89 LEd2d 734.—Crim Law
698(1), 1035(5), 1043(2), 1043(3), 1169.5(1), 1170.5(1),
1170.5(5), 1170.5(6); Homic 1165; Jury 100; Witn 230.

Guzzardi, In re, NDTex, 84 FSupp 294.—Crim Law
394.2(2); Hab Corp 490(4); Searches 31.1, 32.

Gwaltney; National Hotel Co. v., TexCivApp–Texarkana,
127 SW2d 365.—App & E 500(2); Plead 111.2, 111.3,
111.39(2), 111.42(6).

Gwartney v. Dahlin and Fitch, TexCivApp–Fort Worth,
551 SW2d 781.—Divorce 226, 254(1).

G.W.H. v. D.A.H., TexApp–Houston (14 Dist), 650 SW2d
480.—Infants 156, 179.

Gwin v. Griffith, TexApp–Corpus Christi, 394 SW2d
191.—Judgm 181(15.1), 185(2), 185.3(17); Mtg 154(2),
186(4), 186(5), 372(1), 378; Tresp to T T 7; Ven & Pur
242.

Gwinn v. Associated Emp. Lloyds, TexCivApp–Fort
Worth, 280 SW2d 624, ref nre.—Compromise 19(1);
Contracts 93(5); Judgm 181(2); Work Comp 1148, 1152,
1159.

Gwinn; Thomason v., TexCivApp–Amarillo, 184 SW2d
542, writ refused wom.—Evid 568(3); Wills 130, 179,
206, 289, 303(7), 324(1), 327, 400.

GWI PCS 1 Inc., In re, CA5 (Tex), 230 F3d 788, reh and
sug for reh den 245 F3d 792, cert den US v. GWI PCS
1, Inc, 121 SCt 2623, 533 US 964, 150 LEd2d 776.—
Auctions 7; Bankr 2641, 2644, 2650(2), 2726.1(3),
3776.5(1), 3776.5(5), 3781, 3782, 3787; Tel 1037.

GWI PCS 1, Inc.; U.S. v., NDTex, 245 BR 59, aff In re
GWI PCS 1 Inc, 230 F3d 788, reh and sug for reh den
245 F3d 792, cert den 121 SCt 2623, 533 US 964, 150
LEd2d 776.—Bankr 3569, 3775, 3776.5(5), 3781, 3782,
3786.

G-W-L, Inc. v. Juneau, TexCivApp–Beaumont, 486 SW2d
812, ref nre.—Damag 140; Evid 568(7); Garn 9, 251;
Trial 140(2).

G-W-L, Inc. v. Robichaux, Tex, 643 SW2d 392.—Contracts 93(2), 205.15(3), 205.35(4); Sales 10.

G-W-L, Inc. v. Robichaux, TexApp–Beaumont, 622 SW2d
461, ref nre, and writ gr, rev 643 SW2d 392.—Contracts
205.15(3), 205.30; Damag 191, 221(2.1), 221(5.1).

GWM Corp. v. Wilson-Riley, Inc., TexApp–Tyler, 657
SW2d 903.—Acct Action on 14; App & E 846(5), 852,
931(5), 931(6).

G. W. Murphy Industries, Inc.; Hughes Tool Co. v., CA5
(Tex), 491 F2d 923.—Pat 168(3), 226.8, 227, 312(1.7),
312(2), 314(5), 318(3), 319(1), 324.55(2).

G. W. Murphy Industries, Inc.; Salinas v., SDTex, 338
FSupp 1381.—Civil R 1529.

GWR Operating Co.; Taylor v., TexApp–Houston (1
Dist), 820 SW2d 908, writ den.—Antitrust 141, 143(2);
Fraud 64(1); Joint Adv 1.2(1); Judgm 181(33), 185(2);
Mines 101.

GWR Operating Co.; Taylor and Associates v., TexApp–
Houston (1 Dist), 820 SW2d 908. See Taylor v. GWR
Operating Co.

GWR Operating Co.; Tom Taylor and Associates v.,
TexApp–Houston (1 Dist), 820 SW2d 908. See Taylor v.
GWR Operating Co.

G. W. Townsend Lease Service; Appell Petroleum Corp.
v., TexCivApp–Corpus Christi, 375 SW2d 547.—App &
E 846(5), 931(1); Corp 503(2), 513.1; Evid 265(10),
314(1), 591, 593; Mines 80; Fraud 34(6).

Gwynn; Usher v., TexCivApp–San Antonio, 375 SW2d
564, writ gr, aff Ashley v. Usher, 384 SW2d 696, 17
ALR3d 595.—App & E 930(3), 989, 1001(1); Wills 290,
306, 316.1.

GXG, Inc. v. Texacal Oil & Gas, TexApp–Corpus Christi,
977 SW2d 403, reh overr, and review den, and reh of
petition for review den.—App & E 216(7), 863, 1151(1);
Contracts 176(2); Damag 73, 87(1); Deeds 94, 110;
Evid 244(7), 258(1), 397(2), 429, 448; Fraud 27, 32, 59(2);

Judgm 199(1), 199(3.10); Liens 7; Mines 54.5, 55(2), 55(5), 55(8); Princ & A 1, 20(2), 70, 128, 157, 158, 162.

GXG, Inc. v. Texacal Oil & Gas, Inc., TexApp–Corpus Christi, 882 SW2d 850.—App & E 100(2); Inj 163(1), 174.

GX Technology Corp.; Davidoff v., TexApp–Waco, 134 SW3d 514, opinion after remand 2005 WL 1981425, reh overr, and review den.—App & E 337(2), 347(1).

Gyarfas v. U.S., SDTex, 934 FSupp 817. See Andrade v. Chojnacki.

Gym-N-I Playgrounds, Inc. v. Snider, Tex, 220 SW3d 905, reh den.—Antitrust 297; Contracts 1; Fraud 36; Land & Ten 90(2), 125(1), 125(2), 166(6), 196.

Gym-N-I Playgrounds, Inc. v. Snider, TexApp–Austin, 158 SW3d 78, review gr, aff 220 SW3d 905, reh den.— Antitrust 297; Contracts 143(1), 152, 175(1), 176(2); Fraud 36; Judgm 185(6); Land & Ten 24(3), 37, 115(3), 125(2), 162, 166(2); Prod Liab 26.

Gyorkey; Claus v., CA5 (Tex), 674 F2d 427.—Colleges 8.1(1); Consp 8; Const Law 4011; Evid 397(2); Fed Cts 613; Labor & Emp 40(2), 903; Princ & A 22(1); U S 50.5(2), 50.10(4).

G._____ v. State, TexApp–Dallas, 715 SW2d 790. See B------- A------- G------- v. State.

G2, Inc. v. Midwest Gaming, Inc., WDTex, 485 FSupp2d 757.—Fed Cts 13, 43, 47.1, 57; Gaming 68(0.5); Int Liq 116; Lotteries 3; Postal 13.

G4 Trading, Inc. v. NationsBank of Texas, N.A., Tex-App–Houston (1 Dist), 937 SW2d 137.—App & E 901, 970(2), 1003(6), 1056.1(1); Banks 188.5.

H

H., Ex parte, TexApp–Houston (1 Dist), 869 SW2d 496. See E.E.H., Ex parte.

H., Ex parte, TexApp–Houston (14 Dist, 823 SW2d 791. See P.D.H., Ex parte.

H., In Interest of, TexApp–San Antonio, 961 SW2d 550. See J.H., In Interest of.

H., In Interest of, TexApp–Beaumont, 979 SW2d 445. See A.D.H., In Interest of.

H., In Interest of, TexApp–Beaumont, 739 SW2d 490. See S.P.H., In Interest of.

H., In Interest of, TexApp–Beaumont, 661 SW2d 744. See J.D.H., In Interest of.

H., In Interest of, TexApp–Corpus Christi, 843 SW2d 740. See R.M.H., In Interest of.

H., In Interest of, TexApp–Houston (14 Dist, 745 SW2d 424. See M.H., In Interest of.

H., In re, Tex, 973 SW2d 296. See D.A.S., In re.

H., Matter of, TexApp–Fort Worth, 700 SW2d 782. See K.A.H., Matter of.

H., Matter of, TexApp–Austin, 779 SW2d 954. See J.T.H., Matter of.

H., Matter of, TexApp–Austin, 771 SW2d 697. See R.L.H., Matter of.

H., Matter of, TexApp–San Antonio, 974 SW2d 359. See A.L.H., Matter of.

H., Matter of, TexApp–Dallas, 971 SW2d 606. See T.D.H., Matter of.

H., Matter of, TexApp–Texarkana, 913 SW2d 684. See K.B.H., Matter of.

H., Matter of, TexApp–Beaumont, 972 SW2d 928. See J.E.H., Matter of.

H., Matter of, TexApp–Corpus Christi, 846 SW2d 103. See S.H., Matter of.

H., Matter of, TexApp–Corpus Christi, 664 SW2d 415. See R.H., Matter of.

H. v. National Convenience Stores, Inc., TexApp–Houston (1 Dist), 936 SW2d 406. See S.H. v. National Convenience Stores, Inc.

H. v. State, TexApp–Houston (1 Dist), 662 SW2d 42. See V.C.H. v. State.

H. v. State, TexApp–San Antonio, 905 SW2d 726. See R.H. v. State.

H. v. State, TexApp–Houston (14 Dist, 966 SW2d 618. See D.R.H. v. State.

H. v. Stop–N–Go, TexApp–Houston (1 Dist), 936 SW2d 406. See S.H. v. National Convenience Stores, Inc.

Haag; Bank of America v., TexApp–San Antonio, 37 SW3d 55, reh overr.—App & E 761; Estop 95; Evid 385, 389, 397(1); Lost Inst 8(3); Trusts 43(1), 262.

Haag; Cantu v., TexCivApp–San Antonio, 297 SW2d 384. —App & E 1170.7.

Haag v. Cantu, TexCivApp–San Antonio, 282 SW2d 246. —Venue 8.5(8).

Haag; Government Personnel Auto. Ass'n v., TexCiv-App–San Antonio, 131 SW2d 978, writ refused.—App & E 1008.1(11); Insurance 1810, 2663, 3007(1), 3013, 3015, 3549(4).

Haag v. Pugh, TexCivApp–Eastland, 545 SW2d 22.—App & E 731(2), 758.3(9); Interest 30(1), 46(1).

Haag Engineering Co.; Dagley v., TexApp–Houston (14 Dist), 18 SW3d 787.—Antitrust 134, 221; Consp 1.1, 8; Insurance 1654, 1867, 3361, 3415, 3417; Judgm 185(5); Neglig 202, 1692; Torts 212, 244; Trial 139.1(20).

Haak; Falls County Water Control and Imp. Dist. No. 1 v., TexApp–Waco, 220 SW3d 92.—App & E 76(1), 1024.1; Em Dom 253(1), 265(1), 265(3); Judgm 297; Plead 48.

Haan v. Daly, TexCivApp–Waco, 409 SW2d 958, ref nre. —App & E 187(3); Evid 382; Hus & W 25(1); Plead 130, 132; Ven & Pur 327, 328.

Haas, Ex parte, TexCrimApp, 155 SW2d 809, 142 Tex-Crim 621.—Hab Corp 526.

Haas v. ADVO Systems, Inc., CA5 (Tex), 168 F3d 732.— Civil R 1551; Fed Civ Proc 2497.1.

Haas v. Ashford Hollow Community Improvement Ass'n, Inc., TexApp–Houston (14 Dist), 209 SW3d 875. —App & E 837(1), 893(1), 1008.1(2), 1010.2, 1012.1(4); Contracts 313(2); Costs 208; Courts 163, 169(1), 169(3), 170, 184; Covenants 132(2); Plead 111.36, 111.43, 427; Statut 181(1), 206.

Haas v. Carrier Corp., TexCivApp–Houston, 339 SW2d 727.—Food 25; Judgm 181(2); Neglig 1614; Prod Liab 79.

Haas v. Dodson, TexCivApp–Waco, 589 SW2d 193.— Mental H 112, 113.

Haas v. Earley, TexCivApp–Corpus Christi, 443 SW2d 861.—Agric 3.4(2); Land & Ten 124(1).

Haas v. George, TexApp–Texarkana, 71 SW3d 904.—App & E 66, 76(1), 78(1), 856(1), 863, 934(1), 946, 1073(1), 1079, 1135; Atty & C 109; Judgm 181(7), 183, 185(5), 190, 216; Lim of Act 43, 55(3), 95(1), 95(3), 95(17), 104(1), 104(2), 199(1); Pretrial Proc 11, 378; Trial 18.

Haas v. Gulf Coast Natural Gas Co., TexCivApp–Corpus Christi, 484 SW2d 127.—App & E 846(5); Mines 109.

Haas; Jacobsen v., TexApp–Corpus Christi, 688 SW2d 634.—Hab Corp 532(1), 532(2); Mand 54.

Haas; Moody v., TexCivApp–Hous (14 Dist), 493 SW2d 555, 59 ALR3d 1109, writ refused.—Char 37(3), 43, 47; Trusts 169(1).

Haas; Ottis v., TexCivApp–Corpus Christi, 569 SW2d 508, ref nre.—App & E 205, 756, 1060.2, 1078(1), 1078(4), 1079; Mines 73.1(6); Trial 139.1(5.1), 139.1(7).

Haas; Spears v., TexApp–Corpus Christi, 718 SW2d 756. —Divorce 86, 166; Judgm 335(3); Mand 72; Pretrial Proc 25.

Haas v. State, TexCrimApp, 498 SW2d 206.—Crim Law 438(6), 444, 577.8(2), 577.10(1), 577.10(9), 577.10(10), 577.15(3), 577.16(5.1), 713, 730(14), 855(5), 1144.12, 1153(5), 1168(2), 1171.8(1).

Haas v. State, TexCrimApp, 163 SW2d 407, 144 TexCrim 406.—Larc 55.

Haas v. State, TexApp–Waco, 172 SW3d 42, petition stricken, and petition for discretionary review refused. —Arrest 63.5(3.1), 63.5(4), 63.5(9), 68(4); Autos 349(1),

349(2.1), 349(10), 349(17), 349(18), 349.5(7); Crim Law 394.5(4), 1139, 1147, 1153(1), 1158(1); Searches 22, 23, 180.

Haas v. Texas Employment Com'n, TexApp–Dallas, 683 SW2d 462.—Const Law 4027, 4116; Unemp Comp 68, 473, 479.

Haas; U.S. v., CA5 (Tex), 171 F3d 259.—Consp 47(6), 48.2(2); Crim Law 559, 561(1), 568, 772(5), 800(6), 805(1), 822(1), 1139, 1158(1); Health 314, 992; Sent & Pun 736, 761, 996.

Haas v. Voigt, TexApp–San Antonio, 940 SW2d 198, reh overr, and writ den.—App & E 842(1), 854(2); Hus & W 14.3, 266.2(1), 267(0.5); Joint Ten 3, 6.

Haas Drilling Co. v. First Nat. Bank in Dallas, Tex, 456 SW2d 886.—Frds St of 23(1), 33(2), 160; Guar 92(2); Trial 350.4(1).

Haas Drilling Co.; First Nat. Bank in Dallas v., TexCiv-App–Dallas, 446 SW2d 29, rev 456 SW2d 886.—App & E 1062.1; Frds St of 160; Trial 350.4(1), 352.5(3).

Haase v. Glazner, Tex, 62 SW3d 795.—App & E 863, 934(1); Fraud 20, 24, 59(2); Frds St of 119(1); Judgm 181(11).

Haase; Glazner v., TexApp–Texarkana, 61 SW3d 10, review gr, aff in part, rev in part 62 SW3d 795.—Contracts 9(1), 10(1), 56, 85; Corp 1.4(4); Fraud 24, 25, 32, 36; Frds St of 106(1), 108(1), 113(2), 118(1), 118(2); Guar 17; Judgm 181(11), 185(6); Plead 228.23.

Haase v. Greutzmacher, TexCivApp–San Antonio, 521 SW2d 666.—App & E 387(2), 387(3), 395; Courts 23, 37(1); New Tr 155.

Haase v. Herberger, TexApp–Houston (14 Dist), 44 SW3d 267.—Atty & C 112, 113, 153.

Haas' Estate v. Metro-Goldwyn-Mayer, Inc., CA5 (Tex), 617 F2d 1136.—Assign 57, 93.

Haass; Peat Marwick Main v., TexApp–San Antonio, 775 SW2d 698, writ gr, rev 818 SW2d 381.—App & E 930(3), 970(2), 1003(7), 1024.1; Contracts 1, 91, 116(1); Costs 208; Damag 117; Estop 52(1), 52(8), 52.15; Evid 146; Fraud 9, 12; Partners 19, 20, 25, 236, 242(7).

Haass; Peat Marwick Main & Co. v., Tex, 818 SW2d 381.—Contracts 116(1), 118, 327(1); Partners 230.

Habeeb; Morrison v., Tex, 252 SW2d 148, 151 Tex 508.—Gaming 58.

Habeeb; Morrison v., TexCivApp–Galveston, 246 SW2d 217, rev 252 SW2d 148, 151 Tex 508.—App & E 931(1); Gaming 61; Nuis 60.

Haber; Zep Mfg. Corp. v., SDTex, 202 FSupp 847.—Action 6; Fed Cts 343.

Haber Fabrics Corp.; Rylander v., TexApp–Austin, 13 SW3d 845.—Tax 3657.

Haberman; Bitter & Associates v., TexApp–San Antonio, 834 SW2d 383. See J.A. Bitter & Associates v. Haberman.

Haberman v. Equitable Life Assur. Soc. of the U.S., CA5 (Tex), 225 F2d 837.—Fed Cts 744.

Haberman v. Equitable Life Assur. Soc. of the U. S., CA5 (Tex), 224 F2d 401, reh den 225 F2d 837, cert den 76 SCt 322, 350 US 948, 100 LEd 826.—Annuities 17, 33; Corp 661(1); Fed Civ Proc 773; Fed Cts 541; Sec Reg 249.1, 252, 307; Tender 19(1).

Haberman; Flores v., Tex, 915 SW2d 477.—Lis Pen 3(1), 15.

Haberman; Howley By and Through Howley, Estate of v., Tex, 878 SW2d 139.—Mand 43; Pretrial Proc 698.

Haberman; J.A. Bitter & Associates v., TexApp–San Antonio, 834 SW2d 383.—Equity 72(1); Judgm 137; Mand 3(2.1), 4(1), 4(4), 50; New Tr 116.

Haberman; Thompson v., TexApp–San Antonio, 739 SW2d 71.—App & E 671(1), 907(3); Pretrial Proc 41.

Haberman v. U.S., CCA5 (Tex), 131 F2d 1018.—Armed S 40(2).

Haberman; Velasco v., TexApp–San Antonio, 700 SW2d 729.—Divorce 85, 115; Mand 32.

Habern v. Commonwealth Nat. Bank of Dallas, TexCiv-App–Dallas, 479 SW2d 99.—Judgm 185(2), 185.1(4), 185.2(1), 185.3(5), 185.3(16), 189.

Habern; State v., TexApp–Houston (1 Dist), 945 SW2d 225.—Ind & Inf 140(1), 140(2).

Haber Oil Co., Inc., In re, BkrtcyNDTex, 82 BR 435.—Bankr 2853.20(3), 2853.70.

Haber Oil Co., Inc., Matter of, CA5 (Tex), 12 F3d 426.—Bankr 2125, 2156, 2162, 2534, 2543, 3782, 3786, 3787; Contracts 143(3); Fed Civ Proc 636; Fed Cts 412.1, 776, 859; Fraud 12; Trusts 91, 94.5, 102(1), 103(1), 110, 358(1), 371(2).

Haber Oil Co., Inc. v. Stanley Swabbing and Well Service, Inc., TexApp–Beaumont, 741 SW2d 611.—Motions 51, 62; Pretrial Proc 44.1, 434, 435.

Haber Oil Co., Inc. v. Stanley Well Service, Inc., Tex-App–Beaumont, 741 SW2d 611. See Haber Oil Co., Inc. v. Stanley Swabbing and Well Service, Inc.

Haber Oil Co., Inc. v. Swinehart, CA5 (Tex), 12 F3d 426. See Haber Oil Co., Inc., Matter of.

Habets v. Waste Management, Inc., CA5 (Tex), 363 F3d 378.—Contracts 143(2), 147(3), 166; Corp 308(3); Evid 448; Fed Cts 776; U S Mag 25, 27.

Habitat Apartments; Hughes v., Tex, 860 SW2d 872.—Atty & C 62.

Habitat Apartments; Hughes v., TexApp–Dallas, 828 SW2d 794.—App & E 465(1); Costs 264; Execution 7.

Habitat Apartments; LeVada Hughes and Occupants v., TexApp–Dallas, 880 SW2d 5, writ gr, rev 860 SW2d 872.—App & E 852, 977(3), 977(5); Atty & C 62; Clerks of C 67; Const Law 3993; Judgm 106(1), 123(1), 143(3), 145(2), 146, 162(2); New Tr 6.

Habitat, Inc. v. McKanna, TexCivApp–Eastland, 523 SW2d 787.—Mech Liens 183; Mtg 364, 376, 378.

Habluetzel; Mills v., USTex, 102 SCt 1549, 456 US 91, 71 LEd2d 770.—Child 30, 38; Const Law 3195; Lim of Act 4(2).

Haby v. Howard, TexApp–San Antonio, 757 SW2d 34, writ den.—Adv Poss 43(2), 85(1), 104, 112; App & E 934(1); Bound 3(3), 40(1); Deeds 117, 118; Frds St of 63(1); Judgm 181(2), 181(15.1), 185(2), 185(6), 186.

Haby; McFarland v., TexCivApp–Austin, 589 SW2d 521, ref nre.—Contracts 103, 105, 136, 137(1), 137(2), 171(1).

Haby v. Stanolind Oil & Gas Co., CA5 (Tex), 228 F2d 298.—Fed Civ Proc 201; Hus & W 194; Mines 78.1(1), 78.1(9), 78.1(10), 78.2, 78.5, 78.7(4).

Haby v. Stanolind Oil & Gas Co., CA5 (Tex), 225 F2d 723.—Fed Cts 623, 697, 712.

Haby v. Stanolind Oil & Gas Co., NDTex, 120 FSupp 791, rev 228 F2d 298.—Mines 78.1(1), 78.2.

Haby; Teich v., TexCivApp–San Antonio, 408 SW2d 562, ref nre.—Ease 16, 17(1), 18(3), 36(3).

Hachar v. Hachar, TexApp–San Antonio, 153 SW3d 138.—App & E 238(4), 293, 931(1), 984(5), 1010.1(1), 1010.1(2); Costs 194.18, 194.40; Trusts 267, 268.

Hachar; Hachar v., TexApp–San Antonio, 153 SW3d 138.—App & E 238(4), 293, 931(1), 984(5), 1010.1(1), 1010.1(2); Costs 194.18, 194.40; Trusts 267, 268.

Hachar v. Webb County, TexCivApp–San Antonio, 563 SW2d 693, ref nre.—Counties 196(1); Courts 72, 122; Plead 104(1).

Hachar's Dept. Store; Gutierrez v., TexCivApp–San Antonio, 484 SW2d 433, ref nre.—App & E 766; Judgm 185(2), 185.1(8), 185.3(13), 186; Labor & Emp 210.

Hachar's, Inc.; Enterprise-Laredo Associates v., Tex-App–San Antonio, 839 SW2d 822, reh den, writ den with per curiam opinion 843 SW2d 476.—Antitrust 147, 198, 205, 477; App & E 842(2), 1008.1(1), 1010.1(1), 1010.1(2); Contracts 143(2), 176(1), 176(2), 227; Costs 2; Interest 39(2.30), 60; Judges 51(1), 51(2), 51(3); Land & Ten 200, 222, 231(8); Lim of Act 13, 95(1), 95(2), 95(9), 195(3), 197(2), 199(2); Sales 261(1), 261(3).

Hack v. Laney, BkrtcyNDTex, 53 BR 231. See Laney, In re.

Hackathorn v. Decker, CA5 (Tex), 438 F2d 1363.—Hab Corp 289, 452, 795(1), 795(2).

Hackathorn v. Decker, CA5 (Tex), 369 F2d 150, cert den 88 SCt 301, 389 US 940, 19 LEd2d 294, reh den 88 SCt 596, 389 US 1025, 19 LEd2d 674.—Const Law 4667; Courts 100(1); Crim Law 517.2(3), 627.7(2), 700(3); Hab Corp 721(2).

Hackathorn v. Decker, NDTex, 312 FSupp 1304, rev 438 F2d 1363.—Hab Corp 723, 765.1, 897; Sent & Pun 1668.

Hackathorn v. Decker, NDTex, 243 FSupp 22, aff 369 F2d 150, cert den 88 SCt 301, 389 US 940, 19 LEd2d 294, reh den 88 SCt 596, 389 US 1025, 19 LEd2d 674.—Crim Law 16, 531(3); Hab Corp 289, 445, 490(1), 493(3).

Hackathorn v. State, TexCrimApp, 422 SW2d 920, cert den 85 SCt 1570, 381 US 930, 14 LEd2d 688.—Crim Law 338(7), 627.6(4), 627.7(1), 628(2), 698(1), 1166(7); Homic 1134.

Hackbarth v. State, TexCrimApp, 617 SW2d 944.—Crim Law 404.70, 625.10(4), 706(4), 814(8), 1035(2), 1043(2); Rape 33, 53(1), 59(22).

Hackberry Creek Country Club, Inc. v. Hackberry Creek Home Owners Ass'n, TexApp–Dallas, 205 SW3d 46, reh overr, and review den.—App & E 934(1), 1175(1), 1177(7); Contracts 143(1), 143(2), 143(4), 143.5, 147(2), 153, 170(1), 176(2), 315, 326; Judgm 181(19), 183, 185(2), 185(5).

Hackberry Creek Home Owners Ass'n; Hackberry Creek Country Club, Inc. v., TexApp–Dallas, 205 SW3d 46, reh overr, and review den.—App & E 934(1), 1175(1), 1177(7); Contracts 143(1), 143(2), 143(4), 143.5, 147(2), 153, 170(1), 176(2), 315, 326; Judgm 181(19), 183, 185(2), 185(5).

Hack Branch Distributing Co., Inc.; Ash v., TexApp–Waco, 54 SW3d 401, review den (2 pets).—Antitrust 821, 976, 977(5); App & E 430(1), 863, 934(1), 970(2), 1195(1); Courts 97(5); Evid 244(7), 253(1), 267, 318(1), 318(7); Judgm 181(2), 181(15.1), 181(33), 185(3), 185(5), 185.1(2), 185.1(3), 185.1(4); Pretrial Proc 202; Torts 213, 242.

Hackenjos v. Hackenjos, TexApp–Dallas, 204 SW3d 906.—App & E 842(2), 893(1); Divorce 200, 245(3), 247.

Hackenjos; Hackenjos v., TexApp–Dallas, 204 SW3d 906.—App & E 842(2), 893(1); Divorce 200, 245(3), 247.

Hacker; American Universal Inv. Co. v., TexCivApp–Corpus Christi, 611 SW2d 654.—Plead 111.5, 111.42(11), 409(1).

Hacker; Fyfe Cement & Supply Co. v., TexCivApp–Amarillo, 372 SW2d 735, writ dism.—Plead 111.42(4); Sales 273(2).

Hacker v. Hacker, TexCivApp–Galveston, 110 SW2d 923.—Evid 66; Judgm 335(1), 405, 407(1), 447(1).

Hacker; Hacker v., TexCivApp–Galveston, 110 SW2d 923.—Evid 66; Judgm 335(1), 405, 407(1), 447(1).

Hacker; Texas Emp. Ins. Ass'n v., TexCivApp–Fort Worth, 448 SW2d 234, ref nre.—App & E 1170.6; Evid 201, 265(10); Trial 131(1); Work Comp 1610, 1926, 1927, 1968(5).

Hacker v. Whitney Dam Lumber & Const. Co., TexCivApp–Waco, 225 SW2d 225, writ refused.—App & E 1062.1; Contracts 74; Frds St of 23(2), 158(2); Partners 131.

Hackerman; Guertin v., SDTex, 496 FSupp 593.—Action 3; Civil R 1055, 1313, 1330(1); Fed Civ Proc 2497.1; U S 82(1).

Hackett, In re, BkrtcyNDTex, 224 BR 360. See Thompson, In re.

Hackett v. Broadway Nat. Bank, TexCivApp–Waco, 570 SW2d 184.—Bills & N 23; Judgm 189.

Hackett; Burklund v., TexCivApp–Tyler, 575 SW2d 389.—App & E 843(2), 954(1), 954(2); Atty & C 32(12); Inj 11, 132, 135, 138.18, 138.21; Schools 106.23(2); Tax 2711, 2712, 2882.

Hackett; Del Valle Independent School Dist. Bd. of Equalization v., TexCivApp–Waco, 563 SW2d 338, ref

nre.—App & E 959(3); Plead 236(3); Schools 111; Tax 2882.

Hackett v. G.D. Searle & Co., WDTex, 246 FSupp2d 591.—Neglig 238, 259; Prod Liab 46.2.

Hackett v. Housing Authority of City of San Antonio, CA5 (Tex), 750 F2d 1308, cert den 106 SCt 146, 474 US 850, 88 LEd2d 121.—Evid 318(1), 368(12); Fed Civ Proc 2334.

Hackett v. Laird, WDTex, 326 FSupp 1075.—Armed S 22.

Hackett v. State, TexCrimApp, 357 SW2d 391, 172 Tex-Crim 414.—Arrest 63.3; Assault 92(2); Crim Law 656(1), 1166.22(1), 1166.22(4.1).

Hackett v. State, TexApp–Waco, 160 SW3d 588, corrected, and petition for discretionary review refused.—Crim Law 369.5, 673(5), 867, 1169.5(1), 1169.5(3), 1177.5(1); Ind & Inf 113, 159(1); Sent & Pun 1361, 1365, 1367.

Hackett v. U.S., NDTex, 462 FSupp 131, aff 606 F2d 319.—Sheriffs 105; U S 78(9), 141(8).

Hackett; Zglinski v., TexCivApp–Austin, 552 SW2d 933, ref nre.—Tax 2431, 2711, 2712.

Hackey v. State, TexCrimApp, 500 SW2d 520.—Crim Law 1128(1), 1144.17.

Hackfeld v. Hurren, WDTex, 167 BR 429, aff 961 F2d 213.—Antitrust 141, 145; Atty & C 26; Banks 505; Corp 306; Torts 242, 246.

Hackfeld v. Pacific Emp. Ins. Co., TexCivApp–San Antonio, 393 SW2d 720, writ refused.—Work Comp 747.

Hackfeld v. Ryburn, TexCivApp–Tyler, 606 SW2d 340, dism.—App & E 322, 327(2); Char 13, 50.

Hackfeld; Scott v., TexCivApp–Eastland, 263 SW2d 570.—Courts 121(6), 122, 170; Plead 12, 18, 228.7.

Hackleman; McHaney v., TexCivApp–San Antonio, 347 SW2d 822, ref nre.—Accord 16; Elect of Rem 7(1); Estop 119; Frds St of 118(4); Partners 55; Plead 427; Spec Perf 58, 121(3); Trial 351.2(2), 351.2(4).

Hackleman v. State, TexApp–Austin, 919 SW2d 440, reh overr, and petition for discretionary review refused, untimely filed.—Controlled Subs 27, 68, 80, 148(3); Crim Law 586, 594(1), 627.10(8), 943, 944, 1024(5), 1063(1), 1151, 1166(10.10); Double J 29.1, 100.1; Searches 105.1, 112, 116, 117, 191, 199.

Hackler v. H. Kohnstamm & Co. of Tex., TexCivApp–Dallas, 227 SW2d 347.—Exemp 45, 47; Sheriffs 106, 123, 124, 125(1), 163, 169.

Hackman; Tri-Steel Structures, Inc. v., TexApp–Fort Worth, 883 SW2d 391, reh overr, and writ den.—App & E 5, 440, 914(1), 934(1); Const Law 42(2), 4014; Evid 366(2), 366(5); Judgm 297, 335(1), 335(3), 340, 343, 345, 815, 823.

Hackney v. Barnhart, TexCivApp–Hous (1 Dist), 553 SW2d 17.—Corp 121(1), 121(5).

Hackney v. First State Bank of Honey Grove, TexApp–Texarkana, 866 SW2d 59, reh den.—App & E 543, 559, 573; Damag 188(2), 221(7).

Hackney; Jefferson v., USTex, 92 SCt 1724, 406 US 535, 32 LEd2d 285, reh den 93 SCt 178, 409 US 898, 34 LEd2d 156.—Const Law 2970, 3268, 3541; Social S 4.5, 4.15, 9.1, 194.12(2), 194.16(1).

Hackney; Jefferson v., NDTex, 304 FSupp 1332, vac 90 SCt 1517, 397 US 821, 25 LEd2d 807, appeal after remand 92 SCt 1724, 406 US 535, 32 LEd2d 285, reh den 93 SCt 178, 409 US 898, 34 LEd2d 156.—Civil R 1055; Const Law 2646, 3226, 3268; Fed Civ Proc 181; Social S 194.12(2).

Hackney v. Johnson, TexCivApp–El Paso, 601 SW2d 523, ref nre.—Corp 417; Evid 591; Joint Adv 1, 7; Partners 141, 148; Witn 400(1).

Hackney; McClure v., TexCivApp–Austin, 491 SW2d 177.—Social S 194.3(1).

Hackney; Machado v., WDTex, 299 FSupp 644, vac 90 SCt 1347, 397 US 593, 25 LEd2d 592.—Courts 100(1); Social S 8.5, 194.3(2).

Hackney v. Meade, TexCivApp–Austin, 466 SW2d 341, ref nre.—Social S 8.20.

Hackney; Ojeda v., CA5 (Tex), 452 F2d 947.—Fed Civ Proc 2737.13.

Hackney; Ojeda v., NDTex, 319 FSupp 149.—Child S 30; Civil R 1052; Courts 489(1); Social S 194.3(2).

Hackney; Rios v., NDTex, 294 FSupp 885.—Const Law 4116; Social S 194.16(2), 194.20.

Hackney; Robinson v., SDTex, 307 FSupp 1249, appeal dism 90 SCt 1536, 397 US 1082, 26 LEd2d 59.—Decl Judgm 204; Social S 194.21.

Hackney v. State, TexCrimApp, 93 SW2d 446.—Crim Law 15.

Hackney v. State, TexApp–Beaumont, 634 SW2d 337, petition for discretionary review refused.—Crim Law 419(1.5), 656(1), 656(3), 1166.22(4.1), 1169.1(1), 1169.1(9); Rob 17(3).

Hackney; Wilson v., TexCivApp–Austin, 468 SW2d 935.—Const Law 4123; Social S 181.

Hackworth v. Beto, CA5 (Tex), 434 F2d 852.—Const Law 4650, 4671; Crim Law 224, 393(1), 1177.5(2); Hab Corp 490(1), 827; Sent & Pun 1379(5).

Hackworth; First Nat. Bank of Kerrville v., TexApp–San Antonio, 673 SW2d 218.—Abate & R 52, 57; Antitrust 141; App & E 931(3), 994(2), 995, 999(1); Banks 148(2), 148(3), 148(4), 154(8); Damag 87(1), 221(2.1); Interest 39(2.6), 39(2.30); Statut 212.1, 215; Trial 143.

Hackworth; Foster v., TexCivApp–Austin, 164 SW2d 796. —App & E 1010.1(12), 1040(16); Hus & W 25(1), 146, 249(6), 262.1(2), 268(1), 268(5), 270(8); Princ & A 136(1).

Hackworth v. U.S., CA5 (Tex), 423 F2d 1127.—Crim Law 1132, 1433(1), 1580(1), 1580(4), 1580(6).

Hackworth v. U.S., CA5 (Tex), 380 F2d 19, cert den 88 SCt 799, 389 US 1054, 19 LEd2d 848.—Crim Law 740, 773(2), 824(8); Postal 50.

Hackworth; U.S. v., CA5 (Tex), 136 FedAppx 643, cert den 126 SCt 583, 546 US 991, 163 LEd2d 486.—Crim Law 1026.10(4).

Hada v. Hudson, TexApp–Corpus Christi, 694 SW2d 343, set aside.—Contracts 221(1), 221(2); Damag 117, 190; Mines 109; Plead 34(1), 48; Spec Perf 128(1); Trial 219, 350.4(1).

Hada v. James, TexCivApp–Beaumont, 100 SW2d 395.—Bills & N 518(2).

Hadaway v. Lone Star Gas Co., TexCivApp–Fort Worth, 355 SW2d 590, mandamus overr.—App & E 1175(5); Autos 150, 284, 285, 306(8); Neglig 213, 1692.

Hadd v. LSG-Sky Chefs, CA5 (Tex), 272 F3d 298, reh en banc den 31 FedAppx 157.—Action 68; Fed Civ Proc 1951; Fed Cts 543.1, 813; Judges 49(1).

Haddad v. Bagwell, TexCivApp–El Paso, 317 SW2d 781, ref nre.—Alt Disp Res 401, 409; Contracts 177; Lim of Act 13, 28(1); Trial 350.4(1).

Haddad v. Boon, TexCivApp–Amarillo, 609 SW2d 609, ref nre.—App & E 761, 1175(1); Judgm 199(3.5), 199(3.10); Lim of Act 96(2), 195(3), 199(1); New Tr 70; Ref of Inst 45(4.1), 45(6).

Haddad v. Boon, TexCivApp–Amarillo, 557 SW2d 805, appeal after remand 609 SW2d 609, ref nre.—Estop 23.

Haddad; Brown & Root v., Tex, 180 SW2d 339, 142 Tex 624.—App & E 34, 1062.1; Trial 82, 85; Witn 216(3), 379(6).

Haddad v. Brown & Root, TexCivApp–San Antonio, 175 SW2d 269, rev 180 SW2d 339, 142 Tex 624.—Trial 84(1); Witn 216(3).

Haddad v. State, TexApp–Houston (1 Dist), 9 SW3d 454. —Const Law 656, 1030, 1160, 1164, 1512, 1514, 1515, 1521, 1800, 2192, 2202, 2204, 2218, 4292, 4509(20); Crim Law 13.1(1); Mun Corp 598; Obscen 2.5; Statut 61.

Haddad v. State, TexApp–Dallas, 860 SW2d 947, petition for discretionary review refused.—Crim Law 59(1), 342, 552(1), 559, 718, 730(6), 742(1), 867, 1134(2), 1144.13(2.1), 1144.13(6), 1159.2(4), 1159.2(7), 1159.6, 1171.1(1), 1171.1(6); Obscen 5.2, 15, 17.

Haddad v. Tyler Production Credit Ass'n, TexCivApp–Texarkana, 212 SW2d 1006, writ refused.—Land & Ten 33, 76(1), 81.5, 88(1), 91.

Haddad v. Wood, TexApp–El Paso, 949 SW2d 438, reh overr., and review den.—App & E 854(1); Contracts 143(2), 147(2), 147(3); Evid 448; Frds St of 106(1), 119(1); Guar 8.1; Judgm 181(24), 185.3(14).

Hadden v. State, TexApp–Corpus Christi, 829 SW2d 838, reh overr., and petition for discretionary review refused. —Burg 2, 18; Crim Law 706(1), 706(5), 919(1), 1036.1(2), 1043(2), 1044.1(5.1), 1045, 1134(2), 1162, 1165(1), 1169.5(3), 1171.8(1).

Haddix v. Kerss, CA5 (Tex), 203 FedAppx 551.—Civil R 1088(4), 1395(6), 1420; Const Law 4545(2), 4545(3); Prisons 17(1), 17(2); U S Mag 31.

Haddock v. Arnspiger, Tex, 793 SW2d 948.—Health 818; Neglig 1613, 1614, 1620.

Haddock v. Arnspiger, TexApp–Dallas, 763 SW2d 13, writ gr, aff 793 SW2d 948.—App & E 218.2(10), 499(1), 500(1); Health 818, 823(1); Plead 362(2); Trial 351.2(7).

Haddock; Hartford Acc. & Indem. Co. v., TexCivApp–Tyler, 511 SW2d 102, ref nre.—Jury 142; Pretrial Proc 308; Work Comp 840, 1507, 1543, 1648, 1703, 1966, 1968(1).

Haddox v. Futrell, TexCivApp–Waco, 321 SW2d 110.—App & E 218.2(2); Autos 244(6), 244(54), 244(58), 247.

Haddox; Rainwater v., TexCivApp–Amarillo, 544 SW2d 729.—App & E 920(2); Atty & C 62; Damag 204; Pretrial Proc 44.1, 309, 315, 715, 723.1; Trial 14, 18.

Haden v. David J. Sacks, P.C., TexApp–Houston (1 Dist), 222 SW3d 580.—Antitrust 396, 397; App & E 863, 893(1); Atty & C 129(4), 143, 153; Contracts 9(1), 15, 16, 34, 42, 100, 147(2), 176(1); Costs 194.14, 194.32; Damag 71, 73; Evid 384, 397(1), 397(2), 441(1), 448, 463, 593; Judgm 178, 181(16), 185.3(4).

Haden; Dennis v., TexApp–Texarkana, 867 SW2d 48, reh den, and writ den.—App & E 961, 1050.1(1), 1051.1(1), 1056.1(1); Pretrial Proc 40, 42, 44.1, 45, 204, 434.

Haden; Nass v., TexCivApp–Galveston, 87 SW2d 833, writ dism.—New Tr 140(1), 140(2), 157.

Haden Associates, Inc.; Hilton v., TexCivApp–Fort Worth, 458 SW2d 854.—Counties 123; Plead 406(1).

Haden Co v. C I R, CCA5 (Tex), 118 F2d 285, cert den 62 SCt 73, 314 US 622, 86 LEd 500.—Int Rev 3125.

Haden Co.; Riggs v., TexComApp, 94 SW2d 152, 127 Tex 314.—Autos 194(2).

Haden Co. v. Riggs, TexCivApp–Galveston, 84 SW2d 789, aff 94 SW2d 152, 127 Tex 314.—Autos 194(2), 242(5); Contracts 31; Labor & Emp 29.

Haden Co., Inc. v. Johns-Manville Sales Corp., NDTex, 459 FSupp 1250.—Antitrust 592, 847, 882, 977(2), 977(5), 985.

Haden Co., Inc. v. Johns-Manville Sales Corp., Tex, 553 SW2d 759.—Corp 666.

Haden Co., Inc.; Johns-Manville Sales Corp. v., TexCivApp–Fort Worth, 543 SW2d 415, ref nre 553 SW2d 759. —App & E 846(5); Venue 2, 7(5), 15, 22(5).

Haden Co., Inc. v. Mixers, Inc., TexApp–Dallas, 667 SW2d 316.—Cust & U 18; Evid 18, 21; Mech Liens 115(4), 139(3), 159.

Haden Employees' Ass'n v. Lovett, TexCivApp–Galveston, 122 SW2d 230, writ refused.—App & E 846(5); Inj 11, 12, 132, 151, 152, 189; Labor & Emp 2042, 2059, 2135.

Hadley v. International-Great Northern R. Co., TexCivApp–Texarkana, 268 SW2d 738, writ dism.—App & E 1170.7; Evid 591; R R 397(10), 400(12); Witn 319.

Hadley; Investors, Inc. v., TexApp–Austin, 738 SW2d 737, writ den.—Antitrust 286, 364, 369; App & E 931(1), 989, 1003(5); Pretrial Proc 304.

Hadley; Marathon Oil Co. v., TexCivApp–Fort Worth, 107 SW2d 883, writ dism.—Antitrust 525, 597; Const Law 240(9), 990, 3706; Corp 399(4), 513.4; Guar 5; Princ & A 99; Sales 48.

Hadley v. State, TexCrimApp, 294 SW2d 717, 163 TexCrim 571.—Crim Law 636(2), 720(3), 720(8); Larc 59, 64(1).

Hadley v. State, TexCrimApp, 237 SW2d 979.—Crim Law 1094(3).

Hadley v. State, TexCrimApp, 205 SW2d 374, 151 TexCrim 27.—Autos 351.1, 352, 355(6); Crim Law 1091(11).

Hadley v. State, TexApp–Amarillo, 223 SW3d 421, petition for discretionary review refused.—Arrest 63.5(4); Autos 335, 349(2.1).

Hadley v. State, TexApp–Amarillo, 735 SW2d 522, petition for discretionary review refused.—Crim Law 304(11), 394.1(1), 419(6), 422(1), 422(4), 422(6), 423(9), 424(1), 510, 511.1(3), 511.2, 780(3), 1169.2(6); Searches 25.1, 32.

Hadley; Texas Emp. Ins. Ass'n v., TexCivApp–San Antonio, 289 SW2d 809.—Work Comp 1636, 1926, 1968(5).

Hadley v. VAM P T S, CA5 (Tex), 44 F3d 372.—Civil R 1571, 1594; Damag 50.10, 87(2), 215(1), 221(5.1), 221(7), 223; Fed Cts 415, 776, 830, 877; Interest 39(2.40).

Hadnot v. Bay, Ltd., CA5 (Tex), 344 F3d 474.—Alt Disp Res 133(2), 134(1), 134(2), 140, 143, 200, 205, 213(5); Fed Cts 403.

Hadnot; Federal Underwriters Exchange v., TexCivApp–Beaumont, 143 SW2d 653.—Costs 236.

Hadnot v. State, TexCrimApp, 310 SW2d 90, 165 TexCrim 560.—Crim Law 974(2).

Hadnot v. State, TexApp–Houston (1 Dist), 851 SW2d 378, petition for discretionary review refused.—Sent & Pun 1254, 1314.

Hadnot v. State, TexApp–Beaumont, 945 SW2d 278.—Arrest 62, 63.4(2), 63.5(6), 63.5(8), 63.5(9); Autos 349(3), 349(18); Crim Law 394.4(9), 394.5(4), 394.6(5), 412.1(3), 1130(5), 1134(2), 1134(3), 1158(4), 1169.12; Searches 171.

Hadnot v. State, TexApp–Beaumont, 884 SW2d 922.—Crim Law 641.13(1), 641.13(2.1), 747, 1038.1(4), 1134(2); Extort 32.

Hadnot v. State, TexApp–Houston (14 Dist), 14 SW3d 348.—Const Law 4811; Crim Law 1077.3.

Hadnot; Stewart Title Guaranty Co. v., TexApp–Houston (1 Dist), 101 SW3d 642, reh overr, and review den.—App & E 1175(1); Decl Judgm 41; Lim of Act 1, 13, 46(6), 66(6).

Hadnot v. Wenco Distributors, TexApp–Houston (1 Dist), 961 SW2d 232, reh overr.—Mech Liens 1, 115(1), 132(1), 249.

Hadra v. Herman Blum Consulting Engineers, CA5 (Tex), 632 F2d 1242, cert den 101 SCt 1983, 451 US 912, 68 LEd2d 301.—Fed Civ Proc 2315, 2339, 2372.1; Fed Cts 612.1, 826; Interest 39(2.40); Labor & Emp 765, 868(4), 871; Lim of Act 100(11).

Hadra v. Herman Blum Consulting Engineers, NDTex, 74 FRD 113.—Fed Civ Proc 1278, 1685.

Hadwiger; Mid-America Pipeline Co. v., TexCivApp–Amarillo, 471 SW2d 157.—Em Dom 170, 182, 263; Trial 2.

Haeberle v. Texas Intern. Airlines, CA5 (Tex), 739 F2d 1019.—Const Law 2116; Fed Civ Proc 1951, 1974.1.

Haeberle v. Texas Intern. Airlines, CA5 (Tex), 738 F2d 1434.—Contracts 147(1), 176(1), 176(2), 176(5); Evid 397(2), 448, 461(1).

Haeber Roofing Co.; Denison v., TexApp–Corpus Christi, 767 SW2d 862.—App & E 181; Judgm 185(2), 185(5), 185(6); Work Comp 208, 1393, 1432, 2161.

Haecker; Lynn v., TexCivApp–San Antonio, 244 SW2d 539.—App & E 930(1), 1002, 1046.5; Deeds 203; Evid 265(7).

Haecker v. Santa Rosa Medical Center, TexCivApp–San Antonio, 609 SW2d 879.—Acct Action on 13; Judgm 185.3(3).

Haecker v. State, TexCrimApp, 571 SW2d 920.—Ind & Inf 71.1, 71.2(2), 71.2(3), 110(3), 110(4), 110(23).

Haegele v. Southwest Research Institute, CA5 (Tex), 409 F2d 1353.—Labor & Emp 873.

Haegelin; Alaniz v., TexCivApp–Eastland, 384 SW2d 431.—App & E 912, 989; Plead 111.43; Venue 8.5(2).

Haenel v. State, TexCrimApp, 116 SW2d 736, 134 TexCrim 484.—Crim Law 742(1), 1091(2), 1092.14, 1182.

Haerr v. U.S., CA5 (Tex), 240 F2d 533.—Cust Dut 126(4); Searches 13.1, 18.

Haese; H & R Block, Inc. v., Tex, 992 SW2d 437, reh of petition for review overr, on remand 82 SW3d 331, reh overr, and review den, and reh of petition for review den.—App & E 479(1), 484.1, 1080.

Haese; H & R Block, Inc. v., TexApp–Corpus Christi, 82 SW3d 331, reh overr, and review den, and reh of petition for review den.—Atty & C 32(12); Const Law 2091, 3981; Inj 133, 138.3; Parties 35.31, 35.71.

Haese; H & R Block, Inc. v., TexApp–Corpus Christi, 976 SW2d 237, reh overr, and review den, review gr, rev 992 SW2d 437, reh of petition for review overr, on remand 82 SW3d 331, reh overr, and review den, and reh of petition for review den.—App & E 949; Const Law 3981; Parties 35.1, 35.33, 35.35, 35.37, 35.71.

Haese; U.S. v., CA5 (Tex), 162 F3d 359, cert den 119 SCt 1795, 526 US 1138, 143 LEd2d 1022.—Brib 1(1); Const Law 268(10), 4632, 4633, 4689; Crim Law 380, 508(2), 641.13(1), 641.13(6), 706(2), 741(1), 742(1), 1030(1), 1134(3), 1134(10), 1139, 1152(1), 1153(1), 1168(2), 1169.1(1), 1170(1), 1655(7); Witn 2(1).

Haesly v. Whitten, TexCivApp–Waco, 580 SW2d 104.—Accord 24; Atty & C 129(1); Judgm 634, 665, 715(1); Plead 108; Torts 121.

Hafdahl v. Johnson, CA5 (Tex), 251 F3d 528, cert den 122 SCt 629, 534 US 1047, 151 LEd2d 550.—Const Law 4632, 4633; Crim Law 371(12), 419(2.30), 662.1, 662.7, 662.8, 706(2), 1168(2); Hab Corp 481, 490(6), 508.

Hafdahl v. State, TexCrimApp, 805 SW2d 396, reh den, cert den 111 SCt 2250, 500 US 948, 114 LEd2d 491, denial of habeas corpus aff 251 F3d 528, cert den 122 SCt 629, 534 US 1047, 151 LEd2d 550.—Const Law 4594(1); Crim Law 413(1), 700(2.1), 700(3), 700(6), 901, 959, 1077.3, 1092.8; Homic 554, 1003.

Hafer v. Prashner, TexCivApp–Corpus Christi, 413 SW2d 759.—App & E 846(5); Evid 577, 578, 583.

Haffa; Hankins v., TexCivApp–Amarillo, 469 SW2d 733, ref nre.—App & E 961; Mental H 488, 518; Pretrial Proc 44.1, 221; Trusts 103(1).

Haffley; Nationwide Mut. Ins. Co. v., CA5 (Tex), 78 FedAppx 348.—Insurance 3357, 3406, 3426.

Hafford v. State, TexApp–Houston (1 Dist), 989 SW2d 439, petition for discretionary review refused.—Controlled Subs 149; Searches 121.1.

Hafford v. State, TexApp–Fort Worth, 828 SW2d 275, petition for discretionary review refused, cert den 113 SCt 1313, 507 US 931, 122 LEd2d 700.—Arrest 63.4(1), 63.4(2), 63.4(6), 63.4(11), 63.4(13), 68(3).

Hafford v. State, TexApp–Beaumont, 864 SW2d 216.—Crim Law 273(2), 961.

Hafi v. Baker, Tex, 164 SW3d 383, on remand 2005 WL 1907684.—Jury 97(1).

Hafley; County of Real v., TexApp–San Antonio, 873 SW2d 725, writ den.—App & E 80(6); Dedi 1, 15, 16.1, 44; Judgm 185.3(1).

Hafley; Hartford Underwriters Ins. Co. v., TexApp–Austin, 96 SW3d 469, reh overr.—Admin Law 305, 325; Statut 219(1), 219(4); Venue 1.5; Work Comp 833, 1419, 1832, 1964, 1981.

Hafley v. State, TexApp–Dallas, 781 SW2d 642.—Crim Law 772(1), 822(11), 1038.1(4), 1038.1(5); Homic 535, 668; Weap 11(1), 17(1), 17(6).

Hafstienn v. BMW of North America, LLC, CA5 (Tex), 194 FedAppx 209.—Evid 150, 519; Fed Civ Proc 2515.

Hafti v. State, TexCrimApp, 487 SW2d 745.—Crim Law 393(1), 436(5), 614(1), 778(4), 789(4), 1130(2), 1134(3), 1137(5), 1169.5(2); Jury 109, 131(17), 131(18), 133, 136(5); Rob 20, 23(2); Sent & Pun 1379(2), 1788(5).

Hafti v. State, TexCrimApp, 416 SW2d 824, appeal after remand 487 SW2d 745.—Crim Law 365(1), 369.1, 369.2(1), 369.15, 371(1), 374, 1169.11.

Haga, In re, BkrtcyWDTex, 131 BR 320.—Bankr 2052, 2060.1, 2062, 2324, 2325, 3361, 3382.1, 3418, 3420(12), 3422(1).

Haga v. National Union Fire Ins. Co. of Pittsburgh, Pa., BkrtcyWDTex, 131 BR 320. See Haga, In re.

Haga; U.S. v., CA5 (Tex), 821 F2d 1036.—Consp 33(1), 43(12); Crim Law 257, 1167(1); Double J 103; Ind & Inf 1, 117.

Hagaman; Carson v., TexApp–Eastland, 884 SW2d 194, reh den.—App & E 125, 758.3(9), 836, 846(1), 930(3), 989, 1001(3), 1003(7), 1096(1); Judgm 91; Partit 94(1).

Hagaman; Carson v., TexApp–Eastland, 824 SW2d 267, appeal after remand 884 SW2d 194, reh den.—App & E 1173(2); Partit 94(3), 113.

Hagaman v. Hasbro, Inc., SDTex, 710 FSupp 1119.—Trademarks 1136(2), 1241, 1800.

Hagaman v. Morgan, TexApp–Dallas, 886 SW2d 398, writ den.—Adop 20, 21; App & E 387(6), 388; Courts 99(1); Wills 199, 437, 440, 476, 481, 487(1), 498, 695(2).

Hagan v. Acme Drilling & Service Co., TexCivApp–Eastland, 225 SW2d 870.—Mines 114; Plead 111.8, 111.26; Venue 5.2.

Hagan; Adam v., CA5 (Tex), 325 F2d 719.—Hab Corp 285.1.

Hagan v. Anderson, Tex, 513 SW2d 818.—Plead 111.26.

Hagan v. Anderson, TexCivApp–San Antonio, 506 SW2d 298, ref nre 513 SW2d 818.—Liens 18, 22; Plead 49, 104(2), 111.26, 111.39(4), 111.42(4); Venue 15.

Hagan v. Coggins, NDTex, 183 FSupp2d 776, aff 264 F3d 1142, cert den 122 SCt 1082, 534 US 1136, 151 LEd2d 982.—Courts 70; Judges 24, 49(1).

Hagan v. EZ Mfg. Co., CA5 (Tex), 674 F2d 1047.—Fed Civ Proc 2127, 2142.1; Prod Liab 8, 14, 75.1, 79, 82.1, 85, 87.1, 95.

Hagan v. Houston Independent School Dist., CA5 (Tex), 51 F3d 48.—Civil R 1376(5); Consp 13.

Hagan; Hughes Production Co. v., TexCivApp–Texarkana, 144 SW2d 953, writ dism, correct.—App & E 1099(3); Mines 118.

Hagan; Hughes Production Co. v., TexCivApp–El Paso, 114 SW2d 326, writ dism.—Action 50(3); App & E 1036(6), 1066(9); Death 104(4); Mines 118; Neglig 210, 230, 1613; New Tr 100; Stip 14(10).

Hagan; Lipstreu v., TexCivApp–San Antonio, 571 SW2d 36, ref nre.—Ex & Ad 488, 489, 495(5).

Hagan v. McKenna, TexApp–El Paso, 768 SW2d 518, writ den.—Compromise 16(1), 17(2); Contrib 6.

Hagan; Schroller v., TexCivApp–San Antonio, 388 SW2d 278.—Ex & Ad 460; Hus & W 276(7), 276(8).

Hagan v. State, TexCrimApp, 104 SW2d 857, 132 TexCrim 338.—Rec S Goods 8(3).

Hagan v. U.S., CA5 (Tex), 256 F2d 34, cert den 79 SCt 77, 358 US 850, 3 LEd2d 84.—Crim Law 1660; Sent & Pun 563, 1129, 1490.

Hagans, Ex parte, TexCrimApp, 558 SW2d 457.—Const Law 4782, 4783(2), 4783(3); Crim Law 625.15, 625.20, 625.35; Hab Corp 477, 845; Mental H 432.

Hagans; Bair v., TexApp–Houston (1 Dist), 838 SW2d 677, reh den, and writ den.—App & E 961; Pretrial Proc 44.1, 435.

Hagans v. Oliver Machinery Co., CA5 (Tex), 576 F2d 97.—Prod Liab 58, 85, 95.

Hagans v. State, TexCrimApp, 372 SW2d 946.—Const Law 4559; Crim Law 121, 570(1), 673(4), 1056.1(1), 1092.11(2), 1115(2), 1166.16; Homic 1134; Witn 76(3).

Hagans v. Woodruff, TexApp–Houston (14 Dist), 830 SW2d 732.—App & E 997(3), 1067; Brok 101, 102, 106; Fraud 9, 20; Trial 349(1).

Hagans v. Woodruff & Associates, TexApp–Houston (14 Dist, 830 SW2d 732. See Hagans v. Woodruff.

Hagar, Ex parte, TexCrimApp, 434 SW2d 675.—Extrad 24, 29, 36.

Hagar v. McCaskill, TexCivApp–Fort Worth, 98 SW2d 367.—App & E 742(6), 907(3); Home 133.

Hagar v. Martin, TexCivApp–Dallas, 277 SW2d 195, ref nre.—App & E 1011.1(2), 1050.1(11); Evid 429; Mines 51(2), 52, 62.1, 64.

Hagar; Ohlen v., TexCivApp–Fort Worth, 212 SW2d 253, ref nre.—App & E 1003(1), 1003(5); Assault 35; Neglig 1679; Trial 139.1(3), 350.3(5).

Hagar v. Texas Distributors, Inc., TexCivApp–Tyler, 560 SW2d 773, ref nre.—Bills & N 103(1), 516; Fraud 11(1); Judgm 181(2), 181(6), 185.1(3).

Hagar v. Williams, TexCivApp–Amarillo, 593 SW2d 783. —App & E 205, 842(2), 1008.1(1); Evid 208(6); Trial 391; Usury 137, 145, 146.

Hagberg v. City of Pasadena, TexApp–Houston (1 Dist), 224 SW3d 477.—App & E 758.3(1), 762, 1078(1), 1079, 1136; Plead 16; Pretrial Proc 518; Work Comp 52, 1908, 1933, 1981.

Hagco Bldg. Systems, Inc.; Guerrero v., TexApp–San Antonio, 733 SW2d 635.—App & E 766; Can of Inst 24(3); Contracts 262; Judgm 256(1); Ven & Pur 117, 123.

Hage v. Westgate Square Commercial, TexCivApp–Waco, 598 SW2d 709, ref nre.—Contracts 211; Liens 7; Spec Perf 126(1), 129; Ven & Pur 22, 78, 82.

Hagedorn; Alexander v., Tex, 226 SW2d 996, 148 Tex 565.—App & E 842(4), 1008.1(13); Judgm 143(1), 335(1), 335(2), 335(3), 443(1), 444.

Hagedorn; Alexander v., TexCivApp–Austin, 220 SW2d 196, rev 226 SW2d 996, 148 Tex 565.—App & E 1008.1(8.1); Judgm 335(3), 335(4), 403; New Tr 124(1), 163(1); Trial 6(1).

Hagedorn v. Tisdale, TexApp–Amarillo, 73 SW3d 341, rule 537(f) motion gr.—Abate & R 4; App & E 936(2), 1024.1; Costs 2, 194.18, 207; Evid 536, 538; Health 804, 805, 807; Pretrial Proc 435; Statut 181(1), 188.

Hageman/Fritz, Byrne, Head & Harrison, L.L.P. v. Luth, TexApp–Austin, 150 SW3d 617.—App & E 186, 226(2), 835(2), 984(5); Bankr 3411, 3414; Costs 194.16, 194.22, 194.25, 194.40; Decl Judgm 41, 271, 392.1; Judgm 878(2); Trover 72; Venue 13, 84.

Hagemeister v. Vanity Fair Properties, TexCivApp–Tyler, 503 SW2d 879, dism.—App & E 1203(5); Judgm 649, 714(1), 714(2).

Hagen v. Brzozowski, TexCivApp–San Antonio, 336 SW2d 213.—Auctions 9; Fact 53; Sales 263.

Hagen v. Jameson, TexApp–Dallas, 127 SW3d 387.—App & E 204(2), 931(1), 989, 1001(1), 1003(5); Damag 185(3).

Hagen; J. S. Abercrombie Co. v., TexCivApp–Galveston, 238 SW2d 239.—Lim of Act 55(8), 121(2).

Hagen; O'Carter v., WDTex, 184 FSupp 936.—Prisons 15(6).

Hagen v. State, TexCrimApp, 180 SW2d 952, 147 TexCrim 396.—Rob 24.10.

Hagen; Texas Oil & Gas Corp. v., TexApp–Texarkana, 683 SW2d 24, writ gr, aff in part, rev in part 1987 WL 47847, opinion withdrawn 760 SW2d 960, set aside 760 SW2d 960.—Accord 10(1); Corp 1.5(3); Damag 89(2); Elect of Rem 3(1); Evid 142(1); Fraud 7, 9, 10, 13(1), 61, 62; Mines 79.3, 79.7.

Hagen; U.S. v., SDTex, 711 FSupp 879.—Costs 285; Statut 6.

Hagendorf Const. Co., Inc.; Illinois Nat. Ins. Co. v., WDTex, 337 FSupp2d 902.—Insurance 2748(1), 2914, 2915, 2922(1).

Hagenloh; Texas & P. Ry. Co. v., Tex, 247 SW2d 236, 151 Tex 191.—App & E 1091(4), 1175(3); Labor & Emp 2769, 2796, 3056(1).

Hagenloh; Texas & P. Ry. Co. v., TexCivApp–El Paso, 241 SW2d 669, aff 247 SW2d 236, 151 Tex 191.—App & E 231(1), 927(7), 934(1); Assault 40, 42, 43(5); Evid 591; Labor & Emp 2880, 2941, 3045, 3055; Trial 131(3).

Hagens v. State, TexApp–Houston (14 Dist), 979 SW2d 788, reh overr, and petition for discretionary review refused.—Courts 1, 40; Crim Law 38, 641.13(1), 641.13(4), 641.13(7), 656(9), 951(1), 1088.9, 1124(1), 1130(0.5), 1156(1), 1166.10(1), 1166.22(1), 1181.5(3.1), 1181.5(8), 1182, 1186.5, 1189; Homic 1493.

Hager v. Apollo Paper Corp., TexApp–Houston (1 Dist), 856 SW2d 512.—Ack 15; Civil R 1773.

Hager; Cactus Drilling Corp. v., TexCivApp–El Paso, 487 SW2d 758.—Neglig 1037(4), 1286(7), 1670, 1679; Plead 45, 111.5, 111.6, 111.39(4), 111.42(7), 229, 360, 400, 422; Pretrial Proc 692.

Hager v. Carter, TexCivApp–Texarkana, 554 SW2d 956. —Elections 260, 262, 278.

Hager v. Hager, TexCivApp–Eastland, 127 SW2d 234.— Deeds 72(1), 78, 196(3), 211(4); Evid 54.

Hager; Hager v., TexCivApp–Eastland, 127 SW2d 234.— Deeds 72(1), 78, 196(3), 211(4); Evid 54.

Hager v. NationsBank N.A., CA5 (Tex), 167 F3d 245, on remand 1999 WL 1044498.—Fed Cts 776; Labor & Emp 682.

Hager v. Romines, TexApp–Fort Worth, 913 SW2d 733. —Agric 9.5; App & E 866(3); Evid 536, 570; Neglig 202, 1657.

Hager v. State, TexCrimApp, 487 SW2d 723.—Crim Law 393(3), 829(6); Ind & Inf 54.

Hager v. State, TexApp–Eastland, 734 SW2d 180, petition for discretionary review refused.—Crim Law 380, 1169.11; Larc 65; Witn 337(4), 344(5).

Hager v. State ex rel. TeVault, TexCivApp–Beaumont, 446 SW2d 43, ref nre.—App & E 781(1), 802; Mand 187.1, 187.3; Mun Corp 95.

Hagerla; Genador v., TexCivApp–Fort Worth, 369 SW2d 70.—Bound 37(3); New Tr 102(1); Tresp to T T 47(1).

Hager's Flying Service v. Romines, TexApp–Fort Worth, 913 SW2d 733. See Hager v. Romines.

Hagerty; State v., TexCivApp–Dallas, 479 SW2d 729.— Estop 62.2(1); Tax 2764, 2863.

Hagerty; Willingham v., TexCivApp–Amarillo, 553 SW2d 137.—App & E 80(1); Autos 226(3); Statut 188, 205.

Hagerty Partners Partnership v. Livingston, TexApp– Dallas, 128 SW3d 416, review den.—App & E 846(5), 893(1), 1010.1(8.1); Const Law 3964, 3965(10); Courts 12(2.1), 12(2.5), 12(2.10), 12(2.25), 35, 39.

Hagey; Ronnie Loper Chevrolet-Geo, Inc. v., TexApp– Houston (14 Dist), 999 SW2d 81.—Labor & Emp 40(2), 41(1), 55, 57, 863(1).

Haggar; Fudge v., TexCivApp–Texarkana, 621 SW2d 196, ref nre.—Mand 7; Mun Corp 185(3), 185(12).

Haggar Apparel Co. v. Leal, Tex, 154 SW3d 98.—Civil R 1218(3).

Haggar Apparel Co. v. Leal, TexApp–Corpus Christi, 100 SW3d 303, review gr, rev 154 SW3d 98.—App & E 230, 231(9), 1004(1), 1062.1; Civil R 1019(1), 1019(2), 1218(2), 1218(5), 1218(6), 1744, 1753, 1764, 1765, 1772, 1773; Costs 194.18, 198.

Haggar Clothing Co. v. Hernandez, Tex, 164 SW3d 386. —App & E 930(1), 1001(1), 1001(3); Labor & Emp 810, 863(2).

Haggar Clothing Co. v. Hernandez, TexApp–Corpus Christi, 164 SW3d 407, review gr, rev 164 SW3d 386.— App & E 840(4), 882(12), 893(1), 1004(1), 1004(11), 1047(1), 1050.1(1), 1056.1(1), 1182; Const Law 963, 4427; Damag 57.9, 57.11, 95, 97, 99, 140.5, 208(2), 208(4), 208(6); Evid 138, 597; Labor & Emp 755, 809, 810, 861, 862, 863(2), 867, 870, 871, 874; Trial 182, 219, 228(1), 241, 349(2).

Haggar Clothing Co.; Palasota v., CA5 (Tex), 342 F3d 569, reh and reh den 84 FedAppx 472, cert den 124 SCt 1441, 540 US 1184, 158 LEd2d 89, on remand 2005 WL 221221.—Civil R 1204, 1209, 1551; Fed Civ Proc 2142.1, 2608.1; Fed Cts 763.1, 765, 776, 801, 842, 844.

Haggar Co v. Commissioner of Internal Revenue, CCA5 (Tex), 104 F2d 24, cert gr 60 SCt 93, 308 US 533,

84 LEd 449, rev 60 SCt 337, 308 US 389, 84 LEd 340, conformed to 111 F2d 144.—Int Rev 3621, 4260, 4261, 4479.

Haggar Co. v. Helvering, USTex, 60 SCt 337, 308 US 389, 84 LEd 340, conformed to Haggar Company v. Commissioner of Internal Revenue, 111 F2d 144.—Int Rev 3037; Statut 181(2), 184, 223.5(1), 223.5(9), 263.

Haggar Co. v. Rutkiewicz, TexCivApp–Waco, 405 SW2d 462, ref nre.—Interest 39(1), 66; Labor & Emp 178, 267.

Haggar Co. v. U.S. Fire Ins. Co., TexCivApp–Texarkana, 497 SW2d 61.—Insurance 2137(3); Trial 368.

Haggard, Ex parte, TexCrimApp, 501 SW2d 908.—Extrad 36.

Haggard; Betts v., TexCivApp–Tyler, 495 SW2d 602, ref nre.—App & E 171(1); Wills 471, 472, 587(5), 590, 634(1).

Haggard v. Haggard, TexCivApp–Dallas, 550 SW2d 374. —Divorce 178, 223, 252.1, 252.2, 252.3(1), 252.3(2), 281, 286(5), 286(9).

Haggard; Haggard v., TexCivApp–Dallas, 550 SW2d 374. —Divorce 178, 223, 252.1, 252.2, 252.3(1), 252.3(2), 281, 286(5), 286(9).

Haggard; Hutson v., TexCivApp–Beaumont, 475 SW2d 330.—Adop 3, 7.4(2.1), 13, 15.

Haggard; McFadin v., TexCivApp–San Antonio, 398 SW2d 638.—Lim of Act 148(1), 148(3), 199(3).

Haggard v. McFarland, TexComApp, 155 SW2d 797, 137 Tex 542.—Guard & W 92, 103; Infants 34.

Haggard v. McFarland, TexCivApp–Fort Worth, 133 SW2d 313, aff 155 SW2d 797, 137 Tex 542.—Guard & W 89, 92, 100, 103, 104, 107, 164, 173.

Haggard; Mills v., TexApp–Waco, 58 SW3d 164.—App & E 842(2), 846(6), 1001(1), 1010.1(1), 1010.1(2); Execution 251(2); Mtg 335; Trial 388(1).

Haggard; Mills v., TexApp–Waco, 17 SW3d 462, opinion after remand 58 SW3d 164.—App & E 619, 820; Courts 82.

Haggard; Sims v., Tex, 346 SW2d 110, 162 Tex 307.—App & E 878(1), 878(4); Ref of Inst 13(1), 33, 47.

Haggard v. Sims, TexCivApp–Texarkana, 336 SW2d 866, ref nre, and writ gr, rev 346 SW2d 110, 162 Tex 307.— Evid 591; Lim of Act 96(2), 100(1); Ref of Inst 33.

Haggar Ltd., Inc., In re, BkrtcyNDTex, 190 BR 281. See Eddie Haggar Ltd., Inc., In re.

Haggerton v. State, TexCrimApp, 218 SW2d 211, 153 TexCrim 102.—Crim Law 572; Larc 41.

Haggerty; Koppers Co., Inc. v., TexCivApp–Beaumont, 488 SW2d 600, ref nre.—Neglig 1037(7), 1205(7), 1566.

Haggerty v. State, TexCrimApp, 491 SW2d 916.—Crim Law 486(10), 598(2), 603.3(7), 1030(1), 1036.1(2), 1045, 1169.5(4).

Haggerty v. State, TexCrimApp, 490 SW2d 858.—Controlled Subs 100(2); Crim Law 369.2(7), 404.60, 459.

Haggerty v. State, TexApp–Houston (1 Dist), 825 SW2d 545.—Crim Law 622.1(2), 622.2(3), 622.2(8), 641.13(1), 641.13(2.1), 641.13(6), 790, 1148, 1166.10(1).

Haggerty v. Texas Southern University, CA5 (Tex), 391 F3d 653.—Civil R 1037, 1088(4), 1376(6); False Imp 15(1); Fed Cts 574, 776, 915; Mun Corp 747(3); Offic 114.

Haggins v. State, TexCrimApp, 785 SW2d 827.—Infants 20.

Haggins v. State, TexCrimApp, 113 SW2d 192, 133 TexCrim 564.—Crim Law 537, 1169.2(6), 1169.11.

Haggins v. State, TexCrimApp, 113 SW2d 191, 133 TexCrim 562.—Burg 41(1).

Haginas v. Malbis Memorial Foundation, Tex, 354 SW2d 368, 163 Tex 274.—Courts 30; Forci E & D 6(1), 6(2), 43(1), 46; J P 141(4).

Haginas v. Malbis Memorial Foundation, TexCivApp– Houston, 349 SW2d 957, writ gr, aff 354 SW2d 368, 163 Tex 274.—Courts 30; Forci E & D 6(2); Judgm 335(1); J P 141(4); Land & Ten 291(6.5), 291(14).

Hagins; Brown County Life Ins. Co. v., TexCivApp–Amarillo, 110 SW2d 1162.—Action 6; App & E 781(1), 790(3), 873(1), 891.

Hagins v. E-Z Mart Stores, Inc., TexApp–Texarkana, 128 SW3d 383.—App & E 969, 989, 999(3), 1003(7), 1062.1, 1064.1(8), 1182; Evid 219.50, 571(3); Labor & Emp 3040, 3132; Neglig 1011, 1204(1), 1205(7), 1683, 1684, 1710; Trial 182, 228(0.5).

Hagins; U.S. v., CA5 (Tex), 451 F2d 359.—Crim Law 1132, 1147.

Hagle v. Leeder, TexCivApp–Austin, 442 SW2d 908.—Domicile 4(1), 5, 8; Venue 21, 28.

Hagler, Ex parte, TexCrimApp, 284 SW2d 150.—Crim Law 1094(3).

Hagler, Ex parte, TexCrimApp, 278 SW2d 143, 161 Tex-Crim 387.—Extrad 36; Hab Corp 711, 713.

Hagler v. Continental Nat. Bank of Fort Worth, Tex-CivApp–Texarkana, 549 SW2d 250, ref nre.—Inj 22; Mtg 151(3), 154(2), 186(5).

Hagler; Hanover Ins. Co. of New York v., TexCivApp–Dallas, 532 SW2d 136, ref nre.—Insurance 3147, 3153, 3164, 3188, 3191(1), 3191(7), 3191(13), 3198(2).

Hagler; Hillin v., TexCivApp–Fort Worth, 286 SW2d 661.—App & E 688(2), 1004(7); Evid 48, 158(15), 474(16), 474(19), 502.

Hagler; Jordan v., TexApp–Fort Worth, 179 SW3d 217.—App & E 1042(1), 1073(1); Costs 194.40; Decl Judgm 181; Lis Pen 1, 3(1), 15, 20; Plead 228.14, 228.23; Trusts 91.

Hagler; Procter & Gamble Mfg. Co. v., TexApp–Texarkana, 880 SW2d 123, reh den, writ den with per curiam opinion 884 SW2d 771.—App & E 930(3), 989, 1001(3), 1003(6); Libel 44(3), 50, 51(1), 51(4), 101(4).

Hagler v. Proctor & Gamble Mfg. Co., Tex, 884 SW2d 771.—Libel 51(1).

Hagler; Rush v., TexCivApp–Fort Worth, 611 SW2d 718.—Child S 549.

Hagler v. State, TexCrimApp, 288 SW2d 789, 163 Tex-Crim 63.—Crim Law 1090.1(1), 1099.7(1).

Hagler v. State, TexCrimApp, 276 SW2d 269, 161 Tex-Crim 223.—Forg 32; Ind & Inf 32(3).

Hagler v. State, TexCrimApp, 262 SW2d 726, 159 Tex-Crim 265.—Autos 355(6).

Hagman; City of Houston v., TexCivApp–Houston, 347 SW2d 355, ref nre.—App & E 1170.6; Autos 261, 282, 293, 303; Mun Corp 733(2), 757(1), 812(2), 812(6.1), 819(8); Nuis 59; Plead 246(3); Trial 352.4(7).

Hagood v. City of Houston Zoning Bd. of Adjustment, TexApp–Houston (1 Dist), 982 SW2d 17.—App & E 66; Zoning 565, 569, 741.

Hagood's Conoco Service Station v. Faglie, TexCivApp–Waco, 376 SW2d 947.—App & E 79(1), 80(1), 80(6).

Hague v. State, TexCrimApp, 307 SW2d 577, 165 Tex-Crim 393.—Crim Law 364(4), 553, 1037.1(3); Homic 1177.

Hague; Thompson v., TexCivApp–Fort Worth, 430 SW2d 293.—Usury 7, 52.

Hague–Neyland, Ltd., In re, BkrtcyWDTex, 90 BR 246. See Oakgrove Village, Ltd., In re.

Hagy; Dorchester Gas Producing Co. v., TexApp–Amarillo, 748 SW2d 474, writ den, and writ gr, and writ withdrawn, set aside 777 SW2d 709.—App & E 758.3(11); Contracts 155, 169, 170(1); Estop 95; Evid 448; Lim of Act 43, 95(9); Mines 74(10).

Hahn, In re, WDTex, 35 FSupp 114.—Bankr 2802, 3785.1, 3786; Home 70.

Hahn; City of San Antonio v., TexCivApp–Austin, 274 SW2d 162, ref nre.—Mun Corp 180(1), 186(5), 186(6), 194.

Hahn; Craft v., TexCivApp–Eastland, 246 SW2d 897, ref nre.—App & E 274(1), 500(1), 1175(7); Evid 390(1), 433(4); Mines 55(8); Ref of Inst 48; Trial 351.2(2), 351.2(4).

Hahn; Farmers Royalty Holding Co. v., TexCivApp–Galveston, 187 SW2d 930, aff 190 SW2d 62, 144 Tex 316.—Estop 45, 50.

Hahn; Leonard & Harral Packing Co. v., TexCivApp–San Antonio, 571 SW2d 201, ref nre.—App & E 207, 756, 768, 1004(1), 1004(7); Damag 127; Death 97, 99(1); Evid 574; Prod Liab 74; Trial 351.5(6).

Hahn v. State, TexCrimApp, 502 SW2d 724.—Controlled Subs 80, 113; Searches 36.1.

Hahn v. State, TexApp–Houston (14 Dist), 852 SW2d 627, petition for discretionary review refused.—Crim Law 273.1(1), 394.5(4), 394.6(5).

Hahn; Svrcek v., TexCivApp–Galveston, 103 SW2d 840, writ dism.—Em Dom 79, 285; Inj 37, 120.

Hahn v. Texan Nat. Bank of Beaumont, TexCivApp–Beaumont, 88 SW2d 1078.—App & E 773(2).

Hahn; Texas Nat. Bank of Beaumont v., TexCivApp–Beaumont, 84 SW2d 263.—Execution 172(6).

Hahn; U.S. v., CA5 (Tex), 922 F2d 243.—Crim Law 1134(3); Searches 66.

Hahn; U.S. v., CA5 (Tex), 849 F2d 932, reh den U.S. v. Garcia, 856 F2d 191.—Arrest 63.4(16); Cust Dut 126(9.1); Searches 15, 22.

Hahn; U.S. v., TexCivApp–Austin, 563 SW2d 379, writ refused.—U S 146.

Hahn; Wanda Petroleum Co. v., TexCivApp–Corpus Christi, 489 SW2d 428, ref nre.—Autos 227.5.

Hahn v. Whiting Petroleum Corp., TexApp–Corpus Christi, 171 SW3d 307, reh overr.—Judgm 143(2), 143(7), 143(12), 145(4), 146, 153(1), 162(2), 162(4), 169.

Hahn; Wilson County Peanut Co. v., TexCivApp–San Antonio, 364 SW2d 468.—Plead 111.39(7); Princ & A 136(1), 144, 183(1), 190(3); Venue 22(6), 22(8).

Hahn & Clay v. A. O. Smith Corp., CA5 (Tex), 320 F2d 166, cert den 84 SCt 351, 375 US 944, 11 LEd2d 274.—Antitrust 412, 432; Labor & Emp 121, 323(4); Pat 7, 16.10(3), 16.13, 118.21, 165(1), 167(1), 324.5, 324.55(5); Torts 241.

Hahn & Clay v. A. O. Smith Corp., SDTex, 212 FSupp 22, aff 320 F2d 166, cert den 84 SCt 351, 375 US 944, 11 LEd2d 274.—Labor & Emp 121, 323(4); Torts 242.

Hahne v. Hahne, TexApp–Houston (14 Dist), 663 SW2d 77.—Costs 262; Divorce 194; Hus & W 278(1); Judgm 80.

Hahne; Hahne v., TexApp–Houston (14 Dist), 663 SW2d 77.—Costs 262; Divorce 194; Hus & W 278(1); Judgm 80.

Hahnel; Melton v., TexCivApp–Dallas, 347 SW2d 350, ref nre.—Ex & Ad 7.

Haid & Kyle, Inc.; Bracken v., TexCivApp–Dallas, 589 SW2d 501, ref nre.—Judgm 181(29); Mtg 529(8), 529(10).

Haiduk v. Haiduk, TexCivApp–San Antonio, 374 SW2d 323, writ dism.—App & E 846(5); Child S 140(2); Divorce 93(3), 130, 252.3(2), 286(0.5).

Haiduk; Haiduk v., TexCivApp–San Antonio, 374 SW2d 323, writ dism.—App & E 846(5); Child S 140(2); Divorce 93(3), 130, 252.3(2), 286(0.5).

Haidusek; Engbrock v., TexCivApp–Austin, 95 SW2d 520, writ refused.—App & E 1177(7); Home 62, 70, 142(1), 214; Hus & W 273(4); Subrog 41(6).

Haig v. Gittings, TexCivApp–Dallas, 260 SW2d 311.—App & E 954(1); Contracts 215(1); Inj 189.

Haigh v. Calhoun, TexCivApp–Amarillo, 215 SW2d 426, ref nre.—App & E 907(3); Trusts 72, 79, 373.

Haigh v. State, TexCrimApp, 205 SW2d 992, 151 Tex-Crim 189.—Burg 9(1), 41(4); Crim Law 1023(9), 1131(7).

Haight v. Savoy Apartments, TexApp–Houston (1 Dist), 814 SW2d 849, writ den.—App & E 852, 856(1), 863; Judgm 181(11), 181(33), 185(2); Neglig 210, 213, 220, 1089.

Haight v. State, TexCrimApp, 137 SW3d 48.—Const Law 3855; Double J 139.1; States 4.1(2).

Haight v. State, TexApp–San Antonio, 103 SW3d 498, petition for discretionary review refused (2 pets), and petition for discretionary review gr (1 pet), rev 137 SW3d 48.—Arrest 63.4(1), 65; Assault 48; Crim Law 619, 620(3.1), 1035(2), 1144.13(2.1), 1144.13(3), 1159.2(1), 1159.2(2), 1159.2(7), 1159.2(9), 1159.4(2), 1162, 1165(1), 1166(6), 1181.5(1), 1189; Double J 1, 134, 135, 139.1; Extort 4; States 81.

Haight v. State, TexApp–Dallas, 772 SW2d 159, petition for discretionary review refused.—Crim Law 959, 1184(1), 1184(4.1), 1192.

Haight; Waroff v., TexCivApp–Amarillo, 185 SW2d 241, writ refused wom.—Child C 76, 473.

Haigler; Gilbert v., TexCivApp–Houston, 363 SW2d 337, ref nre.—App & E 547(3); Damag 127, 132(3), 208(1); Neglig 1656, 1676; Trial 350.1, 350.6(3), 365.1(1); Witn 347.

Haigood v. State, TexApp–Austin, 814 SW2d 262, petition for discretionary review refused.—Crim Law 108(1).

Haik; Aetna Cas. & Sur. Co. v., TexCivApp–Waco, 442 SW2d 836, writ gr, and rev pursuant to stipulation.—Plead 290(3); Work Comp 838, 1239, 1648.

Haik; Poynter v., TexCivApp–Tyler, 580 SW2d 114.—App & E 846(5); Child S 41, 62, 339(2).

Haikl v. Phillips Semiconductor of America, CA5 (Tex), 115 FedAppx 693.—Fed Civ Proc 1840; Fed Cts 657.

Haile v. Amarillo Nat. Bank, TexCivApp–Amarillo, 283 SW2d 279.—Nova 5, 10.

Haile v. Amarillo Nat. Bank, TexCivApp–Amarillo, 283 SW2d 276.—Nova 3, 12.

Haile v. Federal Land Bank of Houston, TexCivApp–Eastland, 135 SW2d 1024, writ refused.—Home 57.5, 154, 177(1), 181.5.

Haile v. Holtzclaw, Tex, 414 SW2d 916.—Ack 4, 6(2); App & E 1194(2); Deeds 31; Estates 5; Gifts 1, 15; Hus & W 274(1); Mental H 16, 18; Mines 55(1), 55(4); Wills 7, 53(3), 439, 441, 448, 449, 470(1), 486, 577, 611, 618, 865(1), 866.

Haile v. Holtzclaw, TexCivApp–Amarillo, 400 SW2d 603, writ gr, rev 414 SW2d 916.—Ack 6(2), 6(3); App & E 1001(1); Deeds 31, 78, 203, 211(1); Estates 1; Gifts 50; Guard & W 13(3); Mental H 7, 9; Mines 55(1); Remaind 4; Wills 7, 58(2), 63, 439, 441, 448, 470(1), 634(3), 782(3), 800.

Haile v. McDonald, BkrtcyNDTex, 73 BR 877. See McDonald, In re.

Haile v. State, TexCrimApp, 556 SW2d 818.—Sent & Pun 2021.

Haile v. State, TexCrimApp, 95 SW2d 708, 131 TexCrim 17.—Gr Jury 17, 19.

Haile v. Town of Addison, NDTex, 264 FSupp2d 464.—Decl Judgm 300; Fed Civ Proc 2544, 2552.

Haile; U.S. v., CA5 (Tex), 795 F2d 489.—Sent & Pun 1962, 1965, 1974(3).

Hailes; Fidelity & Cas. Co. of New York v., TexApp–El Paso, 969 SW2d 123, review den.—App & E 842(2); Work Comp 2142.15.

Hailes v. Gentry, TexCivApp–El Paso, 520 SW2d 555.—App & E 1170.10; Autos 171(9), 244(11), 244(35), 244(36.1), 244(37); Evid 474(8); Trial 205, 352.18.

Hailey; Barksdale v., TexApp–Fort Worth, 624 SW2d 733, ref nre.—Spec Perf 106(1), 123; Trial 382; Ven & Pur 79.

Hailey; Cohen v., TexCivApp–San Antonio, 280 SW2d 300, ref nre.—App & E 230; Cust & U 18; Trial 360.

Hailey v. Hailey, Tex, 331 SW2d 299, 160 Tex 372.—Child C 467; Courts 247(1), 247(7); Divorce 108, 130, 252.3(2), 252.3(5), 286(0.5); Partit 116(1).

Hailey; Hailey v., Tex, 331 SW2d 299, 160 Tex 372.—Child C 467; Courts 247(1), 247(7); Divorce 108, 130, 252.3(2), 252.3(5), 286(0.5); Partit 116(1).

Hailey v. Hailey, TexApp–Houston (1 Dist), 176 SW3d 374.—App & E 842(2), 931(3), 1008.1(2), 1071.2; Divorce 108, 226, 252.2, 252.3(2), 253(1), 253(3), 286(2); Hus & W 258, 265, 272(4).

Hailey; Hailey v., TexApp–Houston (1 Dist), 176 SW3d 374.—App & E 842(2), 931(3), 1008.1(2), 1071.2; Divorce 108, 226, 252.2, 252.3(2), 253(1), 253(3), 286(2); Hus & W 258, 265, 272(4).

Hailey v. Hailey, TexCivApp–Amarillo, 322 SW2d 575, rev in part 331 SW2d 299, 160 Tex 372.—Child C 7, 76; Divorce 93(1), 124.4, 147, 184(10), 223, 252.1, 252.3(1).

Hailey; Hailey v., TexCivApp–Amarillo, 322 SW2d 575, rev in part 331 SW2d 299, 160 Tex 372.—Child C 7, 76; Divorce 93(1), 124.4, 147, 184(10), 223, 252.1, 252.3(1).

Hailey; Hermes Grain Co. v., TexCivApp–Corpus Christi, 435 SW2d 181.—Plead 111.6, 111.30, 111.44; Pretrial Proc 481; Sales 359(1).

Hailey v. KTBS, Inc., TexApp–Texarkana, 935 SW2d 857.—Damag 50.10; Libel 48(2), 51(5).

Hailey; McWilliams v., TexCivApp–Texarkana, 95 SW2d 985, writ dism.—App & E 218.2(4), 232(3); Autos 244(56); Trial 352.11.

Hailey v. Siglar, TexApp–Texarkana, 194 SW3d 74, reh overr, and review den.—Courts 40, 168, 183, 472.3; Judgm 7.

Hailey v. State, TexCrimApp, 87 SW3d 118, cert den 123 SCt 2218, 538 US 1060, 155 LEd2d 1111, reh den 124 SCt 373, 540 US 941, 157 LEd2d 261.—Crim Law 1028, 1036.1(4).

Hailey v. State, TexApp–Waco, 50 SW3d 636, petition for discretionary review gr, rev 87 SW3d 118, cert den 123 SCt 2218, 538 US 1060, 155 LEd2d 1111, reh den 124 SCt 373, 540 US 941, 157 LEd2d 261.—Assault 2; Autos 411, 414, 419; Crim Law 394.1(2), 1139, 1144.12, 1158(4), 1162, 1168(2); Searches 33, 78.

Hailey v. Texas-New Mexico Power Co., TexApp–Waco, 757 SW2d 833, writ dism woj.—App & E 100(1); Em Dom 186, 258.

Haiman v. Standard Oil Co. of New Jersey, SDTex, 22 FSupp 806.—Seamen 29(5.6).

Haines v. McLean, Tex, 276 SW2d 777, 154 Tex 272.—App & E 839(1); Deeds 119, 140; Mines 54(2); Partit 95.

Haines v. National Union Fire Ins. Co. of Pittsburgh, Pa., SDTex, 812 FSupp 93.—Insurance 1655; Princ & A 132(1), 158; Rem of C 3, 36, 43, 106.

Haines v. State, TexCrimApp, 623 SW2d 367.—Sent & Pun 1318, 1352.

Haines v. State, TexCrimApp, 391 SW2d 58.—Burg 41(1); Ind & Inf 166; Sent & Pun 1299, 1367, 1371, 1381(3), 1381(4).

Haines v. State, TexCrimApp, 116 SW2d 399, 134 TexCrim 524.—Crim Law 508(1), 780(1), 1092.7, 1173.2(6).

Haines; U.S. v., CA5 (Tex), 855 F2d 199.—Const Law 994, 2817; Crim Law 13.2; Sent & Pun 664(2), 664(5).

Hainsworth v. Berry, TexCivApp–Hous (1 Dist), 485 SW2d 934.—App & E 194(1); Inj 144, 147; Plead 129(1).

Hainsworth v. Harris County Com'rs' Court, Tex, 269 SW2d 332, 153 Tex 356, cert den 75 SCt 110, 348 US 874, 99 LEd 688.—Courts 247(8).

Hainsworth v. Harris County Com'rs Court, TexCivApp–Galveston, 265 SW2d 217, ref nre 269 SW2d 332, 153 Tex 356, cert den 75 SCt 110, 348 US 874, 99 LEd 688.—App & E 907(3); Mand 167, 168(4).

Hainsworth v. Martin, TexCivApp–Austin, 386 SW2d 202, ref nre, vac 86 SCt 256, 382 US 109, 15 LEd2d 190, reh den 86 SCt 532, 382 US 1002, 15 LEd2d 491.—Const Law 2586, 2900, 3657, 3658(8); States 27(3), 27(7).

Hainze v. Richards, CA5 (Tex), 207 F3d 795, reh and sug for reh den 216 F3d 1081, cert den 121 SCt 384, 531 US 959, 148 LEd2d 296.—Civil R 1037, 1088(1), 1088(4), 1088(5); Decl Judgm 61, 300; Fed Cts 813, 814.1; Inj 22; Judgm 822(3).

Hair, In re Guardianship of, TexCivApp–Beaumont, 537 SW2d 82, ref nre.—Guard & W 67, 155.

Hair; Bell v., TexApp–Houston (14 Dist), 832 SW2d 55, writ den.—App & E 907(3), 961; Pretrial Proc 3, 486.

Hair; Bell v., TexApp–Houston (14 Dist), 832 SW2d 53, reh den.—App & E 497(1), 621(3).

Hair; McKinney's Estate v., TexCivApp–Waco, 434 SW2d 217, ref nre.—Wills 300, 306.

Hair v. Pennsylvania Life Ins. Co., TexCivApp–Beaumont, 533 SW2d 387, ref nre.—Insurance 3557; Judgm 181(23).

Hair; Young Women's Christian Ass'n of Austin v., TexCivApp–Austin, 165 SW2d 238, writ refused wom.—Action 35; Courts 480(1); Judgm 747(6); Land & Ten 290(2), 290(3), 291(10), 291(18).

Hair Crimpers v. Employers Cas. Co., TexApp–Houston (1 Dist), 699 SW2d 339. See Holmes v. Employers Cas. Co.

Hair Designers of Houston v. Southwestern Bell Telephone Co., TexApp–Houston (1 Dist), 749 SW2d 569. See FDP Corp. v. Southwestern Bell Telephone Co.

Haire; Isthmian Lines, Inc. v., CA5 (Tex), 334 F2d 521.—Release 13(1); Seamen 5, 11(1), 11(6), 19, 24.

Haire v. Isthmian Lines, Inc., SDTex, 231 FSupp 606, aff 334 F2d 521.—Interest 38(1), 39(2.25); Seamen 11(6), 16, 19, 25, 29(5.14).

Haire v. Nathan Watson Co., TexApp–Fort Worth, 221 SW3d 293, reh overr.—Action 13; App & E 766, 856(1), 893(1), 934(1), 1136; Contracts 187(1), 205.15(4), 205.35(1), 205.35(4), 205.40, 326; Courts 4; Judgm 678(2), 707, 714(1), 948(1); Neglig 1502.

Haire; State v., TexCivApp–Austin, 334 SW2d 488, ref nre.—App & E 692(1), 989; Em Dom 131, 133, 134, 149(3), 205, 262(4), 262(5); Evid 471(20), 474(18), 568(4); Trial 114.

Haire; Texas Shop Towel v., TexCivApp–San Antonio, 246 SW2d 482.—Antitrust 421; Assign 18, 58; Contracts 116(1), 188, 202(2); Cust & U 17; Labor & Emp 305.

Hairgrove v. City of Pasadena, TexApp–Houston (1 Dist), 80 SW3d 703, review den, and reh of petition for review den.—Action 3, 13; App & E 863, 893(1), 919; Decl Judgm 209; Mun Corp 979, 987.

Hairgrove v. Cramer Financial Group, Inc., TexApp–Fort Worth, 895 SW2d 874, reh overr, and writ den.—Sec Tran 230.

Hair Naturally; Garner v., TexApp–Austin, 771 SW2d 242. See Garner v. McGinty.

Hairrell v. Texas Prudential Ins. Co., TexCivApp–Galveston, 203 SW2d 689.—App & E 1001(2), 1175(1); Insurance 3013, 3015; Judgm 199(3.10).

Hairston, Ex parte, TexCrimApp, 766 SW2d 790.—Crim Law 273.1(2), 273.1(5), 274(3.1).

Hairston; English v., CA5 (Tex), 888 F2d 1069.—Const Law 4198; Schools 147.2(1).

Hairston; Hart v., CA5 (Tex), 343 F3d 762, reh den.—Civil R 1092, 1358, 1376(7); Fed Civ Proc 2491.5, 2538, 2544; Fed Cts 776.

Hairston v. Oakwood Cemetery Ass'n, TexCivApp–Fort Worth, 94 SW2d 493.—Work Comp 1335, 1717.

Hairston v. Richie, TexCivApp–Fort Worth, 338 SW2d 263.—App & E 1064.1(1); Interest 39(5), 44, 66, 67; Labor & Emp 169; Partners 336(3), 345; Trial 352.16.

Hairston v. State, TexCrimApp, 218 SW2d 1006.—Crim Law 1070.

Haith v. Drake, TexCivApp–Hous (1 Dist), 596 SW2d 194, ref nre.—Forci E & D 6(1), 12(2), 16(3), 38(1), 43(1); Inj 26(9); Land & Ten 290(1), 291(6.5); Tresp to T T 1; Ven & Pur 54.

Haith; Jack Criswell Lincoln-Mercury Inc. v., TexCivApp–Hous (1 Dist), 590 SW2d 616, ref nre.—Antitrust 196, 282, 369, 390; Autos 19.

Haizlip; Blazek v., TexCivApp–Dallas, 413 SW2d 486.—App & E 547(1), 989; Autos 244(11), 244(58); Damag 185(1), 191; Hus & W 216.

Hajdik; Wingate v., Tex, 795 SW2d 717.—App & E 302(1); Corp 190, 202; Trial 335.

Hajdik v. Wingate, TexApp–Houston (1 Dist), 753 SW2d 199, writ gr, aff 795 SW2d 717.—App & E 961; Corp 202, 211(4), 211(5), 506; Plead 236(7); Pretrial Proc 644, 690.

Hajecate; Hobbs v., TexCivApp–Austin, 374 SW2d 351, writ refused.—Action 66; Lim of Act 2(1).

Hajecate; U.S. v., CA5 (Tex), 683 F2d 894, cert den Eisenberg v. US, 103 SCt 2086, 461 US 927, 77 LEd2d 298.—Consp 23.1, 43(1), 43(11); Const Law 4581; Crim Law 1023(8); Fraud 68.10(1); Ind & Inf 121.1(7), 144.1(1); U S 34.

Hajek v. Bill Mowbray Motors, Inc., Tex, 647 SW2d 253.—Const Law 2161, 2174; Courts 247(7).

Hajek v. Bill Mowbray Motors, Inc., TexApp–Corpus Christi, 645 SW2d 827, rev 647 SW2d 253.—Const Law 1527, 2174; Inj 138.75, 147; Libel 6(1), 9(1), 9(7), 19, 30, 33.

Hajek; Machac v., TexCivApp–Corpus Christi, 437 SW2d 325, ref nre.—App & E 281(1); Judgm 199(6); Lim of Act 40(1), 141, 165, 175; Paymt 66(1); Ven & Pur 85.

Hajjar v. State, TexApp–Houston (1 Dist), 176 SW3d 554, petition stricken, and petition for discretionary review refused.—Crim Law 338(7), 419(1.10), 438(3), 438(7), 633(1), 641.13(1), 656(2), 665(1), 700(1), 1030(1), 1035(9), 1037.1(1), 1037.2, 1044.1(8), 1119(1), 1130(2), 1130(5), 1153(1), 1166.22(1), 1166.22(7), 1171.1(1).

Hajovsky; Porter v., TexCivApp–Hous (14 Dist), 537 SW2d 501, ref nre.—App & E 1170.10; Autos 171(9), 242(8), 244(43), 247; Damag 100, 185(1), 187; Neglig 1683.

Hake; Anderson v., TexCivApp–Dallas, 300 SW2d 663.—Acct Action on 14; Judgm 101(2), 185.1(3), 185.2(1).

Hake v. Dilworth, TexCivApp–Waco, 96 SW2d 121, writ dism.—Corp 1.3, 215, 398(1); Costs 241; Courts 475(2); Ex & Ad 93(1), 111(9), 473(4), 473(5); Judgm 243, 252(1); Plead 374.

Hake; Dilworth v., TexCivApp–Waco, 64 SW2d 829, writ dism.—Trademarks 1137(2), 1691, 1800.

Hakemy Bros., Ltd. v. State Bank and Trust Co., Dallas, TexApp–Dallas, 189 SW3d 920, review den.—App & E 760(1), 1079; Banks 132, 117, 118; Labor & Emp 3045, 3047; Plead 233.1, 236(2), 236(7), 237(5), 238(3), 245(1), 245(3), 245(7), 248(17), 258(3); Pretrial Proc 25; Stip 14(3).

Haker, In re, CA5 (Tex), 411 F2d 568.—Bankr 3444.20, 3444.30(2).

Haker; Price v., TexCivApp–Dallas, 419 SW2d 213.—App & E 907(3); Bankr 3353(13); Fraud 38; Judgm 250; Lim of Act 127(13).

Hakim; American Empire Life Ins. Co. v., TexCivApp–El Paso, 312 SW2d 739.—App & E 931(1); Evid 10(2); Plead 111.42(6).

Hakim; Khan v., CA5 (Tex), 201 FedAppx 981.—Estop 68(2); Fed Civ Proc 2651.1; Fed Cts 681.1.

Hakim Daccach; Citizens Ins. Co. of America v., TexApp–Austin, 105 SW3d 712, review gr, rev 217 SW3d 430.—Action 17; App & E 836, 913, 946, 949, 1024.1; Parties 35.1, 35.7, 35.9, 35.13, 35.33, 35.35, 35.41, 35.85.

Halaby; Division of Production, Am. Petroleum Institute v., CA5 (Tex), 307 F2d 363.—Aviation 35.

Halamicek; Carper v., TexCivApp–Tyler, 610 SW2d 556, ref nre.—Partit 46.1.

Halamicek v. Halamicek, TexCivApp–Corpus Christi, 542 SW2d 246, ref nre.—Wills 167, 179, 289, 290, 297(4), 306, 324(4).

Halamicek; Halamicek v., TexCivApp–Corpus Christi, 542 SW2d 246, ref nre.—Wills 167, 179, 289, 290, 297(4), 306, 324(4).

Halamka v. Halamka, TexApp–Texarkana, 799 SW2d 351.—App & E 1008.1(2), 1008.1(5), 1010.1(3); Child C 7, 120, 921(1); Divorce 124.2, 252.3(3), 253(2); Hus & W 232.3, 258, 270(8); Partit 77(4); Trial 382.

Halamka; Halamka v., TexApp–Texarkana, 799 SW2d 351.—App & E 1008.1(2), 1008.1(5), 1010.1(3); Child C 7, 120, 921(1); Divorce 124.2, 252.3(3), 253(2); Hus & W 232.3, 258, 270(8); Partit 77(4); Trial 382.

Hal and Charlie Peterson Foundation; Eoff v., TexApp–San Antonio, 811 SW2d 187.—Antitrust 208, 222, 282; App & E 843(2), 969, 1003(7), 1062.1, 1068(3); Evid 106(1), 219.65; Health 675, 766, 820, 823(3), 823(11), 827; Neglig 284, 431; Trial 127, 215, 219; Witn 217, 388(10).

Halbert, In re, BkrtcyWDTex, 146 BR 185.—Bankr 2297, 2793, 3593, 3594.

Halbert, In re Estate of, TexApp–Texarkana, 172 SW3d 194, reh overr, and review den, and reh of petition for review den.—Wills 212, 435, 740(1), 740(3).

Halbert; City of Dallas v., TexCivApp–Dallas, 246 SW2d 686, ref nre.—Const Law 1066; Courts 1; Mun Corp 623(1); Nuis 3(11); Zoning 6, 321, 351, 355.

Halbert v. City of Sherman, Tex., CA5 (Tex), 33 F3d 526.—Damag 50.10; False Imp 15(2); Fed Civ Proc 828.1, 833, 841; Fed Cts 817; Libel 1, 44(1), 45(1), 50, 51(1), 112(2).

Halbert v. Green, Tex, 293 SW2d 848, 156 Tex 223.—Estop 39; Mines 55(4), 55(8); Ref of Inst 26.

Halbert v. Green, TexCivApp–Eastland, 285 SW2d 767, writ gr, rev 293 SW2d 848, 156 Tex 223.—Mines 55(4), 55(8).

Halbert v. Halbert, TexApp–Tyler, 794 SW2d 535.—App & E 1122(2); Divorce 287.

Halbert; Halbert v., TexApp–Tyler, 794 SW2d 535.—App & E 1122(2); Divorce 287.

Halbert v. Prudential Ins. Co. of America, EDTex, 436 FSupp 543.—Insurance 1809, 2494(2).

Halbert; Seaboard Fire & Marine Ins. Co. v., TexCivApp–El Paso, 173 SW2d 180.—App & E 554(3), 565, 655(3).

Halbert v. Standley, TexCivApp–Waco, 488 SW2d 887, ref nre.—Compromise 21; Contracts 261(1), 321(1); Inj 21.

Halbert v. State, TexCrimApp, 137 SW2d 1010, 138 TexCrim 592.—Crim Law 537, 814(1), 829(2), 1091(4), 1091(10), 1169.1(1); Homic 998, 1345, 1489; Witn 380(2).

Halbert v. State, TexApp–Houston (1 Dist), 881 SW2d 121, petition for discretionary review refused.—Crim Law 577.10(1), 577.10(8), 772(6), 782(16), 1172.1(1), 1173.2(3); Homic 766, 774, 799, 800, 1193, 1197, 1203, 1347, 1480, 1481, 1484.

Halbert v. Sylestine, TexCivApp–Beaumont, 292 SW2d 135.—Pretrial Proc 472, 477.1, 480, 482.1; Venue 8.5(8).

Halbert v. Upper Neches River Municipal Water Authority, TexCivApp–Houston, 367 SW2d 879, ref nre.—App & E 544(3), 719(3), 758.3(3), 1170.7; Em Dom 57, 68, 177, 243(2), 262(5); Plead 354; Trial 76; Witn 266, 267, 270(1), 270(2).

Halbert v. Upshaw, TexCivApp–Eastland, 348 SW2d 254.—Venue 5.3(2).

Halbouty v. Darsey, TexCivApp–Austin, 331 SW2d 835.—Mines 92.26.

Halbouty v. Darsey, TexCivApp–Austin, 326 SW2d 528, ref nre.—Const Law 2632; Mines 48, 92.13, 92.16, 92.26, 92.27, 92.28, 92.29, 92.30, 92.32(1).

Halbouty v. Railroad Commission, Tex, 357 SW2d 364, 163 Tex 417, cert den Dillon v. Halbouty, 83 SCt 185, 371 US 888, 9 LEd2d 122.—Courts 247(1); Mines 47, 92.54, 92.59(1), 92.62.

Halbrook; City of Odessa v., TexCivApp–El Paso, 103 SW2d 223.—Inj 85(1); Mun Corp 120, 601.3, 621.

Halbrook v. State, TexApp–Fort Worth, 31 SW3d 301, petition for discretionary review refused.—Crim Law 407(1), 412.2(4), 641.3(8.1).

Haldeman; Don's Marine, Inc. v., TexCivApp–Corpus Christi, 557 SW2d 826, ref nre.—App & E 846(5); Sales 126(3); Ship 27.

Haldiman, In re Estate of, TexApp–San Antonio, 653 SW2d 337.—Wills 566, 587(1), 704.

Hale, Ex parte, TexCrimApp, 117 SW3d 866.—Pardon 66; Sent & Pun 1130, 1169, 1948, 1953.

Hale, Ex parte, TexCrimApp, 320 SW2d 362, 167 TexCrim 397.—Extrad 31, 34; Hab Corp 729.

Hale, Matter of Marriage of, TexApp–Texarkana, 975 SW2d 694.—App & E 931(1), 946, 989, 1008.1(2), 1012.1(5); Child S 556(1); Divorce 237, 239, 282, 286(3.1).

Hale; Abe I. Brilling Ins. Agency v., TexCivApp–Dallas, 601 SW2d 403.—Acct Action on 10, 13.

Hale v. Allstate Ins. Co., Tex, 344 SW2d 430, 162 Tex 65.—Insurance 2671, 2673.

Hale v. Allstate Ins. Co., TexCivApp–Dallas, 345 SW2d 346, certified question answered 344 SW2d 430, 162 Tex 65.—Insurance 1822, 1834(1), 2655(1), 2673.

Hale; American Cas. & Life Co. v., TexCivApp–Beaumont, 198 SW2d 759.—App & E 1078(1); Evid 67(1); Insurance 1571, 1578, 3381(3), 3384, 3388, 3389, 3426.

Hale; Anderson v., TexCivApp–Fort Worth, 144 SW2d 318.—Estop 72; Mines 54.5.

Hale; Austin v., TexApp–Waco, 711 SW2d 64.—Judgm 185(6); Offic 114, 119; States 79.

Hale; Badouh v., Tex, 22 SW3d 392, reh overr.—Statut 181(1); Wills 651, 717.

Hale v. Badouh, TexApp–Austin, 975 SW2d 419, reh overr, and review gr, aff in part, rev in part 22 SW3d 392, reh overr.—Des & Dist 68; Gifts 24; Judgm 181(15.1); Wills 651, 717.

Hale v. Baker, TexCivApp–El Paso, 397 SW2d 937, ref nre.—App & E 931(1), 989, 1010.1(2), 1177(7); Autos 171(9), 244(34), 244(36.1).

Hale; Brooks v., TexCivApp–Tyler, 457 SW2d 159, ref nre.—App & E 863; Atty & C 76(2); Judgm 181(2), 181(15.1), 185(2), 335(1), 486(1), 710.

Hale v. Burgess, TexApp–Waco, 478 SW2d 856.—App & E 931(1), 989; Neglig 431; Plead 111.42(8).

Hale v. Burns Intern. Sec. Services Corp., CA5 (Tex), 72 FedAppx 100, cert den 124 SCt 1180, 540 US 1165, 157 LEd2d 1212.—Civil R 1168, 1557; Fed Civ Proc 2531.

Hale v. City of Dallas, TexCivApp–Dallas, 335 SW2d 785, ref nre.—High 105(2), 165; Mun Corp 661(1), 755(1), 757(1).

Hale v. City of Los Fresnos, TexApp–Houston (1 Dist), 623 SW2d 745.—Tax 2853, 2918.

Hale v. Colorado River Mun. Water Dist., TexApp–Austin, 818 SW2d 537.—Em Dom 2(1), 84, 114.1; Judgm 181(15.1); Waters 44, 64, 183.5.

Hale v. Corbin, TexCivApp–El Paso, 83 SW2d 726.—App & E 989; Ref of Inst 45(9).

Hale v. Cotton Petroleum Corp., CA5 (Tex), 796 F2d 74.—Fed Cts 644; Princ & A 123(3), 173(3).

Hale; Couch v., TexCivApp–Corpus Christi, 404 SW2d 920.—App & E 930(3), 1001(1), 1003(11), 1062.1; Carr 305(6), 318(7), 320(21), 320(30); Evid 587; Trial 139.1(3), 140(1), 142.

Hale v. County School Trustees of Archer County, TexCivApp–Fort Worth, 207 SW2d 251, ref nre.—Action 57(2); App & E 917(1); Schools 11, 22; Statut 158.

Hale; E-Z Mart Stores, Inc. v., TexApp–Texarkana, 883 SW2d 695, reh den, and writ den.—App & E 930(3), 930(4), 989, 1001(1), 1003(7); Contracts 3, 27, 168; Impl & C C 1; Insurance 1867, 3380; Labor & Emp 79; Trial 350.1, 366; Work Comp 9, 1003, 1058, 1842.

Hale; Fort Worth Lloyds v., TexCivApp–Amarillo, 405 SW2d 639, ref nre.—App & E 930(3), 989, 1050.1(5); Evid 271(18); Insurance 2201; Interest 39(1); Pretrial Proc 388, 407; Trial 219, 350.4(3), 352.9.

Hale; Green v., CA5 (Tex), 433 F2d 324.—Courts 100(1); Fed Civ Proc 1742(1), 1742(3); Fed Cts 34, 290.1, 291, 303, 692, 922, 942; Health 821(5), 823(1), 831; Witn 178(4).

Hale; Green v., TexCivApp–Tyler, 590 SW2d 231.—App & E 901, 930(1), 932(1), 989, 1004(3), 1004(5), 1177(7);

HALE;

Damag 163(1), 166(1), 208(1); Death 60, 67, 68, 69, 77, 95(4), 97, 99(2), 99(3).

Hale; Griffin v., TexComApp, 112 SW2d 1042, 131 Tex 152.—Evid 83(1); Wills 569.

Hale; Griffin v., TexCivApp–Texarkana, 87 SW2d 497, aff 112 SW2d 1042, 131 Tex 152.—Wills 439, 440, 487(2), 590, 608(3.1).

Hale v. Hale, TexCivApp–Austin, 93 SW2d 535, writ dism.—Deeds 25, 121.

Hale; Hale v., TexCivApp–Austin, 93 SW2d 535, writ dism.—Deeds 25, 121.

Hale v. Hale, TexCivApp–Texarkana, 557 SW2d 614.—Divorce 252.3(2); Hus & W 258, 272(5).

Hale; Hale v., TexCivApp–Texarkana, 557 SW2d 614.—Divorce 252.3(2); Hus & W 258, 272(5).

Hale v. Hale, TexCivApp–Eastland, 336 SW2d 934.—Child C 51; Divorce 132(1), 223.

Hale; Hale v., TexCivApp–Eastland, 336 SW2d 934.—Child C 51; Divorce 132(1), 223.

Hale v. Harney, CA5 (Tex), 786 F2d 688.—Civil R 1326(5), 1395(1); Consp 18; Courts 489(1); Fed Civ Proc 2769, 2771(3), 2837.1, 2840.

Hale; Hartford Acc. & Indem. Co. v., Tex, 400 SW2d 310.—Evid 118, 121(1), 208(6); Work Comp 1043, 1389, 1489.

Hale; Hartford Acc. & Indem. Co. v., TexCivApp–San Antonio, 389 SW2d 720, writ gr, rev 400 SW2d 310.—Evid 118, 208(6); Work Comp 1114, 1385, 1389, 1968(3).

Hale v. Herring, TexCivApp–Austin, 102 SW2d 468.—App & E 688(2), 762, 1040(13), 1062.1; Bills & N 516, 518(1); Evid 219(1), 478(1); Trial 351.5(4), 352.5(4), 352.9, 352.11.

Hale; Holt Texas, Ltd. v., TexApp–San Antonio, 144 SW3d 592, opinion after remand 144 SW3d 620.—App & E 984(1); Costs 177, 194.18, 207; Infants 83, 84, 85.

Hale v. Hospice at the Texas Medical Center, TexApp–Beaumont, 96 SW3d 688.—Unemp Comp 473, 478, 500.

Hale; Kacal v., CA5 (Tex), 928 F2d 697. See San Jacinto Sav. & Loan v. Kacal.

Hale; Knorpp v., TexApp–Texarkana, 981 SW2d 469.—Neglig 1001, 1030, 1037(2), 1037(4), 1037(7), 1040(2), 1040(3), 1040(4), 1085, 1538.

Hale; Lake v., TexCivApp–Dallas, 179 SW2d 349.—J P 204.

Hale v. Lavaca County Flood Control Dist., TexCivApp–Houston, 344 SW2d 245.—Const Law 4077; Em Dom 79, 200, 235, 238(2), 242; Evid 83(1); Judgm 497(1), 518.

Hale v. Life Ins. Co. of North America, CA6 (Ky), 750 F2d 547, appeal after remand 795 F2d 22.—Insurance 151(3).

Hale; McDaniel v., TexApp–Amarillo, 893 SW2d 652, reh overr, and writ den.—App & E 1001(1), 1003(7), 1004(3); Evid 43(2), 51; Judgm 143(3), 335(1), 335(2), 335(3), 335(4).

Hale; McFadden v., TexCivApp–Waco, 615 SW2d 345.—Bailm 31(2), 32; Evid 474(16), 568(1); Neglig 1531; Plead 3; Trial 352.4(2).

Hale v. Mann, WDTex, 15 FSupp 1051.—Fed Cts 356, 359.

Hale; Minthorn v., TexCivApp–Beaumont, 372 SW2d 752.—Elections 44, 198, 227(1).

Hale v. Mothershed, TexApp–Texarkana, 715 SW2d 134.—App & E 78(4); Pretrial Proc 699.

Hale; Nuclear Corp. of America v., NDTex, 355 FSupp 193, aff 479 F2d 1045.—Contracts 325; Corp 254, 349; Mech Liens 2, 115(5); Statut 236, 241(2).

Hale; Pacific Mut. Life Ins. Co. of Cal. v., TexCivApp–El Paso, 267 SW 282, writ refused.—Insurance 3580.

Hale v. Pena, TexApp–Fort Worth, 991 SW2d 942, reh overr.—Judgm 181(27), 185(6), 185.2(8), 185.3(1); Mun Corp 747(3); Offic 114.

Hale; Perkins v., TexCivApp–Tyler, 396 SW2d 149, ref nre.—Autos 171(11), 171(13), 244(43); Trial 350.5(1).

Hale v. Ramsey, TexCivApp–Austin, 524 SW2d 436.—App & E 756, 757(3), 758.3(1); 760(1), 760.3, 761, 1079.

Hale; Rasbury v., TexCivApp–El Paso, 131 SW2d 334, writ dism, correct.—Deeds 42, 111; Evid 460(7); Ref of Inst 17(1), 23, 43, 45(5); Trial 358.

Hale v. Realty Acceptance Corp., TexCivApp–Amarillo, 122 SW2d 334.—Estop 52.15; Hus & W 62.

Hale; Republic Ins. Co. v., TexComApp, 99 SW2d 909, 128 Tex 616.—App & E 1069.1; Evid 506; Insurance 2202; New Tr 140(1), 144; Trial 304.

Hale v. Robinson, TexCivApp–Beaumont, 120 SW2d 842.—Venue 70.

Hale v. Schraub, TexCivApp–Austin, 369 SW2d 377, ref nre.—Evid 333(12); High 63, 68, 159(2).

Hale; Segrest v., TexCivApp–Galveston, 164 SW2d 793, writ refused wom.—Bankr 2534, 2576, 2644; Judgm 788(1), 788(2).

Hale v. Sheikholeslam, CA5 (Tex), 724 F2d 1205.—Health 770, 782; Mun Corp 742(4).

Hale; State v., Tex, 146 SW2d 731, 136 Tex 29.—App & E 1177(1); Damag 69; Em Dom 1, 2(1), 2(6), 19, 69, 75, 76, 148, 271, 285, 308; High 23, 80, 165; States 112.1(1), 131, 171, 191.4(6), 191.9(3), 191.9(4); Statut 184; Trial 358, 365.1(1), 365.1(3).

Hale v. State, TexCrimApp, 509 SW2d 637.—Crim Law 1104(6), 1114.1(1), 1120(1).

Hale v. State, TexCrimApp, 330 SW2d 199.—Crim Law 1131(1).

Hale v. State, TexCrimApp, 300 SW2d 75, 164 TexCrim 482.—Assault 96(7); Crim Law 369.2(6), 814(17); Ind & Inf 180; Rape 48(1), 53(5); Witn 350.

Hale v. State, TexCrimApp, 298 SW2d 174.—Crim Law 1090.1(1).

Hale v. State, TexCrimApp, 283 SW2d 762.—Crim Law 1090.1(1).

Hale v. State, TexCrimApp, 229 SW2d 796, 154 TexCrim 630.—Assault 92(4); Evid 506.

Hale v. State, TexCrimApp, 167 SW2d 521.—Crim Law 1090.1(1), 1094(3).

Hale v. State, TexApp–Houston (1 Dist), 694 SW2d 212.—Crim Law 1081(4.1), 1115(1), 1141(2), 1158(1); Judgm 518; Rec S Goods 8(3), 9(1); Sent & Pun 2020, 2021.

Hale v. State, TexApp–Fort Worth, 140 SW3d 801, reh overr, and petition for discretionary review refused.—Crim Law 396(1), 641.13(1), 641.13(2.1), 641.13(6), 920, 959, 1035(7), 1119(1), 1153(1); Rape 40(2), 40(5).

Hale v. State, TexApp–Fort Worth, 139 SW3d 418, appeal after new trial 2006 WL 2507342.—Const Law 3856; Crim Law 662.1, 662.8, 662.10, 662.11, 1044.1(5.1), 1130(5), 1139, 1168(2).

Hale v. State, TexApp–Texarkana, 194 SW3d 39.—Autos 355(13); Crim Law 1144.13(3), 1159.2(2), 1159.2(5), 1159.2(7), 1159.4(1).

Hale v. State, TexApp–Eastland, 220 SW3d 180.—Crim Law 641.3(2), 641.3(3), 641.3(8.1), 641.13(6), 1139, 1158(4).

Hale; State v., TexCivApp–Austin, 96 SW2d 135, mod 146 SW2d 731, 136 Tex 29.—App & E 216(1), 302(6), 672; Em Dom 2(6), 84, 93, 122, 281, 285, 307(4); States 112.1(1), 171, 191.4(5), 191.9(3); Statut 184.

Hale v. Tata Corp., SDTex, 502 FSupp 502.—Rem of C 31, 107(4), 107(7); Seamen 2, 29(5.16); Work Comp 2085.

Hale v. Texas Emp. Ins. Ass'n, Tex, 239 SW2d 608, 150 Tex 215.—App & E 1114, 1122(1); Work Comp 77, 1424.

Hale; Texas Emp. Ins. Ass'n v., Tex, 191 SW2d 472, 144 Tex 432.—Trial 232(2); Work Comp 1922, 1926, 1961.

Hale; Texas Emp. Ins. Ass'n v., TexCivApp–Dallas, 188 SW2d 899, aff 191 SW2d 472, 144 Tex 432.—App & E 216(2), 1064.1(9); Evid 558(2), 558(3); Work Comp 1922, 1926, 1927, 1958, 1968(3), 1968(5), 1969.

Hale; Texas Emp. Ins. Ass'n v., TexCivApp–Amarillo, 242 SW2d 796, ref nre.—Trial 121(2), 129; Work Comp 1396, 1464, 1922, 1926, 1966, 1968(1), 1968(4), 1968(5).

Hale; Texas Emp. Ins. Ass'n v., TexCivApp–Amarillo, 237 SW2d 769, rev 239 SW2d 608, 150 Tex 215.—Work Comp 76, 78, 80, 248, 1438, 1935.

Hale; Texas Emp. Ins. Ass'n v., TexCivApp–Waco, 167 SW2d 575, writ refused.—Trial 29(2); Work Comp 1926, 1968(1).

Hale; Tide Water Oil Co. v., TexCivApp–Texarkana, 92 SW2d 1102, writ dism.—Bound 8, 48(3).

Hale; U.S. v., CA5 (Tex), 155 FedAppx 160.—Crim Law 1042.

Hale; U.S. v., CA5 (Tex), 119 FedAppx 656, cert gr, vac 125 SCt 2309, 544 US 1047, 161 LEd2d 1086, on remand 155 FedAppx 160, reinstated 155 FedAppx 160.—Explos 2; Searches 42.1; Sent & Pun 761.

Hale County; Brittian v., TexCivApp–Amarillo, 297 SW2d 721.—App & E 1010.1(1); High 182; Waters 126(2).

Hale County v. Davis, TexCivApp–Amarillo, 572 SW2d 63, ref nre.—High 88, 89; Inj 1, 34; Judgm 855(1).

Hale County; Thomas v., TexCivApp–Amarillo, 531 SW2d 213.—App & E 954(1); Inj 132, 135, 138.6, 147, 151; Waters 126(2).

Hale County State Bank; Allen v., CA5 (Tex), 725 F2d 290. See Allen, Matter of.

Hale County State Bank v. Bray, TexCivApp–Amarillo, 97 SW2d 337, writ refused.—Evid 43(2); Garn 178.

Hale County, Tex.; Lopez v., NDTex, 797 FSupp 547, aff 113 SCt 954, 506 US 1042, 122 LEd2d 112.—Counties 38; Elections 12(9.1).

Hale-Halsell Co.; Keene v., CCA5 (Tex), 118 F2d 332.—Ex & Ad 423, 430, 439; Fed Cts 7, 287; Fraud Conv 172(1), 229, 230, 255(3); Pretrial Proc 558.

Halepeska v. Callihan Interests, Inc., Tex, 371 SW2d 368, on remand 376 SW2d 932.—App & E 1083(6), 1114; Mines 118; Neglig 452, 553, 554(1), 554(2), 560, 1037(4), 1222, 1562; Trial 133.2.

Halepeska; Callihan Interests, Inc. v., TexCivApp–Eastland, 376 SW2d 932.—Labor & Emp 57; Mines 118.

Halepeska; Callihan Interests, Inc. v., TexCivApp–Eastland, 349 SW2d 758, writ gr, rev 371 SW2d 368, on remand 376 SW2d 932.—Mines 118; Neglig 554(2), 1088.

Hales v. Chubb & Son, Inc., TexApp–Houston (1 Dist), 708 SW2d 597.—App & E 352.1, 387(5), 387(6); Pretrial Proc 699.

Hales; Houston Fire & Cas. Ins. Co. v., TexCivApp–Eastland, 279 SW2d 389, ref nre.—Evid 144, 588; Mech Liens 48; Princ & S 59, 82(1), 161, 162(3).

Hale Supply Co.; Dowdy v., TexCivApp–Fort Worth, 498 SW2d 716.—App & E 758.3(2); Costs 194.32; Mech Liens 115(1), 161(1), 209, 281(1).

Haley, In re, TexApp–Corpus Christi, 174 SW3d 929.—Mand 4(1), 4(4), 12, 154(2).

Haley; Bishop & Babcock Sales Co. v., TexCivApp–Beaumont, 115 SW2d 772.—App & E 1166; Courts 169(2), 170.

Haley v. Boles, TexApp–Tyler, 824 SW2d 796.—Crim Law 641.5(6); Mand 3(2.1), 12, 71.

Haley v. Cockrell, CA5 (Tex), 306 F3d 257, reh and reh den 325 F3d 569, cert gr Dretke v. Haley, 124 SCt 385, 540 US 945, 157 LEd2d 274, vac and remanded 124 SCt 1847, 541 US 386, 158 LEd2d 659, on remand 376 F3d 316.—Crim Law 1134(3), 1429(2), 1534; Hab Corp 319.1, 401, 404, 422, 842, 846.

Haley v. Estelle, CA5 (Tex), 632 F2d 1273, reh den 636 F2d 314.—Hab Corp 864(7), 896, 898(1), 898(2), 899.

Haley v. GPM Gas Corp., TexApp–Amarillo, 80 SW3d 114.—App & E 215(0.5), 215(1), 231(9), 232(0.5), 882(12), 1079; Land & Ten 24(1); Mines 55(2); Pretrial Proc 45; Trial 277.

Haley v. Haley, TexApp–Houston (1 Dist), 713 SW2d 801.—Child C 751; Divorce 253(2).

Haley; Haley v., TexApp–Houston (1 Dist), 713 SW2d 801.—Child C 751; Divorce 253(2).

Haley; Hawkins v., TexApp–Fort Worth, 765 SW2d 914.—Child C 577, 579.

Haley v. Lewis, TexCrimApp, 604 SW2d 194.—Courts 112, 116(1); Crim Law 577.16(1), 577.16(5.1).

Haley; Lingner v., TexCivApp–Amarillo, 277 SW2d 302, dism.—Fraud Conv 305; Statut 223.2(1.1).

Haley; Livingston Ford Mercury, Inc. v., TexApp–Beaumont, 997 SW2d 425.—Acct Action on 10, 13, 14; App & E 1175(1), 1178(1); Judgm 181(15.1), 185(1), 185.3(3); Lim of Act 29(1), 29(3), 53(1).

Haley v. Murray, TexCivApp–Austin, 177 SW2d 333, writ refused wom.—Adv Poss 85(4); Bound 37(1); Deeds 114(1), 115, 117, 118, 119; Ease 36(3); Estop 32(1), 32(3); Evid 460(4).

Haley v. Nickels, TexCivApp–Austin, 235 SW2d 683.—Contracts 217; Judgm 181(33), 186; Neglig 1550, 1571; Princ & A 62(1).

Haley v. Owens, TexCivApp–Texarkana, 483 SW2d 37.—App & E 395.

Haley v. Pagan Lewis Motors, Inc., TexApp–Corpus Christi, 647 SW2d 319, ref nre.—Cons Cred 4; Contracts 153.

Haley v. State, TexCrimApp, 173 SW3d 510.—Crim Law 1042, 1134(2), 1165(1), 1177; Sent & Pun 310, 313, 325; Statut 188.

Haley v. State, TexCrimApp, 811 SW2d 600.—Crim Law 1119(2); Searches 129.

Haley; State v., TexCrimApp, 811 SW2d 597, on remand 816 SW2d 789, petition for discretionary review refused.—Health 331, 333; Searches 47.1.

Haley v. State, TexCrimApp, 480 SW2d 644.—Arrest 63.4(11), 65, 71.1(5), 71.1(6), 71.1(12); Crim Law 394.4(13).

Haley v. State, TexCrimApp, 338 SW2d 468, 170 TexCrim 66.—Crim Law 1036.6, 1037.2, 1044.1(4), 1044.1(5.1).

Haley v. State, TexCrimApp, 303 SW2d 385, 165 TexCrim 48.—Bail 64.

Haley v. State, TexCrimApp, 289 SW2d 771.—Crim Law 1090.1(1).

Haley v. State, TexCrimApp, 247 SW2d 400, 157 TexCrim 150.—Crim Law 366(4), 404.45, 455, 1168(2), 1169.1(10); Rape 51(1); Sent & Pun 1667, 1727.

Haley v. State, TexCrimApp, 208 SW2d 378, 151 TexCrim 392.—Const Law 2507(1); Courts 70.

Haley v. State, TexCrimApp, 191 SW2d 741, 149 TexCrim 75.—Larc 32(3), 33, 60.

Haley v. State, TexCrimApp, 170 SW2d 769, 145 TexCrim 598.—Crim Law 594(3), 1091(5); Witn 344(4).

Haley v. State, TexCrimApp, 170 SW2d 768, 145 TexCrim 597.—Crim Law 598(7).

Haley v. State, TexApp–Austin, 113 SW3d 801, petition for discretionary review dism as untimely filed, and petition for discretionary review gr, aff 173 SW3d 510.—Crim Law 59(1), 59(3), 59(4), 80, 338(7), 796, 1038.1(1), 1043(3), 1134(2), 1139, 1144.1, 1152(2), 1153(1), 1158(1), 1162, 1166.18, 1172.9, 1177; Jury 85, 108; Searches 23, 54, 143.1; Sent & Pun 310, 313, 322.

Haley v. State, TexApp–Houston (14 Dist), 816 SW2d 789, petition for discretionary review refused.—Crim Law 404.60; Ind & Inf 137(1).

Haley v. State, TexApp–Houston (14 Dist), 788 SW2d 892, petition for discretionary review gr, rev 811 SW2d 597, on remand 816 SW2d 789, petition for discretionary review refused.—Crim Law 897(1), 899, 1031(1), 1169.2(1); Health 307, 314, 331, 332; Searches 129.

Haley v. State, TexCivApp–Beaumont, 406 SW2d 477, ref nre.—Em Dom 124, 172, 195, 222(4), 223, 241, 262(5).

Haley; Texaco, Inc. v., TexCivApp–Hous (14 Dist), 610 SW2d 224.—Autos 244(33), 244(34), 244(37), 246(47); Damag 130.1; Jury 131(18); Neglig 530(2), 1744, 1745;

New Tr 44(2), 56, 140(3), 145; Trial 304, 315, 335, 350.6(3), 350.7(9), 351.5(6).

Haley v. Texas Emp. Ins. Ass'n, TexCivApp–Texarkana, 487 SW2d 369, ref nre.—Trial 350.3(8); Work Comp 553.

Haley v. Texas General Indem. Co., TexCivApp–Eastland, 443 SW2d 604.—Work Comp 1962.

Haley; U.S. v., USTex, 83 SCt 11, 371 US 18, 9 LEd2d 1. —Fed Cts 444.

Haley; U.S. v., NDTex, 166 FSupp 336, rev 79 SCt 537, 358 US 644, 3 LEd2d 567, motion den 79 SCt 896, 359 US 977, 3 LEd2d 927, reh den 79 SCt 896, 359 US 981, 3 LEd2d 931.—Agric 3.4(4); Commerce 62.5; Const Law 1066.

Haley v. Young, TexCivApp–Hous (1 Dist), 541 SW2d 217.—App & E 846(5), 907(3); Garn 7, 193, 194; Judgm 17(9); Parties 54; Proc 4.

Haley Transports, Inc.; Knickerbocker v., TexCivApp–El Paso, 386 SW2d 621.—App & E 1061.4; Jury 10; Trial 168, 180.

Halfen; U.S. v., CA5 (Tex), 467 F2d 127.—Jury 29(6); Rec S Goods 2.

Halfen v. U.S., CA5 (Tex), 321 F2d 556, cert den 84 SCt 704, 376 US 934, 11 LEd2d 653.—Crim Law 369.15, 400(4), 673(5); Rec S Goods 8(2), 8(3), 9(1).

Halferty v. Pulse Ambulance Service, CA5 (Tex), 864 F2d 1185, 29 Wage & Hour Cas (BNA) 273. See Halferty v. Pulse Drug Co., Inc.

Halferty v. Pulse Ambulance Service, CA5 (Tex), 826 F2d 2, 28 Wage & Hour Cas (BNA) 495. See Halferty v. Pulse Drug Co., Inc.

Halferty v. Pulse Ambulance Service, CA5 (Tex), 821 F2d 261, 28 Wage & Hour Cas (BNA) 322. See Halferty v. Pulse Drug Co., Inc.

Halferty v. Pulse Drug Co., Inc., CA5 (Tex), 864 F2d 1185, 29 Wage & Hour Cas (BNA) 273.—Fed Cts 754.1, 848; Judges 24; Labor & Emp 2317, 2320.

Halferty v. Pulse Drug Co., Inc., CA5 (Tex), 826 F2d 2, 28 Wage & Hour Cas (BNA) 495, appeal after remand 864 F2d 1185, 29 Wage & Hour Cas (BNA) 273.—Labor & Emp 2371.

Halferty v. Pulse Drug Co., Inc., CA5 (Tex), 821 F2d 261, 28 Wage & Hour Cas (BNA) 322, opinion mod on reh 826 F2d 2, 28 Wage & Hour Cas (BNA) 495, appeal after remand 864 F2d 1185, 29 Wage & Hour Cas (BNA) 273, appeal after remand 864 F2d 1185, 29 Wage & Hour Cas (BNA) 273.—Fed Cts 947; Labor & Emp 2237, 2317, 2371, 2403; Lim of Act 58(1).

Halff; Ellison v., TexCivApp–San Antonio, 94 SW2d 528, writ dism.—Frds St of 50(1), 51; Mal Pros 11; Ven & Pur 343(1).

Halff; Sisk v., TexCivApp–El Paso, 89 SW2d 1079, writ refused.—Mtg 256, 437.

Halfin; Brown v., TexCivApp–Galveston, 294 SW2d 290, ref nre.—Deeds 195; Evid 590; Judgm 256(1); Trusts 44(3), 89(1), 373; Witn 178(1), 181.

Halfin; National Life & Accident Ins. Co. v., TexCivApp–San Antonio, 99 SW2d 997.—App & E 742(1); Courts 169(4).

Halfmann v. USAG Ins. Services, Inc., NDTex, 118 FSupp2d 714.—Fed Cts 241, 289; Insurance 1110; Rem of C 19(1), 25(1); States 18.9, 18.11, 18.41.

Halford, Ex parte, TexCrimApp, 536 SW2d 230.—Const Law 268(2.1), 4674, 4783(2); Courts 100(1).

Halford; Budd v., TexCivApp–Beaumont, 142 SW2d 368. —Wills 337, 340, 355.

Halford v. Perry, TexCivApp–Dallas, 310 SW2d 745.—Trial 350.7(9), 366.

Halford v. State, TexCrimApp, 400 SW2d 339.—Crim Law 768(1), 778(1).

Halford; Yellow Cab Corp. v., TexCivApp–Dallas, 91 SW2d 801, writ dism.—App & E 933(1), 1062.1; Autos 193(14); Damag 221(2.1); New Tr 52, 145; Trial 351.2(2).

Half Price Books, Records, Magazines, Inc.; City of Dallas v., TexApp–Dallas, 883 SW2d 374, appeal after remand Leake v. Half Price Books, Records, Magazines, Inc, 918 SW2d 559.—App & E 93, 934(1); Evid 584(1); Judgm 181(27), 185(2); Mun Corp 188, 747(3); Offic 114.

Half Price Books, Records, Magazines, Inc.; Leake v., TexApp–Dallas, 918 SW2d 559.—App & E 93, 1097(1), 1194(1); Courts 99(1), 99(6); Judgm 183, 185(2); Labor & Emp 3042, 3045, 3055.

Haliburton, Ex parte, TexCrimApp, 755 SW2d 131.—Hab Corp 337, 723.

Haliburton v. City of San Antonio, TexApp–San Antonio, 974 SW2d 779, reh overr.—Judgm 185(2); Lim of Act 58(1), 58(2), 126.5, 195(3).

Haliburton v. Riley, TexCivApp–Waco, 589 SW2d 821.—Judgm 570(3); Pretrial Proc 517.1.

Haliburton v. State, TexCrimApp, 578 SW2d 726.—Crim Law 857(1), 1163(4); Sent & Pun 329, 509.

Haliburton v. State, TexApp–Fort Worth, 80 SW3d 309. —Crim Law 347, 369.2(2), 369.2(3.1), 371(1), 728(1), 728(3), 730(12), 1035(8.1), 1036.2, 1037.1(3), 1153(1); Obst Just 3, 11.

Haliburton v. State, TexApp–Waco, 23 SW3d 192, petition for discretionary review refused.—Crim Law 31.5, 641.13(2.1), 763(1), 775(2); Sent & Pun 558.

Halifax Fire Ins. Co. v. Felton, TexCivApp–Austin, 112 SW2d 269, writ dism.—Costs 238(1); Insurance 3013, 3015, 3571; Trial 90.

Halim v. Ramchandani, TexApp–Houston (14 Dist), 203 SW3d 482.—App & E 213, 232(0.5), 237(5), 237(6), 238(2), 294(1), 302(5), 882(8), 1050.1(12), 1079; Evid 508, 545, 555.2, 555.10.

Halipoto, Matter of, CA5 (Tex), 161 F3d 314. See Trans Chemical Ltd. v. China Nat. Machinery Import and Export Corp.

Halipoto; Maddux v., TexApp–Houston (14 Dist), 742 SW2d 59.—Lim of Act 55(3).

Halipoto; Waguespack v., TexApp–Houston (14 Dist), 633 SW2d 628, writ dism woj.—Pretrial Proc 44.1, 46, 563, 581.

Halkias v. General Dynamics Corp., CA5 (Tex), 137 F3d 333, cert den Bryant v. General Dynamics Corp, 119 SCt 171, 525 US 872, 142 LEd2d 140.—Fed Cts 776; Labor & Emp 3232.

Halkias v. General Dynamics Corp., CA5 (Tex), 31 F3d 224, reh en banc gr, vac on reh 56 F3d 27, on remand 899 FSupp 295, aff 101 F3d 698, on remand 955 FSupp 695, aff 137 F3d 333, cert den Bryant v. General Dynamics Corp, 119 SCt 171, 525 US 872, 142 LEd2d 140, on remand Staudt v Glastron, Inc, 1995 WL 701406, rev 92 F3d 312, reh and sug for reh den 99 F3d 1137.— Const Law 3971, 4182; Fed Cts 409.1, 422.1, 424; Labor & Emp 40(1), 1964, 1998; Lim of Act 6(1), 16, 39(1).

Halkias v. General Dynamics Corp., NDTex, 955 FSupp 695, aff 137 F3d 333, cert den Bryant v. General Dynamics Corp, 119 SCt 171, 525 US 872, 142 LEd2d 140. —Fed Civ Proc 2553; Labor & Emp 3204, 3226.

Halkias v. General Dynamics Corp., NDTex, 899 FSupp 295, aff 101 F3d 698, on remand 955 FSupp 695, aff 137 F3d 333, cert den Bryant v. General Dynamics Corp, 119 SCt 171, 525 US 872, 142 LEd2d 140.—Fed Cts 424.

Halkias v. General Dynamics Corp., NDTex, 825 FSupp 123, aff 31 F3d 224, reh en banc gr, vac on reh 56 F3d 27, on remand 899 FSupp 295, aff 101 F3d 698, on remand 955 FSupp 695, aff 137 F3d 333, cert den Bryant v. General Dynamics Corp, 119 SCt 171, 525 US 872, 142 LEd2d 140, on remand Staudt v Glastron, Inc, 1995 WL 701406, rev 92 F3d 312, reh and sug for reh den 99 F3d 1137, vac 56 F3d 27, on remand 899 FSupp 295, aff 101 F3d 698, on remand 955 FSupp 695, aff 137 F3d 333, cert den 119 SCt 171, 525 US 872, 142 LEd2d

140, on remand 1995 WL 701406, rev 92 F3d 312, reh and sug for reh den 99 F3d 1137.—Fed Civ Proc 1041, 1044, 1049.1; Fed Cts 424; Lim of Act 58(1).

Hall, Ex parte, Tex, 854 SW2d 656.—Child S 440; Const Law 1106; Contempt 20, 78; Divorce 269(2); Hus & W 35, 281, 316.

Hall, Ex parte, TexCrimApp, 995 SW2d 151.—Prisons 15(3).

Hall, Ex parte, TexCrimApp, 696 SW2d 915.—Const Law 4838; Pardon 84.

Hall, Ex parte, TexCrimApp, 546 SW2d 303.—Crim Law 1177.5(1); Hab Corp 725; Sent & Pun 1318, 1327.

Hall, Ex parte, TexCrimApp, 436 SW2d 343.—Sent & Pun 1318.

Hall, Ex parte, TexCrimApp, 258 SW2d 806, 158 TexCrim 646, cert den Hall v. Ellis, 75 SCt 346, 348 US 930, 99 LEd 729, cert den 75 SCt 900, 349 US 966, 99 LEd 1288, cert den 76 SCt 852, 351 US 955, 100 LEd 1478.—Sent & Pun 642.

Hall, Ex parte, TexApp–Dallas, 838 SW2d 674.—Contempt 82; Prisons 15(7).

Hall, Ex parte, TexCivApp–Dallas, 611 SW2d 459.—Child S 474, 497; Const Law 1106, 4494; Contempt 63(1).

Hall, In Interest of, TexApp–Amarillo, 871 SW2d 251.—Child C 905.

Hall, In re, BkrtcySDTex, 128 BR 175.—Bankr 3383.

Hall, In re, BkrtcyWDTex, 368 BR 595.—Bankr 2261, 2264(3).

Hall, In re, TexApp–Waco, 989 SW2d 786.—Mand 3(2.1), 10; Sent & Pun 2283.

Hall, In re, TexApp–Tyler, 112 SW3d 608, reh overr.—Mand 1, 12, 61.

Hall, In re, TexApp–Corpus Christi, 972 SW2d 793, reh overr.—Atty & C 32(12); Mand 4(1), 4(4), 12, 16(1).

Hall v. Aldine Independent School Dist., TexApp–Houston (1 Dist), 95 SW3d 485, review den.—Const Law 990, 1030; Tax 2979.

Hall v. Aloco Oil Co., TexCivApp–Amarillo, 164 SW2d 861, writ refused.—Hus & W 270(5); Judgm 693.

Hall; Amarillo Coca-Cola Bottling Co. v., TexCivApp–Amarillo, 384 SW2d 726.—Prod Liab 78, 84; Venue 22(4).

Hall v. Amoco Oil Co., SDTex, 617 FSupp 111.—Fed Civ Proc 843; Neglig 306; Nuis 3(1); Tresp 40(4).

Hall; Anderson v., TexCivApp–Fort Worth, 137 SW2d 854, dism.—App & E 1172(2); Princ & A 8, 23(5); Sales 52(7), 130(4), 177, 239.

Hall v. Atchison, T. & S. F. Ry. Co., CA5 (Tex), 504 F2d 380.—Death 103(2); Neglig 371, 387, 422, 1693; R R 304, 350(2), 350(3), 350(32).

Hall; Atlas Roofing Co. v., Tex, 245 SW2d 477, 150 Tex 611, opinion conformed to Freelove v. Atas Roofing Company, 245 SW2d 973.—Mand 176; Venue 21, 22(1), 22(6).

Hall v. Barrett, TexCivApp–Fort Worth, 126 SW2d 1045.—Adv Poss 33; Deeds 145; Evid 269(3), 419(2); Gifts 47(1); Hus & W 262.2, 264(4); Judgm 199(1); New Tr 72(4).

Hall v. Baum, Tex, 452 SW2d 699, appeal dism 90 SCt 818, 397 US 93, 25 LEd2d 79.—Const Law 1020, 3644; Courts 95(2); Elections 126(4); Offic 19, 29.

Hall v. Bean, TexCivApp–Beaumont, 582 SW2d 263.—Antitrust 141, 476; Contracts 22(1); Statut 188.

Hall v. Birchfield, TexApp–Texarkana, 718 SW2d 313, writ gr, rev Birchfield v. Texarkana Memorial Hosp, 747 SW2d 361.—Antitrust 392, 393; App & E 882(9), 1026, 1032(1), 1043(6), 1045(1), 1050.1(10), 1050.1(12), 1050.4, 1051.1(2), 1069.1; Atty & C 21.5(1), 21.20; Damag 51, 59, 94, 221(7); Evid 117, 155(10), 219(3), 222(1), 222(2), 243(4), 314(1), 355(4), 472(1), 506, 538, 553(4), 555.4(3); Health 820, 823(1), 823(9), 827, 830, 832; Infants 77, 116, 253; Interest 22(1), 53, 66; Mand 3(3); Neglig 273, 1635; Stip 18(6); Trial 349(2), 350.6(2), 352.5(1), 352.10, 352.16, 366, 412; Witn 37(2).

Hall v. Bleisch, CA5 (Tex), 400 F2d 896, cert den 89 SCt 864, 393 US 1083, 21 LEd2d 775.—Judgm 585(4), 828.15(1), 828.16(4).

Hall v. Board of Adjustment of City of McAllen, TexCivApp–San Antonio, 239 SW2d 647.—Zoning 360, 584.1, 586, 644.1, 646.

Hall v. Board of Firemen's Relief and Retirement Fund Trustees of Houston, TexCivApp–Houston, 351 SW2d 342.—Mun Corp 200(8.1), 200(9), 200(10).

Hall; Borden v., TexCivApp–Beaumont, 255 SW2d 920, ref nre.—Death 2(1); Deeds 90, 99, 108; Evid 384, 395(1), 450(3); Mtg 6, 32(5).

Hall v. Brown, TexCivApp–Waco, 398 SW2d 404.—App & E 1078(1), 1169(7), 1172(3); Damag 40(1), 124(3), 221(2.1); Evid 568(4), 571(7); Interest 56; Trial 351.3, 388(1).

Hall v. Butereg Co., TexCivApp–Amarillo, 114 SW2d 403.—Evid 41; Plead 111.45.

Hall; Calvert v., TexCivApp–Austin, 514 SW2d 778, dism.—Plead 49, 111.43; Tax 3365; Venue 11.

Hall; Carpenter v., SDTex, 352 FSupp 806.—Fed Cts 78, 105, 112; Judges 39, 51(1), 53; Sec Reg 133.

Hall; Carpenter v., SDTex, 311 FSupp 1099.—Bankr 2154.1, 2157; Fed Civ Proc 164, 187; Fed Cts 91; Indem 64; Lim of Act 100(2); Sec Reg 60.16, 60.51.

Hall; Carter v., TexCivApp–Fort Worth, 589 SW2d 502, dism.—Child S 339(2), 339(3), 339(4); Evid 14.

Hall v. C-F Emp. Credit Union, TexCivApp–Texarkana, 536 SW2d 266.—App & E 934(2), 1046.1; Bills & N 489(1), 489(6); Judgm 109; Jury 28(9); Trial 23.

Hall; Chaffin v., TexCivApp–Eastland, 210 SW2d 191, ref nre.—App & E 931(4); Mines 48, 62.1, 73.1(4); Partit 13, 32, 33, 48, 63(1), 77(3).

Hall; Chumley v., TexCivApp–Dallas, 601 SW2d 803.—Child 53, 57, 73.

Hall v. City of Austin, Tex, 450 SW2d 836.—Action 60; App & E 79(1), 80(1), 80(6); Trial 3(1).

Hall; City of Austin v., TexCivApp–Austin, 446 SW2d 330, appeal dism 450 SW2d 836.—Em Dom 56, 64, 235; Pretrial Proc 582, 583.

Hall v. Civil Air Patrol, Inc., CA5 (Tex), 193 FedAppx 298, cert den 127 SCt 2134, 167 LEd2d 864.—Fed Civ Proc 1781, 1837.1.

Hall; Cole v., TexApp–Dallas, 864 SW2d 563, reh den, and writ dism woj.—Action 27(1); App & E 836, 917(1), 960(1), 1078(1); Contracts 68; Labor & Emp 78, 79; Plead 228.23; Torts 432, 433, 454.

Hall; Collins v., Tex, 174 SW2d 50, 141 Tex 433.—App & E 1082(2); Frds St of 74(2); Trusts 44(1).

Hall; Collins v., TexCivApp–Austin, 161 SW2d 311, writ refused wom.—Contracts 232(1), 232(7), 256, 305(1), 324(1), 348; Evid 445(7); Trial 66, 352.10, 352.18.

Hall v. Collins, TexCivApp–Amarillo, 167 SW2d 210, rev 174 SW2d 50, 141 Tex 433.—App & E 758.1; Contracts 138(1); Equity 65(1), 65(2); Frds St of 74(2); Fraud Conv 64(1), 111, 155, 179(1); Judgm 18(2); Plead 403(1); Trusts 48, 56.

Hall v. Collins, TexCivApp–Amarillo, 151 SW2d 338, writ refused.—App & E 1048(2); Trial 75; Witn 139(1), 139(5), 139(9), 173, 178(3).

Hall; Colored Legion Benev. Ass'n v., TexCivApp–Eastland, 87 SW2d 838.—App & E 770(1), 773(4).

Hall v. C.I.R., CA5 (Tex), 406 F2d 706.—Int Rev 3470, 3481, 4503, 4662, 4680.

Hall v. C.I.R., CA5 (Tex), 294 F2d 82.—Int Rev 3626, 4657, 4725, 4743.1, 4744, 4749.

Hall v. Continental Airlines, Inc., SDTex, 127 FSupp2d 811.—Fed Civ Proc 1742(1), 1825; Labor & Emp 1219(2), 1320(6), 1526.

Hall; Continental Cas. Co. v., TexApp–Houston (14 Dist), 761 SW2d 54, writ den, cert den Hall v. CNA Ins Companies, 110 SCt 2174, 495 US 932, 109 LEd2d 503.—Insurance 2278(1), 2350(1).

HALL;

Hall; Cooper v., TexCivApp–Amarillo, 489 SW2d 409, ref nre.—App & E 1024.5; Evid 71, 83(1), 87, 89, 100, 139; Judgm 106(2), 335(1), 335(3), 335(4); Paymt 73(1); Trial 382.

Hall v. Courtney, TexApp–Fort Worth, 919 SW2d 454. See Hall v. Stephenson.

Hall v. Crocker Equipment Leasing, Inc., TexApp–Houston (14 Dist), 737 SW2d 1, writ den.—Sec Tran 230, 240.

Hall v. Dallas Joint-Stock Land Bank of Dallas, Tex-CivApp–Dallas, 95 SW2d 200, writ refused.—Ven & Pur 299(1).

Hall; DeGroot v., TexCivApp–Waco, 526 SW2d 696, ref nre.—App & E 671(1); Child C 778; Infants 179.

Hall; Denman v., Tex, 193 SW2d 515, 144 Tex 633, answer to certified question conformed to 194 SW2d 810.—Brok 43(2); Evid 420(2), 420(3), 444(1).

Hall; Denman v., TexCivApp–Fort Worth, 194 SW2d 810. —Evid 420(3).

Hall; Denman v., TexCivApp–Fort Worth, 191 SW2d 74, certified question answered 193 SW2d 515, 144 Tex 633, answer to certified question conformed to 194 SW2d 810, opinion withdrawn and superseded on reh 194 SW2d 810.—Brok 8(1), 8(3), 40, 86(1); Contracts 34, 42; Evid 420(3), 444(2).

Hall v. Department of Health, Ed., and Welfare, SDTex, 199 FSupp 833.—Lim of Act 125; U S 125(3), 125(6).

Hall; Deposit Guar. Bank v., SDTex, 741 FSupp 1287.— Banks 505; Sales 85(1); Sec Tran 101.

Hall; DeShazo v., TexApp–Houston (14 Dist), 963 SW2d 958, reh overr.—App & E 782; Courts 40.

Hall; Diamond Shamrock Refining Co., L.P. v., Tex, 168 SW3d 164.—App & E 153, 930(1), 1001(1); Neglig 273; Work Comp 2156.

Hall v. Diamond Shamrock Refining Co., L.P., Tex-App–San Antonio, 82 SW3d 5, reh overr, and review gr (2 pets), rev 168 SW3d 164.—App & E 842(1), 930(1), 946, 989, 1001(1), 1001(3), 1003(6), 1050.1(1), 1056.1(1), 1056.1(7); Const Law 2312, 2314; Corp 494, 498; Damag 87(1), 94, 154; Evid 99; Labor & Emp 2825, 2880; Neglig 273, 1659; Plead 373.1; Statut 176; Trial 43, 134, 139.1(3), 140(1), 143.

Hall; Dillard Dept. Stores, Inc. v., Tex, 909 SW2d 491.— Mand 32; Pretrial Proc 19, 331, 403.

Hall; Diversified, Inc. v., TexApp–Houston (1 Dist), 23 SW3d 403, reh overr, and review den.—Deeds 121; Execution 264, 271; Tresp to T T 1, 6.1, 38(1); Ven & Pur 224.

Hall v. Dodson, TexCivApp–Amarillo, 278 SW2d 558.— Child C 908, 921(1), 922(2).

Hall v. D'Oro by Christopher Michael, Inc., NDTex, 475 FSupp 583.—Labor & Emp 258, 262, 2204.

Hall v. Dorsey, TexCivApp–Hous (1 Dist), 596 SW2d 565, ref nre.—Action 58; App & E 345.1, 877(2), 1170.1, 1170.12; Autos 234; Compromise 8(3); New Tr 155; Parties 18, 29.

Hall v. Dow Corning Corp., CA5 (Tex), 114 F3d 73.— Const Law 2315; Fed Cts 776, 802; Health 811; Lim of Act 4(2), 199(1).

Hall; Durant Mill. Co. v., TexCivApp–Amarillo, 284 SW2d 760, ref nre.—Evid 597; Inj 16, 43; Sales 225(4), 234(8).

Hall v. Edlefson, TexCivApp–Waco, 498 SW2d 514, 64 ALR3d 1065.—Neglig 1176.

Hall; Elliott v., TexCivApp–Waco, 337 SW2d 634, writ dism.—Venue 8.5(8).

Hall; Emery Air Freight Corp. v., TexCivApp–Texarkana, 520 SW2d 956.—App & E 1177(6); Venue 22(4).

Hall v. Environmental Chemical Corp., SDTex, 90 FSupp2d 794.—Ship 1, 84(1).

Hall v. Environmental Chemical Corp., SDTex, 64 FSupp2d 638.—Adm 17.1, 20; Const Law 3964; Fed Cts 76, 76.5, 76.35, 96, 101, 104, 105, 111, 1141.

Hall; Exxon Corp. v., NDTex, 480 FSupp 405.—Trademarks 1096(2), 1097.

Hall v. F.A. Halamicek Enterprises, Inc., TexApp–Corpus Christi, 669 SW2d 368.—Judgm 186; Princ & A 14(2), 25(3), 99, 137(1).

Hall; Fannin v., TexCivApp–Tyler, 561 SW2d 952.— Autos 146, 150, 204, 244(58), 245(80), 245(90); Judgm 199(3.2), 199(3.10); Neglig 1541, 1602.

Hall v. Federal Deposit Ins. Corp., SDTex, 741 FSupp 1287. See Deposit Guar. Bank v. Hall.

Hall; Federal Underwriters Exchange v., Tex, 182 SW2d 703, 143 Tex 36.—Work Comp 412, 1485.

Hall; Federal Underwriters Exchange v., TexCivApp–Dallas, 179 SW2d 519, mod 182 SW2d 703, 143 Tex 36. —Work Comp 475, 1009, 1021, 1028, 1481, 1596.

Hall; Fiesta Mart, Inc. v., TexApp–Houston (1 Dist), 886 SW2d 440.—App & E 497(1), 907(3); Costs 2, 177, 208; Infants 83, 115.

Hall; Firestone v., TexCivApp–Fort Worth, 143 SW2d 797.—App & E 78(1), 704.1; Mand 4(1), 53; Trial 356(1).

Hall v. Ford Motor Co., TexCivApp–Corpus Christi, 565 SW2d 592.—Plead 111.9, 111.12; Venue 21.

Hall v. Fowler, TexCivApp–Dallas, 389 SW2d 730.—App & E 223, 934(1); Atty & C 124; Bills & N 92(4), 104; Judgm 185.3(16), 189.

Hall; Fulcher v., TexCivApp–El Paso, 170 SW2d 321.— Attach 178; Autos 19.

Hall; Furr v., TexCivApp–Amarillo, 553 SW2d 666, ref nre.—Abate & R 8(2), 9; App & E 756, 757(1), 758.3(3); Decl Judgm 45, 253, 324; Equity 65(1); Estop 52.10(2), 52.10(3); Ex & Ad 144, 163.

Hall v. Garson, CA5 (Tex), 468 F2d 845.—Const Law 4417; Land & Ten 241.

Hall v. Garson, CA5 (Tex), 430 F2d 430, appeal after remand 468 F2d 845.—Civil R 1318, 1325, 1326(9), 1395(3); Const Law 3020; Fed Cts 47.1, 222, 223, 333, 743, 1002.

Hall; Geigy Chemical Corp. v., TexCivApp–Amarillo, 449 SW2d 115.—Plead 111.3, 111.8, 111.16, 111.37, 111.42(6); Prod Liab 22; Venue 21.

Hall; General Shoe Corp. v., TexCivApp–Texarkana, 123 SW2d 721.—Contracts 9(3), 10(1), 10(4); Damag 23; Princ & A 41(5), 41(6); Sales 418(1).

Hall; George v., Tex, 371 SW2d 874.—App & E 1082(1), 1114, 1178(6); Contracts 186(2).

Hall v. GE Plastic Pacific PTE Ltd., CA5 (Tex), 327 F3d 391.—Estop 68(2); Fed Cts 433, 776.

Hall v. Gillman Inc., CA5 (Tex), 81 F3d 35.—Civil R 1209; Fed Civ Proc 2470, 2497.1; Fed Cts 776.

Hall; Glasgow v., TexApp–Austin, 668 SW2d 863, ref nre. —Antitrust 198, 397; App & E 930(1), 989, 1012.1(5).

Hall v. Goforth, SDTex, 224 BR 580, aff In re Goforth, 179 F3d 390, reh den.—Bankr 2834.

Hall v. Great Nat. Lloyds, Tex, 275 SW2d 88, 154 Tex 200.—App & E 977(5); Embez 9; Insurance 1822, 1832(1), 2706(3).

Hall; Great Nat. Lloyds v., TexCivApp–Fort Worth, 265 SW2d 875, rev 275 SW2d 88, 154 Tex 200.—Crim Law 29(10); Embez 1, 9, 13, 14; Insurance 1088, 1813, 1822, 1832(1), 1851, 2153(1), 2675, 2706(3), 2732, 3579; Larc 15(1), 15(3).

Hall; Grimes v., TexCivApp–Eastland, 211 SW2d 956.— App & E 220, 1022(3); Partit 92, 94(3).

Hall v. Gulf Ins. Co. of Dallas, TexCivApp–Austin, 200 SW2d 450.—App & E 919; Insurance 1812, 1825, 1832(1), 2134(3).

Hall v. Hall, Tex, 308 SW2d 12, 158 Tex 95.—App & E 267(1), 281(1), 747(2), 878(1); Contracts 168, 212(1); Frds St of 44(3), 45(1), 47, 118(3).

Hall; Hall v., Tex, 308 SW2d 12, 158 Tex 95.—App & E 267(1), 281(1), 747(2), 878(1); Contracts 168, 212(1); Frds St of 44(3), 45(1), 47, 118(3).

Hall v. Hall, TexApp–Texarkana, 650 SW2d 101.—Courts 100(1).

Hall; Hall v., TexApp–Texarkana, 650 SW2d 101.— Courts 100(1).

Hall v. Hall, TexCivApp–Dallas, 326 SW2d 594, ref nre.— Antitrust 592; App & E 1009(2); Lim of Act 119(4); Partners 81, 121; Pat 182.

Hall; Hall v., TexCivApp–Dallas, 326 SW2d 594, ref nre. —Antitrust 592; App & E 1009(2); Lim of Act 119(4); Partners 81, 121; Pat 182.

Hall v. Hall, TexCivApp–Waco, 298 SW2d 950, writ gr, rev 308 SW2d 12, 158 Tex 95.—Frds St of 118(3); Judgm 199(3.9); Labor & Emp 57, 863(1); Trial 284.

Hall; Hall v., TexCivApp–Waco, 298 SW2d 950, writ gr, rev 308 SW2d 12, 158 Tex 95.—Frds St of 118(3); Judgm 199(3.9); Labor & Emp 57, 863(1); Trial 284.

Hall v. Hall, TexCivApp–Houston, 352 SW2d 765.—App & E 846(5), 846(5), 931(1), 989, 1051(1), 1078(1); Bills & N 101, 501, 516; Evid 63; Ex & Ad 443(5); Plead 409(1), 409(4); Trial 105(2); Witn 159(14).

Hall; Hall v., TexCivApp–Houston, 352 SW2d 765.—App & E 846(2), 846(5), 931(1), 989, 1051(1), 1078(1); Bills & N 101, 501, 516; Evid 63; Ex & Ad 443(5); Plead 409(1), 409(4); Trial 105(2); Witn 159(14).

Hall v. Hard, Tex, 335 SW2d 584, 160 Tex 565.—App & E 172(1), 931(3), 1178(1); Brok 1, 42; Judgm 199(3.14); Sec Reg 307, 309; Trial 392(1).

Hall; Hard v., TexCivApp–Fort Worth, 318 SW2d 108, rev 335 SW2d 584, 160 Tex 565.—App & E 1050.1(5), 1056.1(6); Brok 43(0.5), 56(3), 57(2), 86(1); Judgm 199(3.14).

Hall; Harris County v., Tex, 172 SW2d 691, 141 Tex 388. —App & E 994(3), 1011.1(1), 1094(2); Autos 38; Counties 80(2); Evid 207(1), 245, 265(18); Offic 110.

Hall; Harris County v., TexCivApp–Galveston, 166 SW2d 729, rev 172 SW2d 691, 141 Tex 388.—App & E 1010.1(1); Counties 80(2), 98(1); Lim of Act 24(2), 28(1).

Hall v. Harris County Child Welfare Unit, TexCivApp– Hous (14 Dist), 533 SW2d 121.—Infants 155, 172, 254.

Hall v. Harris County Water Control & Imp. Dist. No. 50, TexApp–Houston (14 Dist), 683 SW2d 863.—App & E 241; Judgm 181(2), 181(3), 181(15.1), 183, 185(2), 185.3(8); Lim of Act 170; Torts 215, 217, 241, 262, 263; Waters 183.5.

Hall v. Hayes, TexCivApp–El Paso, 441 SW2d 275.—Ack 55(1), 56, 62(2), 62(3); Adop 7.5, 16; App & E 846(5), 934(1); Contracts 93(2), 93(4); Evid 65.

Hall; Hays v., Tex, 488 SW2d 412.—Lim of Act 95(12), 95(13), 104(2).

Hall; Hays v., TexCivApp–Eastland, 477 SW2d 402, writ gr, rev 488 SW2d 412.—Health 830; Lim of Act 104(2), 179(2).

Hall; Helicopteros Nacionales de Colombia, S.A. v., USTex, 104 SCt 1868, 466 US 408, 80 LEd2d 404, on remand 677 SW2d 19.—Const Law 3964, 3965(3), 3965(5); Fed Cts 71, 76.10, 84.

Hall v. Helicopteros Nacionales De Colombia, S.A. (Helicol), Tex, 638 SW2d 870, cert gr 103 SCt 1270, 460 US 1021, 75 LEd2d 493, rev 104 SCt 1868, 466 US 408, 80 LEd2d 404, on remand 677 SW2d 19.—Const Law 3964; Corp 665(1).

Hall; Helicopteros Nacionales De Colombia, S.A. ("Helicol") v., TexCivApp–Hous (1 Dist), 616 SW2d 247, rev 638 SW2d 870, cert gr 103 SCt 1270, 460 US 1021, 75 LEd2d 493, rev 104 SCt 1868, 466 US 408, 80 LEd2d 404, on remand 677 SW2d 19.—App & E 154(3); Corp 665(1), 665(3), 668(4); Courts 12(2.10), 37(3).

Hall; Henderson v., TexCivApp–Galveston, 174 SW2d 985, writ refused wom.—Judgm 747(4); Mines 55(5); Tresp to T T 34; Ven & Pur 89, 212, 231(1), 261(3), 261(6), 278.

Hall v. Houston General Ins. Co., TexApp–Dallas, 663 SW2d 468. See Seay v. Hall.

Hall v. Hudson, TexCivApp–Beaumont, 487 SW2d 434.— Autos 244(44), 244(58); Judgm 199(3.15).

Hall v. Huff, TexApp–Texarkana, 957 SW2d 90, reh overr, and review den.—Abate & R 54; App & E 934(1), 946, 971(2); Death 7, 11; Evid 538, 545, 546; Health 611, 620, 821(2); Judgm 181(33), 183, 185(2); Neglig 371, 379, 380, 384, 387, 421, 423, 431, 432.

Hall; Jackson v., Tex, 214 SW2d 458, 147 Tex 245, conformed to East TexMotor Freight Line v. Jackson, 216 SW2d 686.—App & E 1177(6), 1177(7).

Hall; Jacobini v., TexApp–Fort Worth, 719 SW2d 396, ref nre.—App & E 93, 218.2(3.1), 1001(1), 1001(3); Autos 244(31), 244(32); Death 99(5); New Tr 21; Trial 127, 351.5(1), 420; Witn 336.

Hall; Jarrett v., TexCivApp–Beaumont, 207 SW2d 261.— Contracts 9(3), 259, 271; Interest 31; Trusts 63.5, 83.

Hall; Jordaan v., NDTex, 275 FSupp2d 778.—Courts 509; Divorce 11.5; Fed Civ Proc 2769, 2771(2), 2784, 2790, 2800, 2810, 2812; Fed Cts 198, 1142.

Hall v. Kynerd, TexCivApp–El Paso, 97 SW2d 278, writ dism.—App & E 259, 1165; Appear 8(3); Judgm 160; New Tr 152.

Hall v. Lawlis, Tex, 907 SW2d 493.—Mand 43; Pretrial Proc 388.

Hall; Lawyers Sur. Corp. v., TexCivApp–Hous (14 Dist), 590 SW2d 762, writ refused.—Lim of Act 47(4).

Hall; Lee-Wright, Inc. v., TexApp–Houston (1 Dist), 840 SW2d 572.—App & E 901, 930(3), 969, 989, 999(1), 1003(7); Damag 59, 62(1), 64, 96, 104, 119, 182; Labor & Emp 40(2), 41(1), 41(2), 41(4), 55, 763, 765, 835, 861, 867, 868(3), 868(4), 873, 874; Trial 139.1(3), 140(1), 143, 182, 219, 349(2), 350.2, 351.5(1), 352.1(1), 352.4(1).

Hall; Lewis v., TexCivApp–Fort Worth, 271 SW2d 447, ref nre.—Adv Poss 31; App & E 1036(3); Fraud Conv 249; Judgm 187; Lim of Act 95(8); Notice 6.

Hall; Liska v., TexCivApp–Dallas, 357 SW2d 601.—Child C 26, 76, 555, 567, 577.

Hall v. Lone Star Gas Co., TexApp–Austin, 954 SW2d 174, reh overr, and review den.—Antitrust 141, 363; Contracts 176(2); Ease 61(9.5); Gas 9; Judgm 181(14), 185(6), 189.

Hall; Long v., TexCivApp–Waco, 389 SW2d 683.—Autos 20; Plead 111.12, 111.39(4); Sequest 21; Trover 35.

Hall v. Looney, TexCivApp–Eastland, 106 SW2d 820.— Ten in C 3, 46.

Hall; McArthur v., TexCivApp–Fort Worth, 169 SW2d 724, writ refused wom.—Child 6, 10; Marriage 13, 22, 40(4), 47, 48; Wills 229.

Hall; McCulloch County Elec. Co-op. v., TexCivApp– Austin, 131 SW2d 1019, writ dism, correct.—Electricity 7; Em Dom 2(1.1).

Hall v. McGregor, TexCivApp–Hous (1 Dist), 431 SW2d 369.—Bills & N 120, 527(1); Plead 111.5; Venue 22(4).

Hall v. McKee, TexCivApp–Fort Worth, 179 SW2d 590.— App & E 125, 901, 916(1), 1091(1); J P 147(1), 171(1), 187; Plead 111.9.

Hall; McNamara v., TexApp–Houston (14 Dist), 678 SW2d 578.—Wills 290.

Hall v. McWilliams, TexCivApp–Austin, 404 SW2d 606, ref nre.—Mines 78.1(9), 78.2, 78.5.

Hall; Mahan Volkswagen, Inc. v., TexApp–Houston (1 Dist), 648 SW2d 324, ref nre.—Antitrust 363, 393; App & E 231(1), 231(9), 1004(1), 1004(5); Const Law 2473; Contrib 7; Death 10; Indem 72; New Tr 162(1); Prod Liab 23.1, 27, 75.1, 82.1, 88.5.

Hall; Mangham v., TexApp–Corpus Christi, 564 SW2d 465, ref nre.—App & E 1175(1), 1177(5); Damag 208(1); Tresp 44, 46(3), 47; Trial 216, 352.1(1), 352.16.

Hall; Marshall v., TexApp–Houston (1 Dist), 943 SW2d 180.—Pretrial Proc 35, 358, 386.

Hall; Marshall v., TexCivApp–Beaumont, 151 SW2d 919, dism.—App & E 230; Labor & Emp 2830; Trial 219.

Hall v. Martin, TexApp–Beaumont, 851 SW2d 905, writ den, cert den 114 SCt 1399, 511 US 1018, 128 LEd2d 72.

HALL

59 Tex D 2d—456

—App & E 169, 173(2), 758.1, 854(1), 863, 934(1); Autos 191, 201(1.1), 243(3); Judgm 185(6); Labor & Emp 3082; Neglig 202, 379, 380, 387; Parent & C 11, 13(1).

Hall v. Matthews, TexCivApp–El Paso, 119 SW2d 164.—Bills & N 462(1).

Hall; M.A.W. v., TexApp–Houston (14 Dist), 921 SW2d 911.—Mand 1, 3(1), 4(4), 16(1), 28; Pretrial Proc 382, 411, 414; Witn 208(1), 211(2), 219(1), 219(6), 223.

Hall; Mayo v., TexCivApp–Waco, 571 SW2d 213.—Abate & R 13; Adop 10, 14; Child C 7, 610; Child S 320; Courts 515.

Hall v. Medical Bldg. of Houston, Tex, 251 SW2d 497, 151 Tex 425.—App & E 1083(4); Land & Ten 165(1), 169(6), 169(11); Neglig 1076, 1708, 1714; Trial 350.6(2).

Hall; Medical Bldg. of Houston v., TexCivApp–Galveston, 243 SW2d 409, rev 251 SW2d 497, 151 Tex 425.—Land & Ten 169(6); Neglig 250, 1037(4).

Hall; Megason v., TexCivApp–Texarkana, 434 SW2d 728.—App & E 927(7); Autos 245(2.1), 245(50.1).

Hall v. Mieler, TexApp–Houston (1 Dist), 177 SW3d 278.—App & E 946; Health 804, 809.

Hall v. Miller, TexApp–San Antonio, 147 SW2d 266, writ dism, correct.—Deeds 76; Lim of Act 39(7), 39(11), 100(3), 100(11); Tresp to T T 10; Trusts 95, 143.

Hall v. Mockingbird AMC/Jeep, Inc., Tex, 592 SW2d 913.—App & E 1175(1).

Hall; Mockingbird AMC/Jeep, Inc. v., TexCivApp–Dallas, 583 SW2d 844, rev in part 592 SW2d 913.—Cons Cred 4.

Hall; Monterey Mushrooms, Inc. v., SDTex, 14 FSupp2d 988.—Fed Civ Proc 422; Rem of C 2, 79(1), 107(7).

Hall v. Mosteller, TexCivApp–Austin, 245 SW2d 338, ref nre.—Contracts 163; Sales 261(6), 418(19).

Hall v. Moveable Offshore, Inc., CA5 (Tex), 455 F2d 633, cert den 93 SCt 60, 409 US 850, 34 LEd2d 93.—Neglig 1205(7); Ship 84(3.3), 86(2.5).

Hall v. Muckleroy, TexCivApp–Beaumont, 411 SW2d 390, ref nre.—Nuis 25(2), 31.

Hall v. Mutual Ben. Health & Acc. Ass'n, TexCivApp–Amarillo, 220 SW2d 934, writ refused.—Aviation 2; Insurance 1813, 1822, 1827, 1860, 2588(3).

Hall; National Bulk Carriers v., CCA5 (Tex), 152 F2d 658.—Adm 117; Damag 97, 130.1, 133.

Hall v. National Supply Co., CA5 (Tex), 270 F2d 379.—Autos 242(2), 246(58); Evid 155(11); Fed Civ Proc 828.1, 869; Fed Cts 800; Neglig 1616.

Hall v. O. C. Whitaker Co., Tex, 185 SW2d 720, 143 Tex 397.—App & E 1091(1), 1177(7); Autos 197(7); Labor & Emp 3029.

Hall; O. C. Whitaker Co. v., TexCivApp–Amarillo, 180 SW2d 177, aff 185 SW2d 720, 143 Tex 397.—Autos 197(7); Labor & Emp 3029.

Hall v. Oklahoma Factors, Inc., TexApp–Waco, 935 SW2d 504, reh overr.—App & E 843(2); Courts 91(1), 95(1); Judgm 203, 902, 903, 928.

Hall; Old Lincoln County Mut. Fire Ins. Co. v., TexCivApp–Dallas, 214 SW2d 203.—Venue 3, 8.5(3).

Hall; O'Mara v., TexCivApp–El Paso, 134 SW2d 348.—Evid 441(8); Frds St of 131(1).

Hall; O'Quinn v., TexApp–Corpus Christi, 77 SW3d 452.—App & E 946, 965; Inj 111; Mand 44; Venue 3, 17, 21, 45, 68, 78.

Hall; O'Quinn v., TexApp–Corpus Christi, 77 SW3d 438.—App & E 70(1), 106, 351(1), 352.1, 893(1), 946, 1010.1(8.1), 1181; Evid 1, 43(1); Parties 53; Venue 45, 68; Witn 68.

Hall; Patterson v., Tex, 430 SW2d 483, on remand 439 SW2d 140, ref nre.—App & E 564(2), 564(3).

Hall; Patterson v., TexCivApp–Austin, 439 SW2d 140, ref nre.—Frds St of 129(9); Gifts 25, 49(4), 51; Trial 232(5).

Hall; Patterson v., TexCivApp–Austin, 421 SW2d 921, rev 430 SW2d 483, on remand 439 SW2d 140, ref nre.—App & E 548(6), 564(2), 564(3), 843(4).

Hall; Piwonka v., TexCivApp–Amarillo, 376 SW2d 912, ref nre.—App & E 1062.1; Evid 5(2), 265(7); Inj 5; Waters 126(2).

Hall v. Piwonka, TexCivApp–Amarillo, 357 SW2d 486, writ dism.—Venue 5.5.

Hall v. Price, TexCivApp–Eastland, 148 SW2d 881.—Courts 122; Plead 252(2); Pretrial Proc 554.

Hall; Professional Flooring Supply Co. v., TexApp–Houston (1 Dist), 840SW2d 572. See Lee-Wright, Inc. v. Hall.

Hall v. Professional Leasing Associates, TexCivApp–Dallas, 550 SW2d 392.—Bailm 20, 30, 34; Contracts 245(1); Land & Ten 60, 210.

Hall v. Quarterman, NDTex, 443 FSupp2d 815.—Crim Law 412.2(4); Hab Corp 401, 404, 490(3), 508; Ind & Inf 113; Jury 21.5; Sent & Pun 1642, 1771.

Hall v. Rawls, Tex, 171 SW2d 324, 141 Tex 235.—App & E 1073(1), 1177(5); Evid 460(3), 460(10); Ven & Pur 82.

Hall v. Rawls, TexCivApp–Beaumont, 188 SW2d 807, writ refused wom.—App & E 837(4); Lim of Act 19(3), 39(7); Tresp to T T 10; Trusts 43(2), 60, 135, 140(1), 359(1), 366(3), 371(8).

Hall v. Rawls, TexCivApp–Beaumont, 160 SW2d 1005, rev 171 SW2d 324, 141 Tex 235.—App & E 930(3); Contracts 147(2); Trial 350.8, 351.2(2), 351.2(4), 351.2(5).

Hall; Reeves v., TexCivApp–Austin, 437 SW2d 424.—Accord 1, 7(1); Brok 43(1), 43(3), 84(1), 86(1); Estop 58.

Hall; Republic Nat. Life Ins. Co. v., Tex, 232 SW2d 697, 149 Tex 297.—Insurance 1732, 1740, 1755, 1759, 2000.

Hall; Republic Nat. Life Ins. Co. v., TexCivApp–Fort Worth, 226 SW2d 901, rev 232 SW2d 697, 149 Tex 297.—Alt of Inst 7; App & E 931(1); Contracts 39; Insurance 1749, 1763, 1796, 2005, 2016, 2424, 2445, 3335, 3343.

Hall v. Resolution Trust Corp., CA5 (Tex), 958 F2d 75.—Sec Tran 161, 221.

Hall v. Richardson, SDTex, 362 FSupp 662.—Adop 6; Evid 594; Social S 143.1, 143.55, 147.5, 148.1, 148.5.

Hall v. Robbins, TexApp–Houston (14 Dist), 790 SW2d 417.—Damag 62(3), 109; Ease 61(11).

Hall; Roberts v., TexCivApp–Amarillo, 167 SW2d 621.—Elections 34, 39.1, 244, 287, 288, 291, 298(1); Mun Corp 75, 918(2), 918(5); Plead 228.21.

Hall v. Rogers, TexCivApp–Waco, 620 SW2d 217.—App & E 230, 758.3(9); Contracts 350(3); Trial 277, 355(1).

Hall v. Rutherford, TexApp–San Antonio, 911 SW2d 422, reh overr, and writ den.—Afft 12; App & E 881.1; Atty & C 105, 107, 129(2); Evid 470; Judgm 185(4), 185.1(1), 185.1(3), 185.1(4), 185.1(6), 185.3(4), 186; Pretrial Proc 713.

Hall v. Safeway Stores, Inc., TexCivApp–Eastland, 360 SW2d 536, ref nre.—Neglig 1132.

Hall v. Savings of America, SDTex, 859 FSupp 1032, rev 68 F3d 470, cert den 116 SCt 1265, 516 US 1173, 134 LEd2d 213.—Civil R 1225(1), 1768, 1773; Fed Civ Proc 2183.

Hall v. Schweiker, CA5 (Tex), 660 F2d 116.—Admin Law 386, 416.1; Social S 140.30, 142.5, 143.75, 146.

Hall v. Sears Product Service, NDTex, 792 FSupp 1026.—Admin Law 419; Civil R 1006; Statut 263.

Hall; Seay v., Tex, 677 SW2d 19.—Courts 198, 472.4(2.1); Statut 181(1).

Hall; Seay v., TexApp–Dallas, 663 SW2d 468, writ gr, aff in part, rev in part 677 SW2d 19.—Action 43.1; Const Law 56, 2355; Courts 42(1), 198, 201; Death 10, 31(3.1), 31(5); Judgm 688; Parties 14, 25.

Hall; Shield v., TexCivApp–Eastland, 207 SW2d 997, ref nre.—Alt of Inst 29; App & E 994(3), 1010.1(1); Armed S 34.4(7); Chat Mtg 176(4), 176(6).

Hall; S. H. Kress & Co. v., TexCivApp–Galveston, 154 SW2d 278, writ refused wom.—Labor & Emp 3108; Neglig 1542, 1670, 1708; New Tr 144, 157.

Hall; Smith v., NDTex, 79 FSupp 473.—Fed Civ Proc 502; Fed Cts 84.

Hall; Smith v., Tex, 219 SW2d 441, 147 Tex 634.—Mand 172; Venue 5.1, 7.5(2).

Hall v. Sonic Drive-In of Angleton, Inc., TexApp–Houston (1 Dist), 177 SW3d 636, review den.—App & E 852; Assault 2, 3, 48; Damag 57.21, 57.23(2); Judgm 181(21), 183, 185(2), 185(5), 185.3(21); Labor & Emp 2777, 2784, 2859; Neglig 379, 380, 387, 1001, 1014, 1033, 1036, 1086, 1088, 1089, 1104(6), 1104(7), 1221, 1223, 1593, 1668, 1706.

Hall v. Southern Farm Bureau Cas. Ins. Co., TexApp–Fort Worth, 670 SW2d 775.—Insurance 2657.

Hall v. Southern States Life Ins. Co., TexCivApp–Galveston, 251 SW2d 961.—App & E 766, 773(2).

Hall v. State, TexCrimApp, 225 SW3d 524, reh den.—Crim Law 795(1.5), 795(2.10); Ind & Inf 189(1), 189(2), 191(0.5), 191(4).

Hall v. State, TexCrimApp, 160 SW3d 24, reh den, cert den 125 SCt 2962, 545 US 1141, 162 LEd2d 891, habeas corpus den 443 FSupp2d 815.—Crim Law 1134(2), 1134(3); Hab Corp 508, 710, 725; Sent & Pun 1642, 1754, 1769, 1771, 1772, 1785(2), 1788(5), 1788(8), 1788(11).

Hall v. State, TexCrimApp, 158 SW3d 470.—Assault 96(1); Crim Law 795(1.5), 795(2.5), 795(2.10); Prisons 13(2).

Hall v. State, TexCrimApp, 67 SW3d 870, reh den, cert gr, vac 123 SCt 70, 537 US 802, 154 LEd2d 4, on remand 160 SW3d 24, reh den, cert den 125 SCt 2962, 545 US 1141, 162 LEd2d 891, habeas corpus den 443 FSupp2d 815.—Crim Law 402(1), 412.1(2), 412.2(4), 438(8), 1030(1), 1130(5), 1144.13(7); Sent & Pun 1625, 1628, 1709, 1720, 1789(1).

Hall; State v., TexCrimApp, 829 SW2d 184.—Crim Law 93, 151.1.

Hall v. State, TexCrimApp, 795 SW2d 195.—Searches 111, 117.

Hall v. State, TexCrimApp, 698 SW2d 150.—Crim Law 1081(1).

Hall v. State, TexCrimApp, 661 SW2d 113.—Crim Law 1166.16; Jury 64.

Hall v. State, TexCrimApp, 661 SW2d 101.—Crim Law 1172.2; Obscen 17.

Hall v. State, TexCrimApp, 649 SW2d 627.—Autos 357.

Hall v. State, TexCrimApp, 643 SW2d 738.—Crim Law 394.5(3), 730(8), 730(14); Searches 33.

Hall v. State, TexCrimApp, 640 SW2d 307.—Assault 96(7); Crim Law 763(1), 1037.1(1); Homic 852, 956, 967; Ind & Inf 71.4(5).

Hall v. State, TexCrimApp, 619 SW2d 156.—Crim Law 320, 438(1), 438(5.1), 721(1), 721(3), 730(10); Ind & Inf 171.

Hall v. State, TexCrimApp, 509 SW2d 627.—Crim Law 1170.5(1); Sent & Pun 1953; Witn 345(1), 345(2).

Hall v. State, TexCrimApp, 492 SW2d 950.—Crim Law 641.13(2.1), 641.13(8).

Hall v. State, TexCrimApp, 492 SW2d 512.—Crim Law 719(1), 1037.1(1), 1037.2, 1055, 1130(5), 1171.3.

Hall v. State, TexCrimApp, 490 SW2d 589.—Burg 42(1); Crim Law 393(1), 1036.1(7).

Hall v. State, TexCrimApp, 488 SW2d 788.—Autos 349.5(10).

Hall v. State, TexCrimApp, 488 SW2d 94.—Crim Law 1166.17; Homic 1184; Pardon 28; Sent & Pun 1788(5).

Hall v. State, TexCrimApp, 487 SW2d 721.—Larc 40(2), 62(1).

Hall v. State, TexCrimApp, 485 SW2d 563.—Bail 55, 77(1), 77(2), 79(2), 93.

Hall v. State, TexCrimApp, 475 SW2d 778.—Crim Law 706(7), 749, 1120(3), 1126; Jury 24; Witn 5, 300.

Hall v. State, TexCrimApp, 466 SW2d 762.—Crim Law 339.7(3), 925(1), 1090.1(1), 1166.8; Rob 24.40.

Hall v. State, TexCrimApp, 452 SW2d 490.—Sent & Pun 1960, 2003, 2004, 2018, 2021.

Hall v. State, TexCrimApp, 450 SW2d 90.—Arrest 63.4(1); Burg 41(1); Const Law 266(3.3), 4659(1); Crim Law 339.8(5), 693, 1036.1(7), 1120(1).

Hall v. State, TexCrimApp, 418 SW2d 810.—Crim Law 1144.13(8); Homic 727, 734, 908, 1154, 1325; Sent & Pun 1802.

Hall v. State, TexCrimApp, 402 SW2d 752.—Assault 96(1), 96(7); Crim Law 772(6), 824(3); Homic 1154, 1155, 1387, 1480; Witn 345(1), 345(2).

Hall v. State, TexCrimApp, 394 SW2d 659.—Searches 108.

Hall v. State, TexCrimApp, 373 SW2d 252.—Crim Law 511.1(5), 511.1(9), 511.2; Ind & Inf 87(3).

Hall v. State, TexCrimApp, 347 SW2d 262, 171 TexCrim 227.—Crim Law 394.4(5.1), 1099.6(2.1), 1099.11, 1169.1(8); Searches 121.1.

Hall v. State, TexCrimApp, 310 SW2d 91, 166 TexCrim 10.—Crim Law 932, 1124(1); Rape 51(1).

Hall v. State, TexCrimApp, 301 SW2d 161, 164 TexCrim 573.—Crim Law 1168(1), 1169.2(8), 1169.3; Homic 976, 1014; Infants 69(1).

Hall v. State, TexCrimApp, 297 SW2d 685, 164 TexCrim 142.—Crim Law 673(3), 1168(2); Witn 397.

Hall v. State, TexCrimApp, 292 SW2d 128.—Crim Law 1094(3).

Hall v. State, TexCrimApp, 278 SW2d 297, 161 TexCrim 460.—Burg 41(1); Crim Law 784(1); Sent & Pun 1388.

Hall v. State, TexCrimApp, 274 SW2d 836.—Crim Law 1184(4.1).

Hall v. State, TexCrimApp, 272 SW2d 896, 160 TexCrim 553.—Crim Law 841, 1038.1(7), 1167(1); Rob 4, 20, 24.10.

Hall v. State, TexCrimApp, 263 SW2d 563, 159 TexCrim 342.—Crim Law 1090.13, 1099.7(2).

Hall v. State, TexCrimApp, 257 SW2d 442.—Crim Law 1090.1(1).

Hall v. State, TexCrimApp, 254 SW2d 523, 158 TexCrim 243.—Crim Law 558, 1091(8), 1159.2(3), 1203.26; Homic 1136; Ind & Inf 81(5); Sent & Pun 1325, 1367, 1381(3).

Hall v. State, TexCrimApp, 235 SW2d 638, 155 TexCrim 392.—Crim Law 1171.1(6).

Hall v. State, TexCrimApp, 233 SW2d 582, 155 TexCrim 235.—Arson 37(1); Crim Law 957(1).

Hall v. State, TexCrimApp, 219 SW2d 475, 153 TexCrim 215.—Crim Law 304(2), 338(1), 398(2), 455, 706(3), 1091(8), 1169.1(9), 1169.2(2), 1170.5(1), 1171.1(2.1), 1171.1(6), 1171.8(2); 1187; Homic 993, 1032, 1154.

Hall v. State, TexCrimApp, 206 SW2d 246.—Crim Law 1090.1(1).

Hall v. State, TexCrimApp, 205 SW2d 369, 151 TexCrim 29.—Assault 78, 82, 95.

Hall v. State, TexCrimApp, 199 SW2d 1019.—Crim Law 1090.1(1).

Hall v. State, TexCrimApp, 194 SW2d 561.—Crim Law 1094(3).

Hall v. State, TexCrimApp, 188 SW2d 388, 148 TexCrim 459.—Adultery 4, 5; Witn 58.1.

Hall v. State, TexCrimApp, 188 SW2d 180, 148 TexCrim 457.—Crim Law 994(3), 1086.13, 1090.1(1).

Hall v. State, TexCrimApp, 167 SW2d 532, 145 TexCrim 192.—Crim Law 1097(4), 1144.14; Double J 165; Homic 832; Ind & Inf 189(8).

Hall v. State, TexCrimApp, 162 SW2d 106, 144 TexCrim 193.—Crim Law 1092.7; Larc 55.

Hall v. State, TexCrimApp, 157 SW2d 906, 143 TexCrim 186.—Crim Law 1182.

Hall v. State, TexCrimApp, 150 SW2d 404, 141 TexCrim 607.—Crim Law 366(3), 695(6), 814(17), 829(1), 1091(4), 1166.16, 1169.3; Rape 43(2), 48(1), 51(4); Witn 269(12).

Hall v. State, TexCrimApp, 125 SW2d 293, 136 TexCrim 320.—Crim Law 394.1(4), 419(12), 1169.1(10); Int Liq 248.

Hall v. State, TexCrimApp, 111 SW2d 257, 133 TexCrim 359.—Crim Law 1086.13.

HALL

Hall v. State, TexCrimApp, 110 SW2d 67, 133 TexCrim 254.—Crim Law 1124(3), 1182.

Hall v. State, TexCrimApp, 100 SW2d 375, 131 TexCrim 497.—Crim Law 369.4; Forg 44(0.5).

Hall v. State, TexCrimApp, 95 SW2d 694, 130 TexCrim 516.—Bail 70; Homic 1154.

Hall v. State, TexCrimApp, 94 SW2d 734.—Crim Law 1182.

Hall v. State, TexCrimApp, 81 SW2d 75, 128 TexCrim 232.—Crim Law 1184(4.1).

Hall v. State, TexApp–Houston (1 Dist), 137 SW3d 847, petition for discretionary review refused.—Consp 47(12); Crim Law 37.10(1), 338(7), 438(5.1), 438(6), 1030(3), 1144.13(2.1), 1153(1), 1159.2(1), 1159.2(2), 1159.2(9), 1159.4(1), 1159.4(2); Homic 1134; Sent & Pun 1373.

Hall v. State, TexApp–Houston (1 Dist), 808 SW2d 282.—Const Law 4782; Costs 302.4; Crim Law 273(2), 625(1), 1144.9; Mental H 434; Sent & Pun 604, 645.

Hall; State v., TexApp–Houston (1 Dist), 794 SW2d 916, petition for discretionary review gr, aff 829 SW2d 184.—Crim Law 157.

Hall v. State, TexApp–Houston (1 Dist), 685 SW2d 435, petition for discretionary review refused.—Crim Law 641.10(3), 730(3), 795(1), 795(1.5), 1081(4.1), 1134(2), 1170.5(1), 1171.1(2.1), 1171.1(3); Rob 27(5); Witn 330(1).

Hall v. State, TexApp–Houston (1 Dist), 662 SW2d 37, petition for discretionary review refused.—Const Law 268(8), 4629; Crim Law 552(3), 577.16(8), 632(2), 726, 730(14), 1037.1(1), 1038.1(4), 1134(3), 1166.6, 1171.1(6); Homic 1184, 1185, 1465.

Hall v. State, TexApp–Houston (1 Dist), 646 SW2d 489, rev 661 SW2d 101.—Const Law 4653; Obscen 2.5.

Hall v. State, TexApp–Houston (1 Dist), 630 SW2d 709, petition for discretionary review refused.—Burg 41(1); Crim Law 338(4), 577.1, 795(2.20), 795(2.35).

Hall v. State, TexApp–Fort Worth, 13 SW3d 115, petition for discretionary review refused, and petition for discretionary review gr, review dism as improvidently gr 46 SW3d 264.—Crim Law 388.3, 404.30, 721(3), 728(3), 1043(3), 1134(2), 1171.1(2.1), 1171.5.

Hall v. State, TexApp–Fort Worth, 855 SW2d 894.—Burg 41(8); Sent & Pun 2021.

Hall v. State, TexApp–Fort Worth, 828 SW2d 224.—Arrest 63.4(15); Crim Law 394.6(4), 1043(3).

Hall v. State, TexApp–Fort Worth, 766 SW2d 903.—Crim Law 625.10(2.1), 641.13(1), 641.13(5).

Hall v. State, TexApp–Fort Worth, 745 SW2d 579, petition for discretionary review refused.—Homic 1168; Infants 133; Witn 345(9).

Hall v. State, TexApp–Fort Worth, 663 SW2d 154.—Crim Law 662.7, 1170.5(1), 1170.5(5); Witn 330(1), 363(1), 372(1), 372(2), 374(1), 386.

Hall v. State, TexApp–Austin, 86 SW2d 235, reh overr, and petition for discretionary review refused.—Const Law 4694; Controlled Subs 26, 27, 28, 30, 79, 80, 93; Crim Law 561(1), 741(1), 742(1), 747, 1134(2), 1134(3), 1144.13(2.1), 1159.2(1), 1159.2(7), 1159.6.

Hall v. State, TexApp–San Antonio, 124 SW3d 246, petition for discretionary review refused.—Crim Law 108(1), 449.1, 1043(3), 1120(1), 1137(1); Infants 13.

Hall v. State, TexApp–San Antonio, 935 SW2d 852.—Autos 355(13); Crim Law 273(2), 273(5), 273.1(4), 275, 1167(5), 1177; Sent & Pun 361.

Hall v. State, TexApp–San Antonio, 730 SW2d 7, petition for discretionary review refused.—Crim Law 369.2(6); Larc 6, 40(6).

Hall v. State, TexApp–Dallas, 81 SW3d 927, petition for discretionary review gr, aff 225 SW3d 524, reh den.—Crim Law 83; Ind & Inf 191(0.5).

Hall v. State, TexApp–Dallas, 62 SW3d 918, petition for discretionary review refused.—Crim Law 730(5), 796; Ind & Inf 119, 159(1), 159(2); Sent & Pun 1899.

Hall v. State, TexApp–Texarkana, 161 SW3d 142, reh overr, and petition for discretionary review refused.—Controlled Subs 80; Crim Law 369.1, 369.2(1), 396(1), 407(1), 511.1(1), 511.1(3), 511.2, 511.5, 641.13(1), 641.13(2.1), 641.13(6), 780(1), 1038.1(1), 1038.2, 1119(1), 1134(3), 1144.13(2.1), 1144.13(6), 1159.2(7), 1173.2(6); Witn 350, 406.

Hall v. State, TexApp–Texarkana, 145 SW3d 754.—Assault 54, 56, 96(7), 96(8); Crim Law 814(5), 1038.1(1), 1134(3), 1172.1(1), 1172.6.

Hall v. State, TexApp–Texarkana, 937 SW2d 580, petition for discretionary review refused.—Crim Law 59(1), 507(1), 507(2), 511.2, 780(1), 1028, 1030(1), 1134(3), 1173.2(6); Sent & Pun 329.

Hall v. State, TexApp–Texarkana, 753 SW2d 438, petition for discretionary review gr, rev 795 SW2d 195.—Crim Law 1036.1(1), 1036.1(2), 1043(3), 1044.1(5.1), 1044.2(1), 1155, 1169.1(1); Searches 40.1, 107, 112, 117, 119, 123.1.

Hall v. State, TexApp–Amarillo, 74 SW3d 521.—Arrest 63.5(4), 63.5(6); Crim Law 1031(1), 1036.1(4), 1181.5(7).

Hall v. State, TexApp–Amarillo, 970 SW2d 137, reh overr, and petition for discretionary review refused.—Crim Law 388.5(1), 1144.13(3), 1159.2(2), 1159.2(3), 1159.2(7), 1159.2(8), 1159.3(2), 1159.4(2), 1162, 1169.9; Homic 607, 1141, 1165.

Hall v. State, TexApp–Amarillo, 764 SW2d 19.—Assault 92(5); Crim Law 338(6); Sod 6.

Hall v. State, TexApp–Beaumont, 862 SW2d 710.—Crim Law 29(12), 641.1, 641.13(1), 641.13(2.1), 641.13(6), 641.13(7), 814(5), 1043(3), 1134(2), 1169.2(6); Ind & Inf 159(1); Jury 33(5.15); Tel 1440.

Hall v. State, TexApp–Beaumont, 682 SW2d 608.—Crim Law 719(1), 795(1), 1171.3; Homic 1184, 1186, 1457, 1458.

Hall v. State, TexApp–Waco, 39 SW3d 316.—Crim Law 273(4.1), 273.4(1); Jury 29(6); Sent & Pun 2, 1971(3).

Hall v. State, TexApp–Waco, 829 SW2d 407.—Controlled Subs 82; Crim Law 438(1), 438(8), 444, 1086.4, 1097(4), 1120(9), 1159.1.

Hall v. State, TexApp–Houston (14 Dist), 928 SW2d 186, petition for discretionary review refused.—Controlled Subs 75; Crim Law 394.6(5), 1144.12, 1144.13(3), 1153(1), 1158(4), 1159.2(7); Searches 70.

Hall v. State, TexApp–Houston (14 Dist), 853 SW2d 756, reh den, and petition for discretionary review refused.—Crim Law 273.4(1), 275, 641.13(1), 641.13(7), 1026.10(4).

Hall v. State, TexApp–Houston (14 Dist), 843 SW2d 190.—Autos 352; Crim Law 260.10, 260.11(6), 1144.9, 1144.17; Jury 29(6).

Hall v. State, TexApp–Houston (14 Dist), 783 SW2d 14, petition for discretionary review refused.—Arrest 63.5(4); Controlled Subs 26, 27, 30, 80; Crim Law 394.4(9).

Hall v. State, TexApp–Houston (14 Dist), 778 SW2d 473, petition for discretionary review refused.—Crim Law 627.10(2.1), 627.10(8), 1043(3).

Hall v. State, TexApp–Houston (14 Dist), 736 SW2d 818, petition for discretionary review refused.—Crim Law 93; Mun Corp 190.

Hall v. State, TexApp–Houston (14 Dist), 711 SW2d 108, petition for discretionary review refused.—Crim Law 394.6(4), 438(2), 589(1), 603.2, 627.5(1), 627.5(2), 641.13(1), 665(4), 683(1), 720(7.1), 723(3), 728(2), 730(8), 730(14), 855(1), 1043(3); Infants 20.

Hall v. State, TexApp–Houston (14 Dist), 681 SW2d 867, petition for discretionary review refused.—Burg 42(3); Crim Law 59(3), 552(3), 641.13(2.1), 641.13(6), 1144.13(3), 1159.2(7), 1166.10(1).

Hall v. Stephenson, TexApp–Fort Worth, 919 SW2d 454, reh overr, and writ den.—Antitrust 138, 256, 389(1); App & E 169, 345.1, 758.3(10), 760(1), 775, 852, 863, 893(1), 895(1), 934(1); Atty & C 105, 107, 129(2); Judgm 181(11), 181(15.1), 181(16), 185(2), 185(6), 185.1(1), 185.1(3), 185.2(1), 185.3(4), 186; Lim of Act 55(3), 58(1),

95(16), 118(2), 177(2), 179(2), 193, 199(1); Neglig 202, 273, 371, 379, 380, 387.

Hall v. Stevens, TexCivApp–Dallas, 254 SW 610.—Zoning 774.

Hall; Stratton v., TexCivApp–El Paso, 90 SW2d 865, writ dism.—App & E 500(2); Elections 71.1, 73, 239, 295(1), 305(9); Evid 313.

Hall; Sun Oil Co. (Delaware) v., TexCivApp–Austin, 566 SW2d 696.—Evid 570, 571(1); Plead 111.9, 111.39(4); Venue 7.5(1), 7.5(6).

Hall; Superior Trans-Med, Inc. v., TexApp–Dallas, 683 SW2d 496.—App & E 1177(2); Mand 3(13).

Hall; Syntax, Inc. v., Tex, 899 SW2d 189, as am, on remand 1995 WL 515069.—Tax 2979, 2993.

Hall; Syntax, Inc. v., TexApp–Houston (1 Dist), 881 SW2d 719, reh den, and writ gr, rev and remanded 899 SW2d 189, as am, on remand 1995 WL 515069.—App & E 934(1); Judgm 181(2), 185(2), 185(4), 185.1(3), 185.1(8), 189, 335(1), 489, 501; Tax 2918, 2971, 2979, 3072(3).

Hall; Teixeira v., TexApp–Texarkana, 107 SW3d 805.—Afft 3, 17; App & E 984(4); Convicts 6; Extrad 32; Health 804, 808, 809.

Hall; Teleometrics Intern., Inc. v., TexApp–Houston (1 Dist), 922 SW2d 189, writ den.—Alt Disp Res 114, 133(2), 134(1), 328, 332, 342, 363(4), 363(8), 374(1), 380; Commerce 80.5; Lim of Act 61.

Hall; Tennessee Gas Transmission Co. v., TexCivApp–San Antonio, 277 SW2d 733.—App & E 867(1); Em Dom 205, 224, 262(3), 262(5); Evid 13; Trial 311.

Hall v. Texas & N. O. Ry. Co., CA5 (Tex), 307 F2d 875.—Damag 130.4; Fed Civ Proc 1970.1, 1973; Fed Cts 702, 892, 896.1, 902.

Hall v. Texas Dept. of Public Safety, TexCivApp–Austin, 413 SW2d 470.—App & E 662(3), 883; Autos 144.1(3), 144.2(4), 144.2(5.1), 144.2(9.1), 144.2(10); Exceptions Bill of39(1); Judgm 185(1), 185.2(9).

Hall; Texas Emp. Ins. Ass'n v., TexCivApp–Fort Worth, 295 SW2d 478, ref nre.—Damag 221(4), 221(6); Work Comp 1396, 1968(3).

Hall; Texas Pac. Fidelity & Sur. Co. v., TexCivApp–Eastland, 101 SW2d 1050, writ dism.—Trial 142; Work Comp 934, 1139.

Hall v. Texas State Bank, TexCivApp–Austin, 298 SW2d 188, ref nre.—App & E 1152; Partit 60, 63(2), 86; Ten in C 13, 21; Trial 350.8.

Hall v. Thomas, CA5 (Tex), 190 F3d 693.—Civil R 1090, 1091, 1376(7), 1432; Prisons 17(2); Sent & Pun 1546.

Hall v. Thomas, TexCivApp–Texarkana, 474 SW2d 276, writ dism woj.—Mun Corp 92; Schools 97(4).

Hall v. Timmons, TexApp–Beaumont, 987 SW2d 248, reh overr.—App & E 215(1), 216(1), 756, 760(2); Corp 1.4(4), 1.5(1), 1.7(1), 1.7(2); Damag 135; Labor & Emp 2777, 2883, 2891, 2897.

Hall v. Tomball Nursing Center, Inc., TexApp–Houston (14 Dist), 926 SW2d 617.—App & E 863, 934(1), 954(1); Health 618, 784, 804, 821(2), 823(11); Judgm 185(6), 185.3(21).

Hall v. Tower Land and Investment Co., CA5 (Tex), 512 F2d 481.—Judgm 540, 570(11), 585(2), 587, 713(2).

Hall v. Traders & General Ins. Co., TexCivApp–Dallas, 103 SW2d 390.—Work Comp 289.

Hall v. Treon, TexApp–Beaumont, 39 SW3d 722.—App & E 185(3), 395; Convicts 6; Costs 132(4), 132(5).

Hall v. Tucker, TexCivApp–Eastland, 414 SW2d 766, ref nre.—Ack 6(3); App & E 846(5), 852, 1010.1(3); Hus & W 193, 264(2), 264(5); Ven & Pur 224.

Hall; U.S. v., CA5 (Tex), 455 F3d 508, cert den 127 SCt 2029, 167 LEd2d 772.—Crim Law 37.10(2), 641.13(1), 641.13(7), 1073, 1560.

Hall; U.S. v., CA5 (Tex), 152 F3d 381, reh and sug for reh den 161 F3d 10, cert den 119 SCt 1767, 526 US 1117, 143 LEd2d 797, reh den 120 SCt 15, 527 US 1054, 144 LEd2d 819, post-conviction relief den 2004 WL 1908242,

certificate of appealability den 455 F3d 508, cert den 127 SCt 2029, 167 LEd2d 772.—Const Law 4611, 4745; Crim Law 393(1), 412.1(4), 412.2(4), 519(1), 519(8), 531(3), 590(1), 590(2), 633(1), 641.12(1), 661, 662.3, 734, 741(1), 796, 868, 870, 1030(1), 1039, 1151, 1152(2), 1153(1), 1155, 1158(1), 1158(4), 1166(7), 1168(1), 1168(2); Jury 33(2.10), 33(2.15), 100, 103(14), 107, 108; Sent & Pun 310, 313, 315, 318, 358, 359, 1466, 1660, 1681, 1684, 1752, 1762, 1763, 1772, 1780(3), 1788(10), 1789(3), 1789(9).

Hall; U.S. v., CA5 (Tex), 845 F2d 1281, cert den 109 SCt 155, 488 US 860, 102 LEd2d 126.—Crim Law 59(5), 396(1), 1044.1(7), 1159.2(3), 1159.6; Forg 4, 44(2); Postal 49(1), 49(12).

Hall; U.S. v., CA5 (Tex), 565 F2d 917.—Crim Law 394.6(3), 736(1), 1134(6); Searches 66, 69, 184, 198.

Hall; U.S. v., CA5 (Tex), 545 F2d 1008.—Controlled Subs 148(3).

Hall; U.S. v., CA5 (Tex), 457 F2d 1324.—Crim Law 274(1); Sent & Pun 559(2).

Hall; U.S. v., CA5 (Tex), 440 F2d 1277.—Crim Law 1043(3).

Hall v. U.S., CA5 (Tex), 403 F2d 344, cert den Weatherford Oil Tool Co v. U S, 89 SCt 1306, 394 US 958, 22 LEd2d 560.—Int Rev 4886.

Hall v. U.S., CA5 (Tex), 286 F2d 676, cert den 81 SCt 1087, 366 US 910, 6 LEd2d 236.—Crim Law 59(5), 257, 260.11(4), 260.11(5), 1177, 1192; Embez 4, 44(2).

Hall; U.S. v., CA5 (Tex), 147 FedAppx 403, cert den 126 SCt 1098, 546 US 1122, 163 LEd2d 911.—Crim Law 1042.

Hall; U.S. v., CA5 (Tex), 88 FedAppx 28, appeal after new sentencing hearing 115 FedAppx 219, cert gr, vac 125 SCt 1952, 544 US 996, 161 LEd2d 767, on remand 147 FedAppx 403, cert den 126 SCt 1098, 546 US 1122, 163 LEd2d 911.—Crim Law 1181.5(1); Sent & Pun 787.

Hall v. U. S., CCA5 (Tex), 267 F 795.—Health 314.

Hall; U.S. v., EDTex, 468 FSupp 123.—Arrest 63.1, 63.4(1), 63.4(3), 63.4(7.1), 63.4(8), 63.4(9), 65; Crim Law 211(3), 394.1(1), 394.4(1), 534(1); Searches 24, 47.1, 48, 180, 194, 198.

Hall; U.S. Fidelity & Guaranty Co. v., TexCivApp–Austin, 224 SW2d 268, writ dism.—Work Comp 346, 1927.

Hall v. Universal C.I.T. Credit Corp., TexCivApp–Eastland, 298 SW2d 858.—Inj 147; Receivers 38.

Hall v. Villarreal Development Corp., Tex, 522 SW2d 195.—App & E 1094(1).

Hall v. Villarreal Development Corp., TexCivApp–Corpus Christi, 517 SW2d 326, writ dism 522 SW2d 195.—App & E 931(1), 1008.1(2), 1010.1(1), 1010.2, 1012.1(5); Contracts 175(3), 322(4); Trial 382.

Hall; W. v., TexApp–Houston (14 Dist), 921 SW2d 911. See M.A.W. v. Hall.

Hall; Wagner v., TexCivApp–El Paso, 519 SW2d 488.—Brok 38(7); Princ & A 159(1); Trial 350.3(4), 366; Ven & Pur 322.

Hall; Warren-Bradshaw Drilling Co. v., USTex, 63 SCt 125, 317 US 88, 87 LEd 83.—Commerce 62.44(2), 62.46, 62.62, 62.67; Labor & Emp 2305, 2365, 2385(1), 2387(1).

Hall; Warren-Bradshaw Drilling Co. v., CCA5 (Tex), 124 F2d 42, cert gr 62 SCt 1305, 316 US 660, 86 LEd 1737, aff 63 SCt 125, 317 US 88, 87 LEd 83.—Commerce 62.62, 62.67; Labor & Emp 2298, 2305, 2307, 2387(1).

Hall v. Warren-Bradshaw Drilling Co., NDTex, 40 FSupp 272, mod 124 F2d 42, cert gr 62 SCt 1305, 316 US 660, 86 LEd 1737, aff 63 SCt 125, 317 US 88, 87 LEd 83.—Commerce 62.56, 62.62; Labor & Emp 2236.

Hall v. Weaver, TexCivApp–El Paso, 101 SW2d 1035, writ dism.—App & E 930(4); Autos 245(91); Evid 589; Neglig 1750; Trial 352.5(6), 352.10.

Hall; Weber v., TexApp–Houston (14 Dist), 929 SW2d 138, reh of motion for mandamus overr.—Alt Disp Res 112,

137, 139, 143, 146, 199, 210; Contracts 152; Courts 97(1); Mand 1, 3(1), 4(1), 4(4), 28, 48.

Hall v. Weldon Foods Co., TexCivApp–Fort Worth, 500 SW2d 716.—Dedi 16.1, 20(1); Ease 36(3); Inj 37; Mun Corp 269(1), 657(7).

Hall v. Weller, Hall & Jeffery, Inc., TexCivApp–Hous (1 Dist), 497 SW2d 374, ref nre.—App & E 1172(2); Contracts 167, 175(1); Corp 82, 376; Spec Perf 126(1), 131.

Hall; West v., TexCivApp–Dallas, 608 SW2d 336, ref nre.—Lim of Act 60(3); Partners 70, 225, 259.5.

Hall; Wheat v., CA5 (Tex), 535 F2d 874.—Corp 117; Equity 72(1); Sec Reg 60.28(11), 60.28(13), 156.

Hall v. White, Tex, 525 SW2d 860.—Evid 318(7), 575, 581; Pretrial Proc 77.

Hall v. White, TexCivApp–Hous (1 Dist), 517 SW2d 683, writ gr, rev 525 SW2d 860.—Evid 575, 581, 582(2); Wills 378.

Hall v. White, Getgey, Meyer & Co., LPA, CA5 (Tex), 347 SW3d 576, on remand 2004 WL 1279975, rev in part 465 F3d 587, on remand 2007 WL 1080302, mandate recalled and mod 465 F3d 587, on remand 2007 WL 1080302.—Atty & C 105.5, 112, 129(1), 134(2), 153; Damag 63; Fed Cts 382.1; U S Mag 31.

Hall v. White, Getgey, Meyer Co., LPA, CA5 (Tex), 465 F3d 587, on remand 2007 WL 1080302.—Fed Cts 415, 957; Interest 30(1), 39(2.50).

Hall; Wickham v., CA5 (Tex), 706 F2d 713, reh den 712 F2d 1416.—Armed S 22; Fed Cts 1.1; Hab Corp 524; Mil Jus 896, 1480.

Hall; Williams v., TexCivApp–Austin, 111 SW2d 803.—App & E 210, 1051(1); Evid 472(1); Trial 150.

Hall; Williamson v., TexCivApp–Amarillo, 203 SW2d 265.—Action 36; Inj 37; Tresp to T T 38(1).

Hall v. Wilson, TexCivApp–Texarkana, 215 SW2d 204, ref nre.—Adv Poss 114(1); Improv 4(2); Mtg 372(5); Ven & Pur 242.

Hall; Wolcott v., TexCivApp–Eastland, 111 SW2d 1140.—Ex & Ad 436; Venue 27.

Hall; Wyeth v., TexApp–Beaumont, 118 SW3d 487.—App & E 70(1), 70(6), 78(1), 230, 863, 893(1), 1181; Parties 44, 93(1); Time 2.

Hall; Yetiv v., CA5 (Tex), 132 FedAppx 1.—Arrest 68(4); Civil R 1037, 1351(3), 1376(4), 1376(6); Const Law 4516; Crim Law 59(1); Fed Civ Proc 881, 1837.1; Fed Cts 18; Searches 164.

Hall; Ziebell v., TexCivApp–San Antonio, 220 SW2d 899.—App & E 77(1); Int Liq 104.

Hall; Zimmerman v., TexCivApp–Eastland, 213 SW2d 89, ref nre.—Adv Poss 85(3), 114(1), 115(1), 115(6); App & E 1001(1), 1005(1); Bound 33, 37(3), 37(5).

Hall Acquisitions, Inc., In re, BkrtcySDTex, 181 BR 860. See Mort Hall Acquisition, Inc., In re.

Halladay; O'Donnell v., TexCivApp–El Paso, 152 SW2d 847, writ refused wom.—Courts 472.4(6); Gifts 11, 18(1), 22, 49(5), 52, 62(1); Wills 90.

Halladay Enterprises, Inc., In re, BkrtcySDTex, 5 BR 83.—Bankr 3080; Fed Civ Proc 2654.

Hallan; Stone v., NDTex, 102 FSupp 252.—Pat 168(1), 168(2.1), 168(2.6), 233.1.

Hall & Co. v. Beach, Inc., TexApp–Corpus Christi, 733 SW2d 251. See Frank B. Hall & Co. v. Beach, Inc.

Hall & Co., Inc. v. Buck, TexApp–Houston (14 Dist, 678 SW2d 612. See Frank B. Hall & Co., Inc. v. Buck.

Hall & Northway Advertising, Inc.; Keever v., TexApp–Dallas, 727 SW2d 704.—Judgm 185(1), 185(4), 185.1(1), 185.3(3).

Hallaway v. Thompson, Tex, 226 SW2d 816, 148 Tex 471.—App & E 919; Courts 97(5), 97(6); Labor & Emp 2809, 2817; Lim of Act 1, 125.

Hallaway v. Thompson, TexCivApp–Eastland, 222 SW2d 702, rev 226 SW2d 816, 148 Tex 471.—Bankr 2152.1; Lim of Act 127(11.1), 127(14).

Hallberg v. Hilburn, CA5 (Tex), 434 F2d 90.—Autos 187(5); Fed Cts 848.

Hallbrook; Alldredge v., TexCivApp–El Paso, 122 SW2d 661.—App & E 773(2).

Hall Const. Co., Inc. v. Texas Industries, Inc., TexApp–Dallas, 748 SW2d 533.—Acct Action on 14; App & E 218.2(4), 1043(6); Costs 207, 264; Damag 140, 189; Evid 18; Pretrial Proc 313; Prod Liab 83.

Hallco Texas, Inc. v. McMullen County, Tex, 221 SW3d 50, reh den.—Em Dom 2.1, 81.1, 277, 307(2); Judgm 548, 564(1), 584, 585(2), 585(3), 586(0.5), 713(2), 720, 828.4(2).

Hallco Texas, Inc. v. McMullen County, TexApp–San Antonio, 94 SW3d 735, review gr, aff 221 SW3d 50, reh den.—Em Dom 2(1), 2(1.2), 283, 307(2); Environ Law 432; Judgm 828.16(1).

Hallco Texas, Inc. v. McMullen County, Tex., SDTex, 934 FSupp 238, aff 109 F3d 768.—Const Law 3723, 3895, 4326; Em Dom 2(1), 277; Environ Law 346(1); Fed Cts 14.1.

Hall County; McChristy v., TexCivApp–Amarillo, 140 SW2d 576.—Em Dom 124, 219, 221, 262(5); Evid 555.6(2).

Hall Dadeland Towers Associates v. Hardeman, NDTex, 736 FSupp 1422.—Brok 94, 104; Fraud 4, 13(1), 16; Partners 375; Sec Reg 60.18, 60.27(1), 60.45(1), 265, 278.

Halleman; Alice Roofing and Sheet Metal Works, Inc. v., TexApp–San Antonio, 775 SW2d 869.—Lim of Act 95(1), 95(9); Plead 245(1).

Haller v. State, TexApp–Corpus Christi, 933 SW2d 262.—Crim Law 1072, 1081(2); Sent & Pun 60.

Haller; State v., TexCivApp–San Antonio, 450 SW2d 890, ref nre.—Dedi 19(1).

Haller; Thomas v., TexCivApp–Waco, 214 SW2d 683.—App & E 846(2), 846(5); Plead 111.18; Venue 8.5(2), 22(7).

Hallett v. Houston Northwest Medical Center, Tex, 689 SW2d 888.—App & E 200.

Hallett v. Ponder, TexCivApp–Austin, 376 SW2d 797.—Insurance 3466, 3475(1), 3475(2), 3475(3), 3475(4).

Halley v. Barnhart, CA5 (Tex), 158 FedAppx 645.—Social S 140.70, 142.10, 143.65, 143.85.

Halley; Meacham v., CCA5 (Tex), 103 F2d 967, cert den 60 SCt 86, 308 US 572, 84 LEd 480.—Deeds 121; Estop 71; Evid 65; Fraud 10, 23; Mines 78.1(3); Ven & Pur 224.

Hall Financial Group, Inc. v. DP Partners Ltd. Partnership, CA5 (Tex), 106 F3d 667. See DP Partners Ltd. Partnership, Matter of.

Hall Ford, In re, BkrtcySDTex, 181 BR 860. See Mort Hall Acquisition, Inc., In re.

Hall-Fuston Corp.; International Commercial Bank of China v., TexApp–Beaumont, 767 SW2d 259.—App & E 1177(5); Trial 39.

Halliburton; Fisher v., SDTex, 390 FSupp2d 610, reconsideration den 2005 WL 2001351.—U S 78(1), 78(11), 125(3); Work Comp 262, 2085, 2093.

Halliburton; Johnston Formation Testing Corp. v., CCA5 (Tex), 88 F2d 270, cert den 57 SCt 793, 301 US 690, 81 LEd 1347.—Pat 16.33, 22, 91(2).

Halliburton v. State, TexCrimApp, 528 SW2d 216.—Crim Law 369.1, 369.2(1), 369.2(4), 371(4).

Halliburton v. State, TexApp–San Antonio, 928 SW2d 650, reh overr, and petition for discretionary review refused.—Crim Law 641.4(2), 641.4(4), 641.7(1), 641.10(1), 641.10(2), 641.13(1), 641.13(2.1), 1086.11.

Halliburton v. Texas Indem. Ins. Co., Tex, 213 SW2d 677, 147 Tex 133.—Work Comp 305, 306, 329, 1386, 1710, 1969, 1975.

Halliburton; Texas Indem. Ins. Co. v., TexCivApp–Texarkana, 235 SW2d 499, ref nre.—Admin Law 683; App & E 867(1); New Tr 56, 157; Trial 129, 133.6(1); Work Comp 1932, 1942, 1964.

Halliburton; Texas Indem. Ins. Co. v., TexCivApp–Texarkana, 209 SW2d 775, rev 213 SW2d 677, 147 Tex 133.—App & E 1043(6); Work Comp 305, 1452.

Halliburton Co., In re, Tex, 80 SW3d 566, cert den Myers v. Halliburton Co, 123 SCt 901, 537 US 1112, 154 LEd2d 785.—Alt Disp Res 134(2), 134(6); Labor & Emp 40(2); Mand 4(1).

Halliburton Co. v. Andrews, TexCivApp–Fort Worth, 366 SW2d 240.—App & E 846(2), 846(5); Plead 111.42(8), 427.

Halliburton Co.; Blair v., TexCivApp–El Paso, 456 SW2d 414.—Bills & N 489(1); Judgm 181(11), 185(2), 186.

Halliburton Co. v. C.I.R., CA5 (Tex), 946 F2d 395.—Int Rev 3432, 3441, 3442, 4705.

Halliburton Co.; Hercules Exploration, Inc. v., TexApp–Corpus Christi, 658 SW2d 716, ref nre.—Acct Action on 10, 14; App & E 930(1), 989; Contracts 150; Evid 207(1), 264; Guar 36(1), 38(1); Lim of Act 24(2), 43; Trial 136(1), 350.4(1).

Halliburton Co.; Holleman v., TexCivApp–Fort Worth, 450 SW2d 883.—Evid 418; Judgm 181(6), 181(11).

Halliburton Co. v. Love, CA5 (Tex), 341 F2d 547.—Fed Civ Proc 1973; Mines 118.

Halliburton Co.; McCarty v., TexApp–Eastland, 725 SW2d 817, ref nre.—Estop 37; Mines 112(1), 114, 116, 117.

Halliburton Co. v. N. L. R. B., CA5 (Tex), 409 F2d 496.—Labor & Emp 1736, 1741, 1760, 1878, 1880.

Halliburton Co. v. Olivas, TexCivApp–El Paso, 517 SW2d 349.—App & E 1083(5), 1140(4); Death 95(2), 95(3), 97, 99(4).

Halliburton Co.; Reynolds v., EDTex, 217 FSupp2d 756.—Alt Disp Res 112, 121, 134(2), 143, 146, 195.

Halliburton Co. v. Sanchez, TexApp–San Antonio, 996 SW2d 216, reh overr, and review den.—Damag 50.10, 192; Evid 54, 584(1), 587, 595.

Halliburton Co.; Scherbatskoy v., CA5 (Tex), 125 F3d 288, reh and sug for reh den 135 F3d 142, transf to 178 F3d 1312.—Fed Cts 542, 1137, 1158.

Halliburton Co. v. Schlumberger Technology Corp., CAFed (Tex), 925 F2d 1435, reh den.—Pat 97, 324.54, 324.55(2).

Halliburton Co. v. Schlumberger Technology Corp., SDTex, 722 FSupp 1433.—Pat 319(4), 325.1, 325.11(1), 325.11(2.1), 325.11(4).

Halliburton Co. v. Schlumberger Technology Corp., SDTex, 722 FSupp 324, rev 925 F2d 1435, reh den.—Pat 97, 312(6).

Halliburton Co. v. U.S., NDTex, 611 FSupp 1118.—Int Rev 3038, 4327, 4330.

Halliburton Co.; Wynn v., NDTex, 112 BR 9. See Wynn, In re.

Halliburton Co. Benefits Committee v. Graves, CA5 (Tex), 479 F3d 360.—Labor & Emp 446.

Halliburton Co. Benefits Committee v. Graves, CA5 (Tex), 463 F3d 360, decision clarified on denial of reh 479 F3d 360.—Corp 296, 426(1), 585, 589, 590(1); Labor & Emp 445, 446, 549(1), 630, 678.

Halliburton Co. Benefits Committee v. Graves, CA5 (Tex), 191 FedAppx 248, appeal after remand 463 F3d 360, decision clarified on denial of reh 479 F3d 360.—Fed Cts 595.

Halliburton Energy Services, Inc.; BJ Services Co. v., CAFed (Tex), 338 F3d 1368, reh and reh den, cert den 124 SCt 1878, 541 US 973, 158 LEd2d 467.—Fed Cts 765, 825.1; Pat 62(1), 90(1), 91(1), 91(3), 92, 99, 101(6), 112.5, 314(5), 324.5, 324.55(3.1), 324.55(4), 328(2).

Halliburton Energy Services, Inc.; Emmett Properties, Inc. v., TexApp–Houston (14 Dist), 167 SW3d 365, reh overr, and review den.—Action 13; App & E 242(1), 840(2), 840(4), 893(1), 913; Corp 202, 615.5, 630(2); Evid 508, 555.2, 555.5; Judgm 185.3(1); Neglig 1675.

Halliburton Energy Services, Inc. v. Fleet Nat. Bank f/k/a Summit Bank, SDTex, 334 FSupp2d 930.—Banks 149, 174; Bills & N 201, 327; Fed Civ Proc 2487.

Halliburton Energy Services, Inc.; Henry v., TexApp–Dallas, 100 SW3d 505, reh overr, and review den.—Alt Disp Res 332, 333, 335, 363(8), 374(1); App & E 846(5), 852, 977(1), 977(5).

Halliburton Energy Services, Inc. v. M-I, LLC, EDTex, 456 FSupp2d 811.—Pat 101(6), 112.5, 161, 162, 165(1), 165(4), 165(5), 167(1), 167(1.1), 168(2.1), 328(2).

Halliburton Geophysical Services, Inc.; Guidry v., CA5 (Tex), 976 F2d 938.—Compromise 2, 16(1); Contracts 176(2); Evid 450(5); Fed Cts 776, 859.

Halliburton, Inc.; Fisher v., SDTex, 454 FSupp2d 637.—Const Law 2580.

Halliburton Oil Well Cementing Co.; B. & S. Drilling Co. v., SDTex, 24 FRD 1.—Fed Civ Proc 1472, 1476, 1477, 1483, 1502, 1504, 1511, 1513, 1515.

Halliburton Oil Well Cementing Co.; Bentley v., CA5 (Tex), 174 F2d 788.—Action 38(4); Autos 200; Carr 306(4); Fed Cts 431; Neglig 484; Parties 27, 31; Rem of C 36, 48.2, 49.1(6), 49.1(8), 61(1), 61(2), 107(2).

Halliburton Oil Well Cementing Co.; Bentley v., SDTex, 81 FSupp 323, rev 174 F2d 788.—Rem of C 58.

Halliburton Oil Well Cementing Co.; Blassingame v., TexCivApp–Eastland, 317 SW2d 111.—Explos 7; Neglig 1617.

Halliburton Oil Well Cementing Co.; Cummins v., TexCivApp–El Paso, 319 SW2d 379.—App & E 927(7), 989; Labor & Emp 2944; Neglig 552(1), 554(1), 1205(9), 1314; Trial 139.1(14).

Halliburton Oil Well Cementing Co. v. Groves, TexCivApp–Waco, 308 SW2d 919, ref nre.—App & E 930(1), 1070(2); Death 58(1); Evid 570; Mines 118; Neglig 1579, 1696, 1714, 1719, 1745, 1750; Plead 34(1); Trial 139.1(20), 140(2), 142, 143, 352.4(6), 358.

Halliburton Oilwell Cementing Co.; Head v., CA5 (Tex), 370 F2d 545.—Fed Civ Proc 2011; Fed Cts 896.1, 903; Witn 405(1), 405(2).

Halliburton Oil Well Cementing Co.; Herndon v., TexCivApp–El Paso, 154 SW2d 163, writ refused wom.—App & E 207, 261, 1060.1(6), 1062.1, 1078(1); Labor & Emp 29, 30; Mines 118; Neglig 291, 294, 552(1), 1205(10), 1717, 1720, 1741; Trial 29(2), 232(2), 350.6(6), 351.5(2), 352.4(1).

Halliburton Oil Well Cementing Co.; Larsen v., TexCivApp–Galveston, 105 SW2d 368, writ refused.—App & E 1062.1, 1177(5); Autos 149.

Halliburton Oil Well Cementing Co. v. Millican, CA5 (Tex), 171 F2d 426.—Contracts 108(2); Damag 62(1), 62(3); Mines 125.

Halliburton Oil Well Cementing Co. v. Paulk, CA5 (Tex), 180 F2d 79, cert den 71 SCt 38, 340 US 812, 95 LEd 596.—Indem 31(5), 31(6), 33(5); Labor & Emp 25, 26, 3037.

Halliburton Oil Well Cementing Co.; Rorem v., CA5 (Tex), 246 F2d 427.—Fed Cts 904; Mines 125.

Halliburton Oil Well Cementing Co. v. Schlumberger Well Surveying Corp., CCA5 (Tex), 130 F2d 589, cert den 63 SCt 532, 318 US 758, 87 LEd 1131.—Pat 16.3, 16.29, 98, 118.3(1), 165(2), 229.

Halliburton Oil Well Cementing Co. v. Stellman Transp. Co., SDTex, 123 FSupp 568.—Neglig 1620; Towage 15(2).

Halliburton Services v. First City Energy Finance Co., NDTex, 101 BR 474. See Endrex Exploration Co., In re.

Halliburton Services; Meg Petroleum Corp. v., BkrtcyNDTex, 61 BR 14. See Meg Petroleum Corp., In re.

Halliburton Services v. Pringle, TexCivApp–Corpus Christi, 602 SW2d 110.—App & E 781(1).

Halliburton Services v. Smith Intern. Inc., EDTex, 317 FSupp2d 719, appeal dism, cause remanded 164 FedAppx 976.—Pat 222, 312(1.4), 314(5), 319(1), 323.2(3), 323.2(5), 328(2).

Halliday; Golden v., TexCivApp–Dallas, 339 SW2d 715, writ dism.—Brok 63(1), 88(1); Home 118(3).

Halliday; Hughes v., TexCivApp–Waco, 471 SW2d 88.—Fraud 59(1), 62.

Halliday; U.S. v., CA5 (Tex), 487 F2d 1215, reh den 488 F2d 552.—Controlled Subs 124, 137; Crim Law 394.1(3); Searches 44, 64.

Halliday Real Estate, Inc. v. Murnan, TexApp–Fort Worth, 916 SW2d 585. See Ebby Halliday Real Estate, Inc. v. Murnan.

Halligan v. First Heights, F.S.A., TexApp–Houston (14 Dist), 850 SW2d 801.—App & E 852; Appear 8(1); Judgm 143(3), 145(2), 146, 162(4); Proc 44.

Hall Laboratories, Inc. v. Samuels & Co., CA5 (Tex), 261 F2d 841.—Pat 59, 319(1).

Hall Laboratories, Inc. v. Samuels & Co., NDTex, 151 FSupp 480, rev 261 F2d 841.—Pat 228.1, 312(10), 317, 319(1).

Hall-McGuff Architects; Jetty, Inc. v., TexCivApp–Hous (14 Dist), 595 SW2d 918, ref nre.—Contracts 280(4), 322(4); Corp 1.7(2); Interest 36(1).

Hallman; Allstate Ins. Co. v., Tex, 159 SW3d 640.—Action 6; Decl Judgm 392.1; Insurance 2278(9), 2914.

Hallman v. Allstate Ins. Co., TexApp–Dallas, 114 SW3d 656, reh overr, and review gr, rev 159 SW3d 640.—App & E 223, 1175(1), 1177(6); Evid 584(1); Insurance 1822, 1832(1), 1835(2), 2101, 2275, 2278(9), 2914, 2915, 2922(1).

Hallman v. City of Pampa, TexCivApp–Amarillo, 147 SW2d 543, writ refused.—Estop 62.4; Evid 31; Mun Corp 167, 219, 741.20, 741.55, 812(5).

Hallman; Hogan v., TexApp–Houston (14 Dist), 889 SW2d 332, reh overr, and writ den.—Const Law 2311, 2312, 2314, 2315, 2648, 3006, 3057, 3085, 3105, 3753, 3971; Death 7, 38; Health 604, 811; Lim of Act 4(2), 72(1).

Hallman v. I.N.S., CA5 (Tex), 879 F2d 1244.—U S 146, 147(11.1).

Hallman v. Northwestern Nat. Ins. Co., SDTex, 766 FSupp 575.—Fed Civ Proc 2470.1; Fed Cts 18; Lim of Act 100(6), 100(12).

Hallman v. Safeway Stores, Inc., CA5 (Tex), 368 F2d 400.—Assign 18, 121; Contracts 176(10); Fed Cts 286.1; Perp 4(1); Spec Perf 57, 106(1); Ven & Pur 18(3), 75, 207.

Hallmark, Ex parte, TexCrimApp, 883 SW2d 672, reh den.—Const Law 190, 2789, 2790, 2810; Prisons 15(2).

Hallmark; City Grocery Co. v., TexCivApp–Beaumont, 123 SW2d 988, writ dism.—App & E 901, 1047(1), 1054(1); Chat Mtg 279; Evid 471(29); Set-Off 28(1); Witn 240(4).

Hallmark v. City of Fredericksburg, TexApp–San Antonio, 94 SW3d 703, reh overr, and review den, on remand 2004 WL 5049538, appeal after remand 2005 WL 763264.—Civil R 1345, 1351(1), 1351(4), 1352(1), 1376(6); Mun Corp 745.

Hallmark; General Ins. Co. of America v., TexCivApp–Eastland, 575 SW2d 134, ref nre.—Insurance 2144(3).

Hallmark; Graves v., TexCivApp–Amarillo, 232 SW2d 130, ref nre.—App & E 598; Mech Liens 161(1); Paymt 39(1).

Hallmark v. Hand, TexApp–El Paso, 885 SW2d 471, reh overr, and writ den.—Action 27(1); App & E 930(3), 946, 989, 999(1), 1001(1), 1001(3), 1002, 1003(7), 1062.2, 1097(1), 1195(1); Banks 40, 54(1); Contracts 1, 27, 29; Costs 194.32; Courts 99(1); Damag 23, 56; Interest 39(2.30).

Hallmark v. Hand, TexApp–Corpus Christi, 833 SW2d 603, reh overr, and writ den, appeal after remand 885 SW2d 471, reh overr, and writ den.—Banks 40; Contracts 27, 147(2), 168; Damag 23, 175, 177, 189; Sales 22(1).

Hallmark; Humes v., TexApp–Austin, 895 SW2d 475.—App & E 241, 930(3), 989, 1001(1), 1001(3); Evid 10(2); Trover 39, 40(6), 44, 45, 46, 47.

Hallmark v. Johnson, CA5 (Tex), 118 F3d 1073, cert den Monroe v. Johnson, 118 SCt 576, 522 US 1003, 139 LEd2d 415, reh den 118 SCt 1342, 523 US 1041, 140 LEd2d 502.—Const Law 2790, 2816, 4824, 4829; Hab Corp 513, 818; Prisons 13(7.1), 13(9), 15(5), 15(7).

Hallmark v. Port/Cooper-T. Smith Stevedoring Co., TexApp–Corpus Christi, 907 SW2d 586, reh overr.—App & E 863; Contracts 143(2), 143.5, 147(2), 147(3), 152, 176(1), 176(2); Evid 397(1), 441(1), 445(6); Fraud 7; Judgm 181(19), 183, 185(2); Labor & Emp 40(3), 79, 837; Trusts 134, 140(1), 182.

Hallmark v. State, TexApp–Dallas, 789 SW2d 647, petition for discretionary review refused.—Arrest 63.4(15); Crim Law 404.30, 404.60; Sent & Pun 1381(6).

Hallmark; Stevens v., TexCivApp–Austin, 109 SW2d 1106.—Action 4; Int Liq 256.

Hallmark v. United Fidelity Life Ins. Co., Tex, 286 SW2d 133, 155 Tex 291.—Estop 54; Insurance 3142, 3384, 3388.

Hallmark; United Fidelity Life Ins. Co. v., TexCivApp–Beaumont, 278 SW2d 173, rev 286 SW2d 133, 155 Tex 291.—Insurance 2591, 2607, 3384.

Hallmark Builders, Inc. v. Anthony, TexCivApp–Amarillo, 547 SW2d 681.—Evid 355(3); Impl & C C 91, 102.

Hallmark Builders, Inc. v. Trans-Mix Corp., TexCivApp–Amarillo, 493 SW2d 250, dism.—App & E 499(4), 500(4), 930(3), 989; Estop 85; Trial 366.

Hallmark Cards, Inc. v. McDonald, BkrtcyNDTex, 41 BR 285. See Lane, In re.

Hallmark Contracting, Inc.; Staff Industries, Inc. v., TexApp–Corpus Christi, 846 SW2d 542, reh overr.—App & E 1149; Contracts 143(2), 143.5, 147(2), 169, 170(1), 176(1), 176(2), 231(1); Costs 194.32, 194.50, 207; Decl Judgm 45; Interest 39(3), 50; Mech Liens 224, 227.

Hallmark Elec. Contractors, Inc., In re, BkrtcyWDTex, 116 BR 67.—Jury 25(6).

Hallmark Elec. Contractors, Inc. v. Navasota Valley Elec. Co-op., Inc., BkrtcyWDTex, 116 BR 67. See Hallmark Elec. Contractors, Inc., In re.

Hallmark Personnel of Texas, Inc. v. Franks, TexCivApp–Hous (1 Dist), 562 SW2d 933.—Action 6; Antitrust 413, 417, 432; App & E 781(1), 781(6), 954(1), 954(2); Inj 12, 56, 147; Labor & Emp 121.

Hall Nestletree II Associates, In re, BkrtcySDTex, 112 BR 201.—Bankr 3175, 3204.

Hall Nestletree II Associates; Guaranty Federal Sav. Bank v., BkrtcySDTex, 112 BR 201. See Hall Nestletree II Associates, In re.

Halloran v. Veterans Admin., CA5 (Tex), 874 F2d 315.—Records 52, 58, 63, 66.

Halloway v. State, TexCrimApp, 175 SW2d 258, 146 TexCrim 353.—Autos 354; Crim Law 393(1), 478(1), 939(2), 995(3), 1091(4), 1159.3(6).

Hallowell v. U.S., CA5 (Tex), 197 F2d 926.—Crim Law 641.4(2), 1158(1), 1668(3).

Hall-Page Tire Co.; Continental Nat. Bank v., TexCivApp–Fort Worth, 318 SW2d 127.—Judgm 256(2); Sales 365; Trial 358, 365.2.

Hall's Aero Spraying, Inc. v. Underwriters at Lloyd's, London, CA5 (Tex), 274 F2d 527.—Decl Judgm 347; Insurance 2332, 2333, 2969, 3062, 3554.

Hall's Bayou Realty Corp. v. James, TexCivApp–Galveston, 107 SW2d 1113, writ dism.—App & E 930(1); Damag 108; Trial 278; Waters 125, 126(3).

Halls Clothing Co. v. Ramirez, TexCivApp–El Paso, 184 SW2d 296, dism.—Exemp 139.

Hall Securities Corp.; Hardeman v., NDTex, 736 FSupp 1422. See Hall Dadeland Towers Associates v. Hardeman.

HALTOM

Hallstead; Muecke v., CA5 (Tex), 128 FedAppx 378.—Fed Cts 714.

Hallstead; Muecke v., TexApp–San Antonio, 25 SW3d 221, reh overr.—App & E 78(3), 917(1), 960(1); Lim of Act 180(1), 180(2); Plead 228.14, 228.23.

Hallsville Independent School Dist.; Fields v., CA5 (Tex), 906 F2d 1017, reh den, cert den 111 SCt 676, 498 US 1026, 112 LEd2d 668.—Civil R 1110, 1121, 1527, 1545; Schools 130.

Hallum; City of Dallas v., TexCivApp–Dallas, 285 SW2d 431, ref nre.—Em Dom 90, 100(6), 219, 258, 262(5).

Hallum v. Pinkerton, TexCivApp–Dallas, 267 SW2d 921.—App & E 846(5), 994(3), 1012.1(1); Lim of Act 25(3); Paymt 39(5); Trial 382; Ven & Pur 281(3).

Hallum v. Texas Liquor Control Board, TexCivApp–Dallas, 166 SW2d 175, writ refused.—Courts 80(4); Int Liq 59(2), 106(4); Statut 223.4.

Hall Whispertree Associates; Federal Sav. and Loan Ins. Corp. v., NDTex, 653 FSupp 148.—B & L Assoc 48.

Hallwood Realty Partners, L.P.; HTS Services, Inc. v., TexApp–Houston (1 Dist), 190 SW3d 108.—App & E 842(2), 893(1), 901, 930(1), 989, 994(3), 1008.1(1), 1008.1(2), 1012.1(4); Garn 1, 105, 162, 164.

Halman; Guillot v., TexCivApp–Fort Worth, 91 SW2d 402.—App & E 216(2), 218.2(1), 1068(4); Trial 278.

H.A. Lott, Inc.; Continental Steel Co. v., TexApp–Dallas, 772 SW2d 513, writ den.—Indem 30(1), 31(1), 36, 37, 75.

H. A. Lott Inc. v. Hoisting & Portable Engineers Local No. 450, of Intern. Union of Operating Engineers, AFL-CIO, SDTex, 222 FSupp 993.—Rem of C 58.

H. A. Lott, Inc. v. Pittsburgh Plate Glass Co., TexCivApp–Amarillo, 432 SW2d 583.—Estop 52.10(2), 119; Pub Contr 29; States 108.5.

Halpenny v. City of San Antonio, TexCivApp–San Antonio, 351 SW2d 939.—Mand 23(1).

Halpenny v. Kuykendall, TexCivApp–San Antonio, 345 SW2d 757.—Judgm 183, 185.3(1).

Halpenny v. Maldonado, TexCivApp–San Antonio, 415 SW2d 16.—Bills & N 439.

Halper v. University of the Incarnate Word, TexApp–San Antonio, 90 SW3d 842, reh overr.—Colleges 8(2), 8.1(2), 8.1(6.1); Contracts 166; Fraud 3, 12, 13(1), 20.

Halperin; U.S. v., CA5 (Tex), 441 F2d 612.—Crim Law 429(1); Witn 398(1), 405(1), 406.

Halpin, In re, BkrtcyNDTex, 219 BR 460. See Dragoo, In re.

Halpin; Bank of New York v., BkrtcyNDTex, 219 BR 460. See Dragoo, In re.

Halprin v. State, TexCrimApp, 170 SW3d 111, reh den.—Crim Law 1035(6), 1166.16, 1166.18; Jury 131(13); Sent & Pun 1767, 1789(9).

Halsell v. Dehoyos, Tex, 810 SW2d 371.—App & E 1035; Jury 25(6).

Halsell v. Ferguson, Tex, 202 SW 317, 109 Tex 144, answer to certified question conformed to 203 SW 941.—Mun Corp 601.3.

Halsell; Hooper v., TexCivApp–Amarillo, 143 SW2d 228.—Plead 111.3, 111.4, 111.17.

Halsell v. Local Union No. 5, Bricklayers & Allied Craftsmen, NDTex, 530 FSupp 803, aff 706 F2d 313, cert den 104 SCt 244, 464 US 895, 78 LEd2d 233.—Labor & Emp 1025, 1045(2), 1046(3), 1046(6).

Halsell v. Texas Water Commission, TexCivApp–Austin, 380 SW2d 1, ref nre.—App & E 1051(1); Evid 553(3), 571(1); Jury 19(1); Statut 158, 159, 223.3, 223.4; Waters 78.5, 133, 152(4), 152(7), 152(8), 190.

Halsey, In re, TexApp–Dallas, 646 SW2d 306.—Contempt 20, 70, 81; Crim Law 1077.3.

Halsey; Dallas County v., Tex, 87 SW3d 552.—Courts 57(0.5); Offic 114.

Halsey v. Dallas County, Texas, TexApp–Dallas, 68 SW3d 81, reh overr, and review gr, rev 87 SW3d 552.—

Courts 57(0.5), 57(1); Judges 36; Judgm 185(2), 185(5); Offic 114.

Halsey, Stuart & Co.; City and County of Dallas Levee Imp. Dist. v., TexCivApp–Amarillo, 202 SW2d 957.—App & E 176, 909(6); Interest 38(1), 39(2.30); Levees 9, 11; Lim of Act 50(2).

Halstead v. State, TexApp–Austin, 891 SW2d 11.—Crim Law 398(1), 410, 419(12); Infants 20; Rape 38(1); Witn 360, 389.

Halsted, Ex parte, TexCrimApp, 182 SW2d 479, 147 TexCrim 453.—Const Law 26, 45, 47, 48(1), 50, 240(6.1), 655, 2473, 2474, 3696; Hab Corp 464, 813; Health 103, 105, 111, 163, 164, 176; Statut 47, 49, 63, 195.

Haltenberger; Challenger Sales & Supply v., TexApp–Beaumont, 730 SW2d 453, ref nre.—App & E 846(5); New Tr 99, 102(6), 108(3); Sales 89, 181(11.1); Venue 17.

Halter v. Allied Merchants Bank, TexApp–Beaumont, 751 SW2d 286, writ den.—Mtg 559(4).

Haltom v. Austin Nat. Bank, TexCivApp–Austin, 487 SW2d 201, ref nre.—Wills 467, 601(8).

Haltom v. Haltom's Jewelers, Inc., TexApp–Fort Worth, 691 SW2d 823, ref nre.—Trademarks 1042, 1200(3), 1201(1), 1526.

Haltom v. Leatherwood, TexCivApp–Beaumont, 287 SW2d 744.—Evid 568(1); Plead 111.42(8).

Haltom v. Lykes Bros. S.S. Co., Inc., EDTex, 771 FSupp 179.—Damag 87(1); Death 88, 93; Hus & W 209(3), 209(4).

Haltom; U.S. v., CA5 (Tex), 113 F3d 43.—Sent & Pun 771.

Haltom; Ydrogo v., TexCivApp–Eastland, 302 SW2d 670.—Tresp to T T 40(4), 41(1).

Haltom City; Roberts v., Tex, 543 SW2d 75.—App & E 179(1); Estop 52(1), 52(2); Judgm 181(33); Mun Corp 63.1, 741.55.

Haltom City, City of; DeLeon v., CA5 (Tex), 113 FedAppx 577.—Civil R 1484, 1485; Fed Civ Proc 928; Fed Cts 941.

Haltom City, City of; DeLeon v., CA5 (Tex), 106 FedAppx 909.—Civil R 1351(4), 1358; Consp 18; Judges 36.

Haltom City, City of; Drake v., CA5 (Tex), 106 FedAppx 897.—Civil R 1352(4); Fed Civ Proc 829, 840.

Haltom City, City of; Garcia Guevara v., CA5 (Tex), 106 FedAppx 900.—Civil R 1348, 1351(4); Fed Civ Proc 1838; Prisons 4(4).

Haltom City, City of; Howard-Barrows v., CA5 (Tex), 106 FedAppx 912.—Civil R 1088(4), 1348, 1351(4); Const Law 4788; Costs 302; Crim Law 412.1(4), 641.3(3); Prisons 4(4).

Haltom City, City of; Jane Doe 5 v., CA5 (Tex), 106 FedAppx 906.—Civil R 1088(4), 1348, 1351(4); Fed Civ Proc 1838; Prisons 4(4).

Haltom City, City of; Pederson v., CA5 (Tex), 108 FedAppx 845.—Civil R 1088(4), 1351(4), 1395(6); Const Law 4788, 4806; Costs 302; Crim Law 412.1(4), 641.2(4), 641.3(3).

Haltom City, City of; Soto v., CA5 (Tex), 106 FedAppx 903.—Civil R 1348, 1351(4); Fed Civ Proc 1838; Prisons 4(4).

Haltom City, City of; Whisenant v., CA5 (Tex), 106 FedAppx 915, on remand 2005 WL 283119.—Civil R 1088(4), 1348, 1351(4); Consp 13, 18.

Haltom, City of; Roberts v., TexCivApp–Fort Worth, 529 SW2d 296, writ gr, rev 543 SW2d 75.—Judgm 185.3(21); Mun Corp 733(2), 741.55, 742(5), 816(7).

Haltom City State Bank v. King Music Co., TexCivApp–Fort Worth, 474 SW2d 9, ref nre.—Land & Ten 90(6).

Haltom Medical Investors, L.L.C.; State v., TexApp–Fort Worth, 153 SW3d 664.—App & E 893(1); Health 276; Statut 181(1), 181(2), 184, 188, 212.6, 217.2, 219(1), 223.2(0.5).

Haltom Oil Co. v. Phillips Petroleum Co., CA5 (Tex), 304 F2d 95.—Contracts 152; Sales 75.

Haltom's Jewelers, Inc.; Haltom v., TexApp–Fort Worth, 691 SW2d 823, ref nre.—Trademarks 1042, 1200(3), 1201(1), 1526.

Halton; Cobb v., TexCivApp–Waco, 363 SW2d 388, ref nre.—Autos 244(41.1).

Halton; Employers Ins. of Wausau v., TexApp–Dallas, 792 SW2d 462, writ den.—App & E 961; Judgm 143(2), 146, 185(2); Pretrial Proc 483.

Halverson v. U.S., CA5 (Tex), 972 F2d 654, cert den 113 SCt 1297, 507 US 925, 122 LEd2d 687.—U S 78(5.1).

Halvorson v. National Title & Abstract Co., TexCivApp–Tyler, 391 SW2d 112.—Ease 22; Insurance 2610, 2618.

Ham, Ex parte, TexCrimApp, 423 SW2d 598.—Extrad 29, 36.

Ham, In re Marriage of, TexApp–Texarkana, 59 SW3d 326.—App & E 758.3(11), 1073(1), 1175(1); Appear 8(1); Const Law 4010; Judgm 181(11), 181(15.1), 181(20), 335(1), 335(2), 335(3); Neglig 232, 239; Plead 228.14; Pretrial Proc 621, 695.

Ham; Atchison, T. & S. F. Ry. Co. v., TexCivApp–Austin, 454 SW2d 451, ref nre.—App & E 1004(3), 1004(5), 1057(1), 1140(4); Damag 167; Evid 318(1); Labor & Emp 2824, 2830, 2880, 2881; Neglig 294, 431, 510(1), 1741; Trial 115(3), 313.

Ham v. Blankenship, CA5 (Tex), 194 F2d 430.—Courts 89; Sec Reg 256.1, 293.

Ham; Brewer v., CA5 (Tex), 876 F2d 448.—Fed Cts 855.1; Schools 53(1).

Ham v. Brice, CA5 (Tex), 203 FedAppx 631.—Civil R 1358; Fed Civ Proc 2491.5.

Ham v. Cavette, TexCivApp–Houston, 357 SW2d 438, ref nre.—App & E 846(2), 846(5); Child C 473, 510, 554.

Ham; Freeman v., TexCivApp–Austin, 283 SW2d 438, ref nre.—Autos 181(2).

Ham v. Garvey, TexCivApp–San Antonio, 155 SW2d 976.—Counties 58, 165.

Ham; Korkmas v., TexCivApp–Dallas, 141 SW2d 433.—Damag 39; Plead 236(3); Trial 396(4).

Ham v. La Cienega Music Co., CA5 (Tex), 4 F3d 413.—Const Law 3964, 3965(8); Fed Cts 76.5, 76.10, 76.35, 96, 97, 776.

Ham v. McDonald Well Servicing Co., TexCivApp–Eastland, 364 SW2d 752, ref nre.—App & E 930(3), 989; Autos 245(91); Trial 350.7(9).

Ham; Moore v., TexCivApp–Amarillo, 342 SW2d 825.—App & E 846(2), 846(5), 854(2); Child C 42, 609; Plead 49.

Ham; Phillips Petroleum Co. v., CA5 (Tex), 228 F2d 217.—Mines 5.3, 79.5.

Ham v. State, TexApp–Fort Worth, 855 SW2d 231, reh overr.—Crim Law 795(2.1), 795(2.60), 795(2.90), 829(3), 1159.2(8); Kidnap 36.

Ham v. State, TexApp–Amarillo, 760 SW2d 55.—Crim Law 700(2.1), 700(3).

Ham; Texas Emp. Ins. Ass'n v., TexCivApp–Fort Worth, 333 SW2d 438, ref nre.—Work Comp 597, 1173, 1328, 1927.

Ham; Weaver v., Tex, 232 SW2d 704, 149 Tex 309.—Mun Corp 589; Zoning 4, 27, 151, 490, 679, 747.

Ham; Weaver v., TexApp–Dallas, 429 SW2d 687.—App & E 770(2), 771, 773(4).

Ham v. Weaver, TexCivApp–El Paso, 227 SW2d 286, rev 232 SW2d 704, 149 Tex 309.—Const Law 2642; Zoning 5.1, 27, 29, 151, 153, 157, 171, 604, 672.

Hamacher; Guaranty Bank & Trust Co. v., TexCivApp–Galveston, 112 SW2d 343.—Bills & N 64, 537(2); Contracts 42; Trial 351.5(4).

Hamaker v. American States Ins. Co. of Texas, TexCivApp–Hous (1 Dist), 493 SW2d 893, ref nre.—Autos 144.1(4); Const Law 2414(3); Insurance 1022, 1025(1), 1029, 1722, 1851, 2772, 2807.

Hamamcy v. Texas State Bd. of Medical Examiners, TexApp–Austin, 900 SW2d 423, reh overr, and writ den.—Admin Law 481; Health 223(1).

Hamamcy v. Wyckoff Heights Hosp., TexApp–Fort Worth, 786 SW2d 32, writ den.—Libel 44(1).

Hamann v. Morentin, TexApp–Fort Worth, 660 SW2d 645.—Child C 7, 27, 41, 76, 178, 921(1); Child S 21; Guard & W 29.

Hamann; Texas A & M University at Corpus Christi v., TexApp–Corpus Christi, 3 SW3d 215, review den.—App & E 919; Lim of Act 95(14); Pretrial Proc 622, 681; Statut 181(1), 188.

Hamar v. Ashland, Inc., CA5 (Tex), 211 FedAppx 309.—Civil R 1516; Labor & Emp 762; Princ & A 1.

Hamauei; Trailways Bus System, Inc. v., TexApp–Corpus Christi, 660 SW2d 607, ref nre.—Evid 99; Labor & Emp 1320(6), 1327(3), 1327(4).

Hamberlin v. Longview Bank and Trust Co., TexApp–Texarkana, 770 SW2d 12, writ den.—Ref of Inst 19(1); Ven & Pur 25.

Hamblen v. Horwitz-Texan Theatres Co., TexCivApp–Galveston, 162 SW2d 455.—App & E 954(1); Contracts 121; Corp 1.5(1), 198.1(1).

Hamblen; Mecom v., Tex, 289 SW2d 553, 155 Tex 494.—Mines 74(5); Sec Reg 292.

Hamblen v. Mohr, TexCivApp–Galveston, 171 SW2d 168, writ refused wom.—Labor & Emp 3128, 3132, 3146, 3147, 3159, 3160; Land & Ten 152(10), 164(1), 167(8), 169(10), 170(1); Neglig 1037(4), 1101.

Hamblen; New Amsterdam Cas. Co. v., Tex, 190 SW2d 56, 144 Tex 306.—Insurance 3154, 3168, 3192.

Hamblen; New Amsterdam Cas. Co. v., TexCivApp–Galveston, 186 SW2d 741, rev 190 SW2d 56, 144 Tex 306.—Insurance 1812, 3154, 3168.

Hamblen v. Placid Oil Co., TexCivApp–Waco, 279 SW2d 127, rev Mecom v. Hamblen, 289 SW2d 553, 155 Tex 494.—Brok 1; Mines 74(7), 79.3, 99(3); Sec Reg 253, 292.

Hamblet v. Coveney, TexApp–Houston (1 Dist), 714 SW2d 126, ref nre.—Damag 184; Fraud 6, 9; Frds St of 119(2); Home 96; Trial 219, 263, 268, 333; Trusts 91, 92.5, 94.5, 103(1), 103(3), 110, 373, 374.

Hamborsky v. Hamborsky, TexCivApp–San Antonio, 584 SW2d 330.—Divorce 165(3), 171; Judgm 335(2).

Hamborsky; Hamborsky v., TexCivApp–San Antonio, 584 SW2d 330.—Divorce 165(3), 171; Judgm 335(2).

Hamborsky v. Hamborsky, TexCivApp–San Antonio, 497 SW2d 405.—Divorce 280.

Hamborsky; Hamborsky v., TexCivApp–San Antonio, 497 SW2d 405.—Divorce 280.

Hambric; The Home Ins. Co. v., TexApp–Waco, 906 SW2d 956.—Courts 57(1); Work Comp 1074.

Hambrice v. F. W. Woolworth Co., CA5 (Tex), 290 F2d 557.—Damag 168(1); Evid 472(9); Fed Civ Proc 36; Fed Cts 416; Neglig 1639, 1670.

Hambrick; Beauchamp v., TexApp–Eastland, 901 SW2d 747.—Afft 18; Damag 177, 191; Trial 139.1(17).

Hambrick; Boozier v., TexApp–Houston (1 Dist), 846 SW2d 593.—App & E 142, 874(1); Aviation 223; Judgm 648; Mun Corp 747(3); Offic 114, 116.

Hambrick; Harris County Flood Control Dist. v., TexCivApp–Hous (1 Dist), 433 SW2d 195.—Em Dom 203(1), 205, 262(5); Evid 211, 555.6(10); Trial 260(3).

Hambrick v. State, TexApp–Texarkana, 11 SW3d 241.—Crim Law 670, 697, 1036.1(9), 1042, 1090.15, 1126, 1165(1); Sent & Pun 313.

Hambrick; Thompson v., TexCivApp–Dallas, 508 SW2d 949, ref nre.—Corp 187; Evid 448; Judgm 181(15.1), 181(31).

Hambrick Consol. v. Walker, TexCivApp–Texarkana, 269 SW2d 923.—App & E 989, 1177(7); Bailm 31(1), 31(3).

Hambright; Fort Worth & D. C. Ry. Co. v., TexCivApp–Amarillo, 130 SW2d 436, writ dism, correct.—App & E

843(2); Neglig 1010, 1037(3), 1037(4), 1037(8), 1085, 1088, 1132, 1286(2), 1291(4), 1625, 1717, 1741; R R 275(2); Trial 350.6(4), 352.21.

Hambright v. State, TexCrimApp, 318 SW2d 640.—Crim Law 1097(1), 1097(3), 1097(4).

Hambrosky; Lewis v., TexCivApp–Waco, 417 SW2d 606, ref nre.—Inj 62(1), 114(3), 128(6).

Hamburger v. State Farm Mut. Auto. Ins. Co., CA5 (Tex), 361 F3d 875.—Damag 191, 208(2), 208(5); Evid 601(1); Fed Civ Proc 1275, 1278, 1938.1, 2142.1, 2553, 2608.1; Fed Cts 416, 420; Insurance 2782, 3335, 3336, 3360, 3364.

Hamburg Sav. Bank; Newgard v., TexCivApp–El Paso, 436 SW2d 357.—App & E 499(1); Judgm 181(25), 185.1(3).

Hamby; Jeanes v., TexApp–Dallas, 685 SW2d 695, ref nre.—Accord 5; Evid 419(20); Interest 60; Judgm 185(2), 585(3), 619, 713(2); Lim of Act 55(6); Release 13(4).

Hamby v. Key, TexCivApp–Beaumont, 294 SW2d 169, ref nre.—App & E 927(7); Autos 244(20), 245(24); Trial 350.6(3).

Hamby; Smith v., TexCivApp–Fort Worth, 609 SW2d 866. —Inj 157.

Hamby v. State Farm Mut. Auto. Ins. Co., TexApp–Houston (1 Dist), 137 SW3d 834, review den.—App & E 103, 893(1), 916(1); Courts 26; Insurance 2719(2); Plead 228.14, 228.23.

Hamby Co. v. Palmer, TexApp–Amarillo, 631 SW2d 589. —App & E 172(1), 931(1), 989, 1177(7); J P 174(8); Labor & Emp 180.

Hamby Co. v. Seminole State Bank, Tex, 652 SW2d 939. —Banks 140(3).

Hamby Co. v. Seminole State Bank, TexApp–El Paso, 649 SW2d 81, aff in part, rev in part 652 SW2d 939.— Judgm 181(17).

Hamed; Khraish v., TexApp–Dallas, 762 SW2d 906, writ den.—App & E 100(1); Lis Pen 4, 15.

Hamel, In re, TexApp–San Antonio, 180 SW3d 226.—App & E 82(5); Equity 72(1); Mand 3(1), 4(1), 4(4), 5, 12, 22, 28, 53, 143(2).

Hamel; Bueckner v., TexApp–Houston (1 Dist), 886 SW2d 368, reh den, and writ den.—Accord 1, 15.1; Anim 44; App & E 931(1), 989, 1008.1(3), 1010.1(3), 1012.1(4); Damag 139.

Hamel v. Hamel, TexApp–Beaumont, 161 SW3d 736.— App & E 66, 76(1); Divorce 177.

Hamel; Hamel v., TexApp–Beaumont, 161 SW3d 736.— App & E 66, 76(1); Divorce 177.

Hamel v. State, TexCrimApp, 916 SW2d 491.—Assault 67, 68, 96(2), 96(3); Crim Law 772(6).

Hamel v. State, TexCrimApp, 582 SW2d 424.—Arrest 63.4(16), 63.5(6); Crim Law 412.1(3), 444, 577.1, 1166(7), 1169.5(3); Searches 181.

Hamel v. State, TexApp–Fort Worth, 803 SW2d 878, petition for discretionary review refused.—Crim Law 726; Jury 33(5.15).

Hamer, Matter of Marriage of, TexApp–Amarillo, 906 SW2d 263, reh overr.—Child S 231, 233, 250, 260, 261, 290, 299, 336, 339(2), 363, 556(3).

Hamer; Cook v., Tex, 309 SW2d 54, 158 Tex 164.—App & E 173(6), 1083(3); Evid 317(12); Princ & A 21, 22(1), 22(2); Wills 740(2).

Hamer; Cook v., TexCivApp–Dallas, 302 SW2d 680, aff 309 SW2d 54, 158 Tex 164.—App & E 930(1), 989; Courts 478; Frds St of 68; Partit 5; Wills 439, 462, 463, 470(3), 740(2).

Hamer v. Hamer, TexCivApp–Galveston, 184 SW2d 492. —Child C 26, 122, 144, 451, 943; Divorce 252.1, 252.3(2), 288.

Hamer; Hamer v., TexCivApp–Galveston, 184 SW2d 492. —Child C 26, 122, 144, 451, 943; Divorce 252.1, 252.3(2), 288.

Hamer v. Hope Cottage Children's Bureau, Inc., TexCivApp–Dallas, 389 SW2d 123.—Adop 7.6(2); Infants 154.1, 197, 203.

Hamer; Humble Oil & Refining Co. v., TexCivApp–Beaumont, 167 SW2d 272.—Corp 503(1); Plead 111.40; Princ & A 21, 22(1); R R 22(3); Trial 90, 105(5).

Hames; Fazio v., TexApp–Dallas, 866 SW2d 267.—App & E 522(1), 524, 559, 621(1), 624, 627, 670(1), 757(1).

Hames; General Acc. Fire & Life Assur. Corp. v., TexCivApp–Dallas, 416 SW2d 894.—Work Comp 51, 999, 1034, 1042, 1079, 1790, 1793, 1834, 1981, 1982, 1983.

Hames v. Heckler, CA5 (Tex), 707 F2d 162.—Admin Law 791; Social S 140.30, 143.45, 143.75, 148.5.

Hames; U.S. v., CA5 (Tex), 185 FedAppx 318.—Banks 509.25; Consp 47(5), 47(6); Crim Law 1181.5(8); Fraud 68.10(3), 69(5); Obst Just 16; Postal 49(11); Witn 388(2.1), 389.

Hames; U.S. v., CA5 (Tex), 122 FedAppx 706.—Crim Law 83; Fed Cts 192, 356.

Hames; Wells v., TexCivApp–Hous (14 Dist), 464 SW2d 393, ref nre.—Child 82, 86; Const Law 2970; Courts 91(2); Marriage 13, 50(1).

Hamic v. Harris County W.C. & I.D. No. 36, CA5 (Tex), 184 FedAppx 442.—Civil R 1505(7); Fed Cts 766, 776; Lim of Act 58(1); Waters 183.5.

Hamil; Eastman Oil Well Survey Co. v., TexCivApp–Houston, 416 SW2d 597, ref nre.—Contracts 147(2), 252; Corp 218; Guar 7(1), 9, 42(1), 59, 64, 91.

Hamil; Southwestern Bell Tel. Co. v., TexApp–Fort Worth, 116 SW3d 798.—Damag 113; Tresp 50, 57.

Hamil v. Whitlow Steel Co., Inc., TexCivApp–Hous (14 Dist), 596 SW2d 293.—App & E 1170.7; Bills & N 493(3), 516, 518(1).

Hamill, Ex parte, TexApp–Fort Worth, 718 SW2d 78.— Child S 491; Crim Law 641.2(2), 641.2(4); Trial 21.

Hamill, In re Estate of, TexApp–Amarillo, 866 SW2d 339.—App & E 989; Gifts 4, 15; Infants 78(1), 115; Wills 656, 665, 717, 743.

Hamill v. Bahr, TexCivApp–Galveston, 271 SW2d 319.— App & E 931(6); Bound 35(2); Counties 7; Plead 111.39(4).

Hamill v. Brashear, TexCivApp–Amarillo, 513 SW2d 602, ref nre.—App & E 927(7), 1122(2); Evid 501(3); Infants 78(3); Trial 420; Wills 21, 31, 50, 53(2), 55(1), 55(9), 288(3), 300, 318(1), 324(2), 400.

Hamill v. Burleson, TexCivApp–Amarillo, 278 SW2d 571, ref nre.—App & E 930(1); Contracts 171(1); Evid 471(6); Mines 109; Neglig 1672.

Hamill v. Kitchen, TexCivApp–Amarillo, 182 SW2d 821. —Hus & W 85(1); Plead 102, 111.7; Venue 5.2, 7.5(4).

Hamill v. Level, Tex, 917 SW2d 15.—Pretrial Proc 44.1, 46, 531.

Hamill v. Level, TexApp–Fort Worth, 900 SW2d 457, reh overr, and writ gr, writ 917 SW2d 15.—App & E 854(1), 946, 961; Pretrial Proc 44.1, 46, 309.

Hamill v. Wright, CA5 (Tex), 870 F2d 1032.—Civil R 1057, 1331(6), 1350, 1376(4), 1376(6); Consp 7.5(2); Const Law 4829; Fed Civ Proc 2846; Fed Cts 18.

Hamill & Smith v. Ogden, TexCivApp–Galveston, 163 SW2d 725.—App & E 1069.1; Judgm 198; Partit 9(1); Trial 331.

Hamill & Smith v. Parr, TexCivApp–San Antonio, 173 SW2d 725, writ refused wom.—App & E 207, 231(1), 930(3), 1043(6), 1060.1(4); Mines 101; Trial 121(4), 351.5(1), 352.4(1); Trusts 63.5, 63.9, 79, 89(1), 365(4); Witn 46.

Hamill Drilling Co.; Danciger Oil & Refineries v., Tex, 171 SW2d 321, 141 Tex 153.—Mines 74(5).

Hamilton, Ex parte, TexCrimApp, 376 SW2d 575.—Crim Law 641.12(4).

Hamilton, Ex parte, TexCrimApp, 290 SW2d 673, 163 TexCrim 283.—Crim Law 304(14); Sent & Pun 1132.

Hamilton, In Interest of, TexApp–Corpus Christi, 975 SW2d 758, reh overr, and review den.—App & E 1,

76(1), 935(1); Child S 342, 343; Judgm 321, 328, 386(1), 397.

Hamilton, In re, BkrtcyNDTex, 224 BR 360. See Thompson, In re.

Hamilton, In re, BkrtcyWDTex, 274 BR 266.—Bankr 2159.1, 2325, 3024; Ex & Ad 1.

Hamilton, Matter of, CA5 (Tex), 125 F3d 292.—Bankr 2701, 2702.1, 2705, 3782, 3786, 3790; Mtg 372(1); Notice 5, 6; Ven & Pur 220, 229(1), 229(2), 229(5), 230(1), 231(2), 231(17), 245.

Hamilton, Matter of, CA5 (Tex), 892 F2d 1230.—Bankr 2614; Sec Tran 81.

Hamilton v. Amaimo, TexApp–Houston (1 Dist), 775 SW2d 33.—App & E 80(6).

Hamilton v. Baker, Tex, 214 SW2d 460, 147 Tex 240.—Mines 78.1(3).

Hamilton; Baker v., TexCivApp–Fort Worth, 210 SW2d 634, rev 214 SW2d 460, 147 Tex 240.—Bills & N 23; Mines 78.1(3).

Hamilton; Bandera Independent School Dist. v., Tex-App–San Antonio, 2 SW3d 367, mandamus gr, and review den, subsequent mandamus proceeding In re Bandera Downs, Inc, 1999 WL 792688.—App & E 842(1), 893(1); Auctions 7; Schools 65; Tax 2966.

Hamilton; Beal v., TexApp–Houston (1 Dist), 712 SW2d 873.—Evid 472(1), 506, 538, 571(3); Health 618, 814, 820, 906, 924, 926; Judgm 151, 162(4), 169.

Hamilton; Bill, TexCivApp–Eastland, 90 SW2d 929, writ refused.—Usury 34, 101, 141.

Hamilton; Board of Firemen's Relief and Retirement Fund Trustees of Texarkana v., Tex, 386 SW2d 754.—Const Law 4186; Mun Corp 200(10).

Hamilton; Board of Firemen's Relief and Retirement Fund Trustees of Texarkana v., TexCivApp–Austin, 378 SW2d 361, writ gr, rev 386 SW2d 754.—Mun Corp 196.

Hamilton v. Board of Firemen's Relief and Retirement Fund Trustees of Texarkana, TexCivApp–Texarkana, 408 SW2d 781, ref nre.—Admin Law 744.1, 750; Lim of Act 28(1); Mun Corp 200(2), 200(9), 200(10).

Hamilton v. Booher, TexCivApp–Amarillo, 124 SW2d 184.—Venue 5.1, 7.5(2), 7.5(6), 8.5(5).

Hamilton v. Brown, TexCivApp–San Antonio, 181 SW2d 890, writ refused wom.—Guar 37; Lim of Act 24(1), 46(10).

Hamilton v. Broyhill Furniture Factories, TexCivApp–Waco, 466 SW2d 29, ref nre.—Bills & N 92(5).

Hamilton v. Butler, TexCivApp–Eastland, 397 SW2d 932, ref nre.—Adop 3, 21.

Hamilton v. California Co., TexCivApp–Eastland, 103 SW2d 200, writ dism.—False Imp 31, 39.

Hamilton v. Calvert, TexCivApp–Austin, 235 SW2d 453, writ refused.—Divorce 313.1; Statut 121(7); Tax 3327(1).

Hamilton; Campbell v., TexApp–Dallas, 632 SW2d 633, ref nre.—Princ & A 158.

Hamilton; Campise v., SDTex, 382 FSupp 172, appeal dism 541 F2d 279, cert den 97 SCt 1127, 429 US 1102, 51 LEd2d 552.—Civil R 1004, 1358, 1373, 1376(6), 1376(7), 1462, 1465(1), 1481; Fed Cts 227, 333; Hab Corp 901; Lim of Act 75; Prisons 13(2), 13(5); Sent & Pun 1430, 1553.

Hamilton v. Charles Maund Oldsmobile-Cadillac Co., TexCivApp–Austin, 347 SW2d 944, ref nre.—Autos 20; Hus & W 249(2.1), 254, 264(3), 266.4, 267(4).

Hamilton; Christy v., TexCivApp–Amarillo, 384 SW2d 795.—Mines 125; Plead 48.

Hamilton v. City of Austin, WDTex, 8 FSupp2d 886.—Admin Law 413, 754.1, 763; Environ Law 536, 595(3), 701; Inj 138.1; Statut 219(1).

Hamilton; City of Dallas v., TexApp–Eastland, 132 SW3d 632, reh overr, and petition stricken, and review den.—Admin Law 749, 750, 760, 786, 790, 791, 793; Mun Corp 198(3), 198(5); Offic 72.55(2).

Hamilton; City of San Antonio v., TexApp–San Antonio, 714 SW2d 372, ref nre.—Death 23; Interest 39(2.6); Mun Corp 725, 743, 755(1), 819(1).

Hamilton v. City of Wake Village, EDTex, 593 FSupp 1294.—Civil R 1128; Const Law 1183, 3595, 4165(1), 4171, 4173(4).

Hamilton; Clyde v., Tex, 414 SW2d 434.—App & E 768, 1175(1); Estop 78(3); Ex & Ad 456(3); Life Est 15(1); Mines 48, 54(2); Wills 740(4).

Hamilton v. Clyde, TexCivApp–Waco, 405 SW2d 850, writ gr, rev 414 SW2d 434.—Estop 32(2); Life Est 15(1); Remaind 17(3); Wills 531(2), 740(4).

Hamilton; Coastal States Gas Producing Co. v., TexCiv-App–El Paso, 553 SW2d 659.—Lim of Act 24(2).

Hamilton v. Collett, CA5 (Tex), 83 FedAppx 634, cert den 125 SCt 33, 543 US 809, 160 LEd2d 11.—Civil R 1037; False Imp 13; Fed Cts 574.

Hamilton v. Collins, CA5 (Tex), 905 F2d 825, cert den 111 SCt 244, 498 US 895, 112 LEd2d 203.—Hab Corp 771.

Hamilton v. Craig, TexCivApp–Waco, 257 SW2d 500.—Adop 14, 16; Divorce 168; Hab Corp 536; Infants 231; Judgm 486(1).

Hamilton; Elliott v., TexApp–Beaumont, 767 SW2d 262, writ den.—Judgm 18(1), 675(1).

Hamilton v. Elliott v., TexCivApp–Corpus Christi, 512 SW2d 824.—App & E 230; Judgm 271; Mand 51, 155(1); Trial 355(1), 356(1), 366.

Hamilton v. Empire Gas & Fuel Co., TexComApp, 110 SW2d 561, 134 Tex 377.—App & E 395, 430(1), 911.2, 937(1); Courts 66.1, 89; Judgm 270.

Hamilton v. Empire Gas & Fuel Co., TexCivApp–Texarkana, 85 SW2d 280, aff 110 SW2d 561, 134 Tex 377.—App & E 112; Courts 66.1.

Hamilton v. Fant, TexCivApp–Austin, 422 SW2d 495.—Damag 108, 112; Labor & Emp 3137, 3179(2), 3181(4); Neglig 387, 1225; Tresp 52, 57; Trial 284.

Hamilton v. Federal Deposit Ins. Corp., CA5 (Tex), 939 F2d 1225. See F.D.I.C. v. Hamilton.

Hamilton; F.D.I.C. v., CA5 (Tex), 939 F2d 1225.—Banks 505; Fed Civ Proc 2465.1.

Hamilton v. Federal Land Bank of Houston, TexCiv-App–Galveston, 125 SW2d 1088.—Venue 22(6).

Hamilton v. First Nat. Bank of O'Donnell, TexCivApp–Amarillo, 155 SW2d 626, writ refused wom.—Judgm 715(3); Lim of Act 103(4); Trial 29(1), 114; Trusts 69.

Hamilton v. General Motors Corp., CA5 (Tex), 606 F2d 576, reh den 611 F2d 882, cert den 100 SCt 2990, 447 US 907, 64 LEd2d 856, reh den 101 SCt 288, 449 US 913, 66 LEd2d 141.—Civil R 1142, 1505(2), 1505(3), 1505(6), 1513, 1530, 1535, 1536, 1561, 1562; Fed Cts 425.

Hamilton; Goen v., TexCivApp–Amarillo, 159 SW2d 231.—Brok 43(2), 82(1); Frds St of 148(1); Statut 223.5(4).

Hamilton v. Goodson, TexCivApp–Hous (1 Dist), 578 SW2d 448.—Lim of Act 118(1), 119(1), 119(3), 119(6), 199(1).

Hamilton; Gossett v., TexCivApp–Fort Worth, 133 SW2d 297, writ dism, correct.—Banks 47(1), 63.5; Const Law 632, 633, 1066, 2632, 2734, 2757, 2761, 4410.

Hamilton v. Gregory, TexCivApp–Hous (1 Dist), 482 SW2d 287.—Mand 4(1); Wills 229, 312, 400.

Hamilton v. Grocers Supply Co., Inc., CA5 (Tex), 986 F2d 97.—Civil R 1210, 1539, 1551; Fed Civ Proc 2142.1, 2608.1.

Hamilton v. Grocers Supply Co., Inc., CA5 (Tex), 978 F2d 1441. See Britt v. Grocers Supply Co., Inc.

Hamilton; Gulf, C. & S. F. Ry. Co. v., TexComApp, 89 SW2d 208, 126 Tex 542.—App & E 782; Courts 247(7), 247(8).

Hamilton v. Hamilton, Tex, 280 SW2d 588, 154 Tex 511.—App & E 882(8), 964; Estop 32(1), 78(3); New Tr 9; Partit 9(1); Stip 14(11), 17(3); Trial 105(1); Trusts 30.5(1); Wills 58(2), 59.

Hamilton; Hamilton v., Tex, 280 SW2d 588, 154 Tex 511.
—App & E 882(8), 964; Estop 32(1), 78(3); New Tr 9;
Partit 9(1); Stip 14(11), 17(3); Trial 105(1); Trusts
30.5(1); Wills 58(2), 59.

Hamilton v. Hamilton, TexCivApp–Fort Worth, 592
SW2d 87.—Child C 427, 512.

Hamilton; Hamilton v., TexCivApp–Fort Worth, 592
SW2d 87.—Child C 427, 512.

Hamilton v. Hamilton, TexCivApp–Austin, 363 SW2d
187, ref nre.—Corp 215; Joint Adv 1.2(1); Trial
350.4(1).

Hamilton; Hamilton v., TexCivApp–Austin, 363 SW2d
187, ref nre.—Corp 215; Joint Adv 1.2(1); Trial
350.4(1).

Hamilton v. Hamilton, TexCivApp–Dallas, 292 SW2d
674.—App & E 1199.

Hamilton; Hamilton v., TexCivApp–Dallas, 292 SW2d
674.—App & E 1199.

Hamilton v. Hamilton, TexCivApp–Dallas, 269 SW2d
491, aff 280 SW2d 588, 154 Tex 511.—Action 53(1);
Estop 52(1), 78(1); New Tr 9, 26; Trial 2, 3(2); Wills
58(2), 59, 63.

Hamilton; Hamilton v., TexCivApp–Dallas, 269 SW2d
491, aff 280 SW2d 588, 154 Tex 511.—Action 53(1);
Estop 52(1), 78(1); New Tr 9, 26; Trial 2, 3(2); Wills
58(2), 59, 63.

Hamilton v. H. E. Butt Grocery Store v., TexApp–Corpus
Christi, 632 SW2d 189.—App & E 846(5), 931(1), 989;
Neglig 1104(6); Plead 111.42(7), 111.44; Venue 21.

Hamilton; Henry S. Miller Co. v., TexApp–Houston (1
Dist), 813 SW2d 631.—Antitrust 367, 369, 393; App & E
5, 931(1), 1010.1(3), 1010.2; Damag 194; Judgm 17(8).

Hamilton v. Herrin Transp. Co., TexCivApp–Waco, 343
SW2d 300, ref nre.—App & E 1172(2); Indem 35, 81;
Princ & A 41(6), 47.

Hamilton v. Hi-Plains Truck Brokers, Inc., TexApp–
Amarillo, 23 SW3d 442, reh overr.—App & E 508.

Hamilton; Hirczy v., CA5 (Tex), 190 FedAppx 357, cert
den 127 SCt 1141, 166 LEd2d 893.—Colleges 10; Inj
26(4); Judges 51(2); Records 63.

Hamilton; Houston General Ins. Co. v., TexApp–Beaumont, 634 SW2d 18, dism.—Work Comp 970, 990, 1658,
1728, 1937.

Hamilton v. Jenkins, TexCivApp–San Antonio, 235 SW2d
195, mandamus overr.—App & E 1024.3; Neglig 343;
Plead 111.1, 111.5; Venue 8.5(5), 8.5(6).

Hamilton v. Jones, TexCivApp–Hous (1 Dist), 521 SW2d
350, ref nre.—App & E 758.3(9); Judgm 335(1), 335(3).

Hamilton; Keelin v., TexCivApp–Dallas, 430 SW2d 268.
—App & E 236(2), 918(3), 927(7), 959(3), 989; Contracts
28(3), 29; Plead 229, 236(3), 248(4); Pretrial Proc 723.1.

Hamilton v. Keller, TexCivApp–Eastland, 148 SW2d
1011.—Estop 32(1); Partit 4, 9(1), 14; Remaind 14;
Trusts 110, 296, 361.

Hamilton v. Liles, TexCivApp–Houston, 404 SW2d 342,
ref nre.—App & E 927(7), 989; Health 637; Trial
139.1(7).

Hamilton v. Lyons, CA5 (Tex), 74 F3d 99.—Civil R 1098,
1404; Const Law 4544, 4545(1), 4594(1), 4594(4), 4838;
Crim Law 412.1(1), 412.1(2); Fed Civ Proc 2734; Fed
Cts 830; Pardon 66, 72.1, 80; Prisons 4(4); Sent & Pun
4, 1532, 1574.

Hamilton v. McAmis, TexCivApp–Tyler, 401 SW2d 316.
—Courts 26, 481; Judgm 181(15.1), 518.

Hamilton v. McAmis, TexCivApp–Tyler, 401 SW2d 314.
—App & E 621(1), 627.2.

Hamilton; McCorkle v., TexCivApp–Fort Worth, 150
SW2d 439, writ refused.—Insurance 1365, 1407; Judgm
812(3); Lim of Act 66(15); Mtg 311, 383.

Hamilton v. McCotter, CA5 (Tex), 772 F2d 171, reh den
777 F2d 701.—Crim Law 641.13(1), 641.13(7); Hab
Corp 474, 745.1, 897, 898(1), 898(2); Ind & Inf 4, 33(3).

Hamilton; McKelroy v., TexCivApp–Waco, 130 SW2d
1114.—Contrib 1, 4; Des & Dist 152; Home 99, 123,
142(1); Tax 2730.

Hamilton; Miller Co. v., TexApp–Houston (1 Dist), 813
SW2d 631. See Henry S. Miller Co. v. Hamilton.

Hamilton; Missouri-Kansas-Texas R. Co. v., TexCiv-
App–Dallas, 314 SW2d 114, ref nre.—App & E 1170.1,
1170.6; Death 24, 39, 99(3), 104(4); Evid 539, 539.5(1);
Hus & W 21, 25(1), 268(9), 270(3), 272(2), 273(12);
Neglig 575; Parent & C 7(9); R R 335.5, 347(1); Trial
125(1), 133.6(3.1), 133.6(4), 133.6(5), 352.1(8), 352.20.

Hamilton v. Morris Resources, Ltd., TexApp–San Antonio, 225 SW3d 336, reh overr, and rule 537(f) motion gr.
—App & E 946; Deeds 93, 95, 97; Estop 52(1), 89.1,
92(1), 92(2), 92(3); Lim of Act 44(1), 95(8); Mines 48,
55(4), 55(5), 73.1(2), 79.1(5); Motions 66; Pretrial Proc
746, 752.

Hamilton v. Motor Coach Industries, Inc., TexCivApp–
Texarkana, 569 SW2d 571.—App & E 927(7); Prod
Liab 1, 5, 8, 14, 22, 25, 27, 28, 87.1, 90; Trial 139.1(7).

Hamilton; Mountain States Mut. Cas. Co. v., TexCiv-
App–Eastland, 401 SW2d 303.—Plead 378; Work Comp
1021, 1639, 1920, 1974.

Hamilton; Nealy v., CA5 (Tex), 837 F2d 210.—Atty & C
129(2); Consp 18; Fed Cts 755.

Hamilton v. Newbury, TexCivApp–Dallas, 412 SW2d 801,
ref nre.—Bills & N 128; Courts 12(2.30); Evid 54, 587,
590, 595; Judgm 818(3), 942, 944; Trial 382.

Hamilton; Parr v., TexCivApp–Corpus Christi, 437 SW2d
29.—Abate & R 78, 81; App & E 78(1); Courts 472.2,
475(1), 481; Judgm 480; Plead 111.43, 111.47.

Hamilton v. Perry, TexCivApp–Texarkana, 109 SW2d
1142.—App & E 930(1); Autos 181(1), 244(20).

Hamilton v. Perry, TexCivApp–El Paso, 85 SW2d 846.—
Plead 111.37, 111.42(8); Venue 8.5(5).

Hamilton v. Pilgrim's Pride Employee Group Health
Plan, EDTex, 37 FSupp2d 817.—Insurance 3504, 3509,
3519(2); Labor & Emp 483(1), 483(2), 602(1), 611, 687,
688, 709; Subrog 32.

Hamilton; Podolnick v., Tex, 349 SW2d 715.—Hus & W
62, 90; Judgm 181(15.1); Ven & Pur 53.

Hamilton; Podolnick v., TexCivApp–Austin, 359 SW2d
108, ref nre.—Evid 246; Hus & W 62, 248.5, 262.1(1),
265.5.

Hamilton; Podolnick v., TexCivApp–Austin, 337 SW2d
376, writ gr, rev 349 SW2d 715.—Hus & W 62, 89, 90,
201; Ven & Pur 82.

Hamilton; Powell v., TexCivApp–Waco, 197 SW2d 540.—
Atty & C 145, 167(2), 168; Lim of Act 195(3), 199(1).

Hamilton; Pruett v., TexCivApp–Austin, 263 SW2d 193,
ref nre.—Courts 202(5); Guard & W 9.5, 13(8); Mental
H 157.

Hamilton; Pruett v., TexCivApp–Austin, 259 SW2d 916.
—App & E 781(1); Mental H 152; Supersed 4.

Hamilton; Pruett v., TexCivApp–Austin, 258 SW2d 198,
ref nre.—Inj 138.75.

Hamilton; Realty Portfolio, Inc. v., CA5 (Tex), 125 F3d
292. See Hamilton, Matter of.

Hamilton; Republic Nat. Life Ins. Co. v., TexCivApp–
San Antonio, 373 SW2d 275, ref nre.—Evid 571(9); Insurance 2594(4), 2594(5), 2604, 2607, 2608.

Hamilton v. Robertson, CA5 (Tex), 854 F2d 740.—Fed
Cts 573.

Hamilton v. Robertson, TexApp–Houston (1 Dist), 778
SW2d 474.—Costs 2; Mand 168(4).

Hamilton v. Rodgers, CA5 (Tex), 791 F2d 439.—Civil R
1251, 1351(5), 1359, 1405, 1421, 1528, 1535, 1544, 1553;
Mun Corp 198(1).

Hamilton v. Rogers, SDTex, 573 FSupp 452.—Abate & R
58(1).

Hamilton; San Antonio Loan & Trust Co. v., Tex, 283
SW2d 19, 155 Tex 52.—Mines 73.1(3); Trusts 62, 63.9,
84, 86, 125, 272.1; Wills 684.3(1).

Hamilton v. San Antonio Loan & Trust Co., TexCiv-App–San Antonio, 272 SW2d 384, aff 283 SW2d 19, 155 Tex 52.—Mtg 517; Trusts 84.

Hamilton; S & H Supply Co. v., Tex, 418 SW2d 489.—Bills & N 92(3).

Hamilton v. S & H Supply Co., TexCivApp–Austin, 408 SW2d 773, writ gr, rev 418 SW2d 489.—App & E 1008.1(1); Bills & N 98, 318, 351.

Hamilton v. Scott, TexCivApp–El Paso, 110 SW2d 925.—Tresp to T T 41(1); Trusts 44(3).

Hamilton v. Segue Software Inc., CA5 (Tex), 232 F3d 473.—Fed Civ Proc 2470.1, 2544; Fed Cts 383, 391, 412.1; Fraud 3, 9, 13(1), 16, 17, 64(1); Labor & Emp 40(2), 41(2), 47, 758, 842.

Hamilton v. Shirley-Self Motor Co., TexCivApp–Fort Worth, 202 SW2d 952, ref nre.—Contracts 176(10), 212(1), 212(2), 277(2); Lim of Act 165.

Hamilton; Smith v., TexCivApp–Austin, 237 SW2d 774.—App & E 1039(2.1); Evid 17; Labor & Emp 858, 866, 867, 868(3), 871, 873.

Hamilton; Sneed v., TexCivApp–Beaumont, 299 SW2d 769.—Adv Poss 103, 110(3), 115(2), 115(7); App & E 866(3); Propty 10.

Hamilton v. Southwestern Bell Telephone Co., CA5 (Tex), 136 F3d 1047.—Civil R 1018, 1217, 1218(2), 1218(3), 1218(6), 1220.

Hamilton v. Sowers, TexCivApp–Fort Worth, 554 SW2d 225, dism.—App & E 846(5), 912; Evid 589; Health 821(5); Plead 111.42(7); Venue 72.

Hamilton v. State, TexCrimApp, 831 SW2d 326.—Arrest 63.4(1); Autos 349.5(3).

Hamilton v. State, TexCrimApp, 676 SW2d 120.—Weap 4.

Hamilton v. State, TexCrimApp, 621 SW2d 407.—Crim Law 577.8(1), 577.11(3).

Hamilton v. State, TexCrimApp, 590 SW2d 503.—Arrest 63.3, 63.4(13).

Hamilton v. State, TexCrimApp, 480 SW2d 685.—Homic 1136; Witn 277(3).

Hamilton v. State, TexCrimApp, 438 SW2d 814.—Crim Law 394.4(2), 867, 1167(3); Witn 216(4).

Hamilton v. State, TexCrimApp, 397 SW2d 225.—Const Law 268(7), 4729; Crim Law 147, 404.85; Forg 34(8); Sent & Pun 1260, 1302.

Hamilton v. State, TexCrimApp, 346 SW2d 123.—Mal Mis 12.

Hamilton v. State, TexCrimApp, 305 SW2d 781.—Ind & Inf 41(3).

Hamilton v. State, TexCrimApp, 274 SW2d 699, 161 TexCrim 81.—Crim Law 255.3, 369.6, 1126.

Hamilton v. State, TexCrimApp, 256 SW2d 857.—Crim Law 1094(3).

Hamilton v. State, TexCrimApp, 255 SW2d 509.—Crim Law 1090.1(1).

Hamilton v. State, TexCrimApp, 165 SW2d 737, 145 TexCrim 78.—Arson 30, 37(1), 37(3); Crim Law 422(6), 423(3), 680(1), 1169.2(1), 1169.2(6), 1169.3.

Hamilton v. State, TexCrimApp, 150 SW2d 395, 141 TexCrim 614, cert den 62 SCt 117, 314 US 609, 86 LEd 490.—Crim Law 687(2), 1153(3), 1169.3, 1170.5(5); Gr Jury 8; Homic 1479; Ind & Inf 137(2), 140(2).

Hamilton v. State, TexCrimApp, 136 SW2d 858, 138 TexCrim 360.—Assault 74, 78.

Hamilton v. State, TexCrimApp, 135 SW2d 476, 138 TexCrim 205.—Crim Law 363, 364(4), 519(3), 814(17), 1149, 1169.12; Ind & Inf 133(3).

Hamilton v. State, TexCrimApp, 109 SW2d 1059, 133 TexCrim 228.—Larc 60.

Hamilton v. State, TexCrimApp, 98 SW2d 818.—Crim Law 1094(2.1).

Hamilton v. State, TexCrimApp, 96 SW2d 983, 131 Tex-Crim 88.—Burg 36, 41(1); Crim Law 351(8), 552(3), 1159.3(1).

Hamilton v. State, TexCrimApp, 92 SW2d 442.—Crim Law 1131(1).

Hamilton v. State, TexApp–Houston (1 Dist), 820 SW2d 941.—Autos 332, 335; Double J 132.1, 135, 142, 161.

Hamilton v. State, TexApp–Fort Worth, 804 SW2d 171, petition for discretionary review refused.—Crim Law 847, 950, 951(6), 1044.2(1); Homic 668, 1371.

Hamilton v. State, TexApp–Fort Worth, 772 SW2d 571, petition for discretionary review refused, rev 831 SW2d 326.—Arrest 58; Crim Law 394.4(9), 394.6(5), 783.5, 1134(3), 1172.1(1), 1173.2(9).

Hamilton v. State, TexApp–Dallas, 682 SW2d 322, petition for discretionary review refused.—Crim Law 418(1), 418(2), 1169.1(9).

Hamilton v. State, TexApp–Texarkana, 699 SW2d 576, petition for discretionary review refused.—Crim Law 511.1(3), 511.2; Hab Corp 287.1, 466; Homic 1184, 1186.

Hamilton v. State, TexApp–Beaumont, 663 SW2d 529.—Crim Law 736(2).

Hamilton v. State, TexApp–Eastland, 678 SW2d 90, rev 676 SW2d 120.—Arson 2; Weap 4, 17(1), 17(4), 17(5).

Hamilton v. State, TexApp–Houston (14 Dist), 818 SW2d 880, petition for discretionary review refused.—Crim Law 706(8), 713, 719(1), 722.5, 730(1), 730(13), 790, 1171.1(2.1).

Hamilton; State Bd. of Polygraph Examiners v., Tex-CivApp–Dallas, 594 SW2d 833.—Licens 38; Statut 64(1).

Hamilton; Stekoll Petroleum Co. v., Tex, 255 SW2d 187, 152 Tex 182.—Contracts 25; Frds St of 110(1), 125(2), 156.

Hamilton v. Stekoll Petroleum Co., TexCivApp–Dallas, 250 SW2d 645, rev 255 SW2d 187, 152 Tex 182.—App & E 757(1), 934(1); Frds St of 106(1), 110(1), 112, 113(3), 118(1), 118(2); Judgm 181(19); Mines 74(2).

Hamilton; Texas Dept. of Public Safety v., Tex, 306 SW2d 712, 157 Tex 616.—Autos 144.2(1).

Hamilton; Texas Dept. of Public Safety v., TexCivApp–Eastland, 304 SW2d 719, ref nre 306 SW2d 712, 157 Tex 616.—Autos 144.2(1), 144.2(5.1); Const Law 1007, 4262; Evid 80(1); Judgm 815, 818(1), 818(3), 818(4); Licens 38.

Hamilton v. Texas Dept. of Transp., CA5 (Tex), 85 Fe-dAppx 8.—Civil R 1249(1), 1251, 1553; States 53.

Hamilton v. Texas Dept. of Transp., SDTex, 206 FSupp2d 826, reconsideration den 2001 WL 34109380.—Civil R 1126, 1135, 1246, 1248, 1510.

Hamilton; Texas Emp. Ins. Ass'n v., TexCivApp–Fort Worth, 430 SW2d 216, ref nre.—App & E 1170.6; Trial 121(2), 129, 133.6(8); Work Comp 848, 1628, 1639, 1966, 1968(3), 1968(5).

Hamilton; Texas Emp. Ins. Ass'n v., TexCivApp–Texar-kana, 267 SW2d 216, ref nre.—Work Comp 1930, 1936.

Hamilton; Texas Emp. Ins. Ass'n v., TexCivApp–East-land, 95 SW2d 767, writ dism.—Work Comp 820, 1404, 1964, 1966, 1968(3).

Hamilton; Texas General Indem. Co. v., TexCivApp–San Antonio, 420 SW2d 735, ref nre.—Work Comp 949, 1703, 1968(5).

Hamilton v. Texas Oil & Gas Corp., TexApp–El Paso, 648 SW2d 316, ref nre.—Antitrust 141, 143(2); Contracts 171(1); Costs 194.32; Damag 76, 89(2), 91(3); Mines 101, 109; Neglig 273.

Hamilton v. Travelers Ins. Co., TexCivApp–Texarkana, 116 SW2d 414.—App & E 1144; Judgm 199(3.14); Work Comp 1278.

Hamilton; U.S. v., CA5 (Tex), 440 F3d 693, reh den, cert dism Miles v. US, 126 SCt 2887, 165 LEd2d 914, cert den 127 SCt 176, 166 LEd2d 42.—Crim Law 1042, 1139, 1141(2), 1165(1), 1177, 1178, 1192.

Hamilton; U.S. v., CA5 (Tex), 48 F3d 149.—Crim Law 662.7, 1170.5(1); Fed Cts 404; Witn 345(1), 345(8), 374(1).

Hamilton; U.S. v., CA5 (Tex), 694 F2d 398.—Crim Law 620(6), 1134(3); Ind & Inf 127, 130; Tel 1018(3).

Hamilton v. U.S., CA5 (Tex), 304 F2d 542.—Consp 47(11).

Hamilton v. U.S., CA5 (Tex), 221 F2d 611.—Crim Law 37(1), 37(2.1), 37(3), 37(8), 739.1(2), 742(1), 772(6), 1172.1(2), 1172.1(4), 1173.2(3).

Hamilton v. U.S., CCA5 (Tex), 90 F2d 996.—Crim Law 242(4), 242(5), 242(7), 242(8); Hab Corp 717(1), 848.

Hamilton v. U.S., EDTex, 928 FSupp 684.—Fed Civ Proc 2512; Seamen 29(3), 29(5.14), 29(5.16).

Hamilton; U.S. Life Ins. Co. v., TexCivApp–Waco, 238 SW2d 289, ref nre.—Labor & Emp 866, 869, 2204; Names 17; Torts 388.

Hamilton; Victory v., TexComApp, 91 SW2d 697, 127 Tex 203.—App & E 434, 435, 655(1), 1165.

Hamilton v. Waples-Platter Co., TexCivApp–Fort Worth, 424 SW2d 295.—App & E 927(7), 989; Autos 244(13); Trial 39.

Hamilton v. Williams, TexCivApp–Texarkana, 81 SW2d 265.—App & E 742(1).

Hamilton v. Wilson, TexApp–Amarillo, 223 SW3d 535, reh overr.—App & E 863, 934(1); Evid 547.5, 555.10, 571(3); Health 611, 665; Judgm 185(5), 185.1(4).

Hamilton; Winter v., TexCivApp–Eastland, 214 SW2d 330.—App & E 138, 833(3); Autos 200; Execution 18; Parties 27, 31; Plead 110, 111.2, 111.38, 111.46; Torts 135; Venue 21, 22(6).

Hamilton Air Mart, Inc.; Gibraltar Sav. Ass'n v., TexApp–Dallas, 662 SW2d 632.—App & E 564(3), 564(5).

Hamilton, City of; Gardner v., TexCivApp–Waco, 536 SW2d 422, ref nre.—Em Dom 9, 27, 169.

Hamilton County; Schuman v., TexCivApp–Waco, 436 SW2d 366.—Dedi 44; High 17, 53(2), 159(2).

Hamilton County Elec. Co-op. Ass'n; Ethridge v., TexApp–Waco, 995 SW2d 292.—App & E 863; Judgm 183, 185(2), 185(6), 185.3(21).

Hamilton Energy, Inc.; Truelove v., TexApp–Tyler, 627 SW2d 499, ref nre.—Judgm 183, 189.

Hamilton Independent School Dist.; Lamkin Independent School Dist. v., TexCivApp–Waco, 242 SW2d 828. —Schools 38.

Hamilton Ins. Agency v. Allstate Ins. Co., TexApp–San Antonio, 693 SW2d 735. See Zuniga v. Allstate Ins. Co.

Hamilton Investment Trust v. Hi Fashion Wigs Profit Sharing Trust, TexCivApp–Dallas, 559 SW2d 376.— Plead 111.38, 111.39(2); Venue 46.

Hamilton Inv. Trust; Hi Fashion Wigs Profit Sharing Trust v., TexCivApp–Eastland, 579 SW2d 300.—Usury 2(1).

Hamilton Lane Advisors, Inc.; American Realty Trust, Inc. v., CA5 (Tex), 115 FedAppx 662.—Fed Civ Proc 636, 1755; Fed Cts 76.20, 79, 97.

Hamilton Nat. Bank; Allen v., TexCivApp–Waco, 459 SW2d 955.—App & E 863; Plead 45, 111.12, 111.36; Venue 6.

Hamilton Nat. Bank v. Pool, TexCivApp–Waco, 144 SW2d 670.—Counties 21.5, 167; Mand 102(1); Mun Corp 373(1); Pub Contr 25.

Hamilton Standard Controls, Inc.; Garrett v., CA5 (Tex), 850 F2d 253.—Fed Cts 907, 911; Prod Liab 8, 15.

Hamilton Supply Corp.; Gulf Coast Factors, Inc. v., TexCivApp–Houston, 389 SW2d 341.—Fact 53, 66; Sales 53(1), 168.5(1).

Hamilton Trailer Co.; Guyger v., TexCivApp–Eastland, 304 SW2d 377.—Autos 160(1), 240(1), 244(59), 245(6), 245(91), 246(38); Neglig 1537; Trial 244(4).

Hamiter v. Westmoreland, TexCivApp–Texarkana, 524 SW2d 95.—App & E 1010.1(10); Contracts 176(11); Impl & C C 112.

Hamker v. Diamond Shamrock Chemical Co., CA5 (Tex), 756 F2d 392.—Const Law 2511; Environ Law 226.

Hamlet v. Silliman, TexCivApp–Hous (1 Dist), 605 SW2d 663.—Child C 76, 469, 552.

Hamlet; U.S. v., CA5 (Tex), 480 F2d 556, cert den 94 SCt 452, 414 US 1026, 38 LEd2d 317.—Costs 302.4.

Hamlet; U.S. v., CA5 (Tex), 456 F2d 1284, appeal after remand 480 F2d 556, cert den 94 SCt 452, 414 US 1026, 38 LEd2d 317.—Costs 302.4; Crim Law 1132.

Hamlett v. Holcomb, TexApp–Corpus Christi, 69 SW3d 816.—App & E 223, 863, 934(1); Brok 100, 102; Judgm 181(10), 183, 185(2); Torts 242; Ven & Pur 79, 186.

Hamlett v. State, TexCrimApp, 243 SW2d 166.—Crim Law 1137(5).

Hamlin, Ex parte, TexCrimApp, 152 SW2d 334, 142 TexCrim 185.—Hab Corp 281, 466.

Hamlin; Bryant v., TexCivApp–Dallas, 373 SW2d 837, ref nre, appeal after remand 399 SW2d 572, ref nre.— Courts 198, 202(5); Trial 139.1(17), 178; Wills 324(1), 327.

Hamlin v. Bryant, TexCivApp–Tyler, 399 SW2d 572, ref nre.—Evid 41; Wills 55(1), 158, 163(8), 166(1), 166(7), 166(12), 311, 324(2), 324(3).

Hamlin; City of Midland v., TexCivApp–El Paso, 239 SW2d 159, 25 ALR2d 1048, ref nre.—Evid 14; Mun Corp 724, 725, 745.5, 747(4).

Hamlin v. Gutermuth, TexApp–Houston (14 Dist), 909 SW2d 114, reh overr, and writ den.—Atty & C 105, 129(3).

Hamlin; Martin v., TexCrimApp, 25 SW3d 718.—Hab Corp 603, 689, 819.

Hamlin; Means v., TexCivApp–El Paso, 174 SW2d 499.— Des & Dist 86; Evid 116, 318(1); Lim of Act 48(1); Trusts 44(3), 61(3); Ven & Pur 54, 266(2), 299(3).

Hamlin v. State, TexCrimApp, 510 SW2d 611.—Statut 109.2, 118(1).

Hamlin v. State, TexApp–Houston (1 Dist), 902 SW2d 613.—Crim Law 268, 1134(5), 1152(2), 1158(3), 1166.17; Ind & Inf 179; Jury 97(1), 105(4), 132.

Hamlin v. State, TexApp–Fort Worth, 632 SW2d 203.— Crim Law 641.10(3), 720(6), 720(8), 1169.2(7); Sent & Pun 1367, 1378, 1381(2).

Hamlin; State v., TexApp–Houston (14 Dist), 871 SW2d 796, reh overr, and petition for discretionary review refused.—Arrest 63.5(5), 68(3), 68(4); Crim Law 1158(2), 1158(4).

Hamlin; State v., TexApp–Houston (14 Dist), 871 SW2d 790, petition for discretionary review refused.—Arrest 63.1, 63.5(5), 68(3), 68(4); Crim Law 1148, 1158(4), 1159.2(9), 1159.4(2); Searches 23.

Hamlin, City of; Motor Inv. Co. v., Tex, 179 SW2d 278, 142 Tex 486.—Autos 19, 20; Chat Mtg 2, 201(1); Plead 8(2), 36(1), 36(2); Statut 161(1).

Hamlin Hospital Dist.; Carter v., TexCivApp–Eastland, 538 SW2d 671, ref nre, cert den 97 SCt 1680, 430 US 984, 52 LEd2d 378.—Const Law 2580, 3482, 3657; Health 105.

Hamlin Nat. Bank; Poe v., TexApp–Eastland, 921 SW2d 515, reh overr, and writ den.—Fraud Conv 174(3), 176(1).

Hamm v. Allstate Ins. Co., NDTex, 286 FSupp2d 790.— Contracts 176(2); Fed Cts 373; Insurance 1806, 1808, 2278(17), 2914, 2939.

Hamm v. Berrey, TexCivApp–San Antonio, 419 SW2d 401, ref nre.—Courts 8; Evid 51, 80(1); Judgm 822(1).

Hamm; Catchings v., TexCivApp–Waco, 560 SW2d 194.— Lim of Act 6(1).

Hamm v. Crockett, TexCivApp–Amarillo, 576 SW2d 871. —App & E 846(5), 852; Fraud 3; Plead 111.42(10).

Hamm v. Hamm, TexCivApp–Fort Worth, 159 SW2d 183. —App & E 281(1), 672; Divorce 51, 179, 252.1, 252.2, 252.3(1), 252.3(2), 252.3(3), 253(4), 254(1), 286(0.5).

Hamm; Hamm v., TexCivApp–Fort Worth, 159 SW2d 183.—App & E 281(1), 672; Divorce 51, 179, 252.1, 252.2, 252.3(1), 252.3(2), 252.3(3), 253(4), 254(1), 286(0.5).

Hamm v. Millennium Income Fund, L.L.C., TexApp–Houston (1 Dist), 178 SW3d 256, review den, and reh of petition for review den, cert den 127 SCt 297, 166

HAMM

59 Tex D 2d—470

See Guidelines for Arrangement at the beginning of this Volume

LEd2d 154.—Alt Disp Res 116, 342, 354, 357, 363(1), 363(4), 363(8); App & E 837(1), 966(1); New Tr 18; Plead 78, 130.

Hamm v. State, TexCrimApp, 513 SW2d 85.—Sent & Pun 636, 1064, 2021.

Hamm v. State, TexCrimApp, 177 SW2d 793.—Crim Law 1090.1(1).

Hamm v. State, TexApp–Corpus Christi, 709 SW2d 14.—Crim Law 99, 394.4(9), 1036.1(4), 1044.2(1), 1169.1(8).

Hamm; U.S. v., CA5 (Tex), 659 F2d 624.—Crim Law 274(2), 303.15, 303.30(1).

Hamm; U.S. v., CA5 (Tex), 638 F2d 823, reh gr 644 F2d 354, on reh 659 F2d 624.—Crim Law 303.20, 303.30(1), 303.35(1), 303.50.

Hammack v. Automated Information Management, Inc., NDTex, 981 FSupp 993.—Action 3; U S 120.1.

Hammack v. Baroid Corp., CA5 (Tex), 142 F3d 266.—Fed Cts 543.1, 776, 850.1; Labor & Emp 569(2), 688; Statut 181(1), 184.

Hammack v. Conoco, Inc., TexApp–Houston (1 Dist), 902 SW2d 127, reh overr, and writ den.—App & E 854(1); Judgm 185(2); Labor & Emp 3125, 3155, 3159; Neglig 202, 210, 1011, 1020, 1037(7), 1692.

Hammack v. N L Industries, Inc., CA5 (Tex), 142 F3d 266. See Hammack v. Baroid Corp.

Hammack v. Public Utility Com'n of Texas, TexApp–Austin, 131 SW3d 713, review den, and reh of petition for review den.—Admin Law 314, 325, 481, 791, 793; Const Law 4027, 4371; Electricity 9(2); Pub Ut 195; Statut 219(1).

Hammack v. State, TexApp–Austin, 963 SW2d 199.—Crim Law 994(1), 1081(5), 1081(6); Sent & Pun 1001, 2079.

Hammack; U.S. v., CA5 (Tex), 604 F2d 437.—Arrest 63.4(5), 63.5(3.1), 63.5(4), 63.5(5), 63.5(8).

Hamman v. Boaz Well Service, Inc., TexCivApp–Fort Worth, 620 SW2d 903.—Labor & Emp 29, 30; Torts 140.

Hamman v. Bright & Co., TexApp–Amarillo, 924 SW2d 168, reh overr, and writ gr, vac pursuant to settlement 938 SW2d 718.—App & E 169; Contracts 134; Evid 448; Mines 73.1(4), 74.5; Perp 4(1), 4(3), 4(4).

Hamman v. City of Houston, TexCivApp–Fort Worth, 362 SW2d 402, ref nre.—Dedi 65; Mun Corp 224.

Hamman; Firemen's and Policemen's Civil Service Commission of City of Port Arthur v., Tex, 404 SW2d 308.—Const Law 4172(3); Mun Corp 185(7), 185(12), 216(1).

Hamman; Firemen's and Policemen's Civil Service Commission of City of Port Arthur v., TexCivApp–Beaumont, 393 SW2d 406, writ gr, aff in part, rev in part 404 SW2d 308.—Const Law 2450; Jury 19(12); Mun Corp 185(7), 185(8), 185(10), 185(12).

Hamman; Gaines v., Tex, 358 SW2d 557, 163 Tex 618.—App & E 516; Judgm 178, 181(1), 185(2), 185(6), 185.2(8), 185.3(1); Trusts 103(1).

Hamman; Gaines v., TexCivApp–Fort Worth, 346 SW2d 186, writ gr, rev 358 SW2d 557, 163 Tex 618.—Frds St of 129(1); Trusts 17(3), 103(1).

Hamman v. Geophysical Data Processing Center, Inc., TexCivApp–Corpus Christi, 430 SW2d 840.—App & E 624, 627.2, 628(1).

Hamman v. Hayes, TexCivApp–Beaumont, 391 SW2d 73, writ refused.—Quo W 5.

Hamman v. Ritchie, TexCivApp–Fort Worth, 547 SW2d 698, ref nre.—Acct 20(3); Life Est 21; Lim of Act 182(2); Ten in C 10, 22, 26, 49; Trusts 183, 263, 265, 304, 329, 340; Waste 18; Wills 577, 705.

Hamman v. Southwestern Gas Pipeline, Inc., CA5 (Tex), 832 F2d 55.—Fed Civ Proc 2366.1, 2737.5, 2743.1.

Hamman v. Southwestern Gas Pipeline, Inc., CA5 (Tex), 821 F2d 299, vac in part on reh 832 F2d 55.—Damag 55; Fed Cts 637, 638, 640, 641; Interest 39(2),

39(2.50), 66; Lis Pen 16, 18, 22(2), 24(1); Tresp 46(3), 49, 50.

Hamman v. Southwestern Gas Pipeline, Inc., CA5 (Tex), 721 F2d 140, appeal after remand 821 F2d 299, vac in part on reh 832 F2d 55.—Fed Civ Proc 2531, 2547.1, 2549; Fed Cts 14.1, 932.1; Gas 9.

Hamman v. State, TexCrimApp, 314 SW2d 301, 166 TexCrim 349.—Crim Law 379, 390; Embez 48(2); Gr Jury 2.5.

Hamman; State v., TexCivApp–Houston, 377 SW2d 727.—App & E 970(2); Em Dom 221, 262(1), 262(5); Evid 142(1), 359(1); Trial 194(20), 261.

Hamman Exploration Co.; Gulf Coast Water Co. v., TexCivApp–Galveston, 160 SW2d 92, writ refused.—App & E 931(6); Deeds 101; Ease 1, 36(3).

Hamman Oil and Refining Co.; Mandell v., TexApp–Houston (1 Dist), 822 SW2d 153, writ den.—App & E 169, 215(1), 901, 931(1), 977(5), 989, 994(1), 1012.1(4); Compromise 23(3); Contracts 187(1); Costs 207; Frds St of 44(1), 119(1); Judgm 199(3.7), 199(3.10); Mines 73, 78.1(2), 78.1(3), 78.1(4), 78.1(8), 78.1(11), 79.1(1), 79.7; New Tr 6; Nova 1, 12; Ref of Inst 33.

Hammer, Ex parte, TexCrimApp, 91 SW2d 706.—Hab Corp 823.

Hammer; Ashbrook v., TexCivApp–Amarillo, 106 SW2d 776.—App & E 1177(1); Des & Dist 130; Ex & Ad 7; Lim of Act 102(1); Trover 1; Wills 827, 847(2).

Hammer v. City of Dallas, TexCivApp–Fort Worth, 273 SW2d 646.—App & E 799, 843(1); Em Dom 107, 203(1), 203(7), 224, 262(1); New Tr 150(2).

Hammer v. Dallas Transit Co., Tex, 400 SW2d 885, on remand 404 SW2d 85.—App & E 1094(1); Autos 238(3), 242(4); Neglig 1560; Trial 352.5(6), 365.1(7).

Hammer; Dallas Transit Co. v., TexCivApp–Dallas, 404 SW2d 85.—Damag 96, 132(8), 134(3).

Hammer; Dallas Transit Co. v., TexCivApp–Dallas, 390 SW2d 823, writ gr, rev 400 SW2d 885, on remand 404 SW2d 85.—App & E 232(0.5), 1078(1), 1170.1, 1170.7, 1177(6); Autos 242(7), 244(10); Judgm 18(1), 19, 199(2), 199(3); Trial 350.6(3), 352.1(7), 352.10, 361.

Hammer; N803RA, Inc. v., TexApp–Houston (1 Dist), 11 SW3d 363.—App & E 840(2); Appear 9(1), 9(2); Corp 665(1); Courts 12(2.1), 12(2.5), 12(2.10); Plead 87.

Hammer v. Plumhoff, TexCivApp–Waco, 114 SW2d 438.—Wills 741, 832.

Hammer v. Powers, TexApp–Fort Worth, 819 SW2d 669.—App & E 223, 1024.4; Judgm 185.1(8), 185.3(1); Wills 55(1), 166(1), 667.

Hammer; Tide Water Associated Oil Co. v., TexCivApp–Texarkana, 163 SW2d 232, writ refused.—Lis Pen 24(1), 26(4); Mines 79.1(4).

Hammer; U.S. v., CA5 (Tex), 496 F2d 917.—Judges 24; Sent & Pun 2280.

Hammer & Steel, Inc.; Magana v., SDTex, 206 FSupp2d 848.—Adm 1(3), 20; Fed Cts 5, 32.

Hammerly Oaks, Inc. v. Edwards, Tex, 958 SW2d 387.—Corp 397, 498; Damag 87(1); Evid 587; Land & Ten 169(11); Neglig 1704.

Hammerly Oaks, Inc.; Edwards v., TexApp–Houston (1 Dist), 908 SW2d 270, reh overr, and writ gr, mod 958 SW2d 387.—App & E 215(1), 216(1), 231(1), 231(9), 761, 863, 934(1), 1001(1), 1001(3); Corp 423, 498, 521; Damag 91(3); Neglig 211, 273.

Hammerman & Gainer; Watkins v., TexApp–Austin, 814 SW2d 867.—Afft 9; Antitrust 294; Compromise 18(1); Contracts 245(1); Judgm 181(15.1), 185(5), 185.3(1).

Hammerman & Gainer, Inc. v. Bullock, TexApp–Austin, 791 SW2d 330.—Decl Judgm 216; Tax 3635.

Hammers, Matter of, CA5 (Tex), 988 F2d 32.—Bankr 2125, 2233(3), 2264(1); Const Law 4478; Statut 181(1), 190.

Hammers; Birdo v., TexApp–Tyler, 842 SW2d 700, reh overr, and writ den.—Pretrial Proc 474.

For Later Case History Information, see KeyCite on WESTLAW

Hammers v. I.R.S., CA5 (Tex), 988 F2d 32. See Hammers, Matter of.

Hammers v. State, TexCrimApp, 286 SW2d 636.—Crim Law 1090.1(1).

Hammers v. State, TexCrimApp, 286 SW2d 626.—Crim Law 1090.1(1).

Hammerstein v. Hammerstein, TexCivApp–Fort Worth, 269 SW2d 591.—App & E 768; Divorce 62(2).

Hammerstein; Hammerstein v., TexCivApp–Fort Worth, 269 SW2d 591.—App & E 768; Divorce 62(2).

Hammett v. Arnim, TexCivApp–Houston, 385 SW2d 598.—Ex & Ad 216(2); Impl & C C 34; Witn 159(9).

Hammett; Baker v., TexApp–Texarkana, 789 SW2d 682.—Ex & Ad 35(1), 85(5.1), 315.1.

Hammett v. Fleming, TexCivApp–Austin, 324 SW2d 70, ref nre.—Autos 181(1), 245(87); Judgm 181(12), 185(2), 185.2(9), 185.3(21), 186; Neglig 1717.

Hammett v. Lee, TexApp–Dallas, 730 SW2d 350, writ dism woj.—Hus & W 281; Judgm 203, 219.

Hammett v. McIntire, TexCivApp–Houston, 365 SW2d 844, ref nre.—App & E 628(1), 653(3); Judgm 199(3.10); Trusts 72, 77, 79, 89(1), 136.5.

Hammett v. State, TexCrimApp, 713 SW2d 102, on remand 724 SW2d 946.—Crim Law 1144.12; Witn 337(1), 337(4), 398(3), 405(1), 406.

Hammett v. State, TexCrimApp, 578 SW2d 699, cert dism 100 SCt 2905, 448 US 725, 65 LEd2d 1086.—Costs 302.4; Crim Law 339.6, 404.15, 404.65, 404.80, 419(1.5), 444, 531(3), 641.7(1), 720(9), 726, 1166.16; Homic 850, 1387; Jury 131(4); Mental H 434; Sent & Pun 1752, 1762, 1769; Statut 118(1).

Hammett v. State, TexApp–Fort Worth, 724 SW2d 946.—Crim Law 1169.1(1), 1170.5(1); Witn 406.

Hammett; Taylor Fishing Club v., TexCivApp–Waco, 88 SW2d 127, writ dism.—Fish 5(1); Nav Wat 1(2), 1(3), 1(5), 1(6); Waters 111.

Hammett v. Texas, USTex, 100 SCt 2905, 448 US 725, 65 LEd2d 1086.—Fed Cts 510.

Hammett v. Zimmerman, TexApp–Fort Worth, 804 SW2d 663.—Damag 185(1), 192, 221(7).

Hammit v. Westbrook, TexCivApp–Eastland, 262 SW2d 260.—Autos 368; Witn 400(1).

Hammitt; State v., TexApp–Beaumont, 825 SW2d 131, petition for discretionary review refused.—Arrest 63.5(1), 63.5(4), 63.5(5); Crim Law 338(1), 394.4(12), 1158(4).

Hammock v. State, TexCrimApp, 46 SW3d 889.—Courts 89, 90(6); Crim Law 673(5), 698(1), 824(8), 826.

Hammock v. State, TexApp–Texarkana, 211 SW3d 874.—Controlled Subs 22; Crim Law 1, 1030(3); Ind & Inf 72, 125(20).

Hammon v. Texas & N. O. R. Co., TexCivApp–Tyler, 382 SW2d 155, ref nre, cert den Hammons v. Texas and New Orleans R Co, 86 SCt 73, 382 US 832, 15 LEd2d 76.—App & E 230, 237(2), 760(2), 1045(3), 1062.5, 1170.6; Jury 133; Labor & Emp 2879, 2881; Neglig 1693, 1694.

Hammon v. Wichita County, TexCivApp–Fort Worth, 290 SW2d 545.—Action 65; Em Dom 74, 167(4); Inj 9, 34.

Hammond, Ex parte, TexCrimApp, 540 SW2d 328.—Bail 43, 49(3.1), 49(4); Crim Law 528, 1158(2); Sent & Pun 1670, 1675, 1720.

Hammond, In re, TexApp–El Paso, 155 SW3d 222.—Child S 487; Contempt 63(5), 66(7), 70, 72, 81; Hab Corp 490(1), 528.1, 529, 705.1; Jury 24.5, 29(6).

Hammond v. All Wheel Drive Co., TexApp–Beaumont, 707 SW2d 734.—App & E 179(1); Costs 262; Judgm 185(4); Mtg 369(1), 414.

Hammond; American Nat. Ins. Co. v., TexCivApp–Waco, 91 SW2d 432, writ dism.—App & E 1043(7); Insurance 3379, 3381(5), 3571, 3580; Trial 133.2, 133.6(4).

Hammond v. Barnhart, CA5 (Tex), 132 FedAppx 6.—Social S 147.5.

Hammond v. Barnhart, CA5 (Tex), 124 FedAppx 847, reh den 132 FedAppx 6.—Social S 142.5, 143.60, 145, 145.5.

Hammond v. Chadwick, TexCivApp–Waco, 199 SW2d 547.—Adop 7.6(1), 7.6(3), 7.8(3.1), 11.

Hammond v. City of Dallas, Tex, 712 SW2d 496.—Mun Corp 57, 58, 185(12); Statut 194.

Hammond; City of Dallas v., TexApp–Fort Worth, 691 SW2d 827, writ gr, rev 712 SW2d 496.—App & E 846(5); Mun Corp 185(5), 185(12).

Hammond v. Coastal Rental & Equipment Co., Inc., SDTex, 95 FRD 74.—Fed Civ Proc 1636.1, 1637.

Hammond v. County of Dallas, CA5 (Tex), 970 F2d 1441. See Arrington v. County of Dallas.

Hammond v. Eplen, TexCivApp–Galveston, 216 SW2d 258.—Adop 13; Trial 142, 143.

Hammond v. Hammond, TexApp–Fort Worth, 898 SW2d 406.—Child S 21, 140(2), 231, 234, 251, 339(3), 556(2), 556(3).

Hammond; Hammond v., TexApp–Fort Worth, 898 SW2d 406.—Child S 21, 140(2), 231, 234, 251, 339(3), 556(2), 556(3).

Hammond v. Hammond, TexApp–Beaumont, 688 SW2d 690, dism.—App & E 5; Divorce 178.

Hammond; Hammond v., TexApp–Beaumont, 688 SW2d 690, dism.—App & E 5; Divorce 178.

Hammond v. Hammond, TexCivApp–Fort Worth, 216 SW2d 630.—Corp 553(5), 556, 558, 606, 609, 665(3), 684; Receivers 60.

Hammond; Hammond v., TexCivApp–Fort Worth, 216 SW2d 630.—Corp 553(5), 556, 558, 606, 609, 665(3), 684; Receivers 60.

Hammond v. Hammond, TexCivApp–Fort Worth, 197 SW2d 502.—Divorce 252.1, 252.5(3), 286(0.5).

Hammond; Hammond v., TexCivApp–Fort Worth, 197 SW2d 502.—Divorce 252.1, 252.5(3), 286(0.5).

Hammond v. Hammond, TexCivApp–Galveston, 210 SW2d 829, dism.—App & E 1000; Divorce 161; Judgm 443(1); Lim of Act 39(7), 100(11).

Hammond; Hammond v., TexCivApp–Galveston, 210 SW2d 829, dism.—App & E 1000; Divorce 161; Judgm 443(1); Lim of Act 39(7), 100(11).

Hammond v. Johnson, TexApp–Waco, 647 SW2d 68.—Antitrust 369; App & E 1054(1), 1071.1(5.1).

Hammond v. Katy Independent School Dist., TexApp–Houston (14 Dist), 821 SW2d 174.—App & E 173(2); Civil R 1123, 1351(5); Damag 50.10; Judgm 184, 185(1); Labor & Emp 826; Libel 1, 33, 36; Schools 63(3), 147, 147.51.

Hammond; Pena v., CA5 (Tex), 172 F2d 312.—Judgm 828.5(2).

Hammond v. Rimmer's Estate, TexApp–Eastland, 643 SW2d 222, ref nre.—Damag 185(1).

Hammond; Scroggins v., TexCivApp–Austin, 121 SW2d 629.—J P 162(2), 188(3).

Hammond v. Secretary of Health, Ed. and Welfare, CA5 (Tex), 452 F2d 1205.—Fed Cts 743.

Hammond; Shropshire v., TexCivApp–Fort Worth, 120 SW2d 282.—Mines 74(5), 74(9.1); Trusts 107, 371(8).

Hammond v. Smidth, TexCivApp–Galveston, 286 SW2d 654, writ refused.—Hus & W 152.

Hammond v. State, TexCrimApp, 799 SW2d 741, reh den, motion gr Madden v. Texas, 111 SCt 902, 498 US 1301, 112 LEd2d 1026, cert den 111 SCt 2912, 501 US 1259, 115 LEd2d 1076, denial of habeas corpus aff 35 F3d 559, cert den 115 SCt 1825, 514 US 1097, 131 LEd2d 747.—Const Law 42.1(3), 725; Crim Law 1171.5; Jury 132, 133; Sent & Pun 1780(2); Witn 71.

Hammond v. State, TexCrimApp, 583 SW2d 785.—Rob 27(6).

Hammond v. State, TexCrimApp, 470 SW2d 683.—Crim Law 273(4.1).

Hammond v. State, TexCrimApp, 465 SW2d 748.—Const Law 4711; Crim Law 730(1), 1110(1), 1130(2); Double J 150(1); Larc 40(10); Sent & Pun 505, 1132.

Hammond v. State, TexCrimApp, 293 SW2d 652, 163 TexCrim 471.—Jury 59(1).

Hammond v. State, TexCrimApp, 257 SW2d 304.—Crim Law 1090.1(1).

Hammond v. State, TexCrimApp, 137 SW2d 1042, 138 TexCrim 546.—Crim Law 394.4(12), 419(3), 1186.7.

Hammond v. State, TexCrimApp, 137 SW2d 1025, 138 TexCrim 641.—Crim Law 364(4), 412.1(1), 721(3), 730(12), 1091(8); Int Liq 167, 236(7).

Hammond v. State, TexApp–Dallas, 898 SW2d 6.—Controlled Subs 148(3), 148(4); Searches 113.1.

Hammond v. State, TexApp–Corpus Christi, 664 SW2d 838.—Arrest 63.5(3.1), 63.5(5); Burg 18; Crim Law 1036.4.

Hammond v. State, TexApp–Houston (14 Dist), 942 SW2d 703.—Crim Law 26, 80, 507(1), 519(8), 535(1), 535(2), 641.13(2.1), 641.13(6), 781(3), 847, 881(1), 1038.1(3.1), 1038.3, 1144.13(3), 1159.2(7), 1166.16; Homic 569, 1127, 1165, 1166, 1167, 1177, 1207; Rob 24.20; Witn 88.

Hammond v. State, TexApp–Houston (14 Dist), 746 SW2d 278, petition for discretionary review refused.—Crim Law 1081(2).

Hammond v. Stricklen, TexCivApp–Tyler, 498 SW2d 356, ref nre.—App & E 901, 930(1), 932(1), 989, 1003(1), 1004(3), 1012.1(1), 1177(7); Autos 244(14), 244(45); Courts 106; Damag 96, 127, 132(1); Trial 127; Witn 330(1), 372(1).

Hammond v. Texas, USTex, 111 SCt 902, 498 US 1301, 112 LEd2d 1026. See Madden v. Texas.

Hammond; Texas Emp. Ins. Ass'n v., TexCivApp–Amarillo, 278 SW2d 503.—Work Comp 817, 1374, 1619, 1930.

Hammond v. Travelers Indem. Co., TexCivApp–Hous (14 Dist), 553 SW2d 205.—Princ & S 175, 185.

Hammond; U.S. v., CA5 (Tex), 201 F3d 346, appeal after remand 275 F3d 43.—Crim Law 1139, 1158(1); Labor & Emp 3270, 3283; Sent & Pun 672, 674, 970, 973.

Hammond; U.S. v., CA5 (Tex), 815 F2d 302.—Crim Law 700(10), 1171.1(1).

Hammond; U.S. ex rel. Angelica v., CCA5 (Tex), 99 F2d 557, reh den U.S. ex rel Carlisle v. Hammond, 100 F2d 227, cert den 59 SCt 488, 306 US 638, 83 LEd 1039.—Const Law 2654; Fed Cts 541; Hab Corp 205, 814.

Hammond; U.S. ex rel. Maceo v., CCA5 (Tex), 98 F2d 187.—Crim Law 242(1), 242(5), 242(7), 242(8), 242(11); Hab Corp 702, 712.1, 717(1).

Hammonds, Ex parte, TexCrimApp, 407 SW2d 779.—Hab Corp 509(2); Sent & Pun 1318.

Hammonds, Ex parte, TexCrimApp, 398 SW2d 283.—Hab Corp 230.

Hammonds, Ex parte, TexCrimApp, 230 SW2d 820, 155 TexCrim 82.—Hab Corp 223, 822.

Hammonds; Brown v., CA5 (Tex), 747 F2d 320.—Fed Cts 8.

Hammonds v. Calhoun Distributing Co., Inc., TexCivApp–Texarkana, 584 SW2d 473, ref nre.—Frds St of 63(2), 129(3), 129(5), 129(7), 158(4); Judgm 181(19), 185(2).

Hammonds v. City of Corpus Christi, Tex., CA5 (Tex), 343 F2d 162, cert den 86 SCt 85, 382 US 837, 15 LEd2d 80.—Mun Corp 29(4), 33(9).

Hammonds v. City of Corpus Christi, Tex., SDTex, 226 FSupp 456, aff 343 F2d 162, cert den 86 SCt 85, 382 US 837, 15 LEd2d 80.—Const Law 2508, 2580; Fed Cts 27, 178, 221; Mun Corp 29(2).

Hammonds; Cliett v., CA5 (Tex), 305 F2d 565.—Contempt 4, 20, 21, 22, 28(1), 40, 55, 60(1), 60(3), 61(1), 61(6), 66(8), 70, 72; Inj 218, 223, 232; Judgm 829(1); Witn 302.

Hammonds; Cliett v., CA5 (Tex), 286 F2d 471, cert den 81 SCt 1921, 366 US 960, 6 LEd2d 1253, reh den 82 SCt 27, 368 US 870, 7 LEd2d 71.—Adv Poss 45; Fed Civ Proc 2654, 2656.

Hammonds v. Hammonds, Tex, 313 SW2d 603, 158 Tex 516.—App & E 119, 458(1); Costs 10, 195, 209, 216; Damag 71; Partit 114(3); Receivers 154(1).

Hammonds; Hammonds v., Tex, 313 SW2d 603, 158 Tex 516.—App & E 119, 458(1); Costs 10, 195, 209, 216; Damag 71; Partit 114(3); Receivers 154(1).

Hammonds v. Hammonds, Tex, 285 SW2d 362, 155 Tex 207.—Courts 247(7); Venue 5.3(1), 46.

Hammonds; Hammonds v., Tex, 285 SW2d 362, 155 Tex 207.—Courts 247(7); Venue 5.3(1), 46.

Hammonds v. Hammonds, TexCivApp–Dallas, 583 SW2d 807, dism.—Divorce 224, 226, 252.3(2), 252.3(5), 286(8).

Hammonds; Hammonds v., TexCivApp–Dallas, 583 SW2d 807, dism.—Divorce 224, 226, 252.3(2), 252.3(5), 286(8).

Hammonds v. Hammonds, TexCivApp–Amarillo, 308 SW2d 895, rev 313 SW2d 603, 158 Tex 516.—Costs 169, 251; Receivers 200.

Hammonds; Hammonds v., TexCivApp–Amarillo, 308 SW2d 895, rev 313 SW2d 603, 158 Tex 516.—Costs 169, 251; Receivers 200.

Hammonds v. Hammonds, TexCivApp–Amarillo, 290 SW2d 272.—App & E 1180(2); Equity 35; Partit 53.

Hammonds; Hammonds v., TexCivApp–Amarillo, 290 SW2d 272.—App & E 1180(2); Equity 35; Partit 53.

Hammonds v. Hammonds, TexCivApp–Amarillo, 278 SW2d 380, rev 285 SW2d 362, 155 Tex 207.—App & E 846(5), 1024.3; Partit 10, 43, 63(1); Plead 111.9, 111.38; Venue 22(6).

Hammonds; Hammonds v., TexCivApp–Amarillo, 278 SW2d 380, rev 285 SW2d 362, 155 Tex 207.—App & E 846(5), 1024.3; Partit 10, 43, 63(1); Plead 111.9, 111.38; Venue 22(6).

Hammonds v. Holmes, Tex, 559 SW2d 345.—Judgm 627; Mtg 209.

Hammonds v. Holmes, TexCivApp–Waco, 543 SW2d 20, writ gr, aff in part, rev in part 559 SW2d 345.—Judgm 624, 707, 717; Labor & Emp 3027.

Hammonds v. Houston Elec. Co., TexCivApp–Beaumont, 169 SW2d 765.—Plead 111.18, 111.42(8), 111.42(9).

Hammonds v. Lloyds Fire & Cas. Assur. of San Antonio, TexCivApp–San Antonio, 256 SW2d 223.—App & E 870(2), 874(2), 874(3), 920(1).

Hammonds; Marion v., TexCivApp–Amarillo, 374 SW2d 349.—Sales 389.

Hammonds; Mission Wholesale Grocery Co. v., TexCivApp–San Antonio, 215 SW2d 260, ref nre.—App & E 1008.1(1); Evid 13; Sales 181(12), 397.

Hammonds; Producers Pipe & Supply Co. v., TexCivApp–Texarkana, 143 SW2d 412.—Corp 633, 666; Evid 347.

Hammonds v. Riley, TexCivApp–El Paso, 151 SW2d 602, dism.—Courts 104.

Hammonds v. Roper, TexCivApp–Corpus Christi, 493 SW2d 569, ref nre.—App & E 930(1), 989; Gifts 45, 49(1), 50; Plead 34(1), 132, 381(3), 382(1); Replev 69(3), 69(4).

Hammonds v. Shannon, WDTex, 323 FSupp 681.—Schools 172.

Hammonds v. State, TexCrimApp, 500 SW2d 831.—Crim Law 372(5), 1166.8; Larc 62(2), 65.

Hammonds v. State, TexCrimApp, 320 SW2d 7, 167 TexCrim 228.—Burg 41(1); Crim Law 570(1); Sent & Pun 1381(3).

Hammonds v. State, TexCrimApp, 316 SW2d 423, 166 TexCrim 499.—Controlled Subs 33; Crim Law 511.1(8), 511.2.

Hammonds v. Thomas, TexApp–Texarkana, 770 SW2d 1.—Judgm 181(33), 185.3(21); Time 10(6).

Hammons; Murphy v., Tex, 509 SW2d 845.—App & E 930(1), 989; Autos 244(50), 244(58).

Hammons; Murphy v., TexCivApp–Texarkana, 501 SW2d 442, writ gr, rev 509 SW2d 845.—Autos 244(50).

Hammons v. Sheriff of Jefferson County, Tex., CA5 (Tex), 901 F2d 59.—Pardon 81.

Hammons v. State, TexApp–Fort Worth, 856 SW2d 797, petition for discretionary review refused.—Crim Law 404.65, 633(2), 660, 789(2), 813, 814(1), 1134(3), 1144.13(3), 1159.2(7), 1169.2(1); Jury 131(4), 131(15.1); Rob 11, 17(3), 17(4), 24.15(1).

Hammons v. State, TexApp–San Antonio, 221 SW3d 720, petition for discretionary review gr.—Crim Law 808.5, 1153(1), 1165(1), 1169.2(1), 1170.5(1); Ind & Inf 110(17); Infants 13; Witn 414(2).

Hamm-Tex Distributing Co.; Kelly v., TexCivApp–Waco, 337 SW2d 608, ref nre.—Autos 171(9), 212, 244(46), 244(55), 244(58); Neglig 85(2), 259.

Hamner; Juarez v., TexApp–Tyler, 674 SW2d 856.—App & E 758.3(11), 846(5), 931(1), 989; Contracts 303(4); Ven & Pur 78, 111, 144(1), 186, 341(3).

Hamner v. State, TexApp–Beaumont, 689 SW2d 504, petition for discretionary review refused.—Costs 302.1(4); Crim Law 1166(1).

Hamner v. U.S., CCA5 (Tex), 134 F2d 592.—Consp 27, 43(1), 43(10); War 315, 316.

Hamon v. Allen, TexCivApp–Corpus Christi, 457 SW2d 384.—App & E 1056.5; Home 118(3), 118(5), 119; Spec Perf 1, 7, 8, 95, 96, 99, 101, 119; Trial 178.

Hamon; Shuttle Oil Corp. v., TexCivApp–Beaumont, 477 SW2d 701, ref nre.—Mines 77, 78.1(3).

Hamon v. State, TexCrimApp, 119 SW2d 1057, 135 TexCrim 347.—Crim Law 537, 594(4), 595(9), 675, 1137(5), 1169.11, 1170(4), 1170.5(5); Witn 337(16).

Hamon & Griffith; City of Aransas Pass v., TexCivApp–Fort Worth, 104 SW2d 893, writ dism.—App & E 1062.1; Mun Corp 220(2).

Hamon Operating Co.; Santanna Natural Gas Corp. v., TexApp–Austin, 954 SW2d 885, reh overr, and review den.—App & E 893(1); Damag 15; Elect of Rem 15; Fraud 9, 16; Judgm 181(7), 181(29), 181(33), 185(2), 185(6); Lim of Act 55(5), 95(7), 104(1), 195(5); Princ & A 24; Trover 2, 44, 57, 61.

Hamons; City of Houston v., TexCivApp–Hous (14 Dist), 496 SW2d 662, ref nre.—Em Dom 68, 149(1), 196, 262(5); Mun Corp 1040.

Hamor; General American Life Ins. Co. v., TexCivApp–Amarillo, 95 SW2d 975, writ refused.—Usury 62, 97, 100(1).

Hamor; Texas Emp. Ins. Ass'n v., TexCivApp–Amarillo, 97 SW2d 1041.—App & E 742(1), 742(2), 928(1), 1064.2; Evid 314(1); Trial 83(2), 191(10), 215, 219, 233(2), 295(1), 352.18; Work Comp 1922, 1924, 1968(6).

Hampshire v. Hampshire, TexCivApp–Fort Worth, 485 SW2d 314.—Contracts 28(1), 93(2); Divorce 189; Evid 65, 66; Hus & W 14.3, 49.2(9), 49.2(11).

Hampshire; Hampshire v., TexCivApp–Fort Worth, 485 SW2d 314.—Contracts 28(1), 93(2); Divorce 189; Evid 65, 66; Hus & W 14.3, 49.2(9), 49.2(11).

Hampshire v. State, TexApp–Beaumont, 691 SW2d 38, petition for discretionary review refused.—Crim Law 719(1), 721(3), 726, 1169.1(3), 1171.1(2.1), 1171.3; Homic 1184.

Hampshire Silver Co. v. Hill, TexCivApp–Galveston, 244 SW2d 520.—Corp 644, 657(3), 672(7), 673.

Hampton, In re, Tex, 775 SW2d 629.—Judges 11(5.1).

Hampton v. Atlas Subsidiaries of Tex., Inc., TexCivApp–Beaumont, 475 SW2d 407.—Plead 111.36; Venue 7(6), 16 1/2.

Hampton v. Bowen, CA5 (Tex), 785 F2d 1308.—Social S 124.5, 149.5.

Hampton; Brewer v., TexCivApp–Eastland, 166 SW2d 193.—Mental H 10.1, 372.1, 382.1, 486, 495.

Hampton; Carpenters and Joiners Local Union No. 1097 v., TexCivApp–Tyler, 457 SW2d 299.—Labor & Emp 1670, 1673, 1677(5).

Hampton v. C. D. Shamburger Lumber Co., TexCivApp–Amarillo, 127 SW2d 245, writ dism, correct.—Home 57(3); Judgm 768(1).

Hampton; Central Sur. & Ins. Corp. v., CA5 (Tex), 179 F2d 261.—Decl Judgm 276; Insurance 2748(1); Labor & Emp 23.

Hampton; Commerce Independent School Dist. v., TexCivApp–Eastland, 577 SW2d 740.—Const Law 958.

Hampton; Cooper v., TexCivApp–Amarillo, 123 SW2d 941, writ dism.—Alt of Inst 6, 20; App & E 930(3); Bills & N 378; Lim of Act 174(1), 197(2).

Hampton; Gates v., TexCivApp–Amarillo, 350 SW2d 62. —Frds St of 129(11), 158(4).

Hampton v. Graff Vending Co., CA5 (Tex), 516 F2d 100. —Antitrust 839; Commerce 62.13; Fed Cts 916.1, 943.1.

Hampton v. Graff Vending Co., CA5 (Tex), 478 F2d 527, cert den 94 SCt 69, 414 US 859, 38 LEd2d 109, reh den 94 SCt 609, 414 US 1087, 38 LEd2d 493, appeal after remand 516 F2d 100.—Antitrust 814, 872, 913, 976, 977(5), 980, 995; Fed Cts 860, 947.

Hampton; Graves v., CA5 (Tex), 1 F3d 315.—Civil R 1091, 1375, 1376(8), 1376(9); Fed Civ Proc 1838; Fed Cts 791, 830; Judges 36.

Hampton; Gulf, C. & S. F. Ry. Co. v., TexCivApp–Eastland, 358 SW2d 690, ref nre.—App & E 932(1); Damag 132(3), 167, 208(1); Trial 115(2), 122, 133.2, 133.6(4), 133.6(7).

Hampton v. Hauck, CA5 (Tex), 383 F2d 389.—Crim Law 371(1), 683(2); Witn 337(9).

Hampton v. I.R.S., CA5 (Tex), 913 F2d 180.—Admin Law 229; Civil R 1502, 1513, 1514, 1560; Fed Cts 13.10.

Hampton v. ITT Corp., SDTex, 829 FSupp 202.—Alt Disp Res 134(1), 146; Commerce 80.5.

Hampton v. Jackson, TexCivApp–Eastland, 167 SW2d 543.—Assign 49; J P 61, 72.

Hampton; King v., TexComApp, 113 SW2d 173, 131 Tex 85.—Ven & Pur 267.

Hampton v. King, TexCivApp–Amarillo, 87 SW2d 319, rev 113 SW2d 173, 131 Tex 85.—Estates 10(1); Mech Liens 281(1); Mtg 295(1), 295(2); Nova 3.

Hampton v. Long, EDTex, 686 FSupp 1202.—Courts 489(9); Fed Civ Proc 777, 2785; Fed Cts 420; Judgm 828.15(1), 828.16(4).

Hampton v. Lum, TexCivApp–Texarkana, 544 SW2d 839. —Contracts 143(4); Land & Ten 37, 86(2), 88(2).

Hampton v. McCaig, TexCivApp–Fort Worth, 537 SW2d 527.—Bound 37(3), 39, 43, 45; Tresp 52.

Hampton; McCree v., TexCrimApp, 824 SW2d 578.—Hab Corp 689; Mand 16(1).

Hampton; Malone v., TexApp–Dallas, 182 SW3d 465.—Atty & C 24; Costs 2; Courts 40; Judgm 297, 317, 524, 855(1); New Tr 111, 113, 155; Parties 42, 44.

Hampton v. Minton, TexApp–Austin, 785 SW2d 854, writ den.—Contracts 318, 346(2); Covenants 96(1); Mtg 25(5), 414, 556, 559(3), 559(7); Plead 406(5); Ven & Pur 185, 187, 197, 266(2), 301.

Hampton; National Cas. Co. v., TexCivApp–Dallas, 216 SW2d 614, ref nre.—App & E 1001(1), 1003(6), 1083(1), 1083(6), 1175(5), 1177(7); Courts 91(1), 247(7); Insurance 3571.

Hampton v. Nix, TexCivApp–Texarkana, 281 SW2d 126. —Adv Poss 114(1); App & E 931(6), 1054(1); Tresp to T T 41(1).

Hampton; Revlon, Inc. v., TexCivApp, 551 SW2d 121.—Prod Liab 83.

Hampton v. Sharp, TexCivApp–Hous (1 Dist), 447 SW2d 754, ref nre.—App & E 1170.7; Appear 28; Assault 15, 35; Torts 215, 220.

Hampton v. State, TexCrimApp, 165 SW3d 691.—Crim Law 795(1.5), 795(2.10), 795(2.80), 1144.13(3), 1159.2(7), 1189.

Hampton v. State, TexCrimApp, 109 SW3d 437, on remand 2003 WL 22413968, petition for discretionary review gr, aff 165 SW3d 691.—Crim Law 795(1.5), 795(2.10), 795(2.80).

Hampton v. State, TexCrimApp, 86 SW3d 603, on remand 106 SW3d 846, reh overr.—Crim Law 700(2.1), 700(5), 1134(2), 1139, 1158(1), 1171.1(1); Infants 68.4; Statut 188.

Hampton v. State, TexCrimApp, 511 SW2d 1.—Arrest 63.4(10); Autos 355(1); Crim Law 1169.1(10); Searches 62.

Hampton v. State, TexCrimApp, 402 SW2d 748.—Crim Law 371(3), 633(2); False Pret 38, 41, 49(3); Sent & Pun 1374.

Hampton v. State, TexCrimApp, 290 SW2d 905.—Crim Law 1090.1(1).

Hampton v. State, TexCrimApp, 248 SW2d 488, 157 TexCrim 244.—Autos 355(6); Crim Law 565, 1037.2, 1055, 1098, 1171.1(6); Ind & Inf 162.

Hampton v. State, TexCrimApp, 170 SW2d 748, 145 TexCrim 599.—Crim Law 507(1), 511.1(6.1), 511.2.

Hampton v. State, TexCrimApp, 163 SW2d 198.—Crim Law 1094(3).

Hampton v. State, TexCrimApp, 136 SW2d 820, 138 TexCrim 408.—Larc 64(5).

Hampton v. State, TexCrimApp, 135 SW2d 122, 138 TexCrim 271.—Crim Law 304(2), 1169.2(2), 1170.5(5), 1172.8; Homic 982, 1174, 1321; Ind & Inf 132(3); Witn 370(1).

Hampton v. State, TexCrimApp, 90 SW2d 840.—Crim Law 1182.

Hampton v. State, TexApp–Houston (1 Dist), 66 SW3d 430, petition for discretionary review gr, rev 109 SW3d 437, on remand 2003 WL 22413968, petition for discretionary review gr, aff 165 SW3d 691.—Crim Law 748, 770(2), 795(2.1), 795(2.10); Rape 59(20.1); Sent & Pun 323.

Hampton v. State, TexApp–Houston (1 Dist), 838 SW2d 337, opinion after remand 1994 WL 27365, petition for discretionary review refused.—Crim Law 956(11), 956(13), 957(1), 1043(3), 1181.5(3.1).

Hampton v. State, TexApp–Austin, 121 SW3d 778, petition for discretionary review refused.—Crim Law 393(1), 720(1), 721(4), 1043(2), 1165(1), 1171.1(3); Witn 277(1), 319, 347.

Hampton v. State, TexApp–Texarkana, 977 SW2d 467, petition for discretionary review refused.—Crim Law 661.

Hampton v. State, TexApp–El Paso, 106 SW3d 846, reh overr.—Crim Law 700(2.1), 700(3), 700(5), 1192.

Hampton v. State, TexApp–El Paso, 36 SW3d 921, petition for discretionary review gr, rev 86 SW3d 603, on remand 106 SW3d 846, reh overr.—Crim Law 527, 700(2.1), 700(3), 700(4), 1162, 1169.12; Infants 68.4, 192, 195.

Hampton v. State Farm Mut. Auto. Ins. Co., TexApp–Corpus Christi, 778 SW2d 476.—App & E 395; Autos 244(34), 244(35); Damag 63; Estop 52(8); Insurance 2793(1), 3376; Plead 78, 374.

Hampton; Stewart–Warner Corp. v., CA5 (Tex), 950 F2d 244. See Dedmon v. Stewart-Warner Corp.

Hampton; Stubblefield v., TexCivApp–San Antonio, 295 SW2d 233.—Infants 197, 203.

Hampton v. Texas Dept. of Protective and Regulatory Services, TexApp–El Paso, 138 SW3d 564.—Infants 155, 157, 178, 250, 252.

Hampton v. Thompson, CA5 (Tex), 171 F2d 535.—Admin Law 229; Civil R 1009; Const Law 3250; Labor & Emp 1526.

Hampton; Travelers Ins. Co. v., TexCivApp–Eastland, 414 SW2d 712, ref nre.—Work Comp 696, 1565, 1966, 1968(3).

Hampton v. Union Pacific R. Co., EDTex, 81 FSupp2d 703.—Rem of C 2, 29, 36, 84, 92, 95, 96.1, 107(7), 115.

Hampton v. University of Texas--M.D. Anderson Cancer Center, TexApp–Houston (1 Dist), 6 SW3d 627, reh

overr.—App & E 893(1), 911.3; Courts 35; Mun Corp 847; Plead 104(1); States 112.2(4), 191.1.

Hampton; Weiser v., TexCivApp–Hous (1 Dist), 445 SW2d 224, ref nre.—App & E 302(5); Evid 98, 586(2); Health 908, 926, 927; Judges 24; Trial 171.

Hampton & Kennedy Lumber Co. v. Whitfield, TexCivApp–Texarkana, 213 SW2d 152.—Contrib 6, 9(8); Judgm 252(1); Neglig 484.

Hampton Hardware, Inc. v. Cotter & Co., Inc., NDTex, 156 FRD 630.—Const Law 2091; Fed Civ Proc 177.1.

Hampton Inns, Inc.; Hartnett v., TexApp–San Antonio, 870 SW2d 162, writ den.—Antitrust 355, 397; App & E 197(1), 205, 207, 218.2(10), 231(1); Assign 121; Contracts 176(2); Inn 10.8; Plead 139; Subrog 1, 34, 41(7); Trial 274, 351.2(1.1), 366.

Hampton Oil Co. v. Standard Oil Co. of Kansas, SDTex, 14 FSupp 436.—Adv Poss 16(1), 109.

Hampton Place, Inc.; Cash America Intern., Inc. v., TexApp–Fort Worth, 955 SW2d 469, reh overr, and review den.—App & E 230, 231(1), 241, 1051.1(1), 1051.1(2), 1062.2; Land & Ten 233(3); Trial 252(2).

Hampton State Bank; Aetna Life & Cas. Co. v., TexCivApp–Dallas, 497 SW2d 80, ref nre.—Banks 149; Bills & N 21, 201, 356, 443(1), 497(2); Insurance 2405, 2412; Pretrial Proc 308.

Hampton Terrace Apartments, In re, BkrtcyNDTex, 163 BR 488. See Welker, In re.

Hamra v. Gulden, TexApp–Dallas, 898 SW2d 16, writ dism woj.—Antitrust 397; Compromise 15(1); Damag 63.

Hamrah v. Hamrah, TexCivApp–Dallas, 547 SW2d 308, ref nre.—App & E 113(5), 347(3), 623, 624, 629, 824; Judgm 273(7).

Hamrah; Hamrah v., TexCivApp–Dallas, 547 SW2d 308, ref nre.—App & E 113(5), 347(3), 623, 624, 629, 824; Judgm 273(7).

Hamric v. Kansas City Southern Ry. Co., TexApp–Beaumont, 718 SW2d 916, ref nre.—Autos 252, 264, 289; Judgm 185.3(21).

Hamric Chevrolet, Inc. v. U.S. I.R.S., WDTex, 849 FSupp 500. See Bob Hamric Chevrolet, Inc. v. U.S. I.R.S.

Hamrick, In re, TexApp–Houston (14 Dist), 979 SW2d 851.—Child C 730; Mand 1.

Hamrick v. City of Eustace, EDTex, 732 FSupp 1390.—Civil R 1088(3), 1088(4), 1358, 1376(2), 1376(6), 1420, 1432, 1464; Fed Civ Proc 2191, 2192.1, 2233.

Hamrick; Commercial Cas. Ins. Co. v., TexComApp, 94 SW2d 421, 127 Tex 403.—App & E 719(1), 1062.1.

Hamrick; Houston Livestock Show and Rodeo, Inc. v., TexApp–Austin, 125 SW3d 555, reh overr.—Agric 5; Antitrust 141, 145, 147, 150, 357, 363, 369, 390, 393, 398; App & E 959(3), 971(2), 989, 1001(1), 1001(3), 1003(7), 1004(8), 1024.3, 1043(8), 1097(1), 1144, 1195(1); Costs 194.16, 198, 207, 208, 252, 264; Damag 6, 15, 16, 18, 102, 140.7, 192; Evid 532, 536, 546, 555.2; Libel 117; Lim of Act 43, 95(1), 177(2), 187, 195(3), 197(2), 199(1); Plead 236(4), 236(6); Venue 82.

Hamrick v. Simpler, Tex, 95 SW2d 357, 127 Tex 428.—Const Law 990; Counties 62; Offic 40; Statut 48.

Hamrick v. State, TexCrimApp, 495 SW2d 256.—Arrest 63.4(11).

Hamrick v. Wilhite, TexCivApp–Amarillo, 278 SW2d 578, ref nre.—Explos 8; Neglig 1176.

Hamshire v. De Villeneuve, TexCivApp–Beaumont, 135 SW2d 571.—Home 129(1); Trial 350.2, 350.3(2.1).

Hamshire-Fannett Independent School Dist.; LeLeaux v., Tex, 835 SW2d 49.—Schools 89, 89.8(1), 89.13(1), 89.13(3), 159.5(6).

Hamshire-Fannett Independent School Dist.; LeLeaux v., TexApp–Beaumont, 798 SW2d 20, writ gr, aff 835 SW2d 49.—Schools 89.2, 89.8(1), 89.13(1), 89.13(4).

Hamstein Music Co. v. La Cienega Music Co., CA5 (Tex), 4 F3d 413. See Ham v. La Cienega Music Co.

Hanafin; Hone v., Tex, 104 SW3d 884, on remand 2003 WL 22020778, review den, and reh of petition for review den.—App & E 428(2).

Hanafin; Hone v., TexApp–Dallas, 105 SW3d 15, review gr, rev 104 SW3d 884, on remand 2003 WL 22020778, review den, and reh of petition for review den.—App & E 352.1, 428(2).

Hanafy; U.S. v., CA5 (Tex), 302 F3d 485.—Crim Law 1139; Food 15; Health 314; Trademarks 1787.

Hanafy; U.S. v., NDTex, 124 FSupp2d 1016, aff 302 F3d 485.—Consp 25, 48.3; Crim Law 1144.13(3), 1144.13(5), 1159.2(7), 1159.4(2); Food 15; Rec S Goods 1, 8(3); Trademarks 1787; U S 34.

Hanafy v. U.S., NDTex, 991 FSupp 794.—Const Law 3911, 4416; Deeds 79; Int Rev 4767, 4768.1, 4770, 4781; Ven & Pur 221.

Hanak v. Talon Ins. Agency, Ltd., EDTex, 470 FSupp2d 695.—Contracts 147(1), 187(1); Fed Civ Proc 2466, 2470.1, 2544, 2546; Fed Cts 14.1, 18; Insurance 1110, 1302, 1829, 2209, 2993, 3183, 3361, 3436, 3447; States 18.41.

Hanau, In re Estate of, TexApp–Corpus Christi, 806 SW2d 900, writ den.—Const Law 2314, 4089; Courts 201; Ex & Ad 7.

Hanau v. Betancourt, TexApp–Corpus Christi, 800 SW2d 371.—Ex & Ad 7; Mand 3(2.1), 3(7), 26.

Hanau, Estate of v. Hanau, Tex, 730 SW2d 663, on subsequent appeal In re Estate of Hanau, 806 SW2d 900, writ den.—Hus & W 246, 249(6), 264(7); Wills 435.

Hanau; Hanau, Estate of v., Tex, 730 SW2d 663, on subsequent appeal In re Estate of Hanau, 806 SW2d 900, writ den.—Hus & W 246, 249(6), 264(7); Wills 435.

Hanau, Estate of v. Hanau, TexApp–Corpus Christi, 721 SW2d 515, writ gr, aff in part, rev in part 730 SW2d 663, on subsequent appeal In re Estate of Hanau, 806 SW2d 900, writ den.—Hus & W 249(5), 254, 264(2); Wills 435.

Hanau; Hanau, Estate of v., TexApp–Corpus Christi, 721 SW2d 515, writ gr, aff in part, rev in part 730 SW2d 663, on subsequent appeal In re Estate of Hanau, 806 SW2d 900, writ den.—Hus & W 249(5), 254, 264(2); Wills 435.

Hanby v. Shell Oil Co., EDTex, 144 FSupp2d 673.—Fed Cts 101, 103, 104, 105, 106.5, 144.

Hance, Ex parte, TexCrimApp, 417 SW2d 175.—Sent & Pun 1318.

Hance v. Cogswell, TexCivApp–Austin, 307 SW2d 277.—Judgm 17(2).

Hance; Missouri Pac. R. Co. v., TexCivApp–San Antonio, 310 SW2d 374, ref nre.—Explos 8; Neglig 1045(3), 1537.

Hance v. Stubbs, TexCivApp–Amarillo, 146 SW2d 492, writ refused.—App & E 1195(3); Usury 26, 100(1).

Hance, Scarborough, Wright, Ginsberg & Brusilow, L.L.P. v. Kincaid, TexApp–Amarillo, 70 SW3d 907, reh overr, and review den.—App & E 842(8); Bills & N 28, 116; Contracts 143(1), 143(3), 143.5, 147(2), 152; Mtg 211, 563, 567(1); Ten in C 12.

Hanchett; Baker v., TexCivApp–San Antonio, 134 SW2d 407.—Lim of Act 24(2).

Hanchett v. East Sunnyside Civic League, TexApp–Houston (14 Dist), 696 SW2d 613, ref nre.—Covenants 1, 73, 84, 122, 132(2).

Hancock, In re, BkrtcyEDTex, 126 BR 270.—Bankr 2424, 2574, 2784.1, 2784.4(2), 2794.1; Sec Tran 2, 87, 133, 139.1, 140.

Hancock, In re, TexApp–Fort Worth, 212 SW3d 922, reh overr.—Courts 40; Crim Law 990.1, 994(4), 996(1); Mand 4(1), 12, 53; Prohib 3(1), 5(1); Sent & Pun 34, 1923, 1950.

Hancock; Aiken v., TexApp–San Antonio, 115 SW3d 26, reh overr, and review den.—App & E 854(1); Atty & C 105.5, 106, 107, 129(2).

Hancock; Arquette v., TexApp–San Antonio, 656 SW2d 627, ref nre.—Civil R 1381, 1382; Lim of Act 2(1), 55(1), 55(6), 58(1), 66(1).

Hancock v. Bennett, TexCivApp–Waco, 230 SW2d 328.—Bound 33, 37(1), 37(3), 43.

Hancock v. Booker, TexCivApp–Waco, 608 SW2d 811, ref nre.—Can of Inst 47; Courts 202(5); Deeds 38(1); Insurance 1990; Tresp to T T 6.1, 16, 38(3), 41(3), 47(1).

Hancock v. Bradshaw, TexCivApp–Amarillo, 350 SW2d 955.—Inj 16, 17; Licens 44(2), 56.

Hancock; Bristol-Myers Squibb Co. v., TexApp–Houston (14 Dist), 921 SW2d 917.—Mand 4(1), 4(3), 28; Pretrial Proc 33, 36.1, 44.1; Witn 208(1), 211(2), 219(1), 219(4.1).

Hancock; Bryant v., TexCivApp–Waco, 287 SW2d 525, 58 ALR2d 1348.—Autos 19; Chat Mtg 32; Sales 21, 391(1).

Hancock; Burch v., TexApp–Tyler, 56 SW3d 257.—Acct Action on 9.1, 14; App & E 931(1), 994(1), 1008.1(3), 1010.1(1), 1010.2, 1012.1(5), 1122(2); Corp 325; Princ & A 142, 146(2), 147(2), 148(4), 190(1); Trial 388(1).

Hancock; Cavazos v., TexApp–Amarillo, 686 SW2d 284.—Courts 207.4(2); Judgm 203, 518; J P 155(1), 187.

Hancock; City of Amarillo v., Tex, 239 SW2d 788, 150 Tex 231.—Admin Law 654.1, 655, 656; Const Law 2564, 2644, 4169, 4475; Courts 1; Mun Corp 184(1), 184.1, 185(12), 194, 197, 198(4); Offic 72.41(1).

Hancock; City of Amarillo v., TexCivApp–Amarillo, 233 SW2d 339, rev 239 SW2d 788, 150 Tex 231.—Admin Law 656, 658, 755, 790, 791; App & E 2; Const Law 2541, 4028; Mun Corp 125, 194.

Hancock; City of Lubbock v., TexApp–Amarillo, 940 SW2d 123.—Alt Disp Res 112, 113, 117, 199, 200, 210; Commerce 80.5; Mand 1, 4(1), 28, 172; Ship 39(7); States 18.15.

Hancock v. City of San Antonio, TexApp–San Antonio, 800 SW2d 881, writ den.—App & E 1070(2); Damag 221(7); Gas 15.1, 19, 20(2); Judgm 181(33), 185(1), 185(4), 185.3(21).

Hancock; Cosner v., TexCivApp–El Paso, 149 SW2d 239, writ dism, correct.—App & E 1175(1); Plead 36(2); Sec Reg 253, 260, 268, 298.

Hancock v. Decker, CA5 (Tex), 379 F2d 552.—Const Law 4509(17); Fed Cts 386, 404; Larc 2.

Hancock v. Estelle, CA5 (Tex), 558 F2d 786, reh den 562 F2d 1257.—Crim Law 412.2(2), 531(3).

Hancock; Esteve Cotton Co. v., TexCivApp–Amarillo, 539 SW2d 145, ref nre.—App & E 1051.1(2), 1170.7; Contracts 170(1), 176(2); Evid 129(1), 205(1), 207(1), 211, 265(1), 265(10), 269(1), 448, 461(1), 471(29), 518; Sales 72(1), 87(3), 88; Trial 140(1), 143.

Hancock v. Express One Intern., Inc., TexApp–Dallas, 800 SW2d 634, writ den.—App & E 169, 863; Judgm 181(3), 185(2); Labor & Emp 40(2), 759, 783.

Hancock; First Nat. Bank v., TexCivApp–Amarillo, 60 SW2d 871.—Banks 285.

Hancock; Fricks v., TexApp–Corpus Christi, 45 SW3d 322, reh overr.—App & E 852, 863, 946; Evid 448; Judgm 185(2), 185(3), 185.1(1), 185.1(3), 185.1(4), 185.3(17); Quiet T 1, 10, 10.1, 10.2; Tresp to T T 1, 6, 6.1; Trial 43.

Hancock v. Frost Lumber Industries, Inc., of Texas, TexCivApp–Beaumont, 182 SW2d 747.—Trial 25(9).

Hancock v. Gathright, TexCivApp–Waco, 451 SW2d 591.—App & E 78(4); Judgm 335(1); New Tr 109; Pretrial Proc 698, 699.

Hancock v. Great Am. Ins. Co., TexCivApp–Texarkana, 510 SW2d 687.—Judgm 181(14), 185(2).

Hancock; Gugenheim v., TexCivApp–Amarillo, 231 SW2d 935, ref nre.—Contracts 6; Corp 116; Frds St of 56(4), 74(1); Sales 61, 340.

Hancock; Hlavinka v., TexApp–Corpus Christi, 116 SW3d 412, reh overr, and review den.—App & E 989, 1001(1), 1001(3), 1003(7); Mines 55(2), 55(7), 74(8), 78.1(2).

Hancock v. **Hoegmeyer**, TexCivApp–Beaumont, 119 SW2d 141.—Autos 247; Damag 185(1), 191.

Hancock; **Hollums** v., TexCivApp–Amarillo, 180 SW2d 209.—Brok 49(3), 54, 63(1), 74, 84(1), 88(3).

Hancock; **Jordan** v., TexCivApp–Hous (14 Dist), 508 SW2d 878.—Adop 3, 7.4(2.1), 7.8(1), 7.8(3.1), 7.8(5), 13; App & E 854(1), 931(3); Child C 68, 469.

Hancock v. **Krause**, TexApp–Houston (1 Dist), 757 SW2d 117.—Judgm 181(15.1); Wills 107, 130, 435, 439, 450, 463, 470(1), 491, 506(1).

Hancock; **Liberty Mut. Ins. Co.** v., TexCivApp–Eastland, 427 SW2d 321.—App & E 930(3); Work Comp 1653, 1932.

Hancock v. **Moore**, Tex, 146 SW2d 369, 135 Tex 619.—Tresp to T T 41(3); Waters 93.

Hancock v. **Moore**, TexCivApp–El Paso, 137 SW2d 45, aff 146 SW2d 369, 135 Tex 619.—App & E 1010.1(18); Bound 37(1); Tresp to T T 38(0.5), 41(3); Trial 355(1); Waters 93, 94.

Hancock v. **O. K. Rental Equipment Co.**, TexCivApp–San Antonio, 441 SW2d 955.—Judgm 101(2), 126(1).

Hancock; **Page** v., TexCivApp–Austin, 200 SW2d 421, ref nre.—App & E 1172(1), 1172(2); Contracts 10(4); Damag 40(1), 106; Evid 129(6); New Tr 143(2); Pretrial Proc 67, 81; Sales 418(15); Trial 133.6(7), 352.5(1), 352.5(4).

Hancock v. **Rouse**, TexCivApp–Hous (1 Dist), 437 SW2d 1, ref nre.—Mun Corp 108.1, 108.2; Zoning 4.

Hancock v. **Sammons**, TexCivApp–Fort Worth, 267 SW2d 252, ref nre.—App & E 219(2), 1062.1, 1070(2); Deeds 93; Mtg 39, 608.5; Trial 352.1(2), 352.12, 352.15, 357, 358, 365.1(1), 365.2, 366; Ven & Pur 1.

Hancock v. **Sosbee**, TexCivApp–El Paso, 183 SW2d 284, writ refused.—Brok 43(3); Courts 90(5); Statut 116.

Hancock v. **State**, TexCrimApp, 495 SW2d 222.—Double J 146.

Hancock v. **State**, TexCrimApp, 491 SW2d 139.—Sent & Pun 1966(3), 2004, 2030.

Hancock v. **State**, TexCrimApp, 462 SW2d 36.—Crim Law 531(3), 1044.1(8), 1115(2), 1166.17; Homic 1502; Sent & Pun 1495.

Hancock v. **State**, TexCrimApp, 402 SW2d 906, 18 ALR3d 1113.—Crim Law 394.1(2), 398(2); Ind & Inf 132(1); Larc 5, 55, 59.

Hancock v. **State**, TexCrimApp, 363 SW2d 273.—Crim Law 29(5.5), 564(1); Ind & Inf 110(36); Tresp 79, 88.

Hancock v. **State**, TexCrimApp, 254 SW2d 521.—Crim Law 1090.1(1).

Hancock v. **State**, TexCrimApp, 250 SW2d 220.—Autos 351.1.

Hancock v. **State**, TexCrimApp, 238 SW2d 961, 156 Tex-Crim 83.—Autos 4, 15, 354; Crim Law 1174(2).

Hancock v. **State**, TexCrimApp, 166 SW2d 135, 145 Tex-Crim 108.—Crim Law 1094(2.1).

Hancock v. **State**, TexCrimApp, 150 SW2d 385, 141 Tex-Crim 568.—Crim Law 507(1), 510.

Hancock v. **State**, TexCrimApp, 121 SW2d 337, 135 Tex-Crim 506.—Crim Law 1097(4).

Hancock v. **State**, TexApp–Fort Worth, 756 SW2d 447.—Crim Law 905; Sent & Pun 2090, 2091, 2094.

Hancock v. **State**, TexApp–Austin, 800 SW2d 683, writ den.—Admin Law 704; App & E 70(4); Mand 187.2.

Hancock v. **State**, TexApp–San Antonio, 955 SW2d 369.—Crim Law 273.1(1), 273.1(2), 273.1(4), 273.1(5), 1141(2), 1167(5).

Hancock; **State** v., TexApp–Waco, 35 SW3d 199.—Const Law 975, 4509(13); Crim Law 13.1(1); Gaming 63(1).

Hancock v. **State Bd. of Ins.**, TexApp–Austin, 797 SW2d 379.—Records 65; Statut 219(5), 219(9.1).

Hancock v. **Texaco, Inc.**, TexCivApp–Corpus Christi, 520 SW2d 466, ref nre.—Contracts 143.5, 169; Mines 78.2, 78.3.

Hancock; **Texas & N. O. R. Co.** v., TexCivApp–Beaumont, 134 SW2d 408.—App & E 1175(5); Neglig 1579; R R 398(1).

Hancock; **Texas General Indem. Co.** v., TexCivApp–Fort Worth, 422 SW2d 565.—Work Comp 975, 1001, 1653.

Hancock v. **Walker**, TexApp–Fort Worth, 873 SW2d 422.—Insurance 1571, 3417; Mand 3(2.1), 12, 28, 167.

Hancock; **Wentz** v., TexCivApp–Austin, 236 SW2d 175, writ refused.—App & E 1012.1(1), 1071.6.

Hancock; **White** v., TexCivApp–Fort Worth, 238 SW2d 801.—Equity 57; Evid 419(2), 419(20); Mtg 338; Ven & Pur 265(3).

Hancock v. **Zurich Ins. Co.**, TexCivApp–Beaumont, 361 SW2d 248, ref nre.—Work Comp 1107, 1969.

Hancock East Texas Sanitation, Inc.; **Midkiff** v., TexApp–Beaumont, 996 SW2d 414, opinion after remand 1999 WL 1044353.—App & E 78(1), 1178(1); Judgm 190.

Hancock Fabrics, Inc. v. **Martin**, TexCivApp–Hous (14 Dist), 596 SW2d 186, ref nre.—App & E 901, 932(1), 959(1); Damag 185(1); Indem 68; Neglig 1670; Plead 236(2), 236(3); Tel 830.

Hancock's Estate; **Cross** v., TexCivApp–Amarillo, 176 SW2d 586, writ refused wom.—App & E 20, 1091(1); Courts 202(5); Des & Dist 119(1); Evid 82; Ex & Ad 3(3).

Hancox v. **Peek**, TexCivApp–Fort Worth, 355 SW2d 568, ref nre.—Improv 1; Inj 89(3); Mun Corp 601.1.

Hancox; **State** v., TexApp–Fort Worth, 762 SW2d 312, petition for discretionary review refused.—Crim Law 1024(3).

Hancox; **Texas Emp. Ins. Ass'n** v., Tex, 349 SW2d 102, 162 Tex 565.—Work Comp 1283, 1382, 1927.

Hancox; **Texas Emp. Ins. Ass'n** v., TexCivApp–El Paso, 343 SW2d 720, writ gr, rev 349 SW2d 102, 162 Tex 565.—Work Comp 1283, 1683.

Hand; **Carden** v., NDTex, 407 FSupp 451. See Turner v. American Bar Ass'n.

Hand v. **Dean Witter Reynolds Inc.**, TexApp–Houston (14 Dist), 889 SW2d 483, reh overr, and writ den.—Antitrust 141, 145; App & E 497(1), 712, 719(1), 761, 852, 863, 934(1); Brok 6, 7, 9, 19, 29, 38(3); Fraud 3; Judgm 185(2), 185(6); Neglig 202, 210, 215, 1692; Plead 34(3), 48, 245(7); Princ & A 1, 13; Sales 24, 25, 81(1).

Hand; **Eubanks** v., TexCivApp–Corpus Christi, 578 SW2d 515, ref nre.—App & E 20, 714(1), 719(1), 782; Judgm 489, 518; Wills 355.

Hand v. **Gary**, CA5 (Tex), 838 F2d 1420.—Arrest 58; Civil R 1088(4), 1088(5), 1339; Const Law 3845, 3850, 3873, 3896, 4536; Mal Pros 24(7), 48, 56; Searches 23.

Hand; **Gaskin** v., SDTex, 560 FSupp 930.—Receivers 1, 29(1); Rem of C 97.

Hand; **Hallmark** v., TexApp–El Paso, 885 SW2d 471, reh overr, and writ den.—Action 27(1); App & E 930(3), 946, 989, 999(1), 1001(1), 1001(3), 1002, 1003(7), 1062.2, 1097(1), 1195(1); Banks 40, 54(1); Contracts 1, 27, 29; Costs 194.32; Courts 99(1); Damag 23, 56; Interest 39(2.30).

Hand; **Hallmark** v., TexApp–Corpus Christi, 833 SW2d 603, reh overr, and writ den, appeal after remand 885 SW2d 471, reh overr, and writ den.—Banks 40; Contracts 27, 147(2), 168; Damag 23, 175, 177, 189; Sales 22(1).

Hand v. **Lubbock Production Credit Ass'n**, TexCivApp–Amarillo, 466 SW2d 438, ref nre.—Chat Mtg 41, 133, 158.1; Compromise 20(1).

Hand; **Quanah, A. & P. Ry. Co.** v., TexCivApp–Amarillo, 484 SW2d 390, ref nre.—App & E 766, 1001(1), 1003(5); R R 480(4), 482(1), 482(2).

Hand v. **State ex rel. Yelkin**, TexCivApp–Houston, 348 SW2d 72.—App & E 781(1), 781(4), 802.

Hand; **State ex rel. Yelkin** v., TexCivApp–Houston, 344 SW2d 467, mandamus overr.—Insurance 1152.

Hand v. State ex rel. Yelkin, TexCivApp–Houston, 335 SW2d 410, ref nre 337 SW2d 798, 160 Tex 416.—App & E 863, 954(1); Corp 283(3); Equity 65(1); Inj 70, 80, 132, 135, 138.42, 147; Insurance 1132; Quo W 23, 38.

Hand; State ex rel. Yelkin v., TexCivApp–Houston, 331 SW2d 789, ref nre 333 SW2d 109.—Corp 283(3), 296; Elect of Rem 7(1); Insurance 1034, 1132, 1152; Offic 77; Quo W 38, 48; Venue 22(8).

Hand v. Stevens Transport, Inc. Employee Benefit Plan, TexApp–Dallas, 83 SW3d 286.—Insurance 3545, 3564(3), 3564(8), 3564(9); Labor & Emp 623, 679, 682, 683; Lim of Act 14, 104.5.

Hand v. Tavera, TexApp–San Antonio, 864 SW2d 678, reh den.—Health 197, 576, 658, 810.

Hand; U.S. v., CA5 (Tex), 516 F2d 472, cert den 96 SCt 1427, 424 US 953, 47 LEd2d 359.—Crim Law 1032(1); Searches 45.

Hand; U.S. v., CA5 (Tex), 497 F2d 929, on reh 516 F2d 472, cert den 96 SCt 1427, 424 US 953, 47 LEd2d 359.—Crim Law 105, 394.4(3), 641.13(2.1); Embez 26; Ind & Inf 1, 60, 117, 119; Searches 39.

Hand v. URCARCO, Inc., CA5 (Tex), 27 F3d 1097. See Melder v. Morris.

H & A Investments; Luna v., TexApp–Corpus Christi, 900 SW2d 735.—App & E 863, 934(1); Judgm 185.3(21); Neglig 1172, 1205(8), 1262, 1263.

H And A Land Corp. v. City of Kennedale, Tex., CA5 (Tex), 480 F3d 336.—Const Law 1509, 2209, 2210, 2213; Pub Amuse 9(1).

Handa-Lopez, Inc.; Thompson v., WDTex, 998 FSupp 738.—Const Law 3964, 3965(3), 3965(5), 3965(8); Courts 12(2.1); Fed Cts 76, 77, 81, 84, 96, 101, 103, 104, 106, 122, 144.

H & B Equipment Co., Inc. v. International Harvester Co., CA5 (Tex), 577 F2d 239.—Antitrust 535, 537, 544, 546, 560, 592, 620, 714, 737, 925, 977(1), 977(2), 983, 984; Fed Cts 17.

H & C Communications, Inc. v. Gini's Home Cooking & Bakery, TexApp–San Antonio, 887 SW2d 475. See H & C Communications, Inc. v. Reed's Food Intern., Inc.

H & C Communications, Inc.; Lumpkin v., TexApp–Houston (1 Dist), 755 SW2d 538, writ den 1989 WL 380483.—Courts 91(1); Judgm 181(11), 185(2); Labor & Emp 40(3), 79, 835.

H & C Communications, Inc. v. Reed's Food Intern., Inc., TexApp–San Antonio, 887 SW2d 475, reh den.—App & E 66, 70(8); Statut 203, 206, 223.1.

H&D Tire and Automotive-Hardware Inc. v. Pitney Bowes Inc., CA5 (Tex), 250 F3d 302.—Fed Cts 346.

H&D Tire and Automotive-Hardware, Inc. v. Pitney Bowes Inc., CA5 (Tex), 227 F3d 326, reh and reh den 250 F3d 302, cert den Pitney Bowes Inc v. H & D Tire and Automotive-Hardware, Inc, 122 SCt 214, 534 US 894, 151 LEd2d 152.—Courts 90(2); Fed Cts 337, 338, 346, 542; Rem of C 15, 94, 107(7).

Handel v. Long Trusts, TexApp–Texarkana, 757 SW2d 848.—App & E 1043(6), 1173(2); Evid 242(5); Mines 109; Pretrial Proc 45; Witn 37(2), 41, 45(1), 78.

Handel; Reader's Wholesale Distributors, Inc. v., TexCivApp–Waco, 410 SW2d 803.—Acct Action on 14; Sales 87(3).

Handelman v. Handelman, TexCivApp–Hous (14 Dist), 608 SW2d 298, ref nre.—Bills & N 129(2); Costs 260(5); Notice 9; Plead 182; Stip 16, 18(7).

Handelman; Handelman v., TexCivApp–Hous (14 Dist), 608 SW2d 298, ref nre.—Bills & N 129(2); Costs 260(5); Notice 9; Plead 182; Stip 16, 18(7).

Hander v. San Jacinto Jr. College, CA5 (Tex), 522 F2d 204.—Fed Cts 221, 270.

Hander v. San Jacinto Junior College, CA5 (Tex), 519 F2d 273, decision clarified on denial of reh 522 F2d 204.—Civil R 1479, 1483; Colleges 8.1(3), 8.1(7); Const Law

82(11), 1091, 3627(4), 4223(4); Fed Civ Proc 2737.5; Fed Cts 270, 417; Schools 147.

Hander v. San Jacinto Jr. College, SDTex, 325 FSupp 1019, vac 468 F2d 619, cert den 93 SCt 2268, 411 US 982, 36 LEd2d 957.—Const Law 2400, 2406, 2407; Fed Civ Proc 1741; Fed Cts 62; States 53, 74.

H & H Concrete Co.; Culp v., TexApp–Corpus Christi, 711 SW2d 726. See Culp v. Hawkins.

H. & H. Elec. Co.; General Elec. Supply Corp. v., TexCivApp–Galveston, 259 SW2d 617.—Judgm 153(4).

H & H Meat Products Co., Inc.; Laredo Hides Co., Inc. v., TexCivApp–Corpus Christi, 513 SW2d 210, ref nre.—App & E 1175(5); Contracts 15, 211, 214, 261(3), 261(7), 279(1), 305(1), 313(2); Damag 67, 141; Evid 397(3), 448; Paymt 8(1); Sales 82(4), 99, 190, 194, 195, 411, 420.

H & H Meat Products Co., Inc.; Mid Century Ins. Co. v., TexApp–Corpus Christi, 822 SW2d 747.—App & E 901, 930(3); Insurance 1633, 3092, 3093.

H & H Meat Products, Inc.; Adams v., TexApp–Corpus Christi, 41 SW3d 762.—Acct Action on 9.1, 14; App & E 836, 842(2), 843(2), 852, 893(1), 931(1), 1008.1(2), 1008.1(3), 1010.1(1), 1010.1(3), 1010.2, 1011.1(6), 1012.1(5); Contracts 1, 14, 15, 326; Costs 194.32, 194.36; Damag 22, 117, 189; Em Dom 247(1); Estop 85; Fraud 3, 12, 58(1); Frds St of 23(1), 89(1), 152(2), 159, 161; Guar 91; Impl & C C 30, 60.1; Interest 36(1), 38(2), 39(2.30), 39(2.50), 39(3); Sales 1(1), 161; Trial 398.

H & H Music Co.; McGann v., CA5 (Tex), 946 F2d 401, cert den Greenberg v. H & H Music Co, 113 SCt 482, 506 US 981, 121 LEd2d 387.—Fed Civ Proc 2470.1, 2471; Labor & Emp 400, 563(1), 694, 795.

H & H Music Co.; McGann v., SDTex, 742 FSupp 392, aff 946 F2d 401, certden Greenberg v. H & H Music Co, 113 SCt 482, 506 US 981, 121 LEd2d 387.—Fed Civ Proc 2470; Labor & Emp 403, 411, 445, 554.

H & H Oil Services, Inc. v. National County Mut. Fire Ins. Co., TexApp–Dallas, 687 SW2d 110. See Hunter v. National County Mut. Fire Ins. Co.

H. & I. Imp. Co. v. Three B Co., TexCivApp–Austin, 235 SW2d 461.—Costs 264.

H. & I. Imp. Co. v. Three B. Co., TexCivApp–Austin, 229 SW2d 392, ref nre, motion gr 235 SW2d 461.—Ease 8(2), 36(3).

Handl v. State, TexApp–Houston (14 Dist), 763 SW2d 446, petition for discretionary review refused.—Crim Law 1044.2(1), 1072, 1134(3); Obscen 2.5.

Handler; Cauble v., TexCivApp–Fort Worth, 503 SW2d 362, ref nre.—Replev 249, 298, 301, 305, 306, 336(1), 342, 346; Refer 100(7).

Handley; Alexander v., TexComApp, 146 SW2d 740, 136 Tex 110.—Accord 17; Compromise 11.

Handley; Alexander v., TexCivApp–Dallas, 123 SW2d 379, aff 146 SW2d 740, 136 Tex 110.—Compromise 2, 8(4), 11, 20(2), 24.

Handley; Boswell v., Tex, 397 SW2d 213.—App & E 282, 302(1); Judgm 185(4); Plead 378.

Handley v. Boswell, TexCivApp–Tyler, 386 SW2d 300, aff 397 SW2d 213.—Judgm 185(2), 185(4).

Handley; City of San Antonio v., TexCivApp–San Antonio, 308 SW2d 608, writ refused.—Mun Corp 180(1), 180(3), 186(5), 186(6); Statut 181(1).

Handley v. City of Seagoville, Tex., NDTex, 798 FSupp 1267.—Civil R 1027, 1332(1); Const Law 4111; Fed Cts 411; Mun Corp 747(4).

Handley v. Coker, TexCivApp–Beaumont, 248 SW2d 814, writ refused.—Admin Law 303.1; Schools 22, 36, 37(5).

Handley v. Handley, TexApp–Corpus Christi, 122 SW3d 904, rule 537(f) motion gr.—App & E 946, 989, 1012.1(5); Divorce 132(6), 252.1, 252.2, 253(2), 253(3), 256, 286(5); Hus & W 264(4); Trial 140(1), 143.

Handley; Handley v., TexApp–Corpus Christi, 122 SW3d 904, rule 537(f) motion gr.—App & E 946, 989, 1012.1(5); Divorce 132(6), 252.1, 252.2, 253(2), 253(3), 256, 286(5); Hus & W 264(4); Trial 140(1), 143.

Handley; Missouri Pac. R. Co. v., TexCivApp–San Antonio, 341 SW2d 203.—Damag 98, 102, 127; Labor & Emp 2824.

Handley v. State, TexCrimApp, 480 SW2d 738.—Crim Law 627.6(5), 696(3), 730(1), 730(3), 1038.2, 1038.3, 1130(2); Ind & Inf 119.

Handley; United Fidelity Life Ins. Co. v., TexComApp, 86 SW2d 201, 126 Tex 147.—Insurance 1735, 1764(1).

Handlin v. State, TexCrimApp, 95 SW2d 712, 130 TexCrim 153.—Crim Law 1182.

Handlin v. Stuckey, TexCivApp–Waco, 295 SW2d 463.—App & E 66, 80(6).

Handly, Ex parte, TexCivApp–Hous (14 Dist), 460 SW2d 525.—Contempt 24, 72.

Handly; U.S. v., CA5 (Tex), 591 F2d 1125.—Crim Law 713, 719(3), 720(5), 730(1), 1037.1(1), 1037.1(2), 1169.7, 1170.5(1), 1171.1(3), 1171.2.

H & M Food Systems; International Meat Traders, Inc. v., CA5 (Tex), 70 F3d 836.—Fed Civ Proc 381, 2492; Fed Cts 630.1, 633, 635, 776, 802; Frds St of 127.

H & M Food Systems Co., Inc. v. CKS, Inc., CA5 (Tex), 70 F3d 836. See International Meat Traders, Inc. v. H & M Food Systems.

H & M Food Systems Co., Inc. v. Intertrade, CA5 (Tex), 70 F3d 836. See International Meat Traders, Inc. v. H & M Food Systems.

H & M Wholesale, Inc.; Munoz v., SDTex, 926 FSupp 596.—Civil R 1019(2), 1217, 1218(2), 1218(4), 1218(6), 1225(1), 1225(2), 1417, 1540; Damag 50.10, 192; Fed Civ Proc 2466, 2497.1, 2539, 2544, 2545; Labor & Emp 806, 808, 809, 810, 861, 863(2).

H & N Machining Inc.; Meek v., TexCivApp–Fort Worth, 420 SW2d 227.—Contracts 346(2), 348; Evid 450(6); Frds St of 131(1); Trial 350.4(4).

H & R Block, In re, TexApp–Corpus Christi, 159 SW3d 127, mandamus dism.—Courts 39; Mand 1, 3(2.1), 4(1), 4(4), 45; Parties 35.31, 35.39, 35.44.

H & R Block v. Allen, TexApp–Texarkana, 667 SW2d 181. See Elmore Enterprises v. Allen.

H & R Block, Inc. v. Haese, Tex, 992 SW2d 437, reh of petition for review overr, on remand 82 SW3d 331, reh overr, and review den, and reh of petition for review den.—App & E 479(1), 484.1, 1080.

H & R Block, Inc. v. Haese, TexApp–Corpus Christi, 82 SW3d 331, reh overr, and review den, and reh of petition for review den.—Atty & C 32(12); Const Law 2091, 3981; Inj 133, 138.3; Parties 35.31, 35.71.

H & R Block, Inc. v. Haese, TexApp–Corpus Christi, 976 SW2d 237, reh overr, and review den, review gr, rev 992 SW2d 437, reh of petition for review overr, on remand 82 SW3d 331, reh overr, and review den, and reh of petition for review den.—App & E 949; Const Law 3981; Parties 35.1, 35.33, 35.35, 35.37, 35.71.

H & R Block, Ltd. v. Housden, EDTex, 24 FSupp2d 703. —Rem of C 3, 59.

H & R Block, Ltd. v. Housden, EDTex, 186 FRD 399.—Labor & Emp 2377.

H & R Block of Houston; Meinecke v., CA5 (Tex), 66 F3d 77, reh den, appeal after remand 91 F3d 137.—Civil R 1168, 1201, 1204, 1539, 1545, 1549, 1551; Fed Civ Proc 1706, 1713.1, 2544, 2558; Fed Cts 595, 640, 724, 766, 776, 802.

Handrick; Kirkland v., TexCivApp–San Antonio, 173 SW2d 735, writ refused wom.—Equity 65(1), 65(2); Trusts 95, 100.

Handrick v. State, TexCrimApp, 340 SW2d 296, 170 TexCrim 251.—Autos 355(6).

H & R Oils, Inc. v. Pioneer Am. Ins. Co., TexCivApp–Fort Worth, 541 SW2d 665.—Mines 52, 78.2, 78.6; Receivers 12, 14, 16.

Hands v. Arkon, TexCivApp–Amarillo, 489 SW2d 633, ref nre.—Autos 216, 226(2); Neglig 453, 554(1).

Handsbur; State v., TexCrimApp, 816 SW2d 749.—Sent & Pun 1379(2), 1381(2).

Handsel; Diamond Products Intern., Inc. v., TexApp–Houston (14 Dist), 142 SW3d 491, reh overr.—App & E 361(1), 363, 366, 411, 422, 428(2).

H & S Mechanical Contractors; Perry v., TexCivApp–Amarillo, 578 SW2d 423.—Neglig 371, 379, 380, 387, 1672, 1677, 1693, 1710, 1713; Trial 351.5(5).

Handspur v. State, TexApp–Dallas, 792 SW2d 239, petition for discretionary review gr, rev 816 SW2d 749.—Crim Law 1177.5(2); Sent & Pun 1379(2).

H & S Supply Co., Inc.; Oscar Renda Contracting, Inc. v., TexApp–Waco, 195 SW3d 772, review den.—Lim of Act 130(7).

H & S Water Well Service, Inc.; Dismukes v., TexCivApp–Waco, 439 SW2d 869.—Plead 111.42(7).

Handy, Ex parte, TexCrimApp, 99 SW2d 929, 131 TexCrim 413.—Hab Corp 715.1.

Handy v. Brownlee, CA5 (Tex), 118 FedAppx 850.—Armed S 27(4), 27(5); Civil R 1123, 1218(4), 1220, 1249(1), 1251, 1252.

Handy; General Ins. Corp. v., TexCivApp–San Antonio, 267 SW2d 622, ref nre.—Pretrial Proc 714; Witn 336, 345(7); Work Comp 840, 1653, 1922, 1973, 1988.

Handy; General Life and Acc. Ins. Co. v., TexApp–El Paso, 766 SW2d 370.—Action 60; App & E 218.2(3.1), 231(2), 242(1), 699(2); Insurance 3381(4); Interest 31; Trial 350.4(3).

Handy v. Holman, TexCivApp–Galveston, 281 SW2d 356. —Elections 59, 83, 291, 293(3), 299(0.5); Schools 97(4); Statut 223.2(11).

Handy; Lacquement v., TexApp–Fort Worth, 876 SW2d 932, reh den, and extension of time gr.—App & E 863; Contracts 16, 22(1), 152, 155; Insurance 3335, 3347; Judgm 181(23), 185(2); Princ & A 142, 146(2), 193.

Handy; Rodriguez v., CA5 (Tex), 873 F2d 814.—Civil R 1327, 1345; Fed Civ Proc 2727; Fed Cts 922; Judgm 586(2); U S 50.20, 147(22).

Handy; Rodriguez v., CA5 (Tex), 802 F2d 817, appeal after remand 873 F2d 814.—Fed Cts 541, 574, 600, 659.

Handy v. State, TexCrimApp, 189 SW3d 296.—Crim Law 394.5(4).

Handy v. State, TexCrimApp, 286 SW2d 144.—Crim Law 1090.1(1).

Handy v. State, TexCrimApp, 286 SW2d 143.—Crim Law 1090.1(1).

Handy v. State, TexCrimApp, 268 SW2d 182, 160 TexCrim 258.—Crim Law 339.6, 1172.7; Homic 527; Sent & Pun 1206, 1367, 1371, 1388.

Handy v. State, TexCrimApp, 138 SW2d 541, 139 TexCrim 3.—Crim Law 126(1), 134(1), 134(4), 135; Homic 1134.

Handy v. State, TexCrimApp, 126 SW2d 30, 136 TexCrim 208.—Bail 66; Crim Law 1169.11; Homic 1483; Witn 337(14).

Handy; U.S. v., CA5 (Tex), 222 FedAppx 414.—Arrest 63.5(5).

Handy; U.S. ex rel. Mobley v., CA5 (Tex), 176 F2d 491, cert den 70 SCt 306, 338 US 904, 94 LEd 556, reh den 70 SCt 427, 338 US 945, 94 LEd 583.—Mil Jus 515.

Handy Andy Community Stores of Tex.; Martin v., CA5 (Tex), 214 F2d 10.—Fed Cts 697, 902; Neglig 1670.

Handy Andy, Inc. v. Rademacher, TexApp–San Antonio, 666 SW2d 300.—App & E 930(3), 989; Evid 588; Labor & Emp 256(1), 256(7), 262, 265, 863(1).

Handy Andy, Inc. v. Ruiz, TexApp–Corpus Christi, 900 SW2d 739, reh overr, and writ den.—Garn 153; Judgm 105.1; Plead 287, 288, 409(1).

Handy-Andy, Inc.; Scott v., TexCivApp–San Antonio, 490 SW2d 196, ref nre.—Statut 105(1), 107(1).

Handy Dan v. Scotch Corp., Inc., TexApp–Austin, 753 SW2d 743. See W.R. Grace Co. v. Scotch Corp., Inc.

Handy Dan Hardware, Inc.; Retail Merchants Ass'n of Houston, Inc. v., TexApp–Houston (1 Dist), 696 SW2d 44.—App & E 840(3); Commerce 60(1); Const Law

3027, 3057, 3334, 3682, 3877, 3903, 4263; Courts 89; Sunday 2.

Handy Hardware Wholesale, Inc. v. Harris County Appraisal Dist., TexApp–Houston (1 Dist), 985 SW2d 618.—Tax 2603.

Handy Hardware Wholesale, Inc.; N.L.R.B. v., CA5 (Tex), 542 F2d 935, reconsideration den 1977 WL 4288, cert den 97 SCt 2675, 431 US 954, 53 LEd2d 271.— Const Law 4185; Labor & Emp 1178(1), 1178(2), 1193(1), 1195(5), 1195(8), 1802, 1875, 1884.

Handzlik v. U.S., CA5 (Tex), 93 FedAppx 15.—Armed S 27(4); Civil R 1249(1), 1252; Fed Civ Proc 837, 2497.1.

Haner; Boat Superstore, Inc. v., TexApp–Houston (1 Dist), 877 SW2d 376.—Antitrust 360, 393; App & E 5, 493, 914(1); Damag 194; Proc 133.

Haner v. State, TexCrimApp, 339 SW2d 212, 170 TexCrim 68.—Crim Law 1111(1), 1111(3); Sent & Pun 2021.

Haner v. U.S., CA5 (Tex), 315 F2d 792.—Crim Law 1038.1(6), 1172.3; Int Rev 5261, 5317.

Hanes; Bourland's Estate v., TexCivApp–Corpus Christi, 526 SW2d 156, ref nre.—App & E 187(3); Cert 33(1), 42(8), 46; Plead 360; Pretrial Proc 695; Statut 223.1; Wills 356, 361, 364, 371.

Hanes; Bourland's Estate v., TexCivApp–Corpus Christi, 474 SW2d 592.—Wills 396, 400, 434.

Hanes; Duffey v., TexCivApp–Dallas, 474 SW2d 621, ref nre.—App & E 216(7), 547(2), 548(6), 846(5), 907(3); Trial 366.

Hanes; Rudolph v., TexCivApp–Fort Worth, 111 SW2d 1189.—App & E 656(1), 930(2); Home 57(3); Judgm 948(1), 949(2); Trial 352.1(3), 361.

Hanes; Rudolph v., TexCivApp–Fort Worth, 106 SW2d 743.—App & E 455, 456, 568, 614, 655(3), 938(1); Evid 41, 43(1).

Hanes; Spell v., TexCivApp–Texarkana, 139 SW2d 229, writ dism, correct.—Mines 55(2), 55(4).

Hanes v. State, TexCrimApp, 341 SW2d 428, 170 TexCrim 394.—Burg 41(10); Crim Law 627.9(4), 661, 730(10), 1038.1(3.1).

Hanes v. State, TexCrimApp, 318 SW2d 645.—Crim Law 1087.1(2).

Hanes; Walker v., TexCivApp–Corpus Christi, 570 SW2d 534, ref nre.—Cert 37, 40; Courts 99(3), 202(5); Judgm 181(7), 185(2), 185.3(2); Lim of Act 13, 105(1), 118(2), 119(1), 119(3).

Hanes Corp.; Bohrer v., CA5 (Tex), 715 F2d 213, cert den 104 SCt 1284, 465 US 1026, 79 LEd2d 687.—Civil R 1535, 1551; Fed Civ Proc 2602.

Haney; Benson v., TexCivApp–Eastland, 381 SW2d 138. —Plead 111.42(7); Venue 8.5(5), 8.5(6), 46.

Haney v. Beto, EDTex, 308 FSupp 262.—Crim Law 264.

Haney; Braxton v., TexCivApp–Waco, 82 SW2d 984, writ refused.—Estop 78(2); Princ & A 166(3), 170(2), 175(2), 175(3); Ven & Pur 231(1), 265(3).

Haney v. Cooke County Tax Appraisal Dist., TexApp–Fort Worth, 782 SW2d 349.—Tax 2515.

Haney; Duncan Development, Inc. v., Tex, 634 SW2d 811.—Contracts 229(2); Evid 177.

Haney v. Duncan Development, Inc., TexCivApp–Beaumont, 626 SW2d 61, writ gr, rev 634 SW2d 811.—App & E 1013; Evid 318(3), 555.4(1); Judgm 199(3.14).

Haney v. Fenley, Bate, Deaton and Porter, Tex, 618 SW2d 541.—Partners 195.

Haney v. Fenley, Bate, Deaton, and Porter, TexCivApp–Beaumont, 612 SW2d 208, ref nre 618 SW2d 541.— Partners 54, 195.

Haney v. Haney, TexApp–Houston (14 Dist), 834 SW2d 490, reh den, and writ den.—Child S 214, 341.

Haney; Haney v., TexApp–Houston (14 Dist), 834 SW2d 490, reh den, and writ den.—Child S 214, 341.

Haney v. Henry, TexCivApp–Amarillo, 307 SW2d 649.— Acct Action on 13; Evid 591; Plead 110, 111.18, 111.30, 111.40, 111.42(9); Venue 2, 21, 22(4), 22(6), 31.

Haney v. Logan, TexCivApp–Waco, 393 SW2d 938, writ gr, and writ dism by agreement.—App & E 93; Bills & N 97(1), 518(1); Evid 97.

Haney; Metropolitan Life Ins. Co. v., TexApp–Houston (14 Dist), 987 SW2d 236, reh overr, and review den.— Antitrust 147, 251, 292; App & E 1175(1), 1194(1); Costs 194.25; Damag 15, 37, 38, 100, 190; Fraud 59(1), 59(2), 59(3), 60; Insurance 1651.

Haney v. Minnesota Mut. Life Ins. Co., TexCivApp–Hous (14 Dist), 505 SW2d 325, ref nre.—App & E 230; Contracts 156; Insurance 2007, 2959, 2983, 3125(6); Trial 365.1(5).

Haney; Mortgage Bond Corp. of New York v., TexCivApp–Beaumont, 105 SW2d 488, writ refused.—Wills 111(3), 123(3), 303(1), 421.

Haney v. Purcell Co., Inc., Tex, 770 SW2d 566, on remand 796 SW2d 782, writ den.—Antitrust 294; Contracts 328(1); Fraud 28; Neglig 252.

Haney v. Purcell Co., Inc., TexApp–Houston (1 Dist), 796 SW2d 782, writ den.—App & E 170(1), 181, 206.2, 218.2(3.1), 231(5), 882(8), 989, 1010.1(1); Contracts 205.35(2); Evid 81, 213(1); Fraud 3, 17; Lim of Act 95(9), 197(2); Sales 272; Trial 81, 350.4(2), 350.6(1), 351.5(1).

Haney; Quita, Inc. v., TexApp–Eastland, 810 SW2d 469. —Pretrial Proc 697.

Haney v. State, TexCrimApp, 588 SW2d 913.—Crim Law 1026.10(4), 1169.3.

Haney v. State, TexCrimApp, 544 SW2d 384.—Controlled Subs 10.

Haney v. State, TexCrimApp, 438 SW2d 580.—Crim Law 784(1), 1173.2(10); Forg 16.

Haney v. State, TexCrimApp, 211 SW2d 215, 152 TexCrim 63.—Crim Law 369.6, 1169.11; Int Liq 236(3).

Haney v. State, TexCrimApp, 160 SW2d 931, 144 TexCrim 46.—Crim Law 730(8), 814(1), 1169.2(3); Rob 3, 24.15(2), 27(1), 30.

Haney v. State, TexApp–Fort Worth, 977 SW2d 638, reh overr, and petition for discretionary review refused.— Crim Law 369.2(5), 577.10(1), 577.10(10), 577.15(4), 577.16(4), 577.16(8), 577.16(9), 1043(1), 1139, 1162, 1169.11; Infants 20.

Haney v. State, TexApp–Dallas, 646 SW2d 579.—Crim Law 1134(10), 1184(2); Sent & Pun 2004.

Haney v. State, TexApp–Waco, 951 SW2d 551.—Const Law 4638; Crim Law 507(1), 780(1), 780(3); Sent & Pun 313.

Haney; Temple Trust Co. v., Tex, 126 SW2d 950, 133 Tex 414.—App & E 1010.1(1); Usury 100(1), 117, 137.

Haney; Temple Trust Co. v., Tex, 107 SW2d 368, 133 Tex 414, reh den 126 SW2d 950, 133 Tex 414.—Costs 241.

Haney; Temple Trust Co. v., TexCivApp–Austin, 103 SW2d 1035, aff 107 SW2d 368, 133 Tex 414, reh den 126 SW2d 950, 133 Tex 414.—App & E 747(1); Courts 500; Usury 16, 22, 100(1), 136, 137, 138, 142(2).

Haney; Texas & N. O. R. Co. v., TexCivApp–El Paso, 144 SW2d 677, writ dism, correct.—App & E 1140(2); Damag 128, 132(10); New Tr 140(3); R R 328(5), 348(3), 348(4), 348(5).

Haney v. Texas & N. O. R. Co., TexCivApp–Beaumont, 119 SW2d 714, dism.—Neglig 506(8); R R 327(1), 352.

Haney v. Texas Real Estate Com'n, TexApp–Houston (14 Dist), 789 SW2d 304, writ den.—Brok 4; States 119.

Haney; Texas State Bd. of Medical Examiners v., TexCivApp–Austin, 472 SW2d 550, ref nre.—Health 223(2); Statut 263.

Haney; Thompson v., TexCivApp–Amarillo, 191 SW2d 491.—App & E 185(3), 192.1, 485(1); Child C 7, 413, 610, 637, 906, 921(1).

Haney; Traders & General Ins. Co. v., TexCivApp–Fort Worth, 312 SW2d 690, ref nre.—Damag 221(5.1); Trial 83(2); Work Comp 1926, 1974.

Haney v. Yarbrough, TexCivApp–Amarillo, 112 SW2d 1074.—App & E 218.2(2), 218.2(4), 1175(1); Autos 247.

Haney Elec. Co. v. Hurst, TexCivApp–Dallas, 624 SW2d 602, dism.—App & E 209.1, 215(1), 218.2(4), 1056.1(5), 1062.1; Autos 202.1, 226(3), 234, 243(16); Evid 123(8), 588, 591; Neglig 549(9), 549(10); Pretrial Proc 202; Trial 2, 56; Witn 248(1), 397.

Haney Elec. Co. v. Hurst, TexCivApp–Dallas, 608 SW2d 355.—App & E 465(1).

Hanford v. State, TexCrimApp, 421 SW2d 908.—Crim Law 1171.1(6); Rape 64.

Hanger; Thompson v., CA5 (Tex), 70 F3d 390. See State of Tex. v. Thompson.

Hanger General Contractors v. Greater Swenson Grove Baptist Church, TexCivApp–Austin, 597 SW2d 32.—Contracts 164; Plead 111.3, 307; Venue 7.5(1).

Hangers Dry Cleaner and Laundry, Inc.; Schlobohm v., Tex, 784 SW2d 355. See Schlobohm v. Schapiro.

Hang On III, Inc. v. Gregg County, TexApp–Texarkana, 893 SW2d 724, reh den, and writ dism by agreement.—App & E 863, 954(1), 954(2); Const Law 4095; Inj 16, 76, 85(2), 126; Zoning 321.

Hang On II, Inc. v. Tuckey, TexApp–Fort Worth, 978 SW2d 281.—App & E 1175(1); Labor & Emp 2881; Neglig 371, 379, 380, 383, 387, 1568, 1655, 1675.

Hang On, Inc. v. City of Arlington, CA5 (Tex), 65 F3d 1248.—Const Law 42(1), 230.3(6), 855, 928, 2218, 2239, 2240(1), 3405, 3698; Fed Civ Proc 2481; Int Liq 11, 15; Mun Corp 120, 121; Searches 79.

Hanh H. Duong v. Bank One, N.A., TexApp–Fort Worth, 169 SW3d 246, reh en banc den.—App & E 1136; Banks 148(2); Courts 95(1); Judgm 185(4), 185.3(5); Pretrial Proc 473, 474, 481, 486.

Hanie v. State, TexCrimApp, 208 SW2d 373, 151 TexCrim 395.—Crim Law 400(1), 507(2), 594(1), 1120(1), 1166(7); Homic 975, 976, 1134, 1174.

Hanie v. State, TexApp–Dallas, 820 SW2d 7, petition for discretionary review dism.—Crim Law 1111(2), 1144.1, 1144.10; Jury 21.1, 29(7).

Hankamer v. Delta Leasing & Inv. Corp., TexCivApp–Hous (1 Dist), 481 SW2d 491, ref nre.—App & E 846(5); Bailm 3, 5, 11, 20, 27, 31(3); Costs 194.34; Evid 418.

Hankamer v. Roberts Undertaking Co., Tex, 141 SW2d 587, 135 Tex 139.—Autos 244(40), 245(66).

Hankamer v. Roberts Undertaking Co., TexCivApp–Beaumont, 139 SW2d 865, writ dism 141 SW2d 587, 135 Tex 139.—App & E 1060.1(2.1); Autos 245(66); Plead 36(3); Trial 366.

Hankamer v. State, TexCrimApp, 150 SW2d 794, 142 TexCrim 23.—Crim Law 121, 134(4), 371(2), 406(1), 565, 763(1), 1150, 1166(7), 1169.3; Embez 11(1); Ex & Ad 29(1); Ind & Inf 110(13); Witn 274(2).

Hankamer v. Sumrall, TexCivApp–Beaumont, 257 SW2d 827, ref nre.—Adv Poss 38, 114(1), 114(2), 115(4), 116(3), 116(5); App & E 213; Trial 350.3(2.1), 352.10.

Hankamer v. Templin, Tex, 187 SW2d 549, 143 Tex 572.—Atty & C 14, 61; Crim Law 83; Mand 3(8); Pardon 23.1.

Hankamer; Texas Gas Corp. v., TexCivApp–Houston, 326 SW2d 944, ref nre.—Acct Action on 15; Contracts 147(1), 147(2), 175(2), 291; Costs 194.36; Gas 13(1), 14.6; Princ & A 74, 188.

Hankerson; Russell v., TexApp–Corpus Christi, 771 SW2d 650, writ den.—App & E 1056.1(3); Damag 178, 185(1), 191, 192.

Hankey v. Employer's Cas. Co., TexCivApp–Galveston, 176 SW2d 357.—Action 48(1); Contracts 172; Courts 121(1), 121(2), 122; Damag 89(2); Detinue 1; Insurance 2719(2); Plead 8(1), 8(3), 111.46, 111.48, 246(2); Trover 13, 23, 60.

Hankins; Central Sur. & Ins. Corp. v., TexCivApp–San Antonio, 140 SW2d 360.—App & E 931(1), 1010.1(2), 1175(3); Fact 2.5.

Hankins v. Coca-Cola Bottling Co., Tex, 249 SW2d 1008, 151 Tex 303.—Prod Liab 78.

Hankins; Coca Cola Bottling Co. v., TexCivApp–Fort Worth, 245 SW2d 740, rev 249 SW2d 1008, 151 Tex 303.—Damag 185(3); Prod Liab 78; Trial 27.

Hankins v. Connally, TexCivApp–Waco, 206 SW2d 89, ref nre.—Schools 22, 40, 42(2), 65, 118; Statut 158, 161(1).

Hankins v. Dallas Independent School Dist., NDTex, 698 FSupp 1323.—Civil R 1132; Consp 7.5(1); Const Law 3618(3), 3936, 4198, 4203; Libel 89(3); Records 50, 63; Schools 139.

Hankins; Dunn v., TexCivApp–San Antonio, 127 SW2d 983.—Labor & Emp 233; Partners 32, 55; Plead 218(1).

Hankins; First Continental Life & Acc. Ins. Co. v., TexCivApp–Amarillo, 480 SW2d 244, ref nre.—Insurance 1808, 1809, 1822, 2588(2).

Hankins v. First Nat. Bank of Panhandle, TexCivApp–Amarillo, 287 SW2d 493, ref nre.—Contracts 25.

Hankins v. Griffith, TexApp–Corpus Christi, 773 SW2d 589, writ den.—Release 52, 57(2).

Hankins v. Haffa, TexCivApp–Amarillo, 469 SW2d 733, ref nre.—App & E 961; Mental H 488, 518; Pretrial Proc 44.1, 221; Trusts 103(1).

Hankins v. Harlan, TexCivApp–Waco, 114 SW2d 588, writ dism.—App & E 1172(1); Autos 201(9), 244(61), 247; Damag 19.

Hankins v. P.H., TexApp–Corpus Christi, 1 SW3d 352, petition for discretionary review den.—Schools 177.

Hankins v. State, TexCrimApp, 132 SW3d 380, cert den 125 SCt 358, 543 US 944, 160 LEd2d 256, habeas corpus den 2007 WL 959040.—Crim Law 218(5), 394.1(3), 412.1(3), 412.2(5), 1130(5), 1152(2), 1158(2); Jury 131(2), 131(13); Searches 108, 191; Sent & Pun 1625, 1720, 1740, 1746, 1771, 1780(3).

Hankins v. State, TexCrimApp, 646 SW2d 191, 36 ALR4th 1003.—Crim Law 552(3), 552(4), 784(1), 784(7), 829(15); Sent & Pun 1381(5).

Hankins v. State, TexCrimApp, 295 SW2d 658.—Crim Law 1090.1(1).

Hankins v. State, TexCrimApp, 294 SW2d 850, 163 TexCrim 553.—Crim Law 1097(1), 1097(4), 1097(5), 1099.7(2).

Hankins v. State, TexCrimApp, 294 SW2d 840.—Crim Law 1097(5).

Hankins v. State, TexCrimApp, 251 SW2d 729, 157 TexCrim 562.—Autos 351.1, 355(6); Bail 64; Crim Law 1099.11.

Hankins v. State, TexCrimApp, 183 SW2d 980, 147 TexCrim 644.—Crim Law 419(10), 1092.11(3), 1169.1(9).

Hankins v. State, TexCrimApp, 146 SW2d 195, 140 TexCrim 520.—Crim Law 1144.13(3), 1159.2(10); Rape 53(2); Witn 379(3).

Hankins v. State, TexApp–Austin, 180 SW3d 177, reh overr, and petition for discretionary review refused.—Crim Law 1086.11, 1134(2), 1162, 1168(1), 1170.5(1); Witn 337(21), 337(25), 337(28), 337(31).

Hankins v. State, TexApp–Corpus Christi, 85 SW3d 433.—Const Law 4693; Crim Law 1134(3), 1144.13(2.1), 1149, 1159.2(7), 1167(1); Ind & Inf 60, 71.2(3); Obscen 3, 11.

Hankins; Tello v., TexCivApp–El Paso, 468 SW2d 115.—App & E 773(2).

Hankins; Union Pacific Resources Group, Inc. v., Tex, 111 SW3d 69.—Mines 78.1(8); Parties 35.17, 35.35, 35.37, 35.79.

Hankins; Union Pacific Resources Group, Inc. v., TexApp–El Paso, 51 SW3d 741, reh overr, and review gr, rev 111 SW3d 69.—App & E 4, 169, 170(2), 874(1), 931(1), 946, 949; Atty & C 21.5(1), 21.20, 129(1); Damag 205; Mines 73, 79.1(1), 79.7; Parties 35.1, 35.5, 35.7, 35.9, 35.13, 35.17, 35.31, 35.33, 35.37, 35.79; Trial 18.

Hankins; Union Pacific Resources Group, Inc. v., TexApp–El Paso, 51 SW3d 738.—App & E 68, 70(1).

Hankins; Union Pacific Resources Group, Inc. v., TexApp–El Paso, 41 SW3d 286, opinion after remand 51

SW3d 738, opinion after remand 51 SW3d 741, reh overr, and review gr, rev 111 SW3d 69.—App & E 931(1), 946, 949, 1178(1); Parties 35.5, 35.9, 35.33, 35.35.

Hankins; Winkel v., TexCivApp–Eastland, 585 SW2d 889, dism.—App & E 231(3), 242(4); Libel 103, 112(2), 121(1), 121(2), 125; Trial 75, 86.

Hankla; Lail v., TexCivApp–Eastland, 276 SW2d 340, ref nre.—App & E 930(1); Deeds 109; Evid 215(1); Trusts 77, 79, 90, 373.

Hanks; Ellis v., TexCivApp–Dallas, 478 SW2d 172, ref nre.—App & E 169, 719(1); Counties 47; Elections 1; Int Liq 30; Mand 16(1), 151(2), 185.

Hanks v. GAB Business Services, Inc., Tex, 644 SW2d 707.—Contracts 303(1).

Hanks v. GAB Business Services, Inc., TexApp–Amarillo, 626 SW2d 564, writ gr, rev 644 SW2d 707.—Contracts 175(1), 176(1); Elect of Rem 7(1); Sales 65, 195, 368.

Hanks; Groves v., TexCivApp–Corpus Christi, 546 SW2d 638, ref nre.—App & E 758.3(2), 1175(5), 1177(1), 1178(6); Crops 5; Lim of Act 80, 127(17); Princ & A 81(2); Release 33; Trial 368; Trover 1, 10, 35, 44.

Hanks v. Gulf, C. & S. F. Ry. Co., Tex, 320 SW2d 333, 159 Tex 311.—Witn 406.

Hanks; Gulf, C. & S. F. Ry. Co. v., TexCivApp–Fort Worth, 308 SW2d 165, rev 320 SW2d 333, 159 Tex 311.—Em Dom 262(5); Evid 200, 219(1), 222(1), 265(1).

Hanks v. Lake Towne Apartments, TexApp–Dallas, 812 SW2d 625, writ den.—Forci E & D 6(2); Land & Ten 290(5); Pretrial Proc 508, 517.1.

Hanks v. LaQuey, TexCivApp–Austin, 425 SW2d 396, ref nre.—App & E 1170.7; Autos 181(7), 244(20), 245(44), 246(2.1); Evid 474(9), 492; Trial 350.1, 350.7(5), 352.4(7); Witn 387.

Hanks; McDonald v., TexCivApp–Eastland, 349 SW2d 787, ref nre.—App & E 204(1), 302(3), 1067; Ex & Ad 151; Trial 234(8).

Hanks v. NCNB Texas Nat. Bank, TexApp–Eastland, 815 SW2d 763.—Guar 71, 82(3); Judgm 185.3(10); Plead 129(5).

Hanks v. Rosser, Tex, 378 SW2d 31.—App & E 1175(1); Judgm 106(2), 335(1), 335(2), 335(3).

Hanks; Rosser v., TexCivApp–Beaumont, 369 SW2d 643, writ gr, aff in part, rev in part 378 SW2d 31.—Judgm 138(2), 143(3), 335(2).

Hanks v. Smith, TexApp–Tyler, 74 SW3d 409, reh overr, and review den, and reh of petition for review den.—Admin Law 500; Counties 53; High 62, 63, 77(7), 77(11).

Hanks v. State, TexCrimApp, 137 SW3d 668.—Crim Law 777, 1134(2), 1159.2(1).

Hanks v. State, TexCrimApp, 542 SW2d 413.—Crim Law 56, 660, 826; Homic 530, 823, 824, 1333, 1452.

Hanks v. State, TexCrimApp, 266 SW2d 378.—Crim Law 1090.1(1).

Hanks v. State, TexCrimApp, 151 SW2d 808, 142 TexCrim 186.—Crim Law 323, 448(1), 564(1), 913(1), 1169.6; Rape 48(2), 52(1).

Hanks v. State, TexCrimApp, 147 SW2d 777, 141 TexCrim 166.—Crim Law 1169.2(2), 1186.4(8).

Hanks v. State, TexApp–Houston (1 Dist), 113 SW3d 523.—Extrad 36, 39; Hab Corp 525.1, 729.

Hanks v. State, TexApp–El Paso, 104 SW3d 695, petition stricken, and petition for discretionary review gr, aff 137 SW3d 668.—Crim Law 661, 693, 694, 777, 789(1), 789(2), 795(1.5), 795(2.1), 795(2.10), 795(2.70), 822(1), 1038.1(1), 1144.13(6), 1172.1(1); Ind & Inf 191(0.5), 192.

Hanks v. State, TexApp–Houston (14 Dist), 625 SW2d 433.—Crim Law 438(1), 438(6), 438(7), 675, 1030(1), 1038.1(1), 1038.1(2), 1038.1(4), 1038.3.

Hanks v. Texas Emp. Ins. Ass'n, Tex, 128 SW2d 1, 133 Tex 187.—App & E 2, 564(2), 621(3).

Hanks v. Texas Emp. Ins. Ass'n, TexCivApp–Beaumont, 120 SW2d 831, rev 128 SW2d 1, 133 Tex 187.—App & E 564(2), 621(3); Statut 223.2(24).

Hank's Flite Center, Inc.; Airway Ins. Co. v., Tex, 534 SW2d 878.—App & E 294(1), 758.3(9).

Hank's Flite Center, Inc.; Airway Ins. Co. v., TexCivApp–San Antonio, 527 SW2d 488, writ gr, aff 534 SW2d 878.—App & E 281(1), 758.1.

Hankton v. State, TexApp–Houston (1 Dist), 23 SW3d 540, petition for discretionary review refused.—Controlled Subs 26, 27, 81; Crim Law 369.1, 369.2(1), 370, 371(1), 374, 1153(1), 1162, 1169.1(1), 1169.11.

Hanley v. First Investors Corp., EDTex, 793 FSupp 719.—Fed Civ Proc 2511; Fraud 38; Lim of Act 100(12); Neglig 1507.1; Sec Reg 134, 149, 154.1, 305, 309.

Hanley v. First Investors Corp., EDTex, 761 FSupp 40.—Rem of C 107(1).

Hanley v. First Investors Corp., EDTex, 151 FRD 76.—Fed Civ Proc 241, 776, 786, 1956.

Hanley; Frazin v., TexApp–Dallas, 130 SW3d 373.—App & E 766, 836, 931(1), 961, 1010.1(2); Contracts 326; Mtg 216; Pretrial Proc 45.

Hanley v. Hanley, TexApp–Dallas, 813 SW2d 511.—App & E 961; Costs 2; Evid 43(1); Pretrial Proc 44.1, 46, 221, 225, 226.

Hanley; Hanley v., TexApp–Dallas, 813 SW2d 511.—App & E 961; Costs 2; Evid 43(1); Pretrial Proc 44.1, 46, 221, 225, 226.

Hanley; Litton v., TexApp–Houston (1 Dist), 823 SW2d 428.—App & E 1050.1(1), 1056.1(1); Evid 397(1), 402, 450(10).

Hanley v. Oil Capital Broadcasting Ass'n, Tex, 171 SW2d 864, 141 Tex 243.—Lim of Act 1, 141, 148(2), 148(4), 151(1), 179(3); Plead 228.14.

Hanley v. Oil Capital Broadcasting Ass'n, TexCivApp–Galveston, 167 SW2d 631, rev 171 SW2d 864, 141 Tex 243.—Lim of Act 148(4), 151(4), 179(3).

Hanley; Seaway Products Pipeline Co. v., TexApp–Fort Worth, 153 SW3d 464.—App & E 766; Environ Law 357, 371; Joint Adv 1.1, 1.2(1), 7; Judgm 183, 185.1(4), 185.3(21); Neglig 202, 372, 379, 380, 387, 411, 1000, 1204(1), 1240, 1706; Princ & A 1, 3(2).

Hanley v. State, TexApp–Waco, 921 SW2d 904, petition for discretionary review refused.—Assault 68, 96(2); Const Law 4626; Crim Law 639.4, 1043(2), 1043(3), 1045, 1153(4); Witn 370(4), 372(1), 373.

Hanley v. State, TexApp–Houston (14 Dist), 909 SW2d 117, reh overr.—Crim Law 1166(1); Double J 1, 58, 59, 95.1, 100.1, 105, 107.1; Jury 4, 29(1), 29(3), 29(5), 29(6).

Hanlon, Ex parte, Tex, 406 SW2d 204.—Hab Corp 528.1; Pretrial Proc 72.

Hanlon; LeCroy v., Tex, 713 SW2d 335.—Clerks of C 11; Const Law 2314, 2317; Statut 105(1), 107(1), 107(6), 107(10), 124(1).

Hanlon v. Nelson, TexCivApp–Eastland, 474 SW2d 526, ref nre.—Mun Corp 185(14).

Hanlon v. United Parcel Service, NDTex, 132 FSupp2d 503.—Carr 108; Damag 49.10; Insurance 1103; States 18.15, 18.41; Tresp 16.

Hanlon-Buchanan, Inc.; Hearn v., TexCivApp–Fort Worth, 179 SW2d 364, writ refused wom.—App & E 934(1); Brok 106; Evid 243(1); Judgm 199(3.14); Mines 75; Princ & A 21, 22(1), 25(1), 54, 93, 94, 99, 147(3), 150(2).

Hanmore Development Corp. v. JBK Enterprises, TexApp–Corpus Christi, 776 SW2d 738, writ den.—Lim of Act 95(16), 124; Parties 54, 65(1); Trial 139.1(17).

Hann v. Life & Cas. Ins. Co. of Tenn., TexCivApp–San Antonio, 312 SW2d 261.—App & E 934(1), 1078(1), 1175(1); Insurance 2590(1), 2608; Judgm 199(1), 199(6).

Hann v. State, TexApp–Fort Worth, 771 SW2d 731.—Larc 7; Tresp 84.

Hann v. Texas Dept. of Protective and Regulatory Services, TexApp–El Paso, 969 SW2d 77, reh overr, and review den.—App & E 662(4), 837(1), 931(1), 994(1), 1008.1(2), 1010.1(4), 1010.1(5), 1011.1(1), 1012.1(2), 1012.1(3), 1012.1(5); Infants 156, 172, 178.

Hanna; Calvert v., TexCivApp–Amarillo, 140 SW2d 976. —Home 57.5, 96; Lim of Act 44(4); Mtg 137, 187.1, 191; Tresp to T T 44.

Hanna v. Gardner, CA5 (Tex), 352 F2d 70.—Social S 143.70.

Hanna v. Godwin, TexApp–El Paso, 876 SW2d 454.— Action 13; App & E 151(2), 158(1), 781(1), 781(4), 877(1), 877(2); Const Law 2600; Work Comp 1981.

Hanna v. Goodyear Tire and Rubber, EDTex, 17 FSupp2d 647.—Civil R 1185, 1189; Damag 192; Fed Civ Proc 2142.1, 2152; Labor & Emp 2937.

Hanna v. Goodyear Tire & Rubber, EDTex, 6 FSupp2d 605.—Damag 149; Labor & Emp 866, 870; Lim of Act 55(4), 104.5.

Hanna; Government Emp. Ins. Co. v., TexCivApp–Fort Worth, 219 SW2d 122, ref nre.—Accord 1; Compromise 2; Contracts 22(1); Evid 10(2), 242(1), 461(1); Insurance 1747, 2730, 2732; Princ & A 23(2).

Hanna v. Hanna, TexApp–Houston (1 Dist), 813 SW2d 626.—Child S 215, 558(2).

Hanna; Hanna v., TexApp–Houston (1 Dist), 813 SW2d 626.—Child S 215, 558(2).

Hanna; Hollenbeck v., TexApp–San Antonio, 802 SW2d 412.—Trusts 289, 291; Wills 680.

Hanna v. Home Ins. Co., CA5 (Tex), 281 F2d 298, cert den 81 SCt 751, 365 US 838, 5 LEd2d 747, reh den 81 SCt 1905, 366 US 955, 6 LEd2d 1247.—App & E 653(3); Consp 7.5(1), 7.5(2), 18; Const Law 3000; Courts 509; Fed Cts 221.

Hanna v. Home Ins. Co., TexCivApp–Dallas, 260 SW2d 891, ref nre.—App & E 568, 621(1), 628(1), 628(2).

Hanna; International Services Ins. Co. v., TexCivApp–Eastland, 515 SW2d 175.—Evid 474(19), 474(20).

Hanna; Jones v., TexCivApp–Waco, 264 SW2d 133.—Impl & C C 61; Labor & Emp 2516.

Hanna v. Lattimore, TexComApp, 81 SW2d 496, 125 Tex 243.—Evid 441(8).

Hanna v. Lott, TexApp–Tyler, 888 SW2d 132.—Autos 192(11), 244(31), 247, 249.2; Damag 38, 62(1), 62(2), 106, 113; Infants 105; Pretrial Proc 45.

Hanna v. Meurer, TexApp–Austin, 769 SW2d 680.—App & E 907(2); Pretrial Proc 36.1.

Hanna; National Life & Acc. Ins. Co. v., TexCivApp–Dallas, 195 SW2d 733, ref nre.—App & E 237(2); Evid 528(1); Insurance 2589(1); Trial 351.5(4), 352.4(4), 352.12.

Hanna v. Rio Grande Nat. Life Ins. Co., TexCivApp–Dallas, 181 SW2d 908, writ refused.—App & E 916(1); Insurance 2590(1), 2590(2), 3571.

Hanna v. State, TexCrimApp, 546 SW2d 318.—Consp 48.2(2); Larc 64(8), 70(3).

Hanna v. State, TexCrimApp, 259 SW2d 570, 159 TexCrim 2.—Autos 355(6); Crim Law 1092.14, 1099.10, 1099.13, 1102, 1111(3), 1111(4), 1115(2).

Hanna v. State, TexCrimApp, 135 SW2d 105, 138 TexCrim 183.—Counties 47, 60.

Hanna v. State, TexCrimApp, 94 SW2d 737, 130 TexCrim 360.—Crim Law 465, 784(1); Larc 60.

Hanna v. State, TexCrimApp, 105 SW 793, 52 TexCrim 162.—Civil R 1058.

Hanna v. Turner, TexCivApp–Corpus Christi, 556 SW2d 866.—Child C 554, 577, 638, 921(3).

Hanna v. Vastar Resources, Inc., TexApp–Beaumont, 84 SW3d 372.—Labor & Emp 23; Neglig 1001, 1010, 1011, 1037(4), 1037(7), 1692; Princ & A 1, 3(2), 19.

Hanna v. Wright, TexCivApp–Tyler, 504 SW2d 779.— App & E 882(1), 882(10), 1170.10; Autos 247; Damag 113; Evid 366(1); Trial 350.3(7).

Hannah; Chavez v., TexApp–Austin, 827 SW2d 100, writ den.—Const Law 82(8), 990, 1466, 4232; Elections 24.

Hannah; Hardy v., TexApp–Austin, 849 SW2d 355, reh overr, and writ den.—Action 13; Const Law 540, 542, 556, 725; Judgm 185.1(1).

Hannah; Keene Corp. v., WDTex, 800 FSupp 490.— Const Law 980; Corp 651; Fed Cts 47.1, 269, 272.

Hannah; LaRouche v., Tex, 822 SW2d 632.—Mand 4(5), 74(3).

Hannah; Pennsylvania Nat. Mut. Cas. Ins. Co. v., TexApp–Beaumont, 701 SW2d 67, ref nre.—Trial 350.3(8); Work Comp 302, 1683, 1727.

Hannah; Slagle v., Tex, 837 SW2d 100.—Elections 146, 147.

Hannah v. State, TexApp–Houston (14 Dist), 624 SW2d 750, petition for discretionary review refused by 632 SW2d 151.—Crim Law 339.10(3), 726, 881(2), 1037.1(2), 1043(3), 1109(1).

Hannah v. Stephens, TexCivApp–El Paso, 101 SW2d 823. —High 113(5); Plead 111.9; Venue 7.5(3), 8.5(8), 69.

Hannah v. U.S., CA5 (Tex), 396 F2d 785, cert den 89 SCt 122, 393 US 842, 21 LEd2d 112.—Crim Law 330, 569, 739.1(1).

Hannah v. Walker, TexCivApp–Dallas, 409 SW2d 949, mandamus overr.—App & E 389(3), 571; Offic 30.5.

Hannah Const. Co.; Stephens v., TexCivApp–El Paso, 81 SW2d 729.—Venue 22(6).

Hannan v. City of Coppell, TexCivApp–Dallas, 583 SW2d 817, ref nre.—Zoning 131.

Hannan Trucking, Inc., In re, BkrtcyNDTex, 17 BR 475. —Int Rev 4832, 4855.

Hannasch; Street v., TexCivApp–San Antonio, 410 SW2d 941.—Ex & Ad 202.4; Judgm 181(2), 181(4), 185(4), 185(5), 185.1(4), 185.2(4), 185.3(4); Witn 164(1).

Hannen, Ex parte, TexCrimApp, 230 SW2d 236, 155 TexCrim 10.—Courts 113; Crim Law 996(1).

Hannen, Ex parte, TexCrimApp, 228 SW2d 864, 155 TexCrim 10, opinion set aside on reh 230 SW2d 236, 155 TexCrim 10.—Crim Law 749, 881(3), 980(1), 994(1), 994(4), 995(4), 1184(1); Hab Corp 505, 791; Sent & Pun 401, 1001, 1057.

Hanner; First Continental Life and Acc. Ins. Co. v., TexApp–Beaumont, 658 SW2d 798.—App & E 994(2), 995, 1057(1); Evid 59; Insurance 2445.

Hanner v. State, TexCrimApp, 572 SW2d 702, cert den 99 SCt 1504, 440 US 961, 59 LEd2d 774.—Crim Law 366(3), 517(5), 1038.3, 1045, 1083, 1137(5); Rape 42, 48(1), 59(15); Witn 368.

Hanners v. State Bar of Texas, TexApp–Dallas, 860 SW2d 903, application for writ of error dism.—App & E 758.3(9), 846(5), 914(1), 977(1), 989, 1012.1(4), 1073(2); Atty & C 52, 53(2), 55, 57, 59; Const Law 3993, 3998; Damag 194; Evid 43(1), 43(2); Judgm 109, 140, 145(2); Jury 19(18), 28(9); New Tr 157.

Hanney; Aguirre v., TexCivApp–Galveston, 107 SW2d 917.—Costs 132(5).

Hanney v. State, TexCrimApp, 472 SW2d 776.—Crim Law 698(1), 1119(4).

Hannigan v. First State Bank-Wylie, TexApp–Dallas, 700 SW2d 7, ref nre.—Sec Tran 113.1.

Hannington v. State, TexCrimApp, 832 SW2d 355.—Sent & Pun 1160.

Hannon; Green v., TexCivApp–Texarkana, 369 SW2d 853, ref nre.—Evid 317(1); Ex & Ad 7; Princ & A 1; Spec Perf 24, 68, 70.

Hannon; John P. MaGuire & Co., Inc. v., TexCivApp–Hous (14 Dist), 563 SW2d 844.—App & E 756; Judgm 335(1); Parties 18, 29.

Hannon v. State, TexCrimApp, 475 SW2d 800.—Burg 42(1); Crim Law 507.5, 641.13(2.1), 780(1), 792(1), 867, 1170.5(6), 1172.1(3); Searches 174.

Hannsz v. State, TexCrimApp, 341 SW2d 938, 170 TexCrim 398.—Bail 64.

Hannum; Brown v., WDTex, 50 FSupp 697.—Inj 128(8); Inn 3; War 204, 225.

Hannum v. General Life and Acc. Ins. Co., TexApp–Corpus Christi, 745 SW2d 500.—Evid 366(1); Insurance 2476.

Hanover Bldg. Materials, Inc. v. Guiffrida, CA5 (Tex), 748 F2d 1011.—Fed Cts 419; Insurance 2210; U S 147(11.1).

Hanover Fire Ins. Co. v. Bock Jewelry Co., TexCivApp–Dallas, 435 SW2d 909, ref nre.—App & E 1178(6); Bailm 11; Insurance 2181, 2990, 3050(4), 3051, 3095, 3515(1); Judgm 181(14), 185.3(12); Princ & A 3(1), 136(1).

Hanover Fire Ins. Co. v. Glenn, TexCivApp–Fort Worth, 153 SW2d 993.—App & E 758.3(1), 758.3(2), 758.3(3), 758.3(5), 758.3(9); Insurance 3191(7), 3546, 3571; Trial 350.4(3).

Hanover Fire Ins. Co.; Harris v., CA5 (Tex), 425 F2d 1168.—Insurance 3564(9); Lim of Act 25(2).

Hanover Fire Ins. Co.; Nash v., TexCivApp–Dallas, 92 SW2d 1114, writ dism.—Dep in Court 11.

Hanover Fire Ins. Co. v. Slaughter, TexCivApp–Amarillo, 111 SW2d 362.—Evid 174.5, 318(1), 370(1); Insurance 3167, 3192, 3197, 3201, 3571; Trial 350.1, 350.4(3), 362.

Hanover Fire Ins. Co. of N.Y.; Alexander v., TexCivApp–Eastland, 346 SW2d 667, ref nre.—Home 131; Insurance 3051; Spec Perf 64.

Hanover Ins. Co.; Blue Ridge Ins. Co. v., NDTex, 748 FSupp 470.—Insurance 2663, 2921.

Hanover Ins. Co.; Crawford v., TexCivApp–Waco, 582 SW2d 240.—App & E 1024.4; Judgm 181(3), 181(22), 185(2), 186.

Hanover Ins. Co.; E & L Chipping Co., Inc. v., TexApp–Beaumont, 962 SW2d 272.—Insurance 2265, 2270(2), 2275, 2278(3), 2278(17), 2915, 2919, 3170, 3370.

Hanover Ins. Co. v. Hoch, TexCivApp–Corpus Christi, 469 SW2d 717, ref nre.—Action 60; App & E 688(2), 714(4), 842(7), 930(3), 989; Contracts 93(5); Evid 317(18), 471(7); Insurance 2189, 3025; New Tr 143(5); Pretrial Proc 724; Witn 126, 159(2).

Hanover Ins. Co.; Hogan v., TexCivApp–Fort Worth, 406 SW2d 217, ref nre.—Judgm 185.3(13); Work Comp 204.

Hanover Ins. Co. v. Holleman, TexCivApp–Dallas, 372 SW2d 554, ref nre.—Work Comp 230, 1114, 1132, 1182, 1186, 1461, 1789.

Hanover Ins. Co.; Jackson v., TexCivApp–Waco, 389 SW2d 328.—Work Comp 1105, 1958.

Hanover Ins. Co. v. Johnson, TexCivApp–Waco, 397 SW2d 904, ref nre.—Witn 344(2), 383, 405(2); Work Comp 555, 569, 619.

Hanover Ins. Co.; Miller v., TexApp–Eastland, 718 SW2d 429, ref nre.—Insurance 2793(2).

Hanover Ins. Co.; PAJ, Inc. v., TexApp–Dallas, 170 SW3d 258, review gr.—App & E 1175(1); Contracts 1, 221(2), 315, 317, 318; Insurance 1808, 1863, 3147, 3168.

Hanover Ins. Co.; Park v., TexCivApp–Amarillo, 443 SW2d 940.—Insurance 2142(4), 2144(1), 2165(2).

Hanover Ins. Co. v. Peyson, TexCivApp–Fort Worth, 373 SW2d 701.—App & E 1170.1, 1170.6; Trial 121(2), 131(3); Work Comp 1926, 1968(4).

Hanover Ins. Co. v. Richardson, TexCivApp–Hous (1 Dist), 529 SW2d 608, dism.—App & E 912; Corp 666; Insurance 3559; Plead 111.6, 111.9, 335, 409(1); Venue 7(3).

Hanover Ins. Co. v. Sanford, TexCivApp–Beaumont, 457 SW2d 115.—Corp 666; Plead 111.19.

Hanover Ins. Co. v. Sonfield, TexCivApp–Houston, 386 SW2d 160.—App & E 153, 265(1), 931(1), 931(3); Evid 211; Insurance 2199, 2214, 2219, 2227, 2255.

Hanover Ins. Co. of New York v. Hagler, TexCivApp–Dallas, 532 SW2d 136, ref nre.—Insurance 3147, 3153, 3164, 3188, 3191(1), 3191(7), 3191(13), 3198(2).

Hanover Ins. Co. of New York v. Stevenson, TexComApp, 90 SW2d 822, 127 Tex 186.—Insurance 1929(11), 1935, 3396.

Hanover Mfg. Co. v. Ed Hanover Trailers, Inc., Tex, 434 SW2d 109.—Good Will 6(3); Trademarks 1032, 1042, 1186, 1201(2).

Hanover Mfg. Co.; Ed Hanover Trailers, Inc. v., TexCivApp–Waco, 421 SW2d 144, writ gr, rev 434 SW2d 109.—Good Will 6(4); Trademarks 1200(3), 1526.

Hanover Modular Homes of Taft, Inc. v. Corpus Christi Bank and Trust, TexCivApp–Corpus Christi, 476 SW2d 97.—App & E 493, 914(1); Appear 8(8); Corp 668(14); Evid 334(1); Judgm 17(1), 17(10), 124, 162(2), 951(1); Proc 153.

Hanovia Chemical & Mfg. Co.; Racugno v., TexCivApp–Fort Worth, 110 SW2d 249.—App & E 20; Chat Mtg 138(3); Corp 661(6); Courts 120; J P 174(15).

Hanovice; Henke & Pillot v., TexCivApp–Galveston, 77 SW2d 303.—Antitrust 17, 18; App & E 863; Trademarks 1425, 1705(2), 1800.

Hanovich; Liberty Mut. Ins. Co. v., CA5 (Tex), 171 F2d 168.—Evid 591; Work Comp 1396, 1637, 1724.

Hanratty; Stokley v., TexApp–Houston (14 Dist), 809 SW2d 924.—App & E 836, 931(1), 989, 1010.1(3), 1012.1(5); Bills & N 98, 543; Estop 52.10(2), 52.10(3).

Hanratty v. U.S., CA5 (Tex), 218 F2d 358, cert den 75 SCt 770, 349 US 928, 99 LEd 1259.—Consp 47(3.1); Crim Law 1035(6); Jury 33(1.25); Rec S Goods 8(3).

Hansard; McCaleb v., TexApp–El Paso, 697 SW2d 73.—Child C 531(1), 872; Hab Corp 532(2).

Hansard v. Pepsi–Cola Bottling Group, CA5 (Tex), 865 F2d 1461. See Hansard v. Pepsi-Cola Metropolitan Bottling Co., Inc.

Hansard v. Pepsi-Cola Metropolitan Bottling Co., Inc., CA5 (Tex), 865 F2d 1461, cert den 110 SCt 129, 493 US 842, 107 LEd2d 89, cert den 110 SCt 129, 493 US 842, 107 LEd2d 89.—Civil R 1204, 1539, 1551, 1555, 1556, 1571, 1573, 1576(2); Evid 501(9); Fed Cts 823; Interest 39(2.45).

Hansbro v. Neiderhofer, TexCivApp–Beaumont, 83 SW2d 685.—Counties 52; Mand 72, 81.

Hanschke; Claussen v., TexCivApp–El Paso, 93 SW2d 239, writ refused.—App & E 215(1), 544(1); Fraud 58(4); New Tr 124(1).

Hansel, In re, BkrtcySDTex, 160 BR 66.—Bankr 2832.1, 2902, 2923; Insurance 3120, 3506(2).

Hansel; Regal Const. Co. v., TexCivApp–Hous (1 Dist), 596 SW2d 150, ref nre.—App & E 174; Contracts 175(3), 350(1), 350(2); Corp 202, 209, 617(1), 630(1); Evid 210, 265(1); Judgm 199(3.2), 199(3.9), 199(3.10); Parties 40(1), 76(2).

Hansel & Gretel Children's Shop, Inc.; Sandy Intern., Inc. v., TexApp–Dallas, 775 SW2d 802.—App & E 747(2), 931(1), 996, 1001(1); Courts 472.3; Statut 181(1), 205; Trademarks 1626.

Hanselka v. Lummus Crest, Inc., TexApp–Corpus Christi, 800 SW2d 665.—Neglig 210, 213, 1205(4), 1692; Prod Liab 42.

Hansen v. Academy Corp., TexApp–Houston (1 Dist), 961 SW2d 329, review den, and reh of petition for review overr, appeal after remand 2002 WL 356492, review den (2 pets), and reh of petition for review den.—App & E 832(4), 1097(7), 1212(3); Costs 208; Interest 39(2.20); Stip 1, 14(1), 16, 18(6).

Hansen; Adams v., CA5 (Tex), 906 F2d 192.—Fed Civ Proc 2734; Sent & Pun 1548.

Hansen v. Aon Risk Services of Texas, SDTex, 473 FSupp2d 743.—Civil R 1137, 1166, 1179, 1536, 1545, 1732; Evid 597; Fed Civ Proc 2497.1; Jury 25(6).

Hansen; Baker v., Tex, 679 SW2d 480.—App & E 20, 78(1), 80(3); Judgm 217.

Hansen; Blackmon v., Tex, 169 SW2d 962, 140 Tex 536.—Licens 34; Statut 226; Tax 3318, 3371.

Hansen v. Blackmon, TexCivApp–El Paso, 169 SW2d 955, aff 169 SW2d 962, 140 Tex 536.—States 191.10; Statut 226; Tax 3318, 3371.

Hansen v. Christie, TexCivApp–Galveston, 132 SW2d 910.—Debtor & C 19; Deeds 70(4).

Hansen v. Continental Ins. Co., CA5 (Tex), 940 F2d 971. —Fed Cts 415, 666, 923; Insurance 1117(1); Interest 31, 39(2.6), 39(2.40); Labor & Emp 413, 414, 428, 483(1), 483(2), 638, 676; States 18.51.

Hansen; Dyess v., TexCivApp–Galveston, 151 SW2d 904, writ dism, correct.—App & E 846(5); Home 118(3).

Hansen v. Eagle Mountain-Saginaw Independent School Dist., TexCivApp–Fort Worth, 373 SW2d 817, ref nre.—Judgm 181(15.1), 185(6); Pretrial Proc 478.

Hansen; Gonzalez v., TexCivApp–San Antonio, 505 SW2d 613.—App & E 934(1), 989; Damag 186.

Hansen; Goree v., TexCivApp–Fort Worth, 214 SW2d 824.—App & E 930(1), 1003(5); Autos 244(42), 244(58); Judgm 199(3.17); Trial 215, 352.9.

Hansen v. Hansen, TexCivApp–San Antonio, 110 SW2d 1006.—Divorce 144, 184(1); Trial 215.

Hansen; Hansen v., TexCivApp–San Antonio, 110 SW2d 1006.—Divorce 144, 184(1); Trial 215.

Hansen v. Hansen, TexCivApp–San Antonio, 96 SW2d 548.—Divorce 27(9), 130, 147.

Hansen; Hansen v., TexCivApp–San Antonio, 96 SW2d 548.—Divorce 27(9), 130, 147.

Hansen v. Hidalgo and Cameron Counties Water Control and Imp. Dist. No. Nine, TexCivApp–San Antonio, 319 SW2d 765.—Lim of Act 24(2), 66(15).

Hansen; Huckabee v., TexCivApp–Corpus Christi, 422 SW2d 606, 27 ALR3d 1380.—Wills 570.

Hansen v. Johns-Manville Products Corp., CA5 (Tex), 734 F2d 1036, reh den 744 F2d 94, cert den 105 SCt 1749, 470 US 1051, 84 LEd2d 814, cert den Johns-Manville Sales Corporation v. Hansen, 105 SCt 1750, 470 US 1051, 84 LEd2d 814.—Const Law 260, 3855; Damag 91(1), 91(3), 94, 208(8), 216(1); Death 99(1); Double J 23; Fed Civ Proc 1432.1, 1974.1, 2174, 2339, 2342, 2343, 2372.1; Fed Cts 825.1, 898, 929; Prod Liab 26, 62, 88.

Hansen v. Ken Stoepel Ford, Inc., TexCivApp–San Antonio, 515 SW2d 1.—Lim of Act 51(2).

Hansen; Lopez v., TexApp–Houston (1 Dist), 947 SW2d 587.—App & E 219(2), 846(5), 852; Wills 289, 302(6).

Hansen v. Starr, TexApp–Dallas, 123 SW3d 13, reh overr, and review den.—App & E 671(1), 754(3), 945; Estop 52.10(2); Health 804, 805, 809.

Hansen v. State, TexApp–Houston (1 Dist), 224 SW3d 325, petition for discretionary review refused.—Crim Law 394.1(2), 394.5(4), 1036.1(4), 1144.13(2.1), 1159.2(7); Extort 32; Searches 33.

Hansen v. State, TexApp–Texarkana, 636 SW2d 241.— Crim Law 412.1(4), 829(4); Homic 1458; Ind & Inf 110(17), 138; Witn 277(4).

Hansen v. Sullivan, TexApp–Houston (1 Dist), 886 SW2d 467.—Alt Disp Res 113, 444; Compromise 2; Mand 1, 53, 141, 168(2); Refer 27, 47, 99(1).

Hansen; Texas Employment Commission v., Tex, 342 SW2d 551, 161 Tex 511.—Unemp Comp 101.

Hansen v. Texas Employment Com'n, TexCivApp–Dallas, 332 SW2d 372, writ gr, aff 342 SW2d 551, 161 Tex 511.—Unemp Comp 117.

Hansen v. Texas Local Bd. No. 5, Selective Service System, CA5 (Tex), 444 F2d 532.—Courts 104.

Hansen v. Ware's, Inc., TexCivApp–San Antonio, 324 SW2d 909.—Judgm 181(2); Mun Corp 808(1); Neglig 1088.

Hansford County Com'rs Court; Gumfory v., TexCivApp–Amarillo, 561 SW2d 28, ref nre.—Const Law 725; Counties 18.

Hansler, Matter of, CA5 (Tex), 988 F2d 35.—Judgm 587, 638, 650, 828.21(2).

Hansler v. Mainka, CA5 (Tex), 988 F2d 35. See Hansler, Matter of.

Hansler v. Mainka, TexApp–Corpus Christi, 807 SW2d 3. —Lim of Act 119(3), 195(3), 199(1); Trover 28.

Hanslik v. Dittfurth, TexCivApp–San Antonio, 356 SW2d 495.—App & E 790(3); Venue 28.

Hanslik v. Nickels Ginning Co., TexCivApp–Amarillo, 496 SW2d 788.—Evid 318(1), 593; Fraud 59(3); Plead 45, 111.9, 111.18, 111.42(4); Princ & A 136(2); Trial 105(2).

Hanson; Butler v., Tex, 473 SW2d 934.—Tresp to T T 47(1).

Hanson; Butler v., Tex, 455 SW2d 942, appeal after remand 469 SW2d 713, mod 473 SW2d 934.—Adv Poss 19, 50, 109, 114(2), 115(4); Afft 18; App & E 930(3), 989, 1176(4).

Hanson; Butler v., TexCivApp–El Paso, 469 SW2d 713, mod 473 SW2d 934.—App & E 1097(5).

Hanson; Butler v., TexCivApp–El Paso, 432 SW2d 559, writ gr, rev 455 SW2d 942, appeal after remand 469 SW2d 713, mod 473 SW2d 934.—Adv Poss 11, 19, 29, 31, 114(1), 116(5); App & E 1146.

Hanson; Dipuccio v., TexCivApp–Galveston, 233 SW2d 863.—App & E 1, 143, 882(2); Evid 589; Hus & W 262.1(2), 264(1), 267(1); Spec Perf 33, 106(1), 119.

Hanson; Electronic Data Systems Corp. v., TexApp–Dallas, 792 SW2d 506.—Appear 8(1); Courts 35.

Hanson; Fidelity Union Cas. Co. v., TexCivApp–Galveston, 26 SW2d 395, writ gr, aff 44 SW2d 985, cert den 53 SCt 12, 287 US 599, 77 LEd 522.—Bankr 143(11), 421(1), 433(1).

Hanson; Forrest v., Tex, 424 SW2d 899.—App & E 1082(2); Covenants 101, 130(1), 131; Estop 32(1); Mines 55(4); Trial 66.

Hanson; Foust v., TexCivApp–Beaumont, 612 SW2d 251. —App & E 847(1); Damag 163(4); Equity 65(2); Spec Perf 28(1), 128(1), 129; Ven & Pur 129.

Hanson v. Green, TexCivApp–Texarkana, 339 SW2d 381, writ refused.—Autos 192(2), 192(11), 193(1), 201(1.1).

Hanson v. Guardian Trust Co., TexCivApp–Galveston, 150 SW2d 465, dism.—App & E 839(1); Garn 1, 93, 175, 178, 194.

Hanson v. Hanson, TexApp–Houston (14 Dist), 672 SW2d 274, dism.—Divorce 184(1), 184(6.1), 252.2, 252.3(2), 252.3(5), 254(1), 282, 286(5).

Hanson; Hanson v., TexApp–Houston (14 Dist), 672 SW2d 274, dism.—Divorce 184(1), 184(6.1), 252.2, 252.3(2), 252.3(5), 254(1), 282, 286(5).

Hanson v. Haymann, TexCivApp–Galveston, 280 SW 869, writ dism woj.—Action 50(4.1).

Hanson; Johnson v., TexCivApp–Austin, 575 SW2d 361. —Judgm 217, 304, 306, 323.

Hanson v. Jordan, Tex, 198 SW2d 262, 145 Tex 320.— Const Law 599; Mun Corp 918(1).

Hanson v. Jordan, TexCivApp–Beaumont, 196 SW2d 546, certified question answered 198 SW2d 262, 145 Tex 320. —Mun Corp 918(1).

Hanson; Kelso v., Tex, 388 SW2d 396.—Replev 2, 25, 119, 125, 133; Sequest 20.

Hanson; Kelso v., TexCivApp–Amarillo, 380 SW2d 187, ref nre, rev 388 SW2d 396.—Bailm 18(3); Sequest 21.

Hanson v. Leckey, TexApp–Tyler, 754 SW2d 292, writ den.—Child C 719, 735, 736, 943; Hab Corp 798, 882.

Hanson; Moore v., CA5 (Tex), 325 F2d 784.—Int Rev 4921, 4925.

Hanson v. Pelham, TexCivApp–Eastland, 413 SW2d 394, writ gr, rev Forrest v. Hanson, 424 SW2d 899.—Estop 23, 32(1); Interest 39(3); Mines 55(4); Set-Off 60.

Hanson v. Pittsburgh Plate Glass Industries, Inc., CA5 (Tex), 482 F2d 220, cert den 94 SCt 880, 414 US 1136, 38 LEd2d 761.—Antitrust 913, 963(3).

Hanson v. Polk County Land, Inc., CA5 (Tex), 608 F2d 129, 52 ALR Fed 561.—Fed Civ Proc 2532, 2533.1, 2547.1; Fed Cts 914.

Hanson; Raymond v., TexApp–Dallas, 970 SW2d 175.— Counties 213; Judgm 178, 185(2), 185(6); Mun Corp 741.10; Statut 223.4.

Hanson v. Republic Ins. Co., TexApp–Houston (1 Dist), 5 SW3d 324, petition for review den.—App & E 854(1), 1175(1); Evid 207(1); Insurance 1722, 1809, 1832(2), 1863, 2747, 2764, 2806, 3081, 3349, 3350, 3360.

Hanson; Riverside Chemical Co. v., TexCivApp–Waco, 567 SW2d 880.—Corp 666; Venue 8.5(8).

Hanson v. State, TexCrimApp, 790 SW2d 646.—Crim Law 1070.

Hanson v. State, TexCrimApp, 342 SW2d 648, 170 Tex-Crim 544.—Weap 17(8).

Hanson v. State, TexCrimApp, 336 SW2d 183, 169 Tex-Crim 550.—Int Liq 236(5), 236(7).

Hanson v. State, TexCrimApp, 199 SW2d 163, 150 Tex-Crim 35.—Crim Law 1092.7.

Hanson v. State, TexCrimApp, 139 SW2d 573, 139 Tex-Crim 233.—Crim Law 372(12), 387, 531(3), 594(3), 698(3), 720(6), 722.3, 781(5), 956(4), 1043(2), 1169.11; Forg 44(3).

Hanson v. State, TexApp–Fort Worth, 781 SW2d 445, petition for discretionary review gr, appeal abated 790 SW2d 646.—Autos 332, 355(6); Crim Law 414.

Hanson v. State, TexApp–Austin, 55 SW3d 681, reh overr, and petition for discretionary review refused.—Consp 28(3), 47(8); Crim Law 59(5), 80, 554, 568, 695.5, 795(1.5), 795(2.10), 795(2.50), 814(19), 872.5, 881(1), 1144.13(2.1), 1144.13(6), 1159.2(1), 1159.2(2), 1159.2(7), 1171.3, 1172.1(1); Homic 571, 1167, 1400, 1465; Sent & Pun 1624; Statut 223.2(1.1), 223.2(35), 223.4.

Hanson v. State, TexApp–Waco, 180 SW3d 726, reh overr.—Crim Law 419(14), 662.9, 755.5, 763(1), 1030(2), 1169.1(9); Double J 148; Infants 20.

Hanson; State v., TexApp–Waco, 793 SW2d 270.—Const Law 4506; Extort 25.1; Statut 135.

Hanson v. State, TexApp–Houston (14 Dist), 11 SW3d 285, reh overr, and petition for discretionary review refused.—Crim Law 641.3(1), 641.3(4), 641.10(2), 641.13(1), 641.13(7), 1026.10(3), 1081(2), 1166.10(2).

Hanson; Texas & N. O. R. Co. v., TexCivApp–Galveston, 271 SW2d 309, writ dism.—App & E 994(2), 1003(1), 1003(5), 1004(9); Death 95(4), 99(3), 103(4); Evid 359(3), 380, 586(2); R R 348(2), 348(4); Trial 139.1(3), 140(1); Witn 330(1).

Hanson v. Town of Flower Mound, CA5 (Tex), 679 F2d 497.—Const Law 2583; Courts 90(2); Fed Civ Proc 642, 1742(1), 1742(2), 1832; Fed Cts 172, 219.1, 542, 571, 584, 654, 666, 712; Searches 85; Treaties 7, 8.

Hanson v. Town of Flower Mound, TexCivApp–Fort Worth, 539 SW2d 178.—Mun Corp 956(1); Tax 2167, 2187, 2413, 2420.

Hanson; U.S. v., CA5 (Tex), 801 F2d 757.—Arrest 63.4(1), 63.5(4), 63.5(5), 63.5(9), 68(4); Consp 47(12); Crim Law 394.5(3), 1224(1).

Hanson; U.S. v., CA5 (Tex), 469 F2d 1375.—Controlled Subs 142; Crim Law 394.4(5.1); Cust Dut 126(1); Searches 103.1.

Hanson v. U.S., EDTex, 710 FSupp 1105.—Admin Law 470; Environ Law 136, 145, 175, 626; Nav Wat 1(1), 1(4), 1(6).

Hanson v. Veterans Admin., CA5 (Tex), 800 F2d 1381.—Civil R 1075, 1331(3), 1395(3), 1419.

Hanson Bldg. Materials America, Inc. v. Pennington, CA5 (Tex), 176 FedAppx 577.—Alt Disp Res 146.

Hanson Business Park, L.P. v. First Nat. Title Ins. Co., TexApp–Dallas, 209 SW3d 867, review den.—App & E 870(2), 1175(1); Insurance 1013, 1716, 2610, 2616.

Hanson Galleries; Dinzik v., SDTex, 553 FSupp 547.—Action 69(3); Courts 493(3).

Hanson Industries; American States Ins. Co. v., SDTex, 873 FSupp 17.—Contracts 143.5; Fed Civ Proc 2501; Insurance 1805, 1806, 1822, 2276, 2277, 2278(17), 2278(27), 2278(28), 2913, 2914, 3156, 3160(4), 3167, 3168, 3200; Waters 101.

Hanson Industries North America-Grove Worldwide; Indelco, Inc. v., TexApp–Houston (14 Dist), 967 SW2d 931, review den.—Action 27(1).

Hanson Pipe & Products, Inc. v. Bridge Technologies, LLC, CA5 (Tex), 160 FedAppx 380.—Alt Disp Res 143, 213(4); Fed Cts 79, 82.

Hanson Pipe & Products, Inc. v. Bridge Technologies, LLC, EDTex, 351 FSupp2d 603, aff 160 FedAppx 380.—Alt Disp Res 137, 143; Const Law 3965(5); Copyr 109; Pat 328(2).

Hanson Production Co. v. Americas Ins. Co., CA5 (Tex), 108 F3d 627, reh den.—Insurance 1091(4), 3167, 3168.

Hanson Production Co.; EOG Resources, Inc. v., Tex-App–San Antonio, 94 SW3d 697, reh overr.—App & E 842(8), 893(1); Contracts 143(1), 143.5, 147(2), 164, 170(1), 175(1), 176(2); Deeds 95; Mines 64, 74(3), 74(5).

Hanson Southwest Corp. v. Dal-Mac Const. Co., Tex-CivApp–Dallas, 554 SW2d 712, ref nre.—Contracts 143.5, 221(1), 221(2), 221(3), 284(3), 350(1); Corp 1.5(2), 1.6(2), 1.6(13), 399(4), 429; Costs 194.32; Damag 118, 140; Evid 181, 187, 373(1), 593; Princ & A 190(1); Trial 81.

Hanssard v. Ledbetter, TexCivApp–Waco, 561 SW2d 34.—App & E 1177(9); Venue 2, 3.

Hanssen v. Our Redeemer Lutheran Church, TexApp–Dallas, 938 SW2d 85, reh overr, and reh overr, and writ den.—App & E 758.3(11); Damag 50.10; Evid 589, 590, 594; Judgm 178, 181(2), 185(2), 185(4), 185(5), 185.3(21); Libel 1, 6(1), 23.1, 44(1), 45(1), 48(1), 51(1), 51(4), 51(5), 101(4), 123(8); Pretrial Proc 308; Torts 353.

Hanssen v. Qantas Airways Ltd., CA5 (Tex), 904 F2d 267.—Contracts 143(2), 169, 176(2); Fed Civ Proc 2492.

Hansson v. Harris, TexCivApp–Austin, 252 SW2d 600, ref nre.—Inj 96.

Hanus v. Texas Utilities Co., TexApp–Fort Worth, 71 SW3d 874.—App & E 840(1), 842(4); Electricity 12.1, 16(1); Judgm 183, 185(5); Neglig 202, 210, 221, 301, 1692; Prod Liab 1, 5, 8, 11, 14, 87.1.

Hanvy v. State, TexCrimApp, 162 SW2d 721, 144 Tex-Crim 351.—Crim Law 641.7(1), 824(4), 841, 1038.3, 1056.1(4); Larc 55.

Hanyard; U.S. v., CA5 (Tex), 762 F2d 1226.—Crim Law 1026.10(2.1), 1134(8), 1147, 1429(2), 1576; Prisons 13.3; Sent & Pun 2232, 2305.

Hanyard; W.O.S. Const. Co., Inc. v., Tex, 684 SW2d 675.—Corp 30(5); Plead 291(1).

Hanyard Enterprises, Inc. v. McBeath, TexApp–Austin, 663 SW2d 639. See Bernard Hanyard Enterprises, Inc. v. McBeath.

Hanzel v. Herring, TexApp–Fort Worth, 80 SW3d 167.—App & E 870(2), 1175(1); Bankr 2154.1, 2395; Costs 194.40; Frds St of 110(1); Interpl 5, 15, 17, 18, 21, 35; Judgm 720, 725(1), 750; Jud S 61; Tax 2936.

Hanzelka v. State, TexApp–Austin, 682 SW2d 385.—Crim Law 641.13(1), 641.13(5).

Hanzi v. Bailey, TexApp–San Antonio, 48 SW3d 259, reh overr, and review den.—App & E 893(1), 946, 949; Health 803, 804, 809.

Hapag-Lloyd Aktiengesellschaft; Uncle Ben's Intern. Div. of Uncle Ben's,Inc. v., CA5 (Tex), 855 F2d 215.—Rem of C 19(5); Ship 106(1), 140(1), 142.

Hapgood; West v., Tex, 174 SW2d 963, 141 Tex 576.—Evid 54, 372(10), 383(7); Mines 49, 55(1); Princ & A 119(1), 123(1); Trusts 176, 181(2).

Hapgood; West v., TexCivApp–Fort Worth, 169 SW2d 204, aff 174 SW2d 963, 141 Tex 576.—Adv Poss 1; Mines 49.

Happ v. Happ, TexCivApp–San Antonio, 160 SW2d 227, writ refused wom.—App & E 2, 15, 927(7), 999(1); Divorce 253(2); Evid 211, 265(10); Judgm 199(1), 199(3.5), 199(3.9); Witn 379(5), 397.

Happ; Happ v., TexCivApp–San Antonio, 160 SW2d 227, writ refused wom.—App & E 2, 15, 927(7), 999(1);

Divorce 253(2); Evid 211, 265(10); Judgm 199(1), 199(3.5), 199(3.9); Witn 379(5), 397.

Happ v. State, TexApp–Fort Worth, 958 SW2d 474.—Crim Law 1081(2).

Happner v. State, TexCrimApp, 325 SW2d 390, 168 TexCrim 260.—Crim Law 1036.8; Incest 13, 14.

Happold; C.I.R. v., CCA5 (Tex), 141 F2d 199.—Int Rev 3495.

Happy Cattle Feeders, Inc. v. First Nat. Bank in Canyon, TexCivApp–Amarillo, 618 SW2d 424, ref nre.—Banks 138, 153, 154(8); Judgm 178, 185(2).

Happy Harbor Methodist Home, Inc. v. Cowins, TexApp–Houston (1 Dist), 903 SW2d 884.—App & E 756, 760(1), 761, 763, 1079; Damag 221(7).

Happy Independent School Dist.; Northwest Texas Conference of United Methodist Church v., TexApp–Amarillo, 839 SW2d 140.—Tax 2367, 2369(2), 2381, 2394, 2667, 2692, 2696, 2698, 2703, 2859, 2932.

Happy Indus. Corp. v. American Specialties, Inc., TexApp–Corpus Christi, 983 SW2d 844, review dism woj.—App & E 846(5), 852, 893(1), 1010.1(8.1); Appear 9(2); Const Law 3964, 3965(3), 3965(4); Courts 12(2.1), 12(2.5), 12(2.10), 12(2.20), 12(2.30), 39; Princ & A 1, 3(2), 19, 24.

Happy Mfg. Co., Inc. v. Southern Air & Hydraulics, Inc., NDTex, 572 FSupp 891.—Fed Cts 79, 95, 97.

Happy Motor Co.; Firestone Tire & Rubber Co. v., TexCivApp–Amarillo, 152 SW2d 778.—Lim of Act 148(2), 149(1).

Happy Wheat Growers, Inc.; Tex-Co Grain Co. v., TexCivApp–Amarillo, 542 SW2d 934.—App & E 1010.1(11); Joint Adv 1.1, 1.2(1), 1.12, 1.13, 4(1), 5(3), 7, 8; Partners 20, 52.

Happy Wheat Growers, Inc.; Utica Nat. Bank & Trust Co. v., CA5 (Tex), 558 F2d 279.—Wareh 25(5), 25(8), 34(6), 34(8), 34(9).

Haq v. America's Favorite Chicken Co., TexApp–Corpus Christi, 921 SW2d 728, reh overr, and writ dism woj.—App & E 846(5); Inj 135, 138.1, 138.3, 138.6, 138.9, 138.37, 140.

Haragan; Humphreys v., TexCivApp–Amarillo, 476 SW2d 880.—App & E 927(7), 989; Neglig 1696; Trial 139.1(12), 142, 178.

Haragan; Roberts v., NDTex, 346 FSupp2d 853.—Colleges 9.30(2); Const Law 855, 859, 1517, 1520, 1730, 1735, 1750, 2007, 2010; Fed Cts 12.1.

Haralson v. E.F. Hutton Group, Inc., CA5 (Tex), 919 F2d 1014, reh den.—Brok 31; Consp 8, 9, 19; Contracts 249, 305(1), 312(1); Fed Civ Proc 2488; Fraud 11(1), 18, 20, 23, 35; Fraud Conv 43(1); Impl & C C 3; Nova 10; Paymt 1(2), 59; Sec Tran 231; Sec Reg 27.36, 27.39, 27.41, 27.42, 35.24, 60.41, 60.44, 60.46, 60.48(1), 278, 297, 302; Torts 212, 222, 223, 242; Usury 18, 102(5).

Haralson v. Rumsfeld, NDTex, 391 FSupp2d 442.—Armed S 27(5); Civil R 1243, 1251.

Haralson; Wheeler v., TexComApp, 99 SW2d 885, 128 Tex 429.—App & E 854(1); Trusts 1, 17(5), 35(4).

Harang v. Aetna Life Ins. Co., TexCivApp–Houston, 400 SW2d 810, ref nre.—App & E 236(1), 768, 882(18); Consp 13; Evid 253(1); Insurance 3361, 3504; Judgm 185(2), 185.1(3), 185.1(7), 185.3(21), 186, 297, 316, 340, 381; Lim of Act 55(1), 55(6); Torts 245.

Harang v. State ex rel. City of West Columbia, TexCivApp–Hous (14 Dist), 466 SW2d 8.—Mun Corp 7, 12(1), 12(7), 12(12), 18.

Harben; Doyle v., TexApp–San Antonio, 660 SW2d 586.—Const Law 4410; Sales 283.

Harben; Doyle Motor Co. v., TexApp–San Antonio, 660 SW2d 586. See Doyle v. Harben.

Harbenito Realty Corp. v. Avila, TexCivApp–Corpus Christi, 406 SW2d 523.—Plead 45, 111.18; Venue 22(9).

Harber; Anderson Machinery Co. v., TexCivApp–Austin, 584 SW2d 480.—App & E 238(2), 241, 768; Sales 178(4), 347(3), 359(1).

Harber v. Switzer, TexCivApp–Amarillo, 403 SW2d 843.—App & E 846(5), 931(1); Plead 111.42(2), 111.42(8).

Harberger; Houston v., TexCivApp–Fort Worth, 377 SW2d 673, ref nre.—Estates 1; Wills 6, 441, 470(1), 472, 523, 590, 614(2), 617, 634(3), 634(7), 634(9), 635, 637.

Harberson v. Arledge, TexCivApp–Fort Worth, 438 SW2d 591, ref nre.—Inj 88; Judgm 199(1); Schools 55, 103(1), 110, 111; Tax 2655, 2875.

Harberson v. Lawhon, TexCivApp–Fort Worth, 518 SW2d 840.—App & E 918(3), 959(3), 1041(2); Elections 198, 227(1); Schools 97(4).

Harbert v. Mathis, TexCivApp–Eastland, 230 SW2d 380.—Autos 172(11), 209, 226(1), 244(58); Neglig 422.

Harbert v. Owen, TexApp–Beaumont, 791 SW2d 627.—Costs 194.36.

Harbert v. State, TexCrimApp, 124 SW2d 1005, 136 TexCrim 301.—Crim Law 814(4), 1172.8; Sent & Pun 1250, 1260, 1379(2), 1382, 1400, 1417.

Harbert Energy Corp.; Johnson Southwest, Inc. v., NDTex, 205 BR 823. See Johnson Southwest, Inc., In re.

Harbin v. City of Beaumont, TexCivApp–Beaumont, 146 SW2d 297, writ dism, correct.—Labor & Emp 2784, 2832, 2845, 2875, 2877; Plead 9; Trial 357, 359(1).

Harbin v. Seale, Tex, 461 SW2d 591.—Autos 181(1), 242(1), 242(7), 244(20); Judgm 199(3.10).

Harbin v. Seale, TexCivApp–Dallas, 454 SW2d 271, rev 461 SW2d 591.—App & E 934(1), 1073(1); Autos 181(1); Judgm 199(3.10); Trial 350.6(3).

Harbin v. State, TexCrimApp, 399 SW2d 564.—Crim Law 641.9.

Harbin; Terrill v., TexCivApp–Eastland, 376 SW2d 945, writ dism.—Dead Bodies 1, 3, 9; Venue 8.5(5).

Harbin Citrus Groves; Young v., TexCivApp–San Antonio, 130 SW2d 896, writ refused.—App & E 742(2); Covenants 29; Lim of Act 143(6); Mtg 154(2), 200(3); Tax 2769; Tresp to T T 6.2, 32; Ven & Pur 253, 261(3), 296, 299(1), 299(2), 299(3).

Harbison; American Home Assur. Co. v., TexCivApp–Hous (14 Dist), 576 SW2d 485, writ dism woj.—App & E 931(1), 989; Insurance 2545(1), 2545(4).

Harbison; D. H. Overmyer Co. v., TexCivApp–El Paso, 453 SW2d 368.—Contracts 232(4); Mech Liens 228.

Harbison v. Jeffreys, TexCivApp–El Paso, 353 SW2d 65.—Evid 474(15); Judgm 178, 181(2), 181(11), 185(1), 185(2), 185.2(4); Land & Ten 164(1), 164(2), 164(6), 164(7), 167(7), 170(1).

Harbison; Klinke v., TexCivApp–Amarillo, 248 SW2d 545, aff Petit v. Klinke, 254 SW2d 769, 152 Tex 142.—App & E 262(1), 291, 758.1, 927(7), 997(3); Trial 139.1(17), 243; Wareh 34(9).

Harbison v. McMurray, Tex, 158 SW2d 284, 138 Tex 192.—Const Law 2356; Contempt 40, 66(1); Hab Corp 202, 813, 821.1; Statut 223.2(24).

Harbison v. McMurray, TexCivApp–El Paso, 163 SW2d 680.—Contempt 63(1); Hab Corp 443.1, 528.1; Pretrial Proc 73.

Harbison v. McMurray, TexCivApp–El Paso, 132 SW2d 916, rev 158 SW2d 284, 138 Tex 192.—Hab Corp 813.

Harbison; Service Lloyds Ins. Co. v., Tex, 826 SW2d 930.—Pretrial Proc 304, 305.

Harbison v. Service Lloyds Ins. Co., TexApp–Corpus Christi, 808 SW2d 690, writ gr, rev 826 SW2d 930.—App & E 1051.1(1), 1058(1); Pretrial Proc 40, 42, 45; Work Comp 1703, 1937.

Harbison v. U.S. By and Through I.R.S., CA5 (Tex), 784 F2d 1238. See USLIFE Title Ins. Co. of Dallas on Behalf of Mathews v. Harbison.

Harbison; USLIFE Title Ins. Co. of Dallas on Behalf of Mathews v., CA5 (Tex), 784 F2d 1238.—Int Rev 3520, 5204, 5233, 5246; U S 147(10), 147(21).

Harbison-Fischer Mfg. Co.; Missouri Pacific R. Co. v., CA5 (Tex), 26 F3d 531, am on denial of reh.—Contracts 175(1), 187(1); Environ Law 712; Estop 52(1), 52(4),

52(7), 65, 66; Fed Civ Proc 2533.1, 2544, 2545; Fed Cts 762, 776, 802.

Harbison–Fischer Mfg. Co.; Union Pacific R. Co. v., CA5 (Tex), 26 F3d 531. See Missouri Pacific R. Co. v. Harbison-Fischer Mfg. Co.

Harbison-Fischer Mfg. Co., Inc. v. Mohawk Data Sciences Corp., TexApp–Fort Worth, 823 SW2d 679, writ gr, vac pursuant to settlement 840 SW2d 383.—Alt Disp Res 259, 260, 392, 400; App & E 347(1), 472; Appear 9(1), 22; Const Law 4476; Costs 194.25; Evid 347; Judgm 815, 823; Plead 106(2).

Harbolt v. Department of State, CA5 (Tex), 616 F2d 772, cert den 101 SCt 154, 449 US 856, 66 LEd2d 71.—Records 58.

Harbolt; U.S. v., CA5 (Tex), 491 F2d 78, cert den 95 SCt 86, 419 US 848, 42 LEd2d 78.—Crim Law 641.10(2), 1169.11; Sent & Pun 1480.

Harbolt; U.S. v., CA5 (Tex), 455 F2d 970.—Crim Law 1132; Sent & Pun 20, 56, 276.

Harbord v. Harbord, TexCivApp–Eastland, 397 SW2d 959.—Divorce 135.

Harbord; Harbord v., TexCivApp–Eastland, 397 SW2d 959.—Divorce 135.

Harbor Financial Group, Inc., In re, BkrtcyNDTex, 303 BR 124.—Bankr 2164.1, 2921, 2933; Judgm 567.

Harbor Ins. Co.; Nortex Oil & Gas Corp. v., TexCivApp–Dallas, 456 SW2d 489.—Insurance 1808, 2277, 2396.

Harbor Ins. Co. v. Trammell Crow Co., Inc., CA5 (Tex), 854 F2d 94, cert den 109 SCt 1315, 489 US 1054, 103 LEd2d 584.—Fed Civ Proc 2501, 2543, 2544; Fed Cts 600; Insurance 3145, 3197.

Harbor Ins. Co. v. Urban Const. Co., CA5 (Tex), 990 F2d 195, reh den.—Fed Civ Proc 2481; Fed Cts 611; Insurance 1867, 1887(1), 1892, 3336, 3349; Lim of Act 95(1), 95(9); Ref of Inst 19(1), 32.

Harbor Perfusion, Inc. v. Floyd, TexApp–Corpus Christi, 45 SW3d 713.—App & E 842(2), 893(1), 946, 954(1), 954(2); Inj 12, 26(3), 126, 138.1, 138.6, 138.39, 189.

Harborth; Biliski v., CA5 (Tex), 55 F3d 160, reh den.—Civil R 1090; Const Law 3823; Fed Civ Proc 1772, 1788.10; Fed Cts 13.10, 818.

Harborth; Palfrey v., TexCivApp–San Antonio, 158 SW2d 326, writ refused.—Ex & Ad 7; Lim of Act 83(2), 132, 148(2), 151(1).

Harbour; Beeler v., TexCivApp–Fort Worth, 116 SW2d 927, writ refused.—App & E 909(5); Estates 10(1); Lim of Act 146(3), 148(2), 164, 195(6); Trial 105(1); Ven & Pur 261(1), 279, 281(2).

Harbour; Cogburn v., Tex, 657 SW2d 432.—App & E 500(1).

Harbour v. Cogburn, TexApp–Eastland, 646 SW2d 330, rev 657 SW2d 432.—App & E 242(1), 930(3); Partners 329; Trial 252(2), 350.3(1).

Harbour; Green v., CA5 (Tex), 444 F2d 223.—Courts 104; Fed Cts 743.

Harbour v. Harbour, TexCivApp–Hous (14 Dist), 590 SW2d 828, ref nre, cert den 101 SCt 106, 449 US 834, 66 LEd2d 40.—Bankr 3348, 3348.10, 3420(2), 3422(2).

Harbour; Harbour v., TexCivApp–Hous (14 Dist), 590 SW2d 828, ref nre, cert den 101 SCt 106, 449 US 834, 66 LEd2d 40.—Bankr 3348, 3348.10, 3420(2), 3422(2).

Harbour; Toler v., TexCivApp–Amarillo, 589 SW2d 529, ref nre.—App & E 179(1); Judgm 186, 948(1); Wills 608(1), 608(3.1).

Harbour Heights Development, Inc. v. Seaback, TexCivApp–Hous (14 Dist), 596 SW2d 296.—App & E 863; Judgm 185.3(16), 340.

Harbour Title Co.; Harris v., TexApp–Houston (14 Dist), 49 SW3d 371, review gr, and review withdrawn, and review gr, rev Lehmann v. Har-Con Corp, 39 SW3d 191, on remand 2001 WL 1249730, on remand 76 SW3d 555.—App & E 4, 78(1), 338(1), 780(1), 1178(1); Judgm 187, 190, 303.

Harbrook Tool & Mfg. Co., In re, TexApp–El Paso, 181 SW3d 551, reh overr, and mandamus den.—Mand 1, 3(2.1), 12, 143(2).

Harbuck v. Ramos, TexCivApp–Waco, 371 SW2d 912.—Damag 131(6), 208(2); Neglig 1691.

Harburger; Texas Lloyds Ins. Co. v., TexCivApp–San Antonio, 252 SW2d 957, ref nre.—Evid 313; Insurance 3066.

Harck, Ex parte, TexCrimApp, 274 SW2d 74, 160 TexCrim 602.—Extrad 34; Hab Corp 704, 729.

Harco Energy, Inc., In re, BkrtcyNDTex, 270 BR 658.—Atty & C 70, 72, 101(1), 103; Bankr 2158, 2164.1; Compromise 2, 5(1), 5(3), 8(3), 11, 13, 15(1); Contracts 97(2), 221(1); Estop 68(2), 90(1); Fed Civ Proc 2492; Princ & A 163(1), 166(1); Stip 1.

Harco Energy, Inc. v. Re-Entry People, Inc., TexApp–Amarillo, 23 SW3d 389, reh overr.—App & E 846(5), 931(1), 989, 1010.2; Contracts 15, 16, 47; Corp 1.4(4), 1.7(2), 361, 519(3), 547(4); Fraud 3, 12, 13(3), 20, 25, 59(1); Princ & A 138, 142.

Harco Nat. Ins. Co.; Thompson v., TexApp–Dallas, 120 SW3d 511, reh overr, and review den, and reh of petition for review den, cert den 125 SCt 100, 543 US 876, 160 LEd2d 127.—App & E 856(1); Garn 145, 146, 151, 178; Insurance 2888; Judgm 105.1, 106(9), 183.

Harco Nat. Ins. Co.; Thompson v., TexApp–Dallas, 997 SW2d 607, review den, concurring opinion 1998 WL 652660.—App & E 174, 1010.2, 1175(1); Estop 52(8), 68(2); Garn 1, 2, 7, 105, 194, 248; Judgm 153(3), 159; Motions 15.

Harco Nat. Ins. Co. v. Villanueva, TexApp–Dallas, 765 SW2d 809, writ den.—App & E 989, 994(2), 1001(3), 1002; Insurance 3381(5).

Har-Con Corp. v. Aetna Cas. & Sur. Co., TexApp–Houston (1 Dist), 757 SW2d 153.—Insurance 1929(7); Judgm 181(23), 185.1(3).

Har-Con Corp.; Lehmann v., Tex, 39 SW3d 191, on remand Harris v. Harbour Title Co, 2001 WL 1249730, on remand 76 SW3d 555.—App & E 66, 76(1), 78(1), 79(1), 80(6), 775; Judgm 217.

Har-Con Corp.; Lehmann v., TexApp–Houston (14 Dist), 76 SW3d 555.—App & E 863; Child C 3; Compromise 16(1), 53.1; Contracts 147(2); Indem 25, 27, 28, 30(1), 30(4); Judgm 181(19); Parent & C 1, 7.5, 8; Release 38.

Har-Con Corp.; Lehmann v., TexApp–Houston (14 Dist), 988 SW2d 415.—App & E 78(1), 338(1), 780(1), 1073(1); Judgm 303.

Har-Con Engineering Co., Inc.; Holloway v., TexCivApp–Hous (14 Dist), 563 SW2d 695, ref nre.—App & E 866(3), 1058(1); Prod Liab 86.

Har-Con Engineering, Inc. v. Guthrie, TexCivApp–Fort Worth, 408 SW2d 159, ref nre.—Contracts 175(3); Damag 191.

Harcrow; Red Oak Fishing Club v., TexCivApp–Waco, 460 SW2d 151.—Clubs 12; Land & Ten 37, 72, 86(1).

Harcrow v. Reed, TexCivApp–Waco, 425 SW2d 59, ref nre.—App & E 750(1), 846(5); Fraud Conv 172(1), 179(1).

Harcrow v. W. T. Rawleigh Co., TexCivApp–Eastland, 145 SW2d 925.—Antitrust 980; App & E 1043(6); Commerce 60(1); Contracts 176(1); Paymt 45; Pretrial Proc 79.

Hard; D. C. Hall Transport, Inc. v., Tex, 358 SW2d 117, 163 Tex 504.—App & E 1082(1), 1083(1).

Hard; D. C. Hall Transport, Inc. v., TexCivApp–Fort Worth, 355 SW2d 257, ref nre 358 SW2d 117, 163 Tex 504.—App & E 1213; Brok 86(1), 86(8); Interest 39(3).

Hard; Hall v., Tex, 335 SW2d 584, 160 Tex 565.—App & E 172(1), 931(3), 1178(1); Brok 1, 42; Judgm 199(3.14); Sec Reg 307, 309; Trial 392(1).

Hard v. Hall, TexCivApp–Fort Worth, 318 SW2d 108, rev 335 SW2d 584, 160 Tex 565.—App & E 1050.1(5), 1056.1(6); Brok 43(0.5), 56(3), 57(2), 86(1); Judgm 199(3.14).

HARDACRE

59 Tex D 2d—488

See Guidelines for Arrangement at the beginning of this Volume

Hardacre, In re, BkrtcyNDTex, 338 BR 718.—Bankr 3705; Statut 195, 205.

Hardage, In re, BkrtcyNDTex, 99 BR 738.—Sec Tran 41, 81.

Hardage, In re, BkrtcyNDTex, 69 BR 681, subsequently rev Hardage v. Herring Nat Bank, 837 F2d 1319.—Bankr 2492, 2531, 2794.1, 2796, 2854(5).

Hardage v. Herring Nat. Bank, CA5 (Tex), 837 F2d 1319.—Bankr 2794.1, 2796, 2797.1, 3079, 3790.

Hardage v. Rouly, TexCivApp–Beaumont, 349 SW2d 616, ref nre.—App & E 930(1), 989, 1041(1); Autos 244(49), 244(51), 244(58); Neglig 547, 1602, 1683.

Hardage v. State, TexCrimApp, 552 SW2d 837.—Burg 42(1), 42(3); Larc 64(2).

Hardaway v. State, TexCrimApp, 319 SW2d 336, 167 TexCrim 160.—Crim Law 507(1), 556; Infants 20.

Hardaway v. State, TexApp–San Antonio, 699 SW2d 359, petition for discretionary review refused.—Crim Law 810, 863(2), 1167(3), 1172.4.

Hardaway v. State, TexApp–Amarillo, 939 SW2d 224.—Crim Law 1177; Sent & Pun 238.

Hardaway; U.S. v., CA5 (Tex), 731 F2d 1138, cert den 105 SCt 206, 469 US 865, 83 LEd2d 137.—Int Rev 5264, 5295.

Hardberger v. O'Dell, TexCivApp–Austin, 544 SW2d 522.—App & E 927(7), 989; Autos 242(2), 245(15); Evid 571(10).

Hardberger; State ex rel. Angelini v., Tex, 932 SW2d 489.—Const Law 2391; Judges 3, 8, 10, 11(4); Quo W 1, 3, 10.

Hardbody's of Arlington v. City of Arlington, CA5 (Tex), 65 F3d 1248. See Hang On, Inc. v. City of Arlington.

Hardcastle; Houtex Managing General Agency, Inc. v., TexApp–Houston (1 Dist), 735 SW2d 520, ref nre.—App & E 5, 937(1), 1096(1); Judgm 17(9); Proc 73, 149.

Hardcastle v. Sibley, TexCivApp–El Paso, 107 SW2d 432, writ refused.—App & E 268(2); Conversion 1, 2, 11, 19(2); Ven & Pur 18; Wills 734(2.1).

Hardcastle; T. E. Moor & Co. v., TexCivApp–Beaumont, 421 SW2d 126, ref nre.—Assign 19; Contracts 116(1), 171(1); Labor & Emp 38.

Hardcastle; Von Koenneritz v., TexCivApp–Austin, 231 SW2d 498, ref nre.—Wills 176, 800.

Hardee, Matter of, CA5 (Tex), 137 F3d 337.—Bankr 2956, 3352, 3358, 3782.

Hardee; City of San Antonio v., TexApp–San Antonio, 70 SW3d 207.—Admin Law 124; App & E 768, 863, 916(1); Estop 52(8), 62.4; Mun Corp 29(2), 33(1), 33(4), 33(9); Plead 104(1), 111.39(0.5); Quo W 3, 8; Statut 212.1.

Hardee; Etherington v., CA5 (Tex), 290 F2d 28.—Pat 290(1).

Hardee; Etherington v., SDTex, 182 FSupp 905, aff 290 F2d 28.—Pat 290(1).

Hardee v. I.R.S., CA5 (Tex), 137 F3d 337. See Hardee, Matter of.

Hardee; Standard Life & Acc. Ins. Co. v., TexCivApp–Texarkana, 330 SW2d 544, 78 ALR2d 1040, ref nre.—Insurance 1808, 1822, 1831, 2588(2).

Hardee v. Vincent, TexComApp, 147 SW2d 1072, 136 Tex 99.—Hus & W 249(1), 257, 262.1(5), 262.2, 264(4).

Hardee v. Vincent, TexCivApp–Amarillo, 127 SW2d 333, rev 147 SW2d 1072, 136 Tex 99.—App & E 1010.1(12); Execution 172(4); Hus & W 265.5.

Hardee's Food Systems, Inc.; Neal v., CA5 (Tex), 918 F2d 34, reh den.—Alt Disp Res 112, 113, 139, 145, 213(5), 368; Contracts 164; Fed Cts 403.

Hardee's Restaurants, In re, BkrtcyNDTex, 140 BR 874. See Jim-O-Lette, Inc., In re.

Hardegree v. American & Foreign Ins. Co., TexCivApp–Fort Worth, 449 SW2d 554.—Damag 221(7), 221(8); Work Comp 877, 1919, 1941, 1974.

Hardegree v. State, TexCrimApp, 104 SW2d 24, 132 TexCrim 212.—Autos 355(13).

Hardeman; Hall Dadeland Towers Associates v., NDTex, 736 FSupp 1422.—Brok 94, 104; Fraud 4, 13(1), 16; Partners 375; Sec Reg 60.18, 60.27(1), 60.45(1), 265, 278.

Hardeman v. Hall Securities Corp., NDTex, 736 FSupp 1422. See Hall Dadeland Towers Associates v. Hardeman.

Hardeman v. Judge, TexApp–Fort Worth, 931 SW2d 716, reh overr, and writ den.—App & E 169, 173(1); Home 167; Mental H 236, 261, 262, 264.

Hardeman v. Mitchell, TexCivApp–Tyler, 444 SW2d 651.—Adv Poss 36, 37, 43(8), 68, 86; App & E 758.1, 758.3(3); Deeds 54; Lim of Act 16, 19(1), 19(2), 39(12); Ten in C 15(10).

Hardeman v. Parish, TexApp–El Paso, 730 SW2d 813, ref nre.—Bills & N 132, 452(1); Contracts 164; Estop 52.15, 95.

Hardeman v. State, TexCrimApp, 1 SW3d 689.—Crim Law 1023(10), 1030(1), 1042, 1042.5, 1063(1); Sent & Pun 331, 2033.

Hardeman v. State, TexCrimApp, 552 SW2d 433.—Crim Law 322, 369.2(6), 627.10(5), 627.10(7.1), 633(1), 720(1), 728(2), 868, 935(1), 951(6); Rec S Goods 2, 4, 8(2), 8(3), 8(4); Witn 379(2).

Hardeman v. State, TexApp–Austin, 868 SW2d 404, petition for discretionary review gr, petition for discretionary review dism 891 SW2d 960.—Crim Law 396(1); Witn 345(1), 345(2).

Hardeman v. State, TexApp–Houston (14 Dist), 981 SW2d 773, petition for discretionary review dism, and petition for discretionary review refused, and petition for discretionary review gr, aff 1 SW3d 689.—Crim Law 641.13(7), 1023(3), 1023.5, 1181(1); Sent & Pun 2033.

Hardeman v. Timmins, TexApp–El Paso, 111 SW2d 746, dism.—App & E 731(2).

Hardeman; U.S. v., CA5 (Tex), 933 F2d 278.—Sent & Pun 765, 780, 995.

Harden v. Colonial Country Club, TexApp–Fort Worth, 634 SW2d 56, ref nre.—Assoc 1; Clubs 1, 4, 7; Costs 194.32; Parties 35.33.

Harden v. Federal Farm Mortg. Corp., TexCivApp–Galveston, 223 SW2d 39.—App & E 374(2), 554(2), 931(1); Judgm 259.

Harden v. State, TexCrimApp, 417 SW2d 170.—Arson 5, 37(1); Crim Law 371(7), 511.1(6.1), 564(1), 564(2), 564(3), 663, 808.5.

Harden v. State, TexApp–Dallas, 629 SW2d 119.—Crim Law 371(12), 721(3), 723(1).

Harden; Times-Mirror Co. v., TexApp–Eastland, 628 SW2d 859, ref nre.—App & E 989; Const Law 2164; Libel 48(2), 51(5).

Harden v. U.S. Dept. of Health and Human Services, CA5 (Tex), 979 F2d 1082.—Social S 140.76, 147.

Harden; Universal Life Ins. Co. v., TexCivApp–Waco, 117 SW2d 469, writ dism.—Insurance 3343, 3375, 3571; Plead 216(2); Trial 36.

Harder; City of Gainesville v., Tex, 162 SW2d 93, 139 Tex 155.—Lim of Act 28(1), 119(1), 119(3).

Harder; City of Gainesville v., TexCivApp–Fort Worth, 147 SW2d 959, aff 162 SW2d 93, 139 Tex 155.—App & E 518(1); Lim of Act 119(4), 124, 167(1), 172; Mun Corp 434(5), 565, 586.

Harder; Hartman v., TexCivApp–Amarillo, 322 SW2d 555.—App & E 1052(5); Const Law 4002; Crim Law 393(1); Evid 150; Searches 75.

Harder v. Sanders, Tex, 284 SW2d 144, 155 Tex 149.—App & E 1178(6), 1212(3); Judgm 185.3(1); Tresp to T T 48.

Harder; Sanders v., Tex, 227 SW2d 206, 148 Tex 593.—App & E 1012.1(2), 1175(5), 1177(6); Evid 596(1); Judgm 199(3.8), 868(1); New Tr 16, 70, 72(6); Pretrial Proc 471, 472, 477.1, 482.1, 483; Proc 149; Tresp to T T 44; Trial 352.10.

For Later Case History Information, see KeyCite on WESTLAW

Harder v. Sanders, TexCivApp–Texarkana, 275 SW2d 160, rev 284 SW2d 144, 155 Tex 149.—Action 46, 50(1), 56; App & E 964; Courts 99(1).

Harder; Sanders v., TexCivApp–Texarkana, 223 SW2d 61, rev 227 SW2d 206, 148 Tex 593.—Judgm 162(4); Proc 149.

Hardesty v. Commissioner of Internal Revenue, CCA5 (Tex), 127 F2d 843.—Int Rev 3319, 3360, 4732, 4744; Mines 73.

Hardesty v. Douglas, TexApp–Waco, 894 SW2d 548.—Pretrial Proc 39, 40, 97.

Hardesty v. State, TexCrimApp, 667 SW2d 130.—Crim Law 338(1), 412.1(1), 412.2(3), 698(1), 899, 1134(2); Sent & Pun 2004.

Hardesty v. State, TexCrimApp, 659 SW2d 823.—Infants 68.7(1), 69(7).

Hardesty v. State, TexCrimApp, 656 SW2d 73.—Crim Law 306, 510, 511.1(9), 511.2; Larc 64(6), 64(7).

Hardesty v. State, TexApp–Dallas, 738 SW2d 9, petition for discretionary review refused.—Crim Law 577.10(1), 577.10(4), 577.10(6), 577.15(1), 577.15(3), 577.16(4), 577.16(8), 577.16(9), 1035(1).

Hardgrave v. Texas & P. Ry. Co., TexCivApp–Dallas, 401 SW2d 693, writ gr, rev Texas & Pac Ry Co v. McCleery, 418 SW2d 494.—App & E 934(1), 1002, 1014, 1177(5); Judgm 199(3.10); R R 335.5, 348(2).

Hardi; Stafford v., TexCivApp–Dallas, 464 SW2d 958, ref nre.—Autos 244(12), 244(35).

Hardie, In re, SDTex, 204 BR 944.—Bankr 3352, 3779, 3782, 3786.

Hardie v. State, TexCrimApp, 807 SW2d 319.—Crim Law 407(1), 438.1, 1169.1(10), 1169.12.

Hardie v. State, TexCrimApp, 588 SW2d 936.—Autos 344, 351.1, 352, 355(13), 356, 358; Crim Law 814(1); Ind & Inf 111(1), 119; Sent & Pun 1500.

Hardie v. State, TexCrimApp, 265 SW2d 87.—Crim Law 1090.1(1).

Hardie v. State, TexCrimApp, 264 SW2d 436, 159 Tex-Crim 395.—Crim Law 1094(2.1); Ind & Inf 130.

Hardie v. State, TexCrimApp, 144 SW2d 571, 140 Tex-Crim 368.—Consp 40.3; Crim Law 59(5), 80, 814(17); False Imp 43; Infants 152, 193; Kidnap 18, 31, 40.

Hardie v. State, TexApp–Dallas, 787 SW2d 89, petition for discretionary review gr, aff 807 SW2d 319.—Crim Law 412.2(1), 1169.12.

Hardie v. State, TexApp–Waco, 79 SW3d 625, reh overr, and petition for discretionary review refused.—Controlled Subs 26, 27; Crim Law 507(1), 511.2, 780(1), 780(2), 795(2.1), 795(2.10), 795(2.70), 1134(2), 1172.1(1), 1173.2(6); Ind & Inf 159(1), 159(2), 161(1), 162, 191(0.5).

Hardie; Stewart v., TexApp–Fort Worth, 978 SW2d 203, review den.—App & E 845(2), 893(1), 895(1); Bankr 2154.1, 2323, 2553, 2556, 3022; Estop 68(2); Ex & Ad 15, 420, 423; Lim of Act 121(2); Trial 368.

Hardie v. U.S., CA5 (Tex), 208 F2d 694.—Prost 28.

Hardie v. U.S., I.R.S., SDTex, 204 BR 944. See Hardie, In re.

Hardigree v. Sweetwater Cotton Oil Co., TexCivApp–Eastland, 84 SW2d 756.—App & E 912; Plead 111.17, 111.42(4).

Hardiman v. State, TexCrimApp, 307 SW2d 584.—Int Liq 223(1), 236(3).

Hardiman v. State, TexCrimApp, 279 SW2d 343, 161 TexCrim 640.—Int Liq 236(7).

Hardin, Ex parte, Tex, 344 SW2d 152, 161 Tex 567.—Const Law 4494; Contempt 53, 64.

Hardin, In re, BkrtcyNDTex, 16 BR 810.—Bankr 3705.

Hardin; Best Steel Bldgs., Inc. v., TexCivApp–Tyler, 553 SW2d 122, ref nre.—App & E 242(1), 302(4), 758.1, 930(3), 1004(3), 1170.7; Autos 193(8.1), 193(10), 244(26); Damag 127, 228; Death 77, 83, 86(1), 99(4); Evid 576, 577, 580; Labor & Emp 3046(2), 3061(1).

Hardin; Blankenship v., TexCivApp–Beaumont, 104 SW2d 612, writ dism.—Mines 55(8).

Hardin v. Briscoe, CA5 (Tex), 504 F2d 885.—Fed Civ Proc 1741.

Hardin; Bullock v., TexCivApp–Austin, 578 SW2d 550, ref nre.—App & E 219(2), 1074(3); States 60.1(2), 191.10.

Hardin; Central American Life Ins. Co. v., TexCivApp–Amarillo, 367 SW2d 935, writ gr, aff 374 SW2d 881.—Tax 2128, 2288, 2558.

Hardin v. Central Am. Life Ins. Co., Tex, 374 SW2d 881.—Tax 2128, 2290, 2558.

Hardin; Central Fibre Products Co. v., CCA5 (Tex), 82 F2d 692, cert den 57 SCt 10, 299 US 547, 81 LEd 402, reh den 57 SCt 113, 299 US 620, 81 LEd 457.—Bankr 2281, 2295.1, 3785.1.

Hardin v. Cotton, TexCivApp–Beaumont, 300 SW2d 719, ref nre.—Adv Poss 28; App & E 1036(3); Evid 318(1), 383(7); Ten in C 15(11); Trial 140(2); Trusts 44(3), 373.

Hardin; Durbin v., TexApp–Dallas, 775 SW2d 798, writ den.—Autos 232, 244(1); Evid 314(4).

Hardin; Dyer v., TexCivApp–Amarillo, 323 SW2d 119, ref nre.—App & E 218.2(7), 237(5), 878(6), 930(1), 972, 989, 1032(1), 1060.1(5), 1060.1(7), 1060.1(9); Evid 434(3); Lim of Act 197(2); Ten in C 28(3); Trial 111, 121(1), 125(1), 129; Trusts 109, 374.

Hardin v. Estelle, CA5 (Tex), 484 F2d 944.—Hab Corp 495.

Hardin v. Estelle, WDTex, 365 FSupp 39, aff 484 F2d 944.—Const Law 2793, 4616; Crim Law 637; Hab Corp 338, 495, 705.1; Witn 2(1).

Hardin v. Eubank, TexCivApp–Fort Worth, 245 SW2d 554.—Judgm 19; Partit 12(1), 55(2), 63(3).

Hardin; Federal Union Ins. Co. v., TexCivApp–Amarillo, 115 SW2d 1144.—Estop 111, 112; Insurance 3191(7), 3196, 3197, 3571; Trial 105(2).

Hardin; Friend In Need Ben. Ass'n v., TexCivApp–Dallas, 88 SW2d 1103.—Insurance 2035, 2079, 2082.

Hardin; General Acc. Fire & Life Assur. Corp. v., CA5 (Tex), 290 F2d 862.—Fed Cts 381, 848; Work Comp 1297, 1969.

Hardin v. Hardin, Tex, 597 SW2d 347.—App & E 948, 959(3); Divorce 168, 255; Plead 236(2), 420(1).

Hardin; Hardin v., Tex, 597 SW2d 347.—App & E 948, 959(3); Divorce 168, 255; Plead 236(2), 420(1).

Hardin v. Hardin, TexApp–San Antonio, 681 SW2d 241.—Const Law 3994; Divorce 252.3(1), 252.3(4), 286(5).

Hardin; Hardin v., TexApp–San Antonio, 681 SW2d 241.—Const Law 3994; Divorce 252.3(1), 252.3(4), 286(5).

Hardin v. Hardin, TexApp–Tyler, 932 SW2d 566.—Const Law 3993; Trial 6(1).

Hardin; Hardin v., TexApp–Tyler, 932 SW2d 566.—Const Law 3993; Trial 6(1).

Hardin v. Hardin, TexApp–Houston (14 Dist), 161 SW3d 14, reh overr, vac 2005 WL 310076.—App & E 230, 231(7), 934(1), 946, 1079; Child C 921(1); Child S 88, 192, 233, 339(2), 339(3), 341, 539, 540, 543, 549, 556(1), 556(2), 556(3), 557(4), 603, 610, 612; Const Law 1106; Costs 207.

Hardin; Hardin v., TexApp–Houston (14 Dist), 161 SW3d 14, reh overr, vac 2005 WL 310076.—App & E 230, 231(7), 934(1), 946, 1079; Child C 921(1); Child S 88, 192, 233, 339(2), 339(3), 341, 539, 540, 543, 549, 556(1), 556(2), 556(3), 557(4), 603, 610, 612; Const Law 1106; Costs 207.

Hardin v. Hardin, TexCivApp–San Antonio, 247 SW2d 614.—Child S 11, 240, 444.

Hardin; Hardin v., TexCivApp–San Antonio, 247 SW2d 614.—Child S 11, 240, 444.

Hardin v. Hardin, TexCivApp–Waco, 351 SW2d 268.—Child S 9.

Hardin; Hardin v., TexCivApp–Waco, 351 SW2d 268.—Child S 9.

Hardin v. Hardin, TexCivApp–Eastland, 584 SW2d 384, rev 597 SW2d 347.—Plead 236(2).

HARDIN;

Hardin; Hardin v., TexCivApp–Eastland, 584 SW2d 384, rev 597 SW2d 347.—Plead 236(2).

Hardin; Harry H. Price & Son, Inc. v., NDTex, 299 FSupp 557, vac 425 F2d 1137, cert den 91 SCt 568, 400 US 1009, 27 LEd2d 622.—Admin Law 668; Food 4.1.

Hardin; Harry H. Price & Sons, Inc. v., CA5 (Tex), 425 F2d 1137, cert den 91 SCt 568, 400 US 1009, 27 LEd2d 622.—Admin Law 668; Courts 2; Food 4.1.

Hardin; Hartford Acc. & Indem. Co. v., TexCivApp–Fort Worth, 252 SW2d 752, writ refused.—Work Comp 1279, 1283, 1297, 1726.

Hardin v. Houston Chronicle Pub. Co., CA5 (Tex), 572 F2d 1106.—Antitrust 996; Fed Cts 815; Inj 135, 138.21.

Hardin v. Houston Chronicle Pub. Co., SDTex, 434 FSupp 54, aff 572 F2d 1106.—Antitrust 595, 885, 995, 996; Inj 138.21, 138.37, 147.

Hardin v. Houston Chronicle Pub. Co., SDTex, 426 FSupp 1114, aff 572 F2d 1106.—Antitrust 995, 996; Equity 23; Inj 138.21.

Hardin v. James Talcott Western, Inc., TexCivApp–Waco, 390 SW2d 517, ref nre.—Evid 417(1), 417(9), 417(12), 417(19).

Hardin; Lance Roof Inspection Service, Inc. v., SDTex, 653 FSupp 1097.—Antitrust 421, 432; Contracts 152, 155, 202(2), 210; Cust & U 17; Evid 460(2); Labor & Emp 121, 123.

Hardin; Lewallen v., TexCivApp–Dallas, 563 SW2d 356. —Child S 24, 26, 70, 508(4); Evid 318(7).

Hardin; Mack Trucks, Inc. v., TexCivApp–Waco, 355 SW2d 795.—Plead 111.42(10); Venue 8.5(2).

Hardin; Peavy v., TexCivApp–El Paso, 288 SW 588.—Health 706; Prod Liab 46.2.

Hardin; Ryan v., TexCivApp–Austin, 495 SW2d 345.—App & E 1094(1); Damag 182, 208(4); Trial 131(1), 133.6(4), 139.1(3), 140(1).

Hardin v. State, TexCrimApp, 475 SW2d 254, cert den 92 SCt 2511, 408 US 927, 33 LEd2d 339.—Jury 33(5.15).

Hardin v. State, TexCrimApp, 471 SW2d 60.—Const Law 4674, 4677; Crim Law 1086.11, 1144.1, 1158(4), 1163(1), 1166.8; Witn 2(1), 20.

Hardin v. State, TexCrimApp, 458 SW2d 822.—Burg 2; Crim Law 781(1), 814(20), 1171.8(2), 1173.2(7); Ind & Inf 189(7); Sent & Pun 1251, 1302, 1379(2).

Hardin v. State, TexCrimApp, 453 SW2d 158.—Crim Law 394.4(10), 627.8(3); Judges 50.

Hardin v. State, TexCrimApp, 453 SW2d 156, cert den 91 SCt 375, 400 US 965, 27 LEd2d 385.—Arrest 68(8), 71.1(9); Crim Law 627.9(1), 627.9(5), 1114.1(3), 1169.1(8).

Hardin v. State, TexCrimApp, 387 SW2d 60.—Arrest 63.4(4), 63.4(15), 71.1(6); Controlled Subs 80; Crim Law 814(5).

Hardin v. State, TexCrimApp, 248 SW2d 487, 157 Tex-Crim 283.—Crim Law 1017.

Hardin v. State, TexCrimApp, 101 SW2d 265, 131 Tex-Crim 588.—Int Liq 205(1).

Hardin v. State, TexCrimApp, 101 SW2d 264, 131 Tex-Crim 587.—Int Liq 205(1).

Hardin v. State, TexApp–Fort Worth, 818 SW2d 208.—Autos 349.5(8); Crim Law 790; Searches 49.

Hardin v. State, TexApp–Texarkana, 20 SW3d 84, petition for discretionary review refused.—Crim Law 469, 478(1), 627.8(1), 629(3.1), 629.5(1), 629.5(2), 867, 1035(2), 1044.1(2), 1147, 1148, 1153(1), 1155, 1169.5(1); Sent & Pun 247, 308, 320, 328, 366.

Hardin v. State, TexApp–Houston (14 Dist), 951 SW2d 208.—Crim Law 633(2), 641.13(1), 641.13(2.1), 777, 992, 1035(3), 1044.1(6), 1137(5), 1144.10.

Hardin v. State, TexApp–Amarillo, 254 SW2d 898.—Ack 62(2), 62(4); App & E 996, 1012.1(1); High 8; Ref of Inst 19(1), 45(4.1), 45(5), 47; States 85.

Hardin; Sullivan v., TexCivApp–Amarillo, 102 SW2d 1110.—Ack 37(1); App & E 242(3), 672, 837(11), 1010.2;

Jud S 48; Mtg 342, 375, 378, 390; Plead 53(1); Princ & A 164(1).

Hardin v. Texas Bd. of Pardons and Paroles, TexCivApp–Austin, 554 SW2d 18.—Pardon 78, 92.

Hardin; Transamerica Ins. Co. v., TexCivApp–Fort Worth, 437 SW2d 443, ref nre.—App & E 753(2).

Hardin; Trans-Cold Exp., Inc. v., TexCivApp–Austin, 415 SW2d 431.—Carr 88, 108, 114, 140, 215.1; Evid 318(1), 370(1); Indem 84.

Hardin; U.S. v., CA5 (Tex), 437 F3d 463.—Costs 302.2(2); Crim Law 1139, 1148; Sent & Pun 651, 995.

Hardin v. U.S., CA5 (Tex), 410 F2d 146.—Crim Law 273.1(5), 641.9, 1132.

Hardin; Volunteer State Life Ins. Co. v., Tex, 197 SW2d 105, 145 Tex 245, 168 ALR 337.—Hus & W 249(3), 274(1); Insurance 3470, 3471, 3474, 3479, 3490.

Hardin v. Volunteer State Life Ins. Co., TexCivApp–Dallas, 193 SW2d 554, rev 197 SW2d 105, 145 Tex 245, 168 ALR 337.—Hus & W 249(3), 274(4).

Hardin Associates, Inc. v. Brummett, TexCivApp–Texarkana, 613 SW2d 4.—Contracts 313(1); Costs 194.25, 194.32; Damag 125; Frds St of 44(3), 49; Labor & Emp 256(5), 258, 259, 868(3).

Hardin, City of; Hardin Water Supply Corp. v., Tex, 671 SW2d 505.—Mun Corp 619; Pub Ut 111; Waters 202, 203(6).

Hardin Const. Group, Inc. v. Peeples, TexApp–San Antonio, 945 SW2d 308. See Hardin Const. Group, Inc. v. Strictly Painting, Inc.

Hardin Const. Group, Inc. v. Strictly Painting, Inc., TexApp–San Antonio, 945 SW2d 308, reh overr, and reh of motion for mandamus overr.—Alt Disp Res 137, 141, 213(5); Commerce 80.5; Contracts 9(1), 25, 29; Mand 4(4), 28, 60, 172.

Hardin County v. Trunkline Gas Co., CA5 (Tex), 330 F2d 789, cert den 85 SCt 71, 379 US 848, 13 LEd2d 51. —Const Law 38, 193, 655, 1007; Counties 124(3), 130; Pub Contr 14; States 102, 113.

Hardin County; West Tex. Gulf Pipe Line Co. v., Tex, 321 SW2d 576, 159 Tex 374.—App & E 954(2); Tax 2879(1).

Hardin County; West Texas Gulf Pipe Line Co. v., TexCivApp–Austin, 319 SW2d 155, ref nre 321 SW2d 576, 159 Tex 374.—App & E 931(3); Tax 2510, 2647, 2655, 2699(7), 2882, 2883.

Hardin County Community Supervision and Corrections Dept. v. Sullivan, TexApp–Austin, 106 SW3d 186, review den.—App & E 863; Courts 32, 35, 37(2), 55, 89; Plead 104(1), 111.36, 111.39(0.5).

Hardin County Sav. & Loan Ass'n; Mosley v., TexCivApp–Beaumont, 602 SW2d 82.—App & E 171(1), 173(1); B & L Assoc 40.

Hardin County, Tex. v. Trunkline Gas Co., CA5 (Tex), 311 F2d 882, vac 84 SCt 49, 375 US 8, 11 LEd2d 38, on remand 330 F2d 789, cert den 85 SCt 71, 379 US 848, 13 LEd2d 51.—Counties 113(1); High 88, 99, 105(1).

Harding v. American Stock Exchange, Inc., CA5 (Tex), 527 F2d 1366.—Antitrust 900, 920; Civil R 1028; Sec Reg 88.

Harding; Franklin Offices, Inc. v., TexCivApp–Dallas, 579 SW2d 254.—App & E 846(5); Inj 147; Usury 117.

Harding; Harding v., TexCivApp–San Antonio, 485 SW2d 297.—Jury 28(17); Stip 14(4).

Harding v. Harding, TexCivApp–San Antonio, 485 SW2d 297.—Jury 28(17); Stip 14(4).

Harding v. Harding, TexCivApp–San Antonio, 461 SW2d 235, appeal after remand 485 SW2d 297.—Divorce 227(1), 253(4), 286(9), 287; Hus & W 278(1); Trial 391, 395(5).

Harding; Harding v., TexCivApp–San Antonio, 461 SW2d 235, appeal after remand 485 SW2d 297.—Divorce 227(1), 253(4), 286(9), 287; Hus & W 278(1); Trial 391, 395(5).

Harding v. Kaufman County, TexApp–Tyler, 119 SW3d 428.—Autos 258, 285, 293, 308(4); Mun Corp 847, 857; Neglig 1001, 1037(4), 1051, 1562, 1706.

Harding v. Lewis, TexApp–Corpus Christi, 133 SW3d 693.—Judgm 866.1.

Harding; Lopez v., TexApp–Dallas, 68 SW3d 78.—App & E 962; Pretrial Proc 582, 583, 676.

Harding; Nissan Motor Corp. in U.S.A. v., CA5 (Tex), 739 F2d 1005.—Const Law 977; Fed Cts 41, 42, 43, 47.1, 53, 65.

Harding v. Regent, NDTex, 347 FSupp2d 334.—Fed Civ Proc 1831.

Harding v. Sinclair Pipeline Co., TexCivApp–Hous (14 Dist), 480 SW2d 786, ref nre.—Explos 7; Judgm 185.3(21).

Harding v. Smith, WDTex, 708 FSupp 792. See Birdsong v. Olson.

Harding; Snow v., TexCivApp–San Antonio, 180 SW2d 965, writ refused.—App & E 1015(5), 1053(4), 1078(1); Fraud Conv 62, 95(1), 206(2), 230, 297, 308(1); Inj 118(2); New Tr 99, 105, 144, 157; Trial 304.

Harding v. State, TexCrimApp, 790 SW2d 638, on subsequent appeal 822 SW2d 817, petition for discretionary review refused.—Crim Law 790, 1144.15, 1172.1(2).

Harding v. State, TexCrimApp, 431 SW2d 554.—Crim Law 938(3); Larc 55.

Harding v. State, TexCrimApp, 208 SW2d 892, 151 TexCrim 508.—Crim Law 396(1), 1120(4); Homic 1014, 1154; Witn 337(28).

Harding v. State, TexApp–Houston (1 Dist), 822 SW2d 817, petition for discretionary review refused.—Const Law 2815; Crim Law 1181(2), 1189.

Harding v. State, TexApp–Houston (1 Dist), 691 SW2d 815, petition for discretionary review refused.—Crim Law 795(1), 1144.13(2.1); Rob 24.50, 27(5).

Harding v. State Nat. Bank of El Paso, TexCivApp–El Paso, 387 SW2d 768.—Abate & R 52.

Harding v. Stith, TexCivApp–San Antonio, 88 SW2d 528.—App & E 773(2).

Harding v. Watson, TexCivApp–San Antonio, 91 SW2d 956.—App & E 843(2); Ease 2; Evid 22(1); Waters 197.

Harding v. Wrotenbery, CA5 (Tex), 901 F2d 1270. See Birdsong v. Wrotenbery.

Harding Bros. Oil & Gas Co. v. Jim Ned Independent School Dist., TexCivApp–Eastland, 457 SW2d 102.—Decl Judgm 5.1, 6, 8, 213.1, 214; Equity 66; Schools 107.

Harding Chemicals, Inc.; West Texas Production Credit Ass'n v., TexCivApp–San Antonio, 407 SW2d 950, ref nre.—App & E 1176(1); Contracts 54(1); Frds St of 23(1), 159.

Hardinge v. State, TexCrimApp, 500 SW2d 870.—Arrest 63.1, 63.4(15), 68(3); Searches 24.

Hardin Independent School Dist.; Kirby Lumber Corp. v., TexCivApp–Waco, 351 SW2d 310, ref nre.—Const Law 605, 611, 655; Statut 188; Tax 2300, 2319.

Hardin-Jefferson Independent School Dist.; University Interscholastic League v., TexApp–Beaumont, 648 SW2d 770.—App & E 374(4), 781(4); Inj 147.

Hardin Medical Center; U.S. v., EDTex, 807 FSupp 47. See U.S. v. Contemporary Health Management of Hardin County, Inc.

Hardin Memorial Hospital; Hartman v., TexCivApp–Beaumont, 587 SW2d 55.—Health 770.

Hardin Water Supply Corp. v. City of Hardin, Tex, 671 SW2d 505.—Mun Corp 619; Pub Ut 111; Waters 202, 203(6).

Hardin Water Supply Corp.; City of Hardin v., TexApp–Beaumont, 666 SW2d 354, rev 671 SW2d 505.—Waters 203(6).

Hardison v. A. H. Belo Corp., TexCivApp–Dallas, 247 SW2d 167.—App & E 719(1), 758.1, 919; Frds St of 51; Labor & Emp 835, 858, 873.

Hardison v. Beard, TexCivApp–Dallas, 430 SW2d 53, ref nre.—Damag 163(2); Evid 5(2); Judgm 181(14); Nova 3; Schools 133.5, 135(1), 135(3), 139, 144(4).

Hardison v. State, TexCrimApp, 597 SW2d 355.—Arrest 63.1, 63.4(1).

Hardison v. State, TexCrimApp, 450 SW2d 638.—Crim Law 304(16); Sent & Pun 2003, 2018.

Hardman v. Bertrand, TexCivApp–El Paso, 220 SW2d 363.—App & E 175; Plead 111.3, 111.43.

Hardman v. Dault, TexApp–San Antonio, 2 SW3d 378.—Alt Disp Res 451, 484; App & E 242(1), 242(2); Compromise 21; Contracts 14, 29, 39; Jury 28(5).

Hardman v. State, TexCrimApp, 614 SW2d 123.—Crim Law 273.1(4), 304(1), 429(1), 1042, 1116; Estop 62.1; Sent & Pun 2019, 2021.

Hardmon v. State, TexCrimApp, 218 SW2d 204.—Crim Law 1094(2.1).

Hardrick v. State, TexCrimApp, 155 SW2d 367, 142 TexCrim 520.—Crim Law 1171.5; Homic 877.

Hard Rock Cafe Intern., Inc.; Texas Pig Stands, Inc. v., CA5 (Tex), 966 F2d 956.—Trademarks 1653, 1662.

Hard Rock Cafe Intern., Inc.; Texas Pig Stands, Inc. v., CA5 (Tex), 951 F2d 684, reh den 966 F2d 956.—Fed Cts 813; Judgm 540, 739; Trademarks 1033, 1034, 1036, 1354, 1363, 1365, 1387, 1529, 1615, 1628(2), 1650, 1656(3), 1662, 1689, 1754(2).

Hardt v. Texas Dept. of Corrections, TexCivApp–Austin, 530 SW2d 897.—States 191.2(2), 200; Venue 8.5(8).

Hardtke, Inc. v. Katz, TexApp–Houston (1 Dist), 813 SW2d 548. See Charles L. Hardtke, Inc. v. Katz.

Hardware Dealers Mut. Fire Ins. Co.; Berglund v., TexCivApp–Houston, 381 SW2d 631, rev 393 SW2d 309.—Insurance 1831, 1835(2), 2142(5), 2145, 2165(2), 3571, 3579; Trial 252(14), 350.5(1).

Hardware Dealers Mut. Fire Ins. Co. v. Farmers Ins. Exchange, Tex, 444 SW2d 583.—Insurance 2762(3), 2878, 2923.

Hardware Dealers Mut. Fire Ins. Co. v. Farmers Ins. Exchange, TexCivApp–Hous (14 Dist), 437 SW2d 390, writ gr, rev 444 SW2d 583.—Insurance 2761, 2878.

Hardware Dealers' Mut. Fire Ins. Co. v. King, Tex, 426 SW2d 215.—App & E 1062.2; Trial 350.3(8); Work Comp 110, 1964.

Hardware Dealers Mut. Fire Ins. Co. v. King, TexCivApp–Austin, 408 SW2d 790, writ gr, rev 426 SW2d 215.—App & E 930(1), 989; Work Comp 108, 1427, 1929, 1958, 1968(5).

Hardware Dealers Mut. Fire Ins. Co. v. Ovalle, TexCivApp–Corpus Christi, 470 SW2d 241.—Work Comp 1657.

Hardware Dealers Mut. Fire Ins. Co.; Rio Grande Nat. Life Ins. Co. v., TexCivApp–Amarillo, 209 SW2d 654, ref nre.—Insurance 3042, 3051, 3450, 3451, 3571.

Hardware Dealers Mut. Ins. Co. v. Berglund, Tex, 393 SW2d 309.—Contracts 167; Insurance 1813, 1832(2), 2117, 2142(5), 2145.

Hardware Indem. Ins. Co. of Minn.; Mallard v., TexCivApp–San Antonio, 216 SW2d 263.—Insurance 1896, 2035.

Hardware Mut. Cas. Co.; Bean v., TexCivApp–Beaumont, 349 SW2d 284, ref nre.—App & E 390, 395, 927(7); Evid 54; Work Comp 1357, 1385, 1392, 1396, 1416, 1519, 1703, 1960, 1968(4).

Hardware Mut. Cas. Co. v. Brown, TexCivApp–San Antonio, 390 SW2d 53, ref nre.—App & E 927(7), 934(1), 989; Work Comp 74, 78, 80, 1341, 1424.

Hardware Mut. Cas. Co. v. Buck's Tri-State Irr. Engine Co., Inc., TexCivApp–Amarillo, 500 SW2d 897, ref nre.—App & E 1175(7); Evid 595, 597; Insurance 2136(5), 2201.

Hardware Mut. Cas. Co. v. Clark, TexCivApp–Waco, 360 SW2d 921, writ dism.—Work Comp 1034, 1163, 1890.

Hardware Mut. Cas. Co. v. Courtney, Tex, 363 SW2d 427.—Work Comp 951.

Hardware Mut. Cas. Co. v. Courtney, TexCivApp–Austin, 353 SW2d 299, writ gr, aff 363 SW2d 427.—Work Comp 949.

Hardware Mut. Cas. Co. v. Hicks, TexCivApp–Texarkana, 344 SW2d 907.—Damag 221(3); Work Comp 1173, 1333, 1847.

Hardware Mut. Cas. Co. v. McDonald, TexCivApp–San Antonio, 502 SW2d 602, ref nre.—Work Comp 666.

Hardware Mut. Cas. Co. v. McIntyre, CA5 (Tex), 304 F2d 566, cert den 83 SCt 147, 371 US 878, 9 LEd2d 115, reh den 83 SCt 286, 371 US 931, 9 LEd2d 238.—Fed Cts 340.1, 354, 356.

Hardware Mut. Cas. Co.; Meyer v., TexCivApp–Austin, 383 SW2d 625.—Insurance 3066; Sales 450.

Hardware Mut. Cas. Co.; Minsky v., TexCivApp–Waco, 358 SW2d 664, ref nre.—App & E 930(4); Insurance 2853, 2856; Trial 351.2(2).

Hardware Mut. Cas. Co.; Owen v., CCA5 (Tex), 158 F2d 471.—Work Comp 605, 666, 744.

Hardware Mut. Cas. Co. v. Riddle, TexCivApp–Fort Worth, 142 SW2d 312.—Work Comp 1975.

Hardware Mut. Cas. Co. v. Schantz, CA5 (Tex), 186 F2d 868.—Insurance 2278(21), 2295, 2914, 2934(2); Judgm 243, 310.

Hardware Mut. Cas. Co. v. Schantz, CA5 (Tex), 178 F2d 779.—Decl Judgm 24, 274.1, 276; Fed Cts 284, 336.1.

Hardware Mut. Cas. Co. v. Styron, TexCivApp–Waco, 382 SW2d 799, ref nre.—New Tr 140(1).

Hardware Mut. Cas. Co. v. Wesbrooks, TexCivApp–Amarillo, 511 SW2d 406.—Evid 536, 546; Work Comp 556, 597, 998, 1536, 1546, 1972, 1973, 1975.

Hardware Mut. Cas. Co.; Woods v., TexCivApp–Austin, 141 SW2d 972, writ refused.—Evid 157(6); Marriage 11, 40(6), 40(10); Work Comp 433, 438, 1100.

Hardware Mut. Ins. Co. of Minn.; Prigmore v., TexCivApp–Amarillo, 225 SW2d 897.—Atty & C 64; Bills & N 94(1), 104; Paymt 85(7).

Hardwick v. Austin Gallery of Oriental Rugs, Inc., TexApp–Austin, 779 SW2d 438, writ den.—Antitrust 209; Corp 499, 592; Interest 31; Usury 42, 61, 62, 83, 102(1), 102(2), 102(7), 134, 137, 138, 139, 142(4).

Hardwick; Custom Drapery Co., Inc. v., TexCivApp–Hous (1 Dist), 531 SW2d 160.—Contracts 65.5, 116(1), 116(2), 117(2), 138(1), 141(3), 321(1); Inj 11, 61(2), 63, 126; Labor & Emp 908.

Hardwick v. Houston Lighting and Power Co., TexApp–Houston (1 Dist), 943 SW2d 183.—Judgm 185(2); Libel 1, 44(3), 54.

Hardwick v. Houston Lighting and Power Co., TexApp–Corpus Christi, 881 SW2d 195, reh overr, and writ dism woj, appeal after remand 943 SW2d 183.—App & E 863, 934(1); Judgm 181(1), 181(23), 185(2); Libel 1, 6(1), 10(6), 36, 38(1), 44(1), 44(3), 45(1), 50, 101(1), 101(3), 112(1), 123(2).

Hardwick v. Jackson, TexCivApp–Dallas, 315 SW2d 440.—App & E 758.3(4); Mines 109.

Hardwick v. Nu-Way Oil Co., SDTex, 443 FSupp 940, aff 589 F2d 806, reh den 592 F2d 1190, cert den 100 SCt 70, 444 US 836, 62 LEd2d 46.—Antitrust 839, 887, 963(1), 964; Fed Civ Proc 2484.

Hardwick v. Nu-Way Oil Co., Inc., CA5 (Tex), 589 F2d 806, reh den 592 F2d 1190, cert den 100 SCt 70, 444 US 836, 62 LEd2d 46.—Antitrust 824, 887.

Hardwick v. Pro-Line Boats, Inc., SDTex, 895 FSupp 145.—Adm 4, 18; Commerce 82.30; Nav Wat 1(3), 1(5), 1(7).

Hardwick v. State, TexCrimApp, 287 SW2d 658.—Crim Law 1090.1(1).

Hardwick v. City of Lubbock, TexApp–Amarillo, 150 SW3d 708.—App & E 954(1), 954(2); Em Dom 18.5, 300, 315; Inj 132, 135, 138.1, 138.18.

Hardwicke v. Trinity Universal Ins. Co., TexCivApp–Eastland, 89 SW2d 500.—App & E 544(1), 719(1),

719(6), 722(1), 747(1), 747(3), 759, 878(4); Contracts 50, 334, 354; Judgm 715(3); Trial 404(1).

Hardwicke-Etter Co.; Beall v., TexCivApp–Waco, 460 SW2d 516, writ dism woj.—Evid 461(3); Sales 1(3), 1(4); Venue 7.5(7).

Hardwick's Estate, In re, TexCivApp–Amarillo, 278 SW2d 258, ref nre.—Evid 472(8), 501(3); Wills 55(1), 316.3, 400; Witn 202.

Hardy, Ex parte, TexCrimApp, 230 SW2d 527.—Crim Law 1131(4).

Hardy, Ex parte, TexCivApp–Dallas, 531 SW2d 895.—Contempt 63(3), 63(4).

Hardy, In re, BkrtcyNDTex, 224 BR 360. See Thompson, In re.

Hardy; Amoco Production Co. v., TexApp–Corpus Christi, 628 SW2d 813, dism.—App & E 949; Parties 35.17, 35.79.

Hardy v. Barkley, TexCivApp–Waco, 430 SW2d 555, ref nre.—Autos 227.5, 244(20), 244(36.1).

Hardy v. Calhoun, TexCivApp–Texarkana, 383 SW2d 652.—Zoning 304.1.

Hardy; Carter v., CA5 (Tex), 736 F2d 271.—Fed Cts 937.1.

Hardy; Carter v., CA5 (Tex), 543 F2d 555, reh den 547 F2d 573.—Crim Law 1226(3.1).

Hardy; Carter v., CA5 (Tex), 526 F2d 314, reh den 528 F2d 928, cert den 97 SCt 108, 429 US 838, 50 LEd2d 105.—Civil R 1395(5); Crim Law 1226(3.1); Fed Cts 11; Hab Corp 224.1, 251; Records 11.

Hardy; City of Austin v., TexApp–Corpus Christi, 678 SW2d 495. See Houston Chronicle Pub. Co. v. Hardy.

Hardy; City of San Antonio, By and Through City Public Service Bd. of City of San Antonio v., TexApp–Corpus Christi, 678 SW2d 495. See Houston Chronicle Pub. Co. v. Hardy.

Hardy v. City of Throckmorton, TexCivApp–Eastland, 81 SW2d 567.—App & E 406; Em Dom 263.

Hardy; Ciulla v., TexCivApp–Hous (1 Dist), 431 SW2d 364.—Infants 245.

Hardy v. Construction Systems, Inc., TexCivApp–Hous (14 Dist), 556 SW2d 843, ref nre.—Dep in Court 4; Garn 58, 59.

Hardy; Cornett v., TexCivApp–Beaumont, 241 SW2d 186.—Autos 368; Damag 127, 132(13); Evid 474(15); Labor & Emp 3052, 3074; Trial 352.10.

Hardy v. C. P. I. Sales, Inc., TexCivApp–Hous (1 Dist), 511 SW2d 89.—App & E 302(1), 500(1), 719(1), 758.3(1), 758.3(4), 758.3(9), 768; Judgm 199(3.10); Neglig 1037(4), 1284, 1286(6), 1677, 1683; Trial 349(1).

Hardy; First City Nat. Bank of Houston v., TexCivApp–Corpus Christi, 620 SW2d 732, dism.—App & E 1, 634, 1177(9); Venue 22(4).

Hardy v. Fisher, EDTex, 901 FSupp 228.—Insurance 1117(3), 1654; Labor & Emp 407, 426, 428; States 18.15, 18.41, 18.51.

Hardy v. Fleming, TexCivApp–El Paso, 553 SW2d 790, ref nre.—Judgm 185(2), 632, 713(2), 720.

Hardy v. Gulf Oil Corp., CA5 (Tex), 949 F2d 826.—Adm 31; Contracts 144; Contrib 1, 6, 7, 8; Damag 63; Indem 24, 27, 33(5), 33(8), 61, 67, 69, 72, 74; Torts 135.

Hardy v. Hannah, TexApp–Austin, 849 SW2d 355, reh overr, and writ den.—Action 13; Const Law 540, 542, 556, 725; Judgm 185.1(1).

Hardy; Hernandez v., TexCivApp–Hous (14 Dist), 426 SW2d 258.—Infants 245.

Hardy; Holmes v., CA5 (Tex), 852 F2d 151, cert den 109 SCt 322, 488 US 931, 102 LEd2d 339.—Fed Civ Proc 664, 2734.

Hardy; Houston Chronicle Pub. Co. v., TexApp–Corpus Christi, 678 SW2d 495.—Const Law 2093; Mand 12; Mun Corp 54; Pretrial Proc 43, 433.

Hardy; International Interests, L.P. v., CA5 (Tex), 448 F3d 303, certified question accepted.—Contracts 129(1); Estop 52.10(2); Fed Cts 392, 409.1.

Hardy v. Johns-Manville Sales Corp., CA5 (Tex), 851 F2d 742, reh den 860 F2d 437, reh den Burke v. Johns-Manville Sales Corp, 860 F2d 437, reh den Dartez v Johns-Manville Sales Corp, 860 F2d 437, reh den Overstreet v Johns-Manville Sales Corp, 860 F2d 437, reh den Smith v Johns-Manville Sales Corp, 860 F2d 438, appeal after remand 910 F2d 1291, cert den 112 SCt 2301, 504 US 955, 119 LEd2d 224.—Evid 222(1); Fed Cts 896.1.

Hardy v. Johns-Manville Sales Corp., CA5 (Tex), 681 F2d 334.—Const Law 3953; Evid 14; Fed Cts 420; Judgm 634, 665, 678(1), 707, 715(3), 724; Prod Liab 14.

Hardy v. Johns-Manville Sales Corp., EDTex, 509 FSupp 1353, rev in part 681 F2d 334.—Fed Civ Proc 786, 1264, 1274; Fed Cts 371; Judgm 678(1), 678(2); Prod Liab 23.1, 75.1.

Hardy; Johnson v., CA5 (Tex), 601 F2d 172.—Civil R 1092, 1319; Hab Corp 342, 666.

Hardy v. Johnson, TexCivApp–Fort Worth, 434 SW2d 932.—App & E 758.3(11); Evid 590; Insurance 1929(2), 1929(7); Judgm 185.3(12); Pretrial Proc 308, 434.

Hardy; Laney v., TexCivApp–El Paso, 265 SW2d 609.—App & E 1004(4); Damag 133; Trial 315.

Hardy; Langley v., TexCivApp–Dallas, 293 SW2d 793.—Venue 22(3), 22(6).

Hardy; Lawrence v., TexCivApp–San Antonio, 583 SW2d 795, ref nre.—Autos 227.5, 244(35); Bailm 2, 21; Hus & W 214, 268(9); Neglig 259, 291.

Hardy v. Lubbock County, TexCivApp–Amarillo, 89 SW2d 240.—Counties 57; Sheriffs 64.

Hardy; Lundy v., TexCivApp–Galveston, 146 SW2d 1057.—App & E 1152.

Hardy v. McCorkle, TexApp–Houston (1 Dist), 765 SW2d 910.—Action 57(5), 57(6), 60; Courts 27; Mand 31; Prohib 9, 10(2).

Hardy; Macfadden's Publications v., TexCivApp–Waco, 95 SW2d 1023, writ refused.—App & E 1060.1(2.1); Evid 14; Libel 7(3), 111, 114; Trial 118.

Hardy; McIlhenny v., TexCivApp–Galveston, 226 SW2d 886.—App & E 846(5).

Hardy; McIver v., TexCivApp–Galveston, 146 SW2d 1054.—Contracts 170(1); J P 36(2.1); Ten in C 22.

Hardy v. McMillar, TexCivApp–Waco, 492 SW2d 381.—Plead 111.39(6), 111.43.

Hardy v. Marsh, TexApp–Texarkana, 170 SW3d 865.—App & E 946; Health 618, 804, 809; Statut 227.

Hardy v. Martin, TexCivApp–Texarkana, 439 SW2d 389, writ gr, aff in part, rev in part Mercer v. Hardy, 444 SW2d 593.—Contracts 156; Indem 30(1), 33(5).

Hardy; Martinez v., TexApp–Houston (14 Dist), 864 SW2d 767.—App & E 854(1); Counties 67, 89, 142, 146; Judgm 184, 185(2), 185.1(8), 185.3(21); Labor & Emp 904, 911; Libel 36, 38(1), 50, 50.5, 51(1); Lim of Act 55(4), 55(5), 105(1), 183(1); Mun Corp 218(10), 723; Stip 3, 11, 17(1), 17(3).

Hardy; Mauldin v., TexCivApp–San Antonio, 337 SW2d 434, ref nre.—Child C 469, 473, 559, 567, 637.

Hardy; Mercer v., Tex, 444 SW2d 593.—Indem 33(3).

Hardy; Miller v., TexCivApp–El Paso, 564 SW2d 102, ref nre.—App & E 837(1), 927(7), 989, 1060.1(2.1); Evid 382, 555.3, 555.6(10), 555.10, 558(9); Health 707, 787, 818, 819, 823(5); Neglig 1614; Trial 54(1), 105(1), 105(4).

Hardy v. Mitchell, TexApp–Dallas, 195 SW3d 862, review den.—App & E 984(1); Child C 981; Child 20.12; Costs 2; Parent & C 7(1).

Hardy; Naylor v., TexCivApp–El Paso, 122 SW2d 708.—App & E 930(3); Damag 188(1), 221(6).

Hardy v. Owens–Illinois, Inc., CA5 (Tex), 910 F2d 1291. See Dartez v. Owens-Illinois, Inc.

Hardy; Pan Am. Petroleum Corp. v., TexCivApp–Waco, 370 SW2d 904, ref nre.—Damag 87(1), 91(1); Mines 78.1(6), 78.7(4), 78.7(6), 79.3, 92.59(2).

Hardy v. Port City Ford Truck Sales, Inc., TexApp–Houston (14 Dist), 693 SW2d 578, ref nre.—Jury 25(2), 26.

Hardy v. Proctor & Gamble Mfg. Co., CA5 (Tex), 209 F2d 124.—Fed Civ Proc 2111; Prod Liab 88; Sales 445(1).

Hardy v. Robinson, TexApp–Waco, 170 SW3d 777, rule 537(f) motion gr.—App & E 1010.2, 1175(5); Assign 22, 137; Princ & A 51, 97; Trusts 17(1), 25(1).

Hardy; Rudy v., TexCivApp–Waco, 610 SW2d 565, dism.—Adv Poss 22, 29, 31, 114(1).

Hardy; San Antonio, City of, By and Through Public Service Bd. of City of San Antonio v., TexApp–Corpus Christi, 678 SW2d 495. See Houston Chronicle Pub. Co. v. Hardy.

Hardy; Southwestern Bell Tel. Co. v., TexComApp, 117 SW2d 418, 131 Tex 573.—Autos 290.

Hardy; Southwestern Bell Tel. Co. v., TexCivApp–Beaumont, 91 SW2d 1075, rev 117 SW2d 418, 131 Tex 573.—Autos 290; Tel 813, 825, 834; Trial 120(2).

Hardy v. State, Tex, 102 SW3d 123.—Forfeit 4, 5; Gaming 58, 61, 68(3).

Hardy v. State, TexCrimApp, 213 SW3d 916.—Perj 10.

Hardy; State v., TexCrimApp, 963 SW2d 516, reh den.—Autos 411; Crim Law 1139; Searches 14, 26, 78; Statut 149, 181(2), 188, 212.6, 214, 220; Witn 208(2).

Hardy v. State, TexCrimApp, 610 SW2d 511.—Crim Law 1023(16).

Hardy v. State, TexCrimApp, 496 SW2d 635.—Crim Law 766, 814(3), 1171.2; Searches 183.

Hardy v. State, TexCrimApp, 344 SW2d 451, 171 TexCrim 18.—Crim Law 619, 1120(3); Int Liq 236(11).

Hardy v. State, TexCrimApp, 344 SW2d 450, 171 TexCrim 17.—Int Liq 236(11).

Hardy v. State, TexCrimApp, 343 SW2d 256, 170 TexCrim 580.—Crim Law 1097(1).

Hardy v. State, TexCrimApp, 339 SW2d 899, 170 TexCrim 253.—Crim Law 1134(3); Int Liq 236(7).

Hardy v. State, TexCrimApp, 288 SW2d 63, 162 TexCrim 658.—Crim Law 1044.2(1), 1186.1; Int Liq 236(3), 236(11).

Hardy v. State, TexCrimApp, 283 SW2d 234, 162 TexCrim 166.—Int Liq 236(3).

Hardy v. State, TexCrimApp, 283 SW2d 233, 162 TexCrim 165.—Int Liq 27, 223(1), 236(3).

Hardy v. State, TexCrimApp, 279 SW2d 345, 161 TexCrim 637.—Crim Law 1115(2), 1170.5(1), 1171.1(3); Ind & Inf 122(1).

Hardy v. State, TexCrimApp, 278 SW2d 312, 161 TexCrim 463.—Crim Law 721(6).

Hardy v. State, TexCrimApp, 261 SW2d 172, 159 TexCrim 54.—Crim Law 893, 992, 1144.17, 1186.1.

Hardy v. State, TexCrimApp, 244 SW2d 819, 156 TexCrim 559.—Int Liq 236(3).

Hardy v. State, TexCrimApp, 144 SW2d 904, 140 TexCrim 385.—Crim Law 1133, 1182.

Hardy v. State, TexCrimApp, 118 SW2d 797.—Crim Law 1131(1).

Hardy v. State, TexCrimApp, 113 SW2d 918, 133 TexCrim 619.—Int Liq 223(1), 236(3).

Hardy v. State, TexCrimApp, 93 SW2d 425, 130 TexCrim 173.—Crim Law 968(5).

Hardy; State v., TexApp–Houston (1 Dist), 769 SW2d 353.—Clerks of C 6; Const Law 2350, 2355.

Hardy v. State, TexApp–San Antonio, 52 SW3d 786, petition for discretionary review refused.—Sent & Pun 2021.

Hardy v. State, TexApp–Texarkana, 187 SW3d 232, petition for discretionary review refused.—Crim Law 641.13(6), 641.13(7), 795(1.5), 795(2.10), 795(2.20), 1036.1(5); Rape 51(1), 51(4); Sent & Pun 1279; Statut 176.

Hardy v. State, TexApp–Amarillo, 71 SW3d 535.—Crim Law 433, 1169.1(10).

Hardy v. State, TexApp–Waco, 50 SW3d 689, review gr, aff but criticized 102 SW3d 123.—App & E 838.1, 893(1), 989, 1008.1(5), 1010.1(2); Const Law 4078; Gaming 58, 61.

Hardy v. State, TexApp–Houston (14 Dist), 187 SW3d 678, petition stricken, and petition for discretionary review gr, rev 213 SW3d 916.—Crim Law 1144.13(2.1), 1144.13(6), 1159.2(2), 1159.2(7), 1159.2(9), 1159.3(2), 1159.4(2), 1159.6; Perj 9(0.5), 10, 33(5).

Hardy v. State, TexApp–Houston (14 Dist), 738 SW2d 792, petition for discretionary review refused.—Arrest 63.5(8); Controlled Subs 151.

Hardy v. State, TexApp–Houston (14 Dist), 722 SW2d 164, review gr, cause remanded 726 SW2d 158, on remand 1987 WL 16202.—Courts 100(1); Crim Law 723(1), 790, 810; Jury 33(5.15); Rape 51(7).

Hardy v. State, TexApp–Houston (14 Dist), 681 SW2d 170, appeal after remand 722 SW2d 164, review gr, cause remanded 726 SW2d 158, on remand 1987 WL 16202.—Crim Law 772(1), 814(1), 1038.1(3.1), 1038.1(4); Rape 51(1), 59(20.1).

Hardy; State Dept. of Highways and Public Transp. v., TexCivApp–Tyler, 607 SW2d 611, dism.—Venue 22(10), 72.

Hardy; Texas Emp. Ins. Ass'n v., TexCivApp–Eastland, 81 SW2d 191, writ dism.—App & E 930(3); Compromise 19(1); Trial 358; Work Comp 1162.

Hardy v. University Interscholastic League, CA5 (Tex), 759 F2d 1233.—Const Law 3619, 4226; Rem of C 107(8).

Hardy; University of Texas Medical Branch Hosp. at Galveston v., TexApp–Houston (14 Dist), 2 SW3d 607, reh overr, and review den, and reh of petition for review den.—Mun Corp 745, 847, 854; States 112.1(1), 112.2(4).

Hardy; Walton v., TexCivApp–Waco, 401 SW2d 614, ref nre.—Lim of Act 1; Ten in C 15(7), 15(10), 15(11).

Hardy v. Wernette, TexComApp, 134 SW2d 1032, 134 Tex 229.—Adop 11, 14.

Hardy v. Wernette, TexCivApp–San Antonio, 114 SW2d 951, aff 134 SW2d 1032, 134 Tex 229.—Adop 16.

Hardy; Wilson v., TexCivApp–San Antonio, 309 SW2d 114, ref nre.—Contracts 315, 333(1); Trial 118.

Hardy v. Wise, TexApp–Beaumont, 92 SW3d 650.—App & E 840(4); Const Law 3975, 3981; Covenants 84; Judgm 707; Parties 35.1, 35.17, 35.41, 35.79.

Hardy v. 11702 Memorial, Ltd., TexApp–Houston (1 Dist), 176 SW3d 266, reh overr.—App & E 842(2), 846(5), 931(3), 1010.1(1); Land & Ten 184(2).

Hardy Road 13.4 Joint Venture v. Med Center Bank, TexApp–Houston (1 Dist), 867 SW2d 889, reh den, and writ den, appeal after remand Southwest Guar Trust Co v. Hardy Road 134 Joint Venture, 981 SW2d 951, reh overr, and review den, and reh of petition for review overr.—App & E 852, 856(1), 863; Judgm 181(17), 185(2).

Hardy Road 13.4 Joint Venture; Southwest Guar. Trust Co. v., TexApp–Houston (1 Dist), 981 SW2d 951, reh overr, and review den, and reh of petition for review overr.—Attach 356; Banks 100; Damag 188(1); Decl Judgm 42, 82; Libel 135, 139; Quiet T 54.

Hardy St. Investors v. Texas Water Rights Commission, TexCivApp–Waco, 536 SW2d 85, ref nre.—Admin Law 791; Drains 34, 36(4); Evid 83(1).

Hardy Street Investors; Inverness Forest Imp. Dist. v., TexCivApp–Hous (1 Dist), 541 SW2d 454, ref nre.—App & E 422; Inj 77(1), 88, 128(7); Mand 73(1); Mun Corp 63.5, 712(1), 879, 911, 921(3); Trial 351.2(4); Waters 201.

Hare, In Interest of, TexCivApp–Texarkana, 599 SW2d 856.—Infants 178, 179.

Hare; Cullinan v., TexCivApp–Eastland, 181 SW2d 594. —App & E 1170.9(6); Damag 210(2).

Hare; Gerland's Food Fair, Inc. v., TexCivApp–Hous (1 Dist), 611 SW2d 113, ref nre.—App & E 1013; Corp 507(13); Damag 130.3, 133, 163(1), 185(1), 191, 192; Evid 314(2), 318(2), 373(1), 474(3); Neglig 1524(3); Proc 145.

Hare v. Government Employees Ins. Co., EDTex, 132 FRD 448.—Fed Civ Proc 1366, 1455.

Hare v. Hare, TexApp–Houston (1 Dist), 786 SW2d 747.— App & E 387(1), 784.

Hare; Hare v., TexApp–Houston (1 Dist), 786 SW2d 747. —App & E 387(1), 784.

Hare v. Henderson, CCA5 (Tex), 113 F2d 277, cert den 61 SCt 135, 311 US 697, 85 LEd 451.—Ven & Pur 86, 278.

Hare; Indemnity Ins. Co. of North America v., TexCivApp–Beaumont, 107 SW2d 739, writ refused.—Fraud 31; Work Comp 1131, 2084.

Hare; Leonard v., Tex, 336 SW2d 619, 161 Tex 28.—Elect of Rem 11; Estop 90(1); Work Comp 2138.

Hare; Leonard v., TexCivApp–Texarkana, 325 SW2d 197, writ gr, aff 336 SW2d 619, 161 Tex 28.—Can of Inst 35(1); Labor & Emp 2881, 2941, 3003; Release 57(1).

Hare; O. P. Leonard Trust v., TexCivApp–Texarkana, 305 SW2d 833, dism.—Labor & Emp 3045, 3076, 3077, 3085; Plead 111.18, 111.42(9); Trial 142; Trusts 254.

Hare v. State, TexCivApp, 460 SW2d 124.—Crim Law 354, 429(2), 822(9), 1170(1), 1170(2).

Hare v. State, TexApp–El Paso, 713 SW2d 396, petition for discretionary review refused.—Assault 77; Autos 351.1; Courts 107; Crim Law 273(4.1); Ind & Inf 71.2(3).

Hare; Supreme Forest, Woodmen Circle v., TexCivApp–Amarillo, 105 SW2d 414.—App & E 930(3); Insurance 2986, 3003(11), 3096(2); Princ & A 99.

Hare; U.S. v., CA5 (Tex), 150 F3d 419.—Autos 349(2.1), 349(17), 349.5(3), 349.5(7); Consp 51; Crim Law 444, 622.1(1), 1139, 1148, 1153(1), 1158(1), 1158(4), 1163(1), 1166(3), 1166(6), 1169.11; Sent & Pun 726(3), 752, 764, 765.

Hare; U.S. v., EDTex, 932 FSupp 852.—Controlled Subs 137; Crim Law 627.6(6).

Hare; U.S. v., EDTex, 932 FSupp 843.—Arrest 63.5(6), 71.1(5); Autos 349(14.1), 349(18), 349.5(3), 349.5(4), 349.5(7); Controlled Subs 137, 148(3), 154; Crim Law 394.1(3); Searches 22, 40.1, 47.1, 62, 117, 126, 180, 181, 186, 200.

Harford Mut. Ins. Co. v. Gorbet, CA5 (Tex), 241 F2d 363. —Hus & W 23.5, 266.3; Insurance 1874, 1945, 1952, 1955.

Hargadon v. Cove State Bank, BkrtcyWDTex, 48 BR 33. See Jaggers, In re.

Harger v. Cason, TexCivApp–Waco, 223 SW2d 244.—App & E 765, 1078(3); Dedi 45.

Hargesheimer v. State, TexCrimApp, 182 SW3d 906, on remand 2006 WL 1932597, petition for discretionary review refused.—Crim Law 1023(3), 1073.

Hargesheimer v. State, TexApp–Amarillo, 140 SW3d 443, reh overr, and petition for discretionary review gr, rev 182 SW3d 906, on remand 2006 WL 1932597, petition for discretionary review refused.—Crim Law 1078; Sent & Pun 2094.

Hargesheimer v. State, TexApp–Amarillo, 126 SW3d 658, petition for discretionary review refused, opinion after remand 140 SW3d 443, reh overr, and petition for discretionary review gr, rev 182 SW3d 906, on remand 2006 WL 1932597, petition for discretionary review refused.—Crim Law 1026.10(1).

Hargest; Waters v., TexCivApp–Texarkana, 593 SW2d 364.—Const Law 1338; Costs 60; Relig Soc 14, 24, 27(1), 27(3).

Hargett, Ex parte, TexCrimApp, 819 SW2d 866, on remand 827 SW2d 606, petition for discretionary review refused.—Hab Corp 201, 253, 814.

Hargett, Ex parte, TexApp–Austin, 827 SW2d 606, petition for discretionary review refused.—Crim Law 1137(2); Hab Corp 742.

Hargett v. McDaniel, TexApp–Texarkana, 717 SW2d 688. —Courts 472.2; Elections 258.

Hargett v. State, TexCrimApp, 534 SW2d 909.—Burg 10; Crim Law 338(1), 641.5(3), 721(5).

Hargett v. State, TexCrimApp, 274 SW2d 553.—Crim Law 1090.1(1).

Hargett v. State, TexApp–Tyler, 718 SW2d 923, petition for discretionary review refused by 729 SW2d 748.— Controlled Subs 82.

Hargis, In re, NDTex, 146 BR 176.—Bankr 3192.

Hargis, In re, NDTex, 146 BR 173, appeal after remand 146 BR 176.—Bankr 2103.

Hargis, In re, BkrtcyNDTex, 148 BR 19.—Atty & C 21.5(6); Bankr 3172.1, 3177, 3179, 3185, 3193.

Hargis, In re, BkrtcyNDTex, 73 BR 622, subsequently rev 887 F2d 77, decision clarified on reh 895 F2d 1025, on remand 148 BR 19.—Bankr 2187, 3172.1, 3177, 3178, 3185, 3502.15, 3622.

Hargis, Matter of, CA5 (Tex), 895 F2d 1025, on remand 148 BR 19.—Bankr 2623, 3192.

Hargis, Matter of, CA5 (Tex), 887 F2d 77, decision clarified on reh 895 F2d 1025, on remand 148 BR 19.— Bankr 2558, 2610, 2648, 2701.

Hargis; Iles v., TexCivApp–Beaumont, 120 SW2d 1094.— Inj 22.

Hargis; Iles v., TexCivApp–Beaumont, 120 SW2d 1091.— App & E 397; Elections 154(6); Statut 223.1.

Hargis v. Maryland American General Ins. Co., TexCivApp–Eastland, 567 SW2d 923, ref nre.—App & E 1135; Insurance 2278(21), 3557; Judgm 181(1).

Hargis v. Nance, Tex, 317 SW2d 922, 159 Tex 263.—Wills 136, 302(6), 318(1).

Hargis; Nance v., TexCivApp–Austin, 311 SW2d 465, rev 317 SW2d 922, 159 Tex 263.—App & E 655(1), 655(3), 766; Wills 302(6), 318(1).

Hargis v. Radio Corp. of America, Electronic Components, TexCivApp–Austin, 539 SW2d 230.—Contracts 88; Guar 14, 16(1), 16(2), 16(3), 36(1); Interest 46(1), 47(1).

Hargis; Seligman-Hargis v., TexApp–Dallas, 186 SW3d 582, reh overr.—Child C 730, 816, 918; Child S 559; Contracts 137(2); Divorce 287.

Hargis; Whitehead v., TexCivApp–Beaumont, 119 SW2d 118.—Replev 8(5).

Hargis Bldg. Co.; Kamp v., TexCivApp–Galveston, 238 SW2d 277, ref nre.—App & E 758.3(1); Brok 102; Evid 590, 594; Trial 140(2), 142; Ven & Pur 33, 34; Witn 125, 126, 139(1).

Hargiss v. State, TexCrimApp, 360 SW2d 881, 172 TexCrim 531.—Crim Law 1038.1(3.1), 1172.7; Int Liq 236(7).

Hargiss v. State, TexCrimApp, 339 SW2d 538, 170 TexCrim 164.—Int Liq 223(1), 236(3).

Hargrave v. Fibreboard Corp., CA5 (Tex), 710 F2d 1154. —Corp 1.4(1), 1.4(5), 1.7(2); Fed Civ Proc 2559; Fed Cts 34, 82, 96, 617.

Hargrave v. Lefever, TexApp–San Antonio, 82 SW3d 524. —App & E 937(1); Child C 662; Judgm 584, 713(2).

Hargrave; Regent Care Center Of San Antonio II, Limited Partnership v., TexApp–San Antonio, 202 SW3d 807.—Action 6; App & E 19; Pretrial Proc 502, 508, 518.

Hargrave; Sands Motel v., TexCivApp–Texarkana, 358 SW2d 670, ref nre.—App & E 302(5); Contracts 280(3); Trial 215, 350.4(1), 365.1(5).

Hargrave v. State, TexApp–Houston (1 Dist), 10 SW3d 355, publication ordered, and reh den, and petition for discretionary review refused.—Crim Law 273.1(1), 273.1(2), 275, 1023(3), 1158(1).

Hargrave v. TXU Corp., NDTex, 392 FSupp2d 785.—Fed Civ Proc 103.7; Labor & Emp 534, 678, 699.

Hargrave v. U.S., CA5 (Tex), 242 F2d 752.—Game 9.

Hargrave v. Vaughn, Tex, 18 SW 695, 82 Tex 347.—Prod Liab 46.2.

Hargrave; Wild v., TexCivApp–San Antonio, 565 SW2d 558, dism.—Contracts 24; Evid 417(9), 417(12), 448, 455, 460(3); Frds St of 110(0.5), 110(1), 113(1), 113(3), 118(2).

Hargraves v. Armco Foods, Inc., TexApp–Austin, 894 SW2d 546.—Judgm 181(7), 185(2); Lim of Act 74(1); Mental H 3.1.

Hargraves v. Foodland, TexApp–Austin, 894 SW2d 546. See Hargraves v. Armco Foods, Inc.

Hargraves v. State, TexApp–Dallas, 738 SW2d 743, petition for discretionary review refused.—Crim Law 369.2(1), 371(1), 371(9), 1159.2(7), 1159.2(9); Rape 51(1).

Hargrove, In re, CCA5 (Tex), 96 F2d 168.—Bankr 2184, 2189, 3773, 3779; Fed Cts 522.

Hargrove; Calhoun v., CA5 (Tex), 312 F3d 730, on remand 2003 WL 292140, aff 71 FedAppx 371, cert den 124 SCt 1612, 541 US 908, 158 LEd2d 253.—Civil R 1304, 1395(7), 1463; Const Law 3894, 4823; Fed Civ Proc 657.5(1), 1829, 1835; Fed Cts 776; Sent & Pun 1532, 1533, 1546.

Hargrove; Calhoun v., CA5 (Tex), 71 FedAppx 371, cert den 124 SCt 1612, 541 US 908, 158 LEd2d 253.—Civil R 1454, 1463.

Hargrove v. City of Rotan, TexCivApp–Eastland, 553 SW2d 246.—Mun Corp 747(1).

Hargrove v. Cornett Estate, TexCivApp–San Antonio, 292 SW2d 666, ref nre.—Chat Mtg 148; Judgm 185.1(2); Notice 15.

Hargrove v. Denno, TexApp–San Antonio, 40 SW3d 714. —App & E 946; Health 804, 809.

Hargrove v. Edmont Hotel Co., TexCivApp–Beaumont, 125 SW2d 415.—Frds St of 56(6), 131(1), 140; Land & Ten 46, 48(1); Plead 189.

Hargrove; Faggett v., TexApp–Houston (1 Dist), 921 SW2d 274.—App & E 5, 398.1; Judgm 17(1), 17(9), 162(0.5), 162(2); Proc 133, 135, 152.

Hargrove; First Nat. Bank of Atlanta v., TexCivApp– Texarkana, 503 SW2d 856.—App & E 624; Banks 153; Bills & N 183, 237, 245; Courts 107; Guar 71; Princ & A 177(1).

Hargrove; Herfort v., TexCivApp–Austin, 606 SW2d 359, ref nre.—Venue 2.

Hargrove; Hopper v., TexCivApp–Texarkana, 154 SW2d 978, writ refused.—Lim of Act 127(2.1), 127(12).

Hargrove v. Insurance Inv. Corp., Tex, 176 SW2d 744, 142 Tex 111, conformed to 179 SW2d 383, writ refused wom.—App & E 76(1), 80(3).

Hargrove; Insurance Inv. Corp. v., TexCivApp–San Antonio, 179 SW2d 383, writ refused wom.—App & E 286, 756, 761; Corp 121(4), 121(5); Trial 143.

Hargrove; Insurance Inv. Corp. v., TexCivApp–San Antonio, 171 SW2d 384, rev 176 SW2d 744, 142 Tex 111, conformed to 179 SW2d 383, writ refused wom.—Action 6; App & E 66, 76(1), 80(1), 802; Decl Judgm 1.

Hargrove v. Koepke, TexCivApp–San Antonio, 320 SW2d 53.—Plead 111.33, 111.34.

Hargrove v. Koepke, TexCivApp–Eastland, 210 SW2d 434.—App & E 302(6), 1177(1); Plead 111.3, 111.8, 111.38; Trial 352.4(2); Venue 8.5(3).

Hargrove; McLean v., TexComApp, 162 SW2d 954, 139 Tex 236.—Evid 210; Ex & Ad 44; Partners 245(1); Trusts 103(5), 138.

Hargrove; McLean v., TexCivApp–Texarkana, 144 SW2d 1021, rev 162 SW2d 954, 139 Tex 236.—Evid 210, 272; Pretrial Proc 61.

Hargrove; Morris v., TexCivApp–Austin, 351 SW2d 666, ref nre.—App & E 1041(2); Judgm 190; Libel 38(3); Mal Pros 16, 34.

Hargrove; Oakley v., TexCivApp–Beaumont, 125 SW2d 403.—Venue 8.5(2), 8.5(3).

Hargrove v. Powell, TexApp–San Antonio, 648 SW2d 372. —Corp 431; Sales 418(1), 420.

Hargrove; Rodriguez v., TexApp–San Antonio, 673 SW2d 702.—App & E 1061.4; Libel 123(8).

Hargrove v. State, TexCrimApp, 579 SW2d 238.—Crim Law 1037.1(1); Sent & Pun 308; Sod 6.

Hargrove v. State, TexCrimApp, 501 SW2d 878.—Assault 96(7); Homic 908, 1387.

Hargrove v. State, TexCrimApp, 215 SW2d 887, 152 TexCrim 536.—Crim Law 1087.1(2).

Hargrove v. State, TexApp–Fort Worth, 162 SW3d 313, petition for discretionary review refused.—Crim Law 412.1(4), 412.2(4), 412.2(5), 414, 517.2(2), 641.3(3), 641.3(4), 641.3(6), 1036.1(5), 1134(3), 1153(1), 1158(4), 1169.12.

Hargrove v. State, TexApp–San Antonio, 211 SW3d 379, petition for discretionary review refused.—Controlled Subs 26, 27, 30, 79, 80; Crim Law 338(7), 369.2(3.1), 369.2(7), 1144.13(2.1), 1153(1), 1159.2(1), 1159.2(2), 1169.1(1); Disorderly C 9.

Hargrove v. State, TexApp–Corpus Christi, 774 SW2d 771, petition for discretionary review refused.—Autos 355(6); Const Law 2600; Crim Law 1134(3).

Hargrove v. State, TexApp–Houston (14 Dist), 40 SW3d 556, reh overr, and petition for discretionary review refused.—Autos 316, 349(2.1), 349(3), 349(17), 349.5(3); Const Law 4509(19); Crim Law 394.6(5), 1026.10(4), 1134(3), 1144.12, 1158(4); Statut 188.

Hargrove v. Texas Emp. Ins. Ass'n, TexCivApp–Amarillo, 332 SW2d 121.—App & E 499(4), 969; Trial 273; Work Comp 1926.

Hargrove v. Trinity Universal Ins. Co., Tex, 256 SW2d 73, 152 Tex 243.—Work Comp 52, 1919, 1930, 1942.

Hargrove; Trinity Universal Ins. Co. v., TexCivApp–Amarillo, 256 SW2d 966, rev 256 SW2d 73, 152 Tex 243.—Damag 221(5.1); Work Comp 1942, 1975.

Hargrove v. Underwriters at Lloyd's, London, SDTex, 937 FSupp 595.—Const Law 3964; Courts 12(2.25); Evid 75; Fed Civ Proc 1742(1), 1828, 1831, 1835; Fed Cts 73, 76, 76.5, 76.10, 79, 96; Intern Law 10.9, 10.11.

Hargrove v. U.S., CCA5 (Tex), 139 F2d 1014, cert den 64 SCt 937, 321 US 797, 88 LEd 1085.—Crim Law 1160.

Hargrove; Villa v., TexApp–San Antonio, 110 SW3d 74, review den.—App & E 766; Const Law 245(1), 3754, 4422; Courts 100(1); Health 804, 809.

Hargus v. First Nat. Bank in Port Lavaca, SDTex, 666 FSupp 111, aff 835 F2d 286.—Banks 521.1.

Haring v. Bay Rock Corp., TexApp–San Antonio, 773 SW2d 676.—Contrib 6; Indem 30(1), 30(5), 61, 67.

Hariri; Ramirez v., TexApp–Dallas, 165 SW3d 912.—App & E 893(1), 1010.1(1); Const Law 3962, 3964; Corp 1.4(1), 1.6(9), 1.6(13), 1.7(2); Courts 12(2.1), 12(2.5), 12(2.20), 35, 39.

Harjean Co.; 600 California Corp. v., NDTex, 284 FSupp 843.—Corp 584; Courts 508(1), 508(2.1); Evid 10(1), 12, 20(2); Fed Cts 373, 417; Inj 26(3), 26(5), 128(2), 147.

Harjo; Aetna Cas. & Sur. Co. v., TexApp–Beaumont, 766 SW2d 583.—Work Comp 2247.

Harken Exploration; Rice v., NDTex, 89 FSupp2d 820.—Environ Law 437, 438.

Harken Exploration Co.; Rice v., CA5 (Tex), 250 F3d 264, reh en banc den 263 F3d 167.—Environ Law 437, 441; Fed Cts 776.

Harken Exploration Co. v. Sphere Drake Ins. PLC, CA5 (Tex), 261 F3d 466, reh den.—Fed Civ Proc 2470, 2470.1, 2501, 2533.1, 2543; Fed Cts 372, 382.1, 383, 390, 412.1, 776, 830, 871; Insurance 1713, 1822, 1823, 1832(1), 2264, 2265, 2275, 2278(1), 2278(17), 2325, 2914, 2915, 2922(1), 2934(2), 2939; Interest 31.

Harken Oil & Gas, Inc. v. Sharp, TexApp–Austin, 873 SW2d 750.—Tax 2153, 2540.

Harker v. Coastal Engineering, Inc., TexApp–Corpus Christi, 672 SW2d 517, ref nre.—App & E 994(2), 995, 1004(8), 1070(2); Autos 244(12), 246(39.1), 246(42); Evid 588; New Tr 47; Trial 304; Witn 345(1), 345(2).

Harker Heights, Tex., City of; Collins v., USTex, 112 SCt 1061, 503 US 115, 117 LEd2d 261.—Civil R 1027, 1031, 1126, 1343, 1345, 1352(5), 1395(8); Const Law

Harker Heights, Tex., City of; Collins v., CA5 (Tex), 916 F2d 284, cert gr 111 SCt 1579, 499 US 958, 113 LEd2d 644, aff 112 SCt 1061, 503 US 115, 117 LEd2d 261.—Civil R 1126, 1343, 1351(1).

Harker Heights, Tex., City of, v. Sun Meadows Land, Ltd., TexApp–Austin, 830 SW2d 313. See City of Harker Heights, Tex. v. Sun Meadows Land, Ltd.

Harkey v. deWetter, CA5 (Tex), 443 F2d 828, cert den 92 SCt 109, 404 US 858, 30 LEd2d 100.—Mun Corp 604; Searches 79.

Harkey; Fry v., TexCivApp–San Antonio, 141 SW2d 662, writ dism, correct.—App & E 609, 846(5), 849(1), 927(7); Frds St of 129(3); Lim of Act 44(1); Quiet T 44(3), 47(1); Spec Perf 105(2); Trial 141, 177; Waters 156(1), 156(6), 156(7), 156(9).

Harkey v. Lackey, TexCivApp–Austin, 259 SW2d 641, ref nre.—Hus & W 254, 274(1); Wills 781.

Harkey v. State, TexCrimApp, 251 SW2d 412.—Crim Law 1091(14), 1092.11(3).

Harkey v. State, TexCrimApp, 150 SW2d 808, 142 TexCrim 32.—Crim Law 404.55, 829(1), 1038.1(5), 1038.3; Int Liq 239(7); Searches 191, 199.

Harkey v. State, TexApp–Austin, 785 SW2d 876.—Crim Law 641.3(4), 713, 719(1), 720(5), 726; Jury 105(4), 107, 131(1), 131(2), 131(4), 131(13), 131(15.1), 131(17), 149.

Harkey; Taylor v., TexCivApp–Austin, 145 SW2d 625.—Wills 692(1).

Harkey; Territo v., TexCivApp–Waco, 249 SW2d 251, ref nre.—Costs 91; Princ & A 124(1); Sales 123.

Harkey v. Texas Emp. Ins. Ass'n, Tex, 208 SW2d 919, 146 Tex 504.—Trial 1; Work Comp 1297, 1920, 1929.

Harkey; Texas Emp. Ins. Ass'n v., TexCivApp–El Paso, 208 SW2d 915, aff 208 SW2d 919, 146 Tex 504.—Damag 221(5.1); Trial 351.5(8), 366; Work Comp 1297, 1916, 1920, 1968(1).

Harkins; Alamo Cas. Co. v., TexCivApp–Galveston, 252 SW2d 1014, ref nre.—App & E 931(3); Insurance 2706(3).

Harkins; Christensen v., TexApp–Fort Worth, 740 SW2d 69.—App & E 79(1), 80(6); Courts 202(5); Decl Judgm 392.1.

Harkins v. Crews, TexApp–San Antonio, 907 SW2d 51, reh den, and writ den.—App & E 930(1), 999(1), 999(2), 1003(7); Courts 201, 488(1); Damag 94; Decl Judgm 2, 241, 273, 341.1, 342; Plead 36(1); Wills 171, 173, 176, 184(1), 186, 206, 290, 306, 310, 335, 404, 405, 412.1, 415, 416.

Harkins v. Dever Nursing Home, TexApp–Houston (14 Dist), 999 SW2d 571.—App & E 766.

Harkins v. Indiana Lumbermens Mut. Ins. Co. of Indianapolis, Ind., TexCivApp–Galveston, 234 SW2d 430.—False Pret 7(5); Insurance 1851, 2706(1), 2706(3).

Harkins; Missouri Pac. R. Co. v., TexCivApp–Eastland, 346 SW2d 910, ref nre.—App & E 1170.7, 1170.10; Damag 221(2.1), 221(4); Evid 129(1).

Harkins; Mosley v., TexCivApp–Amarillo, 147 SW2d 309.—App & E 1050.1(11); Evid 213(1); Mal Pros 47, 59(1), 60(3), 71(1); Trial 191(5), 260(6).

Harkins v. Mosley, TexCivApp–Amarillo, 134 SW2d 706.—New Tr 44(2); Trial 349(1), 355(1).

Harkins v. State, TexApp–Fort Worth, 782 SW2d 20.—Controlled Subs 30; Crim Law 469.2, 488, 1036.6, 1147; Searches 47.1; Sent & Pun 2016, 2019, 2020, 2021, 2024.

Harkins; State ex rel. Ownby v., TexApp–Dallas, 705 SW2d 788.—Crim Law 261(1); Double J 56.1; Mand 4(4), 61.

Harkins v. State on Behalf of Mason, TexApp–Houston (14 Dist), 773 SW2d 401.—App & E 870(2); Child S 390, 391, 459; Const Law 2759; Courts 26; Judgm 183, 185.1(1).

Harkins; Underwriters at Lloyds, London v., TexCivApp–Hous (14 Dist), 427 SW2d 659, ref nre.—Contracts

HARLAN

143(3), 152; Insurance 1808, 1822, 2095, 3154, 3160(2), 3167, 3168.

Harkins; Ware v., TexCivApp–Dallas, 249 SW2d 261, ref nre.—Chat Mtg 280.

Harkins; Ware v., TexCivApp–Waco, 228 SW2d 537, ref nre.—Evid 434(8); Refer 99(6); Trial 399.

Harkins & Co.; Robinson v., Tex, 711 SW2d 619.—Evid 272; Pretrial Proc 373.

Harkins & Co.; Robinson v., TexApp–Corpus Christi, 704 SW2d 554, rev 711 SW2d 619.—Autos 247; Evid 272; Pretrial Proc 414; Trial 365.1(1).

Harkins & Co.; Wachtendorf v., TexCivApp–San Antonio, 518 SW2d 599.—App & E 302(1), 1170.1, 1170.6; Trial 306.

Harkins & Munoz; Day v., TexApp–Houston (1 Dist), 961 SW2d 278, reh overr.—Atty & C 112; Health 576, 611, 614, 615, 668, 709(1).

Harkinson; Trammell Crow Co. No. 60 v., Tex, 944 SW2d 631.—Brok 43(2); Estop 85; Torts 251.

Harkinson v. Trammell Crow Co. No. 60, TexApp–Dallas, 915 SW2d 28, writ gr, aff in part, rev in part 944 SW2d 631.—App & E 169; Brok 1, 43(2), 43(3), 66, 74; Consp 8; Frds St of 144; Torts 242, 243.

Harkleroad v. State, TexCrimApp, 257 SW2d 438.—Crim Law 1090.1(1).

Harkless; Safeway Stores, Inc. v., TexCivApp–Tyler, 601 SW2d 534, ref nre.—App & E 930(3), 989; Neglig 1104(6), 1595, 1670.

Harkless v. Sweeny Independent School Dist., CA5 (Tex), 427 F2d 319, cert den 91 SCt 451, 400 US 991, 27 LEd2d 439, on remand 388 FSupp 738, aff in part, rev in part 554 F2d 1353, cert den 98 SCt 507, 434 US 966, 54 LEd2d 452, on remand 466 FSupp 457, aff and remanded 608 F2d 594.—Civil R 1346, 1349, 1359; Courts 91(0.5); Jury 13(12).

Harkless v. Sweeny Independent School Dist., SDTex, 466 FSupp 457, aff and remanded 608 F2d 594.— Interest 39(2.20); Schools 144(3), 144(4).

Harkless v. Sweeny Independent School Dist., SDTex, 278 FSupp 632, rev 427 F2d 319, cert den 91 SCt 451, 400 US 991, 27 LEd2d 439, on remand 388 FSupp 738, aff in part, rev in part 554 F2d 1353, cert den 98 SCt 507, 434 US 966, 54 LEd2d 452, on remand 466 FSupp 457, aff and remanded 608 F2d 594.—Action 53(1); Civil R 1430; Equity 43, 46; Fed Civ Proc 85, 673, 1962; Inj 106; Jury 9, 13(1), 14(1.5), 14(11), 14.5(2.1), 14.5(4), 25(6), 28(1), 28(17), 31.

Harkless v. Sweeny Independent School Dist. of Sweeny, Tex., CA5 (Tex), 554 F2d 1353, cert den 98 SCt 507, 434 US 966, 54 LEd2d 452, on remand 466 FSupp 457, aff and remanded 608 F2d 594.—Civil R 1137; Fed Civ Proc 392, 843; Fed Cts 858; Lim of Act 127(3).

Harkless v. Sweeny Independent School Dist. of Sweeny, Texas, SDTex, 388 FSupp 738, aff in part, rev in part 554 F2d 1353, cert den 98 SCt 507, 434 US 966, 54 LEd2d 452, on remand 466 FSupp 457, aff and remanded 608 F2d 594.—Civil R 1027, 1132, 1133, 1349, 1359, 1390, 1395(8), 1401, 1405, 1421, 1470; Const Law 3869, 4159, 4201, 4202; Fed Civ Proc 281, 392, 839.1, 842, 2252; Fed Cts 219.1, 268.1, 270, 425, 950; Lim of Act 21(3), 39(2); Offic 114, 116; Schools 147.2(2), 147.38, 147.44, 147.47.

Harkless v. Sweeny Independent School Dist. of Sweeny, Tex., SDTex, 300 FSupp 794, rev 427 F2d 319, cert den 91 SCt 451, 400 US 991, 27 LEd2d 439, on remand 388 FSupp 738, aff in part, rev in part 554 F2d 1353, cert den 98 SCt 507, 434 US 966, 54 LEd2d 452, on remand 466 FSupp 457, aff and remanded 608 F2d 594. —Civil R 1376(10); Fed Civ Proc 1837.1; Fed Cts 176, 225.

Harkless v. Sweeny Independent School Dist., Sweeny, Tex., CA5 (Tex), 608 F2d 594.—Civil R 1478, 1487, 1488, 1490; Fed Civ Proc 2742.5; Fed Cts 830.

Harkness, In re, CA5 (Tex), 189 FedAppx 311.—Bankr 2233(3).

Harkness v. Employers Nat. Ins. Co., Tex, 502 SW2d 670.—Venue 7.5(2).

Harkness; Employers Nat. Ins. Co. v., TexCivApp–El Paso, 497 SW2d 645, ref nre 502 SW2d 670.—Plead 45, 111.39(4), 111.42(6); Venue 7.5(2), 7.5(3).

Harkness v. Harkness, TexApp–Beaumont, 709 SW2d 376, dism.—Child C 659; Divorce 85, 105.

Harkness; Harkness v., TexApp–Beaumont, 709 SW2d 376, dism.—Child C 659; Divorce 85, 105.

Harkness v. McQueen, TexCivApp–Beaumont, 232 SW2d 629.—Hus & W 262.1(2), 262.2, 264(2), 264(4), 270(9), 272(5); Trial 140(2); Trusts 357(2); Ven & Pur 226(1), 228(1), 244.

Harkness v. McQueen, TexCivApp–Galveston, 207 SW2d 676.—Action 60; Courts 484, 488(1); Divorce 57, 151, 249.1, 322; Hus & W 249(2.1); Judgm 226, 736; Venue 46.

Harkness v. State, TexApp–Fort Worth, 139 SW3d 4, reh overr.—Weap 17(4).

Harkrider; Freeman v., TexCivApp–Amarillo, 320 SW2d 238.—Autos 168(1), 172(5.1), 201(2); Evid 474(15).

Harkrider; Manhattan Life Ins. Co. v., Tex, 402 SW2d 511.—Insurance 3013.

Harkrider; Manhattan Life Ins. Co. v., TexCivApp–Austin, 396 SW2d 207, ref nre 402 SW2d 511.—Insurance 2445, 2985, 3001, 3015; Trial 352.1(4).

Harkrider v. Morales, TexApp–San Antonio, 686 SW2d 712.—Divorce 322; Hus & W 247, 272(4).

Harkrider; U.S. v., CA5 (Tex), 88 F3d 1408, cert den 117 SCt 446, 519 US 987, 136 LEd2d 342.—Commerce 82.50; Weap 3.

Harkrider Distributing Co.; Differential Development-1994, Ltd. v., SDTex, 470 FSupp2d 727.—Environ Law 444, 445(1), 445(3), 447; Fed Cts 14.1, 18.

Harlan, In re, BkrtcyWDTex, 32 BR 91.—Bankr 2252.1, 2766; Home 76.

Harlan; City of Carrollton v., TexApp–Dallas, 180 SW3d 894, reh overr, and review den.—App & E 863; Courts 35; Em Dom 293(1); Mun Corp 723, 837; Plead 104(1).

Harlan; Hankins v., TexCivApp–Waco, 114 SW2d 588, writ dism.—App & E 1172(1); Autos 201(9), 244(61), 247; Damag 19.

Harlan; Jones v., TexCivApp–El Paso, 109 SW2d 251, dism.—Mun Corp 63.15(1), 155, 159(1).

Harlan; Manning v., TexCivApp–El Paso, 122 SW2d 704, dism.—Atty & C 104; Mun Corp 147, 149(4), 160, 218(11); Offic 41.

Harlan; Petroleum Cas. Co. v., TexCivApp–Eastland, 352 SW2d 342.—Evid 121(1), 123(1); Work Comp 532, 1385, 1526, 1927.

Harlan; Reed v., TexCivApp–Waco, 103 SW2d 236, writ refused.—Ex & Ad 25, 26(2), 29(1), 29(4); Judgm 457, 475.

Harlan v. State, TexCrimApp, 430 SW2d 213.—Autos 415; Crim Law 1130(4); Ind & Inf 10.1(1).

Harlan v. State, TexCrimApp, 416 SW2d 422.—Crim Law 656(3), 663, 1137(5).

Harlan v. State, TexCrimApp, 310 SW2d 78, 165 TexCrim 562.—Crim Law 1081(6).

Harlan v. State, TexCrimApp, 134 SW2d 289, 138 TexCrim 47.—Crim Law 1020.

Harlan v. State, TexApp–Tyler, 975 SW2d 387, petition for discretionary review refused.—Crim Law 577.10(1), 577.10(2), 577.10(3), 577.10(9), 577.10(10), 577.15(1), 577.15(4), 577.16(4), 577.16(8).

Harlan; Texas Indem. Ins. Co. v., TexCivApp–Eastland, 236 SW2d 564, dism.—App & E 901, 920(2), 1032(1); Pretrial Proc 724.

Harlan; U.S. v., CA5 (Tex), 130 F3d 1152.—Crim Law 273(4.1); Weap 6.

Harlan v. U.S., CA5 (Tex), 409 F2d 904.—Int Rev 3763, 3768, 3769.

Harlan v. Vetter, TexApp–Eastland, 732 SW2d 390, ref nre.—Deeds 5, 9, 26, 36, 38(1), 93; Mines 55(2).

Harland; Blackmon v., TexApp–Tyler, 656 SW2d 239, dism.—Elections 269; Quo W 1; Schools 53(5).

Harlandale Bank; Madden v., TexCivApp–Beaumont, 574 SW2d 590, ref nre.—Set-Off 60.

Harlandale Independent School Dist. v. Cornyn, TexApp–Austin, 25 SW3d 328, review den.—App & E 846(5), 852; Courts 89; Records 57; Trial 392(2); Witn 198(1), 200.

Harlandale Independent School Dist. v. Hernandez, TexApp–San Antonio, 994 SW2d 257.—App & E 70(3); Labor & Emp 854; Plead 104(1).

Harlandale Independent School Dist. v. Rodriguez, TexApp–San Antonio, 121 SW3d 88.—App & E 837(1), 893(1), 911.3; Courts 39; Plead 111.36, 111.37; Schools 47, 115, 147.4, 147.44, 147.51.

Harle v. Krchnak, TexCivApp–Hous (1 Dist), 422 SW2d 810, ref nre.—Health 624, 631, 666, 786, 787, 817, 818, 821(2), 821(3), 821(4), 823(5), 825, 832; Neglig 384, 386, 387, 1693.

Harleaux v. Harleaux, TexApp–Dallas, 154 SW3d 925.—Divorce 222, 252.2, 254(2), 269(13); Home 90; Judgm 855(1).

Harleaux; Harleaux v., TexApp–Dallas, 154 SW3d 925.—Divorce 222, 252.2, 254(2), 269(13); Home 90; Judgm 855(1).

Harlem Sav. Bank v. Standard Fire Ins. Co., TexCivApp–Hous (14 Dist), 612 SW2d 710.—Insurance 3044, 3072, 3449.

Harlen v. Pfeffer, TexApp–San Antonio, 693 SW2d 543.—App & E 1171(3); Frds St of 125(3); Judgm 18(2), 112, 143(3), 143(7), 145(2), 145(4), 163; Receivers 36; Trusts 91.

Harlequin Inc.; Southwest Software, Inc. v., CAFed (Tex), 226 F3d 1280.—Courts 96(7); Fed Civ Proc 2313; Fed Cts 629, 764, 765, 825.1, 842, 844, 845; Pat 126, 312(6), 314(5), 314(6), 324.1, 324.60; Statut 188.

Harless v. Bichsel, TexCivApp–San Antonio, 327 SW2d 791.—Mun Corp 185(1), 185(9).

Harless; Brosseau v., TexApp–Dallas, 697 SW2d 56.—Execution 158(1), 158(2); Mand 28, 29, 168(4); Trial 9(1).

Harless; Johnson v., Tex, 651 SW2d 259.—Atty & C 57.

Harless; Merritt v., TexApp–Dallas, 685 SW2d 708.—Courts 207.4(2); Judgm 822(1), 822(3), 823; Mand 141.

Harless; NCF, Inc. v., TexApp–Dallas, 846 SW2d 79.—Judges 25(1), 51(2), 54; Mand 4(1).

Harless v. Niles, TexApp–San Antonio, 100 SW3d 390.—Autos 187(6), 238(2); Judgm 185.3(1); Mun Corp 747(3); Offic 114, 116; States 203.

Harless; Schultz v., TexCivApp–El Paso, 271 SW2d 696.—Damag 112, 174(3); Trial 62(2), 350.6(1).

Harless v. State, TexCrimApp, 473 SW2d 519.—Crim Law 394.4(11).

Harley v. State, TexCrimApp, 165 SW2d 464, 145 TexCrim 26.—Autos 355(13).

Harley-Davidson Motor Co., Inc. v. Young, TexApp–Houston (14 Dist), 720 SW2d 211.—Antitrust 369; App & E 173(2); Judgm 185.1(4), 185.2(9), 185.3(18); Sales 442(5), 442(6).

Harleysville Mut. Ins. Co. v. Frierson, TexCivApp–Hous (14 Dist), 455 SW2d 370.—Work Comp 52, 962, 983, 986, 993, 998, 999, 1001, 1115, 1130, 1135, 1258, 1262.

Harlin; Mooney v., Tex, 622 SW2d 83.—Lim of Act 100(1), 100(13); Notice 6, 14; Wills 206, 423.

Harlin v. Mooney, TexCivApp–Dallas, 604 SW2d 199, rev 622 SW2d 83.—Contracts 328(1); Evid 54; Fraud 38, 64(1); Judgm 181(7); Notice 14; Wills 423.

Harling v. State, TexApp–San Antonio, 899 SW2d 9, reh den, and petition for discretionary review refused.—Bail 51; Crim Law 273.1(5), 274(3.1), 274(9), 641.13(1), 641.13(2.1), 641.13(6), 990.1, 1072, 1081(2); Rape 17; Sent & Pun 1117.

Harlingen Canning Co. v. Commodity Credit Corp., CA5 (Tex), 193 F2d 176.—U S 53(7), 53(17).

Harlingen Canning Co. v. Commodity Credit Corp., SDTex, 93 FSupp 45, aff 193 F2d 176.—Fed Cts 84; U S 53(7).

Harlingen, City of, v. Avila, TexApp–Corpus Christi, 942 SW2d 49. See City of Harlingen v. Avila.

Harlingen, City of; Edmiston v., TexCivApp–San Antonio, 347 SW2d 742, ref nre.—Bound 54(2); Com Law 9; Dedi 19(1), 19(5), 34, 35(5), 47.

Harlingen, City of; Gonzalez v., TexApp–Corpus Christi, 814 SW2d 109, writ den.—Contracts 332(2); Judgm 185(2), 185(6), 185.3(2); Lim of Act 95(16), 179(2), 182(2); Plead 1, 34(3), 48.

Harlingen, City of, v. Lucio, TexApp–Corpus Christi, 770 SW2d 7. See City of Harlingen v. Lucio.

Harlingen, City of; Muniz v., CA5 (Tex), 247 F3d 607.—Const Law 4173(2); Mun Corp 218(10).

Harlingen, City of; Scroggins v., Tex, 114 SW2d 853, 131 Tex 237.—App & E 1114.

Harlingen, City of; Scroggins v., Tex, 112 SW2d 1035, 131 Tex 237, set aside on reh 114 SW2d 853, 131 Tex 237.—Mun Corp 734, 745.5, 747(1), 748; Pub Amuse 76.

Harlingen, City of; State ex rel. Winell v., TexCivApp–San Antonio, 324 SW2d 248, ref nre.—Const Law 190, 225(2), 3483, 4056.

Harlingen, City of; Tamayo v., TexCivApp–Corpus Christi, 618 SW2d 102.—Mun Corp 743.

Harlingen, City of, v. Vega, TexApp–Corpus Christi, 951 SW2d 25. See City of Harlingen v. Vega.

Harlingen Consol. Independent School Dist.; De Leon v., TexCivApp–Corpus Christi, 552 SW2d 922.—Const Law 242.2(6), 3362; Inj 108; Schools 61, 153; Statut 184.

Harlingen Consol. Independent School Dist.; Luna v., TexApp–Corpus Christi, 821 SW2d 442, writ den.—Schools 89.13(1), 89.13(4).

Harlingen Home Health Agency, Inc. v. Diemer, TexCivApp–Hous (14 Dist), 483 SW2d 551.—App & E 712; Judgm 181(11), 186; Records 7.

Harlingen Independent School Dist. v. Dunlap, TexCivApp–San Antonio, 146 SW2d 235, writ refused.—Const Law 4138(1); Equity 65(2); Schools 103(1); Tax 2160.

Harlingen Irrigation Dist. Cameron County No. 1 v. Caprock Communications Corp., TexApp–Corpus Christi, 49 SW3d 520, reh overr, and review den.—Decl Judgm 392.1, 393; Dedi 46, 55, 57; Deeds 97, 143; Em Dom 2(1.1), 85, 318; High 85, 88, 165; Mun Corp 648, 703(1); Tel 788, 800; Tresp 24, 25; Waters 183.5, 242.

Harlingen Mall Co.; Wright Way Const. Co., Inc. v., TexApp–Corpus Christi, 799 SW2d 415, writ den.—App & E 216(1), 230, 231(9), 242(1), 548(6), 1067, 1173(3); Contracts 322(4), 353(8); Estop 120; Princ & S 65; Trial 278, 279, 349(1), 350.2.

Harlingen Nat. Bank; Bank of Southwest N.A., Brownsville v., TexApp–Corpus Christi, 662 SW2d 113.—App & E 71(3), 852, 863, 954(1); Inj 16, 17, 135, 138.9, 151.

Harlingen Nat. Bank; Duval County Ranch Co. v., TexApp–Corpus Christi, 577 SW2d 563.—App & E 553(1), 757(1), 907(3), 907(4), 1032(1).

Harlingen Nat. Bank; Quintanilla v., TexCivApp–Corpus Christi, 612 SW2d 674, ref nre.—Cons Cred 18; Lim of Act 59(1).

Harlingen Nat. Bank; Sechrist-Hall Co. v., TexCivApp–Austin, 368 SW2d 155, ref nre.—Chat Mtg 219.

Harlingen State Bank; Oak Forest Bank of Houston v., TexApp–Corpus Christi, 656 SW2d 589.—Banks 32, 152, 218.

Harlow; Ford v., TexCivApp–Fort Worth, 439 SW2d 682, ref nre.—Gifts 18(1), 31(1); Trover 4; Trusts 69.

Harlow v. Giles, TexApp–Eastland, 132 SW3d 641, review den.—Adv Poss 13, 16(1), 19, 20, 22, 24, 31, 34, 37, 57,

HARMON

86, 88, 114(1), 115(1); App & E 994(3), 1008.1(2), 1010.1(1), 1012.1(3); Evid 588; Trial 382.

Harlow v. Hayes, TexApp–Amarillo, 991 SW2d 24, review den.—Anim 48, 49; App & E 1048(6); Autos 178, 245(21); Evid 558(11); Motions 58; Statut 181(1), 212.6, 212.7.

Harlow; Leyendecker v., TexCivApp–Galveston, 189 SW2d 706, writ refused wom.—Abate & R 81; App & E 186, 216(7), 218.2(1), 232(3), 870(3), 1002, 1170.7; Autos 173(5), 244(14); Damag 49, 130.1, 134(1), 139, 221(5.1); Evid 474(19); Plead 110; Trial 219.

Harlow; McMillen Feeds, Inc. of Tex. v., TexCivApp–Austin, 405 SW2d 123, ref nre.—Anim 44; App & E 1078(1); Damag 67, 139, 208(1), 221(2.1); Evid 318(1), 361, 571(1), 587, 596(1); Interest 39(1); Prod Liab 45; Release 2; Sales 267, 274; Torts 134; Trial 352.9.

Harlow; Norwood v., TexCivApp–Fort Worth, 429 SW2d 670, ref nre.—App & E 927(7); Wills 58(2), 289, 293(1), 324(4).

Harlow v. Southern Farm Bureau Cas. Ins. Co., TexCivApp–Austin, 439 SW2d 365, ref nre.—Evid 571(7); Insurance 2521, 3374, 3375.

Harlow; Southern Pacific Transp. Co. v., TexApp–Corpus Christi, 729 SW2d 946, writ gr, and writ withdrawn, writ den Port Terminal RR Ass'n v. Harlow, 745 SW2d 320.—App & E 901; Corp 498; Damag 100, 216(4); Labor & Emp 2824; New Tr 162(1); Princ & A 159(1); R R 17, 22(1), 22(3), 25.

Harlow v. Swift & Co., TexCivApp–Eastland, 491 SW2d 472, ref nre.—App & E 204(1), 216(1), 237(2), 842(1), 933(1), 1015(5), 1069.1, 1170.7; Costs 42(6); New Tr 157, 163(1); Pretrial Proc 3; Sales 417; Trial 139.1(10), 140(1), 141, 344.

Harlow v. U.S., CA5 (Tex), 301 F2d 361, cert den 83 SCt 25, 371 US 814, 9 LEd2d 56, reh den 83 SCt 204, 371 US 906, 9 LEd2d 167.—Brib 1(1), 11; Consp 43(12), 47(13); Const Law 4565; Crim Law 113, 330, 394.1(3), 402(1), 419(10), 531(3), 569, 573, 575, 576(4), 576(8), 627.9(1), 1166(10.10), 1167(1), 1169.1(9); Double J 136, 151(2), 183.1; Ind & Inf 71.4(3), 121.4; Searches 116, 164; War 32.

Harlow Corp.; Dorchester Gas Producing Co. v., TexApp–Amarillo, 743 SW2d 243, writ den, and writ withdrawn, and reh gr, and writ gr, and vac, and writ withdrawn.—Admin Law 500; App & E 1056.1(4.1), 1064.1(9); Corp 306, 336; Costs 193, 194.40; Damag 221(2.1); Mines 51(3), 51(4), 51(5), 74(5), 92.16, 92.20, 104; Plead 245(6); Trover 72; Venue 50, 84.

Harm v. State, TexCrimApp, 183 SW3d 403.—Crim Law 700(2.1), 700(3), 700(4), 700(6), 700(7).

Harman, In re, BkrtcyNDTex, 243 BR 671.—Bankr 2021.1, 2045, 2234, 2287; Fraud Conv 172(1); Judgm 768(1), 776, 782.

Harman; Braniff Intern. Airways, Inc. v., CA5 (Tex), 202 F2d 928.—Labor & Emp 2845; Work Comp 872, 1927.

Harman; Goodspeed v., NDTex, 39 FSupp2d 787.—Evid 318(7); Statut 230; Tel 1436, 1437, 1451.

Harman; Peavy v., NDTex, 37 FSupp2d 495, aff in part, vac in part, rev in part 221 F3d 158, cert den WFAA–TV, Inc v. Peavy, 121 SCt 2191, 532 US 1051, 149 LEd2d 1023, cert den 121 SCt 2191, 532 US 1051, 149 LEd2d 1023.—Action 18; Commerce 59; Consp 1.1, 13; Const Law 2070, 2134, 2138, 2157; Crim Law 20, 38; Damag 50.10; Fed Civ Proc 2481; Lim of Act 55(1); Tel 1436, 1437, 1440, 1441, 1443, 1448; Torts 253, 340, 341, 346, 350, 357.

Harman; Serna, Inc. v., CA5 (Tex), 742 F2d 186.—Frds St of 127; Sales 384(1), 384(4), 384(7).

Harman v. State, TexApp–Houston (1 Dist), 788 SW2d 193.—Rob 24.15(2).

Harman; United Services Automobile Ass'n v., TexCivApp–San Antonio, 151 SW2d 609, writ dism, correct,

cert den 62 SCt 640, 315 US 807, 86 LEd 1206.—Autos 235(3); Domicile 1; U S 3.

Harmar Bottling Co.; Coca-Cola Co. v., Tex, 218 SW3d 671, reh den.—Antitrust 521, 530, 677, 713, 714, 715, 958, 961, 963(3), 983; Courts 8, 28, 511; Evid 80(1); Intern Law 7; States 5(1); Torts 218, 241, 255.

Harmar Bottling Co.; Coca-Cola Co. v., TexApp–Texarkana, 111 SW2d 287, review gr, rev 218 SW3d 671, reh den.—Antitrust 521, 524, 535, 556, 582, 620, 621, 641, 677, 713, 714, 715, 963(2), 975, 977(2), 977(3), 977(5), 983, 985, 989, 995; App & E 215(1), 230, 930(2), 946, 954(1), 954(2), 971(2), 984(5), 1001(1), 1060.1(1), 1060.1(7); Costs 207, 208; Courts 97(5); Damag 63, 163(2); Evid 535, 536, 546, 555.4(1); Inj 9.

Harmel; Beacon Nat. Ins. Co. v., TexCivApp–Waco, 514 SW2d 480, dism.—Plead 111.18, 111.42(4); Pretrial Proc 481.

Harmes v. Arklatex Corp., Tex, 615 SW2d 177.—App & E 931(3), 1106(4); Interest 39(2.30); Mines 109; Trial 351.2(5), 366.

Harmes; Arklatex Corp. v., TexCivApp–Eastland, 603 SW2d 390, aff in part, rev in part 615 SW2d 177.—App & E 1012.1(9); Trial 352.20.

Harmes v. State, TexApp–San Antonio, 636 SW2d 513, petition for discretionary review refused.—Jury 29(6); Sent & Pun 1373; Stip 5.

Harmon, Matter of, BkrtcyNDTex, 11 BR 162.—Antitrust 402.

Harmon; Alston v., TexCivApp–Galveston, 261 SW2d 199.—Venue 5.3(5).

Harmon; American General Ins. Co. v., TexCivApp–Beaumont, 274 SW2d 741, ref nre.—Evid 265(7); Work Comp 1017, 1020, 1021, 1028.

Harmon; Brazos River Conservation & Reclamation Dist. v., TexCivApp–Eastland, 178 SW2d 281, writ refused wom.—App & E 758.3(1), 946, 1078(1); Em Dom 1, 4, 7, 9, 17, 27, 41, 45, 57, 58, 68, 153, 158, 246(4), 262(5), 300, 307(3), 308; Evid 100, 587; Trial 209, 219, 260(1).

Harmon; Buntion v., TexCrimApp, 827 SW2d 945, reh den.—Crim Law 641.10(1), 641.10(2); Mand 3(3), 12, 61.

Harmon v. City of Dallas, TexCivApp–Dallas, 229 SW2d 825, ref nre.—App & E 282; Mand 73(1), 154(4), 167, 169, 187.4; Plead 228.14, 228.17; Zoning 71.1.

Harmon; Dallas Ry. & Terminal Co. v., TexCivApp–Dallas, 200 SW2d 854, writ refused.—Contrib 5(4), 6.

Harmon v. General Motors Corp., CA5 (Tex), 999 F2d 964, reh den.—Fed Cts 776; Neglig 1037(7), 1045(2), 1045(3), 1706.

Harmon v. Grande Tire Co., Inc., CA5 (Tex), 821 F2d 252.—Autos 244(21), 244(36.1), 247; Damag 51, 208(7); Fed Civ Proc 1856, 2241; Interest 39(2.50).

Harmon v. Harmon, TexApp–Houston (14 Dist), 879 SW2d 213, reh den, and writ den.—Child S 214, 215; Divorce 62(1), 76, 81, 91, 96.1, 143(2), 143(3), 150, 150.1(3), 151, 160, 161, 168, 170; Judgm 126(1), 143(2), 146.

Harmon; Harmon v., TexApp–Houston (14 Dist), 879 SW2d 213, reh den, and writ den.—Child S 214, 215; Divorce 62(1), 76, 81, 91, 96.1, 143(2), 143(3), 150, 150.1(3), 151, 160, 161, 168, 170; Judgm 126(1), 143(2), 146.

Harmon; Hercules v., TexApp–Houston (14 Dist), 864 SW2d 752.—Crim Law 641.10(1), 641.10(2); Mand 3(2.1), 4(3), 10, 61.

Harmon; Lyon v., TexCivApp–San Antonio, 212 SW2d 491.—Brok 43(3), 55(1), 56(3); Courts 90(4).

Harmon; Mayfield v., CA5 (Tex), 941 F2d 346. See Mayfield v. Klevenhagen.

Harmon v. Miller, TexCivApp–Tyler, 530 SW2d 173.—App & E 388, 392, 640.

Harmon v. Overton Refining Co., TexComApp, 110 SW2d 555, 130 Tex 365.—App & E 878(6).

Harmon v. Overton Refining Co., TexComApp, 109 SW2d 457, 130 Tex 365, set aside on reh 110 SW2d 555, 130 Tex 365.—Adv Poss 100(4), 114(2); Partit 8, 9(1); Tresp to T T 4.

Harmon; Overton Refining Co. v., TexCivApp–Amarillo, 81 SW2d 207, rev 109 SW2d 457, 130 Tex 365, set aside on reh 110 SW2d 555, 130 Tex 365, aff 110 SW2d 555, 130 Tex 365.—Adv Poss 43(2), 43(3), 68; App & E 1067; Mines 51(5); Trial 143, 350.3(2.1).

Harmon; Owens v., TexApp–Texarkana, 28 SW3d 177, review den.—Atty & C 112; Judgm 186.

Harmon; Papas v., TexCivApp–Fort Worth, 263 SW2d 269.—Plead 111.3, 111.42(9).

Harmon; Patel v., TexApp–Eastland, 213 SW3d 449.— App & E 946; Health 804, 809.

Harmon v. Schoelpple, TexApp–Houston (14 Dist), 730 SW2d 376.—Divorce 87, 207, 280; Receivers 51.

Harmon v. Sears, Roebuck & Co., TexCivApp–Beaumont, 324 SW2d 92, ref nre.—Labor & Emp 2881, 2883, 2906; Neglig 1575; Trial 350.6(6).

Harmon v. S. H. Kress & Co., SDTex, 78 FSupp 952.— Courts 96(1); Fed Civ Proc 2242; Fed Cts 428; Sales 427.

Harmon v. Sohio Pipeline Co., Tex, 623 SW2d 314, on remand 627 SW2d 498.—App & E 1082(1), 1083(6); Neglig 1621.

Harmon; Sohio Pipeline Co. v., TexApp–Tyler, 627 SW2d 498.—App & E 1001(1); Neglig 1614, 1658.

Harmon; Sohio Pipeline Co. v., TexCivApp–Tyler, 613 SW2d 577, writ gr, rev 623 SW2d 314, on remand 627 SW2d 498.—App & E 1001(1); Ease 64, 69, 71; Evid 241(1); Neglig 1612, 1620.

Harmon v. State, TexCrimApp, 113 SW2d 1240, 134 TexCrim 39.—Int Liq 236(3).

Harmon v. State, TexCrimApp, 100 SW2d 361.—Crim Law 1094(2.1).

Harmon v. State, TexCrimApp, 93 SW2d 437, 130 Tex-Crim 223.—Crim Law 1144.12.

Harmon v. State, TexApp–Beaumont, 951 SW2d 530.— Arrest 63.5(4), 63.5(5), 63.5(7), 63.5(8), 68(2); Crim Law 394.6(5), 1144.12, 1153(1); Searches 13.1, 15, 70.

Harmon v. State, TexApp–Corpus Christi, 649 SW2d 93. —Atty & C 32(4), 42, 112; Crim Law 273.1(4), 516, 538(3).

Harmon v. State, TexApp–Houston (14 Dist), 167 SW3d 610, petition for discretionary review refused.—Crim Law 393(3), 1144.13(2.1), 1144.13(3), 1144.13(6), 1159.2(2), 1159.2(7), 1159.2(8), 1159.2(9), 1159.3(1), 1159.4(1), 1162, 1170.5(5); Rob 24.40; Witn 277(1), 297(1), 300, 305(2).

Harmon v. State, TexApp–Houston (14 Dist), 889 SW2d 521, reh overr, and petition for discretionary review refused.—Afft 11; Crim Law 374, 956(11), 957(3), 959, 1086.13, 1126; False Pret 49(1), 52; Sent & Pun 1060.

Harmon; U.S. v., CA5 (Tex), 156 FedAppx 674.—Crim Law 1166(1); Sent & Pun 736, 2138, 2175.

Harmon; U.S. v., NDTex, 21 FSupp2d 642, aff 202 F3d 265, post-conviction relief den 2001 WL 434914.— Judges 39, 49(1), 50, 51(1), 51(4).

Harmon v. U.S., WDTex, 206 FSupp 225.—Autos 244(34), 244(35), 244(36.1), 244(37), 244(44); Damag 130.1.

Harmon; Williams v., TexApp–Houston (1 Dist), 788 SW2d 192.—Hab Corp 675, 742, 814.

Harmon v. 1401 Elm Street Condominium Ass'n, TexApp–Dallas, 139 SW3d 411, reh overr.—App & E 238(4), 295; Land & Ten 201.

Harmon & Reid v. Quin, TexCivApp–San Antonio, 258 SW2d 441.—Judgm 17(10); Mand 51.

Harmond v. State, TexApp–Houston (1 Dist), 960 SW2d 404.—Controlled Subs 26, 27, 28, 80; Crim Law 1134(1), 1144.13(2.1), 1144.13(5), 1144.13(6), 1159.2(2), 1159.2(7), 1159.2(9).

Harmon Tank Co., Inc.; Guerrero v., TexApp–Amarillo, 55 SW3d 19, review den.—Labor & Emp 26, 936; Sta-

tut 181(1), 181(2), 184, 188, 212.6; Work Comp 195, 204, 2161, 2168.

Harmon Truck Lines, Inc. v. Steele, TexApp–Texarkana, 836 SW2d 262, reh den, and writ dism.—App & E 497(1), 907(2), 907(3); Judgm 17(2), 143(3), 145(2), 146, 162(2), 163.

Harmony Drilling Co., Inc. v. Kreutter, CA5 (Tex), 846 F2d 17.—Fed Civ Proc 2810, 2819, 2828.

Harmony Exploration, Inc.; Aquila Southwest Pipeline, Inc. v., TexApp–San Antonio, 48 SW3d 225, review den.—App & E 253, 863, 930(1), 934(1), 946, 974(0.5), 984(1), 1001(1), 1001(3), 1024.1, 1064.1(1); Com Law 11; Contracts 326; Costs 194.16, 194.18, 207, 264; Damag 40(1), 190; Gas 13(1); Interest 31, 39(2.6), 39(2.10), 39(2.30), 49; Judgm 199(3.10); Plead 228.15, 404; Sales 10, 71(4), 164, 384(1); Trial 139.1(3), 140(1), 143, 251(1), 252(1), 295(1).

Harms v. Ehlers, TexCivApp–Austin, 179 SW2d 582, writ refused.—Ex & Ad 261; Home 103, 153; Judgm 768(1).

Harms; Koch Gathering Systems, Inc. v., TexApp–Corpus Christi, 946 SW2d 453, reh overr, and writ den.— App & E 21, 66, 68, 70(1), 76(1), 352.1, 353, 387(5), 1096(3).

Harms; U.S. v., CA5 (Tex), 442 F3d 367, reh and reh den 214 FedAppx 493, cert den 127 SCt 2875, 167 LEd2d 1152.—Const Law 2817; Crim Law 400(1), 437, 673(2), 1037.1(2), 1139, 1153(1), 1170(1); Ind & Inf 60, 71.2(2), 71.2(4); Postal 35(2), 48(4.1), 49(11), 50; Sent & Pun 664(1), 736, 761, 2160; U S 41; Work Comp 2080.

Harms Marine Service, Inc. v. Swiere, TexCivApp–Beaumont, 411 SW2d 602, ref nre, cert den 88 SCt 227, 389 US 899, 19 LEd2d 223.—App & E 387(2), 387(6), 426, 1062.1; Neglig 387; Seamen 29(1); Trial 350.1, 350.5(2), 351.2(2), 352.1(6), 352.10; Witn 379(7).

Harnden v. McKinney, TexCivApp–San Antonio, 103 SW2d 869.—App & E 930(3); Land & Ten 161(1), 161(3).

Harned v. E-Z Finance Co., Tex, 254 SW2d 81, 151 Tex 641.—Const Law 2503(1), 2503(2), 2507(1); Damag 49, 50.20; Usury 134.

Harned v. State, TexCrimApp, 236 SW2d 808.—Crim Law 1094(3).

Harner v. State, TexApp–Texarkana, 997 SW2d 695.— Crim Law 394.6(5), 412.1(1), 414, 531(2), 641.13(1), 741(3), 795(2.1), 795(2.60), 814(16), 824(11), 1038.1(1), 1038.3, 1119(1), 1134(3), 1144.12, 1153(1), 1158(4).

Harnett, In re, NDTex, 106 FSupp 467.—Aliens 716.

Harnett v. State, TexApp–Austin, 38 SW3d 650, petition for discretionary review refused.—Crim Law 451(1), 462, 469.1, 472, 476.6, 480, 486(1), 486(2), 632(4), 720(2), 720(7.1), 722.5, 723(1), 723(3), 726, 1036.1(1), 1036.1(9), 1036.6, 1043(2), 1043(3), 1044.2(1), 1153(4), 1169.2(1), 1169.5(1), 1169.5(3), 1171.1(2.1), 1171.1(4); Sent & Pun 98.

Harney; Craig v., USTex, 67 SCt 1249, 331 US 367, 91 LEd 1546, conformed to Ex parte Craig, 204 SW2d 842, 150 TexCrim 598.—Const Law 2119, 2121; Contempt 8, 9; Fed Cts 512.

Harney; Garza v., TexApp–Amarillo, 726 SW2d 198.— Child C 802, 816; Mand 11.

Harney; Hale v., CA5 (Tex), 786 F2d 688.—Civil R 1326(5), 1395(1); Consp 18; Courts 489(1); Fed Civ Proc 2769, 2771(3), 2837.1, 2840.

Harney; Shely v., TexCivApp–San Antonio, 163 SW2d 839, writ refused wom.—App & E 216(1), 1003(9.1), 1050.1(12); Libel 110(1), 111.

Harney; State ex rel. Downs v., TexCivApp–San Antonio, 164 SW2d 55, writ refused wom.—Atty Gen 6, 7; Counties 24, 69.2; Quo W 14, 33.

Harney v. Wood, TexCivApp–San Antonio, 160 SW2d 315. —Courts 207.5.

Harnischfeger; Walton v., TexApp–San Antonio, 796 SW2d 225, writ den.—Judgm 185.3(21); Neglig 1692; Prod Liab 49, 85.

Harnischfeger Corp.; Roberts v., CA5 (Tex), 901 F2d 42.
—Evid 219.20(3), 318(7); Prod Liab 81.1.

Harnischfeger Corp. v. Stone, TexApp–Houston (14 Dist), 814 SW2d 263.—Mand 4(1), 12, 32, 187.9(2); Pretrial Proc 97, 171, 182.

Harnly; Phillips Petroleum Co. v., TexCivApp–Amarillo, 348 SW2d 856, ref nre.—App & E 907(3); Bills & N 1; Mines 62.1, 78.1(3), 78.1(9), 78.5; Tender 8; Time 4.

Haro; Morgan v., CA5 (Tex), 112 F3d 788.—Fed Cts 662.1, 664.

Haro v. State, TexCrimApp, 105 SW2d 1093, 132 TexCrim 507.—Burg 41(1); Ind & Inf 110(18); Sent & Pun 1207.

Haro v. State, TexApp–Eastland, 946 SW2d 120, petition for discretionary review refused.—Const Law 2812; Crim Law 1037.1(1); Rape 13, 54(1).

Haro v. Universal Underwriters Ins. Co., TexApp–Houston (14 Dist), 162 SW3d 661, review den.—Insurance 2865, 2866.

Harold v. Houston Yacht Club, TexCivApp–Houston, 380 SW2d 184.—Plead 210, 228.14, 228.23, 354, 360; Pretrial Proc 250, 692, 695.

Harold v. State, TexCrimApp, 303 SW2d 794, 165 TexCrim 78.—Crim Law 912.5; Embez 44(1).

Harold; U.S. v., CA5 (Tex), 531 F2d 704.—Controlled Subs 79, 82.

Harold; U.S. v., CA5 (Tex), 425 F2d 721, cert den 91 SCt 148, 400 US 906, 27 LEd2d 144.—Crim Law 577.15(3), 641.13(2.1), 1170.5(1).

Harold-Elliott Co., Inc. v. K.P./Miller Realty Growth Fund I, TexApp–Houston (1 Dist), 853 SW2d 752, reh den.—App & E 977(1); Corp 507(12); Judgm 139, 143(3), 145(2), 146, 151; New Tr 6.

Harold Munce Toyota, Inc.; Citizens Nat. Bank, Greenville, Tex. v., NDTex, 37 BR 928.—Bankr 2439(1).

Harold Thomas Excavating, Inc.; Landscape Design and Const., Inc. v., TexCivApp–Dallas, 604 SW2d 374, ref nre.—App & E 226(2), 931(6), 1054(1), 1071.6; Contracts 189, 221(1), 221(2), 301, 318.

Harold V. Simpson & Co.; Giddings v., TexCivApp–Waco, 532 SW2d 719.—Acct Action on 13; App & E 192.1, 907(3).

Harold V. Simpson and Co. v. Shuler, CA5 (Tex), 722 F2d 1253. See Shuler, Matter of.

Harp, Ex parte, TexCrimApp, 561 SW2d 180.—Hab Corp 224.1, 285.1; Sent & Pun 2014.

Harp; Reserve Petroleum Co. v., Tex, 226 SW2d 839, 148 Tex 448.—Deeds 42; Evid 48; Mines 55(5), 55(8); Pub Lands 175(2).

Harp; Reserve Petroleum Co. v., TexCivApp–Amarillo, 221 SW2d 366, rev 226 SW2d 839, 148 Tex 448.—Action 46; App & E 931(1); Contracts 322(1); Home 128; Lim of Act 5(3), 19(2), 193; Mines 55(1); Tresp to T T 35(1).

Harp v. State, TexCrimApp, 383 SW2d 176.—Autos 355(6); Crim Law 534(2), 1144.6.

Harp; United Am. Ins. Co. v., TexCivApp–Amarillo, 290 SW2d 392.—Atty & C 72; Fraud 21; Insurance 3015.

Harp; U.S. v., CA5 (Tex), 454 F2d 1161.—Weap 17(1).

Harp v. Valley Forge Life Ins. Co., TexCivApp–San Antonio, 577 SW2d 746, dism.—Insurance 1747.

Harp and Lovelace; H. Molsen & Co., Inc. v., TexCivApp–Amarillo, 516 SW2d 433.—Decl Judgm 271; Plead 111.16, 111.42(4).

Harper, In re, BkrtcyWDTex, 143 BR 682.—Bankr 2021.1, 2422.5(3), 2931, 3034, 3061.

Harper v. Agency Rent-A-Car, Inc., CA5 (Tex), 905 F2d 71, reh den.—Autos 388; Carr 235.1; Fed Cts 910.

Harper v. American Motors Corp., TexApp–Houston (14 Dist), 672 SW2d 44.—Courts 85(1); Time 10(4).

Harper v. Atlas, CA5 (Tex), 197 FedAppx 305.—Fed Civ Proc 2813; Fed Cts 663, 726.

Harper v. Barnhart, CA5 (Tex), 176 FedAppx 562.—Social S 142.5, 143.65, 143.85, 145.5.

Harper; Bass v., Tex, 441 SW2d 825.—Covenants 46; Mines 55(5).

Harper; Bass v., TexCivApp–Fort Worth, 437 SW2d 648, writ gr, rev 441 SW2d 825.—Deeds 90, 120, 141, 143; Mines 55(1), 55(5).

Harper; Berry v., TexCivApp–Texarkana, 111 SW2d 795, writ dism.—Neglig 432; Weap 23(3).

Harper v. Brown, TexComApp, 95 SW2d 1291, 127 Tex 631.—Plead 406(1); Tresp to T T 32.

Harper v. Cadenhead, TexApp–Eastland, 926 SW2d 588, subsequent mandamus proceeding Brownwood Regional Hosp v. Eleventh Court of Appeals, 927 SW2d 24.—Health 271; Mand 4(4); Pretrial Proc 382.

Harper; Campbell v., TexCivApp–Houston, 354 SW2d 629.—Partners 287.

Harper; Catholic Charities of Diocese of Galveston, Inc. v., Tex, 337 SW2d 111, 161 Tex 21.—Adop 3, 7.6(2), 7.6(3); App & E 1175(2).

Harper; Catholic Charities of the Diocese of Galveston, Inc. v., TexCivApp–Eastland, 331 SW2d 761, writ gr, rev 337 SW2d 111, 161 Tex 21.—Abate & R 11; Adop 7.6(3).

Harper; City of Anson v., TexApp–Eastland, 216 SW3d 384.—Action 6; App & E 893(1); Counties 141; Courts 35, 39, 97(1); Decl Judgm 62, 187, 209; Em Dom 2.1, 2.3, 106, 277, 307(2); Inj 74; Mun Corp 723, 733(1), 1016; Plead 104(1); Pretrial Proc 11; Schools 89; States 191.1, 191.10.

Harper v. City of Wichita Falls, TexCivApp–Fort Worth, 105 SW2d 743, writ refused.—Autos 7, 12; Const Law 1066; Evid 14; Mun Corp 657(2), 703(1).

Harper; Commercial Standard Ins. Co. v., TexComApp, 103 SW2d 143, 129 Tex 249, 110 ALR 529.—Insurance 3154, 3192, 3200.

Harper; Creole Production Services, Inc. v., TexApp–Houston (14 Dist), 640 SW2d 727, ref nre.—Antitrust 414; App & E 766, 1170.7; Evid 596(1); Labor & Emp 323(4); Trial 31, 122, 129, 351.2(1.1), 351.2(4).

Harper; Dallas County v., Tex, 913 SW2d 207.—Counties 143.

Harper; Dodd v., TexApp–Houston (1 Dist), 670 SW2d 646.—Contracts 103, 122; Evid 220(2), 588; Guar 25(3); Home 29, 31; Mtg 25(5), 74; Trial 382.

Harper v. Dorsett Brothers, CA5 (Tex), 145 FedAppx 893.—Fed Cts 663.

Harper v. Fikes, TexCivApp–Austin, 336 SW2d 631, ref nre.—Bankr 2532, 2554; Judgm 185(6); Mines 59; Spec Perf 61, 87, 94.

Harper v. FMC Corp., Niagara Chemical Division, TexCivApp–Waco, 407 SW2d 854.—Acct Action on 14; Evid 318(7); Plead 111.42(9).

Harper v. Garlington, TexCivApp–Eastland, 85 SW2d 1098.—Mand 45, 152.

Harper; General Motors Corp. v., TexApp–Eastland, 61 SW3d 118, reh overr, and review den.—App & E 204(7), 930(1), 1001(3); Evid 222(2), 333(7), 555.2, 555.10, 571(6), 571(9); Prod Liab 11, 15, 36, 77.5, 81.5, 83.5; Trial 82, 85, 255(4).

Harper; Golden Rule Ins. Co. v., Tex, 925 SW2d 649.—Inj 26(1), 26(3), 33.

Harper; Golden Rule Ins. Co. v., TexApp–Houston (14 Dist), 905 SW2d 804, writ gr, rev 925 SW2d 649.—App & E 954(1); Courts 516; Inj 26(1), 33, 138.27, 147.

Harper v. Harper, TexApp–Fort Worth, 8 SW3d 782, reh overr, and review den, and reh of petition for review overr.—App & E 756, 760(1), 761; Divorce 248.1; Ex & Ad 455; Hus & W 205(2), 272(2).

Harper; Harper v., TexApp–Fort Worth, 8 SW3d 782, reh overr, and review den, and reh of petition for review overr.—App & E 756, 760(1), 761; Divorce 248.1; Ex & Ad 455; Hus & W 205(2), 272(2).

Harper v. Harper, TexCivApp–Amarillo, 274 SW2d 930.—Adv Poss 57, 60(1), 85(1); Evid 129(3); Gifts 45, 49(4); Tresp to T T 35(1), 47(1); Trial 351.2(4).

HARPER;

Harper; Harper v., TexCivApp–Amarillo, 274 SW2d 930.
—Adv Poss 57, 60(1), 85(1); Evid 129(3); Gifts 45, 49(4); Tresp to T T 35(1), 47(1); Trial 351.2(4).

Harper v. Harris County, Tex., CA5 (Tex), 21 F3d 597, reh den 29 F3d 626.—Arrest 63.4(1), 63.4(2), 68(2); Civil R 1088(2), 1376(6), 1429; Fed Civ Proc 2491.5, 2544; Fed Cts 579, 766, 802; Mun Corp 747(3); Offic 114.

Harper; Hicks Rubber Co. v., Tex, 132 SW2d 579, 134 Tex 89.—App & E 216(2), 499(1).

Harper; Hicks Rubber Co. v., TexCivApp–Waco, 131 SW2d 749, writ dism 132 SW2d 579, 134 Tex 89.—App & E 218.2(7), 699(4), 704.1, 930(2), 1047(5), 1062.1, 1067; Damag 34, 132(3); Neglig 1717; Trial 58, 129.

Harper v. Highway Motor Freight Lines, TexCivApp–Dallas, 89 SW2d 448, writ dism.—Autos 242(5), 242(6), 243(2), 244(26), 245(17), 245(36); Evid 53, 87, 121(1), 123(11), 355(1); Trial 127; Witn 255(2.1).

Harper; Housing Authority of City of El Paso v., TexCivApp–El Paso, 241 SW2d 347.—Mun Corp 191.

Harper v. Johnson, Tex, 345 SW2d 277, 162 Tex 117.—Witn 126, 159(2), 159(3).

Harper v. Johnson, TexCivApp–Texarkana, 331 SW2d 482, writ gr, rev 345 SW2d 277, 162 Tex 117.—Abate & R 55(1); Costs 237; Death 29; Witn 128, 159(2), 173.

Harper v. Killion, Tex, 348 SW2d 521, 162 Tex 481.—Evid 10(2), 51.

Harper v. Killion, TexCivApp–Texarkana, 345 SW2d 309, writ gr, aff 348 SW2d 521, 162 Tex 481.—App & E 912; Evid 3, 4, 10(2), 25(1), 25(2); Venue 8.5(3).

Harper v. Lindsay, CA5 (Tex), 616 F2d 849.—Const Law 3682, 4025, 4260, 4329; Counties 20.5, 21.5; Statut 47.

Harper v. Lindsay, SDTex, 454 FSupp 597, aff in part, rev in part 616 F2d 849.—Const Law 82(10), 1066, 1091, 1176, 1244, 2330, 2438, 2484, 2500; Counties 21.5, 38, 55; Fed Civ Proc 1742(2); Fed Cts 43; Licens 38; Statut 190, 223.1.

Harper; Looney v., TexCivApp–El Paso, 112 SW2d 760.—Venue 5.3(2).

Harper; Madison v., TexCivApp–Amarillo, 395 SW2d 842.—App & E 499(1), 500(1), 931(1), 989; Plead 111.21, 111.42(10).

Harper v. Meyer, TexCivApp–Galveston, 274 SW2d 904, ref nre.—Wills 1, 69, 73, 77, 78, 88(1), 93, 179, 198, 302(7).

Harper; Modern Woodmen of America v., TexComApp, 94 SW2d 156, 127 Tex 489.—App & E 909(6); Insurance 1606, 2079, 3080, 3084, 3093.

Harper v. Newton, TexApp–Waco, 910 SW2d 9, writ gr, rev Dallas County v. Harper, 913 SW2d 207.—App & E 78(1), 80(6), 854(1); Counties 141, 143, 146; Judgm 181(2), 181(7), 183; Libel 48(2); Lim of Act 95(1), 95(6); Mun Corp 847.

Harper v. Over, TexCivApp–Eastland, 101 SW2d 830.—Mtg 372(1); Ven & Pur 238.

Harper; Perkins v., TexCivApp–San Antonio, 330 SW2d 241, ref nre.—App & E 1170.1; Lim of Act 127(12); Ven & Pur 120, 334(1).

Harper; Polk Terrace, Inc. v., TexCivApp–Tyler, 386 SW2d 588, ref nre.—App & E 996; Corp 422(1); Fraud 4, 11(1), 13(2), 22(1), 23, 64(5); Lim of Act 100(1), 197(2); Princ & A 24.

Harper v. Powell, TexApp–Corpus Christi, 821 SW2d 456.—Child S 456; Inj 138.3.

Harper; Sandoval v., TexCivApp–El Paso, 392 SW2d 475, writ dism.—Judgm 181(29), 185(2), 185(5), 186.

Harper; Small v., TexApp–Houston (1 Dist), 638 SW2d 24, ref nre.—Judgm 185.2(1), 185.3(17); Marriage 54.

Harper; Snelling v., TexCivApp–Texarkana, 137 SW2d 222, writ dism, correct.—App & E 1050.1(12); Evid 513(2); Ex & Ad 454; Neglig 552(1), 1037(7), 1050, 1205(1), 1205(7), 1241, 1313; Trial 350.6(2).

Harper; Southern Cal. Petroleum Corp. v., CA5 (Tex), 273 F2d 715.—Courts 493(3), 508(1), 508(2.1); Decl Judgm 276; Judgm 600.1.

Harper v. Springfield, TexCivApp–Waco, 578 SW2d 824, ref nre.—Wills 450, 506(4), 614(6.1).

Harper v. State, TexCrimApp, 533 SW2d 776.—Autos 357; Crim Law 1169.12, 1173.5.

Harper v. State, TexCrimApp, 477 SW2d 31.—Crim Law 59(3), 552(1); Rob 24.15(2).

Harper v. State, TexCrimApp, 366 SW2d 789.—Crim Law 1087.1(2).

Harper v. State, TexCrimApp, 291 SW2d 950, 163 TexCrim 361.—Crim Law 939(1), 941(1), 945(1); Rape 4, 51(4).

Harper v. State, TexCrimApp, 284 SW2d 362, 162 TexCrim 295.—Arrest 63.4(15); Controlled Subs 121, 122.

Harper v. State, TexCrimApp, 277 SW2d 114.—Crim Law 1184(4.1).

Harper v. State, TexCrimApp, 188 SW2d 174, 148 TexCrim 407.—Forg 7(1).

Harper v. State, TexCrimApp, 187 SW2d 570, 148 TexCrim 354.—Const Law 4600, 4664(2); Crim Law 519(5), 1038.1(1), 1038.3, 1090.1(3), 1090.8; Homic 1134.

Harper v. State, TexCrimApp, 162 SW2d 971, 144 TexCrim 385.—Homic 784, 1134, 1481.

Harper v. State, TexCrimApp, 136 SW2d 216.—Crim Law 1182.

Harper v. State, TexCrimApp, 112 SW2d 189, 133 TexCrim 432.—Crim Law 404.70, 423(5), 564(1).

Harper v. State, TexCrimApp, 110 SW2d 67, 133 TexCrim 255.—Assault 80; Crim Law 721(3).

Harper v. State, TexCrimApp, 98 SW2d 191, 131 TexCrim 286.—Crim Law 1182.

Harper v. State, TexApp–Houston (1 Dist), 930 SW2d 625.—Costs 302.2(2), 302.4; Crim Law 351(3), 351(6), 374, 673(5), 796, 829(1), 829(22), 1152(2), 1158(3), 1162, 1165(1), 1170.5(1); Jury 33(5.15); Witn 277(1), 305(2), 319, 337(31).

Harper v. State, TexApp–Houston (1 Dist), 753 SW2d 516, petition for discretionary review refused.—Assault 56, 92(3), 92(4); Crim Law 1115(1); Ind & Inf 125(4.1), 132(1).

Harper v. State, TexApp–Austin, 686 SW2d 738.—Autos 411; Const Law 2812; Crim Law 740; Searches 65; Sent & Pun 138.

Harper v. State, TexApp–Amarillo, 217 SW3d 672.—Arrest 63.5(4), 63.5(7), 68(4); Autos 349(6), 349(16); Crim Law 1139, 1144.1, 1153(1), 1158(1), 1224(1).

Harper v. State, TexApp–Amarillo, 850 SW2d 736, petition for discretionary review refused.—Crim Law 1028, 1077.1(1), 1077.1(4), 1077.2(1), 1077.2(3), 1077.3.

Harper v. State, TexApp–Houston (14 Dist), 704 SW2d 546, petition for discretionary review refused.—Controlled Subs 113; Crim Law 394.6(1), 1035(10); Searches 64, 80.1.

Harper v. State, TexApp–Houston (14 Dist), 696 SW2d 463, appeal after remand 1986 WL 10964.—Sent & Pun 1381(4), 1381(6).

Harper v. State, TexApp–Houston (14 Dist), 675 SW2d 534, petition for discretionary review refused.—Rob 1, 24.10.

Harper v. State, TexApp–Houston (14 Dist), 675 SW2d 529, petition for discretionary review refused.—Sent & Pun 1139.

Harper; State v., TexCivApp–San Antonio, 188 SW2d 400, writ refused, cert den 66 SCt 964, 327 US 805, 90 LEd 1030.—Commerce 77.10(1), 77.10(2); Evid 10(1); Tax 2470, 2853.

Harper; Stone Companies, Inc. v., BkrtcyNDTex, 170 BR 884. See T.F. Stone Companies, Inc., In re.

Harper; Stone Co., Inc. v., CA5 (Tex), 72 F3d 466. See T.F. Stone Co., Inc., Matter of.

Harper; Stowers v., TexCivApp–Tyler, 376 SW2d 34, ref nre.—Contracts 150, 152, 155, 236, 238(2), 247, 248; Estop 52.10(2), 52.10(3), 53, 92(2); Evid 448; Labor & Emp 40(3), 47, 207, 256(17).

Harper v. Swoveland, TexCivApp–Dallas, 591 SW2d 629.
—Ex & Ad 130(1), 138(1).

Harper v. Taylor, TexCivApp–Beaumont, 490 SW2d 227.
—Admin Law 753; Schools 53(5), 63(1).

Harper v. Texas & P. Ry. Co., TexCivApp–Eastland, 146
SW2d 426, writ refused.—Autos 150, 224(1), 224(3),
224(4); R R 327(12).

Harper; Texas Emp. Ins. Ass'n v., TexCivApp–Dallas,
249 SW2d 677, ref nre.—Work Comp 306, 323, 1922,
1924, 1927.

Harper; T.F. Stone Companies, Inc. v., BkrtcyNDTex,
170 BR 884. See T.F. Stone Companies, Inc., In re.

Harper; T.F. Stone Co., Inc. v., CA5 (Tex), 72 F3d 466.
See T.F. Stone Co., Inc., Matter of.

Harper v. Thiokol Chemical Corp., CA5 (Tex), 619 F2d
489.—Civil R 1172, 1176, 1554, 1574.

Harper; Traders & General Ins. Co. v., TexCivApp–
Texarkana, 140 SW2d 593, writ refused.—App & E
882(12); Trial 232(2), 278; Work Comp 1629, 1968(7).

Harper; U.S. v., CA5 (Tex), 448 F3d 732, cert den 127 SCt
285, 166 LEd2d 218.—Crim Law 1024(9), 1139, 1158(1);
Sent & Pun 973.

Harper; U.S. v., CA5 (Tex), 932 F2d 1073, cert den 112
SCt 443, 502 US 970, 116 LEd2d 462.—Bail 97(4); Crim
Law 1134(3), 1139; Sent & Pun 658.

Harper; U.S. v., CA5 (Tex), 901 F2d 471, reh den 907 F2d
146.—Crim Law 273.2(1), 1436; Escape 9.

Harper; U.S. v., EDTex, 360 FSupp2d 833, subsequent
determination 448 F3d 732, cert den 127 SCt 285, 166
LEd2d 218.—Jury 34(7); Sent & Pun 651, 973, 982.

Harper; U.S. Fidelity & Guaranty Co. v., TexCivApp–
Fort Worth, 561 SW2d 630.—App & E 1175(1); Guard
& W 182(3); Subrog 7(4).

Harper v. Welchem, Inc., TexApp–Houston (14 Dist), 799
SW2d 492.—App & E 66, 68, 76(1), 78(1), 782, 937(1);
Courts 39; Judgm 215, 277.1, 524; Motions 62; Plead
106(1); Pretrial Proc 556.1.

Harper; Wells v., TexCivApp–Texarkana, 394 SW2d 540.
—Adv Poss 33, 57, 109.

Harper Bldg. Systems, Inc. v. Upjohn Co., TexCivApp–
Beaumont, 564 SW2d 123, ref nre.—App & E 930(3),
989; Damag 40(1); Judgm 199(3.14); Sales 426, 442(1),
442(5).

Harper Trucks, Inc.; Camp v., CA5 (Tex), 30 F3d 37.
See Camp v. Ruffin.

Harpold; Executors of Tartt's Estate v., TexCivApp–
Hous (14 Dist), 531 SW2d 696, ref nre.—Atty & C 23,
132; Des & Dist 71(7); Ex & Ad 216(2).

Harral v. U.S., WDTex, 81 FSupp 983.—Int Rev 3430.1,
3432.

Harral County Line Independent School Dist.; Lubbock County School Trustees v., TexCivApp–Amarillo,
95 SW2d 204.—Const Law 2488, 2489; Schools 42(2);
Statut 195.

Harred v. Conrad, TexCivApp–Amarillo, 287 SW2d 229,
ref nre.—Bills & N 429; Chat Mtg 72; Judgm 181(2),
181(14), 183.

Harrell, Ex parte, TexCrimApp, 740 SW2d 446. See
Edone, Ex parte.

Harrell, Ex parte, TexCrimApp, 542 SW2d 169.—Forg
17; Health 305; Statut 223.3, 223.4.

Harrell, In re, BkrtcyWDTex, 94 BR 86.—Bankr 3356,
3357(2.1), 3420(9), 3422(4.1), 3422(8), 3422(10.1).

Harrell; Allied Underwriters v., TexCivApp–Eastland,
143 SW2d 621, writ dism, correct.—App & E 758.3(1);
Insurance 3025, 3571; Judgm 256(2).

Harrell v. Alvarez, TexApp–El Paso, 46 SW3d 483.—App
& E 1056.6; Lim of Act 119(3), 195(3); Proc 23, 145.

Harrell v. Atlantic Refining Co., TexCivApp–Waco, 339
SW2d 548, ref nre.—Bound 36(2), 37(3), 40(1), 47(1);
Estop 32(1); Evid 460(3); Mines 74(4), 81; Pretrial
Proc 357.

Harrell v. Bakhaus, TexCivApp–San Antonio, 315 SW2d
685, ref nre.—Contracts 32; Costs 194.34; Mines 58,
73.5, 78.1(3).

Harrell; Benson v., TexCivApp–Fort Worth, 324 SW2d
620, ref nre.—Atty & C 148(2), 165; Contracts 297;
Impl & C C 65; Judgm 185.1(1).

Harrell; Berry v., CCA5 (Tex), 83 F2d 671, cert den 57
SCt 21, 299 US 559, 81 LEd 411.—Mines 74(2), 74(3),
74(6); Receivers 141, 142.

Harrell v. Black, TexCivApp–Waco, 329 SW2d 127, ref
nre.—App & E 80(1); Judgm 178, 181(14), 185.1(3),
185.1(4), 335(4).

Harrell v. Bowen, CA5 (Tex), 862 F2d 471.—Admin Law
413, 462; Social S 124.5, 140.21, 140.30, 140.45, 143.45,
143.80, 143.85, 147, 148.10.

Harrell; Carter v., TexCivApp–Fort Worth, 126 SW2d 43,
writ dism, correct.—Courts 168; Mun Corp 131; Plead
193(3), 205(2).

Harrell v. City of Denton, TexCivApp–Fort Worth, 116
SW2d 423.—Action 6; Em Dom 185, 234(1), 235, 237(7),
238(1).

Harrell v. Colonial Finance Corp., TexCivApp–San Antonio, 341 SW2d 545, ref nre.—Usury 5, 42, 53, 59.

Harrell v. Continental Assur. Co. of Chicago, Ill., Tex-
CivApp–Austin, 381 SW2d 223.—Insurance 1805,
1832(1), 2422.

Harrell; Corzelius v., Tex, 186 SW2d 961, 143 Tex 509.—
Admin Law 9, 390.1, 391, 499, 500; App & E 1175(1);
Const Law 2625(1); Mines 47, 73.1(2), 92.3(2), 92.16,
92.21, 92.54; Pub Ut 141, 169.1, 170.

Harrell; Corzelius v., TexCivApp–Austin, 179 SW2d 419,
writ gr, rev 186 SW2d 961, 143 Tex 509.—Admin Law
499; Const Law 2419, 4475; Courts 207.3; Mines
92.3(2), 92.5(3), 92.44(3), 92.49, 92.54, 92.59(2), 92.64;
Pub Ut 181.

Harrell v. Crabtree, TexCivApp–Eastland, 271 SW2d 130,
ref nre.—Adv Poss 11, 40, 58, 112, 114(1), 115(5); Evid
589.

Harrell v. DCS Equipment Leasing Corp., CA5 (Tex),
951 F2d 1453.—Corp 1.4(4); Evid 146; Fed Civ Proc
2176.4, 2444.1, 2559; Fed Cts 630.1, 829, 901.1, 907;
Partners 370; RICO 79; Witn 292.

Harrell v. Fashing, TexCivApp–El Paso, 562 SW2d 544.
—Mand 60; Mental H 137.1; Pretrial Proc 434.

Harrell v. F. H. Vahlsing, Inc., TexCivApp–San Antonio,
248 SW2d 762, ref nre.—Damag 87(2), 95, 103, 163(1);
Decl Judgm 385; Evid 471(35); Impl & C C 110;
Waters 144.5, 152(2), 152(9).

Harrell; First Nat. Bank of Midlothian v., BkrtcyWD-
Tex, 94 BR 86. See Harrell, In re.

Harrell; Fort Worth Nat. Bank v., TexCivApp–Fort
Worth, 544 SW2d 697, ref nre.—Compromise 15(1);
Evid 397(6); Trial 105(5).

Harrell; Great Nat. Life Ins. Co. v., TexCivApp–Waco,
157 SW2d 427, writ dism.—App & E 1091(1); Insurance
1920, 1936, 3571; J P 174(26).

Harrell v. Harrell, Tex, 692 SW2d 876, on remand 700
SW2d 645.—Divorce 254(2), 322; Hus & W 272(4).

Harrell; Harrell v., Tex, 692 SW2d 876, on remand 700
SW2d 645.—Divorce 254(2), 322; Hus & W 272(4).

Harrell v. Harrell, TexApp–El Paso, 986 SW2d 629.—
Divorce 150.1(3).

Harrell; Harrell v., TexApp–El Paso, 986 SW2d 629.—
Divorce 150.1(3).

Harrell v. Harrell, TexApp–Corpus Christi, 700 SW2d
645.—App & E 900; Hus & W 249(3), 272(4).

Harrell; Harrell v., TexApp–Corpus Christi, 700 SW2d
645.—App & E 900; Hus & W 249(3), 272(4).

Harrell v. Harrell, TexApp–Corpus Christi, 684 SW2d
118, rev 692 SW2d 876, on remand 700 SW2d 645.—
Courts 475(15); Divorce 151, 199.7(10), 252.2, 252.3(4),
254(2), 255, 322; Hus & W 249(3), 272(4); Judgm 335(1),
543, 713(2), 720.

HARRELL;

Harrell; Harrell v., TexApp–Corpus Christi, 684 SW2d 118, rev 692 SW2d 876, on remand 700 SW2d 645.— Courts 475(15); Divorce 151, 199.7(10), 252.2, 252.3(4), 254(2), 255, 322; Hus & W 249(3), 272(4); Judgm 335(1), 543, 713(2), 720.

Harrell v. Harrell, TexCivApp–Corpus Christi, 591 SW2d 324.—Divorce 252.2, 252.3(2), 252.3(3), 286(2), 286(5).

Harrell; Harrell v., TexCivApp–Corpus Christi, 591 SW2d 324.—Divorce 252.2, 252.3(2), 252.3(3), 286(2), 286(5).

Harrell v. Harrell, TexCivApp–Hous (14 Dist), 428 SW2d 370, ref nre.—Child C 553; Hab Corp 636, 902; Infants 198; Judgm 713(2), 958(1).

Harrell; Harrell v., TexCivApp–Hous (14 Dist), 428 SW2d 370, ref nre.—Child C 553; Hab Corp 636, 902; Infants 198; Judgm 713(2), 958(1).

Harrell v. Harrell, TexCivApp–Galveston, 206 SW2d 109. —Divorce 27(3), 124, 127(3), 130, 184(6.1).

Harrell; Harrell v., TexCivApp–Galveston, 206 SW2d 109. —Divorce 27(3), 124, 127(3), 130, 184(6.1).

Harrell v. Hickman, Tex, 215 SW2d 876, 147 Tex 396.— Wills 62, 88(2), 602(1), 634(4.1), 692(1).

Harrell; Hickman v., TexCivApp–Waco, 211 SW2d 374, writ gr, rev 215 SW2d 876, 147 Tex 396.—Contracts 150, 168; Wills 61, 64, 439, 440, 488, 590, 602(1), 692(1), 692(4).

Harrell; Hillkee Corp. v., TexCivApp–Texarkana, 573 SW2d 558, ref nre.—Courts 480(3); Execution 256(1).

Harrell v. Hobbs, TexApp–Tyler, 791 SW2d 310.—Child S 442, 496.

Harrell; Huff v., TexApp–Corpus Christi, 941 SW2d 230, reh overr, and writ den.—App & E 218.2(5.1), 1043(6), 1048(7), 1050.1(11), 1051.1(2); Corp 1.6(6), 269(2), 269(3), 349, 547(4), 627; Estop 52.10(3); Evid 200, 208(1), 208(4), 208(5), 208(6), 264, 265(8), 376(1), 555.3; Fraud 3; Plead 36(1); Trial 39, 74, 350.1, 366; Witn 379(1).

Harrell v. La Salle County, TexCivApp–Eastland, 348 SW2d 853, ref nre.—Courts 475(13); Em Dom 157, 158, 161, 273.

Harrell; Luther Transfer & Storage Co. v., TexCivApp– Hous (1 Dist), 445 SW2d 268.—App & E 1175(7), 1176(3), 1177(1); Evid 318(8).

Harrell; Markwardt v., TexCivApp–Eastland, 430 SW2d 1, ref nre.—Contracts 116(1), 117(2), 117(9), 142; Evid 265(1), 265(10).

Harrell; Maxwell v., TexCivApp–Austin, 183 SW2d 577, writ refused wom.—App & E 747(1), 878(1), 878(6); Hus & W 273(1); Wills 439, 440, 488, 601(2), 692(2), 692(5).

Harrell v. Patel, TexApp–El Paso, 225 SW3d 1, reh overr, and review den.—App & E 204(1), 204(2), 205, 946; Corp 269(3); Stip 1, 3, 14(4), 17(1), 17(3).

Harrell v. Rothschild–Reserve Intern., Inc., CA5 (Tex), 951 F2d 1453. See Harrell v. DCS Equipment Leasing Corp.

Harrell; Scurlock Oil Co. v., TexCivApp–Austin, 443 SW2d 334, ref nre.—Mines 119, 121, 125; Neglig 1657; Prod Liab 85.

Harrell v. State, TexCrimApp, 980 SW2d 661.—Jury 29(5).

Harrell v. State, TexCrimApp, 884 SW2d 154.—Crim Law 374.

Harrell v. State, TexCrimApp, 852 SW2d 521.—Crim Law 562, 1159.2(7); False Pret 4; Larc 7.

Harrell v. State, TexCrimApp, 743 SW2d 229.—Escape 1.

Harrell v. State, TexCrimApp, 725 SW2d 208.—Autos 422.1, 424; Crim Law 1036.1(3.1).

Harrell v. State, TexCrimApp, 659 SW2d 825.—Assault 96(7).

Harrell v. State, TexCrimApp, 643 SW2d 686.—Controlled Subs 62, 65, 84; Crim Law 1038.2, 1171.6; Ind & Inf 60, 71.4(7), 73(1); Sent & Pun 318.

Harrell v. State, TexCrimApp, 386 SW2d 142.—Crim Law 274(3.1), 698(1); Sent & Pun 411.

Harrell v. State, TexCrimApp, 358 SW2d 126, 172 Tex-Crim 418.—Crim Law 535(2), 1176; Rape 52(2).

Harrell v. State, TexCrimApp, 314 SW2d 590, 166 Tex-Crim 384.—Controlled Subs 6.

Harrell v. State, TexCrimApp, 263 SW2d 781.—Crim Law 1097(1).

Harrell v. State, TexCrimApp, 218 SW2d 466, 153 Tex-Crim 141.—Crim Law 338(1); Homic 1553.

Harrell v. State, TexCrimApp, 143 SW2d 941.—Crim Law 1090.1(1).

Harrell v. State, TexCrimApp, 139 SW2d 600, 139 Tex-Crim 272.—Crim Law 608, 1087.1(2).

Harrell v. State, TexCrimApp, 139 SW2d 272, 139 Tex-Crim 150.—Crim Law 1064.5, 1156(1).

Harrell v. State, TexApp–San Antonio, 699 SW2d 319, rev 743 SW2d 229.—Escape 10.

Harrell v. State, TexApp–San Antonio, 693 SW2d 693, petition for discretionary review gr, rev 725 SW2d 208. —Autos 424; Crim Law 1036.1(3.1), 1044.1(5.1), 1169.1(7).

Harrell v. State, TexApp–Beaumont, 679 SW2d 612.— Crim Law 772(1), 814(1), 814(5), 822(1), 1038.1(2), 1172.1(3); Ind & Inf 86(2), 87(2).

Harrell v. State, TexApp–Tyler, 885 SW2d 433, petition for discretionary review gr, rev 884 SW2d 154.—Courts 97(1); Crim Law 369.1, 369.2(1), 369.2(3.1), 371(1), 374, 695(5), 1043(1), 1153(1).

Harrell v. State, TexApp–Tyler, 885 SW2d 427, reh overr, review gr, cause remanded 820 SW2d 800, on remand 885 SW2d 433, petition for discretionary review gr, rev 884 SW2d 154.—Consp 24(1), 24(2), 24.15, 27, 46; Crim Law 369.1, 369.2(1), 1144.13(3), 1159.2(7), 1169.11; RICO 103, 104, 121.

Harrell v. State, TexApp–Houston (14 Dist), 65 SW3d 768, reh overr, and petition for discretionary review refused, habeas corpus dism 2007 WL 1729983.—Const Law 4705, 4728; Crim Law 566, 1144.13(2.1), 1144.13(6), 1159.2(3), 1159.2(7), 1159.2(9), 1159.5; Kidnap 29, 36, 41; Sent & Pun 206.

Harrell v. State, TexApp–Houston (14 Dist), 938 SW2d 162, reh overr, review gr, rev 980 SW2d 661.—Jury 29(5), 32(3), 149.

Harrell v. State, TexApp–Houston (14 Dist), 923 SW2d 104, review gr, vac 930 SW2d 100, on remand 938 SW2d 162, reh overr, review gr, rev 980 SW2d 661.—Crim Law 26, 641.13(1), 641.13(2.1), 641.13(7), 713, 720(6), 720(9), 822(1), 822(7), 1038.1(2), 1134(2), 1172.1(1); Homic 520, 1371, 1387; Jury 29(6); Sent & Pun 1840.

Harrell v. State, TexApp–Houston (14 Dist), 882 SW2d 65, petition for discretionary review refused.—Crim Law 566, 641.13(2.1), 1134(5), 1144.13(3), 1159.2(7); Jury 33(5.15).

Harrell v. State, TexApp–Houston (14 Dist), 834 SW2d 540, reh den, and petition for discretionary review refused.—Const Law 4723; Crim Law 790; Embez 4; Larc 7, 13, 15(1), 40(2), 55, 57, 59, 63.

Harrell v. State, TexApp–Houston (14 Dist), 832 SW2d 154, petition for discretionary review gr, rev 852 SW2d 521.—Crim Law 1038.2; False Pret 4, 52; Sent & Pun 1295, 1367, 1371.

Harrell v. Sunylan Co., TexComApp, 97 SW2d 686, 128 Tex 460.—Evid 588; Interpl 1; Mun Corp 712(2).

Harrell; Texas Housing Co. v., TexCivApp–Dallas, 257 SW2d 484.—Sales 359(2), 365; Trial 351.2(8), 351.5(3).

Harrell v. Thompson, Tex, 165 SW2d 81, 140 Tex 1.— Mand 4(5), 16(1).

Harrell; Thomson v., TexCivApp–San Antonio, 271 SW2d 724.—Adop 7.3, 16; Infants 157, 198, 230.1, 231, 232.

Harrell v. Tilley, TexCivApp–Beaumont, 111 SW2d 736. —App & E 627.2.

Harrell v. Trupin, CA5 (Tex), 951 F2d 1453. See Harrell v. DCS Equipment Leasing Corp.

Harrell; U.S. v., CA5 (Tex), 894 F2d 120, reh den, cert den 111 SCt 101, 498 US 834, 112 LEd2d 72.—Aliens 795(2), 795(4); Crim Law 412.2(2), 412.2(3).

Harrell; Vahlsing v., CA5 (Tex), 178 F2d 622, cert den 71 SCt 39, 340 US 812, 95 LEd 597.—Ease 12(1); Waters 240, 242.

Harrell v. Walsh, TexCivApp–Dallas, 249 SW2d 927, ref nre.—Contracts 1; Frds St of 75; Wills 58(2), 775.

Harrell Drilling Co.; Rozner v., TexCivApp–Galveston, 261 SW2d 190, ref nre.—Autos 173(8), 211, 242(1), 242(2), 242(7), 244(14); Evid 8; Neglig 259.

Harrelson v. Armstrong, TexCivApp–Eastland, 438 SW2d 673.—App & E 554(3).

Harrelson; Bryant v., SDTex, 187 FSupp 738.—Civil R 1027; Consp 1.1, 7.5(1), 7.5(2); Fed Civ Proc 2734; Fed Cts 220, 313, 333; Sent & Pun 1430.

Harrelson v. Davis, TexCivApp–Fort Worth, 415 SW2d 293.—Child C 23, 465, 468, 469, 510.

Harrelson; General & Excess Underwriters, Inc. v., TexCivApp–Waco, 327 SW2d 78, ref nre.—Insurance 1635, 1766, 3066, 3131.

Harrelson; Montana v., CA5 (Tex), 469 F2d 1091.—Fed Cts 925.

Harrelson v. State, TexCrimApp, 692 SW2d 659.—Crim Law 275, 1026.10(4).

Harrelson v. State, TexCrimApp, 511 SW2d 957.—Sent & Pun 12, 1160.

Harrelson v. State, TexCrimApp, 274 SW2d 714, 161 TexCrim 83.—Autos 355(6); Crim Law 382, 1169.1(7), 1173.2(1).

Harrelson v. State, TexApp–El Paso, 668 SW2d 455, petition for discretionary review gr, aff 692 SW2d 659.—Crim Law 1026.10(2.1), 1186.1.

Harrelson v. State, TexApp–Beaumont, 153 SW3d 75, petition for discretionary review refused (4 pets).—Counties 102; Crim Law 37.10(1), 549, 554, 641.13(2.1), 641.13(6), 641.13(7), 720(7.1), 920, 951(1), 1031(1), 1035(8.1), 1036.1(3.1), 1036.7, 1037.1(1), 1038.1(4), 1144.13(2.1), 1144.13(5), 1144.13(6), 1159.2(7); Forg 44(0.5); Records 22.

Harrelson v. State, TexApp–Houston (14 Dist), 654 SW2d 712, petition for discretionary review refused.—Courts 494; Crim Law 627.10(1), 627.10(5), 1034, 1035(2), 1044.2(1); Witn 198(1).

Harrelson; U.S. v., CA5 (Tex), 766 F2d 186.—Consp 28(3); Crim Law 1172.1(3); Homic 549.

Harrelson; U.S. v., CA5 (Tex), 754 F2d 1182, reh den 767 F2d 918.—Consp 28(1); Crim Law 419(2.20), 1177, 1181.5(1); Double J 135, 139.1; Ind & Inf 127, 129(1); Perj 33(1); Sent & Pun 1508.

Harrelson; U.S. v., CA5 (Tex), 754 F2d 1153, reh den 766 F2d 186, cert den 106 SCt 277, 474 US 908, 88 LEd2d 241, cert den 106 SCt 599, 474 US 1034, 88 LEd2d 578, on remand US v. Chagra, 638 FSupp 1389, aff 807 F2d 398, cert den 108 SCt 106, 484 US 832, 98 LEd2d 66.—Consp 28(3), 47(13), 48.2(2); Crim Law 93, 126(1), 427(5), 622, 622.1(2), 622.2(3), 622.2(8), 622.2(11), 814(6), 852, 1036.1(9), 1148, 1152(2), 1166(6), 1166.4, 1166.16, 1169.1(8), 1170.5(1), 1172.6, 1173.2(2); Ind & Inf 124(1), 124(5), 129(1), 130; Judges 49(1), 51(3), 51(4); Jury 116, 131(1); Tel 1473; Witn 190, 192, 201(2), 222.

Harrelson; U.S. v., CA5 (Tex), 713 F2d 1114, cert den El Paso Times, Inc v. US District Court for Western District of Texas, 104 SCt 1318, 465 US 1041, 79 LEd2d 714.—Const Law 2070; Crim Law 868; Jury 76.

Harrelson; U.S. v., CA5 (Tex), 705 F2d 733.—Crim Law 394.6(2), 394.6(4), 394.6(5), 805(1), 809, 829(3), 834(2), 1044.1(5.1), 1044.2(1), 1173.1; Ind & Inf 110(38); Weap 4.

Harrelson v. U.S., CA5 (Tex), 613 F2d 114.—Fed Civ Proc 1758.1, 1759; Fed Cts 818; Inj 26(1), 26(5).

Harrelson; U.S. v., CA5 (Tex), 477 F2d 383, cert den 94 SCt 133, 414 US 847, 38 LEd2d 95, reh den 94 SCt 608,

414 US 1086, 38 LEd2d 492.—Consp 47(11); Crim Law 605, 641.10(1), 780(3).

Harrelson v. U.S., WDTex, 967 FSupp 909.—Crim Law 1570, 1572, 1573; Fed Civ Proc 2750.

Harrelson v. U.S., WDTex, 964 FSupp 227.—Records 32.

Harrelson v. Wright, TexCivApp–Eastland, 339 SW2d 712, writ refused.—Trademarks 1037, 1048, 1086, 1628(2), 1691, 1704(1).

Harrelson Rubber Co.; Strain v., CA5 (Tex), 742 F2d 888.—Fed Cts 312.1, 313, 314, 315, 542.

Harrelson Rubber Co.; Trans Texas Tire v., CA5 (Tex), 742 F2d 888. SeeStrain v. Harrelson Rubber Co.

Harriel v. State, TexCrimApp, 572 SW2d 535.—Crim Law 641.1, 641.6(3), 641.7(1).

Harriford v. State, TexCrimApp, 487 SW2d 351.—Larc 21, 57, 60, 61.

Harrill v. A.J.'s Wrecker Service, Inc., TexApp–Dallas, 27 SW3d 191, reh overr, and review dism woj, appeal after remand 2002 WL 31122160, review den.—App & E 919; Courts 35; Judgm 181(3), 181(15.1), 185(2); Plead 104(1), 248(17); Pretrial Proc 551; States 18.3.

Harrill; U.S. v., CA5 (Tex), 877 F2d 341, reh den.—Banks 509.20; Crim Law 814(5), 1172.6; Ind & Inf 3.

Harrill; U.S. v., CA5 (Tex), 91 FedAppx 356.—Crim Law 1130(6); Judges 49(2); Sent & Pun 299, 2252.

Harrington, Ex parte, TexCrimApp, 148 SW2d 1110, 141 TexCrim 347.—Fines 12.

Harrington, Ex parte, TexApp–Fort Worth, 883 SW2d 396, reh overr, and petition for discretionary review refused.—Const Law 4733(2), 4838; Sent & Pun 2010, 2032, 2085.

Harrington, In re, BkrtcyEDTex, 306 BR 172.—Bankr 2492, 2533, 2553, 2766, 2793, 2801, 2802, 3009.

Harrington v. Aetna Cas. & Sur. Co., TexCivApp–Waco, 489 SW2d 171, ref nre.—App & E 194(1), 758.3(11); Evid 66; Insurance 1902, 1904, 2958, 3008, 3066; Trial 83(2).

Harrington v. Bailey, TexCivApp–Waco, 351 SW2d 946.—Gifts 4, 47(1), 49(3); Princ & A 42.

Harrington v. Board of Adjustment of City of Alamo Heights, Bexar County, TexCivApp–Amarillo, 124 SW2d 401, writ refused.—Autos 395; Const Law 2437; Mun Corp 591; Zoning 13, 152, 481, 490, 506.

Harrington; Cobb v., Tex, 190 SW2d 709, 144 Tex 360, 172 ALR 837.—App & E 1175(6); Autos 97; Decl Judgm 1, 42, 43, 215, 253, 313; Inj 7; Mand 3(2.1); States 191.10; Tax 2776; Trial 368.

Harrington v. Cobb, TexCivApp–Dallas, 185 SW2d 133, aff 190 SW2d 709, 144 Tex 360, 172 ALR 837.—App & E 1175(6); Autos 73, 76; Const Law 2525; Decl Judgm 215, 303; Evid 60; States 191.9(2), 191.10; Statut 245.

Harrington v. C.I.R., CA5 (Tex), 404 F2d 237.—Evid 150, 351; Fed Civ Proc 2011; Int Rev 3495, 3505.

Harrington; F.D.I.C. v., NDTex, 844 FSupp 300.—Banks 54(1); Const Law 46(1); Corp 307, 310(1), 314(0.5); Fed Civ Proc 1721, 1829.

Harrington; Great Southern Life Ins. Co. v., TexCivApp–San Antonio, 171 SW2d 538.—Contracts 143(3); Insurance 1739, 1758, 1766, 3580.

Harrington v. Harrington, TexApp–Houston (1 Dist), 742 SW2d 722.—Divorce 253(2); Hus & W 42; Joint Adv 1.2(7), 1.2(9); Judgm 215, 289; Partners 5.

Harrington; Harrington v., TexApp–Houston (1 Dist), 742 SW2d 722.—Divorce 253(2); Hus & W 42; Joint Adv 1.2(7), 1.2(9); Judgm 215, 289; Partners 5.

Harrington v. Harrington, TexCivApp–Hous (1 Dist), 451 SW2d 797.—Divorce 252.3(2), 252.3(5), 252.4, 253(1), 253(2), 286(5); Hus & W 254, 262.1(2), 262.1(3), 262.2.

Harrington; Harrington v., TexCivApp–Hous (1 Dist), 451 SW2d 797.—Divorce 252.3(2), 252.3(5), 252.4, 253(1), 253(2), 286(5); Hus & W 254, 262.1(2), 262.1(3), 262.2.

Harrington v. Harris, CA5 (Tex), 118 F3d 359, reh and sug for reh den 122 F3d 1068, cert den 118 SCt 603, 522 US 1016, 139 LEd2d 491.—Civil R 1032, 1137, 1305,

1326(1), 1405, 1421, 1544, 1545; Colleges 8(3); Const Law 1928, 1929, 1932, 1990, 2025, 3895, 4171, 4223(3); Evid 595; Fed Civ Proc 2601; Fed Cts 753, 765, 776, 801; Offic 100(1).

Harrington v. Harrison, NDTex, 62 FSupp 449.—Deeds 54, 56(2), 58(1).

Harrington; Ingersoll-Rand Co. v., TexApp–Beaumont, 805 SW2d 597, writ den.—App & E 110, 870(6); Jury 31.2(5); Prod Liab 85; Trial 255(11), 351.2(1.1), 351.5(6), 352.10.

Harrington; Johnson v., TexCivApp–Amarillo, 139 SW2d 202, writ dism, correct.—Nova 1, 12.

Harrington; Kirk v., TexCivApp–Fort Worth, 255 SW2d 557.—Abate & R 81; App & E 882(4); Autos 168(2), 242(6), 242(7), 244(26); Plead 111.39(6), 111.42(8), 111.46, 111.47; Pretrial Proc 481.

Harrington; Natural Gas Pipeline Co. of America v., CA5 (Tex), 246 F2d 915, reh den 253 F2d 231, cert den 78 SCt 992, 356 US 957, 2 LEd2d 1065, cert den 78 SCt 995, 356 US 957, 2 LEd2d 1065.—Accord 1, 11(3); Compromise 5(2); Gas 14.1(3), 14.3(2), 14.3(3), 14.6; Interest 39(4); Pub Ut 181.

Harrington; Natural Gas Pipeline Co. of America v., NDTex, 139 FSupp 452, vac 246 F2d 915, reh den 253 F2d 231, cert den 78 SCt 992, 356 US 957, 2 LEd2d 1065, cert den 78 SCt 995, 356 US 957, 2 LEd2d 1065.—Accord 2(2); Corp 218; Evid 44; Fed Civ Proc 2509; Fed Cts 943.1; Gas 14.1(3), 14.6; Impl & C C 10; Lim of Act 49(4).

Harrington v. North Am. Union Life Ins. Co., TexCivApp–Texarkana, 308 SW2d 580, mandamus overr.—Corp 432(8), 432(12); Plead 111.21; Venue 8.5(2), 22(8).

Harrington; Powers v., TexCivApp–Texarkana, 308 SW2d 234.—App & E 1051(1); Venue 8.5(2).

Harrington v. Railroad Commission, Tex, 375 SW2d 892.—Mines 92.26, 92.32(2), 92.42, 92.52, 92.82, 92.83, 92.86, 94; Pub Ut 172, 183.

Harrington v. Rouw v., TexCivApp–San Antonio, 281 SW2d 746, writ dism.—Elections 298(1); Jury 19(1); Mand 117; Mun Corp 918(1); Plead 228.

Harrington; Safety Cas. Co. v., TexCivApp, 193 SW2d 703, ref nre.—Trial 174; Work Comp 1927, 1932.

Harrington v. Schuble, TexCivApp–Hous (14 Dist), 608 SW2d 253.—Divorce 267; Home 76; Judgm 243; Receivers 133, 134, 137, 138, 139, 199.

Harrington; State v., Tex, 407 SW2d 467, cert den 87 SCt 977, 386 US 944, 17 LEd2d 874.—Mines 92.26, 92.42, 92.82, 94, 97; Trial 71, 255(13).

Harrington v. State, TexCrimApp, 547 SW2d 621.—Child S 26; Crim Law 59(3), 438(4), 438(6), 438(7), 438(8), 552(2); Homic 565, 1172, 1174, 1467; Ind & Inf 180.

Harrington v. State, TexCrimApp, 547 SW2d 616.—Child S 26, 653; Crim Law 369.2(4), 517(5), 698(3), 1036.1(2), 1036.9, 1043(3); Homic 565, 1174; Infants 20.

Harrington v. State, TexCrimApp, 424 SW2d 237.—Burg 46(2); Crim Law 304(1), 393(1), 478(1), 721(3), 763(10), 766, 784(1), 796, 822(4), 822(11), 844(1), 867, 1115(2), 1144.8, 1166.15, 1177.5(1); Sent & Pun 1212, 1381(6).

Harrington v. State, TexCrimApp, 117 SW2d 1091, 135 TexCrim 243.—Crim Law 1114.1(1), 1121(1); Rob 24.50.

Harrington v. State, TexCivApp–Austin, 385 SW2d 411, writ gr, rev 407 SW2d 467, cert den 87 SCt 977, 386 US 944, 17 LEd2d 874.—Admin Law 385.1; App & E 837(2), 970(2), 1041(2), 1047(4), 1051(1); Atty Gen 7; Const Law 4426; Costs 69, 101, 237; Evid 28, 65, 150; Fines 1.3; Mines 92.8, 92.16, 92.23(1), 92.42, 92.56, 94, 97, 100; Penalties 4, 32, 33; Plead 34(3), 248(15), 251, 290(3); Pretrial Proc 246; Statut 223.2(1.1); Trial 71, 194(9), 194(20), 215, 216, 219, 283, 350.1, 350.3(2.1), 350.8.

Harrington v. State, TexCivApp–Austin, 363 SW2d 321, ref nre.—Mines 94.

Harrington v. Texaco, Inc., CA5 (Tex), 339 F2d 814, cert den 85 SCt 1538, 381 US 915, 14 LEd2d 435.—Damag

15, 63, 163(4); Evid 150; Fed Civ Proc 2011, 2723, 2736, 2738; Fed Cts 628, 643, 830, 876; Lim of Act 166; Mines 48, 51(1), 51(3), 51(5), 92.8; Trover 3, 44.

Harrington; Texas Western Securities, Inc. v., TexCivApp–Texarkana, 308 SW2d 237.—App & E 1051(1), 1054(1); Venue 8.5(2).

Harrington; U.S. v., CA5 (Tex), 129 FedAppx 112, cert den 126 SCt 275, 546 US 912, 163 LEd2d 245, reh den, reh den 126 SCt 726, 546 US 1057, 163 LEd2d 622.—Crim Law 1026.10(4).

Harrington v. Walker, TexApp–Fort Worth, 829 SW2d 935, reh den, and writ den.—Wills 487(4), 865(1).

Harrington; Wampler v., TexCivApp–Texarkana, 261 SW2d 883, ref nre.—App & E 931(6), 1061.4; Contracts 108(1), 127(1), 164; Deeds 130, 134, 147; Fraud 64(1); Mines 74(10), 99(3); Partners 96; Trusts 103(5), 336, 343.

Harrington; Watson v., TexCivApp–Austin, 285 SW2d 390.—Plead 110, 111.21.

Harrington v. Western Nat. Bank of Amarillo, TexCivApp–Amarillo, 572 SW2d 769.—Banks 275; Plead 111.38; Propty 7.

Harrington; William B. Morris Co. v., TexCivApp–Texarkana, 454 SW2d 427.—App & E 1177(2); Judgm 181(5.1), 185.2(9).

Harrington v. Young Men's Christian Ass'n of Houston and Harris County, Tex, 452 SW2d 423.—App & E 863; Judgm 181(1), 185(2), 185.3(17).

Harrington v. Young Men's Christian Ass'n of Houston and Harris County, TexCivApp–Hous (1 Dist), 440 SW2d 354, rev 452 SW2d 423.—App & E 465(2); Courts 207.4(2); Covenants 49, 51(2), 52; Mand 57(2).

Harris, Ex parte, TexCrimApp, 946 SW2d 79.—Bail 42; Sent & Pun 1157, 1167.

Harris, Ex parte, TexCrimApp, 825 SW2d 120, reh den.—Sent & Pun 1780(3).

Harris, Ex parte, TexCrimApp, 618 SW2d 369.—Crim Law 393(1), 474, 625.15; Hab Corp 816, 847.

Harris, Ex parte, TexCrimApp, 600 SW2d 791.—Crim Law 1189; Double J 109.

Harris, Ex parte, TexCrimApp, 596 SW2d 893.—Const Law 4813; Crim Law 641.13(1); Hab Corp 475.1, 486(2).

Harris, Ex parte, TexCrimApp, 593 SW2d 330, appeal after remand 596 SW2d 893.—Hab Corp 823, 845.

Harris, Ex parte, TexCrimApp, 592 SW2d 624, appeal after remand 618 SW2d 369.—Const Law 4782; Mental H 432.

Harris, Ex parte, TexCrimApp, 583 SW2d 419.—Double J 150(1).

Harris, Ex parte, TexCrimApp, 495 SW2d 231.—Burg 49; Hab Corp 228.

Harris, Ex parte, TexCrimApp, 460 SW2d 150.—Sent & Pun 1161.

Harris, Ex parte, TexCrimApp, 389 SW2d 668.—Hab Corp 526, 791.

Harris, Ex parte, TexCrimApp, 375 SW2d 453.—Extrad 27, 36; Hab Corp 729.

Harris, Ex parte, TexCrimApp, 225 SW2d 838, 154 TexCrim 209.—Hab Corp 469.

Harris, Ex parte, TexApp–Austin, 733 SW2d 712.—Bail 39, 51, 52, 53.

Harris, Ex parte, TexApp–Corpus Christi, 649 SW2d 389.—Child S 456, 459.

Harris, Ex parte, TexCivApp–Fort Worth, 581 SW2d 545.—Child S 489; Contempt 40; Witn 306, 307.

Harris, In re, BkrtcyEDTex, 111 BR 589.—Bankr 2429(2), 2852.

Harris; Adam v., TexCivApp–Hous (14 Dist), 564 SW2d 152, ref nre.—App & E 216(1); Damag 87(2); Fraud 61; Judgm 518; Trial 255(14), 284, 350.2; Trover 1, 22, 58, 60, 61, 69; Trusts 181(1), 231(1), 265.

Harris; Administrative Committee for the H.E.B. Inv. and Retirement Plan v., EDTex, 217 FSupp2d 759.—

Fed Cts 419; Insurance 3484; Labor & Emp 407, 587; States 18.51.

Harris; Aetna Cas. & Sur. Co. v., TexApp–Houston (1 Dist), 682 SW2d 670.—Mand 26, 53; Pretrial Proc 698.

Harris; Aetna Cas. & Sur. Co. v., TexCivApp–Beaumont, 428 SW2d 112, dism.—App & E 930(3); Damag 221(3); Work Comp 1639.

Harris; Aetna Life Ins. Co. v., TexCivApp–Austin, 83 SW2d 1087, aff 121 SW2d 324, 132 Tex 213.—App & E 207, 688(2); Courts 37(3); Plead 8(8); Work Comp 524, 589, 975, 1287, 1846.

Harris v. Allstate Ins. Co., TexCivApp–Texarkana, 249 SW2d 669, writ refused.—App & E 218.2(1), 1052(5); Insurance 1752, 2693, 2968, 3006, 3024, 3089, 3106; Trial 351.2(4).

Harris; American Exp. Travel Related Services v., Tex-App–Houston (14 Dist), 831 SW2d 531.—Exemp 48(2); Garn 1, 54.

Harris v. American Protection Ins. Co., TexApp–Fort Worth, 158 SW3d 614.—App & E 241, 927(7), 930(3), 989, 1003(5), 1003(7); Contracts 326; Fraud 21, 25; Insurance 2112, 2189, 3335, 3336, 3337, 3345, 3356, 3360, 3363, 3364, 3374, 3381(5), 3513(1), 3514(1), 3514(3), 3515(1); Lim of Act 100(1), 180(7), 199(2); Subrog 1; Trial 139.1(14), 139.1(17).

Harris v. American Red Cross, WDTex, 752 FSupp 737. —Fed Civ Proc 2470.2; Labor & Emp 807, 809.

Harris v. Angelina County, Tex., CA5 (Tex), 31 F3d 331, reh and sug for reh den.—Civil R 1454, 1457(5); Const Law 4544, 4545(1), 4545(4); Fed Cts 265, 272, 776, 850.1; Prisons 4(3), 18(7); Sent & Pun 1532, 1534, 1538.

Harris v. Annuity Bd. of Southern Baptist Convention, TexApp–Corpus Christi, 666 SW2d 346, ref nre.—App & E 173(1), 179(1), 863; Deeds 93; Judgm 181(8), 185(5).

Harris v. A–OK Motel, TexApp–Fort Worth, 818 SW2d 530. See Harris v. Schepp.

Harris v. Apfel, CA5 (Tex), 209 F3d 413.—Atty & C 62; Social S 8.20, 143.60.

Harris v. Archer, TexApp–Amarillo, 134 SW3d 411, reh overr, and review den.—App & E 356, 756, 761, 766, 842(11), 927(7), 969, 1004(11); Const Law 4427; Contracts 97(1), 97(2), 98, 328(1), 352(2); Damag 87(1), 94.1, 94.6, 94.7, 94.8, 208(1), 208(8); Fraud 35; Partners 25, 95, 121, 122, 122.5, 227, 259.5, 264, 277, 311(5).

Harris; Arkla, Inc. v., TexApp–Houston (14 Dist), 846 SW2d 623.—Mand 4(4), 26; Pretrial Proc 33, 34, 35, 41, 44.1, 358, 371, 401, 406, 411, 434; Witn 198(1), 222.

Harris v. Ashland Oil & Refining Co., TexCivApp–El Paso, 315 SW2d 327.—Plead 111.39(2), 111.42(5); Venue 7.5(2), 7.5(3).

Harris v. Atchison, T. & S. F. Ry. Co., CA5 (Tex), 538 F2d 682.—Explos 7; Fed Cts 372, 714, 866; Indem 58, 60, 70; Neglig 503, 570, 1010, 1012, 1020, 1037(4), 1037(7), 1085.

Harris; Autrey v., CA5 (Tex), 639 F2d 1233.—Social S 143.1.

Harris; Baird v., TexApp–Dallas, 778 SW2d 147.—Mand 29.

Harris v. Balderas, TexApp–San Antonio, 27 SW3d 71, reh overr, and review den.—App & E 781(1); Contracts 9(1), 14, 15, 16, 24, 28(0.5), 28(3); Insurance 3350; Judgm 181(19), 486(1).

Harris v. Balderas, TexApp–San Antonio, 949 SW2d 42, reh overr.—App & E 1003(5), 1004(3), 1004(8); Damag 49.10, 96, 132(3), 192.

Harris v. BASF Corp., CA5 (Tex), 81 FedAppx 495.— Civil R 1505(3), 1708; Fed Civ Proc 840, 2553.

Harris v. Belue, TexApp–Tyler, 974 SW2d 386, review den.—App & E 204(2), 866(3), 927(7); Damag 37, 38; Evid 555.10; Health 618, 684, 821(2), 822(3), 825, 826.

Harris v. Beto, CA5 (Tex), 438 F2d 116.—Gr Jury 35; Hab Corp 719, 720, 721(2), 827.

Harris v. Beto, CA5 (Tex), 399 F2d 679.—Crim Law 1069(6), 1077.3; Hab Corp 338, 864(1).

Harris v. Beto, CA5 (Tex), 387 F2d 149, cert den 88 SCt 1662, 391 US 908, 20 LEd2d 424, cert den 88 SCt 1662, 391 US 901, 20 LEd2d 424.—Crim Law 519(8).

Harris v. Beto, CA5 (Tex), 367 F2d 567, on remand 280 FSupp 532, aff 387 F2d 149, cert den 88 SCt 1662, 391 US 908, 20 LEd2d 424, cert den 88 SCt 1662, 391 US 901, 20 LEd2d 424.—Crim Law 520(2), 522(1); Hab Corp 483, 799, 864(4).

Harris v. Beto, NDTex, 280 FSupp 200.—Hab Corp 361, 364, 612.1, 613.

Harris v. Beto, SDTex, 280 FSupp 532, aff 387 F2d 149, cert den 88 SCt 1662, 391 US 908, 20 LEd2d 424, cert den 88 SCt 1662, 391 US 901, 20 LEd2d 424.—Hab Corp 207, 339, 722(2).

Harris; Bishop v., TexApp–Tyler, 669 SW2d 859, dism.— Waters 118, 126(3).

Harris; Blevins v., TexCivApp–Fort Worth, 150 SW2d 813.—Adop 14, 16; App & E 499(1); Child C 553, 555; Hab Corp 532(1), 861.

Harris v. Blue Cross and Blue Shield of Texas, Inc., NDTex, 729 FSupp 49.—Fed Cts 421; Insurance 1117(1); Labor & Emp 407, 662, 702; States 18.51.

Harris; Boney v., TexCivApp–Hous (1 Dist), 557 SW2d 376.—Ex & Ad 227(3); Judgm 183.

Harris v. Borne, TexApp–Houston (1 Dist), 933 SW2d 535.—App & E 387(6), 389(3), 624; Evid 42; Records 7.

Harris; Bowie v., TexCivApp–Waco, 351 SW2d 668, ref nre.—Judgm 648.

Harris; Bradley v., TexCivApp–Waco, 300 SW2d 335.— App & E 1001(1); Impl & C C 99.1; Mech Liens 199, 288(1).

Harris; Brenem v., CA5 (Tex), 621 F2d 688.—Social S 140.30, 143.45, 143.70, 149.

Harris; Brown Exp. v., TexCivApp–San Antonio, 202 SW2d 470.—Carr 134, 135.

Harris; Burkhardt v., TexCivApp–Austin, 200 SW2d 445. —Hus & W 21, 23.5; Trial 382.

Harris v. Callahan, EDTex, 11 FSupp2d 880.—Const Law 3881, 4123; Social S 140.21, 142.5, 143.85, 148.15.

Harris v. Cantu, TexApp–Corpus Christi, 697 SW2d 721, set aside, and writ gr.—App & E 1064.1(8); Autos 244(4); Damag 185(2), 186; Trial 207.

Harris; Cantu v., TexApp–Corpus Christi, 660 SW2d 638. —App & E 846(5), 989; Fixt 1, 6.1; Inj 128(3.1).

Harris; Carson v., TexCivApp–San Antonio, 242 SW2d 777, ref nre.—App & E 931(1); Courts 247(6); Mand 57(1); Names 17; Trademarks 1042, 1113, 1158, 1172, 1198, 1200(3), 1201(1), 1419, 1526, 1629(3), 1800.

Harris; Carter v., CA5 (Tex), 615 F2d 1044.—Social S 143.45, 143.75, 148.5.

Harris; Castle v., TexApp–Corpus Christi, 960 SW2d 140. —Child S 453, 543, 559; Interest 39(2.20).

Harris v. Casualty Reciprocal Exchange, Tex, 632 SW2d 714.—Work Comp 302, 303.

Harris; Casualty Reciprocal Exchange v., TexApp–Waco, 623 SW2d 154, rev 632 SW2d 714.—Work Comp 303.

Harris; Central Bank v., TexApp–Austin, 623 SW2d 807. —Action 3; App & E 179(4); Insurance 1371, 1412.

Harris; Chapman v., TexCivApp–Texarkana, 231 SW2d 549.—App & E 907(3); Child C 42, 275, 413, 414; Divorce 172.

Harris v. Chemical Leaman Tank Lines, Inc., CA5 (Tex), 437 F2d 167.—Fed Civ Proc 184.10; Fed Cts 743; Labor & Emp 1213, 1214, 1218, 1219(2), 1320(1), 1615, 1983, 1996.

Harris v. Christianson-Keithley Co., TexCivApp–Galveston, 303 SW2d 422, ref nre.—App & E 218.2(7), 239, 302(1), 882(3); Chat Mtg 162; Trial 351.2(2), 355(3); Trover 40(1), 42, 53, 66, 70.

HARRIS;

See Guidelines for Arrangement at the beginning of this Volume

Harris; City of Dallas v., TexCivApp–Dallas, 157 SW2d 710, writ refused.—Autos 362, 363; Const Law 4105(4); High 165; Mun Corp 594(1), 658, 703(1), 721(1).

Harris v. City of Fort Worth, Tex, 180 SW2d 131, 142 Tex 600.—Const Law 593; Statut 181(1), 184, 214, 217.1; Tax 2346, 2351, 2355.

Harris; City of Fort Worth v., TexCivApp–Fort Worth, 177 SW2d 308, rev 180 SW2d 131, 142 Tex 600.—Statut 109.11, 126; Tax 2351.

Harris v. City of Houston, CA5 (Tex), 151 F3d 186, reh and sug for reh den 172 F3d 871.—Fed Cts 12.1, 13, 13.25, 723.1, 776, 932.1, 936.

Harris v. City of Houston, SDTex, 10 FSupp2d 721, vac 151 F3d 186, reh and sug for reh den 172 F3d 871.— Const Law 82(8), 1466, 1480, 2970, 3255, 3285; Elections 12(1), 12(2.1), 12(6), 12(8); Mun Corp 29(0.5), 33(10), 35.

Harris; City of Houston v., TexApp–Houston (14 Dist), 192 SW3d 167, reh overr.—App & E 70(3), 1097(1), 1097(8), 1195(1); Courts 37(1), 37(2), 99(1); Mun Corp 742(5), 742(6), 847, 851, 857.

Harris v. City of Houston, Tex., CA5 (Tex), 476 F2d 283. —Rem of C 102.

Harris v. City of Port Arthur, TexCivApp–Austin, 244 SW2d 716.—App & E 80(6).

Harris; City of Wichita Falls v., TexCivApp–Fort Worth, 532 SW2d 653, ref nre.—App & E 1078(1); Mun Corp 176(3.1), 194, 197, 198(1), 198(2), 198(3), 198(4), 216(1); Plead 18, 427; Statut 47.

Harris v. Civil Service Com'n for Mun. Employees of City of Houston, TexApp–Houston (14 Dist), 803 SW2d 729, extension of time to file for writ of error overr.— Admin Law 474, 651, 674, 704; Mun Corp 185(3), 185(12).

Harris v. Cleveland, TexCivApp–Galveston, 294 SW2d 235, dism.—App & E 832(4); Joint Adv 1.2(7), 1.13; Plead 111.18, 111.42(9); Venue 22(1).

Harris v. Cochran, TexCivApp–Texarkana, 288 SW2d 814, ref nre.—App & E 270(1); Autos 244(29), 246(42); Evid 588; Infants 90; Labor & Emp 23, 29; Trial 131(1); Work Comp 231.

Harris v. Cockrell, CA5 (Tex), 313 F3d 238, cert den 124 SCt 1503, 540 US 1218, 158 LEd2d 152, reh den 124 SCt 2933, 542 US 952, 159 LEd2d 836.—Const Law 4566, 4708, 4744(2); Crim Law 641.13(7), 723(3); Hab Corp 497; Judgm 751; Sent & Pun 1762, 1780(3), 1784(4).

Harris v. Cockrell, CA5 (Tex), 84 FedAppx 438, on subsequent appeal 115 FedAppx 731.—Civil R 1395(7); Fed Civ Proc 2491.5.

Harris; Coker v., TexCivApp–Dallas, 281 SW2d 100, ref nre.—Child C 468, 920, 921(1); Judges 49(1).

Harris; Cole v., TexCivApp–Amarillo, 332 SW2d 119.— Wills 55(1), 306, 440, 449, 481, 853, 858(1).

Harris v. Collins, CA5 (Tex), 990 F2d 185, cert den 113 SCt 3069, 509 US 933, 125 LEd2d 746.—Const Law 4623; Courts 100(1); Crim Law 655(8), 1035(5); Homic 1465; Sent & Pun 1784(4).

Harris v. Columbia Broadcasting System, Inc., TexCivApp–Austin, 405 SW2d 613, ref nre.—Corp 642(1); Libel 76; Lim of Act 84(2), 193; Pretrial Proc 473.

Harris; Commercial Credit Corp. v., TexCivApp–Fort Worth, 227 SW2d 886.—Autos 20; Chat Mtg 158.1, 162; Sales 480(1.1).

Harris; Commercial Credit Corp. v., TexCivApp–Fort Worth, 225 SW2d 247.—Autos 20; Venue 8.5(5), 8.5(7).

Harris v. C. I. R., CA5 (Tex), 461 F2d 554.—Evid 77(6); Fed Cts 743; Int Rev 4623.

Harris; Conmark Equipment, Inc. v., TexCivApp–Tyler, 595 SW2d 145.—Judgm 306, 340.

Harris v. Corpus Christi Broadcasting Co., TexCivApp– San Antonio, 333 SW2d 475, ref nre.—Acct Action on 13; Costs 194.32.

Harris v. Coward, TexCivApp–Fort Worth, 573 SW2d 875, ref nre.—Autos 201(10), 240(1), 245(49); Neglig 1698; Trial 252(7).

Harris v. Currie, Tex, 176 SW2d 302, 142 Tex 93.—Deeds 120; Mines 54(2), 55(1), 55(4), 55(6), 74.5; Ten in C 49.

Harris; Currie v., TexCivApp–Austin, 172 SW2d 404, aff 176 SW2d 302, 142 Tex 93.—Mines 55(4), 55(6), 55(7), 74(5), 78.7(6); Ten in C 49; Ven & Pur 196.

Harris; Dallas Cowboys Football Club, Inc. v., TexCivApp–Dallas, 348 SW2d 37.—Antitrust 634; App & E 790(3), 1051(2); Estop 84; Inj 60, 130, 135, 138.37, 158; Judgm 181(21), 199(3.14); Labor & Emp 34(2), 48; New Tr 72(8); Trial 139.1(14), 350.4(4), 355(3).

Harris; Dallas Railway & Terminal Co. v., TexCivApp– Dallas, 81 SW2d 716.—App & E 1068(4); Carr 344, 347; Damag 158(2); Trial 139.1(6), 366.

Harris; Danforth Memorial Hospital v., Tex, 573 SW2d 762.—Pretrial Proc 699.

Harris; Downtown Auto Repair v., TexApp–San Antonio, 715 SW2d 418. SeePalacios v. Harris.

Harris; Elliott v., CA5 (Tex), 205 FedAppx 255.—Fed Civ Proc 1940; Fed Cts 915.

Harris v. Ellis, CA5 (Tex), 204 F2d 685.—Hab Corp 818.

Harris v. Ellis, CA5 (Tex), 194 F2d 604.—Hab Corp 818.

Harris v. Elm Oil Co., TexCivApp–Texarkana, 183 SW2d 216, writ refused wom.—App & E 933(1), 977(1), 1054(1); Courts 493(2); Evid 222(10), 575; Judgm 145(2), 145(4), 335(1), 829(3).

Harris; El Paso City Lines v., TexCivApp–El Paso, 233 SW2d 620.—App & E 994(2), 1004(5), 1004(8); Damag 127, 132(1), 208(1), 208(2).

Harris; El Paso Natural Gas Co. v., TexCivApp–El Paso, 436 SW2d 408, ref nre.—App & E 931(1), 989; Death 14(1), 76; Labor & Emp 2765; Mines 118; Neglig 1011, 1037(7), 1568, 1579, 1652, 1676; Trial 350.6(2).

Harris; Empire Life and Hospital Ins. Co. v., TexCivApp–Austin, 595 SW2d 904.—Const Law 2758; Insurance 1350, 1414; Sec Tran 92.1; Trial 31.

Harris v. Estelle, CA5 (Tex), 583 F2d 775.—Crim Law 1104(1), 1104(3).

Harris v. Estelle, CA5 (Tex), 487 F2d 1293.—Const Law 4809; Courts 100(1); Crim Law 223, 224, 232, 339.8(7), 641.12(1), 641.13(2.1), 641.13(6); Hab Corp 351, 402, 472, 496, 861; Jury 33(1.15), 64.

Harris v. Estelle, CA5 (Tex), 487 F2d 56.—Crim Law 1069(6), 1077.3; Hab Corp 753.

Harris v. Ferguson, Tex, 156 SW2d 135, 137 Tex 592.— App & E 1114; Corp 269(3); Paymt 1(1).

Harris; Ferguson v., TexCivApp–Dallas, 159 SW2d 950.— Corp 90(6).

Harris; Ferguson v., TexCivApp–Dallas, 135 SW2d 595, rev 156 SW2d 135, 137 Tex 592.—Trial 350.3(6), 350.4(1), 350.8.

Harris; Fireman's Fund Ins. Co. v., TexCivApp–Waco, 475 SW2d 325, writ gr.—Insurance 3559; Venue 22(7).

Harris; Fort Worth & D. Ry. Co. v., CA5 (Tex), 230 F2d 680.—Fed Civ Proc 1969, 1976; Fed Cts 611, 621, 628, 641, 875, 906; Labor & Emp 2881.

Harris v. Foster, TexCivApp–Austin, 261 SW2d 860.— Venue 7.5(3), 22(4), 22(6).

Harris; Freedman Packing Co. v., TexCivApp–Galveston, 160 SW2d 130, writ refused wom.—App & E 758.3(1), 1072; Const Law 2653; Courts 247(7); New Tr 109, 128(4), 140(1), 143(1), 152; Plead 13.

Harris; French v., TexApp–Dallas, 658 SW2d 690.—Child S 471; Mand 44; Venue 78.

Harris; Gaebler v., TexCivApp–San Antonio, 625 SW2d 5, ref nre.—App & E 962; Pretrial Proc 581, 582, 583, 584.

Harris v. Galveston County, TexApp–Houston (14 Dist), 799 SW2d 766, writ den.—Counties 143; Health 260; Judgm 181(11), 185(6); Lim of Act 127(1), 127(14); Mun Corp 847.

Harris; General Crude Oil Co. v., TexCivApp–Texarkana, 101 SW2d 1098, writ dism.—Abate & R 19; App

& E 1039(16); Contracts 348, 352(1); Land & Ten 27; Mines 78.4, 78.7(6).

Harris; General Dynamics Corp. v., TexCivApp–Waco, 581 SW2d 300.—Courts 489(1); Divorce 273; States 18.28.

Harris; General Ins. Corp. v., TexCivApp–Dallas, 327 SW2d 651.—Damag 87(1), 87(2); Insurance 2276, 2280, 2914.

Harris v. General Motors Corp., TexApp–San Antonio, 924 SW2d 187, writ den.—App & E 758.1, 1070(2), 1136; Prod Liab 96.5; Trial 186, 194(1), 205.

Harris; G.F.S. Ventures, Inc. v., TexApp–Houston (1 Dist), 934 SW2d 813.—App & E 5, 914(1); Corp 507(12), 507(14), 668(14); Proc 145, 149.

Harris; Gilmer v., TexCivApp–Fort Worth, 460 SW2d 215.—Ex & Ad 7, 15, 25.

Harris v. Glen Falls Group, TexCivApp–Corpus Christi, 478 SW2d 561, ref nre.—Insurance 2019, 2039, 3541.

Harris; Goodloe & Meredith v., TexComApp, 94 SW2d 1141, 127 Tex 583.—Mines 109; Partit 12(1), 16, 62, 63(1), 83, 87.

Harris; Gorsalitz v., TexCivApp–Tyler, 410 SW2d 956, ref nre.—App & E 883; Health 821(2), 823(10).

Harris; Gorsalitz v., TexCivApp–Houston, 360 SW2d 574, appeal after remand 410 SW2d 956, ref nre.—Health 826.

Harris; Great Atlantic Life Ins. Co. v., TexApp–Austin, 723 SW2d 329, dism.—Insurance 1363, 3606, 3631.

Harris; Gribble v., CA5 (Tex), 625 F2d 1173.—Fed Civ Proc 2294, 2366.1, 2658; Fed Cts 653, 657, 658.

Harris; Grimes v., TexApp–Dallas, 695 SW2d 648.—Child C 404; Courts 475(1), 475(15).

Harris v. Gunner, TexCivApp–Fort Worth, 545 SW2d 856.—Plead 34(6), 404; Sales 370, 379, 383, 384(2).

Harris v. Gurley, CCA5 (Tex), 80 F2d 744.—Courts 493(3); Evid 357; Mines 100; Trial 11(3); Trusts 17(3), 43(1), 44(3).

Harris v. Hanover Fire Ins. Co., CA5 (Tex), 425 F2d 1168.—Insurance 3564(9); Lim of Act 25(2).

Harris; Hansson v., TexCivApp–Austin, 252 SW2d 600, ref nre.—Inj 96.

Harris v. Harbour Title Co., TexApp–Houston (14 Dist), 49 SW3d 371, review gr, and review withdrawn, and review gr, rev Lehmann v. Har-Con Corp, 39 SW3d 191, on remand 2001 WL 1249730, on remand 76 SW3d 555.—App & E 4, 78(1), 338(1), 780(1), 1178(1); Judgm 187, 190, 303.

Harris; Harrington v., CA5 (Tex), 118 F3d 359, reh and sug for reh den 122 F3d 1068, cert den 118 SCt 603, 522 US 1016, 139 LEd2d 491.—Civil R 1032, 1137, 1305, 1326(1), 1405, 1421, 1544, 1545; Colleges 8(3); Const Law 1928, 1929, 1932, 1990, 2025, 3895, 4171, 4223(3); Evid 595; Fed Civ Proc 2601; Fed Cts 753, 765, 776, 801; Offic 100(1).

Harris v. Harris, TexApp–Houston (1 Dist), 850 SW2d 241.—Divorce 97, 160; Judgm 107; Plead 34(1).

Harris; Harris v., TexApp–Houston (1 Dist), 850 SW2d 241.—Divorce 97, 160; Judgm 107; Plead 34(1).

Harris v. Harris, TexApp–Dallas, 679 SW2d 75, dism.—App & E 1031(1); Divorce 254(1), 254(2); Judgm 329; Jury 12(1); Ven & Pur 18(3).

Harris; Harris v., TexApp–Dallas, 679 SW2d 75, dism.—App & E 1031(1); Divorce 254(1), 254(2); Judgm 329; Jury 12(1); Ven & Pur 18(3).

Harris v. Harris, TexApp–Houston (14 Dist), 765 SW2d 798, writ den.—Divorce 253(4), 282, 286(9); Hus & W 249(2.1), 249(5), 249(6), 257, 258, 262.1(1), 262.1(3), 262.1(8), 264(2), 264(3), 270(8); Judgm 199(1), 199(3.10); Partners 77; Trial 215, 252(1).

Harris; Harris v., TexApp–Houston (14 Dist), 765 SW2d 798, writ den.—Divorce 253(4), 282, 286(9); Hus & W 249(2.1), 249(5), 249(6), 257, 258, 262.1(1), 262.1(3), 262.1(8), 264(2), 264(3), 270(8); Judgm 199(1), 199(3.10); Partners 77; Trial 215, 252(1).

Harris v. Harris, TexCivApp–Hous (1 Dist), 605 SW2d 684, ref nre.—App & E 205, 242(4), 500(3), 548(5), 907(4); Bankr 3348.10; Divorce 252.2, 255, 285, 286(6.1).

Harris; Harris v., TexCivApp–Hous (1 Dist), 605 SW2d 684, ref nre.—App & E 205, 242(4), 500(3), 548(5), 907(4); Bankr 3348.10; Divorce 252.2, 255, 285, 286(6.1).

Harris v. Harris, TexCivApp–Fort Worth, 174 SW2d 996.—App & E 756, 926(6); Divorce 144, 253(2), 254(1), 286(0.5); Evid 5(2), 20(1); Execution 158(1); Fixt 17; Trial 351.2(2), 366.

Harris; Harris v., TexCivApp–Fort Worth, 174 SW2d 996.—App & E 756, 926(6); Divorce 144, 253(2), 254(1), 286(0.5); Evid 5(2), 20(1); Execution 158(1); Fixt 17; Trial 351.2(2), 366.

Harris v. Harris, TexCivApp–Waco, 562 SW2d 953, dism.—Divorce 252.3(2), 253(2); Hus & W 248; Marriage 50(1).

Harris; Harris v., TexCivApp–Waco, 562 SW2d 953, dism.—Divorce 252.3(2), 253(2); Hus & W 248; Marriage 50(1).

Harris v. Harris, TexCivApp–Houston, 403 SW2d 445, ref nre.—Evid 35, 80(1); Judgm 521, 813, 815, 818(5), 942, 944.

Harris; Harris v., TexCivApp–Houston, 403 SW2d 445, ref nre.—Evid 35, 80(1); Judgm 521, 813, 815, 818(5), 942, 944.

Harris v. Harris, TexCivApp–Galveston, 190 SW2d 489.—Divorce 91, 179, 252.2, 253(2).

Harris; Harris v., TexCivApp–Galveston, 190 SW2d 489.—Divorce 91, 179, 252.2, 253(2).

Harris v. Harris County Hospital Dist., TexCivApp–Hous (1 Dist), 557 SW2d 353.—Health 656, 696, 703(2), 819, 823(14).

Harris; Hartford Acc. & Indem. Co. v., TexCivApp–Eastland, 152 SW2d 857, writ dism.—Damag 221(1), 221(5.1); Trial 352.20, 358; Work Comp 1927, 1930.

Harris; Hartford Acc. & Indem. Co. v., TexCivApp–Eastland, 138 SW2d 277, writ dism, correct.—App & E 692(1); Evid 558(1); Witn 280; Work Comp 1375, 1924, 1961.

Harris; Haskett v., TexCivApp–Corpus Christi, 567 SW2d 841.—App & E 185(1); Contempt 24; Prohib 1, 3(1), 16.

Harris v. Hayles, TexCivApp–Texarkana, 433 SW2d 250.—App & E 865; Judgm 17(3), 130; Proc 80.

Harris; Helms v., TexCivApp–Fort Worth, 281 SW2d 770, ref nre.—Neglig 1162, 1238, 1673; Torts 121.

Harris v. Henley, TexCivApp–Tyler, 493 SW2d 643.—App & E 907(3); Costs 194.32, 194.38.

Harris v. Herbers, TexApp–Houston (1 Dist), 838 SW2d 938.—Adop 9.1; App & E 1010.1(1), 1010.1(5); Const Law 82(10); Infants 155, 156, 178, 179.

Harris; Heritage Manor Apartments v., Tex, 924 SW2d 375. See Walker v. Harris.

Harris; Hester v., CA5 (Tex), 631 F2d 53.—Const Law 4120; Social S 122.5.

Harris; Highlands Underwriters Ins. Co. v., TexCivApp–Tyler, 530 SW2d 350, ref nre.—Work Comp 872, 876.

Harris v. Hines, TexApp–Texarkana, 137 SW3d 898.—App & E 895(2); Wills 435, 439, 440, 456, 470(1), 470(2), 481, 487(1), 487(2), 488, 491, 750, 751, 753, 756, 764, 765, 767, 770.

Harris v. Holbert, TexCivApp–Eastland, 517 SW2d 333.—Judgm 199(3.7), 199(3.17); New Tr 44(2).

Harris v. Holland, TexApp–Texarkana, 867 SW2d 86.—App & E 161; Divorce 252.1, 252.3(1), 252.4, 281, 286(5); Hus & W 265.

Harris; Homan & Crimen, Inc. v., CA5 (Tex), 626 F2d 1201, reh den 633 F2d 582, cert den 101 SCt 1506, 450 US 975, 67 LEd2d 809.—Admin Law 413; Corp 1.3; Health 485, 535(1), 535(2), 535(4), 547, 548, 549, 557(1); Social S 8.20.

Harris; Homestead Lumber Co. v., TexCivApp–Waco, 178 SW2d 161.—App & E 2, 624.

Harris v. Honda, CA5 (Tex), 213 FedAppx 258.—Atty & C 62; Civil R 1506, 1513, 1708, 1709, 1715; Courts 97(5); Fed Civ Proc 1829; Fed Cts 776; Statut 226.

Harris; Horton v., TexCivApp–Tyler, 610 SW2d 819, ref nre.—App & E 1001(1); Deeds 211(1); Hus & W 273(9); Trial 350.3(2.1); Trusts 95, 103(1), 110.

Harris v. Hubbert, TexCivApp–Eastland, 82 SW2d 726, writ refused.—App & E 499(3), 690(3); Bills & N 499, 527(1); Evid 332(7).

Harris; Ianni v., CCA5 (Tex), 111 F2d 833.—Aliens 274, 332.

Harris; Illinois Tool Works, Inc. v., TexApp–Houston (14 Dist), 194 SW3d 529, reh overr.—Action 17; Contracts 129(1), 143(2), 143.5, 147(1), 152, 154, 164, 176(1), 221(1); Labor & Emp 39.

Harris; International Sec. Life Ins. Co. v., TexCivApp–Amarillo, 461 SW2d 222, writ dism woj.—App & E 286; Insurance 3343; Witn 16.

Harris v. Interstate Lumber Co., TexCivApp–Waco, 303 SW2d 950.—App & E 1001(1), 1003(2); Mech Liens 92, 281(1).

Harris; Inwood North Homeowners' Ass'n, Inc. v., Tex, 736 SW2d 632.—Covenants 53, 84; Home 12, 81, 90, 93, 96, 97; Liens 3; Mech Liens 57(1).

Harris; Inwood North Homeowners' Ass'n, Inc. v., Tex-App–Houston (1 Dist), 707 SW2d 127, ref nre, and writ gr, and writ withdrawn, rev 736 SW2d 632.—Covenants 104; Ven & Pur 249.

Harris v. J.B. Hunt Transport, Inc., EDTex, 423 FSupp2d 595.—Labor & Emp 611, 676, 690, 691, 699.

Harris v. Johnson, CA5 (Tex), 376 F3d 414.—Civil R 1088(5); Sent & Pun 1798.

Harris v. Johnson, CA5 (Tex), 81 F3d 535, cert den 116 SCt 1863, 517 US 1227, 134 LEd2d 961.—Const Law 3811, 4744(2); Crim Law 641.13(1), 641.13(2.1); Hab Corp 688, 742, 767, 818; Sent & Pun 1762, 1780(3).

Harris; Johnson v., CA5 (Tex), 612 F2d 993.—Social S 140.41, 143.40, 143.45, 143.55, 143.85, 147, 148.5, 149.5.

Harris v. Johnson, SDTex, 323 FSupp2d 797, vac 376 F3d 414.—Civil R 1088(5), 1090, 1301, 1304, 1311, 1457(1), 1457(5); Hab Corp 462, 507, 508; Sent & Pun 1798.

Harris v. Jones, TexApp–El Paso, 8 SW3d 383.—Mand 3(2.1), 3(5), 7, 12, 187.9(1), 187.9(5), 187.9(6).

Harris v. Jones, TexCivApp–Eastland, 404 SW2d 349, writ refused.—Judgm 585(4).

Harris; Kaname Susuki v., EDTex, 29 FSupp 46.—Aliens 249, 259, 403(1), 403(3); Const Law 2541.

Harris v. Keoun, TexCivApp–Waco, 135 SW2d 194, writ refused.—App & E 1234(1); Elect of Rem 12; Judgm 581.

Harris; Kerr-McGee Chemical Corp. v., CA5 (Tex), 442 F2d 1109.—Lim of Act 46(9).

Harris, Estate of; Kilpatrick v., TexApp–Corpus Christi, 848 SW2d 859, reh overr.—App & E 930(3), 989, 999(1), 1001(1); Frds St of 139(1); Lim of Act 102(8), 127(10); Trusts 103(3); Wills 56, 58(2), 61, 66, 67, 68, 152.

Harris; Kirkpatrick v., TexApp–Dallas, 716 SW2d 124.—Divorce 150.1(3), 177; Lim of Act 127(1); Mand 4(1), 48.

Harris; Kostoff v., TexCivApp–Dallas, 266 SW2d 204, ref nre.—Inj 103, 135, 138.6, 138.75, 163(1), 163(7).

Harris; Kurtz v., SDTex, 245 FSupp 752.—Rem of C 2, 3, 79(1).

Harris v. Laquinta-Redbird Joint Venture, TexCivApp–Texarkana, 522 SW2d 232, 87 ALR3d 372, ref nre.—App & E 927(7), 989; Inn 10.13; Mun Corp 120; Neglig 1599, 1713; Pub Amuse 42, 98, 146, 160; Trial 178.

Harris v. Lebow, TexCivApp–Dallas, 363 SW2d 184, ref nre.—App & E 563, 882(21), 907(3), 1165; Judgm 138(2), 143(2); Tresp 72.

Harris; Legal Sec. Life Ins. Co. v., TexCivApp–Texarkana, 359 SW2d 953, ref nre.—Insurance 3015.

Harris v. Leslie, Tex, 96 SW2d 276, 128 Tex 81.—Courts 247(5); Mand 57(1).

Harris v. Levy, TexCivApp–El Paso, 217 SW2d 154, ref nre.—App & E 217, 842(1), 1015(5), 1050.1(4), 1052(8), 1069.1, 1069.2; Autos 243(12), 245(88), 245(90); Damag 185(1); Trial 307(3).

Harris v. Logue, Tex, 554 SW2d 168.—App & E 854(1).

Harris v. Logue, TexCivApp–Fort Worth, 544 SW2d 932, ref nre 554 SW2d 168.—Judgm 5, 335(1), 335(4); Parties 35.13.

Harris v. Lone Star Motor Co., TexCivApp–El Paso, 106 SW2d 343, writ dism woj.—App & E 544(1), 907(3), 934(1); Trial 141.

Harris; Longoria v., SDTex, 554 FSupp 102.—Civil R 1218(3), 1220, 1330(1), 1448, 1460, 1561; Fed Cts 272.

Harris v. Lykes Bros. S. S. Co., Inc., EDTex, 375 FSupp 1155.—Adm 34.1, 34.2; Equity 75; Release 16, 55, 57(2).

Harris; McDaniel v., CA5 (Tex), 639 F2d 1386.—Social S 143.65, 143.70, 149.5.

Harris; McDowell v., TexCivApp–Dallas, 107 SW2d 647, writ dism.—Hus & W 246; Judgm 725(1), 725(4); Wills 590, 601(5), 656.

Harris; McFarland v., EDTex, 499 FSupp 550.—Social S 143.75.

Harris; McLeod v., Tex, 582 SW2d 772.—Judges 51(4).

Harris v. Marathon Oil Co., WDTex, 948 FSupp 27, aff 108 F3d 332.—Estop 68(2).

Harris; Marshall v., TexApp–Houston (1 Dist), 764 SW2d 34.—Mand 3(2.1), 26; Trial 3(2).

Harris; Mertz v., SDTex, 497 FSupp 1134.—Fed Civ Proc 163, 165, 189; Social S 122.5, 136.

Harris v. Mickel, CA5 (Tex), 15 F3d 428.—Contracts 21; Fed Cts 415, 776; Interest 31, 39(2.50), 49.

Harris; Montgomery v., TexCivApp–Tyler, 565 SW2d 358.—Corp 503(2); Plead 111.42(6); Venue 7.5(3).

Harris v. Moore, TexApp–Austin, 912 SW2d 860.—App & E 224, 238(1), 790(3); Inj 138.1, 147; Judgm 335(3).

Harris v. Moore, TexApp–El Paso, 740 SW2d 14.—Action 60; Courts 24, 475(1), 478.

Harris; Moore Cable Const. v., TexApp–Houston (1 Dist), 934 SW2d 813. See G.F.S. Ventures, Inc. v. Harris.

Harris v. Moore's Trucking, TexApp–Austin, 912 SW2d 860. See Harris v. Moore.

Harris; Moorman v., TexCivApp–San Antonio, 217 SW2d 182.—Brok 43(2).

Harris; Morrow-Thomas, Inc. v., TexCivApp–Eastland, 466 SW2d 323.—App & E 870(2), 930(3), 989; Fraud Conv 300(4).

Harris; Murray v., TexCivApp–Amarillo, 112 SW2d 1091, dism.—Action on Case 4; Libel 80, 85, 87; Sheriffs 18, 21, 86.

Harris; Murray v., TexCivApp–Waco, 208 SW2d 626.—Plead 228.23; Schools 111, 117.

Harris; National Life & Acc. Ins. Co. v., Tex, 107 SW2d 361, 130 Tex 168.—Insurance 2035, 3086, 3093.

Harris; National Life & Accident Ins. Co. v., TexCiv-App–Beaumont, 149 SW2d 286, writ dism, correct.—Insurance 1832(1), 2035, 2063, 2069.

Harris; National Life & Acc. Ins. Co. v., TexCivApp–Eastland, 118 SW2d 838.—App & E 1003(9.1), 1060.1(2.1); Evid 290; Insurance 3016; Trial 106, 115(2), 121(2).

Harris v. National Passenger Railroad Corp., EDTex, 79 FSupp2d 673, aff 234 F3d 707.—Carr 280(3), 316(1.5); Neglig 380, 1613, 1614, 1676, 1713; Prod Liab 76.

Harris v. Nelson, TexApp–Beaumont, 25 SW3d 917, reh overr.—App & E 989, 994(3), 1010.1(1), 1010.2, 1012.1(2), 1012.1(3), 1012.1(4); Statut 181(1); Tresp 46(1), 52, 56; Trusts 104.

Harris; Nevels v., Tex, 102 SW2d 1046, 129 Tex 190, 109 ALR 1464.—Contracts 162; Evid 69; Usury 22, 42, 52, 53, 72, 88.

Harris; Nevels v., TexCivApp–Austin, 95 SW2d 1315, aff 102 SW2d 1046, 129 Tex 190, 109 ALR 1464.—Usury 56, 117.

Harris v. New Amsterdam Cas. Co., TexCivApp–Galveston, 150 SW2d 431, writ dism, correct.—Damag 221(8); Trial 358; Work Comp 1930, 1965.

Harris v. O'Connor, TexCivApp–El Paso, 185 SW2d 993, writ refused wom.—Aband L P 2, 4, 5; Adv Poss 1, 7(2); Bound 6, 24, 35(4); Evid 83(1), 83(3), 177; Intern Law 6; Mines 4; Paymt 66(1); Pub Lands 172.1, 176(1), 197, 201, 202, 203, 204, 206, 209, 210; States 1, 66, 191.8(2), 201; Trial 136(1).

Harris; Oglesby v., TexCivApp–Austin, 130 SW2d 449, writ dism, correct.—Wills 55(7), 163(4), 166(4), 166(5), 327, 384.

Harris; Orange & N. W. R. Co. v., Tex, 89 SW2d 973, 127 Tex 13.—Neglig 1713; R R 350(32); Trial 219.

Harris; Palacios v., TexApp–San Antonio, 715 SW2d 418. —App & E 400.

Harris v. Panhandle & S. F. Ry. Co., TexCivApp–El Paso, 163 SW2d 647, writ refused wom.—Ease 12(1), 25, 30(2); Land & Ten 157(2), 275, 278.

Harris v. Parker College of Chiropractic, CA5 (Tex), 286 F3d 790.—Alt Disp Res 316, 329, 332, 363(6), 374(7); Civil R 1516; Contracts 143.5, 147(2); Fed Cts 412.1.

Harris; Parks v., CA5 (Tex), 614 F2d 83.—Social S 146, 149.5.

Harris; Pearce v., TexCivApp–El Paso, 134 SW2d 859.—Adop 2, 7.2(1), 7.2(2), 7.3, 7.7, 12, 22; Const Law 3974; Des & Dist 30.

Harris v. Philip Morris Inc., CA5 (Tex), 232 F3d 456.—Assault 2; Const Law 2312, 2314; Fed Cts 776; Prod Liab 2, 59.

Harris v. Phillips Pipe Line Co., TexCivApp–Austin, 517 SW2d 361, ref nre.—Contracts 155; Ease 12(1), 24, 42, 47, 54.

Harris; Plant Process Equipment, Inc. v., TexCivApp–Hous (14 Dist), 579 SW2d 53.—App & E 100(1), 954(1), 954(2); Inj 132, 135, 138.31, 150, 157.

Harris v. Plastics Mfg. Co., CA5 (Tex), 617 F2d 438.—Civil R 1421, 1544, 1592; Fed Civ Proc 2847; Fed Cts 915.

Harris; Polk County Motor Co. v., TexCivApp–Beaumont, 350 SW2d 870, writ dism.—Prod Liab 39; Venue 8.5(8).

Harris v. Potts, Tex, 545 SW2d 126.—Frds St of 129(11), 158(4).

Harris v. Potts, TexCivApp–Beaumont, 528 SW2d 321, writ gr, aff 545 SW2d 126.—App & E 927(7); Ven & Pur 19, 44.

Harris; Presbyterian Hospital of Dallas v., CA5 (Tex), 638 F2d 1381, reh den 647 F2d 1121, cert den 102 SCt 476, 454 US 940, 70 LEd2d 248.—Admin Law 744.1, 817.1; Const Law 2136, 2144; Health 535(4), 535(6).

Harris v. Prince, TexComApp, 121 SW2d 983, 132 Tex 231.—Hus & W 79, 80, 198; Insurance 1222(4), 1227(3), 1227(4).

Harris v. Prince, TexCivApp–Fort Worth, 98 SW2d 1022, rev 121 SW2d 983, 132 Tex 231.—B & L Assoc 10; Estop 52(1); Hus & W 62, 198; Insurance 1225(3), 1405; Statut 105(1), 109.5, 113(3).

Harris v. Rabe, TexCivApp–Waco, 375 SW2d 919.—App & E 1001(1), 1010.1(3), 1012.1(5); Ease 12(1), 36(3); Estop 87.

Harris; R. B. Spencer & Co. v., TexCivApp–Amarillo, 171 SW2d 393, writ refused.—Judgm 853(3).

Harris v. Reeves, TexCivApp–Waco, 421 SW2d 689, ref nre.—App & E 1062.1; Autos 244(34), 244(36.1); Death 76; Evid 555.8(1), 581.

Harris v. Reno Oil Co., NDTex, 48 FSupp 908.—Rem of C 13.

Harris v. Rhodes, CA5 (Tex), 94 F3d 196.—Civil R 1326(2), 1326(8); Fed Cts 776.

Harris v. Road Dist. No. 4, San Jacinto County, TexCivApp–Beaumont, 290 SW 875, writ gr, rev 6 SW2d 340.—Bridges 20(2), 20(4), 20(6); Lim of Act 127(13); Pub Contr 6, 14.

Harris v. Robbins, TexCivApp–Amarillo, 302 SW2d 225.—Wills 290, 302(8), 306, 324(4); Witn 139(10).

Harris v. Rose, TexApp–Dallas, 204 SW3d 903.—Action 9; App & E 946, 984(1).

Harris v. Rowe, Tex, 593 SW2d 303.—Accord 1, 4, 23, 26(1); Contracts 153, 164, 169, 170(1), 176(1); Deeds 94.

Harris; Rowe v., TexCivApp–Waco, 576 SW2d 172, rev 593 SW2d 303.—Accord 4, 15.1, 17, 19, 23; App & E 927(7), 989, 997(3); Ven & Pur 352.

Harris v. Royal, TexCivApp–Waco, 446 SW2d 351, ref nre.—Hus & W 258; Trial 351.2(4).

Harris v. St. John the Baptist Parish School Bd, CA5 (Tex), 419 F2d 1211. See Singleton v. Jackson Municipal Separate School Dist.

Harris v. Sanderson, TexCivApp–Eastland, 178 SW2d 315, writ refused wom.—Contracts 93(4); Courts 90(1); Death 25, 75; Fraud 4, 11(1), 12, 13(2), 50; Release 16; Trial 178.

Harris v. Schepp, TexApp–Fort Worth, 818 SW2d 530.—Bankr 3412; Costs 260(5).

Harris; Schlager v., TexApp–Corpus Christi, 805 SW2d 893.—App & E 866(1), 927(3); Bills & N 499, 516, 527(1), 537(1); Plead 291(2).

Harris; Security Ins. Co. v., TexCivApp–Eastland, 478 SW2d 118, ref nre.—Work Comp 1683.

Harris v. Sentry Title Co., Inc., CA5 (Tex), 806 F2d 1278, reh den 812 F2d 1405, reh den Sentry Title Co, Inc v. Ward, 812 F2d 1405, cert den 108 SCt 74, 484 US 818, 98 LEd2d 37, reh den 108 SCt 735, 484 US 1020, 98 LEd2d 683.—Fed Cts 954.

Harris v. Sentry Title Co., Inc., CA5 (Tex), 727 F2d 1368, cert den Ward v. Sentry Title Co, Inc, 104 SCt 2679, 467 US 1226, 81 LEd2d 874, reh den 738 F2d 437, reh den 738 F2d 437, cert den 105 SCt 514, 469 US 1037, 83 LEd2d 404, appeal after remand 806 F2d 1278, reh den 812 F2d 1405, reh den 812 F2d 1405, cert den 108 SCt 74, 484 US 818, 98 LEd2d 37, reh den 108 SCt 735, 484 US 1020, 98 LEd2d 683.—Trusts 92.5, 103(1).

Harris v. Sentry Title Co., Inc., CA5 (Tex), 715 F2d 941, reh den 719 F2d 404, mandate recalled 727 F2d 1368, cert den Ward v. Sentry Title Co, Inc, 104 SCt 2679, 467 US 1226, 81 LEd2d 874, reh den 738 F2d 437, reh den 738 F2d 437, cert den 105 SCt 514, 469 US 1037, 83 LEd2d 404, appeal after remand 806 F2d 1278, reh den 812 F2d 1405, reh den 812 F2d 1405, cert den 108 SCt 74, 484 US 818, 98 LEd2d 37, reh den 108 SCt 735, 484 US 1020, 98 LEd2d 683, cert den 105 SCt 514, 469 US 1037, 83 LEd2d 404.—Equity 65(1); Fed Cts 407.1; Frds St of 55, 71.1, 74(1), 125(1); Impl & C C 3; Trusts 1, 17(1), 17(3), 62, 65, 83, 85.1, 91, 92.5, 95, 103(1), 104, 110.

Harris; Shaw v., CA5 (Tex), 116 FedAppx 499, cert den 125 SCt 1845, 544 US 982, 161 LEd2d 737.—Civil R 1088(5); Consp 7.5(1).

Harris; Shindler v., TexApp–Houston (1 Dist), 673 SW2d 600, ref nre.—App & E 843(2); Bills & N 501; Evid 402; Joint Adv 1, 2, 4(1), 5(2).

Harris; Shirey v., TexCivApp–Fort Worth, 288 SW2d 315.—App & E 395; Cert 1, 5(1); Ex & Ad 501, 510(2), 510(6).

Harris v. Shotwell, TexCivApp–Fort Worth, 490 SW2d 860.—App & E 496; Costs 12, 32(1), 154, 207; Infants 212; Pretrial Proc 501, 517.1.

Harris v. Shoults, TexApp–Fort Worth, 877 SW2d 854, reh overr.—Plead 129(1), 252(2).

Harris; Simmons v., CA5 (Tex), 602 F2d 1233.—Social S 140.30, 143.40, 143.75, 147.

Harris v. Skelly Oil Co., Tex, 352 SW2d 950, 163 Tex 92.—Mines 78.1(7).

Harris; Skelly Oil Co. v., TexCivApp–Texarkana, 341 SW2d 693, writ gr, rev 352 SW2d 950, 163 Tex 92.—App & E 758.3(1), 758.3(3); Mines 78.1(9).

Harris v. State, TexCrimApp, 227 SW3d 83.—Crim Law 1035(10); Searches 199.

Harris v. State, TexCrimApp, 153 SW3d 394.—Crim Law 558; Double J 30.

Harris v. State, TexCrimApp, 843 SW2d 34.—Sent & Pun 2010, 2012, 2018.

Harris v. State, TexCrimApp, 827 SW2d 949, cert den 113 SCt 381, 506 US 942, 121 LEd2d 292, certificate of probable cause den 81 F3d 535, cert den 116 SCt 1863, 517 US 1227, 134 LEd2d 961.—Const Law 3309, 3811, 4594(1), 4657, 4744(2); Crim Law 339.8(3), 339.10(1), 339.11(3), 339.11(5.1), 577.8(2), 577.10(3), 577.15(1), 577.15(3), 577.16(1), 577.16(4), 713, 1036.1(5), 1037.1(2), 1045, 1158(3), 1181(1); Jury 33(5.15); Sent & Pun 1746, 1762, 1780(3), 1789(3).

Harris v. State, TexCrimApp, 790 SW2d 568, reh den.— Courts 85(3); Crim Law 339.10(8), 365(1), 365(3), 870, 1035(5), 1043(3), 1134(3), 1162, 1165(1), 1166.13, 1166.16, 1168(2), 1169.1(8), 1169.5(3), 1169.5(5), 1169.11, 1180; Jury 108; Sent & Pun 1762, 1772.

Harris v. State, TexCrimApp, 784 SW2d 5, cert den 110 SCt 1837, 494 US 1090, 108 LEd2d 966, habeas corpus den Ex parte Harris, 825 SW2d 120, reh den, grant of habeas corpus rev 313 F3d 238, cert den 124 SCt 1503, 540 US 1218, 158 LEd2d 152, reh den 124 SCt 2933, 542 US 952, 159 LEd2d 836, habeas corpus dism In re Harris, 2004 WL 1497714, dissenting opinion 136 SW3d 669.—Crim Law 627.6(1), 713, 723(1), 728(2), 1037.1(1), 1037.1(3), 1043(3), 1045, 1169.2(2); Homic 1458; Jury 75(2), 97(1), 99.7, 105(4), 106, 107, 108; Sent & Pun 1772, 1780(2).

Harris v. State, TexCrimApp, 738 SW2d 207, cert den 108 SCt 207, 484 US 872, 98 LEd2d 158, habeas corpus den 806 FSupp 627, post-conviction relief den 990 F2d 185, cert den 113 SCt 3069, 509 US 933, 125 LEd2d 746.— Crim Law 369.2(4), 374, 507(1), 507(2), 511.1(5), 511.1(7), 511.2, 511.5, 563, 742(2), 780(1), 854(1), 854(2), 854(3), 868, 1039, 1064(6), 1119(1), 1144.8, 1174(4); Double J 108; Homic 511, 1127, 1129; Sent & Pun 323, 1772.

Harris v. State, TexCrimApp, 727 SW2d 537.—Crim Law 698(1); Homic 1184.

Harris v. State, TexCrimApp, 684 SW2d 687.—Crim Law 721(1), 721(3), 721(4).

Harris v. State, TexCrimApp, 661 SW2d 106.—Crim Law 438(5.1), 438(6).

Harris v. State, TexCrimApp, 656 SW2d 481.—Arrest 63.4(12), 71.1(8); Burg 28(3), 42(1), 42(3); Const Law 4629, 4759; Crim Law 698(1), 1038.2, 1115(2), 1130(5); Sent & Pun 1513.

Harris v. State, TexCrimApp, 645 SW2d 447, appeal after remand 790 SW2d 568, reh den.—Crim Law 59(5), 507(1), 552(2), 780(2), 1172.1(5).

Harris v. State, TexCrimApp, 642 SW2d 471, appeal after remand 738 SW2d 207, cert den 108 SCt 207, 484 US 872, 98 LEd2d 158, habeas corpus den 806 FSupp 627, post-conviction relief den 990 F2d 185, cert den 113 SCt 3069, 509 US 933, 125 LEd2d 746.—Crim Law 662.7, 1091(3), 1170.5(1); Witn 330(1), 372(3).

Harris v. State, TexCrimApp, 608 SW2d 229.—Sent & Pun 2003.

Harris v. State, TexCrimApp, 587 SW2d 429.—Crim Law 1044.1(2); Larc 30(1).

Harris v. State, TexCrimApp, 565 SW2d 66.—Crim Law 1043(2), 1184(4.1), 1186.3, 1186.7; Ind & Inf 15(4).

Harris v. State, TexCrimApp, 562 SW2d 463, 100 ALR3d 278.—Rob 11, 24.15(1).

Harris v. State, TexCrimApp, 524 SW2d 65.—Crim Law 511.4.

Harris v. State, TexCrimApp, 522 SW2d 199.—Crim Law 813, 1038.1(1), 1038.1(4).

Harris v. State, TexCrimApp, 516 SW2d 931.—Crim Law 531(3), 534(2), 614(1), 622.2(9), 1043(2); Double J 182.

Harris v. State, TexCrimApp, 505 SW2d 576.—Crim Law 980(1); Sent & Pun 2026.

Harris v. State, TexCrimApp, 500 SW2d 126.—Crim Law 273.1(4).

Harris v. State, TexCrimApp, 499 SW2d 139.—Crim Law 29(8).

Harris v. State, TexCrimApp, 499 SW2d 9.—Autos 332.

Harris v. State, TexCrimApp, 489 SW2d 303.—Crim Law 577.10(1), 577.15(3), 577.16(5.1), 577.16(8); Int Liq 111, 134, 154(1), 223(1), 236(17).

Harris v. State, TexCrimApp, 486 SW2d 573.—Bail 52; Crim Law 38.

Harris v. State, TexCrimApp, 486 SW2d 317.—Const Law 250.2(1), 3816, 4765; Crim Law 737(1), 741(1), 742(1); Jury 24.1.

Harris v. State, TexCrimApp, 486 SW2d 88.—Controlled Subs 80, 97, 113; Crim Law 784(1); Sent & Pun 313.

Harris v. State, TexCrimApp, 485 SW2d 284.—Crim Law 1181(1), 1181.5(8), 1183; Sent & Pun 1610, 1788(11).

Harris v. State, TexCrimApp, 475 SW2d 922.—Const Law 739; Crim Law 717, 730(5).

Harris v. State, TexCrimApp, 474 SW2d 706.—Rape 51(1), 51(3), 51(6).

Harris v. State, TexCrimApp, 473 SW2d 37.—Crim Law 1038.2, 1038.3; Rape 51(3), 54(1).

Harris v. State, TexCrimApp, 471 SW2d 390.—Burg 22; Crim Law 1184(2); Ind & Inf 105, 166.

Harris v. State, TexCrimApp, 466 SW2d 761.—Witn 300, 337(28).

Harris v. State, TexCrimApp, 465 SW2d 175.—Crim Law 532(0.5), 698(1), 736(2), 739.1(1), 1169.12.

Harris v. State, TexCrimApp, 460 SW2d 928.—Crim Law 1166(7), 1170.5(1).

Harris v. State, TexCrimApp, 457 SW2d 903, cert gr 91 SCt 579, 400 US 1003, 27 LEd2d 630, rev 91 SCt 2291, 403 US 947, 29 LEd2d 859, conformed to 485 SW2d 284. —Const Law 4664(2); Crim Law 223, 225, 438(7), 517.2(3), 519(1), 532(0.5), 781(4), 781(5), 796, 815(13), 852, 1064.5, 1169.2(2); Jury 108, 130.

Harris v. State, TexCrimApp, 453 SW2d 838.—Crim Law 339.10(9), 627.6(1), 949(3), 1064.5, 1128(2).

Harris v. State, TexCrimApp, 450 SW2d 629.—Crim Law 457, 1166(7); Ind & Inf 137(1), 137(3).

Harris v. State, TexCrimApp, 441 SW2d 189.—Crim Law 641.13(2.1), 641.13(6); Rape 6, 52(3).

Harris v. State, TexCrimApp, 435 SW2d 502.—Arrest 63.4(6); Crim Law 339.6, 867; Witn 269(15).

Harris v. State, TexCrimApp, 425 SW2d 652.—Crim Law 730(1), 1036.1(3.1), 1037.2, 1044.1(8).

Harris v. State, TexCrimApp, 425 SW2d 642.—Crim Law 366(3), 641.4(1), 1137(5), 1166.12, 1166.22(1); Witn 321.

Harris v. State, TexCrimApp, 416 SW2d 424.—Homic 1345.

Harris v. State, TexCrimApp, 398 SW2d 773.—Homic 1207.

Harris v. State, TexCrimApp, 396 SW2d 880.—Crim Law 636(1).

Harris v. State, TexCrimApp, 376 SW2d 838.—Rob 24.10.

Harris v. State, TexCrimApp, 375 SW2d 310.—Controlled Subs 80; Crim Law 867, 1169.5(1), 1169.5(5).

Harris v. State, TexCrimApp, 370 SW2d 886, vac 84 SCt 1930, 378 US 572, 12 LEd2d 1040, on remand 384 SW2d 349.—Crim Law 736(2), 1056.1(2); Homic 1135, 1207.

Harris v. State, TexCrimApp, 365 SW2d 931.—Mun Corp 639(1).

Harris v. State, TexCrimApp, 358 SW2d 130, 172 Tex-Crim 421.—Crim Law 1170.5(1); Witn 256.

Harris v. State, TexCrimApp, 354 SW2d 155, 172 Tex-Crim 150.—Crim Law 393(3), 394.4(12), 621(2); Rob 23(1).

Harris v. State, TexCrimApp, 333 SW2d 381, 169 Tex-Crim 298.—Bail 77(2).

Harris v. State, TexCrimApp, 333 SW2d 142, 169 Tex-Crim 143.—Crim Law 370, 371(5), 372(12), 1038.2, 1038.3; Forg 44(3).

Harris v. State, TexCrimApp, 331 SW2d 941, 169 Tex-Crim 71.—Sent & Pun 2004.

Harris v. State, TexCrimApp, 294 SW2d 123, 163 TexCrim 519.—Crim Law 566; Int Liq 236(4).

Harris v. State, TexCrimApp, 291 SW2d 953.—Crim Law 1090.1(1).

Harris v. State, TexCrimApp, 289 SW2d 605, 163 TexCrim 183.—Crim Law 665(1), 665(4), 1153(5).

Harris v. State, TexCrimApp, 286 SW2d 936, 162 TexCrim 498.—Burg 41(1); Crim Law 419(10), 517.1(2), 531(2), 730(14), 1169.5(5).

Harris v. State, TexCrimApp, 274 SW2d 688.—Crim Law 1090.1(1).

Harris v. State, TexCrimApp, 254 SW2d 386.—Crim Law 1090.1(1).

Harris v. State, TexCrimApp, 253 SW2d 44, 158 TexCrim 37.—Crim Law 917(2); Homic 1480.

Harris v. State, TexCrimApp, 252 SW2d 947.—Crim Law 1094(3).

Harris v. State, TexCrimApp, 233 SW2d 123, 155 TexCrim 180.—Int Liq 146(3), 207, 236(10).

Harris v. State, TexCrimApp, 199 SW2d 522, 150 TexCrim 137.—Crim Law 402(2); Forg 28(2), 28(5).

Harris v. State, TexCrimApp, 198 SW2d 1020, 150 TexCrim 36.—Crim Law 778(3), 1097(1), 1099.13, 1105(1).

Harris v. State, TexCrimApp, 198 SW2d 459, 149 TexCrim 610.—Int Liq 223(1), 223(2).

Harris v. State, TexCrimApp, 198 SW2d 264, 150 TexCrim 38.—Homic 621, 637, 650, 661(3), 762, 1135, 1563.

Harris v. State, TexCrimApp, 194 SW2d 101, 149 TexCrim 308.—Crim Law 376, 1169.1(6).

Harris v. State, TexCrimApp, 166 SW2d 136.—Crim Law 1094(3).

Harris v. State, TexCrimApp, 165 SW2d 453, 145 TexCrim 28.—Crim Law 1090.8, 1090.14, 1159.3(6).

Harris v. State, TexCrimApp, 149 SW2d 99, 141 TexCrim 447.—Crim Law 90(5); Homic 848, 1134; Ind & Inf 86(2).

Harris v. State, TexCrimApp, 144 SW2d 546, 140 TexCrim 256.—Extort 14, 25.1.

Harris v. State, TexCrimApp, 115 SW2d 936, 134 TexCrim 295.—Crim Law 1086.13.

Harris v. State, TexCrimApp, 109 SW2d 203, 133 TexCrim 129.—Autos 132, 358; Crim Law 1172.9.

Harris v. State, TexCrimApp, 109 SW2d 201, 133 TexCrim 126.—Autos 358; Crim Law 1132, 1172.9.

Harris v. State, TexCrimApp, 97 SW2d 226, 131 TexCrim 223.—Crim Law 791, 814(17); Homic 569, 572(1), 1207.

Harris v. State, TexCrimApp, 95 SW2d 398, 130 TexCrim 518.—Rob 24.10.

Harris v. State, TexApp–Houston (1 Dist), 152 SW3d 786, petition for discretionary review refused.—Autos 330; Crim Law 338(1), 338(7), 661, 795(1.5), 795(2.10), 795(2.55), 1153(1), 1166.6, 1169.1(1), 1170(1), 1170(2); Witn 388(2.1).

Harris v. State, TexApp–Houston (1 Dist), 149 SW3d 285, petition for discretionary review refused.—Crim Law 1072.

Harris; State v., TexApp–Houston (1 Dist), 921 SW2d 376, petition for discretionary review refused.—Sent & Pun 1234.

Harris v. State, TexApp–Houston (1 Dist), 846 SW2d 960, petition for discretionary review refused.—Autos 339, 355(10); Crim Law 432, 436(2), 436(3), 444; Larc 7, 32(6).

Harris v. State, TexApp–Houston (1 Dist), 827 SW2d 49, petition for discretionary review refused.—Arrest 63.5(8), 63.5(9); Crim Law 394.6(5), 1158(4).

Harris v. State, TexApp–Houston (1 Dist), 713 SW2d 773. —Autos 349(2.1); Searches 165.

Harris v. State, TexApp–Houston (1 Dist), 670 SW2d 284. —Crim Law 339.11(1), 1144.13(3), 1184(1); Rape 51(1), 64.

Harris v. State, TexApp–Houston (1 Dist), 638 SW2d 914, petition for discretionary review refused.—Sent & Pun 1379(2).

Harris v. State, TexApp–Houston (1 Dist), 630 SW2d 774. —Crim Law 1028, 1184(3); Searches 161, 164.

Harris v. State, TexApp–Fort Worth, 184 SW3d 801, petition for discretionary review gr, rev 227 SW3d 83.—Controlled Subs 147, 148(4); Crim Law 394.6(5), 1044.1(6), 1134(2), 1134(8), 1179; Searches 38, 111, 112, 113.1, 117, 118.

Harris v. State, TexApp–Fort Worth, 173 SW3d 575.—Controlled Subs 26, 27, 28, 30, 79, 80; Crim Law 394.6(2), 561(1), 632(3.1).

Harris v. State, TexApp–Fort Worth, 122 SW3d 871, petition for discretionary review refused (2 pets).—Crim Law 665(1), 665(3), 665(4), 665(7), 708.1, 713, 721(6), 721.5(1), 721.5(2), 723(1), 723(3), 726, 730(1), 730(14), 1153(5); Jury 85, 107, 131(1), 131(2), 131(8), 131(13); Rape 51(1).

Harris v. State, TexApp–Fort Worth, 958 SW2d 292, petition for discretionary review refused.—Crim Law 947, 961, 965, 1192.

Harris v. State, TexApp–Fort Worth, 700 SW2d 778.—Crim Law 351(8), 406(7), 778(2).

Harris v. State, TexApp–Austin, 125 SW3d 45, reh overr, and petition for discretionary review dism as untimely filed.—Const Law 969, 990, 1030; Crim Law 29(8), 254.1, 1030(2); Statut 188, 189.

Harris v. State, TexApp–Austin, 666 SW2d 537.—Crim Law 1032(5), 1144.13(3); Ind & Inf 60, 110(3), 166; Rape 1, 35(2), 51(1), 59(5).

Harris v. State, TexApp–San Antonio, 891 SW2d 730, petition for discretionary review refused.—Bail 75.2(3); Sent & Pun 2079.

Harris v. State, TexApp–San Antonio, 866 SW2d 316, reh den, and petition for discretionary review refused.—Arrest 63.5(1), 68(3); Crim Law 407(1), 444, 720(1), 720(6), 728(2), 1168(2), 1169.2(6), 1171.1(2.1), 1171.3; Ind & Inf 159(1), 161(1); Sent & Pun 323; Witn 347.

Harris v. State, TexApp–San Antonio, 827 SW2d 442.—Crim Law 951(1).

Harris v. State, TexApp–San Antonio, 818 SW2d 231, opinion after remand 827 SW2d 442.—Courts 26; Crim Law 1017, 1132, 1181.5(3.1); Hab Corp 494.

Harris v. State, TexApp–San Antonio, 771 SW2d 10.—Crim Law 532(0.5), 671, 1168(2).

Harris v. State, TexApp–San Antonio, 733 SW2d 710.—Crim Law 1226(3.1), 1226(4).

Harris v. State, TexApp–Dallas, 887 SW2d 482.—Crim Law 273.1(4), 275, 954(1), 959, 1167(5).

Harris v. State, TexApp–Dallas, 833 SW2d 535, reh den, and petition for discretionary review refused.—Burg 41(1); Crim Law 552(3), 820, 1159.6.

Harris v. State, TexApp–Dallas, 783 SW2d 253.—Controlled Subs 26, 27; Crim Law 753.2(1), 1144.13(3), 1159.2(7); Double J 109; Jury 131(13); Sent & Pun 1300, 1377.

Harris v. State, TexApp–Dallas, 722 SW2d 436.—Homic 997, 1051(2).

Harris v. State, TexApp–Texarkana, 133 SW3d 760, petition for discretionary review refused, habeas corpus den 2007 WL 470647.—Crim Law 363, 366(2), 474.4(3), 481, 1036.5, 1130(2), 1144.13(2.1), 1153(1), 1159.2(2), 1159.2(8), 1168(2), 1169.2(6); Homic 1184.

Harris v. State, TexApp–Texarkana, 913 SW2d 706.—Arrest 58, 63.4(1), 63.5(1), 63.5(2), 63.5(4), 63.5(5); Const Law 3043, 3808; Controlled Subs 8; Crim Law 394.6(5), 1158(4), 1224(1); Sent & Pun 17(3).

Harris v. State, TexApp–Texarkana, 903 SW2d 514.—Crim Law 273.1(4).

Harris v. State, TexApp–Amarillo, 185 SW3d 524.—Obscen 3; Sent & Pun 34, 1800.

Harris v. State, TexApp–Beaumont, 32 SW3d 926, petition for discretionary review refused, cert den 122 SCt 206, 534 US 891, 151 LEd2d 146.—Crim Law 1144.13(2.1), 1144.13(6), 1159.2(2), 1159.2(7); Larc 60.

Harris v. State, TexApp–Waco, 160 SW3d 621, petition stricken.—Crim Law 1035(1), 1042, 1148, 1177; Judges 49(1), 51(2); Sent & Pun 2009, 2030.

Harris v. State, TexApp–Waco, 137 SW3d 829, opinion after remand 160 SW3d 621, petition stricken.—Crim Law 1026.10(2.1), 1073.

Harris v. State, TexApp–Waco, 34 SW3d 609, reh overr, and petition for discretionary review refused.—Crim Law 29(1), 532(0.5), 553, 641.13(1), 641.13(2.1), 641.13(6), 641.13(7), 1037.1(2), 1141(2), 1159.2(2); Double J 150(1), 161; Homic 1213; Ind & Inf 125(4.1), 125(29), 130; Jury 33(1.1), 33(1.15).

Harris v. State, TexApp–Waco, 994 SW2d 927, petition for discretionary review refused.—Controlled Subs 27, 28, 81; Crim Law 394.5(4), 394.6(4), 1139, 1158(4); Searches 171, 172, 180, 181, 183, 184, 186.

Harris v. State, TexApp–Eastland, 54 SW3d 824, reh overr.—Arrest 63.5(4), 63.5(6); Crim Law 1139, 1158(1), 1158(2), 1158(4).

Harris v. State, TexApp–Eastland, 624 SW2d 418, petition for discretionary review gr, aff 661 SW2d 106.—Crim Law 438(6), 438(7), 1171.1(2.1).

Harris v. State, TexApp–Tyler, 986 SW2d 619, reh overr, and petition for discretionary review refused, cert den 119 SCt 1115, 525 US 1178, 143 LEd2d 111.—Autos 352; Const Law 975, 990, 996; Crim Law 577.4, 577.8(2), 577.10(1), 577.10(3), 577.10(4), 577.10(10), 577.15(1), 577.15(3), 577.16(4), 577.16(8), 713, 728(2), 1030(2), 1032(1), 1037.1(1), 1114.1(1), 1139; Larc 7, 32(6); Statut 212.3.

Harris v. State, TexApp–Houston (14 Dist), 204 SW3d 19, petition for discretionary review refused.—Autos 355(6), 359.6; Crim Law 553, 737(1), 741(1), 742(1), 747, 1042.5, 1044.1(1); Sent & Pun 1482, 1483, 1513.

Harris v. State, TexApp–Houston (14 Dist), 164 SW3d 775, petition for discretionary review refused.—Burg 41(1), 41(4), 41(8); Crim Law 553, 747, 1144.13(2.1), 1159.2(7), 1169.2(1), 1169.2(3), 1169.5(3); Double J 1, 23, 144.

Harris v. State, TexApp–Houston (14 Dist), 56 SW3d 52, reh overr, and petition for discretionary review refused, and petition for discretionary review refused (2 pets), appeal after new sentencing hearing 2003 WL 22413493, petition for discretionary review refused.—Crim Law 655(1), 656(1), 656(8), 706(4), 708.1, 713, 717, 719(1), 720(2), 720(7.1), 723(1), 723(3), 726, 1158(1), 1165(1), 1171.1(2.1), 1171.1(3), 1171.1(6); Sent & Pun 57, 308; Witn 198(1).

Harris v. State, TexApp–Houston (14 Dist), 996 SW2d 232.—Crim Law 720(6), 723(1), 730(1), 867, 1134(5), 1158(3), 1171.1(2.1); Jury 33(5.15), 131(3).

Harris v. State, TexApp–Houston (14 Dist), 905 SW2d 708, petition for discretionary review refused.—Controlled Subs 26, 27, 79, 97; Crim Law 700(1), 713, 720(6), 720(7.1), 726, 763(1), 829(1), 1141(1), 1144.13(3), 1148, 1159.2(7), 1171.1(2.1); Jury 131(4), 131(15.1).

Harris v. State, TexApp–Houston (14 Dist), 882 SW2d 61, petition for discretionary review refused.—Crim Law 394.5(4), 394.6(4), 394.6(5), 1158(1); Kidnap 27, 36; Searches 180.

Harris v. State, TexApp–Houston (14 Dist), 799 SW2d 348.—Crim Law 444, 629(1), 1170.5(1).

Harris v. State, TexApp–Houston (14 Dist), 790 SW2d 778, petition for discretionary review refused.—Crim Law 753.2(5); Disorderly C 1.

Harris v. State, TexApp–Houston (14 Dist), 781 SW2d 365, petition for discretionary review refused.—Controlled Subs 26, 27, 30, 79; Sent & Pun 1160.

Harris v. State, TexApp–Houston (14 Dist), 736 SW2d 166.—Crim Law 366(4), 868.

Harris v. State, TexApp–Houston (14 Dist), 681 SW2d 726, petition for discretionary review gr, aff 727 SW2d 537.—Crim Law 145, 1033.2, 1090.3, 1144.6, 1159.2(7); Homic 1134, 1465.

Harris v. State, TexApp–Houston (14 Dist), 629 SW2d 832, petition for discretionary review refused.—Sent & Pun 2021, 2022.

Harris v. State, TexApp–Houston (14 Dist), 629 SW2d 805.—Crim Law 641.13(2.1), 1171.1(3); False Pret 27, 28.

Harris v. State, TexCivApp–Fort Worth, 615 SW2d 330, ref nre.—Mental H 41.

Harris; State v., TexCivApp–Dallas, 342 SW2d 177.—Int Liq 1, 50, 146(6), 246; Statut 219(9.1).

Harris v. State, TexCivApp–Beaumont, 159 SW2d 172.—Tax 3279.

Harris; State ex rel. Wilson v., TexCrimApp, 555 SW2d 470.—Const Law 2357; Convicts 7(2); Prohib 5(2).

Harris v. State of Texas, Walker County, CA5 (Tex), 476 F2d 719.—Hab Corp 479.

Harris; Stegall v., TexCivApp–Eastland, 525 SW2d 214.—Wills 290.

Harris; Storey v., TexCivApp–Dallas, 475 SW2d 848.—Em Dom 171.

Harris v. Strawbridge, TexCivApp–Houston, 330 SW2d 911, ref nre.—Deeds 26, 29, 36, 104, 105, 124(1); Ref of Inst 32; Ten in C 15(7), 15(10); Wills 179, 181, 182, 184(1), 449, 455, 475, 476, 865(1).

Harris v. Sugg, TexCivApp–Austin, 143 SW2d 149, writ dism, correct.—Judgm 142, 145(1), 159, 162(2).

Harris v. Superior Ins. Co., TexCivApp–Eastland, 322 SW2d 665.—App & E 66, 79(1), 80(1), 80(6), 792.

Harris; Taylor v., EDTex, 505 FSupp 153.—Social S 142.5, 149.

Harris; Texas & N. O. R. Co. v., TexCivApp–El Paso, 101 SW2d 640, writ dism.—App & E 1175(5); Judgm 191, 251(1); New Tr 27; Trial 352.4(7).

Harris v. Texas Dept. of Criminal Justice, SDTex, 806 FSupp 627.—Assault 96(1); Const Law 269, 3310, 3833, 4637, 4674, 4769; Courts 100(1); Crim Law 59(4), 641.13(2.1), 700(2.1), 700(4), 1030(1), 1030(2), 1133; Gr Jury 2.5; Hab Corp 313.1, 340, 342, 366, 404, 422, 423, 441, 442, 486(1), 499, 500.1, 508, 703; Jury 33(5.15), 33(5.20), 108, 142; Rob 27(1); Sent & Pun 1624, 1628, 1669, 1670, 1677, 1712, 1720, 1757, 1771, 1772, 1780(3), 1784(4); States 4.1(1).

Harris; Texas Dept. of Public Safety v., TexApp–Fort Worth, 33 SW3d 406.—Autos 144.1(1.11), 144.2(1), 144.2(2.1); Statut 212.6, 212.7.

Harris v. Texas Emp. Ins. Ass'n, TexCivApp–Beaumont, 447 SW2d 211, ref nre.—App & E 758.3(9); Judgm 198, 199(3.10); Work Comp 1657.

Harris v. Texas Vending Commission, TexCivApp–Austin, 486 SW2d 623.—App & E 781(4); Const Law 2604.

Harris v. Thaler, CA5 (Tex), 146 FedAppx 720.—Fed Civ Proc 2734.

Harris v. Thompson Buick, G.M.A.C., Inc., TexCivApp–Tyler, 601 SW2d 757.—App & E 499(1), 500(1); Sec Tran 242.1.

Harris v. Thornton's Dept. Store, TexCivApp–Eastland, 94 SW2d 849.—App & E 843(1), 1060.1(4), 1067; Libel 112(1), 123(3); Trial 219, 255(13), 351.2(6), 351.2(9), 352.20.

Harris; Tidelands Life Ins. Co. v., TexApp–Corpus Christi, 675 SW2d 224, ref nre.—Antitrust 369; App & E 548(2), 573, 907(4), 1032(1); Evid 434(1); Insurance 1565, 3424(2), 3426.

Harris; Timmons v., CA5 (Tex), 629 F2d 416.—Social S 143.75.

Harris v. TMG Life Ins. Co., SDTex, 915 FSupp 869.—Insurance 2460; Labor & Emp 537; Rem of C 25(1), 107(7), 107(11).

Harris v. Traders' & General Ins. Co., TexCivApp–Beaumont, 82 SW2d 750, writ refused.—Labor & Emp 913, 917, 923; Work Comp 1066.

Harris v. Travelers Ins. Co., CCA5 (Tex), 80 F2d 127.—Evid 450(5); Insurance 1729, 1755, 1762, 1766, 2035, 3125(6).

Harris; Trinity River Authority v., TexCivApp–Beaumont, 439 SW2d 670.—Em Dom 149(1); Evid 142(1); Trial 186.

Harris; Tucker v., TexCivApp–Fort Worth, 409 SW2d 955.—Bankr 3353(11), 3357(2.1).

Harris v. Tucker, TexCivApp–Waco, 245 SW2d 992, ref nre.—Adop 13, 15, 16.

Harris v. Tucker, TexCivApp–Waco, 241 SW2d 304.— App & E 458(1); Mand 28, 57(1).

Harris; U.S. v., CA5 (Tex), 434 F3d 767, cert den 126 SCt 1897, 547 US 1104, 164 LEd2d 580.—Crim Law 1026.10(1), 1026.10(2.1), 1026.10(5), 1030(1), 1042, 1139, 1158(1); Sent & Pun 757.

Harris; U.S. v., CA5 (Tex), 420 F3d 467.—Crim Law 1139, 1144.13(2.1), 1144.13(5), 1159.2(7); Rob 3, 24.35.

Harris; U.S. v., CA5 (Tex), 104 F3d 1465, reh and sug for reh den 110 F3d 795, cert den 118 SCt 103, 522 US 833, 139 LEd2d 57.—Crim Law 38, 561(1), 641.13(1), 641.13(7), 863(2), 1030(1), 1038.2, 1039, 1144.13(3), 1159.2(7), 1172.7; Rob 24.20; Sent & Pun 653(2), 754, 755, 761.

Harris; U.S. v., CA5 (Tex), 932 F2d 1529, cert den 112 SCt 270, 502 U.S. 897, 116 LEd2d 223, cert den Shackleford v. US, 112 SCt 324, 502 US 917, 116 LEd2d 265, cert den Townsend v US, 112 SCt 914, 502 US 1049, 116 LEd2d 814, denial of post-conviction relief vac 55 F3d 168.—Autos 349.5(3); Consp 47(12); Const Law 4700; Crim Law 369.2(3.1), 370, 371(1), 622.2(8), 829(3), 1044.2(1), 1177; Homic 757; Jury 24; Sent & Pun 241, 653(2), 658, 672, 764, 783.

Harris v. U.S., CA5 (Tex), 764 F2d 1126.—Corp 1.6(11); Hus & W 270(8); Int Rev 3192, 3620, 4782.1, 4802; Stip 14(10).

Harris; U.S. v., CA5 (Tex), 628 F2d 875.—Fed Civ Proc 411, 1325, 1603, 1951, 2011; Int Rev 4490, 4493, 4494, 4504, 4508, 4512, 4514.

Harris v. U.S., CA5 (Tex), 538 F2d 1226.—Const Law 4172(3), 4178; Postal 10(1).

Harris; U.S. v., CA5 (Tex), 533 F2d 306.—Crim Law 776(4), 1172.1(2).

Harris; U.S. v., CA5 (Tex), 460 F2d 1041, cert den 93 SCt 128, 409 US 877, 34 LEd2d 130.—Commerce 3, 5, 7(2), 62.10(1), 82.10; Crim Law 412.2(2), 412.2(3), 1132; Gaming 60, 62, 63(1), 98(1); States 4.4(1), 4.16(2).

Harris v. U.S., CA5 (Tex), 356 F2d 582.—Crim Law 410, 483; Int Rev 5294, 5295, 5303.

Harris v. U.S., CA5 (Tex), 239 F2d 612.—Crim Law 641.10(1), 641.13(6), 673(5); Postal 48(2), 50, 51.

Harris v. U.S., CA5 (Tex), 216 F2d 953.—Crim Law 1147, 1618(3).

Harris; U.S. v., CA5 (Tex), 217 FedAppx 376.—Sent & Pun 300.

Harris; U.S. v., CA5 (Tex), 213 FedAppx 286.—Sent & Pun 973, 978.

Harris; U.S. v., CA5 (Tex), 193 FedAppx 333, cert den 127 SCt 3053.—Controlled Subs 100(1), 100(2); Sent & Pun 686.

Harris; U.S. v., CA5 (Tex), 158 FedAppx 561.—Crim Law 1077.1(2).

Harris; U.S. v., CA5 (Tex), 152 FedAppx 384.—Crim Law 1042.

Harris; U.S. v., CA5 (Tex), 133 FedAppx 99, cert den 126 SCt 462, 546 US 953, 163 LEd2d 351.—Crim Law 1035(1).

Harris; U.S. v., CA5 (Tex), 96 FedAppx 182, cert gr, vac 125 SCt 1040, 543 US 1105, 160 LEd2d 1023, on remand 133 FedAppx 99, cert den 126 SCt 462, 546 US 953, 163 LEd2d 351.—Controlled Subs 100(9); Sent & Pun 761, 765.

Harris; U.S. v., CA5 (Tex), 85 FedAppx 993, post-conviction relief den 2006 WL 2468717.—Crim Law 1023(11), 1028; Sent & Pun 941.

Harris; U.S. v., CA5 (Tex), 84 FedAppx 467, cert den 124 SCt 2194, 541 US 1056, 158 LEd2d 755.—Sent & Pun 731.

Harris v. U.S., NDTex, 588 FSupp 835, aff 764 F2d 1126. —Int Rev 4775, 4784.

Harris; U.S. v., NDTex, 588 FSupp 835. See Harris v. U.S.

Harris v. U.S., NDTex, 333 FSupp 870.—Aviation 141, 232.5, 233.

Harris; U.S. v., NDTex, 332 FSupp 315.—Commerce 82.10; Const Law 47.

Harris v. U.S., SDTex, 340 FSupp2d 764.—Const Law 4149; Fed Cts 30, 32, 33, 34; Int Rev 4464, 4940; U S 50.1, 50.3, 50.5(1), 78(5.1), 78(14), 125(3), 125(5), 125(6), 125(9).

Harris v. U.S. Dept. of Justice, CA5 (Tex), 680 F2d 1109, reh den 685 F2d 1385, cert den 103 SCt 1209, 459 US 1212, 75 LEd2d 449.—Fed Civ Proc 1741, 2734.

Harris v. U.S. Dept. of Transp., CA5 (Tex), 843 F2d 219. —Civil R 1530.

Harris; U.S. Fidelity & Guaranty Co. v., TexCivApp– Tyler, 489 SW2d 312, ref nre.—App & E 768, 930(3), 989, 1177(7); Work Comp 661, 719, 734, 1581.

Harris v. Varo, Inc., TexApp–Dallas, 814 SW2d 520.— Estop 52.15; Evid 157(1), 159, 161.1; Judgm 183, 185(1), 185(4), 185(6); Work Comp 55, 1045, 2100, 2110, 2162.

Harris v. Ventura, TexCivApp–Beaumont, 582 SW2d 853. —Hus & W 249(6), 262.1(8), 264(2), 264(3), 264(7).

Harris v. Victoria Independent School Dist., CA5 (Tex), 336 F3d 343.—Civil R 1376(10).

Harris v. Victoria Independent School Dist., CA5 (Tex), 168 F3d 216, reh and reh den 336 F3d 343, cert den 120 SCt 533, 528 US 1022, 145 LEd2d 413.—Civil R 1351(1), 1351(5), 1376(2), 1376(10); Const Law 90.1(7.3), 1182, 1184(1), 1190(2), 1928, 1929, 1930, 1989, 1990, 1991; Fed Civ Proc 2543; Fed Cts 776; Offic 114; Schools 147.12.

Harris; Walker v., Tex, 924 SW2d 375.—Land & Ten 164(1), 167(8); Neglig 220, 1019, 1692, 1711.

Harris v. Ware, TexCivApp–Waco, 144 SW2d 647.—App & E 1199, 1206; Costs 279; Execution 97; Judgm 883(1), 883(7).

Harris v. Ware, TexCivApp–Waco, 93 SW2d 598, writ refused.—App & E 878(1), 1236; Hus & W 80, 89; Land & Ten 34(5), 94(2), 112(2); Statut 223.5(0.5); Tender 18, 19(1), 19(2).

Harris; Waring v., TexCivApp–Austin, 221 SW2d 345, writ refused.—Labor & Emp 2927, 2963.

Harris; Warncke v., CA5 (Tex), 619 F2d 412, reh den 624 F2d 1098.—Social S 143.40, 143.65, 147, 148.5, 148.10, 149.5.

Harris; Weathersby v., TexCivApp–Galveston, 244 SW2d 888, ref nre.—App & E 547(3); Can of Inst 52; Deeds 203, 211(5); Impl & C C 98; Judgm 199(3.14); Lim of Act 102(1).

Harris; Wege v., TexCivApp–Amarillo, 420 SW2d 255.— Sales 261(2), 261(3).

Harris v. Wells, TexCivApp–Houston, 335 SW2d 774.— Hus & W 238.1.

Harris v. Western Best, Inc., TexApp–Amarillo, 795 SW2d 347.—Banks 505.

Harris; West Tex. Utilities Co. v., TexCivApp–Eastland, 231 SW2d 558, ref nre.—Electricity 16(7), 18(3), 18(4); Neglig 506(8).

Harris; Whiteman v., TexCivApp–Fort Worth, 123 SW2d 699, writ refused.—Autos 245(33); Judgm 199(3.9), 199(3.10).

Harris; Whitson v., TexApp–Austin, 792 SW2d 206, writ den.—Insurance 1416; Judgm 185(2); Lim of Act 120; Venue 78.

Harris; Whitson v., TexApp–Amarillo, 682 SW2d 423.— Inj 26(1), 192; Insurance 1384, 1413; Plead 111.39(0.5), 111.40.

Harris; Wilks v., TexApp–Waco, 727 SW2d 318.—Bound 42; High 80, 81.

Harris; Williams v., EDTex, 504 FSupp 819.—Social S 124.10, 140.10, 140.30, 142.5, 143.45, 143.50, 143.60, 143.65, 143.75, 147, 148.5.

Harris v. Windsor, Tex, 294 SW2d 798, 156 Tex 324.—App & E 169, 1082(2); Deeds 93; Mines 55(4).

Harris v. Windsor, TexCivApp–Texarkana, 279 SW2d 648, aff 294 SW2d 798, 156 Tex 324.—Deeds 112(1), 143.

Harris v. Winslar, TexCivApp–Waco, 314 SW2d 642.—App & E 930(1), 1001(1); Evid 571(9); Trial 139.1(3), 140(1), 141, 142, 143; Waters 126(2).

Harris; Wohler Livestock Co., Inc. v., NDTex, 487 FSupp 1.—Fed Cts 12.1, 13.

Harris v. Wood, TexCivApp–Beaumont, 85 SW2d 1051, writ dism.—App & E 173(7), 179(1), 846(3), 846(5); Brok 73, 86(1).

Harris v. Wood County Cotton Oil Co., TexCivApp–Texarkana, 222 SW2d 331, ref nre.—Adv Poss 17, 25, 71(1), 93, 94, 101, 114(1); Corp 1.6(8); Mines 79.1(5); Partit 78; Propty 7; Tresp to T T 47(1); Trial 350.3(3).

Harris; Wyman v., TexCivApp–Beaumont, 222 SW2d 297, ref nre.—Bound 2, 6, 8; Costs 230; Covenants 100(1); Judgm 518, 524, 743(2); Tresp to T T 50; Ven & Pur 220.

Harris Adacom Network Services, Inc.; Byrne v., TexApp–Texarkana, 11 SW3d 244, reh overr, and petition for review den, and reh of petition for review overr.—App & E 213, 231(1), 232(0.5), 232(3), 969, 1062.1, 1064.1(10); Trial 352.1(1), 352.1(2).

Harris & Beeman v. Koon, TexCivApp–Fort Worth, 229 SW2d 212.—Corp 503(2); Costs 230; Venue 7.5(2).

Harris and Eliza Kempner Fund; Bramlett v., TexCivApp–Hous (1 Dist), 462 SW2d 104, ref nre.—Adv Poss 29, 30, 33.

Harris & Westmoreland; CPS Intern., Inc. v., TexApp–Texarkana, 784 SW2d 538.—App & E 206.2, 762, 1026, 1056.1(4.1), 1175(1); Atty & C 140, 166(4), 167(2); Costs 264; Judgm 199(3.2), 199(3.5); Set-Off 8(1); Trial 140(2); Witn 269(1).

Harrisburg Nat. Bank v. Geo. C. Vaughan & Sons, TexCivApp–Galveston, 204 SW2d 9, dism.—App & E 659(3); Fraud Conv 3, 43(1), 229; Garn 49, 105; Judgm 29, 705.

Harrisburg Nat. Bank; Geo. C. Vaughan & Sons v., TexCivApp–Galveston, 195 SW2d 613, dism.—Evid 318(6), 324(3); Garn 171; Trial 169, 174.

Harris By and Through Harris v. Spires Council of Co-Owners, TexApp–Houston (1 Dist), 981 SW2d 892.—App & E 223, 242(2), 934(1); Condo 8, 14; Fraud 7; Judgm 181(33), 185(5), 185.1(4), 185.3(21); Neglig 202, 210, 218.

Harris-Childs v. Medco Health Solutions, Inc., CA5 (Tex), 169 FedAppx 913.—Civil R 1137, 1147, 1171, 1244.

Harris Community Health; Carpenter v., NDTex, 154 FSupp2d 928.—Fed Cts 241; Health 607; Labor & Emp 407; Rem of C 2, 25(1), 95, 102, 107(7); States 18.15, 18.51.

Harris Corp.; Dahlgren Mfg. Co. v., NDTex, 399 FSupp 1253.—Decl Judgm 274.1; Fed Civ Proc 1835; Fed Cts 45, 212; Intern Law 10.26; Pat 212(1).

Harris Corp. v. Ericsson Inc., CAFed (Tex), 417 F3d 1241.—Courts 96(7); Fed Civ Proc 2142.1, 2608.1; Fed Cts 611, 765, 773.1, 776; Pat 101(8), 229, 312(6), 312(8), 319(1), 319(3), 324.1, 324.5, 324.54, 324.55(1), 324.60, 325.11(5), 328(2).

Harris Corp.; Ericsson, Inc. v., CAFed (Tex), 352 F3d 1369, reh and reh den, appeal after remand 146 FedAppx 476.—Fed Cts 543.1; Pat 226.6, 312(6), 312(10), 314(5), 318(3), 318(4.1), 324.2, 324.5.

Harris Corp. v. Ericsson Inc., NDTex, 194 FSupp2d 533.—Evid 177; Fed Civ Proc 2508; Pat 66(1.14), 76, 77, 80, 97, 112.5, 314(5), 323.2(5).

Harris County; Adams v., TexCivApp–Hous (14 Dist), 530 SW2d 606, ref nre, appeal dism 97 SCt 34, 429 US 803, 50 LEd2d 63.—Autos 252, 301(3); Const Law 2513; Counties 142; Courts 91(1); States 191.1, 191.8(1); Statut 237.

Harris County v. Allwaste Tank Cleaning, Inc., TexApp–Houston (1 Dist), 808 SW2d 149, writ dism woj.—Environ Law 265; Evid 333(1).

Harris County; Armstrong v., TexApp–Houston (1 Dist), 669 SW2d 323, ref nre.—Const Law 2473, 2474, 2645, 3869, 3894; Evid 24, 29; Judgm 181(27), 185.1(4); Sheriffs 66, 74; Statut 189.

Harris County v. Bassett, TexCivApp–Galveston, 139 SW2d 180, writ refused.—Counties 58; Courts 480(2); Inj 28, 135; Tax 2655, 2656, 2657, 2667.

Harris County v. Black, TexCivApp–Hous (14 Dist), 448 SW2d 859.—App & E 66, 77(1); Judgm 217.

Harris County; Blackwell v., TexApp–Houston (14 Dist), 909 SW2d 135, reh overr, and writ den.—Autos 11, 329; Crim Law 304(12); Judgm 181(2), 185(2), 185.3(13); Mun Corp 184(3), 188, 189(1); Work Comp 383, 617, 619, 626, 649, 1719.

Harris County v. Bruyneel, TexApp–Houston (14 Dist), 787 SW2d 92.—App & E 930(3), 1001(1), 1067; Autos 286, 306(8); Trial 261, 268, 349(2), 351.5(6).

Harris County; Cantu v., TexApp–Houston (1 Dist), 931 SW2d 39, opinion withdrawn and superseded on reh 1997 WL 467030, review den, appeal after remand 26 SW3d 500.

Harris County v. Cantu, TexApp–Tyler, 26 SW3d 500.—App & E 930(1), 1001(3); Autos 273, 276, 304(1), 306(5).

Harris County v. Carr, TexApp–Houston (1 Dist), 11 SW3d 342, reh overr, and rule 537(f) motion dism.—App & E 854(1); Judgm 181(6); Work Comp 2190, 2210, 2216.

Harris County; Carr v., TexApp–Houston (1 Dist), 745 SW2d 531.—Pretrial Proc 44.1, 46, 226, 315.

Harris County; Castro v., TexApp–Houston (1 Dist), 663 SW2d 502, dism.—Lim of Act 1, 121(1), 121(2).

Harris County; Christensen v., USTex, 120 SCt 1655, 529 US 576, 146 LEd2d 621.—Admin Law 413; Labor & Emp 2312, 2322; Statut 195, 219(1).

Harris County v. Estate of Ciccia, TexApp–Houston (1 Dist), 125 SW3d 749, reh overr, and review den.—App & E 428(2), 840(2), 893(1), 916(1); Autos 252, 258, 259, 277.1, 279, 308(4), 308(6); Mun Corp 723, 728; Plead 104(1), 111.37.

Harris County; City of Piney Point Village v., TexCivApp–Hous (1 Dist), 479 SW2d 358, ref nre, appeal dism 93 SCt 1503, 410 US 976, 36 LEd2d 173.—Const Law 2438; Contracts 153; Em Dom 9, 19, 45, 55; Estop 62.4; High 18, 23, 95(1), 99, 105(1), 105(2), 165; Statut 93(7), 223.4.

Harris County v. Collin, TexCivApp–Texarkana, 365 SW2d 187, ref nre.—Dedi 17, 43, 44, 63(2); Evid 147, 472(1), 586(2), 593.

Harris County v. Comstock, TexApp–Houston (14 Dist), 687 SW2d 419, ref nre, appeal dism, cert den 106 SCt 1451, 475 US 1077, 89 LEd2d 709.—Judgm 335(2), 335(3).

Harris County v. Cypress Forest Public Utility Dist. of Harris County, TexApp–Houston (14 Dist), 50 SW3d 551.—App & E 893(1); Counties 39; Courts 39; Mun Corp 723; Plead 104(1), 111.36, 111.37, 111.48; Pretrial Proc 554; Tresp 2.

Harris County; Davidson v., TexCivApp–Hous (1 Dist), 454 SW2d 830, ref nre.—Em Dom 247(2), 262(5); Evid 558(1); Witn 256, 268(1).

Harris County v. Demny, TexApp–Houston (1 Dist), 886 SW2d 330, reh den, and writ den.—App & E 927(7), 969, 989, 1001(1), 1064.1(1); Autos 279, 306(5); Bridges 46(6); Evid 571(1); Trial 139.1(6), 219, 260(8).

Harris County; DeWitt v., Tex, 904 SW2d 650.—Autos 187(3); Labor & Emp 3045; Mun Corp 723, 723.5, 745, 747(3), 847; Offic 114.

Harris County v. DeWitt, TexApp–Houston (14 Dist), 880 SW2d 99, reh den, and writ gr, aff 904 SW2d 650.—Counties 146; Judges 36; Mun Corp 745, 747(3); Offic 114; Sheriffs 99.

Harris County v. Dillard, Tex, 883 SW2d 166.—Counties 146.

Harris County v. Dillard, TexApp–Houston (1 Dist), 841 SW2d 552, reh den, and writ gr, rev 883 SW2d 166.—App & E 231(9), 870(2), 882(12); Autos 230, 244(4), 244(26); Counties 146, 212; Mun Corp 741.30, 745; Neglig 273; Trial 279.

Harris County v. Dowlearn, TexCivApp–Hous (14 Dist), 489 SW2d 140, ref nre.—App & E 5; Const Law 3011, 3057, 3454; Counties 141, 143, 149, 150(2), 198, 213; Mun Corp 723.5; States 119; Statut 195.

Harris County; Doyle v., CA5 (Tex), 74 FedAppx 302.—Const Law 1953; Counties 67.

Harris County; Dubois v., TexApp–Houston (14 Dist), 866 SW2d 787.—App & E 934(1); Counties 143; Judgm 183, 185(1), 185(2), 185(4), 185(6), 185.3(21); Mun Corp 851; Neglig 1194, 1196; Plead 245(1).

Harris County; Dueitt v., TexCivApp–Galveston, 249 SW2d 636, writ refused.—Em Dom 228, 231, 232, 237(1).

Harris County v. Eaton, Tex, 573 SW2d 177.—Autos 279, 306(5); High 194; Mun Corp 798.

Harris County v. Eaton, TexCivApp–Hous (14 Dist), 561 SW2d 245, writ gr, aff 573 SW2d 177.—Autos 264, 277.1, 279, 306(5), 306(7), 306(8), 308(11).

Harris County v. E.B.H., TexApp–Houston (1 Dist), 95 SW3d 719, review den, and reh of petition for review den.—Const Law 2473; Crim Law 1226(3.1), 1226(4).

Harris County v. Emmite, TexCivApp–Hous (1 Dist), 554 SW2d 203, dism.—Counties 125, 129; Mun Corp 249.

Harris County; Felts v., Tex, 915 SW2d 482.—Em Dom 2(1), 91.

Harris County; Felts, TexApp–Houston (14 Dist), 881 SW2d 866, reh den, and writ gr, aff 915 SW2d 482.—Em Dom 2(1), 2(6), 266, 307(2).

Harris County; First Bank of Deer Park v., TexApp–Houston (1 Dist), 804 SW2d 588.—Admin Law 229; Fraud 47; Judgm 185.2(4); Tax 2556, 2696, 2698, 2777, 2780, 2790, 2791.

Harris County; Frank v., CA5 (Tex), 118 FedAppx 799, cert den 125 SCt 2530, 544 US 1062, 161 LEd2d 1112.—Civil R 1189, 1244, 1252, 1351(5); Sheriffs 21.

Harris County v. Franks, TexApp–Houston (1 Dist), 875 SW2d 1, reh den.—Work Comp 1038, 1822, 1829, 1981.

Harris County; Freeman v., TexApp–Houston (1 Dist), 183 SW3d 885, review den.—App & E 893(1), 916(1); Counties 146; Damag 57.1, 57.14, 57.42; Dead Bodies 9; Mun Corp 745, 852; Plead 104(1), 111.37, 111.38.

Harris County; Fuller v., CA5 (Tex), 137 FedAppx 677, appeal after remand 207 FedAppx 450, on remand 2007 WL 1672100.—Const Law 4823; Prisons 17(2); Sent & Pun 1546.

Harris County v. Garza, TexApp–Houston (14 Dist), 971 SW2d 733.—Autos 196; Counties 146; Judgm 199(1), 199(3.10), 256(1); Offic 114; Sheriffs 140.

Harris County v. Gibbons, TexApp–Houston (14 Dist), 150 SW3d 877.—App & E 294(1), 930(3), 1001(1), 1001(3); Autos 187(3), 187(6); Evid 597; Judgm 199(1), 199(3.10), 199(3.17); Mun Corp 189(1), 723, 742(6), 745, 753(1); Offic 114.

Harris County v. Going, TexApp–Houston (1 Dist), 896 SW2d 305, reh overr, and writ den.—Action 1, 3; App & E 866(3), 878(1), 927(7); Civil R 1345, 1351(1), 1376(3), 1376(4), 1719; Const Law 1493; Counties 146; Lim of Act 58(1); Mun Corp 742(2); Trial 142.

Harris County; Goodman v., CA5 (Tex), 443 F3d 464.—Fed Civ Proc 1654; Fed Cts 556, 571, 572.1, 574, 579.

Harris County v. Gordon, Tex, 616 SW2d 167.—App & E 954(1), 954(2); Em Dom 279(2).

Harris County; Gordon v., TexCivApp–Hous (14 Dist), 603 SW2d 294, rev 616 SW2d 167.—App & E 954(1), 954(2); Em Dom 273.

Harris County; Graf v., TexApp–Houston (1 Dist), 877 SW2d 82, writ den.—App & E 934(1); Counties 143; Mun Corp 755(1), 847, 857; Statut 223.4.

Harris County; Gray-Taylor, Inc. v., CA5 (Tex), 569 F2d 893, cert den 99 SCt 351, 439 US 954, 58 LEd2d 344.—Fed Cts 59.

Harris County v. Hall, Tex, 172 SW2d 691, 141 Tex 388.—App & E 994(3), 1011.1(1), 1094(2); Autos 38; Counties 80(2); Evid 207(1), 245, 265(18); Offic 110.

Harris County v. Hall, TexCivApp–Galveston, 166 SW2d 729, rev 172 SW2d 691, 141 Tex 388.—App & E 1010.1(1); Counties 80(2), 98(1); Lim of Act 24(2), 28(1).

Harris County; Heikkila v., TexApp–Tyler, 973 SW2d 333, review den.—Coroners 23; Counties 146; Mun Corp 742(4), 745; Offic 114, 116; States 78.

Harris County; Hein v., TexCivApp–Hous (1 Dist), 557 SW2d 366, ref nre.—Counties 146, 222; States 112.2(2).

Harris County; Hennigan v., TexCivApp–Waco, 593 SW2d 380, ref nre.—App & E 843(1); Atty & C 26, 114; Fraud 3, 16, 60, 61; Judgm 878(1); Plead 406(1).

Harris County v. Hermann Hosp., TexApp–Eastland, 943 SW2d 547, set aside, and writ gr.—Counties 153.5; Mun Corp 870; Prisons 18(6).

Harris County; Holland v., TexComApp, 102 SW2d 196, 129 Tex 118.—Judges 22(8).

Harris County; Holland v., TexCivApp–Galveston, 103 SW2d 1067, certified question answered 102 SW2d 196, 129 Tex 118.—Judges 22(8); Statut 223.2(7).

Harris County v. Howard, TexCivApp–Hous (1 Dist), 494 SW2d 250, ref nre.—App & E 1079; Contracts 147(2), 176(2); Counties 126; Evid 448.

Harris County v. Hunt, TexCivApp–Houston, 388 SW2d 459.—App & E 961; Courts 57(1), 57(2); Estop 92(1); Judgm 181(27), 185(2); Offic 114; Pretrial Proc 92, 122.

Harris County v. Ideal Cement Co., SDTex, 290 FSupp 956.—Counties 208; Fed Cts 268.1, 283, 284, 304.1; Rem of C 26; States 203.

Harris County v. Inter Nos, Ltd., TexApp–Houston (1 Dist), 199 SW3d 363.—App & E 854(1), 946, 970(2); Em Dom 203(1); Pretrial Proc 44.1, 45; Trial 43; Witn 266, 267, 268(1).

Harris County; James v., SDTex, 237 FRD 606.—Witn 214.5, 222.

Harris County v. Jones, TexCivApp–Galveston, 219 SW2d 737, ref nre.—App & E 846(5); Counties 113(1); Lim of Act 60(7); Spec Perf 105(3); Ven & Pur 18.

Harris County; Junemann v., TexApp–Houston (1 Dist), 84 SW3d 689, reh overr, and review den.—App & E 893(1); Autos 187(3), 196; Judgm 181(27), 185.3(1); Mun Corp 188, 723, 742(4), 747(3), 854, 857; Offic 114; Plead 104(1).

Harris County; Kerr v., TexApp–Houston (1 Dist), 177 SW3d 290.—App & E 20, 782; Em Dom 286; Lim of Act 18, 43, 55(7), 95(3).

Harris County v. Lawson, TexApp–Houston (1 Dist), 122 SW3d 276, reh en banc den, and review den, and reh of petition for review den.—Counties 67, 141; Courts 37(1), 39, 40; Mun Corp 723; Offic 61, 66, 72.41(2); Plead 104(1).

Harris County v. Louvier, TexApp–Houston (14 Dist), 956 SW2d 106.—App & E 893(1); Counties 67; Mun Corp 742(6).

Harris County; Lovett v., TexCivApp–Hous (1 Dist), 462 SW2d 405, ref nre.—Dedi 1, 16.1, 18(2), 41; Em Dom 2(1.1); Fences 6; Mun Corp 671(9); Pretrial Proc 480.

Harris County v. McCoy, TexApp–Houston (1 Dist), 804 SW2d 523, writ dism woj.—App & E 215(1); Work Comp 723, 1617, 1855.

HARRIS

59 Tex D 2d—518

See Guidelines for Arrangement at the beginning of this Volume

Harris County v. McFerren, TexApp–Houston (1 Dist), 788 SW2d 76, writ den.—App & E 1001(1), 1024.4; Counties 143, 223; Judgm 199(3.2), 199(3.5), 199(3.7), 199(3.10); Neglig 1040(3).

Harris County; McIncrow v., CA5 (Tex), 878 F2d 835.— Fed Cts 938.

Harris County; Marquart v., TexCivApp–Galveston, 117 SW2d 494, dism.—Contracts 137(2); Statut 223.2(29); Tax 2437, 2440, 2655.

Harris County; Martinez v., TexApp–Houston (1 Dist), 808 SW2d 257, writ den.—Const Law 2314, 3751; Counties 143; Neglig 1002, 1194.

Harris County; MCorp Financial, Inc. v., BkrtcySDTex, 216 BR 596. See MCorp Financial, Inc., In re.

Harris County; Merritt v., TexApp–Houston (14 Dist), 775 SW2d 17, writ den.—Civil R 1326(4), 1351(1), 1351(3), 1351(4), 1360, 1426; Const Law 3847, 3879, 4080; Courts 97(1); Land & Ten 288, 291(17); Sheriffs 11, 77, 88, 111.

Harris County v. Miller, Tex, 576 SW2d 808.—Pretrial Proc 698.

Harris County; Moreau v., CA5 (Tex), 158 F3d 241, cert gr Christensen v. Harris County, 120 SCt 320, 528 US 926, 145 LEd2d 250, aff 120 SCt 1655, 529 US 576, 146 LEd2d 621.—Fed Cts 581, 584; Labor & Emp 2296.

Harris County; Moreau v., SDTex, 945 FSupp 1067, rev 158 F3d 241, cert gr Christensen v. Harris County, 120 SCt 320, 528 US 926, 145 LEd2d 250, aff 120 SCt 1655, 529 US 576, 146 LEd2d 621.—Labor & Emp 2296, 2322, 2323.

Harris County; Nash v., Tex, 63 SW3d 415.—Judgm 190.

Harris County v. Nash, TexApp–Houston (14 Dist), 22 SW3d 46, reh overr, review gr, rev 63 SW3d 415.—App & E 80(6), 337(1); Courts 40; Judgm 190, 217, 297, 303, 340.

Harris County; O'Bryan v., TexCivApp–Hous (14 Dist), 583 SW2d 896, ref nre.—Courts 91(1); Em Dom 234(5), 235, 251; Judgm 335(2).

Harris County v. Ochoa, TexApp–Houston (14 Dist), 881 SW2d 884, reh den, and writ den.—Autos 196; Mun Corp 745, 753(1); Offic 114, 116.

Harris County v. Ogden, TexApp–Beaumont, 84 SW2d 835.—Counties 125; Sheriffs 32.

Harris County; Olson v., TexApp–Houston (1 Dist), 807 SW2d 594, writ den.—App & E 522(1), 1050.1(1), 1056.1(1); Em Dom 91, 138, 200, 255, 262(5).

Harris County v. Patrick, TexApp–Texarkana, 636 SW2d 211.—Counties 224; Trial 314(1), 362.

Harris County v. Progressive Nat. Bank, TexApp–Houston (14 Dist), 93 SW3d 381, review den.—App & E 893(1); Courts 39; Em Dom 293(1); Plead 104(1), 111.37, 111.39(0.5), 111.48; Pretrial Proc 554, 695.

Harris County v. Proler, TexApp–Houston (14 Dist), 29 SW3d 646.—App & E 893(1); Counties 47; Courts 39; Plead 104(1); Sheriffs 76; Statut 181(1), 188, 206, 212.6; Tax 2002.

Harris County; Renken v., TexApp–Houston (14 Dist), 808 SW2d 222.—Const Law 4171; Counties 67; Labor & Emp 50; Offic 110; Sheriffs 21.

Harris County; Rhodia, Inc. v., TexCivApp–Hous (1 Dist), 470 SW2d 415, 49 ALR3d 1229.—App & E 755, 758.1, 768, 954(1); Inj 132, 133, 135, 147, 151; Nuis 80, 84; Plead 404.

Harris County v. Schoenbacher, TexCivApp–Hous (1 Dist), 594 SW2d 106, ref nre.—Counties 80(1); Judgm 181(15.1).

Harris County; Sellers v., Tex, 483 SW2d 242.—Const Law 4410; Interest 3, 20.

Harris County v. Sellers, TexCivApp–Hous (1 Dist), 468 SW2d 950, writ gr, rev 483 SW2d 242.—Const Law 4108; Dep & Escr 31, 33; Dep in Court 4, 9; Em Dom 2(1.1); Interpl 1, 21.

Harris County; Settegast v., TexCivApp–Galveston, 159 SW2d 543, writ refused.—Bonds 48; Counties 99; Lim of Act 28(1); Offic 129.

Harris County v. Shepperd, Tex, 291 SW2d 721, 156 Tex 18.—Autos 28; Const Law 583; High 121; Licens 1, 3; Statut 95(2); Tax 2002.

Harris County; Shields v., TexCivApp–Fort Worth, 248 SW2d 510, ref nre.—Dedi 12, 21, 38, 45; Evid 18, 25(2); Mines 47, 48, 55(1).

Harris County; Simmons v., TexApp–Houston (14 Dist), 917 SW2d 376, reh overr, and writ den.—Costs 198; Mental H 159.

Harris County; Simpson v., TexApp–Houston (14 Dist), 951 SW2d 251.—Counties 143; Neglig 273, 1040(3).

Harris County v. Smith, Tex, 96 SW3d 230.—App & E 1062.1; Damag 221(5.1); Trial 203(1), 252(1), 350.1.

Harris County v. Smith, TexApp–Houston (1 Dist), 66 SW3d 326, reh overr, and review gr, rev 96 SW3d 230. —App & E 840(4), 969, 1066(9); Damag 32, 38, 184, 185(1), 186, 216(1), 216(4), 216(6), 216(7), 216(8); Torts 101; Trial 182, 295(2).

Harris County v. Smoker, TexApp–Houston (1 Dist), 934 SW2d 714, reh overr, and writ den.—App & E 930(3), 1001(3); Damag 62(1), 157(2), 163(2), 214; High 192, 194, 198, 211, 213(2), 214; Neglig 1001, 1222; States 211; Trial 139.1(14), 352.4(1).

Harris County v. Smyly, TexApp–Houston (14 Dist), 130 SW3d 330, reh overr.—App & E 223, 934(1); Counties 146; Judgm 181(27), 185.1(4); Mun Corp 723, 742(1), 742(5), 747(3); Offic 114, 119; Sheriffs 100.

Harris County; Southern Pac. Transp. Co. v., TexCivApp–Hous (1 Dist), 508 SW2d 484, writ refused.—Em Dom 291.

Harris County v. Southern Pac. Transp. Co., TexCivApp–Hous (1 Dist), 457 SW2d 336.—App & E 954(1), 954(2); Em Dom 2(8), 82, 274(5), 292; Inj 132, 135, 138.6, 147; R R 96.

Harris County; Styers v., TexApp–Houston (14 Dist), 838 SW2d 955, reh den, and writ refused.—Lim of Act 31.

Harris County v. Suburban Utility Co., TexCivApp–Hous (1 Dist), 547 SW2d 72.—Action 6; Judgm 180; Pretrial Proc 551; Statut 147, 178.

Harris County v. Sykes, Tex, 136 SW3d 635.—App & E 78(3); Courts 39; Mun Corp 742(4), 745; Plead 104(1), 111.48; Pretrial Proc 690; States 191.4(1).

Harris County; Sykes v., TexApp–Houston (1 Dist), 89 SW3d 661, review gr, rev in part, mod in part 136 SW3d 635.—App & E 893(1), 916(1), 934(1), 1039(6); Counties 146; Judgm 183, 185(2), 185(5), 185.3(2), 570(9), 632; Mun Corp 742(4), 745; Offic 114, 119; Plead 104(1), 111.38, 111.39(0.5), 111.47, 228.14; States 79, 191.10, 203.

Harris County v. Tennessee Products Pipe Line Co., TexCivApp–Houston, 332 SW2d 777.—Const Law 2438; Counties 47; High 88; Statut 184, 223.1.

Harris County v. Texas & N. O. R. Co., TexCivApp–Galveston, 131 SW2d 109, writ dism, correct.—Counties 125; Em Dom 2(6), 70; High 115; Mun Corp 249.

Harris County; Texas Nat. Bank of Baytown v., TexApp–Houston (14 Dist), 765 SW2d 823, writ den.—Tax 2776, 2777, 2779, 2780.

Harris County; Texas Workers' Compensation Com'n v., TexApp–Houston (14 Dist), 132 SW3d 139.—Admin Law 412.1, 413; Judgm 185(5); Work Comp 1094, 1809, 1834, 1911, 1929, 1949.

Harris County; Thomas v., CA5 (Tex), 784 F2d 648, on remand 1987 WL 6258, vac 971 F2d 748, cert den 113 SCt 1275, 507 US 917, 122 LEd2d 669.—Civil R 1376(9); Const Law 1955; Fed Civ Proc 2491.5; Fed Cts 612.1.

Harris County; Thomas v., TexApp–Houston (1 Dist), 30 SW3d 51, rule 537(f) motion gr.—Counties 146; Mun Corp 745; Prisons 17(2).

Harris County v. Vernagallo, TexApp–Houston (14 Dist), 181 SW3d 17, reh overr, and review den.—App & E

For Later Case History Information, see KeyCite on WESTLAW

179(3), 930(1), 994(3), 996, 999(1); Evid 597; Labor & Emp 779, 863(2); Sheriffs 21.

Harris County; Villarreal v., TexApp–Houston (1 Dist), 226 SW3d 537.—App & E 893(1); Counties 141; Em Dom 1, 2.4, 3, 13, 69, 166, 266, 285, 286, 293(1); Mun Corp 723, 742(1); Plead 104(1), 111.38, 111.48; Schools 89; States 191.1.

Harris County v. Walsweer, TexApp–Houston (1 Dist), 930 SW2d 659, reh overr, and writ den.—App & E 852, 866(3), 934(1), 1096(3), 1097(1), 1195(1); Civil R 1348, 1354, 1358; Courts 99(1); Execution 22; Garn 17; Judgm 181(2), 185(2); Mand 12, 14(1), 14(3), 28, 65, 71, 72, 97, 111, 141, 173, 187.9(2); Mun Corp 1038; Offic 119.

Harris County; Walsweer v., TexApp–Houston (1 Dist), 930 SW2d 659. See Harris County v. Walsweer.

Harris County; Walsweer v., TexApp–Eastland, 796 SW2d 269, writ den, cert den 112 SCt 192, 502 US 866, 116 LEd2d 153, opinion withdrawn and superseded on denial of reh 930 SW2d 659, reh overr, and writ den.— App & E 1048(7); Civil R 1031, 1351(1), 1429; Witn 406.

Harris County v. White, TexApp–Texarkana, 823 SW2d 385.—Civil R 1345, 1351(1), 1351(4); Counties 141; Death 91; Prisons 18(1), 18(6).

Harris County v. Wilkinson, TexCivApp–Hous (14 Dist), 540 SW2d 541, ref nre.—App & E 768; Counties 223; Interest 67.

Harris County v. Wilkinson, TexCivApp–Hous (14 Dist), 507 SW2d 848, ref nre, appeal after remand 540 SW2d 541, ref nre.—Clerks of C 72; Counties 154.5; Courts 100(1); Judgm 181(15.1), 185(2).

Harris County v. Williams, TexApp–Houston (1 Dist), 981 SW2d 936, reh overr, and review den, and reh of petition for review overr.—Insurance 1494, 1497; Statut 176, 181(2), 184, 188, 189, 206; Work Comp 2191.

Harris County v. Xerox Corp., TexCivApp–Hous (1 Dist), 619 SW2d 402, ref nre, probable jur noted 102 SCt 1766, 456 US 913, 72 LEd2d 172, rev 103 SCt 523, 459 US 145, 74 LEd2d 323.—Commerce 4, 77.10(1), 77.15(1); Const Law 2473; Counties 190.1; Estop 62.1; Tax 2215, 2712.

Harris County; Zimmelman v., TexApp–Houston (1 Dist), 819 SW2d 178, extension of time to file for writ of error overr.—App & E 852, 856(1); Counties 47, 105(1), 153.5, 196(1); Inj 86; Judgm 181(3), 183; Prisons 1.

Harris County Appraisal Dist.; Alief Independent School Dist. v., TexApp–Houston (1 Dist), 731 SW2d 628, ref nre.—Tax 2603.

Harris County Appraisal Dist.; Antonini v., TexApp–Houston (14 Dist), 999 SW2d 608.—App & E 842(2), 852; Compromise 5(2), 5(3); Contracts 24, 29; Judgm 570(3), 585(2), 591.1, 713(2); 729.

Harris County Appraisal Dist.; Aramco Associated Co. v., TexApp–Texarkana, 33 SW3d 361, review den, and reh of petition for review den.—App & E 852; Const Law 947; Stip 14(10); Tax 2160, 2212, 2216, 2573(1), 2603, 2652, 2666, 2695, 2696, 2810.

Harris County Appraisal Dist.; Beck & Masten Pontiac-GMC, Inc. v., TexApp–Houston (14 Dist), 830 SW2d 291, reh den, and writ den.—App & E 497(1), 863, 907(4), 934(1); Judgm 181(32), 185(2), 185.3(20); Tax 2482, 2571.

Harris County Appraisal Dist.; Benmar Place, L.P. ex rel. Patrick O'Connor & Associates, Inc. v., TexApp–Houston (14 Dist), 997 SW2d 282, reh overr.—App & E 863; Tax 2603, 2699(7).

Harris County Appraisal Dist. v. Bradford Realty, Ltd., TexApp–Houston (14 Dist), 919 SW2d 131.—Tax 2105, 2667, 2697.

Harris County Appraisal Dist.; Braeswood Harbor Partners and Property Owners ex rel. Patrick O'Connor & Associates, Inc. v., TexApp–Houston (1 Dist), 69 SW3d 251.—App & E 66, 76(1); Judgm 190, 326; Tax 2702.

Harris County Appraisal Dist.; Coastal Liquids Transp., L.P. v., Tex, 46 SW3d 880.—Action 13; App & E 832(4); Parties 1, 96(2); Partners 354, 375.

Harris County Appraisal Dist. v. Coastal Liquids Transp., L.P., TexApp–Houston (1 Dist), 7 SW3d 183, review gr, aff in part, rev in part 46 SW3d 880.—Action 13, 34, 35; App & E 854(1); Partners 375; Statut 263, 265, 267(1), 270; Tax 2518, 2641, 2650.

Harris County Appraisal Dist. v. Consolidated Capital Properties IV, TexApp–Amarillo, 795 SW2d 39, writ den.—App & E 338(1); Statut 227; Tax 2697.

Harris County Appraisal Dist.; Deer Park v., SDTex, 963 FSupp 605, aff 132 F3d 1095, cert den 118 SCt 2343, 524 US 938, 141 LEd2d 714.—Const Law 1055; States 18.75; Tax 2089.

Harris County Appraisal Dist.; Deer Park Independent School Dist. v., CA5 (Tex), 132 F3d 1095, cert den 118 SCt 2343, 524 US 938, 141 LEd2d 714.—Commerce 1, 3, 7(2), 62.71, 71.1; States 4.3, 4.4(1), 4.16(1), 4.16(2); Tax 2288.

Harris County Appraisal Dist. v. Dincans, TexApp–Houston (14 Dist), 882 SW2d 75, reh den, and writ den. —Admin Law 229; Evid 71; Statut 212.7; Tax 2367, 2667.

Harris County Appraisal Dist. v. Dipaola Realty Associates, TexApp–Houston (1 Dist), 841 SW2d 487, reh den, and writ den.—Tax 2697.

Harris County Appraisal Dist. v. Drever Partners, Inc., TexApp–Houston (14 Dist), 938 SW2d 196, reh overr.— Tax 2672, 2694.

Harris County Appraisal Dist. v. Duncan, TexApp–Houston (14 Dist), 944 SW2d 706, reh overr, and writ den.—Tax 2678, 2699(5), 2699(11).

Harris County Appraisal Dist.; Galena Park Independent School Dist. v., CA5 (Tex), 132 F3d 1095. See Deer Park Independent School Dist. v. Harris County Appraisal Dist.

Harris County Appraisal Dist.; Handy Hardware Wholesale, Inc. v., TexApp–Houston (1 Dist), 985 SW2d 618.—Tax 2603.

Harris County Appraisal Dist.; Harris County Emergency Services Dist. No. 2 v., TexApp–Houston (14 Dist), 132 SW3d 456, review den.—Action 13; Const Law 695, 725, 726; Counties 208; Parties 1.

Harris County Appraisal Dist. v. Herrin, Tex, 924 SW2d 154.—Tax 2697.

Harris County Appraisal Dist. v. Herrin, TexApp–Houston (14 Dist), 917 SW2d 345, reh overr, and writ gr, mod 924 SW2d 154.—Const Law 2314, 2316; Tax 2641.

Harris County Appraisal Dist.; Himont U.S.A., Inc. v., TexApp–Houston (1 Dist), 904 SW2d 740, reh overr.— Tax 2212, 2466, 2603.

Harris County Appraisal Dist.; Houston Land & Cattle Co., L.C. v., TexApp–Houston (1 Dist), 104 SW3d 622, reh overr, and review den.—App & E 893(1); Tax 2572, 2695.

Harris County Appraisal Dist. v. Johnson, TexApp–Houston (14 Dist), 889 SW2d 531.—App & E 78(1), 80(6), 934(1); Mand 48, 51.

Harris County Appraisal Dist. v. Kempwood Plaza Ltd., TexApp–Houston (1 Dist), 186 SW3d 155, reh overr.—App & E 971(2); Evid 508, 524, 555.2, 555.6(10); Stip 18(6); Tax 2128, 2721.

Harris County Appraisal Dist. v. Krupp Realty Ltd. Partnership, TexApp–Houston (1 Dist), 787 SW2d 513. —Tax 2692.

Harris County Appraisal Dist.; Martin v., TexApp–Houston (14 Dist), 44 SW3d 190, reh overr, and review den, and reh of petition for review den.—App & E 863; Costs 194.16, 194.22; Judgm 185(2); Statut 188, 194; Tax 2168, 2699(11).

Harris County Appraisal Dist.; Marubeni America Corp. v., TexApp–Houston (1 Dist), 168 SW3d 860.— Tax 2603.

Harris County Appraisal Dist. v. Pasadena Property, LP, TexApp–Eastland, 197 SW3d 402, review den.—Const Law 4137, 4138(2); Judgm 181(32); Tax 2308, 2698, 2791.

Harris County Appraisal Dist.; Plexchem Intern., Inc. v., Tex, 922 SW2d930, on remand Houston Independent School Dist v. Plexchem Intern, Inc, 1998 WL 78052.—App & E 758.3(11), 761.

Harris County Appraisal Dist.; Quantum Chemical Corp. v., TexApp–Houston (1 Dist), 962 SW2d 50, on reh in part, and reh overr.—App & E 870(2); Contracts 143(2); Tax 2318.

Harris County Appraisal Dist. v. Reynolds/Texas, J.V., TexApp–El Paso, 884 SW2d 526, reh overr.—App & E 863, 1175(1); Tax 2461, 2602, 2681.

Harris County Appraisal Dist.; Sagemont Plaza Shopping ex rel. O'Connor & Associates, Inc. v., TexApp–Corpus Christi, 30 SW3d 425, review den.—App & E 1071.1(2); Tax 2699(11), 2728.

Harris County Appraisal Dist.; Sheldon Independent School Dist. v., CA5 (Tex), 132 F3d 1095. See Deer Park Independent School Dist. v. Harris County Appraisal Dist.

Harris County Appraisal Dist.; SLW Aviation, Inc. v., TexApp–Houston (1 Dist), 105 SW3d 99.—App & E 845(2), 893(1); Tax 2212, 2463, 2469, 2603; Trial 368.

Harris County Appraisal Dist. v. Southeast Texas Housing Finance Corp., TexApp–Amarillo, 991 SW2d 18.—App & E 836, 842(2), 852, 893(1), 1008.1(1), 1010.1(1), 1010.2, 1012.1(4); Tax 2315.

Harris County Appraisal Dist.; Spring Independent School Dist. v., TexApp–Houston (14 Dist), 889 SW2d 562, reh overr, and writ gr, rev Enron Corp v. Spring Independent School Dist, 922 SW2d 931.—Const Law 655, 990, 1004; Tax 2121, 2127, 2128, 2135, 2286, 2288.

Harris County Appraisal Dist.; Stuckey Diamonds, Inc. v., TexApp–Houston (14 Dist), 93 SW3d 212.—Tax 2699(10), 2728; Trial 392(3), 395(5), 401, 404(6).

Harris County Appraisal Dist.; Taufiq ex rel. Patrick O'Connor & Associates, Inc. v., TexApp–Houston (14 Dist), 6 SW3d 652.—Partners 375; Statut 227; Tax 2642, 2694, 2699(1), 2699(3).

Harris County Appraisal Dist.; Tex-Air Helicopters, Inc. v., TexApp–Texarkana, 15 SW3d 173, review den.—Tax 2699(11).

Harris County Appraisal Dist. v. Texas Eastern Transmission Corp., TexApp–Houston (14 Dist), 99 SW3d 849, review den.—Tax 2603.

Harris County Appraisal Dist. v. Texas Gas Transmission Corp., TexApp–Houston (14 Dist), 105 SW3d 88, review den.—App & E 845(2), 893(1); Statut 181(1), 181(2), 188, 206, 217.4, 220; Tax 2212, 2463, 2464, 2466, 2603; Trial 368.

Harris County Appraisal Dist. v. Texas Nat. Bank of Baytown, TexApp–Houston (1 Dist), 775 SW2d 66.—Admin Law 229; Tax 2640, 2667, 2671, 2696.

Harris County Appraisal Dist.; Tourneau Houston, Inc. v., TexApp–Houston (1 Dist), 24 SW3d 907.—Courts 24, 37(1); Estop 52(8), 62.2(1), 62.2(2); Statut 270; Tax 2650, 2699(4).

Harris County Appraisal Dist. v. Transamerica Container Leasing Inc., TexApp–Houston (1 Dist), 920 SW2d 678, reh overr, and writ den.—App & E 845(2); Commerce 62.71, 62.75, 72, 73; Tax 3400; Trial 368.

Harris County Appraisal Dist. v. Transamerica Container Leasing Inc., TexApp–Houston (1 Dist), 821 SW2d 637, writ den, cert gr, vac 113 SCt 1407, 507 US 969, 122 LEd2d 779, on remand 920 SW2d 678, reh overr, and writ den.—Commerce 62.71, 62.75, 73.

Harris County Appraisal Dist. v. United Investors Realty Trust, TexApp–Houston (14 Dist), 47 SW3d 648, reh overr, and review den, and reh of petition for review den.—Const Law 961, 990, 999; Statut 181(1), 181(2), 184, 190, 217.4, 236, 245; Tax 2128, 2720.

Harris County Appraisal Dist.; Vinmar, Inc. v., Tex, 947 SW2d 554.—Commerce 62.71, 71.1; Tax 2103.

Harris County Appraisal Dist.; Vinmar, Inc. v., TexApp–El Paso, 890 SW2d 493, reh den, and writ gr, rev 947 SW2d 554.—App & E 1079; Commerce 62.71, 62.75, 62.80, 71.1; Const Law 3057, 3564; Tax 2126.

Harris County Appraisal Dist.; Virginia Indonesia Co. v., Tex, 910 SW2d 905, cert den 116 SCt 2523, 518 US 1004, 135 LEd2d 1048.—Commerce 77.15(2).

Harris County Appraisal Dist. v. Virginia Indonesia Co., TexApp–Houston (14 Dist), 871 SW2d 864, reh den, and writ gr, rev 910 SW2d 905, cert den 116 SCt 2523, 518 US 1004, 135 LEd2d 1048.—Commerce 62.71, 77.10(1), 77.15(1); Judgm 181(32); Tax 2100, 2101, 2291, 2369(3), 2392.

Harris County Appraisal Dist.; Weingarten Realty Investors v., TexApp–Houston (14 Dist), 93 SW3d 280.—App & E 856(1), 946, 971(2), 1079; Evid 508, 535, 555.2; Tax 2720, 2721.

Harris County Appraisal Dist. v. West, TexApp–Houston (14 Dist), 708 SW2d 893.—Judgm 321, 386(1); Motions 58.

Harris County Appraisal Dist. v. Westbrook Place Apartments, TexApp–Houston (1 Dist), 787 SW2d 513. See Harris County Appraisal Dist. v. Krupp Realty Ltd. Partnership.

Harris County Appraisal Dist. v. Wilkerson, TexApp–Houston (1 Dist), 911 SW2d 84, reh overr, and writ den.—App & E 662(4), 931(1), 989, 1008.1(1), 1008.1(2), 1010.1(1), 1010.1(3), 1012.1(5); Tax 2524.

Harris County Appraisal Dist. v. Wittig, TexApp–Houston (1 Dist), 881 SW2d 193.—App & E 347(1), 347(2); Courts 30; Pretrial Proc 501.

Harris County Appraisal Dist.; World Houston, Inc. v., TexApp–Houston (14 Dist), 979 SW2d 761. See G.E. American Communication v. Galveston Cent. Appraisal Dist.

Harris County Appraisal Dist. v. World Houston, Inc., TexApp–Houston (14 Dist), 905 SW2d 594.—Statut 188, 190; Tax 2685.

Harris County Appraisal Review Bd. v. General Elec. Corp., TexApp–Houston (14 Dist), 819 SW2d 915, writ den.—App & E 863, 870(2); Const Law 4138(2); Judgm 185(2); Tax 2667, 2670, 2674.

Harris County Bail Bond Bd.; ABD Bonding Co. v., TexApp–Houston (1 Dist), 663 SW2d 615. See Burns v. Harris County Bail Bond Bd.

Harris County Bail Bond Bd.; Austin v., TexApp–Houston (1 Dist), 756 SW2d 65, writ den.—Bail 60.

Harris County Bail Bond Bd. v. Blackwood, Tex, 41 SW3d 123.—Bail 60; Licens 22; New Tr 81.

Harris County Bail Bond Bd. v. Blackwood, TexApp–Houston (1 Dist), 2 SW3d 31, reh overr, and review gr, rev 41 SW3d 123.—App & E 852, 893(1), 931(1), 989, 1010.1(1), 1010.2, 1012.1(4); Bail 60; Statut 181(2), 212.3.

Harris County Bail Bond Bd.; Burns v., CA5 (Tex), 139 F3d 513, reh den.—Bail 60; Civil R 1321, 1345, 1350; Consp 2; Const Law 885, 3879, 3881, 3890, 4282; Fed Civ Proc 1832, 2533.1, 2543, 2544; Fed Cts 425, 427, 776, 802; Lim of Act 95(1), 95(15).

Harris County Bail Bond Bd.; Burns v., TexApp–Houston (1 Dist), 663 SW2d 615.—Bail 60; Const Law 2625(1), 4282.

Harris County Bail Bond Bd.; Burns v., TexApp–Houston (14 Dist), 971 SW2d 102, reh overr.—App & E 863, 934(1), 1175(1); Bail 60; Judgm 185(2).

Harris County Bail Bond Bd. v. Burns, TexApp–Houston (14 Dist), 881 SW2d 61, clarified on denial of reh, and writ den.—Licens 22.

Harris County Bail Bond Bd. v. Burns, TexApp–Houston (14 Dist), 790 SW2d 862, writ den.—Admin Law 468; Licens 38; Mand 4(5).

Harris County Bail Bond Bd. v. John Burns Bail Bonds, TexApp–Houston (14 Dist, 790 SW2d 862. See Harris County Bail Bond Bd. v. Burns.

Harris County Bail Bond Bd.; Pruett v., CA5 (Tex), 489 F3d 217.—Bail 60; Civil R 1414; Const Law 1133, 1535, 1539, 1540, 1541, 1606; Fed Cts 776, 945.

Harris County Bail Bond Bd.; Pruett v., CA5 (Tex), 104 FedAppx 995.—Fed Civ Proc 340; Fed Cts 555.

Harris County Bail Bond Bd.; Pruett v., SDTex, 400 FSupp2d 967, entered 2005 WL 3047787, motion den 2005 WL 3047786, vac 489 F3d 217, subsequent determination 2005 WL 3047789, vac 489 F3d 217, aff in part, rev in part 489 F3d 217.—Bail 60; Civil R 1351(1); Const Law 1020, 1033, 1490, 1491, 1505, 1535, 1536, 1539, 1540, 1541, 1606, 1870, 1879, 2145, 2191, 3000, 3053, 3851; Statut 47, 176, 181(1); Tel 888.

Harris County Bail Bond Bd. v. Pruett, TexApp–Houston (1 Dist), 177 SW3d 260, review gr (3 pets).—App & E 856(1), 893(1), 1175(1); Bail 60; Const Law 984, 1539, 1540, 1541, 1606, 2145; Licens 5; Statut 181(1).

Harris County Bail Bond Bd.; Texas Fire and Cas. Co. v., TexApp–Houston (14 Dist), 684 SW2d 177, ref nre.—Admin Law 386, 387; Bail 60.

Harris County Children Protective Services v. Richker, TexApp–Houston (14 Dist), 2 SW3d 741.—Counties 228; Infants 243, 249, 251, 252; States 191.4(1), 191.6(1).

Harris County Children's Protective Services v. Olvera, TexApp–Houston (14 Dist), 77 SW3d 336, review den.—App & E 984(5), 1097(1), 1192, 1195(1), 1212(1); Atty & C 63, 132; Child C 924; Costs 264; Courts 26, 99(1).

Harris County Children's Protective Services v. Olvera, TexApp–Houston (14 Dist), 971 SW2d 172, review den, and reh of petition for review overr, appeal after remand 77 SW3d 336, review den.—App & E 1198; Child C 947; Infants 83, 116.

Harris County Child Welfare Dept.; Callip v., CA5 (Tex), 757 F2d 1513.—Atty & C 32(7), 77, 88; Fed Civ Proc 1758.1, 1836, 1837.1; Fed Cts 818, 927.

Harris County Child Welfare Unit; Allred v., TexCivApp–Hous (1 Dist), 615 SW2d 803, ref nre.—App & E 1071.6; Evid 53, 89, 597; Infants 155, 178, 180, 252.

Harris County Child Welfare Unit v. Caloudas, TexCivApp–Hous (1 Dist), 590 SW2d 596.—Adop 10, 11, 13; App & E 171(1), 218.2(5.1), 501(1), 930(3), 989; Infants 17; Judgm 270; Trial 349(1).

Harris County Child Welfare Unit; Furlow v., TexCivApp–Hous (1 Dist), 527 SW2d 802.—Adop 4, 13, 15; Child 3, 20.2.

Harris County Child Welfare Unit; Hall v., TexCivApp–Hous (14 Dist), 533 SW2d 121.—Infants 155, 172, 254.

Harris County Civil Service Com'n; Parks v., TexApp–El Paso, 225 SW3d 246.—App & E 1175(1); Judgm 180; Offic 72.44, 72.54, 72.55(2), 72.62, 72.63; Sheriffs 19.

Harris County Com'rs Court; Driscoll v., TexApp–Houston (14 Dist), 688 SW2d 569, ref nre.—Costs 12; Counties 113(5); Dist & Pros Attys 8, 10; Mun Corp 39; Statut 161(1), 188, 212.1, 223.1; Turnpikes 4.

Harris County Com'rs' Court; Hainsworth v., Tex, 269 SW2d 332, 153 Tex 356, cert den 75 SCt 110, 348 US 874, 99 LEd 688.—Courts 247(8).

Harris County Com'rs Court; Hainsworth v., TexCivApp–Galveston, 265 SW2d 217, ref nre 269 SW2d 332, 153 Tex 356, cert den 75 SCt 110, 348 US 874, 99 LEd 688.—App & E 907(3); Mand 167, 168(4).

Harris County Com'rs Court v. Moore, USTex, 95 SCt 870, 420 US 77, 43 LEd2d 32.—Courts 89, 493(2); Fed Cts 41, 43, 58, 480, 997, 999.1, 1002.

Harris County Com'rs Court; Moore v., SDTex, 378 FSupp 1006, probable jur noted 94 SCt 2637, 417 US 928, 41 LEd2d 231, rev 95 SCt 870, 420 US 77, 43 LEd2d 32.—Const Law 206(1), 2920, 3358(1), 4174; Fed Cts 997; J P 8.

Harris County Community Action Ass'n; Jefferies v., CA5 (Tex), 693 F2d 589.—Civil R 1135, 1544.

Harris County Community Action Ass'n; Jefferies v., CA5 (Tex), 615 F2d 1025, appeal after remand 693 F2d 589.—Civil R 1107, 1152, 1165, 1172, 1173, 1231, 1244, 1251, 1536, 1542, 1544, 1545, 1548, 1549, 1554; Fed Cts 612.1, 613, 617, 714, 865, 941, 947.

Harris County Community Action Ass'n; Jeffries v., SDTex, 425 FSupp 1208, aff in part, vac in part 615 F2d 1025, appeal after remand 693 F2d 589.—Civil R 1244, 1251, 1252, 1542, 1548, 1549, 1553.

Harris County Democratic Executive Committee; Hayes v., TexCivApp–Hous (14 Dist), 563 SW2d 884.—Elections 126(3), 126(4); Mand 74(3); Offic 31.

Harris County Democratic Executive Committee; Shipley v., TexApp–Houston (1 Dist), 795 SW2d 766, subsequent mandamus proceeding Correa v. First Court of Appeals, 795 SW2d 704.—Judges 3.

Harris County Democratic Executive Committee; Thiel v., Tex, 534 SW2d 891.—Courts 472.2; Mand 23(1); Statut 178; Time 3, 10(1).

Harris County Dist. Attorney v. Lacafta, TexApp–Houston (14 Dist), 965 SW2d 568.—App & E 662(4), 1008.1(1), 1010.1(2); Crim Law 1226(3.1), 1226(4).

Harris County Dist. Attorney v. Small, TexApp–Houston (1 Dist), 920 SW2d 740, reh overr.—Crim Law 37(1), 37(2.1), 255.2, 752.5, 1134(3), 1144.13(5), 1144.13(6), 1158(1), 1159.2(2), 1226(3.1), 1226(4).

Harris County Dist. Attorney's Office v. Burns, TexApp–Houston (14 Dist), 825 SW2d 198, writ den.—Action 35; Arrest 68(3); Crim Law 1134(6), 1144.1, 1226(3.1); Ind & Inf 142.

Harris County Dist. Attorney's Office v. Dawson, TexApp–Houston (14 Dist), 809 SW2d 359.—Crim Law 1226(4).

Harris County Dist. Attorney's Office v. D.W.B., TexApp–Houston (1 Dist), 860 SW2d 719.—Crim Law 1226(3.1), 1226(4).

Harris County, Dist. Attorney's Office; Green v., CA5 (Tex), 390 F3d 839.—Hab Corp 666, 894.1.

Harris County Dist. Attorney's Office v. Hopson, TexApp–Houston (14 Dist), 880 SW2d 1, reh den.—Crim Law 1226(3.1).

Harris County Dist. Attorney's Office v. Jimenez, TexApp–Houston (1 Dist), 886 SW2d 521, reh den, and writ den.—Crim Law 1226(3.1).

Harris County Dist. Attorney's Office v. J.T.S., Tex, 807 SW2d 572.—Crim Law 1226(3.1), 1226(4); Statut 51, 181(1), 223.1.

Harris County Dist. Attorney's Office v. J.T.S., TexApp–Houston (14 Dist), 790 SW2d 755, writ gr, rev 807 SW2d 572.—Crim Law 1226(3.1).

Harris County Dist. Attorney's Office v. M.G.G., TexApp–Houston (14 Dist), 866 SW2d 796.—Crim Law 1226(3.1).

Harris County Dist. Attorney's Office v. Pennington, TexApp–Houston (1 Dist), 882 SW2d 529.—Crim Law 1226(4).

Harris County Dist. Atty's Office v. R.R.R., TexApp–Houston (14 Dist), 928 SW2d 260.—Crim Law 1226(3.1), 1226(4); Gr Jury 26.

Harris County Eastex Oaks Water and Sewer Dist.; City of Houston v., TexCivApp–Hous (1 Dist), 438 SW2d 941, ref nre.—App & E 758.3(6), 758.3(9), 1040(16), 1056.2, 1078(1); Evid 460(6); Mun Corp 29(4), 33(2), 33(4), 33(9), 33(10), 121; Quo W 5.

Harris County Emergency Corps; Harris County Emergency Service Dist. No.1 v., TexApp–Houston (14 Dist), 999 SW2d 163.—Admin Law 124; App & E 954(1), 954(2); Counties 52; Inj 83.

Harris County Emergency Service Dist. No. 1 v. Harris County Emergency Corps, TexApp–Houston (14 Dist), 999 SW2d 163.—Admin Law 124; App & E 954(1), 954(2); Counties 52; Inj 83.

Harris County Emergency Services Dist. # 1 v. Miller, TexApp–Houston (1 Dist), 122 SW3d 218.—Admin Law 651; Work Comp 51, 1846, 1942.

Harris County Emergency Services Dist. No. 1 v. Miller, TexApp–Houston (1 Dist), 102 SW3d 182, reh gr 102 SW3d 187, vac and superseded on reconsideration en banc 122 SW3d 218.

Harris County Emergency Services Dist. No. 2 v. Harris County Appraisal Dist., TexApp–Houston (14 Dist), 132 SW3d 456, review den.—Action 13; Const Law 695, 725, 726; Counties 208; Parties 1.

Harris County Flood Control Dist. v. Adam, Tex, 66 SW3d 265.—Judgm 217.

Harris County Flood Control Dist. v. Adam, TexApp–Houston (1 Dist), 988 SW2d 423, review den with per curiam opinion 66 SW3d 265.—App & E 76(1), 79(1), 80(6).

Harris County Flood Control Dist. v. Adam, TexApp–Houston (14 Dist), 56 SW3d 665, reh overr, and review dism woj.—App & E 70(2); Courts 39; Em Dom 2(1), 2(10), 266, 293(1), 293(3), 293(4), 307(2); Plead 104(1).

Harris County Flood Control Dist. v. Cohen, TexCivApp–Galveston, 282 SW2d 917, ref nre.—Em Dom 224; Exceptions Bill of54; New Tr 40(1).

Harris County Flood Control Dist.; EPGT Texas Pipeline, L.P. v., TexApp–Houston (1 Dist), 176 SW3d 330, reh overr, and review dism.—App & E 893(1); Contracts 175(1), 187(1); Courts 35; Em Dom 266, 286; Judgm 181(6), 185.3(2); Labor & Emp 29, 58; Levees 10, 19; Mun Corp 723, 745; States 191.1, 191.4(1), 191.8(1).

Harris County Flood Control Dist. v. Glenbrook Patiohome Owners Ass'n, TexApp–Houston (1 Dist), 933 SW2d 570, reh overr, and writ den.—App & E 216(7); Covenants 21, 53, 68, 70, 77.1, 84; Em Dom 2(1), 63, 85, 91, 255, 263, 266, 307(2); Ven & Pur 231(3).

Harris County Flood Control Dist. v. Hambrick, TexCivApp–Hous (1 Dist), 433 SW2d 195.—Em Dom 203(1), 205, 262(5); Evid 211, 555.6(10); Trial 260(3).

Harris County Flood Control Dist. v. Hill, TexCivApp–Houston, 348 SW2d 806, ref nre.—Evid 142(1), 568(4).

Harris County Flood Control Dist.; Hubbard v., TexCivApp–Galveston, 286 SW2d 285, ref nre.—App & E 1002, 1078(1); Em Dom 149(1), 202(1), 224, 255; Evid 142(3), 543(3), 555.6(2), 555.6(7).

Harris County Flood Control Dist.; Johnston v., CA5 (Tex), 869 F2d 1565, reh den, cert den 110 SCt 718, 493 US 1019, 107 LEd2d 738.—Atty & C 21, 21.5(2); Civil R 1249(2), 1487, 1502, 1573, 1594; Const Law 1929, 1952; Evid 571(10); Fed Civ Proc 1855.1; Fed Cts 634, 878, 945; Int Rev 3124; Levees 8.

Harris County Flood Control Dist. v. King, TexCivApp–Galveston, 221 SW2d 361, dism.—Em Dom 148, 262(3).

Harris County Flood Control Dist.; King v., TexCivApp–Galveston, 210 SW2d 438, ref nre.—Const Law 4076; Em Dom 8, 58, 66, 67, 68, 262(3); Plead 11, 228.23; Waters 222.

Harris County Flood Control Dist.; Kothe v., TexCivApp–Houston, 306 SW2d 390.—Deeds 93, 95, 97; Ease 12(1), 42.

Harris County Flood Control Dist. v. Mann, Tex, 140 SW2d 1098, 135 Tex 239.—Const Law 63(2), 2435; Counties 154(1), 158; Levees 2, 5, 34; States 119, 131; Statut 94(1), 103.

Harris County Flood Control Dist. v. Midwest Const. Co., TexApp–Houston (14 Dist), 25 SW3d 722, reh overr, and review den.—Levees 16.

Harris County Flood Control Dist. v. Mihelich, Tex, 525 SW2d 506.—Levees 31, 32; States 112(2).

Harris County Flood Control Dist. v. Mihelich, TexCivApp–Hous (1 Dist), 512 SW2d 393, writ gr, aff 525 SW2d 506.—Levees 10, 31; States 191.1.

Harris County Flood Control Dist.; Musquiz v., TexApp–Houston (1 Dist), 31 SW3d 664, reh overr.—Em Dom 235, 253(1), 255.

Harris County Flood Control Dist. v. PG & E Texas Pipeline, L.P., TexApp–Houston (1 Dist), 35 SW3d 772, review dism woj.—App & E 70(3); Plead 104(1).

Harris County Flood Control Dist. v. Shell Pipe Line Corp., Tex, 591 SW2d 798.—App & E 1010.1(1); Dedi 57; Ease 1; Em Dom 85; High 88.

Harris County Flood Control Dist. v. Shell Pipeline Corp., TexCivApp–Hous (1 Dist), 578 SW2d 495, aff 591 SW2d 798.—Em Dom 69, 85; High 88.

Harris County Flood Control Dist.; State Highway Commission v., TexCivApp–Galveston, 247 SW2d 135, writ refused.—Autos 45.

Harris County Flood Control Dist.; Stuart v., TexCivApp–Hous (14 Dist), 537 SW2d 352, ref nre.—Em Dom 200, 235; Estop 92(4).

Harris County Flood Control Dist.; Taub v., TexApp–Houston (1 Dist), 76 SW3d 406, reh overr, and review den.—App & E 911.3; Counties 141, 212; Courts 32, 37(1), 39; Mun Corp 723; Plead 104(1); States 112(1), 191.4(1), 191.6(1), 191.9(1).

Harris County Fresh Water Supply Dist. No. 1-A; Niles v., TexCivApp–Waco, 339 SW2d 562.—App & E 883; Contracts 342; Waters 183.5.

Harris County Fresh Water Supply Dist. No. 1A; Niles v., TexCivApp–Waco, 336 SW2d 637, writ refused, reh den 339 SW2d 562.—Plead 291(1); Waters 183.5.

Harris County Fresh Water Supply Dist. No. 23; Christie v., TexCivApp–Waco, 317 SW2d 214, ref nre.—Abate & R 23; App & E 330(2); Judgm 253(2); Mun Corp 35; Waters 183.5.

Harris County Fresh Water Supply Dist. No. 23; Ferrell v., TexCivApp–Galveston, 241 SW2d 242.—Elections 10, 29; Waters 183.5.

Harris County Fresh Water Supply Dist. No. 55 v. Carr, Tex, 372 SW2d 523.—Statut 109, 109.2, 109.4, 120(3).

Harris County Hospital Dist.; Clabon v., TexCivApp–Hous (14 Dist), 567 SW2d 71, ref nre.—Judgm 181(2), 181(3), 181(33).

Harris County Hosp. Dist.; Dinh v., TexApp–Houston (1 Dist), 896 SW2d 248, reh overr, and writ dism woj, and reh dism.—App & E 388, 852, 934(1); Const Law 2312, 2314; Judgm 181(33), 185(2); Mun Corp 723.5, 741.30, 741.40(1), 741.40(3), 741.50, 742(6); States 112(2).

Harris County Hosp. Dist.; Dupre v., SDTex, 8 FSupp2d 908.—Civil R 1019(2), 1119, 1217, 1218(2), 1218(3), 1218(6), 1219, 1220, 1221, 1222, 1225(2), 1225(4), 1243, 1246, 1552; Counties 141; Damag 50.10; Mun Corp 723, 723.5.

Harris County Hosp. Dist.; Eber v., SDTex, 130 FSupp2d 847.—Civil R 1019(1), 1019(4), 1218(3), 1218(6), 1384, 1505(3), 1505(4), 1505(5), 1513, 1542; Fed Civ Proc 1684, 1685, 2546, 2770; Fed Cts 424, 427; Lim of Act 74(1), 104.5, 195(3); Time 10(2).

Harris County Hosp. Dist. v. Estrada, TexApp–Houston (1 Dist), 872 SW2d 759, writ den.—App & E 221, 846(5), 852, 931(1), 931(3), 971(2); Counties 141; Death 82, 88, 89, 99(2), 99(4); Evid 536, 538, 546; Health 706, 823(13), 835.

Harris County Hosp. Dist. v. Estrada, TexApp–Houston (1 Dist), 831 SW2d 876.—App & E 337(1), 387(6); New Tr 116.

Harris County Hospital Dist.; Harris v., TexCivApp–Hous (1 Dist), 557 SW2d 353.—Health 656, 696, 703(2), 819, 823(14).

Harris County Hosp. Dist.; Lowe v., TexApp–Houston (14 Dist), 809 SW2d 502.—Const Law 245(1), 3166; States 112(2), 112.2(4).

Harris County Hosp. Dist.; Lowe by Armstrong v., TexApp–Houston (14 Dist, 809 SW2d 502. See Lowe v. Harris County Hosp. Dist.

HARRIS

Harris County Hosp. Dist.; Regis, Estate of, ex rel. McWashington v., TexApp–Houston (14 Dist), 208 SW3d 6.—Health 804, 805.

Harris County Hosp. Dist.; Seamans v., TexApp–Houston (14 Dist), 934 SW2d 393.—Counties 143; Dead Bodies 9; Mun Corp 723.

Harris County Hosp. Dist. v. Shalala, CA5 (Tex), 64 F3d 220.—Admin Law 413, 754.1, 763, 791; Health 535(6); Social S 8.20; Statut 190, 219(6.1).

Harris County Hosp. Dist. v. Shalala, SDTex, 863 FSupp 404, aff 64 F3d 220.—Admin Law 413, 416.1, 741; Health 523, 535(1), 535(4), 541; Statut 190, 219(2).

Harris County Hosp. Dist.; Tomball Hosp. Authority v., TexApp–Houston (14 Dist), 178 SW3d 244, reh overr, and review gr.—Admin Law 228.1, 305; App & E 68, 863; Counties 141; Courts 4, 35, 91(1), 155; Health 507, 512(1); Mun Corp 723, 742(1), 742(6); Plead 104(1); Schools 89; States 191.1, 191.4(1), 191.6(2), 191.8(1).

Harris County Hosp. Dist.; Weeks v., TexApp–Houston (14 Dist), 785 SW2d 169, writ den.—Health 703(2), 770; States 112(1), 112.2(2).

Harris County Hosp. Dist. Auxiliary, Inc., In re, TexApp–Houston (1 Dist), 127 SW3d 155.—App & E 78(1), 79(1), 80(1); Judgm 340; Mand 1, 28, 172, 187.9(1), 187.9(6); Motions 62.

Harris County Houston Ship Channel Nav. Dist.; McCrea v., CA5 (Tex), 423 F2d 605, cert den 91 SCt 189, 400 US 927, 27 LEd2d 186.—Fed Civ Proc 2282.1; Fed Cts 611, 942; Labor & Emp 2773.

Harris County Houston Ship Channel Nav. Dist.; Sivils v., TexCivApp–Hous (14 Dist), 462 SW2d 352.—Nav Wat 8.5.

Harris County-Houston Ship Channel Nav. Dist.; Smith v., Tex, 329 SW2d 845, 160 Tex 292.—Time 10(9).

Harris County-Houston Ship Channel Navigation Dist.; Smith v., TexCivApp–Fort Worth, 330 SW2d 672.—Levees 5; Mun Corp 723; Nav Wat 8.5; Waters 224.

Harris County-Houston Ship Channel Nav. Dist.; South Atlantic & Gulf Coast Dist. of Intern. Longshoremen's Ass'n, Independent v., TexCivApp–Houston, 360 SW2d 181, ref nre, cert den South Atlantic & Gulf Coast District of the International Longshoremen's Association Independent v. Harris County-Houston Ship Channel Navigation District, 83 SCt 1111, 372 US 975, 10 LEd2d 142.—App & E 449.

Harris County-Houston Ship Channel Nav. Dist.; South Atlantic & Gulf Coast Dist. of Intern. Longshoremen's Ass'n, Independent v., TexCivApp–Houston, 358 SW2d 658, ref nre, cert den South Atlantic & Gulf Coast District of the International Longshoremen's Association Independent v. Harris County-Houston Ship Channel Navigation District, 83 SCt 1111, 372 US 975, 10 LEd2d 142.—App & E 954(1); Courts 489(9); Labor & Emp 1345(3), 1420, 1421(1), 1424, 2047, 2111.

Harris County Houston Ship Channel Nav. Dist.; State of Tex. v., CCA5 (Tex), 158 F2d 861.—Em Dom 82, 152(1), 158, 253(1).

Harris County Houston Ship Channel Nav. Dist.; Williams v., Tex, 99 SW2d 276, 128 Tex 411, 110 ALR 59.—Mtg 310; Ven & Pur 230(1).

Harris County Houston Ship Channel Nav. Dist. v. Williams, TexCivApp–Galveston, 87 SW2d 813, rev 99 SW2d 276, 128 Tex 411, 110 ALR 59.—App & E 719(6), 882(3); Mtg 148, 310; Princ & A 177(3.1), 180.

Harris County Inv. Corp. v. Wiggins, TexCivApp–Galveston, 255 SW2d 304, dism.—Courts 30, 39; Judgm 298, 341; Mech Liens 258.

Harris County Medical Soc.; Ford v., CA5 (Tex), 535 F2d 321, cert den 97 SCt 492, 429 US 980, 50 LEd2d 589.—Fed Cts 223.

Harris County Medical Soc.; Guidry v., TexCivApp–Hous (1 Dist), 618 SW2d 844, ref nre.—App & E 1056.1(1), 1056.4; Fraud 52, 58(2); Health 295; Trial 260(6), 352.20; Witn 16.

Harris County Mun. Utility Dist. No. 130; General Motors Acceptance Corp. v., TexApp–Houston (14 Dist), 899 SW2d 821.—Tax 2105, 2697, 2703.

Harris County Mun. Utility Dist. No. 29; Coulson v., TexApp–Houston (14 Dist), 678 SW2d 726, ref nre.—Judgm 335(1); Mand 108; Mun Corp 956(4); Waters 183.5.

Harris County Mun. Utility Dist. No. 48 v. Mitchell, TexApp–Houston (1 Dist), 915 SW2d 859, reh overr, and writ den.—Admin Law 228.1, 662; App & E 756, 931(1), 1008.1(2); Const Law 2450, 2625(1); Contracts 147(2), 176(2); Mun Corp 250, 254, 917(1), 1017, 1040; Waters 183.5.

Harris County Mun. Utility Dist. No. 9, Northwest Harris County; Kaye v., TexApp–Houston (14 Dist), 866 SW2d 791.—App & E 170(2), 173(2), 179(1); Judgm 183, 185(2), 185(6); Mun Corp 30, 33(1); New Tr 26; Statut 176, 181(1), 188, 214.

Harris County Outdoor Advertising Ass'n; City of Houston v., TexApp–Houston (14 Dist), 879 SW2d 322, reh den, and writ den, cert den 116 SCt 85, 516 US 822, 133 LEd2d 42.—App & E 836, 842(2), 931(1), 994(3), 1008.1(2), 1008.1(3), 1010.1(1), 1010.1(3), 1010.2, 1011.1(2), 1012.1(2), 1012.1(5); Civil R 1072, 1422; Const Law 1011, 4135, 4267; Damag 96, 104, 119; Licens 1, 5.5, 7(1), 22; Plead 427.

Harris County Outdoor Advertising Ass'n; City of Houston v., TexApp–Houston (14 Dist), 732 SW2d 42.—App & E 842(2), 984(5); Crim Law 13(1); Mun Corp 65, 1040; Statut 47, 219(1); Zoning 14, 28, 81, 282, 321, 322, 384.1.

Harris County Precinct Four Constable Dept. v. Grabowski, Tex, 922 SW2d 954.—Mun Corp 185(1); Sheriffs 21.

Harris County Republican Executive Committee; Bacon v., TexApp–Houston (14 Dist), 743 SW2d 369.—Elections 126(1).

Harris County Republican Executive Committee; Fisher v., TexApp–Houston (1 Dist), 744 SW2d 339.—Mand 154(3), 154(5).

Harris County Risk Management; Ashley v., TexApp–Corpus Christi, 104 SW3d 905.—App & E 346.1, 346.2, 428(2); Judgm 297, 386(1).

Harris County Sheriff's Dept.; Clark v., TexApp–Houston (14 Dist), 889 SW2d 569.—Jury 142.

Harris County Sheriff's Dept.; Edwards v., SDTex, 864 FSupp 633.—Atty & C 62; Civil R 1345, 1351(4), 1355, 1358, 1395(7); Fed Civ Proc 1758.1, 1759, 1760.

Harris County Sheriff's Dept.; James v., SDTex, 234 FRD 150, opinion withdrawn and superseded 237 FRD 606.

Harris County Sports and Convention Corp.; Ray Ferguson Interests, Inc. v., TexApp–Houston (1 Dist), 169 SW3d 18.—Counties 208; Judgm 585(4); Mun Corp 723, 742(4); Plead 104(1); Set-Off 60.

Harris County Tax Assessor-Collector v. Reed, TexCivApp–Austin, 225 SW2d 586, rev Texas Automotive Dealers Ass'n v. Harris County Tax Assessor-Collector, 229 SW2d 787, 149 Tex 122.—Autos 19; Decl Judgm 294; States 191.10.

Harris County Tax Assessor-Collector v. Reed, TexCivApp–Austin, 210 SW2d 852.—Decl Judgm 62, 253; Plead 111.8, 111.36; States 191.10; Venue 22(9).

Harris County Tax Assessor-Collector; Texas Automotive Dealers Ass'n v., Tex, 229 SW2d 787, 149 Tex 122.—Autos 54, 57.

Harris County, Tex.; Adams v., CA5 (Tex), 452 F2d 994, 14 ALR Fed 659, cert den 92 SCt 2414, 406 US 968, 32 LEd2d 667.—Adm 22.

Harris County, Tex.; Adams v., SDTex, 316 FSupp 938, rev 452 F2d 994, 14 ALR Fed 659, cert den 92 SCt 2414, 406 US 968, 32 LEd2d 667.—Adm 1.20(5), 18, 20, 22; Fed Cts 265, 266.1, 418; States 4.16(3), 112(2), 112.1(1), 191.2(1), 191.4(1).

Harris County, Tex. v. CarMax Auto Superstores Inc., CA5 (Tex), 177 F3d 306.—Const Law 735, 1040, 3057; Courts 508(1), 508(2.1); Fed Cts 611, 617, 623, 755, 815, 937.1, 1145, 1146; Inj 1, 128(1), 138.1, 138.24, 143(1), 192; Judgm 243, 675(1), 677, 678(1), 678(2), 681; Statut 77(1).

Harris County, Tex.; Clanton v., CA5 (Tex), 893 F2d 757. —Civil R 1088(5).

Harris County, Tex. v. Gist, SDTex, 976 FSupp 620.— Fed Cts 12.1, 13; U S 82(2).

Harris County, Tex. v. Gist, SDTex, 976 FSupp 601.— Atty Gen 8; Const Law 994, 2407; Decl Judgm 8, 303; Evid 23(1); Fed Civ Proc 2533.1; Fed Cts 12.1, 13, 14.1, 269, 272; Inj 14, 132, 138.1, 138.66, 147; Statut 39, 190, 195, 196, 200, 219(2), 219(4); U S 82(2).

Harris County, Tex.; Harper v., CA5 (Tex), 21 F3d 597, reh den 29 F3d 626.—Arrest 63.4(1), 63.4(2), 68(2); Civil R 1088(2), 1376(6), 1429; Fed Civ Proc 2491.5, 2544; Fed Cts 579, 766, 802; Mun Corp 747(3); Offic 114.

Harris County, Tex.; Houston Oilers, Inc. v., SDTex, 960 FSupp 1202.—Alt Disp Res 247, 332; Assoc 14; Consp 19; Contracts 187(1); Fraud 3, 13(1), 20; Libel 1, 136; Pub Amuse 26; Ship 80; Torts 242, 243.

Harris County, Tex. v. Jenkins, TexApp–Houston (14 Dist), 678 SW2d 639, ref nre.—App & E 971(6), 1050.1(1), 1050.1(10), 1170.3, 1170.7; Evid 317(2), 318(1); Pretrial Proc 312; Prisons 17(0.5); Witn 336, 345(1).

Harris County, Tex.; Mathes v., SDTex, 96 FSupp2d 650, rev 31 FedAppx 835.—Civil R 1218(4); Const Law 3155; Sheriffs 24.

Harris County, Tex.; Portis v., CA5 (Tex), 632 F2d 486. —Fed Cts 670.

Harris County, Tex.; Rutherford v., CA5 (Tex), 197 F3d 173.—Civil R 1138, 1166, 1536, 1544, 1555, 1563, 1573, 1574; Evid 129(5); Fed Civ Proc 2656, 2658, 2737.4; Fed Cts 681.1, 682, 715, 763.1, 776, 813, 823, 901.1, 913, 915, 941, 944, 945.

Harris County, Tex.; Simi Inv. Co., Inc. v., CA5 (Tex), 236 F3d 240, reh en banc den 256 F3d 323, cert den 122 SCt 550, 534 US 1022, 151 LEd2d 426.—Civil R 1482, 1486; Const Law 978, 3874(1), 3874(2), 3893, 3894, 3895, 4071, 4105(1); Decl Judgm 274.1; Ease 40, 70; Fed Civ Proc 758, 845, 2531, 2741; Fed Cts 6, 177, 763.1, 776, 817, 830, 878; High 85; Nuis 1, 3(1), 4, 29.

Harris County, Tex.; Simi Investment Co., Inc. v., SDTex, 13 FSupp2d 603, vac 236 F3d 240, reh en banc den 256 F3d 323, cert den 122 SCt 550, 534 US 1022, 151 LEd2d 426.—Deeds 144(1); Em Dom 2(1), 106; Fed Cts 13.25; High 18, 85; Lim of Act 55(6); Mun Corp 646; Propty 1; Quiet T 27.

Harris County, Tex.; Staley v., CA5 (Tex), 485 F3d 305. —Civil R 1482; Fed Cts 724, 776, 932.1, 933.

Harris County, Tex.; Staley v., CA5 (Tex), 461 F3d 504, reh en banc gr 470 F3d 1086, on reh 485 F3d 305.— Const Law 1379, 1380; Counties 107; Fed Cts 776, 814.1, 862.

Harris County Tex.; Staley v., CA5 (Tex), 160 FedAppx 410.—Fed Civ Proc 320, 331; Fed Cts 817.

Harris County, Texas; Staley v., SDTex, 332 FSupp2d 1041.—App & E 460(4); Fed Civ Proc 2737.5; Fed Cts 685; Interest 39(3).

Harris County, Texas; Staley v., SDTex, 332 FSupp2d 1030, stay gr 332 FSupp2d 1041, aff 461 F3d 504, reh en banc gr 470 F3d 1086, on reh 485 F3d 305.—Const Law 1295, 1379; Counties 107.

Harris County, Tex.; Staley v., SDTex, 223 FRD 458, aff 160 FedAppx 410.—Const Law 1507; Fed Civ Proc 316, 320, 331; Fed Cts 817.

Harris County, Tex.; Thibodeaux v., CA5 (Tex), 215 F3d 540.—Fed Cts 574, 595.

Harris County, Tex.; Waymire v., CA5 (Tex), 86 F3d 424. —Civil R 1113, 1149, 1185, 1189; Fed Civ Proc 2142.1, 2152; Fed Cts 766, 798, 801.

Harris County, Tex.; Willie v., SDTex, 202 FSupp 549.— Admin Law 229; Civil R 1360, 1391, 1451; Const Law 3267; Decl Judgm 209, 302.1, 329; Fed Civ Proc 186.15; Inj 94, 114(3), 123.

Harris County, Tex.; Willie v., SDTex, 180 FSupp 560.— Civil R 1321; Const Law 1435, 4034; Estop 70(2); Fed Cts 7, 261, 263.

Harris County, Tex.; Xerox Corp. v., USTex, 103 SCt 523, 459 US 145, 74 LEd2d 323.—Commerce 77.15(1); Fed Cts 504.1; Tax 2214, 2215.

Harris County Toll Road Authority; CenterPoint Energy Houston Elec. LLC v., CA5 (Tex), 436 F3d 541, reh and reh den 179 FedAppx 245, cert den 126 SCt 2945, 165 LEd2d 956.—Com Law 11; Fed Cts 812, 830, 947; High 88; Statut 181(1), 206.

Harris County, TX v. Cabazos, TexApp–Houston (1 Dist), 177 SW3d 105.—App & E 893(1); Counties 146; Courts 4, 35, 39; Mun Corp 723, 723.5, 746; Offic 114; Plead 104(1), 111.36, 111.37; States 191.6(1).

Harris County Water Control and Improvement Dist. No. 109; Chase Bank ofTexas, N.A. v., TexApp–Houston (1 Dist), 36 SW3d 654.—App & E 1030.

Harris County Water Control and Imp. Dist. No. 110 v. Texas Water Rights Commission, TexCivApp–Austin, 593 SW2d 852.—Const Law 2340; Mun Corp 276.

Harris County Water Control and Imp. Dist. No. 21; St. Clair v., TexCivApp–Hous (14 Dist), 474 SW2d 545.— Statut 185; Waters 203(5), 203(10), 203(12).

Harris County Water Control & Improvement District # 21; Wilson v., TexApp–Houston (14 Dist), 194 SW3d 551, reh overr, and review den, and reh of petition for review den.—Judgm 181(6), 185(5), 185(6); Mun Corp 723, 745, 847, 854; Offic 114, 119; States 191.1, 191.4(1); Waters 183.5.

Harris County Water Control and Imp. Dist. No. 39 v. Albright, Tex, 263 SW2d 944, 153 Tex 94.—Courts 247(1); Statut 64(1), 64(5), 123(3); Waters 183.5.

Harris County Water Control & Imp. Dist. No. 50; Hall v., TexApp–Houston (14 Dist), 683 SW2d 863.—App & E 241; Judgm 181(2), 181(3), 181(15.1), 183, 185(2), 185.3(8); Lim of Act 170; Torts 215, 217, 241, 262, 263; Waters 183.5.

Harris County Water Control and Imp. Dist. No. 58; Calvert v., TexCivApp–Austin, 368 SW2d 833, ref nre. —States 191.10; Tax 3665.

Harris County Water Control and Imp. Dist. No. 58 v. City of Houston, TexCivApp–Houston, 357 SW2d 789, ref nre.—Const Law 4361, 4372; Evid 25(2); Mun Corp 619; Pub Ut 120; States 66; Waters 183.5, 190, 203(5), 203(6).

Harris County Water Control & Imp. Dist. No. 7; City of Pelly v., Tex, 198 SW2d 450, 145 Tex 443.—Const Law 2687, 2704; Mun Corp 29(4), 33(9), 34, 39, 957(1).

Harris County Water Control and Imp. Dist. No. 7; City of Pelly v., TexCivApp–Galveston, 195 SW2d 241, rev 198 SW2d 450, 145 Tex 443.—Mun Corp 29(4), 33(9), 33(10).

Harris County Water Control and Imp. Dist. No. 70; Home Sav. of America FSB v., TexApp–Houston (14 Dist), 928 SW2d 217, reh overr.—App & E 5, 916(1); Corp 508; Judgm 106(1).

Harris County Water Control and Imp. Dist. No. 84 v. Hornberger, TexCivApp–Hous (1 Dist), 601 SW2d 66, ref nre.—Judgm 134, 139; Waters 183.5.

Harris County Water Control and Imp. Dist. No. 99 v. Duke, TexApp–Houston (1 Dist), 59 SW3d 333.—Damag 15; Elect of Rem 16; Statut 176, 181(1), 181(2), 188, 206, 208, 223.1; Waters 183.5.

Harris County W.C. & I.D. No. 36; Hamic v., CA5 (Tex), 184 FedAppx 442.—Civil R 1505(7); Fed Cts 766, 776; Lim of Act 58(1); Waters 183.5.

Harris County Wrecker Owners for Equal Opportunity v. City of Houston, SDTex, 943 FSupp 711.—Assoc 20(1); Autos 5(1), 43, 61, 62; Commerce 3, 61(1), 63.15;

Fed Civ Proc 103.2, 103.3, 2539; Fed Cts 173; High 165; Mun Corp 53, 590; States 18.3, 18.5, 18.11, 18.13, 18.21; Statut 184, 188, 205.

Harris Cty. Appraisal Dist.; Western Athletic Clubs, Inc. v., TexApp–Amarillo, 56 SW3d 269.—App & E 223, 1175(1); Judgm 181(1), 181(6), 183, 185(2); Tax 2603, 2649.

Harris Data Communications, Inc. v. Dellana, TexApp–Austin, 680 SW2d 641.—Mand 53; Pretrial Proc 372.

Harris-Galveston Coastal Subsidence Dist.; Beckendorff v., Tex, 563 SW2d 239.—App & E 363; Const Law 3509; Levees 2; Licens 1; Waters 101.

Harris-Galveston Coastal Subsidence Dist.; Beckendorff v., TexCivApp–Hous (14 Dist), 558 SW2d 75, ref nre 563 SW2d 239.—Action 6; Const Law 225(2), 655, 1020, 1066, 3037, 3483; Levees 2; Statut 67, 90(1), 219(1); Tax 2002; Waters 101.

Harris Hospital; Clark v., TexCivApp–Fort Worth, 543 SW2d 743.—App & E 1056.4, 1170.7; Health 660, 823(4); Princ & A 159(1); Trial 350.5(1), 366.

Harris Hospital v. Pope, TexCivApp–Fort Worth, 520 SW2d 813, ref nre.—Health 703(2), 823(4).

Harris Hosp. v. Schattman, TexApp–Fort Worth, 734 SW2d 759.—Pretrial Proc 371, 382.

Harris Hospital-Fort Worth; Luckett v., NDTex, 764 FSupp 436.—Fed Cts 34, 230; Rem of C 84, 86(1).

Harris Hospital–Methodist v. Heckler, CA5 (Tex), 730 F2d 391. See Baylor University Medical Center v. Heckler.

Harris Hospital–Methodist v. Schweiker, NDTex, 563 FSupp 1081. See Baylor University Medical Center v. Schweiker.

Harris Hospital--Methodist, Inc.; Diggs v., CA5 (Tex), 847 F2d 270, cert den 109 SCt 394, 488 US 956, 102 LEd2d 383.—Civil R 1110, 1522.

Harris Leasing Co.; O'Kehie v., TexApp–Texarkana, 80 SW3d 316, reh overr.—App & E 230, 1001(1); Contracts 143(2), 143.5, 169, 176(2), 338(1); Costs 194.34, 207; Land & Ten 18(3).

Harris Memorial Methodist Hospital; Southern Health Ass'n v., TexCivApp–Fort Worth, 180 SW2d 169, writ refused wom.—Antitrust 583; Contracts 140, 350(3), 355; Evid 351.

Harris Methodist Affiliated Hospitals; Gunn v., TexApp–Fort Worth, 887 SW2d 248, reh overr, and writ den.—App & E 863, 907(1); Judgm 185(2), 186; Neglig 213, 1001, 1032, 1036, 1037(2), 1037(4), 1086, 1670, 1692.

Harris Methodist, Fort Worth; Mathews v., TexApp–Fort Worth, 834 SW2d 582, reh den, and writ den, cert den 113 SCt 1851, 507 US 1032, 123 LEd2d 474.—Const Law 3989; Pretrial Proc 691, 697, 699.

Harris Methodist Fort Worth v. Sales Support Services Inc. Employee Health Care Plan, CA5 (Tex), 426 F3d 330, on remand 2006 WL 2577826.—Assign 31, 72; Contracts 143(2), 152; Evid 448; Insurance 3564(7); Labor & Emp 591, 633, 677, 678; Lim of Act 66(6).

Harris Methodist Fort Worth; U.S. v., CA5 (Tex), 970 F2d 94.—Civil R 1055; Searches 79, 171, 172.

Harris Methodist Fort Worth Hosp.; Camp v., TexApp–Fort Worth, 983 SW2d 876.—App & E 946, 989, 1003(7); Evid 333(9); Health 197, 258, 658.

Harris Methodist HEB; Scott v., TexApp–Fort Worth, 871 SW2d 548.—Action 13; Dist & Pros Attys 8; Tax 2372, 2380, 2709(2).

Harrison, Ex parte, TexCrimApp, 568 SW2d 339.—Extrad 30, 32, 34, 36.

Harrison, Ex parte, TexCrimApp, 469 SW2d 571.—Extrad 32, 39.

Harrison, Ex parte, TexCrimApp, 297 SW2d 684, 164 TexCrim 145.—Crim Law 1090.1(1), 1099.7(3).

Harrison, Ex parte, TexCrimApp, 122 SW2d 314, 135 TexCrim 611.—Autos 5(3), 7, 12; Dedi 55.

Harrison, Ex parte, TexApp–Austin, 741 SW2d 607.—Child S 444; Const Law 3773; Contempt 71; Courts 92.

Harrison, Ex parte, TexApp–Eastland, 52 SW3d 901.—Crim Law 1226(3.1), 1226(4); Double J 22; Estop 62.2(2).

Harrison, In re, CA5 (Tex), 180 FedAppx 485.—Judgm 828.21(2).

Harrison, In re, TexApp–Texarkana, 187 SW3d 199.—Hab Corp 271; Mand 1, 3(1).

Harrison v. Air Park Estates Zoning Committee, TexCivApp–Dallas, 533 SW2d 108.—App & E 854(1), 954(1); Covenants 1, 71, 73; Inj 147; Ven & Pur 211.

Harrison; Allison v., TexComApp, 156 SW2d 137, 137 Tex 582.—App & E 927(7); Princ & A 69(1), 69(4), 75, 78(6.5); Trusts 111.

Harrison; Allison v., TexCivApp–Galveston, 134 SW2d 399, writ gr, rev and remanded 156 SW2d 137, 137 Tex 582.—App & E 927(7); Contracts 94(1); Fraud 13(1), 18, 20; Princ & A 75.

Harrison; American Cent. Ins. Co. v., TexCivApp–Eastland, 205 SW2d 419, ref nre.—App & E 1050.1(1); Insurance 1790(1), 2171, 2190, 3445, 3496; Partners 135.

Harrison v. Arlington Independent School Dist., NDTex, 717 FSupp 453, aff 891 F2d 904.—Compromise 23(1); Fed Civ Proc 2544; Release 57(2).

Harrison v. Associates Corp. of North America, CA5 (Tex), 917 F2d 195.—Civil R 1135, 1536, 1548; Jury 14(1.5).

Harrison v. Bailey, TexCivApp–Eastland, 260 SW2d 702.—Judgm 324; Lis Pen 25(3); Partners 89, 142(2), 304.

Harrison; Baldwin v., TexApp–Dallas, 765 SW2d 504. See ECC Parkway Joint Venture v. Baldwin.

Harrison; Baldwin Co. v., TexApp–Dallas, 765 SW2d 504. See ECC ParkwayJoint Venture v. Baldwin.

Harrison; Barker v., TexApp–Houston (1 Dist), 752 SW2d 154, writ dism woj.—Evid 265(18); Pretrial Proc 483.

Harrison v. Barngrover, TexCivApp–Beaumont, 118 SW2d 415, writ refused.—App & E 465(2), 1151(2), 1223, 1234(6), 1234(7), 1236, 1239, 1240; Atty & C 96; Bonds 48; Costs 238(2).

Harrison v. Bass Enterprises Production Co., TexApp–Corpus Christi, 888 SW2d 532.—Action 27(1); Fraud 3, 16; Judgm 181(7), 185(2); Lim of Act 43, 46(6), 95(1), 95(3), 95(9), 100(7), 104(1), 104(2); Mines 79.1(1).

Harrison; Bell v., TexCivApp–Dallas, 550 SW2d 369.—Elections 280; Mun Corp 46.

Harrison; Benavides v., TexCivApp–San Antonio, 331 SW2d 251.—App & E 931(6), 1052(5); Evid 474(8); Judgm 829(3).

Harrison v. Benavides, TexCivApp–San Antonio, 327 SW2d 610.—App & E 628(1), 628(2).

Harrison; Boyne v., TexApp–Austin, 647 SW2d 82, writ dism by agreement.—Fed Cts 15; Judgm 634, 713(2), 720, 829(1), 829(3).

Harrison v. Brown, Tex, 422 SW2d 718.—Wills 634(8).

Harrison v. Brown, TexCivApp–Corpus Christi, 416 SW2d 613, ref nre 422 SW2d 718.—Remand 4; Wills 435, 455, 470(1), 634(8).

Harrison v. Bunnell, TexCivApp–Austin, 420 SW2d 777.—Const Law 2340; Mun Corp 12(9), 33(7), 33(10); Quo W 26; States 191.10.

Harrison v. Byrd, CA5 (Tex), 765 F2d 501.—Fed Civ Proc 2470.1, 2491.5, 2642, 2646, 2655; Fed Cts 596, 829.

Harrison; Carmichael v., TexCivApp–Eastland, 165 SW2d 510.—App & E 1064.1(10); Courts 85(2); Evid 473; Trial 215.

Harrison; Carter v., TexApp–Fort Worth, 447 SW2d 704, ref nre.—Judgm 199(3.15); Neglig 213, 384, 387, 452, 453, 454, 503, 504, 506(6), 506(8), 1247, 1296, 1656, 1676.

Harrison; Castro Co-op. Gin Co. v., TexCivApp–Eastland, 272 SW2d 538.—App & E 912, 989; Corp 503(2); Evid 450(8); Plead 111.42(10); Trover 1.

Harrison v. Chesshir, Tex, 320 SW2d 814, 159 Tex 359.—App & E 931(1), 989.

Harrison v. Chesshir, TexCivApp–Amarillo, 322 SW2d 317.—Evid 598(1); Inj 128(7).

Harrison v. Chesshir, TexCivApp–Amarillo, 316 SW2d 909, rev 320 SW2d 814, 159 Tex 359.—App & E 930(1), 989, 1001(1), 1170.6; Const Law 642; Counties 42; Domicile 4(2), 8; Evid 309; Offic 82; Trial 25(4), 350.3(1).

Harrison; City of Houston v., TexApp–Houston (14 Dist), 778 SW2d 916.—Contempt 20; Mand 3(2.1).

Harrison v. City of San Antonio, TexApp–San Antonio, 695 SW2d 271.—Contracts 169, 170(1); Corp 406(2); Frds St of 131(1); Labor & Emp 1073, 1265, 1281, 1304; Plead 427.

Harrison v. City of Victoria, TexApp–Corpus Christi, 730 SW2d 119, 28 Wage & Hour Cas (BNA) 334, ref nre.—Mun Corp 199.

Harrison v. C.I.R., CA5 (Tex), 173 F2d 736.—Assign 108; Int Rev 4817.

Harrison; Cottingham v., TexCivApp–Eastland, 89 SW2d 255, writ dism.—Accord 14; Contracts 57; Evid 441(1), 444(2); Nova 3, 4; Trial 105(5).

Harrison; County of Dallas v., TexApp–Dallas, 759 SW2d 530.—Pretrial Proc 474.

Harrison v. Coutret, TexCivApp–San Antonio, 157 SW2d 454, writ refused wom.—Receivers 92, 93, 100, 214.

Harrison v. Cox, TexCivApp–Fort Worth, 524 SW2d 387, ref nre.—Child S 5, 6, 444, 446, 542, 555; Const Law 191; Statut 267(2).

Harrison v. Craddock, TexCivApp–Galveston, 178 SW2d 296.—Can of Inst 4, 56, 63; Deeds 54, 56(3), 61; Ex & Ad 56, 314(11), 315.6(2), 315.6(3); Lim of Act 39(7); Mental H 382.1; Tresp to T T 4, 6.1, 10; Wills 722, 747.

Harrison; Dairyland County Mut. Ins. Co. of Texas v., TexCivApp–Hous (14 Dist), 578 SW2d 186.—Antitrust 145; Plead 111.3, 111.12, 111.38; Venue 3.

Harrison v. Dallas Court Reporting College, Inc., Tex-CivApp–Dallas, 589 SW2d 813.—Antitrust 367, 389(1), 390, 397; Damag 189, 194; Proc 73, 74, 153.

Harrison; Dallas Joint Stock Land Bank of Dallas v., Tex, 156 SW2d 963, 138 Tex 84.—Covenants 8; Deeds 93, 97, 99; Fraud 22(1), 49; Trial 351.2(2).

Harrison; Dallas Joint Stock Land Bank of Dallas v., TexCivApp–Fort Worth, 135 SW2d 573, rev 156 SW2d 963, 138 Tex 84.—App & E 989; Banks 405; Corp 383, 399(1), 399(2), 400, 432(12); Damag 18; Evid 75, 76, 434(9); Fraud 22(1), 23; Mines 54(2); Princ & A 23(2), 120(2); Torts 115; Tresp to T T 41(1); Ven & Pur 232(1).

Harrison; Dallas Joint Stock Land Bank of Dallas v., TexCivApp–Fort Worth, 131 SW2d 742.—Corp 666; Plead 110, 111.8, 111.9, 111.40; Venue 8.5(2).

Harrison; Darden v., Tex, 511 SW2d 925.—Bills & N 49.

Harrison; Darden v., TexCivApp–Waco, 495 SW2d 49, writ gr, rev 511 SW2d 925.—Bills & N 92(1), 106, 493(3), 516, 518(1).

Harrison; Davenport v., TexApp–Texarkana, 711 SW2d 340.—App & E 241, 863; Judgm 181(6).

Harrison v. Dretke, WDTex, 865 FSupp 385, aff 68 F3d 469.—Const Law 3873, 4820, 4824, 4826; Prisons 13(5), 13(7.1).

Harrison v. Dyson, CA5 (Tex), 492 F2d 1162.—Fed Cts 938.

Harrison v. Energy Gathering, Inc., TexCivApp–Hous (14 Dist), 511 SW2d 78.—App & E 790(3), 802.

Harrison v. Estes Express Lines, CA5 (Tex), 211 Fe-dAppx 261.—Civil R 1505(3), 1505(6).

Harrison v. Facade, Inc., TexCivApp–Dallas, 355 SW2d 543.—App & E 846(2), 846(5); Contracts 147(1); Cust & U 10; Venue 7.5(7).

Harrison v. Federal Energy Regulatory Commission, CA5 (Tex), 567 F2d 308.—Gas 1, 6.

Harrison v. First Nat. Bank, TexComApp, 238 SW 209. —Judgm 784.

Harrison v. Flota Mercante Grancolombiana, S.A., CA5 (Tex), 577 F2d 968.—Adm 1.15, 50, 80; Fed Cts 841, 853, 868, 870.1, 875; Interest 38(1), 39(2.25); Neglig 282, 372, 378, 383, 484; Prod Liab 14, 15, 43; Ship 73, 84(3.2), 84(3.3), 84(6), 85.

Harrison v. Gardner, CA5 (Tex), 369 F2d 172.—Social S 140.60, 143.75.

Harrison v. Gemdrill Intern., Inc., TexApp–Houston (1 Dist), 981 SW2d 714, reh overr, and review den.— Admin Law 501; App & E 846(5), 852, 931(1), 989; Costs 194.16, 207; Damag 124(1); Elect of Rem 1, 15; Judgm 542, 564(1), 577(2); Labor & Emp 222, 254, 256(4), 271, 272, 274, 2350(3).

Harrison; Grays v., TexCivApp–Amarillo, 179 SW2d 1020. —App & E 931(3); New Tr 150(1); Propty 9; Tresp to T T 41(1); Ven & Pur 232(7).

Harrison v. Great American Assur. Co., TexApp–Dallas, 227 SW3d 890.—Insurance 1808, 1810, 1813, 1816, 1822, 1832(1), 1863, 2160(3).

Harrison; Green Tree Acceptance, Inc. v., TexCivApp–Austin, 595 SW2d 608.—App & E 842(1), 931(1), 989; Evid 10(2), 314(1); Plead 111.42(1).

Harrison; Guarantee Mut. Life Ins. Co. v., TexCivApp–Austin, 358 SW2d 404, ref nre.—Estop 54; Statut 212.6, 219(1); Tax 2263, 2562.

Harrison; Harrington v., NDTex, 62 FSupp 449.—Deeds 54, 56(2), 58(1).

Harrison v. Harrison, TexApp–Eastland, 734 SW2d 737. —Guard & W 9.5, 13(4).

Harrison; Harrison v., TexApp–Eastland, 734 SW2d 737. —Guard & W 9.5, 13(4).

Harrison v. Harrison, TexCivApp–San Antonio, 365 SW2d 698, writ dism.—Divorce 252.1, 252.3(2), 286(0.5).

Harrison; Harrison v., TexCivApp–San Antonio, 365 SW2d 698, writ dism.—Divorce 252.1, 252.3(2), 286(0.5).

Harrison v. Harrison, TexCivApp–Eastland, 100 SW2d 780.—Neglig 202, 210, 1037(7); Trial 355(1); Work Comp 2089.

Harrison; Harrison v., TexCivApp–Eastland, 100 SW2d 780.—Neglig 202, 210, 1037(7); Trial 355(1); Work Comp 2089.

Harrison v. Harrison, TexCivApp–Tyler, 597 SW2d 477, ref nre.—App & E 930(3), 989, 994(2), 1001(1), 1002, 1003(5), 1170.7; Evid 584(1); Judgm 199(3.10); Labor & Emp 2765, 2796, 2810, 2832, 2842, 2848, 2881; Neglig 202, 379, 387, 1656, 1676; Trial 127, 142, 215, 350.1; Work Comp 2110, 2133.

Harrison; Harrison v., TexCivApp–Tyler, 597 SW2d 477, ref nre.—App & E 930(3), 989, 994(2), 1001(1), 1002, 1003(5), 1170.7; Evid 584(1); Judgm 199(3.10); Labor & Emp 2765, 2796, 2810, 2832, 2842, 2848, 2881; Neglig 202, 379, 387, 1656, 1676; Trial 127, 142, 215, 350.1; Work Comp 2110, 2133.

Harrison v. Harrison, TexCivApp–Tyler, 495 SW2d 1.— Child C 7, 921(1); Divorce 252.2, 252.5(1), 252.5(3), 286(5); Hus & W 272(5).

Harrison; Harrison v., TexCivApp–Tyler, 495 SW2d 1.— Child C 7, 921(1); Divorce 252.2, 252.5(1), 252.5(3), 286(5); Hus & W 272(5).

Harrison v. Harrison, TexCivApp–Hous (14 Dist), 543 SW2d 176.—App & E 387(1), 388, 846(5); Divorce 62(6), 181; Plead 106(1), 111.42(3).

Harrison; Harrison v., TexCivApp–Hous (14 Dist), 543 SW2d 176.—App & E 387(1), 388, 846(5); Divorce 62(6), 181; Plead 106(1), 111.42(3).

Harrison; HBO, A Div. of Time Warner Entertainment Co., L.P. v., TexApp–Houston (14 Dist), 983 SW2d 31.— App & E 854(1), 863, 934(1); Judgm 181(33), 185(2), 185(5), 185(6), 185.3(21); Libel 23.1, 25, 38(1), 38(4), 48(1), 48(2), 51(5), 112(1), 112(2), 123(8).

Harrison; Houston Independent School Dist. v., Tex-App–Houston (1 Dist), 744 SW2d 298.—App & E 216(3); Work Comp 1417, 1490, 1491.

HARRISON

Harrison; Humble Oil & Refining Co. v., Tex, 205 SW2d 355, 146 Tex 216.—Deeds 90; Estop 95; Mines 55(5), 78.1(3), 78.2, 78.5, 79.1(4).

Harrison; Humble Oil & Refining Co. v., TexCivApp–Galveston, 199 SW2d 786, rev 205 SW2d 355, 146 Tex 216.—App & E 846(2), 846(5); Mines 74.5, 78.1(3).

Harrison v. Humphries, TexCivApp–Amarillo, 567 SW2d 884.—App & E 846(5), 971(2); Evid 544, 546; Labor & Emp 29; Plead 111.3, 111.42(7); Venue 15.

Harrison v. ICT Life Ins. Co., TexCivApp–Fort Worth, 319 SW2d 372, ref nre.—App & E 155; Insurance 1652(2), 1653(1).

Harrison; Ingham v., Tex, 224 SW2d 1019, 148 Tex 380.—Costs 229; Interest 39(3); Mech Liens 310(1); Mtg 581(2).

Harrison v. Ingham, TexCivApp–San Antonio, 223 SW2d 267, rev in part 224 SW2d 1019, 148 Tex 380.—App & E 1008.1(10); Bills & N 165, 350, 351, 497(1), 530, 534, 537(6); Contracts 326; Tender 11.

Harrison v. Jay, Tex, 271 SW2d 388, 153 Tex 460.—Counties 35(3); Elections 83.

Harrison v. Jay, TexCivApp–Eastland, 280 SW2d 636, aff 271 SW2d 388, 153 Tex 460.—Counties 35(3); Elections 71.1.

Harrison; John Hancock Mut. Life Ins. Co. v., TexCivApp–Waco, 82 SW2d 1075, writ dism.—Estop 52.10(1); Usury 34, 69.

Harrison; Jones v., TexApp–San Antonio, 773 SW2d 759, writ den.—Adv Poss 42, 106(2).

Harrison; Jones-Yates Co. v., TexCivApp–Dallas, 96 SW2d 238.—Venue 22(6).

Harrison v. Kell Jones & Son, TexCivApp–Beaumont, 262 SW2d 763.—App & E 80(1).

Harrison; Kemp v., TexCivApp–Hous (14 Dist), 431 SW2d 900, ref nre.—Action 56, 57(1); App & E 949; Atty & C 104; Consp 19; Deeds 17(1); Estop 92(3); Evid 167; Ex & Ad 59; Judgm 128, 185(2), 185.2(1).

Harrison v. King, TexCivApp–San Antonio, 296 SW2d 344, ref nre.—App & E 1170.1, 1170.10; Autos 245(60); Neglig 1537; Trial 352.20.

Harrison; Lambert v., TexCivApp–Waco, 295 SW2d 439, ref nre.—Partners 311(5).

Harrison v. Langlinais, TexCivApp–San Antonio, 312 SW2d 286.—Action 1; Adj Land 10(3).

Harrison v. Leasing Associates, Inc., TexCivApp–Hous (14 Dist), 454 SW2d 808.—Judgm 185(2), 185.3(16); Paymt 55, 59.

Harrison v. Lee Lewis Const., Inc. v., Tex, 70 SW3d 778.—App & E 930(1), 1010.1(3), 1010.2, 1062.1; Neglig 202, 273, 379, 380, 387, 422, 1204(1), 1205(1), 1205(7), 1659, 1672, 1710.

Harrison; Lee Lewis Const., Inc. v., TexApp–Amarillo, 64 SW3d 1, aff 70 SW3d 778.—App & E 930(1), 996, 1001(1), 1003(3), 1004(8); Contrib 1; Damag 32, 49, 97, 102; Death 93, 95(1); Evid 219.50; Indem 20, 29, 30(1); Neglig 273, 371, 380, 387, 1011, 1205(7), 1240, 1659, 1672, 1675, 1680; Work Comp 2142.15, 2142.20.

Harrison v. Life Ins. Co. of Virginia, TexCivApp–Dallas, 121 SW2d 451, writ dism.—Princ & A 99, 124(2), 137(1), 166(1), 173(3), 174; Release 58(2).

Harrison; McEwen v., Tex, 345 SW2d 706, 162 Tex 125.—App & E 347(2); Judgm 135, 138(2), 145(2), 153(1), 335(1), 335(2), 335(3), 386(1).

Harrison v. MacGregor, TexCivApp–Amarillo, 112 SW2d 1095.—App & E 187(3); Princ & A 69(1), 124(2), 160.5; Tresp to T T 28, 35(2), 44.

Harrison v. McKaskle, CA5 (Tex), 959 F2d 22. See Powell v. Estelle.

Harrison v. Manvel Oil Co., Tex, 180 SW2d 909, 142 Tex 669.—Bound 11, 47(1); Estop 90(1); Evid 448, 452; Judgm 526, 527, 712; Tresp to T T 41(1).

Harrison v. Manvel Oil Co., TexCivApp–Beaumont, 179 SW2d 413, rev 180 SW2d 909, 142 Tex 669.—Adv Poss 40; Bound 47(1); Tresp to T T 34, 41(1).

Harrison; Miller v., TexCivApp–Hous (1 Dist), 446 SW2d 372.—App & E 1003(11); Autos 168(6), 242(2), 244(11), 245(16); Trial 105(2).

Harrison v. Missouri-Kansas & T. R. Co. of Texas, TexCivApp–Dallas, 89 SW2d 455, writ dism.—App & E 230, 968, 1004(8), 1070(2); Jury 82(2), 85, 92; New Tr 157; Trial 237(1).

Harrison v. Moore, CA5 (Tex), 178 FedAppx 341.—Civil R 1091.

Harrison v. Nueces Royalty Co., TexCivApp–San Antonio, 163 SW2d 244, writ dism.—Evid 10(2); Plead 111.40; Venue 7.5(2), 7.5(4).

Harrison; Oak Park, Inc. v., TexApp–Eastland, 206 SW3d 133.—Health 804, 809.

Harrison v. Oliver, TexCivApp–Hous (1 Dist), 545 SW2d 229, dism.—Work Comp 1188.

Harrison; Pacific Indem. Co. v., TexCivApp–Dallas, 277 SW2d 256.—Insurance 2706(3).

Harrison v. Parker, Tex, 620 SW2d 102.—Ten in C 15(2).

Harrison; Peacock v., TexCivApp–Austin, 189 SW2d 500, dism.—App & E 1061.4; Attach 279; Brok 48, 54, 85(3), 86(1), 94; Contracts 19; Evid 448, 461(1).

Harrison v. Phillips, SDTex, 185 FSupp 204, aff 289 F2d 927, cert den 82 SCt 62, 368 US 835, 7 LEd2d 37.—Evid 390(4), 397(2); U S 58(4), 60.

Harrison; Pickens v., Tex, 252 SW2d 575, 151 Tex 562.—App & E 232(0.5), 1151(2); Damag 108, 221(1); Land & Ten 142(1); Mines 125; Trial 295(1), 350.1, 350.5(1).

Harrison; Pickens v., TexCivApp–Galveston, 246 SW2d 316, aff 252 SW2d 575, 151 Tex 562.—App & E 989; Evid 318(2); Mines 125; Trial 351.5(5).

Harrison; Pickens v., TexCivApp–Galveston, 231 SW2d 812.—Plead 111.36; Venue 5.5.

Harrison v. Pilot Life Ins. Co., TexCivApp–Fort Worth, 101 SW2d 1027.—App & E 231(5); Mtg 578; Plead 291(2).

Harrison; Plummer v., TexCivApp–Texarkana, 540 SW2d 835, ref nre.—False Imp 22.

Harrison v. Price, TexCivApp–Galveston, 274 SW2d 575, ref nre.—Const Law 2585; Nuis 75.

Harrison; Rayburn v., TexCivApp–El Paso, 269 SW2d 487.—Adv Poss 61; Ex & Ad 115; Tresp to T T 47(3).

Harrison; Reynolds v., TexApp–Tyler, 635 SW2d 845, ref nre.—Judgm 297; Spec Perf 132.

Harrison v. San-Tex Lumber Co., TexCivApp–San Antonio, 459 SW2d 502.—Wills 608(1).

Harrison v. Sea River Maritime, Inc., SDTex, 181 FSupp2d 691.—Seamen 29(1), 29(4).

Harrison; Seddon v., TexCivApp–Houston, 367 SW2d 888, ref nre.—Adv Poss 104; App & E 927(7); Deeds 109; Evid 67(1), 208(1), 591; Land & Ten 18(3); Lost Inst 8(1); Tresp to T T 6.1, 38(1); Trial 350.3(3).

Harrison v. Smith, CA5 (Tex), 83 FedAppx 630.—Civil R 1395(7), 1463.

Harrison; Solomon v., TexCivApp–Dallas, 81 SW2d 164.—App & E 387(3); New Tr 116.3, 119.

Harrison v. Southland Corp., TexCivApp–Dallas, 544 SW2d 692.—False Imp 15(1), 15(2), 31.

Harrison; South Tex. Inv. Co. v., TexCivApp–San Antonio, 194 SW2d 587, ref nre.—App & E 931(1); Can of Inst 55; Deeds 68(2), 211(1); Mental H 508.

Harrison v. Southwest Coaches, TexCivApp–Eastland, 207 SW2d 159, ref nre.—App & E 216(7), 1062.1, 1067, 1069.1; Autos 224(4); Carr 280(1.2), 323, 329, 347; Neglig 453; Trial 255(11), 256(2), 352.4(7).

Harrison v. Stanley, TexApp–Houston (1 Dist), 193 SW3d 581, review den, and reh of petition for review den.—Elections 216.1, 291, 295(1), 305(6), 305(7).

Harrison v. State, TexCrimApp, 205 SW3d 549.—Autos 418, 421; Crim Law 1144.12, 1158(4); Searches 171, 180, 198.

Harrison v. State, TexCrimApp, 187 SW3d 429.—Crim Law 603.3(5), 603.3(7), 954(1), 956(5), 1044.2(1).

Harrison v. State, TexCrimApp, 788 SW2d 18.—Crim Law 641.10(2), 867; Double J 7, 99.

Harrison v. State, TexCrimApp, 767 SW2d 803, on remand 772 SW2d 556, petition for discretionary review gr, rev 788 SW2d 18.—Double J 96.

Harrison v. State, TexCrimApp, 688 SW2d 497.—Crim Law 273.1(4), 1167(5).

Harrison v. State, TexCrimApp, 626 SW2d 518.—Sent & Pun 2021.

Harrison v. State, TexCrimApp, 556 SW2d 811.—Crim Law 516, 517(1), 517(6).

Harrison v. State, TexCrimApp, 555 SW2d 736.—Controlled Subs 26, 30, 80.

Harrison v. State, TexCrimApp, 552 SW2d 151.—Crim Law 641.5(3), 641.13(1), 641.13(2.1), 1166.10(1).

Harrison v. State, TexCrimApp, 516 SW2d 192.—Crim Law 1077.3.

Harrison v. State, TexCrimApp, 501 SW2d 668.—Crim Law 404.70, 517.2(3), 518(3); Stip 18(7).

Harrison v. State, TexCrimApp, 495 SW2d 930.—Crim Law 339.11(2), 1037.1(3), 1170.5(1); Witn 389.

Harrison v. State, TexCrimApp, 491 SW2d 920.—Crim Law 412.2(3), 706(8), 1171.8(2); Witn 390.

Harrison v. State, TexCrimApp, 477 SW2d 583.—Const Law 4509(25); Explos 2.

Harrison v. State, TexCrimApp, 456 SW2d 371.—Crim Law 393(1), 412.1(4), 641.13(8), 1035(1).

Harrison v. State, TexCrimApp, 445 SW2d 216.—Arrest 63.3, 68(13).

Harrison v. State, TexCrimApp, 409 SW2d 848.—Double J 55.

Harrison v. State, TexCrimApp, 350 SW2d 204, 171 TexCrim 329.—Autos 355(6).

Harrison v. State, TexCrimApp, 308 SW2d 519, 165 TexCrim 430.—Autos 355(6); Crim Law 763(1).

Harrison v. State, TexCrimApp, 299 SW2d 297, 164 TexCrim 371.—Crim Law 1064(8), 1090.11.

Harrison v. State, TexCrimApp, 297 SW2d 823.—Ind & Inf 122(4).

Harrison v. State, TexCrimApp, 284 SW2d 367, 162 TexCrim 301.—Burg 36, 41(1); Crim Law 885, 886, 1169.5(1), 1175.

Harrison v. State, TexCrimApp, 275 SW2d 117.—Crim Law 1184(4.1).

Harrison v. State, TexCrimApp, 251 SW2d 413.—Crim Law 1090.1(1).

Harrison v. State, TexCrimApp, 210 SW2d 591, 151 TexCrim 606.—Autos 1, 351.1, 355(8); Crim Law 556, 1032(5).

Harrison v. State, TexCrimApp, 200 SW2d 409, 150 TexCrim 205.—Crim Law 112(7), 554; Larc 71(4).

Harrison v. State, TexCrimApp, 196 SW2d 933, 149 TexCrim 513.—Crim Law 394.4(8).

Harrison v. State, TexCrimApp, 168 SW2d 243, 145 TexCrim 386.—Ind & Inf 114; Sent & Pun 1299, 1367.

Harrison v. State, TexCrimApp, 158 SW2d 780.—Crim Law 1094(2.1).

Harrison v. State, TexCrimApp, 156 SW2d 983, 143 TexCrim 51.—Autos 355(13).

Harrison v. State, TexCrimApp, 150 SW2d 244, 141 TexCrim 526.—Assault 96(3).

Harrison v. State, TexApp–Houston (1 Dist), 7 SW3d 309, petition for discretionary review refused.—Autos 349(17), 349.5(7); Controlled Subs 112, 137; Crim Law 1139, 1141(1), 1158(1); Searches 40.1.

Harrison v. State, TexApp–Houston (1 Dist), 950 SW2d 419, petition for discretionary review refused.—Crim Law 641.13(7), 1144.10; Sent & Pun 1381(2).

Harrison v. State, TexApp–Houston (1 Dist), 788 SW2d 392.—Crim Law 412.2(2).

Harrison v. State, TexApp–Houston (1 Dist), 686 SW2d 220, petition for discretionary review refused.—Crim Law 394.1(1); Rape 51(4); Witn 331.5, 372(1), 374(1), 379(2), 405(1).

Harrison v. State, TexApp–Houston (1 Dist), 663 SW2d 120, petition for discretionary review gr, rev 688 SW2d 497.—Crim Law 273.1(4).

Harrison v. State, TexApp–Fort Worth, 144 SW3d 82, petition for discretionary review gr, rev 205 SW3d 549.—Arrest 63.5(4); Autos 349(6); Crim Law 394.6(4); Searches 24, 180, 183, 184, 198.

Harrison v. State, TexApp–Fort Worth, 766 SW2d 600, petition for discretionary review refused.—Autos 421; Crim Law 713, 717, 721(1), 721(3), 721(6), 726, 728(5), 1171.5.

Harrison v. State, TexApp–Fort Worth, 728 SW2d 902.—Const Law 2545(4), 2823; Crim Law 790.

Harrison v. State, TexApp–San Antonio, 630 SW2d 350.—Crim Law 662.7, 829(3), 834(2); Larc 40(4); Witn 266, 267, 304(3).

Harrison v. State, TexApp–Dallas, 772 SW2d 556, petition for discretionary review gr, rev 788 SW2d 18.—Crim Law 868; Double J 96, 99.

Harrison v. State, TexApp–Dallas, 721 SW2d 904, petition for discretionary review gr, vac 767 SW2d 803, on remand 772 SW2d 556, petition for discretionary review gr, rev 788 SW2d 18.—Atty & C 22; Crim Law 867, 1026.10(4); Double J 59, 99, 202.

Harrison; State v., TexApp–Texarkana, 97 SW3d 810.—App & E 930(2), 1026; Em Dom 134, 150, 202(4), 219, 262(5); Evid 113(16), 142(1), 474(16), 474(18), 501(7), 568(4), 571(7).

Harrison v. State, TexApp–Beaumont, 179 SW3d 629, petition stricken, and petition for discretionary review dism as untimely filed, and review den, and reh of petition for review den.—Mental H 440.

Harrison v. State, TexApp–Beaumont, 148 SW3d 678, appeal after remand 179 SW3d 629, petition stricken, and petition for discretionary review dism as untimely filed, and review den, and reh of petition for review den.—App & E 931(1), 1010.1(5); Evid 596(1); Mental H 439.1, 440.

Harrison v. State, TexApp–Eastland, 929 SW2d 80, reh overr, and petition for discretionary review refused.—Arrest 63.5(1); Controlled Subs 81; Crim Law 665(3), 777, 1144.13(2.1), 1144.13(6), 1159.2(2), 1159.2(7), 1159.2(9), 1173.2(1); Sent & Pun 313, 1988, 1992, 1993.

Harrison v. State, TexApp–Corpus Christi, 76 SW3d 537.—Crim Law 1032(5), 1149; Game 7, 9; Ind & Inf 60, 71.2(2), 71.2(4), 71.3.

Harrison v. State, TexApp–Houston (14 Dist), 843 SW2d 157, petition for discretionary review refused.—Const Law 4767; Crim Law 577.2, 577.10(9), 577.14, 577.16(4).

Harrison v. State, TexApp–Houston (14 Dist), 713 SW2d 760, petition for discretionary review refused.—Crim Law 273.1(2), 1042; Double J 182; Pardon 64.1; Sent & Pun 2123, 2188(4), 2197.

Harrison v. State, TexApp–Houston (14 Dist), 633 SW2d 337.—False Pers 1, 2; Ind & Inf 110(3).

Harrison v. State Highway Dept., TexCivApp–Eastland, 380 SW2d 771, ref nre.—Work Comp 381, 389.

Harrison; Surko v., TexCivApp–Corpus Christi, 391 SW2d 115, ref nre.—Contracts 159, 313(2), 318; Estop 52.10(2), 53; Evid 317(15); Judgm 185(2), 185.3(8), 186; Mines 109.

Harrison v. S/V Wanderer, SDTex, 25 FSupp2d 760.—Fed Civ Proc 2512; Salv 3, 36.

Harrison v. S/V Wanderer, SDTex, 25 FSupp2d 754.—Adm 1.20(2); Contracts 95(1), 114, 189; Contrib 1; Fed Civ Proc 2539; Indem 20, 30(8); Salv 1, 3, 7, 22, 36; Ship 62; Towage 1.

Harrison; Taylor v., TexCivApp–Fort Worth, 445 SW2d 270.—Insurance 3467.

Harrison v. TDCJ-ID, TexApp–Waco, 134 SW3d 490, opinion after remand 2004 WL 1746888, reh overr.—App & E 804.

Harrison v. Texas Bd. of Pardons and Paroles, TexApp–Texarkana, 895 SW2d 807, reh overr, and writ den.

—App & E 854(1), 934(1); Judgm 185(2); Mun Corp 723.5, 745, 847; Pardon 56.

Harrison; Texas Const. Rentals, Inc. v., TexCivApp–Waco, 410 SW2d 482, ref nre.—Sales 441(1), 442(1), 442(6), 447; Trial 356(3), 420.

Harrison v. Texas Dept. of Corrections, EDTex, 694 FSupp 226.—Fed Cts 15; Rem of C 49.1(1).

Harrison v. Texas Dept. of Criminal Justice-Institutional Div., TexApp–Houston (1 Dist), 915 SW2d 882.—Action 3; App & E 863, 984(1); Civil R 1093, 1344, 1350, 1354, 1395(7); Costs 130; Judges 36; Mun Corp 723, 742(4), 742(6); Offic 114; Pretrial Proc 649; Prisons 10; Sent & Pun 1548; States 78, 197, 208.

Harrison v. Texas Dept. of Criminal Justice, Institutional Div., TexApp–Corpus Christi, 164 SW3d 871, reh overr.—Admin Law 651; App & E 984(1); Convicts 6; Costs 128; Prisons 13(10).

Harrison; Texas Emp. Ins. Ass'n v., TexCivApp–Fort Worth, 207 SW2d 168, ref nre.—Trial 208; Work Comp 51, 207, 208, 617, 661, 1927.

Harrison v. Texas Employers Ins. Ass'n, TexApp–Beaumont, 747 SW2d 494, writ den.—App & E 1056.1(1); Witn 270(1), 330(1), 372(1); Work Comp 1396, 1420, 1653, 1703, 1935.

Harrison v. Thompson, CA5 (Tex), 447 F2d 459.—Fed Cts 743; Lim of Act 189.

Harrison; Thompson v., TexCivApp–Waco, 86 SW2d 1093.—High 166; Inj 118(1); Plead 8(6).

Harrison v. Tinney, TexCivApp–Austin, 250 SW2d 631, writ refused.—Evid 400(5); Frds St of 110(1).

Harrison; Tisko v., TexCivApp–Dallas, 500 SW2d 565, ref nre.—Autos 181(1); Const Law 1021, 2489, 3756; Parent & C 7(1), 7(8).

Harrison v. Travelers Ins. Co., EDTex, 347 FSupp 303.—Insurance 2095, 2422, 3374.

Harrison v. Travelers Ins. Co., TexCivApp–Dallas, 442 SW2d 400.—Evid 66, 317(4); Insurance 1634(2), 1635, 1863, 1883, 1885, 1887(1), 1892, 1910, 3084; Judgm 185.3(12); Princ & A 99, 137(1); Ref of Inst 19(1).

Harrison; Tribble v., TexCivApp–Fort Worth, 125 SW2d 383.—App & E 994(3), 1008.1(14).

Harrison v. Tucker, TexCivApp–Fort Worth, 342 SW2d 383, ref nre.—App & E 954(1), 954(2); Const Law 3259; Inj 62(1).

Harrison; U.S. v., CA5 (Tex), 55 F3d 163, cert den 116 SCt 324, 516 US 924, 133 LEd2d 225.—Controlled Subs 31, 68, 81; Crim Law 43.5, 772(6), 795(1.5), 795(2.1), 795(2.5), 795(2.70), 795(2.90).

Harrison; U.S. v., CA5 (Tex), 918 F2d 469.—Arrest 63.5(4), 63.5(6); Const Law 4580; Controlled Subs 116, 117; Crim Law 29(4), 295, 1139, 1158(2), 1158(4); Double J 186; Ind & Inf 7; Searches 165, 198, 201; Sent & Pun 1487.

Harrison; U.S. v., CA5 (Tex), 918 F2d 30.—Const Law 4709; Sent & Pun 941, 1308.

Harrison v. U.S., CA5 (Tex), 708 F2d 1023.—Fraud 16; Lim of Act 95(10.1), 95(12), 104(1), 195(5).

Harrison; U.S. v., CA5 (Tex), 209 FedAppx 390.—Controlled Subs 69; Crim Law 338(7), 412.1(1), 700(3), 700(4), 1177; Cust Dut 126(5); Sent & Pun 764, 990.

Harrison; U.S. v., CA5 (Tex), 108 FedAppx 987, cert gr, vac 125 SCt 2982, 545 US 1137, 162 LEd2d 885, reh den 126 SCt 24, 545 US 1160, 162 LEd2d 927.—Consp 47(12); Crim Law 577.11(6); Ind & Inf 71.4(3).

Harrison; U.S. v., SDTex, 366 BR 656, reconsideration den, and reconsideration den, reconsideration den also published at 2007 WL 1112946, reconsideration den also published at 2007 WL 1675640, motion for stay pending appeal den 2007 WL 1428635.—Bankr 3321; Contempt 2; Fraud Conv 138, 277(1), 278(1), 300(1), 300(3); Int Rev 4857.

Harrison v. Vance, TexApp–Dallas, 34 SW3d 660.—App & E 946, 984(1); Gr Jury 41.10, 41.30; Mand 12; Records 52, 55, 62.

Harrison; Velasquez v., TexApp–Houston (1 Dist), 934 SW2d 767.—App & E 387(2), 387(6).

Harrison; Villiva v., TexCivApp–Beaumont, 102 SW2d 520, writ dism.—Princ & A 3(1), 69(4); Spec Perf 64.

Harrison; Walker v., Tex, 597 SW2d 913.—Judgm 282; Motions 51, 56(1); Pretrial Proc 698.

Harrison v. Williams Dental Group, P.C., TexApp–Dallas, 140 SW3d 912.—Contracts 3, 14, 15, 27, 116(1), 202(2); Trial 140(1).

Harrison; Winsett v., TexCivApp–Texarkana, 101 SW2d 1053.—Land & Ten 252(2), 254(1), 254(2).

Harrison Clinic Hospital; Texas State Bd. of Health v., Tex, 410 SW2d 181.—Health 253.

Harrison Clinic Hospital v. Texas State Bd. of Health, TexCivApp–Fort Worth, 400 SW2d 840, writ gr, aff 410 SW2d 181.—Health 253.

Harrison County v. City of Marshall, TexCivApp–Fort Worth, 253 SW2d 67, writ refused.—Counties 21.5; Dedi 44, 57; High 23, 165; Mun Corp 58, 661(1).

Harrison County v. Clayton, TexCivApp–Beaumont, 587 SW2d 59, ref nre.—Counties 47; Pub Lands 175(0.5).

Harrison County; Gorelick v., TexApp–Texarkana, 720 SW2d 835.—Judgm 634, 678(2), 699(1), 713(2), 720, 829(3).

Harrison County; Smith v., TexApp–Texarkana, 824 SW2d 788.—App & E 846(5); Deeds 70(1), 94, 118; Em Dom 266, 295, 300; Fraud 20, 32, 41; Mines 54(1); Trial 382, 392(3).

Harrison County; Weir v., TexApp–Texarkana, 161 SW2d 322.—Counties 113(1), 114, 125; Impl & C C 34.

Harrison County Clerk; Oliver v., CA5 (Tex), 442 F2d 421, cert den 92 SCt 749, 404 US 1061, 30 LEd2d 750, reh den 92 SCt 1258, 405 US 999, 31 LEd2d 469.—Courts 104; Fed Cts 743.

Harrison County Finance Corp. v. KPMG Peat Marwick, LLP, TexApp–Texarkana, 948 SW2d 941, reh overr, and review gr, rev KPMG Peat Marwick v. Harrison County Housing Finance Corp, 988 SW2d 746.—Accnts 8; Judgm 181(7); Lim of Act 47(1), 95(1), 95(9), 95(10.1).

Harrison County Hosp. Ass'n; Drew v., TexApp–Texarkana, 20 SW3d 244.—Afft 9; App & E 223, 242(2), 854(1), 863, 934(1); Carr 293, 317(1); Judgm 181(33), 183, 185(2), 185(5); Neglig 1001, 1037(4), 1088.

Harrison County Housing Finance Corp.; KPMG Peat Marwick v., Tex, 988 SW2d 746.—App & E 863, 934(1); Judgm 185(2); Lim of Act 95(1), 95(3), 95(10.1), 104(1).

Harrison-Daniels Co. v. Aughtry, TexCivApp–Dallas, 309 SW2d 879.—Damag 40(1); Ven & Pur 350, 351(1).

Harrison Interests, Ltd.; ExxonMobil Pipeline Co. v., TexApp–Houston (14 Dist), 93 SW3d 188, reh overr, and review den (2 pets).—Em Dom 170, 195, 262(1), 262(4).

Harrison Truck Lines, Inc. v. Larson, TexApp–Houston (14 Dist), 663 SW2d 37. See J.V. Harrison Truck Lines, Inc. v. Larson.

Harrison, Walker & Harper, L.L.P.; Nowell v., EDTex, 80 FSupp2d 622.—Civil R 1523, 1530.

Harrison-Wilson-Pearson; Air Conditioning, Inc. v., Tex, 253 SW2d 422, 151 Tex 635.—App & E 927(7); Brok 53, 54, 55(1), 56(3), 57(2), 88(3); Trial 139.1(5.1), 143, 168.

Harrison-Wilson-Pearson; Air Conditioning, Inc. v., TexCivApp–Austin, 250 SW2d 274, rev 253 SW2d 422, 151 Tex 635.—App & E 927(7); Brok 43(2), 43(3), 55(2), 86(4); Trial 139.1(17).

Harris Packaging Corp. v. Baker Concrete Const. Co., TexApp–Houston (1 Dist), 982 SW2d 62, reh overr, and review den.—App & E 866(3); Costs 194.16, 194.36; Neglig 202, 220, 1692; Prod Liab 17.1, 42; Sales 260, 261(6), 262, 273(2), 284(1), 427; Trial 139.1(14), 139.1(17), 168.

Harris Press and Shear, Inc., a Subsidiary of American Hoist and DerrickCo.; Middleton v., CA5 (Tex), 796

F2d 747.—Fed Civ Proc 2182.1; Fed Cts 630.1, 635, 907, 908.1, 912; Prod Liab 81.1, 96.1; Trial 56.

Harris Realty Co. v. Austin, TexComApp, 137 SW2d 19, 134 Tex 484.—Judgm 678(1), 707; Lis Pen 22(2), 25(4).

Harris Realty Co. v. Austin, TexCivApp–Galveston, 118 SW2d 491, aff 137 SW2d 19, 134 Tex 484.—Judgm 785(1).

Harriss v. Norsworthy, TexApp–San Antonio, 869 SW2d 600.—Aviation 238, 240.1; Const Law 2473, 2475; Statut 181(1), 205.

Harriss v. Ritter, Tex, 279 SW2d 845, 154 Tex 474.— Deeds 95; Evid 448, 461(2); Mines 55(4).

Harriss; Ritter v., TexCivApp–Eastland, 267 SW2d 241, mod 279 SW2d 845, 154 Tex 474.—Deeds 90; Evid 458, 461(2); Mines 55(2).

Harrist; Marion v., CA5 (Tex), 363 F2d 139, cert den 87 SCt 960, 386 US 934, 17 LEd2d 807.—Courts 100(1); Hab Corp 490(3).

Harris Trust & Sav. Bank; Robinson v., CCA5 (Tex), 89 F2d 929, cert den 58 SCt 37, 302 US 716, 82 LEd 553.— Bills & N 31; Bonds 1; Corp 471, 480; Fed Cts 757.

Harris, Upham & Co.; Kahn v., Tex, 253 SW2d 647, 151 Tex 655.—Frds St of 82; Gaming 12; States 18.15.

Harris, Upham & Co.; Kahn v., TexCivApp–San Antonio, 247 SW2d 139, aff 253 SW2d 647, 151 Tex 655.—App & E 1051(1); Brok 72, 86(1), 88(6); Contracts 138(6); Evid 22(1); Frds St of 115.3(1); Sales 52(1).

Harris, Upham & Co., Inc. v. Ballantyne, TexCivApp–Dallas, 538 SW2d 153.—Accord 1, 15.1; App & E 989, 994(3), 1008.1(2), 1010.1(6), 1012.1(3); Brok 11; Estop 52.10(3), 52.15; Impl & C C 70.

Harrod v. Grider, TexApp–Beaumont, 701 SW2d 937.— Neglig 1040(4), 1161; Weap 19.

Harrod; Perry v., TexCivApp–Amarillo, 451 SW2d 821, ref nre.—Autos 181(1), 181(2), 244(20).

Harrod v. State, TexApp–Dallas, 203 SW3d 622.—Crim Law 872.5, 1144.13(3), 1144.14, 1159.2(7), 1159.2(10); Homic 683, 774, 942, 1345, 1347, 1480, 1558.

Harrod; State v., TexApp–Dallas, 81 SW3d 904, reh overr, and petition stricken, and petition for discretionary review refused.—Infants 13.5(2); Statut 181(2), 188, 205, 208, 214, 217.4.

Harrold v. First Nat. Bank of Fort Worth, NDTex, 93 FSupp 882.—Char 12; Courts 472.4(6), 489(13), 509; Fed Cts 9; Wills 421.

Harrold v. Ross, TexCivApp–El Paso, 112 SW2d 780, writ dism.—Frds St of 129(5), 129(12), 158(4); Spec Perf 32(3), 43.

Harroll v. State, TexCrimApp, 117 SW2d 103, 135 Tex-Crim 65.—Burg 9(0.5), 41(1), 46(3); Crim Law 552(3).

Harrop Const. Co., Inc.; Electro Associates, Inc. v., TexApp–Houston (1 Dist), 908 SW2d 21, reh overr, and writ den.—Contracts 168; Torts 433.

Harrop Const. Co., Inc.; U.S. ex rel. CMC Steel Fabricators, Inc. v., SDTex, 131 FSupp2d 882, aff 61 FedAppx 120.—Antitrust 272, 389(1), 389(2), 390, 391, 392; Corp 1.5(3), 1.6(2); Damag 22, 190; Fraud 3, 16, 24, 32, 59(1), 59(2), 59(3), 60, 61.

Harroun; Alice Pipe & Supply Co. v., TexCivApp–San Antonio, 195 SW2d 852, ref nre.—App & E 238(1); Bailm 20, 23.

Harroun; Interstate Minerals v., TexCivApp–San Antonio, 173 SW2d 547.—Acct Action on 14; Evid 158(28); Plead 111.2, 111.32, 111.46.

Harry, Ex parte, TexCrimApp, 482 SW2d 197.—Extrad 32, 36, 39.

Harry v. State, TexCrimApp, 299 SW2d 137.—Crim Law 1087.1(2).

Harry; U.S. v., CA5 (Tex), 874 F2d 248.—Sent & Pun 1946.

Harry; University of Texas System v., TexApp–El Paso, 948 SW2d 481.—App & E 1192, 1212(4); Work Comp 1937, 1951.

Harry v. University of Texas System, TexApp–El Paso, 878 SW2d 342, reh den, appeal after remand 948 SW2d 481.—App & E 882(17), 946, 969; Trial 349(1), 350.2, 350.3(8), 352.1(1); Work Comp 1887.

Harry Armstrong Ins. Co.; Hicks v., TexApp–Houston (14 Dist, 708 SW2d 890. See Hicks v. Armstrong.

Harry Brown, Inc. v. McBryde, TexApp–Tyler, 622 SW2d 596.—App & E 230, 231(1); Contracts 95(5), 259; Evid 433(6), 434(8); Trial 84(5).

Harry Cloud Transport, Inc.; State v., Tex, 505 SW2d 798.—Autos 127.

Harry Cloud Transport, Inc. v. State, TexCivApp–Corpus Christi, 500 SW2d 705, dism, and writ gr, rev 505 SW2d 798.—Autos 77, 127; Plead 111.14, 111.17, 111.38, 111.39(4), 111.42(7).

Harry Eldridge Co. v. T. S. Lankford & Sons, Inc., Tex, 371 SW2d 878.—App & E 361(1), 1082(1).

Harry Eldridge Co.; T. S. Lankford & Sons, Inc. v., TexCivApp–Texarkana, 359 SW2d 663, writ dism 371 SW2d 878.—Plead 111.42(4); Venue 22(3).

Harry F. Frey & Co. v. W. D. Lacy Feed Co., TexCivApp–Waco, 272 SW2d 765, writ dism.—App & E 1010.1(3); Contracts 163; Evid 25(2); Plead 111.42(5).

Harry Hines Medical Center, Ltd. v. Wilson, TexApp–Dallas, 656 SW2d 598.—App & E 842(2), 931(4), 1175(6); Costs 198, 208; Judgm 18(0.5), 18(2); Land & Ten 194(2), 195(1), 195(2), 230(2), 230(8), 231(1), 233(1); Trial 427.

Harry Hines Property Venture; Warfield Elec. of Texas, Inc. v., TexApp–Eastland, 871 SW2d 273.—Costs 2.

Harry Hott & Associates, Inc.; Norris v., TexCivApp–Dallas, 612 SW2d 630.—Tax 2936, 3001, 3011, 3063; Tresp to T T 6.1.

Harry H. Price & Son, Inc. v. Hardin, NDTex, 299 FSupp 557, vac 425 F2d 1137, cert den 91 SCt 568, 400 US 1009, 27 LEd2d 622.—Admin Law 668; Food 4.1.

Harry H. Price & Sons, Inc. v. Hardin, CA5 (Tex), 425 F2d 1137, cert den 91 SCt 568, 400 US 1009, 27 LEd2d 622.—Admin Law 668; Courts 2; Food 4.1.

Harry L. Edwards Drilling Co.; McCurdy v., TexCivApp–Galveston, 198 SW2d 609.—Costs 60, 61; Interest 18(1); Mines 48, 101, 109; Ten in C 32.

Harryman v. Estelle, CA5 (Tex), 616 F2d 870, cert den 101 SCt 161, 449 US 860, 66 LEd2d 76.—Crim Law 412.1(4), 412.2(3), 1169.1(1), 1169.12; Hab Corp 775(2).

Harryman v. Estelle, CA5 (Tex), 597 F2d 927, reh gr 602 F2d 1244, on reh 616 F2d 870, cert den 101 SCt 161, 449 US 860, 66 LEd2d 76.—Crim Law 1162, 1169.1(1), 1169.12.

Harryman v. State, TexCrimApp, 522 SW2d 512.—Arrest 63.4(11); Crim Law 363, 364(1), 1036.1(5).

Harry Newton, Inc. v. Broaddus, TexCivApp–Austin, 372 SW2d 950.—Plead 111.39(2); Princ & S 148.

Harry Newton, Inc.; Gulf, C. & S. F. R. Co. v., TexCivApp–Fort Worth, 430 SW2d 223, ref nre.—Labor & Emp 3105(5).

Harry Newton, Inc. v. H. Richards Oil Co., TexCivApp–Austin, 385 SW2d 893.—App & E 1051(1); Contracts 187(5), 236, 249; Corp 52; Evid 265(7); Guar 1; Judgm 707; Plead 45, 111.37, 111.38; Venue 2, 22(6), 22(8).

Harry Newton, Inc.; Vines v., TexCivApp–Hous (1 Dist), 445 SW2d 260, writ dism.—App & E 846(5); Corp 52, 503(1), 666; Plead 111.16, 111.19, 111.42(6); Venue 21.

Harry Payne Motors, Inc.; Davenport v., TexCivApp–Austin, 256 SW2d 245.—Costs 194.36; Trial 350.4(2).

Harry Payne Motors, Inc.; Davenport v., TexCivApp–Austin, 247 SW2d 452.—App & E 1024.3; Plead 111.43; Venue 28.

Harry Wagner Products Co. v. Adams, TexCivApp–Galveston, 258 SW2d 190, ref nre.—Sales 99, 101, 168(4), 181(11.1), 201(4), 221.

Harsch; Kelley v., TexCivApp–Austin, 161 SW2d 563.— Courts 37(3), 472.4(6); Ex & Ad 7; Partit 95; Wills 439, 487(3), 488, 490, 704, 776.

Harsch v. Kelly, TexCivApp–Austin, 184 SW2d 342, writ refused wom.—Courts 475(2), 476; Partit 38, 83; Trial 178; Wills 704.

Harsh v. CPC Intern., Inc., NDTex, 395 FSupp 578.— Antitrust 963(3); Fed Civ Proc 1773.

Harshberger v. Reliable-Aire, Inc., TexCivApp–Corpus Christi, 619 SW2d 478, dism.—App & E 544(2), 554(3); Torts 214, 215, 263; Venue 8.5(3).

Harston v. Kendall County Appraisal Dist., TexApp– San Antonio, 773 SW2d 815.—Tax 2652.

Hart, Ex parte, TexCrimApp, 422 SW2d 446.—Bail 43.

Hart, Ex parte, TexCivApp–Dallas, 524 SW2d 365.— Contempt 24; Divorce 269(1); Hab Corp 730.

Hart, Ex parte, TexCivApp–Dallas, 520 SW2d 952.— Child S 444, 458; Const Law 4494; Contempt 61(1), 64.

Hart, In re, BkrtcyNDTex, 151 BR 84.—Bankr 2558, 3684, 3713.

Hart v. Aetna Cas. and Sur. Co., TexApp–Amarillo, 756 SW2d 27.—App & E 170(1); Insurance 3356; Release 17(2).

Hart; Aetna Ins. Co. v., TexCivApp–Houston, 315 SW2d 169, ref nre.—Work Comp 6, 516, 518, 520, 567, 1419, 1542, 1545.

Hart; Baranowski v., CA5 (Tex), 486 F3d 112.—Civil R 1032, 1406, 1442, 1445; Const Law 1422, 1425, 1427, 3341(2), 4821; Fed Civ Proc 1951; Fed Cts 558, 714, 776, 813; Jury 25(11), 31.2(4); Prisons 4(1), 4(14).

Hart v. Berko, Inc., TexApp–El Paso, 881 SW2d 502, reh den, and writ den.—Antitrust 358, 364, 369; App & E 181, 193(1), 223, 230, 231(9), 267(1), 293, 836, 930(3), 989, 994(2), 999(1), 1001(3), 1003(6), 1026, 1032(3), 1064.1(1), 1064.1(2.1); Damag 221(5.1); Insurance 1672, 1673, 3417, 3426; Interest 39(2.35), 39(2.50); Trial 295(1).

Hart v. Calkins Mfg. Co., Inc., TexApp–Texarkana, 623 SW2d 451.—Judgm 942.

Hart; Campbell v., TexCivApp–Fort Worth, 256 SW2d 255, ref nre.—App & E 907(1); Contracts 252, 253, 256; Judgm 294, 298, 321, 341; Mines 55(8); Trial 350.4(2); Ven & Pur 136, 137.

Hart; Carrington v., TexCivApp–Austin, 703 SW2d 814.— Antitrust 398; Contracts 155, 169, 176(2); Costs 194.32; Evid 43(2); Spec Perf 28(2), 134.

Hart; Citizens Nat. Bank in Ennis v., TexCivApp–Fort Worth, 321 SW2d 319, writ refused.—Garn 105, 178.

Hart v. City of Dallas, TexCivApp–Tyler, 565 SW2d 373. —App & E 954(1); Inj 1; Mun Corp 628; Nuis 33, 59.

Hart; Col-Tex Refining Co. v., TexCivApp–Eastland, 144 SW2d 909, writ refused.—Carr 7; Mines 105(1); Tax 2244.

Hart; Cooper Petroleum Co. v., CA5 (Tex), 379 F2d 777. —Bankr 2607, 2608(1), 2608(2), 2612, 2727(2); Paymt 43.

Hart v. Eason, Tex, 321 SW2d 574, 159 Tex 375.—Evid 383(7); Tresp to T T 44.

Hart; Eason v., TexCivApp–Beaumont, 316 SW2d 945, rev 321 SW2d 574, 159 Tex 375.—App & E 761; Evid 589; Mtg 354; Tresp to T T 38(1), 44.

Hart v. Ehlers, TexCivApp–Houston, 319 SW2d 418.— Contracts 143.5, 147(1); Corp 116, 121(2); Sales 3.1, 28.

Hart v. El Encanto, TexApp–El Paso, 881 SW2d 502. See Hart v. Berko, Inc.

Hart v. Estelle, CA5 (Tex), 634 F2d 987.—Hab Corp 381, 384.

Hart v. Fielden, TexCivApp–Texarkana, 295 SW2d 911, ref nre.—App & E 750(4); Health 823(11).

Hart v. First Federal Sav. & Loan Ass'n of Esterville & Emmettsburg, Iowa, TexApp–Austin, 727 SW2d 723.— Guar 78(2), 97.

Hart v. Floyd, TexCivApp–San Antonio, 558 SW2d 578.— Names 14, 18.

Hart v. Foster, TexCivApp–Fort Worth, 109 SW2d 504, writ dism.—App & E 662(2), 907(3), 1073(1); Judgm 216.

Hart; Gilgon, Inc. v., TexApp–Corpus Christi, 893 SW2d 562, reh overr, and writ den.—App & E 216(1), 216(7), 230, 231(9), 970(2), 977(3), 977(5), 1001(1), 1056.1(3), 1058(1), 1062.2; Autos 193(12), 193(14), 244(26), 246(15), 246(42); Evid 188; Labor & Emp 3046(1); New Tr 6; Trial 277.

Hart v. Gossum, TexApp–Fort Worth, 995 SW2d 958, reh overr.—Mand 187.2, 187.7; Records 62, 63, 65; Witn 199(1).

Hart v. Greis, TexCivApp–Fort Worth, 155 SW2d 997, writ refused wom.—App & E 758.3(8), 882(16), 930(1); Bound 1, 8, 33, 37(1), 37(3), 40(1), 41; Evid 155(8), 157(2); New Tr 44(2); Trial 215, 219, 248.

Hart; Gulf Cas. Co. v., Tex, 175 SW2d 73, 141 Tex 642.— Work Comp 1139.

Hart v. Gulf Cas. Co., TexCivApp–Fort Worth, 170 SW2d 491, rev 175 SW2d 73, 141 Tex 642.—Work Comp 1123, 1139, 1178, 1971.

Hart v. Hairston, CA5 (Tex), 343 F3d 762, reh den.—Civil R 1092, 1358, 1376(7); Fed Civ Proc 2491.5, 2538, 2544; Fed Cts 776.

Hart v. Hart, TexApp–Austin, 705 SW2d 332, ref nre.— Mental H 495.

Hart; Hart v., TexApp–Austin, 705 SW2d 332, ref nre.— Mental H 495.

Hart v. Hart, TexApp–Texarkana, 679 SW2d 80.—App & E 78(2), 78(3).

Hart; Hart v., TexApp–Texarkana, 679 SW2d 80.—App & E 78(2), 78(3).

Hart v. International Tel. & Tel. Corp., TexCivApp–San Antonio, 546 SW2d 660, ref nre.—Lim of Act 43, 46(7).

Hart v. Keller Properties, TexCivApp–Dallas, 567 SW2d 888.—Land & Ten 291(14); Plead 428(3).

Hart; Lane v., TexApp–Eastland, 651 SW2d 419, ref nre. —Child C 36, 526; Divorce 151; Judgm 326.

Hart; Las Chaumiera Apartments v., TexApp–Fort Worth, 832 SW2d 360. See Pipgras v. Hart.

Hart v. Littlejohn, TexCivApp–Austin, 190 SW2d 148.— Contracts 266(1); Sales 82(1), 92, 96, 104.

Hart v. McClusky, TexCivApp–Amarillo, 118 SW2d 1077, writ refused.—Mtg 300.1, 341, 342.

Hart v. McCormack, TexApp–Beaumont, 746 SW2d 330, writ dism woj.—Inj 56.

Hart, Estate of; McNeme v., TexApp–El Paso, 860 SW2d 536, on reh.—Joint Ten 3, 6.

Hart v. Mazda Motors of America, Inc., CA5 (Tex), 521 F2d 193.—Fed Civ Proc 2233; Neglig 530(1).

Hart v. Meadows, TexApp–Texarkana, 302 SW2d 448, ref nre.—Mines 81; Trover 17.

Hart; Meek v., TexApp–El Paso, 611 SW2d 162.—App & E 76(1), 80(3); Courts 202(5).

Hart; Mendiola v., CA5 (Tex), 561 F2d 1207.—Fed Civ Proc 1755.

Hart v. Moore, TexApp–Amarillo, 952 SW2d 90, reh overr, and review den.—App & E 213, 215(1), 216(1), 230, 231(9), 233(2), 233(2), 237(5), 238(2), 292, 294(1), 918(2), 946, 1172(1); Consp 6, 14, 19, 20; Courts 21; Damag 15; Decl Judgm 369; Judgm 198; Land & Ten 48(1); Plead 236(1), 236(7), 276, 279(2), 279(4).

Hart v. National Homes Corp., CA5 (Tex), 668 F2d 791. —Alt Disp Res 374(3); Labor & Emp 1213, 1219(12), 1611(1).

Hart v. Northside Independent School Dist., TexCiv-App–San Antonio, 498 SW2d 459, ref nre.—Schools 106.25(8); Tax 2588, 2935, 2936.

Hart v. O'Brien, CA5 (Tex), 127 F3d 424, reh and sug for reh den 154 F3d 419, cert den 119 SCt 868, 525 US 1103, 142 LEd2d 770.—Arrest 63.4(0.5), 63.4(2), 63.4(17), 65; Bail 42; Civil R 1031, 1088(1), 1088(3), 1088(4), 1088(5), 1376(1), 1376(2), 1376(6), 1376(9); Dam-ag 50.10; Dist & Pros Attys 10; Evid 317(2), 470, 474(1); Extrad 52; False Imp 2, 3, 12, 15(1); Fed Civ Proc 2544; Fed Cts 404, 411, 574, 579, 627.1, 766, 770,

HART

776, 802; Mal Pros 3, 8, 16, 18(1), 27, 40; Mun Corp 747(3); Offic 114; Searches 112; U S Mag 26.

Hart; Page v., TexCivApp–San Antonio, 124 SW2d 399.— App & E 999(1); Courts 104.

Hart; Paschal v., TexCivApp–Waco, 105 SW2d 337.—App & E 173(6); Fixt 1, 29; Frds St of 110(1); Sales 1(3).

Hart; Pipgras v., TexApp–Fort Worth, 832 SW2d 360, reh den, and writ den.—App & E 215(1), 221, 241, 295, 302(6), 930(1), 989, 999(1), 1001(1), 1004(8), 1043(1), 1047(4), 1062.1; Damag 63, 100, 128, 130.1, 132(3), 185(1), 191, 208(3), 208(6); Land & Ten 167(8); Neglig 1037(4), 1127, 1241, 1568, 1670.

Hart; Richardson v., Tex, 185 SW2d 563, 143 Tex 392.— Contracts 170(1); Evid 448; Mines 55(5), 79.1(4).

Hart; Richardson v., TexCivApp–Texarkana, 183 SW2d 235, aff as reformed 185 SW2d 563, 143 Tex 392.— Contracts 170(1); Mines 55(2).

Hart v. Rochelle, TexCivApp–Texarkana, 170 SW2d 245. —Adv Poss 16(1), 27, 44, 57; Lim of Act 195(3).

Hart v. Rogers, TexCivApp–Eastland, 527 SW2d 230, ref nre.—Deeds 56(3); Evid 324(3); Wills 542(1); Witn 159(3), 160(1).

Hart; R. P. Lightfoot Co. v., TexCivApp–Waco, 224 SW2d 726, dism.—Plead 111.8, 111.17; Venue 8.5(5), 8.5(8).

Hart; Sanders v., TexCivApp–Eastland, 171 SW2d 531, writ refused wom.—Des & Dist 90(1); Ex & Ad 3(1), 20(10).

Hart v. Sims, CA5 (Tex), 702 F2d 574.—Bills & N 405, 422(1), 526; Paymt 34.

Hart v. Sinclair Oil & Gas Co., TexCivApp–Waco, 352 SW2d 142, ref nre.—Mines 73, 73.1(6), 79.1(1).

Hart; Southern Pine Lumber Co. v., Tex, 340 SW2d 775, 161 Tex 357.—Adv Poss 34, 100(1), 100(6), 110(3), 117; App & E 1178(1); Deeds 114(1); Evid 273(2), 317(5); Ten in C 13, 15(2); Tresp to T T 41(2); Trial 350.3(3).

Hart; Southern Pine Lumber Co. v., TexCivApp–Fort Worth, 329 SW2d 511, writ gr, rev 340 SW2d 775, 161 Tex 357.—Adv Poss 100(2); Bound 35(3); Ten in C 15(10); Trial 105(5).

Hart v. State, TexCrimApp, 89 SW3d 61.—Larc 55; RICO 107, 121.

Hart v. State, TexCrimApp, 634 SW2d 714.—Controlled Subs 80; Crim Law 671, 791, 795(2.20), 795(2.70), 796; Jury 131(4).

Hart v. State, TexCrimApp, 581 SW2d 675.—Assault 56, 92(4); Crim Law 452(1), 571, 720(1), 1171.1(6); Homic 852; Ind & Inf 189(8).

Hart v. State, TexCrimApp, 537 SW2d 21.—Crim Law 796; Sent & Pun 106.

Hart v. State, TexCrimApp, 463 SW2d 431.—Crim Law 1090.1(1).

Hart v. State, TexCrimApp, 455 SW2d 237.—Crim Law 847; Homic 1134, 1136, 1567; Sent & Pun 82.

Hart v. State, TexCrimApp, 447 SW2d 944.—Crim Law 365(1), 369.15, 371(9), 372(7), 388.5(1), 438(5.1), 627.6(5), 627.7(3), 627.8(3), 695(1), 959, 1035(8.1), 1036.1(1), 1036.2, 1044.1(3), 1090.11, 1120(4), 1130(3), 1169.1(10), 1169.2(1); Witn 274(1), 274(2), 388(1).

Hart v. State, TexCrimApp, 396 SW2d 873.—Controlled Subs 65; Crim Law 1044.1(2), 1050.

Hart v. State, TexCrimApp, 393 SW2d 916.—Assault 92(1); Crim Law 956(1), 1091(7), 1105(1), 1105(2).

Hart v. State, TexCrimApp, 367 SW2d 345.—Crim Law 598(7), 956(4).

Hart v. State, TexCrimApp, 350 SW2d 547, 171 TexCrim 375.—Crim Law 959, 1081(5).

Hart v. State, TexCrimApp, 293 SW2d 659, 163 TexCrim 472.—Crim Law 721(1), 721(3); Int Liq 236(7).

Hart v. State, TexCrimApp, 289 SW2d 271.—Crim Law 1090.1(1).

Hart v. State, TexCrimApp, 215 SW2d 883, 152 TexCrim 537.—Crim Law 306; Int Liq 236(5), 236(7).

Hart v. State, TexCrimApp, 161 SW2d 791, 144 TexCrim 161.—Crim Law 721(6), 724(2).

Hart v. State, TexCrimApp, 141 SW2d 648, 139 TexCrim 650.—Crim Law 814(15), 1169.1(4), 1169.2(2); Jury 33(1), 80; Larc 40(4), 51(1); Sent & Pun 1900; Witn 274(2).

Hart v. State, TexCrimApp, 138 SW2d 818, 139 TexCrim 101.—Crim Law 366(3), 598(6), 1134(3), 1174(2); Rape 43(2), 46, 59(1), 59(20.1).

Hart v. State, TexCrimApp, 122 SW2d 193, 135 TexCrim 565.—Crim Law 1111(4).

Hart v. State, TexCrimApp, 93 SW2d 157, 130 TexCrim 174.—Crim Law 698(1), 783.5, 814(17), 829(1).

Hart v. State, TexApp–Dallas, 682 SW2d 346, petition for discretionary review refused.—Crim Law 351(3); Forg 34(1), 44(1), 48.

Hart v. State, TexApp–Texarkana, 173 SW3d 131.—Crim Law 394.6(4), 404.65, 438(7), 459, 474, 625(3), 625.20, 627.6(3), 627.8(6), 641.3(11), 650, 753.2(2), 911, 923(1), 923(4), 1035(3), 1035(6), 1134(5), 1151, 1152(2), 1153(1), 1156(1), 1158(1), 1158(3), 1163(1), 1166.16, 1167(1); Ind & Inf 171; Jury 97(1), 99.7, 107, 131(4), 131(8), 131(13), 131(18); Searches 180, 183, 184, 198.

Hart v. State, TexApp–Texarkana, 15 SW3d 117, reh overr, and petition for discretionary review refused.— Controlled Subs 27, 34, 82; Crim Law 957(1), 957(2), 1038.1(1).

Hart; State v., TexApp–Beaumont, 753 SW2d 213, writ den.—Environ Law 428, 673; Pretrial Proc 587.

Hart; State v., TexApp–Corpus Christi, 818 SW2d 430.— Const Law 4612; Crim Law 394.6(1), 412.1(2), 414, 577.4, 577.8(2), 577.10(1), 577.10(4), 577.10(7), 577.12(1), 577.12(2), 577.16(4), 594(1), 632(2), 632(4), 730(2), 1035(5), 1115(1), 1129(4), 1130(2), 1130(5), 1166.22(4.1), 1172.1(2); Infants 20.

Hart; State v., TexApp–Houston (14 Dist), 905 SW2d 690, petition for discretionary review refused.—Crim Law 554, 568, 738, 741(1), 742(1), 763(10), 772(6), 911, 935(1), 1144.13(2.1), 1156(1), 1159.2(7); Larc 57, 71(3).

Hart; Stout v., TexCivApp–Amarillo, 202 SW2d 483.— App & E 82(3), 1062.5; Evid 220(4), 314(1); Gifts 49(1), 50; Judgm 198.

Hart; Stretch-O-Rama, Inc. v., EDTex, 79 FSupp2d 660. —Fed Cts 30; Int Rev 4556, 4765, 4769, 4773, 4778, 4793.

Hart; Taylor-Evans Seed Co. v., TexCivApp–Amarillo, 420 SW2d 138.—App & E 989, 1024.3, 1177(7); Contracts 322(3); Corp 503(2).

Hart; Texas & N. O. Ry. Co. v., Tex, 356 SW2d 901, 163 Tex 450, on remand 361 SW2d 237, ref nre.—App & E 1177(6); Autos 227.5; Neglig 530(1), 1683, 1717; R R 307.3, 307.4(3), 346(5.1), 350(5), 350(33).

Hart; Texas & N.O. Ry. Co. v., TexCivApp–Beaumont, 361 SW2d 237, ref nre.—App & E 989, 999(1).

Hart; Texas & N. O. Ry. Co. v., TexCivApp–Beaumont, 350 SW2d 227, writ gr, rev 356 SW2d 901, 163 Tex 450, on remand 361 SW2d 237, ref nre.—App & E 930(1), 989; Damag 132(2), 134(2); R R 348(6.1), 350(33), 351(22), 352; Trial 350.7(9).

Hart v. Texas Dept. of Criminal Justice, CA5 (Tex), 106 FedAppx 244.—Civil R 1376(7); Fed Cts 579.

Hart v. Texas Emp. Ins. Ass'n, TexCivApp–Amarillo, 387 SW2d 706, ref nre.—Judgm 186; Work Comp 1822, 1834.

Hart; Tippett v., Tex, 501 SW2d 874.—Evid 47; Torts 263.

Hart; Tippett v., TexCivApp–Amarillo, 497 SW2d 606, ref nre 501 SW2d 874.—Evid 34; Torts 200, 205, 212, 215, 242, 258, 263, 424, 429; Tresp 10, 50.

Hart v. Traders & General Ins. Co., Tex, 189 SW2d 493, 144 Tex 146.—Courts 90(1); Release 30, 38; Work Comp 1105, 1107.

Hart v. Traders & General Ins. Co., TexCivApp–Fort Worth, 487 SW2d 415, ref nre.—Contracts 152; Insurance 1825, 2669.

Hart v. Traders & General Ins. Co., TexCivApp–Dallas, 185 SW2d 605, aff 189 SW2d 493, 144 Tex 146.—Release 30; Work Comp 306, 316, 1105, 1107, 1160.

Hart v. U.S., CA5 (Tex), 585 F2d 1280, cert den 99 SCt 2882, 442 US 941, 61 LEd2d 310.—Lim of Act 95(8); U S 125(7).

Hart; U.S. v., CA5 (Tex), 566 F2d 977.—Crim Law 264, 1166(3).

Hart; U.S. v., CA5 (Tex), 525 F2d 1199, cert den 96 SCt 3234, 428 US 923, 49 LEd2d 1226.—Cust Dut 126(5).

Hart; U.S. v., CA5 (Tex), 506 F2d 887, vac 95 SCt 2674, 422 U.S. 1053, 45LEd2d 706, on remand 525 F2d 1199, cert den 96 SCt 3234, 428 US 923, 49 LEd2d 1226, on remand US v. Dixon, 525 F2d 1201, cert den 96 SCt 3234, 428 US 923, 49 LEd2d 1226.—Courts 96(7); Cust Dut 126(1), 126(5).

Hart v. U.S., EDTex, 945 FSupp 1009, aff 137 F3d 1349.— Contracts 143(2), 176(2); Deeds 93, 95, 97, 110, 143; Waters 165.

Hart v. U. S. Fidelity & Guaranty Co., CA5 (Tex), 304 F2d 572, cert den 83 SCt 147, 371 US 878, 9 LEd2d 115, reh den 83 SCt 286, 371 US 931, 9 LEd2d 239.—Fed Cts 354.

Hart v. University of Texas at Houston, SDTex, 474 FSupp 465.—Civil R 1532; Fed Cts 265, 269.

Hart v. Van Zandt, Tex, 399 SW2d 791.—App & E 927(7), 989; Evid 538, 544; Health 631, 821(2), 821(3), 822(3), 825, 826; Neglig 384, 386, 387.

Hart v. Van Zandt, TexCivApp–Fort Worth, 383 SW2d 627, writ gr, rev 399 SW2d 791.—App & E 1056.6; Health 623, 631, 674, 814, 821(3), 823(7); Trial 105(2).

Hart; Watson v., TexApp–Austin, 871 SW2d 914.—App & E 389(3), 883; Courts 26, 85(1); Mand 59; Motions 59(1), 62.

Hart; Wichita County v., TexApp–Fort Worth, 989 SW2d 2, reh overr, and review den, and reh of petition for review overr.—App & E 930(1), 946, 970(2), 989, 1001(1), 1001(3), 1003(5), 1056.1(3), 1182; Evid 508, 512; Offic 66; Sheriffs 21; Trial 56.

Hart; Wichita County v., TexApp–Austin, 892 SW2d 912, reh overr, and writ gr, rev 917 SW2d 779, on subsequent appeal 989 SW2d 2, reh overr, and review den, and reh of petition for review overr.—App & E 930(3), 969, 989, 1003(6), 1043(8); Const Law 2503(1), 4410; Courts 40; Damag 49.10, 192; Evid 570, 574; Mun Corp 185(1), 218(10); Offic 2, 66, 72.41(1), 76; Sheriffs 21; Trial 219; Venue 16, 17, 40.

Hart; Wichita County, Tex. v., Tex, 917 SW2d 779, on subsequent appeal 989 SW2d 2, reh overr, and review den, and reh of petition for review overr.—App & E 1043(8); Offic 66, 72.41(1); Statut 190, 223.1, 227; Venue 45.

Hart; Wilson v., TexCivApp–Amarillo, 332 SW2d 107.— App & E 1175(5).

Hart v. Winsett, Tex, 171 SW2d 853, 141 Tex 312.—App & E 1177(6); Lim of Act 5(2), 85(5); Statut 223.5(4), 223.5(6); Ven & Pur 278.

Hart v. Winsett, TexCivApp–Fort Worth, 164 SW2d 783, rev 171 SW2d 853, 141 Tex 312.—Judgm 17(3); Ven & Pur 278.

Hart v. Wright, TexApp–Fort Worth, 16 SW3d 872, reh overr, and review den.—App & E 946, 949; Fraud 3, 17; Health 615, 800, 804, 805, 809, 906, 908.

Hart Auto Sales, Inc. v. Comerica Bank–Texas, TexApp–Eastland, 893 SW2d 705. See Bill Hart Auto Sales, Inc. v. Comerica Bank-Texas.

Hart Creosoting Co.; State v., TexApp–Beaumont, 753 SW2d 213. See State v. Hart.

Hartec Enterprises, Inc., In re, BkrtcyWDTex, 117 BR 865, vac U.S. v. Hartec Enterprises, Inc, 130 BR 929, on remand 130 BR 930.—Bankr 3102.1, 3105.1; U S 71.

Hartec Enterprises, Inc.; U.S. v., CA5 (Tex), 967 F2d 130.—Ind & Inf 179; Larc 5, 7; Statut 241(1); U S 70(10).

Harte-Hanks Communications, Inc.; Villarreal v., TexApp–Corpus Christi, 787 SW2d 131, writ den, cert den 111 SCt 1316, 499 US 923, 113 LEd2d 249.—App & E 1001(3); Libel 123(8).

Harte-Hanks Newspapers; U.S. v., CA5 (Tex), 254 F2d 366, cert den 78 SCt 1385, 357 US 938, 2 LEd2d 1551.— Crim Law 394.6(4); Gr Jury 25, 36.8; Searches 181; Witn 293.

Harte-Hanks Newspapers v. U.S. Officers and Jury, NDTex, 154 FSupp 68, rev 254 F2d 366, cert den 78 SCt 1385, 357 US 938, 2 LEd2d 1551.—Gr Jury 36.8.

Harte-Hanks Newspapers, Inc.; Taylor Communications, Inc. v., Tex, 447 SW2d 401.—Judgm 185.3(8).

Harte-Hanks Newspapers, Inc.; Taylor Communications, Inc. v., TexCivApp–Eastland, 436 SW2d 565, writ gr, aff 447 SW2d 401.—Brok 42, 43(1).

Harte-Hanks Newspapers, Inc.; U.S. v., NDTex, 170 FSupp 227.—Antitrust 795.

Harte-Hanks Television, Inc.; Crumrine v., TexApp–San Antonio, 37 SW3d 124, review den.—Const Law 2077, 2137, 3746; Judgm 185(2); Torts 121, 122, 350, 357.

Harte-Hanks Texas Newspapers, Inc.; Hubert v., TexApp–Austin, 652 SW2d 546, ref nre.—Records 58, 63.

Hartel v. Dishman, Tex, 145 SW2d 865, 135 Tex 600.— Judgm 387, 503, 518; Lim of Act 118(1); Lis Pen 11(1), 22(3), 24(1), 24(2); Ven & Pur 210.

Hartel v. Dishman, TexCivApp–Beaumont, 116 SW2d 891, rev 145 SW2d 865, 135 Tex 600.—Lis Pen 22(3); Mtg 424; Ven & Pur 231(1), 231(9).

Hartel; Texas Emp. Ins. Ass'n v., TexCivApp–Amarillo, 289 SW2d 380, dism.—New Tr 117(1); Work Comp 869, 878, 1660.

Hartely v. Langdon & Co., TexCivApp–Houston, 347 SW2d 749.—Courts 198; Des & Dist 39, 71(7); Escheat 4; Judgm 181(13), 335(2), 335(3), 475, 518, 585(1); Lim of Act 4(2).

Harter, Ex parte, TexCrimApp, 233 SW2d 502, 155 TexCrim 216.—Sent & Pun 1129.

Harter; Hays v., TexCivApp–El Paso, 177 SW2d 797, writ refused.—Trusts 172; Wills 487(4), 488, 567.

Harter; Loy v., TexApp–Texarkana, 128 SW3d 397, reh overr, and review den (2 pets).—Alt Disp Res 113, 139, 143, 146, 210, 380; App & E 80(6), 930(1), 989, 1001(1), 1003(6), 1008.1(2), 1010.1(1); Const Law 3997; Corp 185, 307, 308(1), 310(2), 314(0.5), 315, 318, 319(8), 320(11.5); Evid 208(6), 265(8); Judgm 181(15.1), 185(4), 190, 297, 584; Motions 58; Trial 399.

Hartfiel v. Owen, TexCivApp–El Paso, 618 SW2d 902, ref nre.—App & E 231(7); Evid 357; Health 823(1), 906.

Hartfield v. State, TexCrimApp, 645 SW2d 436.—Const Law 4760; Crim Law 1059(2), 1166.16, 1166.17, 1184(4.1); Jury 33(1), 108.

Hartfield v. State, TexApp–Texarkana, 28 SW3d 69, petition for discretionary review refused.—Crim Law 1043(3), 1084, 1144.13(2.1), 1159.2(2), 1159.2(7); Homic 1143.

Hartford; Abate v., EDTex, 471 FSupp2d 724.—Fed Civ Proc 1439, 2470.4, 2534; Fed Cts 419, 421; Labor & Emp 440, 628, 629(2), 636, 637, 685, 687, 688, 690, 691, 704.

Hartford v. Coolidge-Locher Co., TexCivApp–San Antonio, 314 SW2d 445.—Neglig 1205(7), 1205(8), 1242.

Hartford v. State, TexCrimApp, 289 SW2d 770, 163 TexCrim 152.—Health 164.

Hartford Acc. & Indem. v. Collins, TexApp–Corpus Christi, 895 SW2d 750, reh overr.—App & E 946, 984(1); Work Comp 2247.

Hartford Acc. & Indem. Co. v. Abascal, TexApp–San Antonio, 831 SW2d 559.—App & E 961; Mand 3(11), 172; Pretrial Proc 44.1.

HARTFORD

59 Tex D 2d—534

See Guidelines for Arrangement at the beginning of this Volume

Hartford Acc. & Indem. Co. v. Addison, CCA5 (Tex), 93 F2d 627.—Work Comp 207, 208, 615, 1432, 1615.

Hartford Acc. & Indem. Co.; Anders v., TexCivApp–Amarillo, 141 SW2d 1014.—App & E 758.3(1); Judges 16(1).

Hartford Acc. & Indem. Co.; Associated Indem. Co. v., TexCivApp–Dallas, 524 SW2d 373.—App & E 1175(5); Contracts 138(1); Evid 66; Insurance 3513(3); Subrog 1; Work Comp 208, 1072, 2161.

Hartford Acc. & Indem. Co. v. Baugh, CCA5 (Tex), 87 F2d 240, cert den 57 SCt 670, 300 US 679, 81 LEd 883.—Evid 128, 271(1); Fed Civ Proc 58; Fed Cts 626; Work Comp 1927, 1937.

Hartford Acc. & Indem. Co. v. Black, CA5 (Tex), 194 F2d 1005.—Work Comp 1229.

Hartford Acc. & Indem. Co. v. Black, CA5 (Tex), 193 F2d 971, reh den 194 F2d 1005.—Witn 391; Work Comp 1615, 1847, 1922, 1926, 1929, 1968(6).

Hartford Acc. & Indem. Co. v. Bond, TexCivApp–Eastland, 199 SW2d 293, ref nre.—Evid 125; Work Comp 718, 1922, 1924, 1927.

Hartford Acc. & Indem. Co. v. Buckland, TexApp–Dallas, 882 SW2d 440, writ den.—App & E 846(5), 984(5); Costs 194.12; Work Comp 2191, 2247.

Hartford Acc. & Indem. Co.; Carpenter v., TexCivApp–Fort Worth, 133 SW2d 181.—Work Comp 626.

Hartford Acc. & Indem. Co. v. Carter, CCA5 (Tex), 110 F2d 355.—Evid 128; Trial 178; Work Comp 1392, 1414, 1716, 1937.

Hartford Acc. and Indem. Co.; Centennial Ins. Co. v., TexApp–Houston (14 Dist), 821 SW2d 192.—Insurance 2278(13).

Hartford Acc. & Indem. Co. v. Choate, TexComApp, 89 SW2d 205, 126 Tex 368.—Work Comp 1334, 1335, 1826, 1847.

Hartford Acc. & Indem. Co. v. Christensen, Tex, 228 SW2d 135, 149 Tex 79.—Work Comp 9, 391, 1065, 2100.

Hartford Acc. & Indem. Co. v. Christensen, TexCivApp–Galveston, 223 SW2d 45, rev 228 SW2d 135, 149 Tex 79.—Action 57(1); Admin Law 228.1, 663, 721, 725, 812; Work Comp 2, 1065, 1103, 1105, 1178, 1187, 1319, 1872, 1889, 1942.

Hartford Acc. & Indem. Co. v. Clark, TexCivApp–Waco, 126 SW2d 799, writ dism, correct.—App & E 719(1), 719(6), 731(1); Courts 508(8); Plead 34(3); Rem of C 89(3); Trial 350.8, 362; Work Comp 283, 1323.

Hartford Acc. & Indem. Co.; Coleman v., TexCivApp–Fort Worth, 297 SW2d 236, writ refused.—Work Comp 876, 878.

Hartford Acc. & Indem. Co. v. Contreras, TexCivApp–Hous (1 Dist), 498 SW2d 419, ref nre.—Damag 221(3); Trial 114, 351.2(2), 366; Work Comp 517, 1396, 1490, 1610, 1615, 1855, 1863, 1866, 1937.

Hartford Acc. & Indem. Co. v. Craig, TexCivApp–Dallas, 197 SW2d 148, writ refused.—Courts 121(2), 122.

Hartford Acc. & Indem. Co. v. Crowley, TexCivApp–Waco, 509 SW2d 939, ref nre.—Work Comp 460, 1139, 1408, 1478, 1754.

Hartford Acc. & Indem. Co.; Douglas v., TexCivApp–Waco, 367 SW2d 730, ref nre.—Work Comp 1724.

Hartford Acc. & Indem. Co. v. Douglass, CA5 (Tex), 215 F2d 201.—Fed Cts 911; Insurance 2607, 3579.

Hartford Acc. & Indem. Co. v. Ethridge, TexCivApp–Eastland, 149 SW2d 1040.—App & E 544(1), 616(1).

Hartford Accident & Indemnity Co. v. Farrell, TexCivApp–Fort Worth, 107 SW2d 442, writ dism.—App & E 1175(3); Corp 560(1); Receivers 110, 212.

Hartford Acc. & Indem. Co. v. Ferguson, TexCivApp–Fort Worth, 417 SW2d 376, ref nre.—Trial 233(2); Work Comp 1403, 1653, 1968(1), 1968(3), 1968(4).

Hartford Acc. & Indem. Co. v. Frazier, TexCivApp–Waco, 362 SW2d 417, ref nre.—Evid 177, 506.

Hartford Acc. & Indem. Co. v. Gainesville Nat. Bank in Gainesville, Tex., CCA5 (Tex), 124 F2d 97.—Lim of Act 46(10); Princ & S 145(1).

Hartford Acc. & Indem. Co. v. Gant, TexCivApp–Dallas, 346 SW2d 359.—App & E 766, 931(1), 989; Work Comp 535, 1519, 1536, 1927.

Hartford Acc. & Indem. Co.; Garrett v., TexCivApp–Eastland, 107 SW2d 726.—Lim of Act 130(5); Work Comp 1832, 1874, 1880.

Hartford Acc. & Indem. Co.; Gasch v., CA5 (Tex), 491 F3d 278, reh den.—Fed Cts 30, 31, 776; Insurance 3242; Rem of C 2, 36, 107(7); Work Comp 1072.

Hartford Acc. & Indem. Co.; Gilcrease v., TexCivApp–El Paso, 252 SW2d 715.—Pretrial Proc 78; Trial 358; Work Comp 1385, 1543, 1686, 1924, 1930, 1968(1), 1968(5).

Hartford Acc. & Indem. Co. v. Gladney, TexCivApp–Waco, 335 SW2d 792, ref nre.—App & E 933(1), 977(1); Judgm 335(1), 344; New Tr 6, 118, 152; Work Comp 1859, 1932.

Hartford Acc. & Indem. Co.; Graves v., TexComApp, 161 SW2d 464, 138 Tex 589.—Fraud 13(2); Judgm 199(1); Work Comp 1159, 1162.

Hartford Acc. & Indem. Co. v. Graves, TexCivApp–Eastland, 148 SW2d 859, rev 161 SW2d 464, 138 Tex 589.—Contracts 94(3); Fraud 3; Judgm 198; Work Comp 1154, 1159, 1162.

Hartford Acc. & Indem. Co. v. Haddock, TexCivApp–Tyler, 511 SW2d 102, ref nre.—Jury 142; Pretrial Proc 308; Work Comp 840, 1507, 1543, 1648, 1703, 1966, 1968(1).

Hartford Acc. & Indem. Co. v. Hale, Tex, 400 SW2d 310.—Evid 118, 121(1), 208(6); Work Comp 1043, 1389, 1489.

Hartford Acc. & Indem. Co. v. Hale, TexCivApp–San Antonio, 389 SW2d 720, writ gr, rev 400 SW2d 310.—Evid 118, 208(6); Work Comp 1114, 1385, 1389, 1968(3).

Hartford Acc. & Indem. Co. v. Hardin, TexCivApp–Fort Worth, 252 SW2d 752, writ refused.—Work Comp 1279, 1283, 1297, 1726.

Hartford Acc. & Indem. Co. v. Harris, TexCivApp–Eastland, 152 SW2d 857, writ dism.—Damag 221(1), 221(5.1); Trial 352.20, 358; Work Comp 1927, 1930.

Hartford Acc. & Indem. Co. v. Harris, TexCivApp–Eastland, 138 SW2d 277, writ dism, correct.—App & E 692(1); Evid 558(1); Witn 280; Work Comp 1375, 1924, 1961.

Hartford Acc. & Indem. Co. v. Helms, TexCivApp–Tyler, 467 SW2d 656.—Work Comp 876, 1532, 1660.

Hartford Acc. & Indem. Co. v. Herriage, TexCivApp–Amarillo, 139 SW2d 873.—Work Comp 50, 51, 1009, 1028, 1893.

Hartford Acc. & Indem. Co. v. Hooten, TexCivApp–San Antonio, 531 SW2d 365, ref nre.—Labor & Emp 23; Work Comp 239.

Hartford Acc. & Indem. Co.; Hundley v., CCA5 (Tex), 87 F2d 416.—Work Comp 666.

Hartford Acc. & Indem. Co.; Indiana Lumbermen's Mut. Ins. Co. v., TexCivApp–Waco, 454 SW2d 781, ref nre.—Insurance 2663, 2666, 2694.

Hartford Acc. & Indem. Co. v. Jackson, TexCivApp–Galveston, 201 SW2d 265, ref nre.—Work Comp 1297, 1335, 1644, 1683, 1726.

Hartford Acc. & Indem. Co.; Johnson v., CA5 (Tex), 425 F2d 254.—Fed Cts 743; Work Comp 1539, 1651.

Hartford Acc. & Indem. Co. v. Jones, CCA5 (Tex), 80 F2d 680, cert den 56 SCt 674, 298 US 655, 80 LEd 1381.—Evid 7; Work Comp 550, 771, 1716.

Hartford Acc. and Indem. Co.; Kalmar Industries, AB v., CA5 (Tex), 8 F3d 272. See Jacques v. Kalmar Industries, AB.

Hartford Acc. & Indem. Co.; Leonard v., TexCivApp–Hous (14 Dist), 466 SW2d 794.—Work Comp 876, 1374, 1656, 1671.

For Later Case History Information, see KeyCite on WESTLAW

Hartford Acc. and Indem. Co. v. LTV Corp., CA5 (Tex), 774 F2d 677.—Decl Judgm 165; Fed Civ Proc 2737.5; Insurance 3506(2), 3508.

Hartford Acc. & Indem. Co.; Lucas v., Tex, 552 SW2d 796, on remand 556 SW2d 104.—App & E 930(3), 1001(1); Work Comp 1420.

Hartford Acc. & Indem. Co. v. Lucas, TexCivApp–Tyler, 556 SW2d 104.—Work Comp 1520.

Hartford Acc. & Indem. Co. v. Lucas, TexCivApp–Tyler, 547 SW2d 386, writ gr, rev 552 SW2d 796, on remand 556 SW2d 104.—App & E 930(3); Damag 185(1); Health 821(3); Work Comp 1417, 1492, 1520.

Hartford Acc. & Indem. Co. v. McCardell, Tex, 369 SW2d 331.—App & E 205; Evid 200, 202, 222(1), 265(1), 314(1); Witn 379(1); Work Comp 1385, 1391, 1392, 1919, 1958, 1968(1), 1968(3).

Hartford Acc. & Indem. Co.; McCardell v., TexCivApp–Beaumont, 360 SW2d 831, aff 369 SW2d 331.—App & E 981, 1039(1); New Tr 99, 102(3); Work Comp 1919, 1922, 1932, 1933, 1968(1).

Hartford Acc. & Indem. Co. v. McFarland, TexCivApp–Tyler, 433 SW2d 534, ref nre.—App & E 934(2); Work Comp 512, 514, 547, 548, 1924.

Hartford Acc. & Indem. Co.; McNew v., TexCivApp–Fort Worth, 400 SW2d 808, ref nre.—Judgm 185(2), 185.3(13).

Hartford Acc. and Indem. Co.; Meridian Oil Production, Inc. v., CA5 (Tex), 27 F3d 150, reh and sug for reh den 35 F3d 564.—Insurance 2275, 2278(3), 2926, 3349.

Hartford Acc. & Indem. Co.; Middleton v., CCA5 (Tex), 119 F2d 721.—Fed Civ Proc 35; Fed Cts 651, 691, 791; Statut 159; Work Comp 1283, 1297.

Hartford Acc. & Indem. Co. v. Moore, TexCivApp–Dallas, 102 SW2d 441, writ refused.—Judgm 248, 253(1), 256(2); Work Comp 1943.

Hartford Acc. & Indem. Co. v. Morris, TexCivApp–San Antonio, 233 SW2d 218, ref nre.—App & E 215(1); Insurance 1834(3); Mun Corp 860; Work Comp 1042, 1072, 1619, 1981.

Hartford Acc. & Indem. Co. v. Murphy, CCA5 (Tex), 158 F2d 506.—Damag 221(1); Jury 31.2(4), 31.2(5); Trial 355(3); Work Comp 1028, 1932, 1968(8).

Hartford Acc. & Indem. Co. v. Neal, TexCivApp–Beaumont, 460 SW2d 245, ref nre.—Insurance 3196, 3198(2).

Hartford Acc. & Indem. Co. v. Olivier, CCA5 (Tex), 123 F2d 709.—Evid 118, 126(1).

Hartford Acc. & Indem. Co.; Olson v., Tex, 477 SW2d 859.—Work Comp 517, 571.

Hartford Acc. & Indem. Co. v. Olson, TexCivApp–El Paso, 466 SW2d 373, writ gr, aff 477 SW2d 859.—Work Comp 516, 517, 571, 597, 1536.

Hartford Acc. & Indem. Co. v. Pacific Employers Ins. Co., SDTex, 862 FSupp 160.—Insurance 1808, 2118, 2270(1), 2281(3), 2286, 2396, 3506(1), 3571; Interest 31.

Hartford Acc. & Indem. Co. v. Parrott, TexCivApp–Beaumont, 486 SW2d 405.—App & E 1107, 1175(5), 1177(1), 1177(2), 1177(7); Insurance 1964, 1966, 2047(2), 2692, 2694, 3571; Plead 291(3).

Hartford Acc. & Indem. Co. v. Perry, TexCivApp–Dallas, 228 SW2d 532.—Work Comp 1159.

Hartford Acc. & Indem. Co.; Rangel v., TexApp–Dallas, 821 SW2d 196, writ den.—Judgm 178, 634; Work Comp 1042, 1789, 1793.

Hartford Acc. & Indem. Co. v. Reina, TexCivApp–Amarillo, 441 SW2d 622, ref nre.—Work Comp 1004, 1041, 1042, 1789.

Hartford Acc. & Indem. Co.; Reynolds v., CCA5 (Tex), 107 F2d 892.—Work Comp 1927.

Hartford Acc. & Indem. Co. v. Shelton, TexCivApp–Texarkana, 119 SW2d 118.—Work Comp 1339, 1923, 1929.

Hartford Acc. & Indem. Co. v. Spain, TexCivApp–Tyler, 520 SW2d 853, ref nre.—App & E 863, 934(1); Insurance 1766, 2770, 3577; Plead 123, 127(2).

Hartford Acc. & Indem. Co. v. Stanley, TexCivApp–Eastland, 148 SW2d 856, writ dism, correct.—App & E 938(5), 991; Work Comp 1028.

Hartford Acc. & Indem. Co. v. Swilley, CA5 (Tex), 304 F2d 213.—Estop 87; Insurance 1929(8), 1930.

Hartford Acc. and Indem. Co.; Texas Medical Liability Trust v., TexApp–Waco, 151 SW3d 706, reh overr, and review den.—Insurance 2361, 2914, 2915, 3557; Judgm 665, 713(1), 725(1).

Hartford Acc. and Indem. Co.; Texas Workers' Compensation Com'n v., TexApp–Corpus Christi, 952 SW2d 949, reh overr, and review den.—Parties 47; Records 7; Time 3.5; Work Comp 1869, 1874.

Hartford Acc. and Indem. Co.; Texoma Ag-Products, Inc. v., CA5 (Tex), 755 F2d 445.—Fed Cts 641, 643, 847; Insurance 3349, 3375, 3376, 3381(4), 3381(5).

Hartford Acc. & Indem. Co. v. Thurmond, TexCivApp–Corpus Christi, 527 SW2d 180, ref nre.—App & E 959(3); Plead 236(3); Trial 129, 131(1), 131(2), 133.3, 133.6(3.1); Work Comp 512, 571, 597, 998, 1001, 1325, 1380, 1400, 1490, 1492, 1716, 1717, 1935, 1937, 1939.11(5).

Hartford Acc. & Indem. Co. v. Turner, Tex, 512 SW2d 687.—Insurance 2798, 2799.

Hartford Acc. & Indem. Co. v. Turner, TexCivApp–Hous (1 Dist), 498 SW2d 8, rev 512 SW2d 687.—Insurance 2799.

Hartford Acc. & Indem. Co.; Universal Underwriters Ins. Co. v., TexCivApp–Hous (14 Dist), 487 SW2d 152, ref nre.—App & E 564(4), 653(3), 654, 768; Insurance 2678, 2684.

Hartford Acc. & Indem. Co.; Vaughn v., EDTex, 62 FRD 480.—Fed Civ Proc 1742(3).

Hartford Acc. & Indem. Co. v. Vick, TexCivApp–Amarillo, 155 SW2d 664.—App & E 930(3); Damag 221(3), 221(7); Trial 366; Work Comp 1926, 1964, 1966.

Hartford Acc. & Indem. Co.; Wallace v., Tex, 226 SW2d 612, 148 Tex 503.—Work Comp 1307, 1310, 1927.

Hartford Acc. & Indem. Co.; Wallace v., TexCivApp–Beaumont, 223 SW2d 528, rev 226 SW2d 612, 148 Tex 503.—Work Comp 1310, 1927.

Hartford Acc. & Indem. Co.; Watts v., TexCivApp–Eastland, 140 SW2d 604.—App & E 1071.1(2); Trial 390.

Hartford Acc. & Indem. Co.; Weaver v., Tex, 570 SW2d 367.—Insurance 2919, 3170; Proc 6.

Hartford Accident and Indemnity Company v. Weaver, TexCivApp, 556 SW2d 117, writ gr, aff 570 SW2d 367.—Insurance 3169, 3458(1).

Hartford Acc. & Indem. Co. v. Weeks Drug Store, TexCivApp–Austin, 161 SW2d 153, writ refused wom.—Action 60; Work Comp 2224, 2243.

Hartford Acc. and Indem. Co.; Whitley v., NDTex, 532 FSupp 190, aff 670 F2d 183.—Contracts 175(1); Fed Civ Proc 2543, 2544, 2546; Insurance 1091(12); Lim of Act 2(1), 13, 46(1).

Hartford Acc. & Indem. Co. v. Williams, TexCivApp–Amarillo, 516 SW2d 425, ref nre.—Trial 352.20; Witn 340(1), 344(2), 345(1), 345(2); Work Comp 840, 1491, 1492, 1639, 1662, 1719.

Hartford Acc. & Indem. Co.; Wolverton v., TexCivApp–Amarillo, 254 SW2d 834, ref nre.—Work Comp 1028, 1394, 1581, 1927.

Hartford Acc. & Indem. Co.; Wright v., CA5 (Tex), 580 F2d 809.—Evid 99; Fed Cts 611, 621, 637, 823; Work Comp 1396.

Hartford Acc. & Indem. Co.; X.L. Ins. Co., Ltd. v., TexApp–Beaumont, 918 SW2d 687, case abated, mandamus dism In re XL Ins Co, Ltd, 988 SW2d 741.—Alt Disp Res 112, 143; Insurance 3284.

Hartford Acc. & Indem. Corp. v. Lowery, TexCivApp–Beaumont, 490 SW2d 935, ref nre.—App & E 930(3), 989; Evid 5(2); Insurance 2653, 2663, 2687, 2694, 2695.

Hartford Acc. & Indem. Ins. Co.; Southern Farm Bureau Cas. Ins. Co. v., TexCivApp–Dallas, 620 SW2d 779, ref nre.—Judgm 181(23).

Hartford Cas. Co. v. Cruse, CA5 (Tex), 938 F2d 601, reh den.—Insurance 2275, 2278(21), 2278(23), 2278(29), 2914; Judgm 828.16(1), 828.16(4).

Hartford Cas. Ins. Co. v. Albertsons Grocery Stores, TexApp–Fort Worth, 931 SW2d 729.—App & E 852, 856(1), 863; Judgm 183, 185(2), 186; Subrog 1; Work Comp 2191, 2210, 2216.

Hartford Cas. Ins. Co. v. Budget Rent-A-Car Systems, Inc., TexApp–Dallas, 796 SW2d 763, writ den.—Costs 194.32, 194.40, 194.46; Decl Judgm 45; Insurance 2760, 2761, 2921, 3530.

Hartford Cas. Ins. Co. v. Carroll, TexCivApp–Beaumont, 575 SW2d 578.—Antitrust 145, 221; Insurance 2201, 3586.

Hartford Cas. Ins. Co. v. F.D.I.C., CA5 (Tex), 21 F3d 696.—Admin Law 17, 413, 651, 750, 754.1, 763; Banks 502, 505, 506; Compromise 16(1); Princ & S 173; Statut 263, 267(2).

Hartford Cas. Ins. Co. v. Fields, CA5 (Tex), 926 F2d 501. See Fields, Matter of.

Hartford Cas. Ins. Co.; Industrial Acc. Bd. v., TexApp–Texarkana, 649 SW2d 751.—Work Comp 1056.

Hartford Cas. Ins. Co. v. Lafarge Corp., CA5 (Tex), 61 F3d 389. See Lafarge Corp. v. Hartford Cas. Ins. Co.

Hartford Cas. Ins. Co.; Lafarge Corp. v., CA5 (Tex), 61 F3d 389.—Fed Civ Proc 2501; Fed Cts 774; Insurance 1822, 2270(2), 2275, 2278(21), 2282, 2316, 2913, 2914, 2915, 2922(1), 2922(2), 2923, 3214, 3367, 3585; Interest 31; Records 32.

Hartford Cas. Ins. Co. v. Morton, TexApp–Tyler, 141 SW3d 220, reh overr, and review den.—App & E 173(2), 836, 1175(1); Guard & W 1, 2, 13(6), 13(7), 58, 159; Judgm 183.

Hartford Cas. Ins. Co. v. Phillips, TexCivApp–Texarkana, 575 SW2d 62.—App & E 930(3), 989, 1003(5); Domicile 1, 5; Insurance 2694.

Hartford Cas. Ins. Co. v. Powell, NDTex, 19 FSupp2d 678.—Courts 90(2); Damag 87(1), 91(1); Fed Cts 383, 390, 391; Insurance 2753.

Hartford Cas. Ins. Co. v. Price, NDTex, 435 FSupp2d 566.—Counties 141, 208; Decl Judgm 5.1, 46, 362, 365; Fed Cts 51, 265, 267, 269, 270.

Hartford Cas. Ins. Co.; Russell v., TexCivApp–Austin, 548 SW2d 737, ref nre.—Action 50(4.1); Consp 1.1, 4; Insurance 3335, 3347, 3357, 3542; Princ & A 164(2); Statut 243.

Hartford Cas. Ins. Co.; Sandoval v., TexApp–Amarillo, 653 SW2d 604.—App & E 1008.1(1); Evid 590, 591, 594; Insurance 2732.

Hartford Cas. Ins. Co. v. State, TexApp–Austin, 159 SW3d 212, review den.—App & E 893(1); Banks 19; Bonds 50; Const Law 990, 999, 3847, 3867, 3876, 3879, 3893, 4426; Princ & S 66(1); Statut 176, 181(1), 208.

Hartford Cas. Ins. Co.; Vaughan v., NDTex, 277 FSupp2d 682.—Antitrust 138, 221; Insurance 1867, 3335, 3359, 3390, 3419; Torts 439.

Hartford Cas. Ins. Co. v. Walker County Agency, Inc., TexApp–Corpus Christi, 808 SW2d 681.—Damag 73; Impl & C C 3; Indem 58, 64, 84; Insurance 1644, 1647, 1648, 3417; Judgm 181(23), 186; Princ & A 1, 48, 61(1), 79(9), 99, 101(1), 119(1), 136(1), 150(3); Work Comp 1042, 1061.

Hartford Co. of the Midwest; Gomez v., TexApp–El Paso, 803 SW2d 438, writ den.—App & E 170(1), 756; Contracts 143(2), 143.5, 162; Insurance 1808, 1853, 2120, 2278(16), 2915, 2940.

Hartford Fire Ins. Co. v. Christianson, TexCivApp–Corpus Christi, 395 SW2d 53, ref nre.—App & E 1078(1), 1078(4), 1151(2), 1170.7, 1170.9(5), 1170.10; Evid 113(8), 113(10), 150; Insurance 2199, 2201, 3579; Trial 350.2, 350.4(3).

Hartford Fire Ins. Co. v. Continental Bus System, TexCivApp–Galveston, 274 SW2d 175, writ refused.—Insurance 3525.

Hartford Fire Ins. Co.; Eagle Leasing Corp. v., CA5 (Tex), 540 F2d 1257, reh den 546 F2d 906, reh den 546 F2d 906, cert den 97 SCt 2926, 431 US 967, 53 LEd2d 1063.—Adm 1.20(2); Insurance 1832(1), 1833, 1834(3), 2264.

Hartford Fire Ins. Co.; Eagle Leasing Corp. v., EDTex, 384 FSupp 247, rev 540 F2d 1257, reh den 546 F2d 906, reh den 546 F2d 906, cert den 97 SCt 2926, 431 US 967, 53 LEd2d 1063.—Insurance 1805, 1832(1), 2264, 2270(1), 2367.

Hartford Fire Ins. Co.; F. H. Vahlsing, Inc. v., TexCivApp–San Antonio, 108 SW2d 947, writ dism.—App & E 972; Evid 219(1); Insurance 3512, 3515(1), 3523(1), 3525, 3526(1), 3526(8); Judgm 256(1); Land & Ten 150(1), 152(2), 166(2), 166(10); Trial 106, 108, 313, 350.6(1).

Hartford Fire Ins. Co.; Galveston County v., TexCivApp–Galveston, 231 SW2d 684, writ refused.—Insurance 3191(7).

Hartford Fire Ins. Co.; H. Schumacher Oil Works, Inc. v., CA5 (Tex), 239 F2d 836.—Insurance 1894, 2128, 2143(1), 2199, 2201.

Hartford Fire Ins. Co. v. LaMon, TexCivApp–San Antonio, 149 SW2d 157.—Insurance 3191(12); Trial 141.

Hartford Fire Ins. Co.; Payne v., TexCivApp–Beaumont, 409 SW2d 591, ref nre.—Evid 123(1), 129(1), 130, 134, 138, 506, 555.5; Insurance 2198, 2199, 2201, 3571; Plead 354; Witn 216(1), 391.

Hartford Fire Ins. Co.; Penry v., EDTex, 662 FSupp 792.—Consp 18; RICO 10, 27, 49.

Hartford Fire Ins. Co. v. Rainbow Drilling Co., Inc., TexApp–Houston (14 Dist), 748 SW2d 262.—Costs 32(1); Insurance 2663, 2681.

Hartford Fire Ins. Co.; Rx.com Inc. v., SDTex, 426 FSupp2d 546.—Accord 1; Fed Civ Proc 103.2, 2501, 2537; Insurance 2914, 2928, 2929; Lim of Act 21(1).

Hartford Fire Ins. Co.; Rx.Com Inc. v., SDTex, 364 FSupp2d 609.—Fed Cts 382.1, 383, 390; Insurance 2911, 2919, 2933, 3140.

Hartford Fire Ins. Co. v. Tubb, CA5 (Tex), 242 F2d 921.—Autos 19; Insurance 2706(3).

Hartford Fire Ins. Co.; U.S. ex rel. United Rentals, Inc. v., WDTex, 339 FSupp2d 799.—Estop 52(5); Lim of Act 13, 105(2); U S 67(16.1).

Hartford Fire Ins. Co.; Western Hills Bowling Center, Inc. v., CA5 (Tex), 412 F2d 563.—Fed Cts 765; Insurance 3420, 3427; Neglig 371, 379, 380, 387.

Hartford Ins. Co. v. Branton & Mendelsohn, Inc., TexApp–San Antonio, 670 SW2d 699.—Work Comp 2248, 2251.

Hartford Ins. Co. v. Commerce & Industry Ins. Co., TexApp–Houston (1 Dist), 864 SW2d 648, reh den, and writ den.—App & E 863; Contracts 147(1), 147(3); Evid 384, 405(1); Insurance 1832(2), 2654, 2656, 2659; Judgm 185(2); Trial 105(1).

Hartford Ins. Co. v. Jiminez, TexApp–Houston (1 Dist), 814 SW2d 551.—App & E 205, 548(5), 1071.1(3), 1071.1(7); Damag 105, 188(1), 222.

Hartford Ins. Co. of Midwest; Perry v., EDTex, 198 FSupp2d 836.—Fed Cts 346; Rem of C 74.

Hartford Ins. Co. of Midwest; Perry v., EDTex, 196 FSupp2d 447.—Fed Cts 315; Rem of C 118.

Hartford Ins. Co. of Texas; McGatlin v., TexApp–Texarkana, 94 SW3d 311.—Admin Law 305, 325; App & E 893(1); Courts 35, 37(1); Statut 181(1); Work Comp 1821, 1824.

Hartford Ins. Co. of the Midwest; Bergensen v., TexApp–Houston (1 Dist), 845 SW2d 374, reh den, and writ refused.—Insurance 2786, 2799.

Hartford Ins. Co. of the Midwest; Horihan v., EDTex, 979 FSupp 1073.—Const Law 3964; Courts 12(2.1); Fed Cts 76, 76.5, 76.10, 76.25, 79, 97, 122.

Hartford Ins. ex rel. Blue Line Promotions Inc.; Continental Cas. Co. v., TexApp–Houston (1 Dist), 74 SW3d 432.—App & E 977(5); Judgm 139, 145(4), 146, 151, 153(1), 159; Neglig 202; New Tr 128(1), 140(1).

Hartford Life; Chandler v., CA5 (Tex), 178 FedAppx 365. —Labor & Emp 629(2), 688.

Hartford Life & Accident Ins. Co.; Matney v., CA5 (Tex), 172 FedAppx 571.—Fed Cts 715; Labor & Emp 629(2), 685, 690.

Hartford Life and Acc. Ins. Co.; Pylant v., NDTex, 429 FSupp2d 816, reconsideration den 2006 WL 3247314.— Insurance 2561(2), 2578; Labor & Emp 438, 572, 685, 688, 690.

Hartford Life and Acc. Ins. Co.; Teweleit v., CA5 (Tex), 43 F3d 1005, appeal after remand 95 F3d 45.—Int Rev 3048; Labor & Emp 405, 568.

Hartford Life and Acc. Ins. Co. v. Texas Mun. Group Benefits Risk Pool, CA5 (Tex), 43 F3d 1005. See Teweleit v. Hartford Life and Acc. Ins. Co.

Hartford Life Ins. Co.; McSperitt v., NDTex, 393 FSupp2d 418.—Antitrust 132; Fed Cts 241; Insurance 1117(4), 2578; Labor & Emp 407, 572; Rem of C 19(5), 25(1); States 18.41, 18.51.

Hartford Life Ins. Co.; Mayfield v., WDTex, 699 FSupp 605.—Insurance 1117(1); States 18.41.

Hartford Life Ins. Co.; Mayo v., CA5 (Tex), 354 F3d 400. —Fed Cts 776; Insurance 1091(7), 1791(1), 1791(4), 1791(5), 3560; Lim of Act 28(1), 43, 49(1); Trover 28.

Hartford Life Ins. Co.; Mayo v., SDTex, 220 FSupp2d 794, motion to certify appeal gr 214 FRD 458, aff and remanded 354 F3d 400.—Insurance 1719, 1791(1), 1791(5), 3464.

Hartford Life Ins. Co.; Mayo v., SDTex, 220 FSupp2d 714, motion to certify appeal gr 214 FRD 458, aff and remanded 354 F3d 400.—Action 17; Contracts 145; Courts 8; Decl Judgm 61, 62, 64, 163.1; Fed Civ Proc 2553; Fed Cts 12.1, 409.1; Insurance 1088, 1091(7), 1117(1), 1719, 1791(1), 1791(4), 1791(5), 3466, 3560; Judgm 632, 634, 666, 713(1), 958(1); Labor & Emp 407, 414; Lim of Act 28(1), 50(1), 102(8); States 18.41, 18.51; Trusts 91, 365(5).

Hartford Life Ins. Co.; Mayo v., SDTex, 214 FRD 465.— Fed Civ Proc 164, 1269.1, 1272.1.

Hartford Life Ins. Co.; Mayo v., SDTex, 214 FRD 458.— Fed Civ Proc 311, 314.1, 320, 337; Fed Cts 660.5.

Hartford Livestock Ins. Co.; Wilson v., CA5 (Tex), 193 F2d 752.—Insurance 2160(3), 2202.

Hartford Lloyd's Ins. Co.; Butler & Binion v., TexApp–Houston (14 Dist), 957 SW2d 566, writ den, and reh overr.—Insurance 1808, 1836, 2268, 2278(3), 2310, 2913, 2914, 2915, 2939, 3336; Judgm 185(2).

Hartford Lloyd's Ins. Co.; LaBatt Co. v., TexApp–Corpus Christi, 776 SW2d 795.—Insurance 1808, 1822, 2278(21), 2278(22); Prod Liab 1, 6.

Hartford Lloyd's Ins. Co. v. Teachworth, CA5 (Tex), 898 F2d 1058.—Alt Disp Res 113; Commerce 80.5; Fed Cts 419, 617; Insurance 3247, 3249.

Hartford Lloyd's Ins. Co. v. The Seasons Apartments, CA5 (Tex), 898 F2d 1058. See Hartford Lloyd's Ins. Co. v. Teachworth.

Hartford Steam Boiler Inspection and Ins. Co. v. State, TexApp–Austin, 729 SW2d 372, ref nre.—States 171.

Hartford Underwriters Ins. v. Mills, TexApp–Fort Worth, 110 SW3d 588.—App & E 82(2); Courts 37(2), 39; Judgm 335(1), 335(3), 335(4).

Hartford Underwriters Ins. Co., In re, TexApp–Eastland, 168 SW3d 293.—Work Comp 1981.

Hartford Underwriters Ins. Co. v. Burdine, TexApp–Fort Worth, 34 SW3d 700, reh overr.—Work Comp 55, 984, 1658.

Hartford Underwriters Ins. Co. v. Hafley, TexApp–Austin, 96 SW3d 469, reh overr.—Admin Law 305, 325; Statut 219(1), 219(4); Venue 1.5; Work Comp 833, 1419, 1832, 1964, 1981.

Hartford Underwriters Ins. Co.; Insurance Co. of State of Pennsylvania v., TexApp–Houston (14 Dist), 164 SW3d 747.—Admin Law 417; App & E 1175(1); Work Comp 1114.

Hartford Underwriters Ins. Co.; Royal Ins. Co. of America v., CA5 (Tex), 391 F3d 639.—Insurance 1863, 2285(4), 2285(8), 2391(4), 2919.

Hartford Underwriters Ins. Co.; Tri-Coastal Contractors, Inc. v., TexApp–Houston (1 Dist), 981 SW2d 861, review den.—Evid 405(1); Insurance 2913, 2914, 2915.

Hartgraves; Callison v., TexCivApp–Eastland, 438 SW2d 670.—Autos 242(7), 244(36.1), 244(46); Evid 588; Trial 139.1(3), 140(1).

Hartgraves v. State, TexCrimApp, 374 SW2d 888.—Crim Law 1092.11(1), 1097(6); Ind & Inf 119; Infants 20.

Hartgraves; Stock v., TexCivApp–San Antonio, 236 SW2d 257, writ refused.—Ven & Pur 287, 295.

Hartgraves; Whitt v., TexCivApp–San Antonio, 412 SW2d 344.—App & E 624, 627, 628(1).

Hartgrove; Meuth v., TexApp–Austin, 811 SW2d 626, writ den.—App & E 204(4), 241, 671(4), 671(6), 1043(1); Courts 70; Evid 350, 359(5); Trial 127.

Hartgrove v. Thompson, TexCivApp–Austin, 608 SW2d 349.—App & E 781(1), 781(4).

Harthcock v. Royston, Rayzor, Vickery & Williams LLP., CA5 (Tex), 77 FedAppx 206.—Larc 5.

Harthcock; Zep Mfg. Co. v., TexApp–Dallas, 824 SW2d 654.—App & E 852, 863; Contracts 116(1), 117(2), 117(3), 118, 137(1), 137(4), 142; Judgm 181(1), 181(4), 181(6), 185(2); Labor & Emp 40(2), 40(3), 835, 900; Ref of Inst 11; Torts 212, 220.

Hartigan, In re, TexApp–San Antonio, 107 SW3d 684, reh overr, and mandamus den, and reh of motion for mandamus overr.—Alt Disp Res 119, 134(1), 143, 179, 182(1), 210; Atty & C 129(1); Jury 31.2(1); Mand 4(4), 28, 154(2).

Hartis v. Mason & Hanger Corp., TexApp–Amarillo, 7 SW3d 700.—App & E 854(1), 863; Civil R 1019(1), 1210, 1218(2), 1218(3), 1218(6).

Hartis v. State, TexApp–Houston (14 Dist), 183 SW3d 793.—Arrest 68(3); Crim Law 13(1), 438(8), 678(1), 881(1), 1030(1); Ind & Inf 71.2(3), 125(19.1), 125(20); Obst Just 3, 11, 16.

Hartkopf v. Southland Corp., TexCivApp–Austin, 256 SW2d 241.—Inj 61(2).

Hartland Developers, Inc.; Tips v., TexApp–San Antonio, 961 SW2d 618, reh overr.—App & E 931(1), 1010.1(1), 1010.2, 1012.1(4); Contracts 167, 168, 294, 303(4), 312(1), 313(1), 313(2), 326; Damag 61, 120(3); Interest 31, 39(3).

Hartless v. State, TexCrimApp, 93 SW2d 422.—Crim Law 15.

Hartley v. Brady, TexCivApp–Amarillo, 114 SW2d 406.— App & E 907(3); Inj 138.31; Mines 52.

Hartley v. Coker, TexApp–Corpus Christi, 843 SW2d 743. —Abate & R 4, 8(1), 9; App & E 907(5), 949; Aviation 244; Courts 475(1); Evid 40; Plead 106(2).

Hartley; Giller Industries, Inc. v., TexApp–Dallas, 644 SW2d 183.—App & E 846(5), 1079; Land & Ten 112(2).

Hartley; Pams Advertising Agency, Inc. v., TexCivApp–Waco, 357 SW2d 764.—Frds St of 152(1), 152(2); Venue 22(6).

Hartley v. Schwab, TexCivApp–Amarillo, 564 SW2d 829, ref nre.—Damag 113.

Hartley v. State, TexCrimApp, 382 SW2d 483.—Bail 62, 74(1), 77(1), 79(1); Crim Law 93.

Hartley v. State, TexCrimApp, 334 SW2d 287, 169 TexCrim 341.—Sent & Pun 2006.

Hartley v. State, TexApp–Dallas, 765 SW2d 883, petition for discretionary review refused.—Crim Law 1172.1(2).

Hartley v. U.S., CA5 (Tex), 252 F2d 262.—Int Rev 4330, 4962.

Hartley Independent School Dist.; Roberts v., TexApp–Amarillo, 877 SW2d 506, reh den, and writ den.—Admin Law 229; Schools 147.51.

Hartman, In re, BkrtcyNDTex, 102 BR 90.—Bankr 2576.5(3.1), 3106, 3672; Land & Ten 20; Sec Tran 2, 14.1, 17, 83.

Hartman v. A & F Motor Lines, TexApp–Texarkana, 937 SW2d 575. See Hartman v. Trio Transp., Inc.

Hartman v. American Bar Ass'n, NDTex, 407 FSupp 451. See Turner v. American Bar Ass'n.

Hartman; City of San Antonio v., Tex, 201 SW3d 667.—App & E 361(0.5), 831, 833(1), 833(3); Autos 278; Const Law 2473; Mun Corp 723; Statut 176.

Hartman; City of San Antonio v., TexApp–San Antonio, 155 SW3d 460, reh overr, and review gr, rev 201 SW3d 667.—App & E 893(1), 916(1); Autos 255, 259, 303; Courts 4, 35, 37(1); Mun Corp 723, 728, 742(4), 742(6), 847; Neglig 1011; Plead 111.36, 111.43.

Hartman v. Costales, TexCivApp–Galveston, 145 SW2d 603, writ dism, correct.—App & E 598, 1050.1(3.1); New Tr 28; Trial 54(1), 139.1(5.1); Witn 139(9), 139(11).

Hartman v. Crain, TexCivApp–Houston, 398 SW2d 387. —Hus & W 14.3, 49.3(6), 264(3), 265; Interpl 8(1), 35; Stip 14(10); Trusts 234, 244; Wills 6.

Hartman; Dahl v., TexApp–Houston (14 Dist), 14 SW3d 434, review den.—App & E 962; Assoc 13, 20(1); Decl Judgm 256, 293.1, 296.

Hartman v. Engler, TexCivApp–Waco, 153 SW2d 598.—App & E 846(5); New Tr 99.

Hartman; Fenske v., TexCivApp–Beaumont, 99 SW2d 631.—Trial 194(2), 260(3).

Hartman v. First Nat. Bank, TexCivApp–El Paso, 97 SW2d 969.—App & E 1050.1(10); Chat Mtg 49(1).

Hartman v. Harder, TexCivApp–Amarillo, 322 SW2d 555. —App & E 1052(5); Const Law 4002; Crim Law 393(1); Evid 150; Searches 75.

Hartman v. Hardin Memorial Hospital, TexCivApp–Beaumont, 587 SW2d 55.—Health 770.

Hartman v. Hartman, TexComApp, 138 SW2d 802, 135 Tex 596.—Adv Poss 71(2); App & E 910; Child S 60; Fraud Conv 69(2); Lim of Act 43, 99(2).

Hartman; Hartman v., TexComApp, 138 SW2d 802, 135 Tex 596.—Adv Poss 71(2); App & E 910; Child S 60; Fraud Conv 69(2); Lim of Act 43, 99(2).

Hartman v. Hartman, TexCivApp–Austin, 253 SW2d 480. —Confusion of G 13; Divorce 252.3(1); Hus & W 249(5), 254, 272(5).

Hartman; Hartman v., TexCivApp–Austin, 253 SW2d 480.—Confusion of G 13; Divorce 252.3(1); Hus & W 249(5), 254, 272(5).

Hartman v. Hartman, TexCivApp–Austin, 217 SW2d 872, ref nre.—Ex & Ad 458; Fraud Conv 172(1), 179(1); Hus & W 47(1), 266.3; Judgm 588.

Hartman; Hartman v., TexCivApp–Austin, 217 SW2d 872, ref nre.—Ex & Ad 458; Fraud Conv 172(1), 179(1); Hus & W 47(1), 266.3; Judgm 588.

Hartman v. Hartman, TexCivApp–Austin, 109 SW2d 218, rev 138 SW2d 802, 135 Tex 596.—Adv Poss 71(2), 106(1); Child S 440; Const Law 2503(4); Fraud Conv 74(4), 172(1), 249; Lim of Act 19(3), 44(1).

Hartman; Hartman v., TexCivApp–Austin, 109 SW2d 218, rev 138 SW2d 802, 135 Tex 596.—Adv Poss 71(2), 106(1); Child S 440; Const Law 2503(4); Fraud Conv 74(4), 172(1), 249; Lim of Act 19(3), 44(1).

Hartman; Laros v., Tex, 260 SW2d 592, 152 Tex 518.—Des & Dist 71(7); Ex & Ad 510(5); Judgm 244, 668(1).

Hartman v. Laros, TexCivApp–Galveston, 255 SW2d 310, rev 260 SW2d 592, 152 Tex 518.—Des & Dist 71(7); Judgm 233.

Hartman v. Maryland Cas. Co., TexCivApp–Waco, 417 SW2d 640.—Evid 155(5), 380; Witn 386, 397; Work Comp 1929, 1965, 1968(3), 1968(4).

Hartman; Progressive Ins. Companies v., TexApp–Dallas, 788 SW2d 424.—Interpl 26, 30; Mand 154(9), 168(2); Pretrial Proc 501, 508.

Hartman v. St. Paul Fire and Marine Ins. Co., NDTex, 55 FSupp2d 600.—Insurance 3335, 3379.

Hartman v. St. Paul Fire and Marine Ins. Co., NDTex, 40 FSupp2d 837.—Insurance 3557; Judgm 540.

Hartman v. Sirgo Operating, Inc., TexApp–El Paso, 863 SW2d 764, reh overr, and writ den.—App & E 181; Costs 194.40; Courts 18, 29; Decl Judgm 45, 83, 271, 296, 301; Hus & W 267(0.5); Parties 18, 29.

Hartman v. State, TexCrimApp, 946 SW2d 60, on remand 2 SW3d 490, petition for discretionary review refused, and reh of petition for review den.—Crim Law 388.1, 472.

Hartman v. State, TexCrimApp, 507 SW2d 557.—Crim Law 662.1, 925.5(1).

Hartman v. State, TexCrimApp, 507 SW2d 553.—Assault 82; Crim Law 665(4), 706(3), 1171.8(1); Homic 989(1), 1136; Witn 270(1), 277(4), 281.

Hartman v. State, TexCrimApp, 496 SW2d 582.—Crim Law 304(2), 857(1), 1171.1(6).

Hartman v. State, TexCrimApp, 280 SW2d 739, 162 TexCrim 36.—Autos 355(6); Crim Law 1169.2(2).

Hartman v. State, TexApp–Austin, 144 SW3d 568.—Arrest 63.5(1), 63.5(4), 63.5(7), 63.5(9), 68(4); Autos 349(10), 349(17); Crim Law 1139, 1158(4).

Hartman v. State, TexApp–San Antonio, 2 SW3d 490, petition for discretionary review refused, and reh of petition for review den.—Crim Law 388.1, 486(7), 1169.9.

Hartman v. State, TexApp–San Antonio, 917 SW2d 115, petition for discretionary review gr, rev 946 SW2d 60, on remand 2 SW3d 490, petition for discretionary review refused, and reh of petition for review den.—Autos 357; Const Law 4629; Crim Law 469, 469.1, 475.2(4), 478(1), 480, 700(1), 1147, 1153(1), 1158(4).

Hartman; State v., TexApp–Beaumont, 810 SW2d 22.—Crim Law 273.1(2), 273.2(1), 274(2), 914.

Hartman; State v., TexApp–Corpus Christi, 198 SW3d 829, petition stricken.—Autos 332, 355(6), 413, 419, 422.1, 423; Crim Law 394.6(1), 1036.1(8), 1043(2), 1043(3), 1045, 1128(4), 1165(1), 1169.1(1), 1169.1(10).

Hartman; State v., TexApp–Austin, 338 SW2d 302, ref nre.—Em Dom 149(2.1), 202(1), 262(5); Evid 555.6(2), 558(7); Trial 120(2); Witn 316.

Hartman; Stefka v., TexCivApp–Austin, 120 SW2d 617.—App & E 670(2).

Hartman; Tennessee Gas Pipeline Co. v., TexCivApp–Corpus Christi, 556 SW2d 616.—Courts 207.4(2); Judgm 271; Neglig 1750; Trial 358.

Hartman v. Texaco, Inc., SDTex, 119 FSupp2d 668, aff 273 F3d 1107.—Labor & Emp 407, 426, 429, 555; States 18.51.

Hartman v. Trio Transp., Inc., TexApp–Texarkana, 937 SW2d 575, reh overr, and writ den.—App & E 199; Pretrial Proc 481, 483.

Hartman v. Urban, TexApp–Corpus Christi, 946 SW2d 546, reh overr.—Antitrust 130, 161, 259, 397; App & E 984(1); Const Law 2800; Contracts 167; Neglig 1205(5).

Hartmangruber; Wolf v., TexCivApp–Fort Worth, 162 SW2d 112.—Costs 236; Hus & W 262.1(6), 273(1), 274(1), 274(4); Wills 577, 578(2.1), 578(3), 782(3).

Hartmann, Appeal of, CA5 (Tex), 757 F2d 1580. See Grand Jury Proceedings No. 84-4, In re.

Hartmann v. Solbrig, TexApp–San Antonio, 12 SW3d 587, review den.—App & E 931(1), 1010.2, 1024.1; Costs 194.18, 198, 207; Ex & Ad 15, 35(0.5), 35(19), 219, 456(1); Int Rev 4823; Torts 242; Trial 395(5).

Hartman Newspapers, Inc.; Webb v., TexApp–Houston (14 Dist), 793 SW2d 302.—Contracts 117(2); Inj 2, 138.39, 158.

Hartman Water Well Service, In re, BkrtcyNDTex, 102 BR 90. See Hartman, In re.

Hartmarx Specialty Stores, Inc.; Norris v., CA5 (Tex), 913 F2d 253.—Civil R 1486, 1490, 1492, 1544.

Hartnett v. Adams & Holmes Mort. Co., Inc., TexCiv-App–Texarkana, 539 SW2d 181.—Action 53(1); Ex & Ad 92; Guar 77(2); Pretrial Proc 503; Usury 140.

Hartnett v. Chase Bank of Texas Nat. Ass'n, NDTex, 59 FSupp2d 605.—Civil R 1263, 1505(6), 1523, 1530.

Hartnett v. Hampton Inns, Inc., TexApp–San Antonio, 870 SW2d 162, writ den.—Antitrust 355, 397; App & E 197(1), 205, 207, 218.2(10), 231(1); Assign 121; Contracts 176(2); Inn 10.8; Plead 139; Subrog 1, 34, 41(7); Trial 274, 351.2(1.1), 366.

Hartnett; Powell v., TexCivApp–Eastland, 521 SW2d 896. —App & E 77(2).

Hartnett; Warren v., TexCivApp–Dallas, 561 SW2d 860, ref nre.—App & E 927(7); Evid 536, 572; Trial 139.1(7); Wills 80, 324(2).

Hartney v. State, TexApp–Houston (1 Dist), 823 SW2d 398.—Crim Law 562, 1144.13(2.1), 1144.13(6), 1159.2(7); Tel 1018(4).

Harton; Peoria Life Ins. Co. v., TexCivApp–Dallas, 84 SW2d 864, writ refused.—Usury 22, 34, 72.

Hartrick v. Great American Lloyds Ins. Co., TexApp–Houston (1 Dist), 62 SW3d 270, rule 537(f) motion gr.—App & E 854(1), 1175(1); Contracts 188.5(3); Insurance 1806, 1809, 1810, 1812, 1832(1), 1835(2), 1863, 2101, 2117, 2268, 2269, 2275.

Hartsell; Boreham v., TexApp–Dallas, 826 SW2d 193.—Courts 12(2.1), 35; Judgm 17(3), 162(2); Proc 153.

Hartsell v. Dr. Pepper Bottling Co. of Texas, CA5 (Tex), 207 F3d 269, on remand 2000 WL 1194537.—Fed Civ Proc 2182.1; Fed Cts 630.1, 636, 850.1; Labor & Emp 2307, 2318.

Hartsell v. State, TexApp–Waco, 143 SW3d 233.—Crim Law 1131(0.5), 1144.10.

Hartsell v. Town of Talty, TexApp–Dallas, 130 SW3d 325, clarified on denial of reh, and review den.—App & E 984(5), 1178(6); Costs 194.40; Statut 181(1), 188; Zoning 376.

Hartsfield, Matter of, TexCivApp–Tyler, 531 SW2d 149. —App & E 931(1); Assault 48; Infants 132, 176, 192, 225, 230.1; Obst Just 3.

Hartsfield; Anchor Cas. Co. v., Tex, 390 SW2d 469.—Work Comp 306, 1342, 1453, 1459.

Hartsfield v. Anchor Cas. Co., TexCivApp–Tyler, 383 SW2d 455, rev 390 SW2d 469.—App & E 930(3), 989; Work Comp 509, 1028, 1452, 1870.

Hartsfield v. A. O. Reece & Son, TexCivApp–San Antonio, 144 SW2d 959.—Courts 104.

Hartsfield v. Ferguson, TexApp–Eastland, 109 SW2d 364.—App & E 672; Land & Ten 270(3).

Hartsfield v. McRee Ford, Inc., TexApp–Houston (1 Dist), 893 SW2d 148, reh den, and writ den.—App & E 169, 854(1), 856(1); Autos 173(8); Judgm 185(2), 185(6), 186; Neglig 210, 213, 215, 1692.

Hartsfield; Marino v., TexApp–Beaumont, 877 SW2d 508, reh overr, and writ den.—App & E 302(6), 758.3(11), 882(14), 1001(3); Land & Ten 55(3); Trial 358.

Hartsfield; Marino v., TexApp–Beaumont, 849 SW2d 835, writ gr, rev 868 SW2d 336, on remand 877 SW2d 508, reh overr, and writ den.—App & E 554(1), 624, 627.2; Land & Ten 184(2).

Hartsfield v. State, TexCrimApp, 523 SW2d 683.—Sent & Pun 2021.

Hartsfield v. State, TexCrimApp, 353 SW2d 26, 171 TexCrim 644.—Autos 355(6), 356; Crim Law 761(6), 763(1).

Hartsfield v. State, TexCrimApp, 88 SW2d 714.—Crim Law 1184(5).

Hartsfield v. State, TexApp–Texarkana, 200 SW3d 813, petition for discretionary review refused.—Crim Law

404.11, 404.15, 404.30, 404.36, 1030(1), 1035(1), 1153(1); Dist & Pros Attys 3(4), 8.

Hartsfield v. Wisdom, TexApp–Amarillo, 843 SW2d 221, reh overr, and writ den.—App & E 170(1); Divorce 166; Judgm 181(11), 181(15.1), 335(1), 335(3).

Hartshorn; Aetna Ins. Co. v., CA5 (Tex), 477 F2d 97.—Const Law 3879, 3994; Fed Civ Proc 8.1.

Hartshorn; U.S. v., CA5 (Tex), 163 FedAppx 325, cert den 126 SCt 2313, 164 LEd2d 832.—Const Law 2262, 2815; Crim Law 1023(16), 1026.10(4); Searches 78; Sent & Pun 1983(2), 1983(3), 1996.

Hartson; Durham v., TexCivApp–Austin, 104 SW2d 948. —App & E 907(3); Princ & A 78(3), 81(4), 89(11).

Hartson v. State, TexApp–Texarkana, 59 SW3d 780.—Crim Law 351(10), 370, 371(5), 374, 595(4), 867, 938(1), 938(4), 1043(3), 1063(1), 1144.13(2.1), 1144.13(6), 1151, 1153(1), 1155, 1159.2(2), 1159.2(7); Forg 44(2); Witn 297(13.1), 300, 305(2).

Hartsook; Finley v., CCA5 (Tex), 158 F2d 618.—Courts 202(1); Evid 80(1); Fed Cts 752; Judgm 501; Mental H 172, 195, 196, 251, 256.

Hartsook; Finley v., NDTex, 63 FSupp 97, aff 158 F2d 618.—Jud S 50(1); Mental H 172, 195, 251, 256, 268.

Hartsook v. State, TexCrimApp, 244 SW2d 830, 156 TexCrim 560.—Autos 351.1, 355(6); Crim Law 665(1), 1168(2), 1171.1(2.1).

Hartsough v. Steinberg, TexApp–Dallas, 737 SW2d 408, writ den.—Judgm 185.3(21).

Hartt; Chandler v., TexCivApp–Tyler, 467 SW2d 629, ref nre.—Deeds 63.1, 66, 93, 194(2), 194(3), 194(4), 208(6); Estop 22(2), 29; Partit 2, 9(1), 83.

Hartt; Wasson v., TexCivApp–Dallas, 244 SW2d 258, ref nre.—Brok 40, 42; Release 4.

Hartwell; Swate v., CA5 (Tex), 99 F3d 1282. See Swate, Matter of.

Hartwell v. Texas Consol. Oils, NDTex, 94 FSupp 609.—Fed Civ Proc 101, 312, 315; Parties 40(2), 47; Rem of C 38.

Hartwell; Texas Consol. Oils v., TexCivApp–Dallas, 240 SW2d 324, mandamus overr.—App & E 999(1); Corp 544(2), 553(1), 553(3), 557(4); Receivers 1, 39.

Hartwell's Office World, Inc. v. Systex Corp., TexCiv-App–Hous (14 Dist), 598 SW2d 636, ref nre.—App & E 920(3), 954(1), 954(2); Contracts 116(1); Inj 16, 61(2), 126, 132, 135, 138.39, 140, 147, 152.

Harty; City of Fort Worth v., TexApp–Fort Worth, 862 SW2d 776, reh overr, and writ den.—Mun Corp 180(1), 210; Statut 217.2.

Hartzell v. State, TexCrimApp, 232 SW2d 710.—Crim Law 1094(3).

Hartzell Propeller Co., Inc. v. Alexander, TexCivApp–Waco, 485 SW2d 943, ref nre.—Death 32, 64, 95(1); Prod Liab 5, 11, 15, 27, 34, 83.1.

Hartzell Propeller, Inc. v. Alexander, TexCivApp–Texarkana, 517 SW2d 455.—Costs 216.

Hartzheim; Texas Employment Commission v., TexCivApp–San Antonio, 549 SW2d 770.—Unemp Comp 400, 461.

Hartzog; Commercial Standard Ins. Co. v., TexCivApp–Hous (14 Dist), 619 SW2d 417, ref nre.—Insurance 2893, 2894.

Harvard; U.S. v., CA5 (Tex), 103 F3d 412, cert den 118 SCt 82, 522 US 824, 139 LEd2d 40.—Banks 509.10, 509.25; Const Law 2507(1); Crim Law 673(2), 678(4), 1152(1), 1153(1), 1173.2(1); Ind & Inf 125(20).

Harvel; Flagg Realtors, Inc. v., TexCivApp–Amarillo, 509 SW2d 885, ref nre.—Accord 1, 11(1), 26(3); App & E 747(1), 931(4), 1071.6; Cust & U 1, 19(3); Estop 52.10(2); Evid 265(10), 588; Labor & Emp 256(5), 265, 271, 2204; Trial 382, 395(5), 401.

Harvel v. Harvel, TexCivApp–Hous (1 Dist), 466 SW2d 39.—Divorce 54, 115, 184(12).

Harvel; Harvel v., TexCivApp–Hous (1 Dist), 466 SW2d 39.—Divorce 54, 115, 184(12).

Harvest Communities of Houston, Inc., In re, TexApp–San Antonio, 88 SW3d 343.—Judgm 21; Jury 31.2(1); Pretrial Proc 44.1, 221, 224.

Harvest House Publishers v. Local Church, TexApp–Houston (1 Dist), 190 SW3d 204, reh overr, and review den, and reh of petition for review den, cert den 127 SCt 2987.—Const Law 1292, 1330; Libel 1, 6(1), 19, 21, 123(2); Relig Soc 14, 30.

Harvestons Securities, Inc. v. Narnia Investments, Ltd., TexApp–Houston (14 Dist), 218 SW3d 126, reh overr, and review den.—App & E 5, 865, 914(1), 1177(2); Judgm 17(2); Proc 64, 145, 148, 149; Sec Reg 303.1.

Harvey, Ex parte, TexCrimApp, 846 SW2d 328.—Sent & Pun 373, 1160.

Harvey, Ex parte, TexCrimApp, 495 SW2d 229.—Crim Law 264, 1167(5).

Harvey, Ex parte, TexCrimApp, 459 SW2d 853.—Extrad 36, 39.

Harvey v. Alexander, TexApp–Fort Worth, 671 SW2d 727.—App & E 179(1), 223, 916(1); Costs 194.16, 194.22, 194.34; Judgm 185(6), 185.1(1), 186; Mines 78.2.

Harvey v. Andrist, CA5 (Tex), 754 F2d 569, reh den 758 F2d 651, cert den 105 SCt 2659, 471 US 1126, 86 LEd2d 276.—Civil R 1311, 1319, 1358, 1389; Fed Civ Proc 840, 1852, 1856, 1857, 2011; Fed Cts 663; Witn 8.

Harvey; Armstead v., TexCivApp–Texarkana, 390 SW2d 871.—Autos 245(1); Damag 130.4, 208(1); Trial 134, 139.1(3), 140(1), 140(2).

Harvey v. Bain, TexComApp, 168 SW2d 234, 140 Tex 375.—Plead 111.15, 111.37, 111.39(5).

Harvey v. Bain, TexCivApp–Waco, 169 SW2d 568.—App & E 1175(1); Plead 111.15, 111.39(5).

Harvey v. Blake, CA5 (Tex), 913 F2d 226.—Civil R 1529, 1571; Fed Cts 585.1.

Harvey; Bly v., TexCivApp–Texarkana, 397 SW2d 893, ref nre.—Acct 17(1); Mental H 495, 499, 514; Parties 64; Partit 31, 109(4).

Harvey v. Braniff Intern. Airways, CCA5 (Tex), 164 F2d 521.—Armed S 118(3), 118(5).

Harvey v. Braniff Intern. Airways, NDTex, 70 FSupp 206, aff 164 F2d 521.—Armed S 118(3).

Harvey; Burlington Northern R. Co. v., TexApp–Houston (14 Dist), 717 SW2d 371, ref nre.—Const Law 2473; Evid 536, 544; Labor & Emp 2805; Statut 181(1), 184, 206, 211, 217, 230.

Harvey; Cadle Co. v., TexApp–Fort Worth, 46 SW3d 282, review den.—App & E 984(5); Contracts 164; Costs 194.40; Home 90, 103, 104, 112, 128, 175; Judgm 185(2), 780(2), 785(1), 787; Land & Ten 92(1), 184(2); Ven & Pur 3(4), 54.

Harvey v. Campbell, NDTex, 107 FSupp 757.—Int Rev 3513.

Harvey v. Casebeer, TexCivApp–Tyler, 531 SW2d 206.—App & E 927(7); Bills & N 330, 453, 537(1); Equity 65(1); Trusts 231(2), 344.1.

Harvey v. Chevron U.S.A., Inc., SDTex, 961 FSupp 1017.—Civil R 1166, 1168, 1171, 1244, 1251, 1505(7), 1532, 1549.

Harvey v. Chevron U.S.A. Production Co., SDTex, 961 FSupp 1017. See Harvey v. Chevron U.S.A., Inc.

Harvey v. City of Conroe, TX, SDTex, 148 FSupp2d 783.—Const Law 3040, 3053, 3377, 3785; Crim Law 1222.1.

Harvey; City of Waxahachie v., TexCivApp–Waco, 255 SW2d 549, ref nre.—App & E 1069.1; Mun Corp 741.40(3), 742(1), 821(11), 821(15.1), 821(16), 821(22), 821(24); Trial 304, 311, 315.

Harvey v. Crockett Drilling Co., TexCivApp–Waco, 242 SW2d 952.—Acct Action on 13; Damag 142, 147, 221(6), 221(8); Evid 318(7); Judgm 248; Trial 352.4(1).

Harvey v. Culpepper, TexApp–Corpus Christi, 801 SW2d 596.—App & E 930(3), 970(2), 989, 1001(1), 1003(7), 1050.1(6), 1056.1(3), 1069.2; Damag 101, 133, 134(1), 135, 191, 208(4), 208(5); Evid 356, 506, 553(1), 571(3); Trial 307(3).

Harvey v. Denton, TexCivApp–Eastland, 601 SW2d 121, ref nre.—App & E 218.2(1), 901, 930(3), 932(1), 989; Damag 15; Health 786, 787, 811, 823(5), 832; Lim of Act 4(2), 6(1), 95(12); Statut 263.

Harvey; Dickens v., TexApp–Waco, 868 SW2d 436.—Judgm 181(15.1), 185(2); Lim of Act 55(6), 95(8); Mines 55(2), 55(4), 55(5), 70(1), 79.1(1).

Harvey v. Elder, TexCivApp–San Antonio, 191 SW2d 686, writ refused.—App & E 1061.4; Contracts 93(2); Release 16.

Harvey; Foster v., TexCivApp–Amarillo, 356 SW2d 829.—App & E 1170.6, 1170.7; Covenants 72.1; Evid 543(3).

Harvey v. Harvey, TexApp–Austin, 905 SW2d 760.—Divorce 169, 252.3(4), 254(1), 254(2).

Harvey; Harvey v., TexApp–Austin, 905 SW2d 760.—Divorce 169, 252.3(4), 254(1), 254(2).

Harvey; Heidelberg v., Tex, 368 SW2d 947.—App & E 100(1).

Harvey; Heidelberg v., TexCivApp–El Paso, 391 SW2d 828, ref nre.—Judgm 185(2); Ven & Pur 231(1), 239(6), 242.

Harvey; Heidelberg v., TexCivApp–El Paso, 366 SW2d 121, rev 368 SW2d 947.—Waters 127, 156(8).

Harvey; Holt Oil & Gas Corp. v., CA5 (Tex), 801 F2d 773, cert den 107 SCt 1892, 481 US 1015, 95 LEd2d 499.—Fed Civ Proc 2193, 2214, 2215, 2333.1; Fed Cts 76.5, 76.10, 76.15, 76.30, 626, 641; Mines 109.

Harvey v. Humphreys, TexCivApp–Galveston, 178 SW2d 733, writ refused wom.—Adv Poss 17, 25, 27, 31, 71(1), 101, 104, 112; App & E 1008.1(2); Execution 271; Hus & W 262.1(4), 265, 267(8); Judgm 712, 747(5).

Harvey; Johnson v., EDTex, 382 FSupp 1043, aff 516 F2d 898.—Colleges 8.1(5); Const Law 87, 4200, 4223(5), 4223(6).

Harvey; Jones v., TexCivApp–Texarkana, 380 SW2d 924.—Judgm 335(3); Plead 228.14, 228.16, 228.23; Tresp to T T 32.

Harvey; Lincoln v., TexCivApp–Dallas, 191 SW2d 764.—App & E 20; Contracts 159; Courts 121(4); Decl Judgm 186, 312.1; Judgm 660.

Harvey; Moncrief v., TexApp–Dallas, 805 SW2d 20.—App & E 343.1; Courts 517; Judgm 203, 823; New Tr 124(1).

Harvey v. Morgan, TexCivApp–Austin, 272 SW2d 621, ref nre.—Const Law 3044, 3057, 3290; Evid 20(1); Pub Amuse 5, 27.

Harvey; National Life Co. v., TexCivApp–Amarillo, 159 SW2d 920.—Action 1; Contracts 313(1); Insurance 1938, 1963, 3559.

Harvey v. Nunlist, CA5 (Tex), 499 F2d 335.—Admin Law 751; Offic 72.54; Postal 5.

Harvey v. Parks, TexCivApp–Fort Worth, 493 SW2d 286, ref nre.—Tax 2699(7).

Harvey; Peace v., CA5 (Tex), 207 FedAppx 366.—Armed S 27(4), 27(7); Civil R 1249(1), 1252, 1553; Fed Cts 915.

Harvey v. Pedigo Oil Co., Inc., TexCivApp–Fort Worth, 557 SW2d 167, ref nre.—Acct Action on 10; Costs 207; Propty 5.

Harvey; Peek v., TexCivApp–Texarkana, 599 SW2d 674, dism.—App & E 719(8); Atty & C 20.1; Int Liq 37.

Harvey v. Peters, TexCivApp–Fort Worth, 227 SW2d 867.—Adv Poss 4, 31, 49; Estop 118; Evid 370(4), 372(8); Mun Corp 980(3); Tax 2932, 2935, 2936, 3130, 3174; Ten in C 15(5).

Harvey v. Potter, CA5 (Tex), 202 FedAppx 2, cert den 127 SCt 3016.—Work Comp 1187.

Harvey; Roberts v., TexApp–El Paso, 663 SW2d 525.—App & E 1170.10; Consp 1.1, 6, 19, 21; Evid 601(4).

Harvey; San Antonio Hermann Sons Home Ass'n v., TexCivApp–Austin, 256 SW2d 906, ref nre.—App & E 930(1), 931(3), 1062.1, 1070(2); Damag 134(2); Neglig 1037(4), 1037(5), 1076, 1088, 1289, 1708, 1717; Trial 139.1(3), 140(1), 352.6.

Harvey v. Seale, Tex, 362 SW2d 310.—Land & Ten 164(6), 164(7), 168(1), 169(4), 169(11); Neglig 1037(4), 1040(3).

Harvey; Seale v., TexCivApp–Beaumont, 349 SW2d 292, writ gr, rev 362 SW2d 310.—Land & Ten 168(1).

Harvey; Smith v., TexCivApp–San Antonio, 104 SW2d 938, writ refused.—Sequest 15; Sheriffs 111.

Harvey; Staley v., TexCivApp–Texarkana, 226 SW2d 897, ref nre.—Contracts 9(1), 10(4); Sales 32.

Harvey v. Stanley, TexApp–Fort Worth, 803 SW2d 721, writ den.—App & E 994(2), 1003(3), 1003(7); Evid 574, 588; Health 675, 820, 823(11); Neglig 273, 387; Plead 237(6); Trial 105(3).

Harvey v. Stanley, TexApp–Fort Worth, 783 SW2d 217.— App & E 475.

Harvey v. State, TexCrimApp, 78 SW3d 368, on remand 2002 WL 31525279, petition for discretionary review refused.—Breach of P 15.1.

Harvey v. State, TexCrimApp, 611 SW2d 108, cert den 102 SCt 149, 454 US 840, 70 LEd2d 123.—Crim Law 273.1(4); Sent & Pun 1378, 1388.

Harvey v. State, TexCrimApp, 515 SW2d 108.—Crim Law 1182; Double J 142; Statut 61, 64(6), 109.11, 118(6).

Harvey v. State, TexCrimApp, 487 SW2d 75.—Controlled Subs 73, 80.

Harvey v. State, TexCrimApp, 485 SW2d 907.—Crim Law 324; Sent & Pun 1377, 1378, 1381(5).

Harvey v. State, TexCrimApp, 263 SW2d 788, 159 TexCrim 312.—Crim Law 1131(4).

Harvey v. State, TexCrimApp, 201 SW2d 42, 150 TexCrim 332.—Crim Law 1063(1), 1063(5), 1064(6), 1159.5; Homic 530, 909, 1136, 1326.

Harvey v. State, TexCrimApp, 109 SW2d 474, 133 TexCrim 90.—Crim Law 595(9), 596(1).

Harvey v. State, TexCrimApp, 105 SW2d 664, 132 TexCrim 487.—Forg 44(0.5).

Harvey v. State, TexCrimApp, 104 SW2d 51, 132 TexCrim 214.—Crim Law 784(1); Forg 44(0.5).

Harvey v. State, TexCrimApp, 104 SW2d 26, 132 TexCrim 213.—Forg 28(1).

Harvey v. State, TexCrimApp, 97 SW2d 478, 131 TexCrim 159.—Crim Law 938(4); Homic 1345.

Harvey v. State, TexApp–Houston (1 Dist), 762 SW2d 760, petition for discretionary review refused.—Crim Law 723(1), 823(1).

Harvey v. State, TexApp–Fort Worth, 116 SW3d 816.— Crim Law 1134(2), 1144.13(2.1), 1159.2(1), 1159.2(2), 1159.2(7), 1159.2(8), 1159.2(9), 1159.3(2), 1159.4(1), 1159.6; Mal Mis 9.

Harvey v. State, TexApp–Austin, 48 SW3d 847, reh overr, and petition for discretionary review gr, rev 78 SW3d 368, on remand 2002 WL 31525279, petition for discretionary review refused.—Breach of P 15.1; Crim Law 20, 772(1), 790, 1030(1), 1032(5), 1038.1(2), 1038.1(4), 1134(3), 1172.1(1).

Harvey v. State, TexApp–Dallas, 135 SW3d 712.—Crim Law 1134(2), 1134(3); Double J 5.1, 134; Ind & Inf 71.2(3), 133(1), 171; Obscen 13, 17.

Harvey v. State, TexApp–Texarkana, 173 SW3d 841.— Autos 355(6), 359.4; Crim Law 577.10(1), 577.10(8), 577.10(9), 577.16(2), 577.16(4), 577.16(8), 633(2), 1042, 1086.11, 1130(5), 1144.13(2.1), 1159.2(7), 1181.5(1), 1189; Sent & Pun 31.

Harvey v. State, TexApp–Texarkana, 123 SW3d 623, petition for discretionary review refused.—Const Law 3306; Crim Law 363, 366(6), 633(1), 662.8, 734, 1035(5), 1134(6), 1139, 1147, 1152(2), 1153(1), 1158(3), 1169.2(6); Jury 33(1.15), 33(2.10), 79.3, 97(1), 108; Rape 48(1).

Harvey v. State, TexApp–Texarkana, 887 SW2d 174.— Crim Law 126(1), 126(2).

Harvey v. State, TexApp–Texarkana, 847 SW2d 365.— Controlled Subs 27, 34, 82; Crim Law 753.2(5), 1144.13(6), 1159.2(7).

Harvey v. State, TexApp–Beaumont, 798 SW2d 373.— Crim Law 723(3), 796, 1063(6), 1134(2), 1170.5(6), 1172.9, 1173.2(9); Sent & Pun 106.

Harvey v. State, TexApp–Houston (14 Dist), 97 SW3d 162, reh overr, and petition for discretionary review refused. —Crim Law 641.13(1), 641.13(2.1), 737(1), 1134(5), 1147, 1156(1), 1166.18; Jury 85, 97(1), 105(2); Witn 198(2), 222.

Harvey v. State, TexApp–Houston (14 Dist), 3 SW3d 170, petition for discretionary review refused.—Crim Law 312, 339.8(1), 369.2(1), 369.15, 737(1), 741(1), 742(1), 1144.13(3), 1153(1), 1159.2(1), 1159.2(2), 1159.2(7), 1159.2(9), 1159.4(1), 1159.4(2), 1159.6, 1181.5(1), 1191; Rob 24.15(1).

Harvey v. State, TexApp–Houston (14 Dist), 821 SW2d 389, petition for discretionary review refused.—Const Law 3792, 3819, 4733(2); Crim Law 1038.2, 1172.1(1), 1173.2(1); Double J 31; Sent & Pun 1157, 2019, 2020, 2032, 2041.

Harvey v. State, TexApp–Houston (14 Dist), 681 SW2d 646, petition for discretionary review refused.—Crim Law 641.13(1), 641.13(7).

Harvey v. State, TexApp–Houston (14 Dist), 672 SW2d 23. —Crim Law 1030(1), 1077.3; Witn 2(4).

Harvey v. State, TexApp–Houston (14 Dist), 642 SW2d 222, petition for discretionary review refused, appeal after remand 672 SW2d 23.—Escape 1, 9; Ind & Inf 113.

Harvey v. State, TexCivApp–Dallas, 389 SW2d 692, ref nre.—Em Dom 262(3), 262(5); Evid 358.

Harvey; Stump v., TexCivApp–Fort Worth, 96 SW2d 411. —App & E 1040(5); Pretrial Proc 510; Set-Off 28(1).

Harvey; Texas & N. O. R. Co. v., TexCivApp–Galveston, 146 SW2d 227, writ dism, correct.—Ease 8(4).

Harvey; U.S. v., CA5 (Tex), 897 F2d 1300, cert den 111 SCt 568, 498 US 1003, 112 LEd2d 574, denial of post-conviction relief aff 992 F2d 324, cert den 114 SCt 131, 510 US 843, 126 LEd2d 95.—Arrest 63.5(5), 63.5(8); Crim Law 577.15(3), 577.16(4); Sent & Pun 841; Weap 17(4).

Harvey; U.S. v., CA5 (Tex), 100 FedAppx 262.—Crim Law 1036.1(3.1).

Harvey; U.S. v., NDTex, 131 FSupp 493.—Admin Law 229; Agric 3.4(2).

Harvey; University of North Texas v., TexApp–Fort Worth, 124 SW3d 216, reh overr, and review den, and reh of petition for review den.—App & E 837(1), 893(1), 916(1); Colleges 5; Courts 32; Mun Corp 723, 847, 854; Plead 111.36, 111.37; States 112(2).

Harvey; Vineyard v., TexCivApp–Amarillo, 231 SW2d 921, writ dism.—App & E 837(11); Neglig 1541, 1571, 1602; Trial 105(5), 350.8, 352.9.

Harvey v. Wichita Nat. Bank, TexCivApp–Fort Worth, 113 SW2d 1022.—Courts 484; Garn 71, 84; Judgm 497(1); Statut 167(1).

Harvey v. Wiley, TexCivApp–Waco, 88 SW2d 569.— Judgm 17(1), 120; Lim of Act 182(2).

Harvey; Willis v., TexCivApp–Houston, 349 SW2d 323, ref nre.—Judgm 185(2), 185.3(1); Partners 20, 21, 22, 26.

Harvey Const. Co. v. Robertson-CECO Corp., CA5 (Tex), 10 F3d 300.—Fed Civ Proc 2461; Fed Cts 303, 317, 585.1, 595, 763.1, 776, 947.

Harvey Hubbell, Inc.; Erickson v., NDTex, 593 FSupp 1319.—Prod Liab 27.

Harvey Industries, Inc. v. International Union of Electronic, Elec., Salaried Mach. and Furniture Workers, AFL-CIO; Local 376 FW, EDTex, 715 FSupp 171.— Labor & Emp 968, 1670, 1967; Rem of C 25(1); States 18.3, 18.46, 18.55; Torts 213; Tresp 76.

Harvill, Ex parte, Tex, 415 SW2d 174.—Contempt 6; Judgm 670; Receivers 72, 74.

Harvill; Foster v., TexCivApp–Waco, 353 SW2d 84.—Autos 181(1), 242(1), 245(5), 245(14), 245(24), 245(39), 245(40.1), 245(93); Neglig 273.

Harvill v. State, TexApp–Corpus Christi, 13 SW3d 478.—Child S 6, 650, 669; Crim Law 273.1(4), 273.1(5), 1026.10(2.1), 1130(5), 1177, 1181.5(8); Sent & Pun 34, 1976(3).

Harvill v. State, TexCivApp–Austin, 188 SW2d 869, writ refused.—Const Law 80(1), 2621, 2625(1); Cons Cred 5.1, 17; Licens 7(3); Penalties 1.

Harvill v. Westward Communications, L.L.C., CA5 (Tex), 433 F3d 428.—Civil R 1123, 1147, 1185, 1189, 1243, 1244; Fed Civ Proc 2497.1; Labor & Emp 2305, 2365, 2385(3).

Harvill v. Westward Communications, LLC, EDTex, 311 FSupp2d 573, aff but criticized 433 F3d 428.—Civil R 1123, 1147, 1183, 1185, 1189, 1513, 1516; Fed Civ Proc 2498; Fed Cts 18; Labor & Emp 2296, 2387(4).

Harville v. Anchor-Wate Co., CA5 (Tex), 663 F2d 598.—Contrib 5(6.1); Fed Civ Proc 2176.4, 2236, 2242; Fed Cts 409.1, 410, 870.1; Indem 72, 102; Prod Liab 8, 27, 28, 88.

Harville; Arriola v., CA5 (Tex), 781 F2d 506, cert den 107 SCt 84, 479 US 820, 93 LEd2d 38.—Counties 38; Elections 12(8).

Harville; Siebenlist v., Tex, 596 SW2d 113, on remand 609 SW2d 315.—Autos 245(5).

Harville v. Siebenlist, TexCivApp–Amarillo, 609 SW2d 315.—App & E 231(9), 1003(11); Trial 284.

Harville v. Siebenlist, TexCivApp–Amarillo, 582 SW2d 621, rev 596 SW2d 113, on remand 609 SW2d 315.—Autos 245(40.1); Evid 264; Neglig 273; Trial 349(1), 352.5(5).

Harville; Southern-Plaza Exp., Inc. v., CA5 (Tex), 233 F2d 264.—Carr 123, 131, 132, 134, 136, 137; Damag 188(1); Fed Civ Proc 2176.4.

Harville v. State, TexCrimApp, 591 SW2d 864.—Crim Law 412.2(5), 522(1), 531(3), 532(0.5), 577.1, 736(2); Homic 1186.

Harville v. Twin City Fire Ins. Co., CA5 (Tex), 885 F2d 276.—Insurance 2917, 3367.

Harville; Villanueva v., TexCivApp–San Antonio, 419 SW2d 711.—App & E 548(5); Const Law 4175; Mand 168(3).

Harville Rose Service v. Kellogg Co., CA5 (Tex), 448 F2d 1346, cert den 92 SCt 1248, 405 US 987, 31 LEd2d 453.—Contracts 245(2), 247; Evid 397(2), 413, 441(1), 441(9); Fed Cts 416.

Harvin; De Busk v., CA5 (Tex), 212 F2d 143.—Rem of C 21; U S 47.

Harvison; Henderson 66 Sales, Inc. v., NDTex, 58 FRD 408.—Fed Civ Proc 414, 2441, 2444.1, 2453; Fed Cts 683.

Harward v. State, TexCrimApp, 398 SW2d 127.—Crim Law 796.

Harwath v. Colwell, TexApp–Dallas, 648 SW2d 709.—Antitrust 146(1), 367; Princ & A 79(9).

Harwath v. Hudson, TexApp–Dallas, 654 SW2d 851, ref nre.—Mtg 354, 360.

Harwell, Ex parte, TexCivApp–Waco, 538 SW2d 667.—Atty & C 104; Child S 498; Const Law 1106, 4494; Contempt 61(1), 63(1); Divorce 269(13).

Harwell; Federal Underwriters Exchange v., TexCivApp–Waco, 157 SW2d 460, writ refused wom.—Damag 221(5.1), 221(6); Trial 255(13); Work Comp 813, 1924.

Harwell v. Growth Program, Inc., CA5 (Tex), 459 F2d 461.—Antitrust 920.

Harwell v. Growth Programs, Inc., CA5 (Tex), 451 F2d 240, opinion mod on denial of reh 459 F2d 461, cert den National Association of Securities Dealers, Inc, v. Harwell, 93 SCt 126, 409 US 876, 34 LEd2d 129.—Antitrust 920; Banks 315(1); Contracts 309(1); Evid 65; Exchanges 2, 14; Fed Civ Proc 2490.

Harwell v. Growth Programs, Inc., WDTex, 315 FSupp 1184, rev and remanded 451 F2d 240, opinion mod on denial of reh 459 F2d 461, cert den National Association of Securities Dealers, Inc, v. Harwell, 93 SCt 126, 409 US 876, 34 LEd2d 129.—Antitrust 906; Banks 315(1); Const Law 2406, 4295; Exchanges 4.

Harwell; Horne v., TexCivApp–Austin, 533 SW2d 450, ref nre.—Child C 577, 609, 610; Child S 537.

Harwell; Hutton v., TexCivApp–Fort Worth, 95 SW2d 467.—Lim of Act 4(2), 51(2).

Harwell v. Morris, TexCivApp–Amarillo, 143 SW2d 809.—App & E 747(1); Domicile 5; Elections 72, 74, 151, 154(6), 154(10); Ind & Inf 3; Judges 45.

Harwell; Morrow v., CA5 (Tex), 768 F2d 619, on remand 640 FSupp 225.—Const Law 2311, 3420; Decl Judgm 204; Fed Cts 42; Inj 22, 75, 76; Prisons 4(6), 4(10.1), 4(13); Sent & Pun 1544; U S Mag 23.

Harwell; Morrow v., WDTex, 640 FSupp 225.—Prisons 4(10.1), 4(11), 4(13); U S Mag 13.

Harwell v. Sloane, TexCivApp–Austin, 230 SW2d 558, ref nre.—App & E 846(2); Bound 37(3).

Harwell v. State, TexCrimApp, 377 SW2d 956.—Crim Law 1177; Fences 28(4).

Harwell v. State, TexCrimApp, 286 SW2d 948.—Crim Law 1090.1(1).

Harwell v. State, TexCrimApp, 286 SW2d 946.—Crim Law 1090.1(1).

Harwell v. State, TexCrimApp, 242 SW2d 388, 156 TexCrim 337.—Homic 987, 989(2), 999, 1193; Witn 193, 274(2), 277(4).

Harwell v. State, TexCrimApp, 197 SW2d 349, 149 TexCrim 559.—Crim Law 640, 1092.9; Homic 1134.

Harwell v. State, TexCrimApp, 191 SW2d 36, 149 TexCrim 43.—Crim Law 507(1), 511.1(9); Larc 55.

Harwell v. State, TexCrimApp, 182 SW2d 713, 147 TexCrim 505.—Const Law 2489; Crim Law 1077.2(1).

Harwell v. State Farm Mut. Auto. Ins. Co., Tex, 896 SW2d 170.—App & E 934(1); Estop 52(4); Insurance 2919, 3145, 3147, 3163, 3168, 3191(2), 3200, 3556; Judgm 183, 185(2).

Harwell v. State Farm Mut. Auto. Ins. Co., TexApp–Houston (1 Dist), 782 SW2d 518.—Insurance 2653, 2806.

Harwell v. State Farm Mut. Auto. Ins. Co., TexApp–Fort Worth, 876 SW2d 494, reh overr, and writ gr, aff 896 SW2d 170.—Contracts 327(1); Estop 52(5); Insurance 2919, 3111(2), 3141, 3163, 3168, 3170, 3191(7), 3200.

Harwell v. Ward County, TexCivApp–El Paso, 314 SW2d 868, ref nre.—Counties 59, 217; Evid 95; Offic 114.

Harwell & Harwell v. Clifton, TexCivApp–San Antonio, 307 SW2d 167.—Offic 119; Plead 111.18; Venue 7.5(1), 15, 22(6).

Harwell & Harwell, Inc. v. Rodriguez, TexCivApp–San Antonio, 487 SW2d 388, ref nre.—App & E 204(7), 971(2), 978(3), 1170.6, 1170.7, 1170.11; Evid 364, 375, 383(11), 536, 546; Neglig 1205(9), 1672; New Tr 56; Trial 352.10; Witn 396(2).

Harwell Properties v. Pan American Logistics Center, Inc., TexApp–San Antonio, 945 SW2d 216. See Wayne Harwell Properties v. Pan American Logistics Center, Inc.

Harwood; Binz v., TexCivApp–Fort Worth, 297 SW2d 210, writ refused.—App & E 837(4), 866(1); Stip 14(10); Wills 282, 401.

Harwood; Dezso v., TexCivApp–Austin, 926 SW2d 371, reh overr, and writ den.—App & E 517, 859; Judgm 17(9).

Harwood v. Hines Interests Ltd. Partnership, TexApp–Houston (1 Dist), 73 SW3d 450.—App & E 863, 934(1); Evid 587; Judgm 181(33); Neglig 1037(4).

Harwood v. Hunt, TexCivApp–Beaumont, 473 SW2d 287.—Partit 55(2); Plead 45, 49, 111.3, 111.30; Venue 5.1, 5.2, 5.3(1), 5.3(2), 5.3(6), 7.5(2), 7.5(3), 22(1), 81.

Harwood; International Sec. Life Ins. Co. of Dallas v., TexCivApp–Corpus Christi, 503 SW2d 378.—App & E 1177(7); Insurance 2494(1), 3343, 3571.

Harwood; Lang v., TexCivApp–Waco, 145 SW2d 945.—App & E 757(1), 757(2), 758.3(1), 760(2), 761, 766, 1062.1; Chat Mtg 176(2), 176(5), 292(1); Estop 76; Hus & W 210(2); Plead 291(2), 299, 428(3); Trial 352.4(3).

Harwood v. State, TexCrimApp, 115 SW2d 955, 134 TexCrim 443.—Rob 24.10.

Harwood v. State, TexApp–San Antonio, 961 SW2d 531.—Const Law 4594(1); Crim Law 419(1.5), 661, 662.7, 675, 700(2.1), 700(3), 700(4), 700(6), 700(8), 713, 721(3), 723(1), 730(1), 730(6), 730(10), 730(14), 1091(5), 1153(1), 1168(2), 1170(1), 1170(2), 1170(3), 1171.1(2.1), 1171.1(3), 1171.1(6), 1171.5; Homic 975, 986, 997, 999, 1051(1), 1051(2), 1051(5), 1054; Sent & Pun 117; Witn 270(2).

Harwood & Associates, Inc. v. Texas Bank and Trust, CA5 (Tex), 654 F2d 1073.—Banks 133; Fed Civ Proc 2608.1; Frds St of 17.

Harwood Tire-Arlington, Inc. v. Young, TexApp–Fort Worth, 963 SW2d 881, dism by agreement.—App & E 930(1), 1001(1), 1001(3), 1050.1(1), 1056.1(1); Corp 1.4(1), 1.4(4), 1.5(1), 1.5(3), 1.7(2), 215; Damag 182; Labor & Emp 2881; Lim of Act 126; Neglig 202.

Haryanto v. Saeed, TexApp–Houston (14 Dist), 860 SW2d 913, reh den, and writ den.—App & E 207, 219(2), 232(0.5), 233(2), 237(1), 882(1), 968, 1004(3), 1004(7), 1004(11), 1043(1), 1050.1(1), 1051.1(1), 1051.1(2), 1056.1(1), 1060.1(1); Assault 27, 37, 39; Damag 48, 94, 130, 178; Extort 34; False Imp 23, 36; Jury 131(1), 131(2), 131(6), 131(15.1), 131(17); Pretrial Proc 45, 313; Torts 436; Trial 125(2), 125(4), 131(2), 133.3, 133.6(4), 133.6(5).

Hasbro, Inc., In re, TexApp–Dallas, 97 SW3d 894, set aside 2003 WL 1983720.—Atty & C 24; Costs 2, 221.

Hasbro, Inc.; Hagaman v., SDTex, 710 FSupp 1119.—Trademarks 1136(2), 1241, 1800.

H.A.S. Const. Co.; Pelican Elec., Inc. v., TexApp–Houston (14 Dist), 720 SW2d 241.—App & E 1175(1).

Hasdorff; Davis v., TexCivApp–San Antonio, 207 SW2d 424.—App & E 846(5), 931(1); Autos 372(4); Bailm 31(1), 31(3); Trial 142, 382.

Hasek v. State, TexCrimApp, 384 SW2d 722.—Crim Law 719(1), 1037.1(1), 1171.2.

Hasette; U.S. v., CA5 (Tex), 898 F2d 994.—Cust Dut 126(2).

Hash; Hines v., Tex, 843 SW2d 464.—Abate & R 19; Antitrust 286, 297; App & E 870(2).

Hash v. Hines, TexApp–Amarillo, 796 SW2d 312, writ gr, rev 843 SW2d 464.—Abate & R 19; Antitrust 286.

Hash v. James, TexCivApp–San Antonio, 337 SW2d 506, ref nre.—Tresp to T T 7, 38(1), 41(1); Trial 141.

Hash v. State, TexCrimApp, 141 SW2d 345, 139 TexCrim 532.—Crim Law 730(12), 1171.6; Rape 44, 51(3); Sent & Pun 1422.

Hasha; Foster Cathead Co. v., CA5 (Tex), 382 F2d 761, cert den 88 SCt 819, 390 US 906, 19 LEd2d 872.—Pat 26(1.1), 118.21, 243(1), 324.5.

Hashop v. Rockwell Space Operations Co., SDTex, 867 FSupp 1287.—Civil R 1137, 1243, 1252, 1536; Fed Civ Proc 2470, 2470.1, 2543, 2544, 2552; Labor & Emp 788, 789, 792, 2251, 2266, 2267, 2385(6); Lim of Act 58(1).

Haskell; Anglo-Dutch Petroleum Intern., Inc. v., TexApp–Houston (1 Dist), 193 SW3d 87, reh overr, and review den, and reh of petition for review den.—Assign 65; Contracts 193, 328(1); Judgm 183, 185(2), 185(5), 185.3(2); Sec Reg 11.25, 309; Statut 241(2); Usury 6, 11, 13, 16, 39, 72, 113.

Haskell v. Border City Bank, TexApp–El Paso, 649 SW2d 133.—App & E 185(1); Bills & N 519; Elect of Rem 1, 3(1); Nova 5; Plead 236(1); Proc 158; Release 55.

Haskell County; West Texas Utilities Co. v., TexCivApp–Eastland, 490 SW2d 237.—Em Dom 292; High 159(2); Inj 204; Venue 5.1.

Haskell Independent School Dist. v. Ferguson, TexCivApp–Eastland, 178 SW2d 130, writ refused wom.—App & E 373(1), 499(1), 501(1), 758.3(1), 758.3(11), 878(1), 1052(5).

Haskell Nat. Bank; Ferguson v., TexCivApp–Eastland, 127 SW2d 242.—Banks 130(1).

Haskell Nat. Bank of Haskell v. Ferguson, TexCivApp–Eastland, 155 SW2d 427.—Inj 26(5); Judgm 720, 745; Prohib 9.

Haskell Tel. Co.; U.S. v., NDTex, 42 FSupp 498.—Atty & C 141; Courts 493(3); Int Rev 4775, 4794.1, 4800.

Hasker v. State, TexApp–Houston (1 Dist), 725 SW2d 443.—Crim Law 339.7(4), 339.8(4), 339.10(6.1), 339.10(7), 1169.1(5).

Haskett v. Butts, TexApp–Waco, 83 SW3d 213, review den, and reh of petition for review den.—App & E 215(1), 215(3), 216(1), 930(1), 989, 1001(1), 1001(3), 1003(6), 1026, 1050.1(11); Damag 51; Health 684, 706, 830.

Haskett v. Harris, TexCivApp–Corpus Christi, 567 SW2d 841.—App & E 185(1); Contempt 24; Prohib 1, 3(1), 16.

Haskin, Ex parte, TexApp–Corpus Christi, 801 SW2d 12.—Contempt 61(5); Hab Corp 445, 447, 462.

Haskins v. Cherry, TexCivApp–Dallas, 202 SW2d 691, writ refused.—Work Comp 367, 2097.

Haskins v. Finks, TexCivApp–Eastland, 470 SW2d 717, ref nre.—Judgm 162(4).

Haskins v. First City Nat. Bank of Lufkin, TexApp–Beaumont, 698 SW2d 754.—Deeds 145, 165.

Haskins v. Montgomery Ward & Co., Inc., SDTex, 73 FRD 499.—Fed Civ Proc 161.1, 165, 181; Garn 248.

Haskins v. Panhandle & S. F. Ry. Co., TexCivApp–Amarillo, 89 SW2d 831, writ dism.—Carr 320(1); Trial 178.

Haskins v. State, TexApp–Corpus Christi, 960 SW2d 207.—Autos 332, 355(6), 359; Crim Law 553, 741(1), 742(1), 1144.12, 1170.5(1), 1177; Witn 360.

Haskins; U.S. v., EDTex, 773 FSupp 965, aff 983 F2d 1061.—Arrest 63.5(4); Autos 349(5), 349(17), 349.5(3); Searches 180, 181.

Haskins v. Winters, TexApp–Dallas, 641 SW2d 603, ref nre.—Ease 14(2), 15.1, 16, 17(1), 17(5), 18(1), 18(4), 61(12); Estop 83(1).

Haskit; Webb v., TexCivApp, 25 SW 161, writ refused.—Bankr 263, 268.

Haslam Lumber Co.; Davis v., TexCivApp–Beaumont, 213 SW2d 771, ref nre.—App & E 839(1); Inj 138.31; Logs 3(7), 3(10), 3(11), 3(15); Tresp 52.

Haslam Lumber Co.; Jumonville Pipe & Machinery Co. v., TexCivApp–Beaumont, 129 SW2d 386.—Contracts 94(3); Sales 34, 411, 417.

Hasley v. Estelle, SDTex, 425 FSupp 227.—Sent & Pun 1318, 2014.

Hasley; Ray v., CA5 (Tex), 214 F2d 366.—Abate & R 10.1; Action 69(3); Fed Cts 420; Judgm 580, 828.10(2), 958(1).

Hasley v. State, TexCrimApp, 442 SW2d 739.—Crim Law 406(1), 562, 661; Larc 59; Sent & Pun 1318; Stip 19.

Hasley v. State, TexApp–Beaumont, 786 SW2d 733, petition for discretionary review refused.—Controlled Subs 82; Crim Law 386, 444, 698(3), 1177.5(2), 1203.27.

Hasley v. State, TexApp–Beaumont, 670 SW2d 362.—Crim Law 742(1); Escape 10.

Hass v. Aetna Ins. Co., TexCivApp–Fort Worth, 391 SW2d 756, ref nre.—Evid 271(20); Princ & S 77, 156.

Hass v. State, TexCrimApp, 790 SW2d 609.—Controlled Subs 146; Crim Law 1028; Searches 112.

Hass; U.S. v., CA5 (Tex), 199 F3d 749, cert den 121 SCt 34, 531 US 812, 148 LEd2d 14.—Crim Law 1134(3), 1147, 1192.

Hass; U.S. v., CA5 (Tex), 150 F3d 443, reh den, appeal after remand 199 F3d 749, cert den 121 SCt 34, 531 US 812, 148 LEd2d 14, appeal after remand 281 F3d 1279.—Consp 24(1), 24(2), 24.5, 45, 47(12); Crim Law 369.2(3.1), 374, 1169.5(2); Sent & Pun 1209, 1286, 1302.

Hassan v. Lubbock Independent School Dist., CA5 (Tex), 55 F3d 1075, cert den 116 SCt 532, 516 US 995, 133 LEd2d 438.—Civil R 1376(2), 1376(5), 1376(7); Const Law 82(12), 4209(3); Fed Civ Proc 2470, 2470.4, 2543; Fed Cts 585.1, 776; Schools 169, 169.5.

Hassan; U.S. v., CA5 (Tex), 83 F3d 693.—Crim Law 394.1(3), 394.6(5), 1139, 1158(4), 1181.5(7).

Hassbrock v. Barnhart, SDTex, 457 FSupp2d 736.—Social S 140.76, 147, 147.5, 148.15, 175.20.

Hassell; American Rolling Mill Co. v., TexCivApp–Fort Worth, 234 SW2d 290.—Ref of Inst 46.

Hassell v. Board of Nurse Examiners, TexApp–Austin, 695 SW2d 284.—Admin Law 676, 749; Health 223(1).

Hassell v. Brotherhood of Locomotive Firemen and Enginemen, TexComApp, 87 SW2d 468, 126 Tex 256, conformed to 93 SW2d 789.—App & E 987(1); Insurance 2561(5), 2578.

Hassell; Brotherhood of Locomotive Firemen and Enginemen v., TexCivApp–Dallas, 93 SW2d 789.—Insurance 2561(1).

Hassell v. Com. Cas. & Ins. Co., Tex, 184 SW2d 917, 143 Tex 353.—Insurance 1604, 1607; Venue 8.5(2).

Hassell v. Croft, TexCivApp–Waco, 324 SW2d 272, ref nre.—Evid 478(1); Wills 166(1), 324(3).

Hassell; Delhi Gas Pipeline Corp. v., TexApp–Tyler, 730 SW2d 159.—Decl Judgm 392.1.

Hassell v. Frey, Tex, 117 SW2d 413, 131 Tex 578.—Wills 58(2), 435, 439, 440, 441, 487(1), 506(1), 506(5), 608(1), 608(3.1).

Hassell; Frey v., TexCivApp–El Paso, 97 SW2d 970, rev 117 SW2d 413, 131 Tex 578.—Wills 439, 601(2).

Hassell v. Great Southern Life Ins. Co., TexCivApp–Galveston, 103 SW2d 442, writ dism.—Insurance 2027.

Hassell; Green v., TexApp–Tyler, 764 SW2d 391.—Child C 602; Mand 26.

Hassell v. Missouri Pacific R. Co., TexApp–Tyler, 880 SW2d 39, reh den and writ den.—App & E 863, 934(1); Courts 97(1); Judgm 181(7), 185(2), 185(5); Labor & Emp 2806, 2817; Lim of Act 95(2), 95(4.1), 95(5), 179(2), 193, 197(2), 199(1).

Hassell v. New England Mut. Life Ins. Co., TexCivApp–Waco, 506 SW2d 727, writ refused.—App & E 523.1, 926(8).

Hassell v. Pruner, TexCivApp–Amarillo, 286 SW2d 266, ref nre.—App & E 930(1), 989, 1001(1); Trial 25(2), 59(2); Wills 52(1), 155.1, 163(1), 164(1), 166(1), 166(12), 324(3), 400.

Hassell v. State, TexCrimApp, 607 SW2d 529.—Crim Law 367, 415(1), 1169.11.

Hassell v. State, TexCrimApp, 194 SW2d 400, 149 TexCrim 333.—Autos 137, 351.1.

Hassell v. State, TexCrimApp, 194 SW2d 270.—Crim Law 1090.1(1).

Hassell v. Union Pacific R. Co., TexApp–Tyler, 880 SW2d 39. See Hassell v. Missouri Pacific R. Co.

Hassell; U.S. v., CA5 (Tex), 82 FedAppx 372.—Fed Civ Proc 2444.1; Int Rev 4912.

Hassell v. U.S., NDTex, 203 FRD 241.—Action 5; Atty & C 62; Fed Civ Proc 414, 425, 441, 1855.1; Int Rev 4457, 4464, 5006.

Hassell Const. Co., Inc. v. Stature Commercial Co., Inc., TexApp–Houston (14 Dist), 162 SW3d 664, on remand 2006 WL 3480099.—App & E 1008.1(2), 1010.2; Contracts 322(1), 343, 344; Costs 194.32, 207; Plead 76, 78, 87.

Hassenflu v. Pyke, CA5 (Tex), 491 F2d 1094.—Fed Civ Proc 1762; Fed Cts 708.

Hassenpflug, Ex parte, TexApp–Fort Worth, 754 SW2d 835.—Extrad 37.

Hassett; Soliz v., CA5 (Tex), 71 FedAppx 331.—Civil R 1094; Prisons 4(6), 4(11), 13.3.

Hassler v. Carson County, CA5 (Tex), 111 FedAppx 728.—Civil R 1088(5), 1454.

Hassler v. State, TexCrimApp, 473 SW2d 513.—Crim Law 517.2(3), 1134(2).

Hassler v. Texas Gypsum Co., Inc., TexCivApp–Dallas, 525 SW2d 53.—Acct Action on 13, 14; App & E 907(3); Corp 325, 361; Judgm 101(2); Plead 312.

Hasslocher v. Heger, TexApp–San Antonio, 670 SW2d 689, ref nre.—App & E 1064.1(6); Joint Adv 1.2(4), 1.15; Trial 352.1(3).

Hasslocher; Newman v., TexCivApp–San Antonio, 242 SW2d 822.—Dep & Escr 26; Ven & Pur 154.

Hastert; Burris v., TexCivApp–San Antonio, 191 SW2d 811, writ refused.—Ven & Pur 21, 22, 28, 128.

Hastey v. Bush, CA5 (Tex), 100 FedAppx 319.—Const Law 695; Judges 49(1).

Hastey v. Bush, CA5 (Tex), 82 FedAppx 370.—Anim 3.5(3); Const Law 1310; Fed Civ Proc 1837.1; Fed Cts 768.1.

Hastey v. Humphries, TexCivApp–Amarillo, 576 SW2d 159, ref nre.—Labor & Emp 3094(2), 3105(9); Plead 123.

Hastie v. Rodriguez, TexApp–Corpus Christi, 716 SW2d 675, ref nre.—Damag 51; Death 44, 89.

Hasting; Bowles v., CCA5 (Tex), 146 F2d 94.—War 155, 158, 160, 162.

Hasting; Schnitzendable v., TexCivApp–San Antonio, 97 SW2d 715.—App & E 840(1), 1033(4); Ease 10(1), 30(1), 30(2); Lim of Act 32(1); Partit 4, 9(1), 9(2).

Hasting v. Texas & Pacific Ry. Co., TexCivApp–El Paso, 313 SW2d 344.—App & E 671(2), 719(8); New Tr 144; R R 337(1).

Hasting; Texas & Pac. Ry. Co. v., TexCivApp–El Paso, 282 SW2d 758, ref nre.—App & E 1062.2; R R 327(7), 334, 335(5), 337(6), 347(1), 347(10), 350(32), 351(16); Trial 350.5(2), 350.7(6).

Hasting; Texas Farm Bureau Underwriters v., TexCivApp–El Paso, 449 SW2d 283.—Insurance 3191(12); Plead 251.

Hastings; American Cas. & Life Ins. Co. v., TexCivApp–Waco, 300 SW2d 754, ref nre.—App & E 930(1), 1001(1), 1177(7); Insurance 1652(2); Trial 142.

Hastings v. American General Ins. Co., TexCivApp–San Antonio, 547 SW2d 360, ref nre.—Costs 252; High 110, 113(5); Interest 39(1); Paymt 39(1), 47(1); Trial 350.8.

Hastings v. Champer, TexCivApp–Texarkana, 139 SW2d 863.—App & E 1050.1(3.1); Evid 441(1), 441(8), 448, 461(1).

Hastings v. De Leon, TexCivApp–San Antonio, 532 SW2d 147, ref nre.—Courts 91(1); Neglig 1040(3), 1040(4), 1104(5).

Hastings; Dixon v., CA5 (Tex), 202 FedAppx 750.—Const Law 4824; Hab Corp 253; Prisons 13(7.1), 13(8).

Hastings v. Houston Shell & Concrete, TexCivApp–Hous (1 Dist), 596 SW2d 142, ref nre.—Frds St of 44(1), 119(1); Lim of Act 127(3).

Hastings; Maples v., TexCivApp–Amarillo, 97 SW2d 507.—Land & Ten 233(2).

Hastings v. North East Independent School Dist., CA5 (Tex), 615 F2d 628.—Fed Civ Proc 1271, 1278; Fed Cts 769, 820.

Hastings v. Pichinson, TexCivApp–San Antonio, 370 SW2d 1.—Deeds 43, 75; Land & Ten 32; Mines 73, 78.2, 78.5, 78.7(1).

Hastings v. Royal-Globe Ins. Companies, TexCivApp–San Antonio, 521 SW2d 869.—Insurance 2921, 2933, 3549(3), 3557; Lim of Act 24(2), 43, 46(1); Plead 111.39(1).

Hastings; Sanchez v., Tex, 898 SW2d 287.—Lim of Act 105(2).

Hastings; Sanchez v., TexApp–San Antonio, 880 SW2d 471, reh den, and writ gr, rev 898 SW2d 287.—Atty & C 129(1); Judgm 185(2); Lim of Act 95(11), 104(1).

Hastings v. Selby Oil & Gas Co., USTex, 63 SCt 1114, 319 US 348, 87 LEd 1443, reh den 63 SCt 1443, 320 US 214, 87 LEd 1851.—Fed Cts 7.

Hastings v. State, TexApp–Austin, 82 SW3d 493, reh overr, and petition for discretionary review refused.— Crim Law 824(2), 1038.2, 1144.13(3), 1159.2(1), 1159.2(7), 1159.6; Obst Just 16.

Hastings v. State, TexApp–San Antonio, 755 SW2d 183, petition for discretionary review refused.—Crim Law 996(1), 1172.1(2); Jury 33(1.15), 33(5.15), 120.

Hastings v. State, TexApp–Dallas, 641 SW2d 332, petition for discretionary review refused.—Crim Law 770(2), 784(1), 787(1), 800(1), 1120(1), 1169.2(3), 1171.5; Sent & Pun 1377, 1379(2); Witn 318.

Hastings v. State, TexApp–Amarillo, 20 SW3d 786, petition for discretionary review refused.—Controlled Subs 100(1); Crim Law 1037.1(2), 1169.1(1), 1169.11; Sent & Pun 309, 329, 1408.

Hastings v. Thweatt, TexCivApp–Austin, 425 SW2d 661. —Bailm 14(1), 31(3).

Hastings; Tran v., CA5 (Tex), 98 FedAppx 296.—Courts 100(1); Hab Corp 285.1.

Hastings Mfg. Co.; Gaines Motor Sales Co. v., TexCivApp–Fort Worth, 104 SW2d 548, writ dism.—Evid 419(1), 419(15), 432, 448; Sales 348(1), 354(9).

Hastings Oil Co. v. Texas Co., Tex, 234 SW2d 389, 149 Tex 416.—App & E 874(2); Courts 26; Inj 48; Mines 52.

Hastings Oil Co. v. Texas Co., TexCivApp–Galveston, 227 SW2d 317, aff 234 SW2d 389, 149 Tex 416.—App & E 78(3), 843(2), 954(1), 954(2), 1041(2); Inj 135, 138.31, 144, 152, 153.

Hasty v. A & B Const. Co., TexCivApp–San Antonio, 612 SW2d 267.—New Tr 165; Trial 14.

Hasty; Gunter v., TexCivApp–Waco, 422 SW2d 198, ref nre.—Lim of Act 122.

Hasty v. Johnson, CA5 (Tex), 103 FedAppx 816.—Civil R 1395(7); Fed Civ Proc 1788.10; Prisons 17(2); Sent & Pun 1546; U S Mag 31.

Hasty v. McKnight, TexCivApp–Texarkana, 460 SW2d 949, ref nre.—Deeds 93, 120; Mines 55(4), 62.1.

Hasty v. Rust Engineering Co., CA5 (Tex), 726 F2d 1068.—Courts 96(3); Fed Cts 386.

Hasty; Ward v., TexCivApp–Austin, 295 SW2d 433.— Autos 20; Chat Mtg 68; Evid 386(1); Sales 313.

Hasty Inc. v. Inwood Buckhorn Joint Venture, TexApp–Dallas, 908 SW2d 494, writ den.—App & E 204(1), 842(2), 984(1), 984(5), 989, 994(3), 1008.1(2), 1012.1(2), 1012.1(5), 1012.1(9), 1032(2), 1050.1(1), 1050.1(11); Contracts 143(2), 143.5, 147(1), 152, 169, 176(2); Costs 12, 32(1), 32(2), 32(3), 194.12, 194.40, 207; Decl Judgm 2, 142, 186; Land & Ten 37, 76(4), 86(1), 154(3); Pretrial Proc 45.

Hatch, Ex parte, Tex, 410 SW2d 773.—Child S 232, 240, 399, 444, 446, 456, 459, 461, 470.

Hatch v. Davis, TexCivApp–Corpus Christi, 621 SW2d 443, ref nre.—App & E 1079; Costs 194.32, 252; Courts 57(2); Penalties 1.

Hatch; Edwards v., TexCivApp–Waco, 106 SW2d 741.— Bills & N 92(3), 443(4); Judgm 243.

Hatch; Kubena v., Tex, 193 SW2d 175, 144 Tex 627.— Judgm 28; Tax 2736, 2918, 2927, 2929, 2936.

Hatch v. Kubena, TexCivApp–Austin, 190 SW2d 175, rev 193 SW2d 175, 144 Tex 627.—Home 105, 206; Judgm 279, 485, 526; Tax 2927, 2929, 3162(2), 3162(4).

Hatch v. National Cash Register Corp., TexCivApp–San Antonio, 105 SW2d 1114.—App & E 927(7); Contracts 99(1); Sales 52(1), 52(5.1), 121.

Hatch v. Sallas, TexCivApp–Beaumont, 263 SW2d 610.— App & E 933(1), 1015(1), 1069.1; New Tr 144.

Hatch v. State, TexCrimApp, 958 SW2d 813.—Jury 29(5).

Hatch v. State, TexApp–Dallas, 923 SW2d 98, petition for discretionary review gr, rev 958 SW2d 813.—Crim Law 872.5; Jury 149.

Hatch; Texas Life Ins. Co. v., TexCivApp–Eastland, 167 SW2d 802, writ refused wom.—Atty & C 141; Evid 474(3), 570, 571(1), 574; Insurance 1758, 3015, 3375; Stip 14(1); Trial 356(5).

Hatch v. Turner, Tex, 193 SW2d 668, 145 Tex 17.—Ex & Ad 453(2); Insurance 1768, 1844, 1845(1), 2097, 2098, 2431, 3065, 3125(2), 3488.

Hatch v. Turner, TexCivApp–Texarkana, 191 SW2d 701, rev 193 SW2d 668, 145 Tex 17.—Evid 80(1); Insurance 2431, 3488.

Hatch v. Wal-Mart Stores Inc., CA5 (Tex), 200 FedAppx 310.—Fed Civ Proc 2545, 2546; Torts 351; Trover 4.

Hatch v. Williams, TexApp–Waco, 110 SW3d 516.—Adv Poss 114(1); App & E 179(2), 197(1), 846(5), 852, 931(1), 977(5), 989, 1008.1(2), 1010.1(1), 1010.1(2), 1010.2, 1012.1(3), 1012.1(4), 1182; Equity 72(1); Estop 52.10(2), 54, 90(1); New Tr 6, 26, 97, 103; Ref of Inst 17(2), 19(1), 22, 23, 32; Tresp to T T 33.

Hatchel; Watts v., TexCivApp–Beaumont, 249 SW2d 69. —Child C 26, 68, 76, 641, 784, 914, 921(1).

Hatchell v. State, TexApp–Beaumont, 679 SW2d 614.— Crim Law 1170.5(1); Witn 75.

Hatcher, Ex parte, TexCrimApp, 894 SW2d 364.—Pardon 67, 70.1, 71; Prisons 15(3), 15(5); Sent & Pun 1157.

Hatcher v. Budget Rent-A-Car Systems, Inc., CA5 (Tex), 617 F2d 91.—Antitrust 214.

Hatcher; Cadenhead v., TexApp–Fort Worth, 13 SW3d 861, reh overr.—App & E 173(13), 1073(1); Judgm 181(24), 183, 185(2); Land & Ten 164(1), 164(3), 164(6), 167(8).

Hatcher v. City of Galveston, TexApp–Houston (1 Dist), 775 SW2d 37.—Judgm 181(33); Mun Corp 741.40(1).

Hatcher v. Continental Southland Sav. & Loan Ass'n, TexComApp, 80 SW2d 299, 124 Tex 601.—B & L Assoc 33(5), 33(21).

Hatcher; Hatley v., TexCivApp–Dallas, 376 SW2d 943.— App & E 173(1), 931(3); Atty & C 140; Lim of Act 197(4); Trial 140(1), 382.

Hatcher v. Jack Miller Milling Corp., TexCivApp–Texarkana, 501 SW2d 439, ref nre.—Corp 99(2).

Hatcher; Lord v., TexCivApp–Galveston, 83 SW2d 758, writ dism.—App & E 724(2); Wills 55(1), 324(2), 386.

Hatcher v. Mewbourn, TexCivApp–Texarkana, 457 SW2d 151, ref nre.—Autos 146, 150, 160(1), 244(36.1), 245(15); Neglig 380.

Hatcher v. State, TexComApp, 81 SW2d 499, 125 Tex 84, 98 ALR 1213.—Lim of Act 12(2), 28(1); Schools 65, 92(1).

Hatcher v. State, TexApp–Texarkana, 916 SW2d 643, reh overr, and petition for discretionary review refused.— Crim Law 394.6(5), 1158(4); Searches 58.

Hatcher; Texas Emp. Ins. Ass'n v., TexCivApp–Waco, 365 SW2d 641, ref nre.—App & E 927(7), 934(1); Work Comp 1385, 1396, 1719.

Hatcher; U.S. v., CA5 (Tex), 423 F2d 1086, cert den 91 SCt 45, 400 US 848, 27 LEd2d 86.—Crim Law 365(1), 369.1, 370, 371(1), 372(14), 673(5), 1166(6).

Hatcher v. Weatherall, TexCivApp–Texarkana, 551 SW2d 179.—App & E 262(1), 302(5), 1010.1(10); Contracts 156; Interest 39(3); Sales 75.

Hatcher; Westinghouse Electric Elevator Co. v., CCA5 (Tex), 133 F2d 109.—Labor & Emp 3137; Neglig 1205(8), 1633, 1639, 1708.

Hatcher Cleaning Co. v. Comerica Bank-Texas, TexApp–Fort Worth, 995 SW2d 933.—App & E 852; Banks 148(0.5), 148(3), 148(4); Judgm 181(17).

Hatchet v. Nettles, CA5 (Tex), 201 F3d 651.—Fed Civ Proc 2734.

Hatchett v. State, TexApp–Houston (14 Dist), 930 SW2d 844, petition for discretionary review refused.—Assault 56, 92(3); Crim Law 1036.1(1), 1036.2, 1134(3), 1144.13(3), 1158(3), 1159.2(7), 1178; Jury 33(5.15).

Hatchett v. State, TexCivApp–Eastland, 211 SW2d 771.— Em Dom 201, 262(5).

Hatchett; U.S. v., CA5 (Tex), 923 F2d 369, on remand 765 FSupp 349.—Crim Law 1042, 1134(3), 1177, 1181.5(8); Sent & Pun 674, 783, 804, 976.

Hatchett; U.S. v., CA5 (Tex), 224 FedAppx 434.—Banks 509.25; Jury 34(6).

Hatchett; U.S. v., WDTex, 765 FSupp 349.—Sent & Pun 362.

Hatchett; U.S. v., WDTex, 741 FSupp 622, aff U.S. v. Soto, 952 F2d 400.—Sent & Pun 650, 654, 860, 985.

Hatchett v. Williams, TexCivApp–Hous (1 Dist), 437 SW2d 334, ref nre, cert den 90 SCt 437, 396 US 963, 24 LEd2d 427.—Antitrust 535, 537, 575, 625; Commerce 60(1); Contracts 325; Cust Dut 93; Guar 12; Sales 168.5(1); Trial 350.4(2).

Hatfield, Ex parte, TexCrimApp, 238 SW2d 788, 156 TexCrim 92.—Crim Law 994(4); Hab Corp 503.1; Sent & Pun 1125, 1130, 1138, 1300.

Hatfield v. Anthony Forest Products Co., CA5 (Tex), 642 F2d 175.—Damag 132(1); Death 99(4); Work Comp 1065, 2100, 2136.

Hatfield; AutoNation, Inc. v., TexApp–Houston (14 Dist), 186 SW3d 576, reh overr.—Courts 516; Inj 26(1), 26(3), 33, 138.1, 157, 204.

Hatfield v. Board of Firemen, Policemen and Fire Alarm Operators Pension Fund, TexCivApp–El Paso, 472 SW2d 319.—Mun Corp 187(2), 187(9).

Hatfield v. Brown & Root, Inc., EDTex, 245 FSupp 733.—Seamen 29(5.14).

Hatfield v. Christoph, TexCivApp–Waco, 539 SW2d 396.—Divorce 399(1); Interest 39(3); Judgm 273(1), 326.

Hatfield v. City of Port Arthur, TexCivApp–Beaumont, 598 SW2d 669.—Abate & R 15; App & E 1190; Inj 114(2); Mand 7; Plead 106(1), 108, 111.48.

Hatfield; CU Lloyd's of Texas v., TexApp–Houston (14 Dist), 126 SW3d 679, review den.—Contracts 143(2); Corp 1.3; Evid 448; Insurance 1810, 1813, 1832(2), 2268, 2269, 2278(13), 2914.

Hatfield; Decker v., TexApp–Eastland, 798 SW2d 637, writ dism woj.—Evid 555.3.

Hatfield; Gritzman v., TexCivApp–Dallas, 439 SW2d 468.—Plead 111.23; Venue 5.3(5).

Hatfield; Marin v., CA5 (Tex), 546 F2d 1230.—Divorce 231; Fed Cts 8; U S 125(9).

Hatfield v. Quantum Chemical Corp., SDTex, 920 FSupp 108.—Civil R 1019(2), 1217, 1218(3), 1218(4).

Hatfield v. Scott, CA5 (Tex), 306 F3d 223, reh den.—Const Law 947; Em Dom 2(1.1), 81.1; Fed Cts 574, 766, 776.

Hatfield v. State, TexCrimApp, 377 SW2d 647.—Assault 92(4), 96(7); Crim Law 564(1), 564(2), 564(3), 1098, 1144.6.

Hatfield v. State, TexCrimApp, 276 SW2d 829, 161 TexCrim 362.—Arrest 63.4(12); Crim Law 622.1(2), 890, 992, 1169.1(8), 1169.1(10), 1184(1); Rob 24.40; Searches 164; Sent & Pun 1367.

Hatfield v. State, TexCrimApp, 243 SW2d 34, 156 TexCrim 425.—Homic 1490.

Hatfield v. State, TexCrimApp, 188 SW2d 175.—Crim Law 1094(3).

Hatfield v. State, TexApp–Dallas, 747 SW2d 1.—Const Law 3831, 4756; Crim Law 1043(3); Jury 80.

Hatfield-Holcomb, Inc.; Patterson v., TexCivApp–Waco, 582 SW2d 899.—App & E 253, 930(3); Impl & C C 34, 100; Plead 34(1), 404.

Hathaway; Carson v., TexApp–El Paso, 997 SW2d 760.—App & E 946; Child S 32, 231, 341, 357, 549, 556(1).

Hathaway v. General Mills, Inc., Tex, 711 SW2d 227, 69 ALR4th 1139.—Labor & Emp 47, 265.

Hathaway; General Mills, Inc. v., TexApp–Dallas, 694 SW2d 96, writ gr, rev 711 SW2d 227, 69 ALR4th 1139.—Judgm 199(3.14); Labor & Emp 40(2), 40(3), 169, 173.

Hathaway; Gilbreath v., TexApp–Beaumont, 108 SW3d 365, review den.—Damag 38, 134(1); Neglig 440(1), 1741; Trial 351.5(6).

Hathaway; Louis Thames Chevrolet Co. v., TexApp–Houston (1 Dist), 712 SW2d 602.—App & E 218.2(3.1), 237(5), 238(2), 302(1), 1070(2); Autos 242(6), 244(31).

Hathaway; Miller v., TexCivApp–Austin, 477 SW2d 655.—Life Est 12.

Hathaway v. New York Cas. Co., CCA5 (Tex), 152 F2d 684.—Work Comp 1297, 1927.

Hathaway; Russell v., NDTex, 423 FSupp 833.—Courts 96(4); Elections 21; Fed Cts 1013.

Hathaway v. Tascosa Country Club, Inc., TexApp–Amarillo, 846 SW2d 614, reh den.—App & E 189(1); Judgm 181(33), 189; Neglig 332; Pub Amuse 78, 82, 84.

Hathaway; Thames Chevrolet Co. v., TexApp–Houston (1 Dist), 712 SW2d 602. See Louis Thames Chevrolet Co. v. Hathaway.

Hathcock v. Acme Truck Lines, Inc., CA5 (Tex), 262 F3d 522, reh den, cert den 122 SCt 1298, 535 US 928, 152 LEd2d 210.—Int Rev 4376, 4849; Labor & Emp 30; Tax 3260.

Hathcock; Herring v., TexApp–El Paso, 643 SW2d 235.—Neglig 202, 1076; Venue 8.5(8).

Hathcock; U.S. v., CA5 (Tex), 441 F2d 197.—Witn 2(1), 18.

Hathcox, In re, TexApp–Texarkana, 981 SW2d 422.—App & E 893(1); Child S 5, 440, 472; Courts 85(3); Divorce 317; Judgm 106(1), 132, 191.

Hathorn, Ex parte, TexCrimApp, 189 SW2d 1021, 148 TexCrim 576.—Bail 43.

Hathorn v. Sivers, TexApp–Houston (14 Dist), 962 SW2d 284.—Child S 323; Parent & C 2(5).

Hathorn v. State, TexCrimApp, 848 SW2d 101, reh den, cert den 113 SCt 3062, 509 US 932, 125 LEd2d 744, reh den 114 SCt 28, 509 US 946, 125 LEd2d 779, habeas corpus den Ex parte Hathorn, 2006 WL 2615525.—Burg 41(4); Const Law 4559, 4745; Crim Law 126(1), 126(2), 135, 327, 641.4(1), 641.4(2), 641.13(2.1), 641.13(6), 713, 726, 761(2), 763(10), 790, 1077.3, 1150, 1152(2), 1159.5, 1166.16; Homic 598, 1165; Ind & Inf 127, 132(1), 138; Jury 33(2.15), 97(1), 108, 110(14); Sent & Pun 204, 1675, 1720, 1780(3).

Hathorne v. State, TexCrimApp, 459 SW2d 826, cert den 91 SCt 1398, 402 US 914, 28 LEd2d 657.—Crim Law 1090.11; Ind & Inf 137(7); Judges 47(1); Sent & Pun 313, 1364, 1373, 1376.

Hatke v. State, TexCrimApp, 455 SW2d 310.—Crim Law 525, 532(0.5), 842, 938(2), 945(1), 1037.1(2).

Hatley; Adcock v., TexCivApp–Eastland, 162 SW2d 1017.—App & E 1135; Princ & A 170(3).

Hatley v. American Quarter Horse Ass'n, CA5 (Tex), 552 F2d 646.—Anim 16.1, 44; Antitrust 545, 567, 572, 620, 920; Assoc 8, 20(1); Const Law 4445; Courts 489(2); Fed Cts 340.1.

Hatley; Bexar County v., Tex, 150 SW2d 980, 136 Tex 354.—Counties 54, 57, 122(1), 152, 162, 196(7); Evid 83(4).

Hatley v. Bexar County, TexCivApp–San Antonio, 144 SW2d 695, mod 150 SW2d 980, 136 Tex 354.—Counties 152, 162; Plead 129(1).

Hatley; Central and Southern Freight Lines, Inc. v., TexCivApp–Texarkana, 614 SW2d 864.—Corp 503(1), 666.

Hatley; Digby v., TexCivApp–San Antonio, 574 SW2d 186.—Game 3; Land & Ten 80(1), 80(3); Licens 43, 58(3); Plead 78, 427.

Hatley v. Hatcher, TexCivApp–Dallas, 376 SW2d 943.—App & E 173(1), 931(3); Atty & C 140; Lim of Act 197(4); Trial 140(1), 382.

Hatley; Illey v., TexApp–San Antonio, 693 SW2d 506, ref nre.—App & E 878(1), 878(2), 949; Autos 246(39.1), 246(57); Damag 148, 191; Neglig 291.

Hatley; Kassen v., Tex, 887 SW2d 4.—App & E 169; Health 770; Judgm 181(27), 181(33), 185(2); Mun Corp 723; Offic 114, 116; States 79, 112.2(2).

Hatley v. Kassen, TexApp–Dallas, 859 SW2d 367, writ gr, aff in part, rev in part 887 SW2d 4.—Action 6; App & E 854(1), 927(7), 934(1), 997(3); Compromise 16(1); Health 703(2), 770, 819, 823(14); Judges 36; Judgm 178, 185(2), 186; Mun Corp 847; Offic 114, 116; States 79; Trial 139.1(16), 139.1(17), 168.

Hatley; Receiver for Citizen's Nat. Assur. Co. v., TexApp–Austin, 852 SW2d 68.—Contracts 147(2); Release 13(3), 25, 31; Work Comp 2248.

Hatley v. Schmidt, TexCivApp–San Antonio, 471 SW2d 440, ref nre.—App & E 344; Parties 54, 65(1); Plead 252(2).

Hatley v. State, TexCrimApp, 533 SW2d 27.—Crim Law 683(1); Homic 997.

Hatley v. State, TexCrimApp, 206 SW2d 1017, 151 TexCrim 280.—Crim Law 304(6), 564(5), 726, 1091(8), 1091(11), 1165(2), 1170.5(6).

Hatley v. State, TexCrimApp, 109 SW2d 1062, 133 TexCrim 232.—Autos 355(13); Crim Law 720(9), 723(1), 1171.1(2.1).

Hatley v. State, TexApp–Texarkana, 206 SW3d 710.— Contracts 147(2), 169, 176(1), 176(2); Crim Law 273.1(2), 511.1(2.1), 511.1(7), 511.2, 511.3, 511.4, 1036.2, 1159.4(2); Evid 448; Homic 1207.

Hatmaker; Slattery v., TexCivApp–San Antonio, 255 SW2d 334.—Child S 100, 204.

Hatridge; Day & Zimmermann, Inc. v., TexApp–Texarkana, 831 SW2d 65, reh den, and writ den.—App & E 930(3), 1001(3); Courts 7; Evid 99; Frds St of 44(3), 49; Judgm 199(3.5); Labor & Emp 7, 38, 40(2), 50, 57, 79, 862; States 18.46.

Hatridge v. Day & Zimmermann, Inc., TexApp–Texarkana, 789 SW2d 654, appeal after remand 831 SW2d 65, reh den, and writ den.—Civil R 1703; Labor & Emp 757, 968, 1146; Libel 68; States 18.15, 18.46.

Hatridge v. Home Life & Acc. Ins. Co., TexCivApp– Dallas, 246 SW2d 666.—App & E 909(5); Const Law 26, 642, 1120; Insurance 1721; Usury 4, 52, 53, 78, 119.

Hatt; Luong v., NDTex, 979 FSupp 481.—Civil R 1093, 1095, 1412; Const Law 4828; Prisons 13(5), 13.5(1); Sent & Pun 1537.

Hatteberg v. Hatteberg, TexApp–Houston (1 Dist), 933 SW2d 522, reh overr.—App & E 662(4), 931(1), 946, 966(1), 989, 994(3), 1008.1(1), 1008.1(2), 1010.1(1), 1010.2, 1012.1(2), 1012.1(3), 1012.1(5), 1043(7); Child S 145, 148, 214, 215, 339(1), 556(1); Divorce 145, 235, 253(3), 286(5); Pretrial Proc 721, 724; Trial 382.

Hatteberg; Hatteberg v., TexApp–Houston (1 Dist), 933 SW2d 522, reh overr.—App & E 662(4), 931(1), 946, 966(1), 989, 994(3), 1008.1(1), 1008.1(2), 1010.1(1), 1010.2, 1012.1(2), 1012.1(3), 1012.1(5), 1043(7); Child S 145, 148, 214, 215, 339(1), 556(1); Divorce 145, 235, 253(3), 286(5); Pretrial Proc 721, 724; Trial 382.

Hatteberg v. Red Adair Co., Inc. Employees' Profit Sharing Plan and its Related Trust, CA5 (Tex), 79 FedAppx 709.—Fed Civ Proc 81, 1877.1, 1962; Judges 49(1); Labor & Emp 436, 461, 466, 482, 493, 563(5), 597, 643, 648, 715, 795, 797; Lim of Act 99(1).

Hatten v. City of Houston, TexCivApp–Houston, 373 SW2d 525, ref nre.—Action 16, 18; App & E 66, 80(6), 624, 1043(7); Const Law 961, 2356, 4361, 4372; Courts 78, 475(13); Decl Judgm 211, 251, 319, 344, 345.1, 392.1, 395; Evid 5(2); Jury 10, 12(1.1), 14(12.5), 19(1), 31.1; Mun Corp 108.6, 122.1(2), 122.1(4), 911, 917(1), 918(3); Plead 8(20); Pretrial Proc 711, 716, 723.1; Statut 64(1); Waters 203(3), 203(10).

Hatten; Lone Star Steel Co. v., TexApp–Texarkana, 104 SW3d 323, reh den.—Labor & Emp 806, 810, 863(2).

Hatten v. Mohr Chevrolet Co., TexCivApp–Dallas, 366 SW2d 945.—App & E 934(1); Fraud 43; Plead 34(1); Usury 111(3).

Hatten v. Rains, CA5 (Tex), 854 F2d 687, cert den 109 SCt 3156, 490 US 1106, 104 LEd2d 1019.—Const Law 82(8), 977, 1440, 1464, 1466, 1477, 3071, 3095, 3098(3), 3653; Fed Cts 172; Judges 4, 7.

Hatten; Rose v., TexCivApp–Houston, 417 SW2d 456.— App & E 80(1); Divorce 162, 249.1, 254(1); Judgm 526, 528.

Hatten v. State, TexCrimApp, 71 SW3d 332, on remand 89 SW3d 160.—Crim Law 641.2(2), 641.4(1), 641.4(2), 641.7(1); Sent & Pun 2009, 2014.

Hatten v. State, TexApp–Texarkana, 89 SW3d 160.—Sent & Pun 2014.

Hatten v. State, TexApp–Texarkana, 32 SW3d 868, petition for discretionary review gr, rev 71 SW3d 332, on remand 89 SW3d 160.—Sent & Pun 1914, 2014.

Hatten v. State, TexApp–Corpus Christi, 978 SW2d 608, aff and remanded, opinion after remand 1998 WL 34201880.—Crim Law 625.10(2.1), 625.15, 1144.9; Mental H 432.

Hatten; State ex rel. Vance v., TexCrimApp, 600 SW2d 828.—Const Law 3819; Mand 61; Sent & Pun 1825, 1827, 1853, 1936.

Hatten; State ex rel. Vance v., TexCrimApp, 508 SW2d 625.—Courts 207.4(1.1), 247(2); Crim Law 1192; Mand 61.

Hattenbach, In re, TexApp–Waco, 999 SW2d 636.—Child C 751; Child S 504, 509(1); Mand 3(3), 28, 172; Statut 176, 181(1), 188, 206.

Hatter; Chaffino v., TexCivApp–Waco, 410 SW2d 924.— App & E 302(5); Autos 247; Trial 358.

Hatter; State Board of Registration for Professional Engineers v., TexCivApp–Waco, 139 SW2d 171.—App & E 1172(1).

Hatter; State Bd. of Registration for Professional Engineers v., TexCivApp–Waco, 139 SW2d 169.—Licens 38; Mand 142.

Hatter v. Worst, TexCivApp–Amarillo, 390 SW2d 293, ref nre.—Admin Law 229; Counties 18; Judgm 181(2), 181(27), 185(2), 185.2(9), 185.3(1); Mand 72.

Hatteras v. Southwestern Bell Telephone Co., CA5 (Tex), 774 F2d 1341.—Civil R 1304; Const Law 3912, 4370; Tel 897.

Hatterick; Ervay-Canton Apartments v., TexCivApp– Fort Worth, 239 SW2d 150, ref nre.—App & E 1062.1; Evid 150, 188, 194; Trial 39, 350.6(1), 352.1(3).

Hattersley v. State, TexCrimApp, 487 SW2d 354, stay den 93 SCt 1376, 410 US 923, 35 LEd2d 585, cert den 93 SCt 1900, 411 US 932, 36 LEd2d 391.—Controlled Subs 75, 118; Crim Law 260.11(2).

Hattman; Goshorn v., TexCivApp–Beaumont, 387 SW2d 422, ref nre.—App & E 230, 1003(11), 1170.6, 1170.7; Autos 168(6), 171(8), 171(11); Damag 191; Evid 351.

Hatton, In re, CA5 (Tex), 96 FedAppx 941.—Bankr 2187, 3771.

Hatton; Brennan v., CA5 (Tex), 474 F2d 9, 20 Wage & Hour Cas (BNA) 1166, cert den 94 SCt 132, 414 US 826, 21 Wage & Hour Cas (BNA) 298, 38 LEd2d 60.— Commerce 62.51; Labor & Emp 2269.

Hatton; Burgess v., TexCivApp–Beaumont, 209 SW2d 999, writ refused.—Deeds 15, 17(4), 18, 19; Hus & W 70, 80; Stip 14(10); Tresp to T T 38(1); Trial 45(1); Wills 88(6).

Hatton v. Burgess, TexCivApp–Beaumont, 167 SW2d 260, writ refused wom.—Adv Poss 60(3), 115(5); Deeds 38(1); Judgm 21.

Hatton; Commercial Credit Equipment Corp. v., NDTex, 429 FSupp 997.—Contrib 4; Guar 36(5), 36(9), 62, 71, 100; Sec Tran 240; Subrog 7(1).

Hatton v. Gonzalez, TexCivApp–Corpus Christi, 541 SW2d 197.—Judgm 143(2), 151, 153(1), 160.

Hatton v. Grigar, TexApp–Houston (14 Dist), 66 SW3d 545, rule 537(f) motion den.—App & E 173(5), 846(5), 852, 989, 994(1), 1008.1(3), 1010.1(1), 1010.2, 1012.1(4), 1122(2); Costs 194.40; Dedi 1, 15, 16.1, 17, 18(2), 20(5), 30.1, 41, 45, 55; High 1, 5.

Hatton v. Highlands Ins. Co., TexApp–Tyler, 631 SW2d 787.—New Tr 143(2), 157; Work Comp 1727, 1797.

Hatton; Hodgson v., SDTex, 348 FSupp 895, 20 Wage & Hour Cas (BNA) 549.—Commerce 62.49; Labor & Emp 2227.

Hatton v. State, TexCrimApp, 217 SW2d 1021, 153 Tex-Crim 94.—Larc 46, 59.

Hatton v. State, TexCrimApp, 93 SW2d 444.—Crim Law 1182.

Hatton v. State Bd. of Control, Tex, 204 SW2d 390, 146 Tex 160.—Mental H 41, 47.1, 48, 59.1, 60, 61.

Hatton; Texas Emp. Ins. Ass'n v., Tex, 255 SW2d 848, 152 Tex 199.—Trial 115(3); Work Comp 1022.1, 1926, 1983.

Hatton; Texas Emp. Ins. Ass'n v., TexCivApp–El Paso, 252 SW2d 754, rev 255 SW2d 848, 152 Tex 199.—Trial 186, 194(19), 233(2); Work Comp 546, 1686, 1926, 1932, 1968(3).

Hatton v. Turner, TexCivApp–Tyler, 622 SW2d 450.—App & E 1010.1(3); Lim of Act 103(4); Trusts 91, 95, 103(1), 110, 365(5); Witn 159(3).

Hatz; Rosas v., TexApp–Waco, 147 SW3d 560.—Antitrust 161, 162; App & E 242(2), 275, 1058(2); Brok 102; Fraud 13(1), 13(3), 16; Judgm 178, 181(18), 185(4), 189.

Hatzenbuehler, In re, BkrtcyNDTex, 282 BR 828.—Bankr 2233(3).

Hatzenbuehler v. Call, TexApp–San Antonio, 894 SW2d 68, reh overr, and writ den.—Usury 6, 16, 48, 113.

Haubold v. Intermedics, Inc., CA5 (Tex), 11 F3d 1333, reh den.—Fed Cts 611; Labor & Emp 41(4), 576, 612, 688.

Hauck; Andrade v., CA5 (Tex), 452 F2d 1071.—Civil R 1395(7); Const Law 2330, 4827; Convicts 6; Fed Cts 743.

Hauck; Cameron v., CA5 (Tex), 383 F2d 966, cert den 88 SCt 777, 389 US 1039, 19 LEd2d 828.—Const Law 250.2(1), 3789, 4581, 4637, 4715; Crim Law 5, 731; False Pret 1, 12, 34, 49(6); Fed Civ Proc 56; Ind & Inf 191(5); Larc 1, 12, 34.

Hauck; Carlson Boat Works v., TexCivApp–Hous (1 Dist), 459 SW2d 887.—App & E 5; Proc 133, 153.

Hauck; Cruz v., CA5 (Tex), 762 F2d 1230.—Civil R 1479, 1482, 1486, 1490; Equity 72(1); Fed Civ Proc 2742.5; Fed Cts 830; Release 33.

Hauck; Cruz v., CA5 (Tex), 627 F2d 710.—Fed Civ Proc 164.5, 171, 173, 186.10; Fed Cts 12.1; Prisons 4(11), 4(13).

Hauck; Cruz v., CA5 (Tex), 515 F2d 322, cert den Andrade v. Hauck, 96 SCt 1118, 424 US 917, 47 LEd2d 322.—Decl Judgm 342; Fed Civ Proc 1872, 1873, 1875.1, 1891; Fed Cts 13.15, 622, 947; Prisons 4(10.1), 4(13), 12; U S Mag 20, 21.

Hauck; Cruz v., CA5 (Tex), 475 F2d 475, 23 ALR Fed 1, appeal after remand 515 F2d 322, cert den Andrade v. Hauck, 96 SCt 1118, 424 US 917, 47 LEd2d 322.—Civil R 1094; Crim Law 641.13(3); Prisons 4(2.1), 4(10.1), 4(13).

Hauck; Cruz v., WDTex, 345 FSupp 189, rev 475 F2d 475, 23 ALR Fed 1, appeal after remand 515 F2d 322, cert den Andrade v. Hauck, 96 SCt 1118, 424 US 917, 47 LEd2d 322.—Const Law 321, 2325; Prisons 4(13), 17.5.

Hauck; Guerrero v., CA5 (Tex), 502 F2d 579.—Fed Civ Proc 1773, 1827.1.

Hauck v. Gulf, C. & S. F. Ry. Co., TexCivApp–Dallas, 246 SW2d 913, ref nre.—Carr 51, 177(1), 177(4).

Hauck; Hampton v., CA5 (Tex), 383 F2d 389.—Crim Law 371(3), 683(2); Witn 337(9).

Hauck; Motor Truck Sales Co. v., TexCivApp–San Antonio, 388 SW2d 214, ref nre.—Autos 20, 383; Sheriffs 114.

Hauck; Piper v., CA5 (Tex), 532 F2d 1016.—Fed Cts 635, 637; U S Mag 14, 21.

Hauck; Powers v., CA5 (Tex), 399 F2d 322.—Const Law 3811, 4626; Crim Law 1166.9; Hab Corp 342; Sent & Pun 1668.

Hauck v. Price, TexCivApp–Houston, 374 SW2d 463.—App & E 230, 233(1), 1015(5), 1069.1; Trial 304, 306.

Hauck; Reyes v., WDTex, 339 FSupp 195.—Civil R 1420; Prisons 12, 13(3); Sent & Pun 1546.

Hauck; Sabine Pilot Service, Inc. v., Tex, 687 SW2d 733.—App & E 934(1); Courts 91(1); Judgm 185(6); Labor & Emp 782, 786, 861, 863(2).

Hauck v. Sabine Pilots, Inc., TexApp–Beaumont, 672 SW2d 322, writ gr, aff Sabine Pilot Service, Inc v. Hauck, 687 SW2d 733.—App & E 863, 934(1), 989; Courts 91(1); Labor & Emp 858.

Hauck; Sawyer v., WDTex, 245 FSupp 55.—Const Law 3867, 4563; Infants 232.

Hauerwas; Flesher Const. Co., Inc. v., TexCivApp–Dallas, 491 SW2d 202.—App & E 345.1, 758.3(3), 758.3(11), 1024.4; Contracts 322(5), 352(1); Costs 194.18, 194.32; Impl & C C 99.1; New Tr 11(1).

Haufler Equipment; White Farm Equipment Co. v., CA5 (Tex), 792 F2d 526. See White Farm Equipment Co. v. Kupcho.

Haufler Equipment Co.; Ruby Switch Ranch v., TexApp–San Antonio, 665 SW2d 208. See Syed v. Haufler Equipment Co.

Haufler Equipment Co.; Syed v., TexApp–San Antonio, 665 SW2d 208.—App & E 977(5); New Tr 159; Trial 136(1).

Haug v. Franklin, TexApp–Austin, 690 SW2d 646.—Action 6; Admin Law 701; Colleges 6(5), 9.30(5); Const Law 947, 3866, 3875, 3879.

Haugen, Ex parte, TexApp–El Paso, 752 SW2d 612.—Mental H 436.1.

Hauger v. State, TexCrimApp, 386 SW2d 800.—Bail 64.

Haught v. Agricultural Production Credit Ass'n, TexApp–Tyler, 39 SW3d 252.—App & E 236(1), 840(2), 863, 893(1), 989, 994(1), 996, 1010.1(4), 1011.1(1), 1011.1(2), 1012.1(2), 1012.1(5); Const Law 3964; Corp 121(7), 316(1), 452, 457, 458; Courts 12(2.1), 12(2.5), 12(2.10), 12(2.15), 12(2.20), 12(2.25), 35, 489(9); Proc 157.

Haught v. Maceluch, CA5 (Tex), 681 F2d 291, reh den 685 F2d 1385.—Damag 51; Fed Civ Proc 828.1, 882; Fed Cts 764, 765, 798, 801; Health 618, 819, 823(9), 826.

Haughton v. Blackships, Inc., CA5 (Tex), 462 F2d 788.—Damag 60, 63; Fed Cts 868; Seamen 11(6).

Haughton v. Blackships, Inc., SDTex, 334 FSupp 317, rev 462 F2d 788.—Damag 60, 100, 130.3, 185(1); Seamen 11(6), 29(2), 29(4).

Haughton v. Houston Belt & Terminal Ry. Co., TexCivApp–Houston, 317 SW2d 102.—App & E 927(1); Evid 123(10); Neglig 1717; Plead 34(3); R R 344(5), 348(1), 350(7.1), 350(11), 350(13); Trial 139.1(6), 142; Witn 392(1).

Haughton v. State, TexCrimApp, 805 SW2d 405, on remand 816 SW2d 803.—Witn 414(2).

Haughton v. State, TexApp–Houston (14 Dist), 816 SW2d 803.—Crim Law 1162, 1169.1(10).

Haughton v. State, TexApp–Houston (14 Dist), 751 SW2d 899, petition for discretionary review gr, rev 805 SW2d 405, on remand 816 SW2d 803.—Crim Law 720(5), 721(3), 1159.2(7); Rape 52(1); Witn 414(2).

Haugland; Prudential Securities, Inc. v., TexApp–El Paso, 973 SW2d 394, reh overr, and review den.—Bills & N 516, 517; Compromise 20(1), 23(1), 23(3); Contracts 326; Damag 22, 36.

Hauglum v. Durst, TexApp–Corpus Christi, 769 SW2d 646.—App & E 226(2), 302(5), 1058(1); Contracts 313(2); Costs 194.32; Damag 11; Evid 213(1); Hus & W 17; Libel 130, 136, 139.

Hauk; Leghart v., WDTex, 25 FSupp2d 748.—Arrest 68(2); Civil R 1376(6); Fed Civ Proc 2491.5; Mun Corp 747(3); Offic 114.

Haun v. Steigleder, TexApp–San Antonio, 868 SW2d 387.—App & E 469, 1223, 1225, 1234(7).

Haun v. Steigleder, TexApp–San Antonio, 830 SW2d 833.—App & E 79(1), 80(6), 112; Bankr 2462; Judgm 217.

Haunschild; Texas Emp. Ins. Ass'n v., TexCivApp–Amarillo, 527 SW2d 270, ref nre.—Statut 105(1), 107(1), 109.2, 114(2), 188, 212.1, 212.6; Work Comp 845.

Haupt v. Atwood Oceanics, Inc., CA5 (Tex), 681 F2d 1058, reh den 688 F2d 840, reh den Atwood Oceanics, Inc v. Shaffer, 688 F2d 840.—Damag 212; Fed Civ Proc 2016, 2179; Fed Cts 637; Prod Liab 23.1.

Haupt v. Coldwell, TexCivApp–El Paso, 500 SW2d 563.—Bills & N 488, 489(1), 524; Judgm 185.3(16); Lost Inst 1.

Haupt; James v., TexCivApp–Tyler, 573 SW2d 285, ref nre.—Trial 133.6(6), 350.1, 350.8; Wills 52(1), 289, 302(1), 312, 317, 318(1), 323, 333, 486.

Haupt, Inc.; Tarrant County Water Control and Imp. Dist. No. One v., Tex, 854 SW2d 909, on remand 870 SW2d 350.—Em Dom 2(7); Mines 55(6), 62.1, 73.1(6).

Haupt, Inc. v. Tarrant County Water Control and Imp. Dist. No. One, TexApp–Waco, 870 SW2d 350.—Em Dom 2(1), 300, 315; Mines 55(6).

Haupt, Inc. v. Tarrant County Water Control and Imp. Dist. No. One, TexApp–Waco, 833 SW2d 697, reh den, and writ gr, rev 854 SW2d 909, on remand 870 SW2d 350.—App & E 1180(3); Em Dom 2(1), 2(7), 263, 266, 319.

Hauptmann; Rowen v., TexCivApp–Eastland, 352 SW2d 158.—Tax 2909, 2936.

Hauser; Cebell v., TexCivApp–San Antonio, 112 SW2d 285, writ dism.—Abate & R 28; App & E 173(6); Plead 216(1); Ven & Pur 254(1), 261(1), 261(2), 261(3).

Hauser; Dyer v., TexCivApp–El Paso, 100 SW2d 787.—Torts 140; Venue 22(9).

Hauser; Magness By and Through Magness, Estate of v., TexApp–Houston (1 Dist), 918 SW2d 5, writ den.—App & E 934(1); Judgm 185(2); Lim of Act 55(3), 199(1).

Hauser; Weber v., TexCivApp–San Antonio, 486 SW2d 609.—Courts 202(5).

Hausladen v. Hausladen, TexCivApp–Dallas, 388 SW2d 952.—Divorce 12, 34, 49(2), 51, 54, 55, 62(6), 129(16), 130, 135, 184(6.1), 184(7), 184(10).

Hausladen; Hausladen v., TexCivApp–Dallas, 388 SW2d 952.—Divorce 12, 34, 49(2), 51, 54, 55, 62(6), 129(16), 130, 135, 184(6.1), 184(7), 184(10).

Hausler; Boothe v., Tex, 766 SW2d 788.—App & E 1043(6); Pretrial Proc 312.

Hausler; Boothe v., TexApp–Houston (1 Dist), 762 SW2d 304, rev 766 SW2d 788.—Pretrial Proc 304, 313.

Hausler v. Hausler, TexApp–Waco, 636 SW2d 874.—Divorce 150, 179, 252.3(2), 286(2).

Hausler; Hausler v., TexApp–Waco, 636 SW2d 874.—Divorce 150, 179, 252.3(2), 286(2).

Hausman; Carpenter v., TexCivApp–San Antonio, 601 SW2d 88.—Courts 207.1, 207.3, 209(2); Mtg 338.

Hausman v. Hausman, TexApp–San Antonio, 199 SW3d 38.—Child 1, 14, 58, 64; Equity 3; Estop 52(8), 52.15.

Hausman; Hausman v., TexApp–San Antonio, 199 SW3d 38.—Child 1, 14, 58, 64; Equity 3; Estop 52(8), 52.15.

Hausman; Mitchell v., CA5 (Tex), 261 F2d 778.—Labor & Emp 2418, 2424.

Hausman v. State, TexCrimApp, 480 SW2d 721.—Controlled Subs 26, 30, 80.

Hausman; U.S. v., CA5 (Tex), 894 F2d 686, cert den 111 SCt 92, 498 US 830, 112 LEd2d 64.—Crim Law 577.15(4), 1026.10(5); Ind & Inf 7.

Hausmann v. Texas Sav. & Loan Ass'n, TexCivApp–El Paso, 585 SW2d 796, ref nre.—App & E 172(3), 362(1), 1177(1), 1177(6); Evid 71; Mtg 330, 353, 354, 369(3), 369(6), 369(8); Trial 219.

Hausmann; U.S. v., CA5 (Tex), 711 F2d 615.—Crim Law 400(1), 778(6), 1044.1(2), 1158(1), 1187; Fraud 69(3), 69(4), 69(6), 69(7).

Hausman Packing Co. v. Badwey, TexCivApp–San Antonio, 147 SW2d 856, writ refused.—Autos 181(1), 181(2), 224(1); Neglig 1037(4).

Haussecker; Childs v., Tex, 974 SW2d 31.—Judgm 181(16), 650, 720; Lim of Act 1, 43, 55(4), 95(1), 95(2), 95(4.1), 95(5), 199(1); Work Comp 2103.

Haussecker v. Childs, TexApp–El Paso, 935 SW2d 930, reh overr, and writ gr, aff 974 SW2d 31.—Atty & C 105, 107; Judgm 181(16); Lim of Act 95(1), 95(3), 95(5).

Hausser v. Mulligan, TexComApp, 107 SW2d 870, 130 Tex 117.—Sheriffs 32.

Havana Painting Co., Inc.; Avila v., TexApp–Houston (14 Dist), 761 SW2d 398, writ den.—Atty & C 117, 129(2), 129(4); Costs 260(5).

Havard; Brown v., Tex, 593 SW2d 939.—Contracts 93(1); Evid 450(3); Lim of Act 96(2); Mines 55(8); Ref of Inst 32.

Havard v. Brown, TexCivApp–San Antonio, 577 SW2d 757, aff 593 SW2d 939.—App & E 930(1), 989; Deeds 119; Evid 461(5); Mines 55(8).

Havard v. State, TexCrimApp, 800 SW2d 195, reh gr, and reh den.—Crim Law 134(4), 369.2(4), 438(4), 627.7(2), 698(3), 706(6), 894, 1043(2), 1043(3); Double J 163; Homic 672, 1139, 1141, 1395, 1403, 1557; Jury 108; Sent & Pun 1772, 1780(3), 1784(4).

Havard v. State, TexApp–Beaumont, 972 SW2d 200.—Burg 29; Crim Law 553, 1144.13(3), 1144.13(6), 1159.2(7), 1159.3(2), 1159.6.

Havard v. State, TexApp–Beaumont, 705 SW2d 366.—Crim Law 577.10(4).

Havard v. State, TexApp–Corpus Christi, 925 SW2d 290.—Jury 29(6).

Havel v. State, TexCrimApp, 360 SW2d 878, 172 TexCrim 584.—Autos 355(6); Crim Law 1099.10; Witn 266.

Havelka v. State, TexApp–Eastland, 224 SW3d 787.—Controlled Subs 28, 67, 77; Crim Law 27.

Haven; Texas American Bank/West Side v., TexApp–Fort Worth, 728 SW2d 102, dism.—Divorce 87.

Havener; Medlin v., TexCivApp–Fort Worth, 98 SW2d 863.—Land & Ten 150(1), 164(2), 167(2); Plead 214(1); Pub Amuse 98.

Havens v. Ayers, TexApp–Houston (1 Dist), 886 SW2d 506.—App & E 5, 363; Estop 68(2); Guar 1, 32; Judgm 184, 335(1); Plead 36(1), 36(2), 291(1), 291(2); Proc 145.

Havens v. Dallas Power & Light Co., TexCivApp–Dallas, 256 SW2d 689, ref nre.—Electricity 16(1), 16(5); Judgm 181(4); Neglig 233, 259.

Havens; Frazier v., TexApp–Houston (14 Dist), 102 SW3d 406, reh overr.—Afft 17; App & E 1050.1(1), 1056.1(1), 1056.1(3); Corp 1.6(9); Estop 52.10(2), 52.10(3), 119; Impl & C C 30; Lim of Act 129; Plead 427; Trial 43.

Havens v. Guetersloh, TexCivApp–Amarillo, 255 SW2d 233, ref nre.—App & E 1033(5), 1062.2, 1068(2); Autos 244(44), 245(49); Trial 352.18.

Havens v. Lee, TexApp–Houston (1 Dist), 694 SW2d 1.—Mand 154(4), 154(9).

Havens v. Tomball Community Hosp., TexApp–Houston (1 Dist), 793 SW2d 690, writ den.—Damag 49, 50, 50.10, 149; Judgm 181(11), 186.

Havenstrite; Maynard v., CA5 (Tex), 727 F2d 439.—Fed Cts 915; Sent & Pun 1988.

Haverfield Co. v. Siegel, TexCivApp–San Antonio, 366 SW2d 790, writ refused.—App & E 758.1; Costs 230; Fixt 27(2).

Haverkamp v. Willingham, TexCivApp–Dallas, 281 SW2d 362.—Plead 111.42(7).

Haverkamp v. Willingham Drilling Co., TexCivApp–Dallas, 281 SW2d 359.—Plead 111.39(6), 111.42(7).

Haverkorn; Warren v., TexCivApp–Fort Worth, 191 SW2d 793.—Adv Poss 60(4), 85(4); App & E 846(5),

1008.1(14), 1175(1); Hus & W 248, 249(2.1), 265; Land & Ten 66(2); Witn 159(6).

Haverlah; Republic Ins. Co. v., TexCivApp–Austin, 565 SW2d 587.—Insurance 2131.

Haverlah's Estate; Pierce v., TexCivApp–Tyler, 428 SW2d 422, ref nre.—Contracts 95(1), 95(5), 100; Judgm 181(7), 185(2), 185.3(2), 186; Lim of Act 20, 97, 195(3); Trover 28.

Haverlah's Estate v. U. S., CA5 (Tex), 464 F2d 512, cert den Brown v. US, 93 SCt 560, 409 US 1061, 34 LEd2d 513.—Int Rev 4172(3), 4172(5).

Haverlah's Estate v. U. S., EDTex, 327 FSupp 243, rev 464 F2d 512, cert den Brown v. US, 93 SCt 560, 409 US 1061, 34 LEd2d 513.—Int Rev 4172(3).

Havertys Furniture Cos, Inc.; Flanagan v., WDTex, 484 FSupp2d 580.—Civil R 1484, 1592; Fed Civ Proc 2737.3; Labor & Emp 2403.

Haves; R. H. Sanders Corp. v., TexCivApp–Dallas, 541 SW2d 262.—Contracts 143.5, 147(3), 167; Corp 199; Inj 17, 18, 138.42.

Haviland v. W. U. Tel. Co., SDTex, 119 FSupp 438.—Action 27(2); Banks 188.5; Courts 39; Rem of C 75, 76, 102; Tel 699.

Havins; Anderson v., TexCivApp–Amarillo, 595 SW2d 147, dism.—Antitrust 144, 150, 358, 369, 390, 397; App & E 758.3(9), 930(3), 931(3), 989, 1001(1), 1003(6); Evid 434(1), 434(11), 588, 590; Trial 139.1(3), 140(1), 350.4(2); Ven & Pur 194, 329, 341(5).

Havins; Canavespe v., TexCivApp–Fort Worth, 478 SW2d 166.—App & E 548(5), 946; Child C 400, 531(1), 553, 555, 567, 662, 920, 921(4).

Havins v. Dallas Ry. & Terminal Co., TexCivApp–Dallas, 130 SW2d 878, writ refused.—Statut 223.4; Urb R R 23.1, 24, 26, 30.

Havins v. First Nat. Bank of Paducah, TexApp–Amarillo, 919 SW2d 177.—Evid 5(1), 20(1); Sec Tran 230, 231, 240.

Havis v. Havis, TexApp–Corpus Christi, 657 SW2d 921, dism.—Child S 140(2), 342, 556(1); Divorce 188, 192, 223, 225, 226, 286(9).

Havis; Havis v., TexApp–Corpus Christi, 657 SW2d 921, dism.—Child S 140(2), 342, 556(1); Divorce 188, 192, 223, 225, 226, 286(9).

Havis v. Rhea, SDTex, 143 BR 690. See Rhea, In re.

Havlen v. McDougall, Tex, 22 SW3d 343.—App & E 901; Divorce 252.3(4); Judgm 185(5); States 18.28, 18.29, 18.51; Statut 176.

Havlen; McDougall v., TexApp–San Antonio, 980 SW2d 767, reh overr, and review gr, rev 22 SW3d 343.—Divorce 254(1), 322; Equity 72(1); Estop 52.15; Hus & W 272(4); Partit 13, 22, 26, 44; States 18.29.

Havlir & Associates, Inc. v. Tacoa, Inc., NDTex, 810 FSupp 752. See John Havlir & Associates, Inc. v. Tacoa, Inc.

Havner v. E-Z Mart Stores, Inc., Tex, 825 SW2d 456, on remand 832 SW2d 368, reh den, and writ gr, and writ withdrawn, writ den 846 SW2d 286.—App & E 833(1), 930(3); Death 76; Evid 544; Neglig 379, 380, 422.

Havner; E-Z Mart Stores, Inc. v., TexApp–Texarkana, 832 SW2d 368, reh den, and writ gr, and writ withdrawn, writ den 846 SW2d 286.—App & E 1001(1); Courts 247(1); Evid 571(9).

Havner; E-Z Mart Stores, Inc. v., TexApp–Texarkana, 797 SW2d 116, writ gr, rev 825 SW2d 456, on remand 832 SW2d 368, reh den, and writ gr, and writ withdrawn, writ den 846 SW2d 286.—Death 76; Evid 501(1), 501(9), 555.5; Neglig 379, 380, 433, 1676.

Havner v. Meno, TexApp–Austin, 867 SW2d 130, reh overr.—Admin Law 387, 469.1, 470, 706; Schools 61, 147.42.

Havner; Merrell Dow Pharmaceuticals, Inc. v., Tex, 953 SW2d 706, reh overr, dissenting opinion 956 SW2d 532, cert den 118 SCt 1799, 523 US 1119, 140 LEd2d 939.—

App & E 842(7), 930(3), 1001(3); Evid 150, 546, 555.2, 570, 596(1); Prod Liab 15, 82.1, 83, 87.1.

Havner; Merrell Dow Pharmaceuticals, Inc. v., TexApp–Corpus Christi, 907 SW2d 535, on reh, and reh overr, and writ gr, rev 953 SW2d 706, reh overr, dissenting opinion 956 SW2d 532, cert den 118 SCt 1799, 523 US 1119, 140 LEd2d 939.—App & E 930(1), 930(3), 970(2), 989, 999(1), 1003(3), 1004(11), 1047(1), 1050.1(7); Const Law 4427; Courts 100(1); Damag 87(1), 91(3); Evid 434(5), 508, 512, 536, 538, 555.7, 555.10, 557, 570, 571(9), 588; Judgm 185(2); Pretrial Proc 44.1; Prod Liab 15, 83; Trial 90, 98, 321.5.

Havron v. Havron, TexCivApp–Amarillo, 301 SW2d 949.—Child C 510, 578, 641.

Havron; Havron v., TexCivApp–Amarillo, 301 SW2d 949.—Child C 510, 578, 641.

Hawes; Brown v., TexApp–Austin, 764 SW2d 855.—Elect of Rem 3(1); Plead 210, 228.14, 228.17; Spec Perf 116.9.

Hawes v. Central Texas Production Credit Ass'n, Tex, 503 SW2d 234.—App & E 931(4); Fraud Conv 115(1), 302, 310.

Hawes v. Central Texas Production Credit Ass'n, TexCivApp–Austin, 492 SW2d 714, writ gr, aff 503 SW2d 234.—App & E 1070(2), 1078(1); Fraud Conv 156(1).

Hawes v. State, TexApp–Houston (1 Dist), 125 SW3d 535, reh overr.—Arrest 63.5(4); Autos 349(2.1); Crim Law 394.6(4), 394.6(5), 1134(2), 1139, 1144.12, 1162, 1169.12.

Hawk, In re, TexApp–Houston (14 Dist), 5 SW3d 874.—New Tr 1, 6, 161(1); Trial 66, 67; Wills 337, 355.

Hawk; American Institute of Real Estate Appraisers v., TexCivApp–Hous (14 Dist), 436 SW2d 359.—App & E 843(2), 954(1); Assoc 10, 20(1); Const Law 4445; Inj 135, 147, 208; Judgm 17(3).

Hawk v. E.K. Arledge, Inc., TexApp–Eastland, 107 SW3d 79, reh gr in part, and review den, and reh of petition for review den.—Banks 505; Costs 17, 34, 194.40; Judgm 7, 16, 472, 486(1); Tax 2925, 2991, 3072(5), 3081, 3153; Tresp to T T 1, 50.

Hawk v. State, TexCrimApp, 482 SW2d 183.—Crim Law 393(1), 407(1), 720(6).

Hawk v. Texas Dept. of Public Safety, TexApp–Houston (1 Dist), 678 SW2d 88.—Autos 144.2(4), 144.2(8); Judgm 185.3(1).

Hawk; Todd v., CA5 (Tex), 72 F3d 443.—Civil R 1376(1), 1398.

Hawk; Todd v., NDTex, 861 FSupp 35, rev 66 F3d 320, rev 72 F3d 443.—Fed Civ Proc 392; Offic 119; U S 127(1).

Hawk & Buck Co. v. Cassidy, TexCivApp–Amarillo, 164 SW2d 245.—Corp 18, 40, 503(1), 503(3).

Hawker; Ablon v., TexCivApp–Dallas, 200 SW2d 265, ref nre.—App & E 931(1); Autos 372(2), 372(4); Bailm 14(1), 31(1), 31(3); Damag 113, 139; Insurance 3526(7); Parties 52; War 165.

Hawkeye-Security Ins. Co.; Keane v., TexApp–Houston (1 Dist), 786 SW2d 802.—Insurance 3614.

Hawkins, Ex parte, TexCrimApp, 6 SW3d 554.—Double J 134, 145; Rob 1.

Hawkins, Ex parte, TexCrimApp, 722 SW2d 424.—Hab Corp 864(3); Infants 20.

Hawkins, Ex parte, TexApp–El Paso, 885 SW2d 586.—Contempt 2, 3, 20, 66(1); Hab Corp 613.

Hawkins, Ex parte, TexCivApp–Texarkana, 545 SW2d 599.—Contempt 63(1), 64; Hab Corp 529, 678.1.

Hawkins, In re, BkrtcyNDTex, 113 BR 315.—Partners 271.

Hawkins, In re Estate of, TexApp–Fort Worth, 187 SW3d 182.—App & E 852; Costs 208; Ex & Ad 314(13), 456(1).

Hawkins v. Aetna Cas. & Sur. Co., TexCivApp–Fort Worth, 355 SW2d 537, ref nre.—Trial 311; Work Comp 1651, 1724, 1932, 1974.

Hawkins; All Am. Bus Lines v., TexCivApp–Eastland, 188 SW2d 992, writ refused wom.—Autos 60, 107(2); Commerce 14.10(1).

Hawkins; American Recreational Markets General Agency, Inc. v., TexApp–Houston (14 Dist), 846 SW2d 476, reh den.—App & E 1070(2); Damag 87(2), 221(7); Fraud 66; Judgm 199(1); Trial 360.

Hawkins v. Anderson, TexApp–Dallas, 672 SW2d 293.—Courts 169(6); Plead 4, 15, 175, 228.14, 241, 244.

Hawkins v. B. & G. Const. & Ditching Co., TexCivApp–Waco, 289 SW2d 340.—App & E 1177(2); Partners 327(1).

Hawkins v. Campbell, TexCivApp–San Antonio, 226 SW2d 891, ref nre.—Brok 7, 8(3), 38(4); Evid 588; Fraud 11(1), 17, 23, 50, 58(1), 58(4); Lim of Act 100(13).

Hawkins v. Coleman, CA5 (Tex), 475 F2d 1278.—Inj 135.

Hawkins v. Coleman, NDTex, 376 FSupp 1330.—Const Law 4212(2); Schools 177.

Hawkins v. Collier, TexCivApp–Galveston, 235 SW2d 528.—App & E 707(1); Damag 37, 38, 43, 50, 134(1); Labor & Emp 2881, 2918; Plead 252(2); Trial 215, 352.9.

Hawkins v. Collins, CA5 (Tex), 980 F2d 975, reh den 985 F2d 555, cert den 113 SCt 1147, 506 US 1089, 122 LEd2d 498.—Hab Corp 898(1).

Hawkins v. Commission for Lawyer Discipline, TexApp–El Paso, 988 SW2d 927, reh overr, and review den, cert den 120 SCt 1426, 529 US 1022, 146 LEd2d 317.—Admin Law 390.1; App & E 181, 235, 248, 842(1), 846(5), 893(1), 930(1), 994(2), 1001(1), 1001(3), 1002, 1003(3), 1003(7), 1073(1); Atty & C 23, 32(2), 44(1), 48, 49, 53(2), 54, 58; Const Law 965, 975, 4273(3); Courts 85(2); Statut 47, 223.4.

Hawkins v. Community Health Choice, Inc., TexApp–Austin, 127 SW3d 322.—Admin Law 441; App & E 852, 856(1), 893(1); Mand 12, 14(1), 14(3), 71; States 108.

Hawkins; Culberson v., TexCivApp–Houston, 321 SW2d 140.—App & E 931(9); Bills & N 226, 237, 495, 519.

Hawkins; Culp v., TexApp–Corpus Christi, 711 SW2d 726, ref nre.—Acct Action on 13; Judgm 185(1); Pretrial Proc 483.

Hawkins v. Dallas County Hosp. Dist., TexApp–Austin, 150 SW3d 535.—Health 487(4); Statut 188, 190, 206, 208.

Hawkins v. Ehler, TexApp–Fort Worth, 100 SW3d 534.—App & E 842(2), 852, 893(1), 931(1), 989, 1008.1(2), 1010.1(1), 1010.1(2), 1010.2; Contracts 152; Costs 32(2); Deeds 123; Divorce 11.5, 224, 249.2, 252.4, 253(2); Estates 5; Evid 597; Frds St of 119(1); Land & Ten 127.

Hawkins v. El Paso First Health Plans, Inc., TexApp–Austin, 214 SW3d 709.—App & E 893(1), 916(1); Decl Judgm 272; Health 462, 471(8), 487(1); Mun Corp 742(1); Plead 104(1); States 191.4(1), 191.9(2).

Hawkins; Endres v., TexCivApp–Fort Worth, 348 SW2d 547.—App & E 80(6); Plead 111.48, 228.23.

Hawkins; Equal Access for El Paso, Inc. v., WDTex, 428 FSupp2d 585.—Assoc 20(1); Civil R 1027, 1029, 1052, 1307, 1330(6); Const Law 42.2(1), 3550; Fed Civ Proc 103.2, 103.3, 103.4; Fed Cts 660.5, 1145; Health 487(2), 510; Inj 114(2).

Hawkins v. Estelle, SDTex, 364 FSupp 394.—Const Law 4761.

Hawkins v. Everts, TexCivApp–Fort Worth, 91 SW2d 1086, writ refused.—App & E 185(1), 519, 1030; Appear 19(1); Mtg 32(1), 32(3), 33(1), 37(2), 38(1).

Hawkins; Federal Mortg. Co. v., Tex, 111 SW2d 1062, 131 Tex 56.—Courts 90(1).

Hawkins; Federal Mortg. Co. v., TexCivApp–Fort Worth, 95 SW2d 744, rev 111 SW2d 1062, 131 Tex 56.—Mtg 25(6); Usury 42, 88, 100(1).

Hawkins; First Dallas Petroleum, Inc. v., TexCivApp–Dallas, 727 SW2d 640.—App & E 5, 176, 181, 859, 865, 934(1); Fraud 49, 58(1); Judgm 112, 126(1); Pretrial Proc 44.1, 46.

Hawkins; First Dallas Petroleum, Inc. v., TexApp–Dallas, 715 SW2d 168.—App & E 79(1); Parties 65(1); Proc 63.

Hawkins; Foremost Ins. Co. v., TexCivApp–Waco, 336 SW2d 901, ref nre.—Insurance 2719(2), 2720.

Hawkins v. Frank Gillman Pontiac, CA5 (Tex), 102 FedAppx 394, motion gr Yang v. Yu, 130 P3d 729.—Damag 57.58; Fed Civ Proc 2497.1.

Hawkins v. Franklin, TexCivApp–Eastland, 567 SW2d 596.—App & E 863; Corp 121(4).

Hawkins v. Frazar, CA5 (Tex), 376 F3d 444, on remand Frew v. Hawkins, 401 FSupp2d 619, aff 457 F3d 432, cert den 127 SCt 1039, 166 LEd2d 714.—Fed Cts 573, 576.1, 769.

Hawkins; Frew v., EDTex, 401 FSupp2d 619, aff Frazar v. Ladd, 457 F3d 432, cert den 127 SCt 1039, 166 LEd2d 714.—Fed Civ Proc 2397.1, 2397.4, 2397.6.

Hawkins v. Frick-Reid Supply Corp., CCA5 (Tex), 154 F2d 88.—Contracts 176(1), 176(2); Fed Civ Proc 680, 2552; Sales 54, 58, 88.

Hawkins v. Friendship Missionary Baptist Church, TexApp–Houston (14 Dist), 69 SW3d 756.—Const Law 1328, 1329, 1330; Relig Soc 14.

Hawkins v. Gilger, TexCivApp–Houston, 399 SW2d 203, writ dism.—Courts 39; Plead 110, 111.23; Venue 5.3(1).

Hawkins v. Graham, TexCivApp–San Antonio, 81 SW2d 754, writ refused.—Execution 171(4).

Hawkins v. Groom, TexApp–Eastland, 893 SW2d 123.—Tax 2445.

Hawkins v. Haley, TexApp–Fort Worth, 765 SW2d 914.—Child C 577, 579.

Hawkins v. Hawkins, TexApp–Austin, 999 SW2d 171.—App & E 161, 162(3); Armed S 34.2(3), 34.5(4); Divorce 172.

Hawkins; Hawkins v., TexApp–Austin, 999 SW2d 171.—App & E 161, 162(3); Armed S 34.2(3), 34.5(4); Divorce 172.

Hawkins v. Hawkins, TexApp–Tyler, 626 SW2d 332.—App & E 557, 1177(9); Child C 907; Divorce 186.

Hawkins; Hawkins v., TexApp–Tyler, 626 SW2d 332.—App & E 557, 1177(9); Child C 907; Divorce 186.

Hawkins v. Hawkins, TexCivApp–El Paso, 612 SW2d 683.—Divorce 252.3(3).

Hawkins; Hawkins v., TexCivApp–El Paso, 612 SW2d 683.—Divorce 252.3(3).

Hawkins v. Hawkins, TexCivApp–Eastland, 515 SW2d 738, dism.—Hab Corp 636, 902; Judgm 654; Plead 409(1), 427; Pretrial Proc 517.1.

Hawkins; Hawkins v., TexCivApp–Eastland, 515 SW2d 738, dism.—Hab Corp 636, 902; Judgm 654; Plead 409(1), 427; Pretrial Proc 517.1.

Hawkins; H. E. Butt Grocery Co. v., TexCivApp–Corpus Christi, 594 SW2d 187.—App & E 846(5), 854(1), 989; Neglig 1076, 1095, 1104(6), 1670.

Hawkins; Hemus & Co. v., SDTex, 452 FSupp 861.—Evid 142(1); Fed Civ Proc 2737.5; Mines 79.1(1), 79.3, 79.7.

Hawkins v. Henderson County, EDTex, 22 FSupp2d 573, aff 180 F3d 265.—Const Law 3881, 3912, 4078; Controlled Subs 178, 181, 185; Courts 493(1); Em Dom 2(1.1), 180; Forfeit 5; Rem of C 21; U S 135.

Hawkins; Home Furniture Co. v., TexCivApp–Dallas, 84 SW2d 830, writ dism.—Damag 208(8); New Tr 76(1); Trial 350.3(6), 351.5(3); Trover 40(6), 60.

Hawkins v. Hood, TexCivApp–Amarillo, 331 SW2d 954, writ dism.—Divorce 139; Mand 190; Pretrial Proc 501.

Hawkins v. Houston Transit Co., TexCivApp–Galveston, 227 SW2d 604, ref nre.—Autos 227(1); Neglig 530(1), 1571; Trial 350.7(5), 350.7(9).

Hawkins v. Howard, TexApp–Dallas, 97 SW3d 676.—Compromise 5(1); Judgm 27, 72, 91; New Tr 140(1), 157.

Hawkins; Kelso v., TexCivApp–Austin, 293 SW2d 807, ref nre.—Evid 472(8), 474(4), 501(3), 537; Plead 374; Wills 286, 288(3), 324(2).

Hawkins v. Kysor Industries Corp., TexCivApp–Hous (14 Dist), 562 SW2d 565.—Lim of Act 31.

Hawkins v. Lynaugh, CA5 (Tex), 862 F2d 487, cert gr, vac 110 SCt 1313, 494 US 1013, 108 LEd2d 489.—Crim Law 641.13(5); Hab Corp 315, 689, 818, 896, 897, 898(2), 899.

Hawkins v. Lynaugh, CA5 (Tex), 862 F2d 482, appeal after remand 862 F2d 487, cert gr, vac 110 SCt 1313, 494 US 1013, 108 LEd2d 489.—Hab Corp 896, 898(1).

Hawkins v. Lynaugh, CA5 (Tex), 844 F2d 1132, reh den 849 F2d 1471, cert den 109 SCt 247, 488 US 900, 102 LEd2d 236.—Crim Law 519(1), 519(9), 520(2), 523; Hab Corp 719, 768, 775(1); Homic 1184, 1186.

Hawkins; McCarthy ex rel. Travis v., CA5 (Tex), 381 F3d 407, reh and reh den 391 F3d 676.—Civil R 1330(1), 1330(6), 1391; Const Law 975; Fed Cts 269, 272, 574, 753, 776; States 191.10.

Hawkins v. McCowan, TexCivApp–Dallas, 246 SW2d 322, writ refused.—Impl & C C 42; Partit 63(3), 89; Ten in C 13; Witn 140(19).

Hawkins v. Maxfield, TexCivApp–Dallas, 318 SW2d 492. —App & E 1008.1(1), 1177(8); Evid 589.

Hawkins v. M.B. Anderson and Associates, TexApp–Dallas, 672 SW2d 293. See Hawkins v. Anderson.

Hawkins; Miller v., CA5 (Tex), 73 FedAppx 56.—Civil R 1088(5).

Hawkins v. National Ass'n of Securities Dealers Inc., CA5 (Tex), 149 F3d 330.—Fed Cts 207; Rem of C 107(8), 108; Sec Reg 40.15.

Hawkins; Parker v., TexApp–Corpus Christi, 668 SW2d 444.—Brok 8(3); Evid 588.

Hawkins; Providence Washington Ins. Co. v., TexCivApp–Waco, 340 SW2d 874.—Insurance 2138(1).

Hawkins v. Puderbaugh, TexCivApp–Hous (14 Dist), 617 SW2d 758.—Frds St of 110(0.5), 110(1), 118(2).

Hawkins; Richard v., TexCivApp–Dallas, 272 SW2d 421, ref nre.—Trial 121(1); Witn 331.5.

Hawkins v. Rudco Oil & Gas Co., TexCivApp–Texarkana, 187 SW2d 230, writ refused wom.—Adv Poss 91, 95, 104, 114(1), 115(1); App & E 264, 927(7), 934(1), 1001(1); Trial 139.1(3), 194(10), 215, 219.

Hawkins; Rudman v., TexCivApp–Eastland, 226 SW2d 491.—Hus & W 80; Plead 111.15, 111.37; Venue 7.5(8).

Hawkins v. Safety Cas. Co., Tex, 207 SW2d 370, 146 Tex 381.—Work Comp 1283, 1297, 1927.

Hawkins v. Safety Cas. Co., TexCivApp–Beaumont, 204 SW2d 866, rev 207 SW2d 370, 146 Tex 381.—Work Comp 1683.

Hawkins v. Schroeter, TexCivApp–San Antonio, 212 SW2d 843.—Action 2, 50(3); Hus & W 249(2.1), 260; Venue 8.5(3), 8.5(5), 16 1/2.

Hawkins v. State, TexCrimApp, 135 SW3d 72, on remand 2005 WL 1654738, petition for discretionary review dism as untimely filed, and petition for discretionary review refused.—Crim Law 13(1), 723(1), 730(1), 867, 1155, 1162, 1171.1(2.1), 1177.

Hawkins v. State, TexCrimApp, 891 SW2d 257, on remand 910 SW2d 176.—Infants 13.

Hawkins v. State, TexCrimApp, 758 SW2d 255.—Arrest 63.5(4), 63.5(5); Crim Law 394.1(2); Searches 28, 80.1.

Hawkins v. State, TexCrimApp, 660 SW2d 65, denial of habeas corpus aff 980 F2d 975, reh den 985 F2d 555, cert den 113 SCt 1147, 506 US 1089, 122 LEd2d 498.—Arrest 63.4(2), 63.4(12), 63.4(15); Const Law 4594(1); Crim Law 300, 347, 412(4), 412.2(5), 438(4), 438(5.1), 474, 531(3), 532(0.5), 641.13(1), 641.13(7), 706(2), 728(5), 781(5), 824(4), 1035(3), 1035(6), 1141(2), 1166(10.10), 1170.5(3), 1170.5(6), 1171.5, 1171.8(1), 1173.1; Homic 845, 1165, 1387, 1395; Jury 107, 108; Sent & Pun 1720, 1750, 1760, 1762, 1772.

Hawkins v. State, TexCrimApp, 656 SW2d 70.—Crim Law 755.5; Sec Reg 326, 328, 329.

Hawkins v. State, TexCrimApp, 628 SW2d 71.—Crim Law 273(4.1), 414, 519(8), 625.10(3), 641.10(3), 641.12(1), 1035(5), 1037.1(1), 1044.2(1), 1119(1), 1134(3), 1137(5); Ind & Inf 137(6); Jury 109; Quo W 1; Rape 5, 21.

Hawkins v. State, TexCrimApp, 613 SW2d 720, cert den 102 SCt 422, 454 US 919, 70 LEd2d 231, reh den 102 SCt 660, 454 US 1093, 70 LEd2d 632.—Courts 104; Crim Law 404.11, 448(3), 517.1(2), 520(2), 531(3), 641.4(1), 641.4(4), 641.4(5), 700(3), 722.3, 1115(2), 1130(2), 1133, 1134(7), 1159.5, 1165(1), 1166.16, 1169.9, 1171.6, 1186.6; Prisons 4(13); Sent & Pun 1745; Stip 8, 14(4).

Hawkins v. State, TexCrimApp, 605 SW2d 586.—Assault 56, 92(3), 96(7); Crim Law 55.

Hawkins v. State, TexCrimApp, 579 SW2d 923.—Crim Law 1038.1(3.1).

Hawkins v. State, TexCrimApp, 535 SW2d 359.—Crim Law 29(15); Weap 4.

Hawkins v. State, TexCrimApp, 515 SW2d 275.—Crim Law 1077.1(4).

Hawkins v. State, TexCrimApp, 509 SW2d 607.—Crim Law 339.11(6), 1169.2(2), 1171.1(3); Rape 40(2), 51(4).

Hawkins v. State, TexCrimApp, 505 SW2d 578.—Crim Law 698(1), 899, 1169.11; Sod 6.

Hawkins v. State, TexCrimApp, 467 SW2d 465.—Burg 41(3), 42(3); Crim Law 847.

Hawkins v. State, TexCrimApp, 450 SW2d 349.—Crim Law 674, 1137(5).

Hawkins v. State, TexCrimApp, 447 SW2d 680.—Crim Law 867; Larc 40(11).

Hawkins v. State, TexCrimApp, 426 SW2d 879.—Crim Law 1035(6), 1131(7).

Hawkins v. State, TexCrimApp, 424 SW2d 907.—Const Law 268(10), 4629, 4673, 4693; Crim Law 1038.2, 1038.3.

Hawkins v. State, TexCrimApp, 424 SW2d 634, appeal reinstated 426 SW2d 879.—Crim Law 1081(4.1).

Hawkins v. State, TexCrimApp, 416 SW2d 428.—Crim Law 1130(4), 1132.

Hawkins v. State, TexCrimApp, 397 SW2d 78.—Crim Law 1090.1(3), 1184(3).

Hawkins v. State, TexCrimApp, 386 SW2d 536.—Crim Law 1094(2.1).

Hawkins v. State, TexCrimApp, 383 SW2d 416.—Larc 31.

Hawkins v. State, TexCrimApp, 283 SW2d 396.—Crim Law 1090.1(1).

Hawkins v. State, TexCrimApp, 266 SW2d 385.—Crim Law 1090.1(1).

Hawkins v. State, TexCrimApp, 255 SW2d 875, 158 Tex-Crim 406.—Crim Law 273.3, 935(1).

Hawkins v. State, TexCrimApp, 238 SW2d 779, 156 Tex-Crim 122.—Crim Law 609, 956(5), 1169.5(2); Larc 55.

Hawkins v. State, TexCrimApp, 183 SW2d 170.—Crim Law 1094(3).

Hawkins v. State, TexCrimApp, 178 SW2d 520.—Crim Law 1094(3).

Hawkins v. State, TexCrimApp, 125 SW2d 580, 136 Tex-Crim 413.—Crim Law 586, 911, 925(1), 1151; Health 163, 164, 186(4), 187; Ind & Inf 110(3), 111(1).

Hawkins v. State, TexApp–Houston (1 Dist), 89 SW3d 674, petition for discretionary review refused.—Crim Law 26, 322, 444, 661, 1153(1); Sent & Pun 313; Weap 4.

Hawkins v. State, TexApp–Houston (1 Dist), 792 SW2d 491.—Assault 92(5); Crim Law 363, 366(6), 643, 720(7.1), 1028, 1109(1), 1159.4(6); Ind & Inf 137(1); Jury 131(4).

Hawkins v. State, TexApp–Fort Worth, 910 SW2d 176.—Crim Law 338(7), 438(5.1), 438(6), 1156(1); Ind & Inf 60, 71.4(12), 110(3); Infants 13, 20.

Hawkins v. State, TexApp–Fort Worth, 871 SW2d 539.—Controlled Subs 30, 69; Crim Law 338(1), 338(7), 369.2(1), 1153(1).

HAWKINS

Hawkins v. State, TexApp–Fort Worth, 855 SW2d 881, reh overr, and petition for discretionary review gr, rev 891 SW2d 257, on remand 910 SW2d 176.—Infants 13.

Hawkins v. State, TexApp–Fort Worth, 745 SW2d 511, petition for discretionary review refused.—Crim Law 872, 889, 1169.2(1), 1169.2(3), 1175, 1208.1(1); States 5(2); Weap 11(0.5).

Hawkins v. State, TexApp–Fort Worth, 692 SW2d 592, petition for discretionary review refused.—Crim Law 577.8(1), 577.16(8), 577.16(9).

Hawkins v. State, TexApp–Fort Worth, 644 SW2d 764, petition for discretionary review gr, rev 758 SW2d 255. —Arrest 63.4(18); Controlled Subs 138; Crim Law 720(7.1); Searches 15.

Hawkins v. State, TexApp–Fort Worth, 644 SW2d 762.— Crim Law 1130(4).

Hawkins v. State, TexApp–Dallas, 793 SW2d 291, petition for discretionary review refused.—Const Law 3309; Crim Law 720(7.1), 1043(3), 1115(2); Jury 33(5.15), 120.

Hawkins v. State, TexApp–Dallas, 783 SW2d 288, appeal after remand 793 SW2d 291, petition for discretionary review refused.—Crim Law 1181.5(3.1); Jury 33(5.15), 142.

Hawkins v. State, TexApp–Dallas, 687 SW2d 48, petition for discretionary review refused.—Controlled Subs 31, 81; Crim Law 1144.13(8), 1159.2(10).

Hawkins v. State, TexApp–Amarillo, 853 SW2d 598, reh den.—Arrest 63.1, 63.4(4), 63.4(18), 63.5(4), 63.5(5), 63.5(8), 63.5(9); Crim Law 394.6(5), 1158(4); Searches 36.1, 172.

Hawkins v. State, TexApp–Beaumont, 964 SW2d 767, petition for discretionary review refused.—Const Law 945; Crim Law 493, 940, 945(2), 957(1), 1030(2).

Hawkins v. State, TexApp–Beaumont, 807 SW2d 874, petition for discretionary review refused.—Crim Law 719(1), 720(8), 790, 1130(5).

Hawkins v. State, TexApp–Beaumont, 766 SW2d 840, petition for discretionary review refused, appeal after remand 807 SW2d 874, petition for discretionary review refused.—Crim Law 1172.8.

Hawkins v. State, TexApp–Beaumont, 744 SW2d 641, petition for discretionary review gr, vac 761 SW2d 23, on remand 766 SW2d 840, petition for discretionary review refused, appeal after remand 807 SW2d 874, petition for discretionary review refused.—Arrest 63.5(2), 63.5(8).

Hawkins v. State, TexApp–Waco, 214 SW3d 668.—Crim Law 31.10, 1144.13(2.1), 1144.13(6), 1159.2(1), 1159.2(2), 1159.2(7), 1159.3(5), 1191; Larc 17.

Hawkins v. State, TexApp–Tyler, 968 SW2d 382, petition for discretionary review refused, and reh overr.—Crim Law 394.6(5), 1134(6), 1153(1), 1158(4); Searches 13.1, 28, 42.1, 43, 44, 45, 171, 186, 192.1.

Hawkins v. State, TexApp–Corpus Christi, 112 SW3d 340.—Crim Law 1023(16), 1042, 1068.5, 1077.3, 1134(10); Sent & Pun 2003, 2038.

Hawkins v. State, TexApp–Corpus Christi, 99 SW3d 890, petition for discretionary review gr (1 pet), and petition for discretionary review refused (1 pet), rev 135 SW3d 72, on remand 2005 WL 1654738, petition for discretionary review dism as untimely filed, and petition for discretionary review refused.—Controlled Subs 26, 27, 28, 30, 79, 80; Crim Law 663, 689, 719(1), 719(3), 720(2), 720(6), 720(7.1), 723(1), 723(3), 726, 730(1), 730(8), 730(14), 755.5, 770(2), 1037.1(1), 1141(2), 1162, 1163(1), 1165(1), 1171.1(2.1), 1171.1(6), 1171.3.

Hawkins v. State, TexApp–Corpus Christi, 865 SW2d 97, reh overr, and petition for discretionary review refused. —Autos 356, 414, 415, 421, 422.1; Crim Law 1158(4).

Hawkins v. State, TexApp–Houston (14 Dist), 742 SW2d 61.—Autos 355(10).

Hawkins v. State, TexCivApp–Houston, 401 SW2d 301.— Infants 250.

Hawkins v. State Agr. Stabilization and Conservation Committee, CA5 (Tex), 252 F2d 570.—Agric 3.4(2).

Hawkins v. State Agriculture Stabilization and Conservation Committee, SDTex, 149 FSupp 681, aff 252 F2d 570.—Admin Law 400, 411; Agric 3.4(2); Evid 13, 23(1).

Hawkins; State Farm Mut. Auto. Ins. Co. v., EDTex, 962 FSupp 984.—Insurance 2675.

Hawkins; Sulphur Springs Water Dist. v., TexCivApp–Tyler, 519 SW2d 272.—App & E 719(1), 758.1; Em Dom 172, 241; Judgm 301.

Hawkins; Sunburst Condominiums v., TexApp–Corpus Christi, 711 SW2d 726. See Culp v. Hawkins.

Hawkins; Texas & New Orleans R. Co. v., TexCivApp–San Antonio, 112 SW2d 1107, writ dism.—App & E 1175(8); Release 17(2).

Hawkins v. Texas Co., Tex, 209 SW2d 338, 146 Tex 511. —Admin Law 744.1, 746, 784.1, 791; Mines 92.27, 92.28, 92.38, 92.39, 92.40; Pub Ut 187.

Hawkins v. Texas Co., TexCivApp–Austin, 203 SW2d 1003, aff 209 SW2d 338, 146 Tex 511.—App & E 1058(1); Mines 92.40.

Hawkins; Texas Dept. of Criminal Justice v., TexApp–Dallas, 169 SW3d 529.—App & E 893(1), 911.3; Courts 32, 39; Mun Corp 723, 847, 854; Plead 104(1); States 112.2(4).

Hawkins; Texas Emp. Ins. Ass'n v., Tex, 369 SW2d 305. —Work Comp 847, 1929, 1968(7), 1969.

Hawkins; Texas Emp. Ins. Ass'n v., TexCivApp–Amarillo, 387 SW2d 469, ref nre.—Work Comp 847, 849, 1639.

Hawkins; Texas Emp. Ins. Ass'n, TexCivApp–Amarillo, 363 SW2d 788, aff 369 SW2d 305.—App & E 989, 1177(7); Work Comp 1654, 1929, 1937.

Hawkins v. Texas Oil and Gas Corp., TexApp–Waco, 724 SW2d 878, ref nre.—Costs 194.40; Decl Judgm 5.1, 8, 26, 45, 187; Estop 35; Interpl 34; Mines 55(2), 55(4), 55(5), 58, 79.1(1), 79.1(5).

Hawkins v. Trinity Baptist Church, TexApp–Tyler, 30 SW3d 446, reh overr.—App & E 863, 934(1); Atty & C 105; Const Law 1328, 1340(1); Fraud 7; Judgm 181(7), 181(33), 183, 185(2), 185(5), 185(6); Partners 70; Relig Soc 30; Trusts 173.

Hawkins v. Twin Montana, Inc., TexApp–Fort Worth, 810 SW2d 441.—App & E 458(1), 489; Mines 52, 55(4), 78.1(11); Proc 154; Receivers 8, 35(1).

Hawkins; Ulrickson v., TexApp–Fort Worth, 696 SW2d 704, ref nre.—App & E 1212(1); Mental H 139, 141, 156.

Hawkins; U.S. v., CA5 (Tex), 87 F3d 722, cert den 117 SCt 408, 519 US 974, 136 LEd2d 321.—Crim Law 1023(11), 1030(1), 1139, 1147, 1158(1); Sent & Pun 723, 730, 814, 815, 820, 821, 825, 838, 841, 995.

Hawkins; U.S. v., CA5 (Tex), 69 F3d 11, cert den 116 SCt 1053, 516 US 1163, 134 LEd2d 198.—Crim Law 1134(3), 1139, 1158(1); Sent & Pun 797, 900, 908; Weap 17(8).

Hawkins; U.S. v., CA5 (Tex), 658 F2d 279.—Crim Law 566, 1166.16, 1177; Double J 134; Jury 131(13); RICO 5; Sent & Pun 67, 374, 559(3).

Hawkins; U.S. v., CA5 (Tex), 492 F2d 771, cert den 95 SCt 629, 419 US 1052, 42 LEd2d 647.—Sent & Pun 1167.

Hawkins v. U.S., CA5 (Tex), 458 F2d 1153.—Crim Law 1132, 1177; Embez 11(1); Sent & Pun 643, 2333.

Hawkins; U.S. v., CA5 (Tex), 425 F2d 252.—Crim Law 260.11(2), 260.12.

Hawkins v. U.S., CA5 (Tex), 417 F2d 1271, cert den 90 SCt 917, 397 US 914, 25 LEd2d 95.—Crim Law 422(9), 1037.1(2), 1171.8(2); Witn 288(2).

Hawkins v. U.S., EDTex, 324 FSupp 223, aff 458 F2d 1153.—Crim Law 1426(1), 1455; Sent & Pun 645, 2276, 2279, 2305.

Hawkins v. Upjohn Co., EDTex, 890 FSupp 609.—Consp 18; Fed Civ Proc 1771, 1829, 1831, 1835; Prod Liab 46.1, 46.2; States 18.65.

Hawkins v. Upjohn Co., EDTex, 890 FSupp 601.—Consp 1.1, 3; Const Law 3964; Courts 12(2.1); Fed Cts 74, 76, 76.5, 76.10, 76.20, 76.25, 76.35, 94, 96.

Hawkins v. Van Zandt County Appraisal Dist., TexApp–Eastland, 834 SW2d 619, reh den, and writ den.—Tax 2322.

Hawkins v. Volkmann, Estate of, TexApp–San Antonio, 898 SW2d 334, reh overr, and writ den.—App & E 984(1); Atty & C 24; Costs 2; Courts 202(5); Ex & Ad 22(3), 122(1), 431(1); Judges 25(2), 51(2), 53; Judgm 650; Wills 396, 400, 410.

Hawkins v. Walvoord, TexApp–El Paso, 25 SW3d 882, review den.—App & E 852, 863; Atty & C 31; Contempt 40, 41.1; Courts 55; Dist & Pros Attys 10; Judges 36; Judgm 183; Lim of Act 95(3); Neglig 371, 379, 380, 383, 386, 1655; Offic 114; RICO 62, 65; Sheriffs 99; Torts 119.

Hawkins; Weems v., TexCivApp–Amarillo, 278 SW2d 439, ref nre.—Adv Poss 4, 25; Mines 55(7), 73.1(2).

Hawkins; Wood Motor Co. v., TexCivApp–Texarkana, 226 SW2d 487.—Contracts 145, 164; Corp 503(2); Plead 111.15, 111.42(5), 111.42(6); Venue 7.5(7).

Hawkins Ins. Agency; American Recreational Markets General Agency, Inc. v., TexApp–Houston (14 Dist, 846 SW2d 476. See American Recreational Markets General Agency, Inc. v. Hawkins.

Hawkins Service Co.; Western Steel Co. v., TexApp–Corpus Christi, 760 SW2d 725. See Western Steel Co. v. Coast Inv. Corp.

Hawk Leasing Co., Inc. v. Texas Workforce Com'n, TexApp–Dallas, 971 SW2d 598.—Const Law 2317, 2600; Judgm 21; Labor & Emp 2354, 2355.

Hawks v. Davis, TexCivApp–Beaumont, 307 SW2d 121.—Infants 200, 230.1.

Hawks; Else v., TexCivApp–Amarillo, 284 SW2d 413, ref nre.—App & E 927(7), 997(3); Neglig 1708, 1714; Trial 139.1(17).

Hawks; Taylor v., TexCivApp–El Paso, 129 SW2d 1203, writ dism, correct.—App & E 1039(17).

Hawley; Columbia Rio Grande Regional Healthcare, L.P. v., TexApp–Corpus Christi, 188 SW3d 838.—App & E 840(4), 930(1), 969, 1003(7), 1004(5), 1051.1(2), 1067, 1079; Evid 146, 538, 547.5, 555.10, 571(9), 571(10); Health 633, 822(3), 823(8), 827, 830; Interest 30(3); Neglig 431, 432, 1741; Trial 43, 143, 182, 203(1), 232(1), 250, 350.2.

Hawley v. Ground Water Conservation Dist. No. 2, Tex, 306 SW2d 352, 157 Tex 643.—Const Law 2970; Waters 216.

Hawley; Ground Water Conservation Dist. No. 2 v., TexCivApp–Amarillo, 304 SW2d 764, ref nre 306 SW2d 352, 157 Tex 643.—Const Law 639, 2970, 3057, 3470; Statut 64(2); Waters 216, 226.

Hawley v. State, TexCrimApp, 252 SW2d 933, 158 TexCrim 61, writ refused.—Crim Law 419(10), 763(6); Ind & Inf 137(6); Sent & Pun 1369; Witn 414(1).

Hawley v. State Dept. of Highways and Public Transp. for State of Tex., TexApp–Amarillo, 830 SW2d 278.—Autos 256, 258.

Hawley v. U.S., CA5 (Tex), 170 F2d 858.—Crim Law 1182.

Hawley Independent School District; Moreland v., TexComApp, 168 SW2d 660, 140 Tex 391.—App & E 861; Mand 18, 185; Venue 8.5(5), 22(6).

Hawley Independent School Dist.; Moreland v., TexCivApp–Eastland, 169 SW2d 227.—Courts 247(7).

Hawley Independent School Dist.; Moreland v., TexCivApp–Eastland, 163 SW2d 892, opinion supplemented 169 SW2d 227.—Autos 244(32); Evid 574; Plead 111.17, 111.38, 111.39(6), 111.42(8); Venue 22(4), 22(6).

Hawn, In re, BkrtcySDTex, 149 BR 450, aff in part Hawn v. American Nat Bank, 1996 WL 142521.—Int Rev 4767, 4772, 4781; Mines 47; Sec Tran 90, 115.1, 133, 144, 168.

Hawn; First Nat. Bank in Dallas v., TexCivApp–Dallas, 392 SW2d 377, ref nre.—Abate & R 64; Parties 59(3), 60.

Hawn; Griffin v., Tex, 341 SW2d 151, 161 Tex 422.—Em Dom 75; States 191.4(6), 191.10.

Hawn v. Hawn, TexCivApp–Eastland, 574 SW2d 883, ref nre.—Estop 78(1); Partners 165, 374; Pretrial Proc 481, 691; Release 57(1); Spec Perf 25, 62, 134.

Hawn; Hawn v., TexCivApp–Eastland, 574 SW2d 883, ref nre.—Estop 78(1); Partners 165, 374; Pretrial Proc 481, 691; Release 57(1); Spec Perf 25, 62, 134.

Hawnco, Inc.; City of Farmers Branch v., TexCivApp–Dallas, 435 SW2d 288, ref nre.—App & E 71(3), 954(1); Const Law 2642; Inj 135; Mand 4(1), 4(3), 178; Mun Corp 61, 62, 63.15(1), 63.20, 151; Offic 27, 110; Zoning 5.1, 151.

Hawn Lumber Co.; Aetna Casualty & Sur. Co. v., Tex, 98 SW2d 167, 128 Tex 296.—App & E 1173(2).

Hawn Lumber Co.; Aetna Cas. & Sur. Co. v., Tex, 97 SW2d 460, 128 Tex 296, opinion mod on denial of reh 98 SW2d 167, 128 Tex 296.—Evid 23(1); Mun Corp 347(1); Paymt 43; Princ & S 113; Pub Contr 58, 59, 60; Schools 81(2).

Hawn Lumber Co.; Davis v., TexCivApp–Dallas, 193 SW2d 263.—App & E 1; Home 13, 36, 122, 129(1), 164; Hus & W 243.

Haworth; City of Dallas v., TexCivApp–Dallas, 218 SW2d 264, ref nre.—App & E 846(5); Int Liq 106(2), 261; Zoning 274, 394.

Haworth v. Haworth, TexApp–Houston (14 Dist), 795 SW2d 296.—Divorce 169, 254(2); Judgm 526.

Haworth; Haworth v., TexApp–Houston (14 Dist), 795 SW2d 296.—Divorce 169, 254(2); Judgm 526.

Haworth v. State, TexCrimApp, 88 SW2d 115, 129 TexCrim 428.—Autos 316.

Hawryluk; Chopra v., TexApp–El Paso, 892 SW2d 229, reh overr, and writ den.—App & E 934(1); Health 618, 821(2); Judgm 181(3), 181(33), 183, 185(2), 185.1(4), 185.3(21).

Haws, In re, BkrtcySDTex, 158 BR 965.—Bankr 2043(1), 2043(2), 2043(3), 2048.2, 3568(1); Fed Cts 31.

Haws; Reynolds v., TexApp–Fort Worth, 741 SW2d 582, writ den.—Parties 66; Zoning 569, 582.1, 586, 587, 590.

Haws; Schneider v., TexApp–Amarillo, 118 SW3d 886.—Evid 571(3); Health 611, 619, 625, 631, 651, 664, 821(3), 821(4), 821(5), 823(4).

Haws & Garrett General Contractors, Inc.; Everman Corp. v., TexCivApp–Fort Worth, 578 SW2d 539.—App & E 768, 930(1), 1003(10); Judgm 199(3.10), 199(3.15); Labor & Emp 3096(5); Trial 350.1, 352.5(5).

Haws & Garrett General Contractors, Inc. v. Gorbett Bros. Welding Co., Tex, 480 SW2d 607.—Contracts 3, 16, 27; Impl & C C 1; Indem 104.

Haws & Garrett General Contractors, Inc. v. Gorbett Bros. Welding Co., TexCivApp–Fort Worth, 471 SW2d 595, writ gr, set aside 480 SW2d 607.—Contracts 348, 350(1); Indem 27; Labor & Emp 25.

Haws & Garrett General Contractors, Inc.; Knox-Evans Const. Co. v., TexCivApp–Hous (1 Dist), 503 SW2d 669.—App & E 1024.3; Evid 570, 572; Plead 111.16, 111.42(6).

Hawsey v. Louisiana Dept. of Social Services, TexApp–Houston (1 Dist), 934 SW2d 723, reh overr, and writ den.—App & E 662(4), 846(5), 1008.1(1); Const Law 3964; Courts 12(2.1), 35, 511; Judgm 815; Offic 114; States 5(1).

Hawthorne, Ex parte, TexCrimApp, 207 SW2d 408, 151 TexCrim 283.—Hab Corp 825.1.

Hawthorne, In re, NDTex, 45 FSupp 374.—Bankr 2762.1, 2797.1, 2802, 3786; Home 5, 18, 154, 158, 162(1).

Hawthorne v. Anchor Cas. Co., SDTex, 53 FSupp 475.—Fed Cts 93; Work Comp 1022.1, 1028.

Hawthorne; Besing v., CA5 (Tex), 981 F2d 1488. See Besing, Matter of.

Hawthorne; Cain v., TexCivApp–Amarillo, 404 SW2d 90, ref nre.—App & E 989, 1170.7; Autos 242(2), 244(34), 244(35), 244(40); Witn 268(2).

Hawthorne v. Countrywide Home Loans, Inc., TexApp–Austin, 150 SW3d 574, reh overr.—App & E 173(2); Contracts 143(2), 164; Evid 452; Judgm 178; Mtg 201.

Hawthorne v. Fisher, NDTex, 33 FSupp 891.—Agric 3.3(4); Const Law 2438, 2488; Inj 46, 76, 114(3), 118(3); Offic 1; Tresp 25.

Hawthorne v. Guenther, TexApp–Beaumont, 917 SW2d 924, reh overr, and writ den.—Action 57(5); App & E 221, 237(5), 238(2), 294(1), 295, 676, 854(2), 946, 966(1), 1003(7); Courts 100(1); Damag 91(1); Fraud 7, 61; Partners 70, 79, 121; Pretrial Proc 713, 715, 724; Trial 3(5.1).

Hawthorne v. Hillin, TexCivApp–Waco, 463 SW2d 266.—Schools 107; Tax 2128, 2160.

Hawthorne; International-Great Northern R. Co. v., TexComApp, 116 SW2d 1056, 131 Tex 622, cert den 59 SCt 487, 306 US 63, 83 LEd 1040.—App & E 843(2), 1015(5), 1094(1); Labor & Emp 2877, 3006; Neglig 372; Trial 350.5(4), 350.6(6), 352.12, 352.18.

Hawthorne; International-Great Northern R. Co. v., TexCivApp–Waco, 90 SW2d 895, aff 116 SW2d 1056, 131 Tex 622, cert den 59 SCt 487, 306 US 63, 83 LEd 1040. —Labor & Emp 2824, 2975, 3010; Trial 304, 350.2, 351.5(8), 352.12.

Hawthorne v. La-Man Constructors, Inc., TexApp–Beaumont, 672 SW2d 255.—Contempt 23; Mand 1, 3(2.1), 16(1), 71, 72, 111, 151(2), 154(2), 154(3), 168(4), 185, 187.4, 187.7; Mun Corp 1038.

Hawthorne; Marion v., TexCivApp–Amarillo, 376 SW2d 889.—App & E 1062.4; Damag 221(5.1); Trial 351.2(9).

Hawthorne; Roby v., TexCivApp–Dallas, 84 SW2d 1108, writ dism.—Costs 93, 240, 246.5, 254(5), 264; Statut 181(1), 202, 203, 223.2(24).

Hawthorne v. Star Enterprise, Inc., TexApp–Texarkana, 45 SW3d 757, review den, on subsequent appeal 2003 WL 21705370, reh overr, and review den.—App & E 970(2); Judgm 181(21), 185(3), 185(6), 185.1(4), 185.3(13); Labor & Emp 782, 784.

Hawthorne v. Texas & N. O. R. Co., TexCivApp–Beaumont, 84 SW2d 1015.—R R 364, 395, 396(1), 396(2), 400(1).

Hawthorne; Texas Elec. Service Co. v., TexCivApp–Fort Worth, 135 SW2d 531, writ dism, correct.—Autos 173(5), 245(17); Neglig 210.

Hawthorne v. Texas Liquor Control Board, TexCivApp–Eastland, 113 SW2d 577.—Int Liq 41.

Hawthorne v. U.S., CCA5 (Tex), 115 F2d 805.—Agric 1; Fed Civ Proc 2466; U S 125(3).

Hawthorne; U.S. v., NDTex, 31 FSupp 827, aff 115 F2d 805.—Admin Law 422; Const Law 951; U S 40, 125(9), 130(7), 135.

Hawthorne-Seving, Inc.; Reames v., TexApp–Dallas, 949 SW2d 758, review den, and reh of petition for review overr.—Const Law 2315; Fixt 1, 15; Improv 1; Lim of Act 4(2), 30; Prod Liab 71.5.

Hay v. Beto, CA5 (Tex), 467 F2d 1388.—Hab Corp 369.

Hay v. City of Irving, Tex., CA5 (Tex) F2d 796.—Civil R 1420, 1462; Consp 19; Fed Cts 597, 907, 940.

Hay v. Shell Oil Co., TexApp–Corpus Christi, 986 SW2d 772, reh overr, and review den, and reh of petition for review overr.—App & E 1073(1); Judgm 183, 185(2); Lim of Act 43, 46(6), 95(1), 95(9), 104(1), 104(2), 197(1); Mines 79.7.

Hay v. State, TexCrimApp, 472 SW2d 157.—Crim Law 656(4), 656(9).

Hay v. State, TexCrimApp, 436 SW2d 153.—Arrest 63.4(18), 71.1(5), 71.1(6); Autos 349(8); Burg 46(1); Crim Law 394.1(1), 394.4(9), 436(4), 656(1), 698(1), 1036.1(1), 1044.1(5.1).

Hay v. State, TexCrimApp, 265 SW2d 107.—Crim Law 1090.1(1).

Hay v. State, TexCrimApp, 237 SW2d 987, 155 TexCrim 604.—Burg 36; Crim Law 598(2), 719(1), 720(8), 722.4, 808.5, 1091(4), 1091(8).

Hay; U.S. v., CA5 (Tex), 702 F2d 572.—Crim Law 1443, 1612(1), 1652, 1656; Sent & Pun 2221.

Hay; U.S. v., CA5 (Tex), 685 F2d 919.—Crim Law 1116.

Hay; U.S. v., NDTex, 187 FSupp2d 653.—Crim Law 577.3, 577.8(2), 577.10(1), 577.12(1).

Hay v. U.S., NDTex, 263 FSupp 813.—Int Rev 3014, 3037, 3038, 3048, 3080, 3273, 3472, 3475, 4006, 4009; Trusts 272.1, 274(1), 280.

Hay v. Waldron, CA5 (Tex), 834 F2d 481.—Civil R 1395(7); Prisons 4(7), 13(2), 13(3), 13(5); U S Mag 23, 26, 27.

Haydel v. State, TexCrimApp, 183 SW2d 470.—Crim Law 1094(2.1).

Haydell; Woods v., CA5 (Tex), 178 F2d 914.—Hus & W 238.3; War 216, 222.

Hayden, Ex parte, TexCrimApp, 215 SW2d 620, 152 TexCrim 517.—Const Law 591, 593; Crim Law 995(1); J P 31; Sent & Pun 1801; Statut 105(1), 109, 126, 181(1), 205.

Hayden, In re, BkrtcyNDTex, 248 BR 519.—Bankr 3372.14, 3375, 3376(4), 3403(1), 3405(13); Fed Cts 420; Judgm 634, 713(1), 720, 724, 828.21(2).

Hayden v. American Honda Motor Co., Inc., TexApp–Tyler, 835 SW2d 656.—App & E 110, 113(1), 873(1), 873(3); Bankr 3414; Judgm 585(4), 634, 707, 713(2), 800(1).

Hayden v. American Honda Motor Co., Inc., TexApp–Tyler, 835 SW2d 652, opinion withdrawn and superseded on reh 835 SW2d 656.—App & E 110, 113(1), 873(2), 873(3); Bankr 3413.1; Judgm 585(4), 707, 713(2), 800(1).

Hayden v. Bowen, CA5 (Tex), 404 F2d 682, cert den 89 SCt 1995, 395 US 933, 19 Wage & Hour Cas (BNA) 5, 23 LEd2d 448.—Commerce 62.43, 62.57; Fed Cts 921; Labor & Emp 2220(2), 2290(3), 2325.

Hayden v. City of Houston, TexCivApp–Fort Worth, 305 SW2d 798, ref nre.—App & E 172(1), 863, 954(1), 954(2); Aviation 217; Evid 31; Franch 1; Mun Corp 57, 59, 276, 722, 993(2).

Hayden v. Dallas County, TexCivApp–Dallas, 143 SW2d 990.—Commerce 14.6, 14.10(1), 54.5; Corp 657(3); Counties 116, 118, 120, 124(2).

Hayden v. Dunlap, TexCivApp–Dallas, 84 SW2d 306.—Fraud 12, 25, 49.

Hayden v. First Nat. Bank of Mt. Pleasant, Tex., CA5 (Tex), 595 F2d 994.—Fed Civ Proc 2497.1.

Hayden; Holland v., TexApp–Houston (14 Dist), 901 SW2d 763, reh overr, and writ den.—App & E 213, 232(0.5), 237(5), 238(2), 241, 294(1), 302(1), 302(6), 930(3); Atty & C 129(2); Damag 15, 190, 221(8).

Hayden v. Liberty Mut. Fire Ins. Co., Tex, 786 SW2d 260, on remand 805 SW2d 932.—Courts 101.

Hayden; Liberty Mut. Fire Ins. Co. v., TexApp–Beaumont, 805 SW2d 932.—App & E 1177(2); Pretrial Proc 474.

Hayden; Liberty Mut. Fire Ins. Co. v., TexApp–Beaumont, 779 SW2d 877, rev 786 SW2d 260, on remand 805 SW2d 932.—Judgm 181(5.1), 181(21), 186; Pretrial Proc 476; Time 8.5, 10(2).

Hayden v. Lowe, TexCivApp–Fort Worth, 239 SW2d 211, writ refused.—Contracts 123(1); U S 53(8).

Hayden v. Middleton, TexCivApp–Beaumont, 135 SW2d 281.—Courts 201; Wills 260, 302(2), 368, 376, 698.

Hayden v. State, TexCrimApp, 66 SW3d 269, reh den.—Crim Law 374, 1144.1.

Hayden v. State, TexApp–Texarkana, 13 SW3d 69, petition for discretionary review gr, and petition for discretionary review refused, rev 66 SW3d 269, reh den.—Crim Law 369.2(2), 374, 747, 1130(5), 1134(2), 1134(3), 1159.3(1), 1169.11; Infants 20.

Hayden v. State, TexApp–Beaumont, 753 SW2d 461.—Controlled Subs 80; Crim Law 436(3), 662.40.

Hayden v. State, TexApp–Eastland, 155 SW3d 640, petition for discretionary review refused.—Crim Law 304(1), 338(7), 351(2), 366(4), 369.2(2), 369.2(6), 641.13(1), 641.13(6), 706(3), 1134(8); Rob 7, 24.50.

Hayden v. State, TexApp–Corpus Christi, 818 SW2d 194. —Burg 2; Crim Law 273(4.1), 274(1), 274(2), 274(4), 274(8), 641.13(1), 641.13(5), 1134(2); False Pret 4, 26.

Hayden v. State, TexApp–Houston (14 Dist), 928 SW2d 229, petition for discretionary review refused.—Crim Law 1130(5), 1153(1); Ind & Inf 119, 167; Infants 20; Sent & Pun 311.

Hayden v. Texas-U.S. Chemical Co., CA5 (Tex), 681 F2d 1053, on remand 557 FSupp 382.—Fed Cts 941, 943.1; Labor & Emp 685.

Hayden v. Texas-U.S. Chemical Co., EDTex, 557 FSupp 382.—Fed Cts 424; Labor & Emp 405, 412, 427, 441, 571, 573, 618, 621, 687, 717; States 18.51.

Hayden; U.S. v., CA5 (Tex), 898 F2d 966.—Const Law 3809, 4729; Sent & Pun 1201, 1210.

Hayden v. U. S., CCA5 (Tex), 284 F 852.—Int Rev 5285.

Haydon v. Newman, TexApp–Amarillo, 162 SW2d 1041.—Chat Mtg 169, 208, 213, 265.

Haye v. State, TexCrimApp, 634 SW2d 313.—Const Law 1066, 1178; Mun Corp 631(1), 640.

Hayek v. Western Steel Co., Tex, 478 SW2d 786.—Const Law 642; Interest 39(1); Mech Liens 5, 113(1), 115(1), 161(1); Statut 209.

Hayek v. Western Steel Co., TexCivApp–Corpus Christi, 469 SW2d 206, writ gr, aff 478 SW2d 786.—Interest 22(1), 39(1), 44; Mech Liens 3, 113(1), 132(4), 304(1); Statut 223.1.

Hayek; Western Steel Co. v., TexCivApp–Corpus Christi, 452 SW2d 732.—App & E 854(1); Plead 111.3, 111.18, 111.42(5); Venue 22(3), 22(4), 22(6), 26.

Hayes, Ex parte, TexCrimApp, 97 SW2d 952, 131 TexCrim 255.—Crim Law 1182.

Hayes, Ex parte, TexApp–Fort Worth, 931 SW2d 721, petition for discretionary review refused.—Const Law 617; Double J 7, 59, 97.

Hayes, In re, CA5 (Tex), 194 FedAppx 217.—Ven & Pur 229(1), 232(8).

Hayes, In re, BkrtcyEDTex, 127 BR 795.—Bankr 3321, 3322.

Hayes; Ad West Marketing, Inc. v., CA5 (Tex), 745 F2d 980.—Const Law 3964, 3965(4); Fed Civ Proc 2444.1, 2451.1.

Hayes; Arzate v., TexApp–El Paso, 915 SW2d 616, reh overr, and appeal dism.—App & E 387(2), 946, 949; Atty & C 21.15, 21.20; Mand 4(4).

Hayes v. Bouligny, TexCivApp–Corpus Christi, 420 SW2d 800.—Bills & N 464, 465, 493(3); Contracts 334, 346(2); Evid 178(1), 185(2); Lost Inst 23(2), 23(3); Plead 290(3).

Hayes v. Brotherhood of Ry. and Airline Clerks/Allied Services Div., CA5 (Tex), 734 F2d 219.—Labor & Emp 1007, 1219(2).

Hayes v. Brotherhood of Ry. and Airline Clerks/Allied Services Div., CA5 (Tex), 727 F2d 1383, reh den 734 F2d 219, cert den 105 SCt 336, 469 US 935, 83 LEd2d 272, leave to file for reh den 105 SCt 944, 469 US 1182, 83 LEd2d 956.—Labor & Emp 1219(2).

Hayes; Brotherhood of R. R. Trainmen v., TexCivApp–San Antonio, 130 SW2d 1078, writ dism, correct.—App & E 294(1); Insurance 3002, 3014, 3117.

Hayes v. Caltex Petroleum Corp., SDTex, 332 FSupp 1205.—Fed Cts 81, 84.

Hayes v. City of Beaumont, TexCivApp–Beaumont, 190 SW2d 835, writ refused wom.—Schools 32, 52, 103(2), 106.23(2); Tax 2883.

Hayes; Commercial Standard Ins. Co. v., Tex, 142 SW2d 897, 135 Tex 288.—Work Comp 1927.

Hayes v. Commercial Standard Ins. Co., TexCivApp–Fort Worth, 140 SW2d 250, writ refused 142 SW2d 897, 135 Tex 288.—Work Comp 1192, 1238, 1285, 1927, 1969.

Hayes v. Diaz, CA5 (Tex), 78 FedAppx 353.—Evid 146; Fed Civ Proc 2338.1; Prisons 4(11).

Hayes; Dollison v., TexApp–Texarkana, 79 SW3d 246.—Damag 32, 49.10, 50, 97, 102, 130.3, 132(3), 163(1), 185(1), 221(7); Evid 568(1).

Hayes v. Easter, TexCivApp–Texarkana, 437 SW2d 652. —App & E 1012.1(12); Bills & N 520; Trial 382.

Hayes v. E.T.S. Enterprises, Inc., TexApp–Amarillo, 809 SW2d 652, writ den.—App & E 854(1); Contracts 93(1); Judgm 185(5), 185.3(14); Release 16.

Hayes v. First Trust Joint Stock Land Bank of Chicago, TexCivApp–Fort Worth, 111 SW2d 1172, writ dism. —Home 5, 33, 55, 70, 73, 81, 90, 95, 96.

Hayes; First Trust Joint Stock Land Bank of Chicago v., TexCivApp–Waco, 90 SW2d 331.—App & E 863; Inj 135; Mtg 335, 338.

Hayes v. Floyd, TexApp–Beaumont, 881 SW2d 617.—App & E 949; Mand 3(2.1), 4(1), 4(4), 12, 26.

Hayes v. Foodmaker, Inc., CA5 (Tex), 634 F2d 802.—U S Mag 20, 26.

Hayes; Gerhart v., CA5 (Tex), 217 F3d 320, reh den, cert den 121 SCt 573, 531 US 1014, 148 LEd2d 491.— Colleges 8.1(3); Const Law 1183, 1947, 2021.

Hayes; Gerhart v., CA5 (Tex), 201 F3d 646, opinion superseded in part on denial of reh 217 F3d 320, reh den, cert den 121 SCt 573, 531 US 1014, 148 LEd2d 491, cert den 121 SCt 573, 531 US 1014, 148 LEd2d 491.—Const Law 3879, 4172(6); Fed Cts 753, 766; States 53.

Hayes; Golden State Mut. Life Ins. Co. v., TexCivApp–Waco, 301 SW2d 147, ref nre.—App & E 930(1), 1001(1), 1177(7); Insurance 2578, 3571; Plead 34(1), 406(5).

Hayes v. Gulf Oil Corp., CA5 (Tex), 821 F2d 285.—Fed Cts 93; Judgm 825, 829(1).

Hayes; Gulf States Theatres of Texas v., TexCivApp–Beaumont, 534 SW2d 406, ref nre.—App & E 931(1), 989, 1010.1(1), 1010.1(3); Land & Ten 49(3), 105, 112.5.

Hayes; Gulf States Theatres of Texas, Inc. v., TexCivApp–Beaumont, 518 SW2d 604.—App & E 846(5), 854(1), 931(3), 989; Contracts 202(2); Labor & Emp 111; Princ & A 8.

Hayes; Hall v., TexCivApp–El Paso, 441 SW2d 275.—Ack 55(1), 56, 62(2), 62(3); Adop 7.5, 16; App & E 846(5), 934(1); Contracts 93(2), 93(4); Evid 65.

Hayes; Hamman v., TexCivApp–Beaumont, 391 SW2d 73, writ refused.—Quo W 5.

Hayes; Harlow v., TexApp–Amarillo, 991 SW2d 24, review den.—Anim 48, 49; App & E 1048(6); Autos 178, 245(21); Evid 558(11); Motions 58; Statut 181(1), 212.6, 212.7.

Hayes v. Harris County Democratic Executive Committee, TexCivApp–Hous (14 Dist), 563 SW2d 884.— Elections 126(3), 126(4); Mand 74(3); Offic 31.

Hayes v. Hayes, TexApp–Texarkana, 920 SW2d 344, writ den.—App & E 395, 798, 801(1); Const Law 4013(3), 4426, 4494; Contempt 2, 61(4); Courts 27, 78; Execution 373.1.

Hayes; Hayes v., TexApp–Texarkana, 920 SW2d 344, writ den.—App & E 395, 798, 801(1); Const Law 4013(3), 4426, 4494; Contempt 2, 61(4); Courts 27, 78; Execution 373.1.

Hayes v. Hayes, TexCivApp–Corpus Christi, 378 SW2d 375, writ dism.—Divorce 223, 227(2), 252.1, 252.2, 252.3(1), 252.3(3), 252.4, 286(0.5); Evid 353(9); Hus & W 49.2(10).

Hayes; Hayes v., TexCivApp–Corpus Christi, 378 SW2d 375, writ dism.—Divorce 223, 227(2), 252.1, 252.2, 252.3(1), 252.3(3), 252.4, 286(0.5); Evid 353(9); Hus & W 49.2(10).

Hayes; Hernandez v., TexApp–San Antonio, 931 SW2d 648, reh overr, and writ den.—Const Law 328, 2311, 2312, 2314; Libel 36, 38(1); Torts 121, 122.

Hayes v. Home Indem. Co., TexCivApp–Houston, 354 SW2d 600, ref nre.—Trial 352.10; Work Comp 1543, 1696, 1958, 1962.

Hayes; Lott v., TexCivApp–Waco, 433 SW2d 514, writ refused.—App & E 78(4).

Hayes; Manning v., CA5 (Tex), 212 F3d 866, cert den 121 SCt 1401, 532 US 941, 149 LEd2d 345.—Fed Cts 374, 419, 776; Insurance 1117(1), 3462, 3481(2); Labor & Emp 407, 579, 580, 582, 583; States 18.41, 18.51.

Hayes; Moore v., TexCivApp–El Paso, 144 SW2d 373.— Plead 111.40, 111.42(10).

Hayes; Most Worshipful Grand Lodge Free & Accepted Masons of Texas v., TexCivApp–Dallas, 82 SW2d 411. —Fraud 35; Insurance 1848, 3089, 3090, 3393, 3464.

Hayes; NCNB Texas Nat. Bank v., BkrtcyEDTex, 127 BR 795. See Hayes, In re.

Hayes v. Nichols, TexCivApp–Eastland, 203 SW2d 274.— App & E 231(9), 1062.1; Contracts 350(1); Trial 219, 366.

Hayes v. Norman, TexCivApp–Corpus Christi, 383 SW2d 477, ref nre.—Action 60; App & E 79(1), 80(6), 257, 964; Judgm 181(14), 185.3(16).

Hayes; Northeast Independent School Dist. v., TexApp– San Antonio, 727 SW2d 26.—Work Comp 846, 847, 1654.

Hayes v. Packard Bell, Nec., EDTex, 193 FSupp2d 910. —Tel 1342.

Hayes; P & M Crane Co. v., CA5 (Tex), 930 F2d 424, reh den 935 F2d 1293, reh den Suderman Stevedores v. Green, 935 F2d 1293.—Work Comp 803, 844, 1624, 1636, 1939.4(4).

Hayes v. Patrick, TexApp–Fort Worth, 71 SW3d 516.— App & E 171(1), 863, 934(1); Game 6; Judgm 181(27), 185(2), 185.3(2); Offic 114; States 112.1(3).

Hayes v. Patrick, TexApp–Fort Worth, 45 SW3d 110, reh overr, and review den, and reh of petition for review den.—App & E 70(8), 863; Courts 185; Game 6; Judgm 185(2), 185(5), 185.3(1); Mun Corp 747(3); Offic 114.

Hayes v. Pennock, TexCivApp–Beaumont, 192 SW2d 169, ref nre.—App & E 1212(1); Deeds 56(2), 56(4), 186; Plead 354; Witn 140(4), 202, 205, 222.

Hayes v. Pin Oak Petroleum, Inc., TexApp–Austin, 798 SW2d 668, writ den.—Courts 97(1); Judgm 185(2), 524, 526, 619, 634, 713(2), 829(3).

Hayes; Process Operators, Inc. v., TexCivApp–Tyler, 566 SW2d 93.—App & E 846(5), 989, 1012.1(3); Labor & Emp 34(2); Plead 427.

Hayes; Renck v., TexCivApp–Austin, 224 SW2d 909.— Chat Mtg 176(1).

Hayes v. Rinehart, TexApp–Eastland, 65 SW3d 286.— Evid 384, 397(1), 434(8); Gifts 4, 15, 49(1), 49(5).

Hayes v. Roux Laboratories, Inc., TexCivApp–Eastland, 443 SW2d 621.—Judgm 185.3(8); Release 12(3), 38.

Hayes v. Royala, Inc., EDTex, 180 BR 476.—Bankr 2103, 2130.

Hayes; RSR Corp. v., TexApp–Dallas, 673 SW2d 928, dism.—App & E 946, 949; Neglig 371; Parties 35.1, 35.17, 35.79.

Hayes v. Secretary of Health, Ed. and Welfare, CA5 (Tex), 413 F2d 997.—Adop 6; Social S 137.5.

Hayes; Smith v., TexCivApp–Fort Worth, 597 SW2d 488. —App & E 389(2), 389(3), 624.

Hayes v. Snoddy, TexCivApp–El Paso, 583 SW2d 479.— Wills 703, 725.

Hayes v. Solomon, CA5 (Tex), 597 F2d 958, reh den 602 F2d 1246, cert den 100 SCt 1028, 444 US 1078, 62 LEd2d 761.—Antitrust 520, 560, 621, 650, 958, 963(1), 964, 972(3), 977(2); Fed Cts 402; Judgm 591.1; Monop 28(7.7).

Hayes; Southern Pac. Co. v., TexCivApp–Corpus Christi, 391 SW2d 463, ref nre.—Em Dom 147, 149(5), 219, 262(5); Trial 191(11).

Hayes v. State, TexCrimApp, 161 SW3d 507.—Crim Law 1134(3); Homic 1054.

Hayes v. State, TexCrimApp, 85 SW3d 809.—Const Law 4594(1); Crim Law 338(7), 438(5.1), 438(7), 700(3), 1153(1), 1165(1), 1169.1(10); Sent & Pun 1720, 1789(6).

Hayes v. State, TexCrimApp, 728 SW2d 804.—Assault 67, 96(3); Crim Law 770(2), 795(2.30), 814(1), 829(5); Neglig 1659, 1725.

Hayes v. State, TexCrimApp, 560 SW2d 671.—Crim Law 330; Sent & Pun 2006, 2021.

Hayes v. State, TexCrimApp, 502 SW2d 158.—Crim Law 339.11(2), 517.3(1), 1169.12.

Hayes v. State, TexCrimApp, 495 SW2d 897.—Bail 77(1).

Hayes v. State, TexCrimApp, 484 SW2d 922.—Crim Law 274(6), 274(8), 641.13(2.1), 1130(5), 1170(1), 1178.

Hayes v. State, TexCrimApp, 464 SW2d 832.—Crim Law 829(15); Larc 60, 64(1).

Hayes v. State, TexCrimApp, 449 SW2d 233.—Crim Law 1126, 1130(4).

Hayes v. State, TexCrimApp, 353 SW2d 25, 171 TexCrim 646.—Homic 1154, 1377.

Hayes v. State, TexCrimApp, 334 SW2d 442, 169 TexCrim 439.—Sent & Pun 1014, 1066, 2021.

Hayes v. State, TexCrimApp, 288 SW2d 771, 162 TexCrim 660.—Autos 356; Crim Law 713, 784(1), 814(17).

Hayes v. State, TexCrimApp, 288 SW2d 508.—Crim Law 1090.1(1).

Hayes v. State, TexCrimApp, 288 SW2d 501.—Crim Law 1097(5).

Hayes v. State, TexCrimApp, 252 SW2d 200.—Crim Law 1090.1(1).

Hayes v. State, TexCrimApp, 214 SW2d 631, 152 TexCrim 422.—Crim Law 1086.14, 1090.1(3); Homic 1134.

Hayes v. State, TexCrimApp, 172 SW2d 98, 146 TexCrim 113.—Crim Law 730(11), 1169.5(3).

Hayes v. State, TexCrimApp, 115 SW2d 960, 134 TexCrim 444.—Autos 359; Crim Law 1144.17.

Hayes v. State, TexApp–Houston (1 Dist), 124 SW3d 781, reh overr, and petition for discretionary review gr, aff 161 SW3d 507.—Crim Law 26, 795(1.5), 795(2.10), 1043(3), 1144.13(2.1), 1144.13(6), 1153(1), 1159.2(1), 1159.2(2); Homic 565, 708, 1051(1), 1054, 1056, 1148, 1457; Ind & Inf 189(8).

Hayes v. State, TexApp–Houston (1 Dist), 709 SW2d 780. —Crim Law 938(1), 1042, 1134(3); Sent & Pun 115(1), 117; Witn 297(13.1).

Hayes v. State, TexApp–Houston (1 Dist), 630 SW2d 820. —Forg 48.

Hayes v. State, TexApp–Austin, 132 SW3d 147.—Arrest 63.5(1), 63.5(4), 63.5(5), 68(4); Controlled Subs 81; Crim Law 741(1), 742(1), 795(2.10), 795(2.70), 1139, 1158(4), 1159.4(1), 1187, 1189, 1224(1); Double J 107.1, 108; Searches 23.

Hayes v. State, TexApp–Dallas, 740 SW2d 887.—Homic 1080(3), 1080(4), 1080(8), 1082, 1084.

Hayes v. State, TexApp–Amarillo, 166 SW3d 899, petition for discretionary review refused.—Crim Law 620(6), 620(7), 1030(1), 1035(2), 1144.9.

Hayes v. State, TexApp–Amarillo, 634 SW2d 359.—Autos 320, 355(6), 355(13), 357, 419; Crim Law 347, 388.2, 438(1), 444, 627.8(6), 675, 814(17); Searches 31.1, 44.

Hayes v. State, TexApp–Beaumont, 672 SW2d 246.— Const Law 4509(25); Crim Law 13.1(1), 1130(5); Weap 3, 6.

Hayes v. State, TexApp–Eastland, 656 SW2d 926.—Burg 41(1).

Hayes; Storey v., TexCivApp–San Antonio, 448 SW2d 179, writ dism.—Evid 472(8), 474(4), 478(1), 506, 510; Wills 400.

Hayes v. Super-Cold Southwest Co., TexCivApp–Dallas, 285 SW2d 402.—Venue 7.5(4).

Hayes; Texas & N. O. R. Co. v., Tex, 293 SW2d 484, 156 Tex 148.—App & E 712; Labor & Emp 2777, 2784, 2879, 2881; Trial 350.7(7), 351.4.

Hayes; Texas & N. O. R. Co. v., TexCivApp–Austin, 284 SW2d 776, aff 293 SW2d 484, 156 Tex 148.—App & E 1004(5), 1062.2, 1078(1); Damag 208(1); Labor & Emp 2824, 2881; Trial 350.7(1).

Hayes v. Texas Dept. of Public Safety, TexCivApp–Hous (1 Dist), 498 SW2d 35, ref nre.—Autos 132; Const Law 48(1), 990, 3102; Judgm 476.

Hayes; Texas Employers' Ins. Ass'n v., TexApp–Houston (14 Dist), 654 SW2d 804.—App & E 136; Work Comp 554, 571, 600, 1536, 1728, 1988.

Hayes v. Texas Employers' Ins. Ass'n, TexCivApp–Amarillo, 254 SW 501, writ refused.—Divorce 375.

Hayes v. Texas General Indem. Co., TexCivApp–Texarkana, 298 SW2d 618.—Work Comp 1400.

Hayes; Texas Indem. Ins. Co. v., TexCivApp–Amarillo, 106 SW2d 760.—Work Comp 1300, 1683.

Hayes v. Travelers Ins. Co., TexCivApp–Waco, 358 SW2d 254, writ refused.—Partners 213(2); Work Comp 235.

Hayes; U.S. v., CA5 (Tex), 32 F3d 171.—Crim Law 1139, 1181.5(8); Sent & Pun 2101, 2143.

Hayes v. U.S., CA5 (Tex), 899 F2d 438.—Aviation 122, 141, 151, 153, 176.1; Damag 191; Fed Cts 824, 866, 871; Neglig 202, 213, 231, 233, 259, 1577, 1579, 1656, 1692; U S 78(12), 78(14); Witn 79(1).

Hayes; U.S. v., CA5 (Tex), 595 F2d 258, reh den 598 F2d 620, cert den 100 SCt 138, 444 US 866, 62 LEd2d 89.—Consp 28(3), 47(12); Controlled Subs 10.

Hayes; U.S. v., CA5 (Tex), 589 F2d 811, reh den 591 F2d 1343, cert den 100 SCt 93, 444 US 847, 62 LEd2d 60.—Civil R 1808; Const Law 4506; Crim Law 11, 26, 31, 37.10(1), 37.10(2), 60, 625.10(3), 625.15, 641.13(5), 829(16), 1030(1), 1038.2, 1083, 1147, 1158(2); Double J 186; Ind & Inf 10.1(1); Judgm 828.8; Mental H 432; Sent & Pun 35, 56, 1483; Stip 14(7).

Hayes v. U.S., CA5 (Tex), 464 F2d 1252.—Consp 43(8); Crim Law 1436, 1478, 1498, 1618(10).

Hayes; U.S. v., CA5 (Tex), 444 F2d 472, cert den 92 SCt 210, 404 US 882, 30 LEd2d 163.—Crim Law 371(1), 641.13(2.1), 1037.1(2), 1171.1(3).

Hayes v. U.S., CA5 (Tex), 416 F2d 23.—Crim Law 1132, 1433(1).

Hayes v. U.S., CA5 (Tex), 323 F2d 954.—Crim Law 1655(6), 1667, 1668(1).

Hayes v. U.S., CA5 (Tex), 258 F2d 400, cert den 79 SCt 87, 358 US 856, 3 LEd2d 89, cert den 79 SCt 610, 359 US 928, 3 LEd2d 630.—Crim Law 1077.1(2), 1077.1(3).

Hayes; U.S. v., CA5 (Tex), 118 FedAppx 856.—Crim Law 465, 720(5), 723(3), 726, 1036.6.

Hayes; U.S. v., SDTex, 468 FSupp 179.—Const Law 4782, 4783(1), 4783(2); Crim Law 625.25, 625.35, 1166(12), 1409, 1412, 1443, 1498, 1612(1), 1613, 1615, 1618(5), 1668(1), 1668(2); Hab Corp 705.1, 898(1); Mental H 434.

Hayes; U.S. v., SDTex, 293 FSupp 628, aff 416 F2d 23.—Crim Law 1433(1); Judges 51(1).

Hayes; U.S. v., SDTex, 293 FSupp 625, aff 416 F2d 23.—Crim Law 641.7(1), 1447, 1449, 1618(10).

Hayes v. Western Weighing and Inspection Bureau, CA5 (Tex), 838 F2d 1434.—Const Law 4185; Labor & Emp 1576, 1612.

Hayes v. White, TexCivApp–Corpus Christi, 384 SW2d 895, ref nre.—Chat Mtg 6, 255; Gifts 41; Judgm 715(2); Trover 16.

Hayes v. Williams, SDTex, 341 FSupp 182.—Civil R 1098; Courts 509; Elections 18, 90; Fed Cts 52, 998, 1011; Offic 27; Rem of C 70; Sent & Pun 1286; States 28(1).

Hayes v. Wissel, TexApp–Fort Worth, 882 SW2d 97.—Courts 12(2.10), 12(2.30), 35.

Hayes-Jenkins; Monumental Life Ins. Co. v., CA5 (Tex), 403 F3d 304.—Antitrust 221; Estop 52.10(2), 52.15, 119; Fed Civ Proc 2491.9, 2501, 2507; Fed Cts 776; Insurance 1625, 3081, 3128; Mtg 201.

Hayes Wheels Intern., Inc.; Lozano v., TexApp–Corpus Christi, 933 SW2d 245, reh overr.—Judgm 17(3), 17(9), 101(1), 102, 162(2).

Haygood; Fort Worth Lloyds v., Tex, 246 SW2d 865, 151 Tex 149.—Work Comp 1072, 2191, 2247, 2251.

Haygood; Fort Worth Lloyds v., TexCivApp–Galveston, 238 SW2d 835, rev 246 SW2d 865, 151 Tex 149.—Work Comp 2213.

Haygood v. State, TexApp–San Antonio, 127 SW3d 805, reh overr, and petition for discretionary review refused. —Const Law 4594(1); Crim Law 636(4), 700(2.1), 700(4), 700(5), 938(1), 943, 959, 1036.1(9), 1090.8, 1120(3), 1166.14; Homic 1181.

Hayhoe v. Henegar, TexApp–Eastland, 172 SW3d 642.—App & E 1151(2); Damag 191; Evid 544, 545, 546, 555.10, 571(10), 574; Interest 39(2.50), 39(3).

Hayhurst v. Henry, NDTex, 102 FSupp 306.—Fed Cts 295; Work Comp 2158, 2223, 2224.

Hayhurst v. Paylor, TexCivApp–Amarillo, 293 SW2d 531.—Deeds 61; Wills 88(4).

Hayhurst; Plains Common Consol. School Dist. No. 1 of Yoakum County v., TexCivApp–Amarillo, 122 SW2d 322.—Admin Law 132; Const Law 642; Inj 138.54; Offic 40, 54, 62, 104; Schools 48(7), 53(4), 61, 63(1), 63(2).

Haykel v. State, TexCrimApp, 255 SW2d 1014, 158 TexCrim 359.—Burg 41(1); Crim Law 698(1), 1036.1(5), 1054(1), 1169.2(5).

Hayles v. General Motors Corp., SDTex, 82 FSupp2d 650.—Judgm 185.3(21); Neglig 1610, 1613, 1614, 1619; Prod Liab 6, 8, 11, 15, 36, 76, 77.5; Sales 284(1).

Hayles; Harris v., TexCivApp–Texarkana, 433 SW2d 250.—App & E 865; Judgm 17(3), 130; Proc 80.

Hayles v. State, TexCrimApp, 507 SW2d 213.—Crim Law 394.5(3), 577, 1170.5(1); Witn 37(4).

Hayles v. State, TexApp–Beaumont, 644 SW2d 762.—Crim Law 749.

Hayles; U.S. v., CA5 (Tex), 492 F2d 125, cert gr, vac 95 SCt 168, 419 US 892, 42 LEd2d 136.—Dist & Pros Attys 8; Double J 186; Searches 178, 198.

Hayles; U.S. v., CA5 (Tex), 471 F2d 788, cert den 93 SCt 2159, 411 US 969, 36 LEd2d 690.—Counterfeit 18; Crim Law 412(3), 412(4), 739.1(1), 1169.12; Searches 119.

Hayman v. Dowda, TexCivApp–Fort Worth, 233 SW2d 466.—App & E 692(1), 931(1), 981; Mines 55(2); New Tr 99, 102(3), 102(8), 105, 108(1); Ref of Inst 19(1), 43, 44, 45(6).

Hayman; Dowda v., TexCivApp–Fort Worth, 221 SW2d 1016, writ refused.—App & E 878(2); Lim of Act 39(12); Mines 55(5); Ven & Pur 230(1).

Hayman v. Hayman, TexCivApp–Tyler, 512 SW2d 71.—App & E 66, 76(1), 78(4), 792.

Hayman; Hayman v., TexCivApp–Tyler, 512 SW2d 71.—App & E 66, 76(1), 78(4), 792.

Hayman Co. General Contractors, Inc.; Island on Lake Travis, Ltd. v., TexApp–Austin, 834 SW2d 529, reh overr, and writ den, and writ withdrawn, and writ gr, vac pursuant to settlement 848 SW2d 84.—Alt Disp Res 115, 144, 230, 328, 332, 334, 342, 371, 374(5).

Haymann; Hanson v., TexCivApp–Galveston, 280 SW 869, writ dism woj.—Action 50(4.1).

Haymes; Clifton v., TexCivApp–Eastland, 608 SW2d 272.—Pretrial Proc 699.

Haymes; Maucini v., TexCivApp–Fort Worth, 231 SW2d 757, mandamus overr.—Plead 111.2, 111.3, 111.4, 111.5, 111.6, 111.42(8).

Haymes; Mower v., TexApp–Houston (1 Dist), 780 SW2d 896.—App & E 961; Pretrial Proc 44.1, 314, 315.

Haynen; Dufner v., TexCivApp–San Antonio, 263 SW2d 662, ref nre.—App & E 766; Wills 62, 64, 450, 470(1), 601(2), 800.

Haynes; Balli v., CA5 (Tex), 804 F2d 306.—Civil R 1090; Prisons 17(1).

Haynes v. Beceiro, TexApp–San Antonio, 219 SW3d 24, review den.—Assault 11; Fraud 3, 9, 16; Health 907, 908.

Haynes; Butler v., TexCivApp–Beaumont, 426 SW2d 642, ref nre.—App & E 837(1), 1069.1; New Tr 56; Trial 344.

Haynes v. City of Abilene, Tex, 659 SW2d 638.—App & E 1001(1), 1003(5); Em Dom 2(6), 146, 303; Mun Corp 122.1(2), 299, 439, 502(1), 502(3), 511(2).

Haynes; City of Abilene v., TexApp–Eastland, 645 SW2d 928, writ gr, rev 659 SW2d 638.—Mun Corp 429, 513(7).

Haynes v. City of Beaumont, TexApp–Texarkana, 35 SW3d 166.—Action 2; App & E 173(2), 223, 232(0.5), 863, 949, 1079; Civil R 1304, 1343, 1345, 1351(1), 1376(1), 1376(2), 1407, 1765; Const Law 1929, 1947, 4172(1), 4172(6); Costs 2; Judgm 181(1), 181(27), 183, 185(5), 185.1(2), 185.1(4), 185.2(5), 189; Labor & Emp 40(2), 388; Mun Corp 218(3), 218(8); Offic 60, 114; Plead 34(1), 228, 263.

Haynes v. City of Quanah, TexCivApp–Amarillo, 610 SW2d 842, ref nre.—Zoning 22.

Haynes; City of Waco v., TexCivApp–Waco, 562 SW2d 546.—Mun Corp 805(2), 808(3), 821(6), 821(23.1); Neglig 1037(4).

Haynes v. Clanton, TexCivApp–El Paso, 257 SW2d 789, writ dism by agreement.—Ex & Ad 18, 35(1), 35(2).

Haynes; Crais v., TexApp–Waco, 867 SW2d 412.—App & E 497(1), 635(1), 659(3).

Haynes v. Dallas County Jr. College Dist., NDTex, 386 FSupp 208.—Const Law 90.1(1.4), 702, 1189(1), 1190(1), 1967, 2007, 2011, 4224(12); Fed Cts 994, 1002, 1011; Schools 169.

Haynes; Duncan Coffee Co. v., TexCivApp–El Paso, 129 SW2d 1163.—Corp 503(1).

Haynes v. Dunn, TexCivApp–Waco, 518 SW2d 880, ref nre.—Adv Poss 42, 57, 63(4), 85(1); App & E 78(1), 843(3), 1170.6; Estop 23, 32(1).

Haynes v. Eanes, TexCivApp–Eastland, 152 SW2d 799.—Bills & N 493(3), 516, 518(1); Compromise 16(2).

Haynes; Eanes v., TexCivApp–Eastland, 135 SW2d 190.—App & E 755, 1175(1); Courts 121(5), 122.

Haynes v. Edwards, Tex, 698 SW2d 97.—Wills 358.

Haynes; Edwards v., TexApp–Houston (14 Dist), 690 SW2d 50, rev 698 SW2d 97.—Adop 6, 7.1; Courts 202(5); Wills 220, 358.

Haynes; F & N Taxi v., TexCivApp–Galveston, 262 SW2d 117, ref nre.—Carr 295.2, 318(4).

Haynes v. Felder, CA5 (Tex), 239 F2d 868.—Aband L P 10; Fed Civ Proc 2536.1; Fed Cts 1.1, 288, 622; Statut 181(1).

Haynes; Fielder v., TexCivApp–Fort Worth, 97 SW2d 328, writ dism.—Frds St of 63(1); Ven & Pur 257.

Haynes; First City Nat. Bank of Paris v., TexCivApp–Texarkana, 614 SW2d 605.—Damag 91(1), 91(3), 221(5.1); Interest 31, 47(1); Trial 366; Trusts 262.

Haynes; Garcia v., TexCivApp–Beaumont, 99 SW2d 433.—Venue 22(8).

Haynes v. Haynes, TexApp–Dallas, 180 SW3d 927.—Divorce 249.2, 254(1); Hus & W 278(1), 278(3).

Haynes; Haynes v., TexApp–Dallas, 180 SW3d 927.—Divorce 249.2, 254(1); Hus & W 278(1), 278(3).

Haynes v. Haynes, TexApp–Houston (14 Dist), 178 SW3d 350, reh overr, and review den, and reh of petition for review den.—App & E 1079; Courts 489(9); Fed Cts 241; Insurance 1117(1); Labor & Emp 407; States 18.15, 18.41, 18.51; Torts 203, 244.

Haynes; Haynes v., TexApp–Houston (14 Dist), 178 SW3d 350, reh overr, and review den, and reh of petition for review den.—App & E 1079; Courts 489(9); Fed Cts 241; Insurance 1117(1); Labor & Emp 407; States 18.15, 18.41, 18.51; Torts 203, 244.

Haynes v. Haynes, TexCivApp, 191 SW2d 81, writ dism.—Child C 275, 920.

Haynes; Haynes v., TexCivApp, 191 SW2d 81, writ dism.—Child C 275, 920.

Haynes v. Henderson, TexCivApp–Austin, 345 SW2d 857, ref nre.—App & E 931(6), 1170.7; Evid 317(18); Frds St of 44(1); Wills 184(3), 184(4), 476, 566.

Haynes v. McIntosh, TexApp–Corpus Christi, 776 SW2d 784, writ den.—App & E 763, 907(4); Divorce 322; Hus & W 249(3), 272(4).

Haynes; McKain v., TexApp–Texarkana, 203 SW2d 970.—Neglig 232, 1010, 1713, 1717; Trial 365.1(1).

Haynes v. Martinez, TexCivApp–Amarillo, 260 SW2d 369, ref nre.—Autos 226(2), 245(66); Neglig 440(1).

Haynes; Morales v., CA5 (Tex), 890 F2d 708.—Const Law 4149; Int Rev 4464.

Haynes v. Pennzoil Co., CA5 (Tex), 207 F3d 296.—Civil R 1135, 1243, 1252, 1536, 1541; Fed Civ Proc 2497.1.

Haynes v. Rederi A/S Aladdin, CA5 (Tex), 362 F2d 345, cert den 87 SCt 731, 385 US 1020, 17 LEd2d 557.—Adm 117, 118.7(5); Atty & C 155; Damag 133; Fed Cts 850.1, 866; Interest 39(3), 47(1); Ship 84(5); Work Comp 2085, 2251.

Haynes v. Rederi A/S Aladdin, SDTex, 254 FSupp 185, aff 362 F2d 345, cert den 87 SCt 731, 385 US 1020, 17 LEd2d 557.—Damag 130.3, 133, 134(1); Fed Civ Proc 2736, 2737.5, 2741; Ship 84(3.2), 84(5), 86(2.5); Work Comp 2243.

Haynes; Reynolds v., TexCivApp–Eastland, 425 SW2d 29, ref nre.—Land & Ten 54, 152(4), 192(1), 192(2), 231(8); Ten in C 29.

Haynes v. Rippetoe, TexCivApp–Eastland, 203 SW2d 628, ref nre 203 SW2d 630.—Mand 28, 44, 187.1, 187.8.

Haynes v. Rippetoe, TexCivApp–Eastland, 198 SW2d 768.—Courts 207.4(2).

Haynes; San Angelo Life & Acc. Ass'n v., TexCivApp–Austin, 106 SW2d 363, writ dism.—Insurance 1606, 1663, 1758, 2957, 2958, 3095, 3096(2).

Haynes v. Scott, CA5 (Tex), 116 F3d 137.—Fed Civ Proc 2734.

Haynes v. Southwest Natural Gas Co., CCA5 (Tex), 123 F2d 1011.—Mines 78.2, 78.7(4), 79.3.

Haynes v. State, TexCrimApp, 627 SW2d 710.—Crim Law 347, 404.70, 629.5(2), 723(3), 1036.1(8), 1036.2, 1166.16; Witn 374(1), 389.

Haynes v. State, TexCrimApp, 567 SW2d 518.—Crim Law 419(1), 419(3), 1169.1(9).

Haynes v. State, TexCrimApp, 498 SW2d 950.—Crim Law 720(7.1), 1171.3; Rape 4, 40(1), 40(3), 40(4), 51(4).

Haynes v. State, TexCrimApp, 482 SW2d 191.—Crim Law 419(11), 656(1), 921, 1166.22(4.1), 1171.1(3).

Haynes v. State, TexCrimApp, 475 SW2d 739.—Controlled Subs 79; Crim Law 394.4(5.1), 400(10), 419(1.5); Searches 23, 30, 75, 126, 147.1; Witn 298.

Haynes v. State, TexCrimApp, 468 SW2d 375, cert den 92 SCt 1180, 405 US 956, 31 LEd2d 233.—Crim Law 217, 1115(1), 1144.1; Sent & Pun 313.

Haynes v. State, TexCrimApp, 466 SW2d 780.—Crim Law 1109(3), 1130(2).

Haynes v. State, TexCrimApp, 359 SW2d 52, 172 Tex-Crim 470.—Homic 1155.

Haynes v. State, TexCrimApp, 317 SW2d 945, 167 Tex-Crim 68.—Crim Law 956(4); Homic 1136, 1193; Jury 120.

Haynes v. State, TexCrimApp, 284 SW2d 736.—Crim Law 1070.

Haynes v. State, TexCrimApp, 283 SW2d 57.—Crim Law 1070.

Haynes v. State, TexCrimApp, 200 SW2d 824, 150 Tex-Crim 337.—Autos 355(6), 359; Crim Law 800(2), 881(1), 1033.2, 1090.3, 1159.2(3).

Haynes v. State, TexCrimApp, 143 SW2d 617, 140 Tex-Crim 52.—Crim Law 394.5(2), 424(1), 564(2), 564(3), 1056.1(1), 1090.14, 1159.5; Rec S Goods 7(3), 8(3).

Haynes v. State, TexCrimApp, 98 SW2d 815, 131 Tex-Crim 317.—Crim Law 1086.13.

Haynes v. State, TexApp–Houston (1 Dist), 727 SW2d 294, petition for discretionary review gr, petition for discretionary review dism 794 SW2d 35.—Crim Law 641.13(1), 641.13(6), 660, 724(1); Witn 405(1), 406.

Haynes v. State, TexApp–Houston (1 Dist), 663 SW2d 118, petition for discretionary review refused.—Crim Law 722.5, 1134(3), 1171.6.

Haynes v. State, TexApp–Austin, 790 SW2d 824.—Crim Law 641.13(1), 641.13(2.1), 641.13(5), 641.13(6).

Haynes v. State, TexApp–Waco, 85 SW3d 855, petition for discretionary review refused, habeas corpus gr Ex parte Haynes, 2003 WL 1821487.—Crim Law 774, 1036.1(3.1), 1169.1(3), 1169.2(1), 1169.2(2); Homic 996, 1506.

Haynes v. Stripling, TexApp–Eastland, 812 SW2d 397.—Const Law 2663, 2759; Hus & W 247, 266.1.

Haynes; Texas State Bd. of Medical Examiners v., TexCivApp–Tyler, 388 SW2d 258.—App & E 846(5), 994(3), 1010.1(3), 1012.1(2); Health 223(2).

Haynes; Trans-State Pavers, Inc. v., TexApp–Beaumont, 808 SW2d 727, writ den.—App & E 232(2), 878(2), 1056.1(5); Autos 305(10); Const Law 309(1), 3974; Evid 146, 155(1); Insurance 3526(5); Judgm 243; Neglig 1634; Plead 36(1); Witn 406.

Haynes v. U.S., USTex, 88 SCt 722, 390 US 85, 19 LEd2d 923.—Const Law 45, 2525; Crim Law 393(1), 1181(1), 1186.1; Fed Cts 458; Int Rev 4311, 5265; Statut 217.4.

Haynes; U.S. v., CA5 (Tex), 573 F2d 236, cert den 99 SCt 154, 439 US 850, 58 LEd2d 153.—Crim Law 656(7), 858(3), 1039, 1166.22(4.1), 1174(6); Int Rev 5263.55, 5312, 5313.

Haynes v. U.S., CA5 (Tex), 415 F2d 347, cert den 90 SCt 600, 396 US 1024, 24 LEd2d 518.—Crim Law 1036.4, 1037.1(2), 1044.1(6), 1171.3; Searches 62.

Haynes v. U.S., CA5 (Tex), 372 F2d 651, cert gr 87 SCt 2130, 388 US 908, 18 LEd2d 1347, rev 88 SCt 722, 390 US 85, 19 LEd2d 923.—Crim Law 273.4(1), 393(1), 1026.10(4); Int Rev 5251.

Haynes v. U.S., CA5 (Tex), 339 F2d 30, cert den 85 SCt 926, 380 US 924, 13 LEd2d 809.—Controlled Subs 7, 100(2); Crim Law 393(1), 1429(1), 1429(2), 1451, 1493, 1650.

Haynes v. U.S., CA5 (Tex), 319 F2d 620.—Controlled Subs 39; Crim Law 37(5), 37(8), 1028; Int Rev 5262.

Haynes; U.S. v., EDTex, 120 FSupp2d 615.—Crim Law 589(1), 632(2); Judges 32.

Haynes; Vermillion v., Tex, 215 SW2d 605, 147 Tex 359.—App & E 959(3); Home 143; Autos at 184; Partit 63(1), 87, 97; Plead 236(3); Ten in C 28(3).

Haynes v. Vermillion, TexCivApp–Fort Worth, 242 SW2d 444, ref nre.—Home 36, 57(3), 140; Hus & W 249(2.1); Partit 86, 87; Ten in C 15(10), 28(7).

Haynes; Vermillion v., TexCivApp–Texarkana, 211 SW2d 781, rev 215 SW2d 605, 147 Tex 359.—App & E 1010.1(18); Covenants 13, 37; Home 57(1); Lim of Act 184; Wills 837, 839, 847(2).

Haynes; Warthan v., Tex, 288 SW2d 481, 155 Tex 413.—Hus & W 249(3), 265; Insurance 3402, 3485, 3490.

Haynes v. Warthan, TexCivApp–Texarkana, 272 SW2d 140, rev 288 SW2d 481, 155 Tex 413.—Hus & W 254, 276(3); Insurance 3468.

Haynes; Whitaker v., TexCivApp–Beaumont, 128 SW2d 532, writ dism, correct.—App & E 730(1), 1067; Trial 219.

Haynes; Wise v., TexCivApp–Texarkana, 103 SW2d 477.—Evid 205(1), 208(2), 208(6), 220(6), 230(3), 272; Tresp to T T 47(2); Trusts 110, 357(2); Witn 205.

Haynes; Young v., TexCivApp–Galveston, 295 SW2d 536.—Contracts 256; Estop 110, 115; Judgm 198, 199(1), 251(1).

Haynes & Boone v. Bowser Bouldin, Ltd., Tex, 896 SW2d 179.—Antitrust 389(2); App & E 930(3); Damag 18, 20, 22, 141, 184; Neglig 384, 385, 422.

Haynes & Boone v. Bowser Bouldin, Ltd., TexApp–San Antonio, 864 SW2d 662, reh den, and writ gr, vac 896 SW2d 179.—Antitrust 138, 256, 389(1), 389(2), 390, 393; App & E 231(9), 930(3), 994(2), 996, 1001(3), 1003(3),

1003(6), 1004(11); Const Law 4427; Costs 264; Damag 94, 221(5.1).

Haynes & Boone, L.L.P.; Brents v., TexApp–Dallas, 53 SW3d 911, review den, and reh of petition for review den.—App & E 934(1); Judgm 181(7), 185(2); Lim of Act 55(3), 95(11), 199(1).

Haynes & Boone, L.L.P.; Brents v., TexApp–Dallas, 10 SW3d 772, review gr, vac 52 SW3d 733, on remand 53 SW3d 911, review den, and reh of petition for review den.—Judgm 181(7), 185(2); Lim of Act 55(3), 95(11), 104.5, 199(1).

Haynes & Boone, L.L.P. v. Chason, TexApp–Tyler, 81 SW3d 307, reh overr, and review den.—App & E 866(3), 930(1), 1001(1), 1001(3); Damag 50.10; Trial 139.1(14).

Haynes & Boone, L.L.P.; Lee v., TexApp–Dallas, 129 SW3d 192, reh overr, and review den, and reh of petition for review den.—App & E 966(1); Judgm 185.1(4), 185.3(13), 186; Labor & Emp 810, 863(2); Pretrial Proc 477.1.

Haynes B. Ownby Drilling Co. v. McClure, TexCivApp–Austin, 264 SW2d 204, ref nre.—App & E 1062.2, 1069.1; Damag 221(2.1); Evid 113(21), 175; Trial 350.6(1), 351.2(4), 352.10.

Haynes Brinkley & Co.; Mendez v., TexApp–San Antonio, 705 SW2d 242, ref nre.—Judgm 665, 666, 678(1), 678(2), 720, 725(1), 956(1).

Haynes Drilling Co.; Railroad Commission of Texas v., TexCivApp–Austin, 94 SW2d 200.—App & E 1175(1), 1177(6); Mines 92.68.

Haynes Oil Corp.; Federal Tender Board No. 1. v., CCA5 (Tex), 80 F2d 468.—Mines 92.5(3).

Haynie, Ex parte, TexApp–Houston (14 Dist), 793 SW2d 317.—Child S 494; Hab Corp 529.

Haynie; C. I. T. Corp. v., TexCivApp–Eastland, 135 SW2d 618.—App & E 1175(1); Bankr 2062, 2492, 2514, 2701; Chat Mtg 129, 182, 188(1); Judgm 770.

Haynie; Douthitt v., TexCivApp–Waco, 398 SW2d 831, ref nre.—Wills 55(1), 155.1, 166(5), 166(7).

Haynie v. General Leasing Co., Inc., TexCivApp–Dallas, 538 SW2d 244.—App & E 157, 781(7); Courts 99(4); Inj 133, 138.6, 147, 148(1), 157.

Haynie v. Gibson Distributing Co., Inc.-Permian Basin, BkrtcyWDTex, 40 BR 767. See Gibson Distributing Co., Inc.-Permian Basin, In re.

Haynie; Lunsford v., CA5 (Tex), 175 F2d 603.—Bankr 2050, 2154.1, 2671, 2726.1(1); Trusts 84.

Haynie; St. Paul Fire & Marine Ins. Co. v., TexCivApp–Waco, 389 SW2d 488.—App & E 302(3); Evid 318(3).

Haynie v. State, TexCrimApp, 751 SW2d 878.—Crim Law 1181.5(3.1).

Haynie v. State, TexCrimApp, 275 SW2d 114.—Crim Law 1090.1(1).

Haynie v. State, TexCrimApp, 252 SW2d 161.—Crim Law 1094(3).

Haynie v. Wasson, TexCivApp–Austin, 324 SW2d 239.—App & E 770(1); Judgm 822(1).

Haynie Wire Line Service, Inc.; J.C. Kinley Co. v., TexApp–Houston (1 Dist), 705 SW2d 193, ref nre.—Contracts 176(9); Lim of Act 197(2); Pat 212(1).

Haynie Wire Line Service, Inc.; Kinley Co. v., TexApp–Houston (1 Dist),705 SW2d 193. See J.C. Kinley Co. v. Haynie Wire Line Service, Inc.

Haynsworth; Leeper v., TexApp–El Paso, 179 SW3d 742.—Judgm 103, 140; Pretrial Proc 587, 676, 678.

Haynsworth v. Lloyd's of London, SDTex, 933 FSupp 1315, aff 121 F3d 956, reh and sug for reh den 129 F3d 614, cert den 118 SCt 1513, 523 US 1072, 140 LEd2d 666.—Alt Disp Res 113, 134(1), 134(3), 140, 199, 203; Contracts 127(4), 129(1); Fed Cts 45; Judgm 707, 713(2).

Haynsworth v. The Corporation, CA5 (Tex), 121 F3d 956, reh and sug for reh den 129 F3d 614, cert den 118 SCt 1513, 523 US 1072, 140 LEd2d 666.—Contracts

HAYS

127(4), 129(1), 141(1); Fed Civ Proc 1828, 2553; Fed Cts 410, 820.

Hays; American Cas. & Life Co. v., TexCivApp–Waco, 150 SW2d 816, dism.—Insurance 1809, 1832(1), 3002.

Hays; Ashley v., SDTex, 647 FSupp 251.—Fed Civ Proc 2546; Labor & Emp 563(1), 563(3), 687.

Hays v. Brandon, TexCivApp–Fort Worth, 245 SW2d 381. —Child C 76, 906, 910; Child S 397.

Hays v. Department of Public Safety, TexCivApp–Eastland, 301 SW2d 276, writ dism.—App & E 1043(7); Autos 144.1(1.11), 144.2(5.1), 326; Pretrial Proc 713.

Hays; Doherty v., TexCivApp–Austin, 225 SW2d 1021.— App & E 907(3); Frds St of 138(2).

Hays v. Dumraese, TexCivApp–San Antonio, 153 SW2d 225, writ refused wom.—App & E 1056.1(1); Evid 236(1), 236(3); Frds St of 129(9); Hus & W 263, 264(5); Tax 3134; Witn 150(2), 150(3).

Hays; Erwin v., TexCivApp–Texarkana, 267 SW2d 884, ref nre.—Judgm 199(3.7); Trial 139.1(6); Trusts 92.5, 110.

Hays v. First State Bank of Dell City, TexCivApp–El Paso, 377 SW2d 210, ref nre.—Bills & N 140, 537(8); Princ & A 36, 50; Princ & S 128(2).

Hays; Gates v., TexCivApp–San Antonio, 95 SW2d 1020, writ dism.—Elect of Rem 7(1); Elections 269; Offic 83; Quo W 11.

Hays v. Hall, Tex, 488 SW2d 412.—Lim of Act 95(12), 95(13), 104(2).

Hays v. Hall, TexCivApp–Eastland, 477 SW2d 402, writ gr, rev 488 SW2d 412.—Health 830; Lim of Act 104(2), 179(2).

Hays v. Harter, TexCivApp–El Paso, 177 SW2d 797, writ refused.—Trusts 172; Wills 487(4), 488, 567.

Hays v. Hays, TexCivApp–El Paso, 123 SW2d 968.—Child C 182, 188, 850; Child S 159, 254; Divorce 51, 111.

Hays; Hays v., TexCivApp–El Paso, 123 SW2d 968.— Child C 182, 188, 850; Child S 159, 254; Divorce 51, 111.

Hays v. H. J. Hogan, Inc., TexCivApp–Austin, 474 SW2d 330.—App & E 1008.1(2), 1011.1(4); Damag 140; Impl & C C 112.

Hays v. Hughes, TexCivApp–Austin, 106 SW2d 724, writ refused.—Judgm 326.

Hays v. Kessler, TexCivApp–Dallas, 564 SW2d 496.— Mand 15, 74(3), 164(3).

Hays; Littlefield v., TexCivApp–Amarillo, 609 SW2d 627. —Const Law 990, 2315, 3051, 3458; Insurance 3560; Lim of Act 4(2), 95(12).

Hays; McCulloch County v., TexCivApp–Austin, 366 SW2d 877, ref nre.—App & E 931(1), 954(1), 954(2), 1010.1(1); High 159(1); Inj 1.

Hays v. McKemie, TexCivApp–Austin, 185 SW2d 484.— Plead 111.38, 111.46.

Hays v. McMillan, NDTex, 418 FSupp 116, aff 560 F2d 204.—Fed Cts 1146; Judgm 674, 715(1).

Hays v. McNeice, TexApp–Amarillo, 641 SW2d 695.— Judgm 181(7).

Hays v. Marble, TexCivApp–Amarillo, 213 SW2d 329, writ dism.—Des & Dist 84; Frds St of 116(10); Hus & W 187, 251, 274(1); Princ & A 163(1), 175(1), 175(3); Spec Perf 10(1), 24, 35, 114(6), 123; Ten in C 3, 43, 44; Ven & Pur 159.

Hays; Meadows v., TexCivApp–Waco, 137 SW2d 838.— App & E 623, 1126.

Hays v. Monfort, Inc., NDTex, 160 FSupp2d 746.—Labor & Emp 2316.

Hays v. Nabours, TexCivApp–Eastland, 193 SW2d 893, ref nre.—App & E 173(9), 1001(1); Courts 475(2); Ex & Ad 59.

Hays v. Nelson, TexCivApp–Fort Worth, 400 SW2d 12.— App & E 989, 1177(7); Gifts 49(5); Judgm 199(3.9), 199(3.10).

Hays v. Old, TexCivApp–Texarkana, 385 SW2d 464, ref nre.—Abate & R 81; Infants 197; Plead 228.15, 304, 432.

Hays; Pipkin v., TexCivApp–Austin, 482 SW2d 59, ref nre.—Int Rev 4141, 4812, 4824; Tax 3302; Wills 450.

Hays v. Spangenberg, TexCivApp–Austin, 94 SW2d 899. —App & E 984(2); Costs 12, 32(3), 103, 177; Lim of Act 24(1), 60(11); Mental H 373, 387, 391; Subrog 1, 23(2), 23(4), 26, 33(3).

Hays v. Sparks, TexCivApp–Dallas, 566 SW2d 115.— Fraud 59(1); Plead 111.21, 111.42(10); Venue 8.5(2).

Hays v. Starling, TexCivApp–Fort Worth, 619 SW2d 14. —App & E 171(1), 218.2(1); Contracts 346(12).

Hays v. State, TexCrimApp, 480 SW2d 635.—Assault 92(3); Crim Law 364(1), 448(11), 800(1), 1120(3), 1170(2).

Hays v. State, TexCrimApp, 284 SW2d 366.—Crim Law 1090.1(1).

Hays v. State, TexCrimApp, 254 SW2d 1003, 158 TexCrim 269.—Int Liq 224, 236(7).

Hays v. State, TexCrimApp, 211 SW2d 216, 152 TexCrim 65.—Crim Law 877; Homic 1207.

Hays v. State, TexCrimApp, 158 SW2d 69, 143 TexCrim 164.—Crim Law 1094(2.1).

Hays v. State, TexCrimApp, 103 SW2d 374, 132 TexCrim 165.—Int Liq 239(1).

Hays v. State, TexCrimApp, 92 SW2d 249.—Crim Law 15.

Hays v. State, TexCrimApp, 84 SW2d 1008, 129 TexCrim 156.—Burg 45; Crim Law 814(16), 829(4), 841, 842, 1038.1(1).

Hays v. State, TexApp–San Antonio, 933 SW2d 659.— Crim Law 1144.17, 1147; Sent & Pun 2004, 2021, 2022, 2029.

Hays; State v., TexCivApp–Dallas, 361 SW2d 401, ref nre. —App & E 758.3(6), 766, 1050.1(8.1); Em Dom 222(4); Evid 142(1).

Hays v. State, TexCivApp–Dallas, 342 SW2d 167, ref nre. —Em Dom 262(5); Evid 142(1), 555.6(10); Waters 154(1).

Hays v. Sullins, TexCivApp–El Paso, 442 SW2d 494, writ gr, and writ dism by agreement.—App & E 930(3), 989; Judgm 178, 181(2), 190; Land & Ten 25.3, 231(6).

Hays v. Texarkana & Fort Smith Ry. Co., TexCivApp–Texarkana, 87 SW2d 1106, writ refused.—R R 94(1), 109, 113(3).

Hays; Texas Employment Commission v., Tex, 360 SW2d 525.—Courts 247(8); Unemp Comp 40, 200, 211, 216, 470, 583.

Hays; Texas Employment Commission v., TexCivApp–Austin, 353 SW2d 924, writ gr, rev 360 SW2d 525.— Unemp Comp 211, 486.

Hays v. The Texan, Inc., TexCivApp–Fort Worth, 174 SW2d 1006.—Inn 10.1, 10.9; Neglig 202, 387.

Hays; U.S. v., CA5 (Tex), 872 F2d 582.—Crim Law 369.1, 408, 1153(1), 1169.7, 1169.11, 1169.12.

Hays; Wilson v., TexCivApp–Waco, 544 SW2d 833, ref nre.—Sales 52(5.1), 391(7), 418(3), 418(7).

Hays; Zavala-Dimmit Counties Water Imp. Dist. No. 1 v., TexComApp, 153 SW2d 463, 137 Tex 338.—Judgm 707, 739; Waters 224, 226, 230(1).

Hays; Zavala-Dimmit Counties Water Imp. Dist. No. 1 v., TexCivApp–San Antonio, 128 SW2d 535, aff 153 SW2d 463, 137 Tex 338.—Waters 226, 227.

Hays & Martin, L.L.P. v. Ubinas-Brache, TexApp–Dallas, 192 SW3d 631, reh overr, and review den.—Admin Law 303.1, 305, 325; App & E 1079; Costs 194.18, 194.32, 207; Courts 35, 155; Work Comp 1141.

Hays Consol. Independent School Dist.; Valero Transmission Co. v., TexApp–Austin, 704 SW2d 857, ref nre. —Statut 181(1), 184, 217, 223.1; Tax 2642, 2678, 2850, 2855.

Hays Consol. Independent School Dist. v. Valero Transmission Co., TexApp–Austin, 645 SW2d 542, ref

HAYS

nre, and ref nre.—App & E 1073(1); Plead 78, 123; Schools 106.12(7); Tax 2647, 2699(11), 2722, 2723, 2727, 2859.

Hays County v. Alexander, TexApp–Austin, 640 SW2d 73.—Counties 54; Em Dom 2(6), 166; High 18, 52, 71, 79.1, 95(1), 105(1).

Hays County v. Hays County Water Planning Partnership, TexApp–Austin, 106 SW3d 349.—App & E 893(1), 984(5); Assoc 20(1); Const Law 2314, 2600, 2601; Costs 194.40; Counties 47, 49, 52, 58, 208; Decl Judgm 111, 209, 313, 387; High 103.1; Mun Corp 170; States 191.4(1), 191.9(2).

Hays County v. Hays County Water Planning Partnership, TexApp–Austin, 69 SW3d 253.—Action 6; Admin Law 124; App & E 68, 70(0.5), 71(3), 863, 874(1); Counties 52, 59; Mun Corp 92, 170; Plead 16.

Hays County; Hood v., TexApp–Austin, 836 SW2d 327.—Admin Law 229; Tax 2642, 2650, 2692; Trial 45(2).

Hays County Appraisal Dist. v. Mayo Kirby Springs, Inc., TexApp–Austin, 903 SW2d 394, reh overr, appeal after remand 1997 WL 703124, reh overr.—Const Law 718, 2314, 2376, 2450; Tax 2105.

Hays County Appraisal Dist. v. Robinson, TexApp–Austin, 809 SW2d 328.—Tax 2523.

Hays County Appraisal Dist. v. Southwest Texas State University, TexApp–Austin, 973 SW2d 419, rule 537(f) motion gr.—Tax 2300, 2315, 2347, 2389.

Hays County Guardian v. Supple, CA5 (Tex), 969 F2d 111, reh den 974 F2d 169, cert den 113 SCt 1067, 506 US 1087, 122 LEd2d 371.—Civil R 1376(5); Colleges 9.30(2); Const Law 1505, 1510, 1564, 1681, 1730, 1735, 1738, 1745, 1746, 1751, 1870, 2007, 2008, 2010, 2015, 2070, 2079; Fed Cts 269, 776; Offic 116; Rem of C 101.1, 107(9).

Hays County, Texas; Hays County Water Planning Partnership v., TexApp–Austin, 41 SW3d 174, reh overr, and review den, and reh of petition for review den.—App & E 863; Const Law 1926; Counties 52; Mun Corp 92; Statut 174, 176, 188.

Hays County, Tex.; Stefanoff v., CA5 (Tex), 154 F3d 523, reh den.—Civil R 1376(2), 1376(4), 1376(7); Const Law 2270, 2276, 3041, 3053, 3824; Prisons 15(3).

Hays County Water Planning Partnership; Hays County v., TexApp–Austin, 106 SW3d 349.—App & E 893(1), 984(5); Assoc 20(1); Const Law 2314, 2600, 2601; Costs 194.40; Counties 47, 49, 52, 58, 208; Decl Judgm 111, 209, 313, 387; High 103.1; Mun Corp 170; States 191.4(1), 191.9(2).

Hays County Water Planning Partnership; Hays County v., TexApp–Austin, 69 SW3d 253.—Action 6; Admin Law 124; App & E 68, 70(0.5), 71(3), 863, 874(1); Counties 52, 59; Mun Corp 92, 170; Plead 16.

Hays County Water Planning Partnership v. Hays County, Texas, TexApp–Austin, 41 SW3d 174, reh overr, and review den, and reh of petition for review den.—App & E 863; Const Law 1926; Counties 52; Mun Corp 92; Statut 174, 176, 188.

Hayse v. Seaboard Fire & Marine Ins. Co., TexCivApp–Fort Worth, 562 SW2d 282, ref nre.—Work Comp 535.

Hays Furniture Co.; Johnson v., TexCivApp–Waco, 233 SW2d 934.—App & E 1151(2); Bills & N 534; Hus & W 21, 23, 24; Princ & A 14(2), 24.

Hayslip v. State, TexCrimApp, 502 SW2d 119.—Controlled Subs 65, 98; Crim Law 507(4), 1036.1(3.1), 1038.1(1), 1038.3, 1130(2).

Hayter v. City of Mount Vernon, CA5 (Tex), 154 F3d 269.—Civil R 1376(6); Evid 546; Fed Civ Proc 2491.5, 2515, 2539; Fed Cts 557, 823; Mal Pros 16.

Hayter; Commercial Nat. Bank in Nacogdoches v., TexCivApp–Tyler, 473 SW2d 561, ref nre.—Trusts 182, 239; Wills 488, 684.2(1), 684.3(1), 703.

Hayter v. Fern Lake Fishing Club, TexCivApp–Beaumont, 318 SW2d 912.—App & E 954(1); Clubs 5; Corp 54; Inj 138.1, 138.31, 163(7).

Hayter; Lucas v., TexCivApp–San Antonio, 376 SW2d 790, writ dism.—App & E 918(1), 1041(2); Forci E & D 43(4), 43(8), 45; Judgm 217; Proc 6; Trial 13(2).

Hayter v. State, TexCrimApp, 541 SW2d 435.—Crim Law 419(1.5), 419(11), 1169.1(9).

Hayter v. State, TexCrimApp, 244 SW2d 514.—Crim Law 1090.1(1).

Hayter; Texas Real Estate Commission v., TexCivApp–San Antonio, 338 SW2d 771.—Judgm 181(5.1).

Hayter Lumber Co. v. Winder, TexCivApp–Beaumont, 295 SW2d 730, writ dism.—App & E 207, 544(1), 616(1), 1053(1); Damag 127, 132(3), 208(6).

Hayton v. Eichelberger, BkrtcySDTex, 100 BR 861. See Eichelberger, In re.

Hayton; Eichelberger v., TexApp–Houston (1 Dist), 814 SW2d 179, writ den.—App & E 66, 70(0.5), 71(3), 78(1); Divorce 85, 270, 286(1); Inj 148(1), 148(4).

Hayton v. State, TexCrimApp, 256 SW2d 853, 158 TexCrim 455.—Crim Law 1094(3), 1099.7(3), 1099.10.

Hayward, Ex parte, TexCrimApp, 711 SW2d 652.—Burg 49; Const Law 2332, 2473; Sent & Pun 1157, 1169.

Hayward; City of Corpus Christi v., CCA5 (Tex), 111 F2d 637, cert den 61 SCt 30, 311 US 670, 85 LEd 430.—Fed Cts 293.1, 384; Judgm 828.3; Mun Corp 918(1), 931.

Hayward v. City of Corpus Christi, TexCivApp–Waco, 195 SW2d 995, ref nre.—Equity 62, 87(1); Judgm 540, 570(4), 678(1), 720, 829(3); Lim of Act 48(6), 103(2); Mun Corp 254, 918(1), 949, 954, 955(1.1), 1000(4); Paymt 84(2).

Hayward v. Commercial Concepts Corp., TexApp–Dallas, 748 SW2d 305.—App & E 852; Brok 54, 82(1); Pretrial Proc 481; Sales 3.1, 87(3).

Hayward v. Duiker, TexCivApp–Eastland, 276 SW2d 320.—Bills & N 489(6).

Hayward; Pratt v., TexCivApp–Texarkana, 151 SW2d 874.—Wills 55(1), 155.1, 324(3).

Hayward v. Southwest Arkansas Elec. Co-op. Corp., EDTex, 476 FSupp 1008.—Death 7, 8, 88, 89, 95(1); Fed Cts 372, 410, 431.

Hayward v. State, TexCrimApp, 158 SW3d 476, on remand 2006 WL 162582.—Crim Law 795(2.10), 795(2.50), 824(3); Double J 161.

Hayward v. State, TexApp–Houston (14 Dist), 117 SW3d 5, reh overr, and petition for discretionary review gr, rev 158 SW3d 476, on remand 2006 WL 162582.—Assault 96(1); Const Law 4582; Crim Law 59(1), 59(3), 80, 552(3), 553, 741(1), 742(1), 795(1.5), 795.2(1), 795(2.10), 1134(3), 1144.13(2.1), 1144.13(6), 1159.2(1), 1159.2(2), 1159.2(7), 1159.6, 1172.1(1), 1173.2(4); Homic 1134; Ind & Inf 191(0.5), 191(4).

Hayward v. VR Business Brokers, TexApp–Dallas, 748 SW2d 305. See Hayward v. Commercial Concepts Corp.

Haywood, Ex parte, TexCrimApp, 550 SW2d 292.—Hab Corp 474; Rob 17(5).

Haywood, Ex parte, TexCrimApp, 498 SW2d 351.—Bail 51.

Haywood; Caro v., TexCivApp–Austin, 585 SW2d 354.—Acct Action on 10; App & E 854(1); Costs 194.32, 194.38.

Haywood; Crawford v., TexCivApp–Corpus Christi, 392 SW2d 387.—App & E 1056.1(1); Land & Ten 109(4), 230(8), 230(9), 231(8).

Haywood; Nye v., TexCivApp–San Antonio, 182 SW2d 14.—New Tr 99; Tresp to T T 35(2), 38(2).

Haywood v. Southwestern Elec. Power Co., CA5 (Tex), 708 F2d 163.—Fed Civ Proc 2178, 2215; Indem 30(1), 33(4), 103.

Haywood v. State, TexCrimApp, 507 SW2d 756.—Crim Law 345, 627.6(2), 627.6(5), 627.7(1), 627.7(3), 706(2), 1037.1(1), 1037.1(2), 1130(5); Rob 20, 24.40; Sent & Pun 1367, 1381(2).

Haywood v. State, TexCrimApp, 482 SW2d 855.—Controlled Subs 82, 100(2); Crim Law 404.60, 720(1), 730(11), 772(6), 867.

Haywood v. State, TexCrimApp, 159 SW2d 503, 143 TexCrim 459.—Crim Law 1094(3).

Haywood v. State, TexCrimApp, 136 SW2d 866, 138 TexCrim 413.—Infants 152.

Haywood; Texas Emp. Ins. Ass'n v., Tex, 266 SW2d 856, 153 Tex 242.—New Tr 31; Trial 133.6(7); Witn 311; Work Comp 1926.

Haywood; Texas Emp. Ins. Ass'n v., TexCivApp–Amarillo, 266 SW2d 499, rev 266 SW2d 856, 153 Tex 242.—App & E 1003(5); New Tr 31; Trial 131(2), 312(2); Work Comp 1652, 1926, 1929, 1968(5).

Haywood v. Texas Emp. Ins. Ass'n, TexCivApp–Houston, 383 SW2d 866.—App & E 544(1); Work Comp 1392, 1974.

Haywood; University of Texas System v., TexCivApp–Austin, 546 SW2d 147.—Trial 82, 83(1); Work Comp 1654.

Haywood, Jordan, McCowan of Dallas, Inc. v. Bank of Houston, TexApp–Houston (14 Dist), 835 SW2d 738, reh den.—App & E 989, 1003(5), 1003(7); Corp 432(12); Princ & A 96, 99.

Haywood, Rice & William Venture; Arkla Exploration Co. v., TexApp–Texarkana, 863 SW2d 112, reh overr, and writ dism by agreement.—Admin Law 501; Judgm 470; Mines 92.16, 92.32(2), 92.49; Pub Ut 194.

Hazar; Crossmark, Inc. v., TexApp–Dallas, 124 SW3d 422, review den.—Alt Disp Res 113, 251, 255, 263, 266, 312, 328, 329, 330, 332, 354, 357, 359, 363(5), 363(5), 368, 374(1), 374(8), 379; Contracts 116(1); Damag 76, 80(1).

Hazard v. State, TexCrimApp, 93 SW2d 435.—Crim Law 1131(1).

Hazel; Bowen v., TexApp–Texarkana, 723 SW2d 795.—Courts 472.3, 475(2); Ex & Ad 85(8).

Hazel v. Magnet Cove Barium Corp., TexCivApp–Texarkana, 411 SW2d 748.—Judgm 181(26), 186.

Hazel v. State, TexCrimApp, 534 SW2d 698.—Crim Law 1130(2); Ind & Inf 189(1); Searches 69; Weap 4, 6, 17(4).

Hazelip v. Horridge, SDTex, 127 BR 798. See Horridge, In re.

Hazeltine v. U.S., CA5 (Tex), 486 F2d 219, reh den 488 F2d 1055.—Crim Law 1181.5(8).

Hazelton v. City of Grand Prairie, Tex., NDTex, 8 FSupp2d 570.—Arrest 63.4(2); Civil R 1031, 1088(4), 1345, 1351(1), 1376(2), 1376(6), 1382, 1395(5), 1395(6), 1432; Const Law 3936; False Imp 13; Fed Cts 18; Lim of Act 124; Offic 114.

Hazelton; Colonial Life Ins. Co. of America v., TexApp–Dallas, 711 SW2d 305, ref nre.—Insurance 2460.

Hazelwood; Baumler v., Tex, 347 SW2d 560, 162 Tex 361.—App & E 1062.1; Autos 244(58); Neglig 387.

Hazelwood; Baumler v., TexCivApp–Dallas, 339 SW2d 75, writ gr, rev 347 SW2d 560, 162 Tex 361.—App & E 1003(11), 1015(5); Autos 242(8), 244(42), 244(58); Trial 365.1(7).

Hazelwood; Borger v., TexCivApp–Texarkana, 199 SW2d 223.—Action 1; Contracts 138(1); Plead 111.9; Venue 22(4), 22(6).

Hazelwood v. City of Cooper, TexCivApp–Texarkana, 87 SW2d 776, writ refused.—Mun Corp 993(2), 993(3), 995(2).

Hazelwood v. Jinkins, TexCivApp–Hous (1 Dist), 580 SW2d 33.—Child S 9, 70, 82, 85, 100, 236, 341, 363, 557(1); Trial 392(1), 395(5).

Hazelwood v. Mandrell Industries Co., Ltd., TexCivApp–Hous (1 Dist), 596 SW2d 204, ref nre.—Contracts 108(1); Labor & Emp 2792; Work Comp 11.

Hazelwood v. State, TexApp–Corpus Christi, 838 SW2d 647.—Atty & C 62; Crim Law 641.1, 641.4(1), 641.10(3), 1169.2(7), 1177.5(1); Sent & Pun 1355.

Hazelwood; Womack v., TexCivApp–Dallas, 271 SW2d 699, ref nre.—App & E 989; Autos 244(42), 244(58); New Tr 68.4(5).

Hazen v. Cooper, TexApp–Houston (14 Dist), 786 SW2d 519, appeal after remand 1994 WL 699078, writ den, cert den 116 SCt 1677, 517 US 1189, 134 LEd2d 780.—Judgm 185.3(1); Wills 660.

Hazen v. Pickett, TexCrimApp, 581 SW2d 694.—Mand 4(1).

Hazkell v. State, TexCrimApp, 616 SW2d 204.—Obst Just 11.

Hazle v. McDonald, TexCivApp–Dallas, 449 SW2d 343.—Fraud 3, 11(1), 50; Judgm 185(5), 185.3(21), 186.

Hazle; McGriff v., TexCivApp–Eastland, 201 SW2d 92.—App & E 846(2), 846(5); Execution 45; Hus & W 230; Plead 111.21, 111.25, 111.26, 111.42(10); Venue 5.4; Wills 671.

Hazlewood; Eagle Lincoln-Mercury Inc. v., TexCivApp–Fort Worth, 391 SW2d 180, ref nre.—Neglig 210, 1022, 1037(4), 1140, 1226, 1288, 1530, 1562.

Hazlewood; Phillips Petroleum Co. v., CA5 (Tex), 534 F2d 61, reh den 581 F2d 267.—Assign 73; Interest 20; Interpl 35.

Hazlewood; Phillips Petroleum Co. v., NDTex, 409 FSupp 1193, aff 534 F2d 61, reh den 581 F2d 267.—Contracts 187(1); Fed Cts 24, 352; Interest 39(1); Interpl 35; Land & Ten 79(1); Mines 74(3).

Hazlitt; Alamo Nat. Bank of San Antonio v., TexCivApp–El Paso, 92 SW2d 315, writ dism.—Neglig 1314, 1533, 1708; Trial 122.

Hazlitt; Provident Life & Acc. Ins. Co. v., Tex, 216 SW2d 805, 147 Tex 426.—App & E 1172(1); Plead 228.14; Pretrial Proc 741.

Hazlitt v. Provident Life & Acc. Ins. Co., TexCivApp–San Antonio, 212 SW2d 1012, aff 216 SW2d 805, 147 Tex 426.—App & E 863; Insurance 3191(7), 3571; Judgm 178, 197; Plead 228.19.

H.B.; S. v., TexApp–Corpus Christi, 767 SW2d 860. See S.A.B.S. v. H.B.

H.B.; S.A.B.S. v., TexApp–Corpus Christi, 767 SW2d 860.—Child C 609; Child S 234.

HBA East, Ltd. v. JEA Boxing Co., Inc., TexApp–Houston (1 Dist), 796 SW2d 534, writ den, cert den 111 SCt 2828, 501 US 1218, 115 LEd2d 998.—App & E 241, 302(1); Bankr 2395, 2396; Courts 85(2), 85(3); Plead 85(4); Rem of C 94, 103; Statut 202, 206.

HB & WM, Inc. v. Smith, TexApp–San Antonio, 802 SW2d 279.—App & E 914(1), 1203(1); Judgm 17(2), 17(10); Proc 153.

H.B. Leasing Co., In re, EDTex, 188 BR 810.—Bankr 2053, 2541, 3107, 3115.1, 3770; Mtg 171(1), 271, 272; Statut 188; Ven & Pur 231(1), 231(16.1), 233.

HBO, A Div. of Time Warner Entertainment Co., L.P. v. Harrison, TexApp–Houston (14 Dist), 983 SW2d 31.—App & E 854(1), 863, 934(1); Judgm 181(33), 185(2), 185(5), 185(6), 185.3(21); Libel 23.1, 25, 38(1), 38(4), 48(1), 48(2), 51(5), 112(1), 112(2), 123(8).

HBO, A Division of Time Warner Entertainment Co., L.P. v. Huckabee, TexApp–Houston (14 Dist), 995 SW2d 152, review gr, aff 19 SW3d 413.—App & E 856(1), 863, 1175(1); Judgm 181(33); Libel 4, 51(5), 101(1), 112(2).

H. by Gabert v. Messick, TexApp–Fort Worth, 828 SW2d 226. See R.M.H. by Gabert v. Messick.

H.B. Zachry Co.; BASF Fina Petrochemicals Ltd. Partnership v., TexApp–Houston (1 Dist), 168 SW3d 867, review den.—App & E 148, 893(1); Costs 194.16, 194.22; Courts 85(2), 85(3); Pretrial Proc 134.

H.B. Zachry Co.; Carlyle Joint Venture v., TexApp–San Antonio, 802 SW2d 814, writ den.—Joint Adv 7.

H. B. Zachry Co. v. Ceco Steel Products Corp., TexCivApp–Eastland, 404 SW2d 113, ref nre.—Contracts 312(1), 322(3); Costs 194.32; Damag 6, 221(5.1); Evid

H. B.

59 Tex D 2d—564

See Guidelines for Arrangement at the beginning of this Volume

113(8); Impl & C C 98; Interest 39(1), 50; Trial 352.5(4), 352.10, 352.21; Trover 40(4).

H. B. Zachry Co. v. Fullilove, TexCivApp–El Paso, 177 SW2d 980, writ refused wom.—Damag 91(3); Labor & Emp 2825.

H.B. Zachry Co. v. Gonzalez, Tex, 847 SW2d 246.— Pretrial Proc 312.

H. B. Zachry Co. v. Maerz, TexCivApp–San Antonio, 223 SW2d 552.—Judgm 72.

H.B. Zachry Co.; Martinez v., TexApp–Houston (1 Dist), 976 SW2d 746, review den.—Judgm 185(2); Work Comp 2089, 2129.

H. B. Zachry Co.; Mitchell v., USTex, 80 SCt 739, 362 US 310, 4 LEd2d 753.—Commerce 62.40, 62.44(1), 62.44(2), 62.51; Fed Cts 459; Labor & Emp 2220(1).

H. B. Zachry Co. v. Mitchell, CA5 (Tex), 262 F2d 546, cert gr 80 SCt 52, 361 US 807, 4 LEd2d 57, aff 80 SCt 739, 362 US 310, 4 LEd2d 753.—Commerce 62.44(1), 62.51; Labor & Emp 2220(1), 2220(2), 2238.

H. B. Zachry Co. v. N. L. R. B., CA5 (Tex), 377 F2d 670. —Const Law 4185; Labor & Emp 1743(1), 1860.

H. B. Zachry Co.; Pipe Line Workers Local No. 38 v., TexCivApp–Beaumont, 276 SW2d 876, ref nre.—Labor & Emp 1677(1), 2071, 2111, 2112, 2114; Trial 351.5(1), 366; Venue 17, 21.

H.B. Zachry Co. v. Quinones, CA5 (Tex), 206 F3d 474.— Admin Law 507; Statut 219(2), 219(4), 219(6.1); Work Comp 827, 1740, 1822, 1910, 1964, 1981.

H. B. Zachry Co.; Raney v., TexCivApp–San Antonio, 285 SW2d 955.—Corp 423.

H. B. Zachry Co. v. Ruckman, TexCivApp–San Antonio, 348 SW2d 251.—Plead 111.42(7).

H. B. Zachry Co. v. Sanford Independent School Dist. v., TexCivApp–Amarillo, 393 SW2d 402, ref nre.—Schools 102; Tax 2403.

H. B. Zachry Co. v. Terry, CA5 (Tex), 195 F2d 185, cert den 73 SCt 14, 344 US 819, 97 LEd 637, reh den 73 SCt 163, 344 US 882, 97 LEd 683.—Equity 44; Interest 39(1); Jury 14(3); Labor & Emp 207, 256(9).

H. B. Zachry Co. v. Thibodeaux, Tex, 364 SW2d 192, on remand 368 SW2d 776, ref nre.—App & E 79(1), 1163.

H. B. Zachry Co.; Thibodeaux v., TexCivApp–San Antonio, 368 SW2d 776, ref nre.—App & E 78(1), 419(1); Mun Corp 806(3).

H. B. Zachry Co.; Thibodeaux v., TexCivApp–San Antonio, 361 SW2d 579, cause remanded 364 SW2d 192, on remand 368 SW2d 776, ref nre.—App & E 79(1), 494, 509.

H. B. Zachry Co. v. Travelers Indem. Co., CA5 (Tex), 391 F2d 43.—Contracts 220, 303(1), 309(1).

H. B. Zachry Co. v. Travelers Indem. Co., NDTex, 262 FSupp 237, aff in part, rev in part 391 F2d 43.— Contracts 143(4), 147(1), 199(1), 205.40, 284(4), 300(1), 303(5), 309(1), 322(1), 322(3); Damag 120(3); Evid 333(1), 442(5), 448; Fed Civ Proc 2726.1; U S 67(6), 70(8).

H.B. Zachry Co. v. Waller Creek, Ltd., CA5 (Tex), 867 F2d 228. See Waller Creek, Ltd., Matter of.

H.B. Zachry Co. v. Waller Parking Garage, Ltd., CA5 (Tex), 867 F2d 228. See Waller Creek, Ltd., Matter of.

H.B. Zachry Co., Inc.; Fluor Daniel, Inc. v., TexApp–Corpus Christi, 1 SW3d 166, reh overr, and petition for review den, and reh of petition for review overr, on remand 2001 WL 35832899, appeal dism 2001 WL 1000711, appeal after remand 2005 WL 2559773, review den.—Judgm 570(9), 713(2), 715(1), 715(3), 720, 724, 829(3).

H.C., In Interest of, TexApp–San Antonio, 942 SW2d 661. —Infants 155, 156, 157, 172, 179, 203, 248.1, 250, 252.

HCA Deer Park Hosp.; Anderson v., SDTex, 834 FSupp 183.—Civil R 1101, 1122, 1137, 1138, 1238, 1535, 1536, 1544, 1545, 1573.

HCA Health Services of Texas, Inc.; Berel v., TexApp–Houston (1 Dist), 881 SW2d 21, reh overr, and writ den.

—App & E 852; Health 260, 782; Judgm 181(33); Labor & Emp 58, 3125, 3137; Neglig 1011; Statut 4, 174, 188, 214.

HCA Health Services of Texas, Inc.; Cummings v., TexApp–Houston (14 Dist), 799 SW2d 403.—Judgm 181(7), 185(2), 185(5), 185.1(3).

HCA Health Services of Texas, Inc.; Fiore v., TexApp–Fort Worth, 915 SW2d 233, reh overr, and writ den.— App & E 863, 901, 934(1); Const Law 328, 990, 2312, 2314, 2315; Lim of Act 4(2), 55(3), 95(12).

HCA Health Services of Texas, Inc. v. Salinas, Tex, 838 SW2d 246.—Mand 24, 44; Venue 76, 82.

HCA Health Services of Texas, Inc.; Washington v., CA5 (Tex), 152 F3d 464, cert gr, vac 119 SCt 2388, 527 US 1032, 144 LEd2d 790, on remand 199 F3d 192.— Civil R 1019(2), 1217, 1218(2), 1218(3); Statut 219(1), 219(2), 219(3), 219(4), 219(5), 219(6.1).

HCA Health Services of Texas, Inc.; Washington v., SDTex, 906 FSupp 386, rev 95 F3d 45, appeal after remand 152 F3d 464, cert gr, vac 119 SCt 2388, 527 US 1032, 144 LEd2d 790, on remand 199 F3d 192.—Civil R 1218(3), 1220, 1221, 1243, 1251, 1540, 1544, 1545, 1552, 1555; Courts 97(1); Damag 50.10; Fed Civ Proc 2470, 2497.1, 2543, 2546.

HCA Health Services of Texas, Inc.; Wells v., TexApp–Fort Worth, 806 SW2d 850, writ den.—App & E 207, 237(1), 882(1), 961, 970(2), 972, 1026, 1060.1(1); Evid 150; Pretrial Proc 40, 42, 45; Trial 106.

HCA, Inc.; Clark v., TexApp–El Paso, 210 SW3d 1.—Evid 536; Health 603, 618, 804.

HCA Inc.; Lavergne v., EDTex, 452 FSupp2d 682.—Civil R 1101, 1109, 1112, 1113, 1118, 1135, 1137, 1243, 1528, 1532, 1541; Fed Civ Proc 2470, 2470.4, 2531, 2538, 2547.1, 2553; U S Mag 27, 31.

HCA, Inc.; Miller ex rel. Miller v., Tex, 118 SW3d 758.— Assault 2; Health 906, 907, 911, 915; Infants 2, 156; Parent & C 1, 7(12).

HCA, Inc. v. Miller ex rel. Miller, TexApp–Houston (14 Dist), 36 SW3d 187, review gr, aff 118 SW3d 758.— Child C 20; Const Law 4391; Health 684, 903, 910, 911, 914, 915, 917; Infants 13.

HCA Management Co., Inc.; Blumberg v., CA5 (Tex), 848 F2d 642, reh den, cert den 109 SCt 789, 488 US 1007, 102 LEd2d 781.—Civil R 1505(3), 1505(6), 1507, 1535.

HCA Medical Center of Plano; Easterly v., TexApp–Dallas, 772 SW2d 211. See Easterly v. HSP of Texas, Inc.

HCA Spring Branch Medical Center; Washington v., CA5 (Tex), 152 F3d 464. See Washington v. HCA Health Services of Texas, Inc.

HCA Spring Branch Medical Center; Washington v., SDTex, 906 FSupp 386. See Washington v. HCA Health Services of Texas Inc.

H.C.B. Mechanical, Inc.; Chubb Lloyds Ins. Co. of Texas v., TexApp–Houston (1 Dist), 190 SW3d 89, rule 537(f) motion dism.—Evid 555.4(2); Neglig 371, 379, 380, 387, 1675, 1676, 1678.

H. C. Burt & Co. v. French Independent School Dist., TexCivApp–Beaumont, 99 SW2d 429.—Venue 22(10).

H. C. Burt & Co. v. Littlefield Independent School Dist., TexCivApp–Amarillo, 104 SW2d 110.—Schools 97(10).

HCC Credit Co. of Arlington, Inc.; Skinner v., TexCivApp–Fort Worth, 498 SW2d 708.—App & E 932(1); Damag 221(1); Evid 1, 18, 20(1), 69, 83(1).

HCCI-San Antonio, Inc.; Cortez ex rel. Estate of Puentes v., Tex, 159 SW3d 87.—App & E 200, 230, 232(0.5), 968, 1045(3); Jury 85, 97(1), 131(2), 131(4), 131(6), 131(13).

HCCI-San Antonio, Inc.; Cortez ex rel. Estate of Puentes v., TexApp–San Antonio, 131 SW3d 113, review gr, aff 159 SW3d 87.—App & E 200, 215(1), 1056.1(1), 1056.4, 1058(1), 1061.4; Damag 15, 57.20, 57.21, 57.22,

For Later Case History Information, see KeyCite on WESTLAW

57.23(1), 63, 192, 208(6); Death 10, 82, 103(4); Judgm
199(1), 199(3.15); Jury 97(1), 133; Labor & Emp 3045,
3049(3), 3055; Trial 139.1(14), 139.1(17), 168, 356(5).

H.C. Distributors, Inc.; Microsoft Corp. v., CA5 (Tex),
145 FedAppx 864.—Fed Cts 669.

HCFCO, Inc. v. Northway Mobile Home Park, TexApp–
Waco, 750 SW2d 23. See HCFCO, Inc. v. White.

HCFCO, Inc. v. White, TexApp–Waco, 750 SW2d 23.—
New Tr 140(1); Proc 145, 149.

HC Gun & Knife Shows, Inc. v. City of Houston, CA5
(Tex), 201 F3d 544, reh den.—Damag 176; Fed Civ
Proc 1852, 2608.1; Fed Cts 776, 819, 820, 823, 895, 915;
Mun Corp 592(1); Weap 3.

HCI Acquisition Corp.; Crystal Media, Inc. v., TexApp–
San Antonio, 773 SW2d 732.—Inj 152, 173; Mtg 413;
Plead 303, 422.

HCI Chemicals (USA), Inc. v. Henkel KGaA, CA5 (Tex),
966 F2d 1018.—Fed Civ Proc 2011; Fed Cts 628; Sales
168(2), 168.5(6), 418(9), 418(19), 429.

HCI, Inc.; Pileco, Inc. v., TexApp–Houston (1 Dist), 735
SW2d 561, ref nre.—Accord 11(2), 11(3); Costs 194.38.

H. C. Price Co.; Carlton v., CA5 (Tex), 640 F2d 573.—
Costs 194.12; Damag 191; Evid 571(10); Fed Civ Proc
2313, 2377, 2737.5; Fed Cts 644, 929; Interest 39(2.6),
39(2.50).

H. C. Price Co. v. Compass Ins. Co., NDTex, 483 FSupp
171.—Contracts 147(1); Insurance 1835(2), 2278(15),
3556; Judgm 489.

HCRA of Texas, Inc. v. Johnston, TexApp–Fort Worth,
178 SW3d 861.—App & E 174, 300, 930(1), 989, 994(1),
1001(1), 1001(3), 1003(3), 1004(1), 1004(5), 1135; Damag
43, 91.5(1), 97, 102, 127.9, 163(1), 185(1); Death 31(1),
77, 93, 99(1), 99(2); Evid 571(9); Health 823(4); New Tr
65.

H.C.S., In re, TexApp–San Antonio, 219 SW3d 33.—Action 13; Child 15; Plead 104(1), 111.37.

H.D.H., In re, TexApp–Beaumont, 127 SW3d 921.—Atty
& C 86; Costs 260(4); Infants 246.

H.D. Industries, Inc.; Lozano v., TexApp–El Paso, 953
SW2d 304.—App & E 930(1), 1001(1), 1001(3), 1002,
1003(7), 1062.1; Neglig 549(8); Prod Liab 6, 8, 10, 11,
14, 48, 85, 87.1; Trial 350.5(2), 350.5(4), 350.7(10),
352.16, 356(5).

H. Dittlinger Roller Mills Co.; Colman v., TexCivApp–
Galveston, 181 SW2d 604.—Plead 111.15, 111.42(2),
111.46; Venue 7.5(8).

H D , Jr., In re, TexCivApp–Amarillo, 511 SW2d 615.—
Adop 16; App & E 916(1); Judgm 20, 335(3); Plead
228.17, 228.19, 228.23; Pretrial Proc 691.

H. D. Lee Mercantile Co. v. Thompson, TexCivApp–
Dallas, 161 SW2d 581.—Courts 472.4(3); Fraud Conv
182(5); Trusts 233, 348; Venue 2, 22(6).

H. D. O., In re, TexCivApp–Eastland, 580 SW2d 421.—
App & E 931(1), 994(3); Child C 7, 28, 176, 525, 554,
641; Const Law 3738, 4389; Infants 12, 132, 155, 201,
243.

H. D. Snow Housemoving, Inc. v. Moyers, TexCivApp–
Fort Worth, 581 SW2d 809.—Home 154, 214; Mtg
32(2).

H. E. Abbott & Sons, Inc.; Royal Indem. Co. v., Tex, 399
SW2d 343.—Insurance 2663, 2664, 2694.

H. E. Abbott & Sons, Inc.; Royal Indem. Co. v., TexCiv-
App–Austin, 392 SW2d 359, writ gr, rev 399 SW2d 343.
—App & E 930(1); Autos 243(12); Evid 151(1); Insur-
ance 2664, 2693, 2694.

Heaberlin v. Joaquin Independent School Dist. No. 38,
TexCivApp–Beaumont, 95 SW2d 1339.—Schools 147.42.

Heacker v. Southwestern Bell Tel. Co., CA5 (Tex), 270
F2d 505.—Fed Cts 421; Work Comp 51, 611, 1719,
2084, 2144.

Head, Ex parte, TexCivApp–Eastland, 102 SW2d 1101.—
App & E 842(1), 1024.3; Venue 68.

Head, In re Estate of, TexApp–Texarkana, 165 SW3d
897.—App & E 5, 138, 148, 428(2); Wills 265.1, 395.

Head; Barbour v., SDTex, 200 FSupp2d 687.—Copyr 88.

Head; Barbour v., SDTex, 178 FSupp2d 758.—Copyr
12(3), 50.30, 53(1), 83(3.1), 89(2); Fed Civ Proc 2544,
2552; Lim of Act 95(7), 104.5.

Head; City of Longview v., TexApp–Tyler, 33 SW3d 47.
—App & E 893(1), 1097(1), 1195(1); Const Law 2600;
Courts 4, 99(6); Crim Law 83, 86; Decl Judgm 1, 2, 8,
61, 124.1, 272, 273, 294, 302.1, 387; Dist & Pros Attys 1;
Inj 85(2); Plead 104(1).

Head v. City of Shoreacres, TexCivApp–Waco, 401 SW2d
703, ref nre.—Zoning 385.

Head v. Coleman, TexCivApp–Waco, 470 SW2d 380, ref
nre.—Autos 226(1), 227.5, 245(13); Damag 185(1); Neglig 1656, 1676.

Head; DeMuth v., TexCivApp–Dallas, 378 SW2d 389, ref
nre.—Bills & N 232; Evid 418; Judgm 186; Ven & Pur
281(1).

Head v. Halliburton Oilwell Cementing Co., CA5 (Tex),
370 F2d 545.—Fed Civ Proc 2011; Fed Cts 896.1, 903;
Witn 405(1), 405(2).

Head v. Head, TexApp–Beaumont, 739 SW2d 635, writ
den.—Divorce 164, 252.3(4); Hus & W 272(1).

Head; Head v., TexApp–Beaumont, 739 SW2d 635, writ
den.—Divorce 164, 252.3(4); Hus & W 272(1).

Head v. Kearney, EDTex, 142 FSupp 569.—Hab Corp
632.1; Pardon 72.1.

Head; Kirk v., Tex, 152 SW2d 726, 137 Tex 44.—Courts
23; Evid 208(1), 208(6), 265(8); Judgm 16; Partit 38, 62,
64.

Head; Kirk v., TexCivApp–Fort Worth, 132 SW2d 125, aff
152 SW2d 726, 137 Tex 44.—App & E 210, 262(2),
662(1), 933(4); Ex & Ad 221(6), 237; Judgm 955; Partit
57, 77(3), 89; Plead 15; Trial 33.

Head v. Newton, TexCivApp–Hous (14 Dist), 596 SW2d
209.—Libel 7(16), 112(1); Plead 111.42(2), 111.42(4),
111.42(7).

Head; Panhandle Const. Co. v., TexCivApp–Amarillo,
134 SW2d 779, writ refused.—Home 5, 141(1), 142(1),
154, 161, 168, 181(1).

Head v. Roberts, TexCivApp–Fort Worth, 291 SW2d 483.
—App & E 87(4); Const Law 3953; Partners 376;
Receivers 32, 35(1), 38.

Head v. State, TexCrimApp, 4 SW3d 258.—Crim Law
419(1), 419(2), 1134(2).

Head v. State, TexCrimApp, 419 SW2d 375.—Courts 107;
Crim Law 393(1); Ind & Inf 171; Sent & Pun 1304,
1352.

Head v. State, TexCrimApp, 267 SW2d 419, 160 TexCrim
42.—Crim Law 369.2(8), 519(8), 1172.7; Rape 52(1).

Head v. State, TexCrimApp, 214 SW2d 305, 152 TexCrim
355.—Crim Law 814(17); Larc 68(1).

Head v. State, TexCrimApp, 183 SW2d 570, 147 TexCrim
594.—Const Law 3106, 4509(1), 4509(15); Infants 132;
Witn 45(2).

Head v. State, TexCrimApp, 96 SW2d 981, 131 TexCrim
96.—Arrest 63.1; Autos 10; Breach of P 1(1).

Head v. State, TexApp–Corpus Christi, 82 SW3d 735,
petition for discretionary review refused.—Crim Law
394.6(5), 1153(1), 1158(1); Searches 26, 161, 162, 164.

Head; Stowe v., TexApp–Tyler, 728 SW2d 120.—Ease
36(3); Lim of Act 95(7); Mines 55(2).

Head; Taylor v., TexCivApp–Texarkana, 414 SW2d 542,
ref nre.—New Tr 75(4).

Head; Texas Indem. Ins. Co. v., TexCivApp–El Paso, 89
SW2d 283, writ dism.—Damag 221(5.1); Work Comp
819.

Head v. Thomason, TexCivApp–Eastland, 430 SW2d 369,
ref nre.—Covenants 51(2).

Head; Turnbow v., TexCivApp–Eastland, 158 SW2d 854.
—Frds St of 125(2), 138(4); Plead 228.23; Spec Perf 39;
Tresp to T T 47(1).

Head v. Twelfth Court of Appeals, Tex, 811 SW2d 570.—
App & E 771.

Head; U.S. v., CA5 (Tex), 693 F2d 353.—Arrest 63.5(4), 63.5(9); Cust Dut 126(2); Searches 49, 62.

Head v. U.S. Inspect DFW, Inc., TexApp–Fort Worth, 159 SW3d 731.—Antitrust 128, 140, 147, 161, 162, 205, 255, 259, 363; App & E 223; Contracts 1, 205.10; Costs 194.14, 194.32, 194.36; Damag 74, 76; Judgm 181(15.1), 185(5), 185(6); Sales 261(1), 261(6), 405, 427.

Head; Weaver v., TexApp–Texarkana, 984 SW2d 744, appeal after remand City of Longview v. Head, 33 SW3d 47.—Courts 89, 155; Decl Judgm 84; Inj 138.48.

Head; Wollman v., SDTex, 176 FSupp 563, aff Head v. Wollmann, 272 F2d 298.—Bills & N 516; Contracts 177, 318, 328(1); Evid 355(1), 450(1); Lim of Act 24(1); Mines 101; Princ & A 97, 132(1).

Head v. Wollmann, CA5 (Tex), 272 F2d 298.—Bills & N 527(2); Chat Mtg 255; Guar 25(3); Mtg 218.1; Plgs 55; Princ & A 132(1).

Head v. W. T. Rawleigh Co., TexCivApp–Amarillo, 152 SW2d 463, writ dism.—App & E 267(1), 301, 302(1), 758.1; Execution 198.

Head & Guild Equipment Co. v. Bond, TexCivApp–Beaumont, 470 SW2d 909.—App & E 930(3), 989, 1140(4), 1170.1; Evid 211; Interest 39(1); Sales 441(3), 441(4), 442(2), 442(5).

Head Indus. Coatings and Services, Inc.; Maryland Ins. Co. v., Tex, 938 SW2d 27, on remand 981 SW2d 305, reh overr, and review den.—Insurance 2926, 2933, 3350.

Head Indus. Coatings & Services, Inc. v. Maryland Ins. Co., TexApp–Texarkana, 981 SW2d 305, reh overr, and review den.—App & E 226(2), 857.1; Costs 279; Insurance 3347, 3396; Interest 31, 39(2.15), 39(2.30).

Head Indus. Coatings and Services, Inc.; Maryland Ins. Co. v., TexApp–Texarkana, 906 SW2d 218, writ den, and writ gr, rev 938 SW2d 27, on remand 981 SW2d 305, reh overr, and review den.—Antitrust 221; App & E 172(3), 215(1), 756, 758.1, 761, 836, 883, 930(3), 989, 1001(3), 1003(6), 1003(7), 1070(2); Compromise 100, 101; Const Law 3759, 4426; Corp 1.1(2), 397, 428(1); Fraud 7; Indem 57; Insurance 1634(1), 1638, 1644, 3091, 3335, 3336, 3342, 3347, 3349, 3359, 3374, 3379, 3381(5), 3417, 3419; Interest 38(1), 60; Princ & A 48, 61(1), 71, 159(1), 177(1); Trial 358.

Headley v. State, TexCrimApp, 386 SW2d 290.—Autos 355(6); Crim Law 1171.2.

Head Oil Production Co.; Durkay v., EDTex, 112 BR 825.—Action 69(3); Fed Cts 47.1.

Headquarters Corp.; Texas Vending Commission v., TexCivApp–Austin, 505 SW2d 402, ref nre.—Const Law 2403, 2500; Licens 7(1).

Headrick, Ex parte, TexApp–Fort Worth, 997 SW2d 348. —Hab Corp 466, 814.

Headrick, Ex parte, TexApp–Fort Worth, 948 SW2d 554, petition for discretionary review gr, vac Headrick v. State, 988 SW2d 226, on remand 997 SW2d 348.— Admin Law 501; Autos 144.2(1).

Headrick v. Fair, TexCivApp–Eastland, 99 SW2d 653.— Sales 218.5.

Headrick v. State, TexCrimApp, 988 SW2d 226, on remand Ex parte Headrick, 997 SW2d 348.—Double J 6; Hab Corp 201, 222, 271, 291, 441; Judgm 713(1).

Headrick v. State, TexCrimApp, 491 SW2d 912.—Larc 60.

Headrick; U.S. v., CA5 (Tex), 963 F2d 777.—Crim Law 1139, 1147, 1158(1); Sent & Pun 665, 2004, 2033, 2038.

Heads v. Beto, CA5 (Tex), 468 F2d 240, cert den 93 SCt 1454, 410 US 969, 35 LEd2d 704.—Crim Law 371(4); Hab Corp 490(1), 490(6).

Heads v. State, TexCrimApp, 301 SW2d 159.—Crim Law 1090.1(1).

Heads v. State, TexCrimApp, 301 SW2d 157.—Crim Law 1090.1(1).

Headspeth v. State, TexCrimApp, 151 SW2d 807, 142 TexCrim 139.—Int Liq 236(7), 239(2).

Headstream v. Gailey, TexCivApp–Amarillo, 192 SW2d 795, ref nre.—Bound 25, 46(2).

Headstream v. Mangum, TexCivApp–Amarillo, 174 SW2d 496.—App & E 719(8), 770(1); Autos 214, 245(90).

Headstream v. Mangum, TexCivApp–Amarillo, 149 SW2d 625.—App & E 901, 1210(1).

Headstream v. Mangum, TexCivApp–Amarillo, 129 SW2d 1155.—App & E 755, 1114; Costs 236; J P 159(1).

Heafner; Frost National Bank v., TexApp–Houston (1 Dist), 12 SW3d 104, reh overr, and review den, and reh of petition for review den.—Antitrust 220; App & E 758.3(9); Banks 148(0.5), 148(2), 154(9), 227(3), 229; Damag 5, 15, 18, 89(2), 118; Evid 595; Fraud 3, 12, 50, 58(3); Trial 139.1(3).

Heafner; Lavely v., TexApp–Houston (14 Dist), 976 SW2d 896.—Action 6; App & E 781(1); Decl Judgm 8, 61, 92.1; Pretrial Proc 674.

Heafner & Associates v. Koecher, TexApp–Houston (1 Dist), 851 SW2d 309, opinion after remand 1994 WL 389030, writ den.—App & E 1031(1); Divorce 150, 184(1); Trial 388(1), 392(1).

Heagy; Texas State Hotel, Inc. v., TexApp–Houston (14 Dist), 650 SW2d 503.—Civil R 1710.

Heal; State v., Tex, 917 SW2d 6.—App & E 846(5); Em Dom 91, 106, 203(1), 219, 221.

Heal; State v., TexApp–Dallas, 884 SW2d 864, writ gr, rev 917 SW2d 6.—Em Dom 122, 138, 202(4), 262(5); Evid 245.

Heald v. State, TexCrimApp, 92 SW2d 1042, 130 TexCrim 178.—Crim Law 956(10), 1158(1), 1174(5).

Heald v. Texas Real Estate Recovery Fund, TexApp–Fort Worth, 669 SW2d 179.—App & E 931(1), 989, 1008.1(1), 1008.1(2), 1010.1(2), 1012.1(5); Brok 4.

Healey; Disbrow v., TexApp–Houston (1 Dist), 982 SW2d 189.—App & E 1062.1; Atty & C 166(1), 167(2); Evid 571(7), 590, 594; Jury 9, 34(3); Trial 139.1(17), 349(2), 350.1.

Healey; Mannix Co. v., CA5 (Tex), 341 F2d 1009.—Pat 36.2(3), 51(2), 66(1.5), 324.5.

Healey; Roberts v., TexApp–Houston (14 Dist), 991 SW2d 873, reh overr, and review den, and reh of petition for review overr.—Antitrust 134, 138, 141, 162, 256, 363; Atty & C 63, 64, 109, 112; Damag 51; Judgm 183, 185.3(4); Neglig 202, 375, 379, 380, 383, 387, 433, 1526, 1568, 1713.

Healey, State ex rel., v. McMeans, TexCrimApp, 884 SW2d 772. See State ex rel. Healey v. McMeans.

Health and Human Services Com'n; Dallas Healthcare, Inc. v., NDTex, 921 FSupp 426.—Admin Law 229, 662; Health 509, 556(3).

Health and Human Services Com'n; Texas Health Care Ass'n v., TexApp–Austin, 949 SW2d 544.—Costs 194.40; Health 489, 505(2).

Health & Tennis Corp. of America v. Jackson, TexApp–San Antonio, 928 SW2d 583, reh overr, and writ dism woj.—App & E 863, 949; Atty & C 22; Parties 35.1, 35.9, 35.13, 35.17, 35.33, 35.35, 35.37, 35.61.

Health & Tennis Corp. of America, Inc.; Burkart v., TexApp–Dallas, 730 SW2d 367, 79 ALR4th 119.—App & E 843(2), 883; Neglig 1583, 1670, 1677.

Health Ben. Management Cost Containment, Inc.; Walker v., NDTex, 860 FSupp 1163.—Insurance 3349, 3360; Rem of C 3, 25(1), 107(7); States 18.11.

Healthcare Cable Systems, Inc. v. Good Shepherd Hosp., Inc., TexApp–Tyler, 180 SW3d 787.—App & E 863, 893(1); Contracts 1, 143(1), 143(2), 143(3), 143.5, 152, 170(1), 175(1), 176(2); Evid 448; Judgm 181(19), 185(2), 185(6).

Health Care Centers of Texas, Inc. v. Nolen, TexApp–Waco, 62 SW2d 813.—App & E 422, 428(1), 784, 930(1), 1001(3); Motions 62; New Tr 165.

Healthcare Centers of Texas, Inc. v. Rigby, TexApp–Houston (14 Dist), 97 SW3d 610, reh overr, and review den (2 pets).—App & E 430(1), 930(1), 989, 999(3), 1004(3); Damag 32, 49, 49.10, 51, 97, 102, 208(1); Evid 265(7), 265(8); Health 662, 766, 831, 832; Neglig 375, 379, 380, 383, 387; New Tr 77(2); Plead 36(1); Statut 228.

Healthcare Centers of Texas, Inc.; Simmons v., Tex-App–Texarkana, 55 SW3d 674.—App & E 758.3(11), 852, 854(1), 863, 1136; Judgm 181(7), 186; Lim of Act 43, 55(1), 55(3), 95(12), 105(1), 197(1).

Healthcare Intern., Inc.; L & B Hosp. Ventures, Inc. v., CA5 (Tex), 894 F2d 150, reh den 901 F2d 1110, cert den 111 SCt 55, 498 US 815, 112 LEd2d 30.—Fed Civ Proc 2511.

Healthcare San Antonio, Inc.; Zuniga v., TexApp–San Antonio, 94 SW3d 778.—Health 804, 809.

Health Care Service Corp.; Quality Infusion Care, Inc. v., TexApp–Houston (1 Dist), 224 SW3d 369.—App & E 1073(1); Contracts 143(2), 143.5, 147(1), 147(2), 152, 155, 176(2); Costs 194.16, 194.32, 207; Evid 448; Health 942, 946, 957; Insurance 2501, 2521, 2533, 3114, 3504.

Health Care Service Corp. v. Tap Pharmaceutical Products, Inc., EDTex, 274 FSupp2d 807.—Fed Cts 191, 205; Impl & C C 3, 4; Labor & Emp 403, 407, 461, 488, 493, 646; Rem of C 25(1), 79(1); States 18.15, 18.51.

Healthco, Inc.; Cunningham v., CA5 (Tex), 824 F2d 1448.—Antitrust 143(2); Bankr 2157, 2554; Contracts 187(1), 353(10); Damag 15, 140; Fed Civ Proc 846, 2236, 2331; Fed Cts 630.1; Frds St of 158(4); Sales 52(5.1).

Health Discovery Corp., In re, TexApp–Waco, 148 SW3d 163.—Courts 207.3.

Health Discovery Corp. v. Williams, TexApp–Waco, 148 SW3d 167.—App & E 954(1), 954(2); Inj 138.1, 138.3, 138.18, 138.42.

Healthmark Partners, L.L.C.; Figueroa v., SDTex, 125 FSupp2d 209.—Fed Cts 417; Rem of C 3, 107(7).

Healthmark Partners, L.L.C.; Thomas v., TexApp–Houston (14 Dist), 93 SW3d 465, review den, and reh of petition for review overr.—Health 800, 804, 809.

Healthpoint, Ltd. v. Ethex Corp., WDTex, 273 FSupp2d 817.—Antitrust 22, 62, 103(1), 104(2), 105, 110(1); Equity 65(1), 65(2), 65(3); Fed Civ Proc 2493; Health 308, 314; Inj 132, 138.1, 138.6, 138.9, 147, 152; Trademarks 1530, 1531.

Healthpoint, Ltd. v. Stratus Pharmaceuticals, Inc., WDTex, 273 FSupp2d 871.—Antitrust 22, 24, 27, 81, 103(1), 110(1); Estop 68(2); Fed Civ Proc 2493.

Healthpoint, Ltd. v. Stratus Pharmaceuticals, Inc., WDTex, 273 FSupp2d 769.—Antitrust 22, 23, 28, 47, 103(1), 104(1), 104(2), 105, 110(1); Equity 65(1), 65(3); Health 301, 319; Inj 132, 138.1, 138.9, 147, 152.

Health Source Home Care, Inc.; 2616 South Loop L.L.C. v., TexApp–Houston (14 Dist), 201 SW3d 349.—App & E 1010.2, 1012.1(1), 1071.2, 1182; Impl & C C 30, 58; Judgm 522, 747(6); Land & Ten 50, 130(2), 171(3), 172(2); Princ & A 1, 23(5), 96, 99, 100(2), 123(11), 163(1), 173(3).

Healthsouth Corp.; Ballard v., NDTex, 147 FSupp2d 529.—Civil R 1224, 1228, 1229; Fed Civ Proc 2497.1.

HealthTexas Medical Group of San Antonio; Zamora-Quezada v., WDTex, 34 FSupp2d 433.—Civil R 1018, 1019(3), 1042, 1045, 1053, 1331(6), 1395(1); Fed Civ Proc 2491.5; Health 535(1), 535(2), 556(3); Insurance 1518.

HealthTrust, Inc.-The Hosp. Co.; Austin v., Tex, 967 SW2d 400.—Labor & Emp 776.

Healthtrust, Inc. - The Hosp. Co.; Austin v., TexApp–Corpus Christi, 951 SW2d 78, reh overr, and writ gr, aff 967 SW2d 400.—Courts 91(1); Labor & Emp 776.

Healy; Emco, Inc. v., TexCivApp–Texarkana, 602 SW2d 309.—Contracts 103, 138(4); Corp 99(1).

Healy v. Masters, TexCivApp–Fort Worth, 504 SW2d 594. —Lim of Act 143(3).

Healy; Morgan v., TexCivApp–Fort Worth, 614 SW2d 186, ref nre.—Usury 53.

Healy v. Wick Bldg. Systems, Inc., TexCivApp–Dallas, 560 SW2d 713, ref nre.—Garn 153, 165, 178, 180, 187; Judgm 162(4), 163; New Tr 140(1); Trial 388(1).

Heaner, Ex parte, TexCrimApp, 729 SW2d 756.—Hab Corp 715.1.

Heaner; Houston Sash and Door Co., Inc. v., Tex, 577 SW2d 217.—Guar 5, 77(2), 78(1); Usury 32, 82, 137, 138, 140, 143.

Heaner v. Houston Sash & Door Co., Inc., TexCivApp–Waco, 560 SW2d 525, writ gr, aff in part, rev in part 577 SW2d 217.—Usury 125, 137, 138, 144, 145.

Heaney; Barker v., TexCivApp–San Antonio, 82 SW2d 417, writ dism.—Evid 597; Health 632, 671, 818, 825, 908, 910.

Heaney v. U.S. Veterans Admin., CA5 (Tex), 756 F2d 1215.—Action 35; Civil R 1462; Fed Cts 171; U S 36.

Heard, Ex parte, Tex, 372 SW2d 942.—Child S 487, 497; Divorce 269(11), 269(13).

Heard, Ex parte, TexCrimApp, 275 SW2d 119, 161 Tex-Crim 133.—Crim Law 553.

Heard, In re, BkrtcyWDTex, 84 BR 454.—Bankr 2481, 2482.

Heard; Alberti v., SDTex, 600 FSupp 443, stay den 606 FSupp 478, aff 790 F2d 1220, reh den 799 F2d 992.— Civil R 1090; Contempt 20; Prisons 4(2.1), 4(3), 4(6), 12, 13(1), 17(0.5); Sent & Pun 1537.

Heard v. Bauman, Tex, 443 SW2d 715.—Adop 3, 7.4(6); Child S 82.

Heard; Bauman v., TexCivApp–Fort Worth, 442 SW2d 416, writ gr, aff 443 SW2d 715.—Adop 4; Child S 24, 32.

Heard v. Bell, TexCivApp–El Paso, 434 SW2d 222.— Child S 27, 76, 175, 577, 638.

Heard; Bichsel v., TexCivApp–San Antonio, 328 SW2d 462.—App & E 436, 1175(7), 1180(1); Decl Judgm 209; Inj 16, 77(2); Labor & Emp 40(2).

Heard; Carter v., CA5 (Tex), 593 F2d 10.—Civil R 1395(7); Decl Judgm 294.

Heard v. City of Dallas, TexCivApp–Dallas, 456 SW2d 440, 62 ALR3d 190, ref nre.—App & E 931(1), 989, 994(3), 1008.1(2), 1008.1(7), 1010.2, 1012.1(5); Mun Corp 120; Statut 181(1), 219(2); Trial 392(3), 404(1); Zoning 288, 786.

Heard v. City of Houston, TexCivApp–Hous (1 Dist), 529 SW2d 560.—Costs 194.16, 194.25; Fed Civ Proc 2737.14; Mun Corp 184.1; Offic 11.7.

Heard v. City Water Bd., BkrtcyWDTex, 84 BR 454. See Heard, In re.

Heard; Clark v., SDTex, 538 FSupp 800.—Arrest 65; Crim Law 218(3); False Imp 2, 7(3), 15(1), 35, 36.

Heard v. Commodity Products Co., TexCivApp–Fort Worth, 214 SW2d 701.—App & E 1178(1); Venue 7.5(7).

Heard; Corrigan v., TexCivApp–San Antonio, 225 SW2d 446, ref nre.—App & E 231(1), 548(4), 548(5), 548(6), 758.3(2), 758.3(9); Contracts 95(1); Evid 130, 134; Impl & C C 75; Trover 32(1); Witn 414(1).

Heard; Curry v., CA5 (Tex), 819 F2d 130, cert den 108 SCt 330, 484 US 944, 98 LEd2d 357.—Fed Civ Proc 551; Lim of Act 122.

Heard; Foster v., TexApp–Houston (1 Dist), 757 SW2d 464.—Mand 32; Pretrial Proc 33, 373, 410.

Heard v. Gomez, CA5 (Tex), 321 F2d 88.—Const Law 4810.

Heard; Gomez v., SDTex, 218 FSupp 228, aff 321 F2d 88. —Const Law 4810; Crim Law 641.10(2).

Heard v. Heard, TexCivApp–Galveston, 305 SW2d 231, writ refused.—App & E 347(1), 387(3), 508, 937(4); Courts 82, 85(2); Judgm 280.

Heard; Heard v., TexCivApp–Galveston, 305 SW2d 231, writ refused.—App & E 347(1), 387(3), 508, 937(4); Courts 82, 85(2); Judgm 280.

Heard; Hilliard v., TexApp–Houston (1 Dist), 666 SW2d 584.—Mand 26, 32.

HEARD

See Guidelines for Arrangement at the beginning of this Volume

Heard v. Houston General Ins. Co., TexCivApp–Waco, 553 SW2d 830.—Judgm 198; Work Comp 1489, 1492, 1769.

Heard v. Houston Gulf Gas Co., CCA5 (Tex), 78 F2d 189, cert den 56 SCt 178, 296 US 643, 80 LEd 457.— Equity 87(1); Mines 74(6); Spec Perf 3, 32(2); Trial 11(3).

Heard v. Houston Post, TexApp–Houston (1 Dist), 684 SW2d 210. See Heard v. Houston Post Co.

Heard v. Houston Post Co., TexApp–Houston (1 Dist), 684 SW2d 210, ref nre.—App & E 374(4); Courts 89; Records 52, 60, 63.

Heard v. Howard, TexCivApp–Fort Worth, 215 SW2d 364.—Evid 318(6), 320; Mines 109.

Heard v. Incalcaterra, TexApp–Houston (1 Dist), 702 SW2d 272, ref nre.—Admin Law 786, 812; Offic 72.22, 72.51, 72.55(2), 72.58(1), 72.63.

Heard v. J. & C. Drilling Co., TexCivApp–San Antonio, 124 SW2d 866.—Judgm 17(9).

Heard; Jenke v., SDTex, 375 FSupp 650.—Hab Corp 337, 351.

Heard; King v., CA5 (Tex), 310 F2d 127, cert den 84 SCt 114, 375 US 854, 11 LEd2d 81.—Hab Corp 715.1, 846.

Heard; Kisro v., TexCivApp–Hous (1 Dist), 547 SW2d 322. —Garn 88.

Heard v. Liberty Mut. Fire Ins. Co., TexApp–El Paso, 828 SW2d 457, writ den.—Work Comp 1981.

Heard; McCarty v., SDTex, 381 FSupp 1290.—Crim Law 577.10(1), 577.10(3), 577.10(7), 577.15(2), 577.15(4), 577.16(4), 577.16(5.1).

Heard; McGrew v., TexApp–Houston (1 Dist), 779 SW2d 455.—Courts 37(1); Mand 1, 52; New Tr 116.2, 155; Pretrial Proc 513.

Heard; Mitchell v., TexCivApp–San Antonio, 98 SW2d 832.—App & E 237(1), 1171(6); Damag 221(4); False Imp 39; Judgm 199(3.9); Trial 215.

Heard v. Moore, TexApp–Texarkana, 101 SW3d 726, review den.—Action 66; App & E 756, 757(1), 1079; Judgm 584, 586(1), 591.1, 704; Parties 55.

Heard; Newby v., TexCivApp–Fort Worth, 341 SW2d 563. —Adop 7.6(1).

Heard; Port v., CA5 (Tex), 764 F2d 423.—Const Law 250.5, 1415, 3464; Crim Law 42; Fed Cts 13; Hab Corp 253, 528.1; Witn 186, 188, 304(1), 304(3).

Heard; Port v., SDTex, 594 FSupp 1212, aff 764 F2d 423. —Const Law 889, 2488, 3036, 3053, 3464; Courts 508(7); Crim Law 42; Evid 83(1); Gr Jury 26, 36.1, 36.2, 36.3(2), 36.4(2), 36.5(1), 36.9(1), 36.9(2); Hab Corp 385; Ind & Inf 5, 10.2(2); Witn 1, 50, 66, 292, 304(1), 304(3).

Heard; Richie v., Tex, 611 SW2d 419.—Mand 53.

Heard v. Roos, TexApp–Corpus Christi, 885 SW2d 592, reh overr.—App & E 758.3(9), 989, 999(1), 1003(7); Ease 15.1, 18(1), 18(2), 18(4), 36(3); Trial 139.1(3), 140(1), 143.

Heard; Schlang v., CA5 (Tex), 691 F2d 796, appeal dism, cert den 103 SCt 2419, 461 US 951, 77 LEd2d 1310.— Const Law 965; Crim Law 641.6(3), 1119(1); Double J 52; Hab Corp 224.1, 374.1, 491, 670(7), 845; Ind & Inf 55.

Heard; Shelton v., CA5 (Tex), 696 F2d 1127, on reconsideration 707 F2d 200.—Hab Corp 320, 374.1, 377.

Heard; Skaggs v., SDTex, 172 FSupp 813.—Mines 73, 74(3), 79.3.

Heard; Smith v., CA5 (Tex), 315 F2d 692, cert den 84 SCt 154, 375 US 883, 11 LEd2d 113.—Const Law 4664(1); Courts 96(7); Crim Law 517.1(3), 519(1), 519(8), 522(1), 736(2); Hab Corp 722(2), 846.

Heard; Smith v., SDTex, 214 FSupp 909, aff 315 F2d 692, cert den 84 SCt 154, 375 US 883, 11 LEd2d 113.—Const Law 4664(2); Crim Law 519(8), 531(3); Hab Corp 367.

Heard; Smith v., TexApp–San Antonio, 980 SW2d 693, reh overr, and review den.—Antitrust 138, 212, 256; App & E 901; Atty & C 105, 109, 112, 129(2), 129(4);

Judgm 180, 181(16); Plead 234, 236(2), 236(7), 245(1), 258(1).

Heard v. State, Tex, 204 SW2d 344, 146 Tex 139.—Adv Poss 7(2), 11, 13, 14, 31; Judgm 485, 501; Nav Wat 36(4).

Heard v. State, TexCrimApp, 665 SW2d 488.—Autos 357; Crim Law 1038.1(2).

Heard v. State, TexCrimApp, 416 SW2d 427.—Sent & Pun 1238, 1242.

Heard v. State, TexCrimApp, 267 SW2d 150, 160 TexCrim 88, aff Ex parte Heard, 275 SW2d 119, 161 TexCrim 133.—Crim Law 1168(1); Larc 27, 59.

Heard v. State, TexCrimApp, 232 SW2d 854.—Crim Law 1131(4).

Heard v. State, TexCrimApp, 184 SW2d 285, 148 TexCrim 19.—Crim Law 695(6); Int Liq 236(11); Sent & Pun 1286, 1379(2), 1381(3).

Heard v. State, TexApp–Texarkana, 887 SW2d 94, petition for discretionary review refused.—Crim Law 53, 56, 592, 636(1), 636(2), 641.13(1), 641.13(2.1), 641.13(6), 641.13(7), 1038.1(6), 1144.13(2.1), 1151, 1152(1), 1159.2(7), 1159.6, 1172.1(3); Homic 541, 1184, 1387; Jury 146.

Heard v. State, TexApp–Corpus Christi, 995 SW2d 317, petition for discretionary review refused.—Crim Law 627.10(1), 627.10(8), 1162, 1166(10.10); Homic 1181, 1184.

Heard v. State, TexApp–Houston (14 Dist), 701 SW2d 298, petition for discretionary review refused.—Arrest 65; Crim Law 792(1), 792(2), 1038.1(7), 1038.2, 1038.3; Ind & Inf 137(6).

Heard; State v., TexCivApp–Austin, 199 SW2d 191, aff 204 SW2d 344, 146 Tex 139.—Adv Poss 7(2), 7(3), 13, 16(1), 31, 60(1); App & E 1010.1(6); Bound 13; Courts 90(1); Judgm 743(2); Nav Wat 36(1), 37(8).

Heard v. State, TexCivApp–Beaumont, 149 SW2d 237.— Plead 45, 111.1; States 200.

Heard; State Bar of Tex. v., Tex, 603 SW2d 829.—Atty & C 4, 39, 57; Courts 207.4(2); Mand 3(1), 4(3), 4(4), 53, 141, 152, 172; Plead 4.

Heard; Stevens v., CA5 (Tex), 674 F2d 320.—Civil R 1090, 1098; Fed Cts 652.1, 666; Inj 118(3).

Heard; Stuart v., SDTex, 359 FSupp 921.—Civil R 1395(7); Fed Cts 227, 244, 998, 999.1; Prisons 12.

Heard; Tennessee Gas & Transmission Co. v., TexCivApp–San Antonio, 190 SW2d 518.—Plead 111.3, 111.38; Venue 5.5.

Heard; Texas Compensation Ins. Co. v., CCA5 (Tex), 93 F2d 548.—Damag 221(7); Judgm 256(2); Work Comp 1975.

Heard v. Texas Compensation Ins. Co., CCA5 (Tex), 87 F2d 30.—Work Comp 391, 1187, 1846, 1872, 1917.

Heard v. Town of Refugio, Tex, 103 SW2d 728, 129 Tex 349.—Adv Poss 7(2); Nav Wat 1(2), 36(1), 37(1), 37(8); Pub Lands 224.5; Waters 87.

Heard; Town of Refugio v., TexCivApp–San Antonio, 124 SW2d 1015, writ dism, correct.—Adv Poss 40; Quiet T 10.2, 10.4; Tresp to T T 7, 9.

Heard; Town of Refugio v., TexCivApp–San Antonio, 95 SW2d 1008, rev in part 103 SW2d 728, 129 Tex 349.— Adv Poss 7(2); Dedi 53; Deeds 93; Judgm 128; Nav Wat 1(2), 36(1), 36(2), 37(4), 37(7).

Heard; Toyota Motor Sales, U.S.A., Inc. v., TexApp–Houston (14 Dist), 774 SW2d 316, writ withdrawn.— Pretrial Proc 35.

Heard; Turbodyne Corp. v., Tex, 720 SW2d 802.—Pretrial Proc 33, 373, 381, 406.

Heard; Turbodyne Corp. v., TexApp–Houston (14 Dist), 698 SW2d 703, subsequent mandamus proceeding 720 SW2d 802.—Mand 28, 32; Pretrial Proc 41, 373.

Heard; Williams v., SDTex, 568 FSupp 89.—Fed Civ Proc 2737.6, 2742.5.

Heard; Williams v., SDTex, 533 FSupp 1153, aff in part 703 F2d 555.—Civil R 1037, 1326(8), 1376(6), 1421; Offic 114.

Heard & Heard; Connor v., TexCivApp–San Antonio, 242 SW2d 205, ref nre.—App & E 528(1), 1015(5), 1056.6, 1069.1; Autos 244(36.1), 244(44); New Tr 47, 163(1); Trial 115(2), 352.21; Witn 345(2).

Heard & Heard v. Kuhnert, TexCivApp–San Antonio, 155 SW2d 817.—App & E 837(5); Autos 240(1); Neglig 1713; Plead 111.17, 111.42(2), 111.42(8); Princ & A 159(1); Trial 350.5(3); Venue 8.5(1), 8.5(3), 8.5(4), 8.5(6), 14, 17.

Heard & Jones Drug Stores, Inc.; Liberty Mut. Ins. Co. v., TexCivApp–Amarillo, 446 SW2d 911.—Evid 272, 309; Plead 111.19, 111.42(10).

Heard, Goggan, Blair & Williams; First City v., TexApp–Houston (1 Dist), 827 SW2d 462. See City of Houston v. First City.

Heard, Goggan, Blair & Williams; Gonzalez v., TexApp–Corpus Christi, 923 SW2d 764, reh overr, and writ den.—Judgm 181(2), 181(27), 185(2); Mun Corp 723; Offic 114.

Heard, Goggan, Blair & Williams; Nine Greenway Ltd. v., TexApp–Houston (1 Dist), 875 SW2d 784, writ den.—App & E 167, 174; Judgm 526; Land & Ten 49(2); Parties 76(1).

Hearing, Ex parte, TexApp–Texarkana, 125 SW3d 778.—Extrad 39.

Hearks; Maryland Cas. Co. v., Tex, 190 SW2d 62, 144 Tex 317.—App & E 930(1); Evid 570; Trial 311; Work Comp 1932, 1969.

Hearks; Maryland Cas. Co. v., TexCivApp–Beaumont, 188 SW2d 262, aff 190 SW2d 62, 144 Tex 317.—New Tr 140(3); Trial 350.3(8), 352.10, 352.20; Witn 257; Work Comp 1416, 1594, 1665, 1932, 1939.4(3).

Hearld v. Barnes and Spectrum Emergency Care, EDTex, 107 FRD 17.—Const Law 3984; Fed Civ Proc 2758, 2769, 2790, 2828.

Hearld v. State, TexCrimApp, 271 SW2d 286.—Crim Law 1097(1), 1099.7(2).

Hearn, In re, CA5 (Tex), 418 F3d 444.—Hab Corp 898(3).

Hearn, In re, CA5 (Tex), 389 F3d 122.—Hab Corp 679, 690.

Hearn, In re, CA5 (Tex), 376 F3d 447, decision clarified on denial of reh 389 F3d 122, opinion after remand 418 F3d 444.—Courts 90(2); Hab Corp 205, 603, 679, 690.

Hearn, In re, TexApp–San Antonio, 137 SW3d 681, reh overr.—Costs 146, 208; Mand 3(2.1), 4(1), 4(4), 12, 42; Motions 17, 40.

Hearn v. Ellis, TexCivApp–Beaumont, 504 SW2d 518, ref nre.—App & E 930(3), 989; Autos 244(59); Trial 18, 29(2).

Hearn v. Frazier, TexCivApp–Eastland, 241 SW2d 171.—App & E 218.2(3.1), 218.2(7); Evid 351; Ten in C 3, 4, 38(7).

Hearn v. Frazier, TexCivApp–Eastland, 228 SW2d 582, writ dism.—Abate & R 82; Mines 113; Partners 89; Plead 111.36, 111.37; Venue 5.2, 6.

Hearn v. Gulf Coast Rod, Reel and Gun Club, CA5 (Tex), 153 F3d 190. See Gordon v. State of Tex.

Hearn v. Hanlon-Buchanan, Inc., TexCivApp–Fort Worth, 179 SW2d 364, writ refused wom.—App & E 934(1); Brok 106; Evid 243(1); Judgm 199(3.14); Mines 75; Princ & A 21, 22(1), 25(1), 54, 93, 94, 99, 147(3), 150(2).

Hearn, Estate of v. Hearn, TexApp–Houston (1 Dist), 101 SW3d 657, review den.—Ref of Inst 19(1); Statut 176, 188; Trusts 57, 112; Wills 63, 77.

Hearn; Hearn, Estate of v., TexApp–Houston (1 Dist), 101 SW3d 657, review den.—Ref of Inst 19(1); Statut 176, 188; Trusts 57, 112; Wills 63, 77.

Hearn v. Hearn, TexCivApp–Tyler, 449 SW2d 141.—App & E 846(5); Child S 82, 159, 202, 556(1); Divorce 200, 221, 223, 252.1, 252.2, 252.3(2), 253.3(5), 286(5).

Hearn; Hearn v., TexCivApp–Tyler, 449 SW2d 141.—App & E 846(5); Child S 82, 159, 202, 556(1); Divorce 200, 221, 223, 252.1, 252.2, 252.3(2), 253.3(5), 286(5).

Hearn v. Internal Revenue Agents, NDTex, 623 FSupp 263.—Const Law 1071; Fed Cts 414; Searches 164; U S 50.5(4), 50.10(3).

Hearn v. Internal Revenue Agents, NDTex, 597 FSupp 966.—Fed Cts 229; Int Rev 4637, 4917, 4920, 4921; Searches 84, 113.1, 114, 125, 141, 200.

Hearn; Mrs. Baird's Bread Co. v., Tex, 300 SW2d 646, 157 Tex 159.—App & E 1069.1, 1170.7; New Tr 143(5), 145.

Hearn v. Mrs. Baird's Bread Co., TexCivApp–Dallas, 295 SW2d 689, rev 300 SW2d 646, 157 Tex 159.—App & E 1015(2), 1069.1; Autos 243(4), 245(14); Evid 14; Trial 62(2), 202, 304.

Hearn v. Ralph Sollitt & Sons Const. Co., TexCivApp–Texarkana, 93 SW2d 551.—App & E 1178(8); Contracts 187(1); Courts 122; Labor & Emp 265.

Hearn v. Short, SDTex, 327 FSupp 33.—Courts 508(7); Decl Judgm 276; Fed Cts 997.

Hearn v. State, TexCrimApp, 483 SW2d 461.—Crim Law 486(4), 489, 814(17).

Hearn v. State, TexCrimApp, 411 SW2d 543.—Autos 418, 421; Crim Law 655(1), 736(1), 1119(3).

Hearn v. State, TexCrimApp, 391 SW2d 437.—Crim Law 1090.1(1).

Hearn; Texas General Indem. Co. v., TexApp–Beaumont, 830 SW2d 257.—Elect of Rem 3(1), 7(1); Work Comp 1383.

Hearne v. AmWest Sav. Ass'n, TexApp–Fort Worth, 951 SW2d 950.—Civil R 1019(3), 1019(4), 1218(3); Courts 97(6).

Hearne v. Barnhart, CA5 (Tex), 111 FedAppx 256.—Social S 142.5.

Hearne v. Bradshaw, Tex, 312 SW2d 948, 158 Tex 453.—App & E 846(5), 883, 1177(2); Covenants 104; Deeds 143, 145; Hus & W 193; Tresp to T T 47(1).

Hearne v. Bradshaw, TexCivApp–Dallas, 305 SW2d 618, aff 312 SW2d 948, 158 Tex 453.—Covenants 122; Deeds 145; Hus & W 193.

Hearne; Cofer v., TexCivApp–Austin, 459 SW2d 877, ref nre.—Atty & C 30; Estop 115.

Hearne v. Dow-Badische Chemical Co., SDTex, 224 FSupp 90.—Const Law 3965(3), 3965(4); Corp 642(1), 668(1); Fed Civ Proc 495; Torts 103.

Hearne; Rauch v., TexCivApp–Waco, 189 SW2d 342, writ refused wom.—Estop 118; Lim of Act 13.

Hearne v. State, TexCrimApp, 534 SW2d 703.—Crim Law 519(9).

Hearne v. State, TexCrimApp, 500 SW2d 851, appeal after remand 534 SW2d 703.—Crim Law 528, 781(1).

Hearne v. State, TexCrimApp, 192 SW2d 155.—Crim Law 1090.1(1).

Hearne v. State, TexApp–Houston (1 Dist), 80 SW3d 677, reh overr.—Autos 355(6); Crim Law 1144.13(2.1), 1159.2(1), 1159.2(2), 1159.2(7).

Hearne; Steinbach v., TexCivApp–Amarillo, 278 SW2d 285.—Ex & Ad 436; Venue 22(1), 22(7).

Hearne; Tokar v., CA5 (Tex), 699 F2d 753, reh den 704 F2d 1251, cert den 104 SCt 146, 464 US 844, 78 LEd2d 137.—Armed S 28.

Hearne; White v., TexCivApp–Waco, 514 SW2d 765.—Elections 154(10), 289.

Hearne, City of; Bland v., TexCivApp–Waco, 95 SW2d 979.—Courts 120; Electricity 11.5(1).

Hearne, City of; Lastor v., TexApp–Waco, 810 SW2d 742, writ den.—Mun Corp 156; Offic 66; Statut 183, 189, 190.

Hearne, City of, v. Williams, TexApp–Waco, 715 SW2d 375. See City of Hearne v. Williams.

Hearne Sand & Gravel Co.; Gifford-Hill & Co. v., TexCivApp–Waco, 183 SW2d 766.—Plead 34(1), 111.15; Venue 7.5(3), 8.5(7).

Hearne Sand & Gravel Co. v. McKinney, TexCivApp–Waco, 106 SW2d 1099.—App & E 1002; Sales 52(1), 52(5.1).

Hearon, Ex parte, TexApp–Waco, 3 SW3d 650.—Hab Corp 613.

Hearon v. Jackson, TexCivApp–Texarkana, 109 SW2d 230, writ dism.—App & E 1050.1(6); Evid 263(3), 276, 354(22); Sequest 21; Witn 178(1), 178(3), 181, 395.

Hearon; Mims v., TexCivApp–Dallas, 248 SW2d 754.—App & E 1033(4), 1036(3); Bailm 35; Interest 26; Judgm 675(1), 694; Lim of Act 24(2); Trial 350.3(2.1), 352.5(2), 352.5(3), 352.10; Wareh 16, 24(7), 25(1), 34(3), 34(7), 34(8).

Hearrean v. State, TexCrimApp, 146 SW2d 379, 140 TexCrim 527.—Crim Law 419(10); False Pret 38, 49(3).

Hearrell; Moseley v., Tex, 171 SW2d 337, 141 Tex 280.—Partit 14, 26.

Hearrell v. Moseley, TexCivApp–Texarkana, 168 SW2d 317, rev 171 SW2d 337, 141 Tex 280.—App & E 1177(1); Mines 97, 100; Partit 13.

Hearst Communications, Inc.; Lowe v., CA5 (Tex), 487 F3d 246.—Courts 509; Judgm 828.6; Records 32; Torts 350, 355, 357, 377, 411.

Hearst Communications, Inc.; Lowe v., WDTex, 414 FSupp2d 669, aff 487 F3d 246.—Const Law 1545, 1627, 2070; Damag 57.20, 57.21, 57.22, 57.25(3), 208(6); Fed Civ Proc 1832, 1835; Torts 350, 351, 357, 377.

Hearst Communications, Inc.; Truex v., SDTex, 96 FSupp2d 652.—Fed Civ Proc 2498; Labor & Emp 790, 2254, 2266.

Hearst Corp.; Arlen v., TexApp–Houston (1 Dist), 4 SW3d 326, reh overr, and petition for review den, and reh of petition for review overr.—Autos 194(1); Labor & Emp 3130, 3134, 3141; Neglig 1010, 1011.

Hearst Corp.; Barbouti v., TexApp–Houston (1 Dist), 927 SW2d 37, on reh, and writ den.—App & E 761, 854(1), 934(1); Judgm 185(2), 185(6); Libel 55.

Hearst Corp.; Cain v., Tex, 878 SW2d 577, answer to certified question conformed to 35 F3d 562.—Torts 353.

Hearst Corp.; E.E.O.C. v., CA5 (Tex), 103 F3d 462.—Civil R 1506.

Hearst Corp.; Gonzales v., TexApp–Houston (14 Dist), 930 SW2d 275.—App & E 866(3), 927(7); Libel 51(5), 104(1), 112(2); Trial 139.1(14), 139.1(17), 142, 143, 168.

Hearst Corp.; Hogan v., TexApp–San Antonio, 945 SW2d 246.—Const Law 1230, 1545, 1554, 1570, 2070; Crim Law 1226(2); Damag 50.10, 208(6); Death 21, 31(1); Torts 350, 357.

Hearst Corp. v. Skeen, Tex, 159 SW3d 633.—Const Law 2163, 2169, 2170; Judgm 185.3(21); Libel 51(5), 101(1), 101(5), 112(2).

Hearst Corp. v. Skeen, TexApp–Fort Worth, 130 SW3d 910, reh overr, review gr, rev 159 SW3d 633.—App & E 863; Const Law 1622, 2161, 2165; Judgm 181(6), 181(33), 185(5), 185.3(21); Libel 1, 6(1), 7(2), 19, 36, 38(1), 41, 43, 45(1), 48(1), 49, 50.5, 51(4), 51(5), 54, 55, 112(2), 123(2).

Hearst Entertainment, Inc.; Bloom v., CA5 (Tex), 33 F3d 518, reh den.—Contracts 143(2), 152, 156, 176(2), 189, 203; Cust & U 15(1), 15(2); Evid 450(5), 461(5); Fed Cts 776.

Heart & Vascular Institute of Texas; First Professionals Ins. Co., Inc. v., TexApp–San Antonio, 182 SW3d 6, reh overr, and review den.—Contracts 143(2), 143.5, 169, 176(2); Insurance 1808, 1836, 2266.

Heartfield; Barret v., TexCivApp–Beaumont, 140 SW2d 942, writ refused.—Land & Ten 109(1), 172(1), 190(1), 195(2), 233(3), 258.

Heartfield; Brooks v., TexCivApp–Beaumont, 2 SW2d 510.—Trademarks 1425, 1540.

Heartfield v. Heartfield, CA5 (Tex), 749 F2d 1138.—Child C 744, 745; Child S 507; Courts 508(2.1); Fed Cts 8, 15.

Heartfield; Heartfield v., CA5 (Tex), 749 F2d 1138.—Child C 744, 745; Child S 507; Courts 508(2.1); Fed Cts 8, 15.

Heartfield v. State, TexCrimApp, 470 SW2d 895.—Crim Law 706(3), 720(6), 730(1), 730(14); Jury 75(2); Witn 277(4).

Hearth, Inc. v. Department of Public Welfare, CA5 (Tex), 617 F2d 381.—Fed Cts 243.

Hearth, Inc. v. Department of Public Welfare, CA5 (Tex), 612 F2d 981, opinion mod 617 F2d 381.—Fed Cts 243.

Heart Hosp. IV, L.P. v. King, TexApp–Austin, 116 SW3d 831, reh overr, and review den.—Admin Law 651; App & E 893(1); Courts 4, 39; Lim of Act 104.5, 130(7); Pretrial Proc 582; Unemp Comp 461, 462.

Heart Hosp. of Austin v. Matthews, TexApp–Austin, 212 SW3d 331, review gr.—App & E 68; Health 804, 809; Statut 208, 212.6, 212.7.

Hearthshire Braeswood Plaza Ltd. Partnership v. Bill Kelly Co., TexApp–Houston (14 Dist), 849 SW2d 380, reh den, and writ den.—Alt Disp Res 113, 119, 133(2), 134(3), 134(6), 137, 144, 196, 199, 200, 203, 210, 213(5); App & E 836, 852, 931(1), 1010.1(3), 1024.1; Contracts 1, 22(2), 99(3); Plead 111.39(1), 111.47.

Hearthwood II Owners Ass'n, Inc.; Brown v., TexApp–Houston (14 Dist), 201 SW3d 153, reh overr, and review den.—App & E 223, 267(1), 852, 855, 863, 934(1), 1079; Evid 596(1); Judgm 183, 185(5), 185.1(4), 185.3(8), 185.3(14), 185.3(21); Neglig 210, 1692.

Heartland Federal Sav. & Loan Ass'n v. Briscoe Enterprises, Ltd., II, CA5 (Tex), 994 F2d 1160. See Briscoe Enterprises, Ltd., II, Matter of.

Heartland Federal Sav. and Loan Ass'n v. Briscoe Enterprises Ltd., II, NDTex, 138 BR 795. See Briscoe Enterprises Ltd., II, In re.

Heartland Federal Sav. and Loan Ass'n; Galveston Independent School Dist. v., SDTex, 159 BR 198.—Bankr 2582, 2852, 2853.30; Interest 31; Judgm 735; Statut 223.4; Tax 2733, 2763, 2787, 2810, 3211, 3212, 3216, 3218, 3220.

Heartland Federal Sav. & Loan Ass'n v. Regalridge Apartments, CA5 (Tex), 994 F2d 1160. See Briscoe Enterprises, Ltd., II, Matter of.

Heartland Healthcare Center; Flowerette v., NDTex, 903 FSupp 1042.—Fed Cts 241, 246; Labor & Emp 757; Rem of C 25(1), 79(1), 103, 107(11); States 18.46.

Heartland Wireless Communications, Inc.; Coates v., NDTex, 100 FSupp3d 417.—Sec Reg 60.45(1), 60.51.

Heartland Wireless Communications, Inc.; Coates v., NDTex, 55 FSupp3d 628.—Fed Civ Proc 636, 1789, 1827.1; Sec Reg 60.45(1), 60.51.

Heartland Wireless Communications, Inc.; Coates v., NDTex, 26 FSupp2d 910.—Fed Civ Proc 636, 821; Sec Reg 60.18, 60.45(1), 60.47, 60.48(2), 60.51.

Heart of Texas Pizza, L.L.C.; Caballero v., TexApp–San Antonio, 70 SW3d 180.—App & E 777, 781(6).

HeartPlace v. Mallick, TexApp–Texarkana, 978 SW2d 209. See Dallas Cardiology Associates, P.A. v. Mallick.

Hearty; Rodriguez v., SDTex, 121 FSupp 125.—Autos 235(4); Rem of C 79(1).

Heasley, In re, BkrtcyNDTex, 217 BR 82.—Bankr 2021.1, 2253, 2254, 2363.1.

Heat Energy Advanced Technology, Inc. v. West Dallas Coalition for Environmental Justice, TexApp–Austin, 962 SW2d 288, review den.—Admin Law 497, 791; Environ Law 630, 652, 656, 661, 665, 678.

Heath v. Boyd, Tex, 175 SW2d 214, 141 Tex 569.—Arrest 62, 63.1; False Imp 7(3), 8, 39.

Heath v. Boyd, TexCivApp–Austin, 171 SW2d 396, rev 175 SW2d 214, 141 Tex 569.—Arrest 63.3; False Imp 31, 39; High 63.

Heath v. Brown, CA5 (Tex), 858 F2d 1092.—Civil R 1404, 1482, 1490; Fed Cts 917.

Heath v. Brown, CA5 (Tex), 807 F2d 1229, appeal after remand 858 F2d 1092.—Civil R 1482.

Heath; Chapel Hill Independent School Dist. v., TexCivApp–Waco, 272 SW2d 377.—App & E 395, 564(5).

Heath; Charlie Hillard, Inc. v., TexApp–Fort Worth, 624 SW2d 758.—Cons Cred 4, 17.

Heath v. City of Abilene, TexCivApp–Eastland, 337 SW2d 180.—Judgm 185.3(20).

Heath v. City of Abilene, TexCivApp–Eastland, 337 SW2d 179.—Judgm 185.2(9).

Heath; City of Cleburne v., TexCivApp–Waco, 304 SW2d 417.—App & E 547(1), 846(5); Em Dom 224; New Tr 140(3).

Heath; Crow v., TexCivApp–Corpus Christi, 516 SW2d 225, ref nre.—Jud S 48; Mtg 335, 369(2), 369(3), 369(7), 375.

Heath; Diversion Lake Club v., Tex, 86 SW2d 441, 126 Tex 129.—Com Law 12; Fish 3; Nav Wat 1(1), 1(2), 16, 36(1).

Heath v. Elliston, TexCivApp–Amarillo, 145 SW2d 243, writ dism, correct.—Brok 55(2); Judgm 199(3.7), 199(3.9), 199(3.14).

Heath v. Elliston, TexCivApp–Amarillo, 135 SW2d 512.—App & E 458(1), 468.

Heath; Fulford v., TexCivApp–Amarillo, 212 SW2d 649, ref nre.—Adv Poss 13, 16(1), 112, 114(1), 114(2); App & E 989, 1011.1(4), 1012.1(3); Bound 3(2), 20(1), 33, 37(3), 37(5).

Heath; Gelfand v., TexCivApp–Texarkana, 124 SW2d 1017.—App & E 719(1), 752, 759.

Heath v. Gilbreath, TexCivApp–El Paso, 536 SW2d 404.—Venue 7.5(1), 7.5(3).

Heath v. Herron, TexApp–Houston (14 Dist), 732 SW2d 748, writ den.—Antitrust 256; Atty & C 112, 129(2); Damag 49.10; Elect of Rem 1, 7(1); Evid 591; Judgm 707, 713(1); Torts 109.

Heath; Jackson v., TexCivApp–San Antonio, 325 SW2d 453.—Adv Poss 58, 71(3), 82, 86.

Heath v. Johnson, CA5 (Tex), 70 FedAppx 193, cert den 124 SCt 1433, 540 US 1190, 158 LEd2d 99.—Fed Cts 612.1.

Heath; Producers' & Refiners' Corp. of Texas v., TexCivApp–Austin, 81 SW2d 533, writ dism.—Judgm 829(3); States 191.5; Tax 2776, 2777.

Heath; San Antonio Fence Co. v., TexCivApp–San Antonio, 287 SW2d 524.—App & E 1175(6); Contracts 176(8); Judgm 199(3.14).

Heath; Scholz v., TexApp–Waco, 642 SW2d 554.—App & E 989, 1170.10; Decl Judgm 345.1, 369; Deeds 112(1), 140, 141; Estop 12; Evid 448, 450(3); Mines 55(2), 55(7); Trial 401.

Heath v. State, TexCrimApp, 817 SW2d 335.—Crim Law 1042, 1136, 1192; Sent & Pun 34, 2005.

Heath v. State, TexCrimApp, 375 SW2d 909.—Assault 92(5); Crim Law 364(4), 814(8).

Heath v. State, TexCrimApp, 276 SW2d 534, 161 TexCrim 323.—Crim Law 394.4(2), 1083; Gaming 75(1), 98(5).

Heath v. State, TexCrimApp, 244 SW2d 815, 156 TexCrim 563.—Crim Law 393(1), 1120(4); Ind & Inf 86(2).

Heath v. State, TexCrimApp, 210 SW2d 586, 151 TexCrim 609.—Crim Law 438(5.1), 556, 786(1), 1173.2(7); Homic 847.

Heath v. State, TexCrimApp, 164 SW2d 677, 144 TexCrim 491.—Crim Law 1090.1(3), 1097(5).

Heath v. State, TexApp–Fort Worth, 778 SW2d 208, petition for discretionary review gr, rev 817 SW2d 335.—Crim Law 1147; Sent & Pun 2004, 2006, 2018, 2020, 2021.

Heath; Traders & General Ins. Co. v., TexCivApp–Galveston, 197 SW2d 130, ref nre.—App & E 1062.1; Damag 221(2.1); Trial 215, 232(3), 357; Work Comp 840, 1922, 1927, 1929, 1969.

Heath; United North & South Development Co. v., TexCivApp–Austin, 78 SW2d 650, writ refused.—Const Law 4140.

Heath; U.S. v., CA5 (Tex), 978 F2d 879, cert den Cheng v. US, 113 SCt 1643, 507 US 1004, 123 LEd2d 265.—Crim Law 1038.1(2), 1038.1(4).

Heath; U.S. v., CA5 (Tex), 970 F2d 1397, reh den 976 F2d 732, reh den 978 F2d 879, cert den Cheng v. US, 113 SCt 1643, 507 US 1004, 123 LEd2d 265, cert den 113 SCt 1643, 507 US 1004, 123 LEd2d 265.—Banks 509.10, 509.25; Crim Law 419(2), 478(1), 720(5), 745, 865(1.5), 867, 1038.1(4), 1038.1(6), 1043(2), 1043(3), 1170(1), 1174(1); Fraud 68; Ind & Inf 128, 129(1); Rec S Goods 4, 8(4); Witn 396(1), 414(1).

Heath; Ware v., TexCivApp–Fort Worth, 237 SW2d 362.—Insurance 1001, 3567.

Heath & Stich, Inc.; City of San Antonio v., TexCivApp–Waco, 567 SW2d 56, ref nre.—Contracts 155, 156; Mun Corp 374(1).

Heath, City of, v. King, TexApp–Dallas, 705 SW2d 812. See City of Heath v. King.

Heathcoat v. State, TexApp–San Antonio, 709 SW2d 303.—Crim Law 369.2(6); Ind & Inf 189(11); Rob 24.15(2), 27(5).

Heathcock v. State, TexCrimApp, 494 SW2d 570.—Crim Law 273.1(4), 1167(5).

Heatherly; J. Weingarten, Inc. v., TexCivApp–Hous (14 Dist), 450 SW2d 693.—Corp 503(1); Plead 111.16; Venue 8.5(8); Work Comp 2110, 2122.

Heath Furniture Co. No. 2; Bennett v., TexCivApp–Eastland, 390 SW2d 505.—App & E 930(1), 996; Judgm 199(3.10); Mal Pros 42.

Heathington; A.V.I., Inc. v., TexApp–Amarillo, 842 SW2d 712, reh overr, and writ den.—Antitrust 286, 359, 360, 368, 369, 390; App & E 984(5), 1144; Costs 194.18, 207; Interest 1, 39(2.6), 39(2.20); Judgm 199(3.4), 199(3.10).

Heathington v. Heathington Lumber Co., TexCivApp–Amarillo, 420 SW2d 252, ref nre.—Corp 30(6); Lim of Act 53(4); Partners 259.5, 297.

Heathington v. Heathington Lumber Co., TexCivApp–Amarillo, 398 SW2d 822, appeal after remand 420 SW2d 252, ref nre.—App & E 927(1), 927(7), 934(1); Frds St of 51; Lim of Act 28(1), 53(4), 199(1); Partners 53, 61, 62, 259, 329.

Heathington v. State, TexApp–Amarillo, 705 SW2d 326.—Autos 144.2(5.1), 356, 357; Crim Law 796, 1173.2(4).

Heathington; Texas & P. Ry. Co. v., TexCivApp–Fort Worth, 119 SW2d 713.—Costs 132(6), 276.

Heathington; Texas & P. Ry. Co. v., TexCivApp–Fort Worth, 115 SW2d 495.—Costs 194.30; Damag 3; Plead 228.14; R R 408, 415(3), 425, 439(2), 446(1), 446(10); Trial 215, 219, 350.6(4), 352.1(8), 352.4(8), 352.5(7), 352.9, 352.17.

Heathington; U.S. v., CA5 (Tex), 545 F2d 972.—Consp 40.4, 48.2(2); Crim Law 772(6).

Heathington Lumber Co.; Heathington v., TexCivApp–Amarillo, 420 SW2d 252, ref nre.—Corp 30(6); Lim of Act 53(4); Partners 259.5, 297.

Heathington Lumber Co.; Heathington v., TexCivApp–Amarillo, 398 SW2d 822, appeal after remand 420 SW2d 252, ref nre.—App & E 927(1), 927(7), 934(1); Frds St of 51; Lim of Act 28(1), 53(4), 199(1); Partners 53, 61, 62, 259, 329.

Heath Motor Co.; Springer v., TexCivApp–San Antonio, 261 SW2d 757.—Princ & A 25(3), 123(6).

Heatley; Coven v., TexApp–Austin, 715 SW2d 739, ref nre.—App & E 241, 1035; Pretrial Proc 583, 587, 590.1, 591.

Heaton; Allred v., TexCivApp–Waco, 336 SW2d 251, ref nre, appeal dism, cert den 81 SCt 293, 364 US 517, 5 LEd2d 265, reh den 81 SCt 459, 364 US 944, 5 LEd2d 375.—Colleges 9.15, 9.35(1); Const Law 2974; Decl Judgm 210; Inj 78; Parties 1, 35.87.

Heaton v. Bristol, TexCivApp–Waco, 317 SW2d 86, writ refused, appeal dism, cert den 79 SCt 802, 359 US 230, 3 LEd2d 765, reh den 79 SCt 1123, 359 US 999, 3 LEd2d 987.—Colleges 9.15; Const Law 1033, 2920, 3396; Mand 10, 12, 79; Plead 8(3), 228.14; Statut 219(3), 223.5(1), 223.5(6).

Heaton; Burnaman v., Tex, 240 SW2d 288, 150 Tex 333. —App & E 1178(8); Atty & C 85, 101(1); Compromise 15(2); Judgm 72, 80, 88, 361, 567.

Heaton; Burnaman v., TexCivApp–San Antonio, 231 SW2d 1006, rev 240 SW2d 288, 150 Tex 333.—App & E 1008.1(9); Compromise 5(1), 5(3); Trial 350.4(1).

Heaton; H. E. Butt Grocery Co. v., TexCivApp–Waco, 547 SW2d 75.—Evid 471(2), 471(19); Neglig 1670; Plead 111.12; Witn 240(8).

Heaton; Hunt v., Tex, 643 SW2d 677.—Tresp to T T 1, 6.1, 35(1), 36, 41(1).

Heaton; Hunt v., TexApp–Beaumont, 631 SW2d 549, writ gr, aff 643 SW2d 677.—Statut 181(2), 184, 206, 227; Tresp to T T 36.

Heaton v. State, TexCrimApp, 292 SW2d 119.—Bail 63.1.

Heaton v. State, TexCrimApp, 87 SW2d 256, 129 TexCrim 365.—Crim Law 400(1); Hus & W 266.4; Larc 55, 60.

Heaton; Witt v., TexApp–Beaumont, 10 SW3d 435.— Judgm 181(7); Lim of Act 118(2), 119(1), 119(3).

Heaton Cattle Co.; U.S. Fire Ins. Co. v., TexCivApp–Beaumont, 462 SW2d 388, ref nre.—Insurance 3580.

Heatransfer Corp. v. Volkswagenwerk, A. G., CA5 (Tex), 553 F2d 964, reh den 562 F2d 1257, cert den 98 SCt 1282, 434 US 1087, 55 LEd2d 792.—Antitrust 534, 553, 557, 558, 569, 571, 575, 641, 644, 687, 775, 908, 910, 958, 963(1), 963(3), 964, 976, 977(1), 977(2), 977(3), 977(4), 980, 981, 983, 984, 985; Fed Cts 856; Jury 32(2).

Heat Research Corp.; Welch v., CA5 (Tex), 644 F2d 487. —Neglig 221, 1692; Prod Liab 24.

Heavin v. State, TexCrimApp, 299 SW2d 135, 164 TexCrim 334.—Autos 355(6).

Heavy Haulers v. Nicholson, TexCivApp–Galveston, 277 SW2d 250, ref nre.—App & E 79(1), 807; Autos 201(5).

Heavy Haulers, Inc. v. Precise, TexCivApp–Texarkana, 348 SW2d 653, ref nre.—App & E 930(1); Autos 227(1), 244(3), 244(36.1), 244(59); Neglig 530(1), 1683.

H.E.B.; Ramos v., SDTex, 27 FSupp 342, 27 Wage & Hour Cas (BNA) 1147. See Ramos v. H.E. Butt Grocery Co.

Hebberd; White v., TexCivApp–El Paso, 89 SW2d 482.— Hus & W 115, 134, 249(5), 258, 265; Wills 695(2), 702, 703, 759(4), 792(1), 792(4), 800, 841.

Hebbronville Auction & Commission Co.; Miller v., TexCivApp–San Antonio, 558 SW2d 128.—Plead 111.18, 111.42(9).

Hebbronville Utilities; Quilliam v., TexCivApp–San Antonio, 241 SW2d 225, ref nre.—Corp 56, 189(10), 189(12), 200, 283(1), 297.

HEB Chrome Plating; Waite Hill Services, Inc. v., Tex, 959 SW2d 182. See Waite Hill Services, Inc. v. World Class Metal Works, Inc.

HEB Chrome Plating; Waite Hill Services, Inc. v., TexApp–Fort Worth, 935 SW2d 197. See Waite Hill Services, Inc. v. World Class Metal Works, Inc.

Heberling v. State, TexCrimApp, 834 SW2d 350.—Controlled Subs 34, 82; Crim Law 663, 1038.1(2), 1038.1(5), 1134(2).

Heberling v. State, TexApp–Houston (1 Dist), 814 SW2d 183, petition for discretionary review gr, aff 834 SW2d 350.—Controlled Subs 45, 74, 82.

Hebert, Ex parte, TexCrimApp, 579 SW2d 486.—Bail 44(3.1); Hab Corp 712.1.

Hebert, Ex parte, TexCrimApp, 256 SW2d 571, 158 TexCrim 456.—Hab Corp 729.

Hebert v. Continental Land Corp., TexCivApp–Waco, 513 SW2d 948.—App & E 1024.4; Judgm 185(2).

Hebert; Cuchia v., TexCivApp–Beaumont, 133 SW2d 140, writ refused.—Lim of Act 24(1); Mun Corp 519(6).

Hebert; D/S Ove Skou v., CA5 (Tex), 365 F2d 341, cert den Southern Stevedoring & Contracting Co v. D/S Ove Skou, 91 SCt 139, 400 US 902, 27 LEd2d 139.—Adm 118.7(1), 118.7(5); Contracts 187(1); Indem 69, 75, 76; Ship 84(3.2), 84(6), 86(2.5).

Hebert v. D/S Ove Skou, EDTex, 232 FSupp 277, aff in part, rev in part 365 F2d 341, cert den Southern Stevedoring & Contracting Co v. D/S Ove Skou, 91 SCt 139, 400 US 902, 27 LEd2d 139.—Damag 130.4; Ship 86(2.5).

Hebert; General Motors Corp. v., TexCivApp–Hous (1 Dist), 501 SW2d 950, ref nre.—App & E 933(6), 1045(1); Death 15; Fraud 58(1); Insurance 3526(5); Jury 139; Statut 181(2).

Hebert; Jefferson County Drainage Dist. No. 7 v., TexCivApp–Austin, 244 SW2d 535, ref nre.—App & E 1062.2; Damag 221(1); Evid 208(2); Trial 350.6(1), 350.8, 351.5(5), 352.4(1); Waters 119(2).

Hebert v. Loveless, TexCivApp–Beaumont, 474 SW2d 732, ref nre.—App & E 837(11); Evid 314(1), 314(2); Food 25; Prod Liab 8, 15, 82.1; Trial 105(2).

Hebert v. McFaddin, Tex, 105 SW2d 650, 129 Tex 499.— Bound 37(1).

Hebert v. McFaddin, Tex, 104 SW2d 475, 129 Tex 499, reh den 105 SW2d 650, 129 Tex 499.—App & E 1094(1), 1094(5), 1095; Bound 37(3).

Hebert; McFaddin v., TexCivApp–Beaumont, 100 SW2d 140, rev 104 SW2d 475, 129 Tex 499, reh den 105 SW2d 650, 129 Tex 499.—App & E 843(2), 882(14), 1097(1), 1213; Trial 350.2, 352.9, 355(1).

Hebert v. Monsanto Co., CA5 (Tex), 682 F2d 1111.—Civil R 1544, 1554, 1592.

Hebert v. Monsanto Co., Texas City, Tex., CA5 (Tex), 580 F2d 178.—Fed Cts 574.

Hebert v. Monsanto Co., Texas City, Tex., CA5 (Tex), 576 F2d 77, opinion vac on reh 580 F2d 178.

Hebert v. Pan American Van Lines, Inc., TexApp–Houston (14 Dist), 681 SW2d 221.—App & E 932(1), 989, 1004(4); Damag 185(1); Evid 570, 594.

Hebert v. Probate Court No. One of Harris County, TexCivApp–Hous (14 Dist), 466 SW2d 849.—Courts 155; Prohib 1, 3(1), 3(2), 3(3).

Hebert; Rio Bravo Oil Co. v., Tex, 106 SW2d 242, 130 Tex 1, motion gr 58 SCt 52, cert den 58 SCt 366, 302 US 759, 82 LEd 588, reh den 58 SCt 475, 302 US 780, 82 LEd 603.—App & E 1206; Judgm 713(2), 715(2), 717, 720, 725(1); Lis Pen 24(1); Prohib 5(3).

Hebert v. Shrake, TexCivApp–Hous (1 Dist), 492 SW2d 605.—Pretrial Proc 597; Trial 14.

Hebert v. State, TexCrimApp, 586 SW2d 529.—Crim Law 419(2.40), 814(1), 1036.5; Rape 2.

Hebert v. State, TexCrimApp, 255 SW2d 201, 158 TexCrim 271.—Crim Law 1130(4).

Hebert v. State, TexCrimApp, 249 SW2d 925, 157 TexCrim 504.—Crim Law 394.1(1), 394.4(6), 419(12); Searches 111.

Hebert v. State, TexCrimApp, 114 SW2d 549, 134 TexCrim 112.—Int Liq 140, 221, 223(1), 236(7).

Hebert v. State, TexApp–Houston (1 Dist), 836 SW2d 252, petition for discretionary review refused.—Const Law 4594(8); Crim Law 700(9), 1153(1), 1170.5(1); Witn 88.

Hebert v. State, TexApp–Beaumont, 853 SW2d 207, petition for discretionary review refused.—Crim Law 641.13(1), 641.13(2.1).

Hebert; Texas Dept. of Human Resources v., TexCivApp–Waco, 621 SW2d 466.—Child S 497; Contempt 66(1).

Hebert; Time Warner Entertainment Co. L.P. v., TexApp–Houston (1 Dist), 916 SW2d 47, appeal decided 1996 WL 112115.—App & E 70(8).

Hebert; U.S. v., CA5 (Tex), 131 F3d 514, cert den 118 SCt 1571, 523 US 1101, 140 LEd2d 804.—Arrest 63.4(2),

63.4(15); Crim Law 1030(1), 1038.1(2), 1038.1(4), 1139, 1152(1), 1165(3), 1173.1; Extort 32, 33; Rob 24.20; Sent & Pun 590, 644; Weap 17(4).

Hebert v. U.S., CA5 (Tex), 53 F3d 720.—Fed Cts 12.1, 13, 776; U S 127(2).

Hebert; U.S. v., CA5 (Tex), 753 F2d 1301. See U.S. v. Antone.

Hebert v. U.S., EDTex, 862 FSupp 137, aff 53 F3d 720.— U S 125(10.1), 127(2).

Hebert; Wirtz v., CA5 (Tex), 368 F2d 139.—Labor & Emp 2228.

Hebert; Wirtz v., SDTex, 239 FSupp 705, rev 368 F2d 139.—Labor & Emp 2228, 2291, 2312, 2319.

Hebert Undertaking Co. v. Ozen, TexCivApp–Beaumont, 99 SW2d 1013.—App & E 773(2).

HEB Federal Credit Union; Hunt v., BkrtcyWDTex, 215 BR 505. See Hunt, In re.

HEB Federal Credit Union; Osherow v., BkrtcyWDTex, 215 BR 505. See Hunt, In re.

H. E. B. Foods, Inc. v. Moore, TexCivApp–Corpus Christi, 599 SW2d 126.—App & E 846(5); Neglig 1104(6), 1595; Plead 111.42(7).

HEB Food Store No. 4; Gray v., TexApp–Corpus Christi, 941 SW2d 327, reh overr, and writ den.—App & E 879; Judgm 181(33), 185.3(21); Libel 33, 36, 51(1).

H. E. B. Food Stores v. Atchison, TexCivApp–Waco, 383 SW2d 954.—Plead 111.42(7).

H. E. B. Food Stores v. Mercado, TexCivApp–Beaumont, 486 SW2d 591.—App & E 912; Neglig 1037(4), 1583, 1613, 1614; Plead 111.30, 111.39(6), 111.42(7), 111.42(9); Venue 22(4), 22(6).

H. E. B. Food Stores v. Rodgers, TexCivApp–Eastland, 385 SW2d 626.—App & E 1175(5); Plead 111.9, 111.42(3), 111.42(6), 111.42(7).

H. E. B. Food Stores v. Slaughter, TexCivApp–Corpus Christi, 484 SW2d 794, dism.—Neglig 1037(4), 1104(6), 1595, 1708; Plead 111.42(7).

H.E.B. Food Stores, Inc. v. Flores, TexApp–Corpus Christi, 661 SW2d 297, dism.—Neglig 1037(4), 1076, 1077, 1088, 1579, 1595; Plead 111.12, 111.42(7).

H.E.B. Food Stores, Inc.; Hukill v., TexApp–Corpus Christi, 756 SW2d 840.—App & E 989, 1001(1), 1003(5), 1003(7), 1003(10), 1064.1(8); Neglig 1741, 1742.

H. E. B. Food Stores, Inc. v. Warncke, TexCivApp–San Antonio, 444 SW2d 954.—App & E 846(5), 934(2), 989; Neglig 1717; Plead 111.42(7).

H. E. B. Grocery Co.; Contreras v., TexCivApp–San Antonio, 328 SW2d 469, writ refused.—Neglig 1289.

H.E.B., Inc.; Morrow v., Tex, 714 SW2d 297.—App & E 946; Pretrial Proc 313.

H.E.B., Inc. v. Morrow, TexApp–Corpus Christi, 704 SW2d 93, rev 714 SW2d 297.—App & E 961, 1032(1), 1043(6); Pretrial Proc 45, 309, 312, 313, 719.

Hebisen v. Clear Creek Independent School Dist., TexApp–Houston (14 Dist), 217 SW3d 527, reh overr.—App & E 497(1), 846(5), 931(1), 934(1); Const Law 4138(2); Refer 1, 100(6); Statut 227; Tax 2861, 2862.

Hebisen v. Nassau Development Co., TexApp–Houston (14 Dist), 754 SW2d 345, writ den.—Action 27(1); App & E 237(1), 238(2), 1177(7); Fraud 20, 58(3), 61; Frds St of 110(1), 110(3); Land & Ten 216, 231(8), 238.

Hebisen v. State, TexCivApp–Hous (1 Dist), 615 SW2d 866.—Atty & C 54, 56, 57, 117.

HEB Ministries, Inc. v. Texas Higher Educ. Coordinating Bd., TexApp–Austin, 114 SW3d 617, reh overr, and review gr.—App & E 893(1); Colleges 1, 2; Const Law 655, 990, 999, 1030, 1290, 1291, 1295, 1300, 1303, 1307, 1310, 1363, 1371, 1389, 1512, 1514, 1515, 1541, 2005; Statut 181(1), 212.3, 212.7.

HEB Nursing Center v. Texas Dept. of Human Services, TexApp–Austin, 926 SW2d 823. See Sensitive Care, Inc. v. Texas Dept. of Human Services.

H.E.B. Pantry Foods; Olsen v., EDTex, 196 FSupp2d 436.—Civil R 1184, 1185, 1189, 1243, 1528, 1541, 1544; Fed Civ Proc 2497.1.

H-Ebrahimi; Ayati-Ghaffari v., TexApp–Dallas, 109 SW3d 915.—App & E 920(2), 946, 966(1), 1030; Divorce 145; Pretrial Proc 715.

H.E. Butt Co.; Wilhite v., TexApp–Corpus Christi, 812 SW2d 1.—App & E 497(1), 559, 638, 863, 1073(5); Consp 1.1, 2; Judgm 186, 190, 217, 282; Labor & Emp 40(2), 50, 835, 840; Motions 56(1); Torts 341, 350, 351, 353, 354.

H. E. Butt Food Stores, Inc. v. Vera, TexCivApp–San Antonio, 516 SW2d 287.—Atty & C 86; Neglig 1022; Plead 111.42(7).

H. E. Butt Foundation; Green v., CA5 (Tex), 217 F2d 553.—Bankr 2050, 2553; Contracts 278(1); Mech Liens 113(1); Propty 10.

H.E. Butt Grocery Co., In re, TexApp–Houston (14 Dist), 17 SW3d 360.—Alt Disp Res 112, 113, 117, 124, 134(1), 134(3), 134(5), 139, 143, 146, 191, 198, 199, 210, 382; Contracts 1, 10(1), 114, 143(2), 176(2); Evid 384, 397(1), 398; Indem 30(1); Judgm 634, 715(1), 948(1), 956(1), 958(2); Labor & Emp 412, 425, 483(2), 554, 695; Mand 26, 28, 60; States 18.15; Work Comp 1045.

H.E. Butt Grocery Co. v. Bay, Inc., TexApp–Corpus Christi, 808 SW2d 678, writ den.—App & E 23, 185(1), 236(1), 237(4), 1078(2); Interest 38(1); Judgm 128, 217, 222, 223.

H.E. Butt Grocery Co. v. Bilotto, Tex, 985 SW2d 22.—Damag 210(1); Neglig 1746; Trial 194(1), 219, 352.17.

H.E. Butt Grocery Co. v. Bilotto, TexApp–San Antonio, 928 SW2d 197, reh overr, and writ gr, aff 985 SW2d 22.—App & E 969; Courts 85(3); Neglig 1746; Trial 228(1), 335.

H. E. Butt Grocery Co.; Bosquez v., TexCivApp–Corpus Christi, 586 SW2d 680, ref nre.—Neglig 1670, 1679; Trial 112, 365.1(6).

H. E. Butt Grocery Co. v. Bradfield, TexCivApp–San Antonio, 396 SW2d 254.—Neglig 1286(5); Plead 111.42(4).

H. E. Butt Grocery Co. v. Brown, TexCivApp–Austin, 381 SW2d 201.—Plead 111.42(4).

H. E. Butt Grocery Co. v. Bruner, TexCivApp–Waco, 530 SW2d 340, writ dism by agreement.—Courts 89; Evid 75, 76, 78, 87, 89; Neglig 1639, 1670, 1693.

H. E. Butt Grocery Co. v. Calvert, TexCivApp–Austin, 388 SW2d 727, ref nre.—Tax 3646.

H.E. Butt Grocery Co.; Cline v., SDTex, 79 FSupp2d 730.—Alt Disp Res 113, 134(1), 143, 182(2), 210; Labor & Emp 1542; Work Comp 1045, 1316.

H. E. Butt Grocery Co.; Cuellar v., TexApp–Corpus Christi, 397 SW2d 873.—App & E 773(2).

H.E. Butt Grocery Co. v. Currier, TexApp–Corpus Christi, 885 SW2d 175.—Action 60; App & E 70(4), 76(1), 78(1), 949; Mand 32; Pretrial Proc 33, 153.1.

H. E. Butt Grocery Co. v. Davis, TexCivApp–Austin, 451 SW2d 559.—Corp 503(1); Plead 111.35, 111.42(7).

H. E. Butt Grocery Co. v. Dillingham, TexCivApp–Corpus Christi, 417 SW2d 373.—Neglig 1104(6); Plead 111.43.

H. E. Butt Grocery Co. v. Dorn, TexCivApp–San Antonio, 494 SW2d 239.—Neglig 1037(4), 1289; Plead 111.17, 111.42(7).

H.E. Butt Grocery Co.; Flores v., TexApp–Corpus Christi, 802 SW2d 53.—App & E 5, 859; Pretrial Proc 44.1, 46.

H.E. Butt Grocery Co.; Foster v., TexCivApp–San Antonio, 548 SW2d 769, ref nre.—Assault 13, 43(2), 67, 96(3); Plead 111.42(9); Venue 22(1).

H. E. Butt Grocery Co.; Garcia v., TexCivApp–Corpus Christi, 461 SW2d 439.—Judgm 185.3(21).

H.E. Butt Grocery Co. v. Godawa, TexApp–Corpus Christi, 763 SW2d 27.—Neglig 1037(1), 1037(4), 1076, 1077, 1088, 1104(3), 1670.

H.E. BUTT

H.E. Butt Grocery Co.; Gonzales v., CA5 (Tex), 226 FedAppx 342.—Civil R 1049; Consp 7.5(1); Damag 57.25(2).

H.E. Butt Grocery, Co.; Gonzalez v., TexApp–Corpus Christi, 667 SW2d 188.—App & E 1107.

H.E. Butt Grocery Co.; Guevara v., TexApp–San Antonio, 82 SW3d 550, review den.—App & E 893(1); Civil R 1004, 1708, 1717, 1732.

H. E. Butt Grocery Co. v. Hawkins, TexCivApp–Corpus Christi, 594 SW2d 187.—App & E 846(5), 854(1), 989; Neglig 1076, 1095, 1104(6), 1670.

H. E. Butt Grocery Co. v. Heaton, TexCivApp–Waco, 547 SW2d 75.—Evid 471(2), 471(19); Neglig 1670; Plead 111.12; Witn 240(8).

H. E. Butt Grocery Co.; Hersh v., TexCivApp–San Antonio, 338 SW2d 174, ref nre.—Judgm 178, 185(2), 185.3(21), 186.

H. E. Butt Grocery Co. v. Israel, TexCivApp–Waco, 544 SW2d 769.—Neglig 1102, 1286(1), 1289; Plead 111.42(8).

H.E. Butt Grocery Co. v. Jefferson County Appraisal Dist., Tex, 922 SW2d 941.—Tax 2135, 2432, 2443.

H. E. Butt Grocery Co. v. Johnson, TexCivApp–San Antonio, 226 SW2d 501, ref nre.—App & E 1062.1, 1064.1(11); Evid 268; Neglig 1076, 1104(6), 1571, 1708; Trial 240, 350.1, 350.2.

H. E. Butt Grocery Co. v. Justice, TexCivApp–Waco, 484 SW2d 628, ref nre.—Covenants 49, 52.

H. E. Butt Grocery Co. v. Justice, TexCivApp–Waco, 473 SW2d 77.—Venue 5.4.

H. E. Butt Grocery Co.; Karam v., TexCivApp–San Antonio, 527 SW2d 481, ref nre.—Antitrust 575, 591.

H. E. Butt Grocery Co. v. Keeble, TexCivApp–Corpus Christi, 444 SW2d 358.—Plead 111.3, 111.42(1), 111.42(2).

H. E. Butt Grocery Co. v. Kirkwood, TexCivApp–Corpus Christi, 384 SW2d 790.—Plead 111.42(7).

H.E. Butt Grocery Co. v. Lansdown, TexCivApp–Waco, 567 SW2d 608.—Plead 111.42(7).

H.E. Butt Grocery Co.; Larson v., TexApp–Corpus Christi, 769 SW2d 694, writ den.—App & E 961; Mand 32; Pretrial Proc 19, 44.1, 721, 723.1.

H. E. Butt Grocery Co. v. Logue, TexCivApp–Waco, 370 SW2d 418, mandamus overr.—Prohib 3(3), 5(3), 9.

H. E. Butt Grocery Co. v. Marroquin, TexCivApp–San Antonio, 466 SW2d 837.—Neglig 1037(4), 1104(6); Plead 111.42(7).

H. E. Butt Grocery Co.; Martinez v., TexCivApp–San Antonio, 379 SW2d 94.—App & E 1032(1), 1069.1; Trial 309, 351.2(4), 352.5(5).

H.E. Butt Grocery Co. v. Moody's Quality Meats, Inc., TexApp–Corpus Christi, 951 SW2d 33, reh overr, and review den.—Antitrust 413, 417, 418, 432.

H.E. Butt Grocery Co.; Morehead v., TexCivApp–Austin, 333 SW2d 428, ref nre.—Evid 5(2); Judgm 181(33); Neglig 1288.

H.E. Butt Grocery Co. v. National Union Fire Ins. Co. of Pittsburgh, Pa., CA5 (Tex), 150 F3d 526, reh and sug for reh den 159 F3d 1358.—Contracts 143(1), 143(2), 176(2); Insurance 1806, 1808, 1809, 1813, 1850, 2275, 2281(2).

H.E. Butt Grocery Co. v. Navarro, TexApp–Corpus Christi, 658 SW2d 842.—Neglig 1037(4), 1076; Plead 111.42(7).

H. E. Butt Grocery Co. v. Neely, TexCivApp–San Antonio, 417 SW2d 759.—App & E 1177(1); Evid 237, 243(2); Libel 75; Plead 111.1, 111.17.

H.E. Butt Grocery Co.; Nevills v., TexApp–Beaumont, 38 SW3d 294, reh overr, and review den, and reh of petition for review den.—App & E 927(7); Neglig 1095, 1562, 1708; Trial 139.1(7).

H.E. Butt Grocery Co. v. Newell, TexApp–Corpus Christi, 664 SW2d 116.—App & E 931(1), 989; Neglig 1037(4), 1076, 1077, 1088; Plead 111.42(7).

H.E. Butt Grocery Co.; Ortiz v., TexApp–San Antonio, 673 SW2d 660.—App & E 846(5); Neglig 1620; Plead 111.42(8).

H.E. Butt Grocery Co. v. Paez, TexApp–Corpus Christi, 742 SW2d 824, writ den.—App & E 1070(2); Damag 210(1); New Tr 143(1); Trial 352.17.

H.E. Butt Grocery Co. v. Pais, TexApp–San Antonio, 955 SW2d 384.—Evid 207(1); Judgm 304, 305, 306, 325; New Tr 58, 143(1); Trial 340(1), 344.

H. E. Butt Grocery Co. v. Pena, TexCivApp–Austin, 592 SW2d 956.—App & E 989; Evid 100; Neglig 1076, 1104(7); Plead 111.39(4), 111.42(6).

H. E. Butt Grocery Co. v. Perez, TexCivApp–San Antonio, 408 SW2d 576.—Anim 66.9, 74(2), 74(3); Corp 503(2); Damag 56.20, 185(1); Plead 111.42(7).

H. E. Butt Grocery Co. v. Quick, TexCivApp–San Antonio, 442 SW2d 798, ref nre.—App & E 930(3), 1170.6, 1170.10; Damag 143(3); Neglig 1077(4), 1670; Trial 125(4), 129, 350.5(2), 350.6(1), 350.6(2), 350.7(1).

H. E. Butt Grocery Co. v. Quick, TexCivApp–San Antonio, 396 SW2d 541.—Neglig 1012, 1076, 1077, 1286(1), 1683.

H.E. Butt Grocery Co.; Ramirez v., TexApp–Waco, 909 SW2d 62, reh overr, and writ den.—Antitrust 141, 145, 363; App & E 230, 927(7), 1064.1(1), 1067, 1068(5); Neglig 200, 383, 1000, 1001, 1032, 1076, 1086, 1742; Trial 75, 76, 143, 295(1).

H.E. Butt Grocery Co.; Ramos v., SDTex, 632 FSupp 342, 27 Wage & Hour Cas (BNA) 1147.—Rem of C 13.

H.E. Butt Grocery Co.; Regalado v., TexApp–San Antonio, 863 SW2d 107.—Atty & C 148(1); Costs 246.5; Judgm 185(2); Work Comp 203, 208, 1217, 1221, 1988.

H.E. Butt Grocery Co. v. Resendez, Tex, 988 SW2d 218.—Neglig 1001, 1104(7); 1670.

H.E. Butt Grocery Co. v. Resendez, TexApp–Corpus Christi, 989 SW2d 768, reh overr, review gr, rev 988 SW2d 218.—App & E 934(1), 989, 999(1), 1003(6), 1004(3), 1050.1(1), 1056.1(1), 1182; Courts 26; Damag 97, 102, 132(7), 135, 208(1), 221(7); Neglig 1001, 1670, 1679; Trial 33, 43, 62(1).

H. E. Butt Grocery Co. v. Reyna, TexApp–Corpus Christi, 632 SW2d 890.—App & E 846(5), 912, 931(1), 989; Plead 111.9, 111.12, 111.39(6); Venue 8.5(8), 21.

H. E. Butt Grocery Co. v. Rodriguez, TexCivApp–Corpus Christi, 441 SW2d 215.—Neglig 1104(6); Plead 111.42(7).

H.E. Butt Grocery Co.; Rosales v., TexApp–San Antonio, 905 SW2d 745, writ den.—App & E 80(1), 187(2), 236(1), 843(2), 882(4), 1043(8); Venue 28, 68.

H. E. Butt Grocery Co. v. Russell, TexCivApp–Waco, 391 SW2d 571, ref nre.—Neglig 1077, 1104(2), 1104(6), 1104(7).

H.E. Butt Grocery Co. v. Saldivar, TexApp–Corpus Christi, 752 SW2d 701.—False Imp 2, 31.

H.E. Butt Grocery Co.; Serna v., TexApp–San Antonio, 21 SW3d 330, reh den.—Action 35; App & E 893(1), 919; Courts 97(5); Tax 3700, 3704, 3707.

H. E. Butt Grocery Co. v. Shachet, TexCivApp–Eastland, 384 SW2d 427.—Plead 111.42(7).

H. E. Butt Grocery Co. v. Sheppard, TexCivApp–Austin, 137 SW2d 823, writ refused, appeal dism 61 SCt 52, 311 US 608, 85 LEd 385, reh den 61 SCt 134, 311 US 727, 85 LEd 473.—Corp 1.3; Licens 8(1), 15(8); Statut 245.

H. E. Butt Grocery Co.; S. K. Y. Inv. Corp. v., TexCivApp–Corpus Christi, 440 SW2d 885.—Contracts 314; Cust & U 14, 15(1), 16; Judgm 181(2), 185(2), 185.1(4), 185.3(14), 186; Land & Ten 103(3).

H.E. Butt Grocery Co.; Smith v., TexApp–Beaumont, 18 SW3d 910, review den.—Alt Disp Res 134(1), 134(6), 146, 186, 191, 199, 205, 210.

H. E. Butt Grocery Co.; Snead v., TexCivApp–Waco, 397 SW2d 332.—App & E 302(5); Neglig 1679, 1683, 1717, 1750.

H. E. Butt Grocery Co.; Sneed v., TexCivApp–Corpus Christi, 569 SW2d 555, ref nre.—App & E 961, 1170.1.

H.E. Butt Grocery Co. v. Snodgrass, TexApp–Corpus Christi, 655 SW2d 241.—App & E 930(1); Neglig 1037(4), 1076, 1088; Plead 111.42(7).

H.E. Butt Grocery Co. v. Stastny, TexApp–Corpus Christi, 645 SW2d 314.—Neglig 1037(4); Plead 111.9, 111.42(7); Venue 8.5(8), 21.

H. E. Butt Grocery Co. v. Tester, TexCivApp–Corpus Christi, 498 SW2d 683.—App & E 694(1), 758.3(9), 768; Neglig 1076, 1085, 1104(6), 1595; Plead 111.12.

H.E. Butt Grocery Co.; Turner v., TexApp–Austin, 645 SW2d 936.—App & E 621(1), 624, 627.

H.E. Butt Grocery Co.; United Farm Workers, AFL-CIO v., TexCivApp–Corpus Christi, 590 SW2d 600.—Antitrust 537; App & E 190(2), 609, 624, 846(5), 954(1); Const Law 90.1(7.1), 1622, 1850, 1921; Inj 63, 151; Labor & Emp 1403, 2059, 2121, 2136.

H.E. Butt Grocery Co. v. U.S., WDTex, 108 FSupp2d 709.—Fed Civ Proc 2514; Int Rev 3102, 3536, 4479.

H. E. Butt Grocery Co. v. Vaught, TexCivApp–San Antonio, 413 SW2d 940, writ dism.—Neglig 1104(1), 1670; Plead 111.3, 111.4.

H.E. Butt Grocery Co.; Villarreal v., TexApp–Corpus Christi, 742 SW2d 725, writ dism woj.—App & E 387(2), 389(3).

H.E. Butt Grocery Co. v. Warner, Tex, 845 SW2d 258, on remand 856 SW2d 591.—App & E 1062.2; Neglig 1542; Trial 352.1(6).

H.E. Butt Grocery Co.; Warner v., TexApp–Waco, 820 SW2d 819, writ gr, rev 845 SW2d 258, on remand 856 SW2d 591.—App & E 969, 1062.1; Trial 352.1(1), 352.1(5).

H.E. Butt Grocery Co.; Warner v., TexApp–Corpus Christi, 856 SW2d 591.—Neglig 1001, 1032, 1086, 1735; Trial 260(8).

H.E. Butt Grocery Co. v. Williams, TexApp–San Antonio, 751 SW2d 554.—Mand 172; Pretrial Proc 371, 372, 386.

H. E. Butt Grocery Co.; Wilson v., TexApp–Corpus Christi, 758 SW2d 904.—Autos 197(7); Judgm 183, 185(5), 185(6), 185.3(21); Labor & Emp 3031(1), 3045.

H.E. Butt Grocery Co.; Zimmerman v., CA5 (Tex), 932 F2d 469, reh den 937 F2d 607, cert den 112 SCt 591, 502 US 984, 116 LEd2d 615.—Contracts 1; Fed Cts 776, 850.1; Frds St of 44(3); Labor & Emp 40(2), 50, 57, 835.

H. E. Butt Grocery Store v. Hamilton, TexApp–Corpus Christi, 632 SW2d 189.—App & E 846(5), 931(1), 989; Neglig 1104(6); Plead 111.42(7), 111.44; Venue 21.

H. E. Butt Grocery Stores, Inc. v. Norwood, TexCiv-App–San Antonio, 504 SW2d 920.—Neglig 1037(4), 1076, 1579; Plead 111.42(7).

H.E. Butt Stores, Inc.; Flores v., TexApp–Corpus Christi, 791 SW2d 160, writ den.—Judgm 185(1), 185(2), 185(6); Neglig 1104(3), 1568; Pretrial Proc 483.

Hechler; Parker v., TexCivApp–Hous (14 Dist), 473 SW2d 243.—App & E 846(5); Plead 111.42(1), 111.42(7).

Hecht, In re, TexSpecCtRev, 213 SW3d 547.—Const Law 3905, 4034, 4426; Judges 11(2), 11(7), 11(8); Statut 176, 181(1), 181(2), 184, 188, 200, 206, 208, 217.2, 235, 241(1).

Hecht; Dillard Dept. Stores, Inc. v., TexApp–El Paso, 225 SW3d 109, review gr, and vac pursuant to settlement.—App & E 294(1), 930(1), 969, 1001(1), 1001(3); Evid 597; Labor & Emp 810, 826, 870, 874.

Hecht; Howell v., TexApp–Dallas, 821 SW2d 627, writ den.—Action 3, 6; Evid 208(4); Judgm 183, 185.3(21); Libel 6(1), 48(3), 51(1), 51(5), 55, 112(2).

Hecht; Streller v., TexApp–Houston (14 Dist), 859 SW2d 114, reh den, and writ den.—Fraud 3, 59(1); Frds St of 119(2); Judgm 183.

HECI Exploration Co. v. Clajon Gas Co., TexApp–Austin, 843 SW2d 622, reh overr, and writ den.—App & E 253; Atty & C 20.1, 21.5(1), 21.10, 21.20; Const Law 3954; Contracts 211, 212(2); Costs 194.40; Gas 14.1(3); Judgm 181(19); Mines 92.54; Sales 85(1), 177.

HECI Exploration Co. v. Neel, Tex, 982 SW2d 881, reh overr.—Contracts 168; Impl & C C 3; Judgm 668(1), 675(1), 677, 678(1), 679, 681, 707, 713(1), 725(1); Lim of Act 49(1), 95(1), 95(7), 95(9), 100(11); Mines 73.1(2), 78.1(2), 78.1(11), 79.1, 121; Notice 5.

HECI Exploration Co.; Neel v., TexApp–Austin, 942 SW2d 212, reh overr, and writ gr, rev in part 982 SW2d 881, reh overr.—App & E 854(1); Fraud 38; Impl & C C 55; Judgm 181(7), 181(24), 684; Lim of Act 28(1), 47(2), 49(1), 55(5), 95(1), 95(3), 199(1); Mines 47, 73, 73.1(2), 73.1(4), 78.1(1), 78.1(2), 78.1(11), 78.7(1), 79.1(1), 121.

HECI Exploration Co., Employees' Profit Sharing Plan v. Holloway, CA5 (Tex), 862 F2d 513. See HECI Exploration Co., Inc., Matter of.

HECI Exploration Co. Employees' Profit Sharing Plan; Holloway v., NDTex, 76 BR 563, aff Matter of HECI Exploration Co, Inc, 862 F2d 513.—Bankr 2043(2), 2045, 2047, 2058.1, 2548, 2927, 3770, 3774.1, 3779; Fed Cts 611, 714, 742; Labor & Emp 636; Stip 1, 3.

HECI Exploration Co., Inc., Matter of, CA5 (Tex), 862 F2d 513.—Bankr 3770, 3782, 3784, 3786; Fed Civ Proc 928; Fed Cts 612.1, 714; Labor & Emp 540; Stip 3.

Heck, Ex parte, TexCrimApp, 434 SW2d 855.—Hab Corp 526; Ind & Inf 87(3).

Heck v. Plumb, TexApp–Fort Worth, 665 SW2d 495.—App & E 66, 80(1), 80(6), 97.

Heck v. State, TexCrimApp, 507 SW2d 737.—Arrest 63.4(18), 64, 70(2), 71.1(1); Const Law 3809; Controlled Subs 80; Crim Law 1106(2).

Heckathorn v. Tate, TexCivApp–Amarillo, 355 SW2d 845.—App & E 1002; Damag 185(1); Trial 140(2).

Heckathorne v. State, TexApp–Houston (14 Dist), 697 SW2d 8, petition for discretionary review refused.—Assault 83, 92(5); Crim Law 366(3), 920, 938(1), 1063(1), 1088.1, 1153(2), 1169.2(6); Witn 40(1), 45(2).

Heck Co. of Texas, Inc. v. Temple Nat. Bank, CA5 (Tex), 748 F2d 982. See Starcraft Co., A Div. of Bangor Punta Operations, Inc. v. C.J. Heck Co. of Texas, Inc.

Hecker v. Wal-Mart Stores, Inc., CA5 (Tex), 33 F3d 531.—Records 7.

Heckerman; American Motors Acceptance Corp. v., TexCivApp–El Paso, 332 SW2d 345, writ dism.—Bills & N 220, 342, 370, 451(1); Judgm 185.2(9), 185.3(16).

Heckert v. American Cas. Co., TexCivApp–Dallas, 129 SW2d 424.—App & E 770(1); Evid 265(2); Insurance 2608; Trial 140(1).

Heckert v. State, TexCrimApp, 612 SW2d 549.—Crim Law 347, 369.2(3.1), 404.70, 438(4), 438(5.1); Homic 504, 1141, 1558.

Heckle; Burns v., TexCivApp–Austin, 193 SW2d 983.—Fed Cts 1140; War 205.

Heckler; Austin, City of, Texas/Brackenridge Hosp. v., WDTex, 574 FSupp 582. See City of Austin, Texas/Brackenridge Hosp. v. Heckler.

Heckler; Austin, Tex., City of, Brackenridge Hosp. v., CA5 (Tex), 753 F2d 1307. See City of Austin, Tex., Brackenridge Hosp. v. Heckler.

Heckler; Bain v., NDTex, 596 FSupp 253.—Social S 140.30, 142.20, 143.55, 143.65, 149.

Heckler; Banegas v., WDTex, 587 FSupp 549.—Admin Law 479; Social S 140.30, 142.5, 149.

Heckler; Barajas v., CA5 (Tex), 738 F2d 641.—Admin Law 786, 791; Social S 140.21, 140.30, 143.65, 143.75, 148.15, 175.15.

Heckler; Baylor University Medical Center v., CA5 (Tex), 758 F2d 1052.—Admin Law 390.1, 391, 392.1, 402; Equity 72(1), 84; Fed Civ Proc 751; Fed Cts 616; Health 535(1), 547, 548, 556(1); Statut 219(1), 219(4).

Heckler; Baylor University Medical Center v., CA5 (Tex), 730 F2d 391.—Health 535(4).

Heckler; Burris v., NDTex, 598 FSupp 573.—Social S 142.30; U S 147(10), 147(18).

Heckler; Byerly v., CA5 (Tex), 744 F2d 1143.—Social S 140.80, 143.45, 143.55, 143.75, 143.85.

Heckler; Carry v., CA5 (Tex), 750 F2d 479.—Social S 140.30, 143.65, 143.85, 148.1, 149.

Heckler; City of Austin, Tex., Brackenridge Hosp. v., CA5 (Tex), 753 F2d 1307.—Health 535(4), 549.

Heckler; City of Austin, Texas/Brackenridge Hosp. v., WDTex, 574 FSupp 582, aff 753 F2d 1307.—Health 535(2), 535(4).

Heckler; Conlon by Conlon v., CA5 (Tex), 719 F2d 788. —Child S 225; Child 21(2), 36; Courts 12(2.1); Divorce 62(5), 65, 169, 201, 354, 362; Fed Civ Proc 462, 470.1, 2393; Fed Cts 76, 76.35; Judgm 815; Marriage 13; Social S 137, 143.2.

Heckler; Curtis v., EDTex, 579 FSupp 1026.—Social S 140.21, 149.

Heckler; Davis v., CA5 (Tex), 759 F2d 432.—Social S 140.10, 140.30, 149.5.

Heckler; Davis v., CA5 (Tex), 748 F2d 293.—Social S 140.21, 142, 149.5.

Heckler; Dellolio v., CA5 (Tex), 705 F2d 123.—Admin Law 791; Social S 140.21, 140.30, 140.45, 140.50, 143.31, 143.45, 143.80, 143.85, 148.1, 148.5, 148.15, 149.5.

Heckler; Edwards v., NDTex, 573 FSupp 66.—Social S 142.20, 143.40, 143.65, 148.5, 148.20.

Heckler; Estran v., CA5 (Tex), 745 F2d 340.—Social S 140.21.

Heckler; Fleshman on Behalf of Fleshman v., CA5 (Tex), 709 F2d 999, cert den 104 SCt 727, 464 US 1049, 79 LEd2d 188.—Social S 8.20, 175.20, 175.30.

Heckler; Flores v., CA5 (Tex), 755 F2d 401.—Fed Civ Proc 2464; Social S 143.60, 145, 149.5.

Heckler; Garza v., CA5 (Tex), 771 F2d 871.—Social S 149.5.

Heckler; Green v., CA5 (Tex), 742 F2d 237.—Mand 1, 4(1), 72; Social S 145, 175.30.

Heckler; Hames v., CA5 (Tex), 707 F2d 162.—Admin Law 791; Social S 140.30, 143.45, 143.75, 148.5.

Heckler; Harris Hospital–Methodist v., CA5 (Tex), 730 F2d 391. See Baylor University Medical Center v. Heckler.

Heckler; Hernandez v., CA5 (Tex), 704 F2d 857.—Social S 140.21, 143.35, 143.65, 143.85.

Heckler; Johnson v., CA5 (Tex), 767 F2d 180.—Social S 140.30, 142.10, 143.85, 147.5, 149, 149.5.

Heckler; Lawler v., CA5 (Tex), 761 F2d 195.—Social S 149.5.

Heckler; Loya v., CA5 (Tex), 707 F2d 211.—Social S 140.30, 143.45, 143.65, 143.85, 148.10.

Heckler; Martin v., SDTex, 617 FSupp 1078.—Admin Law 412.1; Social S 137, 140.

Heckler; Martinez v., CA5 (Tex), 735 F2d 795.—Social S 143.85, 148.5.

Heckler; Memorial Hosp. System v., CA5 (Tex), 769 F2d 1043.—Health 556(2).

Heckler; Mercy Hosp. of Laredo v., CA5 (Tex), 777 F2d 1028.—Admin Law 390.1, 391, 413, 797; Health 529, 535(4), 556(3).

Heckler; Miller v., EDTex, 601 FSupp 1471.—Decl Judgm 272; Fed Cts 178; Health 556(1); Mand 1, 7, 105; Statut 219(1).

Heckler; Pena on Behalf of Zamora v., WDTex, 606 FSupp 958.—Social S 124.5, 143.1, 143.2, 143.4, 147, 148.10.

Heckler; Perez v., CA5 (Tex), 777 F2d 298.—Social S 143.85.

Heckler; Plowman for Children of Welch v., EDTex, 625 FSupp 1577.—Social S 142.5, 143.2, 149.

Heckler; Ransom v., CA5 (Tex), 715 F2d 989.—Social S 140.21, 143.45, 143.65, 143.70, 148.1.

Heckler; Segovia v., CA5 (Tex), 768 F2d 596.—Social S 143.4, 148.5.

Heckler; Sewell v., CA5 (Tex), 764 F2d 291.—Social S 140.55.

Heckler; Stone v., CA5 (Tex), 752 F2d 1099.—Social S 140.21, 142.5, 143.65, 149.5.

Heckler; Stone v., CA5 (Tex), 715 F2d 179, 70 ALR Fed 771.—Insurance 2595(1); Social S 135.1, 148.1.

Heckler; Sun Towers, Inc. v., CA5 (Tex), 725 F2d 315, cert den 105 SCt 100, 469 US 823, 83 LEd2d 45.—Corp 1.3, 182.1(1); Health 535(4), 547, 556(2), 557(2), 557(5); Judgm 702, 715(1); Statut 219(1), 219(6.1).

Heckler; Taylor v., CA5 (Tex), 742 F2d 253.—Social S 143.75.

Heckler; Totten v., CA5 (Tex), 742 F2d 237. See Green v. Heckler.

Heckler; U.S. v., CA5 (Tex), 165 FedAppx 360.—Crim Law 1655(6).

Heckler; Vasquez v., CA5 (Tex), 736 F2d 1053.—Social S 149.5.

Heckler; White v., CA5 (Tex), 740 F2d 390.—Social S 140.21, 140.70, 143.70, 143.85.

Heckler; Wilkerson v., EDTex, 623 FSupp 191.—Social S 143.85.

Heckman; Coca Cola Bottling Co. v., TexCivApp–Dallas, 113 SW2d 201.—App & E 930(2), 1140(1), 1177(5); Damag 32, 158(1), 216(10), 221(2.1); Food 25; Trial 350.5(2), 350.6(2), 352.15.

Heckman; Crittenden v., TexCivApp–San Antonio, 185 SW2d 495.—App & E 768; Hus & W 272(4).

Heckmann; Vinson v., CA5 (Tex), 940 F2d 114.—Civil R 1445; Fed Civ Proc 2820; Judges 51(4); Pardon 56.

Hector v. Barnhart, SDTex, 337 FSupp2d 905.—Social S 140.30, 142.5, 142.10, 143.60, 143.65, 143.85, 147, 147.5, 148.15.

Hector v. Christus Health Gulf Coast, TexApp–Houston (14 Dist), 175 SW3d 832, review den.—App & E 893(1); Health 800, 804, 805, 818; Neglig 1610, 1613, 1614, 1620.

Hector v. State, TexCrimApp, 246 SW2d 212, 157 TexCrim 11.—Crim Law 706(5).

Hector v. Thaler, TexApp–Houston (1 Dist), 927 SW2d 95, reh overr, and writ den.—App & E 371, 1194(2); Judges 51(4); Prisons 17(1).

Hector v. Thaler, TexApp–Houston (1 Dist), 862 SW2d 176, appeal after remand 927 SW2d 95, reh overr, and writ den.—Pretrial Proc 622, 652, 673, 678; Prisons 10.

Hector Martinez and Co. v. Southern Pac. Transp. Co., CA5 (Tex), 606 F2d 106, reh den 609 F2d 1008, cert den 100 SCt 2962, 446 US 982, 64 LEd2d 838.—Carr 103, 105(1), 106, 124; Compromise 12; Damag 62(1).

Hedberg; Holt v., TexCivApp–Fort Worth, 316 SW2d 955. —Lim of Act 39(7), 74(2); Mental H 15, 16.

Heddin v. Delhi Gas Pipeline Co., Tex, 522 SW2d 886.— Em Dom 124, 131, 200, 202(1), 219, 262(5); Evid 359(1).

Heddin; Delhi Gas Pipeline Co. v., TexCivApp–Tyler, 509 SW2d 954, writ gr, aff 522 SW2d 886.—App & E 1170.7; Em Dom 124, 202(1).

Heddin; Delhi Gas Pipeline Co. v., TexCivApp–Tyler, 508 SW2d 417.—App & E 1170.1, 1170.7; Em Dom 262(5); Evid 131, 161.1, 174.1, 318(1), 318(4), 318(6); Trial 105(2), 105(5).

Heddington Ins. Ltd.; Westchester Fire Ins. v., SDTex, 883 FSupp 158, aff 84 F3d 432.—Contracts 143(1), 143(2); Insurance 1191, 1808, 1810, 1845(2), 2101, 2110, 2111(3), 2112, 2285(1), 2396, 2725, 3517, 3523(1), 3523(4).

Heden v. Hill, SDTex, 937 FSupp 1230.—Consp 1.1; Fed Civ Proc 2481, 2508, 2515; Fraud 6, 7, 64(1); Libel 6(1); Pat 90(7), 92; Postal 35(2), 35(3); RICO 5, 10, 29, 73; Tel 1014(11).

Heden v. Hill, SDTex, 937 FSupp 1222.—Pat 92.

Heder; Central Power & Light Co. v., TexCivApp–San Antonio, 133 SW2d 795.—App & E 758.1, 758.3(2), 763, 766.

Hedge v. Bryan, TexCivApp–Tyler, 425 SW2d 866, ref nre.—App & E 989, 1003(6), 1003(11), 1177(7); Evid 207(1), 207(2); New Tr 44(1), 44(2), 140(3); Trial 306.

Hedgecoke Ins. Agency; Horn v., TexApp–Amarillo, 836 SW2d 296, reh den, and writ den.—Insurance 1669, 3451.

Hedgecroft v. City of Houston, Tex, 244 SW2d 632, 150 Tex 654.—Mun Corp 967(1); Tax 2300, 2341.

Hedgecroft v. City of Houston, TexCivApp–Galveston, 239 SW2d 828, rev 244 SW2d 632, 150 Tex 654.—Mun Corp 957(1), 958, 967(1); Tax 2187, 2300.

Hedgeman v. Berwind Ry. Service Co., TexCivApp–Hous (14 Dist), 512 SW2d 827, ref nre.—Elect of Rem 9; Work Comp 1061, 2084, 2107.

Hedges; Cox v., TexCivApp–Eastland, 344 SW2d 919, ref nre.—Autos 244(28); Trial 404(1).

Hedges v. Rudeloff, SDTex, 196 FSupp 475.—Fed Civ Proc 8.1; Rem of C 30, 37, 107(4).

Hedges v. State, TexCrimApp, 136 SW2d 607, 138 TexCrim 456.—Plead 237(8).

Hedges v. State, TexCrimApp, 136 SW2d 606, 138 TexCrim 453.—Plead 248(3).

Hedgpeth v. Gartman, Tex, 135 SW2d 86, 134 Tex 260.—Courts 247(5).

Hedgpeth; Gartman v., TexComApp, 157 SW2d 139, 138 Tex 73, 138 ALR 666.—Libel 15, 19, 41, 86(1), 86(4), 97; Plead 214(1).

Hedgpeth v. Gartman, TexCivApp–Waco, 136 SW2d 641, certificate dism 135 SW2d 86, 134 Tex 260, rev 157 SW2d 139, 138 Tex 73, 138 ALR 666.—Libel 19, 80, 81, 86(1); Plead 214(1).

Hedick v. Lone Star Steel Co., TexCivApp–Texarkana, 277 SW2d 925, ref nre.—Contracts 163; Deeds 90, 93, 108, 120, 145, 153, 155, 166; Mines 55(1), 55(4).

Hedicke v. State, TexCrimApp, 779 SW2d 837, cert den 110 SCt 840, 493 US 1044, 107 LEd2d 836.—Crim Law 338(6), 466, 1042, 1177, 1178; Sent & Pun 308, 319; Witn 274(2).

Hedley; duPont v., Tex, 570 SW2d 384, on remand 580 SW2d 662, ref nre.—Brok 42.

Hedley v. duPont, TexCivApp–Hous (14 Dist), 580 SW2d 662, ref nre.—Acct 1; Mines 55(8); Trusts 347, 371(2).

Hedley v. duPont, TexCivApp–Hous (14 Dist), 558 SW2d 72, writ gr, rev 570 SW2d 384, on remand 580 SW2d 662, ref nre.—Brok 3; Courts 29; Sec Reg 253; Spec Perf 114(1); Statut 230; Tresp to T T 12.

Hedley Feedlot, Inc. v. Weatherly Trust, TexApp–Amarillo, 855 SW2d 826, reh gr, and reh overr, and writ den.—Antitrust 141, 142, 147, 161, 205, 282, 294, 355, 363, 367, 369, 389(2), 390, 397; App & E 758.3(1), 930(3), 989, 1001(1), 1003(7), 1026, 1062.1; Damag 142, 153, 189, 208(1), 210(1), 218, 221(5.1); Fraud 59(2), 59(3); Parties 18, 29, 50; Plead 374; Princ & A 99, 101(1), 119(1), 131, 158, 159(1); Trial 230, 352.1(1), 352.1(3); Trusts 217.3(7), 246, 250, 257, 366(1).

Hedley Independent School Dist v. Doneghy, TexCivApp–Amarillo, 358 SW2d 724.—App & E 347(1), 627.2.

Hedrick; Carrick v., TexCivApp–Amarillo, 351 SW2d 659.—App & E 758.3(10), 761, 766, 1051(1); Evid 123(10), 207(4), 317(9), 340(1); Witn 388(2.1), 388(8).

Hedrick; Coffman v., TexCivApp–Hous (1 Dist), 437 SW2d 60, ref nre.—Lim of Act 55(3).

Hedrick; Demary v., TexCivApp–Beaumont, 153 SW2d 496.—App & E 14(2).

Hedrick; Galley v., TexCivApp–Amarillo, 127 SW2d 978.—App & E 846(5), 907(3); Courts 39, 163; Inj 118(2); Judgm 16; Land & Ten 127.

Hedrick; Hidalgo County Water Control and Imp. Dist. No. 7 v., CA5 (Tex), 226 F2d 1, cert den Hidalgo County Water Control and Improvement District No 7 v. Hedrick, 76 SCt 469, 350 US 983, 100 LEd 851.—Em Dom 84; Fed Cts 161, 162, 191; Treaties 7, 8; Waters 142.

Hedrick; Ochiltree County v., TexCivApp–Amarillo, 366 SW2d 866, ref nre.—Counties 125, 152; Impl & C C 30.

Hedrick v. State, TexApp–Corpus Christi, 759 SW2d 8.—Infants 20.

Hedrick; Villarreal v., TexCivApp–Corpus Christi, 579 SW2d 41, dism.—Elections 289, 298(1), 299(1), 305(6).

Hedrick; Williams v., TexCivApp–Beaumont, 131 SW2d 187, writ dism, correct.—Judgm 878(1), 880; Mtg 151(5), 535(2); Ten in C 47.

Hedrick Sav. Bank of Hedrick, Iowa; Andrews v., TexCivApp–Galveston, 103 SW2d 838.—Appear 19(4); Evid 43(2), 80(1), 348(2); Plead 35, 291(1).

H. E. D. Sales, Inc. v. Szelc, TexCivApp–Hous (14 Dist), 596 SW2d 299, aff in part, rev in part Torregrossa v. Szelc, 603 SW2d 803.—Corp 1.4(2), 1.7(2); Plead 237(6); Sales 283.

Hedspeth v. State, TexCrimApp, 160 SW2d 928, 143 TexCrim 627.—Ind & Inf 162.

Hedtke v. Transport Ins. Co., TexCivApp–San Antonio, 383 SW2d 474, ref nre.—Evid 334(4); Stip 14(7); Work Comp 1424.

Hedwig Village Planning and Zoning Com'n, City of; Howeth Investments, Inc. v., CA5 (Tex), 113 FedAppx 11.—Rem of C 107(11).

Hedwig Village, Tex., City of; Ramie v., CA5 (Tex), 765 F2d 490, reh den 770 F2d 1081, cert den 106 SCt 809, 474 US 1062, 88 LEd2d 784.—Civil R 1351(1), 1417; Const Law 1210, 1212, 1225.

Heelco Corp., In re, BkrtcyWDTex, 167 BR 445.—Bankr 2048.2, 2103, 2130; Jury 19(9).

Heep Petroleum, Inc.; Navasota Resources, Ltd. v., TexApp–Austin, 212 SW3d 463.—App & E 893(1), 931(3), 1010.1(1), 1010.2; Const Law 3964, 3965(5); Corp 432(12), 665(1); Courts 12(2.1), 12(2.5), 12(2.10), 15, 35.

Heerema v. State, TexApp–Dallas, 786 SW2d 532.—Weap 4.

Heeremac; Shell Offshore, Inc. v., SDTex, 33 FSupp2d 1111.—Action 2; Decl Judgm 322; Fed Cts 95.

HeereMac Vof; Den Norske Stats Oljeselskap As v., CA5 (Tex), 241 F3d 420, cert den Statoil ASA v. HeereMac vof, 122 SCt 1059, 534 US 1127, 151 LEd2d 967, reh den 122 SCt 1597, 535 US 1012, 152 LEd2d 512.—Antitrust 945; Fed Civ Proc 1831, 1832, 1835; Fed Cts 776.

Heeth; Rudi's Automotive Corp. v., TexCivApp–Hous (1 Dist), 509 SW2d 428.—Acct Action on 3, 10, 14; Costs 194.38; Evid 354(5); Insurance 1669.

Heffelman; Kemp v., TexApp–Houston (1 Dist), 713 SW2d 751.—Health 823(1); Judgm 185.3(21).

Heffernan; City of Galveston v., Tex, 155 SW2d 912, 138 Tex 16.—Courts 247(7).

Heffernan v. Ryan, TexCivApp–Galveston, 163 SW2d 911, writ refused wom.—App & E 231(2), 846(2), 846(5), 880(2); Contracts 346(10); Partners 219(1); Plead 388.

Heffernon; U.S. v., CA5 (Tex), 314 F3d 211, 188 ALR Fed 769.—Const Law 4657, 4658(1), 4658(3); Crim Law 339.8(6), 366(6), 633(1), 655(1), 656(1), 656(2), 735, 1139, 1147, 1153(1), 1158(1), 1158(4), 1166.22(2), 1169.1(1), 1169.2(6); Rape 51(7); Sent & Pun 756, 833, 841, 844.

Heffington; Cities Service Oil Co. v., TexCivApp–Austin, 108 SW2d 334.—Bailm 31(3); Sales 199, 201(1), 218.

Heffington v. Gillespie, TexCivApp–Fort Worth, 176 SW2d 205.—Ex & Ad 124, 142, 438(8), 451(2).

Heffington v. Hellums, TexCivApp–Austin, 212 SW2d 245, ref nre.—App & E 832(1); Assign 10, 18; Contracts 261(1), 270(1); Evid 318(1); Mines 52, 109; Trial 105(2).

Heffington; U.S. v., CA5 (Tex), 682 F2d 1075, cert den Giella v. US, 103 SCt 734, 459 US 1108, 74 LEd2d 957.—Consp 47(4), 48.2(1); Const Law 4692; Crim Law 42, 406(1), 427(4), 662.10, 769, 792(1), 1118; Double J 139.1; Gr Jury 34; Ind & Inf 144.1(2); Tel 1018(4); Witn 2(1).

Heffron; Focke, Wilkens & Lange v., TexCivApp–Galveston, 197 SW 1027, writ refused.—Mun Corp 621.

Heflebower; Mayborn v., CCA5 (Tex), 145 F2d 864, cert den 65 SCt 1087, 325 US 854, 89 LEd 1975.—Armed S 20.11.

Hefley v. Hefley, TexApp–Tyler, 859 SW2d 120, reh den. —Child C 512; Infants 82; New Tr 99.

Hefley; Hefley v., TexApp–Tyler, 859 SW2d 120, reh den. —Child C 512; Infants 82; New Tr 99.

Hefley v. Sentry Ins. Co., TexApp–San Antonio, 131 SW3d 63, reh overr, and review den, and reh of petition for review den.—App & E 946, 960(1); Plead 38.5, 228.14, 228.23; Work Comp 1847.

Hefley v. State, TexCrimApp, 489 SW2d 115.—Crim Law 419(1.10), 726, 1036.5, 1130(2); Rob 24.20.

Hefley v. State, TexCivApp–Fort Worth, 480 SW2d 810. —App & E 671(4), 1047(1); Evid 474(4), 558(9); Mental H 13, 18, 438; Witn 266.5.

Hefley-Stedman Motor Co.; Humbles v., TexCivApp–Austin, 127 SW2d 515.—Hus & W 268(4).

Heflin, Ex parte, TexCrimApp, 267 SW2d 556, 160 Tex-Crim 92.—Hab Corp 717(1).

Heflin v. Big Spring Independent School Dist., TexCiv-App–Eastland, 453 SW2d 211.—Courts 472.3.

Heflin; E. R. Squibb & Sons, Inc. v., TexCivApp–Beaumont, 579 SW2d 19, ref nre.—App & E 930(3), 989; Death 99(2); Evid 213(1); Prod Liab 83.

Heflin v. Fort Worth & D. C. Ry. Co., TexCivApp–Fort Worth, 207 SW2d 114, ref nre.—New Tr 143(5), 144.

Heflin v. State, TexCrimApp, 574 SW2d 554.—Crim Law 363, 369.8.

Heflin v. State, TexCrimApp, 274 SW2d 681, 161 Tex-Crim 41.—Crim Law 350, 363, 366(3), 516; Infants 20; Searches 181; Witn 266.

Heflin v. State, TexApp–Austin, 640 SW2d 58, petition for discretionary review refused.—Crim Law 393(1), 414, 474, 486(6), 641.3(11), 790, 1166(12), 1169.3; Jury 106, 110(14); Mental H 434; Witn 268(1).

Heflin v. Stiles, TexApp–Fort Worth, 663 SW2d 131.—Action 70; Judgm 181(24); Land & Ten 75(3), 76(3).

Heflin v. Wilson, TexCivApp–Beaumont, 297 SW2d 864, writ refused.—App & E 1045(1); Jury 110(10); Statut 85(3).

Hefner, Ex parte, EDTex, 599 FSupp 95.—Const Law 885, 1106; Contempt 61(1), 63(1), 63(3); Fed Civ Proc 103.4; Hab Corp 528.1.

Hefner v. Alexander, CA5 (Tex), 779 F2d 277.—Antitrust 902; Const Law 715; Courts 489(1); Fed Cts 14.1, 18, 55.

Hefner; Employers Mut. Cas. Co. v., TexCivApp–Dallas, 254 SW2d 565.—Insurance 2295, 2362.

Hefner v. Grievance Committee for Dist. 1-A, State Bar of Texas, TexApp–Dallas, 708 SW2d 43.—Atty & C 36(1).

Hefner; Horn v., TexApp–Texarkana, 115 SW3d 255.—App & E 989, 1001(1), 1001(2), 1003(7); Autos 167(1), 167(2), 171(13), 206, 244(2.1); Evid 150, 359(6), 574.

Hefner v. Metropolitan Life Ins. Co., EDTex, 329 FSupp 356.—Const Law 2414(3); Insurance 2583.

Hefner v. Republic Indem. Co. of America, SDTex, 773 FSupp 11.—Fed Cts 412.1, 419; Insurance 2278(3), 3167, 3168, 3549(3).

Hefner v. State, TexApp–Houston (1 Dist), 934 SW2d 855, reh overr, and petition for discretionary review refused. —Obscen 3, 17.

Hefner v. State, TexApp–Dallas, 735 SW2d 608, petition for discretionary review refused.—Crim Law 673(2), 695(2), 814(1), 1038.2, 1043(1), 1119(1), 1178; Ind & Inf 132(1), 179; Larc 63, 76, 78; Sent & Pun 1973(2).

Hefner; Tashnek v., TexCivApp–Galveston, 282 SW2d 298, ref nre.—App & E 1050.1(5); Can of Inst 58; Contracts 94(1); Evid 155(7); Records 2; Ven & Pur 1, 39, 54, 108, 123, 127.

Heft; Goolsbee v., TexCivApp–Tyler, 549 SW2d 34.—Child C 283, 285, 923(5).

Hegar; Carter v., TexCivApp–Austin, 595 SW2d 612.—Acct Action on 12; App & E 219(2); Costs 194.32, 194.38.

Hegar v. State, TexApp–Houston (1 Dist), 11 SW3d 290. —Crim Law 369.1, 371(3), 627.6(6), 1036.1(8), 1040, 1043(3), 1134(8), 1159.5, 1163(1), 1166.16; False Pret 49(1); Jury 32(3), 33(4), 149.

Hegar v. Tucker, TexCivApp–Galveston, 274 SW2d 752, ref nre.—Contracts 26, 29, 32, 155, 156; Evid 318(2), 423(3); Land & Ten 22(1), 37, 136.

Hegdal v. State, TexCrimApp, 488 SW2d 782.—Controlled Subs 148(4); Searches 108, 116, 118.

Heger; Hasslocher v., TexApp–San Antonio, 670 SW2d 689, ref nre.—App & E 1064.1(6); Joint Adv 1.2(4), 1.15; Trial 352.1(3).

Heggen v. Pemelton, Tex, 836 SW2d 145, mod on reh.—Divorce 252.3(1), 256; Home 1, 90; Hus & W 258.

Heggins v. City of Dallas, Tex., NDTex, 469 FSupp 739. —Inj 80, 138.51; Mun Corp 80.

Heggins v. State, TexCrimApp, 620 SW2d 603.—Int Liq 236(1).

Heggy v. American Trading Employee Retirement Account Plan, TexApp–Houston (14 Dist), 123 SW3d 770, reh overr, and review den.—App & E 1096(3), 1097(1), 1175(1), 1195(1); Courts 99(1); Interest 39(2.40); Interpl 1, 6, 13, 18, 21, 23, 35; Labor & Emp 407, 712, 717; Plead 76; States 18.15.

Heggy v. American Trading Employee Retirement Account Plan, TexApp–Houston (14 Dist), 56 SW3d 280, appeal after remand 123 SW3d 770, reh overr, and review den.—App & E 856(1), 893(1), 934(1); Courts 91(1), 97(1); Divorce 252.3(2); Judgm 185(2); Labor & Emp 407, 583, 687; States 18.29, 18.51.

Hegi; English v., TexCivApp–Amarillo, 337 SW2d 860.—Autos 244(47); Damag 100, 130.3, 163(1), 208(4), 221(5.1); Trial 139.1(3), 141, 350.2, 350.7(3.1).

Hegna v. Islamic Republic of Iran, CA5 (Tex), 376 F3d 485, reh and reh den 121 FedAppx 59.—Amb & C 3; Intern Law 10.33, 10.35; Treaties 8.

Hegwood v. Kindrick, SDTex, 264 FSupp 720.—Const Law 3849, 3867, 3875, 3879, 4464, 4465; Hab Corp 331; Infants 205.

Heibel v. Bermann, TexCivApp–Houston, 407 SW2d 945. —App & E 1152; Judgm 187; Work Comp 2178.

Heid; Bolash v., TexApp–San Antonio, 733 SW2d 698.—Marriage 13, 40(6), 50(2), 50(4), 50(5).

Heid Bros. v. Bray, TexCivApp–El Paso, 7 SW2d 165, writ dism woj.—App & E 230, 742(1), 978(3); Damag 139; Negl 121(5); New Tr 44(3), 143(2); Prod Liab 77, 88; Trial 352(1).

Heid Bros. v. Dawson, TexCivApp–El Paso, 117 SW2d 481.—Execution 275(3), 344.

Heid Bros.; Dawson v., TexCivApp–El Paso, 94 SW2d 201.—App & E 71(4).

Heid Bros. v. Mueller-Huber Grain Co., TexCivApp–El Paso, 185 SW2d 470.—App & E 912; Assoc 20(1); Corp 503(2); Partners 195; Plead 111.3, 409(1); Statut 223.5(4).

Heid Bros. v. Smiley, TexCivApp–Texarkana, 166 SW2d 181, writ refused wom.—App & E 500(1); Courts 85(2), 97(1); Evid 400(3); Sales 353(5), 353(8); Trial 355(1).

Heid Bros. v. Smiley, TexCivApp–Texarkana, 144 SW2d 952.—Evid 10(2); Venue 7.5(7).

Heid by Heid; Bayne v., TexApp–Houston (1 Dist), 638 SW2d 40.—Judgm 185.3(2), 942.

Heidelberg v. Harvey, Tex, 368 SW2d 947.—App & E 100(1).

Heidelberg v. Harvey, TexCivApp–El Paso, 391 SW2d 828, ref nre.—Judgm 185(2); Ven & Pur 231(1), 239(6), 242.

Heidelberg v. Harvey, TexCivApp–El Paso, 366 SW2d 121, rev 368 SW2d 947.—Waters 127, 156(8).

Heidelberg v. State, TexCrimApp, 144 SW3d 535, application for writ of habeas corpus held in abeyance Ex parte

Heidelberg, 2006 WL 1751186, opinion after remand 2006 WL 3306880, reh den.—Crim Law 407(1), 1043(3).

Heidelberg v. State, TexApp–Houston (1 Dist), 112 SW3d 658, reh overr, and petition for discretionary review gr, aff 144 SW3d 535, application for writ of habeas corpus held in abeyance Ex parte Heidelberg, 2006 WL 1751186, opinion after remand 2006 WL 3306880, reh den.—Crim Law 407(1), 726, 1036.1(1), 1036.1(5), 1043(3), 1045, 1169.2(2).

Heidelberg v. State, TexApp–Houston (14 Dist), 36 SW3d 668.—Crim Law 396(1), 474.3(1), 632(4), 660, 672, 691, 693, 696(2), 696(7), 1036.1(1), 1044.1(5.1), 1130(5), 1137(2), 1137(5), 1153(1).

Heidenreich v. State, TexCrimApp, 168 SW2d 254, 145 TexCrim 468.—Crim Law 351(3), 814(8); Larc 1, 18, 55, 76.

Heidingsfelder v. Rodgers, TexCivApp–Galveston, 96 SW2d 147.—Evid 80(1), 84; Judgm 913, 915; Stip 18(1).

Heidingsfelder v. State, TexCrimApp, 81 SW2d 510, 128 TexCrim 351.—Crim Law 139, 361(1), 363, 364(5), 413(1), 413(2), 589(2), 687(1), 687(2), 730(4).

Heidle v. State, TexCrimApp, 86 SW2d 641, 129 TexCrim 201.—Bail 64; Crim Law 475, 476.6, 720(9), 1044.1(4), 1092.11(3), 1120(4), 1169.1(3), 1169.2(2), 1171.1(2.1).

Heidmar, Inc. v. Anomina Ravennate Di Armamento Sp.A. of Ravenna, SDTex, 993 FSupp 990, vac 132 F3d 264.—Adm 28, 47, 48; Contracts 141(1), 206; Mar Liens 1; Ship 51(8).

Heidmar, Inc. v Anomina Ravennate Di Armanento Sp.A. of Ravenna, CA5 (Tex), 132 F3d 264.—Adm 47; Fed Cts 574.

Heidrick; Ellis v., TexCivApp–San Antonio, 154 SW2d 293, writ refused wom.—App & E 911.3; Chat Mtg 169, 176(4); Evid 10(2); Lim of Act 55(5); Time 9(2), 11.

Heidtman v. County of El Paso, CA5 (Tex), 171 F3d 1038.—Fed Civ Proc 1278, 2737.4, 2737.11; Labor & Emp 2255, 2385(7), 2387(10), 2390(4).

Heien v. Crabtree, Tex, 369 SW2d 28.—Adop 6, 20.

Heien v. Crabtree, TexCivApp–Amarillo, 364 SW2d 271, aff 369 SW2d 28.—Adop 6, 22; Evid 315.1; Judgm 185(1), 185.3(1).

Height; Brewer v., TexCivApp–Amarillo, 219 SW2d 516.—App & E 954(1), 954(2); Courts 122; Inj 132, 135, 138.24, 144, 147.

Heights Funeral Home v. McClain, TexCivApp–Beaumont, 288 SW2d 839, ref nre.—Judgm 91, 634, 651, 660, 720, 725(1); Parties 50; Plead 142.

Heights Funeral Home, Inc. v. N. L. R. B., CA5 (Tex), 385 F2d 879.—Labor & Emp 1680, 1734, 1735, 1741, 1754, 1755, 1759, 1820.

Heights Hospital v. Patterson, TexCivApp–Waco, 269 SW2d 810, writ refused.—Const Law 190; Health 961.

Heights Hosp.; Peralta v., USTex, 108 SCt 896, 485 U.S. 80, 99 LEd2d 75. See Peralta v. Heights Medical Center, Inc.

Heights Hosp.; Peralta v., TexApp–Houston (1 Dist), 715 SW2d 721. See Peralta v. Heights Medical Center, Inc.

Heights Medical Center, Inc.; Peralta v., USTex, 108 SCt 896, 485 US 80, 99 LEd2d 75, on remand 1988 WL 83861, writ den.—Judgm 17(9).

Heights Medical Center, Inc.; Peralta v., TexApp–Houston (1 Dist), 715 SW2d 721, ref nre, probable jur noted 107 SCt 2458, 481 US 1067, 95 LEd2d 868, rev 108 SCt 896, 485 US 80, 99 LEd2d 75, on remand 1988 WL 83861, writ den.—Judgm 335(3).

Heights Muffler Co.; Emsco Screen Pipe Co. of Tex. v., TexCivApp–Hous (14 Dist), 420 SW2d 179.—Contracts 170(1); Cust & U 12(2), 19(3); Sales 429.

Heights Sav. and Loan Ass'n; Munoz v., TexCivApp–Texarkana, 319 SW2d 945, dism.—Judgm 185.3(15).

Heights Sav. Ass'n v. Cordes, TexCivApp–Houston, 412 SW2d 372.—App & E 499(1), 554(1), 905, 907(3), 930(3), 931(3); Bills & N 63, 132, 318, 538(1), 539; Evid 420(3), 420(7); Trial 388(1), 392(1).

Heights Sav. Ass'n; Hennigan v., TexCivApp–Hous (1 Dist), 576 SW2d 126, ref nre.—Cons Cred 2, 50; Judgm 185(2); Lim of Act 40(1), 41; Mtg 201, 262.

Heights Sav. Ass'n; Morgan v., EDTex, 761 FSupp 35.—B & L Assoc 23(8).

Heights Sav. Ass'n; Morgan v., EDTex, 741 FSupp 620.—Banks 505; B & L Assoc 42(3), 42(17).

Heights State Bank of Houston; Anderson v., TexCivApp–Galveston, 244 SW2d 374, writ refused.—Judgm 181(15.1).

Heikkila; Fort Bend County v., TexApp–Houston (1 Dist), 921 SW2d 395, appeal after remand 1998 WL 418045.—App & E 70(8); Counties 146; Judgm 185.3(2); Offic 114; States 112.1(1).

Heikkila v. Harris County, TexApp–Tyler, 973 SW2d 333, review den.—Coroners 23; Counties 146; Mun Corp 742(4), 745; Offic 114, 116; States 78.

Heil, In re, BkrtcyNDTex, 141 BR 112.—Bankr 3131, 3137; Const Law 4478.

Heil v. Rudd, TexCivApp–Amarillo, 291 SW2d 351, ref nre.—Labor & Emp 2848, 2875, 2877, 2879, 2961, 3003.

Heil v. Washichek, TexCivApp–San Antonio, 369 SW2d 510.—Deeds 194(3), 211(1); Witn 159(5).

Heiland Research Corp.; Saldibar v., SDTex, 32 FSupp 248.—Rem of C 2, 79(2.1), 79(6), 103, 107(6).

Heilbron; Myricks v., TexCivApp–Texarkana, 170 SW2d 827.—Frds St of 63(4); Lim of Act 48(7), 166; Tresp to T T 47(3); Ven & Pur 105(1), 125, 257.

Heilbron v. Stubblefield, TexCivApp–El Paso, 203 SW2d 986, ref nre.—App & E 1010.1(1); Evid 594; Partners 83, 86; Trial 142.

Heil Co.; Daberko v., CA5 (Tex), 681 F2d 445, reh den 685 F2d 1385, rehden American International Adjustment Co, Inc v. Heil Co, 685 F2d 1385.—Prod Liab 8, 11, 27, 36, 40.

Heil Co. v. Grant, TexCivApp–Tyler, 534 SW2d 916, ref nre.—App & E 930(3), 1170.7; Contrib 5(1), 5(2), 5(6.1); Death 10, 31(6), 31(7), 31(8), 93; Indem 58, 59; Judgm 609; Neglig 551, 554(2); Prod Liab 15, 27, 49, 75.1, 85; Witn 128, 129, 158.

Heil Co. v. Polar Corp., TexApp–Fort Worth, 191 SW3d 805, review den, and reh of petition for review den.—Action 27(1); App & E 893(1); Contracts 143(2), 147(2), 152, 176(2); Corp 120; Fraud 32; Indem 33(2), 40; Judgm 181(11), 183, 185.3(5); Lim of Act 47(1); Torts 112, 118.

Heiliger v. State, TexCrimApp, 471 SW2d 411.—Crim Law 1109(3).

Heiligmann v. State, TexApp–San Antonio, 980 SW2d 713.—Crim Law 273.1(1), 273.1(2), 274(3.1), 275, 1026.10(4).

Heiling, Ex parte, TexCrimApp, 82 SW2d 644, 128 TexCrim 399.—Statut 68, 77(1), 103.

Heilner; Southwest Craft Center v., TexApp–San Antonio, 670 SW2d 651, ref nre.—App & E 931(1), 971(2), 1010.1(3); Bailm 31(1), 31(3); Estop 78(3), 83(1), 102; Evid 474(19); Fraud 58(4); Indem 105; Judgm 527.

Heil-Quaker Corp. v. Mischer Corp., TexApp–Houston (14 Dist), 863 SW2d 210, reh den, and writ gr, vac pursuant to settlement 877 SW2d 300.—App & E 930(3), 1001(1), 1003(7); Const Law 4427; Corp 522; Joint Adv 5(1), 5(3); Torts 211, 213, 214, 219, 242.

Heim; City of San Antonio v., TexApp–Austin, 932 SW2d 287, reh overr, and writ den.—App & E 171(1), 1004(11), 1140(1), 1182; Damag 130.1; Mun Corp 185(1), 185(15); Offic 65, 66.

Heim; Panhandle Const. Co. v., TexCivApp–Amarillo, 84 SW2d 869.—Mun Corp 519(5), 519(6).

Heim; Travelers Ins. Co. v., TexCivApp–Texarkana, 413 SW2d 796.—App & E 930(1); Trial 106; Work Comp 1532, 1671, 1968(5).

Heiman v. State, TexApp–Houston (1 Dist), 923 SW2d 622, petition for discretionary review refused.—Crim

Law 369.2(1), 369.2(2), 369.8, 386, 641.13(1), 641.13(6), 1030(1), 1036.1(8), 1036.8, 1043(2); Witn 414(1).

Heimann v. National Elevator Industry Pension Fund, CA5 (Tex), 187 F3d 493, appeal after remand 248 F3d 1142.—Const Law 2474; Damag 50.10; Decl Judgm 26, 61, 99, 272, 312.1, 314, 385, 386.1; Fed Civ Proc 1773, 1837.1; Fed Cts 241, 763.1, 776; Labor & Emp 402, 403, 407, 510, 534, 577, 634, 643, 649, 676, 794, 797, 857, 863(2); Rem of C 25(1); States 18.5, 18.15, 18.51; Statut 209.

Heimer; Kelly v., TexCivApp–San Antonio, 312 SW2d 430, ref nre.—Estop 54; Mech Liens 61; Partners 32, 35.

Heim-Hall; Erickson v., TexApp–San Antonio, 172 SW3d 664.—Const Law 2315; Lim of Act 4(2), 199(1).

Heimlich v. First Bank N.A., CA5 (Tex), 80 FedAppx 947.—Fed Cts 630.1; Mal Pros 72(2).

Heimlich v. State, TexApp–Houston (14 Dist), 988 SW2d 382, petition for discretionary review refused.—Larc 60.

Heimlich v. State ex rel. Abbott, TexApp–Austin, 107 SW3d 643, rule 537(f) motion gr, on remand 2003 WL 25537507.—States 111, 193.

Hein; Burrus Mills, Inc. v., TexCivApp–Dallas, 378 SW2d 85, writ dism.—Contracts 143(1), 147(3); Venue 2, 7.5(3), 21.

Hein; Burrus Mills, Inc. v., TexCivApp–Houston, 399 SW2d 950, ref nre.—Acct Action on 12, 14; App & E 1177(2); Evid 67(1); Paymt 63(2).

Hein v. Harris County, TexCivApp–Hous (1 Dist), 557 SW2d 366, ref nre.—Counties 146, 222; States 112.2(2).

Hein v. U.S. Immigration and Naturalization Service, CA5 (Tex), 456 F2d 1239.—Aliens 651, 696; Const Law 3072.

Heinatz v. Allen, Tex, 217 SW2d 994, 147 Tex 512.—Courts 107; Mines 48; Wills 441, 456, 560(1).

Heinatz; Allen v., TexCivApp–Austin, 212 SW2d 987, aff 217 SW2d 994, 147 Tex 512.—Wills 441, 560(1).

Heincelman v. State, TexApp–Eastland, 56 SW2d 799.—Autos 349(3), 349(17), 349(18); Crim Law 1134(3), 1134(6), 1139, 1144.12, 1158(4); Searches 172, 180, 181, 197.

Heine, Ex parte, TexCrimApp, 254 SW2d 790, 158 TexCrim 248.—Autos 133, 134.

Heine; Holt Atherton Industries, Inc. v., Tex, 835 SW2d 80.—App & E 931(1), 1010.1(2), 1178(6); Damag 103, 190, 194; Judgm 112, 143(3), 143(4), 145(2), 146, 151, 159, 163.

Heine; Holt Atherton Industries, Inc. v., TexApp–Corpus Christi, 797 SW2d 250, writ gr, aff in part, rev in part 835 SW2d 80.—App & E 865, 957(1), 1010.1(3); Damag 140, 190; Judgm 111, 112, 143(2), 143(4), 146, 162(2), 162(4), 220, 248.

Heine v. Schendel, TexApp–Corpus Christi, 797 SW2d 278, writ den.—Atty & C 77; Usury 20, 72.

Heine v. Texas Dept. of Public Safety, TexApp–Austin, 92 SW3d 642, review den.—App & E 969; Const Law 3953, 4008, 4531; Convicts 6; Crim Law 1226(3.1), 1226(4).

Heineken USA, Inc.; Glazer's Wholesale Distributors, Inc. v., TexApp–Dallas, 95 SW3d 286, review gr, judgment vac, and remanded by agreement.—Alt Disp Res 112, 114, 117, 132, 143, 191, 205, 213(3), 213(4), 357, 380; App & E 941, 945, 946; Const Law 990, 1030, 2311, 2312, 2314, 2352, 2450, 2570; Contracts 143(3), 147(2), 152, 176(2); Int Liq 124; Judgm 540, 584; Jury 25(2), 26, 31.2(1); Mand 1, 3(2.1), 4(1), 12, 26, 28; States 18.15.

Heinen; Donaubauer v., TexCivApp–Austin, 132 SW2d 166, aff Wright v. Donaubauer, 154 SW2d 637, 137 Tex 473.—Can of Inst 37(5); Frds St of 50(2); Plead 34(3); Ven & Pur 82.

Heiner v. Homeland Realty Co., TexCivApp–Waco, 100 SW2d 793.—Evid 383(7), 590; Mtg 341, 342, 350, 356, 362; Trial 140(2).

Heinrich; City of El Paso v., TexApp–El Paso, 198 SW3d 400, review gr.—App & E 863, 893(1); Courts 40; Decl Judgm 252.1; Mun Corp 187(10), 723, 724, 725; States 191.1, 191.4(1), 191.9(2).

Heinrich; J.C. Penney Life Ins. Co. v., TexApp–San Antonio, 32 SW3d 280, reh overr, and review den.—App & E 949, 984(1), 984(5), 1030; Costs 194.40, 252; Divorce 66.5; Estop 52.15, 95; Insurance 3360, 3406, 3479, 3585; Interest 39(2.55); Marriage 55; Notice 5; Statut 181(1), 188; Trial 386(1).

Heinrich v. Texas Bitulithic Co., TexCivApp–Texarkana, 324 SW2d 600.—Judgm 198.

Heinrich; Weeks v., TexCivApp–Corpus Christi, 447 SW2d 688, ref nre.—App & E 216(1), 757(1), 758.3(10), 760(2), 1078(1); Damag 221(1); Health 823(10), 827; New Tr 73, 143(2); Trial 41(5), 215, 260(8), 350.3(1), 365.1(6), 365.3; Witn 9.

Heinrich v. Wharton County Livestock, Inc., TexCivApp–Corpus Christi, 557 SW2d 830, ref nre.—Estop 52.10(2); Joint Adv 1.2(1), 1.15, 4(1); Sales 202(8), 218.5, 234(8), 324(3).

Heinrich v. Winkler, TexCivApp–Austin, 112 SW2d 751.—App & E 1177(6).

Heinrichs v. Evins Personnel Consultants, Inc., No. One, Tex, 486 SW2d 935.—Princ & A 146(1), 188; Sales 130(0.5).

Heinrichs; Evins-Personnel Consultants, Inc. No. One v., TexCivApp–Austin, 477 SW2d 413, writ gr, rev 486 SW2d 935.—Can of Inst 35(1); Contracts 176(8), 177; Corp 210; Princ & A 188; Sales 130(0.5), 130(3).

Heinrichs v. State, TexCrimApp, 263 SW2d 777, 159 TexCrim 293.—Game 9.

Heins v. Beaumont Independent School Dist., EDTex, 525 FSupp 367, aff 690 F2d 903.—Const Law 4202; Schools 147.12, 147.31, 147.36, 147.38, 147.40(1).

Heins; Sowell v., TexCivApp–Dallas, 466 SW2d 862, ref nre.—Wills 449, 687(1), 866.

Heins v. State, TexApp–Houston (14 Dist), 157 SW3d 457.—Crim Law 790, 822(1), 1038.1(2), 1134(2), 1134(3), 1172.1(1), 1173.2(2); Weap 9, 17(6).

Heinsohn v. Trans-Con Adjustment Bureau, TexApp–Fort Worth, 939 SW2d 793, reh overr, and writ den.—Damag 210(1); Labor & Emp 806, 808, 810, 861, 863(2), 873; Trial 139.1(5.1), 139.1(17), 140(1), 142, 178.

Heinz; Champlin Petroleum Co. v., TexApp–Corpus Christi, 665 SW2d 544, ref nre.—Corp 666; Plead 111.19, 111.42(1), 111.42(6); Venue 2.

Heinz; U.S. v., CA5 (Tex), 983 F2d 609, reh den 988 F2d 1215.—Atty & C 32(12); Crim Law 394.1(2), 641.3(3), 641.12(1).

Heinzelmann; Cullum v., TexCivApp–Eastland, 352 SW2d 516, ref nre.—App & E 930(1); Bound 37(1); Tresp to T T 52.

Heinzman v. Coon, Tex, 290 SW2d 219, 155 Tex 569.—Ex & Ad 55; Judgm 822(3); Life Est 21; Powers 4; Wills 616(5).

Heinzman; Coon v., TexCivApp–San Antonio, 281 SW2d 461, rev 290 SW2d 219, 155 Tex 569.—Ex & Ad 315.1, 315.6(1), 315.6(2), 508(1); Judgm 545; Wills 698, 705.

Heiringhoff v. State, TexApp–El Paso, 130 SW3d 117, reh overr, and petition for discretionary review refused.—Crim Law 795(1.5), 795(2.1), 795(2.20), 795(2.26), 1042, 1137(1); Environ Law 756; Ind & Inf 191(0.5); Sent & Pun 1963, 1983(3).

Heironimus v. Tate, TexCivApp–Austin, 355 SW2d 76, ref nre.—Trusts 21(2); Wills 184(1), 488, 684.10(1).

Heirs and Beneficiaries of Watkins; King v., TexApp–Tyler, 624 SW2d 252, ref nre.—Adop 6, 17; App & E 758.3(9), 930(3), 1170.7; Decl Judgm 364, 369; Evid 474.5; Trial 140(1), 182, 350.1.

Heirs and Unknown Heirs of Barrow v. Champion Paper & Fibre Co., TexCivApp–Beaumont, 327 SW2d 338, ref nre.—Bound 52; Deeds 38(1), 38(3), 90, 109, 121; Evid 318(1), 318(7), 358.

Heisdorf and Nelson Farms; Atwood Hatcheries v., CA5 (Tex), 357 F2d 847.—Const Law 3964, 3965(4); Corp 665(1); Fed Cts 76, 76.30.

Heise; Broders v., Tex, 924 SW2d 148.—App & E 946, 971(2); Evid 508, 536, 538, 544, 545, 546.

Heise v. Presbyterian Hosp. of Dallas, TexApp–Eastland, 888 SW2d 264, reh den, and writ gr, rev Broders v. Heise, 924 SW2d 148.—App & E 970(2), 1056.1(1), 1056.1(3); Evid 538, 544; Pretrial Proc 304.

Heiselbetz v. State, TexCrimApp, 906 SW2d 500, reh den. —Crim Law 412(1), 517(5), 530, 553, 586, 590(2), 741(1), 1130(5), 1134(5), 1144.13(3), 1151, 1152(2), 1159.2(3), 1159.2(7), 1159.3(2); Homic 1137, 1139, 1172; Jury 47, 85, 103(3), 105(4), 107, 108, 131(4), 131(10), 131(13), 133; Sent & Pun 1658, 1720, 1750, 1757.

Heiser v. Eckerd Corp., TexApp–Fort Worth, 983 SW2d 313.—App & E 733, 852, 854(1); Judgm 185(2), 185.3(13); Labor & Emp 3049(3); Libel 30, 100(1).

Heisey v. Booth, TexCivApp–Fort Worth, 476 SW2d 782, writ dism woj.—Judgm 674; Parties 56.

Heiskala v. Johnson Space Center Federal Credit Union, SDTex, 474 FSupp 448.—B & L Assoc 23(2); Consp 7.5(1), 7.5(2), 18; Const Law 1225, 1909, 1947, 3941, 3942; Searches 33.

Heiskell; Greenstreet v., TexApp–Amarillo, 960 SW2d 713.—Judges 51(2).

Heiskell; Greenstreet v., TexApp–Amarillo, 940 SW2d 831, reh overr, and rule 537(f) motion overr, reh den 960 SW2d 713.—App & E 5; Courts 37(3), 41.

Heiskell v. Heiskell, TexCivApp–Amarillo, 412 SW2d 774. —Child C 76, 531(1), 553, 554, 565, 567, 635, 637, 659.

Heiskell; Heiskell v., TexCivApp–Amarillo, 412 SW2d 774.—Child C 76, 531(1), 553, 554, 565, 567, 635, 637, 659.

Heiskell v. State, TexCrimApp, 522 SW2d 477.—Crim Law 1026.10(6), 1028; Sent & Pun 2009, 2021.

Heissner v. Koons, TexApp–Dallas, 679 SW2d 112.— Child S 508(3); Pretrial Proc 248.1.

Heissner; Putnam v., TexCivApp–Austin, 220 SW2d 701. —Can of Inst 35(1), 37(6); Fraud 12; Trusts 59(1).

Heissner; Sevine v., Tex, 224 SW2d 184, 148 Tex 345.— Partit 116(1); Ten in C 9; Trusts 7, 43(1), 109, 362.

Heissner; Sevine v., TexCivApp–Austin, 262 SW2d 218, ref nre.—Trial 351.2(1.1), 426; Trusts 37.5, 43(3), 373.

Heissner; Sevine v., TexCivApp–Austin, 220 SW2d 704, rev 224 SW2d 184, 148 Tex 345.—App & E 927(7); Trusts 92.5, 110, 347.

Heister v. Western Shamrock Corp., TexApp–Waco, 50 SW3d 643.—App & E 79(1); Judgm 216, 217.

Heisterberg v. Standridge, TexApp–Austin, 656 SW2d 138.—Divorce 252.3(4), 261, 322; Hus & W 249(3).

Heitchew; Franklin Life Ins. Co. v., CCA5 (Tex), 146 F2d 71, cert den 65 SCt 914, 324 US 865, 89 LEd 1421. —Evid 59, 89; Fed Cts 774; Insurance 2445, 2605, 2608; Trial 234(7), 237(4).

Heitkamp v. Dyke, CA5 (Tex), 943 F2d 1435. See Dyke, Matter of.

Heitkamp; Dyke v., SDTex, 119 BR 536. See Dyke, In re.

Heitkamp v. Dyke, BkrtcySDTex, 99 BR 343. See Dyke, In re.

Heitkamp v. Krueger, TexCivApp–Austin, 265 SW2d 655, ref nre.—App & E 1071.1(7); Autos 193(5), 193(6); Labor & Emp 3049(2).

Heitkamp; Salazar v., CA5 (Tex), 193 FedAppx 281.— Bankr 3781.

Heitman v. State, TexCrimApp, 815 SW2d 681, on remand 836 SW2d 840.—Const Law 18.

Heitman v. State, TexApp–Fort Worth, 836 SW2d 840.— Searches 58, 66.

Heitman v. State, TexApp–Fort Worth, 776 SW2d 324, petition for discretionary review gr, rev 815 SW2d 681, on remand 836 SW2d 840.—Searches 23, 58, 65, 66.

Heitman v. State, TexApp–Dallas, 789 SW2d 607, petition for discretionary review refused.—Crim Law 394.4(6); Searches 112, 113.1, 117, 118, 196, 200.

Heitmann v. Buenger, TexCivApp–Galveston, 207 SW2d 163, ref nre.—App & E 846(2), 846(5), 934(2); Decl Judgm 9; Hus & W 217; Judgm 456(2).

Heitmann Bering-Cortes Co.; Del Bosque v., Tex, 474 SW2d 450.—Carr 349; Neglig 294, 510(1).

Heitmann Bering-Cortes Co.; Del Bosque v., TexCivApp–Hous (1 Dist), 468 SW2d 522, writ gr, aff 474 SW2d 450.—App & E 1070(2); Carr 349.

Heitschmidt v. City of Houston, CA5 (Tex), 161 F3d 834. —Civil R 1088(2), 1376(6); Fed Civ Proc 2553; Offic 114; Searches 40.1.

Hejkal; Forbes v., TexCivApp–Dallas, 271 SW2d 435, dism.—App & E 216(1); Evid 318(1); Witn 380(6), 388(6), 388(7.1), 396(3).

Hejl, In re, BkrtcyWDTex, 85 BR 399.—Bankr 2131.

Hejl v. State of Tex., CA5 (Tex), 664 F2d 1273, cert den 102 SCt 1987, 456 US 933, 72 LEd2d 452, reh den 102 SCt 2286, 456 US 1001, 73 LEd2d 1296.—Fed Civ Proc 1758.1; Fed Cts 818.

Hejl; Texas Dept. of Health v., TexApp–Austin, 635 SW2d 656.—App & E 79(1).

Hejl; Texas Dept. of Health v., TexCivApp–Austin, 607 SW2d 34.—App & E 781(1), 781(4), 802.

Hejl v. U.S., CA5 (Tex), 449 F2d 124.—Fed Cts 743; U S 113, 127(2).

Hejl v. Wirth, Tex, 343 SW2d 226, 161 Tex 609.—Bound 14, 33; Tresp to T T 6.1, 47(3).

Hejl v. Wirth, TexCivApp–Austin, 334 SW2d 498, writ gr, rev 343 SW2d 226, 161 Tex 609.—Adv Poss 114(1); Bound 14, 40(2); Tresp to T T 27.

Hekimain; U.S. v., CA5 (Tex), 975 F2d 1098.—Crim Law 273.1(4), 1167(5).

Helber v. State, TexApp–Houston (1 Dist), 915 SW2d 955. —Autos 144.1(1), 144.1(1.11), 332; Double J 1, 21, 24, 25, 132.1, 135, 142; Statut 190.

Helbert; Service Mut. Ins. Co. v., TexCivApp–San Antonio, 157 SW2d 720, writ refused.—Work Comp 665.

Helbing v. Texas Dept. of Water Resources, TexApp–Austin, 713 SW2d 134.—Admin Law 749, 750; Environ Law 196, 230, 682.

Held v. List Laundry & Dry Cleaners, TexCivApp–El Paso, 109 SW2d 1029.—App & E 773(2).

Held v. Missouri Pac. R. Co., SDTex, 373 FSupp 996.— Civil R 1242, 1244, 1506, 1511, 1513, 1517, 1568; Const Law 2974; Fed Cts 21, 225; Inj 132, 138.18, 147, 151, 152; Labor & Emp 1597, 1599.

Held v. Missouri Pac. R. Co., SDTex, 64 FRD 346.— Compromise 55, 59, 67; Fed Civ Proc 164, 172, 174, 184.15.

Held v. State, TexApp–Houston (14 Dist), 948 SW2d 45, petition for discretionary review refused.—Arrest 63.5(4); Autos 349(6), 349(12), 421; Crim Law 478(1), 480, 485(1); Jury 33(5.15).

Heldenfels; Hernandez v., Tex, 374 SW2d 196.—App & E 1043(6), 1050.1(1); Autos 155, 201(10), 245(4), 245(70); Neglig 1040(3), 1125, 1205(9); Pretrial Proc 713, 726; Propty 7.

Heldenfels v. Hernandez, TexCivApp–Waco, 366 SW2d 641, writ gr, rev 374 SW2d 196.—Autos 155; Neglig 1040(3), 1205(9).

Heldenfels v. Montgomery, TexCivApp–San Antonio, 157 SW2d 998, writ dism.—App & E 999(3), 1064.1(10); Costs 238(1); Courts 85(2); Labor & Emp 3046(3), 3049(4); Neglig 307, 506(2); Trial 215, 219, 352.9.

Heldenfels Bros.; Rains v., TexCivApp–Corpus Christi, 443 SW2d 280, ref nre.—App & E 1062.2, 1170.10; Autos 243(3), 243(7), 244(5), 244(41.1), 244(58), 247; Damag 34; Death 76; Labor & Emp 3096(4); Neglig 282, 285, 502(3).

Heldenfels Bros., Inc. v. City of Corpus Christi, Tex, 832 SW2d 39.—App & E 931(1); Impl & C C 3, 30; Mun Corp 245, 249, 374(1).

Heldenfels Bros., Inc.; City of Corpus Christi v., Tex-App–Corpus Christi, 802 SW2d 35, writ gr, aff 832 SW2d 39.—App & E 1008.1(2); Contracts 186(2); Evid 143, 597; Impl & C C 3, 30, 34; Mech Liens 13; Mun Corp 249, 373(2), 374(1), 374(4).

Heldenfels Bros., Inc. v. First Nat. Bank of Hallettsville, TexApp–Corpus Christi, 657 SW2d 883, ref nre.—Banks 134(7).

Heldenfels Bros., Inc.; Parks and Wildlife Dept. of State of Tex. v., TexApp–San Antonio, 647 SW2d 39.—Appear 9(1), 9(2); Plead 111.42(8), 409(1); States 200.

Heldenfels Bros., Inc.; Saenz v., CA5 (Tex), 183 F3d 389.—Civil R 1351(4); Const Law 3869, 3910, 4048, 4542; Sheriffs 99.

Heldt; Light v., TexCivApp–San Antonio, 349 SW2d 271, ref nre.—Judgm 181(2), 181(5.1), 185(2), 186.

Heldt v. McCreary, TexCivApp–Corpus Christi, 399 SW2d 181.—App & E 758.3(9), 931(1), 989; Neglig 554(1), 554(2); Plead 111.36, 111.42(7), 111.43.

Heldt; Magnolia Petroleum Co. v., TexCivApp–Texarkana, 236 SW2d 255.—Corp 458, 503(2); Plead 111.16.

Heldt v. Martin, TexCivApp–Austin, 368 SW2d 9, writ dism woj.—Plead 111.36.

Heldt v. Southwestern Bell Tel. Co., TexCivApp–Corpus Christi, 482 SW2d 352.—Autos 290, 306(2), 306(7); Evid 376(9); Mun Corp 120, 680(1); Statut 263; Tel 813.

Heldt Bros. Trucks v. Alvarez, TexCivApp–San Antonio, 477 SW2d 691, writ refused.—App & E 345.1, 387(3); New Tr 118, 152, 155; Time 9(8), 10(7).

Heldt Bros. Trucks v. Alvarez, TexCivApp–San Antonio, 461 SW2d 448, writ dism woj.—Plead 111.6, 111.38, 228.15.

Heldt Bros. Trucks; Crosby v., TexCivApp–San Antonio, 394 SW2d 235.—Abate & R 81; Appear 8(1), 8(3), 17, 23; Plead 110; Venue 17.

Heldt Bros. Trucks v. McCollum, TexCivApp–San Antonio, 293 SW2d 214.—App & E 912, 989; Plead 111.42(8).

Heldt Bros. Trucks v. Silva, TexCivApp–Corpus Christi, 464 SW2d 931.—App & E 912, 1024.3; Appear 19(1), 23; Plead 48, 111.3, 111.16, 111.18, 111.39(4), 111.42(1), 111.42(3), 290(1); Pretrial Proc 76.1; Venue 21, 22(6), 32(1).

Heldt Bros. Trucks v. Tesoro Petroleum Corp., TexCivApp–San Antonio, 462 SW2d 631, writ dism.—Plead 111.42(8).

Helena Chemical Co., In re, TexApp–Waco, 134 SW3d 378.—Judgm 340, 397; Mand 3(2.1), 12.

Helena Chemical Co. v. Wilkins, Tex, 47 SW3d 486.—Alt Disp Res 114, 152, 181; Antitrust 138, 161, 162, 369, 391; App & E 930(1), 971(2), 1001(1); Damag 40(1), 112, 188(1), 188(2), 190; Evid 508, 535, 536, 542, 546, 555.2, 555.4(1), 557; Sales 441(3); Statut 174, 176, 184, 188, 205, 207, 226, 227.

Helena Chemical Co. v. Wilkins, TexApp–San Antonio, 18 SW3d 744, review gr, aff 47 SW3d 486.—Alt Disp Res 113, 155, 216; Antitrust 166, 369; App & E 893(1), 911.3, 919, 970(2), 971(2), 984(1); Damag 40(1), 118, 190; Evid 536, 542, 555.4(1), 555.4(2), 556, 557, 571(6); Fraud 11(1); Interest 49, 54; Sales 261(6), 267, 441(3); Statut 181(1), 181(2).

Helena Chemical Corp.; Condit Chemical & Grain Co., Inc. v., CA5 (Tex), 789 F2d 1101.—Fed Cts 373, 412.1; Frds St of 149.

Helena Laboratories Corp. v. Alpha Scientific Corp., EDTex, 483 FSupp2d 538.—Fed Civ Proc 928; Pat 235(2), 328(2).

Helena Laboratories Corp. v. N. L. R. B., CA5 (Tex), 557 F2d 1183.—Admin Law 314; Const Law 4185; Labor & Emp 1454, 1491, 1711, 1741, 1773, 1878, 1879, 1928, 1935, 1936, 1937, 1938.

Helena Laboratories Corp.; SmithKline Diagnostics, Inc. v., CAFed (Tex), 926 F2d 1161.—Pat 312(1.7), 312(10), 314(6), 318(1), 318(3), 319(1).

Helena Laboratories Corp.; SmithKline Diagnostics, Inc. v., CAFed (Tex), 859 F2d 878, sug for reh declined, on remand 1989 WL 418791, aff 926 F2d 1161.—Pat 16.33, 92, 97, 165(4), 229.

Helena Laboratories Corp.; Smithkline Diagnostics, Inc. v., EDTex, 662 FSupp 622, aff in part, mod in part and rev in part 859 F2d 878, sug for reh declined, on remand 1989 WL 418791, aff 926 F2d 1161.—Pat 16(3), 16.33, 112.1, 165(2), 165(3), 167(1), 226.6, 229, 230, 237, 312(4), 328(2).

Helena Laboratories Corp. v. Snyder, Tex, 886 SW2d 767.—Hus & W 323.1; Torts 200.

Helena Laboratories, Inc.; Snyder v., TexApp–Beaumont, 877 SW2d 35, rehoverr, and writ gr, rev Helena Laboratories Corp v. Snyder, 886 SW2d 767.—App & E 854(1); Judgm 181(33); Torts 200.

Helene Curtis Industries, Inc. v. Pruitt, CA5 (Tex), 385 F2d 841, cert den 88 SCt 1806, 391 US 913, 20 LEd2d 652.—Evid 5(2); Fed Civ Proc 2142.1, 2152, 2608.1; Fed Cts 391, 409.1, 428, 641, 798, 801, 843, 847; Health 325; Jury 31; Neglig 1612; Prod Liab 4, 5, 8, 9, 11, 14, 15, 18, 20, 24, 27, 44, 76, 77, 82.1, 83, 88; Sales 280.

Helen of Troy Corp.; United Parcel Service v., TexCivApp–El Paso, 536 SW2d 415.—App & E 1024.4; Contracts 97(1); Judgm 180, 181(3), 181(6), 185(1), 185.3(8), 186; Plead 228.14.

Helen of Troy L.P.; I & JC Corp. v., TexApp–El Paso, 164 SW3d 877, review den.—App & E 219(2), 842(2), 852, 854(1), 931(4), 989, 1008.1(1), 1008.1(2), 1010.1(1), 1010.2, 1012.1(5), 1024.3, 1071.2; Const Law 3964; Corp 1.5(2), 1.5(3), 1.6(9), 1.7(2), 665(1); Courts 12(2.1), 12(2.5), 12(2.10), 32, 35, 39; Trademarks 1435.

Helen of Troy, L.P. v. Zotos Corp., WDTex, 235 FRD 634.—Evid 9; Fed Civ Proc 1278, 2531, 2539, 2545.

Helen of Troy Nevada Corp.; Lara v., WDTex, 218 FRD 504.—Fed Civ Proc 1361.

Helfand v. Coane, TexApp–Houston (1 Dist), 12 SW3d 152, reh overr, and review den, and reh of petition for review den.—App & E 961, 1043(6); Libel 38(1), 38(5); Pretrial Proc 24, 40, 384.1, 401.

Helfer v. Helfer, TexCivApp–Fort Worth, 342 SW2d 8.—Divorce 54, 124.1, 124.5, 127(1).

Helfer; Helfer v., TexCivApp–Fort Worth, 342 SW2d 8.—Divorce 54, 124.1, 124.5, 127(1).

Helfer v. Texas Emp. Ins. Ass'n, TexCivApp–San Antonio, 467 SW2d 687.—App & E 907(3); Judgm 654.

Helfman Motors, Inc. v. Stockman, TexCivApp–Fort Worth, 616 SW2d 394, ref nre.—Action 60; Antitrust 369, 390, 398; App & E 1073(2); Corp 506, 507(14); Damag 184, 194; Proc 133.

Helfrich; Griffin v., TexCivApp–Waco, 312 SW2d 422.—Judgm 743(1); Mines 55(4), 55(8).

Helfrich; Morin v., TexApp–Houston (1 Dist), 930 SW2d 733.—App & E 242(1); Judgm 181(11), 185(2), 185(6), 185.1(4), 186; Lim of Act 55(3).

Helge v. American Central Life Ins. Co., TexCivApp–Austin, 124 SW2d 191, writ dism, correct.—App & E 1073(7); Courts 472.4(2.1), 475(2); Ex & Ad 533; Home 129(1), 129(2); Mtg 282(1), 292(1), 416, 594(3).

Helicoid Gage Division of Am. Chain & Cable Co. v. Howell, TexCivApp–Hous (14 Dist), 511 SW2d 573, ref nre.—Damag 132(14), 133, 134(1); Prod Liab 8, 15, 26, 27, 55, 75.1, 96.1.

Helicopteros Nacionales de Colombia, S.A. v. Hall, USTex, 104 SCt 1868, 466 US 408, 80 LEd2d 404, on remand 677 SW2d 19.—Const Law 3964, 3965(3), 3965(5); Fed Cts 71, 76.10, 84.

Helicopteros Nacionales De Colombia, S.A. (Helicol); Hall v., Tex, 638 SW2d 870, cert gr 103 SCt 1270, 460 US 1021, 75 LEd2d 493, rev 104 SCt 1868, 466 US 408,

80 LEd2d 404, on remand 677 SW2d 19.—Const Law 3964; Corp 665(1).

Helicopteros Nacionales De Colombia, S.A. ("Helicol") v. Hall, TexCivApp–Hous (1 Dist), 616 SW2d 247, rev 638 SW2d 870, cert gr 103 SCt 1270, 460 US 1021, 75 LEd2d 493, rev 104 SCt 1868, 466 US 408, 80 LEd2d 404, on remand 677 SW2d 19.—App & E 154(3); Corp 665(1), 665(3), 668(4); Courts 12(2.10), 37(3).

Helland v. Oppenheimer, TexCivApp–San Antonio, 102 SW2d 299, writ refused.—App & E 1056.1(6); Evid 423(6), 441(11), 443(2).

Helland v. Western Const. Co., TexCivApp–San Antonio, 516 SW2d 437.—Plead 45, 111.18, 111.39(4); Princ & A 136(2); Venue 19.

Helle, Ex parte, TexCivApp–Corpus Christi, 477 SW2d 379.—Child C 531(1); Contempt 21, 63(1); Courts 472.1; Plead 97; Pretrial Proc 501, 502, 506.1, 508, 509, 517.1.

Helle; Coastal Banc SSB v., Tex, 988 SW2d 214, on remand 48 SW3d 796, reh overr, and review den.—App & E 23, 388; Records 7.

Helle; Coastal Banc SSB v., TexApp–Corpus Christi, 48 SW3d 796, reh overr, and review den.—App & E 66, 76(1), 344, 946, 977(5); Const Law 3974, 3993, 4010; Judgm 123(1), 128, 138(3), 143(2), 146; Trial 6(1).

Helle; Coastal Bank SSB v., TexApp–Corpus Christi, 989 SW2d 1, reh overr, rev 988 SW2d 214, on remand 48 SW3d 796, reh overr, and review den.—App & E 395.

Helle v. Hightower, TexApp–Austin, 735 SW2d 650, writ den.—Admin Law 390.1; Agric 9.3; Statut 190.

Hellenguard, Ex parte, TexCrimApp, 622 SW2d 875.—Bail 52.

Hellenic Investment Fund, Inc. v. Det Norske Veritas, CA5 (Tex), 464 F3d 514.—Alt Disp Res 141; Contracts 127(4); Estop 92(2); Fed Cts 776, 874.

Hellenic Inv., Inc. v. Kroger Co., TexApp–Houston (1 Dist), 766 SW2d 861.—Contracts 175(1), 187(1); Cust & U 10, 15(1); Evid 457; Inj 62(2), 114(2), 128(3.1), 189.

Hellenic Lines, Limited; Mpiliris v., CA5 (Tex), 440 F2d 1163.—Courts 104; Fed Cts 743.

Hellenic Lines, Ltd.; Mpiliris v., SDTex, 323 FSupp 865, aff 440 F2d 1163.—Death 18(1), 82, 91, 93, 95(1), 95(3); Domicile 8; Fed Cts 574; Interest 39(2.25); Intern Law 10.45(2); Judgm 665, 677, 678(1), 678(2), 681, 830.1; Marriage 3, 12.1, 18, 23, 40(2), 40(10); Seamen 29(2), 29(5), 29(5.1), 29(5.2), 29(5.3).

Hellenic Lines, Limited; Southern Stevedoring & Contracting Co. v., CA5 (Tex), 388 F2d 267.—Fed Cts 850.1, 868; Indem 69, 102; Ship 110, 143.

Hellenic Lines, Ltd.; Viator v., EDTex, 558 FSupp 700.—Damag 132(1); Ship 84(2), 84(3.3), 84(5).

Heller v. American Indus. Properties Reit, WDTex, 156 FSupp2d 645.—Corp 584; Partners 370, 376.

Heller v. Armstrong World Industries, Inc., TexApp–Dallas, 708 SW2d 18, ref nre.—Antitrust 397, 398; App & E 216(1), 1062.4.

Heller Financial, Inc. v. Grammco Computer Sales, Inc., CA5 (Tex), 71 F3d 518.—Action 27(1); Damag 23; Fed Civ Proc 2194.1; Fed Cts 765, 776, 871, 896.1, 901.1; Fraud 31, 61; Judgm 540, 567, 704; RICO 26, 28, 29, 31; Sec Tran 3.1, 111, 161.

Helleson v. State, TexApp–Fort Worth, 5 SW3d 393, reh overr, and petition for discretionary review refused.—Crim Law 713, 717, 730(5), 795(2.1), 1037.1(1), 1037.1(2), 1037.1(4), 1037.2, 1171.1(2.1); Ind & Inf 191(7); Obst Just 7, 16.

Hellman v. Huebner, TexCivApp–Galveston, 234 SW2d 117, ref nre.—Hus & W 265; Tax 2930, 3063.

Hellman v. Kincy, TexApp–Fort Worth, 632 SW2d 216.—App & E 842(2), 1010.1(10), 1010.2; Evid 596(1); Infants 155, 178.

Hellman v. Mateo, Tex, 772 SW2d 64.—Judgm 181(7), 185.3(2); Lim of Act 4(2).

Hellman v. Mateo, TexApp–Houston (1 Dist), 751 SW2d 623, writ den, and writ withdrawn, and writ gr, rev 772

SW2d 64.—App & E 170(1); Judgm 185(2); Lim of Act 46(6), 55(3), 95(2), 95(12), 100(11).

Hellums; Heffington v., TexCivApp–Austin, 212 SW2d 245, ref nre.—App & E 832(1); Assign 10, 18; Contracts 261(1), 270(1); Evid 318(1); Mines 52, 109; Trial 105(2).

Hellums v. Hellums, TexCivApp–Eastland, 335 SW2d 390, ref nre.—Divorce 252.5(1).

Hellums; Hellums v., TexCivApp–Eastland, 335 SW2d 390, ref nre.—Divorce 252.5(1).

Hellums v. State, TexApp–Austin, 831 SW2d 545.—Crim Law 553, 785(6); Infants 20; Rape 54(4).

Hellyer v. Wig Imports, Inc. of the Southwest, TexCivApp–Eastland, 458 SW2d 492.—App & E 846(5); Equity 65(3); Trademarks 1704(8), 1704(9).

Helm; Capco and Capco Contractors, Inc. v., TexApp–Dallas, 725 SW2d 525. See Prade v. Helm.

Helm; Highland Underwriters Ins. Co. v., TexApp–Eastland, 449 SW2d 548.—Evid 380; Trial 83(1); Work Comp 1491, 1937.

Helm; International Sec. Life Ins. Co. v., TexCivApp–Tyler, 447 SW2d 956.—Insurance 2494(1), 3360.

Helm; Kingston v., TexApp–Corpus Christi, 82 SW3d 755, reh overr, and review den.—App & E 854(5), 927(7); Corp 1.4(4), 306, 397; Fraud 32; Princ & A 159(1); Trial 139.1(12), 139.1(14), 139.1(17), 169.

Helm; Prade v., TexApp–Dallas, 725 SW2d 525.—App & E 230, 231(1); Pretrial Proc 44.1.

Helm v. Reserve Life Ins. Co., TexCivApp–Galveston, 230 SW2d 566.—Insurance 2477, 3571.

Helm; Sovereign Camp, W. O. W. v., TexCivApp–El Paso, 94 SW2d 521, writ refused.—Action 53(1).

Helm v. Swan, TexApp–San Antonio, 61 SW3d 493, review den, and reh of petition for review den.—App & E 863, 934(1), 970(2); Evid 508, 555.2, 555.10; Health 633; Judgm 185(5).

Helmcamp v. Interfirst Bank Wichita Falls, N.A., TexApp–Fort Worth, 685 SW2d 794, ref nre.—Bills & N 49; Judgm 181(6), 181(26).

Helmcamp; Texas Bank and Trust in Wichita Falls v., TexCivApp–Fort Worth, 506 SW2d 667.—Banks 116(4), 130(1).

Helmcamp Ins. Agency; Green v., TexCivApp–Hous (1 Dist), 499 SW2d 730, ref nre.—Elect of Rem 3(4); Estop 85; Lim of Act 55(1), 55(3); Torts 117; Trial 366.

Helmer v. Texas Farmers Ins. Co., TexApp–Fort Worth, 632 SW2d 194.—Insurance 3426, 3447.

Helmerich & Payne, Inc.; Gray v., TexApp–Amarillo, 834 SW2d 579, reh overr, and writ den.—Courts 95(1); Mines 58, 73.1(2), 78.1(9), 92.26.

Helmerich and Payne, Inc.; Yarbrough v., TexCivApp–Hous (14 Dist), 616 SW2d 444.—Corp 116; Trial 356(5).

Helmerich & Payne International Drilling Co.; Southeast Texas Industriesv., TexApp–San Antonio, 70 SW3d 181, reh overr.—Judgm 183, 185(2), 185.3(13); Plead 130.

Helmerich & Payne Intern. Drilling Co. v. Swift Energy Co., TexApp–Houston (14 Dist), 180 SW3d 635, reh overr, and rule 537(f) motion gr, on remand 2006 WL 4009595.—Contracts 143(1), 143(2), 143(3), 143.5, 147(2), 147(3), 162, 169, 176(2); Decl Judgm 395; Insurance 2282, 3425; Mines 109.

Helmerich-Payne, Inc., v. Debus, TexCivApp–Fort Worth, 148 SW2d 243.—App & E 1001(1), 1010.1(2); Fences 27.

Helmick; Shary v., TexCivApp–San Antonio, 90 SW2d 302, writ dism.—App & E 218.2(2); Plead 34(2); Princ & A 156; Trial 351.2(4); Ven & Pur 123.

Helm-Lary Ford, Inc.; Dairyland County Mut. Ins. Co. v., TexCivApp–Fort Worth, 560 SW2d 529.—Judgm 181(23).

Helmle v. State, TexApp–Houston (14 Dist), 746 SW2d 301, petition for discretionary review refused.—Crim Law 1026.10(3); Sent & Pun 2090.

HELMS

Helms, Ex parte, Tex, 259 SW2d 184, 152 Tex 480.—Child S 508(3); Const Law 1106; Contempt 24; Divorce 408.1; Hab Corp 528.1, 529, 730.

Helms v. Day, TexCivApp–Fort Worth, 215 SW2d 356, dism.—Bills & N 452(1), 452(3), 518(1), 537(1); Evid 474(3); Health 579, 619, 624, 625, 821(1), 951; Plead 422.

Helms v. D. Gonzalez and Associates, TexApp–Eastland, 885 SW2d 535. See Helms v. Gonzalez.

Helms; Dill v., TexCivApp–Waco, 468 SW2d 608, ref nre. —Contracts 319(1), 323(3); Costs 194.32; Damag 124(4); Impl & C C 124; Trial 352.4(1).

Helms v. Ehe, SDTex, 279 FSupp 132.—Rem of C 1, 2, 30, 31, 38, 41.

Helms v. Gonzalez, TexApp–Eastland, 885 SW2d 535.—App & E 852; Health 752; Judgm 185(2).

Helms v. Guthrie, TexCivApp–Fort Worth, 573 SW2d 855, ref nre.—Mines 55(2), 55(4), 79.1(3).

Helms v. Harris, TexCivApp–Fort Worth, 281 SW2d 770, ref nre.—Neglig 1162, 1238, 1673; Torts 121.

Helms; Hartford Acc. & Indem. Co. v., TexCivApp–Tyler, 467 SW2d 656.—Work Comp 876, 1532, 1660.

Helms; Hines v., CA5 (Tex), 78 FedAppx 360.—Civil R 1326(8); Fed Civ Proc 2734.

Helms v. Home Imp. Loan Co., TexCivApp–Dallas, 294 SW2d 165, writ dism.—Venue 7.5(4).

Helms v. Home Owners' Loan Corp., Tex, 103 SW2d 128, 129 Tex 121.—Corp 374, 383, 405; U S 53(11).

Helms; Manning v., TexCivApp–Dallas, 387 SW2d 476.—Plead 111.42(4), 111.42(8).

Helms; Men's Wearhouse v., TexApp–Houston (1 Dist), 682 SW2d 429, ref nre, cert den 106 SCt 38, 474 US 804, 88 LEd2d 31.—App & E 554(1), 907(3), 932(1), 1008.1(1).

Helms; Puckett v., TexCivApp–Galveston, 166 SW2d 210.—Child C 921(1), 922(5).

Helms v. Southwestern Bell Telephone Co., CA5 (Tex), 794 F2d 188.—Antitrust 224; Tel 916(1).

Helms v. State, TexCrimApp, 493 SW2d 227.—Crim Law 423(9), 814(17), 1045; Homic 1184; Witn 397.

Helms v. State, TexCrimApp, 484 SW2d 925.—Controlled Subs 80; Crim Law 273.4(1), 273.4(2), 641.13(8), 661, 1086.1; Stip 7.

Helms v. State, TexCrimApp, 402 SW2d 759.—Bail 64.

Helms v. State, TexCrimApp, 210 SW2d 169.—Crim Law 1094(3).

Helms v. State, TexCrimApp, 99 SW2d 303, 131 TexCrim 358.—Crim Law 721(5), 761(11).

Helms v. Texas Alcoholic Beverage Com'n, TexApp–Corpus Christi, 700 SW2d 607.—Admin Law 669.1, 670, 676, 683, 754.1, 788, 789, 790, 791; App & E 931(6); Const Law 230.3(5), 990, 1030, 3695; Int Liq 69, 70, 71; Statut 47.

Helms; U.S. v., CA5 (Tex), 897 F2d 1293, cert den 111 SCt 257, 498 US 900, 112 LEd2d 215.—Crim Law 577.10(5), 577.10(8), 622.2(1), 656(2), 878(4), 1166(6); Ind & Inf 196(1); Jury 149; Postal 35(8), 49(11), 51; Sent & Pun 1508; Tel 1014(6).

Helms; U.S. v., CA5 (Tex), 467 F2d 1085.—Crim Law 841, 1038.1(2), 1038.1(5).

Helms v. U.S., CA5 (Tex), 340 F2d 15, cert den 86 SCt 33, 382 US 814, 15 LEd2d 62.—Crim Law 726, 814(1), 1030(1), 1038.1(5), 1130(4), 1162; Int Rev 5302.

Helms v. U.S., NDTex, 231 FSupp 961.—Autos 244(36.1), 244(37); Damag 102, 132(1).

Helms v. Universal Atlas Cement Co., CA5 (Tex), 202 F2d 421, cert den 74 SCt 74, 346 US 858, 98 LEd 372.—Damag 91(3); Death 93, 103(4); Labor & Emp 2825; Neglig 273, 275.

Helms; West Texas State Bank of Snyder v., TexCivApp–Eastland, 326 SW2d 47.—Home 162(1), 181.5.

Helmsley-Spear of Texas, Inc. v. Blanton, TexApp–Houston (14 Dist), 699 SW2d 643.—Lis Pen 3(1), 20.

Helmus v. State, TexCrimApp, 397 SW2d 437.—Ind & Inf 73(1), 125(29).

Helotes, City of; Grothues v., TexApp–San Antonio, 928 SW2d 725.—Const Law 996, 999, 1020, 1066; Environ Law 355, 368, 384; Inj 85(2); Mun Corp 120, 122.1(2), 589, 595, 607, 633(1); States 4.4(2); Statut 174, 195.

Helping Hands Lifeline Foundation, Inc.; United Way of San Antonio, Inc.v., TexApp–San Antonio, 949 SW2d 707, supplemented on reh, and reh overr, and writ den.—App & E 231(3), 231(7), 1050.1(12), 1173(1); Damag 140, 184, 191; Evid 471(1), 472(1), 506, 555.9, 568(1).

Helpinstill v. Regions Bank, TexApp–Texarkana, 33 SW3d 401, reh overr, and review den, and reh of petition for review den.—App & E 930(1), 989, 1001(1), 1001(3), 1003(6), 1062.1, 1067, 1068(3); Partners 217(3), 218(2).

Helpman v. U.S., CA5 (Tex), 373 F2d 401.—Crim Law 1618(3).

Helscher; United Gas Pipe Line Co. v., TexCivApp–San Antonio, 259 SW2d 735.—App & E 613(2); Exceptions Bill of 32(3).

Helsley v. Anderson, TexCivApp–Dallas, 519 SW2d 130. —Contracts 313(1); Equity 72(1), 87(1); Estop 116; Spec Perf 93, 105(3); Ven & Pur 75, 78, 185.

Helsley v. State, TexCrimApp, 80 SW2d 962, 128 TexCrim 205.—Sent & Pun 1379(2), 1379(4).

Helstrom; Travelers Ins. Co. v., TexCivApp–Waco, 351 SW2d 321, ref nre.—App & E 1062.1; Damag 221(4); Work Comp 1404, 1615, 1628, 1658, 1662, 1671.

Heltcel v. State, TexCrimApp, 583 SW2d 791.—Controlled Subs 30, 67, 80.

Helton v. City of Burkburnett, TexCivApp–Fort Worth, 619 SW2d 23, ref nre, appeal dism 102 SCt 2002, 456 US 940, 72 LEd2d 462.—Const Law 228.2, 3697, 3902, 4093.

Helton v. Clements, CA5 (Tex), 832 F2d 332.—Const Law 1905, 4165(2), 4172(1), 4172(6); Fed Cts 427; Lim of Act 95(15), 192(2), 192(4); Offic 72.12, 72.16(1).

Helton v. Clements, CA5 (Tex), 787 F2d 1016.—Fed Cts 589.

Helton; Dallas Railway & Terminal Co. v., TexCivApp–Dallas, 145 SW2d 655, writ dism, correct.—App & E 500(2); Autos 245(60), 245(65), 245(66); Damag 158(1); Trial 226.

Helton; Farmers & Merchants State Bank of Shamrock v., TexCivApp–Amarillo, 278 SW2d 352, ref nre.—Ex & Ad 46; Insurance 3471, 3484; Plead 111.42(4).

Helton; Kerr-McGee Corp. v., Tex, 133 SW3d 245.—App & E 232(2), 842(7), 930(1), 1175(5), 1177(1), 1177(7); Evid 555.2, 555.4(1), 555.9, 570; Mines 78.1(11), 78.7(2), 78.7(4), 78.7(6); Trial 76, 84(2).

Helton; Kerr-McGee Corp. v., TexApp–Amarillo, 134 SW3d 204, reh overr, and review gr, rev 133 SW3d 245. —App & E 232(2); Evid 555.9; Interest 39(2.20), 56; Mines 73, 78.1(1), 78.1(11), 78.7(4).

Helton v. Kimbell, TexApp–Fort Worth, 621 SW2d 675.—App & E 236(1), 497(1), 554(1), 846(6), 934(2); Courts 85(1); Judgm 340; Mines 56; Parties 40(1), 42, 43, 44, 65(1); Receivers 35(1), 59, 60, 139.

Helton v. Luse & Fosdick Drilling Co., TexCivApp–Eastland, 147 SW2d 831.—App & E 1072; New Tr 56; Waters 74.

Helton; Paluxy Asphalt Co. v., TexCivApp–Galveston, 144 SW2d 453, writ dism, correct.—App & E 1175(5); Damag 6, 208(1); Evid 7, 13; Torts 135; Waters 46, 49.

Helton v. Railroad Com'n of Texas, TexApp–Houston (1 Dist), 126 SW3d 111, reh overr, and review den, and reh of petition for review den.—Admin Law 651, 724; Courts 4; Mines 92.79; States 191.4(1), 191.10.

Helton; Stanley v., TexCivApp–Fort Worth, 451 SW2d 299.—Aband L P 2; App & E 302(1); Tresp 6.

Helton v. State, TexCrimApp, 670 SW2d 644.—Atty & C 32(13); Crim Law 641.7(1).

Helton v. State, TexCrimApp, 300 SW2d 87, 164 TexCrim 488.—Searches 126.

Helton v. State, TexApp–Houston (1 Dist), 886 SW2d 465, petition for discretionary review refused.—Crim Law 273.2(2), 273.3.

Helton v. State, TexApp–Beaumont, 909 SW2d 298, reh overr, and petition for discretionary review refused.— Crim Law 273.1(3), 275, 641.13(5), 1156(1).

Helton v. State, TexApp–Beaumont, 738 SW2d 734, petition for discretionary review refused.—Crim Law 566, 731, 1137(5), 1169.3, 1224(3).

Helton v. State, TexApp–Beaumont, 635 SW2d 824, aff 670 SW2d 644.—Crim Law 300, 641.10(3); Sent & Pun 1286, 1333.

Helton; Todd v., Tex, 495 SW2d 213.—Mand 187.10; Mun Corp 12(8).

Helton v. Todd, TexCivApp–Fort Worth, 481 SW2d 910, writ gr, rev 495 SW2d 213.—Mun Corp 12(8).

Helton v. U.S., CA5 (Tex), 302 F2d 558.—Crim Law 264, 1147; Postal 51; Sent & Pun 2220.

Helton v. U.S., CA5 (Tex), 231 F2d 654.—Crim Law 778(3).

Helton v. U.S., CA5 (Tex), 221 F2d 338.—Const Law 4666; Crim Law 317, 369.1, 393(1), 394.2(2), 407(1), 407(2), 867, 1169.5(1), 1169.5(5), 1169.11, 1186.4(1).

Helton; U.S. v., CA5 (Tex), 203 FedAppx 682.—Controlled Subs 100(6); Crim Law 273.1(2), 1026.10(2.1), 1130(5); Sent & Pun 973.

Helton; U.S. v., CA5 (Tex), 115 FedAppx 687, cert gr, vac 125 SCt 1714, 544 US 946, 161 LEd2d 520, on remand 161 FedAppx 382, opinion reinstated 161 FedAppx 382. —Sent & Pun 979.

Helton Oil Co.; Bunnett/Smallwood & Co. v., TexCivApp–Amarillo, 577 SW2d 291.—Contracts 175(3), 187(3); Costs 194.38; Indem 97; Judgm 217; New Tr 13; Plead 387, 427; Trial 79.

Heltzel v. State, TexCrimApp, 462 SW2d 289.—Crim Law 1130(2), 1137(5).

Helvering; F. H. E. Oil Co. v., USTex, 60 SCt 26, 308 US 104, 84 LEd 109.—Statut 223.5(2).

Helvering; Haggar Co. v., USTex, 60 SCt 337, 308 U.S. 389, 84 LEd 340, conformed to Haggar Company v. Commissioner of Internal Revenue, 111 F2d 144.—Int Rev 3037; Statut 181(2), 184, 223.5(1), 223.5(9), 263.

Helvering v. Hutchings, USTex, 61 SCt 653, 312 US 393, 85 LEd 909.—Statut 188.

Helvering v. Sabine Transp. Co., USTex, 63 SCt 569, 318 US 306, 87 LEd 773.—Evid 23(1).

Helvey; Conder v., TexCivApp–Fort Worth, 430 SW2d 374.—Adop 5, 15.

Helvey; State v., TexCivApp–Tyler, 375 SW2d 744.—Em Dom 262(5); Evid 113(16), 555.6(1), 555.6(10).

Helvey; Stefek v., TexCivApp–Corpus Christi, 601 SW2d 168, ref nre.—App & E 627, 846(5), 1074(3); Lim of Act 145(1), 150(1); Trial 392(2), 405(2).

Helvir Oil Co.; East Texas Refining Co. v., TexCivApp–Dallas, 82 SW2d 392, writ dism.—Mines 74(3), 74(10); Plead 165.

Helwani v. Learjet Acquisition Corp., CA5 (Tex), 966 F2d 179. See Wenche Siemer v. Learjet Acquisition Corp.

Helwick v. Laird, CA5 (Tex), 438 F2d 959.—Armed S 20.6(3), 20.9(5), 22; Const Law 4246.

Helwick v. Laird, WDTex, 318 FSupp 878, rev 438 F2d 959.—Armed S 20.6(3), 20.9(5), 22; Hab Corp 712.1, 728.

Helwig; First Nat. Bank, Giddings v., TexCivApp–Austin, 464 SW2d 953.—App & E 1177(2); Princ & S 115(1).

Helwig v. State, TexApp–Houston (1 Dist), 661 SW2d 295, petition for discretionary review refused.—Crim Law 369.1, 369.2(2), 369.2(7), 726.

Hem; Benyo v., TexApp–Houston (1 Dist), 833 SW2d 714. —App & E 345.1, 387(6), 395.

H. E. McMasters Co.; Donahue Inv. Co. v., TexCivApp–El Paso, 301 SW2d 330, ref nre.—Sales 480(0.5).

Hemanes v. State, TexCrimApp, 238 SW2d 777.—Crim Law 1087.1(2).

Hemanes v. State, TexCrimApp, 85 SW2d 251.—Crim Law 1086.13, 1106(2).

Hemby, Ex parte, TexCrimApp, 765 SW2d 791, reh den. —Courts 100(1).

Hemenway Co., Inc. v. Sequoia Pac. Realco, TexCivApp–San Antonio, 590 SW2d 545, ref nre.—App & E 989, 1001(1), 1177(7); Contracts 32; Estop 52.10(3), 118; Evid 383(7).

Hemingway v. Robertson, TexApp–Houston (1 Dist), 778 SW2d 199.—Child C 733, 736; Child S 506(4); Const Law 3965(1); Divorce 164, 229; Mand 1, 32.

Hemingway v. STAR SAVANNAH, MV, EDTex, 198 FSupp2d 855.—Adm 118.4; Ship 79; Wharves 22.

Hemingway v. Vessel Star Savannah, EDTex, 200 FRD 572.—Fed Civ Proc 824, 828.1, 833, 840, 843.

Hemmeline v. State, TexCrimApp, 314 SW2d 833, 166 TexCrim 458.—Crim Law 719(1), 1092.11(3), 1171.3.

Hemmeline v. State, TexCrimApp, 310 SW2d 97, 165 TexCrim 583.—Crim Law 980(1).

Hemmenway v. Skibo, TexApp–Beaumont, 498 SW2d 9, ref nre.—App & E 302(4), 1060.6; Autos 245(82); Evid 43(3); Neglig 535(14); Trial 106, 365.1(7); Witn 414(2).

Hemmi, Ex parte, TexCrimApp, 274 SW2d 413.—Hab Corp 729.

Hemmings v. U.S., SDTex, 842 FSupp 935.—Fed Civ Proc 777; Inj 26(4); Int Rev 4916, 4925, 5246.

Hemmitt, Ex parte, TexCivApp–Hous (14 Dist), 580 SW2d 51.—Child S 497; Hab Corp 529.

Hemness; Walles v., TexCivApp–Fort Worth, 600 SW2d 407.—Ack 25; Princ & A 29.5.

Hempel; Dismukes v., TexCivApp–Beaumont, 91 SW2d 770.—Venue 8.5(1).

Hempfling; Krider v., TexCivApp–Galveston, 137 SW2d 83.—App & E 683, 882(8); Bound 3(3); Deeds 38(1); Evid 83(1), 155(5); Ex & Ad 305; New Tr 99, 102(1), 150(1), 150(4).

Hemphill v. Cayce, TexCivApp–Fort Worth, 197 SW2d 137.—Covenants 69(2), 72.1, 77.1; Inj 62(1), 62(3), 128(6); Judgm 586(1).

Hemphill v. Greater Houston Bank, TexCivApp–Hous (14 Dist), 537 SW2d 124.—Judgm 185(2), 185.3(2), 185.3(16); Set-Off 29(1), 60.

Hemphill v. Junious, TexCivApp–Houston, 372 SW2d 580.—Princ & A 37, 64(1).

Hemphill v. Meyers, TexCivApp–Austin, 469 SW2d 327, mandamus overr.—Autos 167(3); Trial 356(3).

Hemphill v. S & Q Clothiers, TexCivApp–Fort Worth, 579 SW2d 564.—App & E 761, 934(2); Cons Cred 50, 66; Costs 194.18, 194.32; Trial 393(1).

Hemphill v. State, TexCrimApp, 505 SW2d 560.—Crim Law 312, 553, 557, 738; Homic 1021, 1136, 1329.

Hemphill v. State, TexCrimApp, 467 SW2d 412.—Crim Law 412(5); Rape 38(1).

Hemphill v. State, TexCrimApp, 252 SW2d 166.—Crim Law 1087.1(2).

Hemphill v. State, TexCrimApp, 110 SW2d 64, 133 TexCrim 257.—Crim Law 1168(2); Homic 612, 1086, 1178.

Hemphill v. State, TexApp–Austin, 634 SW2d 78, petition for discretionary review refused.—Witn 367(1), 372(2).

Hemphill v. State, TexApp–Houston (14 Dist), 826 SW2d 730, petition for discretionary review refused, untimely filed.—Crim Law 438(8), 662.40, 698(3), 1043(3), 1144.13(2.1), 1159.2(7); Sod 6.

Hemphill Bus Sales, Inc., In re, BkrtcyEDTex, 259 BR 865.—Bankr 2422.5(4.1), 3031.

Hemphill County v. Adams, Tex, 408 SW2d 926.—Lim of Act 11(2).

Hemphill County v. Adams, TexCivApp–Amarillo, 416 SW2d 855, ref nre.—Counties 227.

Hemphill County v. Adams, TexCivApp–Amarillo, 406 SW2d 267, rev 408 SW2d 926.—Lim of Act 11(2), 25(2), 28(1).

Hemphill County v. Adams, TexCivApp–Eastland, 390 SW2d 546.—Judgm 185(2), 185.3(1), 186.

Hemphill County; Baker & Taylor Drilling Co. v., TexCivApp–Amarillo, 378 SW2d 370.—App & E 1180(2).

Hemphill County; Baker & Taylor Drilling Co. v., TexCivApp–Amarillo, 376 SW2d 66.—App & E 1177(6); Plead 111.39(6), 111.42(8); Princ & A 22(1), 22(2); Venue 18, 21.

Hemphill County v. Rathjen, TexCivApp–Eastland, 389 SW2d 365.—Lim of Act 28(1).

Hemphill County; Williams v., TexCivApp–Amarillo, 254 SW2d 839.—App & E 232(3), 1177(6); Autos 244(35); Evid 471(1); Trial 277, 349(1), 352.5(6); Venue 8.5(5).

Hemphill-McCombs Ford, Inc. v. Kellner, TexCivApp–San Antonio, 419 SW2d 887.—App & E 233(1), 930(3); Fraud 62.

Hemphill, Texas, City of; Jerge v., CA5 (Tex), 80 FedAppx 347.—Fed Civ Proc 2497.1.

Hemphill, Texas, City of; Jerge v., EDTex, 224 FSupp2d 1086, rev and remanded 80 FedAppx 347.—Civil R 1121, 1137, 1169, 1185, 1189, 1405, 1505(7), 1506, 1528, 1536, 1545, 1549, 1555; Fed Civ Proc 2497.1; Labor & Emp 826; Mun Corp 218(10).

Hempstead; D & B, Inc. v., TexApp–Beaumont, 715 SW2d 857.—App & E 901, 907(3); Sales 384(1).

Hempstead; Wilcox v., TexApp–Fort Worth, 992 SW2d 652.—App & E 230, 231(1), 231(7), 242(2), 499(1), 500(1); Judgm 181(33), 185(6), 185.3(21).

Hempstead, City of, v. Kmiec, TexApp–Houston (1 Dist), 902 SW2d 118. See City of Hempstead v. Kmiec.

Hemsell; Johnson v., TexCivApp–Texarkana, 93 SW2d 476.—Brok 82(4); Trial 352.4(1).

Hemsell v. Summers, TexCivApp–Amarillo, 153 SW2d 305.—App & E 933(1), 1069.1; New Tr 143(5), 157; Trial 59(1), 59(2), 350.5(3).

Hemsell v. Summers, TexCivApp–Amarillo, 138 SW2d 865.—App & E 216(1); Autos 201(1.1); Damag 221(5.1); Death 86(1), 86(2), 88, 89, 95(3), 103(4), 104(4), 104(6); Evid 5(2), 383(11); Neglig 375, 1675; Trial 114, 133.1, 191(11), 215, 350.5(3), 351.5(5), 351.5(6), 352.4(7), 352.10.

Hemus & Co. v. Hawkins, SDTex, 452 FSupp 861.—Evid 142(1); Fed Civ Proc 2737.5; Mines 79.1(1), 79.3, 79.7.

Hemyari; Stephens v., TexApp–Dallas, 216 SW3d 526, review den.—Bankr 2442, 2462; Judgm 181(25).

Henage v. State, TexCrimApp, 352 SW2d 122, 171 TexCrim 541.—Crim Law 1116.

Henager; Employers Cas. Co. v., TexApp–Dallas, 852 SW2d 655, reh den, and writ den.—App & E 758.1, 1008.1(2); Work Comp 907, 984, 2215, 2251.

Henan Oil Tools, Inc. v. Engineering Enterprises, Inc., SDTex, 262 FSupp 629.—Fed Civ Proc 1952, 1954.1, 1959.1.

Henao; U.S. v., EDTex, 835 FSupp 926, aff U.S. v. Ramirez, 22 F3d 1095, cert den 115 SCt 430, 513 US 965, 130 LEd2d 343, aff 22 F3d 1095.—Arrest 63.5(3.1), 68(4); Autos 349(2.1), 349(18), 349.5(3); Crim Law 394.6(5); Searches 171, 177, 183.

Hence, In re, BkrtcySDTex, 358 BR 294, aff Hence v. Indian Cave Park Partnership, 2007 WL 1176787.—Bankr 2164.1, 3710(6), 3711(3), 3711(5), 3715(14); Bills & N 37, 129(2); Contracts 152, 155; Interest 37(2), 67.

Hencerling v. Texas A & M University, TexApp–Houston (1 Dist), 986 SW2d 373, review den.—Colleges 5; Damag 36; States 1, 112(1), 112(2), 191.4(1), 191.10.

Hencey v. State, TexApp–San Antonio, 904 SW2d 160.—Crim Law 1177; Sent & Pun 2014.

Henck; Elliott v., TexCivApp–Galveston, 223 SW2d 292, ref nre.—Atty & C 11(12); Damag 77, 78(6), 79(5), 80(3), 81, 85; Frds St of 110(1), 110(4); Ven & Pur 351(1).

Henckel; Moreno v., CA5 (Tex), 431 F2d 1299.—Civil R 1304, 1315; Const Law 3030; Decl Judgm 366; Fed Cts 3.1, 42, 44, 48, 53, 58; Mun Corp 724; Statut 184.

Hendershot v. Amarillo Nat. Bank, TexCivApp–Amarillo, 476 SW2d 919.—Evid 588, 595; Spec Perf 8, 87, 117, 121(11).

Henderson, Ex parte, TexCrimApp, 645 SW2d 469.—Const Law 4829; Pardon 72.1; Prisons 15(5), 15(6).

Henderson, Ex parte, TexCrimApp, 565 SW2d 50.—Bail 52; Hab Corp 823.

Henderson, Ex parte, TexCivApp–El Paso, 512 SW2d 37.—Child C 862, 906, 970; Hab Corp 528.1; Judgm 485.

Henderson, Ex parte, TexCivApp–Beaumont, 300 SW2d 189.—Child S 489, 497, 542; Contempt 66(1); Hab Corp 528.1, 711, 730.

Henderson, In re, CA5 (Tex), 462 F3d 413.—Hab Corp 894.1, 898(1), 898(3); Sent & Pun 1642.

Henderson, In re, CCA5 (Tex), 100 F2d 820.—Bankr 2251, 2263.

Henderson, In re, WDTex, 168 BR 151, aff 18 F3d 1305, cert den Belknap v. Henderson, 115 SCt 573, 513 US 1014, 130 LEd2d 490.—Bankr 2784.1, 2785, 2787, 2792, 3782; Home 5.

Henderson, In re, BkrtcyNDTex, 364 BR 906.—Bankr 2222.1, 2233(1), 2261.

Henderson, In re, BkrtcyNDTex, 352 BR 439.—Bankr 2422.5(4.1), 3671.

Henderson, In re, BkrtcyWDTex, 155 BR 157, rev 168 BR 151, aff 18 F3d 1305, cert den Belknap v. Henderson, 115 SCt 573, 513 US 1014, 130 LEd2d 490.—Bankr 2784.1, 2785, 2792; Home 5, 103, 104, 187; Judgm 754, 772, 778.

Henderson, In re, BkrtcyWDTex, 133 BR 813.—Bankr 2582, 2702.1, 2800, 2829; Int Rev 4772, 4782.1.

Henderson, In re, TexApp–Houston (1 Dist), 133 SW3d 380.—Contempt 20, 75, 79.

Henderson, In re, TexApp–Amarillo, 982 SW2d 566.—Child C 725; Child S 502, 509(1).

Henderson, Matter of, CA5 (Tex), 18 F3d 1305, cert den Belknap v. Henderson, 115 SCt 573, 513 US 1014, 130 LEd2d 490.—Bankr 2784.1, 2785, 2792; Home 103; Judgm 777.

Henderson; Amberson v., TexCivApp–San Antonio, 127 SW2d 553, writ refused.—App & E 460(2); Waters 225.

Henderson v. Applegate, TexCivApp–Fort Worth, 203 SW2d 548, ref nre.—Infants 77, 78(1); Jury 25(2); Mental H 122, 487, 488; Parties 21.

Henderson v. AT & T Corp., SDTex, 933 FSupp 1326.—Civil R 1101, 1118, 1168, 1200, 1203, 1505(3), 1505(4), 1505(6), 1505(7), 1517, 1537, 1539, 1549, 1551; Fed Civ Proc 2497.1, 2515, 2553; Lim of Act 55(1).

Henderson v. AT & T Corp., SDTex, 918 FSupp 1059.—Fed Civ Proc 81, 82.1; Fed Cts 101, 103, 104, 105, 106, 144.

Henderson; Baker v., TexComApp, 153 SW2d 465, 137 Tex 266.—App & E 1094(1); Covenants 29, 49, 51(2).

Henderson; Baker v., TexCivApp–Austin, 125 SW2d 660, aff 153 SW2d 465, 137 Tex 266.—App & E 909(2); Inj 109, 128(6).

Henderson; Barfield v., TexCivApp–Corpus Christi, 471 SW2d 633, ref nre.—Liens 7; Nav Wat 8.5; Pub Contr 56, 58; States 101.

Henderson v. Barrett, TexCivApp–Waco, 376 SW2d 432, ref nre.—Evid 178(12), 186(6); Wills 296, 303(4), 306; Witn 164(11).

Henderson v. Belknap, CA5 (Tex), 18 F3d 1305. See Henderson, Matter of.

Henderson v. Belknap, WDTex, 168 BR 151. See Henderson, In re.

Henderson v. Beto, NDTex, 309 FSupp 244.—Arrest 63.4(13), 63.5(5), 71, 71.1(1), 71.1(2.1); Crim Law 394.4(2); Hab Corp 381, 442, 490(3), 497, 668, 767; Searches 13.1, 15.

HENDERSON;

Henderson; Bonner v., CA5 (Tex), 147 F3d 457.—Fed Civ Proc 1772; Fed Cts 776; RICO 34, 36, 39.

Henderson v. Book, TexCivApp–San Antonio, 128 SW2d 117, writ refused.—Estop 22(2), 26, 30, 32(2); Mtg 534.

Henderson; Bormaster v., TexApp–Houston (14 Dist), 624 SW2d 655.—Antitrust 134, 138, 169, 369; App & E 931(1), 989, 1008.1(5), 1158, 1177(7); Evid 536, 547, 547.5, 570, 571(9), 572, 588; Sales 261(1), 441(1), 441(3); Trial 382.

Henderson; Brisco Bros. v., TexCivApp–Corpus Christi, 443 SW2d 923.—App & E 846(5); Plead 111.42(5).

Henderson; Brown v., TexApp–Corpus Christi, 941 SW2d 190.—Antitrust 357; Damag 87(2); Judgm 544, 590(3), 639, 720.

Henderson; Brown Express v., TexCivApp–San Antonio, 142 SW2d 585, writ dism, correct.—App & E 204(1), 218.2(1), 758.3(1), 758.3(7), 843(2); Trial 215, 352.18; Witn 379(11), 389.

Henderson; Brown Foundation Repair and Consulting, Inc. v., TexApp–Dallas, 719 SW2d 229.—Antitrust 203, 369; Damag 189.

Henderson; Burkholder v., TexCivApp–El Paso, 97 SW2d 297, writ dism.—Estop 3(2); Lim of Act 127(4); Plead 229.

Henderson; Cadle Co. v., TexApp–San Antonio, 982 SW2d 543.—App & E 173(10), 223; Assign 31; Banks 508; Contracts 236, 246; Judgm 183, 185(2); Lim of Act 165.

Henderson; Capitol Steel & Iron Co. v., TexCivApp–Amarillo, 239 SW2d 851.—App & E 931(1), 989, 994(3), 1008.2, 1010.1(5), 1056.2; Evid 148, 378(5); Mech Liens 160.

Henderson v. Central Power and Light Co., TexApp–Corpus Christi, 977 SW2d 439, reh overr, and review den, and reh of petition for review overr.—Antitrust 134, 135(1), 141, 143(2), 147, 290, 292, 363, 369; App & E 747(2), 901, 934(1), 1024.4, 1175(2); Contracts 303(4), 313(1); Electricity 17; Judgm 199(3.5); Pub Ut 119.1; Stip 3.

Henderson v. Chambers, TexApp–Austin, 208 SW3d 546. —Divorce 254(2); Judgm 7, 16, 470, 509, 511, 512, 514, 518.

Henderson; CHCA East Houston, L.P. v., TexApp–Houston (14 Dist), 99 SW3d 630.—Action 13; App & E 174, 330(1), 878(6); Assoc 20(1); Corp 506; Evid 393(1); Land & Ten 224, 231(1), 231(8); Parties 1, 80(7), 84(6), 94(2); Plead 290(1).

Henderson; Cherokee Village v., TexCivApp–Hous (1 Dist), 538 SW2d 169, dism.—App & E 78(1); Courts 28; Joint Adv 7; Partners 17, 20; Plead 111.42(9); Venue 24, 42.

Henderson; City of Beaumont v., TexCivApp–Beaumont, 349 SW2d 301.—App & E 1045(1); Mun Corp 755(1), 757(1), 763(2), 768(3), 785; Trial 133.6(4), 215.

Henderson v. City of Cross Plains, TexCivApp–Eastland, 235 SW2d 936, writ refused.—Gas 20(2).

Henderson; City of Houston v., TexCivApp–Hous (14 Dist), 506 SW2d 731.—App & E 274(7), 766; Autos 286, 306(4), 306(5), 306(8); Costs 260(4); Evid 586(2); Neglig 1717; Nuis 43.

Henderson v. City of Longview, TexCivApp–El Paso, 111 SW2d 740.—Inj 46, 138.46.

Henderson v. Cockrell, CA5 (Tex), 333 F3d 592, cert den 124 SCt 1170, 540 US 1163, 157 LEd2d 1208.—Crim Law 641.13(2.1), 641.13(6); Hab Corp 403, 404, 406, 422, 500.1, 766, 773, 818.

Henderson; Continental Oil Co. v., TexCivApp–Fort Worth, 180 SW2d 998, writ refused wom.—Corp 214; Costs 236; Judgm 378; New Tr 108(2), 161(2).

Henderson; Cope v., TexCivApp–Texarkana, 460 SW2d 183.—Jury 25(6), 28(6); Mand 3(8), 168(2), 173; Mun Corp 12(8), 12(9).

Henderson; Corchine v., TexCivApp–Dallas, 70 SW2d 766.—Antitrust 9.

Henderson v. Couch, TexCivApp–Eastland, 274 SW2d 844.—Action 60; App & E 1032(1); Contracts 177, 187(1); Labor & Emp 29; Mech Liens 115(4), 164(1).

Henderson v. Cummings, TexCivApp–El Paso, 147 SW2d 850.—App & E 758.3(1), 767(1).

Henderson; Daniel v., TexCivApp–El Paso, 183 SW2d 242, aff Southern Trust & Mortgage Co v. Daniel, 184 SW2d 465, 143 Tex 321.—Mtg 529(3), 600(3); Trusts 198, 231(2).

Henderson v. Democratic Executive Committee of Falls County, TexCivApp–Waco, 164 SW2d 192.—App & E 782; Elections 83, 298(1).

Henderson; DePue v., TexApp–Houston (14 Dist), 801 SW2d 178.—J P 158(3).

Henderson; Diles v., TexApp–Corpus Christi, 76 SW3d 807, reh overr.—App & E 5, 859, 863, 946, 984(1); Costs 132(1), 132(6), 133.

Henderson v. Dixon v., CA5 (Tex), 186 FedAppx 426.—Civil R 1105, 1126, 1544; Evid 146; Fed Civ Proc 840, 841, 1938.1; Fed Cts 614, 893; Jury 25(6); U S Mag 31.

Henderson; Dixon v., TexCivApp–Texarkana, 267 SW2d 869.—App & E 170(1); Hus & W 273(8.1), 273(10); Lim of Act 186.1; Mines 49, 55(2); Ten in C 15(7), 15(10).

Henderson v. Dretke, CA5 (Tex), 164 FedAppx 506, subsequent determination 460 F3d 654, cert den 127 SCt 1383, 167 LEd2d 160.—Crim Law 641.13(6), 823(5); Hab Corp 486(2), 816, 818, 824.

Henderson; Duran v., TexApp–Texarkana, 71 SW3d 833, reh overr, and review den.—Fraud Conv 1, 51(1), 52(1), 248, 296; Home 17, 57(1), 154; Lim of Act 1, 95(1), 100(3), 100(12), 165, 199(1).

Henderson v. Duran, TexApp–Waco, 39 SW3d 392, reh overr.—App & E 80(6); Judgm 183, 187, 190.

Henderson; F. B. McIntire Equipment Co. v., TexCivApp–Fort Worth, 472 SW2d 566, ref nre.—App & E 242(4), 1050.1(7), 1050.1(12), 1051(2); Damag 130.1; Evid 471(3), 496; Labor & Emp 26; Neglig 1717; Trial 83(1); Witn 236(1); Work Comp 2089.

Henderson; F.D.I.C. v., CA5 (Tex), 61 F3d 421.—Banks 55(2), 508; B & L Assoc 48; Fed Civ Proc 2173.1(1); Fed Cts 911; Lim of Act 6(9), 58(4), 58(5).

Henderson; F.D.I.C. v., EDTex, 849 FSupp 495, aff 61 F3d 421.—Action 27(5); Corp 306; Fed Civ Proc 2487; Fraud 7, 38; Lim of Act 6(9), 21(1), 55(1), 58(4), 58(5); Neglig 273, 1507.1.

Henderson; First State Bank of Monahans v., TexCivApp–El Paso, 377 SW2d 96.—Judgm 181(17), 185.1(3), 185.1(4), 185.2(3).

Henderson; Fisher v., NDTex, 105 FRD 515.—Fed Civ Proc 1278, 1366, 1451, 1636.1, 1758.1.

Henderson v. Floyd, Tex, 891 SW2d 252.—Atty & C 19, 21.15, 21.20.

Henderson v. Ford Motor Co., Tex, 519 SW2d 87.—Neglig 552(1); Prod Liab 11, 27, 36, 40, 83.5; Torts 126.

Henderson v. Ford Motor Co., TexCivApp–Amarillo, 547 SW2d 663.—Fraud 6, 7, 18, 33, 50; Sales 255, 267, 427, 437(1), 442(1).

Henderson; Ford Motor Co. v., TexCivApp–Beaumont, 500 SW2d 709, writ gr, rev 519 SW2d 87.—Prod Liab 26, 40, 73.5.

Henderson v. Fort Worth Independent School Dist., CA5 (Tex), 526 F2d 286, appeal after remand 574 F2d 1210, reh gr 579 F2d 376, on reh 584 F2d 115, cert den 99 SCt 1996, 441 US 906, 60 LEd2d 375.—Const Law 703, 977, 3062, 3644, 3648; Elections 18, 21; Fed Cts 13.20.

Henderson v. Frio County, TexCivApp–San Antonio, 362 SW2d 406.—Afft 18; App & E 1047(1); Dedi 1, 15, 16.1, 17, 41, 43, 44; Trial 350.3(1).

Henderson; Garrard v., TexCivApp–Dallas, 209 SW2d 225.—Home 1, 17, 18, 31, 32, 33, 154; Infants 47, 59, 62; Receivers 12.

Henderson; Gibson v., TexCivApp–Galveston, 136 SW2d 634.—App & E 846(2), 846(5); Autos 193(1), 193(11).

HENDERSON;

59 Tex D 2d—588

See Guidelines for Arrangement at the beginning of this Volume

Henderson; Gifford-Hill & Co. v., TexCivApp–Texarkana, 81 SW2d 274, writ dism woj, and writ gr, and writ dism.—App & E 218.2(4), 218.2(5.1), 994(1), 1015(5), 1050.1(6); Autos 305(6); Damag 130.3; New Tr 143(2); Trial 131(2), 219.

Henderson v. Goodwin, TexCivApp–Beaumont, 368 SW2d 800.—Adv Poss 10, 100(4), 115(2), 115(3); Trial 219, 350.3(3).

Henderson; Grogan v., TexCivApp–Texarkana, 313 SW2d 315, ref nre.—App & E 197(7); Hus & W 254, 255, 274(4); Insurance 3445; Lim of Act 5(3), 102(1); Plead 427; Trial 351.2(4).

Henderson; Gulfcraft, Inc. v., TexCivApp–Galveston, 300 SW2d 768.—App & E 70(6), 704.2; Autos 193(10); Labor & Emp 23, 29; Plead 111.36, 111.42(8), 111.44.

Henderson v. Gunter, Tex, 328 SW2d 868, 160 Tex 267.—App & E 1142, 1177(1), 1177(5), 1177(6); Bound 35(1), 35(4), 37(3); Ref of Inst 13(1).

Henderson; Gunter v., TexCivApp–Austin, 320 SW2d 221, aff 328 SW2d 868, 160 Tex 267.—App & E 1177(6); Bound 33.

Henderson v. Hall, TexCivApp–Galveston, 174 SW2d 985, writ refused wom.—Judgm 747(4); Mines 55(5); Tresp to T T 34; Ven & Pur 89, 212, 231(1), 261(3), 261(6), 278.

Henderson; Hare v., CCA5 (Tex), 113 F2d 277, cert den 61 SCt 135, 311 US 697, 85 LEd 451.—Ven & Pur 86, 278.

Henderson; Haynes v., TexCivApp–Austin, 345 SW2d 857, ref nre.—App & E 931(6), 1170.7; Evid 317(18); Frds St of 44(1); Wills 184(3), 184(4), 476, 566.

Henderson v. Henderson, TexApp–Corpus Christi, 694 SW2d 31, ref nre.—App & E 846(5), 852, 931(6); Deeds 192, 206; Lim of Act 95(2), 95(8), 199(1); Plead 34(1), 48; Quiet T 34(1); Ref of Inst 19(1), 32.

Henderson; Henderson v., TexApp–Corpus Christi, 694 SW2d 31, ref nre.—App & E 846(5), 852, 931(6); Deeds 192, 206; Lim of Act 95(2), 95(8), 199(1); Plead 34(1), 48; Quiet T 34(1); Ref of Inst 19(1), 32.

Henderson v. Henderson, TexCivApp–Austin, 259 SW2d 780.—Divorce 189, 223, 253(2), 286(0.5).

Henderson; Henderson v., TexCivApp–Austin, 259 SW2d 780.—Divorce 189, 223, 253(2), 286(0.5).

Henderson v. Henderson, TexCivApp–San Antonio, 425 SW2d 363, writ dism.—Divorce 249.1, 322; Hus & W 272(4).

Henderson; Henderson v., TexCivApp–San Antonio, 425 SW2d 363, writ dism.—Divorce 249.1, 322; Hus & W 272(4).

Henderson v. Henderson, TexCivApp–Texarkana, 236 SW2d 154.—App & E 927(7), 995; Gifts 25, 50; Ten in C 55(5).

Henderson; Henderson v., TexCivApp–Texarkana, 236 SW2d 154.—App & E 927(7), 995; Gifts 25, 50; Ten in C 55(5).

Henderson v. Herrington, TexCivApp–Houston, 366 SW2d 677, ref nre.—Adv Poss 33, 85(4); Tresp to T T 6.1, 41(2).

Henderson v. Heyer-Schulte Corp. of Santa Barbara, TexCivApp–Hous (1 Dist), 600 SW2d 844, ref nre.—App & E 1064.1(8); Evid 512, 560; Health 820.

Henderson v. Holland, TexCivApp–Austin, 348 SW2d 396.—Venue 8.5(8).

Henderson; Housing Authority of City of Galveston v., TexCivApp–Galveston, 267 SW2d 843.—Em Dom 202(1), 205, 262(4), 262(5); Evid 535, 543(3), 545, 546; Trial 76; Witn 245, 282.5.

Henderson; Huckaby v., TexApp–Houston (1 Dist), 635 SW2d 129, ref nre.—App & E 242(1), 692(1), 930(3); Can of Inst 46; Deeds 207; Trial 350.1.

Henderson, Estate of; InterFirst Bank of Fort Worth, N.A. v., TexApp–El Paso, 719 SW2d 641.—Courts 484, 485; Wills 307.

Henderson; International Sec. Life Ins. Co. v., Tex, 455 SW2d 200.—Autos 197(7); Corp 503(1).

Henderson; International Sec. Life Ins. Co. v., TexCivApp–Waco, 450 SW2d 758, rev 455 SW2d 200.—Plead 111.42(1), 111.42(8).

Henderson; Jeanes v., CA5 (Tex), 703 F2d 855.—Evid 384, 450(8), 518; Fed Cts 907; Fraud 7, 9, 58(2); Libel 130, 139; Mines 74(6); Sec Reg 60.37, 300.

Henderson; Jeanes v., Tex, 688 SW2d 100.—Courts 97(1); Fed Cts 14.1, 23; Judgm 181(33), 540, 634, 720, 724, 829(1).

Henderson v. Jimmerson, TexCivApp–Texarkana, 234 SW2d 710, ref nre.—App & E 758.1, 1051.1(1); Evid 230(2), 230(3), 242(1), 273(3), 313, 314(1); Frds St of 63(5); Hus & W 21, 23.5, 24, 25(1); Mtg 37(2); Plead 252(2); Princ & A 115(1), 171(1), 175(3); Trusts 43(3).

Henderson v. Jock, TexApp–Tyler, 864 SW2d 576.—App & E 5.

Henderson v. Johnson, CA5 (Tex), 201 FedAppx 284.—Civil R 1395(7); Fed Civ Proc 2531; Prisons 4(9).

Henderson v. Johnson, NDTex, 1 FSupp2d 650.—Hab Corp 603.

Henderson; Johnson v., TexCivApp–Eastland, 132 SW2d 458.—App & E 23, 799, 901, 907(3); Autos 235(4); Insurance 3517; Judgm 137; Sheriffs 119.

Henderson; Kellahin v., CCA5 (Tex), 81 F2d 128, cert den 57 SCt 13, 299 US 551, 81 LEd 406.—Deeds 196(2), 211(3), 211(4); Gifts 49(2).

Henderson; Ken Pruitt Buick Co. v., TexCivApp–Eastland, 545 SW2d 261.—Courts 170.

Henderson v. KRTS, Inc., TexApp–Houston (1 Dist), 822 SW2d 769.—App & E 946, 954(1); Const Law 2128, 2131; Inj 138.3, 138.6, 138.9, 138.21, 151; Tel 1136.

Henderson; Lang v., Tex, 215 SW2d 585, 147 Tex 353.—Evid 5(2); Land & Ten 164(1), 169(11); Neglig 233, 259, 1717.

Henderson; Lang v., TexCivApp–Dallas, 211 SW2d 972, rev 215 SW2d 585, 147 Tex 353.—Land & Ten 164(6), 164(7), 168(1), 168(2), 169(0.5), 169(1).

Henderson; Lee v., EDTex, 75 FSupp2d 591.—Civil R 1513, 1530; Fed Civ Proc 417.

Henderson v. L.G. Balfour Co., CA5 (Tex), 852 F2d 818, cert den 109 SCt 3216, 492 US 906, 106 LEd2d 566.—Labor & Emp 79, 836, 843, 866.

Henderson v. Life and Cas. Ins. Co. of Tennessee, TexCivApp–Fort Worth, 574 SW2d 634.—Insurance 2530, 2578.

Henderson v. Little, TexCivApp–Amarillo, 248 SW2d 759, ref nre.—App & E 1010.1(18); Contracts 164; Estop 38, 45; Mines 54(2), 55(2).

Henderson v. Lomax, TexCivApp–Waco, 559 SW2d 466, ref nre.—Em Dom 147, 158; Evid 574; Mines 55(6).

Henderson v. Love, TexApp–Texarkana, 181 SW3d 810.—Const Law 994, 999, 1007, 1020, 1030, 2489, 2494, 2661, 2668, 2671, 2672, 2763, 4426; Cons Cred 2; Fines 1.3; Statut 241(1).

Henderson v. McCarter, TexCivApp–Galveston, 200 SW2d 889, writ dism.—Divorce 139.

Henderson v. Mason, TexCivApp–El Paso, 386 SW2d 879.—App & E 863, 930(1), 989; Evid 591; Health 624, 625, 631, 670, 817, 821(4), 821(5), 823(1); Trial 139.1(17).

Henderson; Mitchell v., TexCivApp–Dallas, 90 SW2d 1117.—App & E 773(2).

Henderson; Modern Homes Const. Co. v., TexCivApp–Waco, 407 SW2d 21, ref nre.—Home 57(2).

Henderson v. Moore, Tex, 190 SW2d 800, 144 Tex 398.—Perp 4(1), 4(2), 4(12).

Henderson v. Moore, TexCivApp–Waco, 189 SW2d 59, aff 190 SW2d 800, 144 Tex 398.—Clerks of C 67; Perp 4(1), 4(2), 4(11), 4(12); Wills 366, 374, 439, 440, 447, 450, 470(1), 473, 486.

Henderson v. Morris, TexCivApp–Amarillo, 476 SW2d 471.—Autos 171(9), 244(11), 244(34); Neglig 504.

Henderson v. Nevada County Superior Court, State of Cal., CA5 (Tex), 431 F2d 704.—Fed Cts 743.

For Later Case History Information, see KeyCite on WESTLAW

Henderson v. New York Life, Inc., NDTex, 991 FSupp 527.—Civil R 1019(2), 1218(3), 1225(2), 1225(3), 1225(4), 1513, 1516, 1540; Damag 50.10; Fed Civ Proc 2497.1.

Henderson v. Nitschke, TexCivApp–Eastland, 470 SW2d 410, 46 ALR3d 1369, ref nre.—App & E 78(1), 223, 232(0.5), 758.3(11), 863, 1175(2); Land & Ten 92(1).

Henderson v. Norfolk Southern Corp., CA5 (Tex), 55 F3d 1066.—Autos 244(2.1); Damag 91(1), 91(3); Evid 571(3); Fed Cts 776, 844, 848, 850.1, 866; R R 114(2).

Henderson v. O'Neill, Tex, 797 SW2d 905.—Venue 63.

Henderson; Otto Goedecke, Inc. v., TexCivApp–Amarillo, 388 SW2d 728, ref nre, appeal after remand 430 SW2d 120, ref nre.—Damag 62(4), 163(2); Sales 418(1), 418(2), 418(3), 418(7).

Henderson v. Otto Goedecke, Inc., TexCivApp–Tyler, 430 SW2d 120, ref nre.—Sales 415, 417, 418(1), 418(4), 418(7).

Henderson; Page v., TexComApp, 106 SW2d 673, 129 Tex 652.—Hus & W 270(9).

Henderson v. Parker, Tex, 728 SW2d 768.—Wills 440, 470(2), 523, 524(3).

Henderson; Parker v., TexApp–Houston (14 Dist), 712 SW2d 224, writ gr, rev 728 SW2d 768.—Death 5; Wills 439, 448, 449, 470(1), 470(2), 548, 648.

Henderson; Pearson v., TexCivApp–Hous (1 Dist), 422 SW2d 256.—Lim of Act 121(2).

Henderson v. Perry, EDTex, 399 FSupp2d 756, probable jur noted League of United Latin American Citizens v. Perry, 126 SCt 827, 546 US 1074, 163 LEd2d 705, probable jur noted Travis County, Tex v Perry, 126 SCt 827, 546 US 1074, 163 LEd2d 705, probable jur noted Jackson v Perry, 126 SCt 827, 546 US 1074, 163 LEd2d 705, probable jur noted GI Forum of Texas v Perry, 126 SCt 829, 546 US 1075, 163 LEd2d 705, miscellaneous rulings 126 SCt 844, 546 US 1083, 163 LEd2d 720, miscellaneous rulings 126 SCt 844, 546 US 1083, 163 LEd2d 720, miscellaneous rulings 126 SCt 844, 546 US 1083, 163 LEd2d 720, miscellaneous rulings 126 SCt 845, 546 US 1083, 163 LEd2d 720, and 126 SCt 1186, 546 US 1149, 163 LEd2d 1127, and 126 SCt 1186, 546 US 1149, 163 LEd2d 1127, and 126 SCt 1186, 546 US 1149, 163 LEd2d 1127, and 126 SCt 1186, 546 US 1149, 163 LEd2d 1127, and 126 SCt 1296, 546 US 1163, 163 LEd2d 1147, and 126 SCt 1607, 547 US 1017, 164 3.—Const Law 3658(3), 3658(5); U S 10.

Henderson v. Pipkin Grocery Co., TexCivApp–El Paso, 268 SW2d 703, writ dism.—Evid 54; Neglig 1076, 1088, 1670, 1708.

Henderson v. Priest, TexCivApp–Dallas, 591 SW2d 635, ref nre.—Divorce 254(1); Evid 415.

Henderson v. Quarterman, CA5 (Tex), 460 F3d 654, cert den 127 SCt 1383, 167 LEd2d 160.—Courts 100(1); Crim Law 412.2(4), 641.2(1), 641.3(4), 641.3(6), 641.13(2.1), 641.13(7); Hab Corp 364, 401, 404, 450.1, 452, 486(5), 842, 846.

Henderson; Richardson v., TexCivApp–Waco, 424 SW2d 510, ref nre.—Autos 244(43), 244(58), 247; Trial 350.6(3), 352.5(6).

Henderson v. Rowe, TexCivApp–Austin, 93 SW2d 589, writ dism.—App & E 1064.1(6); Evid 113(1); Exch of Prop 8(4), 8(5).

Henderson; Satanta Oil Co. v., TexApp–El Paso, 855 SW2d 888.—Mines 73.1(6).

Henderson; Schwertner v., TexCivApp–Waco, 575 SW2d 358, dism.—Plead 111.6, 111.36; Venue 5.5.

Henderson v. Shackelford, TexApp–Amarillo, 671 SW2d 687.—Child C 552; Hab Corp 532(1).

Henderson v. Shackelford, TexCivApp–El Paso, 87 SW2d 824.—Trial 206.

Henderson v. Shell Oil Co., Tex, 208 SW2d 863, 146 Tex 467, cert den 69 SCt 233, 335 US 884, 93 LEd 423.—App & E 1091(1); Atty & C 106; Guard & W 2; Mental H 111, 113, 123, 128, 131, 270; Motions 59(1).

Henderson v. Shell Oil Co., Tex, 182 SW2d 994, 143 Tex 142.—App & E 66, 76(1), 78(2); Mental H 481.1.

Henderson v. Shell Oil Co., TexCivApp–Fort Worth, 202 SW2d 492, aff 208 SW2d 863, 146 Tex 467, cert den 69 SCt 233, 335 US 884, 93 LEd 423.—App & E 931(1); Guard & W 79; Jury 19(1); Mental H 108.1, 109, 110, 111, 112, 121.1, 123, 131, 133, 146.1, 264, 270; Mines 74(2); Proc 69; States 12.

Henderson v. Shell Oil Co., TexCivApp–Fort Worth, 179 SW2d 386, rev 182 SW2d 994, 143 Tex 142.—Cert 70(5), 70(6); Mental H 10.1, 494, 517.

Henderson v. Sims, TexCivApp–Tyler, 591 SW2d 593.—App & E 934(1), 989, 1024.4; Wills 163(1), 163(6), 166(12).

Henderson v. Smith, TexCivApp–Fort Worth, 354 SW2d 429.—App & E 930(1); Autos 208, 245(39), 245(80); Trial 139.1(3), 140(1), 142, 143.

Henderson v. Soash, TexCivApp–Amarillo, 157 SW2d 161.—App & E 569(3); Exceptions Bill of32(3); Judges 25(1), 32; Judgm 199(5), 298, 341; New Tr 165.

Henderson v. Sotelo, CA5 (Tex), 761 F2d 1093.—Const Law 4165(1), 4172(6); Fed Cts 421; Mun Corp 67(1), 192, 218(1).

Henderson; Stanley v., TexComApp, 162 SW2d 95, 139 Tex 160.—Courts 475(2); Ex & Ad 294, 490; Receivers 14; Wills 174, 472.

Henderson v. Stanley, TexCivApp–Waco, 150 SW2d 152, rev 162 SW2d 95, 139 Tex 160.—Evid 65; Ex & Ad 81, 138(4), 490; Receivers 19, 29(1); Wills 439, 440, 450, 462, 470(1), 706.

Henderson v. State, TexCrimApp, 962 SW2d 544, reh den, cert den 119 SCt 437, 525 US 978, 142 LEd2d 357, habeas corpus den 2004 WL 5295477, certificate of appealability den 164 FedAppx 506, subsequent determination 460 F3d 654, cert den 127 SCt 1383, 167 LEd2d 160, aff 460 F3d 654, cert den 127 SCt 1383, 167 LEd2d 160.—Const Law 3781, 4664(2); Courts 85(3), 97(5); Crim Law 371(4), 374, 393(1), 519(1), 520(2), 520(7), 531(3), 1030(2), 1035(8.1), 1043(3), 1139, 1158(1), 1159.4(2); Gr Jury 36.3(2); Homic 523; Sent & Pun 1624, 1652, 1827; Witn 198(1), 201(1), 201(2).

Henderson v. State, TexCrimApp, 826 SW2d 156, on remand 1992 WL 193575, petition for discretionary review refused.—Crim Law 1035(5); Sent & Pun 1379(2).

Henderson v. State, TexCrimApp, 661 SW2d 721, 51 ALR4th 787.—Gaming 98(4).

Henderson v. State, TexCrimApp, 619 SW2d 175.—Jury 29(6); Sent & Pun 1373.

Henderson v. State, TexCrimApp, 617 SW2d 697.—Crim Law 1037.1(3), 1038.1(2), 1038.1(3.1), 1043(2), 1043(3), 1171.8(2); Witn 274(2), 337(27).

Henderson v. State, TexCrimApp, 600 SW2d 788.—Escape 1, 9.

Henderson v. State, TexCrimApp, 593 SW2d 954.—Crim Law 594(1), 796, 867.

Henderson v. State, TexCrimApp, 592 SW2d 613.—Ind & Inf 101.

Henderson v. State, TexCrimApp, 560 SW2d 645.—Controlled Subs 29.

Henderson v. State, TexCrimApp, 552 SW2d 464.—Crim Law 1186.1; Sent & Pun 1318.

Henderson v. State, TexCrimApp, 519 SW2d 654.—Crim Law 273(4.1).

Henderson v. State, TexCrimApp, 487 SW2d 88.—Crim Law 1036.1(4); Rob 24.15(1).

Henderson v. State, TexCrimApp, 422 SW2d 175.—Arrest 63.3, 63.4(18), 71.1(2.1); Burg 23.

Henderson v. State, TexCrimApp, 420 SW2d 613.—Int Liq 249.

Henderson v. State, TexCrimApp, 402 SW2d 180.—Crim Law 829(18), 1037.1(3), 1092.11(3), 1092.12; Homic 1134, 1483.

Henderson v. State, TexCrimApp, 362 SW2d 322.—Ind & Inf 110(18); Larc 2, 21.

HENDERSON

59 Tex D 2d—590

See Guidelines for Arrangement at the beginning of this Volume

Henderson v. State, TexCrimApp, 353 SW2d 226, 172 TexCrim 75.—Crim Law 393(1), 404.60, 534(1), 537; Searches 184.

Henderson v. State, TexCrimApp, 347 SW2d 622, 171 TexCrim 244.—Homic 1134.

Henderson v. State, TexCrimApp, 332 SW2d 705, 169 TexCrim 206.—Crim Law 959, 1166.18, 1174(2); Homic 920, 1134, 1136, 1483.

Henderson v. State, TexCrimApp, 318 SW2d 898, 167 TexCrim 112.—Crim Law 1177; Sent & Pun 34, 1425.

Henderson v. State, TexCrimApp, 301 SW2d 131.—Crim Law 1090.1(1).

Henderson v. State, TexCrimApp, 298 SW2d 145.—Crim Law 1081(1).

Henderson v. State, TexCrimApp, 295 SW2d 215, 163 TexCrim 573.—Autos 355(6); Crim Law 723(3), 925.5(3), 1144.15; Ind & Inf 166.

Henderson v. State, TexCrimApp, 289 SW2d 274, 163 TexCrim 153.—Crim Law 351(3); Larc 51(2), 65; Witn 379(9).

Henderson v. State, TexCrimApp, 243 SW2d 708.—Crim Law 1090.1(1).

Henderson v. State, TexCrimApp, 243 SW2d 179.—Crim Law 1090.1(1).

Henderson v. State, TexCrimApp, 228 SW2d 158, 154 TexCrim 584.—Crim Law 364(4), 448(1); Homic 1136.

Henderson v. State, TexCrimApp, 227 SW2d 821, 154 TexCrim 376.—Crim Law 857(1), 957(3), 1176; Homic 1139.

Henderson v. State, TexCrimApp, 226 SW2d 635.—Crim Law 1099.10.

Henderson v. State, TexCrimApp, 198 SW2d 268, 149 TexCrim 619.—Crim Law 404.70, 1166(7); Gr Jury 30; Homic 976, 1205; Ind & Inf 140(2).

Henderson v. State, TexCrimApp, 192 SW2d 446, 149 TexCrim 167.—Crim Law 622, 755.5, 884, 893; Rob 27(1).

Henderson v. State, TexCrimApp, 192 SW2d 273, 149 TexCrim 160.—Crim Law 814(17), 1091(4), 1169.5(5); Homic 1091(4); Witn 260.

Henderson v. State, TexCrimApp, 165 SW2d 196, 144 TexCrim 616.—Crim Law 1134(3).

Henderson v. State, TexCrimApp, 152 SW2d 743, 142 TexCrim 337.—Crim Law 419(1.5), 603.2, 683(1), 1111(3), 1166.15, 1166.22(3), 1171.3; Jury 82(3); Witn 277(3).

Henderson v. State, TexCrimApp, 127 SW2d 902, 137 TexCrim 18.—Crim Law 264, 636(9).

Henderson v. State, TexCrimApp, 114 SW2d 881, 134 TexCrim 130.—Mayhem 5.

Henderson v. State, TexCrimApp, 106 SW2d 291, 132 TexCrim 596.—Crim Law 695(6), 925(1), 925.5(3), 1156(5), 1169.2(1), 1169.2(8); Homic 976, 988(2), 989(1).

Henderson v. State, TexCrimApp, 94 SW2d 467, 130 TexCrim 409.—Crim Law 354, 452(2), 486(6); Rob 23(1).

Henderson v. State, TexCrimApp, 92 SW2d 454.—Crim Law 15.

Henderson v. State, TexApp–Houston (1 Dist), 29 SW3d 616, reh overr, and petition for discretionary review refused.—Autos 355(6), 355(14), 359; Crim Law 338(1), 338(7), 553, 641.13(1), 742(1), 1086.11, 1119(1), 1147; Sent & Pun 313.

Henderson v. State, TexApp–Houston (1 Dist), 965 SW2d 710, reh overr, and petition for discretionary review refused.—Arrest 68(4); Crim Law 1139; Searches 171, 172.

Henderson v. State, TexApp–Houston (1 Dist), 822 SW2d 171.—App & E 107; Crim Law 488.

Henderson v. State, TexApp–Fort Worth, 77 SW3d 321, reh overr.—Crim Law 417(6), 419(1.10), 469, 476, 477.1, 478(1), 479, 480, 486(1), 1134(8), 1147, 1153(1), 1153(2), 1159.2(3); Homic 1145; Ind & Inf 69.

Henderson v. State, TexApp–Fort Worth, 816 SW2d 845.—Const Law 3306; Crim Law 421(6), 1036.1(6), 1134(5), 1166.17, 1169.2(2); Jury 33(5.15).

Henderson v. State, TexApp–Austin, 208 SW3d 593, petition for discretionary review refused.—Crim Law 1035(1); Jury 34(7).

Henderson v. State, TexApp–Austin, 14 SW3d 409.—Autos 411, 422.1, 423, 424; Crim Law 388.1, 436(1), 486(2), 661, 662.1, 662.8, 730(11).

Henderson v. State, TexApp–Austin, 758 SW2d 694, review gr, cause remanded, and review withdrawn, and review gr, review dism as improvidently gr 812 SW2d 322.—Sent & Pun 1862, 2006, 2021; Statut 223.3.

Henderson v. State, TexApp–San Antonio, 673 SW2d 662.—Crim Law 438(1), 438(4), 438(5.1), 438(6), 438(7), 641.2(1), 641.13(1), 641.13(6), 698(1), 1144.13(3), 1159.2(7); Homic 795, 1134, 1193, 1345.

Henderson v. State, TexApp–San Antonio, 669 SW2d 385.—App & E 931(1), 989; Controlled Subs 184.

Henderson v. State, TexApp–Dallas, 132 SW3d 112, habeas corpus den 2006 WL 3779750.—Crim Law 1004, 1023(3), 1043(3); Hab Corp 291.

Henderson v. State, TexApp–Texarkana, 13 SW3d 107.—Crim Law 641.4(2), 641.4(4), 641.7(1), 641.9, 1036.2; Witn 300, 305(1), 305(2).

Henderson v. State, TexApp–El Paso, 906 SW2d 589, reh overr, and petition for discretionary review refused.—Assault 67, 68; Crim Law 338(1), 338(7), 1153(1), 1162, 1170(1); Homic 757, 766, 787, 794, 799, 800, 975, 986, 1050, 1053(1), 1054, 1062, 1478.

Henderson v. State, TexApp–Beaumont, 725 SW2d 790, petition for discretionary review refused.—Crim Law 577.8(2), 577.10(3), 577.11(4).

Henderson v. State, TexApp–Waco, 864 SW2d 227, petition for discretionary review refused.—Arrest 63.4(2), 63.4(11).

Henderson v. State, TexApp–Waco, 786 SW2d 62.—Sent & Pun 323, 372, 1381(3).

Henderson v. State, TexApp–Waco, 666 SW2d 522.—Crim Law 577.8(1), 890, 1186.1; Rob 17(3), 30; Sent & Pun 373, 1058.

Henderson v. State, TexApp–Corpus Christi, 82 SW3d 750, reh overr, and petition stricken, and petition for discretionary review refused.—Crim Law 394.1(3), 693, 938(1), 942(2), 944, 1036.1(4), 1038.1(1), 1038.1(3.1), 1044.1(6), 1172.1(1), 1172.1(3).

Henderson v. State, TexApp–Houston (14 Dist), 971 SW2d 755.—Crim Law 409(5), 1144.13(3), 1159.2(7); Rob 24.15(2).

Henderson v. State, TexApp–Houston (14 Dist), 825 SW2d 746, petition for discretionary review refused.—Crim Law 20, 23, 345, 347, 568, 741(1), 772(6), 795(2.1), 830, 1144.13(3), 1159.2(7), 1159.6; Homic 908, 1205, 1492; Ind & Inf 189(8).

Henderson v. State, TexApp–Houston (14 Dist), 788 SW2d 621, review gr, rev 826 SW2d 156, on remand 1992 WL 193575, petition for discretionary review refused.—Crim Law 224, 429(1), 444; Jury 33(5.15), 120, 121.

Henderson v. State, TexApp–Houston (14 Dist), 704 SW2d 536, petition for discretionary review refused.—Crim Law 641.13(2.1), 641.13(5), 641.13(6), 641.13(7), 800(1), 823(1), 1119(1), 1120(1), 1144.17, 1166.10(1).

Henderson v. State, TexApp–Houston (14 Dist), 681 SW2d 173, petition for discretionary review refused.—Controlled Subs 34; Sent & Pun 2009, 2021.

Henderson; Stauffer v., Tex, 801 SW2d 858.—Joint Ten 6, 14.

Henderson; Stauffer v., TexApp–Amarillo, 746 SW2d 533, writ gr, aff 801 SW2d 858.—Joint Ten 6.

Henderson v. Sterrett, CA5 (Tex), 447 F2d 981.—Fed Civ Proc 1825; Fed Cts 743.

For Later Case History Information, see KeyCite on WESTLAW

Henderson v. **Stone**, TexCivApp–Texarkana, 95 SW2d 772, writ dism.—App & E 80(6); Judgm 342(2), 501, 686; Partit 95.

Henderson; **Stone City Attractions, Inc.** v., TexCivApp–Austin, 571 SW2d 206, ref nre.—App & E 1073(7); Partners 264, 305, 306, 336(3).

Henderson; **Teemac** v., CA5 (Tex), 298 F3d 452.—Admin Law 413, 751, 791; Civil R 1505(4), 1505(6), 1510; Fed Cts 776, 794, 813, 817, 947; Lim of Act 104.5, 195(3).

Henderson v. **Terrell**, WDTex, 24 FSupp 147.—Const Law 1039, 4290; Courts 101; Fed Cts 6; Mines 92.3(2), 92.49, 92.54, 92.62, 92.63.

Henderson v. **Texas Commerce Bank-Midland, N.A.**, TexApp–El Paso, 837 SW2d 778, reh overr, and writ den.—Antitrust 145; App & E 934(1), 1024.4; Contracts 221(1), 278(2); Estop 85; Judgm 199(3.10); Trial 147.

Henderson; **Texas Co.** v., TexCivApp–El Paso, 154 SW2d 911.—J P 174(15).

Henderson v. **Texas Turnpike Authority**, TexCivApp–Dallas, 308 SW2d 199, writ refused.—Em Dom 166, 235, 238(1).

Henderson; **Thomas** v., TexApp–Beaumont, 795 SW2d 847, writ den.—App & E 1178(6); Mines 49; Tresp to T T 50.

Henderson; **Thompson** v., TexApp–Houston (1 Dist), 927 SW2d 323, appeal after remand 1999 WL 417330.—Pretrial Proc 552.

Henderson; **Thompson** v., TexApp–Dallas, 45 SW3d 283, review den, and reh of petition for review den.—App & E 9, 113(1); Equity 64; Judgm 335(1), 335(2).

Henderson; **Tinkle** v., TexApp–Tyler, 777 SW2d 537, writ den.—App & E 1043(1); Pretrial Proc 40, 45, 282, 305, 312.

Henderson; **Tinkle** v., TexApp–Tyler, 730 SW2d 163, writ refused.—Const Law 2314, 2315, 3971; Judgm 181(7); Lim of Act 4(2).

Henderson v. **Travelers Ins. Co.**, Tex, 544 SW2d 649.—App & E 866(3), 927(7), 989; Trial 142; Work Comp 554, 571, 1536, 1716.

Henderson v. **Travelers Ins. Co.**, TexCivApp–Beaumont, 533 SW2d 407, writ gr, rev 544 SW2d 649.—Work Comp 1904, 1927.

Henderson; **Trio Transport, Inc.** v., TexCivApp–Amarillo, 413 SW2d 806, ref nre.—Neglig 235, 1550, 1578, 1610, 1625, 1658, 1677, 1685.

Henderson; **Tyler** v., TexCivApp–Fort Worth, 162 SW2d 170, writ refused wom.—App & E 934(2); Evid 65; Execution 345; Judgm 138(2), 151; Jud S 53; Mech Liens 298; Plead 8(15), 214(1), 214(4); Time 9(6).

Henderson v. **U.S.**, USTex, 116 SCt 1638, 517 US 654, 134 LEd2d 880, on remand 1996 WL 34317931.—Fed Civ Proc 21, 411; Lim of Act 118(2), 119(3); U S 110, 136, 147(5).

Henderson; **U.S.** v., CA5 (Tex), 254 F3d 543.—Crim Law 1139, 1158(1); Sent & Pun 686, 726(3).

Henderson; **U.S.** v., CA5 (Tex), 72 F3d 463.—Crim Law 273.1(2), 274(1), 274(3.1), 641.13(2.1), 641.13(5), 1004, 1026.10(2.1), 1149.

Henderson v. **U.S.**, CA5 (Tex), 51 F3d 574, cert gr 116 SCt 493, 516 US 983, 133 LEd2d 419, rev 116 SCt 1638, 517 US 654, 134 LEd2d 880, on remand 1996 WL 34317931.—Adm 117; U S 136.

Henderson; **U.S.** v., CA5 (Tex), 19 F3d 917, reh den, cert den 115 SCt 207, 513 US 877, 130 LEd2d 137.—Banks 509.10, 509.15, 509.20, 509.25; Const Law 4714; Crim Law 1147; Double J 29.1, 134; Frds St of 119(2); Sent & Pun 606, 664(6), 736, 989; Witn 414(2).

Henderson; **U.S.** v., CA5 (Tex), 565 F2d 900.—Crim Law 393(1), 713, 1037.1(2).

Henderson v. **U.S.**, CA5 (Tex), 446 F2d 557.—Crim Law 1132; Double J 115; Sent & Pun 1163.

Henderson v. **U.S.**, CA5 (Tex), 425 F2d 134.—Consp 47(5); Crim Law 29(5.5), 844(1), 1159.2(7), 1172.2; Postal 35(2), 35(6), 35(8), 50; Tel 1018(4), 1021.

Henderson; **U.S.** v., CA5 (Tex), 375 F2d 36, cert den 88 SCt 335, 389 US 953, 19 LEd2d 362.—Int Rev 3071, 3396, 3420, 3442.

Henderson; **U.S.** v., CA5 (Tex), 274 F2d 419.—Bankr 2124.1, 2125, 2184, 2854(2), 2854(3.1), 2854(7), 2854(8), 3501, 3837.

Henderson v. **U.S.**, CA5 (Tex), 261 F2d 909.—Controlled Subs 39; Crim Law 37(8); Int Rev 5259.

Henderson v. **U.S.**, CA5 (Tex), 206 F2d 300, cert den 74 SCt 274, 346 US 915, 98 LEd 410.—Arrest 65, 71.1(4.1); Controlled Subs 75, 86; Int Rev 5295.

Henderson v. **U.S.**, CA5 (Tex), 203 F2d 81.—Wareh 36.

Henderson v. **U.S.**, CA5 (Tex), 200 F2d 35.—Consp 47(12); Crim Law 1169.5(2), 1169.7.

Henderson; **U.S.** v., CA5 (Tex), 209 FedAppx 401.—Int Rev 4508; Witn 298.

Henderson; **U.S.** v., CA5 (Tex), 100 FedAppx 302.—Weap 4.

Henderson v. **U.S.**, NDTex, 949 FSupp 473.—Int Rev 4855, 4856, 5343.

Henderson v. **U.S. Veterans Admin.**, CA5 (Tex), 790 F2d 436.—Civil R 1525.

Henderson v. **Vanderwal**, TexApp–Beaumont, 403 SW2d 489, writ dism.—Libel 134, 139.

Henderson v. **Viesca**, TexApp–San Antonio, 922 SW2d 553, writ den.—App & E 893(1), 931(1), 999(1), 999(2), 1003(7), 1010.2, 1011.1(2), 1012.1(2); Evid 571(1), 574; Mental H 176, 180.1, 181, 185, 233, 251, 256, 301, 306, 309; Pretrial Proc 15, 40, 45.

Henderson v. **Weisser**, TexCivApp–Corpus Christi, 375 SW2d 571.—Child C 911.

Henderson v. **Wellmann**, TexApp–Houston (1 Dist), 43 SW3d 591.—App & E 863, 883, 930(1), 934(1); Damag 50.10, 208(6); Libel 38(1), 112(1).

Henderson; **Wells** v., TexCivApp–Beaumont, 78 SW2d 683, writ refused.—Evid 596(1).

Henderson; **West Lumber Co.** v., TexCivApp–Beaumont, 238 SW 710, writ gr, mod 252 SW 1044.—Mental H 48.

Henderson; **West Texas Utilities Co.** v., TexCivApp–Austin, 126 SW2d 699, writ refused.—Adv Poss 115(1); Bound 40(1), 54(1).

Henderson; **West Texas Utilities Co.** v., TexCivApp–Austin, 106 SW2d 370.—Bound 40(1).

Henderson; **Whelan** v., TexCivApp–El Paso, 137 SW2d 150, writ dism, correct.—Adv Poss 114(1); App & E 1069.1; New Tr 56; Trial 215, 219, 304, 337, 350.3(3), 352.9, 352.10.

Henderson v. **Wietzikoski**, TexApp–Waco, 841 SW2d 101, writ den.—Child 31; Const Law 2314, 3409.

Henderson; **Williams** v., TexCivApp–Hous (1 Dist), 580 SW2d 37.—App & E 1010.2, 1012.1(3); Bills & N 375, 519; Mtg 218.1, 375.

Henderson v. **Willmon**, TexCivApp–Texarkana, 407 SW2d 24, writ dism.—App & E 846(2), 846(5); Mun Corp 809(2); Neglig 1656, 1676; Plead 111.42(7); Trial 388(2).

Henderson; **Woodrow** v., TexApp–Texarkana, 783 SW2d 281.—Adv Poss 60(4), 85(1); Judgm 181(15.1); Tresp to T T 6.1.

Henderson v. **Youngblood**, TexCivApp–El Paso, 512 SW2d 35.—App & E 949; Jury 9, 10, 19.10(1), 26.

Henderson-Bridges, Inc. v. White, TexApp–Corpus Christi, 647 SW2d 375.—App & E 846(5), 989; Judges 24; Labor & Emp 256(9); Witn 246(2).

Henderson Broadcasting Corp. v. Houston Sports Ass'n, Inc., SDTex, 659 FSupp 109.—Antitrust 604, 699; Tel 1159(1).

Henderson Broadcasting Corp. v. Houston Sports Ass'n, Inc., SDTex, 647 FSupp 292.—Antitrust 534, 592, 604; Fed Civ Proc 2515.

Henderson Broadcasting Corp. v. Houston Sports Ass'n, Inc., SDTex, 541 FSupp 263.—Antitrust 604, 976.

Henderson, City of; Newton v., CA5 (Tex), 47 F3d 746, reh den.—Labor & Emp 2305.

Henderson Clay Products v. U.S., CA5 (Tex), 377 F2d 349.—Int Rev 3472, 4475, 4537.

Henderson Clay Products; U.S. v., CA5 (Tex), 324 F2d 7, cert den 84 SCt 1182, 377 US 917, 12 LEd2d 186.—Int Rev 3490, 3491, 3492, 3505, 4537, 4961, 5007, 5008, 5095.

Henderson Clay Products v. U.S., EDTex, 252 FSupp 1013, aff 377 F2d 349.—Int Rev 4475, 4537.

Henderson Clay Products v. U.S., EDTex, 199 FSupp 304, rev 324 F2d 7, cert den 84 SCt 1182, 377 US 917, 12 LEd2d 186.—Int Rev 3492, 3505, 5004, 5007, 5008.

Henderson Clay Products, Inc.; Dorney v., TexApp-Texarkana, 838 SW2d 314, reh den, and writ den.—Corp 630(2); Judgm 713(1), 715(1), 720, 724, 829(3); Lim of Act 127(11.1), 127(12); Mines 74(8), 78.1(3).

Henderson Clay Products, Inc.; SCD Production Co. v., TexApp-Texarkana,838 SW2d 314. See Dorney v. Henderson Clay Products, Inc.

Henderson Co. v. Thompson, USTex, 57 SCt 447, 300 US 258, 81 LEd 632.—Const Law 240(8), 2511, 2672, 2747, 3697, 3711; Fed Cts 389; Mines 92.3(2), 92.49.

Henderson Co. v. Thompson, WDTex, 14 FSupp 328, aff 57 SCt 447, 300 US 258, 81 LEd 632.—Const Law 990, 2672, 2970; Mines 92.2, 92.3(2), 92.13.

Henderson Co. v. Thompson, WDTex, 12 FSupp 519.—Const Law 46(2), 4084, 4290; Courts 101; Fed Cts 178, 297; Inj 118(4), 147; Mines 52, 92.2.

Henderson County; Hawkins v., EDTex, 22 FSupp2d 573, aff 180 F3d 265.—Const Law 3881, 3912, 4078; Controlled Subs 178, 181, 185; Courts 493(1); Em Dom 2(1.1), 180; Forfeit 5; Rem of C 21; U S 135.

Henderson County; Howard v., TexCivApp-Dallas, 116 SW2d 479, writ refused.—Counties 47, 69.2, 152, 204(1), 206(1).

Henderson County; Maples v., TexCivApp-Dallas, 259 SW2d 264, ref nre.—Adv Poss 8(2); App & E 301, 1050.1(2), 1056.2; Counties 49, 53; Evid 5(2); High 64, 79.1, 79.2, 95.1; Nav Wat 4.

Henderson County; Rhyne v., CA5 (Tex), 973 F2d 386, reh den.—Civil R 1088(4), 1332(4), 1345, 1351(1), 1404, 1420; Const Law 4337; Fed Cts 18; Prisons 17(2).

Henderson County Appraisal Dist. v. HL Farm Corp., TexApp-Eastland, 956 SW2d 672.—Courts 91(1), 100(1); Tax 2640, 2790.

Henderson County Appraisal Dist.; HL Farm Corp. v., TexApp-Tyler, 894 SW2d 830, appeal after remand 956 SW2d 672.—Const Law 3116; Tax 2137.

Henderson Drilling Corp. v. Perez, TexCivApp-San Antonio, 304 SW2d 172.—Autos 242(5), 242(6), 245(36).

Henderson Family Partnership, Ltd.; Temple-Inland Forest Products Corp. v., Tex, 958 SW2d 183.—Mines 55(4).

Henderson Family Partnership, Ltd.; Temple-Inland Forest Products Corp. v., TexApp-Beaumont, 911 SW2d 531, reh overr, and writ gr, rev 958 SW2d 183.—App & E 842(8); Mines 47, 55(2), 55(4).

Henderson Hardware Co.; Brinegar v., TexCivApp-Austin, 95 SW2d 740.—App & E 781(4); J P 43(1), 141(2).

Henderson Oil Co. v. City of Port Arthur, Tex., CA5 (Tex), 806 F2d 1273. See Peter Henderson Oil Co. v. City of Port Arthur, Tex.

Henderson 66 Sales, Inc. v. Harvison, NDTex, 58 FRD 408.—Fed Civ Proc 414, 2441, 2444.1, 2453; Fed Cts 683.

Hendes v. Gale, TexCivApp-San Antonio, 376 SW2d 922, ref nre.—Deeds 99, 110, 124(0.5); Lim of Act 60(6), 95(8); Ref of Inst 19(1).

Hendley; Hersh v., TexApp-Fort Worth, 626 SW2d 151.—App & E 218.2(1), 1062.1; Evid 474(6), 547, 571(3); Health 814, 821(2), 821(3), 822(3), 823(7), 827; Neglig 1741; Plead 430(2); Trial 194(16), 365.1(6).

Hendley v. State, TexCrimApp, 313 SW2d 296.—Crim Law 996(1); Larc 30(1).

Hendley v. State, TexApp-Houston (1 Dist), 783 SW2d 750.—Crim Law 304(1), 665(1), 665(4), 1043(2), 1153(5); Sent & Pun 2001, 2002, 2003, 2019, 2021, 2026.

Hendley v. State, TexApp-Tyler, 649 SW2d 105.—Crim Law 778(4).

Hendon v. Glover, TexApp-Beaumont, 761 SW2d 120, writ den.—Damag 15; Fraud 58(3); Interest 66; Mtg 298(3).

Hendren v. Paxson, TexApp-El Paso, 951 SW2d 496.—Crim Law 1007; Mand 3(2.1), 4(4), 10, 12.

Hendren; Tucker v., BkrtcyWDTex, 133 BR 819. See Tucker, In re.

Hendrick v. Beto, SDTex, 302 FSupp 380.—Hab Corp 385, 691.1, 799.

Hendrick v. Beto, SDTex, 253 FSupp 994, aff 360 F2d 618.—Const Law 3780, 4555; Courts 489(2); Crim Law 633(1), 980(1); Hab Corp 227.

Hendrick v. Hendrick, TexCivApp-Amarillo, 222 SW2d 281.—Child S 153; Divorce 189, 228, 252.3(2), 252.5(1), 253(1), 282, 286(0.5); Hus & W 249(1), 249(2.1), 249(5), 254, 262.1(1), 262.2.

Hendrick; Hendrick v., TexCivApp-Amarillo, 222 SW2d 281.—Child S 153; Divorce 189, 228, 252.3(2), 252.5(1), 253(1), 282, 286(0.5); Hus & W 249(1), 249(2.1), 249(5), 254, 262.1(1), 262.2.

Hendrick; Hodge v., TexCivApp-Eastland, 97 SW2d 722. —App & E 837(3); Inj 132, 147; Land & Ten 114(3); Princ & A 123(11).

Hendrick; Humphrey v., TexCivApp-Dallas, 88 SW2d 777.—App & E 805.

Hendrick v. McMorrow, TexApp-Beaumont, 852 SW2d 22.—App & E 863, 1043(8); Venue 1.5, 24, 45.

Hendrick v. State, TexCrimApp, 488 SW2d 814.—Stip 14(10).

Hendrick v. State, TexCrimApp, 341 SW2d 935, 170 TexCrim 399.—Burg 41(1).

Hendrick v. State, TexApp-Houston (1 Dist), 731 SW2d 147, petition for discretionary review refused.—Crim Law 406(2), 1167(1); Larc 30(8).

Hendrick v. Voss, TexCivApp-Dallas, 334 SW2d 308.—Adop 7.6(3), 13; App & E 1074(3); Child C 400, 413; Hab Corp 534, 731, 744, 816, 823, 841, 847.

Hendrick-Long Pub. Co.; Droste v., TexApp-Austin, 573 SW2d 589.—App & E 66, 78(1), 79(1), 80(1), 80(6).

Hendrick Medical Center, In re, TexApp-Eastland, 87 SW3d 773.—Health 804; Mand 3(2.1), 12.

Hendrick Medical Center v. Howell, TexApp-Dallas, 690 SW2d 42.—Courts 99(3); Mand 4(1).

Hendrick Medical Center; Malone v., TexApp-Eastland, 846 SW2d 951, reh den, and writ den.—Health 821(2), 821(3); Judgm 181(11), 185(2), 185(5), 185(6), 185.3(21).

Hendrick Medical Center; Nafrawi v., NDTex, 676 FSupp 770.—Antitrust 977(2); Const Law 4187; Health 273.

Hendrick Memorial Hospital; Maryland Cas. Co. v., TexCivApp-Eastland, 169 SW2d 965.—Statut 243; Work Comp 962, 986, 1001.

Hendrick Memorial Hospital, Inc.; Chandler v., TexCivApp-Eastland, 317 SW2d 248, ref nre.—App & E 1010.1(3); Civil R 1071; Const Law 3465, 3954; Evid 65; Ex & Ad 221(4.1), 255, 267, 437(7), 451(2); Judgm 18(2), 729; Lim of Act 43, 74(1), 187; Mental H 250, 377; Plead 404.

Hendrick Memorial Hospital (State Report Title: Maryland Cas. Co. v. Hendricks Memorial Hosp.); Maryland Cas. Co. v., TexComApp, 169 SW2d 969, 141 Tex 23.—Evid 47; Judgm 666; Work Comp 9, 52, 962, 976, 986, 1061, 1792.

Hendricks, Ex parte, TexCrimApp, 470 SW2d 192.—Extrad 36.

Hendricks; Batte v., TexApp-Dallas, 137 SW3d 790, reh overr, and review den.—Autos 192(11), 244(31).

Hendricks v. Bauer, TexApp-Beaumont, 709 SW2d 774, ref nre.—False Imp 15(1), 15(3); Labor & Emp 3045.

Hendricks v. Board of Trustees of Spring Branch Independent School Dist., TexCivApp–Hous (1 Dist), 525 SW2d 930, ref nre.—Mand 10; Records 31.

Hendricks; Briggs v., TexCivApp–Galveston, 197 SW2d 511.—Covenants 49; Evid 20(1); Inj 62(1), 114(2).

Hendricks v. City of Sherman, TexCivApp–Fort Worth, 220 SW2d 189, ref nre.—Costs 241; Equity 66; Judgm 18(2); Mun Corp 978(10); Tax 2743, 2936, 3068, 3176, 3179.

Hendricks v. C.I.R., CA5 (Tex), 406 F2d 269.—Int Rev 3092, 3270, 4623.

Hendricks; Cooper Concrete Co. v., TexCivApp–Dallas, 386 SW2d 221.—Contracts 350(1); Damag 123, 188(1), 221(5.1); Judgm 199(3.10), 199(3.14); Trial 350.4(1), 360.

Hendricks; Cotton Belt R.R. v., TexApp–Texarkana, 768 SW2d 865.—App & E 232(0.5), 930(3), 1177(8); Corp 432(1), 493; Libel 10(6); States 18.15.

Hendricks v. Curry, Tex, 401 SW2d 796.—Adop 7.6(1), 7.6(3); Child C 407; Infants 154.1, 156, 157, 177, 196, 254.

Hendricks v. Curry, TexCivApp–Fort Worth, 389 SW2d 181, writ gr, rev 401 SW2d 796.—Adop 7.2(1), 7.6(2), 7.8(3.1), 15; Child C 9; Infants 18, 131, 154.1, 157, 172, 173.1, 177, 191, 194.1, 196, 197, 200, 222, 226, 230.1, 231, 251, 252, 253; Judges 29.

Hendricks; Dallas Railway & Terminal Co. v., TexComApp, 166 SW2d 116, 140 Tex 93.—App & E 1050.1(7); Evid 208(6); Plead 93(3).

Hendricks; Dallas Railway & Terminal Co. v., TexCivApp–Dallas, 154 SW2d 899, rev 166 SW2d 116, 140 Tex 93.—App & E 1001(1), 1004(14), 1050.1(7); Carr 320(8), 320(19); Damag 95, 96, 130.1, 213; Evid 208(6); New Tr 74, 140(3); Trial 141, 350.6(4).

Hendricks; Gaubert v., NDTex, 679 FSupp 622.—B & L Assoc 23(8), 48; Fed Civ Proc 343.

Hendricks v. Hendricks, TexCivApp–Hous (1 Dist), 535 SW2d 668, ref nre.—Const Law 3410; Divorce 199.7(5), 394(1), 400(1), 405, 413.1.

Hendricks; Hendricks v., TexCivApp–Hous (1 Dist), 535 SW2d 668, ref nre.—Const Law 3410; Divorce 199.7(5), 394(1), 400(1), 405, 413.1.

Hendricks v. Kopecky, TexCivApp–Dallas, 133 SW2d 837, writ dism, correct.—App & E 1040(6), 1061.4; Courts 114; Elect of Rem 3(1); Hus & W 187; Tresp to T T 4, 16.

Hendricks v. Moore, Tex, 297 SW2d 811, 156 Tex 570.—Sales 52(5.1), 129, 348(1), 418(1).

Hendricks; Moore v., TexCivApp–Amarillo, 290 SW2d 758, rev 297 SW2d 811, 156 Tex 570.—Sales 150(1), 166(1); Trial 350.4(2).

Hendricks; Owen v., Tex, 433 SW2d 164, 30 ALR3d 929. —Brok 43(3).

Hendricks; Owen v., TexCivApp–Eastland, 426 SW2d 955, writ gr, aff 433 SW2d 164, 30 ALR3d 929.—Brok 43(2), 43(3); Frds St of 158(3); Judgm 185(1).

Hendricks; Richardson v., TexCivApp–El Paso, 109 SW2d 363.—Home 81; Land & Ten 61, 242.

Hendricks; Sinclair Houston Federal Credit Union v., TexCivApp–Galveston, 268 SW2d 290, 44 ALR2d 1234, ref nre.—Accord 17, 26(1); Gaming 26(5), 30, 43, 50(1); Impl & C C 25; Insurance 3526(8); Plead 236(5); Princ & A 136(1); Replev 8(1); Trial 26, 68(1).

Hendricks v. State, TexCrimApp, 640 SW2d 932.—Crim Law 597(3), 627.6(1), 627.6(5), 629(5), 713, 721(3), 721.5(1), 721.5(2), 726, 728(4), 730(1), 1043(3), 1171.1(2.1), 1171.1(3).

Hendricks v. State, TexCrimApp, 508 SW2d 633.—Crim Law 507(1), 780(1), 1173.2(6).

Hendricks v. State, TexApp–Fort Worth, 727 SW2d 816. —Arson 37(1); Crim Law 534(1), 535(2), 1167(1); Ind & Inf 139.

Hendricks; Sutter v., TexCivApp–Dallas, 575 SW2d 308, ref nre.—App & E 216(3), 232(3); Child C 554, 650, 904, 920.

Hendricks v. Swift, TexCivApp–El Paso, 142 SW2d 601. —App & E 66, 78(1), 930(1).

Hendricks v. Thornton, TexApp–Beaumont, 973 SW2d 348, reh overr, and review den.—Accnts 8, 9, 10.1; Antitrust 141, 145, 258; App & E 766, 863; Consp 1.1; Contracts 326; Contrib 1; Evid 571(3); Fraud 3, 20, 30; Judgm 181(5.1), 181(7), 181(11), 181(14), 181(33), 183, 185(2), 185(5), 185.3(1), 190; Lim of Act 43, 95(1), 95(10.1), 100(1), 100(7), 100(11), 104(1), 127(3); Plead 228.2; Sec Reg 278.

Hendricks v. Todora, TexApp–Dallas, 722 SW2d 458, writ gr, and writ withdrawn, and ref nre.—Evid 506; Land & Ten 167(8); Neglig 1024, 1037(4), 1070, 1078, 1088, 1089, 1162.

Hendricks; U.S. v., CA5 (Tex), 661 F2d 38.—Const Law 4580; Crim Law 577.8(2), 577.11(4), 577.12(2), 577.16(4), 1035(7); Jury 135.

Hendricks v. Williams, TexCivApp–Corpus Christi, 485 SW2d 304.—App & E 858; Judgm 174; New Tr 24, 155.

Hendricks & Peralta, Inc.; Texas Cookie Co. v., TexApp–Corpus Christi, 747 SW2d 873, writ den.—Action 3; Antitrust 145, 150, 161, 162, 264, 290, 363, 364, 368, 390, 397; App & E 215(1), 216(1), 218.2(1), 226(2), 930(2), 1026, 1052(2), 1053(6); Contracts 312(1); Evid 130, 134; Fraud 25.

Hendrickson; Kines v., TexCivApp–Waco, 153 SW2d 645. —Plead 111.18, 111.46.

Hendrickson; Mansell v., TexCivApp–Houston, 417 SW2d 908, writ dism by agreement.—Autos 244(36.1); Death 99(4), 99(5); Evid 92, 94; Stip 14(12); Trial 350.6(3).

Hendrickson; Security Ben. Ass'n v., TexCivApp–El Paso, 94 SW2d 1257.—Insurance 2081, 2083, 2093.

Hendrickson v. Swyers, TexApp–San Antonio, 9 SW3d 298, petition for review den.—App & E 893(1); Nuis 6, 40; Statut 181(1).

Hendrix; Appleby v., TexApp–Beaumont, 673 SW2d 295. —Antitrust 208; App & E 846(5); Venue 7.5(7).

Hendrix; Bass v., SDTex, 931 FSupp 523.—Antitrust 131, 141, 144, 147, 257, 292, 367; Const Law 1628; Contracts 168, 186(1), 188; Damag 49.10, 50.10, 56; Fed Civ Proc 2466, 2535, 2543, 2544; Fraud 13(3), 25, 59(3), 60; Insurance 1867; Neglig 202, 210, 213, 215, 219, 273, 276, 321; Torts 432, 433.

Hendrix v. Bell Helicopter Textron Inc., NDTex, 634 FSupp 1551.—Prod Liab 14, 34.

Hendrix v. Bexar County Hosp. Dist., TexApp–San Antonio, 31 SW3d 661, review den.—Counties 146; Mun Corp 723, 854.

Hendrix; Brown v., EDTex, 228 FSupp 698, vac Richard v. Christ, 377 F2d 460.—Schools 13(11).

Hendrix; Caraway v., TexCivApp–Waco, 389 SW2d 611. —Venue 21.

Hendrix; City of Houston v., TexCivApp–Austin, 374 SW2d 764, ref nre.—Em Dom 149(2.1); Evid 5(2), 486, 568(4).

Hendrix; C-Loc Retention Systems, Inc. v., TexApp–Houston (14 Dist), 993 SW2d 473.—App & E 846(5), 852, 893(1), 1008.1(8.1); Const Law 3964, 3965(3), 3965(4); Courts 12(2.1), 12(2.5), 12(2.10), 12(2.15), 35, 39.

Hendrix; Dallas Ry. & Terminal Co. v., TexCivApp–Dallas, 261 SW2d 610.—App & E 1178(6); Damag 20, 32, 163(1); Neglig 387, 431; Work Comp 2234, 2243.

Hendrix v. Everett, TexCivApp–Austin, 214 SW2d 667.— Sales 201(4); Venue 8.5(1), 8.5(5).

Hendrix v. Gabrysch, TexCivApp–San Antonio, 190 SW2d 516.—App & E 499(4), 699(1); Lim of Act 197(2); Mines 81; Mtg 364, 378; Subrog 23(2).

Hendrix v. Hendrix, TexCivApp–Beaumont, 457 SW2d 123.—App & E 1, 564(3), 907(3), 1135, 1177(9).

Hendrix; Hendrix v., TexCivApp–Beaumont, 457 SW2d 123.—App & E 1, 564(3), 907(3), 1135, 1177(9).

Hendrix; Hendrix' Estate v., TexCivApp–Waco, 440 SW2d 312, appeal after remand 457 SW2d 123.—Action 60; App & E 337(3), 989; Deeds 78.

Hendrix; Herrmann v., TexCivApp–El Paso, 145 SW2d 649.—App & E 554(3); Brok 61(1), 61(4).

Hendrix; Jackson v., TexCivApp–Fort Worth, 494 SW2d 652.—App & E 554(1), 557, 569(2), 907(3), 931(1).

Hendrix v. Jones-Lake Const. Co., TexCivApp–Corpus Christi, 570 SW2d 546, ref nre.—Judgm 199(3.9), 199(3.10); Neglig 1286(1), 1571, 1672, 1680, 1717.

Hendrix v. Lynaugh, CA5 (Tex), 888 F2d 336.—Hab Corp 252, 253.

Hendrix v. Matlock, CA5 (Tex), 782 F2d 1273.—Civil R 1088(2).

Hendrix v. Memorial Hosp. of Galveston County, CA5 (Tex), 776 F2d 1255.—Civil R 1530; Lim of Act 121(2).

Hendrix v. Port Terminal R.R. Ass'n, TexApp–Houston (1 Dist), 196 SW3d 188, reh overr.—App & E 856(1), 1073(1); Judgm 181(21), 183, 185(5); Labor & Emp 2753, 2757, 2801; States 18.21.

Hendrix v. State, TexCrimApp, 474 SW2d 230.—Burg 41(4), 41(8); Crim Law 393(1), 693, 695(2), 723(3), 1043(3), 1166(10.10), 1171.1(6).

Hendrix v. State, TexCrimApp, 459 SW2d 634.—Crim Law 404.75, 625.10(2.1), 863(1), 1038.2, 1038.3, 1137(3).

Hendrix v. State, TexCrimApp, 147 SW2d 247.—Crim Law 1182.

Hendrix v. State, TexApp–Waco, 86 SW3d 762.—Crim Law 1131(1).

Hendrix v. State, TexApp–Houston (14 Dist), 150 SW3d 839, petition for discretionary review refused.—Crim Law 678(1), 795(1.5), 795(2.10), 795(2.80), 872.5, 1038.1(2), 1044.1(1), 1134(3), 1134(3), 1172.1(5); Ind & Inf 87(7), 176, 191(8); Sent & Pun 506; Statut 220.

Hendrix' Estate v. Hendrix, TexCivApp–Waco, 440 SW2d 312, appeal after remand 457 SW2d 123.—Action 60; App & E 337(3), 989; Deeds 78.

Hendrix Mfg. Co. v. N. L. R. B., CA5 (Tex), 321 F2d 100. —Labor & Emp 1465, 1470, 1472, 1473(4), 1491, 1719, 1728, 1757, 1773, 1794, 1825, 1857, 1879, 1881, 1882, 1886, 1950(1).

Hendrixson v. State, TexApp–Beaumont, 679 SW2d 616. —Crim Law 553; Sent & Pun 2003, 2021, 2022.

Hendron v. Yount-Lee Oil Co, CCA5 (Tex), 108 F2d 759, cert den 61 SCt 21, 311 US 664, 85 LEd 426.—Fed Cts 178.

Hendron v. Yount-Lee Oil Co., TexCivApp–Texarkana, 119 SW2d 171, writ refused.—Adv Poss 13, 60(4), 70; Execution 256(1); Lim of Act 70(1).

Hendry v. Hendry, TexCivApp–Austin, 238 SW2d 821.— App & E 71(4), 792; Divorce 207.

Hendry; Hendry v., TexCivApp–Austin, 238 SW2d 821.— App & E 71(4), 792; Divorce 207.

Henefield; U.S. v., CA5 (Tex), 143 FedAppx 586.—Crim Law 1077.3, 1177, 1181.5(8); Sent & Pun 661.

Henegar; Graham v., CA5 (Tex), 640 F2d 732, 24 Wage & Hour Cas (BNA) 1294, reh den 646 F2d 566.—Fed Cts 974.1, 979, 1139.

Henegar; Hayhoe v., TexApp–Eastland, 172 SW3d 642.— App & E 1151(2); Damag 191; Evid 544, 545, 546, 555.10, 571(10), 574; Interest 39(2.50), 39(3).

Henery; Meyer v., TexCivApp–Austin, 400 SW2d 933.— App & E 1035, 1073(2); Judgm 109; Jury 10, 31.2(4).

Henery v. Schraub, TexCivApp–San Antonio, 370 SW2d 98.—Judgm 340.

Henger v. Cotton, Tex, 316 SW2d 719, 159 Tex 139.—App & E 1172(3); Judgm 181(33).

Henger; Cotton v., TexCivApp–Dallas, 312 SW2d 299, rev 316 SW2d 719, 159 Tex 139.—Action 57(5); App & E 373(1), 396, 747(2); Gas 16, 17; Judgm 185.3(21); Labor & Emp 30; Work Comp 2168.

Henger v. Sale, Tex, 365 SW2d 335.—Corp 297.

Henger v. Sale, TexCivApp–Waco, 357 SW2d 774, aff in part, rev in part 365 SW2d 335.—Corp 316(1), 316(4), 320(11), 404(2), 545(3).

Henger; Smith v., Tex, 226 SW2d 425, 148 Tex 456, 20 ALR2d 853.—Abate & R 68; App & E 139, 143, 334(1), 930(1), 1114; Damag 221(2.1); Neglig 506(8), 1011, 1018, 1204(1), 1205(7), 1296, 1683, 1710, 1714, 1717; Trial 350.6(6), 350.8, 366; Work Comp 2237, 2247.

Henger v. Smith, TexCivApp–El Paso, 222 SW2d 422, rev 226 SW2d 425, 148 Tex 456, 20 ALR2d 853.—Neglig 414, 1204(1), 1205(7), 1240, 1672, 1680.

Hengst; Jarbet Co. v., TexCivApp–Austin, 260 SW2d 88. —Damag 178, 208(3), 208(4); Evid 379, 539; Neglig 1658, 1672, 1680, 1683; Trial 114, 122, 125(3), 352.1(6); Work Comp 2243, 2251.

Hengy; Dallas County Levee Imp. Dist. No. 6 v., Tex, 202 SW2d 918, 146 Tex 95.—App & E 1177(1); Levees 34; Tax 2424.

Hengy v. Dallas County Levee Imp. Dist. No. 6, TexCivApp–Dallas, 233 SW2d 157, ref nre.—Levees 25; Tax 2431, 2709(2).

Hengy v. Dallas County Levee Imp. Dist. No. 6, TexCivApp–Waco, 199 SW2d 230, aff 202 SW2d 918, 146 Tex 95.—Const Law 196, 4138(2); Evid 23(1), 178(3); Levees 9, 20, 25, 27; Tax 2140.

Henke v. First Southern Properties, Inc., TexCivApp–Waco, 586 SW2d 617, ref nre.—Interest 17; Judgm 18(1); Mtg 372(3); Subrog 23(6).

Henke v. Peoples State Bank of Hallettsville, TexApp–Corpus Christi, 6 SW3d 717, reh overr, and review dism woj.—App & E 66, 71(3), 125, 882(18), 882(20), 948, 954(4); Inj 160, 161, 163(1), 163(7), 174, 189, 204.

Henke v. State, TexApp–Corpus Christi, 730 SW2d 117, petition for discretionary review refused.—Larc 55.

Henke; Tanglewood Homes Ass'n, Inc. v., TexApp–Houston (1 Dist), 728 SW2d 39, ref nre, appeal after remand 1989 WL 49084, writ den.—App & E 635(1); Costs 194.40; Covenants 1, 5, 72.1; Decl Judgm 184, 394; Equity 66; Inj 62(3), 128(6); Statut 212.6.

Henke; U.S. v., CA5 (Tex), 775 F2d 641.—Cust Dut 126(2), 126(3.1), 126(9.1).

Henke & Pillot v. Amalgamated Meat Cutters & Butchers Workmen, Etc., No. 408, TexCivApp–Galveston, 109 SW2d 1088, writ dism.—App & E 931(3); Labor & Emp 997, 1236, 1344, 2059, 2121, 2122.

Henke & Pillot v. Hanovice, TexCivApp–Galveston, 77 SW2d 303.—Antitrust 17, 18; App & E 863; Trademarks 1425, 1705(2), 1800.

Henke & Pillot, Division of Kroger Co.; Luvual v., TexCivApp–Houston, 366 SW2d 831, ref nre.—App & E 554(1), 934(1), 970(2); Autos 201(1.1), 243(5), 247; Evid 123(8), 243(4), 272; Judgm 199(3.10); Neglig 1713; Trial 45(1), 48, 350.5(5); Witn 406.

Henke & Pillot, Inc.; Beard v., TexCivApp–Beaumont, 314 SW2d 844.—Neglig 1104(7), 1708.

Henke Grain Co. v. Keenan, TexApp–Corpus Christi, 658 SW2d 343.—App & E 934(1), 1050.1(10); Bankr 2088; Costs 207; Fact 31; Judgm 217; Pretrial Proc 476, 483; Rem of C 95.

Henkel KGaA v. Empresa Naviera Santa, S.A., CA5 (Tex), 966 F2d 1018. See HCI Chemicals (USA), Inc. v. Henkel KGaA.

Henkel KGaA; HCI Chemicals (USA), Inc. v., CA5 (Tex), 966 F2d 1018.—Fed Civ Proc 2011; Fed Cts 628; Sales 168(2), 168.5(6), 418(9), 418(19), 429.

Henley, Ex parte, TexCrimApp, 229 SW2d 810, 154 Tex-Crim 558.—Hab Corp 652, 721(1).

Henley; Briggs v., TexCivApp–Eastland, 319 SW2d 453. —Brok 40, 56(3).

Henley v. City of Dallas, TexCivApp–Dallas, 583 SW2d 952.—Mun Corp 186(5).

Henley; Davis v., TexCivApp–Hous (1 Dist), 471 SW2d 883, ref nre.—Infants 116; Judgm 220.

Henley v. Dillard Dept. Stores, NDTex, 46 FSupp2d 587.—Torts 384, 385, 387, 388.

Henley v. Ellis, CA5 (Tex), 228 F2d 657.—Hab Corp 452, 721(1), 773.

Henley; Harris v., TexCivApp–Tyler, 493 SW2d 643.—App & E 907(3); Costs 194.32, 194.38.

Henley; Lopez v., CA5 (Tex), 416 F3d 455.—Aliens 710; Statut 219(1), 219(2).

Henley v. Moore, CA5 (Tex), 218 F2d 589.—Hab Corp 746.

Henley v. Moore, CA5 (Tex), 199 F2d 752, cert den 73 SCt 500, 344 US 931, 97 LEd 716.—Hab Corp 825.1.

Henley v. State, TexCrimApp, 576 SW2d 66.—Const Law 4559, 4599, 4600, 4754; Crim Law 126(1), 854(2); Jury 131(1).

Henley v. State, TexCrimApp, 387 SW2d 877.—Controlled Subs 65; Crim Law 785(11), 1166(10.10), 1173.2(8); Ind & Inf 71.4(7), 111(1), 119; Searches 164.

Henley v. State, TexApp–Corpus Christi, 644 SW2d 950, petition for discretionary review refused.—Crim Law 781(1), 855(5), 1166.18; Jury 83(1), 85, 100, 107, 108, 131(7), 131(16); Sent & Pun 40, 74.

Henley; Travelers Ins. Co. v., TexCivApp–Beaumont, 328 SW2d 944.—Trial 358, 360; Work Comp 1927.

Henn v. City of Amarillo, Tex, 301 SW2d 71, 157 Tex 129.—Counties 54, 57; Courts 61, 63; Em Dom 241.

Henn; City of Amarillo v., TexCivApp–Amarillo, 297 SW2d 732, rev 301 SW2d 71, 157 Tex 129.—Courts 63; Estop 62.4, 62.8; Judgm 11.

Henneberger v. Sheahan, TexCivApp–Dallas, 278 SW2d 497, ref nre.—App & E 692(1); Gifts 50, 51, 52; Witn 140(4), 178(3).

Henneke v. Andreas, TexCivApp–Austin, 473 SW2d 221, ref nre.—Ven & Pur 57; Wills 184(4), 435, 439, 488, 725.

Henneman; Deviney v., TexCivApp–Amarillo, 366 SW2d 688.—App & E 790(3), 991; Autos 244(43).

Hennemuth v. Weatherford, TexCivApp–Waco, 278 SW2d 271, ref nre.—Contracts 295(1), 350(1); Home 98; Mech Liens 163, 310(1), 310(3).

Hennessee Homes, Inc.; Industrial Indem. Co. v., TexCivApp–Hous (1 Dist), 465 SW2d 955, ref nre.—Insurance 2278(21), 2278(28), 2296.

Hennessy v. Bell, TexApp–Corpus Christi, 775 SW2d 650, writ den.—App & E 170(1); Mtg 298(3), 572.

Hennessey v. Skinner, TexApp–Houston (14 Dist), 698 SW2d 382.—Antitrust 145, 152, 360, 393, 397, 398; Costs 207; Interest 31, 39(2.30).

Hennessey v. State, TexApp–Houston (14 Dist), 732 SW2d 387, petition for discretionary review refused.—Arrest 63.4(2), 63.4(7.1), 63.4(8), 63.4(9), 63.4(16), 63.5(4); Searches 40.1.

Hennessey v. Vanguard Ins. Co., TexApp–Amarillo, 895 SW2d 794, reh overr, and writ den.—Alt Disp Res 501; Antitrust 134, 147, 168, 221; App & E 174, 179(1), 654, 758.1, 934(1); Estop 110; Insurance 3262, 3360; Judgm 181(15.1), 181(23), 185(2), 185.3(12).

Hennessey & Associates, Inc.; Smith v., TexApp–San Antonio, 103 SW3d 567.—Antitrust 138, 162; Judgm 185(4), 185.3(1), 185.3(21).

Hennessey Motorsports, Inc.; T-N-T Motorsports, Inc. v., TexApp–Houston (1 Dist), 965 SW2d 18, reh overr, and petition dism.—Antitrust 413, 417, 418, 419; App & E 874(2), 920(3), 954(1), 954(2); Inj 138.1, 138.3, 138.6, 138.18, 138.33, 147, 163(7); Labor & Emp 121, 305.

Hennessy; Grice v., TexCivApp–San Antonio, 327 SW2d 629.—App & E 688(3), 740(1), 929, 1070(2); Neglig 1683, 1750; Trial 355(1), 358, 426.

Hennessy v. Marshall, TexApp–Dallas, 682 SW2d 340.—Judgm 830.1; Mand 23(1), 26, 32, 178.

Hennessy v. Miller, TexCivApp–Austin, 356 SW2d 818.—Autos 83, 84, 105; Princ & A 97.

Hennessy v. Estate of Perez, TexApp–Houston (1 Dist), 725 SW2d 507.—Judgm 180, 181(33); Neglig 371, 387.

Hennessy v. State, TexCrimApp, 660 SW2d 87.—Controlled Subs 93; Crim Law 394.6(4), 1169.1(8); Searches 115.1, 117.

Hennessy Industries, Inc.; Cantrell v., TexApp–Tyler, 829 SW2d 875, rehden, and writ den, cert den Coats Co v. Cantrell, 113 SCt 2347, 508 US 912, 124 LEd2d 256.—App & E 1031(1), 1043(6); Pretrial Proc 371; Prod Liab 81.1, 87.1.

Hennig, Ex parte, TexCivApp–Dallas, 559 SW2d 401.—Child S 487; Contempt 79; Hab Corp 529, 730.

Hennig v. Gardner, NDTex, 276 FSupp 622.—Social S 142.5, 143.50, 143.55, 143.60.

Hennig; McLennan and Hill Counties Tehuacana Creek Water Control Dist. No. 1 v., TexCivApp–Waco, 469 SW2d 590.—Em Dom 265(3), 265(5).

Hennigan v. Chargers Football Co., CA5 (Tex), 431 F2d 308.—Contracts 143(2), 143.5, 170(1), 176(1), 176(2), 217, 220, 221(1); Evid 448; Fed Cts 786.

Hennigan v. Harris County, TexCivApp–Waco, 593 SW2d 380, ref nre.—App & E 843(1); Atty & C 26, 114; Fraud 3, 16, 60, 61; Judgm 878(1); Plead 406(1).

Hennigan v. Heights Sav. Ass'n, TexCivApp–Hous (1 Dist), 576 SW2d 126, ref nre.—Cons Cred 2, 50; Judgm 185(2); Lim of Act 40(1), 41; Mtg 201, 242.

Hennigan v. Hennigan, Tex, 677 SW2d 495.—Costs 263; Execution 402(1).

Hennigan; Hennigan v., Tex, 677 SW2d 495.—Costs 263; Execution 402(1).

Hennigan v. Hennigan, TexApp–Houston (14 Dist), 666 SW2d 322, dism, ref nre 677 SW2d 495.—Exemp 48(2); Receivers 6, 67.

Hennigan; Hennigan v., TexApp–Houston (14 Dist), 666 SW2d 322, dism, ref nre 677 SW2d 495.—Exemp 48(2); Receivers 6, 67.

Hennigan v. I.P. Petroleum Co., Inc., Tex, 858 SW2d 371.—Civil R 1715; Evid 211; Judgm 185.3(1).

Hennigan v. I.P. Petroleum Co., Inc., TexApp–Beaumont, 848 SW2d 276, writ gr, rev in part 858 SW2d 371.—Civil R 1708; Consp 1.1; Damag 49.10, 50.10; Evid 210; Judgm 185(2), 185.1(4); Labor & Emp 40(2); Lim of Act 127(1).

Hennigan; Jenkins v., TexApp–Beaumont, 298 SW2d 905, ref nre.—App & E 232(3), 1062.1, 1068(1); Autos 245(24); Death 82, 99(2); Evid 508, 555.8(1); Plead 236(3), 236(7); Trial 109, 114, 124, 133.6(1), 133.6(4), 244(4), 352.4(1), 352.21, 366; Witn 255(2.1).

Hennigan; Lee v., CA5 (Tex), 98 FedAppx 286.—Prisons 4(4), 17(1), 17(2); Sent & Pun 1546; U S Mag 21.

Hennigan; South Main Kennel Ass'n v., TexCivApp–Galveston, 100 SW2d 1076.—Gaming 68(0.5).

Hennig Production Co., Inc.; Baker Hughes Oilfield Operations, Inc. v., TexApp–Houston (14 Dist), 164 SW3d 438.—Alt Disp Res 113, 230, 235, 316, 325, 328, 329, 330, 357, 363(8), 374(1), 374(5), 376, 379; Costs 260(1), 260(5), 261; Damag 188(1), 188(2); Interest 39(2.6); Trial 388(2).

Henning v. Cox, CCA5 (Tex), 148 F2d 586.—Fed Cts 930; Joint Adv 1.2(3); Judgm 828.14(7), 828.20(1); Trusts 107.

Henning v. Henning, TexApp–Houston (14 Dist), 889 SW2d 611, reh overr, and writ den.—App & E 497(1), 638; Courts 113; Divorce 151, 183.

Henning; Henning v., TexApp–Houston (14 Dist), 889 SW2d 611, reh overr, and writ den.—App & E 497(1), 638; Courts 113; Divorce 151, 183.

Henning v. Jefferson Standard Life Ins. Co., CCA5 (Tex), 129 F2d 225.—Insurance 2016; Ref of Inst 19(1), 45(14).

Henninger, In re, BkrtcyNDTex, 336 BR 733.—Bankr 2606.1, 2609, 2610, 2612, 2620.

Henninger; Jackson v., TexCivApp–Austin, 482 SW2d 323.—App & E 931(6), 1010.1(3); Deeds 68(1.5), 196(1), 203, 211(1); Parties 59(2).

Hennings; Cravey v., TexApp–San Antonio, 705 SW2d 368.—Ex & Ad 22(1), 22(3), 122(1).

Hennington v. State, TexCrimApp, 149 SW2d 587, 141 TexCrim 449.—Assault 96(1), 96(5); Crim Law 377; Witn 274(2).

Hennington v. State, TexApp–Eastland, 144 SW3d 42, petition for discretionary review refused.—Crim Law 1191; Judges 16(2).

Henpil, Inc.; McCabe v., EDTex, 889 FSupp 983.—Corp 1.4(1), 1.4(2), 1.5(1), 1.5(3), 1.6(13); Damag 50.10; Fed Cts 286.1, 296.1, 300, 316.1, 318; Insurance 1117(4); Joint Adv 1.1, 1.2(1), 7; Labor & Emp 407, 2801; Land & Ten 165(1), 167(1); Neglig 1011, 1037(4); Rem of C 25(1), 36, 107(7); States 18.15, 18.46, 18.47, 18.51; Unemp Comp 10; Work Comp 1045.

Henrich v. State, TexCrimApp, 694 SW2d 341, on remand 697 SW2d 841, petition for discretionary review refused, cert den 107 SCt 3183, 482 US 913, 96 LEd2d 672.—Crim Law 394.1(2).

Henrich v. State, TexApp–Dallas, 697 SW2d 841, petition for discretionary review refused, cert den 107 SCt 3183, 482 US 913, 96 LEd2d 672.—Crim Law 398(1), 412.1(2); Searches 180, 181.

Henrich v. State, TexApp–Dallas, 666 SW2d 185, petition for discretionary review on remand 694 SW2d 341, on remand 697 SW2d 841, petition for discretionary review refused, cert den 107 SCt 3183, 482 US 913, 96 LEd2d 672.—Atty & C 32(2), 32(12); Crim Law 412.2(4).

Henrichson; Holt v., TexCivApp–San Antonio, 321 SW2d 146, ref nre.—Bills & N 400, 422(1).

Henrichson; Simon v., TexCivApp–Corpus Christi, 394 SW2d 249, ref nre.—App & E 1064.1(2.1); Covenants 72.1, 108(2); Decl Judgm 184; Trial 350.3(1), 366.

Henriksen; U.S. v., CA5 (Tex), 564 F2d 197.—Const Law 268(8), 4689; Crim Law 700(10).

Henrickson v. Potter, CA5 (Tex), 327 F3d 444, reh den, cert den 124 SCt 579, 540 US 1018, 157 LEd2d 432.—Civil R 1116(3), 1302, 1505(3), 1505(7).

Henrie; Compton v., Tex, 364 SW2d 179.—App & E 900; Jury 97(1); New Tr 44(2), 56, 140(3); Trial 304.

Henrie v. Compton, TexCivApp–Fort Worth, 357 SW2d 589, rev 364 SW2d 179.—Jury 39, 105(1); New Tr 27, 56.

Henrie; McGeorge v., TexCivApp–Texarkana, 94 SW2d 761.—Mtg 187.1, 193, 199(1), 199(2).

Henrietta Independent School Dist.; Fry v., TexCivApp–Fort Worth, 98 SW2d 245.—App & E 374(2).

Henriksen v. State, TexCrimApp, 500 SW2d 491.—Costs 302.3; Crim Law 339.7(3), 339.11(2), 369.15, 398(1), 599, 627.5(2), 666.5, 822(1), 956(1), 1115(1), 1130(4), 1130(5), 1134(3), 1147, 1166.16; Jury 109.

Henriksen, Inc.; N.L.R.B. v., CA5 (Tex), 481 F2d 1156.—Labor & Emp 1473(1), 1473(4), 1743(1), 1760, 1763, 1773, 1832.

Henrikson v. Guzik, CA5 (Tex), 249 F3d 395.—Prisons 14; Statut 188, 205, 206, 219(1).

Henriquez v. Cemex Management, Inc., TexApp–Houston (1 Dist), 177 SW3d 241, review den.—App & E 179(1), 758.3(11), 852, 854(1); Frds St of 44(3), 113(3), 118(1), 118(4), 158(3); Judgm 185(2), 185(5), 185(6), 185.3(21); Labor & Emp 40(2), 50; Libel 1, 6(1), 10(6), 19, 21, 41, 45(2), 50.5, 51(1), 51(4), 123(2), 123(8).

Henrise v. Horvath, NDTex, 174 FSupp2d 493, aff in part 45 FedAppx 323.—Civil R 1351(1), 1351(5), 1407; Consp 18; Const Law 1446; Mun Corp 185(1).

Henrise v. Horvath, NDTex, 94 FSupp2d 768.—Civil R 1345, 1351(1), 1395(1); Fed Civ Proc 642, 1772.

Henrise v. Horvath, NDTex, 94 FSupp2d 765.—Civil R 1398; Fed Civ Proc 1273.

Henri Studios, Inc.; Ballou v., CA5 (Tex), 656 F2d 1147.—Death 58(2), 77, 97; Evid 150, 188; Fed Cts 416, 823, 871, 901.1, 941.

Henry, Ex parte, Tex, 215 SW2d 588, 147 Tex 315.—Antitrust 940; Const Law 655, 1920, 1921, 1922, 2450;

Contempt 21; Hab Corp 528.1; Inj 110; Labor & Emp 1345(2), 1393, 2020, 2061, 2086.

Henry, Ex parte, Tex, 126 SW2d 1, 132 Tex 575.—Elections 216.1, 293(3), 300; Quo W 55, 58; Witn 21.

Henry, In re, BkrtcyNDTex, 183 BR 748.—Bankr 2766, 2776, 2787, 2789, 2796, 2821.

Henry, In re, Tex, 154 SW3d 594.—Child S 20, 497, 603; Const Law 1106; Contempt 63(1), 64; Divorce 269(3), 269(13), 321.5; Fines 11; Hab Corp 528.1.

Henry v. Aetna Cas. and Sur. Co., TexApp–Texarkana, 633 SW2d 583, ref nre.—Insurance 3164, 3191(2), 3191(4), 3191(10).

Henry v. American Airlines, Inc., TexCivApp–Eastland, 413 SW2d 123.—App & E 1062.2; Carr 318(8); Neglig 1695, 1750.

Henry; Boone v., TexCivApp–Fort Worth, 151 SW2d 323.—App & E 1001(1), 1003(4); Breach of M P 35; Evid 5(2); Trial 120(2), 128, 133.6(6), 252(20).

Henry; Bradley v., TexCivApp–Fort Worth, 239 SW2d 404.—Infants 81, 113; Judgm 681.

Henry v. Cash Today, Inc., SDTex, 199 FRD 566.—Fed Civ Proc 161.2, 163, 164, 172, 174, 182.5.

Henry v. Chubb Lloyds Ins. Co. of Texas, TexApp–Corpus Christi, 895 SW2d 810, reh overr, and writ den.—Courts 100(1); Insurance 3390; Judgm 576(1), 651, 660, 713(2), 720.

Henry; City of Sherman v., Tex, 928 SW2d 464, cert den 117 SCt 1098, 519 US 1156, 137 LEd2d 230.—Admin Law 791; Adultery 1; Const Law 1050, 1065, 1094, 1212, 1213, 1238, 1248, 1258, 1263; Mun Corp 184.1; Offic 72.55(2), 72.70.

Henry; City of Sherman v., TexApp–Dallas, 910 SW2d 542, writ gr, rev 928 SW2d 464, cert den 117 SCt 1098, 519 US 1156, 137 LEd2d 230.—Admin Law 669.1, 744.1, 796; App & E 719(1), 863, 893(1), 1175(1); Const Law 617, 984, 1050, 1053, 1079, 1210, 1214, 1216, 1217, 1253, 1258; Costs 194.16; Judgm 178, 181(2), 181(6), 181(27), 183, 185(2), 185.3(4); Mun Corp 124(1), 184.1; Offic 72.44, 72.70.

Henry; Cline v., TexCivApp–Dallas, 239 SW2d 205, ref nre.—Home 15, 74, 90, 103, 109, 139, 167, 168; Mines 48; Tent in C 1, 35, 37.

Henry v. Cockrell, CA5 (Tex), 327 F3d 429, cert den 124 SCt 408, 540 US 956, 157 LEd2d 293.—Hab Corp 319.1, 382, 818.

Henry v. Cullum Companies, Inc., TexApp–Amarillo, 891 SW2d 789, reh overr, and writ den.—Antitrust 141, 145, 150, 363; Judgm 178, 185(2), 185(6), 215, 277.1, 282.

Henry; Cunningham v., TexCivApp–Texarkana, 231 SW2d 1013, ref nre.—Mun Corp 49, 114, 164; Statut 158, 159.

Henry v. Curb, TexCivApp–Eastland, 430 SW2d 29, ref nre.—Wills 467, 601(8).

Henry v. Custard, TexCivApp–Waco, 213 SW2d 862.—Deeds 38(1), 114(5); Evid 460(7).

Henry; Dallas Bldg. & Loan Ass'n v., TexCivApp–Fort Worth, 98 SW2d 1030, writ dism.—Home 115(1), 122, 129(1), 131; Mental H 375; Tresp to T T 38(3); Trial 317, 397(1).

Henry; Delhi-Taylor Oil Corp. v., Tex, 416 SW2d 390, cert den 88 SCt 592, 389 US 1021, 19 LEd2d 667, reh den 88 SCt 1023, 390 US 975, 19 LEd2d 1192.—Explos 7; Labor & Emp 2901; Neglig 1037(4), 1037(7), 1085, 1205(7).

Henry; Delhi-Taylor Oil Corp. v., TexCivApp–Corpus Christi, 403 SW2d 885, writ gr, rev 416 SW2d 390, cert den 88 SCt 592, 389 US 1021, 19 LEd2d 667, reh den 88 SCt 1023, 390 US 975, 19 LEd2d 1192.—App & E 1064.1(8), 1170.7; Damag 132(7); Explos 7; Neglig 213, 1037(4), 1037(7), 1284, 1286(6), 1313, 1562; Trial 127, 366.

Henry v. Dillard Dept. Stores, Inc., Tex, 70 SW3d 808.—Work Comp 1949.

Henry v. **Dillard Dept. Stores, Inc.**, TexApp–San Antonio, 21 SW3d 414, reh overr, review gr, rev 70 SW3d 808.—Work Comp 999, 1001, 1042.

Henry v. **Estelle**, CA5 (Tex), 688 F2d 407.—Hab Corp 819.

Henry; **Evans v.**, TexCivApp–San Antonio, 230 SW2d 620.—App & E 931(6); Infants 56, 57(1), 102; Trial 82.

Henry v. **Felici**, TexApp–Corpus Christi, 758 SW2d 836, writ den.—App & E 1060.6; Evid 219(3); Health 823(1).

Henry v. **Gentry Plumbing & Heating Co.**, CA5 (Tex), 704 F2d 863.—Work Comp 1029, 1790, 1805, 1809.

Henry; **Glover v.**, TexApp–Eastland, 749 SW2d 502.—App & E 1064.1(9), 1173(2); Evid 383(0.5); Hus & W 254, 256, 264(5), 270(9); Trial 205.

Henry v. **Gonzalez**, TexApp–San Antonio, 18 SW3d 684, reh overr, and review dism by agreement.—Alt Disp Res 114, 134(1), 139, 140, 143, 178, 182(1), 191, 199, 210, 374(7); App & E 893(1), 949; Contracts 143.5, 162; Jury 31.2(1); States 18.15.

Henry v. **Halliburton Energy Services, Inc.**, TexApp–Dallas, 100 SW3d 505, reh overr, and review den.—Alt Disp Res 332, 333, 335, 363(8), 374(1); App & E 846(5), 852, 977(1), 977(5).

Henry; **Haney v.**, TexCivApp–Amarillo, 307 SW2d 649.—Acct Action on 13; Evid 591; Plead 110, 111.18, 111.30, 111.40, 111.42(9); Venue 2, 21, 22(4), 22(6), 31.

Henry; **Hayhurst v.**, NDTex, 102 FSupp 306.—Fed Cts 295; Work Comp 2158, 2223, 2224.

Henry v. **Henry**, TexApp–Houston (14 Dist), 48 SW3d 468.—App & E 931(1), 946, 994(1), 1008.1(2), 1010.1(1), 1010.1(2), 1010.2, 1011.1(2), 1012.1(2), 1012.1(3); Child C 952; Divorce 27(0.5), 27(1), 28, 130, 184(10), 200, 252.3(2), 252.3(4), 252.3(5), 253(2), 282, 286(5), 286(9), 287, 288; Hus & W 265.

Henry; **Henry v.**, TexApp–Houston (14 Dist), 48 SW3d 468.—App & E 931(1), 946, 994(1), 1008.1(2), 1010.1(1), 1010.1(2), 1010.2, 1011.1(2), 1012.1(2), 1012.1(3); Child C 952; Divorce 27(0.5), 27(1), 28, 130, 184(10), 200, 252.3(2), 252.3(4), 252.3(5), 253(2), 282, 286(5), 286(9), 287, 288; Hus & W 265.

Henry v. **Henson**, TexCivApp–Texarkana, 174 SW2d 270, writ refused.—Autos 181(1), 181(2); Statut 226.

Henry v. **Houston Lighting & Power Co.**, TexApp–Houston (1 Dist), 934 SW2d 748, reh overr, and writ den.—App & E 934(1); Gas 20(4); Judgm 185(6); Neglig 202, 371, 379, 380, 383, 387, 423, 431, 432.

Henry v. **Independent American Sav. Ass'n**, CA5 (Tex), 857 F2d 995.—B & L Assoc 48; Fed Cts 681.1; Rem of C 20, 49.1(1), 118.

Henry v. **Insurance Co. of North America**, TexApp–Houston (14 Dist), 879 SW2d 366.—Costs 194.16; Garn 191.

Henry v. **Johnson**, CA5 (Tex), 444 F2d 541, cert den 92 SCt 726, 404 US 1041, 30 LEd2d 734.—Courts 104; Fed Cts 743.

Henry v. **Kaufman County Development Dist. No. 1**, TexApp–Austin, 150 SW3d 498, review gr, and remanded by agreement.—Counties 22, 174, 192; Courts 89; Decl Judgm 44; Drains 66, 67; Mun Corp 405, 956(1); Statut 206; Tax 2060, 3611.

Henry v. **LaGrone**, TexApp–Amarillo, 842 SW2d 324, reh overr.—App & E 946; Courts 483, 484, 486; Mand 28.

Henry v. **Lincoln Income Life Ins. Co.**, TexCivApp–Fort Worth, 405 SW2d 167.—Insurance 1732, 1766, 1785, 1797.

Henry; **Low v.**, Tex, 221 SW3d 609.—App & E 232(0.5), 840(1), 946, 984(1), 1178(6); Atty & C 24; Costs 2; New Tr 152; Plead 16, 53(1).

Henry v. **Low**, TexApp–Corpus Christi, 132 SW3d 180, review gr, rev 221 SW3d 609.—App & E 856(1), 984(1); Atty & C 24; Const Law 4426; Costs 2; Plead 16.

Henry v. **McConnell**, TexCivApp–Waco, 400 SW2d 344.—App & E 719(8); Pat 212(1).

Henry; **Maxwell v.**, SDTex, 815 FSupp 213.—Civil R 1345, 1389, 1394, 1398; Fed Civ Proc 1772, 1829; Libel 48(1), 100(7), 112(2).

Henry v. **Mr. M Convenience Stores, Inc.**, TexCivApp–Hous (14 Dist), 543 SW2d 393, ref nre.—Action 60; App & E 949; Quiet T 10.2, 10.3, 30(3); Spec Perf 97(1), 106(1); Ven & Pur 188.

Henry; **Moore v.**, TexApp–Houston (1 Dist), 960 SW2d 82.—App & E 863; Mand 82; Records 62.

Henry v. **Mrs. Baird's Bakeries, Inc.**, TexCivApp–Fort Worth, 475 SW2d 288, ref nre.—Damag 130.1; Mun Corp 808(1), 818(9), 819(4); Neglig 1635; Witn 404.

Henry; **O'Banion v.**, TexComApp, 96 SW2d 233, 128 Tex 59.—Fraud Conv 57(3), 96(2).

Henry; **Pirtle v.**, TexCivApp–Tyler, 486 SW2d 585, ref nre.—Adv Poss 19, 28, 33, 57, 68, 71(1).

Henry v. **Powers**, TexCivApp–Hous (1 Dist), 447 SW2d 738.—Contracts 143(2), 147(2), 169, 170(1), 175(2), 311; Evid 384, 427, 448, 459(1), 461(1); Joint Ten 6; Trial 105(5).

Henry v. **Premier Healthstaff**, TexApp–Fort Worth, 22 SW3d 124.—Judgm 185(2), 185(5); Lim of Act 105(1).

Henry; **Pritchard v.**, TexCivApp–San Antonio, 200 SW2d 651, ref nre.—Autos 155, 244(36.1); Evid 265(18).

Henry; **Pritchett v.**, TexCivApp–Beaumont, 287 SW2d 546, writ dism.—Trusts 95.

Henry; **Railway Mail Mut. Ben. Ass'n v.**, Tex, 182 SW2d 798, 143 Tex 89.—Courts 107; Evid 20(1); Insurance 1236, 2079.

Henry v. **Railway Mail Mut. Ben. Ass'n**, TexCivApp–Fort Worth, 179 SW2d 333, rev 182 SW2d 798, 143 Tex 89.—Courts 107; Evid 80(1); Insurance 1022, 1126, 1851, 2018, 2079, 3417, 3585.

Henry; **R. B. Butler, Inc. v.**, TexCivApp–Waco, 589 SW2d 190, ref nre.—Adj Land 7; App & E 387(2), 387(6), 395, 846(5), 882(18); Indem 57; Judgm 186.

Henry v. **Reinle**, TexCivApp–Waco, 245 SW2d 743, ref nre.—Hus & W 249(5), 251, 258.

Henry v. **Reno**, TexCivApp–Eastland, 401 SW2d 118, ref nre.—Judgm 807; Proc 71; Venue 7.5(5), 22(5).

Henry v. **Rivera**, TexApp–San Antonio, 783 SW2d 766.—Child C 100, 577, 601, 730, 733, 736, 749.

Henry v. **Rountree**, TexCivApp–Dallas, 354 SW2d 604, ref nre.—Ease 32, 36(1), 36(3).

Henry v. **Rust**, TexCivApp–Beaumont, 85 SW2d 1084, writ dism.—Abate & R 81; App & E 758.3(5); Ex & Ad 22(2); Lim of Act 82.

Henry; **San Antonio Public Service Co. v.**, TexCivApp–San Antonio, 102 SW2d 479.—App & E 994(2), 1005(4); Evid 8.

Henry v. **Schweitzer**, TexCivApp–San Antonio, 435 SW2d 941, ref nre.—Brok 52, 60, 65(6); Contracts 98.

Henry v. **State**, TexCrimApp, 729 SW2d 732.—Courts 100(1); Crim Law 1035(5), 1192; Jury 33(5.20), 120, 121.

Henry v. **State**, TexCrimApp, 567 SW2d 7.—Crim Law 720(7.1); Rob 23(1); Witn 355.

Henry v. **State**, TexCrimApp, 446 SW2d 876.—Crim Law 231.

Henry v. **State**, TexCrimApp, 433 SW2d 430.—Crim Law 339.6, 577, 1038.1(1), 1038.3, 1090.13, 1119(4), 1166(7); Rob 24.15(1); Sent & Pun 312.

Henry v. **State**, TexCrimApp, 300 SW2d 79, 164 TexCrim 199, 164 TexCrim 433.—Crim Law 390, 808.5, 1173.2(3); Homic 1333, 1348, 1371, 1391, 1473.

Henry v. **State**, TexCrimApp, 279 SW2d 877, 162 TexCrim 6.—Crim Law 996(1), 1184(1).

Henry v. **State**, TexCrimApp, 246 SW2d 891, 157 TexCrim 88.—Homic 505, 727, 732, 908, 1155, 1161, 1193, 1325.

Henry v. **State**, TexCrimApp, 237 SW2d 980.—Crim Law 1090.1(1).

Henry v. **State**, TexCrimApp, 207 SW2d 76, 151 TexCrim 284.—Crim Law 413(1), 720(9), 726, 730(8), 763(23),

829(5), 1037.2, 1091(5), 1111(3); Homic 997, 1051(1), 1051(2), 1051(4), 1484.

Henry v. State, TexCrimApp, 194 SW2d 264, 149 Tex-Crim 321.—Crim Law 757(1), 758, 763(1), 829(5).

Henry v. State, TexCrimApp, 149 SW2d 115, 141 Tex-Crim 486.—Crim Law 303.10, 438(5.1), 438(7), 621(2), 770(2), 798.5, 814(1), 1099.10, 1137(1), 1174(2); Riot 1.

Henry v. State, TexCrimApp, 143 SW2d 961, 140 Tex-Crim 143.—Crim Law 1097(1), 1097(4), 1137(5).

Henry v. State, TexCrimApp, 129 SW2d 676.—Crim Law 1182.

Henry v. State, TexCrimApp, 123 SW2d 347, 136 Tex-Crim 22.—Crim Law 778(12), 814(3); Homic 796, 1479, 1484.

Henry v. State, TexCrimApp, 111 SW2d 722, 133 Tex-Crim 435.—Crim Law 1091(11), 1124(1), 1124(3).

Henry v. State, TexCrimApp, 103 SW2d 761, 132 Tex-Crim 196.—Crim Law 784(1).

Henry v. State, TexCrimApp, 103 SW2d 377, 132 Tex-Crim 148.—Crim Law 938(3), 941(2), 945(1); Rape 59(8).

Henry v. State, TexCrimApp, 101 SW2d 1024.—Crim Law 1094(3).

Henry v. State, TexApp–Houston (1 Dist), 916 SW2d 57, petition for discretionary review refused.—Sent & Pun 1238.

Henry v. State, TexApp–Houston (1 Dist), 738 SW2d 332, petition for discretionary review refused.—Crim Law 662.7, 700(1); Homic 1167.

Henry v. State, TexApp–Houston (1 Dist), 728 SW2d 894.—Const Law 2545(4); Crim Law 790.

Henry v. State, TexApp–Fort Worth, 828 SW2d 312, petition for discretionary review refused.—Crim Law 338(7), 369.2(4); Ind & Inf 180.

Henry; State v., TexApp–San Antonio, 25 SW3d 260.—Crim Law 1023(3); Double J 3; Ind & Inf 15(1); Judgm 650, 751.

Henry v. State, TexApp–Dallas, 948 SW2d 338.—Crim Law 1077.3, 1130(3); Larc 23; Sent & Pun 1416.

Henry v. State, TexApp–Beaumont, 732 SW2d 443.—Crim Law 1038.2.

Henry v. State, TexApp–Beaumont, 729 SW2d 362, petition for discretionary review refused.—Crim Law 419(1.5), 438(3); Infants 20.

Henry v. State, TexApp–Corpus Christi, 797 SW2d 281, petition for discretionary review refused.—Crim Law 1144.13(2.1), 1159.2(7); Game 7.

Henry v. State, TexApp–Houston (14 Dist), 800 SW2d 612.—Crim Law 1035(6); Jury 105(4), 131(8), 131(15.1); Rob 1, 6, 24.10.

Henry; Tarrant County Hosp. Dist. v., TexApp–Fort Worth, 52 SW3d 434.—App & E 174, 893(1), 916(1); Civil R 1116(1); Const Law 4426; Counties 129, 141, 143, 146, 215, 222; Courts 4, 35, 37(1); Mand 3(2.1), 4(1), 4(4), 28, 59, 143(2), 190; Mun Corp 254, 723, 723.5, 742(1), 742(4), 854, 1016; Plead 104(1); Pretrial Proc 44.1; States 191.1, 191.4(1), 191.6(2), 191.8(1), 208; Statut 181(1), 188, 190, 223.4.

Henry v. Texas Emp. Ins. Ass'n, TexCivApp–Texarkana, 279 SW2d 614.—App & E 846(2), 846(5); Plead 111.21, 111.39(8), 111.42(10).

Henry v. Texas Tech University, NDTex, 466 FSupp 141.—Civil R 1517, 1520, 1544; Fed Civ Proc 176, 184.10, 186.15; Fed Cts 265, 268.1, 269, 270.

Henry; Toshiba Intern. Corp. v., TexApp–Texarkana, 152 SW3d 774, reh overr.—Hus & W 209(3), 209(4); Prod Liab 5, 6, 8, 10, 11, 14, 24, 48, 75.1.

Henry; Tudor v., TexCivApp–Amarillo, 278 SW2d 874, writ refused.—Frds St of 110(3), 118(1), 125(2); Spec Perf 39.

Henry; U.S. v., CA5 (Tex), 417 F3d 493, cert den 126 SCt 673, 546 US 1025, 163 LEd2d 542.—Crim Law 1042, 1139; Sent & Pun 661, 705.

Henry; U.S. v., CA5 (Tex), 372 F3d 714.—Autos 349(17), 349(18), 349.5(4); Crim Law 1042, 1130(2).

Henry; U.S. v., CA5 (Tex), 288 F3d 657, cert den 123 SCt 224, 537 US 902, 154 LEd2d 176.—Crim Law 273(4.1), 1032(5), 1139; Ind & Inf 55, 60; Sent & Pun 908; Weap 17(1).

Henry; U.S. v., CA5 (Tex), 113 F3d 37.—Crim Law 273.1(4).

Henry; U.S. v., CA5 (Tex), 749 F2d 203.—Crim Law 37(1), 37(3), 37(4), 330, 554, 569, 738, 739.1(1), 739.1(2), 772(6).

Henry; U.S. v., CA5 (Tex), 727 F2d 1373, on reh 749 F2d 203.—Const Law 4286; Controlled Subs 6; Crim Law 37(8), 371(1), 371(12).

Henry; U.S. Cas. Co. v., TexCivApp–Waco, 367 SW2d 405, ref nre.—App & E 863; Work Comp 615, 678, 683, 686, 1564.

Henry v. Walter Bennett, Inc., TexCivApp–El Paso, 135 SW2d 1073, writ dism, correct.—App & E 281(1), 758.3(1), 758.3(9), 758.3(11), 766; Trial 273.

Henry; Weems v., TexCivApp–Fort Worth, 375 SW2d 791.—App & E 554(1).

Henry v. Williams, TexCivApp–Beaumont, 132 SW2d 633.—Home 216; Tresp 67.

Henry; Zable v., TexApp–Dallas, 649 SW2d 136.—Home 118(5), 128.

Henry & Peters, P.C.; Bland v., TexApp–Tyler, 763 SW2d 5, writ den.—Contracts 116(1).

Henry Bldg., Inc.; II Deerfield Ltd. Partnership v., TexApp–San Antonio, 41 SW3d 259, review den.—App & E 863, 930(3), 931(5), 931(8), 970(2), 989, 999(1), 1001(1), 1001(3), 1003(1), 1003(5), 1003(6), 1004(1), 1010.1(1); Compromise 20(1); Contracts 221(1), 221(2), 303(4), 321(1); Costs 194.32; Evid 146; Subrog 1; Trial 43.

Henry C. Beck Co. v. Arcrete, Inc., TexCivApp–Dallas, 515 SW2d 712, dism.—Contracts 29; Corp 503(2); Venue 22(4).

Henry C. Beck Co. v. C. I. R., CA5 (Tex), 433 F2d 309.—Int Rev 3725, 3747.

Henry C. Beck Co.; Jenkins v., Tex, 449 SW2d 454.—Accord 1, 11(2); Judgm 181(19), 185(2).

Henry C. Beck Co.; Jenkins v., TexCivApp–Dallas, 440 SW2d 85, rev 449 SW2d 454.—Accord 7(1), 10(1), 11(2); App & E 267(1), 1073(1).

Henry C. Beck Co.; Ramos v., TexApp–Dallas, 711 SW2d 331.—App & E 173(2); Judgm 181(11), 181(33), 185(2), 185(6), 185.2(1), 185.3(13), 185.3(21); Labor & Emp 40(2), 835; Libel 1, 7(1), 23.1, 44(3), 47, 51(4), 101(4); Pretrial Proc 673.

Henry Hydrocarbon, Inc.; Norman v., TexCivApp–Eastland, 588 SW2d 831.—App & E 781(4).

Henry I. Siegel Co.; Holliday v., TexApp–Houston (14 Dist), 643 SW2d 519, writ gr, aff 663 SW2d 824.—Corp 349; Trial 393(2).

Henry I. Siegel Co., Inc. v. Holliday, Tex, 663 SW2d 824.—Corp 349, 547(4), 628.

Henry P. Roberts Investments, Inc. v. Kelton, TexApp–Corpus Christi, 881 SW2d 952.—Pretrial Proc 358, 373, 379.

Henry Schein, Inc. v. Stromboe, Tex, 102 SW3d 675.—Antitrust 169; App & E 803, 913; Contracts 144; Courts 247(7); Parties 35.1, 35.9, 35.17, 35.31, 35.35, 35.69, 35.71; Pretrial Proc 676; Prod Liab 62; Sales 262; Torts 103.

Henry Schein, Inc. v. Stromboe, TexApp–Austin, 28 SW3d 196, reh overr, and review dism woj, and withdrawn, and reh of petition for review gr, rev 102 SW3d 675.—App & E 913, 949, 1036(1); Contracts 144; Parties 35.9, 35.13, 35.17, 35.33, 35.37, 35.69, 35.71.

Henry's Diner, Inc.; De La Paz v., NDTex, 946 FSupp 484.—Witn 184(1), 196.1.

Henry S. Miller Co.; Albritton v., TexCivApp–Dallas, 608 SW2d 693, ref nre.—Fraud 36; Judgm 181(18), 183, 185.3(7), 185.3(8), 186.

Henry S. Miller Co. v. Bynum, Tex, 836 SW2d 160.—Antitrust 389(1), 390; Pretrial Proc 45, 224, 313.

Henry S. Miller Co. v. Bynum, TexApp–Houston (1 Dist), 797 SW2d 51, writ gr, aff 836 SW2d 160.—Antitrust 198, 389(1), 389(2), 390; App & E 499(1); Brok 102, 106; Pretrial Proc 313.

Henry S. Miller Co. v. Evans, Tex, 452 SW2d 426.—Divorce 255; Evid 390(1), 429; Fraud Conv 210, 213; Hus & W 249(5), 262.1(4), 264(4); Sheriffs 88, 111, 139(2), 143, 170; Trusts 88.

Henry S. Miller Co.; Evans v., TexCivApp–Austin, 413 SW2d 954.—Plead 111.47; Sheriffs 132; Statut 223.4.

Henry S. Miller Co.; Evans v., TexCivApp–Waco, 440 SW2d 317, writ gr, rev 452 SW2d 426.—Evid 390(1), 434(3); Execution 124; Home 190; Sheriffs 106; Trusts 88.

Henry S. Miller Co. v. Hamilton, TexApp–Houston (1 Dist), 813 SW2d 631.—Antitrust 367, 369, 393; App & E 5, 931(1), 1010.1(3), 1010.2; Damag 194; Judgm 17(8).

Henry S. Miller Co. v. Shoaf, TexCivApp–Eastland, 434 SW2d 243, ref nre.—Home 57(3), 216.

Henry S. Miller Co.; Stephens v., TexApp–Dallas, 667 SW2d 250, writ dism by agreement.—Afft 2; App & E 344, 347(1), 395; Judgm 215, 282, 397.

Henry S. Miller Co. v. Stephens, TexCivApp–Dallas, 587 SW2d 491, ref nre, appeal after remand 667 SW2d 250, writ dism by agreement.—Spec Perf 87, 95.

Henry S. Miller Co. v. Treo Enterprises, Tex, 585 SW2d 674.—Brok 3, 42.

Henry S. Miller Co. v. Treo Enterprises, TexCivApp–Texarkana, 573 SW2d 553, aff 585 SW2d 674.—Bills & N 129(2); Brok 42, 82(4); Corp 383.

Henry S. Miller Co. v. Ulmer, SDTex, 701 FSupp 598.—Brok 71.

Henry S. Miller Co.; Vail v., TexCivApp–Dallas, 592 SW2d 410.—Contracts 176(2); Evid 448; Joint Adv 2.

Henry S. Miller Co.; Wood v., Tex, 597 SW2d 332.—Mtg 123, 209, 375; Subrog 12.

Henry S. Miller Co. v. Wood, TexCivApp–Texarkana, 584 SW2d 302, aff 597 SW2d 332.—App & E 841; Mtg 123, 209, 372(1), 375; Subrog 31(4); Trial 368.

Henry S. Miller Management Corp. v. Houston State Associates, TexApp–Houston (1 Dist), 792 SW2d 128, writ den.—Action 60; Antitrust 367; App & E 151(6), 756, 760(1), 766; Judgm 199(3.10), 252(1); Land & Ten 34(2).

Henry S. Miller Management, Corp.; Story v., TexApp–Houston (1 Dist), 630 SW2d 839.—App & E 223; Judgm 185(4), 186.

Henry S. Miller Realty Trust v. Bobby McGees Conglomeration of Dallas, Inc., TexCivApp–Dallas, 582 SW2d 566, ref nre.—Land & Ten 200.3.

Henry S. Miller Residential Service Corp. v. Arthur, TexApp–Dallas, 671 SW2d 670.—App & E 994(3), 1008.1(4), 1010.1(3), 1011.1(1); Brok 53.

Henry S. Miller Residential Services, Inc.; Klein v., NDTex, 94 FRD 651.—Antitrust 535, 963(1), 977(1), 984; Fed Civ Proc 161, 164, 165, 181.5.

Henry S. Miller Residential Services, Inc.; Klein v., NDTex, 82 FRD 6.—Atty & C 66; Champ 4(1); Compromise 66.1; Const Law 3981; Fed Civ Proc 164, 1600(2), 2737.13.

Henry Wu, Inc. v. Rex Machinery Movers, Inc., TexApp–El Paso, 802 SW2d 96, writ den.—Costs 2; Pretrial Proc 44.1, 314, 316, 434, 435.

Hensarling, In re, TexCivApp–Tyler, 590 SW2d 639.—App & E 930(3), 989, 1003(4); Evid 570, 588; Wills 31, 155.1, 324(2), 324(3).

Hensarling v. Southern States Life Ins. Co., TexCivApp–Waco, 269 SW2d 555, ref nre.—App & E 879; Estop 52(1); Mtg 37(2), 38(1), 183, 335.

Hensarling v. State, TexCrimApp, 829 SW2d 168.—Witn 71.

Hensarling; Thrasher v., TexCivApp–Waco, 406 SW2d 515.—App & E 596, 694(1), 907(3), 907(4).

Henschen v. City of Houston, Tex., CA5 (Tex), 959 F2d 584.—Civil R 1395(1), 1456, 1462; Const Law 2602; Fed Cts 12.1, 13, 13.10.

Henshaw v. Kroenecke, Tex, 656 SW2d 416, on remand 671 SW2d 117, ref nre.—Contracts 116(1), 142; Damag 80(1); Partners 230; Trial 105(4).

Henshaw v. Kroenecke, TexApp–Houston (1 Dist), 671 SW2d 117, ref nre.—App & E 1079; Partners 263.

Henshaw v. Texas Emp. Ins. Ass'n, TexCivApp–Amarillo, 282 SW2d 928, ref nre.—Work Comp 719, 1922, 1927, 1929.

Henshaw v. Texas Natural Resources Foundation, Tex, 216 SW2d 566, 147 Tex 436.—Contracts 170(1), 261(1), 318; Mines 101.

Henshaw v. Texas Natural Resources Foundation, TexCivApp–San Antonio, 212 SW2d 241, rev 216 SW2d 566, 147 Tex 436.—Estates 1; Trusts 1, 136.

Henslee; Acrey v., TexCivApp–Amarillo, 279 SW2d 925.—Execution 258, 275(3); Sheriffs 120.

Henslee v. Alexander, TexCivApp–Eastland, 469 SW2d 318.—Hus & W 268(9), 270(2); Lim of Act 124.

Henslee; Bowman v., TexCivApp–Fort Worth, 373 SW2d 292, ref nre.—Judgm 185.3(17).

Henslee; Daniel v., TexCivApp–Dallas, 94 SW2d 197.—App & E 1177(1); Plead 111.3.

Henslee v. First Nat. Bank of Whitewright, TexCivApp–Dallas, 314 SW2d 881.—App & E 707(2); Bills & N 245, 250; Evid 403; Judgm 181(25); Plead 258(3); Princ & S 190(6).

Henslee v. State, TexCivApp–Dallas, 375 SW2d 474, ref nre.—App & E 395, 733, 767(2); Em Dom 202(4), 254, 257.

Henslee v. U.S., CA5 (Tex), 262 F2d 750, cert den 79 SCt 942, 359 US 984, 3 LEd2d 933.—Crim Law 4, 113; False Pret 11; Fraud 69(1); Ind & Inf 75(1); States 4.19.

Henslee v. U.S., CA5 (Tex), 246 F2d 190.—Crim Law 925.5(1), 925.5(4).

Hensler, In re, TexApp–Waco, 27 SW3d 719.—Mand 156.

Hensler v. District Four Grievance Committee of State Bar of Texas, CA5 (Tex), 790 F2d 390.—Fed Cts 41, 55.

Hensley, Ex parte, TexCrimApp, 285 SW2d 720, 162 TexCrim 348.—Controlled Subs 6; Statut 63, 135.

Hensley, Ex parte, TexCrimApp, 145 SW2d 573, 140 TexCrim 450.—Hab Corp 526.

Hensley v. Amber Sky, Inc., TexApp–Beaumont, 624 SW2d 774.—Pretrial Proc 698.

Hensley v. City Bank & Trust Co., TexCivApp–Tyler, 495 SW2d 282, ref nre.—App & E 931(1), 1010.1(1), 1011.1(4), 1177(7); Bills & N 491, 516.

Hensley; Cleveland v., TexCivApp–Texarkana, 548 SW2d 473.—Evid 165(2), 273(2), 427; Land & Ten 66(1), 66(2), 66(3).

Hensley; Cullen Center Bank & Trust v., CA5 (Tex), 102 F3d 1411. See Criswell, Matter of.

Hensley v. Fort Worth & D. Ry. Co., TexCivApp–Fort Worth, 408 SW2d 761, ref nre, cert den 88 SCt 51, 389 US 823, 19 LEd2d 75.—App & E 1067; Labor & Emp 2887; Neglig 1619, 1620, 1695; Trial 199, 352.1(9).

Hensley; Gossett v., TexCivApp–Dallas, 94 SW2d 903.—App & E 882(1); Courts 1; Mines 100; Partners 325(2).

Hensley v. Hensley, TexCivApp–El Paso, 496 SW2d 929.—Divorce 252.1, 252.2, 286(5).

Hensley; Hensley v., TexCivApp–El Paso, 496 SW2d 929.—Divorce 252.1, 252.2, 286(5).

Hensley v. Jones, TexCivApp–Hous (14 Dist), 492 SW2d 283.—App & E 1151(1); Bills & N 516, 534; Judgm 185(4).

Hensley v. Lubbock Nat. Bank, TexCivApp–Amarillo, 561 SW2d 885.—App & E 901, 927(7); Cons Cred 4, 33.1; Damag 163(1); Evid 265(1); Fraud 28; Sec Tran 230, 242.1; Trial 139.1(7), 141.

Hensley; Millers Mut. Fire Ins. Co. of Tex. v., TexCiv-App–Fort Worth, 414 SW2d 488.—Insurance 1806, 1810, 1814, 1832(1), 1836, 1877, 1929(2), 1935.

Hensley v. Salinas, Tex, 583 SW2d 617.—App & E 302(1); Judgm 72; New Tr 157.

Hensley v. Salinas, TexCivApp–Waco, 577 SW2d 383, rev 583 SW2d 617.—App & E 554(1); Judgm 72; New Tr 140(1), 157.

Hensley; State v., TexCrimApp, 866 SW2d 28, on remand 1994 WL 88047.—Crim Law 1072, 1181(2), 1192; Double J 132.1.

Hensley v. State, TexCrimApp, 851 SW2d 867, on remand 858 SW2d 13, review gr, vac 866 SW2d 28, on remand 1994 WL 88047.—Crim Law 1181.5(3.1).

Hensley v. State, TexCrimApp, 494 SW2d 816.—Crim Law 394.4(13); Searches 62, 165; Sent & Pun 1400.

Hensley v. State, TexCrimApp, 388 SW2d 424, cert den 86 SCt 173, 382 US 882, 15 LEd2d 122.—Crim Law 371(9), 372(7), 507(7); Infants 20.

Hensley v. State, TexCrimApp, 224 SW2d 245, 153 TexCrim 616.—Crim Law 875(3), 875(4), 881(2), 881(3), 1081(1).

Hensley v. State, TexCrimApp, 202 SW2d 675.—Crim Law 1090.1(1).

Hensley; State v., TexApp–Beaumont, 858 SW2d 13, review gr, vac 866 SW2d 28, on remand 1994 WL 88047.—Crim Law 1181.5(3.1).

Hensley; State v., TexApp–Beaumont, 810 SW2d 20, petition for discretionary review gr, vac 851 SW2d 867, on remand 858 SW2d 13, review gr, vac 866 SW2d 28, on remand 1994 WL 88047.—Double J 142.

Hensley; Tondre v., TexCivApp–San Antonio, 223 SW2d 671.—App & E 1122(2), 1175(5); Elections 83; Evid 158(19); Schools 38; Tax 2054; Trial 83(3).

Hensley v. United Transports, Inc., NDTex, 346 FSupp 1108.—Fed Cts 14.1, 16, 202; Labor & Emp 1213, 1214, 1219(10), 1219(12), 1319, 1321; Lim of Act 24(1), 39(1).

Hensley; Wiggins v., TexCivApp–Beaumont, 114 SW2d 914, writ dism.—Costs 216, 220; Judgm 314.

Hensley; Wiggins v., TexCivApp–Beaumont, 90 SW2d 572, writ dism.—Deeds 38(1); Tresp to T T 6.1, 41(1).

Hensley Elec. Steel Co., Inc.; International Ins. Co. in New York v., TexCivApp–Waco, 497 SW2d 64.—Autos 1; Insurance 2136(5).

Hensley Enterprises, Inc. v. Great Southwest Fire Ins., TexCivApp–Eastland, 499 SW2d 742.—Insurance 3054(1), 3072; Trial 284, 350.4(3), 366.

Hensley Equipment Co. v. Esco Corp., CA5 (Tex), 386 F2d 442.—Pat 324.60.

Hensley Equipment Co. v. Esco Corp., CA5 (Tex), 383 F2d 252, am, reh den 386 F2d 442.—Antitrust 587(1), 587(2), 587(3), 682, 732; Decl Judgm 323; Pat 3, 16.17, 36.1(3), 36.2(9), 46, 66(1.19), 167(1), 191, 255, 283(1), 310.8, 324.55(5).

Hensley Equipment Co.; Esco Corp. v., NDTex, 251 FSupp 631, aff in part, rev in part 383 F2d 252, am, reh den 386 F2d 442.—Antitrust 977(2), 977(3); Decl Judgm 323; Equity 65(1); Pat 16.1, 16.14, 17(1), 36.2(9), 37, 74, 112.1, 222, 234, 255, 286, 312(6), 319(1), 328(2).

Henson, Ex parte, TexCrimApp, 731 SW2d 97.—Sent & Pun 1168.

Henson, Ex parte, TexCrimApp, 639 SW2d 700.—Hab Corp 670(1), 689, 729.

Henson, Ex parte, TexCrimApp, 408 SW2d 233.—Extrad 36.

Henson, Ex parte, TexCrimApp, 278 SW2d 166, 161 TexCrim 427.—Sent & Pun 1132.

Henson, Ex parte, TexApp–Texarkana, 131 SW3d 645.—Bail 39, 51, 52; Crim Law 1148.

Henson, Guardianship of, TexCivApp–Corpus Christi, 551 SW2d 136, ref nre.—App & E 934(1), 989, 1024.4; Guard & W 1, 10, 11, 13(1), 13(8); Judgm 199(3.10).

Henson, In re, TexApp–Texarkana, 120 SW3d 926.—Mand 1, 3(2.1), 12, 60.

Henson v. American Eagle Ins. Co., TexApp–Fort Worth, 832 SW2d 145, reh overr.—Insurance 1867, 3419.

Henson v. B & W Finance Co., TexCivApp–Tyler, 401 SW2d 261.—Evid 568(1); Land & Ten 190(1), 195(2), 231(1).

Henson v. Barnhart, EDTex, 373 FSupp2d 674.—Social S 142.10, 143.60, 143.65, 147, 147.5, 148.15.

Henson v. Bell Helicopter Textron, Inc., CA5 (Tex), 128 FedAppx 387.—Civil R 1218(6), 1505(7); Labor & Emp 355, 386.

Henson v. Brown, TexCivApp–Austin, 524 SW2d 412.—Child 37.

Henson v. Citizens Bank of Irving, TexCivApp–Eastland, 549 SW2d 446.—Pretrial Proc 226.

Henson v. City of Corpus Christi, TexCivApp–San Antonio, 258 SW2d 343, writ refused.—Judgm 181(32); Tax 2837.

Henson; Connecticut Indem. Co. v., TexCivApp–Houston, 388 SW2d 300.—Work Comp 840, 849, 1490, 1491, 1633, 1639, 1653, 1724.

Henson v. Estate of Crow, Tex, 734 SW2d 648.—Ex & Ad 420.

Henson v. Denison, TexCivApp–Fort Worth, 546 SW2d 898.—Const Law 975; Inj 126, 132, 157; Land & Ten 277(0.5); Nuis 59, 80, 84.

Henson v. Ellis, CA5 (Tex), 217 F2d 134.—Hab Corp 818.

Henson v. Ellis, CA5 (Tex), 199 F2d 952, cert den 73 SCt 499, 344 US 930, 97 LEd 715, cert den 75 SCt 541, 348 US 976, 99 LEd 760.—Hab Corp 818.

Henson v. Estelle, CA5 (Tex), 641 F2d 250, reh den 645 F2d 71, cert den 102 SCt 603, 454 US 1056, 70 LEd2d 593.—Hab Corp 603, 706, 768, 864(1).

Henson v. Grayford Oil Corp. (Oil & Gas Energy, Inc.), TexCivApp–Dallas, 549 SW2d 7, ref nre.—Action 70; Contracts 52, 309(1); Corp 187, 190, 404(1); Elect of Rem 11; Spec Perf 4, 117.

Henson; Great Southwest Life Ins. Co. v., TexCivApp–El Paso, 401 SW2d 89, ref nre.—App & E 758.1; Insurance 1747.

Henson; Henry v., TexCivApp–Texarkana, 174 SW2d 270, writ refused.—Autos 181(1), 181(2); Statut 226.

Henson v. Henson, TexCivApp–Austin, 181 SW2d 285.—Venue 7.5(3), 8.5(1), 8.5(2), 8.5(7).

Henson; Henson v., TexCivApp–Austin, 181 SW2d 285.—Venue 7.5(3), 8.5(1), 8.5(2), 8.5(7).

Henson v. Jarmon, TexApp–Tyler, 758 SW2d 368.—Child 82; Const Law 3184; Des & Dist 74.

Henson; Lowe v., TexCivApp–Amarillo, 190 SW2d 423.—Alt of Inst 5(1), 16, 29; App & E 931(1), 1010.1(1), 1011.1(6).

Henson; McCarty v., CA5 (Tex), 749 F2d 1134.—Const Law 1482; Schools 53(1).

Henson; Prudential Ins. Co. of America v., TexApp–Eastland, 753 SW2d 415.—Contrib 9(5); Trial 352.1(1), 352.1(6).

Henson; Rains County v., TexCivApp–Amarillo, 183 SW2d 689, writ refused.—Courts 90(1); Evid 43(3); Pub Lands 173(14); Ven & Pur 181.

Henson; Socony Vacuum Oil Co. v., TexCivApp, 183 SW2d 256, writ refused.—Seamen 29(5.14).

Henson v. Southern Farm Bureau Cas. Ins. Co., Tex, 17 SW3d 652.—Insurance 2793(1), 2816; Interest 39(2.35).

Henson v. Southwest Airlines Co., TexApp–Dallas, 180 SW3d 841, reh overr, and review den, cert den 127 SCt 258, 166 LEd2d 201.—Carr 408(1); Mal Pros 0.7; States 18.3, 18.5, 18.15, 18.21.

Henson v. State, TexCrimApp, 683 SW2d 702.—Crim Law 713, 720(5), 721(3).

Henson; State v., TexCrimApp, 573 SW2d 548.—Courts 39, 247(2).

Henson v. State, TexCrimApp, 530 SW2d 584.—Crim Law 577, 1035(1), 1130(2), 1181.5(9).

Henson v. State, TexCrimApp, 502 SW2d 719.—Controlled Subs 75, 115; Searches 65.

Henson v. State, TexCrimApp, 452 SW2d 448.—Assault 96(7); Crim Law 531(2), 531(3), 589(1), 627.8(5), 1151.

Henson v. State, TexCrimApp, 275 SW2d 651, 161 TexCrim 177.—Autos 358; Crim Law 749.

Henson v. State, TexCrimApp, 266 SW2d 864, 159 TexCrim 647.—Crim Law 388.2, 393(1), 519(1), 519(3), 519(8), 522(1), 531(3), 532(0.5), 730(7), 1184(4.1).

Henson v. State, TexCrimApp, 252 SW2d 711, 158 TexCrim 5.—Weap 17(4).

Henson v. State, TexCrimApp, 217 SW2d 415.—Crim Law 1094(3).

Henson v. State, TexCrimApp, 207 SW2d 386, 151 TexCrim 297.—Burg 41(1); Crim Law 394.5(2).

Henson v. State, TexCrimApp, 201 SW2d 56, 150 TexCrim 340.—Crim Law 1092.4, 1092.8.

Henson v. State, TexCrimApp, 200 SW2d 1007, 150 TexCrim 344.—Crim Law 379, 695(5), 938(1), 939(1), 944, 945(1), 945(2), 958(1), 1156(3), 1169.5(5), 1176; Homic 1004.

Henson v. State, TexCrimApp, 160 SW2d 258, 143 TexCrim 628.—Crim Law 598(6), 603.2, 1092.11(3); Rob 24.10.

Henson v. State, TexCrimApp, 135 SW2d 999, 138 TexCrim 362.—Burg 45; Crim Law 605, 911, 913(3), 1156(1).

Henson v. State, TexCrimApp, 116 SW2d 393, 134 TexCrim 472.—Crim Law 369.1, 586, 594(4), 1151; Weap 6.

Henson v. State, TexCrimApp, 81 SW2d 680, 128 TexCrim 402.—Crim Law 1077.2(3), 1097(6), 1101.

Henson v. State, TexApp–Houston (1 Dist), 734 SW2d 119, petition for discretionary review refused.—Crim Law 641.13(2.1), 641.13(7); Sent & Pun 1379(2).

Henson v. State, TexApp–Houston (1 Dist), 638 SW2d 504.—Crim Law 304(1), 1038.1(1), 1038.1(2), 1038.1(4), 1038.1(5), 1166.16; Jury 83(1); Sent & Pun 1064, 1129, 1139.

Henson v. State, TexApp–Dallas, 794 SW2d 385, petition for discretionary review refused, appeal after remand 1992 WL 76510, petition for discretionary review refused.—Crim Law 412.1(1), 412.1(2), 412.1(4), 519(3), 519(9), 1134(2), 1159.2(2), 1165(1), 1169.1(1), 1177; Homic 1184, 1186; Sent & Pun 308, 309, 312, 318.

Henson v. State, TexApp–El Paso, 885 SW2d 485.—Extrad 36, 39.

Henson v. State, TexApp–Tyler, 173 SW3d 92, petition for discretionary review refused.—Crim Law 44, 552(1), 1030(1), 1030(2), 1035(6), 1130(5), 1144.13(1), 1152(2), 1166.16, 1166.18; Infants 13, 20; Jury 85, 97(1), 107, 131(1), 131(2), 131(3), 131(8), 131(13).

Henson v. State, TexApp–Corpus Christi, 915 SW2d 186. —Atty & C 11(1); Crim Law 388.2, 394.1(2), 394.5(4), 394.6(4), 475.2(2), 486(8), 511.1(8), 511.2, 553, 641.1, 641.13(1), 641.13(2.1), 641.13(4), 641.13(6), 742(2), 822(1), 1038.2, 1134(2), 1139, 1144.13(2.1), 1153(1), 1158(4), 1159.2(7), 1159.4(2), 1166.10(1), 1172.1(1), 1173.2(1), 1173.2(6); Searches 23, 24, 165, 171, 172, 174, 180, 186.

Henson v. State, TexApp–Houston (14 Dist), 650 SW2d 432, aff 683 SW2d 702.—Crim Law 721(5), 1134(3), 1169.2(3); Jury 149; Sent & Pun 2010.

Henson; Texas Dept. of Transp. v., TexApp–Houston (14 Dist), 843 SW2d 648, reh den, and writ den.—Autos 279; Neglig 1040(3).

Henson; Texas Emp. Ins. Ass'n v., TexCivApp–Beaumont, 569 SW2d 516.—Pretrial Proc 202; Work Comp 1389, 1703, 1968(3).

Henson v. Texas Farm Bureau Mut. Ins. Co., TexApp–Amarillo, 989 SW2d 837, reh overr, and review gr, aff 17 SW3d 652.—Insurance 2782; Interest 39(2.35).

Henson; Texas Indem. Ins. Co. v., TexCivApp–Beaumont, 172 SW2d 113, writ refused.—Work Comp 1103, 1424.

Henson v. Tom, TexCivApp–Texarkana, 473 SW2d 258, ref nre.—App & E 927(7), 989; Health 631, 674, 823(7); Venue 21, 50, 72.

Henson v. U.S., SDTex, 338 FSupp 599.—Int Rev 3340, 3377, 5095.

Henson-El v. Rogers, CA5 (Tex), 923 F2d 51, cert den 111 SCt 2863, 501 US 1235, 115 LEd2d 1030.—Civil R 1379; Const Law 2789; Fed Civ Proc 2734; Lim of Act 6(1).

Hensz v. Linnstaedt, TexCivApp–Corpus Christi, 501 SW2d 463.—Adv Poss 11, 13, 42, 68, 112, 114(1); Judgm 181(2).

Henthorn v. Swinson, CA5 (Tex), 955 F2d 351, cert den 112 SCt 2974, 504 US 988, 119 LEd2d 593.—Fed Civ Proc 2734; Prisons 4(9), 4(10.1), 4(12), 9.

Henthorn; Texas Emp. Ins. Ass'n v., TexCivApp–Amarillo, 240 SW2d 392, ref nre.—App & E 1170.1; Damag 221(5.1); Evid 54; Trial 350.2, 350.5(4); Work Comp 1922, 1974.

Henthorn v. Tyler, TexCivApp–Amarillo, 266 SW2d 484. —Child C 719, 766; Domicile 5; Evid 35.

Henthorn; U.S. v., CA5 (Tex), 815 F2d 304.—Const Law 257.5, 4523; Crim Law 369.2(3.1), 371(1), 622.2(8), 706(2), 1148; Jury 131(17).

Henton, Ex parte, TexCrimApp, 468 SW2d 850.—Hab Corp 469.

Henton v. State, TexApp–Houston (1 Dist), 893 SW2d 165.—Crim Law 552(3), 553, 1144.13(3), 1159.2(1), 1159.2(7), 1159.6; Sent & Pun 1840, 1848, 1902.

Hentzen v. Oldt, TexCivApp–Dallas, 298 SW2d 272.— Plead 111.42(3), 252(2).

Henwood; Attebery v., TexCivApp–Texarkana, 177 SW2d 95, writ refused wom.—R R 307.3, 307.4(1), 402; Trial 350.6(4), 352.4(8).

Henwood v. Bennett, TexCivApp–Texarkana, 154 SW2d 922, writ refused wom.—App & E 1175(5); R R 329, 335(1).

Henwood v. Gary, TexCivApp–Fort Worth, 196 SW2d 958, ref nre.—Labor & Emp 2862; Trial 350.6(6), 352.1(1).

Henwood v. Gilliam, TexCivApp–Dallas, 207 SW2d 904, writ refused.—App & E 930(1), 1001(1); Neglig 231, 503, 1717; R R 328(8), 346(5.1), 350(1), 350(26).

Henwood v. Kolb, TexCivApp–Eastland, 157 SW2d 947.— App & E 66, 78(6).

Henwood; McCasland v., TexCivApp–Texarkana, 213 SW2d 555, ref nre.—App & E 1001(1), 1010.1(3), 1069.1; Evid 380, 383(10).

Henwood; Massingill v., TexComApp, 159 SW2d 118, 138 Tex 317.—App & E 966(1), 1062.1, 1067; Neglig 1741; R R 348(1), 348(4), 348(5), 350(7.1), 350(11), 350(12); Trial 219.

Henwood v. Massingill, TexCivApp–Beaumont, 138 SW2d 554, rev 159 SW2d 118, 138 Tex 317.—R R 350(32), 351(21).

Henwood v. Moore, TexCivApp–Texarkana, 203 SW2d 973.—App & E 1004(8), 1151(2); Damag 95, 132(1), 216(4); New Tr 74.

Henwood v. Neal, TexCivApp–Amarillo, 198 SW2d 125.— App & E 930(1), 989, 994(2), 996, 1001(1), 1003(3); Labor & Emp 2842, 2881; Trial 315.

Henwood v. Polis & Hagan, TexCivApp–San Antonio, 231 SW2d 720.—App & E 994(3), 995; Bankr 2152.1; Carr 134, 135; Plead 36(3).

Henwood v. Richardson, TexCivApp–Texarkana, 163 SW2d 256, writ refused wom.—App & E 231(1), 1064.1(5); Death 41; R R 346(6), 348(8); Trial 133.6(7), 351.5(2).

Henwood; Tye v., TexCivApp–Texarkana, 153 SW2d 184, writ refused wom.—Labor & Emp 2879, 2881.

Henwood; Vanover v., TexComApp, 150 SW2d 785, 136 Tex 348.—App & E 878(1), 878(4), 930(3); R R 277.5; Trial 232(2), 356(3).

Henwood v. Vanover, TexCivApp–Fort Worth, 126 SW2d 1036, rev 150 SW2d 785, 136 Tex 348.—Plead 216(1); R R 277.5, 282(1.1); Trial 356(3).

Henwood; Webster v., TexCivApp–Waco, 134 SW2d 333. —Neglig 1579; R R 346(1), 346(7), 350(32).

Henwood; Wilson v., TexCivApp–Amarillo, 337 SW2d 194, ref nre.—Judgm 181(6), 540, 627, 678(1), 678(2); Release 55.

Hepner v. State, TexApp–Austin, 966 SW2d 153.—Crim Law 334, 338(7), 388.1, 388.2, 469.1, 494, 552(3), 671, 1043(3), 1045, 1153(1), 1169.1(7); Homic 1165, 1184.

Hepperle v. Johnston, CA5 (Tex), 590 F2d 609.—Fed Civ Proc 1366, 1758.1; Fed Cts 818, 893; Judges 49(1), 51(3), 51(4).

Hepperle v. Johnston, CA5 (Tex), 544 F2d 201.—Fed Civ Proc 1754, 1771, 1773; Lim of Act 55(6).

Hepperle v. Southern Methodist University, CA5 (Tex), 526 F2d 1257.—Courts 104; Fed Cts 557, 660.5.

Hepworth v. State, TexCrimApp, 120 SW2d 250, 135 TexCrim 301.—Forg 44(0.5), 44(2).

Hera; Voelker v., TexCivApp–Texarkana, 616 SW2d 647. —Bills & N 137(1), 139(1), 139(2); Judgm 181(26), 185(2).

Herald v. State, TexApp–Amarillo, 67 SW3d 292.—Crim Law 1144.17, 1147; Sent & Pun 2003, 2020.

Herald-Post Pub. Co. v. Hervey, TexCivApp–El Paso, 282 SW2d 410, ref nre.—Libel 4, 6(1), 10(1), 10(3), 19, 123(2).

Herald-Post Pub. Co., Inc. v. Hill, Tex, 891 SW2d 638.— App & E 1175(1); Libel 123(8).

Herald-Post Pub. Co.; Hill v., TexApp–El Paso, 877 SW2d 774, reh den, and writ gr, aff in part, rev in part 891 SW2d 638.—App & E 173(2), 863; Judgm 185(2); Libel 1, 9(3), 19, 21, 33, 38(1), 38(5), 49, 51(2), 55, 123(2).

Herald Pub. Co., Inc.; Kantor v., TexApp–Tyler, 645 SW2d 625, ref nre.—App & E 989; Judgm 335(1), 335(2), 335(3); New Tr 82; Princ & A 177(1).

Herald Pub. Co., Inc.; Kantor v., TexApp–Tyler, 632 SW2d 656.—App & E 462.1, 469; Courts 207.3, 207.5; Execution 16; Judgm 335(4); Supersed 1.

Heras v. State, TexApp–El Paso, 786 SW2d 72.—Crim Law 641.13(2.1), 1130(6), 1167(1); Ind & Inf 69, 166, 184.

Herbage v. Snoddy, TexApp–Houston (1 Dist), 864 SW2d 695, reh den, and writ den.—App & E 662(4), 842(2), 1008.1(1), 1008.1(2); Ven & Pur 79.

Herber v. Sanders, TexCivApp–Amarillo, 336 SW2d 783. —Contracts 176(10); Mines 53, 54(2), 55(2); Spec Perf 101; Ven & Pur 18(3), 78.

Herberger; Haase v., TexApp–Houston (14 Dist), 44 SW3d 267.—Atty & C 112, 113, 153.

Herberger v. Shanbaum, CA5 (Tex), 897 F2d 801, cert den 111 SCt 60, 498 US 817, 112 LEd2d 35.—Exemp 49.

Herberger v. Shanbaum, CA5 (Tex), 853 F2d 1307. See McLaughlin v. Lindemann.

Herberman, In re, BkrtcyWDTex, 122 BR 273.—Bankr 2558, 3008.1, 3021, 3026, 3151, 3622; Const Law 1102; Fed Civ Proc 131.

Herberman; U.S. v., CA5 (Tex), 583 F2d 222.—Crim Law 113, 633(1), 700(2.1), 713, 719(1), 719(3), 753.2(3.1), 753.2(6), 1144.13(2.1); Fraud 68.10(3), 69(5).

Herbers; Harris v., TexApp–Houston (1 Dist), 838 SW2d 938.—Adop 9.1; App & E 1010.1(1), 1010.1(5); Const Law 82(10); Infants 155, 156, 178, 179.

Herbert v. City of Forest Hill, TexApp–Fort Worth, 189 SW3d 369.—Civil R 1118, 1128, 1137, 1138, 1243, 1251, 1252, 1743, 1744; Courts 97(5); Mun Corp 185(1).

Herbert v. City of Wichita Falls, Tex., CA5 (Tex), 48 F3d 919. See York v. City of Wichita Falls, Tex.

Herbert; Collins v., TexCivApp–Galveston, 219 SW2d 814, ref nre.—Adv Poss 114(1); App & E 846(2), 846(5); Frds St of 142; Ref of Inst 19(1), 45(4.1).

Herbert v. Greater Gulf Coast Enterprises, Inc., Tex-App–Houston (1 Dist), 915 SW2d 866, reh overr.—App

& E 859, 914(1), 931(1), 1010.1(3), 1010.2, 1178(1); Const Law 3964, 3967; Courts 15; Damag 94, 194; Impl & C C 30, 55; Judgm 112; Mech Liens 115(1); Proc 64, 134.

Herbert v. Gulf Coast Enterprises, TexApp–Houston (1 Dist), 915 SW2d 866. See Herbert v. Greater Gulf Coast Enterprises, Inc.

Herbert v. Herbert, Tex, 754 SW2d 141, on remand 774 SW2d 1, writ den.—App & E 999(1), 1003(5), 1094(1); Divorce 286(8).

Herbert; Herbert v., Tex, 754 SW2d 141, on remand 774 SW2d 1, writ den.—App & E 999(1), 1003(5), 1094(1); Divorce 286(8).

Herbert v. Herbert, TexApp–Fort Worth, 774 SW2d 1, writ den.—App & E 989, 1003(5), 1003(7); Spec Perf 121(11); Trial 365.1(1).

Herbert; Herbert v., TexApp–Fort Worth, 774 SW2d 1, writ den.—App & E 989, 1003(5), 1003(7); Spec Perf 121(11); Trial 365.1(1).

Herbert v. Herbert, TexApp–Fort Worth, 699 SW2d 717, ref nre, and writ gr, and writ withdrawn, rev 754 SW2d 141, on remand 774 SW2d 1, writ den.—App & E 93, 758.3(1), 846(5), 1012.1(5); Divorce 177, 179, 254(2), 255; Hus & W 279(1), 281.

Herbert; Herbert v., TexApp–Fort Worth, 699 SW2d 717, ref nre, and writ gr, and writ withdrawn, rev 754 SW2d 141, on remand 774 SW2d 1, writ den.—App & E 93, 758.3(1), 846(5), 1012.1(5); Divorce 177, 179, 254(2), 255; Hus & W 279(1), 281.

Herbert; International Life Ins. Co. v., TexCivApp–Waco, 334 SW2d 525, ref nre.—Can of Inst 37(6); Contracts 94(1), 94(2), 98, 100; Fraud 1, 18, 58(1), 64(1); Insurance 1727, 2065, 2069, 3015, 3611(2); Parties 51(4), 52.

Herbert v. Polly Ranch Homeowners Ass'n, TexApp–Houston (1 Dist), 943 SW2d 906, reh overr.—Covenants 49, 51(2); Evid 390(1), 397(1); Trial 105(1).

Herbert v. Smith, TexCivApp–Austin, 183 SW2d 191, writ refused wom.—App & E 877(4); Lim of Act 44(2); Lis Pen 22(5); Tax 2901, 2949, 2953, 2962, 2982, 2996, 3096; Ven & Pur 242.

Herbert v. State, TexApp–Houston (1 Dist), 827 SW2d 507.—Autos 355(10); Crim Law 1159.2(7).

Herbert v. State, TexApp–El Paso, 631 SW2d 585.—Assault 56, 89.

Herbert; U.S. v., CA5 (Tex), 860 F2d 620, cert den 109 SCt 2074, 490 US 1070, 104 LEd2d 639, reh den 109 SCt 3268, 492 US 927, 106 LEd2d 613.—Sent & Pun 1309; Statut 217.4.

Herbert Rosenthal Jewelry Corp.; Statler Hotels v., TexCivApp–Dallas, 351 SW2d 579, ref nre.—App & E 544(3), 692(1), 1057(1); Corp 642(1); Evid 333(1); Inn 11(12); Interest 39(1), 44; Trial 127, 388(3).

Herblin; Staley v., TexApp–Dallas, 188 SW3d 334, reh overr, and review den.—App & E 946, 949; Compromise 5(3), 18(1), 21, 22; Judgm 72, 181(19).

Herbort v. State, TexCrimApp, 422 SW2d 456.—Autos 351.1; Crim Law 643, 1081(4.1), 1081(6), 1086.13, 1087.1(2), 1097(4), 1131(7).

Herbort v. Weinheimer, TexCivApp–San Antonio, 293 SW2d 673.—Venue 21, 22(6), 32(2).

Herbsleb v. Duty, TexCivApp–Waco, 367 SW2d 958.—Costs 194.38.

Herbst v. Martinez, TexCivApp–San Antonio, 307 SW2d 633.—Adv Poss 115(1); App & E 927(7); Bound 40(1), 46(3); Partit 63(1); Propty 9.

Herbst v. Scott, CA5 (Tex), 42 F3d 902, cert den 115 SCt 2590, 515 US 1148, 132 LEd2d 838.—Hab Corp 230, 253, 319.1, 320, 351, 843, 898(2), 898(4), 899.

Herbst v. Sheppard, TexApp–Corpus Christi, 995 SW2d 310, review den.—Ex & Ad 7, 250; Impl & C C 30, 46; Wills 58(1).

Herbst v. State, TexApp–Beaumont, 941 SW2d 371, reh overr.—Crim Law 126(2), 641.13(1), 641.13(2.1),

641.13(6), 867, 899, 941(1), 958(6), 1036.1(4), 1119(1), 1156(3); Infants 20.

Herbster; Chapa v., TexApp–Tyler, 653 SW2d 594.—App & E 766, 842(2), 1010.1(3); Contracts 164; Mtg 329, 335, 353, 354, 369(2), 369(7), 572; Trial 397(2).

Herby's Foods, Inc., In re, BkrtcyNDTex, 134 BR 207, subsequently aff 2 F3d 128.—Bankr 2164.1, 2967.5, 2968; Fed Civ Proc 2655.

Herby's Foods, Inc., Matter of, CA5 (Tex), 2 F3d 128.—Bankr 2125, 2967.1, 2967.5, 2968, 2972.

Herby's Foods, Inc.; Summit Coffee Co. v., CA5 (Tex), 2 F3d 128. See Herby's Foods, Inc., Matter of.

Herby's Foods, Inc. v. Summit Coffee Co., Inc., BkrtcyNDTex, 134 BR 207. See Herby's Foods, Inc., In re.

Herceg v. Hustler Magazine, Inc., CA5 (Tex), 814 F2d 1017, 94 ALR Fed 1, cert den 108 SCt 1219, 485 US 959, 99 LEd2d 420.—Const Law 90.1(1), 1506, 1545, 2070; Fed Cts 755.

Herceg v. Hustler Magazine, Inc., SDTex, 583 FSupp 1566.—Fed Civ Proc 630, 654.1, 1144; Torts 424, 447.

Herceg v. Hustler Magazine, Inc., SDTex, 565 FSupp 802.—Neglig 1518; Torts 447.

Herco, Inc.; Smith v., TexApp–Corpus Christi, 900 SW2d 852, writ den.—Antitrust 134, 141, 161, 162, 353, 369, 389(1), 390; App & E 930(3), 989, 1001(1), 1001(3), 1003(7); Damag 15, 117; Fraud 58(1); Indem 67; Interest 39(2), 39(2.20), 39(6); Sales 38(1); Ven & Pur 351(3).

Hercules v. Harmon, TexApp–Houston (14 Dist), 864 SW2d 752.—Crim Law 641.10(1), 641.10(2); Mand 3(2.1), 4(3), 10, 61.

Hercules Concrete Pumping Service, Inc. v. Bencon Management and General Contracting Corp., TexApp–Houston (1 Dist), 62 SW3d 308, review den.—App & E 5, 914(1); Judgm 17(10); Proc 149.

Hercules Exploration, Inc. v. Halliburton Co., TexApp–Corpus Christi, 658 SW2d 716, ref nre.—Acct Action on 10, 14; App & E 930(3), 989; Contracts 150; Evid 207(1), 264; Guar 36(1), 38(1); Lim of Act 24(2), 43; Trial 136(1), 350.4(1).

Hercules, Inc. v. Eilers, TexCivApp–Beaumont, 458 SW2d 221, ref nre.—App & E 757(1), 766, 930(3), 931(1), 989; Pretrial Proc 306.1; R R 229(1), 275(1), 275(4).

Hercules, Inc.; Steuber Co., Inc. v., CA5 (Tex), 646 F2d 1093.—Contracts 176(1); Fed Civ Proc 2126.1, 2127, 2142.1, 2146, 2608.1, 2609; Fed Cts 433; Sales 161, 182(1); Wareh 34(9).

Hercules Offshore Corp.; Shanks v., SDTex, 58 FSupp2d 743.—Fed Civ Proc 2512; Seamen 2, 29(5.3).

Hercules Oil Co. v. Thompson, WDTex, 10 FSupp 988.—Commerce 61(1); Fed Cts 10.1; Inj 75; Mines 92.2, 92.3(2).

Herd, In Interest of, TexCivApp–Amarillo, 537 SW2d 950, ref nre.—Adop 13, 15; Child C 7, 76, 178; Evid 597; Guard & W 13(1), 13(4); Infants 222.

Herd; Adams v., TexCivApp–Waco, 526 SW2d 295.—Adop 13; Infants 154.1, 156, 177; Stip 3.

Herd v. State, TexCrimApp, 136 SW2d 220, 138 TexCrim 309.—Crim Law 881(1).

Herder; Seydler v., TexCivApp–El Paso, 361 SW2d 411, ref nre.—App & E 846(2), 846(5); Estop 28, 35; Home 57(3); Hus & W 264(1), 267(1).

Hereden; U.S. v., CA5 (Tex), 464 F2d 611, cert den 93 SCt 472, 409 US 1028, 34 LEd2d 322.—Crim Law 354, 773(2).

Heredia; Moron v., TexApp–Corpus Christi, 133 SW3d 668.—App & E 863, 934(1); Judgm 185(4), 185(5), 185.1(8), 185.3(21), 189.

Heredia v. State, TexCrimApp, 528 SW2d 847.—Crim Law 641.12(1), 855(1), 857(2), 1174(1), 1174(2); Searches 183; Sent & Pun 1379(2).

Heredia v. State, TexCrimApp, 508 SW2d 629.—Crim Law 633(2), 1166.20.

Heredia v. State, TexCrimApp, 493 SW2d 238.—Crim Law 538(3), 1186.1.

Heredia v. State, TexCrimApp, 468 SW2d 833.—Controlled Subs 148(3), 149; Searches 121.1; Sent & Pun 1257.

Heredia; U.S. v., CA5 (Tex), 173 FedAppx 337.—Controlled Subs 81; Crim Law 370, 371(1).

Heredia; U.S. v., SDTex, 677 FSupp 895.—Cust Dut 126(1), 126(3.1).

H.E. Reeves, Inc.; Better Const., Inc. v., TexApp–San Antonio, 675 SW2d 612.—App & E 564(3).

H.E. Reeves, Inc. v. Laredo Ready Mix, Inc., SDTex, 589 FSupp 132.—Antitrust 544, 625, 716, 972(3), 977(2); Commerce 62.13, 62.14; Fed Civ Proc 1838, 2470, 2470.2, 2484, 2492, 2544, 2547.1, 2549.

Hereford; Banks v., TexCivApp–Dallas, 601 SW2d 108.—Ex & Ad 3(1).

Hereford v. Farrar, TexCivApp–Austin, 469 SW2d 16, ref nre.—Health 138, 157; Mand 28, 72.

Hereford v. Sharp, TexCivApp–Dallas, 559 SW2d 99.—Mtg 122, 398.

Hereford; Sisco v., TexApp–San Antonio, 694 SW2d 3, ref nre, appeal after remand Briones v. Solomon, 769 SW2d 312, writ den.—App & E 968, 989, 1032(1), 1045(1), 1079, 1170.10; Costs 32(1); Ease 15.1, 36(1), 53, 54, 71; Equity 46; Jury 136(3); Trial 358.

Hereford v. State, TexCrimApp, 380 SW2d 120.—Sent & Pun 1118.

Hereford v. State, TexCrimApp, 299 SW2d 138.—Crim Law 1090.1(1).

Hereford v. Tilson, Tex, 200 SW2d 985, 145 Tex 600.—Frds St of 110(3), 158(3).

Hereford v. Tilson, TexCivApp–Amarillo, 198 SW2d 275, rev 200 SW2d 985, 145 Tex 600.—App & E 598; Contracts 172; Frds St of 110(1), 110(4), 158(3); Land & Ten 92(1); Spec Perf 57.

Hereford, City of; Robinson v., TexCivApp–Amarillo, 324 SW2d 313, ref nre.—Judgm 185(6), 185.3(21), 186; Mun Corp 733(1), 741.20, 741.25, 741.50, 741.55.

Hereford Independent School Dist. v. Bell, NDTex, 454 FSupp 143.—Elections 12(1), 12(8).

Hereford Independent School Dist.; Woodward v., NDTex, 421 FSupp 93.—Civil R 1133, 1448, 1471, 1487; Const Law 3869; Fed Cts 222; Schools 147.2(1), 147.6, 147.40(2), 147.44.

Hereford Land Co. v. Globe Industries, Inc., TexCivApp–Tyler, 387 SW2d 771, ref nre.—App & E 954(1), 954(2), 1043(5); Corp 316(0.5), 523; Estates 1; Evid 419(2); Execution 172(6); Inj 132, 135, 151, 152; Trusts 1, 26, 62, 69, 129.

Hereford State Bank; McCullen v., CA5 (Tex), 214 F2d 185.—Corp 149; Trover 11.

Herera v. State, TexCrimApp, 109 SW2d 195, 133 TexCrim 132.—Crim Law 595(1).

Herff Jones Co.; Hillin v., CA5 (Tex), 443 F2d 363.—Fed Cts 743, 865; Labor & Emp 835.

Herford v. State, TexCrimApp, 447 SW2d 924.—Crim Law 1081(5).

Herford v. State, TexApp–Fort Worth, 139 SW3d 733.—Crim Law 1144.17, 1177.

Herfort v. Hargrove, TexCivApp–Austin, 606 SW2d 359, ref nre.—Venue 2.

Herfort; Home Decorators v., CA5 (Tex), 179 F2d 398.—Inj 135.

Herfurth v. City of Dallas, TexCivApp–Dallas, 410 SW2d 453, ref nre.—App & E 768; Em Dom 149(1), 262(3), 262(5); Evid 99, 143, 560; Trial 55; Witn 405(1).

Hergert v. State, TexApp–Beaumont, 197 SW3d 394.—Crim Law 641.13(7), 1023(16), 1026.10(4), 1028, 1042, 1044.1(1), 1134(3), 1162; Sent & Pun 2024, 2026, 2033.

Hergesheimer v. State, TexCrimApp, 141 SW2d 598, 139 TexCrim 427.—Crim Law 519(9), 530.

Hergotz; Currie v., TexCivApp–Austin, 250 SW2d 247.—App & E 694(1).

Herider; Magness v., TexCivApp–Tyler, 392 SW2d 383.—Venue 7.5(7).

Herider Farm Processing, Inc. v. City of Nacogdoches, TexCivApp–Tyler, 573 SW2d 297, ref nre.—App & E 954(1); Inj 132, 135, 138.21, 157.

Herider Farms-El Paso, Inc. v. Criswell, TexCivApp–El Paso, 519 SW2d 473, ref nre.—Damag 91(1); Estop 52.10(3), 52.15, 119; Fraud 31; Judgm 181(6), 181(21), 185(2); Labor & Emp 111, 114(2), 155(2), 908; Princ & A 163(1); Torts 215, 217, 441.

Herider Farms, Inc.; W. G. Tufts and Son v., TexCivApp–Tyler, 485 SW2d 300, ref nre.—Costs 194.22, 194.32; Sales 430, 447; Trial 350.2.

Herider Farms, Inc.; W. G. Tufts and Son v., TexCivApp–Tyler, 461 SW2d 257.—App & E 912, 931(1), 1011.1(4); Corp 503(2); Plead 111.16, 111.39(4).

Hering v. Norbanco Austin I, Ltd., TexApp–Austin, 735 SW2d 638, writ den.—Garn 101.

Hering; Texas Power & Light Co. v., Tex, 224 SW2d 191, 148 Tex 350.—App & E 719(2), 1026, 1032(1); Em Dom 203(2), 205, 262(5).

Hering; Texas Power & Light Co. v., TexCivApp–Waco, 218 SW2d 301, aff 224 SW2d 191, 148 Tex 350.—App & E 1032(1); Em Dom 255; New Tr 140(3).

Hering; Texas Power & Light Co. v., TexCivApp–Waco, 178 SW2d 162.—Em Dom 126(1).

Heritage Administrative Co., Inc.; Dent Zone Network, L.L.C. v., CA5 (Tex), 87 FedAppx 341.—Trademarks 1158.

Heritage Bank v. Redcom Laboratories, Inc., CA5 (Tex), 250 F3d 319, also published at 2001 WL 34906864, cert den 122 SCt 468, 534 US 997, 151 LEd2d 384.—Banks 191.10, 191.15, 191.20, 191.25; Evid 207(1); Fed Civ Proc 751; Fed Cts 303, 612.1; Inj 123, 205; Rem of C 11, 36, 107(7), 107(9).

Heritage Bldg. Co.; Tigrett v., TexCivApp–Texarkana, 533 SW2d 65, ref nre.—Contracts 51, 52; Work Comp 392.

Heritage Bldg. Systems, Inc., In re, TexApp–Beaumont, 185 SW3d 539.—Alt Disp Res 114, 116, 143, 191, 461; App & E 946; Commerce 80.5; Mand 28.

Heritage Cablevision of Dallas, Inc.; Missouri-Kansas-Texas R. Co. v., TexApp–Dallas, 783 SW2d 273.—Estop 52.10(2), 52.10(3), 52.10(4); Tel 1214, 1222.

Heritage Group Holding Corp.; Heritage Life Ins. Co. v., TexApp–Dallas, 751 SW2d 229, writ den.—App & E 387(6); Contracts 303(1); Decl Judgm 45; Insurance 1151.

Heritage Housing Corp. v. Ferguson, TexApp–Dallas, 674 SW2d 363, ref nre.—Antitrust 367, 389(1), 389(2), 390, 393; Spec Perf 129.

Heritage Housing Corp. v. Ferguson, TexApp–Dallas, 651 SW2d 272.—App & E 472.

Heritage Housing Development, Inc. v. Carr, TexApp–Houston (1 Dist), 199 SW3d 560.—App & E 930(1), 1001(1), 1001(3), 1177(7); Health 662, 780, 784; Joint Adv 1.2(1), 7; Labor & Emp 26, 3027, 3031(1), 3037, 3045, 3125.

Heritage Life Ins. Co.; American Heritage Life Ins. Co. v., CA5 (Tex), 494 F2d 3.—Admin Law 501; Antitrust 16, 19, 61, 135(1); Fed Cts 860; Judgm 565, 570(1), 634, 720; Trademarks 1032, 1034, 1036, 1037, 1309, 1314, 1322, 1326, 1360, 1362, 1369, 1421, 1426, 1608, 1621, 1623, 1627, 1628(1), 1628(2), 1630, 1690.

Heritage Life Ins. Co. v. Heritage Group Holding Corp., TexApp–Dallas, 751 SW2d 229, writ den.—App & E 387(6); Contracts 303(1); Decl Judgm 45; Insurance 1151.

Heritage Manor Apartments v. Harris, Tex, 924 SW2d 375. See Walker v. Harris.

Heritage Manor, Inc. v. Tidball, TexApp–San Antonio, 724 SW2d 952.—App & E 681; Labor & Emp 2815, 2832, 2848, 2879, 2881; Neglig 1720, 1741; Plead 236(3); Trial 232(5).

Heritage Manor of Blaylock Properties, Inc. v. Peterson, TexApp–Dallas, 677 SW2d 689, ref nre.—Costs 194.32; Subrog 10(1); Work Comp 1063, 1065.

Heritage Manor of Blaylock Properties, Inc. v. Peterson & Associates, TexApp–Dallas, 677 SW2d 689. See Heritage Manor of Blaylock Properties, Inc. v. Peterson.

Heritage Organization, L.L.C., In re, BkrtcyNDTex, 354 BR 407.—Atty & C 11(1), 11(2.1), 11(12); Bankr 2133, 2162, 2164.1; Bills & N 28, 51, 113, 115, 116, 120, 122, 445, 453, 472.1, 495, 516, 519, 537(1); Contracts 1, 137(1), 164, 171(1), 238(1), 245(1), 326; Contrib 4; Corp 428(6); Estop 52.10(2), 52.10(3), 119; Evid 158(2), 402, 448; Ex & Ad 225(1), 225(3); Frds St of 131(1).

Heritage Organization, L.L.C., In re, BkrtcyNDTex, 350 BR 733.—Bankr 3047(2), 3063.1, 3066(6).

Heritage Organization, L.L.C., In re, BkrtcyNDTex, 322 BR 285, aff in part, rev in part 2006 WL 2642204.—Alt Disp Res 230, 235, 312, 314, 316, 329, 354, 363(9), 374(1), 386; Bankr 2088; Records 32.

Heritage Resources, Inc. v. Anschutz Corp., TexApp–El Paso, 689 SW2d 952, ref nre.—Contracts 143(2), 176(2), 212(1), 212(2); Joint Adv 5(3); Mines 101.

Heritage Resources, Inc. v. Hill, TexApp–El Paso, 104 SW3d 612.—App & E 226(2), 230, 758.1, 763, 840(4), 842(2), 852, 893(1), 949, 989, 1008.1(2), 1010.1(1), 1012.1(5), 1071.2, 1175(5), 1177(7), 1207(3); Costs 194.18, 194.40, 207, 208; Decl Judgm 394.

Heritage Resources, Inc.; Hill v., TexApp–El Paso, 964 SW2d 89, reh overr, and review den, and reh of petition for review overr, appeal after remand 104 SW3d 612.—Admin Law 501; App & E 187(2), 218.2(5.1), 242(1), 253, 970(2), 984(1), 984(5), 989, 1001(3), 1047(1), 1050.1(1), 1056.1(1); Bankr 2395; Contracts 236, 237(1); Costs 13, 194.16, 194.18, 194.25, 194.32, 194.40; Damag 15, 89(2), 114, 137; Decl Judgm 10, 142, 148, 368; Evid 48; Fraud 3, 12, 32, 35, 50, 58(3), 59(2); Frds St of 63(2), 129(1), 131(1); Judgm 951(1); Libel 132, 136, 139; Lim of Act 43, 55(1), 55(5), 110, 127(3), 127(4), 127(7), 127(11.1), 127(12), 127(16); Mines 48, 73.1(3), 101; Neglig 219; Plead 252(1); Torts 114, 212, 213, 214, 215, 217, 219, 220, 222, 241, 242, 253, 255, 258, 262, 263, 277; Trial 56.

Heritage Resources, Inc. v. NationsBank, Tex, 939 SW2d 118.—Contracts 143(1), 143(2), 143.5, 152, 176(2); Mines 73, 79.1(1), 79.1(3), 79.3, 79.7.

Heritage Resources, Inc. v. Nationsbank, TexApp–El Paso, 895 SW2d 833, reh overr, and writ gr, rev 939 SW2d 118.—Mines 73, 79.1(3), 79.3, 79.7.

Heritage Sav. Ass'n; Lewis v., TexCivApp–Austin, 502 SW2d 943.—B & L Assoc 3.5(2).

Heritage Soc. of Washington County v. Neumann, TexApp–Houston (14 Dist), 771 SW2d 563, writ den.—Zoning 358.1, 385, 441, 565, 621, 746.

Heritage Southwest Medical Group, P.A., In re, BkrtcyNDTex, 309 BR 916.—Bankr 2048.4, 2162; Fed Cts 47.5; Health 556(3).

Herlitz, Inc.; McClelland v., NDTex, 704 FSupp 749.—Civil R 1515, 1532; Fed Civ Proc 2734; Lim of Act 118(2).

Herman, In re, CA5 (Tex), 211 FedAppx 320.—Lim of Act 167(1).

Herman, In re, NDTex, 56 FSupp 733.—Armed S 3; Hab Corp 258; Mil Jus 515.

Herman, In re, BkrtcyEDTex, 315 BR 399.—Judgm 754, 768(1); Statut 181(1), 181(2), 184, 188.

Herman, In re, BkrtcyEDTex, 315 BR 381, aff Neely v. Herman, 2005 WL 5015557, aff 211 FedAppx 320.—Bankr 2157, 2432, 2784.1, 2785, 2786; Courts 509; Judgm 518; Lim of Act 21(1), 46(1), 46(3), 72(1); Trusts 62, 63.9, 72, 83.

Herman; American Airlines, Inc. v., CA5 (Tex), 176 F3d 283.—Admin Law 704; Fed Cts 574; U S 64.20.

Herman; Brown v., TexApp–Austin, 852 SW2d 91.—App & E 4; Courts 91(1); Mand 3(2.1), 4(1), 31.

Herman v. **Express Sixty-Minutes Delivery Service, Inc.**, CA5 (Tex), 161 F3d 299, reh and reh den 174 F3d 200.—Fed Cts 865; Labor & Emp 2225, 2235, 2236, 2347, 2387(1).

Herman; **Fort Hood Barbers Ass'n v.**, CA5 (Tex), 137 F3d 302.—Admin Law 390.1, 763, 797; Labor & Emp 63, 2185, 2338, 2350(2), 2357.

Herman v. **Johnson**, CA5 (Tex), 98 F3d 171, cert den 117 SCt 1262, 520 US 1123, 137 LEd2d 341.—Hab Corp 496, 818; Jury 131(8).

Herman; **Leddon v.**, TexCivApp–Fort Worth, 402 SW2d 512.—Adop 7.6(1), 7.6(3), 15, 16; Infants 154.1, 198, 203, 230.1, 232; Judgm 17(2).

Herman; **Magnolia Petroleum Co. v.**, TexCivApp–Austin, 295 SW2d 430, ref nre.—Trial 116.

Herman v. **Millicovsky**, SDTex, 834 FSupp 182.—Damag 49.10; Fed Cts 303; Rem of C 36.

Herman; **Milton v.**, TexApp–Austin, 947 SW2d 737, subsequent mandamus proceeding In re Graham, 971 SW2d 56.—Courts 198, 201, 486; Mand 3(3), 4(1), 28.

Herman; **Phelps v.**, TexCivApp–San Antonio, 150 SW2d 287, writ refused.—Bankr 2852.

Herman v. **Rountree**, TexCivApp–Fort Worth, 162 SW2d 144.—App & E 516, 564(3), 568, 578.

Herman v. **Shell Oil Co.**, TexApp–Houston (14 Dist), 93 SW3d 605.—App & E 854(1), 1175(1); Decl Judgm 184; Deeds 171(1); Ven & Pur 18(1), 18(3), 231(3), 231(16.1).

Herman; **Shook v.**, TexApp–Dallas, 759 SW2d 743, writ den, and writ withdrawn, and writ gr, and writ withdrawn, and writ den.—Health 623, 631, 811, 821(2); Judgm 185.2(8), 185.3(21); Lim of Act 55(3).

Herman; **Society of Separationists, Inc. v.**, CA5 (Tex), 959 F2d 1283, cert den 113 SCt 191, 506 US 866, 121 LEd2d 135.—Civil R 1332(6), 1333(6); Courts 508(1); Fed Civ Proc 103.2, 103.3; Inj 11.

Herman; **Society of Separationists, Inc. v.**, CA5 (Tex), 939 F2d 1207, reh en banc gr 946 F2d 1573, on reh 959 F2d 1283, cert den 113 SCt 191, 506 US 866, 121 LEd2d 135.

Herman; **State Dept. of Highways and Public Transp. v.**, TexCivApp–Texarkana, 578 SW2d 442, dism.—Em Dom 287; Plead 111.23, 111.38; States 200.

Herman; **Stuart v.**, TexCivApp–Fort Worth, 157 SW2d 939.—Plead 111.3; Venue 5.3(2).

Herman v. **Tyson Products, Inc.**, EDTex, 82 FSupp2d 631.—Labor & Emp 2274.

Herman & MacLean v. **Huddleston**, USTex, 103 SCt 683, 459 US 375, 74 LEd2d 548, on remand 705 F2d 775.—Sec Reg 27.34, 60.34, 60.37, 60.63(1).

Herman & Maclean; **Huddleston v.**, CA5 (Tex), 705 F2d 775.—Fed Cts 896.1, 939.

Herman & MacLean; **Huddleston v.**, CA5 (Tex), 640 F2d 534, cert gr 102 SCt 1766, 456 US 914, 72 LEd2d 173, aff in part, rev in part 103 SCt 683, 459 US 375, 74 LEd2d 548, on remand 705 F2d 775.—Contrib 5(1), 5(6.1); Evid 155(8), 333(1), 352(1), 506, 531; Fed Civ Proc 1408, 2174, 2234.1; Fed Cts 415, 433; Refer 3; Sec Reg 25.70, 25.75, 27.50, 60.27(2), 60.45(1), 60.47, 60.48(1), 60.57, 60.62, 60.63(1), 60.63(4), 148, 154.1, 155, 157.1, 256.1.

Herman **Blum Consulting Engineers; Hadra v.**, CA5 (Tex), 632 F2d 1242, cert den 101 SCt 1983, 451 US 912, 68 LEd2d 301.—Fed Civ Proc 2315, 2339, 2372.1; Fed Cts 612.1, 826; Interest 39(2.40); Labor & Emp 765, 868(4), 871; Lim of Act 100(11).

Herman **Blum Consulting Engineers; Hadra v.**, NDTex, 74 FRD 113.—Fed Civ Proc 1278, 1685.

Herman **G. West, Inc.; International Ins. Co. v.**, TexApp–Fort Worth, 649 SW2d 824.—Judgm 178, 183, 184.

Herman **J. Smith General Contractors, Inc. v. Riverdrive Mall, Inc.**, TexCivApp–Waco, 513 SW2d 951.—Inj 111; Venue 22(10).

Hermann; **American Airlines, Inc. v.**, NDTex, 971 FSupp 1096, rev 176 F3d 283.—Civil R 1522.

Hermann; **Dallmeyer v.**, TexCivApp–Hous (14 Dist), 437 SW2d 367.—Estates 2, 8; Wills 602(2), 608(1).

Hermann v. **Hermann**, TexCivApp–Beaumont, 359 SW2d 222, writ dism.—Divorce 130, 252.5(1).

Hermann; **Hermann v.**, TexCivApp–Beaumont, 359 SW2d 222, writ dism.—Divorce 130, 252.5(1).

Hermann **Hosp. v. Aetna Life Ins. Co.**, TexApp–Houston (14 Dist), 803 SW2d 351, writ den.—App & E 387(3); Insurance 1117(3); States 18.15, 18.41.

Hermann **Hosp. v. Central States, Southeast and Southwest Areas Health and Welfare Fund**, SDTex, 962 FSupp 993.—Fraud 31; Labor & Emp 407, 685, 688; States 18.15, 18.51.

Hermann **Hosp.; Harris County v.**, TexApp–Eastland, 943 SW2d 547, set aside, and writ gr.—Counties 153.5; Mun Corp 870; Prisons 18(6).

Hermann **Hosp.; Johnson v.**, TexCivApp–Houston (14 Dist), 659 SW2d 124, ref nre.—Evid 536, 538; Health 820; Pretrial Proc 205; Trial 55, 62(1).

Hermann **Hosp. v. Liberty Life Assur. Co. of Boston**, TexApp–Houston (14 Dist), 696 SW2d 37, ref nre.—App & E 170(1), 989; Assign 1; Contracts 39, 187(1); Insurance 1995, 1996, 3436, 3488; Mal Pros 39.

Hermann **Hosp. v. Martinez**, TexApp–Houston (14 Dist), 990 SW2d 476, reh overr, and review den.—Damag 51, 57.29; Death 89; Health 961; Mun Corp 743; Parent & C 7(1).

Hermann **Hosp. v. MEBA Medical and Benefits Plan**, CA5 (Tex), 959 F2d 569.—Estop 90(2); Fed Cts 612.1, 917, 950; Fraud 31; Labor & Emp 591, 592, 678; States 18.15.

Hermann **Hosp. v. MEBA Medical & Benefits Plan**, CA5 (Tex), 845 F2d 1286, appeal after remand 959 F2d 569.—Labor & Emp 407, 591, 678; States 18.51.

Hermann **Hosp.; Members Mut. Ins. Co. v.**, Tex, 664 SW2d 325.—Health 961; Insurance 2274.

Hermann **Hosp.; Members Mut. Ins. Co. v.**, TexApp–Houston (14 Dist), 659 SW2d 132, rev 664 SW2d 325.—Health 961; Insurance 2260, 2775; Statut 181(2).

Hermann **Hosp. v. National Standard Ins. Co.**, TexApp–Houston (1 Dist), 776 SW2d 249, writ den.—Estop 52(7); Insurance 3424, 3424(2); Judgm 181(23); Neglig 481.

Hermann **Hosp. v. Pan American Life Ins. Co.**, SDTex, 932 FSupp 899.—Insurance 1117(3); Labor & Emp 407; States 18.15, 18.51.

Hermann **Hosp. v. Thu Nga Thi Tran**, TexApp–Houston (14 Dist), 730 SW2d 56.—App & E 781(4); Inj 12, 140, 147.

Hermann **Hosp. v. Vardeman**, TexApp–Houston (1 Dist), 775 SW2d 866.—Costs 194.25; Interest 39(2.20).

Hermann **Hosp.; Watts v.**, TexApp–Houston (1 Dist), 962 SW2d 102.—Health 197, 258, 658; Judgm 185.1(8), 185.3(1), 189.

Hermann **Hosp. Estate; Chambers v.**, TexApp–Houston (1 Dist), 961 SW2d 177, reh and reh den, and error gr, and error den, opinion withdrawn and superseded on overruling of reh Van Horn v. Chambers, 970 SW2d 542, cert den 119 SCt 546, 525 US 1019, 142 LEd2d 454, rev 970 SW2d 542, cert den 119 SCt 546, 525 US 1019, 142 LEd2d 454.—Afft 3; Health 615; Judgm 185.3(21); Neglig 218, 220, 234, 282; Work Comp 55, 1061, 2084.

Hermann **Hosp. Estate v. Coffee**, BkrtcySDTex, 103 BR 825. See Coffee, In re.

Hermansen v. **U.S.**, CA5 (Tex), 230 F2d 173.—Postal 35(9), 49(11).

Hermansen v. **U.S.**, CA5 (Tex), 228 F2d 495, reh den 230 F2d 173, cert den 76 SCt 781, 351 US 924, 100 LEd 1455.—Crim Law 814(1); Ind & Inf 71.2(1); Postal 48(8), 49(11).

Herman **Siegel, Inc.; Crawford Undertaking Co. v.**, TexCivApp–Waco, 230 SW2d 590, writ dism.—App & E 994(3), 1008.1(4); Chat Mtg 168, 170(1), 175.1, 177(1), 225(2), 249, 255; Evid 242(1), 244(2); Sales 480(6).

HERMES;

Hermes; Cappetta v., TexApp–San Antonio, 222 SW3d 160, reh overr.—App & E 946, 962; Pretrial Proc 581, 678, 682.1, 697, 699.

Hermes Grain Co. v. Hailey, TexCivApp–Corpus Christi, 435 SW2d 181.—Plead 111.6, 111.30, 111.44; Pretrial Proc 481; Sales 359(1).

Hermleigh Co-op. Gin & Supply Co.; Ruppert v., Tex-CivApp–Eastland, 133 SW2d 305.—Evid 157(1), 157(3), 171.

Hermosillo v. State, TexCrimApp, 475 SW2d 252.—Crim Law 421(1), 1165(1); Larc 65.

Hermosillo v. State, TexApp–Fort Worth, 903 SW2d 60, petition for discretionary review refused.—Crim Law 26, 38, 330, 414, 772(6), 814(8), 1115(2), 1141(1), 1141(2), 1158(1), 1158(3); Jury 33(5.15); Statut 212.6.

Herms v. State, TexCrimApp, 87 SW2d 717, 129 TexCrim 448.—Crim Law 1037.1(4); Homic 1321.

Hermsen Design Associates, Inc.; Minturn Advertising, Inc. v., NDTex, 728 FSupp 430.—Trademarks 1038, 1039, 1058, 1081, 1086, 1095, 1097, 1098, 1102, 1104, 1110, 1111, 1112, 1113.

Hern v. State, TexCrimApp, 892 SW2d 894, cert den 115 SCt 2252, 515 US 1105, 132 LEd2d 259.—Crim Law 947; Double J 60.1.

Hern v. State, TexApp–Houston (1 Dist), 862 SW2d 179, petition for discretionary review gr, aff 892 SW2d 894, cert den 115 SCt 2252, 515 US 1105, 132 LEd2d 259.—Crim Law 273.1(2), 274(3.1); Double J 57, 81, 107.1.

Hern v. State, TexApp–Houston (1 Dist), 849 SW2d 924, opinion withdrawn and superseded on reh 862 SW2d 179, petition for discretionary review gr, aff 892 SW2d 894, cert den 115 SCt 2252, 515 US 1105, 132 LEd2d 259.

Hernaiz; Doncaster v., TexApp–San Antonio, 161 SW3d 594.—Action 12; App & E 242(2), 499(1), 500(1), 970(2), 984(5), 1050.1(1), 1056.1(1), 1071.6; Bills & N 452(3); Compromise 6(1), 21; Contracts 143(2); Costs 194.18, 198, 207; Equity 72(1); Estop 52.15, 83(1), 87; Evid 450(5); Judgm 183, 185(3), 185(4), 185.3(16), 189; Lim of Act 21(1), 148(1), 148(3), 151(1), 151(4), 199(3); Torts 125; Trial 401.

Hernandez, Ex parte, Tex, 827 SW2d 858.—Contempt 64; Inj 232.

Hernandez, Ex parte, TexCrimApp, 953 SW2d 275, cert den Hernandez v. Texas, 118 SCt 1093, 522 US 1135, 140 LEd2d 149.—Courts 95(1); Double J 24; Hab Corp 824.

Hernandez, Ex parte, TexCrimApp, 906 SW2d 931.—Crim Law 872.5; Double J 99; Jury 32(3), 149.

Hernandez, Ex parte, TexCrimApp, 845 SW2d 913.—Sent & Pun 1157.

Hernandez, Ex parte, TexCrimApp, 758 SW2d 594.—Sent & Pun 545, 1159, 1160, 1174.

Hernandez, Ex parte, TexCrimApp, 705 SW2d 700.—Crim Law 1023(16), 1026.10(2.1); Hab Corp 670(9); Sent & Pun 2079, 2086.

Hernandez, Ex parte, TexCrimApp, 698 SW2d 670.—Controlled Subs 100(2); Hab Corp 793.

Hernandez, Ex parte, TexCrimApp, 486 SW2d 299.—Extrad 32.

Hernandez, Ex parte, TexCrimApp, 420 SW2d 708.—Extrad 36.

Hernandez, Ex parte, TexCrimApp, 364 SW2d 688.—Sent & Pun 2034, 2281.

Hernandez, Ex parte, TexApp–Eastland, 165 SW3d 760.—Crim Law 1226(3.1); Pardon 22, 23.1, 24; Statut 181(2), 190, 217.4.

Hernandez, Ex parte, TexApp–Eastland, 726 SW2d 651.—Child S 497.

Hernandez, In re, BkrtcyEDTex, 149 BR 441.—Bankr 3708(9); Trover 10.

Hernandez, In re, BkrtcySDTex, 282 BR 200.—Bankr 3568(3), 3569, 3713, 3715(10), 3718(3).

Hernandez, In re, BkrtcySDTex, 150 BR 29.—Bankr 2650(4), 2705; Judgm 828.21(2).

Hernandez, In re, BkrtcyWDTex, 263 BR 523.—Bankr 3713.

Hernandez, In re, BkrtcyWDTex, 208 BR 872.—Bankr 3353(1), 3353(2), 3353(3.15), 3353(10), 3353(14), 3353(15), 3420(4.1), 3420(11); Statut 205.

Hernandez, In re, BkrtcyWDTex, 131 BR 61.—Exemp 45.

Hernandez, In re Estate of, TexApp–El Paso, 112 SW3d 304, reh overr, and review den.—App & E 181; Const Law 4088; Ex & Ad 380(2.5), 380(3), 438(8).

Hernandez v. Aldridge, CA5 (Tex), 902 F2d 386, cert den 111 SCt 962, 498 US 1086, 112 LEd2d 1049.—Civil R 1530.

Hernandez v. Aldridge, CA5 (Tex), 866 F2d 800, cert gr, vac 110 SCt 1314, 494 US 1013, 108 LEd2d 490, on remand 902 F2d 386, cert den 111 SCt 962, 498 US 1086, 112 LEd2d 1049.—Civil R 1530.

Hernandez v. Allen, TexCivApp–Tyler, 429 SW2d 643, ref nre.—App & E 1170.10; Autos 244(14), 244(34).

Hernandez v. Almendarez, TexCivApp–Eastland, 137 SW2d 1059.—App & E 232(3), 1062.1; Autos 240(1); Trial 350.7(8), 352.4(7).

Hernandez v. Alta Verde Industries, Inc., TexApp–San Antonio, 666 SW2d 499, ref nre.—App & E 863, 934(2); Deeds 143; Evid 269(3), 424; Frds St of 129(11); Gifts 25, 49(4); Land & Ten 66(2); Stip 14(10); Tresp to T T 41(1); Trial 350.3(3).

Hernandez v. Altenberg, TexApp–San Antonio, 904 SW2d 734, reh overr, and writ den.—App & E 866(3), 927(7); Estop 59, 63; Evid 78, 538, 544, 547.5, 571(9); Health 821(2), 821(3), 826; Trial 143.

Hernandez; Amato v., TexApp–Houston (1 Dist), 981 SW2d 947, reh overr, and review den.—App & E 347(3), 914(1); Garn 7; Proc 28, 64, 152, 153.

Hernandez v. American Appliance Mfg. Corp., TexApp–Corpus Christi, 827 SW2d 383, writ den.—App & E 213, 836, 930(1), 930(3), 989, 1001(1), 1001(3), 1003(7), 1068(1), 1175(1), 1177(8); Damag 221(7); Prod Liab 53, 86.

Hernandez; American Nat. Ins. Co. v., TexCivApp–San Antonio, 104 SW2d 525.—Evid 334(4); Insurance 3016, 3381(4).

Hernandez v. American Tel. and Tel. Co., TexApp–El Paso, 198 SW3d 288.—Judgm 181(21); Labor & Emp 807, 809, 810, 861, 863(2).

Hernandez v. Barnhart, CA5 (Tex), 202 FedAppx 681.—Social S 142.5, 143.65; U S 147(18).

Hernandez v. Baucum, TexCivApp–San Antonio, 344 SW2d 498, ref nre.—App & E 1048(6); Damag 97; Trial 116, 121(2), 131(3).

Hernandez v. Baucum, TexCivApp–San Antonio, 338 SW2d 481.—App & E 417(1); New Tr 155.

Hernandez; Baylor College of Medicine v., TexApp–Houston (14 Dist), 208 SW3d 4, reh overr, and review den, and reh of petition for review den.—App & E 23, 68, 70(3), 70(8); Health 770; Judgm 181(6); Mun Corp 745; Offic 114, 119; Statut 181(2), 188, 190, 214.

Hernandez; Best Inv. Co. v., TexCivApp–Dallas, 479 SW2d 759, ref nre.—App & E 766, 1170.7; Deeds 38(1); Evid 215(1); Stip 17(2); Tresp to T T 38(2), 40(4), 40(5), 40(7); Trial 29(1), 29.1; Trusts 42, 43(1).

Hernandez v. Beto, CA5 (Tex), 443 F2d 634, cert den 92 SCt 201, 404 US 897, 30 LEd2d 174.—Const Law 4669; Crim Law 633(1), 641.13(2.1), 1137(8), 1162, 1166.8.

Hernandez; Bexar County Nat. Bank of San Antonio v., Tex, 716 SW2d 938.—Sec Tran 240.

Hernandez v. Bexar County Nat. Bank of San Antonio, TexApp–Corpus Christi, 710 SW2d 684, ref nre 716 SW2d 938.—App & E 173(2), 173(12), 181, 688(2), 1079; Guar 20, 63, 72, 77(1); Sec Tran 230.

Hernandez v. **Big 4 Inc.**, SDTex, 241 FSupp2d 715.—Contracts 143(2), 147(3), 176(2); Evid 461(1); Indem 27, 30(1), 30(5), 104.

Hernandez v. **Borjas**, TexApp–Fort Worth, 734 SW2d 776.—App & E 846(5); Guard & W 13(3), 25.

Hernandez v. **Braddock**, TexApp–Corpus Christi, 641 SW2d 359.—App & E 1004(5), 1140(4); Damag 130.1, 132(1); New Tr 140(3), 143(2), 157.

Hernandez v. **Calle**, TexApp–San Antonio, 963 SW2d 918.—App & E 173(1); Health 823(1); Judgm 181(1), 185(2), 185.3(21).

Hernandez v. **Cantu**, BkrtcySDTex, 150 BR 29. See Hernandez, In re.

Hernandez; **Cartlidge v.**, TexApp–Houston (14 Dist), 9 SW3d 341.—App & E 846(5), 852, 863, 893(1), 1012.1(7.1); Const Law 3964, 3965(5), 3967; Courts 12(2.1), 12(2.5), 12(2.10), 12(2.25), 35.

Hernandez v. **Casillas**, SDTex, 520 FSupp 389.—Aliens 329, 341; Estop 52.10(2).

Hernandez v. **Castillo**, TexCivApp–San Antonio, 309 SW2d 938, writ refused.—App & E 560; Costs 256(2).

Hernandez v. **Castillo**, TexCivApp–San Antonio, 303 SW2d 508, ref nre, mandate am 309 SW2d 938, writ refused.—Autos 181(1), 245(24); Trial 352.15.

Hernandez v. **Central Power and Light**, SDTex, 880 FSupp 494.—Courts 26; Rem of C 3, 43, 102, 107(4).

Hernandez; **Chapa v.**, TexCivApp–Corpus Christi, 587 SW2d 778.—Guard & W 13(1), 13(4), 13(8); Witn 321.

Hernandez; **Chisos Mining Co. v.**, TexCivApp–El Paso, 96 SW2d 292, writ dism.—App & E 1066(7); Labor & Emp 2856, 2879, 2883, 2884, 2889, 2897.

Hernandez v. **Ciba-Geigy Corp. USA**, SDTex, 200 FRD 285.—Action 3; Fed Civ Proc 636; Fraud 3, 16; Princ & A 1; Prod Liab 23.1, 46.2, 73; Treaties 12, 13.

Hernandez; **City of El Paso v.**, TexApp–El Paso, 16 SW3d 409, review den.—Mun Corp 723.5, 724, 747(1), 747(4), 847, 852, 857.

Hernandez v. **City of Ft. Worth**, Tex, 617 SW2d 923.—App & E 758.1, 1095; Mun Corp 180(1).

Hernandez; **City of Ft. Worth v.**, TexCivApp–Fort Worth, 608 SW2d 826, ref nre 617 SW2d 923.—App & E 878(6); Mun Corp 180(1).

Hernandez; **City of San Antonio v.**, TexApp–San Antonio, 53 SW3d 404, review den.—Civil R 1376(2); Judgm 185(2); Mun Corp 747(3), 847; Offic 114.

Hernandez; **Coastal Mart, Inc. v.**, TexApp–Corpus Christi, 76 SW3d 691, review dism by agreement.—App & E 930(1), 989, 1001(1), 1001(3), 1003(5), 1003(6), 1004(8); Civil R 1179, 1743, 1744, 1765, 1772, 1773; Labor & Emp 868(3), 873; Pretrial Proc 42.

Hernandez; **Corpus Christi Area Teachers Credit Union v.**, TexApp–San Antonio, 814 SW2d 195.—App & E 932(1), 1041(3); Damag 128; Fraud 30, 50, 58(1), 62, 65(1); Plead 238(1), 258(1).

Hernandez v. **Crawford Bldg. Material Co.**, CA5 (Tex), 321 F3d 528, reh and reh den 64 FedAppx 419, cert den 124 SCt 82, 540 US 817, 157 LEd2d 34.—Civil R 1242, 1243, 1245; Fed Cts 630.1.

Hernandez v. **Cremer**, CA5 (Tex), 913 F2d 230, reh den 925 F2d 1461.—Aliens 211, 329, 665; Const Law 977, 2553, 3875, 3921, 4036; Fed Cts 12.1.

Hernandez v. **De La Rosa**, TexApp–El Paso, 172 SW3d 78, reh overr.—Autos 192(11).

Hernandez; **DeLeon v.**, TexApp–Houston (14 Dist), 814 SW2d 531.—App & E 863, 934(1), 1024.4; Assault 2, 42; Hus & W 322, 323.1, 332; Judgm 185(6).

Hernandez; **Delgado v.**, TexApp–Corpus Christi, 951 SW2d 97.—App & E 867(1), 901, 977(5); Const Law 3974, 3993; Evid 71, 87, 89; New Tr 6, 84; Trial 6(1).

Hernandez; **Delgado v.**, TexCivApp–El Paso, 390 SW2d 498.—Frds of 23(3); Trial 350.4(2).

Hernandez v. **Del Ray Chemical Intern., Inc.**, TexApp–Houston (14 Dist), 56 SW3d 112.—App & E 1008.1(1), 1008.1(2), 1010.1(1), 1010.1(2), 1010.2; Judgm 540, 584, 585(5), 591.1, 603, 678(1), 678(2), 739.

Hernandez v. **Dominguez**, Tex, 405 SW2d 57.—Partit 34, 81, 95.

Hernandez v. **Dominguez**, TexCivApp–El Paso, 399 SW2d 385, ref nre 405 SW2d 57.—App & E 93; Ease 15.1; Estop 101; Ten in C 45, 55(9); Tresp to T T 47(1).

Hernandez v. **Dretke**, CA5 (Tex), 125 FedAppx 528, cert den 125 SCt 2969, 545 US 1143, 162 LEd2d 894.—Const Law 4669; Crim Law 1169.11; Hab Corp 490(6).

Hernandez; **Eagle Life Ins. Co. v.**, TexApp–El Paso, 743 SW2d 671, writ den.—App & E 374(4).

Hernandez v. **Earney**, WDTex, 558 FSupp 1256.—Dist & Pros Attys 10; Evid 43(1); Fed Civ Proc 2734; Hab Corp 441; Judges 36.

Hernandez; **EDCO Production, Inc. v.**, TexApp–San Antonio, 794 SW2d 69, writ den.—Damag 37, 133, 186; Labor & Emp 3141; Mines 118; Neglig 1011, 1204(1), 1693, 1699.

Hernandez v. **Estelle**, CA5 (Tex), 788 F2d 1154, reh den 793 F2d 1287.—Civil R 1098, 1376(7); Const Law 2293, 4821.

Hernandez v. **Estelle**, CA5 (Tex), 711 F2d 619.—Hab Corp 862.1; U S Mag 27.

Hernandez v. **Estelle**, CA5 (Tex), 674 F2d 313.—Const Law 268(10), 4689; Hab Corp 719, 845, 846.

Hernandez v. **Exxon Corp.**, SDTex, 943 FSupp 740.—Civil R 1118, 1122, 1135, 1137, 1138, 1535, 1536, 1544, 1545; Contracts 176(2); Fed Civ Proc 2497.1.

Hernandez v. **Forbes Chevrolet Co.**, TexApp–Corpus Christi, 680 SW2d 75, writ gr, and dism as moot.—Cons Cred 16; Contracts 153, 175(1); Sec Tran 186, 222.

Hernandez v. **Ford Motor Co.**, SDTex, 390 FSupp2d 602.—Damag 57.27, 57.29.

Hernandez; **Freeman v.**, TexCivApp–Dallas, 521 SW2d 108.—App & E 854(1), 1175(1), 1177(1), 1177(2), 1177(7); Ref of Inst 19(2); Usury 117.

Hernandez; **Furr's, Inc. v.**, TexCivApp–El Paso, 579 SW2d 320, dism.—Plead 111.39(2), 111.42(6), 111.42(7).

Hernandez v. **Furr's Supermarkets, Inc.**, TexApp–El Paso, 924 SW2d 193, reh overr, and writ den.—Judgm 181(7), 185(2); Lim of Act 1, 121(1), 121(2).

Hernandez v. **Garrison**, CA5 (Tex), 916 F2d 291, reh den 928 F2d 403.—Hab Corp 231, 688, 847; Pardon 48.1; Sent & Pun 15, 17(1).

Hernandez; **Glunz v.**, TexApp–San Antonio, 908 SW2d 253, reh overr, and writ den.—Judgm 17(1), 486(1), 489, 497(1), 499, 501, 518.

Hernandez; **Goldston Corp. v.**, TexApp–Corpus Christi, 714 SW2d 350, ref nre.—App & E 237(6), 901, 931(3), 931(6), 932(1); Damag 2, 32, 100, 130.1, 132(1), 132(6.1), 134(1), 185(1).

Hernandez v. **Great Am. Ins. Co. of New York**, Tex, 464 SW2d 91.—Contrib 5(1); Indem 35, 57; Insurance 3350; Lim of Act 55(2), 56(1).

Hernandez v. **Great Am. Ins. Co. of New York**, TexCivApp–Corpus Christi, 456 SW2d 729, rev 464 SW2d 91.—Action 1, 27(1); Insurance 3380; Lim of Act 55(1).

Hernandez v. **Gulf Group Lloyds**, Tex, 875 SW2d 691.—Contracts 318; Insurance 1713, 1806, 2793(2).

Hernandez; **Gulf Group Lloyds v.**, TexApp–San Antonio, 876 SW2d 162, writ gr, rev 875 SW2d 691.—Insurance 2793(2).

Hernandez; **Haggar Clothing Co. v.**, Tex, 164 SW2d 386.—App & E 930(1), 1001(1), 1001(3); Labor & Emp 810, 863(2).

Hernandez; **Haggar Clothing Co. v.**, TexApp–Corpus Christi, 164 SW3d 407, review gr, rev 164 SW3d 386.—App & E 840(4), 882(12), 893(1), 1004(8), 1004(11), 1047(1), 1050.1(1), 1056.1(1), 1182; Const Law 963, 4427; Damag 57.9, 57.11, 95, 97, 99, 140.5, 208(2), 208(4), 208(6); Evid 138, 597; Labor & Emp 755, 809, 810, 861, 862, 863(2), 867, 870, 871, 874; Trial 182, 219, 228(1), 241, 349(2).

Hernandez v. Hardy, TexCivApp–Hous (14 Dist), 426 SW2d 258.—Infants 245.

Hernandez; Harlandale Independent School Dist. v., TexApp–San Antonio, 994 SW2d 257.—App & E 70(3); Labor & Emp 854; Plead 104(1).

Hernandez v. Hayes, TexApp–San Antonio, 931 SW2d 648, reh overr, and writ den.—Const Law 328, 2311, 2312, 2314; Libel 36, 38(1); Torts 121, 122.

Hernandez v. Heckler, CA5 (Tex), 704 F2d 857.—Social S 140.21, 143.35, 143.65, 143.85.

Hernandez v. Heldenfels, Tex, 374 SW2d 196.—App & E 1043(6), 1050.1(1); Autos 155, 201(10), 245(4), 245(70); Neglig 1040(3), 1125, 1205(9); Pretrial Proc 713, 726; Propty 7.

Hernandez; Heldenfels v., TexCivApp–Waco, 366 SW2d 641, writ gr, rev 374 SW2d 196.—Autos 155; Neglig 1040(3), 1205(9).

Hernandez v. Hernandez, TexApp–Corpus Christi, 703 SW2d 250.—Divorce 151, 252.3(2); Hus & W 248.5, 258; Plead 427.

Hernandez; Hernandez v., TexApp–Corpus Christi, 703 SW2d 250.—Divorce 151, 252.3(2); Hus & W 248.5, 258; Plead 427.

Hernandez v. Hernandez, TexCivApp–San Antonio, 611 SW2d 732.—App & E 1170.7; Evid 267, 314(1); Ten in C 15(1), 15(2), 15(7), 15(10).

Hernandez; Hernandez v., TexCivApp–San Antonio, 611 SW2d 732.—App & E 1170.7; Evid 267, 314(1); Ten in C 15(1), 15(2), 15(7), 15(10).

Hernandez v. Hill Country Telephone Co-op., Inc., CA5 (Tex), 849 F2d 139, reh den 853 F2d 925.—Civil R 1312, 1487, 1502, 1529, 1530, 1548, 1574, 1593; Jury 25(6).

Hernandez v. Hines, NDTex, 159 FSupp2d 378.—Civil R 1039, 1057, 1373, 1376(1), 1376(2), 1395(1); Infants 226.

Hernandez v. Home Sav. Ass'n of Dallas County, CA5 (Tex), 606 F2d 596.—Estop 62.2(4); U S 53(9), 53(19).

Hernandez v. Home Sav. Ass'n of Dallas County, NDTex, 425 FSupp 835, rev 606 F2d 596.—B & L Assoc 38(5).

Hernandez v. Home Sav. Ass'n of Dallas County, NDTex, 411 FSupp 858, motion den 425 FSupp 835, rev 606 F2d 596.—Estop 62.2(4); Interpl 35; U S 53(9).

Hernandez v. Houston Independent School Dist., TexCivApp–Austin, 558 SW2d 121, ref nre.—Aliens 114, 121, 126; App & E 1079; Const Law 947, 1021, 1076, 2970, 2972, 2973, 3013, 3062, 3903, 3921, 4205; Schools 17, 148(1).

Hernandez v. Houston Lighting & Power Co., TexApp–Houston (14 Dist), 795 SW2d 775.—Action 60; Electricity 19(1), 19(4); Evid 3, 14, 51; Plead 228.14.

Hernandez v. H. S. Anderson Trucking Co., TexCivApp–Beaumont, 370 SW2d 909, ref nre.—App & E 1062.1; Autos 1, 243(2); Evid 546.

Hernandez v. Igloo Products Corp. Retirement Plan, SDTex, 868 FSupp 200.—Fed Civ Proc 2466, 2544; Labor & Emp 438, 585, 592, 688.

Hernandez v. Immigration and Naturalization Service, CA5 (Tex), 539 F2d 384.—Aliens 384, 386, 392.

Hernandez; International Ins. Co. v., TexApp–Corpus Christi, 659 SW2d 922.—Costs 260(1); Work Comp 554, 566, 571, 598, 966, 998, 1042, 1492, 1633.

Hernandez; Jackson v., Tex, 285 SW2d 184, 155 Tex 249.—Evid 385, 419(1), 419(2); Lim of Act 39(11); Tresp to T T 10; Trusts 17(3), 43(1), 43(3), 88, 373.

Hernandez; Jackson v., TexCivApp–Galveston, 274 SW2d 131, aff 285 SW2d 184, 155 Tex 249.—Lim of Act 39(11); Trusts 1, 43(1), 44(3), 62, 63.9, 72, 75, 77.

Hernandez; Janes v., CA5 (Tex), 215 F3d 541, reh and sug for reh den 232 F3d 212, cert den Bastrop County v. Janes, 121 SCt 858, 531 US 1113, 148 LEd2d 772.—Civil R 1351(4), 1352(4); Convicts 6.

Hernandez v. JLG Industries, Inc., TexApp–San Antonio, 905 SW2d 778.—App & E 543, 1177(9).

Hernandez v. Jobe Concrete Products, Inc., CA5 (Tex), 282 F3d 360.—Rem of C 107(9); States 18.51; Work Comp 406.

Hernandez v. Johnson, CA5 (Tex), 248 F3d 344, cert den Baiza Hernandez v. Cockrell, 122 SCt 621, 534 US 1043, 151 LEd2d 543.—Crim Law 683(1); Sent & Pun 1716.

Hernandez v. Johnson, CA5 (Tex), 213 F3d 243, cert den 121 SCt 400, 531 US 966, 148 LEd2d 308.—Crim Law 53, 641.13(1), 641.13(2.1), 641.13(7), 706(2), 796; Hab Corp 486(5), 768, 818; Homic 821; Sent & Pun 1712, 1773, 1780(3).

Hernandez v. Johnson, CA5 (Tex), 108 F3d 554, cert den 118 SCt 447, 522 US 984, 139 LEd2d 383.—Crim Law 641.5(0.5), 641.13(6), 641.13(7), 818; Hab Corp 205, 688, 746, 841.

Hernandez v. Kasco Ventures, Inc., TexApp–El Paso, 832 SW2d 629.—Antitrust 141, 150; App & E 170(1), 863, 901; Fixt 1, 4, 6.1; Judgm 181(11), 181(24), 185(2), 185(6); Land & Ten 164(2), 165(1); Prod Liab 16, 23.1, 48.

Hernandez; Kimbell, Inc. v., TexCivApp–El Paso, 572 SW2d 784.—App & E 846(5), 912, 989; Plead 111.42(7), 111.44.

Hernandez v. Koch Machinery Co., TexApp–Houston (1 Dist), 16 SW3d 48, reh overr, and review den, and reh of petition for review den.—App & E 302(1), 840(1); Judgm 335(1), 335(2), 335(3); Lim of Act 18, 43; Prod Liab 71.5.

Hernandez v. Kroger Co., Tex, 711 SW2d 3.—Trial 350.6(1).

Hernandez v. Kroger Co., TexApp–Houston (14 Dist), 706 SW2d 335, rev 711 SW2d 3.—Trial 350.6(2), 352.4(6).

Hernandez; Kroger Stores, Inc. v., TexCivApp–Dallas, 549 SW2d 16.—Evid 75; Neglig 1708.

Hernandez v. Lautensack, TexApp–Fort Worth, 201 SW3d 771, reh overr, and review den.—Antitrust 284; App & E 843(2); Costs 194.25, 194.44, 207, 208; Damag 123, 140, 191; Trial 66, 68(1).

Hernandez v. Light Pub. Co., TexCivApp–San Antonio, 245 SW2d 553, writ refused.—App & E 758.1; Jury 28(6); Trial 3(1).

Hernandez; Lopez v., TexCivApp–Corpus Christi, 595 SW2d 180.—App & E 768; Autos 172(1), 172(2), 244(12); Evid 584(1), 587, 597; Trial 350.2, 366.

Hernandez v. Lucas, SDTex, 254 FSupp 901.—Fed Cts 275, 282, 289, 292, 313.

Hernandez v. Lukefahr, TexApp–Houston (14 Dist), 879 SW2d 137.—App & E 523.1, 837(9); Evid 571(3); Health 603, 769; Judgm 178, 185(2), 185.1(8), 185.3(21); Neglig 201, 275, 284.

Hernandez; McCoy v., CA5 (Tex), 203 F3d 371.—Civil R 1437; Fed Civ Proc 2117; Fed Cts 420, 764, 765, 776, 822, 908.1; Judgm 666, 668(1), 675(1), 677, 678(1), 681, 713(1), 725(1), 828.8; Offic 119.

Hernandez v. Malakoff Fuel Co., TexCivApp–Dallas, 109 SW2d 356, writ dism.—App & E 1056.1(10); Labor & Emp 2832, 2889; Neglig 453; Work Comp 2113, 2129.

Hernandez; Martinez v., TexCivApp–San Antonio, 394 SW2d 667, ref nre.—App & E 1175(1); Autos 171(8), 208, 242(1), 245(80), 245(90); Evid 588; Neglig 213, 503, 504.

Hernandez v. Maxwell, CA5 (Tex), 905 F2d 94.—Civil R 1304, 1311, 1395(6), 1396.

Hernandez v. Meno, TexApp–Austin, 828 SW2d 491, writ den.—Admin Law 513; Schools 147.42.

Hernandez v. Mid-Loop, Inc., TexApp–San Antonio, 170 SW3d 138.—App & E 920(1), 946, 961; Pretrial Proc 44.1, 46, 226, 435.

Hernandez; Miller v., TexApp–Dallas, 708 SW2d 25.—App & E 345.1, 346.2.

Hernandez v. Montgomery Ward & Co., Tex, 652 SW2d 923, on remand 661 SW2d 159.—App & E 242(1); Courts 472.2; Trial 271, 274, 278, 366.

Hernandez; Montgomery Ward & Co. v., TexApp–Corpus Christi, 661 SW2d 159.—App & E 1001(1), 1003(5); False Imp 2, 31, 36, 39.

Hernandez; Montgomery Ward & Co. v., TexApp–Corpus Christi, 644 SW2d 758, rev 652 SW2d 923, on remand 661 SW2d 159.—App & E 231(1), 232(0.5), 974(1); False Imp 2; Trial 352.4(2), 352.10, 366.

Hernandez; Moseley v., TexApp–Corpus Christi, 797 SW2d 240.—Parties 35.9, 35.61; Plead 210, 228.14, 228.23.

Hernandez v. M/V Rajaan, CA5 (Tex), 848 F2d 498.—Ship 86(3).

Hernandez v. M/V Rajaan, CA5 (Tex), 841 F2d 582, opinion corrected on denial of reh 848 F2d 498, cert den Dianella Shipping Corp v. Hernandez, 109 SCt 530, 488 US 981, 102 LEd2d 562, cert den 109 SCt 837, 488 US 1030, 102 LEd2d 970.—Damag 15, 63, 100, 101, 130.1, 135; Fed Cts 929; Interest 31, 39(2.25); Ship 84(1), 84(2), 84(3.3), 86(3), 208, 209(3).

Hernandez v. N. L. R. B., CA5 (Tex), 505 F2d 119, reh den 509 F2d 576.—Labor & Emp 1691, 1855.

Hernandez v. National Restoration Technologies, L.L.C., Tex, 211 SW3d 309, on remand 2007 WL 2127721.—App & E 428(2).

Hernandez v. Nissan Motor Corp. in U.S.A., TexApp–El Paso, 740 SW2d 894, writ den.—Prod Liab 77.5, 83.5.

Hernandez v. Nueces County Medical Soc. Community Blood Bank, TexApp–Corpus Christi, 779 SW2d 867.—Judgm 181(33); Prod Liab 46.1.

Hernandez; Perez v., TexApp–Corpus Christi, 658 SW2d 697.—App & E 852, 1079; Costs 32(1), 208; Damag 1; Ten in C 29.1, 30; Trusts 102(1), 374, 377; Usury 12, 50, 111(1).

Hernandez; Perez v., TexCivApp–San Antonio, 317 SW2d 81, ref nre.—Evid 20(1); Judgm 181(33), 185.3(21); Labor & Emp 3137, 3159; Neglig 1037(7).

Hernandez v. Phelps Dodge Refining Corp., CA5 (Tex), 572 F2d 1132.—Civil R 1544, 1548.

Hernandez v. Powell, NDTex, 424 FSupp 479.—Civil R 1548, 1574.

Hernandez; Reed v., CA5 (Tex), 114 FedAppx 609.—Counties 67; Damag 57.58; Fed Civ Proc 1373, 2541; Fraud 58(1).

Hernandez v. Reno, CA5 (Tex), 91 F3d 776, reh den.—Aliens 154, 177, 207, 411; Fed Civ Proc 2582; Statut 181(1), 219(2), 219(4).

Hernandez v. Robledo, TexCivApp–Dallas, 236 SW2d 242.—Bound 43; Judgm 251(1), 255.

Hernandez v. Ruiz, SDTex, 812 FSupp 734.—Action 3; Labor & Emp 2702, 2729; Statut 184, 217.

Hernandez v. San Antonio Independent School Dist., TexCivApp–San Antonio, 598 SW2d 334.—Elections 126(1), 172.

Hernandez; Sanchez v., TexCivApp–San Antonio, 456 SW2d 497, ref nre.—App & E 837(1), 1008.1(3); Contracts 346(10); Paymt 73(1).

Hernandez; Sears, Roebuck and Co. v., BkrtcyWDTex, 208 BR 872. See Hernandez, In re.

Hernandez v. Seventh Day Adventist Corp., Ltd., TexApp–San Antonio, 54 SW3d 335.—Judgm 830.1.

Hernandez; Shockome v., TexCivApp–Corpus Christi, 587 SW2d 535.—Child 12, 13, 20.8, 58.

Hernandez v. Simbeck, TexCivApp–San Antonio, 553 SW2d 13.—App & E 846(5), 854(1); Gifts 49(4); Trial 382.

Hernandez v. Smith, CA5 (Tex), 552 F2d 142.—Damag 91(3); Health 629, 656, 661, 823(9), 831.

Hernandez; Sonic Drive-In of Raymondville, Texas, Inc. v., TexApp–Corpus Christi, 797 SW2d 254, writ den.—Admin Law 413, 749, 761, 791; Const Law 4116; Unemp Comp 304, 497.

Hernandez; Southern Pacific Transp. Co. v., TexApp–San Antonio, 804 SW2d 557, writ den, cert den 112 SCt 406, 502 US 952, 116 LEd2d 355.—App & E 610, 654,

930(3), 1064.1(2.1), 1064.1(7); Courts 97(1); Labor & Emp 2796, 2897; Trial 349(2).

Hernandez v. Southern Pacific Transp. Co., TexApp–Corpus Christi, 641 SW2d 947.—App & E 218.2(1), 843(2), 866(3), 930(3), 989, 1003(5), 1069.3; Neglig 371, 378, 387, 503, 504, 506(1); New Tr 56; Prod Liab 23.1, 85; Trial 133.6(8), 312(1), 315, 350.1, 350.6(6), 351.5(8).

Hernandez v. Spencer, CA5 (Tex), 780 F2d 504.—Action 69(5); Civil R 1311.

Hernandez v. Starr County Hosp. Dist., SDTex, 30 FSupp2d 970.—Health 197, 258, 658.

Hernandez v. State, TexCrimApp, 176 SW3d 821.—Crim Law 374, 1169.11.

Hernandez v. State, TexCrimApp, 161 SW3d 491, reh den.—Crim Law 37(1), 37(2.1), 330, 558, 569, 739.1(1), 739.1(2), 1139, 1159.5.

Hernandez v. State, TexCrimApp, 127 SW3d 768, on remand 2005 WL 283607.—Crim Law 157, 159; Ind & Inf 55, 71.2(3); Statut 184.

Hernandez v. State, TexCrimApp, 116 SW3d 26.—Crim Law 304(1), 388.1, 388.2, 472.

Hernandez v. State, TexCrimApp, 109 SW3d 491.—Crim Law 661.

Hernandez v. State, TexCrimApp, 60 SW3d 106, on remand 80 SW3d 63.—Crim Law 1177.

Hernandez v. State, TexCrimApp, 988 SW2d 770, on remand 2000 WL 1231508.—Crim Law 641.13(7).

Hernandez v. State, TexCrimApp, 939 SW2d 173, on remand 1997 WL 33641950.—Courts 89; Crim Law 511.1(3), 511.2, 511.4, 511.5.

Hernandez v. State, TexCrimApp, 929 SW2d 11.—Sent & Pun 1351.

Hernandez v. State, TexCrimApp, 861 SW2d 908.—Rape 17; Statut 189.

Hernandez v. State, TexCrimApp, 842 SW2d 294.—Autos 144.2(5.1).

Hernandez v. State, TexCrimApp, 819 SW2d 806, reh den, cert den 112 SCt 2944, 504 US 974, 119 LEd2d 568, denial of habeas corpus aff 108 F3d 554, cert den 118 SCt 447, 522 US 984, 139 LEd2d 383.—Crim Law 364(3.1), 388.2, 412.1(2), 412.1(4), 556, 568, 629.5(1), 736(2), 781(1), 781(4), 795(1), 795(2.10), 814(16), 1171.1(2.1), 1171.1(3); Homic 542, 668, 1137, 1141, 1143, 1387, 1458; Ind & Inf 189(8); Jury 33(2.15), 33(5.15); Prisons 4(7); Sent & Pun 318, 1756, 1760, 1769.

Hernandez v. State, TexCrimApp, 805 SW2d 409, reh den, cert den 111 SCt 2275, 500 US 960, 114 LEd2d 726, dism of habeas corpus aff 248 F3d 344, cert den Baiza Hernandez v. Cockrell, 122 SCt 621, 534 US 1043, 151 LEd2d 543.—Crim Law 393(1), 396(1), 412.2(3), 637, 706(3), 783.5, 867; Witn 305(2).

Hernandez v. State, TexCrimApp, 800 SW2d 523.—Crim Law 1177; Sent & Pun 312, 319; Witn 37(4).

Hernandez v. State, TexCrimApp, 785 SW2d 825.—Crim Law 1077.2(2), 1109(3).

Hernandez v. State, TexCrimApp, 757 SW2d 744, appeal after remand 819 SW2d 806, reh den, cert den 112 SCt 2944, 504 US 974, 119 LEd2d 568, denial of habeas corpus aff 108 F3d 554, cert den 118 SCt 447, 522 US 984, 139 LEd2d 383.—Crim Law 749, 1152(2); Homic 1184, 1186; Jury 107, 108, 132.

Hernandez v. State, TexCrimApp, 746 SW2d 237.—Crim Law 1134(3).

Hernandez v. State, TexCrimApp, 726 SW2d 53.—Crim Law 641.13(1), 641.13(2.1), 641.13(6), 1166.10(1).

Hernandez v. State, TexCrimApp, 698 SW2d 679, on remand 704 SW2d 488.—Controlled Subs 74.

Hernandez v. State, TexCrimApp, 669 SW2d 734.—Statut 64(6), 143.

Hernandez v. State, TexCrimApp, 651 SW2d 746, on remand 665 SW2d 181, petition for discretionary review refused.—Crim Law 507(7).

Hernandez v. State, TexCrimApp, 643 SW2d 397, cert den 103 SCt 3128, 462 US 1144, 77 LEd2d 1379.—Crim

Law 586, 590(2), 1034, 1035(6), 1151, 1152(2), 1153(2), 1166.16, 1170.5(1); Homic 1152; Jury 40, 75(1), 108, 109; Sent & Pun 1675; Witn 39, 79(1), 240(2).

Hernandez v. State, TexCrimApp, 613 SW2d 287.—Sent & Pun 1968(2), 2003.

Hernandez v. State, TexCrimApp, 603 SW2d 848.—Crim Law 223.

Hernandez v. State, TexCrimApp, 600 SW2d 793.—Bail 60, 80; Crim Law 394.1(1), 394.1(2).

Hernandez v. State, TexCrimApp, 599 SW2d 614.—Crim Law 828, 1042.

Hernandez v. State, TexCrimApp, 578 SW2d 731.—Crim Law 511.1(7), 511.2.

Hernandez v. State, TexCrimApp, 563 SW2d 947.—Crim Law 1166.18; Jury 107.

Hernandez v. State, TexCrimApp, 556 SW2d 337.—Const Law 3856, 4732; Crim Law 260.11(2), 577.4, 577.10(1), 577.16(4), 1134(3), 1177; Sent & Pun 1962, 1963, 2019, 2021, 2025.

Hernandez v. State, TexCrimApp, 548 SW2d 904.—Crim Law 394.4(13); Cust Dut 126(10); Searches 46.

Hernandez v. State, TexCrimApp, 538 SW2d 127.—Controlled Subs 27, 30, 80; Crim Law 698(1), 1159.4(2), 1170.5(1); Sent & Pun 2020, 2021.

Hernandez v. State, TexCrimApp, 532 SW2d 612.—Crim Law 1141(2); Witn 344(2), 351.

Hernandez v. State, TexCrimApp, 530 SW2d 563.—Const Law 4535; Controlled Subs 67; Crim Law 31, 388.2, 494, 577.8(2), 641.7(1), 1166.22(1), 1166.22(2), 1169.5(3), 1556; Hab Corp 690; Sent & Pun 1367, 1371, 1386, 1388.

Hernandez v. State, TexCrimApp, 523 SW2d 410.—Arrest 63.4(13), 63.5(3.1), 63.5(4), 63.5(6).

Hernandez v. State, TexCrimApp, 517 SW2d 782.—Controlled Subs 68, 80.

Hernandez v. State, TexCrimApp, 508 SW2d 853.—Crim Law 1166.16; Jury 131(6).

Hernandez v. State, TexCrimApp, 507 SW2d 209.—Crim Law 655(1), 656(9), 938(1), 1166.22(2), 1166.22(4.1), 1166.22(7).

Hernandez v. State, TexCrimApp, 506 SW2d 884.—Crim Law 699, 1171.4; Jury 42, 110(14), 131(2); Witn 277(4), 302, 305(2).

Hernandez v. State, TexCrimApp, 492 SW2d 466.—Crim Law 586, 1035(6), 1130(5); Homic 1186.

Hernandez v. State, TexCrimApp, 484 SW2d 754.—Controlled Subs 68; Crim Law 349, 370, 673(5), 1115(1), 1153(1).

Hernandez v. State, TexCrimApp, 468 SW2d 387.—Const Law 4506; Crim Law 371(1), 372(14), 486(9), 673(5), 1169.5(2), 1169.5(3); Double J 6; Mal Mis 1, 4, 8, 9, 10.

Hernandez v. State, TexCrimApp, 450 SW2d 340.—Crim Law 1023(11), 1081(5).

Hernandez v. State, TexCrimApp, 437 SW2d 831, cert den 89 SCt 2148, 395 US 987, 23 LEd2d 775.—Const Law 75, 2572; Courts 100(1); Crim Law 518(1), 867; Searches 126; Witn 270(2).

Hernandez v. State, TexCrimApp, 435 SW2d 520, cert den 90 SCt 112, 396 US 866, 24 LEd2d 120.—Arrest 63.4(8), 63.4(14), 71.1(3); Controlled Subs 80; Crim Law 627.10(4), 632(5), 1120(1).

Hernandez v. State, TexCrimApp, 425 SW2d 653.—Crim Law 412.2(3), 531(3).

Hernandez v. State, TexCrimApp, 397 SW2d 68.—Homic 1171.

Hernandez v. State, TexCrimApp, 396 SW2d 889.—Crim Law 1092.4, 1092.9; Rape 51(1).

Hernandez v. State, TexCrimApp, 378 SW2d 311.—Autos 355(13); Crim Law 662.80, 1038.1(2), 1038.3.

Hernandez v. State, TexCrimApp, 375 SW2d 285.—Crim Law 822(8); Homic 727, 739, 908, 1154.

Hernandez v. State, TexCrimApp, 367 SW2d 676.—Bail 64.

Hernandez v. State, TexCrimApp, 367 SW2d 675.—Bail 64.

Hernandez v. State, TexCrimApp, 366 SW2d 575.—Crim Law 723(1), 730(14); Homic 1333; Sent & Pun 34.

Hernandez v. State, TexCrimApp, 334 SW2d 299, 169 TexCrim 418.—Crim Law 486(8), 507(1), 507(4), 852; Witn 394.

Hernandez v. State, TexCrimApp, 324 SW2d 558, 168 TexCrim 194.—Int Liq 236(7), 236(9), 236(11).

Hernandez v. State, TexCrimApp, 320 SW2d 829, 167 TexCrim 487.—Crim Law 720(10), 723(3); Sent & Pun 1352.

Hernandez v. State, TexCrimApp, 307 SW2d 88, 165 TexCrim 329.—Burg 41(1); Crim Law 814(16), 1173.2(7).

Hernandez v. State, TexCrimApp, 294 SW2d 837.—Crim Law 1087.1(2).

Hernandez v. State, TexCrimApp, 286 SW2d 935.—Crim Law 1090.1(1).

Hernandez v. State, TexCrimApp, 286 SW2d 137.—Crim Law 1090.1(1).

Hernandez v. State, TexCrimApp, 272 SW2d 376.—Bail 64.

Hernandez v. State, TexCrimApp, 263 SW2d 552, 159 TexCrim 313.—Crim Law 641.7(1).

Hernandez v. State, TexCrimApp, 262 SW2d 507.—Crim Law 1090.1(1).

Hernandez v. State, TexCrimApp, 262 SW2d 200, 159 TexCrim 178.—Crim Law 1090.13.

Hernandez v. State, TexCrimApp, 255 SW2d 219, 158 TexCrim 296.—Controlled Subs 75, 142; Crim Law 394.4(6); Searches 112, 117, 123.1, 126, 191, 199.

Hernandez v. State, TexCrimApp, 251 SW2d 531, 160 TexCrim 72, cert gr 74 SCt 52, 346 US 811, 98 LEd 339, rev 74 SCt 667, 347 US 475, 98 LEd 866.—Const Law 3013, 3306; Gr Jury 2.5; Jury 33(1), 33(1.15).

Hernandez v. State, TexCrimApp, 248 SW2d 749, 157 TexCrim 322.—Autos 351.1.

Hernandez v. State, TexCrimApp, 247 SW2d 260, 157 TexCrim 112.—Crim Law 1090.1(1), 1159.5; Homic 530, 532, 909, 1136, 1210.

Hernandez v. State, TexCrimApp, 189 SW2d 876, 148 TexCrim 566.—Crim Law 737(1), 741(1), 742(1); Larc 57, 71(3).

Hernandez v. State, TexCrimApp, 172 SW2d 696, 146 TexCrim 196.—Ind & Inf 52(1).

Hernandez v. State, TexCrimApp, 138 SW2d 1069.—Crim Law 1182.

Hernandez v. State, TexCrimApp, 133 SW2d 584, 138 TexCrim 4.—Crim Law 641.4(4), 641.7(1).

Hernandez v. State, TexCrimApp, 129 SW2d 301, 137 TexCrim 343.—Controlled Subs 80, 97; Crim Law 369.2(8), 394.5(3), 481, 772(6), 1086.13; Searches 171, 172.

Hernandez v. State, TexApp–Houston (1 Dist), 127 SW3d 206, petition for discretionary review refused.—Crim Law 388.1, 472, 486(2), 488, 641.13(1), 641.13(6), 956(1), 1036.1(9), 1042, 1045, 1134(3), 1144.13(2.1), 1153(1), 1153(2), 1159.5, 1159.6; Homic 668, 673; Sent & Pun 104, 319, 323, 364.

Hernandez v. State, TexApp–Houston (1 Dist), 53 SW3d 742, petition for discretionary review refused.—Crim Law 469, 478(1), 1035(10), 1043(1), 1043(2), 1147, 1153(1), 1153(2).

Hernandez v. State, TexApp–Houston (1 Dist), 976 SW2d 753, reh overr, petition for discretionary review refused 980 SW2d 652.—Crim Law 1153(4), 1162, 1170.5(1); Witn 337(8), 337(9), 337(25), 337(28).

Hernandez v. State, TexApp–Houston (1 Dist), 827 SW2d 54.—Crim Law 273.4(1), 274(3.1), 274(8), 274(9), 275, 1026.10(4), 1159.6.

Hernandez v. State, TexApp–Houston (1 Dist), 817 SW2d 744.—Crim Law 338(1), 338(7), 369.1, 369.2(1), 371(1), 1130(5), 1153(1).

Hernandez v. State, TexApp–Houston (1 Dist), 782 SW2d 512, petition for discretionary review refused.—Const Law 4723; Crim Law 790, 847, 1172.1(2).

Hernandez v. State, TexApp–Fort Worth, 114 SW3d 58, petition for discretionary review refused.—Crim Law 412(4), 412.2(2), 720(2), 720(6), 721(3), 722.3, 723(3), 726, 730(1), 919(3), 919(4), 1134(2), 1162, 1169.2(3), 1169.2(6), 1169.12, 1171.1(2.1).

Hernandez v. State, TexApp–Fort Worth, 939 SW2d 692, reh overr, and petition for discretionary review refused. —Crim Law 721(3), 726, 1144.13(3), 1159.2(2), 1159.2(8), 1159.2(9), 1159.3(2), 1191; Homic 1184, 1186.

Hernandez v. State, TexApp–Fort Worth, 931 SW2d 49. —Crim Law 719(3), 726, 730(1).

Hernandez v. State, TexApp–Fort Worth, 903 SW2d 109, reh overr, and petition for discretionary review refused, and petition for discretionary review refused.—Assault 80, 92(2); Crim Law 44, 553, 562, 1134(2), 1144.13(2.1), 1159.2(7), 1159.6; Ind & Inf 119, 120; Obst Just 1, 16.

Hernandez v. State, TexApp–Fort Worth, 895 SW2d 508, petition for discretionary review refused.—Crim Law 795(2.5), 795(2.10), 1043(2), 1134(3), 1144.13(3), 1159.2(1), 1159.2(7); Homic 527, 528, 1184, 1185, 1457, 1458; Ind & Inf 189(1).

Hernandez v. State, TexApp–Fort Worth, 891 SW2d 744, petition for discretionary review refused.—Crim Law 130, 139, 369.2(1), 371(12), 795(1.5), 795(2.10), 814(20), 1139, 1153(1), 1166(4); Rob 27(6).

Hernandez v. State, TexApp–Austin, 149 SW3d 761, petition for discretionary review gr, rev 161 SW3d 491, reh den.—Crim Law 37(1), 37(2.1), 37(3), 37(8), 330, 569, 739.1(1), 739.1(2), 1159.5.

Hernandez v. State, TexApp–Austin, 986 SW2d 817, petition for discretionary review refused.—Crim Law 273.1(1), 273.1(4), 642, 1026.10(1), 1035(3), 1072, 1081(2).

Hernandez v. State, TexApp–Austin, 983 SW2d 867, petition for discretionary review refused.—Autos 335, 349(2.1); Crim Law 394.5(4), 1139.

Hernandez v. State, TexApp–Austin, 978 SW2d 137, petition for discretionary review refused.—Costs 302.2(2); Crim Law 412.2(5), 899.

Hernandez v. State, TexApp–Austin, 973 SW2d 787, petition for discretionary review refused.—Crim Law 372(7), 1153(1); Ind & Inf 87(7); Infants 20.

Hernandez v. State, TexApp–Austin, 952 SW2d 59, review gr, vac 957 SW2d 851, on remand 1998 WL 132930. —Const Law 656, 2370, 2450, 4646, 4756; Crim Law 412.2(3), 412.2(5), 414, 517(6), 519(9), 520(1), 520(2), 522(1), 531(1), 531(3), 641.12(1), 671, 906, 932, 959, 1035(5), 1084, 1134(3), 1153(1), 1158(4), 1162, 1166.18; Jury 39, 131(18).

Hernandez v. State, TexApp–Austin, 768 SW2d 5.—Larc 7; Sent & Pun 2020.

Hernandez v. State, TexApp–Austin, 692 SW2d 190, petition for discretionary review refused by 709 SW2d 1, cert den 107 SCt 207, 479 US 860, 93 LEd2d 137.— Crim Law 1174(5); Homic 852; Ind & Inf 60, 65, 71.2(2), 71.4(5), 115.

Hernandez v. State, TexApp–San Antonio, 219 SW3d 6, petition for discretionary review gr.—Crim Law 662.1, 662.7, 662.8, 673(3), 700(1), 706(3), 706(4), 720(6), 730(3), 1037.1(1), 1037.2, 1044.1(8); Witn 380(3).

Hernandez v. State, TexApp–San Antonio, 198 SW3d 257, petition for discretionary review refused.—Crim Law 59(4), 59(5), 80, 323, 564(2), 564(3), 641.13(1), 641.13(2.1), 769, 772(6), 814(19), 824(4), 1038.2, 1038.3, 1119(1), 1134(2), 1144.6, 1144.10, 1144.13(2.1), 1159.2(7), 1159.2(9), 1159.4(1), 1159.6, 1175; Homic 1166, 1207.

Hernandez v. State, TexApp–San Antonio, 107 SW3d 41, reh overr, and petition for discretionary review refused. —Arrest 63.5(3.1), 63.5(9); Autos 332; Crim Law 412(4), 412.2(2), 778(3), 781(1), 835, 1130(5), 1134(2), 1139, 1158(4); Jury 131(13).

Hernandez v. State, TexApp–San Antonio, 18 SW3d 699, reh overr, and petition for discretionary review gr, aff 109 SW3d 491.—Autos 351.1, 359; Crim Law 369.2(7), 633(2), 661, 1026.10(5).

Hernandez v. State, TexApp–San Antonio, 969 SW2d 440, petition for discretionary review refused.—Crim Law 770(2), 795(1), 795(1.5), 795(2.1), 795(2.10), 795(2.50), 1109(3), 1144.13(1); Homic 607, 683, 766, 800, 1166, 1458, 1474, 1479, 1480, 1484; Ind & Inf 191(4).

Hernandez v. State, TexApp–San Antonio, 963 SW2d 921, petition for discretionary review refused.—Arrest 68(4); Crim Law 394.6(4), 394.6(5), 1139, 1144.9, 1158(4).

Hernandez v. State, TexApp–San Antonio, 904 SW2d 808, petition for discretionary review gr, aff Ex parte Hernandez, 953 SW2d 275, cert den 118 SCt 1093, 522 US 1135, 140 LEd2d 149.—Double J 1, 24; Prisons 13(2).

Hernandez v. State, TexApp–San Antonio, 894 SW2d 807, reh overr, and petition for discretionary review refused. —Crim Law 1026.10(4), 1026.10(8), 1072, 1131(4), 1132.

Hernandez; State v., TexApp–San Antonio, 842 SW2d 306, reh den, and petition for discretionary review refused, cert den 113 SCt 3049, 509 US 927, 125 LEd2d 733, on subsequent appeal 894 SW2d 807, reh overr, and petition for discretionary review refused.—Crim Law 412.1(1), 412.1(2), 412.2(4), 641.1, 641.3(3), 641.3(4).

Hernandez; State v., TexApp–San Antonio, 830 SW2d 631.—Crim Law 577.10(3), 577.10(10), 577.16(8).

Hernandez; State v., TexApp–San Antonio, 802 SW2d 894.—Child S 233, 250, 255, 356, 361, 496.

Hernandez v. State, TexApp–San Antonio, 783 SW2d 764. —Statut 188; Tresp 77.

Hernandez v. State, TexApp–San Antonio, 773 SW2d 761. —Autos 355(6); Crim Law 552(1), 1144.13(3), 1159.2(7).

Hernandez v. State, TexApp–San Antonio, 740 SW2d 594, petition for discretionary review refused.—Crim Law 126(2), 128, 295, 730(16), 739(4), 867.

Hernandez v. State, TexApp–San Antonio, 739 SW2d 957, petition for discretionary review refused.—Controlled Subs 27, 30, 80.

Hernandez v. State, TexApp–San Antonio, 665 SW2d 181, petition for discretionary review refused.—Crim Law 224, 511.2, 590(2), 594(3); Rape 54(1).

Hernandez v. State, TexApp–San Antonio, 656 SW2d 630. —Crim Law 1144.13(2.1); Rob 24.15(1).

Hernandez v. State, TexApp–San Antonio, 648 SW2d 751. —Crim Law 1077.3, 1097(1), 1104(1), 1129(1).

Hernandez v. State, TexApp–San Antonio, 636 SW2d 617, rev 651 SW2d 746, on remand 665 SW2d 181, petition for discretionary review refused.—Crim Law 507(1), 510, 511.1(1), 511.1(3), 511.2, 511.10; Rape 52(2), 54(1), 54(2).

Hernandez v. State, TexApp–San Antonio, 636 SW2d 611. —Crim Law 627.8(6), 1166(10.10).

Hernandez v. State, TexApp–San Antonio, 626 SW2d 876. —Crim Law 695(6), 1038.1(3.1), 1043(3), 1090.14; Sent & Pun 1379(2).

Hernandez v. State, TexApp–Dallas, 927 SW2d 644, review gr, rev 929 SW2d 11.—Sent & Pun 1234, 1237, 1256, 1259, 1424; Statut 181(1), 181(2), 184, 188, 189, 190.

Hernandez v. State, TexApp–Dallas, 774 SW2d 319, petition for discretionary review refused, appeal after remand 1992 WL 14006, petition for discretionary review refused.—Crim Law 723(1), 956(12), 957(1), 957(3), 957(5), 1036.1(1), 1037.1(2), 1134(3), 1159.2(7), 1159.3(1), 1174(2), 1177; Homic 1193, 1194, 1480.

Hernandez v. State, TexApp–Dallas, 748 SW2d 324, petition for discretionary review refused.—Const Law 2815; Sent & Pun 506, 546, 634.

Hernandez v. State, TexApp–Texarkana, 84 SW3d 26, petition for discretionary review refused.—Crim Law 273.1(5), 641.13(1), 641.13(5), 641.13(7), 953, 956(1), 956(2), 956(4), 959, 994(1), 1086.11, 1134(3).

Hernandez; State v., TexApp–Texarkana, 64 SW3d 548.—Arrest 68(4); Autos 349(2.1), 349(18); Crim Law 1139, 1153(1); Searches 171, 180, 181, 183.

Hernandez v. State, TexApp–Texarkana, 13 SW3d 78.—Autos 355(6), 411; Crim Law 412.1(4), 412.2(3), 438(8), 566, 1144.13(6), 1169.1(10), 1169.12.

Hernandez v. State, TexApp–Texarkana, 956 SW2d 699.—Controlled Subs 27, 34, 82; Crim Law 627.10(3), 627.10(7.1), 737(1), 741(1), 742(1), 1144.13(3), 1144.13(6), 1159.2(2), 1159.2(7).

Hernandez v. State, TexApp–Texarkana, 867 SW2d 900.—Arrest 63.1; Autos 349(3), 349(8), 349.5(6), 349.5(7); Const Law 4594(1), 4594(3), 4594(6), 4594(8); Controlled Subs 28, 30, 79, 80; Crim Law 627.8(6), 629(1), 700(9), 865(2), 922(3), 1155; Searches 12, 65.

Hernandez v. State, TexApp–Amarillo, 205 SW3d 555, petition for discretionary review refused.—Crim Law 338(1), 394.6(5), 433, 1153(1), 1162; Searches 24, 171, 181, 186, 194, 197, 201; Witn 52(7).

Hernandez v. State, TexApp–Amarillo, 80 SW3d 63.—Crim Law 394.1(1), 1162, 1163(1), 1165(1), 1177.

Hernandez v. State, TexApp–Amarillo, 13 SW3d 492, reh overr, and petition for discretionary review gr, opinion dissenting to overruling of reh 23 SW3d 122, rev 60 SW3d 106, on remand 80 SW3d 63.—Arrest 63.5(4), 63.5(6), 68(4); Autos 328, 349(2.1); Controlled Subs 29, 67, 74; Courts 97(5); Crim Law 338(1), 349, 369.2(1), 369.2(7), 394.4(1), 394.4(9), 404.65, 720(2), 720(6), 720(7.1), 723(3), 726, 730(8), 730(14), 1139, 1153(1), 1158(1), 1162, 1169.1(1), 1169.5(1), 1169.5(3), 1169.11; Searches 24, 165, 192.1.

Hernandez v. State, TexApp–Amarillo, 810 SW2d 843, petition for discretionary review gr, rev 842 SW2d 294.—Autos 144.2(5.1); Crim Law 769, 770(2); Sent & Pun 1872(2), 1891, 1902.

Hernandez v. State, TexApp–Amarillo, 670 SW2d 686.—Crim Law 1104(6), 1106(3).

Hernandez v. State, TexApp–Amarillo, 649 SW2d 720.—Assault 56, 92(3).

Hernandez v. State, TexApp–El Paso, 24 SW3d 846, reh overr, and petition for discretionary review refused.—Const Law 42.2(2), 3310, 3833, 4574, 4626, 4815; Crim Law 639.1, 1130(5); Gr Jury 8.

Hernandez v. State, TexApp–El Paso, 946 SW2d 108.—Crim Law 772(6), 814(8); Ind & Inf 189(11); Rob 1, 11, 22.

Hernandez v. State, TexApp–El Paso, 943 SW2d 930, petition for discretionary review refused, and petition for discretionary review gr, rev 988 SW2d 770, on remand 2000 WL 1231508.—Crim Law 641.13(2.1), 641.13(7), 1134(3), 1166.10(1).

Hernandez v. State, TexApp–El Paso, 939 SW2d 665, reh overr, and petition for discretionary review refused.—Crim Law 444, 663, 1169.1(10), 1169.2(7).

Hernandez v. State, TexApp–El Paso, 914 SW2d 218, petition for discretionary review refused.—Crim Law 633(1), 635, 772(6), 855(5), 1035(5), 1037.1(1), 1037.1(2), 1130(5), 1173.3; Homic 757, 1490.

Hernandez v. State, TexApp–El Paso, 885 SW2d 597.—Crim Law 273.1(1), 273.1(3), 273.1(4), 273.2(1), 273.2(1), 274(1), 274(4), 274(9), 641.13(5), 641.13(6), 1101, 1134(2), 1144.4, 1144.10, 1144.17.

Hernandez v. State, TexApp–El Paso, 825 SW2d 765.—Crim Law 338(1), 350, 599, 698(1), 698(3), 706(8), 1036.1(2), 1043(1), 1043(2), 1044.2(1), 1144.12, 1151, 1171.8(1); Sent & Pun 310.

Hernandez v. State, TexApp–El Paso, 730 SW2d 816, petition for discretionary review refused.—Crim Law 577.11(2), 577.11(4), 1044.1(1).

Hernandez v. State, TexApp–El Paso, 663 SW2d 5, petition for discretionary review gr, petition for discretionary review dism 746 SW2d 237.—Crim Law 577.8(1), 577.10(7), 594(1), 1036.9, 1151, 1166(7), 1169.1(7), 1169.3; Searches 70.

Hernandez v. State, TexApp–Beaumont, 10 SW3d 812, reh overr, and petition for discretionary review refused.—Const Law 4694, 4742; Crim Law 388.5(1), 511.2, 511.5, 511.9, 561(1), 795(2.1), 795(2.5), 795(2.10), 1030(2), 1038.3, 1134(3), 1159.5, 1172.1(1), 1172.1(3); Homic 1165, 1181, 1182, 1207, 1404, 1456; Kidnap 36; Sent & Pun 1655, 1660.

Hernandez v. State, TexApp–Beaumont, 862 SW2d 193, petition for discretionary review refused.—Crim Law 622.2(2), 641.5(3), 642, 1166.13.

Hernandez v. State, TexApp–Beaumont, 628 SW2d 145.—Crim Law 641.10(1), 641.10(2), 1110(3); Sent & Pun 359, 1400, 1406.

Hernandez v. State, TexApp–Waco, 203 SW3d 477, reh overr, and petition for discretionary review refused, petition stricken 2007 WL 677820.—Assault 59, 65, 82; Crim Law 338(7), 369.2(1), 371(1), 371(9), 374, 1036.1(8), 1153(1).

Hernandez v. State, TexApp–Waco, 191 SW3d 370.—Crim Law 338(1), 356, 661, 1030(2), 1036.1(9), 1043(1), 1043(2).

Hernandez v. State, TexApp–Waco, 938 SW2d 503, reh overr, and petition for discretionary review refused.—Controlled Subs 82; Crim Law 569, 620(1), 925(1), 925.5(1), 1086.10, 1115(2), 1156(5), 1159.2(1), 1159.2(2), 1166.18; Tel 1440.

Hernandez v. State, TexApp–Waco, 914 SW2d 226.—Crim Law 338(7), 369.2(2), 369.2(4), 371(1), 371(4), 374, 693, 698(3), 867, 1045, 1130(2), 1130(5), 1139, 1153(1), 1162, 1165(1), 1169.5(1), 1169.11; Homic 975.

Hernandez v. State, TexApp–Waco, 808 SW2d 536.—Controlled Subs 6, 34, 68, 82; Crim Law 561(1), 693, 713, 720(7.1), 730(1), 792(3), 1030(1), 1044.1(1), 1044.2(1), 1137(3), 1158(3), 1166(1.10), 1171.1(3), 1182; Jury 33(5.15), 120.

Hernandez v. State, TexApp–Waco, 704 SW2d 909.—Sent & Pun 1980(2), 2003, 2030.

Hernandez v. State, TexApp–Eastland, 118 SW3d 469, petition for discretionary review refused.—Crim Law 412.1(1), 412.1(2), 438(1), 438(6); Homic 1184.

Hernandez v. State, TexApp–Eastland, 74 SW3d 73, petition for discretionary review gr, rev 127 SW3d 768, on remand 2005 WL 283607.—Crim Law 159, 1134(3).

Hernandez v. State, TexApp–Eastland, 841 SW2d 569, reh den, and petition for discretionary review refused.—Crim Law 562, 847, 1159.2(7); Larc 65.

Hernandez v. State, TexApp–Tyler, 897 SW2d 488.—Crim Law 419(1.5), 652, 661, 693, 698(3), 1134(2), 1165(1), 1170.5(1); Witn 345(1), 345(8), 350, 406.

Hernandez; State v., TexApp–Tyler, 801 SW2d 8.—Crim Law 925(5), 957(2), 1041.

Hernandez; State v., TexApp–Tyler, 776 SW2d 598.—Crim Law 1106(2).

Hernandez v. State, TexApp–Corpus Christi, 190 SW3d 856, reh overr.—Burg 29, 41(1), 41(3), 41(4), 41(6); Crim Law 394.6(4), 881(1), 1042.5, 1134(2), 1134(6), 1139, 1144.12, 1158(4), 1162, 1177.5(1), 1192; Ind & Inf 125(19.1); Searches 171; Sent & Pun 367, 1364, 1373.

Hernandez v. State, TexApp–Corpus Christi, 69 SW3d 211.—Obst Just 16.

Hernandez v. State, TexApp–Corpus Christi, 55 SW3d 701, petition for discretionary review gr, aff 116 SW3d 26, on subsequent appeal 2005 WL 1705638.—Crim Law 388.1, 480, 488, 1153(2), 1153(6); Sent & Pun 2019.

Hernandez v. State, TexApp–Corpus Christi, 52 SW3d 268, reh overr.—Crim Law 59(1), 80, 369.2(1), 369.2(3.1), 371(12), 372(14), 511.1(4), 511.2, 511.3, 511.5, 511.9, 553, 641.13(1), 641.13(2.1), 641.13(6), 661, 1134(2), 1134(8), 1144.13(2.1), 1144.13(6), 1159.2(2), 1159.2(7), 1159.2(9), 1159.4(2); Homic 570; Ind & Inf 72; RICO 121.

Hernandez v. State, TexApp–Corpus Christi, 28 SW3d 660, clarified on denial of rearg, and reh overr, and petition for discretionary review refused.—Assault 92(5); Crim Law 273.1(2), 641.13(1), 641.13(2.1),

641.13(5), 641.13(7), 867, 1030(2), 1134(2), 1155; Double J 1, 2, 5.1, 161; Jury 97(1), 125; Kidnap 35, 36, 39.

Hernandez v. State, TexApp–Corpus Christi, 989 SW2d 796, opinion after remand 2000 WL 34249514, petition for discretionary review refused, habeas corpus gr in part Ex parte Hernandez, 2004 WL 3259022.—Crim Law 939(1), 956(4), 959, 1156(1).

Hernandez v. State, TexApp–Corpus Christi, 907 SW2d 654, reh overr, and petition for discretionary review gr, rev 939 SW2d 173, on remand 1997 WL 33641950.— Crim Law 507(1), 511.1(3), 511.1(7), 511.2, 1144.13(1), 1144.13(2.1).

Hernandez v. State, TexApp–Corpus Christi, 900 SW2d 835, reh overr.—Crim Law 371(12), 374, 1134(6); Witn 268(1).

Hernandez v. State, TexApp–Corpus Christi, 805 SW2d 858.—Crim Law 1036.1(2), 1119(4), 1119(5), 1169.5(1), 1169.5(2), 1174(2).

Hernandez v. State, TexApp–Corpus Christi, 799 SW2d 507, petition for discretionary review refused.—Atty & C 76(4); Crim Law 641.13(1), 641.13(2.1), 641.13(6), 641.13(7).

Hernandez v. State, TexApp–Corpus Christi, 791 SW2d 301, petition for discretionary review refused.—Controlled Subs 80; Crim Law 627.9(2.1), 627.9(4), 665(2), 719(1), 720(1), 720(7.1), 722.3, 1166(10.10), 1168(2), 1171.3, 1171.6; Ind & Inf 137(3).

Hernandez v. State, TexApp–Corpus Christi, 772 SW2d 274.—Crim Law 470(1), 476.1, 1153(1).

Hernandez v. State, TexApp–Corpus Christi, 771 SW2d 596.—Crim Law 1172.1(2).

Hernandez v. State, TexApp–Corpus Christi, 767 SW2d 902, petition for discretionary review gr, aff 800 SW2d 523.—Crim Law 1036.1(2), 1044.2(1), 1045, 1177; Sent & Pun 312.

Hernandez v. State, TexApp–Corpus Christi, 761 SW2d 483.—Crim Law 552(3), 741(6); Perj 33(8).

Hernandez v. State, TexApp–Corpus Christi, 750 SW2d 902.—Crim Law 517.3(4).

Hernandez v. State, TexApp–Corpus Christi, 742 SW2d 841, appeal after remand 767 SW2d 902, petition for discretionary review gr, aff 800 SW2d 523.—Crim Law 728(2), 795(2.10); Homic 1380, 1458; Ind & Inf 189(8).

Hernandez v. State, TexApp–Corpus Christi, 730 SW2d 35, petition for discretionary review gr, vac 761 SW2d 8, on remand 771 SW2d 596.—Crim Law 790, 866.

Hernandez v. State, TexApp–Corpus Christi, 713 SW2d 697, petition for discretionary review gr, rev 751 SW2d 513.—Const Law 2357; Crim Law 577.2; Statut 109.5, 109.11, 118(1).

Hernandez v. State, TexApp–Corpus Christi, 704 SW2d 488.—Controlled Subs 121; Searches 47.1.

Hernandez v. State, TexApp–Corpus Christi, 697 SW2d 764.—Ind & Inf 173.

Hernandez v. State, TexApp–Corpus Christi, 665 SW2d 842, petition for discretionary review gr, rev 698 SW2d 679, on remand 704 SW2d 488.—Controlled Subs 67, 68, 74, 75; Crim Law 409(5), 478(1).

Hernandez v. State, TexApp–Houston (14 Dist), 171 SW3d 347, reh overr, and petition for discretionary review refused.—Crim Law 59(3), 59(5), 80, 338(7), 369.2(4), 371(1), 371(4), 371(12), 413(1), 417(15), 419(2.20), 720(2), 720(6), 723(3), 726, 795(1.5), 795(2.1), 795(2.10), 795(2.50), 1043(3), 1134(2), 1153(1), 1159.2(3), 1171.1(2.1), 1171.3; Homic 1167.

Hernandez v. State, TexApp–Houston (14 Dist), 804 SW2d 168, petition for discretionary review refused.— Assault 59; Rape 4, 14, 51(4).

Hernandez v. State, TexApp–Houston (14 Dist), 754 SW2d 321, petition for discretionary review gr, aff 861 SW2d 908.—Crim Law 369.8, 438(4); Rape 17, 40(5).

Hernandez v. State Bar of Texas, TexApp–Corpus Christi, 812 SW2d 75.—App & E 719(8), 1008.1(2); Atty & C 39, 57, 58, 60.

Hernandez v. State of Tex., USTex, 74 SCt 667, 347 US 475, 98 LEd 866.—Const Law 3057, 3250, 3306, 3830; Ind & Inf 140(2); Jury 33(1), 120.

Hernandez v. Sullivan, WDTex, 757 FSupp 795.—Judges 47(2).

Hernandez v. Telles, TexApp–El Paso, 663 SW2d 91.— App & E 195; Compromise 2, 3, 6(2), 15(1), 23(3).

Hernandez v. Texas & N. O. R. Co., TexCivApp–San Antonio, 124 SW2d 188.—R R 400(5).

Hernandez; Texas Dept. of Human Resources v., TexCivApp–Corpus Christi,595 SW2d 189, ref nre, appeal dism Herrera v. Hernandez, 101 SCt 848, 449 US 1072, 66 LEd2d 795.—Child 30, 31, 38; Lim of Act 4(2), 72(1), 165.

Hernandez v. Texas Dept. of Human Services, CA5 (Tex), 91 FedAppx 934.—Fed Cts 266.1.

Hernandez v. Texas Dept. of Ins., TexApp–Austin, 923 SW2d 192.—Admin Law 504, 681.1; App & E 344; Insurance 1620.

Hernandez v. Texas Dept. of Public Safety, TexCivApp–Eastland, 398 SW2d 157, ref nre.—Autos 144.2(9.1); Judgm 185.3(1).

Hernandez v. Texas Employers Ins. Ass'n, TexApp–Corpus Christi, 783 SW2d 250.—Work Comp 521, 523, 532, 1417.

Hernandez; Texas Farmers Ins. Co. v., TexApp–Amarillo, 649 SW2d 121, ref nre.—Costs 194.22, 207; Evid 272; Insurance 3571, 3585; Interest 39(2.35); Pretrial Proc 718; Trial 350.4(3).

Hernandez; Texas General Indem. Co. v., TexCivApp–San Antonio, 388 SW2d 334.—Work Comp 840, 1652.

Hernandez v. Texas Liquor Control Bd., TexCivApp–San Antonio, 317 SW2d 552.—Int Liq 68(0.5), 70, 75(7).

Hernandez v. Texas Workers' Compensation Ins. Fund, TexApp–Eastland, 946 SW2d 904, reh overr.—Admin Law 663; Work Comp 1829, 1832.

Hernandez v. Texas Workforce Com'n, TexApp–San Antonio, 18 SW3d 678, reh overr.—Unemp Comp 290, 473, 478, 480, 481, 483, 486, 491(1).

Hernandez v. Tokai Corp., Tex, 2 SW3d 251, answer to certified question conformed to 189 F3d 489.—Prod Liab 8, 11, 15, 27, 59, 87.1, 88.

Hernandez; Transamerica Ins. Co. of Texas v., TexApp–Corpus Christi, 769 SW2d 608, writ den.—Work Comp 840, 847, 850, 857, 860, 1376, 1418, 1629, 1630, 1637.

Hernandez v. Travelers Indem. Co. of Rhode Island, TexApp–El Paso, 855 SW2d 786.—Work Comp 201, 551, 1074.

Hernandez v. Travelers Ins. Co., CA5 (Tex), 489 F2d 721, reh den 493 F2d 664, cert den 95 SCt 78, 419 US 844, 42 LEd2d 73.—Fed Cts 301.

Hernandez; Travelers Ins. Co. v., CA5 (Tex), 276 F2d 267.—Fed Cts 389; Work Comp 51, 976, 998.

Hernandez v. Union Nat. Bank of Arkansas, BkrtcyED-Tex, 149 BR 441. See Hernandez, In re.

Hernandez; U.S. v., CA5 (Tex), 477 F3d 210.—Aliens 441; Arrest 63.5(4); Crim Law 1139; Cust Dut 126(2).

Hernandez; U.S. v., CA5 (Tex), 457 F3d 416.—Consp 28(3), 47(12); Crim Law 577.10(1), 577.10(9), 577.12(1), 577.12(2), 577.15(4), 577.16(4), 577.16(8), 1023(11), 1119(1), 1130(5), 1139, 1158(1), 1159.2(1); Sent & Pun 327, 726(3), 726(5), 996.

Hernandez; U.S. v., CA5 (Tex), 291 F3d 313.—Crim Law 1139, 1177, 1181.5(8); Sent & Pun 359.

Hernandez; U.S. v., CA5 (Tex), 279 F3d 302.—Arrest 68(4); Crim Law 1130(5), 1139, 1144.12, 1158(4); Searches 180, 182, 183.

Hernandez; U.S. v., CA5 (Tex), 234 F3d 252.—Crim Law 273.1(1), 273.1(4), 1139; Hab Corp 475.1.

Hernandez; U.S. v., CA5 (Tex), 116 F3d 725.—Crim Law 1665; Sent & Pun 905.

Hernandez; U.S. v., CA5 (Tex), 92 F3d 309, reh and sug for reh den 100 F3d 955, cert den 117 SCt 1437, 520 US

1170, 137 LEd2d 544.—Crim Law 769, 822(1), 829(4), 1134(2), 1152(1), 1171.1(3).

Hernandez; U.S. v., CA5 (Tex), 64 F3d 179.—Crim Law 1042; Sent & Pun 630, 631, 635, 665, 802.

Hernandez; U.S. v., CA5 (Tex), 17 F3d 78.—Crim Law 273.1(2), 1192; Sent & Pun 941, 996.

Hernandez; U.S. v., CA5 (Tex), 996 F2d 62, opinion withdrawn and superseded 17 F3d 78.

Hernandez; U.S. v., CA5 (Tex), 976 F2d 929, cert den 113 SCt 2352, 508 US 914, 124 LEd2d 261.—Cust Dut 126(1), 126(4), 126(9.1); Searches 22.

Hernandez; U.S. v., CA5 (Tex), 962 F2d 1152.—Consp 24(2), 43(12), 47(12); Controlled Subs 81; Crim Law 510, 622.1(2), 622.2(3), 622.2(4), 770(2), 778(1), 1044.1(7), 1126, 1166(6), 1173.1; Ind & Inf 166; Witn 297(1).

Hernandez; U.S. v., CA5 (Tex), 943 F2d 1.—Aliens 799; Sent & Pun 820, 996.

Hernandez; U.S. v., CA5 (Tex), 911 F2d 981.—Controlled Subs 162, 189; Forfeit 9.

Hernandez; U.S. v., CA5 (Tex), 901 F2d 1217.—Arrest 63.5(9), 71.1(5); Autos 60, 111, 349(4), 349(15), 349.5(3), 349.5(11); Searches 60.1.

Hernandez; U.S. v., CA5 (Tex), 891 F2d 521, cert den 110 SCt 1935, 495 US 909, 109 LEd2d 298.—Crim Law 723(1), 726, 867, 1037.1(2); Ind & Inf 110(38).

Hernandez; U.S. v., CA5 (Tex), 842 F2d 82, reh den 846 F2d 752.—Controlled Subs 71, 97; Crim Law 412(3), 428, 622.2(10), 636(2).

Hernandez; U.S. v., CA5 (Tex), 825 F2d 846, cert den 108 SCt 1032, 484 US 1068, 98 LEd2d 996.—Arrest 63.4(8), 63.4(12), 63.4(15), 68(3), 71.1(1), 71.1(8); Crim Law 394.6(4), 1134(3), 1158(4).

Hernandez; U.S. v., CA5 (Tex), 750 F2d 1256.—Const Law 4838; Crim Law 421(6), 1169.1(9); Pardon 43; Sent & Pun 605.

Hernandez; U.S. v., CA5 (Tex), 662 F2d 289.—Crim Law 1177; Weap 17(4).

Hernandez; U.S. v., CA5 (Tex), 591 F2d 1019.—Crim Law 30.

Hernandez; U.S. v., CA5 (Tex), 580 F2d 188, on reh 591 F2d 1019.—Controlled Subs 81; Courts 96(4); Sent & Pun 604.

Hernandez; U.S. v., CA5 (Tex), 484 F2d 86.—Controlled Subs 28, 81.

Hernandez; U.S. v., CA5 (Tex), 453 F2d 297.—Armed S 20.9(2).

Hernandez; U.S. v., CA5 (Tex), 441 F2d 157, cert den 92 SCt 150, 404 US 847, 30 LEd2d 84.—Crim Law 394.3, 423(1), 424(1), 425, 673(2), 700(3), 706(2), 1169.7; Ind & Inf 132(3); Int Rev 5319; Tel 1436.

Hernandez; U.S. v., CA5 (Tex), 438 F2d 676, cert den 91 SCt 1679, 402 US 976, 29 LEd2d 141.—Controlled Subs 6; Crim Law 570(1).

Hernandez v. U.S., CA5 (Tex), 256 F2d 342, cert den 79 SCt 80, 358 US 851, 3 LEd2d 85.—Crim Law 1476, 1528, 1534.

Hernandez; U.S. v., CA5 (Tex), 210 FedAppx 431.—Crim Law 1042; Jury 34(8); Sent & Pun 686.

Hernandez; U.S. v., CA5 (Tex), 202 FedAppx 708.—Consp 28(3); Controlled Subs 80.

Hernandez; U.S. v., CA5 (Tex), 200 FedAppx 283.—Const Law 4664(2); Crim Law 412.1(4), 412.2(3), 412.2(5).

Hernandez; U.S. v., CA5 (Tex), 193 FedAppx 338.—Aliens 441; Crim Law 394.5(2).

Hernandez; U.S. v., CA5 (Tex), 156 FedAppx 624, cert den 126 SCt 1178, 546 US 1155, 163 LEd2d 1136.—Crim Law 394.4(6).

Hernandez; U.S. v., CA5 (Tex), 151 FedAppx 297.—Crim Law 641.13(7), 1119(1).

Hernandez; U.S. v., CA5 (Tex), 139 FedAppx 612, cert den 126 SCt 779, 546 US 1050, 163 LEd2d 604.—Crim Law 1042.

Hernandez; U.S. v., CA5 (Tex), 86 FedAppx 739, cert den 125 SCt 177, 543 US 858, 160 LEd2d 96.—Sent & Pun 299, 300, 301.

Hernandez v. U.S., NDTex, 313 FSupp 349.—Child S 113; Damag 48, 95, 131(1), 132(11), 133, 135; Death 81, 82, 86(1), 87, 89, 95(1), 95(3); Explos 8; Infants 72(2); Neglig 373, 386, 506(8); Parent & C 7(1).

Hernandez; U.S. v., SDTex, 347 FSupp2d 375.—Aliens 292; Const Law 268(5), 4689; Crim Law 700(10); Witn 2(1).

Hernandez; U.S. Fidelity & Guaranty Co. v., TexCiv-App–Eastland, 410 SW2d 224, ref nre.—App & E 930(1), 989; Damag 221(5.1); Plead 228.23; Work Comp 1492, 1929, 1967, 1968(1).

Hernandez v. U.S. Finance Co., TexCivApp–Waco, 441 SW2d 859, writ dism.—App & E 213, 216(6), 237(3), 291; Nova 12; Trial 351.2(4); Usury 12, 32, 117.

Hernandez; U.S. Fire Ins. Co. v., TexApp–Corpus Christi, 918 SW2d 576, reh overr, and writ den.—Work Comp 2190, 2191, 2248, 2251.

Hernandez v. Valls, TexApp–San Antonio, 656 SW2d 153. —Guard & W 8.

Hernandez; Vasquez v., TexApp–San Antonio, 844 SW2d 802, writ dism woj, appeal after remand 1995 WL 555715.—App & E 173(2); Judgm 185(2), 185(6); Mun Corp 747(3); Offic 114.

Hernandez; Villarreal v., TexApp–San Antonio, 943 SW2d 101.—App & E 770(1), 771.

Hernandez; Watson v., TexCivApp–Amarillo, 374 SW2d 326, writ dism.—Chat Mtg 158.1; Plead 111.42(7); Venue 8.5(7).

Hernandez-Antonio; U.S. v., CA5 (Tex), 214 FedAppx 369.—Crim Law 1134(3); Jury 34(7); Sent & Pun 796.

Hernandez-Arredondo; U.S. v., CA5 (Tex), 167 FedAppx 998, cert den Hernandez-Perez v. US, 126 SCt 2914, 165 LEd2d 934.—Crim Law 1163(1).

Hernandez-Avalos; U.S. v., CA5 (Tex), 251 F3d 505, cert den 122 SCt 305, 534 US 935, 151 LEd2d 226.—Aliens 273, 274, 376.

Hernandez Balderrama v. U.S., CA5 (Tex), 419 F2d 1279, cert den 90 SCt 1508, 397 US 1068, 25 LEd2d 689.— Armed S 20.8(5).

Hernandez-Bautista; U.S. v., CA5 (Tex), 293 F3d 845.— Controlled Subs 31, 80; Crim Law 59(5), 1139.

Hernandez-Bautista; U.S. v., WDTex, 159 FSupp2d 410, aff 293 F3d 845.—Controlled Subs 81; Crim Law 1144.13(2.1), 1159.2(1), 1159.2(7), 1159.6.

Hernandez-Beltran; U.S. v., CA5 (Tex), 867 F2d 224, cert den 109 SCt 2439, 490 US 1094, 104 LEd2d 995.— Controlled Subs 31, 68, 81, 100(2); Crim Law 59(5).

Hernandez-Beltran; U.S. v., CA5 (Tex), 169 FedAppx 195, cert den Salgado-Brito v. US, 126 SCt 2952, 165 LEd2d 969.—Sent & Pun 793.

Hernandez Camacho; U.S. v., CA5 (Tex), 779 F2d 227, cert den 106 SCt 1981, 476 US 1119, 90 LEd2d 664.— Sent & Pun 313.

Hernandez-Cartagena; U.S. v., CA5 (Tex), 145 FedAppx 899, cert den Medina-Teniente v. US, 126 SCt 839, 546 US 1080, 163 LEd2d 714.—Crim Law 1042.

Hernandez Castellanos v. Bridgestone Corp., SDTex, 215 FSupp2d 862, reconsideration den.—Fed Cts 275; Rem of C 36, 107(7).

Hernandez-Castillo v. Moore, CA5 (Tex), 436 F3d 516, cert den 127 SCt 40, 166 LEd2d 18.—Aliens 54.3(4), 216, 384, 398, 404; Const Law 188.

Hernandez-Castillo v. Moore, WDTex, 402 FSupp2d 749, vac 436 F3d 516, cert den 127 SCt 40, 166 LEd2d 18.— Aliens 282(4); Fed Cts 13; Hab Corp 235, 257.

Hernandez-Coronado; U.S. v., CA5 (Tex), 39 F3d 573.— Sent & Pun 673, 675.

Hernandez-Davila; Castro v., TexApp–Corpus Christi, 694 SW2d 575.—App & E 989, 1012.1(5); Autos 155, 240(1), 244(3); Neglig 258, 259, 1560, 1693, 1720.

Hernandez-de la Torre; U.S. v., CA5 (Tex), 169 FedAppx 890, cert den 127 SCt 142, 166 LEd2d 103.—Crim Law 1042; Fed Cts 462.

Hernandez-Echeveste; U.S. v., CA5 (Tex), 105 FedAppx 544, appeal after remand 161 FedAppx 428.—Crim Law 1181.5(3.1); Jury 117.

Hernandez ex rel. Hernandez v. Texas Dept. of Protective and Regulatory Services, CA5 (Tex), 380 SW2d 872. —Civil R 1027, 1305, 1376(1), 1376(2), 1376(3); Const Law 3896, 3911, 4404; Fed Cts 542, 554.1, 574, 766, 776, 802; Infants 17; Offic 114, 116; States 79.

Hernandez Flores; U.S. v., CA5 (Tex), 155 FedAppx 745. —Crim Law 1026.10(4).

Hernandez-Franco; U.S. v., CA5 (Tex), 167 FedAppx 986, cert den Salazar-Palacios v. US, 126 SCt 2309, 164 LEd2d 829.—Crim Law 1177; Jury 34(7); Sent & Pun 973.

Hernandez-Gonzalez; U.S. v., CA5 (Tex), 405 F3d 260.— Crim Law 1030(1), 1042, 1133.

Hernandez-Gonzalez; U.S. v., CA5 (Tex), 169 FedAppx 207.—Crim Law 1134(3).

Hernandez-Gonzalez; U.S. v., CA5 (Tex), 119 FedAppx 668, reh den 405 F3d 260, cert den 126 SCt 202, 546 US 890, 163 LEd2d 201.—Crim Law 1042.

Hernandez-Grimaldo; U.S. v., CA5 (Tex), 145 FedAppx 52, cert den Rodriguez-Mendez v. US, 126 SCt 1076, 546 US 1114, 163 LEd2d 896.—Crim Law 1042.

Hernandez Guerreo v. State, TexApp–Corpus Christi, 773 SW2d 775.—Autos 355(13).

Hernandez-Guevara; U.S. v., CA5 (Tex), 162 F3d 863, cert den 119 SCt 1375, 526 US 1059, 143 LEd2d 534.— Crim Law 300, 369.2(1), 370, 371(1), 374, 695.5, 708.1, 720(7.1), 722.5, 731, 801, 824(8), 1030(1), 1035(9), 1035(10), 1043(3), 1134(2), 1134(3), 1139, 1141(2), 1152(1), 1153(1), 1154, 1155, 1156(1), 1158(1), 1166.22(1), 1166.22(2), 1171.1(1), 1171.1(2.1), 1181.5(8), 1184(4.1); Sent & Pun 651, 1940.

Hernandez-Hernandez; U.S. v., CA5 (Tex), 142 FedAppx 834.—Crim Law 1042.

Hernandez-Hernandez; U.S. v., WDTex, 291 FSupp2d 490.—Aliens 773; Crim Law 113.

Hernandez-Juarez; U.S. v., CA5 (Tex), 138 FedAppx 640. —Crim Law 1042, 1181.5(8).

Hernandez-Landaverde; U.S. v., SDTex, 65 FSupp2d 567. —Aliens 770, 773, 794, 795(2); Crim Law 20, 21, 312; Ind & Inf 60.

Hernandez-Martinez; U.S. v., CA5 (Tex), 485 F3d 270, reh den.—Crim Law 1030(1), 1042.

Hernandez-Martinez; U.S. v., CA5 (Tex), 165 FedAppx 372, cert den Lopez-Martinez v. US, 126 SCt 2314, 164 LEd2d 833, appeal after new sentencing hearing 230 FedAppx 429.—Crim Law 1177, 1181.5(8); Sent & Pun 661.

Hernandez-Mesa; U.S. v., CA5 (Tex), 146 FedAppx 727, cert den Villarreal-Gonsalez v. US, 126 SCt 637, 546 US 1009, 163 LEd2d 516.—Crim Law 1042; Sent & Pun 780.

Hernandez-Neave; U.S. v., CA5 (Tex), 291 F3d 296.— Crim Law 1139, 1147, 1158(1).

Hernandez Nodarse v. U.S., SDTex, 166 FSupp2d 538.— Aliens 219, 220, 334, 463, 469.

Hernandez-Palacios; U.S. v., CA5 (Tex), 838 F2d 1346.— Commerce 82.10; Consp 24(1), 24(8), 44.2, 47(12); Controlled Subs 28, 79, 81, 86; Crim Law 478(1), 1038.1(3.1).

Hernandez-Perez; U.S. v., CA5 (Tex), 166 FedAppx 758, cert den 126 SCt 2914, 165 LEd2d 934.—Crim Law 1181.5(8); Sent & Pun 661.

Hernandez-Rodarte; U.S. v., CA5 (Tex), 141 FedAppx 251.—Aliens 795(4); Crim Law 1036.2, 1036.6.

Hernandez-Rodriguez v. Pasquarell, CA5 (Tex), 118 F3d 1034.—Admin Law 419; Aliens 153, 211, 216, 300, 322, 404; Const Law 186, 2382; Courts 100(1); Fed Cts 924.1; Hab Corp 461; Statut 219(6.1).

Hernandez-Rodriguez; U.S. v., CA5 (Tex), 467 F3d 492, cert den 127 SCt 1350, 167 LEd2d 143.—Sent & Pun 781, 793.

Hernandez-Rodriguez; U.S. v., CA5 (Tex), 135 FedAppx 661.—Sent & Pun 793.

Hernandez-Rodriguez; U.S. v., CA5 (Tex), 95 FedAppx 92.—Consp 47(12); Controlled Subs 81; Crim Law 1044.2(2), 1137(1).

Hernandez-Rodriguez; U.S. v., NDTex, 170 FSupp2d 700.—Aliens 216, 379, 773, 795(4); Const Law 4438.

Hernandez-Romero; U.S. v., CA5 (Tex), 195 FedAppx 283, cert den Amaya-Melgoza v. US, 127 SCt 1012, 166 LEd2d 763.—Jury 34(7).

Hernandez-Valadez; U.S. v., CA5 (Tex), 86 FedAppx 714. —Controlled Subs 69, 81, 86.

Hernandez-Vasquez; U.S. v., CA5 (Tex), 73 FedAppx 65. —Jury 34(1).

Hernandez-Vela; U.S. v., CA5 (Tex), 533 F2d 211.—Crim Law 627.10(2.1), 1163(1), 1165(1); Sent & Pun 275, 362.

Hernandez-Zuniga; U.S. v., CA5 (Tex), 215 F3d 483, cert den 121 SCt 628, 531 US 1038, 148 LEd2d 537.—Arrest 63.5(1); Crim Law 1139, 1158(4); Cust Dut 126(2); Searches 171, 173.1.

Hernden; Fleming v., TexCivApp–El Paso, 564 SW2d 157, ref nre.—App & E 865; Appear 26; Judgm 17(9), 123(1), 143(2), 145(2), 162(2); Proc 105, 153, 166.

Hernden v. State, TexCrimApp, 505 SW2d 546.—Bail 77(2), 79(1).

Hernden v. State, TexApp–San Antonio, 865 SW2d 521.— App & E 1010.2; Bail 77(1).

Herndon; Chandler v., TexCivApp–Corpus Christi, 450 SW2d 703, ref nre.—Joint Adv 1.2(1); Mines 101.

Herndon v. Cocke, TexCivApp–El Paso, 138 SW2d 298.— App & E 781(4); Courts 122; Execution 109, 172(2), 172(4), 172(6); Plead 228.23.

Herndon v. C.I.R., CA5 (Tex), 175 F2d 55.—Int Rev 3098, 3271, 4655, 4744.

Herndon; Fee v., CA5 (Tex), 900 F2d 804, cert den 111 SCt 279, 498 US 908, 112 LEd2d 233.—Civil R 1394; Const Law 4210, 4214; Fed Cts 763.1, 794; Schools 147, 176.

Herndon; Fee v., TexApp–Houston (14 Dist), 837 SW2d 834.—App & E 961; Pretrial Proc 303, 313.

Herndon v. First Nat. Bank of Tulia, TexApp–Amarillo, 802 SW2d 396, writ den.—Antitrust 141, 358; App & E 1136; Banks 226; Contracts 95(1), 168.

Herndon v. G. C. McBride, Inc., TexCivApp–Eastland, 342 SW2d 10.—Lim of Act 55(7).

Herndon v. Halliburton Oil Well Cementing Co., TexCivApp–El Paso, 154 SW2d 163, writ refused wom.— App & E 207, 261, 1060.1(6), 1062.1, 1078(1); Labor & Emp 29, 30; Mines 118; Neglig 291, 294, 552(1), 1205(10), 1717, 1720, 1741; Trial 29(2), 232(2), 350.6(6), 351.5(2), 352.4(1).

Herndon v. Herndon, WDTex, 491 FSupp 53.—Fed Cts 23, 78.

Herndon; Herndon v., WDTex, 491 FSupp 53.—Fed Cts 23, 78.

Herndon v. Housing Authority of City of Dallas, TexCivApp–Dallas, 261 SW2d 221, writ refused.—Em Dom 203(7), 222(4).

Herndon; Mecklin v., TexCivApp–Texarkana, 325 SW2d 824, writ dism woj.—Child C 641.

Herndon; Parr v., TexCivApp–Fort Worth, 294 SW2d 162, ref nre.—App & E 499(1), 930(1); Autos 245(42), 245(59); Damag 95, 130.1; Trial 83(1), 350.7(3.1), 351.5(2).

Herndon v. Sentry Ins., TexCivApp–Dallas, 615 SW2d 249, ref nre.—Insurance 2137(1), 2153(1).

Herndon; Siegert v., TexApp–Houston (1 Dist), 961 SW2d 348, reh overr.—App & E 223, 267(1); Judgm 181(15.1), 183.

Herndon; State v., TexCrimApp, 215 SW3d 901.—Crim Law 895, 911, 912.5, 913(1), 918(1), 961, 1028, 1133, 1134(6), 1147, 1156(1).

Herndon v. State, TexCrimApp, 787 SW2d 408.—Controlled Subs 80.

Herndon v. State, TexCrimApp, 679 SW2d 520.—Const Law 4733(2); Sent & Pun 2024.

Herndon v. State, TexCrimApp, 543 SW2d 109.—Crim Law 417(1), 491(1), 552(3), 1158(4); Gaming 98(3).

Herndon v. State, TexCrimApp, 272 SW2d 532, 160 TexCrim 500.—Int Liq 205(2).

Herndon v. State, TexApp–Houston (1 Dist), 627 SW2d 502, petition for discretionary review gr, aff 679 SW2d 520.—Sent & Pun 2024.

Herndon v. State, TexApp–Fort Worth, 767 SW2d 510, petition for discretionary review refused.—Controlled Subs 34; Crim Law 1159.2(7).

Herndon; State v., TexApp–Corpus Christi, 115 SW3d 231, reh overr, and petition for discretionary review gr, vac 215 SW3d 901.—Crim Law 918(10), 949(1), 949(3).

Herndon; Traders & General Ins. Co. v., TexCivApp–El Paso, 95 SW2d 540, writ dism.—App & E 729; Damag 221(3), 221(4), 221(5.1); Work Comp 1268.

Herndon; U.S. v., CA5 (Tex), 7 F3d 55.—Crim Law 273(4.1), 1167(5).

Herndon Marine Products, Inc.; Liberty Seafood, Inc. v., CA5 (Tex), 38 F3d 755. See Liberty Seafood, Inc., Complaint of.

Herndon Marine Products, Inc.; Rivera v., TexApp–Corpus Christi, 895 SW2d 430, reh overr, and writ den. —App & E 866(3), 901, 1062.2; Seamen 29(5.14), 29(5.16), 29(5.17); Ship 80; Trial 349(1).

Herndon Marine Products, Inc. v. San Patricio County Appraisal Review Bd., TexApp–Corpus Christi, 695 SW2d 29, ref nre.—Const Law 4138(1); Judgm 185(2), 185(5), 185(6), 185.3(20); Notice 15; Tax 2105, 2678, 2680, 2694, 2695.

Herod v. Baptist Foundation of Texas, TexApp–Eastland, 89 SW3d 689.—Corp 294; Estop 85, 118; Fraud 3, 12; Frds St of 49, 131(1); Judgm 183, 189; Labor & Emp 34(1), 40(1), 40(2), 50, 55.

Herod; City of Corsicana v., TexApp–Waco, 768 SW2d 805.—App & E 231(1); Ease 38; Em Dom 136, 194, 202(1), 255, 262(5); Evid 373(1), 555.6(7); Plead 245(3), 258(3); Trial 131(2).

Herod v. Davidson, TexApp–Houston (14 Dist), 650 SW2d 501.—Adop 11; Guard & W 10; Parties 40(1), 40(2), 48.

Herod v. DeKalb Energy Co., CA5 (Tex), 158 F3d 312. See Gasmark Ltd. Liquidating Trust v. Louis Dreyfus Natural Gas Corp.

Herod; Dreyfus Natural Gas Corp. v., CA5 (Tex), 158 F3d 312. See Gasmark Ltd. Liquidating Trust v. Louis Dreyfus Natural Gas Corp.

Herod; Fidelity Management Co. v., TexCivApp–Corpus Christi, 600 SW2d 380.—Land & Ten 108(1).

Herod v. Grapeland Joint Account, TexCivApp–Waco, 366 SW2d 623, ref nre.—Mines 78.1(7).

Herod; Louis Dreyfus Natural Gas Corp. v., CA5 (Tex), 158 F3d 312. See Gasmark Ltd. Liquidating Trust v. Louis Dreyfus Natural Gas Corp.

Herod; U.S. v., CA5 (Tex), 152 FedAppx 337.—Crim Law 1181.5(8); Health 989; Postal 49(11); Sent & Pun 758, 2103.

Herold; Ayoub v., TexCivApp–El Paso, 287 SW2d 539, ref nre.—App & E 169; Des & Dist 147; Trusts 43(3), 44(1), 44(3), 63; Witn 159(2).

Herold v. City of Austin, TexCivApp–Austin, 310 SW2d 368, ref nre.—App & E 934(1); Judgm 178, 185.3(2), 185.3(8); Licens 19(3).

Herold; Sanders v., TexApp–Houston (1 Dist), 217 SW3d 11, reh overr.—App & E 863, 934(1); Infants 59; Judgm 181(1), 181(2), 181(6); Neglig 210, 273, 1692, 1694; Parent & C 13.5(2), 13.5(4); Witn 309.

Herold v. Texas Venetian Blind Co., TexCivApp–Dallas, 203 SW2d 691.—Plead 111.16, 111.18.

Heron, Burchette, Ruckert & Rothwell; Compton v., BkrtcySDTex, 93 BR 513. See Powers, In re.

Heron Financial Corp. v. U.S. Testing Co., Inc., TexApp–Austin, 926 SW2d 329, reh overr, and writ den.—Judgm 181(7), 181(29), 185(2); Lim of Act 1, 46(6), 55(1), 55(2), 95(1), 95(2), 95(3), 95(7), 95(9), 199(1).

Herr; City of La Joya v., TexApp–Corpus Christi, 41 SW3d 755.—App & E 934(1); Autos 196, 244(16); Judgm 185(2), 185(6), 185.3(1); Mun Corp 742(1), 745, 747(3); Offic 114, 119.

Herr; Farney v., TexCivApp–Fort Worth, 358 SW2d 758. —Autos 181(1), 181(7), 192(11), 197(5).

Herrada; U.S. v., CA5 (Tex), 887 F2d 524, cert den 110 SCt 2565, 495 US 958, 109 LEd2d 748.—Const Law 1003; Costs 285; Statut 6.

Herre v. Morris, TexCivApp–Fort Worth, 251 SW2d 260. —Child C 63, 921(1); Hab Corp 532(1), 731, 798, 841.

Herren; Ballinger v., TexCivApp–Fort Worth, 332 SW2d 131.—App & E 846(5), 930(1), 991, 1015(5); New Tr 144, 157; Trial 315.

Herren v. Hollingsworth, Tex, 167 SW2d 735, 140 Tex 263.—Sec Reg 243.1, 253, 260, 306.

Herren v. Hollingsworth, TexCivApp–Galveston, 188 SW2d 706, writ refused wom.—App & E 194(6); Brok 82(1); Costs 256(4); Evid 419(11); Frds St of 72(1), 110(1), 125(1), 125(2), 131(1); Plead 18.

Herren v. Hollingsworth, TexCivApp–Galveston, 161 SW2d 511, rev 167 SW2d 735, 140 Tex 263.—Sec Reg 292, 298.

Herren; Johnson v., TexCivApp–Texarkana, 374 SW2d 253.—Acct St 8; Contracts 170(2); Estop 90(3); Labor & Emp 207, 214.

Herren; Roddy v., TexCivApp–Galveston, 125 SW2d 1057. —Autos 171(8), 206, 208, 244(43), 244(58); Courts 104.

Herren v. U.S., SDTex, 317 FSupp 1198, aff 443 F2d 1363. —Int Rev 4327, 4330; Statut 184, 211, 217.3, 217.4, 228, 245; Tax 2300.

Herrera, Ex parte, TexCrimApp, 828 SW2d 8.—Sent & Pun 1798.

Herrera, Ex parte, TexCrimApp, 819 SW2d 528, reh den, cert den Herrera v. Texas, 112 SCt 1074, 502 US 1085, 117 LEd2d 279.—Hab Corp 725.

Herrera, Ex parte, TexCrimApp, 608 SW2d 683.—Ind & Inf 87(2).

Herrera, Ex parte, TexCrimApp, 493 SW2d 809.—Hab Corp 509(2), 791; Sent & Pun 1260, 1318, 2014.

Herrera, Ex parte, TexApp–Corpus Christi, 750 SW2d 923.—Hab Corp 741, 814.

Herrera, Ex parte, TexApp–Houston (14 Dist), 820 SW2d 54.—Child S 444; Const Law 4495; Contempt 63(1), 64; Hab Corp 528.1.

Herrera, In re, TexCivApp–Amarillo, 402 SW2d 782, writ gr, rev 409 SW2d 395.—Child C 22, 279, 510; Hab Corp 701.1.

Herrera; Allen v., TexCivApp–San Antonio, 257 SW2d 753.—Admin Law 744.1, 791; App & E 770(1); Mun Corp 185(5), 185(7), 185(12).

Herrera; American Finance and Inv. Co. v., TexApp–El Paso, 20 SW3d 829.—Ex & Ad 115, 148, 167, 388(5); Wills 561(1).

Herrera; Baker Marine Corp. v., TexApp–Corpus Christi, 704 SW2d 58, ref nre.—App & E 1051.1(2); Damag 208(2); Evid 363, 544; Jury 136(2), 136(3).

Herrera v. Balmorhea Feeders, Inc., TexCivApp–El Paso, 539 SW2d 84, ref nre.—App & E 930(2), 930(3); Neglig 1714, 1742; Trial 252(1), 352.5(5), 356(3), 356(7), 366.

Herrera v. Carlson, CA5 (Tex), 862 F2d 1157. See Herrera v. Millsap.

Herrera v. Collins, USTex, 113 SCt 853, 506 US 390, 122 LEd2d 203, reh den 113 SCt 1628, 507 US 1001, 123 LEd2d 186.—Const Law 48(4.1), 4646; Crim Law 308,

561(1), 951(1); Hab Corp 462, 493(2), 494, 753, 897, 898(1).

Herrera v. Collins, CA5 (Tex), 954 F2d 1029, cert gr 112 SCt 1074, 502 US 1085, 117 LEd2d 279, aff 113 SCt 853, 506 US 390, 122 LEd2d 203, reh den 113 SCt 1628, 507 US 1001, 123 LEd2d 186.—Crim Law 700(3), 938(1), 1402, 1536; Hab Corp 462, 494, 745.1, 818, 896; Sent & Pun 1798.

Herrera v. Collins, CA5 (Tex), 904 F2d 944, cert den 111 SCt 307, 498 US 925, 112 LEd2d 260.—Const Law 4658(4); Crim Law 339.6, 339.7(3), 339.7(4), 339.10(8); Hab Corp 490(2).

Herrera v. CTS Corp., SDTex, 183 FSupp2d 921.—Civil R 1018, 1218(4), 1225(2), 1225(3); Fed Civ Proc 2497.1, 2539; Statut 226.

Herrera; Export Ins. Co. v., TexCivApp–Corpus Christi, 426 SW2d 895, ref nre.—Damag 39, 89(2), 91(1); Insurance 1641, 1743, 1903, 2014, 2128, 2201, 3381(5), 3580.

Herrera; Firefighters' & Police Officers' Civil Service Com'n of City ofHouston v., TexApp–Houston (1 Dist), 981 SW2d 728, reh overr, and review den.—Admin Law 229; App & E 1008.1(1); Interest 31, 66; Mun Corp 184(1), 197, 199, 216(1), 217.3(5), 1040; Offic 72.70.

Herrera v. FMC Corp., TexApp–Houston (14 Dist), 672 SW2d 5, ref nre.—App & E 230, 1012.1(3); Evid 506, 512; Prod Liab 81.1, 85, 90; Trial 56.

Herrera v. Gibbs, TexCivApp–El Paso, 499 SW2d 912.— App & E 1170.7, 1170.9(8), 1170.10; Autos 20; Estop 75; Evid 273(5); Trial 352.20; Trover 17, 40(3), 40(4), 40(6), 46, 57.

Herrera; Golleher v., TexApp–Amarillo, 651 SW2d 329.— Autos 150, 206, 244(34), 244(35); Evid 555.4(2), 555.8(1), 570.

Herrera v. Herrera, Tex, 409 SW2d 395.—Child C 23, 42, 68, 275, 452, 510, 921(1); Hab Corp 636.

Herrera; Herrera v., Tex, 409 SW2d 395.—Child C 23, 42, 68, 275, 452, 510, 921(1); Hab Corp 636.

Herrera; Medina v., Tex, 927 SW2d 597.—Const Law 2312, 2314; Elect of Rem 1; Insurance 3513(3); Labor & Emp 3045; Work Comp 17, 680, 2084, 2093, 2105, 2106, 2107, 2168, 2171, 2190.

Herrera; Medina v., TexApp–Houston (14 Dist), 905 SW2d 624, reh overr, and writ gr, aff in part, rev in part 927 SW2d 597.—App & E 901, 934(1); Work Comp 2093, 2105, 2106, 2107, 2109, 2168.

Herrera v. Millsap, CA5 (Tex), 862 F2d 1157.—Civil R 1088(4); Fed Cts 766.

Herrera v. Santos, CA5 (Tex), 883 F2d 385. See de Jesus Benavides v. Santos.

Herrera v. Seton Northwest Hosp., TexApp–Austin, 212 SW3d 452, rule 537(f) motion gr.—App & E 946, 977(3), 977(5); Const Law 656, 657, 990, 1030, 2314, 2315, 2489, 2494, 3989; Health 800, 804, 805; New Tr 102(1); Statut 212.1.

Herrera v. State, TexCrimApp, 682 SW2d 313, cert den 105 SCt 2665, 471 US 1131, 86 LEd2d 282, denial of habeas corpus aff 904 F2d 944, cert den 111 SCt 307, 498 US 925, 112 LEd2d 260, habeas corpus den Ex parte Herrera, 819 SW2d 528, reh den, cert den 112 SCt 1074, 502 US 1085, 117 LEd2d 279, grant of habeas corpus rev 954 F2d 1029, cert gr 112 SCt 1074, 502 US 1085, 117 LEd2d 279, aff 113 SCt 853, 506 US 390, 122 LEd2d 203, reh den 113 SCt 1628, 507 US 1001, 123 LEd2d 186, stay gr 828 SW2d 8, habeas corpus den 860 SW2d 106.—Crim Law 339.11(7), 369.2(4), 1141(2), 1169.1(5), 1169.1(9), 1169.11; Homic 1076, 1080(3), 1080(4), 1082, 1094; Sent & Pun 1756, 1762, 1765.

Herrera v. State, TexCrimApp, 623 SW2d 940.—Ind & Inf 180.

Herrera v. State, TexCrimApp, 561 SW2d 175.—Controlled Subs 30, 75, 80, 154.

Herrera v. State, TexCrimApp, 513 SW2d 71.—Controlled Subs 6; Crim Law 1184(4.1); Sent & Pun 31, 1802.

Herrera v. State, TexCrimApp, 462 SW2d 597.—Crim Law 742(2), 1090.9; Witn 78.

Herrera v. State, TexCrimApp, 319 SW2d 709, 167 TexCrim 282.—Larc 55.

Herrera v. State, TexCrimApp, 261 SW2d 706, 159 TexCrim 175.—Crim Law 510, 814(15), 854(9); Homic 787, 1193, 1479.

Herrera v. State, TexCrimApp, 256 SW2d 851, 158 TexCrim 505.—Crim Law 531(3), 627.5(5); Embez 8.

Herrera v. State, TexCrimApp, 157 SW2d 363, 143 TexCrim 96.—Crim Law 1036.1(1), 1036.1(8), 1037.1(1), 1038.1(5), 1137(3); Rape 4.

Herrera v. State, TexCrimApp, 124 SW2d 147, 136 TexCrim 88.—Crim Law 134(2), 537, 781(5); Homic 1163.

Herrera v. State, TexCrimApp, 101 SW2d 811, 131 TexCrim 647.—Afft 5.

Herrera v. State, TexApp–Houston (1 Dist), 11 SW3d 412, petition for discretionary review refused.—Crim Law 338(7), 717, 814(1), 1144.12, 1144.15, 1165(1), 1171.1(2.1), 1171.1(3).

Herrera v. State, TexApp–Fort Worth, 756 SW2d 120, petition for discretionary review refused.—Double J 144.

Herrera; State v., TexApp–Austin, 25 SW3d 326, on remand 2000 WL 35465929, new trial den 2001 WL 35923779, rev and remanded 2002 WL 185476.—App & E 223; Judgm 95, 173, 197; Pretrial Proc 583; Trial 15.

Herrera v. State, TexApp–San Antonio, 12 SW3d 607.— Crim Law 273.1(2), 1026.10(4).

Herrera v. State, TexApp–San Antonio, 915 SW2d 94, application for writ of habeas corpus held in abeyance Ex parte Herrera, 2006 WL 2846426.—Crim Law 20, 568, 703, 823(5), 1030(1), 1144.13(2.1), 1152(1), 1159.3(2), 1159.4(2), 1171.1(2.1); Jury 131(2), 131(3), 131(4), 131(13); Obst Just 1, 16, 18.

Herrera v. State, TexApp–San Antonio, 848 SW2d 244.— Crim Law 661, 863(2), 1035(2), 1037.1(1), 1038.1(1), 1038.1(3.1), 1153(1), 1172.1(1), 1174(5); Homic 1051(1), 1059; Jury 142.

Herrera v. State, TexApp–Texarkana, 80 SW3d 283, reh overr, and petition for discretionary review refused.— Arrest 63.4(2), 63.5(4); Autos 349(1), 349(10), 349(17), 349(18); Crim Law 1134(2), 1144.12, 1158(4), 1169.1(8); Searches 184.

Herrera v. State, TexApp–Amarillo, 665 SW2d 497, petition for discretionary review refused.—Arrest 63.4(2), 63.4(17), 63.5(1), 63.5(2), 63.5.3(1), 63.5(4), 63.5(9), 68(4); Autos 418; Crim Law 394.4(9), 394.6(5), 412.1(1), 412.2(5), 414, 923(2), 925(1), 1156(5); Jury 131(1); Searches 192.1.

Herrera v. State, TexApp–El Paso, 24 SW3d 844, reh overr.—Const Law 725; Crim Law 1134(3).

Herrera; State v., TexApp–El Paso, 754 SW2d 795.— Double J 131, 166.1.

Herrera v. State, TexApp–Waco, 656 SW2d 148.—Sent & Pun 2003, 2021.

Herrera v. State, TexApp–Corpus Christi, 951 SW2d 197. —Crim Law 1144.17; Sent & Pun 2001, 2003, 2004, 2011, 2013, 2020.

Herrera v. State, TexApp–Corpus Christi, 756 SW2d 882. —Crim Law 1134(3).

Herrera v. State, TexApp–Corpus Christi, 745 SW2d 527, petition for discretionary review refused.—Arrest 63.4(2), 63.4(16), 71.1(5), 71.1(6); Sent & Pun 2019.

Herrera v. State, TexApp–Houston (14 Dist), 194 SW3d 656, petition for discretionary review refused.—Crim Law 517.1(3), 520(1), 520(2), 1139, 1158(4).

Herrera; State Office of Risk Management v., TexApp–Amarillo, 189 SW3d 405.—Work Comp 1874.

Herrera; Talbert v., TexCivApp–San Antonio, 353 SW2d 948.—App & E 913; Estop 91(2).

Herrera v. Talbert, TexCivApp–San Antonio, 316 SW2d 952.—Abate & R 7; App & E 113(1); Judgm 297, 340; New Tr 155.

Herrera v. Texas Employers' Ins. Ass'n, TexApp–San Antonio, 653 SW2d 359.—Work Comp 1874, 1881, 1883.

Herrera; U.S. v., CA5 (Tex), 412 F3d 577.—Crim Law 641.13(1), 641.13(2.1), 641.13(5), 1139, 1181.5(6).

Herrera; U.S. v., CA5 (Tex), 313 F3d 882, cert den 123 SCt 1375, 537 US 1242, 155 LEd2d 213, denial of post-conviction relief rev 412 F3d 577.—Crim Law 1044.1(7), 1044.2(1), 1134(3).

Herrera; U.S. v., CA5 (Tex), 289 F3d 311, reh gr, opinion vac 300 F3d 530, on reh 313 F3d 882, cert den 123 SCt 1375, 537 US 1242, 155 LEd2d 213, denial of post-conviction relief rev 412 F3d 577.—Consp 24(1), 24(2), 28(3), 43(12), 47(2), 47(12), 48.1(1); Controlled Subs 81; Courts 96(5); Crim Law 44, 510, 1144.13(2.1), 1144.13(3), 1144.13(5), 1144.13(8), 1159.2(1), 1159.2(7), 1159.2(10), 1159.6, 1167(1); Ind & Inf 171; Statut 188, 217.2, 217.4, 241(1); Weap 4, 17(4).

Herrera; U.S. v., CA5 (Tex), 600 F2d 502.—Aliens 797; Crim Law 356, 419(2.20), 1189; Witn 414(1).

Herrera; U.S. v., CA5 (Tex), 474 F2d 1049, cert den 94 SCt 77, 414 US 861, 38 LEd2d 111.—Costs 302.1(1).

Herrera; U.S. v., CA5 (Tex), 455 F2d 157.—Crim Law 627.10(5), 673(2), 1132, 1169.1(9); Jury 131(13).

Herrera v. U.S., CA5 (Tex), 384 F2d 525, cert den 88 SCt 1425, 390 US 1031, 20 LEd2d 288.—Crim Law 569.

Herrera; U.S. v., CA5 (Tex), 171 FedAppx 446.—Consp 47(12); U S 34; Witn 88.

Herrera; U.S. v., CA5 (Tex), 70 FedAppx 208, opinion after remand 82 FedAppx 872, cert den 124 SCt 2049, 541 US 1001, 158 LEd2d 514.—Crim Law 1131(7), 1181.5(3.1).

Herrera; U.S. v., NDTex, 29 FSupp2d 756.—Bail 73.1(1); Fed Cts 3.1; Statut 181(2), 188, 190, 205, 208, 214; U S Mag 27.

Herrera; Wembley Inv. Co. v., Tex, 11 SW3d 924, on remand 2000 WL 1100872, petition stricken, and review den.—Evid 71; Judgm 335(1), 335(2); New Tr 155; Pretrial Proc 513.

Herrera v. Wembley Inv. Co., TexApp–Dallas, 12 SW3d 83, review gr, rev 11 SW3d 924, on remand 2000 WL 1100872, petition stricken, and review den.—App & E 76(1); Insurance 3512, 3526(5); Judgm 131, 140, 178, 217, 335(1), 335(2), 335(3); Subrog 1, 33(1); Work Comp 2191, 2242.

Herrera v. Yellow Freight System, Inc., CA5 (Tex), 505 F2d 66, reh den 518 F2d 1407, cert gr Teamsters Local Union 657 v. Rodriguez, 96 SCt 2200, 425 US 990, 48 LEd2d 814, cert den Lee Way Motor Freight, Inc v Resendis, 96 SCt 2201, 425 US 991, 48 LEd2d 815, reh gr, vac 97 SCt 2669, 431 US 952, 53 LEd2d 268, on remand 560 F2d 1285, on remand 560 F2d 1285, reh den 568 F2d 1367, vac East Texas Motor Freight System Inc v Rodriguez, 97 SCt 1891, 431 US 395, 52 LEd2d 453, on remand 560 F2d 1286, vac 97 SCt 2669, 431 US 952, 53 LEd2d 268, on remand 560 F2d 1285, on remand 560 F2d 1285, reh den 568 F2d 1367.—Civil R 1135, 1535, 1545, 1548.

Herrera v. Zinberg, TexCivApp–San Antonio, 287 SW2d 695, ref nre.—App & E 1070(2); Trial 360.

Herrera-Mendez; U.S. v., CA5 (Tex), 215 FedAppx 377, cert den 127 SCt 3077.—Aliens 799; Ind & Inf 113.

Herrera-Montes; U.S. v., CA5 (Tex), 490 F3d 390.—Crim Law 1139; Sent & Pun 781, 793.

Herrera-Nunez; U.S. v., CA5 (Tex), 184 FedAppx 362, cert den 127 SCt 271, 166 LEd2d 208.—Crim Law 1042.

Herrera-Ochoa; U.S. v., CA5 (Tex), 245 F3d 495.—Aliens 795(4); Crim Law 304(1), 394.4(9), 1139, 1144.13(2.1), 1144.13(3), 1144.13(5), 1158(1), 1159.2(7).

Herrera-Solorzano; U.S. v., CA5 (Tex), 114 F3d 48, appeal after remand US v. Altamirana-Lopez, 158 F3d 583, cert den 119 SCt 845, 525 US 1090, 142 LEd2d 699. —Aliens 799.

Herrera-Torres; U.S. v., CA5 (Tex), 145 FedAppx 909, cert den 126 SCt 838, 546 US 1080, 163 LEd2d 713.— Crim Law 1042.

Herrera-Trejo; U.S. v., CA5 (Tex), 169 FedAppx 225, cert gr, vac Gutierrez-Tovar v. US, 127 SCt 828, 166 LEd2d 662, on remand US v Villa-Gutierrez, 222 FedAppx 393, on remand US v Gonzalez-Silva, 228 FedAppx 413, on remand US v Lozano-Mireles, 224 FedAppx 431.— Aliens 770; Sent & Pun 780.

Herrero v. State, TexApp–Houston (14 Dist), 124 SW3d 827.—Crim Law 26, 534(1), 535(2), 538(3), 553, 730(1), 741(1), 742(1), 867, 1134(2), 1144.13(2.1), 1144.13(3), 1144.13(6), 1155, 1159.2(2), 1159.2(7), 1159.2(8), 1159.2(9), 1159.3(1), 1159.3(5), 1170.5(6); Homic 511, 1184, 1186.

Herriage; Hartford Acc. & Indem. Co. v., TexCivApp–Amarillo, 139 SW2d 873.—Work Comp 50, 51, 1009, 1028, 1893.

Herriage v. State, TexCrimApp, 256 SW2d 411.—Crim Law 1090.1(1).

Herriage v. State, TexCrimApp, 255 SW2d 516, 158 Tex-Crim 362.—Autos 425; Crim Law 796, 819, 1090.13, 1171.8(2); Witn 274(2).

Herrick v. State, TexApp–Houston (1 Dist), 825 SW2d 215.—Crim Law 507(1), 507(2), 742(2).

Herrick Co. Steel Products; Cox v., TexCivApp–San Antonio, 356 SW2d 197.—Evid 417(9); Venue 7.5(2), 7.5(3).

Herrin, Ex parte, TexCrimApp, 537 SW2d 33.—Crim Law 641.2(4), 641.4(1), 641.12(1), 951(1); Hab Corp 613; Ind & Inf 35.

Herrin v. Bunge, TexCivApp–Houston, 336 SW2d 281.— App & E 172(3), 1140(4); Evid 8; Fixt 4, 21, 27(1), 35(2), 35(6).

Herrin; California Fina Group, Inc. v., CA5 (Tex), 379 F3d 311.—Alt Disp Res 213(5), 412, 414.

Herrin; California Fina Group, Inc. v., NDTex, 278 FSupp2d 808, aff 379 F3d 311.—Alt Disp Res 412.

Herrin; Commercial Standard Ins. Co. v., TexCivApp–Eastland, 515 SW2d 163.—App & E 846(5), 852, 1010.1(3); Insurance 2129; Plead 45, 111.42(4), 427.

Herrin v. Falcon, TexCivApp–Beaumont, 198 SW2d 117, ref nre.—App & E 757(3), 933(1), 1062.2; Autos 173(4), 173(5), 244(14), 247; Death 99(4); Infants 78(1); Neglig 259, 409; New Tr 144.

Herrin; Harris County Appraisal Dist. v., Tex, 924 SW2d 154.—Tax 2697.

Herrin; Harris County Appraisal Dist. v., TexApp–Houston (14 Dist), 917 SW2d 345, reh overr, and writ gr, mod 924 SW2d 154.—Const Law 2314, 2316; Tax 2641.

Herrin v. Kelly, TexCivApp–Waco, 429 SW2d 195.—Acct Action on 13; App & E 302(1); Judgm 185.3(3); Neglig 1664; Trial 140(1).

Herrin v. Medical Protective Co., TexApp–Texarkana, 89 SW3d 301, review den.—Antitrust 145, 150; App & E 934(1); Fraud 3, 7, 64(1); Insurance 1563, 1900, 1929(3), 3417, 3424; Judgm 181(23), 185.3(12); Lim of Act 95(1), 95(9), 95(16), 100(12); Torts 433.

Herrin; Nacalina Lumber Co. v., TexCivApp–Beaumont, 445 SW2d 613.—Plead 111.42(7).

Herrin v. Newton Cent. Appraisal Dist., EDTex, 706 FSupp 511.—Civil R 1563, 1573, 1574.

Herrin v. Newton Cent. Appraisal Dist., EDTex, 687 FSupp 1072.—Civil R 1123, 1171, 1176, 1349, 1359, 1448, 1455, 1473, 1479, 1736, 1769, 1773; Const Law 3424.

Herrin v. Standard Fire Ins. Co., TexCivApp–Hous (14 Dist), 466 SW2d 798, ref nre.—Work Comp 888, 893.

Herrin v. State, TexCrimApp, 125 SW3d 436, reh den.— Crim Law 44, 730(8), 881(1), 1144.13(2.1), 1159.2(7), 1184(3); Homic 604, 607, 1165; Sent & Pun 1667, 1788(11).

Herrin v. State, TexCrimApp, 525 SW2d 27.—Crim Law 641.12(1), 1091(1), 1092.11(1), 1114.1(1).

Herrin v. State, TexCrimApp, 115 SW2d 942, 134 TexCrim 296.—Autos 355(2); Crim Law 1087.1(2), 1131(7).

Herrin v. State, TexApp–Dallas, 668 SW2d 896.—Courts 106; Crim Law 1071, 1133, 1181.5(1).

Herrin; Taylor v., TexCivApp–Galveston, 127 SW2d 945. —Equity 57; Ven & Pur 54, 101, 104, 216, 284.

Herrin; Tejas Gas Corp. v., Tex, 716 SW2d 45.—Estop 92(4).

Herrin; Tejas Gas Corp. v., TexApp–Texarkana, 705 SW2d 177, rev 716 SW2d 45.—Em Dom 171, 196, 198(2), 202(1); Evid 555.4(3).

Herrin v. Treon, NDTex, 459 FSupp2d 525.—Civil R 1358, 1376(2); Const Law 3849, 4545(3), 4820, 4821; Fed Civ Proc 2491.5; Fed Cts 265; Offic 114; Prisons 10; Sent & Pun 1532, 1533, 1537, 1546, 1553.

Herring, Ex parte, Tex, 438 SW2d 801.—Const Law 4494; Hab Corp 528.1.

Herring, Ex parte, TexCrimApp, 271 SW2d 657, 160 TexCrim 357, cert den Herring v. Ellis, 76 SCt 309, 350 US 938, 100 LEd 819.—Hab Corp 441; Sent & Pun 1160.

Herring, Ex parte, TexCrimApp, 245 SW2d 705, 156 TexCrim 624.—Hab Corp 228.

Herring, In re, TexApp–San Antonio, 221 SW3d 729.—Child C 606, 650, 661; Mand 3(2.1), 4(4), 12.

Herring, In re Estate of, TexApp–Corpus Christi, 983 SW2d 61, reh overr.—Execution 405, 406(1); Ex & Ad 431(1); Hus & W 273(1), 273(2), 273(4); Receivers 8, 42, 51.

Herring, In re Estate of, TexApp–Corpus Christi, 970 SW2d 583.—Fraud 6; Hus & W 265; Judgm 185(2), 185(4); Lim of Act 100(1), 100(3), 100(7), 100(11); Plead 287; Pretrial Proc 472, 473, 474, 477.1, 483, 486.

Herring v. Bank of America, N.A., TexApp–Houston (1 Dist), 176 SW3d 513.—App & E 893(1); Ex & Ad 264(1); Statut 176.

Herring v. Blakeley, Tex, 385 SW2d 843.—Divorce 252.3(2), 252.3(4), 254(1), 287; Hus & W 249(1), 249(2.1), 249(3), 254; Propty 2.

Herring; Blakeley v., TexCivApp–Tyler, 374 SW2d 677, writ gr, rev 385 SW2d 843.—Divorce 267, 322.

Herring; Bocquet v., Tex, 972 SW2d 19.—App & E 946, 984(5), 1182; Costs 194.12, 194.40, 208.

Herring v. Bocquet, TexApp–San Antonio, 21 SW3d 367. —App & E 989, 1012.1(4); Costs 207; Evid 571(7).

Herring v. Bocquet, TexApp–San Antonio, 933 SW2d 611, review gr, rev 972 SW2d 19, on remand 21 SW3d 367.— App & E 984(5); Costs 194.18, 194.40, 208.

Herring; Brown v., TexCivApp–Eastland, 466 SW2d 664, ref nre.—App & E 1045(3); Autos 244(41.1); Evid 555.8(2).

Herring; Chicago Fraternal Life Ins. Ass'n v., TexCivApp–Waco, 104 SW2d 901.—Accord 1, 5, 20; App & E 1236; Fraud 13(2); Insurance 2082, 3384, 3388, 3390.

Herring v. Dunigan Tool & Supply Co., TexCivApp–Eastland, 361 SW2d 474.—App & E 989; Des & Dist 83.

Herring v. Estelle, CA5 (Tex), 491 F2d 125, reh den 493 F2d 664.—Crim Law 273.1(4), 641.13(1), 641.13(5).

Herring; First Nat. Life Ins. Co. v., TexCivApp–Waco, 318 SW2d 119.—App & E 196, 201(1), 256, 285, 554(3), 907(3), 918(3), 959(3); Const Law 4426; Judgm 284; Plead 236(2), 365(3).

Herring; Gardner v., TexApp–Amarillo, 21 SW3d 767, reh overr.—Admin Law 124; Costs 194.44; Judgm 181(15.1); Schools 57.

Herring v. Garnett, TexCivApp–Hous (1 Dist), 463 SW2d 52, ref nre.—Autos 201(5).

Herring; Hale v., TexCivApp–Austin, 102 SW2d 468.— App & E 688(2), 762, 1040(13), 1062.1; Bills & N 516, 518(1); Evid 219(1), 478(1); Trial 351.5(4), 352.5(4), 352.9, 352.11.

Herring; Hanzel v., TexApp–Fort Worth, 80 SW3d 167.— App & E 870(2), 1175(1); Bankr 2154.1, 2395; Costs

194.40; Frds St of 110(1); Interpl 6, 15, 17, 18, 21, 35; Judgm 720, 725(1), 750; Jud S 61; Tax 2936.

Herring v. Hathcock, TexApp–El Paso, 643 SW2d 235.— Neglig 202, 1076; Venue 8.5(8).

Herring; Howard v., TexCivApp–Amarillo, 324 SW2d 266. —Autos 244(51), 244(58), 245(26.1); New Tr 10, 56.

Herring; McMahan v., TexCivApp–El Paso, 348 SW2d 679, writ dism.—App & E 1024.3; Labor & Emp 30, 57; Plead 111.42(9).

Herring v. Moore, CA5 (Tex), 735 F2d 797.—Int Rev 4637, 4916, 4920, 5245, 5388.

Herring; Owen v., TexCivApp–Austin, 330 SW2d 500.— Insurance 1408; Venue 22(1), 22(7).

Herring; Peveto v., TexCivApp–Beaumont, 198 SW2d 921.—Adv Poss 25, 27, 31, 36, 38, 58, 97, 115(1), 115(3); Trial 140(2), 180.

Herring; Republic Bankers Life Ins. Co. v., TexCivApp–Waco, 463 SW2d 743.—App & E 218.2(3.1), 218.2(7); Insurance 3575; Judgm 199(3.10), 199(5); New Tr 164; Trial 357, 388(2).

Herring v. Schingler, TexCivApp–Beaumont, 101 SW2d 394, writ dism.—Anim 66.5(2), 74(3), 74(4), 74(8).

Herring v. State, TexCrimApp, 202 SW3d 764.—Rob 24.15(2).

Herring v. State, TexCrimApp, 147 SW3d 390.—Crim Law 1165(1), 1169.11.

Herring v. State, TexCrimApp, 659 SW2d 391.—Crim Law 814(1); Ind & Inf 93, 193; Lewd 1.

Herring v. State, TexCrimApp, 573 SW2d 232.—Mal Mis 9.

Herring v. State, TexCrimApp, 440 SW2d 649.—Crim Law 134(2), 641.12(1), 863(2), 1039, 1169.1(5); Sent & Pun 1899.

Herring v. State, TexCrimApp, 371 SW2d 884.—Weap 17(4).

Herring v. State, TexCrimApp, 302 SW2d 428, 165 TexCrim 4.—Jury 103(1), 103(5).

Herring v. State, TexCrimApp, 273 SW2d 421, 160 TexCrim 597.—Ind & Inf 32(3).

Herring v. State, TexCrimApp, 148 SW2d 416, 141 TexCrim 281.—Crim Law 331, 518(1), 778(7), 1172.2.

Herring v. State, TexCrimApp, 132 SW2d 418, 137 TexCrim 502.—Crim Law 1099.8, 1099.11.

Herring v. State, TexCrimApp, 130 SW2d 294, 137 TexCrim 20.—Mand 169.

Herring v. State, TexApp–Houston (1 Dist), 752 SW2d 169, cause remanded 758 SW2d 283, on remand 1989 WL 17133, petition for discretionary review refused.— Crim Law 374, 641.13(6), 1169.4, 1172.1(2), 1184(2); Ind & Inf 132(5).

Herring v. State, TexApp–Austin, 738 SW2d 18, petition for discretionary review refused, untimely filed.—Const Law 2545(4), 4594(1); Crim Law 700(2.1), 700(4), 790.

Herring v. State, TexApp–Dallas, 633 SW2d 905, petition for discretionary review gr, aff 659 SW2d 391.—Crim Law 59(1), 59(5), 568; Ind & Inf 71.4(12); Lewd 1.

Herring v. State, TexApp–Amarillo, 147 SW3d 425, petition for discretionary review gr, aff 147 SW3d 390.— Crim Law 412.2(2), 633(2), 742(1), 1153(1), 1169.1(1), 1169.11.

Herring v. State, TexApp–Waco, 160 SW3d 618, petition for discretionary review gr, rev 202 SW3d 764, cert den 127 SCt 2107, 167 LEd2d 822.—Crim Law 260.11(4), 1119(1), 1134(2), 1184(3); Ind & Inf 159(1).

Herring v. State, TexApp–Corpus Christi, 758 SW2d 849, petition for discretionary review refused, cert den 110 SCt 247, 493 US 896, 107 LEd2d 197.—Arrest 63.4(12), 63.4(16), 63.5(6); Crim Law 596(3), 721.5(2), 726, 1114.1(1), 1116, 1169.5(3); Jury 133; Rob 17(7); Searches 65, 68; Sent & Pun 1311, 1314, 1325, 1381(2).

Herring v. Telectronics Pacing Systems, Inc., TexApp–Beaumont, 964 SW2d 753, review den.—Antitrust 132; App & E 852, 1178(1); Prod Liab 46.1; States 18.65.

HERRING;

Herring; Texas Dept. of Corrections v., Tex, 513 SW2d 6.—App & E 1177(4); Judgm 181(11), 183; Pretrial Proc 242, 246; States 112.2(4), 190.

Herring v. Texas Dept. of Corrections, TexCivApp–Hous (14 Dist), 500 SW2d 718, writ gr, aff 513 SW2d 6.—Atty Gen 7; Judgm 181(2), 181(6), 183; Pretrial Proc 246.

Herring v. Welborn, TexApp–San Antonio, 27 SW3d 132, reh overr, and review den.—App & E 893(1), 920(3), 941, 984(1); Costs 2, 260(4), 260(5); Courts 4, 26, 40, 200.5, 201, 472.4(1), 472.4(2.1); Ex & Ad 436; Inj 111, 135, 138.18, 152; Pretrial Proc 552, 690; Venue 1.5.

Herring Nat. Bank; Hardage v., CA5 (Tex), 837 F2d 1319.—Bankr 2794.1, 2796, 2797.1, 3079, 3790.

Herring v. Nat. Bank of Vernon; National Liberty Ins. Co. v., TexCivApp–Amarillo, 135 SW2d 219, writ dism, correct.—App & E 758.3(9); Insurance 1834(1), 2205, 3151, 3153, 3168; Trial 352.4(4), 355(1).

Herrington; Ames v., TexCivApp–Eastland, 139 SW2d 183, writ dism, correct.—App & E 1062.1; Elect of Rem 3(1); Guard & W 33, 178, 180; Judgm 592, 614(3), 627, 670, 678(1), 678(2), 713(2); Neglig 1713; Trial 352.10.

Herrington; Henderson v., TexCivApp–Houston, 366 SW2d 677, ref nre.—Adv Poss 33, 85(4); Tresp to T T 6.1, 41(2).

Herrington v. Herrington, TexCivApp–Waco, 482 SW2d 407.—App & E 627.3.

Herrington; Herrington v., TexCivApp–Waco, 482 SW2d 407.—App & E 627.3.

Herrington v. Hiller, CA5 (Tex), 883 F2d 411.—Evid 146; Fed Cts 823, 901.1; Health 820.

Herrington; Independent Eastern Torpedo Co. v., Tex-ComApp, 95 SW2d 377, 128 Tex 17.—App & E 734, 837(3); Insurance 3525; Work Comp 2186, 2191.

Herrington; Loyd v., Tex, 182 SW2d 1003, 143 Tex 135.—Labor & Emp 3157, 3159.

Herrington; Loyd v., TexCivApp–Fort Worth, 178 SW2d 694, rev 182 SW2d 1003, 143 Tex 135.—App & E 930(2), 1026, 1050.1(7), 1052(5), 1060.4; Explos 7; Labor & Emp 3052, 3053, 3095, 3148, 3159; Trial 18, 129, 133.6(5).

Herrington v. Luce, TexCivApp–Tyler, 491 SW2d 478.—Mech Liens 118, 126.

Herrington v. McDonald, Tex, 174 SW2d 307, 141 Tex 441.—Partit 43; Plead 111.9, 111.27.

Herrington v. Pelkey, TexCivApp–Beaumont, 424 SW2d 507, ref nre.—Brok 43(3); Estop 118; Home 118(3); Hus & W 24, 265.

Herrington; Ridenour v., TexApp–Waco, 47 SW3d 117, review den.—Judgm 178, 181(2), 183, 185(5); Mines 78.1(8), 78.1(9).

Herrington v. Sandcastle Condominium Ass'n, TexApp–Houston (14 Dist), 222 SW3d 99.—Condo 12; Decl Judgm 329; Judgm 252(1); Plead 1, 427.

Herrington v. State, TexCrimApp, 534 SW2d 331.—Const Law 2637; Sent & Pun 1969(2), 2003, 2021.

Herrington v. State, TexCrimApp, 89 SW2d 991, 129 TexCrim 567.—Crim Law 844(2), 942(1), 1092.11(1); Homic 1154; Witn 48(1), 48(3).

Herrington; Young v., TexCivApp–Austin, 312 SW2d 685.—Evid 357; Gas 9; Plead 111.42(7); Venue 8.5(8).

Herring-Turner Hardware Co. v. Park, TexCivApp–Waco, 123 SW2d 983.—App & E 65, 1091(3); J P 159(1), 174(8); Paymt 39(5), 61, 71.

Herrin Petroleum Transport Equipment Corp. v. Railroad Commission of Texas, TexCivApp–Waco, 619 SW2d 588, ref nre.—Admin Law 461; Autos 105, 106; Carr 8.

Herrin Transfer & Warehouse Co.; Savage v., TexCivApp–Galveston, 219 SW2d 101.—Perj 12; Plead 111.3, 111.39(4); Venue 21.

Herrin Transp. Co. v. Andrews, TexCivApp–Waco, 233 SW2d 891.—Evid 10(2), 314(1); Plead 111.42(8); Trial 105(2).

Herrin Transp. Co.; Bickham v., TexCivApp–Houston, 344 SW2d 953.—App & E 1170.6; Autos 244(12), 244(34), 244(35); Evid 5(2); Trial 19.

Herrin Transp. Co.; Francis v., Tex, 432 SW2d 710, appeal after remand 473 SW2d 664.—Courts 95(2), 97(6); Death 8, 39, 51; Lim of Act 120, 126, 165.

Herrin Transp. Co.; Francis v., TexCivApp–Hous (1 Dist), 473 SW2d 664.—App & E 758.3(9), 1070(2); Autos 193(1), 242(1), 244(36.1), 245(50.1); Plead 20, 127(1); Trial 350.5(3), 352.5(6).

Herrin Transp. Co.; Francis v., TexCivApp–Hous (14 Dist), 423 SW2d 610, writ gr, rev 432 SW2d 710, appeal after remand 473 SW2d 664.—Death 8, 11, 38, 39; Lim of Act 1, 2(1), 104.5, 165, 166; Neglig 204.

Herrin Transp. Co. v. Gregory, TexCivApp–Waco, 384 SW2d 787.—Autos 244(2.1), 244(41.1); Witn 414(2).

Herrin Transp. Co.; Hamilton v., TexCivApp–Waco, 343 SW2d 300, ref nre.—App & E 1172(2); Indem 35, 81; Princ & A 41(6), 47.

Herrin Transp. Co.; Hilburn v., TexCivApp–Dallas, 197 SW2d 149.—Autos 78; Contracts 168.

Herrin Transp. Co.; Marmion v., TexCivApp–Beaumont, 127 SW2d 558, writ refused.—Judgm 399.

Herrin Transp. Co. v. Marmion, TexCivApp–Beaumont, 113 SW2d 291.—App & E 80(1); Carr 12(1), 69(4); Trial 397(1).

Herrin Transp. Co. v. Parker, TexCivApp–Hous (1 Dist), 425 SW2d 876, ref nre.—App & E 901, 918(3); Autos 243(1); Neglig 1541; New Tr 108(4); Plead 238(3); Trial 350.7(1).

Herrin Transp. Co. v. Peterson, TexCivApp–Galveston, 216 SW2d 245, writ refused.—App & E 1045(1), 1060.6; Damag 96, 130.3; Jury 71, 137(1); New Tr 53.1, 56.

Herrin Transp. Co. v. Pursley, TexCivApp–Beaumont, 424 SW2d 660, ref nre.—App & E 216(1), 231(7), 1052(5); Autos 244(34), 244(36.1); Damag 132(3).

Herrin Transp. Co.; Railroad Commission v., TexCivApp–Austin, 262 SW2d 426, ref nre.—Admin Law 461, 481, 482; Autos 82, 83.

Herrin Transp. Co.; Red Ball Motor Freight v., NDTex, 98 FSupp 248.—Admin Law 763; Commerce 83, 85(1), 85.27(1), 85.28(3), 152, 168.

Herrin Transp. Co. v. Robert E. Olson Co., TexCivApp–San Antonio, 325 SW2d 826.—Carr 90, 185(3); Costs 194.32.

Herrin Transp. Co. v. Sheldon, TexCivApp–Amarillo, 209 SW2d 943.—Carr 131, 135, 185(1), 185(3).

Herrin Transp. Co. v. Southeastern Elec. Co., TexCivApp–Houston, 310 SW2d 343.—App & E 931(1), 1071.5; Carr 106, 147, 159(1), 165.

Herrin Transp. Co. v. U.S., SDTex, 297 FSupp 529.—Commerce 108, 168.

Herrman; Maher v., TexApp–Fort Worth, 69 SW3d 332, reh overr, and review den.—App & E 173(10), 230, 231(1); Judgm 181(6), 181(7), 183, 185(2), 185.3(2); Lim of Act 121(1), 121(2), 187; Trial 136(1).

Herrmann v. Hendrix, TexCivApp–El Paso, 145 SW2d 649.—App & E 554(3); Brok 61(1), 61(4).

Herrmann v. Lindsey, TexApp–San Antonio, 136 SW3d 286.—App & E 223; Contracts 93(5), 138(1); Deeds 18, 19, 69; Ref of Inst 16.

Herrmann; Mergenthaler Linotype Co. v., TexCivApp–Fort Worth, 217 SW2d 122, ref nre.—Contracts 346(2); Evid 448; Sales 85(1).

Herrmann; Mergenthaler Linotype Co. v., TexCivApp–Fort Worth, 211 SW2d 633.—Corp 52, 661(6), 666; Plead 36(2).

Herrmann & Andreas Ins. Agency, Inc. v. Appling, TexApp–Corpus Christi, 800 SW2d 312.—App & E 231(1); Costs 2, 194.44; Evid 222(2), 222(4); Judgm 181(23).

Herrmann Holdings Ltd. v. Lucent Technologies Inc., CA5 (Tex), 302 F3d 552.—Contracts 9(1), 143.5, 280(1); Corp 582; Courts 97(5); Fed Civ Proc 636, 824, 833,

834, 839.1, 851; Fed Cts 372, 383, 390, 391, 611, 763.1, 776, 794, 817, 915; Fraud 3, 12, 41; Sec Reg 278.

Herrmann's Estate v. C.I.R., CA5 (Tex), 235 F2d 440.— Int Rev 4206.10, 4206.20.

Herrod, Ex parte, TexCrimApp, 175 SW2d 87, 146 Tex-Crim 360.—Sent & Pun 1157.

Herrod v. State, TexCrimApp, 650 SW2d 814.—Crim Law 304(17); Judges 7, 15(1), 16(1), 18.

Herron, Ex parte, TexCrimApp, 790 SW2d 623.—Double J 149.

Herron; A. B. C. Storage & Moving Co. v., TexCivApp-Galveston, 138 SW2d 211, writ dism, correct.—App & E 970(2), 1060.1(2.1), 1140(1); Autos 245(59), 246(22); Damag 221(5.1); Death 99(2), 99(3); Evid 123(10), 317(9); Trial 48, 122, 350.2, 351.5(6), 352.4(1).

Herron v. Bowen, CA5 (Tex), 788 F2d 1127.—Social S 142.16; U S 147(10), 147(18).

Herron v. City of Abilene, TexCivApp-Eastland, 528 SW2d 349, writ refused.—Admin Law 749; Mun Corp 185(12).

Herron; City of Silsbee v., TexCivApp-Beaumont, 484 SW2d 154, ref nre.—Zoning 321, 323, 324, 325, 327, 329.1.

Herron v. Cockrell, CA5 (Tex), 78 FedAppx 429.—Fed Civ Proc 2734.

Herron v. Continental Airlines, Inc., CA5 (Tex), 73 F3d 57.—Rem of C 19(1), 21.

Herron; Heath v., TexApp-Houston (14 Dist), 732 SW2d 748, writ den.—Antitrust 256; Atty & C 112, 129(2); Damag 49.10; Elect of Rem 1, 7(1); Evid 591; Judgm 707, 713(1); Torts 109.

Herron v. Herron, CA5 (Tex), 255 F2d 589.—Fed Civ Proc 1754, 1826, 2471, 2516, 2533.1; Fed Cts 893.

Herron; Herron v., CA5 (Tex), 255 F2d 589.—Fed Civ Proc 1754, 1826, 2471, 2516, 2533.1; Fed Cts 893.

Herron; Keaton McCrary Cotton Co., Inc. v., TexCivApp-Amarillo, 529 SW2d 630.—Contracts 147(3); Evid 448; Land & Ten 328(1), 328(3), 330(1), 332; Sales 170.

Herron v. Lackey, Tex, 556 SW2d 246.—Interest 39(3).

Herron v. Lackey, TexCivApp-Beaumont, 554 SW2d 708, aff as reformed 556 SW2d 246.—App & E 1151(2), 1153; Contracts 303(4), 322(5), 354, 355; Mech Liens 157(3), 163.

Herron v. Patrolman # 1, CA5 (Tex), 111 FedAppx 710. —Civil R 1319, 1463.

Herron v. State, TexCrimApp, 86 SW3d 621, habeas corpus dism by Ex parte Herron, 2006 WL 1412259.— Const Law 3309; Crim Law 59(5), 394.6(5), 412(4), 412.2(4), 412.2(5), 511.1(1), 511.2, 641.13(1), 641.13(2.1), 641.13(6), 780(0.5), 780(1), 1038.2, 1134(3), 1152(2), 1158(1), 1158(3), 1169.12, 1173.2(6); Jury 33(2.15), 33(5.15), 108.

Herron v. State, TexCrimApp, 485 SW2d 558.—Crim Law 412.2(3), 517.2(3).

Herron v. State, TexCrimApp, 203 SW2d 225, 150 Tex-Crim 475.—Crim Law 1098; Ind & Inf 122(4).

Herron; State v., TexApp-Fort Worth, 53 SW3d 843.— Crim Law 258, 260.11(4), 386, 1158(1), 1226(3.1).

Herron v. State, TexApp-Dallas, 821 SW2d 329.—Const Law 2507(1); Crim Law 1226(3.1); Ind & Inf 10.2(1), 144.1(3).

Herron; Texas Emp. Ins. Ass'n v., TexCivApp-Corpus Christi, 569 SW2d 549.—App & E 930(3), 989; Work Comp 1283, 1286, 1292, 1295, 1335, 1382, 1683.

Herron; U.S. v., CA5 (Tex), 825 F2d 50.—Consp 40.4, 47(6); Tel 1014(2), 1014(8).

Herron; U.S. v., CA5 (Tex), 816 F2d 1036, opinion superseded 825 F2d 50.

Herr-Voss Corp. v. Delta Brands, Inc., NDTex, 900 FSupp 34, aff in part, vac in part 101 F3d 714, reh den. —Pat 16(2), 16.5(1), 16.14, 34, 36.1(3), 36.1(4), 36.2(1), 75, 76, 81, 98, 99, 101(2), 101(4), 112.1, 112.6, 159, 161, 165(1), 165(2), 167(1.1), 167(2), 226.6, 235(2), 237, 314(5), 325.11(3).

Herschap; Laurel v., TexApp-San Antonio, 5 SW3d 799. —App & E 837(10); Judgm 185.3(21); Neglig 1085, 1202(1), 1205(7); New Tr 157.

Herschap v. Moore, TexCivApp-San Antonio, 430 SW2d 843.—Evid 594; Plead 111.42(7); Trial 140(2); Venue 8.5(8).

Herschbach v. City of Corpus Christi, TexApp-Corpus Christi, 883 SW2d 720, reh overr, and writ den.—Admin Law 133; App & E 223, 854(1), 863, 934(1); Contracts 1, 332(2); Estop 52(1), 52(4), 52(8), 52.10(1), 52.10(2), 52.10(3), 52.15, 92(1), 92(2); Evid 207(1), 265(7); Judgm 19, 181(15.1), 183, 185(2); Mun Corp 200(1), 200(4), 200(7), 200(8.1), 723, 724, 725, 745; Neglig 371, 387; Princ & A 1; States 112(1), 112(2), 191.1, 191.8(3); Stip 1, 6, 7, 14(1), 17(3); Trusts 4, 173, 179.

Herschbach; City of Corpus Christi v., TexCivApp-Corpus Christi, 536 SW2d 653, ref nre.—Mun Corp 199; Statut 230, 270; Work Comp 60, 907, 1113.

Herschberg v. Herschberg, TexApp-Corpus Christi, 994 SW2d 273, reh overr.—Divorce 146, 212, 215, 227(2), 252.3(1), 281, 286(4), 287, 288.

Herschberg; Herschberg v., TexApp-Corpus Christi, 994 SW2d 273, reh overr.—Divorce 146, 212, 215, 227(2), 252.3(1), 281, 286(4), 287, 288.

Hersey, In re Estate of, TexApp-Amarillo, 223 SW3d 457.—App & E 68, 77(2); Ex & Ad 239.

Hersey; Lee v., TexApp-Amarillo, 223 SW3d 439, review den.—App & E 836, 863, 893(1), 934(1); Consp 20; Corp 182.4(6); Courts 4, 24, 37(1), 201; Damag 87(2); Evid 597; Ex & Ad 435; Fraud 58(1); Judgm 27; Trial 139.1(14), 139.1(17).

Hersey's Guardianship, In re, TexCivApp-San Antonio, 93 SW2d 810, writ gr, set aside Holland v. Bailey, 127 SW2d 446, 133 Tex 150.—Domicile 5, 10; Judges 47(1).

Hersh v. H. E. Butt Grocery Co., TexApp-San Antonio, 338 SW2d 174, ref nre.—Judgm 178, 185(2), 185.3(21), 186.

Hersh v. Hendley, TexApp-Fort Worth, 626 SW2d 151.— App & E 218.2(1), 1062.1; Evid 474(6), 547, 571(3); Health 814, 821(2), 821(3), 822(3), 823(7), 823(11), 827; Neglig 1741; Plead 430(2); Trial 194(16), 365.1(6).

Hersh; U.S. v., CA5 (Tex), 415 F2d 835.—Crim Law 911, 1083, 1132.

Hersh v. U.S., NDTex, 347 BR 19.—Atty & C 32(3); Bankr 2022, 3030; Const Law 42.2(1), 855, 976, 1518, 1600, 2040; Fed Civ Proc 103.2; Fed Cts 34; Licens 5; Statut 188.

Hershey; Armendariz v., CA5 (Tex), 413 F2d 1006.— Action 6; Const Law 2600; Fed Cts 724.

Hershey; Armendariz v., WDTex, 295 FSupp 1351, appeal dism 413 F2d 1006.—Armed S 20.6(1), 20.9(3); Const Law 2621; Fed Cts 11, 343.

Hershey; Green v., CA5 (Tex), 422 F2d 1319.—Fed Cts 724, 743.

Hershey; Green v., NDTex, 302 FSupp 43, appeal dism 422 F2d 1319.—Armed S 20.6(1).

Hershey v. Praxair, Inc., SDTex, 969 FSupp 429.—Civil R 1218(2), 1218(4), 1225(2), 1225(3); Fed Civ Proc 2497.1.

Hershey v. Praxair, Inc., SDTex, 948 FSupp 29.—Civil R 1505(7), 1516; Consp 18.

Hershey v. UCISCO, Inc., SDTex, 969 FSupp 429. See Hershey v. Praxair, Inc.

Hershey v. Ucisco, Inc., SDTex, 948 FSupp 29. See Hershey v. Praxair, Inc.

Hershey; Walsh v., TexCivApp-Fort Worth, 472 SW2d 954, ref nre.—App & E 221, 302(1), 1062.1, 1078(1); Autos 171(9), 226(2), 244(34), 244(36.1); Damag 221(2.1); Parent & C 7(1), 7(9); Trial 349(1), 351.2(1.1).

Herskowitz; Ince v., TexApp-Houston (1 Dist), 630 SW2d 762, ref nre.—Judgm 185.3(16).

Herter v. Wolfe, TexApp-Houston (1 Dist), 961 SW2d 1, writ den.—App & E 758.3(9), 846(5), 852, 931(1), 989,

1010.1(3), 1012.1(5); Atty & C 129(2); Contracts 317, 318.

Hertz Corp.; Carr v., TexApp–Corpus Christi, 737 SW2d 12.—Autos 387; Judgm 185(4), 185.1(1), 185.3(21).

Hertz Corp.; Dodge v., CA5 (Tex), 124 FedAppx 242.—Civil R 1138, 1179.

Hertz Corp.; Johnson v., SDTex, 316 FSupp 961.—Civil R 1557; Fed Civ Proc 2734.

Hertz Corp.; N.L.R.B. v., CA5 (Tex), 449 F2d 711.—Fed Cts 743; Labor & Emp 1454, 1478, 1740, 1760, 1772, 1931.

Hertz Corp. v. Pap, NDTex, 923 FSupp 914, aff 98 F3d 1339.—Autos 144.1(4); Insurance 1726, 1774, 2674, 2675, 2737, 3111(1), 3111(2).

Hertz Corp. v. Robineau, TexApp–Austin, 6 SW3d 332.—App & E 1175(1); Insurance 1004, 2109, 2761.

Hertz Corp. v. State Dept. of Highways and Public Transp., TexApp–Austin, 728 SW2d 917.—App & E 863, 954(1); Inj 130, 138.18, 138.31.

Hertz Equipment Rental Co.; Southwestern Bell Telephone Co. v., TexCivApp–Fort Worth, 533 SW2d 853, ref nre.—App & E 1175(1); Autos 155, 201(1.1); Neglig 387.

Hertz Equipment Rental Corp.; Zoner v., TexCivApp–Hous (14 Dist), 523 SW2d 765, ref nre.—App & E 999(3), 1043(1); Bailm 21; Judgm 181(21), 185(2), 708; Labor & Emp 3096(5), 3105(5), 3143, 3181(5); Work Comp 2168.

Hertz Penske Truck Rental and Leasing; Jobe v., TexApp–Dallas, 882 SW2d447. See Jobe v. Penske Truck Leasing Corp.

Hervey v. Flores, TexApp–El Paso, 975 SW2d 21, reh overr, and review den, and reh of petition for review overr.—App & E 78(1), 80(6), 343.1, 347(1), 842(2), 870(2), 893(1), 1010.1(3), 1010.1.8(.1), 1012.1(5); Courts 30; Judgm 181(14), 297.

Hervey v. Forse, TexCivApp–Beaumont, 253 SW2d 701.—J P 92, 159(11), 159(12), 163, 164(3), 164(4), 169, 183(1).

Hervey; Herald-Post Pub. Co. v., TexCivApp–El Paso, 282 SW2d 410, ref nre.—Libel 4, 6(1), 10(1), 10(3), 19, 123(2).

Hervey v. Passero, Tex, 658 SW2d 148.—Interest 39(2.20).

Hervey v. Passero, TexApp–El Paso, 648 SW2d 344, aff in part as mod, rev in part 658 SW2d 148.—App & E 218.2(4); Brok 8(3), 71, 86(1); Contracts 29, 143(2), 147(1), 176(1), 176(2); Evid 448; Interest 39(2.30); New Tr 162(1); Trial 350.4(1), 350.4(4).

Hervey v. State, TexApp–Waco, 131 SW3d 561.—Crim Law 641.13(1), 641.13(2.1), 641.13(7), 1030(1), 1032(1), 1119(1).

Hervey; W. L. Moody Cotton Co. v., TexCivApp–San Antonio, 97 SW2d 275, writ dism.—App & E 1001(1); Cust & U 21; Ex & Ad 433, 451(2).

Herwald v. Schweiker, CA5 (Tex), 658 F2d 359.—Civil R 1304; Fed Cts 815; Inj 22, 138.75, 151.

Herweck's Paint & Wallpaper Co. v. C. I. T. Corp., CCA5 (Tex), 123 F2d 989.—Bills & N 516; Princ & A 171(4), 186, 190(3).

Herwig v. State, TexCrimApp, 138 SW2d 549, 138 TexCrim 645.—Crim Law 878(4); Ind & Inf 71.4(2).

Herzberg; U.S. v., CA5 (Tex), 558 F2d 1219, cert den 98 SCt 417, 434 US 930, 54 LEd2d 290.—Crim Law 338(7), 390, 1153(1), 1170.5(5); Postal 49(11); Witn 344(2), 345(5), 349, 383, 405.16.

Herzik; U.S. Fidelity & Guaranty Co. v., TexCivApp–Houston, 359 SW2d 914, ref nre.—Work Comp 396, 518, 554, 1283, 1297, 1519, 1726, 1927, 1969.

Herzing v. Metropolitan Life Ins. Co., TexApp–Corpus Christi, 907 SW2d 574, reh overr, and writ den.—Antitrust 390; App & E 231(1), 843(1), 1050.1(1), 1056.1(1), 1056.1(3), 1064.1(1); Corp 202; Damag 15, 117, 178; Evid 146, 148, 244(13); Insurance 1638; Trial 43.

Herzog; Mattern v., Tex, 367 SW2d 312.—App & E 1082(1); Contracts 153; Perp 1, 3, 4(1), 4(6), 6(1), 6(5), 6(15); Wills 447, 725.

Herzog v. Mattern, TexCivApp–Texarkana, 359 SW2d 86, aff 367 SW2d 312.—Perp 6(15); Wills 439, 601(1).

Herzog Services, Inc.; Burlington Northern & Santa Fe Ry. Co. v., NDTex, 990 FSupp 503.—Fed Cts 102, 103, 104, 143, 144; Rem of C 14.

Herzstein v. Bonner, TexCivApp–Amarillo, 215 SW2d 661, ref nre.—App & E 758.3(7), 1010.1(1); Contracts 32, 353(2); Damag 221(5.1); Sales 415; Trial 352.16.

Herzstein v. Echols and Lynn, TexCivApp–Dallas, 517 SW2d 355.—Ven & Pur 143, 185, 335, 341(3).

Hesbrook v. State, TexCrimApp, 202 SW2d 677, 150 TexCrim 476.—False Pret 11, 39, 49(2).

Hesbrook v. State, TexCrimApp, 194 SW2d 262, 149 TexCrim 314.—Crim Law 980(1); False Pret 8, 49(4).

Hesbrook v. State, TexCrimApp, 194 SW2d 260, 149 TexCrim 310.—Crim Law 273.2(2); False Pret 8, 49(4).

Hess, In re, BkrtcyNDTex, 61 BR 977.—Bankr 2558; Mines 54.5.

Hess v. American States Ins. Co., TexCivApp–Amarillo, 589 SW2d 548.—App & E 218.2(5.1), 242(1); Plead 78; Princ & S 185, 190(9); Trial 351.2(4).

Hess v. Bank of Oklahoma, Oklahoma City, N.A., BkrtcyNDTex, 61 BR 977. See Hess, In re.

Hess v. Cockrell, CA5 (Tex), 281 F3d 212.—Fed Civ Proc 2643.1, 2647.1, 2651.1, 2653; Hab Corp 802.

Hess; Hughes v., Tex, 172 SW2d 301, 141 Tex 511.—Contracts 138(1); Estop 92(2); Execution 273; Ex & Ad 87, 122(1); Lim of Act 142, 148(3), 164; Ven & Pur 210, 267.

Hess; Hughes v., TexCivApp–Austin, 166 SW2d 718, aff in part, mod in part 172 SW2d 301, 141 Tex 511.—Ex & Ad 122(1); Judgm 785(1); Lim of Act 142, 143(6), 151(1), 151(4).

Hess; Latimer v., TexCivApp–Texarkana, 183 SW2d 996, writ refused.—Ease 1, 18(1), 22; Licens 44(3); Ven & Pur 230(1).

Hess v. McLean Feedyard, Inc., TexApp–Amarillo, 59 SW3d 679, review den.—App & E 223, 238(1), 856(1), 863, 893(1), 934(1), 971(2); Evid 555.2, 555.5; Judgm 183, 185(2), 185(3), 185(5), 185.1(4), 185.3(21).

Hess; Shelton v., SDTex, 599 FSupp 905.—Atty & C 21.10, 32(3), 32(12).

Hess v. State, TexCrimApp, 528 SW2d 842.—Crim Law 1032(5); Ind & Inf 87(2).

Hess v. State, TexCrimApp, 328 SW2d 308, 168 TexCrim 425.—Crim Law 723(1), 1171.1(2.1), 1171.1(6); Rob 24.15(1).

Hess v. State, TexCrimApp, 168 SW2d 250, 145 TexCrim 343.—Crim Law 1128(2); Int Liq 138.

Hess v. State, TexApp–Fort Worth, 224 SW3d 511, reh overr, and petition for discretionary review refused.—Crim Law 755.5, 759(1), 761(3), 762(3), 811(2), 1038.1(1), 1134(2), 1172.1(1), 1172.3.

Hess v. State, TexApp–Fort Worth, 953 SW2d 837, reh overr, and petition for discretionary review refused.—Crim Law 211(1), 214, 899, 1026.10(4), 1137(2); Ind & Inf 81(1), 81(2), 161(1); Sent & Pun 313.

Hess v. Young, TexCivApp–Waco, 160 SW2d 574.—App & E 843(3), 1050.1(1); Evid 536, 573; Plead 111.9, 111.15, 111.36.

Hessbrook v. Lennon, CA5 (Tex), 777 F2d 999.—Admin Law 229; U S 50.10(3), 78(5.1).

Hessbrook v. State, TexCrimApp, 421 SW2d 907.—Crim Law 301; False Pret 49(3).

Hessbrook; U.S. v., CA5 (Tex), 555 F2d 468, cert den 98 SCt 417, 434 US 930, 54 LEd2d 290.—Crim Law 868.

Hessbrook; U.S. v., CA5 (Tex), 504 F2d 1375, cert den 95 SCt 1450, 420 US 1006, 43 LEd2d 764.—False Pers 6, 7; False Pret 49(1).

Hess Die Mold, Inc. v. American Plasti-Plate Corp., TexApp–Tyler, 653 SW2d 927.—App & E 548(2), 554(1), 882(17), 907(3), 1015(4), 1079; Damag 5.

Hesse; Missouri Pac. R. Co. v., TexCivApp–San Antonio, 417 SW2d 379, ref nre.—App & E 977(5); New Tr 6, 108(1), 108(5).

Hesse; U.S. v., CA5 (Tex), 576 F2d 1110.—Bail 75.2(1), 79(2).

Hesse Envelope Co.; Weber v., TexCivApp–Dallas, 342 SW2d 652.—App & E 846(5); Contracts 116(2), 117(1), 117(3), 141(1), 141(3), 303(1).

Hesseltine v. Goodyear Tire & Rubber Co., EDTex, 391 FSupp2d 509.—Equity 72(1); Estop 52(1), 52.10(2), 119; Labor & Emp 2312, 2315, 2316, 2322, 2327, 2385(3).

Hesser v. Hesser, TexApp–Houston (1 Dist), 842 SW2d 759, reh den, and writ den.—App & E 5, 859, 934(3); Courts 4; Divorce 166, 254(1), 271; Judgm 335(1), 335(2), 386(1), 386(3); Mand 53.

Hesser; Hesser v., TexApp–Houston (1 Dist), 842 SW2d 759, reh den, and writ den.—App & E 5, 859, 934(3); Courts 4; Divorce 166, 254(1), 271; Judgm 335(1), 335(2), 386(1), 386(3); Mand 53.

Hesser v. Schuble, TexApp–Houston (1 Dist), 842 SW2d 759. See Hesser v. Hesser.

Hess, Inc. v. Garcia, TexCivApp–Eastland, 358 SW2d 391.—App & E 1170.7; Damag 221(2.1); Seamen 29(1), 29(2), 29(5.14), 29(5.16); Trial 18, 352.5(5), 352.10.

Hesskew v. Texas Dept. of Public Safety, TexApp–Tyler, 144 SW3d 189.—Admin Law 790, 791, 793; Afft 17; Autos 144.2(9.6), 349(2.1); Crim Law 559.

Hess Oil & Chemical Corp.; McKenzie Equipment Co. v., Tex, 451 SW2d 230.—Bailm 11, 14(1).

Hess Oil & Chemical Corp.; McKenzie Equipment, Inc. v., TexCivApp–Hous (14 Dist), 446 SW2d 903, rev McKenzie Equipment Co v. Hess Oil & Chemical Corp, 451 SW2d 230.—Bailm 14(1).

Hess Oil & Chemical Corp. v. N. L. R. B., CA5 (Tex), 415 F2d 440, cert den Oil, Chemical and Atomic Workers Intern Union AFL–CIO v. NLRB, 90 SCt 920, 397 US 916, 25 LEd2d 97.—Labor & Emp 1121, 1124, 1125, 1483(4), 1769.

Hesson; Wichita Falls & S. R. Co. v., TexCivApp–Eastland, 151 SW2d 270, writ dism, correct.—App & E 1175(5); Judgm 18(2); Plead 8(1); R R 314, 329, 338.4, 347(7), 348(1), 348(2).

Hesston Corp.; Deere & Co. v., CA5 (Tex), 440 F2d 904, cert den 92 SCt 67, 404 US 829, 30 LEd2d 58.—Pat 1.

Hesston Corp.; Deere & Co. v., NDTex, 316 FSupp 866, aff 440 F2d 904, cert den 92 SCt 67, 404 US 829, 30 LEd2d 58.—Pat 1, 16.13, 26(1), 36.2(1), 36.2(3), 51(1), 66(2), 112.3(4).

Hestand v. Johnson County, TexCivApp–Waco, 206 SW2d 665.—App & E 243.1; Dedi 12, 15, 16.1, 41, 44; Hus & W 262.1(5).

Hestand Kimbell Grocery Co. v. Forrest, TexCivApp–El Paso, 151 SW2d 882.—App & E 1177(7); Partners 213(2).

Hester, Matter of, CA5 (Tex), 899 F2d 361.—Bankr 2131, 3765, 3768; Mand 57(1).

Hester; Callahan v., TexCivApp–Eastland, 181 SW2d 294, writ refused wom.—App & E 207, 1011.1(8.1), 1015(5), 1050.1(7); Damag 132(8); Evid 555.10; New Tr 47, 140(3); Trial 313; Work Comp 2110.

Hester; City of Waco v., TexApp–Waco, 805 SW2d 807, writ den.—App & E 837(7); Civil R 1351(1), 1351(4), 1420, 1484; Damag 130.1, 221(8); Mun Corp 742(5), 745, 747(3); Neglig 371, 379, 380, 387; Prisons 17(4); Sent & Pun 1437, 1439, 1537.

Hester; Cluck v., Tex, 521 SW2d 845.—Cert 5(1); Courts 202(5), 472.2.

Hester v. Friedkin Companies, Inc., TexApp–Houston (14 Dist), 132 SW3d 100, review den.—App & E 218.2(5.1), 863, 866(3), 934(1); Impl & C C 30, 60.1; Judgm 199(3.10).

Hester v. Harris, CA5 (Tex), 631 F2d 53.—Const Law 4120; Social S 122.5.

Hester v. Hester, CA5 (Tex), 171 F2d 477.—Armed S 77(5), 77(19).

Hester; Hester v., CA5 (Tex), 171 F2d 477.—Armed S 77(5), 77(19).

Hester v. Hester, TexCivApp–Fort Worth, 205 SW2d 115. —App & E 846(2), 846(5), 931(3); Gifts 4, 15, 18(1), 21, 47(2), 49(1); Plead 111.42(2), 111.42(4).

Hester; Hester v., TexCivApp–Fort Worth, 205 SW2d 115. —App & E 846(2), 846(5), 931(3); Gifts 4, 15, 18(1), 21, 47(2), 49(1); Plead 111.42(2), 111.42(4).

Hester v. Hester, TexCivApp–Tyler, 413 SW2d 448.—App & E 989, 994(1), 1008.1(1); Divorce 27(18), 130, 147, 184(6.1).

Hester; Hester v., TexCivApp–Tyler, 413 SW2d 448.— App & E 989, 994(1), 1008.1(1); Divorce 27(18), 130, 147, 184(6.1).

Hester v. Keefer, TexCivApp–Waco, 497 SW2d 642.—App & E 387(2), 387(3); New Tr 155.

Hester v. Kemper Military School, TexCivApp–Fort Worth, 138 SW2d 833.—Bills & N 94(1); Home 122.

Hester; King v., CA5 (Tex), 200 F2d 807.—Des & Dist 71(6); Estop 47; Evid 288; Judgm 490(1); Mines 49, 55(1), 55(4), 55(7), 55(8), 101; Pub Lands 178(1); Ven & Pur 231(14).

Hester v. NCNB Texas Nat. Bank, CA5 (Tex), 899 F2d 361. See Hester, Matter of.

Hester; Nesmith v., TexCivApp–Austin, 522 SW2d 605.— App & E 724(4), 854(1), 1078(1).

Hester; Root v., TexCivApp–Eastland, 309 SW2d 480, writ refused.—App & E 554(1), 554(3), 564(3), 907(3); Tresp to T T 46.

Hester v. Ross, Banks, May, Cron and Cavin, TexCivApp–Waco, 492 SW2d 378.—Fraud 27; Guar 53(1), 87; Plead 129(3); Princ & S 99, 101(1), 157.

Hester; Sanchez v., TexApp–Corpus Christi, 911 SW2d 173, reh overr.—Bankr 2395, 2462; Equity 72(1); Mand 4(4), 53, 143(1); Motions 61, 62; Pretrial Proc 693.1.

Hester v. State, TexCrimApp, 544 SW2d 129.—Burg 42(1); Crim Law 29(14), 108(1), 394.4(10), 519(8), 531(3), 538(3), 1158(4); Searches 116; Sent & Pun 548, 568.

Hester v. State, TexCrimApp, 535 SW2d 354.—Crim Law 532(0.5), 1114.1(1), 1132, 1134(1), 1147.

Hester v. State, TexCrimApp, 287 SW2d 477.—Crim Law 1090.1(1).

Hester v. State, TexCrimApp, 277 SW2d 709.—Crim Law 1094(3).

Hester v. State, TexCrimApp, 273 SW2d 420.—Crim Law 1094(3).

Hester v. State, TexCrimApp, 244 SW2d 813.—Crim Law 1020.

Hester v. State, TexApp–Dallas, 909 SW2d 174, appeal after remand 1998 WL 131277.—Assault 56, 92(3); Crim Law 572, 741(1), 742(1), 1144.13(2.1), 1159.2(7); Ind & Inf 189(11); Rob 24.15(2), 24.40, 24.50.

Hester v. State, TexApp–Dallas, 859 SW2d 95.—Const Law 3809, 4841; Costs 308, 314, 318; Crim Law 273(4.1), 273.2(1), 641.13(5), 1081(2), 1086.11; Fines 1.5; Statut 214.

Hester v. State, TexCivApp–El Paso, 497 SW2d 501, ref nre.—App & E 300, 345.1; Em Dom 203(5), 205, 221, 255, 262(1), 262(2), 262(5); Evid 113(8); New Tr 117(1), 138.

Hester; Vela v., TexCivApp–San Antonio, 280 SW2d 369, ref nre.—Adv Poss 27, 36, 43(3), 115(4).

Hester v. Weaver, TexCivApp–Eastland, 252 SW2d 214, writ refused.—Deeds 90; Judgm 178, 181(15.1), 183; Mines 55(5); Pretrial Proc 473.

Hester & Wise v. Chinn, TexCivApp–Galveston, 162 SW2d 450.—Banks 126; Contracts 350(2); Impl & C C 5; Lim of Act 24(2); Trial 350.4(1).

Hestilow; United Services Auto. Ass'n v., Tex, 777 SW2d 378. See Stracener v. United Services Auto. Ass'n.

Hestilow; United Services Auto. Ass'n v., TexApp–San Antonio, 754 SW2d 754, writ gr, aff Stracener v. United Services Auto Ass'n, 777 SW2d 378.—Insurance 2772, 2788, 2799, 2839, 2846.

Heston; Anyah v., CA5 (Tex), 74 FedAppx 300.—Aliens 343; Const Law 4438; Hab Corp 282, 521.

Heston; Whittley v., TexApp–San Antonio, 954 SW2d 119. —Evid 555.10; Health 618, 821(2); Judgm 183, 185.3(21).

Heth v. Heth, TexApp–Fort Worth, 661 SW2d 303, dism, and reh overr.—Divorce 59.

Heth; Heth v., TexApp–Fort Worth, 661 SW2d 303, dism, and reh overr.—Divorce 59.

Hetmaniak v. Avis Rent-A-Car System, Inc., TexCiv-App–Hous (14 Dist), 459 SW2d 723.—Autos 172(6), 244(44); Trial 352.12, 352.21.

Hetrick v. Air Logistics, Inc., SDTex, 55 FSupp2d 663.— Damag 130.1, 132(3), 133, 134(2), 226; Interest 27, 31, 39(2.25).

Hetrick v. State, TexCivApp–Amarillo, 87 SW2d 887.— Int Liq 260, 261, 275; Nuis 6, 19.

Hettich v. State, TexCrimApp, 95 SW2d 113, 130 Tex-Crim 580.—Crim Law 366(1), 741(1), 1159.3(6), 1169.2(6); Homic 1385, 1391.

Hettig & Co. v. Union Mut. Life Ins. Co., CA5 (Tex), 781 F2d 1141.—Fed Civ Proc 2488.

Hettler, In re, TexApp–Amarillo, 110 SW3d 152, mandamus den.—Mand 24, 63.

Hettler v. Travelers Lloyds Ins. Co., TexApp–Amarillo, 190 SW3d 52, reh overr, and review den.—App & E 223, 852, 1175(1); Insurance 2290, 2310, 2311, 2911, 2914, 2915; Judgm 183, 185(2); Libel 123(2).

Hetzel v. Bethlehem Steel Corp., CA5 (Tex), 50 F3d 360. —Antitrust 132; Fed Civ Proc 923, 2532; Fed Cts 433, 761, 766, 927; States 18.3, 18.84; Work Comp 2085.

Heublein Inc.; Tarrant Distributors Inc. v., CA5 (Tex), 127 F3d 375.—Accnts 6.1; Compromise 13; Fed Cts 776, 859.

Heuermann; Allen v., TexCivApp–Hous (1 Dist), 444 SW2d 646, ref nre.—Courts 202(5); Ex & Ad 256(6).

Heufelder; Beaumont Broadcasting Corp. v., TexCiv-App–Fort Worth, 328 SW2d 470.—Venue 3, 8.5(1), 16, 21.

Heusinger Hardware Co. v. First Nat. Bank of San Antonio, TexCivApp–Eastland, 367 SW2d 710, ref nre. —App & E 916(1); Banks 174; Contracts 150; Judgm 185.3(16), 186; Lim of Act 24(2).

Heusinger Hardware Co. v. Frost Nat. Bank of San Antonio, TexCivApp–Eastland, 364 SW2d 851.—App & E 854(3); Banks 165, 169, 175(2); Judgm 181(17); Plead 228.20, 291(2), 422; Princ & A 109(0.5), 109(4).

Hevi-Duty Elec.; Pearson v., TexCivApp–Hous (1 Dist), 618 SW2d 784, ref nre.—Electricity 16(1), 18(1); Prod Liab 10, 14, 15, 87.1.

Hevolow; Texas Employers Ins. Ass'n v., TexCivApp–El Paso, 136 SW2d 931, writ dism, correct.—App & E 218.2(10), 499(1), 553(1), 930(3); Trial 82, 351.2(7); Work Comp 892, 1653, 1656, 1920, 1924, 1968(3), 1969.

Hewes; Roberson v., CA5 (Tex), 701 F2d 418.—Fed Civ Proc 1741; Prisons 4(10.1).

Hewett v. Leppanen, TexCivApp–San Antonio, 148 SW2d 970.—Plead 111.3, 111.17, 111.42(8).

Hewgley; Norsworthy v., TexCivApp–El Paso, 234 SW2d 126, writ refused.—App & E 917(1); Courts 91(1); Frds St of 63(2), 113(3); Mines 55(4).

Hewin; U.S. v., CA5 (Tex), 877 F2d 3.—Sent & Pun 726(1), 976.

Hewitt; Brown v., TexCivApp–Galveston, 143 SW2d 223, writ refused.—Mtg 401(1).

Hewitt v. Chadwick, TexApp–Texarkana, 760 SW2d 333. —Damag 51.

Hewitt v. Citizens Sav. Bank & Trust Co. of St. Johnsbury, Vt., TexCivApp–Austin, 119 SW2d 1073, writ dism, correct.—Usury 22, 66, 100(1).

Hewitt; Johnson v., TexCivApp–Hous (1 Dist), 539 SW2d 239.—Decl Judgm 112, 241; Wills 76, 80, 206, 215, 288(1), 357, 384, 657.

Hewitt v. Nielsen, TexCivApp–Austin, 553 SW2d 248.— App & E 78(1), 79(1), 80(6); Judgm 216, 217.

Hewitt; Scott v., Tex, 90 SW2d 816, 127 Tex 31, 103 ALR 977.—Forci E & D 6(1); Hus & W 79; Land & Ten 118(1); Mtg 544(5).

Hewitt; Service Station Equipment Co. v., TexCivApp–Dallas, 282 SW 286, writ dism woj.—App & E 733; Bankr 263; Fixt 35(2), 35(3).

Hewitt v. State, TexCrimApp, 152 SW2d 352.—Crim Law 1090.1(1).

Hewitt v. State, TexApp–Fort Worth, 734 SW2d 745, petition for discretionary review refused.—Autos 332, 421; Crim Law 564(1), 713, 720(7.1), 795(2.1), 795(2.55), 814(4), 1036.1(3.1), 1137(5), 1169.3, 1169.5(2); Ind & Inf 125(41).

Hewitt v. U.S., CA5 (Tex), 377 F2d 921, 22 ALR3d 1.— Fed Civ Proc 2146; Fed Cts 798; Int Rev 4831, 5205, 5219.25.

Hewitt; U.S. v., CA5 (Tex), 145 FedAppx 876, cert den 126 SCt 815, 546 US 1069, 163 LEd2d 641.—Crim Law 1031(4).

Hewlett; CNL Financial Corp. v., TexCivApp–Beaumont, 539 SW2d 176, ref nre.—App & E 877(2), 877(3); Guar 87; Judgm 118; Plead 87.

Hewlett v. Hewlett, TexCivApp–Waco, 486 SW2d 107, writ dism woj, cert den 94 SCt 48, 414 US 877, 38 LEd2d 122, reh den 94 SCt 611, 414 US 1088, 38 LEd2d 494.—Child S 9, 231, 363, 555, 556(3).

Hewlett; Hewlett v., TexCivApp–Waco, 486 SW2d 107, writ dism woj, cert den 94 SCt 48, 414 US 877, 38 LEd2d 122, reh den 94 SCt 611, 414 US 1088, 38 LEd2d 494.—Child S 9, 231, 363, 555, 556(3).

Hewlett v. Texas Alcoholic Beverage Commission, TexCivApp–Waco, 492 SW2d 686, ref nre.—Int Liq 10(2), 11, 70, 71, 75(7), 99; Plead 36(5), 129(2).

Hewlett Knitting Mills, Inc. v. Flying Tiger Line, Inc., TexApp–Dallas, 669 SW2d 412.—Carr 159(2), 405(3).

Hewlett Packard, In re, TexApp–Austin, 212 SW3d 356, mandamus den.—Mand 1, 4(1), 4(4), 28; Pretrial Proc 33, 41, 66.

Hewlett-Packard Co. v. Benchmark Electronics, Inc., TexApp–Houston (14 Dist), 142 SW3d 554, review den. —App & E 856(1); Contracts 143(1), 143(2), 143(4), 176(1), 176(2), 212(2); Evid 264, 448; Judgm 181(8), 183, 185(2), 185.3(2), 185.3(18); Lim of Act 14; Sales 82(2), 82(3).

Hewlett-Packard Co.; Bullock v., Tex, 628 SW2d 754.— Admin Law 391; Const Law 4026, 4140; Tax 2540, 3211.

Hewlett-Packard Co. v. Bullock, TexCivApp–Austin, 619 SW2d 33, rev 628 SW2d 754.—Tax 2445, 2543, 3214.

Hexamer v. Foreness, CA5 (Tex), 997 F2d 93.—U S 147(6), 147(7), 147(10).

Hexamer v. Foreness, CA5 (Tex), 981 F2d 821.—Fed Cts 192, 192.5; Rem of C 102.

Hexamer; Foreness v., TexApp–Dallas, 971 SW2d 525, review den, cert den 119 SCt 240, 525 US 904, 142 LEd2d 197.—App & E 1175(1); Child S 503; Courts 4; Garn 1, 18; Judgm 495(1), 497(1), 499; States 18.5, 18.9, 18.28, 18.35; U S 125(9).

Hexcel Corp. v. Advanced Textiles, Inc., WDTex, 716 FSupp 974, aff 960 F2d 155, reh den, and sug for reh declined.—Equity 65(1); Pat 129(2).

Hexcel Corp. v. Conap, Inc., TexApp–Fort Worth, 738 SW2d 359, writ den.—App & E 387(1), 387(2), 387(6), 417(1), 803, 1074(3).

Hexemer v. Farm & Home Sav. & Loan Ass'n of Missouri, TexCivApp–Fort Worth, 115 SW2d 458, dism. —Ack 55(2); B & L Assoc 2, 33(5), 33(8), 38(6); Estop 92(3); Lim of Act 48(7).

Hext; Brooks v., TexCivApp–Beaumont, 392 SW2d 500.—Wills 364, 366.

Hext v. Central Educ. Agency, TexApp–Austin, 909 SW2d 252, reh overr.—Evid 383(3), 387(8), 417(3).

Hext v. Price, TexApp–Amarillo, 847 SW2d 408, reh den.—App & E 302(5); Costs 194.40; Interest 31; Life Est 5, 23, 28.

Hext; U.S. v., CA5 (Tex), 444 F2d 804.—Fed Cts 413; U S 53(7).

Hext; U.S. v., SDTex, 298 FSupp 226, rev 444 F2d 804.—Chat Mtg 170(1), 177(4); Const Law 2478; Indem 57, 64; Statut 158, 159; U S 53(7); Wareh 2, 13, 25(5).

Hexter; Jackson v., TexCivApp–Dallas, 372 SW2d 570.—Compromise 16(1); Costs 260(4).

Hexter; Neiman-Marcus Co. v., TexCivApp–Dallas, 412 SW2d 915, ref nre.—Antitrust 591; App & E 1172(1); Decl Judgm 296; Land & Ten 37, 44(2), 80(1), 134(2).

Hexter; O'Hara v., TexCivApp–Dallas, 584 SW2d 310.—App & E 1056.3; Evid 265(8), 448; Plead 36(1); Witn 160(1), 178(1), 181.

Hexter; O'Hara v., TexCivApp–Dallas, 550 SW2d 379, ref nre, appeal after remand 584 SW2d 310.—Judgm 138(1), 139, 145(4), 162(2), 162(4), 169.

Hexter v. Powell, TexCivApp–Dallas, 475 SW2d 857, ref nre.—App & E 301; Damag 67; Fraud 61; Interest 31; Labor & Emp 219, 258, 259.

Hexter & Lobello; Reynolds-Penland Co. v., TexCivApp–Dallas, 567 SW2d 237, writ dism by agreement.—App & E 946; Contracts 93(2), 175(1); Jury 13(1), 13(5.1); Land & Ten 86(1), 86(2).

Hexter Title & Abstract Co.; Bar Ass'n of Dallas v., TexCivApp–Fort Worth, 175 SW2d 108, aff Hexter Title & Abstract Co v. Grievance Committee, Fifth Congressional Dist, State Bar of Texas, 179 SW2d 946, 142 Tex 506, 157 ALR 268.—Abate & R 18; App & E 1175(6); Assoc 19; Atty & C 63; Corp 377.5; Courts 78; Inj 68, 114(1), 114(2).

Hexter Title & Abstract Co. v. Grievance Committee, Fifth Congressional Dist., State Bar of Texas, Tex, 179 SW2d 946, 142 Tex 506, 157 ALR 268.—Atty & C 11(3), 11(13); Corp 377.5; Inj 114(2).

Heyden Newport Chemical Corp. v. Southern General Ins. Co., Tex, 387 SW2d 22.—Autos 238(2), 240(2); Insurance 2914, 2915, 2921, 2941.

Heyden Newport Chemical Corp., Newport Industries Division v. Southern General Ins. Co., TexCivApp–Beaumont, 376 SW2d 821, writ gr, rev 387 SW2d 22.—Insurance 2660.

Heydrick; Upshur County v., TexCivApp–Eastland, 221 SW2d 326, ref nre.—Contracts 242; Mines 4, 55(7), 58; Princ & A 101(1).

Heyduck v. State, TexApp–Houston (1 Dist), 814 SW2d 156.—Const Law 18; Double J 1, 132.1, 136, 142.

Heyer v. North East Independent School Dist., TexApp–San Antonio, 730 SW2d 130, ref nre.—Schools 89.8(1), 89.13(4).

Heyer-Schulte Corp. of Santa Barbara; Henderson v., TexCivApp–Hous (1 Dist), 600 SW2d 844, ref nre.—App & E 1064.1(8); Evid 512, 560; Health 820.

Heyl; Western Inn Corp. v., TexCivApp–Fort Worth, 452 SW2d 752, ref nre.—Corp 210, 316(1), 316(4), 320(1), 615.5; Evid 318(2); Fraud 38; Judgm 668(1), 678(1), 701, 713(2); Set-Off 60; Trusts 102(1), 365(5).

Heyland; Hoffman, McBryde & Co., P.C. v., TexApp–Dallas, 74 SW3d 906, review den, appeal after remand 2004 WL 1626543.—Judgm 753, 754, 768(1), 772, 785(1), 787.

Heyn v. Massachusetts Bonding & Insurance Co., TexCivApp–Dallas, 110 SW2d 261, writ dism woj.—Const Law 2350; Courts 42(4); Guard & W 15, 25, 137; Judges 36, 37; Lim of Act 174(2).

Heyser; Hightower Oil & Refining Corp. v., TexCivApp–Austin, 135 SW2d 202.—Lim of Act 180(2), 180(3).

H.E.Y. Trust v. Popcorn Express Co., Inc., TexApp–Houston (14 Dist), 35 SW3d 55, reh overr, and review den.—Aviation 227; Brok 3, 42; Land & Ten 127; Licens 43, 44(2).

Heyward; Republic Nat. Life Ins. Co. v., Tex, 536 SW2d 549.—Crim Law 308; Evid 59, 60, 87; Insurance 1825, 2590(1), 2593, 2595(1), 2595(2), 2604, 2605, 2608.

Heyward v. Republic Nat. Life Ins. Co., TexCivApp–San Antonio, 527 SW2d 807, writ gr, aff 536 SW2d 549.—Insurance 2593, 2595(1), 2595(2), 2604, 2605, 2608; Trial 139.1(14), 139.1(17), 142, 143, 178.

Heyward; Republic Nat. Life Ins. Co. v., TexCivApp–Eastland, 568 SW2d 879, ref nre.—App & E 758.3(7), 930(3), 1024.1; Costs 194.18; Evid 594; Insurance 2607; Trial 194(11), 350.8; Witn 269(2.1), 269(14), 319, 364, 367(1), 372(2).

Heywood-Wakefield Co. v. Brady, TexComApp, 101 SW2d 224, 128 Tex 371.—App & E 1126.

HFI, Ltd. Partnership; Faulconer, Inc. v., TexApp–Tyler, 970 SW2d 36. See Vernon E. Faulconer, Inc. v. HFI, Ltd. Partnership.

HFI, Ltd. Partnership; Vernon E. Faulconer, Inc. v., TexApp–Tyler, 970 SW2d 36, reh overr.—Alt Disp Res 329, 330, 374(1); Costs 260(1), 260(4); New Tr 155.

H.G., In re, TexApp–San Antonio, 993 SW2d 211.—Infants 230.1, 250, 251, 252.

H. G. Berning, Inc.; Blunt v., TexCivApp–Dallas, 211 SW2d 773, writ refused.—Autos 217(5), 218, 245(72), 245(74); Neglig 1602, 1717.

H. G. Berning, Inc. v. Waggoner, TexCivApp–Beaumont, 247 SW2d 570.—Acct Action on 13, 14, 15; Acct St 1, 19(3); Plead 237(3).

H. G. Brelsford & Associates v. Bankston Rentals, Inc., TexCivApp–Eastland, 573 SW2d 604.—Judgm 181(29).

H.G. Sledge, Inc. v. Prospective Inv. and Trading Co., Ltd., TexApp–Austin, 36 SW3d 597, review den.—Admin Law 412.1, 413, 750, 791; App & E 863, 893(1), 911.3; Courts 35; Mines 74(3), 78.1(11), 92.8, 92.21, 92.32(1), 92.35, 92.40; Plead 104(1).

H.G.V. v. State, TexApp–San Antonio, 646 SW2d 623.—Infants 68.7(1), 243.

H. Heller & Co., Inc. v. Louisiana-Pacific Corp., TexApp–Houston (14 Dist), 209 SW3d 844, review den.—Const Law 3964, 3965(4); Courts 12(2.1), 12(2.5), 12(2.10), 12(2.15), 12(2.30), 511; Judgm 815, 818(1), 818(3), 820, 823; States 5(1).

H. Hentz & Co.; Lange v., NDTex, 418 FSupp 1376.—Brok 19, 38(4); Fed Cts 207; Neglig 259; Sec Reg 40.15.

H. Hentz & Co., Inc.; First Nat. Bank in Grand Prairie v., TexCivApp–Waco, 498 SW2d 478.—App & E 1146; Brok 72; Corp 120; Interest 46(1); Princ & A 85, 171(1), 171(7).

H.H. Holloway Trust v. Outpost Estates Civic Club Inc., TexApp–Houston (1 Dist), 135 SW3d 751, reh overr, and review den, and reh of petition for review den.—App & E 758.1, 1008.1(2); Covenants 20, 79(3), 84.

Hibbard v. Don Love, Inc., SDTex, 584 FSupp 2.—Civil R 1530.

Hibbard; Texas State Life Ins. Co. v., TexCivApp–Fort Worth, 128 SW2d 833.—App & E 1126.

Hibbard; Younger Bros. v., TexCivApp–Galveston, 201 SW2d 624.—App & E 1004(8), 1140(1); Damag 132(3).

Hibbard Office World, Inc. v. F. Jay, a Corp., TexCivApp–Tyler, 580 SW2d 55.—App & E 79(1), 80(6).

Hibbert; Bryant v., TexApp–Austin, 639 SW2d 718.—Atty & C 132; Infants 155.

Hibbs v. Johnson, TexCivApp–Amarillo, 342 SW2d 642.—Em Dom 224; Mand 3(1), 172; New Tr 4.

Hibbetts v. State, TexCrimApp, 123 SW2d 898, 136 TexCrim 170.—Crim Law 780(2), 918(10), 1097(6); Embez 21, 41, 44(5), 48(4).

Hibbitts; Bank of Woodson v., TexApp–Eastland, 626 SW2d 133, ref nre.—Mtg 121, 319(3).

Hibbitts; Woodson State Bank v., TexCivApp–Eastland, 606 SW2d 339.—App & E 79(1), 80(6).

Hibbler v. Knight, TexApp–Houston (1 Dist), 735 SW2d 924, ref nre.—Evid 591; Hus & W 29(9); Stip 14(10); Wills 88(1), 114, 290.

Hibbler v. Walker, TexCivApp–Texarkana, 598 SW2d 19. —Plead 111.39(4); Venue 7.5(4).

Hibbler v. Walker, TexCivApp–Hous (14 Dist), 593 SW2d 398.—App & E 883, 916(1); Courts 475(1); Plead 110, 111.35; Pretrial Proc 222; Trial 45(1).

Hibernia Corp.; Service Asset Management Co. v., ED–Tex, 80 FSupp2d 626.—Rem of C 2, 79(1), 107(11).

Hibernia Nat. Bank, In re, TexApp–Corpus Christi, 21 SW3d 908.—Banks 274; Mand 3(2.1), 12; States 18.19.

Hibernia Nat. Bank; Garza v., TexApp–Houston (1 Dist), 227 SW3d 233.—App & E 430(1).

Hibler v. Hibler, TexApp–San Antonio, 813 SW2d 524, writ den.—Child C 36, 574; Child S 45, 54, 239, 470.

Hibler; Hibler v., TexApp–San Antonio, 813 SW2d 524, writ den.—Child C 36, 574; Child S 45, 54, 239, 470.

Hibler; Security Ben. Ass'n v., TexCivApp–Amarillo, 107 SW2d 470, writ dism by agreement.—Insurance 1743, 1801, 1848, 2986, 3083, 3096(2).

Hice v. Cole, TexCivApp–Beaumont, 295 SW2d 661.—App & E 253, 694(1); Inj 208, 210; Judgm 21, 307, 317.

Hice v. State, TexCrimApp, 491 SW2d 910.—Crim Law 404.60, 852, 1174(1), 1174(2).

Hice v. State, TexCrimApp, 235 SW2d 182.—Crim Law 1070.

Hick v. Bexar County, Tex., WDTex, 973 FSupp 653, aff Hicks v. Bexar County, 137 F3d 1352.—Civil R 1031, 1036, 1056, 1088(5), 1304, 1315, 1336, 1345, 1348, 1351(1), 1351(2), 1351(4), 1351(6), 1352(4), 1354, 1355, 1358, 1376(1), 1376(2), 1376(4), 1376(5), 1376(6), 1376(8), 1398, 1407; Consp 7.5(1), 18; Const Law 82(6.1); Dist & Pros Attys 1; Fed Civ Proc 657.5(2), 1264, 2756.1, 2765, 2769, 2771(5), 2790, 2810, 2812, 2827; Fed Cts 411; Judges 36; Schools 55.

Hickerson v. State, TexCrimApp, 928 SW2d 561. See Gray v. State.

Hickerson v. State, TexCrimApp, 286 SW2d 437, 162 TexCrim 446.—Crim Law 719(3), 720(5), 1171.3.

Hickerson v. State, TexCrimApp, 275 SW2d 801, 161 TexCrim 140.—Crim Law 594(1), 605, 626, 1166(7); Statut 231.

Hickerson; U.S. v., CA5 (Tex), 489 F3d 742.—Crim Law 589(1), 594(1), 598(2), 598(8), 620(6), 1144.15, 1148, 1151, 1166(6).

Hickey v. Arkla Industries, Inc., CA5 (Tex), 699 F2d 748, 69 ALR Fed 692.—Civil R 1110, 1112, 1551.

Hickey v. Arkla Industries, Inc., CA5 (Tex), 688 F2d 1009, opinion vac on reh 699 F2d 748, 69 ALR Fed 692. —Civil R 1110, 1551.

Hickey v. Arkla Industries, Inc., CA5 (Tex), 624 F2d 35. —Civil R 1598, 1599.

Hickey v. Arkla Industries, Inc., CA5 (Tex), 615 F2d 239, on reh 624 F2d 35, appeal after remand 688 F2d 1009, opinion vac on reh 699 F2d 748, 69 ALR Fed 692.—Fed Civ Proc 2533.1.

Hickey v. Couchman, TexApp–Corpus Christi, 797 SW2d 103, writ den.—App & E 761, 842(7), 931(1), 989, 1010.1(1), 1010.1(3), 1012.1(3), 1012.1(4), 1012.1(5), 1071.1(5.1); Bankr 2395, 2604, 3414; Execution 51; Exemp 37, 44; Sheriffs 106, 130, 137(1), 137(4), 138(1), 138(5), 139(5), 140; Trial 388(1).

Hickey v. Hickey, TexCivApp–Eastland, 203 SW2d 568.— Divorce 186; Evid 43(3); Plead 110, 111.42(2), 111.42(4).

Hickey; Hickey v., TexCivApp–Eastland, 203 SW2d 568. —Divorce 186; Evid 43(3); Plead 110, 111.42(2), 111.42(4).

Hickey v. Irving Independent School Dist., CA5 (Tex), 976 F2d 980, motion den 986 F2d 916.—Fed Civ Proc 2734; Fed Cts 425, 776; Lim of Act 72(1); U S Mag 13.

Hickey v. Johnson, TexApp–Houston (14 Dist), 672 SW2d 33.—Adop 6, 7.1, 15, 21; App & E 842(1), 1001(1); Trial 203(1).

Hickey; Kidd v., TexCivApp–El Paso, 237 SW2d 389, ref nre.—Mines 5.2(3).

Hickey; McClain v., TexCivApp–Texarkana, 418 SW2d 588, ref nre.—App & E 384(2), 419(1), 1175(1), 1176(1); Judgm 72, 87, 91; Stip 6.

Hickey v. NCNB Texas Nat. Bank, NDTex, 763 FSupp 896.—Banks 508; Courts 100(1).

Hickey; Redden v., TexCivApp–Waco, 327 SW2d 778.— App & E 882(14), 1062.1; Partit 92; Trial 350.3(2.1), 350.8.

Hickey; Redden v., TexCivApp–Waco, 308 SW2d 225, ref nre.—App & E 77(1); Jury 10, 14(10); Partit 70, 73, 94(2), 95.

Hickey; Rose's Heirs v., TexCivApp–Waco, 336 SW2d 753.—Hus & W 262.1(2), 264(2), 264(4).

Hickey v. Sibley, TexCivApp–Waco, 304 SW2d 165.— Appear 19(5), 24(13).

Hickey v. Spangler, TexCivApp–Texarkana, 358 SW2d 216, ref nre, appeal after remand 401 SW2d 721.— Mines 78.1(9), 78.7(4); Trial 350.3(2.1).

Hickey; Spangler v., TexCivApp–Tyler, 401 SW2d 721.— Action 60.

Hickey; State v., TexCivApp–Waco, 97 SW2d 713.— Clerks of C 32.

Hickey & Co.; U.S. v., NDTex, 70 FSupp 13, aff 168 F2d 752, cert den 69 SCt 138, 335 US 867, 93 LEd 412.— Const Law 4279; War 36, 59.

Hickie; Rogers v., TexCivApp–Eastland, 376 SW2d 413, writ gr, aff Carr v. Rogers, 383 SW2d 383.—Wills 435, 440, 449, 579, 587(1).

Hickman, In re, CA5 (Tex), 260 F3d 400.—Bankr 3377.

Hickman v. Adams, TexApp–Houston (14 Dist), 35 SW3d 120, reh overr.—Convicts 6; Crim Law 1148; Judgm 570(1), 654.

Hickman; American Hydrocarbon Corp. v., TexCivApp–Texarkana, 393 SW2d 197.—Judgm 185.1(8), 185.3(1), 186; New Tr 26, 124(1), 128(1).

Hickman v. American Pawn and Jewelry, Inc., TexApp–Texarkana, 972 SW2d 144.—App & E 934(1); Judgm 185(2); Labor & Emp 2772; Neglig 210, 213, 1019, 1161, 1162, 1692.

Hickman v. American Pawn Superstore, TexApp–Texarkana, 972 SW2d 144. See Hickman v. American Pawn and Jewelry, Inc.

Hickman v. Board of Regents of University of Texas System, TexCivApp–Austin, 552 SW2d 616, writ refused.—App & E 954(1), 954(2); Inj 135, 138.21, 147.

Hickman v. Bowen, CA5 (Tex), 803 F2d 1377.—Social S 175.20, 175.30.

Hickman; Bright v., EDTex, 96 FSupp2d 572.—Civil R 1442, 1447; Fed Civ Proc 2734; U S Mag 27, 31.

Hickman v. City of Dallas, NDTex, 475 FSupp 137.— Const Law 1464, 1472, 1473, 1925, 4166(2); Mun Corp 142.

Hickman; Connecticut General Life Ins. Co. v., TexCivApp–Fort Worth, 150 SW2d 121, writ refused.—Insurance 1096, 3153.

Hickman v. Cooper, TexCivApp–Eastland, 210 SW2d 858, ref nre.—App & E 1010.1(13); Damag 62(4); Plead 376; Trial 351.5(4); Ven & Pur 114, 118, 123.

Hickman; Craddock v., TexCivApp–Eastland, 546 SW2d 126.—App & E 1175(1); Damag 134(1), 187, 221(5.1); Trial 350.1.

Hickman; Dawson v., TexCivApp–Texarkana, 95 SW2d 1319.—App & E 931(6); Bound 35(3), 37(1); Partit 8; Tresp to T T 27; Ven & Pur 230(1); Waters 89.

Hickman; Deen v., USTex, 79 SCt 1, 358 US 57, 3 LEd2d 28.—Fed Cts 513; Mand 58.

Hickman v. Durham, TexCivApp–Eastland, 213 SW2d 569, ref nre.—App & E 216(1); Assault 43(2); Crim Law 763(23); Trial 278.

Hickman v. Finlay, TexCivApp–Austin, 392 SW2d 147, writ refused.—Autos 181(2), 244(6).

Hickman; First Nat. Bank v., TexCivApp–Austin, 89 SW2d 838, writ refused.—Hus & W 265, 266.3, 269.

Hickman v. Fox Television Station, Inc., CA5 (Tex), 177 FedAppx 427.—Fed Civ Proc 1451, 1758.1.

Hickman v. Fox Television Station, Inc., SDTex, 231 FRD 248, aff 177 FedAppx 427.—Fed Civ Proc 1278, 1741, 1758.1, 1759, 1837.1, 1991.

Hickman; Harrell v., Tex, 215 SW2d 876, 147 Tex 396.—Wills 62, 88(2), 602(1), 634(4.1), 692(1).

Hickman v. Harrell, TexCivApp–Waco, 211 SW2d 374, writ gr, rev 215 SW2d 876, 147 Tex 396.—Contracts 150, 168; Wills 61, 64, 439, 440, 488, 590, 602(1), 692(1), 692(4).

Hickman v. Hickman, Tex, 234 SW2d 410, 149 Tex 439.—App & E 931(1); Ex & Ad 298; Exemp 4, 30, 40, 44, 45, 55.

Hickman; Hickman v., Tex, 234 SW2d 410, 149 Tex 439.—App & E 931(1); Ex & Ad 298; Exemp 4, 30, 40, 44, 45, 55.

Hickman v. Hickman, TexCivApp–Eastland, 244 SW2d 681, ref nre.—Evid 380, 537, 555.10; Wills 53(9), 55(5), 55(10), 164(5), 293(3), 386, 400.

Hickman; Hickman v., TexCivApp–Eastland, 244 SW2d 681, ref nre.—Evid 380, 537, 555.10; Wills 53(9), 55(5), 55(10), 164(5), 293(3), 386, 400.

Hickman v. Hickman, TexCivApp–Eastland, 228 SW2d 565, aff 234 SW2d 410, 149 Tex 439.—App & E 931(1); Autos 1; Ex & Ad 194(7); Exemp 30, 40, 43, 44, 45, 55.

Hickman; Hickman v., TexCivApp–Eastland, 228 SW2d 565, aff 234 SW2d 410, 149 Tex 439.—App & E 931(1); Autos 1; Ex & Ad 194(7); Exemp 30, 40, 43, 44, 45, 55.

Hickman; Mercantile Nat. Bank at Dallas v., TexCivApp–Amarillo, 80 SW2d 488.—Mun Corp 955(1.5).

Hickman v. Moya, TexApp–Waco, 976 SW2d 360, reh overr, and review den, and reh of petition for review overr, cert den 119 SCt 2348, 527 US 1009, 144 LEd2d 245.—Records 52, 64.

Hickman v. Myers, TexApp–Fort Worth, 632 SW2d 869, ref nre.—Health 684, 686, 830; Plead 228.14.

Hickman; Park North General Hosp. v., TexApp–San Antonio, 703 SW2d 262, ref nre.—Health 656, 660, 672; Trial 350.6(2), 352.4(5); Venue 50.

Hickman v. Rawls, TexApp–Dallas, 638 SW2d 100, ref nre.—Corp 1.4(1), 1.4(3), 1.6(1), 1.6(2).

Hickman v. Richter, TexCivApp–Galveston, 243 SW2d 466.—App & E 874(2), 954(1), 954(2); Ease 1, 18(1), 18(2), 18(4), 26(3), 61(6); Inj 135.

Hickman v. Rusk State Hospital, TexCivApp–Waco, 242 SW2d 913, writ refused.—App & E 20; Courts 247(2); Mental H 60.

Hickman v. Smith, TexCivApp–Austin, 238 SW2d 838, writ refused.—Adop 13; Infants 230.1; Jury 10, 19.10(1), 34(1).

Hickman v. State, TexCrimApp, 548 SW2d 736.—Crim Law 1181.5(9); Sent & Pun 1302, 1381(4).

Hickman v. State, TexCrimApp, 342 SW2d 752.—Crim Law 1087.1(2).

Hickman v. State, TexCrimApp, 132 SW2d 598, 137 TexCrim 616.—Crim Law 1137(1), 1169.5(2), 1169.9; Rape 4, 43(2), 51(4), 52(1), 57(1).

Hickman v. State, TexApp–Houston (1 Dist), 835 SW2d 244, reh den, and petition for discretionary review refused.—Controlled Subs 29, 80, 100(1); Crim Law 1189.

Hickman v. Sullivan, TexCivApp–Beaumont, 128 SW2d 457, writ dism, correct.—Autos 244(44), 245(81); Trial 351.5(6), 352.13.

Hickman v. U.G. Lively, SDTex, 897 FSupp 955.—Civil R 1351(1); Fed Civ Proc 417, 1837.1, 2470.1, 2543, 2544, 2546; Mun Corp 723, 847; States 112.1(1).

Hickman; U.S. v., CA5 (Tex), 374 F3d 275, cert gr, vac 125 SCt 1043, 543 US 1110, 160 LEd2d 1041, on remand

159 FedAppx 553, cert den 126 SCt 1598, 547 US 1032, 164 LEd2d 321.—Courts 99(1); Crim Law 1134(2), 1180, 1192; Sent & Pun 341, 664(5), 1101, 1139, 2200.

Hickman; U.S. v., CA5 (Tex), 331 F3d 439, appeal after new sentencing hearing 282 FSupp2d 528, aff 374 F3d 275, cert gr, vac 125 SCt 1043, 543 US 1110, 160 LEd2d 1041, on remand 159 FedAppx 553, cert den 126 SCt 1598, 547 US 1032, 164 LEd2d 321.—Const Law 2789, 2790, 2810, 2845; Crim Law 568, 772(1), 1030(1), 1038.1(4), 1042, 1166.17; Health 979, 980, 981; Insurance 3652; Sent & Pun 2143.

Hickman; U.S. v., CA5 (Tex), 151 F3d 446, reh gr, vac 165 F3d 1020, cert dism 119 SCt 923, 525 US 1131, 142 LEd2d 972, cert dism McCray v. US, 119 SCt 1161, 526 US 1013, 143 LEd2d 226, on reh 179 F3d 230, cert den Gasaway v US, 120 SCt 2194, 530 US 1203, 147 LEd2d 232, cert den Chopane v US, 120 SCt 2195, 530 US 1203, 147 LEd2d 232, cert den Limbrick v US, 120 SCt 2195, 530 US 1203, 147 LEd2d 232, cert den 120 SCt 2195, 530 US 1203, 147 LEd2d 232, cert den 120 SCt 2195, 530 US 1203, 147 LEd2d 232.—Consp 24(1), 24.5, 27, 40.1, 40.3, 47(2), 47(3.1); Crim Law 100(1), 339.7(3), 339.10(2), 339.10(3), 339.10(9), 510, 517(5), 528, 562, 622.2(6), 627.10(1), 627.10(2.1), 627.10(5), 665(1), 665(2), 665(3), 1038.2, 1038.3, 1139, 1144.13(3), 1144.13(5), 1147, 1153(5), 1158(4), 1159.2(7), 1162, 1168(2), 1169.7, 1177; Rob 1, 24.40; Sent & Pun 578, 598, 675, 730, 761; Weap 17(4).

Hickman; U.S. v., CA5 (Tex), 159 FedAppx 553, cert den 126 SCt 1598, 547 US 1032, 164 LEd2d 321.—Fed Cts 462.

Hickman; U.S. v., SDTex, 282 FSupp2d 528, aff 374 F3d 275, cert gr, vac 125 SCt 1043, 543 US 1110, 160 LEd2d 1041, on remand 159 FedAppx 553, cert den 126 SCt 1598, 547 US 1032, 164 LEd2d 321.—Sent & Pun 689.

Hickman; Williamson v., TexCivApp–Austin, 391 SW2d 171.—Wills 337, 400.

Hickok; Beets v., TexApp–Tyler, 701 SW2d 281.—Adv Poss 116(1); App & E 1062.2; Ten in C 15(7), 15(10); Trial 260(1), 351.5(3).

Hickok; Toledo Soc. for Crippled Children v., Tex, 261 SW2d 692, 152 Tex 578, 43 ALR2d 553, cert den 74 SCt 631, 347 US 936, 98 LEd 1086.—Conversion 2; Judgm 815; Mines 48; Propty 6; Wills 2.

Hickok; Toledo Soc. for Crippled Children v., TexCivApp–Eastland, 252 SW2d 739, rev 261 SW2d 692, 152 Tex 578, 43 ALR2d 553, cert den 74 SCt 631, 347 US 936, 98 LEd 1086.—Hus & W 246; Remaind 1, 4; Wills 634(18).

Hickok Producing & Development Co. v. Texas Co., CCA5 (Tex), 128 F2d 183.—Corp 1.7(2); Fed Cts 848; Lim of Act 50(1), 104(1), 104(2); Mines 79.7.

Hickombottom v. State, TexCrimApp, 486 SW2d 951.—Crim Law 369.15, 1169.11.

Hickox v. Hickox, TexCivApp–El Paso, 151 SW2d 913.—Accord 1; App & E 1177(6); Bills & N 49, 437, 438; Compromise 2, 22; Trial 25(7.1), 350.4(1), 351.2(3.1), 352.1(4).

Hickox; Hickox v., TexCivApp–El Paso, 151 SW2d 913.—Accord 1; App & E 1177(6); Bills & N 49, 437, 438; Compromise 2, 22; Trial 25(7.1), 350.4(1), 351.2(3.1), 352.1(4).

Hicks; Allstate Ins. Co. v., TexApp–Amarillo, 134 SW3d 304, reh overr.—App & E 852, 856(1), 1175(1); Contracts 143(2), 176(2); Insurance 2264, 2275, 2914, 2915, 2922(1); Judgm 183, 185(2).

Hicks v. Armstrong, TexApp–Houston (14 Dist), 708 SW2d 890, writ dism, and writ withdrawn, and ref nre.—Judgm 335(1).

Hicks v. Armstrong Ins. Co., TexApp–Houston (14 Dist, 708 SW2d 890. See Hicks v. Armstrong.

Hicks v. Atlatl Royalty Corp., TexCivApp–Texarkana, 109 SW2d 1108.—App & E 743(1), 748.

HICKS

Hicks v. Baylor University Medical Center, TexApp–Dallas, 789 SW2d 299, writ den.—App & E 852; Judgm 185(2); Labor & Emp 50, 51.

Hicks v. Brooks, TexCivApp–Tyler, 504 SW2d 942, ref nre.—App & E 219(2), 907(3); Infants 197, 211, 221; Judgm 335(2); New Tr 91.

Hicks v. Brown, TexComApp, 151 SW2d 790, 136 Tex 399.—App & E 232(0.5), 1173(1); Autos 242(7); Neglig 1538, 1568, 1713; Trial 232(5), 352.5(5), 352.9.

Hicks v. Brown, TexCivApp–Amarillo, 128 SW2d 884, mod 151 SW2d 790, 136 Tex 399.—App & E 1050.1(10), 1062.2; Autos 168(2), 245(14); Evid 318(6), 558(11); Neglig 440(1), 1541; Trial 208, 219, 244(1), 273, 350.1, 350.5(2), 350.7(1), 350.7(2), 350.7(5), 352.5(7), 352.21, 424.

Hicks v. Brysch, WDTex, 989 FSupp 797.—Civil R 1094, 1351(1), 1354, 1376(1), 1376(2), 1376(4), 1376(5), 1376(8), 1407, 1450; Const Law 2325, 3232, 4827; Convicts 6; Courts 509; Fed Civ Proc 657.5(1), 657.5(2), 1264, 1758.1, 1824, 2411, 2415, 2461, 2535, 2538, 2539, 2544, 2545, 2546, 2552, 2553, 2734; Fed Cts 5, 48; Inj 1, 16; Mand 141; Plead 41; U S Mag 14.

Hicks; Burbridge v., TexCivApp–Galveston, 286 SW2d 678.—Inj 163(1), 163(3), 163(5).

Hicks; Campbell v., TexCivApp–Fort Worth, 83 SW2d 1013, writ dism.—App & E 1051(3); Evid 576, 579, 580; Lim of Act 195(3), 197(1); Trial 136(1).

Hicks v. Canessa, TexApp–El Paso, 825 SW2d 542.—Health 611, 620, 656, 820, 823(7); Judgm 185(6).

Hicks v. Charles Pfizer & Co. Inc., EDTex, 466 FSupp2d 799.—Evid 314(1), 318(1), 361, 372(1), 381; Fed Civ Proc 2515, 2545.

Hicks v. Charles Pfizer & Co. Inc., EDTex, 368 FSupp2d 628.—Prod Liab 1, 46.4; Sales 427.

Hicks; City of Dublin v., TexCivApp–Eastland, 120 SW2d 872.—App & E 729; Damag 39, 153, 221(2.1), 221(5.1); Trial 215, 350.3(4), 350.8.

Hicks v. City of Houston, TexApp–Corpus Christi, 641 SW2d 352.—Judgm 713(2), 715(2), 720.

Hicks v. City of Houston, TexApp–Hous (1 Dist), 524 SW2d 539, ref nre.—Adv Poss 14; Ease 17(4), 26(1), 30(1); Mun Corp 85, 657(4), 657(5).

Hicks v. Continental Carbon Paper Mfg. Co. of Dallas, TexCivApp–Waco, 380 SW2d 737, ref nre 382 SW2d 910.—Abate & R 37; Corp 349, 361, 599, 608, 615.5.

Hicks v. Crowley Maritime Corp., SDTex, 538 FSupp 285, aff 707 F2d 514, aff Bishop v. Crowley Maritime Corp, 707 F2d 514, aff Hildebran v Crowley Maritime Corp, 707 F2d 514.—Labor & Emp 2563; Seamen 16, 29(1), 29(2), 29(4), 29(5.14).

Hicks; Ditmore Land & Cattle Co. v., Tex, 290 SW2d 499, 155 Tex 596.—App & E 879; Judgm 335(1), 335(4); Tax 2930, 3072(2).

Hicks; Ditmore Land & Cattle Co. v., TexCivApp–Eastland, 282 SW2d 753, mod 290 SW2d 499, 155 Tex 596.—Judgm 243; Tax 2930, 3157, 3171, 3179.

Hicks v. Duncan, TexApp–Houston (1 Dist), 651 SW2d 871, petition for discretionary review refused by 662 SW2d 3.—Courts 27; Mand 12, 61.

Hicks; Espinoza v., TexApp–El Paso, 984 SW2d 274.—App & E 863; Electricity 17; Judgm 185(2); Labor & Emp 3125.

Hicks v. First Nat. Bank in Dalhart, TexApp–Amarillo, 778 SW2d 98, writ den.—Action 70; Const Law 3953; Garn 7; Judgm 153(1), 335(1); Pretrial Proc 583.

Hicks v. Fleming Companies, Inc., CA5 (Tex), 961 F2d 537, 124 ALR Fed 777.—Labor & Emp 483(1).

Hicks v. Fleming Companies, Inc., SDTex, 802 FSupp 39, aff 961 F2d 537, 124 ALR Fed 777.—Labor & Emp 483(1).

Hicks v. Flores, TexApp–Amarillo, 900 SW2d 504.—Judgm 143(3), 145(2), 146, 159; Plead 85(5).

Hicks v. Fredericks, TexCivApp–Beaumont, 286 SW2d 315.—App & E 688(1), 704.1; New Tr 40(4); Trial 273, 278.

Hicks v. Frost, TexCivApp–El Paso, 195 SW2d 606, ref nre.—App & E 929, 1003(10), 1068(1); Autos 201(10), 204, 243(3), 243(17); Evid 474(4), 478(3); Judgm 199(3.7); Neglig 510(1), 530(1); Trial 41(2), 235(4), 350.7(3.1).

Hicks v. Garner, CA5 (Tex), 69 F3d 22.—Civil R 1098; Const Law 1422, 1424; Fed Civ Proc 2734; Fed Cts 830; Prisons 4(14).

Hicks v. Glenn, TexCivApp–Amarillo, 155 SW2d 828.—Carr 408(4); Judgm 244.

Hicks; Hardware Mut. Cas. Co. v., TexCivApp–Texarkana, 344 SW2d 907.—Damag 221(3); Work Comp 1173, 1333, 1847.

Hicks v. Harry Armstrong Ins. Co., TexApp–Houston (14 Dist, 708 SW2d 890. See Hicks v. Armstrong.

Hicks v. Hicks, TexCivApp–Dallas, 546 SW2d 71.—Divorce 255, 322; Hus & W 249(3), 262.1(4), 262.2, 264(4), 264(7).

Hicks; Hicks v., TexCivApp–Dallas, 546 SW2d 71.—Divorce 255, 322; Hus & W 249(3), 262.1(4), 262.2, 264(4), 264(7).

Hicks v. Hicks, TexCivApp–Eastland, 395 SW2d 400.—Venue 5.3(6).

Hicks; Hicks v., TexCivApp–Eastland, 395 SW2d 400.—Venue 5.3(6).

Hicks v. Hightower, TexCivApp–Beaumont, 122 SW2d 289.—App & E 544(1), 719(2), 758.3(4); Schools 97(4).

Hicks; H. Molsen & Co., Inc. v., TexCivApp–El Paso, 550 SW2d 354, ref nre.—Frds St of 144.

Hicks; Hodge v., Tex, 233 SW2d 557, 149 Tex 390.—Child 11; Marriage 50(1).

Hicks; Hodge v., TexCivApp–Dallas, 229 SW2d 893, aff 233 SW2d 557, 149 Tex 390.—App & E 1008.1(8.1); Marriage 40(10).

Hicks; Hollums v., TexCivApp–Amarillo, 179 SW2d 824, writ refused wom.—Judgm 681; Mtg 191, 538, 553; Receivers 147.

Hicks; Home Indem. Co. of New York, N. Y. v., TexCivApp–Beaumont, 488 SW2d 614, dism.—Insurance 3559.

Hicks v. Hoover, TexCivApp–Dallas, 410 SW2d 534.—App & E 1078(1), 1170.7; Evid 373(2).

Hicks v. Hoover, TexCivApp–Waco, 422 SW2d 613, ref nre.—Fraud Conv 314; Lim of Act 39(11).

Hicks v. Humble Oil & Refining Co., TexApp–Houston (14 Dist), 970 SW2d 90, reh overr, and review den.—Admin Law 412.1; App & E 223, 1079; Const Law 190; Environ Law 408; Fraud 16; Neglig 1238, 305, 1011, 1025; Nuis 3(1), 27; Statut 263; Waters 104.

Hicks v. Industrial Underwriters Ins. Co., TexCivApp–Waco, 582 SW2d 216.—App & E 930(3), 989; Work Comp 1492.

Hicks v. Johnson, CA5 (Tex), 186 F3d 634, cert den 120 SCt 976, 528 US 1132, 145 LEd2d 844.—Hab Corp 364, 401, 404, 422, 768, 818; Jury 33(5.15).

Hicks v. Jones, CA5 (Tex), 453 F2d 400.—Hab Corp 319.1, 827.

Hicks; Knight v., TexCivApp–Amarillo, 505 SW2d 638, ref nre.—App & E 1170.1, 1170.9(8); Brok 43(2), 43(3), 53, 56(3), 65(1), 85(7), 86(1), 86(4), 88(1); Princ & A 23(5), 123(6); Statut 181(2), 183.

Hicks; Kovac v., TexCivApp–Eastland, 416 SW2d 496, ref nre.—Health 821(5); Trial 388(2).

Hicks v. Lamar Consol. Independent School Dist., TexApp–Eastland, 943 SW2d 540, reh overr.—Admin Law 229; App & E 863; Civil R 1320, 1715; Const Law 963; Schools 147.51.

Hicks v. Loveless, TexApp–Dallas, 714 SW2d 30, ref nre.—Covenants 1, 49, 72.1, 84; Deeds 67, 194(3).

Hicks v. Matthews, Tex, 266 SW2d 846, 153 Tex 177.—App & E 1175(1), 1177(1), 1177(2), 1177(7); Arrest 70(2); False Imp 8, 31, 39; Judgm 199(3.9); Trial 351.2(2), 365.1(4).

Hicks v. Matthews, TexCivApp–Beaumont, 261 SW2d 207, rev 266 SW2d 846, 153 Tex 177.—App & E 1140(1),

HICKS

1140(4); Autos 336; False Imp 7(1), 8, 22, 31, 33, 36; Trial 351.2(4).

Hicks; Mayfield v., TexCivApp–Dallas, 575 SW2d 571, ref nre.—Damag 78(6), 80(3); Evid 181; Guar 16(1), 16(2), 25(1), 27, 36(9), 41, 78(1), 79, 92(1); Trial 350.4(1).

Hicks v. Price, TexCivApp–Galveston, 81 SW2d 116.— Execution 18; Judgm 768(1), 782, 847.

Hicks v. Rapides Grocery Co., TexCivApp–El Paso, 101 SW2d 1042.—Evid 80(1); Int Liq 329(2); Judgm 101(2).

Hicks; Reed v., TexCivApp–Amarillo, 489 SW2d 958, 66 ALR3d 598, ref nre.—Autos 181(2).

Hicks v. Ricardo, TexApp–Houston (1 Dist), 834 SW2d 587, reh den.—App & E 977(5), 989, 1001(1), 1003(6); Damag 48, 58, 102, 163(1), 208(6), 221(7); New Tr 6, 75(2).

Hicks; Rice Food Market, Inc. v., TexApp–Houston (1 Dist), 111 SW3d 610, review den, and review gr, and withdrawn, and review den.—App & E 930(1), 1001(1); Neglig 1001, 1030, 1031, 1037(4), 1088, 1089, 1593, 1670, 1706, 1708.

Hicks v. Secretary of Health, Ed. and Welfare, NDTex, 424 FSupp 485.—Social S 140.70, 143.45, 143.55.

Hicks v. Shively, TexCivApp–Beaumont, 137 SW2d 102. —Abate & R 40; Ex & Ad 524(1); Lim of Act 125.

Hicks v. Sias, TexCivApp–Beaumont, 102 SW2d 460, writ refused.—Courts 8, 29; Execution 272(1); Judgm 16, 17(3), 489, 490(2); Proc 83; States 5(1).

Hicks v. Smith, TexCivApp–Fort Worth, 330 SW2d 641, ref nre.—Contracts 10(1), 54(1), 75(2), 154, 155, 171(3), 236, 284(1), 350(2); Costs 194.32; Evid 450(7); Interest 39(3).

Hicks v. Southwestern Settlement & Development Corp., TexCivApp–Beaumont, 214 SW2d 315, ref nre.— Adv Poss 100(6), 114(3); App & E 1043(6), 1058(1); Debtor & C 7; Tax 3107; Tresp to T T 10, 44.

Hicks v. Southwestern Settlement & Development Corp., TexCivApp–Beaumont, 188 SW2d 915, writ refused wom.—Abate & R 27; Judgm 666, 680; Parties 18, 29, 35, 35.79, 51(1); Ten in C 55(1), 55(3), 55(9); Tresp to T T 6.1, 26, 32, 47(1).

Hicks v. Southwestern Settlement & Development Corp., TexCivApp–Eastland, 181 SW2d 982.—App & E 66, 78(1), 870(1).

Hicks; Stanley v., TexCivApp–Waco, 272 SW2d 917.— App & E 799, 1091(1), 1091(2), 1201(6); J P 119.2, 141(4).

Hicks; Stansbury v., TexCivApp–Fort Worth, 396 SW2d 526.—Action 57(7); App & E 76(1); Judgm 217, 335(1).

Hicks v. State, TexCrimApp, 860 SW2d 419, reh den, cert den 114 SCt 2725, 512 US 1227, 129 LEd2d 848.—Crim Law 338(7), 388.1, 388.2, 412.2(4), 412.2(5), 438(7), 438(8), 671, 1169.1(1), 1169.2(6), 1169.12; Gr Jury 35; Ind & Inf 69, 184.

Hicks v. State, TexCrimApp, 664 SW2d 329.—Crim Law 1042.

Hicks v. State, TexCrimApp, 587 SW2d 422.—Crim Law 13.2; Rob 11, 27(6).

Hicks v. State, TexCrimApp, 545 SW2d 805.—Controlled Subs 113, 124; Crim Law 361(1), 394.4(12), 394.4(13), 404.60, 419(1), 723(3), 729, 865(1), 865(2), 1169.1(8), 1169.2(8), 1171.1(6), 1178; Searches 41, 117; Sent & Pun 312, 1296, 1297; Witn 274(2).

Hicks v. State, TexCrimApp, 544 SW2d 424.—Crim Law 1077.2(1), 1077.2(3), 1104(1).

Hicks v. State, TexCrimApp, 525 SW2d 177.—Crim Law 721(1), 721(6), 1134(2), 1171.5.

Hicks v. State, TexCrimApp, 508 SW2d 400.—Crim Law 404.15, 404.65, 590(2), 632(5), 1174(5); Ind & Inf 127.

Hicks v. State, TexCrimApp, 493 SW2d 833.—Crim Law 377, 407(2), 1036.1(9), 1037.2, 1043(3); Ind & Inf 119, 137(1).

Hicks v. State, TexCrimApp, 489 SW2d 912.—Controlled Subs 30, 80; Crim Law 863(2).

Hicks v. State, TexCrimApp, 487 SW2d 137.—Crim Law 577.

Hicks v. State, TexCrimApp, 482 SW2d 186.—Crim Law 429(1), 627.9(1), 1120(3); Rob 24.50; Witn 270(2), 283.

Hicks v. State, TexCrimApp, 476 SW2d 671.—Crim Law 273.4(4).

Hicks v. State, TexCrimApp, 476 SW2d 670.—Sent & Pun 2004, 2021.

Hicks v. State, TexCrimApp, 452 SW2d 465.—Crim Law 1166(10.10).

Hicks v. State, TexCrimApp, 389 SW2d 950.—Crim Law 371(8); Rob 22, 24.50, 27(6).

Hicks v. State, TexCrimApp, 355 SW2d 189, 172 TexCrim 195.—Crim Law 867, 1174(1).

Hicks v. State, TexCrimApp, 318 SW2d 652, 167 TexCrim 115.—Crim Law 419(12), 577, 1166(7).

Hicks v. State, TexCrimApp, 251 SW2d 409, 158 TexCrim 45.—Autos 349(6), 355(6); Const Law 4655; Crim Law 956(2), 956(13).

Hicks v. State, TexCrimApp, 224 SW2d 712.—Crim Law 1094(2.1).

Hicks v. State, TexCrimApp, 208 SW2d 365.—Crim Law 1090.1(1), 1094(2.1).

Hicks v. State, TexCrimApp, 183 SW2d 566, 147 TexCrim 606.—Crim Law 1023(9).

Hicks v. State, TexCrimApp, 167 SW2d 522, 145 TexCrim 259.—Int Liq 238(5).

Hicks v. State, TexCrimApp, 83 SW2d 349, 128 TexCrim 595.—Crim Law 687(1), 742(1), 763(8), 814(17), 890, 893; Rec S Goods 7(5), 9(2); Witn 48(1), 53(4).

Hicks v. State, TexApp–Houston (1 Dist), 837 SW2d 686. —Crim Law 419(3), 641.13(1), 641.13(2.1), 641.13(6), 721(1), 721(3), 721(6), 1030(1), 1159.2(7), 1166.10(1), 1169.2(2), 1171.1(5); Rob 7, 24.15(1), 24.50; Weap 4.

Hicks v. State, TexApp–Houston (1 Dist), 815 SW2d 299. —Crim Law 721(1), 721(3), 730(10), 867, 1129(4), 1134(3), 1162, 1171.5.

Hicks v. State, TexApp–Houston (1 Dist), 723 SW2d 238. —Assault 56, 92(3); Jury 131(4).

Hicks v. State, TexApp–Houston (1 Dist), 630 SW2d 829, petition for discretionary review refused.—Crim Law 586, 814(1), 1036.1(3.1), 1044.2(1), 1159.6, 1166(2), 1166(7); Gr Jury 2.5, 41.10; Homic 1181, 1465; Ind & Inf 137(3); Witn 344(1).

Hicks v. State, TexApp–Houston (1 Dist), 630 SW2d 766, petition for discretionary review refused.—Crim Law 641.13(1), 641.13(6); Witn 318.

Hicks v. State, TexApp–Fort Worth, 722 SW2d 257, petition for discretionary review gr, petition for discretionary review dism with per curiam opinion 779 SW2d 408. —Jury 75(2), 131(13), 131(17).

Hicks v. State, TexApp–San Antonio, 18 SW3d 743.— Autos 351.1.

Hicks v. State, TexApp–San Antonio, 901 SW2d 614, petition for discretionary review refused.—Crim Law 339.7(3), 339.7(4), 339.10(1), 339.10(2), 339.11(3), 339.11(5.1), 369.8, 641.13(1), 641.13(2.1), 641.13(6), 956(1), 1044.2(1), 1166.22(1), 1166.22(2), 1169.2(3), 1169.5(3).

Hicks v. State, TexApp–Texarkana, 183 SW3d 869, petition for discretionary review gr.—Assault 48, 91.7; Crim Law 1134(2), 1144.13(2.1), 1159.2(2), 1159.2(7).

Hicks v. State, TexApp–Texarkana, 968 SW2d 425, petition for discretionary review refused.—Crim Law 273.2(1), 273.2(2), 905, 1134(3); Double J 57.

Hicks v. State, TexApp–Amarillo, 204 SW3d 505.—Crim Law 795(2.10), 795(2.35), 1042; Sent & Pun 335.

Hicks v. State, TexApp–Beaumont, 753 SW2d 419.—Crim Law 394.1(3), 394.4(6); Searches 28.

Hicks v. State, TexApp–Waco, 151 SW3d 672, petition for discretionary review refused.—Crim Law 641.4(1), 641.7(1), 1077.3, 1134(10), 1137(2), 1139, 1590.

Hicks v. State, TexApp–Waco, 999 SW2d 417, rev on reh, and petition for discretionary review refused.—Crim Law 273.1(2), 303.15, 303.45; Ind & Inf 144.2, 196(1).

Hicks v. State, TexApp–Tyler, 721 SW2d 399.—Crim Law 339.9(3), 438(3), 444, 478(1), 1121(1).

Hicks v. State, TexApp–Houston (14 Dist), 15 SW3d 626, reh overr, and petition for discretionary review refused.—Const Law 665, 667; Crim Law 957(1), 957(2), 1030(1), 1038.1(3.1), 1043(2), 1130(5); Infants 13; Sent & Pun 1209, 1422, 1482, 1483, 1513.

Hicks v. State, TexApp–Houston (14 Dist), 864 SW2d 693. —Crim Law 27, 370, 371(1); Ind & Inf 119, 159(1), 167.

Hicks v. State, TexCivApp–Hous (14 Dist), 422 SW2d 539, ref nre.—Atty & C 38, 53(2); Trial 350.3(1).

Hicks v. Sunray Oil Co., CCA5 (Tex), 139 F2d 937.—Fed Cts 793; Spec Perf 123.

Hicks; Taylor v., TexApp–Fort Worth, 691 SW2d 839.—Divorce 254(1); Judgm 21.

Hicks; Texas Dept. of Public Safety v., TexCivApp–Waco, 439 SW2d 894.—Autos 144.2(4); Dist & Pros Attys 9.

Hicks; Texas Emp. Ins. Ass'n v., TexCivApp–Amarillo, 237 SW2d 699, ref nre.—App & E 901, 931(3), 1015(5), 1032(1); New Tr 144; Trial 122, 129, 350.5(4); Work Comp 1728, 1904, 1965, 1966, 1968(1).

Hicks; Texas Emp. Ins. Ass'n v., TexCivApp–Eastland, 271 SW2d 460, dism.—App & E 232(2); New Tr 140(3); Trial 76; Work Comp 1696, 1927.

Hicks; Texas General Indem. Co. v., TexCivApp–Tyler, 472 SW2d 547.—Evid 208(2); Witn 383; Work Comp 1391, 1392, 1630, 1703, 1974.

Hicks v. Texas Municipal Power Agency, TexCivApp–Hous (14 Dist), 548 SW2d 949, ref nre.—Em Dom 8, 20(5), 186, 318; Mun Corp 272.

Hicks v. Thompson, TexCivApp–Waco, 207 SW2d 1000.—Admin Law 500, 501; Labor & Emp 1597, 1599; Plead 201, 228.14.

Hicks; Traders & General Ins. Co. v., TexCivApp–Austin, 94 SW2d 824.—Work Comp 862, 1326, 1336, 1619, 1724, 1728.

Hicks; Trinity Reserve Life Ins. Co. v., TexCivApp–Dallas, 297 SW2d 345.—Can of Inst 47; Insurance 2958, 3001, 3015, 3096(2), 3339, 3375; Trial 352.20.

Hicks; U.S. v., CA5 (Tex), 389 F3d 514, reh den, cert den 126 SCt 1022, 546 US 1089, 163 LEd2d 853, reh den 126 SCt 1459, 546 US 1226, 164 LEd2d 153.—Arrest 68(9), 68(10); Const Law 4728; Crim Law 338(7), 472, 478(1), 486(1), 486(2), 488, 561(1), 566, 1134(3), 1139, 1144.13(3), 1153(1), 1158(1), 1158(2), 1158(4), 1159.2(7), 1169.1(1), 1169.1(2.1); Homic 546, 659; Judgm 828.5(3); Jury 34(6); Sent & Pun 643, 653(2), 973; Weap 17(3).

Hicks; U.S. v., CA5 (Tex), 980 F2d 963, cert den Canty v. US, 113 SCt 1618, 507 US 998, 123 LEd2d 178, cert den 113 SCt 2417, 508 US 941, 124 LEd2d 640.—Aviation 16; Const Law 855, 859, 1170, 1514, 1559, 1561, 1830.

Hicks; U.S. v., CA5 (Tex), 945 F2d 107.—Controlled Subs 40; Crim Law 1438, 1572.

Hicks v. U.S., CA5 (Tex), 787 F2d 1018.—Int Rev 3551.

Hicks; U.S. v., CA5 (Tex), 153 FedAppx 346, cert den 126 SCt 1824, 547 US 1091, 164 LEd2d 555, appeal after new sentencing hearing 202 FedAppx 27, cert den 127 SCt 1317, 167 LEd2d 127.—Crim Law 274(3.1), 1181.5(8); Double J 28.

Hicks; U.S. v., NDTex, 420 FSupp 533.—Consp 45; Const Law 2362, 2503(5); Courts 82; Crim Law 113, 622.2(1), 622.2(3), 622.3; Witn 52(1), 52(7), 54, 75, 76(3).

Hicks; U.S. v., NDTex, 137 FSupp 564.—Lim of Act 6(1), 58(1); U S 53(13.1), 53(14), 133.

Hicks v. Wallis Lumber Co., TexCivApp–San Antonio, 137 SW2d 93.—Judgm 335(1), 335(3).

Hicks v. Western Funding, Inc., TexApp–Houston (1 Dist), 809 SW2d 787, writ den.—App & E 907(3); Costs 260(4).

Hicks; World Oil Co. v., TexComApp, 103 SW2d 962, 129 Tex 297.—Jury 37; New Tr 140(3), 162(2), 162(3).

Hicks v. Wright, TexCivApp–Tyler, 564 SW2d 785, ref nre.—App & E 930(3), 989, 1003(5); Consp 2, 19; Corp 1.4(3), 1.7(2), 417; Damag 87(2), 184; Fraud 11(1), 41; Release 18, 38, 58(1); Subrog 25, 33(1).

Hicks v. Wyeth–Ayerst Laboratories Co., EDTex, 899 FSupp 312. See Norplant Contraceptive Products Liability Litigation, In re.

Hicks; Young v., Tex, 559 SW2d 343.—App & E 1178(6).

Hicks v. Young, TexCivApp–Eastland, 553 SW2d 1, aff in part, rev in part 559 SW2d 343.—High 159(2); Inj 204.

Hicksbaugh Lumber Co. v. Fidelity & Cas. Co. of New York, TexCivApp–Galveston, 177 SW2d 802.—Autos 19; Insurance 2677, 3066.

Hicks Bros. Const. Co. of Abilene, Inc.; Skinny's, Inc. v., TexCivApp–Eastland, 602 SW2d 85.—App & E 173(16), 931(1), 931(6), 961, 989, 1008.1(2), 1010.1(4), 1012.1(1); Contracts 28(3); Evid 351; Mech Liens 139(3), 277(4), 292; Trover 23.

Hicks Bldg. & Equipment Co. v. Buice, Tex, 371 SW2d 44.—App & E 362(1), 365(1).

Hicks Bldg. & Equipment Co.; Buice v., TexCivApp–Waco, 369 SW2d 624, ref nre 371 SW2d 44.—Autos 244(11); Damag 185(1).

Hickson v. Allison, TexApp–Waco, 928 SW2d 677.—Const Law 2325; Pretrial Proc 652; Prisons 4(13).

Hickson v. City of Van Alstyne, TexApp–Dallas, 195 SW2d 571.—Const Law 946; Mun Corp 972(4), 973; Stip 6.

Hickson v. Martinez, TexApp–Dallas, 707 SW2d 919, ref nre 716 SW2d 499.—Carr 318(1); Evid 363, 382, 555.10, 571(3); Health 823(1), 827.

Hickson v. Moya, TexApp–Waco, 926 SW2d 397.—App & E 946, 984(1); Costs 128, 133.

Hicks–Ponder Co.; N.L.R.B. v., CA5 (Tex), 458 F2d 19.—Labor & Emp 1743(1), 1913.

Hicks–Ponder Co. v. N. L. R. B., CA5 (Tex), 424 F2d 538, cert den 91 SCt 48, 400 US 825, 27 LEd2d 53.—Fed Cts 743; Labor & Emp 1735, 1740.

Hicks Rubber Co.; Employers Cas. Co. v., TexCivApp–Waco, 160 SW2d 96, rev Traders & General Ins Co v. Hicks Rubber Co v, 169 SW2d 142, 140 Tex 586.—Insurance 2678, 3111(2), 3347, 3349; Judgm 198; Neglig 1694; Trial 355(3).

Hicks Rubber Co. v. Harper, Tex, 132 SW2d 579, 134 Tex 89.—App & E 216(2), 499(1).

Hicks Rubber Co. v. Harper, TexCivApp–Waco, 131 SW2d 749, writ dism 132 SW2d 579, 134 Tex 89.—App & E 218.2(7), 699(4), 704.1, 930(2), 1047(5), 1062.1, 1067; Damag 34, 132(3); Neglig 1717; Trial 58, 129.

Hicks Rubber Co. v. Port Iron & Supply Co., TexCivApp–Beaumont, 252 SW2d 987, mandamus overr.—Evid 174.4; Plead 111.42(2); Sales 66, 382; Venue 7.5(7).

Hicks Rubber Co.; Traders & General Ins. Co. v., Tex, 169 SW2d 142, 140 Tex 586.—Insurance 2270(1), 2285(1), 2285(4), 2285(5), 3530.

Hicks Rubber Co., Distributors v. Stacy, TexCivApp–Austin, 133 SW2d 249.—Trover 4, 5, 9(8), 32(6).

Hicks Rubber Co. of Waco; Stahr v., TexCivApp–Waco, 122 SW2d 1112, dism.—App & E 1032(1), 1069.1.

Hicks Thomas & Lilienstern, L.L.P.; Valley Forge Ins. Co. v., TexApp–Houston (1 Dist), 174 SW3d 254, review den.—App & E 881.1; Insurance 1806, 1808, 1809, 1813, 1832(2), 1836, 1863, 2142(5); Waters 115.

Hi-Class Business Systems of America, Inc.; Case Corp. v., TexApp–Dallas, 184 SW3d 760, reh overr, and review den.—App & E 852, 854(4), 930(1), 946, 1001(1), 1001(3); Contracts 168, 315, 326; Copyr 107; Damag 40(1); Evid 267, 314(1), 317(2), 351; Fraud 59(2), 59(3), 60; Frds St of 49, 119(1); Judgm 185(2), 185(5), 185(6); Plead 427; Trial 43, 48, 85.

Hico County Line Independent School Dist.; Erath County School Trustees v., TexCivApp–Eastland, 247 SW2d 564, writ refused.—Courts 475(1); Schools 42(2).

Hico Independent School Dist.; Braune v., CA5 (Tex), 736 F2d 243. See Wells v. Hico Independent School Dist.

Hico Independent School Dist.; Wells v., CA5 (Tex), 736 F2d 243, cert dism Hico Independent School District v. Wells, 106 SCt 11, 473 US 901, 87 LEd2d 672.—Civil R 1438, 1465(1), 1474(1); Const Law 90.1(7.3), 1150, 1995, 3874(2), 4040, 4161, 4162, 4173(1), 4201, 4202; Fed Civ Proc 2182.1; Fed Cts 630.1, 641, 757, 865, 908.1; Schools 133.5.

Hidalgo, In Interest of, TexApp–Texarkana, 938 SW2d 492.—App & E 230; Child C 272, 409, 465, 467, 468, 510, 618; Child S 55, 146, 195, 543; Social S 139.

Hidalgo v. Lechuga, TexCivApp–El Paso, 407 SW2d 545, ref nre.—Adv Poss 47; App & E 760(2); Frds St of 158(4); Infants 24; Lim of Act 187; Tresp to T T 46.

Hidalgo v. State, TexCrimApp, 983 SW2d 746.—Crim Law 641.2(2), 641.3(2), 641.3(3), 641.3(11); Infants 68.7(3).

Hidalgo v. State, TexApp–San Antonio, 945 SW2d 313, petition for discretionary review gr, aff 983 SW2d 746. —Crim Law 1144.13(2.1), 1159.2(7), 1159.2(9), 1159.4(2), 1451; Homic 561(2), 1168, 1181; Infants 68.7(3), 68.7(4), 68.8; Sent & Pun 1789(3).

Hidalgo v. Surety Sav. & Loan Ass'n, Tex, 487 SW2d 702, appeal after remand 502 SW2d 220, 78 ALR3d 1012.—Judgm 181(26), 185.1(4).

Hidalgo v. Surety Sav. & Loan Ass'n, Tex, 462 SW2d 540, appeal after remand 481 SW2d 208, rev 487 SW2d 702, appeal after remand 502 SW2d 220, 78 ALR3d 1012.—Evid 383(7); Judgm 185(1), 185.3(16).

Hidalgo v. Surety Sav. and Loan Ass'n, TexCivApp–El Paso, 502 SW2d 220, 78 ALR3d 1012.—App & E 80(1); Judgm 183, 185.3(16); Mtg 376.

Hidalgo v. Surety Sav. & Loan Ass'n, TexCivApp–El Paso, 481 SW2d 208, rev 487 SW2d 702, appeal after remand 502 SW2d 220, 78 ALR3d 1012.—App & E 223; Bills & N 327, 370; Const Law 945; Judgm 185.1(2), 185.2(8).

Hidalgo v. Surety Sav. & Loan Ass'n, TexCivApp–El Paso, 457 SW2d 341, rev 462 SW2d 540, appeal after remand 481 SW2d 208, rev 487 SW2d 702, appeal after remand 502 SW2d 220, 78 ALR3d 1012.—App & E 863, 934(1); Judgm 185.3(2), 185.3(16); Mtg 426.

Hidalgo; U.S. v., CA5 (Tex), 226 FedAppx 391.—Consp 40.1, 47(12), 48.2(2); Crim Law 438.1, 569, 662.40, 1169.10.

Hidalgo and Cameron Counties Water Control and Imp. Dist. No. Nine; Hansen v., TexCivApp–San Antonio, 319 SW2d 765.—Lim of Act 24(2), 66(15).

Hidalgo and Cameron Counties Water Control and Improvement Dist. No. 9 v. American Rio Grande Land & Irrigation Co., CCA5 (Tex), 103 F2d 509, cert den American Rio Grande Land & Irrigation Co v. Hidalgo and Cameron County Water Control and Imp Dist No 9, 60 SCt 88, 308 US 573, 84 LEd 481.—Bankr 2851, 2899, 2955, 3790; Const Law 48(4.1), 4372; Statut 105(1), 107(6), 121(1); Waters 216, 228, 231.

Hidalgo and Cameron Counties Water Control and Imp. Dist. No. 9 v. Maverick County Water Control and Imp. Dist. No. 1, TexCivApp–San Antonio, 349 SW2d 768, writ dism.—Ease 1, 3(1); Plead 111.23; Venue 5.3(1), 5.3(2), 5.5, 16.

Hidalgo and Cameron Counties Water Control and Improvement Dist. No. 9 v. Starley, Tex, 373 SW2d 731.—Judges 45.

Hidalgo, Chambers & Co. v. Federal Deposit Ins. Corp., TexApp–Waco, 790 SW2d 700, writ den.—App & E 543, 562, 1177(9); Courts 85(2).

Hidalgo County; American Indem. Co. v., TexCivApp–San Antonio, 146 SW2d 1076, writ refused.—Action 50(3); Appear 12; Lim of Act 124; Proc 6.

Hidalgo County; Bazan ex rel. Bazan v., CA5 (Tex), 246 F3d 481.—Arrest 68(2); Civil R 1376(2), 1407; Fed Civ Proc 2491.5; Fed Cts 574, 776.

Hidalgo County; Fonseca v., TexCivApp–Corpus Christi, 527 SW2d 474, ref nre.—App & E 854(2), 1008.1(2), 1011.1(12), 1170.10; Atty & C 77; Can of Inst 3, 5; Compromise 8(4), 19(2); Em Dom 241; Judgm 368; Trial 382, 394(1), 404(1).

Hidalgo County v. Gonzalez, TexApp–Corpus Christi, 128 SW3d 788.—App & E 70(8); Autos 187(1); Counties 141, 146; Mun Corp 745, 747(3), 847; Offic 114, 119; Sheriffs 99, 100; States 78.

Hidalgo County; Griffin v., TexCivApp–San Antonio, 185 SW2d 234, writ refused wom.—App & E 758.1; Atty & C 151; Compromise 18(2); Counties 128.

Hidalgo County; Hidalgo County Water Control & Improvement Dist. No. 1 v., TexCivApp–San Antonio, 134 SW2d 464, writ refused.—App & E 1172(1); Bridges 7, 21(2); Mand 90, 94; Waters 216, 228.

Hidalgo County; Hogan v., TexCivApp–San Antonio, 246 SW2d 709.—Action 60; Counties 89; Lim of Act 197(2); Pretrial Proc 713, 714, 719; Refer 79.

Hidalgo County v. Jackson, CCA5 (Tex), 119 F2d 108.— Lim of Act 24(2), 51(3), 102(2), 103(2), 141.

Hidalgo County v. Johnstone, TexCivApp–Eastland, 137 SW2d 825, writ dism, correct.—Em Dom 180; High 64.

Hidalgo County v. Parker, TexApp–Corpus Christi, 83 SW3d 362, review den.—App & E 66, 68; Counties 141, 146; Judgm 181(6); Mun Corp 723; Offic 114.

Hidalgo County v. Pate, TexCivApp–Corpus Christi, 443 SW2d 80, ref nre.—Adv Poss 13, 50; App & E 1010.1(3), 1135; Deeds 93, 97; Ease 1; Estop 54, 62.3; Evid 419(1), 419(2), 441(1), 591; Nova 1; Trusts 43(1), 88, 89(1).

Hidalgo County; Sheppard v., Tex, 90 SW2d 811, 126 Tex 550.—App & E 1107.

Hidalgo County; Southern Surety Co. v., TexComApp, 83 SW2d 313, 125 Tex 390.—Banks 89; Counties 98(1), 101(7).

Hidalgo County; Yturria Town & Imp. Co. v., TexCivApp–San Antonio, 125 SW2d 1092.—App & E 1032(1); Evid 372(11); High 14, 17, 64; Jury 66(1).

Hidalgo County; Yturria Town & Imp. Co. v., TexCivApp–San Antonio, 114 SW2d 917.—App & E 456, 477, 488(2).

Hidalgo County Appraisal Dist. v. Engfar N.V., TexApp–Corpus Christi, 756 SW2d 754.—Tax 2063; Treaties 7, 8.

Hidalgo County Appraisal Dist.; Sharyland Water Supply Corp. v., Tex, 804 SW2d 894. See North Alamo Water Supply Corp. v. Willacy County Appraisal Dist.

Hidalgo County Appraisal Dist.; Sharyland Water Supply Corp. v., TexApp–Corpus Christi, 783 SW2d 297, writ den, and writ withdrawn, and writ gr, aff North Alamo Water Supply Corp v. Willacy County Appraisal Dist, 804 SW2d 894.—Admin Law 669.1; App & E 845(2); Stip 14(10); Tax 2288, 2300, 2338, 2339, 2392, 2696.

Hidalgo County Appraisal Review Dist.; Mission Palms Retirement Housing,Inc. v., TexApp–Corpus Christi, 896 SW2d 819, reh overr.—Char 48(1); Evid 48; States 18.3, 18.5, 18.7, 18.15; Tax 2300, 2339, 2392.

Hidalgo County Bank & Trust Co. v. Goodwin, TexCivApp–San Antonio, 137 SW2d 161, writ dism, correct.— App & E 927(7), 989; Banks 90, 119; Lim of Act 103(4), 199(1); Trusts 1, 41, 373.

Hidalgo County Com'rs Court v. Mancias, TexApp–Corpus Christi, 885 SW2d 268. See Leo v. Mancias.

Hidalgo County Drainage Dist. No. 1; Security Development Co. v., TexCivApp–Amarillo, 124 SW2d 178.—

Deeds 38(1), 137, 140, 143; Drains 18, 20, 75; Lim of Act 66(12).

Hidalgo County Grand Jury Com'rs; Ciudadanos Unidos De San Juan v., CA5 (Tex), 622 F2d 807, cert den 101 SCt 1479, 450 US 964, 67 LEd2d 613.—Const Law 919, 977, 980, 1050, 3000, 3039, 3053, 3054, 3833; Fed Civ Proc 1741; Fed Cts 12.1, 13; Gr Jury 2.5, 5.

Hidalgo County, Texas; Gonzalez v., CA5 (Tex), 489 F2d 1043.—Const Law 947, 948, 4417, 4480; Contracts 1.

Hidalgo County Water Control and Imp. Dist. No. 1 v. Boysen, TexCivApp–San Antonio, 354 SW2d 420, writ refused.—Judges 45, 47(1), 56.

Hidalgo County Water Control & Improvement Dist. No. 1 v. Hidalgo County, TexCivApp–San Antonio, 134 SW2d 464, writ refused.—App & E 1172(1); Bridges 7, 21(2); Mand 90, 94; Waters 216, 228.

Hidalgo County Water Control & Imp. Dist. No. 1; Texas Agr. Ass'n of Edinburg v., CCA5 (Tex), 125 F2d 829, cert den Abraham v. Hidalgo County Water Control and Improvement Dist No 1, 63 SCt 35, 317 US 643, 87 LEd 518, reh den 63 SCt 199, 317 US 709, 87 LEd 565.—Bankr 2251; Fed Cts 862; Mand 115, 119; Waters 230(1), 230(2).

Hidalgo County Water Control & Improvement Dist. No. 1; Texas Agricultural Ass'n of Edinburg v., SDTex, 36 FSupp 314, rev 125 F2d 829, cert den Abraham v. Hidalgo County Water Control and Improvement Dist No 1, 63 SCt 35, 317 US 643, 87 LEd 518, reh den 63 SCt 199, 317 US 709, 87 LEd 565.—Bankr 2251; Contracts 105; Fed Civ Proc 2334; Waters 228.5, 230(6).

Hidalgo County Water Control and Imp. Dist. No. 1 v. Van Horn, TexComApp, 84 SW2d 699, 125 Tex 486.—App & E 564(3), 624, 1126.

Hidalgo County Water Control & Imp. Dist. No. 12; Brady v., TexComApp, 91 SW2d 1058, 127 Tex 123.—App & E 1177(7); Mand 116; Waters 227.

Hidalgo County Water Control and Improvement Dist. No. 12; Holderman v., CCA5 (Tex), 142 F2d 792.—Mun Corp 942, 948(1); Waters 230(6).

Hidalgo County Water Control and Imp. Dist. No. 12; Laycock v., CCA5 (Tex), 142 F2d 789, 155 ALR 460, cert den 65 SCt 68, 323 US 731, 89 LEd 587.—Judgm 414; Mand 1, 15, 103.

Hidalgo County Water Control and Imp. Dist. No. 16 v. Hippchen, CA5 (Tex), 233 F2d 712.—Deeds 90, 140, 143; Ease 2, 14(3); Waters 156(4).

Hidalgo County Water Control and Imp. Dist. No. 16; Pickens v., TexCivApp–San Antonio, 284 SW2d 784.—Courts 475(8); Decl Judgm 45, 389; Em Dom 172, 241.

Hidalgo County Water Control and Imp. Dist. No. 18; State v., TexCivApp–Corpus Christi, 443 SW2d 728, ref nre.—Const Law 4101; Treaties 8; Waters 128, 130, 133, 140, 142, 151, 152(1), 152(8), 152(11), 152(12).

Hidalgo County Water Control and Imp. Dist. No. 6; Arnold H. Bruner & Co. v., TexCivApp–San Antonio, 371 SW2d 932, writ dism.—App & E 846(5); Plead 111.36, 111.43; Venue 7.5(1), 7.5(6).

Hidalgo County Water Control and Imp. Dist. No. 7 v. Hedrick, CA5 (Tex), 226 F2d 1, cert den Hidalgo County Water Control and Improvement District No 7 v. Hedrick, 76 SCt 469, 350 US 983, 100 LEd 851.—Em Dom 84; Fed Cts 161, 162, 191; Treaties 7, 8; Waters 142.

Hidalgo County Water Dist. No. 1; Castillo v., TexApp–Corpus Christi, 771 SW2d 633, extension of time to file for writ of error overr.—Const Law 990, 2312, 2314, 3057, 3753, 4421; Death 9, 31(1), 81.

Hidalgo County Water Imp. Dist. Number Six; Anderson v., TexCivApp–San Antonio, 251 SW2d 761, ref nre.—Inj 143(1), 152.

Hidalgo County Water Imp. Dist. No. Two v. Cameron County Water Control & Imp. Dist. No. Five, TexCivApp–San Antonio, 250 SW2d 941.—App & E 458(3);

Courts 204, 206(17.3), 207.3, 207.5; Refer 47; Waters 152(12).

Hidalgo County Water Imp. Dist. No. Two v. Dean, TexCivApp–San Antonio, 366 SW2d 703, ref nre.—Estop 68(5); Tax 2935, 2995, 2996.

Hidalgo County Water Imp. Dist. No. Two; Dean v., TexCivApp–San Antonio, 320 SW2d 29, ref nre.—Estop 22(2), 23, 27(1), 32(1), 43, 68(5); Judgm 185(2); Mines 55(1), 62.1.

Hidalgo County Water Imp. Dist. No. 2 v. Blalock, Tex, 301 SW2d 593, 157 Tex 206.—Courts 207.4(1.1), 207.4(2); Judges 42, 44; Mand 145, 151(1).

Hidalgo County Water Imp. Dist. No. 2 v. Cameron County Water Control & Imp. Dist. No. 5, TexCivApp–San Antonio, 253 SW2d 294, ref nre.—Inj 132, 133; Parties 18, 29, 35.61; Waters 152(3), 152(4), 152(5).

Hidalgo County Water Imp. Dist. No. 2 v. Feick, TexCivApp–Beaumont, 111 SW2d 742, dism.—Contracts 131; Mun Corp 867(2); Pub Contr 4; Waters 228.5.

Hidalgo County Water Improvement Dist. No. 2; Fonseca v., CA5 (Tex), 496 F2d 109.—Fed Cts 998, 1000; Time 9(1).

Hidalgo County Water Improvement Dist. No. 2; Jimenez v., CA5 (Tex), 496 F2d 113, on remand 68 FRD 668, aff 96 SCt 1423, 424 US 950, 47 LEd2d 357.—Fed Cts 999.1.

Hidalgo County Water Improvement Dist. No. 2; Jimenez v., SDTex, 68 FRD 668, aff 96 SCt 1423, 424 US 950, 47 LEd2d 357.—Const Law 2486, 2580, 2970, 3039, 3057, 3635; Evid 83(1); Mun Corp 28, 455; Waters 182, 183.5.

Hidalgo County Water Imp. Dist. No. 2; Kolberg v., TexCivApp–San Antonio, 110 SW2d 961.—Lim of Act 55(7), 197(1).

Hidalgo County Water Imp. Dist. No. 2; Snell v., SDTex, 507 FSupp 834.—Const Law 3869, 3874(3), 4165(1), 4171; Fed Cts 421; Labor & Emp 40(2).

Hidalgo County Water Imp. Dist. No. 6; Guelker v., TexCivApp–San Antonio, 269 SW2d 551, ref nre.—App & E 679(1); Waters 144.5, 153, 154(1), 154(2), 256.

Hidalgo Distributing Co. v. Safeway Stores, TexCivApp–San Antonio, 204 SW2d 523.—App & E 1039(13); Sales 397.

Hidalgo Guarantee Abstract Co. v. City of Edinburg, TexCivApp–El Paso, 181 SW2d 597, writ refused.—Mun Corp 966(1); Tax 2167, 2176.

Hidalgo-Peralta; U.S. v., CA5 (Tex), 166 FedAppx 762.—Sent & Pun 637.

Hidalgo Pub. Co.; Trevino v., TexApp–Corpus Christi, 805 SW2d 862.—Const Law 4011; Judgm 184.

Hidden Oaks Ltd. v. City of Austin, CA5 (Tex), 138 F3d 1036, reh den.—Civil R 1482, 1484, 1487; Const Law 3874(2), 4074, 4080, 4360; Contracts 176(1); Damag 189; Em Dom 2(1.1), 277, 300; Estop 68(2); Evid 474(16), 543(3), 546; Fed Civ Proc 2182.1; Fed Cts 630.1, 712, 714, 764, 774, 776, 798, 823, 825.1, 826, 830, 842, 843, 844, 859; Health 392; Mun Corp 247, 250.

Hidden Valley Airpark Ass'n, Inc.; Etheredge v., TexApp–Fort Worth, 169 SW3d 378, review den.—App & E 5; Const Law 4011; Judgm 178, 183, 184; Motions 22; Pretrial Proc 477.1, 482.1; Proc 64, 82.

Hidden Valley Airpark Ass'n, Inc.; Lott v., TexApp–Fort Worth, 49 SW3d 604.—App & E 428(2).

Hidden Valley Civic Club v. Brown, TexApp–Houston (14 Dist), 702 SW2d 665.—Inj 138.37, 147.

Hidden Valley Civic Club; Malik v., TexCivApp–Hous (1 Dist), 601 SW2d 59, ref nre, cert den 101 SCt 1513, 450 US 980, 67 LEd2d 814.—App & E 387(3), 387(6), 395; Time 10(7).

Hidden Valley Moving and Storage, Inc.; Franyutti v., WDTex, 325 FSupp2d 775.—Antitrust 132; Carr 108; Fed Cts 241, 246; Fraud 31; Rem of C 25(1); States 18.15.

Hide-A-Way Lake Club, Inc.; Butler v., TexApp–Eastland, 730 SW2d 405, ref nre.—App & E 758.3(11); Clubs 5; Evid 268.

Hide-A-Way Lake Club, Inc.; McGonagill v., TexCivApp–Tyler, 566 SW2d 371.—App & E 863, 954(1); Inj 1, 12, 14, 16, 138.21, 147, 151.

Hide-A-Way Lake Club, Inc.; Robertson v., TexApp–Tyler, 856 SW2d 841.—App & E 5, 136, 859; Pretrial Proc 506.1.

Hideca Petroleum Corp. v. Tampimex Oil Intern., Ltd., TexApp–Houston (1 Dist), 740 SW2d 838.—Contracts 190; Corp 1.4(4), 1.5(1), 1.5(2), 1.6(3), 1.7(2); Costs 194.36; Fraud 12; Frds St of 158(2), 158(3), 158(4); Neglig 219; Princ & A 138, 146(2), 147(0.5), 190(3); Torts 242.

Hidi; Fireman's Fund County Mut. Ins. Co. v., Tex, 13 SW3d 767.—Insurance 1203, 2688; Statut 181(1), 195.

Hidi v. State and County Mut. Fire Ins. Co., TexApp–Austin, 988 SW2d 441, rev Fireman's Fund County Mut Ins Co v. Hidi, 13 SW3d 767.—Insurance 1003, 1203, 2688; Statut 176, 181(1).

Hidro Gas Juarez, S.A. v. U.S., WDTex, 790 FSupp 1302. See Central De Gas De Chihuahua, S.A. v. U.S.

Hiebert v. Weiss, TexApp–Fort Worth, 622 SW2d 150, ref nre.—Pretrial Proc 384.1.

Hieby; Moffitt v., Tex, 229 SW2d 1005, 149 Tex 161.— Food 3; Sales 89, 199, 200(1), 200(2), 387.

Hieby; Moffitt v., TexCivApp–San Antonio, 225 SW2d 441, rev 229 SW2d 1005, 149 Tex 161.—Nova 1, 4, 11; Sales 61, 87(1), 217, 218, 387.

Hielscher v. State, TexCrimApp, 511 SW2d 305.—Crim Law 784(1), 814(17).

Hierholzer; Texas Emp. Ins. Ass'n v., TexCivApp–Austin, 207 SW2d 178, ref nre.—Evid 20(1), 590; Work Comp 813, 816, 961, 984, 1041, 1410, 1611, 1639, 1937.

Hiester, Ex parte, Tex, 572 SW2d 300.—Child S 491; Const Law 4494.

Hiett v. Biondi, NDTex, 389 FSupp 1132.—Schools 13(2).

Hiett; U.S. v., CA5 (Tex), 581 F2d 1199, reh den 585 F2d 520.—Crim Law 726, 1171.7; Int Rev 5292; Witn 347.

Hiett v. U.S., CA5 (Tex), 415 F2d 664, cert den 90 SCt 941, 397 US 936, 25 LEd2d 117.—Const Law 1529, 1573; Crim Law 13.1(1); Postal 14, 27, 35(1); Statut 63.

Hi Fashion Wigs Profit Sharing Trust; Hamilton Investment Trust v., TexCivApp–Dallas, 559 SW2d 376.— Plead 111.38, 111.39(2); Venue 46.

Hi Fashion Wigs Profit Sharing Trust v. Hamilton Inv. Trust, TexCivApp–Eastland, 579 SW2d 300.—Usury 2(1).

Higbee v. Carter, TexCivApp–Beaumont, 444 SW2d 841, ref nre.—Autos 244(36.1).

Higbie v. State, TexCrimApp, 780 SW2d 228.—Autos 349(9); Crim Law 1134(3); Searches 23.

Higbie v. State, TexApp–Dallas, 723 SW2d 802, petition for discretionary review gr, aff 780 SW2d 228.—Arrest 68(4); Autos 349(9), 349.5(3); Searches 192.1.

Higbie Roth Const. Co. v. Houston Shell & Concrete, TexApp–Houston (1 Dist), 1 SW3d 808, reh overr, and petition for review den.—Antitrust 134, 138, 221, 389(1), 389(2); App & E 863, 883, 893(1), 895(2), 916(1); Judgm 181(11), 185(2); Neglig 202, 213, 215, 1692; Work Comp 2142.20.

Higdon; Anderson v., TexApp–Waco, 695 SW2d 320, ref nre.—App & E 215(1), 231(9), 232(3), 500(1), 548(5), 757(1), 760(2), 1068(4); Death 14(1); Health 702; Mun Corp 182, 747(3); Offic 116; Pretrial Proc 380; Sheriffs 105; Witn 196.4.

Higdon v. Channell, TexCivApp–El Paso, 109 SW2d 254, dism.—Brok 55(1), 86(4).

Higdon v. Shelton Motor Co., Tex, 157 SW2d 627, 138 Tex 121.—Labor & Emp 249; Plead 34(1), 34(3).

Higdon; Shelton Motor Co. v., TexCivApp–Eastland, 140 SW2d 905, rev 157 SW2d 627, 138 Tex 121.—Contracts

1, 47; Courts 80(1), 85(3); Labor & Emp 249; Plead 8(3), 34(4), 48.

Higdon v. State, TexCrimApp, 436 SW2d 541.—Crim Law 1134(3), 1134(8); Hab Corp 826(1).

Higdon v. State, TexApp–Houston (1 Dist), 764 SW2d 308, petition for discretionary review refused.—Crim Law 655(1), 698(1), 859, 868, 1166.22(2).

Higdon; Tucker v., TexCivApp–El Paso, 115 SW2d 973.— Courts 104.

Higdon; U.S. v., CA5 (Tex), 832 F2d 312, cert den 108 SCt 1051, 484 US 1075, 98 LEd2d 1013.—Crim Law 1035(7); Rob 1, 7, 24.50.

Higdon; Woodward v., TexApp–Waco, 643 SW2d 470, ref nre.—App & E 544(1), 907(3); New Tr 44(1), 56, 157.

Higganbotham's Estate, In re, TexCivApp, 192 SW2d 285.—Courts 202(5); Guard & W 15, 25, 49, 58, 137, 159, 163; Judgm 548; Jury 12(3).

Higginbotham, Ex parte, TexCrimApp, 382 SW2d 927.— Crim Law 641.12(4), 641.13(8).

Higginbotham, Ex parte, TexApp–Fort Worth, 768 SW2d 4.—Divorce 206.

Higginbotham v. Alexander Trust Estate, TexCivApp–Eastland, 129 SW2d 352, writ refused.—Ex & Ad 7.

Higginbotham v. Allwaste, Inc., TexApp–Houston (14 Dist), 889 SW2d 411, reh overr, and writ den, and reh dism.—Damag 50.10, 192; Judgm 181(21), 185(1), 185(2), 189; Labor & Emp 782.

Higginbotham; Bagley v., TexCivApp–Beaumont, 353 SW2d 868, ref nre.—Inj 16, 51.

Higginbotham v. Bagley, TexCivApp–Beaumont, 346 SW2d 142, writ dism.—Adv Poss 57; App & E 846(2), 846(5), 931(6), 1054(1); Bound 37(5); Stip 14(10).

Higginbotham v. Barnhart, CA5 (Tex), 405 F3d 332, appeal after remand 163 FedAppx 279.—Social S 145.5, 146, 147, 148.15.

Higginbotham v. Barnhart, CA5 (Tex), 163 FedAppx 279.—Social S 143.65, 143.80.

Higginbotham v. Bemis Co., Inc., TexApp–Beaumont, 722 SW2d 511.—App & E 78(4).

Higginbotham; City of El Paso v., TexApp–El Paso, 993 SW2d 819.—Judgm 181(27), 185(2); Mun Corp 747(4); Offic 114, 116, 119.

Higginbotham v. Clues, TexApp–Houston (14 Dist), 730 SW2d 129.—Inj 163(1).

Higginbotham v. Collateral Protection, Inc., TexApp–Houston (1 Dist), 859 SW2d 487, reh den, and writ den. —App & E 946, 966(1); Jury 25(6), 25(8), 26, 28(17); Pretrial Proc 713, 714.

Higginbotham v. Concho County School Trustees, TexCivApp–Austin, 220 SW2d 213, ref nre.—Admin Law 701, 725; Schools 42(2); Statut 208.

Higginbotham v. Davis, TexApp–Waco, 35 SW3d 194, review den.—Bound 1, 3(1), 40(1), 43; Judgm 181(15.1); Tresp to T T 47(1).

Higginbotham v. Davis, TexCivApp–Dallas, 221 SW2d 290.—Courts 200.7.

Higginbotham v. Fort Worth Nat. Bank, TexCivApp–Fort Worth, 172 SW2d 402, writ refused.—App & E 758.1; Home 117, 118(3).

Higginbotham v. General Life and Acc. Ins. Co., Tex, 796 SW2d 695, on remand 817 SW2d 830, writ den.— Evid 17; Insurance 3569.

Higginbotham; General Life and Acc. Ins. Co. v., TexApp–Fort Worth, 817 SW2d 830, writ den.—App & E 936(2); Damag 227; Insurance 3374, 3375; Interest 31, 39(2.35); Judgm 143(3), 145(2), 146, 151, 153(1), 160.

Higginbotham; General Life and Acc. Ins. Co. v., TexApp–Fort Worth, 750 SW2d 19, writ gr, rev 796 SW2d 695, on remand 817 SW2d 830, writ den.—Judgm 17(1), 17(9).

Higginbotham; Grimmett v., TexApp–Tyler, 907 SW2d 1, reh overr, and writ den.—Partners 1, 18, 44, 53.

Higginbotham; Housing Authority of City of Dallas v., Tex, 143 SW2d 79, 135 Tex 158, 130 ALR 1053, answer

See Guidelines for Arrangement at the beginning of this Volume

to certified question conformed to 143 SW2d 95.—Admin Law 9, 330; Const Law 2400, 2408, 2409, 2427(1), 2437, 2898; Em Dom 14, 17, 56, 67, 68, 191(3); Health 357, 358; Mun Corp 266, 407(2), 717.5(1); States 119; Statut 221; Tax 2289.

Higginbotham; Housing Authority of City of Dallas v., TexCivApp–Dallas, 143 SW2d 95.—Courts 475(8); Mun Corp 717.5(1).

Higginbotham v. International-Great Northern R. Co., TexCivApp–Amarillo, 99 SW2d 338, writ dism.—App & E 930(1); New Tr 42(2), 145; R R 327(1), 351(12.1), 352.

Higginbotham; J. Weingarten, Inc. v., TexCivApp–Beaumont, 523 SW2d 450, ref nre.—App & E 930(3), 989; Damag 63, 130.3; Judgm 253(1); Labor & Emp 2842, 2848, 2881; Work Comp 2133.

Higginbotham; Loving County v., TexCivApp–Eastland, 115 SW2d 1110, dism.—App & E 930(3), 1033(3), 1062.1; Counties 2, 50; Evid 54, 87, 94, 340(1), 372(7); Judgm 497(1), 720; Pub Lands 173(14), 173(18), 173(19); Statut 120(1), 195; Tresp to T T 35(0.5); Trial 84(3.1), 350.3(3), 366.

Higginbotham v. O'Keeffe, TexCivApp–Amarillo, 340 SW2d 350, ref nre.—App & E 758.1, 846(5), 863, 1002, 1015(5), 1060.1(1), 1060.1(5), 1064.1(9), 1140(3); Autos 244(12), 244(36.1), 244(44), 245(5); Damag 127, 215(1); Death 99(4); Evid 588; Neglig 1656, 1676; New Tr 56, 140(3), 163(2); Trial 139.1(3), 140(1), 142, 194(16).

Higginbotham v. Ritchie, TexCivApp–Fort Worth, 367 SW2d 210.—App & E 1003(11), 1177(8); Autos 159; Neglig 291, 293, 403, 421.

Higginbotham; Smith v., TexComApp, 158 SW2d 481, 138 Tex 227.—App & E 907(3), 1197; Judgm 163.

Higginbotham; Smith v., TexCivApp–Fort Worth, 112 SW2d 770.—Judgm 142, 163, 335(1).

Higginbotham; Smith v., TexCivApp–Dallas, 141 SW2d 752, aff 158 SW2d 481, 138 Tex 227.—App & E 907(3); Judgm 163, 164; Partners 219(1); Trusts 265.

Higginbotham v. State, TexCrimApp, 807 SW2d 732.—Crim Law 1162, 1169.12.

Higginbotham v. State, TexCrimApp, 497 SW2d 299.—Crim Law 273(4.1), 995(1), 1086.9; Sent & Pun 1100, 1108.

Higginbotham v. State, TexApp–Fort Worth, 919 SW2d 502, reh overr, and petition for discretionary review refused.—Burg 42(3), 42(4); Crim Law 369.2(6), 814(1), 1134(2), 1144.13(2.1), 1159.2(7).

Higginbotham v. State, TexApp–Houston (14 Dist), 769 SW2d 265, petition for discretionary review gr, and petition for discretionary review dism, rev 807 SW2d 732.—Crim Law 412.2(4), 412.2(5), 414, 641.3(4), 720(5), 1169.12, 1172.9; Homic 1210; Sent & Pun 238, 240.

Higginbotham v. State Farm Mut. Auto. Ins. Co., CA5 (Tex), 103 F3d 456, reh den.—Action 27(1); Antitrust 221, 282; Fed Cts 666; Insurance 1560, 3336, 3339, 3347, 3350, 3359, 3360, 3374; Neglig 219.

Higginbotham; Stripling v., TexCivApp–Waco, 353 SW2d 48, ref nre.—Bankr 2369.

Higginbotham; U.S. v., CA5 (Tex), 137 FedAppx 665, cert den 126 SCt 498, 546 US 968, 163 LEd2d 377.—Crim Law 1042, 1192.

Higginbotham; U.S. v., CA5 (Tex), 113 FedAppx 641, cert gr, vac 125 SCt 1749, 544 US 958, 161 LEd2d 599, on remand 137 FedAppx 665, cert den 126 SCt 498, 546 US 968, 163 LEd2d 377.—Controlled Subs 81; Crim Law 1169.11.

Higginbotham & Associates, Inc. v. Caddo Lanes, TexApp–Texarkana, 738 SW2d 45. See Higginbotham & Associates, Inc. v. Greer.

Higginbotham & Associates, Inc. v. Greer, TexApp–Texarkana, 738 SW2d 45, writ den.—Antitrust 369; Insurance 1669, 1673.

Higginbotham-Bailey-Logan Co. v. Bellah, TexCivApp–Fort Worth, 79 SW2d 907.—Attach 357.

Higginbotham-Bailey-Logan Co.; Rodriguez v., Tex, 160 SW2d 234, 138 Tex 476.—App & E 1178(1); Judgm 199(3.6), 199(3.9).

Higginbotham-Bailey-Logan Co.; Rodriguez v., TexCivApp–San Antonio, 172 SW2d 991, writ refused.—App & E 1212(3); Trial 351.2(1.1), 351.2(5).

Higginbotham-Bailey-Logan Co.; Rodriguez v., TexCivApp–San Antonio, 144SW2d 993, aff Westbrook v. Landa, 160 SW2d 232, rev 160 SW2d 234, 138 Tex 476.—App & E 854(5), 931(4); Judgm 199(3.14), 256(2); Trial 351.2(3.1), 351.2(5), 355(1).

Higginbotham-Bartlett Co.; Commercial Standard Ins. Co. v., TexCivApp–Eastland, 164 SW2d 63, writ refused.—Mech Liens 315.

Higginbotham Bartlett Co.; Dockrey v., TexCivApp–Eastland, 493 SW2d 254.—Acct Action on 10, 14; Costs 194.38.

Higginbotham-Bartlett Co. v. Powell, TexCivApp–Amarillo, 270 SW 193, writ dism woj.—Bankr 423(1); Fraud 12, 16; Home 107; Sales 43(2), 44.

Higginbotham Bros. & Co. v. Callaway, TexCivApp–Eastland, 170 SW2d 333.—App & E 989; Evid 590; Lim of Act 119(1), 197(1), 197(3).

Higginbotham Bros. & Co.; Tomlinson v., TexCivApp–Eastland, 229 SW2d 920.—Const Law 642; Mech Liens 128, 187, 262(1), 271(1); Mtg 151(3), 154(2), 186(5).

Higginbotham Enterprises, Inc. v. Clues, TexApp–Houston (14 Dist, 730 SW2d 129. See Higginbotham v. Clues.

Higgins, Ex parte, TexCrimApp, 338 SW2d 717, 170 TexCrim 21.—Extrad 34.

Higgins; Arando v., TexCivApp–El Paso, 220 SW2d 291, ref nre.—App & E 1060.1(3); Damag 163(4), 221(2.1); Trial 115(2), 311.

Higgins v. Barnhart, SDTex, 288 FSupp2d 811.—Social S 140.21, 140.25, 140.45, 140.70, 142.5, 143.45, 143.60, 148.15.

Higgins v. Dallas County Child Welfare Unit, TexCivApp–Dallas, 544 SW2d 745.—Evid 380; Infants 156, 178, 179, 209; Neglig 1612.

Higgins v. Higgins, TexCivApp–Austin, 246 SW2d 271.—Evid 265(10); Marriage 18, 51; Trial 141.

Higgins; Higgins v., TexCivApp–Austin, 246 SW2d 271.—Evid 265(10); Marriage 18, 51; Trial 141.

Higgins v. Higgins, TexCivApp–Eastland, 458 SW2d 498.—Divorce 252.1, 286(9); Evid 208(6), 265(8); Hus & W 49.2(6), 250, 251, 262.1(2), 270(9).

Higgins; Higgins v., TexCivApp–Eastland, 458 SW2d 498.—Divorce 252.1, 286(9); Evid 208(6), 265(8); Hus & W 49.2(6), 250, 251, 262.1(2), 270(9).

Higgins v. Intraworld Development Corp., TexCivApp–Hous (1 Dist), 498 SW2d 234.—Trover 44, 46, 61, 66.

Higgins v. Millsap, TexCivApp–Austin, 121 SW2d 469.—App & E 301; Home 129(1), 154, 177(2).

Higgins v. Mossler Acceptance Co., TexCivApp–Galveston, 140 SW2d 532, dism.—App & E 662(3), 1177(1); Usury 22, 59, 139, 142(4).

Higgins v. Pittsburgh-Des Moines Co., SDTex, 635 FSupp 1182.—Rem of C 30, 36, 39, 43, 107(2), 107(7).

Higgins v. Randall County Sheriff's Office, Tex, 193 SW3d 898, on remand 2006 WL 2418823.—App & E 389(1), 389(2).

Higgins v. Robertson, TexCivApp–Amarillo, 210 SW2d 250, ref nre.—App & E 562; Autos 20; Chat Mtg 83, 84, 89, 283.

Higgins v. Smith, TexApp–Houston (14 Dist), 722 SW2d 825.—Contracts 337(2); Costs 194.32, 207; Damag 194; Judgm 101(1); Plead 48.

Higgins; South Texas Development Co. v., TexCivApp–Galveston, 110 SW2d 997, writ refused.—App & E 1195(3).

Higgins v. Standard Lloyds, TexCivApp–Galveston, 149 SW2d 143, writ dism.—App & E 927(7), 989, 1175(1); Courts 169(5); Damag 113; Insurance 2733.

Higgins v. State, TexCrimApp, 515 SW2d 268.—Controlled Subs 26, 27, 68, 80; Crim Law 552(3).

Higgins v. State, TexCrimApp, 473 SW2d 493.—Crim Law 412.2(2).

Higgins v. State, TexCrimApp, 97 SW2d 700.—Crim Law 1182.

Higgins v. State, TexApp–Texarkana, 924 SW2d 739, petition for discretionary review refused.—Crim Law 412.1(1), 414, 683(1), 790, 855(1), 857(1), 957(3), 959, 961, 1036.1(2), 1043(1), 1144.15, 1153(1), 1156(1); Homic 997; Witn 37(2).

Higgins v. State, TexApp–Houston (14 Dist), 764 SW2d 311, petition for discretionary review refused.—Crim Law 147, 1144.6.

Higgins v. State, TexCivApp–Fort Worth, 591 SW2d 646.—Courts 200; Mental H 33.

Higgs; Ali v., CA5 (Tex), 892 F2d 438.—Civil R 1379; Fed Cts 616; Judgm 570(4); Lim of Act 6(7), 75.

Higgs v. Amarillo Postal Emp. Credit Union, TexCivApp–Amarillo, 358 SW2d 761.—App & E 931(1), 931(3); Fraud Conv 280; Garn 109.

Higgs v. Farmer, TexCivApp–Fort Worth, 234 SW2d 1021.—Deeds 15, 17(1), 179, 181, 182; Estop 115; Witn 159(12), 180, 181.

Higgs; Spaulding v., TexCivApp–Austin, 254 SW2d 208, ref nre.—Deeds 31, 90, 93, 105.

Higgs v. State, TexApp–Houston (14 Dist), 680 SW2d 497, rev Breazeale v. State, 683 SW2d 446, on remand 1986 WL 10860, petition for discretionary review refused.—Jury 29(6).

Higgs; Taylor v., TexApp–Eastland, 764 SW2d 935, writ den.—App & E 1035; Libel 123(3).

High v. Braniff Airways, Inc., CA5 (Tex), 592 F2d 1330.—Civil R 1599; Fed Civ Proc 2397.2, 2397.5; Fed Cts 763.1.

High; Dallas Railway & Terminal Co. v., Tex, 103 SW2d 735, 129 Tex 219.—Death 15; Neglig 575.

High; Dallas Railway & Terminal Co. v., TexCivApp–El Paso, 97 SW2d 965, rev 103 SW2d 735, 129 Tex 219.—Hus & W 260; Neglig 575; Urb R R 26.

High; Erickson v., TexCivApp–Hous (14 Dist), 517 SW2d 702, writ refused.—App & E 907(3).

High v. E-Systems Inc., CA5 (Tex), 459 F3d 573, reh and reh den 213 FedAppx 366.—Insurance 2571; Labor & Emp 403, 441, 555, 574(2), 611, 688.

High v. Glameyer, TexCivApp–Hous (14 Dist), 428 SW2d 872, ref nre.—Deeds 90, 100, 110, 112(0.5); Hus & W 48(4).

High v. Karell, TexCivApp–Fort Worth, 346 SW2d 920.—Plead 111.3; Venue 4, 5.5.

High v. State, TexCrimApp, 964 SW2d 637, on remand 998 SW2d 642, petition for discretionary review refused.—Courts 102(1); Crim Law 273.1(4), 1167(5).

High v. State, TexCrimApp, 573 SW2d 807.—Crim Law 1077.1(2), 1077.3.

High v. State, TexCrimApp, 253 SW2d 874, 158 TexCrim 148.—Crim Law 351(1), 351(3), 721(3), 1171.2; Rob 27(3).

High v. State, TexApp–Houston (1 Dist), 998 SW2d 642, petition for discretionary review refused.—Crim Law 1162, 1167(5).

High v. State, TexApp–Houston (1 Dist), 962 SW2d 53, vac 964 SW2d 637, on remand 998 SW2d 642, petition for discretionary review refused.—Crim Law 273.1(4), 273.1(5), 275, 1031(4), 1167(5).

High Crest Realty Co.; Western Management Corp. v., TexCivApp–Fort Worth, 331 SW2d 365, writ refused.—App & E 846(5); Covenants 72.1.

High Island Independent School Dist.; Matthews v., SDTex, 991 FSupp 840.—Civil R 1183, 1184, 1185, 1243, 1252, 1351(1), 1351(2), 1376(2), 1376(10), 1513, 1532, 1549; Const Law 1928; Fed Civ Proc 1772; Schools 55, 147.12; Statut 226.

Highland Capital Management, L.P. v. Ryder Scott Co., TexApp–Houston (1 Dist), 212 SW3d 522, reh overr, and review den (2 pets).—App & E 893(1), 895(1); Bankr 2154.1, 2533, 2553, 2556; Venue 2, 8.5(1), 8.5(2), 8.5(8), 33.

Highland Church of Christ v. Powell, Tex, 640 SW2d 235, on remand 644 SW2d 177, ref nre.—App & E 158(1), 158(2); Judgm 875.

Highland Church of Christ v. Powell, TexApp–Eastland, 644 SW2d 177, ref nre.—App & E 931(1), 934(1), 989; Courts 89; Judgm 199(1), 199(3.9); Tax 2355, 2369(1), 2389, 2394.

Highland Church of Christ v. Powell, TexApp–Eastland, 633 SW2d 324, writ gr, rev 640 SW2d 235, on remand 644 SW2d 177, ref nre.—Action 6.

Highland Farms Corp. v. Fidelity Trust Co. of Houston, TexComApp, 82 SW2d 627, 125 Tex 474.—Contracts 170(1); Judgm 504(1); Mand 15; New Tr 155.

Highland Farms Corp.; Fidelity Trust Co. of Houston v., TexCivApp–Galveston, 109 SW2d 1014, writ dism.—Const Law 2503(1), 3998; Courts 100(1); Judgm 237(4), 335(4), 414, 460(1), 720.

Highland Hills Apartments; Kennedy v., TexApp–Dallas, 905 SW2d 325.—Forci E & D 6(1), 16(3); Land & Ten 291(16).

Highland Hills Drive Apartments; Johnson v., Tex, 568 SW2d 661.—Land & Ten 125(1).

Highland Hills Drive Apartments; Johnson v., TexCivApp–Dallas, 552 SW2d 493, ref nre 568 SW2d 661.—Forci E & D 6(1), 6(2); Judgm 747(6); Land & Ten 125(1), 125(2).

Highland Hills, Ltd., In re, NDTex, 232 BR 868.—Bankr 2164.1, 3782.

Highland Hills, Ltd., In re, BkrtcyNDTex, 232 BR 864, aff 232 BR 868.—Bankr 2877, 3101.

Highland Ins. Co.; Wayne Duddlesten, Inc. v., TexApp–Houston (1 Dist), 110 SW3d 85, review den.—Antitrust 221; App & E 863, 931(1), 960(1), 1012.1(4); Atty & C 63; Fraud 7; Insurance 1628, 1629, 1866; Judgm 181(11); Plead 228.14; Pretrial Proc 622; Work Comp 1061, 1063, 1072.

Highland Memorial Park; Jones v., TexCivApp–San Antonio, 242 SW2d 250.—Equity 3; Nuis 3(7), 23(1), 33; Waters 107(2), 107(3).

Highland Park, Inc.; Parker v., Tex, 565 SW2d 512.—Land & Ten 167(8), 169(11); Neglig 502(1), 503, 506(8), 549(9), 1012, 1020, 1286(1), 1286(7), 1289, 1717.

Highland Park, Inc. v. Parker, TexCivApp–Eastland, 545 SW2d 275, writ gr, rev 565 SW2d 512.—App & E 293; Neglig 1037(4), 1289.

Highland Park Independent School Dist.; David Graham Hall Foundation v., TexCivApp–Dallas, 371 SW2d 762, ref nre.—Pretrial Proc 581; Tax 2290, 2299, 2341, 2342, 2394, 2588, 2859.

Highland Park Independent School Dist.; Humphrey v., NDTex, 361 FSupp 451, aff 489 F2d 1311.—Const Law 4202; Fed Civ Proc 184.5.

Highland Park Independent School Dist. v. Loring, TexCivApp–Dallas, 323 SW2d 469.—Schools 106.1.

Highland Park Independent School Dist.; Newton v., TexCivApp–Austin, 361 SW2d 916.—App & E 547(2); Evid 590; Schools 106.12(8).

Highland Park Independent School Dist.; Republic Ins. Co. v., Tex, 125 SW2d 270, 133 Tex 545.—App & E 802.

Highland Park Independent School Dist.; Republic Ins. Co. v., TexComApp, 171 SW2d 342, 141 Tex 224.—Schools 102, 103(1), 105, 106.1; Tax 2764.

Highland Park Independent School Dist. v. Republic Ins. Co., TexCivApp–Dallas, 162 SW2d 1056, rev 171 SW2d 342, 141 Tex 224.—Const Law 2560, 2621, 4138(2); Schools 102, 103(1), 106.1, 106.12(1), 106.12(7), 106.12(8), 106.12(11); Tax 2243, 2445, 2535, 2714, 2901, 3212.

Highland Park Independent School District; Republic Ins. Co. v., TexCivApp–Dallas, 123 SW2d 784, writ dism 125 SW2d 270, 133 Tex 545.—App & E 837(4), 866(3); Evid 43(2), 333(4); Schools 103(1), 106.12(7), 106.43(1); Tax 2558, 2590, 2611, 2709(2), 2853; Tender 26.

Highland Park Independent School Dist.; Stein v., TexCivApp–Texarkana, 574 SW2d 807, dism.—App & E 1201(1).

Highland Park Independent School Dist.; Stein v., TexCivApp–Texarkana, 540 SW2d 551, ref nre, appeal after remand 574 SW2d 807, dism.—Judgm 181(6); Mun Corp 736; Nuis 25(1), 29, 46; Schools 62, 89, 116.

Highland Park Independent School Dist. v. Thomas, TexCivApp–Dallas, 139 SW2d 299.—Execution 69; Ex & Ad 91, 212, 272; Tax 2738, 2924.

Highland Park Independent School Dist. of Dallas County; Republic Ins. Co. v., Tex, 102 SW2d 184, 129 Tex 55.—App & E 1095; Const Law 996; Schools 103(1); Tax 2220, 2288, 2470, 2558, 2680.

Highland Park Independent School Dist. of Dallas County v. Republic Ins. Co., TexCivApp–Dallas, 80 SW2d 1053, rev 102 SW2d 184, 129 Tex 55.—Tax 2709(2).

Highland Park Shopping Village v. Trinity Universal Ins. Co., TexApp–Dallas, 36 SW3d 916.—Insurance 2361.

Highland Park State Bank v. Continental Nat. Bank of Fort Worth, TexCivApp–Fort Worth, 300 SW2d 304, ref nre.—App & E 1170.10; Chat Mtg 47, 49(1), 150(1), 157(2), 170(1), 178(3), 219; Trial 352.10.

Highland Park State Bank; Eichman v., TexCivApp–Eastland, 345 SW2d 352, writ refused.—Chat Mtg 26, 262(1).

Highland Park State Bank v. Salazar, TexCivApp–San Antonio, 555 SW2d 484, ref nre.—App & E 80(1); Assign 31; Exemp 37; Liens 1; Work Comp 1097, 1098.

Highland Park State Bank; Scott v., TexCivApp–Fort Worth, 218 SW2d 877, ref nre.—Banks 150; Home 206; Hus & W 80.

Highland Park Subdivision Residents v. Central Educ. Agency, TexApp–Austin, 775 SW2d 500, writ den.—Schools 39.

Highland Park, Town of; Loftis v., TexApp–Eastland, 893 SW2d 154.—App & E 854(1); Const Law 3869, 3874(1), 3874(2), 4156; Contracts 170(1); Labor & Emp 40(2), 50, 835; Mun Corp 218(1).

Highland Park, Town of; Newton v., TexCivApp–Dallas, 282 SW2d 266, ref nre.—App & E 1172(1); Estop 52.15, 61, 62.4, 62.5, 62.8, 70(2), 115; Inj 89(2); Judgm 18(2), 19, 199(1); Mun Corp 601.1, 623(1), 623(4), 628; Nuis 1, 3(1), 59; Trial 351.2(4), 352.12; Zoning 273.1, 741.

Highland Resources, Inc.; Brooks v., TexCivApp–Hous (14 Dist), 440 SW2d 401, ref nre 446 SW2d 6.—App & E 758.3(11); Costs 205.

Highland Resources, Inc. v. Federal Power Commission, CA5 (Tex), 537 F2d 1336.—Gas 6; Pub Ut 149.

Highlands Cable Television, Inc. v. Wong, TexCivApp–Austin, 547 SW2d 324, ref nre.—Bills & N 534; Guar 105; New Tr 99; Princ & S 182, 190(1).

Highlands Ins. Co.; Adami v., TexCivApp–San Antonio, 512 SW2d 737.—App & E 930(3); Work Comp 1063.

Highlands Ins. Co.; Ausaf v., TexApp–Houston (1 Dist), 2 SW3d 363, review den.—Work Comp 1396, 1872, 1895, 1911.

Highlands Ins. Co. v. Baugh, TexCivApp–Eastland, 605 SW2d 314.—App & E 930(3), 989, 1079, 1140(2); Evid 222(1), 237, 590; Judgm 199(1); New Tr 161(1); Trial 356(1), 362; Work Comp 998, 1318, 1334, 1392, 1397, 1487, 1643, 1723, 1724, 1937.

Highlands Ins. Co.; Blankenship v., TexCivApp–Dallas, 594 SW2d 147, ref nre.—Statut 195, 219(9.1); Work Comp 408, 495, 496, 501, 502, 918.

Highlands Ins. Co.; Bogard v., TexCivApp–El Paso, 601 SW2d 957.—Work Comp 306, 316.

Highlands Ins. Co.; Castro v., TexCivApp–Corpus Christi, 401 SW2d 689.—App & E 1160.

Highlands Ins. Co. v. City of Galveston By and Through Its Bd. of Trustees of Galveston Wharves, TexApp–Houston (14 Dist), 721 SW2d 469, ref nre.—Insurance 1009, 1010, 1822, 1836, 2090, 2125, 2133, 2137(1), 2260, 2277, 2349.

Highlands Ins. Co. v. Clements, TexApp–Corpus Christi, 422 SW2d 218, ref nre.—Work Comp 1497.

Highlands Ins. Co.; Criton Corp. v., TexApp–Houston (14 Dist), 809 SW2d 355, writ den.—App & E 994(3), 1008.1(2), 1012.1(2), 1012.1(4); Contracts 322(4); Costs 194.32; Interest 39(3); Plead 4.

Highlands Ins. Co. v. Currey, TexApp–Houston (14 Dist), 773 SW2d 750, writ den.—Judgm 181(21), 185(1), 185.3(13), 186; Work Comp 1167, 1946, 1949.

Highlands Ins. Co. v. Daniel, TexApp–Tyler, 410 SW2d 491, ref nre.—States 18.49; Work Comp 996, 1042, 1097, 1637, 1926, 1929.

Highlands Ins. Co.; Hatton v., TexApp–Tyler, 631 SW2d 787.—New Tr 143(2), 157; Work Comp 1727, 1797.

Highlands Ins. Co.; Hill v., TexApp–Hous (1 Dist), 433 SW2d 247, ref nre.—App & E 934(1); Judgm 178, 181(2), 185(2), 185.3(13); Work Comp 598, 600, 1536.

Highlands Ins. Co.; Hopkins v., TexApp–Houston, 838 SW2d 819, reh overr.—Antitrust 221; App & E 223, 242(1); Contracts 168; Insurance 1865, 1867, 1938, 3423; Judgm 181(6), 181(11), 181(23), 181(33), 185(2); Labor & Emp 911; Torts 212, 220.

Highlands Ins. Co.; Houston Petroleum Co. v., TexApp–Houston (1 Dist), 830 SW2d 153, writ den.—Insurance 1808, 1822, 1835(2), 2277, 2307, 2315, 2914, 2915.

Highlands Ins. Co.; Kelley-Coppedge, Inc. v., Tex, 980 SW2d 462, reh overr.—App & E 179(1); Insurance 1808, 1810, 2278(17).

Highlands Ins. Co. v. Kelley-Coppedge, Inc., TexApp–Fort Worth, 950 SW2d 415, reh overr, and review gr, rev 980 SW2d 462, reh overr.—App & E 845(2), 863; Insurance 2278(17).

Highlands Ins. Co. v. Lumbermen's Mut. Cas. Co., TexApp–Austin, 794 SW2d 600.—Parties 42.

Highlands Ins. Co.; Martinez v., Tex, 644 SW2d 442.—Interest 39(2.20).

Highlands Ins. Co. v. Martinez, TexApp–Houston (1 Dist), 638 SW2d 507, ref nre 644 SW2d 442.—Work Comp 1001, 1041.

Highlands Ins. Co. v. National Union Fire Ins. Co. of Pittsburgh, CA5 (Tex), 27 F3d 1027, reh den, cert den 115 SCt 903, 513 US 1112, 130 LEd2d 786.—Costs 194.16; Fed Cts 621, 630.1, 631; Fraud 7, 59(1); Insurance 3508.

Highlands Ins. Co. v. New England Ins. Co., TexApp–San Antonio, 811 SW2d 276.—Insurance 3517; Judgm 185.2(4).

Highlands Ins. Co. v. New England Ins. Co., TexApp–San Antonio, 811 SW2d 272.—Insurance 3512, 3513(4), 3517, 3522.

Highlands Ins. Co.; Weaver v., TexApp–Houston (1 Dist), 4 SW3d 826.—App & E 863; Contracts 143(2), 147(2), 176(2), 190; Judgm 181(19).

Highlands Ins. Co. v. Youngblood, TexApp–Beaumont, 820 SW2d 242, writ den.—App & E 930(3), 989, 999(1), 1001(1); Work Comp 726.

Highlands Management Co., Inc. v. First Interstate Bank of Texas, N.A., TexApp–Houston (14 Dist), 956 SW2d 749, review den.—App & E 93, 242(2), 500(1); Covenants 49, 52, 134; Estop 85; Evid 448, 450(3).

Highlands of McKamy IV and V Community Ass'n v. Housing Authority of City of Dallas, CA5 (Tex), 129 F3d 831. See Walker v. City of Mesquite, Tex.

Highlands State Bank; Gentry v., TexApp–Houston (14 Dist), 633 SW2d 590, writ refused.—Judgm 181(22), 185.2(3), 185.2(9); Sec Tran 240.

Highlands State Bank v. Gonzales, TexCivApp–Waco, 340 SW2d 828.—Garn 32.

Highlands Underwriters Ins. Co.; Camarillo v., TexApp–Beaumont, 625 SW2d 11.—Const Law 245(4), 1020, 3057, 3603; Work Comp 803, 1239, 1257, 1287.

Highlands Underwriters Ins. Co. v. Carabajal, TexCivApp–Corpus Christi, 503 SW2d 336.—App & E 1140(4); Trial 306; Work Comp 975, 976, 998, 1362, 1418, 1653, 1945.

Highlands Underwriters Ins. Co. v. Harris, TexCivApp–Tyler, 530 SW2d 350, ref nre.—Work Comp 872, 876.

Highlands Underwriters Ins. Co. v. McGrath, TexCivApp–El Paso, 485 SW2d 593.—Evid 268; Work Comp 697, 1363, 1390.

Highlands Underwriters Ins. Co. v. Martin, TexCivApp–Beaumont, 442 SW2d 770.—App & E 1165; Trial 68(1); Work Comp 1968(1), 1974.

Highlands Underwriters Ins. Co. v. Martinez, TexCivApp–Waco, 441 SW2d 666, ref nre.—Work Comp 208, 1707.

Highlands Underwriters Ins. Co.; Vaughn v., TexCivApp–Hous (1 Dist), 445 SW2d 234, ref nre.—Judgm 181(21); Work Comp 617, 661, 719, 723.

Highlands Underwriters Ins. Co.; Winters v., TexApp–Houston (14 Dist), 693 SW2d 729.—Work Comp 1729.

Highland Underwriters Ins. Co. v. Helm, TexCivApp–Eastland, 449 SW2d 548.—Evid 380; Trial 83(1); Work Comp 1491, 1937.

Highland Village, Texas, City of; Myers v., EDTex, 269 FSupp2d 850.—Civil R 1351(1), 1351(5), 1376(2), 1376(10), 1407; Const Law 963, 1182, 1928, 1929, 1934, 1955; Fed Civ Proc 2497.1; Mun Corp 185(1).

Highland Village, Texas, City of; Myers v., EDTex, 212 FRD 324.—Fed Civ Proc 1600(3); Witn 198(1), 201(1), 201(2), 219(1), 219(3), 222.

Highlite Broadcasting Co.; Sargent v., TexCivApp–Austin, 466 SW2d 866.—App & E 750(7); Contracts 236, 303(4); Corp 1.4(1); Judgm 185.3(18); Sales 1(3), 89.

High Plains Distributor v. Texas Liquor Control Bd., TexCivApp–Amarillo, 318 SW2d 681.—Evid 265(10); Int Liq 108.5, 108.10(8); Stip 16.

High Plains Natural Gas Co.; City of Perryton v., TexCivApp–Fort Worth, 413 SW2d 740.—Venue 7.5(1), 7.5(3).

High Plains Natural Gas Co. v. City of Perryton, TexCivApp–Amarillo, 434 SW2d 203.—Plead 111.40; Venue 15.

High Plains Natural Gas Co.; Railroad Commission of Texas v., Tex, 628 SW2d 753.—Gas 14.4(8).

High Plains Natural Gas Co.; Railroad Commission of Texas v., TexCivApp–Austin, 613 SW2d 46, ref nre 628 SW2d 753.—Gas 14.4(8); Pub Ut 128.

High Plains Natural Gas Co. v. Railroad Commission of Tex., TexCivApp–Austin, 467 SW2d 532, ref nre.—Admin Law 793; Gas 14.1(3), 14.4(12), 14.5(8); Pub Ut 194; Statut 211, 226.

High Plains Underground Water Conservation Dist. No. 1; Bryson v., Tex, 297 SW2d 117, 156 Tex 405.—Courts 247(1), 247(8).

High Plains Underground Water Conservation Dist. No. 1; Lewis Cox & Son,Inc. v., TexCivApp–Amarillo, 538 SW2d 659, ref nre.—Counties 216; Estop 62.2(1), 62.3, 62.4; Lim of Act 11(1), 11(2), 11(3); Waters 224, 256.

High Plains Underground Water Conservation Dist. No. 1; South Plains Lamesa Railroad, Ltd. v., TexApp–Amarillo, 52 SW3d 770.—App & E 1175(1); Const Law 2340; Costs 194.40; Judgm 181(6), 183, 185(2); Statut 212.1, 212.7; Waters 5, 101, 183.5.

High Plains Underground Water Conservation Dist. No. 1; Sun Oil Co. v., TexCivApp–Amarillo, 426 SW2d 347.—App & E 78(2); Plead 45, 111.39(4); Venue 15.

High Plains Wire Line Services, Inc. v. Hysell Wire Line Service, Inc., TexApp–Amarillo, 802 SW2d 406.—

App & E 179(1), 931(4), 989, 1010.1(3), 1012.1(5); Costs 194.32; Damag 113, 116, 137, 188(1), 191; Trover 40(4), 40(6), 43.1, 66, 72.

Highpoint of Montgomery Corp. v. Vail, TexApp–Houston (1 Dist), 638 SW2d 624, ref nre.—Bills & N 129(1), 129(2); Contracts 227; Evid 177, 181.

Highpoint Village Apartments; Cattin v., TexApp–Fort Worth, 26 SW3d 737, review dism woj.—Forci E & D 6(1), 16(3), 43(0.5), 43(1), 43(7); Land & Ten 291(18).

Highrabedian; Tillerson v., TexApp–Hous (14 Dist), 503 SW2d 398, ref nre.—Insurance 1701, 1704, 1790(1), 1790(7), 3445.

Highrise, Inc.; Edmunds v., TexApp–Houston (1 Dist), 715 SW2d 377, writ refused.—Const Law 3603; Work Comp 19, 2084.

Highsmith; Emeritus Corp. v., TexApp–San Antonio, 211 SW3d 321, reh overr, and review den, and reh of petition for review den.—Asylums 40; Health 800, 804, 809.

Highsmith v. Southwestern Medical Foundation, NDTex, 116 FSupp 958.—Em Dom 322.

Highsmith v. Tyler State Bank & Trust Co., TexCivApp–Texarkana, 194 SW2d 142, writ refused.—App & E 414, 846(2), 846(5), 1008.2; Jury 25(2), 28(3); Wills 300, 400; Witn 173.

High Standard, Inc.; Anderegg v., CA5 (Tex), 825 F2d 77, reh den 830 F2d 1126, cert den 108 SCt 1046, 484 US 1073, 98 LEd2d 1009.—Compromise 5(3); Fed Cts 617, 917; Stip 7.

Hight, Ex parte, TexCrimApp, 132 SW2d 262, 137 TexCrim 462.—Hab Corp 817.1.

Hight v. Dublin Veterinary Clinic, TexApp–Eastland, 22 SW3d 614, reh overr, and petition for discretionary review den.—Action 27(1); Antitrust 161; App & E 863, 934(1), 946; Evid 78, 89, 508, 536, 545, 546, 555.2; Health 710, 818; Judgm 183, 185(5), 185.1(4), 185.3(21); Torts 109, 114.

Hight v. Jim Bass Ford, Inc., TexCivApp–Austin, 552 SW2d 490, writ gr, and writ withdrawn, and ref nre.—Cons Cred 3.1, 16, 17, 56; Statut 241(1).

Hight v. State, Tex, 483 SW2d 256.—Infants 68.8.

Hight; State v., TexCrimApp, 907 SW2d 845.—Crim Law 905.

Hight; State v., TexApp–Houston (14 Dist), 879 SW2d 111, reh den, and petition for discretionary review gr, rev 907 SW2d 845.—Crim Law 905, 954(1).

Hight v. State, TexCivApp–Hous (1 Dist), 473 SW2d 348, ref nre, ref nre 483 SW2d 256, appeal dism 93 SCt 702, 409 US 1071, 34 LEd2d 660.—Crim Law 1131(4); Infants 68.8, 152.

Hightower, Ex parte, TexApp–Dallas, 877 SW2d 17, reh den, and writ dism woj.—Child S 444, 603; Const Law 1106; Contempt 30, 66(7), 68; Hab Corp 203, 493(1), 528.1, 705.1, 711; Infants 114; Mand 172.

Hightower; American General Ins. Co. v., TexCivApp–Eastland, 279 SW2d 397, ref nre.—Trial 260(5), 352.5(8); Work Comp 1374, 1385, 1615.

Hightower; American General Ins. Co. v., TexCivApp–Eastland, 264 SW2d 481, ref nre.—Work Comp 997, 1377, 1460, 1619.

Hightower; Big D Auto Auction, Inc. v., TexCivApp–Eastland, 368 SW2d 881.—Auctions 11; Bailm 30, 31(1), 31(3).

Hightower v. City of Tyler, TexCivApp–El Paso, 134 SW2d 404, writ refused.—Em Dom 280.

Hightower v. C.I.R., CA5 (Tex), 187 F2d 535.—Int Rev 4743.1.

Hightower; Employers Mut. Liability Ins. Co. of Wis. v., TexCivApp–Houston, 366 SW2d 701.—Work Comp 1653.

Hightower; Federal Underwriters Exchange v., TexCivApp–Fort Worth, 161 SW2d 338, writ refused.—Work Comp 1414, 1526, 1974.

Hightower; Federal Underwriters Exchange v., TexCiv-App–Fort Worth, 142 SW2d 963, writ dism, correct.—Damag 221(3), 221(5.1), 221(6); Trial 350.1; Work Comp 517, 547, 548, 550, 1025, 1028, 1927, 1929, 1930, 1932, 1965.

Hightower; Fletcher v., CA5 (Tex), 381 F2d 371.—Fed Civ Proc 1832.

Hightower; Helle v., TexApp–Austin, 735 SW2d 650, writ den.—Admin Law 390.1; Agric 9.3; Statut 190.

Hightower; Hicks v., TexCivApp–Beaumont, 122 SW2d 289.—App & E 544(1), 719(2), 758.3(4); Schools 97(4).

Hightower; Hudson v., TexCivApp–Austin, 394 SW2d 46, ref nre.—App & E 1048(7); Autos 243(4); Witn 398(1), 405(2).

Hightower v. Kellam, TexCivApp–San Antonio, 118 SW2d 657.—App & E 66, 78(3), 792.

Hightower v. Kidde-Fenwal, Inc., CA5 (Tex), 159 FedAppx 555.—Torts 242.

Hightower v. McFarland, CA5 (Tex), 355 F2d 468.—Fed Cts 225.

Hightower; Manzell v., TexCivApp–Texarkana, 159 SW2d 552.—Frds St of 129(1), 144; Lim of Act 13.

Hightower v. Members Mut. Ins. Co., TexCivApp–Waco, 494 SW2d 285.—Insurance 2813; Neglig 1713; Plead 111.16, 111.42(8).

Hightower v. Nocedal, TexCivApp–Hous (14 Dist), 429 SW2d 657.—Child C 26, 554, 555, 921(4).

Hightower; O'Con v., TexCivApp–San Antonio, 268 SW2d 321, writ refused.—App & E 548(2); Contracts 273; Sales 127.

Hightower v. Saxton, TexApp–Waco, 54 SW3d 380, reh overr.—Health 804, 805, 823(12); Judgm 185.1(4), 185.3(21), 186.

Hightower; Siglar v., CA5 (Tex), 112 F3d 191.—Civil R 1090, 1463; Fed Civ Proc 2734; Fed Cts 818; Prisons 13(4); Sent & Pun 1548.

Hightower; Smith v., CA5 (Tex), 693 F2d 359.—Civil R 1415; Const Law 2097; Courts 508(1), 508(7); Fed Cts 850.1, 855.1, 870.1; Gr Jury 1.

Hightower v. State, TexCrimApp, 822 SW2d 48.—Crim Law 641.12(2), 662.65, 1170.5(1); Witn 228.

Hightower v. State, TexCrimApp, 629 SW2d 920.—Crim Law 412.1(4), 599, 603.2, 629.5(3), 720(2), 720(6), 722.5, 723(3), 726, 1036.2, 1043(2), 1148; Marriage 13, 50(1), 51; Rob 11, 17(3), 17(5), 24.15(1).

Hightower v. State, TexCrimApp, 476 SW2d 327.—Crim Law 1036.1(6); Ind & Inf 180.

Hightower v. State, TexCrimApp, 389 SW2d 674.—Autos 355(2); Crim Law 561(1).

Hightower v. State, TexApp–Eastland, 736 SW2d 949, petition for discretionary review gr, aff 822 SW2d 48.—Crim Law 415(1), 662.1, 662.3, 667(1), 671; Searches 114; Witn 228.

Hightower v. State, TexCivApp–Dallas, 156 SW2d 327, writ refused.—Evid 5(2); Gaming 58.

Hightower v. State Com'r of Educ., TexApp–Austin, 778 SW2d 595.—Schools 47, 147.2(1).

Hightower v. Texas Hosp. Ass'n, CA5 (Tex), 73 F3d 43.—Fed Cts 744.

Hightower v. Texas Hosp. Ass'n, CA5 (Tex), 65 F3d 443, reh den 73 F3d 43.—Fed Civ Proc 2470, 2535, 2546; Fed Cts 205, 766, 776, 802; Labor & Emp 403, 416, 417; Statut 174, 188, 205, 217.2.

Hightower; Uvalde Rock Asphalt Co. v., TexComApp, 166 SW2d 681, 140 Tex 200, 143 ALR 1366.—Courts 93(1); Home 118(3).

Hightower; Uvalde Rock Asphalt Co. v., TexComApp, 144 SW2d 533, 135 Tex 410.—Courts 247(5).

Hightower; Uvalde Rock Asphalt Co. v., TexCivApp–Beaumont, 154 SW2d 940, rev 166 SW2d 681, 140 Tex 200, 143 ALR 1366.—Can of Inst 46; Home 117, 146; Lim of Act 146(3); Mun Corp 373(7).

Hightower Oil & Refining Co. v. Castor, TexCivApp–Austin, 177 SW2d 311.—App & E 232(2), 275; Bills & N 48.1, 241, 518(1); Mines 62.1, 74(5), 74(10); Plead 406(5).

Hightower Oil & Refining Corp.; Collier v., TexCivApp–Eastland, 225 SW2d 462.—App & E 1169(6); Mines 109.

Hightower Oil & Refining Corp. v. Heyser, TexCivApp–Austin, 135 SW2d 202.—Lim of Act 180(2), 180(3).

Hightower Petroleum Corp. v. Story, TexCivApp–Fort Worth, 236 SW2d 679, writ refused.—App & E 263(1), 544(1); Corp 661(2).

Hightower, State ex rel., v. Smith, Tex, 671 SW2d 32. See State ex rel. Hightower v. Smith.

High Voltage Engineering Corp. v. Potentials, Inc., WDTex, 398 FSupp 18, aff 519 F2d 1375.—Pat 177, 255.

Highwarden v. State, TexApp–Houston (14 Dist), 846 SW2d 479, petition for discretionary review gr, review dism as improvidently gr 871 SW2d 726.—Arrest 63.4(3); Autos 349(3), 349(6); Const Law 617; Crim Law 394.5(4), 1134(10).

Highway Cas. Co. v. Reid, TexCivApp–Fort Worth, 311 SW2d 484, ref nre.—Work Comp 307, 1393, 1459, 1966.

Highway Contractors, Inc. v. West Texas Equipment Co., Inc., TexCivApp–Amarillo, 617 SW2d 791.—Estop 68(2); Judgm 181(6), 183, 185.1(4), 186; Lim of Act 58(6); Plead 76; Tax 3704.

Highway Contractors, Inc. v. West Texas Equipment Co., Inc., TexCivApp–Amarillo, 584 SW2d 382, appeal after remand 617 SW2d 791.—App & E 79(1), 80(1), 80(3); Judgm 217, 233.

Highway Dept.; Moorlane Co. v., TexCivApp–Amarillo, 384 SW2d 415, ref nre.—Em Dom 2(6).

Highway Ins. Underwriters; Baker v., TexCivApp–El Paso, 209 SW2d 979, ref nre.—App & E 758.1; Insurance 1980(1); Witn 323; Work Comp 1065, 1072, 1360, 1831, 1920, 1924, 1958, 1968(8).

Highway Insurance Underwriters; Board of Ins. Com'rs v., TexCivApp–Austin, 169 SW2d 541.—Insurance 1049, 1206(2); Judgm 627; Stip 14(1).

Highway Ins. Underwriters v. Coleman, TexCivApp–Beaumont, 239 SW2d 131, ref nre.—Work Comp 1532, 1653, 1926, 1958, 1968(5).

Highway Ins. Underwriters v. Dempsey, TexCivApp–Amarillo, 232 SW2d 117, ref nre.—Evid 558(7); Trial 125(1); Witn 372(1); Work Comp 1926, 1968(5).

Highway Ins. Underwriters v. Griffith, TexCivApp–Austin, 290 SW2d 950, ref nre.—Garn 164, 173; Insurance 3120, 3191(12), 3200; Pretrial Proc 387; Trial 178.

Highway Ins. Underwriters v. J. H. Robinson Truck Lines, TexCivApp–Galveston, 272 SW2d 904, ref nre.—Insurance 2888, 3120, 3503(1).

Highway Ins. Underwriters; Jones v., TexCivApp–Galveston, 253 SW2d 1018, ref nre.—Insurance 3336, 3350, 3381(5); Neglig 231.

Highway Ins. Underwriters; Le Beau v., Tex, 187 SW2d 73, 143 Tex 589.—Trial 350.3(8), 352.18, 356(3); Work Comp 197, 1919, 1926.

Highway Ins. Underwriters v. Le Beau, TexCivApp–Fort Worth, 184 SW2d 671, rev 187 SW2d 73, 143 Tex 589.—App & E 662(3), 1050.1(1); Evid 474(3), 477(2), 501(2); Trial 125(1), 125(4), 129, 356(1); Work Comp 197, 516, 1330, 1334, 1340, 1385, 1396, 1733, 1919, 1927, 1962.

Highway Ins. Underwriters v. Lufkin-Beaumont Motor Coaches, TexCivApp–Beaumont, 215 SW2d 904, ref nre.—App & E 989, 1060.1(1); Atty & C 109; Evid 77(3); Insurance 2928, 2934(1), 3347, 3350, 3370, 3379, 3381(3), 3382; Princ & A 73, 79(1); Trial 142, 260(1), 352.1(4).

Highway Ins. Underwriters v. Matthews, TexCivApp–Galveston, 246 SW2d 214, ref nre.—Evid 553(1); Work Comp 51, 1385, 1404, 1615, 1638, 1644, 1924, 1927.

Highway Ins. Underwriters; Pattison v., TexCivApp–Galveston, 292 SW2d 694, ref nre.—App & E 761, 766;

HILD

Judgm 178, 181(1), 181(2), 185(1), 185(2), 185.3(2); Parties 78, 82.

Highway Ins. Underwriters; Pattison v., TexCivApp–Galveston, 278 SW2d 207, ref nre.—Abate & R 28; Action 50(10); App & E 173(1), 916(1), 1050.1(7), 1060.6, 1064.1(7); Can of Inst 35(1), 37(4), 37(6); Hus & W 265; Insurance 3354, 3367, 3389, 3549(3); Release 4; Trial 127, 140(1), 233(2); Witn 372(2); Work Comp 2234.

Highway Ins. Underwriters v. Phillips, TexCivApp–Texarkana, 234 SW2d 278.—Work Comp 1924, 1926, 1968(5).

Highway Ins. Underwriters; Pritchett v., Tex, 309 SW2d 46, 158 Tex 116.—App & E 544(1); Autos 20; Trial 219, 350.4(3).

Highway Ins. Underwriters; Pritchett v., TexCivApp–Texarkana, 304 SW2d 585, aff in part, rev in part 309 SW2d 46, 158 Tex 116.—App & E 232(0.5); Trial 352.16.

Highway Ins. Underwriters v. Pyeatt, TexCivApp–Fort Worth, 234 SW2d 457, mandamus overr.—Assoc 20(1); Corp 503(1); Insurance 3559; Joint-St Co 19; Venue 7.5(3).

Highway Ins. Underwriters; Railroad Commission v., TexCivApp–Austin, 124 SW2d 413.—Admin Law 305; Const Law 2620; Insurance 1126, 1137.

Highway Ins. Underwriters v. Reed, TexCivApp–Austin, 221 SW2d 925.—Insurance 1211(3), 3559, 3567.

Highway Ins. Underwriters v. Roberts, TexCivApp–Fort Worth, 224 SW2d 903, ref nre.—App & E 989, 1002, 1003(5); New Tr 163(2); Work Comp 1489, 1932, 1939.1, 1968(5).

Highway Ins. Underwriters v. Smyrl, TexCivApp–Austin, 267 SW2d 265, ref nre.—Work Comp 1283, 1683, 1726, 1930.

Highway Ins. Underwriters v. Spradlin, TexCivApp–Eastland, 190 SW2d 181, writ refused wom.—Trial 121(2); Witn 379(7); Work Comp 1385, 1389, 1926, 1927, 1929, 1937.

Highway Ins. Underwriters v. Stephens, TexCivApp–Eastland, 208 SW2d 677, ref nre.—App & E 1062.5; Damag 221(5.1); Work Comp 1630.

Highway Motor Freight Lines; Harper v., TexCivApp–Dallas, 89 SW2d 448, writ dism.—Autos 242(5), 242(6), 243(2), 244(26), 245(17), 245(36); Evid 53, 87, 121(1), 123(11), 355(1); Trial 127; Witn 255(2.1).

Highway Motor Freight Lines v. Slaughter, TexCivApp–Dallas, 84 SW2d 533.—App & E 854(2), 1051(1); Corp 503(2); Evid 121(6); Plead 111.37, 111.40, 111.41; Venue 22(7), 72.

Highway Safety Devices, Inc.; Amerace Esna Corp. v., NDTex, 330 FSupp 313.—Pat 36.1(3), 36.1(5), 36.2(9), 97, 112.1, 237, 238, 239, 240, 312(1.1), 312(1.2), 312(6).

Highway Transp. Co. v. Southwestern Greyhound Lines, TexCivApp–Austin, 124 SW2d 433, writ refused.—Admin Law 452.1, 470, 744.1; App & E 1152; Const Law 4363; Costs 238(2).

Highway Trucking Co.; Cormier v., TexCivApp–San Antonio, 312 SW2d 406.—Action 53(2); Judgm 597.

Higle; City of San Antonio v., TexApp–San Antonio, 685 SW2d 682, ref nre.—App & E 1052(8), 1053(1), 1053(3), 1170.1; Damag 187, 221(5.1); Evid 245; Judgm 199(3.10), 199(3.15); Mun Corp 742(5), 742(6), 747(3); Neglig 1698; Trial 261, 350.3(5); Witn 389.

Higle v. Craig, TexCivApp–Waco, 296 SW2d 948.—App & E 1010.1(3); Autos 244(11), 244(43).

Higley, Matter of Marriage of, TexCivApp–Amarillo, 575 SW2d 432.—App & E 966(1); Divorce 145, 252.3(1), 256, 258, 286(5); Hus & W 257; Judgm 855(1); Pretrial Proc 713.

Higley; Westwood Development Co. v., CA5 (Tex), 266 F2d 555.—Rem of C 21, 24.

Higman Marine Services, Inc. v. BP Amoco Chemical Co., SDTex, 114 FSupp2d 593.—Alt Disp Res 112, 113, 134(1), 134(5), 139, 143, 191, 200, 203, 210; Contracts 143.5, 206; Fed Cts 403; States 18.15.

Higman Towing Co. v. Dredge Tom James, EDTex, 637 FSupp 925.—Collision 75(1), 75(9), 75(11), 77; Nav Wat 16, 19; Ship 11.

Hignett v. State, TexCrimApp, 341 SW2d 166, 170 TexCrim 342.—Crim Law 535(2), 703, 741(3), 784(1), 1180; Homic 1154, 1155; Witn 372(2).

Hignett v. State, TexCrimApp, 328 SW2d 300, 168 TexCrim 380.—Crim Law 706(7), 1171.8(1).

Hignite v. State, TexCrimApp, 522 SW2d 210.—Crim Law 112(1), 564(1), 564(2).

Hijar; SCI Texas Funeral Services, Inc. v., TexApp–El Paso, 214 SW3d 148, reh overr.—Action 3, 13; Antitrust 290; App & E 874(1), 913; Contracts 103, 138(1), 326; Courts 4; Impl & C C 3, 55, 61; Parties 35.13.

Hilal, In re, CA5 (Tex), 226 FedAppx 381.—Bankr 3776.5(5), 3781.

Hilal v. Gatpandan, TexApp–Corpus Christi, 71 SW3d 403, reh overr.—App & E 5, 846(5), 859; Compromise 5(3), 20(1); Judgm 109, 335(3); Trial 6(1).

Hilatex, Inc. v. State, TexCivApp–Houston, 401 SW2d 269, ref nre.—App & E 1170.11; Judgm 28; Motions 53, 62; New Tr 155, 165.

Hilbig; Chambers v., CA5 (Tex), 63 F3d 358. See Moore v. Morales.

Hilbig, State ex rel., v. McDonald, TexApp–San Antonio, 877 SW2d 469. See State ex rel. Hilbig v. McDonald.

Hilbig, State ex rel., v. McDonald, TexApp–San Antonio, 839 SW2d 854. See State ex rel. Hilbig v. McDonald.

Hilbish v. State, TexCrimApp, 485 SW2d 554.—Bail 42; Ind & Inf 2(4); Jury 31.3(1); Sent & Pun 2004, 2021.

Hilb, Rogal & Hamilton Co. of Texas v. Wurzman, TexApp–Dallas, 861 SW2d 30, reh overr.—App & E 71(3), 170(1), 946, 954(1); Com Law 11; Inj 16, 17, 138.3, 138.6, 138.18, 138.33, 138.39, 140, 190, 195, 197.

Hilbun; Intratex Gas Co. v., TexCivApp–Hous (1 Dist), 485 SW2d 364.—App & E 544(1); Em Dom 201, 222(2), 223, 224, 262(5).

Hilburn v. Blount, TexCivApp–Amarillo, 206 SW2d 878.—Child C 400, 555, 920, 921(1); Hab Corp 532(1), 731, 841, 844.

Hilburn v. Brazos Elec. Power Co-op., Inc., TexApp–Eastland, 683 SW2d 58, ref nre.—Em Dom 235.

Hilburn v. Butz, CA5 (Tex), 463 F2d 1207, cert den 93 SCt 1359, 410 US 942, 35 LEd2d 608.—Agric 3.1.

Hilburn; Hallberg v., CA5 (Tex), 434 F2d 90.—Autos 187(5); Fed Cts 848.

Hilburn v. Herrin Transp. Co., TexCivApp–Dallas, 197 SW2d 149.—Autos 78; Contracts 168.

Hilburn v. Jennings, Tex, 698 SW2d 99.—Wills 230.

Hilburn; Jennings v., TexApp–Dallas, 690 SW2d 298, rev 698 SW2d 99.—Const Law 3975; Courts 42(4), 202(1); Wills 270.

Hilburn v. State, TexCrimApp, 269 SW2d 379.—Crim Law 1090.1(1).

Hilburn v. State, TexApp–Fort Worth, 946 SW2d 885.—Crim Law 1023(3).

Hilburn; Wells v., TexComApp, 98 SW2d 177, 129 Tex 11.—Life Est 8; Mtg 6, 33(5), 39, 608.5.

Hilco Elec. Co-op.; Double Diamond, Inc. v., TexApp–Waco, 195 SW3d 336, review den.—Electricity 11.4.

Hilco Elec. Co-op., Inc.; Double Diamond, Inc. v., TexApp–Waco, 127 SW3d 260, on subsequent appeal 195 SW3d 336, review den.—Acct Action on 14; App & E 80(6), 856(1); Contracts 27, 29, 238(2), 242; Electricity 8.1(3); Frds St of 49; Impl & C C 30, 60.1; Judgm 181(19).

Hilco Elec. Co-op., Inc. v. Midlothian Butane Gas Co., Inc., Tex, 111 SW3d 75.—Electricity 2.1; Statut 194.

Hilco Elec. Co-op., Inc.; Midlothian Butane Gas Co., Inc. v., TexApp–Waco, 43 SW3d 677, review gr, aff but criticized 111 SW3d 75.—Electricity 2.1.

Hild v. State, TexCrimApp, 94 SW2d 733, 130 TexCrim 362.—Brib 6(4).

Hild; Valley Municipal Utility Dist. No. 2 v., TexCivApp–Hous (1 Dist), 578 SW2d 827.—Plead 111.45, 111.47; Venue 77.

Hildebrand v. Honeywell, Inc., CA5 (Tex), 622 F2d 179.—Fed Civ Proc 839.1, 1721, 1788.6, 1837.1, 1838; Fed Cts 32.

Hildebrand; Hurr v., TexCivApp–Houston, 388 SW2d 284, ref nre.—Adv Poss 57, 109; Bound 25, 33, 37(1); Des & Dist 75.

Hildebrandt Engineering Co.; Swonke v., TexCivApp–Waco, 389 SW2d 355, ref nre.—Autos 244(45); R R 245, 327(1), 327(7).

Hilderbrand v. Lumbroff, TexCivApp–Dallas, 140 SW2d 317, writ refused.—Hus & W 262.1(8).

Hildreth v. State, TexCrimApp, 83 SW2d 332, 128 TexCrim 601.—Crim Law 722.4, 730(16); Homic 968, 988(1), 990, 1002.

Hildyard v. Fannel Studio, Inc., TexCivApp–Corpus Christi, 547 SW2d 332, ref nre.—App & E 624, 629; Judgm 185(2), 186, 335(1), 335(2), 335(3).

Hileman v. City of Dallas, Tex., CA5 (Tex), 115 F3d 352.—Civil R 1218(3).

Hilgenberg v. Elam, Tex, 198 SW2d 94, 145 Tex 437.—Autos 193(5); Labor & Emp 26, 3029, 3038(1), 3105(5).

Hilgenberg v. Elam, TexCivApp–Eastland, 192 SW2d 799, aff 198 SW2d 94, 145 Tex 437.—Autos 193(5), 194(1), 244(29); Labor & Emp 29.

Hi-Line Elec. Co. v. Dowco Elec. Products, CA5 (Tex), 765 F2d 1359.—Contracts 137(3), 137(4); Labor & Emp 909; Torts 212, 214, 242.

Hi-Line Elec. Co. v. Travelers Ins. Companies, Tex, 593 SW2d 953.—Courts 107.

Hi-Line Elec. Co. v. Travelers Ins. Companies, TexCivApp–Dallas, 587 SW2d 488, ref nre 593 SW2d 953.—Antitrust 141, 290, 292.

Hi-Line Elec. Co., Inc. v. Cryer, TexApp–Houston (14 Dist), 659 SW2d 118.—App & E 854(1), 954(2); Contracts 141(1); Inj 138.39, 147.

Hilker v. Agricultural Bond & Credit Corp., TexCivApp–Amarillo, 96 SW2d 544, writ dism.—App & E 1052(5), 1062.1; Chat Mtg 48, 229(2); Corp 642(7), 672(7), 673; Evid 75, 215(1), 474(19); Trial 307(3).

Hill, Ex parte, NDTex, 36 FSupp 191.—Crim Law 996(1); Fed Civ Proc 2656; Hab Corp 510(1); Sent & Pun 1129.

Hill, Ex parte, TexCrimApp, 208 SW3d 462.—Const Law 4838; Pardon 46, 60.

Hill, Ex parte, TexCrimApp, 863 SW2d 488.—Crim Law 641.13(6).

Hill, Ex parte, TexCrimApp, 571 SW2d 900.—Hab Corp 509(1); Sent & Pun 1345, 1352, 1400.

Hill, Ex parte, TexCrimApp, 528 SW2d 259.—Atty & C 112; Crim Law 641.13(7), 1069(6).

Hill, Ex parte, TexCrimApp, 528 SW2d 125.—Crim Law 1189; Hab Corp 864(5).

Hill, Ex parte, TexCrimApp, 417 SW2d 404.—Hab Corp 510(1); Sent & Pun 1318.

Hill, Ex parte, TexCrimApp, 318 SW2d 83, 167 TexCrim 95, cert den Hill v. Texas, 80 SCt 200, 361 US 897, 4 LEd2d 153.—Sent & Pun 1388.

Hill, Ex parte, TexCrimApp, 285 SW2d 763.—Crim Law 1090.1(1).

Hill, Ex parte, TexCrimApp, 262 SW2d 507, 159 TexCrim 238.—Hab Corp 823.

Hill, Ex parte, TexCrimApp, 160 SW2d 929, 144 TexCrim 52.—Courts 247(2); Crim Law 1018; Hab Corp 841; Tel 799.

Hill, Ex parte, TexCrimApp, 114 SW2d 247, 134 TexCrim 40.—Courts 472.2.

Hill, Ex parte, TexApp–Austin, 48 SW3d 283, petition for discretionary review refused.—Double J 132.1, 146, 201.

Hill, In re, BkrtcyNDTex, 19 BR 375.—Bankr 2186, 2402(1), 2465.2, 2467, 2675, 2676.

Hill, In re, BkrtcySDTex, 328 BR 490.—Bankr 2253, 2264(1).

Hill, In re, TexCivApp–Dallas, 611 SW2d 457.—Const Law 4493, 4494; Divorce 269(1).

Hill, Matter of, CA5 (Tex), 972 F2d 116.—Bankr 2802, 3784, 3786, 3788; Home 18, 214; Work Comp 416.

Hill, Matter of Estate of, TexApp–Amarillo, 761 SW2d 527.—Wills 229, 319.

Hill, Matter of Marriage of, TexApp–Amarillo, 893 SW2d 753, reh overr, and writ den.—Crim Law 814(1); Infants 203.

Hill v. Aldrich, TexCivApp–San Antonio, 242 SW2d 465, dism.—App & E 169; Contracts 346(12); Ex & Ad 449; Frds St of 75, 125(2); Wills 59.

Hill v. American Airlines, Inc., CA5 (Tex), 479 F2d 1057.—Civil R 1312, 1544; Fed Civ Proc 176, 184.10.

Hill; American Cas. Co. of Reading, Pennsylvania v., TexApp–Dallas, 194 SW3d 162, review den.—App & E 866(3), 931(1), 946, 970(2), 1010.1(1), 1010.2; Work Comp 868, 869, 1396, 1911, 1933, 2005.

Hill v. American Nat. Can Company/Foster Forbes Glass Div., NDTex, 952 FSupp 398.—Civil R 1502; Labor & Emp 1253, 1266.

Hill; Associates Inv. Co. v., TexCivApp–Austin, 221 SW2d 365, dism.—Usury 32, 138.

Hill; Avila v., TexCivApp–Amarillo, 497 SW2d 541.—Child C 42, 68, 76, 921(1).

Hill v. Bartlette, TexApp–Texarkana, 181 SW3d 541.—Accord 3(3), 10(1), 11(1); Atty & C 63, 64; Death 7, 31(1); Estop 52(4), 52.15; Ex & Ad 87; Judgm 185.3(2); Lim of Act 13.

Hill v. Bellville General Hosp., TexApp–Houston (1 Dist), 735 SW2d 675.—App & E 621(1); Judgm 72, 181(11), 181(33), 186; Mun Corp 741.10; Plead 246(3).

Hill v. Beto, CA5 (Tex), 422 F2d 840.—Double J 183.1, 186; Hab Corp 765.1, 827.

Hill v. Beto, CA5 (Tex), 412 F2d 831.—Crim Law 532(0.5).

Hill v. Beto, CA5 (Tex), 390 F2d 640, cert den 89 SCt 491, 393 US 1007, 21 LEd2d 472.—Crim Law 29(4); Double J 186; Hab Corp 369.

Hill v. Binford, TexCivApp–Galveston, 91 SW2d 488.—Bankr 2361, 2537, 2775.

Hill v. Blanco Nat. Bank, TexCivApp–Galveston, 179 SW2d 999, writ refused wom.—Insurance 1208(1), 1208(2), 1211(3), 1211(4), 2080.

Hill v. Board of Adjustment of City of Castle Hills, TexCivApp–San Antonio, 301 SW2d 490, writ refused.—Zoning 212, 414.1, 618.

Hill v. Board of Trustees, TexApp–Austin, 40 SW3d 676.—Admin Law 229, 480.1, 483, 669.1.

Hill; Booker v., TexCivApp–Waco, 570 SW2d 460.—App & E 5, 347(2), 1024.4; Judgm 181(3), 184, 185(2), 951(1).

Hill; Boutell v., TexCivApp–El Paso, 498 SW2d 713.—Frds St of 44(2); Partners 321, 336(3).

Hill; Brewer v., NDTex, 453 FSupp 67.—Civil R 1376(8), 1376(9); Dist & Pros Attys 10; Fed Civ Proc 1537.1; Judges 49(1); Receivers 168.

Hill v. Brockman, TexCivApp–Fort Worth, 351 SW2d 934.—Ref of Inst 19(2), 45(7).

Hill v. Budget Finance & Thrift Co., TexCivApp–Dallas, 383 SW2d 79.—App & E 882(15), 1046.5, 1170.9(3); Damag 63, 163(2), 184.

Hill v. Burnet County Sheriff's Dept., TexApp–Austin, 96 SW3d 436, reh overr, and review den.—App & E 863, 893(1), 911.3; Courts 32; Offic 69.2, 69.7; Plead 104(1), 111.36; Sheriffs 24; States 191.6(1), 191.6(2).

Hill; Calhoun v., TexCivApp–Eastland, 607 SW2d 951.—Judgm 199(3.2), 199(3.10); Labor & Emp 2927.

Hill v. Calvert, TexCivApp–Austin, 307 SW2d 618, ref nre.—App & E 1152; Inj 129(1).

Hill v. Caparino, TexCivApp–Houston, 370 SW2d 760.—Judgm 185.1(3), 185.2(9); Pretrial Proc 474, 482.1, 483.

Hill v. Carr, TexCivApp–Austin, 307 SW2d 828.—Parties 18, 29; States 87, 168.5.

Hill v. Cheek, CA5 (Tex), 230 F2d 104.—Autos 181(1), 229.5, 240(1), 246(2.1), 246(36); Fed Cts 937.1; Statut 226.

Hill v. Childers, TexCivApp–Waco, 268 SW2d 203, ref nre.—Sales 200(1), 342, 384(2); Trover 4, 44.

Hill; Citizens Nat. Bank of Dallas v., Tex, 505 SW2d 246.—Banks 119, 129, 130(1), 133, 153.

Hill v. Citizens Nat. Bank of Dallas, TexCivApp–Tyler, 495 SW2d 615, writ gr, rev 505 SW2d 246.—Banks 129, 134(4); Elect of Rem 3(4); Joint Adv 1.2(1), 1.12; Judgm 199(3.2), 199(3.9), 199(3.10); Nova 1, 12; Paymt 16(1), 67(1).

Hill; City of Amarillo v., TexCivApp–Amarillo, 278 SW2d 332.—Autos 211, 244(36.1), 245(66); Compromise 4, 16(1); Neglig 440(1).

Hill v. City of Castle Hills, TexCivApp–San Antonio, 282 SW2d 891, writ refused.—Inj 89(3), 138.31; Zoning 771, 784.

Hill v. City of Cedar Hill, TexCivApp–Dallas, 427 SW2d 672.—Inj 11.

Hill v. City of El Paso, Tex., CA5 (Tex), 437 F2d 352.— Civil R 1350, 1360; Courts 508(2.1); Fed Cts 41, 43, 56, 65.

Hill; City of Fort Worth v., TexCivApp–Fort Worth, 306 SW2d 817, ref nre.—App & E 281(1), 863, 866(3); Mun Corp 821(6), 821(19).

Hill; City of Galveston v., Tex, 519 SW2d 103.—Mun Corp 722.

Hill; City of Galveston v., Tex, 246 SW2d 860, 151 Tex 139.—App & E 882(16), 907(3), 1032(1); Trial 127.

Hill v. City of Galveston, TexCivApp–Galveston, 241 SW2d 229, rev 246 SW2d 860, 151 Tex 139.—App & E 1039(5.1); Commerce 48; Evid 5(2); Work Comp 2142.30.

Hill v. City of Greenville, Tex., NDTex, 696 FSupp 1123, 28 Wage & Hour Cas (BNA) 1575.—Labor & Emp 789, 790, 827, 2219, 2264(1), 2292(2).

Hill v. City of Houston, SDTex, 991 FSupp 847.—Civil R 1394, 1395(1); Consp 2; Const Law 3040, 3936; Mun Corp 723, 747(3); Sent & Pun 1433, 1436.

Hill; City of Houston v., TexApp–Houston (1 Dist), 792 SW2d 176, writ dism by agreement.—App & E 876; Judgm 335(1), 335(3); Mand 3(4), 3(8), 3(11), 168(2), 168(4); Mun Corp 1038.

Hill; City of Houston, Tex. v., USTex, 107 SCt 2502, 482 US 451, 96 LEd2d 398.—Const Law 90.1(1), 1490, 1814; Fed Cts 53, 56, 461, 755; Mun Corp 121, 592(1).

Hill v. City of Houston, Tex., CA5 (Tex), 789 F2d 1103, probable jur noted 107 SCt 58, 479 US 811, 93 LEd2d 17, aff 107 SCt 2502, 482 US 451, 96 LEd2d 398, appeal dism, cert den 107 SCt 3222, 483 US 1001, 97 LEd2d 729.—Const Law 799, 1141; Courts 489(2); Mun Corp 594(2).

Hill v. City of Houston, Tex., CA5 (Tex), 764 F2d 1156, on reh 789 F2d 1103, probable jur noted 107 SCt 58, 479 US 811, 93 LEd2d 17, aff 107 SCt 2502, 482 US 451, 96 LEd2d 398, appeal dism, cert den 107 SCt 3222, 483 US 1001, 97 LEd2d 729.—Const Law 82(4), 795, 855, 859, 1014, 1144, 1163, 1520, 1521, 1522; Fed Civ Proc 103.2.

Hill v. City of Seven Points, CA5 (Tex), 230 F3d 167, appeal after remand 31 FedAppx 835.—Fed Cts 542; U S Mag 12.1, 31.

Hill; City of Stephenville v., TexCivApp–Eastland, 443 SW2d 412, ref nre.—App & E 1050.1(3.1), 1067; Inj 130; Judgm 199(3.14).

Hill v. Clayton, TexApp–Corpus Christi, 827 SW2d 570.— App & E 292, 302(5), 930(1), 994(2), 1003(3), 1003(5), 1003(7); Damag 96, 130.4, 221(7).

Hill v. Connors, TexCivApp–Amarillo, 219 SW2d 587.— App & E 846(5), 1024.3; Plead 110, 111.8, 111.42(7), 111.42(8); Venue 8.5(6).

Hill v. Cooper, TexCivApp–Austin, 307 SW2d 638.—App & E 931(1), 931(5), 931(6).

Hill; Copeland v., TexCivApp–Austin, 126 SW2d 567.— Contracts 35; Labor & Emp 57, 858, 871.

Hill; Dallas Fountain & Fixture Co. v., TexCivApp– Dallas, 330 SW2d 648, ref nre.—App & E 302(1), 662(1), 683, 758.3(5), 758.3(6), 758.3(10); Judgm 248; Trial 352.4(4).

Hill v. Dallas Ry. & Terminal Co., TexCivApp–Dallas, 235 SW2d 522, ref nre.—Electricity 16(2), 16(5); Neglig 1694.

Hill; David v., SDTex, 401 FSupp2d 749.—Civil R 1090, 1092, 1304, 1336, 1352(1), 1355, 1358, 1395(7), 1420; Const Law 4824; Convicts 6; Fed Civ Proc 657.5(1), 1773, 1829, 1835; Sent & Pun 1532, 1533, 1537, 1548.

Hill; Davis v., TexCivApp–San Antonio, 371 SW2d 917, writ dism.—Plead 104(2), 111.18, 290(3); Venue 7.5(6).

Hill v. Davis, TexCivApp–San Antonio, 227 SW2d 381, ref nre.—Trial 351.2(6), 352.4(1); Wills 289, 302(2), 305, 317, 360.

Hill v. Davis, TexCivApp–Eastland, 392 SW2d 596, ref nre.—Armed S 108.1; Mines 54(2); Ref of Inst 19(2), 47; Spec Perf 22.

Hill; Ector County v., Tex, 843 SW2d 477. See Ector County v. Stringer.

Hill v. Ector County, TexApp–El Paso, 825 SW2d 180, writ gr, rev Ector County v. Stringer, 843 SW2d 477.— App & E 179(1); Estop 62.3; Interest 39(2.6); Sheriffs 28, 131.

Hill; El Paso County v., TexApp–El Paso, 754 SW2d 267, writ den.—Const Law 2478; Sheriffs 21, 32.

Hill v. El Paso Nat. Bank, TexCivApp–El Paso, 511 SW2d 421.—Wills 687(1).

Hill; Employees Retirement System v., TexCivApp– Waco, 557 SW2d 819, ref nre.—Admin Law 676, 744.1, 750, 754.1, 791; Evid 318(1); States 64.1(6).

Hill v. Enerlex, Inc., TexApp–Eastland, 969 SW2d 120, reh overr, and review den.—Judgm 185(6); Tax 2736, 3070; Venue 5.1.

Hill v. Engel, TexCivApp–Waco, 89 SW2d 219, writ refused.—Estop 115; Mech Liens 73(2), 76, 262(2), 279, 281(1).

Hill v. Estelle, CA5 (Tex), 653 F2d 202, cert den 102 SCt 577, 454 US 1036, 70 LEd2d 481.—Const Law 4587, 4700; Crim Law 273.1(1), 273.1(4), 274(4), 641.13(5), 1177; Hab Corp 442.

Hill v. Estelle, CA5 (Tex), 537 F2d 214.—Const Law 3420; Convicts 4(3), 4(7), 17(1).

Hill v. Estelle, SDTex, 423 FSupp 690, aff 543 F2d 754.— Civil R 1395(7); Fed Civ Proc 1781; Inj 26(5); Prisons 13(4).

Hill v. Evans, TexCivApp–Austin, 414 SW2d 684, ref nre. —Const Law 556; Evid 84.

Hill; Ferguson v., CA5 (Tex), 846 F2d 20.—Civil R 1554; Fed Cts 848, 913, 922.

Hill; Flatt v., TexCivApp–Dallas, 379 SW2d 926, ref nre. —App & E 1004(5), 1170.6; Damag 132(14); Release 12(1), 31; Trial 127, 133.3.

Hill v. Floating Decks of America, Inc., TexCivApp–San Antonio, 590 SW2d 723.—Acct Action on 11, 13; Afft 3, 12.

Hill v. Forrest & Cotton, Inc., TexCivApp–Eastland, 555 SW2d 145, ref nre.—Const Law 3454, 3971; Contrib 9(3); Death 38, 39; Indem 96; Lim of Act 4(2), 6(1), 30; Statut 4, 236.

Hill v. Foster, Tex, 186 SW2d 343, 143 Tex 482.—Ack 6(3), 29, 37(1), 43.1, 46, 61; App & E 1094(2); Ven & Pur 228(4), 231(15).

Hill v. Foster, TexCivApp–Amarillo, 181 SW2d 299, aff 186 SW2d 343, 143 Tex 482.—Ack 29, 37(2), 60; App & E 934(2), 1010.1(1); Deeds 25, 45, 193; Hus & W 194; Names 16(1), 16(2); Tresp to T T 6.1.

Hill v. Fourteenth Court of Appeals, Tex, 695 SW2d 554. —Elections 305(4).

Hill; Freeman v., TexCivApp–Hous (1 Dist), 419 SW2d 923, ref nre.—Estop 118; Sales 238; Trover 40(3).

HILL

Hill v. Galveston Housing Authority, TexCivApp–Hous (1 Dist), 593 SW2d 741.—App & E 758.1; Land & Ten 169(7).

Hill; Gardner v., EDTex, 195 FSupp2d 832.—Civil R 1345, 1351(1), 1352(4), 1354, 1376(2), 1376(6), 1432; False Imp 15(1); Fed Civ Proc 2491.5, 2515; Mun Corp 747(3).

Hill v. General Elec. Credit Corp., TexCivApp–San Antonio, 434 SW2d 457.—Contracts 187(1); Lim of Act 41.

Hill; General Exchange Ins. Corp. v., TexCivApp–El Paso, 131 SW2d 287.—Infants 78(1); Plead 111.5, 228.14, 311, 409(3).

Hill v. G E Power Systems, Inc., CA5 (Tex), 282 F3d 343.—Alt Disp Res 112, 182(1), 191, 193, 196, 205, 213(2), 213(3), 213(5); Fed Cts 812.

Hill v. Gibson Discount Center, TexCivApp–Amarillo, 437 SW2d 289, ref nre.—App & E 954(2); Const Law 48(1), 990, 1002; Evid 594; Sunday 2, 29(1).

Hill; Graham v., WDTex, 444 FSupp 584.—Const Law 42(1), 42.2(1), 795, 990, 1016, 1497, 1520, 2190, 2225, 2249, 2250; Courts 97(6), 508(1), 508(7); Decl Judgm 64, 124.1; Fed Cts 12.1, 31; Obscen 2.1, 2.5, 15.

Hill; Hampshire Silver Co. v., TexCivApp–Galveston, 244 SW2d 520.—Corp 644, 657(3), 672(7), 673.

Hill; Harris County Flood Control Dist. v., TexCivApp–Houston, 348 SW2d 806, ref nre.—Evid 142(1), 568(4).

Hill; Heden v., SDTex, 937 FSupp 1230.—Consp 1.1; Fed Civ Proc 2481, 2508, 2515; Fraud 6, 7, 64(1); Libel 6(1); Pat 90(7), 92; Postal 35(2), 35(3); RICO 5, 10, 29, 73; Tel 1014(11).

Hill; Heden v., SDTex, 937 FSupp 1222.—Pat 92.

Hill; Herald-Post Pub. Co., Inc. v., Tex, 891 SW2d 638.— App & E 1175(1); Libel 123(8).

Hill v. Herald-Post Pub. Co., Inc., TexApp–El Paso, 877 SW2d 774, reh den, and writ gr, aff in part, rev in part 891 SW2d 638.—App & E 173(2), 863; Judgm 185(2); Libel 1, 9(3), 19, 21, 33, 38(1), 38(5), 49, 51(2), 55, 123(2).

Hill; Heritage Resources, Inc. v., TexApp–El Paso, 104 SW3d 612.—App & E 226(2), 230, 758.1, 763, 840(4), 842(2), 852, 893(1), 949, 989, 1008.1(2), 1010.1(1), 1012.1(5), 1071.2, 1175(5), 1177(7), 1207(3); Costs 194.18, 194.40, 207, 208; Decl Judgm 394.

Hill v. Heritage Resources, Inc., TexApp–El Paso, 964 SW2d 89, reh overr, and review den, and reh of petition for review overr, appeal after remand 104 SW3d 612.— Admin Law 501; App & E 187(2), 218.2(5.1), 242(1), 253, 970(2), 984(1), 984(5), 989, 1001(3), 1047(1), 1050.1(1), 1056.1(1); Bankr 2395; Contracts 236, 237(1); Costs 13, 194.16, 194.18, 194.25, 194.32, 194.40; Damag 15, 89(2), 114, 137; Decl Judgm 10, 142, 148, 368; Evid 48; Fraud 3, 12, 32, 35, 50, 58(3), 59(2); Frds St of 63(2), 129(1), 131(1); Judgm 951(1); Libel 132, 136, 139; Lim of Act 43, 55(1), 55(5), 110, 127(3), 127(4), 127(7), 127(11.1), 127(12), 127(16); Mines 48, 73.1(3), 101; Neglig 219; Plead 252(1); Torts 114, 212, 213, 214, 215, 217, 219, 220, 222, 241, 242, 253, 255, 258, 262, 263, 271; Trial 56.

Hill v. Highlands Ins. Co., TexCivApp–Hous (1 Dist), 433 SW2d 247, ref nre.—App & E 934(1); Judgm 178, 181(2), 185(2), 185.3(13); Work Comp 598, 600, 1536.

Hill v. Hill, TexApp–Dallas, 819 SW2d 570, writ den.— Child S 45, 239, 290, 446; Hus & W 281.

Hill; Hill v., TexApp–Dallas, 819 SW2d 570, writ den.— Child S 45, 239, 290, 446; Hus & W 281.

Hill v. Hill, TexApp–Amarillo, 971 SW2d 153.—App & E 173(1), 931(1), 989, 1010.2, 1012.1(4); Divorce 150, 252.3(4), 253(4), 282; Hus & W 262.1(8), 264(4), 264(7); Trial 394(1), 404(1).

Hill; Hill v., TexApp–Amarillo, 971 SW2d 153.—App & E 173(1), 931(1), 989, 1010.2, 1012.1(4); Divorce 150, 252.3(4), 253(4), 282; Hus & W 262.1(8), 264(4), 264(7); Trial 394(1), 404(1).

Hill v. Hill, TexApp–Amarillo, 623 SW2d 779, ref nre.— Home 141(1), 143; Life Est 5, 16, 19.

Hill; Hill v., TexApp–Amarillo, 623 SW2d 779, ref nre.— Home 141(1), 143; Life Est 5, 16, 19.

Hill v. Hill, TexCivApp–Hous (1 Dist), 423 SW2d 943.— Child C 175, 182, 188, 471, 920; Pretrial Proc 718, 724.

Hill; Hill v., TexCivApp–Hous (1 Dist), 423 SW2d 943.— Child C 175, 182, 188, 471, 920; Pretrial Proc 718, 724.

Hill v. Hill, TexCivApp–Austin, 599 SW2d 691.—Child C 605, 609, 610; Judgm 90, 91.

Hill; Hill v., TexCivApp–Austin, 599 SW2d 691.—Child C 605, 609, 610; Judgm 90, 91.

Hill v. Hill, TexCivApp–Beaumont, 205 SW2d 82.—App & E 194(1); Divorce 37(18), 66, 130; Evid 23(1), 43(2), 471(2); Marriage 50(1); Plead 111.3, 376.

Hill; Hill v., TexCivApp–Beaumont, 205 SW2d 82.—App & E 194(1); Divorce 37(18), 66, 130; Evid 23(1), 43(2), 471(2); Marriage 50(1); Plead 111.3, 376.

Hill v. Hill, TexCivApp–Waco, 249 SW2d 654, ref nre.— Divorce 252.1, 252.3(2), 286(0.5).

Hill; Hill v., TexCivApp–Waco, 249 SW2d 654, ref nre.— Divorce 252.1, 252.3(2), 286(0.5).

Hill v. Hill, TexCivApp–Houston, 404 SW2d 641.—Child C 176, 182, 216, 400, 471, 525, 921(3); Judgm 21.

Hill; Hill v., TexCivApp–Houston, 404 SW2d 641.—Child C 176, 182, 216, 400, 471, 525, 921(3); Judgm 21.

Hill; Hollis v., TexCivApp–Houston, 232 F3d 460.—Corp 3, 174, 182.3, 182.4(5), 187, 190, 296, 307, 310(1), 597, 640; Fed Cts 382.1, 390, 391; Labor & Emp 40(1).

Hill; Horton v., TexCivApp–Galveston, 95 SW2d 751, writ dism.—App & E 742(4), 901.

Hill; Hyltin-Manor Funeral Home, Inc. v., TexCivApp–San Antonio, 304 SW2d 469.—Judgm 17(10).

Hill v. Imperial Sav., WDTex, 852 FSupp 1354.—Banks 502, 505, 508; B & L Assoc 42(6), 42(16); Contracts 9(1), 147(1), 176(1), 211; Costs 194.18; Fed Civ Proc 2737.1; Fraud 3, 20, 59(1); Libel 139; Lis Pen 15, 20; Ref of Inst 16, 17(1), 21, 50; Spec Perf 5, 8, 28(2), 65; States 18.19; Ven & Pur 44.

Hill; James v., TexApp–Fort Worth, 753 SW2d 839.— Trial 351.2(7).

Hill v. James, TexCivApp–Austin, 307 SW2d 619.—App & E 801(1), 1152; Inj 129(1).

Hill v. J. C. Penney Co., Inc., CA5 (Tex), 688 F2d 370, 25 Wage & Hour Cas (BNA) 974.—Civil R 1549; Interest 39(2.40); Labor & Emp 2476, 2478(3), 2481(5), 2481(7), 2482(2), 2485(1).

Hill v. Johnson, CA5 (Tex), 210 F3d 481, cert den 121 SCt 2001, 532 US 1039, 149 LEd2d 1004.—Const Law 4594(1), 4594(4); Crim Law 700(6), 706(2), 1159.6; Hab Corp 450.1, 452, 480, 500.1, 688, 818, 883.1.

Hill v. Johnson, CA5 (Tex), 114 F3d 78.—Hab Corp 818, 864(1).

Hill; Johnson v., TexCivApp–Texarkana, 301 SW2d 239. —Bound 8; Tresp to T T 44.

Hill v. Jones, TexApp–Houston (14 Dist), 773 SW2d 55.— Mental H 118, 135.

Hill v. Joseffy, TexCivApp–San Antonio, 259 SW2d 760, writ refused.—Des & Dist 26, 47(1), 47(3); Ex & Ad 14; Wills 150.

Hill v. Kelsey, TexCivApp–Dallas, 89 SW2d 1017, writ dism.—App & E 187(3); Frds St of 33(2); Hus & W 203; Parties 80(5).

Hill; Kelsey v., TexCivApp–Texarkana, 433 SW2d 241.— App & E 719(1); Judgm 5; Parties 18, 29; Wills 700.

Hill; Kilgarlin v., USTex, 87 SCt 820, 386 US 120, 17 LEd2d 771, reh den 87 SCt 1300, 386 US 999, 18 LEd2d 352.—Const Law 3658(6); Inj 189; States 27(6), 27(10).

Hill; King v., Tex, 172 SW2d 298, 141 Tex 294.—App & E 1177(8); Ten in C 15(6), 15(7); Tresp to T T 35(1).

Hill; King v., TexComApp, 157 SW2d 881, 138 Tex 187.— App & E 837(2), 1082(2), 1114; Mtg 608.5; Tresp to T T 35(1), 35(2).

Hill; King v., TexCivApp–Galveston, 167 SW2d 628, aff 172 SW2d 298, 141 Tex 294.—Home 119, 216; Tresp to T T 46; Trial 358.

Hill; King v., TexCivApp–Galveston, 136 SW2d 632, rev 157 SW2d 881, 138 Tex 187.—Mtg 37(2); Tresp to T T 35(1), 47(1).

Hill v. Leschber, TexCivApp–Austin, 235 SW2d 236.— App & E 907(3); Sales 355(3); Trial 360, 365.1(5), 365.2.

Hill v. Lester, TexCivApp–Fort Worth, 91 SW2d 1152, writ dism.—App & E 883; Evid 87; Judgm 335(1), 335(3), 414; Trial 351.5(1).

Hill; Lewis v., TexCivApp–Amarillo, 409 SW2d 946.— Impl & C C 55; Partners 83, 336(3).

Hill; Lewis v., TexCivApp–Tyler, 429 SW2d 572.—Costs 244; Interest 39(3), 39(5); Partners 308.

Hill; Lewis Boggus Motors, Inc. v., TexCivApp–Waco, 340 SW2d 957, writ dism.—Plead 111.30.

Hill; Lindner v., Tex, 691 SW2d 590.—App & E 931(3), 1010.1(8.1); Dedi 1, 2, 20(1), 45, 63(1).

Hill; Lindner v., TexApp–San Antonio, 673 SW2d 611, writ gr, aff 691 SW2d 590.—App & E 170(1), 1008.1(2), 1010.1(3), 1010.1(4), 1012.1(3); Dedi 1, 2, 15, 17, 39, 44, 45; Statut 11.

Hill; Lone Star Ford, Inc. v., TexApp–Houston (14 Dist), 879 SW2d 116, reh den, and extension of time gr.— Antitrust 147, 193, 390, 393, 397; App & E 231(9), 232(3), 930(3), 1001(1); Damag 57.9, 57.10, 130; Trial 139.1(3), 140(1), 143; Trover 1, 3, 40(1), 40(4).

Hill v. Lopez, TexApp–Amarillo, 858 SW2d 563.—Mand 4(3), 4(4), 11, 53.

Hill v. Lower Colorado River Authority, TexCivApp– Austin, 568 SW2d 473, ref nre.—Atty Gen 9; Char 49; States 191.10; Waters 152(5).

Hill v. McCaa, TexCivApp–Waco, 367 SW2d 381, ref nre. —Can of Inst 39, 43; Contracts 318, 346(2); Estop 115; Land & Ten 108(1).

Hill v. McClellan, CA5 (Tex), 490 F2d 859.—Civil R 1326(4), 1326(9), 1326(10), 1376(8); Consp 7.5(3), 18; Courts 509.

Hill; MacConnell v., TexCivApp–Corpus Christi, 569 SW2d 524.—Damag 185(1); Neglig 8(1), 535(4), 1684, 1745, 1746.

Hill; McCorvey v., CA5 (Tex), 385 F3d 846, cert den 125 SCt 1387, 543 US 1154, 161 LEd2d 119.—Const Law 977; Fed Civ Proc 2662; Fed Cts 12.1, 1011; Statut 152, 158.

Hill v. McDaniel, TexCivApp–Eastland, 129 SW2d 321, writ refused.—App & E 773(4), 846(5).

Hill; McDonald v., TexCivApp–Beaumont, 401 SW2d 160. —App & E 773(2).

Hill; McFarland & Tondre v., BkrtcySDTex, 122 BR 306. See Texas General Petroleum Corp., In re.

Hill; McVey v., TexApp–Austin, 691 SW2d 67, ref nre.— Mines 58.

Hill; Maryland Cas. Co. v., TexCivApp–San Antonio, 91 SW2d 391, writ dism.—App & E 232(3); Evid 20(1), 528(1); Trial 85, 133.6(4), 351.5(2).

Hill v. Meadows, TexCivApp–El Paso, 476 SW2d 705.— Evid 589, 590.

Hill; Melton, TexCivApp–Dallas, 311 SW2d 496, writ dism woj.—Plead 111.10, 111.42(4), 111.42(9); Trial 66, 68(1); Venue 22(4), 22(6), 22(8).

Hill; Mihovil v., TexCivApp–Galveston, 118 SW2d 615.— App & E 931(3); Gaming 58.

Hill v. Milani, Tex, 686 SW2d 610.—Lim of Act 85(2).

Hill v. Milani, TexApp–Austin, 678 SW2d 203, writ gr, aff 686 SW2d 610.—App & E 173(10); Judgm 181(7), 185.2(3); Lim of Act 84(2), 85(2); Motions 39.

Hill v. Miller, Tex, 714 SW2d 313.—Courts 247(7), 247(8).

Hill; Miller v., TexApp–Houston (14 Dist), 698 SW2d 372, writ gr, and writ withdrawn, cause dism 714 SW2d 313. —App & E 1010.2; Elections 291, 295(1).

Hill; Mission Ins. Co. v., TexApp–Texarkana, 679 SW2d 578, ref nre.—App & E 867(1), 977(1); Courts 78; Judgm 143(5), 162(2); New Tr 13, 85, 117(1), 124(1).

Hill v. Mobile Auto Trim, Inc., Tex, 725 SW2d 168.— Contracts 47, 65.5, 116(1), 116(2), 141(1); Inj 138.39.

Hill v. Mobile Auto Trim, Inc., TexApp–Dallas, 704 SW2d 384, writ gr, rev 725 SW2d 168.—App & E 954(1); Inj 138.18, 147, 151.

Hill; Moore v., CA5 (Tex), 487 F2d 221.—Hab Corp 666, 861.

Hill v. Moore, TexCivApp–Austin, 268 SW2d 488.—Abate & R 34; Autos 245(14), 245(80); Hus & W 222; Judgm 5.

Hill v. Moore, TexCivApp–Amarillo, 278 SW2d 472.—App & E 387(3), 1002; Autos 211, 242(1), 244(14), 244(26), 245(36); Evid 123(11), 185(1); Judgm 565; Trial 139.1(7), 143.

Hill; Morton v., TexCivApp, 355 SW2d 269, ref nre.— Tresp to T T 27; Trial 397(2), 397(5); Wills 775, 865(1).

Hill v. National Food Ins. Program, CA5 (Tex), 812 F2d 253. See Lee, In re Estate of.

Hill; Neinast v., TexCivApp–Galveston, 206 SW2d 625.— App & E 758.3(10); Consp 19; Fraud 58(1); Hus & W 262.1(1), 270(9); Sales 19; Trial 156(3), 366.

Hill; Neon Signs & Service v., TexCivApp–Galveston, 251 SW2d 570.—App & E 863.

Hill; Ogilvie v., TexCivApp–Texarkana, 563 SW2d 846, ref nre.—Contracts 217, 318; Frds St of 110(1), 118(2); Judgm 181(29); Ref of Inst 19(2), 46; Ven & Pur 79.

Hill; O'Hair v., CA5 (Tex), 641 F2d 307, reh gr 652 F2d 423, on reh 675 F2d 680, on remand 1984 WL 251621.— Assoc 20(1); Civil R 1421; Const Law 839, 915, 2591; Decl Judgm 124.1; Fed Civ Proc 103.2, 103.6, 679; Fed Cts 43; Inj 14, 16, 32, 105(1).

Hill; Oxford v., TexCivApp–Austin, 558 SW2d 557, writ refused.—Const Law 1391, 1490, 2407, 2408, 2425(3), 3851; Licens 7(1); States 191.10.

Hill v. Palestine Independent School Dist., TexApp– Tyler, 113 SW3d 14, reh overr, and review den.—Admin Law 124; App & E 852; Const Law 4025; Schools 147.34(2), 147.38.

Hill v. Palms, TexCivApp–Amarillo, 237 SW2d 455.— Anim 66.5(2), 74(8).

Hill; Pan American Fire & Cas. Co. v., TexCivApp–El Paso, 586 SW2d 187, ref nre.—Work Comp 816, 818, 820, 827, 842, 1172, 1677, 1683.

Hill v. Parker, TexCivApp–Texarkana, 239 SW2d 219, ref nre.—App & E 994(3), 1010.1(1), 1012.1(7.1); Deeds 72(1); Mines 55(8).

Hill; Payless Cashways, Inc. v., TexApp–Dallas, 139 SW3d 793.—App & E 517; Bankr 2442; Corp 507(13); Judgm 162(2), 162(4); Motions 62; Proc 145.

Hill; Peaslee-Gaulbert Corp. v., TexCivApp–Dallas, 311 SW2d 461.—Hus & W 264(2), 264(3); Trial 404(5).

Hill v. Perel, TexApp–Houston (1 Dist), 923 SW2d 636, reh overr.—Action 17; App & E 852, 934(1); Const Law 3964; Corp 665(0.5); Costs 260(1), 260(4), 260(5); Courts 12(2.5); Judgm 181(2), 185(2), 185.1(3); Lim of Act 2(1).

Hill v. Pierce, TexApp–El Paso, 729 SW2d 340, ref nre.— Antitrust 398.

Hill; Printing Industries of Gulf Coast v., SDTex, 382 FSupp 801, stay gr 95 SCt 19, 419 US 805, 42 LEd2d 33, probable jur noted 95 SCt 677, 419 US 1088, 42 LEd2d 679, vac 95 SCt 2670, 422 US 937, 45 LEd2d 664.—Const Law 655, 727, 855, 1460, 1545, 1553, 1600, 1709; Elections 24; Statut 47.

Hill; Rachal v., CA5 (Tex), 435 F2d 59, cert den 91 SCt 2203, 403 US 904, 29 LEd2d 680.—Fed Cts 914; Judgm 585(3), 634, 666; Sec Reg 14.13, 18.25.

Hill; Radford v., TexCivApp–Dallas, 185 SW2d 129, writ refused wom.—App & E 1053(2); Evid 273(3), 314(1); Witn 275(1), 275(2.1), 275(6), 395, 414(2).

Hill v. Reynolds Trust, TexCivApp–Fort Worth, 137 SW2d 195.—App & E 216(1), 301, 758.3(1); New Tr 152; Trover 66.

Hill v. Rich, TexCivApp–Austin, 522 SW2d 597, ref nre.— Judgm 185(2), 185.3(19); Pretrial Proc 75, 201.1; Spec Perf 117; Ven & Pur 16(1).

Hill v. **Richardson**, CA5 (Tex), 463 F2d 773.—Social S 143.55.

Hill; **Roberson Farm Equipment Co. v.**, TexCivApp–Texarkana, 514 SW2d 796, ref nre.—App & E 555, 614, 641, 644(2), 655(3), 656(1), 907(3), 1074(3); Judgm 525; Plead 427; Trial 393(1).

Hill; **Robinson v.**, Tex, 507 SW2d 521.—Const Law 990, 1030; Licens 1; States 109; Statut 61, 68, 77(1), 93(2), 105(1), 108, 109, 109.2, 121(1).

Hill v. **Robinson**, TexCivApp–Tyler, 592 SW2d 376, ref nre.—App & E 226(1), 1064.1(11); Costs 12, 177; Crim Law 417(15); Death 104(1); Evid 272, 276; Judgm 203; Trial 194(1), 203(1), 217, 308.

Hill v. **Sabine Pipe & Supply Co.**, TexCivApp–Texarkana, 272 SW2d 769, ref nre.—Judgm 199(3.15); Neglig 371, 372.

Hill; **Salazar v.**, TexCivApp–Corpus Christi, 551 SW2d 518, ref nre.—App & E 930(3), 989, 999(1); Autos 242(7), 244(12), 244(34), 244(35), 245(15), 245(49), 245(66); Neglig 1726, 1750; Trial 142.

Hill v. **Sargent**, TexCivApp–Dallas, 615 SW2d 300.—App & E 1071.6; Const Law 1329, 1331; Relig Soc 8, 14.

Hill v. **Schuhart**, TexCivApp–Amarillo, 391 SW2d 579, writ refused.—Agric 3.3(1).

Hill v. **Schultz**, TexCivApp–Galveston, 248 SW2d 535, ref nre.—Sales 89, 479.2(1), 481.

Hill; **Sibley v.**, TexCivApp–El Paso, 331 SW2d 227.—Contracts 143(3); Mines 101; Partit 14, 22; Perp 6(1).

Hill v. **Silsbee Independent School Dist.**, EDTex, 933 FSupp 616.—Civil R 1346, 1351(5), 1376(2), 1376(10); Const Law 1932, 1947, 1991, 2000, 3865, 3874(1), 3874(2), 4040, 4157, 4165(1), 4171, 4173(4), 4198, 4199, 4203, 4255; Fed Civ Proc 2545; Schools 147.2(1), 147.9, 147.12, 147.38.

Hill; **Sims v.**, TexCivApp–Hous (14 Dist), 567 SW2d 912.—Partners 213(2), 217(2); Plead 38.5, 76; Pretrial Proc 472.

Hill v. **Singing Hills Funeral Home, Inc.**, NDTex, 77 FRD 746.—Civil R 1517, 1532; Fed Civ Proc 184.10, 184.25.

Hill v. **Smith**, TexCivApp–Dallas, 181 SW2d 1015.—App & E 927(7); Marriage 13, 50(1), 51.

Hill v. **Snider**, BkrtcySDTex, 62 BR 382. See Snider, In re.

Hill; **Socialist Workers Party v.**, CA5 (Tex), 483 F2d 554, reh den 485 F2d 688.—Const Law 977, 1686; Elections 21; Fed Cts 491, 541.

Hill; **Solana v.**, TexCivApp–Eastland, 348 SW2d 481, ref nre.—App & E 1069.1; Autos 150, 201(1.1); New Tr 56, 157; Trial 304.

Hill v. **Spencer & Son, Inc.**, TexApp–Texarkana, 973 SW2d 772.—App & E 934(1), 1175(1), 1175(2); Contracts 245(1); Deeds 94; Evid 211, 265(10); Logs 3(11), 3(15); Ref of Inst 20, 25.

Hill; **Starling v.**, TexCivApp–Waco, 121 SW2d 648.—App & E 1177(7); Consp 19, 21.

Hill v. **State**, TexCrimApp, 90 SW3d 308.—Crim Law 295, 867, 1030(2), 1086.11; Double J 59, 96, 99, 132.1; Jury 29(5), 149.

Hill v. **State**, TexCrimApp, 955 SW2d 96.—Bail 75.2(3), 77(1); Judgm 185(2).

Hill v. **State**, TexCrimApp, 913 SW2d 581.—Assault 56; Crim Law 1042, 1137(2); Sent & Pun 80, 306, 323, 375.

Hill v. **State**, TexCrimApp, 827 SW2d 860, cert den 113 SCt 297, 506 US 905, 121 LEd2d 221.—Const Law 3309; Crim Law 1035(5), 1134(3), 1158(3); Jury 33(5.15), 117; Statut 220.

Hill v. **State**, TexCrimApp, 765 SW2d 794.—Controlled Subs 92, 96; Crim Law 1173.2(3).

Hill v. **State**, TexCrimApp, 719 SW2d 199, on remand 721 SW2d 953.—Crim Law 1158(1); Sent & Pun 2020.

Hill v. **State**, TexCrimApp, 692 SW2d 716.—Arrest 63.4(12); Crim Law 339.10(8), 394.1(3), 1169.1(5).

Hill v. **State**, TexCrimApp, 690 SW2d 900.—Courts 107; Crim Law 577.10(9).

Hill v. **State**, TexCrimApp, 686 SW2d 184.—Crim Law 641.9, 1035(7).

Hill v. **State**, TexCrimApp, 641 SW2d 543.—Crim Law 1044.2(1), 1169.1(10).

Hill v. **State**, TexCrimApp, 640 SW2d 879.—Crim Law 1038.1(4); Rob 27(6).

Hill v. **State**, TexCrimApp, 633 SW2d 520.—Crim Law 695.5, 1036.1(8).

Hill v. **State**, TexCrimApp, 608 SW2d 932.—Crim Law 829(1); Forg 44(1), 44(3); Witn 342, 344(1), 344(3), 345(1), 352, 363(1).

Hill v. **State**, TexCrimApp, 585 SW2d 713.—Crim Law 1173.2(3); Homic 1400.

Hill v. **State**, TexCrimApp, 576 SW2d 642.—Crim Law 1038.1(3.1).

Hill v. **State**, TexCrimApp, 568 SW2d 338.—Rob 17(3), 17(5).

Hill v. **State**, TexCrimApp, 544 SW2d 411.—Ind & Inf 71.1, 87(2), 137(1), 169, 176.

Hill v. **State**, TexCrimApp, 521 SW2d 253.—Burg 11; Ind & Inf 190.

Hill v. **State**, TexCrimApp, 518 SW2d 810.—Crim Law 363, 364(3.1), 726, 1171.1(3).

Hill v. **State**, TexCrimApp, 504 SW2d 484.—Crim Law 700(2.1), 720(9), 1169.3, 1171.1(1); Homic 1136; Statut 64(6).

Hill v. **State**, TexCrimApp, 496 SW2d 606.—Homic 1483.

Hill v. **State**, TexCrimApp, 493 SW2d 847.—Crim Law 656(9), 957(3); Homic 1567; Jury 24, 90; Sent & Pun 1495.

Hill v. **State**, TexCrimApp, 493 SW2d 530.—Crim Law 531(3).

Hill v. **State**, TexCrimApp, 487 SW2d 64.—Crim Law 1130(4); Jury 33(5.15).

Hill v. **State**, TexCrimApp, 480 SW2d 670.—Crim Law 507.5, 720(1), 721(3), 911, 938(1), 945(1), 1124(1), 1156(1); Incest 13, 14; Witn 40(1), 77.

Hill v. **State**, TexCrimApp, 480 SW2d 200, cert den 93 SCt 694, 409 US 1078, 34 LEd2d 667.—Crim Law 633(1), 641.7(2), 1042; Sent & Pun 2014, 2024, 2025.

Hill v. **State**, TexCrimApp, 479 SW2d 288.—Crim Law 1186.6.

Hill v. **State**, TexCrimApp, 472 SW2d 124.—Crim Law 1203.27; Sent & Pun 1310.

Hill v. **State**, TexCrimApp, 466 SW2d 791.—Crim Law 706(3), 787(1), 814(17), 1038.2, 1038.3; Rob 24.15(2).

Hill v. **State**, TexCrimApp, 456 SW2d 699.—Crim Law 418(1); Homic 1154.

Hill v. **State**, TexCrimApp, 447 SW2d 420.—Crim Law 730(8), 730(12); Jury 149.

Hill v. **State**, TexCrimApp, 434 SW2d 864.—Larc 62(1).

Hill v. **State**, TexCrimApp, 429 SW2d 481, cert den 89 SCt 384, 393 US 955, 21 LEd2d 367.—Crim Law 517.2(1), 517.2(2), 531(1), 532(0.5), 534(2), 608, 1035(7); Mental H 434.

Hill v. **State**, TexCrimApp, 420 SW2d 408.—Burg 41(1); Crim Law 363, 364(1), 364(3.1), 364(4), 404.50, 419(2.10), 792(2), 1119(4).

Hill v. **State**, TexCrimApp, 403 SW2d 797.—Crim Law 938(4), 939(1), 1120(3), 1182; Homic 1136.

Hill v. **State**, TexCrimApp, 403 SW2d 421.—Burg 41(1); Crim Law 394.5(3), 661, 695(2), 814(16), 1171.2; Stip 14(10).

Hill v. **State**, TexCrimApp, 398 SW2d 944.—Crim Law 1116; Double J 186; Rob 24.15(1).

Hill v. **State**, TexCrimApp, 393 SW2d 901.—Atty & C 31; Crim Law 577, 641.6(3), 641.13(4), 1166.10(1).

Hill v. **State**, TexCrimApp, 375 SW2d 306.—Crim Law 945(1), 1090.16, 1099.6(3), 1099.10, 1133, 1144.19.

Hill v. **State**, TexCrimApp, 368 SW2d 215.—Autos 355(6).

Hill v. **State**, TexCrimApp, 365 SW2d 184, 170 TexCrim 313.—Crim Law 1087.1(2).

Hill v. State, TexCrimApp, 364 SW2d 381.—Crim Law 371(3), 1056.1(2), 1092.7; False Pret 4, 49(1).

Hill v. State, TexCrimApp, 356 SW2d 321, 172 TexCrim 268.—Crim Law 1036.4; Larc 40(4).

Hill v. State, TexCrimApp, 334 SW2d 303, 169 TexCrim 414.—Int Liq 236(7).

Hill v. State, TexCrimApp, 332 SW2d 579, 169 TexCrim 104.—Crim Law 1032(3), 1032(4); Ind & Inf 196(2); Statut 107(3).

Hill v. State, TexCrimApp, 321 SW2d 583, 167 TexCrim 512.—Autos 355(6).

Hill v. State, TexCrimApp, 319 SW2d 318, 167 TexCrim 229.—Crim Law 627.7(3), 763(1), 785(12), 1169.5(2); Homic 1177.

Hill v. State, TexCrimApp, 310 SW2d 588, 166 TexCrim 13.—Crim Law 641.2(3).

Hill v. State, TexCrimApp, 299 SW2d 140.—Crim Law 1090.1(1).

Hill v. State, TexCrimApp, 297 SW2d 679, 164 TexCrim 146.—Int Liq 242.

Hill v. State, TexCrimApp, 294 SW2d 844.—Crim Law 1094(2.1).

Hill v. State, TexCrimApp, 294 SW2d 840.—Crim Law 1090.1(1).

Hill v. State, TexCrimApp, 290 SW2d 677, 163 TexCrim 331.—Crim Law 429(1), 1036.1(6); Int Liq 55, 120; Sent & Pun 1260.

Hill v. State, TexCrimApp, 278 SW2d 842, 161 TexCrim 540, cert den 75 SCt 773, 349 US 930, 99 LEd 1261.—Crim Law 394.4(4), 800(2); Explos 5.

Hill v. State, TexCrimApp, 264 SW2d 953, 159 TexCrim 501.—Crim Law 572, 641.12(1).

Hill v. State, TexCrimApp, 261 SW2d 849, 159 TexCrim 150.—Explos 5.

Hill v. State, TexCrimApp, 256 SW2d 93, 158 TexCrim 313.—Autos 359, 425; Const Law 2815, 2816; Crim Law 419(12), 488; Double J 22.

Hill v. State, TexCrimApp, 247 SW2d 114.—Crim Law 1090.1(1).

Hill v. State, TexCrimApp, 239 SW2d 618.—Crim Law 1090.1(1).

Hill v. State, TexCrimApp, 224 SW2d 880.—Crim Law 1086.14, 1090.1(1).

Hill v. State, TexCrimApp, 217 SW2d 1009, 153 TexCrim 105.—Crim Law 404.70, 655(1), 656(8), 857(2), 954(3), 956(1), 957(1), 957(3), 1144.10, 1166.22(3), 1169.1(3), 1169.3, 1170(2).

Hill v. State, TexCrimApp, 212 SW2d 143, 152 TexCrim 248.—Crim Law 134(4), 394.4(1), 590(2), 591, 1151, 1169.3.

Hill v. State, TexCrimApp, 207 SW2d 413, 151 TexCrim 299.—Ind & Inf 47, 51(1), 161(4).

Hill v. State, TexCrimApp, 194 SW2d 266, 149 TexCrim 324.—Ind & Inf 171; Sent & Pun 1381(1).

Hill v. State, TexCrimApp, 184 SW2d 283, 147 TexCrim 660.—Crim Law 1090.16, 1094(2.1).

Hill v. State, TexCrimApp, 174 SW2d 733, 146 TexCrim 333.—Crim Law 1070.

Hill v. State, TexCrimApp, 171 SW2d 880, 146 TexCrim 333, cert dism 64 SCt 72, 320 US 806, 88 LEd 487.—Const Law 199, 2784, 2789, 2790, 2793, 2810, 2811, 2812; Crim Law 146, 160; Gr Jury 3; Ind & Inf 137(2).

Hill v. State, TexCrimApp, 161 SW2d 80, 144 TexCrim 57.—Crim Law 402(1), 1091(11), 1098, 1134(2), 1170.5(1); Homic 1139, 1174; Witn 240(4).

Hill v. State, TexCrimApp, 158 SW2d 810, 143 TexCrim 412.—Crim Law 510; Gaming 85(1), 98(1).

Hill v. State, TexCrimApp, 157 SW2d 369, 144 TexCrim 415, cert gr 62 SCt 1048, 316 US 655, 86 LEd 1735, rev 62 SCt 1159, 316 US 400, 86 LEd 1559.—Const Law 4574; Crim Law 322, 726, 730(12), 730(14), 872.5, 957(1), 957(2); Gr Jury 5, 8; Ind & Inf 137(2), 140(2); Witn 277(4), 337(16).

Hill v. State, TexCrimApp, 149 SW2d 93, 141 TexCrim 169.—Crim Law 338(1), 1169.1(10); Double J 150(3).

Hill v. State, TexCrimApp, 121 SW2d 996, 135 TexCrim 567.—Burg 16; Crim Law 1169.11.

Hill v. State, TexCrimApp, 114 SW2d 1180, 134 TexCrim 163.—Crim Law 419(6), 450, 470(1), 470(2), 473, 1120(3), 1169.9; Homic 1096, 1178; Jury 67(2).

Hill v. State, TexCrimApp, 111 SW2d 259, 133 TexCrim 398.—Crim Law 1097(1).

Hill v. State, TexCrimApp, 108 SW2d 912, 133 TexCrim 92.—Crim Law 814(17), 836, 1092.9, 1133, 1173.2(3); Homic 1193, 1491, 1567; Sent & Pun 72.

Hill v. State, TexCrimApp, 97 SW2d 202, 131 TexCrim 161.—Crim Law 1120(1); Witn 53(4), 76(3), 398(1).

Hill v. State, TexCrimApp, 95 SW2d 106, 130 TexCrim 585.—Crim Law 594(4), 808.5, 925.5(3), 1163(6).

Hill v. State, TexCrimApp, 94 SW2d 168.—Crim Law 1131(1).

Hill v. State, TexCrimApp, 91 SW2d 348.—Crim Law 15.

Hill v. State, TexCrimApp, 87 SW2d 719, 129 TexCrim 451.—Crim Law 517(1), 923(4), 1166.17.

Hill v. State, TexApp–Houston (1 Dist), 902 SW2d 57, petition for discretionary review refused.—Crim Law 394.6(5), 520(1), 520(2), 1042, 1153(1), 1158(4); Sent & Pun 2011.

Hill v. State, TexApp–Houston (1 Dist), 832 SW2d 724.—Crim Law 419(1), 419(1.5), 510, 511.1(1), 511.1(3), 511.2, 511.5, 1169.1(9).

Hill v. State, TexApp–Houston (1 Dist), 748 SW2d 314, petition for discretionary review refused.—Crim Law 1038.1(4); Homic 1051(5), 1054.

Hill v. State, TexApp–Houston (1 Dist), 666 SW2d 663, petition for discretionary review gr, aff 686 SW2d 184.—Crim Law 374, 641.4(4), 641.9, 641.10(1), 641.10(3), 641.13(6), 1038.1(3.1); Witn 18.

Hill v. State, TexApp–Fort Worth, 99 SW3d 248, reh overr, and petition for discretionary review refused.—Crim Law 330, 739(1), 772(6), 1128(2), 1144.13(2.1), 1159.2(7), 1159.2(8), 1159.3(2); Homic 942, 1202, 1473, 1558.

Hill v. State, TexApp–Fort Worth, 897 SW2d 533.—Crim Law 1134(3), 1144.13(3), 1159.1, 1159.2(1), 1159.2(2), 1159.2(7); False Imp 43; Statut 181(1), 188, 208, 217.4, 219(2).

Hill v. State, TexApp–Fort Worth, 881 SW2d 897, petition for discretionary review gr, aff 913 SW2d 581.—Child S 100, 113; Crim Law 562, 796, 1134(2), 1137(2), 1144.13(2.1), 1144.13(3), 1159.2(1), 1159.2(7), 1159.2(9); Infants 13, 20; Sent & Pun 77, 80, 373.

Hill v. State, TexApp–Fort Worth, 852 SW2d 769, petition for discretionary review refused.—Crim Law 29(9), 369.13, 374, 1169.11; Infants 13, 20.

Hill v. State, TexApp–Fort Worth, 834 SW2d 452. See Routledge v. State.

Hill v. State, TexApp–Fort Worth, 750 SW2d 2, petition for discretionary review refused, untimely filed.—Crim Law 1032(1); Forg 26.

Hill v. State, TexApp–Fort Worth, 704 SW2d 599.—Crim Law 1023(16); Sent & Pun 2091.

Hill v. State, TexApp–Austin, 760 SW2d 369.—Bail 4, 97(1); Ind & Inf 6.

Hill v. State, TexApp–Dallas, 788 SW2d 858.—Crim Law 625.10(2.1), 625.15.

Hill v. State, TexApp–Dallas, 787 SW2d 74, petition for discretionary review gr, aff and remanded 827 SW2d 860, cert den 113 SCt 297, 506 US 905, 121 LEd2d 221.—Crim Law 1144.13(2.1), 1158(1); Jury 33(5.15), 33(5.20).

Hill v. State, TexApp–Dallas, 775 SW2d 754, petition for discretionary review refused.—Const Law 3309, 3832; Jury 121.

Hill v. State, TexApp–Dallas, 730 SW2d 86.—Crim Law 577.10(9), 577.14, 577.16(7); Double J 59; Forg 16, 44(1).

HILL

59 Tex D 2d—646

See Guidelines for Arrangement at the beginning of this Volume

Hill v. State, TexApp–Dallas, 672 SW2d 302, denial of post-conviction relief aff 2005 WL 729942.—Crim Law 720(2), 720(6), 721.5(1), 730(11); Rape 54(1).

Hill v. State, TexApp–Dallas, 658 SW2d 705, review gr, cause remanded 663 SW2d 457, on remand 672 SW2d 302, denial of post-conviction relief aff 2005 WL 729942. —Rape 51(5), 54(1), 54(3).

Hill v. State, TexApp–Texarkana, 213 SW3d 533.—Crim Law 577.4, 577.10(1), 577.15(4), 577.16(4), 577.16(7), 635, 1134(2), 1136, 1139, 1158(1); Sent & Pun 637, 1064, 1139.

Hill v. State, TexApp–Texarkana, 30 SW3d 505.—Crim Law 790, 822(1), 1038.1(1), 1038.1(3.1), 1134(2).

Hill v. State, TexApp–Texarkana, 783 SW2d 257.—Crim Law 438(3), 1091(11).

Hill v. State, TexApp–Amarillo, 79 SW3d 682, petition for discretionary review refused.—Double J 96, 97.

Hill v. State, TexApp–Amarillo, 883 SW2d 765, reh den, and petition for discretionary review refused.—Crim Law 59(1), 59(3), 80, 312; Infants 13, 20.

Hill v. State, TexApp–Amarillo, 644 SW2d 849.—Arson 37(3); Const Law 268(5), 4594(4); Crim Law 59(1), 351(10), 369.2(3.1), 436(2), 436(7), 444, 511.1(1), 511.1(3), 511.1(6.1), 511.2, 552(3), 741(1), 1159.6, 1178.

Hill v. State, TexApp–El Paso, 679 SW2d 173.—Crim Law 789(3), 789(4); Homic 1152.

Hill v. State, TexApp–Beaumont, 161 SW3d 771.—Controlled Subs 22, 23, 77; Ind & Inf 60, 66, 71.2(1), 71.2(3).

Hill v. State, TexApp–Beaumont, 888 SW2d 255.—Crim Law 369.2(4), 374, 778(5), 783.5, 1036.1(8); Homic 1181, 1385.

Hill v. State, TexApp–Beaumont, 774 SW2d 102, petition for discretionary review refused.—Crim Law 1169.5(5).

Hill v. State, TexApp–Waco, 3 SW3d 249, petition for discretionary review refused.—Courts 85(3); Crim Law 1036.2, 1088.10; Infants 13; Witn 77.

Hill v. State, TexApp–Waco, 929 SW2d 607, reh overr.— Crim Law 1026.10(1).

Hill v. State, TexApp–Waco, 920 SW2d 468, reh overr, and petition for discretionary review gr, rev 955 SW2d 96.—App & E 863, 934(1); Bail 77(1), 77(2); Judgm 181(6), 181(15.1), 185(2), 185.3(1).

Hill v. State, TexApp–Eastland, 844 SW2d 937.—Assault 48.

Hill v. State, TexApp–Eastland, 817 SW2d 816, petition for discretionary review refused.—Crim Law 419(1.5), 1036.5, 1044.2(1), 1169.1(9), 1169.5(1), 1169.5(5).

Hill v. State, TexApp–Tyler, 78 SW3d 374, reh overr, and petition for discretionary review refused, appeal after new trial 2004 WL 2158030, petition for discretionary review refused.—Crim Law 394.6(5), 412.1(4), 412.2(3), 412.2(4), 412.2(5), 414, 527, 1036.1(6), 1044.1(6), 1044.2(1), 1134(3), 1139, 1144.12, 1158(4); Infants 192.

Hill v. State, TexApp–Tyler, 721 SW2d 953.—Crim Law 1144.13(3); Sent & Pun 2021.

Hill v. State, TexApp–Tyler, 718 SW2d 751, remanded 719 SW2d 199, on remand 721 SW2d 953.—Home 99; Sent & Pun 2003, 2006, 2018.

Hill v. State, TexApp–Tyler, 673 SW2d 890, dism.—Sent & Pun 1952.

Hill v. State, TexApp–Corpus Christi, 647 SW2d 306, petition for discretionary review refused.—Costs 302.2(2), 302.3; Crim Law 438(5.1), 438(7), 478(1), 720(2), 720(6), 720(9), 1166(10.10), 1169.5(1), 1169.5(2), 1169.9.

Hill v. State, TexApp–Houston (14 Dist), 135 SW3d 267, petition for discretionary review refused.—Arrest 63.4(2), 63.5(4), 63.5(9); Autos 349(17); Crim Law 1139, 1144.1, 1158(2).

Hill v. State, TexApp–Houston (14 Dist), 951 SW2d 244.— Arrest 63.4(2), 63.4(4), 63.5(4), 63.5(5), 63.5(7), 68(3); Courts 97(6); Crim Law 394, 394.6(5), 1144.12, 1153(1), 1224(1); Searches 22, 181.

Hill v. State, TexApp–Houston (14 Dist), 755 SW2d 197, petition for discretionary review refused.—Arrest 63.4(15); Controlled Subs 27, 28, 30, 80, 131; Crim Law 552(3), 562, 641.13(1), 641.13(2.1), 641.13(5), 641.13(6), 713, 720(2), 720(7.1), 723(3), 728(2), 1159.6, 1171.1(2.1); Searches 30, 47.1, 49.

Hill v. State, TexApp–Houston (14 Dist), 681 SW2d 765, review refused, decision disapproved in part 690 SW2d 900.—Crim Law 339.8(5), 577.10(9).

Hill v. State, TexApp–Houston (14 Dist), 666 SW2d 130.— Crim Law 507(1), 511.1(2.1), 511.1(3), 511.1(9), 511.2, 511.5, 742(2), 780(2), 1184(2); Sent & Pun 1286, 1379(2), 1381(3), 1381(6).

Hill v. State, TexApp–Houston (14 Dist), 659 SW2d 94.— Crim Law 720(5), 1171.3.

Hill v. State, TexApp–Houston (14 Dist), 643 SW2d 417, aff 641 SW2d 543.—Crim Law 394.2(1), 394.6(1), 1043(1), 1043(2), 1044.2(1), 1169.1(1), 1169.1(5), 1169.1(8), 1169.1(10), 1184(1), 1184(2).

Hill v. State, TexApp–Houston (14 Dist), 625 SW2d 803, petition for discretionary review gr, aff 640 SW2d 879. —Courts 90(7); Crim Law 339.10(6.1), 339.10(9), 772(1), 805(3), 1115(2), 1129(2); Larc 1; Rob 17(1), 24.15(1), 27(5); Witn 318.

Hill; State v., TexCivApp–Austin, 452 SW2d 58.—App & E 907(4), 1170.1, 1170.7.

Hill v. State, TexCivApp–San Antonio, 454 SW2d 429.— Infants 175.1.

Hill v. State, TexCivApp–Texarkana, 289 SW2d 801.— Em Dom 201, 203(1).

Hill v. State Farm Lloyds, CA5 (Tex), 79 FedAppx 644. —Insurance 3579, 3580.

Hill v. State of Tex., USTex, 62 SCt 1159, 316 US 400, 86 LEd 1559.—Const Law 961, 3000, 3310; Double J 108; States 4.1(2).

Hill; State Reserve Life Ins. Co. v., TexCivApp–Austin, 93 SW2d 485.—Insurance 2037.

Hill v. Steinberger, TexApp–Houston (1 Dist), 827 SW2d 58.—App & E 852, 934(1); Divorce 166, 254(2); Evid 265(7); Judgm 185(2), 185(6), 335(1), 335(2), 335(3).

Hill v. Sterrett, TexCivApp–Dallas, 252 SW2d 766, ref nre.—Counties 23, 47, 113(1), 113(6); Decl Judgm 124.1; High 90, 93, 95(1); Statut 8.5(1).

Hill v. Stone, USTex, 95 SCt 1637, 421 US 289, 44 LEd2d 172, reh den 95 SCt 2617, 422 US 1029, 45 LEd2d 686. —Courts 100(1); Elections 15; Mun Corp 918(1).

Hill v. Sutton, TexCivApp–Beaumont, 281 SW2d 231.— Venue 7.5(7).

Hill; Templeton v., TexCivApp–Waco, 497 SW2d 948.— App & E 79(1), 80(6).

Hill v. Texaco, Inc., CA5 (Tex), 674 F2d 447.—Ship 84(3.2), 86(2.3).

Hill v. Texaco, Inc., SDTex, 499 FSupp 470, rev 674 F2d 447.—Ship 84(5); Work Comp 1671.

Hill v. Texas Council Risk Management Fund, TexApp–Texarkana, 20 SW3d 209, reh overr, and petition for review den.—Action 6; Insurance 1004, 2776; Mun Corp 226; Statut 188, 205, 211, 223.1.

Hill v. Texas, New Mexico & Oklahoma Coaches, Inc., Tex, 272 SW2d 91, 153 Tex 581.—App & E 1064.1(5), 1140(4); Carr 321(1); Damag 221(5.1).

Hill; Texas, N. M. & Okl. Coaches v., TexCivApp–Amarillo, 277 SW2d 178, ref nre.—Carr 318(4).

Hill; Texas, N. M. & Okl. Coaches v., TexCivApp–Amarillo, 266 SW2d 412, rev 272 SW2d 91, 153 Tex 581. —Carr 317(1), 318(4), 321(1); Damag 221(5.1); Neglig 213, 387.

Hill v. Texas Water Quality Bd., TexCivApp–Austin, 568 SW2d 738, ref nre.—Atty Gen 4, 7; Const Law 915; States 191.4(2).

Hill v. The Praetorians, TexCivApp–Waco, 219 SW2d 564, ref nre.—Const Law 642; Mech Liens 146, 149(1), 149(3), 279; Mtg 151(3), 257.

For Later Case History Information, see KeyCite on WESTLAW

Hill v. Thomas, TexCivApp–Beaumont, 140 SW2d 875, writ dism, correct.—App & E 1067; Deeds 188, 196(2), 211(3); Fraud 49; Plead 34(3).

Hill v. Thompson & Knight, TexApp–Dallas, 756 SW2d 824.—Bills & N 489(6); Costs 263; Judgm 185.3(16).

Hill v. Thrasher, TexCivApp–Austin, 196 SW2d 461, ref nre.—Wills 439, 440, 487(1), 840.

Hill; Traders & General Ins. Co. v., TexCivApp–Beaumont, 161 SW2d 1101, writ refused wom.—App & E 760(2); Damag 221(6); Trial 351.5(1); Work Comp 1396, 1490, 1683, 1919.

Hill; Traders & General Ins. Co. v., TexCivApp–Eastland, 104 SW2d 603, writ dism.—App & E 724(4), 1060.1(1), 1060.1(10); Trial 114, 121(2).

Hill; Travelers Ins. Co. v., Tex, 351 SW2d 530, 163 Tex 81.—Work Comp 1034.

Hill v. Travelers Ins. Co., TexCivApp–Amarillo, 401 SW2d 120.—Work Comp 1660, 1927, 1969.

Hill; Travelers Ins. Co. v., TexCivApp–Houston, 344 SW2d 208, writ gr, aff 351 SW2d 530, 163 Tex 81.—Work Comp 1034, 1036, 1041, 1042.

Hill; Tucker v., TexCivApp–Hous (14 Dist), 577 SW2d 321, ref nre.—Wills 121, 123(3), 302(1).

Hill v. Turner, TexCivApp–Eastland, 165 SW2d 489.—Elections 152, 154(1).

Hill; U.S. v., CA5 (Tex), 258 F3d 355, cert den 122 SCt 575, 534 US 1033, 151 LEd2d 447.—Sent & Pun 698, 973.

Hill; U.S. v., CA5 (Tex), 42 F3d 914, reh and sug for reh den 50 F3d 1035, cert den 116 SCt 130, 516 US 843, 133 LEd2d 79.—Crim Law 1134(2), 1136, 1139, 1158(1), 1177; Sent & Pun 630, 736.

Hill; U.S. v., CA5 (Tex), 19 F3d 984, cert den 115 SCt 320, 513 US 929, 130 LEd2d 281.—Crim Law 394.1(3); Searches 47.1, 49, 124, 148, 149.

Hill; U.S. v., CA5 (Tex), 468 F2d 899.—Rec S Goods 1, 8(3).

Hill; U.S. v., CA5 (Tex), 463 F2d 235, cert den 93 SCt 297, 409 US 952, 34 LEd2d 223.—Const Law 4679; Crim Law 706(7), 742(3), 1132.

Hill; U.S. v., CA5 (Tex), 368 F2d 617.—Fed Cts 799; Int Rev 4849, 5200, 5203, 5206, 5219.25, 5228, 5235; Princ & S 82(2).

Hill v. U.S., CA5 (Tex), 363 F2d 176.—Crim Law 867, 1169.1(2.1), 1169.3, 1169.5(1), 1169.5(5); Int Rev 5263.35, 5294, 5313; Witn 377.

Hill; U.S. v., CA5 (Tex), 174 F2d 61.—U S 111(4), 144.

Hill; U.S. v., CA5 (Tex), 171 F2d 404, opinion withdrawn in part on rearg 174 F2d 61.—Fed Civ Proc 86, 1951, 2573; U S 111(1), 111(2), 111(4).

Hill; U.S. v., CA5 (Tex), 142 FedAppx 836.—Obscen 2.5.

Hill; U.S. v., CA5 (Tex), 139 FedAppx 622.—Crim Law 330, 1035(1), 1042.

Hill; U.S. v., NDTex, 537 FSupp 677.—Int Rev 4490, 4500.

Hill v. U.S., NDTex, 74 FSupp 129, set aside 171 F2d 404, opinion withdrawn in part on rearg 174 F2d 61, aff as mod 174 F2d 61.—Fed Civ Proc 1835; Insurance 3517; U S 111(2), 111(4), 111(8), 135.

Hill; Utilities Natural Gas Corp. v., TexCivApp–Dallas, 239 SW2d 431, ref nre.—Action 40, 45(1), 60; App & E 1026, 1046.1, 1050.1(5), 1058(1); Evid 441(1); Frds St of 72(1); Labor & Emp 255, 256(5), 265; Trial 3(4), 351.2(3.1).

Hill; Uvalde Const. Co. v., Tex, 175 SW2d 247, 142 Tex 19.—Explos 12; Neglig 386, 387, 1537.

Hill v. Uvalde Const. Co., TexCivApp–Eastland, 151 SW2d 283.—Plead 111.16, 111.42(6).

Hill v. Victoria County Drainage Dist. No. 3, CA5 (Tex), 441 F2d 416.—Decl Judgm 389.

Hill v. Villarreal, TexCivApp–San Antonio, 383 SW2d 463, ref nre.—Mun Corp 63.15(3); Nuis 31, 33, 34, 36, 84.

Hill v. Villarreal, TexCivApp–Waco, 362 SW2d 348, ref nre, appeal after remand 383 SW2d 463, ref nre.—Estop 62.4; Nuis 21, 23(2), 32.

Hill v. Walker, TexCivApp–Eastland, 479 SW2d 121.—App & E 934(1), 989, 1079, 1170.9(4); Autos 244(43), 244(58); New Tr 60.

Hill v. Wallace, TexCivApp–Austin, 253 SW2d 464, dism.—Wills 440, 531(1), 531(3).

Hill v. Watts, TexApp–Beaumont, 801 SW2d 176, writ den.—Deeds 70(1); Ven & Pur 196, 198.

Hill; Waukee v., TexCivApp–El Paso, 99 SW2d 1047, writ refused.—Frds St of 56(5), 71.1; Trusts 17(3).

Hill v. W. E. Brittain, Inc., TexCivApp–Fort Worth, 405 SW2d 803.—Autos 150, 168(1), 172(5.1), 201(3), 245(60); Evid 597; Judgm 199(3.9), 199(3.17), 199(5); Motions 19; Trial 18, 180.

Hill; Weldon v., TexApp–Fort Worth, 678 SW2d 268, ref nre.—Abate & R 7; Courts 472.4(6), 475(1), 484, 487(1), 488(1); Ex & Ad 7; Judgm 749; Wills 218, 702, 703.

Hill v. Wesco Materials Corp., TexCivApp–Fort Worth, 382 SW2d 786.—Autos 197(1), 197(7).

Hill; Western Minerals, Inc. v., TexCivApp–Amarillo, 441 SW2d 677.—App & E 302(5); Sales 422; Trial 358.

Hill; Wheat v., TexCivApp–San Antonio, 317 SW2d 575, writ refused.—Wills 440, 470(1), 471, 614(2), 695(2).

Hill v. Wheat, TexCivApp–San Antonio, 304 SW2d 599.—App & E 66, 79(1), 80(1), 80(6).

Hill v. Whiteside, TexApp–Fort Worth, 749 SW2d 144, writ den.—Bound 3(7), 25, 32, 36(5), 37(3), 53; Plead 236(7); Pretrial Proc 313.

Hill; Williams v., TexCivApp–Dallas, 396 SW2d 911.—Contracts 82, 91, 100; Judgm 185(2), 185.1(3), 185.2(4), 185.3(2); Release 9, 12(2).

Hill; Williams v., TexCivApp–Dallas, 392 SW2d 759.—App & E 23, 344, 345.1, 356, 396.

Hill; Williams v., TexCivApp–Tyler, 496 SW2d 748, ref nre.—App & E 989; Autos 201(1.1), 201(2), 206, 226(2), 244(36.1); Neglig 371, 387, 1683.

Hill v. Winkleman, SDTex, 377 FSupp 738.—Civil R 1465(1).

Hill v. Winn Dixie Texas, Inc., Tex, 849 SW2d 802.—App & E 1064.1(8); Neglig 1741; Trial 252(8).

Hill v. Winn Dixie Texas, Inc., TexApp–Texarkana, 824 SW2d 311, writ den 849 SW2d 802.—App & E 989, 1122(2); Neglig 1679, 1741; Trial 182, 219, 349(2).

Hill v. Wolfe, TexCivApp–El Paso, 184 SW2d 489, writ refused wom.—Autos 20; Chat Mtg 83, 133; Const Law 2632.

Hill; Yellow Cab Corp. of Dallas v., TexCivApp–Dallas, 111 SW2d 1193.—App & E 383, 455.

Hill; Zielinski v., CA5 (Tex), 972 F2d 116. See Hill, Matter of.

Hill; Zurich Gen. Acc. & Liability Ins. Co. v., TexCivApp–Texarkana, 251 SW2d 948, ref nre.—Death 2(1); Work Comp 1410, 1924, 1969.

Hilla v. State, TexApp–Houston (1 Dist), 832 SW2d 773, petition for discretionary review refused.—Arrest 63.4(12), 63.4(16), 63.5(7); Crim Law 1152(2); Jury 131(8), 131(13), 131(17).

Hillaire v. U.S., CA5 (Tex), 438 F2d 128.—Crim Law 273.3, 1132, 1481.

Hillan; U.S. v., NDTex, 381 FSupp 1171.—Searches 16, 33, 47.1.

Hilland v. Arnold, TexApp–Texarkana, 856 SW2d 240.—App & E 1003(7); Damag 43, 185(1).

Hilland; Continental Southern Lines, Inc. v., Tex, 528 SW2d 828.—App & E 1178(2); Corp 505; Lim of Act 6(11), 121(2), 126, 138.

Hilland; Continental Trailways, Inc. v., TexCivApp–Hous (14 Dist), 516 SW2d 279, writ gr, rev Continental Southern Lines, Inc v. Hilland, 528 SW2d 828.—Lim of Act 121(1), 121(2).

HILL &

Hill & Combs v. First Nat. Bank of San Angelo, Tex., CCA5 (Tex), 139 F2d 740.—Contracts 166, 176(1); Evid 448, 450(7); U S 74.2.

Hill & Combs; First Nat. Bank of San Angelo, Tex. v., TexCivApp–Austin, 177 SW2d 75.—Plead 111.43.

Hill & Combs; Seligmann v., TexCivApp–San Antonio, 338 SW2d 178, ref nre.—Assign 41, 73, 85.

Hill and Griffith Co. v. Bryant, TexApp–Tyler, 139 SW3d 688, review den (2 pets).—App & E 961, 989; Atty & C 77; Costs 2; Pretrial Proc 13, 15, 30, 31, 32, 44.1, 375, 434; Prod Liab 14.

Hill & Hill Exterminators; Collier v., TexCivApp–Houston, 322 SW2d 329, 73 ALR2d 1141.—App & E 218.2(2), 230, 928(3); Neglig 306, 404, 1599, 1676, 1683; Trial 352.10, 356(5), 365.3.

Hill & Hill Exterminators, Inc.; McKnight v., Tex, 689 SW2d 206.—Antitrust 367, 369; App & E 930(3), 989; Evid 548; Trial 139.1(7), 139.1(8).

Hill & Hill Exterminators, Inc. v. McKnight, TexApp–Houston (14 Dist), 678 SW2d 515, writ gr, aff 689 SW2d 206.—Antitrust 130, 369, 390; App & E 930(1), 989.

Hill & Hill Motor Co.; General Am. Cas. Co. v., TexCivApp–Galveston, 269 SW2d 818.—Insurance 1832(1), 2652, 2885.

Hill & Hill Truck Line v. Van Schoubroek, TexCivApp–Galveston, 233 SW2d 167.—App & E 932(1), 1004(3); Damag 132(7), 221(5.1); New Tr 44(1), 152.

Hill & Hill Truck Line, Inc.; Carter v., SDTex, 259 FSupp 429, 19 Wage & Hour Cas (BNA) 134.—Courts 489(9); Rem of C 13.

Hill & Hill Truck Line, Inc.; Mitchell v., SDTex, 183 FSupp 463.—Labor & Emp 2290(5).

Hill & Hill Truck Line, Inc. v. Owens, TexCivApp–Beaumont, 514 SW2d 74, ref nre.—Autos 180, 244(18), 245(67.1); Damag 134(2); Neglig 1696, 1714; New Tr 27, 56.

Hill & Hill Truck Line, Inc. v. Powell, TexCivApp–Waco, 319 SW2d 128.—Costs 234; Land & Ten 148(1), 148(4), 154(3), 157(5), 160(2), 184(2); Lim of Act 46(6).

Hillard v. C.I.R., CA5 (Tex), 281 F2d 279.—Int Rev 3233, 3236, 4731, 4736.

Hillblom v. Continental Air Lines, Inc., SDTex, 61 BR 758. See Continental Air Lines, Inc., In re.

Hillblom; Continental Air Lines, Inc. v., SDTex, 61 BR 758. See Continental Air Lines, Inc., In re.

Hillburn v. State, TexApp–Amarillo, 627 SW2d 546.—Crim Law 1042; Sent & Pun 2019, 2021.

Hill Chemicals Co. v. Miller, Tex, 462 SW2d 568.—App & E 628(1).

Hill Chemicals Co. v. Miller, TexCivApp–Texarkana, 459 SW2d 905, rev 462 SW2d 568.—App & E 23, 436, 564(1), 622, 624, 627, 628(1), 628(2); New Tr 155.

Hillcoat Properties, Inc.; Esquivel v., WDTex, 484 FSupp2d 582.—Commerce 62.43, 62.44(1), 62.49, 62.61; Fed Civ Proc 2498, 2553; Labor & Emp 2232, 2236.

Hill Const. Co. v. Dealers Elec. Supply Co., TexApp–Beaumont, 790 SW2d 805. See Don Hill Const. Co. v. Dealers Elec. Supply Co.

Hill Constructors, Inc. v. Stonhard, Inc., TexApp–Houston (1 Dist), 833 SW2d 742, writ den.—Contracts 143(2), 155, 198(2), 232(2), 312(5); Costs 260(5); Judgm 185(2).

Hill Country Life Ins. Co.; American Ben. Life Ins. Co. v., TexCivApp–Fort Worth, 582 SW2d 227, ref nre.—Insurance 1401.

Hill Country Memorial Hosp.; Durst v., TexApp–San Antonio, 70 SW3d 233.—App & E 946, 971(2), 1050.1(1), 1056.1(1); Atty & C 32(12); Evid 535, 536, 544, 546, 560; Pretrial Proc 356.1, 410, 434; Witn 208(1).

Hill Country Spring Water of Texas, Inc. v. Krug, TexApp–San Antonio, 773 SW2d 637, writ den.—Const Law 885, 3965(4); Courts 517; Ex & Ad 441; Judgm 815, 818(1), 944; Parties 94(1).

Hill Country Telephone Co-op., Inc.; Hernandez v., CA5 (Tex), 849 F2d 139, reh den 853 F2d 925.—Civil R 1312, 1487, 1502, 1529, 1530, 1548, 1574, 1593; Jury 25(6).

Hill County; Crain v., TexCivApp–Waco, 613 SW2d 367, ref nre.—App & E 218.2(1), 218.2(7), 1170.7.

Hill County; Hill Farm, Inc. v., Tex, 436 SW2d 320.—Estop 62.3; High 12, 153, 167; Mun Corp 668, 680(4), 692, 703(1); Nuis 63.

Hill County; Hill Farm, Inc. v., TexCivApp–Waco, 425 SW2d 414, ref nre, and writ gr, aff 436 SW2d 320.—Counties 49, 216; Dist & Pros Attys 7(1); Estop 62.3; Evid 265(9); High 88, 159(1), 159(2), 165, 167; Nuis 63; Pretrial Proc 479, 483.

Hill County; Parks v., TexCivApp–Waco, 387 SW2d 956.—App & E 171(3), 173(2), 187(3), 846(5); Ease 61(7); Evid 591; High 52, 158.

Hill County; Patten v., TexCivApp–Waco, 297 SW 918, writ dism woj.—Bankr 154, 155, 295, 309, 315(1); Judgm 883(12); Partners 219(2); Torts 22.

Hill County v. Sheppard, Tex, 178 SW2d 261, 142 Tex 358.—Const Law 19, 2390; Dist & Pros Attys 1; Statut 48.

Hillcrest Baptist Medical Center; Sosebee v., TexApp–Waco, 8 SW3d 427, reh overr, and review den.—App & E 223, 934(1); Const Law 328, 2312, 3015; Damag 51; Death 15, 31(7); Judgm 181(33), 185(5), 186.

Hillcrest Baptist Medical Center v. Wade, TexApp–Waco, 172 SW3d 55, review gr, and cause dism.—Health 611, 804, 809.

Hillcrest Memorial Park of Dallas; Wilcox v., Tex, 701 SW2d 842.—Sales 441(3).

Hillcrest Memorial Park of Dallas; Wilcox v., TexApp–Dallas, 696 SW2d 423, ref nre 701 SW2d 842.—Sales 285(1), 285(2).

Hillcrest State Bank v. Bankers Leasing Corp. of Texas, TexCivApp–Dallas, 544 SW2d 727, ref nre.—Sec Tran 24, 25, 205.

Hillcrest State Bank of University Park; Ballard v., TexCivApp–Dallas, 592 SW2d 373, ref nre.—App & E 1050.2; Cons Cred 16, 17, 19; Interest 31, 39(2.55), 39(3); Trial 365.1(1).

Hillcrest State Bank of University Park; Costello v., TexCivApp–Dallas, 380 SW2d 780.—Inj 135, 147; Mtg 338; Trusts 25(1).

Hillcrest State Bank of University Park v. Evis-Southwest, Inc., TexCivApp–Fort Worth, 402 SW2d 276, ref nre 409 SW2d 841.—Banks 148(1), 148(4), 154(1), 154(6), 154(8); Interest 19(1); Stip 14(10).

Hillcrest State Bank of University Park; Flurry v., TexCivApp–Texarkana, 401 SW2d 857, ref nre.—Banks 181; Bills & N 131; Usury 42, 100(1).

Hillcrest State Bank of University Park; Miller & Miller Auctioneers, Inc. v., TexCivApp–Dallas, 430 SW2d 61.—App & E 619, 679(2), 901; Corp 503(2); Plead 15, 45, 111.15, 111.18, 111.21, 111.30, 404; Venue 19, 22(4).

Hillcrest State Bank of University Park; Steine v., TexCivApp–Dallas, 423 SW2d 443.—Bailm 30; Fraud 12, 50, 58(1).

Hillegust v. Amerada Petroleum Corp., TexCivApp–Beaumont, 282 SW2d 892, ref nre.—Decl Judgm 327.1; Mines 55(7), 78.1(7).

Hilleman; Wiggins v., TexCivApp–Dallas, 327 SW2d 774, ref nre.—Home 103, 107; Inj 150.

Hillen v. Hooker Const. Co., TexCivApp–Waco, 484 SW2d 113.—Neglig 1612, 1620, 1658, 1677, 1695.

Hill Engineering, Inc.; Davis v., CA5 (Tex), 549 F2d 314, reh den 554 F2d 1065.—Adm 32.1, 39; Damag 99, 226; Evid 571(10); Fed Civ Proc 536; Fed Cts 77, 101, 714, 868, 875; Seamen 2, 11(4), 29(1), 29(2), 29(5.4), 29(5.5), 29(5.12), 29(5.14).

Hill Equipment Co. v. Merryman, TexApp–Austin, 771 SW2d 207. See Gene Hill Equipment Co. v. Merryman.

Hiller; Herrington v., CA5 (Tex), 883 F2d 411.—Evid 146; Fed Cts 823, 901.1; Health 820.

Hiller v. Manufacturers Product Research Group of North America, Inc., CA5 (Tex), 59 F3d 1514, reh den. —Antitrust 368, 389(2), 391, 392; Damag 190; Fed Cts 901.1, 945; Frds St of 119(1), 119(2).

Hiller v. Prosper Tex, Inc., TexCivApp–Hous (1 Dist), 437 SW2d 412.—Bills & N 129(2); Mtg 302, 338.

Hillerby v. State, TexCrimApp, 155 SW2d 609.—Crim Law 1182.

Hillery Apartments v. O'Neill, TexApp–Houston (1 Dist), 782 SW2d 942. See Sherwood Lane Associates v. O'Neill.

Hilley; Carson v., TexCivApp–Fort Worth, 484 SW2d 457. —Courts 478; Plead 111.42(4); Receivers 177.

Hilley v. Hilley, Tex, 342 SW2d 565, 161 Tex 569.—Gifts 1; Hus & W 248.5, 249(1), 254, 266.2(2); States 18.69.

Hilley; Hilley v., Tex, 342 SW2d 565, 161 Tex 569.—Gifts 1; Hus & W 248.5, 249(1), 254, 266.2(2); States 18.69.

Hilley v. Hilley, TexCivApp–Waco, 327 SW2d 467, writ gr, aff 342 SW2d 565, 161 Tex 569.—Hus & W 254, 266.1; Trusts 30.5(1).

Hilley; Hilley v., TexCivApp–Waco, 327 SW2d 467, writ gr, aff 342 SW2d 565, 161 Tex 569.—Hus & W 254, 266.1; Trusts 30.5(1).

Hilley v. Hilley, TexCivApp–Waco, 305 SW2d 204, ref nre.—Courts 39; Decl Judgm 276, 311.

Hilley; Hilley v., TexCivApp–Waco, 305 SW2d 204, ref nre.—Courts 39; Decl Judgm 276, 311.

Hill Farm, Inc. v. Hill County, Tex, 436 SW2d 320.— Estop 62.3; High 12, 153, 167; Mun Corp 668, 680(4), 692, 703(1); Nuis 63.

Hill Farm, Inc. v. Hill County, TexCivApp–Waco, 425 SW2d 414, ref nre, and writ gr, aff 436 SW2d 320.— Counties 49, 216; Dist & Pros Attys 7(1); Estop 62.3; Evid 265(9); High 88, 159(1), 159(2), 165, 167; Nuis 63; Pretrial Proc 479, 483.

Hillhaven, Inc. v. Care One, Inc., TexCivApp–Fort Worth, 620 SW2d 788, ref nre.—Contracts 16; Inj 200; Interpl 35; Land & Ten 37, 83(2), 86(1).

Hill, Heard, O'Neal, Gilstrap & Goetz, P.C.; Diversified Financial Systems, Inc. v., Tex, 63 SW3d 795, on remand 99 SW3d 349, on remand 2004 WL 5138054.— App & E 344; Judgm 217.

Hill, Heard, O'Neal, Gilstrap & Goetz, P.C.; Diversified Financial Systems, Inc. v., TexApp–Fort Worth, 99 SW3d 349, on remand 2004 WL 5138054.—App & E 854(4), 946, 970(2); Banks 505; Bills & N 150(1), 157, 169.1; Evid 354(1), 376(1); Judgm 181(7), 181(22), 181(26), 185.3(16); Lim of Act 25(3), 124.

Hill, Heard, O'Neal, Gilstrap & Goetz, P.C.; Diversified Financial Systems, Inc. v., TexApp–Fort Worth, 3 SW3d 616, reh overr, review gr, rev 63 SW3d 795, on remand 99 SW3d 349, on remand 2004 WL 5138054.— Action 60; App & E 78(1), 79(1), 80(1), 428(2); Parties 65(1).

Hillhouse v. Allumbaugh, TexCivApp–Fort Worth, 238 SW2d 799.—Wills 369, 371.5, 373.1.

Hillhouse v. Allumbaugh, TexCivApp–Eastland, 258 SW2d 826, ref nre.—App & E 1099(1); Judgm 306, 326.

Hillhouse; Daimlerchrysler Corp. v., TexApp–San Antonio, 161 SW3d 541, reh overr, and review gr, judgment vac, and remanded by agreement.—App & E 204(7), 230, 994(2), 1003(3); Damag 101, 127.71(2), 191, 208(5); Evid 508, 555.2, 555.4(2), 555.10, 571(6); Prod Liab 11, 14, 15, 36, 75.1, 82.1, 83.5, 87.1.

Hilliard, Ex parte, TexCrimApp, 687 SW2d 316.—Crim Law 273.4(1), 577.7, 577.8(1), 577.10(5), 577.10(8), 577.11(2), 577.16(8), 577.16(9); Hab Corp 479.

Hilliard, Ex parte, TexCrimApp, 538 SW2d 135.—Double J 150(1); Hab Corp 275.1, 276.

Hilliard; Arredondo v., TexApp–San Antonio, 904 SW2d 754, reh overr, and writ gr, rev Baptist Memorial Hosp System v. Arredondo, 922 SW2d 120.—App & E 863;

Const Law 2315, 3871, 3879, 3895, 3971; Death 15, 21, 38, 39; Judgm 185(2), 185.1(4); Lim of Act 4(2), 104(1), 104(2), 195(5).

Hilliard v. Bennett, TexApp–Corpus Christi, 925 SW2d 338, subsequent mandamus proceeding In re Bennett, 960 SW2d 35, reh overr, cert den In re Hilliard, 119 SCt 66, 525 US 823, 142 LEd2d 52.—Atty & C 36(2); Const Law 3992; Costs 2; Judges 24; Pretrial Proc 506.1, 508, 517.1, 520.

Hilliard v. Beto, CA5 (Tex), 494 F2d 35.—Hab Corp 747.

Hilliard v. Beto, CA5 (Tex), 465 F2d 829, opinion vac 494 F2d 35.—Hab Corp 747, 864(3).

Hilliard v. Board of Pardons and Paroles, CA5 (Tex), 759 F2d 1190.—Civil R 1097, 1376(7), 1395(7); Const Law 82(13), 3823; Fed Civ Proc 1837.1.

Hilliard v. Heard, TexApp–Houston (1 Dist), 666 SW2d 584.—Mand 26, 32.

Hilliard v. Hilliard, TexApp–Dallas, 725 SW2d 722.— Evid 207(1), 265(7); Hus & W 262.1(1), 262.2, 264(4).

Hilliard; Hilliard v., TexApp–Dallas, 725 SW2d 722.— Evid 207(1), 265(7); Hus & W 262.1(1), 262.2, 264(4).

Hilliard v. Hines, TexCivApp–Tyler, 403 SW2d 442.— App & E 387(3), 387(6), 395, 640.

Hilliard v. Home Builders Supply Co., TexCivApp–Fort Worth, 399 SW2d 198, ref nre.—App & E 547(3), 553(2); Atty & C 166(3), 167(2); Costs 194.18; Evid 222(2); Home 57(1), 57(3), 97, 214; Mech Liens 73(6), 280(3), 290(5), 310(3); Trial 256(4), 284, 350.3(2.1).

Hilliard v. Messina, TexCivApp–Eastland, 404 SW2d 824. —App & E 846(5), 907(3); Tresp to T T 47(1).

Hilliard; Projects American Corp. v., TexApp–Tyler, 711 SW2d 386.—Evid 12; Mand 73(1); Statut 161(1); Zoning 45, 375.1.

Hilliard v. Smith Bros., TexCivApp–San Antonio, 159 SW2d 166.—Lim of Act 127(9); Mun Corp 485(1); Plead 291(2).

Hilliard v. State, TexCrimApp, 513 SW2d 28.—Crim Law 1119(1); Homic 522, 580, 588, 603, 1165, 1174, 1322.

Hilliard v. State, TexCrimApp, 401 SW2d 814, cert den 87 SCt 310, 385 US 941, 17 LEd2d 220, reh den 87 SCt 726, 385 US 1021, 17 LEd2d 561.—Crim Law 29(1), 29(5.5), 1077.2(1); False Pret 7(5), 49(1); Gr Jury 26; Ind & Inf 191(5).

Hilliard v. State, TexCrimApp, 340 SW2d 494, 170 Tex-Crim 290.—Controlled Subs 80; Crim Law 404.60, 1159.3(1), 1159.4(3).

Hilliard v. State, TexCrimApp, 291 SW2d 731.—Crim Law 1094(3).

Hilliard v. State, TexCrimApp, 208 SW2d 378, 151 Tex-Crim 398.—Int Liq 205(2).

Hilliard v. State, TexApp–Fort Worth, 881 SW2d 917.— Crim Law 369.1, 438(5.1), 683(1), 706(5), 1134(3), 1153(1), 1168(2), 1169.1(10), 1171.8(2); Witn 267, 269(7), 270(1), 274(1), 277(1), 301, 337(1), 344(2), 350, 367(1), 372(1).

Hilliard v. State, TexApp–Austin, 652 SW2d 602, petition for discretionary review refused, untimely filed.—Crim Law 577.10(7), 577.10(8), 577.16(5.1), 577.16(8); Ind & Inf 71.2(1), 71.4(12), 110(3), 125(20), 137(6); Infants 20.

Hilliard v. Watson, TexCivApp–Texarkana, 170 SW2d 310, writ refused.—App & E 1051.1(1); Hab Corp 532(1), 731.

Hilliard v. Wilkerson, TexCivApp–Fort Worth, 492 SW2d 292, ref nre, and writ gr, and dism.—Const Law 2473, 2489; Mun Corp 34; Statut 190, 223.5(4).

Hillier v. Howard, TexCivApp–Eastland, 131 SW2d 1002, writ refused.—Evid 590; Home 57(3).

Hillier; Ussery v., TexCivApp–El Paso, 234 SW2d 121, dism.—App & E 185(2), 758.1; Nova 2.

Hillin v. Hagler, TexCivApp–Fort Worth, 286 SW2d 661. —App & E 688(2), 1004(7); Evid 48, 158(15), 474(16), 474(19), 502.

Hillin; Hawthorne v., TexCivApp–Waco, 463 SW2d 266. —Schools 107; Tax 2128, 2160.

Hillin v. Herff Jones Co., CA5 (Tex), 443 F2d 363.—Fed Cts 743, 865; Labor & Emp 835.

Hillin; Porras v., TexCivApp–El Paso, 448 SW2d 532, ref nre.—App & E 1069.2; Trial 81, 307(3), 312(2).

Hillin; Purvis Oil Corp. v., TexApp–El Paso, 890 SW2d 931.—App & E 842(2), 863, 936(2), 984(5); Contracts 143(1), 143(2), 147(2), 147(3), 153, 227; Costs 194.18, 194.40, 198, 199, 207, 264; Estop 52.10(2), 52.10(4); Judgm 185(2), 185(4); Mines 101; Pretrial Proc 313.

Hillin v. State, TexCrimApp, 808 SW2d 486.—Ind & Inf 159(1).

Hillis; Gulf, C. & S. F. Ry. Co. v., TexCivApp–Waco, 320 SW2d 687.—App & E 1050.1(10); Carr 104; Evid 113(16), 333(7).

Hillis v. Stephen F. Austin State University, CA5 (Tex), 665 F2d 547, reh den 669 F2d 729, cert den 102 SCt 2906, 457 US 1106, 73 LEd2d 1315.—Civil R 1421; Colleges 8.1(1), 8.1(3), 8.1(5), 8.1(6.1); Const Law 90.1(7.3), 1989, 2019, 4223(5).

Hillis v. Stephen F. Austin State University, EDTex, 486 FSupp 663, rev 665 F2d 547, reh den 669 F2d 729, cert den 102 SCt 2906, 457 US 1106, 73 LEd2d 1315.— Colleges 7, 8.1(4.1), 8.1(5), 8.1(7); Const Law 90.1(7.3), 1435, 1989, 2019; Fed Cts 268.1.

Hillje, In re Estate of, TexApp–San Antonio, 830 SW2d 689.—App & E 5, 403, 907(4); Costs 260(5); Wills 356, 367.

Hillkee Corp. v. Harrell, TexCivApp–Texarkana, 573 SW2d 558, ref nre.—Courts 480(3); Execution 256(1).

Hillkee, Inc. v. Navarro Sav. Ass'n, TexApp–Waco, 632 SW2d 374.—App & E 233(1), 267(1), 274(7); Judgm 185.3(15).

Hill Lines; U.S. v., CA5 (Tex), 175 F2d 770.—Autos 245(67.1); Fed Cts 866; Neglig 1717.

Hillman v. Barnhart, CA5 (Tex), 170 FedAppx 909.— Social S 142.5, 142.10, 143.65, 143.85.

Hillman; Freeman v., TexCivApp–Amarillo, 173 SW2d 657.—App & E 1069.1; Trial 313.

Hillman v. Graves, TexCivApp–San Antonio, 134 SW2d 436.—Estop 22(2); Evid 419(2); Fraud 4, 12, 35, 64(2); Mtg 297.

Hillman v. Hillman, TexComApp, 157 SW2d 143, 138 Tex 111.—Partit 69, 89.

Hillman; Hillman v., TexComApp, 157 SW2d 143, 138 Tex 111.—Partit 69, 89.

Hillman v. Hillman, TexCivApp–Austin, 135 SW2d 802, rev 157 SW2d 143, 138 Tex 111.—Des & Dist 113; Partit 69.

Hillman; Hillman v., TexCivApp–Austin, 135 SW2d 802, rev 157 SW2d 143, 138 Tex 111.—Des & Dist 113; Partit 69.

Hillman; McLean v., TexCivApp–Amarillo, 352 SW2d 310.—Contracts 164; Land & Ten 49(2); Sales 59, 82(1).

Hillman; Sonken-Galamba Corp. v., TexCivApp–Amarillo, 111 SW2d 853, dism.—App & E 231(1), 1039(13), 1050.1(1), 1051(1); Evid 99, 143; Labor & Emp 2883, 2889; Plead 192(5); Trial 191(11); Work Comp 2124, 2135.

Hillman Distributing Co.; Greggs v., SDTex, 719 FSupp 552.—Civil R 1122, 1150, 1395(8); Fed Civ Proc 827, 1829.

Hillman Distributing Co.; Hilton v., TexApp–Texarkana, 12 SW3d 846.—App & E 552, 907(4), 1031(4), 1056.1(1).

Hillman-Kelley v. Pittman, TexCivApp–El Paso, 489 SW2d 689.—App & E 499(1), 1175(5); Neglig 551, 554(1), 554(2), 1719; Prod Liab 85; Trial 352.1(6).

Hillmer v. Farmers Royalty Holding Co., CA5 (Tex), 196 F2d 124.—Home 112, 123.

Hillock Homes, Inc. v. Claflin, CA5 (Tex), 761 F2d 1088. See Claflin, Matter of.

Hillock Homes, Inc.; Claflin v., TexApp–Austin, 645 SW2d 629, ref nre.—Spec Perf 7, 8, 16, 129.

Hill Production Co. v. Sherrill, TexCivApp–Eastland, 613 SW2d 508.—Tresp 56, 57, 68(1).

Hills; Richardson v., TexCivApp–Beaumont, 104 SW2d 151, writ dism.—Prisons 10; Sheriffs 99.

Hills v. State, TexCrimApp, 524 SW2d 692.—Crim Law 421(6).

Hills and Dales v. Reeves, TexCivApp–San Antonio, 459 SW2d 672, writ dism.—Mun Corp 12(8).

Hillsboro, City of; Barnes v., TexCivApp–Waco, 504 SW2d 939.—Evid 471(14), 505, 568(1); Judgm 185(2), 185(5), 185.2(1); Mental H 13; Mun Corp 812(10), 1021.

Hillsboro, City of; Combined Am. Ins. Co. v., TexCivApp–Waco, 421 SW2d 488, ref nre.—Costs 241; Inj 11; Mun Corp 592(1).

Hillsboro, City of; Gay v., Tex, 545 SW2d 765.—App & E 609.

Hillsboro, City of; Gay v., TexCivApp–Waco, 536 SW2d 425, writ gr, rev 545 SW2d 765.—App & E 596, 926(8).

Hillsboro Independent School Dist.; Campbell v., TexCivApp–Waco, 203 SW2d 663.—Autos 187(2); Courts 89; Schools 89.2.

Hillsboro Independent School Dist.; Doe v., CA5 (Tex), 113 F3d 1412.—Civil R 1065, 1066, 1326(6); Schools 89.2.

Hillsboro Independent School Dist.; Doe v., CA5 (Tex), 81 F3d 1395, reh gr, opinion vac, on reh 113 F3d 1412.

Hillsboro Independent School Dist.; D.S.A., Inc. v., Tex, 973 SW2d 662, appeal after remand 999 SW2d 887, review den.—Damag 91(3); Fraud 13(3), 25, 32, 36, 59(2).

Hillsboro Independent School Dist.; D.S.A., Inc. v., TexApp–Waco, 999 SW2d 887, review den.—App & E 1195(1), 1207(3); Costs 264; Interest 39(2.6).

Hillsboro Independent School Dist.; D.S.A., Inc. v., TexApp–Waco, 975 SW2d 1, rev 973 SW2d 662, appeal after remand 999 SW2d 887, review den.—App & E 232(3); Damag 140; Fraud 13(3), 32; Lim of Act 95(2), 95(16); Neglig 273, 1659, 1672; Schools 85.

Hillsboro State Bank; Smith v., TexCivApp–Galveston, 253 SW2d 897.—New Tr 86, 98.

Hillsdale Gravel Co. v. Dennehy Const. Co., TexCivApp–Eastland, 185 SW2d 583, writ refused wom.—App & E 239, 296, 877(1), 1010.1(1); Assign 72; Contracts 147(3); Corp 410, 413; Garn 105, 191, 206, 217; Mech Liens 108, 109.

Hills Fitness Center, Inc.; Williams v., TexApp–Texarkana, 705 SW2d 189, ref nre.—Antitrust 225, 363.

Hillside Bank & Trust Co.; Faulkner v., TexCivApp–Waco, 526 SW2d 274, ref nre.—App & E 927(7), 997(3); Banks 189.

Hill's, Inc.; Todd v., TexCivApp–Fort Worth, 383 SW2d 250, ref nre.—Neglig 1104(7), 1670.

Hillsman v. State, TexApp–Houston (14 Dist), 999 SW2d 157, petition for discretionary review refused.—Arrest 63.4(2), 63.4(16); Controlled Subs 115; Crim Law 394.5(4); Searches 47.1, 49.

Hillsman; U.S. v., CA5 (Tex), 480 F3d 333.—Crim Law 641.3(2), 641.3(4), 863(2), 1039, 1139, 1163(2), 1166.10(1).

Hillson Steel Products, Inc. v. Wirth Ltd., TexCivApp–Hous (1 Dist), 538 SW2d 162.—App & E 5; Corp 507(13); Judgm 123(1), 124, 126(1); Plead 310; Proc 148; Sales 22(4).

Hill, State ex rel., v. Pirtle, TexCrimApp, 887 SW2d 921. See State ex rel. Hill v. Pirtle.

Hill-Tex Communications, Inc.; City of Jacksonville v., TexCivApp–Tyler, 613 SW2d 76.—App & E 242(1), 242(2).

Hilltop Auto Salvage v. Housholder, TexApp–Eastland, 722 SW2d 217. See Chandler v. Housholder.

Hilltop Baptist Temple, Inc. v. Williamson County Appraisal Dist., TexApp–Austin, 995 SW2d 905, review den, and reh of petition for review overr.—Judgm 540, 580, 663, 713(2), 720.

Hilltop Drilling & Production, Inc.; Pipeline Services, Inc. v., TexApp–Fort Worth, 651 SW2d 416.—Venue 7.5(2), 7.5(8).

Hilltop Village, Inc. v. Kerrville Independent School Dist., Tex, 426 SW2d 943.—Tax 2300, 2338, 2340, 2341, 2343.

Hilltop Village, Inc. v. Kerrville Independent School Dist., TexCivApp–San Antonio, 487 SW2d 167, ref nre. —Tax 2343.

Hilltop Village, Inc. v. Kerrville Independent School Dist., TexCivApp–San Antonio, 410 SW2d 824, writ gr, aff 426 SW2d 943.—Asylums 2; Tax 2291, 2300, 2343, 2392.

Hill Tower, Inc. v. Department of Navy, NDTex, 718 FSupp 568.—Records 68.

Hill Tower, Inc. v. Department of Navy, NDTex, 718 FSupp 562.—Fed Civ Proc 1600(3); Records 54, 57.

Hilltown Property Owners Ass'n, Inc.; Continental Homes Co. v., TexCivApp–Fort Worth, 529 SW2d 293. —Propty 4; Receivers 12, 35(1), 42.

Hillyer, Ex parte, TexCrimApp, 372 SW2d 342.—Mental H 436.1.

Hi-Lo Auto Supply, L.P. v. Beresky, TexApp–Beaumont, 986 SW2d 382, mandamus den.—Action 13; App & E 949; Parties 35.9, 35.13, 35.17, 35.41, 35.71.

Hilpold, Ex parte, TexComApp, 97 SW2d 947, 128 Tex 281.—Contempt 82.

Hilsher v. Merrill Lynch, Pierce, Fenner & Smith, Inc., TexApp–Houston (14 Dist), 717 SW2d 435.—App & E 171(1), 172(1), 203.3, 218.2(10), 971(2), 1026, 1062.2; Com Fut 30; Damag 221(7); Evid 541, 546; Trial 350.4(4), 351.2(6), 351.5(1), 352.1(1).

Hilshire Village; Raub v., TexCivApp–Hous (14 Dist), 463 SW2d 261, ref nre.—App & E 564(3), 712, 907(3).

Hilshire Village, Village of; Frost v., TexCivApp–Houston, 403 SW2d 836, ref nre.—App & E 846(5); Evid 177; Zoning 21, 30, 137, 643, 653.

Hilson v. State, TexCrimApp, 475 SW2d 788.—Controlled Subs 148(4); Searches 143.1, 145.1.

Hilson v. State, TexApp–Houston (1 Dist), 751 SW2d 279. —Crim Law 641.13(7), 1032(7); Ind & Inf 173, 180; Larc 6, 59; Sent & Pun 1381(4).

Hilt v. Hooper, TexCivApp–Galveston, 203 SW2d 334.— Adop 6, 17.

Hilt v. Kirkpatrick, TexCivApp–Waco, 538 SW2d 849.— Child C 606, 637, 650, 733, 766.

Hilt; Martin v., TexCivApp–Waco, 289 SW2d 304.—Evid 461(1).

Hilton v. Atlantic Refining Co., CA5 (Tex), 327 F2d 217. —Fed Civ Proc 203; Fed Cts 289; Tresp to T T 26, 27.

Hilton; Atlantic Richfield Co. v., TexCivApp–Tyler, 437 SW2d 347, ref nre, cert den 90 SCt 221, 396 US 905, 24 LEd2d 182.—Estop 58, 59; Evid 264; Mines 59, 78.1(9), 78.1(10), 78.2, 78.5, 78.7(3.1); Rem of C 118; Stip 18(1).

Hilton; Commercial Cas. Ins. Co. v., TexComApp, 87 SW2d 1081, 126 Tex 497, reh den 89 SW2d 1116, 126 Tex 497.—Work Comp 1123, 1130, 1144, 1148, 1153, 1187, 1730.

Hilton v. Gray, TexCivApp–Dallas, 103 SW2d 1002.— Mun Corp 586.

Hilton v. Haden Associates, Inc., TexCivApp–Fort Worth, 458 SW2d 854.—Counties 123; Plead 406(1).

Hilton v. Hillman Distributing Co., TexApp–Texarkana, 12 SW3d 846.—App & E 552, 907(4), 1031(4), 1056.1(1).

Hilton v. Hilton, TexApp–Houston (14 Dist), 678 SW2d 645.—App & E 161; Divorce 179, 203, 252.3(2), 252.3(3), 252.3(5), 253(2), 281, 282; Hus & W 264(4), 265, 268(1).

Hilton; Hilton v., TexApp–Houston (14 Dist), 678 SW2d 645.—App & E 161; Divorce 179, 203, 252.3(2), 252.3(3), 252.3(5), 253(2), 281, 282; Hus & W 264(4), 265, 268(1).

Hilton; Hollifield v., TexCivApp–Fort Worth, 515 SW2d 717, ref nre.—Home 122, 154, 162(1), 168, 181.5; Mech Liens 14.

Hilton v. Musebeck Shoe Co., Inc., TexCivApp–Austin, 505 SW2d 341, ref nre.—Acct Action on 14.

Hilton; Peltier Enterprises, Inc. v., TexApp–Tyler, 51 SW3d 616, reh overr, and review den, and reh of

petition for review den.—Antitrust 135(1), 138, 162; App & E 863, 946, 985; Fraud 3, 16, 18, 20; Parties 35.5, 35.7, 35.17, 35.71; Torts 219.

Hilton v. Southwestern Bell Telephone Co., CA5 (Tex), 936 F2d 823, cert den 112 SCt 913, 502 US 1048, 116 LEd2d 813.—Civil R 1218(2), 1228; Fed Cts 776; Statut 194.

Hilton; State v., Tex, 412 SW2d 41.—Em Dom 238(6), 262(5).

Hilton v. State, TexCrimApp, 443 SW2d 844.—Crim Law 1147; Sent & Pun 2004.

Hilton v. State, TexCrimApp, 443 SW2d 843.—Crim Law 578, 938(3), 951(1), 959; Forg 44(3).

Hilton v. State, TexCrimApp, 324 SW2d 5, 168 TexCrim 119.—Int Liq 236(4).

Hilton v. State, TexCrimApp, 301 SW2d 133, 164 Tex-Crim 456.—Crim Law 369.6; Int Liq 236(6.5).

Hilton v. State, TexCrimApp, 273 SW2d 873, 160 Tex-Crim 638.—Crim Law 736(2), 1090.19, 1134(3); Infants 20.

Hilton v. State, TexCrimApp, 235 SW2d 178, 155 Tex-Crim 393.—Crim Law 1171.1(3); Homic 1325, 1474.

Hilton v. State, TexCrimApp, 191 SW2d 875, 149 Tex-Crim 22.—Big 2, 8; Witn 191, 380(2).

Hilton v. State, TexApp–Fort Worth, 659 SW2d 154, petition for discretionary review refused.—Assault 92(5); Crim Law 59(3), 347, 552(1), 552(3), 560, 772(6), 814(1), 829(20).

Hilton v. State, TexApp–Texarkana, 975 SW2d 788, petition for discretionary review refused.—Crim Law 59(1), 508(9), 510, 568, 738, 742(2), 780(1), 792(1), 1134(8), 1144.13(3), 1159.2(1), 1159.2(6), 1159.2(7), 1159.2(9), 1159.3(1), 1159.4(2), 1165(1), 1173.2(1), 1173.2(6); Larc 57.

Hilton v. State, TexApp–Beaumont, 870 SW2d 209, opinion after remand 1996 WL 355163.—Crim Law 1181.5(6).

Hilton v. State, TexApp–Houston (14 Dist), 879 SW2d 74, petition for discretionary review refused.—Crim Law 260.11(4), 814(1), 820, 847, 1134(3), 1144.13(2.1), 1144.13(3), 1159.2(1), 1159.2(7), 1159.2(9), 1159.4(1), 1167(4); Ind & Inf 159(1), 159(2), 167; Larc 1, 40(6), 55.

Hilton; State v., TexCivApp–Waco, 405 SW2d 715, writ gr, rev 412 SW2d 41.—App & E 1170.1, 1170.6, 1170.7; Em Dom 149(1), 201, 262(5); Evid 568(4); Jury 66(1); Trial 25(1); Witn 270(2).

Hilton v. Texas Inv. Bank, N.A., TexApp–Houston (14 Dist), 650 SW2d 545.—Judgm 180, 181(6), 185(6).

Hilton Center, Inc.; Sekaly v., TexCivApp–Waco, 340 SW2d 827.—App & E 554(1); Costs 194.22; Judgm 101(1), 101(2), 220.

Hilton Credit Corp.; Kirksey v., TexCivApp–Waco, 340 SW2d 565.—Plead 111.38, 111.39(2).

Hilton Hotels Corp.; Howell v., TexApp–Houston (1 Dist), 84 SW3d 708, reh overr, and petition stricken, and review den, and reh of petition for review den.— App & E 856(1), 1073(1); Corp 1.4(1), 1.4(4), 1.7(2), 215; Judgm 183, 185.3(5); Partners 67, 70.

Hilton Hotels Corp.; Walkoviak v., TexCivApp–Hous (14 Dist), 580 SW2d 623, ref nre.—App & E 230; Judgm 181(3), 181(33), 185(2), 185(3); Neglig 62(3), 1078, 1162.

Hilts v. State, TexCrimApp, 476 SW2d 283.—Sent & Pun 2003, 2025; Sheriffs 95.

Hiltz v. State, TexCrimApp, 443 SW2d 851.—Crim Law 1177.

Hilyard v. State, TexApp–Houston (1 Dist), 43 SW3d 574. —Crim Law 1026.10(1), 1026.10(2.1).

Hilzendager v. Methodist Hospital, TexCivApp–Hous (1 Dist), 596 SW2d 284, 9 ALR4th 145.—Health 656, 696, 823(4); Neglig 1599.

Hime v. City of Galveston, TexCivApp–Waco, 268 SW2d 543, ref nre.—Mun Corp 186(1), 199; Statut 199.

Hime v. State, TexApp–Houston (14 Dist), 998 SW2d 893, petition for discretionary review refused.—Arrest 63.5(4), 63.5(5); Autos 349(6), 355(6).

Himes v. American Home Fence Co., Tex, 379 SW2d 290.—Courts 89; Judgm 181(15.1), 185.3(4).

Himes; American Home Fence Co. v., TexCivApp–Tyler, 374 SW2d 777, ref nre 379 SW2d 290.—Acct Action on 10, 13; Judgm 181(15.1); Plead 296.

Himont U.S.A., Inc. v. Harris County Appraisal Dist., TexApp–Houston (1 Dist), 904 SW2d 740, reh overr.—Tax 2212, 2466, 2603.

Hinchliffe v. Texas Co., TexCivApp–Austin, 182 SW2d 368, writ refused, cert den 65 SCt 1085, 325 US 850, 89 LEd 1971.—Mines 92.39, 92.41.

Hinckley; Eggers v., TexApp–Dallas, 683 SW2d 473.—Elect of Rem 3(4); Estop 68(2); Interest 39(2.15), 39(2.30); Joint Adv 2, 8; Princ & A 99.

Hinckley v. Eggers, TexCivApp–Dallas, 587 SW2d 448, ref nre.—Bills & N 151, 152, 157, 164, 166; Evid 459(1).

Hinde v. Hinde, Tex, 701 SW2d 637.—App & E 66, 76(1), 80(1), 80(2).

Hinde; Hinde v., Tex, 701 SW2d 637.—App & E 66, 76(1), 80(1), 80(2).

Hinde v. Hinde, TexApp–Fort Worth, 689 SW2d 519, writ gr, rev 701 SW2d 637.—Divorce 186; Judgm 21.

Hinde; Hinde v., TexApp–Fort Worth, 689 SW2d 519, writ gr, rev 701 SW2d 637.—Divorce 186; Judgm 21.

Hinde; Texas Real Estate Commission v., TexApp–Fort Worth, 627 SW2d 537.—Brok 1, 3.

Hinderliter; Fox v., TexApp–San Antonio, 222 SW3d 154.—Health 804, 805, 809; Pretrial Proc 508, 512, 516, 517.1.

Hinderliter Industries, Inc., In re, BkrtcyEDTex, 228 BR 848.—Bankr 2970; Contracts 143(1), 143.5; Corp 468.1.

Hindes v. U.S., CA5 (Tex), 371 F2d 650, cert den 87 SCt 1307, 386 US 992, 18 LEd2d 337.—Int Rev 3629.1, 5049.

Hindes v. U.S., CA5 (Tex), 326 F2d 150, cert den 84 SCt 1168, 377 US 908, 12 LEd2d 178, on remand 246 FSupp 147, aff in part, rev in part and remanded 371 F2d 650, cert den 87 SCt 1307, 386 US 992, 18 LEd2d 337.—Fed Civ Proc 2514, 2534, 2556.

Hindes v. U.S., WDTex, 246 FSupp 147, aff in part, rev in part and remanded 371 F2d 650, cert den 87 SCt 1307, 386 US 992, 18 LEd2d 337.—Corp 1.6(11); Int Rev 3179, 3198, 3203, 3225, 3402, 3563, 4957, 5041.

Hindes v. U.S., WDTex, 214 FSupp 583, rev 326 F2d 150, cert den 84 SCt 1168, 377 US 908, 12 LEd2d 178, on remand 246 FSupp 147, aff in part, rev in part and remanded 371 F2d 650, cert den 87 SCt 1307, 386 US 992, 18 LEd2d 337.—Int Rev 3186.

Hindley v. State, TexCrimApp, 166 SW2d 704, 145 TexCrim 176.—Crim Law 1094(2.1).

Hindley v. State, TexCrimApp, 166 SW2d 703, 145 TexCrim 174.—Crim Law 1094(2.1); Int Liq 236(11).

Hindman v. City of Paris, Tex., CA5 (Tex), 746 F2d 1063.—Civil R 1429; Crim Law 211(1); Fed Civ Proc 2148.1; Fed Cts 637.

Hindman v. State, TexCrimApp, 463 SW2d 1.—Crim Law 1020.

Hindman v. State, TexCrimApp, 211 SW2d 182, 152 TexCrim 75.—Crim Law 720(5), 742(1); Rape 13, 17, 54(1), 57(1), 59(11); Witn 379(1), 379(9).

Hindman v. State Dept. of Highways & Public Transp., TexApp–Tyler, 906 SW2d 43, reh overr, and writ den.—Autos 258, 273.

Hindman; Texas Dept. of Public Safety v., TexApp–Fort Worth, 989 SW2d 28.—Admin Law 683, 749, 754.1, 763, 791; Autos 349(2.1), 349(5).

Hindman v. Texas Lime Co., Tex, 305 SW2d 947, 157 Tex 592.—Damag 6; Land & Ten 170(1), 170(4); Nuis 49(5); Trial 3(4), 352.10.

Hindman; Texas Lime Co. v., TexCivApp–Waco, 300 SW2d 112, writ gr, aff 305 SW2d 947, 157 Tex 592.—

Action 50(3); App & E 1039(13), 1062.1; Damag 221(5.1); Land & Ten 169(11), 170(4); Nuis 33, 48, 49(2), 50(1); Plead 1, 228.14.

Hinds; Bates v., NDTex, 334 FSupp 528.—Const Law 4202; Fed Civ Proc 2737.6; Schools 144(3), 147.38, 147.47.

Hinds; Biggs v., TexCivApp–Amarillo, 177 SW2d 288, writ refused wom.—App & E 1008.2; Evid 589; Hus & W 264(5), 264(7).

Hinds v. Biggs, TexCivApp–Amarillo, 142 SW2d 902.—App & E 1040(10); Lim of Act 40(1), 40(2); Mines 50, 74(8); Paymt 60(1).

Hinds, Estate of; C.I.R. v., CA5 (Tex), 180 F2d 930.—Int Rev 4159(3), 4686.

Hinds v. Dallas Independent School Dist., NDTex, 188 FSupp2d 664.—Civil R 1027, 1335; Consp 15; Const Law 1204, 1435, 2085; Evid 43(3); Fed Civ Proc 2466, 2470, 2470.1, 2470.4, 2543, 2544, 2545, 2546, 2552, 2553; Mal Pros 0.5, 14.

Hinds; Darrah v., TexApp–Fort Worth, 720 SW2d 689, ref nre.—App & E 236(1); Libel 38(1), 38(2), 41, 50.5, 51(1).

Hinds v. Hinds, TexCivApp–San Antonio, 491 SW2d 448.—Abate & R 13; Child C 732, 733.

Hinds; Hinds v., TexCivApp–San Antonio, 491 SW2d 448.—Abate & R 13; Child C 732, 733.

Hinds; Killough v., Tex, 338 SW2d 707, 161 Tex 178.—Adv Poss 11, 60(4); Judgm 185.2(3); Land & Ten 66(2); Mines 49.

Hinds v. Killough, TexCivApp–Amarillo, 332 SW2d 101, ref nre, and writ gr, rev 338 SW2d 707, 161 Tex 178.—Adv Poss 22, 36, 47, 60(4), 80(2), 115(1); Judgm 181(15.1).

Hinds v. Madison, TexCivApp–San Antonio, 424 SW2d 61, ref nre.—Inj 22; Land & Ten 92(1).

Hinds v. Parmley, TexCivApp–Beaumont, 315 SW2d 159.—Adv Poss 110(3), 114(1); Bound 5, 37(5), 46(1); Deeds 90.

Hinds v. Southwestern Sav. Ass'n of Houston, TexCivApp–Beaumont, 562 SW2d 4, ref nre.—Judgm 185.3(5); Lim of Act 66(9).

Hinds v. State, TexApp–Dallas, 970 SW2d 33.—Crim Law 369.2(5), 1169.1(2.1).

Hinds; Texas Dept. of Human Services v., TexApp–El Paso, 860 SW2d 893, reh overr, and writ gr, rev 904 SW2d 629.—Damag 48, 100, 187, 192, 208(1), 226; Interest 39(2.6); Offic 66; States 53, 79, 191.9(1); Statut 212.6, 212.7.

Hinds; Texas Dept. of Human Services of State of Tex. v., Tex, 904 SW2d 629.—App & E 216(7), 1067; Civil R 1536; Labor & Emp 785, 861, 863(2); Offic 66, 72.61; States 53.

Hindsman v. Willis, TexCivApp–Texarkana, 125 SW2d 1073, writ dism, correct.—Adv Poss 71(2); App & E 931(1); Hus & W 274(1); Ten in C 15(1), 15(5), 15(7).

Hine v. State, TexCrimApp, 622 SW2d 872.—Tel 1018(4).

Hineline v. State, TexCrimApp, 502 SW2d 703.—Controlled Subs 73, 75.

Hine Pontiac Co.; Smith v., TexCivApp–Waco, 328 SW2d 919, writ refused.—Judgm 145(3).

Hinerman v. Gunn Chevrolet, TexApp–San Antonio, 877 SW2d 806, reh den, and writ gr, rev in part 898 SW2d 817.—App & E 854(1); Judgm 181(21); Labor & Emp 810, 863(2).

Hinerman; Gunn Chevrolet, Inc. v., Tex, 898 SW2d 817.—Labor & Emp 807; Work Comp 2088.

Hines v. AC and S, Inc., NDTex, 128 FSupp2d 1003.—Rem of C 25(2), 79(1), 107(7).

Hines v. Aetna Cas. and Sur. Co., TexApp–Houston (1 Dist), 754 SW2d 803, writ den.—Work Comp 862, 876.

Hines v. Bankers Life and Cas. Co., TexCivApp–Hous (14 Dist), 572 SW2d 804.—Insurance 3564(7); Judgm 181(3), 181(7), 181(23), 185(1), 185(2).

Hines v. **Beto**, CA5 (Tex), 473 F2d 1034, reh den 474 F2d 1347, cert den 94 SCt 93, 414 US 870, 38 LEd2d 89.—Hab Corp 490(2), 722(1).

Hines v. **Bevers**, TexCivApp–Amarillo, 105 SW2d 388, writ dism.—App & E 713(1); Jury 25(2); Mental H 123, 128, 138, 155, 295, 304; Plead 8(9), 18.

Hines; **Bitner v.**, TexCivApp–Galveston, 293 SW2d 540.—App & E 912; Crim Law 59(1), 59(2), 59(4); Neglig 1620; Venue 8.5(4).

Hines v. **Boothe**, CA5 (Tex), 841 F2d 623.—Civil R 1395(7).

Hines; **Bowman Biscuit Co. of Tex. v.**, Tex, 251 SW2d 153, 151 Tex 370.—Sales 255.

Hines; **Bowman Biscuit Co. of Tex. v.**, TexCivApp–Dallas, 240 SW2d 467, certified question answered 251 SW2d 153, 151 Tex 370.—Corp 503(2); Pretrial Proc 479, 481, 483; Sales 255.

Hines v. **Commission for Lawyer Discipline**, TexApp–Corpus Christi, 28 SW3d 697.—App & E 93, 854(1), 930(1), 931(3), 1010.2, 1011.1(1), 1011.1(6), 1012.1(4); Atty & C 53(2); Evid 597.

Hines v. **Davison**, TexCivApp–Waco, 381 SW2d 360.—Trial 26.

Hines; **Dean v.**, TexCivApp–Texarkana, 100 SW2d 194.—App & E 1008.1(8.1); Names 18; Plead 388.

Hines v. **Evergreen Cemetery Ass'n**, TexApp–Texarkana, 865 SW2d 266.—Antitrust 134, 141, 150, 363; App & E 919; Pretrial Proc 695.

Hines; **Gibson v.**, TexCivApp–Waco, 511 SW2d 546.—Child C 7, 42, 76, 276, 908, 921(1).

Hines v. **Graham**, NDTex, 320 FSupp2d 511.—Civil R 1036, 1090, 1098, 1358, 1376(7), 1395(7), 1463; Const Law 1422, 3823, 3825, 4824; Fed Civ Proc 41, 1700, 2734; Prisons 4(5), 13(6).

Hines; **Harris v.**, TexApp–Texarkana, 137 SW3d 898.—App & E 895(2); Wills 435, 439, 440, 456, 470(1), 470(2), 481, 487(1), 487(2), 488, 491, 750, 751, 753, 756, 764, 765, 767, 770.

Hines v. **Hash**, Tex, 843 SW2d 464.—Abate & R 19; Antitrust 286, 297; App & E 870(2).

Hines; **Hash v.**, TexApp–Amarillo, 796 SW2d 312, writ gr, rev 843 SW2d 464.—Abate & R 19; Antitrust 286.

Hines v. **Helms**, CA5 (Tex), 78 FedAppx 360.—Civil R 1326(8); Fed Civ Proc 2734.

Hines; **Hernandez v.**, NDTex, 159 FSupp2d 378.—Civil R 1039, 1057, 1373, 1376(1), 1376(2), 1395(1); Infants 226.

Hines; **Hilliard v.**, TexCivApp–Tyler, 403 SW2d 442.—App & E 387(3), 387(6), 395, 640.

Hines; **McCormick v.**, TexCivApp–Amarillo, 503 SW2d 333.—App & E 23, 66, 76(1), 80(3), 80(6), 792.

Hines; **McCormick v.**, TexCivApp–Amarillo, 498 SW2d 58, dism.—Contracts 113(5); Judgm 518; Pretrial Proc 517.1, 518; Spec Perf 73; Trusts 162, 167, 254; Venue 22(3).

Hines; **Maricle v.**, TexCivApp–Fort Worth, 247 SW2d 611.—Ease 5, 8(2), 36(1), 36(3).

Hines v. **Massachusetts Mut. Life Ins. Co.**, CA5 (Tex), 43 F3d 207.—Labor & Emp 478, 484(1), 565, 795, 797.

Hines v. **Massachusetts Mut. Life Ins. Co.**, TexCivApp–Fort Worth, 174 SW2d 94.—Accord 7(1), 10(1), 20; App & E 854(5); Compromise 5(2), 6(1), 8(4); Princ & A 148(4); Trial 351.2(8), 352.9.

Hines v. **Massey**, TexApp–Beaumont, 79 SW3d 269.—App & E 389(1), 984(1); Const Law 3228, 3302, 3823; Costs 128, 129, 133; Trial 21.

Hines; **Midkiff v.**, TexApp–Houston (1 Dist), 866 SW2d 328, reh den.—Judgm 181(33), 185.3(21); Neglig 202, 210, 213, 220, 371, 379, 380, 387, 433, 1019, 1692.

Hines v. **Nelson**, TexCivApp–Tyler, 547 SW2d 378.—Action 6; App & E 1003(11); Autos 172(7), 192(11), 201(1.1), 242(1), 242(2), 243(3), 244(31), 244(40), 245(15), 249; Evid 555.4(3); Trial 105(3).

Hines v. **Parks**, TexComApp, 96 SW2d 970, 128 Tex 289.—App & E 878(1); Judgm 199(1), 199(5); Notice 9.

Hines; **Parks v.**, TexCivApp–Amarillo, 314 SW2d 431.—App & E 912; Autos 244(36.1); Neglig 371, 380, 387; Plead 111.42(4); Venue 8.5(8).

Hines v. **Pointer**, TexCivApp–Fort Worth, 523 SW2d 733, ref nre.—Adv Poss 43(6), 114(1); App & E 216(7), 232(0.5), 499(1), 704.2; Estop 43, 44, 47; Ten in C 4, 15(1), 15(7), 15(10), 43, 44; Tresp to T T 7, 9, 11, 35(1).

Hines v. **Sands**, TexCivApp–Fort Worth, 312 SW2d 275.—Execution 41; Garn 32; Trusts 12, 28, 135, 136, 148, 152.

Hines; **Seaboard Fire & Marine Ins. Co. of New York v.**, TexCivApp–Texarkana, 142 SW2d 538, writ dism.—Insurance 2046(2).

Hines; **Simpson v.**, CA5 (Tex), 903 F2d 400.—Civil R 1376(6); Fed Cts 574, 755.

Hines; **Simpson v.**, EDTex, 730 FSupp 753, aff in part, rev in part, dism in part 903 F2d 400.—Civil R 1088(4), 1376(1), 1376(6), 1394; Const Law 4545(3).

Hines; **Simpson v.**, EDTex, 729 FSupp 526.—Gr Jury 41.50(1), 41.50(6).

Hines v. **State**, TexCrimApp, 75 SW3d 444, on remand 2003 WL 21710575.—Crim Law 29(13); Kidnap 36; Statut 188, 214, 217.4, 219(1).

Hines v. **State**, TexCrimApp, 906 SW2d 518.—Lewd 1; Statut 214, 241(1).

Hines v. **State**, TexCrimApp, 653 SW2d 817.—Crim Law 1038.2; Rape 59(15).

Hines v. **State**, TexCrimApp, 571 SW2d 322.—Controlled Subs 67; Crim Law 369.15, 695(1), 1169.11; Ind & Inf 171.

Hines v. **State**, TexCrimApp, 515 SW2d 670.—Autos 316, 355(13); Crim Law 90(5), 388.2; Homic 1174; Ind & Inf 19; Statut 158; Witn 274(1), 274(2).

Hines v. **State**, TexCrimApp, 495 SW2d 252.—Crim Law 603.2, 603.3(7), 614(1), 741(1), 742(1), 814(17), 885, 938(1), 951(1).

Hines v. **State**, TexCrimApp, 458 SW2d 666.—Burg 11, 29, 41(10); Const Law 266(3.2), 4658(1); Crim Law 351(3).

Hines v. **State**, TexCrimApp, 362 SW2d 652.—Crim Law 304(20); Int Liq 139, 236(6.5), 249.

Hines v. **State**, TexCrimApp, 360 SW2d 890, 172 TexCrim 586.—Infants 20.

Hines v. **State**, TexCrimApp, 327 SW2d 755, 168 TexCrim 381.—Bail 77(1).

Hines v. **State**, TexCrimApp, 292 SW2d 131.—Crim Law 1114.1(3).

Hines v. **State**, TexCrimApp, 268 SW2d 459, 160 TexCrim 284.—Crim Law 396(2), 720(7.1), 721.5(1), 1169.2(1); Infants 20; Witn 40(1), 45(2), 79(2).

Hines v. **State**, TexCrimApp, 248 SW2d 156, 157 TexCrim 205.—Autos 351.1; Crim Law 369.1, 1169.11.

Hines v. **State**, TexCrimApp, 162 SW2d 108.—Crim Law 1094(2.1).

Hines v. **State**, TexApp–Houston (1 Dist), 646 SW2d 469, petition for discretionary review refused.—Crim Law 351(3), 369.1, 1038.1(4), 1044.1(5.1), 1166.6.

Hines v. **State**, TexApp–Fort Worth, 144 SW3d 90.—Crim Law 641.13(1), 641.13(2.1), 641.13(7), 1119(1), 1166.10(1).

Hines v. **State**, TexApp–Fort Worth, 942 SW2d 785.—Crim Law 857(1), 862, 1155.

Hines v. **State**, TexApp–Texarkana, 3 SW3d 618, petition for discretionary review refused.—Crim Law 925(1), 925(5), 956(11), 957(1), 1141(1).

Hines v. **State**, TexApp–Texarkana, 978 SW2d 169.—Crim Law 511.1(1), 511.1(3), 511.1(4), 511.2, 511.7, 789(4), 822(1), 1038.1(1), 1134(1), 1144.13(2.1), 1144.13(3), 1159.2(1), 1159.2(2), 1159.2(7), 1159.2(9), 1159.3(1), 1165(1), 1172.1(1), 1172.2, 1189; Homic 908, 1141, 1165; Ind & Inf 110(3), 196(5).

Hines v. **State**, TexApp–Texarkana, 880 SW2d 178, petition for discretionary review gr, aff 906 SW2d 518.—Lewd 1.

Hines v. State, TexApp–Beaumont, 976 SW2d 912.—Controlled Subs 29, 67, 80.

Hines v. State, TexApp–Corpus Christi, 822 SW2d 790, petition for discretionary review refused.—Const Law 4587; Crim Law 273.1(4), 273.4(1).

Hines v. State, TexApp–Houston (14 Dist), 40 SW3d 705, petition for discretionary review gr, rev 75 SW3d 444, on remand 2003 WL 21710575.—Crim Law 1144.13(3), 1159.2(7); Kidnap 17, 18, 36; Statut 181(2), 184, 188, 190, 226.

Hines v. State, TexApp–Houston (14 Dist), 38 SW3d 805, habeas corpus den 2005 WL 1924185.—Crim Law 388.3, 472, 488, 494, 1130(5), 1134(2), 1139, 1144.13(2.1), 1153(1), 1159.2(7); Jury 31.3(1).

Hines v. Taylor, TexCivApp–Hous (14 Dist), 476 SW2d 81.—Frds St of 129(11), 158(1); Inj 147; Spec Perf 108.

Hines v. Tenneco Chemicals, Inc., CA5 (Tex), 728 F2d 729.—Const Law 2315; Lim of Act 4(2), 6(9).

Hines v. Tenneco Chemicals, Inc., SDTex, 546 FSupp 1229, aff 728 F2d 729.—Fed Cts 372, 409.1, 422.1; Lim of Act 2(1), 55(1), 55(4), 95(5), 199(1); Prod Liab 3, 5, 6; Sales 55, 255, 260, 441(2); Torts 103.

Hines v. Texas, CA5 (Tex), 129 FedAppx 100.—Fed Cts 629; Jury 33(1.1), 33(5.15).

Hines v. Texas, CA5 (Tex), 76 FedAppx 564.—Civil R 1092; Fed Cts 266.1, 269; U S Mag 31.

Hines v. Texas Tel. & Tel. Co., TexCivApp–Tyler, 490 SW2d 953.—App & E 949, 1152; Parties 35.13, 35.61; Tel 1243.

Hines v. Thomas, TexCivApp–Dallas, 164 SW2d 59.—Acct St 4, 7; Interest 47(1); Mines 101.

Hines; U.S. v., CA5 (Tex), 563 F2d 737.—Crim Law 552(3), 1044.1(7); Rec S Goods 1, 8(3).

Hines v. Wilson, TexCivApp–Amarillo, 197 SW2d 840, ref nre.—App & E 916(1); Lim of Act 39(7), 95(1), 100(11), 179(1), 179(2); Mtg 335.

Hines Interests Ltd. Partnership; Harwood v., TexApp–Houston (1 Dist), 73 SW3d 450.—App & E 863, 934(1); Evid 587; Judgm 181(33); Neglig 1037(4).

Hines Nurseries, Inc.; Johnson v., NDTex, 950 FSupp 175.—Damag 50.10; Estop 68(2).

Hines Wholesale Nurseries; Fort Bend Cent. Appraisal Dist. v., TexApp–Texarkana, 844 SW2d 857, reh overr, and writ den.—App & E 863, 1175(1); Pretrial Proc 483; Tax 2706.

Hingst v. Providian Nat. Bank, SDTex, 124 FSupp2d 449.—Fed Cts 241; Pretrial Proc 517.1; Rem of C 17, 107(7).

Hininger v. Case Corp., CA5 (Tex), 23 F3d 124, reh den 32 F3d 568, cert den 115 SCt 728, 513 US 1079, 130 LEd2d 632.—Prod Liab 17.1; Sales 255.

Hink; Lopez v., TexApp–Houston (14 Dist), 757 SW2d 449.—Judgm 185(4), 185.1(3); Lim of Act 104(2).

Hinkle v. Adams, TexApp–Texarkana, 74 SW3d 189.—App & E 766; Corp 1.4(4), 1.7(2), 306, 325, 615.5, 617(1); Joint Adv 1.2(1), 1.12, 1.15; Judgm 183.

Hinkle; Bell v., TexCivApp–Hous (14 Dist), 607 SW2d 936, ref nre, cert den 102 SCt 115, 454 US 826, 70 LEd2d 100.—Child 86.

Hinkle; Bell v., TexCivApp–Hous (14 Dist), 562 SW2d 35, ref nre, appeal after remand 607 SW2d 936, ref nre, cert den 102 SCt 115, 454 US 826, 70 LEd2d 100.—Courts 198, 472.4(1), 472.4(2.1); Tresp to T T 23.

Hinkle v. Dretke, CA5 (Tex), 86 FedAppx 687.—Hab Corp 486(4).

Hinkle; Federal Underwriters Exchange v., TexCivApp–Fort Worth, 187 SW2d 122, writ refused wom.—App & E 301, 837(2), 989, 1003(6), 1075, 1078(1); Work Comp 416, 428, 492, 1262, 1485, 1919, 1920, 1924, 1927.

Hinkle; Federal Underwriters Exchange v., TexCivApp–Fort Worth, 167 SW2d 307, writ refused wom.—Work Comp 423, 1013, 1919, 1926, 1964, 1968(5), 1976.

Hinkle v. Federal Underwriters Exchange, TexCivApp–Fort Worth, 152 SW2d 387, writ refused wom.—Work Comp 419, 492, 1919, 1922, 1924, 1965.

Hinkle v. Hinkle, TexApp–Dallas, 223 SW3d 773.—App & E 930(1), 933(1), 977(5), 989, 994(2), 999(1), 1001(1), 1001(3), 1003(6); Child C 452, 462, 512.

Hinkle; Hinkle v., TexApp–Dallas, 223 SW3d 773.—App & E 930(1), 933(1), 977(5), 989, 994(2), 999(1), 1001(1), 1001(3), 1003(6); Child C 452, 462, 512.

Hinkle; Lubbock Nat. Bank v., TexCivApp–Amarillo, 397 SW2d 285, ref nre.—Courts 90(1); Mech Liens 173, 195.

Hinkle v. State, TexCrimApp, 442 SW2d 728.—Crim Law 99, 134(2), 673(5), 675, 695(2), 695(4), 875(1), 886, 1043(3), 1115(2), 1116, 1129(4), 1130(3), 1137(5), 1166(10.10); Homic 834, 835, 1136; Sent & Pun 2327.

Hinkle v. State, TexApp–San Antonio, 934 SW2d 146, reh overr, and petition for discretionary review refused.—Crim Law 273.1(1), 273.1(4), 274(2), 274(8), 275.

Hinkle v. State, TexApp–Beaumont, 779 SW2d 504, petition for discretionary review refused.—Crim Law 444, 552(3), 671, 693, 713, 730(1), 730(3), 784(1), 789(3), 1171.1(3), 1172.1(2); Homic 1174, 1184, 1184.5; Ind & Inf 113; Sent & Pun 240.

Hinkle; Texas Alcoholic Beverage Commission v., TexCivApp–Austin, 493 SW2d 257, ref nre.—Int Liq 108.5, 108.10(2), 108.10(3).

Hinkle; Texas Emp. Ins. Ass'n v., TexCivApp–El Paso, 308 SW2d 543, ref nre.—Damag 221(3).

Hinkley, In re, SDTex, 89 BR 608, aff Hinkley v. Robinson, 875 F2d 859.—Bankr 2127.1, 2162, 2822.1, 2925.1; Bills & N 49, 472.1, 476(2), 477, 478; Contracts 128(1); Fed Civ Proc 742, 2411; Jury 19(9).

Hinkley, In re, BkrtcySDTex, 58 BR 339, aff 89 BR 608, aff Hinkley v. Robinson, 875 F2d 859.—Bankr 2043(2), 2052, 2921, 2923, 2926, 2928; Bills & N 52, 92(5), 104, 106; Fed Civ Proc 2415, 2417, 2418.1; Jury 19(9); Lim of Act 12(1), 25(3), 182(5); Princ & S 5.

Hinkley; Hunte v., TexApp–Houston (14 Dist), 731 SW2d 570, ref nre.—Health 782; Judgm 185.3(21), 186.

Hinkley; Robinson v., SDTex, 89 BR 608. See Hinkley, In re.

Hinkley; Robinson v., BkrtcySDTex, 58 BR 339. See Hinkley, In re.

Hinkley v. State, TexCrimApp, 389 SW2d 667.—Arson 11, 37(1); Crim Law 517.2(2); Searches 172.

Hinkley v. Texas State Bd. of Medical Examiners, TexApp–Austin, 140 SW3d 737, reh overr, and review den.—Admin Law 749, 750, 754.1, 763, 790, 791, 793; Health 218, 219, 223(1).

Hinkson; La Neve v., TexCivApp–Eastland, 271 SW2d 467, ref nre.—Judgm 181(2); Lim of Act 95(1), 95(8), 96(2), 99(1), 195(5).

Hinkson v. Lorenzo Independent School Dist., TexCivApp–Amarillo, 109 SW2d 1008, dism.—Schools 106.12(3), 106.12(8), 106.42; Tax 2607, 2709(1).

Hinman; McCarty v., TexCivApp–Dallas, 342 SW2d 29.—Plead 111.5, 111.42(3); Venue 22(1).

Hinn v. Continental Nat. Bank of Ft. Worth, TexCivApp–Fort Worth, 495 SW2d 290.—Bills & N 485.

Hinn v. Continental Nat. Bank of Ft. Worth, TexCivApp–Fort Worth, 495 SW2d 286.—Bills & N 485; Plead 111.15, 290(3); Venue 7.5(4).

Hinn; Irick v., TexCivApp–Amarillo, 104 SW2d 76.—Bankr 2160, 2367, 2374; Plead 129(1).

Hinnant; Lynch Davidson & Co. v., TexCivApp–San Antonio, 93 SW2d 532.—Courts 478.

Hino Gas Sales, Inc.; B. Cantrell Oil Co. v., TexApp–Corpus Christi, 756 SW2d 781.—Contracts 116(1); Labor & Emp 922.

Hino Gas Sales, Inc.; Cantrell Oil Co. v., TexApp–Corpus Christi, 756 SW2d 781. See B. Cantrell Oil Co. v. Hino Gas Sales, Inc.

Hino Gas Sales, Inc.; Lone Star Propane Co. v., Tex-App–Corpus Christi, 756 SW2d 781. See B. Cantrell Oil Co. v. Hino Gas Sales, Inc.

Hinojos; Big Bend Flying Service, Inc. v., TexCivApp–El Paso, 489 SW2d 694.—Neglig 1037(4), 1037(7); Plead 111.17.

Hinojos v. Railroad Retirement Bd., CA5 (Tex), 323 F2d 227.—Marriage 13, 50(1); Social S 171.1, 172.

Hinojosa, In re Estate of, TexApp–El Paso, 866 SW2d 67. See Hinojosa v. Hinojosa.

Hinojosa v. Allstate Ins. Co., TexCivApp–Amarillo, 520 SW2d 936.—Insurance 1779; Judgm 185(2).

Hinojosa; Boyattia v., TexApp–Dallas, 18 SW3d 729, review den.—App & E 863, 934(1); Autos 196; Counties 93; Judgm 178, 181(27), 185(2), 185(5); Lim of Act 118(2), 119(3), 121(2); Neglig 379, 380, 387, 422, 423; Parties 66; Plead 34(1); Proc 23, 63.

Hinojosa; Cameron County v., TexApp–Corpus Christi, 760 SW2d 742.—App & E 557; Pretrial Proc 41, 371.

Hinojosa v. Castellow Chevrolet Oldsmobile, Inc., Tex-App–Corpus Christi, 678 SW2d 707, ref nre.—App & E 842(2), 842(8), 1008.1(7), 1010.1(3), 1012.1(5); Assign 100; Cons Cred 12, 16, 17, 18; Evid 265(8); Plead 374; Sec Tran 228.

Hinojosa v. City of Kingsville, Texas, SDTex, 266 FSupp2d 562.—Fed Cts 13; Inj 132, 138.1, 138.69.

Hinojosa v. City of Terrell, Tex., CA5 (Tex), 864 F2d 401, cert den 110 SCt 80, 493 US 822, 107 LEd2d 46.—Fed Civ Proc 2491.5.

Hinojosa v. City of Terrell, Tex., CA5 (Tex), 834 F2d 1223, appeal after remand 864 F2d 401, cert den 110 SCt 80, 493 US 822, 107 LEd2d 46.—Assault 2; Civil R 1088(1), 1088(4); Fed Civ Proc 2602.

Hinojosa v. Columbia/St. David's Healthcare System, L.P., TexApp–Austin, 106 SW3d 380.—App & E 223; Evid 477(2), 574, 584(1); Judgm 183, 185(1), 185.3(21).

Hinojosa; Cruz v., TexApp–San Antonio, 12 SW3d 545, reh overr, and petition for review overr.—App & E 949, 1001(3), 1003(5), 1050.1(1), 1050.1(11), 1051.1(1), 1056.1(1), 1058(1), 1069.2; Atty & C 19, 21, 21.5(1); Courts 23, 74; Evid 571(3); Prod Liab 83.5; Trial 43.

Hinojosa v. Edgerton, Tex, 447 SW2d 670.—App & E 1177(9); Lim of Act 39(7); Records 9(1).

Hinojosa v. Edgerton, TexCivApp–San Antonio, 429 SW2d 636, writ gr, rev 447 SW2d 670.—Lim of Act 39(7), 195(3).

Hinojosa v. Garcia, TexCivApp–San Antonio, 260 SW2d 711.—App & E 781(4); Costs 232.

Hinojosa v. Hinojosa, TexApp–El Paso, 866 SW2d 67.—App & E 78(1), 80(6).

Hinojosa; Hinojosa v., TexApp–El Paso, 866 SW2d 67.—App & E 78(1), 80(6).

Hinojosa v. Hinojosa, TexCivApp–San Antonio, 294 SW2d 910.—Plead 293; Venue 5.3(2), 5.4.

Hinojosa; Hinojosa v., TexCivApp–San Antonio, 294 SW2d 910.—Plead 293; Venue 5.3(2), 5.4.

Hinojosa v. Housing Authority of City of Corpus Christi, TexApp–Corpus Christi, 896 SW2d 833, reh overr, and writ dism woj.—Abate & R 19; Antitrust 286; App & E 1050.1(1), 1051.1(1); Const Law 4083, 4112; Health 807; Land & Ten 291(0.5), 291(1), 291(18).

Hinojosa v. Housing Authority of the City of Laredo, TexApp–San Antonio, 940 SW2d 763.—Contracts 143.5, 156; Mun Corp 717.5(6).

Hinojosa v. Jim Hogg County, Tex., CA5 (Tex), 730 F2d 1009. See McBee v. Jim Hogg County, Tex.

Hinojosa v. Jones, TexCivApp–San Antonio, 154 SW2d 275.—App & E 1060.1(7).

Hinojosa v. Jostens Inc., CA5 (Tex), 128 FedAppx 364, cert den 126 SCt 650, 546 US 1015, 163 LEd2d 525.—Civil R 1218(3), 1218(6), 1552; Labor & Emp 462, 797.

Hinojosa v. King, CA5 (Tex), 71 FedAppx 363.—Fed Civ Proc 2734.

Hinojosa; Land Rover U.K., Ltd. v., Tex, 210 SW3d 604.—App & E 1024.1; Infants 77, 83, 85, 115.

Hinojosa v. Longoria, TexCivApp–San Antonio, 381 SW2d 140, writ dism.—Elections 278; Time 9(2).

Hinojosa v. Love, TexCivApp–Corpus Christi, 496 SW2d 224.—App & E 187(3); Bills & N 120, 457; Parties 34.

Hinojosa v. Perez, SDTex, 214 FSupp2d 703.—Fed Cts 192.5, 241; Health 556(1); Rem of C 25(1), 82, 86(1).

Hinojosa; Point Isabel Independent School Dist. v., TexApp–Corpus Christi, 797 SW2d 176, writ den.—Admin Law 124; App & E 931(1), 989, 1010.1(3); Costs 194.40; Courts 89; Schools 57, 133.1(1).

Hinojosa; Saenz v., TexCivApp–San Antonio, 268 SW2d 476.—Evid 54; Plead 111.42(8).

Hinojosa; Salmon v., TexCivApp–San Antonio, 538 SW2d 22.—Autos 193(8.1), 242(6), 244(26).

Hinojosa v. San Isidro Independent School Dist., TexCivApp–San Antonio, 273 SW2d 656.—App & E 907(2); Plead 4, 106(1); Schools 115.

Hinojosa; Shultz v., CA5 (Tex), 432 F2d 259, 19 Wage & Hour Cas (BNA) 625.—Labor & Emp 2236, 2324, 2333, 2385(1), 2418, 2421, 2422.

Hinojosa v. South Texas Drilling & Exploration, Inc., TexApp–San Antonio, 727 SW2d 320.—Damag 51; Judgm 181(11).

Hinojosa v. State, TexCrimApp, 4 SW3d 240, habeas corpus den 2004 WL 2434353, certificate of appealability den 141 FedAppx 395, cert den 126 SCt 1569, 547 US 1022, 164 LEd2d 305, habeas corpus dism by Ex parte Hinojosa, 2006 WL 2370240.—Crim Law 211(1), 213, 321, 388.1, 388.2, 394.6(4), 566, 867, 1120(2), 1144.13(3), 1153(1), 1159.2(1), 1159.2(2), 1169.5(2); Homic 1184; Rape 51(7); Searches 112; Sent & Pun 1610, 1789(8); Treaties 7, 8, 13.

Hinojosa v. State, TexCrimApp, 230 SW2d 231.—Crim Law 1094(3).

Hinojosa v. State, TexCrimApp, 206 SW2d 1011, 151 TexCrim 301.—Crim Law 273.3, 1083, 1099.2, 1128(4), 1134(2), 1182, 1186.1.

Hinojosa v. State, TexCrimApp, 180 SW2d 626, 147 Tex-Crim 340.—Rob 24.55.

Hinojosa v. State, TexApp–Austin, 648 SW2d 380, petition for discretionary review refused.—False Pret 38; Larc 8, 33; Schools 63(3).

Hinojosa v. State, TexApp–San Antonio, 685 SW2d 374.—Crim Law 577.8(2).

Hinojosa v. State, TexApp–Beaumont, 780 SW2d 299, petition for discretionary review refused.—Crim Law 790, 1035(5), 1038.1(3.1), 1170.5(1), 1172.1(2), 1172.1(5), 1177; Jury 33(5.15); Witn 350.

Hinojosa v. State, TexApp–Corpus Christi, 875 SW2d 339.—Const Law 3855; Controlled Subs 93; Crim Law 1144.13(2.1), 1144.13(6), 1159.2(7), 1167(4); Double J 59; Ind & Inf 159(1).

Hinojosa v. State, TexApp–Corpus Christi, 788 SW2d 594, petition for discretionary review refused.—Crim Law 444, 633(2), 709, 721(1), 721(3), 721(6), 726, 728(2), 728(5), 1035(10), 1036.1(8), 1036.2, 1036.5, 1043(3), 1044.1(5.1), 1166.6, 1170.5(6), 1171.1(2.1), 1171.1(3), 1171.5; Witn 367(1), 370(1), 373.

Hinojosa v. State, TexApp–Corpus Christi, 744 SW2d 319, petition for discretionary review refused.—Const Law 2545(4), 4723; Crim Law 790, 1173.2(3); Homic 799, 1483, 1485.

Hinojosa v. State, TexApp–Corpus Christi, 659 SW2d 914, petition for discretionary review refused.—Crim Law 339.10(9), 438(3), 641.13(1), 641.13(2.1), 641.13(6), 1035(7), 1038.1(6), 1166.10(1); Rob 24.40.

Hinojosa v. State, TexApp–Corpus Christi, 657 SW2d 510.—Rape 51(1).

Hinojosa v. State, TexApp–Houston (14 Dist), 995 SW2d 955.—Crim Law 338(7), 369.1, 1086.11, 1144.12, 1153(1), 1169.2(3); Infants 20.

Hinojosa; State Farm Mut. Auto. Ins. Co. v., TexCiv-App–Waco, 367 SW2d 933, ref nre.—Estop 118; Insurance 3191(1).

Hinojosa; State Farm Mut. Auto. Ins. Co. v., TexCiv-App–Waco, 346 SW2d 914, ref nre, appeal after remand 367 SW2d 933, ref nre.—App & E 843(2); Insurance 3155, 3191(1); Trial 118.

Hinojosa v. Stephens, TexCivApp–Hous (14 Dist), 461 SW2d 232, ref nre.—Autos 246(58); Neglig 530(1), 1571, 1683.

Hinojosa v. Tagle, TexApp–Corpus Christi, 667 SW2d 927.—Const Law 3881, 4010; Judgm 106(2); Pretrial Proc 46.

Hinojosa; Teran v., TexApp–Corpus Christi, 929 SW2d 37. See Teran v. Valdez.

Hinojosa; U.S. v., CA5 (Tex), 484 F3d 337.—Crim Law 1139, 1158(1); Sent & Pun 677, 736, 2134, 2146.

Hinojosa; U.S. v., CA5 (Tex), 349 F3d 200, reh den, cert den 124 SCt 2405, 541 US 1070, 158 LEd2d 975, post-conviction relief den 2006 WL 237079.—Crim Law 394.4(6), 1139, 1144.13(2.1), 1144.13(5), 1158(1), 1158(2), 1158(4), 1159.2(7); Searches 193; Sent & Pun 1273; Weap 4, 17(4).

Hinojosa; U.S. v., CA5 (Tex), 958 F2d 624, appeal from denial of post-conviction relief dism US v. Lerma, 20 F3d 466, dism of habeas corpus aff 99 F3d 1135.—Commerce 82.6, 82.10; Controlled Subs 40, 87; Crim Law 59(5), 1036.8, 1126, 1152(2), 1158(3); Jury 33(5.15), 42, 85, 105(1); Sent & Pun 752, 973.

Hinojosa; Wal-Mart Stores, Inc. v., TexApp–Corpus Christi, 827 SW2d 43.—App & E 930(3), 934(1), 1001(3); Judgm 199(3.10); Neglig 1001, 1222, 1670.

Hinojosa; Yeary v., TexCivApp–Houston, 307 SW2d 325, ref nre.—Lim of Act 125; Work Comp 2216, 2221, 2225, 2228, 2237, 2240, 2242.

Hinojosa-Lopez; U.S. v., CA5 (Tex), 130 F3d 691.—Aliens 799; Crim Law 273(4.1), 1134(3), 1139, 1158(1).

Hinote v. Oil, Chemical and Atomic Workers Intern. Union, AFL-CIO, Local 4-23, TexApp–Houston (14 Dist), 777 SW2d 134, writ den.—App & E 110, 218.2(5.1), 232(3), 233(1), 233(2), 1175(1); Damag 191; Evid 193, 359(5); Labor & Emp 1078, 1986(3), 1986(4); Torts 200; Trial 350.1.

Hinrichs v. Texas & N. O. R. Co., TexCivApp–Fort Worth, 153 SW2d 859, writ refused wom.—Evid 225, 272, 355(5), 370(4); Witn 387, 390.

Hinrichsen, In re Guardianship of, TexApp–Houston (1 Dist), 99 SW3d 773.—App & E 931(1), 1010.1(1), 1010.1(5), 1011.1(1); Mental H 105, 135.

Hinshaw v. Doffer, CA5 (Tex), 785 F2d 1260.—Civil R 1088(2), 1358, 1404, 1420, 1429, 1463, 1464, 1465(1).

Hinshaw; Perry v., Tex, 633 SW2d 503.—Wills 435, 523.

Hinshaw; Perry v., TexApp–Fort Worth, 625 SW2d 751, rev 633 SW2d 503.—Wills 440, 449, 478, 523, 547, 552(3), 858(1).

Hinsley, In re, CA5 (Tex), 201 F3d 638.—Fed Civ Proc 2470.1, 2481; Fed Cts 542, 611, 666, 776; Fraud Conv 14, 77, 300(7), 308(1); Lim of Act 104(1), 195(3), 197(1).

Hinsley v. Continental Trailways Bus System, TexCiv-App–Galveston, 302 SW2d 668.—App & E 204(1), 692(1); Evid 129(1), 380.

Hinsley; Scotsman-Norwood Co., Inc. v., TexCivApp–Hous (1 Dist), 515 SW2d 347.—App & E 954(1), 954(2); Inj 135, 147.

Hinsley v. State, TexApp–Dallas, 722 SW2d 476.—Crim Law 577.8(2), 577.14, 577.16(9), 730(1), 730(14), 730(15); Searches 102, 111.

Hinson; American Interstate Ins. Co. v., TexApp–Beaumont, 172 SW3d 108, review den, and reh of petition for review den.—App & E 901, 994(2); Evid 100, 150, 588; Work Comp 798, 1604, 1923, 1924, 1964.

Hinson v. Connecticut General Life Ins. Co., TexCiv-App–Beaumont, 83 SW2d 810, writ dism.—Insurance 2561(5).

Hinson v. Hinson, Tex, 280 SW2d 731, 154 Tex 561.—Wills 72, 73, 98, 199, 317, 400.

Hinson; Hinson v., Tex, 280 SW2d 731, 154 Tex 561.—Wills 72, 73, 98, 199, 317, 400.

Hinson v. Hinson, TexCivApp–Galveston, 273 SW2d 116, rev 280 SW2d 731, 154 Tex 561.—Wills 69, 73, 93, 98.

Hinson; Hinson v., TexCivApp–Galveston, 273 SW2d 116, rev 280 SW2d 731, 154 Tex 561.—Wills 69, 73, 93, 98.

Hinson; Hutcherson v., TexCivApp–Tyler, 557 SW2d 814.—App & E 302(1), 758.3(3).

Hinson; Hutcherson v., TexCivApp–Tyler, 543 SW2d 719, ref nre.—App & E 564(3), 624.

Hinson; Lasater v., TexCivApp–Fort Worth, 84 SW2d 874.—Execution 272(1); Ven & Pur 230(1), 231(1).

Hinson v. Noble, TexCivApp–Fort Worth, 122 SW2d 1082.—App & E 846(5); Contracts 143(2), 147(2), 155, 164, 170(1); Mines 73.2, 78.1(9).

Hinson v. SS Paros, SDTex, 461 FSupp 219.—Death 82, 95(1), 95(3); Ship 84(3.3); Work Comp 2190, 2197, 2245, 2251.

Hinson v. State, TexCrimApp, 547 SW2d 277.—Arrest 63.5(4), 63.5(5); Crim Law 394.4(9); Searches 82.

Hinson v. State, TexCrimApp, 272 SW2d 514.—Crim Law 1090.1(1).

Hinson v. State, TexCrimApp, 211 SW2d 750, 152 Tex-Crim 159.—Crim Law 507(7), 511.1(10).

Hinson v. State, TexCrimApp, 162 SW2d 979, 144 Tex-Crim 390.—Child S 666.

Hinson v. State, TexApp–Waco, 166 SW3d 331, reh overr, and petition for discretionary review refused.—Crim Law 641.13(7).

Hinson v. State, TexCivApp–Austin, 245 SW2d 755.—Mines 1, 5.2(3), 5.3.

Hinson; State Highway Dept. v., TexCivApp–Corpus Christi, 517 SW2d 308, ref nre.—App & E 927(7), 989; Autos 172(6), 201(1.1); Damag 62(2); Neglig 386, 387, 1656, 1676.

Hinson v. Thompson, TexApp–Beaumont, 112 SW3d 766.—App & E 66, 68, 79(1), 366.

Hinson; Tri-State Ass'n of Credit Men v., Tex, 146 SW2d 723, 136 Tex 1.—App & E 1178(8).

Hinson; Tri-State Ass'n of Credit Men v., Tex, 144 SW2d 881, 136 Tex 1, reh overr 146 SW2d 723, 136 Tex 1.—App & E 1078(3); Lim of Act 180(5), 182(2); Trial 404(2).

Hinson; Tri-State Ass'n of Credit Men v., TexCivApp–El Paso, 117 SW2d 158, rev 144 SW2d 881, 136 Tex 1, reh overr 146 SW2d 723, 136 Tex 1.—Lim of Act 150(1), 180(2).

Hinson; U.S. v., CA5 (Tex), 429 F3d 114, cert den 126 SCt 1804, 547 US 1083, 164 LEd2d 540.—Crim Law 1134(10); Jury 24.1, 34(7).

Hinson; Victory v., TexComApp, 102 SW2d 194, 129 Tex 30.—Tax 2172, 2568.

Hinson; W. U. Tel. Co. v., TexCivApp–Amarillo, 222 SW2d 636, ref nre.—App & E 216(1), 736, 1050.1(1); Evid 18; Neglig 431, 451, 1541; Tel 699, 708, 710, 711; Trial 350.5(5), 351.2(2).

Hinterlong, In re, TexApp–Fort Worth, 109 SW3d 611, mandamus den, and petition for writ of mandamus stayed, and reh of motion for mandamus overr.—App & E 946; Const Law 990, 1030, 2312, 2314, 3957; Crim Law 1222.1; Equity 64, 72(1); Mand 1, 4(1), 4(4), 11, 28, 143(1), 143(2); Offic 119; Pretrial Proc 33, 40, 41; Schools 89.2, 147; Witn 185, 216(4).

Hinton; Davis v., TexCivApp–Tyler, 374 SW2d 723, ref nre.—Covenants 72.1, 103(1), 103(3); Inj 62(1), 113, 128(6).

Hinton v. Entex Inc., EDTex, 93 FRD 336.—Fed Civ Proc 1272.1.

Hinton v. Federal Nat. Mortg. Ass'n, SDTex, 957 FSupp 101.—Atty & C 155, 175.

Hinton v. Federal Nat. Mortg. Ass'n, SDTex, 945 FSupp 1052, aff 137 F3d 1350.—Antitrust 221; Contracts 168,

187(1); Dep & Escr 13; Gifts 4, 17.1; Mtg 200(1), 201, 211; Trusts 30.5(1); U S 53(9).

Hinton; Hudson v., TexCivApp–Dallas, 435 SW2d 211.— Contracts 152; Corp 120; Indem 31(2), 31(5); Judgm 185.3(8); Lim of Act 56(2); Tax 2431.

Hinton; McLeod v., TexCivApp–Waco, 422 SW2d 235.— Ease 5, 8(2), 18(1), 36(3), 61(9); High 17, 68.

Hinton v. Meador, TexCivApp–El Paso, 97 SW2d 251, rev Wilson v. Hinton, 116 SW2d 365, 131 Tex 593.—Bills & N 140; Mech Liens 206.

Hinton; Safety Cas. Co. v., TexCivApp–Beaumont, 197 SW2d 226, ref nre.—Damag 221(4); Trial 29(2); Work Comp 514, 1929.

Hinton; Spurlock v., TexCivApp–Dallas, 225 SW2d 203. —Mines 59, 78.1(2), 78.1(4), 78.7(1), 78.7(5).

Hinton v. State, TexCrimApp, 626 SW2d 781.—Crim Law 339.6, 369.2(6), 404.50, 721.5(3), 1169.11.

Hinton v. State, TexCrimApp, 147 SW2d 798.—Crim Law 1182.

Hinton v. State, TexCrimApp, 129 SW2d 670, 137 TexCrim 352.—Crim Law 450, 451(3), 661, 696(2), 703, 720(1), 720(7.1), 721(5), 721(6), 763(12), 772(4), 829(4), 1169.1(2.1), 1169.9, 1170.5(3), 1170.5(6), 1171.1(2.1); Gaming 101; Ind & Inf 176.

Hinton v. State, TexCrimApp, 120 SW2d 1053, 135 TexCrim 400.—Crim Law 784(1); Int Liq 224.

Hinton v. State, TexCrimApp, 116 SW2d 733, 134 TexCrim 527.—Int Liq 200.

Hinton v. State, TexCrimApp, 116 SW2d 391, 134 TexCrim 528.—Int Liq 211.

Hinton v. U.S., CA5 (Tex), 232 F2d 485.—Crim Law 641.4(2), 1618(10); Sent & Pun 1381(6).

Hinton; University of Texas at Austin v., TexApp–Austin, 822 SW2d 197.—App & E 230, 683, 714(5), 907(5), 970(2), 1050.1(1), 1050.1(2), 1056.1(1), 1060.6, 1070(2), 1195(1); Colleges 10; Evid 359(6); Jury 131(13); Mun Corp 723; Neglig 1001, 1620; Pretrial Proc 45; States 112.2(1), 171; Trial 127.

Hinton v. Uvalde Paving Co., TexCivApp–Dallas, 77 SW2d 733, writ refused.—Mun Corp 485(5).

Hinton v. Uvalde Paving Co., TexCivApp–Waco, 118 SW2d 317, writ refused.—App & E 205, 692(1); Judgm 725(4), 735, 910(2).

Hinton; Wilson v., Tex, 116 SW2d 365, 131 Tex 593.— Home 55; Mech Liens 51, 86.

Hinton Drilling Co. v. Zuniga, TexApp–Tyler, 784 SW2d 442. See W.B. Hinton Drilling Co. v. Zuniga.

Hintz v. Beto, CA5 (Tex), 379 F2d 937.—Courts 100(1); Crim Law 517.2(2), 641.13(1), 641.13(2.1), 641.13(3).

Hintz; Kingery v., TexApp–Houston (14 Dist), 124 SW3d 875, reh overr, and mandamus den.—Marriage 4.1, 5, 19, 40(1); Parent & C 16.

Hintz v. State, TexCrimApp, 396 SW2d 411.—Crim Law 518(3), 532(0.5), 590(2), 641.7(1), 778(5), 814(17), 878(2), 1037.1(4).

Hinze v. State, TexCrimApp, 352 SW2d 954.—Crim Law 1090.1(1).

Hipes; Chisholm v., TexCivApp–Amarillo, 552 SW2d 519. —Brok 43(3); Frds St of 110(1); Judgm 181(2); Lim of Act 96(2); Paymt 48; Ref of Inst 32.

Hipfner v. Anderson, TexCivApp–Fort Worth, 258 SW2d 357, ref nre.—App & E 1050.1(10); Autos 245(67.1), 245(83); Neglig 1693.

Hi-Plains Haulers, Inc.; Pan Am. Ins. Co. v., Tex, 350 SW2d 644, 163 Tex 1.—Work Comp 2191, 2234, 2240, 2247, 2251.

Hi-Plains Haulers, Inc.; Pan Am. Ins. Co. v., TexCivApp–Amarillo, 341 SW2d 191, writ gr, rev 350 SW2d 644, 163 Tex 1.—Stip 18(7); Work Comp 2210, 2242, 2247, 2251.

Hi-Plains Hospital v. U.S., CA5 (Tex), 670 F2d 528, 70 ALR Fed 217.—Int Rev 4068, 4071.

Hi-Plains Truck Brokers, Inc.; Hamilton v., TexApp–Amarillo, 23 SW3d 442, reh overr.—App & E 508.

Hipolito v. Hipolito, TexApp–Dallas, 200 SW3d 805, reh overr, and review den.—App & E 946; Divorce 237, 286(3.1); Statut 181(1), 188, 205, 212.6, 212.7.

Hipolito; Hipolito v., TexApp–Dallas, 200 SW3d 805, reh overr, and review den.—App & E 946; Divorce 237, 286(3.1); Statut 181(1), 188, 205, 212.6, 212.7.

Hipolito-Alcantar; U.S. v., CA5 (Tex), 145 FedAppx 910, cert den Ramirez-Garcia v. US, 126 SCt 497, 546 US 967, 163 LEd2d 376.—Crim Law 1042.

Hi-Port, Inc. v. American Intern. Specialty Lines Ins. Co., SDTex, 22 FSupp2d 596, aff 162 F3d 93.—Insurance 2269, 2278(21), 2278(24), 2278(29).

Hipp v. Donald, TexCivApp–Fort Worth, 220 SW2d 268, ref nre.—Action 66; Courts 1, 37(1); Judgm 16, 470, 489, 501, 503.

Hipp v. Fall, TexCivApp–Galveston, 213 SW2d 732, ref nre.—Bankr 3079; Hus & W 249(2.1), 249(5), 264(4), 273(1), 274(1); Judgm 704; Lim of Act 5(3); Mtg 226; Partit 83, 85, 86, 87; Trusts 134.

Hipp; Griffith v., BkrtcyNDTex, 71 BR 643. See Hipp, Inc., In re.

Hipp v. J.D. Lowrie Well Service, Inc., TexApp–Corpus Christi, 800 SW2d 668, writ den.—App & E 204(4), 930(3), 989, 1001(1), 1003(5), 1003(7); Damag 185(1).

Hipp; Moss v., Tex, 387 SW2d 656.—Chat Mtg 107, 109; Evid 590; Liens 22.

Hipp v. Moss, TexCivApp–Amarillo, 380 SW2d 168, rev 387 SW2d 656.—Autos 20; Chat Mtg 21, 22, 41, 139; Evid 589.

Hipp; State v., TexApp–Austin, 832 SW2d 71, reh overr, and writ den, and writ gr, rev State v. Dowd, 867 SW2d 781.—Courts 39; Em Dom 170, 192, 195, 196, 198(1), 198(2), 262(4).

Hippchen; Hidalgo County Water Control and Imp. Dist. No. 16 v., CA5 (Tex), 233 F2d 712.—Deeds 90, 140, 143; Ease 2, 14(3); Waters 156(4).

Hipp, Inc., In re, BkrtcyNDTex, 71 BR 643, subsequently remanded 859 F2d 374.—Bills & N 90, 157, 332, 429; Sec Tran 22.

Hipp, Inc., In re Estate of, BkrtcyNDTex, 96 BR 656.— Bankr 3032.1, 3079, 3103.2, 3115.1; Bills & N 438.

Hipp, Inc., Matter of, CA5 (Tex), 5 F3d 109.—Bankr 2045, 2134, 2374; Contempt 60(3), 61(1); Fed Cts 812; Inj 219; Judges 49(1), 51(3), 51(4).

Hipp, Inc., Matter of, CA5 (Tex), 895 F2d 1503, reh den, appeal after remand 5 F3d 109.—Bankr 2134.

Hipp, Inc., Matter of, CA5 (Tex), 859 F2d 374.—Bankr 3771, 3777.

Hipp, Inc.; Oles v., CA5 (Tex), 859 F2d 374. See Hipp, Inc., Matter of.

Hipp, Inc., Estate of; Phoenix Grain, Inc. v., BkrtcyNDTex, 96 BR 656. See Hipp, Inc., In re Estate of.

Hips; Jones-Holt Enterprises, Inc. v., TexApp–San Antonio, 643 SW2d 773.—App & E 920(3); Inj 138.39, 147.

Hirabayashi v. North Main Bar-B-Q, Inc., TexApp–Fort Worth, 977 SW2d 704, reh overr, and review den.— Neglig 1011, 1019, 1020, 1022, 1076, 1151, 1152.

Hirad v. State, TexApp–Houston (14 Dist), 14 SW3d 351, petition for discretionary review refused.—Assault 53, 82; Crim Law 1137(3); Ind & Inf 191(0.5).

Hiram Clarke Civic Club, Inc. v. Lynn, CA5 (Tex), 476 F2d 421.—Environ Law 585, 589, 595(2), 689.

Hiram Walker Inc.; Freeman v., TexApp–Beaumont, 790 SW2d 842. See McGuire v. Joseph E. Seagram & Sons, Inc.

Hirczy v. Hamilton, CA5 (Tex), 190 FedAppx 357, cert den 127 SCt 1141, 166 LEd2d 893.—Colleges 10; Inj 26(4); Judges 51(2); Records 63.

Hirczy v. Hirczy, TexApp–Corpus Christi, 838 SW2d 783, reh overr, and writ den.—App & E 846(5), 948, 984(1); Child C 41, 921(3), 945, 947, 949; Child S 556(1); Child 20.3; Const Law 947, 966; Costs 177; Divorce 179, 188, 221; Infants 116.

Hirczy; Hirczy v., TexApp–Corpus Christi, 838 SW2d 783, reh overr, and writ den.—App & E 846(5), 948, 984(1); Child C 41, 921(3), 945, 947, 949; Child S 556(1); Child 20.3; Const Law 947, 966; Costs 177; Divorce 179, 188, 221; Infants 116.

Hirdler v. Boyd, TexApp–San Antonio, 702 SW2d 727, ref nre.—App & E 1064.2; Evid 336(1), 351, 357, 382; Trial 186, 295(9); Wills 163(1), 166(5).

Hirko; U.S. v., SDTex, 447 FSupp2d 734.—Consp 32; Crim Law 1083; Judgm 713(1), 713(2), 725(1), 751, 956(1); Sec Reg 193; Tel 1014(2); U S 34.

Hiroms v. Scheffey, TexApp–Houston (14 Dist), 76 SW3d 486.—App & E 233(1), 497(1), 611, 969, 1026; Health 624, 660; Trial 295(2).

Hironymous v. Allison, TexApp–Corpus Christi, 893 SW2d 578, reh overr, and writ den, and reh dism.—App & E 226(2), 930(3), 989, 994(3), 1001(1), 1002, 1003(3), 1003(7); Damag 113, 116, 130; Neglig 273; Wareh 34(8).

Hirras v. Amtrak, CA5 (Tex), 95 F3d 396. See Hirras v. National R.R. Passenger Corp.

Hirras v. Amtrak, CA5 (Tex), 44 F3d 278. See Hirras v. National R.R. Passenger Corp.

Hirras v. Amtrak, CA5 (Tex), 10 F3d 1142. See Hirras v. National R.R. Passenger Corp.

Hirras v. Amtrak, WDTex, 826 FSupp 1062. See Hirras v. National R.R. Passenger Corp.

Hirras v. National R.R. Passenger Corp., CA5 (Tex), 95 F3d 396.—Civil R 1149, 1185, 1189; Damag 50.10; Fed Civ Proc 2544; Fed Cts 766, 776, 802.

Hirras v. National R.R. Passenger Corp., CA5 (Tex), 44 F3d 278, appeal after remand 95 F3d 396.—Damag 49.10, 50.10; Labor & Emp 757, 1515, 1523, 1524, 1967; States 18.15, 18.46, 18.49.

Hirras v. National R.R. Passenger Corp., CA5 (Tex), 10 F3d 1142, cert gr, vac 114 SCt 2732, 512 US 1231, 129 LEd2d 855, on remand 44 F3d 278, appeal after remand 95 F3d 396.—Damag 49.10, 50.10; Fed Cts 589; Labor & Emp 1524, 1535, 1536, 1575; States 18.15, 18.46.

Hirras v. National R.R. Passenger Corp., WDTex, 826 FSupp 1062, aff 10 F3d 1142, cert gr, vac 114 SCt 2732, 512 US 1231, 129 LEd2d 855, on remand 44 F3d 278, appeal after remand 95 F3d 396.—Fed Civ Proc 1829; Labor & Emp 1523, 1536.

Hirsch, In re, BkrtcyNDTex, 224 BR 360. See Thompson, In re.

Hirsch; Anderson v., TexCivApp–Amarillo, 112 SW2d 535, writ refused.—App & E 758.3(4); Bills & N 443(3); Mech Liens 14; Plead 236(3), 236(4); Usury 34, 60.

Hirsch v. Dearing, TexCivApp–Galveston, 151 SW2d 949.—App & E 984(5); Atty & C 140; Costs 194.18; Evid 265(8); Garn 191; Plead 36(7).

Hirsch; Fuentes v., TexCivApp–El Paso, 472 SW2d 288, ref nre.—Adv Poss 80(1); Deeds 112(2), 137, 140; Stip 18(7); Ven & Pur 233.

Hirsch v. Hirsch, TexApp–El Paso, 770 SW2d 924.—App & E 216(1); Divorce 252.1, 252.3(1), 253(1), 256, 286(5); Plead 427; Trial 352.4(1).

Hirsch; Hirsch v., TexApp–El Paso, 770 SW2d 924.—App & E 216(1); Divorce 252.1, 252.3(1), 253(1), 256, 286(5); Plead 427; Trial 352.4(1).

Hirsch; Minchen v., TexCivApp–Beaumont, 295 SW2d 529, ref nre.—App & E 931(6); Contracts 163; Deeds 93, 95; Mines 54.5, 55(1), 55(5).

Hirsch; Santa Fe R. Co. v., TexCivApp–Beaumont, 429 SW2d 624, ref nre.—App & E 909(1); Trial 365.1(8).

Hirsch v. State, TexCrimApp, 90 SW2d 256, 129 TexCrim 571.—Anim 29.

Hirsch; Stillman v., Tex, 99 SW2d 270, 128 Tex 359.—App & E 1, 281(1), 544(1), 719(1), 722(1), 745, 747(2), 758.1, 758.3(1), 759; Courts 80(4).

Hirsch; Stillman v., TexCivApp–Galveston, 84 SW2d 501, aff 99 SW2d 270, 128 Tex 359.—App & E 181, 263(1),

263(3), 281(1), 291, 719(1), 719(8); Frds St of 20; Lim of Act 56(1); New Tr 114; Trial 350.4(1), 352.4(4), 352.12.

Hirsch v. Texas Lawyers' Ins. Exchange, TexApp–El Paso, 808 SW2d 561, writ den.—Contracts 108(1); Corp 397, 428(7); Insurance 2266, 2391(2), 3168, 3191(7).

Hirsch & Westheimer, P.C.; Moore Landrey, L.L.P. v., TexApp–Houston (1 Dist), 126 SW3d 536.—App & E 428(2); Judgm 297, 340; Motions 59(3).

Hirschfeld Steel Co., Inc. v. Kellogg Brown & Root, Inc., TexApp–Houston (14 Dist), 201 SW3d 272.—Action 6; App & E 205, 213, 232(2), 242(2); Contracts 218, 221(1), 221(2), 295(1), 354; Costs 194.32; Decl Judgm 26, 143.1, 392.1.

Hirschhorn; U.S. v., CA5 (Tex), 649 F2d 360.—Arrest 58; Crim Law 394.6(3); Int Rev 5126, 5270, 5295; Searches 118.

Hirschi; Nixon v., Tex, 136 SW2d 583, 134 Tex 415.—App & E 930(3); Home 213; Trial 351.2(2).

Hirschi; Nixon v., TexComApp, 132 SW2d 89, rearg gr, opinion withdrawn.—Courts 93(1); Home 99.5, 115(2), 116, 122, 177(2); Subrog 23(3); Ven & Pur 232(1).

Hirschi v. Nixon, TexCivApp–Fort Worth, 103 SW2d 833, rev 136 SW2d 583, 134 Tex 415.—Home 122.

Hirschi v. State, TexCrimApp, 683 SW2d 415.—Crim Law 1172.1(3); Riot 1, 3, 7.

Hirschman; Department of Public Safety v., TexApp–Waco, 169 SW3d 331, review den.—Admin Law 683, 749, 750, 788, 790, 791, 793; Autos 144.1(1.20), 144.2(1), 144.2(3), 349(6).

Hirth v. Metropolitan Life Ins. Co., CA5 (Tex), 189 FedAppx 292.—Labor & Emp 427, 445.

Hirtz v. State of Tex., CA5 (Tex), 974 F2d 663.—Fed Cts 266.1, 272, 623.

Hirtz v. State of Tex., SDTex, 773 FSupp 6, vac 974 F2d 663.—Ease 38, 53; Em Dom 2(10); Nav Wat 33, 36(1), 36(3), 41(1).

Hisaw & Associates General Contractors, Inc. v. Cornerstone Concrete Systems, Inc., TexApp–Fort Worth, 115 SW3d 16, reh overr, and review den, and reh of petition for review den.—Alt Disp Res 251, 316, 319, 362(1), 362(2), 374(1), 374(5), 382; App & E 946, 949; Parties 42, 43, 93(2).

Hisaw & Associates General Contractors, Inc.; Sutton v., TexApp–Dallas, 65 SW3d 281, reh overr, and review den.—App & E 5, 842(1), 859, 989, 1010.1(1), 1010.1(2), 1010.1(3), 1010.2, 1012.1(4); Contracts 321(2), 326; Fraud 3, 58(1), 58(4); Impl & C C 30, 33.1; Indem 122.

Hise v. State, TexCrimApp, 640 SW2d 271.—Burg 26; Crim Law 1134(8); Sent & Pun 2003, 2024, 2025.

Hisel; Shoreline, Inc. v., TexApp–Corpus Christi, 115 SW3d 21, reh overr, and review den.—App & E 5, 78(1), 79(1), 80(1), 859; Civil R 1118, 1740, 1765, 1769; Evid 265(2); Judgm 128, 217, 223.

Hiser v. State, TexApp–Houston (14 Dist), 830 SW2d 338.—Crim Law 394.6(5), 531(3), 532(0.5), 1153(1).

Hisey v. State, TexApp–Houston (1 Dist), 207 SW3d 383.—Crim Law 1188; Double J 1, 108, 109.

Hisey v. State, TexApp–Houston (1 Dist), 129 SW3d 649, petition for discretionary review dism with per curiam opinion 161 SW3d 502.—Crim Law 822(1), 1038.1(1), 1038.1(3.1), 1134(2), 1141(2), 1144.15, 1165(1), 1172.1(1), 1172.1(3); Homic 1450.

Hiskett; Wells v., TexCivApp–Texarkana, 288 SW2d 257, ref nre.—Corp 1.3, 1.4(3), 1.6(8), 1.7(2), 29(1), 100, 182.1(3), 202, 383, 397, 505, 660; Evid 73; Hus & W 257, 264(4); States 5(2); Trial 351.2(4), 358; Trusts 373.

Hisler v. Channelview Bank, TexCivApp–Hous (14 Dist), 538 SW2d 200.—App & E 5; Proc 52.

Hislop v. State, TexApp–Texarkana, 64 SW3d 544.—Crim Law 406(1), 444, 1169.12.

Hispanic Educ. Committee v. Houston Independent School Dist., SDTex, 886 FSupp 606, aff 68 F3d 467.—Admin Law 124, 125; Const Law 1435, 1490, 1553, 1555, 1775, 1969, 3272; Schools 55, 57, 63(1).

Hispanic Housing & Educ. Corp. v. Chicago Title Ins. Co., TexApp–Houston (1 Dist), 97 SW3d 150, review den.—Abstr of T 3; Insurance 1729, 1867, 3424.

Hiss v. Great North American Companies, Inc., TexApp–Dallas, 871 SW2d 218.—App & E 863, 870(4), 954(1); Inj 138.3; Trial 5.

Hitachi, Ltd.; Motorola, Inc. v., WDTex, 750 FSupp 1319, vac 923 F2d 868.—Compromise 20(1); Contracts 127(4), 147(1), 147(2), 155; Fraud 16, 17, 50, 58(1); Pat 36(2), 36(3), 66(1.14), 97, 112.1, 211(1), 219(1), 235(2), 312(6), 317, 318(2), 318(3), 319(1); Torts 103, 202, 242, 263.

Hitachi Shin Din Cable, Ltd. v. Cain, TexApp–Texarkana, 106 SW3d 776.—Afft 3, 17; App & E 846(5), 893(1); Appear 9(2); Const Law 3964; Corp 1.6(9), 665(1); Courts 12(2.1), 12(2.5), 12(2.10), 35, 39.

Hitchcock; Betts v., TexCivApp–Amarillo, 197 SW2d 878.—Damag 188(2); War 119, 165.

Hitchcock; Brown v., TexCivApp–Austin, 235 SW2d 478, writ refused.—Mines 92.23(1), 92.26.

Hitchcock v. Cassel, TexCivApp–Austin, 275 SW2d 205, ref nre.—Divorce 322; Estop 58, 77; Hus & W 265, 272(1); Ten in C 13, 15(5), 15(7), 15(10).

Hitchcock v. City of Killeen, TexCivApp–Eastland, 553 SW2d 22.—Judgm 702; Zoning 775, 783.

Hitchcock v. Garvin, TexApp–Dallas, 738 SW2d 34.—Judgm 181(33), 185.2(4); Schools 89.13(4).

Hitchcock; James v., TexCivApp–San Antonio, 309 SW2d 909, ref nre.—Adv Poss 114(1); Bound 3(6); Evid 358; Partit 10; Tresp to T T 11, 38(2), 41(1), 41(2).

Hitchcock; James v., TexCivApp–San Antonio, 294 SW2d 859.—Inj 138.31, 142, 147, 157.

Hitchcock v. Pearce, TexCivApp–Waco, 348 SW2d 408.—Plead 111.42(8).

Hitchcock; Simmons v., TexCivApp–El Paso, 283 SW2d 84.—App & E 931(6); Child C 463, 510, 554, 578, 632, 634, 641, 921(4), 923(4).

Hitchcock v. Sojourner Drilling Corp., TexCivApp–Eastland, 360 SW2d 444, ref nre.—Const Law 4084; Mines 79.1(4).

Hitchcock v. State, TexCrimApp, 612 SW2d 930.—Crim Law 673(5), 1173.2(9).

Hitchcock v. State, TexCrimApp, 388 SW2d 428.—Crim Law 770(2).

Hitchcock v. State, TexApp–Texarkana, 118 SW3d 844, reh overr, and petition for discretionary review refused.—Arrest 63.5(4), 63.5(8), 63.5(9); Controlled Subs 123, 137; Crim Law 394.1(3), 394.4(14), 394.5(4), 1044.2(1); Searches 45, 47.1.

Hitchcock; U.S. v., CA5 (Tex), 115 FedAppx 703.—Aliens 798.

Hitchcock; Welder v., TexCivApp–Corpus Christi, 617 SW2d 294, ref nre.—Des & Dist 72, 74, 81.

Hitchcock, City of; Nebout v., SDTex, 71 FSupp2d 702.—Civil R 1031, 1343, 1345, 1351(1), 1352(4), 1395(5); Fed Civ Proc 941, 943; Mun Corp 723.

Hitchcock Independent School Dist.; Goins v., SDTex, 424 FSupp2d 902.—Fed Cts 25, 241; Rem of C 1, 11, 19(1), 25(1), 89(1).

Hitchcock Independent School Dist.; James v., TexApp–Houston (1 Dist), 742 SW2d 701, writ den.—Const Law 4198; Decl Judgm 6, 7, 210; Judgm 181(11), 181(27), 185.1(2); Plead 228.14; Schools 57, 136.

Hitchcock I.S.D.; Goins v., SDTex, 191 FSupp2d 860, aff 65 FedAppx 508.—Civil R 332, 1011, 1116(2), 1170, 1305, 1330(5), 1359, 1395(8), 1502, 1527; Const Law 1553, 1928, 1929, 1932, 1990, 2000; Damag 50.10; Fed Civ Proc 1872, 1877.1; Offic 119; Schools 147.12.

Hitchcock Properties, Inc. v. Levering, TexApp–Houston (1 Dist), 776 SW2d 236, writ den.—Brok 43(2); Decl Judgm 45.

Hite, In re, TexApp–Corpus Christi, 700 SW2d 713, ref nre.—Mines 55(4); Wills 324(1), 440, 450, 456, 481, 490, 564(2), 587(1), 704, 721.

Hite v. Maritime Overseas Corp., EDTex, 380 FSupp 222.—Neglig 1020, 1037(7); Ship 73, 84(1), 84(5).

Hite v. Maritime Overseas Corp., EDTex, 375 FSupp 233.—Work Comp 260, 2085.

Hite v. State, TexCrimApp, 650 SW2d 778.—Crim Law 878(4); Larc 64(1).

Hite v. State, TexApp–Houston (14 Dist), 653 SW2d 455, rev 650 SW2d 778.—Burg 42(1); Crim Law 1144.13(2.1); Larc 64(1), 64(5).

Hi–Tech Electronics; Satellite Earth Stations East, Inc. v., TexApp–Eastland, 756 SW2d 385. See Satellite Earth Stations East, Inc. v. Davis.

Hi–Tech Towing; Amelia's Automotive, Inc. v., TexApp–San Antonio, 921 SW2d 767. See Amelia's Automotive, Inc. v. Rodriguez.

Hitt, Ex parte, TexCrimApp, 301 SW2d 920.—Crim Law 1094(3).

Hitt v. Bell, TexCivApp–Austin, 141 SW2d 726.—Appear 8(8); Lim of Act 118(1), 122, 197(1), 199(1).

Hitt v. Bell, TexCivApp–Austin, 111 SW2d 1164.—Judgm 17(1), 17(9), 145(2); Proc 52.

Hitt v. Carter, TexCivApp–Eastland, 115 SW2d 1154, dism.—Bailm 31(3), 33; Princ & A 101(1).

Hitt v. City of Pasadena, CA5 (Tex), 561 F2d 606.—Civil R 1343; Fed Civ Proc 1773, 1832, 1836, 1837.1, 1838; Fed Cts 936.

Hitt v. Connell, CA5 (Tex), 301 F3d 240.—Admin Law 501; Civil R 1125, 1421; Const Law 1435, 1446, 1449; Damag 49.10, 192; Evid 134, 380; Fed Cts 425, 427, 433, 813, 823, 945; Lim of Act 58(1), 95(15); Offic 72.33(1); Witn 406.

Hitt; Dumitrov v., TexCivApp–Hous (14 Dist), 601 SW2d 472, ref nre.—Ex & Ad 216(2), 510(2).

Hitt v. Dumitrov, TexCivApp–Hous (14 Dist), 598 SW2d 355.—Evid 472(1), 568(1); Ex & Ad 35(15).

Hitt v. East Texas Theatres, TexCivApp–Texarkana, 203 SW2d 963.—Corp 432(12), 433(1); Labor & Emp 3047; Trial 139.1(20).

Hitt v. Mabry, TexApp–San Antonio, 687 SW2d 791.—App & E 230, 863, 931(1), 989; Inj 12, 22, 118(1), 189, 192; Judgm 252(1).

Hitt v. Morris, TexCivApp–El Paso, 250 SW2d 408, mandamus overr.—Partners 17, 53, 325(2); Receivers 26.

Hitt; O'Connell v., TexApp–Corpus Christi, 730 SW2d 16.—Antitrust 397; Costs 194.16, 194.48, 198.

Hitt; Pompano Properties v., TexApp–Corpus Christi, 730 SW2d 16. See O'Connell v. Hitt.

Hitt v. State, TexCrimApp, 548 SW2d 732.—Const Law 4666; Crim Law 393(1).

Hitt v. State, TexCrimApp, 391 SW2d 438.—Crim Law 1052; Forg 44(3).

Hitt v. State, TexCrimApp, 311 SW2d 239, 166 TexCrim 58.—Autos 355(6), 359.

Hitt v. State, TexApp–Austin, 53 SW3d 697, petition for discretionary review refused.—Const Law 2370, 2403; Courts 78, 80(2), 85(1); Crim Law 369.2(1), 369.2(5), 374, 474.3(1), 474.4(4), 695.5, 741(1), 742(1), 747, 1036.1(2), 1036.1(9), 1036.6, 1043(2), 1043(3), 1045, 1090.8, 1134(6), 1144.12, 1144.13(1), 1144.13(2.1), 1144.13(6), 1159.2(2), 1168(2), 1169.2(1), 1169.2(8); Infants 20.

Hitt; Texas Emp. Ins. Ass'n v., TexCivApp–Galveston, 125 SW2d 323.—Damag 221(6), 221(8); Trial 76, 90, 219, 273, 352.1(9), 352.9; Witn 286(2); Work Comp 512, 515, 597, 849, 858, 863, 1020, 1313, 1922, 1924, 1926, 1929.

Hitt v. U.S., NDTex, 296 FSupp 633.—Int Rev 4339.

Hitton v. State, TexCrimApp, 117 SW2d 90, 135 TexCrim 67.—Autos 355(8); Crim Law 775(3), 829(7), 899.

Hittson v. State, TexCrimApp, 114 SW2d 881, 134 TexCrim 131.—Autos 355(13).

Hittson v. State, TexCrimApp, 97 SW2d 951, 131 TexCrim 228.—Autos 351.1.

Hitzelberger; Long v., TexCivApp–Eastland, 602 SW2d 321.—Partit 14, 22.

Hitzelberger v. Samedan Oil Corp., TexApp–Waco, 948 SW2d 497, reh overr, and review den, and reh of petition for review overr.—App & E 842(2), 893(1), 989, 1008.1(2), 1012.1(4); Compromise 5(1), 7.1, 15(1), 21; Contracts 143(2), 176(2), 318; Evid 448; Mines 73, 73.1(5), 73.5, 77, 78.1(3), 78.2, 79.1(2), 79.1(5), 79.3, 79.6.

Hitzeman; Lacy v., TexCivApp–Fort Worth, 190 SW2d 764.—Child C 76, 719, 767, 921(1); Evid 80(2); Hab Corp 532(2), 687, 847.

Hitzeman; Lacy v., TexCivApp–Fort Worth, 188 SW2d 711.—App & E 458(2); Hab Corp 821.1.

Hitzfeld; Burg v., TexCivApp–San Antonio, 89 SW2d 272, writ dism.—Debtor & C 16; Home 108, 182; Subrog 17.

Hi–Way Auto Parts II v. Longo, TexApp–Fort Worth, 909 SW2d 618. See Bown v. Longo.

Hi–Way Billboards, Inc.; N.L.R.B. v., CA5 (Tex), 500 F2d 181.—Labor & Emp 1483(1).

Hi–Way Billboards, Inc.; N.L.R.B. v., CA5 (Tex), 473 F2d 649.—Labor & Emp 1483(1), 1767(1), 1945.

Hi–Way Equipment Co.; Baldwin-Lima-Hamilton Corp. v., SDTex, 250 FSupp 574.—Pat 16(2), 25, 26(1.1), 26(2), 74, 165(1), 168(2.1), 243(1), 291, 325.11(4).

Hix v. Billingsley, TexCivApp–Galveston, 195 SW2d 219. —Estop 87; Mines 99(3).

Hix v. De Phillipi, TexCivApp–Galveston, 216 SW2d 643, ref nre.—App & E 1010.1(2), 1010.1(3); Home 162(1), 181(3), 181.5; Judgm 106(5); Plead 258(1).

Hix; Guillot v., Tex, 838 SW2d 230.—Subrog 33(1), 38, 41(3); Work Comp 2191, 2210, 2215, 2216.

Hix v. Guillot, TexApp–Houston (14 Dist), 812 SW2d 400, writ gr, aff 838 SW2d 230.—Work Comp 2216.

Hix v. Robertson, TexApp–Waco, 211 SW3d 423.—Decl Judgm 300, 395; Judgm 185.3(1); Nav Wat 1(1), 1(3), 1(6), 39(2).

Hix v. Tuloso-Midway Independent School Dist., Tex-CivApp–Corpus Christi, 489 SW2d 706, ref nre.—App & E 934(1); Const Law 4202; Schools 133.6(1), 133.6(5), 135(3), 147.4, 147.6, 147.12, 147.38, 147.40(2), 147.51.

Hix v. U.S. Army Corps. of Engineers, CA5 (Tex), 155 FedAppx 121.—Fed Civ Proc 1742(2), 1837.1; U S 78(12).

Hix; Western Nat. Bank of Amarillo v., TexCivApp–Amarillo, 533 SW2d 859.—Banks 275.

Hix; White v., TexCivApp–El Paso, 104 SW2d 136, writ dism.—App & E 846(5); Lim of Act 145(5); Partners 157(3), 183(6), 258(8); Trusts 44(3); Ven & Pur 242.

Hix v. Wirt, TexCivApp–Waco, 220 SW2d 530, ref nre.— App & E 230, 978(2); Autos 243(1); Evid 220(1), 471(3), 471(11); Trial 76, 121(5).

Hixon; Armstrong v., TexApp–Corpus Christi, 206 SW3d 175, reh overr, and review den, and reh of petition for review den.—Adop 23; App & E 854(4), 863, 893(1), 946, 984(5), 1047(1); Costs 194.40, 208; Decl Judgm 1, 8, 61; Judgm 178; Statut 181(1), 188, 190, 205, 212.4; Trial 43; Wills 437, 440, 470(1), 487(2), 488, 491, 497(5), 707(1).

Hixon v. State, TexCrimApp, 523 SW2d 711.—Const Law 240(1), 2970, 3701; Mun Corp 595, 611, 663(1), 703(1).

Hixson v. Cox, TexApp–Dallas, 633 SW2d 330, ref nre.— Accord 10(1), 11(1), 11(2), 11(3).

Hixson v. Pride of Texas Distributing Co., Inc., Tex-App–Fort Worth, 683 SW2d 173.—App & E 724(4), 754(1), 930(3), 989, 994(2), 1001(1), 1001(3), 1002, 1003(1), 1003(4), 1003(5), 1079, 1177(7); Corp 349; Fraud Conv 47, 267, 299(1).

Hixson v. Salem Corp., TexApp–Texarkana, 673 SW2d 345, ref nre.—Judgm 181(7).

Hixson v. State, TexCrimApp, 383 SW2d 932.—Autos 355(6).

Hixson v. State, TexApp–Corpus Christi, 1 SW3d 160.— Const Law 2332, 2390; Crim Law 1032(1); Ind & Inf 7.

Hixson v. State, TexApp–Corpus Christi, 969 SW2d 150, reh overr, review gr, cause remanded 979 SW2d 330, on remand 1 SW3d 160.—Ind & Inf 7.

Hi-Yield Chemical Co.; Mozer v., CA5 (Tex), 234 F2d 906, cert den 77 SCt 327, 352 US 952, 1 LEd2d 243.— Fed Cts 914; Sales 441(3).

Hjalmarson v. Langley, TexApp–Waco, 840 SW2d 153.— Costs 2; Courts 1, 2, 30, 40; Pretrial Proc 506.1, 520.

H. J. Cohn Furniture (No. 2) Co. v. Texas Western Financial Corp., CA5 (Tex), 544 F2d 886.—Corp 99(1), 99(2), 468.1.

H. J. Heinz Co. v. Ashley, TexCivApp–Galveston, 291 SW2d 427.—App & E 1053(3), 1060.6, 1140(1), 1140(4); Autos 243(1); Damag 132(7), 163(4), 187, 208(4).

H.J. Heinz Co.; Coghlan v., NDTex, 851 FSupp 815.— Civil R 1218(3), 1769.

H.J. Heinz Co.; Coghlan v., NDTex, 851 FSupp 808.— Civil R 1019(3), 1218(3); Fed Civ Proc 2470.1, 2497.1, 2544, 2546, 2547.1, 2552.

H. J. Hogan, Inc.; Hays v., TexCivApp–Austin, 474 SW2d 330.—App & E 1008.1(2), 1011.1(4); Damag 140; Impl & C C 112.

H.J. Justin & Sons, Inc.; Stanley v., TexApp–Fort Worth, 672 SW2d 327, ref nre.—Evid 450(6); Labor & Emp 41(2), 58.

HJS Industries, Inc.; Tuscarora Corp. v., TexApp–Corpus Christi, 794 SW2d 435, writ den.—Antitrust 134, 141, 147, 264, 291, 363; App & E 218.2(5.1), 866(3); Contracts 176(1), 176(2), 316(1); Corp 445.1; Neglig 321; Torts 424.

H.K. Global Trading, Ltd.; Khaledi v., TexApp–San Antonio, 126 SW3d 273.—App & E 190(2), 863, 920(3), 954(1), 1024.2; Inj 16, 34, 132, 135, 138.3, 138.6, 138.18, 138.37, 140, 147, 148(1), 148(2), 157, 189, 204; Mtg 159, 186(6), 311, 338.

H. Kohnstamm & Co. of Tex. v. Burleson, TexCivApp–El Paso, 237 SW2d 319.—Home 70, 214, 216.

H. Kohnstamm & Co. of Tex.; Hackler v., TexCivApp–Dallas, 227 SW2d 347.—Exemp 45, 47; Sheriffs 106, 123, 124, 125(1), 163, 169.

H.K. Porter Co., Inc.; Epps v., NDTex, 601 FSupp 399. See Young v. Armstrong World Industries, Inc.

H.K. Porter Co., Inc.; Friend v., NDTex, 601 FSupp 399. See Young v. Armstrong World Industries, Inc.

H.K. Porter Co., Inc.; Lane v., NDTex, 601 FSupp 399. See Young v. Armstrong World Industries, Inc.

H.K. Porter Co., Inc.; Luster v., NDTex, 601 FSupp 399. See Young v. Armstrong World Industries, Inc.

H.K. Porter Co., Inc.; Noble v., NDTex, 601 FSupp 399. See Young v. Armstrong World Industries, Inc.

H.K. Porter Co., Inc.; Oder v., NDTex, 601 FSupp 399. See Young v. Armstrong World Industries, Inc.

H.K. Porter Co., Inc.; Owens v., NDTex, 601 FSupp 399. See Young v. Armstrong World Industries, Inc.

H.K. Porter Co., Inc.; Phillips v., NDTex, 601 FSupp 399. See Young v. Armstrong World Industries, Inc.

H.K. Porter Co., Inc.; Roper v., NDTex, 601 FSupp 399. See Young v. Armstrong World Industries, Inc.

Hlavaty v. State, TexCrimApp, 275 SW2d 818.—Crim Law 1203.26.

Hlavinka v. Griffin, TexApp–Corpus Christi, 721 SW2d 521.—App & E 931(1); Pretrial Proc 223, 517.1; Trial 382.

Hlavinka v. Hancock, TexApp–Corpus Christi, 116 SW3d 412, reh overr, and review den.—App & E 989, 1001(1), 1001(3), 1003(7); Mines 55(2), 55(7), 74(8), 78.1(2).

Hlawiczka v. Fitch, TexCivApp–Galveston, 197 SW2d 135, ref nre.—Frds St of 116(5).

H. L. Brown & Associates, Inc. v. McMahon, TexCiv-App–Tyler, 525 SW2d 553.—Adv Poss 11, 13, 19, 22, 24, 27, 28, 33, 57, 70, 114(1); App & E 931(1), 989, 1177(7).

H. L. "Brownie" Choate, Inc. v. Southland Drilling Co., Tex, 447 SW2d 676.—Accord 11(1), 26(3).

H. L. "Brownie" Choate, Inc. v. Southland Drilling Co., TexCivApp–San Antonio, 441 SW2d 672, rev 447 SW2d 676.—Accord 1, 10(1), 11(2), 11(3).

H. L. Butler & Son v. Walpole, TexCivApp–Austin, 239 SW2d 653, ref nre.—App & E 930(1), 989; Damag 138; Evid 474(18); High 118; Labor & Emp 3077, 3179(4); Trial 118, 125(1), 133.1, 350.1.

HLC Properties, Inc., In re, BkrtcyNDTex, 55 BR 685.—Bankr 3071.

HL Farm Corp.; Henderson County Appraisal Dist. v., TexApp–Eastland, 956 SW2d 672.—Courts 91(1), 100(1); Tax 2640, 2790.

HL Farm Corp. v. Henderson County Appraisal Dist., TexApp–Tyler, 894 SW2d 830, appeal after remand 956 SW2d 672.—Const Law 3116; Tax 2137.

HL Farm Corp. v. Self, Tex, 877 SW2d 288.—Const Law 990, 3012, 3057, 3116; Tax 2523.

HL Farm Corp. v. Self, TexApp–Dallas, 820 SW2d 372, writ gr, rev 877 SW2d 288.—App & E 93; Atty & C 32(7); Const Law 3013, 3355, 3560; Judgm 185(2); Tax 2106, 2121, 2135.

H. L. H. v. State, TexCivApp–Austin, 560 SW2d 536.—Infants 68.7(3).

H. L. H. Enterprises, Inc.; McGregor v., CA5 (Tex), 470 F2d 188, cert den 94 SCt 127, 414 US 824, 38 LEd2d 58.—Sec Reg 60.63(1).

H. L. Hunt, Inc.; Cooper v., TexCivApp–Texarkana, 87 SW2d 763.—Judgm 713(3).

H. L. McRae Co. v. Hooker Const. Co., TexCivApp–Austin, 579 SW2d 62.—App & E 493, 635(2), 1203(1); Appear 8(3), 8(8), 19(1), 24(5); Courts 37(3); Proc 80.

H. L. McRae Co. v. Hooker Const. Co., TexCivApp–Austin, 564 SW2d 142.—App & E 395.

H. L. Peterson Co. v. Applewhite, CA5 (Tex), 383 F2d 430.—Courts 493(3); Fed Civ Proc 776; Fed Cts 23, 24, 914; Fraud 4, 6, 58(1), 59(1); Lim of Act 134.

H. L. Peterson Co.; Griffin v., TexCivApp–Dallas, 427 SW2d 140.—Action 70; App & E 707(1), 1073(1); Bailm 3; Evid 168, 400(6); Judgm 181(1), 186; Sales 38(3), 90, 267.

H.L.S. Energy Co., Inc., Matter of, CA5 (Tex), 151 F3d 434.—Bankr 2871, 2874, 2965, 2972, 3009, 3134, 3594; Mines 92.56.

HLW Enterprises of Texas, Inc., In re, BkrtcyWDTex, 157 BR 592.—Bankr 2182.1; Int Rev 4767, 4769, 4775, 4778, 4788.1; Mech Liens 115(1).

H.M.B. Const. Co.; Martin v., CA5 (Tex), 279 F2d 495.—Fed Civ Proc 2646; Fed Cts 829.

H. M. Cohen Lumber & Bldg. Co.; Croft v., TexCivApp–Galveston, 107 SW2d 1040, writ dism.—App & E 773(3), 999(1); Contracts 286.

H. M. Cohen Lumber & Bldg. Co. v. McCalla, TexCivApp–Galveston, 142 SW2d 685.—Mand 151(1).

H. M. Cohen Lumber & Building Co. v. Panos, TexCivApp–Beaumont, 154 SW2d 206, writ refused wom.—App & E 706(3); Contracts 127(2); New Tr 152, 163(1); Trial 215, 304, 352.12.

H.M.J.H., In re, TexApp–Dallas, 209 SW3d 320.—App & E 877(2); Infants 221, 222, 242.

H. Molsen & Co.; Cotton Concentration Co. v., TexCivApp–Texarkana, 454 SW2d 255, rev Toyo Cotton Co v. Cotton Concentration Co, 461 SW2d 116.—App & E 833(5).

H. Molsen & Co., Inc.; Davis v., TexCivApp–Tyler, 545 SW2d 889.—App & E 302(3), 500(1), 1170.9(2.1); Contracts 147(2), 147(3); Evid 461(1); Sales 359(1).

H. Molsen & Co., Inc. v. E. W. Settle, TexCivApp–Dallas, 534 SW2d 376.—Judgm 654; Plead 111.17, 111.42(6), 111.42(7).

H. Molsen & Co., Inc. v. Harp and Lovelace, TexCivApp–Amarillo, 516 SW2d 433.—Decl Judgm 271; Plead 111.16, 111.42(4).

H. Molsen & Co., Inc. v. Hicks, TexCivApp–El Paso, 550 SW2d 354, ref nre.—Frds St of 144.

H. Molsen & Co., Inc.; Lambert v., TexCivApp–Waco, 551 SW2d 151, ref nre.—Action 43.1, 50(4.1), 56, 60;

App & E 949, 1035; Interest 39(2.30); Parties 14, 25; Trial 350.2, 352.14.

H. Molsen & Co., Inc. v. Raines, TexCivApp–El Paso, 534 SW2d 146, writ dism.—App & E 768, 912, 989; Cust & U 15(1); Plead 111.16; Sales 87(3); Venue 7.5(3), 7.5(7).

H. Molsen & Co., Inc. v. Williamson, TexCivApp–Dallas, 510 SW2d 366.—Decl Judgm 295, 301; Plead 110; Venue 22(1), 22(4), 22(6).

H. Morgan Daniel Seafoods, Inc.; Hodgson v., CA5 (Tex), 433 F2d 918, 19 Wage & Hour Cas (BNA) 816.—Const Law 2600; Fed Cts 850.1; Labor & Emp 2399.

H. M. R. Const. Co. v. Wolco of Houston, Inc., TexCivApp–Hous (14 Dist), 422 SW2d 214, ref nre.—Contracts 198(1), 326; Contrib 3, 5(6.1), 9(6); Indem 25; Labor & Emp 3125, 3128, 3135, 3160; Neglig 1205(9).

HMS Aviation v. Layale Enterprises, S.A., TexApp–Fort Worth, 149 SW3d 182, reh overr.—App & E 846(5), 893(1), 1010.1(1), 1024.3; Appear 9(1), 9(2), 9(5); Const Law 3963, 3964, 3965(4), 3966, 3974; Courts 11, 12(2.1), 12(2.5), 12(2.10), 12(2.25), 15, 17, 35, 39; Judgm 804, 805, 812(1).

HMT Const. Services, Inc.; Lazenby v., TexApp–Beaumont, 944 SW2d 54, reh overr, and writ den.—Work Comp 78, 80, 391, 2084, 2107, 2136.

H. N. C. Realty Co.; F. M. Stigler, Inc. v., TexCivApp–Dallas, 595 SW2d158, rev Land Title Co of Dallas, Inc v. F M Stigler, Inc, 609 SW2d 754.—Contracts 143(2), 176(2); 346(3); Princ & A 96, 97, 99, 147(2), 148(4), 166(1), 171(1), 189(4).

HNC Realty Co.; Willowood Condominium Ass'n, Inc. v., CA5 (Tex), 531 F2d 1249.—Contracts 9(1), 39.

HNG Oil Co.; Goudie v., TexApp–El Paso, 711 SW2d 716, ref nre.—App & E 934(1), 989, 1062.1; Judgm 199(3.10); Labor & Emp 561, 696(1).

HNG Oil Co.; Hunt v., TexApp–Corpus Christi, 791 SW2d 191, writ den.—Mines 51(5), 73.1(6).

HNG Oil Co.; Parker v., TexApp–Corpus Christi, 732 SW2d 754.—Ref of Inst 17(2), 19(1).

HNG Oil Co.; Robbins v., TexApp–Beaumont, 878 SW2d 351, writ dism woj.—Courts 89, 91(0.5), 97(1); Deeds 113, 118, 119; Evid 384, 390(1), 397(1); Judgm 625, 666, 714(1), 715(1), 829(3); Mines 79.7, 81; Perp 6(1).

Ho v. State, TexApp–Houston (1 Dist), 856 SW2d 495, reh den.—Crim Law 105, 304(1), 338(1), 829(3), 1032(7), 1033.1, 1044.1(1); Ind & Inf 38, 41(2), 41(3), 161(1), 196(1); Obscen 1.1, 5.1, 5.2, 16, 17, 20.

Ho v. State, TexApp–Houston (14 Dist), 171 SW3d 295, reh overr, and petition for discretionary review refused.—Crim Law 338(1), 338(7), 340, 347, 598(2), 662.7, 730(8), 867, 911, 938(1), 939(2), 1035(10), 1036.1(9), 1043(3), 1044.1(2), 1147, 1153(1), 1153(4), 1155, 1156(3), 1169.5(5); Sent & Pun 312; Witn 267, 372(1).

Ho; U.S. v., CA5 (Tex), 311 F3d 589, reh den, cert den 123 SCt 2274, 539 US 914, 156 LEd2d 129, appeal after new sentencing hearing 132 FedAppx 560.—Commerce 7(2), 82.6; Crim Law 1139; Environ Law 735, 744, 751; Sent & Pun 734, 752.

Ho v. University of Texas at Arlington, TexApp–Amarillo, 984 SW2d 672, review den.—Action 2; App & E 863, 934(1), 949, 1079; Atty & C 62; Civil R 1067(5), 1731, 1733; Colleges 5, 8(1), 9.35(3.1), 9.35(4), 10; Const Law 642, 953, 1021, 3020, 3034, 3040, 3053, 3060, 3081, 3867, 3893, 3912, 4224(7), 4224(11); Evid 314(1), 318(7); Fraud 3, 4.5, 7, 16, 17, 64(1), 64(2); Judgm 181(2), 181(6), 181(27), 185(2), 185(3), 185.1(3), 185.3(1), 185.3(21), 203, 216, 217, 345; Lim of Act 16, 39(1), 165; New Tr 99; States 78, 191.4(1), 191.10, 208; Trial 9(1).

Ho v. Wolfe, TexApp–Amarillo, 688 SW2d 693.—App & E 173(6), 984(5); Evid 52; Sales 1(4), 75, 89, 92, 168(4), 181(13), 182(1), 182(4).

Hoag; Evans v., TexApp–Houston (14 Dist), 711 SW2d 744, ref nre.—App & E 499(1); Judgm 183; Lim of Act 124; Plead 252(2); Pretrial Proc 511.

Hoag v. State, TexCrimApp, 728 SW2d 375.—Arrest 63.1, 63.4(15), 63.5(1), 63.5(4), 63.5(5), 63.5(6), 63.5(7), 63.5(9), 68(3).

Hoag v. State, TexApp–Fort Worth, 959 SW2d 311.—Crim Law 273(4.1), 1031(4).

Hoag v. State, TexApp–San Antonio, 693 SW2d 718, petition for discretionary review gr, rev 728 SW2d 375.—Arrest 63.1, 63.4(1), 63.4(3), 63.4(11), 63.4(13), 63.5(3.1), 63.5(4), 63.5(5), 63.5(6), 68(3); Crim Law 1144.12, 1158(4).

Hoag v. State, TexApp–Corpus Christi, 791 SW2d 342.—Arrest 71.1(3); Controlled Subs 122; Crim Law 394.4(3), 394.4(4).

Hoagland; Bass v., CA5 (Tex), 172 F2d 205, cert den 70 SCt 57, 338 US 816, 94 LEd 494.—Const Law 4010; Evid 90; Fed Civ Proc 1053.1, 1055; Fed Cts 420; Hab Corp 447; Judgm 104, 113, 486(1), 495(1), 501, 518, 525, 720; Jury 12(3), 16(1), 28(3), 28(5), 31.

Hoagland v. Finholt, TexApp–Dallas, 773 SW2d 740.—Contracts 54(1), 88; Joint Adv 1.11; Partners 70, 353.

Hoagland v. State, TexCrimApp, 541 SW2d 442.—Crim Law 1099.6(2.1).

Hoagland v. State, TexCrimApp, 494 SW2d 186.—Crim Law 629.5(5), 720(6), 722.5, 730(14), 863(1), 1038.3; Infants 20; Witn 4.

Hoai Le v. State, TexApp–Corpus Christi, 963 SW2d 838. See Nam Hoai Le v. State.

Hoak v. Ferguson, TexCivApp–Fort Worth, 255 SW2d 258, ref nre.—Ease 16, 18(2), 18(3), 22, 31, 36(1), 36(3), 55.

Hoang; Spellman v., TexApp–San Antonio, 887 SW2d 480.—App & E 345.1, 387(2); New Tr 153.

Hoang v. State, TexCrimApp, 939 SW2d 593, on remand 1997 WL 404010.—Crim Law 739(3), 772(4), 1173.2(2), 1179.

Hoang v. State, TexCrimApp, 872 SW2d 694, cert den Luan Van Hoang v. Texas, 115 SCt 177, 513 US 863, 130 LEd2d 112.—Const Law 4590; Courts 472.2; Crim Law 273.1(2), 1663; Double J 28, 52, 60.1, 105; Hab Corp 223, 256, 687; Judgm 660.5, 951(1).

Hoang v. State, TexApp–Dallas, 810 SW2d 6, petition for discretionary review gr, aff 872 SW2d 694, cert den Luan Van Hoang v. Texas, 115 SCt 177, 513 US 863, 130 LEd2d 112.—Crim Law 98, 273.1(2), 289.1, 295; Double J 5.1, 52, 112.1; Hab Corp 274, 466; Infants 196; Judgm 470, 751; Sent & Pun 1163.

Hoang v. State, TexApp–Texarkana, 997 SW2d 678.—Crim Law 655(1), 656(1), 656(2), 656(3), 656(9), 1035(8.1), 1166.22(1).

Hoang v. State, TexApp–Houston (14 Dist), 825 SW2d 729, petition for discretionary review refused.—Agric 1; Const Law 990; Crim Law 641.13(1), 641.13(2.1), 641.13(6), 641.13(7); Jury 29(6).

Hoarel Sign Co. v. Dominion Equity Corp., TexApp–Amarillo, 910 SW2d 140, reh overr, and writ den.—Bankr 2515, 2571; Equity 43; Improv 1; Judgm 181(7), 181(15.1); Liens 1, 7; Lim of Act 6(1), 51(2), 151(4), 167(1); Mech Liens 260(1); Mtg 151(3).

Hobart; Coca Cola Bottling Co. of Houston v., TexCivApp–Hous (14 Dist), 423 SW2d 118, ref nre.—App & E 392; Costs 241; Damag 132(8); Indem 72, 102; Neglig 1586, 1614, 1620, 1624; Prod Liab 8, 41, 75.1, 76, 84.

Hobart Corp.; Sharp v., TexApp–Austin, 957 SW2d 650, reh overr.—Commerce 69(1); Costs 194.40; Tax 2233, 2699(11), 2727; Trial 393(3).

Hobbs, Ex parte, TexCrimApp, 410 SW2d 787.—Extrad 36, 39.

Hobbs, Ex parte, TexCrimApp, 364 SW2d 239.—Hab Corp 723.

Hobbs, Ex parte, TexCrimApp, 157 SW2d 397, 143 TexCrim 100.—Const Law 3512; Hab Corp 291, 464; Mun Corp 635; Zoning 9, 29, 33, 61.

Hobbs, In re, BkrtcyNDTex, 333 BR 751.—Bankr 3251, 3271, 3273.1, 3274, 3276.1, 3278.1, 3279, 3280, 3281, 3285, 3315(1), 3315(2), 3317(1), 3317(5).

Hobbs; Bamford v., SDTex, 569 FSupp 160.—Antitrust 969; Const Law 3962, 3963, 3964, 3965(3), 3965(10); Corp 1.6(9); Fed Civ Proc 412, 492, 497, 500; Fed Cts 76, 76.15, 76.20, 79, 85, 97, 417.

Hobbs v. Bass, TexCivApp–Texarkana, 279 SW2d 480, ref nre.—Frds St of 110(1), 118(2).

Hobbs v. Downing, TexCivApp–Amarillo, 147 SW2d 284.—Fraud Conv 229; J P 159(1).

Hobbs v. Grant, TexCivApp–Austin, 314 SW2d 351, ref nre.—App & E 1060.1(7); Autos 216; Damag 130.2; Neglig 554(1); Trial 9(1), 90, 191(11), 194(20), 215, 350.7(3.1).

Hobbs v. Hajecate, TexCivApp–Austin, 374 SW2d 351, writ refused.—Action 66; Lim of Act 2(1).

Hobbs; Harrell v., TexApp–Tyler, 791 SW2d 310.—Child S 442, 496.

Hobbs v. Hobbs, TexApp–Dallas, 691 SW2d 75, dism.—Divorce 139.5, 145, 146, 179, 183; Evid 208(1), 265(8); Pretrial Proc 676.

Hobbs; Hobbs v., TexApp–Dallas, 691 SW2d 75, dism.—Divorce 139.5, 145, 146, 179, 183; Evid 208(1), 265(8); Pretrial Proc 676.

Hobbs v. Hutson, TexApp–Texarkana, 733 SW2d 269, writ den.—Judgm 185.3(14); Mines 55(5).

Hobbs v. Jackson, TexCivApp–Fort Worth, 313 SW2d 348.—App & E 773(2).

Hobbs v. Slayton, TexCivApp–Texarkana, 265 SW2d 838, ref nre.—App & E 1170.6; Damag 134(1), 221(2.1); New Tr 143(2); Trial 125(5), 133.6(7).

Hobbs; Standifer Bros. v., TexCivApp–Texarkana, 98 SW2d 231, writ dism.—App & E 907(3); Tresp 40(4).

Hobbs v. State, TexCrimApp, 175 SW3d 777.—Burg 41(3); Crim Law 29(5.5).

Hobbs v. State, TexCrimApp, 548 SW2d 884.—Crim Law 45; Homic 851, 852; Ind & Inf 60, 109, 171, 196(5).

Hobbs v. State, TexCrimApp, 433 SW2d 700.—Crim Law 1114.1(1).

Hobbs v. State, TexCrimApp, 407 SW2d 791.—Autos 349.5(10); Crim Law 554, 1031(1), 1130(2); Weap 17(1), 17(4).

Hobbs v. State, TexCrimApp, 352 SW2d 836, 171 TexCrim 607.—Sent & Pun 1381(4).

Hobbs v. State, TexCrimApp, 227 SW2d 570, 154 TexCrim 341.—Assault 78, 91; Weap 17(4).

Hobbs; State v., TexApp–San Antonio, 824 SW2d 317, petition for discretionary review refused.—Crim Law 394.4(2), 394.4(6).

Hobbs v. State, TexApp–Beaumont, 778 SW2d 185.—Crim Law 641.4(1), 641.4(4).

Hobbs v. State, TexApp–Houston (14 Dist), 650 SW2d 449, petition for discretionary review refused.—Crim Law 374, 633(1), 867, 1169.5(1), 1174(1).

Hobbs; Traveler's Ins. Co. of Hartford, Conn. v., TexCivApp–San Antonio, 222 SW2d 168.—Evid 83(2); Trial 352.4(9); Work Comp 1360, 1597, 1919.

Hobbs v. Triangle Supply Co., TexCivApp–Eastland, 378 SW2d 726.—Acct Action on 13; App & E 1041(3); Corp 30(6).

Hobbs; Trujillo v., CA5 (Tex), 137 FedAppx 663.—Fed Civ Proc 2734; Prisons 17(2); Sent & Pun 1546; U S Mag 21.

Hobbs v. U.S., CA5 (Tex), 73 FedAppx 54.—Civil R 1376(8).

Hobbs v. U.S. ex rel. Russell, CA5 (Tex), 209 F3d 408.—Int Rev 4482; Records 31; Statut 158, 223.4.

Hobbs Mfg. Co.; Pinkard v., TexCivApp–Fort Worth, 168 SW2d 539, dism.—App & E 173(6), 877(2), 884, 1070(1); Costs 234; Judgm 668(1); Sequest 12, 17, 20.

Hobbs Trailers v. J. T. Arnett Grain Co., Inc., Tex, 560 SW2d 85.—Evid 393(1); Lim of Act 41; Sales 4(1).

Hobbs Trailers; J. T. Arnett Grain Co., Inc. v., TexCiv-App–Waco, 540 SW2d 441, writ gr, rev 560 SW2d 85.—Evid 434(8); Fraud 31, 58(1); Lim of Act 41.

Hobbs Trailers; McCauley v., TexCivApp–Fort Worth, 357 SW2d 494.—B & L Assoc 1; Cons Cred 5.1.

Hobbs Trailers, A Div. of Fruehauf Corp.; Marine Drilling Co. v., TexApp–Corpus Christi, 697 SW2d 831, ref nre.—Sec Tran 94, 138, 141.

Hobby v. Commissioner of Internal Revenue, CCA5 (Tex), 97 F2d 731.—Int Rev 4655, 4657.

Hobby; Farrar v., USTex, 113 SCt 566, 506 US 103, 121 LEd2d 494.—Civil R 1459, 1461, 1462, 1482, 1487.

Hobby; Grammar v., TexCivApp–San Antonio, 276 SW2d 311, ref nre.—Judgm 118, 143(2), 153(1), 162(4).

Hobdy v. Lewis, TexCivApp–Fort Worth, 409 SW2d 428.—Child S 255, 555.

Hobert's Estate; Marshall v., TexCivApp–Eastland, 315 SW2d 604, writ refused.—Courts 200.7, 202(5); Ex & Ad 7; Statut 181(1), 190.

Hoblinski; McIntyre v., TexCivApp–Waco, 333 SW2d 697, writ refused.—Schools 111.

Hoblitzelle; City of University Park v., TexCivApp–Dallas, 150 SW2d 169, writ dism, correct, appeal dism, cert den 62 SCt 806, 315 US 781, 86 LEd 1188.—Admin Law 456; Mand 178; Mun Corp 63.15(3), 63.20; Zoning 21.5, 432, 608.1, 609, 618.

Hoblitzelle; Glass v., TexCivApp–Dallas, 83 SW2d 796, writ dism.—Action 10; Antitrust 9, 580, 977(3); App & E 954(1); Commerce 62.7; Inj 135.

Hoboken Web Services LLC; Blastmyresume.com LP v., CA5 (Tex), 214 FedAppx 423.—Fed Civ Proc 1636.1.

Hobrecht v. Malone & Hyde, Inc., TexApp–San Antonio, 685 SW2d 739. See Malone & Hyde, Inc. v. Hobrecht.

Hobrecht; Malone & Hyde, Inc. v., TexApp–San Antonio, 685 SW2d 739, writ gr, set aside.—App & E 930(3), 989, 1001(1), 1140(2), 1177(7); Damag 185(1), 208(4); Death 31(8), 81, 82, 86(1), 95(1), 95(3), 97, 99(1), 99(4); Health 606; Hus & W 209(3), 209(4); Jury 136(3); New Tr 77(2), 162(1), 162(3); Parties 64.

Hobson; Browning-Ferris, Inc. v., TexApp–Houston (14 Dist), 967 SW2d 543, review den.—App & E 999(3); Neglig 371, 379, 380, 383, 387, 1677, 1713.

Hobson; Buckner Const., Inc. v., TexApp–Houston (14 Dist), 793 SW2d 74. See D.A. Buckner Const., Inc. v. Hobson.

Hobson; D.A. Buckner Const., Inc. v., TexApp–Houston (14 Dist), 793 SW2d 74.—Costs 2; Mand 4(3), 28; Plead 352; Pretrial Proc 622.

Hobson v. Moore, Tex, 734 SW2d 340.—Pretrial Proc 33, 286.

Hobson; Scrivner v., TexApp–Houston (1 Dist), 854 SW2d 148.—App & E 945; Mand 1, 40, 168(2), 187.9(5); Pretrial Proc 358; Witn 198(1), 199(2), 204(2).

Hobson v. Shelton, TexCivApp–Waco, 302 SW2d 268, ref nre.—Life Est 15(1), 23; Wills 439, 450, 616(1), 616(6).

Hobson v. State, TexCrimApp, 644 SW2d 473.—Crim Law 772(6), 795(2.1); Homic 668, 669, 672, 1451, 1458.

Hobson v. State, TexCrimApp, 438 SW2d 571.—Crim Law 737(2), 742(1), 1035(10), 1170(1); Homic 1333.

Hobson v. State, TexApp–Corpus Christi, 627 SW2d 532, petition for discretionary review gr, aff 644 SW2d 473.—Crim Law 211(3), 519(8), 530, 566, 698(1), 723(3), 730(14); Homic 839, 843, 845, 1458.

Hobson; Weeks v., TexApp–Houston (1 Dist), 877 SW2d 478.—J P 157(3); Mand 168(2), 168(4).

Hobson & Associates, Inc. v. First Print, Inc., TexApp–Amarillo, 798 SW2d 617.—Garn 64, 248; Judgm 181(14).

Hobyl v. State Of Texas, TexApp–Houston (1 Dist), 152 SW3d 624, petition for discretionary review gr, petition for discretionary review dism 193 SW3d 903.—Const Law 4723; Crim Law 796, 1144.13(2.1), 1159.2(1), 1159.2(2); Obst Just 7, 16.

Hoch; Hanover Ins. Co. v., TexCivApp–Corpus Christi, 469 SW2d 717, ref nre.—Action 60; App & E 688(2),

714(4), 842(7), 930(3), 989; Contracts 93(5); Evid 317(18), 471(7); Insurance 2189, 3025; New Tr 143(5); Pretrial Proc 724; Witn 126, 159(2).

Hoch v. Hoch, Tex, 168 SW2d 638, 140 Tex 475.—Adop 18, 21, 25; Ex & Ad 17(2), 17(7); Statut 126, 226.

Hoch; Hoch v., Tex, 168 SW2d 638, 140 Tex 475.—Adop 18, 21, 25; Ex & Ad 17(2), 17(7); Statut 126, 226.

Hoch v. Hoch, TexCivApp–San Antonio, 162 SW2d 433, rev 168 SW2d 638, 140 Tex 475.—Adop 3, 18, 20; Ex & Ad 17(1), 17(2), 17(7), 20(10).

Hoch; Hoch v., TexCivApp–San Antonio, 162 SW2d 433, rev 168 SW2d 638, 140 Tex 475.—Adop 3, 18, 20; Ex & Ad 17(1), 17(2), 17(7), 20(10).

Hochberg v. Schick Inv. Co., TexCivApp–Fort Worth, 469 SW2d 474.—Corp 584.

Hochheim Prairie Farm Mut. Ins. Ass'n, In re, TexApp–Beaumont, 115 SW3d 793.—Insurance 3357, 3379; Pretrial Proc 122, 402.

Hochheim Prairie Farm Mut. Ins. Ass'n v. Burnett, TexApp–Fort Worth, 698 SW2d 271.—App & E 989, 994(2), 1001(1), 1002, 1003(5), 1003(7); Costs 207; Evid 474(18), 543(3), 555.6(1); Insurance 2171, 2175, 2201, 3585; Pretrial Proc 313; Trial 351.5(4).

Hochheim Prairie Farm Mut. Ins. Ass'n; Campion v., TexApp–Corpus Christi, 644 SW2d 795, ref nre.—App & E 761; Insurance 2185; Interest 39(2.35); Judgm 199(1).

Hochheim Prairie Farm Mut. Ins. Ass'n v. Campion, TexCivApp–Corpus Christi, 581 SW2d 254, ref nre, appeal after remand 644 SW2d 795, ref nre.—App & E 1056.1(9); Insurance 1712, 2194, 2200; Judgm 199(3.13).

Hochheim Prairie Farm Mut. Ins. Ass'n; Favor v., TexApp–San Antonio, 939 SW2d 180, reh overr, and writ den.—Antitrust 251; App & E 907(2), 948; Insurance 3567; Plead 238(3).

Hochheim Prairie Farm Mut. Ins. Ass'n; Tweedell v., TexApp–Corpus Christi, 1 SW3d 304.—Antitrust 141, 143(2), 251, 291, 363; Insurance 1651; Judgm 185(2).

Hochheim Prairie Farm Mut. Ins. Ass'n; Tweedell v., TexApp–Corpus Christi, 962 SW2d 685, reh overr, review gr, vac 997 SW2d 277, on remand 1 SW3d 304.—Antitrust 141, 251, 363; Insurance 3417.

Hochman; J. Weingarten, Inc. v., TexCivApp–Hous (1 Dist), 487 SW2d 159, ref nre.—App & E 1060.1(1); Neglig 1656, 1670, 1679; Trial 108.5; Witn 276.

Hochman v. State, TexCrimApp, 171 SW2d 130, 146 TexCrim 23.—Crim Law 370.

Hochman v. State, TexCrimApp, 170 SW2d 756, 146 TexCrim 23, motion overr 171 SW2d 130, 146 TexCrim 23.—Crim Law 511.9(9), 511.2, 824(8), 857(1); Larc 27; Rec S Goods 6, 8(4), 9(1).

Hochmetal Africa (PTY), Ltd. v. Metals, Inc., TexCivApp–Corpus Christi, 566 SW2d 715.—Evid 207(1), 207(2); Plead 111.39(1), 111.42(1).

Ho Chong Tsao v. Immigration and Naturalization Service, CA5 (Tex), 538 F2d 667, cert den 97 SCt 1176, 430 US 906, 51 LEd2d 582.—Aliens 352, 423.

Hock v. Salaices, TexApp–San Antonio, 982 SW2d 591.—App & E 949; Judgm 92, 178, 181(2), 183, 185.1(4).

Hockaday v. Texas Dept. of Criminal Justice, Pardons and Paroles Div., SDTex, 914 FSupp 1439.—Admin Law 229; Civil R 1126, 1344, 1348, 1514, 1715, 1719; Consp 2, 7.5(1); Damag 50.10, 54; Fed Civ Proc 2497.1, 2542.1, 2546; Fed Cts 265; Labor & Emp 40(2), 50, 782; Lim of Act 105(1); Mun Corp 723; Neglig 273; Offic 66; States 112.1(1), 112.2(1), 191.1, 191.4(1), 191.8(1).

Hockett; Owens v., Tex, 251 SW2d 957, 151 Tex 503.—Dedi 16.1, 39, 44.

Hockett v. Owens, TexCivApp–Dallas, 247 SW2d 412, rev 251 SW2d 957, 151 Tex 503.—Dedi 1, 41, 44; Ease 5, 8(2), 8(4), 36(1), 36(3).

Hockless; Pinchback v., TexComApp, 164 SW2d 19, 139 Tex 536.—App & E 1189; Costs 105, 116, 132(6).

HOCKLESS;

59 Tex D 2d—664

See Guidelines for Arrangement at the beginning of this Volume

Hockless; Pinchback v., TexComApp, 158 SW2d 997, 138 Tex 306.—Adv Poss 44, 80(2), 93, 116(1); App & E 1064.1(2.1); Deeds 111; Trial 352.18.

Hockless; Pinchback v., TexCivApp–Beaumont, 137 SW2d 864, rev 158 SW2d 997, 138 Tex 306.—Adv Poss 60(1), 85(2), 85(4), 95, 109, 114(1), 114(2); Deeds 111; Estop 22(2); Lost Inst 16.

Hockley County; Cochran County v., TexCivApp–Amarillo, 158 SW2d 102, writ refused.—Counties 8.

Hockley County Appraisal Dist.; Devon Energy Production, L.P. v., TexApp–Amarillo, 178 SW3d 879, reh overr, and review den.—Tax 2400, 2402, 2723.

Hockley County Seed & Delinting, Inc.; Southwestern Inv. Co. v., Tex, 516 SW2d 136.—Usury 88, 139.

Hockley County Seed & Delinting, Inc.; Southwestern Inv. Co. v., TexCivApp–Amarillo, 511 SW2d 724, ref nre 516 SW2d 136.—App & E 989, 996; Evid 461(1); Ref of Inst 41; Stip 14(1), 14(8), 14(12); Trial 397(1); Usury 1, 9, 42, 52, 77, 111(1), 113, 115, 117, 125.

Hockley County Seed & Delinting, Inc. v. Southwestern Inv. Co., TexCivApp–Amarillo, 476 SW2d 38, ref nre, appeal after remand 511 SW2d 724, ref nre 516 SW2d 136.—Statut 262, 263, 265; Usury 7.

Hockman v. Lowe's Estate, TexApp–Beaumont, 624 SW2d 719, ref nre.—Des & Dist 43.

Hockman v. Westward Communications, LLC, CA5 (Tex), 407 F3d 317.—Civil R 1123, 1147, 1149, 1185, 1189, 1243, 1244, 1245, 1246, 1541; Fed Civ Proc 2546; Fed Cts 776.

Hockman v. Westward Communications, LLC, CA5 (Tex), 122 FedAppx 734.—Civil R 1123, 1147, 1185, 1189, 1243, 1244, 1245, 1246, 1250, 1541; Fed Civ Proc 2546; Fed Cts 776; Labor & Emp 826.

Hockman v. Westward Communications, L.L.C., ED-Tex, 282 FSupp2d 512, aff 407 F3d 317, aff 122 FedAppx 734.—Civil R 1123, 1147, 1175, 1183, 1185, 1189, 1243, 1245, 1246, 1535, 1541.

Hock Shop; Colony Ins. Co. v., TexApp–Dallas, 728 SW2d 848. See ColonyIns. Co. v. H.R.K., Inc.

Hoctel; U.S. v., CA5 (Tex), 154 F3d 506, reh and sug for reh den 170 F3d 185.—Crim Law 273.4(1), 1026.10(2.1).

Hocut; Rio Grande Valley Telephone Co. v., TexCiv-App–El Paso, 93 SW2d 167, writ dism.—Damag 91(3); Death 103(4); Judgm 243; Neglig 273; Trial 253(4).

Hocutt v. Prudential Ins. Co. of America, TexCivApp–Texarkana, 501 SW2d 347.—Insurance 2439, 3081, 3117.

Hocutt v. State, TexApp–Fort Worth, 927 SW2d 201, reh overr, and petition for discretionary review refused.—Crim Law 1042, 1177, 1181.5(8); Ind & Inf 113; Pardon 54; Sent & Pun 238, 240.

Hodas v. Scenic Oaks Property Ass'n, TexApp–San Antonio, 21 SW3d 524, reh overr, and petition for review den.—App & E 173(2); Covenants 21, 49, 68, 134.

Hodde v. Anderson, TexCivApp–Galveston, 105 SW2d 332.—Land & Ten 180(3).

Hodde; Young v., Tex, 682 SW2d 236.—App & E 223.

Hodde v. Young, TexApp–Houston (14 Dist), 672 SW2d 45, ref nre 682 SW2d 236.—App & E 66, 78(1), 80(6), 185(1), 719(3); Judgm 185(6), 186.

Hoddeson v. Conroe Ear, Nose and Throat Associates, P.A., TexApp–Beaumont, 751 SW2d 289.—Contracts 117(2).

Hodel; Prager v., CA5 (Tex), 793 F2d 730, cert den 107 SCt 581, 479 US 988, 93 LEd2d 584.—Admin Law 763; Mines 92.5(2).

Hodge, Ex parte, Tex, 389 SW2d 463.—Const Law 4494; Contempt 53; Hab Corp 253.

Hodge, Ex parte, TexCrimApp, 258 SW2d 323, 158 Tex-Crim 549.—Sent & Pun 1132.

Hodge, Ex parte, TexCivApp–Dallas, 611 SW2d 468.—Child S 180, 470; Const Law 3881, 4494; Contempt 63(1).

Hodge v. BSB Investments, Inc., TexApp–Dallas, 783 SW2d 310, writ den.—App & E 934(1); Labor & Emp 806; Work Comp 391, 392.

Hodge v. Ellis, Tex, 277 SW2d 900, 154 Tex 341.—App & E 173(2), 176; Evid 390(4); Hus & W 249(6), 256, 262.1(3), 262.1(4), 262.1(5), 262.2, 273(12); Wills 577, 783, 802(2).

Hodge v. Ellis, TexCivApp–Fort Worth, 268 SW2d 275, aff in part, rev in part 277 SW2d 900, 154 Tex 341.—App & E 1050.1(3.1), 1050.1(12); Estates 1; Evid 222(6), 390(4), 423(6), 505; Home 136; Hus & W 249(1), 249(6), 254, 255, 256, 257, 262.1(3), 262.1(5), 262.2, 264(2), 264(4), 264(5), 264(7), 270(7); Trial 136(1); Trusts 86; Wills 486, 665, 792(1).

Hodge v. Fly, TexCivApp–San Antonio, 105 SW2d 778.—Chat Mtg 219.

Hodge; Fort Worth Independent School Dist. v., TexCivApp–Fort Worth, 96 SW2d 1113.—Em Dom 170, 223; Evid 586(3).

Hodge; Green v., TexCivApp–Waco, 102 SW2d 500.—Execution 172(7), 174, 177.

Hodge v. Hendrick, TexCivApp–Eastland, 97 SW2d 722.—App & E 837(3); Inj 132, 147; Land & Ten 114(3); Princ & A 123(11).

Hodge v. Hicks, Tex, 233 SW2d 557, 149 Tex 390.—Child 11; Marriage 50(1).

Hodge v. Hicks, TexCivApp–Dallas, 229 SW2d 893, aff 233 SW2d 557, 149 Tex 390.—App & E 1008.1(8.1); Marriage 40(10).

Hodge; Holy Spirit Ass'n for Unification of World Christianity v., NDTex, 582 FSupp 592.—Const Law 814, 1228, 1389, 1517, 1870, 1872, 1873, 1879; Fed Civ Proc 2464; Mun Corp 594(2), 621.

Hodge v. Lower Colorado River Authority, TexCivApp–Austin, 163 SW2d 855, writ dism by agreement.—Counties 141; Levees 10; Mun Corp 724, 725, 733(4).

Hodge; McLain v., TexCivApp–Waco, 474 SW2d 772, ref nre.—Prod Liab 23.1, 60.5, 71, 81.1, 86.5, 95.5; Trial 178.

Hodge v. McLean Trucking Co., CA5 (Tex), 607 F2d 1118.—Civil R 1141, 1544, 1564; Fed Civ Proc 163, 337.

Hodge v. Northern Trust Bank of Texas, N.A., TexApp–Eastland, 54 SW3d 518, review den, and reh of petition for review den.—Banks 119, 129, 133, 134(7), 152, 153, 154(1), 154(2); Judgm 181(11), 185(2), 185.1(3), 185.1(4); Lim of Act 1, 16, 46(6), 72(1), 95(1), 95(7), 100(7); Notice 5; Plead 251; Trover 1.

Hodge; Oates v., TexApp–Dallas, 713 SW2d 361.—Evid 461(1); Insurance 3465, 3492.

Hodge; Owen v., TexApp–Houston (1 Dist), 874 SW2d 301.—App & E 356; Costs 260(4); Pretrial Proc 698.

Hodge v. Prince, NDTex, 730 FSupp 747, aff 923 F2d 853.—Const Law 1205, 1435, 4827; Fed Civ Proc 2741; Prisons 4(10.1), 4(11), 4(12), 4(13).

Hodge v. Quik-Pik Icehouse, TexCivApp–San Antonio, 445 SW2d 266.—Neglig 1104(5), 1104(6), 1133, 1670.

Hodge; Reserve Petroleum Co. v., Tex, 213 SW2d 456, 147 Tex 115, 7 ALR2d 288.—Ack 62(4); Estop 32(1); Home 123; Mines 55(1), 55(8).

Hodge; Reserve Petroleum Co. v., TexCivApp–Galveston, 209 SW2d 220, rev 213 SW2d 456, 147 Tex 115, 7 ALR2d 288.—App & E 999(1); Home 123.

Hodge v. Smith, TexApp–Houston (1 Dist), 856 SW2d 212, writ den.—App & E 863; Judgm 181(7), 181(11), 185(2); Lim of Act 119(3); Plead 4; Pretrial Proc 100; Proc 64, 149.

Hodge v. State, TexCrimApp, 631 SW2d 754.—Controlled Subs 74; Crim Law 398(1), 436(2), 713, 723(1), 730(1), 1043(3), 1169.5(3); Sent & Pun 94, 313; Witn 367(3), 372(1), 374(1).

Hodge v. State, TexCrimApp, 527 SW2d 289.—Ind & Inf 86(3).

Hodge v. State, TexCrimApp, 506 SW2d 870.—Crim Law 351(9), 369.1, 369.2(1).

For Later Case History Information, see KeyCite on WESTLAW

Hodge v. State, TexCrimApp, 488 SW2d 779.—Crim Law 719(1), 730(1), 730(14), 1171.1(1), 1171.1(3).

Hodge v. State, TexCrimApp, 297 SW2d 138, 164 TexCrim 69.—Crim Law 147; Ind & Inf 87(1).

Hodge v. State, TexCrimApp, 283 SW2d 941.—Crim Law 1090.1(1).

Hodge v. State, TexCrimApp, 214 SW2d 469, 152 TexCrim 395.—Crim Law 419(1.5), 720(1), 736(1), 1169.1(10); Int Liq 236(20).

Hodge v. State, TexCrimApp, 176 SW2d 946, 146 TexCrim 571.—Crim Law 936(1).

Hodge v. State, TexCrimApp, 141 SW2d 947, 139 TexCrim 655.—Crim Law 1104(2), 1110(8), 1133; Int Liq 236(7).

Hodge v. State, TexCrimApp, 128 SW2d 1205, 137 TexCrim 195.—Crim Law 1020.

Hodge v. State, TexCrimApp, 126 SW2d 669.—Crim Law 1090.1(1).

Hodge v. State, TexCrimApp, 126 SW2d 652, 136 TexCrim 532.—Crim Law 351(3), 1169.2(4), 1171.6; Larc 55.

Hodge v. State, TexApp–Houston (1 Dist), 824 SW2d 304, petition for discretionary review refused.—Crim Law 264, 1166(3).

Hodge v. State, TexApp–Dallas, 756 SW2d 353.—Crim Law 275, 1031(1), 1031(4), 1115(1), 1137(1), 1167(3); Ind & Inf 55, 65, 71.1, 71.3, 110(3), 110(26), 137(6).

Hodge v. State, TexApp–Amarillo, 896 SW2d 340, petition for discretionary review refused.—Crim Law 1035(5), 1063(1), 1134(5), 1147; Jury 42.

Hodge v. State, TexApp–Eastland, 940 SW2d 316, petition for discretionary review refused.—Crim Law 374, 396(1), 478(1), 693, 698(1), 723(3), 729, 1043(3); Homic 981, 1021; Jury 33(5.15); Witn 318.

Hodge v. State, TexApp–Corpus Christi, 626 SW2d 837, petition for discretionary review refused.—Crim Law 1043(3), 1172.7; Forg 34(2), 44(3).

Hodge v. Taylor, TexCivApp–Fort Worth, 87 SW2d 533, writ dism.—Wills 300, 386, 434.

Hodge v. Taylor, TexCivApp–Fort Worth, 85 SW2d 799. —App & E 374(2).

Hodge Boats and Motors v. King, TexCivApp–Beaumont, 578 SW2d 890, ref nre.—Sales 255, 439, 441(3); Trial 139.1(4), 142.

Hodge Boats & Motors, Inc.; Anderson v., TexApp–Beaumont, 814 SW2d 894, writ den.—Const Law 328, 2312, 2314; Corp 617(2), 630(0.5); Jury 31.2(1).

Hodges, Ex parte, Tex, 625 SW2d 304.—Contempt 20; Receivers 82.

Hodges, Ex parte, Tex, 109 SW2d 964, 130 Tex 280.—Contempt 63(1); Divorce 172, 182, 200, 269(13); Hab Corp 529.

Hodges, Ex parte, TexCrimApp, 314 SW2d 581, 166 TexCrim 433.—Crim Law 311, 573, 625(1), 625.10(1), 625.35, 641.12(1), 1023(3); Hab Corp 477, 797; Mental H 432.

Hodges, Matter of Estate of, TexApp–Amarillo, 725 SW2d 265, ref nre.—Ex & Ad 3(1), 27, 488, 490; Wills 219, 478, 651, 656, 665, 740(1).

Hodges v. Alford, TexCivApp–Eastland, 194 SW2d 293.—App & E 273(10), 1060.1(3); Autos 245(66); Damag 113; Trial 115(2), 352.10.

Hodges v. Arlington Neuropsychiatric Center, Inc., TexApp–Fort Worth, 628 SW2d 536, ref nre.—Health 273.

Hodges; Ayers v., TexCivApp–Tyler, 517 SW2d 589.—App & E 172(1); Contracts 1, 346(2); Ven & Pur 112(1), 118, 133, 136, 334(5).

Hodges; Bow v., TexCivApp–Texarkana, 101 SW2d 1043. —Debtor & C 13.1; Exemp 91, 93; Land & Ten 262(8); Plead 377.

Hodges v. Braun, TexApp–Dallas, 654 SW2d 542, ref nre. —Contracts 143(3), 274; Evid 589; Partners 53, 217(2).

Hodges v. Brazos County Water Control and Imp. Dist. No. 1, Big Creek, Brazos County, TexCivApp–Hous (1 Dist), 449 SW2d 861, ref nre.—Decl Judgm 124.1, 345.1.

Hodges v. Casey, Tex, 646 SW2d 175.—Plead 111.4, 111.18.

Hodges; Casey v., TexApp–Houston (1 Dist), 640 SW2d 314, rev 646 SW2d 175.—Plead 111.4, 111.18, 111.37; Venue 2, 17, 22(6).

Hodges v. Central Bank & Trust Co., TexCivApp–Texarkana, 463 SW2d 41.—App & E 544(3), 564(3), 907(3).

Hodges; City of Taylor v., Tex, 186 SW2d 61, 143 Tex 441.—App & E 845(2); Assign 90; Counties 216; Impl & C C 6, 70, 71; Paymt 84(2).

Hodges; City of Taylor v., TexCivApp–Austin, 183 SW2d 664, aff in part, rev in part 186 SW2d 61, 143 Tex 441.—Evid 65; Paymt 82(3), 84(2); Subrog 26.

Hodges v. Cofer, TexCivApp–Hous (1 Dist), 449 SW2d 836, ref nre.—Elections 275; Levees 34.

Hodges v. Coke County, TexCivApp–Amarillo, 197 SW2d 886.—Counties 215; Statut 208; Venue 5.3(1), 5.4, 5.5.

Hodges v. Coke County, TexCivApp–Amarillo, 196 SW2d 935, motion overr 197 SW2d 886.—Counties 208, 215; Statut 231; Venue 2.

Hodges v. Cole, TexCivApp–Amarillo, 117 SW2d 822.—App & E 1001(1); Estop 52.10(2), 63, 111, 115; Sales 288(6), 428, 437(3), 441(1), 445(1).

Hodges v. Delta Airlines, Inc., CA5 (Tex), 44 F3d 334.—Aviation 101; Carr 311; States 18.3, 18.5, 18.11, 18.17, 18.21.

Hodges v. Delta Airlines, Inc., CA5 (Tex), 4 F3d 350, reh en banc gr 12 F3d 426, on reh 44 F3d 334.

Hodges; Dillon v., CA5 (Tex), 804 F2d 1384.—Pub Lands 174, 175(5), 175(7), 176(2); Stip 18(4); Tresp to T T 26, 44.

Hodges; Dockeray v., CA5 (Tex), 129 FedAppx 59.—Fed Civ Proc 2734; Fed Cts 612.1.

Hodges; Drummond v., TexCivApp–Dallas, 417 SW2d 740.—App & E 989; Evid 537; Health 823(5), 825, 908, 927; Trial 105(2).

Hodges; Gulf Ins. Co. v., TexCivApp–Amarillo, 513 SW2d 267.—Damag 221(3); Trial 215, 256(12); Work Comp 836, 1021, 1624, 1662, 1671, 1724, 1961, 1964, 1969.

Hodges v. Hodges, TexCivApp–Fort Worth, 207 SW2d 943.—Atty & C 140; Divorce 130, 147, 149, 150, 184(6.1), 184(10), 221; Evid 555.6(1).

Hodges; Hodges v., TexCivApp–Fort Worth, 207 SW2d 943.—Atty & C 140; Divorce 130, 147, 149, 150, 184(6.1), 184(10), 221; Evid 555.6(1).

Hodges v. Hodges, TexCivApp–Amarillo, 111 SW2d 779. —App & E 1008.2, 1010.1(1); Divorce 227(2), 253(1), 253(2); Evid 543(2), 570, 571(7).

Hodges; Hodges v., TexCivApp–Amarillo, 111 SW2d 779. —App & E 1008.2, 1010.1(1); Divorce 227(2), 253(1), 253(2); Evid 543(2), 570, 571(7).

Hodges; Johnson v., TexCivApp–Fort Worth, 121 SW2d 371, dism.—App & E 230, 237(2), 544(1); Autos 246(22), 246(57); Neglig 1713; Trial 76, 90, 92, 295(1).

Hodges v. Joseph E. Seagram & Sons, Inc., CA5 (Tex), 418 F2d 563.—Damag 221(8); Fed Cts 743.

Hodges v. Keystone Shipping Co., SDTex, 578 FSupp 620.—Damag 87(1); Fed Civ Proc 2345.1, 2372.1, 2377, 2610; Seamen 11(1), 11(6), 11(8), 11(9).

Hodges v. Leach, TexCivApp–Amarillo, 214 SW2d 837.—Accession 1; App & E 562, 598, 1152; Chat Mtg 136, 138(1), 177(4), 225(1), 283; Sales 202(1), 300.

Hodges v. Liggett Group Inc., SDTex, 60 FSupp2d 627. —Rem of C 25(1).

Hodges; Loughry v., TexCivApp–Fort Worth, 215 SW2d 669, ref nre.—App & E 930(1), 932(1), 1026, 1053(2); Damag 95, 132(13), 208(1), 216(8); Evid 589; Labor & Emp 3003, 3006; Neglig 502(1), 506(8), 1717; Trial 133.6(2), 191(11); Work Comp 2121.

Hodges v. Mack Trucks Inc., CA5 (Tex), 474 F3d 188.—Evid 539, 571(6); Fed Cts 391, 428, 641, 765, 776, 801,

823, 866, 896.1, 901.1; Prod Liab 81.5, 88.5; Work Comp 2191, 2247, 2248, 2249, 2251.

Hodges v. Nix, TexCivApp–Galveston, 225 SW2d 576, ref nre.—App & E 564(3), 655(3); Neglig 1088, 1204(1); Trial 357.

Hodges; North East Texas Motor Lines v., TexCivApp–Dallas, 141 SW2d 386, aff Northeast Texas Motor Lines, Inc v. Hodges, 158 SW2d 487, 138 Tex 280.—App & E 930(2), 1033(4); Autos 246(60); Evid 474(19), 498.5, 568(4); Trial 350.5(3), 351.5(1), 351.5(6), 352.5(6).

Hodges; Northeast Texas Motor Lines, Inc. v., TexCom-App, 158 SW2d 487, 138 Tex 280.—App & E 882(1), 882(14), 1082(1); Trial 351.5(1), 351.5(6).

Hodges v. Peden, TexApp–Houston (14 Dist), 634 SW2d 8. —Costs 192, 209; Evid 167; Receivers 29(1), 197, 198(1), 198(2).

Hodges v. Pemberton, TexCivApp–Fort Worth, 442 SW2d 420.—Divorce 130; Fraud Conv 172(2); Hus & W 6(4), 264(1); Marriage 50(1).

Hodges v. Plasky, TexCivApp–Austin, 300 SW2d 955, ref nre.—App & E 930(2), 1062.1; Damag 186, 187; Trial 252(20), 366.

Hodges v. Price, TexCivApp–Galveston, 163 SW2d 868, writ refused wom.—Lim of Act 25(1), 28(1), 127(3), 127(4); Paymt 39(1), 39(5), 44.

Hodges; Recon Exploration, Inc. v., TexApp–Dallas, 798 SW2d 848.—App & E 68, 946, 954(1); Com Law 11; Inj 1, 132, 135, 138.3, 138.9, 138.39, 140, 147.

Hodges; Roberts v., TexCivApp–Amarillo, 401 SW2d 332, ref nre.—Const Law 3964, 3965(7); Evid 80(1), 265(2), 265(17); Judgm 815, 942, 944, 951(1); Proc 70.

Hodges; Sammons v., TexCivApp–Amarillo, 95 SW2d 734. —Aband L P 4; Contracts 108(2); Trial 350.3(2.1).

Hodges; Sitz v., TexCivApp–Amarillo, 278 SW2d 400.—App & E 253; Land & Ten 61, 105, 108(1), 112.5; Tresp to T T 4, 32.

Hodges; Southern Underwriters v., TexCivApp–Waco, 141 SW2d 707, writ refused.—Action 71; App & E 949, 1032(1), 1040(1); Plead 228.16; Trial 68(2); Work Comp 52, 74, 811, 1424, 1919, 1924, 1926, 1965.

Hodges v. Star Lumber & Hardware Co., Inc., TexCivApp–Amarillo, 544 SW2d 185.—Mtg 375.

Hodges; State v., Tex, 92 SW3d 489.—App & E 839(1), 893(1); Civil R 1417; Const Law 82(8), 1461, 1464, 1466, 1477, 4232; Judges 3; Offic 19, 25; Statut 181(1), 181(2), 184, 190, 208.

Hodges v. State, TexCrimApp, 604 SW2d 152.—Const Law 2415(3); Controlled Subs 6, 9, 22, 65, 145; Crim Law 273.1(4), 1026.10(4), 1184(4.1); Gr Jury 2.5.

Hodges v. State, TexCrimApp, 489 SW2d 916.—Bail 55, 77(2), 79(1).

Hodges v. State, TexCrimApp, 430 SW2d 204.—Ind & Inf 87(2).

Hodges v. State, TexCrimApp, 417 SW2d 178.—Crim Law 994(1), 1086.13, 1130(2); Sent & Pun 201.

Hodges v. State, TexCrimApp, 401 SW2d 241.—Autos 355(6); Crim Law 899.

Hodges v. State, TexCrimApp, 383 SW2d 421.—Rob 24.15(1).

Hodges v. State, TexCrimApp, 380 SW2d 631.—Crim Law 1094(2.1).

Hodges v. State, TexCrimApp, 321 SW2d 307, 167 TexCrim 490.—Homic 1134.

Hodges v. State, TexCrimApp, 272 SW2d 902, 160 TexCrim 579.—Homic 555, 1134, 1492.

Hodges v. State, TexCrimApp, 218 SW2d 1006.—Crim Law 1094(2.1).

Hodges v. State, TexCrimApp, 209 SW2d 611, 151 TexCrim 511.—Crim Law 564(1), 1144.13(7); Int Liq 223(1), 236(3).

Hodges v. State, TexCrimApp, 160 SW2d 262, 143 TexCrim 573.—Crim Law 510, 511.2, 1173.2(4); Rec S Goods 7(6), 8(3), 9(1), 9(2).

Hodges v. State, TexCrimApp, 149 SW2d 111, 141 TexCrim 493.—Crim Law 394.4(11), 412(5); Int Liq 236(9).

Hodges v. State, TexCrimApp, 140 SW2d 179, 139 TexCrim 274.—Bail 63.1; Crim Law 1097(5); Ind & Inf 137(1).

Hodges v. State, TexCrimApp, 137 SW2d 25, 138 TexCrim 509.—Crim Law 881(1).

Hodges v. State, TexCrimApp, 135 SW2d 996, 138 TexCrim 296.—False Pret 49(4).

Hodges v. State, TexCrimApp, 132 SW2d 863, 137 TexCrim 527.—Crim Law 370, 507(1), 742(2), 814(17); Rec S Goods 3, 8(4).

Hodges v. State, TexApp–Fort Worth, 651 SW2d 386.—Crim Law 1077.3; Homic 999, 1182, 1186.

Hodges v. State, TexApp–Corpus Christi, 116 SW3d 289, reh overr, and petition for discretionary review refused. —Crim Law 273(4.1), 273.4(1), 274(8), 275, 636(1), 636(3), 641.3(2), 641.3(3), 641.3(4), 641.4(2), 641.13(7), 1036.1(4), 1153(1), 1163(2), 1166.10(1), 1181.5(8).

Hodges v. State, TexApp–Houston (14 Dist), 629 SW2d 850.—Crim Law 721(1), 721(3), 1045, 1171.5.

Hodges v. State, TexCivApp–Austin, 539 SW2d 394.—App & E 345.1.

Hodges v. State, TexCivApp–Austin, 198 SW2d 150.—Courts 85(2); Int Liq 275, 278.

Hodges v. State, TexCivApp–Texarkana, 437 SW2d 447, ref nre.—Em Dom 202(4); Evid 142(1), 555.6(10).

Hodges v. State, TexCivApp–Texarkana, 403 SW2d 207, ref nre.—App & E 971(2); Em Dom 222(4), 262(5); Evid 201, 543(3), 546, 555.6(2), 555.6(3), 568(1), 571(7); Pretrial Proc 379.

Hodges; Texan Development Co. v., TexCivApp–Amarillo, 237 SW2d 436.—App & E 1024.3; Plead 53(1); Quiet T 7(2), 13, 30(3), 34(5); Tresp to T T 13; Venue 5.1, 5.3(2).

Hodges; Texas Employment Com'n v., TexApp–Dallas, 734 SW2d 427.—Unemp Comp 477, 486, 500.

Hodges v. Thompson, TexApp–Fort Worth, 932 SW2d 717.—Int Liq 32(1); Statut 181(1), 212.6, 227.

Hodges; Thompson v., TexCivApp–San Antonio, 237 SW2d 757, ref nre.—Assault 26, 35; Labor & Emp 3096(8); Trial 350.5(2), 351.5(1), 351.5(7), 352.4(8).

Hodges; Treadaway v., TexCivApp–Amarillo, 125 SW2d 385.—App & E 662(1); Execution 254; Trial 388(1).

Hodges; U.S. v., CA5 (Tex), 628 F2d 350.—Sent & Pun 605, 644, 2221, 2256, 2329; Weap 4.

Hodges; U.S. v., CA5 (Tex), 559 F2d 1389.—Crim Law 1141(2), 1192.

Hodges; U.S. v., CA5 (Tex), 547 F2d 951, appeal after remand 559 F2d 1389.—Sent & Pun 294, 295.

Hodges; U.S. v., CA5 (Tex), 502 F2d 586.—Crim Law 622.2(7), 633(1); Double J 151(2).

Hodges; U.S. v., CA5 (Tex), 489 F2d 212.—Crim Law 627.7(3); Sent & Pun 2013, 2021.

Hodges v. U.S., CA5 (Tex), 223 F2d 140.—Crim Law 1167(1); Int Rev 4243, 5290, 5295.

Hodges; Wells v., TexCivApp–San Antonio, 604 SW2d 218.—App & E 1062.1; Bailm 5, 27, 33; Trial 352.1(1).

Hodges; Western Cottonoil Co. v., CA5 (Tex), 218 F2d 158.—Divorce 254(1); Fed Civ Proc 212; Fed Cts 786, 846; Nuis 49(4).

Hodges; Wheelways Ins. Co. v., TexApp–Texarkana, 872 SW2d 776.—Antitrust 397; App & E 836, 852, 930(3), 1001(1), 1175(1), 1177(8); Costs 194.18, 194.32; Damag 49.10, 71, 127; Insurance 1165, 1172, 1292, 2911, 2933, 2934(3), 2934(4), 2941, 3357, 3579, 3585; Interest 39(2.35).

Hodges; Wilson v., Tex, 904 SW2d 628. See Wilson v. Burford.

Hodges v. Wilson, TexApp–Tyler, 885 SW2d 253. See Burford v. Wilson.

Hodges' Estate; Turner v., TexCivApp–Fort Worth, 219 SW2d 522, ref nre.—Evid 478(1), 501(1), 502; Trial 82; Wills 248, 292, 322, 384; Witn 139(4), 180, 181, 183.

Hodges Food Stores, Inc. v. Gulf Ins. Co., TexCivApp–Dallas, 441 SW2d 309.—Insurance 3234, 3502.

Hodges, Grant & Kaufmann v. U.S. Government, Dept. of the Treasury, I.R.S., CA5 (Tex), 768 F2d 719.—Fed Civ Proc 1600(3), 1615.1; Int Rev 4517; Witn 204(2), 206, 219(3), 222.

Hodges, Grant & Kaufmann v. U.S. Government, Dept. of Treasury, I.R.S., CA5 (Tex), 762 F2d 1299.—Fed Civ Proc 320; Int Rev 4510.

Hodges Tire Co. v. Kemp, TexCivApp–Fort Worth, 334 SW2d 627.—App & E 1175(3), 1177(6); Evid 8; Neglig 387, 406, 1625, 1702; Trial 350.6(5), 360.

Hodgkins v. Bryan, TexApp–Houston (14 Dist), 99 SW3d 669, reh overr.—App & E 223; Death 17; Health 623, 631, 633, 822(3); Judgm 183, 185.1(2), 185.1(4), 185.3(21); Neglig 371, 379, 380, 387; Plead 76.

Hodgkins v. Pickett, TexCivApp–Fort Worth, 344 SW2d 461.—Covenants 72.1; Dedi 55.

Hodgkins v. Sansom, TexCivApp–Fort Worth, 135 SW2d 759, writ dism, correct.—Judgm 650, 702, 713(2); Schools 53(2).

Hodgkiss; U.S. v., CA5 (Tex), 116 F3d 116, cert gr, vac 118 SCt 597, 522 US 1012, 139 LEd2d 486.—Crim Law 627.7(3), 1035(2), 1043(1), 1044.2(1), 1158(2), 1166(10.10), 1181.5(5).

Hodgson v. American Bank of Commerce, CA5 (Tex), 447 F2d 416, 20 Wage & Hour Cas (BNA) 148, 20 Wage & Hour Cas (BNA) 185.—Fed Cts 853, 858; Labor & Emp 2461, 2462, 2463, 2481(2), 2482(1), 2486(1), 2486(2).

Hodgson v. Behrens Drug Co., CA5 (Tex), 475 F2d 1041, 20 Wage & Hour Cas (BNA) 1152, cert den Behrens Drug Co v. Brennan, 94 SCt 121, 414 US 822, 21 Wage & Hour Cas (BNA) 298, 38 LEd2d 55.—Fed Cts 865; Labor & Emp 2461, 2463, 2466, 2481(2), 2482(1); Lim of Act 58(1).

Hodgson v. Brookhaven General Hospital, CA5 (Tex), 470 F2d 729, 20 Wage & Hour Cas (BNA) 991.—Fed Cts 950; Labor & Emp 2483(2), 2486(2).

Hodgson v. Brookhaven General Hospital, CA5 (Tex), 436 F2d 719, 19 Wage & Hour Cas (BNA) 822, on remand 20 Wage & Hour Cas (BNA) 54, aff 470 F2d 729, 20 Wage & Hour Cas (BNA) 991, appeal after remand 470 F2d 729, 20 Wage & Hour Cas (BNA) 991.—Civil R 1509, 1549; Fed Civ Proc 2251; Fed Cts 941; Labor & Emp 2463, 2464, 2466, 2468, 2481(5), 2486(2).

Hodgson v. Burnett, CA5 (Tex), 455 F2d 213, 20 Wage & Hour Cas (BNA) 448.—Fed Civ Proc 2498.

Hodgson v. Charles Martin Inspectors of Petroleum, Inc., CA5 (Tex), 459 F2d 303, 20 Wage & Hour Cas (BNA) 596.—Fed Civ Proc 1925.1; Witn 216(4).

Hodgson v. Crotty Bros. Dallas, Inc., CA5 (Tex), 450 F2d 1268, 19 Wage & Hour Cas (BNA) 1073, 20 Wage & Hour Cas (BNA) 204.—Labor & Emp 2252, 2269.

Hodgson v. Ewing, CA5 (Tex), 451 F2d 526, 20 Wage & Hour Cas (BNA) 328.—Commerce 62.44(2); Labor & Emp 2252, 2273, 2274, 2367.

Hodgson v. First Victoria Nat. Bank, CA5 (Tex), 446 F2d 47, 20 Wage & Hour Cas (BNA) 132.—Fed Cts 858.

Hodgson v. Good Shepherd Hospital, EDTex, 327 FSupp 143, 19 Wage & Hour Cas (BNA) 1067.—Labor & Emp 2486(2).

Hodgson v. Griffin & Brand of McAllen, Inc., CA5 (Tex), 471 F2d 235, 20 Wage & Hour Cas (BNA) 1051, reh den 472 F2d 1405, cert den Griffin & Brand of McAllen, Inc v. Brennan, 94 SCt 43, 414 US 819, 21 Wage & Hour Cas (BNA) 298, 38 LEd2d 51.—Labor & Emp 2227, 2228, 2387(7), 2418.

Hodgson v. Hatton, SDTex, 348 FSupp 895, 20 Wage & Hour Cas (BNA) 549.—Commerce 62.49; Labor & Emp 2227.

Hodgson v. H. Morgan Daniel Seafoods, Inc., CA5 (Tex), 433 F2d 918, 19 Wage & Hour Cas (BNA) 816.—Const Law 2600; Fed Cts 850.1; Labor & Emp 2399.

Hodgson v. Local Union No. 920, Indus. and Allied Workers and Helpers, Intern. Broth. of Teamsters, Chauffeurs, Warehousemen and Helpers of America, EDTex, 327 FSupp 1284.—Labor & Emp 1062, 1065, 1066(3).

Hodgson v. Parke, SDTex, 324 FSupp 1297, 19 Wage & Hour Cas (BNA) 978.—Commerce 62.63; Labor & Emp 2418, 2421, 2432(4).

Hodgson v. Union de Permisionarios Circulo Rojo, S. de R. L., SDTex, 331 FSupp 1119, 20 Wage & Hour Cas (BNA) 325.—Courts 9; Labor & Emp 2371, 2415, 2418, 2421.

Hodgson v. University of Texas Medical Branch at Galveston, SDTex, 953 FSupp 168, aff 158 F3d 584.—Civil R 1105; Const Law 990, 4870; Fed Cts 265.

Hodgson v. Wittenburg, CA5 (Tex), 464 F2d 1219, 20 Wage & Hour Cas (BNA) 784.—Labor & Emp 2274.

Hodnett; Forgus v., Tex, 405 SW2d 337.—Autos 181(1), 181(5).

Hodnett; Forgus v., TexCivApp–Eastland, 401 SW2d 104, ref nre 405 SW2d 337.—Autos 181(1), 181(5), 244(20).

Hodnett; Texas Emp. Ins. Ass'n v., TexCivApp–Fort Worth, 216 SW2d 301, ref nre.—Trial 105(1); Work Comp 975, 1924, 1958, 1968(3), 1968(7), 1982.

Hodnett; U.S. v., CA5 (Tex), 537 F2d 828, reh den 540 F2d 1086.—Crim Law 683(2), 1037.1(1), 1038.1(2); Witn 345(1), 345(7), 372(2).

Hodorowski v. Ray, CA5 (Tex), 844 F2d 1210.—Civil R 1373, 1376(1), 1376(2), 1376(3); Offic 114.

Hodson v. Keiser, TexApp–El Paso, 81 SW3d 363.—App & E 930(1), 946, 949, 1010.1(1); Child S 21, 202, 231, 342, 550, 556(1).

Hodson; Texas Employment Commission v., TexCivApp–Waco, 346 SW2d 665, ref nre.—Unemp Comp 154.

H. O. Dyer, Inc. v. Steele, TexCivApp–Hous (1 Dist), 489 SW2d 686.—App & E 236(2), 949; Autos 372(3.1); Bailm 14(1), 30, 31(1); Costs 193; Plead 228.23, 246(3); Pretrial Proc 310.1.

Hoechst Celanese Chemical Group, Inc.; Richard v., CA5 (Tex), 355 F3d 345, reh and reh den 91 FedAppx 975, cert den 125 SCt 46, 543 US 917, 160 LEd2d 201.—Civil R 1326(4), 1326(5), 1326(7), 1326(9); Const Law 3981; Courts 509; RICO 83.

Hoechst Celanese Chemical Group, Inc.; Richard v., EDTex, 208 FRD 575, aff in part 355 F3d 345, reh and reh den 91 FedAppx 975, cert den 125 SCt 46, 543 US 917, 160 LEd2d 201.—Courts 509; Fed Civ Proc 103.2, 103.3, 171, 179, 182.5, 839.1, 1828; Fed Cts 178.5, 241, 243, 246; Fraud 50, 29.

Hoechst Celanese Chemical Group, Inc.; Turco v., SDTex, 906 FSupp 1120, aff 101 F3d 1090, reh and sug for reh den 108 F3d 335.—Civil R 1019(2), 1217, 1218(2), 1218(4), 1220, 1225(2), 1225(3), 1225(4), 1240, 1540; Fed Civ Proc 2497.1, 2543, 2544.

Hoechst Celanese Chemical, Inc.; Conner v., CA5 (Tex), 211 FedAppx 257.—Civil R 1203; Fed Civ Proc 2497.1.

Hoechst Celanese Corp.; Anderson v., BkrtcyEDTex, 173 BR 1000. See U.S. Brass Corp., In re.

Hoechst Celanese Corp.; Armstrong v., BkrtcyEDTex, 173 BR 1000. See U.S. Brass Corp., In re.

Hoechst Celanese Corp. v. Arthur Bros., Inc., TexApp–Corpus Christi, 882 SW2d 917, writ den.—App & E 843(2), 930(3), 989, 1001(3), 1047(1); Contracts 202(1); Damag 40(1), 94, 184; Estop 85; Fraud 12, 20, 58(1), 58(3), 59(1), 60, 61, 62.

Hoechst Celanese Corp.; Ashley v., BkrtcyEDTex, 173 BR 1000. See U.S. Brass Corp., In re.

Hoechst Celanese Corp. v. BP Chemicals Ltd., CAFed (Tex), 78 F3d 1575, cert den 117 SCt 275, 519 US 911, 136 LEd2d 198.—Fed Civ Proc 2236, 2602, 2839; Fed Cts 846; Pat 157(1), 159, 175, 226.10, 227, 232, 312(1.1), 312(3.1), 314(5), 319(3), 323.1, 324.1, 324.5, 328(2).

Hoechst Celanese Corp. v. BP Chemicals Ltd., SDTex, 846 FSupp 542, aff 78 F3d 1575, cert den 117 SCt 275,

519 US 911, 136 LEd2d 198.—Fed Cts 685; Interest 31, 39(2.20), 56; Pat 17(3), 33, 97, 230, 312(2), 312(3.1), 314(5), 317, 319(3), 328(2).

Hoechst Celanese Corp. v. BP Chemicals Ltd., SDTex, 844 FSupp 336, aff in part, vac in part 65 F3d 188.— Contracts 143(2), 152, 176(2); Fed Civ Proc 2470.1, 2539; Pat 90(1), 112.1, 112.3(4), 211(1), 314(5), 323.2(3).

Hoechst Celanese Corp.; Clarke v., BkrtcyEDTex, 173 BR 1000. See U.S. Brass Corp., In re.

Hoechst Celanese Corp. v. Compton, TexApp–Houston (14 Dist), 899 SW2d 215, reh overr, and writ den.—App & E 169, 170(1), 758.3(9), 901, 930(3), 996, 999(1), 1001(1), 1001(3); Autos 5(5), 252, 258, 279, 306(2), 306(4); Evid 584(1); Labor & Emp 29, 55, 58, 3040, 3137, 3162, 3179(2); Nuis 4, 61.

Hoechst Celanese Corp.; Cox v., BkrtcyEDTex, 173 BR 1000. See U.S. Brass Corp., In re.

Hoechst Celanese Corp.; Daniels v., BkrtcyEDTex, 173 BR 1000. See U.S. Brass Corp., In re.

Hoechst Celanese Corp.; Dunn v., BkrtcyEDTex, 173 BR 1000. See U.S. Brass Corp., In re.

Hoechst Celanese Corp.; Greentree at the Gardens v., BkrtcyEDTex, 173 BR 1000. See U.S. Brass Corp., In re.

Hoechst Celanese Corp.; Hutchinson v., BkrtcyEDTex, 173 BR 1000. See U.S. Brass Corp., In re.

Hoechst Celanese Corp.; Johnson v., BkrtcyEDTex, 173 BR 1000. See U.S. Brass Corp., In re.

Hoechst Celanese Corp.; Johnson v., TexApp–Corpus Christi, 127 SW3d 875, reh overr.—App & E 856(1); Civil R 1004, 1166, 1708, 1714, 1744; Courts 97(1); Judgm 181(21).

Hoechst Celanese Corp.; Kolton v., BkrtcyEDTex, 173 BR 1000. See U.S. Brass Corp., In re.

Hoechst Celanese Corp.; McWhorter v., BkrtcyEDTex, 173 BR 1000. See U.S. Brass Corp., In re.

Hoechst-Celanese Corp. v. Mendez, Tex, 967 SW2d 354. —Labor & Emp 3141; Neglig 1011, 1013, 1204(1).

Hoechst Celanese Corp.; Nelson v., BkrtcyEDTex, 173 BR 1000. See U.S. Brass Corp., In re.

Hoechst Celanese Corp.; Patterson v., BkrtcyEDTex, 173 BR 1000. See U.S. Brass Corp., In re.

Hoechst Celanese Corp.; Phillips v., BkrtcyEDTex, 173 BR 1000. See U.S. Brass Corp., In re.

Hoechst Celanese Corp.; Pineforest Motel v., Bkrtcy-EDTex, 173 BR 1000. See U.S. Brass Corp., In re.

Hoechst Celanese Corp.; Ryan v., BkrtcyEDTex, 173 BR 1000. See U.S. Brass Corp., In re.

Hoechst Celanese Corp.; Stolarski v., BkrtcyEDTex, 173 BR 1000. See U.S. Brass Corp., In re.

Hoechst Celanese Corp.; Strutz v., BkrtcyEDTex, 173 BR 1000. See U.S. Brass Corp., In re.

Hoechst Celanese Corp.; Summit Properties Inc. v., CA5 (Tex), 214 F3d 556, reh en banc den 228 F3d 411, cert den 121 SCt 896, 531 US 1132, 148 LEd2d 802.— Prod Liab 15; RICO 62.

Hoechst-Celanese Corp.; Summit Properties, Inc. v., SDTex, 125 FSupp2d 205, aff 214 F3d 556, reh en banc den 228 F3d 411, cert den 121 SCt 896, 531 US 1132, 148 LEd2d 802.—Fed Civ Proc 1771; Fed Cts 18; RICO 3, 62.

Hoechst Celanese Corp.; Turco v., CA5 (Tex), 101 F3d 1090, reh and sug for reh den 108 F3d 335.—Civil R 1217, 1218(4); Fed Civ Proc 2497.1, 2535; Fed Cts 776.

Hoechst Celanese Plastics Co. v. Arthur Bros., Inc., TexApp–Corpus Christi, 882 SW2d 917. See Hoechst Celanese Corp. v. Arthur Bros., Inc.

Hoechst Corp. v. Kirk, TexApp–Eastland, 859 SW2d 651. See Aktiengesellschaft v. Kirk.

Hoecker; Odinot v., TexCivApp–Galveston, 228 SW2d 318.—Sales 442(1).

Hoeffner v. State, TexCrimApp, 163 SW2d 198, 144 Tex-Crim 354.—Crim Law 1087.1(2).

Hoefs; Beatty v., TexCivApp–Austin, 229 SW2d 430.— Plead 111.37; Venue 5.5.

Hoefs; Shook v., TexCivApp–El Paso, 302 SW2d 446.— Plead 111.42(7).

Hoegmeyer; Hancock v., TexCivApp–Beaumont, 119 SW2d 141.—Autos 247; Damag 185(1), 191.

Hoel; Jones v., EDTex, 211 FSupp2d 823.—Courts 507; Fed Cts 41, 47.1, 65, 419; Insurance 1101, 1385; States 18.41.

Hoelscher v. GFH Financial Services, Inc., TexApp–Dallas, 814 SW2d 842, extension of time to file for writ of error overr.—Antitrust 136; App & E 878(1), 918(1); Evid 18; Plead 234, 245(1), 258(1), 262.

Hoeme v. Jeoffroy, CCA5 (Tex), 100 F2d 225.—Pat 112.1, 294, 295, 301(1), 303.

Hoeneke v. Lehman, TexCivApp–San Antonio, 542 SW2d 728.—Elections 311, 317.4, 323; Penalties 2; Statut 223.5(4).

Hoenig; Langston v., TexCivApp–Fort Worth, 494 SW2d 615, ref nre.—Partners 311(1); Wills 98, 692(5).

Hoenig v. Texas Commerce Bank, N.A., TexApp–San Antonio, 939 SW2d 656, reh overr, and extension of time gr.—App & E 1010.1(1), 1010.1(16); Contrib 5(6.1); Land & Ten 118(4), 278.10(1), 278.10(3); Neglig 380, 387, 433; Trover 2, 9(3.1), 9(5); Trusts 205, 235, 267, 268.

Hoenig; U.S. v., CA5 (Tex), 79 FedAppx 8, post-conviction relief den 2006 WL 2993262.—Crim Law 590(1).

Hoerchler; Omick v., TexApp–San Antonio, 809 SW2d 758, writ den.—Child S 506(4), 506(5); Judgm 815, 829(1), 928.

Hoerster; Giberson v., TexCivApp–Austin, 339 SW2d 730, writ dism.—Social S 140.3.

Hoerster; Lewis v., TexCivApp–San Antonio, 92 SW2d 537.—Inj 36(2).

Hoerster; Morris v., Tex, 370 SW2d 451.—Courts 207.4(2).

Hoerster; Morris v., TexCivApp–Austin, 377 SW2d 841.— Atty Gen 6; Evid 43(1); Mand 82, 151(2); Records 52.

Hoerster; Morris v., TexCivApp–Austin, 368 SW2d 639, ref nre 370 SW2d 451, cert den 84 SCt 676, 376 US 919, 11 LEd2d 614.—App & E 78(1); Courts 207.4(2).

Hoerster; Morris v., TexCivApp–Austin, 348 SW2d 642, ref nre.—Mental H 21; Pretrial Proc 382; States 191.10.

Hoerster v. Wilke, Tex, 158 SW2d 288, 138 Tex 263.— Adv Poss 71(2); Lim of Act 39(7), 100(11).

Hoerster v. Wilke, TexCivApp–Austin, 140 SW2d 952, aff 158 SW2d 288, 138 Tex 263.—Adv Poss 71(1); App & E 989, 1002; Deeds 56(2); Lim of Act 39(7), 99(3), 100(11), 100(13); Partners 34, 44, 216(2), 218(4); Trial 350.3(2.1), 351.2(4); Ven & Pur 261(1).

Hoestenbach v. Hoestenbach, TexCivApp–El Paso, 388 SW2d 255.—App & E 846(5); Divorce 166.

Hoestenbach; Hoestenbach v., TexCivApp–El Paso, 388 SW2d 255.—App & E 846(5); Divorce 166.

Hoey v. San Antonio Real Estate Bd., TexCivApp–San Antonio, 297 SW2d 214.—Assoc 7; Brok 4.

Hoey v. Solt, TexCivApp–San Antonio, 236 SW2d 244.— Autos 172(1), 172(7), 201(1.1), 245(2.1); Trial 142.

Hofer v. Lavender, Tex, 679 SW2d 470.—Damag 87(1), 93; Death 31(1), 31(3.1).

Hofer; Lavender v., TexApp–Corpus Christi, 658 SW2d 812, writ gr, rev 679 SW2d 470.—Damag 87(1), 93; Death 31(5), 31(6), 55, 88, 89, 93; Des & Dist 74; Plead 236(3).

Hofer; Willacy County Water Control & Improvement Dist. No. 1 v., TexCivApp–El Paso, 149 SW2d 1114.— App & E 1008.1(8.1); Hus & W 273(9), 276(6); Princ & A 137(1), 173(3).

Hoff; Lacy v., TexApp–Houston (14 Dist), 633 SW2d 605, ref nre.—Zoning 245, 353.1, 372.6, 373.1, 381.5, 440.1.

Hoff v. North Am. Aviation, NDTex, 67 FSupp 375.— Labor & Emp 2261.

Hoff v. Nueces County, Tex, 153 SW3d 45.—App & E 893(1), 1080; Counties 208; Courts 97(5); Fed Cts 265, 266.1, 269, 418.

Hoff; Nueces County v., TexApp–Corpus Christi, 105 SW3d 208, reh overr, review gr, rev 153 SW3d 45.—App & E 837(1), 893(1), 919; Counties 208; Mun Corp 723, 742(4); Plead 104(1), 111.48; Schools 89; States 191.1, 191.4(1), 191.9(1), 191.9(2), 208.

Hoff v. Westhoff, TexCivApp–Galveston, 102 SW2d 293, writ refused.—Inj 12; Mun Corp 993(3).

Hoffart v. State, TexApp–Houston (14 Dist), 686 SW2d 259, writ refused, cert den 107 SCt 95, 479 US 824, 93 LEd2d 46, reh den 107 SCt 478, 479 US 977, 93 LEd2d 423.—Const Law 1179, 1811; Crim Law 627.6(1), 734, 772(6), 1043(2), 1090.8, 1130(5); Sent & Pun 1971(2); Tresp 77, 88, 89.

Hoffbrau Steakhouse, Inc.; Mainland Sav. Ass'n v., TexApp–Houston (14 Dist), 659 SW2d 101.—Evid 417(12), 460(5); Frds St of 72(1), 110(1); Spec Perf 22, 29(2); Ven & Pur 22.

Hoffer v. Eastland Nat. Bank, TexCivApp–Eastland, 169 SW2d 275.—Bills & N 87, 338, 338.5, 371, 452(3), 537(3); Contracts 50; Evid 76; Frds St of 14; Hus & W 131(1), 235(2); Impl & C C 91, 121.

Hoffer v. Eastland Nat. Bank, TexCivApp–Eastland, 153 SW2d 345.—Venue 22(6).

Hoffert v. General Motors Corp., CA5 (Tex), 656 F2d 161, reh den 660 F2d 497, reh den Cochrane & Bresnahan, PA v. Smith, 660 F2d 497, cert den 102 SCt 2037, 456 US 961, 72 LEd2d 485.—Atty & C 147; Fed Civ Proc 2737.4; Fed Cts 12.1.

Hoffert v. State, TexCrimApp, 623 SW2d 141.—Crim Law 369.2(1), 673(5); Sent & Pun 312, 313; Witn 274(1), 274(2), 355.

Hoffman; Amateur Athletic Foundation of Los Angeles v., TexApp–Dallas, 893 SW2d 602.—Judges 51(1), 51(2), 56; Mand 3(3), 42.

Hoffman; Beken v., TexCivApp–Galveston, 196 SW2d 548, ref nre.—Estop 118; Tresp to T T 6.1, 11, 38(1), 41(1), 41(2).

Hoffman v. Burroughs Corp., NDTex, 571 FSupp 545.—Contracts 127(4), 206; Fed Cts 95, 121, 146, 412.1.

Hoffman; Burton v., TexApp–Austin, 959 SW2d 351.—App & E 962; Pretrial Proc 674, 697.

Hoffman; Bynum, TexCivApp–Beaumont, 101 SW2d 600.—Dedi 43; High 1, 213(1), 213(2).

Hoffman; City of Austin v., TexCivApp–Austin, 379 SW2d 103, writ dism by agreement.—App & E 1056.1(3); Autos 201(1.1), 223(2), 226(2); Damag 132(3), 191, 208(3); Evid 510, 536, 537, 546; Neglig 85(2), 85(3); Plead 245(6); Trial 255(13).

Hoffman v. City of Mt. Pleasant, TexComApp, 89 SW2d 193, 126 Tex 632.—Mun Corp 236; Pub Contr 6.

Hoffman; City of Victoria v., TexApp–Corpus Christi, 809 SW2d 603, writ den.—Estop 52.10(2), 62.4; Execution 18; Garn 17; Mun Corp 742(4).

Hoffman; Continental Supply Co. v., TexComApp, 144 SW2d 253, 135 Tex 552.—Commerce 54.5; Corp 661(3), 672(5).

Hoffman v. Continental Supply Co., TexCivApp–Eastland, 120 SW2d 851, mod 144 SW2d 253, 135 Tex 552.—Corp 672(1), 672(5), 672(7); Mines 74(2), 113, 116.

Hoffman v. Davis, TexComApp, 100 SW2d 94, 128 Tex 503.—Counties 124(1), 196(4); Parties 3.

Hoffman v. Deck Masters, Inc., TexApp–Corpus Christi, 662 SW2d 438.—App & E 1024.1; Costs 194.14; Damag 140; Impl & C C 30, 55, 64; New Tr 44(1), 52; Stip 14(1), 14(12); Trial 340(1), 344, 350.1.

Hoffman; Dyna Span Corp. v., TexApp–Dallas, 754 SW2d 341, subsequent mandamus proceeding Hoffman v. Fifth Court of Appeals, 756 SW2d 723.—Pretrial Proc 403, 411.

Hoffman v. Elliott, Tex, 476 SW2d 845.—Mun Corp 33(9), 33(10); Quo W 5.

Hoffman v. Elliott, TexCivApp–Hous (1 Dist), 473 SW2d 675, ref nre 476 SW2d 845.—Mand 74(2); Mun Corp 33(10).

Hoffman v. Fifth Court of Appeals, Tex, 756 SW2d 723. —Pretrial Proc 411.

Hoffman v. French, Limited, TexCivApp–Corpus Christi, 394 SW2d 259, ref nre.—App & E 846(5), 882(16), 1015(5), 1170.6; Autos 249; Damag 87(2), 177, 185(1), 191; New Tr 52, 140(3), 145.

Hoffman v. Godlin, TexCivApp–El Paso, 128 SW2d 865. —Abate & R 81, 82; Mines 99(2); Partners 108, 110.

Hoffman v. Hoffman, TexApp–Fort Worth, 821 SW2d 3. —Appear 9(1); Child C 404; Divorce 59, 65, 201; Plead 106(1).

Hoffman; Hoffman v., TexApp–Fort Worth, 821 SW2d 3. —Appear 9(1); Child C 404; Divorce 59, 65, 201; Plead 106(1).

Hoffman v. Hoffman, TexApp–Corpus Christi, 805 SW2d 848, writ den.—Child C 554; Child S 40, 47, 230, 231, 234, 240, 355, 363, 556(3).

Hoffman; Hoffman v., TexApp–Corpus Christi, 805 SW2d 848, writ den.—Child C 554; Child S 40, 47, 230, 231, 234, 240, 355, 363, 556(3).

Hoffman v. Hoffman, TexCivApp–San Antonio, 153 SW2d 275.—App & E 846(5); Divorce 49(2), 130.

Hoffman; Hoffman v., TexCivApp–San Antonio, 153 SW2d 275.—App & E 846(5); Divorce 49(2), 130.

Hoffman v. Irizarry, TexApp–Dallas, 673 SW2d 674, dism.—Wills 93, 292, 384, 486, 487(1), 487(5).

Hoffman; Julian v., TexCivApp–Dallas, 520 SW2d 935.— Courts 207.4(2); New Tr 155; Time 10(7).

Hoffman v. Kramer, CA5 (Tex), 362 F3d 308.—Labor & Emp 1006, 1076, 1078.

Hoffman v. Kramer, SDTex, 185 FSupp2d 700, aff 362 F3d 308.—Labor & Emp 1066(3), 1073, 1076, 1078, 1201.

Hoffman; Love v., Tex, 499 SW2d 295.—Home 68.

Hoffman v. Love, TexCivApp–Dallas, 494 SW2d 591, ref nre 499 SW2d 295.—Home 68, 103, 109, 154, 176, 192, 202.

Hoffman v. Love, TexCivApp–Texarkana, 523 SW2d 503. —Interest 22(1).

Hoffman; National Union Fire Ins. Co. of Pittsburgh, Pa. v., TexApp–Dallas, 746 SW2d 305.—Pretrial Proc 41, 185, 403, 406, 410, 411; Witn 223.

Hoffman v. Overton Refining Co., TexCivApp–Texarkana, 110 SW2d 93.—Contracts 303(4); Mines 49, 75.

Hoffman; Paul Stanley Leasing Co. v., TexApp–Dallas, 651 SW2d 440.—App & E 1176(6); Corp 520; Pretrial Proc 693.1.

Hoffman v. Prudential Ins. Co. of America, TexApp–Houston (14 Dist), 624 SW2d 626.—Insurance 2460.

Hoffman; Republic Bankers Life Ins. Co. v., TexCivApp–Dallas, 483 SW2d 268.—Insurance 2959, 2985, 3015.

Hoffman; Rubin v., TexApp–Dallas, 843 SW2d 658.— Judges 51(2), 51(4), 56; Mand 3(3).

Hoffman; Salgo v., TexCivApp–Dallas, 521 SW2d 922.— App & E 1175(1), 1192, 1208(1); Courts 87; Mand 5, 16(1), 58, 151(1).

Hoffman; Salgo v., TexCivApp–Dallas, 515 SW2d 756.— App & E 1192.

Hoffman v. State, TexCrimApp, 514 SW2d 248.—Crim Law 450, 627.7(3), 627.8(3), 627.9(2.1), 824(8), 1036.1(2), 1166(10.10), 1170.5(1); Witn 271(1), 337(4), 344(2), 388(5), 389, 392(1), 405(1), 405(2).

Hoffman v. State, TexCrimApp, 397 SW2d 461.—Autos 355(6); Crim Law 487, 1091(8).

Hoffman v. State, TexCrimApp, 185 SW2d 729, 148 TexCrim 216.—Crim Law 507(1).

Hoffman v. State, TexCrimApp, 113 SW2d 1246, 134 TexCrim 41.—Crim Law 1097(5), 1184(2).

Hoffman v. State, TexApp–Fort Worth, 877 SW2d 501.— Crim Law 1184(1).

Hoffman; State v., TexApp–Austin, 999 SW2d 573.—Crim Law 1139; Weap 4, 17(1).

Hoffman v. State, TexApp–Waco, 922 SW2d 663, reh overr, and petition for discretionary review refused.—Crim Law 274(8), 409(5), 538(3), 713, 720(7.1), 723(1), 1035(5), 1134(2), 1158(3), 1166.16; Ind & Inf 176; Infants 20; Jury 108.

Hoffman v. State, TexApp–Houston (14 Dist), 874 SW2d 138, petition for discretionary review refused.—Crim Law 1165(1), 1177; Sent & Pun 313.

Hoffman v. State, TexApp–Houston (14 Dist), 687 SW2d 495, petition for discretionary review gr, rev 751 SW2d 512.—Crim Law 577.7, 577.10(7), 577.15(3), 577.16(9).

Hoffman v. State, TexCivApp–Dallas, 219 SW2d 539.—Gaming 67, 68(0.5); Inj 102; Lotteries 2, 3.

Hoffman v. Texas Commerce Bank Nat. Ass'n, TexApp–Houston (14 Dist), 846 SW2d 336, reh den, and writ den.—App & E 961; Judgm 143(2), 153(1); Pretrial Proc 302, 476, 486; Wills 21, 50, 155.1, 314.

Hoffman v. Tolbert, TexCivApp–Texarkana, 327 SW2d 604.—App & E 931(6), 1054(1); Lost Inst 8(3); Mines 55(8); Tresp to T T 11.

Hoffman v. Trinity Industries, Inc., TexApp–Beaumont, 979 SW2d 88, reh overr, and review dism by agreement.—Judgm 181(21); Labor & Emp 26; Work Comp 2084.

Hoffman v. U.S. Dept. of Housing and Urban Development, CA5 (Tex), 519 F2d 1160.—Civil R 1343, 1362, 1364; Const Law 947; Fed Cts 991, 993.1, 1004.1; U S 53(15).

Hoffman v. U.S. Department of Housing and Urban Development, NDTex, 371 FSupp 576, aff 519 F2d 1160.—Civil R 1325, 1326(9).

Hoffman; Veltmann v., TexCivApp–San Antonio, 621 SW2d 441.—Mtg 335.

Hoffman v. Wall, TexCivApp–Texarkana, 602 SW2d 324, ref nre.—App & E 931(3); Lim of Act 55(8), 118(1), 195(3), 197(1).

Hoffman-La Roche, Inc. v. Zeltwanger, TexApp–Corpus Christi, 69 SW3d 634, review gr, rev 144 SW3d 438.—App & E 216(7), 230, 242(1), 766, 843(2), 930(1), 930(3), 989, 1001(3), 1003(6), 1004(11); Civil R 1104, 1147, 1182, 1185, 1708, 1765; Damag 49.10, 50.10, 91(1), 94, 208(6); Labor & Emp 139(4); Lim of Act 58(1).

Hoffman, McBryde & Co., P.C. v. Heyland, TexApp–Dallas, 74 SW3d 906, review den, appeal after remand 2004 WL 1626543.—Judgm 753, 754, 768(1), 772, 785(1), 787.

Hoffmann v. Chapman, TexCivApp–El Paso, 170 SW2d 496, writ refused wom.—Adv Poss 60(1); Contracts 14; Deeds 114(1); Evid 100, 587; Ex & Ad 388(5); Land & Ten 1; Ven & Pur 232(9).

Hoffmann v. Dandurand, TexApp–Dallas, 180 SW3d 340.—Const Law 3964; Corp 1.4(4), 1.5(1), 1.7(2), 306; Courts 12(2.1), 12(2.5), 12(2.10), 12(2.20), 15, 25, 35, 39; Plead 16.

Hoffmann v. Dandurand, TexApp–Dallas, 143 SW3d 555, appeal after remand 180 SW3d 340.—App & E 1071.6; Courts 12(5), 39; Names 16(1); Plead 111.36, 111.44; Trial 401.

Hoffmann; Eppenauer v., TexCivApp–Eastland, 115 SW2d 478.—Mines 110; Plead 48; Venue 7.5(3).

Hoffmann-La Roche Inc.; Gerber v., SDTex, 392 FSupp2d 907.—Evid 219.65; Fed Civ Proc 928, 2653, 2655; Health 687(3); Prod Liab 1, 8, 11, 14, 15, 46.1, 46.2, 87.1; Sales 267, 284(1).

Hoffmann-La Roche, Inc. v. Kwasnik, TexApp–El Paso, 109 SW3d 21, reh overr.—Const Law 3964; Courts 12(2.1), 12(2.5), 12(2.10), 12(2.25), 35; Trial 388(2).

Hoffmann-La Roche Inc. v. Zeltwanger, Tex, 144 SW3d 438.—App & E 238(2); Civil R 1104, 1182, 1704, 1714; Courts 97(1); Damag 57.21, 57.22, 57.24, 57.55, 57.58, 208(6).

Hoffmeyer v. Hoffmeyer, TexApp–Eastland, 869 SW2d 667, reh den, and writ den.—App & E 863, 934(1); Parent & C 11.

Hoffmeyer; Hoffmeyer v., TexApp–Eastland, 869 SW2d 667, reh den, and writ den.—App & E 863, 934(1); Parent & C 11.

Hoffpauir; Hoxsey v., CA5 (Tex), 180 F2d 84, cert den 70 SCt 841, 339 US 953, 94 LEd 1366.—Atty & C 130, 181, 182(2), 192(1); Courts 37(3); Fed Cts 407.1; Judgm 721.

Hoffpauir v. State, TexCrimApp, 596 SW2d 139.—Crim Law 627.9(1), 627.9(4).

Hoffpuir v. Hoxsey, NDTex, 82 FSupp 14, rev 180 F2d 84, cert den 70 SCt 841, 339 US 953, 94 LEd 1366.—Judgm 721, 812(3).

Hoffrichter v. Brookhaven Country Club Corp., TexCivApp–Dallas, 448 SW2d 843, ref nre.—App & E 927(7); Labor & Emp 40(2), 58.

Hofheinz; Buie v., TexCivApp–Galveston, 254 SW2d 852.—Impl & C C 65.

Hofheinz; Gottlieb v., TexCivApp–Hous (1 Dist), 523 SW2d 7, dism.—Elections 212, 227(1), 270, 280, 285(1), 285(3); Judgm 178.

Hofheinz; Ptacek v., TexCivApp–Galveston, 128 SW2d 872, writ refused.—Waters 183.5.

Hofheinz; Ramirez v., CA5 (Tex), 619 F2d 442.—Civil R 1522, 1536, 1545, 1548; Fed Civ Proc 2262.1, 2282.1; Fed Cts 941.

Hofheinz v. U.S., CA5 (Tex), 511 F2d 661.—Int Rev 5066.

Hofheinz; Universal Amusement Co., Inc. v., CA5 (Tex), 646 F2d 996, reh den 655 F2d 1131.—Civil R 1376(1), 1376(2).

Hofheinz; Universal Amusement Co., Inc. v., CA5 (Tex), 616 F2d 202, on rearg 646 F2d 996, reh den 655 F2d 1131.—Civil R 1376(1), 1376(4), 1376(9), 1479, 1480, 1482.

Hofheinz; Zbranek v., EDTex, 730 FSupp 758.—Fed Cts 528; Rem of C 107(8).

Hofheinz; Zbranek v., EDTex, 727 FSupp 324.—Rem of C 2, 17, 79(1), 103, 107(4).

Hofland v. Elgin-Butler Brick Co., TexApp–Corpus Christi, 834 SW2d 409.—App & E 758.3(9), 931(1), 989, 1010.1(1), 1010.1(3), 1012.1(5); Lim of Act 43, 66(14), 95(1), 95(7), 197(2); Trover 4, 9(1), 9(5), 40(4), 40(5).

Hofland v. Fireman's Fund Ins. Co., TexApp–Corpus Christi, 907 SW2d 597, reh overr.—App & E 842(2), 852; Contracts 143(2), 143.5, 147(3), 152, 176(1), 176(2); Insurance 1808, 2278(11), 2278(13).

Hofmann, In re, BkrtcyWDTex, 248 BR 90.—Bankr 2090, 2091; Rem of C 107(11).

Hofmann, In re, BkrtcyWDTex, 248 BR 79.—Bankr 2041.1, 2045, 2089, 2091, 2532, 2537, 3444.30(1), 3444.50(2).

Hofmann; Weidel v., TexCivApp–Austin, 269 SW2d 945, ref nre.—App & E 991; Evid 589; Mines 55(7); Ref of Inst 45(4.1).

Hofmann Paint Mfg. Co. v. Paint Cottage, Inc., TexCivApp–Austin, 473 SW2d 954.—App & E 230; Garn 42, 106, 191.

Hofmayer, Ex parte, Tex, 420 SW2d 137.—Hab Corp 613, 614(1).

Hofrock; Thornton v., TexCivApp–Austin, 609 SW2d 883.—App & E 930(3); Bailm 9; Trial 351.2(2).

Hofstadter; Andy Machinery Co., Inc. v., TexApp–Corpus Christi, 721 SW2d 472.—Bailm 21; Trover 13, 60, 70.

Hogan, Ex parte, TexCrimApp, 556 SW2d 352.—Hab Corp 500.1.

Hogan, Ex parte, TexApp–Houston (1 Dist), 916 SW2d 82, habeas corpus den.—Child S 470, 487, 497, 498, 538; Const Law 4494; Contempt 44, 63(1), 64, 66(8); Courts 114.

Hogan, In re, BkrtcyNDTex, 346 BR 715.—Bankr 2892.1, 2894, 2895.1, 2897.1, 2900(1), 3413.1, 3708(1), 3715(10).

HOGARD;

Hogan, Matter of, CA5 (Tex), 707 F2d 209.—Bankr 3351.1.

Hogan; Air Control Engineering, Inc. v., TexCivApp–Dallas, 477 SW2d 941.—App & E 173(2), 231(1), 930(3); Explos 7; Neglig 232, 236; Trial 352.5(3).

Hogan v. Beckel, TexApp–San Antonio, 783 SW2d 307, writ den.—Pretrial Proc 124, 127, 226.

Hogan; Century Ins. Co., Limited, of Edinburgh, Scotland v., TexCivApp–Austin, 135 SW2d 224.—Evid 590, 592; Insurance 2201, 2202, 3164, 3179, 3191(5), 3191(7), 3571; Plead 291(2), 291(3), 301(3).

Hogan v. C I R, CCA5 (Tex), 141 F2d 92, cert den 65 SCt 36, 323 US 710, 89 LEd 571.—Int Rev 3013.1, 3070, 3140, 3470, 3498, 3500, 4700.

Hogan v. City of Houston, CA5 (Tex), 819 F2d 604.—Civil R 1395(7).

Hogan v. City of Tyler, TexCivApp–Tyler, 602 SW2d 555, ref nre.—Em Dom 191(1), 317(1); Estop 92(4); Judgm 518; Tresp to T T 25.

Hogan v. Credit Motors, Inc., TexApp–San Antonio, 827 SW2d 392, writ den with per curiam opinion 841 SW2d 360.—App & E 544(1), 1030; Exceptions Bill of5; Pretrial Proc 45, 309, 747.1.

Hogan v. Cunningham, TexCivApp–Amarillo, 278 SW2d 265.—App & E 1010.1(8.1), 1060.1(1); Damag 33, 213; Judgm 198; Neglig 1240, 1672; Trial 255(4).

Hogan v. Estelle, NDTex, 417 FSupp 9, aff 537 F2d 238, cert den 97 SCt 794, 429 US 1065, 50 LEd2d 782.—Crim Law 641.13(2.1); Hab Corp 771.

Hogan v. G., C. & S. F. Ry. Co., TexCivApp–Beaumont, 411 SW2d 815, writ refused.—App & E 21, 22; Courts 247(2).

Hogan v. Hallman, TexApp–Houston (14 Dist), 889 SW2d 332, reh overr, and writ den.—Const Law 2311, 2312, 2314, 2315, 2648, 3006, 3057, 3085, 3105, 3753, 3971; Death 7, 38; Health 604, 811; Lim of Act 4(2), 72(1).

Hogan v. Hanover Ins. Co., TexCivApp–Fort Worth, 406 SW2d 217, ref nre.—Judgm 185.3(13); Work Comp 204.

Hogan v. Hearst Corp., TexApp–San Antonio, 945 SW2d 246.—Const Law 1230, 1545, 1554, 1570, 2070; Crim Law 1226(2); Damag 50.10, 208(6); Death 21, 31(1); Torts 350, 357.

Hogan v. Hidalgo County, TexCivApp–San Antonio, 246 SW2d 709.—Action 60; Counties 89; Lim of Act 197(2); Pretrial Proc 713, 714, 719; Refer 79.

Hogan v. J. Higgins Trucking, Inc., TexApp–Dallas, 197 SW3d 879, rule 537(f) motion gr.—App & E 242(2), 852, 856(1), 863, 866(3), 934(1); Autos 197(1); Judgm 181(33), 185.1(8), 189; States 18.61.

Hogan v. Kraft Foods, CA5 (Tex), 969 F2d 142.—Antitrust 132; Contracts 324(1); Damag 50.10; Fed Civ Proc 2744; Insurance 1117(2); Labor & Emp 679, 711; Lim of Act 66(6), 104(1); States 18.15, 18.51.

Hogan; McCarty v., TexCivApp–Fort Worth, 121 SW2d 499, writ dism.—App & E 1002, 1011.1(1), 1011.1(2); Damag 157(1); Evid 597; Mines 119, 125; Neglig 250; Trial 139.1(17).

Hogan v. Malone Lumber, Inc., EDTex, 800 FSupp 1441.—Const Law 3963; Fed Cts 71, 104, 105, 113, 144; Work Comp 2145.

Hogan v. Midland County Com'rs Court, CA5 (Tex), 680 F2d 1101.—Civil R 1395(7); Fed Civ Proc 657.5(3), 1139, 1788.10, 2734.

Hogan v. Morris, CA5 (Tex), 424 F2d 424.—Fed Cts 743; Judgm 828.12, 828.20(3).

Hogan; Myrtle Springs Reverted Independent School Dist. v., TexApp–Texarkana, 705 SW2d 707, ref nre, cert den 107 SCt 1350, 480 US 906, 94 LEd2d 520.—Damag 56; Labor & Emp 866, 867, 868(3); Schools 136, 147.4, 147.54.

Hogan; Panhandle & S. F. Ry. Co. v., TexCivApp–Amarillo, 388 SW2d 320, ref nre.—Neglig 1706; R R 73(4), 133(3), 134(1).

Hogan; Perna v., TexApp–Houston (14 Dist), 162 SW3d 648.—App & E 1008.1(1), 1010.1(3), 1012.1(5), 1024.3, 1071.2; Const Law 3964, 3965(3); Courts 12(2.1), 12(2.5), 12(2.10), 12(2.15), 12(2.25), 15, 35, 39.

Hogan v. Price, TexCivApp–Texarkana, 274 SW2d 745, ref nre.—Lim of Act 60(6).

Hogan v. Roop, TexCivApp–Waco, 500 SW2d 936.—Infants 156.

Hogan v. San Antonio Express-News, TexApp–San Antonio, 945 SW2d 246. See Hogan v. Hearst Corp.

Hogan v. State, TexCrimApp, 631 SW2d 159.—Arrest 63.1; Crim Law 394.4(9).

Hogan v. State, TexCrimApp, 572 SW2d 526.—Crim Law 641.13(7), 1077.3.

Hogan v. State, TexCrimApp, 529 SW2d 515.—Burg 29; Sent & Pun 327, 385, 1381(6), 1387.

Hogan v. State, TexCrimApp, 496 SW2d 594, cert den 94 SCt 81, 414 US 862, 38 LEd2d 112.—Const Law 3800, 4789(2); Costs 302.4; Crim Law 48, 331, 479, 633(1), 800(2), 805(3), 814(17), 844(1); Homic 1172, 1174, 1177, 1210; Jury 131(13), 149.

Hogan v. State, TexCrimApp, 393 SW2d 898.—Crim Law 763(1); False Pret 7(2), 38, 51; Ind & Inf 191(5).

Hogan v. State, TexCrimApp, 264 SW2d 113, 159 TexCrim 343.—Crim Law 814(17); Int Liq 236(7); Searches 181.

Hogan v. State, TexCrimApp, 178 SW2d 525, 147 TexCrim 75.—Crim Law 673(5); Larc 70(1).

Hogan v. State, TexApp–San Antonio, 943 SW2d 80, petition for discretionary review refused, habeas corpus gr Ex parte Hogan, 2003 WL 1846049.—Crim Law 721(3), 730(10), 938(1), 942(1).

Hogan v. State, TexApp–Houston (14 Dist), 954 SW2d 875, reh overr, and petition for discretionary review refused.—Autos 332; Crim Law 304(1), 394.6(4), 1120(9).

Hogan v. Stoepler, TexCivApp–Austin, 82 SW2d 1000.—Wills 203, 277, 289.

Hogan; Tabor v., TexApp–Amarillo, 955 SW2d 894, reh overr.—App & E 989, 1010.1(1), 1010.2; Const Law 2540, 2570, 2572; Counties 58; Courts 1; Dedi 44, 46.

Hogan; Texas-New Mexico Power Co. v., TexApp–Waco, 824 SW2d 252, writ den.—Em Dom 170.

Hogan v. Turland, Tex, 428 SW2d 316.—Courts 247(2).

Hogan v. Turland, TexCivApp–Austin, 430 SW2d 720.—Courts 207.4(1.1); Crim Law 1026.10(2.1), 1026.10(6).

Hogan v. Turland, TexCivApp–Austin, 419 SW2d 383, rev 428 SW2d 316, appeal reinstated 430 SW2d 720.—Action 18; Courts 247(2).

Hogan; U.S. v., CA5 (Tex), 771 F2d 82, appeal decided 779 F2d 296.—Crim Law 1170.5(1).

Hogan; U.S. v., CA5 (Tex), 763 F2d 697, opinion withdrawn in part 771 F2d 82, appeal decided 779 F2d 296. —Crim Law 622, 622.3, 627.6(4), 627.8(4), 692, 899, 1028, 1043(1), 1158(1), 1166(6), 1170.5(1); Witn 321, 323, 379(1), 380(5.1).

Hogan; Wagner v., TexCivApp–Eastland, 161 SW2d 849. —App & E 761; Judgm 526, 527; Ven & Pur 302.

Hogan; Waits v., TexCivApp–Texarkana, 220 SW2d 915, ref nre.—App & E 842(1); Carr 282; Evid 14; Lim of Act 127(5); New Tr 140(3), 157.

Hogan v. W. H. Norris Lumber Co., TexCivApp–Waco, 90 SW2d 585.—Contracts 236, 245(2); Fraud 12; Mech Liens 290(2).

Hogans v. State, TexCrimApp, 176 SW3d 829.—Crim Law 1023(3), 1023(16), 1134(3), 1134(10); Sent & Pun 2024.

Hogan Systems, Inc. v. Cybresource Intern., Inc., CA5 (Tex), 158 F3d 319, reh and sug for reh den 165 F3d 25. —Antitrust 417, 420; Copyr 48, 49, 67.3, 90(2); Fed Cts 776.

Hogard; O'Hern v., TexApp–Houston (14 Dist), 841 SW2d 135.—Antitrust 199; Judgm 181(15.1).

Hogden; Robertson Truck Lines, Inc. v., TexCivApp–Beaumont, 487 SW2d 401, ref nre.—App & E 205; Pretrial Proc 75.

Hoge v. Lopez, TexCivApp–San Antonio, 394 SW2d 816. —App & E 302(1); Fixt 34, 35(2); Land & Ten 160(3).

Hogenson v. Williams, TexCivApp–Texarkana, 542 SW2d 456.—Assault 2, 10, 43(1), 43(2), 48; Schools 169, 176; Trial 219.

Hogg v. Jaeckle, TexCivApp–Tyler, 561 SW2d 568.—Evid 445(3); Land & Ten 184(2).

Hogg v. Professional Pathology Associates, P.A., TexCivApp–Hous (14 Dist), 598 SW2d 328, dism.—App & E 954(1); Inj 111, 135, 138.39; Venue 2, 22(6).

Hogg v. Rust Indus. Cleaning Services, Inc., EDTex, 896 FSupp 655.—Rem of C 15, 102, 107(7).

Hogg v. Smith, TexCivApp–Texarkana, 157 SW2d 165, writ refused wom.—App & E 238(2), 544(2); Trial 358.

Hogg v. State, TexCrimApp, 220 SW2d 134, 153 TexCrim 342.—Sent & Pun 2255.

Hogg v. State, TexCrimApp, 202 SW2d 238, 150 TexCrim 406.—Crim Law 53, 730(8), 854(6), 1171.1(2.1).

Hogg v. State, TexCrimApp, 141 SW2d 340, 139 TexCrim 411.—Crim Law 1099.7(2), 1099.8, 1099.10, 1182.

Hogg; Talbott v., TexCivApp–Amarillo, 298 SW2d 883, writ dism.—App & E 719(5), 758.1, 1056.3; Evid 121(1), 123(2), 230(3), 591; Pretrial Proc 477.1, 480; Trusts 44(2), 44(3).

Hogg; Tide Water Associated Oil Co. v., TexCivApp–El Paso, 294 SW2d 725, ref nre.—Mines 53, 62.1.

Hogg v. Washington Nat. Ins. Co., TexCivApp–Tyler, 503 SW2d 325.—App & E 500(4), 930(3), 1070(2); Insurance 2445, 3580; Trial 344, 358.

Hogg v. Washington Nat. Ins. Co., TexCivApp–Tyler, 495 SW2d 25.—App & E 387(3), 392, 503; New Tr 155, 163(1).

Hoggard; Keel v., TexCivApp–Waco, 590 SW2d 939.— Bills & N 489(7); Evid 419(1), 419(2), 419(20); Fraud 6, 7; Lim of Act 48(1), 51(2), 100(2), 182(5); Plead 228.15; Release 57(1), 57(2).

Hoggard v. Snodgrass, TexApp–Dallas, 770 SW2d 577.— Atty & C 19, 21.5(1), 21.10, 21.20, 32(4), 32(13); Mand 1, 4(1), 28, 42, 176.

Hogge; Fudge v., TexApp–Dallas, 323 SW2d 663.— Adv Poss 6; Bound 14; Covenants 79(2); Dedi 19(5), 50; Lim of Act 14, 47(2), 100(11); Waters 111.

Hogge v. Kimbrow, TexApp–Beaumont, 631 SW2d 603.— Child C 554, 634, 637, 654, 658, 904.

Hoggett v. Brown, TexApp–Houston (14 Dist), 971 SW2d 472, review den, and reh of petition for review overr.— App & E 964, 984(5), 1062.5, 1071.1(5.1), 1079; Consp 1.1; Corp 174, 180, 289, 297, 307, 310(1), 397, 513.4, 583, 584; Costs 194.12, 194.40, 207; Fraud 7, 16, 17, 50; Judges 49(2), 51(2); Judgm 199(1), 199(3.2), 199(3.10); Partners 125; Torts 222, 223, 242; Trial 18, 29(1), 29.1, 107, 295(1), 349(1), 352.4(1); Trusts 91, 95.

Hoggett; Kidd v., TexCivApp–San Antonio, 331 SW2d 515, ref nre.—App & E 931(3); Damag 3, 91(1); Libel 131, 135, 136, 139; Mines 73.5, 78.1(3); Tresp 40(1).

Hoggett; Uzzell v., TexCivApp–San Antonio, 430 SW2d 846, ref nre.—App & E 1177(6); Contracts 170(1); Land & Ten 134(1).

Hoggett v. Wright, TexCivApp–San Antonio, 374 SW2d 690, ref nre.—App & E 1177(1), 1177(7); Lim of Act 39(5); Stip 14(10); Tresp to T T 38(2), 41(2).

Hoggett v. Zimmerman, Axelrad, Meyer, Stern and Wise, P.C., TexApp–Houston (14 Dist), 63 SW3d 807, reh overr.—Alt Disp Res 184, 259, 263, 279, 355; Pretrial Proc 714, 715.

Hogrobrooks v. Williams, TexCivApp–Fort Worth, 324 SW2d 916.—App & E 286.

Hogsett v. Dallas Mortg. Securities Co., TexCivApp–Dallas, 110 SW2d 135, writ dism woj.—Corp 619, 621(1); Trusts 160(2), 162, 369.

Hogstrom; Yates v., TexCivApp–Hous (14 Dist), 444 SW2d 851.—Adv Poss 65(2), 106(1), 109, 115(5); App & E 282, 302(1); Bound 48(3).

Hogue v. Blue Bell Creameries, L.P., TexApp–Texarkana, 922 SW2d 566, reh overr, writ den with per curiam opinion 930 SW2d 88.—App & E 907(4), 930(3), 989, 1003(1), 1064.1(1), 1064.1(2.1); Labor & Emp 807, 810, 861, 863(2); Trial 182, 228(1), 241.

Hogue v. Blue Bell Ice Cream, Inc., TexApp–Texarkana, 922 SW2d 566. See Hogue v. Blue Bell Creameries, L.P.

Hogue; Boyd v., TexCivApp–Amarillo, 224 SW2d 301.— Plead 104(2), 111.23, 111.39(2), 111.42(11); Venue 5.5, 15, 16.

Hogue; Budget Rent-A-Car Conroe/Woodlands v., TexApp–Beaumont, 104 SW3d 236.—Autos 390; Judgm 185.3(2).

Hogue v. City of Bowie, TexCivApp–Fort Worth, 209 SW2d 807, ref nre.—Inj 24, 123; Mun Corp 846.

Hogue v. Coit, TexCivApp–Fort Worth, 196 SW2d 346, ref nre.—Ex & Ad 236, 237; Judgm 270, 272, 286.

Hogue; Columbia Medical Center of Las Colinas, Inc. v., TexApp–Dallas, 132 SW3d 671, reh gr, and review withdrawn (2 pets), and review gr.—App & E 893(1), 930(1), 969, 974(0.5), 989, 1001(1), 1001(3), 1003(7), 1004(1), 1064.1(1), 1067, 1079; Damag 94.1, 94.6; Death 77, 85, 86(1), 88, 89, 93, 99(1); Evid 571(10); Health 657, 675, 834(1); Interest 29; Neglig 273, 1659; New Tr 74; Trial 182, 203(1), 219, 220, 349(2), 350.2.

Hogue v. El Paso Products Co., TexCivApp–El Paso, 507 SW2d 246, ref nre.—App & E 927(7); Neglig 1101, 1204(1), 1566, 1612, 1613, 1625, 1670, 1696; Trial 139.1(8).

Hogue v. Glover, TexCivApp–Waco, 302 SW2d 757, ref nre.—Clubs 6, 11; Covenants 49, 69(1), 84; Dedi 60; Inj 89(3), 128(6); Nav Wat 1(3), 37(2), 37(4); Waters 61.

Hogue v. Hogue, TexCivApp–Dallas, 242 SW2d 673.— Divorce 27(1), 62(1), 124.3, 127(4), 130, 184(6.1), 184(10); Domicile 3, 4(1), 4(2), 10; Marriage 1.

Hogue; Hogue v., TexCivApp–Dallas, 242 SW2d 673.— Divorce 27(1), 62(1), 124.3, 127(4), 130, 184(6.1), 184(10); Domicile 3, 4(1), 4(2), 10; Marriage 1.

Hogue v. Johnson, CA5 (Tex), 131 F3d 466, cert den 118 SCt 1297, 523 US 1014, 140 LEd2d 334.—Courts 90(2); Fed Cts 502; Hab Corp 205, 381, 401, 403, 405.1, 422, 423, 424, 431, 453, 508, 770; Sent & Pun 94, 313, 1660, 1681, 1762.

Hogue v. Kroger Store No. 107, TexApp–Houston (1 Dist), 875 SW2d 477, reh den, and writ den.—App & E 989, 999(1), 1003(6); Atty & C 32(12); Damag 130.3; Evid 558(7); Trial 186, 194(16); Witn 208(1), 267, 268(1), 372(1).

Hogue; Masterson v., TexApp–Tyler, 842 SW2d 696, reh overr.—Costs 260(1), 260(4), 260(5); Gifts 47(1); Judgm 185(1); Pretrial Proc 483; Trusts 72, 86.

Hogue v. National Bank of Commerce of San Antonio, TexCivApp–Eastland, 562 SW2d 291, ref nre.—Elections 317.2, 323.

Hogue v. Propath Laboratory, Inc., TexApp–Fort Worth, 192 SW3d 641, review den, and reh of petition for review den.—Antitrust 222, 353; App & E 754(1), 852, 927(7), 933(1), 977(5); Const Law 2312, 2315; Contracts 205.25; Fraud 30, 38; Health 705, 780, 811; Lim of Act 4(2), 95(12); New Tr 6, 17; Sales 246; Trial 139.1(14), 139.1(17).

Hogue v. Royse City, Tex., CA5 (Tex), 939 F2d 1249.— Fed Civ Proc 2771(5), 2840; Fed Cts 420, 666; Judgm 713(2), 720, 828.10(1), 828.15(1).

Hogue v. Scott, NDTex, 874 FSupp 1486, aff 131 F3d 466, cert den 118 SCt 1297, 523 US 1014, 140 LEd2d 334.— Const Law 2805, 4629; Costs 302.4; Courts 100(1); Crim Law 126(1), 368(3), 641.13(1), 641.13(2.1), 641.13(6), 641.13(7), 700(2.1), 700(3), 706(4), 720.5, 723(3), 789(4), 800(6); Hab Corp 314, 319.1, 320, 352, 364, 381,

403, 421, 422, 452, 453, 490(1), 495, 497, 501, 505, 742, 770; Homic 576; Jury 33(2.10), 45, 97(1), 99.1, 108, 130, 136(4); Sent & Pun 1626, 1681, 1745, 1762, 1780(1).

Hogue v. State, TexCrimApp, 711 SW2d 9, cert den 107 SCt 329, 479 US 922, 93 LEd2d 301, habeas corpus den 874 FSupp 1486, aff 131 F3d 466, cert den 118 SCt 1297, 523 US 1014, 140 LEd2d 334.—Const Law 3811, 4744(2); Crim Law 485(1); Homic 832, 850; Jury 108, 136(4); Sent & Pun 1681; Witn 345(8).

Hogue v. State, TexCrimApp, 487 SW2d 756.—Crim Law 1144.17; Sent & Pun 2021.

Hogue v. State, TexCrimApp, 234 SW2d 687, 155 TexCrim 310.—Crim Law 586, 621(2), 1111(3), 1114.1(2), 1159.5, 1171.8(2); Jury 136(5); Witn 350.

Hogue v. State, TexCrimApp, 231 SW2d 419.—Crim Law 1094(3).

Hogue v. State, TexApp–Tyler, 752 SW2d 585, petition for discretionary review refused.—Autos 351.1, 418, 421; Crim Law 721(3), 1167(3), 1171.5; Ind & Inf 65, 71.4(2), 110(3).

Hogue v. United Olympic Life Ins. Co., CA5 (Tex), 39 F3d 98, reh and sug for reh den 46 F3d 68, cert den 115 SCt 2248, 515 US 1103, 132 LEd2d 256.—Antitrust 161, 369; Fed Cts 611; Insurance 1008, 1564, 1934, 2005, 2039, 3360; Rem of C 119.

Hogue; U.S. v., CA5 (Tex), 132 F3d 1087, on remand U.S. v. Meeks, 1998 WL 320270.—Crim Law 255.4, 308, 328, 561(1), 753.3, 1134(8); Ind & Inf 144.2.

Hogue v. U.S., CA5 (Tex), 287 F2d 99, cert den 82 SCt 369, 368 US 932, 7 LEd2d 195, reh den 82 SCt 441, 368 US 972, 7 LEd2d 402.—Crim Law 1431; Prisons 13.3; Sent & Pun 462, 1798.

Hogue v. Wilkinson, TexCivApp–Texarkana, 291 SW2d 750.—Infants 50, 58(1), 58(2); Judgm 181(19), 185.3(8), 694; Princ & A 136(3).

Hohenberg Bros. Co. v. George E. Gibbons & Co., Tex, 537 SW2d 1.—Contracts 218, 221(1); Sales 85(1).

Hohenberg Brothers Co. v. George E. Gibbons & Co., TexCivApp–Corpus Christi, 526 SW2d 570, writ gr, rev 537 SW2d 1.—App & E 1170.10; Contracts 147(2), 176(2), 221(2), 245(2); Evid 397(1), 461(1); Fraud 58(2); Sales 379, 383.

Hohenberger; Beckman v., TexCivApp–San Antonio, 104 SW2d 529, writ dism.—Brok 74, 86(1), 88(14).

Hohenberger v. Osborne, TexCivApp–Beaumont, 113 SW2d 255, writ dism.—Damag 130.2; New Tr 144.

Hohenberger v. Schnitzer, TexCivApp–San Antonio, 235 SW2d 466, writ refused.—App & E 846(2); Brok 66; Costs 240; Cust & U 19(3); Decl Judgm 143.1, 344, 347, 390.

Hohenberger; Sumners v., TexCivApp–San Antonio, 356 SW2d 804, ref nre.—Contracts 9(1), 25; Fraud 61; Plead 360.

Hohenstein v. State, TexApp–Houston (1 Dist), 723 SW2d 244.—Mental H 41.

Hohman; Camden Oil Co. v., TexCivApp–Beaumont, 476 SW2d 708.—Plead 110, 111.2; Proc 157.

Hohman; University of Texas Medical Branch at Galveston v., TexApp–Houston (1 Dist), 6 SW3d 767, review dism woj.—Admin Law 229; App & E 863; Consp 1.1; Damag 50.10; Health 264, 266; Judgm 181(27); Labor & Emp 826; Libel 2; Lim of Act 58(1); Mun Corp 723, 723.5; Offic 69.7, 72.41(2), 114, 119; Plead 104(1); Pretrial Proc 554, 690; States 53, 79, 112.2(2), 191.6(1), 191.9(1), 191.10; Statut 212.6, 212.7; Torts 330.

Hohmann v. Gillespie County, TexCivApp–San Antonio, 104 SW2d 573.—App & E 773(2).

Hohmann; Langehennig v., TexComApp, 163 SW2d 402, 139 Tex 452.—Hus & W 262.1(1); Wills 6, 72, 87, 184(1), 215, 309, 467.

Hohmann; Langehennig v., TexCivApp–San Antonio, 365 SW2d 203, ref nre.—App & E 934(1), 989; Judgm 185(6), 185.1(3), 185.2(1), 185.2(4), 186; Lim of Act 20, 44(1); Wills 742.

Hohmann v. Langehennig, TexCivApp–El Paso, 153 SW2d 1011, aff 163 SW2d 402, 139 Tex 452.—Wills 6, 72, 99, 184(1), 440, 441, 481, 675.

Hohn v. State, TexCrimApp, 538 SW2d 619.—Const Law 250.2(3), 3801; Infants 13, 20; Rape 54(1).

Hohn v. State, TexApp–Beaumont, 951 SW2d 535, petition for discretionary review refused, post-conviction relief den In re Hohn, 2004 WL 1119207.—Crim Law 273.4(1), 374, 1026.10(4); Ind & Inf 87(7), 176.

Hoing; Stripling v., TexCivApp–Fort Worth, 203 SW2d 1016.—App & E 776, 912, 1024.3; Evid 76; Plead 111.37, 111.42(7); Princ & A 23(2); Venue 8.5(5).

Hoisington v. Box, TexCivApp–San Antonio, 237 SW2d 1003, ref nre.—Covenants 103(1); Inj 132, 138.31, 152.

Hoisting & Portable Engineers Local No. 450, of Intern. Union of Operating Engineers, AFL-CIO; H. A. Lott Inc. v., SDTex, 222 FSupp 993.—Rem of C 58.

Hoisting and Portable Engineers Local 450 of Intern. Union of Operating Engineers, AFL-CIO; Pence Const. Corp. v., CA5 (Tex), 484 F2d 398, cert den 94 SCt 896, 414 US 1144, 39 LEd2d 99.—Fed Cts 421, 901.1; Labor & Emp 1311, 1386.

Hoitt v. State, TexApp–Texarkana, 30 SW3d 670, petition for discretionary review refused.—Bail 42; Const Law 3227, 3788; Crim Law 1167(4), 1177, 1181.5(8); Ind & Inf 159(1), 198; Sent & Pun 1064, 1155, 1157; Statut 223.4.

Hoitt v. State, TexApp–Texarkana, 28 SW3d 162, petition for discretionary review gr, petition for discretionary review dism with per curiam opinion 65 SW3d 59.—Assault 48, 92(2); Crim Law 80, 361(1), 369.2(1), 369.2(4), 371(1), 371(12), 372(14), 769, 814(1), 1134(2), 1144.13(3), 1147, 1153(1), 1159.2(2), 1159.2(7), 1159.2(9), 1159.3(1), 1189; Ind & Inf 119; Mun Corp 180(1); Sent & Pun 1061.

Hokanson; Algorde Oil Co. v., TexCivApp–Eastland, 179 SW2d 350, writ refused wom.—Evid 157(1); Torts 135; Waters 49.

Hoke v. Poser, Tex, 384 SW2d 335.—App & E 773(3); Damag 34, 216(4), 221(6).

Hoke; Wyatt v., TexCivApp–Beaumont, 149 SW2d 1019.—Execution 172(4).

Hoker; U.S. v., CA5 (Tex), 483 F2d 359.—Crim Law 656(2), 1166.22(1).

H.O.K. Investments, Inc.; Elm Creek Owners Ass'n v., TexApp–San Antonio, 12 SW3d 495, reh overr.—App & E 893(1), 949; Const Law 3867, 3874(1), 3879, 3981; Parties 35.9, 35.44.

Hokr v. Burgett, TexCivApp–Fort Worth, 489 SW2d 928.—Autos 168(1), 244(58).

Hokr v. State, TexCrimApp, 545 SW2d 463.—Arrest 70(2); Bail 48, 77(2), 90.

Holbein; Atlantic Richfield Co. v., TexApp–Dallas, 672 SW2d 507, ref nre.—App & E 758.1, 758.3(3); Estop 68(2); Gas 14.1(3); Mines 79.3, 79.7.

Holbein v. Austral Oil Co., Inc., CA5 (Tex), 609 F2d 206.—Mines 79.1(1), 79.3, 87.

Holbein Family Mineral Trust; Bright & Co. v., TexApp–San Antonio, 995 SW2d 742, reh overr, and review den.—Action 12; App & E 177, 1043(6); Lim of Act 62, 63, 148(1), 148(3), 199(3); Mines 79.7.

Holberg; Short, TexApp–Houston (14 Dist), 731 SW2d 584.—App & E 907(3); Judgm 106(9), 126(1), 126(2), 130, 143(3), 145(2), 146, 153(1), 162(2), 163.

Holberg v. State, TexCrimApp, 38 SW3d 137, reh den, cert den 122 SCt 394, 534 US 972, 151 LEd2d 298.—Const Law 1017, 1298, 1299, 1416; Crim Law 1030(2), 1430; Sent & Pun 1623; Statut 216.

Holberg v. Teal Const. Co., TexApp–Houston (14 Dist), 879 SW2d 358.—App & E 931(1), 989, 1001(1), 1003(7), 1010.2; Fraud 58(2); Guar 91; Princ & A 158, 159(2).

Holberg; Texas Employment Commission v., Tex, 440 SW2d 38.—Unemp Comp 180, 193, 195, 436, 439, 493(8).

Holberg; Texas Employment Commission v., TexCiv-App–Beaumont, 434 SW2d 733, writ gr, aff in part, rev in part 440 SW2d 38.—Unemp Comp 62, 203, 219, 220, 486.

Holberg & Co. v. Citizens Nat. Assur. Co., TexApp–Houston (1 Dist), 856 SW2d 515.—Action 13, 14; Assoc 16; Costs 260(4), 260(5); Judgm 310.

Holbert v. City of Amarillo, TexCivApp–Amarillo, 294 SW2d 243, ref nre.—Adv Poss 114(1); Tax 2936, 3162(1), 3162(3).

Holbert; Harris v., TexCivApp–Eastland, 517 SW2d 333. —Judgm 199(3.7), 199(3.17); New Tr 44(2).

Holbert v. State, TexCrimApp, 457 SW2d 286.—Crim Law 622.2(8), 656(5), 721(3), 726, 730(10), 814(17), 1170.5(1), 1171.6; Witn 242, 244, 380(5.1).

Holbrook, Ex parte, TexCrimApp, 609 SW2d 541.—Controlled Subs 65; Ind & Inf 59, 73(1), 110(3).

Holbrook, Ex parte, TexCrimApp, 606 SW2d 925.—Autos 351.1; Hab Corp 474; Statut 223.4.

Holbrook; Birdo v., TexApp–Fort Worth, 775 SW2d 411, writ den.—Convicts 6; Evid 43(1); Inj 26(3); Pretrial Proc 477.1; Trial 21.

Holbrook v. City of El Paso, TexCivApp–El Paso, 377 SW2d 669, ref nre.—App & E 768, 854(2), 920(3), 954(1), 954(2); Autos 104; Inj 135.

Holbrook v. C. I. R., CA5 (Tex), 450 F2d 134, reh den 451 F2d 1350.—Int Rev 3071, 3487, 3488, 3560, 3571; Subrog 1, 41(6).

Holbrook v. Guynes, TexApp–Houston (1 Dist), 827 SW2d 487, writ gr, aff Guynes v. Galveston County, 861 SW2d 861.—App & E 713(1); Dist & Pros Attys 9.

Holbrook; National Life & Acc. Ins. Co. v., CCA5 (Tex), 100 F2d 780, cert den 59 SCt 822, 307 US 624, 83 LEd 1502.—Insurance 1732, 1735, 1755, 1767, 1818.

Holbrook; Parker v., TexApp–Houston (1 Dist), 647 SW2d 692, ref nre.—Judgm 181(33); Libel 36, 38(1), 41, 51(2), 101(4).

Holbrook; Prater v., TexCivApp–Beaumont, 283 SW2d 263.—App & E 969, 1170.6; Autos 201(2), 244(35); Damag 132(3); Trial 18.

Holbrook; Prater v., TexCivApp–Beaumont, 251 SW2d 547.—App & E 994(1), 1071.5; Autos 247; Plead 111.42(8), 111.44; Venue 8.5(3), 8.5(4).

Holbrook v. Southland Life Ins. Co., TexCivApp–Galveston, 129 SW2d 448.—App & E 927(7); Insurance 1638, 1755, 2019.

Holbrook v. State, TexCrimApp, 257 SW2d 441.—Crim Law 1094(3).

Holbrook v. State, TexCivApp–Eastland, 355 SW2d 235, ref nre.—Em Dom 106, 201, 203(1), 222(5).

Holbrook; U.S. v., CA5 (Tex), 571 F2d 335.—Arrest 63.5(6); Cust Dut 126(4).

Holcek; Conditt v., TexCivApp–Fort Worth, 203 SW2d 295, ref nre.—Evid 54, 318(2); War 155.

Holcemback v. Holcemback, TexCivApp–Eastland, 580 SW2d 877.—Divorce 252.3(5); Hus & W 264(5).

Holcemback; Holcemback v., TexCivApp–Eastland, 580 SW2d 877.—Divorce 252.3(5); Hus & W 264(5).

Holchak; Clark v., Tex, 254 SW2d 101, 152 Tex 26.—Mines 55(7).

Holchak v. Clark, TexCivApp–San Antonio, 284 SW2d 399, writ refused.—Mines 55(7); Ref of Inst 16.

Holchak; Clark v., TexCivApp–San Antonio, 247 SW2d 463, rev 254 SW2d 101, 152 Tex 26.—Mines 55(7).

Holcim (Texas) Ltd. Partnership v. Humboldt Wedag, Inc., TexApp–Waco, 211 SW3d 796, reh overr, and rule 537(f) motion gr.—Alt Disp Res 116, 117, 137, 141, 179, 182(1), 213(3), 363(1), 363(4); Commerce 80.5; Mand 60; States 18.15.

Holcomb, In re, Tex, 186 SW3d 553.—Elections 126(1), 158.

Holcomb v. Atlantic Refining Co., TexCivApp–Austin, 172 SW2d 523, writ refused wom.—Mines 58, 92.28, 92.29, 92.35, 92.40.

Holcomb v. Brown, TexCivApp–Tyler, 473 SW2d 595.—Judgm 713(2), 720.

Holcomb; Cate v., TexCivApp–Texarkana, 370 SW2d 422, ref nre.—Autos 181(2), 244(20), 244(37).

Holcomb; City of Dallas v., Tex, 383 SW2d 585.—Evid 560.

Holcomb; City of Dallas v., TexCivApp–Dallas, 381 SW2d 347, ref nre 383 SW2d 585.—App & E 928(4), 1170.1; Em Dom 75, 133, 201, 222(4), 238(6), 262(5); Evid 560.

Holcomb v. City of Dallas, TexCivApp–Texarkana, 315 SW2d 454, ref nre.—Em Dom 170, 222(1), 243(2); Tresp 30, 50, 52.

Holcomb v. City of Fort Worth, TexCivApp–Fort Worth, 175 SW2d 427, writ refused.—Courts 91(1); Em Dom 119(1).

Holcomb v. Copeland, TexCivApp–El Paso, 118 SW2d 932.—App & E 773(2).

Holcomb; Hamlett v., TexApp–Corpus Christi, 69 SW3d 816.—App & E 223, 863, 934(1); Brok 100, 102; Judgm 181(10), 183, 185(2); Torts 242; Ven & Pur 79, 186.

Holcomb v. Holcomb, TexApp–Dallas, 803 SW2d 411, writ den.—App & E 1003(5), 1003(6); Wills 152, 153, 155.1, 166(1), 166(2), 230.

Holcomb; Holcomb v., TexApp–Dallas, 803 SW2d 411, writ den.—App & E 1003(5), 1003(6); Wills 152, 153, 155.1, 166(1), 166(2), 230.

Holcomb; Jashinski v., WDTex, 482 FSupp2d 785.—Armed S 5(4), 22(3); Hab Corp 258, 523, 652.

Holcomb v. Newton, TexCivApp–Texarkana, 226 SW2d 670, writ refused.—Wills 105, 486, 489(5).

Holcomb v. Prudential Ins. Co. of America, CA5 (Tex), 673 F2d 102.—Insurance 2545(4).

Holcomb v. Randall's Food Markets, Inc., TexApp–Houston (1 Dist), 916 SW2d 512, writ den.—Judgm 185(2), 185(6); Neglig 202, 210, 213, 215, 220, 1162, 1692.

Holcomb; Schuhmacher Co. v., Tex, 177 SW2d 951, 142 Tex 332.—App & E 1062.2; Autos 201(0.5), 244(61); Trial 350.1, 350.5(3), 351.5(6), 352.4(1), 352.13, 365.1(1), 365.1(7).

Holcomb; Schuhmacher Co. v., TexCivApp–Austin, 174 SW2d 637, aff 177 SW2d 951, 142 Tex 332.—App & E 1062.2; Autos 227.5, 245(93); Trial 350.5(5), 351.5(6), 365.1(7).

Holcomb; Simplex Elec. Corp. v., TexApp–Austin, 949 SW2d 446, reh overr, and review den.—Statut 181(1), 190, 206, 219(1), 219(4); Work Comp 1304.

Holcomb v. State, TexCrimApp, 745 SW2d 903.—Crim Law 619, 1032(1), 1167(2); Ind & Inf 127, 128, 129(1), 130, 132(7), 137(1).

Holcomb v. State, TexCrimApp, 597 SW2d 373.—Crim Law 393(1), 402(2); Forg 28(1); Ind & Inf 72.

Holcomb v. State, TexCrimApp, 573 SW2d 814.—Burg 3, 19; Ind & Inf 60.

Holcomb v. State, TexCrimApp, 523 SW2d 661.—Crim Law 686(2), 1114.1(1), 1128(2).

Holcomb v. State, TexCrimApp, 484 SW2d 938, cert den 93 SCt 1404, 410 US 940, 35 LEd2d 606.—Arrest 63.1, 71.1(1); Const Law 266(3.2), 4680; Crim Law 364(1), 404.65, 693, 1169.1(8).

Holcomb v. State, TexCrimApp, 484 SW2d 935, cert den 93 SCt 1404, 410 US 940, 35 LEd2d 606.—Arrest 63.4(1), 71.1(2.1); Const Law 266(3.2), 4658(2); Courts 100(1); Crim Law 1077.3, 1169.1(8).

Holcomb v. State, TexCrimApp, 484 SW2d 929, cert den 93 SCt 1404, 410 US 940, 35 LEd2d 606.—Const Law 266(3.5), 4658(2); Courts 100(1); Crim Law 365(1), 394.5(2), 641.3(10), 1036.1(7), 1077.3, 1169.1(8); Searches 164; Sent & Pun 545; Witn 240(6).

Holcomb v. State, TexCrimApp, 356 SW2d 932, 172 Tex-Crim 392.—Crim Law 134(2); Rob 24.15(2); Searches 164.

Holcomb v. State, TexCrimApp, 356 SW2d 670, 172 Tex-Crim 294.—Rob 24.15(2); Searches 164.

Holcomb v. State, TexCrimApp, 356 SW2d 669, 172 Tex-Crim 292.—Rob 24.15(2); Searches 164.

Holcomb v. State, TexCrimApp, 242 SW2d 887.—Crim Law 1090.1(1).

Holcomb v. State, TexApp–Houston (1 Dist), 696 SW2d 190, petition for discretionary review gr, aff as reformed 745 SW2d 903.—Crim Law 29(1), 29(12), 620(7); Ind & Inf 125(2), 132(2), 196(7); Jury 29(6); Rape 1, 20, 24, 29, 51(1); Sod 5.

Holcomb v. State, TexApp–Austin, 146 SW3d 723.—Const Law 947, 2781, 2784, 2789, 2790, 2793, 2812, 2815; Sent & Pun 1802, 1811, 1812, 1817, 1977(2), 2057, 2094; Statut 181(1), 181(2), 188, 189.

Holcomb; U.S. v., CA5 (Tex), 797 F2d 1320.—Commerce 82.6; Consp 23.1, 40.1, 47(1), 47(2), 47(3.1); Crim Law 59(1), 622, 622.2(6), 622.2(7), 622.2(10); Prost 23, 28.

Holcombe; Beal v., CA5 (Tex), 193 F2d 384, cert den 74 SCt 783, 347 US 974, 98 LEd 1114.—Const Law 3041, 3250, 3267; Courts 101.

Holcombe; Beal v., SDTex, 103 FSupp 218, rev 193 F2d 384, cert den 74 SCt 783, 347 US 974, 98 LEd 1114.—Civil R 1054.

Holcombe v. City of Houston, TexCivApp–Houston, 351 SW2d 69.—App & E 564(3); Em Dom 150, 205, 247(1), 247(2), 262(1); Evid 142(1), 142(2), 142(3); Trial 412.

Holcombe v. Grota, Tex, 102 SW2d 1041, 129 Tex 100, 110 ALR 234.—Clerks of C 6; Courts 55; Mand 76, 168(2); Mun Corp 126, 180(3); Offic 40.

Holcombe; Grota v., TexCivApp–Galveston, 97 SW2d 301, rev 102 SW2d 1041, 129 Tex 100, 110 ALR 234.—App & E 1040(2); Courts 55; Mand 76; Mun Corp 215; Plead 214(1).

Holcombe; Kavanagh v., TexCivApp–Houston, 312 SW2d 399, ref nre.—Admin Law 749, 750; App & E 554(1), 907(3); Mun Corp 180(2).

Holcombe v. Levy, TexCivApp–Galveston, 301 SW2d 507, ref nre.—Judges 3; Mun Corp 79, 125, 158, 217.3(1); Statut 181(1), 184, 206.

Holcombe; Ryan v., TexCivApp–Texarkana, 170 SW2d 838.—Plead 205(1), 228.14; Spec Perf 114(2).

Holcombe; State v., TexCrimApp, 187 SW3d 496, cert den 127 SCt 176, 166 LEd2d 41.—Const Law 1524, 3905, 4506, 4509(8); Crim Law 13.1(1); Mun Corp 594(2); Statut 188.

Holcombe v. State, TexCrimApp, 448 SW2d 493.—Burg 41(1); Sent & Pun 1161.

Holcombe v. State, TexCrimApp, 424 SW2d 635.—Crim Law 320, 633(2); Sent & Pun 313, 1292, 1381(3).

Holcombe v. State, TexCrimApp, 375 SW2d 914.—Crim Law 1086.13.

Holcombe; State v., TexApp–Fort Worth, 145 SW3d 246, reh overr, and petition for discretionary review gr, aff 187 SW3d 496, cert den 127 SCt 176, 166 LEd2d 41.—Const Law 859, 1066, 1133, 1140, 1141, 1164, 1504, 1505, 1512, 1840; Crim Law 13.1(1), 1139, 1153(1), 1158(4); Mun Corp 594(2).

Holcroft v. Wheatley, TexCivApp–Amarillo, 112 SW2d 298, dism.—Lim of Act 143(6), 167(1).

Holdaway v. State, TexCrimApp, 505 SW2d 262.—Controlled Subs 33; Crim Law 507(4), 739.1(2).

Holdbrook v. California Federal Bank, NDTex, 905 FSupp 367.—Antitrust 132; Fed Civ Proc 2544; Fed Cts 419, 421; Fraud 31; Labor & Emp 407, 413, 421; States 18.15, 18.51.

Holdeman v. Masters, Mates and Pilots Pension Plan, SDTex, 749 FSupp 155.—Fed Civ Proc 2470.1, 2543, 2544, 2546; Labor & Emp 542.

Holden, Ex parte, Tex, 190 SW2d 485, 144 Tex 295.—Const Law 4494.

Holden, Ex parte, TexApp–Houston (1 Dist), 774 SW2d 957.—Bail 51, 52.

Holden, Ex parte, TexApp–Dallas, 719 SW2d 678.—Extrad 34, 39.

Holden v. Boynton, TexCivApp–San Antonio, 170 SW2d 323, writ refused wom.—Adv Poss 22, 31; Land & Ten 66(2).

Holden v. Capri Lighting, Inc., TexApp–Amarillo, 960 SW2d 831.—App & E 169, 970(1); Corp 445.1; Evid 35, 51, 80(1).

Holden v. City of Boerne, TexCivApp–San Antonio, 252 SW2d 474, ref nre.—Mun Corp 89, 111(1), 122.1(4), 508(2).

Holden; City of Houston v., TexCivApp–Eastland, 336 SW2d 193, ref nre.—Autos 230, 245(50.1), 245(67.1); Damag 38, 134(3), 163(1), 208(1); Mun Corp 741.15.

Holden; Dahlberg v., Tex, 238 SW2d 699, 150 Tex 179.—App & E 1177(1), 1177(7); Contracts 9(1), 153; Deeds 38(1), 38(6), 95, 120; Propty 9; Ten in C 55(1), 55(6); Tresp to T T 41(1).

Holden v. Dahlberg, TexCivApp–San Antonio, 228 SW2d 889, aff 238 SW2d 699, 150 Tex 179.—Deeds 38(6); Mtg 131; Ten in C 8; Tresp to T T 13, 38(1).

Holden v. Gibbons, TexCivApp–Austin, 101 SW2d 837, writ dism.—App & E 201(2), 1046.5, 1050.1(2), 1056.4, 1062.2; Home 213, 214; Trial 350.1, 350.3(2.1), 351.5(1), 351.5(3), 352.5(3).

Holden; Keller Industries, Inc. v., CA5 (Tex), 514 F2d 1269.—Accord 26(3); Contracts 1; Fed Civ Proc 1941.

Holden; Partin v., TexApp–Austin, 663 SW2d 883.—Partit 1, 46.1, 113.

Holden v. Phillips, TexCivApp–Texarkana, 132 SW2d 419.—Elections 271, 300; Schools 38.

Holden v. State, TexCrimApp, 201 SW3d 761, reh den.—Crim Law 959, 1156(1).

Holden v. State, TexCrimApp, 641 SW2d 919.—Costs 302.1(4); Rob 27(1).

Holden v. State, TexApp–Waco, 205 SW3d 587.—Crim Law 1139, 1158(4); Searches 28, 162.

Holden v. State, TexApp–Houston (14 Dist), 628 SW2d 166, petition for discretionary review gr, and review dism as improvidently gr.—Crim Law 1170.5(1); Witn 337(4), 337(23), 345(1), 345(7), 349.

Holden v. Weidenfeller, TexApp–San Antonio, 929 SW2d 124, reh overr, and writ den.—App & E 843(1), 931(1), 989, 1008.1(2), 1010.1(3), 1011.1(7); Ease 15.1, 16, 36(1); Estop 83(1), 98(1), 118; Evid 506, 508.

Holden Business Forms Co. v. Columbia Medical Center of Arlington Subsidiary, L.P., TexApp–Fort Worth, 83 SW3d 274.—App & E 863, 1175(1); Insurance 3504; Judgm 185(2), 185(6).

Holden Corp. v. Verheul, TexApp–Corpus Christi, 769 SW2d 629. See Wayne C. Holden Corp. v. Verheul.

Holder, Ex parte, TexCrimApp, 227 SW2d 807, 154 TexCrim 255, cert den Holder v. State of Tex, 71 SCt 22, 340 US 837, 95 LEd 614.—Crim Law 641.7(1); Hab Corp 709.

Holder, In re, BkrtcySDTex, 356 BR 184.—Autos 144.1(1), 144.1(4); Bankr 2402(2.1), 2461, 3377.

Holder v. Bennett, BkrtcyNDTex, 126 BR 869. See Bennett, In re.

Holder v. Central Freight Lines, Inc., TexCivApp–Waco, 429 SW2d 191.—App & E 1060.1(1); Trial 133.6(4).

Holder v. Gerant Industries, Inc., BkrtcyNDTex, 165 BR 22. See Omni Video, Inc., In re.

Holder v. Holder, TexApp–El Paso, 808 SW2d 197.—App & E 113(5), 346.2; Courts 30; Divorce 177, 283.

Holder; Holder v., TexApp–El Paso, 808 SW2d 197.—App & E 113(5), 346.2; Courts 30; Divorce 177, 283.

Holder v. Holder, TexCivApp–Texarkana, 582 SW2d 598.—App & E 374(4), 1177(9).

Holder; Holder v., TexCivApp–Texarkana, 582 SW2d 598.—App & E 374(4), 1177(9).

Holder v. Holder, TexCivApp–Tyler, 528 SW2d 113.—Child S 383, 391, 537, 555; Contempt 66(1); Judgm 91.

Holder; Holder v., TexCivApp–Tyler, 528 SW2d 113.—Child S 383, 391, 537, 555; Contempt 66(1); Judgm 91.

Holder; Houston v., CA5 (Tex), 60 F3d 230. See Omni Video, Inc., Matter of.

Holder; Lavigne v., TexApp–Fort Worth, 186 SW3d 625. —Contracts 152; Ease 1; Inj 135, 138.1, 138.6, 138.18; Mtg 274, 335, 338.

Holder; McClain v., TexCivApp–Galveston, 279 SW2d 105, ref nre.—Des & Dist 5, 52(1); Evid 461(1); Hus & W 6(1), 14.1, 14.4, 68, 79, 110, 149(1); Joint Ten 1; Wills 6.

Holder v. Martin, TexCivApp–Beaumont, 131 SW2d 165. —App & E 273(6), 882(1), 882(16); Damag 130.1, 216(1), 221(1); Trial 115(1), 129; Witn 347.

Holder; Mellon Mortg. Co. v., Tex, 5 SW3d 654, reh overr.—Autos 370; Neglig 1162.

Holder v. Mellon Mortg. Co., TexApp–Houston (14 Dist), 954 SW2d 786, reh overr, and review gr, rev 5 SW3d 654, reh overr.—App & E 232(0.5), 1056.1(3); Autos 370; Evid 272, 333(1), 506; Judgm 181(15.1), 181(33), 185.1(4), 185.3(21); Mun Corp 120, 723, 747(3); Neglig 259, 1019, 1025, 1040(3), 1045(2), 1045(3), 1162; Statut 176, 212.3, 219(2).

Holder; Nicholas v., TexCivApp–San Antonio, 244 SW2d 313, ref nre.—Breach of M P 7, 23; Divorce 320; Frds St of 44(1); Statut 184, 206.

Holder v. Porter, TexApp–Waco, 845 SW2d 442.—Judgm 181(27); Offic 114.

Holder v. Prudential Ins. Co. of America, CA5 (Tex), 951 F2d 89.—Insurance 2485; Labor & Emp 717.

Holder v. Scott, TexCivApp–Texarkana, 396 SW2d 906, ref nre.—App & E 662(4); Divorce 167, 375, 376; Evid 80(1); Judgm 27, 455, 486(1); Partit 62.

Holder; Smith v., TexApp–El Paso, 756 SW2d 9.—Contempt 66(1).

Holder v. State, TexCrimApp, 643 SW2d 718.—Crim Law 720(7.1), 790; Infants 13; Rape 1; Sent & Pun 1504.

Holder v. State, TexCrimApp, 618 SW2d 80.—Crim Law 1023(3), 1134(8).

Holder v. State, TexCrimApp, 571 SW2d 885.—Sent & Pun 2021.

Holder v. State, TexCrimApp, 469 SW2d 184.—Crim Law 1077.1(2).

Holder v. State, TexCrimApp, 406 SW2d 436.—Mental H 432, 434; Sent & Pun 2004, 2025.

Holder v. State, TexCrimApp, 354 SW2d 153, 172 TexCrim 153.—Autos 355(6); Crim Law 564(1).

Holder v. State, TexCrimApp, 143 SW2d 613, 140 TexCrim 55.—Crim Law 720(8), 855(7), 956(12), 956(13), 1133, 1166.18, 1169.11; Witn 277(2.1).

Holder v. State, TexApp–Austin, 837 SW2d 802, petition for discretionary review refused.—Assault 56; Const Law 4658(3), 4664(2), 4690; Crim Law 339.8(5), 393(3), 404.11, 404.65, 488, 641.3(10), 814(1); Ind & Inf 159(2); Rob 24.15(2); Witn 414(2).

Holder; Texas Power & Light Co. v., TexCivApp–Tyler, 385 SW2d 873, ref nre 393 SW2d 821.—App & E 237(1), 1001(1), 1170.7, 1170.9(3); Electricity 1, 9(1), 14(1), 15(2), 16(1), 16(2), 16(4), 16(5), 16(7), 17, 19(5), 19(7), 19(12), 19(13); Evid 5(2), 219.25(1); Neglig 421, 423, 431, 1037(2), 1037(6), 1037(7), 1045(2), 1694, 1717; Plead 236(3), 236(6); Statut 223.4; Trial 352.10.

Holder; Thomas v., TexApp–Tyler, 836 SW2d 351.—App & E 962; Assault 2; Costs 128; Prisons 10.

Holder; U.S. v., CA5 (Tex), 150 FedAppx 347, cert den 126 SCt 1398, 546 US 1199, 164 LEd2d 100.—Crim Law 1035(1).

Holder; U.S. v., CA5 (Tex), 109 FedAppx 673, cert gr, vac 125 SCt 1093, 543 US 1115, 160 LEd2d 1061, on remand 150 FedAppx 347, cert den 126 SCt 1398, 546 US 1199, 164 LEd2d 100.—Crim Law 662.3; Sent & Pun 726(3).

Holder v. U.S., EDTex, 285 FSupp 380.—Sent & Pun 1800, 1802, 1812, 2001, 2014, 2026.

Holder v. Wilson, BkrtcyNDTex, 49 BR 19. See Wilson, In re.

Holder v. Wood, Tex, 714 SW2d 318.—Const Law 191; Sales 429.

Holder-McDonald v. Chicago Title Ins. Co., TexApp–Dallas, 188 SW3d 244, reh overr, and review den.—App & E 754(1), 893(1), 930(3); Dep & Escr 13; Evid 571(7), 574; Fraud 58(1), 62; Trial 358.

Holderman v. Hidalgo County Water Control and Improvement Dist. No. 12, CCA5 (Tex), 142 F2d 792.—Mun Corp 942, 948(1); Waters 230(6).

Holding v. State, TexCrimApp, 460 SW2d 133.—Autos 355(13); Crim Law 437, 475.

Holditch v. Standard Acc. Ins. Co., CA5 (Tex), 208 F2d 721.—Work Comp 654, 669.

Holdman v. State, TexCrimApp, 399 SW2d 361.—Crim Law 1005, 1092.1, 1092.12; Homic 1134.

Holdridge v. State, TexCrimApp, 707 SW2d 18.—Crim Law 564(1), 564(2), 564(3), 1144.6.

Holdridge v. State, TexCrimApp, 158 SW2d 72, 143 TexCrim 165.—Crim Law 1097(4).

Holdridge v. State, TexApp–Waco, 684 SW2d 766, petition for discretionary review gr, aff 707 SW2d 18.—Crim Law 577.16(8), 1117.

Holdridge v. Thornburgh, NDTex, 804 FSupp 876.—Civil R 1207, 1522.

Holdsworth v. Guthrie Trust, TexApp–San Antonio, 712 SW2d 177, ref nre.—Adv Poss 4, 57, 117; App & E 989, 1010.1(9); Judgm 251(1).

Hole; Texas A & M University v., TexApp–Waco, 194 SW3d 591, reh overr, and review den.—Action 6; Colleges 9.30(7); Const Law 2601; Decl Judgm 66, 272.

Holeman v. Director, Federal Emergency Management Agency, NDTex, 699 FSupp 98.—Insurance 3179; U S 78(10).

Holeman v. Elliott, SDTex, 732 FSupp 726, aff 927 F2d 601, cert den 112 SCt 59, 502 US 812, 116 LEd2d 35.—Civil R 1376(8); Courts 509; Fed Cts 48; Judgm 828.5(1).

Holeman v. Greyhound Corp., TexCivApp–Houston, 396 SW2d 507, ref nre.—App & E 866(3), 927(1), 989; Carr 280(1), 302(1), 316(1.5), 387; Neglig 259, 1614; Trial 350.5(2), 350.6(4).

Holeman v. Landmark Chevrolet Corp., TexApp–Houston (14 Dist), 989 SW2d 395, review den, and reh of petition for review overr.—Antitrust 141, 150, 363, 367; App & E 969, 1001(1), 1003(6), 1056.1(1), 1056.1(4.1), 1064.1(1), 1182; Evid 129(1), 134; Judgm 199(3.10); Trial 182, 295(1).

Holeman v. National Business Institute, Inc., TexApp–Houston (14 Dist), 94 SW3d 91, reh overr, and review den, and reh of petition for review den.—App & E 171(1), 172(1), 949; Contracts 1, 101(1), 116(1), 127(4), 129(1), 141(1), 206; Labor & Emp 34(1), 40(1).

Holford, Matter of, CA5 (Tex), 896 F2d 176.—Bankr 2399, 2671.

Holford v. Powers, CA5 (Tex), 896 F2d 176. See Holford, Matter of.

Holford v. State, TexApp–Houston (1 Dist), 177 SW3d 454, petition for discretionary review refused.—Crim Law 338(7), 438(1), 438(5.1), 438(6), 438(7), 798(0.5), 814(1), 872.5, 881(1), 1038.1(3.1), 1134(2), 1134(3), 1153(1), 1172.1(1); Homic 1421.

Holgin v. State, TexCrimApp, 480 SW2d 405.—Crim Law 1130(2), 1134(3), 1170.5(6); Witn 337(22), 345(2).

Holgin v. Texas Employers Ins. Ass'n, TexApp–Fort Worth, 790 SW2d 97, writ den.—Admin Law 793; New Tr 102(5); Work Comp 1375, 1492, 1717, 1723, 1794, 1795, 1800, 1911, 1939.6.

Holguin; State v., TexCrimApp, 861 SW2d 919.—Double J 135, 146.

Holguin v. Twin Cities Services, Inc., TexApp–El Paso, 750 SW2d 817.—Contracts 10(3).

Holguin; Villalobos v., Tex, 208 SW2d 871, 146 Tex 474. —Autos 71, 73, 78, 104, 107(2); Inj 204, 208; Mun Corp 23.

Holguin v. Villalobos, TexCivApp–El Paso, 212 SW2d 498, aff in part, rev in part 208 SW2d 871, 146 Tex 474.—App & E 1172(1); Autos 78, 107(2); Mun Corp 23.

Holguin v. Ysleta Del Sur Pueblo, TexApp–El Paso, 954 SW2d 843, reh overr, and review den.—App & E 934(1); Const Law 2442; Indians 27(1), 27(6), 32(2), 32(4.1), 32(5), 32(9); Int Liq 5.1, 283; Judgm 186.

Holguin Enterprises v. Twin Cities Services, Inc., TexApp–El Paso, 750 SW2d 817. See Holguin v. Twin Cities Services, Inc.

Holick v. Smith, Tex, 685 SW2d 18.—Child C 3; Const Law 4393; Infants 132, 157, 178, 232, 248.1.

Holiday v. Barnhart, SDTex, 460 FSupp2d 790.—Social S 140.21, 140.30, 142.5, 142.10, 143.60, 143.65, 143.80, 147, 147.5, 148.15.

Holiday; Pierce v., TexApp–Texarkana, 155 SW3d 676.—App & E 863, 934(1); Judgm 178, 181(2), 181(6), 181(21), 183, 185(6); Labor & Emp 2859; Neglig 1001, 1037(4); Work Comp 2129, 2133.

Holiday v. Red Ball Motor Freight, Inc., SDTex, 399 FSupp 81.—Civil R 1390, 1517; Labor & Emp 1210, 1219(5).

Holiday v. State, TexApp–Houston (1 Dist), 14 SW3d 784, petition for discretionary review refused, cert den 121 SCt 1491, 532 US 960, 149 LEd2d 377.—Crim Law 59(3), 59(5), 417(15), 662.1, 662.8, 795(2.10), 795(2.50), 1035(5), 1134(2); Homic 908, 1141.

Holiday v. State, TexApp–Houston (1 Dist), 983 SW2d 326, reh overr, and petition for discretionary review refused.—Crim Law 1023(3), 1134(8).

Holiday Hills Retirement and Nursing Center, Inc.; Yeldell v., Tex, 701 SW2d 243.—Pretrial Proc 304, 312; Work Comp 652, 654.

Holiday Hills Retirement and Nursing Center, Inc. v. Yeldell, TexApp–Fort Worth, 686 SW2d 770, writ gr, rev 701 SW2d 243.—Labor & Emp 2797, 3005; Pretrial Proc 304, 312.

Holiday Hill Stone Products, Inc. v. Peek, TexCivApp–San Antonio, 387 SW2d 731.—Contracts 117(0.5), 117(2), 118, 316(1); Inj 199.

Holiday Hospitality Franchising, Inc.; Patel v., NDTex, 172 FSupp2d 821.—Abate & R 19; Antitrust 286, 357, 367; Estop 53, 85, 107; Fed Civ Proc 636.

Holiday Inn; Weber v., EDTex, 42 FSupp2d 693.—Civil R 1118, 1530, 1557; Fed Civ Proc 2734; U S Mag 27, 31.

Holiday Inn, Inc.; Purvis v., TexCivApp–Eastland, 588 SW2d 794, rev 595 SW2d 103.—Labor & Emp 3096(8), 3100(2).

Holiday Inn (Lubbock Plaza); Tarbox v., BkrtcyNDTex, 183 BR 122. See Ferguson, In re.

Holiday Inns, Inc. v. Airport Holiday Corp., NDTex, 493 FSupp 1025, aff 683 F2d 931.—Trademarks 1656(3), 1658, 1665(1).

Holiday Inns, Inc. v. Alberding, CA5 (Tex), 683 F2d 931.—Fed Cts 612.1; Stip 14(10); Trademarks 1653, 1658, 1665(1).

Holiday Inns, Inc.; Cantu v., TexApp–Corpus Christi, 910 SW2d 113, reh overr, and writ den.—Judgm 185.3(1); Plead 298, 301(1), 301(3), 302, 303.

Holiday Inns, Inc.; Garrity v., TexApp–Amarillo, 664 SW2d 854, ref nre.—App & E 621(1), 624, 627.2, 628(2).

Holiday Inns, Inc.; Michaels v., SDTex, 716 FSupp 294.—Action 6.

Holiday Inns, Inc.; Poe v., EDTex, 800 FSupp 1439.—Const Law 190; Fed Civ Proc 755, 2481, 2515, 2544; Int Liq 283; Lim of Act 70(1), 180(2).

Holiday Inns, Inc.; Pope v., CA5 (Tex), 464 F2d 1303.—Fed Civ Proc 2608.1; Inn 10.7, 10.15; Neglig 1288.

Holiday Inns, Inc. v. State, TexApp–Amarillo, 931 SW2d 614, reh overr, and writ den.—App & E 1024.3, 1069.1; Em Dom 106, 142, 201, 202(1), 221, 255, 262(5); Evid 142(3), 359(6), 543(3), 555.6(3); Jury 33(5.15); Trial 125(1).

Holiday Inns of America; Griffin v., Tex, 496 SW2d 535.—Judgm 585(4), 587, 588, 592, 713(2), 720.

Holiday Inns of America; Griffin v., TexCivApp–Austin, 480 SW2d 506, writ gr, aff 496 SW2d 535.—Judgm 588, 634, 713(2).

Holiday Inns of America; Griffin v., TexCivApp–Austin, 452 SW2d 517.—Contracts 295(1), 303(5), 322(4); Damag 123, 159(6).

Holiday Inns of America, Inc.; Chief Freight Lines Co. v., TexCivApp–Dallas, 469 SW2d 413.—App & E 1177(6); Carr 114, 140; Trial 401.

Holiday Inn–Trends; Broadcast Music, Inc. v., EDTex, 872 FSupp 348. See Broadcast Music, Inc. v. Penny.

Holiday Lincoln Mercury, Inc.; Brownlee v., TexApp–Fort Worth, 675 SW2d 817.—Autos 43, 244(26); Insurance 2684, 3145.

Holiday Lodge Nursing Home, Inc. v. Huffman, TexCivApp–Texarkana, 430 SW2d 826.—App & E 846(5), 1010.1(2); Labor & Emp 2840, 2923; Plead 111.42(7).

Holiday Wines & Spirits, Inc.; Pan American Nat. Bank v., TexCivApp–Hous (1 Dist), 580 SW2d 7, ref nre.—App & E 547(2), 846(5); Interest 39(2.20).

Holien v. Briggs, TexCivApp–Fort Worth, 344 SW2d 891.—Child C 554, 637, 921(1).

Holifield v. Coronado Bldg., Inc., TexCivApp–Hous (14 Dist), 594 SW2d 214.—Antitrust 141; Contracts 205.35(2), 312(5); Lim of Act 24(1), 24(6).

Holifield v. Cosden Petroleum Corp., TexCivApp–El Paso, 170 SW2d 500.—App & E 79(2).

Holifield; Lone Star Gas Co. v., TexCivApp–Fort Worth, 150 SW2d 282.—App & E 1177(7); Damag 111, 159(8), 163(4), 221(2.1); Evid 593; Gas 18, 20(2), 20(3); Judgm 18(1); Plead 245(4).

Holifield v. National Cylinder Gas Division of Chemetron Corp., TexCivApp–Waco, 542 SW2d 218, ref nre.—Courts 100(1); Prod Liab 71.5; Work Comp 2216.

Holifield v. State, TexCrimApp, 599 SW2d 836.—Crim Law 686(1), 687(1); Homic 1473.

Holifield v. State, TexCrimApp, 538 SW2d 123.—Crim Law 933; Judges 47(1), 51(1).

Holifield v. State, TexApp–Beaumont, 856 SW2d 575, petition for discretionary review refused.—Crim Law 396(1), 396(2), 1137(1), 1137(5); Sent & Pun 308.

Holifield v. State, TexApp–Beaumont, 827 SW2d 623, petition for discretionary review gr, vac 843 SW2d 572, on remand 856 SW2d 575, petition for discretionary review refused.—Crim Law 695(5), 698(1); Sent & Pun 313.

Holifield; Verschoyle v., TexComApp, 123 SW2d 878, 132 Tex 516.—App & E 361(2); Evid 318(2), 343(7); High 113(4); Judgm 252(5); Mech Liens 51; Plead 48, 387; Subrog 23(8), 26.

Holifield; Verschoyle v., TexCivApp–Austin, 90 SW2d 907, mod 123 SW2d 878, 132 Tex 516.—App & E 544(1), 931(6); Bills & N 534; High 113(1), 113(4); Princ & A 158; Princ & S 55; Subrog 26.

Holik; Holmes v., TexCivApp–Galveston, 238 SW2d 260, dism.—Brok 7, 46, 55(3).

Holinone, Inc. v. International Hole-In-One Club, Inc., CA5 (Tex), 466 F2d 504.—Fed Cts 815; Trademarks 1704(2), 1704(3).

Holinone, Inc. v. International Hole-In-One Club, Inc., SDTex, 341 FSupp 1241, decision supplemented 1972 WL 19401, aff 466 F2d 504.—Inj 132, 147; Trademarks 1033, 1034, 1360, 1704(8), 1704(9).

Holitzke v. Holitzke, TexCivApp–Tyler, 476 SW2d 360, dism.—App & E 846(5); Child C 7, 76, 921(1).

Holitzke; Holitzke v., TexCivApp–Tyler, 476 SW2d 360, dism.—App & E 846(5); Child C 7, 76, 921(1).

Holk v. Biard, TexApp–Texarkana, 920 SW2d 803, reh overr, and reh of motion for mandamus overr.—Alt Disp Res 114, 134(3), 199, 203, 342, 354, 357, 362(3), 363(6), 363(8), 379; Judgm 851; Mand 4(4).

HOLK

Holk v. USA Managed Care Organization, Inc., TexApp–Austin, 149 SW3d 769.—App & E 846(5), 893(1); Appear 2; Const Law 3964, 3965(3), 3965(5); Corp 665(0.5); Courts 12(2.5), 12(2.10), 12(2.15), 35, 37(3), 39; Proc 157.

Holladay; Burlington Industries v., TexCivApp–Amarillo, 372 SW2d 730.—Plead 111.42(2), 111.42(4), 111.42(8).

Holladay v. CW & A, Inc., TexApp–Corpus Christi, 60 SW3d 243, reh overr, and review den.—App & E 1010.1(1), 1010.2; Judgm 948(1); Mech Liens 115(1); Plead 78, 427.

Holladay v. Intercontinental Industries, Inc., TexCivApp–Austin, 476 SW2d 779, ref nre.—Const Law 3869, 4295, 4475; Sec Reg 244, 270.

Holladay v. Perez De Rios, TexCivApp–San Antonio, 562 SW2d 16.—App & E 846(5); Plead 111.12, 111.42(8).

Holladay v. State, TexCrimApp, 805 SW2d 464.—Arrest 63.5(4), 63.5(5), 63.5(7).

Holladay v. State, TexCrimApp, 709 SW2d 194.—Crim Law 508(9), 510, 511.2, 780(4).

Holladay v. State, TexCrimApp, 95 SW2d 119, 130 TexCrim 591.—Crim Law 644, 665(2), 666.5, 742(1), 1119(1), 1120(3), 1120(4); Incest 14; Witn 340(3), 374(1).

Holladay v. State, TexCrimApp, 95 SW2d 118, 130 TexCrim 588.—Crim Law 382, 444, 644, 666.5; Witn 373, 374(1).

Holladay v. State, TexApp–Houston (1 Dist), 682 SW2d 434, petition for discretionary review gr, rev 709 SW2d 194.—Crim Law 507(1), 780(2), 780(3), 1043(1).

Holladay v. State, TexApp–Houston (14 Dist), 755 SW2d 501, petition for discretionary review gr, aff 805 SW2d 464.—Arrest 63.5(4), 63.5(5), 63.5(7); Crim Law 899, 1036.1(1).

Hollan v. Hollan, TexCivApp–Galveston, 187 SW2d 423.—Divorce 124.3, 179, 184(12); Hus & W 3(1).

Hollan; Hollan v., TexCivApp–Galveston, 187 SW2d 423.—Divorce 124.3, 179, 184(12); Hus & W 3(1).

Hollan v. State, TexCivApp–Fort Worth, 308 SW2d 122, ref nre.—App & E 877(2); Ease 8(1), 8(4), 14(1), 37, 38; Nav Wat 37(4), 37(8), 39(3); Statut 181(1), 184; Tresp to T T 16, 38(1), 47(3).

Holland, Ex parte, Tex, 790 SW2d 568.—Child S 444.

Holland, Ex parte, TexCrimApp, 183 SW2d 975, 147 TexCrim 619.—Hab Corp 274.

Holland, Ex parte, TexApp–Dallas, 807 SW2d 827, writ dism woj.—Child S 470, 489; Judges 16(0.5), 31, 51(2), 51(4).

Holland, In re, BkrtcyNDTex, 48 BR 874.—Bankr 3348.15, 3349, 3350(2), 3350(4).

Holland, In re, BkrtcyWDTex, 85 BR 735.—Bankr 2129, 2131, 3539.1.

Holland; American Pub. Co. v., TexCivApp–Austin, 89 SW2d 286.—Plead 111.24, 111.42(4).

Holland v. Bailey, TexComApp, 127 SW2d 446, 133 Tex 150.—App & E 781(4).

Holland; Barfield v., TexApp–Tyler, 844 SW2d 759, reh den, and writ den.—Costs 194.25, 194.40; Estop 70(1); Lim of Act 44(2), 95(8); Mines 49, 55(1); Partit 12(1); Ten in C 33, 44, 45; Ven & Pur 239(1).

Holland; Bavarian Autohaus, Inc. v., TexCivApp–Hous (1 Dist), 570 SW2d 110.—Antitrust 195, 389(2); App & E 865; Corp 507(13); Costs 207; Damag 6; Evid 113(16), 474(16), 543(1); Judgm 951(1); Proc 133, 145, 164(4).

Holland; Bethurum v., TexApp–Amarillo, 771 SW2d 719.—App & E 80(6), 797(1), 934(1), 934(2); Judgm 186.

Holland v. Beto, SDTex, 309 FSupp 784.—Civil R 1311, 1315; Fed Civ Proc 656; Prisons 4(9).

Holland; Bussan v., TexCivApp–Fort Worth, 235 SW2d 657.—Mand 26, 28, 51.

Holland; Bute v., TexCivApp–El Paso, 155 SW2d 69, writ refused wom.—Contracts 278(1), 333(6); Mines 74(5), 74(9.1); Trial 350.3(2.1), 352.4(3).

Holland; City of Fort Worth v., TexApp–Fort Worth, 748 SW2d 112, writ den.—App & E 204(1), 204(4); Neglig 1613, 1614, 1621; Waters 209.

Holland v. City of Houston, SDTex, 41 FSupp2d 678, appeal dism 237 F3d 632.—Arrest 68(2); Autos 187(2), 201(1.1); Civil R 1031, 1088(2), 1304, 1324, 1330(1), 1335, 1343, 1345, 1351(1), 1351(4), 1352(1), 1352(4), 1354, 1376(1), 1376(2), 1394, 1397; Compromise 17(2); Fed Civ Proc 2491.5, 2515; Judgm 702; Mun Corp 188, 723, 723.5, 728, 739(2), 744, 745, 747(3), 847, 854; Offic 114, 116.

Holland v. Collins, CA5 (Tex), 962 F2d 417, cert den 113 SCt 3043, 509 US 925, 125 LEd2d 729.—Sent & Pun 1780(3), 1789(3).

Holland v. Collins, TexCivApp–Amarillo, 457 SW2d 177, ref nre.—Autos 206, 244(2.1), 244(40), 244(41.1), 244(58), 245(2.1); Neglig 504, 1560.

Holland v. Commonwealth Finance Corp., TexCivApp–Texarkana, 118 SW2d 364.—App & E 1175(1); Estop 76; Evid 584(1); Stip 14(10); Tresp to T T 41(1); Trial 35.

Holland v. De Leon, TexCivApp–San Antonio, 118 SW2d 489, writ refused.—Autos 227.5, 244(12), 245(15), 247; Neglig 440(1), 1741.

Holland; Eitel v., CA5 (Tex), 798 F2d 815, reh den 801 F2d 398.—Fed Cts 48.

Holland; Eitel v., CA5 (Tex), 787 F2d 995, on reh 798 F2d 815, reh den 801 F2d 398.—Civil R 1376(8); Consp 7.5(1), 18; Const Law 3954; Fed Cts 41, 48, 727; Judges 36.

Holland; Ellender v., TexCivApp–Beaumont, 221 SW2d 990, ref nre.—Adv Poss 14, 34, 38, 103; Propty 7; Tresp to T T 41(1).

Holland; Employers Reinsurance Corp. v., Tex, 347 SW2d 605, 162 Tex 394.—Damag 221(7); Work Comp 803, 858.

Holland; Fate v., TexCivApp–El Paso, 115 SW2d 1032, writ dism.—Lim of Act 148(2), 164.

Holland v. Fidelity & Deposit Co. of Maryland, TexApp–Corpus Christi, 623 SW2d 469.—App & E 181, 226(2); Indem 42; Lim of Act 56(3).

Holland v. First Nat. Bank in Dallas, TexCivApp–Dallas, 597 SW2d 406, dism.—App & E 1041(4); Bills & N 139(3); Guar 35, 36(3), 53(1), 86, 87, 89; Lim of Act 46(10), 48(1); Plead 233, 261, 280; Pretrial Proc 713, 723.1.

Holland v. Fleming, TexApp–Houston (1 Dist), 728 SW2d 820, ref nre.—Land & Ten 86(1), 92(1); Ven & Pur 18(1).

Holland v. Florey, TexCivApp–Texarkana, 151 SW2d 926.—Princ & S 200(7).

Holland v. Foley Bros. Dry Goods Co., TexCivApp–Texarkana, 324 SW2d 430, writ refused.—App & E 387(3), 395; New Tr 155.

Holland v. GEXA Corp., CA5 (Tex), 161 FedAppx 364.—Fed Cts 18; Sec Reg 25.56, 25.62(3), 60.37.

Holland v. Gibbs, TexApp–Austin, 388 SW2d 295, ref nre.—App & E 854(2), 931(1); Can of Inst 34(1); Deeds 211(3); Des & Dist 83; Lim of Act 39(7), 100(11).

Holland; Harris v., TexApp–Texarkana, 867 SW2d 86.—App & E 161; Divorce 252.1, 252.3(1), 252.4, 281, 286(5); Hus & W 265.

Holland v. Harris County, TexComApp, 102 SW2d 196, 129 Tex 118.—Judges 22(8).

Holland v. Harris County, TexCivApp–Galveston, 103 SW2d 1067, certified question answered 102 SW2d 196, 129 Tex 118.—Judges 22(8); Statut 223.2(7).

Holland v. Hayden, TexApp–Houston (14 Dist), 901 SW2d 763, reh overr, and writ den.—App & E 213, 232(0.5), 237(5), 238(2), 241, 294(1), 302(1), 302(6), 930(3); Atty & C 129(2); Damag 15, 190, 221(8).

Holland; Henderson v., TexCivApp–Austin, 348 SW2d 396.—Venue 8.5(8).

Holland v. Holland, BkrtcyNDTex, 48 BR 874. See Holland, In re.

Holland; Holland v., BkrtcyNDTex, 48 BR 874. See Holland, In re.

Holland v. Kem Mfg. Corp., TexCivApp–Hous (14 Dist), 550 SW2d 125.—App & E 773(2).

Holland; Kennedy v., TexCivApp–Galveston, 267 SW2d 283.—Ex & Ad 219.9.

Holland; King v., TexApp–Corpus Christi, 884 SW2d 231, reh overr, and writ den.—App & E 852, 863, 934(1), 962; Judgm 181(7), 185(2), 185.1(8), 190; Lim of Act 95(1), 199(1); Pretrial Proc 583, 587, 588, 693.1.

Holland v. Kiper, TexApp–Tyler, 696 SW2d 588, ref nre. —App & E 187(3), 218.2(1), 1062.1, 1062.2; Mines 55(5); Trial 350.3(2.1), 351.5(1), 352.1(3).

Holland v. Lansdowne-Moody Co., TexCivApp–Waco, 269 SW2d 478.—Chat Mtg 162; Corp 398(1), 410; Judgm 185.2(7), 185.3(21); Princ & A 70; Sales 475.

Holland; Laskowski v., TexCivApp–Eastland, 358 SW2d 230.—Venue 5.3(8), 22(4).

Holland; Leatherwood v., TexCivApp–Fort Worth, 375 SW2d 517, ref nre.—App & E 215(1), 900, 969; Judgm 270, 397, 538; Trial 18, 133.6(4).

Holland v. Lesesne, TexCivApp–San Antonio, 350 SW2d 859, ref nre.—App & E 302(1), 1041(2), 1170.6; Damag 221(4); Fraud 7; Plead 236(3); Trial 352.1(1), 352.5(4); Trover 4, 13, 47, 57, 60; Trusts 99, 371(2), 373.

Holland; Lloyd v., TexApp–Houston (14 Dist), 659 SW2d 103.—Judgm 181(30), 185(2), 185(3), 185(5), 185.2(9); Spec Perf 28(1).

Holland; National Auto. & Cas. Ins. Co. v., TexCivApp– Dallas, 483 SW2d 28.—Alt Disp Res 363(8), 383.

Holland; Parker v., Tex, 444 SW2d 581.—Judgm 129, 140, 335(3).

Holland; Pearson v., TexCivApp–Dallas, 136 SW2d 920, writ refused.—Action 57(6); Courts 202(5).

Holland; Penn v., TexCivApp–Galveston, 105 SW2d 351, writ refused.—R R 69.

Holland; Peterson v., TexCivApp–Texarkana, 189 SW2d 94, writ refused.—Adv Poss 31, 60(6), 71(1), 112; Bound 22; Deeds 93; Mines 49; R R 63, 69, 73(1).

Holland; Pippin v., TexCivApp–Fort Worth, 146 SW2d 266.—App & E 1001(1), 1008.1(2); Elections 291, 295(1); Schools 38.

Holland; Preferred Life Ins. Co. v., TexCivApp–Beaumont, 280 SW2d 653.—Insurance 2476.

Holland v. Pyramid Life Ins. Co. of Little Rock, CA5 (Tex), 199 F2d 926.—Insurance 1791(1), 2066, 3490, 3629; Lim of Act 96(2), 100(11), 104(2).

Holland; Ruenbuhl v., TexCivApp–Galveston, 250 SW2d 455.—Adop 17; App & E 931(6), 1010.1(3).

Holland; Sisttie v., TexCivApp–Tyler, 374 SW2d 803.— App & E 80(6); Judgm 217, 233.

Holland; South End Development Co. v., TexCivApp– Galveston, 248 SW2d 1013.—Courts 207.1; Decl Judgm 295; Mand 31; Prohib 11.

Holland; State v., Tex, 221 SW3d 639.—App & E 836, 863, 893(1), 916(1); Courts 247(7); Em Dom 2.1, 2.34; Plead 104(1), 111.36, 111.43; States 107, 191.4(1), 191.9(1), 191.9(3).

Holland v. State, TexCrimApp, 802 SW2d 696.—Crim Law 662.8, 1043(3), 1179; Infants 12, 20.

Holland v. State, TexCrimApp, 761 SW2d 307, cert den 109 SCt 1560, 489 US 1091, 103 LEd2d 863, denial of habeas corpus aff 962 F2d 417, cert den 113 SCt 3043, 509 US 925, 125 LEd2d 729.—Crim Law 273(1), 273.1(1), 273.1(4), 275, 485(1), 641.12(1), 641.13(2.1), 641.13(5), 641.13(7), 1043(3), 1129(3), 1134(3), 1177; Jury 24, 45, 91, 107, 108; Sent & Pun 1772, 1780(3), 1788(5).

Holland v. State, TexCrimApp, 623 SW2d 651.—Ind & Inf 41(2), 122(2), 122(3), 122(4).

Holland v. State, TexCrimApp, 484 SW2d 719.—Crim Law 867.

Holland v. State, TexCrimApp, 481 SW2d 410.—Crim Law 730(1), 730(3), 1036.2, 1144.17.

Holland v. State, TexCrimApp, 415 SW2d 186.—Crim Law 364(3.1), 1169.1(9).

Holland v. State, TexCrimApp, 356 SW2d 687, 172 TexCrim 296.—Homic 1154.

Holland v. State, TexCrimApp, 253 SW2d 51.—Crim Law 1094(3).

Holland v. State, TexCrimApp, 246 SW2d 889, 157 TexCrim 86.—Crim Law 1137(3).

Holland v. State, TexCrimApp, 216 SW2d 228, 152 TexCrim 552.—Courts 90(4); Crim Law 552(3), 566, 1092.4, 1092.8, 1092.11(1), 1092.12, 1186.1; Homic 564, 1134.

Holland v. State, TexCrimApp, 146 SW2d 400, 140 TexCrim 529.—Crim Law 829(1), 1090.14, 1090.16.

Holland v. State, TexCrimApp, 95 SW2d 399, 131 TexCrim 48.—Crim Law 673(1), 823(16), 1169.5(2); Larc 55.

Holland v. State, TexCrimApp, 94 SW2d 1164.—Crim Law 1131(1).

Holland v. State, TexApp–Fort Worth, 820 SW2d 221, petition for discretionary review refused, and petition for discretionary review gr, rev 845 SW2d 914.—Crim Law 719(1), 730(1), 1171.1(3); Sent & Pun 313, 1900.

Holland v. State, TexApp–Fort Worth, 622 SW2d 904.— Crim Law 427(5), 444, 599, 603.3(9), 1151; Larc 64(1), 65.

Holland v. State, TexApp–Austin, 112 SW3d 251.—Crim Law 273.1(2), 274(3.1).

Holland; State v., TexApp–Austin, 808 SW2d 556. See State v. Nolan.

Holland v. State, TexApp–Austin, 770 SW2d 56, petition for discretionary review gr, aff 802 SW2d 696.—Crim Law 412.2(2), 518(1), 531(3), 662.8; Infants 12, 20.

Holland v. State, TexApp–Dallas, 788 SW2d 112, petition for discretionary review refused.—Arrest 62, 63.1, 63.4(17), 63.4(18).

Holland v. State, TexApp–Beaumont, 729 SW2d 366.— Burg 41(3); Crim Law 938(1), 944, 951(6); Sent & Pun 1344.

Holland; State v., TexApp–Corpus Christi, 161 SW3d 227, review gr, rev, case dism 221 SW3d 639.—App & E 863, 893(1); Em Dom 2.1, 2.34, 266, 307(2); Plead 104(1), 111.34, 111.36, 111.37, 111.38, 111.43; States 191.4(1), 191.9(3).

Holland v. State, TexApp–Houston (14 Dist), 654 SW2d 745, aff 653 SW2d 820.—Burg 16, 29, 41(1); Const Law 266(3.3), 4659(1); Crim Law 511.1(1), 511.1(2.1), 511.1(3), 511.1(9), 511.3, 511.5, 814(17), 1036.1(9), 1043(3).

Holland; State v., TexCivApp–Tyler, 453 SW2d 871.— App & E 930(3), 989; Em Dom 149(1), 150; Evid 555.6(3), 555.9.

Holland v. Taylor, Tex, 270 SW2d 219, 153 Tex 433.— Action 13; App & E 719(1); Const Law 2508; Elections 121(1), 154(9).

Holland v. Taylor, TexCivApp–Beaumont, 270 SW2d 215, rev 270 SW2d 219, 153 Tex 433.—Elections 121(1), 154(1).

Holland; Texas Public Utilities Corp. v., TexCivApp– Fort Worth, 123 SW2d 1028, writ dism.—Elections 298(1); Mun Corp 918(1).

Holland; U.S. v., CA5 (Tex), 26 F3d 26.—Crim Law 1139; Sent & Pun 793.

Holland; U.S. v., CA5 (Tex), 850 F2d 1048.—Const Law 4733(2); Crim Law 982.9(6), 1134(10); Sent & Pun 2009, 2024, 2026.

Holland v. U.S., SDTex, 94 FSupp2d 787, aff 251 F3d 157. —Int Rev 3124, 3143; Nuis 3(1), 3(2), 4.

Holland v. Vela De Pena, TexCivApp–San Antonio, 343 SW2d 750, writ refused.—Mines 78.1(3).

Holland v. Wal-Mart Stores, Inc., Tex, 1 SW3d 91.—App & E 223, 230, 882(19); Costs 194.22, 208; Labor & Emp 866, 880.

Holland; Wal-Mart Stores, Inc. v., TexApp–Tyler, 956 SW2d 590, reh overr, and reh overr, and review gr, withdrawn, and reh gr, and review gr, opinion superseded 1 SW3d 91, rev in part 1 SW3d 91.—App & E 173(12), 226(2), 932(1), 994(3), 1004(3), 1004(5), 1004(8); Damag 32, 38, 48, 50, 96, 134(2); Labor & Emp 810, 863(2), 871, 880; Plead 78, 387, 402, 403(1), 403(2), 404, 427; Work Comp 1138, 1163.

Holland; Williams v., TexApp–Dallas, 740 SW2d 59.—Divorce 85.

Holland American Ins. Co.; Federal Deposit Ins. Corp. v., TexApp–El Paso, 759 SW2d 786, writ den.—Insurance 3512, 3515(1), 3560.

Holland Elec. Co.; Taylor v., TexCivApp–Beaumont, 386 SW2d 598, writ dism.—Electricity 19(5), 19(12); Neglig 1550, 1568; Pretrial Proc 726.

Hollander v. Capon, TexApp–Houston (1 Dist), 853 SW2d 723, reh den, and writ den.—Child S 451, 472, 558(4); Contracts 321(1); Interest 37(2); Lim of Act 2(1), 46(6), 51(2); Plead 245(1), 258(1).

Holland Mortg. and Inv. Corp.; Bellatti v., TexApp–Texarkana, 838 SW2d 261, reh den.—App & E 930(3), 1001(1), 1024.4; Damag 163(1); Judgm 199(3.5), 199(3.9).

Holland Mortg. and Inv. Corp. v. Bone, TexApp–Houston (1 Dist), 751 SW2d 515, ref nre.—Antitrust 209, 363, 369; App & E 1001(3); Lim of Act 6(1); Mtg 211; Trial 350.4(4).

Holland Page, Inc. v. Capitol Truck & Trailer Co., Inc., TexCivApp–Beaumont, 518 SW2d 441, ref nre.—Appear 8(1), 8(4), 8(5); Autos 368.

Holland Page, Inc.; Darr Equipment Co. v., TexCivApp–Austin, 355 SW2d 595, writ dism.—Judgm 725(3); Plead 111.42(4); Sequest 21.

Holland Page, Inc. v. Darr Equipment Co., TexCivApp–Amarillo, 351 SW2d 586.—Costs 193; Sequest 15; Venue 7.5(6).

Holland Page Industries, Inc.; Pewthers' Estate v., TexCivApp–Austin, 443 SW2d 392, ref nre.—Abate & R 75(1); Compromise 5(3), 23(2); Judgm 17(1).

Hollandsworth; Pan Am. Production Co. v., TexCivApp–Austin, 294 SW2d 205, ref nre.—Action 60; Compromise 15(1); Contracts 164; Judgm 673; Mines 92.32(1), 92.40.

Hollandsworth Drilling Co.; Graham v., TexCivApp–Texarkana, 169 SW2d 1001, writ refused wom.—App & E 989; Evid 236(6); Home 133; Trial 140(1).

Holland Texas Hypotheek Bank of Amsterdam, Holland v. Nolen, TexCivApp–San Antonio, 110 SW2d 230.—Courts 480(3).

Hollar v. Jowers, TexCivApp–Eastland, 310 SW2d 721, ref nre.—Can of Inst 27, 35(2); Deeds 72(1), 196(3), 211(1), 211(4); Parties 1, 18, 29, 80(1), 84(1), 97(1).

Hollaway v. Hollaway, TexApp–Houston (1 Dist), 792 SW2d 168, writ den.—Divorce 8, 162, 170, 184(12), 254(1), 286(9); Hus & W 278(1).

Hollaway; Hollaway v., TexApp–Houston (1 Dist), 792 SW2d 168, writ den.—Divorce 8, 162, 170, 184(12), 254(1), 286(9); Hus & W 278(1).

Hollaway v. Woodley, CA5 (Tex), 203 FedAppx 563.—Civil R 1209, 1551.

Hollebeke; Azopardi v., TexCivApp–Waco, 428 SW2d 167.—App & E 387(3), 425, 516; New Tr 155.

Hollebeke; Ussery v., TexCivApp–El Paso, 391 SW2d 497, ref nre.—Contracts 93(4), 134, 138(1); Covenants 104; Deeds 19, 69; Equity 7; Evid 66; Fraud 10; Lim of Act 95(8), 155(1); Mines 5.2(3), 54(1), 54(4), 55(1); Spec Perf 25.

Hollech; Seigle v., TexApp–Houston (14 Dist), 892 SW2d 201.—App & E 962; Pretrial Proc 581, 596.

Holleman; Biddle v., TexCivApp–Waco, 375 SW2d 314.—Lim of Act 19(1); Ref of Inst 43.

Holleman; Edwards v., Tex, 862 SW2d 580, on remand 893 SW2d 115, reh den, and writ den.—Mtg 218.24, 377.

Holleman; Edwards v., TexApp–Houston (1 Dist), 893 SW2d 115, reh den, and writ den.—App & E 241, 930(3), 1001(3), 1062.1; Costs 208; Evid 571(7); Fraud 61; Mtg 209, 377; Trial 295(1); Trusts 315(1).

Holleman; Edwards v., TexApp–Houston (1 Dist), 842 SW2d 704, reh den, and writ gr, rev 862 SW2d 580, on remand 893 SW2d 115, reh den, and writ den.—Costs 252; Mtg 377.

Holleman v. Halliburton Co., TexCivApp–Fort Worth, 450 SW2d 883.—Evid 418; Judgm 181(6), 181(11).

Holleman; Hanover Ins. Co. v., TexCivApp–Dallas, 372 SW2d 554, ref nre.—Work Comp 230, 1114, 1132, 1182, 1186, 1461, 1789.

Holleman v. Mission Trace Homeowners Ass'n, TexCivApp–San Antonio, 556 SW2d 632.—Assoc 5; Covenants 1, 84.

Holleman; National Resort Communities, Inc. v., TexCivApp–Austin, 594 SW2d 195, ref nre.—App & E 989; Can of Inst 8, 34(4); Contracts 94(1); Evid 588; Fraud 12, 38; Ven & Pur 44, 123.

Holleman v. State, TexCrimApp, 259 SW2d 197.—Crim Law 1087.1(2).

Holleman v. State, TexCrimApp, 185 SW2d 442.—Crim Law 1090.1(1).

Holleman v. State, TexApp–Amarillo, 945 SW2d 232, reh overr, and petition for discretionary review refused.—Crim Law 577.1; Ind & Inf 196(1).

Holleman Const. Co. Inc.; Carpenters am and Restated Health Ben. Fund v., CA5 (Tex), 751 F2d 763.—Contracts 147(1), 176(2); Evid 448; Fed Cts 754.1, 859, 865; Labor & Emp 1247.

Hollen v. Leadership Homes, Inc., TexCivApp–El Paso, 502 SW2d 837.—App & E 846(5), 1010.1(3); Contracts 205.35(2), 322(3), 324(1); Evid 590; Frds St of 125(1); Impl & C C 91; Trial 382.

Hollen v. State, TexCrimApp, 117 SW3d 798.—Autos 359.

Hollen v. State, TexApp–Fort Worth, 87 SW3d 151, reh overr, and petition for discretionary review gr, rev 117 SW3d 798, cert den 124 SCt 2022, 541 US 992, 158 LEd2d 499.—Crim Law 369.1, 633(2), 661, 1165(1), 1169.11; Stip 1, 3, 14(4), 17(1), 17(3).

Hollen v. State Farm Mut. Auto. Ins. Co., Tex, 551 SW2d 46.—Insurance 3523(3); Judgm 73.

Hollen; State Farm Mut. Auto. Ins. Co. v., TexCivApp–Hous (14 Dist), 543 SW2d 178, writ gr, rev 551 SW2d 46.—App & E 145; Evid 589; Judgm 185(6), 185.3(12).

Hollenbeck, In re, BkrtcySDTex, 166 BR 291.—Bankr 3352, 3422(10.1); Estop 62(1), 62.1, 62.2(4); Int Rev 3038, 3048, 4458, 4464, 4840, 4841.

Hollenbeck v. Estelle, CA5 (Tex), 672 F2d 451, reh den 679 F2d 250, cert den 103 SCt 383, 459 US 1019, 74 LEd2d 514.—Crim Law 641.13(6); Witn 88.

Hollenbeck v. Hanna, TexApp–San Antonio, 802 SW2d 412.—Trusts 289, 291; Wills 680.

Hollenbeck; LaChance v., TexApp–Austin, 695 SW2d 618, ref nre.—App & E 842(2), 852, 966(1); Costs 260(5); Damag 22, 23; Equity 65(2); Impl & C C 3, 30, 40; New Tr 108(3); Pretrial Proc 713, 726; Ven & Pur 351(7).

Hollenbeck v. U.S. I.R.S., BkrtcySDTex, 166 BR 291. See Hollenbeck, In re.

Hollern; Lowe v., TexApp–Dallas, 784 SW2d 737.—Mand 175.

Hollestelle v. Hollestelle, TexCivApp–Amarillo, 371 SW2d 121, ref nre.—Child C 658, 660, 924; Trial 358.

Hollestelle; Hollestelle v., TexCivApp–Amarillo, 371 SW2d 121, ref nre.—Child C 658, 660, 924; Trial 358.

Holley, Ex parte, TexCrimApp, 339 SW2d 903, 170 TexCrim 206.—Hab Corp 474; Sent & Pun 1299.

Holley v. Adams, TexApp, 544 SW2d 367.—Child C 68, 76, 467, 469, 914; Child S 59; Infants 178.

Holley v. Adams, TexCivApp–Austin, 532 SW2d 694, writ gr, rev 544 SW2d 367.—Child C 48, 452, 469; Child S 26, 59.

Holley v. **Central Auto Parts**, TexCivApp–Austin, 347 SW2d 341, ref nre.—Fraud 11(1), 49; Prod Liab 77.5, 88.5; Sales 262.5.

Holley v. **Corbell**, TexCivApp–Eastland, 443 SW2d 63.— App & E 758.1, 758.3(2), 1029; Bills & N 115; Fraud 31.

Holley; **Fox v.**, TexCivApp–Eastland, 155 SW2d 395.— App & E 387(2); New Tr 155.

Holley v. **Grigg**, TexApp–Eastland, 65 SW3d 289.—Contracts 2, 93(1), 93(5), 129(1), 143(2), 143.5, 176(2), 193; Evid 207(1), 265(7); Judgm 181(2); Ref of Inst 17(1); Wills 88(1).

Holley v. **Holley**, TexApp–Houston (1 Dist), 864 SW2d 703, reh den, and writ den.—App & E 907(4); Child S 233, 254, 339(2), 339(3), 356, 364, 474, 485, 539, 555, 556(1); Courts 26; Evid 43(2), 43(3).

Holley; **Holley v.**, TexApp–Houston (1 Dist), 864 SW2d 703, reh den, and writ den.—App & E 907(4); Child S 233, 254, 339(2), 339(3), 356, 364, 474, 485, 539, 555, 556(1); Courts 26; Evid 43(2), 43(3).

Holley v. **Hooper**, TexCivApp–Austin, 205 SW2d 120, ref nre.—Evid 448, 450(8); Spec Perf 130.

Holley v. **Kitty Hawk, Inc.**, NDTex, 200 FRD 275.—Fed Civ Proc 179, 187.

Holley; **Locus Const. Co., Inc. v.**, TexCivApp–Dallas, 524 SW2d 357.—Corp 308(11), 319(7); Impl & C C 60.1; Trial 366.

Holley v. **Mucher**, TexCivApp–Texarkana, 165 SW2d 1015, writ refused wom.—Des & Dist 82, 86; Estop 92(3); Evid 187, 471(29); Frds St of 129(4).

Holley v. **NL Industries/NL Acme Tool Co.**, TexApp– Austin, 718 SW2d 813, ref nre.—Mines 109.

Holley; **Old Nat. Life Ins. Co. v.**, TexCivApp–Fort Worth, 216 SW2d 676.—App & E 931(6); Insurance 2607, 3015.

Holley v. **Painters Local Union No. 318**, TexCivApp– Fort Worth, 376 SW2d 44, ref nre.—App & E 395, 758.3(11), 931(1), 989, 1010.1(3); Labor & Emp 1047(3), 1047(4), 1049, 1050, 1051, 1203, 1209(2), 1295(2).

Holley; **Pressley v.**, TexCivApp–Fort Worth, 507 SW2d 869, ref nre.—App & E 1064.1(4); Autos 181(1), 181(2), 246(1); Judgm 199(3.2), 199(3.7).

Holley; **Ratliff v.**, TexCivApp–Eastland, 482 SW2d 347, ref nre.—Autos 245(49), 245(66).

Holley; **Shearrer v.**, TexApp–San Antonio, 952 SW2d 74. —App & E 842(2); Trusts 31, 134, 139.1, 140(3), 154.

Holley; **Smith v.**, TexApp–San Antonio, 827 SW2d 433, writ den.—Libel 44(1), 44(3), 45(1), 47, 50, 50.5, 51(1).

Holley v. **State**, TexCrimApp, 766 SW2d 254.—Homic 1418.

Holley v. **State**, TexCrimApp, 582 SW2d 115.—Crim Law 369.2(5), 1169.11.

Holley v. **State**, TexCrimApp, 502 SW2d 151.—Crim Law 394.4(9), 1043(2).

Holley v. **State**, TexCrimApp, 366 SW2d 570.—Autos 355(5); Crim Law 665(4), 1092.12, 1131(7).

Holley v. **State**, TexCrimApp, 353 SW2d 437, 172 Tex-Crim 98.—Larc 65.

Holley v. **State**, TexCrimApp, 275 SW2d 112.—Crim Law 1090.1(1).

Holley v. **State**, TexCrimApp, 274 SW2d 828.—Crim Law 1087.1(2), 1090.1(1).

Holley v. **State**, TexApp–Amarillo, 713 SW2d 381, petition for discretionary review gr, rev 766 SW2d 254.—Crim Law 1036.8, 1038.1(2); Homic 581, 603, 1134, 1418.

Holley v. **State**, TexApp–Houston (14 Dist), 167 SW3d 546, petition for discretionary review refused.—Crim Law 1030(2), 1042, 1139; Obst Just 11; Sent & Pun 1502.

Holley; **U.S. v.**, CA5 (Tex), 23 F3d 902, reh and sug for reh den 30 F3d 1496, cert den 115 SCt 635, 513 US 1043, 130 LEd2d 542, cert den Haass v. US, 115 SCt 737, 513 US 1083, 130 LEd2d 639.—Brib 3, 11; B & L Assoc 23(8); Consp 47(4); Crim Law 627.7(3), 700(1), 801, 806(1), 1139, 1159.2(7), 1159.2(8), 1166(10.10),

1167(4), 1169.1(2.1), 1172.8; Ind & Inf 159(1), 159(2); Sent & Pun 2175; Witn 366.

Holley; **U.S. v.**, CA5 (Tex), 986 F2d 100, reh den 990 F2d 1254, cert den 114 SCt 77, 510 US 821, 126 LEd2d 45.— Crim Law 577.14, 1139, 1155, 1158(1); Double J 7, 59, 99.

Holley; **U.S. v.**, CA5 (Tex), 942 F2d 916, appeal after remand 986 F2d 100, reh den 990 F2d 1254, cert den 114 SCt 77, 510 US 821, 126 LEd2d 45.—Crim Law 798(0.5), 1173.2(1); Perj 11(1), 11(2), 36.

Holley; **U.S. v.**, CA5 (Tex), 818 F2d 351.—Sent & Pun 1506; Weap 4.

Holley v. **Watts**, Tex, 629 SW2d 694.—App & E 768; Plead 111.42(11); Usury 11.

Holley; **Watts v.**, TexCivApp–Austin, 622 SW2d 583, rev 629 SW2d 694.—App & E 768, 989; Usury 31, 102(1), 113, 117.

Holley; **Williams v.**, TexApp–Waco, 653 SW2d 639, ref nre.—Const Law 3953, 3974; Judgm 138(3), 335(2); Land & Ten 55(3), 148(4), 232, 238.

Holliday v. **Anderson**, TexCivApp–Waco, 428 SW2d 479. —Alt of Inst 6, 12, 29; Bills & N 64.

Holliday; **Drollinger v.**, TexCivApp–Waco, 117 SW2d 562. —App & E 213, 719(4), 743(1); Land & Ten 109(1), 230(8); Trial 350.3(2.1).

Holliday; **Erwin v.**, TexComApp, 112 SW2d 177, 131 Tex 69.—Appear 26; Courts 18; Evid 65; Judgm 17(3); Proc 48, 84; Propty 6.

Holliday v. **Erwin**, TexCivApp–San Antonio, 85 SW2d 355, aff 112 SW2d 177, 131 Tex 69.—Can of Inst 4; Courts 12(2.1); Mines 74(3).

Holliday v. **Henry I. Siegel Co.**, TexApp–Houston (14 Dist), 643 SW2d 519, writ gr, aff 663 SW2d 824.—Corp 349; Trial 393(2).

Holliday; **Henry I. Siegel Co., Inc. v.**, Tex, 663 SW2d 824.—Corp 349, 547(4), 628.

Holliday v. **Holliday**, TexApp–Houston (14 Dist), 642 SW2d 280.—Child S 8, 364, 440, 450, 496, 498.

Holliday; **Holliday v.**, TexApp–Houston (14 Dist), 642 SW2d 280.—Child S 8, 364, 440, 450, 496, 498.

Holliday v. **Holliday**, TexCivApp–Corpus Christi, 453 SW2d 512.—App & E 564(5), 901; Divorce 184(4).

Holliday; **Holliday v.**, TexCivApp–Corpus Christi, 453 SW2d 512.—App & E 564(5), 901; Divorce 184(4).

Holliday; **Rexford v.**, TexApp–Houston (1 Dist), 807 SW2d 356.—App & E 78(1); Sequest 16, 17, 21.

Holliday; **Siegel Co., Inc. v.**, Tex, 663 SW2d 824. See Henry I. Siegel Co., Inc. v. Holliday.

Holliday v. **Smith**, TexCivApp–Corpus Christi, 458 SW2d 106, ref nre.—App & E 333; Decl Judgm 241; Judgm 180, 183; Wills 439, 455, 464, 466, 470(1), 472, 587(1).

Holliday v. **Smith**, TexCivApp–Corpus Christi, 422 SW2d 791, ref nre.—App & E 233(1); Evid 82, 591; Lim of Act 73(3), 118(2); Trial 252(18); Wills 260, 270, 317, 360.

Holliday v. **State**, TexCrimApp, 482 SW2d 215.—Crim Law 1131(5), 1131(7).

Holliday v. **State**, TexCrimApp, 90 SW2d 839.—Crim Law 1182.

Holliday v. **Taylor**, TexCivApp–Waco, 249 SW2d 941, ref nre.—Partners 14, 55.

Holliday; **United Fidelity Life Ins. Co. v.**, TexCivApp– Amarillo, 226 SW2d 139, ref nre.—App & E 1004(13), 1050.4, 1060.4; New Tr 162(1); Witn 252; Work Comp 2122.

Holliday, **City of, v. Wood**, TexApp–Fort Worth, 914 SW2d 175. See City of Holliday v. Wood.

Holliday Ins. Agency, Inc.; **Sabine Towing & Transp. Co., Inc. v.**, TexApp–Texarkana, 54 SW3d 57, reh overr, and review den.—Lim of Act 43, 95(1), 100(1), 100(11), 100(12).

Hollie v. **State**, TexApp–Houston (1 Dist), 962 SW2d 302, petition for discretionary review gr, review dism as improvidently gr 984 SW2d 263.—Crim Law 1042, 1134(2); Sent & Pun 34, 1976(2).

Hollie v. State, TexApp–Fort Worth, 967 SW2d 516, petition for discretionary review refused.—Crim Law 865(1), 865(1.5), 867.

Hollie; Waters v., TexApp–Fort Worth, 642 SW2d 90.—Antitrust 141.

Hollifield v. Beto, CA5 (Tex), 372 F2d 478.—Crim Law 522(1); Hab Corp 715.1.

Hollifield v. Hilton, TexCivApp–Fort Worth, 515 SW2d 717, ref nre.—Home 122, 154, 162(1), 168, 181.5; Mech Liens 14.

Hollifield v. Hollifield, TexApp–Austin, 925 SW2d 153.—App & E 758.3(2), 758.3(3), 766, 946; Child S 21, 231, 234, 253, 258, 290, 377, 539, 543, 556(1).

Hollifield; Hollifield v., TexApp–Austin, 925 SW2d 153.—App & E 758.3(2), 758.3(3), 766, 946; Child S 21, 231, 234, 253, 258, 290, 377, 539, 543, 556(1).

Hollifield v. State, TexCivApp–Fort Worth, 545 SW2d 267.—Mental H 45.

Holligan; Pierson v., TexCivApp–Waco, 497 SW2d 637, dism.—Contracts 94(1); Evid 434(8); Fraud 31; Venue 8(2).

Holliman; Fullerton v., TexApp–Eastland, 730 SW2d 168, ref nre.—App & E 747(3); Child S 343; Hus & W 279(1), 280, 281; Judgm 654.

Holliman; Fullerton v., TexApp–Eastland, 721 SW2d 478, dism.—Child S 390.

Holliman v. Leander Independent School Dist., TexApp–Austin, 679 SW2d 92, ref nre.—Work Comp 1615, 1729, 1937.

Holliman v. State, TexCrimApp, 485 SW2d 912.—Bail 51, 53.

Holliman v. State, TexApp–Texarkana, 762 SW2d 656.—App & E 846(5); Mental H 41, 45.

Holliman v. State, TexApp–Waco, 692 SW2d 120, petition for discretionary review refused.—Const Law 699, 3781, 4509(9); Controlled Subs 6, 34, 67, 74, 82.

Holliman v. State, TexApp–Houston (14 Dist), 879 SW2d 85.—Crim Law 713, 719(1), 720(7.1), 721(3), 730(7), 730(14), 772(6), 1171.1(2.1), 1171.1(6), 1171.3, 1171.5.

Hollimon; Blackmon v., TexApp–San Antonio, 847 SW2d 614, writ den.—App & E 852; Death 39.

Hollin v. State, TexApp–Houston (1 Dist), 227 SW3d 117.—Autos 332, 343, 344; Crim Law 1026.10(4), 1042, 1139; Homic 576; Statut 223.2(1.1), 223.4.

Hollines v. Estelle, WDTex, 569 FSupp 146, aff 714 F2d 136, reh den 718 F2d 1096.—Const Law 4534, 4580, 4693; Courts 100(1); Crim Law 577.4, 577.8(2), 577.10(10), 577.12(2), 577.15(1), 577.16(4), 577.16(9), 641.13(1), 641.13(2.1), 641.13(3), 641.13(6); Hab Corp 361, 486(1), 493(1), 603, 721(2), 746; Ind & Inf 42.

Hollinger v. State, TexCrimApp, 344 SW2d 695, 171 TexCrim 32.—Crim Law 1036.2; Larc 65.

Hollinger v. State, TexApp–Tyler, 911 SW2d 35, petition for discretionary review refused.—Crim Law 1134(2), 1153(2); Infants 20; Witn 39, 40(1), 227.

Hollingshead; Texas Emp. Ins. Assn. v., TexCivApp–Eastland, 282 SW2d 305, writ refused.—Work Comp 877.

Hollingsworth v. American Trading Co., TexCivApp–Dallas, 156 SW2d 290.—Neglig 1076, 1088, 1104(7).

Hollingsworth v. Cities Service Oil Co., TexCivApp–Beaumont, 199 SW2d 266, writ refused, cert den 68 SCt 83, 332 US 774, 92 LEd 359.—Fed Cts 386; Judgm 198; Lim of Act 2(4), 28(1).

Hollingsworth v. City of Dallas, TexApp–Dallas, 931 SW2d 699, writ den.—App & E 173(2); Judgm 181(1), 185(2); Mun Corp 64, 65, 111(2), 120, 592(1); Statut 181(1), 181(2), 184, 206, 223.1; Zoning 771, 789.

Hollingsworth; Herren v., Tex, 167 SW2d 735, 140 Tex 263.—Sec Reg 243.1, 253, 260, 306.

Hollingsworth; Herren v., TexCivApp–Galveston, 188 SW2d 706, writ refused wom.—App & E 194(6); Brok 82(1); Costs 256(4); Evid 419(11); Frds St of 72(1), 110(1), 125(1), 125(2), 131(1); Plead 18.

Hollingsworth; Herren v., TexCivApp–Galveston, 161 SW2d 511, rev 167 SW2d 735, 140 Tex 263.—Sec Reg 292, 298.

Hollingsworth v. Hollingsworth, TexCivApp–Amarillo, 441 SW2d 619.—Action 60; Venue 21, 32(2).

Hollingsworth; Hollingsworth v., TexCivApp–Amarillo, 441 SW2d 619.—Action 60; Venue 21, 32(2).

Hollingsworth; Houston & North Tex. Motor Freight Lines v., TexCivApp–Fort Worth, 213 SW2d 747.—App & E 912; Corp 503(3); Evid 54, 591; Venue 8.5(5).

Hollingsworth v. King, TexApp–Amarillo, 810 SW2d 772, writ den with per curiam opinion 816 SW2d 340.—Anim 48; App & E 714(5); Evid 1, 51; Judgm 185(4), 185.3(21), 934(1).

Hollingsworth v. Kohler, TexCivApp–Waco, 195 SW2d 563.—Child C 9, 76, 460; Judgm 19.

Hollingsworth; Musick v., TexCivApp–Houston, 373 SW2d 503.—App & E 758.2, 954(1); Inj 135, 151, 157.

Hollingsworth v. Northwestern Nat. Ins. Co., TexCivApp–Texarkana, 522 SW2d 242.—Acct Action on 10, 13; Contracts 346(10); Judgm 248; Plead 387, 427.

Hollingsworth; Sears, Roebuck & Co. v., Tex, 293 SW2d 639, 156 Tex 176.—App & E 761, 1089(2); Pretrial Proc 44.1, 224, 226.

Hollingsworth v. Sears, Roebuck & Co., TexCivApp–Austin, 286 SW2d 182, aff 293 SW2d 639, 156 Tex 176.—Witn 16.

Hollingsworth; Seastrunk Rendering Co. v., TexCivApp–Austin, 177 SW2d 1014.—App & E 843(2); Inj 204, 219; Nuis 36.

Hollingsworth v. State, TexCrimApp, 419 SW2d 854.—Autos 355(13); Crim Law 552(3), 1081(6).

Hollingsworth v. State, TexCrimApp, 205 SW2d 604, 151 TexCrim 108.—Crim Law 1099.7(2).

Hollingsworth v. State, TexApp–Austin, 15 SW3d 586.—Arrest 68(4); Costs 302.2(2), 302.4; Crim Law 376, 465, 726, 1124(1), 1139, 1147, 1158(4), 1159.2(7), 1171.1(1), 1171.1(3); Obst Just 5, 16; Searches 28.

Hollingsworth; State v., TexApp–Austin, 784 SW2d 461, writ den, cert den 111 SCt 2237, 500 US 942, 114 LEd2d 479, reh den 112 SCt 12, 501 US 1269, 115 LEd2d 1097.—Mines 5.2(2.1).

Hollingsworth; Taylor v., Tex, 176 SW2d 733, 142 Tex 158.—Hus & W 152, 162, 266.2(1), 266.3, 269.

Hollingsworth; Taylor v., TexCivApp–Galveston, 169 SW2d 519, aff 176 SW2d 733, 142 Tex 158.—Hus & W 249(1), 250, 251, 255, 264(4).

Hollingsworth; Williams v., Tex, 568 SW2d 130.—Judgm 72; Wills 307, 340.

Hollingsworth v. Williams, TexCivApp–Texarkana, 559 SW2d 111, writ gr, rev 568 SW2d 130.—Ex & Ad 7; Wills 288(3), 311.

Hollingsworth v. Williamson, TexCivApp–Waco, 300 SW2d 194, ref nre.—Adv Poss 114(1); App & E 933(4), 1015(5); Ease 5, 8(4), 36(1), 36(3); New Tr 44(3), 47, 56, 157.

Hollingsworth; Wright v., CA5 (Tex), 260 F3d 357.—Civil R 1319; Lim of Act 105(1).

Hollingsworth; Wright v., CA5 (Tex), 201 F3d 663, reh and reh gr 225 F3d 777, remanded 253 F3d 839, rev on reh 260 F3d 357.

Hollingsworth Roofing Co. v. Morrison, TexApp–Fort Worth, 668 SW2d 872.—Abate & R 19; Antitrust 286, 392; App & E 931(1), 989, 1010.1(2), 1012.1(5); Contracts 322(4); Damag 108, 163(1), 189; Trial 139.1(8).

Hollins, In re, BkrtcyNDTex, 286 BR 310.—Bankr 3369, 3371(1), 3403(4).

Hollins, In re, BkrtcyNDTex, 185 BR 523.—Bankr 2853.30, 3560, 3564; Interest 31.

Hollins; Aatco Transmission Co. v., TexApp–Houston (1 Dist), 682 SW2d 682.—App & E 1008.1(1), 1008.1(4), 1050.1(11); Autos 372(4); Bailm 11, 31(1); Evid 313, 474(19), 588; Trial 105(2).

Hollins v. Beto, CA5 (Tex), 467 F2d 951, conformed to 373 FSupp 1246, aff Williams v. Estelle, 500 F2d 1183, cert den 95 SCt 813, 419 US 1125, 42 LEd2d 827, aff 503 F2d 1373.—Crim Law 633(1); Hab Corp 864(1).

Hollins v. Beto, SDTex, 373 FSupp 1246, aff Williams v. Estelle, 500 F2d 1183, cert den 95 SCt 813, 419 US 1125, 42 LEd2d 827, aff 503 F2d 1373.—Const Law 4615; Courts 100(1); Crim Law 633(1), 641.13(2.1), 660; Hab Corp 481, 720.

Hollins v. Estelle, CA5 (Tex), 503 F2d 1373.—Courts 100(1); Crim Law 1166.8.

Hollins v. Lone Star Gas Co., TexCivApp–Beaumont, 308 SW2d 276, ref nre.—Work Comp 1151.

Hollins v. Rapid Transit Lines, Inc., Tex, 440 SW2d 57.—Courts 95(1); Fraud Conv 216; Judgm 181(15.1).

Hollins v. Rapid Transit Lines, Inc., TexCivApp–Hous (14 Dist), 430 SW2d 57, writ gr, rev 440 SW2d 57.—Corp 542(1), 547(4); Fraud Conv 215, 241(2); Judgm 178, 181(2), 186.

Hollins v. State, TexCrimApp, 805 SW2d 475, on remand 1991 WL 168601, denial of post-conviction relief aff 2004 WL 1472240, petition for discretionary review refused.—Crim Law 859, 1030(1), 1039.

Hollins v. State, TexCrimApp, 571 SW2d 873.—Crim Law 855(1), 1043(3), 1130(2), 1167(1); Ind & Inf 137(4); Sent & Pun 1367, 1371.

Hollins v. State, TexCrimApp, 427 SW2d 865.—Bail 79(1), 88, 89(1).

Hollins v. State, TexCrimApp, 411 SW2d 366.—Crim Law 796, 854(9), 1038.1(1), 1056.1(1); Larc 64(1).

Hollins v. State, TexCrimApp, 187 SW2d 577, 148 TexCrim 388.—Crim Law 409(5), 720(6).

Hollins v. State, TexApp–Houston (1 Dist), 876 SW2d 923.—Crim Law 417(15), 713, 720(6), 720(8); Witn 17.

Hollins v. State, TexApp–Houston (1 Dist), 661 SW2d 211.—Crim Law 412(1), 419(1).

Hollins v. State, TexApp–Dallas, 734 SW2d 194, petition for discretionary review gr, rev 805 SW2d 475, on remand 1991 WL 168601, denial of post-conviction relief aff 2004 WL 1472240, petition for discretionary review refused.—Crim Law 859, 868, 1064(8), 1174(1).

Hollins; U.S. v., CA5 (Tex), 97 FedAppx 477.—Crim Law 641.13(7), 1440(1); Sent & Pun 643, 644.

Hollis v. Beto, CA5 (Tex), 352 F2d 550, cert den 86 SCt 639, 382 US 1020, 15 LEd2d 534.—Hab Corp 721(1), 722(2), 823; Sent & Pun 1, 2273.

Hollis v. Bo-Mac Contractors, Inc., SDTex, 35 FSupp2d 536.—Fed Cts 101, 104, 105, 113, 144.

Hollis v. Boone, TexCivApp–El Paso, 315 SW2d 350.—App & E 394(1), 655(3), 664(3), 1203(1); Assoc 1; Corp 2, 503(1); Fraud Conv 314; Plead 111.39(2), 111.42(5), 111.42(6); Sales 230, 233(2); Venue 7.5(1), 7.5(2).

Hollis v. Bowen, CA5 (Tex), 832 F2d 865.—Social S 140.55, 143.70.

Hollis; Charter Oak Fire Ins. Co. v., TexCivApp–Hous (14 Dist), 511 SW2d 583, ref nre.—Work Comp 1323, 1334, 1500, 1717.

Hollis; City of Wichita Falls v., TexCivApp–Fort Worth, 539 SW2d 180, ref nre.—App & E 564(3).

Hollis; Colbert v., TexApp–Dallas, 102 SW3d 445.—App & E 70(8), 780(1), 837(1), 870(2), 907(1), 934(1); Judgm 181(6), 185.3(13), 189; Offic 114, 119; States 78.

Hollis v. Connecticut General Life Ins. Co., TexCivApp–Beaumont, 99 SW2d 428, writ refused.—Insurance 3167.

Hollis v. Ellis, CA5 (Tex), 261 F2d 230, cert den 79 SCt 883, 359 US 971, 3 LEd2d 837, reh den 79 SCt 1124, 359 US 999, 3 LEd2d 987.—Crim Law 286.5(1), 990.3; Hab Corp 333, 721(2); Sent & Pun 34.

Hollis v. Ellis, SDTex, 201 FSupp 616.—Crim Law 1166(2), 1166.16; Sent & Pun 348.

Hollis; Gulf Stevedore Corp. v., CA5 (Tex), 427 F2d 160, cert den 91 SCt 63, 400 US 831, 27 LEd2d 62.—Work Comp 898.

Hollis; Gulf Stevedore Corp. v., SDTex, 298 FSupp 426, aff 427 F2d 160, cert den 91 SCt 63, 400 US 831, 27 LEd2d 62.—Work Comp 869, 898, 1042, 1665, 1893, 1939.4(4).

Hollis v. Hill, CA5 (Tex), 232 F3d 460.—Corp 3, 174, 182.3, 182.4(5), 187, 190, 296, 307, 310(1), 597, 640; Fed Cts 382.1, 390, 391; Labor & Emp 40(1).

Hollis v. Hollis, TexCivApp–Amarillo, 508 SW2d 179.—Child C 577, 767, 784; Child S 502, 506(2), 509(1); Divorce 398; Evid 80(1).

Hollis; Hollis v., TexCivApp–Amarillo, 508 SW2d 179.—Child C 577, 767, 784; Child S 502, 506(2), 509(1); Divorce 398; Evid 80(1).

Hollis v. Hollis, TexCivApp–Amarillo, 226 SW2d 129, dism.—Fraud Conv 181(1); Hus & W 238.7, 270(5); Judgm 16, 486(1), 497(1), 511, 513, 514, 693; Marriage 60(5), 65.

Hollis; Hollis v., TexCivApp–Amarillo, 226 SW2d 129, dism.—Fraud Conv 181(1); Hus & W 238.7, 270(5); Judgm 16, 486(1), 497(1), 511, 513, 514, 693; Marriage 60(5), 65.

Hollis; Kelso Marine, Inc. v., CA5 (Tex), 449 F2d 342.—Courts 104; Fed Cts 743.

Hollis; Kelso Marine, Inc. v., SDTex, 316 FSupp 1271, aff 449 F2d 342.—Admin Law 791; Work Comp 93.

Hollis v. McCammon, Morris & Pickens, TexCivApp–Fort Worth, 86 SW2d 652, writ dism.—Libel 42(2), 83.

Hollis; Pardue Const. Co. v., TexCivApp–Beaumont, 204 SW2d 860, writ refused.—Autos 244(59); Neglig 1683.

Hollis; Rockport Yacht & Supply Co., Inc. v., SDTex, 371 FSupp 1229.—Work Comp 904, 1111, 1703, 1914.

Hollis v. Rumph, TexCivApp–Fort Worth, 90 SW2d 884.—Mines 52.

Hollis v. State, TexCrimApp, 509 SW2d 372.—Crim Law 1044.1(8), 1054(1), 1129(3); Jury 110(14).

Hollis v. State, TexCrimApp, 436 SW2d 341.—Crim Law 1130(4).

Hollis v. State, TexCrimApp, 351 SW2d 233, 171 TexCrim 523, cert den 82 SCt 952, 369 US 862, 8 LEd2d 20, reh den 82 SCt 1252, 370 US 906, 8 LEd2d 402.—Homic 1567.

Hollis v. State, TexCrimApp, 257 SW2d 309.—Crim Law 1094(3).

Hollis v. State, TexCrimApp, 161 SW2d 794, 144 TexCrim 165.—Int Liq 238(2), 239(2).

Hollis v. State, TexCrimApp, 151 SW2d 597, 142 TexCrim 36.—Crim Law 1081(2).

Hollis v. State, TexApp–Austin, 219 SW3d 446.—Arrest 63.4(2), 63.4(13), 63.4(17); Crim Law 338(7), 394.5(2), 412(4), 412.2(3), 438(3), 474.5, 478(1), 633(1), 641.13(1), 641.13(2.1), 641.13(6), 1169.2(2), 1169.11, 1169.12; Searches 26, 162, 164.

Hollis v. State, TexApp–Dallas, 971 SW2d 653, petition for discretionary review refused.—Crim Law 1023(3), 1134(6); Searches 60.1, 61, 62, 63, 64.

Hollis v. State, TexApp–Tyler, 673 SW2d 597.—Crim Law 625.15, 625.20, 762(1), 1030(1), 1043(3), 1166.6, 1169.5(2), 1192; Homic 1371; Mental H 434.

Hollis v. State, TexApp–Tyler, 633 SW2d 947, petition for discretionary review refused, appeal after remand 673 SW2d 597.—Const Law 4783(3); Crim Law 364(0.5), 394.4(3), 404.30, 404.70, 577.16(3), 586, 594(1), 625.15, 625.20, 663, 713, 720(5), 720(9), 730(14), 867, 1168(2); Searches 184, 201.

Hollis; Strachan Shipping Co. v., CA5 (Tex), 460 F2d 1108, 19 ALR Fed 793, cert den Lewis, v. Strachan Shipping Co, 93 SCt 114, 409 US 887, 34 LEd2d 144, reh den 93 SCt 307, 409 US 1002, 34 LEd2d 263, and 96 SCt 159, 423 US 885, 46 LEd2d 116.—Work Comp 983, 1003, 1090, 1990, 2016.

Hollis; Strachan Shipping Co. v., SDTex, 323 FSupp 1122, aff in part, rev in part 460 F2d 1108, 19 ALR Fed 793, cert den Lewis, v. Strachan Shipping Co, 93 SCt 114, 409 US 887, 34 LEd2d 144, reh den 93 SCt 307, 409

US 1002, 34 LEd2d 263, and 96 SCt 159, 423 US 885, 46 LEd2d 116.—Work Comp 46, 47, 48, 2016.

Hollis v. Tarrant County, TexComApp, 114 SW2d 240, 131 Tex 172.—Counties 74(2).

Hollis v. Tarrant County, TexComApp, 102 SW2d 1055, 129 Tex 176.—App & E 34.

Hollis; Tarrant County v., TexCivApp–Fort Worth, 89 SW2d 835, rev 114 SW2d 240, 131 Tex 172.—App & E 742(1), 759, 1151(2); Counties 74(2).

Hollis v. U.S., CA5 (Tex), 323 F3d 330.—Evid 571(3), 574; Fed Cts 776, 850.1, 943.1; Health 611, 620, 821(2), 823(1), 906, 911; U S 78(14).

Hollis v. Winfree, TexCivApp–Beaumont, 216 SW2d 625, ref nre.—Princ & S 196, 198; Replev 122.

Hollister, In re, BkrtcyNDTex, 13 BR 178.—Bankr 3353(1), 3353(1.45), 3353(14), 3354.1, 3422(4.1); Contracts 143(1); Fraud 12; Sales 85(1).

Hollister v. Palmer Independent School Dist., TexApp–Waco, 958 SW2d 956.—App & E 5, 557, 934(3); Proc 64, 133, 135, 153; Schools 106.12(4).

Hollmann; Ector County v., TexApp–El Paso, 901 SW2d 687.—Costs 194.40; Judges 22(5); Statut 217.4.

Hollock v. State, TexCrimApp, 431 SW2d 553.—Crim Law 264, 275.

Holloman v. City of Georgetown, TexCivApp–Austin, 526 SW2d 682, ref nre.—App & E 301, 758.3(9); Contracts 176(2); Damag 60; Mun Corp 374(4), 375; Trial 351.2(1.1), 352.10.

Holloman v. C. I. R., CA5 (Tex), 551 F2d 987, acquiescence recommended RE: JOSEPH L HOLLOMAN, ET UX, 1982 WL 213059.—Int Rev 3524, 3525.

Holloman v. Denson, TexApp–Waco, 640 SW2d 417, ref nre.—App & E 846(5); Brok 96; Const Law 3699; Penalties 2, 8, 38.

Holloman; Lawson v., TexCivApp–San Antonio, 238 SW2d 987, ref nre.—Brok 43(3); Evid 158(26); Plead 96.

Holloman v. State, TexApp–Amarillo, 948 SW2d 349.—Assault 67, 96(3); Crim Law 772(6), 1134(3).

Holloman v. State, TexApp–Beaumont, 942 SW2d 773.—Crim Law 665(5); Sent & Pun 277, 278.

Holloman; U.S. v., CA5 (Tex), 109 F3d 1053. See U.S. v. Landerman.

Hollomon v. O. Mustad & Sons (USA), Inc., EDTex, 196 FSupp2d 450.—Antitrust 414, 418; Contracts 143(2), 143.5, 147(1), 169, 176(2), 202(1); Evid 448; Fed Civ Proc 2492, 2493; Joint Adv 1.2(1), 1.12.

Hollomon v. State, TexApp–Fort Worth, 675 SW2d 351, petition for discretionary review refused.—Extrad 59.

Hollomon v. State, TexApp–Austin, 633 SW2d 939, petition for discretionary review refused.—Arrest 63.4(6), 63.5(4), 63.5(5), 68(3); Crim Law 474.2, 519(8), 531(3), 1170(2); Homic 674.

Hollon v. Alexander, TexCivApp–San Antonio, 282 SW2d 126.—Sales 359(3).

Hollon v. Mathis Independent School Dist., CA5 (Tex), 491 F2d 92.—Fed Cts 757; Inj 22, 132, 157.

Hollon v. Mathis Independent School Dist., SDTex, 358 FSupp 1269, vac 491 F2d 92.—Schools 164.

Hollon v. Oy, EDTex, 898 FSupp 433. See Norplant Contraceptive Products Liability Litigation, In re.

Hollon v. Rethaber, TexApp–San Antonio, 643 SW2d 783.—App & E 181; Child C 632; Divorce 223.

Holloway, Ex parte, TexCivApp–Dallas, 490 SW2d 624.—Child S 23, 24, 429, 444, 459, 496; Hus & W 279(1).

Holloway, In re, CA5 (Tex), 800 F2d 479. See Holloway v. Walker.

Holloway, In re, BkrtcyEDTex, 247 BR 197.—Bankr 2185, 3159, 3165, 3181, 3182, 3187(1), 3194, 3196, 3205.

Holloway, Matter of, CA5 (Tex), 955 F2d 1008, reh den.—Bankr 2608(2), 2648; Fraud Conv 162.2.

Holloway v. Allison, TexCivApp–Tyler, 494 SW2d 612.—App & E 1010.1(1); Child C 551, 553, 560, 921(4).

Holloway; Atchison, T. & S. F. Ry. Co. v., TexCivApp–Beaumont, 479 SW2d 700, ref nre.—Evid 578; Neglig 530(1), 1745; R R 338.4, 348(6.1); Trial 350.7(6), 350.7(7), 350.7(9); Venue 61.

Holloway v. Atlantic Richfield Co., TexApp–Tyler, 970 SW2d 641.—Consp 2; Judgm 181(19), 713(2), 720, 735; Mines 109.

Holloway v. Avalon Residential Care Homes, Inc., CA5 (Tex), 107 FedAppx 398.—Labor & Emp 2757; States 18.46.

Holloway; Braxton v., CA5 (Tex), 246 F2d 953.—Acct 18; Evid 411.

Holloway; Browning v., TexCivApp–Dallas, 620 SW2d 611, ref nre.—Accord 17; App & E 835(2); Compromise 11, 16(1), 20(1), 21; Jury 14.5(3), 25(8), 26, 28(5); Stip 19.

Holloway v. Butler, TexApp–Houston (1 Dist), 828 SW2d 810, writ den.—Const Law 1004, 2403; Costs 189, 190.

Holloway; Butler v., TexApp–Houston (1 Dist), 757 SW2d 810. See Holloway v. Texas Medical Ass'n.

Holloway v. Butler, TexApp–Houston (14 Dist), 662 SW2d 688, ref nre.—Libel 26.1, 27, 107(1); Lim of Act 43, 55(6), 95(1.5), 95(6).

Holloway; Central Power & Light Co. v., TexCivApp–Corpus Christi, 431 SW2d 436.—Ease 12(1), 50; Electricity 9(1).

Holloway; Chickasha Cotton Oil Co. v., TexCivApp–Amarillo, 378 SW2d 695, ref nre.—App & E 930(9), 996; Damag 6, 132(1), 133; Labor & Emp 3096(10); Neglig 253, 552(1), 554(1), 1037(4), 1090, 1314, 1533, 1668.

Holloway; Coal Operators' Cas. Co. v., TexCivApp–Beaumont, 398 SW2d 421, ref nre.—App & E 930(1); Work Comp 858, 1385, 1404, 1653, 1964, 1974.

Holloway v. Currie, TexCivApp–Waco, 388 SW2d 435.—Adop 13, 15.

Holloway v. Dannenmaier, TexCivApp–Fort Worth, 581 SW2d 765, dism.—Antitrust 200; Venue 7.5(6).

Holloway v. Fifth Court of Appeals, Tex, 767 SW2d 680.—Mand 4(4); Prohib 3(2), 3(3), 5(1), 16.

Holloway; First Texas Joint Stock Land Bank v., TexCivApp–Amarillo, 77 SW2d 301.—Banks 405.

Holloway v. Gunnell, CA5 (Tex), 685 F2d 150.—Admin Law 229; Fed Civ Proc 1741, 1742(5), 1773; Fed Cts 74, 95; Sent & Pun 1539, 1545, 1549, 1553.

Holloway v. Har-Con Engineering Co., Inc., TexCivApp–Hous (14 Dist), 563 SW2d 695, ref nre.—App & E 866(3), 1058(1); Prod Liab 86.

Holloway; HECI Exploration Co., Employees' Profit Sharing Plan v., CA5 (Tex), 862 F2d 513. See HECI Exploration Co., Inc., Matter of.

Holloway v. HECI Exploration Co. Employees' Profit Sharing Plan, NDTex, 76 BR 563, aff Matter of HECI Exploration Co, Inc, 862 F2d 513.—Bankr 2043(2), 2045, 2047, 2058.1, 2548, 2927, 3770, 3774.1, 3779; Fed Cts 611, 714, 742; Labor & Emp 636; Stip 1, 3.

Holloway v. Holloway, TexApp–Dallas, 671 SW2d 51, dism.—App & E 837(1), 934(2); Divorce 143(2), 172, 179, 184(4), 194, 252.3(2), 252.3(3), 253(4), 287; Estop 68(2); Evid 148, 178(8), 207(1), 211; Hus & W 254, 255, 258, 264(2), 264(3), 264(5), 264(7), 268(1), 270(7), 270(8), 270(9); Pretrial Proc 690; Trusts 110.

Holloway; Holloway v., TexApp–Dallas, 671 SW2d 51, dism.—App & E 837(1), 934(2); Divorce 143(2), 172, 179, 184(4), 194, 252.3(2), 252.3(3), 253(4), 287; Estop 68(2); Evid 148, 178(8), 207(1), 211; Hus & W 254, 255, 258, 264(2), 264(3), 264(5), 264(7), 268(1), 270(7), 270(8), 270(9); Pretrial Proc 690; Trusts 110.

Holloway; International Bankers Life Ins. Co. v., Tex, 368 SW2d 567.—App & E 1001(3), 1178(6); Consp 1.1, 4, 13, 19, 21; Corp 307, 310(1), 314(1), 314(2), 314(3), 315, 316(1), 319(0.5), 319(7); Damag 89(1); Evid 253(2); Lim of Act 95(18), 199(1).

Holloway v. International Bankers Life Ins. Co., TexCivApp–Fort Worth, 354 SW2d 198, writ gr, rev 368

See Guidelines for Arrangement at the beginning of this Volume

SW2d 567.—Consp 19, 20; Corp 1.7(2), 317(0.5), 319(7), 428(5), 428(11); Damag 87(2), 91(1); Insurance 1132; Trusts 308, 374.

Holloway; John R. Thompson Co. v., CA5 (Tex), 366 F2d 108.—Fed Cts 860; Trademarks 1042, 1104, 1137(1), 1287, 1363, 1426, 1526, 1691, 1714(2), 1754(2).

Holloway v. Kelley, BkrtcySDTex, 151 BR 790. See Kelley, In re.

Holloway v. Lynaugh, CA5 (Tex), 838 F2d 792, cert den 109 SCt 104, 488 US 838, 102 LEd2d 80.—Crim Law 273.1(4); Sent & Pun 1372, 1373.

Holloway; Manhattan Fire & Marine Ins. Co. v., Tex-CivApp–Austin, 359 SW2d 203, ref nre.—Insurance 2134(2), 3073; Judgm 185(2).

Holloway v. Matagorda County, Tex, 686 SW2d 100.—Em Dom 255.

Holloway v. Matagorda County, TexApp–Corpus Christi, 667 SW2d 324, writ gr, aff 686 SW2d 100.—Ease 55; Em Dom 150, 181, 184, 205, 221, 262(5), 317(2); Impl & C C 3.

Holloway; Navarro v., CA5 (Tex), 826 F2d 335. See Browning v. Navarro.

Holloway v. Oguejiofor, CA5 (Tex), 166 FedAppx 751.—Fed Civ Proc 1788.10; Fed Cts 726; Prisons 17(2); Sent & Pun 1546.

Holloway v. Skinner, Tex, 898 SW2d 793, reh overr.—Corp 397; Labor & Emp 904; Torts 212, 223, 242.

Holloway v. Skinner, TexApp–Austin, 860 SW2d 217, reh overr, and writ gr, rev 898 SW2d 793, reh overr.—App & E 930(3), 989; Corp 306; Torts 212, 220, 223, 242, 258, 263.

Holloway; Smith v., TexCivApp–Austin, 115 SW2d 427.—Banks 77(4); Equity 56; Evid 441(5), 465.

Holloway; Smith v., TexCivApp–San Antonio, 91 SW2d 680.—Jury 16(1); Plead 111.18, 111.43, 111.47; Venue 22(8).

Holloway; Spivey v., TexApp–Houston (1 Dist), 902 SW2d 46.—App & E 5, 914(1); Appear 20; Divorce 81, 183.

Holloway v. Starnes, TexApp–Dallas, 840 SW2d 14, reh den, and writ den, cert den 114 SCt 93, 510 US 828, 126 LEd2d 60, cert den Flojo Trading Corp v. Browning, 114 SCt 93, 510 US 828, 126 LEd2d 60.—App & E 854(1); Courts 97(1); Judgm 232, 245, 335(1), 336, 349, 354, 392(2), 486(1), 489, 525, 540, 644, 713(2), 720, 739, 829(3), 957.

Holloway; Starnes v., TexApp–Dallas, 779 SW2d 86, writ den.—Action 58; App & E 76(1), 78(1), 93, 242(1), 1008.1(1), 1175(2), 1180(1), 1180(2); Const Law 3992; Courts 70, 474, 475(1), 487(7), 488(1); Judgm 178, 181(1), 346, 486(1), 619, 649, 713(2), 829(1); Plead 106(2); Trial 388(2).

Holloway v. State, TexCrimApp, 781 SW2d 605.—Crim Law 1134(10).

Holloway v. State, TexCrimApp, 780 SW2d 787, reh den. —Crim Law 393(1), 412.2(4), 412.2(5), 641.1, 641.3(6), 1169.12.

Holloway v. State, TexCrimApp, 751 SW2d 866.—Crim Law 532(0.5), 695.5, 1153(1); Sod 6.

Holloway v. State, TexCrimApp, 691 SW2d 608, cert gr, vac 106 SCt 1508, 475 US 1105, 89 LEd2d 908, on remand 780 SW2d 787, reh den.—Crim Law 339.10(9), 339.11(5.1), 438(4), 438(5.1), 485(2), 517.2(2), 532(0.5), 641.1, 641.4(1), 700(3), 867; Jury 107, 108; Sent & Pun 1772.

Holloway v. State, TexCrimApp, 666 SW2d 104.—Crim Law 304(1), 304(16), 1130(5), 1166.18; Jury 83(1); Rob 24.15(1); Sent & Pun 2021.

Holloway v. State, TexCrimApp, 613 SW2d 497, appeal after remand 691 SW2d 608, cert gr, vac 106 SCt 1508, 475 US 1105, 89 LEd2d 908, on remand 780 SW2d 787, reh den.—Crim Law 469, 469.1, 472, 478(1), 481, 486(2), 486(6), 695(4), 736(1).

Holloway v. State, TexCrimApp, 583 SW2d 376.—Tresp 89.

Holloway v. State, TexCrimApp, 525 SW2d 165.—Crim Law 59(1), 552(2), 627.6(5), 627.8(6), 720(8), 723(3), 726, 730(1), 1037.2, 1045, 1166(10.10); Rob 24.20.

Holloway v. State, TexCrimApp, 362 SW2d 325.—Crim Law 371(3), 371(12), 372(9), 396(1); False Pret 49(3).

Holloway v. State, TexCrimApp, 324 SW2d 886, 168 TexCrim 264.—Assault 97.

Holloway v. State, TexCrimApp, 288 SW2d 86.—Crim Law 1087.1(2).

Holloway v. State, TexCrimApp, 256 SW2d 573.—Crim Law 1070.

Holloway v. State, TexCrimApp, 237 SW2d 303, 155 TexCrim 484.—Autos 351.1.

Holloway v. State, TexCrimApp, 184 SW2d 479, 148 TexCrim 33.—Crim Law 273(2), 517(5), 625(1), 1030(1), 1111(3), 1128(2).

Holloway v. State, TexCrimApp, 178 SW2d 688, 147 TexCrim 106.—Crim Law 1005, 1099.10, 1101.

Holloway v. State, TexCrimApp, 132 SW2d 272.—Crim Law 1090.1(1).

Holloway v. State, TexCrimApp, 111 SW2d 251, 133 TexCrim 359.—Crim Law 949(2).

Holloway; State v., TexApp–Houston (1 Dist), 886 SW2d 482, reh den, and petition for discretionary review refused, cert den 116 SCt 318, 516 US 922, 133 LEd2d 220.—Crim Law 1035(5), 1137(1); Jury 45.

Holloway v. State, TexApp–Fort Worth, 695 SW2d 112, petition for discretionary review gr, aff 751 SW2d 866. —Crim Law 741(1), 1130(0.5), 1159.2(7); Jury 131(4), 131(15.1); Rape 40(2), 51(1), 54(1), 55; Witn 297(1), 344(1), 405(1).

Holloway v. State, TexApp–Austin, 115 SW3d 797.—Const Law 3788, 3809; Crim Law 1144.1, 1144.17; Sent & Pun 1160.

Holloway v. State, TexApp–Beaumont, 698 SW2d 745, petition for discretionary review refused.—Autos 355(13).

Holloway v. Texas Medical Ass'n, TexApp–Houston (1 Dist), 757 SW2d 810, writ den.—Const Law 90.1(5), 2168; Libel 42(1), 74, 112(1), 128.

Holloway; Travelers Indem. Co. of Rhode Island v., CA5 (Tex), 17 F3d 113, reh den.—Fed Cts 776; Insurance 2274, 2276, 2914.

Holloway; U.S. v., CA5 (Tex), 1 F3d 307, reh den.—Crim Law 620(7), 1044.2(2), 1147, 1148, 1167(2); Ind & Inf 125(2); Sent & Pun 77.

Holloway; U.S. v., CA5 (Tex), 962 F2d 451.—Arrest 63.1, 63.4(16), 63.5(5), 68(3); Crim Law 1134(1), 1134(3).

Holloway; Vance v., Tex, 689 SW2d 403.—Acct Action on 13.

Holloway; Vanguard Production v., Tex, 689 SW2d 403. See Vance v. Holloway.

Holloway v. Walker, CA5 (Tex), 811 F2d 263.—Atty & C 58; Contempt 40; Fed Civ Proc 2843.

Holloway v. Walker, CA5 (Tex), 800 F2d 479.—Amb & C 3, 8.

Holloway v. Walker, CA5 (Tex), 790 F2d 1170.—Const Law 3844, 3910, 3911, 3912, 3937.

Holloway v. Walker, CA5 (Tex), 784 F2d 1294.—Civil R 1484.

Holloway v. Walker, CA5 (Tex), 784 F2d 1287, reh den 790 F2d 1170, reh den 800 F2d 479, cert den 107 SCt 571, 479 US 984, 93 LEd2d 576.—Consp 7.5(1); Const Law 3992; Fed Cts 18, 244.

Holloway v. Walker, CA5 (Tex), 765 F2d 517, reh den 773 F2d 1236, cert den 106 SCt 605, 474 US 1037, 88 LEd2d 583, appeal after remand 784 F2d 1287, reh den 790 F2d 1170, reh den 800 F2d 479, cert den 107 SCt 571, 479 US 984, 93 LEd2d 576.—Civil R 1376(8), 1395(1); Fed Cts 269, 272, 555, 574; Judges 36.

Holloway; Wohlfahrt v., TexApp–Houston (14 Dist), 172 SW3d 630, reh overr, and petition stricken, and review den (2 pets), and reh of petition for review den, cert den 127 SCt 666, 166 LEd2d 514.—App & E 232(0.5), 422,

1097(1); Atty & C 130, 167(2), 167(3); Costs 216, 254(1), 264; Evid 584(1); Impl & C C 30; Lim of Act 193, 195(3).

Holloway v. Zapara, TexCivApp–San Antonio, 412 SW2d 943.—Land & Ten 195(2).

Holloway-Houston, Inc. v. Gulf Coast Bank & Trust Co., TexApp–Houston (1 Dist), 224 SW3d 353, reh overr.—App & E 852; Sec Tran 188, 190.

Holloway's Unknown Heirs v. Whatley, TexComApp, 131 SW2d 89, 133 Tex 608, 123 ALR 843.—Deeds 93, 95; Mines 48, 54(2).

Holloway's Unknown Heirs v. Whatley, TexCivApp–Beaumont, 104 SW2d 646, aff 131 SW2d 89, 133 Tex 608, 123 ALR 843.—Deeds 90, 93, 95, 109; Mines 48, 54(2).

Hollowell v. State, TexCrimApp, 571 SW2d 179.—Crim Law 627.8(6), 720(8), 1144.17, 1166(10.10).

Hollums; Glenn v., CCA5 (Tex), 80 F2d 555.—Bankr 2062, 2397(2); Execution 264; Fed Cts 407.1.

Hollums v. Glenn, TexCivApp–Austin, 82 SW2d 731, writ dism.—App & E 1011.1(1); Mech Liens 73(2), 76.

Hollums v. Hancock, TexCivApp–Amarillo, 180 SW2d 209.—Brok 49(3), 54, 63(1), 74, 84(1), 88(3).

Hollums v. Hicks, TexCivApp–Amarillo, 179 SW2d 824, writ refused wom.—Judgm 681; Mtg 191, 538, 553; Receivers 147.

Hollums; Sharkey v., TexCivApp–Amarillo, 400 SW2d 353, ref nre.—App & E 1170.7; Frds St of 56(6); Land & Ten 157(2); Sales 359(2); Trover 4, 5, 10, 61.

Holly v. Bluebonnet Exp. Co., TexCivApp–Galveston, 275 SW2d 737, ref nre.—App & E 1122(2); Autos 247; Trial 350.1, 350.6(3).

Holly v. Cannady, TexApp–Dallas, 669 SW2d 381.—App & E 846(5), 931(1), 989, 1011.1(1); Libel 1, 51(1); Plead 111.42(7).

Holly v. Craig, TexCivApp–Fort Worth, 334 SW2d 586.—Plead 111.42(8); Venue 5.5, 21.

Holly v. Metropolitan Transit Authority, CA5 (Tex), 213 FedAppx 343.—Fed Civ Proc 1751.

Holly v. State, TexCrimApp, 494 SW2d 178.—Crim Law 1181.5(8); Sent & Pun 343, 344.

Holly v. State, TexCrimApp, 460 SW2d 136.—Ind & Inf 41(3), 51(1), 51(2).

Holly v. State, TexCrimApp, 297 SW2d 181.—Crim Law 1090.1(1).

Holly Farms of Texas, Inc.; Johnson v., TexApp–Amarillo, 731 SW2d 641.—App & E 1071.6; Autos 198(3), 226(3), 227.5; Death 57, 89; Hus & W 21, 25(1), 260; Neglig 575; Princ & A 96, 99.

Hollyfield, Ex parte, TexCrimApp, 88 SW2d 112, 129 TexCrim 412.—Licens 7(1); Mun Corp 111(1).

Hollyfield v. Rovenger, TexCivApp–Waco, 262 SW2d 114, ref nre.—Evid 43(2); Judgm 743(2); Partit 83.

Hollymatic Corp.; Roy B. Taylor Sales, Inc. v., CA5 (Tex), 28 F3d 1379, cert den 115 SCt 779, 513 US 1103, 130 LEd2d 673.—Antitrust 529, 541, 569, 571, 582, 641, 977(2), 977(3); Fed Cts 574.

Hollymatic Corp.; Taylor Sales, Inc. v., CA5 (Tex), 28 F3d 1379. See Roy B. Taylor Sales, Inc. v. Hollymatic Corp.

Holly Sugar Co. of Hereford v. Aguirre, TexCivApp–Amarillo, 487 SW2d 421, ref nre.—App & E 996, 1062.2; Autos 245(39), 245(55); Neglig 1032, 1076, 1706; Trial 140(2), 350.7(2), 351.5(5).

Holly Sugar Corp.; Benavides v., TexCivApp–San Antonio, 302 SW2d 946, dism.—Plead 111.42(9); Venue 22(6).

Holly Sugar Corp.; Trevino v., CA5 (Tex), 811 F2d 896.—Civil R 1138, 1139, 1417, 1421, 1484, 1492, 1584, 1592, 1599; Fed Civ Proc 165, 184.10, 2737.3, 2804, 2826; Fed Cts 817.

Hollywood; U.S. v., CA5 (Tex), 138 FedAppx 661, cert den 126 SCt 635, 546 US 1008, 163 LEd2d 514.—Crim Law 1042.

Hollywood; U.S. v., CA5 (Tex), 117 FedAppx 905, cert gr, vac 125 SCt 1716, 544 US 946, 161 LEd2d 522, on remand 138 FedAppx 661, cert den 126 SCt 635, 546 US 1008, 163 LEd2d 514.—Crim Law 274(3.1).

Hollywood Calling v. Public Utility Com'n of Texas, TexApp–Austin, 805 SW2d 618.—Admin Law 387, 391, 750; Tel 614, 756.

Hollywood Fantasy Corp. v. Gabor, CA5 (Tex), 151 F3d 203.—Contracts 22(1), 23, 24, 29, 250, 328(3); Damag 30, 45, 140, 190; Evid 540; Fed Cts 433, 612.1, 763.1, 776, 823; Judges 49(2), 51(2).

Hollywood Marine, Inc.; Intercontinental Terminals, Co. v., TexApp–Houston (1 Dist), 630 SW2d 861, ref nre.—Garn 109, 146; Judgm 181(15.1).

Hollywood Marine, Inc.; U.S. v., CA5 (Tex), 625 F2d 524, cert den 101 SCt 2336, 451 US 994, 68 LEd2d 855.—Environ Law 214.

Hollywood Marine, Inc.; U.S. v., SDTex, 519 FSupp 688.—Environ Law 214, 223.

Hollywood Marine, Inc.; U.S. v., SDTex, 487 FSupp 1211, rev 625 F2d 524, cert den 101 SCt 2336, 451 US 994, 68 LEd2d 855.—Towage 19.

Hollywood Overhead Door Co. of Fort Worth; Gage v., TexCivApp–Fort Worth, 482 SW2d 406, ref nre.—Mech Liens 115(4).

Hollywood Youths, Inc. v. Mistrot, CA5 (Tex), 246 F2d 399.—Bankr 2297.

Holm; Employers Cas. Co. v., TexCivApp–Houston, 393 SW2d 363.—Evid 5(2); Insurance 1823, 1832(1), 1835(2), 2090, 2140, 2141, 2142(6), 2146, 2156.

Hol-Main Corp. v. Dissen, TexCivApp–Corpus Christi, 531 SW2d 912.—App & E 770(1), 773(2), 794.1, 1127.

Holman; Bernardoni v., TexCivApp–Galveston, 177 SW2d 321, writ refused.—Lim of Act 28(1).

Holman v. Dow, TexCivApp–Beaumont, 467 SW2d 547, ref nre.—Acct 18; Assign 59, 73, 90, 137; Corp 399(4), 406(2), 406(4); Joint Adv 1.2(4), 1.15; Partners 17, 20, 44.

Holman; Handy v., TexCivApp–Galveston, 281 SW2d 356.—Elections 59, 83, 291, 293(3), 299(0.5); Schools 97(4); Statut 223.2(11).

Holman v. Holman, TexCivApp–Eastland, 189 SW2d 76.—Divorce 207; Inj 143(1), 143(2), 144, 148(1), 152; Receivers 37.

Holman; Holman v., TexCivApp–Eastland, 189 SW2d 76.—Divorce 207; Inj 143(1), 143(2), 144, 148(1), 152; Receivers 37.

Holman v. Meridian Oil, Inc., TexApp–San Antonio, 988 SW2d 802, reh overr, and review den.—App & E 235, 901, 1175(1); Contracts 168, 176(2); Damag 78(6); Judgm 185.3(14); Mines 73, 73.5; Quiet T 7(2).

Holman; Pit Const. Co. v., TexCivApp–Beaumont, 438 SW2d 662.—Autos 290.

Holman v. Richardson, EDTex, 323 FSupp 606.—Social S 137.5.

Holman v. State, TexCrimApp, 474 SW2d 247.—Controlled Subs 113; Crim Law 394.4(12), 661, 865(2), 1166(1).

Holman v. State, TexCrimApp, 471 SW2d 394.—Burg 41(8).

Holman v. State, TexApp–Houston (1 Dist), 697 SW2d 824.—Crim Law 351(1), 823(4), 1043(1), 1172.6; Homic 558, 559; Sent & Pun 300.

Holman v. State, TexApp–Houston (1 Dist), 680 SW2d 894.—Const Law 4636; Crim Law 44, 813, 822(1), 1134(2); Homic 559, 852, 1404; Jury 31.3(1).

Holman v. State, TexApp–Fort Worth, 730 SW2d 881.—Crim Law 1173.2(3); Homic 1345, 1349, 1479.

Holman v. State, TexApp–Fort Worth, 666 SW2d 672. See Wilson v. State.

Holman v. State, TexApp–Dallas, 636 SW2d 18, petition for discretionary review refused.—Jury 64.

Holman v. State, TexApp–Beaumont, 772 SW2d 530.— Crim Law 126(1), 728(4), 730(3), 1150, 1152(2); Jury 33(5.15), 120, 121.

Holman v. Stephen F. Austin Hotel, TexCivApp–Austin, 599 SW2d 679, dism.—App & E 71(4).

Holman; Swafford v., TexCivApp–Dallas, 446 SW2d 75, ref nre.—Action 60; App & E 934(1), 949, 1073(1); Atty & C 26; Chat Mtg 283, 291; Execution 7, 213, 360; Judgm 178, 183, 713(3).

Holman; Tompkins v., TexCivApp–Austin, 537 SW2d 98, ref nre.—Judgm 747(4); Tresp to T T 6.1, 10, 12, 35(1).

Holman; Travelers Indem. Co. v., CA5 (Tex), 330 F2d 142.—Contracts 143(1), 170(1); Costs 194.16; Estop 85; Insurance 1091(4), 1642, 1741, 1748, 1768, 2270(1), 2295, 3081, 3092, 3131, 3349, 3585.

Holman; Williams v., TexCivApp–Texarkana, 524 SW2d 809.—Evid 589; Land & Ten 152(2), 164(2), 167(3); Plead 111.36, 111.39(6), 111.42(7), 111.43.

Holmans v. Transource Polymers, Inc., TexApp–Fort Worth, 914 SW2d 189, reh overr, and writ den.—App & E 842(1); Com Law 11; Const Law 990; Jury 12(1.1), 14(2); Labor & Emp 239, 2173(2); Statut 176, 181(1), 181(2), 222.

Holman Shipping, Inc.; Eurasia Intern., Ltd. v., CA5 (Tex), 411 F3d 578.—Adm 102, 114.

Holmberg v. State, TexApp–Houston (1 Dist), 931 SW2d 3, petition for discretionary review refused.—Autos 144.2(1); Crim Law 394.6(1).

Holmes, Ex parte, TexCrimApp, 754 SW2d 676.—Courts 70; Evid 41; Statut 146, 157, 169, 206.

Holmes, Ex parte, TexCrimApp, 397 SW2d 458.—Hab Corp 861.

Holmes, In re, BkrtcyNDTex, 121 BR 505.—Bankr 3271, 3286.

Holmes v. American General Ins. Co., TexCivApp–Beaumont, 263 SW2d 615.—App & E 1001(3), 1002, 1003(5); Work Comp 1927.

Holmes; Anderson v., CA5 (Tex), 63 F3d 358. See Moore v. Morales.

Holmes; Bradshaw v., TexCivApp–Amarillo, 246 SW2d 296, ref nre.—App & E 846(5), 931(3), 934(2), 989; Ten in C 1, 4, 14, 15(4), 15(10).

Holmes v. Cagle, TexCivApp–Amarillo, 356 SW2d 814, ref nre.—Neglig 1037(4); Prod Liab 40.

Holmes v. Campsey, TexCivApp–Fort Worth, 415 SW2d 25.—Evid 271(10), 313, 314(1).

Holmes v. Canlen Management Corp., TexCivApp–El Paso, 542 SW2d 199.—Judgm 181(11), 186; Land & Ten 182, 184(2); Pretrial Proc 308.

Holmes v. Cessna Aircraft Co., CA5 (Tex), 11 F3d 63.— Fed Civ Proc 2740, 2741, 2742.1; Fed Cts 830.

Holmes v. Clow, TexCivApp–Tyler, 533 SW2d 99.—App & E 931(1), 989, 1010.1(6), 1010.1(11); Corp 1.4(3), 1.4(4), 1.6(3), 1.7(2); Trial 382, 401, 404(1).

Holmes; Coleman v., CA5 (Tex), 789 F2d 1206.—Fed Civ Proc 417; Fed Cts 668, 669.

Holmes; Comet Motor Freight Lines v., TexCivApp–Waco, 175 SW2d 464, writ refused wom.—App & E 931(1), 1011.1(1), 1012.1(2), 1177(7); Autos 242(1), 242(2), 242(7), 244(6); Neglig 1652, 1656.

Holmes; Comet Motor Freight Lines v., TexCivApp–Eastland, 203 SW2d 233, ref nre.—Autos 244(6), 244(36.1); Evid 54, 87; Neglig 213, 387, 1652, 1656, 1676.

Holmes; Commercial Cas. Ins. Co. v., TexCivApp–Austin, 206 SW2d 882, ref nre.—Insurance 2732, 3182, 3185; Perj 1.

Holmes v. Concord Homes, Ltd., TexApp–Texarkana, 115 SW3d 310, reh overr.—App & E 205, 226(2), 230, 232(0.5), 232(2), 232(3), 242(1), 927(1), 930(1), 989, 999(1), 1001(1), 1001(3), 1003(6), 1051.1(2), 1062.2, 1182; Costs 198, 207, 208; Trial 350.1.

Holmes v. Cooley, TexCivApp–Austin, 308 SW2d 150, ref nre.—App & E 395, 1010.1(1), 1015(2); Autos 206,

226(1), 246(58); Damag 50, 163(4), 210(1); New Tr 56, 144, 159; Trial 351.5(6), 352.4(1).

Holmes v. Cox, TexCivApp–Texarkana, 380 SW2d 917.— Venue 7.5(5).

Holmes; Culberson County v., TexCivApp–El Paso, 513 SW2d 126.—Statut 100(2).

Holmes; Dallas County v., TexApp–Dallas, 62 SW3d 326. —App & E 840(4), 930(1), 994(1), 999(1), 1001(1), 1001(3), 1002, 1003(6), 1122(2); Counties 67; Labor & Emp 806, 861, 863(2); Trial 182, 230, 241, 260(9).

Holmes v. Dallas Intern. Bank, TexApp–Dallas, 718 SW2d 59, ref nre.—App & E 173(2), 863; Judgm 185.2(4), 185.3(10), 186; Usury 22.

Holmes v. Delhi-Taylor Oil Corp., TexCivApp–San Antonio, 337 SW2d 479, writ gr, rev 344 SW2d 420, 162 Tex 39.—Inj 110; Mines 92.44(1).

Holmes v. Eckels, TexApp–Houston (1 Dist), 731 SW2d 101, ref nre.—Dist & Pros Attys 9.

Holmes v. Employers Cas. Co., TexApp–Houston (1 Dist), 699 SW2d 339, ref nre.—Insurance 2374, 2914.

Holmes v. Energy Catering Services, LLC, SDTex, 270 FSupp2d 882.—Adm 32.1, 32.2, 32.10(5); Fed Cts 45, 79, 97, 101, 103, 104, 105, 144, 819; Seamen 29(5.5).

Holmes; First Nat. Bank of Amarillo v., BkrtcyNDTex, 121 BR 505. See Holmes, In re.

Holmes; Green Tree Acceptance, Inc. v., TexApp–Fort Worth, 803 SW2d 458, writ den.—Antitrust 201, 367, 369; App & E 931(1), 1008.1(2), 1008.1(3), 1177(8); Corp 428(1).

Holmes v. Greyhound Lines, Inc., CA5 (Tex), 757 F2d 1563.—Labor & Emp 1219(4); Lim of Act 127(1), 127(11.1), 127(12), 170.

Holmes; Hammonds v., Tex, 559 SW2d 345.—Judgm 627; Mtg 209.

Holmes; Hammonds v., TexCivApp–Waco, 543 SW2d 20, writ gr, aff in part, rev in part 559 SW2d 345.—Judgm 624, 707, 717; Labor & Emp 3027.

Holmes v. Hardy, CA5 (Tex), 852 F2d 151, cert den 109 SCt 322, 488 US 931, 102 LEd2d 339.—Fed Civ Proc 664, 2734.

Holmes v. Holik, TexCivApp–Galveston, 238 SW2d 260, dism.—Brok 7, 46, 55(3).

Holmes v. Holmes, TexCivApp–San Antonio, 301 SW2d 677.—App & E 77(1); Child C 426; Child S 210; Divorce 87, 184(1), 214(0.5).

Holmes; Holmes v., TexCivApp–San Antonio, 301 SW2d 677.—App & E 77(1); Child C 426; Child S 210; Divorce 87, 184(1), 214(0.5).

Holmes v. Holmes, TexCivApp–Beaumont, 588 SW2d 674.—App & E 970(1); Assault 13, 35, 43(2); Trial 41(5), 219.

Holmes; Holmes v., TexCivApp–Beaumont, 588 SW2d 674.—App & E 970(1); Assault 13, 35, 43(2); Trial 41(5), 219.

Holmes v. Holmes, TexCivApp–Waco, 447 SW2d 423.— Deeds 120; Divorce 179, 252.3(3); Hus & W 249(2.1); Wills 614(1).

Holmes; Holmes v., TexCivApp–Waco, 447 SW2d 423.— Deeds 120; Divorce 179, 252.3(3); Hus & W 249(2.1); Wills 614(1).

Holmes v. Jackson, TexCivApp–Waco, 200 SW2d 276.— App & E 1043(8); Child C 601; Evid 43(2); Hus & W 221; Judgm 335(1), 373, 455; Plead 110.

Holmes v. J. C. Penney Co., Tex, 382 SW2d 472.—App & E 1026, 1062.1; Neglig 1714; Trial 350.2, 351.5(1).

Holmes; J. C. Penney Co. v., TexCivApp–Dallas, 378 SW2d 105, writ gr, rev 382 SW2d 472.—App & E 931(1), 996, 1062.1; Neglig 452, 1230, 1571; Trial 350.6(2), 352.3, 352.5(5), 352.12.

Holmes v. Kent, Tex, 221 SW3d 622.—Schools 146(4); Trusts 91.

Holmes; Kent v., TexApp–Texarkana, 139 SW3d 120, review gr, rev 221 SW3d 622.—Contracts 93(1); Courts 89; Divorce 169, 252.3(4), 254(1), 261, 282; Hus & W

249(3), 279(6); Judgm 91, 181(15.1); Lim of Act 58(1); Ref of Inst 17(1), 20; Schools 146(3); Statut 219(1), 219(4); Trusts 103(3).

Holmes v. Klein, TexCivApp–Amarillo, 84 SW2d 521, writ dism.—Bills & N 499, 534; Chat Mtg 174(1).

Holmes v. Lawrence, TexCivApp–San Antonio, 118 SW2d 900, dism.—App & E 706(3); Trial 397(1).

Holmes; Louisiana Pacific Corp. v., TexApp–San Antonio, 94 SW3d 834, review den.—Adv Poss 34, 36, 37, 38, 60(1), 60(3), 112, 115(3); App & E 1001(3); Bound 25; Land & Ten 66(2).

Holmes v. McKnight, TexCivApp–Corpus Christi, 373 SW2d 541.—Mines 73.1(3), 75, 78.2.

Holmes v. McMichael, TexCivApp–Texarkana, 430 SW2d 824.—App & E 846(5), 934(2), 1129; Mtg 37(2), 38(1).

Holmes; Magaha v., TexApp–Houston (1 Dist), 886 SW2d 447.—Atty & C 11(2.1), 11(12), 11(13).

Holmes v. Morales, Tex, 924 SW2d 920.—App & E 93, 1175(1); Courts 1, 89; Records 51, 60; Statut 223.4.

Holmes v. Morales, TexApp–Austin, 906 SW2d 570, reh overr, and writ gr, rev 924 SW2d 920.—Const Law 58, 2330, 2332, 2390; Records 50, 51, 54.

Holmes v. National Football League, NDTex, 939 FSupp 517.—Alt Disp Res 328, 332; Fed Civ Proc 1829, 1832; Fraud 31; Labor & Emp 1326, 1549(5), 1569, 1574, 1575, 1592, 1601, 1608, 1610(1), 1619, 1623(1), 1967; States 18.15, 18.46, 18.53.

Holmes; Nationwide Ins. Co. v., TexApp–San Antonio, 842 SW2d 335. See Nationwide Mut. Ins. Co. v. Holmes.

Holmes; Nationwide Mut. Ins. Co. v., TexApp–San Antonio, 842 SW2d 335, reh den, and writ den.—Antitrust 221, 364, 369, 389(1), 393, 397; App & E 930(3), 1003(7); Costs 194.10, 194.16; Damag 87(2); Insurance 3349.

Holmes; Nawas v., TexCivApp–Waco, 541 SW2d 283.— Bills & N 63, 426, 452(1), 511, 518(1), 537(2); Evid 420(3), 420(7).

Holmes v. Olson, Tex, 587 SW2d 678.—Cons Cred 61.1; Courts 97(5).

Holmes; Olson v., TexCivApp–Austin, 571 SW2d 211, ref nre 587 SW2d 678.—Cons Cred 50; Courts 97(5).

Holmes v. Ottawa Truck, Inc., TexApp–El Paso, 960 SW2d 866, reh overr, and review den.—Judgm 181(1), 183.

Holmes; Payne v., TexCivApp–Fort Worth, 151 SW2d 359, writ dism, correct.—App & E 216(1), 218.2(7), 1175(1); Mines 109.

Holmes; Perry v., CA5 (Tex), 152 FedAppx 404.—Civil R 1088(5); Fed Civ Proc 2734; Lim of Act 58(1).

Holmes v. P.K. Pipe & Tubing, Inc., TexApp–Houston (1 Dist), 856 SW2d 530.—Antitrust 360; App & E 179(1), 662(4), 842(2), 931(1), 1008.1(2), 1010.1(1), 1012.1(4); Damag 91(1); Fraud 3, 16, 22(1), 36, 58(4), 59(1), 60; Land & Ten 130(2), 171(1), 171(3), 213(5); Lim of Act 100(11), 100(12).

Holmes v. Red Arrow Freight Lines, TexCivApp–Waco, 466 SW2d 343, writ dism.—Plead 111.42(8).

Holmes; Resolution Trust Corp. v., SDTex, 846 FSupp 1310.—B & L Assoc 42(6); Fed Civ Proc 2658; Lim of Act 4(2), 11(1), 58(5); States 18.15, 18.19.

Holmes; Resolution Trust Corp. v., SDTex, 839 FSupp 449.—B & L Assoc 42(1), 42(6), 42(16); Fed Civ Proc 2470.1, 2539, 2544; Lim of Act 58(5).

Holmes; Richardson v., TexCivApp–Beaumont, 525 SW2d 293, ref nre.—App & E 930(3), 989, 1064.1(9); Damag 59; Death 64, 72, 78, 91, 99(4); Health 632, 823(5), 827.

Holmes; Roberts v., TexCivApp–Eastland, 412 SW2d 947. —App & E 1003(9.1); Trial 351.2(4), 365.1(4), 366.

Holmes; Rodriguez v., CA5 (Tex), 963 F2d 799.—Fed Cts 425, 427; Lim of Act 130(5).

Holmes; Rodriguez v., TexCivApp–San Antonio, 556 SW2d 125.—App & E 863; Health 770, 813; Judgm 186.

Holmes; Rutherford v., TexCivApp–Austin, 599 SW2d 668, dism.—App & E 170(1), 499(1); Cons Cred 51, 52; Plead 427.

Holmes; Shaw v., TexCivApp–Waco, 524 SW2d 74.— Contracts 28(3), 90; Evid 588; Trial 382.

Holmes; Smith v., TexApp–Austin, 53 SW3d 815, appeal after remand 2003 WL 1561321, reh overr, and review den.—App & E 977(1); Const Law 3993, 4010; Judgm 138(3), 162(4), 163; New Tr 140(1).

Holmes v. Southern Pac. Co., TexCivApp–El Paso, 98 SW2d 1048.—App & E 688(2), 727; New Tr 44(1), 140(2).

Holmes; Stansberry v., CA5 (Tex), 613 F2d 1285, reh den 616 F2d 568, cert den 101 SCt 240, 449 US 886, 66 LEd2d 112.—Const Law 1176, 4096; Crim Law 13.1(1); Em Dom 2(1.2); Mun Corp 594(2); Zoning 76, 288, 609.

Holmes v. State, TexCrimApp, 502 SW2d 728.—Crim Law 695(4); Sent & Pun 1900.

Holmes v. State, TexCrimApp, 493 SW2d 795.—Crim Law 695(2), 1036.1(2), 1043(3), 1169.3.

Holmes v. State, TexCrimApp, 398 SW2d 121.—Crim Law 1090.13, 1171.3; Homic 1134.

Holmes v. State, TexCrimApp, 333 SW2d 842, 169 Tex-Crim 343, cert den 81 SCt 240, 364 US 905, 5 LEd2d 197.—Crim Law 665(1), 665(4), 721(3), 1119(5), 1174(2); Rape 64.

Holmes v. State, TexCrimApp, 305 SW2d 588, 165 Tex-Crim 220.—Crim Law 366(4); Infants 20.

Holmes v. State, TexCrimApp, 146 SW2d 400, 140 Tex-Crim 619.—Crim Law 730(1), 763(24), 783(1), 822(1), 822(8), 822(11), 1091(2), 1111(3), 1137(2); Homic 1492; Sent & Pun 1900.

Holmes v. State, TexCrimApp, 123 SW2d 343, 136 Tex-Crim 26.—Crim Law 1128(1).

Holmes v. State, TexCrimApp, 120 SW2d 595, 136 Tex-Crim 26, reh den 123 SW2d 343, 136 TexCrim 26.— Crim Law 394.5(2), 598(6); Larc 62(2).

Holmes v. State, TexApp–Fort Worth, 873 SW2d 123.— Crim Law 1144.13(8), 1159.5; Ind & Inf 119, 167, 171; Kidnap 15, 32, 36.

Holmes v. State, TexApp–Texarkana, 938 SW2d 488.— Crim Law 577.10(8), 577.10(10), 577.15(3), 577.16(4), 938(3), 945(2), 1139.

Holmes v. State, TexApp–Texarkana, 830 SW2d 263.— Crim Law 20, 795(1.5), 795(2.10); Homic 527, 659, 709, 807, 1458, 1474, 1476, 1478, 1483, 1484; Ind & Inf 189(4).

Holmes v. State, TexApp–Amarillo, 634 SW2d 762.— Double J 31; Sent & Pun 2004, 2007.

Holmes v. State, TexApp–Waco, 135 SW3d 178.—Crim Law 304(1), 388.1, 478(1), 1043(1), 1043(2), 1153(2).

Holmes v. State, TexApp–Waco, 962 SW2d 663, reh overr, and petition for discretionary review refused, untimely filed.—Controlled Subs 80, 126; Crim Law 369.2(2), 374, 394.1(1), 394.1(3), 412(4), 673(5), 678(1), 678(3), 713, 719(1), 720(1), 720(7.1), 753.2(3.1), 777, 783.5, 790, 800(1), 800(2), 814(1), 814(4), 814(5), 1134(2), 1144.1, 1162, 1169.5(3), 1169.11, 1171.3; Searches 40.1, 42.1, 45.

Holmes v. State, TexApp–Waco, 752 SW2d 700.—Crim Law 406(2); Sent & Pun 2003, 2021.

Holmes v. State, TexApp–Houston (14 Dist), 223 SW3d 728.—Crim Law 777, 1172.1(1), 1173.2(9).

Holmes v. State, TexApp–Houston (14 Dist), 795 SW2d 815, petition for discretionary review refused.—Arrest 63.4(15); Chem Dep 9.

Holmes v. State, TexApp–Houston (14 Dist), 681 SW2d 812.—Crim Law 1130(5); Sent & Pun 1379(2), 1381(4).

Holmes v. State Dept. of Public Welfare, CA5 (Tex), 370 F2d 371.—Fed Cts 269.

Holmes v. Steger, Tex, 339 SW2d 663, 161 Tex 242.— Courts 247(1), 247(8).

Holmes v. Texas A&M University, CA5 (Tex), 145 F3d 681.—Civil R 1384; Fed Cts 425, 611, 612.1, 763.1, 776; Lim of Act 95(15), 105(1).

Holmes; Texas Emp. Ins. Ass'n v., Tex, 196 SW2d 390, 145 Tex 158, answer to certified question conformed to Texas Employers' Insurance Ass'n v. Holmes, 196 SW2d 1023.—Statut 219(9.1); Work Comp 50, 862.

Holmes v. Tibbs, TexCivApp–Corpus Christi, 542 SW2d 487.—Child S 62, 84, 200, 508(4), 556(1); Evid 67(1).

Holmes v. Travelers Ins. Co., TexCivApp–Galveston, 148 SW2d 270, writ refused.—Work Comp 110, 170, 172, 181, 185, 250.

Holmes; U.S. v., CA5 (Tex), 406 F3d 337, cert den 126 SCt 375, 546 US 871, 163 LEd2d 163.—Consp 23.1, 24.5, 47(1), 47(2), 47(5); Crim Law 423(1), 641.13(1), 662.8, 662.11, 662.60, 713, 723(1), 730(14), 938(1), 942(1), 945(2), 1030(1), 1035(1), 1035(7), 1035(10), 1037.1(2), 1042, 1119(1), 1130(5), 1141(2), 1144.13(2.1), 1148, 1156(1), 1158(1), 1159.2(1), 1159.2(7), 1159.2(8), 1159.6, 1163(1), 1166(1), 1166(10.10), 1171.1(2.1); Jury 34(6), 34(7); Postal 35(2), 49(11); Sent & Pun 661, 761.

Holmes; U.S. v., CA5 (Tex), 614 F2d 985.—Const Law 1295, 1298, 1299, 1300, 1303, 1304, 1310, 1386(2); Int Rev 4493, 4495, 4512.

Holmes; U.S. v., SDTex, 110 FSupp 233.—Crim Law 974(2); Extort 30; Ind & Inf 71.2(1).

Holmes; VanZandt v., TexApp–Waco, 689 SW2d 259.—App & E 863, 866(1), 927(1); Bound 26, 27, 44; Pretrial Proc 551; Tresp to T T 42.1; Trial 139.1(14), 382.

Holmes; W. T. Carter & Bro. v., TexComApp, 113 SW2d 1225, 131 Tex 365.—Adv Poss 13, 34, 36, 63(2), 98, 112.

Holmes; W. T. Carter & Bro. v., TexCivApp–Beaumont, 85 SW2d 993, rev 113 SW2d 1225, 131 Tex 365.—Tresp to T T 41(1), 45(1).

Holmes; Zurich General Acc. & Liability Ins. Co. v., TexCivApp–Beaumont, 291 SW2d 373, ref nre.—Evid 20(1); Work Comp 904, 932, 1619.

Holmes Enterprises, Inc. v. John Bankston Const. & Equipment Rental, Inc., TexApp–Beaumont, 664 SW2d 832. See James Holmes Enterprises, Inc. v. John Bankston Const. & Equipment Rental, Inc.

Holmes' Estate; C.I.R. v., USTex, 66 SCt 257, 326 U.S. 480, 90 LEd 228, reh den Commissioner of Internal Revenue v. Holmes' Estate, 66 SCt 519, 327 US 813, 90 LEd 1037, on remand 1946 WL 6244.—Int Rev 4149.10, 4159(6), 4200.

Holmes' Estate; C.I.R. v., CCA5 (Tex), 148 F2d 740, cert gr Commissioner of Internal Revenue v. Holmes' Estate, 66 SCt 40, 326 US 702, 90 LEd 413, rev 66 SCt 257, 326 US 480, 90 LEd 228, reh den 66 SCt 519, 327 US 813, 90 LEd 1037, on remand 1946 WL 6244.—Int Rev 4159(6).

Holmes, State ex rel., v. Denson, TexCrimApp, 671 SW2d 896. See State ex rel. Holmes v. Denson.

Holmes, State ex rel., v. Honorable Court of Appeals for Third Dist., TexCrimApp, 885 SW2d 389. See State ex rel. Holmes v. Honorable Court of Appeals for Third Dist.

Holmes, State ex rel., v. Klevenhagen, TexCrimApp, 819 SW2d 539. See State ex rel. Holmes v. Klevenhagen.

Holmes, State ex rel., v. Kolenda, TexApp–Houston (1 Dist), 756 SW2d 39. See State ex rel. Holmes v. Kolenda.

Holmes, State ex rel., v. Lanford, TexApp–Houston (14 Dist, 837 SW2d 705. See State ex rel. Holmes v. Lanford.

Holmes, State ex rel., v. Lanford, TexApp–Houston (14 Dist, 764 SW2d 593. See State ex rel. Holmes v. Lanford.

Holmes, State ex rel., v. Salinas, TexCrimApp, 784 SW2d 421. See State ex rel. Holmes v. Salinas.

Holmes, State ex rel., v. Salinas, TexApp–Houston (14 Dist, 774 SW2d 421. See State ex rel. Holmes v. Salinas.

Holmes, State ex rel., v. Shaver, TexApp–Texarkana, 824 SW2d 285. See State ex rel. Holmes v. Shaver.

Holmgram; Buchman v., TexCivApp–Fort Worth, 81 SW2d 177.—Cons Cred 4.

Holmquest v. Priesmeyer, TexCivApp–Hous (1 Dist), 574 SW2d 173.—Antitrust 223; App & E 518(6), 758.1, 835(2), 846(5); Contracts 175(3), 229(3), 322(4), 346(2).

Holmquist; Banegas v., TexCivApp–El Paso, 535 SW2d 410.—Work Comp 450.

Holmquist v. Occidental Life Ins. Co. of California, TexCivApp–Hous (14 Dist), 536 SW2d 434, ref nre.—App & E 223, 232(0.5), 1175(2); Insurance 1812, 3360, 3467, 3480; Interpl 35.

Holmstrom v. Lee, TexApp–Austin, 26 SW3d 526.—Decl Judgm 385; Ease 3(1), 5, 12(1), 14(1), 15.1, 38, 42, 48(2), 48(6), 51; Judgm 18(1); Mtg 372(1); Plead 1, 72, 76, 397.

Holmstrom; Rinn v., TexCivApp–Austin, 243 SW2d 862. —App & E 994(3), 1008.2; Autos 150, 226(1), 242(8), 243(17), 244(43), 244(58), 245(80); Costs 32(2).

Holmstrom; Rodriguez v., TexApp–Austin, 627 SW2d 198.—Antitrust 393, 397; Costs 252; Judgm 335(1), 335(2), 335(3), 335(4); Review 8.

Holoye; Starkey v., TexApp–Hous (14 Dist), 536 SW2d 438, ref nre.—App & E 80(3); Deeds 136; Divorce 252.5(1), 321 1/2; Mtg 12; Partit 13.

Holson; Bisbee v., TexCivApp–Eastland, 109 SW2d 289. —App & E 773(2), 773(4).

Holson v. Bisbee, TexCivApp–Eastland, 97 SW2d 510, writ refused.—App & E 1177(6); Contracts 214.

Holst; American Speedreading Academy, Inc. v., TexCivApp–Beaumont, 496 SW2d 133.—App & E 920(3), 931(3), 954(1); Contracts 117(3); Inj 135, 147; Reports 1.

Holst v. Newsletters, Inc., TexCivApp–Hous (1 Dist), 578 SW2d 420, ref nre.—App & E 447, 456.

Holstead; Drake v., TexApp–Beaumont, 757 SW2d 909.—App & E 1047(1); Evid 51; New Tr 68.4(6).

Holstein v. Federal Debt Management, Inc., TexApp–Houston (1 Dist), 902 SW2d 31.—App & E 93, 852, 934(1); Banks 508; Judges 53; Judgm 181(2), 181(7), 185(2), 185.3(2); Lim of Act 58(1), 119(3).

Holstein v. Grier, TexCivApp–San Antonio, 262 SW2d 954.—Courts 78; Damag 208(5); Trial 41(5).

Holstein; Texaco, Inc. v., CA5 (Tex), 793 F2d 1448. See Pin v. Texaco, Inc.

Holstein; U.S. v., CA5 (Tex), 435 F2d 144, cert den Wolfe v. US, 91 SCt 1229, 401 US 993, 28 LEd2d 530, cert den 91 SCt 1240, 401 US 993, 28 LEd2d 531.—Controlled Subs 86; Crim Law 393(1), 1132; Cust Dut 134.

Holstein and Kappert, G.m.b.H.; Lodge & Shipley Co. v., SDTex, 322 FSupp 1039.—Pat 16.4, 26(1.1), 27(1), 36.1(1), 36.1(3), 36.2(3), 36.2(9), 112.1, 112.3(1), 112.3(3), 178, 234, 237, 241, 312(1.1).

Holstine v. Connecticut General Life Ins. Co., EDTex, 338 FSupp 817.—Insurance 2589(1), 2605.

Holston v. Implement Dealers Mut. Fire Ins. Co., CA5 (Tex), 206 F2d 682.—Insurance 3554, 3564(1), 3564(3), 3564(4).

Holston v. Sloan, TexCivApp–El Paso, 620 SW2d 255.—Const Law 4187; Health 275.

Holsworth v. Czeschin, TexApp–Corpus Christi, 632 SW2d 643.—App & E 925(2); Costs 194.18; Labor & Emp 256(1).

Holt, In re, BkrtcyNDTex, 310 BR 675.—Assault 2; Bankr 2163, 3374(1), 3374(2), 3374(4), 3374(5), 3374(7), 3374(9); Damag 57.22, 57.23(1), 57.23(2), 57.25(1); False Imp 2.

Holt; Allied Vista, Inc. v., TexApp–Houston (14 Dist), 987 SW2d 138, reh overr, and review den.—App & E 1001(3); Damag 95, 103, 117, 186, 208(1), 210(1); Estop 85; Fraud 12, 13(3), 59(2), 59(3); Labor & Emp 40(2), 866.

Holt; Angelina Cas. Co. v., Tex, 362 SW2d 99.—Work Comp 1958, 1968(6).

HOLT;

Holt; Angelina Cas. Co. v., TexCivApp–Waco, 351 SW2d 627, writ gr, rev 362 SW2d 99.—Work Comp 1615, 1619, 1661, 1929, 1932, 1974.

Holt; Bagley v., TexCivApp–Texarkana, 430 SW2d 817, ref nre.—Elections 27, 227(1), 305(7); Schools 38, 39.

Holt; Beach, Bait & Tackle, Inc., Store No. 2 v., TexApp–Houston (14 Dist), 693 SW2d 684.—Corp 507(12); Judgm 123(1); Proc 74, 136, 152, 153.

Holt v. City Nat. Bank of Bryan, TexCivApp–Waco, 273 SW2d 902, ref nre.—Banks 133; Hus & W 262.1(3), 265.

Holt v. City of Lubbock, TexCivApp–Eastland, 390 SW2d 500.—App & E 901; Evid 589; Plead 45, 111.23, 111.30, 111.38, 111.39(6); Venue 5.5, 8.5(5), 22(4), 22(9).

Holt v. City of San Antonio, TexCivApp–San Antonio, 547 SW2d 715, ref nre.—Inj 85(2), 204; Licens 7(1).

Holt v. City of San Marcos, TexCivApp–Austin, 288 SW2d 802, ref nre.—App & E 203.2, 930(3), 931(1), 1051(1), 1060.1(2.1); Em Dom 167(3); Mun Corp 733(2), 845(4); New Tr 140(3); Trial 114; Witn 379(6).

Holt v. Collins, TexCivApp–Waco, 131 SW2d 813, writ dism, correct.—App & E 207, 930(1); Consp 19; Trial 131(3), 139.1(12).

Holt v. Community Development & Const. Corp., TexCivApp–Beaumont, 575 SW2d 395, ref nre.—App & E 1050.1(9); Evid 181.

Holt; Crawford v., TexCivApp–Dallas, 92 SW2d 1144.—Courts 475(2).

Holt; De Leon v., TexCivApp–Austin, 322 SW2d 659.—Action 45(1); Time 9(1), 9(3).

Holt v. D'Hanis State Bank, TexApp–San Antonio, 993 SW2d 237.—Atty & C 76(1); Banks 67; Judgm 184; Lim of Act 119(3), 195(3).

Holt v. Drake, TexCivApp–Eastland, 505 SW2d 650.—Trial 194(9); Wills 245; Witn 139(10).

Holt; Eason v., CA5 (Tex), 73 F3d 600, appeal after remand 114 F3d 1182.—Fed Civ Proc 1773, 1832, 1835, 2734; Fed Cts 776; Sent & Pun 1548.

Holt v. Elliott Industries, Inc., TexApp–Fort Worth, 711 SW2d 435.—Judgm 181(30).

Holt v. Employers' Liability Assur. Corp., TexCivApp–Waco, 423 SW2d 620.—Judgm 185.3(12).

Holt; Employers Reinsurance Corp. v., Tex, 410 SW2d 633.—Work Comp 1765, 1773, 1834, 1916.

Holt v. Employers Reinsurance Corp., TexCivApp–Houston, 393 SW2d 329, writ gr, aff 410 SW2d 633.—Judgm 181(21); Work Comp 1330, 1687, 1689, 1690, 1765, 1829, 1834, 1916.

Holt v. Epley, TexApp–Amarillo, 894 SW2d 511, reh overr, and writ den.—App & E 179(1); Const Law 328, 2315; Damag 49.10; Judgm 185(2); Lim of Act 55(3).

Holt; Ewing v., TexApp–Fort Worth, 835 SW2d 274.—Child S 120, 302, 364.

Holt v. Farley, TexCivApp–Texarkana, 350 SW2d 659.—Execution 172(2), 172(4).

Holt v. Federal Deposit Ins. Corp., CA5 (Tex), 868 F2d 146. See CTS Truss, Inc., Matter of.

Holt v. Federal Deposit Ins. Corp., CA5 (Tex), 859 F2d 357. See CTS Truss, Inc., Matter of.

Holt v. Federal Deposit Ins. Corp., BkrtcyWDTex, 99 BR 742. See Instrument Sales & Service, Inc., In re.

Holt v. F.F. Enterprises, TexApp–Amarillo, 990 SW2d 756, review den, and reh of petition for review overr.—App & E 389(2), 389(3); Atty & C 62; Courts 85(2); Statut 181(2), 206.

Holt; First State Bank of Monahans, Tex. v., BkrtcyWDTex, 41 BR 132. See McDaniel, In re.

Holt v. Fuller Cotton Oil Co., TexCivApp–Amarillo, 175 SW2d 272, writ refused wom.—Neglig 1036, 1040(3), 1051, 1066, 1076, 1090, 1175, 1176.

Holt; General Office Outfitters, Inc. v., TexApp–Dallas, 670 SW2d 748.—App & E 496; Corp 507(12); Judgm 162(2).

Holt v. Giles, Tex, 240 SW2d 991, 150 Tex 351.—Mines 5.2(3).

Holt; Gist v., TexCivApp–Beaumont, 173 SW2d 216, writ refused wom.—App & E 387(3), 395, 653(1), 662(1), 668, 670(1).

Holt v. Hedberg, TexCivApp–Fort Worth, 316 SW2d 955.—Lim of Act 39(7), 74(2); Mental H 15, 16.

Holt v. Henrichson, TexCivApp–San Antonio, 321 SW2d 146, ref nre.—Bills & N 400, 422(1).

Holt v. Holt, TexCivApp–Dallas, 620 SW2d 650.—Child S 62, 234, 339(5).

Holt; Holt v., TexCivApp–Dallas, 620 SW2d 650.—Child S 62, 234, 339(5).

Holt v. Holt, TexCivApp–Waco, 271 SW2d 477, ref nre.—Damag 89(2), 189.

Holt; Holt v., TexCivApp–Waco, 271 SW2d 477, ref nre.—Damag 89(2), 189.

Holt; Hooper v., TexCivApp–Texarkana, 416 SW2d 916.—App & E 1177(5); Autos 208; Courts 92; Judgm 199(3), 199(3.17); Trial 365.1(7).

Holt v. International Great Northern R. Co., TexCivApp–Texarkana, 152 SW2d 472.—App & E 544(3); Evid 82; Trial 358, 365.2.

Holt v. JTM Industries, Inc., CA5 (Tex), 89 F3d 1224, reh and sug for reh den 105 F3d 658, cert den 117 SCt 1821, 520 US 1229, 137 LEd2d 1029.—Civil R 1243, 1244, 1522; Fed Civ Proc 2151, 2608.1; Fed Cts 776, 798, 801; Statut 223.2(19).

Holt; Keele v., CA5 (Tex), 171 F2d 480.—Armed S 108.1; Fed Cts 192, 855.1.

Holt; Leatherman v., TexCivApp–Eastland, 212 SW2d 1004.—Adv Poss 115(1); Deeds 121; Tresp to T T 6.1.

Holt; Liberty Trust Co. Employees Profit Sharing Trust v., WDTex, 130 BR 467. See Liberty Trust Co., Matter of.

Holt v. Lone Star Gas Co., TexApp–Fort Worth, 921 SW2d 301, reh overr.—App & E 934(1); Civil R 1104, 1106, 1216, 1218(3), 1744; Courts 97(1); Judgm 181(21), 185(2).

Holt v. Lowden, TexCivApp–Fort Worth, 140 SW2d 318.—App & E 218.2(5.1), 758.1; Carr 205, 216, 230(13); Evid 534, 571(9).

Holt; Manley v., TexCivApp–Amarillo, 161 SW2d 857, writ refused wom.—Evid 314(1), 324(1), 593; Judgm 199(3.9); Spec Perf 13, 114(1), 121(3), 128(2); Ven & Pur 33.

Holt v. Manley, TexCivApp–Amarillo, 146 SW2d 773.—App & E 1178(8); Frds St of 129(3), 139(4), 140; Trial 350.4(2); Ven & Pur 37(1), 44, 85, 185.

Holt; MAPCO, Inc. v., TexCivApp–Amarillo, 476 SW2d 70, ref nre.—App & E 1050.1(1); Em Dom 64, 203(1), 219, 262(2), 262(5); Evid 142(2), 317(2), 546.

Holt; MAPCO, Inc. v., TexCivApp–Amarillo, 476 SW2d 64, ref nre.—App & E 1050.1(1); Em Dom 64, 219, 262(5); Evid 142(2), 188, 495, 546; New Tr 31.

Holt v. Marshall, TexCivApp–Fort Worth, 222 SW2d 1018, ref nre.—App & E 863, 927(7); Garn 171.

Holt; Morris v., Tex, 714 SW2d 311.—App & E 218.2(10); Trial 365.1(1).

Holt v. Owen Elec. Supply, Inc., TexApp–Houston (1 Dist), 722 SW2d 22.—Guar 91; Partners 125, 165.

Holt v. Preload Technology, Inc., TexApp–El Paso, 774 SW2d 806.—Const Law 2312, 4186; Work Comp 19, 2162.

Holt v. Purviance, TexCivApp–Dallas, 347 SW2d 321, ref nre.—App & E 230, 387(3), 758.3(4), 1047(5); Contracts 322(4); Damag 221(2.1); New Tr 152; Pretrial Proc 723.1.

Holt; Rawls v., TexCivApp–El Paso, 193 SW2d 536, ref nre, and writ refused wom.—App & E 907(3); Fraud 23; Sales 179(4), 266, 288(2), 439, 441(3); Trial 350.4(2), 352.7, 356(1), 356(3), 365.3.

Holt v. Ray, TexCivApp–Eastland, 435 SW2d 568.—Autos 201(6), 242(1), 242(7); Neglig 379, 384, 386, 387, 431, 1713; Torts 119.

Holt v. **Reproductive Services, Inc.**, TexApp–Corpus Christi, 946 SW2d 602, reh overr, and writ den.—App & E 836, 917(1), 946, 960(1); Land & Ten 164(1), 167(8), 169(3); Neglig 202, 220, 1037(4), 1070, 1692; Pretrial Proc 622.

Holt; **Reynolds v.**, TexCivApp–Waco, 474 SW2d 506.— Evid 174.5, 222(2); Spec Perf 76.

Holt v. **State**, TexCrimApp, 887 SW2d 16.—Autos 349(9).

Holt v. **State**, TexCrimApp, 538 SW2d 125.—Arrest 63.4(8), 71.1(5).

Holt v. **State**, TexCrimApp, 487 SW2d 725.—Crim Law 1130(2); Witn 337(28).

Holt v. **State**, TexCrimApp, 378 SW2d 323.—Crim Law 736(2), 781(4), 1169.12.

Holt v. **State**, TexCrimApp, 289 SW2d 293, 163 TexCrim 65.—Crim Law 1184(1); Rob 24.15(1), 30; Sent & Pun 1057.

Holt v. **State**, TexCrimApp, 208 SW2d 643, 151 TexCrim 399.—Crim Law 519(2), 522(1), 736(2); Fed Cts 506.

Holt v. **State**, TexCrimApp, 160 SW2d 957, 144 TexCrim 88.—Arrest 63.1; Crim Law 394.4(9), 406(1), 429(3); Rec S Goods 6.

Holt v. **State**, TexCrimApp, 160 SW2d 944, 144 TexCrim 62.—Arrest 71.1(6); Crim Law 59(1), 59(3), 351(3), 775(3), 1172.1(2), 1172.1(4); False Pret 16, 23.

Holt v. **State**, TexCrimApp, 121 SW2d 370, 135 TexCrim 441.—Crim Law 1097(5), 1184(1).

Holt; **State v.**, TexApp–Fort Worth, 852 SW2d 47, reh den, and petition for discretionary review gr, rev 887 SW2d 16.—Autos 349(9); Searches 23.

Holt v. **State**, TexApp–Austin, 683 SW2d 92.—Crim Law 386.

Holt v. **State**, TexApp–San Antonio, 912 SW2d 294, reh overr, and petition for discretionary review refused.— Const Law 3309; Crim Law 377, 1153(4), 1158(1), 1158(3); Jury 33(5.15); Witn 372(1), 372(2), 373, 405(1).

Holt v. **State**, TexApp–San Antonio, 724 SW2d 914.— Arrest 63.5(6); Crim Law 511.1(2.1), 511.1(3), 511.1(9), 511.2; Searches 66.

Holt v. **State**, TexApp–Amarillo, 195 SW3d 795.—Autos 355(6); Crim Law 1043(1).

Holt v. **State**, TexApp–Waco, 64 SW3d 434.—Crim Law 1020.5, 1077.3.

Holt v. **State**, TexApp–Tyler, 899 SW2d 22.—Crim Law 637, 723(1), 723(3), 857(1), 1165(1), 1177.5(1); Sent & Pun 1302, 1364, 1371.

Holt; **Sun Operating Ltd. Partnership v.**, TexApp–Amarillo, 984 SW2d 277, reh den, and reh den, and review den, and reh overr.—App & E 930(1), 1064.1(2.1); Contracts 143(3), 152, 309(1); Estop 92(1), 92(2); Mines 73, 73.5, 75, 78.1(3), 78.1(9), 78.7(5).

Holt; **Swanson v.**, TexComApp, 87 SW2d 1090, 126 Tex 383, appeal after remand 97 SW2d 285.—App & E 344.

Holt; **Swanson v.**, TexCivApp–Texarkana, 97 SW2d 285. —App & E 181, 302(1), 302(6), 745, 750(5), 866(3); New Tr 71, 128(5); Trial 143.

Holt; **Swartout v.**, TexCivApp–Waco, 272 SW2d 756, ref nre.—Evid 43(1); Health 821(2), 821(3), 823(5); Jury 10, 131(1); New Tr 140(3).

Holt; **Tejas Trail Property Owners Ass'n v.**, TexCivApp–Fort Worth, 516 SW2d 441.—App & E 704.2, 852, 934(2), 1071.1(5.1), 1071.6, 1078(5); Estop 118; Judgm 289; Trial 395(1).

Holt; **Texas Elec. Service Co. v.**, TexCivApp–Fort Worth, 249 SW2d 662, ref nre.—App & E 930(1); Electricity 14(1), 16(1), 16(5), 16(7); Labor & Emp 29, 2765, 3159, 3162, 3164; Neglig 1010, 1011, 1037(7), 1204(1).

Holt v. **Texas-New Mexico Pipeline Co.**, CCA5 (Tex), 145 F2d 862, cert den 65 SCt 1570, 325 US 879, 89 LEd 1996.—Labor & Emp 3155, 3159, 3160, 3161; Neglig 1037(4), 1037(7), 1204(1).

Holt v. **Trantham**, TexCivApp–Fort Worth, 575 SW2d 83, ref nre.—Elections 19, 29, 33 1/2, 45; Estop 62.4; Mun Corp 159(1).

Holt; **U.S. v.**, NDTex, 397 FSupp 1397, aff in part, vac in part U.S. v. Bailey, 537 F2d 845, cert den Harstrom v US, 97 SCt 764, 429 US 1051, 50 LEd2d 767.—Const Law 4728; Crim Law 1177; Sent & Pun 8, 116, 1361, 1362.

Holt v. **Wheeler**, TexCivApp–Galveston, 301 SW2d 678, dism.—Const Law 191; Insurance 1384; Plead 111.42(1); Venue 3.

Holt; **York v.**, TexCivApp–Fort Worth, 144 SW2d 415.— Hab Corp 532(1), 662.1, 803, 891.

Holt v. **York**, TexCivApp–Waco, 335 SW2d 390, ref nre.— Marriage 58(1), 58(7), 59.

Holt Atherton Industries, Inc. v. **Heine**, Tex, 835 SW2d 80.—App & E 931(1), 1010.1(2), 1178(6); Damag 103, 190, 194; Judgm 112, 143(3), 143(4), 145(2), 146, 151, 159, 163.

Holt Atherton Industries, Inc. v. **Heine**, TexApp–Corpus Christi, 797 SW2d 250, writ gr, aff in part, rev in part 835 SW2d 80.—App & E 865, 957(1), 1010.1(3); Damag 140, 190; Judgm 111, 112, 143(2), 143(4), 146, 162(2), 162(4), 220, 248.

Holt Co. of Texas v. **OCE, Inc.**, TexApp–San Antonio, 971 SW2d 618. See B.D. Holt Co. v. OCE, Inc.

Holten; **Michiana Easy Livin' Country, Inc. v.**, Tex, 168 SW3d 777, reh den.—App & E 185(1), 498.1, 499(1), 712, 775, 907(2), 914.3; Atty & C 32(14); Const Law 3962, 3964, 3965(1), 3965(4), 3968; Contracts 127(4); Corp 665(1); Courts 12(2.1), 25, 39; Stip 6, 7, 9.

Holten; **Michiana Easy Livin' Country Inc. v.**, TexApp–Houston (1 Dist), 127 SW3d 89, reh overr, and review gr, rev 168 SW3d 777, reh den.—App & E 836, 840(2), 846(5), 893(1), 907(1); Appear 9(2); Const Law 3964, 3965(3), 3965(4); Courts 12(2.1), 12(2.5), 12(2.10), 12(2.25), 12(2.30), 32, 35.

Holter v. **Employers Mut. Fire Ins. Co.**, TexCivApp–Hous (14 Dist), 520 SW2d 435.—Insurance 2801, 2806, 3582.

Holtermann v. **Conrad**, TexCivApp–San Antonio, 143 SW2d 791, dism.—Bills & N 92(1), 96, 493(3), 537(3).

Holt Helicopters, Inc.; **AIG Aviation, Inc. v.**, TexApp–San Antonio, 198 SW3d 276, review den.—App & E 893(1), 931(1), 996; Courts 91(1); Insurance 3048, 3062, 3064(1), 3070, 3336, 3361, 3381(5).

Holt Machinery Co.; **Butler v.**, TexApp–San Antonio, 741 SW2d 169, writ gr, and writ withdrawn, and writ den, opinion corrected on denial of reh 739 SW2d 958.—Cons Cred 67; Contracts 176(9); Interest 1; Sales 5; Usury 32, 42, 43, 48, 61, 125.

Holt Machinery Co.; **Travelers Indem. Corp. v.**, TexCivApp–El Paso, 554 SW2d 12.—Judgm 181(14), 183; Plead 210, 216(1).

Holt Oil & Gas Corp. v. **Harvey**, CA5 (Tex), 801 F2d 773, cert den 107 SCt 1892, 481 US 1015, 95 LEd2d 499.— Fed Civ Proc 2193, 2214, 2215, 2333.1; Fed Cts 76.5, 76.10, 76.15, 76.30, 626, 641; Mines 109.

Holton; **City of Alamo v.**, TexApp–Corpus Christi, 934 SW2d 833, reh overr.—App & E 70(8), 78(1), 93; Costs 260(1), 260(4), 260(5); Judgm 181(6); Mun Corp 218(10), 745; Offic 66, 114, 119.

Holton v. **Hutchinson**, TexCivApp–Fort Worth, 90 SW2d 1103.—Evid 222(1), 222(2), 265(18), 474(8); Plead 111.4, 111.9.

Holton v. **Mohon**, NDTex, 684 FSupp 1407.—Arrest 63.4(15); Autos 349(6); Civil R 1088(4), 1351(4), 1358, 1376(1), 1376(6), 1376(7), 1464; Crim Law 393(1), 412.2(2); Searches 55.

Holton v. **State**, TexCrimApp, 158 SW2d 772, 143 TexCrim 415, cert den 62 SCt 1311, 316 US 703, 86 LEd 1771.—Crim Law 633(1), 641.1, 641.7(1), 1090.1(3), 1139; Rob 24.10; States 4.4(1).

Holt's Sporting Goods Co. of Lubbock v. **American Nat. Bank of Amarillo**, TexCivApp–Amarillo, 400 SW2d 943, writ dism.—Banks 134(1); Garn 130, 191.

Holt's Sporting Goods Store; Dill v., TexCivApp–Houston, 323 SW2d 644.—Neglig 1595, 1708.

Holt Texas, Ltd. v. Hale, TexApp–San Antonio, 144 SW3d 592, opinion after remand 144 SW3d 620.—App & E 984(1); Costs 177, 194.18, 207; Infants 83, 84, 85.

Holtzclaw v. DSC Communications Corp., CA5 (Tex), 255 F3d 254.—Civil R 1104, 1118, 1217, 1218(4), 1220, 1243, 1246; Fed Civ Proc 2466, 2470, 2497.1; Fed Cts 762, 776; Labor & Emp 794, 795, 797, 863(2).

Holtzclaw; Haile v., Tex, 414 SW2d 916.—Ack 4, 6(2); App & E 1194(2); Deeds 31; Estates 5; Gifts 1, 15; Hus & W 274(1); Mental H 16, 18; Mines 55(1), 55(4); Wills 7, 53(3), 439, 441, 448, 449, 470(1), 486, 577, 611, 618, 865(1), 866.

Holtzclaw; Haile v., TexCivApp–Amarillo, 400 SW2d 603, writ gr, rev 414 SW2d 916.—Ack 6(2), 6(3); App & E 1001(1); Deeds 31, 78, 203, 211(1); Estates 1; Gifts 50; Guard & W 13(3); Mental H 7, 9; Mines 55(1); Remaind 4; Wills 7, 58(2), 63, 439, 441, 448, 470(1), 634(3), 782(3), 800.

Holtzclaw v. State, TexCrimApp, 451 SW2d 505.—Crim Law 255, 1036.2, 1169.1(10), 1169.9, 1170.5(5).

Holtzclaw; Traders & General Ins. Co. v., TexCivApp–El Paso, 111 SW2d 759, writ dism.—Evid 345(1), 383(3); Trial 219, 312(1), 339(3).

Holtzinger v. Estelle, CA5 (Tex), 488 F2d 517.—Courts 514; Pardon 76; Prisons 15(1), 15(3).

Holtzinger v. State, TexCrimApp, 284 SW2d 158, 162 TexCrim 231.—Crim Law 855(7), 928, 1114.1(1).

Holtzman v. Holtzman, TexApp–Texarkana, 993 SW2d 729, reh overr, and review den.—App & E 78(1), 79(1), 80(1), 82(5), 983(3); Bankr 3388; Garn 118, 186; Judgm 91, 217, 855(1).

Holtzman; Holtzman v., TexApp–Texarkana, 993 SW2d 729, reh overr, and review den.—App & E 78(1), 79(1), 80(1), 82(5), 983(3); Bankr 3388; Garn 118, 186; Judgm 91, 217, 855(1).

Holtzman v. State, TexApp–Houston (14 Dist), 866 SW2d 728, petition for discretionary review refused.—Sent & Pun 2010.

Holub v. Nortex Oil & Gas Corp., TexCivApp–Eastland, 330 SW2d 491.—App & E 79(1), 80(1), 80(6).

Holub v. Reno, SDTex, 934 FSupp 817. See Andrade v. Chojnacki.

Holub v. Sword S. S. Line, CCA5 (Tex), 132 F2d 206.—Ship 80, 86(2.5).

Holub v. U.S., SDTex, 934 FSupp 817. See Andrade v. Chojnacki.

Holubec v. Brandenberger, Tex, 111 SW3d 32, on remand Carl BRANDENBURGER, Individually and as Next Friend of Payton Brandenburger, and Carson Brandenburger Minors, Kathy Brandenburger, and First Mason II, Ltd, Plaintiffs, v. David HOLUBEC and Mary Holubec, Defendants, 2005 WL 4889891, aff in part, rev in part 214 SW3d 650.—App & E 231(9), 1062.2; Inj 118(5), 189; Lim of Act 1, 43, 55(5), 95(1), 95(7), 165; Nuis 4, 34.

Holubec v. Brandenberger, TexApp–Austin, 214 SW3d 650.—App & E 946, 954(1); Damag 91.5(3); Inj 17, 106, 128(1), 189; Nuis 23(1), 23(2), 33, 37, 50(6); Tresp 56; Trial 134.

Holubec v. Brandenburger, TexApp–Austin, 58 SW3d 201, reh overr, and review den, and reh of petition for review gr, and withdrawn, and review gr, rev 111 SW3d 32, on remand 2005 WL 4889891, aff in part, rev in part 214 SW3d 650.—App & E 232(3), 1067; Inj 17, 130; Lim of Act 55(5), 195(3), 197(1); Nuis 23(1), 23(2), 25(2), 34.

Holveck v. Phoenix Indem. Co., NDTex, 101 FSupp 537.—Work Comp 1831.

Holway v. Holway, TexCivApp–El Paso, 506 SW2d 643.—Judgm 273(1), 273(3).

Holway; Holway v., TexCivApp–El Paso, 506 SW2d 643.—Judgm 273(1), 273(3).

Holy Cross Church of God in Christ v. Wolf, Tex, 44 SW3d 562.—App & E 1175(1); Banks 505, 508; Bills & N 129(2); Evid 264, 265(7); Judgm 181(7); Lim of Act 48(1), 199(1); Mtg 218.11, 306, 423; Stip 3.

Holy Cross Church of God in Christ; Wolf v., TexApp–Tyler, 49 SW3d 1, review gr, rev 44 SW3d 562.—Action 13; App & E 174, 934(1), 1172(5), 1175(1), 1178(1); Bills & N 129(2); Courts 40; Judgm 181(25), 185(2), 186; Lim of Act 43, 48(1), 195(3), 199(1); Mtg 216, 341; Stip 3.

Holyfield v. Guaranty Title & Trust Co., SDTex, 22 FSupp 896.—Courts 493(3), 509; Ex & Ad 519(1), 522, 524(2).

Holyfield v. Members Mut. Ins. Co., Tex, 572 SW2d 672.—Insurance 2654.

Holyfield v. Members Mut. Ins. Co., TexCivApp–Dallas, 566 SW2d 28, ref nre 572 SW2d 672.—Insurance 2005, 2652, 2826.

Holy Land Foundation For Relief and Development; U.S. v., CA5 (Tex), 445 F3d 771, reh en banc gr 470 F3d 572, opinion reinstated in part on reh 493 F3d 469.—Attach 1; Courts 90(2); Execution 15, 130, 145, 146(1), 146(2); Fed Civ Proc 103.2, 103.3; Fed Cts 543.1, 544, 743, 776, 814.1; Forfeit 5; Garn 9, 64; Inj 132, 143(1), 150, 163(1); Intern Law 10.31, 10.35.

Holy Spirit Ass'n for Unification of World Christianity v. Alley, NDTex, 460 FSupp 346.—Const Law 1160, 1163, 1170, 1527, 1879; Fed Civ Proc 2470.3.

Holy Spirit Ass'n for Unification of World Christianity v. Hodge, NDTex, 582 FSupp 592.—Const Law 814, 1228, 1389, 1517, 1870, 1872, 1873, 1879; Fed Civ Proc 2464; Mun Corp 594(2), 621.

Holzapfel v. Brueggman, TexCivApp–Corpus Christi, 404 SW2d 916, ref nre.—App & E 719(1), 761, 1060.1(2.1), 1062.2; Judgm 186, 713(1); Trial 139.1(14).

Holzapfel; Smith v., EDTex, 739 FSupp 1089.—Civil R 1088(4), 1420; Const Law 4545(3); Prisons 13(4); Sent & Pun 1433.

Holzapfel; Wimer v., EDTex, 868 FSupp 844.—Antitrust 537, 546, 556, 575, 714, 715; Autos 370; Civil R 1376(2), 1376(6), 1422; Const Law 1464, 3867, 4040, 4105(4), 4156; Contracts 175(1).

Homan, Ex parte, TexApp–Tyler, 963 SW2d 543, petition for discretionary review gr, and reh overr, dism Homan v. State, 962 SW2d 599.—Bail 49(5).

Homan v. Commissioner of Social Sec. Admin., EDTex, 84 FSupp2d 814.—Social S 140.5, 140.21, 140.41, 143.40, 143.60.

Homan; Gutierrez-Morales v., CA5 (Tex), 461 F3d 605.—Aliens 347, 385; Const Law 3921, 4438.

Homan; Gutierrez-Morales v., CA5 (Tex), 455 F3d 537, opinion withdrawn and superseded 461 F3d 605.—Aliens 347, 385, 388; Const Law 3921, 4438.

Homan v. Hughes, TexCrimApp, 708 SW2d 449.—Crim Law 1026.10(4), 1083; Mand 4(4), 61, 141; Sent & Pun 2305.

Homan v. State, TexCrimApp, 19 SW3d 847.—Homic 541, 555, 581, 598.

Homan v. State, TexCrimApp, 662 SW2d 372.—Crim Law 308, 561(1), 1035(5); Jury 105(2), 107.

Homan v. U.S., CA5 (Tex), 464 F2d 555.—Sent & Pun 537.

Homan & Crimen, Inc. v. Harris, CA5 (Tex), 626 F2d 1201, reh den 633 F2d 582, cert den 101 SCt 1506, 450 US 975, 67 LEd2d 809.—Admin Law 413; Corp 1.3; Health 485, 535(1), 535(2), 535(4), 547, 548, 549, 557(1); Social S 8.20.

Homan & Crimen, Inc.; Wallace v., TexCivApp–El Paso, 584 SW2d 322, ref nre.—Lim of Act 4(2), 6(10); Statut 107(1), 107(2), 109.2.

Homann, Ex parte, TexApp–Austin, 780 SW2d 933.—Crim Law 1155; Double J 99.

Homann; Kinnard v., TexApp–Austin, 750 SW2d 30, writ den.—Admin Law 417; Brok 19.

Homann & Fielder Real Estate; Kinnard v., TexApp–Austin, 750 SW2d 30. See Kinnard v. Homann.

Homart Development Co.; Awad Texas Enterprises, Inc. v., TexCivApp–Dallas, 589 SW2d 817.—App & E 765, 770(1), 772, 852, 931(3), 934(1); Contracts 42, 46, 218; Land & Ten 24(1), 25.3.

Homart Development Co. v. Blanton, TexApp–Houston (1 Dist), 755 SW2d 158.—Judgm 137, 163, 176.

Homart Development Corp.; Cox's Bakeries of North Dakota, Inc. v., TexCivApp–Dallas, 515 SW2d 326.—App & E 901; Land & Ten 112(1), 161(1), 161(3), 172(1), 180(6), 190(1), 231(1), 233(3).

Homayun v. Cravener, SDTex, 39 FSupp2d 837.—Admin Law 419; Aliens 216, 249; Const Law 190, 191; Hab Corp 521, 603; Statut 181(1), 219(4), 263.

Homcare Health Services, Inc.; Floca v., CA5 (Tex), 845 F2d 108.—Civil R 1535, 1536, 1571, 1573.

Homco, Inc.; Chapman v., CA5 (Tex), 886 F2d 756, cert den 110 SCt 1784, 494 US 1067, 108 LEd2d 785.—Lim of Act 95(15).

Homco, Inc.; Chapman v., NDTex, 708 FSupp 787, aff 886 F2d 756, cert den 110 SCt 1784, 494 US 1067, 108 LEd2d 785.—Civil R 1209, 1383, 1505(4), 1530; Lim of Act 46(7), 58(1).

Home; Chapman v., TexCivApp–Fort Worth, 561 SW2d 265.—Adop 7.1, 7.3, 7.5, 7.8(1), 13, 14.

Home and Hearth Plano Parkway, L.P., In re, BkrtcyNDTex, 320 BR 596.—Bankr 2162, 2164.1, 2534, 2535(4), 2851, 2852; Contracts 168; Judgm 636; Mtg 211, 363, 375, 376.

Home and Hearth Sugarland, L.P.; City of Sugar Land v., TexApp–Eastland, 215 SW3d 503, review den.—App & E 760(1), 840(4), 863, 934(1), 946, 970(2); Em Dom 124, 131, 134, 136, 138, 200, 202(4), 203(2), 222(4), 255; Evid 508, 535, 543(3), 544, 555.2, 555.4(2), 555.6(2), 555.6(7), 555.9; Trial 43, 182.

Home Ben. Ass'n v. Allee, TexCivApp–Beaumont, 128 SW2d 417.—Insurance 2016, 3559, 3582.

Home Ben. Ass'n v. Aycock, TexCivApp–Waco, 88 SW2d 655, writ refused.—Insurance 2080, 2082.

Home Ben. Ass'n v. Gayle, TexCivApp–Waco, 147 SW2d 280.—Debtor & C 10; Interest 45; Lim of Act 100(1), 197(2).

Home Ben. Ass'n v. Griffin, TexCivApp–Waco, 98 SW2d 862.—App & E 1002; Insurance 2445.

Home Ben. Ass'n v. Springer, TexCivApp–Texarkana, 104 SW2d 172.—Insurance 2561(3), 2578.

Home Ben. Ass'n v. Springer, TexCivApp–Texarkana, 93 SW2d 606.—Insurance 3559.

Home Benev. Soc. v. Keeter, TexCivApp–Eastland, 82 SW2d 1084, writ dism.—Accord 7(1), 10(1), 26(3); App & E 846(2), 846(5); Insurance 3571.

Home Benev. Soc. v. Reed, TexCivApp–Austin, 81 SW2d 153.—Trial 352.10.

Home Box Office, Inc.; Personal Preference Video, Inc. v., CA5 (Tex), 986 F2d 110, reh den 992 F2d 326.—Tel 1248(1); Torts 212, 220, 242.

Home Builders Lumber Co. v. C.I.R., CCA5 (Tex), 165 F2d 1009.—Int Rev 3186, 4747.

Home Builders Supply Co.; Hilliard v., TexCivApp–Fort Worth, 399 SW2d 198, ref nre.—App & E 547(3), 553(2); Atty & C 166(3), 167(2); Costs 194.18; Evid 222(2); Home 57(1), 57(3), 97, 214; Mech Liens 73(6), 280(3), 290(5), 310(3); Trial 256(4), 284, 350.3(2.1).

Home Bldg. & Loan Co.; Yates v., TexCivApp–Beaumont, 103 SW2d 1081.—Evid 215(1); Home 13, 35, 165, 168; Hus & W 156; Mech Liens 184, 281(1); Mtg 490, 581(2); Plead 127(2), 301(1).

Home Capital Collateral, Inc. v. F.D.I.C., CA5 (Tex), 96 F3d 760.—Admin Law 723; B & L Assoc 42(6), 42(16); Fed Civ Proc 1773; Fed Cts 29.1, 763.1, 776.

Home Centers of America, Inc.; Pro Hardware, Inc. v., SDTex, 607 FSupp 146.—Trademarks 1024, 1067, 1081,

1084, 1086, 1096(3), 1097, 1102, 1110, 1111, 1112, 1363, 1419, 1609, 1629(2), 1691, 1704(2), 1800.

Home Club, Inc. v. Barlow, TexApp–San Antonio, 818 SW2d 192.—Alt Disp Res 182(1); Mand 42.

Homecoming Financial Network, Inc.; Doss v., TexApp–Corpus Christi, 210 SW3d 706, reh overr, and petition stricken, and petition stricken, and petition stricken.—App & E 76(1), 852; Contracts 326; Costs 194.16, 194.40; Damag 120(1); Decl Judgm 25, 272, 392.1; Impl & C C 3, 4, 10, 13, 22; Judgm 181(25).

Homecraft Land Development, Inc.; Howell v., TexApp–Dallas, 749 SW2d 103, writ den.—Antitrust 369, 397; Contracts 164; Costs 194.40; Dep & Escr 11, 20; Fraud 25; Judgm 359; Witn 13.

Home Decorators v. Herfort, CA5 (Tex), 179 F2d 398.—Inj 135.

Home Depot U.S.A., Inc.; Chretien v., SDTex, 169 FSupp2d 670.—Fed Cts 101, 103, 104, 105, 113, 144, 819.

Home Depot, U.S.A., Inc. v. Federal Ins. Co., EDTex, 241 FSupp2d 702, aff 85 FedAppx 988.—Fed Civ Proc 2501; Insurance 1835(2), 2098, 2117, 2268, 2269, 2361, 2362, 2914.

Home Depot USA, Inc.; McDowell v., CA5 (Tex), 126 FedAppx 168.—Civil R 1252; Fed Cts 714.

Home Depot U.S.A., Inc.; Martin v., WDTex, 369 FSupp2d 887.—Antitrust 203; Negllg 404, 460, 462; Prod Liab 15, 17.1, 42; Sales 261(6), 285(1), 427.

Home Depot U.S.A., Inc.; Martin v., WDTex, 225 FRD 198.—Fed Civ Proc 182.5.

Home Federal Sav. & Loan Ass'n; Georgetown Associates, Ltd. v., TexApp–Houston (14 Dist), 795 SW2d 252, writ dism woj.—App & E 78(1); Guar 75; Judgm 181(22), 183; Mtg 209, 360, 369(2), 375.

Home Fire & Marine Ins. Co. of Cal.; Neas v., NDTex, 135 FSupp 205.—Insurance 1822, 1831, 1832(1), 2137(3).

Home for Aged Masons; Langford v., TexCivApp–Fort Worth, 617 SW2d 778.—Asylums 4; Labor & Emp 40(2), 861.

Home Fund, Inc. v. Denton Federal Sav. & Loan Ass'n, TexCivApp–Fort Worth, 485 SW2d 845.—App & E 373(1), 387(3), 428(2), 621(1), 622, 627.2; New Tr 117(2), 155.

Home Fund, Inc. v. Garland, TexCivApp–Fort Worth, 520 SW2d 939, ref nre.—App & E 544(3), 548(5), 549(3), 549(4), 555, 624, 627; Inj 261.

Home Furniture Co.; Bond v., TexCivApp–Waco, 516 SW2d 224.—Contracts 187(1); Venue 7.5(4).

Home Furniture Co. v. Hawkins, TexCivApp–Dallas, 84 SW2d 830, writ dism.—Damag 208(8); New Tr 76(1); Trial 350.3(6), 351.5(3); Trover 40(6), 60.

Home Health Agency, Inc.; U.S. v., NDTex, 862 FSupp 129.—Fed Civ Proc 2543, 2544, 2546, 2552; Health 539, 541, 556(3).

Home Health Reimbursement & Health Care Financing Admin.; AHN Homecare, L.L.C. v., BkrtcyNDTex, 222 BR 804. See AHN Homecare, LLC, In re.

Home Imp. Loan Co. v. Brewer, TexCivApp–Dallas, 318 SW2d 673, ref nre.—Exemp 57; Garn 157, 158; Home 170, 171, 197, 209.

Home Imp. Loan Co.; Helms v., TexCivApp–Dallas, 294 SW2d 165, writ dism.—Venue 7.5(4).

Home Imp. Loan Co. v. Johnson, TexCivApp–El Paso, 294 SW2d 418, ref nre.—Ack 6(3), 25; Home 116, 118(3), 122; Hus & W 57.

Home Imp. Loan Co. v. Lowe, TexCivApp–Fort Worth, 324 SW2d 939.—Ack 49; Judgm 181(15.1), 185.2(8).

Home Imp. Loan Co. v. Pruitt, TexCivApp–Texarkana, 345 SW2d 452, ref nre.—Home 119; Mech Liens 73(6).

Home Imp. Loan Co.; Tatum v., TexCivApp–Waco, 300 SW2d 215.—Venue 7.5(4), 21.

Home Indem. Co.; Applegate v., TexApp–Texarkana, 705 SW2d 157, dism.—Work Comp 1677, 1729.

HOME

Home Indem. Co.; Ashley v., TexApp–Amarillo, 685 SW2d 780, ref nre.—Work Comp 1357, 1581.

Home Indem. Co.; Burton v., TexCivApp–El Paso, 531 SW2d 665, ref nre.—App & E 5; Work Comp 1954.

Home Indem. Co.; Coty v., TexCivApp–Waco, 494 SW2d 645.—Work Comp 1671.

Home Indem. Co. v. Draper, TexCivApp–Hous (1 Dist), 504 SW2d 570, ref nre.—App & E 237(2); Damag 221(3); Evid 67(1), 417(7), 448, 461(1), 471(28), 543(2), 548; Plead 236(6), 238(3); Trial 31, 352.10; Work Comp 970, 998, 1432, 1968(3).

Home Indem. Co. v. Eason, TexApp–Houston (14 Dist), 635 SW2d 593.—Work Comp 998, 1728.

Home Indem. Co. v. Edwards, TexCivApp–Fort Worth, 488 SW2d 561, ref nre.—Marriage 11, 40(10); New Tr 99; Work Comp 1476, 1792, 1932.

Home Indem. Co.; Eulich v., TexCivApp–Dallas, 503 SW2d 846, ref nre.—Insurance 1826, 2098, 2278(22).

Home Indem. Co.; Foremost County Mut. Ins. Co. v., CA5 (Tex), 897 F2d 754, reh den 902 F2d 955.—Insurance 2355, 3350, 3517; Subrog 27.

Home Indem. Co.; Foster v., TexApp–Dallas, 757 SW2d 481.—Judgm 181(21).

Home Indem. Co.; Fuller, TexCivApp–Austin, 427 SW2d 97, ref nre.—Evid 264; Insurance 2278(29), 2369; Plead 69, 280, 283.

Home Indem. Co.; Garcia v., TexCivApp–Amarillo, 474 SW2d 535.—Work Comp 1922, 1958, 1968(5), 1974.

Home Indem. Co. v. Garcini, TexApp–Houston (1 Dist), 757 SW2d 77, writ den.—Work Comp 900, 1552.

Home Indem. Co. v. Giles, TexCivApp–Austin, 392 SW2d 568.—App & E 854(2); Insurance 3141.

Home Indem. Co. v. Gonzalez, TexCivApp–San Antonio, 383 SW2d 857, ref nre.—App & E 999(1); Insurance 2412.

Home Indem. Co.; Hayes v., TexCivApp–Houston, 354 SW2d 600, ref nre.—Trial 352.10; Work Comp 1543, 1696, 1958, 1962.

Home Indem. Co. v. Humble Oil & Refining Co., Tex, 317 SW2d 515, 159 Tex 224.—Insurance 2760.

Home Indem. Co. v. Humble Oil & Refining Co., TexCivApp–Dallas, 314 SW2d 861, ref nre 317 SW2d 515, 159 Tex 224.—Autos 144.1(4), 200; Insurance 2760, 3517.

Home Indem. Co.; Johnson v., TexCivApp–Texarkana, 401 SW2d 871, ref nre.—Judgm 185.3(12).

Home Indem. Co.; Kay v., CA5 (Tex), 337 F2d 898.—Courts 121(2), 122, 493(3); Fed Cts 421; Work Comp 1036, 1826.

Home Indem. Co. v. Lopez, TexApp–El Paso, 724 SW2d 855.—Work Comp 880, 1828.

Home Indem. Co. v. McKay, TexCivApp–San Antonio, 543 SW2d 171, mandamus overr.—Work Comp 1930.

Home Indem. Co. v. Martin, TexCivApp–Eastland, 399 SW2d 941, ref nre.—App & E 1170.7; Insurance 3381(5); Labor & Emp 57; Neglig 1672, 1678.

Home Indem. Co.; Martinez v., TexApp–Fort Worth, 647 SW2d 102, ref nre.—Trial 352.7; Work Comp 845, 966, 995, 1287, 1382, 1726, 1987.

Home Indem. Co. v. Mosqueda, Tex, 473 SW2d 456.—Infants 11; Work Comp 73, 1034, 1041.

Home Indem. Co. v. Mosqueda, TexCivApp–Corpus Christi, 464 SW2d 902, writ gr, rev 473 SW2d 456.—Dep in Court 1; Guard & W 20, 127; Interest 31, 39(2.20), 44, 47(1); Parties 80(2), 80(3); Work Comp 1003, 1004, 1034, 1041, 1042, 1789, 1981.

Home Indem. Co.; Mosqueda v., TexCivApp–Corpus Christi, 443 SW2d 901, ref nre, appeal after remand 464 SW2d 902, writ gr, rev 473 SW2d 456.—Venue 46; Work Comp 2, 1165, 1792, 1867, 1868, 1871, 1874, 1881, 1885.

Home Indem. Co. v. Muncy, TexCivApp–Tyler, 449 SW2d 312, ref nre.—Insurance 2756(4); Interest 39(3); Judgm 304, 331; Trial 392(0.5).

Home Indem. Co.; Nealy v., TexApp–Houston (14 Dist), 770 SW2d 592.—App & E 345.1; Work Comp 1174.

Home Indem. Co.; O'Dell v., TexCivApp–Amarillo, 449 SW2d 485, ref nre.—Work Comp 558, 571, 845, 1364, 1536.

Home Indem. Co.; Oliver v., CA5 (Tex), 470 F2d 329.—Fed Civ Proc 2658; Fed Cts 585.1, 659, 683.

Home Indem. Co. v. Overstreet, Tex, 704 SW2d 14.—Work Comp 1951.

Home Indem. Co.; Overstreet v., Tex, 678 SW2d 916, on remand 696 SW2d 188, ref nre 704 SW2d 14, appeal after remand 747 SW2d 822, writ den.—Judgm 181(21), 185(5).

Home Indem. Co.; Overstreet v., TexApp–Dallas, 747 SW2d 822, writ den.—App & E 199; Work Comp 1167, 1174.

Home Indem. Co.; Overstreet v., TexApp–Dallas, 696 SW2d 188, ref nre 704 SW2d 14, appeal after remand 747 SW2d 822, writ den.—Costs 60, 241; Work Comp 1113.

Home Indem. Co.; Overstreet v., TexApp–Dallas, 669 SW2d 825, rev 678 SW2d 916, on remand 696 SW2d 188, ref nre 704 SW2d 14, appeal after remand 747 SW2d 822, writ den.—Elect of Rem 10, 15; Evid 265(7); Judgm 185(1), 185(2), 185(4); Pretrial Proc 476, 483.

Home Indem. Co. v. Pate, TexApp–Houston (1 Dist), 866 SW2d 277, reh den, and application for writ of error withdrawn.—App & E 169, 852, 863; Atty & C 26; Judgm 185(2); Work Comp 2188, 2251.

Home Indem. Co. v. Pate, TexApp–Houston (1 Dist), 814 SW2d 497, writ den, appeal after remand 866 SW2d 277, reh den, and application for writ of error withdrawn.—App & E 854(1), 856(1); Courts 97(1); Judgm 634, 829(3); Trover 11, 22; Work Comp 2251.

Home Indem. Co.; Peebles v., TexCivApp–San Antonio, 617 SW2d 274.—App & E 930(3), 989, 1003(5); Work Comp 974, 998.

Home Indem. Co. v. Rios, TexCivApp–Austin, 617 SW2d 798, ref nre.—Work Comp 1981.

Home Indem. Co.; Sauceda v., TexApp–Eastland, 631 SW2d 256, dism.—Work Comp 1832.

Home Indem. Co.; Slayter v., TexCivApp–Hous (14 Dist), 426 SW2d 632, ref nre.—App & E 204(1); Work Comp 1847.

Home Indem. Co.; Smith v., TexApp–Fort Worth, 683 SW2d 559.—Elect of Rem 3(1); Judgm 185(6), 185.3(13); Pretrial Proc 481, 482.1, 483; Work Comp 1113, 1255, 1288, 1683, 1937.

Home Indem. Co. v. Thompson, TexCivApp–Texarkana, 407 SW2d 530.—App & E 1078(1); Work Comp 2203, 2213, 2251.

Home Indem. Co.; Treybig v., TexApp–Dallas, 632 SW2d 896, ref nre.—Work Comp 1262, 1920.

Home Indem. Co. v. Tyler, TexCivApp–Hous (14 Dist), 522 SW2d 594, ref nre.—App & E 662(2); Insurance 2772, 2803, 2813.

Home Indem. Co.; U.S. for Use and Benefit of Rufus A. Walker & Co. v., WDTex, 346 FSupp 1406.—U S 67(12).

Home Indem. Co.; West v., TexCivApp–Beaumont, 444 SW2d 786.—App & E 232(3); Trial 277; Work Comp 693, 719, 1929, 1958.

Home Indem. Co.; Willeford v., TexCivApp–Texarkana, 411 SW2d 640.—Insurance 1822, 1832(2), 2590(4).

Home Indem. Co.; Williams v., TexApp–Houston (14 Dist), 722 SW2d 786.—Work Comp 433.

Home Indem. Co. of New York; Garrity v., CCA5 (Tex), 84 F2d 484.—Work Comp 1335, 1683.

Home Indem. Co. of New York v. Peters, CCA5 (Tex), 86 F2d 916.—Equity 365; Fed Cts 7, 14.1.

Home Indem. Co. of New York, N. Y. v. Hicks, TexCivApp–Beaumont, 488 SW2d 614, dism.—Insurance 3559.

Home Ins. Co. v. Bates Well Service, Inc., TexCivApp–El Paso, 560 SW2d 138, dism.—Plead 111.6, 111.9, 111.16, 111.42(6), 427.

Home Ins. Co. v. Blancas, TexApp–Corpus Christi, 713 SW2d 192.—Work Comp 1396, 1648.

Home Ins. Co. v. Brownlee, TexCivApp–Eastland, 480 SW2d 491.—Evid 420(1), 425, 432; Insurance 2132, 3051.

Home Ins. Co. v. Burkhalter, TexCivApp–Texarkana, 473 SW2d 318.—Trial 350.3(8), 366; Work Comp 571, 1536, 1968(7).

Home Ins. Co.; Connally v., TexCivApp–Amarillo, 525 SW2d 252, ref nre.—Estop 52.15, 112, 116, 119; Insurance 3565(2); Trial 178.

Home Ins. Co.; Cox v., NDTex, 637 FSupp 300.—Labor & Emp 2463, 2467, 2481(5).

Home Ins. Co.; Dabney v., Tex, 643 SW2d 386.—Autos 181(1), 181(2), 201(1.1); Damag 63; Insurance 2790, 2806.

Home Ins. Co. v. Davis, TexApp–Texarkana, 642 SW2d 268.—App & E 1177(7); Evid 570; Work Comp 548, 556, 1530, 1676.

Home Ins. Co.; DeAnda v., Tex, 618 SW2d 529.—App & E 974(1), 1114; Work Comp 1216, 1221, 1239, 1240, 1678, 1758, 1940.

Home Ins. Co. v. DeAnda, TexCivApp–Eastland, 599 SW2d 124, rev 618 SW2d 529.—Work Comp 1230, 1676.

Home Ins. Co. v. Dickey, TexCivApp–Amarillo, 552 SW2d 552.—App & E 846(5), 1024.3; Plead 111.21; Work Comp 1072, 1188, 1591.

Home Ins. Co. v. Espinoza, TexApp–Corpus Christi, 644 SW2d 44, ref nre.—App & E 345.1, 387(6).

Home Ins. Co. v. Fouche, TexCivApp–Texarkana, 149 SW2d 977.—Insurance 2719(2), 2732; Trial 352.5(4).

Home Ins. Co.; Freeport Operators, Inc. v., TexApp–Houston (14 Dist), 666 SW2d 566.—Action 6; Const Law 2600, 3989; Decl Judgm 45, 161; Judgm 570(12).

Home Ins. Co. v. Garcia, TexApp–El Paso, 74 SW3d 52, reh overr.—App & E 930(1), 946, 948, 969, 984(5), 989, 999(1), 1001(1), 1001(3), 1003(3), 1003(5), 1003(7); Trial 279, 284; Work Comp 1624, 1672, 1861, 1981.

Home Ins. Co.; Gibson & Associates, Inc. v., NDTex, 966 FSupp 468.—Insurance 2274, 2275, 2277, 2278(8), 2278(21), 2316, 2915.

Home Ins. Co. v. Gillum, TexApp–Corpus Christi, 680 SW2d 844, ref nre.—App & E 969; Trial 232(5), 350.2, 350.3(8); Witn 388(2.1); Work Comp 957, 1369, 1383, 1389, 1687, 1696, 1703, 1728, 1904, 1937.

Home Ins. Co. v. Greene, Tex, 453 SW2d 470.—App & E 1060.1(1).

Home Ins. Co. v. Greene, TexCivApp–Texarkana, 443 SW2d 326, aff 453 SW2d 470.—App & E 80(1); Insurance 3164; Judgm 313, 326, 526; Trial 131(1).

Home Ins. Co.; Hanna v., CA5 (Tex), 281 F2d 298, cert den 81 SCt 751, 365 US 838, 5 LEd2d 747, reh den 81 SCt 1905, 366 US 955, 6 LEd2d 1247.—App & E 653(3); Consp 7.5(1), 7.5(2), 18; Const Law 3000; Courts 509; Fed Cts 221.

Home Ins. Co.; Hanna v., TexCivApp–Dallas, 260 SW2d 891, ref nre.—App & E 568, 621(1), 628(1), 628(2).

Home Ins. Co.; McNeal v., TexCivApp–Galveston, 112 SW2d 339.—Autos 193(1), 193(10), 193(11).

Home Ins. Co. v. Marsh, TexApp–El Paso, 790 SW2d 749.—Atty & C 21, 21.5(5), 21.20.

Home Ins. Co.; Matthews v., TexApp–Houston (1 Dist), 916 SW2d 666, reh overr, and writ den.—Insurance 1810, 1823, 1826, 1845(2), 2266, 3337, 3349; Judgm 181(2), 185(2).

Home Ins. Co. v. Scott, TexCivApp–El Paso, 152 SW2d 413, dism.—Insurance 3015, 3164, 3179, 3571; Judgm 251(1); Plead 228.14, 228.18.

Home Ins. Co. v. Smith, TexCivApp–Waco, 482 SW2d 395.—App & E 301, 499(4), 501(4); Work Comp 840, 847, 849, 1660.

Home Ins. Co. v. Williams, TexCivApp–Fort Worth, 84 SW2d 876, writ dism.—App & E 232(3), 920(2); Insurance 3146; Pretrial Proc 718.

Home Ins. Co., New York v. Barbee, TexCivApp–Galveston, 166 SW2d 370.—Plead 111.19, 111.42(6), 111.46, 293.

Home Ins. Co., New York, v. Springer, TexCivApp–Fort Worth, 131 SW2d 412.—Contracts 143(3), 167; Insurance 1832(1), 3066.

Home Ins. Co., N. Y. v. Privitt, TexCivApp–Fort Worth, 120 SW2d 294, dism.—Evid 265(17); Insurance 2200, 3072; Judgm 251(2); Ref of Inst 19(1), 36(3), 44, 45(14).

Home Ins. Co., N. Y. v. Rose, Tex, 255 SW2d 861, 152 Tex 222.—Insurance 1822; Time 9(1), 9(10).

Home Ins. Co., N. Y., v. Rose, TexCivApp–Amarillo, 255 SW2d 238, rev 255 SW2d 861, 152 Tex 222.—Insurance 1832(1), 1836; Time 9(10).

Home Ins. Co. of Illinois; General Agents Ins. Co. of America, Inc. v., TexApp–San Antonio, 21 SW3d 419, review dism by agreement.—App & E 232(3), 842(1), 946, 949, 969; Estop 68(2); Insurance 3517, 3526(10); Trial 367.

Home Ins. Co. of Indiana v. Banda, TexApp–San Antonio, 736 SW2d 812, writ den.—App & E 846(5); Elect of Rem 7(1); Interest 66; Work Comp 847, 848, 998, 1041, 1464, 1536, 1639, 1703, 1847.

Home Ins. Co. of Indiana v. Walsh, SDTex, 854 FSupp 458.—Insurance 2278(9), 2391(2).

Home Ins. Co. of New York v. Cox, TexCivApp–Waco, 264 SW2d 149, rev 269 SW2d 343, 153 Tex 421.—Insurance 1832(1), 2704.

Home Ins. Co. of N.Y. v. Enloe, TexCivApp–Amarillo, 287 SW2d 235, ref nre.—Insurance 1813, 2202, 2281(1), 2295.

Home Ins. Co. of New York; Finger v., TexCivApp–Houston, 379 SW2d 950.—Insurance 3048, 3070; Judgm 181(5.1), 185(2), 185.3(12).

Home Ins. Co. of New York v. Lake Dallas Gin Co., TexComApp, 93 SW2d 388, 127 Tex 479.—Insurance 1634(1), 1635, 3043, 3084, 3091, 3096(1), 3112, 3120, 3451.

Home Ins. Co. of New York v. Roberts, TexComApp, 100 SW2d 91, 129 Tex 178.—Insurance 1633, 3084, 3085, 3092.

Home Ins. Co. of New York v. Young, TexCivApp–Fort Worth, 97 SW2d 360, writ dism.—Insurance 1835(1), 3071, 3100(1), 3104, 3130, 3131, 3132, 3515(2), 3525; Trial 352.12.

Home Ins. Co. of N. Y. v. Dacus, TexCivApp–Texarkana, 239 SW2d 182.—App & E 216(1), 241, 263(3), 500(1), 1050.2; Insurance 3015, 3195, 3571; Plead 291(3); Trial 133.6(5), 207, 350.4(3); Witn 379(8.1).

Home Ins. Co. of N. Y. v. Tydal Co., CCA5 (Tex), 152 F2d 309, reh den 157 F2d 851.—Evid 523, 524, 525; Fed Civ Proc 2194.1, 2232.1; Fed Cts 631; Insurance 3579; Trial 194(11), 217, 240, 260(1).

Home Ins. Indem. Co. v. Gutierrez, TexCivApp–Corpus Christi, 409 SW2d 450, ref nre.—App & E 170(1); Cust & U 5, 19(3); Paymt 16(1), 21, 22; Tender 11, 13(1); Work Comp 1003, 1034, 1042, 1789, 1981.

Home Interiors & Gifts, Inc. v. Strayhorn, TexApp–Austin, 175 SW3d 856, review den, and reh of petition for review den.—App & E 1175(1); Commerce 12, 62.71, 62.80, 69(1); Judgm 183; Statut 176, 181(1); Tax 2125, 2540, 2543.

Home Interiors & Gifts, Inc. v. Veliz, TexApp–Corpus Christi, 725 SW2d 295.—App & E 267(1); Judgm 297.

Home Interiors & Gifts, Inc. v. Veliz, TexApp–Corpus Christi, 695 SW2d 35, ref nre.—App & E 213; Autos 244(26), 246(15); Damag 100, 186, 187; Judgm 203; Labor & Emp 23, 29.

Homeland Realty Co.; Heiner v., TexCivApp–Waco, 100 SW2d 793.—Evid 383(7), 590; Mtg 341, 342, 350, 356, 362; Trial 140(2).

HOMELAND

59 Tex D 2d—696

See Guidelines for Arrangement at the beginning of this Volume

Homeland Realty Co. v. Wheelock, TexCivApp–El Paso, 119 SW2d 167.—Mtg 278.

Homeland Realty Co.; Wimberly v., TexCivApp–Dallas, 131 SW2d 423.—App & E 386(1); Mand 57(2).

Home Life & Acc. Ins. Co.; Hatridge v., TexCivApp–Dallas, 246 SW2d 666.—App & E 909(5); Const Law 26, 642, 1120; Insurance 1721; Usury 4, 52, 53, 78, 119.

Home Life & Acc. Ins. Co. v. Phillips-Dupre Hospital, TexCivApp–Amarillo, 287 SW2d 503.—Insurance 1831, 3463, 3559; Plead 111.19.

Home Life Ins. Co. v. Abrams Square II, Ltd., NDTex, 95 BR 51.—Bankr 2124.1, 2374, 2443, 3776.1.

Home Life Ins. Co.; Adamson v., CA5 (Tex), 508 F2d 766.—Fed Cts 901.1; Insurance 3090, 3131, 3365.

Home Loan Corp. v. Texas American Title Co., TexApp–Houston (14 Dist), 191 SW3d 728, reh overr, and review den, and reh of petition for review den.—Dep & Escr 13; Fraud 7, 17; Judgm 181(15.1).

Home Lumber Co.; Bogel v., TexCivApp–Dallas, 283 SW2d 794, ref nre.—Mech Liens 93, 304(1).

Home Marketing Servicing, Inc.; SAS & Associates, Inc. v., TexApp–Dallas, 168 SW3d 296, reh overr, and review den, and reh of petition for review den.—App & E 930(1), 930(3), 1003(6), 1004(1), 1004(13), 1024.1, 1182; Const Law 4427; Costs 194.18, 207, 208, 264; Damag 94.6, 96, 104, 119; Evid 96(2), 474(20), 555.9, 571(5); Fraud 58(1), 62; Land & Ten 148(4); Plead 144.

Home of Holy Infancy v. Kaska, Tex, 397 SW2d 208.—Child 1, 9, 11, 20.2, 21(2).

Home of Holy Infancy; Kaska v., TexCivApp–Austin, 387 SW2d 944, writ gr, aff 397 SW2d 208.—Hab Corp 662.1, 801.

Homeowners Ass'n for Values Essential to Neighborhoods, (HAVEN); Collin County, Tex. v., CA5 (Tex), 915 F2d 167.—Decl Judgm 272, 299.1, 302.1.

Homeowners Ass'n for Values Essential to Neighborhoods (HAVEN); Collin County, Tex. v., NDTex, 716 FSupp 953, vac, cause dism 915 F2d 167.—Counties 52; Decl Judgm 272, 274.1, 300, 302.1, 312.1, 313, 345.1; Environ Law 577, 597, 599, 600, 602, 604(2), 604(7), 689; Fed Cts 13.25, 51, 241.

Homeowners Ass'n for Values Essential to Neighborhoods (HAVEN); Collin County, Tex. v., NDTex, 654 FSupp 943.—Atty & C 32(11); Civil R 1395(1), 1398; Const Law 42.2(1), 4320; Counties 88; Fed Civ Proc 1752.1, 2783(5); Mal Pros 48; Offic 114, 119; Proc 168, 171.

Homeowners Ass'n for Values Essential to Neighborhoods, (HAVEN) v. Farris, CA5 (Tex), 915 F2d 167. See Collin County, Tex. v. Homeowners Ass'n for Values Essential to Neighborhoods, (HAVEN).

Home Owners Funding Corp.; Chislum v., TexApp–Corpus Christi, 803 SW2d 800, writ den.—Antitrust 369; App & E 931(1), 989, 1054(1); Bills & N 453, 501; Judgm 614(3), 678(5); Pretrial Proc 483; States 18.19; Statut 263, 265, 267(1); Trial 382, 391, 395(1).

Home Owners Funding Corp. of America v. Allison, NDTex, 756 FSupp 290.—Rem of C 82, 84, 100.

Home Owners Funding Corp. of America v. Allison Mobile Homes, NDTex, 756 FSupp 290. See Home Owners Funding Corp. of America v. Allison.

Home Owners Funding Corp. of America v. Scheppler, TexApp–Corpus Christi, 815 SW2d 884.—App & E 346.2, 846(5), 863, 984(1); Atty & C 24; Costs 2.

Homeowners Home Imp. Co. v. Longoria, TexApp–San Antonio, 494 SW2d 132. See Enell Corp. v. Longoria.

Home Owners' Loan Corp.; Carter v., TexCivApp–El Paso, 123 SW2d 437, writ refused.—Mtg 306, 461, 464; U S 53(14).

Home Owners' Loan Corp. v. Cilley, TexCivApp–Amarillo, 125 SW2d 313, writ refused.—App & E 907(5), 931(3); Hus & W 25(3); Lim of Act 143(1); Ten in C 39, 43, 46, 52.

Home Owners' Loan Corp. v. Creed, CCA5 (Tex), 108 F2d 153.—Bankr 2026; Statut 162.

Home Owners' Loan Corp.; Dodson v., TexCivApp–El Paso, 123 SW2d 435.—Corp 632; Mtg 464; U S 3, 53(9), 53(14).

Home Owners' Loan Corporation; Gough v., TexCivApp–El Paso, 135 SW2d 771, writ dism, correct.—Hus & W 273(11); Mtg 153; Ven & Pur 220.

Home Owners' Loan Corp.; Helms v., Tex, 103 SW2d 128, 129 Tex 121.—Corp 374, 383, 405; U S 53(11).

Home Owners' Loan Corp. v. Netterville, TexComApp, 132 SW2d 93, 134 Tex 30.—Home 177(1), 177(2).

Home Owners' Loan Corp. v. Netterville, TexCivApp–Beaumont, 110 SW2d 628, rev 132 SW2d 93, 134 Tex 30.—Estop 74(1); Home 118(5), 122, 129(2), 177(2); Ven & Pur 261(4).

Home Owners Loan Corp.; Pullen v., TexCivApp–Fort Worth, 168 SW2d 878.—Ex & Ad 271, 355.

Home Owners' Loan Corp.; Quinn v., TexCivApp–Dallas, 125 SW2d 1063, writ dism.—Statut 109.11; Venue 7.5(1), 7.5(4).

Home Owners' Loan Corp.; Roberson v., TexCivApp–Dallas, 147 SW2d 949, writ dism, correct.—Evid 265(18); Home 1, 29, 31, 32, 169, 213; Mtg 461; U S 53(9), 53(17).

Home Owners' Loan Corp.; Scarborough v., TexCivApp–Amarillo, 161 SW2d 886, writ refused wom.—Home 13, 97, 122, 165, 168.

Home Owners' Loan Corp. v. Williams, TexCivApp–San Antonio, 168 SW2d 325, writ refused.—Lim of Act 11(4); U S 53(9), 53(14).

Home Owners Loan Corp.; Zachary v., TexCivApp–Galveston, 117 SW2d 153, writ dism.—App & E 765, 907(3), 934(2), 989; Judgm 197, 301; Trial 180.

Homeowners Mortgage and Equity, Inc., In re, CA5 (Tex), 354 F3d 372.—Bankr 2163, 2183, 3782, 3784, 3786, 3787; Contracts 176(1), 176(2), 194, 217; Damag 117, 184.

Home Owners Warranty Corp.; Scholl v., TexApp–San Antonio, 810 SW2d 464.—Costs 32(2), 194.46; Judgm 199(3.14).

Home Petroleum Corp.; Simpson v., CA5 (Tex), 770 F2d 499.—Evid 94; Fed Cts 416; Labor & Emp 3094(2).

Homeplace Homes, Inc.; National Environmental Service Co., Inc. v., TexApp–San Antonio, 961 SW2d 632.—App & E 842(2), 893(1), 931(1), 1010.2, 1011.1(2), 1011.1(6), 1012.1(4); Contracts 247; Costs 220; Damag 140; Interest 13.

Homer; Western Union Tel. Co. v., TexComApp, 166 SW2d 684, 140 Tex 193.—App & E 1067; Tel 687, 706, 710.

Homer; Western Union Tel. Co. v., TexCivApp–Fort Worth, 157 SW2d 659, aff 166 SW2d 684, 140 Tex 193.—App & E 216(2); Damag 49; Tel 706, 707, 708, 710; Trial 219, 352.10.

Home Reader Service, Inc. v. Grappi, TexCivApp–Dallas, 446 SW2d 95, ref nre.—Contracts 217, 352(6); Damag 190; Trial 420.

Homeright Co. v. Exchange Warehouses, Inc., TexCivApp–Tyler, 526 SW2d 241, ref nre.—App & E 80(4), 960(1); Bailm 30; Judgm 564(2), 569, 570(3); Plead 228.19, 228.23.

H. O. Merren & Co. v. A. H. Belo Corp., NDTex, 228 FSupp 515, aff 346 F2d 568.—Fed Civ Proc 2515, 2543; Fed Cts 431; Libel 6(1), 19, 48(1), 123(2).

Homes v. Alwattari, TexApp–Fort Worth, 33 SW3d 376, reh overr, and review den, and reh of petition for review den.—Action 35; Antitrust 199, 203, 282, 286, 369, 389(1), 389(2), 390; App & E 758.3(1), 842(1), 930(1), 989; Trial 105(4).

Homes v. Cull, TexApp–Fort Worth, 173 SW3d 565, review gr.—Alt Disp Res 182(1), 182(2), 210, 222, 269, 329, 335, 357, 363(8), 363(9); Interest 39(3); Judgm 181(6), 185(5); Trial 388(2).

For Later Case History Information, see KeyCite on WESTLAW

Homes; Delfino v., TexApp–Houston (1 Dist), 223 SW3d 32, reh overr.—Damag 6; Judgm 185.3(18), 199(5).

Home Sav. Ass'n v. Bevers, TexApp–Amarillo, 745 SW2d 504.—Abate & R 8(2); Banks 191.15, 191.30; Courts 474, 475(1); Mand 4(2), 28, 39.

Home Sav. Ass'n; de la Fuente v., TexApp–Corpus Christi, 669 SW2d 137.—Antitrust 223, 290, 358, 369; App & E 1008.1(1), 1008.1(7), 1010.2, 1012.1(5), 1177(1); Assign 100; Banks 451; Bills & N 342, 487, 527(1); Cons Cred 4, 17, 18; Costs 207; Evid 265(8); New Tr 72(8).

Home Sav. Ass'n v. Guerra, Tex, 733 SW2d 134.—Antitrust 291; Cons Cred 61.1.

Home Sav. Ass'n v. Guerra, TexApp–San Antonio, 720 SW2d 636, writ gr, aff in part, rev in part 733 SW2d 134.—Antitrust 223, 291, 294, 365; App & E 1062.2; Assign 138; Cons Cred 17; Evid 265(8); Pretrial Proc 313; States 18.15.

Home Sav. Ass'n v. Ramirez, TexCivApp–Corpus Christi, 600 SW2d 911, ref nre.—App & E 954(1); Courts 472.7; Forci E & D 6(1), 6(2); Inj 7, 26(9); Mtg 191.

Home Sav. Ass'n v. Southern Union Gas Co., TexCivApp–El Paso, 486 SW2d 386, ref nre.—App & E 1173(2); Const Law 642; Mech Liens 116; Mtg 151(3); Sec Tran 94.

Home Sav. Ass'n v. Tappan Co., CA5 (Tex), 403 F2d 201.—Contracts 221(1), 221(3).

Home Sav. Ass'n Family Development Corp.; J & K Properties, Inc. v., TexApp–Dallas, 741 SW2d 470. See Shenandoah Associates v. J & K Properties, Inc.

Home Sav. Ass'n of Dallas County; Crow v., Tex, 522 SW2d 457.—App & E 930(3); Usury 1, 13, 53, 55.

Home Sav. Ass'n of Dallas County v. Crow, TexCivApp–Dallas, 514 SW2d 160, writ gr, aff 522 SW2d 457.—Contracts 99(1); Trial 350.1, 350.3(1); Usury 6, 16, 55, 57, 72, 82, 117.

Home Sav. Ass'n of Dallas County; Hernandez v., CA5 (Tex), 606 F2d 596.—Estop 62.2(4); U S 53(9), 53(19).

Home Sav. Ass'n of Dallas County; Hernandez v., NDTex, 425 FSupp 835, rev 606 F2d 596.—B & L Assoc 38(5).

Home Sav. Ass'n of Dallas County; Hernandez v., NDTex, 411 FSupp 858, motion den 425 FSupp 835, rev 606 F2d 596.—Estop 62.2(4); Interpl 35; U S 53(9).

Home Sav. Ass'n Service Corp. v. Martinez, TexApp–San Antonio, 788 SW2d 52, writ den.—Antitrust 161, 203, 209, 291, 364; Can of Inst 3, 5, 6.

Home Sav. of America, F.A. v. Van Cleave Development Co., Inc., TexApp–San Antonio, 737 SW2d 58.—App & E 852, 954(1); Inj 138.3; Mtg 143, 413.

Home Sav. of America FSB v. Harris County Water Control and Imp. Dist. No. 70, TexApp–Houston (14 Dist), 928 SW2d 217, reh overr.—App & E 5, 916(1); Corp 508; Judgm 106(1).

Home Service Cas. Ins. Co. v. Barry, TexCivApp–Waco, 277 SW2d 280, ref nre.—App & E 1008.3(1); Insurance 1835(2), 2703.

Home Service Finance Co. v. White, TexCivApp–Austin, 86 SW2d 815, writ dism.—App & E 304; Chat Mtg 292(1), 292(2); Evid 550(1).

Homes, Inc., In re, BkrtcySDTex, 57 BR 967. See Kay Homes, Inc., In re.

Homes of St. Mark; Ainsworth v., TexCivApp–Hous (1 Dist), 530 SW2d 877.—App & E 285; Hab Corp 532(2); Judgm 335(3); Plead 228.23.

Homes of St. Mark; Cochrane v., TexApp–Houston (14 Dist), 687 SW2d 394.—Infants 205, 251.

Home State Bank v. Cavett, TexCivApp–Austin, 518 SW2d 584.—App & E 931(1), 989, 996, 1008.1(2), 1010.1(1), 1010.1(3); Guar 6; Mtg 86(3).

Home State County Mut. Ins. Co. v. Acceptance Ins. Co., TexApp–Amarillo, 958 SW2d 263.—App & E 1175(1); Insurance 2098, 2278(13), 2681, 2893.

Homestate Sav. Ass'n; Westwind Exploration, Inc. v., Tex, 696 SW2d 378.—Banks 191.10, 191.15, 191.20, 191.30; Contracts 147(2), 153, 154, 176(1).

Homestate Sav. Ass'n v. Westwind Exploration, Inc., TexApp–Eastland, 684 SW2d 788, writ gr, aff 696 SW2d 378.—Banks 191.10, 191.20; Contracts 143.5, 147(2); Plead 236(3); Trial 136(3).

Homestead Bank; Dameris v., TexCivApp–Hous (1 Dist), 495 SW2d 52.—App & E 863, 934(1); Bills & N 426, 437; Contracts 235; Evid 402, 468; Judgm 181(2), 181(26), 185(2); Paymt 30.

Homestead Bldg. & Loan Ass'n v. Loukas, TexCivApp–Beaumont, 110 SW2d 246.—B & L Assoc 2, 6(2), 14(1).

Homestead Bldg. & Loan Ass'n v. Youngblood, TexCivApp–Beaumont, 111 SW2d 827.—B & L Assoc 14(1), 14(4), 14(6), 41(2); Trial 140(2).

Homestead Fire Ins. Co. v. Simpson, TexCivApp–Fort Worth, 91 SW2d 960, writ dism.—App & E 1032(1), 1039(16); Insurance 3571.

Homestead Lumber Co. v. Harris, TexCivApp–Waco, 178 SW2d 161.—App & E 2, 624.

Homestead Mobile Homes, Inc. v. Foremost Corp. of America, NDTex, 603 FSupp 767.—Antitrust 575, 583, 972(3); Insurance 1106(1); States 18.41.

Homestead Studio Suites Hotels; McCoy v., CA5 (Tex), 177 FedAppx 442.—Antitrust 226; Civil R 1046, 1071; Consp 19; Inn 9.

Homestead Studio Suites Hotels; McCoy v., SDTex, 390 FSupp2d 577, aff 177 FedAppx 442.—Antitrust 135(1), 226; Civil R 1009, 1010, 1033(1), 1044, 1046, 1071, 1075; Consp 7.5(1), 7.5(2); Contracts 326; Inn 9.

Hometown Real Estate Co.; Century 21 Real Estate Corp. v., TexApp–Texarkana, 890 SW2d 118, reh overr, and writ den.—Antitrust 128, 135(1), 135(2), 136, 138, 141, 161, 162, 266, 268, 297, 363, 367, 369, 389(1), 389(2), 390, 393; App & E 179(1), 232(0.5), 930(2), 930(3), 968, 969, 989, 999(1), 1026, 1048(1); Evid 143, 597; Jury 133; Trial 18, 41(1).

Home Transp. Co.; Courville v., TexCivApp–Beaumont, 497 SW2d 788, ref nre.—Autos 160(1), 201(1.1), 279.

Home Transp. Co.; Railroad Com'n of Texas v., TexApp–Austin, 670 SW2d 319.—Admin Law 412.1, 753; Autos 104; Carr 10, 18(1), 18(2); Decl Judgm 206, 344.

Home Transp. Co.; Railroad Com'n of Texas v., TexApp–Austin, 643 SW2d 512, rev 654 SW2d 432, on remand 670 SW2d 319.—App & E 66; Carr 12(11); Judgm 217.

Home Transp. Co.; Roy L. Jones, Inc. v., CA5 (Tex), 422 F2d 179.—Contracts 176(2); Indem 101, 104.

Home Transp. Co., Inc.; Railroad Com'n of Texas v., Tex, 654 SW2d 432, on remand 670 SW2d 319.—App & E 80(3); Carr 18(2).

Homfeld v. Pence, TexCivApp–El Paso, 487 SW2d 224.—Adop 3, 7.4(6), 7.8(3.1), 11, 13; Child S 24, 160; Elect of Rem 7(1); Estop 91(1); Evid 265(2).

Hominick; Park v., TexCivApp–Corpus Christi, 522 SW2d 533.—App & E 374(2); Ex & Ad 109(1), 513(9).

Hom Investments v. Ryder System, Inc., TexApp–Houston (14 Dist, 928 SW2d 190. See Marshall v. Ryder System, Inc.

Homme v. Varing, TexApp–Beaumont, 852 SW2d 74.—Courts 176, 176.5; Trial 168, 173, 383.

Hommel; Ligon v., TexCivApp–Waco, 189 SW2d 23.—Autos 12; Evid 5(2); Venue 8.5(3).

Hommel; San Benito Cash & Carry Bldg. Materials, Inc. v., TexCivApp–Corpus Christi, 474 SW2d 324.—New Tr 143(4).

Hommel v. Southwestern Greyhound Lines, TexCivApp–Fort Worth, 195 SW2d 803.—Autos 146, 151, 173(1), 173(4), 238(3); Neglig 259; Plead 53(2), 228.14; Stip 14(10).

Hom-Ond Food Stores v. Voigt, TexCivApp–San Antonio, 115 SW2d 981, writ dism.—App & E 173(13),

237(5), 301, 729, 750(4), 1002, 1062.1; Damag 130.1; Neglig 1708; Trial 350.6(2), 351.5(5), 352.10, 352.21.

Homsey v. University Gardens Racquet Club, TexApp–El Paso, 730 SW2d 763, ref nre.—Covenants 1, 74, 103(3).

Homsy v. Floyd, CA5 (Tex), 51 F3d 530. See Vitek, Inc., Matter of.

Honaker; Main Place Custom Homes, Inc. v., TexApp–Fort Worth, 192 SW3d 604, reh overr, and review den, and reh of petition for review den.—Antitrust 138, 161, 203, 369, 396, 397; App & E 842(2), 931(1), 983(3), 989, 994(3), 1008.1(1), 1008.1(2), 1008.1(3), 1010.1(1), 1010.1(2), 1010.2, 1012.1(2), 1071.6, 1151(2), 1153; Costs 194.25, 194.32, 198; Damag 15, 57.22, 57.42, 192, 221(8); Elect of Rem 5; Evid 18, 587, 597; Execution 402(1), 402(2), 402(3), 402(5); Trial 401, 404(6).

Honaker v. Reeves County Water Improvement Dist. No. 1, TexCivApp–El Paso, 152 SW2d 454, writ refused.—Waters 43, 249, 256.

Honc v. State, TexCrimApp, 767 SW2d 787, on remand 783 SW2d 773, petition for discretionary review refused.—Crim Law 1134(3), 1181.5(8); Ind & Inf 130.

Honc v. State, TexApp–Corpus Christi, 783 SW2d 773, petition for discretionary review refused.—Crim Law 1186.1.

Honc v. State, TexApp–Corpus Christi, 698 SW2d 218, petition for discretionary review gr, rev 767 SW2d 787, on remand 783 SW2d 773, petition for discretionary review refused.—Assault 59, 74, 75, 92(5); Crim Law 273.4(1), 1167(1), 1181.5(8); Ind & Inf 119, 167, 176; Infants 13, 20.

Honda; Harris v., CA5 (Tex), 213 FedAppx 258.—Atty & C 62; Civil R 1506, 1513, 1708, 1709, 1715; Courts 97(5); Fed Civ Proc 776; Statut 226.

Honda Motor Co., Ltd.; Rosales v., CA5 (Tex), 726 F2d 259, 78 ALR Fed 883.—Fed Civ Proc 53, 1954.1.

Honda of America Mfg., Inc. v. Norman, TexApp–Houston (1 Dist), 104 SW3d 600, reh overr, and review den, and reh of petition for review den.—App & E 930(1), 999(1), 1001(1), 1003(6); Evid 571(6), 588; Prod Liab 11, 15, 83.5; Trial 140(1).

Honda of Midland, In re, BkrtcyNDTex, 82 BR 439. See Mid-West Motors, Inc., In re.

Honda of Midland; First City Nat. Bank of Midland v., BkrtcyNDTex, 82 BR 439. See Mid-West Motors, Inc., In re.

Hondo, City of; Bodnow Corp. v., Tex, 721 SW2d 839.—App & E 870(2); Pretrial Proc 44.1.

Hondo Creek Cattle Co.; Barrera v., TexApp–Corpus Christi, 132 SW3d 544, reh overr.—App & E 883, 1008.1(1), 1008.1(2), 1079; Em Dom 2.1, 2.10(3); Lim of Act 4(2), 43, 55(5), 95(1), 165.

Hondo Drilling Co.; N.L.R.B. v., CA5 (Tex), 428 F2d 943.—Admin Law 385.1, 386, 400; Labor & Emp 1191(1), 1195(1), 1659, 1680, 1681, 1714.

Hondo Drilling Co.; Shawnee Intern., N.V. v., CA5 (Tex), 742 F2d 234.—Fed Civ Proc 1824, 2533.1; Mal Pros 10, 14, 52.

Hondo Drilling Co., N. S. L.; N.L.R.B. v., CA5 (Tex), 525 F2d 864, reh den 528 F2d 928, cert den 97 SCt 63, 429 US 818, 50 LEd2d 78, reh den 97 SCt 509, 429 US 987, 50 LEd2d 599.—Labor & Emp 1113, 1128, 1224, 1231, 1490(2).

Hondo Livestock Hauling; Barker v., TexCivApp–Corpus Christi, 614 SW2d 846.—App & E 770(1); Carr 194.

Hondo Nat. Bank v. Gill Sav. Ass'n, CA5 (Tex), 696 F2d 1095.—Action 3; Fed Cts 18; Inj 22.

Hondo Oil and Gas Co. v. Texas Crude Operator, Inc., CA5 (Tex), 970 F2d 1433.—Contracts 27, 236; Costs 194.32; Estop 52(8); Fed Cts 830; Frds St of 131(1); Indem 20, 54, 71; Interest 39(2.20); Mines 109; Princ & S 180, 185.

Hondo's, In re, BkrtcySDTex, 60 BR 353. See Fleming-Roberts Corp., Ltd., In re.

Hondo's Truck Stop Cafe, Inc. v. Clemmons, TexApp–Corpus Christi, 716 SW2d 725.—Neglig 549(5), 549(10).

Hone v. Hanafin, Tex, 104 SW3d 884, on remand 2003 WL 22020778, review den, and reh of petition for review den.—App & E 428(2).

Hone v. Hanafin, TexApp–Dallas, 105 SW3d 15, review gr, rev 104 SW3d 884, on remand 2003 WL 22020778, review den, and reh of petition for review den.—App & E 352.1, 428(2).

Honea v. Coca Cola Bottling Co., Tex, 183 SW2d 968, 143 Tex 272, 160 ALR 1445.—Corp 432(12); Evid 317(9), 596(1); Neglig 1612, 1631; Prod Liab 78, 81.1.

Honea v. Coca Cola Bottling Co., TexCivApp–El Paso, 182 SW2d 512, rev 183 SW2d 968, 143 Tex 272, 160 ALR 1445.—Evid 5(2), 7; Neglig 1568; Prod Liab 76, 78, 81.1; Trial 171, 174.

Honea; Jennings v., TexCivApp–Waco, 389 SW2d 360.—Child S 293, 339(2), 339(4), 555.

Honea v. Lee, Tex, 352 SW2d 717, 163 Tex 129.—App & E 1082(1).

Honea; Lee v., TexCivApp–Fort Worth, 349 SW2d 110, ref nre 352 SW2d 717, 163 Tex 129.—Home 154; Insurance 3442.

Honea v. Morgan Drive Away, Inc., TexApp–Eastland, 997 SW2d 705.—App & E 1073(1); Judgm 185(1), 185(2), 185(4), 185.3(21); Lim of Act 31, 95(1), 95(4.1), 187, 195(3); Plead 234.

Honea; Palmer v., TexCivApp–Waco, 324 SW2d 929.—App & E 719(3); Judgm 17(1).

Honea v. SGS Control Services Inc., EDTex, 859 FSupp 1025.—Civil R 1137, 1138, 1513, 1516, 1523, 1536, 1545; Damag 49, 50.10; Fed Civ Proc 2470.1, 2497.1, 2543, 2544, 2546; Jury 10.

Honea v. State, TexCrimApp, 585 SW2d 681.—Crim Law 13.1(1), 25, 406(1), 517(5), 531(3), 532(0.5), 535(2), 627.8(6), 737(1), 781(6), 814(17), 938(1), 938(3), 1038.3; Rob 2, 11, 20, 24.10.

Honea v. U.S., CA5 (Tex), 344 F2d 798.—Courts 87; Crim Law 633(1), 1167(1); False Pers 1, 2; False Pret 1, 2, 5, 27, 35, 49(2); Ind & Inf 19, 55, 60, 71.2(4), 110(4); Statut 147.

Honea III; Washburn v., TexCivApp–Waco, 553 SW2d 956.—App & E 989; Contracts 322(5); Partners 121; Trial 382.

Honerkamp; City of Brenham v., TexApp–Austin, 950 SW2d 760, reh overr, and review den, and reh of petition for review overr.—App & E 231(9), 232(3), 907(5), 970(2); Damag 49.10, 130.1; Labor & Emp 866; Mun Corp 218(10); Offic 66; Trial 350.8, 352.1(3).

Honett, In re, BkrtcyEDTex, 116 BR 495.—Bankr 2427, 3708(8).

Honey v. State, TexCrimApp, 102 SW3d 224, 132 TexCrim 98.—Crim Law 829(18), 1036.1(8), 1091(7), 1091(11); Homic 1154; Witn 277(2.1).

Honeycutt, In re, TexCivApp–Texarkana, 337 SW2d 631.—Infants 222.

Honeycutt v. Billingsley, TexApp–Houston (1 Dist), 992 SW2d 570, reh overr, and review den, and reh of petition for review overr.—Accord 1, 2(0.5), 26(1); App & E 1001(3), 1003(5); Atty & C 150, 157.1, 160, 166(1), 166(2), 168; Costs 194.32, 208; Nova 1, 2, 3, 12.

Honeycutt; B.T. Healthcare, Inc. v., TexApp–Amarillo, 196 SW3d 296.—Damag 32, 63, 97, 163(1), 163(2), 185(1); Health 826, 830, 832; Neglig 1718.

Honeycutt v. Doss, Tex, 410 SW2d 772.—App & E 345.2, 356, 833(1).

Honeycutt; Doss v., TexCivApp–Waco, 406 SW2d 504, ref nre 410 SW2d 772.—Evid 383(7); Lis Pen 22(4); Mtg 308, 335; Ven & Pur 299(1), 299(3).

Honeycutt; Fleming v., TexCivApp–Texarkana, 205 SW2d 137.—Child C 42, 76, 554, 921(1); Hab Corp 731.

Honeycutt; K-Mart Corp. v., Tex, 24 SW3d 357.—App & E 854(1), 970(2); Evid 507, 508, 512, 513(1), 528(1), 546.

Honeycutt v. KMart Corp., TexApp–Corpus Christi, 1 SW3d 239, reh overr, and review gr, rev 24 SW3d 357. —App & E 961, 1043(6), 1056.1(3); Evid 506, 508, 538, 555.2, 555.7.

Honeycutt v. Long, CA5 (Tex), 861 F2d 1346.—Civil R 1517, 1531; Fed Cts 612, 612.1; Lim of Act 124.

Honeycutt; Murphy v., TexCivApp–Texarkana, 199 SW2d 298, writ refused.—Lim of Act 43; Wills 470(3), 481, 689.

Honeycutt v. State, TexCrimApp, 627 SW2d 417.—Autos 351.1; Crim Law 13(1), 20, 23; Ind & Inf 88; Mun Corp 111(2), 592(1), 639(1), 643; Statut 199.

Honeycutt v. State, TexCrimApp, 499 SW2d 662.—Arrest 63.1, 63.3, 63.4(3); Autos 349(12).

Honeycutt v. State, TexCrimApp, 248 SW2d 124, 157 TexCrim 206.—Crim Law 918(3), 922(7), 925.5(3), 956(13); Homic 908, 1154, 1155.

Honeycutt v. State, TexCrimApp, 199 SW2d 657, 150 TexCrim 140.—Counties 165, 168(3), 170(1); Forg 7(5), 12(0.5).

Honeycutt v. State, TexApp–San Antonio, 82 SW3d 545, petition for discretionary review refused.—Crim Law 273.2(1), 516, 538(3), 554, 1030(2); Double J 28, 132.1, 161, 162.

Honeycutt v. State, TexApp–Houston (14 Dist), 690 SW2d 64, petition for discretionary review refused.—Lewd 1.

Honeycutt; Stolz v., TexApp–Houston (14 Dist), 42 SW3d 305.—App & E 171(1), 226(1), 226(2), 842(2), 893(1), 1008.1(2), 1012.1(4); Mech Liens 94, 95, 115(1), 191, 226, 227, 228, 245(1), 304(1), 310(1); Pretrial Proc 697.

Honeywell, Inc.; Alpha Marketing, Inc. v., TexApp–Dallas, 690 SW2d 35, writ gr, and writ withdrawn, and ref nre.—Damag 85; Judgm 181(19), 185(2).

Honeywell, Inc.; Boyd Intern., Ltd. v., CA5 (Tex), 837 F2d 1312.—Antitrust 286, 360; Fed Cts 616.

Honeywell, Inc.; Hildebrand v., CA5 (Tex), 622 F2d 179. —Fed Civ Proc 839.1, 1721, 1788.6, 1837.1, 1838; Fed Cts 32.

Honeywell, Inc. v. Imperial Condominium Ass'n, Inc., TexApp–Dallas, 716 SW2d 75.—Antitrust 130, 203, 390; App & E 1024.1, 1078(1); Costs 194.25; Evid 434(11).

Honeywell, Inc.; Pegram v., CA5 (Tex), 361 F3d 272, on remand 2004 WL 1844820.—Civil R 1118, 1119, 1135, 1218(3), 1218(6), 1379, 1383, 1413, 1708; Contracts 326; Estop 85; Fed Civ Proc 2497.1; Fed Cts 425, 611, 614, 617, 915; Insurance 1702; Labor & Emp 552(2); Lim of Act 58(1).

Honeywell, Inc.; Simon v., CA5 (Tex), 642 F2d 754.— Civil R 1405, 1542; Fed Cts 703, 922.

Honeywell Intern., Inc.; Armstrong v., SDTex, 198 FSupp2d 899.—Bankr 2045, 2088.

Honeywell Intern., Inc.; Bain v., EDTex, 257 FSupp2d 879, reconsideration den 2003 WL 21003661.—Damag 51, 89(1); Death 84, 87, 88, 89; Fed Civ Proc 2515; Parent & C 7(0.5), 7.5.

Honeywell Intern., Inc.; Bain v., EDTex, 257 FSupp2d 872.—Damag 2; Death 8; Domicile 1; Prod Liab 3.

Honeywell Intern., Inc.; Bain ex rel. Bain v., EDTex, 167 FSupp2d 932.—Aviation 10; Fed Cts 316.1; Neglig 210; Rem of C 2, 36, 103, 107(7).

Honeywell Intern., Inc. v. Phillips Petroleum Co., CA5 (Tex), 415 F3d 429.—Corp 445.1; Fed Cts 15, 18, 218, 776, 973.

Hong v. Bennett, TexApp–Fort Worth, 209 SW3d 795.— Afft 18; App & E 854(4), 907(4), 946, 970(2), 1050.1(1), 1050.1(12), 1056.1(1); Damag 191; Evid 318(7), 536, 543.5.

Hong; Chu v., TexApp–Fort Worth, 185 SW3d 507, reh overr, and review gr.—Fraud Conv 3, 8, 101, 308(1), 314, 319; Hus & W 265.

Hong v. Smith, CA5 (Tex), 129 F3d 824, reh den 137 F3d 1353.—Fed Cts 697.

Honhorst v. University of North Texas, TexApp–Fort Worth, 983 SW2d 872.—App & E 863; Colleges 5, 8(1);

Courts 91(1); Judgm 185(2), 185.3(2); Labor & Emp 857; States 191.2(1), 191.4(1), 191.6(1), 191.9(1), 191.10.

Honigfeld v. State, TexCrimApp, 330 SW2d 622, 168 TexCrim 560.—Int Liq 236(9), 238(1).

Honish; Merit Drilling Co. v., TexApp–Corpus Christi, 715 SW2d 87, ref nre.—Action 27(1); App & E 959(1); Contracts 187(1), 205.15(3), 205.15(4); Damag 63; Interest 39(2.50), 66; Plead 229, 236(2).

Honnoll; Fireman's Fund Ins. Co. of San Francisco, Cal. v., TexCivApp–Waco, 128 SW2d 96.—App & E 1003(5), 1003(9.1); Evid 588.

Honolulu Oil Corp.; Texas Pac. Coal & Oil Co. v., CA5 (Tex), 241 F2d 920.—Impl & C C 10; Mines 74(5).

Honolulu Oil Corp. v. Texas Pac. Coal & Oil Co., NDTex, 141 FSupp 322, aff 241 F2d 920.—Mines 73.5, 74(5).

Honorable Court of Appeals for Third Dist.; State ex rel. Holmes v., TexCrimApp, 885 SW2d 389, reh den, on remand Texas Bd of Pardons and Paroles v. Graham, 878 SW2d 684.—Courts 480(1); Hab Corp 494; Mand 1, 3(1), 4(4), 12, 53, 61; Motions 7.

Honorable Court of Appeals for Third Dist.; Texas Bd. of Pardons and Paroles v., TexCrimApp, 885 SW2d 389. See State ex rel. Holmes v. Honorable Court of Appeals for Third Dist.

Honorable Court of Criminal Appeals and All of Its Active Justices; Nabelek v., CA5 (Tex), 112 FedAppx 948.—Mand 60.

Honorable First Court of Appeals; Granada Corp. v., Tex, 844 SW2d 223.—App & E 842(8); Mand 4(4), 32, 172; Pretrial Proc 403; Witn 201(2), 204(2), 219(3).

Honorable Fourth Supreme Judicial Dist.; Peeples v., Tex, 701 SW2d 635.—Pretrial Proc 33, 401, 411.

Honorable Governor of Texas; Boswell v., NDTex, 138 FSupp2d 782.—Atty & C 62; Fed Civ Proc 657.5(1), 673, 1041, 1825, 1838; Militia 19; States 208.

Honorable Second Court of Appeals; Street v., Tex, 756 SW2d 299.—Insurance 3549(5); Lim of Act 55(2), 106; Mand 4(1), 4(3), 12; Plead 106(2).

Honorable Thirteenth Court of Appeals; Griffin Industries, Inc. v., Tex, 934 SW2d 349.—App & E 389(1), 389(3); Const Law 2317; Costs 128; Evid 96(1), 584(1).

Honore v. Douglas, CA5 (Tex), 833 F2d 565.—Admin Law 651; Colleges 8.1(6.1); Const Law 4223(6); Fed Civ Proc 2497.1, 2546; Offic 72.41(1).

Honsaker, Matter of, TexCivApp–Dallas, 539 SW2d 198, ref nre.—Const Law 4466; Double J 33; Infants 68.7(2), 68.7(3), 68.7(4), 198.

Honsinger v. Honsinger, TexCivApp–Amarillo, 153 SW2d 317.—Deeds 181, 208(1).

Honsinger; Honsinger v., TexCivApp–Amarillo, 153 SW2d 317.—Deeds 181, 208(1).

Honts v. Shaw, TexApp–Austin, 975 SW2d 816.—App & E 1008.1(1); Elections 37, 154(1), 154(9.1), 158, 227(8), 291, 305(6).

Hoobler v. State, TexCrimApp, 730 SW2d 755.—Crim Law 1166(1); Jury 29(2).

Hoobler v. State, TexApp–Houston (1 Dist), 695 SW2d 785, petition for discretionary review gr, rev 730 SW2d 755.—Crim Law 1035(1).

Hood, Ex parte, TexCrimApp, 211 SW3d 767.—Hab Corp 273, 287.1, 461, 821.1, 894.1, 898(2), 898(3); Statut 181(2), 188, 200, 208, 212.6.

Hood, In re, TexApp–Houston (1 Dist), 113 SW3d 525.— Child C 423, 552, 617; Mand 4(1), 4(4); Pretrial Proc 44.1.

Hood; Acceptance Ins. Co. v., EDTex, 895 FSupp 131.— Insurance 2278(11), 2295, 2914, 2915.

Hood v. Adams, TexCivApp–Amarillo, 334 SW2d 206.— Damag 109, 110, 208(3); Judgm 305; Tresp 46(3), 56, 57, 58; Trial 398, 401.

Hood v. Amarillo Nat. Bank, Tex, 815 SW2d 545.—App & E 80(6); Bankr 2395; Execution 172(2).

HOOD

Hood v. **Amarillo Nat. Bank**, TexApp–Amarillo, 807 SW2d 807, writ den, and writ gr, and writ withdrawn, rev 815 SW2d 545.—Bankr 2396; Execution 7, 172(2); Judgm 524.

Hood; **Bennett v.**, TexCivApp–Beaumont, 238 SW2d 587. —Des & Dist 71(6); Marriage 50(1), 52; Tresp to T T 45(1); Trial 96, 194(10); Witn 139(4).

Hood; **Brand v.**, TexCivApp–Texarkana, 85 SW2d 347, writ dism.—Banks 80(2), 80(10); Const Law 2355; Lim of Act 195(3).

Hood v. **Cockrell**, CA5 (Tex), 72 FedAppx 171.—Hab Corp 364, 461, 486(1), 823.

Hood; **Commercial Standard Fire & Marine Ins. Co. v.**, TexCivApp–Tyler, 474 SW2d 522, ref nre.—Work Comp 110, 172, 173, 1427.

Hood v. **Dretke**, CA5 (Tex), 93 FedAppx 665, cert den 125 SCt 255, 543 US 836, 160 LEd2d 58.—Crim Law 641.13(7).

Hood; **F. E. Prince Co. v.**, TexCivApp–Texarkana, 106 SW2d 1080.—Garn 148, 178.

Hood v. **First Nat. Bank of Panhandle**, TexCivApp–Amarillo, 410 SW2d 449, ref nre.—App & E 1008.1(7), 1010.1(1); Bills & N 250, 517; Evid 420(7), 441(1).

Hood v. **Glenn**, TexCivApp–Austin, 98 SW2d 1036.—Pretrial Proc 690.

Hood; **Hawkins v.**, TexCivApp–Amarillo, 331 SW2d 954, writ dism.—Divorce 139; Mand 190; Pretrial Proc 501.

Hood v. **Hays County**, TexApp–Austin, 836 SW2d 327.—Admin Law 229; Tax 2642, 2650, 2692; Trial 45(2).

Hood v. **Hood**, TexCivApp–Amarillo, 153 SW2d 247.—App & E 1062.1; Trial 140(2); Trusts 95, 359(2), 373.

Hood; **Hood v.**, TexCivApp–Amarillo, 153 SW2d 247.—App & E 1062.1; Trial 140(2); Trusts 95, 359(2), 373.

Hood v. **James**, CA5 (Tex), 256 F2d 895.—Bankr 2234; Contracts 143(3); Fed Cts 32; Joint-St Co 21.

Hood; **Jordan v.**, TexCivApp–Hous (1 Dist), 610 SW2d 215.—Venue 5.3(2).

Hood; **Kanz v.**, TexApp–Waco, 17 SW3d 311, review gr, and withdrawn, and review den, and reh of petition for review den.—App & E 1010.1(1), 1012.1(4); Ex & Ad 35(18), 37(1), 37(4), 314(12).

Hood v. **Laning**, TexCivApp–San Antonio, 415 SW2d 953. —Explos 12.

Hood; **Miller v.**, TexCivApp–Corpus Christi, 536 SW2d 278, ref nre.—App & E 1070(2); Const Law 45; Counties 129, 141, 144; Health 605, 770, 786, 787, 825, 835; Judgm 470; Labor & Emp 26, 58.

Hood; **National County Mut. Fire Ins. Co. v.**, TexApp–Houston (14 Dist), 693 SW2d 638.—Decl Judgm 345.1; Evid 43(3), 43(4); Judgm 185.2(4).

Hood; **Panhandle Const. Co. v.**, TexCivApp–Austin, 114 SW2d 632, writ refused.—App & E 1071.1(5.1); Lim of Act 13.

Hood v. **Phillips**, Tex, 554 SW2d 160.—Evid 508; Health 623, 624, 626, 821(4), 825, 927; Pretrial Proc 382; Trial 352.1(6).

Hood v. **Phillips**, TexCivApp–Beaumont, 537 SW2d 291, writ gr, aff 554 SW2d 160.—Health 665, 820, 827, 908; Trial 350.6(2), 350.8; Witn 196.4.

Hood; **Ryland Group, Inc. v.**, Tex, 924 SW2d 120.—Judgm 185(2), 185.1(3), 185.1(4).

Hood v. **Ryland Group, Inc.**, TexApp–Beaumont, 911 SW2d 931, reh overr, and writ gr, rev 924 SW2d 120.—App & E 934(1); Judgm 181(5.1), 185(2), 185.1(4), 185.3(2), 185.3(21); Lim of Act 30, 104(1), 104(2), 195(3); Plead 36(1); Trial 136(1).

Hood v. **Seay**, TexCivApp–El Paso, 529 SW2d 101.—Plead 111.23, 111.42(11).

Hood; **Siegel v.**, TexCivApp–San Antonio, 119 SW2d 120, writ dism.—App & E 1001(1); Contracts 322(2), 323(1).

Hood; **Smith v.**, TexCivApp–Eastland, 143 SW2d 646.—Plead 225(1).

Hood v. **State**, TexCrimApp, 185 SW3d 445, reh den, cert den 127 SCt 927, 166 LEd2d 714.—Crim Law 1042, 1179; Sent & Pun 115(4).

Hood v. **State**, TexCrimApp, 158 SW3d 480, cert den 125 SCt 2976, 545 US 1146, 162 LEd2d 899.—Crim Law 1590.

Hood v. **State**, TexCrimApp, 607 SW2d 567.—False Pret 32.

Hood v. **State**, TexCrimApp, 490 SW2d 549.—Crim Law 364(3.1), 1035(3), 1115(2).

Hood v. **State**, TexCrimApp, 458 SW2d 662.—Jury 24.1; Sent & Pun 2004.

Hood v. **State**, TexCrimApp, 342 SW2d 436, 170 TexCrim 511.—Bail 77(2).

Hood v. **State**, TexCrimApp, 334 SW2d 302, 169 TexCrim 422.—Ind & Inf 127.

Hood v. **State**, TexCrimApp, 100 SW2d 1014, 131 TexCrim 500.—Int Liq 205(1).

Hood v. **State**, TexApp–Austin, 828 SW2d 87.—Crim Law 396(1), 396(2), 424(1), 854(1), 854(2), 1039, 1119(5), 1144.13(3), 1144.13(6), 1159.2(7), 1159.6, 1163(6), 1169.1(9), 1169.7, 1174(4); Statut 190, 212.6, 227.

Hood v. **State**, TexApp–Austin, 705 SW2d 844.—Burg 28(3); Sent & Pun 1381(6).

Hood v. **State**, TexApp–Dallas, 638 SW2d 622.—Autos 355(11); Crim Law 323, 408, 564(1).

Hood v. **State**, TexApp–Texarkana, 860 SW2d 931.—Burg 16, 41(1), 41(4), 41(6), 42(1), 42(4), 45; Crim Law 552(3), 814(19), 1144.13(1), 1144.13(3), 1144.13(6), 1159.2(7), 1173.2(1).

Hood v. **State**, TexApp–Amarillo, 944 SW2d 743, appeal after new trial 2004 WL 573827, reh overr, and petition for discretionary review gr, aff 185 SW3d 445, reh den, cert den 127 SCt 927, 166 LEd2d 714.—Crim Law 398(3), 1153(1), 1170(1); Rape 40(2), 40(5).

Hood v. **State**, TexCivApp–Amarillo, 90 SW2d 1101, writ dism.—Inj 122; Statut 184.

Hood v. **Tenneco Texas Life Ins. Co.**, CA5 (Tex), 739 F2d 1012.—Antitrust 535, 544, 557, 558, 583, 976, 977(2).

Hood; **Texas Co. v.**, CCA5 (Tex), 161 F2d 618, cert den 68 SCt 206, 332 US 829, 92 LEd 403.—Autos 244(35), 245(13), 245(60); Evid 98, 586(3), 594, 595.

Hood v. **Texas Indem. Ins. Co.**, Tex, 209 SW2d 345, 146 Tex 522.—Evid 568(1), 570; Work Comp 511, 546, 598, 1418, 1529, 1924, 1968(8), 1975.

Hood; **Texas Indem. Ins. Co. v.**, TexCivApp–San Antonio, 208 SW2d 658, rev 209 SW2d 345, 146 Tex 522.—Work Comp 546, 1529, 1975.

Hood; **Texas Real Estate Commission v.**, TexCivApp–Eastland, 617 SW2d 838, ref nre.—App & E 719(8); Brok 4.

Hood v. **U.S.**, CA5 (Tex), 326 F2d 33.—Contempt 60(1), 60(3).

Hood v. **Wal-Mart Stores, Inc.**, Tex, 216 SW3d 829.—App & E 389(1).

Hood & Hall Co.; **Evans Young Wyatt, Inc. v.**, TexCivApp–Waco, 517 SW2d 313, ref nre.—Accord 27; App & E 215(1), 1069.1; Land & Ten 112.5, 160(4), 233(2); Trial 317.

Hood County; **Anderson v.**, TexApp–Fort Worth, 958 SW2d 448, reh overr.—Work Comp 1232, 1234, 1236.

Hood County Sand & Gravel Co.; **Adams v.**, TexCivApp–Fort Worth, 354 SW2d 593, ref nre.—App & E 218.2(3.1); Damag 6; Sequest 21.

Hood Industries Inc.; **Kirby Forest Industries Inc. v.**, CA5 (Tex), 10 F3d 1173. See Folks v. Kirby Forest Industries Inc.

Hood Industries Inc. v. **Knight**, CA5 (Tex), 10 F3d 1173. See Folks v. Kirby Forest Industries Inc.

Hood Industries Inc. v. **Knight's Machinery Removal**, CA5 (Tex), 10 F3d 1173. See Folks v. Kirby Forest Industries Inc.

Hood Lanco, Inc.; Manhattan Const. Co. v., TexApp–Houston (14 Dist), 762 SW2d 617, writ den.—Action 60; Indem 33(5); Judgm 184.

Hoodye v. Bruusgaard Krosterud Skibs A/S Drammen, Norway, SDTex, 197 FSupp 697.—Corp 642(1); Ship 50.

Hooe v. Texas Fire & Cas. Underwriters, TexCivApp–Waco, 151 SW2d 310.—App & E 623, 624, 1126; Stip 6.

Hooey; Fowler v., TexCrimApp, 573 SW2d 241.—Crim Law 1068.5, 1081(1); Hab Corp 814, 817.1; Mand 60; Prisons 13.3.

Hooey; Smith v., USTex, 89 SCt 575, 393 US 374, 21 LEd2d 607.—Const Law 3856; Crim Law 577.2.

Hoof; U.S. v., CA5 (Tex), 119 FedAppx 603, cert gr, vac 125 SCt 2278, 544 US 1030, 161 LEd2d 1055.—Autos 349(17), 349(18); Searches 181.

Hoog v. State, TexApp–San Antonio, 87 SW3d 740, review den, and reh of petition for review den.—Anim 3.5(8); Forfeit 3, 5; Rob 4; Statut 181(1), 188, 205.

Hooge; Matlock v., TexCivApp–San Antonio, 365 SW2d 386, ref nre.—Autos 181(1), 181(2).

Hook v. Morrison Milling Co., CA5 (Tex), 38 F3d 776, reh and sug for reh den 43 F3d 672.—Fed Cts 812; Labor & Emp 407, 2801; Rem of C 19(5), 107(9), 118; States 18.46, 18.47, 18.51.

Hooker; Anderson v., TexCivApp–El Paso, 420 SW2d 235, ref nre.—App & E 931(4), 989, 1177(7); Health 905, 906, 908, 926; New Tr 56, 140(3), 157.

Hooker v. Bodine, TexCivApp–Eastland, 232 SW2d 371. —Wills 290, 324(4).

Hooker v. Hoover, NDTex, 882 FSupp 574.—Atty & C 157.1.

Hooker v. Kirk, TexCivApp–Waco, 379 SW2d 407.—Plead 343.

Hooker v. Roberts, TexCivApp–Eastland, 330 SW2d 493. —App & E 846(6); Judgm 272; Trial 388(2).

Hooker v. State, TexCrimApp, 621 SW2d 597.—Crim Law 134(1), 552(1), 552(3), 1134(3), 1166(4); Neglig 144.

Hooker v. State, TexCrimApp, 388 SW2d 951.—Autos 355(6).

Hooker v. State, TexApp–Beaumont, 932 SW2d 712.— Autos 355(6); Crim Law 444, 1134(2), 1169.2(7); Jury 76.

Hooker; Texas Planting Seed Ass'n v., TexCivApp–Corpus Christi, 386 SW2d 348.—App & E 1178(8); Plead 45, 104(2), 111.3, 111.8, 402.

Hooker v. Williamson, Tex, 60 Tex 524.—Partners 83.

Hooker Const. Co.; Hillen v., TexCivApp–Waco, 484 SW2d 113.—Neglig 1612, 1620, 1658, 1677, 1695.

Hooker Const. Co.; H. L. McRae Co. v., TexCivApp–Austin, 579 SW2d 62.—App & E 493, 635(2), 1203(1); Appear 8(3), 8(8), 19(1), 24(5); Courts 37(3); Proc 80.

Hooker Const. Co.; H. L. McRae Co. v., TexCivApp–Austin, 564 SW2d 142.—App & E 395.

Hooker Contracting Co., Inc.; Meza v., TexApp–San Antonio, 104 SW3d 111.—Judgm 181(7), 185(2), 185.3(2); Lim of Act 118(2), 119(3); Proc 63; Stip 6.

Hooker Industries, Inc.; Stein v., TexCivApp–San Antonio, 545 SW2d 487, ref nre.—Corp 33.

Hookie v. State, TexApp–Texarkana, 136 SW3d 671.— Autos 342.1; Const Law 665, 667, 700, 975, 990, 1030, 1033, 3057, 3078, 3823; Crim Law 23, 1042, 1159.3(2); Homic 708, 709; Sent & Pun 1825.

Hooks, Ex parte, Tex, 415 SW2d 166.—Child S 5, 444, 446, 459.

Hooks v. Army and Air Force Exchange Service, NDTex, 944 FSupp 503.—Fed Civ Proc 657.5(1); Fed Cts 34; Labor & Emp 1613, 1996; U S 125(30), 131.

Hooks v. Brown, TexCivApp–Austin, 348 SW2d 104, ref nre.—App & E 1048(7), 1050.1(3.1), 1060.1(1); Breach of M P 15; Can of Inst 24(1), 24(2), 34(1), 51, 58, 59; Deeds 74, 75, 78, 196(3), 202, 203, 211(0.5), 211(3); Equity 67, 84; Judges 39; Lim of Act 127(8); New Tr

108(2); Pretrial Proc 717.1, 726; Trial 352.1(3); Trover 22; Witn 16.

Hooks v. Cook, TexCivApp–Houston, 345 SW2d 592, ref nre.—Bound 53.

Hooks v. East Texas Pulp & Paper Co., Tex, 369 SW2d 308.—Tax 2564, 2712.

Hooks; East Tex. Pulp & Paper Co. v., TexCivApp–Beaumont, 359 SW2d 955, rev 369 SW2d 308.—Schools 111; Tax 2609, 2647, 2676.

Hooks v. Fourth Court of Appeals, Tex, 808 SW2d 56.— Courts 207.4(2); Em Dom 187, 246(2), 265(5); Mand 4(4), 43; Pretrial Proc 501.

Hooks v. Hooks, TexCivApp–El Paso, 139 SW2d 305.— Child S 60, 70, 140(2), 556(1), 557(3).

Hooks; Hooks v., TexCivApp–El Paso, 139 SW2d 305.— Child S 60, 70, 140(2), 556(1), 557(3).

Hooks v. Quarterman, CA5 (Tex), 224 FedAppx 352.— Hab Corp 603.

Hooks v. State, TexCrimApp, 860 SW2d 110, on remand 877 SW2d 338.—Sent & Pun 372, 373.

Hooks v. State, TexCrimApp, 202 SW2d 675.—Crim Law 1090.1(1).

Hooks v. State, TexApp–Dallas, 877 SW2d 338.—Crim Law 273.1(1).

Hooks v. State, TexApp–Dallas, 838 SW2d 643, reh den, and petition for discretionary review gr, rev 860 SW2d 110, on remand 877 SW2d 338.—Crim Law 273.1(2), 1181.5(8); Sent & Pun 373, 1911.

Hooks v. State, TexApp–Texarkana, 203 SW3d 861, petition for discretionary review refused.—Crim Law 1134(3), 1139, 1158(4), 1177, 1524, 1534, 1590, 1602.

Hooks v. State, TexApp–Texarkana, 44 SW3d 607, petition for discretionary review refused, cert den 122 SCt 1977, 535 US 1085, 152 LEd2d 1034, denial of postconviction relief aff 203 SW3d 861, petition for discretionary review refused, dism of habeas corpus vac 224 FedAppx 352.—Autos 355(13); Crim Law 438(7), 469.2, 591, 1043(2), 1134(1), 1134(2), 1144.13(2.1), 1144.13(6), 1153(1), 1159.2(1), 1159.2(2), 1159.2(7), 1159.4(2), 1159.6, 1187, 1189.

Hooks v. State, TexApp–Amarillo, 659 SW2d 449.—Crim Law 1023(16).

Hooks v. State, TexApp–Beaumont, 144 SW3d 652.— Const Law 2821; Crim Law 1030(2), 1043(2), 1134(3); Double J 22; Mental H 433(2).

Hooks v. State, TexApp–Eastland, 73 SW3d 398, reh overr.—Crim Law 394.6(5), 526, 641.13(1), 641.13(6), 796, 1158(4); Infants 69(5).

Hooks v. Texas Dept. of Water Resources, Tex, 611 SW2d 417, on remand 645 SW2d 874, ref nre.—Environ Law 656, 657.

Hooks v. Texas Dept. of Water Resources, TexApp–Austin, 645 SW2d 874, ref nre.—Environ Law 228, 656, 666, 673, 682, 690.

Hooks v. Texas Dept. of Water Resources, TexCivApp–Austin, 602 SW2d 389, rev 611 SW2d 417, on remand 645 SW2d 874, ref nre.—Admin Law 310, 665.1, 666, 668; App & E 151(1), 151(6); Const Law 2607; Environ Law 651, 656; Statut 223.2(1.1).

Hooks v. U.S., CA5 (Tex), 375 F2d 212.—Crim Law 1158(4), 1170.5(1); Witn 380(5.1).

Hooks v. Vanderburg, TexCivApp–Fort Worth, 328 SW2d 467.—Deeds 82, 194(3); Hus & W 270(11).

Hooks; Williams v., TexCivApp–Beaumont, 333 SW2d 184.—App & E 294(1); Ref of Inst 17(2), 22, 45(4.1).

Hooks & Matteson Enterprises, Inc.; Line Enterprises, Inc. v., TexApp–Amarillo, 659 SW2d 113.—Antitrust 17, 18, 39, 41, 83, 88, 105; App & E 204(1), 232(2), 974(1), 1043(1), 1064.1(9), 1177(5); Inj 14, 130, 208; Trial 219, 351.2(4), 352.1(2).

Hooks Indus., Inc.; Fairmont Supply Co. v., TexApp–Houston (1 Dist), 177 SW3d 529, reh overr, and review den.—App & E 226(2), 893(1), 1050.1(1), 1051(1), 1051.1(1); Contracts 206; Costs 208.

HOOKS

See Guidelines for Arrangement at the beginning of this Volume

Hooks Tel. Co. v. Town of Leary, TexCivApp–Texarkana, 370 SW2d 749, ref nre.—Tel 794.

Hooks Tel. Co. v. Town of Leary, TexCivApp–Texarkana, 352 SW2d 755.—App & E 900, 931(1); Inj 24; Mun Corp 662, 680(1); Tel 789, 794.

Hooper, Ex parte, TexCrimApp, 319 SW2d 320, 167 TexCrim 232.—Hab Corp 712.1.

Hooper, Ex parte, TexCrimApp, 312 SW2d 673, 166 TexCrim 189.—Hab Corp 861.

Hooper; Alpha v., CA5 (Tex), 440 F3d 670.—Civil R 1351(4), 1358, 1412; Evid 146.

Hooper; Alpha v., CA5 (Tex), 100 FedAppx 999.—Fed Cts 557.

Hooper v. Bell, TexCivApp–San Antonio, 210 SW2d 870, ref nre.—Contracts 252, 256, 261(6), 312(1), 318; Sales 1(4), 89, 116, 384(2).

Hooper v. Chittaluru, TexApp–Houston (14 Dist), 222 SW3d 103, review den (2 pets), and reh of petition for review den.—App & E 205, 854(4), 970(2), 989, 1056.1(1), 1056.1(3), 1058(1); Evid 528(0.5), 535, 571(9); Health 675, 706, 822(3); Pretrial Proc 45; Trial 56, 93.

Hooper v. Chrysler Motors Corp., CA5 (Tex), 325 F2d 321, cert den 84 SCt 1647, 377 US 967, 12 LEd2d 736.—Fed Civ Proc 1758.1.

Hooper v. Courtney, TexCivApp–Amarillo, 258 SW2d 124, ref nre.—Lim of Act 197(2); Trusts 138.

Hooper v. Courtney, TexCivApp–Amarillo, 256 SW2d 462.—App & E 882(8), 1029, 1053(2), 1056.1(4.1), 1170.7, 1170.9(2.1), 1178(6); Equity 65(2); Evid 546; Trial 194(9), 244(3), 295(12), 350.3(2.1); Trusts 138, 372(3), 373.

Hooper v. Deisher, TexCivApp–Amarillo, 113 SW2d 966.—Arrest 66(2); False Imp 7(3); Venue 8.5(5).

Hooper v. F.D.I.C., CA5 (Tex), 785 F2d 1228.—Fed Cts 668.

Hooper; Federal Deposit Ins. Corp. v., CA5 (Tex), 785 F2d 1228. See Hooper v. F.D.I.C.

Hooper; First Nat. Bank of Seminole v., Tex, 104 SW3d 83.—Fraud Conv 88.

Hooper; First Nat. Bank of Seminole, Texas v., TexApp–El Paso, 48 SW3d 802, reh overr, and review den, and reh of petition for review gr, and withdrawn, and review gr, rev 104 SW3d 83.—App & E 842(1), 969, 989, 1001(1), 1002, 1003(2), 1003(3), 1003(7); Fraud Conv 77, 186, 272, 273, 277(1), 283, 297, 300(1), 309(1), 314; Jury 13(5.1); Trial 202.

Hooper v. Great Am. Indem. Co., CCA5 (Tex), 102 F2d 739.—Work Comp 51, 606, 1370, 1719.

Hooper v. Halsell, TexCivApp–Amarillo, 143 SW2d 228.—Plead 111.3, 111.4, 111.17.

Hooper; Hilt v., TexCivApp–Galveston, 203 SW2d 334.—Adop 6, 17.

Hooper; Holley v., TexCivApp–Austin, 205 SW2d 120, ref nre.—Evid 448, 450(8); Spec Perf 130.

Hooper v. Holt, TexCivApp–Texarkana, 416 SW2d 916.—App & E 1177(5); Autos 208; Courts 92; Judgm 199(3), 199(3.17); Trial 365.1(7).

Hooper v. Hooper, TexCivApp–Amarillo, 403 SW2d 215, writ dism.—Divorce 252.1, 252.3(2), 252.3(3).

Hooper; Hooper v., TexCivApp–Amarillo, 403 SW2d 215, writ dism.—Divorce 252.1, 252.3(2), 252.3(3).

Hooper; Lohmann v., TexCivApp–Beaumont, 87 SW2d 803.—Estop 52.15, 95, 118, 119.

Hooper v. Mercantile Bank & Trust, TexApp–San Antonio, 762 SW2d 383.—App & E 223; Bills & N 516, 534; Guar 91; Judgm 185(1), 185(3), 185.2(5), 185.3(16).

Hooper; Miller v., TexCivApp–Amarillo, 94 SW2d 230.—Damag 173(2), 208(4); Evid 332(3), 472(2), 501(10); Trial 352.9.

Hooper v. M M Cattle Co., TexCivApp–Amarillo, 278 SW2d 170, ref nre.—Neglig 1177.

Hooper v. Morgan Leasing Corp., TexCivApp–Fort Worth, 509 SW2d 957.—App & E 1152; Judgm 194; Mal Pros 38, 47.

Hooper; Phillips Petroleum Co. v., CCA5 (Tex), 164 F2d 743.—Explos 9; Neglig 1076, 1284, 1287.

Hooper v. Pitney Bowes, Inc., TexApp–Texarkana, 895 SW2d 773, writ den.—Damag 50.10, 192; Labor & Emp 2926, 3049(3), 3055; Libel 44(3), 50, 51(4), 71, 74, 91, 101(4), 112(1), 125.

Hooper; Porter v., TexCivApp–Waco, 529 SW2d 837.—App & E 846(5).

Hooper v. Ranger County Mut. Ins. Co., TexCivApp–Texarkana, 487 SW2d 856.—Insurance 1743, 2647; Judgm 181(23).

Hooper v. Ryan, TexCivApp–Waco, 581 SW2d 237.—Bills & N 48.1, 52, 459; Contrib 6; Release 28(1).

Hooper v. Sanford, TexApp–Tyler, 968 SW2d 392, reh overr.—App & E 1061.2; Health 807.

Hooper; Security & Communications Systems, Inc. v., TexCivApp–Dallas, 575 SW2d 606.—App & E 173(7), 218.2(1), 930(3), 989, 1001(1), 1003(5); Costs 194.32; Judgm 199(3.10); Labor & Emp 256(5), 265; Princ & A 189(4); Trial 350.4(4).

Hooper v. State, TexCrimApp, 214 SW3d 9.—Assault 56, 91.12; Crim Law 59(1), 552(1), 552(3), 552(4), 559, 560, 562, 881(1), 1134(2), 1144.13(2.1), 1144.13(5), 1159.2(7), 1159.2(8), 1159.2(9), 1159.3(2), 1159.6.

Hooper v. State, TexCrimApp, 786 SW2d 295. See Arnold v. State.

Hooper v. State, TexCrimApp, 557 SW2d 122.—Crim Law 1144.10, 1186.1.

Hooper v. State, TexCrimApp, 533 SW2d 762.—Arrest 63.4(18), 71.1(4.1), 71.1(7); Crim Law 394.4(6); Searches 120, 192.1.

Hooper v. State, TexCrimApp, 516 SW2d 941.—Arrest 63.4(1), 63.4(2), 63.4(11), 63.5(6), 71.1(2.1); Rob 24.10; Searches 40.1, 41, 44.

Hooper v. State, TexCrimApp, 494 SW2d 846.—Witn 346, 363(1), 374(2).

Hooper v. State, TexCrimApp, 487 SW2d 349.—Crim Law 507.5, 1038.1(7), 1038.4.

Hooper v. State, TexCrimApp, 329 SW2d 878, 168 TexCrim 506.—Weap 17(4).

Hooper v. State, TexCrimApp, 284 SW2d 355.—Crim Law 1087.1(2).

Hooper v. State, TexCrimApp, 272 SW2d 103, 160 TexCrim 441.—Autos 359; Crim Law 1177.5(2).

Hooper v. State, TexApp–Houston (1 Dist), 788 SW2d 24.—Autos 355(10).

Hooper v. State, TexApp–Austin, 106 SW3d 270, reh overr.—Const Law 655, 656, 990, 1030, 1131, 4509(9); Controlled Subs 6; Crim Law 13.1(1), 1030(1), 1030(2); Statut 188.

Hooper v. State, TexApp–Waco, 170 SW3d 736, petition for discretionary review gr, remanded 214 SW3d 9.—Assault 91.12; Crim Law 59(5), 80, 552(2), 1134(2), 1144.13(2.1), 1144.13(5), 1144.13(6), 1144.13(7), 1159.2(7), 1159.3(2), 1159.4(2), 1159.6.

Hooper; Sturdevant v., TexCivApp–Waco, 101 SW2d 379, writ dism.—App & E 1056.4; Autos 244(26), 245(28).

Hooper; Texas Cas. Ins. Co. v., TexCivApp–Waco, 448 SW2d 258.—Work Comp 1028, 1927.

Hooper v. Torres, TexApp–El Paso, 790 SW2d 757, writ den.—App & E 934(2), 1058(1); Evid 356, 538; Lim of Act 197(1); Trial 351.2(2).

Hooper; U.S. v., CA5 (Tex), 429 F2d 583.—Crim Law 1031(5), 1132.

Hoopes; Southern Underwriters v., TexCivApp–Galveston, 120 SW2d 924, dism.—Evid 54, 552; Work Comp 1536, 1546, 1924.

Hoople Jordan Const. Co.; Shaw Equipment Co. v., TexCivApp–Dallas, 428 SW2d 835.—App & E 213; Chat Mtg 72; Contracts 93(2), 94(5); Estop 119; Evid 400(6); Fraud 35; Sales 38(3), 50, 52(5.1), 52(7), 53(3).

Hoops; U.S. v., CA5 (Tex), 132 FedAppx 21.—Jury 34(7); Sent & Pun 736.

Hooser v. Barnett, TexCivApp–Texarkana, 87 SW2d 519. —Courts 481.

Hooser; Wilson v., TexCivApp–Waco, 573 SW2d 601, ref nre.—Autos 372(1); Bailm 2, 9, 31(1).

Hoot v. Brewer, TexApp–Houston (1 Dist), 640 SW2d 758. —Elections 120, 144; Mand 1, 74(3), 168(4).

Hoot v. Quality Ready-Mix Co., TexCivApp–Corpus Christi, 438 SW2d 421.—App & E 989, 1010.1(1); Atty & C 140; Costs 194.38; Interest 22(1); Sales 357(1), 359(1); Tender 12(2); Trial 382, 388(4).

Hoot v. State, TexCrimApp, 194 SW2d 97, 149 TexCrim 316.—Ind & Inf 87(3), 123.

Hooten v. City of Gatesville, TexCivApp–Waco, 130 SW2d 1067.—Mun Corp 857; Neglig 1655.

Hooten v. Dunbar, TexCivApp–Beaumont, 347 SW2d 775, ref nre.—App & E 232(0.5); Evid 506, 507; Trial 82, 84(1), 84(2).

Hooten v. Enriquez, TexApp–El Paso, 863 SW2d 522, reh overr.—App & E 946; Const Law 2540, 2541, 2560; Costs 194.40; Counties 47, 58, 63, 82, 93, 159, 160; Courts 89; Evid 12, 51; Inj 189, 204; Mand 76; Records 51.

Hooten; Enriquez v., TexApp–El Paso, 857 SW2d 153.— App & E 374(4), 460(4); Inj 220.

Hooten v. Fleckenstein, TexApp–Tyler, 836 SW2d 300, writ dism woj.—App & E 934(1); Const Law 2315; Lim of Act 4(2).

Hooten; Hartford Acc. & Indem. Co. v., TexCivApp–San Antonio, 531 SW2d 365, ref nre.—Labor & Emp 23; Work Comp 239.

Hooten v. State, TexCrimApp, 170 SW2d 744, 145 TexCrim 556.—Crim Law 1091(5), 1170(1); Int Liq 239(1), 239(2).

Hooten v. State, TexApp–Fort Worth, 689 SW2d 328.— Crim Law 364(4), 706(3), 728(5), 867, 1044.2(1); Sent & Pun 308.

Hooten; U.S. v., CA5 (Tex), 942 F2d 878, reh den.—Crim Law 273.1(2), 1134(3), 1139, 1181.5(8); Sent & Pun 275, 282, 293, 299, 300, 726(3), 765, 930, 973, 995, 2264.

Hooten; U.S. v., CA5 (Tex), 933 F2d 293.—Banks 509.10; Brib 1(1); B & L Assoc 23(8); Crim Law 1158(1), 1167(1); Ind & Inf 7, 15(1); Larc 6, 46; Sent & Pun 678, 765.

Hooten v. U.S., CA5 (Tex), 405 F2d 1167.—Em Dom 107.

Hooters, Inc. v. City of Texarkana, Tex., EDTex, 897 FSupp 946.—Civil R 1457(7); Estop 62.4; Inj 138.1, 138.3, 138.6; Licens 20, 38; Zoning 288.

Hootman; Chapman v., TexApp–Houston (14 Dist), 999 SW2d 118.—App & E 498.1, 499(1); Atty & C 148(3); Contracts 143(2), 147(2), 176(2); Costs 260(1), 260(4), 260(5), 261; Evid 448.

Hoots v. State, TexCrimApp, 501 SW2d 134.—Infants 20.

Hoots v. State, TexCrimApp, 346 SW2d 607, 171 TexCrim 178.—Autos 355(6); Crim Law 578, 598(1), 598(7), 603.2.

Hoover, Ex parte, TexCrimApp, 298 SW2d 579, 164 TexCrim 251.—Hab Corp 526, 711, 713, 729.

Hoover, Ex parte, TexCrimApp, 245 SW2d 966.—Hab Corp 224.1.

Hoover, Ex parte, TexCivApp–San Antonio, 245 SW2d 557.—Hab Corp 613.

Hoover, Ex parte, TexCivApp–El Paso, 520 SW2d 483.— Const Law 4494; Hab Corp 445.

Hoover v. Barker, TexCivApp–Austin, 507 SW2d 299, ref nre.—App & E 66, 79(1), 80(1), 80(6), 93, 218.2(1), 230, 237(1), 242(2), 302(5), 712, 729, 758.3(9), 1079; Corp 361; Costs 112(1), 137, 194.32; Judges 49(1); Jury 136(3), 139; Nova 10; Plead 228.14; Pretrial Proc 511; Sales 87(3); Trial 131(2), 351.2(8), 365.1(4).

Hoover v. Barker, TexCivApp–Austin, 476 SW2d 126, dism.—Plead 111.38, 111.42(6); Venue 22(1), 22(8).

Hoover v. Beto, CA5 (Tex), 467 F2d 516, cert den 93 SCt 703, 409 US 1086, 34 LEd2d 673.—Courts 100(1); Crim Law 59(2), 80, 517(5), 517.1(2), 528, 532(0.5), 534(1),

662.8, 673(4), 1086.11, 1169.12; Searches 182, 201; Witn 5.

Hoover v. Beto, CA5 (Tex), 439 F2d 913, on reh 467 F2d 516, cert den 93 SCt 703, 409 US 1086, 34 LEd2d 673.— Courts 100(1); Crim Law 423(1), 528, 662.10, 899; Fed Civ Proc 56; Hab Corp 705.1; Judgm 828.21(1); Searches 172, 182, 194; Witn 380(3).

Hoover v. Beto, SDTex, 306 FSupp 980, rev 439 F2d 913, on reh 467 F2d 516, cert den 93 SCt 703, 409 US 1086, 34 LEd2d 673, aff 467 F2d 516, cert den 93 SCt 703, 409 US 1086, 34 LEd2d 673.—Courts 100(1); Crim Law 673(4); Hab Corp 708, 716, 775(1).

Hoover v. Byrd, CA5 (Tex), 801 F2d 740, reh den 805 F2d 1030.—Obscen 1.4, 2.5.

Hoover v. Cooke, TexCivApp–Corpus Christi, 566 SW2d 19, ref nre.—Trusts 91, 102(1), 103(1), 110.

Hoover; Dade v., TexApp–Dallas, 191 SW3d 886, review den, and reh of petition for review den.—App & E 1079; Judgm 185.3(15), 350; Mtg 218.8, 218.17.

Hoover; Dyegard Land Partnership v., TexApp–Fort Worth, 39 SW3d 300.—App & E 856(1), 863, 1175(2); Covenants 49, 69(1), 69(3), 73; Decl Judgm 342; Judgm 183, 185(2), 189, 190; Mines 48.

Hoover v. El Paso Nat. Bank, TexCivApp–El Paso, 498 SW2d 276, ref nre.—Joint Ten 4; Partit 13.

Hoover v. General Crude Oil Co., Tex, 212 SW2d 140, 147 Tex 89.—App & E 927(7); Decl Judgm 187; Mines 78.3, 78.4; Ven & Pur 101.

Hoover v. General Crude Oil Co., TexCivApp–Galveston, 206 SW2d 139, rev 212 SW2d 140, 147 Tex 89.—Contracts 176(1); Mines 74(3), 74.5, 78.1(9), 78.2, 78.4; Trial 136(3).

Hoover, Estate of; Goode v., TexApp–El Paso, 828 SW2d 558, writ den.—Wills 167, 174, 290.

Hoover v. Gregory, TexApp–Dallas, 835 SW2d 668, reh den, and writ den.—Fraud 38; Judgm 185(2); Lim of Act 21(1), 46(6), 95(1), 99(1), 100(12), 106, 179(2), 182(2), 183(5); Plead 34(1).

Hoover; Hicks v., TexCivApp–Dallas, 410 SW2d 534.— App & E 1078(1), 1170.7; Evid 373(2).

Hoover; Hicks v., TexCivApp–Waco, 422 SW2d 613, ref nre.—Fraud Conv 314; Lim of Act 39(11).

Hoover v. Hooker, NDTex, 882 FSupp 574.—Atty & C 157.1.

Hoover v. Horton, TexCivApp–Amarillo, 209 SW2d 646.— Adj Land 8; Neglig 250, 1010; Plead 111.1, 111.23, 111.42(7), 111.42(11); Venue 5.5, 8.5(6).

Hoover v. Johnson, CA5 (Tex), 193 F3d 366.—Const Law 4637; Crim Law 798(0.5); Hab Corp 452, 842.

Hoover v. Kern, CA5 (Tex), 466 F2d 543.—Hab Corp 638.

Hoover v. Larkin, TexApp–Houston (1 Dist), 196 SW3d 227, review den.—Antitrust 256, 367, 390, 397; App & E 854(1); Atty & C 105.5, 112, 129(2), 153; Judgm 183.

Hoover v. Materi, TexCivApp–El Paso, 515 SW2d 406, ref nre.—App & E 863; Partit 88, 109(2), 111(3), 114(2).

Hoover; Moore v., TexCivApp–San Antonio, 150 SW2d 96. —App & E 913; Autos 195(2), 195(5.1), 234; Venue 8.5(3), 22(4).

Hoover v. Morales, CA5 (Tex), 164 F3d 221.—Colleges 8(1); Const Law 1517, 1536, 1537, 1929, 1934, 2017, 2019; Fed Cts 43, 53, 776, 815, 862; Inj 132, 138.1, 152; States 209.

Hoover; Morse v., TexCivApp–Amarillo, 105 SW2d 682.— Contracts 128(1); Courts 66.1; Plead 111.34; Venue 5.3(8), 5.4, 21.

Hoover; Puckett v., Tex, 202 SW2d 209, 146 Tex 1.—App & E 1008.1(14); Contracts 305(1); Deeds 56(2), 64, 65, 99; Dep & Escr 13; Evid 66; Mines 55(1); Spec Perf 10(1).

Hoover; Puckett v., TexCivApp–Amarillo, 197 SW2d 602, aff 202 SW2d 209, 146 Tex 1.—App & E 909(5), 1054(1); Deeds 56(1); Evid 66; Mines 55(2); Quiet T 43; Spec Perf 10(1).

Hoover v. Redwine, TexCivApp–Fort Worth, 363 SW2d 485.—App & E 931(6); Hus & W 264(4), 267(8); Ven & Pur 231(2), 232(1).

Hoover; S.E.C. v., SDTex, 903 FSupp 1135.—Sec Reg 60.28(4), 60.28(11), 60.28(12), 60.28(13), 60.70.

Hoover v. Sims, TexApp–Houston (1 Dist), 792 SW2d 171, writ den.—App & E 1010.2; Courts 202(5); Wills 439, 449, 470(2).

Hoover; Spires v., TexCivApp–El Paso, 466 SW2d 344, ref nre.—Joint Ten 1; Partit 10, 14, 22, 26, 77(4).

Hoover v. State, TexCrimApp, 603 SW2d 882, cert den 101 SCt 878, 449 US 1087, 66 LEd2d 814.—Crim Law 412.2(2).

Hoover v. State, TexCrimApp, 449 SW2d 60.—Crim Law 412.2(2), 719(1), 720(9), 1036.2, 1044.1(5.1), 1169.3, 1171.1(2.1), 1171.3; Homic 956, 1205; Witn 345(2).

Hoover v. State, TexCrimApp, 390 SW2d 758.—Crim Law 510, 763(1), 780(4), 811(2); Rob 3, 20, 24.10, 24.20, 24.45; Searches 178.

Hoover v. State, TexCrimApp, 355 SW2d 527.—Crim Law 1020.

Hoover v. State, TexCrimApp, 279 SW2d 859, 161 Tex-Crim 642.—Const Law 1389.

Hoover v. State, TexCrimApp, 253 SW2d 868.—Crim Law 1090.1(1).

Hoover v. State, TexCrimApp, 298 SW 438, 107 TexCrim 600.—Crim Law 724(1).

Hoover v. State, TexApp–Houston (14 Dist), 736 SW2d 158, petition for discretionary review refused.—Crim Law 1167(1); Ind & Inf 167; Rec S Goods 7(6), 8(3).

Hoover v. State, TexApp–Houston (14 Dist), 707 SW2d 144, on reconsideration 736 SW2d 158, petition for discretionary review refused.—Crim Law 369.9, 444, 1043(2), 1169.1(10), 1169.11, 1170.5(1); Ind & Inf 71.4(8), 180; Rec S Goods 8(3); Witn 318.

Hoover; Sullivan v., TexApp–San Antonio, 782 SW2d 305. —Antitrust 353; App & E 901; Contracts 329, 332(2); Fraud 38; Lim of Act 58(1), 127(3).

Hoover v. Texas Dept. of Public Safety, TexCivApp–Dallas, 305 SW2d 228.—Autos 144.2(2.1), 144.2(3), 144.3; Mand 5, 184.

Hoover; Texas Emp. Ins. Ass'n v., TexCivApp–Dallas, 382 SW2d 174, ref nre.—Work Comp 1633, 1653.

Hoover; U.S. v., CA5 (Tex), 727 F2d 387.—Crim Law 37.10(1), 37.10(2); Dist & Pros Attys 8.

Hoover v. U.S., CA5 (Tex), 358 F2d 87, cert den 87 SCt 50, 385 US 822, 17 LEd2d 59.—Crim Law 822(16), 1172.1(3); Ind & Inf 110(3), 110(30); Int Rev 5317.

Hoover; Warren Mfg. Co. v., TexCivApp–Amarillo, 223 SW2d 524.—Corp 503(2); Princ & A 164(1); Sales 4(4), 202(1).

Hoover; Whitsel v., TexCivApp–Amarillo, 120 SW2d 930, writ dism.—Atty & C 104; Des & Dist 84; Fraud 7, 9, 11(2), 12, 23, 50, 58(1).

Hoover v. Wukasch, Tex, 254 SW2d 507, 152 Tex 111.—Frds St of 110(1), 110(3), 116(5), 125(1); Judgm 181(24).

Hoover v. Wukasch, TexCivApp–Austin, 274 SW2d 458, ref nre.—Land & Ten 150(1), 172(2), 188(1).

Hoover; Wukasch v., TexCivApp–Austin, 247 SW2d 593, aff 254 SW2d 507, 152 Tex 111.—Frds St of 116(10), 125(3); Land & Ten 24(3), 49(1), 62(1), 195(1).

Hoover & Son v. O. M. Franklin Serum Co., Tex, 444 SW2d 596.—Health 307; Prod Liab 46.2.

Hoover, Bax & Shearer; Baca v., TexApp–Houston (14 Dist), 823 SW2d 734, writ den.—App & E 446, 946, 949, 1145, 1208(1); Garn 1, 7, 64, 71, 187; Impl & C C 4; Pretrial Proc 501, 508, 509.

Hoover, Bax & Slovacek, L.L.P., In re, TexApp–El Paso, 6 SW3d 646.—Action 60; Contracts 147(1), 147(3), 152, 162, 175(1); Mand 1, 3(1), 4(1), 4(4), 12, 26, 28, 172.

Hoover, Bax & Slovacek, L.L.P; Deutsch v., TexApp–Houston (14 Dist), 97 SW3d 179, reh overr.—Action 53(2); Antitrust 256, 397; App & E 173(10), 500(1), 714(5), 870(2), 883, 927(7), 973, 997(3), 1061.4, 1079;

Atty & C 105.5, 106, 114, 129(2), 153, 157.1, 167(2); Costs 194.22; Courts 91(1); Fraud 65(1); Lim of Act 184; Neglig 1720; Plead 245(3), 258(3), 261; Trial 182.

Hoover, Bax & Slovacek, L.L.P.; Walton v., TexApp–El Paso, 149 SW3d 834, review gr, aff in part, rev in part Hoover Slovacek LLP v. Walton, 206 SW3d 557, on remand 2007 WL 416694, vac 2007 WL 416694.—App & E 171(1), 1178(1); Atty & C 76(1), 130, 134(1), 134(2), 142.1, 143, 144, 147; Contracts 134; Damag 118.

Hoover Const. Co.; Sullivan v., TexApp–San Antonio, 782 SW2d 305. See Sullivan v. Hoover.

Hoover Slovacek LLP v. Walton, Tex, 206 SW3d 557, on remand Walton/ Hoover, Bax & Slovacek, LLP v. Hoover, Bax & Slovacek, LLP /Walton, 2007 WL 416694.—Atty & C 62, 76(1), 106, 123(1), 134(2), 143, 144, 146.1, 147, 148(1), 148(2), 167(2); Contracts 1.

Hopcus v. Tredway, TexCivApp–Dallas, 244 SW2d 857.—Venue 8.5(2).

Hope, Ex parte, TexCrimApp, 374 SW2d 441.—Fed Cts 502; Hab Corp 484.

Hope, Ex parte, TexCrimApp, 228 SW2d 171, 154 Tex-Crim 456.—Crim Law 641.7(1), 1167(6); Hab Corp 288, 441, 474.

Hope v. Allstate Ins. Co., TexApp–Fort Worth, 719 SW2d 634, ref nre.—App & E 203; Insurance 1563, 1565, 3417; Interest 39(2.6), 60.

Hope v. Baumgartner, TexApp–Fort Worth, 111 SW3d 775.—App & E 893(1); Ex & Ad 91, 111(1), 268; Statut 188.

Hope; Cox Feedlots, Inc. v., TexCivApp–San Antonio, 498 SW2d 436, ref nre.—Carr 207(1), 207(2); Contracts 137(1), 138(1), 138(2).

Hope; Crawford v., TexApp–Amarillo, 898 SW2d 937, reh overr, and writ den.—App & E 946, 969, 999(1), 1003(7), 1056.1(3); Evid 571(3); Health 631, 823(13), 827; Neglig 384; Pretrial Proc 313; Trial 188.

Hope; Pickens v., TexApp–San Antonio, 764 SW2d 256, writ den.—Mines 47, 55(4), 55(5), 68(1), 78.1(2); Princ & A 48, 69(1).

Hope; Republic Ins. Co. v., TexCivApp–Waco, 557 SW2d 603.—App & E 232(2); Contracts 164; Evid 571(7); Insurance 2128, 3110(2).

Hope v. Seahorse, Inc., SDTex, 651 FSupp 976.—Damag 130.1, 226; Death 82, 83, 86(1), 87, 95(1); Health 823(8); U S 78(14).

Hope v. Secretary of Health, Ed. and Welfare, EDTex, 347 FSupp 1048.—Social S 140.21, 140.35, 143.55, 145.5, 148.5, 149.

Hope v. State, TexCrimApp, 126 SW2d 30.—Crim Law 1070.

Hope; Texas General Indem. Co. v., TexCivApp–Eastland, 461 SW2d 481, ref nre.—Evid 380; Trial 194(19); Work Comp 1653.

Hope; U.S. v., CA5 (Tex), 102 F3d 114.—Crim Law 394.6(4), 637, 698(1), 1139, 1144.12, 1144.13(2.1), 1152(1), 1158(4), 1169.1(10), 1181.5(2); Searches 66.

Hope v. U.S., CA5 (Tex), 691 F2d 786.—Int Rev 4155, 4159(2), 4185.

Hope v. Village of Laguna Vista, TexApp–Corpus Christi, 721 SW2d 463, ref nre.—Mun Corp 57, 417(2).

Hope Cottage-Children's Bureau, Inc.; Carrell v., TexCivApp–Eastland, 425 SW2d 898, ref nre.—Divorce 70; Hab Corp 662.1, 844; Infants 197.

Hope Cottage Children's Bureau, Inc.; Hamer v., TexCivApp–Dallas, 389 SW2d 123.—Adop 7.6(2); Infants 154.1, 197, 203.

Hope Garcia Lancarte, Inc.; Marshall v., CA5 (Tex), 632 F2d 1196, 24 Wage & Hour Cas (BNA) 1133.—Fed Cts 666; Interest 39(2.40); Labor & Emp 2387(1), 2387(6).

Hopes; U.S. v., CA5 (Tex), 286 F3d 788, cert den 123 SCt 138, 537 US 889, 154 LEd2d 151.—Arrest 63.5(5), 63.5(8); Crim Law 1139, 1144.12, 1158(4).

Hope's Financial Management v. Chase Manhattan Mortg. Corp., TexApp–Dallas, 172 SW3d 105, reh overr, and review den.—App & E 760(2), 854(1), 1079, 1136; Atty & C 62; Judgm 185(5).

Hopf v. Hopf, TexApp–Houston (14 Dist), 841 SW2d 898, reh den.—Divorce 252.1, 252.3(2), 252.3(3), 286(5), 286(9), 287; Hus & W 248.5, 249(2.1), 249(3).

Hopf; Hopf v., TexApp–Houston (14 Dist), 841 SW2d 898, reh den.—Divorce 252.1, 252.3(2), 252.3(3), 286(5), 286(9), 287; Hus & W 248.5, 249(2.1), 249(3).

Hopfer v. Commercial Ins. Co. of Newark, New Jersey, TexCivApp–Eastland, 606 SW2d 354, ref nre.—App & E 901, 1032(1); Insurance 2445, 3579; Witn 379(1).

Hopgood; Alton v., SDTex, 994 FSupp 827, aff 168 F3d 196, reh den.—Civil R 1305, 1336, 1356, 1376(2), 1376(5), 1432; Const Law 1086; Offic 119.

Hopingardner; Nagel v., TexCivApp–Hous (14 Dist), 464 SW2d 472.—Adv Poss 17, 19, 21, 85(2), 115(5); App & E 1048(7); Evid 200, 211, 254, 265(1); Witn 379(1), 379(8.1), 388(2.1).

Hopkins, Ex parte, TexCrimApp, 610 SW2d 479.—Hab Corp 288, 825.1.

Hopkins, Ex parte, TexCrimApp, 399 SW2d 551.—Judges 47(1).

Hopkins, Ex parte, TexCrimApp, 368 SW2d 223.—Hab Corp 823.

Hopkins, In re, BkrtcyNDTex, 131 BR 308.—Bankr 2954.1, 2957, 3341, 3352, 3358; Fed Civ Proc 2470.2; Int Rev 4831; Statut 188, 209, 216, 217.2.

Hopkins, In re, TexApp–Houston (14 Dist), 181 SW3d 919.—Elections 126(1); Equity 54.

Hopkins v. Actions, Inc. of Brazoria County, SDTex, 985 FSupp 706.—Labor & Emp 778, 858; U S 120.1, 122.

Hopkins; American Coach Co. v., TexCivApp–Waco, 355 SW2d 83, ref nre.—App & E 1151(2); Sales 279, 442(1).

Hopkins; American Ins. Co. v., TexCivApp–Dallas, 89 SW2d 293.—Insurance 1836, 2028, 3571.

Hopkins; Brown v., TexApp–Corpus Christi, 921 SW2d 306.—Agric 9.5; App & E 933(1), 970(2), 977(3), 977(5), 989, 1003(7), 1026, 1050.1(1), 1050.1(10), 1060.1(1), 1060.1(5), 1060.6; Evid 314(1), 317(2); New Tr 72(9), 81, 99, 102(6), 108(4); Plead 362(5); Trial 43, 127; Work Comp 2234, 2238.

Hopkins v. City of Dallas, TexCivApp–Fort Worth, 106 SW2d 783, writ refused.—App & E 781(4), 799.

Hopkins; Clifton v., TexApp–Waco, 107 SW3d 755.—Banks 100; Fraud 3, 12, 27; Judgm 185(5); Trusts 272.1.

Hopkins v. Cockrell, CA5 (Tex), 325 F3d 579, cert den 124 SCt 430, 540 US 968, 157 LEd2d 314.—Const Law 3855; Crim Law 412.1(4), 412.2(4), 412.2(5), 519(1), 519(3), 523, 641.13(6); Hab Corp 490(3).

Hopkins v. Daniels, TexCivApp–Texarkana, 571 SW2d 413, ref nre.—App & E 846(5); Divorce 174; Evid 158(8); Tresp to T T 23.

Hopkins; De Shong Motor Freight Lines v., TexCivApp–Amarillo, 99 SW2d 1033.—Autos 107(2).

Hopkins; Ector County Independent School Dist. v., TexCivApp–El Paso, 518 SW2d 576.—Admin Law 229; App & E 833(3); Const Law 3937, 4212(2); Evid 383(7); Inj 108; Schools 177; Time 9(1.5).

Hopkins; Eubank v., TexCivApp–Dallas, 238 SW2d 720, ref nre.—App & E 1015(5); Trial 108.5.

Hopkins; Eubanks v., TexCivApp–Amarillo, 203 SW2d 277.—Neglig 250; Plead 111.39(2), 111.42(8); Venue 8.5(6).

Hopkins; Farrier v., TexComApp, 112 SW2d 182, 131 Tex 75.—Evid 418; Princ & A 145(3).

Hopkins; Fireman's Fund Indem. Co. v., TexCivApp–San Antonio, 119 SW2d 394.—Work Comp 877, 1930.

Hopkins v. First Nat. Bank at Brownsville, Tex, 551 SW2d 343.—Courts 247(7); Guar 34, 36(3), 77(2), 78(1); Venue 7.5(3).

Hopkins v. First Nat. Bank at Brownsville, TexCivApp–Corpus Christi, 546 SW2d 84, ref nre 551 SW2d 343.—Venue 7.5(3).

Hopkins; Gann v., TexCivApp–San Antonio, 119 SW2d 110.—App & E 1176(1); Judgm 137; Mand 50.

Hopkins; General Motors Corp. v., Tex, 548 SW2d 344.—App & E 1177(1); Evid 527, 571(9); Prod Liab 8, 15, 27, 28, 72.1, 75.1, 82.1, 83.5, 88.5.

Hopkins; General Motors Corp. v., TexCivApp–Hous (1 Dist), 535 SW2d 880, writ gr, aff 548 SW2d 344.—App & E 846(5), 930(3), 989, 1069.1; Prod Liab 8, 15, 27, 36, 83.5; Trial 140(1), 315, 358.

Hopkins; Grigsby v., TexCivApp–Fort Worth, 218 SW2d 275, writ refused.—Atty & C 192(1); Costs 194.10; Quiet T 54.

Hopkins; Gulf Coast Chemical Co. v., TexCivApp–Dallas, 145 SW2d 928.—App & E 1010.1(1), 1010.1(8.1); Autos 372(3.1), 372(4); Larc 1.

Hopkins v. Gunter Hotel Corp., TexCivApp–San Antonio, 147 SW2d 973, writ dism, correct.—App & E 688(2), 750(1), 989, 1056.4; Damag 130.4, 140.7.

Hopkins v. Highlands Ins. Co., TexApp–El Paso, 838 SW2d 819, reh overr.—Antitrust 221; App & E 223, 242(1); Contracts 168; Insurance 1865, 1867, 1938, 3423; Judgm 181(6), 181(11), 181(23), 181(33), 185(2); Labor & Emp 911; Torts 212, 220.

Hopkins v. Hopkins, TexApp–Dallas, 708 SW2d 31, ref nre.—Des & Dist 82; Wills 121, 123(1), 206, 302(1), 740(1).

Hopkins; Hopkins v., TexApp–Dallas, 708 SW2d 31, ref nre.—Des & Dist 82; Wills 121, 123(1), 206, 302(1), 740(1).

Hopkins v. Hopkins, TexApp–Corpus Christi, 853 SW2d 134.—Child C 28, 76, 100, 101, 120, 175, 177, 178, 921(3); Child S 21, 556(1); Infants 2; Propty 2; Statut 188.

Hopkins; Hopkins v., TexApp–Corpus Christi, 853 SW2d 134.—Child C 28, 76, 100, 101, 120, 175, 177, 178, 921(3); Child S 21, 556(1); Infants 2; Propty 2; Statut 188.

Hopkins v. Hopkins, TexCivApp–Fort Worth, 539 SW2d 242, dism.—Child S 56, 202, 222, 390, 549; Divorce 184(12), 201, 226, 270, 286(9).

Hopkins; Hopkins v., TexCivApp–Fort Worth, 539 SW2d 242, dism.—Child S 56, 202, 222, 390, 549; Divorce 184(12), 201, 226, 270, 286(9).

Hopkins v. Hopkins, TexCivApp–Texarkana, 335 SW2d 879.—Child C 733, 742; Divorce 124, 124.3, 161.

Hopkins; Hopkins v., TexCivApp–Texarkana, 335 SW2d 879.—Child C 733, 742; Divorce 124, 124.3, 161.

Hopkins v. Hopkins, TexCivApp–Corpus Christi, 540 SW2d 783.—App & E 961; Const Law 2648, 3879, 3953, 4244, 4386; Divorce 2, 4, 85, 144, 179, 223, 252.2, 285, 286(2), 286(5); Em Dom 2(1.1); Marriage 1; Pretrial Proc 19, 354; Trial 279.

Hopkins; Hopkins v., TexCivApp–Corpus Christi, 540 SW2d 783.—App & E 961; Const Law 2648, 3879, 3953, 4244, 4386; Divorce 2, 4, 85, 144, 179, 223, 252.2, 285, 286(2), 286(5); Em Dom 2(1.1); Marriage 1; Pretrial Proc 19, 354; Trial 279.

Hopkins; Hudson v., TexApp–Tyler, 799 SW2d 783.—Judgm 185(4), 185.3(1); Wills 493.

Hopkins v. J. E. Foster & Son, Inc., TexCivApp–Beaumont, 360 SW2d 180.—Contracts 318; Evid 18; Mines 54(2).

Hopkins; Liberty Mut. Ins. Co. v., TexApp, 422 SW2d 203, ref nre.—Damag 221(5.1); Trial 351.5(1), 352.11; Work Comp 678, 683, 1564, 1929.

Hopkins; McCarley v., TexApp–Houston (1 Dist), 687 SW2d 510.—App & E 854(5), 1056.4; Corp 30(6); Damag 184; Evid 352(1); Impl & C C 98; Trial 139.1(14), 139.1(17).

Hopkins; Main v., TexCivApp–Amarillo, 229 SW2d 820.—Contracts 313(1); Land & Ten 22(4); Lim of Act 46(6).

Hopkins v. Malcolm Hinkle, Inc., TexCivApp–Amarillo, 431 SW2d 371.—Acct Action on 7; App & E 994(1),

1012.1(8); Estop 3(3), 91(1); Impl & C C 111; Sales 360(1).

Hopkins v. NCNB Texas Nat. Bank, TexApp–Fort Worth, 822 SW2d 353.—Abate & R 8(2), 9; App & E 949, 1071.1(2); Trial 388(2).

Hopkins; Nolte v., TexCivApp–San Antonio, 212 SW2d 885.—App & E 1169(10); Evid 22(1).

Hopkins; Parks v., TexApp–Fort Worth, 677 SW2d 791. —Mand 154(2).

Hopkins v. Pence, TexCivApp–El Paso, 322 SW2d 321.— App & E 544(2), 1070(2).

Hopkins v. Robertson, TexCivApp–Fort Worth, 138 SW2d 310, writ refused.—Courts 475(2); Hus & W 267(1); Pretrial Proc 73; Sales 218; Trial 351.5(1), 352.4(1); Trover 69; Witn 164(2), 178(2).

Hopkins; Simpson v., TexCivApp–Waco, 439 SW2d 898, ref nre.—Deeds 194(2), 194(5); Judgm 250; Trial 253(5), 350.4(1).

Hopkins v. Spring Independent School Dist., Tex, 736 SW2d 617.—Schools 89.11(1), 89.13(1); Statut 188.

Hopkins v. Spring Independent School Dist., TexApp– Houston (14 Dist), 706 SW2d 325, writ gr, aff 736 SW2d 617.—Lim of Act 72(1); Schools 89.13(3), 147, 159.5(6).

Hopkins v. Standard Fire Ins. Co., TexCivApp–Hous (1 Dist), 554 SW2d 270.—App & E 930(3); Trial 351.2(1.1), 351.2(3.1), 351.2(5), 366; Work Comp 1717, 1866, 1906, 1923.

Hopkins v. State, TexCrimApp, 46 SW3d 896.—Ind & Inf 87(3).

Hopkins v. State, TexCrimApp, 480 SW2d 212.—Crim Law 448(1), 449.1, 469, 470(2), 474.3(1), 867, 1159.2(1), 1169.5(1), 1170.5(6).

Hopkins v. State, TexCrimApp, 290 SW2d 239.—Crim Law 1090.1(1).

Hopkins v. State, TexCrimApp, 282 SW2d 232, 162 Tex-Crim 103.—Autos 355(6); Crim Law 899.

Hopkins v. State, TexCrimApp, 207 SW2d 626, 151 Tex-Crim 304.—Crim Law 1087.1(2), 1094(2.1), 1097(5), 1131(7).

Hopkins v. State, TexApp–Texarkana, 628 SW2d 496.— Sent & Pun 308, 315.

Hopkins v. State, TexApp–Houston (14 Dist), 864 SW2d 119, reh den, and reh overr, and petition for discretionary review refused.—Burg 9(2), 41(4); Crim Law 741(1), 742(1), 1159.1, 1159.2(4), 1159.6.

Hopkins v. State, TexApp–Houston (14 Dist), 753 SW2d 413.—Weap 17(4).

Hopkins v. Stice, CA5 (Tex), 916 F2d 1029, reh den.— Civil R 1376(2), 1376(10), 1421; Offic 66, 114; States 64.1(1).

Hopkins v. Texas Power & Light Co., TexCivApp– Dallas, 514 SW2d 143.—Electricity 18(1); Neglig 1040(3), 1045(3), 1050, 1052, 1205(1), 1205(7), 1205(9), 1314.

Hopkins; Tower View, Inc. v., TexApp–San Antonio, 679 SW2d 632, ref nre.—App & E 930(3), 989, 1001(1), 1003(5); Brok 46, 48, 53, 54, 55(1), 56(3), 86(4), 88(3); Contracts 147(1), 152.

Hopkins; U.S. v., CA5 (Tex), 916 F2d 207.—B & L Assoc 23(8); Consp 24(1), 28(3), 33(1), 47(2), 47(3.1); Crim Law 29(3), 29(5.5), 371(1), 586, 589(1), 598(4), 599, 1151; Elections 319, 329; Sent & Pun 2188(4).

Hopkins; U.S. v., CA5 (Tex), 433 F2d 1041, cert den 91 SCt 1252, 401 US 1013, 28 LEd2d 550.—Crim Law 412.1(3), 412.2(5), 1044.2(1); Searches 18.

Hopkins v. U.S., CA5 (Tex), 431 F2d 429.—Courts 100(1); Crim Law 1132, 1618(3); Sent & Pun 359.

Hopkins v. U.S., CA5 (Tex), 423 F2d 1206, appeal after remand 431 F2d 429.—Crim Law 1181.5(3.1).

Hopkins; U.S. v., CA5 (Tex), 196 FedAppx 309.—Crim Law 273.1(1).

Hopkins v. U.S., NDTex, 173 FSupp 245.—Em Dom 300, 305.

Hopkins v. U.S. (I.R.S.), BkrtcyNDTex, 131 BR 308. See Hopkins, In re.

Hopkins; Wofford v., WDTex, 45 FSupp 257.—Rem of C 79(2.1), 79(8).

Hopkins County Hosp. Dist. v. Allen, TexApp–Texarkana, 760 SW2d 341.—App & E 216(1), 232(3), 882(13); Damag 54, 130.1, 185(2).

Hopkins County Tax Appraisal Dist.; Rusk Industries, Inc. v., TexApp–Texarkana, 818 SW2d 111, writ gr, and writ den, and writ withdrawn.—App & E 901, 989, 1008.1(2), 1012.1(5), 1071.1; Tax 2523, 2645, 2706, 2726, 2728.

Hopmann v. Southern Pacific Transp. Co., TexCivApp– Tyler, 581 SW2d 532, cert den 100 SCt 146, 444 US 870, 62 LEd2d 94.—Const Law 4186; Labor & Emp 2802, 2805.

Hopp v. James, TexCivApp–San Antonio, 470 SW2d 716. —App & E 136; Child C 903.

Hoppe, In re, BkrtcyEDTex, 259 BR 852.—Bankr 2125, 2157, 2954.1, 2956; Statut 181(1), 181(2).

Hoppe v. Godeke, TexApp–Austin, 774 SW2d 368, writ den.—Divorce 252.3(4); Hus & W 249(3); Offic 101.5(1).

Hoppe v. Hoppe, TexApp–Houston (14 Dist), 703 SW2d 224, ref nre.—Wills 290, 306.

Hoppe; Hoppe v., TexApp–Houston (14 Dist), 703 SW2d 224, ref nre.—Wills 290, 306.

Hoppe v. Hughes, TexCivApp–Amarillo, 577 SW2d 773, ref nre.—App & E 302(6); Autos 153, 244(10), 244(31); Courts 85(3); Evid 547, 568(1), 571(1).

Hoppe; Inwood Nat. Bank of Dallas v., TexCivApp– Texarkana, 596 SW2d 183, 20 ALR4th 206, ref nre.— Bankr 3412; Hus & W 268(1), 269; Lim of Act 25(3), 127(3).

Hoppe v. Sauter, TexCivApp–Texarkana, 416 SW2d 912, ref nre.—Adv Poss 29, 114(1).

Hoppenfeld v. Crook, TexCivApp–Austin, 498 SW2d 52, ref nre.—App & E 837(4); Courts 12(2.1), 12(2.5), 12(2.20), 35; Fraud 20.

Hopper v. Brittain, TexCivApp–Hous (14 Dist), 612 SW2d 636.—Adop 7.1, 13, 15; App & E 989; Parent & C 1.

Hopper; Cruz v., CA5 (Tex), 73 FedAppx 62.—Civil R 1326(10).

Hopper v. Dretke, CA5 (Tex), 106 FedAppx 221, cert den 125 SCt 1621, 544 US 914, 161 LEd2d 297.—Crim Law 412.1(4), 412.2(4), 641.13(6); Hab Corp 818.

Hopper v. Ford Motor Co. Ltd., SDTex, 837 FSupp 840. —Fed Civ Proc 1825; Fed Cts 45, 86.

Hopper v. Hargrove, TexCivApp–Texarkana, 154 SW2d 978, writ refused.—Lim of Act 127(2.1), 127(12).

Hopper v. Hopper, TexCivApp–Dallas, 270 SW2d 256, dism.—App & E 882(8); Divorce 252.5(1); Hus & W 248.5; Trusts 43(1), 44(1).

Hopper; Hopper v., TexCivApp–Dallas, 270 SW2d 256, dism.—App & E 882(8); Divorce 252.5(1); Hus & W 248.5; Trusts 43(1), 44(1).

Hopper v. Hopper, TexCivApp–Dallas, 264 SW2d 444.— App & E 624, 797(3).

Hopper; Hopper v., TexCivApp–Dallas, 264 SW2d 444.— App & E 624, 797(3).

Hopper v. J. C. Penney Co., TexCivApp–Fort Worth, 371 SW2d 750, ref nre.—Evid 219(1), 219.25(1); Neglig 1037(4), 1110(1), 1230, 1286(1), 1289, 1679.

Hopper; Jones v., TexCivApp–Hous (14 Dist), 506 SW2d 768.—Evid 121(1), 126(1); Princ & A 22(2).

Hopper; Maryland Cas. Co. v., TexCivApp–El Paso, 237 SW2d 411.—App & E 76(1), 1151(2); Insurance 2278(29), 2290, 2295, 3585; Judgm 28.

Hopper v. Mayeaux, SDTex, 545 FSupp 1174.—Const Law 3965(1); Fed Cts 76, 76.30, 386, 387.

Hopper v. Midland County, TexCivApp–El Paso, 500 SW2d 552, writ dism, and order set aside, and ref nre. —Const Law 2513; Counties 141, 143; Courts 91(1); Judgm 185.3(2).

Hopper; O'Carolan v., TexApp–Austin, 71 SW3d 529.—Child S 87; Divorce 199, 199.7(2), 215, 219, 252.1, 252.2, 286(5); Trial 382.

Hopper v. Safeguard Business Systems, Inc., TexApp–San Antonio, 787 SW2d 624.—App & E 447; Inj 157.

Hopper v. State, TexApp–El Paso, 86 SW3d 676.—Crim Law 1144.13(2.1), 1159.2(7), 1159.3(1), 1159.4(1); Obst Just 16.

Hopper; State v., TexApp–El Paso, 842 SW2d 817.—Arrest 63.4(18), 63.5(4); Autos 349(3), 349(6), 349(17), 349.5(3); Crim Law 394.5(4), 394.6(5), 1134(2), 1134(3), 1134(6), 1158(4).

Hopper v. State, TexApp–Houston (14 Dist), 882 SW2d 1, reh den, and petition for discretionary review refused.—Crim Law 700(3), 1156(1), 1158(1); Jury 142.

Hopper & Associates/Safeguard v. Safeguard Business Systems, Inc., TexApp–San Antonio, 787 SW2d 624. See Hopper v. Safeguard Business Systems, Inc.

Hopper Laboratories, Inc. v. Stanbio Laboratories, Inc., WDTex, 310 FSupp 30.—Pat 80, 289(2.1).

Hopperstad Builders, Inc.; Woodard v., TexCivApp–Corpus Christi, 554 SW2d 726, ref nre.—App & E 931(3); Evid 42; Judgm 151, 159, 335(1), 335(3); Trial 15.

Hoppes v. State, TexApp–Houston (1 Dist), 725 SW2d 532.—Crim Law 396(1), 396(2), 854(2), 854(7), 1171.1(1), 1174(4).

Hopson, Ex parte, TexCrimApp, 688 SW2d 545.—Crim Law 273.1(2), 1184(3), 1184(4.1).

Hopson, In re, SDTex, 324 BR 284.—Bankr 3713; Statut 188, 190.

Hopson v. Gulf Oil Corp., Tex, 237 SW2d 352, 150 Tex 1.—App & E 878(1), 878(6), 1003(9.1); Courts 97(5); Jury 37; Neglig 371, 379, 380, 387; Seamen 29(1), 29(5.1), 29(5.16); Trial 350.6(2), 352.20.

Hopson v. Gulf Oil Corp., TexCivApp–Beaumont, 237 SW2d 323, rev in part 237 SW2d 352, 150 Tex 1.—App & E 218.2(2), 232(0.5), 301, 882(3), 1140(1); Damag 221(2.1), 221(5.1); Jury 37; Seamen 11(1), 11(6), 11(7), 11(9), 29(2), 29(5.14), 29(5.16); Trial 140(2), 232(2), 352.20, 357.

Hopson; Harris County Dist. Attorney's Office v., TexApp–Houston (14 Dist), 880 SW2d 1, reh den.—Crim Law 1226(3.1).

Hopson; Pruter v., TexApp–Beaumont, 710 SW2d 92.—Costs 260(5); Damag 134(1).

Hopson; Threadgill v., TexCivApp–El Paso, 458 SW2d 538, ref nre.—App & E 843(2), 1170.9(2.1).

Hopson Towing Co., Inc.; Galveston County Nav. Dist. No. 1 v., CA5 (Tex), 92 F3d 353.—Adm 121; Fed Civ Proc 2737.1, 2737.3, 2737.14.

Hopson Towing Co., Inc.; Galveston County Nav. Dist. No. 1 v., SDTex, 877 FSupp 363, rev 92 F3d 353.—Adm 124; Fed Civ Proc 2737.5; Ship 81(1), 81(2), 86(2.3), 86(2.5).

Hopwood v. Phillips, TexCivApp–Houston, 329 SW2d 459, ref nre.—App & E 781(4).

Hopwood; Phillips v., TexCivApp–Houston, 329 SW2d 452, ref nre.—App & E 930(1); Corp 428(7); Judgm 18(2), 375, 443(1), 460(4), 461(5), 463; Partners 159.

Hopwood v. State, TexCrimApp, 285 SW2d 743.—Crim Law 1090.1(1).

Hopwood v. State of Texas, CA5 (Tex), 236 F3d 256, reh and reh den 248 F3d 1141, cert den 121 SCt 2550, 533 US 929, 150 LEd2d 717.—Civil R 1452, 1462, 1482, 1486, 1487, 1488; Courts 96(3), 99(1); Fed Cts 776, 814.1, 855.1, 870.1, 893, 917, 951.1.

Hopwood v. State of Tex., CA5 (Tex), 78 F3d 932, reh and sug for reh den 84 F3d 720, motion gr Texas v. Hopwood, 116 SCt 2545, 518 US 1016, 135 LEd2d 1066, cert den Thurgood Marshall Legal Soc v Hopwood, 116 SCt 2580, 518 US 1033, 135 LEd2d 1094, cert den 116 SCt 2581, 518 US 1033, 135 LEd2d 1095, appeal after remand 95 F3d 53, on remand 999 FSupp 872, aff in part, rev in part 236 F3d 256, reh and reh den 248 F3d

1141, cert den 121 SCt 2550, 533 US 929, 150 LEd2d 717.—Civil R 1033(3), 1401, 1452; Colleges 9.15; Const Law 3078, 3250, 3280(3); Damag 163(1); Fed Civ Proc 1837.1; Fed Cts 542, 555, 725, 814.1, 850.1, 917, 935.1, 937.1.

Hopwood v. State of Tex., CA5 (Tex), 21 F3d 603.—Fed Civ Proc 316, 321, 331.

Hopwood v. State of Tex., WDTex, 999 FSupp 872, aff in part, rev in part 236 F3d 256, reh and reh den 248 F3d 1141, cert den Texas v. Hopwood, 121 SCt 2550, 533 US 929, 150 LEd2d 717.—Civil R 1033(3), 1418, 1462, 1463, 1464, 1482, 1486, 1487, 1488; Colleges 9.15; Const Law 3280(3); Evid 555.4(1), 571(10).

Hopwood v. State of Tex., WDTex, 861 FSupp 551, rev 78 F3d 932, reh and sug for reh den 84 F3d 720, motion gr Texas v. Hopwood, 116 SCt 2545, 518 US 1016, 135 LEd2d 1066, cert den Thurgood Marshall Legal Soc v Hopwood, 116 SCt 2580, 518 US 1033, 135 LEd2d 1094, cert den 116 SCt 2581, 518 US 1033, 135 LEd2d 1095, appeal after remand 95 F3d 53, on remand 999 FSupp 872, aff in part, rev in part 236 F3d 256, reh and reh den 248 F3d 1141, cert den 121 SCt 2550, 533 US 929, 150 LEd2d 717.—Colleges 9.15; Const Law 915, 1030, 3252, 3280(3).

Horace; U.S. v., CA5 (Tex), 227 FedAppx 350.—Crim Law 730(14), 1037.1(2); Weap 17(6).

Horace Mann Life Ins. Co.; Price v., TexCivApp–Amarillo, 590 SW2d 644.—Contracts 176(10), 212(2); Insurance 1806, 2050; Judgm 178, 181(23).

Horace Mann Mut. Ins. Co. v. Andress' Estate, TexCivApp–Amarillo, 525 SW2d 47.—Evid 506, 528(2), 555.10; Insurance 2589(1), 2607; Trial 178.

Horak v. Pullman, Inc., CA5 (Tex), 764 F2d 1092.—Prod Liab 15, 48.

Horany; Cantu v., TexApp–Dallas, 195 SW3d 867.—App & E 223, 714(5), 854(4), 948, 949; Atty & C 105.5, 109, 129(2); Judgm 185.3(4).

Hord; Crabbe v., TexCivApp–Fort Worth, 536 SW2d 409, ref nre, cert den 97 SCt 1554, 430 US 932, 51 LEd2d 776.—Judgm 335(2), 335(3), 335(4); Jury 28(9).

Hord; U.S. v., CA5 (Tex), 6 F3d 276, cert den 114 SCt 1551, 511 US 1036, 128 LEd2d 200.—Banks 119, 124, 150, 509.10, 509.20, 509.25; Crim Law 1134(3), 1144.13(3), 1144.13(5), 1159.2(7); Ind & Inf 127, 129(1).

Hord; West v., TexCivApp–El Paso, 81 SW2d 740.—Ex & Ad 222(1), 225(1), 431(2).

Horelica v. Fiserv Solutions, Inc., TexApp–San Antonio, 123 SW3d 492.—Labor & Emp 355, 365, 389(2).

Horgan; Pope v., SDTex, 538 FSupp 808.—Int Rev 4458; Offic 114.

Horihan v. Hartford Ins. Co. of the Midwest, EDTex, 979 FSupp 1073.—Const Law 3964; Courts 12(2.1); Fed Cts 76, 76.5, 76.10, 76.25, 79, 97, 122.

Horine v. Kellam, TexCivApp–San Antonio, 123 SW2d 439.—Elections 269, 279; Mun Corp 918(5).

Horine; Walker v., TexApp–Corpus Christi, 695 SW2d 572.—App & E 619, 635(1); Atty & C 112; Contracts 16, 40, 147(2), 176(2); Evid 448; Frds St of 118(2); Judgm 181(6), 185(1), 185.2(4), 185.3(2), 185.3(14); Spec Perf 17.

Horinek v. State, TexApp–Fort Worth, 977 SW2d 696, petition for discretionary review refused.—Crim Law 1159.3(2); Homic 1174.

Horizon Battery Technologies, Ltd.; Electrosource, Inc. v., CA5 (Tex), 176 F3d 867.—Const Law 3964, 3965(3); Fed Cts 34, 76, 76.5, 76.10, 76.30, 86, 776.

Horizon Casket Group, Inc.; York Group, Inc. v., SDTex, 459 FSupp2d 567.—Antitrust 19, 22, 29, 84; Contracts 117(1), 326; Fed Civ Proc 2492; Trademarks 1196.

Horizon/CMS Healthcare Corporation v. Auld, Tex, 34 SW3d 887.—App & E 970(2), 1047(1), 1051.1(2); Com Law 14; Const Law 2314; Damag 67, 154; Evid 207(1), 265(7), 265(8); Health 624, 834(1); Interest 39(2.50);

Plead 16, 34(1), 48, 228; Statut 64(1), 64(7), 181(1), 195, 223.4; Witn 406.

Horizon/CMS Healthcare Corp. v. Auld, TexApp–Fort Worth, 985 SW2d 216, review gr (2 pets), aff in part, rev in part 34 SW3d 887.—App & E 216(1), 241, 242(2), 304, 428(2), 1001(1), 1001(3), 1004(3), 1047(1), 1079; Const Law 949, 963, 2311, 2314; Damag 151, 184; Evid 333(1); Health 604, 820, 832, 834(1); Interest 39(2.50); Neglig 1637; Plead 34(1), 36(2), 78, 372, 427; Statut 181(1), 181(2), 188, 192; Trial 130; Witn 406.

Horizon/CMS Healthcare Corp.; Fuqua v., NDTex, 199 FRD 200, reconsideration den.—Fed Civ Proc 1278, 1636.1, 2757, 2820.

Horizon/CMS Healthcare Corp., Inc. v. Fischer, Tex, 111 SW3d 67.—Health 804.

Horizon Concepts, Inc. v. City of Balch Springs, CA5 (Tex), 789 F2d 1165.—Const Law 228.2, 3512, 4096; Zoning 28, 42, 436.1.

Horizon Creditcorp; Shumway v., TexApp–Houston (1 Dist), 768 SW2d 387, writ gr, rev 801 SW2d 890.—Bills & N 48.1, 129(2), 516; Judgm 185.3(16).

Horizon Credit Corp.; Shumway v., Tex, 801 SW2d 890. —Bills & N 129(2), 394, 422(1).

Horizon Health Care; Farpella-Crosby v., CA5 (Tex), 97 F3d 803.—Civil R 1147, 1149, 1185, 1549, 1574, 1575(1); Fed Civ Proc 2608.1.

Horizon Oil & Gas Co.; Transwestern Pipeline Co. v., TexApp–Dallas, 809 SW2d 589, writ dism woj.—Alt Disp Res 134(3), 135, 137, 182(1), 182(2), 210, 213(5); Contracts 227.

Horizon Petroleum Co. v. Barges Dixie 162,234 and 236, CA5 (Tex), 753 F2d 382.—Ship 104, 116.

Horizon Properties; Welch v., TexApp–Amarillo, 876 SW2d 218. See Welch v. McDougal.

Horizon Properties Corp. v. Martinez, TexCivApp–El Paso, 513 SW2d 264, ref nre.—App & E 1071.1(2); Costs 194.18; Impl & C C 91; Judges 32; Trial 420.

Horizon Resources, Inc. v. Putnam, TexApp–Corpus Christi, 976 SW2d 268, reh overr.—Contracts 147(2), 152, 154; Land & Ten 37; Mines 73, 79.3.

Horizontal Holes, Inc. v. River Valley Enterprises, Inc., TexApp–Dallas, 197 SW3d 834, reh overr.—Costs 194.16, 194.32; Mun Corp 348.

Horlock v. Horlock, TexCivApp–Hous (1 Dist), 593 SW2d 743, ref nre.—Hus & W 249(5); Judgm 191, 331.

Horlock; Horlock v., TexCivApp–Hous (1 Dist), 593 SW2d 743, ref nre.—Hus & W 249(5); Judgm 191, 331.

Horlock v. Horlock, TexCivApp–Hous (14 Dist), 614 SW2d 478, ref nre.—App & E 747(4); Divorce 252.4, 321 1/2; Fraud 33; Hus & W 254, 262.2, 272(1); Lim of Act 55(1), 195(3); Partners 122.5; Plead 427; Ten in C 10, 15(2), 21; Torts 307; Trover 13.

Horlock; Horlock v., TexCivApp–Hous (14 Dist), 614 SW2d 478, ref nre.—App & E 747(4); Divorce 252.4, 321 1/2; Fraud 33; Hus & W 254, 262.2, 272(1); Lim of Act 55(1), 195(3); Partners 122.5; Plead 427; Ten in C 10, 15(2), 21; Torts 307; Trover 13.

Horlock v. Horlock, TexCivApp–Hous (14 Dist), 533 SW2d 52, writ dism woj.—Divorce 252.2, 252.3(2), 252.3(3), 253(2); Fraud 4; Hus & W 249(6), 262.1(1), 262.1(3), 262.1(5), 264(4), 265, 272(5).

Horlock; Horlock v., TexCivApp–Hous (14 Dist), 533 SW2d 52, writ dism woj.—Divorce 252.2, 252.3(2), 252.3(3), 253(2); Fraud 4; Hus & W 249(6), 262.1(1), 262.1(3), 262.1(5), 264(4), 265, 272(5).

Horlock; Romero v., TexCivApp–Hous (14 Dist), 425 SW2d 679, ref nre.—Labor & Emp 2870, 3148; Neglig 1037(4), 1204(1); Trial 350.6(6).

Horman v. State, TexCrimApp, 423 SW2d 317.—Crim Law 304(16); Sent & Pun 2004.

Hormel Foods, Inc.; Logan v., CAFed (Tex), 217 FedAppx 942, reh den.—Pat 101(2), 159, 168(2.1), 328(4).

Horn, Ex parte, TexCrimApp, 97 SW2d 698.—Hab Corp 823, 844.

Horn, In re, BkrtcyEDTex, 264 BR 848.—Bankr 2052, 2091.

Horn v. Atchison, T. & S. F. Ry. Co., TexCivApp–Beaumont, 519 SW2d 894, ref nre.—App & E 218.2(4), 1026, 1052(5); Courts 97(5); Labor & Emp 2879, 2881; Trial 82, 140(2), 366.

Horn v. Beto, CA5 (Tex), 423 F2d 583.—Fed Cts 742; Hab Corp 364.

Horn v. Builders Supply Co. of Longview, TexCivApp–Tyler, 401 SW2d 143, ref nre.—App & E 621(1), 622, 624, 627.2; Contracts 39; Judgm 199(3.14); Labor & Emp 40(1), 40(2); Partners 83, 351, 366, 370, 376.

Horn; Burkhart v., TexCivApp–San Antonio, 369 SW2d 680.—Decl Judgm 65, 66, 68, 342; Tresp to T T 6.1, 11, 38(2).

Horn; Dumas v., TexCivApp–Texarkana, 529 SW2d 88, ref nre.—App & E 930(3), 989; Autos 213, 242(8); Neglig 453, 1675.

Horn v. First Bank of Houston, TexCivApp–Hous (14 Dist), 530 SW2d 864.—Evid 314(1), 373(1); Judgm 185(2), 185.1(8), 185.3(5).

Horn v. Hedgecoke Ins. Agency, TexApp–Amarillo, 836 SW2d 296, reh den, and writ den.—Insurance 1669, 3451.

Horn v. Hefner, TexApp–Texarkana, 115 SW3d 255.—App & E 989, 1001(1), 1001(2), 1003(7); Autos 167(1), 167(2), 171(13), 206, 244(2.1); Evid 150, 359(6), 574.

Horn v. Maples, TexApp–San Antonio, 407 SW2d 867. —App & E 554(1); Hus & W 222; Ven & Pur 285(2).

Horn v. Maples, TexCivApp–El Paso, 441 SW2d 221.—Judgm 589(2); Ven & Pur 285(4).

Horn; Marchbanks v., TexCivApp–Eastland, 203 SW2d 649, ref nre.—Evid 265(10); Hus & W 85(5).

Horn; Moore v., TexCivApp–Beaumont, 359 SW2d 947, ref nre.—Adv Poss 114(1); App & E 727, 842(7), 907(1), 930(1), 989, 1170.7; Evid 208(2), 271(20), 318(8), 372(3), 450(2).

Horn v. Nationwide Financial Corp., TexCivApp–San Antonio, 574 SW2d 218, ref nre.—Cons Cred 4, 17.

Horn; Pickle v., TexCivApp–Beaumont, 87 SW2d 802.—Gifts 45, 49(4).

Horn v. Richardson, TexCivApp–Fort Worth, 90 SW2d 886.—Ex & Ad 261.

Horn; Roebuck v., TexApp–Beaumont, 74 SW3d 160.—App & E 983(3), 1074(2), 1178(1), 1203(1); Execution 396, 402(1), 402(5).

Horn v. Sankary, TexCivApp–Fort Worth, 161 SW2d 156. —App & E 874(3); Courts 475(2); Ex & Ad 224; Home 147; Hus & W 274(1); Receivers 14, 18.

Horn; Shannon v., TexCivApp–Fort Worth, 92 SW2d 1090, writ dism.—App & E 1062.1; Neglig 530(1); Trial 215, 352.4(7), 352.5(6), 352.10.

Horn; Smith v., TexCivApp–Beaumont, 137 SW2d 44, dism.—Bailm 34.

Horn v. State, TexCrimApp, 647 SW2d 283.—Assault 58, 92(3), 96(3); Extort 25.1.

Horn v. State, TexCrimApp, 505 SW2d 269.—Crim Law 1171.2.

Horn v. State, TexCrimApp, 491 SW2d 170.—Crim Law 414, 693, 717, 720(7.1), 730(8); Names 16(2); Obscen 20.

Horn v. State, TexCrimApp, 463 SW2d 14.—Assault 78.

Horn v. State, TexCrimApp, 113 SW2d 892, 133 TexCrim 620.—Crim Law 1090.7; Larc 55.

Horn v. State, TexApp–Houston (1 Dist), 856 SW2d 509, petition for discretionary review refused.—Rob 24.15(2).

Horn v. State, TexApp–Fort Worth, 699 SW2d 714.—Crim Law 412.2(3), 414, 796, 1137(5); Sent & Pun 1361, 1364, 1367.

Horn v. State Farm Ins. Co., TexCivApp–Tyler, 567 SW2d 266.—Damag 128; New Tr 74.

Horn v. Tuller, TexCivApp–Hous (1 Dist), 524 SW2d 597. —Guar 91; Judgm 185(1), 186.

Horn; Wallace v., TexCivApp–Corpus Christi, 506 SW2d 325, ref nre.—Land & Ten 164(1), 167(8), 170(1); Nuis 1, 3(1), 61.

Horn v. White, TexCivApp–Beaumont, 129 SW2d 1210.— Libel 16, 18.

Horn Advertising, Inc.; Sibley v., TexCivApp–Dallas, 505 SW2d 417, ref nre, cert den 95 SCt 1129, 420 US 929, 43 LEd2d 400.—Sec Reg 11.45, 25.56, 60.45(1), 269, 294, 307, 308.

Hornbeak; National Bankers Life Ins. Co. v., TexCivApp–Waco, 266 SW2d 228.—Insurance 1835(2), 2494(1), 2532.

Hornbeck Offshore Services, Inc.; Dinger v., SDTex, 968 FSupp 1185.—U S 78(12).

Hornbeck Offshore (1984) Corp., Complaint of, CA5 (Tex), 981 F2d 752, reh den.—Alt Disp Res 191, 192, 196, 213(5); Fed Cts 951.1.

Hornbeck Offshore (1984) Corp. v. Coastal Carriers Corp., CA5 (Tex), 981 F2d 752. See Hornbeck Offshore (1984) Corp., Complaint of.

Hornberger; Harris County Water Control and Imp. Dist. No. 84 v., TexCivApp–Hous (1 Dist), 601 SW2d 66, ref nre.—Judgm 134, 139; Waters 183.5.

Hornblower and Weeks-Hemphill, Noyes v. D & G Supply & Maintenance Co., Inc., NDTex, 390 FSupp 715.—Brok 24(2), 36; Corp 237, 306, 340(1), 402, 432(12); Princ & A 123(7).

Hornblower & Weeks-Hemphill, Noyes, Inc. v. Crane, TexCivApp–Corpus Christi, 586 SW2d 582, ref nre.— Brok 30, 36; Impl & C C 22; Lim of Act 28(1), 49(1), 129, 166; Princ & A 171(1).

Hornblower, Weeks, Noyes & Trask, Inc. v. Reedy, TexCivApp–Dallas, 587 SW2d 433, ref nre.—App & E 161, 162(2), 781(1), 781(7); Judgm 123(1), 882; Tender 13(1).

Hornbuckle v. Arco Oil and Gas Co., CA5 (Tex), 770 F2d 1321, cert den 106 SCt 1198, 475 US 1016, 89 LEd2d 312.—Fed Civ Proc 1758.1.

Hornbuckle v. Arco Oil & Gas Co., CA5 (Tex), 732 F2d 1233, appeal after remand 770 F2d 1321, cert den 106 SCt 1198, 475 US 1016, 89 LEd2d 312.—Atty & C 32(10), 32(14); Fed Civ Proc 1592, 1723.1, 1728, 1951, 1991, 2726.1, 2737.5, 2757; Fed Cts 947.

Hornburg; Abraxas Petroleum Corp. v., TexApp–El Paso, 20 SW3d 741.—Acct Action on 10, 14; Action 27(1); App & E 215(1), 216(1), 946, 984(5); Contracts 114, 143(2), 143.5, 147(2), 170(1), 176(2), 227, 326; Costs 194.40; Damag 22, 95, 103, 117, 120(1), 208(1), 212; Estop 52.10(2); Evid 584(1); Mines 78.1(8), 109; Neglig 219, 234; Torts 433; Waste 1, 3, 8.

Hornby v. Hunter, TexCivApp–Corpus Christi, 385 SW2d 473.—Libel 2, 5, 7(13), 25, 33, 42(2), 48(1), 56(1), 75, 101(3); Plead 111.24, 111.42(4).

Horne, In re, BkrtcyEDTex, 277 BR 712.—Bankr 2233(3), 2236, 2402(1), 2828.1.

Horne, In re, BkrtcyEDTex, 277 BR 320.—Bankr 2233(3), 3716.30(11).

Horne; Atkins v., TexCivApp–Hous (14 Dist), 470 SW2d 229.—Abate & R 77; App & E 203.3, 1051(1); Ex & Ad 443(1), 450; Lim of Act 182(7); Witn 141.

Horne v. Charter Nat. Ins. Co., TexCivApp–Fort Worth, 614 SW2d 182, ref nre.—Judgm 181(23), 183; Princ & A 24.

Horne v. Harwell, TexCivApp–Austin, 533 SW2d 450, ref nre.—Child C 577, 609, 610; Child S 537.

Horne v. Moody, TexCivApp–San Antonio, 146 SW2d 505, writ dism, correct.—Bound 3(8), 6, 36(1), 37(1); Courts 90(1); Judgm 634.

Horne; Moore v., TexCivApp–Austin, 136 SW2d 638, writ dism, correct.—Wills 156, 163(1), 166(8), 166(12), 384.

Horne; National Aid Life Ass'n v., Tex, 155 SW2d 910, 137 Tex 597.—Insurance 2027, 2035.

Horne; National Aid Life Ass'n v., TexCivApp–Beaumont, 135 SW2d 254, rev 155 SW2d 910, 137 Tex 597.— App & E 1171(2); Courts 170; Insurance 3015.

Horne; National Aid Life Ass'n v., TexCivApp–Beaumont, 133 SW2d 981, on reh 135 SW2d 254, rev 155 SW2d 910, 137 Tex 597.—Courts 168.

Horne v. Rodgers, TexCivApp–Eastland, 134 SW2d 332. —App & E 773(4).

Horne v. Ross, TexApp–San Antonio, 777 SW2d 755.— Ease 3(1), 17(4); Inj 200.

Horne v. Salado Creek Development Co., TexCivApp– Beaumont, 576 SW2d 659, ref nre.—Fraud 49, 50, 59(1), 64(3).

Horne v. State, TexCrimApp, 749 SW2d 74.—Arson 37(1).

Horne v. State, TexCrimApp, 608 SW2d 680.—Sent & Pun 1872(3).

Horne v. State, TexCrimApp, 607 SW2d 556.—Crim Law 739(1), 1168(1); Homic 1349.

Horne v. State, TexCrimApp, 508 SW2d 643.—Crim Law 519(1), 531(3), 531(4); Sent & Pun 57, 1260.

Horne v. State, TexCrimApp, 506 SW2d 596.—Crim Law 531(3), 660, 1137(2), 1166.22(2).

Horne v. State, TexCrimApp, 434 SW2d 366.—Crim Law 511.2.

Horne v. State, TexApp–Fort Worth, 46 SW3d 391, petition for discretionary review refused.—Assault 92(5); Crim Law 1134(8), 1144.13(2.1), 1159.2(7), 1159.2(9).

Horne v. State, TexApp–San Antonio, 693 SW2d 653, petition for discretionary review gr, rev 749 SW2d 74.— Arson 25.

Horne; U.S. v., CA5 (Tex), 210 FedAppx 421.—Crim Law 1192; Jury 34(10); Sent & Pun 973.

Horne; U.S. v., CA5 (Tex), 141 FedAppx 247, appeal after new sentencing hearing 210 FedAppx 421.—Crim Law 1181.5(8).

Horne; U.S. v., CA5 (Tex), 117 FedAppx 327, cert gr, vac 125 SCt 1749, 544 US 958, 161 LEd2d 599, on remand 141 FedAppx 247, appeal after new sentencing hearing 210 FedAppx 421.—Const Law 4729; Int Rev 5295; Sent & Pun 1361, 1381(2); Weap 17(4).

Horne; Womacks v., TexCivApp–Waco, 300 SW2d 765.— App & E 230, 930(1), 989, 1170.7; Autos 244(44), 244(58).

Horne Children Maintenance and Educational Trust; Crozier v., TexCivApp–San Antonio, 597 SW2d 418, ref nre.—App & E 959(3); Contracts 169, 338(1); Evid 384, 441(8), 448; Judgm 18(1), 248; Plead 236(3), 236(6); Ven & Pur 49, 123, 329.

Horne Motors v. Latimer, TexCivApp–Dallas, 148 SW2d 1000, writ dism, correct.—App & E 1064.1(9); Autos 186, 201(9), 201(10), 227.5, 246(57); Corp 1.3, 1.6(10); Labor & Emp 2924; Neglig 431, 575; Trial 219, 352.4(1), 352.4(6), 352.10, 352.18.

Horner v. Bourland, CA5 (Tex), 724 F2d 1142.—Contracts 93(1), 93(5); Frds St of 108(4), 131(1); Spec Perf 8, 64, 133; Ven & Pur 31, 170.

Horner v. Reed, TexApp–San Antonio, 756 SW2d 34.— Mand 3(1), 4(4), 61; Sent & Pun 1972(2).

Horner v. Rowan Companies, Inc., SDTex, 153 FRD 597.—Atty & C 32(12); Fed Civ Proc 2795; Witn 208(1), 219(4.1).

Horner v. Seiders, TexCivApp–Austin, 371 SW2d 416, ref nre.—App & E 627.2; Judgm 340.

Horner v. State, TexCrimApp, 508 SW2d 371.—Crim Law 666(1), 721(3), 730(14), 1171.5.

Horner v. State, TexCrimApp, 149 SW2d 586, 141 TexCrim 496.—Crim Law 1131(1).

Horner; State v., TexApp–Dallas, 936 SW2d 668, petition for discretionary review refused.—Const Law 4580; Crim Law 145.5, 577.8(2), 1024(3); Ind & Inf 7.

Horner v. State, TexApp–Corpus Christi, 129 SW3d 210, reh overr, and petition for discretionary review refused, cert den 125 SCt 2905, 545 US 1116, 162 LEd2d 298.— Crim Law 121, 134(2), 367, 629(3.1), 629.5(1), 629.5(2),

641.13(2.1), 641.13(6), 662.8, 1036.5, 1045, 1148, 1150, 1153(1).

Horning; Duncan v., TexCivApp–Dallas, 587 SW2d 471. —Evid 470; Health 631, 637; Judgm 185(3), 185(4), 185.3(21).

Hornor & Co.; Winkler Const. Co. v., TexCivApp–San Antonio, 580 SW2d 401, ref nre.—App & E 230; Assign 58, 138.

Hornsby v. Bartz, TexCivApp–El Paso, 230 SW2d 360.— Deeds 139; Quiet T 10.2; Ven & Pur 231(1).

Hornsby; Chambers v., TexApp–Houston (14 Dist), 21 SW3d 446.—App & E 901, 934(1); Judgm 181(6), 185(5); Offic 114, 116; Sheriffs 111.

Hornsby v. Conoco, Inc., CA5 (Tex), 777 F2d 243, reh den 780 F2d 532.—Civil R 1168, 1204, 1505(3).

Hornsby v. Crystal Beach Park, TexCivApp–San Antonio, 41 SW2d 82, writ dism woj.—Nuis 35.

Hornsby v. Hornsby, TexComApp, 93 SW2d 379, 127 Tex 474.—Bankr 2513, 2534, 2546, 2573; Hus & W 269, 279(3).

Hornsby; Hornsby v., TexComApp, 93 SW2d 379, 127 Tex 474.—Bankr 2513, 2534, 2546, 2573; Hus & W 269, 279(3).

Hornsby v. Houston Electric Co., TexCivApp–Galveston, 125 SW2d 346, writ dism, correct.—App & E 218.2(1), 719(8); Autos 245(91); New Tr 163(2); Trial 352.10; Witn 321, 331.5.

Hornsby; Leitch v., Tex, 935 SW2d 114.—App & E 930(3), 1001(3); Corp 1.6(13), 306; Damag 185(1); Evid 568(1); Labor & Emp 2778, 2784, 2881; Neglig 371, 387, 400, 1675.

Hornsby; Leitch v., TexApp–San Antonio, 885 SW2d 243, writ gr, rev 935 SW2d 114.—App & E 930(3), 1001(1), 1003(5), 1003(7), 1182; Corp 1.6(13), 306, 325; Labor & Emp 113, 2782, 2840, 2848, 2858, 2881, 2883, 2902, 2921, 2950, 2983, 2990, 3026, 3074; Neglig 200, 236, 371, 387; Princ & A 159(2).

Hornsby; Leon's Shoe Stores, Inc. v., TexCivApp–Waco, 306 SW2d 402.—False Imp 7(4), 15(3); Torts 109, 135.

Hornsby; Saunders v., TexCivApp–Amarillo, 173 SW2d 795, writ refused wom.—Adv Poss 11, 86; Judgm 174; Lim of Act 39(5); Mines 55(2), 55(7); New Tr 164.

Hornsby v. State, TexApp–Houston (1 Dist), 65 SW3d 801.—Crim Law 1077.2(1), 1077.2(3), 1148.

Hornsby; Supreme Forest Woodmen Circle v., TexCivApp–Fort Worth, 107 SW2d 393.—Contracts 318; Insurance 2079, 2082; Trial 350.8.

Hornsby; U.S. v., CA5 (Tex), 88 F3d 336.—Const Law 4711; Crim Law 1139, 1158(1); Sent & Pun 596, 635, 653(2), 964, 1381(3).

Hornsby Heavy Hardware Co. v. Prichard, TexCivApp–Fort Worth, 119 SW2d 410, dism.—App & E 345.1; Trial 352.10.

Hornsby Oil Co., Inc. v. Champion Spark Plug Co., Inc., CA5 (Tex), 714 F2d 1384.—Antitrust 535, 541, 553, 556, 557, 558, 592, 981; Judgm 828.9(5).

Horridge, In re, SDTex, 127 BR 798.—Bankr 3271, 3286.

Horridge; Hazelip v., SDTex, 127 BR 798. See Horridge, In re.

Horrmachea v. State, TexCrimApp, 117 SW2d 66.—Crim Law 1182.

Horrocks v. City of Grand Prairie, Tex, 704 SW2d 17.— Mun Corp 185(12).

Horrocks; City of Grand Prairie v., TexApp–Dallas, 692 SW2d 129, rev 704 SW2d 17.—Mun Corp 185(12); Offic 72.40.

Horrocks v. Horrocks, TexCivApp–Dallas, 608 SW2d 733. —Judgm 185(2), 185(6), 185.3(17); Ten in C 15(7), 15(10).

Horrocks; Horrocks v., TexCivApp–Dallas, 608 SW2d 733.—Judgm 185(2), 185(6), 185.3(17); Ten in C 15(7), 15(10).

Horrocks v. Texas Dept. of Transp., Tex, 852 SW2d 498. —App & E 1153.

Horrocks; Texas Dept. of Transp. v., TexApp–Dallas, 841 SW2d 413, reh den, and writ gr, rev 852 SW2d 498.— App & E 930(3), 989, 1001(1), 1001(3), 1003(7); Autos 258, 273; Plead 403(1), 403(2); States 112.2(2), 209, 211.

Horseshoe Bay Resort Sales Co. v. Lake Lyndon B. Johnson Imp. Corp., TexApp–Austin, 53 SW3d 799, reh overr, and review den.—App & E 199, 989, 1010.1(1), 1043(6); Decl Judgm 237; Judgm 297; Lim of Act 43, 55(6); Trademarks 1021, 1024, 1028, 1030, 1033, 1034, 1036, 1037, 1038, 1039, 1046, 1047(1), 1048, 1081, 1092, 1110, 1111, 1116, 1166, 1420, 1421, 1459, 1463, 1470, 1554, 1629(2), 1689, 1690, 1691, 1755, 1756; Trial 43.

Horseshoe Operating Co.; Guaranty Federal Sav. & Loan Ass'n v., TexApp–Dallas, 748 SW2d 519, writ den, and writ withdrawn, and writ gr, aff in part, rev in part Guaranty Federal Sav Bank v. Horseshoe Operating Co, 793 SW2d 652.—Action 60; App & E 302(6); Banks 189; Bills & N 209, 443(2), 446; Gaming 19(1); Judgm 181(26); Stip 8.

Horseshoe Operating Co.; Guaranty Federal Sav. Bank v., Tex, 793 SW2d 652.—Action 60; App & E 949; Banks 139, 189; Bills & N 313; Parties 40(2), 44.

Horsley, Ex parte, TexCrimApp, 460 SW2d 906.—Hab Corp 526.

Horsley v. Johnson, CA5 (Tex), 197 F3d 134.—Hab Corp 313.1, 320, 378, 401, 843, 895.

Horsley v. Phillips, TexCivApp–Waco, 126 SW2d 703.— Fraud Conv 57(1), 159(1), 221, 299(13), 301(3); Lim of Act 39(1), 100(2), 100(13), 197(2).

Horsley-Layman v. Adventist Health System/Sunbelt, Inc., TexApp–Fort Worth, 221 SW3d 802, reh overr, and review den.—Bankr 2154.1, 2325, 3022; Estop 52.10(2), 52.10(3), 68(2); Judgm 185(5).

Horsley-Layman v. Angeles, TexApp–Fort Worth, 90 SW3d 926, review den.—Health 804, 805, 809.

Horsley-Layman v. Angeles, TexApp–Texarkana, 968 SW2d 533, appeal after remand 90 SW3d 926, review den.—Const Law 655, 3754, 4422; Health 804, 808, 819.

Horst v. State, TexApp–Amarillo, 758 SW2d 311, petition for discretionary review refused.—Crim Law 273(3), 627.10(2.1), 693, 855(8), 868, 928, 1163(6), 1174(5); Ind & Inf 159(2), 189(8); Witn 257.10.

Horstman; State v., TexApp–Fort Worth, 829 SW2d 903, petition for discretionary review gr, rev State v. Duke, 865 SW2d 466.—Crim Law 1043(3), 1134(3); Ind & Inf 15(4), 60, 65, 110(3), 110(4), 137(6), 142; RICO 102, 120.

Horta v. D & C Motors, TexApp–Houston (1 Dist), 671 SW2d 720. See Horta v. Tennison.

Horta v. Tennison, TexApp–Houston (1 Dist), 671 SW2d 720.—Antitrust 130, 369; App & E 233(2), 931(1), 931(5), 989, 1010.1(1); Evid 273(1), 314(1).

Hortenstine v. Jackson, TexCivApp–Amarillo, 289 SW2d 613, ref nre.—Action 68; Judgm 5; Parties 80(1), 80(2), 84(1), 84(2).

Hortenstine; Jones v., TexCivApp–Amarillo, 291 SW2d 761, writ dism by agreement.—App & E 655(1), 758.1, 758.3(1), 758.3(2), 758.3(3), 1035; Bills & N 443(2), 459, 473; Judgm 181(6), 185.3(16), 186.

Hortenstine v. McKlemurry, TexCivApp–Waco, 402 SW2d 946, ref nre.—App & E 302(1).

Hortenstine v. McKlemurry, TexCivApp–Eastland, 425 SW2d 691, ref nre.—App & E 1050.1(11); Tresp to T T 40(4), 41(2).

Hortex, Inc.; Mann Mfg., Inc. v., CA5 (Tex), 439 F2d 403.—Fed Cts 1143, 1144, 1150; Inj 210.

Hortex Inc.; Williamson-Dickie Mfg. Co. v., CA5 (Tex), 504 F2d 983.—Fed Civ Proc 2280; Fed Cts 751; Pat 16(1), 37, 46, 112.1, 112.3(1), 312(1.2), 324.54, 325.11(2.1).

Hortex Mfg. Co. v. N. L. R. B., CA5 (Tex), 364 F2d 302. —Labor & Emp 1787, 1951.

Hortman v. Ransom Industries, CA5 (Tex), 92 FedAppx 978.—Labor & Emp 809, 827.

Horton, In re, BkrtcyNDTex, 224 BR 360. See Thompson, In re.

Horton, In re, BkrtcyNDTex, 95 BR 436.—Int Rev 5205, 5233.

Horton, In re, BkrtcySDTex, 152 BR 912.—Bankr 3353(1.55), 3353(12.10), 3353(14.25), 3355(2.1), 3357(2.1), 3360, 3422(11).

Horton; Amberson v., TexCivApp–San Antonio, 255 SW2d 580, ref nre.—App & E 930(1), 1043(1), 1073(7), 1140(4); Partners 108, 121.

Horton; American Cas. Co. v., TexCivApp–Dallas, 152 SW2d 395, dism.—Contracts 127(1), 127(3); Insurance 2555, 2556, 2558(1), 2561(2), 2568, 2578.

Horton v. Armstrong, TexCivApp–Texarkana, 330 SW2d 498.—App & E 1177(6).

Horton; Associated Grocers of Colorado, Inc. v., BkrtcySDTex, 152 BR 912. See Horton, In re.

Horton; A. Y. Creager Co. v., TexCivApp–El Paso, 96 SW2d 790.—Usury 13.

Horton v. Bank One, N.A., CA5 (Tex), 387 F3d 426, cert den 126 SCt 1164, 546 US 1149, 163 LEd2d 1127.—Fed Cts 281, 301, 417, 611, 617; Statut 209, 212.5, 220.

Horton v. Beto, SDTex, 274 FSupp 97.—Hab Corp 374.1, 509(1).

Horton v. City of Houston, Tex., CA5 (Tex), 179 F3d 188, reh den, cert den 120 SCt 530, 528 US 1021, 145 LEd2d 411, appeal after remand 89 FedAppx 903, cert den 125 SCt 48, 543 US 813, 160 LEd2d 17.—Const Law 1512, 1514, 1517, 1518, 1735, 2142; Fed Civ Proc 2481; Tel 1230.

Horton v. City of Smithville, CA5 (Tex), 117 FedAppx 345.—Const Law 3516, 4093; Em Dom 2.10(6), 277; Fed Cts 915; Zoning 761, 762.

Horton v. Cockrell, CA5 (Tex), 70 F3d 397, reh den.—Fed Civ Proc 2734; Fed Cts 830; Prisons 17(5); Sent & Pun 1532, 1537.

Horton v. Cook, TexCivApp–Austin, 538 SW2d 221, ref nre.—Int Liq 16.

Horton; Dallas Railway & Terminal Co. v., TexCivApp–Dallas, 119 SW2d 122, writ dism.—App & E 1024.5; Damag 216(3); Evid 20(2); New Tr 56; Trial 223, 311, 362.

Horton; Davenport v., TexCivApp–San Antonio, 111 SW2d 729.—App & E 846(2), 1011.1(9).

Horton v. Denny's Inc., TexCivApp–Tyler, 128 SW3d 256, review den.—App & E 994(2), 1003(3), 1003(5), 1003(7), 1004(1); Damag 127.1, 127.28, 208(1); Evid 570, 588.

Horton v. Dental Capital Leasing Corp., TexApp–Texarkana, 649 SW2d 655.—App & E 731(5), 1170.6; Sec Tran 2, 25; Trial 25(4), 350.8.

Horton; Diamond Offshore Management Co. v., TexApp–Houston (1 Dist), 193 SW3d 76, review den.—Adm 1.20(1); App & E 999(1), 1001(1); Labor & Emp 2781; Seamen 29(5.14), 29(5.16).

Horton; Donalson v., TexCivApp–Amarillo, 256 SW2d 693, ref nre.—App & E 253, 1071.6; Judgm 18(2); Trial 388(1), 388(4), 392(4), 393(1), 396(3), 397(4).

Horton; Employers Ins. of Wausau v., TexApp–Texarkana, 797 SW2d 677.—App & E 232(0.5), 236(1), 969; Const Law 3603, 4186; Costs 260(1); Jury 31.2(1); Trial 9(1), 26; Work Comp 1696.

Horton v. Goose Creek Independent School Dist., CA5 (Tex), 693 F2d 524.—Schools 169.5.

Horton v. Goose Creek Independent School Dist., CA5 (Tex), 690 F2d 470, reh den 693 F2d 524, cert den Goose Creek Consolidated Independent School District v. Horton, 103 SCt 3536, 463 US 1207, 77 LEd2d 1387.—Const Law 4210; Fed Civ Proc 161.1, 162, 164, 165, 171, 172, 187.5, 2515; Fed Cts 761, 817; Schools 169, 169.5; Searches 22, 23, 55, 192.1.

Horton; Gulf Oil Corp. v., TexCivApp–Amarillo, 143 SW2d 132.—Contracts 147(1); Land & Ten 55(2), 157(4); Waste 1.

Horton v. Harris, TexCivApp–Tyler, 610 SW2d 819, ref nre.—App & E 1001(1); Deeds 211(1); Hus & W 273(9); Trial 350.3(2.1); Trusts 95, 103(1), 110.

Horton v. Hill, TexCivApp–Galveston, 95 SW2d 751, writ dism.—App & E 742(4), 901.

Horton; Hoover v., TexCivApp–Amarillo, 209 SW2d 646.—Adj Land 8; Neglig 250, 1010; Plead 111.1, 111.23, 111.42(7), 111.42(11); Venue 5.5, 8.5(6).

Horton v. Horton, TexApp–Fort Worth, 965 SW2d 78, reh overr.—App & E 78(1), 863, 870(2), 934(1), 1079; Judgm 199(3.5), 199(3.7), 199(3.10); Trial 139.1(6), 139.1(7), 139.1(14), 139.1(17), 420; Wills 21, 32, 50, 52(1), 53(2), 55(1), 55(6), 155, 156, 163(1), 166(1), 166(2).

Horton; Horton v., TexApp–Fort Worth, 965 SW2d 78, reh overr.—App & E 78(1), 863, 870(2), 934(1), 1079; Judgm 199(3.5), 199(3.7), 199(3.10); Trial 139.1(6), 139.1(7), 139.1(14), 139.1(17), 420; Wills 21, 32, 50, 52(1), 53(2), 55(1), 55(6), 155, 156, 163(1), 166(1), 166(2).

Horton v. Horton, TexApp–Fort Worth, 625 SW2d 78, ref nre.—Child C 609, 637, 650; Const Law 976, 3993.

Horton; Horton v., TexApp–Fort Worth, 625 SW2d 78, ref nre.—Child C 609, 637, 650; Const Law 976, 3993.

Horton v. Liberty Mut. Ins. Co., USTex, 81 SCt 1570, 367 US 348, 6 LEd2d 890, reh den 82 SCt 24, 368 US 870, 7 LEd2d 70.—Fed Cts 334, 335, 340.1, 350.1, 417, 455.1; Work Comp 1914.

Horton; Liberty Mut. Ins. Co. v., CA5 (Tex), 275 F2d 148, cert gr 81 SCt 79, 364 US 814, 5 LEd2d 46, aff 81 SCt 1570, 367 US 348, 6 LEd2d 890, reh den 82 SCt 24, 368 US 870, 7 LEd2d 70.—Const Law 2474; Fed Cts 6, 352, 354, 421; Work Comp 1262, 1826, 1867, 1893.

Horton; Lowrance v., Tex, 959 SW2d 620.—Divorce 194.

Horton v. Mills County, TexCivApp–Austin, 468 SW2d 876.—App & E 768, 1036(1); Em Dom 170, 196, 262(5).

Horton v. Montgomery Ward & Co., Inc., TexApp–San Antonio, 827 SW2d 361, writ den.—Damag 50.10; Fraud 3; Judgm 185(2), 185.1(4); Labor & Emp 50, 51, 2921; Neglig 201, 273; Torts 115; Work Comp 2093.

Horton; Morgan v., TexApp–Dallas, 675 SW2d 602.—Divorce 252.3(4), 254(1), 255, 322.

Horton v. Nacogdoches Independent School Dist., EDTex, 81 FSupp2d 707.—Bankr 2091, 2154.1; Rem of C 2, 44, 79(1), 101.1, 107(7).

Horton; O'Sullivan Industries, Inc. v., CA5 (Tex), 732 F2d 1258. See U.S. v. Westside Bank.

Horton; Ramos v., TexCivApp–El Paso, 456 SW2d 565.—App & E 882(1); Hus & W 204, 221; Judgm 693, 724.

Horton; Reid v., TexCivApp–Amarillo, 278 SW2d 626, ref nre.—Child C 22, 77, 413, 553, 555, 641, 921(1), 921(5).

Horton v. Robinson, TexApp–El Paso, 776 SW2d 260.—App & E 174, 878(6); Consp 19, 20; Contracts 227; Corp 30(1), 202, 406(1), 423; Costs 194.32; Damag 91(1), 94; Fraud 7, 30; Inj 70; Interest 39(2.30); Plead 290(3); Princ & A 163(1).

Horton v. Schultz, TexCivApp–San Antonio, 148 SW2d 252.—App & E 1062.1; Damag 174(1), 221(2.1); Trial 219.

Horton; Sinclair Pipe Line Co. v., TexCivApp–Beaumont, 323 SW2d 656.—Plead 111.42(1).

Horton; Smith v., TexCivApp–San Antonio, 134 SW2d 320.—App & E 781(4), 1175(1); Offic 80.

Horton; Smith v., TexCivApp–Texarkana, 485 SW2d 824, dism.—App & E 984(5); Divorce 197, 198, 225.

Horton v. State, TexCrimApp, 780 SW2d 247. See Ladner v. State.

Horton v. State, TexCrimApp, 621 SW2d 632.—Burg 29; Crim Law 1136, 1184(1); Sent & Pun 2004, 2025.

Horton v. State, TexCrimApp, 333 SW2d 380, 169 TexCrim 210.—Crim Law 1036.2; Witn 274(2).

Horton v. State, TexCrimApp, 165 SW2d 739.—Crim Law 1094(3).

Horton v. State, TexCrimApp, 116 SW2d 394, 134 TexCrim 529.—Crim Law 1091(10), 1091(11), 1092.16.

Horton v. State, TexCrimApp, 105 SW2d 669, 132 TexCrim 488.—Int Liq 139.

Horton v. State, TexCrimApp, 58 SW2d 833, 123 TexCrim 237.—Controlled Subs 65.

Horton v. State, TexApp–Austin, 78 SW3d 701, petition for discretionary review refused.—Crim Law 412(4), 414, 517.2(3), 519(2), 1139, 1144.12, 1153(1), 1158(4); Infants 68.4, 174.

Horton v. State, TexApp–Austin, 16 SW3d 848.—Arrest 63.5(7), 63.5(8), 63.5(9), 68(3), 68(4); Autos 349(10), 349.5(10); Searches 67.1, 70.

Horton v. State, TexApp–Waco, 986 SW2d 297.—Courts 91(1); Crim Law 369.2(1), 369.3, 371(12), 438(1), 438(6), 438(7), 511.2, 511.7, 512, 1153(1), 1162, 1165(1), 1169.1(10), 1169.2(1), 1169.11, 1172.6.

Horton, Estate of; State v., TexApp–Tyler, 4 SW3d 53.— States 112(2), 112.2(1), 112.2(2).

Horton v. State, TexApp–Tyler, 880 SW2d 22, petition for discretionary review refused.—Crim Law 59(1); Homic 1207.

Horton v. State, TexApp–Tyler, 790 SW2d 671. See Ladner v. State.

Horton v. State, TexApp–Houston (14 Dist), 754 SW2d 747.—Autos 355(1); Crim Law 552(3), 560.

Horton; State v., TexCivApp–Beaumont, 454 SW2d 847, ref nre.—Bound 32, 33, 37(1); Tresp to T T 6.1, 38(1).

Horton v. State Dept. of Ins. Receiver J. Robert Hunter, TexApp–Austin, 905 SW2d 59.—Insurance 1407, 1412, 1503, 1508, 3367, 3391.

Horton v. Stone, TexCivApp–Waco, 268 SW2d 247.—App & E 304, 386(1), 729.

Horton; Texas Candy & Nut Co. v., TexCivApp–Dallas, 235 SW2d 518, ref nre.—App & E 499(2), 1172(1); Evid 314(1); Joint Adv 1.15; Princ & A 123(7), 189(1); Sales 415, 417; Trial 60(1); Trusts 210.

Horton; Texas Workers' Compensation Com'n v., TexApp–Beaumont, 187 SW3d 282.—App & E 173(2), 863, 893(1), 911.3; Inj 138.46; Mun Corp 742(4); Plead 111.48, 130; States 191.1, 191.4(1), 191.9(1), 191.10, 209; Work Comp 966, 981.

Horton; Trickey v., TexCivApp–San Antonio, 143 SW2d 145.—Plead 111.18, 111.38, 111.39(7).

Horton; Trinity Universal Ins. Co. v., TexCivApp–Eastland, 363 SW2d 376.—Evid 434(11); Insurance 2412; Judgm 181(23), 185(2), 185.1(3), 185.1(4), 186.

Horton; U.S. v., CA5 (Tex), 646 F2d 181, reh den 655 F2d 1131, cert den102 SCt 516, 454 US 970, 70 LEd2d 388, cert den Estes v. US, 102 SCt 1274, 455 US 919, 71 LEd2d 459.—Consp 40.1, 47(1); Crim Law 37.15(2), 273.1(2), 422(2), 423(1), 427(2), 427(5), 428, 577.2, 620(3.1), 620(4), 620(5), 622.2(1), 622.2(6), 824(1), 923(2), 1038.1(1), 1038.2, 1044.1(1); Jury 97(1), 99.1.

Horton; U.S. v., CA5 (Tex), 488 F2d 374, reh den 488 F2d 552, cert den 94 SCt 2405, 416 US 993, 40 LEd2d 772.— Arrest 63.4(9), 63.4(10); Controlled Subs 28, 31, 81; Crim Law 552(3), 1144.13(3), 1153(1), 1159.6; Searches 173.1, 180, 181, 183, 194.

Horton; Vinson v., TexCivApp–Texarkana, 207 SW2d 432.—Contracts 175(1); Evid 10(2), 460(7); Plead 111.3; Venue 7.5(1), 7.5(7).

Horton; Weisz v., TexCivApp–Galveston, 148 SW2d 219, writ dism, correct.—App & E 672, 714(1), 758.1, 1135; Labor & Emp 251; Set-Off 1.

Horton; Wilhite v., TexCivApp–Dallas, 116 SW2d 807.— Autos 240(1), 242(5); Plead 111.36, 111.42(8); Venue 8.5(5).

Horton; Woods v., CA5 (Tex), 171 F2d 545.—War 224.

Horton & Horton; Jones v., CCA5 (Tex), 100 F2d 345.— Chat Mtg 129; Mar Liens 37(3); Mtg 1; Ship 32.

Horton & Horton Bldg. Materials Co.; Quarles v., TexCivApp–Waco, 336 SW2d 267.—App & E 554(3), 907(3).

Horton & Horton Custom Works, Inc.; Fidelity & Cas. Co. of New York v., TexCivApp–Fort Worth, 462 SW2d 613, ref nre.—Contracts 297; Insurance 2941.

Horton & Horton, Inc.; Creekmore v., TexCivApp–Hous (14 Dist), 487 SW2d 148, ref nre.—Autos 242(6); Judgm 181(21), 185.3(13).

Horton & Horton, Inc.; Mitsui O. S. K. Lines, K. K. v., CA5 (Tex), 480 F2d 1104.—Collision 129, 134; Damag 6; Fed Civ Proc 2353; Fed Cts 828, 871.

Horton & Horton, Inc. v. The Robert E. Hopkins, CA5 (Tex), 269 F2d 914, cert den 80 SCt 589, 361 US 961, 4 LEd2d 543.—Adm 109; Collision 95(3), 105(6), 144.

Horton & Horton, Inc. v. T/S J. E. Dyer, CA5 (Tex), 428 F2d 1131, cert den 91 SCt 461, 400 US 993, 27 LEd2d 441.—Adm 118.6(1), 118.7(5); Contrib 5(6.1); Ship 86(2.5).

Horvath v. Baylor University Medical Center, TexApp–Dallas, 704 SW2d 866.—App & E 989, 994(2), 1002, 1003(7); Evid 333(1); Health 656, 823(1).

Horvath; Henrise v., NDTex, 174 FSupp2d 493, aff in part 45 FedAppx 323.—Civil R 1351(1), 1351(5), 1407; Consp 18; Const Law 1446; Mun Corp 185(1).

Horvath; Henrise v., NDTex, 94 FSupp2d 768.—Civil R 1345, 1351(1), 1395(1); Fed Civ Proc 642, 1772.

Horvath; Henrise v., NDTex, 94 FSupp2d 765.—Civil R 1398; Fed Civ Proc 1273.

Horvath v. State, TexApp–Fort Worth, 884 SW2d 789.— Crim Law 1101.

Horvatich v. Texas Dept. of Protective and Regulatory Services, TexApp–Austin, 78 SW3d 594.—App & E 931(1), 1008.1(1), 1008.1(2), 1010.1(1), 1010.1(2), 1012.1(4); Infants 155, 178, 248.1.

Horwitz; Diggles v., TexApp–Beaumont, 765 SW2d 839, writ den.—Judgm 185.3(21); Prod Liab 60.5.

Horwitz v. Finkelstein, TexCivApp–Amarillo, 196 SW2d 951, ref nre.—App & E 1078(1); Judgm 335(1), 335(2), 335(3); New Tr 155; Plead 214(1).

Horwitz v. Finkelstein, TexCivApp–Amarillo, 189 SW2d 895, writ refused wom.—App & E 907(3), 954(1), 954(2), 954(4); Inj 135, 147, 161.

Horwitz v. Finkelstein, TexCivApp–Amarillo, 182 SW2d 751, writ refused.—App & E 564(2), 622; New Tr 155; Stip 6.

Horwitz-Texan Theatres Co.; Hamblen v., TexCivApp–Galveston, 162 SW2d 455.—App & E 954(1); Contracts 121; Corp 1.5(1), 198.1(1).

Horwood; Wagner & Brown, Ltd. v., Tex, 58 SW3d 732, on remand 2004 WL 321682.—App & E 422; Lim of Act 1, 95(1), 95(9), 104(1).

Horwood v. Wagner & Brown, Ltd., TexApp–El Paso, 61 SW3d 1, rev 58 SW3d 732, on remand 2004 WL 321682. —App & E 409, 852, 863; Judgm 181(7), 185(2); Lim of Act 95(1), 95(9).

Hosack v. Cassidy, TexCivApp–Corpus Christi, 543 SW2d 202.—App & E 758.3(3), 758.3(9), 882(6); Contracts 103; Evid 158(16), 589; Int Rev 4823; Int Liq 327(1); Plead 129(2).

Hosch; Goodpasture, Inc. v., TexCivApp–Hous (1 Dist), 568 SW2d 662, dism.—Negllg 306, 1613, 1614, 1617, 1621, 1625, 1664; Plead 111.12, 111.16, 111.42(7).

Hosch; U.S. v., CA5 (Tex), 577 F2d 963.—Arrest 63.5(6); Cust Dut 126(4).

Hosea v. McMahon, CA5 (Tex), 226 FedAppx 341.—Social S 149.

Hosea v. State, TexCrimApp, 290 SW2d 907, 163 Tex-Crim 335.—Crim Law 683(1), 1170(1); Rape 52(1).

Hosea v. State, TexApp–Houston (14 Dist), 802 SW2d 763. —Crim Law 1023(2), 1023(3), 1023(9), 1081(2).

Hosein v. Gonzales, CA5 (Tex), 452 F3d 401.—Aliens 667; Decl Judgm 62, 341.1, 345.1; Fed Civ Proc 103.2, 103.3; Fed Cts 759.1.

Hosek, In re, BkrtcyWDTex, 136 BR 672.—Exemp 37; Insurance 1020; Statut 147, 176, 179.

Hosek, In re, BkrtcyWDTex, 124 BR 239, reconsideration den 136 BR 672.—Exemp 35.

Hose Pro Connectors, Inc. v. Parker Hannifin Corp., TexApp–Houston (14 Dist), 889 SW2d 555.—Acct Action on 2, 9.1, 12, 14; App & E 836, 931(1), 989, 1010.1(2), 1012.1(5).

HOTCHKISS

Hosey v. County of Victoria, TexApp–Corpus Christi, 852 SW2d 963.—App & E 389(1).

Hosey v. County of Victoria, TexApp–Corpus Christi, 832 SW2d 701.—App & E 78(4), 946; Atty & C 62; Jury 26; New Tr 157; Pretrial Proc 581, 583, 590.1, 676, 683, 715, 716.

Hosey v. First Nat. Bank of Goliad, TexCivApp–Corpus Christi, 595 SW2d 629, dism.—App & E 154(4); Costs 260(5).

Hosey; McBride v., TexCivApp–El Paso, 197 SW2d 372, ref nre.—Inn 9; War 204.

Hosey v. State, TexApp–Corpus Christi, 760 SW2d 778, petition for discretionary review refused.—Crim Law 713, 722.3, 1043(3), 1171.1(2.1), 1172.9; Double J 105, 107.1; Larc 41; Rob 1, 11, 24.15(1).

Hosier; Loper v., TexCivApp–Dallas, 148 SW2d 889, writ dism, correct.—App & E 76(2), 134(1), 347(1), 622, 937(1); Judgm 22.

Hosken, Ex parte, TexCivApp–Beaumont, 480 SW2d 18. —Child S 444, 497; Const Law 4494; Contempt 2, 4, 40, 72, 81; Hab Corp 462, 528.1, 529.

Hoskins, Ex parte, TexCrimApp, 227 SW2d 820, 154 TexCrim 379.—Sent & Pun 1014.

Hoskins, In re, TexCivApp–Amarillo, 198 SW2d 460, ref nre.—Child C 413; Infants 191, 196, 203, 230.1, 250; Judgm 725(1); Jury 21.3.

Hoskins v. Bekins Van Lines, CA5 (Tex), 343 F3d 769, 199 ALR Fed 743.—Antitrust 132; Carr 108, 147, 155, 158(1); Fed Cts 241, 776; Rem of C 25(1); States 18.3, 18.21.

Hoskins; Bell v., TexCivApp–Dallas, 357 SW2d 585.— App & E 692(1); Child C 76, 553, 632, 637, 914, 920, 922(2), 923(4).

Hoskins v. Carpenter, TexCivApp–El Paso, 201 SW2d 606, ref nre.—App & E 692(1), 1003(9.1), 1040(13), 1050.1(3.1); Autos 20; Exceptions Bill of17; Ex & Ad 221(2), 451(2); Gifts 16; Paymt 59; Trial 84(1), 140(1), 141.

Hoskins; City of Dallas v., TexCivApp–Dallas, 193 SW2d 533, ref nre.—Mun Corp 200(7), 200(11).

Hoskins v. Commissioner of Internal Revenue, CCA5 (Tex), 84 F2d 627.—Int Rev 3054, 3564; Schools 72; Tax 2006.

Hoskins; Davis v., TexCivApp–Fort Worth, 531 SW2d 424.—Ex & Ad 17(1), 17(2); Wills 206, 386.

Hoskins v. State, TexCrimApp, 425 SW2d 825.—Crim Law 273.2(1), 980(1), 1134(8), 1147; Sent & Pun 2004, 2021.

Hoskins v. State, TexCrimApp, 373 SW2d 248.—Crim Law 1097(5), 1099.10, 1144.19.

Hoskins v. State, TexCrimApp, 194 SW2d 955, 149 TexCrim 386.—Larc 55, 68(1).

Hoskins; Sutphen v., TexCivApp–Amarillo, 442 SW2d 921, ref nre.—Land & Ten 105.

Hoskins; U.S. v., CA5 (Tex), 910 F2d 309.—Crim Law 274(3.1), 274(9), 641.13(5), 641.13(7), 1480.

Hosler; Welborn-Hosler v., TexApp–Houston (14 Dist), 870 SW2d 323.—Appear 10; Child C 606, 703, 707, 719, 744, 745; Child S 323, 339(1); Divorce 81, 159.1; Notice 14; States 18.28.

Hospice at the Texas Medical Center; Hale v., TexApp–Beaumont, 96 SW3d 688.—Unemp Comp 473, 478, 500.

Hospice in the Pines; Fence v., TexApp–Beaumont, 4 SW3d 476, review den.—Health 611, 614, 615, 618, 656, 663, 782, 821(2), 825; Judgm 181(33), 185.3(21); Labor & Emp 3045; Princ & A 159(1).

Hospital Affiliates Intern., Inc.; Gertner v., CA5 (Tex), 602 F2d 685.—Fed Civ Proc 215, 2492.

Hospital Ass'n of Southern Pac. Lines in Texas and Louisiana v. Gianelloni, TexCivApp–Beaumont, 431 SW2d 949.—Assoc 20(1); Stip 14(12); Trial 350.4(4).

Hospital Consultants, Inc. v. Potyka, TexCivApp–San Antonio, 531 SW2d 657, ref nre.—Contracts 116(1), 116(2), 116(3), 117(2), 141(1); Corp 448(3).

Hospital Corp. Intern., Ltd.; Ferguson v., CA5 (Tex), 776 F2d 105.—Work Comp 186, 2100.

Hospital Corp. Intern., Ltd.; Ferguson v., CA5 (Tex), 769 F2d 268, reh den 776 F2d 105.—Elect of Rem 7(1); Work Comp 186, 2099, 2100.

Hospital Corp. Intern., Ltd.; Ferguson v., EDTex, 573 FSupp 438. See Rabjohns v. Hospital Corp. Intern., Ltd.

Hospital Corp. Intern., Ltd.; Rabjohns v., EDTex, 573 FSupp 438, aff Ferguson v. Hospital Corp Intern, Ltd, 769 F2d 268, reh den 776 F2d 105.—Elect of Rem 7(1); Work Comp 2100.

Hospital Corp. of America; American Development Intern. Corp. v., NDTex, 188 BR 925. See American Development Intern. Corp., In re.

Hospital Corp. of America; Conway v., TexCivApp–Texarkana, 577 SW2d 534, ref nre, appeal dism 100 SCt 22, 444 US 803, 62 LEd2d 16.—Zoning 131, 133, 134.1, 167.1, 193.

Hospital Corp. of America v. Farrar, TexApp–Fort Worth, 733 SW2d 393.—Mand 3(2.1), 12; Pretrial Proc 65.

Hospital Corp. of America; Johnson v., CA5 (Tex), 95 F3d 383.—Antitrust 537, 556, 976, 977(1), 977(2); Assoc 20(1); Corp 202; Fed Civ Proc 103.2, 103.3; Fed Cts 848, 850.1; Health 235, 275; Libel 133, 135; Lim of Act 124; Torts 212, 220, 245.

Hospital Corp. of America; Rea v., NDTex, 892 FSupp 821, aff in part, vac in part, rev in part Johnson v. Hospital Corp of America, 95 F3d 383.—Antitrust 535, 556, 593; Fraud 20; Health 273, 274, 275; Libel 76, 135, 139; Torts 245.

Hospital Housekeeping Systems of Houston, Inc.; McGaskey v., SDTex, 942 FSupp 1118.—Insurance 1117(1); Labor & Emp 407, 414, 635, 650, 682, 683, 757; States 18.49, 18.51.

Hospitality House, Inc. v. Gilbert, CA5 (Tex), 298 F3d 424.—Compromise 21; Fed Cts 3.1, 25, 31, 542, 574, 770, 776.

Hospitals v. Continental Cas. Co., TexApp–Austin, 109 SW3d 96, review den, and reh of petition for review den. —App & E 852, 893(1); Lim of Act 1; Work Comp 1001.

Hospital Sciences of Northern Cal., Inc. v. Medical Computer Systems, Inc., TexCivApp–Waco, 482 SW2d 699.—Plead 111.3, 111.18, 111.42(3), 111.42(9).

Hoss; American Sav. & Loan Ass'n of Brazoria County v., SDTex, 716 FSupp 979.—Rem of C 79(1), 82.

Hoss v. Fabacher, TexCivApp–Hous (1 Dist), 578 SW2d 454.—Bills & N 6, 7, 153, 157, 472.1, 474.

Hoss v. State, TexApp–Houston (14 Dist), 735 SW2d 899. —Controlled Subs 26, 27, 30, 79, 81.

Hossley v. Roadway Exp., Inc., TexCivApp–Beaumont, 419 SW2d 396, ref nre.—Carr 159(1); Judgm 185.1(4), 185.3(7).

Hoster; Thursland v., TexApp–Houston (1 Dist), 713 SW2d 757.—Deeds 192; Judgm 181(29); Tresp to T T 38(2).

Hoster; U.S. v., CA5 (Tex), 988 F2d 1374, appeal after new sentencing hearing 16 F3d 1216, appeal after remand 70 F3d 1267.—Crim Law 273.1(4), 1042, 1130(6), 1134(3), 1158(1); Sent & Pun 653(5), 668, 670, 686, 738, 765, 777.

Hostetter v. State, TexCrimApp, 527 SW2d 544.—Crim Law 419(1.5), 698(1), 1104(3), 1104(5), 1169.1(9); Witn 266.

Hostetter v. State, TexCrimApp, 117 SW2d 110, 135 TexCrim 22.—Crim Law 1088.12, 1182.

Hosxie v. State, TexCrimApp, 667 SW2d 539.—Crim Law 1167(1); Rape 29.

Hotchkin; Dickson v., CA5 (Tex), 202 F2d 426.—Fed Cts 724.

Hotchkiss v. Texas Emp. Ins. Ass'n, TexCivApp–Amarillo, 479 SW2d 336.—App & E 854(5); Trial 139.1(17),

HOTCHKISS

142; Work Comp 2, 11, 51, 1217, 1222, 1224, 1239, 1250, 1262, 1491, 1492, 1726.

Hotel & Restaurant Employees' International Alliance & Bartenders' International League of America v. Longley, TexCivApp–Eastland, 160 SW2d 124.—App & E 719(2), 753(2), 755, 773(1), 773(4); Const Law 1114, 1119, 1121(3), 1554; Inj 57, 94, 95; Labor & Emp 1376.

Hotel and Restaurant Employees International Alliance, Local No. 808; Tipton v., TexCivApp–Galveston, 149 SW2d 1028.—App & E 499(1), 500(1), 863; Inj 147; Labor & Emp 1376, 1379, 1386, 2045, 2050.

Hotel Dieu Hospital v. Huerta, Tex, 639 SW2d 462.—App & E 1177(6).

Hotel Dieu Hosp.; Huerta v., TexApp–El Paso, 636 SW2d 208, review gr, rev 639 SW2d 462.—Courts 100(1); Health 827; Trial 215.

Hotel Longview v. Pittman, TexCivApp–Texarkana, 276 SW2d 915, ref nre.—Atty & C 69, 72, 77; Contracts 19, 28(1); Estop 107, 110, 116; Land & Ten 82, 105; Plead 78; Princ & A 99, 147(3); Release 36; Trial 351.2(3.1); Witn 321.

Hotel Networks Corp.; Southwest Intelecom, Inc. v., TexApp–Austin, 997 SW2d 322, review den.—App & E 893(1); Contracts 127(4), 206.

Hotel Partners v. Craig, TexApp–Dallas, 993 SW2d 116, reh overr, and review den.—App & E 671(4), 842(1), 893(1), 911.3, 914.3, 1024.3; Appear 9(1); Const Law 3964; Courts 12(2.1), 12(2.5), 12(2.10), 12(2.20), 35.

Hotel Partners v. KPMG Peat Marwick, TexApp–Dallas, 847 SW2d 630, writ den.—App & E 842(2), 893(1), 1010.1(3), 1010.1(8.1), 1012.1(5); Appear 9(2); Courts 11, 12(2.1), 12(2.5), 12(2.10), 12(5), 35; Proc 48.

Hotel Ramada of Nevada; Kahn v., CA5 (Tex), 799 F2d 199.—Fed Cts 341; Inn 11(11).

Hotels.com; Taubenfeld v., NDTex, 385 FSupp2d 587.—Fed Civ Proc 1838; Sec Reg 60.27(1), 60.27(5), 60.27(7), 60.28(11), 60.28(13), 60.40, 60.46, 60.53.

Hotels.com, L.P. v. Canales, TexApp–San Antonio, 195 SW3d 147.—App & E 893(1), 913, 949; Inn 4; Parties 35.1, 35.7, 35.13, 35.33, 35.35, 35.71.

Hot-Hed Inc., In re, CA5 (Tex), 477 F3d 320, on remand Hot-Hed, Inc v. Safe House Habitats, Ltd, 2007 WL 556862.—Antitrust 16; Fed Cts 242.1; Mand 26; Rem of C 2, 19(1), 25(1), 107(7), 107(9); Trademarks 1420, 1421, 1583, 1584, 1800.

Hotman v. State, TexCivApp–Austin, 217 SW2d 890.—App & E 843(2), 931(6), 1008.1(8.1); Evid 183(4).

Hot-Mix, Inc.; Kettlewell v., TexCivApp–Hous (1 Dist), 566 SW2d 663.—Civil R 1326(7); Const Law 4324; Environ Law 265; Inj 200; Nuis 23(3), 34.

Hot Shot Messenger Service, Inc. v. State, TexApp–Austin, 818 SW2d 905.—App & E 5; Corp 507(12), 507(13); Proc 133, 148, 152, 153.

Hot Shot Messenger Service, Inc. v. State, TexApp–Austin, 798 SW2d 413, writ den.—App & E 1010.1(8.1); Evid 71, 89, 587.

Hot Spot Detectors, Inc. v. Farmers Supply Co. of Hartley, TexCivApp–Amarillo, 401 SW2d 109, ref nre.—Evid 265(7); Neglig 386, 1537; Prod Liab 81.1, 85.

Hott v. Pearcy/Christon, Inc., TexApp–Dallas, 663 SW2d 851, ref nre.—Contracts 10(5), 275; Estop 78(3), 87; Fraud 20; Judgm 186; Ven & Pur 18(1), 18(3), 18(4).

Hottell v. Hottell, TexCivApp–San Antonio, 454 SW2d 880.—App & E 80(6).

Hottell; Hottell v., TexCivApp–San Antonio, 454 SW2d 880.—App & E 80(6).

Hotton Aviation Co., Inc.; Cessna Aircraft Co. v., TexCivApp–Eastland, 620 SW2d 231, ref nre.—App & E 80(1).

Hotvedt v. Schlumberger Ltd. (N.V.), CA5 (Tex), 942 F2d 294, reh den 946 F2d 893.—Fed Cts 45, 818; Lim of Act 130(1), 130(5), 130(7).

Hotvedt v. Schlumberger Ltd. (N.V.), CA5 (Tex), 914 F2d 79, question certified 925 F2d 119, opinion with-

drawn and superseded on reh 942 F2d 294, reh den 946 F2d 893.—Corp 666; Fed Cts 45; Lim of Act 130(1), 130(6).

Hotze v. Brown, TexApp–Houston (14 Dist), 9 SW3d 404, review gr (2 pets), aff in part, rev in part Brown v. Todd, 53 SW3d 297.—Action 13; Aliens 133; App & E 66, 71(3), 913, 954(1); Corp 499; Ex & Ad 420; Infants 70; Inj 138.6, 138.9, 138.18, 138.46; Mental H 472.1; Mun Corp 990, 1017, 1027; Parties 1.

Houchin v. Godell, TexApp–Fort Worth, 635 SW2d 427.—App & E 638, 758.3(5), 907(4); Plead 228.14; Trover 32(4).

Houchins; Anderson v., TexCivApp–Galveston, 99 SW2d 1029.—Inj 256; Int Liq 6, 250.

Houchins v. Plainos, Tex, 110 SW2d 549, 130 Tex 413.—Const Law 619; Int Liq 24, 30; Statut 183.

Houchins; Plainos v., TexCivApp–Galveston, 106 SW2d 745, rev 110 SW2d 549, 130 Tex 413.—Const Law 632, 633; Int Liq 30, 41; Statut 161(1).

Houchins v. Scheltz, TexCivApp–Hous (14 Dist), 590 SW2d 745.—Accord 1, 15.1, 23, 25(2); App & E 241, 839(1), 1128.1; Assign 90; Decl Judgm 300; Judgm 181(11), 181(16), 185(2), 186, 540, 564(1), 587, 713(2), 720, 735; Trusts 147(1).

Houck v. Kroger Co., TexApp–Hous (14 Dist), 555 SW2d 803, ref nre.—App & E 954(1); Decl Judgm 258; Inj 36(1), 132, 135, 138.21, 138.31, 138.37; Land & Ten 86(1), 92(2).

Houck; Robbins v., TexCivApp–Galveston, 251 SW2d 429, ref nre.—Corp 401; Dedi 12, 19(5); Evid 387(4), 442(1), 443(1); Frds St of 158(3).

Houck v. Southern Pac. Ry. Co., CCWDTex, 38 F 226.—Civil R 1048.

Houck v. State Farm Mut. Auto. Ins. Co., TexCivApp–Beaumont, 394 SW2d 222, ref nre.—Insurance 3145, 3147, 3155, 3160(2), 3160(4), 3167, 3169, 3198(1); Princ & A 177(3.1), 178(1).

Houdaille Industries, Inc. v. Cunningham, Tex, 502 SW2d 544.—Pretrial Proc 379, 383.

Houdaille Industries, Inc.; State v., Tex, 632 SW2d 723.—Autos 128; Plead 228.14.

Houdaille Industries, Inc.; State v., TexCivApp–Hous (14 Dist), 617 SW2d 802, rev 632 SW2d 723.—Autos 127, 128; Carr 8; Statut 188.

Houde; U.S. v., CA5 (Tex), 596 F2d 696, reh den 604 F2d 671, cert den 100 SCt 452, 444 US 965, 62 LEd2d 377.—Consp 27, 28(3), 47(2), 47(12), 51; Controlled Subs 81; Courts 90(2); Crim Law 59(1), 578, 586, 589(1), 627.8(6), 713, 720(1), 726, 730(1), 1144.13(2.1), 1144.13(3), 1144.13(5), 1151.

Hough, In re, CA5 (Tex), 128 FedAppx 369.—Bankr 3779.

Hough v. Grapotte, TexComApp, 90 SW2d 1090, 127 Tex 144.—App & E 1050.1(1); Trial 350.2, 350.3(2.1).

Hough; Howland v., Tex, 570 SW2d 876.—Adv Poss 112; Bound 1, 3(3), 6; Lost Inst 1; Tresp to T T 38(1).

Hough; Howland v., TexCivApp–Eastland, 553 SW2d 162, writ gr, rev 570 SW2d 876.—App & E 1056.1(4.1); Tresp to T T 12, 38(3), 40(4), 41(1).

Hough v. Johnson, TexApp–Austin, 456 SW2d 775.—Pretrial Proc 66, 73, 221; Stip 3, 16, 17(2).

Hough v. McMillan, TexCivApp–Waco, 351 SW2d 609, ref nre.—Autos 181(2).

Hough; Sears, Roebuck & Co. v., TexCivApp–Hous (14 Dist), 421 SW2d 714.—App & E 930(1), 989, 996, 1002; Evid 201, 317(2), 471(17); Prod Liab 5; Sales 441(3), 442(1); Trial 105(1).

Hough v. State, TexApp–Texarkana, 929 SW2d 484, petition for discretionary review refused.—Arson 2, 25; Crim Law 26, 412.1(1), 412.1(4), 520(8), 534(1), 535(1), 535(2), 538(3); Ind & Inf 125(19.1).

Hough v. State, TexApp–Beaumont, 828 SW2d 97, petition for discretionary review refused.—Controlled Subs 6, 74; Crim Law 721(5), 726, 1171.1(2.1), 1171.1(6), 1171.5.

Hough; U.S. v., CA5 (Tex), 561 F2d 594, reh den 564 F2d 416.—Crim Law 273(4.1), 274(2).

Hougham v. State, TexCrimApp, 659 SW2d 410.—Crim Law 438(6), 577.16(1), 577.16(9), 665(1), 720(5), 728(3), 1043(2), 1168(2).

Houghtling v. Dusch, TexCivApp–Dallas, 413 SW2d 478. —App & E 213, 216(1), 221, 740(1), 1004(7); Autos 244(44), 244(58).

Houghton; American Standard, Inc. v., CA5 (Tex), 777 F2d 1042. See Seal Offshore, Inc. v. American Standard, Inc.

Houghton; American Standard, Inc. v., CA5 (Tex), 736 F2d 1078. See Seal Offshore, Inc. v. American Standard, Inc.

Houghton v. Brungardt, TexCivApp–El Paso, 89 SW2d 440.—Inj 118(3).

Houghton v. Fox, TexCivApp–El Paso, 93 SW2d 781.— Gaming 58.

Houghton; Millar v., CA5 (Tex), 115 F3d 348.—Fed Civ Proc 2559.

Houghton v. Port Terminal R.R. Ass'n, TexApp–Houston (14 Dist), 999 SW2d 39.—App & E 840(4), 969, 970(2), 1024.3, 1045(3), 1058(1), 1064.1(5), 1079; Courts 97(1); Evid 508, 535, 536, 544, 545, 546, 555.2; Jury 97(1), 105(1), 131(8), 133; Labor & Emp 2781, 2862, 2880, 2881, 2883, 2897; Trial 202, 241.

Houghton v. State, TexCrimApp, 345 SW2d 535, 171 TexCrim 91.—Crim Law 338(1), 380.

Houghton v. Texas State Life Ins. Co., CCA5 (Tex), 166 F2d 848, cert den 69 SCt 44, 335 US 822, 93 LEd 376.— Armed S 114(2), 115(4), 119; Fed Cts 935.1.

Houghton v. Texas State Life Ins. Co., NDTex, 68 FSupp 21, rev 166 F2d 848, cert den 69 SCt 44, 335 US 822, 93 LEd 376.—Armed S 115(1), 119, 122(6).

Houghton; U.S. v., NDTex, 388 FSupp 773.—Crim Law 273.4(1); Evid 5(2); Fed Civ Proc 2734.

Houghton v. Wholesale Electronic Supply, TexCivApp– Waco, 435 SW2d 216, ref nre.—Costs 194.16, 194.22; Damag 71; Land & Ten 48(2), 112(1), 134(3), 150(2), 210.

Houk v. C.I.R., CA5 (Tex), 173 F2d 821.—Assign 90; Int Rev 3420.

Houk Air Conditioning, Inc. v. Mortgage & Trust, Inc., TexCivApp–Waco, 517 SW2d 593.—Mech Liens 45; Mtg 151(3).

Houle v. U.S., CA5 (Tex), 493 F2d 915.—Sent & Pun 98, 100.

Houle v. U.S., CA5 (Tex), 463 F2d 1137.—Controlled Subs 68; Crim Law 29(8), 255.1, 412.2(3), 1132; Ind & Inf 144; Sent & Pun 1490.

Houle; U.S. v., CA5 (Tex), 428 F2d 816, cert den 91 SCt 127, 400 US 882, 27 LEd2d 120.—Controlled Subs 39, 68, 86; Crim Law 393(1), 1132; Cust Dut 125, 134.

Houlihan v. State, TexCrimApp, 579 SW2d 213.—Action 16; Const Law 2486; Crim Law 1017, 1023(14), 1192; Mand 28; Sent & Pun 1872(2), 1891, 1893.

Houlihan v. State, TexCrimApp, 551 SW2d 719, cert den 98 SCt 481, 434 US 955, 54 LEd2d 313.—Crim Law 394.1(3), 478(1); Sent & Pun 2006, 2021, 2022.

Houlihan Production Co. v. Seidler, WDTex, 125 BR 466. See HST Gathering Co., In re.

Houlis; Smith v., TexCivApp–Waco, 228 SW2d 900.— Trademarks 1704(1), 1707(6).

Houltin; U.S. v., CA5 (Tex), 566 F2d 1027, reh den 572 F2d 320, cert den 99 SCt 97, 439 US 826, 58 LEd2d 118, reh den 99 SCt 600, 439 US 997, 58 LEd2d 671, cert den Phillips v. US, 99 SCt 97, 439 US 826, 58 LEd2d 118, reh den 99 SCt 600, 439 US 998, 58 LEd2d 671.— Crim Law 394.1(1), 394.1(3), 394.4(1); Double J 6, 86, 108, 109.

Houltin; U.S. v., CA5 (Tex), 553 F2d 991.—Double J 186.

Houltin; U.S. v., CA5 (Tex), 525 F2d 943, reh den 533 F2d 1135, cert gr, vac in part Croucher v. United States, 97 SCt 725, 429 US 1034, 50 LEd2d 745, on remand 553

F2d 991, appeal after remand 566 F2d 1027, reh den 572 F2d 320, cert den 99 SCt 97, 439 US 826, 58 LEd2d 118, reh den 99 SCt 600, 439 US 997, 58 LEd2d 671, cert den Phillips v US, 99 SCt 97, 439 US 826, 58 LEd2d 118, reh den 99 SCt 600, 439 US 998, 58 LEd2d 671.—Crim Law 394.1(1), 394.1(3), 394.4(1), 394.5(2), 394.5(4), 394.6(4); Double J 151(1), 151(2).

Houma Industries, Inc. v. Energy Catering Services, Inc., CA5 (Tex), 35 F3d 1008. See Bertram v. Freeport McMoran, Inc.

Hourani, In re, TexApp–Houston (14 Dist), 20 SW3d 819. —Courts 70, 85(1); Judges 51(1), 51(2), 56; Mand 3(3), 4(4), 26, 28, 29; Statut 181(1), 181(2), 184, 188, 190, 206, 212.7.

Hourani; Value Recovery Group, Inc. v., SDTex, 115 FSupp2d 761.—Action 66; Fed Cts 241; Rem of C 2, 19(1), 25(1), 79(1), 102, 103, 107(7).

Hourigan v. Hourigan, TexCivApp–El Paso, 635 SW2d 556.—Child S 70, 85, 87; Divorce 252.2, 253(2), 286(2).

Hourigan; Hourigan v., TexCivApp–El Paso, 635 SW2d 556.—Child S 70, 85, 87; Divorce 252.2, 253(2), 286(2).

Hou-Scape, Inc. v. Lloyd, TexApp–Houston (1 Dist), 945 SW2d 202.—Alt Disp Res 112, 113, 119, 121, 123, 137, 143; Commerce 80.5; Mand 3(1), 60.

Housden; H & R Block, Ltd. v., EDTex, 24 FSupp2d 703.—Rem of C 3, 59.

Housden; H & R Block, Ltd. v., EDTex, 186 FRD 399.— Labor & Emp 2377.

Housden v. State, TexCrimApp, 98 SW2d 181, 131 TexCrim 256.—Crim Law 665(4), 703, 722.3, 725, 1057; Homic 1551.

House, Ex parte, TexCrimApp, 276 SW2d 846, 161 TexCrim 368.—Sent & Pun 384, 1129, 1175, 2032, 2034.

House, In re, TexApp–Amarillo, 65 SW3d 694.—Hab Corp 201, 287.1, 288, 289, 674.1, 814.

House v. Brackins, TexCivApp–Dallas, 130 SW2d 917.— App & E 907(3); Insurance 3441, 3447, 3454; Interpl 31.

House v. C. I. R., CA5 (Tex), 453 F2d 982.—Int Rev 3033, 3895; Statut 211.

House; Cooper v., TexCivApp–Tyler, 422 SW2d 261.— App & E 931(3), 989, 1011.1(4); Plead 111.12, 111.42(8).

House v. House, TexCivApp–Texarkana, 222 SW2d 337. —Adop 6, 17; App & E 994(3); Work Comp 451.

House; House v., TexCivApp–Texarkana, 222 SW2d 337. —Adop 6, 17; App & E 994(3); Work Comp 451.

House v. Humble Oil & Refining Co., TexCivApp– Beaumont, 97 SW2d 314, writ refused.—Deeds 120; Ex & Ad 367, 383, 388(2), 388(6), 397; Jud S 34.1.

House v. Kirby Lumber Corp., EDTex, 113 FSupp 322.— Rem of C 61(2), 102.

House v. Republicbank Brownwood, TexApp–Eastland, 641 SW2d 663.—Wills 529.

House v. State, TexCrimApp, 947 SW2d 251.—Crim Law 1037.1(1), 1171.1(1), 1179.

House v. State, TexCrimApp, 310 SW2d 339, 166 TexCrim 41.—Sent & Pun 2021.

House v. State, TexCrimApp, 233 SW2d 862, 155 TexCrim 275.—Crim Law 419(1), 457.

House v. State, TexCrimApp, 189 SW2d 497, 148 TexCrim 542.—Crim Law 594(1).

House v. State, TexCrimApp, 94 SW2d 1158, 130 TexCrim 520.—Crim Law 706(3), 1099.13.

House v. State, TexCrimApp, 81 SW2d 708, 128 TexCrim 404.—Crim Law 1038.1(1), 1066, 1169.1(3); Homic 1380.

House v. State, TexApp–Texarkana, 733 SW2d 278, petition for discretionary review refused.—Crim Law 938(1), 940, 942(1), 944.

House v. State, TexApp–Eastland, 880 SW2d 512, review gr, cause remanded.—Autos 355(8).

House v. State, TexApp–Houston (14 Dist), 222 SW3d 497, reh overr.—App & E 931(1), 1010.1(1); Mental H 36, 41, 440.

HOUSE

59 Tex D 2d—716

See Guidelines for Arrangement at the beginning of this Volume

House v. State, TexApp–Houston (14 Dist), 105 SW3d 182, petition for discretionary review refused, habeas corpus den 2006 WL 1875957.—Rob 4, 24.10.

House v. State, TexApp–Houston (14 Dist), 909 SW2d 214, petition for discretionary review gr, aff 947 SW2d 251.—Atty & C 22; Crim Law 379, 380, 698(3), 1036.1(2), 1169.2(1); Sent & Pun 312; Witn 350, 405(1), 405(2).

House; U.S. v., CA5 (Tex), 144 FedAppx 416, cert den 126 SCt 1078, 546 US 1115, 163 LEd2d 897.—Crim Law 273(4.1).

House v. U.S., CA5 (Tex), 80 FedAppx 316.—Hab Corp 632.1.

House; Wilson v., TexCivApp–Amarillo, 131 SW2d 995.—Atty & C 189, 190(2), 190(3), 192(2).

House; W. L. MacAtee & Sons v., TexComApp, 153 SW2d 460, 137 Tex 259.—Mech Liens 48, 108, 115(5).

House; W. L. Macatee & Sons v., TexCivApp–Galveston, 131 SW2d 785, rev 153 SW2d 460, 137 Tex 259.—App & E 1178(6); Mech Liens 115(5).

House v. 22 Texas Services, Inc., SDTex, 60 FSupp2d 602.—Const Law 3964, 3965(3), 3965(10); Corp 1.4(1), 1.4(2), 1.4(3), 1.7(2); Courts 12(2.5), 12(2.15); Fed Cts 76, 76.5, 76.10, 76.20, 79, 96.

House Builders, Inc. v. First Business Inv. Corp., TexCivApp–Waco, 448 SW2d 829, ref nre.—Corp 591; Lim of Act 58(1).

House Grain Co. v. Obst, TexApp–Corpus Christi, 659 SW2d 903, ref nre.—Alt Disp Res 113, 115, 210, 222, 325, 328, 335, 362(1), 363(6), 363(7), 374(5).

Household Credit Services, Inc. v. Dragoo, BkrtcyND–Tex, 219 BR 460. See Dragoo, In re.

Household Credit Services, Inc. v. Driscol, TexApp–El Paso, 989 SW2d 72, review den, and reh of petition for review den.—Antitrust 212, 291, 369; App & E 181, 207, 237(1), 930(1), 930(2), 989, 1001(1), 1001(3), 1002, 1003(3), 1003(5), 1003(7), 1004(1), 1004(11), 1060.1(2.1), 1151(2), 1175(1); Corp 397, 521; Damag 15, 48, 50.10, 50.20, 94, 100, 102, 130.1, 186, 187, 192, 216(3), 221(8); Estop 90(1); Judgm 707, 715(1); Labor & Emp 29; Neglig 1635; Princ & A 99; Torts 115, 332, 340, 438, 452; Trial 295(1).

Household Credit Services, Inc.; Waxler v., TexApp–Dallas, 106 SW3d 277, supplemented on denial of reh.—Judgm 185(2); Lim of Act 5(1), 43, 55(1), 55(2), 199(1); Neglig 202, 460.

Household Finance Corp. of Dallas v. Reyes, TexCivApp–Texarkana, 408 SW2d 739, writ dism.—App & E 907(3); Garn 42, 193.

Household Furniture Co.; Illich v., TexCivApp–El Paso, 103 SW2d 873, writ refused.—Exemp 4; Hus & W 269.

Household Goods Carriers' Bureau; Terrell v., CA5 (Tex), 494 F2d 16, reh den 496 F2d 878, cert dism 95 SCt 246, 419 US 987, 42 LEd2d 260.—Antitrust 963(1), 963(2), 976, 977(1), 984, 985; Courts 99(1); Evid 570; Fed Cts 916.1, 917, 950.

Household Goods Carriers' Bureau v. Terrell, CA5 (Tex), 452 F2d 152, appeal after remand 494 F2d 16, reh den 496 F2d 878, cert dism 95 SCt 246, 419 US 987, 42 LEd2d 260.—Action 53(1); Antitrust 958, 975, 977(3), 984; Fed Civ Proc 2011, 2173, 2173.1(1); Fed Cts 625, 630.1, 945.

Household Goods Carriers' Bureau v. Terrell, CA5 (Tex), 417 F2d 47, on reh 452 F2d 152, appeal after remand 494 F2d 16, reh den 496 F2d 878, cert dism 95 SCt 246, 419 US 987, 42 LEd2d 260.—Antitrust 968, 975, 977(3), 985; Damag 6, 163(1), 184; Fed Cts 774; Monop 28(7.7).

Household Intern., Inc.; Baldwin v., TexApp–Houston (14 Dist), 36 SW3d 273, rule 537(f) motion den.—App & E 1010.1(8.1); Const Law 3964, 3965(3); Corp 1.6(9), 665(0.5), 665(1), 672(1); Courts 12(2.1), 12(2.5), 12(2.10), 12(2.15), 12(2.25), 35, 39.

Houseman, In re, TexApp–Beaumont, 66 SW3d 368, corrected.—Mand 3(2.1), 4(4), 12, 40, 154(2), 154(9); Witn 206, 217, 219(3), 220, 221, 223.

Houseman v. Decuir, Tex, 283 SW2d 732, 155 Tex 127.—App & E 1060.1(1); Trial 114, 133.6(4).

Houseman; Decuir v., TexCivApp–Beaumont, 310 SW2d 591, ref nre.—Adv Poss 114(1); Judgm 199(3.14); Tresp to T T 38(1).

Houseman v. Decuir, TexCivApp–Beaumont, 281 SW2d 103, rev 283 SW2d 732, 155 Tex 127.—App & E 999(1); New Tr 72(9).

Houseman v. Mahin, Tex, 390 SW2d 732.—Child C 602; Plead 111.3, 111.12, 111.18; Venue 21, 22(4).

Houseman v. Mahin, TexCivApp–El Paso, 385 SW2d 437, writ gr, rev 390 SW2d 732.—App & E 907(3); Child C 7, 550, 579, 600, 661, 922(6); Domicile 10; Plead 45, 111.18; Venue 22(6), 22(7).

Houseman; Ward v., TexCivApp–Beaumont, 240 SW2d 456, writ refused.—Trial 356(4); Wills 166(1).

House of Doors, Inc.; Steves & Sons, Inc. v., TexApp–San Antonio, 749 SW2d 172, writ den.—Exemp 50(1); Garn 7.

House of Falcon, Inc. v. Gonzalez, TexCivApp–Corpus Christi, 583 SW2d 902.—Contracts 175(1), 187(1); Indem 81, 93; Lim of Act 141, 146(1), 148(1).

House of God Day Care v. Jim Snell Master Plumber, Inc., TexApp–Beaumont, 699 SW2d 705.—Time 10(9).

House of Lloyd, Inc.; Bullock v., TexApp–Austin, 797 SW2d 133, writ gr,rev Sharp v. House of Lloyd, Inc, 815 SW2d 245.—Statut 181(1), 219(1), 223.5(1), 245; Tax 2229.

House of Lloyd, Inc.; Sharp v., Tex, 815 SW2d 245.—Statut 181(2), 184, 223.5(2); Tax 2233, 2540.

House of Tobacco, Inc. v. Calvert, Tex, 394 SW2d 654.—Action 6; Const Law 3902, 4332; Licens 7(1), 38; Tax 3605.

House of Tobacco, Inc. v. Calvert, TexCivApp–Austin, 387 SW2d 74, writ gr, rev 394 SW2d 654.—Const Law 4332.

House of Vacuums Inc.; Scott Fetzer Co. v., CA5 (Tex), 381 F3d 477.—Trademarks 1081, 1085, 1098, 1106, 1110, 1420, 1421, 1429(1), 1459, 1461, 1463, 1466, 1467, 1523(1), 1523(2), 1610, 1619, 1629(2), 1629(4), 1691, 1754(2), 1756, 1800.

Houser v. Accurate Transmisson, TexApp–Austin, 968 SW2d 542. See Houser v. Smith.

Houser v. Dretke, CA5 (Tex), 395 F3d 560.—Const Law 4829; Hab Corp 818.

Houser v. Dretke, CA5 (Tex), 178 FedAppx 443.—Hab Corp 691.1.

Houser v. Sears, Roebuck & Co., CA5 (Tex), 627 F2d 756, 58 ALR Fed 87.—Civil R 1539, 1551; Fed Civ Proc 2608.1.

Houser v. Smith, TexApp–Austin, 968 SW2d 542.—App & E 854(1), 1047(1); Labor & Emp 3040, 3041, 3042, 3043; Neglig 202, 210, 215, 220, 1692.

Houser; State v., Tex, 156 SW2d 968, 138 Tex 28.—Mun Corp 972(4); Tax 2680, 2695, 2699(7), 2699(8), 2931, 2932, 2933.

Houser v. State, TexApp–Houston (14 Dist), 762 SW2d 219, petition for discretionary review refused.—Crim Law 374, 723(3), 1171.1(2.1); Sent & Pun 1381(3), 1381(6).

Houser; State v., TexCivApp–Texarkana, 137 SW2d 800, rev 156 SW2d 968, 138 Tex 28.—Tax 2160, 2515, 2937.

Houser v. Sunshine Laundries & Dry Cleaning Corp., TexCivApp–San Antonio, 438 SW2d 117, ref nre.—App & E 999(1), 1062.1, 1177(5), 1177(7); Damag 95, 96, 130.4; Neglig 1531, 1541; Plead 367(4); Trial 139.1(3), 140(1), 350.6(3), 366.

House the Homeless, Inc. v. Widnall, CA5 (Tex), 94 F3d 176, cert den 117 SCt 1434, 520 US 1169, 137 LEd2d 541.—Fed Cts 30, 776, 815; Fixt 1, 7; Inj 135, 138.1, 138.66; Social S 9.5.

For Later Case History Information, see KeyCite on WESTLAW

HOUSING

Housewright v. State, TexCrimApp, 573 SW2d 233.—Crim Law 632(2), 951(1), 974(2), 1144.17; Sent & Pun 205.

Housewright v. State, TexCrimApp, 225 SW2d 417, 154 TexCrim 101.—Crim Law 393(1), 438(8), 1091(4).

Housh; Ferguson v., TexCivApp–Galveston, 227 SW2d 590, writ refused.—Decl Judgm 366; Mines 74(5), 74(10); Ref of Inst 6.

Housholder; Chandler v., TexApp–Eastland, 722 SW2d 217, ref nre.—Antitrust 128, 195.

Housholder; Hilltop Auto Salvage v., TexApp–Eastland, 722 SW2d 217. See Chandler v. Housholder.

Housing Authority, City of Edgewood v. Sanders, TexApp–Tyler, 693 SW2d 2, ref nre.—Forci E & D 43(7); J P 148.

Housing Authority of City of Austin; Blackshear Residents Organization v., WDTex, 347 FSupp 1138.—Admin Law 417; Civil R 1082, 1302, 1331(3), 1419, 1448, 1453; Fed Civ Proc 186.15; Statut 219(6.1); U S 82(3.2).

Housing Authority of City of Austin, Tex.; Caro v., TexApp–Austin, 794 SW2d 901, writ den.—Land & Ten 94(2), 290(2); States 18.9; U S 82(3.5).

Housing Authority of City of Corpus Christi; Hinojosa v., TexApp–Corpus Christi, 896 SW2d 833, reh overr, and writ dism woj.—Abate & R 19; Antitrust 286; App & E 1050.1(1), 1051.1(1); Const Law 4083, 4112; Health 807; Land & Ten 291(0.5), 291(1), 291(18).

Housing Authority of City of Corpus Christi; Ibarra v., TexApp–Corpus Christi, 791 SW2d 224, writ den.—Const Law 4083; Land & Ten 291(16).

Housing Authority of City of Corpus Christi v. Massey, TexApp–Corpus Christi, 878 SW2d 624.—Estop 118; Judgm 489, 521, 540, 634, 713(2), 715(1), 720, 724, 739; Mun Corp 717.5(8).

Housing Authority of City of Crystal City v. Lopez, TexApp–Austin, 955 SW2d 152, reh overr.—App & E 171(1), 930(1), 1001(3), 1003(6), 1003(7), 1004(11), 1140(2), 1182; Damag 192; Labor & Emp 776, 867, 871; Mun Corp 218(10); Offic 76.

Housing Authority of City of Dallas v. Baylor, CA5 (Tex), 858 F2d 1071. See Walker v. City of Mesquite.

Housing Authority of City of Dallas; Blackman v., Tex, 254 SW2d 103, 152 Tex 21.—App & E 629; Time 10(1), 10(9).

Housing Authority of City of Dallas v. Blackman, TexCivApp–Dallas, 254 SW2d 548, aff 254 SW2d 103, 152 Tex 21.—Em Dom 150; Holidays 5; Sunday 30(1); Time 10(9).

Housing Authority of City of Dallas v. Brown, TexCivApp–Dallas, 256 SW2d 656.—App & E 242(2); Em Dom 148, 262(4), 262(5); Evid 18, 474(18); New Tr 120.

Housing Authority of City of Dallas; Crockett v., TexCivApp–Dallas, 274 SW2d 187.—Costs 257; Damag 15; Deeds 38(1); Em Dom 191(6), 254; Estop 92(4).

Housing Authority of City of Dallas; Crowell v., Tex, 495 SW2d 887.—Contracts 114; Land & Ten 164(1).

Housing Authority of City of Dallas; Crowell v., TexCivApp–Tyler, 483 SW2d 864, writ gr, rev 495 SW2d 887.—Contracts 108(1), 114; Land & Ten 164(1).

Housing Authority of City of Dallas v. Dixon, TexCivApp–Dallas, 250 SW2d 636, ref nre.—Em Dom 247(2), 247(4), 249, 258, 262(5).

Housing Authority of City of Dallas; Herndon v., TexCivApp–Dallas, 261 SW2d 221, writ refused.—Em Dom 203(7), 222(4).

Housing Authority of City of Dallas v. Higginbotham, Tex, 143 SW2d 79, 135 Tex 158, 130 ALR 1053, answer to certified question conformed to 143 SW2d 95.—Admin Law 9, 330; Const Law 2400, 2408, 2409, 2427(1), 2437, 2898; Em Dom 14, 17, 56, 67, 68, 191(3); Health 357, 358; Mun Corp 266, 407(2), 717.5(1); States 119; Statut 221; Tax 2289.

Housing Authority of City of Dallas v. Higginbotham, TexCivApp–Dallas, 143 SW2d 95.—Courts 475(8); Mun Corp 717.5(1).

Housing Authority of City of Dallas; Highlands of McKamy IV and V Community Ass'n v., CA5 (Tex), 129 F3d 831. See Walker v. City of Mesquite, Tex.

Housing Authority of City of Dallas v. Hubbard, TexCivApp–Dallas, 274 SW2d 165.—App & E 304; Em Dom 133, 149(2.1), 202(2), 221, 255; Evid 142(1); Trial 84(1).

Housing Authority of City of Dallas v. Hubbell, TexCivApp–Dallas, 325 SW2d 880, ref nre.—App & E 1050.2, 1062.1, 1172(2), 1178(6); Contracts 221(1), 326; Damag 218, 221(5.1); Extort 34; Labor & Emp 3141; Mun Corp 362(2), 374(4), 374(6), 1040; Refer 7(1); Torts 242, 436; Trial 350.5(1), 352.5(3), 352.5(4), 352.12.

Housing Authority of City of Dallas; Loumparoff v., TexCivApp–Dallas, 261 SW2d 224.—App & E 201(2), 231(7); Em Dom 124, 191(6), 195, 201, 222(4), 255, 257, 262(2); Evid 113(16), 379, 474(18), 543(3); Trial 66; Witn 280.

Housing Authority of City of Dallas; McCord v., TexCivApp–Dallas, 234 SW2d 108, ref nre 236 SW2d 115, 149 Tex 587.—Em Dom 9; Mun Corp 282(1).

Housing Authority of City of Dallas; Miers v., Tex, 266 SW2d 842, 153 Tex 236, answer to certified question conformed to 268 SW2d 325, ref nre.—Courts 247(5); Em Dom 191(6), 241.

Housing Authority of City of Dallas; Miers v., TexCivApp–Fort Worth, 268 SW2d 796, ref nre.—Em Dom 237(1); Judgm 181(1), 185.3(1); Records 7.

Housing Authority of City of Dallas; Miers v., TexCivApp–Dallas, 266 SW2d 487, certified question answered 266 SW2d 842, 153 Tex 236, answer to certified question conformed to 268 SW2d 325, ref nre.—Const Law 4076; Em Dom 3, 17, 19, 40, 77, 124, 172, 191(6), 196, 205, 255, 262(1), 262(5); Evid 366(2); Mun Corp 213; Stip 14(7).

Housing Authority of City of Dallas; Miers v., TexCivApp–El Paso, 268 SW2d 325, ref nre.—Em Dom 263.

Housing Authority of City of Dallas v. Nealy, TexCivApp–Austin, 252 SW2d 967.—Em Dom 205; Evid 142(3).

Housing Authority of City of Dallas; Shambry v., Tex, 255 SW2d 184, 152 Tex 122.—App & E 1082(1).

Housing Authority of City of Dallas v. Shambry, TexCivApp–Austin, 252 SW2d 963, ref nre 255 SW2d 184, 152 Tex 122.—Em Dom 148, 202(4), 205, 262(4); Evid 142(3), 555.6(10).

Housing Authority of City of Dallas v. Sutton, TexCivApp–Austin, 252 SW2d 968.—Em Dom 205; Evid 142(3).

Housing Authority of City of Dallas; Thomas v., Tex, 264 SW2d 93, 153 Tex 137, cert den 75 SCt 29, 348 US 818, 99 LEd 645.—Em Dom 188.

Housing Authority of City of Dallas; Thomas v., TexCivApp–Eastland, 258 SW2d 428, rev 264 SW2d 93, 153 Tex 137, cert den 75 SCt 29, 348 US 818, 99 LEd 645.—Em Dom 76.

Housing Authority of City of Dallas; Townsend v., TexCivApp–Amarillo, 277 SW2d 211, ref nre.—Em Dom 17; Fraud 64(1); Mun Corp 221, 225(1); Princ & A 124(1); Trial 139.1(7), 178, 350.1, 350.2, 365.3.

Housing Authority of City of Dallas; U.S. Dept. of Housing and Urban Development v., CA5 (Tex), 912 F2d 819. See Walker v. U.S. Dept. of Housing and Urban Development.

Housing Authority of City of Dallas; Vilbig v., TexCivApp–Dallas, 287 SW2d 323, ref nre.—Corp 434, 439; Deeds 211(3); Em Dom 17, 55, 198(2), 322, 325; Mun Corp 225(3).

Housing Authority of City of Dallas; Wooten v., CA5 (Tex), 723 F2d 390.—Civil R 1482.

Housing Authority of City of Dallas, Tex. v. Northland Ins. Co., NDTex, 333 FSupp2d 595.—Insurance 2927, 2929, 3120, 3335.

Housing Authority of City of El Paso; Brooks v., TexApp–El Paso, 926 SW2d 316, reh overr.—App & E 275, 931(1), 1008.1(2), 1010.2, 1050.1(1), 1056.1(1), 1079, 1106(2), 1106(5), 1177(8); Evid 351, 355(1), 373(1); Mun Corp 717.5(8).

Housing Authority of City of El Paso; Chavez v., CA5 (Tex), 973 F2d 1245.—Const Law 1443, 3523, 3905, 4080, 4112; Fed Cts 850.1; Mun Corp 717.5(6); U S 82(3.5).

Housing Authority of City of El Paso; Chavez v., TexApp–El Paso, 897 SW2d 523, writ den, cert den 116 SCt 1674, 517 US 1188, 134 LEd2d 778.—App & E 373(1), 387(1), 387(3), 387(6), 388, 389(1), 395, 428(1); Trial 388(1), 388(2).

Housing Authority of City of El Paso; Chavez v., TexApp–El Paso, 876 SW2d 416, on reconsideration 897 SW2d 523, writ den, cert den 116 SCt 1674, 517 US 1188, 134 LEd2d 778.—App & E 387(6), 775.

Housing Authority of City of El Paso v. City of El Paso, TexApp–El Paso, 141 SW3d 663, reh overr.—App & E 920(3), 946, 954(1), 954(2); Inj 132, 135, 138.1, 138.3, 138.6; Mun Corp 192.

Housing Authority of City of El Paso; De La O v., WDTex, 316 FSupp2d 481, aff in part, vac in part, remanded 417 F3d 495, cert den 126 SCt 808, 546 US 1062, 163 LEd2d 629.—Civil R 1305; Const Law 1021, 1739, 1747, 1751, 1765, 1871, 3051, 3476, 3523; Mun Corp 717.5(4).

Housing Authority of City of El Paso; Gomez v., WDTex, 805 FSupp 1363, aff 20 F3d 1169, cert den 115 SCt 198, 513 US 873, 130 LEd2d 129.—U S 70(5), 82(3.2), 82(3.5).

Housing Authority of City of El Paso v. Guerra, TexApp–El Paso, 963 SW2d 946, reh overr, and review den, and reh of petition for review overr.—App & E 969, 1001(3), 1004(1); Labor & Emp 753, 808, 810, 861, 863(2), 867, 871, 874; Trial 352.1(1).

Housing Authority of City of El Paso v. Harper, TexCivApp–El Paso, 241 SW2d 347.—Mun Corp 191.

Housing Authority of City of El Paso; Portillo v., TexApp–El Paso, 652 SW2d 568.—Judgm 181(11); Neglig 1010, 1071; R R 276(3).

Housing Authority of City of El Paso; Potomac Leasing Co. v., TexApp–El Paso, 743 SW2d 712, writ den.—Usury 33.

Housing Authority of City of El Paso v. Rangel, TexApp–El Paso, 131 SW3d 542, reh overr, and review gr, judgment rev, and remanded by agreement.—App & E 863, 893(1), 916(1); Mun Corp 218(10); Offic 61, 66, 110; Plead 104(1).

Housing Authority of City of El Paso; Renteria v., TexApp–El Paso, 96 SW3d 454, reh overr, and review den.—App & E 171(1); Courts 35; Mun Corp 742(4), 847, 848; Plead 104(1); States 191.4(1).

Housing Authority of City of El Paso v. Rodriguez-Yepez, Tex, 843 SW2d 475.—Pretrial Proc 41.

Housing Authority of City of El Paso v. Rodriguez-Yepez, TexApp–El Paso, 828 SW2d 499, writ den with per curiam opinion 843 SW2d 475.—App & E 232(0.5); Pretrial Proc 24, 249.

Housing Authority of City of El Paso; Valenzuela v., TexCivApp–El Paso, 520 SW2d 406, ref nre.—Forci E & D 43(2).

Housing Authority of City of El Paso; Vasquez v., CA5 (Tex), 271 F3d 198, reh gr, opinion vac 289 F3d 350.—Const Law 863, 1150, 1490, 1502, 1686, 1730, 1737, 1745, 1749, 1751, 1765; Fed Cts 776; Mun Corp 717.5(1).

Housing Authority of City of El Paso; Vasquez v., WDTex, 103 FSupp2d 927, rev and remanded 271 F3d 198, reh gr, opinion vac 289 F3d 350.—Civil R 1305, 1394; Const Law 1141, 1178, 1737, 1739, 1746, 1747,

1765, 3060, 3523, 3635; Elections 309; Mun Corp 717.5(1).

Housing Authority of City of El Paso v. Yepez, TexApp–El Paso, 790 SW2d 730, motion den, and writ dism woj.—Inj 32, 138.27.

Housing Authority of City of El Paso, Tex.; de la O v., CA5 (Tex), 417 F3d 495, cert den 126 SCt 808, 546 US 1062, 163 LEd2d 629.—Const Law 977, 1502, 1751, 1765, 1876; Fed Civ Proc 2539; Fed Cts 12.1; Inj 22; Mun Corp 717.5(4).

Housing Authority of City of Galveston v. Henderson, TexCivApp–Galveston, 267 SW2d 843.—Em Dom 202(1), 205, 262(4), 262(5); Evid 535, 543(3), 545, 546; Trial 76; Witn 245, 282.5.

Housing Authority of City of Galveston; Norris v., SDTex, 980 FSupp 885.—Civil R 1128, 1405; Contracts 143(2), 152, 176(1), 186(1); Fed Civ Proc 2497.1; Labor & Emp 40(2), 110, 835, 861, 873; Mun Corp 192, 218(3), 218(10), 229; Princ & A 136(1); States 108, 191.4(1), 191.6(1), 191.8(1).

Housing Authority of City of Grapeland; Forward v., TexApp–Tyler, 864 SW2d 167, reh den.—App & E 840(4); Pretrial Proc 41, 250, 714.

Housing Authority of City of Harlingen; Barajas v., TexApp–Corpus Christi, 882 SW2d 853.—App & E 173(2), 852; Contracts 143(2), 176(2); Judgm 183; Mun Corp 717.5(6).

Housing Authority of City of Harlingen v. State ex rel. Velasquez, TexCivApp–Corpus Christi, 539 SW2d 911, ref nre.—Action 2, 13; App & E 1010.1(3); Mun Corp 717.5(1); Offic 94.

Housing Authority of City of Harlingen v. Valdez, TexApp–Corpus Christi, 841 SW2d 860, reh overr, and writ den.—Civil R 1715; Costs 199, 260(5); Decl Judgm 8, 45, 83, 272, 314.

Housing Authority of City of Houston; Mortellaro v., TexCivApp–Waco, 316 SW2d 813, ref nre.—Em Dom 231.

Housing Authority of City of Houston; Ramirez Co., Inc. v., TexApp–Houston (14 Dist), 777 SW2d 167.—Impl & C C 92, 121; Judgm 185.3(8); Mun Corp 249, 374(1).

Housing Authority of City of San Antonio; Adames v., TexCivApp–San Antonio, 392 SW2d 806, ref nre.—Land & Ten 164(1).

Housing Authority of City of San Antonio; Hackett v., CA5 (Tex), 750 F2d 1308, cert den 106 SCt 146, 474 US 850, 88 LEd2d 121.—Evid 318(1), 368(12); Fed Civ Proc 2334.

Housing Authority of City of San Antonio; Marshall v., Tex, 198 SW3d 782.—Action 6; App & E 714(5), 781(1), 781(7), 1175(1); Costs 196; Forci E & D 6(2); Land & Ten 291(14), 291(18); Mun Corp 717.5(8).

Housing Authority of City of San Antonio; Marshall v., TexApp–San Antonio, 183 SW3d 689, reh overr, and review gr, vac 198 SW3d 782.—Const Law 2317; Land & Ten 289, 291(18).

Housing Authority of City of San Antonio v. Newton, TexCivApp–Waco, 235 SW2d 197.—Contracts 176(10); Cust & U 19(3); Lim of Act 46(3); Mun Corp 220(8).

Housing Authority of City of San Antonio, Tex.; Benavides v., CA5 (Tex), 238 F3d 667, reh den.—Fed Cts 12.1, 13, 612.1, 724.

Housing Authority of City of Taylor; Marshall v., WDTex, 866 FSupp 999, aff 51 F3d 1045.—Admin Law 413; Fed Civ Proc 2470.1, 2543, 2544, 2546, 2552; Infants 50, 58(1), 102; U S 82(2), 82(3.2).

Housing Authority of City of Uvalde; Perez v., CA5 (Tex), 95 FedAppx 51.—Const Law 1947, 4172(6); Mun Corp 192.

Housing Authority of City of Victoria; Transamerica Ins. Co. v., TexApp–Corpus Christi, 669 SW2d 818, ref nre.—Contracts 284(4), 295(1); Lim of Act 47(3); Mun Corp 345, 348; Princ & S 76; Pub Contr 41.

Housing Authority of City of Victoria, Tex.; Campbell & Son Const. Co., Inc. v., TexApp–Corpus Christi, 655 SW2d 271.—App & E 854(1), 912; Corp 1.4(1), 1.7(2); Venue 22(1), 22(4), 22(6).

Housing Authority of El Paso v. Lira, TexCivApp–El Paso, 282 SW2d 746, ref nre.—Contracts 105; Em Dom 126(1), 148; Home 128; Spec Perf 25.

Housing Authority of Texas City; Tex-Craft Builders, Inc. v., TexCivApp–Waco, 404 SW2d 337.—Contracts 328(1), 346(15), 349(1); Damag 189; Plead 78.

Housing Authority of the City of El Paso; Gomez v., TexApp–El Paso, 148 SW3d 471, reh overr, and review den, cert den 126 SCt 379, 546 US 872, 163 LEd2d 166. —App & E 893(1); Civil R 1304, 1326(1), 1343, 1345, 1351(1), 1355, 1376(4), 1395(3); Const Law 4112; Courts 35, 39; Mun Corp 745; Plead 104(1), 111.48; States 191.1, 191.4(1), 191.10.

Housing Authority of the City of Galveston; Norris v., SDTex, 962 FSupp 96.—Damag 50.10; Mun Corp 218(10).

Housing Authority of the City of Laredo; Hinojosa v., TexApp–San Antonio, 940 SW2d 763.—Contracts 143.5, 156; Mun Corp 717.5(6).

Housing, Inc.; Arthur, Ross and Peters v., CA5 (Tex), 508 F2d 562.—Fed Cts 84.

Housland, Inc.; Campos v., SDTex, 824 FSupp 100.— Rem of C 3, 25(1), 79(1), 107(11).

Housman v. State, TexCrimApp, 230 SW2d 541, 155 TexCrim 49.—Abort 9; Crim Law 365(1), 451(1), 476, 655(1), 656(3), 698(1), 706(3), 713.

Houssiere v. Houssiere, TexCivApp–San Antonio, 389 SW2d 533.—App & E 728(3); Divorce 51, 127(3), 127(4), 130, 146, 150, 184(6.1), 184(7), 223, 227(1), 252.3(2).

Houssiere; Houssiere v., TexCivApp–San Antonio, 389 SW2d 533.—App & E 728(3); Divorce 51, 127(3), 127(4), 130, 146, 150, 184(6.1), 184(7), 223, 227(1), 252.3(2).

Houston, In re, TexApp–Houston (14 Dist), 92 SW3d 870. —Const Law 1106, 4494; Contempt 20, 40, 55, 60(3), 61(4), 63(1), 63(3), 63(5), 81; Execution 421; Hab Corp 504, 528.1; Inj 219, 223, 230(2), 230(3), 230(4); Judgm 524.

Houston; Atlanta Life Ins. Co. v., TexCivApp–El Paso, 92 SW2d 1108, writ dism.—Insurance 2037.

Houston; Cole v., TexCivApp–Fort Worth, 152 SW2d 522, mod 162 SW2d 404, 139 Tex 150.—Adop 6, 8, 16, 21; Ex & Ad 17(3), 236; Wills 384.

Houston; Curnutte v., TexCivApp–San Antonio, 163 SW2d 675, writ refused wom.—Usury 119.

Houston; Davis v., TexApp–Fort Worth, 734 SW2d 210.— Child 34.

Houston v. Edgeworth, CA5 (Tex), 993 F2d 51. See Edgeworth, Matter of.

Houston v. Ellis, CA5 (Tex), 267 F2d 43.—Crim Law 1158(1).

Houston v. Ellis, CA5 (Tex), 252 F2d 186.—Hab Corp 751; Sent & Pun 348.

Houston v. Estelle, CA5 (Tex), 569 F2d 372, reh den 572 F2d 320.—Const Law 268(8), 4629; Crim Law 713, 720(1), 720(6), 730(1); Hab Corp 380.1, 385, 401, 421, 481, 497.

Houston v. Grocers Supply Co., Inc., TexApp–Houston (14 Dist), 625 SW2d 798.—App & E 1073(1); Evid 351; Judgm 185.3(21); Libel 41, 45(1), 51(1), 123(8).

Houston; Gulf Coast Regional Blood Center v., TexApp–Fort Worth, 745 SW2d 557.—Const Law 1231, 3986; Pretrial Proc 19, 27.1, 40, 382; Records 32.

Houston v. Harberger, TexCivApp–Fort Worth, 377 SW2d 673, ref nre.—Estates 1; Wills 6, 441, 470(1), 472, 523, 590, 614(2), 617, 634(3), 634(7), 634(9), 635, 637.

Houston v. Holder, CA5 (Tex), 60 F3d 230. See Omni Video, Inc., Matter of.

Houston v. Interstate Circuit, TexCivApp–Galveston, 132 SW2d 903.—App & E 920(3), 954(2); Evid 157(1); Inj 98(1); Libel 19.

Houston; Mergele v., TexCivApp–San Antonio, 436 SW2d 951, ref nre.—Acct Action on 10; App & E 612(1); Costs 194.38; Evid 498.5, 543(4); New Tr 26; Partners 311(1); Plead 236(1), 236(3).

Houston v. Mike Black Auto Sales, Inc., TexApp–Corpus Christi, 788 SW2d 696.—Antitrust 141, 196, 363, 390; App & E 927(7), 997(3).

Houston v. Moore Inv. Co., TexApp–Hous (1 Dist), 559 SW2d 850.—Contracts 143(2); Mines 55(4), 79.1(3); Plead 238(1), 258(5).

Houston v. Nelson, TexApp–Corpus Christi, 147 SW3d 589.—Admin Law 790, 791; Schools 130, 133.6(5), 133.6(6); Statut 219(1), 219(4).

Houston v. Northwest Village, Ltd., TexApp–Amarillo, 113 SW3d 443.—Judgm 181(33); Land & Ten 167(8), 168(1), 169(11).

Houston; Professional Microfilming, Inc. v., TexApp–Fort Worth, 661 SW2d 767.—Mand 28; Pretrial Proc 377.

Houston v. Randolph, TexCivApp–Amarillo, 88 SW2d 1051.—Abate & R 15.

Houston; Richardson Lifestyle Ass'n v., TexApp–Dallas, 853 SW2d 796, reh den, and writ den.—Condo 7; Contracts 143(2), 143.5, 147(2), 147(3), 152, 176(1).

Houston; Riedel v., TexCivApp–Waco, 534 SW2d 937, ref nre.—Deeds 165; Em Dom 274(4); States 191.9(4).

Houston v. Schuhmann, TexCivApp–Amarillo, 92 SW2d 1086, writ refused.—Wills 439, 476, 524(2), 524(8).

Houston v. Shaw Transports Co., TexCivApp–Galveston, 296 SW2d 631.—App & E 544(3); Autos 247; Evid 215(1); Neglig 451; Witn 275(1).

Houston v. Shear, TexCivApp–Austin, 210 SW 976, writ gr, and writ dism.—Bankr 11, 216, 438; Corp 547(1); Evid 43(4); Execution 250, 251(2), 268, 278; Subrog 22, 26.

Houston; Shivers Well Service, Inc. v., TexApp–Fort Worth, 736 SW2d 251.—Mand 3(2.1), 3(3).

Houston; Southwestern Life Ins. Co. v., TexCivApp–Fort Worth, 121 SW2d 619, writ refused.—App & E 1175(6); Contracts 143(2), 143(3), 143.5, 147(2); Costs 42(6), 236; Insurance 1832(1), 2430, 2434(1), 2440; Stip 8.

Houston v. State, TexCrimApp, 846 SW2d 848.—Crim Law 1072.

Houston v. State, TexCrimApp, 663 SW2d 455.—Crim Law 1144.13(2.1).

Houston v. State, TexCrimApp, 652 SW2d 389.—Crim Law 1170.5(1).

Houston v. State, TexCrimApp, 626 SW2d 43.—Witn 321, 380(5.1).

Houston v. State, TexCrimApp, 556 SW2d 345.—Double J 52, 148; Ind & Inf 191(2).

Houston v. State, TexCrimApp, 527 SW2d 551.—Controlled Subs 8, 62.

Houston v. State, TexCrimApp, 506 SW2d 907.—Arrest 63.4(8), 71.1(3); Crim Law 814(17), 855(7), 1130(5).

Houston v. State, TexCrimApp, 503 SW2d 540.—Crim Law 404.65, 726, 730(1), 1037.2, 1170.5(1), 1171.3.

Houston v. State, TexCrimApp, 496 SW2d 94.—Crim Law 855(5); Jury 131(8).

Houston v. State, TexCrimApp, 490 SW2d 851.—Crim Law 1034, 1044.1(1), 1166(7).

Houston v. State, TexCrimApp, 486 SW2d 365.—Sent & Pun 2006, 2030.

Houston v. State, TexCrimApp, 486 SW2d 363.—Burg 28(1), 41(3); Crim Law 829(3), 1167(1); Ind & Inf 159(4).

Houston v. State, TexCrimApp, 446 SW2d 309.—Crim Law 1130(3).

Houston v. State, TexCrimApp, 428 SW2d 353.—Arrest 63.4(11), 71.1(2.1); Crim Law 394.4(9), 720(8), 796, 1037.1(1), 1037.2, 1044.1(8); Rob 24.15(2).

Houston v. State, TexCrimApp, 426 SW2d 868.—Crim Law 304(5), 564(1); Rob 24.15(2).

Houston v. State, TexCrimApp, 298 SW2d 127, 164 Tex-Crim 202.—Crim Law 1169.3; Prost 28.

Houston v. State, TexCrimApp, 287 SW2d 643, 162 Tex-Crim 551, cert den 76 SCt 1042, 351 US 975, 100 LEd 1492, reh den 77 SCt 28, 352 US 861, 1 LEd2d 72, motion den 77 SCt 152, 352 US 905, 1 LEd2d 115.—Crim Law 570(1), 720(1), 723(2), 1137(1); Jury 29(2), 29(5), 32(1), 75(1), 149.

Houston v. State, TexCrimApp, 203 SW2d 621, 150 Tex-Crim 410.—Rob 24.50.

Houston v. State, TexCrimApp, 169 SW2d 184, 145 Tex-Crim 437.—Int Liq 236(5), 239(1).

Houston v. State, TexCrimApp, 158 SW2d 1004, 143 TexCrim 460.—Autos 316, 346, 356, 357; Crim Law 781(8), 789(4), 814(1), 814(3), 814(16), 814(20), 829(1), 1172.3, 1181(2); Ind & Inf 137(6).

Houston v. State, TexApp–Houston (1 Dist), 743 SW2d 751.—Jury 149.

Houston v. State, TexApp–Fort Worth, 638 SW2d 160, petition for discretionary review refused.—Crim Law 641.13(1), 641.13(6), 822(1), 1036.1(8).

Houston v. State, TexApp–Austin, 208 SW3d 585.—Courts 97(1); Crim Law 338(7), 369.1, 396(1), 409(5), 641.13(1), 1119(1), 1134(3), 1137(5), 1144.10, 1163(2); Hab Corp 295.

Houston v. State, TexApp–Austin, 185 SW3d 917, petition for discretionary review refused.—Crim Law 412.2(2), 412.2(4), 419(3), 518(2), 867, 1155, 1169.1(9), 1169.5(1).

Houston v. State, TexApp–Waco, 832 SW2d 180, petition for discretionary review dism, and petition for discretionary review gr, petition for discretionary review dism with per curiam opinion 846 SW2d 848.—Crim Law 338(7), 369.2(2), 369.2(5).

Houston v. State, TexApp–Corpus Christi, 652 SW2d 472.—Crim Law 1181.5(8); Larc 40(6).

Houston v. State, TexApp–Corpus Christi, 636 SW2d 7, remanded 640 SW2d 605, on remand 652 SW2d 472.—Crim Law 460; Larc 59.

Houston v. State, TexApp–Houston (14 Dist), 201 SW3d 212.—Crim Law 273.1(2), 273.1(4), 273.1(5), 274(3.1), 274(8), 274(9), 641.7(1), 1086.4, 1130(5), 1134(2), 1144.1, 1147; Sent & Pun 60.

Houston v. State, TexApp–Houston (14 Dist), 916 SW2d 705.—Mal Mis 1; Sent & Pun 1311, 1314, 1326.

Houston v. State, TexApp–Houston (14 Dist), 735 SW2d 903, petition for discretionary review refused.—Crim Law 37(1), 372(13), 796, 1038.1(3.1).

Houston v. State, TexApp–Houston (14 Dist), 667 SW2d 157.—Crim Law 307, 552(1), 552(3), 641.13(1), 641.13(2.1), 728(2), 822(1), 822(7), 944, 1144.13(3), 1144.13(5), 1144.13(6); Homic 1184.

Houston; Tortuguero Logging Operation, Limited v., TexCivApp–San Antonio, 349 SW2d 315, ref nre.—Accord 7(1); Damag 163(2); Evid 81; Interest 39(3); Logs 8(5).

Houston; U.S. v., CA5 (Tex), 364 F3d 243, reh den 115 FedAppx 766.—Crim Law 1139, 1158(1); Sent & Pun 705, 731, 793, 962.

Houston; U.S. v., CA5 (Tex), 745 F2d 333, cert den 105 SCt 1369, 470 US 1008, 84 LEd2d 388.—Crim Law 1042; Sent & Pun 235, 294.

Houston; White v., TexCivApp–El Paso, 103 SW2d 1073, writ dism.—Partners 131, 145, 146(2), 217(1), 258(2), 258(8); Venue 7.5(4).

Houston v. Zeller, CA5 (Tex), 91 FedAppx 956.—Civil R 1354; Prisons 17(2); Sent & Pun 1546.

Houston Agr. Credit Corp.; Carlton v., TexCivApp–Austin, 376 SW2d 363, writ dism.—App & E 912; Mtg 427(4); Plead 111.6, 111.47; Venue 17, 22(6).

Houston Agr. Credit Corp.; Turner v., TexCivApp–Hous (1 Dist), 601 SW2d 61, ref nre.—Can of Inst 3, 24(1), 52; Evid 442(1); Fraud 3, 59(1).

Houston Agricultural Credit Corp. v. U.S., CA5 (Tex), 736 F2d 233.—U S 147(4), 147(10), 147(21).

Houston Aircraft Co. v. Citizens State Bank, Houston, TexCivApp–Galveston, 184 SW2d 335.—Alt of Inst 8, 20.

Houston-American Finance Corp.; Jemerson v., TexCivApp–Dallas, 351 SW2d 574.—App & E 302(1); Usury 142(5).

Houston-American Finance Corp. v. Travis, TexCivApp–Dallas, 343 SW2d 323, ref nre.—App & E 281(1), 758.2, 766, 886; Damag 50, 56.20, 133; Lim of Act 55(1); Trial 352.5(3), 352.5(5), 366.

Houston-American Life Ins. Co. v. Tate, TexCivApp–Waco, 358 SW2d 645.—Abate & R 52; Antitrust 583; App & E 1140(1); Corp 1.4(1), 1.4(3), 1.6(13); Damag 94, 184, 189.5; Insurance 1611, 1613; Torts 453.

Houston & North Tex. Motor Freight Lines; Dallas General Drivers, Warehousemen & Helpers, Local Union No. 745 v., Tex, 245 SW2d 481, 151 Tex 24.—Labor & Emp 2125.

Houston & North Tex. Motor Freight Lines v. Elliott, NDTex, 63 FSupp 577.—Inj 12, 16; Labor & Emp 987, 2016, 2028, 2057; Statut 208; War 402.

Houston & North Tex. Motor Freight Lines v. Hollingsworth, TexCivApp–Fort Worth, 213 SW2d 747.—App & E 912; Corp 503(3); Evid 54, 591; Venue 8.5(5).

Houston & North Texas Motor Freight Lines v. Johnson, Tex, 166 SW2d 78, 140 Tex 166.—Admin Law 124; Autos 82, 105; Pub Ut 150.

Houston & North Texas Motor Freight Lines v. Johnson, TexCivApp–Galveston, 159 SW2d 905, rev 166 SW2d 78, 140 Tex 166.—Autos 105; Const Law 3874(1), 3902, 4475; Propty 11; Pub Ut 147; Statut 219(1).

Houston & North Tex. Motor Freight Lines v. Local No. 745, International Brotherhood of Teamsters, NDTex, 27 FSupp 154.—Contempt 45; Inj 230(1).

Houston & North Texas Motor Freight Lines v. Local No. 745, Intern. Broth. of Teamsters, Chauffeurs, Stablemen and Helpers of America, NDTex, 27 FSupp 262.—Contempt 2; Labor & Emp 2034, 2084, 2087, 2135, 2164.

Houston & North Tex. Motor Freight Lines v. Phares, NDTex, 19 FSupp 420.—Commerce 55; Const Law 1011, 2488, 2489.

Houston & North Texas Motor Freight Lines, Inc.; Ward v., TexCivApp–Texarkana, 308 SW2d 98.—App & E 499(3), 1056.4, 1062.2.

Houston & North Tex. Motor Freight Lines, Inc. v. Watson, TexCivApp–Waco, 293 SW2d 207.—App & E 846(2), 846(5), 931(3); Plead 111.42(8); Venue 8.5(8).

Houston & T. C. R. Co. v. Werline, TexCivApp–Dallas, 84 SW2d 288, writ dism.—Carr 290, 318(3), 320(1), 320(30); Neglig 236, 372, 386, 387, 1550.

Houston & West Texas Oil Co. v. Storey, TexCivApp–El Paso, 117 SW2d 832, writ dism by agreement.—Evid 129(6); Mines 99(2).

Houston Aristocrat Apartments, Ltd.; Jones v., TexCivApp–Hous (1 Dist), 572 SW2d 1, ref nre.—Land & Ten 152(3), 162, 164(2).

Houston Authority, Port of; City of Seabrook v., TexApp–Houston (1 Dist), 199 SW3d 403, review gr.—App & E 70(3), 782, 863, 893(1), 916(1); Courts 4; Em Dom 55; Plead 104(1), 111.48; Statut 176, 181(1), 188, 205, 206, 212.7, 243.

Houston Authority, Port of; Guillory v., Tex, 845 SW2d 812, motion to stay mandate den, cert den 114 SCt 75, 510 US 820, 126 LEd2d 43.—Adm 1.20(5); Fed Cts 270; Nav Wat 8.5.

Houston Authority, Port of, v. Guillory, TexApp–Houston (1 Dist), 814 SW2d 119. See Port of Houston Authority v. Guillory.

Houston Authority, Port of, v. Intercontinental Transport (ICT) B.V., CA5 (Tex), 998 F2d 316. See Rockwell International Corp. v. M/V Incotrans Spirit.

Houston Authority, Port of; Kamani v., CA5 (Tex), 702 F2d 612.—Adm 1.20(1), 22; Fed Cts 269, 939; States 112.2(2), 197.

Houston Authority, Port of; Kamani v., TexApp–Houston (14 Dist), 725 SW2d 336.—Assign 22; Evid 222(1); Indem 69; Mun Corp 741.15; Nav Wat 14(2); Ship 84(6), 85.

Houston Authority, Port of; Lynch v., TexApp–Houston (14 Dist), 671 SW2d 954, ref nre.—App & E 170(1), 170(2), 179(4), 843(2), 1073(1), 1170.7; Const Law 243.2, 613, 2513, 3759; Courts 91(1); Evid 207(1); Nav Wat 8.5; States 191.6(1), 212.

Houston Authority, Port of; Manchester Terminal Corp. v., TexApp–Houston (14 Dist), 783 SW2d 292.—App & E 80(6).

Houston Authority, Port of; Perry v., SDTex, 118 FSupp2d 770, aff 31 FedAppx 153.—Const Law 3874(1), 3874(2), 3874(3), 4255, 4256; Nav Wat 14(2).

Houston Authority, Port of; Richmond Printing v., TexApp–Houston (14 Dist), 996 SW2d 220.—Contracts 134; Estop 62.1, 62.6; Mand 1, 7, 71, 72, 84, 187.9(5); Nav Wat 14(2); Pub Contr 14.

Houston Authority, Port of; Yang Ming Line v., TexApp–Houston (1 Dist), 833 SW2d 750.—App & E 984(1); Costs 2.

Houston Aviation Products Co. v. Gulf Ports Crating Co., TexCivApp–Hous (1 Dist), 422 SW2d 844, ref nre. —App & E 927(7), 997(3); Bailm 11, 31(1), 31(3).

Houston Avocado Co., Inc. v. Monterey House, Inc., BkrtcySDTex, 71 BR 244. See Monterey House, Inc., In re.

Houston B. & T. Ry. Co.; Adams v., TexCivApp–Houston, 405 SW2d 838.—App & E 1003(5), 1012.1(1), 1177(7); Labor & Emp 2824; Trial 395(5), 401.

Houston B. & T. Ry. Co.; Russell v., TexCivApp–Beaumont, 363 SW2d 160, ref nre.—App & E 761; R R 275(1), 278(2).

Houston Bank & Trust Co. v. Auguste, TexCivApp–Houston, 405 SW2d 800.—App & E 77(2).

Houston Bank & Trust Co.; Flex v., TexCivApp–Hous (14 Dist), 489 SW2d 126.—Bankr 3422(6); Bills & N 534.

Houston Bank & Trust Co. v. Great Southern Life Ins. Co., TexCivApp–Galveston, 232 SW2d 163, rev Board of Ins Com'rs v. Great Southern Life Ins Co, 239 SW2d 803, 150 Tex 258.—Insurance 1008, 1716, 1765.

Houston Bank & Trust Co.; Lange v., TexCivApp–Galveston, 194 SW2d 797, ref nre.—App & E 996; Trusts 38; Wills 663, 667.

Houston Bank & Trust Co. v. Lansdowne, TexCivApp–Galveston, 201 SW2d 834, ref nre.—App & E 931(6); Courts 89; Partners 3, 75; Wills 439, 440, 450, 455, 476, 487(2), 565(1).

Houston Bank & Trust Co. v. Lee, TexCivApp–Houston, 345 SW2d 320, dism.—Courts 475(1), 475(6); Hus & W 272(3); Mental H 163.1, 518; Statut 214.

Houston Bank & Trust Co.; Mundy & Co. v., TexCivApp–Galveston, 254 SW2d 793.—Garn 88, 193.

Houston Baptist University; Massey v., TexApp–Houston (1 Dist), 902 SW2d 81, reh overr, and writ den, and reh dism.—App & E 854(1); Frds St of 43, 44(3); Judgm 185(2); Labor & Emp 40(2), 40(3), 903, 911; Torts 212, 220, 228.

Houston Baseball Ass'n; Williams v., TexCivApp–Galveston, 154 SW2d 874.—Pub Amuse 83, 128.

Houston Bellaire, Ltd. v. TCP LB Portfolio I, L.P., TexApp–Houston (1 Dist), 981 SW2d 916.—App & E 893(1), 984(5), 996; Costs 194.40, 208; Ease 16, 17(5), 18(1).

Houston Belt & Terminal Co. v. Chance, TexCivApp–Eastland, 332 SW2d 430, ref nre.—App & E 927(7); Neglig 1694, 1717; R R 282(3), 282(7.1).

Houston Belt & Terminal Ry.; Wood v., CA5 (Tex), 958 F2d 95.—Fed Cts 766; Labor & Emp 1219(1), 1219(4), 1319, 1322; Lim of Act 95(14).

Houston Belt & Terminal Ry. Co. v. Burmester, TexCivApp–Houston, 309 SW2d 271, ref nre.—Autos 181(1), 181(2), 242(1); Carr 277; Damag 132(3); Indem 69; Labor & Emp 922; New Tr 20, 27.

Houston Belt & Terminal Ry. Co. v. Clark, TexComApp, 143 SW2d 373, 135 Tex 388.—Tax 2317.

Houston Belt & Terminal Ry. Co. v. Clark, TexCivApp–Austin, 122 SW2d 356, aff 143 SW2d 373, 135 Tex 388.—Courts 97(6); Tax 2233, 2300, 2392.

Houston Belt & Terminal R. Co. v. Connell Rice & Sugar Co., CA5 (Tex), 411 F2d 1220, cert den 90 SCt 905, 397 US 908, 25 LEd2d 89.—Carr 100(1).

Houston Belt & Terminal Ry. Co.; Cross v., TexCivApp–Houston, 351 SW2d 84, 96 ALR2d 1, ref nre.—App & E 1048(6), 1050.1(10), 1051(3), 1060.1(4), 1068(1); Evid 318(4), 558(11); New Tr 41(2); Trial 29(2), 105(4), 120(2), 350.3(8).

Houston Belt & Terminal Ry. Co.; Fraser v., CA5 (Tex), 430 F2d 934.—Courts 104; Fed Cts 743.

Houston Belt & Terminal Ry. Co.; Green v., TexCivApp–Hous (14 Dist), 558 SW2d 127.—Evid 506, 546.

Houston Belt & Terminal Ry. Co.; Haughton v., TexCivApp–Houston, 317 SW2d 102.—App & E 927(1); Evid 123(10); Neglig 1717; Plead 34(3); R R 344(5), 348(1), 350(7.1), 350(11), 350(13); Trial 139.1(6), 142; Witn 392(1).

Houston Belt & Terminal Ry. Co. v. J. Weingarten, Inc., TexCivApp–Hous (1 Dist), 421 SW2d 431, ref nre. —App & E 882(18); Contracts 303(1), 318; Contrib 5(6.1); Indem 30(1), 31(1), 31(2), 31(4), 33(7), 65; Judgm 248; New Tr 127; R R 216; Trial 351.2(4).

Houston Belt & Terminal Ry. Co.; Otto v., CA5 (Tex), 444 F2d 219, cert den 92 SCt 449, 404 US 984, 30 LEd2d 368.—Courts 104; Fed Cts 743.

Houston Belt & Terminal Ry. Co.; Otto v., SDTex, 319 FSupp 262, aff 444 F2d 219, cert den 92 SCt 449, 404 US 984, 30 LEd2d 368.—Labor & Emp 1613, 1625.

Houston Belt & Terminal Ry. Co. v. Texas & N. O. R. Co., Tex, 289 SW2d 217, 155 Tex 407.—App & E 840(1), 1043(5); Inj 151, 152.

Houston Belt & Terminal Ry. Co.; Texas & N. O. R. Co. v., TexCivApp–Houston, 308 SW2d 912.—Contracts 147(2); Decl Judgm 143.1, 385; R R 138.

Houston Belt & Terminal R. Co. v. Texas & N. O. R. Co., TexCivApp–Galveston, 279 SW2d 386, rev 289 SW2d 217, 155 Tex 407.—Decl Judgm 393.

Houston Belt & Terminal Ry. Co.; Texas & N. O. R. Co. v., TexCivApp–Galveston, 227 SW2d 610.—Admin Law 228.1; App & E 1176(6); Const Law 55, 2365; Pub Ut 181.

Houston Belt & Terminal Ry. Co.; U.S. v., CA5 (Tex), 210 F2d 421.—R R 229(1), 229(3.1), 229(8), 254(2), 254(6).

Houston Belt & Terminal Ry. Co. v. U.S., SDTex, 153 FSupp 3, aff 78 SCt 560, 356 US 23, 2 LEd2d 578.—Carr 33.

Houston Belt & Terminal Ry. Co. v. Wherry, TexCivApp–Hous (1 Dist), 548 SW2d 743, ref nre, appeal dism 98 SCt 497, 434 US 962, 54 LEd2d 447.—App & E 215(1); Evid 265(18), 357; Libel 1, 7(1), 10(6), 23.1, 39, 74, 101(1), 101(4), 112(1), 112(2), 118, 119, 120(2), 121(1), 123(2); Trial 105(4), 351.3, 351.5(1), 352.5(3), 352.20.

Houston Boxing Club, Inc.; George v., TexCivApp–Hous (14 Dist), 423 SW2d 128, ref nre.—Contracts 218, 252, 278(1); Corp 1.4(4); Estop 78(5); Release 38.

Houston Brokerage, Inc.; McDonald v., TexApp–Corpus Christi, 928 SW2d 633, reh overr, and writ den, cert den 118 SCt 54, 522 US 811, 139 LEd2d 19.—Antitrust 132; App & E 852, 901, 934(1); Courts 97(1); Insurance 1117(3), 1654; Judgm 181(6), 185(2), 540, 627, 632, 634,

707, 713(1), 720, 725(1), 829(3); Labor & Emp 407; States 18.15, 18.41, 18.51.

Houston Bldg. & Loan Ass'n; Wiedeman v., TexCivApp–Beaumont, 120 SW2d 882, writ dism.—Home 177(1).

Houston Bldg. Co.; Westheimer Transfer & Storage Co. v., TexCivApp–Galveston, 198 SW2d 465, ref nre.—Indem 59, 68; Labor & Emp 3046(3), 3049(4).

Houston Bldg. Service, Inc. v. American General Fire and Cas. Co., TexApp–Houston (1 Dist), 799 SW2d 308, writ den.—Fixt 1, 7; Insurance 2278(19), 2278(21).

Houston Business Forms, Inc.; Carr v., TexApp–Houston (14 Dist), 794 SW2d 849.—App & E 837(6), 969, 1067; Hus & W 204, 235(3); Plead 234, 236(7).

Houston Cable TV, Inc. v. Inwood West Civic Ass'n, Tex, 860 SW2d 72.—App & E 1185; Courts 107.

Houston Cable TV, Inc. v. Inwood West Civic Ass'n, Inc., TexApp–Houston (14 Dist), 839 SW2d 497, reh den, and motion den, and writ gr, and writ withdrawn, set aside, opinion not vac 860 SW2d 72.—App & E 181, 235, 930(1), 959(3), 989, 1001(1); Corp 1.4(1), 1.5(1), 1.7(2); Damag 89(2); Fraud 61; Interest 31, 35; Lost Inst 1; Plead 236(3), 238(3), 245(3), 258(3); Tel 1209, 1248(1); Trial 351.2(4).

Houston Cas. Co. v. Certain Underwriters at Lloyd's London, SDTex, 51 FSupp2d 789, aff 252 F3d 1357.—Action 17; Contracts 144; Decl Judgm 161, 361.1; Estop 110; Fed Civ Proc 2737.1, 2737.5; Fed Cts 409.1; Insurance 1091(14), 1164, 2955, 2958, 2959, 2960, 2963, 2964, 2965, 2966, 2996, 3585, 3603, 3609, 3619; Princ & A 96, 99; Ref of Inst 2, 19(1).

Houston Cas. Co.; Siemens AG v., TexApp–Dallas, 127 SW3d 436, petition stricken, and review dism.—App & E 1097(1), 1195(1); Const Law 3964; Corp 665(4); Courts 12(2.1), 12(2.5), 35, 99(1), 99(6).

Houston Cellular Corp.; Chair King, Inc. v., CA5 (Tex), 131 F3d 507.—Action 3; Courts 489(1); Fed Cts 4, 5, 161, 191, 542, 755; Statut 184, 188, 205, 208, 217.1.

Houston Cellular Telephone Co.; Cellular Marketing, Inc. v., TexApp–Houston (14 Dist), 838 SW2d 331, reh den, and writ den.—App & E 846(5), 946, 961; Const Law 4426; Motions 66; Pretrial Proc 44.1, 46.

Houston Cellular Telephone Co.; Cellular Marketing, Inc. v., TexApp–Houston (14 Dist), 784 SW2d 734.—App & E 100(2), 876, 954(4); Inj 169, 174.

Houston Central Industries; Import Systems Intern., Inc. v., SDTex, 752 FSupp 745.—Wareh 31, 32.

Houston Chamber of Commerce; Railroad Commission of Texas v., TexComApp, 78 SW2d 591, 124 Tex 375.—Const Law 2500.

Houston Chapter, Associated General Contractors of America, Inc.; N. L. R. B. v., CA5 (Tex), 349 F2d 449, cert den 86 SCt 648, 382 US 1026, 15 LEd2d 540.—Commerce 62.34; Labor & Emp 1125, 1256.

Houston Chemical Services, Inc.; Smith v., TexApp–Austin, 872 SW2d 252, reh overr, and writ gr, and writ withdrawn, and writ den.—Admin Law 445, 468, 488, 512, 753; Const Law 4025, 4326; Environ Law 272, 360, 365, 370, 378, 380, 381, 389, 644, 656, 661, 673, 685; States 28(2).

Houston Chronicle Pub. Co., In re, TexApp–Houston (14 Dist), 64 SW3d 103, reh overr.—Const Law 665, 859, 2085, 2100, 2114; Crim Law 633(1); Mand 3(3), 14(1), 14(3), 22, 23(1), 28.

Houston Chronicle Pub. Co.; Allen v., TexCivApp–Galveston, 109 SW2d 1135, writ dism woj.—Libel 6(1), 19, 42(1), 42(2).

Houston Chronicle Pub. Co.; Barbouti v., TexApp–Houston (1 Dist), 927 SW2d 37. See Barbouti v. Hearst Corp.

Houston Chronicle Pub. Co. v. Bergman, TexCivApp–Galveston, 128 SW2d 114, writ dism, correct.—Com Law 12; Judgm 743(2); Lis Pen 7; Statut 239.

Houston Chronicle Pub. Co.; Cain v., Tex, 878 SW2d 577. See Cain v. Hearst Corp.

Houston Chronicle Pub. Co. v. City of Houston, Tex, 536 SW2d 559.—App & E 228; Crim Law 1226(2).

Houston Chronicle Pub. Co.; City of Houston v., TexApp–Houston (1 Dist), 673 SW2d 316.—Courts 89; Crim Law 1226(4); Judgm 715(1), 948(1); Mand 3(1), 14(3), 71, 141, 167; Records 60, 62; Trial 394(1).

Houston Chronicle Pub. Co. v. City of Houston, TexCivApp–Hous (14 Dist), 620 SW2d 833.—Autos 7; Const Law 1033, 1036, 1512, 1514, 1515, 1536, 1537, 1735, 1759, 2070, 3039, 3051, 3476, 4034, 4105(5).

Houston Chronicle Pub. Co. v. City of Houston, TexCivApp–Hous (14 Dist), 531 SW2d 177, 82 ALR3d 1, ref nre 536 SW2d 559.—Am Cur 1; App & E 329; Const Law 967, 1550, 2070, 2077, 4594(1); Crim Law 1226(2); Records 51, 54; Statut 47, 181(1), 188, 219(9.1), 223.4.

Houston Chronicle Pub. Co. v. City of League City, Tex., CA5 (Tex), 488 F3d 613.—Civil R 1333(6), 1482; Const Law 855, 1871, 2079; Fed Civ Proc 103.2, 103.3; Fed Cts 12.1, 776, 814.1, 830, 932.1; Mun Corp 626, 703(1).

Houston Chronicle Pub. Co. v. Crapitto, TexApp–Houston (14 Dist), 907 SW2d 99.—Action 6; App & E 138; Const Law 90.1(3), 500, 1050, 2087, 2107; Mand 1, 4(1), 4(4), 28, 53, 61, 168(2), 172.

Houston Chronicle Pub. Co. v. Dean, TexApp–Houston (1 Dist), 792 SW2d 273.—Crim Law 635; Mand 12, 61; Prohib 16.

Houston Chronicle Pub. Co. v. Edwards, TexApp–Beaumont, 956 SW2d 813, reh overr.—Crim Law 1226(2); Mand 29; Records 32.

Houston Chronicle Pub. Co.; E.E.O.C. v., CA5 (Tex), 103 F3d 462. See E.E.O.C. v. Hearst Corp.

Houston Chronicle Pub. Co. v. Flowers, TexCivApp–Beaumont, 413 SW2d 435.—Libel 7(11), 7(19), 9(1); Plead 111.34, 111.42(4), 111.45; Pretrial Proc 581, 583.

Houston Chronicle Pub. Co.; Gonzales v., TexApp–Houston (14 Dist, 930 SW2d 275. See Gonzales v. Hearst Corp.

Houston Chronicle Pub. Co.; Hardin v., CA5 (Tex), 572 F2d 1106.—Antitrust 996; Fed Cts 815; Inj 135, 138.21.

Houston Chronicle Pub. Co.; Hardin v., SDTex, 434 FSupp 54, aff 572 F2d 1106.—Antitrust 595, 885, 995, 996; Inj 138.21, 138.37, 147.

Houston Chronicle Pub. Co.; Hardin v., SDTex, 426 FSupp 1114, aff 572 F2d 1106.—Antitrust 995, 996; Equity 23; Inj 138.21.

Houston Chronicle Pub. Co. v. Hardy, TexApp–Corpus Christi, 678 SW2d 495.—Const Law 2093; Mand 12; Mun Corp 54; Pretrial Proc 43, 433.

Houston Chronicle Pub. Co.; Houston Independent School Dist. v., TexApp–Houston (1 Dist), 798 SW2d 580, writ den.—Const Law 188; Records 50, 58, 68; Statut 219(9.1), 263, 265, 270.

Houston Chronicle Pub. Co.; Houston Typographical Union No. 87 v., CA5 (Tex), 384 F2d 881.—Labor & Emp 1549(18).

Houston Chronicle Pub. Co. v. Houston Typographical Union No. 87, SDTex, 272 FSupp 974, aff 384 F2d 881. —Labor & Emp 1549(18).

Houston Chronicle Pub. Co.; Houston Typographical Union No. 87 v., TexCivApp–Eastland, 397 SW2d 948, ref nre.—App & E 302(1); Labor & Emp 1595(2).

Houston Chronicle Pub. Co. v. Kleindienst, SDTex, 364 FSupp 719.—Const Law 90.1(1.3), 2070, 2276; Fed Civ Proc 103.4; Prisons 4(6).

Houston Chronicle Pub. Co.; Lachmann v., TexCivApp–Austin, 375 SW2d 783, ref nre.—App & E 1071.6; Corp 306; Princ & A 19; Trial 392(2).

Houston Chronicle Pub. Co.; McCullagh v., CA5 (Tex), 211 F2d 4, cert den 75 SCt 44, 348 US 827, 99 LEd 652. —Libel 6(1), 9(5), 16; Torts 330.

Houston Chronicle Pub. Co. v. McMaster, TexCrimApp, 598 SW2d 864.—Hab Corp 741, 752.1.

Houston Chronicle Pub. Co. v. McNair Trucklease, Inc., TexCivApp–Hous (1 Dist), 519 SW2d 924, ref nre. —App & E 846(5); Contracts 32, 45, 46; Corp 1.6(9); Damag 59, 60, 62(4), 117, 120(2), 163(2); Interest 39(2.30).

Houston Chronicle Pub. Co. v. Mattox, Tex, 767 SW2d 695.—Const Law 77, 2470, 2563, 2621; Mand 82; Records 50, 62.

Houston Chronicle Pub. Co.; Mort Keshin & Co., Inc. v., TexApp–Houston (14 Dist), 992 SW2d 642.—App & E 842(2), 1008.1(8.1), 1010.1(8.1), 1012.1(7.1); Const Law 3964, 3965(3), 3965(8); Corp 665(1), 672(1); Courts 12(2.1), 12(2.5), 12(2.10), 12(2.15), 12(2.20), 12(5), 35, 39.

Houston Chronicle Pub. Co. v. Shaver, TexCrimApp, 630 SW2d 927.—Const Law 2314; Crim Law 635; Mand 61; Prohib 9.

Houston Chronicle Pub. Co. v. Stewart, TexApp–Houston (1 Dist), 668 SW2d 727, dism.—Corp 306; Libel 1, 48(2), 51(5); Plead 111.9, 111.42(4.1); Venue 22(6).

Houston Chronicle Pub. Co.; Taylor v., TexCivApp– Hous (1 Dist), 473 SW2d 550, ref nre.—Libel 9(1), 19, 123(2).

Houston Chronicle Pub. Co. v. Thomas, TexApp–Houston (1 Dist), 196 SW3d 396.—Action 6; App & E 19, 78(1); Const Law 2600; Decl Judgm 61, 65, 66, 209, 392.1; Mand 187.5, 187.9(2).

Houston Chronicle Pub. Co. v. U.S., CA5 (Tex), 481 F2d 1240, 24 ALR Fed 718, cert den 94 SCt 867, 414 US 1129, 38 LEd2d 754.—Fed Civ Proc 2152, 2236, 2242, 2608.1; Int Rev 3198, 3405, 3430.1, 3442, 3460, 3470, 3477, 3478, 3480, 3482, 3485, 3505, 5095.

Houston Chronicle Pub. Co. v. U.S., SDTex, 339 FSupp 1314, aff 481 F2d 1240, 24 ALR Fed 718, cert den 94 SCt 867, 414 US 1129, 38 LEd2d 754.—Int Rev 3483.

Houston Chronicle Pub. Co.; Westbrook v., TexComApp, 102 SW2d 197, 129 Tex 95.—Courts 247(5); Libel 48(2).

Houston Chronicle Pub. Co.; Winters v., Tex, 795 SW2d 723.—Labor & Emp 40(2), 776, 782, 794.

Houston Chronicle Pub. Co.; Winters v., TexApp–Houston (1 Dist), 781 SW2d 408, writ gr, aff 795 SW2d 723.— Labor & Emp 777.

Houston Chronicle Pub. Co. v. Woods, TexApp–Beaumont, 949 SW2d 492.—Courts 472.2; Mand 3(3), 4(4), 12, 61; Records 32; Searches 101; Statut 181(1), 188, 190, 217.4.

Houston Citizens Bank & Trust Co.; Chilicote Land Co. v., TexCivApp–El Paso, 525 SW2d 941.—App & E 714(1), 768; Judges 54, 56.

Houston Citizens Bank & Trust Co.; Laswell v., TexApp–Houston (14 Dist), 640 SW2d 701.—Judgm 800(1).

Houston Citizens Bank & Trust Co.; Straughan v., TexCivApp–Hous (1 Dist), 580 SW2d 29.—Action 60; Banks 119; Judgm 178, 185.2(4), 185.3(16); Set-Off 60.

Houston-Citizens Bank & Trust Co.; Williams v., TexCivApp–Hous (14 Dist), 531 SW2d 434, ref nre.—Lim of Act 119(1), 119(3), 195(3).

Houston City Council; Houston Peace Coalition v., SDTex, 310 FSupp 457.—Const Law 1059, 1762, 1864, 4105(5); Mun Corp 703(2).

Houston, City of, v. Aber, TexApp–Houston (14 Dist, 770 SW2d 89. See City of Houston v. Aber.

Houston, City of; Abercrombie Interests, Inc. v., TexApp–Corpus Christi, 830 SW2d 305. See Josephine E. Abercrombie Interests, Inc. v. City of Houston.

Houston, City of; Affiliated Capital Corp. v., CA5 (Tex), 793 F2d 706.—Fed Cts 415; Interest 39(3).

Houston, City of; Affiliated Capital Corp. v., CA5 (Tex), 735 F2d 1555,reh den 741 F2d 766, cert den Gulf Coast Cable Television Co v. Affiliated Capital Corp, 106 SCt 788, 474 US 1053, 88 LEd2d 766, cert den 106 SCt 788, 474 US 1053, 88 LEd2d 766, appeal after remand 793

F2d 706.—Antitrust 905(1), 905(2), 977(1), 977(2), 980; Fed Civ Proc 2217; Mun Corp 170.

Houston, City of; Affiliated Capital Corp. v., CA5 (Tex), 700 F2d 226, reh gr 714 F2d 25, on reh 735 F2d 1555, reh den 741 F2d 766, cert den Gulf Coast Cable Television Co v. Affiliated Capital Corp, 106 SCt 788, 474 US 1053, 88 LEd2d 766, cert den 106 SCt 788, 474 US 1053, 88 LEd2d 766, appeal after remand 793 F2d 706.— Antitrust 535, 537, 541, 552, 604, 968.

Houston, City of; Affiliated Capital Corp. v., SDTex, 519 FSupp 991, rev 700 F2d 226, reh gr 714 F2d 25, on reh 735 F2d 1555, reh den 741 F2d 766, cert den Gulf Coast Cable Television Co v. Affiliated Capital Corp, 106 SCt 788, 474 US 1053, 88 LEd2d 766, cert den 106 SCt 788, 474 US 1053, 88 LEd2d 766, appeal after remand 793 F2d 706.—Antitrust 902, 903, 904, 905(2), 977(2), 977(3), 979, 995; Fed Civ Proc 2217.

Houston, City of; Alamo Barge Lines, Inc. v., Tex, 453 SW2d 132.—Tax 2859.

Houston, City of; Albright v., Tex, 677 SW2d 487.—App & E 1082(2).

Houston, City of, v. All Discount Signs, TexApp–Houston (14 Dist, 771 SW2d 703. See City of Houston v. De Trapani.

Houston, City of; Allen v., TexCivApp–Waco, 397 SW2d 331.—Mun Corp 966(1); Schools 102; Tax 2198.

Houston, City of; Alpha Enterprises, Inc. v., TexCivApp–Houston, 411 SW2d 417, ref nre, cert den 88 SCt 565, 389 US 1005, 19 LEd2d 601, reh den 88 SCt 814, 390 US 913, 19 LEd2d 887.—Explos 1; Mun Corp 111(2), 592(1).

Houston, City of, v. Anderson, TexApp–Houston (1 Dist), 841 SW2d 449. See City of Houston v. Anderson.

Houston, City of; Armstrong v., TexCivApp–Galveston, 272 SW2d 556, rev City of Houston v. Culmore, 278 SW2d 825, 154 Tex 376.—Action 60; Em Dom 96, 157, 223; Trial 350.1.

Houston, City of; Barefield v., TexApp–Houston (14 Dist), 846 SW2d 399, reh den, and writ den.—Detectives 4; Int Liq 285; Mun Corp 740(1), 747(3); Neglig 213, 220, 1019, 1161; Pub Amuse 113, 156.

Houston, City of; Barshop v., Tex, 442 SW2d 682.—App & E 1082(1); Em Dom 124, 131, 222(4), 262(5).

Houston, City of; Barto Watson, Inc. v., TexApp–Houston (1 Dist), 998 SW2d 637, reh overr, and petition for discretionary review den, and reh of petition for review overr.—App & E 918(1), 919; Courts 32, 35; Em Dom 2(1), 2(1.1), 266, 293(3), 307(2); Plead 106(1), 228.14, 228.23, 243; Pretrial Proc 677.

Houston, City of; Bates v., TexCivApp–Galveston, 189 SW2d 17, writ refused wom.—Em Dom 2(1.1), 2(1.2), 13, 277, 293(1); Mun Corp 723.5, 736, 741.20, 741.25, 742(4), 745.5, 747(2); Nuis 7.

Houston, City of; Bellew v., TexCivApp–Hous (1 Dist), 456 SW2d 185, ref nre.—Const Law 2642; Inj 85(1).

Houston, City of; Benningfield v., CA5 (Tex), 157 F3d 369, cert den 119 SCt 1457, 526 US 1065, 143 LEd2d 543.—Civil R 1376(10); Consp 2, 7.5(2), 13; Const Law 1184(1), 1184(2), 1184(3), 1928, 1929, 1930, 1955, 2137; Damag 50.10; Fed Civ Proc 2491.5, 2497.1, 2515; Fed Cts 766, 776, 802; Labor & Emp 904; Mun Corp 218(10), 744, 747(1); Torts 241.

Houston, City of; Benton v., TexCivApp–Hous (1 Dist), 605 SW2d 679.—App & E 954(1); Evid 67(1), 211; Inj 9, 102, 132, 138.21; Nuis 69, 80, 84.

Houston, City of; Blanton v., Tex, 353 SW2d 412, 163 Tex 224.—App & E 1157.5.

Houston, City of; Blanton v., TexCivApp–Houston, 350 SW2d 947, writ gr, vac 353 SW2d 412, 163 Tex 224.— Decl Judgm 209, 369; Inj 80; Mand 100; Mun Corp 35, 36(2), 111(4), 917(1).

Houston, City of; Bowie v., Tex, 261 SW2d 450, 152 Tex 533.—Mun Corp 733(2).

Houston, City of; Bowie v., TexCivApp–Galveston, 259 SW2d 765, ref nre 261 SW2d 450, 152 Tex 533.—Labor & Emp 2878; Mun Corp 733(2), 745.5.

Houston, City of; Brannen v., TexCivApp–Galveston, 153 SW2d 676, writ refused.—Judgm 335(2), 335(4), 405, 407(1), 447(1); New Tr 44(1).

Houston, City of; Brown v., TexApp–Waco, 8 SW3d 331, reh overr, and review den, and reh of petition for review den.—Aviation 232.1; Mun Corp 723, 728, 741.25; Neglig 202, 210, 1692; States 191.9(7).

Houston, City of; Burgess v., CA5 (Tex), 718 F2d 151.—Civil R 1321, 1351(1), 1394, 1395(1), 1396; Consp 18; Const Law 82(6.1); Fed Cts 797; Mun Corp 62, 85, 733(4).

Houston, City of; Burlington Northern and Santa Fe Ry. Co. v., TexApp–Houston (14 Dist), 171 SW3d 240, reh overr, and rule 537(f) motion gr.—Action 6; Courts 185; Em Dom 46, 47(1), 252; Mun Corp 53, 723, 1016; R R 6; States 18.3, 18.11, 18.21, 191.4(1).

Houston, City of; Burnett v., TexApp–Hous (14 Dist), 442 SW2d 919, writ refused.—Courts 91(2); Mun Corp 724, 745.5, 747(3).

Houston, City of; Butcher v., SDTex, 813 FSupp 515.—Aviation 51, 232.1; Rem of C 25(1); States 18.17.

Houston, City of; Campbell v., TexCivApp–Hous (14 Dist), 464 SW2d 372.—App & E 233(2), 846(5); Evid 31, 51, 586(2), 586(3); Mun Corp 79; Tax 2859.

Houston, City of; Campos v., CA5 (Tex), 113 F3d 544.—Elections 12(1), 12(3); Mun Corp 80.

Houston, City of; Campos v., CA5 (Tex), 968 F2d 446, reh den 966 F2d 674, cert den 113 SCt 971, 506 US 1050, 122 LEd2d 126.—Const Law 980; Elections 12(6), 12(7), 12(8), 12(9.1); Fed Cts 1013; Mun Corp 80.

Houston, City of; Campos v., SDTex, 800 FSupp 504. See U.S. v. City of Houston.

Houston, City of; Campos v., SDTex, 776 FSupp 304, vac 968 F2d 446, reh den 966 F2d 674, cert den 113 SCt 971, 506 US 1050, 122 LEd2d 126.—Mun Corp 80.

Houston, City of; Carter v., TexCivApp–Galveston, 255 SW2d 336.—App & E 954(1), 954(2); Em Dom 76; Inj 135, 138.9, 138.21, 138.66.

Houston, City of, v. Cascades, Inc., TexApp–Houston (14 Dist, 730 SW2d 59. See City of Houston v. Cascades, Inc.

Houston, City of; Cash v., TexCivApp–Hous (14 Dist), 426 SW2d 624, ref nre.—Admin Law 749, 750, 791; Mand 28, 72, 168(4); Mun Corp 184.1, 197.

Houston, City of, v. Cavazos, TexApp–Houston (14 Dist, 811 SW2d 231. See City of Houston v. Cavazos.

Houston, City of; CEDA Corp. v., TexApp–Houston (1 Dist), 817 SW2d 846, writ den.—Antitrust 397; App & E 843(3), 984(5); Judgm 199(1), 199(3.10); Mun Corp 723; Plead 262; Torts 121, 141.

Houston, City of; Centamore v., SDTex, 9 FSupp2d 717.—Civil R 1343, 1345, 1351(1), 1352(1), 1352(4); Fed Civ Proc 2491.5, 2515; Mun Corp 723; Neglig 433.

Houston, City of, v. Chambers, TexApp–Houston (14 Dist, 899 SW2d 306. See City of Houston v. Chambers.

Houston, City of; Chapman v., TexApp–Houston (14 Dist), 839 SW2d 95, writ den.—App & E 497(1), 907(4); Bridges 41(1); Colleges 5; Pretrial Proc 486; States 112.2(2), 191.1.

Houston, City of; Chapman v., TexCivApp–Galveston, 101 SW2d 348, rev 123 SW2d 652, 132 Tex 443.—Estop 62.4; Lim of Act 145(3); Mun Corp 281(1).

Houston, City of; Chen v., CA5 (Tex), 206 F3d 502, cert den 121 SCt 2020, 532 US 1046, 149 LEd2d 1017.—Const Law 1466, 1482, 2920, 3125, 3285, 3658(6), 3659; Elections 12(1), 12(6), 15; Fed Cts 766, 802; Mun Corp 80; U S 10.

Houston, City of; Chen v., SDTex, 9 FSupp2d 745, aff 206 F3d 502, cert den 121 SCt 2020, 532 US 1046, 149 LEd2d 1017.—Const Law 1482, 3285, 3658(1), 3658(6);

Elections 12(6), 12(9.1); Fed Civ Proc 103.2, 103.3, 2481; Mun Corp 80.

Houston, City of, v. Chic Lounge, TexApp–Houston (14 Dist, 730 SW2d 62. See City of Houston v. MEF Enterprises, Inc.

Houston, City of; City of Galena Park v., TexCivApp–Galveston, 133 SW2d 162, writ refused.—Mun Corp 29(4), 35, 39; Quo W 5.

Houston, City of; City of Webster v., TexApp–Houston (14 Dist), 855 SW2d 176, reh den, and writ den.—App & E 930(1), 930(3), 989, 994(2), 999(1), 1001(1), 1003(3), 1003(6); Bound 1, 20(1); Mun Corp 33(2), 33(6), 120; Trial 143.

Houston, City of; Clear Creek Basin Authority v., TexCivApp–Hous (1 Dist), 573 SW2d 839, writ gr, rev 589 SW2d 671.—App & E 241; Environ Law 223, 695, 700; Judgm 181(3), 181(15.1).

Houston, City of; Cohen v., TexCivApp–Galveston, 185 SW2d 450.—App & E 1015(5); Const Law 2310, 2315; Evid 53, 87; Judgm 18(1), 18(2), 19, 287; Tax 2857; Trial 21.

Houston, City of; Cole v., TexCivApp–Hous (14 Dist), 442 SW2d 445.—Labor & Emp 868(3); Lim of Act 50(2); Mun Corp 122.1(2), 170, 217.3(2), 218(2), 218(6), 218(8), 218(10), 743, 1040.

Houston, City of; Concerned Community Involved Development, Inc. v., TexApp–Houston (14 Dist), 209 SW3d 666, reh overr, and review den.—Action 13; Admin Law 124; App & E 840(1), 893(1), 916(1); Const Law 2630, 3869, 3874(1); Courts 32; Decl Judgm 299.1, 300; Em Dom 2.1, 95, 104, 106, 286; High 115, 167; Mun Corp 663(1); Plead 104(1), 111.48; Records 63.

Houston, City of; Cornett v., TexCivApp–Houston, 404 SW2d 602.—Antitrust 670; Covenants 79(3), 84; Estop 37; Inj 128(6), 147; Perp 4(4).

Houston, City of; Corporate Funding, Inc. v., TexApp–Texarkana, 686 SW2d 630, ref nre.—Judgm 181(32), 185.3(20), 186.

Houston, City of; Corry v., SDTex, 832 FSupp 1095.—Rem of C 100, 103.

Houston, City of, v. Crabb, TexApp–Houston (14 Dist, 905 SW2d 669. See City of Houston v. Crabb.

Houston, City of; Crawford v., TexApp–Houston (1 Dist), 600 SW2d 891, ref nre.—Admin Law 489.1, 651, 701; App & E 2; Const Law 2649, 4028; Decl Judgm 5.1, 209, 272; Mun Corp 185(0.5), 185(12); Statut 264.

Houston, City of; Crawford v., TexCivApp–Waco, 414 SW2d 212, ref nre.—Mun Corp 184(1), 216(1).

Houston, City of; Crawford v., TexCivApp–Hous (14 Dist), 487 SW2d 179, ref nre.—App & E 803; Mun Corp 185(12), 218(9).

Houston, City of; Cronin v., TexCivApp–Hous (1 Dist), 505 SW2d 329, ref nre.—Mun Corp 221.

Houston, City of; Cyiark v., SDTex, 976 FSupp 591.—Civil R 1455, 1482, 1487, 1488, 1490.

Houston, City of; Dancer v., Tex, 384 SW2d 340.—App & E 1094(1); Mun Corp 733(1), 741.50, 742(5), 747(3).

Houston, City of; Davis v., TexApp–Houston (1 Dist), 869 SW2d 493, reh den, and writ den.—Covenants 51(2), 103(2); Deeds 110.

Houston, City of; Derr Const. Co. v., TexApp–Houston (14 Dist), 846 SW2d 854.—App & E 852; Contracts 114, 143(2), 143.5, 147(1), 176(2), 187(1); Indem 25, 27, 33(5); Judgm 181(19), 185.3(8); Release 1, 5, 25, 38.

Houston, City of, v. De Trapani, TexApp–Houston (14 Dist, 771 SW2d 703. See City of Houston v. De Trapani.

Houston, City of; Dickey v., Tex, 501 SW2d 293.—Em Dom 253(1); Judgm 335(3), 350.

Houston, City of; Dickey v., TexCivApp–Hous (14 Dist), 494 SW2d 648, ref nre 501 SW2d 293.—Const Law 4077; Courts 247(2); Em Dom 252, 253(3).

Houston, City of; Dilley v., Tex, 222 SW2d 992, 148 Tex 191.—App & E 1175(5); Mun Corp 733(1), 733(2), 745.5, 747(2).

Houston, City of; Dilley v., TexCivApp–Galveston, 217 SW2d 459, rev 222 SW2d 992, 148 Tex 191.—Mun Corp 733(2).

Houston, City of; Duckett v., Tex, 495 SW2d 883.—Judgm 181(27), 185.3(1); Mun Corp 197.

Houston, City of; Dykes v., Tex, 406 SW2d 176.—Dedi 47; Em Dom 267; Mand 72, 98(1); Mun Corp 269(1), 281(1), 658, 661(1), 661(2), 663(1), 671(1.1).

Houston, City of; Earl Hayes Rents Cars and Trucks v., TexCivApp–Hous (1 Dist), 557 SW2d 316, ref nre.—App & E 934(2); Aviation 224; Contracts 313(2); Interest 30(1).

Houston, City of; Edwards v., CA5 (Tex), 78 F3d 983.—Fed Civ Proc 311, 314.1, 315, 316, 317, 320, 321, 337, 921, 1722, 1729, 1837.1, 1953, 2646, 2659; Fed Cts 541, 544, 545.1, 555, 561, 574, 652.1, 776, 811, 817, 829; Judgm 707.

Houston, City of; Edwards v., CA5 (Tex), 37 F3d 1097, reh and sug for reh gr 49 F3d 1048, on reh 78 F3d 983.

Houston, City of; Eller Media Co. v., TexApp–Houston (1 Dist), 101 SW3d 668, reh overr, and review den.—App & E 893(1), 931(1), 989, 1008.1(1), 1008.1(2), 1010.1(1), 1010.2, 1012.1(4); Const Law 1541, 1678; Em Dom 2(1), 2(1.2), 307(2); Zoning 14, 81, 282.

Houston, City of; Ethio Exp. Shuttle Service, Inc. v., TexApp–Houston (14 Dist), 164 SW3d 751, reh overr.—App & E 863, 893(1), 916(1); Mun Corp 723, 724, 725, 742(4), 742(5).

Houston, City of; Evans v., CA5 (Tex), 246 F3d 344.—Civil R 1009, 1135, 1201, 1209, 1243, 1244, 1252, 1351(1), 1351(5), 1502, 1536, 1539, 1744; Fed Civ Proc 2497.1, 2543, 2544; Fed Cts 776; Mun Corp 218(10).

Houston, City of; Federal Lanes, Inc. v., TexApp–Houston (1 Dist), 905 SW2d 686, reh overr, and writ den.—App & E 345.1, 387(2), 782; Pretrial Proc 697, 699; Stip 1, 17(1), 17(3).

Houston, City of, v. First City, TexApp–Houston (1 Dist), 827 SW2d 462. See City of Houston v. First City.

Houston, City of; Foote v., TexCivApp–Houston, 361 SW2d 247, ref nre.—Pretrial Proc 554.

Houston, City of; Forbes v., TexCivApp–Houston, 356 SW2d 709.—Mand 16(1), 71, 72, 98(1), 187.9(5); Mun Corp 63.1, 657(1).

Houston, City of; Forbes v., TexCivApp–Galveston, 304 SW2d 542, ref nre, cert den 78 SCt 1151, 357 US 905, 2 LEd2d 1156.—Mun Corp 33(2), 33(10), 34, 112(3), 871, 995(2); Statut 77(1), 135; Waters 216.

Houston, City of; Ft. Worth & Denver Ry. Co. v., TexApp–Houston (14 Dist), 672 SW2d 299, ref nre.—Em Dom 47(1), 149(5), 196, 201, 262(4); R R 96.

Houston, City of; Gano v., TexApp–Houston (14 Dist), 834 SW2d 585, reh den, and writ den.—Tax 2699(11).

Houston, City of; Garcia v., CA5 (Tex), 201 F3d 672.—Civil R 1137, 1171, 1536, 1544, 1548, 1560, 1587, 1590, 1594; Fed Cts 763.1, 799, 830, 847, 878.

Houston, City of; Garcia v., TexApp–El Paso, 799 SW2d 496, writ den.—App & E 989; Autos 242(6), 245(30); Judgm 199(3.3).

Houston, City of; Gardner v., TexApp–Houston, 320 SW2d 715.—Mun Corp 741.50, 816(11).

Houston, City of; Garner v., TexCivApp–Houston, 323 SW2d 659.—Evid 18, 25(2); Health 955, 961; Judgm 181(15.1).

Houston, City of, v. Garrett, TexApp–Houston (14 Dist, 816 SW2d 800. See City of Houston v. Garrett.

Houston, City of; General Motors Acceptance Corp. v., TexApp–Houston (14 Dist), 857 SW2d 731.—App & E 5; Pretrial Proc 676, 697.

Houston, City of; George v., TexCivApp–Hous (1 Dist), 465 SW2d 387, writ gr, rev 479 SW2d 257.—Mun Corp 736, 745.5, 849, 857; Nuis 44, 72.

Houston, City of; Glen Oaks Utilities, Inc. v., CA5 (Tex), 280 F2d 330.—Action 69(3); Courts 493(3); Fed Cts 411, 573, 576.1; Judgm 828.10(2).

Houston, City of; Glen Oaks Utilities, Inc. v., Tex, 340 SW2d 783, 161 Tex 417, on remand 360 SW2d 549, ref nre.—Admin Law 651; Const Law 4361; Inj 118(3), 138.48, 151; Mun Corp 619.

Houston, City of; Glen Oaks Utilities, Inc. v., TexCivApp–Waco, 334 SW2d 469, writ gr, rev 340 SW2d 783, 161 Tex 417, on remand 360 SW2d 549, ref nre.—App & E 655(1), 927(3); Inj 85(2); Mun Corp 619.

Houston, City of; Glover v., TexCivApp–Hous (14 Dist), 590 SW2d 799.—App & E 989, 999(1), 1001(1), 1003(4), 1008.1(13), 1078(1); Autos 304(1), 304(3), 306(8), 308(10), 308(11); Neglig 1713.

Houston, City of; Gobel v., TexCivApp–Hous (1 Dist), 455 SW2d 776, ref nre.—Autos 187(2), 247; Judgm 199(3.7); Mun Corp 734; Neglig 1717; Trial 139.1(3), 140(1), 350.6(3).

Houston, City of, v. Goings, TexApp–Houston (14 Dist, 795 SW2d 829. See City of Houston v. Goings.

Houston, City of; Greanias v., TexApp–Houston (1 Dist), 841 SW2d 411.—Mand 103, 187.6.

Houston, City of; Hamman v., TexCivApp–Fort Worth, 362 SW2d 402, ref nre.—Dedi 65; Mun Corp 224.

Houston, City of; Harris v., CA5 (Tex), 151 F3d 186, reh and sug for reh den 172 F3d 871.—Fed Cts 12.1, 13, 13.25, 723.1, 776, 932.1, 936.

Houston, City of; Harris v., SDTex, 10 FSupp2d 721, vac 151 F3d 186, reh and sug for reh den 172 F3d 871.—Const Law 82(8), 1466, 1480, 2970, 3255, 3285; Elections 12(1), 12(2.1), 12(6), 12(8); Mun Corp 29(0.5), 33(10), 35.

Houston, City of, v. Harris County Outdoor Advertising Ass'n, TexApp–Houston (14 Dist), 879 SW2d 322. See City of Houston v. Harris County Outdoor Advertising Ass'n.

Houston, City of, v. Harris County Outdoor Advertising Ass'n, TexApp–Houston (14 Dist, 732 SW2d 42. See City of Houston v. Harris County Outdoor Advertising Ass'n.

Houston, City of; Harris County Water Control and Imp. Dist. No. 58 v., TexCivApp–Houston, 357 SW2d 789, ref nre.—Const Law 4361, 4372; Evid 25(2); Mun Corp 619; Pub Ut 120; States 66; Waters 183.5, 190, 203(5), 203(6).

Houston, City of; Harris County Wrecker Owners for Equal Opportunity v., SDTex, 943 FSupp 711.—Assoc 20(1); Autos 5(1), 43, 61, 62; Commerce 3, 61(1), 63.15; Fed Civ Proc 103.2, 103.3, 2539; Fed Cts 173; High 165; Mun Corp 53, 590; States 18.3, 18.5, 18.11, 18.13, 18.21; Statut 184, 188, 205.

Houston, City of, v. Harrison, TexApp–Houston (14 Dist, 778 SW2d 916. See City of Houston v. Harrison.

Houston, City of; Hatten v., TexCivApp–Houston, 373 SW2d 525, ref nre.—Action 16, 18; App & E 66, 80(6), 624, 1043(7); Const Law 961, 2356, 4361, 4372; Courts 78, 475(13); Decl Judgm 211, 251, 319, 344, 345.1, 392.1, 395; Evid 5(2); Jury 10, 12(1.1), 14(12.5), 19(1), 31.1; Mun Corp 108.6, 122.1(2), 122.1(4), 911, 917(1), 918(3); Plead 8(20); Pretrial Proc 711, 716, 723.1; Statut 64(1); Waters 203(3), 203(10).

Houston, City of; Hayden v., TexCivApp–Fort Worth, 305 SW2d 798, ref nre.—App & E 172(1), 863, 954(1), 954(2); Aviation 217; Evid 31; Franch 1; Mun Corp 57, 59, 276, 722, 993(2).

Houston, City of; HC Gun & Knife Shows, Inc. v., CA5 (Tex), 201 F3d 544, reh den.—Damag 176; Fed Civ Proc 1852, 2608.1; Fed Cts 776, 819, 820, 823, 895, 915; Mun Corp 592(1); Weap 3.

Houston, City of; Heard v., TexCivApp–Hous (1 Dist), 529 SW2d 560.—Costs 194.16, 194.25; Fed Civ Proc 2737.14; Mun Corp 184.1; Offic 11.7.

Houston, City of; Hedgecroft v., Tex, 244 SW2d 632, 150 Tex 654.—Mun Corp 967(1); Tax 2300, 2341.

Houston, City of; Hedgecroft v., TexCivApp–Galveston, 239 SW2d 828, rev 244 SW2d 632, 150 Tex 654.—Mun Corp 957(1), 958, 967(1); Tax 2187, 2300.

Houston, City of; Heitschmidt v., CA5 (Tex), 161 F3d 834.—Civil R 1088(2), 1376(6); Fed Civ Proc 2553; Offic 114; Searches 40.1.

Houston, City of; Hicks v., TexApp–Corpus Christi, 641 SW2d 352.—Judgm 713(2), 715(2), 720.

Houston, City of; Hicks v., TexCivApp–Hous (1 Dist), 524 SW2d 539, ref nre.—Adv Poss 14; Ease 17(4), 26(1), 30(1); Mun Corp 85, 657(4), 657(5).

Houston, City of; Hill v., SDTex, 991 FSupp 847.—Civil R 1394, 1395(1); Consp 2; Const Law 3040, 3936; Mun Corp 723, 747(3); Sent & Pun 1433, 1436.

Houston, City of, v. Hill, TexApp–Houston (1 Dist), 792 SW2d 176. See City of Houston v. Hill.

Houston, City of; Hogan v., CA5 (Tex), 819 F2d 604.—Civil R 1395(7).

Houston, City of; Holcombe v., TexCivApp–Houston, 351 SW2d 69.—App & E 564(3); Em Dom 150, 205, 247(1), 247(2), 262(1); Evid 142(1), 142(2), 142(3); Trial 412.

Houston, City of; Holland v., SDTex, 41 FSupp2d 678, appeal dism 237 F3d 632.—Arrest 68(2); Autos 187(2), 201(1.1); Civil R 1031, 1088(2), 1304, 1324, 1330(1), 1335, 1343, 1345, 1351(1), 1351(4), 1352(1), 1352(4), 1354, 1376(1), 1376(2), 1394, 1397; Compromise 17(2); Fed Civ Proc 2491.5, 2515; Judgm 702; Mun Corp 188, 723, 723.5, 728, 739(2), 744, 745, 747(3), 847, 854; Offic 114, 116.

Houston, City of; Houston Chronicle Pub. Co. v., Tex, 536 SW2d 559.—App & E 228; Crim Law 1226(2).

Houston, City of; Houston Chronicle Pub. Co. v., TexCivApp–Hous (14 Dist), 620 SW2d 833.—Autos 7; Const Law 1033, 1036, 1512, 1514, 1515, 1536, 1537, 1735, 1759, 2070, 3039, 3051, 3476, 4034, 4105(5).

Houston, City of; Houston Chronicle Pub. Co. v., TexCivApp–Hous (14 Dist), 531 SW2d 177, 82 ALR3d 1, ref nre 536 SW2d 559.—Am Cur 1; App & E 329; Const Law 967, 1550, 2070, 2077, 4594(1); Crim Law 1226(2); Records 51, 54; Statut 47, 181(1), 188, 219(9.1), 223.4.

Houston, City of; Houston Crane Rentals, Inc. v., TexCivApp–Hous (1 Dist), 454 SW2d 216, ref nre.—Judgm 185(2), 185.3(20); 186; Mun Corp 79, 978(1), 978(10); Schools 106; Tax 2446, 2587, 2858.

Houston, City of; Houston Endowment, Inc. v., TexCivApp–Hous (14 Dist), 468 SW2d 540, ref nre.—App & E 1097(1); Const Law 3483; Mun Corp 38; Tax 2126.

Houston, City of, v. Houston Gulf Coast Bldg. and Const. Trades Council, TexApp–Houston (1 Dist), 710 SW2d 181. See City of Houston v. Houston Gulf Coast Bldg. and Const. Trades Council.

Houston, City of; Houston Independent School Dist. v., Tex, 443 SW2d 49.—Courts 247(7).

Houston, City of, v. Houston Police Officers Ass'n, TexApp–Houston (14 Dist, 715 SW2d 145. See City of Houston v. Houston Police Officers Ass'n.

Houston, City of, v. Houston Police Patrolmen's Union, CA5 (Tex), 37 F3d 1097. See Edwards v. City of Houston.

Houston, City of; Houston Professional Fire Fighters' Ass'n v., TexApp–Houston (1 Dist), 177 SW3d 95.—Mun Corp 197, 217.3(2).

Houston, City of, v. Howard, TexApp–Houston (14 Dist, 786 SW2d 391. See City of Houston v. Howard.

Houston, City of, v. Hughes, CA5 (Tex), 37 F3d 1097. See Edwards v. City of Houston.

Houston, City of; Hunter-Reed v., SDTex, 244 FSupp2d 733.—Civil R 1505(4), 1530, 1532, 1535; Equity 64; Evid 318(1), 318(7); Fed Civ Proc 1837.1, 2539, 2545; Lim of Act 104.5.

Houston, City of; Hutson v., TexCivApp–Hous (14 Dist), 418 SW2d 911, ref nre.—App & E 854(5); Autos 273, 293; Mun Corp 741.15, 788.

Houston, City of; Huynh v., TexApp–Houston (14 Dist), 874 SW2d 184, petition for discretionary review gr, aff in part, remanded in part 901 SW2d 480, on remand 928 SW2d 698.—Ind & Inf 196(1); Jury 29(6).

Houston, City of; Hynes v., TexCivApp–Galveston, 263 SW2d 839, ref nre.—Mun Corp 185(10), 185(12).

Houston, City of; Interstate Materials Corp. v., TexCivApp–Galveston, 236 SW2d 653, ref nre.—Mun Corp 248(1), 722; Spec Perf 19.

Houston, City of; Jackson v., TexCivApp–Hous (14 Dist), 595 SW2d 907, ref nre.—Mun Corp 180(1), 184(2).

Houston, City of; Jaimes v., TexApp–Houston (14 Dist), 687 SW2d 460, ref nre.—Autos 297; Contrib 7.

Houston, City of; James v., TexApp–Houston (14 Dist), 138 SW3d 433, reh overr.—Const Law 1947; Judgm 654, 668(2), 715(2), 715(3), 720, 725(1), 958(2).

Houston, City of; Joachimi v., TexApp–Houston (1 Dist), 712 SW2d 861.—Negligg 1037(4), 1089, 1095, 1127, 1568, 1670.

Houston, City of; John Corp. v., CA5 (Tex), 214 F3d 573.—Const Law 280, 978, 1050, 3000, 3855, 4076; Em Dom 2(1.1), 266, 277; Fed Cts 242.1, 776; Sent & Pun 1436, 1580.

Houston, City of; Johnson v., TexApp–Houston (14 Dist), 203 SW3d 7, reh overr, and review den.—Civil R 1243, 1252; Judgm 181(27), 185.3(2); Lim of Act 119(3), 199(1); Mun Corp 218(3).

Houston, City of; Johnson v., TexApp–Houston (14 Dist), 928 SW2d 251, reh overr.—App & E 205, 215(1), 712, 941, 1056.1(1); Evid 129(1), 138, 139, 146; Mun Corp 218(10); Offic 72.45(1); Trial 43.

Houston, City of; Johnson v., TexApp–Houston (14 Dist), 813 SW2d 227, writ gr, and writ withdrawn, and writ den.—Death 7, 10, 29, 32, 85.

Houston, City of; Jolar Cinema of Houston, Inc. v., TexApp–Houston (1 Dist), 695 SW2d 353.—App & E 843(2), 954(1); Const Law 1590, 2208; Inj 128(8), 151; Obscen 2.1.

Houston, City of; Jones v., Tex, 976 SW2d 676.—App & E 387(6), 389(1).

Houston, City of; Jones v., TexApp–Houston (1 Dist), 907 SW2d 871, reh overr, and writ den.—App & E 863, 1175(1); Judgm 185(6), 720, 725(1), 956(1), 956(5); Mun Corp 65, 126, 186(5), 217.3, 220(2).

Houston, City of; Jones v., TexCivApp–Tyler, 380 SW2d 761.—Em Dom 149(2.1), 222(4), 262(5); Evid 555.6(10).

Houston, City of; Josephine E. Abercrombie Interests, Inc. v., TexApp–Corpus Christi, 830 SW2d 305, reh overr, and writ den.—Judgm 185(2); Mun Corp 723, 725.

Houston, City of; Kahng v., SDTex, 485 FSupp2d 787.—Civil R 1035, 1395(1); Const Law 967, 3035, 3039, 3040, 3053.

Houston, City of; Kiel v., TexCivApp–Hous (14 Dist), 558 SW2d 69, ref nre.—Equity 87(2); Lim of Act 24(2); Mun Corp 194, 197.

Houston, City of, v. Kilburn, Tex, 849 SW2d 810. See City of Houston v. Kilburn.

Houston, City of, v. Kilburn, TexApp–Houston (14 Dist, 838 SW2d 344. See City of Houston v. Kilburn.

Houston, City of; Kirschke v., TexCivApp–Houston, 330 SW2d 629, ref nre, appeal dism 81 SCt 242, 364 US 474, 5 LEd2d 221, reh den 81 SCt 377, 364 US 939, 5 LEd2d 371.—Em Dom 2(1), 2(1.1), 90; Inj 77(1); Mand 87; Mun Corp 621, 728.

Houston, City of; Kubosh v., TexApp–Houston (1 Dist), 96 SW3d 606, review den.—Lim of Act 55(5), 197(1); Trover 28.

Houston, City of; Kubosh v., TexApp–Houston (1 Dist), 2 SW3d 463, reh overr, and petition for review den, appeal after remand 96 SW3d 606, review den.—Action 6; Decl Judgm 84, 273; Judges 36; Judgm 181(7); Mun Corp 979, 1016.

Houston, City of, v. L & P Sales and Service, TexApp–Houston (1 Dist), 788 SW2d 419. See City of Houston v. Muse.

Houston, City of; Lawyers Trust Co. v., Tex, 359 SW2d 887.—Dedi 55, 65; Deeds 134, 144(1), 166, 168.

Houston, City of; Layne Texas Co. v., TexCivApp–Houston, 306 SW2d 424, writ refused.—Decl Judgm 319.

Houston, City of, v. Leach, TexApp–Houston (14 Dist, 819 SW2d 185. See City of Houston v. Leach.

Houston, City of; Lee v., Tex, 807 SW2d 290, subsequent mandamus proceeding 842 SW2d 646.—Const Law 2474; Mun Corp 180(2), 180(3), 182, 184(1), 184.1, 194, 197.

Houston, City of, v. Lee, TexApp–Houston (1 Dist), 762 SW2d 180. See City of Houston v. Lee.

Houston, City of; Leroy v., CA5 (Tex), 906 F2d 1068.—Elections 12(10); Fed Civ Proc 2737.4; Fed Cts 830, 949.1, 956.1; Interest 39(2.45).

Houston, City of; Leroy v., CA5 (Tex), 831 F2d 576, reh den 836 F2d 1346, cert den 108 SCt 1735, 486 US 1008, 100 LEd2d 199, on subsequent appeal 906 F2d 1068.—Elections 12(9.1), 12(10); Mun Corp 80.

Houston, City of; Leroy v., SDTex, 648 FSupp 537, rev 831 F2d 576, reh den 836 F2d 1346, cert den 108 SCt 1735, 486 US 1008, 100 LEd2d 199, on subsequent appeal 906 F2d 1068.—Elections 12(10); Mun Corp 80.

Houston, City of; LeRoy v., SDTex, 592 FSupp 415.—Judges 39, 40.

Houston, City of; Leroy v., SDTex, 584 FSupp 653.—Civil R 1482.

Houston, City of; Lethu Inc. v., TexApp–Houston (1 Dist), 23 SW3d 482, review den.—Ease 40; Em Dom 85, 95, 106, 266, 315; High 85; Judgm 181(33), 183; Mun Corp 736; Nuis 2, 3(1), 4.

Houston, City of; Loos v., TexCivApp–Houston, 375 SW2d 952, ref nre.—Mun Corp 106(1), 108.10, 197, 217.3(1).

Houston, City of; Lurie v., TexCivApp–Galveston, 220 SW2d 320, rev 224 SW2d 871, 148 Tex 391, 14 ALR2d 61.—App & E 231(1), 465(2); Const Law 1066, 1112(2); Mun Corp 63.15(1), 605, 623(1), 623(4); Nuis 62, 85; Trial 350.2, 352.1(3), 366.

Houston, City of, v. Lyons Realty, Ltd., TexApp–Houston (1 Dist), 710 SW2d 625. See City of Houston v. Lyons Realty, Ltd.

Houston, City of; McCarthy v., TexCivApp–Corpus Christi, 389 SW2d 159, ref nre.—App & E 927(7), 1048(6), 1052(5); Deeds 160, 165, 168; Ease 1; Em Dom 271; Evid 461(4); Levees 9; Witn 276.

Houston, City of; McConney v., CA5 (Tex), 863 F2d 1180.—Arrest 70(1); Bail 42; Civil R 1351(4), 1376(6); Fed Cts 625, 752.

Houston, City of, v. McDonald, TexApp–Houston (14 Dist, 946 SW2d 419. See City of Houston v. McDonald.

Houston, City of; McDonald v., TexCivApp–Hous (14 Dist), 577 SW2d 800, ref nre.—Autos 293; Mun Corp 58, 122.1(2), 741.15, 741.50, 741.55.

Houston, City of; McGaughy v., CA5 (Tex), 77 FedAppx 280.—Civil R 1376(6); Fed Cts 915; Searches 42.1.

Houston, City of; McGovern v., TexCivApp–Hous (1 Dist), 478 SW2d 229, ref nre.—Dedi 11, 18(1), 29, 38, 39, 47, 63(1); Ease 2, 30(1).

Houston, City of; McGregor v., TexCivApp–Hous (14 Dist), 528 SW2d 620, ref nre.—Mun Corp 197.

Houston, City of; McLendon v., Tex, 267 SW2d 805, 153 Tex 318.—Mun Corp 741.30.

Houston, City of; McLendon v., TexCivApp–Galveston, 261 SW2d 461, rev 267 SW2d 805, 153 Tex 318.—Mun Corp 741.30.

Houston, City of; Maguire Oil Co. v., CA5 (Tex), 143 F3d 205.—Fed Civ Proc 2757, 2769, 2800; Fed Cts 813; Rem of C 107(9), 107(11).

Houston, City of; Maguire Oil Co. v., TexApp–Texarkana, 69 SW3d 350, reh overr, and review den, and reh

of petition for review overr, on remand 2005 WL 4889981.—App & E 863, 901, 934(1); Const Law 885, 915, 3045; Em Dom 2(1), 106, 131, 266; Estop 52(1), 62.4, 85, 89.1, 92(1), 119; Fraud 13(3); Judgm 181(7), 181(15.1), 185(2), 185(5), 185(6), 185.3(1), 185.3(2); Mun Corp 120, 626, 722, 724; Statut 181(1), 188, 219(1); Zoning 377, 762.

Houston, City of, v. Malone, TexApp–Houston (14 Dist, 828 SW2d 567. See City of Houston v. Malone.

Houston, City of; Malone v., TexCivApp–Galveston, 278 SW2d 204, ref nre.—Courts 472.1; Decl Judgm 128, 273, 385; Inj 105(2).

Houston, City of, v. MEF Enterprises, Inc., TexApp–Houston (14 Dist, 730 SW2d 62. See City of Houston v. MEF Enterprises, Inc.

Houston, City of, v. Meister, TexApp–Houston (14 Dist, 882 SW2d 29. See City of Houston v. Meister.

Houston, City of; MGJ Corp. v., TexCivApp–Hous (1 Dist), 544 SW2d 171, ref nre.—App & E 954(1), 954(2); Courts 26; Dedi 4; Deeds 120, 139, 142; Ease 3(1), 38, 52; Estop 25; Frds St of 60(1), 63(3); Inj 48, 135, 138.1, 138.31, 138.46, 147, 151; Tresp 10.

Houston, City of; Michna v., TexCivApp–Hous (1 Dist), 534 SW2d 728, ref nre.—App & E 1198; Judgm 713(2); Mand 187.10.

Houston, City of; Michna v., TexCivApp–Hous (1 Dist), 521 SW2d 331, appeal after remand 534 SW2d 728, ref nre.—Lim of Act 61; Mun Corp 180(3), 186(1), 217.3(4), 217.6.

Houston, City of; Mikkilineni v., TexApp–Houston (1 Dist), 4 SW3d 298, review den, appeal decided 2000 WL 19641, review den, cert den 121 SCt 196, 531 US 882, 148 LEd2d 137.—App & E 389(1).

Houston, City of, v. Mitchell, TexApp–Houston (14 Dist, 737 SW2d 370. See City of Houston v. Mitchell.

Houston, City of; Mokwa v., TexApp–Houston (1 Dist), 741 SW2d 142, writ den.—Admin Law 229; Lim of Act 18; Mun Corp 182, 184(3), 186(5), 186(6).

Houston, City of, v. Moore, TexApp–Houston (14 Dist, 732 SW2d 28. See City of Houston v. Moore.

Houston, City of; Moran v., TexApp–Houston (14 Dist), 58 SW3d 159, review den.—Mun Corp 185(12); Statut 188, 195, 212.1, 212.7.

Houston, City of; Morris v., SDTex, 894 FSupp 1062, aff Campos v. City of Houston, 113 F3d 544.—Mun Corp 80.

Houston, City of; Morris v., TexCivApp–Hous (14 Dist), 466 SW2d 851.—App & E 690(1), 692(1), 1048(1), 1074(3), 1170.7; Mun Corp 796, 818(1); Trial 352.21.

Houston, City of; Mossy Oldsmobile, Inc. v., TexCivApp–Hous (1 Dist), 562 SW2d 890.—App & E 597(1), 624.

Houston, City of, v. Muse, TexApp–Houston (1 Dist), 788 SW2d 419. See City of Houston v. Muse.

Houston, City of; Nehoc Land Co. v., TexCivApp–Houston, 342 SW2d 42, ref nre.—Courts 68; Em Dom 205, 241, 243(1), 246(2); Evid 474(18); Judges 31, 32; Judgm 191, 573.

Houston, City of; Neiman-Marcus Co. v., TexCivApp–Galveston, 109 SW2d 543, writ refused.—Const Law 3036, 4294; Inj 85(2), 126, 130; Licens 5.5, 7(1).

Houston, City of; New Jerusalem Baptist Church, Inc. v., TexCivApp–Hous (14 Dist), 598 SW2d 666.—Covenants 72.1, 108(1), 111, 122.

Houston, City of, v. Newsom, TexApp–Houston (14 Dist, 858 SW2d 14. See City of Houston v. Newsom.

Houston, City of; Nine Hundred Main v., TexCivApp–Galveston, 150 SW2d 468, writ dism, correct.—Fixt 15; Improv 1; Land & Ten 157(2), 157(4); Mun Corp 966(1).

Houston, City of; Nixon v., TexCivApp–Hous (14 Dist), 560 SW2d 447, ref nre.—Const Law 4172(3); Mun Corp 120, 182, 185(11).

Houston, City of; Nugent v., SDTex, 159 FSupp2d 529.—Civil R 1118, 1384; Fed Civ Proc 2497.1; Labor & Emp 1295(1); Mun Corp 184(2), 197; Statut 176, 181(1), 188, 206.

Houston, City of; N.W. Enterprises Inc. v., CA5 (Tex), 372 F3d 333.—Const Law 2205; Fed Cts 683, 932.1; Pub Amuse 9(2).

Houston, City of; N.W. Enterprises Inc. v., CA5 (Tex), 352 F3d 162, on reh in part 372 F3d 333, cert den Ice Embassy, Inc v. City of Houston, Tex, 125 SCt 416, 543 US 958, 160 LEd2d 321.—Const Law 1526, 1528, 1590, 2204, 2208, 2209, 2212, 2213, 2215, 2216, 2225, 2233, 2243; Courts 90(1); Em Dom 2.10(1); Fed Cts 660.20, 915; Inj 7; Mun Corp 592(1), 602; Pub Amuse 3, 9(1), 9(2), 9(3), 47, 49; Zoning 131, 278.1.

Houston, City of; N.W. Enterprises, Inc. v., SDTex, 27 FSupp2d 754, affin part, rev in part, dism in part 352 F3d 162, on reh in part 372 F3d 333, cert den Ice Embassy, Inc v. City of Houston, Tex, 125 SCt 416, 543 US 958, 160 LEd2d 321.—Admin Law 797; Const Law 795, 874, 1135, 1145(3), 1153, 1244, 1402, 1514, 1518, 1564, 2204, 2205, 2208, 2209, 2212, 2213, 2217, 2218, 2225, 2233, 2243, 3698; Em Dom 2(1.2); Evid 18, 318(3), 366(2); Fed Civ Proc 101, 320, 827, 842, 2491.5, 2553; Fed Cts 13.25, 56; Mun Corp 592(1); Pub Amuse 3, 9(1), 9(2), 9(3), 45, 48, 49; Records 3; Zoning 136.

Houston, City of; Olabisiomotosho v., CA5 (Tex), 185 F3d 521, reh den.—Autos 349(18); Civil R 1351(1), 1351(4), 1376(4); Const Law 4544, 4545(1), 4545(2), 4545(4); Mun Corp 747(3); Prisons 10.

Houston, City of; Oldfield v., TexApp–Houston (14 Dist), 15 SW3d 219, reh overr, and review den.—Contracts 143(2); Covenants 49, 72.1; Estop 52.15; Judgm 181(15.1); Mun Corp 724, 725, 735; Trial 136(3).

Houston, City of; Ostrewich v., TexCivApp–Hous (14 Dist), 419 SW2d 247.—Mun Corp 741.10, 741.15, 741.50, 812(2), 812(6.1).

Houston, City of; Overton v., TexCivApp–Hous (1 Dist), 564 SW2d 400, ref nre.—Action 6; Contracts 167; Judgm 866.1; Lim of Act 24(1), 24(2), 28(1), 196(1); Mand 107.

Houston, City of, v. Palace Video, TexApp–Houston (14 Dist, 737 SW2d 370. See City of Houston v. Mitchell.

Houston, City of; Park 'N Fly of Tex., Inc. v., SDTex, 327 FSupp 910.—Commerce 12, 14.10(1), 62; Const Law 241, 3686; Courts 508(7); Decl Judgm 276; Evid 20(2); Mun Corp 122.1(2).

Houston, City of; Peoples Nat. Utility Co. v., CA5 (Tex), 837 F2d 1366.—Fed Cts 28.

Houston, City of; Phillips v., TexApp–Houston (14 Dist), 993 SW2d 357.—Admin Law 683, 754.1, 781, 787; Mun Corp 185(5).

Houston, City of; Phillips v., TexCivApp–Waco, 572 SW2d 797.—App & E 1177(5); Evid 325.

Houston, City of; Pineda v., CA5 (Tex), 291 F3d 325, reh den, cert den 123 SCt 892, 537 US 1110, 154 LEd2d 782.—Civil R 1351(1), 1351(4), 1352(4), 1420; Fed Cts 18.

Houston, City of; Pineda v., SDTex, 124 FSupp2d 1057, dism 252 F3d 1355, aff 291 F3d 325, reh den, cert den 123 SCt 892, 537 US 1110, 154 LEd2d 782.—Civil R 1305, 1343, 1345, 1351(1), 1351(4), 1352(1), 1352(4); Const Law 3045, 3250, 3251, 3299; Controlled Subs 130, 137; Crim Law 37.10(2); Fed Civ Proc 2491.5; Searches 26, 42.1, 45, 181, 183, 184, 192.1, 198, 201.

Houston, City of; Pineda v., SDTex, 124 FSupp2d 1037.—Arrest 63.4(2), 68(2); Civil R 1304, 1376(2), 1376(6), 1395(6), 1398; Const Law 4537; False Imp 13; Fed Civ Proc 2491.5; Offic 114; Searches 25.1, 42.1.

Houston, City of; Piotrowski v., CA5 (Tex), 237 F3d 567, reh en banc den 251 F3d 159, cert den 122 SCt 53, 534 US 820, 151 LEd2d 23.—Civil R 1039, 1088(1), 1343, 1351(1), 1352(1), 1352(4), 1352(6), 1379, 1401, 1420; Const Law 3040, 3041, 4048, 4049, 4050, 4111; Fed Civ

Proc 2127, 2142.1, 2152, 2608.1, 2609; Fed Cts 425, 427, 776; Lim of Act 95(15), 104(1), 105(1).

Houston, City of; Piotrowski v., CA5 (Tex), 51 F3d 512.—Civil R 1027, 1039, 1088(1), 1345, 1351(1), 1379, 1395(5); Const Law 3941, 4048; Fed Civ Proc 1837.1; Fed Cts 425, 427, 776; Lim of Act 95(1), 95(15), 180(7).

Houston, City of; Plaster v., TexApp–Houston (1 Dist), 721 SW2d 421.—App & E 846(5), 852; Crim Law 412.1(1); Mun Corp 185(1); Witn 390.

Houston, City of; Pope v., TexCivApp–Waco, 559 SW2d 905, ref nre.—Const Law 4331; Mun Corp 605.

Houston, City of; Precast Structures, Inc. v., TexApp–Houston (14 Dist), 942 SW2d 632, appeal after remand 60 SW3d 331, motion to dismiss den, and review den.—App & E 893(1); Em Dom 106, 138, 170, 172, 221.

Houston, City of; Pressey v., SDTex, 701 FSupp 594, rev 898 F2d 1018, reh den.—Damag 210(4); Fed Cts 415; Interest 39(2.45), 56.

Houston, City of; Pruitt v., TexCivApp–Hous (1 Dist), 548 SW2d 90.—Admin Law 656; Mand 72, 75; Mun Corp 184(1), 184.1, 197.

Houston, City of; Raeburn v., TexCivApp–Waco, 346 SW2d 488, ref nre.—Mun Corp 854.

Houston, City of; Religious of Sacred Heart of Texas v., Tex, 836 SW2d 606.—Em Dom 131, 133, 138, 255.

Houston, City of, v. Religious of the Sacred Heart of Texas, TexApp–Houston (1 Dist), 811 SW2d 734. See City of Houston v. Religious of the Sacred Heart of Texas.

Houston, City of; Renault, Inc. v., TexCivApp–Waco, 415 SW2d 948, rev 431 SW2d 322.—Em Dom 2(6), 69, 87, 277; Lim of Act 55(5); Mun Corp 835.

Houston, City of; Reyes v., TexApp–Houston (1 Dist), 4 SW3d 459, petition for review den.—App & E 911.3; Autos 278, 279, 301(3); Courts 4, 32, 35, 37(1); Mun Corp 723; Plead 104(1).

Houston, City of, v. Riner, TexApp–Houston (1 Dist), 896 SW2d 317. See City of Houston v. Riner.

Houston, City of; Rivas v., TexApp–Houston (14 Dist), 19 SW3d 901, review den.—Autos 196, 244(1).

Houston, City of; Rivas v., TexApp–Houston (14 Dist), 17 SW3d 23, reh overr, opinion supplemented on denial of reh 19 SW3d 901, review den.—App & E 863, 893(1), 934(1); Autos 187(2), 196, 242(1), 243(1); Evid 54, 587; Judgm 199(3.7), 199(3.10); Mun Corp 745; Offic 114.

Houston, City of, v. River Oaks Garden Club v., Tex, 370 SW2d 851.—Tax 2338, 2339, 2347, 2352, 2354.

Houston, City of, v. Robinson, TexApp–Houston (1 Dist), 837 SW2d 262. See City of Houston v. Robinson.

Houston, City of; Rodriguez v., SDTex, 250 FSupp2d 691.—Civil R 1184, 1185, 1188, 1189, 1528, 1549; Evid 333(1); Fed Civ Proc 2497.1.

Houston, City of; Rosenblatt v., TexApp–Corpus Christi, 31 SW3d 399, review den, cert den 121 SCt 2218, 532 US 1067, 150 LEd2d 211.—Admin Law 482; App & E 497(1), 756, 1079; Const Law 1505, 2204, 2225; Courts 97(1); Judgm 540, 713(2), 720, 829(3); Mun Corp 120; Statut 174, 181(1), 188; Zoning 86, 278.1, 387, 436.1, 626.

Houston, City of; Ross v., TexApp–Houston (1 Dist), 807 SW2d 336, writ den.—Mun Corp 739(2).

Houston, City of; Rothkopf v., TexCivApp–Hous (14 Dist), 612 SW2d 77.—App & E 954(1); Nuis 84, 87.

Houston, City of; Safe Water Foundation of Texas v., TexApp–Houston (1 Dist), 661 SW2d 190, ref nre, appeal dism 105 SCt 55, 469 US 801, 83 LEd2d 6.—Const Law 82(6.1); Mun Corp 992, 1000(5); Waters 196.

Houston, City of; Sam Bassett Lumber Co. v., Tex, 198 SW2d 879, 145 Tex 492.—App & E 1176(1); Counties 24; Lim of Act 165; Mun Corp 72, 79, 978(6); Schools 106.12(3); States 109; Statut 223.4; Tax 2128.

Houston, City of; Sam Bassett Lumber Co. v., TexCivApp–Galveston, 194 SW2d 114, rev 198 SW2d 879, 145 Tex 492.—App & E 1040(10); Const Law 632; Mun Corp 79, 957(4), 971(4), 972(2), 978(9); Plead 228.14;

Schools 103(1), 106.1; Statut 64(1); Tax 2121, 2140, 2713.

Houston, City of; Sanders v., SDTex, 543 FSupp 694, aff 741 F2d 1379.—Arrest 58, 63.4(1), 70(1), 70(2); Bail 42, 49(4); Crim Law 223, 228, 641.12(1), 1224(1); Inj 77(1); Mun Corp 742(5).

Houston, City of, v. Savely, TexApp–Houston (1 Dist), 708 SW2d 879. See City of Houston v. Savely.

Houston, City of; Scanlan v., TexCivApp–Galveston, 137 SW2d 204, writ dism, correct.—App & E 954(3); Dedi 44; Em Dom 308.

Houston, City of; Schulman v., Tex, 412 SW2d 34.—Mun Corp 992.

Houston, City of; Schulman v., TexCivApp–Tyler, 406 SW2d 219, ref nre.—Inj 11, 77(1); Mun Corp 607, 733(1), 736, 993(2), 1000(0.5), 1000(5); Nuis 3(1), 19.

Houston, City of; Schultz v., TexCivApp–Hous (14 Dist), 551 SW2d 494.—Afft 3; Judgm 185.3(21); Mun Corp 723.5, 724, 734, 741.15, 741.50.

Houston, City of; Scott v., SDTex, 613 FSupp 34.—Civil R 1140, 1395(8), 1405, 1421, 1532, 1535, 1548.

Houston, City of; Scott v., TexCivApp–Hous (14 Dist), 595 SW2d 909, ref nre.—Mun Corp 184(2).

Houston, City of; SDJ, Inc. v., CA5 (Tex), 841 F2d 107.—Courts 96(3), 107.

Houston, City of; SDJ, Inc. v., CA5 (Tex), 837 F2d 1268, reh den 841 F2d 107, cert den MEF Enterprises, Inc v. City of Houston, 109 SCt 1310, 489 US 1052, 103 LEd2d 579.—Const Law 1518, 1520, 1529, 2208, 2210, 2212, 2215, 2233, 2237, 2248, 3384, 3405, 3695, 4092, 4289; Em Dom 2(1.2); Int Liq 11, 15; Zoning 6, 27, 28, 76, 81, 86, 602.

Houston, City of; SDJ, Inc. v., SDTex, 636 FSupp 1359, aff 837 F2d 1268, reh den 841 F2d 107, cert den MEF Enterprises, Inc v. City of Houston, 109 SCt 1310, 489 US 1052, 103 LEd2d 579.—Const Law 230.3(5), 725, 855, 1176, 1244, 1504, 1505, 1512, 1514, 1515, 1545, 1790, 2209, 2216, 2233, 2240(2), 2243, 3695, 4092; Em Dom 2(1.2); Int Liq 11, 112; Mun Corp 111(2), 111(4), 111(7), 591, 592(1), 594(2); Obscen 2.5; Statut 109.2, 114(1); Zoning 21, 42, 84.

Houston, City of; Settegast v., Tex, 113 SW2d 1221, 131 Tex 138.—Mun Corp 918(5).

Houston, City of; Sharp v., CA5 (Tex), 164 F3d 923, reh den.—Civil R 1149, 1189, 1351(1), 1421, 1549, 1555; Const Law 1184(1), 1184(2), 1955; Fed Civ Proc 2142.1, 2152; Fed Cts 629, 776, 798, 801; Mun Corp 180(2).

Houston, City of; Sharp v., SDTex, 960 FSupp 1164.—Civil R 1119, 1189, 1244, 1249(1), 1252, 1351(5), 1502, 1537; Const Law 1928, 1932; Fed Civ Proc 2497.1; Mun Corp 180(1).

Houston, City of; Shoppers Fair of North Houston, Inc. v., TexCivApp–Eastland, 406 SW2d 86, ref nre.—Inj 85(1), 151; Mun Corp 121.

Houston, City of; Simpson v., TexCivApp–Galveston, 260 SW2d 94, ref nre.—Judgm 559, 648; Mun Corp 185(10), 185(12), 216(1); Trial 139.1(9).

Houston, City of; Sjolander v., TexCivApp, 551 SW2d 166.—Em Dom 2(1.1), 300, 302.

Houston, City of; Smith v., TexApp–Houston (14 Dist), 960 SW2d 326.—Mun Corp 741.15, 741.55; Pretrial Proc 481.

Houston, City of; Smith v., TexApp–Houston (14 Dist), 693 SW2d 753, ref nre.—Decl Judgm 255; Em Dom 2(11); Mun Corp 466.

Houston, City of; Smith v., TexCivApp–Hous (1 Dist), 552 SW2d 945.—Const Law 4171; Mun Corp 216(1), 217.2, 218(3), 218(8), 218(9).

Houston, City of, v. Southwest Concrete Const., Inc., TexApp–Houston (14 Dist, 835 SW2d 728. See City of Houston v. Southwest Concrete Const., Inc.

Houston, City of; SpawGlass Const. Corp. v., TexApp–Houston (14 Dist), 974 SW2d 876, review den.—Action

6; App & E 1175(1); Decl Judgm 6, 8, 61; Mun Corp 332.

Houston, City of; Spiegel v., CA5 (Tex), 636 F2d 997, reh den 641 F2d 879.—Inj 85(1), 138.6, 138.57, 147, 157; Mun Corp 742(2).

Houston, City of; Spillers v., TexApp–Houston (1 Dist), 777 SW2d 181, writ den.—App & E 1001(1), 1003(7); Work Comp 803, 1357, 1374, 1643, 1939.3.

Houston, City of; Stahl v., TexCivApp–Houston, 397 SW2d 318, ref nre.—Mun Corp 197.

Houston, City of; Starks v., TexCivApp–Hous (1 Dist), 448 SW2d 698, ref nre.—Autos 306(2); Evid 201, 211, 265(10), 265(13), 265(15), 265(17), 591.

Houston, City of; State v., TexCivApp–Galveston, 140 SW2d 277, writ refused.—Counties 190.1; Tax 2275, 2278.

Houston, City of; State ex rel. Richmond Plaza Civic Ass'n v., TexCivApp–Galveston, 270 SW2d 235, ref nre.—Mun Corp 34, 36(1), 36(2), 36(3), 120, 966(4); Waters 201, 203(1), 203(3), 203(12).

Houston, City of; Stecher v., TexCivApp–Galveston, 272 SW2d 925, ref nre.—Decl Judgm 128; Inj 85(2), 123; Statut 212.1.

Houston, City of; Steele v., Tex, 603 SW2d 786.—Mun Corp 628, 739(1), 742(4), 742(5); Plead 228.23.

Houston, City of; Steele v., TexCivApp–Hous (14 Dist), 577 SW2d 372, rev 603 SW2d 786.—App & E 596, 671(4), 926(8); Autos 187(2); Mun Corp 742(4), 745.5, 847.

Houston, City of; Strickland v., TexCivApp–Hous (14 Dist), 608 SW2d 285, ref nre.—Autos 230; Estop 62.4.

Houston, City of; Stuart v., TexCivApp–Hous (14 Dist), 419 SW2d 702, ref nre.—Judgm 326, 335(1); New Tr 12; Pretrial Proc 698, 699.

Houston, City of; Sugar Babes v., CA5 (Tex), 841 F2d 107. See SDJ, Inc. v. City of Houston.

Houston, City of; Sugar Babes v., CA5 (Tex), 837 F2d 1268. See SDJ, Inc. v. City of Houston.

Houston, City of; Sugar Babes v., SDTex, 636 FSupp 1359. See SDJ, Inc. v. City of Houston.

Houston, City of, v. Swindall, TexApp–Houston (1 Dist), 960 SW2d 413. See City of Houston v. Swindall.

Houston, City of; Taxpayers' Ass'n of Harris County v., Tex, 105 SW2d 655, 129 Tex 627.—Mun Corp 108.1, 108.6, 108.9, 124(6), 215, 867(1), 868(3).

Houston, City of; Taxpayers' Ass'n of Harris County v., TexCivApp–Galveston, 100 SW2d 1066, writ gr 105 SW2d 655, 129 Tex 627.—Mun Corp 108.6, 108.10, 162, 220(1), 867(1).

Houston, City of; Taxpayers' Political Action Committee v., TexCivApp–Hous (1 Dist), 596 SW2d 147.—Mand 10, 12, 74(1); Mun Corp 46.

Houston, City of; Temple v., TexApp–Houston (1 Dist), 189 SW3d 816.—App & E 893(1), 916(1); Counties 141; Courts 4, 35; Mun Corp 187(10), 220(9), 723, 724, 725; Plead 104(1); Schools 89; States 191.1, 191.4(1).

Houston, City of; Texas Employment Commission v., TexCivApp–Hous (1 Dist), 616 SW2d 255, ref nre 618 SW2d 329.—Admin Law 750; Autos 5(5); Judgm 181(15.1), 185(3); Statut 188; Unemp Comp 457, 497.

Houston, City of, v. Thomas, TexApp–Houston (1 Dist), 838 SW2d 296. See City of Houston v. Thomas.

Houston, City of; Thompson v., TexCivApp–Houston, 410 SW2d 813, ref nre.—Tax 2712, 2714, 2882, 2883.

Houston, City of; Thordson v., Tex, 815 SW2d 550.—Pretrial Proc 699.

Houston, City of; Thordson v., TexApp–Houston (14 Dist), 809 SW2d 905, writ gr, rev and remanded 815 SW2d 550.—App & E 946; Const Law 3984; Pretrial Proc 699.

Houston, City of; Todaro v., TexApp–Houston (14 Dist), 135 SW3d 287.—App & E 893(1), 916(1); Autos 252, 253; Mun Corp 723, 723.5; Plead 104(1), 111.36, 111.37; States 191.4(1).

Houston, City of; Todd v., TexCivApp–Hous (1 Dist), 508 SW2d 140, ref nre.—Judgm 186; Mun Corp 185(12).

Houston, City of; Trail Enterprises, Inc. v., SDTex, 907 FSupp 250.—Em Dom 277; Fed Civ Proc 1742(1); Fed Cts 51.

Houston, City of; Trail Enterprises, Inc. v., TexApp– Houston (14 Dist), 957 SW2d 625, review den, and reh of petition for review overr, cert den 119 SCt 802, 525 US 1070, 142 LEd2d 663, reh den 119 SCt 1099, 525 US 1172, 143 LEd2d 98.—App & E 78(1), 1175(1); Const Law 190, 2672, 2701, 3057, 3532, 3895, 3898, 4323; Em Dom 2(1), 2(7), 266, 288(1); Environ Law 178; Estop 62.1, 62.6; Judgm 181(11), 185(2), 185(5), 185(6); Lim of Act 43, 44(2), 55(5); Mines 92.13, 92.23(1); Mun Corp 111(1), 111(3), 122.1(2), 595, 597, 600; Plead 48.

Houston, City of; Trevino v., TexApp–Houston (1 Dist), 695 SW2d 289, ref nre.—Work Comp 1041, 1383.

Houston, City of; True Distance, Inc. v., TexApp–Houston (1 Dist), 756 SW2d 813. See Young v. City of Houston.

Houston, City of; Truong v., TexApp–Houston (1 Dist), 99 SW3d 204, reh overr.—App & E 544(1), 635(1), 907(3); Covenants 21, 49, 73, 134; Equity 65(1); Estop 62.1, 62.4; Inj 62(1); Judgm 183; Mun Corp 57, 1018; Plead 106(1); Zoning 6, 26, 27, 481, 507, 761, 764.

Houston, City of; Tuesday Morning, Inc. v., TexCivApp– Hous (1 Dist), 557 SW2d 322.—Inj 157.

Houston, City of; Turvey v., Tex, 602 SW2d 517.— Counties 142; Mun Corp 725, 733(2), 745, 794.

Houston, City of; Tyra v., Tex, 822 SW2d 626.—Mun Corp 67(1); Statut 267(1).

Houston, City of, v. Tyra, TexApp–Houston (14 Dist, 786 SW2d 457. See City of Houston v. Tyra.

Houston, City of; U.S. v., SDTex, 800 FSupp 504.— Elections 12(9.1).

Houston, City of; United Water Services, Inc. v., TexApp–Houston (1 Dist), 137 SW3d 747, review gr, rev 201 SW3d 690.—App & E 893(1); Courts 4, 35, 91(1); Mun Corp 254, 723, 724, 725, 742(5); Plead 104(1); States 191.4(1), 191.8(1).

Houston, City of; Valentino v., TexApp–Houston (1 Dist), 674 SW2d 813, ref nre.—Admin Law 786, 788, 791; Mun Corp 185(6), 185(7), 185(8), 185(10), 185(12).

Houston, City of; Vara v., TexCivApp–Hous (14 Dist), 583 SW2d 935, ref nre, appeal dism 101 SCt 54, 449 US 807, 66 LEd2d 11.—Mun Corp 30, 65.

Houston, City of; Vela v., CA5 (Tex), 276 F3d 659.— Costs 194.18; Fed Civ Proc 2737.4; Fed Cts 12.1, 611, 617, 723.1, 724, 830, 878; Labor & Emp 2240, 2242, 2250, 2251, 2255, 2267, 2292(2), 2338, 2357, 2385(6), 2405, 2406; Statut 263, 265, 266, 267(1).

Houston, City of; Vela v., TexApp–Houston (1 Dist), 186 SW3d 49.—App & E 934(1); Mun Corp 218(10); Offic 66.

Houston, City of, v. Vitek, TexApp–Houston (14 Dist, 849 SW2d 882. See City of Houston v. Vitek.

Houston, City of; Waddy v., TexApp–Houston (1 Dist), 834 SW2d 97, reh den, and writ den.—App & E 173(2), 194(1), 223, 837(9), 852, 856(1), 863, 907(4); Em Dom 1, 2(1), 266, 288(1), 307(2); Judgm 181(11), 183, 185(2), 185.3(1); Lim of Act 32(1), 44(2), 95(7), 195(3); Tresp 35.

Houston, City of; Walker v., SDTex, 341 FSupp 1124.— Decl Judgm 303; Fed Civ Proc 184.5, 241, 256; Fed Cts 93, 221, 223, 993.1.

Houston, City of; Walker v., SDTex, 341 FSupp 1117.— Fed Cts 991, 997, 1002.

Houston, City of; Walker v., Tex, 617 SW2d 673.—Mun Corp 79.

Houston, City of; Walker v., TexCivApp–Hous (14 Dist), 466 SW2d 607.—Mun Corp 185(3), 185(8), 185(10), 185(12), 198(3), 198(4); Statut 184.

Houston, City of; Walton v., Tex, 421 SW2d 902.—Mun Corp 296(2).

Houston, City of; Walton v., TexCivApp–Waco, 409 SW2d 917, writ gr, rev 421 SW2d 902.—App & E 846(5); Const Law 4061; High 113(1); Mun Corp 407(1), 413(1), 436.1, 449(3), 455, 485(1), 513(7), 733(2).

Houston, City of; Washington v., TexApp–Texarkana, 874 SW2d 791.—App & E 854(1), 863, 934(2); Judges 36; Judgm 181(11), 183, 185(1), 185(2), 185(4), 185.1(3); Mun Corp 747(4), 847, 854; Plead 48.

Houston, City of; Watts v., TexApp–Houston (1 Dist), 126 SW3d 97.—Admin Law 796; App & E 1175(1); Decl Judgm 41; Mun Corp 185(12), 198(3), 198(4), 199; Statut 176, 181(1), 181(2), 188, 206.

Houston, City of; Watts v., TexCivApp–Galveston, 196 SW2d 553, writ refused.—Assign 9; Dedi 53; Deeds 134, 144(1), 145; Trial 141; Wills 7, 624.

Houston, City of; Webster v., CA5 (Tex), 739 F2d 993.— Civil R 1420.

Houston, City of; Webster v., CA5 (Tex), 735 F2d 838, on reh 739 F2d 993.—Civil R 1351(1), 1395(6), 1437.

Houston, City of; Webster v., CA5 (Tex), 689 F2d 1220, reh gr 711 F2d 35, on reh 735 F2d 838, on reh 739 F2d 993.—Civil R 1420, 1461, 1465(1).

Houston, City of; Wells v., SDTex, 613 FSupp 479, aff 788 F2d 1563, cert den 107 SCt 218, 479 US 864, 93 LEd2d 147, reh den 107 SCt 681, 479 US 1022, 93 LEd2d 731.—Civil R 1544, 1548; Const Law 4171; Mun Corp 185(3), 185(4).

Houston, City of, v. West Capital Financial Services Corp., TexApp–Houston (1 Dist), 961 SW2d 687. See City of Houston v. West Capital Financial Services Corp.

Houston, City of; White Top Cab Co. v., TexCivApp– Hous (14 Dist), 440 SW2d 732.—Admin Law 701; Autos 83, 84, 104, 142; Mun Corp 108.7.

Houston, City of; Whitton v., SDTex, 676 FSupp 137.— Const Law 4111.

Houston, City of, v. Willow Run Public Service, Inc., TexApp–Houston (1 Dist), 714 SW2d 150. See City of Houston v. Willow Run Public Service, Inc.

Houston, City of; Wilson Oil Co. v., SDTex, 907 FSupp 250. See Trail Enterprises, Inc. v. City of Houston.

Houston, City of; Wilson Oil Co. v., TexApp–Houston (14 Dist, 957 SW2d 625. See Trail Enterprises, Inc. v. City of Houston.

Houston, City of, v. Wolfe, TexApp–Houston (14 Dist, 712 SW2d 228. See City of Houston v. Wolfe.

Houston, City of; Wolfe v., TexCivApp–Hous (14 Dist), 595 SW2d 909, ref nre.—Mun Corp 184(2).

Houston, City of; Wones v., TexCivApp–Galveston, 281 SW2d 133.—Mun Corp 741.40(2), 742(4).

Houston, City of; Woodland v., CA5 (Tex), 940 F2d 134, on remand 918 FSupp 1047, vac 1996 WL 752803.— Const Law 1210, 1257; Mun Corp 1036.

Houston, City of; Woodland v., SDTex, 918 FSupp 1047, vac 1996 WL 752803.—Const Law 1050, 1066, 1210, 1212, 1216, 1217, 1257, 3007, 3053, 3877; Fed Civ Proc 161, 172, 184.5; Inj 77(1); Mun Corp 217.3(1); Offic 8.

Houston, City of; Woodland v., SDTex, 731 FSupp 1304, vac 940 F2d 134, on remand 918 FSupp 1047, vac 1996 WL 752803.—Const Law 1257; Inj 77(1); Mun Corp 184(2), 197.

Houston, City of; Young v., TexApp–Houston (1 Dist), 756 SW2d 813, writ den.—Mun Corp 870; States 119.

Houston, City of, Civic Center, v. Dudley, CA5 (Tex), 800 F2d 491. See Nash v. City of Houston Civic Center.

Houston Civic Center, City of; Nash v., CA5 (Tex), 800 F2d 491, reh den 805 F2d 1030.—Civil R 1544, 1545, 1549; Mun Corp 218(1).

Houston Civic Opera Ass'n; Conrick v., TexCivApp– Amarillo, 99 SW2d 382.—Corp 306, 310(1), 331, 360(1), 544(2).

Houston Coca-Cola Bottling Co. v. Kelley, CCA5 (Tex), 131 F2d 627.—Fed Civ Proc 1968, 2313, 2345.1; Fed Cts 753, 872, 875.

Houston Community College; Sessum v., SDTex, 94 FRD 316.—Civil R 1544, 1545; Fed Civ Proc 161, 162, 164, 165, 171, 173, 177.1, 184.10.

Houston Community College System; Govant v., TexApp–Houston (14 Dist), 72 SW3d 69, reh overr.—Colleges 8(1), 8.1(4.1), 8.1(5); Const Law 3627(4), 3879, 4165(1), 4223(4); Offic 114.

Houston Community College System; Kacher v., SDTex, 974 FSupp 615.—Civil R 1113, 1225(2), 1351(2), 1351(5); Colleges 8(1); Estop 68(1), 68(2); Fed Civ Proc 2497.1; Fed Cts 411.

Houston Community College System; Lin v., TexApp–Amarillo, 948 SW2d 328, reh overr, and writ den.—Admin Law 452.1; App & E 205, 1043(1), 1050.1(1), 1056.1(1); Deeds 111; Em Dom 68, 131, 148, 150, 167(4), 170, 176, 184, 191(1), 191(3), 191(6), 202(1), 221, 223, 255, 262(4), 262(5); Evid 571(7).

Houston Community College System; Mosley v., SDTex, 951 FSupp 1279.—Civil R 1118, 1135, 1376(2), 1376(5), 1379, 1395(8), 1465(2), 1736; Colleges 5, 8(1); Const Law 3006, 3847, 4040, 4223(2), 4223(3); Fed Civ Proc 840, 841, 842, 2491.5, 2544.

Houston Community College System v. Schneider, TexApp–Houston (1 Dist), 67 SW3d 241, review den.—Work Comp 1887.

Houston Community Hosp. v. Blue Cross and Blue Shield of Texas, Inc., CA5 (Tex), 481 F3d 265.—Fed Cts 572.1, 574, 576.1.

Houston Compressed Steel Corp. v. State, TexCivApp–Hous (1 Dist), 456 SW2d 768.—Admin Law 228.1, 386; App & E 242(2), 436, 447, 863, 1097(8); Const Law 47, 975, 1066, 1111, 4324; Environ Law 90, 246, 272, 664; Health 358; Inj 102, 157; Nuis 84; States 18.31; Statut 47; Trial 13(2).

Houston Contracting Co.; Mallett v., TexCivApp–Beaumont, 388 SW2d 216, ref nre.—Dedi 16.1, 17, 20(1), 38, 39; High 68, 160(3).

Houston Contracting Co. v. Texas & P. Ry. Co., TexCivApp–Beaumont, 361 SW2d 251.—R R 22(1), 343.

Houston Contractors Ass'n v. Metropolitan Transit Authority of Harris County, SDTex, 993 FSupp 545.—Const Law 726, 975, 3039, 3054, 3055, 3289, 3402, 3677; Counties 116.

Houston Contractors Ass'n v. Metropolitan Transit Authority of Harris County, SDTex, 945 FSupp 1013.—Civil R 1457(7); Const Law 726, 3041, 3050.

Houston Corrugated Box Co., Inc.; Solomon v., CA5 (Tex), 526 F2d 389.—Antitrust 537, 545, 563, 976, 977(2), 992; Fed Civ Proc 1695, 2461, 2484, 2547.1.

Houston Corrugated Box Co., Inc. v. Sunbelt Nat. Bank, SDTex, 127 BR 158. See Texas Corrugated Box Corp., In re.

Houston Cotton Exchange Bldg Co v. C I R, CCA5 (Tex), 134 F2d 323.—Int Rev 3834.

Houston County v. Leo L. Landauer & Associates, Inc., TexCivApp–Tyler, 424 SW2d 458, ref nre.—App & E 296, 930(1), 1073(1); Contracts 176(10), 212(2), 213(1), 303(4), 317; Counties 224; Judgm 198, 199(1), 199(3.7); Trial 142.

Houston County; Overstreet v., TexCivApp–Houston, 365 SW2d 409, ref nre.—App & E 954(2); Counties 116, 123, 127; Pub Contr 41; States 102.

Houston County Jail; Lewis v., EDTex, 876 FSupp 861.—Civil R 1088(4); Dist & Pros Attys 10; False Imp 20(1); Fed Civ Proc 2470.4, 2543; Mal Pros 42.

Houston County, Texas; Gaston v., EDTex, 202 FSupp2d 564.—Civil R 1352(1), 1376(2); Const Law 3488, 3938, 4830; Fed Cts 15; Mun Corp 740(1).

Houston County, Texas; Gaston v., EDTex, 196 FSupp2d 445.—Civil R 1304; Const Law 4830; Counties 146.

Houston Crane Rentals, Inc. v. City of Houston, TexCivApp–Hous (1 Dist), 454 SW2d 216, ref nre.—Judgm 185(2), 185.3(20), 186; Mun Corp 79, 978(1), 978(10); Schools 106; Tax 2446, 2587, 2858.

Houston Credit Sales Co. v. City of Trinity, TexCivApp–Waco, 269 SW2d 579, ref nre.—Hawk & P 1, 2; Mun Corp 594(1); Nuis 61.

Houston Credit Sales Co. v. English, TexCivApp–Waco, 139 SW2d 163.—Contracts 117(2), 262, 270(1); Inj 138.39.

Houston Crushed Concrete, Inc. v. Concrete Recycling Corp., TexApp–Houston (14 Dist), 879 SW2d 258, reh den.—Appear 8(1), 24(1).

Houston Dairy; McDonald v., TexApp–Houston (1 Dist), 813 SW2d 238, appeal after remand 1994 WL 418974, writ den.—Costs 128.

Houston Deepwater Land Co. v. Scofield, SDTex, 110 FSupp 394.—Int Rev 3233, 3250.

Houston Distributing Co., Inc.; Cavender v., TexApp–Houston (1 Dist), 176 SW3d 71, review den.—Courts 89; Labor & Emp 807.

Houston Drapery Mfrs., Inc. v. Frank Kasmir Associates, Inc., TexCivApp–Waco, 538 SW2d 161.—App & E 907(4); Plead 111.42(5), 111.42(10).

Houston Drywall, Inc. v. Construction Systems, Inc., TexCivApp–Hous (1 Dist), 541 SW2d 220.—Garn 7, 40, 42, 59; Judgm 73, 335(1).

Houston, E. & T. Ry. Co. v. Snow, TexCivApp–Beaumont, 201 SW 224.—App & E 1004(8).

Houston Elec. Co. v. Dorsett, Tex, 194 SW2d 546, 145 Tex 95.—App & E 917(1); Damag 52, 149.

Houston Elec. Co.; Dorsett v., TexCivApp–Galveston, 191 SW2d 514, aff 194 SW2d 546, 145 Tex 95.—Damag 52, 56.20, 149, 208(6).

Houston Elec. Co.; Hammonds v., TexCivApp–Beaumont, 169 SW2d 765.—Plead 111.18, 111.42(8), 111.42(9).

Houston Electric Co.; Hornsby v., TexCivApp–Galveston, 125 SW2d 346, writ dism, correct.—App & E 218.2(1), 719(8); Autos 245(91); New Tr 163(2); Trial 352.10; Witn 321, 331.5.

Houston Elec. Co. v. Lee, TexComApp, 162 SW2d 692, 139 Tex 166.—App & E 1069.1.

Houston Elec. Co.; Lee v., TexCivApp–Beaumont, 152 SW2d 379, aff 162 SW2d 692, 139 Tex 166.—App & E 1069.1; Evid 123(11); Trial 313; Urb R R 30.

Houston Electric Co.; Lipscomb v., TexCivApp–Galveston, 149 SW2d 1042.—App & E 1061.4; Carr 320(25); Neglig 1550, 1579, 1599, 1656, 1675; Release 17(2); Trial 178.

Houston Elec. Co. v. McLeroy, TexComApp, 163 SW2d 1062, 139 Tex 170.—App & E 1069.1, 1094(1); Autos 246(57).

Houston Elec. Co. v. McLeroy, TexCivApp–Galveston, 153 SW2d 617, rev 163 SW2d 1062, 139 Tex 170.—App & E 929, 1001(1), 1015(1), 1069.1, 1072; Autos 243(5), 244(14), 244(35), 245(66); Evid 129(1), 129(6); Neglig 440(1).

Houston Elec. Co.; Montgomery v., TexComApp, 144 SW2d 251, 135 Tex 538.—App & E 1094(5); Autos 247; Neglig 530(1); Trial 365.1(7).

Houston Elec. Co. v. Montgomery, TexCivApp–Galveston, 123 SW2d 943, rev 144 SW2d 251, 135 Tex 538.—App & E 171(1), 840(4), 882(3); Autos 238(10), 247; Trial 350.6(1), 350.7(9).

Houston Elec. Co.; Walker v., TexCivApp–Galveston, 155 SW2d 973, writ refused.—Autos 175(3), 244(43), 245(67.1), 247; Trial 358, 365.1(1), 365.2.

Houston Elec. Distributing Co., Inc. v. MBB Enterprises, TexApp–Houston (14 Dist), 703 SW2d 206.—Mech Liens 130(2), 279.

Houston Emergicare, Inc.; Flynn v., TexApp–Houston (1 Dist), 869 SW2d 403, reh overr, and writ den.—Health 752, 800.

Houston Endowment Inc. v. Atlantic Richfield Co., TexApp–Houston (14 Dist), 972 SW2d 156, rule 537(f) motion gr.—App & E 758.1; Judgm 181(7), 185(2); Lim of Act 46(6), 95(1), 95(9), 104(1).

Houston Endowment, Inc.; City of Houston v., TexCivApp–Hous (1 Dist), 438 SW2d 935, ref nre.—Mun Corp 33(9).

Houston Endowment, Inc.; City of Houston v., TexCivApp–Hous (1 Dist), 428 SW2d 706, ref nre, motion den 438 SW2d 935, ref nre.—Mun Corp 29(1), 29(4), 33(1), 35; Quo W 5.

Houston Endowment, Inc. v. City of Houston, TexCivApp–Hous (14 Dist), 468 SW2d 540, ref nre.—App & E 1097(1); Const Law 3483; Mun Corp 38; Tax 2126.

Houston Endowment, Inc.; City of Pasadena v., TexCivApp–Hous (14 Dist), 438 SW2d 152, ref nre.—Const Law 990, 4056; Mun Corp 29(2), 29(4), 33(2), 33(9), 63.10; Quo W 5; Tax 2135, 2140, 2640, 2712.

Houston Endowment, Inc. v. U.S., CA5 (Tex), 606 F2d 77.—Int Rev 3232, 3234, 3249, 3250, 3251, 5111.1.

Houston Engineers, Inc.; Bowen-Itco, Inc. v., SDTex, 192 FSupp 223, rev 310 F2d 522, cert den 83 SCt 875, 372 US 930, 9 LEd2d 734.—Pat 3, 16(4), 36.1(3), 36.1(4), 36.2(1), 112.1, 144, 178, 237, 240, 245(1), 248, 290(1).

Houston Farms Development Co v. U S, CCA5 (Tex), 131 F2d 577, reh den 132 F2d 861.—Int Rev 3014, 3501.

Houston Federation of Teachers, Local 2415 v. Houston Independent School Dist., Tex, 730 SW2d 644.—Admin Law 229; App & E 100(1); Inj 138.54.

Houston Federation of Teachers, Local 2415; Houston Independent School Dist. v., TexApp–Houston (1 Dist), 715 SW2d 369, writ gr, rev 730 SW2d 644.—Admin Law 229; Labor & Emp 2030; Schools 63(1).

Houston Fire & Cas. Ins. Co.; Atlas Assur. Co. v., TexCivApp–Amarillo, 324 SW2d 943, writ dism.—Action 60; App & E 327(6), 912, 1024.3, 1046.1; Decl Judgm 271; Venue 21, 22(7).

Houston Fire & Cas. Ins. Co. v. Biber, TexCivApp–San Antonio, 146 SW2d 442, writ dism, correct.—App & E 989; Evid 54, 597; Work Comp 642, 1338, 1359, 1360, 1362, 1535.

Houston Fire & Cas. Ins. Co.; Billington v., TexCivApp–Fort Worth, 226 SW2d 494, mandamus overr.—App & E 927(7); Libel 6(1), 6(2), 15, 19, 33, 86(1), 86(2), 123(2).

Houston Fire & Cas. Ins. Co. v. Brittian, Tex, 402 SW2d 509.—Evid 575, 577, 581; Work Comp 1968(3).

Houston Fire & Cas. Ins. Co. v. Brittian, TexCivApp–Beaumont, 392 SW2d 604, writ gr, rev 402 SW2d 509.—Damag 221(7); Evid 575; Trial 352.14; Work Comp 1624, 1964, 1966, 1974.

Houston Fire & Cas. Ins. Co. v. Col-Tex Refining Co., TexCivApp–Eastland, 231 SW2d 468.—High 113(5).

Houston Fire & Cas. Ins. Co. v. Dieter, Tex, 409 SW2d 838.—Work Comp 2, 11, 949, 1847, 1922.

Houston Fire & Cas. Ins. Co.; Dieter v., TexCivApp–Amarillo, 403 SW2d 222, writ gr, rev 409 SW2d 838.—Work Comp 1847.

Houston Fire & Cas. Ins. Co. v. E. E. Cloer General Contractor, CA5 (Tex), 217 F2d 906.—Contracts 198(1); Princ & S 59, 65, 66(1), 69; U S 67(4), 67(11).

Houston Fire & Cas. Ins. Co. v. Farm Air Service, Inc., TexCivApp–Austin, 325 SW2d 860, ref nre.—Work Comp 304, 348, 349, 1065, 1101.

Houston Fire & Cas. Ins. Co.; Farm Air Service, Inc. v., TexCivApp–Austin, 309 SW2d 510.—Corp 503(2); Plead 111.16, 111.42(6).

Houston Fire & Cas. Ins. Co. v. Ford, TexCivApp–Texarkana, 241 SW2d 158, ref nre.—App & E 207, 758.1; Trial 131(3); Witn 287(1); Work Comp 1922, 1926, 1958, 1968(5).

Houston Fire & Cas. Ins. Co. v. Gerhardt, TexCivApp–San Antonio, 281 SW2d 176.—App & E 78(1); Courts 207.4(2); Mand 25, 28, 70, 73(1); Trial 355(1).

Houston Fire & Cas. Ins. Co. v. Hales, TexCivApp–Eastland, 279 SW2d 389, ref nre.—Evid 144, 588; Mech Liens 48; Princ & S 59, 82(1), 161, 162(3).

Houston Fire & Cas. Ins. Co. v. Howell, Tex, 484 SW2d 582.—App & E 883; Damag 221(8); Trial 365.1(6); Work Comp 1974.

Houston Fire & Cas. Ins. Co.; Howell v., TexCivApp–Waco, 474 SW2d 924, writ gr, rev 484 SW2d 582.—Damag 221(8); Work Comp 1943.

Houston Fire & Cas. Ins. Co.; Johnson v., TexCivApp–El Paso, 275 SW2d 140, ref nre.—Work Comp 1615.

Houston Fire & Cas. Ins. Co. v. Kahn, Tex, 359 SW2d 892.—Insurance 2588(2).

Houston Fire & Cas. Ins. Co. v. Kahn, TexCivApp–Houston, 355 SW2d 221, writ gr, rev 359 SW2d 892.—Evid 5(2); Insurance 2673, 2817.

Houston Fire & Cas. Ins. Co.; Kincheloe v., TexCivApp–Texarkana, 289 SW2d 833.—Stip 17(1); Work Comp 1172, 1385, 1702.

Houston Fire & Cas. Ins. Co.; Lambert v., TexCivApp–Beaumont, 260 SW2d 691, ref nre.—Work Comp 1269, 1279, 1283, 1297, 1552, 1683, 1927.

Houston Fire & Cas. Ins. Co.; Lambert v., TexCivApp–Beaumont, 254 SW2d 405.—App & E 564(3), 644(2).

Houston Fire & Cas. Ins. Co.; Lee v., Tex, 530 SW2d 294.—Work Comp 1283, 1286, 1297, 1335, 1382, 1726.

Houston Fire & Cas. Ins. Co. v. Lee, TexCivApp–Texarkana, 521 SW2d 739, writ gr, rev 530 SW2d 294.—Work Comp 1283, 1297, 1382, 1920.

Houston Fire & Cas. Ins. Co. v. Miller, TexCivApp–El Paso, 237 SW2d 461.—App & E 981; New Tr 6, 101, 108(1); Work Comp 1061, 1800.

Houston Fire & Cas. Ins. Co.; Mims v., TexCivApp–Texarkana, 362 SW2d 880.—Insurance 3098, 3374.

Houston Fire & Cas. Ins. Co.; Muro v., TexCivApp–San Antonio, 329 SW2d 326, ref nre.—App & E 110, 747(2), 842(7), 934(1); Evid 555.4(5), 568(1), 570, 574, 588; Trial 125(1), 133.3, 140(1), 143; Work Comp 803, 1404, 1653, 1927.

Houston Fire & Cas. Ins. Co.; Muro v., TexCivApp–San Antonio, 310 SW2d 420, ref nre.—Work Comp 872, 1402, 1968(8).

Houston Fire & Cas. Ins. Co. v. Nichols, Tex, 435 SW2d 140.—App & E 1177(2); Insurance 2171.

Houston Fire & Cas. Ins. Co. v. Nichols, TexCivApp–El Paso, 428 SW2d 458, writ gr, rev 435 SW2d 140.—App & E 758.3(8), 930(1), 989, 1001(1), 1003(9.1), 1177(7); Insurance 1634(1), 1906, 2136(3), 2171, 3015; Trial 352.5(4).

Houston Fire & Cas. Ins. Co.; Palo Pinto General Hospital v., TexCivApp–Eastland, 471 SW2d 437, ref nre.—Judgm 632.

Houston Fire & Cas. Ins. Co. v. Parker, TexCivApp–Amarillo, 341 SW2d 495, ref nre.—Contracts 147(1); Work Comp 1065, 1067.

Houston Fire & Cas. Ins. Co. v. Pritchard & Abbott, Tex, 283 SW2d 728, 155 Tex 120.—App & E 758.3(4), 1094(1); Contracts 98; Insurance 1766, 1902, 1915, 2762(1), 3580.

Houston Fire & Cas. Ins. Co. v. Pritchard & Abbott, TexCivApp–Fort Worth, 272 SW2d 392, aff 283 SW2d 728, 155 Tex 120.—Insurance 1713, 1738, 1748, 1894, 1902, 1906, 2770.

Houston Fire & Cas. Ins. Co. v. Riesel Independent School Dist., TexCivApp–Waco, 375 SW2d 323, ref nre.—App & E 1062.1; Contracts 147(3), 164; Princ & S 117; Schools 81(2), 84, 85, 86(2); Trial 350.4(1), 352.4(4).

Houston Fire & Cas. Ins. Co.; Skelly Oil Co. v., TexCivApp–El Paso, 322 SW2d 419, ref nre.—App & E 934(1); Work Comp 1044, 2210, 2213.

Houston Fire & Cas. Ins. Co.; Spears v., TexCivApp–Galveston, 215 SW2d 896, writ refused.—Work Comp 462.

Houston Fire & Cas. Ins. Co. v. U. S. by and for Use of First State Bank of Denton, Tex., CA5 (Tex), 217 F2d 734.—Assign 137; U S 67(5.1).

Houston Fire & Cas. Ins. Co. v. U.S. for Use and Benefit of Trane Co., CA5 (Tex), 217 F2d 727.—U S 67(13).

Houston Fire & Cas. Ins. Co. v. Walker, Tex, 260 SW2d 600, 152 Tex 503.—App & E 544(2), 547(2), 554(3); Judgm 199(3.9).

Houston Fire & Cas. Ins. Co.; Walker v., TexCivApp–Galveston, 254 SW2d 429, rev 260 SW2d 600, 152 Tex 503.—App & E 930(3); Insurance 3580; Judgm 199(3.10), 276; Trial 343.

Houston Fire & Cas. Ins. Co.; Yellow Transit Freight Lines v., TexCivApp–Amarillo, 254 SW2d 891, ref nre.—Insurance 2891, 2893.

Houston Fire Fighters', City of, v. Morris, TexApp–Houston (14 Dist), 949 SW2d 474. See City of Houston Fire Fighters' v. Morris.

Houston Firefighters' Relief and Retirement Fund; City of Houston v., TexApp–Houston (1 Dist), 196 SW3d 271, rule 537(f) motion gr.—Colleges 5; Counties 141; Lim of Act 58(1); Mun Corp 200(1), 200(2), 200(4), 200(8.1), 200(10), 723; Schools 89; States 191.1, 191.9(2), 191.10; Statut 184, 227, 263, 277.

Houston Firemen's Relief and Retirement Fund; Williams v., TexApp–Houston (1 Dist), 121 SW3d 415, reh overr.—Admin Law 200, 228.1, 229, 651, 657.1; Const Law 188, 190, 665, 672, 709, 3053, 3078, 3596, 4172(5); Courts 89; Decl Judgm 201; Judgm 564(2), 707, 713(1), 715(3), 948(1); Mun Corp 176(3.1), 200(1), 200(3), 200(10), 724, 725, 745.5; Offic 101.5(1), 114; States 191.4(1), 191.6(2), 191.9(1); Statut 68, 77(1), 93(10), 181(2), 270.

Houston First American Sav. v. Musick, Tex, 650 SW2d 764.—App & E 878(4); Estop 32(1), 50; Evid 208(1), 265(1), 265(7), 265(8), 383(7); Mtg 333, 352.1, 353, 372(5), 374; Trial 105(1).

Houston First American Sav. Ass'n; Grubbs v., CA5 (Tex), 730 F2d 236.—Bankr 3711(3), 3711(4), 3711(5), 3711(6).

Houston First American Sav. Ass'n; Grubbs v., CA5 (Tex), 718 F2d 694, reh gr 718 F2d 699, on reh 730 F2d 236.—Bankr 3711(6).

Houston First Sav. Ass'n; Gerst v., TexCivApp–Austin, 422 SW2d 514.—Banks 6; B & L Assoc 3.1(1), 3.5(2), 3.5(3).

Houston Fishing Tools Co.; Delta (Delaware) Petroleum & Energy Corp. v., TexApp–Houston (1 Dist), 670 SW2d 295.—Acct Action on 13; App & E 188; Interest 37(2); Judgm 184.

Houston Fishing Tools Co.; Page Petroleum, Inc. v., Tex, 853 SW2d 505. See Dresser Industries, Inc. v. Page Petroleum, Inc.

Houston Freightliner, Matter of, CA5 (Tex), 948 F2d 976. See Worldwide Trucks, Inc., Matter of.

Houston Freightliner Truck Sales; Mercedes–Benz Credit Corp. v., CA5 (Tex), 948 F2d 976. See Worldwide Trucks, Inc., Matter of.

Houston Freightways, Inc.; Houston Pipe Coating Co., Inc. v., TexApp–Houston (14 Dist), 679 SW2d 42, ref nre.—App & E 569(1), 865, 1177(9); Corp 507(13); Proc 133.

Houston Furniture Distributors, Inc. v. Bank of Woodlake, N. A., TexCivApp–Hous (1 Dist), 562 SW2d 880.—Bills & N 534; Guar 36(2), 38(1), 89; Judgm 181(26), 185(2), 185.2(1), 185.3(2); Usury 52, 82, 83.

Houston-Galveston Area Council; Robinson v., SDTex, 566 FSupp 370.—Const Law 1109, 1947, 4170, 4171, 4172(1), 4172(6); Offic 76.

Houston Gas & Fuel Co. v. Perry, TexComApp, 91 SW2d 1052, 127 Tex 102.—Death 86(1); Interest 39(2); Work Comp 2186, 2205, 2243, 2249.

Houston General Ins. Co. v. Association Cas. Ins. Co., TexApp–Tyler, 977 SW2d 634.—App & E 870(2); Equity 64; Judgm 181(15.1), 181(23), 183; Statut 219(1); Subrog 1; Work Comp 1067, 1074.

Houston General Ins. Co. v. Ater, TexApp–El Paso, 843 SW2d 225, reh overr.—Judges 7, 51(2), 53, 56; Mand 3(1).

Houston General Ins. Co. v. Campbell, TexApp–Corpus Christi, 964 SW2d 691, reh overr, and review den, and reh of petition for review den.—Work Comp 11, 52, 597, 1072, 1981, 2191, 2195, 2210, 2247, 2251.

Houston General Ins. Co.; Dalton's Best Maid Products, Inc. v., TexApp–Fort Worth, 855 SW2d 272.—Insurance 2395, 2396; Judgm 185(2).

Houston General Ins. Co.; DiFrancesco v., TexApp–Texarkana, 858 SW2d 595, reh den.—Contracts 98, 143(2); Insurance 1887(2), 2660, 2677; Trial 358.

Houston General Ins. Co.; Hall v., TexApp–Dallas, 663 SW2d 468. See Seay v. Hall.

Houston General Ins. Co. v. Hamilton, TexApp–Beaumont, 634 SW2d 18, dism.—Work Comp 970, 990, 1658, 1728, 1937.

Houston General Ins. Co.; Heard v., TexCivApp–Waco, 553 SW2d 830.—Judgm 198; Work Comp 1489, 1492, 1769.

Houston General Ins. Co.; Jones v., TexApp–Waco, 736 SW2d 860, writ den.—Insurance 1914; Statut 181(1), 185, 212.7, 219(4); Work Comp 1069, 1075.

Houston General Ins. Co.; Jones v., TexApp–Waco, 624 SW2d 363.—Judgm 181(23).

Houston General Ins. Co. v. Lane Wood Industries, Inc., TexCivApp–Fort Worth, 571 SW2d 384.—App & E 1010.1(1), 1062.1; Cust & U 10; Estop 54, 55; Impl & C C 1; Insurance 1669, 1671, 1882, 3092, 3103; Ref of Inst 19(1), 45(14), 46.

Houston General Ins. Co.; Lujan v., Tex, 756 SW2d 295.—App & E 1128.1; Work Comp 710.

Houston General Ins. Co. v. Lujan, TexApp–El Paso, 740 SW2d 34, writ gr, rev 756 SW2d 295.—Work Comp 617, 710.

Houston General Ins. Co. v. Metcalf, TexApp–Tyler, 642 SW2d 79, ref nre.—Work Comp 2247.

Houston General Ins. Co.; Mission Ins. Co. v., CA5 (Tex), 923 F2d 53. See Barnes v. Mission Ins. Co.

Houston General Ins. Co.; Mitchell v., TexCivApp–Fort Worth, 620 SW2d 730.—Trial 350.3(8); Work Comp 51, 1724.

Houston General Ins. Co. v. Owens, TexApp–Amarillo, 653 SW2d 93, ref nre.—Evid 264; Insurance 2100, 2660, 3367, 3571; Trial 351.2(3.1).

Houston General Ins. Co. v. Pegues, TexCivApp–Texarkana, 514 SW2d 492, ref nre.—Evid 570, 572, 574; Work Comp 1490, 1491, 1492, 1504, 1548, 1593.

Houston General Ins. Co. v. Realex Group, N.V., CA5 (Tex), 776 F2d 514.—Fed Cts 755; Insurance 3626.

Houston General Ins. Co.; Saldana v., TexCivApp–Hous (1 Dist), 610 SW2d 807, ref nre.—App & E 544(3); Trial 352.5(8); Work Comp 809, 1383, 1389, 1533, 1624, 1723, 1728, 1776, 1937.

Houston General Ins. Co. v. Teague, TexCivApp–Waco, 531 SW2d 457, ref nre.—Work Comp 845, 1030.1(1).

Houston General Ins. Co.; Uribe v., TexApp–San Antonio, 849 SW2d 447.—App & E 719(8), 863, 1073(1); Judgm 183, 217.

Houston General Ins. Co. v. Vera, TexApp–Corpus Christi, 638 SW2d 102, ref nre.—App & E 931(1), 989; Work Comp 809, 842, 845, 1130, 1221, 1250, 1288, 1381, 1492, 1543, 1629, 1679, 1853.

Houston General Ins. Group; Johnston v., TexApp–Fort Worth, 636 SW2d 278.—App & E 1151(2); Equity 72(1); Insurance 1735, 2009, 2060; Plead 20.

Houston General Lloyds; Thornhill v., TexApp–Fort Worth, 802 SW2d 127.—App & E 863, 934(1); Insurance 2278(16), 2914; Judgm 185(2).

Houston General Lloyds Ins. Co. v. Stricklin, TexCivApp–Dallas, 538 SW2d 178, dism.—Insurance 3559; Plead 111.39(4).

Houston Geophysical Co.; Klostermann v., TexCivApp–San Antonio, 315 SW2d 664, writ refused.—Mines 121.

Houston Gulf Coast Bldg.; City of Houston v., TexApp–Houston (1 Dist), 697 SW2d 850.—Admin Law 417; Const Law 70.1(1), 2470, 2540, 2541.

Houston Gulf Coast Bldg. and Const. Trades Council; City of Houston v., TexApp–Houston (1 Dist), 710 SW2d 181, ref nre.—Labor & Emp 2354.

Houston Gulf Coast Bldg. Trades Council, AFL-CIO; Potter v., CA5 (Tex), 482 F2d 837.—Labor & Emp 1379, 1403, 1410, 2059, 2119.

Houston Gulf Coast Bldg. Trades Council, AFL-CIO; Potter v., SDTex, 363 FSupp 1, mod 482 F2d 837.—Labor & Emp 1659, 1693, 1694, 1696(1), 1696(3), 1816; Statut 223.2(19).

Houston Gulf Gas Co.; Heard v., CCA5 (Tex), 78 F2d 189, cert den 56 SCt 178, 296 US 643, 80 LEd 457.—Equity 87(1); Mines 74(6); Spec Perf 3, 32(2); Trial 11(3).

Houston-Gulf Inv. Corp., I; La Hacienda Sav. Ass'n v., TexApp–San Antonio, 759 SW2d 195.—Judgm 181(29); Sec Tran 141.

Houston Health Club, Inc.; Rickey v., TexApp–Texarkana, 863 SW2d 148, reh den, and writ gr, and writ withdrawn, writ den with per curiam opinion 888 SW2d 812.—Antitrust 145, 225; App & E 719(1); Contracts 105; Indem 30(1); Release 1, 13(1), 38.

Houston Health Clubs, Inc.; Danesh v., TexApp–Houston (1 Dist), 859 SW2d 535, reh den, and writ refused.—Lim of Act 118(1).

Houston Health Clubs, Inc. v. First Court of Appeals, Tex, 722 SW2d 692.—Judgm 128, 140, 217.

Houston Heating & Air Conditioning, Inc. v. Semands, TexCivApp–Waco, 318 SW2d 777, dism.—Evid 10(2); Plead 111.16; Venue 7.5(3).

Houston Heavy Equipment Co., Inc. v. Gould, SDTex, 198 BR 693.—Bankr 2608(1), 2608(2), 2616(1), 2616(4), 2616(5).

Houston Helicopters, Inc. v. Canadian Helicopters Ltd., SDTex, 901 FSupp 1225.—Const Law 3964, 3965(4); Evid 373(1); Fed Civ Proc 1831, 1835, 2466, 2470.1, 2492, 2543, 2547.1, 2552; Fed Cts 44, 45, 76, 76.5, 76.10, 76.30, 86, 96.

Houstonian, Inc.; Campos v., SDTex, 824 FSupp 100. See Campos v. Housland, Inc.

Houston Ice & Brewing Co. v. Fields, TexCivApp–Amarillo, 81 SW2d 234.—App & E 737, 742(1), 742(2), 742(3), 743(1), 758.1; Plead 293.

Houston Ice & Brewing Co.; Joseph Schlitz Brewing Co. v., USTex, 39 SCt 401, 250 US 28, 63 LEd 822.—Antitrust 35, 37.

Houston Ice & Brewing Co.; Joseph Schlitz Brewing Co. v., CCA5 (Tex), 241 F 817, 154 CCA 519, cert gr 38 SCt 316, 246 US 659, 62 LEd 542, aff 39 SCt 401, 250 US 28, 63 LEd 822.—Trademarks 1001.

Houston Independent School Dist.; Bluitt v., SDTex, 236 FSupp2d 703.—Civil R 1009, 1031, 1033(1), 1041, 1071, 1304, 1305, 1307, 1312, 1335, 1345, 1351(1), 1351(5), 1354, 1376(1), 1376(2), 1376(10), 1394, 1398, 1530, 1535, 1539; Const Law 3039, 3041, 3099, 3278(6), 3867, 3869, 3879, 3893, 3895, 4165(1), 4166(1), 4172(1), 4172(6), 4173(3), 4190, 4200, 4202, 4203; Fed Civ Proc 1837.1, 2491.5; Fed Cts 18, 270, 411; Lim of Act 95(1); Schools 147.9, 147.31, 147.34(1), 147.38.

Houston Independent School Dist. v. Bobby R., CA5 (Tex), 200 F3d 341, cert den 121 SCt 55, 531 US 817, 148 LEd2d 23.—Schools 148(2.1), 148(3), 154(4), 155.5(2.1), 155.5(4).

Houston Independent School Dist.; Brady v., CA5 (Tex), 113 F3d 1419, sug for reh den 121 F3d 706.—Const Law 1928, 1932, 1942; Offic 66.

Houston Independent School Dist.; Brookshire v., TexCivApp–Hous (14 Dist), 508 SW2d 675.—Autos 1, 37; Schools 89.8(1); Statut 179, 188, 195, 199, 212.6.

Houston Independent School Dist.; Broussard v., CA5 (Tex), 403 F2d 34.—Fed Cts 744.

Houston Independent School Dist.; Broussard v., CA5 (Tex), 395 F2d 817, reh den 403 F2d 34.—Const Law 945; Schools 13(2), 13(14), 154(1).

Houston Independent School Dist.; Broussard v., SDTex, 262 FSupp 266, aff 395 F2d 817, reh den 403 F2d 34.—Schools 13(4), 13(7), 13(12), 13(14).

Houston Independent School Dist.; Brown v., SDTex, 763 FSupp 905, aff 957 F2d 866, cert den 113 SCt 198, 506 US 868, 121 LEd2d 140.—Civil R 1346, 1349, 1530; Const Law 4202; Schools 89, 133.14.

Houston Independent School Dist.; Brown v., TexApp–Houston (14 Dist), 123 SW3d 618, review den.—Autos 187(1); Insurance 2677; Schools 89.8(1).

Houston Independent School Dist.; Caramanian v., TexApp–Houston (14 Dist), 829 SW2d 814.—Admin Law 229; App & E 93, 554(1), 846(5), 852, 907(3), 1031(1); Schools 147.51.

Houston Independent School Dist.; Cheek v., CA5 (Tex), 108 FedAppx 935.—Fed Civ Proc 2553.

Houston Independent School Dist. v. City of Houston, Tex, 443 SW2d 49.—Courts 247(7).

Houston Independent School Dist.; City of Houston v., TexCivApp–Hous (14 Dist), 436 SW2d 568, mod 443 SW2d 49.—App & E 94; Const Law 2970; Counties 105(1); Equity 27; Evid 83(2); Mun Corp 122.1(2), 122.1(3), 601.1, 601.2, 601.3.

Houston Independent School Dist.; Coleman v., CA5 (Tex), 113 F3d 528, appeal after remand 202 F3d 264.—Civil R 1041, 1355, 1359, 1376(2), 1376(10); Consp 7.5(1); Const Law 3251; Fed Cts 574, 776, 802.

Houston Independent School Dist.; Davis v., TexApp–Houston (14 Dist), 654 SW2d 818.—Elect of Rem 1, 16; Judgm 181(2), 181(3); Schools 63(3), 89.2, 137; Work Comp 2084.

Houston Independent School Dist.; Goodie v., TexApp–Houston (14 Dist), 57 SW3d 646, review den.—Schools 47, 147.34(1), 147.40(1), 147.44.

Houston Independent School Dist.; Graham v., SDTex, 335 FSupp 1164.—Civil R 1395(2); Const Law 1976, 1978, 4209(3); Fed Civ Proc 1826; Schools 169.

Houston Independent School Dist.; Greater Houston Chapter of Am. Civil Liberties Union v., CA5 (Tex), 391 F2d 599.—Fed Cts 727.

Houston Independent School Dist.; Hagan v., CA5 (Tex), 51 F3d 48.—Civil R 1376(5); Consp 13.

Houston Independent School Dist. v. Harrison, TexApp–Houston (1 Dist), 744 SW2d 298.—App & E 216(3); Work Comp 1417, 1490, 1491.

Houston Independent School Dist.; Hernandez v., TexCivApp–Austin, 558 SW2d 121, ref nre.—Aliens 114, 121, 126; App & E 1079; Const Law 947, 1021, 1076, 2970, 2972, 2973, 3013, 3062, 3903, 3921, 4205; Schools 17, 148(1).

Houston Independent School Dist.; Hispanic Educ. Committee v., SDTex, 886 FSupp 606, aff 68 F3d 467.—Admin Law 124, 125; Const Law 1435, 1490, 1553, 1555, 1775, 1969, 3272; Schools 55, 57, 63(1).

Houston Independent School Dist. v. Houston Chronicle Pub. Co., TexApp–Houston (1 Dist), 798 SW2d 580, writ den.—Const Law 188; Records 50, 58, 68; Statut 219(9.1), 263, 265, 270.

Houston Independent School Dist.; Houston Federation of Teachers, Local 2415 v., Tex, 730 SW2d 644.—Admin Law 229; App & E 100(1); Inj 138.54.

Houston Independent School Dist. v. Houston Federation of Teachers, Local 2415, TexApp–Houston (1 Dist), 715 SW2d 369, writ gr, rev 730 SW2d 644.—Admin Law 229; Labor & Emp 2030; Schools 63(1).

Houston Independent School Dist. v. Houston Teachers Ass'n, TexCivApp–Hous (14 Dist), 617 SW2d 765.—App & E 781(4), 843(1).

Houston Independent School Dist.; Ibarra v., SDTex, 84 FSupp2d 825.—Action 2; Compromise 2; Consp 2; Const Law 963, 1188, 1430, 1435, 1440, 1447, 1481, 1494, 1928, 1929, 2002, 3874(2), 4156, 4198; Release 1, 15, 55; Schools 63(1).

Houston Independent School Dist.; Jackson v., TexApp–Houston (14 Dist), 994 SW2d 396.—Admin Law 229; App & E 984(1); Civil R 1731; Const Law 3874(2); Costs 12; Decl Judgm 2, 61, 82, 91, 210; Impl & C C 55, 60.1; Judgm 185(2), 185.3(13); Lim of Act 58(1); Schools 61, 63(5), 126; Trusts 91, 94.5.

Houston Independent School Dist.; Jarmon v., SDTex, 805 FSupp 24.—Admin Law 501; Judgm 540, 713(1), 828.15(1).

Houston Independent School Dist.; Jason D.W. by Douglas W. v., CA5 (Tex), 158 F3d 205.—Fed Cts 776, 830, 878; Schools 155.5(5).

Houston Independent School Dist.; Johnson v., SDTex, 930 FSupp 276.—Civil R 1028, 1351(1), 1356, 1386, 1536, 1541; Const Law 1925, 1929, 1934, 1990, 3618(3), 3867, 3869, 3893, 3895, 3912, 4173(4), 4190, 4198, 4199, 4202, 4203; Fed Cts 425, 427; Lim of Act 95(15); Schools 63(1).

Houston Independent School Dist.; Jones v., CA5 (Tex), 979 F2d 1004.—Fed Civ Proc 2515; Fed Cts 766; Libel 44(3); Mun Corp 723; Rem of C 82, 101.1; Schools 63(3), 89, 89.3, 89.8(1).

Houston Independent School Dist.; Jones v., SDTex, 805 FSupp 476, aff 979 F2d 1004.—Civil R 1027, 1305; Const Law 3618(1), 3618(5), 3874(2), 3874(3), 4162, 4173(3), 4200, 4201; Labor & Emp 40(2), 782; Libel 44(3), 71; Schools 62, 63(3), 133, 135(3), 147.14, 147.51.

Houston Independent School Dist.; Lopez v., CA5 (Tex), 817 F2d 351.—Civil R 1345, 1351(2), 1352(2), 1418; Fed Civ Proc 2491.5; Fed Cts 270.

Houston Independent School Dist.; Lopez v., CA5 (Tex), 124 FedAppx 234.—Civil R 1588, 1590.

Houston Independent School Dist.; Madison v., SDTex, 47 FSupp2d 825, aff 207 F3d 658.—Civil R 1376(2), 1432; Const Law 1553, 1997, 4200, 4202; Schools 147.12, 147.34(1), 147.38, 147.44.

Houston Independent School Dist.; Mathews v., SDTex, 595 FSupp 445.—Civil R 1513, 1517; Fed Civ Proc 2497.1.

Houston Independent School Dist.; Miller v., TexApp–Houston (1 Dist), 51 SW3d 676, reh overr, and review den, and reh of petition for review den, cert den 122 SCt 1203, 535 US 905, 152 LEd2d 142.—Admin Law 484.1, 791; Schools 147.16, 147.40(1), 147.42, 147.44; Statut 219(1).

Houston Independent School Dist.; Mitchison v., TexApp–Houston (14 Dist), 803 SW2d 769, writ den.—Admin Law 229; App & E 233(2), 671(1), 714(1), 714(5); Inj 14, 16, 17; Schools 47, 61, 147.44, 147.51.

Houston Independent School Dist.; Montoya v., TexApp–Houston (1 Dist), 177 SW3d 332.—App & E 893(1), 916(1); Mun Corp 723, 742(4); Schools 89.13(1), 89.13(3), 89.13(6).

Houston Independent School Dist.; Noyl Corp. v., TexCivApp–Houston, 317 SW2d 756.—App & E 846(5), 1015(1); Em Dom 224, 262(2); New Tr 56, 140(3), 143(5), 157.

Houston Independent School Dist.; Perry v., TexApp–Houston (1 Dist), 902 SW2d 544, reh overr, and writ dism woj.—App & E 863; Const Law 3869, 4173(1), 4203; Contracts 176(1); Judgm 181(11), 185(1), 185(2), 185.1(1); Schools 136, 147.2(1), 147.28, 147.34(1).

Houston Independent School Dist.; Pierson v., TexApp–Houston (14 Dist), 698 SW2d 377, ref nre.—App & E 93, 151(6); Assoc 18; Contrib 5(5); Indem 57; Judgm 185(2), 185(6); Princ & A 8, 131; Schools 89, 89.8(1), 147.

Houston Independent School Dist.; Rivera v., CA5 (Tex), 349 F3d 244.—Civil R 1345, 1351(1), 1351(2); Const Law 4048, 4050, 4211; Fed Cts 411; Schools 89.11(1).

Houston Independent School Dist.; Roberts v., TexApp–Houston (1 Dist), 788 SW2d 107, writ den.—Admin Law 311; Const Law 1210, 1266, 4025, 4190, 4202, 4209(3); Schools 133, 147.14, 147.31.

Houston Independent School Dist.; Romeike v., TexCivApp–Waco, 368 SW2d 895.—Const Law 2722; Schools 136.

Houston Independent School Dist.; Ross v., CA5 (Tex), 699 F2d 218.—Fed Civ Proc 828.1, 830, 834, 849, 1061; Fed Cts 817; Schools 13(4), 13(19), 13(20), 13(21).

Houston Independent School Dist.; Ross v., CA5 (Tex), 583 F2d 712.—Schools 13(6), 13(20).

Houston Independent School Dist.; Ross v., CA5 (Tex), 559 F2d 937, on remand 457 FSupp 18, aff in part, vac in part 583 F2d 712.—Fed Cts 41, 46, 62, 946, 1141; Schools 13(12), 13(20).

Houston Independent School Dist. v. Ross, CA5 (Tex), 282 F2d 95.—Schools 13(9).

Houston Independent School Dist.; Ross v., SDTex, 457 FSupp 18, aff in part, vac in part 583 F2d 712.—Schools 13(4), 13(7), 13(20).

Houston Independent School Dist.; Ross v., SDTex, 81 FRD 532.—Fed Civ Proc 2737.12.

Houston Independent School Dist.; Salvaggio v., TexApp–Houston (14 Dist), 752 SW2d 189, writ den.—Const Law 4138(3); Tax 2777, 2855, 3211, 3220.

Houston Independent School Dist.; Salvaggio v., TexApp–Houston (14 Dist), 709 SW2d 306, dism.—App & E 949; Decl Judgm 305; Parties 35.9; Schools 107; Tax 2777.

Houston Independent School Dist. v. Schwartz, TexApp–Houston (14 Dist, 709 SW2d 306. See Salvaggio v. Houston Independent School Dist.

Houston Independent School Dist.; Scott v., TexApp–Houston (14 Dist), 641 SW2d 255, ref nre.—Trial 202, 219; Work Comp 1728.

Houston Independent School Dist. v. Southwestern Bell Tel. Co., TexCivApp–Austin, 376 SW2d 375, ref nre, and writ gr, rev 397 SW2d 419.—Mun Corp 111(6), 116, 120, 121, 122.1(2), 619; Tel 982.

Houston Independent School Dist.; Southwestern Bell Telephone Co. v., Tex, 397 SW2d 419.—Mun Corp 619; Pub Ut 111; Statut 109.2, 211; Tel 926, 927, 954, 982.

Houston Independent School Dist.; Sullivan v., CA5 (Tex), 475 F2d 1071, reh den 475 F2d 1404, cert den 94 SCt 461, 414 US 1032, 38 LEd2d 323.—Const Law 90.1(1.4), 1977, 4212(2); Inj 205, 210, 231; Schools 169, 172.

Houston Independent School Dist.; Sullivan v., SDTex, 333 FSupp 1149, vac 475 F2d 1071, reh den 475 F2d 1404, cert den 94 SCt 461, 414 US 1032, 38 LEd2d 323. —Civil R 1452; Const Law 1050, 1526, 1976, 4212(2); Inj 205, 223, 226, 230(3), 232; Schools 169, 177.

Houston Independent School Dist.; Sullivan v., SDTex, 307 FSupp 1328, opinion supplemented 333 FSupp 1149, vac 475 F2d 1071, reh den 475 F2d 1404, cert den 94 SCt 461, 414 US 1032, 38 LEd2d 323.—Civil R 1316, 1317; Const Law 82(12), 90.1(1.4), 892, 1150, 1189(1), 1430, 1510, 1976, 1986, 3905, 4209(3), 4212(2); Decl Judgm 210; Fed Civ Proc 187.5; Inj 22, 85(2), 108; Schools 169, 171, 172, 177; Statut 47.

Houston Independent School Dist.; Swanson v., TexApp–Houston (14 Dist), 800 SW2d 630, writ den.—Const Law 4202; Schools 131, 136, 147.34(1), 147.38.

Houston Independent School Dist.; Taub v., TexCivApp–Eastland, 339 SW2d 227, ref nre.—App & E 761, 930(1), 989; Em Dom 136, 149(6), 202(2), 223, 262(5); Evid 142(1); Witn 276.

Houston Independent School Dist.; Taxpayers' Ass'n of Harris County v., TexCivApp–Galveston, 81 SW2d 815, writ dism.—Schools 90, 103(4), 111, 144(4); Statut 158.

Houston Independent School Dist.; White v., SDTex, 815 FSupp 1016.—Civil R 1204, 1208, 1539, 1544, 1551; Fed Civ Proc 2497.1.

Houston Independent School Dist.; W., Jason, by Douglas W. v., CA5 (Tex), 158 F3d 205. See Jason D.W. by Douglas W. v. Houston Independent School Dist.

Houston Independent School Dist.; Wright v., CA5 (Tex), 569 F2d 1383.—Fed Civ Proc 21; Schools 147.2(2), 147.44.

Houston Independent School Dist.; Wright v., CA5 (Tex), 486 F2d 137, reh den 487 F2d 1401, reh den 489 F2d 1312, cert den Brown v. Houston Independent School District, 94 SCt 3173, 417 US 969, 41 LEd2d 1140.—Const Law 1354(2); Schools 164.

Houston Independent School Dist.; Wright v., SDTex, 393 FSupp 1149, vac 569 F2d 1383.—Admin Law 229; Civil R 1359; Counties 141; Fed Cts 268.1, 270; Mun Corp 724, 725; Schools 19(1), 21, 25, 47, 92(1), 147.2(1), 147.2(2), 147.47; States 191.1.

Houston Independent School Dist.; Wright v., SDTex, 366 FSupp 1208, aff486 F2d 137, reh den 487 F2d 1401, reh den 489 F2d 1312, cert den Brown v. Houston Independent School District, 94 SCt 3173, 417 US 969, 41 LEd2d 1140.—Inj 118(1).

Houston Independent School Dist. v. 1615 Corp., TexApp–Houston (14 Dist), 217 SW3d 631, reh overr, and petition stricken, and review den.—App & E 863; Decl Judgm 44, 392.1; Tax 2785, 2792.

Houston Indus. Welding School, Inc.; Joe T. Presswood, Inc. v., TexCivApp–Hous (1 Dist), 585 SW2d 763, ref nre.—App & E 989; Auctions 9, 11; Bailm 18(1); Interest 39(1).

Houston Industries, Inc.; Creel v., TexApp–Houston (1 Dist), 124 SW3d 742.—Action 27(1); Contracts 143(2), 143.5, 152, 155, 169, 170(1); Corp 308(3), 308(11); Evid 398, 427, 448.

Houston Industries Inc.; Norton v., CA5 (Tex), 106 FedAppx 209.—Civil R 1137, 1171, 1252; Damag 57.58.

Houston Insulation Contractors Ass'n v. N. L. R. B., USTex, 87 SCt 1278, 386 US 664, 18 LEd2d 389, reh den 87 SCt 2047, 387 US 938, 18 LEd2d 1005, reh den 87 SCt 2047, 387 US 938, 13 LEd2d 1005.—Labor & Emp 1403, 1413.

Houston Insulation Contractors Ass'n v. N. L. R. B., CA5 (Tex), 357 F2d 182, cert gr Houston Insulation Contractors Association v. National Labor Relations Board, 87 SCt 53, 385 US 811, 17 LEd2d 53, cert gr 87 SCt 93, 385 US 811, 17 LEd2d 53, aff in part, rev in part 87 SCt 1278, 386 US 664, 18 LEd2d 389, reh den 87 SCt 2047, 387 US 938, 18 LEd2d 1005, reh den 87 SCt 2047, 387 US 938, 13 LEd2d 1005.—Contracts 187(1); Labor & Emp 1261, 1403, 1407, 1410, 1413, 1414, 1775, 1782.

Houston Insulation Contractors Ass'n v. N. L. R. B., CA5 (Tex), 339 F2d 868.—Labor & Emp 1697, 1841.

Houston Intern. Hosp.; Berel v., TexCivApp–Houston (1 Dist), 881 SW2d 21. See Berel v. HCA Health Services of Texas, Inc.

Houston Intern. Televideo, Inc. v. Technicolor, Inc., SDTex, 647 FSupp 554.—Contracts 141(1), 206; Fed Cts 104.

Houston Inv. Bankers Corp. v. First City Bank of Highland Village, TexApp–Houston (14 Dist), 640 SW2d 660.—Judgm 753, 767, 772; Mtg 378; Subrog 31(4).

Houston Inv. Realty Trust; Gulf Freeway Lumber Co. v., TexCivApp–Hous (14 Dist), 452 SW2d 39.—App & E 1010.1(1); Evid 400(2); Joint-St Co 18; Princ & A 136(2); Ven & Pur 25, 44, 79, 331.

Houston Ladder Mfg. Co. v. Slats-O-Wood Awning Co., TexCivApp–Galveston, 228 SW2d 278, writ refused.—App & E 302(6); Sales 405.

Houston Land & Cattle Co., L.C. v. Harris County Appraisal Dist., TexApp–Houston (1 Dist), 104 SW3d 622, reh overr, and review den.—App & E 893(1); Tax 2572, 2695.

Houston Land & Trust Co.; Cameron v., TexCivApp–Galveston, 175 SW2d 468, writ refused wom.—Evid 474(4); Wills 55(1), 165(1), 166(5), 324(3).

Houston Land & Trust Co. v. Campbell, TexCivApp–El Paso, 105 SW2d 430, writ refused.—App & E 374(2); Ex & Ad 33; Trusts 191(1); Wills 439, 440, 470(1), 750, 751, 753, 755, 756.

Houston Lawyers' Ass'n v. Attorney General of Texas, USTex, 111 SCt 2376, 501 US 419, 115 LEd2d 379, on remand League of United Latin American Citizens, Council No 4434 v. Clements, 986 F2d 728, reh gr, on reh 999 F2d 831, cert den League of United Latin American Citizens v Attorney General of Texas, 114 SCt 878, 510 US 1071, 127 LEd2d 74, cert den Wood v Attorney General of Texas, 114 SCt 878, 510 US 1071, 127 LEd2d 74, cert den Attorney General of Texas v Entz, 114 SCt 878, 510 US 1071, 127 LEd2d 74.—Elections 12(3).

Houston Legal Foundation; Scruggs v., TexCivApp–Hous (1 Dist), 475 SW2d 604, writ refused.—Corp 377.5.

Houston Legal Foundation; Touchy v., Tex, 432 SW2d 690, appeal after remand Scruggs v. Houston Legal Foundation, 475 SW2d 604, writ refused.—Atty & C 11(2.1), 32(5), 62; Const Law 1440, 2042, 3684(1), 4273(1); Inj 89(1), 114(2), 123; Plead 111.47, 228.14.

Houston Legal Foundation; Touchy v., TexCivApp–Waco, 417 SW2d 625, rev 432 SW2d 690, appeal after remand Scruggs v. Houston Legal Foundation, 475 SW2d 604, writ refused.—App & E 854(1); Atty & C 32(2), 32(7), 47.1, 50; Corp 377.5.

Houston Life Ins. Co. v. Dabbs, Tex, 125 SW2d 1041, 132 Tex 566.—Corp 597; Insurance 1123, 3365, 3379.

Houston Life Ins. Co. v. Dabbs, TexComApp, 81 SW2d 42, 125 Tex 100.—App & E 396, 428(2).

Houston Life Ins. Co. v. Dabbs, TexCivApp–Galveston, 95 SW2d 484, mod 125 SW2d 1041, 132 Tex 566.—App & E 930(3); Evid 351, 471(13); Insurance 1120, 2568, 3125(6), 3365, 3571; Plead 228.14; Trial 351.2(4); Witn 270(2).

Houston Light and Power Co.; Cochrane v., SDTex, 996 FSupp 657.—Civil R 1135, 1136, 1137, 1138, 1141, 1147, 1166, 1171, 1175, 1185, 1189, 1245, 1246, 1250, 1505(7); Damag 50.10, 54; Labor & Emp 2461, 2468; Work Comp 2084.

Houston Light and Power Co.; Uherek v., SDTex, 997 FSupp 789.—Compromise 2; Fed Civ Proc 2492; Release 1, 2, 9, 12(1), 13(1), 15, 18, 20, 21, 55.

Houston Lighting & Power; Andrews v., TexApp–Houston (14 Dist), 820 SW2d 411, writ den.—App & E 934(1), 1024.4; Autos 193(8.1), 193(10); Judgm 199(3.10); Labor & Emp 3045, 3061(1).

Houston Lighting & Power; Davis v., SDTex, 990 FSupp 515.—Alt Disp Res 113, 200; Labor & Emp 1549(1), 1549(17).

Houston Lighting and Power; One Call Systems, Inc. v., TexApp–Houston (14 Dist), 936 SW2d 673, reh overr, and writ den.—App & E 204(1), 213, 216(1), 237(1), 237(2), 237(5), 238(2), 294(1), 302(5), 1001(3); Costs 194.32, 194.40.

Houston Lighting & Power Co., In re, Tex, 976 SW2d 671.—Judges 51(1).

Houston Lighting & Power Co.; Adams v., Tex, 314 SW2d 826, 158 Tex 551.—Em Dom 149(6), 150, 224, 263; New Tr 58, 66, 68.1.

Houston Lighting & Power Co. v. Adams, TexCivApp–Waco, 316 SW2d 461, ref nre.—Em Dom 150, 221; Evid 568(1).

HOUSTON

Houston Lighting & Power Co. v. Adams, TexCivApp–Waco, 309 SW2d 537, rev 314 SW2d 826, 158 Tex 551.—Em Dom 224.

Houston Lighting & Power Co. v. Allen & Coon Const. Co., TexApp–Beaumont, 634 SW2d 875.—Contrib 6; Work Comp 2205, 2251.

Houston Lighting & Power Co.; Almeda Mall, Inc. v., CA5 (Tex), 615 F2d 343, cert den 101 SCt 208, 449 US 870, 66 LEd2d 90.—Antitrust 534, 535, 558, 560, 600, 621, 645, 695, 963(1), 963(3), 977(2); Electricity 11(2), 11.5(2).

Houston Lighting & Power Co.; Arcola Sugar Mills Co. v., TexCivApp–Galveston, 153 SW2d 628, writ refused wom.—Electricity 11.5(1); Em Dom 10(1), 55, 196, 263; Statut 223.2(27).

Houston Lighting & Power Co.; Arcola Sugar Mills Co. v., TexCivApp–Galveston, 146 SW2d 199.—App & E 560, 571, 1165; Mand 3(1), 10, 12.

Houston Lighting & Power Co.; Arcola Sugar Mills Co. v., TexCivApp–Galveston, 142 SW2d 626.—Mand 178.

Houston Lighting & Power Co.; Arends v., SDTex, 969 FSupp 424.—Fed Civ Proc 2492; Release 2, 6, 12(1), 13(1), 15, 18, 55, 57(1).

Houston Lighting & Power Co. v. Atchison, Topeka, & Santa Fe Ry. Co., Tex, 890 SW2d 455.—Indem 27, 30(1), 33(7); Labor & Emp 2785.

Houston Lighting & Power Co. v. Atchison, Topeka & Santa Fe Ry. Co., TexApp–Texarkana, 863 SW2d 141, reh den, and writ gr, rev 890 SW2d 455.—App & E 930(3), 989, 991; Contracts 175(1), 218, 221(1); Indem 30(1), 31(1), 31(2), 33(7), 93; Labor & Emp 2801, 2855; Prod Liab 5, 16.

Houston Lighting & Power Co. v. Auchan USA, Inc., Tex, 995 SW2d 668.—Electricity 11.1(3).

Houston Lighting & Power Co.; Auchan USA, Inc. v., TexApp–Houston (1 Dist), 961 SW2d 197, reh overr, and review gr, rev 995 SW2d 668.—Contracts 114; Electricity 11.1(3); Judgm 181(19), 185(2); Pub Ut 111, 114.

Houston Lighting & Power Co.; Aycock v., TexCivApp–Galveston, 175 SW2d 710, writ refused wom.—Ease 58(3); Electricity 14(1); Em Dom 14, 35, 124, 126(1), 191(1), 195, 201, 202(1), 202(4), 204, 222(5), 223, 262(2), 318, 319.

Houston Lighting & Power Co. v. Boyd, Tex, 115 SW2d 593, 131 Tex 323.—New Tr 117(2), 117(3).

Houston Lighting & Power Co. v. Boyd, TexCivApp–Galveston, 114 SW2d 934.—Com Law 9; Courts 207.4(2); New Tr 117(2), 117(3).

Houston Lighting & Power Co.; Boyles v., Tex, 464 SW2d 359.—App & E 719(11); Evid 558(4).

Houston Lighting & Power Co. v. Boyles, TexCivApp–Beaumont, 456 SW2d 714, writ gr, rev 464 SW2d 359.—App & E 1050.1(1); Em Dom 68, 203(1), 219, 262(5), 318, 319; Evid 558(1), 558(4), 570; Trial 260(5), 311; Witn 4.

Houston Lighting & Power Co.; Brinton v., TexCivApp–Galveston, 175 SW2d 707, writ refused wom.—Em Dom 167(4), 170.

Houston Lighting & Power Co. v. Brooks, Tex, 336 SW2d 603, 161 Tex 32.—Electricity 15(2), 16(5), 19(3); Neglig 213, 387.

Houston Lighting & Power Co. v. Brooks, TexCivApp–Houston, 319 SW2d 427, rev 336 SW2d 603, 161 Tex 32.—App & E 930(1); Damag 132(1); Electricity 14(1), 15(1), 15(2), 16(4), 16(7), 18(1), 19(2), 19(4), 19(5), 19(9); Neglig 251, 1717; Plead 11; Trial 350.6(2), 351.5(2).

Houston Lighting & Power Co.; Calvert v., TexCivApp–Austin, 369 SW2d 502, ref nre.—Statut 223.5(1); Tax 2540.

Houston Lighting & Power Co.; City of Austin v., TexApp–Dallas, 844 SW2d 773, writ den.—Action 27(1); Antitrust 135(1), 136, 203; App & E 216(1), 930(2), 960(1), 994(2), 999(1), 1002, 1003(5), 1003(7), 1050.1(1), 1050.1(11), 1051.1(1), 1056.1(1); Contracts 147(1), 147(3), 168, 169, 176(1), 193, 322(4), 353(6), 353(8); Evid 314(1), 361; Plead 228.14, 228.20; Torts 109; Trial 182, 202, 205, 219, 295(1).

Houston Lighting & Power Co.; City of Houston v., TexCivApp–Hous (14 Dist), 530 SW2d 866, ref nre.—Electricity 11.3(1), 11.3(7); Evid 265(2); Inj 143(1), 147; Judges 42, 51(1); Mun Corp 167.

Houston Lighting & Power Co. v. City of San Antonio, TexApp–Houston (1 Dist), 896 SW2d 366, reh overr, and writ dism woj.—Alt Disp Res 112, 113, 182(1), 210, 211, 213(3); Parties 40(2), 44.

Houston Lighting & Power Co. v. City of Wharton, TexApp–Houston (1 Dist), 101 SW3d 633, reh overr, and review den, and reh of petition for review den.—App & E 893(1), 1001(1); Contracts 143(2); Electricity 8.1(4); Equity 72(1), 84, 87(2); Judgm 199(1); Mun Corp 1025; Stip 14(1), 14(4), 17(1), 17(3), 18(4).

Houston Lighting & Power Co.; Cloud v., TexCivApp–Galveston, 199 SW2d 260, ref nre.—App & E 216(2); Electricity 18(1), 19(12).

Houston Lighting & Power Co.; Coastal Indus. Water Authority v., TexCivApp–Hous (14 Dist), 564 SW2d 389.—Courts 480(1); Decl Judgm 322; Em Dom 268, 271, 293(2).

Houston Lighting and Power Co.; Coleman v., SDTex, 984 FSupp 576.—Civil R 1502, 1514.

Houston Lighting & Power Co.; Danawala v., CA5 (Tex), 14 F3d 251.—Damag 50.10; Libel 45(1), 45(2), 50.5, 51(1), 112(2).

Houston Lighting & Power Co.; Darden v., TexApp–San Antonio, 936 SW2d 25, reh overr.—App & E 837(10), 934(1); Neglig 1010, 1011.

Houston Lighting & Power Co.; Destec Energy, Inc. v., TexApp–Austin, 966 SW2d 792.—App & E 1071.1(1); Electricity 8.1(1), 8.1(4); Statut 181(2), 228.

Houston Lighting & Power Co. v. Dickinson Independent School Dist., TexApp–Texarkana, 794 SW2d 402, writ den.—Courts 247(2); Judgm 715(1), 720, 724, 956(1); Schools 111; Tax 2526, 2699(7), 2699(8), 2699(9), 2699(11), 2728, 2777.

Houston Lighting & Power Co. v. Dickinson Independent School Dist., TexApp–Houston (14 Dist), 641 SW2d 302, ref nre.—Admin Law 104, 749; App & E 984(1), 1107; Costs 252; Equity 66; Evid 545, 546, 555.6(2); Interest 39(3); Schools 103(1); Tax 2445, 2446, 2728, 2762, 2763, 2780, 2836, 2859, 3216, 3221.

Houston Lighting & Power Co.; Edmunds v., TexCivApp–Hous (14 Dist), 472 SW2d 797, ref nre.—Contracts 16, 32; Electricity 11(3); Judgm 181(12), 185.3(8).

Houston Lighting & Power Co. v. Eller Outdoor Advertising Co. of Texas, TexApp–Houston (1 Dist), 635 SW2d 133, ref nre.—Contrib 5(5); Indem 91; Work Comp 2084, 2142.11, 2142.20, 2158, 2191.

Houston Lighting & Power Co.; Federated Dept. Stores, Inc. v., TexApp–Houston (1 Dist), 646 SW2d 509.—Electricity 11.1(1), 11.1(2); Judgm 185(2), 185(6).

Houston Lighting & Power Co. v. Fisher, TexCivApp–Hous (14 Dist), 559 SW2d 682, ref nre.—App & E 1060.1(1); Em Dom 169, 262(5); Evid 113(19), 314(2); Trial 114, 121(2), 133.6(3.1).

Houston Lighting & Power Co.; Fleming v., Tex, 143 SW2d 923, 135 Tex 463.—Electricity 8.1(1).

Houston Lighting & Power Co.; Fleming v., Tex, 138 SW2d 520, 135 Tex 463, reh den 143 SW2d 923, 135 Tex 463, cert den Houston Lighting & Power Co v. City of West University Place, 61 SCt 836, 313 US 560, 85 LEd 1520.—Electricity 8.1(1); Mun Corp 63.20.

Houston Lighting & Power Co. v. Fleming, TexCivApp–Galveston, 128 SW2d 487, rev 138 SW2d 520, 135 Tex 463, reh den 143 SW2d 923, 135 Tex 463, cert den 61 SCt 836, 313 US 560, 85 LEd 1520.—Const Law 134, 2341, 2715, 2888; Electricity 8.1(1); Mun Corp 111(2), 226, 244(2), 269(2), 269(3), 589, 620, 649, 673, 676, 680(1), 722, 956(1).

HOUSTON

Houston Lighting & Power Co.; Goeke v., Tex, 797 SW2d 12.—Admin Law 486, 784.1; Electricity 8.1(4).

Houston Lighting & Power Co.; Goeke v., TexApp–Austin, 761 SW2d 835, writ gr, rev 797 SW2d 12.—Admin Law 485, 507, 746, 784.1, 819, 820; Electricity 8.1(1), 8.1(4).

Houston Lighting and Power Co.; Hardwick v., TexApp–Houston (1 Dist), 943 SW2d 183.—Judgm 185(2); Libel 1, 44(3), 54.

Houston Lighting and Power Co.; Hardwick v., TexApp–Corpus Christi, 881 SW2d 195, reh overr, and writ dism woj, appeal after remand 943 SW2d 183.—App & E 863, 934(1); Judgm 181(1), 181(23), 185(2); Libel 1, 6(1), 10(6), 36, 38(1), 44(1), 44(3), 45(1), 50, 101(1), 101(3), 112(1), 123(2).

Houston Lighting & Power Co.; Henry v., TexApp–Houston (1 Dist), 934 SW2d 748, reh overr, and writ den.—App & E 934(1); Gas 20(4); Judgm 185(6); Neglig 202, 371, 379, 380, 383, 387, 423, 431, 432.

Houston Lighting & Power Co.; Hernandez v., TexApp–Houston (14 Dist), 795 SW2d 775.—Action 60; Electricity 19(1), 19(4); Evid 3, 14, 51; Plead 228.14.

Houston Lighting & Power Co. v. International Broth. of Elec. Workers, Local Union No. 66, CA5 (Tex), 71 F3d 179, cert den 117 SCt 52, 519 US 809, 136 LEd2d 16.—Alt Disp Res 374(1); Labor & Emp 1549(19), 1578, 1580, 1592, 1595(11), 1619, 1623(1).

Houston Lighting & Power Co. v. International Broth. of Elec. Workers, Local Union No. 66, SDTex, 825 FSupp 135. See Polly v. Houston Lighting & Power Co.

Houston Lighting & Power Co. v. International Broth. of Elec. Workers, Local Union No. 66, SDTex, 803 FSupp 1. See Polly v. Houston Lighting & Power Co.

Houston Lighting & Power Co. v. Klein Independent School Dist., TexApp–Houston (14 Dist), 739 SW2d 508, writ den.—Admin Law 229, 664; App & E 638, 1050.1(11), 1069.2, 1079; Em Dom 194, 195, 196, 198(1), 222(1), 223, 238(1), 262(5), 274(1), 277, 304; Evid 333(1); Plead 34(1); Trial 307(3).

Houston Lighting & Power Co. v. Landry, TexApp–Houston (14 Dist), 709 SW2d 693, mandamus conditionally gr Klein Independent School Dist v. Fourteenth Court of Appeals, 720 SW2d 87.—Courts 209(2); Em Dom 257, 258.

Houston Lighting & Power Co.; Long v., SDTex, 902 FSupp 130.—Costs 32(2), 194.14; Insurance 3375, 3379; Labor & Emp 682, 710, 711, 712, 720.

Houston Lighting & Power Co.; Lynn v., TexApp–Houston (14 Dist), 820 SW2d 57.—Electricity 11.1(2).

Houston Lighting & Power Co. v. Office Emp. Intern. Union, Local No. 129, AFL-CIO v., TexCivApp–Austin, 314 SW2d 315, ref nre.—Const Law 90.1(7.1), 1921; Equity 65(2); Evid 593; Labor & Emp 983, 1354, 2100, 2101, 2110, 2111, 2114.

Houston Lighting & Power Co. v. O'Neill, TexApp–Houston (1 Dist), 896 SW2d 366. See Houston Lighting & Power Co. v. City of San Antonio.

Houston Lighting & Power Co.; Pena v., CA5 (Tex), 154 F3d 267.—Estop 68(2).

Houston Lighting & Power Co.; Pena v., SDTex, 978 FSupp 694, aff 154 F3d 267.—Civil R 1218(4); Estop 68(2).

Houston Lighting & Power Co.; Polly v., SDTex, 825 FSupp 135.—Civil R 1185, 1192, 1194, 1555; Labor & Emp 1599.

Houston Lighting & Power Co.; Polly v., SDTex, 803 FSupp 1, report and recommendation adopted in part 825 FSupp 135.—Assault 21; Civil R 1184, 1185, 1187, 1244; Fed Civ Proc 2497.1, 2544, 2546; Labor & Emp 2936, 3040, 3045, 3061(1); Lim of Act 31.

Houston Lighting & Power Co.; Public Utility Com'n of Texas v., Tex, 748 SW2d 439, appeal dism 109 SCt 36, 488 US 805, 102 LEd2d 16, on remand In re

Houston Lighting and Power Co, 1990 WL 711923.—Const Law 2601; Electricity 11.3(4); Pub Ut 128.

Houston Lighting & Power Co. v. Public Utility Com'n of Texas, TexApp–Austin, 843 SW2d 718. See Office of Public Utility Counsel v. Public Utility Com'n of Texas.

Houston Lighting & Power Co.; Public Utility Com'n of Texas v., TexApp–Austin, 778 SW2d 195.—App & E 954(1); Inj 16, 138.46; Witn 219(1), 219(3).

Houston Lighting and Power Co.; Public Utility Com'n of Texas v., TexApp–Austin, 715 SW2d 98, writ gr, aff in part, rev in part 748 SW2d 439, appeal dism 109 SCt 36, 488 US 805, 102 LEd2d 16, on remand In re Houston Lighting and Power Co, 1990 WL 711923.—Admin Law 305, 462, 763, 815, 819; Electricity 11.3(1), 11.3(3), 11.3(4), 11.3(6), 11.3(7); Pub Ut 128, 129, 147, 194.

Houston Lighting & Power Co.; Public Utility Com'n of Texas v., TexApp–Austin, 645 SW2d 645, ref nre.—Admin Law 491, 496; Electricity 11.3(6).

Houston Lighting & Power Co. v. Railroad Commission of Texas, Tex, 529 SW2d 763, 84 ALR3d 531.—Gas 13(1), 13(2), 13(3); Pub Ut 145.1.

Houston Lighting & Power Co.; Reece v., CA5 (Tex), 79 F3d 485, cert den 117 SCt 171, 519 US 864, 136 LEd2d 112.—Civil R 1118, 1703, 1744; Damag 50.10; Fed Cts 776; Labor & Emp 1243; States 18.15, 18.46, 18.49.

Houston Lighting & Power Co. v. Reed, TexCivApp–Houston, 365 SW2d 26, ref nre.—App & E 207, 1170.1, 1170.6, 1170.9(6); Autos 245(23), 245(57); Damag 49, 52, 54, 132(14); Neglig 216; Trial 125(4), 125(5), 283, 350.5(2), 350.7(8).

Houston Lighting and Power Co.; Reeves v., TexApp–Houston (1 Dist), 4 SW3d 374, petition for review den, and reh of petition for review overr.—App & E 223, 714(1), 714(5), 934(1); Lim of Act 95(14).

Houston Lighting & Power Co. v. Reynolds, Tex, 765 SW2d 784.—Electricity 13, 16(4).

Houston Lighting & Power Co. v. Reynolds, TexApp–Houston (1 Dist), 712 SW2d 761, writ gr, rev 765 SW2d 784.—App & E 179(1), 267(1); Damag 89(1), 91(3); Electricity 13, 14(1), 19(5), 19(6.1), 19(9), 19(12); Interest 66; Jury 136(3); Prod Liab 5, 14, 23.1, 87.1; Trial 350.7(10), 351.2(2), 351.2(4), 351.2(10).

Houston Lighting & Power Co. v. Russo Properties, Inc., TexApp–Houston (1 Dist), 710 SW2d 711.—App & E 230, 709, 907(4), 1074(3); Costs 194.18, 194.25, 194.38; Exceptions Bill of 8.

Houston Lighting & Power Co.; Salley v., TexApp–Houston (1 Dist), 801 SW2d 230, writ den.—App & E 760(1), 760(2), 907(2); Costs 260(5), 263.

Houston Lighting & Power Co.; Searcy v., CA5 (Tex), 907 F2d 562, reh den, cert den 111 SCt 438, 498 US 970, 112 LEd2d 421, reh den 111 SCt 718, 498 US 1042, 112 LEd2d 707.—Civil R 1331(6); Fed Civ Proc 103.2, 103.4, 2771(2), 2771(5), 2848; Fed Cts 621, 722, 830; U S 53(16).

Houston Lighting & Power Co.; Smith v., TexApp–Houston (1 Dist), 7 SW3d 287.—App & E 430(2), 719(1), 854(1), 1136.

Houston Lighting and Power Co. v. State, TexApp–Houston (14 Dist), 925 SW2d 312, reh overr, and writ den.—Dedi 53, 58; Em Dom 85, 147; Pub Ut 114.

Houston Lighting & Power Co.; State v., TexApp–Corpus Christi, 609 SW2d 263, ref nre.—Joint Adv 1.1, 1.2(1), 1.2(4), 1.2(9), 1.15; Partners 1, 3, 5, 17, 44; Tax 2168, 2197, 2315.

Houston Lighting & Power Co.; Stewart v., SDTex, 998 FSupp 746.—Civil R 1123, 1137, 1147, 1171, 1172, 1185, 1189, 1505(7), 1522; Damag 50.10; Work Comp 2084.

Houston Lighting & Power Co.; Stott v., TexCivApp–Hous (14 Dist), 453 SW2d 364.—App & E 1170.6; Autos 244(43); Trial 133.2.

Houston Lighting and Power Co. v. Sue, TexApp–Corpus Christi, 644 SW2d 835, ref nre.—App & E

932(2), 989, 1001(1), 1001(2), 1003(4), 1170.1, 1170.7; Corp 498; Damag 91(1), 94; Evid 219(3); Tresp 30, 46(1), 56, 58; Witn 331.5, 383, 405(1).

Houston Lighting & Power Co. v. Taber, TexCivApp–Galveston, 221 SW2d 339, ref nre.—App & E 1050.1(7); Electricity 19(3), 19(5); Evid 219.50; Neglig 502(2), 1571, 1617, 1652, 1683; New Tr 31.

Houston Lighting and Power Co.; Taylor v., SDTex, 756 FSupp 297.—Civil R 1135, 1168, 1252, 1536, 1549; Damag 50.10; Labor & Emp 40(3), 763, 914, 917; Libel 36, 51(1).

Houston Lighting & Power Co. v. Tenn-Tex Alloy & Chemical Corp., Tex, 400 SW2d 296.—Contracts 143.5; Electricity 11(2).

Houston Lighting & Power Co. v. Tenn-Tex Alloy & Chemical Corp., TexCivApp–Waco, 390 SW2d 328, writ gr, rev 400 SW2d 296.—Electricity 11.5(2).

Houston Lighting and Power Co.; Uherek v., SDTex, 997 FSupp 796.—Civil R 1590, 1592, 1594, 1595.

Houston Lighting & Power Co.; West v., TexCivApp–Hous (1 Dist), 483 SW2d 352.—Atty & C 62; Em Dom 201, 202(4), 205, 221, 222(1), 222(2), 241, 262(5); Evid 215(5), 332(3), 591.

Houston Lighting & Power Co. v. Wheelabrator Coal Services Co., TexApp–Houston (14 Dist), 788 SW2d 933. —App & E 856(1), 863, 907(5), 934(1), 1153; Contracts 187(1); Indem 31(3), 33(5); Judgm 181(19).

Houston Lighting & Power Co.; Williams v., SDTex, 980 FSupp 879.—Civil R 1019(2), 1019(3), 1218(3), 1226, 1513, 1516, 1517.

Houston Lighting and Power Co.; Wolfenberger v., TexApp–Houston (1 Dist), 73 SW3d 444, reh overr, and review den, and reh of petition for review den.—App & E 719(1); Electricity 17; Indem 68, 94; Judgm 181(33); Neglig 1263.

Houston Lighting & Power Co.; Young v., SDTex, 11 FSupp2d 921.—Civil R 1119, 1122, 1135, 1137, 1147, 1166, 1185, 1243, 1246, 1252, 1544, 1549, 1592, 1744; Damag 50.10; Fed Civ Proc 2497.1, 2546; Release 38, 55, 57(1); Work Comp 2093.

Houston Livestock Show and Rodeo, Inc. v. Hamrick, TexApp–Austin, 125 SW3d 555, reh overr.—Agric 5; Antitrust 141, 145, 147, 150, 357, 363, 369, 390, 393, 398; App & E 959(3), 971(2), 989, 1001(1), 1001(3), 1003(7), 1004(8), 1024.3, 1043(8), 1097(1), 1144, 1195(1); Costs 194.16, 198, 207, 208, 252, 264; Damag 6, 15, 16, 18, 102, 140.7, 192; Evid 532, 536, 546, 555.2; Libel 117; Lim of Act 43, 95(1), 177(2), 187, 195(3), 197(2), 199(1); Plead 236(4), 236(6); Venue 82.

Houston Loan & Investment Co. v. Abernathy, Tex-ComApp, 117 SW2d 1089, 131 Tex 601, answer to certified question conformed to 119 SW2d 157, 131 Tex 601.—Hus & W 62, 86, 90.

Houston Loan & Investment Co. v. Abernathy, TexCiv-App–Galveston, 119 SW2d 157, 131 Tex 601.—Hus & W 86.

Houston Lumber Supply Co. v. Wockenfuss, TexCiv-App–Houston, 386 SW2d 330, ref nre.—App & E 1170.6; Evid 570, 571(7); Home 29, 31, 33, 57(3); Impl & C C 30, 63, 110, 121, 123, 124; Mech Liens 14, 93; New Tr 140(3); Trial 351.2(4).

Houston Maritime Ass'n; N.L.R.B. v., CA5 (Tex), 426 F2d 584.—Labor & Emp 1212, 1501, 1728, 1880.

Houston Maritime Ass'n; N.L.R.B. v., CA5 (Tex), 337 F2d 333.—Labor & Emp 1255, 1447, 1734, 1736, 1780, 1916.

Houston Maritime Ass'n v. South Atlantic & Gulf Coast Dist. of Intern. Longshoremen's Ass'n, TexCiv-App–Houston, 367 SW2d 705.—App & E 903(3), 989, 1001(1); Decl Judgm 147; Judgm 199(3); Labor & Emp 1327(4), 2057.

Houston Materials Co.; Blackmon & Associates, Inc. v., TexCivApp–Hous (1 Dist), 507 SW2d 838.—Princ & S 159, 161.

Houston Materials Co.; Jones v., TexCivApp–Hous (14 Dist), 477 SW2d 694.—Acct Action on 13; Judgm 185.3(3); Plead 234, 236(2), 258(1).

Houston Mercantile Exchange Corp. v. Dailey Petroleum Corp., TexApp–Houston (14 Dist), 930 SW2d 242. —App & E 169, 719(1), 930(3), 1001(1), 1001(3), 1180(2); Consp 20; Damag 87(2), 184, 190; Evid 570, 595.

Houston Milling Co. v. Carlock, TexCivApp–Eastland, 183 SW2d 1013.—Neglig 218; Plead 111.10, 111.46; Venue 22(6).

Houston Mobilfone, Inc. v. Public Utility Commission, TexCivApp–Eastland, 565 SW2d 323.—Admin Law 722.1; Pub Ut 189, 192; Statut 212.1.

Houston Mun. Employees Pension System v. Abbott, TexApp–Texarkana, 192 SW3d 862, review den.—Mun Corp 92; Records 55, 58, 63.

Houston Mun. Employees Pension System v. Ferrell, TexApp–Houston (1 Dist), 177 SW3d 502, review gr.— Admin Law 228.1, 229, 303.1, 325; App & E 70(3), 893(1), 916(1); Courts 40, 155, 183, 472.3; Decl Judgm 9, 41, 122.1, 126, 207.1, 293.1, 302.1, 385, 390, 392.1; Judgm 702, 707; Mun Corp 187(10), 220(9), 723; States 191.1, 191.10.

Houston Mun. Employees Pension System; Thayer v., TexApp–Houston (1 Dist), 95 SW3d 573.—App & E 782, 863; Courts 37(1), 39; Mun Corp 220(9), 254, 723; Plead 104(1); States 191.6(1).

Houston Nat. Bank v. Adair, Tex, 207 SW2d 374, 146 Tex 387.—Banks 100; Neglig 1025, 1076, 1110(2), 1670, 1685, 1708.

Houston Nat. Bank; Adair v., TexCivApp–Galveston, 203 SW2d 782, rev 207 SW2d 374, 146 Tex 387.—Neglig 1037(3), 1076, 1088, 1670, 1708, 1717; Trial 156(2), 156(3); Zoning 62.1.

Houston Nat. Bank v. Biber, TexCivApp–Hous (14 Dist), 613 SW2d 771, ref nre.—App & E 181; Banks 119, 134(4), 134(7), 154(1), 154(8); Evid 318(1); Interest 39(2.50), 64.1; Trial 219, 232(5); Trover 2, 16, 60, 67.

Houston Nat. Bank; Dorsey v., TexCivApp–Waco, 338 SW2d 540, writ refused.—Bills & N 6, 32, 201.

Houston Nat. Bank v. Farris, TexCivApp–Waco, 549 SW2d 420, dism.—Banks 275; Mines 78.1(11); Venue 4, 5.5.

Houston Nat. Bank; Gillette v., TexCivApp–Galveston, 139 SW2d 646, writ dism, correct.—Corp 123(14), 126, 149; Estop 72; Trover 70.

Houston Nat. Bank; Ginther-Davis Center, Ltd. v., Tex-CivApp–Hous (1 Dist), 600 SW2d 856, ref nre.—Inj 14; Mtg 83, 86(3), 395, 413.

Houston Nat. Bank; Nishimatsu Const. Co., Ltd. v., CA5 (Tex), 515 F2d 1200.—Evid 418; Fed Civ Proc 81, 774, 2411, 2441, 2444.1; Fed Cts 20.1, 24, 313, 763.1; Princ & A 136(2).

Houston Nat. Bank; Thaxton v., TexCivApp–Hous (14 Dist), 439 SW2d 455.—App & E 1151(1); Judgm 21, 181(24), 524; Land & Ten 235, 258, 259, 265(1).

Houston Nat. Bank; Wing v., TexCivApp–Houston, 413 SW2d 843, ref nre.—Hus & W 262.1(1); Plead 182.

Houston Nat. Bank, Houston, Tex.; Phillips v., CCA5 (Tex), 108 F2d 934.—Assign 72; Contracts 156; Ship 56; Statut 194.

Houston Natural Gas Co.; Barnett v., TexCivApp–El Paso, 617 SW2d 305, ref nre.—App & E 173(2); Lim of Act 121(2), 126.

Houston Natural Gas Co. v. Kluck, Tex, 163 SW2d 618, 139 Tex 491.—App & E 1001(1); Gas 20(4).

Houston Natural Gas Co. v. Kluck, TexCivApp–Galveston, 154 SW2d 504, aff 163 SW2d 618, 139 Tex 491.— App & E 1003(10); Evid 587, 595; Gas 20(2), 20(6); Neglig 1539; Plead 53(1); Trial 358.

Houston Natural Gas Corp. v. C.I.R., CA5 (Tex), 173 F2d 461.—Int Rev 3136, 3680.

Houston Natural Gas Corp. v. Janak, Tex, 422 SW2d 159.—App & E 1114.

Houston Natural Gas Corp. v. Janak, TexCivApp–Waco, 416 SW2d 484, mod 422 SW2d 159.—App & E 1178(6); Evid 265(10), 317(6); Fraud 12, 13(1), 20, 25, 36, 50, 58(1); Labor & Emp 3096(4).

Houston Natural Gas Corp.; Leslie v., TexCivApp–Galveston, 280 SW2d 353, ref nre, cert den 77 SCt 43, 352 US 829, 1 LEd2d 50.—App & E 712; Carr 39, 198; Courts 206(17.3); Gas 14.1(1), 14.1(2), 14.1(3), 14.6; Judgm 185.3(11); Plead 356.

Houston Natural Gas Corp.; N.L.R.B. v., CA5 (Tex), 478 F2d 467, reh den 480 F2d 924, cert den 94 SCt 575, 414 US 1067, 38 LEd2d 472.—Labor & Emp 1178(2), 1792, 1793, 1857, 1880.

Houston Natural Gas Corp. v. Nueces County Water Imp. Dist. No. 1, TexCivApp–San Antonio, 157 SW2d 170.—Corp 446; Equity 65(2); Gas 9; Inj 135; Labor & Emp 2059, 2060; Waters 228, 228.5.

Houston Natural Gas Corp. v. Pearce, TexCivApp–Houston, 311 SW2d 899, ref nre.—App & E 854(2), 1012.1(4); Damag 111, 138; Evid 560, 570, 571(7); Lim of Act 55(7), 195(3); Neglig 1656, 1676, 1680, 1717, 1750; Tresp 35; Trial 142, 382, 404(6).

Houston Natural Gas Corp.; Railroad Commission v., Tex, 289 SW2d 559, 155 Tex 502.—Const Law 969, 2426, 2473, 4361; Corp 391; Evid 522; Gas 14.2, 14.4(4), 14.5(6), 14.5(9); Judgm 180; Mun Corp 619; Pub Ut 119.1, 124, 127, 129, 169.1, 194.

Houston Natural Gas Corp.; Railroad Commission v., TexCivApp–Austin, 186 SW2d 117, writ refused wom.—App & E 781(4), 870(4); Decl Judgm 4, 5.1, 43, 111, 122.1, 125, 206; Gas 14.2, 14.3(3), 14.5(9); Statut 176, 219(9.1), 220.

Houston Natural Gas Corp.; Southern Community Gas Co. v., TexCivApp–San Antonio, 197 SW2d 488, writ refused.—Assign 19.

Houston Natural Gas Corp. v. Southwestern Apparel, Inc., TexCivApp–Austin, 558 SW2d 950, dism.—Plead 111.42(9); Tax 3635, 3704.

Houston Natural Gas Corp. v. Wyatt, TexCivApp–Eastland, 359 SW2d 257.—Mun Corp 993(2).

Houston North Hosp. Properties v. Telco Leasing, Inc., CA5 (Tex), 688 F2d 408.—Fed Civ Proc 1432.1, 2470.1; Fed Cts 409.1; Jury 25(8); Torts 422.

Houston North Hosp. Properties v. Telco Leasing, Inc., CA5 (Tex), 680 F2d 19, on reh 688 F2d 408.—Contracts 1, 95(1); Fed Civ Proc 2515; Torts 436.

Houston North Properties v. White, TexApp–Houston (1 Dist), 731 SW2d 719, dism.—Courts 207.1, 475(1); Judges 51(2); Prohib 5(2).

Houston North Shore Ry. Co. v. Tyrrell, Tex, 98 SW2d 786, 128 Tex 248, 108 ALR 1508.—App & E 861; Courts 475(8); Em Dom 45, 58, 170, 171, 191(5), 197; Parties 92(1).

Houston Northwest Medical Center; Hallett v., Tex, 689 SW2d 888.—App & E 200.

Houston Northwest Medical Center; Hughes v., TexApp–Houston (1 Dist), 647 SW2d 5, dism.—Corp 320(4); Inj 26(1), 27; Lis Pen 3(1), 3(3), 20.

Houston Northwest Medical Center, Inc.; Hughes v., TexApp–Houston (1 Dist), 680 SW2d 838, ref nre, cert den 106 SCt 571, 474 US 1020, 88 LEd2d 555.—App & E 901, 930(3), 989, 1001(1), 1079, 1177(7); Corp 307, 320(11); Damag 6, 141; Decl Judgm 385; Judgm 252(1); Mal Pros 47; Torts 212, 242, 263; Trusts 102(1); Witn 216(1).

Houston Northwest Medical Center Survivor, Inc.; Bright v., CA5 (Tex), 934 F2d 671, 30 Wage & Hour Cas (BNA) 609, cert den 112 SCt 882, 502 US 1036, 30 Wage & Hour Cas (BNA) 1176, 116 LEd2d 786.—Fed Civ Proc 2498; Labor & Emp 2320.

Houston Northwest Medical Center Survivor, Inc.; Bright v., CA5 (Tex), 888 F2d 1059, 29 Wage & Hour Cas (BNA) 905, reh gr 898 F2d 968, 29 Wage & Hour Cas (BNA) 1258, on reh 934 F2d 671, 30 Wage & Hour

Cas (BNA) 609, cert den 112 SCt 882, 502 US 1036, 30 Wage & Hour Cas (BNA) 1176, 116 LEd2d 786.

Houston Northwest Medical Center Survivor, Inc. v. King, TexApp–Houston (1 Dist), 788 SW2d 179.—Damag 221(8); Labor & Emp 870; Work Comp 2157.

Houston Northwest Partners, Ltd., In re, TexApp–Austin, 98 SW3d 777, mandamus dism.—Courts 202(1).

Houston Oil & Minerals Corp.; Beakley v., TexCivApp–Eastland, 600 SW2d 396, ref nre.—Neglig 1612, 1614.

Houston Oil & Minerals Corp.; Enserch Corp. v., TexApp–Houston (1 Dist), 743 SW2d 654, writ den.—Contracts 229(1); Gas 14.1(1), 14.1(3).

Houston Oil & Minerals Corp. v. Enserch Corp., TexApp–Houston (14 Dist), 732 SW2d 419, ref nre.—App & E 934(1); Gas 14.1(3); Judgm 181(29), 185(2).

Houston Oil and Refining, Inc. v. U.S. F.E.R.C., CAFed (Tex), 95 F3d 1126, reh den, in banc sug declined, cert den Imparato v. FERC, 117 SCt 1819, 520 US 1228, 137 LEd2d 1028.—Admin Law 305, 683; Const Law 2623; Fed Cts 1140; Jury 19(1); War 108, 109, 110.1, 133.1, 136, 138, 163.

Houston Oil Co. v. Biskamp, TexCivApp–Beaumont, 99 SW2d 1007, writ dism.—App & E 931(1); Deeds 45; Hus & W 198; Lim of Act 39(12); Mental H 333, 382.1.

Houston Oil Co.; Tyler v., TexCivApp–Beaumont, 135 SW2d 307.—Adv Poss 96.

Houston Oil Co. of Tex.; American Republics Corp. v., CA5 (Tex), 173 F2d 728, cert den 70 SCt 101, 338 US 858, 94 LEd 526.—Estop 22(2), 70(2); Evid 450(3), 450(5); Fed Cts 877.

Houston Oil Co. of Tex.; American Republics Corp. v., TexCivApp–Galveston, 198 SW2d 956, ref nre.—App & E 907(3); Mines 58, 59, 74(5), 74(8).

Houston Oil Co. of Texas; Duke v., TexCivApp–Beaumont, 128 SW2d 480, writ dism, correct.—Adv Poss 27, 28, 57, 104, 112; App & E 996; Evid 100, 587; Trial 139.1(20), 142.

Houston Oil Co. of Tex.; Kirby v., TexCivApp–Beaumont, 241 SW2d 198, writ refused.—Judgm 743(2); Tresp to T T 10.

Houston Oil Co. of Texas; Kirby v., TexCivApp–Beaumont, 200 SW2d 246, writ refused, cert den 68 SCt 86, 332 US 772, 92 LEd 357, reh den 68 SCt 152, 332 US 820, 92 LEd 397.—App & E 1026; Home 212; Hus & W 270(5); Judgm 681.

Houston Oil Co. of Texas v. Kirkindall, Tex, 145 SW2d 1074, 136 Tex 103.—Ack 6(3); Evid 461(1), 461(3); Frds St of 68; Hus & W 70; Partit 4, 5, 8, 9(1); Ven & Pur 228(1), 229(1).

Houston Oil Co. of Texas v. Lawson, TexCivApp–Galveston, 175 SW2d 716, writ refused.—Const Law 42(2), 190, 725, 2429, 2675, 2718, 4140; Statut 64(8), 251; Tax 2060, 2103, 2107, 2136, 2153, 2233, 3249.

Houston Oil Co. of Texas; Morgan v., TexCivApp–San Antonio, 84 SW2d 312.—App & E 672, 846(3), 846(5); Mines 78.6, 78.7(4).

Houston Oil Co. of Tex. v. Moss, Tex, 284 SW2d 131, 155 Tex 157.—Adv Poss 25, 48, 101; Land & Ten 5(1), 66(1); Mines 55(7).

Houston Oil Co. of Tex.; Moss v., TexCivApp–Beaumont, 273 SW2d 925, rev 284 SW2d 131, 155 Tex 157.—Adv Poss 43(8), 115(1); Costs 234; Evid 332(1), 332(3); Mines 49, 64; Tresp to T T 16, 25.

Houston Oil Co. of Tex.; Paul v., TexCivApp–Waco, 211 SW2d 345, ref nre.—Action 45(1), 50(2), 50(4.1), 60; App & E 946; Deeds 20.1, 25, 78, 90, 93, 97, 110, 188; Hus & W 273(8.1); Notice 12, 13; Plead 8(6), 228.23, 312; Tresp to T T 32; Ven & Pur 230(1).

Houston Oil Co. of Tex.; Reeves v., TexCivApp–Beaumont, 230 SW2d 255, ref nre.—Adv Poss 43(4), 51, 57, 101; App & E 237(5), 683, 843(2), 989, 1071.2, 1122(1); Estop 32(1); Evid 43(3), 317(5), 353(7); Frds St of 158(1), 158(4); Judgm 470; Lis Pen 22(1); Mines 55(2), 55(7), 55(8); Tresp to T T 35(1), 38(1), 40(5), 41(1).

Houston Oil Co. of Texas; Sabine Hardwood Co. v., CCA5 (Tex), 87 F2d 279, cert den 57 SCt 922, 301 US 694, 81 LEd 1350.—Trial 11(3).

Houston Oil Co. of Texas; Sabine Hardwood Co. v., EDTex, 14 FSupp 743, aff 87 F2d 279, cert den 57 SCt 922, 301 US 694, 81 LEd 1350.—Fed Civ Proc 1995; Fed Cts 7, 31.

Houston Oil Co. of Tex. v. Skeeler, TexCivApp–Amarillo, 178 SW2d 740.—Adv Poss 19, 27; Trial 260(5).

Houston Oil Co. of Tex.; Wiggins v., TexCivApp–Beaumont, 203 SW2d 252, ref nre.—Adv Poss 16(1), 21, 70, 110(3), 114(1), 115(7); Evid 230(1).

Houston Oil Co. of Texas; Zeppa v., TexCivApp–Texarkana, 113 SW2d 612, writ refused.—Bound 9; Contracts 170(1); Mines 73, 73.1(1), 73.2.

Houston Oil Co of Texas; Reed v., CCA5 (Tex), 132 F2d 748, cert den 63 SCt 1032, 319 US 743, 87 LEd 1699, reh den 63 SCt 1315, 319 US 784, 87 LEd 1727.—Fed Cts 927.

Houston Oilers; Smith v., CA5 (Tex), 87 F3d 717. See Smith v. Houston Oilers, Inc.

Houston Oilers, Inc. v. Floyd, TexCivApp–Hous (1 Dist), 518 SW2d 836, ref nre.—Contracts 278(1); Release 25, 38.

Houston Oilers, Inc. v. Harris County, Tex., SDTex, 960 FSupp 1202.—Alt Disp Res 247, 332; Assoc 14; Consp 19; Contracts 187(1); Fraud 3, 13(1), 20; Libel 1, 136; Pub Amuse 26; Ship 80; Torts 242, 243.

Houston Oilers, Inc.; Matuszak v., TexCivApp–Hous (14 Dist), 515 SW2d 725.—Antitrust 601; App & E 863, 954(1), 954(3), 1011.1(1), 1170.1, 1170.7; Contracts 116(1); Courts 489(8); Inj 147.

Houston Oilers, Inc.; Smith v., CA5 (Tex), 87 F3d 717, cert den 117 SCt 510, 519 US 1008, 136 LEd2d 400.—Assault 2; Damag 50.10; Extort 34; Labor & Emp 968; States 18.15, 18.46; Torts 423, 436.

Houston Oilers, Inc.; Spain v., TexCivApp–Hous (14 Dist), 593 SW2d 746.—Alt Disp Res 182(1); Courts 97(5); Labor & Emp 1550.

Houston Oil Field Material Co.; Alexander v., TexCivApp–Tyler, 386 SW2d 540, ref nre.—App & E 223; Bills & N 485, 488, 489(6); Evid 91; Judgm 181(26), 185(6), 185.3(16); Plead 378.

Houston Oil Field Material Co. v. Claypool, CA5 (Tex), 269 F2d 134.—Pat 70, 118.21, 312(6), 314(1), 324.5, 324.55(2).

Houston Oil Field Material Co.; Claypool v., SDTex, 166 FSupp 173, rev 269 F2d 134.—Pat 112.3(3), 118.21, 233.1, 312(1.2).

Houston Oil Field Material Co.; Phinney v., CA5 (Tex), 252 F2d 357.—Fed Cts 656; Int Rev 3879.

Houston Oil Fields Ass'n; Ross v., TexCivApp–Galveston, 88 SW2d 586, writ dism.—Adv Poss 19; App & E 931(1), 989; Bound 3(7), 37(1); Evid 460(4).

Houston Orthopedic Associates; Burkhardt v., TexApp–Houston (14 Dist), 795 SW2d 221, writ den.—App & E 1024.4; Health 823(7).

Houston Orthopedic Center; Trevino v., TexApp–Houston (14 Dist), 831 SW2d 341, reh den, and writ den.—App & E 846(5), 901; Judgm 72; Motions 47; New Tr 6; Pretrial Proc 502.

Houston Orthopedic Center; Trevino v., TexApp–Houston (14 Dist), 782 SW2d 515, appeal after remand 831 SW2d 341, reh den, and writ den.—Judgm 181(33), 185.2(4).

Houston Osteopathic Hospital v. Meisler, TexCivApp–Hous (14 Dist), 441 SW2d 636.—Exch of Prop 6, 8(4); Ven & Pur 261(3).

Houston Oxygen Co. v. Davis, TexComApp, 161 SW2d 474, 139 Tex 1, 140 ALR 868.—App & E 970(2), 1084, 1172(5); Evid 118, 122(6), 314(1); Parent & C 7(6), 7(11).

Houston Oxygen Co. v. Davis, TexCivApp–Beaumont, 145 SW2d 300, rev 161 SW2d 474, 139 Tex 1, 140 ALR

868.—Autos 200, 201(10), 246(22); Damag 132(12), 221(5.1); Evid 314(2); Infants 115; Judgm 252(3); Jury 72(3); Parent & C 5(1), 7(6); Trial 26, 121(2), 232(3), 232(5); Witn 388(1), 414(1).

Houston Packing Co. v. Benson, TexCivApp–Eastland, 114 SW2d 429.—App & E 1001(1); Evid 588; Labor & Emp 3105(8); New Tr 99, 102(1), 102(6), 103, 140(1).

Houston Packing Co. v. Spivey, TexCivApp, 333 SW2d 423.—App & E 931(1); Evid 121(2), 185(1), 361, 474(20); Princ & A 99, 104(2), 123(1); Sales 434, 441(1), 441(2), 441(4).

Houston Peace Coalition v. Houston City Council, SDTex, 310 FSupp 457.—Const Law 1059, 1762, 1864, 4105(5); Mun Corp 703(2).

Houston Petroleum Co. v. Highlands Ins. Co., TexApp–Houston (1 Dist), 830 SW2d 153, writ den.—Insurance 1808, 1822, 1835(2), 2277, 2307, 2315, 2914, 2915.

Houston Pilots v. Goodwin, TexCivApp–Galveston, 178 SW2d 308, dism.—Commerce 56; Evid 65; Pilots 1, 2.5, 5, 14; Plead 111.7; Venue 8.5(5).

Houston Pipe Coating Co., Inc. v. Houston Freightways, Inc., TexApp–Houston (14 Dist), 679 SW2d 42, ref nre.—App & E 569(1), 865, 1177(9); Corp 507(13); Proc 133.

Houston Pipe Line Co. v. BHP Petroleum (Americas), Inc., TexApp–Houston (14 Dist), 785 SW2d 398, writ den.—Atty & C 21.20; Gas 14.1(1), 14.1(3), 14.6.

Houston Pipe Line Co. v. Brown, TexCivApp–Houston, 361 SW2d 884, ref nre.—Em Dom 223, 246(2); Inj 51, 113.

Houston Pipe Line Co. v. Dwyer, Tex, 374 SW2d 662.—App & E 863; Ease 12(1); Gas 9; Judgm 181(2), 185.3(17).

Houston Pipe Line Co.; Dwyer v., TexCivApp–Houston, 364 SW2d 736, writ gr, aff 374 SW2d 662.—Ease 48(5); Gas 9.

Houston Pipe Line Co.; Gulf Fleet Supply Vessels Inc. v., CA5 (Tex), 71F3d 198. See Corpus Christi Oil & Gas Co. v. Zapata Gulf Marine Corp.

Houston Pipeline Co.; Ludewig v., TexApp–Corpus Christi, 773 SW2d 610, writ den.—Ease 61(8); Em Dom 187, 196, 223, 263, 304.

Houston Pipeline Co.; Ludewig v., TexApp–Corpus Christi, 737 SW2d 15.—App & E 100(2), 190(2); Gas 9.

Houston Pipe Line Co. v. Oxy Petroleum, Inc., TexCivApp–Corpus Christi, 597 SW2d 57, dism.—Action 1; Corp 503(2); Damag 11; Gas 13(1).

Houston Pipe Line Co. v. Peddy, TexCivApp–Galveston, 292 SW2d 364, ref nre.—Labor & Emp 29, 2765, 3128.

Houston Pipeline Co.; Russ Mitchell, Inc. v., TexCivApp–Galveston, 219 SW2d 109, ref nre.—App & E 218.2(2), 758.3(1), 758.3(7), 766; Damag 78(1), 79(1); Evid 441(7); Gas 9; Pretrial Proc 77; Trial 62(2).

Houston Pipeline Co.; Taub v., TexApp–Texarkana, 75 SW3d 606, reh overr, and review den, and reh of petition for review den.—Adv Poss 13, 58; App & E 232(0.5), 852, 863, 893(1), 901, 934(1); Consp 1.1, 5; Contracts 326; Corp 423; Damag 22, 117, 120(1), 189; Estates 1; Estop 52(1), 52.10(3), 92(2); Fraud 3, 9, 10; Judgm 181(2), 185(2).—Plead 111.42(4); Libel 130, 135; Lim of Act 43, 46(6), 55(5), 95(1), 95(7), 95(9), 104(1), 104(2); Mines 48, 49, 51(1), 55(7), 73.1(3), 78.7(6); Neglig 202.

Houston Pipeline Co.; U.S. v., CA5 (Tex), 37 F3d 224.—Fed Civ Proc 2554; Int Rev 3336, 3800.1.

Houston Pipe Line Co. v. U.S., SDTex, 838 FSupp 1160, aff US v. Houston Pipeline Co, 37 F3d 224.—Int Rev 3800.1, 3803.

Houston Pipe Line Co.; Walton Transp. Co. v., TexCivApp–Houston, 358 SW2d 744, ref nre.—App & E 846(5); Carr 194, 196; Wareh 10.

Houston Pipeline Co. v. Ybanez, TexCivApp–Austin, 368 SW2d 140, dism.—Plead 111.42(4); Venue 8.5(8), 32(2).

Houston Pipeline Co. LP v. Bank of America, N.A., TexApp–Houston (1 Dist), 213 SW3d 418.—App & E 23,

HOUSTON

See Guidelines for Arrangement at the beginning of this Volume

223, 781(2); Bankr 2391, 2392, 2394.1, 2395, 2396, 2397(1), 2402(1), 2462, 2532, 2535(1), 2535(2), 2541, 2547, 2553; Judgm 16.

Houston Pizza Ventures, Inc.; Prigmore v., SDTex, 189 FSupp2d 635.—Civil R 1118, 1119, 1145, 1147, 1184, 1185, 1189, 1528; Damag 50.10; States 18.15.

Houston Plastic Products, Inc.; Aut-O-Cel Co. v., TexCivApp–Waco, 411 SW2d 749, ref nre.—Attach 374; Bailm 16; Sales 441(3).

Houston Plumbing Supply Co., Inc. v. Ornelas Plumbing Supply Co., Inc., TexApp–El Paso, 636 SW2d 608. —Abate & R 7, 8(1), 8(2), 9; Plead 106(2), 111.39(1).

Houston Police Dept. v. Berkowitz, TexApp–Houston (1 Dist), 95 SW3d 457, reh overr, and review den.—Crim Law 1226(3.1), 1226(4).

Houston Police Dept.; Metzger v., TexApp–Houston (14 Dist), 846 SW2d 383, reh den, and writ den.—Crim Law 632(4), 1166(1), 1226(4).

Houston Police Officers Ass'n; City of Houston v., TexApp–Houston (14 Dist), 715 SW2d 145.—Const Law 58; Mun Corp 180(1), 182.

Houston Police Officers Pension Bd.; Nichols v., TexCivApp–Waco, 335 SW2d 261, ref nre.—Mun Corp 176(3.1), 186(5), 187(7), 220(2).

Houston Police Officers' Union v. City of Houston, Tex., CA5 (Tex), 330 F3d 298, cert den Marticiuc v. City of Houston, Tex, 124 SCt 300, 540 US 879, 157 LEd2d 143.—Admin Law 416.1; Labor & Emp 2322; Statut 209, 219(1), 219(2), 219(4).

Houston Police Officers' Union; Paul v., TexApp–Houston (14 Dist), 76 SW3d 108, reh overr, and review den.—Labor & Emp 1178(2); Statut 179.

Houston Police Patrolmen's Union; City of Houston v., CA5 (Tex), 37 F3d1097. See Edwards v. City of Houston.

Houston, Port of, Authority v. West, TexApp–Houston (1 Dist), 782 SW2d 337. See Port of Houston Authority v. West.

Houston Post; Cook v., CA5 (Tex), 616 F2d 791.—Civil R 1088(5), 1376(9); Consp 7.5(1), 13; Const Law 3865, 4534; Dist & Pros Attys 10.

Houston Post; Covington v., TexApp–Houston (14 Dist), 743 SW2d 345.—Libel 68, 76; Torts 329, 354, 413.

Houston Post; Heard v., TexApp–Houston (1 Dist), 684 SW2d 210. See Heard v. Houston Post Co.

Houston Post Co.; Gibler v., TexCivApp–Houston, 310 SW2d 377, ref nre.—App & E 934(1); Judgm 181(4), 181(33), 186; Libel 5, 25, 33, 48(1), 89(1).

Houston Post Co.; Heard v., TexApp–Houston (1 Dist), 684 SW2d 210, ref nre.—App & E 374(4); Courts 89; Records 52, 60, 63.

Houston Post Co.; Johnson v., TexApp–Houston (14 Dist), 807 SW2d 613, writ den.—Libel 19, 123(2).

Houston Post Co.; Land Liquidators of Texas, Inc. v., TexApp–Houston (14 Dist), 630 SW2d 713.—Acct Action on 10; App & E 171(3); Judgm 185.1(3).

Houston Post Co.; Leatherwood v., CA5 (Tex), 59 F3d 533.—Civil R 1217, 1218(4); Fed Civ Proc 2142.1, 2146, 2151, 2608.1; Fed Cts 765.

Houston Post Co. v. U.S., SDTex, 79 FSupp 199.—Admin Law 749; Tel 644, 1137.

Houston Post Pension Plan; May v., CA5 (Tex), 898 F2d 1068.—Fed Cts 543.1; Labor & Emp 563(1).

Houston Press Co.; Morin v., TexCivApp–El Paso, 103 SW2d 1087.—App & E 1171(6); Libel 36; Lim of Act 127(12).

Houston Printing Co. v. Hunter, TexCivApp–Fort Worth, 105 SW2d 312, writ dism, aff 106 SW2d 1043, 129 Tex 652.—App & E 916(1); Libel 80, 97, 123(2), 124(8); Plead 34(2); Trial 241, 307(3), 350.3(4).

Houston Printing Co. v. Pulitzer Pub. Co. v., CCA5 (Tex), 11 F2d 834, cert den 47 SCt 91, 273 US 694, 71 LEd 844.—Antitrust 16; Trademarks 1036, 1425, 1716, 1800.

Houston Printing Co.; Pulitzer Pub. Co. v., SDTex, 4 F2d 924, aff 11 F2d 834, cert den 47 SCt 91, 273 US 694, 71 LEd 844.—Trademarks 1000, 1186, 1241, 1356, 1419, 1426.

Houston Printing Corp.; American Weekly v., CCA5 (Tex), 134 F2d 447, reh den 135 F2d 733.—Contracts 10(4); Sales 77(1), 77(2), 166(1), 188.

Houston Printing Corp.; Evans v., TexCivApp–Galveston, 217 SW2d 85, ref nre.—App & E 866(3), 1052(8), 1068(3); Judgm 193; Jury 34(1); Libel 19, 123(2), 123(7); Trial 178.

Houston Produce Terminal, Inc.; Gill v., TexCivApp–Hous (14 Dist), 444 SW2d 800, ref nre.—Corp 254, 629; Damag 221(2.1), 221(7); Frds St of 64; Trial 350.3(1), 352.20.

Houston Professional Fire Fighters' Ass'n v. City of Houston, TexApp–Houston (1 Dist), 177 SW3d 95.—Mun Corp 197, 197.3(2).

Houston Raceway Park, Inc.; Dixon v., TexApp–Houston (1 Dist), 874 SW2d 760.—App & E 173(2), 596; Autos 289; High 199; Judgm 185(2); Neglig 202, 1019.

Houston Refuse Disposal, Inc.; Adler Paper Stock, Inc. v., TexApp–Houston (1 Dist), 930 SW2d 761, writ den.—Antitrust 161, 198; App & E 989, 999(1), 1003(5).

Houston R.E. Income Properties XV, Ltd. v. Waller County Appraisal Dist., TexApp–Houston (1 Dist), 123 SW3d 859.—App & E 232(0.5); Tax 2514, 2515, 2517, 2703, 2728.

Houston Sash & Door Co.; Bergman Drive-In, Inc. v., TexCivApp–Galveston, 256 SW2d 661, ref nre.—Corp 414(1), 425(0.5).

Houston Sash & Door Co., Inc. v. Davidson, TexCivApp–Beaumont, 509 SW2d 690, ref nre.—Elect of Rem 9, 14; Evid 209, 265(9); Plead 53(1), 53(2), 111.42(4); Venue 16 1/2, 22(1), 22(4).

Houston Sash and Door Co., Inc. v. Heaner, Tex, 577 SW2d 217.—Guar 5, 77(2), 78(1); Usury 32, 82, 137, 138, 140, 143.

Houston Sash & Door Co., Inc.; Heaner v., TexCivApp–Waco, 560 SW2d 525, writ gr, aff in part, rev in part 577 SW2d 217.—Usury 125, 137, 138, 144, 145.

Houston Shell & Concrete; Hastings v., TexCivApp–Hous (1 Dist), 596 SW2d 142, ref nre.—Frds St of 44(1), 119(1); Lim of Act 127(3).

Houston Shell & Concrete; Higbie Roth Const. Co. v., TexApp–Houston (1 Dist), 1 SW3d 808, reh overr, and petition for review den.—Antitrust 134, 138, 221, 389(1), 389(2); App & E 863, 883, 893(1), 895(2), 916(1); Judgm 181(11), 185(2); Neglig 202, 213, 215, 1692; Work Comp 2142.20.

Houston Shell and Concrete; Texas Gulf Coast Const. Co. v., TexCivApp–Hous (1 Dist), 517 SW2d 650, ref nre.—App & E 428(2), 430(1); New Tr 117(1).

Houston Shell & Concrete Co v. Kingsley Constructors, Inc., TexApp–Houston (14 Dist), 987 SW2d 184.—Contracts 353(6); Evid 366(1), 373(1), 373(2); Interest 37(2).

Houston Shell & Concrete Co. v. Minella, TexCivApp–Galveston, 269 SW2d 953, ref nre.—Contracts 187(1); Estop 85.

Houston Shell & Concrete, Division of McDonough Co.; W. Cecil Sisson Mortg. Co. v., CA5 (Tex), 256 F2d 420.—Bankr 2133, 3768.

Houston Shoe Hospital v. State, TexCivApp–Hous (14 Dist), 423 SW2d 624.—Judgm 185.3(20); Pretrial Proc 481; Tax 2510, 2699(7).

Houston Shopping News Co. v. N.L.R.B., CA5 (Tex), 554 F2d 739.—Labor & Emp 1103, 1112, 1915, 1936.

Houston Singing Soc.; Glass v., TexCivApp–Galveston, 192 SW2d 300.—App & E 215(2), 301; Evid 141; Neglig 1631, 1635.

Houston Sports Ass'n; Friedman v., TexApp–Houston (1 Dist), 731 SW2d 572, ref nre.—App & E 232(0.5), 289; Judgm 199(3.5); Pub Amuse 109(2), 147.

Houston Sports Ass'n; Johnson v., TexCivApp–Hous (1 Dist), 615 SW2d 781, ref nre.—App & E 930(1), 974(1), 1001(1); Neglig 232; Trial 349(2), 350.6(2), 351.2(6), 352.18.

Houston Sports Ass'n v. Russell, TexCivApp–Hous (14 Dist), 450 SW2d 741, ref nre.—App & E 930(1), 989; Neglig 1037(4), 1086, 1683, 1708; New Tr 162(1), 163(2).

Houston Sports Ass'n, Inc. v. Astro-Card Co., Inc., SDTex, 520 FSupp 1178.—Equity 72(1); Estop 95; Trademarks 1651, 1715(1).

Houston Sports Ass'n, Inc.; Henderson Broadcasting Corp. v., SDTex, 659 FSupp 109.—Antitrust 604, 699; Tel 1159(1).

Houston Sports Ass'n, Inc.; Henderson Broadcasting Corp. v., SDTex, 647 FSupp 292.—Antitrust 534, 592, 604; Fed Civ Proc 2515.

Houston Sports Ass'n, Inc.; Henderson Broadcasting Corp. v., SDTex, 541 FSupp 263.—Antitrust 604, 976.

Houston's Restaurant, Inc.; Johnson v., CA5 (Tex), 167 FedAppx 393.—Labor & Emp 367(5).

Houston State Associates; Henry S. Miller Management Corp. v., TexApp–Houston (1 Dist), 792 SW2d 128, writ den.—Action 60; Antitrust 367; App & E 151(6), 756, 760(1), 766; Judgm 199(3.10), 252(1); Land & Ten 34(2).

Houston State Associates; Miller Management Corp. v., TexApp–Houston (1 Dist), 792 SW2d 128. See Henry S. Miller Management Corp. v. Houston State Associates.

Houston State Bank; Bradley v., TexCivApp–Hous (14 Dist), 588 SW2d 618, ref nre.—App & E 866(3), 927(7), 989; Compromise 24; Evid 434(12); Fraud 28; Usury 52, 62, 83.

Houston Steel Drum Co.; Mulcahy v., TexCivApp–Austin, 402 SW2d 817.—Corp 29(1), 615.5; Parties 38, 40(1), 40(2), 44, 48; Quo W 1, 16, 19, 33, 34, 40.

Houston Street Corporation v. Commissioner of Internal Revenue, CCA5 (Tex), 84 F2d 821.—Int Rev 4645, 4648.

Houston's Wild West, Inc. v. Salinas, TexApp–Houston (14 Dist), 690 SW2d 30, ref nre.—Corp 392, 507(12).

Houston Symphony Soc.; Bures v., CA5 (Tex), 503 F2d 842.—Const Law 3935; Labor & Emp 1218, 2023, 2044, 2106.

Houston Teachers Ass'n; Houston Independent School Dist. v., TexCivApp–Hous (14 Dist), 617 SW2d 765.—App & E 781(4), 843(1).

Houston Technical Ceramics, Inc. v. Iwao Jiki Kogyo Co., Ltd., SDTex, 742 FSupp 387.—Fed Cts 86.

Houston Technical Ceramics, Inc. v. Shinagawa Refractories Co., SDTex, 745 FSupp 406.—Fed Cts 76.5, 76.30, 86, 417.

Houston, Tex., City of; Alnoa G. Corp. v., CA5 (Tex), 563 F2d 769, cert den 98 SCt 1610, 435 US 970, 56 LEd2d 62.—Fed Cts 27.

Houston, Tex., City of; Angeles, City of, Mission Church v., SDTex, 716FSupp 982. See City of Angeles Mission Church v. City of Houston, Tex.

Houston, Tex., City of; Brown v., CA5 (Tex), 337 F3d 539.—Civil R 1351(5); Fed Civ Proc 2546; Fed Cts 776, 802.

Houston, Tex., City of; City of Angeles Mission Church v., SDTex, 716 FSupp 982.—Const Law 90.1(4), 1033, 1036, 1504, 1506, 1545, 1879, 3526(5); Mun Corp 661(2).

Houston, Texas, City of; Crawford v., SDTex, 386 FSupp 187.—Civil R 1027, 1126, 1128, 1320, 1326(11), 1349, 1376(10), 1390, 1395(8), 1448; Consp 7.5(1), 18, 21; Const Law 1928, 1934, 3476, 4166(2), 4172(6); Fed Civ Proc 1773, 1829, 1835, 1837.1; Offic 114.

Houston, Tex., City of; Duncantell v., SDTex, 333 FSupp 973.—Elections 11, 15, 21; Fed Civ Proc 164, 176; Fed Cts 161; Mun Corp 124(3).

Houston, Tex., City of; Garrett v., CA5 (Tex), 102 FedAppx 863.—Civil R 1395(8), 1514, 1523.

Houston, Tex., City of; Harris v., CA5 (Tex), 476 F2d 283.—Rem of C 102.

Houston, Tex., City of; Henschen v., CA5 (Tex), 959 F2d 584.—Civil R 1395(1), 1456, 1462; Const Law 2602; Fed Cts 12.1, 13, 13.10.

Houston, Tex., City of, v. Hill, USTex, 107 SCt 2502, 482 US 451, 96 LEd2d 398. See City of Houston, Tex. v. Hill.

Houston, Tex., City of; Hill v., CA5 (Tex), 789 F2d 1103, probable jur noted 107 SCt 58, 479 US 811, 93 LEd2d 17, aff 107 SCt 2502, 482 US 451, 96 LEd2d 398, appeal dism, cert den 107 SCt 3222, 483 US 1001, 97 LEd2d 729.—Const Law 799, 1141; Courts 489(2); Mun Corp 594(2).

Houston, Tex., City of; Hill v., CA5 (Tex), 764 F2d 1156, on reh 789 F2d 1103, probable jur noted 107 SCt 58, 479 US 811, 93 LEd2d 17, aff 107 SCt 2502, 482 US 451, 96 LEd2d 398, appeal dism, cert den 107 SCt 3222, 483 US 1001, 97 LEd2d 729.—Const Law 82(4), 795, 855, 859, 1014, 1144, 1163, 1520, 1521, 1522; Fed Civ Proc 103.2.

Houston, Tex., City of; Horton v., CA5 (Tex), 179 F3d 188, reh den, cert den 120 SCt 530, 528 US 1021, 145 LEd2d 411, appeal after remand 89 FedAppx 903, cert den 125 SCt 48, 543 US 813, 160 LEd2d 17.—Const Law 1512, 1514, 1517, 1518, 1735, 2142; Fed Civ Proc 2481; Tel 1230.

Houston, Tex., City of; Houston Police Officers' Union v., CA5 (Tex), 330 F3d 298, cert den Marticiuc v. City of Houston, Tex, 124 SCt 300, 540 US 879, 157 LEd2d 143.—Admin Law 416.1; Labor & Emp 2322; Statut 209, 219(1), 219(2), 219(4).

Houston, Tex., City of; International Soc. for Krishna Consciousness of Houston, Inc. v., CA5 (Tex), 689 F2d 541.—Const Law 1228, 1389, 1440, 1873; Mun Corp 594(2); Statut 47.

Houston, Tex., City of; International Soc. for Krishna Consciousness of Houston, Inc. v., SDTex, 482 FSupp 852, rev 689 F2d 541.—Civil R 1482; Const Law 82(6.1), 1158, 1163, 1170, 1290, 1328, 1389, 1440, 1524, 1526, 1873, 1879, 4277; Mun Corp 594(2); Statut 47.

Houston, Tex., City of; Johnston v., CA5 (Tex), 14 F3d 1056.—Civil R 1395(6), 1398; Fed Civ Proc 2491.5, 2544; Fed Cts 766.

Houston, Tex., City of; Julian v., CA5 (Tex), 314 F3d 721.—Civil R 1201, 1513, 1514, 1523, 1530, 1555, 1560, 1563, 1564, 1571, 1574, 1576(2); Fed Civ Proc 2176.3, 2182.1, 2252; Fed Cts 763.1, 776, 813, 822.

Houston, Tex., City of; Paz v., SDTex, 748 FSupp 480.—Courts 489(1); Fed Civ Proc 2497.1, 2543, 2544, 2546; Fed Cts 191, 420; Judgm 634, 828.16(1), 828.16(3); Mun Corp 185(2), 185(12).

Houston, Tex., City of; Pratt v., CA5 (Tex), 247 F3d 601, on subsequent appeal 66 FedAppx 525, cert den 124 SCt 543, 540 US 1005, 157 LEd2d 411.—Civil R 1118, 1135, 1536; Fed Civ Proc 2497.1, 2543; Fed Cts 776.

Houston, Tex., City of; Santos v., SDTex, 852 FSupp 601.—Antitrust 641, 902, 903; Autos 61; Commerce 62.10(2); Const Law 990, 2480, 3043, 3057, 3682, 3686, 3869, 3877, 4157, 4367.

Houston, Tex., City of; Standard-Triumph Motor Co. v., SDTex, 220 FSupp 732, vac 347 F2d 194, cert den 86 SCt 539, 382 US 974, 15 LEd2d 466.—Commerce 77.10(2), 77.10(3).

Houston, Tex., City of; Whitaker v., CA5 (Tex), 963 F2d 831.—Fed Civ Proc 839.1, 840, 1838, 2575; Fed Cts 562, 590.

Houston, Tex., City of; Williamson v., CA5 (Tex), 148 F3d 462.—Civil R 1189, 1528, 1549, 1553; Fed Civ Proc 2608.1, 2609.

Houston, Tex., City of; Young v., CA5 (Tex), 906 F2d 177.—Civil R 1014, 1137, 1138, 1511, 1536, 1555; Consp 7.5(2).

Houston Textile Co. v. C.I.R., CA5 (Tex), 173 F2d 464.—Int Rev 3039, 4132.

Houston Textile Mills v. Montgomery, TexCivApp–Galveston, 83 SW2d 754, writ refused.—Labor & Emp 3105(10); Neglig 1101.

Houston Title Co. v. Ojeda De Toca, TexApp–Houston (14 Dist), 733 SW2d 325, writ gr, rev Ojeda de Toca v. Wise, 748 SW2d 449, on remand Wise v DeToca, 761 SW2d 467.—Antitrust 294; Fraud 23; Insurance 2610; Ven & Pur 230(1).

Houston Title Co.; Sumerlin v., TexApp–Houston (14 Dist), 808 SW2d 724, writ den.—App & E 179(1); Judgm 181(11).

Houston Title Guaranty Co. v. Fontenot, TexCivApp–Houston, 339 SW2d 347, ref nre.—Atty & C 141; Bound 46(1), 46(3); Insurance 1831, 1834(1), 2610, 2612, 2614, 2616, 2618, 2632, 2635, 2639.

Houston Tour & Charter Service, Inc.; State v., Tex, 460 SW2d 113.—Autos 74, 78.

Houston Tour & Charter Service, Inc. v. State, TexCivApp–Austin, 451 SW2d 244, rev 460 SW2d 113.—Autos 78.

Houston Transit Ben. Ass'n v. Carrington, TexCivApp–Hous (14 Dist), 590 SW2d 744.—Inj 138.42.

Houston Transit Co.; Bennevendo v., TexCivApp–Galveston, 238 SW2d 271, ref nre.—App & E 927(7); Carr 280(1.2), 284, 305(6), 316(1); Neglig 386, 387.

Houston Transit Co. v. Charon, TexCivApp–Houston, 390 SW2d 394.—App & E 758.3(10), 768, 930(1), 989, 1001(1), 1078(6); Autos 244(38).

Houston Transit Co.; Edwards v., TexCivApp–Waco, 342 SW2d 787, ref nre.—Autos 245(81), 247; New Tr 56, 140(3).

Houston Transit Co. v. Falls, TexCivApp–Houston, 332 SW2d 446.—App & E 80(1).

Houston Transit Co. v. Farrack, TexCivApp–Houston, 403 SW2d 184.—App & E 1170.7, 1170.10; Autos 63; Damag 221(5.1); Evid 123(11); Labor & Emp 2772, 3003; Trial 350.6(3), 358; Work Comp 52, 148, 186, 2110.

Houston Transit Co. v. Felder, Tex, 208 SW2d 880, 146 Tex 428.—Assault 38, 43(5); Labor & Emp 3055, 3056(1), 3096(8), 3105(8); Trial 194(16), 233(1).

Houston Transit Co.; Felder v., TexCivApp–Galveston, 203 SW2d 831, aff 208 SW2d 880, 146 Tex 428.—App & E 766, 927(7); Assault 40, 43(5); Labor & Emp 3049(1), 3056(1), 3056(2), 3105(8), 3106(3).

Houston Transit Co. v. Goldston, TexCivApp–Galveston, 217 SW2d 435.—App & E 768; Damag 221(2.1); Insurance 3406; Trial 108.5, 352.10.

Houston Transit Co.; Hawkins v., TexCivApp–Galveston, 227 SW2d 604, ref nre.—Autos 227(1); Neglig 530(1), 1571; Trial 350.7(5), 350.7(9).

Houston Transit Co. v. McQuade, TexCivApp–Galveston, 223 SW2d 64, writ refused.—App & E 927(7); Carr 247, 303(6), 343, 347.

Houston Transit Co.; Smith v., TexCivApp–Galveston, 215 SW2d 187, ref nre.—App & E 978(3); Autos 242(2), 244(55), 245(74); New Tr 128(4), 143(2).

Houston Transit Co. v. Steele, TexCivApp–Waco, 324 SW2d 912, ref nre.—Autos 156, 244(33), 245(50.1), 247; Damag 132(3); Indem 66; Neglig 213.

Houston Transit Co.; Zalta v., TexCivApp–Houston, 384 SW2d 914.—Autos 169, 226(2), 244(34), 244(36.1), 244(44).

Houston Transit Co. v. Zimmerman, TexCivApp–Galveston, 200 SW2d 848, ref nre.—App & E 927(7), 934(1), 1068(2); Carr 247, 303(6), 305(4), 316(1), 317(1), 318(8), 344; Damag 221(2.1), 221(5.1), 221(6); Neglig 1741.

Houston Transp. Co. v. Grimm, TexCivApp–Galveston, 168 SW2d 892, writ refused wom.—App & E 1064.1(8); Damag 38, 132(14); Evid 7; Explos 7; Trial 119, 140(1), 199, 251(9).

Houston Trial Reports, Inc. v. LRP Publications, Inc., SDTex, 85 FSupp2d 663.—Fed Cts 101, 103, 104, 105, 113, 143, 144.

Houston, Tx., City of; Kossman Contracting Co., Inc. v., CA5 (Tex), 128 FedAppx 376.—Fed Cts 656.

Houston Typographical Union No. 87 v. Houston Chronicle Pub. Co., CA5 (Tex), 384 F2d 881.—Labor & Emp 1549(18).

Houston Typographical Union No. 87; Houston Chronicle Pub. Co. v., SDTex, 272 FSupp 974, aff 384 F2d 881.—Labor & Emp 1549(18).

Houston Typographical Union No. 87 v. Houston Chronicle Pub. Co., TexCivApp–Eastland, 397 SW2d 948, ref nre.—App & E 302(1); Labor & Emp 1595(2).

Houston United Cas. Ins. Co.; Betco Scaffolds Co., Inc. v., TexApp–Houston (14 Dist), 29 SW3d 341.—Contracts 176(2); Insurance 1808, 1835(2), 1863, 2152, 3336, 3337, 3353, 3359, 3361, 3417.

Houston Village Builders, Inc. v. Falbaum, TexApp–Houston (14 Dist), 105 SW3d 28, reh overr, and review den, and mandamus den.—Alt Disp Res 222, 335.

Houston Welfare Rights Organization; Chapman v., USTex, 99 SCt 1905, 441 US 600, 60 LEd2d 508, on remand Houston Welfare Rights Org'n v. Chapman, 599 F2d 111.—Civil R 1305; Fed Cts 220, 226, 228, 243; Social S 2; Statut 184.

Houston Welfare Rights Organization, Inc. v. Vowell, CA5 (Tex), 555 F2d 1219, cert gr Chapman v. Houston Welfare Rights Organization, 98 SCt 1232, 434 US 1061, 55 LEd2d 761, rev 99 SCt 1905, 441 US 600, 60 LEd2d 508, on remand Houston Welfare Rights Org'n v Chapman, 599 F2d 111.—Fed Cts 228, 268.1; Social S 194.1, 194.12(2), 194.12(3).

Houston Welfare Rights Organization, Inc. v. Vowell, SDTex, 391 FSupp 223, rev 555 F2d 1219, cert gr Chapman v. Houston Welfare Rights Organization, 98 SCt 1232, 434 US 1061, 55 LEd2d 761, rev 99 SCt 1905, 441 US 600, 60 LEd2d 508, on remand Houston Welfare Rights Org'n v Chapman, 599 F2d 111.—Civil R 1395(1); Fed Civ Proc 189; Fed Cts 197, 228, 244; Social S 194.1, 194.7(2), 194.7(3), 194.12(1), 194.12(2), 194.12(3), 194.18.

Houston West Corp.; CoTemp, Inc. v., TexApp–Houston (14 Dist), 222 SW3d 487, reh overr.—App & E 209.1, 1079; Labor & Emp 3027, 3040, 3042, 3043; Neglig 220, 371, 379, 380, 383, 387, 1019; Parent & C 13.5(4).

Houston Yacht Club; Harold v., TexCivApp–Houston, 380 SW2d 184.—Plead 210, 228.14, 228.23, 354, 360; Pretrial Proc 250, 692, 695.

Houston Zoning Bd. of Adjustment, City of; Hagood v., TexApp–Houston (1 Dist), 982 SW2d 17.—App & E 66; Zoning 565, 569, 741.

Houtchens v. Kyle's Grocery Corp., TexCivApp–Eastland, 390 SW2d 325, ref nre.—Neglig 1104(6), 1595, 1670.

Houtchens; Matthews v., TexCivApp–Fort Worth, 576 SW2d 880.—App & E 223; Divorce 252.2, 322; Evid 80(1); Judgm 181(20), 185(2), 736.

Houtchens v. Matthews, TexCivApp–Fort Worth, 557 SW2d 581, dism.—App & E 846(5); Child S 5, 6, 177, 242, 364, 452, 496; Equity 84; Estop 52(1), 52.15; Judgm 866.1.

Hou-Tex Const. Co. v. Williams, TexCivApp–Waco, 417 SW2d 597, ref nre.—App & E 171(1); Bills & N 529, 530, 534; Mtg 335, 338.

Hou-Tex, Inc. v. Landmark Graphics, TexApp–Houston (14 Dist), 38 SW3d 103.—Afft 3, 9; Antitrust 161, 291, 292; App & E 223, 232(2), 863, 934(1); Judgm 185(2), 185(6), 185.1(4), 189; Neglig 1692; Prod Liab 17.1; Sales 255, 260, 267, 284(1); Torts 118.

Houtex Managing General Agency, Inc. v. Hardcastle, TexApp–Houston (1 Dist), 735 SW2d 520, ref nre.—App & E 5, 937(1), 1096(1); Judgm 17(9); Proc 73, 149.

Hou-Tex Printers, Inc. v. Marbach, TexApp–Houston (14 Dist), 862 SW2d 188.—Acct Action on 9.1, 10, 11, 13; Judgm 185(1), 185(3), 185.3(16).

Hou-Tex Products, Inc.; Baxter Const. Co., Inc. v., TexApp–Houston (1 Dist), 718 SW2d 355, ref nre.— Mech Liens 132(1).

Houtex Ready Mix Concrete & Materials v. Eagle Const. & Environmental Services, L.P., TexApp– Houston (1 Dist), 226 SW3d 514.—App & E 840(1), 907(1), 946, 984(1), 989, 1024.1, 1030; Costs 2; Judgm 185(2), 540, 544, 584, 585(2), 591.1, 619, 639, 665, 713(1), 713(2), 725(1), 744; Plead 236(2), 245(7), 258(5).

Hou-Tex Sheet Metal; Baxter Const. Co., Inc. v., Tex-App–Houston (1 Dist), 718 SW2d 355. See Baxter Const. Co., Inc. v. Hou-Tex Products, Inc.

Houth; State v., TexCrimApp, 845 SW2d 853.—Double J 1, 131, 142.

Houth; State v., TexApp–Houston (1 Dist), 810 SW2d 852, petition for discretionary review gr, aff 845 SW2d 853. —Double J 142.

Houts v. Barton, TexApp–Houston (1 Dist), 657 SW2d 924.—App & E 524; Interest 39(2.30); Judgm 199(3.7).

Hovar; State v., TexApp–Houston (14 Dist, 761 SW2d 66. See State v. Goebel.

Hovas v. O'Brien, TexApp–Houston (14 Dist), 654 SW2d 801, ref nre.—Contracts 50, 51, 53, 74, 237(2); Evid 177, 351.

Hovenden v. Tenbush, TexCivApp–San Antonio, 529 SW2d 302.—App & E 837(1); Judgm 181(33), 185(2); Prod Liab 25, 42, 87.1; Sales 260, 262.5.

Hovenkamp; May v., TexCivApp–Fort Worth, 293 SW2d 496.—New Tr 56.

Hovermale, Ex parte, TexApp–San Antonio, 636 SW2d 828.—Courts 100(1); Judgm 470; States 18.3.

Hoverson; DirecTV, Inc. v., NDTex, 319 FSupp2d 735.— Const Law 4412; Copyr 109; States 18.81, 18.87; Tel 1251, 1298.

Hovey; Vega Petroleum Corp. v., TexCivApp–Eastland, 604 SW2d 388.—App & E 1002; Evid 571(7); Mines 78.7(4); New Tr 65.

Hovey Petroleum Co.; Thompson v., Tex, 236 SW2d 491, 149 Tex 554.—Admin Law 485; Autos 83.

Hovey Petroleum Co.; Thompson v., TexCivApp–Austin, 232 SW2d 146, rev 236 SW2d 491, 149 Tex 554.—Admin Law 449, 486, 746, 764.1; Autos 82, 83, 84.

Hovila v. State, TexCrimApp, 562 SW2d 243, cert den 99 SCt 1058, 439 US 1135, 59 LEd2d 97.—Crim Law 656(9), 1035(5), 1035(9), 1115(2); Jury 108; Sent & Pun 1720, 1789(9).

Hovila v. State, TexCrimApp, 532 SW2d 293, appeal after remand 562 SW2d 243, cert den 99 SCt 1058, 439 US 1135, 59 LEd2d 97.—Jury 108, 131(18).

Ho Wah Genting Kintron Sdn Bhd v. Leviton Mfg. Co., Inc., TexApp–San Antonio, 163 SW3d 120, reh overr.— App & E 185(1); Const Law 3964, 3965(3), 3965(4); Corp 47, 665(1), 672(1), 673; Courts 12(2.1), 12(2.10); Evid 267, 314(1), 318(2).

Howard, Ex parte, TexCrimApp, 685 SW2d 672.—Crim Law 90(1), 1026.10(4).

Howard, Ex parte, TexCrimApp, 591 SW2d 906.—Hab Corp 483.

Howard, Ex parte, TexCrimApp, 447 SW2d 160.—Jury 29(6); Sent & Pun 558.

Howard, Ex parte, TexCrimApp, 347 SW2d 721, 171 TexCrim 278.—Crim Law 90(3).

Howard, Ex parte, TexCrimApp, 289 SW2d 277.—Extrad 36.

Howard, Ex parte, TexApp–San Antonio, 191 SW3d 201, reh overr.—Hab Corp 201, 223, 251, 287.1, 289, 291, 861.

Howard, In re, BkrtcyWDTex, 65 BR 498.—Banks 505; Const Law 2500; Home 90, 105, 196.

Howard; American Paper Stock Co. v., Tex, 528 SW2d 576.—Interest 39(3).

Howard v. American Paper Stock Co., TexCivApp–Fort Worth, 523 SW2d 744, aff as reformed 528 SW2d 576.— Autos 193(8.1), 242(6), 244(36.1); Damag 185(1); Interest 39(1); Labor & Emp 3046(2).

Howard; Associated Emp. Lloyds v., Tex, 294 SW2d 706, 156 Tex 277.—Work Comp 1116.

Howard; Associated Emp. Lloyds v., TexCivApp–Waco, 288 SW2d 861, rev 294 SW2d 706, 156 Tex 277.—Work Comp 1142, 1152, 1159.

Howard v. Bachman, TexCivApp–Eastland, 524 SW2d 414.—Autos 247; Neglig 452, 549(6).

Howard; Baker v., TexApp–Waco, 799 SW2d 450.—Contracts 29, 32; Usury 42, 138.

Howard; Baldridge v., TexApp–Dallas, 708 SW2d 62, ref nre.—Const Law 2315; Health 811; Judgm 181(7); Lim of Act 4(2), 6(1), 195(1).

Howard; Barnes v., TexCivApp–Waco, 317 SW2d 117.— Brok 8(3), 43(2).

Howard; Bennett v., Tex, 170 SW2d 709, 141 Tex 101.— Damag 87(1), 89(1), 91(1), 91(3); Death 103(4); Work Comp 2149.

Howard v. Bennett, TexCivApp–Fort Worth, 165 SW2d 919, rev 170 SW2d 709, 141 Tex 101.—Labor & Emp 2975, 3009; Neglig 273; Work Comp 2157.

Howard v. Beto, CA5 (Tex), 466 F2d 1356, cert den 93 SCt 1428, 410 US 956, 35 LEd2d 689.—Crim Law 641.13(1), 641.13(2.1), 641.13(5).

Howard v. Beto, CA5 (Tex), 446 F2d 1370, appeal after remand 466 F2d 1356, cert den 93 SCt 1428, 410 US 956, 35 LEd2d 689.—Hab Corp 747, 827.

Howard v. Beto, CA5 (Tex), 375 F2d 441.—Hab Corp 486(1).

Howard; Billingsley v., CA5 (Tex), 196 FedAppx 258.— Fed Civ Proc 1837.1; Prisons 17(2); Sent & Pun 1546.

Howard; Birch v., TexCivApp–Tyler, 435 SW2d 945, ref nre.—App & E 1069.1; Evid 222(2); New Tr 140(3); Witn 379(3).

Howard; Blakeley v., TexCivApp–Dallas, 387 SW2d 96, ref nre.—App & E 302(1), 989; Costs 194.32; Judgm 199(3.14); Pretrial Proc 375; Trial 350.2, 350.3(1), 350.4(1), 352.5(4).

Howard v. Bolin Warehouses, Inc., TexCivApp–Texarkana, 422 SW2d 489.—App & E 302(4), 499(4), 501(4), 994(3); Fraud Conv 296, 298(1); Judgm 199(3.14); New Tr 106, 153, 156; Sales 360(2); Trial 344.

Howard v. Brizendine, TexCivApp–Beaumont, 546 SW2d 136.—Child S 506(5).

Howard; Brown v., TexCivApp–San Antonio, 285 SW2d 752, ref nre.—Neglig 301, 401; Prod Liab 43; Sales 255, 274.

Howard v. Burkholder, TexCivApp–Amarillo, 281 SW2d 764, writ dism.—Can of Inst 1, 24(1), 37(4); Plead 36(2); Sales 124, 130(3).

Howard; Burnett v., TexCivApp–Hous (1 Dist), 466 SW2d 16.—App & E 931(4); Autos 172(5.1), 172(6), 227.5, 244(44), 244(58).

Howard v. Chris-Craft Corp., EDTex, 562 FSupp 932.— Compromise 8(1), 8(3), 20(2), 21, 23(3); Damag 32, 117; Fed Civ Proc 2737.5; Interest 39(1).

Howard; City of Austin v., TexCivApp–Austin, 158 SW2d 556, writ refused wom.—App & E 997(3), 1177(1), 1178(6); Courts 107; Damag 110, 112; Em Dom 92, 112, 298, 300, 303, 307(3), 307(4); Evid 219(2), 470, 471(24), 472(11), 474(11); Mun Corp 733(2); Plead 427; Torts 135; Trial 121(4), 133.6(5), 351.5(1), 352.5(1), 352.12.

Howard v. City of Garland, CA5 (Tex), 917 F2d 898.— Const Law 3512; Zoning 86.

Howard; City of Houston v., TexApp–Houston (14 Dist), 786 SW2d 391, writ den.—App & E 846(5); Damag 187; Labor & Emp 2858; Mun Corp 848, 857; Neglig 1011, 1683; Plead 16, 34(4).

Howard v. City of Kerrville, TexApp–San Antonio, 75 SW3d 112, review den.—App & E 1175(1); Costs 194.14, 194.22, 194.32; Em Dom 2(1), 2(10), 277, 316; Judgm 185(2).

HOWARD;

Howard; City of Terrell v., TexComApp, 111 SW2d 692, 130 Tex 459.—Const Law 2314; Mun Corp 741.10, 741.20, 812(2).

Howard; City of Terrell v., TexCivApp–Dallas, 85 SW2d 283, rev 111 SW2d 692, 130 Tex 459.—Mun Corp 111(2), 759(1), 763(1), 806(2), 821(12.1), 821(14), 821(19), 821(22); Trial 219, 296(12).

Howard; City of Texarkana v., TexApp–Texarkana, 633 SW2d 596, ref nre.—Zoning 1, 35, 151, 162, 654, 675, 707.

Howard v. Clack, TexCivApp–Dallas, 589 SW2d 748.— Mand 66, 76; Mun Corp 159(1).

Howard; Collin County Motor Co. v., TexCivApp–Dallas, 121 SW2d 460, dism.—Autos 193(10); Trial 133.6(8).

Howard; Combs v., TexCivApp–Fort Worth, 131 SW2d 206.—Wills 96, 215, 220, 284, 290, 296, 297(1), 306, 309, 384; Witn 80, 126, 138.

Howard v. Combs, TexCivApp–Fort Worth, 113 SW2d 221.—App & E 927(7); Evid 314(1); Wills 58(1), 58(2), 64, 96, 290, 296, 306, 324(4), 386.

Howard v. Commonwealth Bldg. & Loan Ass'n, Tex-ComApp, 94 SW2d 144, 127 Tex 365.—App & E 878(6), 1175(5).

Howard; Covington v., TexCivApp–Waco, 347 SW2d 802, ref nre.—App & E 1062.1; Trial 352.21.

Howard; Davis v., TexCivApp–Austin, 436 SW2d 225.— App & E 688(1), 931(1), 1073(1); Execution 192, 194(3); Fraud Conv 206(1); Judgm 143(11), 145(2).

Howard; Denton County v., TexApp–Fort Worth, 22 SW3d 113.—App & E 863, 893(1); Costs 260(5); Counties 63, 208, 227; Courts 35; Labor & Emp 29; Mun Corp 723, 742(4); Plead 104(1); Pretrial Proc 554; States 191.1, 191.4(1), 191.6(1), 191.9(1).

Howard v. Dretke, CA5 (Tex), 157 FedAppx 667.—Hab Corp 483, 679; Sent & Pun 1789(2), 1798.

Howard v. Dretke, CA5 (Tex), 125 FedAppx 560.—Hab Corp 486(2).

Howard v. East Texas Baptist University, TexApp–Texarkana, 122 SW3d 407.—App & E 966(1); Colleges 5; Judgm 185.3(21), 186; Neglig 1194; Statut 176, 181(1), 205.

Howard; Employers Mut. Liability Ins. Co. of Wis. v., TexCivApp–Waco, 286 SW2d 302, writ refused.—Work Comp 1069, 1074.

Howard; Everest Reinsurance Co. v., TexApp–Austin, 950 SW2d 800, review den.—Inj 223; Insurance 1384; Rem of C 3, 11, 109, 111.

Howard v. Faberge, Inc., TexApp–Houston (1 Dist), 679 SW2d 644, 46 ALR4th 1185, ref nre.—App & E 207, 1050.1(1), 1050.2, 1056.1(1), 1056.1(10), 1060.1(1), 1060.2, 1064.1(1), 1067, 1070(2); Evid 219.35, 219.65; Prod Liab 75.1, 81.1; Trial 110.

Howard v. Fiesta Texas Show Park, Inc., TexApp–San Antonio, 980 SW2d 716, reh overr, and review den, and reh of petition for review overr.—Antitrust 353; Hus & W 209(3), 209(4), 220; Judgm 185(2); Lim of Act 31, 43, 55(4), 84(2), 87(3), 95(1), 95(1.5), 95(4.1), 199(1); Neglig 1507.1; Parent & C 7(0.5), 7.5.

Howard; First Nat. Bank of Beaumont v., Tex, 229 SW2d 781, 149 Tex 130.—Wills 684.10(4), 684.10(5).

Howard; First Nat. Bank of Beaumont v., TexCivApp–Beaumont, 223 SW2d 694, aff in part, rev in part 229 SW2d 781, 149 Tex 130.—Atty & C 140; Evid 314(1); Wills 684.2(5), 684.10(3.1), 684.10(4), 684.10(5).

Howard; Fisher v., TexCivApp–Dallas, 389 SW2d 482.— Action 60; Attach 248, 322; Bills & N 103(1), 129(3), 395, 489(6), 534; Evid 413, 416, 423(6), 441(11), 444(6); Fraud 49; Judgm 185.2(4), 185.3(16).

Howard v. Fred Jones of Texas, Inc., TexCivApp–Amarillo, 295 SW2d 545, writ dism.—Damag 117; Evid 441(9); Sales 114, 422, 481.

Howard v. French-Brown Floors Co., TexCivApp–Dallas, 542 SW2d 709.—App & E 934(2), 1010.1(1); Contracts 28(3), 175(3); Costs 194.32, 194.36, 207; Trial 382.

Howard; Fuentes v., TexCivApp–El Paso, 423 SW2d 420, writ dism.—App & E 846(5), 931(1), 989; Elections 10, 216.1, 227(8), 291, 295(1), 305(6); Statut 176.

Howard; General Acc. Ins. Co. of America v., TexApp–Houston (14 Dist, 813 SW2d 557. See Potomac Ins. Co. v. Howard.

Howard v. General Cable Corp., CA5 (Tex), 674 F2d 351. —Damag 63, 163(4); Fed Civ Proc 1975, 2182.1, 2183, 2610; Prod Liab 77.5, 83.5, 88.5.

Howard; General Motors Acceptance Corp. v., Tex, 487 SW2d 708.—Action 61; Libel 73, 75; Plead 111.24, 111.42(4).

Howard; General Motors Acceptance Corp. v., TexCivApp–Beaumont, 474 SW2d 929, writ gr, aff 487 SW2d 708.—Libel 6(3), 100(7); Plead 111.24.

Howard v. Gonzales, CA5 (Tex), 658 F2d 352.—Civil R 1412, 1420, 1423, 1437; Courts 90(2); Fed Cts 637, 756.1, 761, 892, 893, 903, 908.1; Witn 337(28), 379(9).

Howard; Graham v., TexCivApp–Galveston, 249 SW2d 639.—App & E 999(1); Hus & W 21, 24; Princ & A 14(2).

Howard; Gregg v., TexCivApp–Houston, 365 SW2d 686, writ dism.—App & E 1050.1(10); Evid 317(2); Relig Soc 31(1), 31(5).

Howard; Haby v., TexApp–San Antonio, 757 SW2d 34, writ den.—Adv Poss 43(2), 85(1), 104, 112; App & E 934(1); Bound 3(3), 40(1); Deeds 117, 118; Frds St of 63(1); Judgm 181(2), 181(15.1), 185(2), 185(6), 186.

Howard; Harris County v., TexCivApp–Hous (1 Dist), 494 SW2d 250, ref nre.—App & E 1079; Contracts 147(2), 176(2); Counties 126; Evid 448.

Howard; Hawkins v., TexApp–Dallas, 97 SW3d 676.— Compromise 5(1); Judgm 27, 72, 91; New Tr 140(1), 157.

Howard; Heard v., TexCivApp–Fort Worth, 215 SW2d 364.—Evid 318(1), 320; Mines 109.

Howard v. Henderson County, TexCivApp–Dallas, 116 SW2d 479, writ refused.—Counties 47, 69.2, 152, 204(1), 206(1).

Howard; Herring v., TexCivApp–Amarillo, 324 SW2d 266. —Autos 244(51), 244(58), 245(26.1); New Tr 10, 56.

Howard; Hillier v., TexCivApp–Eastland, 131 SW2d 1002, writ refused.—Evid 590; Home 57(3).

Howard v. Howard, TexApp–San Antonio, 670 SW2d 737. —App & E 66; Bankr 2395, 2401, 2443; Divorce 151, 177.

Howard; Howard v., TexApp–San Antonio, 670 SW2d 737.—App & E 66; Bankr 2395, 2401, 2443; Divorce 151, 177.

Howard v. Howard, TexCivApp–Hous (1 Dist), 459 SW2d 901.—Marriage 4.1, 13, 40(4), 50(1), 50(5).

Howard; Howard v., TexCivApp–Hous (1 Dist), 459 SW2d 901.—Marriage 4.1, 13, 40(4), 50(1), 50(5).

Howard v. Howard, TexCivApp–Austin, 102 SW2d 473, writ refused.—App & E 544(2); Assault 26, 44; Trial 352.5(5), 358, 365.1(6).

Howard; Howard v., TexCivApp–Austin, 102 SW2d 473, writ refused.—App & E 544(2); Assault 26, 44; Trial 352.5(5), 358, 365.1(6).

Howard v. Howard, TexCivApp–Texarkana, 158 SW2d 591, writ refused.—Insurance 3474, 3477.

Howard; Howard v., TexCivApp–Texarkana, 158 SW2d 591, writ refused.—Insurance 3474, 3477.

Howard v. INA County Mut. Ins. Co., TexApp–Dallas, 933 SW2d 212, writ den.—App & E 863, 893(1), 1175(1), 1178(1); Insurance 1823, 1851, 1883, 1887(1), 2774, 2775, 2778, 3336, 3337, 3349, 3360; Judgm 185(2), 185(6), 185.3(12); Ref of Inst 19(1).

Howard; International Sec. Life Ins. Co. v., TexCivApp–Waco, 456 SW2d 765, ref nre.—App & E 192.1, 193(1), 761; Insurance 2494(1), 2532, 3575; Plead 18.

Howard v. Jackson Elec. Co-op., Inc., TexCivApp–Waco, 430 SW2d 689, ref nre.—Electricity 15(2), 18(1); Land & Ten 164(7); Neglig 554(1), 1012, 1037(4).

Howard; John Hancock Mut. Life Ins. Co. v., TexCiv-App–Waco, 85 SW2d 986, writ refused.—Damag 95; Mtg 351, 353, 369(7), 369(8).

Howard; Kinman v., TexCivApp–Waco, 465 SW2d 400.—Assign 19; Contracts 177; Ven & Pur 214(2).

Howard; Koll Real Estate Group, Inc. v., TexApp–Houston (14 Dist), 130 SW3d 308.—Corp 665(1).

Howard; Ledbetter v., TexCivApp–Waco, 395 SW2d 951.—Covenants 108(1), 130(1), 130(4); Damag 62(4); Lim of Act 129; Ven & Pur 302.

Howard; Lee v., TexCivApp–Eastland, 483 SW2d 922, ref nre.—Neglig 530(1), 549(10); Trial 352.20, 366; Weap 23(2), 23(3).

Howard; Lehman v., TexCivApp–Waco, 133 SW2d 800.—App & E 882(12); Judgm 678(1), 699(1); Witn 138, 178(4).

Howard v. Lemmons, CA5 (Tex), 547 F2d 290.—Fed Civ Proc 1824; Fed Cts 244.

Howard v. Leonard, TexCivApp–San Antonio, 185 SW2d 490, writ refused wom.—Execution 272(2); Judgm 788(2).

Howard; Lutz v., TexCivApp–Eastland, 181 SW2d 869.—Cert 70(8); Wills 259, 384, 824.

Howard v. McCulley, TexApp–Dallas, 686 SW2d 650, ref nre.—Wills 448, 547, 657.

Howard; McDuff v., TexCivApp–Amarillo, 430 SW2d 953, ref nre.—App & E 248, 931(1); Damag 39, 139; Fences 17; Neglig 421, 1656, 1676.

Howard; Memorial Medical Center of East Texas v., TexApp–Austin, 975 SW2d 691, reh overr, and review den, and reh of petition for review overr.—Insurance 2933; Work Comp 1072.

Howard; Mills v., TexCivApp–Amarillo, 228 SW2d 906.—Abate & R 13; Action 69(2); Child C 401, 404, 725, 730, 733; Domicile 5.

Howard; Modica v., TexCivApp–Beaumont, 161 SW2d 1093.—App & E 273(10); Trial 258(1), 350.7(4), 351.2(6), 352.15.

Howard; Montague County v., TexCivApp–Fort Worth, 590 SW2d 833.—App & E 172(1); High 159(2); Plead 36(3).

Howard; Morrison v., TexCivApp–Austin, 261 SW2d 910, ref nre.—Covenants 102(1), 102(2); Lim of Act 47(2); Mines 49.

Howard; National County Mut. Fire Ins. Co. v., Tex-App–Fort Worth, 749 SW2d 618, writ den.—App & E 1050.1(11); Damag 51, 130.3, 135, 168(1), 178; Decl Judgm 362; Hus & W 209(4); Jury 131(8); Trial 18.

Howard v. Neary, TexCivApp–Waco, 485 SW2d 591.—Wills 616(7).

Howard v. Nolan County, TexCivApp–Eastland, 319 SW2d 947.—Counties 103; Em Dom 4, 280; Fraud 16; States 85.

Howard v. Northwest Airlines, Inc., SDTex, 793 FSupp 129.—Action 3; Carr 311; Rem of C 19(5), 107(1); States 18.21.

Howard v. O'Neal, TexCivApp–Eastland, 246 SW2d 907, ref nre.—Contracts 10(1); Evid 213(1); Frds St of 56(6); Trusts 17(3), 92.5.

Howard; Panhandle & S. F. Ry. Co. v., TexCivApp–Amarillo, 397 SW2d 300.—Labor & Emp 2854, 2859, 2860, 2881, 2976, 3006; Neglig 554(1); Trial 194(7), 252(9).

Howard; Patrick v., TexApp–Austin, 904 SW2d 941.—App & E 854(1); Judgm 185(2); Lim of Act 55(1), 95(1), 95(4.1), 95(7), 104(1), 104(2), 199(2); Pretrial Proc 714.

Howard v. Phillips, TexApp–Fort Worth, 728 SW2d 448.—App & E 232(1), 236(2), 497(1), 544(1), 635(4), 679(2), 905, 977(1), 1041(1); New Tr 140(1).

Howard; Pierce Estates v., TexCivApp–Beaumont, 100 SW2d 749, writ dism.—Deeds 38(1), 93, 111.

Howard; Potomac Ins. Co. v., TexApp–Houston (14 Dist), 813 SW2d 557.—Interest 39(2.35).

Howard v. Preston State Bank, TexCivApp–Fort Worth, 402 SW2d 250, ref nre.—Chat Mtg 225(1); Judgm 181(25), 186, 189.

Howard v. Pullicino, TexCivApp–Austin, 519 SW2d 254.—App & E 768; Child C 577, 914, 923(4).

Howard v. Riley, TexApp–Fort Worth, 749 SW2d 618. See National County Mut. Fire Ins. Co. v. Howard.

Howard v. Rodgers, TexCivApp–Waco, 475 SW2d 298.—App & E 302(6), 930(3), 989; Electricity 19(5).

Howard v. Salmon, Tex, 359 SW2d 882.—App & E 1060.1(1); Wills 323, 400.

Howard v. Salmon, TexCivApp–Fort Worth, 359 SW2d 120, writ gr, rev 359 SW2d 882.—App & E 1003(5); Evid 584(3); Trial 140(1); Wills 298, 300, 400; Witn 315.

Howard v. Sears, TexCivApp–Amarillo, 196 SW2d 105, ref nre.—Accord 26(3); App & E 151(5), 882(3), 930(1), 930(2), 989, 1002, 1046.5, 1052(8); Contracts 99(3), 317, 322(3); Evid 471(26); Partners 161; Trial 133.6(3.1).

Howard; Shore v., NDTex, 414 FSupp 379.—Civil R 1009, 1071, 1128, 1376(8), 1390, 1394, 1395(8); Consp 13, 18; Const Law 4172(6); Courts 55, 89; Judges 36, 38; Offic 114; Sent & Pun 1988; Statut 227.

Howard v. Simons, TexCivApp–Dallas, 285 SW2d 478, ref nre.—Brok 1, 3, 42; Mines 48; Statut 236, 241(1).

Howard; Stalnaker v., TexCivApp–Galveston, 230 SW2d 563, writ dism.—App & E 832(6); Contracts 175(3), 346(12); Damag 140; Plead 427; Set-Off 28(2).

Howard v. State, TexCrimApp, 153 SW3d 382, reh den, cert den 126 SCt 1429, 546 US 1214, 164 LEd2d 132.—Crim Law 641.13(1), 641.13(6), 721(3); Sent & Pun 1642, 1720, 1780(2), 1788(5), 1789(9).

Howard v. State, TexCrimApp, 941 SW2d 102, reh gr, and on reh, and reh den, cert den 122 SCt 1935, 535 US 1065, 152 LEd2d 840, for denial of stay of execution, see 2005 WL 2453274, stay den 157 FedAppx 667.—Crim Law 641.3(4), 865(1), 865(1.5), 865(2), 867, 1134(2), 1152(2), 1158(1), 1158(3), 1163(1), 1166.6, 1166.7; Jury 85, 105(4), 108, 131(1), 131(4), 131(8), 131(15.1), 131(17), 132, 142; Sent & Pun 1658, 1754, 1779(1), 1780(3), 1784(4), 1788(9).

Howard v. State, TexCrimApp, 690 SW2d 252.—Crim Law 273.1(2); J P 2, 20; Statut 188, 217.2.

Howard v. State, TexCrimApp, 667 SW2d 524.—Crim Law 1167(4); Ind & Inf 159(1).

Howard v. State, TexCrimApp, 617 SW2d 191.—Crim Law 394.4(9); Mun Corp 594(2).

Howard v. State, TexCrimApp, 599 SW2d 597.—Arrest 63.5(6); Crim Law 899, 1169.2(1); Searches 47.1.

Howard v. State, TexCrimApp, 505 SW2d 306.—Crim Law 627.6(2), 627.6(4), 627.7(1), 627.7(3), 726, 857(2), 1036.2, 1166(10.10), 1174(2); Witn 287(1).

Howard v. State, TexCrimApp, 495 SW2d 252.—Sent & Pun 2010.

Howard v. State, TexCrimApp, 484 SW2d 927.—Crim Law 1037.1(3); Homic 909, 1205.

Howard v. State, TexCrimApp, 484 SW2d 903.—Crim Law 862, 956(11), 1174(2).

Howard v. State, TexCrimApp, 480 SW2d 191.—Crim Law 1043(2), 1130(2), 1166(1); Ind & Inf 137(6); Witn 337(27).

Howard v. State, TexCrimApp, 453 SW2d 155.—Rob 24.15(1).

Howard v. State, TexCrimApp, 453 SW2d 154.—Crim Law 404.65.

Howard v. State, TexCrimApp, 453 SW2d 153.—Crim Law 730(15).

Howard v. State, TexCrimApp, 453 SW2d 150.—Arrest 68(5), 70(1); Crim Law 394.4(2), 1203.27; Sent & Pun 1379(2).

Howard v. State, TexCrimApp, 430 SW2d 214.—Crim Law 1099.10.

Howard v. State, TexCrimApp, 429 SW2d 155.—Crim Law 1181.5(9); Sent & Pun 1057, 1426.

HOWARD

Howard v. State, TexCrimApp, 420 SW2d 706.—Crim Law 570(1), 625.15, 656(8), 741(1), 742(1), 1035(8.1), 1166.22(2); False Pret 38, 49(1).

Howard v. State, TexCrimApp, 389 SW2d 669.—Crim Law 1097(4), 1099.6(3), 1099.7(1), 1099.10.

Howard v. State, TexCrimApp, 387 SW2d 387, cert den 87 SCt 847, 386 US 928, 17 LEd2d 787.—Crim Law 867, 1038.1(1), 1056.1(1); Sent & Pun 1371; Weap 17(4).

Howard v. State, TexCrimApp, 383 SW2d 597.—Crim Law 1065, 1090.12.

Howard v. State, TexCrimApp, 357 SW2d 403, 172 TexCrim 352.—Homic 1479.

Howard v. State, TexCrimApp, 340 SW2d 293, 170 TexCrim 348.—Crim Law 572.

Howard v. State, TexCrimApp, 308 SW2d 45, 165 TexCrim 466.—Crim Law 590(2), 916, 1064.5; Rob 24.10.

Howard v. State, TexCrimApp, 282 SW2d 874, 162 TexCrim 130.—Jury 31.3(1); Rob 24.10.

Howard v. State, TexCrimApp, 276 SW2d 815.—Crim Law 1090.1(1).

Howard v. State, TexCrimApp, 273 SW2d 416, 160 TexCrim 576.—Crim Law 1167(1); Ind & Inf 41(3).

Howard v. State, TexCrimApp, 257 SW2d 713.—Crim Law 1094(3).

Howard v. State, TexCrimApp, 254 SW2d 396.—Crim Law 1090.1(1).

Howard v. State, TexCrimApp, 252 SW2d 173, 157 TexCrim 602.—Crim Law 464, 1175.

Howard v. State, TexCrimApp, 247 SW2d 112, 157 TexCrim 114.—Autos 355(14); Crim Law 1086.14.

Howard v. State, TexCrimApp, 233 SW2d 849.—Crim Law 1090.1(1).

Howard v. State, TexCrimApp, 230 SW2d 213, 155 TexCrim 36.—Autos 354; Crim Law 384.

Howard v. State, TexCrimApp, 186 SW2d 817, 148 TexCrim 291.—Crim Law 882, 1169.2(6).

Howard v. State, TexCrimApp, 178 SW2d 691, 147 TexCrim 88.—Crim Law 726, 1171.7.

Howard v. State, TexCrimApp, 94 SW2d 176, 130 TexCrim 312.—Crim Law 1098.

Howard v. State, TexApp–Houston (1 Dist), 962 SW2d 119, petition for discretionary review refused.—Courts 97(1); Crim Law 422(1), 423(3), 427(4), 427(5), 1036.2, 1165(1), 1169.11; Homic 1181; Sent & Pun 313.

Howard v. State, TexApp–Fort Worth, 145 SW3d 327.—Child S 663; Crim Law 569, 1134(2), 1134(3), 1144.13(6), 1159.2(2), 1191.

Howard v. State, TexApp–Fort Worth, 137 SW3d 282, petition for discretionary review refused.—Autos 355(6), 359; Crim Law 1134(2), 1144.13(2.1), 1158(1), 1159.2(1), 1159.2(2).

Howard v. State, TexApp–Fort Worth, 766 SW2d 907.—Crim Law 633(1), 655(1), 890; Judges 49(1).

Howard v. State, TexApp–Fort Worth, 713 SW2d 414, petition for discretionary review gr, petition for discretionary review refused 789 SW2d 280, reh den.—Controlled Subs 27; Crim Law 369.2(1), 370, 371(1), 419(2.40), 1044.2(1).

Howard v. State, TexApp–Fort Worth, 706 SW2d 168, petition for discretionary review refused.—Ind & Inf 121.1(2); Sent & Pun 2003, 2006.

Howard v. State, TexApp–Austin, 972 SW2d 121.—Controlled Subs 73, 81; Crim Law 507(1), 510, 511.2, 641.13(1), 641.13(2.1), 780(1), 1038.1(1), 1038.2, 1134(2), 1144.13(6), 1173.2(6).

Howard v. State, TexApp–Austin, 966 SW2d 821, petition for discretionary review refused.—Crim Law 641.5(2.1), 641.5(3), 641.5(4), 641.5(5), 641.13(2.1), 660, 749, 814(19), 1035(7), 1134(2), 1166.10(3); Homic 1207; Sent & Pun 373.

Howard; State v., TexApp–Austin, 838 SW2d 926.—Crim Law 721(1), 721(3), 721(6), 721.5(1), 919(4), 950, 954(1).

Howard v. State, TexApp–San Antonio, 982 SW2d 536, review dism as improvidently gr by 11 SW3d 241.—Crim Law 857(1), 1155, 1156(1), 1166.16; Jury 33(2.10), 149.

Howard v. State, TexApp–San Antonio, 830 SW2d 785, petition for discretionary review refused.—Const Law 4705, 4733(2); Sent & Pun 2032.

Howard v. State, TexApp–Dallas, 227 SW3d 794, petition for discretionary review refused.—Arrest 63.1; Autos 349(11); Crim Law 1139, 1144.12, 1153(1), 1158(1).

Howard; State v., TexApp–Dallas, 172 SW3d 190, reh overr.—Const Law 1512, 1514, 2201, 2202, 2218, 4034; Crim Law 20, 21; Pub Amuse 9(1).

Howard v. State, TexApp–Dallas, 667 SW2d 265, petition for discretionary review gr, aff 690 SW2d 252.—Crim Law 90(1), 641.13(1), 641.13(6).

Howard v. State, TexApp–Texarkana, 932 SW2d 216, reh overr, and petition for discretionary review refused.—Arrest 63.4(2), 63.4(4), 63.4(18), 63.5(2), 63.5(4), 63.5(5); Crim Law 394.6(4), 1134(6), 1144.12, 1153(1), 1158(4).

Howard v. State, TexApp–Texarkana, 633 SW2d 536.—Arrest 63.5(2), 63.5(3.1), 63.5(4), 63.5(5).

Howard v. State, TexApp–Amarillo, 945 SW2d 303.—Crim Law 417(15), 422(5), 1169.1(9).

Howard; State v., TexApp–Amarillo, 908 SW2d 602.—Crim Law 899, 1023(1), 1023(3), 1024(1); Statut 192.

Howard v. State, TexApp–Amarillo, 896 SW2d 401, petition for discretionary review refused.—Crim Law 713, 723(1), 726, 1171.1(4); Sent & Pun 313, 323.

Howard v. State, TexApp–Beaumont, 894 SW2d 104, petition for discretionary review refused.—Crim Law 641.13(1), 641.13(5), 641.13(6), 641.13(7), 920, 1088.17, 1144.10.

Howard v. State, TexApp–Beaumont, 890 SW2d 514.—Controlled Subs 40, 74, 87; Crim Law 564(1), 1159.2(7).

Howard v. State, TexApp–Beaumont, 704 SW2d 575.—Gr Jury 5, 39; Offic 43; Statut 223.2(0.5).

Howard v. State, TexApp–Waco, 888 SW2d 166, petition for discretionary review refused.—Autos 349(1), 349(5), 349(8), 349(17), 349.5(3), 349.5(9); Controlled Subs 80; Crim Law 394.6(5), 620(6), 724(1), 814(1), 814(3), 1148, 1159.2(10), 1166(6), 1171.1(6); Ind & Inf 125(4.1), 132(3); Searches 165.

Howard v. State, TexApp–Houston (14 Dist), 744 SW2d 640.—Autos 411, 422.1.

Howard v. State, TexApp–Houston (14 Dist), 650 SW2d 460, petition for discretionary review gr, aff 667 SW2d 524.—Crim Law 1032(1), 1167(4); Homic 607, 852; Ind & Inf 119, 120, 159(1).

Howard v. State, TexApp–Houston (14 Dist), 625 SW2d 440.—Assault 96(7); Crim Law 586, 603.3(7), 605, 829(1), 1038.1(2), 1063(1), 1064(1); Homic 1479.

Howard; Sudderth v., TexCivApp–Amarillo, 560 SW2d 511, ref nre.—App & E 499(1), 846(6), 1078(1); Can of Inst 24(1); Equity 66; Home 110, 122; Mtg 608.5; Trial 273.

Howard; Terry v., TexCivApp–Dallas, 546 SW2d 66.—App & E 241, 709; Costs 194.48, 197; Pretrial Proc 501; Quiet T 54.

Howard; Texas Dept. of Assistive and Rehabilitative Services v., TexApp–Austin, 182 SW3d 393, review den.—App & E 930(1), 994(2), 1002, 1003(3), 1003(7), 1003(9.1), 1012.1(7.1); Evid 597; Labor & Emp 863(2); Offic 61, 66; States 53.

Howard v. Texas Dept. of Human Resources, TexApp–Dallas, 677 SW2d 667.—Child S 440, 496, 498; Contempt 20.

Howard v. Texas Dept. of Human Services, TexApp–Corpus Christi, 791 SW2d 313.—Atty & C 21, 21.5(2), 21.20.

Howard; Texas Real Estate Commission v., TexCivApp–Hous (1 Dist), 538 SW2d 429, ref nre.—Admin Law 324, 744.1, 763, 790; App & E 854(1); Brok 3; Notice 10.

Howard v. Thompson-White Lumber Co., TexCivApp–Galveston, 266 SW2d 242, ref nre.—Autos 217(6), 247.

Howard; U.S. v., CA5 (Tex), 106 F3d 70.—Controlled Subs 130; Crim Law 1139, 1158(1), 1158(2), 1158(4); Searches 42.1, 71, 192.1, 201.

Howard v. U.S., CA5 (Tex), 711 F2d 729.—Fed Civ Proc 2547.1; Int Rev 4849, 5204, 5205, 5219.25, 5228.

Howard v. U.S., CA5 (Tex), 580 F2d 716.—Const Law 4611; Crim Law 641.13(1), 1451, 1481.

Howard; U.S. v., CA5 (Tex), 506 F2d 865.—Crim Law 868, 957(1), 1163(6).

Howard; U.S. v., CA5 (Tex), 483 F2d 229, cert den 94 SCt 850, 414 US 1116, 38 LEd2d 744.—Const Law 4637; Crim Law 393(1), 1170(1).

Howard v. U.S., CA5 (Tex), 441 F2d 271.—Courts 104; Fed Cts 71.

Howard v. U S, CA5 (Tex), 261 F2d 729.—Crim Law 573.

Howard v. U.S., CA5 (Tex), 232 F2d 274.—Courts 96(7); Crim Law 48, 570(1), 740, 773(2).

Howard v. U.S., CA5 (Tex), 229 F2d 602, vac on reh 232 F2d 274.—Crim Law 46, 570(1), 773(2), 822(1).

Howard; U.S. v., CA5 (Tex), 127 FedAppx 692, cert den 126 SCt 147, 546 US 863, 163 LEd2d 146.—Sent & Pun 1508; Weap 17(4).

Howard; U.S. v., CA5 (Tex), 81 FedAppx 511, cert den 124 SCt 2050, 541 US 1002, 158 LEd2d 517, post-conviction relief den Battles v. US, 2005 WL 1745473, post-conviction relief den 2005 WL 3312600.—Consp 47(12); Controlled Subs 81; Crim Law 772(6); Sent & Pun 726(3), 752.

Howard; U.S. v., SDTex, 471 FSupp2d 772.—Consp 41; Crim Law 881(3), 1181.5(1); Postal 35(9).

Howard v. U.S. Dept. of Defense, CAFed (Tex), 354 F3d 1358.—Armed S 5(6); Const Law 3057, 3163; Fed Cts 13.

Howard; USLIFE Title Ins. Co. of Dallas v., TexCiv-App–Amarillo, 603 SW2d 322.—Corp 503(2); Evid 43(3); Plead 111.16, 111.22, 111.39(2); Venue 7.5(3).

Howard v. Weisberg, TexCivApp–Dallas, 583 SW2d 920. —Acct Action on 11, 13; Contracts 335(2).

Howard v. Western Chevrolet Co., TexCivApp–Eastland, 372 SW2d 378, writ dism.—Insurance 1704; Pretrial Proc 480; Trial 350.4(3).

Howard v. Wilburn, TexCivApp–San Antonio, 351 SW2d 345, ref nre.—App & E 989, 1062.1, 1062.2, 1064.1(8), 1068(1); Autos 244(6), 244(50).

Howard; York v., TexCivApp–Waco, 521 SW2d 344.— Covenants 49, 51(2), 79(3), 84, 122.

Howard v. Young, TexCivApp–Amarillo, 210 SW2d 241, ref nre.—Ease 22; Equity 6; Lim of Act 60(10); Quiet T 34(5); Ref of Inst 19(1), 36(1).

Howard-Associated-Page Services, Inc.; London Prop-erties, Inc. v., TexCivApp–San Antonio, 474 SW2d 580. —Plead 110, 111.8, 111.42(6), 292.

Howard-Barrows v. City of Haltom City, CA5 (Tex), 106 FedAppx 912.—Civil R 1088(4), 1348, 1351(4); Const Law 4788; Costs 302; Crim Law 412.1(4), 641.3(3); Prisons 4(4).

Howard Broadcasting Corp.; Lee v., TexCivApp–Hous-ton, 305 SW2d 629, writ dism by agreement.—Atty & C 140; Bills & N 126, 534; Contracts 170(1); Inj 147, 151; Mtg 338.

Howard Bros. Discount Stores, Inc.; Scronce v., CA5 (Tex), 679 F2d 1204.—Prod Liab 60.5, 75.1, 86.5, 87.1.

Howard Corp.; Lone Star Gas Co. v., Tex, 568 SW2d 129. —Gas 14.6.

Howard Corp.; Lone Star Gas Co. v., TexCivApp–Texar-kana, 556 SW2d 372, writ gr, and writ withdrawn, ref nre 568 SW2d 129.—App & E 1008.1(2); Contracts 147(1); Costs 194.16, 194.22, 194.32, 194.36; Gas 14.1(3); Sales 77(1).

Howard County; Robinson v., TexCivApp–Eastland, 287 SW2d 234, ref nre.—App & E 1032(2), 1050.1(1), 1056.1(1); Em Dom 262(5).

Howard County Hospital Authority; Thomas v., Tex, 498 SW2d 146.—App & E 395; Health 105.

Howard County Hospital Authority; Thomas v., TexCiv-App–Eastland, 489 SW2d 403, ref nre 498 SW2d 146.— App & E 395; Health 105; Mun Corp 3; Tax 2290.

Howard County Refining Co.; Reeves v., NDTex, 33 FSupp 90.—Labor & Emp 33, 34(1), 40(1), 1236, 2298, 2387(4), 2390(3), 2393; Penalties 3.

Howard Elec. and Mechanical Inc.; Baker Industries, Inc. v., CA5 (Tex), 794 F2d 965, cert den 107 SCt 402, 479 US 931, 93 LEd2d 355.—Fed Cts 668.

Howard Gardiner, Inc.; Zoeller v., TexCivApp–Amarillo, 585 SW2d 920, ref nre.—Evid 434(9); Judgm 185(2), 185.3(13).

Howard Gault & Son, Inc. v. First Nat. Bank of Here-ford, TexCivApp–Amarillo, 541 SW2d 235.—Banks 140(1), 154(8); Partners 17, 32, 44.

Howard Gault & Son, Inc. v. First Nat. Bank of Here-ford, TexCivApp–Amarillo, 523 SW2d 496.—App & E 79(1), 792; Judgm 217.

Howard Gault & Son, Inc. v. Metcalf, TexCivApp–Amarillo, 529 SW2d 317.—Action 60; App & E 66, 977(1); Judgm 203; Mand 28, 50; New Tr 6, 8.

Howard Gault Co. v. Texas Rural Legal Aid, Inc., CA5 (Tex), 848 F2d 544.—Civil R 1326(4), 1326(5), 1326(9), 1326(11), 1373, 1374, 1376(2), 1464; Const Law 708, 1164, 1449, 1850, 1920; Fed Civ Proc 103.2; Fed Cts 5, 12.1; Labor & Emp 997, 1345(2), 2046, 2090, 2122.

Howard Gault Co. v. Texas Rural Legal Aid, Inc., NDTex, 615 FSupp 916, aff in part, rev in part 848 F2d 544.—Action 3; Civil R 1027, 1037, 1056, 1307, 1326(9), 1326(11), 1401, 1441, 1462, 1463, 1464, 1465(1); Consp 7.5(1); Const Law 90.1(7.1), 672, 699, 708, 808, 1140, 1141, 1520, 1557, 1562, 1801, 1807, 1850, 1917, 1921; Courts 489(2); Crim Law 641.3(3); Inj 150, 200, 257, 261; Labor & Emp 1345(1), 1345(2), 1345(3), 2084.

Howard-Glendale Funeral Home; Roy v., TexApp–Houston (1 Dist), 820 SW2d 844, writ den.—App & E 994(2), 999(1), 1001(1), 1003(5), 1003(7); Dead Bodies 9; Sales 441(2); Trial 252(2), 260(9).

Howard Hughes Medical Institute v. Lummis, TexCiv-App–Hous (14 Dist), 596 SW2d 171, ref nre.—Atty & C 21, 21.5(1); Const Law 2604.

Howard Hughes Medical Institute v. Neff, TexApp–Houston (14 Dist), 640 SW2d 942, ref nre.—Char 37(3), 50; Evid 264, 266, 317(4), 318(2), 372(1); Wills 219, 232, 289, 302(8), 303(6), 324(4), 344, 348.

Howard Johnson, Inc. of Tex.; Arlington Hotel and Motel Ass'n v., TexCivApp–Fort Worth, 397 SW2d 555, ref nre.—Admin Law 658; Inj 114(2); Turnpikes 4.

Howard Kenyon Dredging Co.; Fate-Root-Heath Co. v., TexCivApp–Galveston, 117 SW2d 547, writ dism by agreement.—App & E 927(3); Commerce 54.5.

Howard Love Machinery Supply, Inc.; Colonial Fast Freight Lines, Inc. v., EDTex, 838 FSupp 308.—Carr 4, 189, 192; Interest 39(2.20), 44.

Howard Love Pipeline Supply Co., In re, BkrtcyEDTex, 253 BR 781.—Bankr 3009, 3030, 3152, 3181, 3182, 3187(4), 3190, 3192, 3203(1), 3203(7), 3205.

Howard Motor Co.; Mabry Foundry & Mach. Co. v., TexCivApp–Beaumont, 422 SW2d 238.—Autos 173(8), 201(5); Judgm 181(33), 185(2), 185.1(1), 185.3(21).

Howard M. Smith Co. of Amarillo; Barfield v., Tex, 426 SW2d 834.—Equity 87(2); Estop 52(1), 54, 55, 95, 116; Land & Ten 39, 227; Lim of Act 102(1).

Howard M. Smith Co. of Amarillo; Barfield v., TexCiv-App–Amarillo, 415 SW2d 667, writ gr, rev 426 SW2d 834.—App & E 931(1), 1010.1(1), 1010.1(3), 1010.2, 1012.1(1); Estop 53, 54, 90(2), 95; Evid 595; Notice 3.

Howard P. Foley Co. v. Cox, TexApp–Houston (14 Dist), 679 SW2d 58.—App & E 497(1), 671(6), 1071.2; Contrib 5(6.1); Indem 33(1), 33(4), 33(5), 72; Judgm 256(2); Prod Liab 23.1; Trial 335, 388(4); Work Comp 2240.

Howard P. Foley Co.; Employers Cas. Co. v., CCA5 (Tex), 158 F2d 363.—Indem 31(5), 33(5).

Howard-Reed Oil Co.; La Rocca v., TexCivApp–Beaumont, 277 SW2d 769.—Contracts 117(2), 207, 256, 312(4); Inj 61(2).

Howard S. v. Friendswood Independent School Dist., SDTex, 454 FSupp 634.—Civil R 1330(2); Inj 147; Schools 115, 148(2.1); U S 82(2).

Howard Thornton Ford, Inc. v. Fitzpatrick, CA5 (Tex), 892 F2d 1230. See Hamilton, Matter of.

Howard Trucking Co., Inc.; Nichols v., TexApp–Beaumont, 839 SW2d 155.—App & E 1050.1(1), 1056.1(1); Evid 146.

Howarton; British American Ins. Co. v., TexCivApp–Houston (1 Dist), 877 SW2d 347, reh den, and writ dism by agreement.—App & E 930(3), 1001(3), 1003(7), 1058(1); Pretrial Proc 744, 746; Work Comp 1166, 1262, 1265, 1530, 1846, 1859.

Howarton v. Minnesota Mining and Mfg., Inc., TexApp–Eastland, 133 SW3d 820, reh overr.—App & E 223, 934(1); Electricity 17; Judgm 181(2), 183, 185(5), 185(6); Labor & Emp 3141, 3181(5); Neglig 202, 1000, 1011, 1018, 1037(7), 1086.

Howdeshell v. Stanbery, TexCivApp–Dallas, 122 SW2d 1118.—App & E 151(2).

Howe, Ex parte, TexCivApp–Hous (1 Dist), 457 SW2d 642.—Child S 458; Contempt 79; Hab Corp 528.1, 529.

Howe v. Barnhart, SDTex, 285 FSupp2d 837.—Social S 175.30.

Howe v. Citizens Memorial Hospital of Victoria County, TexCivApp–Corpus Christi, 426 SW2d 882, writ gr, rev Constant v. Howe, 436 SW2d 115.—App & E 927(7), 989; Counties 142; Evid 383(12); Health 256, 631, 818, 821(4), 826.

Howe; Constant v., Tex, 436 SW2d 115.—App & E 927(7); Health 699.

Howe v. Howe, TexCivApp–Eastland, 223 SW2d 944, writ refused.—App & E 387(2), 430(1); Motions 33.

Howe; Howe v., TexCivApp–Eastland, 223 SW2d 944, writ refused.—App & E 387(2), 430(1); Motions 33.

Howe; Kilgore v., TexCivApp–Amarillo, 204 SW2d 1005. —App & E 281(1), 293, 758.2; Autos 247; Trial 358.

Howe v. Kroger Co., TexCivApp–Dallas, 598 SW2d 929.— Evid 318(7); Judgm 185.1(4); Land & Ten 167(2); Neglig 1010, 1037(4).

Howe v. Laird, CA5 (Tex), 456 F2d 233.—Armed S 22; Fed Cts 743.

Howe; Polk County v., TexCivApp–Eastland, 248 SW2d 189, ref nre.—Bound 3(3), 3(4), 37(3), 37(4), 54(6); Courts 90(1); Tresp to T T 6.1; Trial 187(1), 194(10).

Howe; Red Arrow Freight Lines, Inc. v., TexCivApp–Corpus Christi, 480 SW2d 281, ref nre.—App & E 846(5), 1010.1(3); Carr 52(2), 60, 132, 134; Trial 382.

Howe; Roberts v., TexCivApp–Dallas, 125 SW2d 617.— Receivers 198(1), 198(2).

Howe; Silva v., TexCivApp–Corpus Christi, 608 SW2d 840, ref nre.—Health 686, 830; Lim of Act 55(4).

Howe; South Fort Worth State Bank v., TexCivApp–Fort Worth, 361 SW2d 447.—Garn 88.

Howe v. State, TexCrimApp, 380 SW2d 617.—Crim Law 1036.1(4); Rob 24.10.

Howe v. State, TexCrimApp, 380 SW2d 616.—Crim Law 1036.1(4); Rob 24.10.

Howe v. State, TexCrimApp, 380 SW2d 615.—Crim Law 1043(1); Rob 24.10.

Howe v. State, TexApp–Austin, 874 SW2d 895.—Arrest 63.5(4), 63.5(5), 68(4); Crim Law 394.6(4), 394.6(5), 519(8), 1134(3), 1153(1), 1158(4), 1224(1); Searches 171, 180, 182, 183, 184, 198.

Howe; State v., TexCivApp–Amarillo, 91 SW2d 487.—Em Dom 253(1); Judgm 18(2).

Howe; Varner v., TexApp–El Paso, 860 SW2d 458, reh overr, subsequent mandamus proceeding 888 SW2d 511. —App & E 499(4), 1026; Child S 212, 213, 539, 556(2), 558(1), 610; Divorce 85, 145, 184(12); Evid 536; Pretrial Proc 44.1, 254, 303, 312, 313, 434.

Howe & Wise; City of Houston v., TexCivApp–Houston, 373 SW2d 781, ref nre.—App & E 1212(1); Equity 54; Evid 211; Fraud 11(1), 22(1), 36, 58(1), 58(4); Lim of Act 100(11); Mun Corp 364, 374(1), 374(4); Witn 276.

Howe & Wise; City of Houston v., TexCivApp–Houston, 323 SW2d 134, ref nre.—App & E 882(8), 989, 1001(1), 1003(5), 1062.4, 1172(2); Contracts 176(1); Evid 450(5), 450(6); Mun Corp 249, 351, 374(1), 374(4), 1040; Trial 350.4(4).

Howe-Baker Engineers, Inc.; Penn v., CA5 (Tex), 898 F2d 1096, reh den.—Labor & Emp 539, 544, 686, 687, 696(1).

Howe Grain and Mercantile Co.; Hughes v., TexCivApp–Dallas, 162 SW 1187.—Trademarks 1800.

Howe Homes, Inc. v. Rogers, TexApp–Austin, 818 SW2d 901. See Jim Howe Homes, Inc. v. Rogers.

Howell, Ex parte, TexCrimApp, 488 SW2d 123, appeal dism Howell v. Jones, 94 SCt 114, 414 US 803, 38 LEd2d 38, reh den 94 SCt 558, 414 US 1052, 38 LEd2d 341, and 96 SCt 1151, 424 US 936, 47 LEd2d 343.— Const Law 3773, 4494; Contempt 31, 60(3), 71; Judges 39; Jury 24.5.

Howell, Ex parte, TexCrimApp, 120 SW2d 264, 135 TexCrim 305.—Bail 53.

Howell, Ex parte, TexApp–Houston (1 Dist), 843 SW2d 241.—Child S 444, 482, 487, 496; Contempt 66(7); Jury 24.5.

Howell, In re, BkrtcySDTex, 148 BR 269.—Bankr 3155, 3177.

Howell; Airline Motor Coaches v., TexCivApp–Beaumont, 195 SW2d 713, ref nre.—App & E 1051(1), 1060.1(7); Damag 221(5.1); New Tr 26, 40(1); Trial 120(2), 350.5(5), 352.4(7), 412; Witn 216(3).

Howell v. American Live Stock Ins. Co., CA5 (Tex), 483 F2d 1354.—Insurance 1091(2); Witn 369, 372(1), 372(2).

Howell v. American Pub. Co., TexApp–Eastland, 983 SW2d 79.—Judgm 185(5), 185.3(21).

Howell; Boman v., TexCivApp–Fort Worth, 618 SW2d 913.—Courts 1, 472.1, 472.4(6), 475(2).

Howell v. Bowden, TexCivApp–Dallas, 368 SW2d 842, ref nre.—App & E 233(2), 882(8), 1070(2), 1073(1); Damag 103, 127; Evid 213(2), 522; Frds St of 51, 52, 109; Good Will 1; Partners 120, 277, 280, 325(1), 338; Trial 79, 284, 351.2(4), 352.4(1).

Howell; Bradley v., TexCivApp–Fort Worth, 126 SW2d 547, writ dism, correct.—Contracts 143(3); Dep & Escr 13; Evid 75; Frds St of 56(6); Guard & W 44; Home 168; Mines 57; Spec Perf 39, 120, 121(4), 126(2), 126(3), 127(1); Ten in C 49; Trial 352.4(4), 352.5(4).

Howell; Bridges v., TexCivApp–El Paso, 122 SW2d 665. —Wills 1, 155.1, 159, 163(1), 341.

Howell v. Burch, TexCivApp–Texarkana, 616 SW2d 685, ref nre.—Evid 146, 591; Judgm 243, 743(2); New Tr 44(1); Plead 236(7); Trial 18.

Howell; Burnett v., TexCivApp–El Paso, 294 SW2d 410, ref nre.—App & E 854(5), 927(7); Autos 181(2).

Howell; Cameron County Water Improvement Dist. No. 1 v., TexCivApp–San Antonio, 112 SW2d 543, writ refused.—Bills & N 140, 453.

Howell; Chevron Oil Co. v., TexCivApp–Dallas, 407 SW2d 525, ref nre.—Equity 51(3); Mines 6, 52.

Howell; Christie, Mitchell & Mitchell Co. v., TexCivApp–Fort Worth, 359 SW2d 658, ref nre.—Damag 221(2.1); Mines 78.2, 78.7(4), 78.7(5).

Howell v. City of Dallas, TexCivApp–Waco, 549 SW2d 36, ref nre.—Judgm 181(3); Tax 2777, 2780.

Howell v. City Towing Associates, Inc., TexApp–San Antonio, 717 SW2d 729, ref nre.—Carr 235.1, 280(1.2), 281, 282; Judgm 181(33), 186.

Howell v. Coca-Cola Bottling Co. of Lubbock, Inc., Tex, 599 SW2d 801.—App & E 282.

Howell v. Coca-Cola Bottling Co. of Lubbock, Inc., TexCivApp–Amarillo, 595 SW2d 208, ref nre 599 SW2d

801.—App & E 285, 499(1), 500(1), 502(1); Lim of Act 121(2), 126, 165; Plead 228.23.

Howell v. Colorado Interstate Gas Co., CA5 (Tex), 312 F2d 198.—Mines 73.1(8).

Howell v. Colorado Interstate Gas Corp., NDTex, 202 FSupp 119, aff 312 F2d 198.—Fed Cts 32, 299; Licens 28, 32.1, 34; Mines 73.1(8), 87.

Howell v. Commissioner of Internal Revenue, CCA5 (Tex), 140 F2d 765, cert den 64 SCt 1048, 322 US 735, 88 LEd 1569.—Int Rev 3254, 3260; Mines 73.1(4).

Howell v. Continental Cas. Co., TexCivApp–Galveston, 110 SW2d 210, dism.—Evid 463; Work Comp 1418, 1927.

Howell v. Dallas County Child Welfare Unit, TexApp– Dallas, 710 SW2d 729, ref nre, cert den 107 SCt 1898, 481 US 1018, 95 LEd2d 505.—Const Law 3739, 4016; Infants 245, 246.

Howell v. Dixon, TexCivApp–Austin, 89 SW2d 243.—App & E 1177(2); Plead 111.5, 111.15.

Howell; Fant v., Tex, 547 SW2d 261.—App & E 1097(1); Ven & Pur 176.

Howell; Fant v., TexCivApp–Austin, 537 SW2d 350, writ gr, rev 547 SW2d 261.—Tresp to T T 10, 19; Ven & Pur 54, 218.

Howell; Fant v., TexCivApp–Austin, 410 SW2d 294, writ dism.—Covenants 101; Evid 208(2), 265(8); Judgm 183, 185.1(3); Spec Perf 126(1); Ven & Pur 54, 129(1), 191, 202.

Howell v. Ferguson Enterprises, Inc., CA5 (Tex), 93 FedAppx 12.—Fed Cts 625; Labor & Emp 2233.

Howell v. Fifth Court of Appeals, Tex, 689 SW2d 396.— Courts 209(2).

Howell v. Finley, TexCivApp–Texarkana, 489 SW2d 953, ref nre.—Evid 424, 441(8).

Howell; Finley v., TexCivApp–Texarkana, 320 SW2d 25. —App & E 758.1; Em Dom 9, 237(7), 242, 273; Judgm 16, 470.

Howell; First Bankers Ins. Co. v., TexCivApp–Amarillo, 446 SW2d 711.—App & E 1170.6; Insurance 2532, 3545, 3585, 3586; Judgm 28; Trial 9(1), 350.4(4).

Howell v. First Federal Sav. & Loan Ass'n of New Braunfels, TexCivApp–San Antonio, 383 SW2d 484, ref nre.—App & E 907(3), 1170.6; Evid 384; Jury 25(11); Plead 291(2).

Howell v. Fort Worth Stockyards Co., CCA5 (Tex), 108 F2d 593.—Neglig 1288.

Howell; Gifford v., TexCivApp–Amarillo, 119 SW2d 578, dism.—Health 619, 625, 825.

Howell; Greenberg, Benson, Fisk and Fielder, P.C. v., TexApp–Dallas, 685 SW2d 694.—Judges 51(4); Mand 28, 48, 51.

Howell; Greenberg, Fisk & Fielder v., TexApp–Dallas, 676 SW2d 431.—Judges 51(4).

Howell v. Hecht, TexApp–Dallas, 821 SW2d 627, writ den.—Action 3, 6; Evid 208(4); Judgm 183, 185.3(21); Libel 6(1), 48(3), 51(1), 51(5), 55, 112(2).

Howell; Helicoid Gage Division of Am. Chain & Cable Co. v., TexCivApp–Hous (14 Dist), 511 SW2d 573, ref nre.—Damag 132(14), 133, 134(1); Prod Liab 8, 15, 26, 27, 55, 75.1, 96.1.

Howell; Hendrick Medical Center v., TexApp–Dallas, 690 SW2d 42.—Courts 99(3); Mand 4(1).

Howell v. Hilton Hotels Corp., TexApp–Houston (1 Dist), 84 SW3d 708, reh overr, and petition stricken, and review den, and reh of petition for review den.—App & E 856(1), 1073(1); Corp 1.4(1), 1.4(4), 1.7(2), 215; Judgm 183, 185.3(5); Partners 67, 70.

Howell v. Homecraft Land Development, Inc., TexApp– Dallas, 749 SW2d 103, writ den.—Antitrust 369, 397; Contracts 164; Costs 194.40; Dep & Escr 11, 20; Fraud 25; Judgm 359; Witn 13.

Howell; Houston Fire & Cas. Ins. Co. v., Tex, 484 SW2d 582.—App & E 883; Damag 221(8); Trial 365.1(6); Work Comp 1974.

Howell v. Houston Fire & Cas. Ins. Co., TexCivApp– Waco, 474 SW2d 924, writ gr, rev 484 SW2d 582.— Damag 221(8); Work Comp 1943.

Howell v. Howell, Tex, 210 SW2d 978, 147 Tex 14.—App & E 861; Divorce 144; Trial 352.5(2).

Howell; Howell v., Tex, 210 SW2d 978, 147 Tex 14.—App & E 861; Divorce 144; Trial 352.5(2).

Howell v. Howell, TexCivApp–Corpus Christi, 522 SW2d 606.—App & E 1125.

Howell; Howell v., TexCivApp–Corpus Christi, 522 SW2d 606.—App & E 1125.

Howell v. Howell, TexCivApp–Galveston, 206 SW2d 616, certified question answered 210 SW2d 978, 147 Tex 14. —Divorce 124.1, 144, 149, 184(6.1), 184(9).

Howell; Howell v., TexCivApp–Galveston, 206 SW2d 616, certified question answered 210 SW2d 978, 147 Tex 14. —Divorce 124.1, 144, 149, 184(6.1), 184(9).

Howell v. Jones, CA5 (Tex), 516 F2d 53, reh den 521 F2d 815, cert den 96 SCt 1116, 424 US 916, 47 LEd2d 321, reh den 96 SCt 1687, 425 US 945, 48 LEd2d 189.— Const Law 1225, 1440; Contempt 60(2), 61(1); Courts 107; Crim Law 641.12(1); Fed Cts 452; Hab Corp 528.1, 777; Judges 39; Witn 21, 198(2).

Howell; Jones v., TexCivApp–Dallas, 107 SW2d 661.— App & E 1002.

Howell v. Kelly, TexCivApp–Hous (1 Dist), 534 SW2d 737.—App & E 907(3); Atty & C 147, 148(1), 150, 166(1), 167(4); Contracts 324(1), 344, 348.

Howell; King v., TexCivApp–Fort Worth, 120 SW2d 298. —App & E 662(2); Wills 440, 470(1), 522, 524(2), 529.

Howell v. Knox, TexCivApp–Austin, 211 SW2d 324, ref nre.—App & E 1056.1(9); Debtor & C 12; Evid 341; Insurance 1211(3), 1372; Lim of Act 58(1); Names 14; Plead 291(2).

Howell v. Liles, TexCivApp–Amarillo, 246 SW2d 260.— Estop 23.

Howell v. Loftis, TexCivApp–Amarillo, 299 SW2d 954.— App & E 863; Lim of Act 24(4), 29(2); Plead 111.36, 111.39(5), 111.42(5); Venue 7.5(3).

Howell v. Mauzy, TexApp–Austin, 899 SW2d 690, writ den.—Abate & R 4; Admin Law 381; App & E 241, 854(1), 863, 934(1), 1024.3; Costs 194.40; Counties 28; Courts 23, 74, 75, 474, 475(1); Decl Judgm 45, 323; Elections 317.4, 317.5; Judges 30, 56; Judgm 10, 185(2); Plead 16, 34(1), 34(3), 106(1), 106(2); Statut 181(1), 188, 241(1), 267(1); Stip 14(10); Venue 28, 31.

Howell v. Mauzy, TexApp–Austin, 774 SW2d 274, writ den.—App & E 80(3).

Howell; Miller v., TexCivApp–Fort Worth, 234 SW2d 925.—Action 16; Courts 7; Des & Dist 8; Partit 43; Partners 68(1), 68(2), 76, 243, 244, 246, 318, 320, 342; Plead 111.8; Venue 2, 5.2, 5.3(1), 15.

Howell; Mills v., TexCivApp–Austin, 416 SW2d 453.— App & E 138, 141, 868; Courts 23; Decl Judgm 66, 291, 390.

Howell v. Missouri-Kansas-Texas R. Co., TexCivApp– Eastland, 380 SW2d 842, ref nre.—App & E 1062.1; Evid 359(1); R R 352; Trial 352.10, 352.21.

Howell v. Murray Mortg. Co., TexApp–Amarillo, 890 SW2d 78, reh den, and writ den.—App & E 1078(1); Contracts 10(1), 143.5; Ex & Ad 91; Judgm 181(2), 181(25), 183; Mtg 211, 334, 335, 403; Perp 6(1).

Howell v. National Bank of Commerce, TexCivApp–San Antonio, 181 SW2d 837, writ refused.—Banks 189, 190; Lim of Act 28(1).

Howell; Olton State Bank v., TexCivApp–Amarillo, 105 SW2d 287.—Courts 39; Garn 124; Judgm 16, 17(1), 472.

Howell; Perl v., TexApp–Dallas, 650 SW2d 523, ref nre.— Hus & W 275; Wills 58(2), 62, 578(1).

Howell; Pyramid Drilling Co. v., TexCivApp–Texarkana, 173 SW2d 250, writ refused wom.—Chat Mtg 170(1), 282; Corp 428(6); Evid 441(5).

Howell; Rogers v., TexCivApp–Dallas, 592 SW2d 402, ref nre.—App & E 71(3), 863, 954(1); Inj 138.21, 144, 145, 147; Mtg 413.

Howell v. Rosser, TexCivApp–Amarillo, 81 SW2d 1100, writ refused.—App & E 770(2); Ven & Pur 130(8).

Howell v. Sanders, TexCivApp–Waco, 383 SW2d 874, ref nre.—App & E 1003(11); Autos 244(34), 244(36.1), 245(50.1); Damag 143, 146, 185(1), 188(1); Trial 350.6(3), 350.7(3.1).

Howell v. State, TexCrimApp, 175 SW3d 786, reh den, on remand 2006 WL 2450920.—Crim Law 859, 1147, 1155.

Howell v. State, TexCrimApp, 563 SW2d 933.—Crim Law 264, 641.13(1), 641.13(2.1), 641.13(5), 775(3), 1035(6), 1036.2, 1038.1(3.1), 1038.1(4), 1038.3, 1044.1(2), 1181.5(9); Sent & Pun 1382, 1388, 1389.

Howell v. State, TexCrimApp, 478 SW2d 468.—False Pret 49(1).

Howell v. State, TexCrimApp, 352 SW2d 110, 171 Tex-Crim 545.—Autos 355(6); Crim Law 364(3.1), 918(10), 1038.1(7), 1166.15; Jury 103(6).

Howell v. State, TexCrimApp, 350 SW2d 933, 171 Tex-Crim 403.—Bail 55, 75.2(1).

Howell v. State, TexCrimApp, 240 SW2d 779.—Autos 355(6); Crim Law 338(1), 1169.2(2).

Howell v. State, TexCrimApp, 224 SW2d 228, 154 Tex-Crim 8.—Arrest 63.4(15); Crim Law 404.65, 444, 715, 720(1), 1037.1(1), 1092.11(3), 1092.12, 1169.5(2); Rob 11, 20, 23(3), 24.15(2), 27(1).

Howell v. State, TexCrimApp, 176 SW2d 186, 146 Tex-Crim 454.—Crim Law 419(11); Witn 68, 227.

Howell v. State, TexCrimApp, 152 SW2d 341, 142 Tex-Crim 191.—Big 11; Crim Law 421(1).

Howell v. State, TexCrimApp, 146 SW2d 747, 140 Tex-Crim 627.—Crim Law 273.2(2); Embez 21.

Howell v. State, TexCrimApp, 112 SW2d 740, 133 Tex-Crim 566.—Crim Law 511.1(9); Larc 40(11).

Howell v. State, TexCrimApp, 109 SW2d 1064, 133 Tex-Crim 234.—Crim Law 511.1(9); Witn 357.

Howell v. State, TexCrimApp, 100 SW2d 714, 131 Tex-Crim 501.—Burg 41(1).

Howell v. State, TexCrimApp, 88 SW2d 706, 129 TexCrim 475.—Rob 24.10.

Howell v. State, TexCrimApp, 84 SW2d 238, 129 TexCrim 96.—Crim Law 552(3); Rec S Goods 8(3).

Howell v. State, TexApp–Houston (1 Dist), 827 SW2d 586.—Crim Law 1119(1).

Howell v. State, TexApp–Houston (1 Dist), 757 SW2d 513, petition for discretionary review refused.—Const Law 4694; Crim Law 1144.15, 1172.1(2); Homic 667, 668, 938, 1458; Ind & Inf 189(8).

Howell v. State, TexApp–Houston (1 Dist), 661 SW2d 293.—Crim Law 288, 1173.2(1); Homic 1465.

Howell v. State, TexApp–Fort Worth, 906 SW2d 248, reh overr, and petition for discretionary review refused.—Controlled Subs 30, 45, 80; Crim Law 59(5), 1144.13(3), 1159.2(7), 1159.2(8), 1159.2(9), 1159.2(10), 1159.3(2).

Howell v. State, TexApp–Fort Worth, 627 SW2d 836, petition for discretionary review refused.—Forg 44(0.5), 48.

Howell v. State, TexApp–Austin, 149 SW3d 686, petition for discretionary review gr, rev 175 SW3d 786, reh den, on remand 2006 WL 2450920.—Crim Law 859, 863(1), 1162, 1174(1).

Howell; State v., TexApp–Dallas, 871 SW2d 237.—Const Law 2600; Crim Law 303.15, 577.16(1), 1192; Ind & Inf 144.1(1).

Howell v. State, TexApp–Texarkana, 723 SW2d 755.—Const Law 1306, 1308, 1329, 1343; Crim Law 1035(5); Schools 160.

Howell v. State, TexApp–El Paso, 795 SW2d 27, petition for discretionary review refused.—Ind & Inf 127, 130; Sent & Pun 311, 313, 1381(3).

Howell v. State, TexApp–Corpus Christi, 754 SW2d 396.—Sent & Pun 2010.

Howell v. State, TexApp–Houston (14 Dist), 709 SW2d 337, petition for discretionary review refused.—Crim Law 339.7(3), 339.7(4), 339.8(3), 339.8(4), 339.10(10).

Howell v. State, TexCivApp–Tyler, 559 SW2d 432, ref nre.—Atty & C 22, 48, 49, 54; Const Law 240(7), 3684(1), 4273(3).

Howell v. State Bar of Texas, CA5 (Tex), 843 F2d 205, reh den 849 F2d 1471, cert den 109 SCt 531, 488 US 982, 102 LEd2d 563.—Atty & C 1.

Howell v. State Bar of Texas, CA5 (Tex), 710 F2d 1075, cert den 104 SCt 2152, 466 US 950, 80 LEd2d 538, appeal after remand 843 F2d 205, reh den 849 F2d 1471, cert den 109 SCt 531, 488 US 982, 102 LEd2d 563.—Courts 509.

Howell v. State Bar of Texas, CA5 (Tex), 674 F2d 1027, cert gr, vac 103 SCt 1515, 460 US 1065, 75 LEd2d 942, on remand 710 F2d 1075, cert den 104 SCt 2152, 466 US 950, 80 LEd2d 538, appeal after remand 843 F2d 205, reh den 849 F2d 1471, cert den 109 SCt 531, 488 US 982, 102 LEd2d 563.—Fed Cts 42, 1142; Judgm 828.16(4).

Howell v. Supreme Court of Texas, CA5 (Tex), 885 F2d 308, reh den, cert den 110 SCt 3213, 496 US 936, 110 LEd2d 661.—Fed Civ Proc 2771(16), 2774(4); Fed Cts 1142.

Howell; Texas & N. O. R. Co. v., TexCivApp–Beaumont, 176 SW2d 787.—App & E 1177(8); Damag 132(1); R R 356(1), 400(6), 400(11), 400(14).

Howell v. Texas & Pac. Ry. Co., TexCivApp–Eastland, 243 SW2d 186.—R R 482(3).

Howell; Texas & P. Ry. Co. v., TexCivApp–Eastland, 117 SW2d 857, writ dism.—App & E 1177(6); Neglig 1037(4), 1313, 1594; R R 275(1), 278(2), 282(5), 282(9).

Howell v. Texas Dept. of Criminal Justice, TexApp–Texarkana, 28 SW3d 125.—App & E 863, 949; Courts 26; Judgm 181(6), 185(2), 540, 562, 570(1), 585(1), 829(3), 948(1); Plead 109, 111.47.

Howell; Texas Distillers, Inc. v., TexCivApp–San Antonio, 409 SW2d 888, ref nre.—Evid 207(1), 265(13); Judgm 185(6).

Howell; Texas Emp. Ins. Ass'n v., TexCivApp–Dallas, 107 SW2d 391, writ dism.—App & E 151(1); Work Comp 1981, 1983, 1985.

Howell; Texas Prudential Ins. Co. v., TexCivApp–Dallas, 119 SW2d 1100.—Insurance 1759, 3084, 3091, 3117.

Howell v. Texas Workers' Compensation Com'n, TexApp–Austin, 143 SW3d 416, review den (2 pets).—Admin Law 228.1, 229; App & E 186, 226(1), 295, 756, 760(1), 893(1), 949, 984(1), 984(5), 1079; Atty & C 24; Const Law 2311, 2314, 2317, 2600, 2673, 4426; Costs 2, 194.40, 207, 208; Courts 4, 475(1), 516; Decl Judgm 44, 61, 66, 85, 126, 271, 303, 322, 341.1, 387; Inj 9, 12, 26(3), 26(4), 32, 111; Jury 9, 25(2), 25(6), 26; Mand 1; Pretrial Proc 44.1; Work Comp 991.5, 999, 1001.

Howell v. Thomas, CA5 (Tex), 566 F2d 469, reh den 570 F2d 949, cert den 99 SCt 98, 439 US 826, 58 LEd2d 119, reh den 99 SCt 600, 439 US 997, 58 LEd2d 671.—Contempt 38; Courts 90(2); Hab Corp 528.1.

Howell v. Thompson, Tex, 839 SW2d 92.—Bankr 2462.

Howell v. Thompson, TexCivApp–Galveston, 190 SW2d 597.—Adop 6, 17.

Howell v. TS Communications, Inc., TexApp–Dallas, 209 SW3d 921.—Insurance 1702, 3549(3); Judgm 111, 112, 185(2), 185(5), 237(4).

Howell v. T S Communications, Inc., TexApp–Dallas, 130 SW3d 515, as am nunc pro tunc, on remand 2005 WL 4890197, aff 209 SW3d 921.—App & E 1079; Contracts 187(1); Judgm 181(19), 181(33).

Howell v. Union Producing Co., CA5 (Tex), 392 F2d 95.—Contracts 1, 147(1); Fed Cts 388.1; Mines 73, 73.1(1), 73.1(2), 75, 79.1(5); Partit 9(1).

Howell; U.S. v., CA5 (Tex), 719 F2d 1258, cert den 104 SCt 2683, 467 US 1228, 81 LEd2d 878.—Const Law 90.1(1), 1832; Crim Law 577.8(1), 577.10(8), 577.11(6),

1144.13(3), 1144.13(5), 1177; Homic 736, 868; Ind & Inf 60, 125(19.1).

Howell; Valley Steel Products Co. v., TexApp–Houston (1 Dist), 775 SW2d 34.—Guar 89, 91.

Howell v. Wallace, Tex, 707 SW2d 876. See Wallace v. Howell.

Howell; Wallace v., Tex, 707 SW2d 876.—Judges 4; Offic 18.

Howell; Wiedeman v., TexCivApp–Austin, 276 SW2d 380, ref nre.—Contracts 75(2).

Howell v. Wilson, TexCivApp–El Paso, 323 SW2d 61, ref nre.—Adv Poss 61, 85(3); Evid 271(18), 318(1); Hus & W 14.1, 16; Judgm 178; Lim of Act 103(3); Trusts 138, 365(3).

Howell v. Witts, TexCivApp–Dallas, 424 SW2d 19, ref nre.—Atty & C 129(2); Estop 68(2); Evid 265(7); Judgm 185.2(4); Partners 61.

Howell; Young v., TexCivApp–Texarkana, 236 SW2d 247. —App & E 932(1), 1066(9); Damag 148, 191, 208(1), 216(9).

Howell; Zerr v., TexCivApp–San Antonio, 88 SW2d 116.— Partners 327(1); Plead 34(3); Trover 4, 23.

Howell; Zerr v., TexCivApp–San Antonio, 84 SW2d 867, writ refused.—Chat Mtg 100, 126, 219.

Howell Aviation Services v. Aerial Ads, Inc., TexApp–Dallas, 29 SW3d 321.—App & E 1; Costs 260(5); Courts 176.5; Statut 223.4.

Howell Crane Service, U.S. for Use and Ben. of, v. U.S. Fidelity & Guar. Co., CA5 (Tex), 861 F2d 110. See U.S. for Use and Ben. of Howell Crane Service v. U.S. Fidelity & Guar. Co.

Howell Crude Oil Co. v. Donna Refinery Partners, Ltd., TexApp–Houston (14 Dist), 928 SW2d 100, reh overr, and writ den.—Action 27(1); Antitrust 147, 161, 162, 282, 292, 363, 364, 369, 389(1), 389(2), 391, 396; App & E 836, 930(3), 969, 984(1), 989, 999(1), 1001(1), 1003(7), 1079; Costs 194.25, 194.32; Damag 36, 40(1), 189, 190, 221(7); Fraud 58(1); Judgm 199(3.10); Torts 118; Trial 182, 219, 295(1), 349(2).

Howell Crude Oil Co. v. Tana Oil & Gas Corp., TexApp–Corpus Christi, 860 SW2d 634.—Action 43.1; Alt Disp Res 113, 133(2), 135, 143, 145, 182(2), 192, 211; App & E 66; Sales 10, 22(4), 23(4).

Howell Hydrocarbons, Inc. v. Adams, CA5 (Tex), 897 F2d 183, reh den.—Bankr 2043(2), 2053; Evid 318(1); Fed Civ Proc 2470.1, 2544, 2545; Fraud 9; Judgm 634, 668(1), 670, 675(1), 677, 678(1), 681, 739; Postal 35(2), 35(10); RICO 3, 10, 27, 31, 79; Tel 1014(2), 1014(8).

Howell Petroleum Corp.; Geosearch, Inc. v., CA5 (Tex), 819 F2d 521.—Fed Civ Proc 2197, 2211, 2242; Fraud 20, 28, 36, 58(4), 64(5).

Howell Petroleum Corp. v. Kramer, TexApp–Corpus Christi, 647 SW2d 723.—App & E 837(1), 1177(5); Costs 260(1); Plead 110, 111.35, 111.39(2), 111.39(4), 111.42(1), 307, 310; Trial 39.

Howell Petroleum Corp. v. Weaver, CA5 (Tex), 780 F2d 1198.—Fed Civ Proc 636.

Howell Petroleum Corp. v. Weaver, CA5 (Tex), 776 F2d 1302, reh den 780 F2d 1198.—RICO 69.

Howell Refining Co. v. N. L. R. B., CA5 (Tex), 400 F2d 213.—Labor & Emp 1175, 1177, 1193(1), 1195(1), 1195(8).

Howerton, In re, BkrtcyNDTex, 23 BR 58.—Bankr 2182.1, 2189, 3027, 3184.

Howerton, In re, BkrtcyNDTex, 21 BR 621, opinion supplemented 23 BR 58.—Annuities 16; Bankr 2547, 2779, 3109; Exemp 4, 50(1); Insurance 1006, 1011; Trusts 12, 152.

Howerton; City of Fort Worth v., Tex, 236 SW2d 615, 149 Tex 614.—Const Law 655, 2630; Mun Corp 75.

Howerton v. City of Fort Worth, TexCivApp–Fort Worth, 231 SW2d 993, aff 236 SW2d 615, 149 Tex 614.— Const Law 611, 655, 2645; Mun Corp 67(5), 176(3.1); Statut 94(1); Tax 2016.

Howerton v. Designer Homes by Georges, Inc., CA5 (Tex), 950 F2d 281, reh den.—Assign 125; B & L Assoc 42(6); Contracts 350(1); Fed Civ Proc 103.5; Fed Cts 616, 850.1.

Howerton; Sandles v., TexApp–Dallas, 163 SW3d 829.— Costs 194.18, 207; Health 804, 805, 809; Motions 15.

Howerton v. Tomlinson, TexCivApp–Waco, 421 SW2d 494, ref nre.—Brok 86(8); Contracts 147(3); Evid 450(6), 461(1).

Howery v. Allstate Ins. Co., CA5 (Tex), 243 F3d 912, reh den, cert den 122 SCt 459, 534 US 993, 151 LEd2d 377. —Fed Civ Proc 1742(3); Fed Cts 5, 30, 31, 34, 161, 241, 243, 286.1, 297, 300, 311, 315, 318; Rem of C 15, 19(1), 47, 107(7).

Howery v. State, TexCrimApp, 528 SW2d 230.—Controlled Subs 82; Crim Law 507(4), 1144.17, 1166.22(2); Sent & Pun 2021.

Howes v. State, TexApp–Texarkana, 120 SW3d 903, petition for discretionary review refused.—Autos 357, 359, 422.1; Crim Law 394.6(5), 777, 1153(1), 1158(3), 1158(4), 1166.18, 1173.2(9); Jury 107.

Howe State Bank v. Crookham, TexApp–Dallas, 873 SW2d 745.—Courts 475(2).

Howe State Bank; Williams v., TexApp–Dallas, 702 SW2d 675.—Judgm 181(33); Mal Pros 36.

Howeth, Ex parte, TexCrimApp, 609 SW2d 540.—Controlled Subs 65; Hab Corp 509(2), 792.1.

Howeth; Christian v., TexCivApp–Fort Worth, 522 SW2d 700, ref nre.—Courts 182.1, 185, 472.2; Judgm 525.

Howeth v. Davenport, TexCivApp–San Antonio, 311 SW2d 480, ref nre.—Acct Action on 8; App & E 962; Bills & N 537(1); Evid 441(11); Pretrial Proc 583, 587.

Howeth; Foster v., TexApp–Beaumont, 112 SW3d 773.— App & E 223, 1079; Mal Pros 0.5, 24(4), 35(1).

Howeth; INA of Texas v., TexApp–Houston (1 Dist), 755 SW2d 534.—Work Comp 552, 597, 618, 1490, 1533, 1598, 1653, 1728, 1939.11(9), 1988.

Howeth v. Massey, TexCivApp–Eastland, 429 SW2d 513, ref nre.—Autos 244(44).

Howeth v. State, TexCrimApp, 645 SW2d 787.—Autos 355(1); Const Law 4693; Crim Law 304(12); Mun Corp 642(1); Stip 1.

Howeth v. State, TexApp–Austin, 635 SW2d 636, petition for discretionary review gr, rev 645 SW2d 787.—Autos 351.1; Crim Law 421(1); Mun Corp 646.

Howeth; Trinity Universal Ins. Co. v., TexCivApp–Texarkana, 419 SW2d 704.—Insurance 3564(3), 3564(7), 3565(1), 3565(3).

Howeth Investments, Inc.; Brown v., TexApp–Houston (1 Dist), 820 SW2d 900, writ den.—App & E 870(2), 962; Pretrial Proc 697.

Howeth Investments, Inc. v. City of Hedwig Village Planning and Zoning Com'n, CA5 (Tex), 113 FedAppx 11.—Rem of C 107(11).

Howeth Investments, Inc.; City of Hedwig Village Planning and Zoning Com'n v., TexApp–Houston (1 Dist), 73 SW3d 389, reh overr.—Action 6, 13; Courts 4, 39; Judgm 181(6); Plead 101, 104(1), 111.37; Zoning 432.

Howeth Investments, Inc.; Memorial Executive Suites v., TexApp–Houston (1 Dist), 820 SW2d 900. See Brown v. Howeth Investments, Inc.

Howeth Investments, Inc. v. White, TexApp–Houston (1 Dist), 227 SW3d 205.—Action 70; App & E 756; Evid 265(7); Judgm 181(5.1), 187, 190, 524.

Howie; Maryland Cas. Co. v., TexCivApp–San Antonio, 94 SW2d 220, writ dism.—App & E 719(1), 1008.1(1); Judgm 198; Trial 352.9, 358.

HOW Ins. Co. v. Patriot Financial Services of Texas, Inc., TexApp–Austin, 786 SW2d 533, writ den.—Antitrust 141, 145, 360, 363, 367, 369; App & E 232(0.5), 1004(3), 1177(1); Damag 49, 49.10, 163(1), 192; Fraud 11(1), 12, 58(1), 58(2), 58(4).

Howk v. State, TexCrimApp, 135 SW2d 719, 138 TexCrim 275.—Crim Law 402(1); False Pret 32, 38.

Howk v. State, TexApp–Beaumont, 969 SW2d 46.—Crim Law 369.2(1), 369.2(5), 438(2), 565, 1043(2), 1144.12, 1144.13(3), 1153(1), 1159.2(7), 1171.3; Ind & Inf 87(7); Searches 148.

Howland v. Hough, Tex, 570 SW2d 876.—Adv Poss 112; Bound 1, 3(3), 6; Lost Inst 1; Tresp to T T 38(1).

Howland v. Hough, TexCivApp–Eastland, 553 SW2d 162, writ gr, rev 570 SW2d 876.—App & E 1056.1(4.1); Tresp to T T 12, 38(3), 40(4), 41(1).

Howland v. State, TexCrimApp, 990 SW2d 274, cert den 120 SCt 207, 528 US 887, 145 LEd2d 174, reh den 120 SCt 2000, 529 US 1125, 146 LEd2d 823, habeas corpus dism by 2005 WL 2266613.—Crim Law 369.2(5).

Howland v. State, TexCrimApp, 151 SW2d 601, 142 Tex-Crim 37.—Atty & C 11(13); Ind & Inf 41(2), 111(1).

Howland v. State, TexApp–Houston (1 Dist), 966 SW2d 98, petition for discretionary review gr, aff 990 SW2d 274, cert den 120 SCt 207, 528 US 887, 145 LEd2d 174, reh den 120 SCt 2000, 529 US 1125, 146 LEd2d 823, habeas corpus dism 2005 WL 2266613.—Crim Law 338(7), 369.1, 641.13(1), 641.13(2.1), 641.13(6), 661, 695.5, 698(3), 1119(1), 1144.12, 1153(1), 1169.2(3); Statut 181(2), 190, 214.

Howle v. Camp Amon Carter, Tex, 470 SW2d 629.—Char 45(2).

Howle v. Camp Amon Carter, TexCivApp–Fort Worth, 462 SW2d 624, rev 470 SW2d 629.—Char 45(2); Const Law 4420; Courts 91(1).

Howle v. Howle, TexCivApp–Tyler, 422 SW2d 252.—App & E 854(1); Divorce 255; Hus & W 272(4), 272(5); Improv 3; Judgm 719.

Howle; Howle v., TexCivApp–Tyler, 422 SW2d 252.—App & E 854(1); Divorce 255; Hus & W 272(4), 272(5); Improv 3; Judgm 719.

Howle; U.S. v., CA5 (Tex), 537 F2d 1302.—Cust Dut 126(5).

Howlett, Ex parte, TexApp–Eastland, 900 SW2d 937, petition for discretionary review refused.—Crim Law 150.

Howlett v. State, TexCrimApp, 994 SW2d 663.—Crim Law 772(4), 1180, 1192; Mal Mis 5.

Howlett v. State, TexApp–El Paso, 700 SW2d 751, petition for discretionary review refused.—Crim Law 211(3), 218(4), 394.1(3), 394.4(9), 413(1), 419(2.20), 1035(8.1), 1166.22(2); Homic 1184; Searches 61, 62, 123.1, 178.

Howlett v. State, TexApp–Eastland, 946 SW2d 870, petition for discretionary review refused, rev 994 SW2d 663.—Courts 99(1), 99(6); Crim Law 145.5, 507(1), 507(2), 772(4), 800(1), 800(2), 1134(2), 1134(8), 1173.2(2); Mal Mis 10; Searches 113.1, 114, 121.1, 147.1, 148, 149.

Howley v. State, TexApp–Houston (1 Dist), 943 SW2d 152.—Assault 92(1); Crim Law 412(4), 517(7), 1134(2), 1134(3), 1144.13(2.1), 1169.12.

Howley By and Through Howley, Estate of v. Haberman, Tex, 878 SW2d 139.—Mand 43; Pretrial Proc 698.

H. O. Wooten Grocer Co.; Foster v., TexCivApp–Eastland, 273 SW2d 461.—Courts 121(5); Plead 110.

H. O. Wooten Grocer Co.; Twaddell v., TexComApp, 106 SW2d 266, 130 Tex 42.—Antitrust 582; Fraud Conv 47.

Howse; F.D.I.C. v., SDTex, 802 FSupp 1554.—Atty & C 26; Banks 54(1), 505, 508; Corp 202, 206(2), 206(4), 307, 320(4); Fed Civ Proc 1772, 1821, 1825, 1829; Fed Cts 4, 14.1, 19, 20.1, 23, 230, 414; Lim of Act 41; Set-Off 6, 41; States 18.19.

Howse; Federal Deposit Ins. Corp. v., SDTex, 736 FSupp 1437.—Banks 501, 508; Fed Cts 422.1; Lim of Act 6(1), 46(6), 55(1), 58(1), 58(5), 95(1), 95(3), 95(9), 95(18), 100(12); Statut 255.

Howsley; Employers' Fire Ins. Co. v., TexCivApp–Amarillo, 432 SW2d 578.—Insurance 1813, 2142(5), 2145, 2155(1).

Howsley v. Gilliam, Tex, 517 SW2d 531.—Homic 751; Neglig 230, 238, 259, 510(6).

Howsley v. Gilliam, TexCivApp–El Paso, 503 SW2d 628, writ gr, rev 517 SW2d 531.—Const Law 2473; Crim Law 29(10); Death 21; Judgm 185(4).

Howsley; Talley v., Tex, 176 SW2d 158, 142 Tex 81.—Estop 32(1), 41, 47; Fraud 12; Mines 54.5, 55(4); Mtg 284; Trusts 91, 95.

Howsley; Talley v., TexCivApp–Eastland, 170 SW2d 240, aff 176 SW2d 158, 142 Tex 81.—Covenants 57, 58, 68, 71; Estop 23, 32(1); Mines 54.5, 55(4); Trusts 91, 94.5.

Howsley & Jacobs v. Kendall, Tex, 376 SW2d 562.—App & E 207, 1060.1(7); Evid 201; Partners 219(1); Trial 106, 121(4).

Howsley & Jacobs v. Kendall, TexCivApp–Eastland, 364 SW2d 836, ref nre, and writ gr, rev 376 SW2d 562.—App & E 1060.3, 1062.1; Evid 126(1), 126(5); Explos 10; Partners 169.

Howth v. City of Beaumont, TexCivApp–Beaumont, 118 SW2d 350.—Mun Corp 956(2), 971(4), 972(3), 978(9).

Howth v. Farrar, CCA5 (Tex), 94 F2d 654, reh den 95 F2d 1005, cert den 59 SCt 75, 305 US 599, 83 LEd 380.—Adv Poss 40, 78, 82; Life Est 8; Perp 4(6); Remaind 17(2); Wills 353.

Howth v. French Independent School Dist., TexCivApp–Beaumont, 115 SW2d 1036, aff 134 SW2d 1036, 134 Tex 211.—Mun Corp 978(6); Schools 103(1), 106.12(3); Tax 2853; Trial 398.

Howth; French Independent School Dist. of Jefferson County v., TexComApp, 134 SW2d 1036, 134 Tex 211.—Schools 106.4(1), 106.12(11); Tax 2467.

Howth; J.I. Case Threshing Mach. Co. v., Tex, 293 SW 800, 116 Tex 434.—Bills & N 338.5.

Howth v. J.I. Case Threshing Mach. Co., TexCivApp–Dallas, 280 SW 238, writ den 293 SW 800, 116 Tex 434.—Bills & N 338.5.

Howth; Shell Oil Co. v., Tex, 159 SW2d 483, 138 Tex 357.—Adv Poss 71(2), 115(1); App & E 1176(3); Can of Inst 35(1); Courts 472.4(2.1); Hus & W 273(1), 273(9); Judgm 19; Libel 139; Lim of Act 39(12), 165; Mines 73.1(2), 73.1(4), 77; Mtg 32(3), 39, 143; Ven & Pur 269, 287.

Howth; Shell Petroleum Corp. v., TexCivApp–Beaumont, 135 SW2d 197.—Costs 230.

Howth; Shell Petroleum Corp. v., TexCivApp–Beaumont, 133 SW2d 253, mod Shell Oil Co v. Howth, 159 SW2d 483, 138 Tex 357.—Adv Poss 115(1); App & E 389(3), 719(6), 1178(6); Can of Inst 35(1); Damag 72, 177; Deeds 69; Evid 18; Infants 24; Libel 139; Mines 51(1), 55(3), 57, 60, 73.1(2), 73.1(4); Mtg 32(2), 38(1); Ten in C 22; Ven & Pur 269.

Howth; Tolivar v., TexCivApp–Beaumont, 100 SW2d 1090, writ dism.—App & E 728(1), 728(2), 1048(5); Evid 359(2); Trial 194(9), 208, 244(2); Wills 292, 302(1), 303(7), 329(3); Witn 268(1), 340(3), 372(2), 393(2).

Howton; U.S. v., CA5 (Tex), 688 F2d 272.—Crim Law 627.8(4), 641.5(7), 734, 1036.1(8); Obst Just 5.

Howze v. City of Austin, CA5 (Tex), 917 F2d 208.—Const Law 4173(4); Health 266.

Howze v. Garrison, TexCivApp–Waco, 363 SW2d 381, writ refused.—Autos 144.1(4).

Howze v. Surety Corp. of America, Tex, 584 SW2d 263.—Interest 46(1); Licens 26; Princ & S 66(1), 123(1), 123(3).

Howze v. Surety Corp. of America, TexCivApp–Austin, 564 SW2d 834, rev 584 SW2d 263.—Princ & S 66(1), 145(3), 157.

Howze; Young v., TexCivApp–Amarillo, 216 SW2d 988.—App & E 770(1); Frds St of 125(2); Ven & Pur 343(2).

Hoxie Implement Co., Inc. v. Baker, TexApp–Amarillo, 65 SW3d 140, reh overr, and review den.—Acct Action on 8; App & E 209, 226(2), 230, 232(0.5); Costs 194.40, 198; Decl Judgm 392.1; Interest 50; Paymt 8(1); Trial

351.2(1.1); Usury 6, 11, 12, 13, 15, 16, 31, 42, 72, 113, 115, 117, 125.

Hoxsey v. Fishbein, NDTex, 83 FSupp 282.—Libel 48(1), 54, 112(1).

Hoxsey v. Hoffpauir, CA5 (Tex), 180 F2d 84, cert den 70 SCt 841, 339 US 953, 94 LEd 1366.—Atty & C 130, 181, 182(2), 192(1); Courts 37(3); Fed Cts 407.1; Judgm 721.

Hoxsey; Hoffpuir v., NDTex, 82 FSupp 14, rev 180 F2d 84, cert den 70 SCt 841, 339 US 953, 94 LEd 1366.—Judgm 721, 812(3).

Hoxsey v. State, TexCrimApp, 159 SW2d 886, 143 Tex-Crim 508.—Crim Law 338(1), 384, 448(12), 714, 1091(5), 1170(1); Health 164, 186(4); Jury 131(4).

Hoxsey Cancer Clinic; U.S. v., CA5 (Tex), 198 F2d 273, cert den 73 SCt 496, 344 US 928, 97 LEd 714, reh den 73 SCt 642, 345 US 914, 97 LEd 1348, cert den 74 SCt 220, 346 US 897, 98 LEd 398.—Evid 314(2), 568(1); Inj 126, 128(8).

Hoxsey Cancer Clinic; U.S. v., NDTex, 94 FSupp 464, rev 198 F2d 273, cert den 73 SCt 496, 344 US 928, 97 LEd 714, reh den 73 SCt 642, 345 US 914, 97 LEd 1348, cert den 74 SCt 220, 346 US 897, 98 LEd 398.—Health 311, 313; Inj 109, 128(8).

Hoy v. State, TexCrimApp, 509 SW2d 605.—Autos 324.

Hoy v. State, TexCrimApp, 115 SW2d 629, 134 TexCrim 226.—Health 105, 164, 186(5); Jury 95, 132.

Hoye v. Like, TexApp–Amarillo, 958 SW2d 234.—Anim 21.1, 23(2); App & E 930(1), 1001(3); Bailm 1, 5, 31(1), 31(3); Lim of Act 129; Plead 140.

Hoye v. Shepherds Glen Land Co., Inc., TexApp–Dallas, 753 SW2d 226, writ den.—App & E 173(2); Covenants 1, 103(2).

Hoyer v. State, TexCrimApp, 339 SW2d 680, 170 TexCrim 170.—Bail 64.

Hoyle v. Dopslauf, TexCivApp–Galveston, 256 SW2d 457, ref nre.—Mines 78.7(4).

Hoyle v. State, TexCrimApp, 672 SW2d 233.—Crim Law 778(2).

Hoyle v. State, TexCrimApp, 230 SW2d 541.—Crim Law 1090.1(1).

Hoyle v. State, TexCrimApp, 223 SW2d 231, 153 TexCrim 548.—Crim Law 396(1), 419(12), 1091(1), 1091(8), 1169.1(10).

Hoyle v. State, TexApp–Fort Worth, 738 SW2d 362, petition for discretionary review refused.—Crim Law 1099.7(4).

Hoyle v. State, TexApp–Houston (14 Dist), 650 SW2d 97, writ gr, and reh gr, rev 672 SW2d 233.—Crim Law 324; Ind & Inf 71.4(1), 110(19), 137(6); Obscen 2.5, 20.

Hoyle; Texas & P. Ry. Co. v., TexCivApp–El Paso, 421 SW2d 442, ref nre.—App & E 1003(5), 1062.2; Damag 221(2.1); Neglig 510(5); R R 312.3, 334, 348(2), 348(4), 348(6.1); Trial 358.

Hoyler v. City of Longview, TexCivApp–Texarkana, 129 SW2d 416.—New Tr 44(2), 44(4), 56.

Hoyos v. State, TexCrimApp, 982 SW2d 419.—Crim Law 662.7, 1134(2); Witn 363(1), 370(3), 372(1).

Hoyos v. State, TexApp–Houston (14 Dist), 951 SW2d 503, petition for discretionary review gr, aff 982 SW2d 419.—Crim Law 662.7, 942(2), 945(2), 959, 1036.2, 1043(1), 1115(1), 1156(1), 1168(2); Ind & Inf 113; Rob 24.40, 24.45; Sent & Pun 373; Witn 267, 270(2), 363(1), 367(1), 372(2).

Hoyt; Alaniz v., TexApp–Corpus Christi, 105 SW3d 330.—App & E 68, 79(1), 80(1), 223, 529(1), 761, 766, 782, 1057(1), 1073(1); Courts 35, 39; Judgm 178, 183, 185(1), 185(4), 185.1(8), 185.3(21); Libel 1, 4, 6(1), 7(1), 7(16), 9(1), 10(0.5), 11.1, 19, 21, 24, 25, 30, 32, 34, 36, 38(1), 48(1), 49, 50.5, 51(1), 101(4), 112(2), 123(2); Torts 121, 122; Witn 219(1).

Hoyt v. Geist, TexCivApp–Houston, 364 SW2d 461.—App & E 1170.10; Covenants 103(1), 136; Inj 62(1); Trial 395(5), 395(7).

Hoyt v. Hoyt, TexCivApp–Dallas, 351 SW2d 111, writ dism.—Courts 101; Divorce 151, 252.1, 252.2, 254(1).

Hoyt; Hoyt v., TexCivApp–Dallas, 351 SW2d 111, writ dism.—Courts 101; Divorce 151, 252.1, 252.2, 254(1).

Hoyt v. INA of Texas, TexApp–Waco, 752 SW2d 628, writ den.—App & E 1177(9).

Hoyt; Parker v., TexCivApp–Galveston, 105 SW2d 1112, writ dism.—App & E 173(2), 221, 1046.1; Mal Pros 69; Trial 50.

Hoyt; Williams v., CA5 (Tex), 556 F2d 1336, reh den 562 F2d 1258, cert den 98 SCt 1530, 435 US 946, 55 LEd2d 544, reh den 98 SCt 2258, 436 US 915, 56 LEd2d 416.—Civil R 1420, 1423, 1424; Fed Civ Proc 241; Fed Cts 106, 626, 630.1, 895, 906; Prisons 4(3).

Hoyt; Williams v., EDTex, 372 FSupp 1314.—Fed Cts 79, 92, 133.

Hoyt R. Matise Co. v. Zurn, CA5 (Tex), 754 F2d 560.—Brok 50, 60, 71, 78, 103; Contracts 24, 170(1); Fed Civ Proc 2350.1; Fed Cts 772, 825.1; Ven & Pur 16(4), 17.

H----, P.C.; Resolution Trust Corp. v., NDTex, 128 FRD 647.—Atty & C 63; Fed Civ Proc 1600(3).

H. P. Drought & Co.; Booth v., TexCivApp–Waco, 89 SW2d 432, writ dism.—App & E 933(1); Des & Dist 146; Home 38, 39, 70; New Tr 52, 140(3).

H--- P. F--- v. B--- D--- P---, TexCivApp–San Antonio, 479 SW2d 124, ref nre.—Const Law 3881; Infants 198, 230.1, 232.

HP–84 Nursery Associates, Inc.; Marré v., CA5 (Tex), 117 F3d 297. See Marre v. U.S.

HP–84 Nursery Associates, Inc. v. U.S., CA5 (Tex), 117 F3d 297. See Marre v. U.S.

H.R., In re, TexApp–San Antonio, 87 SW3d 691.—App & E 931(1), 946, 949, 966(1), 1008.1(3); Infants 155, 178, 204, 205, 212, 248.1, 252.

H.R.A., Matter of, TexApp–Beaumont, 790 SW2d 102.—Assault 65; Crim Law 260.11(4), 553, 1158(1); Infants 176, 198.

Hrabar; Welch v., TexApp–Houston (14 Dist), 110 SW3d 601, review den, and reh of petition for review den.—App & E 756, 761; Costs 194.32, 207; Damag 189; Judgm 540, 563(2), 565, 570(3), 584, 585(0.5), 634, 649, 654, 665, 666, 672, 713(1), 720, 725(1), 731, 948(1), 951(1), 956(1).

Hradesky v. C. I. R., CA5 (Tex), 540 F2d 821.—Const Law 4149; Int Rev 3377, 3460, 4578, 4645, 4655; Judges 51(3).

Hranicky v. Trojanowsky, TexCivApp–Galveston, 153 SW2d 649, writ refused wom.—App & E 989, 1062.1; Autos 244(26), 245(79); Evid 171; New Tr 64; Pretrial Proc 715, 724; Trial 192.

H.R.C., In re, TexApp–El Paso, 153 SW3d 266.—Infants 223.1, 250, 251, 252.

H. Richards Oil Co.; Harry Newton, Inc. v., TexCivApp–Austin, 385 SW2d 893.—App & E 1051(1); Contracts 187(5), 236, 249; Corp 52; Evid 265(7); Guar 1; Judgm 707; Plead 45, 111.37, 111.38; Venue 2, 22(6), 22(8).

H. Richards Oil Co. v. W. S. Luckie, Inc., TexCivApp–Austin, 391 SW2d 135, ref nre.—Costs 32(3), 194.36; Evid 222(10); Paymt 38(1), 39(5), 41(2), 44; Princ & S 73, 86, 159; Sales 187.

H.R.K., Inc.; Colony Ins. Co. v., TexApp–Dallas, 728 SW2d 848.—Decl Judgm 165; Insurance 2278(21), 2913, 2914, 2921.

H.R.M., In re, Tex, 209 SW3d 105, on remand 2007 WL 707553.—App & E 994(2); Infants 157, 205, 252; Pardon 47.

H.R.M., In re, TexApp–Houston (14 Dist), 221 SW3d 94, review gr, rev 209 SW3d 105, on remand 2007 WL 707553.—App & E 1010.1(5); Infants 132, 155, 157, 178, 180, 248.1.

H.R. Management and La Plaza, Ltd.; Adams v., TexApp–San Antonio, 696 SW2d 256.—App & E 607(1).

H.R.

H.R. Management Co.; Nix v., TexApp–San Antonio, 733 SW2d 573, ref nre.—App & E 1043(1), 1048(7); Pretrial Proc 45; Witn 344(5), 349.

H. R. M., Inc.; C. H. Harrison Co. v., TexCivApp–Waco, 412 SW2d 912, ref nre.—App & E 295, 302(1); High 110.

Hrnciar; City of Shamrock v., TexCivApp–Eastland, 453 SW2d 898, ref nre.—App & E 78(1), 281(1), 692(1), 758.2, 758.3(2), 766; Estop 62.6; Trial 350.3(1), 366.

Hrncirik, In re, BkrtcyNDTex, 138 BR 835.—Bankr 2766, 2778, 2787, 2788; Exemp 45; Sec Tran 146.

Hrncirik v. Farmers Nat. Bank of Seymour, Tex., BkrtcyNDTex, 138 BR 835. See Hrncirik, In re.

HRN, Inc.; Shell Oil Co. v., Tex, 144 SW3d 429.—Sales 1.5, 78.

HRN, Inc. v. Shell Oil Co., TexApp–Houston (14 Dist), 102 SW3d 205, reh overr, and review gr, rev 144 SW3d 429.—App & E 934(1), 962; Contracts 95(1), 95(3); Costs 2; Judgm 181(29), 185(5), 185.1(4), 185.3(2), 185.3(8); Pretrial Proc 44.1, 315, 435; Release 18; Sales 78; Statut 211.

Hromas v. Miller, TexCivApp–Dallas, 148 SW2d 968.— Venue 7.5(4), 22(6), 27.

H. Ron White and Associates v. Tricontinental Leasing Corp., TexCivApp–Dallas, 760 SW2d 23. See White v. Tricontinental Leasing Corp.

H. Rothstein & Sons; Southern Pac. Co. v., TexCivApp– San Antonio, 304 SW2d 383, ref nre.—Carr 95, 98, 99, 104.

H. Rouw Co.; Gaylord Container Division of Crown Zellerbach Corp. v., Tex, 392 SW2d 118.—Bills & N 98; Judgm 181(2), 181(26).

H. Rouw Co. v. Gaylord Container Division of Crown Zellerbach Corp., TexCivApp–Corpus Christi, 385 SW2d 481, rev 392 SW2d 118.—Bills & N 140; Judgm 185(2), 185.3(16), 186.

H. Rouw Co.; McDonald v., TexCivApp–Austin, 195 SW2d 162, ref nre.—Food 3.

H. Rouw Co.; Missouri Pac. R. Co. v., CA5 (Tex), 258 F2d 445, cert den 79 SCt 315, 358 US 929, 3 LEd2d 302, reh den The H Rouw Company v. Missouri Pacific Railroad Company, 79 SCt 605, 359 US 932, 3 LEd2d 634.—Carr 109, 135.

H. Rouw Co. v. Railway Exp. Agency, TexCivApp–San Antonio, 238 SW2d 223, writ refused.—Carr 160.

H. Rouw Co. v. Railway Exp. Agency, TexCivApp–El Paso, 154 SW2d 143, writ refused.—App & E 758.3(2), 801(1); Commerce 80; Const Law 2506; Corp 634; Courts 28.

H. Rouw Co.; Texas & N. O. R. Co. v., TexCivApp–San Antonio, 271 SW2d 666, writ dism.—Carr 105(1), 135, 183, 186; Judgm 243.

H. Rouw Co. v. Texas & N. O. R. Co., TexCivApp–San Antonio, 260 SW2d 130.—Carr 32(2.1), 160; Statut 218.

H. Rouw Co. v. Texas & N. O. R. Co., TexCivApp–San Antonio, 260 SW2d 69.—Action 55; Inj 19, 26(4).

H. Rouw Co.; Texas & N. O. R. Co. v., TexCivApp–San Antonio, 225 SW2d 425, writ dism.—App & E 1047(1), 1050.1(6), 1050.1(9).

H. Rouw Co. v. Texas Citrus Commission, Tex, 247 SW2d 231, 151 Tex 182.—Const Law 2925, 3580; Licens 1, 7(3), 19(1).

H. Rouw Co. v. Thompson, TexCivApp–San Antonio, 297 SW2d 241.—Carr 130; Pretrial Proc 79; R R 17.

H. Rouw Co.; Thompson v., TexCivApp–San Antonio, 237 SW2d 662, ref nre.—Carr 76, 105(1), 135; Commerce 8(1.5), 12, 61(2).

H. Rouw Co. v. Thompson, TexCivApp–San Antonio, 194 SW2d 120, writ refused.—Dedi 55, 57; Em Dom 100(2).

Hruska; City of Houston v., Tex, 283 SW2d 739, 155 Tex 139.—Mun Corp 741.55.

Hruska; City of Houston v., TexCivApp–Waco, 272 SW2d 778, rev 283 SW2d 739, 155 Tex 139.—Equity 65(1); Estop 52(1); Mun Corp 741.55.

Hruska v. First State Bank of Deanville, Tex, 747 SW2d 783.—Bills & N 534; Estop 52(7), 52.10(1); Home 177(2); Liens 7.

Hruska v. First State Bank of Deanville, TexApp– Houston (1 Dist), 727 SW2d 732, writ gr, aff in part, rev in part 747 SW2d 783.—App & E 232(2); Bills & N 534; Fraud 7, 50; Home 97, 177(2); Hus & W 212; Liens 7.

HSAM Inc. v. Gatter, TexApp–San Antonio, 814 SW2d 887, writ dism by agreement.—Cons Cred 13, 18; Equity 34, 65(1).

HSA Mortg. Co. v. Gatter, TexApp–San Antonio, 814 SW2d 887. See HSAM Inc. v. Gatter.

H. S. Anderson Trucking Co.; Hernandez v., TexCiv-App–Beaumont, 370 SW2d 909, ref nre.—App & E 1062.1; Autos 1, 243(2); Evid 546.

H. Schumacher Oil Works, Inc. v. Hartford Fire Ins. Co., CA5 (Tex), 239 F2d 836.—Insurance 1894, 2128, 2143(1), 2199, 2201.

H. S. H., Inc.; Letsos v., TexCivApp–Waco, 592 SW2d 665, ref nre.—App & E 218.2(1), 262(1), 1003(9.1); Evid 215(5), 222(10), 265(1), 318(1), 318(3), 352(1); Fraud Conv 295.1, 300(1), 308(1).

H------ S------, Jr., Matter of, TexCivApp–Amarillo, 564 SW2d 446.—Infants 131, 197.

H.S.M. Acquisitions, Inc. v. West, TexApp–Corpus Christi, 917 SW2d 872, reh overr, and writ den.—App & E 173(2), 230, 758.1, 852, 863; Indem 81, 84; Judgm 91, 185(5), 185.1(2), 185.1(3), 185.1(4), 186, 297; Motions 58; Torts 217, 243.

HSM Kennewick, L.P., In re, BkrtcyNDTex, 347 BR 569.—Bankr 2391, 2395, 2535(1); Corp 1.3, 182.1(1); Ltd Liab Cos 36; Partners 76.

H.S.N., In re, TexApp–Corpus Christi, 69 SW3d 829.— App & E 946, 984(5); Child C 7, 121, 176, 637, 921(3), 921(4), 940, 943, 952; Child S 9, 234, 339(5), 448, 556(1), 600, 603.

HSP Foods, Inc.; Peerenboom v., TexApp–Waco, 910 SW2d 156.—App & E 223, 863, 934(1); Judgm 185.1(8), 185.3(21); Labor & Emp 2775(2); Neglig 202, 371, 379, 380, 383, 387, 1036, 1037(2), 1037(6), 1040(2), 1045(3), 1050, 1052, 1076, 1078, 1088, 1711, 1713, 1714.

HSP of Texas, Inc.; Easterly v., TexApp–Dallas, 772 SW2d 211.—Antitrust 208; Health 656; Prod Liab 5, 46.1; Sales 10, 246, 262.5.

HS Resources, Inc. v. Wingate, CA5 (Tex), 327 F3d 432. —Fed Civ Proc 224, 1747, 2471, 2533.1, 2557; Fed Cts 776, 818; Mines 73, 78.1(7); Paymt 82(1), 82(2).

HST Gathering Co., In re, WDTex, 125 BR 466.—Bankr 3771.

HST Gathering Co. v. Motor Service, Inc., TexApp– Corpus Christi, 683 SW2d 743.—App & E 846(5), 957(1); Judgm 135, 139, 143(5), 143(11), 145(2), 145(4), 146, 169.

Hsu; Wang v., TexApp–Houston (14 Dist), 899 SW2d 409, reh overr, and writ den.—App & E 113(2), 343.1, 346.2; Judgm 203, 297, 336, 340, 399, 868(1); New Tr 155.

H.T. Bartlett Builders, In re, BkrtcyWDTex, 149 BR 446. See Bartlett, In re.

H. T. Cab Co. v. Ginns, TexCivApp–Galveston, 280 SW2d 360, ref nre.—App & E 1036(2); Carr 247, 283(3), 316(1), 318(1), 318(12); Hus & W 260, 273(12).

H. T. D. Inv. Corp. v. Reeves, TexCivApp–Dallas, 413 SW2d 840.—App & E 1010.1(1); Brok 86(1).

H. Tebbs, Inc. v. Silver Eagle Distributors, Inc., Tex-App–Austin, 797 SW2d 80.—Admin Law 470, 673; Decl Judgm 306; Int Liq 124; Judgm 72, 90; Parties 38.

HTM Restaurants, Inc. v. Goldman, Sachs & Co., Tex-App–Houston (14 Dist), 797 SW2d 326, writ den.— Fraud 3, 16, 17, 23, 36; Land & Ten 130(1), 130(2); Pretrial Proc 481.

HTS Services, Inc. v. Hallwood Realty Partners, L.P., TexApp–Houston (1 Dist), 190 SW3d 108.—App & E 842(2), 893(1), 901, 930(1), 989, 994(3), 1008.1(1), 1008.1(2), 1012.1(4); Garn 1, 105, 162, 164.

HTT Headwear, Ltd.; Metromarketing Services, Inc. v., TexApp–Houston (14 Dist), 15 SW3d 190.—Accord 1, 11(1), 11(3), 22(2); Const Law 976; Frds St of 43, 46, 49, 159; Judgm 181(19), 185.3(8); Princ & A 81(1), 89(1); Statut 188, 190, 214.

Huag, In re, TexApp–Houston (1 Dist), 175 SW3d 449, reh overr.—Const Law 70.1(2); Mand 1, 28; Pretrial Proc 25, 91, 97, 155; Statut 176, 181(1), 181(2), 188, 195, 205, 206, 212.3, 212.6, 212.7.

Huang v. Don McGill Toyota, Inc., TexApp–Houston (14 Dist), 209 SW3d 674, reh overr.—Accord 1, 2(0.5), 10(1), 20, 23; Antitrust 194, 369; App & E 846(5), 866(1), 931(1), 931(5), 1008.1(1), 1008.1(2); Bailm 31(3); Fraud 58(1), 59(2), 59(3); Trial 388(3).

Huang; McGowen v., TexApp–Texarkana, 120 SW3d 452, reh overr, and review den.—Health 770; Judgm 540, 564(1), 565, 569, 570(3), 585(2), 654, 675(1), 677, 678(1), 678(2), 681, 686, 694; Mun Corp 745; Pretrial Proc 501, 517.1, 518.

Huawei Technologies, Co., Ltd.; Cisco Systems, Inc. v., EDTex, 266 FSupp2d 551.—Copyr 85; Inj 138.33.

Hubacek v. Ennis State Bank, Tex, 325 SW2d 124, 159 Tex 576.—App & E 1080, 1091(1), 1094(5).

Hubacek v. Ennis State Bank, Tex, 317 SW2d 30, 159 Tex 166, on remand 322 SW2d 409, writ dism 325 SW2d 124, 159 Tex 576.—App & E 1114; Bills & N 241, 281; Contracts 245(1), 245(2); Evid 384, 441(1), 441(11).

Hubacek; Ennis State Bank v., TexCivApp–Waco, 322 SW2d 409, writ dism 325 SW2d 124, 159 Tex 576.—Chat Mtg 278.

Hubacek; Ennis State Bank v., TexCivApp–Waco, 308 SW2d 60, rev 317 SW2d 30, 159 Tex 166, on remand 322 SW2d 409, writ dism 325 SW2d 124, 159 Tex 576.—App & E 230, 237(5), 238(2); Bills & N 300; Evid 441(1), 441(11).

Hubacek v. Manufacturers Cas. Ins. Co., TexCivApp–Waco, 247 SW2d 173, ref nre.—Contracts 95(4); Costs 230; Estop 52(1), 70(2); Judgm 5; Sheriffs 118, 157(4).

Hubacek; State v., TexApp–Fort Worth, 840 SW2d 751, reh den, and petition for discretionary review refused.—Autos 349(9).

Hubbard, Ex parte, TexCrimApp, 225 SW2d 196, 154 TexCrim 57.—Hab Corp 745.1, 812, 814, 841, 894.1.

Hubbard, Ex parte, TexCrimApp, 218 SW2d 209, 153 TexCrim 112.—Hab Corp 288, 296.

Hubbard, Ex parte, TexCrimApp, 209 SW2d 608, 151 TexCrim 514.—Bail 49.

Hubbard, In re, BkrtcyNDTex, 161 BR 173.—Bankr 3358, 3568(2), 3568(3).

Hubbard, In re, BkrtcySDTex, 333 BR 377, reconsideration den In re Salazar, 339 BR 622, appeal den Salazar v. Heitkamp, 193 FedAppx 281.—Bankr 2222.1, 2233(1), 2257, 3008.1, 3030, 3200; Statut 188, 189.

Hubbard, In re, BkrtcySDTex, 333 BR 373.—Bankr 2162, 2222.1; Statut 188, 189.

Hubbard, In re, BkrtcySDTex, 332 BR 285.—Bankr 2222.1, 2233(1); Statut 188, 189.

Hubbard, In re, BkrtcyWDTex, 96 BR 739.—Bankr 2323, 2324, 3273.1, 3274, 3278.1, 3279, 3282.1, 3284, 3286, 3288.1, 3315(1), 3315(2).

Hubbard; A. F. Day Const. Co. v., TexComApp, 141 SW2d 945, 135 Tex 228.—Cust & U 10.

Hubbard; A. F. Day Const. Co. v., TexCivApp–El Paso, 122 SW2d 698, rev 141 SW2d 945, 135 Tex 228.—App & E 1062.2; Contracts 221(1).

Hubbard v. Ammerman, CA5 (Tex), 465 F2d 1169, cert den 93 SCt 967, 410 US 910, 35 LEd2d 272.—Courts 508(2.1); Elections 12(9.1), 270, 273, 275; Fed Civ Proc 181; Fed Cts 5, 243, 433.

Hubbard; Barnsdall Oil Co. v., Tex, 109 SW2d 960, 130 Tex 476.—App & E 122, 878(6).

Hubbard v. Belton Independent School Dist., TexCivApp–Austin, 554 SW2d 4.—App & E 1024.4; Judgm 185.3(20).

Hubbard v. Blue Cross & Blue Shield Ass'n, CA5 (Tex), 42 F3d 942, cert den 115 SCt 2276, 515 US 1122, 132 LEd2d 280.—Fed Cts 14.1, 18, 595; Insurance 1117(3); Labor & Emp 407, 643; Rem of C 25(1); States 18.7, 18.15, 18.51.

Hubbard; Cale's Clean Scene Carwash, Inc. v., TexApp–Houston (14 Dist), 76 SW3d 784.—App & E 863, 930(1), 989, 1001(3); Costs 194.32, 207; Evid 590; Judgm 199(3.3); Stip 19.

Hubbard v. Cannon, TexCivApp–Beaumont, 124 SW2d 888, writ refused.—App & E 907(3).

Hubbard v. Capital Southwest Corp., TexCivApp–Waco, 448 SW2d 571.—Corp 1.4(1), 1.5(1), 1.5(2), 1.6(3), 380.

Hubbard; Carr v., TexApp–Houston (1 Dist), 664 SW2d 151, ref nre.—App & E 390, 846(5), 1071.1(2), 1106(5), 1169(7).

Hubbard; Consolidated Underwriters v., TexCivApp–Beaumont, 107 SW2d 908, writ refused.—App & E 1039(1); Work Comp 1241, 1252, 1323, 1829, 1916, 1919, 1937.

Hubbard v. Dalbosco, TexApp–Houston (1 Dist), 888 SW2d 224, reh den, writ den with per curiam opinion 907 SW2d 453.—Torts 121, 212, 220, 242.

Hubbard; Elmore v., TexCivApp–Beaumont, 332 SW2d 765, ref nre.—Adv Poss 110(3), 114(1); App & E 231(1), 758.3(5), 1062.1; Deeds 78; Evid 175; Judgm 199(3.14); Lim of Act 39(12); Mtg 37(2), 38(1); Trial 350.3(3).

Hubbard v. EMIS Software, Inc., CA5 (Tex), 44 F3d 348. See Thrift v. Hubbard, Estate of.

Hubbard v. Faulks, TexCivApp–Fort Worth, 159 SW2d 919.—App & E 389(3).

Hubbard v. Fidelity & Cas. Co. of N.Y., TexCivApp–Dallas, 285 SW2d 890, ref nre.—Judgm 139, 143(2), 143(3), 145(2), 153(1).

Hubbard; Graham v., TexCivApp–Beaumont, 406 SW2d 747.—Tresp to T T 38(2); Ven & Pur 228(3).

Hubbard v. Gray Tool Co., TexCivApp–Waco, 307 SW2d 599, ref nre.—Neglig 251, 1696; Prod Liab 47.

Hubbard v. Harris County Flood Control Dist., TexCivApp–Galveston, 286 SW2d 285, ref nre.—App & E 1002, 1078(1); Em Dom 149(1), 202(1), 224, 255; Evid 142(3), 543(3), 555.6(2), 555.6(7).

Hubbard; Housing Authority of City of Dallas v., TexCivApp–Dallas, 274 SW2d 165.—App & E 304; Em Dom 133, 149(2.1), 202(2), 221, 255; Evid 142(1); Trial 84(1).

Hubbard; James v., TexApp–San Antonio, 21 SW3d 558. —Action 6; App & E 19; Breach of P 18, 21; Divorce 172; Judgm 191, 215, 217, 276.

Hubbard; James v., TexApp–San Antonio, 985 SW2d 516. —Breach of P 21; Inj 189.

Hubbard; Jones v., TexCivApp–Waco, 302 SW2d 493, ref nre.—Bills & N 92(1); Evid 423(6); Judgm 185.2(1), 185.3(16); Parties 51(4); Princ & S 182; Trial 141.

Hubbard v. Lagow, Tex, 567 SW2d 489, on remand 576 SW2d 163, ref nre.—App & E 148; Bankr 3771.

Hubbard v. Lagow, TexCivApp–Austin, 576 SW2d 163, ref nre.—Judgm 18(1); Sec Tran 221, 223, 228, 232.

Hubbard v. Lagow, TexCivApp–Austin, 559 SW2d 133, writ gr, rev 567 SW2d 489, on remand 576 SW2d 163, ref nre.—App & E 138, 148; Parties 35.3.

Hubbard; Munke v., TexCivApp–Austin, 281 SW2d 165.— Damag 190.

Hubbard; Norris v., TexApp–Houston (1 Dist), 841 SW2d 538.—App & E 497(1), 1135.

Hubbard; North River Ins. Co. v., CA5 (Tex), 391 F2d 863.—Fed Civ Proc 2142.1; Fed Cts 842, 865; Work Comp 1360, 1581.

Hubbard v. Parkman, TexCivApp–Waco, 398 SW2d 401, ref nre.—Adv Poss 112, 114(1).

Hubbard; Poolquip–McNeme, Inc. v., BkrtcyWDTex, 96 BR 739. See Hubbard, In re.

Hubbard; Reisberg v., TexCivApp–Eastland, 326 SW2d 605.—Home 158; Judgm 735, 777.

Hubbard; Republic Bankers Life Ins. Co. v., TexCiv-App–Amarillo, 424 SW2d 519.—Insurance 3559; Plead 45.

Hubbard v. Shankle, TexApp–Fort Worth, 138 SW3d 474, review den.—App & E 863, 934(1); Contracts 1, 16, 47, 74; Estop 85; Fraud 3, 6, 7, 27; Frds St of 119(1); Impl & C C 2.1, 3; Judgm 178, 183, 185(2), 185(5); Trusts 1, 21(2), 25(1), 37, 62, 65, 72, 89(5), 91, 103(1), 107.

Hubbard; Southern Pac. Co. v., Tex, 297 SW2d 120, 156 Tex 525.—App & E 207; New Tr 31.

Hubbard; Southern Pac. Co. v., TexCivApp–El Paso, 290 SW2d 547, rev 297 SW2d 120, 156 Tex 525.—App & E 207, 1060.1(1), 1060.1(6); Damag 185(1); New Tr 31; Trial 122, 131(2), 133.3.

Hubbard v. State, TexCrimApp, 892 SW2d 909, on remand 903 SW2d 892.—Crim Law 855(1), 858(3).

Hubbard v. State, TexCrimApp, 798 SW2d 798.—Double J 97; Ind & Inf 132(7), 133(10).

Hubbard v. State, TexCrimApp, 739 SW2d 341, on remand 770 SW2d 31, petition for discretionary review refused.—Crim Law 641.8, 641.10(2), 1077.3.

Hubbard v. State, TexCrimApp, 579 SW2d 930.—Rob 11.

Hubbard v. State, TexCrimApp, 496 SW2d 924.—Crim Law 339.7(4), 379, 438(3), 641.3(9), 1035(2), 1166(10.10), 1169.1(5).

Hubbard v. State, TexCrimApp, 490 SW2d 849.—Burg 42(1); Searches 69.

Hubbard v. State, TexCrimApp, 390 SW2d 782.—Crim Law 730(13); Homic 1134.

Hubbard v. State, TexCrimApp, 320 SW2d 835, 167 TexCrim 379.—Autos 355(13).

Hubbard v. State, TexCrimApp, 287 SW2d 664.—Crim Law 1090.1(1).

Hubbard v. State, TexCrimApp, 217 SW2d 1019, 153 TexCrim 143.—Crim Law 770(2), 1169.12; Homic 1492.

Hubbard v. State, TexApp–Houston (1 Dist), 896 SW2d 359.—Controlled Subs 34, 46, 82; Crim Law 59(1), 552(1), 553, 1134(3), 1144.13(2.1), 1159.2(7), 1159.4(2), 1159.6; Sent & Pun 1139.

Hubbard v. State, TexApp–Fort Worth, 903 SW2d 892.—Crim Law 1162, 1165(1), 1169.1(1), 1177; Sent & Pun 313.

Hubbard v. State, TexApp–Fort Worth, 809 SW2d 316, petition for discretionary review gr, aff in part, rev in part 892 SW2d 909, on remand 903 SW2d 892.—Crim Law 338(1), 855(1), 858(3), 1153(1), 1174(2), 1174(6); Sent & Pun 207, 240, 313, 316, 1762, 1789(9); Statut 267(2).

Hubbard v. State, TexApp–Dallas, 770 SW2d 31, petition for discretionary review refused.—Const Law 4523, 4629; Costs 302.1(1); Courts 97(1); Crim Law 36.6, 37(2.1), 37(8), 444, 569, 627.6(3), 641.13(2.1), 641.13(7), 717, 720(1), 720(6), 722.3, 722.5, 723(3), 726, 739.1(1), 747, 772(6), 1109(3), 1137(1).

Hubbard v. State, TexApp–Dallas, 668 SW2d 419, petition for discretionary review gr, case remanded 739 SW2d 341, on remand 770 SW2d 31, petition for discretionary review refused.—Brib 1(1); Crim Law 641.10(3), 730(1), 730(3).

Hubbard v. State, TexApp–Dallas, 649 SW2d 167.—Crim Law 641.13(7), 1130(4).

Hubbard v. State, TexApp–Texarkana, 133 SW3d 797, reh overr, and petition for discretionary review refused.—Crim Law 38, 772(6); Homic 1493.

Hubbard v. State, TexApp–Beaumont, 753 SW2d 496, petition for discretionary review gr, aff 798 SW2d 798.—Crim Law 290; Double J 59, 95.1, 96, 99; Hab Corp 466.

Hubbard v. State, TexApp–Waco, 814 SW2d 402.—Bail 75.3, 77(1); Costs 194.25; Interest 39(2.20), 39(3).

Hubbard v. State, TexApp–Houston (14 Dist), 912 SW2d 842.—Crim Law 586, 590(2), 959, 1034, 1156(1), 1166(7).

Hubbard v. State, TexApp–Houston (14 Dist), 841 SW2d 33.—Hab Corp 223.

Hubbard v. State Mut. Life Assur. Companies of America, EDTex, 832 FSupp 1079.—Fed Civ Proc 2533.1, 2544, 2546; Insurance 1117(3); Labor & Emp 407, 425; Rem of C 25(1); States 18.51.

Hubbard v. Suniland Furniture Co., TexCivApp–Galveston, 302 SW2d 688, ref nre.—Hus & W 19(1), 19(9), 235(4); Trial 356(3).

Hubbard v. Tallal, TexComApp, 92 SW2d 1022, 127 Tex 242.—App & E 80(1), 802; Judgm 335(1), 335(3).

Hubbard; Tarrant County Water Control and Imp. Dist. No. 1 v., Tex, 433 SW2d 681.—Em Dom 146, 195.

Hubbard; Tarrant County Water Control and Imp. Dist. No. 1 v., TexCivApp–Tyler, 426 SW2d 330, writ gr, set aside 433 SW2d 681.—App & E 681; Em Dom 145(1), 149(2.1), 149(7), 150, 191(1), 194, 195, 224, 262(1), 262(4); Evid 474(16), 486, 488, 498.5, 501(7).

Hubbard; Texarkana Nat. Bank v., TexCivApp–Beaumont, 114 SW2d 389, writ dism.—Contracts 187(1); Debtor & C 10; Ex & Ad 434(1.1); Judgm 747(1); Mtg 309(3), 319(3); Release 12(1), 13(1); Wills 718.

Hubbard; Texas Emp. Ins. Ass'n v., Tex, 518 SW2d 529.—Work Comp 1297.

Hubbard v. Texas Employers Ins. Ass'n, TexCivApp–Texarkana, 510 SW2d 649, writ gr, rev Texas Emp Ins Ass'n v. Hubbard, 518 SW2d 529.—Judgm 185.3(13); Work Comp 1297.

Hubbard v. Texas Indem. Ins. Co., TexCivApp–El Paso, 136 SW2d 627.—App & E 758.3(1), 1040(9); Plead 252(2); Work Comp 1124, 1139, 1923.

Hubbard; Texas Indem. Ins. Co. v., TexCivApp–Waco, 138 SW2d 626, writ dism, correct.—App & E 1047(1); Infants 81, 82, 115; Trial 41(1), 312(1); Work Comp 51, 230, 452, 492, 619, 626, 642, 1446, 1478, 1571, 1619, 1719, 1919, 1920, 1958, 1967.

Hubbard, Estate of; Texas Soc., Daughters of the American Revolution, Inc. v., TexApp–Texarkana, 768 SW2d 858.—Pretrial Proc 582, 599, 676, 678, 690.

Hubbard, Estate of; Thrift v., CA5 (Tex), 44 F3d 348, reh den.—Contracts 143(2), 169, 175(3), 176(2); Corp 1.4(4), 1.6(3), 1.7(2); Fed Civ Proc 673, 674, 1925.1, 1938.1, 2174; Fed Cts 776, 813, 825.1; Interest 39(2.6), 39(2.30), 47(1), 60; Torts 212, 213, 215; Usury 6, 16, 22.

Hubbard; Thrift v., TexApp–San Antonio, 974 SW2d 70, reh den, and review den.—App & E 1064.1(2.1); Mal Pros 3, 18(1), 20, 32, 35(1), 56, 64(1), 64(2), 69, 71(2).

Hubbard; U.S. v., CA5 (Tex), 480 F3d 341.—Crim Law 1139; Infants 13; Obscen 18.1; Sent & Pun 95, 698; Statut 188, 201(1).

Hubbard; Walling v., TexCivApp–Houston, 389 SW2d 581, ref nre, and writ dism woj.—Des & Dist 81; Ex & Ad 7, 216(2), 219.9, 429, 458, 473(1), 473(4), 489, 495(1), 495(3), 495(5), 495(6), 495(7), 496(1), 511(3); Tax 3302, 3344.

Hubbard By and Through Hubbard v. Buffalo Independent School Dist., WDTex, 20 FSupp2d 1012.—Const Law 1291, 1343, 3006, 3617(1), 3620; Schools 45, 178.

Hubbard Enterprises, Inc.; Rimade Ltd. v., CA5 (Tex), 388 F3d 138.—Corp 1.4(3), 1.4(4), 1.6(2), 1.6(3); Fed Cts 776, 850.1; Fraud 17.

Hubbard Independent School Dist.; Foster v., TexCivApp–Waco, 619 SW2d 607, ref nre.—App & E 926(1); Judgm 185(5); Schools 103(1), 106.12(8).

Hubbell v. Donaldson, TexCivApp–Eastland, 243 SW2d 867.—Evid 478(1); Trial 350.2, 351.2(6).

Hubbell; Housing Authority of City of Dallas v., TexCivApp–Dallas, 325 SW2d 880, ref nre.—App & E 1050.2, 1062.1, 1172(2), 1178(6); Contracts 221(1), 326; Damag 218, 221(5.1); Extort 34; Labor & Emp 3141; Mun Corp 362(2), 374(4), 374(6), 1040; Refer 7(1); Torts 242, 436; Trial 350.5(1), 352.5(3), 352.5(4), 352.12.

Hubbell v. Lambert, TexCivApp–Fort Worth, 352 SW2d 518.—Plead 111.42(9).

Hubbell; U.S. v., CA5 (Tex), 323 F2d 197.—Atty & C 155; Int Rev 4767, 4773, 4783; Interpl 35.

Hubbell Steel Corp. v. Cook, BkrtcyEDTex, 126 BR 261. See Cook, In re.

Hubbell Steel Corp.; Cook v., BkrtcyEDTex, 126 BR 261. See Cook, In re.

Hubberd v. Crude Oil Marketing & Trading Co., TexCivApp–San Antonio, 119 SW2d 161, writ refused.—Interpl 2, 8(1), 11, 24, 35; Plead 127(2).

Hubbert; Harris v., TexCivApp–Eastland, 82 SW2d 726, writ refused.—App & E 499(3), 690(3); Bills & N 499, 527(1); Evid 332(7).

Hubbert v. State, TexCrimApp, 297 SW2d 180.—Crim Law 1090.1(1).

Hubbert v. State, TexApp–Texarkana, 91 SW3d 457, petition stricken, and petition for discretionary review refused.—Crim Law 1134(2), 1134(3); Sent & Pun 1948, 2009, 2012, 2018.

Hubble v. Burchard, TexCivApp–Corpus Christi, 396 SW2d 537.—App & E 1177(8); Labor & Emp 251, 256(1), 256(3).

Hubble v. Lone Star Contracting Corp., TexApp–Fort Worth, 883 SW2d 379, reh overr, and writ den.—App & E 989, 1008.1(2), 1012.1(7.1); Contracts 216, 313(1), 322(4); Lim of Act 50(1), 197(1); Mech Liens 260(6).

Hubble; Wilmans v., TexCivApp–Waco, 153 SW2d 228, writ refused wom.—App & E 931(1), 1011.1(19); Trial 382.

Hubbs; First Nat. Bank of Bellaire v., TexCivApp–Hous (1 Dist), 566 SW2d 375.—App & E 1177(2); Banks 119, 133, 134(1), 143(7), 154(1), 154(5); Trover 2.

Hubby v. U. S., CCA5 (Tex), 150 F2d 165.—Controlled Subs 21, 76; Crim Law 369.1, 369.2(1), 552(3).

Hubby-Reese Co., Inc.; Kinsey v., TexCivApp–Waco, 530 SW2d 846.—Paymt 39(5).

Hubenak v. San Jacinto Gas Transmission Co., Tex, 141 SW3d 172.—Courts 37(1); Em Dom 170, 178.5, 191(5).

Hubenak v. San Jacinto Gas Transmission Co., TexApp–Houston (1 Dist), 65 SW3d 791, reh overr, and review gr (4 pets), aff 141 SW3d 172.—Em Dom 170, 172, 191(1), 195, 235.

Hubenak v. San Jacinto Gas Transmission Co., TexApp–Eastland, 37 SW3d 133, reh overr, and review den, and reh of petition for review den.—Em Dom 170, 198(1); Judgm 181(15.1); Plead 111.36.

Huber v. Buder, TexCivApp–Fort Worth, 434 SW2d 177, ref nre.—App & E 931(5), 931(6), 1039(1); Child C 612, 614, 632; Child S 342; Courts 37(3); Equity 400; Refer 20; Trial 382, 397(2).

Huber; City of Houston v., TexCivApp–Houston, 311 SW2d 488.—App & E 205, 692(1); Em Dom 158, 170, 204, 235, 238(3), 238(4), 238(6), 259, 262(5); Evid 555.6(10).

Huber; Dibrell v., CA5 (Tex), 226 FedAppx 332.—Civil R 1395(8).

Huber; Massachusetts Newton Buying Corp. v., TexApp–Houston (14 Dist), 788 SW2d 100.—App & E 493; Corp 668(4), 668(13), 673; Judgm 17(2), 162(2).

Huber; Maxx, No. 275 v., TexApp–Houston (14 Dist, 788 SW2d 100. See Massachusetts Newton Buying Corp. v. Huber.

Huber v. Ryan, Tex, 627 SW2d 145.—App & E 907(3); Damag 220; Trial 358.

Huber; Ryan v., TexCivApp–Fort Worth, 618 SW2d 887, rev 627 SW2d 145.—App & E 554(1); Damag 221(7).

Huber; Schulenburg Mut. Life Ins. Ass'n v., TexCivApp–Galveston, 147 SW2d 277.—App & E 931(3); Insurance 1832(1), 2589(1).

Huber v. State, TexCrimApp, 207 SW2d 383, 151 TexCrim 306.—Crim Law 1086.14, 1092.9, 1099.7(3).

Huber; T.J. Maxx, No. 275 v., TexApp–Houston (14 Dist, 788 SW2d 100. See Massachusetts Newton Buying Corp. v. Huber.

Huber; West Tex. Utilities Co. v., TexCivApp–Eastland, 292 SW2d 702, ref nre.—Contracts 324(1).

Huber; Williams v., TexApp–Houston (14 Dist), 964 SW2d 84.—Health 611; Judgm 183, 185(2), 185.1(1), 185.3(21); Pretrial Proc 304.

Huber Contracting, Ltd., In re, BkrtcyWDTex, 347 BR 205.—Bankr 2606.1; Mech Liens 3, 115(1), 116, 198; Sec Tran 8.1, 11.1, 144.

Huber Corp. v. Positive Action Tool of Ohio Co., Inc., SDTex, 881 FSupp 279. See J.M. Huber Corp. v. Positive Action Tool of Ohio Co., Inc.

Huber Corp. v. Positive Action Tool of Ohio Co., Inc., SDTex, 879 FSupp 705. See J.M. Huber Corp. v. Positive Action Tool of Ohio Co., Inc.

Huber Corp. v. Santa Fe Energy Resources, Inc., TexApp–Houston (14 Dist, 871 SW2d 842. See J.M. Huber Corp. v. Santa Fe Energy Resources, Inc.

Huber, Formagus, Holstead and Guidry Ins., Inc.; Do v., TexApp–Beaumont, 728 SW2d 852.—Insurance 1673; Trial 178.

Huber, Hunt & Nichols, Inc.; Gilbert v., TexApp–San Antonio, 672 SW2d 9, ref nre 671 SW2d 869.—App & E 345.1, 395.

Huber, Hunt, Nichols, Inc.; Gilbert v., Tex, 671 SW2d 869.—App & E 338(2); Pretrial Proc 698.

Hubert v. Collard, TexCivApp–Austin, 141 SW2d 677, writ dism, correct.—Aband L P 5; Bailm 7, 32; Fixt 15, 33; Judgm 256(2); Lim of Act 65(1); Mines 86, 112(2).

Hubert v. Davis, TexApp–Tyler, 170 SW3d 706.—App & E 893(1); Covenants 1, 49, 134; Ease 1, 12(1), 12(2), 12(3), 25, 26(1), 37, 40, 42; Frds St of 113(2); Nav Wat 46(2).

Hubert v. Harte-Hanks Texas Newspapers, Inc., TexApp–Austin, 652 SW2d 546, ref nre.—Records 58, 63.

Hubert v. Illinois State Assistance Com'n, TexApp–Houston (14 Dist), 867 SW2d 160, reh den.—App & E 907(1); Bills & N 452(1); Const Law 3989; Judgm 183, 185(2), 185(6); Plead 245(1), 258(1).

Hubert; Jackson v., Tex, 234 SW2d 414, 149 Tex 451.—Attach 64; Courts 472.3, 472.7; Des & Dist 119(1); Ex & Ad 202, 289, 454; Garn 61; J P 39(3), 46(1), 48; Wills 830.

Hubert v. Jackson, TexCivApp–Waco, 229 SW2d 842, rev 234 SW2d 414, 149 Tex 451.—Courts 472.4(4); Des & Dist 130; Ex & Ad 271, 289; Wills 841.

Hubert v. State, TexCrimApp, 299 SW2d 293, 164 TexCrim 372.—Crim Law 1097(1), 1099.10.

Hubert v. State, TexApp–Houston (1 Dist), 652 SW2d 585, petition for discretionary review refused.—Crim Law 641.13(1), 641.13(2.1), 775(1), 1038.2; Ind & Inf 71.4(8), 188, 189(11); Rob 24.10.

Hubert; Walker v., TexCivApp–Austin, 337 SW2d 390.—App & E 959(3); Lim of Act 184; Plead 236(1), 259.

Hubert Burda Media, Inc.; Fielding v., CA5 (Tex), 415 F3d 419.—Const Law 3964, 3965(8); Corp 1.5(1); Courts 12(2.1); Fed Civ Proc 1269.1; Fed Cts 76.25, 82, 86, 94, 96, 417, 776, 820, 895.

Hubert Lumber Co. v. Baumgart, TexCivApp–Hous (1 Dist), 464 SW2d 728.—Lim of Act 28(1), 197(1); Lis Pen 22(1); Mech Liens 260(6).

Hubert Lumber Co. v. King, TexCivApp–Hous (1 Dist), 468 SW2d 503, ref nre.—Mech Liens 61, 170, 173; Mtg 151(3).

Hubicki v. Festina, Tex, 226 SW3d 405.—App & E 914(1); Judgm 17(1), 17(9), 99; Proc 73, 82, 150.

Hubicki v. Festina, TexApp–Dallas, 156 SW3d 897, reh overr, review gr, rev 226 SW3d 405.—App & E 5, 859, 865, 931(1), 989, 1010.1(1); Damag 140, 194; Fraud 3, 12, 32, 50, 58(1), 58(3); Proc 73, 82, 145.

Hubler; Bank of America, N.A. v., TexApp–Waco, 211 SW3d 859, reh overr, and review gr, judgment vac, and remanded by agreement.—Action 27(1); App & E 219(2); Banks 129, 139, 231; Contracts 326; Costs 194.16, 194.32, 207; Evid 474(17); Negilg 463.

Hubler v. City of Corpus Christi, TexCivApp–Corpus Christi, 564 SW2d 816, ref nre.—App & E 917(1), 960(1); Em Dom 1, 2(1), 2(1.1), 2(10), 63, 138, 147, 266, 293(1); Lim of Act 19(1), 32(2), 180(2), 194.1; Plead 228.14, 228.23; Pretrial Proc 690.

Hubler; Oshman v., TexApp–Corpus Christi, 730 SW2d 6, ref nre.—Costs 260(5); Interest 39(3).

Hubler v. Oshman, TexApp–Corpus Christi, 700 SW2d 694.—App & E 946, 1010.1(1); Evid 588; Plead 236(3), 241; Spec Perf 65, 97(1), 114(4), 126(2), 131; Ven & Pur 170.

Hubler v. State, TexCrimApp, 437 SW2d 571.—Crim Law 1184(4.1).

Hubler v. State, TexCrimApp, 226 SW2d 867.—Crim Law 1094(3).

Huckabay v. Hughes Tool Co., TexCivApp–Galveston, 122 SW2d 233, dism.—Work Comp 2084, 2107.

Huckabay v. Irving Health Care System, TexApp–Dallas, 879 SW2d 64. See Huckabay v. Irving Hosp. Authority.

Huckabay v. Irving Health Care System, TexApp–Dallas, 802 SW2d 758. See Huckabay v. Irving Hosp. Foundation.

Huckabay v. Irving Hosp. Authority, TexApp–Dallas, 879 SW2d 64, writ gr, and writ vac, and writ dism by agreement.—Const Law 2473; Courts 92; Health 834(1).

Huckabay v. Irving Hosp. Foundation, TexApp–Dallas, 802 SW2d 758, writ den, appeal after remand 879 SW2d 64, writ gr, and writ vac, and writ dism by agreement.—App & E 863; Health 823(12); Judgm 181(5.1), 181(11), 181(33), 185(2), 185.3(21); Mun Corp 741.50.

Huckabay v. Moore, CA5 (Tex), 142 F3d 233.—Civil R 1113, 1116(2), 1147, 1505(7), 1507, 1527, 1532, 1719, 1740, 1764, 1765; Damag 50.10; Fed Civ Proc 2470, 2497.1, 2538; Fed Cts 714, 766, 802, 915.

Huckabee v. Hansen, TexCivApp–Corpus Christi, 422 SW2d 606, 27 ALR3d 1380.—Wills 570.

Huckabee; HBO, A Division of Time Warner Entertainment Co., L.P. v., TexApp–Houston (14 Dist), 995 SW2d 152, review gr, aff 19 SW3d 413.—App & E 856(1), 863, 1175(1); Judgm 181(33); Libel 4, 51(5), 101(1), 112(2).

Huckabee v. Industrial Underwriters Ins. Co., TexCivApp–Amarillo, 465 SW2d 185.—Work Comp 998, 1653.

Huckabee; Lomas & Nettleton Co. v., Tex, 558 SW2d 863, reh den.—Elect of Rem 3(4), 15.

Huckabee v. Lomas & Nettleton Co., TexCivApp–Waco, 550 SW2d 371, rev 558 SW2d 863, reh den.—Elect of Rem 15.

Huckabee; N. R. C., Inc. v., TexCivApp–Austin, 539 SW2d 375, ref nre.—Fraud 12; Ven & Pur 33, 36(1).

Huckabee v. State, TexCivApp–Beaumont, 431 SW2d 927, ref nre.—App & E 971(2); Em Dom 107, 262(5); Evid 317(6), 501(7), 546, 555.6(6).

Huckabee v. Time Warner Entertainment Co. L.P., Tex, 19 SW3d 413.—Const Law 2170; Judgm 185(2), 185(5), 185.3(21), 186, 934(1); Libel 4, 10(4), 49, 51(5), 112(2), 128.

Huckabee; U.S. Fire Ins. Co. v., TexCivApp–Eastland, 452 SW2d 565, ref nre.—Trial 131(1); Work Comp 1533, 1630, 1653.

Huckabee; Waddell v., TexApp–Houston (1 Dist), 807 SW2d 455, subsequent mandamus proceeding 813 SW2d 503, reh of motion for mandamus overr.—App & E 80(6); Divorce 143(1), 143(2), 150.1(1); Judgm 216; Mand 1, 4(1), 4(3), 4(4), 10, 12, 28, 53, 147, 172; Refer 35.

Huckaby v. A.G. Perry & Son, Inc., TexApp–Texarkana, 20 SW3d 194, review den.—App & E 205, 216(1), 232(2), 882(8), 970(2), 1001(3), 1050.1(1), 1050.1(4), 1056.1(1); Autos 201(9), 243(5), 243(16), 244(11), 245(14); Evid 146, 219.25(2), 219.75(1), 359(1), 542; Neglig 1635; Pretrial Proc 3; Trial 43, 56, 79.

Huckaby v. Gans & Smith Ins. Agency, Inc., EDTex, 293 FSupp2d 715.—Rem of C 36, 107(7).

Huckaby v. Henderson, TexApp–Houston (1 Dist), 635 SW2d 129, ref nre.—App & E 242(1), 692(1), 930(3); Can of Inst 46; Deeds 207; Trial 350.1.

Huckaby v. Huckaby, TexCivApp–Hous (1 Dist), 436 SW2d 601, ref nre.—Wills 290, 297(4), 306, 324(4), 331(2).

Huckaby; Huckaby v., TexCivApp–Hous (1 Dist), 436 SW2d 601, ref nre.—Wills 290, 297(4), 306, 324(4), 331(2).

Huckaby v. State, TexCrimApp, 253 SW2d 49.—Crim Law 1090.1(1).

Huckaby; U.S. v., CA5 (Tex), 776 F2d 564, reh den 780 F2d 532, cert den 106 SCt 1468, 475 US 1085, 89 LEd2d 724.—Int Rev 4490, 4512, 4513.

Huckaby v. U.S. Dept. of Treasury, CA5 (Tex), 804 F2d 297.—Int Rev 4482, 5342.

Huckaby v. U.S. Dept. of Treasury, I.R.S., CA5 (Tex), 794 F2d 1041, reh den 804 F2d 297.—Int Rev 4482, 4515.

Huckaby; Westerfeld v., Tex, 474 SW2d 189.—Trusts 30.5(1); Wills 91.

Huckaby; Westerfeld v., TexCivApp–Hous (1 Dist), 462 SW2d 324, writ gr, aff 474 SW2d 189.—Trusts 30.5(1); Wills 91.

Huckeby v. Frozen Food Exp., CA5 (Tex), 555 F2d 542. —Civil R 1530; Fed Civ Proc 1827.1, 2575; Fed Cts 521, 526.1, 530, 599, 600, 660.1, 660.5; Mand 1, 4(1).

Huckeby v. Frozen Food Exp., NDTex, 427 FSupp 967, 23 Wage & Hour Cas (BNA) 212.—Civil R 1168, 1549, 1553; Labor & Emp 2463, 2481(7).

Huckeby v. Lawdermilk, TexApp–Eastland, 709 SW2d 331.—Child C 602; Child S 242, 460; Divorce 223.

Hucker v. City of Beaumont, EDTex, 147 FSupp2d 565. —Evid 508, 545, 555.2.

Hucker v. City of Beaumont, EDTex, 144 FSupp2d 696. —Civil R 1351(1), 1352(1), 1398; Fed Civ Proc 2491.5, 2515; Mun Corp 723; Offic 114.

Huckert v. State, TexCrimApp, 264 SW2d 121, 159 Tex-Crim 368.—Autos 355(6), 357; Crim Law 656(1), 706(3), 720(7.1), 1166.22(7).

Huckin v. Connor, TexApp–Houston (14 Dist), 928 SW2d 180, reh overr, and writ den.—Afft 1, 12; App & E 852, 1079; Estop 68(2); Judgm 185.1(3), 185.1(4).

Huckleberry; American Nat. Ins. Co. v., NDTex, 638 FSupp 233.—Insurance 1091(1), 3484, 3557.

Huckleberry v. Iverson Supply Co., TexCivApp–El Paso, 325 SW2d 445, ref nre.—Contracts 155; Cust & U 20; Princ & A 23(1), 123(11), 149(1), 150(2); Trial 365.1(5); Witn 319.

Huckleberry v. Wilson, TexCivApp–El Paso, 284 SW2d 205, dism.—Ven & Pur 79, 341(4).

Huckman v. Campbell, TexCivApp–San Antonio, 255 SW2d 591.—App & E 544(1), 554(2), 554(3), 907(3).

Huckman v. Campbell, TexCivApp–San Antonio, 252 SW2d 604, mandamus overr.—App & E 624.

Hudco Pub. Co., Inc.; Southwest Offset, Inc. v., CA5 (Tex), 622 F2d 149.—Const Law 3964; Corp 665(1); Fed Cts 84, 96, 97, 387.

Huddle v. Cleveland, TexCivApp–San Antonio, 297 SW2d 737, ref nre.—Adv Poss 60(1); Ven & Pur 80, 93, 267, 269.

Huddle v. Huddle, Tex, 696 SW2d 895, on remand 1986 WL 9866, dism.—Jury 25(6), 26.

Huddle; Huddle v., Tex, 696 SW2d 895, on remand 1986 WL 9866, dism.—Jury 25(6), 26.

Huddle v. Huddle, TexApp–Houston (14 Dist), 687 SW2d 58, ref nre, and writ withdrawn, and writ gr, rev 696 SW2d 895, on remand 1986 WL 9866, dism.—App & E 949; Jury 25(2), 25(6), 26.

Huddle; Huddle v., TexApp–Houston (14 Dist), 687 SW2d 58, ref nre, and writ withdrawn, and writ gr, rev 696

SW2d 895, on remand 1986 WL 9866, dism.—App & E 949; Jury 9, 25(2), 25(6), 26.

Huddle v. Huddle, TexCivApp–Waco, 614 SW2d 630.—Anim 26(5); App & E 916(3); Plead 111.26, 111.38, 111.43; Venue 5.2.

Huddle; Huddle v., TexCivApp–Waco, 614 SW2d 630.—Anim 26(5); App & E 916(3); Plead 111.26, 111.38, 111.43; Venue 5.2.

Huddlen v. State, TexCrimApp, 424 SW2d 633.—Burg 41(1); Crim Law 698(1).

Huddleston, Ex parte, TexCrimApp, 194 SW2d 401, 149 TexCrim 388.—Crim Law 641.5(1), 641.7(1), 995(1), 1144.1; Hab Corp 288, 448.1, 535; Infants 68.7(2); Sent & Pun 1895, 1905.

Huddleston, In re, BkrtcyEDTex, 120 BR 399.—Atty & C 21.5(6); Bankr 3030.

Huddleston v. Allen, TexCivApp–Beaumont, 85 SW2d 1094.—Deeds 38(1), 111.

Huddleston; B. B. Smith Co. v., TexCivApp–San Antonio, 545 SW2d 559, ref nre.—Spec Perf 121(11); Ven & Pur 79.

Huddleston v. Case Power & Equipment Co., TexApp–Dallas, 748 SW2d 102.—Acct Action on 13; Plead 228.14, 301(1).

Huddleston; City of Amarillo v., Tex, 152 SW2d 1088, 137 Tex 226.—App & E 1015(1), 1069.1; Trial 347, 355(1), 365.2.

Huddleston v. City of Amarillo, TexCivApp–Amarillo, 131 SW2d 1095, rev 152 SW2d 1088, 137 Tex 226.—App & E 1015(5), 1069.1; Trial 306.

Huddleston; Crown Const. Co., Inc. v., TexApp–San Antonio, 961 SW2d 552.—App & E 173(2), 223, 343.1; Contracts 16; Equity 65(1); Judgm 185.3(14); Land & Ten 86(1), 86(2), 86(3).

Huddleston v. Dallas Power & Light Co., TexCivApp–Fort Worth, 93 SW2d 199, writ dism.—Electricity 16(1), 16(5), 16(6); Land & Ten 164(1).

Huddleston v. Fergeson, TexCivApp–Amarillo, 564 SW2d 448.—Evid 384, 442(6); Judgm 251(1), 252(1); Propty 10; Trial 105(1); Ven & Pur 143, 157, 341(2), 341(3).

Huddleston; Herman & MacLean v., USTex, 103 SCt 683, 459 US 375, 74 LEd2d 548, on remand 705 F2d 775.—Sec Reg 27.34, 60.34, 60.37, 60.63(1).

Huddleston v. Herman & Maclean, CA5 (Tex), 705 F2d 775.—Fed Cts 896.1, 939.

Huddleston v. Herman & MacLean, CA5 (Tex), 640 F2d 534, cert gr 102 SCt 1766, 456 US 914, 72 LEd2d 173, aff in part, rev in part 103 SCt 683, 459 US 375, 74 LEd2d 548, on remand 705 F2d 775.—Contrib 5(1), 5(6.1); Evid 155(8), 333(1), 352(1), 506, 531; Fed Civ Proc 1408, 2174, 2234.1; Fed Cts 415, 433; Refer 3; Sec Reg 25.70, 25.75, 27.50, 60.27(2), 60.45(1), 60.47, 60.48(1), 60.57, 60.62, 60.63(1), 60.63(4), 148, 154.1, 155, 157.1, 256.1.

Huddleston v. Huddleston, TexCivApp–Waco, 346 SW2d 931, ref nre.—Child C 7, 76, 413, 555, 921(1); Divorce 165(5.5); Trial 397(2).

Huddleston; Huddleston v., TexCivApp–Waco, 346 SW2d 931, ref nre.—Child C 7, 76, 413, 555, 921(1); Divorce 165(5.5); Trial 397(2).

Huddleston v. Jackson, TexCivApp–Waco, 322 SW2d 23, ref nre.—App & E 215(1), 218.2(7), 263(1), 930(1); Des & Dist 90(4); Estop 110.

Huddleston; Kunz v., TexCivApp–El Paso, 546 SW2d 685, ref nre.—Partners 70, 346; Trial 232(2), 350.3(1).

Huddleston v. Maurry, TexApp–Dallas, 841 SW2d 24, writ dism woj.—App & E 70(8), 93; Autos 196; Judgm 181(27), 181(33), 185(4); Mun Corp 747(3); Offic 116.

Huddleston; Missouri-Kansas-Texas R. Co. v., TexCivApp–Fort Worth, 384 SW2d 731, ref nre.—App & E 1170.3, 1170.6, 1170.7; Neglig 291; Trial 125(1), 351.5(1).

Huddleston; National Realty v., TexApp–Austin, 886 SW2d 526. See NRC, Inc. v. Huddleston.

Huddleston v. Nelson Bunker Hunt Trust Estate, NDTex, 117 BR 231, aff 935 F2d 1290.—Bankr 3555, 3566.1, 3567.

Huddleston v. Nelson Bunker Hunt Trust Estate, NDTex, 109 BR 197.—Bankr 3781; Const Law 4008, 4478; Fed Civ Proc 2393; Fed Cts 12.1, 29.1, 541, 723.1; Witn 293.5.

Huddleston v. Nelson Bunker Hunt Trust Estate, NDTex, 102 BR 71.—Bankr 3777, 3790.

Huddleston; NRC, Inc. v., TexApp–Austin, 886 SW2d 526, reh overr.—Antitrust 390; App & E 930(3), 989, 1003(6); Damag 15; Dep & Escr 13; Fraud 62.

Huddleston v. Pace, TexApp–San Antonio, 790 SW2d 47, writ den.—Costs 194.10, 194.14, 194.16, 194.25, 194.32, 194.34; Damag 48, 49.10, 221(8); Judgm 251(1); Land & Ten 172(2).

Huddleston; Republic Natural Gas Co. v., TexCivApp–San Antonio, 120 SW2d 319.—Lim of Act 13.

Huddleston v. Speegle, TexCivApp–Waco, 557 SW2d 178, ref nre.—Judgm 143(2), 153(1), 162(2); New Tr 116.3, 152; Trial 21.

Huddleston v. State, TexCrimApp, 661 SW2d 111.—Ind & Inf 110(42); Kidnap 32, 36, 39.

Huddleston v. State, TexApp–Houston (1 Dist), 997 SW2d 319.—Crim Law 273(4.1); Witn 52(7).

Huddleston; State v., TexApp–Austin, 164 SW3d 711.—Arrest 63.5(4), 68(4); Autos 335, 349(2.1); Crim Law 394.6(5), 1028, 1030(1), 1036.1(4), 1134(6), 1139, 1158(4).

Huddleston; Stelzer v., TexCivApp–Tyler, 526 SW2d 710, dism.—Elections 55, 271, 298(1); Mun Corp 89; Schools 97(4).

Huddleston; Stewart Title Co. v., Tex, 608 SW2d 611.—Divorce 252.4.

Huddleston; Stewart Title Co. v., TexCivApp–San Antonio, 598 SW2d 321, ref nre 608 SW2d 611.—Decl Judgm 342; Divorce 252.4; Fraud 50.

Huddleston; Tatum v., TexApp–Texarkana, 711 SW2d 367.—App & E 842(10), 1004(8); Damag 163(1), 185(1).

Huddleston v. Texas Commerce Bank, N.A., TexApp–Dallas, 756 SW2d 343, writ den.—App & E 758.1; Bankr 2393, 2462; Estop 110; Mtg 375.

Huddleston; Texas Dept. of Public Safety v., TexCivApp–Dallas, 529 SW2d 559.—App & E 781(4).

Huddleston v. Traders & General Ins. Co., TexCivApp–Texarkana, 465 SW2d 418, ref nre.—Insurance 3155, 3165.

Huddleston; U.S. v., CA5 (Tex), 929 F2d 1030.—Crim Law 273.1(2), 1134(3); Sent & Pun 824, 995.

Huddleston; V. J. Keefe, Inc. v., TexCivApp–Beaumont, 459 SW2d 224.—App & E 216(1), 231(9), 1170.9(6); Damag 163(1), 221(6).

Huddleston v. Western Nat. Bank, TexCivApp–Amarillo, 577 SW2d 778, ref nre.—Banks 45; Corp 190; Jury 25(2), 26, 28(6); Parties 35.13; Plead 301(3), 422; Pretrial Proc 644.

Huddleston Co., Inc., In re, BkrtcyEDTex, 120 BR 399. See Huddleston, In re.

Huddy v. Fruehauf Corp., CA5 (Tex), 953 F2d 955, reh den, cert den 113 SCt 89, 506 US 828, 121 LEd2d 52.—Fed Cts 409.1, 776; Prod Liab 3.

Hudenburg v. Neff, TexApp–Houston (14 Dist), 643 SW2d 517, ref nre, cert den 104 SCt 348, 464 US 937, 78 LEd2d 313.—App & E 223, 934(1); Judgm 184.

Hudgens v. Bain Equipment & Tube Sales, Inc., TexCivApp–Corpus Christi, 459 SW2d 873.—Partners 195; Plead 111.38; Sales 369; Venue 7.5(7).

Hudgens v. Goen, TexApp–Fort Worth, 673 SW2d 420, ref nre.—Antitrust 43, 103(1); Judgm 199(1); Trademarks 1104, 1420, 1437, 1696, 1714(3).

Hudgens; Mercantile Nat. Bank at Dallas v., TexCivApp–Fort Worth, 412 SW2d 364, ref nre.—Contracts 74, 348; Damag 71, 71.5; Frds St of 14, 23(2), 158(1); Guar 25(3); Princ & A 123(3).

Hudgens v. Mutual Ben. Health & Acc. Ass'n, TexCiv-App–Fort Worth, 207 SW2d 447, ref nre.—Insurance 2062.

Hudgens; Schleicher County v., TexCivApp–El Paso, 255 SW2d 927.—Lim of Act 41; Pub Lands 173(14); Ven & Pur 93, 176, 341(5).

Hudgens; Seale v., TexCivApp–San Antonio, 538 SW2d 459, dism.—Princ & S 182; Subrog 7(7); Venue 7(6).

Hudgens v. State, TexCrimApp, 709 SW2d 648.—Crim Law 1181.5(8).

Hudgens v. State, TexApp–Dallas, 675 SW2d 588, petition for discretionary review gr, aff as reformed 709 SW2d 648.—Controlled Subs 8; Crim Law 219, 1189.

Hudgens v. Texas Cas. Ins. Co., TexCivApp–Amarillo, 491 SW2d 230, writ dism by agreement.—Judgm 185.1(2); Work Comp 1065.

Hudgens v. Texas Cas. Ins. Co., TexCivApp–Amarillo, 465 SW2d 832, ref nre.—App & E 624; Judgm 183, 193.

Hudgeons v. State, TexCrimApp, 384 SW2d 720.—Crim Law 366(3); Obscen 17.

Hudgins, In re, BkrtcyEDTex, 188 BR 938, aff Security Bank of Whitesboro v. Hudgins, 1998 WL 34262016.—Bankr 2422.5(1), 2422.5(5), 2424, 2430.1; Compromise 5(1), 7.1, 11, 13; Contracts 15, 32, 35, 218, 221(1), 221(2), 227, 309(1), 317; Inj 150; Mtg 413; Records 32.

Hudgins; Edwards v., TexCivApp–Waco, 347 SW2d 745.—App & E 1177(7); Deeds 211(1); Evid 474(4); New Tr 44(2).

Hudgins; Hunt v., TexCivApp–Waco, 168 SW2d 703.—Const Law 1065, 1107, 1114, 1280; Inj 94, 123, 128(9); Trial 351.2(4).

Hudgins; James v., TexApp–El Paso, 876 SW2d 418, writ den.—App & E 497(1), 557, 758.1, 901, 907(3), 946; Costs 260(1), 260(4); Evid 536, 546.

Hudgins; Kinser v., TexCivApp–Austin, 275 SW2d 847.—Guard & W 25; Infants 10; Mental H 116.1.

Hudgins v. Krawetz, TexCivApp–San Antonio, 558 SW2d 131.—Dep & Escr 21; Plead 49, 111.23, 111.38.

Hudgins v. Lincoln Nat. Life Ins. Co., EDTex, 144 FSupp 192.—Deeds 90, 93, 120; Evid 20(1); Mines 55(4), 79.3; Partit 19.

Hudgins v. Security Bank of Whitesboro, BkrtcyED-Tex, 188 BR 938. See Hudgins, In re.

Hudgins; Stoner v., TexCivApp–Fort Worth, 568 SW2d 898, ref nre.—App & E 1064.2, 1151(1), 1158, 1177(8); Damag 63, 186; Statut 181(1), 184; Trial 194(15).

Hudgins; Texas Emp. Ins. Ass'n v., TexCivApp–Waco, 294 SW2d 446, ref nre.—Work Comp 51, 1286, 1920, 1927, 1958, 1966, 1968(6).

Hudgins; Weddle v., TexCivApp–Tyler, 470 SW2d 218, ref nre.—App & E 302(5); Autos 178, 244(41.1); Damag 139.

Hudiburg v. Crown Life Ins. Co., TexCivApp–Fort Worth, 600 SW2d 376, ref nre.—Insurance 1772, 2570.

Hudiburg Chevrolet, Inc.; General Motors Corp. v., Tex, 199 SW3d 249, reh den.—Indem 72, 81; Judgm 181(15.1); Prod Liab 23.1, 24.

Hudiburg Chevrolet, Inc. v. General Motors Corp., Tex-App–Dallas, 114 SW3d 680, reh overr, and review gr (2 pets), aff in part, rev in part 199 SW3d 249, reh den.—App & E 852, 856(1); Const Law 2604; Indem 72; Judgm 181(15.1), 183, 185.3(1); Neglig 202, 371, 379, 380, 384, 387.

Hudiburg Chevrolet, Inc. v. Globe Indem. Co., Tex, 394 SW2d 792, on remand 396 SW2d 954.—Insurance 2153(1), 2706(1), 2733; Judgm 199(3.13); Larc 3(3), 8.

Hudiburg Chevrolet, Inc. v. Globe Indem. Co., TexCiv-App–Fort Worth, 396 SW2d 954.—Insurance 2732.

Hudiburg Chevrolet, Inc. v. Globe Indem. Co., TexCiv-App–Fort Worth, 383 SW2d 65, writ gr, aff in part, rev in part 394 SW2d 792, on remand 396 SW2d 954.—Insurance 2652, 2660, 2699.

Hudiburgh v. Palvic, TexCivApp–Beaumont, 274 SW2d 94, ref nre.—App & E 1175(5); Autos 242(6), 244(11),

245(30), 247; Damag 216(8); Evid 589, 596(1); Labor & Emp 55, 3045, 3094(4), 3096(7), 3105(7); Trial 133.6(6).

Hudler v. Hudler, TexCivApp–Austin, 229 SW2d 853.—App & E 87(7); Divorce 254(2); Judgm 135, 139, 216.

Hudler; Hudler v., TexCivApp–Austin, 229 SW2d 853.—App & E 87(7); Divorce 254(2); Judgm 135, 139, 216.

Hudler-Tye Const., Inc. v. Pettijohn & Pettijohn Plumbing, Inc., TexApp–Fort Worth, 632 SW2d 219.—Estop 90(1); Garn 87, 88, 96; Proc 145.

Hudman; City of Sherman v., TexApp–Dallas, 996 SW2d 904, review gr, judgment vac, and remanded by agreement.—App & E 842(2), 863, 893(1), 916(1); Courts 35; Decl Judgm 212; Elections 3, 10, 227(1), 278; Mun Corp 58, 61, 108.1, 108.3; Plead 104(1); Pretrial Proc 554; Statut 188; Trial 404(6).

Hudman v. John Deere Co., TexCivApp–Dallas, 620 SW2d 752.—Plead 111.9, 111.15, 111.42(5).

Hudman; Mutual Ben. Health and Acc. Ass'n v., Tex, 398 SW2d 110.—Insurance 2589(1), 2589(2), 2590(1).

Hudman; Mutual Ben. Health & Acc. Ass'n v., TexCiv-App–Austin, 385 SW2d 509, writ gr, rev 398 SW2d 110.—Evid 5(2); Insurance 2588(2), 2589(1), 2590(1), 2607, 2653.

Hudmon v. Foster, TexCivApp–Austin, 210 SW 262, writ gr, rev 231 SW 346.—App & E 1008.1(1).

Hudnall v. State, TexCrimApp, 432 SW2d 910.—Crim Law 1184(2).

Hudnall v. Tyler Bank & Trust Co., Tex, 458 SW2d 183.—App & E 934(2); Banks 153, 154(1); Judgm 185(2), 185.3(5); Set-Off 33(1).

Hudnall v. Tyler Bank & Trust Co., TexCivApp–Tyler, 448 SW2d 503, rev 458 SW2d 183.—App & E 934(1); Banks 121, 130(1), 133, 153; Bills & N 496(2), 523, 524; Contracts 252, 253; Evid 67(1); Judgm 185(2); Propty 9.

Hudnell; Jones v., CA5 (Tex), 210 FedAppx 427.—Prisons 4(1), 4(5), 17(2).

Hudnell; Ward v., CA5 (Tex), 366 F2d 247, 5 ALR Fed 955.—Armed S 34(2); Fed Civ Proc 1829, 1835; U S 47.

Hudson, Ex parte, Tex, 917 SW2d 24.—Contempt 70; Double J 34; Inj 218, 232.

Hudson, Ex parte, TexCrimApp, 655 SW2d 206.—Sent & Pun 1169, 1173, 1174.

Hudson, Ex parte, TexCrimApp, 328 SW2d 96, 168 Tex-Crim 345.—Sent & Pun 1132.

Hudson, Ex parte, TexCrimApp, 283 SW2d 956, 162 TexCrim 210.—Burg 49.

Hudson, In re, BkrtcyNDTex, 182 BR 741, aff 107 F3d 355.—Bankr 2164.1, 3348.25, 3349; Child S 23, 129; Child 30, 75; Fed Civ Proc 2470, 2470.1, 2539, 2544; Judgm 632, 634, 636, 663, 668(1), 715(1), 720, 724, 828.21(2).

Hudson, Matter of, CA5 (Tex), 107 F3d 355.—Bankr 3341, 3349, 3350(6), 3420(2), 3422(11), 3779, 3782, 3789.1.

Hudson; AEP Texas Cent. Co. v., WDTex, 441 FSupp2d 810.—Electricity 11(4), 11.3(1), 11.3(6); States 18.73.

Hudson; AEP Texas North Co. v., WDTex, 389 FSupp2d 759, aff 473 F3d 581.—Electricity 11(4), 11.3(1), 11.3(4), 11.3(6); Fed Civ Proc 2500.5, 2534, 2543; States 18.3, 18.73.

Hudson v. Arkansas Louisiana Gas Co., TexApp–Texarkana, 626 SW2d 561, ref nre.—Em Dom 1; Judgm 181(2), 181(3), 181(7), 185(2), 185(5), 186.

Hudson; Bach v., TexCivApp–Corpus Christi, 596 SW2d 673.—Contracts 99(2); Deeds 68(1.5), 211(1); Evid 67(2), 103, 132, 524; Wills 31, 55(1).

Hudson v. Blackwell, TexCivApp–Fort Worth, 151 SW2d 889, dism.—App & E 771, 773(2).

Hudson v. Buddie's Super Markets, Inc., TexCivApp–Fort Worth, 488 SW2d 143.—App & E 758.3(2), 758.3(11), 766, 854(2), 1078(1).

Hudson; Buehring v., TexCivApp–Galveston, 219 SW2d 810, writ refused.—App & E 218.2(5.1); Home 128; Judgm 199(3.14); Ven & Pur 21, 350.

Hudson v. Caffey, TexCivApp–Texarkana, 179 SW2d 1017, writ refused wom.—Deeds 90, 144(1), 158, 165; Ex & Ad 439.

Hudson; Carson v., TexCivApp–Austin, 398 SW2d 321.—Mun Corp 200(8.1), 200(10); Statut 174.

Hudson; City of San Angelo Fire Dept. v., TexApp–Austin, 179 SW3d 695.—App & E 68, 863, 893(1); Autos 187(2), 187(6); Judgm 185(2), 185(5), 185(6), 185.1(4), 185.3(2); Mun Corp 723, 742(4), 744; Offic 114.

Hudson; City of San Saba v., TexCivApp–Austin, 95 SW2d 1312.—Deeds 195, 210.

Hudson v. Continental Bus System, Inc., TexCivApp–Texarkana, 317 SW2d 584, ref nre.—Carr 234, 306(1), 306(4), 307(4); Judgm 185.3(8).

Hudson; Cook v., TexCivApp–Eastland, 558 SW2d 522.—App & E 629.

Hudson v. Cooper, TexApp–Houston (14 Dist), 162 SW3d 685.—App & E 847(1), 989, 994(2), 999(1), 1001(1); Atty & C 76(1), 130, 167(2); Impl & C C 65, 110, 121; Trial 139.1(14).

Hudson; Cottonwood Valley Home Owners Ass'n v., TexApp–Eastland, 75 SW3d 601.—Assoc 12; Covenants 100(2); Motions 10.

Hudson; Dixon v., TexCivApp–El Paso, 304 SW2d 166, writ refused.—Waters 183.5.

Hudson; Don Drum Real Estate Co. v., TexCivApp–Dallas, 465 SW2d 409.—Brok 60, 63(1); Contracts 143(1), 143(3); Evid 441(1), 442(1), 443(1), 448, 461(1).

Hudson v. Ernest Allen Motor Co., TexCivApp–Amarillo, 115 SW2d 1167, dism.—Autos 242(6), 245(31).

Hudson; Espinosa v., TexCivApp–Tyler, 531 SW2d 248.—App & E 758.3(9), 989, 1177(7); Autos 244(36.1), 245(50.1).

Hudson v. Gaines, TexCivApp–Corpus Christi, 501 SW2d 734.—App & E 934(1), 1001(1), 1073(1); Dedi 12, 15, 31, 44; High 1, 7(1), 17; Judgm 199(3.7), 199(3.14); New Tr 72(6); Trial 139.1(6).

Hudson; Garvin v., TexCivApp–Texarkana, 353 SW2d 508, ref nre.—Deeds 120, 137, 141.

Hudson v. Gooden, TexCivApp–Waco, 546 SW2d 931.—Partit 89.

Hudson; Hada v., TexApp–Corpus Christi, 694 SW2d 343, set aside.—Contracts 221(1), 221(2); Damag 117, 190; Mines 109; Plead 34(1), 48; Spec Perf 128(1); Trial 219, 350.4(1).

Hudson; Hall v., TexCivApp–Beaumont, 487 SW2d 434.—Autos 244(44), 244(58); Judgm 199(3.15).

Hudson; Harwath v., TexApp–Dallas, 654 SW2d 851, ref nre.—Mtg 354, 360.

Hudson v. Hightower, TexCivApp–Austin, 394 SW2d 46, ref nre.—App & E 1048(7); Autos 243(4); Witn 398(1), 405(2).

Hudson v. Hinton, TexCivApp–Dallas, 435 SW2d 211.—Contracts 152; Corp 120; Indem 31(2), 31(5); Judgm 185.3(8); Lim of Act 56(2); Tax 2431.

Hudson v. Hopkins, TexApp–Tyler, 799 SW2d 783.—Judgm 185(4), 185.3(1); Wills 493.

Hudson v. Hudson, TexApp–Houston (14 Dist), 763 SW2d 603.—Divorce 252.3(4); Hus & W 249(3), 262.2.

Hudson; Hudson v., TexApp–Houston (14 Dist), 763 SW2d 603.—Divorce 252.3(4); Hus & W 249(3), 262.2.

Hudson v. Hudson, TexCivApp–Fort Worth, 217 SW2d 694.—Divorce 254(1), 287.

Hudson; Hudson v., TexCivApp–Fort Worth, 217 SW2d 694.—Divorce 254(1), 287.

Hudson v. Hudson, TexCivApp–Austin, 308 SW2d 140.—App & E 77(1); Divorce 249.2, 284, 286(0.5); Judges 24.

Hudson; Hudson v., TexCivApp–Austin, 308 SW2d 140.—App & E 77(1); Divorce 249.2, 284, 286(0.5); Judges 24.

Hudson v. Hudson, TexCivApp–Eastland, 265 SW2d 137, ref nre.—Adv Poss 115(5); Evid 589.

Hudson; Hudson v., TexCivApp–Eastland, 265 SW2d 137, ref nre.—Adv Poss 115(5); Evid 589.

Hudson; Industrial Acc. Bd. of Tex. v., TexCivApp–Austin, 246 SW2d 715.—Mand 73(1); Work Comp 949, 1834.

Hudson v. International Exterminator Corp., TexCivApp–Austin, 256 SW2d 123, ref nre.—App & E 954(1); Contracts 10(1), 53, 117(2), 241; Inj 138.39, 147.

Hudson v. Johnson, CA5 (Tex), 242 F3d 534.—Const Law 4824; Hab Corp 513, 816, 842, 848; Prisons 15(7).

Hudson; Kelley v., TexApp–Tyler, 644 SW2d 98.—Covenants 79(3); Frds St of 56(1); Inj 138.21, 138.37; Zoning 786, 789.

Hudson v. Markum, TexApp–Dallas, 948 SW2d 1, error den.—App & E 930(1), 1001(3), 1003(6); Child 67, 73; Witn 246(1).

Hudson v. Markum, TexApp–Dallas, 931 SW2d 336, appeal after remand 948 SW2d 1, error den.—Child S 232, 320; Child 67.

Hudson; Martin Van Voorhies Associates v., TexApp–Houston (14 Dist, 683 SW2d 809. See Van Voorhies v. Hudson.

Hudson; Methodist Hospital v., TexCivApp–Hous (14 Dist), 465 SW2d 439, ref nre.—Health 659, 835; Neglig 1533, 1562; Trial 351.2(2), 365.1(6).

Hudson; Nathan v., TexApp–Dallas, 376 SW2d 856, ref nre.—App & E 758.1, 931(1), 989, 1010.1(3); Trial 404(1); Trusts 217.1, 372(1), 372(3).

Hudson v. Norwood, TexCivApp–Eastland, 147 SW2d 826, writ dism, correct.—Adv Poss 114(1); App & E 336.1; Courts 169(1); Judgm 8, 470; Ven & Pur 89, 93, 257.

Hudson; Pesina v., TexApp–Amarillo, 132 SW3d 133.—Autos 158, 192(11); Judgm 181(33), 185(5); Neglig 202.

Hudson v. Raggio & Raggio, Inc., CA5 (Tex), 107 F3d 355. See Hudson, Matter of.

Hudson; Raggio & Raggio, Inc. v., BkrtcyNDTex, 182 BR 741. See Hudson, In re.

Hudson; Ramseur v., TexCivApp–Austin, 190 SW2d 576.—App & E 989, 994(3); Autos 244(35); Plead 111.42(2), 111.42(8).

Hudson v. San Antonio Independent School Dist., Tex, 95 SW2d 673, 127 Tex 517.—Schools 97(4).

Hudson; San Antonio Independent School Dist. v., TexCivApp–San Antonio, 92 SW2d 527, aff 95 SW2d 673, 127 Tex 517.—App & E 323(2); Schools 97(4).

Hudson; Sartin v., TexCivApp–Fort Worth, 143 SW2d 817.—Abate & R 27; Elections 126(7); Estop 90(1), 99, 114; Inj 80, 118(1), 118(2), 120; Mand 1, 10, 154(2), 154(4), 163.

Hudson; Senter v., TexApp–Fort Worth, 28 SW3d 153, reh overr.—Crim Law 1076(1).

Hudson v. Smith, TexCivApp–Houston, 391 SW2d 441, ref nre.—App & E 205, 286, 548(5), 1056.1(6); Atty & C 141, 165, 166(1); Costs 194.25, 194.32; Evid 248(1), 248(2), 368(6); Plead 356; Princ & A 169(2); Trial 46(2), 48; Witn 205, 221, 379(5).

Hudson; Southwestern Bell Telephone v., TexApp–Beaumont, 728 SW2d 899.—App & E 846(5), 961; Damag 131(1); Pretrial Proc 455.

Hudson v. State, TexCrimApp, 675 SW2d 507.—Crim Law 339.8(6), 698(3), 720(7.1), 728(2), 730(1), 730(12), 770(3), 1037.1(3), 1038.1(2), 1144.13(3), 1159.2(7), 1159.6, 1169.2(1); Mal Mis 9.

Hudson v. State, TexCrimApp, 662 SW2d 957.—Arrest 68(10); Courts 100(1).

Hudson v. State, TexCrimApp, 588 SW2d 348.—Arrest 71.1(8); Const Law 4460; Searches 18, 24, 25.1, 63, 64, 192.1.

Hudson v. State, TexCrimApp, 510 SW2d 583.—Autos 355(6).

Hudson v. State, TexCrimApp, 453 SW2d 149.—Burg 41(1).

Hudson v. State, TexCrimApp, 453 SW2d 147.—Autos 349.5(7); Controlled Subs 67; Crim Law 478(1), 577.10(10), 1171.1(3); Mand 61; Sent & Pun 313.

Hudson v. State, TexCrimApp, 435 SW2d 528.—Crim Law 1130(4).

Hudson v. State, TexCrimApp, 418 SW2d 813.—Crim Law 553, 893; Homic 1180; Witn 409.

Hudson v. State, TexCrimApp, 361 SW2d 388, 172 Tex-Crim 565.—Crim Law 1169.3.

Hudson v. State, TexCrimApp, 341 SW2d 448, 170 Tex-Crim 400.—Crim Law 778(5), 1169.3; Int Liq 236(7).

Hudson v. State, TexCrimApp, 334 SW2d 446, 169 Tex-Crim 377.—Controlled Subs 80; Sent & Pun 1848.

Hudson v. State, TexCrimApp, 261 SW2d 712.—Crim Law 1090.1(1).

Hudson v. State, TexCrimApp, 245 SW2d 259, 156 Tex-Crim 612.—Crim Law 1111(3), 1133, 1159.1.

Hudson v. State, TexCrimApp, 244 SW2d 834, 156 Tex-Crim 566.—Embez 9, 10; Larc 8, 15(1).

Hudson v. State, TexCrimApp, 243 SW2d 841, 156 Tex-Crim 612, reh den 245 SW2d 259, 156 TexCrim 612.—Crim Law 1090.8; Ind & Inf 125(31); Int Liq 223(1), 236(20); Witn 216(4).

Hudson v. State, TexCrimApp, 237 SW2d 302, 155 Tex-Crim 485.—Bail 70; Crim Law 1099.13.

Hudson v. State, TexCrimApp, 144 SW2d 893, 140 Tex-Crim 297.—Crim Law 925.5(1), 925.5(3).

Hudson; State v., TexApp–Houston (1 Dist), 915 SW2d 879, petition for discretionary review refused.—Sent & Pun 1205.

Hudson v. State, TexApp–Houston (1 Dist), 638 SW2d 45, petition for discretionary review refused.—Burg 19; Crim Law 789(4), 795(2.35), 814(17), 1038.1(6).

Hudson v. State, TexApp–Fort Worth, 145 SW3d 323, petition for discretionary review refused.—Assault 96(4); Crim Law 772(6), 1177; Sent & Pun 238, 239.

Hudson v. State, TexApp–Fort Worth, 642 SW2d 562, petition for discretionary review refused.—Burg 42(3); Crim Law 394.4(12), 404.30, 404.75, 552(3), 560, 661, 1144.13(2.1); Searches 28, 60.1.

Hudson v. State, TexApp–Fort Worth, 629 SW2d 227.—Assault 56; Crim Law 369.1, 485(1), 486(2), 726, 1171.1(3); Ind & Inf 71.2(2), 108; Rob 17(1), 24.15(1); Witn 37(4).

Hudson v. State, TexApp–Austin, 643 SW2d 162, petition for discretionary review refused.—Controlled Subs 75, 80, 97; Crim Law 814(2).

Hudson v. State, TexApp–Dallas, 737 SW2d 838, petition for discretionary review refused.—Infants 13.

Hudson v. State, TexApp–Dallas, 675 SW2d 320, petition for discretionary review refused.—Crim Law 553, 641.13(3), 1037.2, 1045, 1134(5), 1166.16; Larc 40(6), 55, 57.

Hudson v. State, TexApp–Texarkana, 128 SW3d 367, habeas corpus den 2006 WL 1050657.—Controlled Subs 26, 27, 28, 30, 80; Crim Law 636(1), 636(2), 641.13(1), 641.13(2.1), 641.13(7), 720(2), 720(6), 723(3), 726, 868, 1039, 1114.1(1), 1119(1), 1139, 1144.13(2.1), 1144.17, 1158(1), 1159.2(2), 1159.2(7), 1159.6, 1171.1(2.1), 1174(1), 1174(5); Sent & Pun 345.

Hudson v. State, TexApp–Waco, 205 SW3d 600, petition for discretionary review refused.—Arrest 63.5(4), 68(4); Crim Law 412.1(4), 412.2(3), 1023(3), 1026.10(4); Searches 28.

Hudson v. State, TexApp–Tyler, 956 SW2d 103.—Assault 67, 96(3); Crim Law 95, 814(8), 824(4), 1144.8, 1158(3); Jury 33(5.15).

Hudson v. State, TexApp–Tyler, 794 SW2d 883.—Crim Law 622.2(3), 622.5, 721(3), 795(1.5), 795(2.20), 829(3), 1043(3), 1044.2(1), 1045; Ind & Inf 191(0.5).

Hudson v. State, TexApp–Houston (14 Dist), 179 SW3d 731.—Assault 91.8; Crim Law 363, 366(6), 419(1.10), 553, 662.8, 772(2), 800(1), 867, 1038.1(1), 1038.1(2), 1038.1(6), 1134(2), 1144.13(2.1), 1144.13(6), 1153(1), 1155, 1159.2(2), 1159.2(7), 1159.2(9), 1159.4(2), 1169.5(3).

Hudson v. State, TexApp–Houston (14 Dist), 112 SW3d 794, petition for discretionary review refused.—Crim

Law 338(1), 338(7), 369.1, 369.2(1), 369.2(4), 371(1), 683(1), 698(1), 1036.1(8), 1134(2), 1153(1), 1169.11.

Hudson v. State, TexApp–Houston (14 Dist), 799 SW2d 314, petition for discretionary review refused.—Burg 41(8); Crim Law 761(6), 761(9), 789(1), 844(2), 1037.1(2), 1159.1.

Hudson v. State, TexApp–Houston (14 Dist), 772 SW2d 180, petition for discretionary review refused.—Crim Law 273.1(4), 273.1(5), 275; Sent & Pun 1800.

Hudson; Texas Cable & Telecommunications Ass'n v., WDTex, 458 FSupp2d 309.—Const Law 656, 969, 975, 978, 980, 981; States 18.3.

Hudson v. Texas Children's Hosp., TexApp–Houston (1 Dist), 177 SW3d 232.—Judges 51(2), 51(4).

Hudson v. Texas Racing Com'n, CA5 (Tex), 455 F3d 597.—Const Law 4292; Pub Amuse 33, 35(2).

Hudson; United Employers Cas. Co. v., TexCivApp–Texarkana, 152 SW2d 451.—App & E 882(14), 1062.1; Damag 221(5.1).

Hudson; U.S. v., CA5 (Tex), 982 F2d 160, cert den 114 SCt 100, 510 US 831, 126 LEd2d 67.—Crim Law 36.6, 330, 569, 734, 769, 772(6), 835, 1134(3), 1159.5, 1172.1(1), 1173.2(1), 1173.2(3).

Hudson; U.S. v., CA5 (Tex), 601 F2d 797, reh den 605 F2d 554.—Cust Dut 126(2).

Hudson; U.S. v., CA5 (Tex), 431 F2d 468, cert den 91 SCt 575, 400 U.S. 1011, 27 LEd2d 624, cert den White v. US, 91 SCt 577, 400 US 1011, 27 LEd2d 624.—Const Law 1415; Controlled Subs 39; Crim Law 393(1), 1132.

Hudson; Vanderford v., TexCivApp–Hous (14 Dist), 619 SW2d 432, ref nre.—Judgm 181(24), 185(2).

Hudson; Van Voorhies v., TexApp–Houston (14 Dist), 683 SW2d 809, ref nre.—App & E 174; Parties 88(1), 96(2).

Hudson v. Vasquez, TexApp–Corpus Christi, 941 SW2d 334.—App & E 70(8); Civil R 1088(4); Judgm 181(27); Mun Corp 747(3); Offic 114; Plead 52(2).

Hudson v. Wakefield, Tex, 711 SW2d 628.—App & E 173(2), 863, 1096(1), 1097(1), 1195(1), 1201(1), 1212(4).

Hudson v. Wakefield, Tex, 645 SW2d 427, appeal after remand 711 SW2d 628.—Contracts 221(1); Ven & Pur 79.

Hudson v. Wakefield, TexApp–Waco, 635 SW2d 216, writ gr, rev 645 SW2d 427, appeal after remand 711 SW2d 628.—Spec Perf 31.

Hudson v. West Central Drilling Co., TexCivApp–Eastland, 195 SW2d 387, ref nre.—App & E 929; Neglig 547; New Tr 44(1), 56, 140(3), 157; Trial 304, 311.

Hudson v. Winn, TexApp–Houston (1 Dist), 859 SW2d 504, reh den, and writ den.—App & E 927(6), 994(3), 996, 997(3), 1008.1(3), 1012.1(2); Courts 40; Detectives 4; Judgm 99; Neglig 259, 387, 409; Pretrial Proc 474, 483; Torts 368; Tresp 46(1).

Hudson & Eads, Inc. v. Enlow, TexCivApp–Fort Worth, 302 SW2d 479.—Corp 503(1); Plead 111.3, 111.16.

Hudson and Hudson Realtors v. Savage, TexCivApp–Tyler, 545 SW2d 863.—App & E 501(1); Fraud 59(1), 60; Plead 111.9, 111.12, 111.42(1), 111.42(6), 111.42(10).

Hudson Buick, Pontiac, GMC Truck Co. v. Gooch, TexApp–Tyler, 7 SW3d 191, reh overr, and review den, and reh of petition for review overr.—App & E 946, 969, 1064.1(1), 1064.1(10), 1070(1); Autos 19, 20, 186, 245(36); Evid 384, 397(1), 400(3); Judgm 256(2); Propty 7, 9; Sales 10, 54, 199.

Hudson Energy Co., Inc.; National Union Fire Ins. Co. of Pittsburgh, Pa.v., Tex, 811 SW2d 552.—Insurance 1832(1), 1835(2), 2098, 2332.

Hudson Energy Co., Inc.; National Union Fire Ins. Co. of Pittsburgh, Pa.v., TexApp–Texarkana, 780 SW2d 417, writ den, and writ withdrawn, and writ gr, aff 811 SW2d 552.—App & E 1050.1(2); Contracts 143(2); Insurance 1854, 1929(2), 2131, 3336, 3360, 3376; Trial 62(1), 136(3), 352.5(1), 365.1(1).

Hudson Engineering Corp. v. C.I.R., CA5 (Tex), 183 F2d 180.—Int Rev 3505.

Hudson Engineering Corp.; Green v., TexCivApp–Fort Worth, 305 SW2d 201, ref nre.—App & E 1170.6; Trial 115(1), 115(2), 131(1).

Hudson Engineering Corp.; Texas Emp. Ins. Ass'n v., TexCivApp–San Antonio, 245 SW2d 523.—App & E 387(3), 1050.1(7), 1062.1, 1062.5, 1070(2); Neglig 1717.

Hudson Gas & Oil Corp.; Coleman v., Tex, 455 SW2d 701.—Mines 118.

Hudson Gas & Oil Corp.; Coleman v., TexCivApp–Beaumont, 444 SW2d 807, aff 455 SW2d 701.—Mines 118.

Hudson Gas & Oil Corp.; Coleman v., TexCivApp–Beaumont, 403 SW2d 482, ref nre, appeal after remand 444 SW2d 807, aff 455 SW2d 701.—App & E 76(2), 695(2), 927(7); Mines 118.

Hudson Oaks, Town of; State ex rel. City of Weatherford v., TexCivApp–Eastland, 610 SW2d 550, ref nre, appeal after remand 646 SW2d 610, ref nre.—Mun Corp 18.

Hudson Sales Corp.; McMorries v., TexCivApp–El Paso, 233 SW2d 938.—Const Law 90.1(1), 1845, 4034; Equity 16, 23; Inj 57, 94, 98(2).

Hudson Sales Corp. v. Waldrip, CA5 (Tex), 211 F2d 268, cert den 75 SCt 34, 348 US 821, 99 LEd 648.—Antitrust 977(3), 979.

Hudson's Bay Co.; Buckspan v., CCA5 (Tex), 22 F2d 721, cert den 48 SCt 321, 276 US 628, 72 LEd 739.—Trademarks 1425.

Hudson Underwriters Agency of Franklin Fire Ins. Co. v. Ablon, TexCivApp–Dallas, 203 SW2d 584, dism.—App & E 1036(1); Insurance 3526(5); Parties 50, 51(4).

Hudson Waterways Corp. v. Coastal Marine Service, Inc., EDTex, 436 FSupp 597.—Adm 1.11; Contracts 103, 114, 189, 205.15(4); Indem 50, 69, 81, 83; Seamen 29(2); Ship 76, 84(6).

Hudspeth; Griffith v., TexCivApp–San Antonio, 378 SW2d 153.—Autos 245(39); New Tr 140(3); Trial 304.

Hudspeth v. Hudspeth, TexApp–San Antonio, 756 SW2d 29, writ den.—App & E 272(1); Wills 618, 628, 706.

Hudspeth; Hudspeth v., TexApp–San Antonio, 756 SW2d 29, writ den.—App & E 272(1); Wills 618, 628, 706.

Hudspeth v. Hudspeth, TexApp–San Antonio, 673 SW2d 248, ref nre, appeal after remand 756 SW2d 29, writ den.—Judgm 185(2), 524, 585(3), 619, 634, 713(2), 715(3), 739, 958(1).

Hudspeth; Hudspeth v., TexApp–San Antonio, 673 SW2d 248, ref nre, appeal after remand 756 SW2d 29, writ den.—Judgm 185(2), 524, 585(3), 619, 634, 713(2), 715(3), 739, 958(1).

Hudspeth v. Hudspeth, TexCivApp–Amarillo, 206 SW2d 863.—App & E 719(1), 758.3(1), 758.3(2), 758.3(3), 758.3(7), 901, 930(2), 1032(1), 1046.1; Marriage 60(7), 60(8).

Hudspeth; Hudspeth v., TexCivApp–Amarillo, 206 SW2d 863.—App & E 719(1), 758.3(1), 758.3(2), 758.3(3), 758.3(7), 901, 930(2), 1032(1), 1046.1; Marriage 60(7), 60(8).

Hudspeth v. Hudspeth, TexCivApp–Amarillo, 198 SW2d 768, ref nre.—Divorce 252.3(2); Hus & W 249(6), 254, 255, 257, 259, 262.1(5); Marriage 40(1), 40.1(1), 50(1).

Hudspeth; Hudspeth v., TexCivApp–Amarillo, 198 SW2d 768, ref nre.—Divorce 252.3(2); Hus & W 249(6), 254, 255, 257, 259, 262.1(5); Marriage 40(1), 40.1(1), 50(1).

Hudspeth v. Investor Collection Services Ltd. Partnership, TexApp–San Antonio, 985 SW2d 477, reh overr.—App & E 223; Banks 505; Bills & N 489(6); Judgm 185.3(16).

Hudspeth; Lester v., Tex, 184 SW2d 467, 143 Tex 279.—Mun Corp 480, 579.

Hudspeth; Lester v., TexCivApp–El Paso, 183 SW2d 220, rev 184 SW2d 467, 143 Tex 279.—Mech Liens 298; Mun Corp 579.

Hudspeth v. State, TexCrimApp, 207 SW2d 885, 151 TexCrim 307.—Crim Law 1094(2.1), 1099.10, 1104(3).

Hudspeth v. State, TexApp–Amarillo, 31 SW3d 409, petition for discretionary review refused.—Crim Law 641.13(6), 1077.1(2); Obst Just 4, 8, 16, 21.

Hudspeth v. Stoker, TexApp–San Antonio, 644 SW2d 92, writ refused.—App & E 852; Insurance 3481(3); Trusts 91, 95, 103(1), 103(3).

Hudspeth v. U.S., CA5 (Tex), 519 F2d 1055.—Fed Cts 479; Int Rev 3393, 3418.

Hudspeth v. U.S., CA5 (Tex), 223 F2d 848.—Crim Law 564(1).

Hudspeth v. U.S., NDTex, 394 FSupp 181, aff 519 F2d 1055.—Int Rev 3393, 3418.

Hudspeth County Conservation and Reclamation Dist. No. 1; Dwyer v., TexCivApp–El Paso, 83 SW2d 391, writ dism.—Levees 27.

Hudspeth County Conservation and Reclamation Dist. No. 1; Dwyer v., TexCivApp–El Paso, 83 SW2d 388.—Const Law 2754, 2775; Levees 2, 10, 27; Statut 63.

Hudspeth County Conservation & Reclamation Dist. No. 1; Gill v., TexCivApp–El Paso, 88 SW2d 517.—App & E 837(1), 843(2); Evid 6; Inj 132, 135, 138.15; Waters 177(1).

Hudspeth County Conservation and Reclamation Dist. No. 1 v. Robbins, CA5 (Tex), 213 F2d 425, cert den Hudspeth County Conservation and Reclamation District No 1 v. Robbins, 75 SCt 56, 348 US 833, 99 LEd 657.—Const Law 2564; U S 47, 125(24), 125(26); Waters 222.

Hudspeth County Underground Water Conservation Dist. No. 1; Guitar Holding Co., L.P. v., TexApp–El Paso, 209 SW3d 172, review gr.—Admin Law 749, 750, 791, 793; App & E 984(1); Const Law 3057, 3509; Contracts 171(1); Costs 32(2), 194.14, 194.18, 198, 207; Statut 64(1), 181(1), 188, 205, 219(1), 219(4); Waters 133, 145, 152(12), 152(13), 183.5.

Hudspeth County Underground Water Conservation Dist. No. 1; Guitar Holding Co., L.P. v., TexApp–El Paso, 209 SW3d 146, review gr.—Admin Law 749, 750, 791, 793; App & E 984(1); Const Law 3057, 3509; Contracts 171(1); Costs 32(2), 194.14, 194.18, 198, 207; Statut 64(1), 181(1), 188, 205, 219(1), 219(4); Waters 133, 145, 152(12), 152(13), 183.5.

Hudstan Oil Corp.; Mellette v., TexCivApp, 243 SW2d 438, ref nre.—App & E 70(8); Evid 317(4); Frds St of 73; Judgm 178; Mines 74(10), 99(2); Trial 169, 178; Trusts 1, 17(1), 17(3), 44(3), 91, 110; Ven & Pur 220, 242.

Hueber; Railway Exp. Agency v., TexCivApp–San Antonio, 191 SW2d 710.—App & E 1012.1(1); Carr 110, 134, 153.

Huebner; Delhi-Taylor Oil Corp. v., CA5 (Tex), 342 F2d 418.—Autos 245(50.1), 246(39.1); Death 72.

Huebner; Hellman v., TexCivApp–Galveston, 234 SW2d 117, ref nre.—Hus & W 265; Tax 2930, 3063.

Huebner; Miller v., TexCivApp–Hous (14 Dist), 474 SW2d 587, ref nre.—Joint Adv 5(2); Trial 365.1(4); Trusts 91, 95, 103(1), 110.

Huebner; Missouri Pacific R. Co. v., TexApp–Corpus Christi, 704 SW2d 353, ref nre.—App & E 230, 231(3), 1060.6; Death 99(4); Evid 219(3); Labor & Emp 2881; Trial 114, 131(1), 252(20); Witn 374(1).

Huebner; Nellums v., TexCivApp–Amarillo, 347 SW2d 845.—Judgm 185.2(4), 185.2(7), 185.3(15).

Huebner; Pace v., TexCivApp–Eastland, 610 SW2d 561, ref nre.—New Tr 157.

Huebsch Mfg. Co. v. Coleman, TexCivApp–Amarillo, 113 SW2d 639.—Cert 60; Chat Mtg 138(3), 157(3); Exemp 93; J P 194(1).

Huelsebusch v. Roensch, TexCivApp–Austin, 141 SW2d 732, writ dism, correct.—App & E 1172(1); Des & Dist 119(1), 152; Trial 36.

Huerta, Ex parte, TexCrimApp, 692 SW2d 681.—Crim Law 274(3.1).

Huerta; Chisos Mining Co. v., Tex, 171 SW2d 867, 141 Tex 289.—Autos 197(7); Labor & Emp 3047.

Huerta; Gorges Foodservice, Inc. v., TexApp–Corpus Christi, 964 SW2d 656, reh overr, and review withdrawn.—App & E 205, 232(0.5), 1001(3), 1003(6), 1004(8), 1004(13), 1050.1(1), 1056.1(1), 1056.1(7), 1079, 1182; Civil R 1221, 1715, 1744, 1749, 1753, 1765, 1769, 1772, 1773; Costs 197; Damag 50.10, 54, 56.20, 91(1), 94, 100, 192; Evid 213(2), 597; Interest 39(2.20), 39(2.40), 39(2.45); Labor & Emp 810, 854, 863(2), 866, 867, 868(3), 870, 871; Plead 34(3), 387; Trial 43.

Huerta; Hotel Dieu Hospital v., Tex, 639 SW2d 462.—App & E 1177(6).

Huerta v. Hotel Dieu Hosp., TexApp–El Paso, 636 SW2d 208, review gr, rev 639 SW2d 462.—Courts 100(1); Health 827; Trial 215.

Huerta; Meru v., TexApp–Corpus Christi, 136 SW3d 383. —App & E 863; Contracts 9(1), 15, 16, 25, 28(3), 29; Evid 219(1); Judgm 181(6), 183, 185(2), 185.3(2); Labor & Emp 175; Lim of Act 199(1).

Huerta v. State, TexCrimApp, 390 SW2d 770.—Controlled Subs 80; Crim Law 438(3), 507(4), 957(3), 1169.2(6).

Huerta v. State, TexCrimApp, 308 SW2d 876, 165 TexCrim 527.—Crim Law 565, 875(1), 1092.11(3).

Huerta v. State, TexApp–San Antonio, 933 SW2d 648.—Assault 92(2), 95; Crim Law 774, 1043(3), 1130(5), 1134(8), 1144.13(6), 1159.2(2).

Huerta v. State, TexApp–Corpus Christi, 709 SW2d 21.—Crim Law 519(8); Sent & Pun 2019, 2021.

Huerta v. State, TexApp–Corpus Christi, 635 SW2d 847, petition for discretionary review refused.—Crim Law 552(3), 656(9), 792(2), 1038.1(1), 1038.1(3.1), 1043(2), 1043(3), 1166.22(1); Homic 1134, 1184, 1186.

Huerta; U.S. v., CA5 (Tex), 182 F3d 361, cert den 120 SCt 1238, 528 US 1191, 146 LEd2d 105.—Crim Law 1030(1), 1042, 1139, 1158(1), 1177; Sent & Pun 299, 300, 665, 761, 977.

Huerta; U.S. v., CA5 (Tex), 181 FedAppx 397, post-conviction relief den 2007 WL 2193963.—Jury 34(8); Sent & Pun 670, 765.

Hues; Smith v., TexCivApp–Hous (14 Dist), 540 SW2d 485, ref nre.—App & E 719(8); Bills & N 403; Contracts 211, 323(1); Frds St of 131(1); Spec Perf 6, 28(1), 30, 31, 57, 97(3), 121(3); Ven & Pur 3(4), 18(1), 78, 187.

Hues v. Warren Petroleum Co., TexApp–Houston (14 Dist), 814 SW2d 526, writ den.—App & E 954(1); Em Dom 2(1), 2(1.1), 266, 288(1); Inj 1, 9, 46, 118(1), 118(5), 135; Lim of Act 32(1), 55(5), 95(1), 95(7).

Hueschen v. Dunn, TexCivApp–San Antonio, 219 SW2d 586.—App & E 931(1); Trusts 7.

Huett v. State, TexApp–Dallas, 970 SW2d 119.—Assoc 1; Crim Law 1144.13(2.1), 1144.13(3), 1144.13(6), 1158(1), 1159.2(1), 1159.2(2), 1159.2(7), 1159.2(9), 1159.3(2), 1159.4(2), 1181.5(3.1); Embez 44(4), 44(6); Fraud 7.

Huett v. State, TexApp–Dallas, 672 SW2d 533, petition for discretionary review refused.—Const Law 82(4), 1160, 3905; Crim Law 13.1(1), 763(1); Sec Reg 244, 323; Statut 47; Witn 345(8).

Huey v. Brand, TexCivApp–Amarillo, 92 SW2d 505, aff Borger v. Brand, 118 SW2d 303, 131 Tex 614.—Banks 80(7); Contracts 108(1), 141(1); Dep & Escr 37; Indem 28, 111; Mtg 25(3); Princ & S 59; Subrog 1, 7(2).

Huey; Church & Dwight Co., Inc. v., TexApp–San Antonio, 961 SW2d 560, reh overr, and review den.—Antitrust 138, 161, 205, 291, 363, 369; App & E 970(2), 1001(3), 1003(7), 1050.1(1), 1056.1(1); Evid 222(2), 268, 318(1), 333(7); Neglig 379, 380; Sales 255, 261(1), 261(6), 273(3), 284(1); Trial 43, 54(1).

Huey; Davis v., Tex, 620 SW2d 561.—Covenants 1, 49, 51(2), 84.

Huey; Davis v., Tex, 571 SW2d 859, appeal after remand 608 SW2d 944, rev 620 SW2d 561.—App & E 365(1), 714(1), 846(5), 863, 920(1), 946, 954(1), 954(2), 1082(1), 1089(1); Inj 135, 152.

Huey; Davis v., TexCivApp–Austin, 608 SW2d 944, rev 620 SW2d 561.—App & E 883, 901, 1032(1), 1069.2; Covenants 49, 51(2), 77.1, 118, 137; Inj 62(1), 62(3), 127, 128(6), 130; Jury 66(1), 79.1; Trial 28(1), 110, 133.6(4), 217, 307(1).

Huey v. Davis, TexCivApp–Austin, 556 SW2d 860, writ gr, rev 571 SW2d 859, appeal after remand 608 SW2d 944, rev 620 SW2d 561.—Contracts 284(4); Covenants 1, 84.

Huey v. Huey, TexApp–Dallas, 200 SW3d 851.—App & E 1079; Child C 603, 908; Venue 33.

Huey; Huey v., TexApp–Dallas, 200 SW3d 851.—App & E 1079; Child C 603, 908; Venue 33.

Huey v. State, TexCrimApp, 155 SW2d 61, 142 TexCrim 522.—Crim Law 475, 1097(1), 1099.10, 1133, 1172.1(5); Witn 52(8), 268(6), 268(16).

Huey v. State, TexCrimApp, 139 SW2d 271, 139 TexCrim 152.—Crim Law 789(3).

Huey v. State, TexCrimApp, 101 SW2d 580, 132 TexCrim 14.—Crim Law 1172.1(2); Embez 42, 47.

Huey; Texas Employment Commission v., Tex, 342 SW2d 544, 161 Tex 500.—Unemp Comp 101.

Huey v. Texas Employment Com'n, TexCivApp–Dallas, 332 SW2d 366, writ gr, aff 342 SW2d 544, 161 Tex 500. —Unemp Comp 117.

Huey & Philp Hardware Co.; Fowzer v., TexCivApp–Dallas, 99 SW2d 1100, writ dism.—Appear 8(7); Inj 106; Judgm 16, 447(1), 447(2), 447(3); Receivers 151.

Huey & Philp Hardware Co. v. McNeil, TexCivApp–Fort Worth, 111 SW2d 1205, writ dism.—App & E 1001(1); Autos 240(2), 243(4); Damag 216(6); Trial 120(1), 121(1), 125(1), 127, 203(1), 208, 350.3(7); Witn 393(1).

Huey & Philp Hardware Co. v. Shepperd, Tex, 251 SW2d 515, 151 Tex 462.—Tax 2494, 2495, 2541.

Huey & Philp Hardware Co.; Shepperd v., TexCivApp–Austin, 246 SW2d 644, rev 251 SW2d 515, 151 Tex 462. —Tax 2541.

Huey & Philp Hardware Co.; Texas Steel Co. v., TexCivApp–Fort Worth, 110 SW2d 964.—Receivers 55, 57, 77(2), 154(1), 155.

Huey & Philp Hardware Co.; Texas Steel Co. v., TexCivApp–El Paso, 79 SW2d 636, writ dism.—Receivers 102.

Huey L. Cheramie, Inc.; Scott v., TexApp–Houston (14 Dist), 833 SW2d 240.—App & E 863; Const Law 3964, 3965(3); Corp 665(1); Courts 12(2.1), 12(2.5), 12(2.10), 35.

Huey T. Littleton Claims Services of Texas, Inc.; Pederson v., EDTex, 158 FSupp2d 773.—Fed Cts 18, 301, 342.

Huff, Ex parte, TexCrimApp, 583 SW2d 774.—Forg 28(3); Hab Corp 474.

Huff, Ex parte, TexCrimApp, 579 SW2d 245.—Const Law 4783(3); Crim Law 625.10(2.1).

Huff, Ex parte, TexCrimApp, 316 SW2d 896, 166 TexCrim 508.—Hab Corp 509(1); Sent & Pun 1309.

Huff, In re Estate of, TexApp–Texarkana, 15 SW3d 301. —App & E 893(1), 946, 970(4); Courts 26; Estop 68(2); Ex & Ad 20(0.5); Statut 181(1), 181(2), 184, 188, 206, 212.6, 212.7; Trial 66, 377(1); Wills 412.1, 416.

Huff; Barney v., TexCivApp–Austin, 326 SW2d 617, ref nre.—Courts 26; Evid 43(3); Judgm 670; Wills 229, 230, 238, 245, 256, 357, 434.

Huff; Capps v., TexCivApp–Eastland, 427 SW2d 121.—Bills & N 48.1, 527(1), 534.

Huff; Carver v., TexCivApp–Amarillo, 283 SW2d 317, ref nre.—App & E 1010.1(3), 1012.1(3); Divorce 151, 254(2), 255.

Huff v. Citizens' Sav. Bank & Trust Co. of St. Johnsbury, Vt., TexCivApp–Austin, 81 SW2d 1043.—Usury 85.

Huff v. Fidelity Union Life Ins. Co., Tex, 312 SW2d 493, 158 Tex 433.—Costs 194.25, 194.32; Insurance 1652(3); Lim of Act 127(4); Plead 228.

Huff; Fidelity Union Life Ins. Co. v., TexCivApp–Waco, 305 SW2d 209, rev 312 SW2d 493, 158 Tex 433.—Damag 71.5; Insurance 1652(3).

Huff; Graham v., TexCivApp–Dallas, 384 SW2d 904.—Contracts 245(1), 245(2); Evid 384; Frds St of 112; Mines 79.1(5); Venue 5.3(8), 22(4), 26, 41.

Huff; Hall v., TexApp–Texarkana, 957 SW2d 90, reh overr, and review den.—Abate & R 54; App & E 934(1), 946, 971(2); Death 7, 11; Evid 538, 545, 546; Health 611, 620, 821(2); Judgm 181(33), 183, 185(2); Neglig 371, 379, 380, 384, 387, 421, 423, 431, 432.

Huff v. Harrell, TexApp–Corpus Christi, 941 SW2d 230, reh overr, and writ den.—App & E 218.2(5.1), 1043(6), 1048(7), 1050.1(11), 1051.1(2); Corp 1.6(6), 269(2), 269(3), 349, 547(4), 627; Estop 52.10(3); Evid 200, 208(1), 208(4), 208(5), 208(6), 264, 265(8), 376(1), 555.3; Fraud 3; Plead 36(1); Trial 39, 74, 350.1, 366; Witn 379(1).

Huff v. Huff, Tex, 648 SW2d 286.—Child S 225, 451.

Huff; Huff v., Tex, 648 SW2d 286.—Child S 225, 451.

Huff v. Huff, Tex, 124 SW2d 327, 132 Tex 540.—Ex & Ad 111(3), 488, 501.

Huff; Huff v., Tex, 124 SW2d 327, 132 Tex 540.—Ex & Ad 111(3), 488, 501.

Huff v. Huff, TexApp–Beaumont, 634 SW2d 5, writ gr, aff 648 SW2d 286.—Child S 451.

Huff; Huff v., TexApp–Beaumont, 634 SW2d 5, writ gr, aff 648 SW2d 286.—Child S 451.

Huff v. Huff, TexCivApp–Waco, 554 SW2d 841, dism.—Divorce 249.2; Hus & W 29(9).

Huff; Huff v., TexCivApp–Waco, 554 SW2d 841, dism.—Divorce 249.2; Hus & W 29(9).

Huff v. Huff, TexCivApp–Eastland, 98 SW2d 442, rev 124 SW2d 327, 132 Tex 540.—App & E 930(3); Ex & Ad 109(1), 111(1), 111(3), 111(9), 488.

Huff; Huff v., TexCivApp–Eastland, 98 SW2d 442, rev 124 SW2d 327, 132 Tex 540.—App & E 930(3); Ex & Ad 109(1), 111(1), 111(3), 111(9), 488.

Huff v. Insurance Co. of North America, TexCivApp–Fort Worth, 394 SW2d 849, ref nre.—App & E 544(3); Work Comp 880, 1846, 1922, 1958, 1968(4).

Huff v. International Longshoremen's Ass'n, Local No. 24, CA5 (Tex), 799 F2d 1087.—Fed Civ Proc 2662; Fed Cts 668, 669.

Huff; Oklahoma Furniture Mfg. Co. v., TexCivApp–Beaumont, 414 SW2d 739.—App & E 1004(1); Damag 130.1, 130.3, 208(1), 208(4); Evid 5(2).

Huff v. Patrick, TexCivApp–Austin, 114 SW2d 598.—App & E 509, 782, 900.

Huff v. Reid, TexCivApp–San Antonio, 109 SW2d 212, dism.—App & E 389(1), 389(3), 456, 985.

Huff; Reilly v., TexCivApp–San Antonio, 335 SW2d 275.—App & E 1050.1(3.1); Des & Dist 25.1; Estates 1; Remaind 1; Wills 498, 597(1), 607(1), 634(4.1).

Huff; Reynosa v., TexApp–San Antonio, 21 SW3d 510.—App & E 852, 893(1), 934(1); Health 576, 611, 614, 615, 618, 684; Judgm 178, 185(5), 185(6).

Huff; Satterfield v., TexApp–Austin, 768 SW2d 839, writ den.—Divorce 85.

Huff v. Simpson, TexCivApp–Fort Worth, 111 SW2d 1186.—App & E 766.

Huff v. Southwestern Life Ins. Co., TexCivApp–Eastland, 95 SW2d 498, writ refused.—Insurance 1808, 2037.

Huff v. Speer, TexCivApp–Hous (1 Dist), 554 SW2d 259, ref nre.—App & E 750(7), 1011.1(1); Bills & N 444, 520; Contracts 86, 318; Labor & Emp 34(2), 265.

Huff v. Stafford, TexCivApp–Dallas, 429 SW2d 620, writ dism.—App & E 927(1); Child C 23, 76, 452, 509, 510; Trial 139.1(17), 143.

Huff v. State, TexCrimApp, 807 SW2d 325.—Crim Law 1134(10), 1181.5(6).

Huff v. State, TexCrimApp, 576 SW2d 645.—Crim Law 1170.5(1); Witn 389.

Huff v. State, TexCrimApp, 560 SW2d 652.—Crim Law 363, 419(12), 1169.2(6); Sent & Pun 1379(2).

Huff v. State, TexCrimApp, 492 SW2d 532.—Larc 55, 64(1), 64(4), 64(6).

Huff v. State, TexCrimApp, 257 SW2d 310.—Crim Law 1090.1(1).

Huff v. State, TexCrimApp, 239 SW2d 1007, 156 TexCrim 194.—Food 18, 21.

Huff v. State, TexCrimApp, 165 SW2d 717, 145 TexCrim 82.—Crim Law 696(2), 1036.1(8), 1038.3, 1043(2), 1044.1(4).

Huff v. State, TexCrimApp, 109 SW2d 172.—Crim Law 1182.

Huff v. State, TexApp–Houston (1 Dist), 677 SW2d 229, petition for discretionary review refused.—Crim Law 1038.1(3.1), 1038.1(6); Rape 2.

Huff v. State, TexApp–Houston (1 Dist), 630 SW2d 711, petition for discretionary review refused.—Controlled Subs 29, 74.

Huff v. State, TexApp–Dallas, 897 SW2d 829, petition for discretionary review refused.—Crim Law 338(1), 338(7), 436(3), 436(6), 444, 662.1, 662.8, 662.40, 713, 730(1), 730(12), 772(6), 814(5), 1130(5), 1153(1), 1170(2), 1171.1(2.1); Larc 15(1), 35, 40(2), 62(2), 78.

Huff v. State, TexApp–Amarillo, 630 SW2d 909.—Crim Law 43, 59(1), 795(2.26), 885; False Pret 49(1).

Huff v. State, TexApp–Corpus Christi, 678 SW2d 236.—Crim Law 412.2(3), 412.2(4), 436(3), 531(3), 577.16(9), 1172.1(3); Ind & Inf 71.4(1), 110(38), 125(1), 196(7); Weap 17(1).

Huff v. State, TexApp–Corpus Christi, 660 SW2d 635, petition for discretionary review refused.—Crim Law 713, 720.5, 772(6), 787(2), 829(1), 1171.1(3); Infants 13, 20.

Huff v. State, TexCivApp–San Antonio, 84 SW2d 1014, writ dism.—App & E 1127.

Huff; State v., TexCivApp–Amarillo, 491 SW2d 216.—App & E 260(3), 554(1); Crim Law 42; Plead 111.12, 111.14, 111.17, 111.42(8); Witn 293.5, 302, 307.

Huff v. State, TexCivApp–El Paso, 93 SW2d 231.—App & E 931(1); Execution 220; Hus & W 273(10); Jud S 47; Tresp to T T 38(1), 41(1).

Huff v. Tippit, TexCivApp–San Antonio, 452 SW2d 523.—Contracts 9(1), 207, 215(1); Inj 61(2), 113, 138.39, 205.

Huff; U.S. v., CA5 (Tex), 370 F3d 454, reh den, postconviction relief den 2006 WL 456265.—Crim Law 1042; Jury 24; Sent & Pun 665, 1343, 1378, 1381(7).

Huff; U.S. v., CA5 (Tex), 637 F2d 368, cert den 102 SCt 312, 454 US 859, 70 LEd2d 156.—Jury 29(6).

Huff; U.S. v., CA5 (Tex), 409 F2d 1225, cert den 90 SCt 123, 396 US 857, 24 LEd2d 108.—Crim Law 48, 444, 624, 736(1), 1132.

Huff v. U.S., CA5 (Tex), 301 F2d 760, cert den 83 SCt 289, 371 US 922, 9 LEd2d 230.—Consp 43(6), 47(1), 47(5); Crim Law 419(2.10), 829(1), 1036.2, 1169.5(2), 1177; Ind & Inf 121.2(9); Tel 1014(5), 1014(8), 1014(9), 1017, 1018(4), 1021.

Huff v. U.S., CA5 (Tex), 273 F2d 56.—Crim Law 371(12), 394.2(2), 448(16), 753.2(7), 1169.9; Cust Dut 134; Fed Civ Proc 23.

Huff v. U.S., CA5 (Tex), 175 F2d 678.—Damag 6; Fed Cts 917; U S 141(5.1), 142.

Huff; U.S. v., CA5 (Tex), 134 FedAppx 697, cert den 126 SCt 1345, 546 US 1176, 164 LEd2d 59.—Crim Law 1042; Searches 70; Sent & Pun 765.

Huff; U.S. v., CCA5 (Tex), 165 F2d 720, 1 ALR2d 854.—Contracts 309(1); U S 70(5), 70(7), 70(22.1), 70(32), 74(3), 127(1).

Huff; U.S. v., SDTex, 36 FSupp 18.—Fed Civ Proc 426, 427.

Huff; Wilson N. Jones Memorial Hosp. v., TexApp–Dallas, 188 SW3d 215, reh overr, and review den.—App & E 954(1), 954(2); Inj 132, 135, 138.1, 138.6, 138.9, 147.

Huff; Zable v., TexCivApp–Amarillo, 432 SW2d 717.—Bailm 31(3); Plead 111.4; Venue 22(4).

Huffaker; Jones v., TexApp–Beaumont, 701 SW2d 935.—Lim of Act 87(5), 119(0.5), 119(3), 193.

Huffaker v. Lea County Elec. Co-op., Inc., TexCivApp–Amarillo, 344 SW2d 915, ref nre.—Electricity 9(1), 9(2); Plead 111.1.

Huffaker; Whitaker v., TexApp–El Paso, 790 SW2d 761, writ den.—App & E 189(1), 1073(1); Compromise 20(1); Consp 19; Ex & Ad 538; Judgm 185.2(1).

Huffco Petroleum Corp. v. Transcontinental Gas Pipe Line Corp., SDTex, 681 FSupp 400.—Alt Disp Res 355; Fed Cts 198.

Huffco Petroleum Corp. v. Trunkline Gas Co., TexApp–Houston (14 Dist), 769 SW2d 672, writ den.—Judgm 181(19).

Huffeldt v. Competition Drywall, Inc., TexApp–Houston (14 Dist), 750 SW2d 272.—New Tr 140(1).

Hufferd v. Lerma, TexCivApp–San Antonio, 107 SW2d 1007.—App & E 187(1); Bills & N 489(7).

Huffhines v. State Farm Lloyds, TexApp–Houston (14 Dist), 167 SW3d 493.—App & E 893(1); Insurance 2275, 2277, 2396, 2914, 2915, 2922(1).

Huffhines Steel Co.; Marshall v., NDTex, 488 FSupp 995, aff Donovan v. Huffines Steel Co, 645 F2d 288.—Admin Law 385.1, 413; Labor & Emp 2600; Statut 219(1).

Huffhines Steel Co.; Marshall v., NDTex, 478 FSupp 986.—Fed Cts 201.1; Labor & Emp 2600; Searches 103.1.

Huffine v. Tomball Hosp. Authority, TexApp–Houston (14 Dist), 983 SW2d 300.—App & E 78(1).

Huffine v. Tomball Hosp. Authority, TexApp–Houston (14 Dist), 979 SW2d 795.—App & E 223, 852, 863; Judgm 157.1, 183, 184, 185(2), 185(5), 186; Mun Corp 741.30, 741.40(1); New Tr 140(1).

Huffines; Camtex Oil Corp. v., TexCivApp–Texarkana, 273 SW2d 471.—Corp 666; Plead 111.3.

Huffines; Hyde Corp. v., Tex, 314 SW2d 763, 158 Tex 566, reh den 1958 WL 91272, cert den 79 SCt 223, 358 US 898, 3 LEd2d 148.—Abate & R 12; Am Cur 3; Antitrust 418; Courts 489(3), 489(4); Inj 4, 56, 190; Pat 1, 182, 211(1), 214.

Huffines; Hyde Corp. v., TexCivApp–Fort Worth, 303 SW2d 865, aff 314 SW2d 763, 158 Tex 566, reh den 1958 WL 91272, cert den 79 SCt 223, 358 US 898, 3 LEd2d 148.—App & E 1001(1); Courts 493(3); Pat 182, 214.

Huffines v. Mercury Life & Health Co., TexCivApp–San Antonio, 185 SW2d 239.—Costs 232; Insurance 1070.

Huffines v. State, TexApp–Dallas, 646 SW2d 612, petition for discretionary review refused.—Crim Law 577.11(5); Double J 98, 107.1, 115; Extrad 59; Weap 3.

Huffines v. Swor Sand & Gravel Co., Inc., TexApp–Fort Worth, 750 SW2d 38.—App & E 93; Contracts 303(1), 309(1), 323(1); Mines 68(1).

Huffines Steel Co.; Donovan v., CA5 (Tex), 645 F2d 288.—Labor & Emp 2601.

Huffington v. Doughtie, TexCivApp–Galveston, 113 SW2d 343.—App & E 833(3); Equity 72(1), 87(1); Ten in C 15(2), 15(5), 15(7), 15(10); Tresp to T T 25, 35(2); Trial 351.2(4).

Huffington v. Enstar Corp., SDTex, 589 FSupp 624.—Action 3; Pub Ut 211.

Huffington; Parks v., TexCivApp–Hous (14 Dist), 616 SW2d 641, ref nre.—App & E 66, 70(0.5), 78(1), 79(1), 80(1), 870(1).

Huffington v. Texas & N. O. R. Co., TexCivApp–Austin, 376 SW2d 388, ref nre.—R R 459(1), 461.

Huffington v. Upchurch, Tex, 532 SW2d 576.—Aband L P 2, 4; App & E 1177(3), 1177(6); Mines 98, 99(1); Partners 70, 121.

Huffington v. Upchurch, TexCivApp–Hous (14 Dist), 523 SW2d 44, writ gr, aff in part, rev in part 532 SW2d 576.—App & E 931(4); Estop 68(1), 68(2); Mines 99(1), 99(2), 99(3); New Tr 159; Parties 96(3); Trial 350.3(1), 366; Trusts 103(5).

Huffman, Ex parte, TexCrimApp, 415 SW2d 408.—Crim Law 641.8; Sent & Pun 1318.

Huffman, Ex parte, TexApp–San Antonio, 9 SW3d 302.—Crim Law 1023(16); Hab Corp 275.1, 814.

Huffman; A.L.G. Enterprises v., TexApp–Corpus Christi, 660 SW2d 603, aff as reformed 672 SW2d 230.—Contracts 93(5); Ven & Pur 44.

Huffman; A.L.G. Enterprises, Inc. v., Tex, 672 SW2d 230.—App & E 1178(6).

Huffman v. Beto, CA5 (Tex), 434 F2d 819, cert den 91 SCt 964, 401 US 946, 28 LEd2d 229.—Hab Corp 719.

Huffman v. Beto, CA5 (Tex), 414 F2d 1094, appeal after remand 434 F2d 819, cert den 91 SCt 964, 401 US 946, 28 LEd2d 229.—Hab Corp 491, 795(1), 799.

Huffman v. Beto, CA5 (Tex), 382 F2d 777, appeal after remand 414 F2d 1094, appeal after remand 434 F2d 819, cert den 91 SCt 964, 401 US 946, 28 LEd2d 229.—Crim Law 1004; Hab Corp 500.1.

Huffman v. Beto, SDTex, 260 FSupp 63.—Crim Law 273.2(2), 641.1, 641.4(1), 641.4(2), 641.4(3), 641.10(1); Estop 52.10(2); Hab Corp 311, 482.1, 701.1, 702, 703, 705.1, 706, 714, 721(1), 745.1.

Huffman; Burdine v., SDTex, 229 FSupp2d 704.—Civil R 1450; Crim Law 641.10(1); Fed Cts 43, 46, 49.

Huffman v. City of Arlington, TexCivApp–Fort Worth, 619 SW2d 425, ref nre.—Tax 2436.

Huffman; Cox v., Tex, 319 SW2d 295, 159 Tex 298.—Brok 50, 79; Trial 358, 366.

Huffman v. Cox, TexCivApp–Austin, 315 SW2d 319, rev 319 SW2d 295, 159 Tex 298.—Brok 9, 50, 87, 89; Costs 194.32.

Huffman v. Estelle, CA5 (Tex), 536 F2d 1106.—Const Law 1100(3), 3811, 4837; Pardon 28.

Huffman v. Estelle, CA5 (Tex), 524 F2d 926.—Hab Corp 864(5).

Huffman; Fischer v., TexCivApp–Amarillo, 254 SW2d 878.—App & E 1078(5); Judgm 304, 306, 326.

Huffman; Fletcher v., TexCivApp–Fort Worth, 149 SW2d 313.—Chat Mtg 250; Consp 21; Mal Pros 40.

Huffman; Goodstein v., TexCivApp–Dallas, 222 SW2d 259, writ refused.—Contracts 1; Covenants 1, 71.

Huffman; Holiday Lodge Nursing Home, Inc. v., TexCivApp–Texarkana, 430 SW2d 826.—App & E 846(5), 1010.1(2); Labor & Emp 2840, 2923; Plead 111.42(7).

Huffman v. Huffman, Tex, 339 SW2d 885, 161 Tex 267.—Wills 94, 435, 439, 440, 449, 467, 478, 579, 704.

Huffman; Huffman v., Tex, 339 SW2d 885, 161 Tex 267.—Wills 94, 435, 439, 440, 449, 467, 478, 579, 704.

Huffman v. Huffman, TexCivApp–Fort Worth, 329 SW2d 139, writ gr, aff 339 SW2d 885, 161 Tex 267.—Wills 1, 69, 73, 78, 94, 435, 440, 470(3), 478, 487(2), 535, 865(1).

Huffman; Huffman v., TexCivApp–Fort Worth, 329 SW2d 139, writ gr, aff 339 SW2d 885, 161 Tex 267.—Wills 1, 69, 73, 78, 94, 435, 440, 470(3), 478, 487(2), 535, 865(1).

Huffman v. Huffman, TexCivApp–Amarillo, 408 SW2d 248.—Child C 27, 76; Courts 475(15); Venue 21.

Huffman; Huffman v., TexCivApp–Amarillo, 408 SW2d 248.—Child C 27, 76; Courts 475(15); Venue 21.

Huffman v. Mobil Oil Corp., CA5 (Tex), 554 F2d 1361.—Work Comp 108, 119, 1939.11(3), 2164.

Huffman v. Saenz, TexCivApp–Corpus Christi, 447 SW2d 508, ref nre.—App & E 843(2), 930(3), 989; Labor & Emp 2879, 2881; Work Comp 2110.

Huffman; S.E.C. v., CA5 (Tex), 996 F2d 800, 119 ALR Fed 789, reh den 4 F3d 992.—Fed Cts 414; Impl & C C 4; Sec Reg 150.1, 177; U S 75.5.

HUGGINS

Huffman v. Southern Underwriters, Tex, 128 SW2d 4, 133 Tex 354.—Autos 142; Labor & Emp 835, 2764; Parent & C 7(4); Work Comp 5, 51, 52, 367, 1072, 1130, 1139.

Huffman; Southern Underwriters v., TexCivApp–Galveston, 114 SW2d 926, rev 128 SW2d 4, 133 Tex 354.— Autos 116; Work Comp 11, 773.

Huffman v. State, TexCrimApp, 746 SW2d 212.—Crim Law 438(1), 438(8), 444, 1170.5(3), 1170.5(6); Homic 1165; Sent & Pun 316, 1720, 1756, 1772; Witn 390.

Huffman v. State, TexCrimApp, 726 SW2d 155.—Weap 17(1).

Huffman v. State, TexCrimApp, 479 SW2d 62.—Const Law 268(9), 4632; Crim Law 304(16), 938(1), 939(1), 958(1), 1094(1), 1124(1), 1170.5(1); Rob 24.25; Witn 345(1), 367(1), 388(2.1), 388(9.1), 388(10).

Huffman v. State, TexCrimApp, 450 SW2d 858, vac in part 92 SCt 2860, 408 US 936, 33 LEd2d 753, reh den 93 SCt 90, 409 US 897, 34 LEd2d 155, on remand Stanley v. State, 490 SW2d 828.—Crim Law 1130(2), 1166.17; Jury 108, 131(10); Witn 79(1).

Huffman v. State, TexCrimApp, 331 SW2d 325.—Crim Law 1131(5).

Huffman v. State, TexCrimApp, 245 SW2d 265.—Crim Law 1090.1(1).

Huffman v. State, TexApp–Houston (1 Dist), 676 SW2d 677, petition for discretionary review refused.—Crim Law 273.1(1), 273.1(2), 273.1(4), 641.13(5).

Huffman v. State, TexApp–Austin, 691 SW2d 726.—Crim Law 450, 637, 641.10(3), 789(3), 1038.1(1), 1038.1(5), 1077.3, 1169.5(2), 1169.11; Homic 938, 1152, 1345, 1346, 1458.

Huffman v. State, TexApp–El Paso, 775 SW2d 653, petition for discretionary review refused.—Courts 100(1); Crim Law 351(1), 552(3), 1159.6, 1172.1(2); Homic 1016, 1187; Ind & Inf 184.

Huffman; Webb v., TexCivApp–Amarillo, 320 SW2d 893, ref nre.—App & E 1036(3); Autos 198(4), 242(6), 245(93); Death 42.

Huffman; Wilson v., CA5 (Tex), 818 F2d 1135. See Missionary Baptist Foundation of America, Matter of.

Huffman; Wilson v., BkrtcyNDTex, 48 BR 885. See Missionary Baptist Foundation of America, Inc., In re.

Huffman; Worm v., TexCivApp–San Antonio, 244 SW2d 899, ref nre.—Evid 383(2).

Huffman Independent School Dist.; First Nat. Bank of Bellaire v., TexApp–Houston (14 Dist), 770 SW2d 571, writ den, cert den 110 SCt 1838, 494 US 1091, 108 LEd2d 967.—Const Law 4138(2); Liens 1; Tax 2105, 2106, 2672.

Huffmeister v. State, TexCrimApp, 341 SW2d 928, 170 TexCrim 460.—Crim Law 394.4(7), 1172.6; Searches 164.

Huffmeyer v. Mann, TexApp–Corpus Christi, 49 SW3d 554.—App & E 79(1), 80(6), ·854(1), 863, 934(1); Corp 559(3); Judgm 185(2); Partners 325(3), 325(4); Receivers 1, 8, 10, 16, 30, 65, 70, 73, 77(1), 77(2), 77(3), 78, 80; Trover 1.

Huffstetler v. State, TexCrimApp, 322 SW2d 624, 168 TexCrim 16.—Crim Law 406(1), 603.2, 814(1), 1169.3; Rob 24.10.

Huffstutlar v. Koons, TexApp–Dallas, 789 SW2d 707.— Child C 733, 736, 743; Hab Corp 532(2), 674.1; Judgm 495(1), 497(1), 499; Mand 4(1), 12, 60.

Huffstutler; American Mannex Corp. v., CA5 (Tex), 329 F2d 449.—Bankr 2050, 2063, 2151, 2374, 3066(1), 3066(6); Contracts 262.

Huffstutler v. Bergland, CA5 (Tex), 607 F2d 1090.— Agric 2; Const Law 4173(3), 4173(4); U S 36, 125(9).

Huffstutler; California Oil Co. v., CA5 (Tex), 322 F2d 596.—Bankr 2371(1), 3836.

Huffstutler; State v., TexApp–Austin, 871 SW2d 955.— App & E 930(1), 1001(1), 1122(2); Em Dom 221, 224;

Evid 570; Judgm 199(1), 199(3.5), 199(3.9), 199(3.10); Trial 139.1(14), 352.4(1).

Huffstutler; Stone v., CA5 (Tex), 227 F2d 217, cert den 76 SCt 788, 351 US 931, 100 LEd 1460.—Bankr 3771, 3789.1, 3837.

Hufft; Garvin v., TexCivApp–Dallas, 243 SW2d 391, ref nre.—App & E 300, 387(2), 468, 485(1); Child C 7, 42, 76, 409, 473, 904; New Tr 116.2, 155.

Hufo Oils; Colorado Interstate Gas Co. v., CA5 (Tex), 802 F2d 133, reh den 806 F2d 261.—Fed Cts 13; Mines 109.

HUFO Oils; Colorado Interstate Gas Co. v., WDTex, 626 FSupp 38, aff 802 F2d 133, reh den 806 F2d 261.— Decl Judgm 143.1; Mines 109.

Hufo Oils; Pan Eastern Exploration Co. v., CA5 (Tex), 855 F2d 1106, reh den.—Corp 1.4(1), 1.5(1), 1.5(2), 1.6(3), 397; Fed Civ Proc 2242; Fed Cts 714, 847, 937.1; Mines 51(1), 51(4), 84; Torts 126; Trover 1, 34(2).

Hufo Oils; Pan Eastern Exploration Co. v., CA5 (Tex), 798 F2d 837.—Fed Cts 572.1, 574, 584, 589.

Hufo Oils v. Railroad Com'n of Texas, TexApp–Austin, 717 SW2d 405, writ den.—Admin Law 481; Mines 92.54, 92.62; New Tr 10.

Hufstedler v. Barnett, TexCivApp–Amarillo, 182 SW2d 504, writ refused wom.—Adv Poss 25, 55, 60(4), 76, 93; Estop 61; Land & Ten 15, 56(2), 68; Statut 63; Tresp 35.

Hufstedler v. General American Life Ins. Co., TexCivApp–Austin, 82 SW2d 759, writ refused.—Mtg 567(1), 594(3).

Hufstedler v. Glenn, TexCivApp–Austin, 82 SW2d 733.— App & E 1140(1); Home 29, 47, 97, 213; Mech Liens 76; Mun Corp 434(5).

Hufstedler v. Sides, TexCivApp–Amarillo, 165 SW2d 1006, writ refused.—Adv Poss 18, 19, 44, 82, 95, 115(4); Corp 300, 432(1), 432(4), 444; Evid 16; Trial 177.

Hufstetler; Schuett v., TexCivApp–Hous (14 Dist), 608 SW2d 787.—Acct Action on 13, 14, 15.

Hufstetler; U.S. v., CA5 (Tex), 496 F2d 1184.—Courts 100(1); Crim Law 394.4(3).

Hug; Dorsett v., CA5 (Tex), 98 FedAppx 298.—Fed Cts 753, 915; Judges 49(1); RICO 28.

Hugg, Ex parte, TexApp–Amarillo, 636 SW2d 862, petition for discretionary review refused.—Bail 44(3.1), 53; Crim Law 1148.

Huggins; Cambridge Oil Co. v., TexApp–Corpus Christi, 765 SW2d 540, writ den.—Contracts 143.5, 147(1), 176(2), 318; Damag 87(1), 87(2), 89(2); Fraud 7; Mines 73, 74(8), 79.7.

Huggins; Chambers v., TexApp–Houston (14 Dist), 709 SW2d 219.—Contracts 93(5), 147(3), 175(1), 176(2); Deeds 69, 93, 120, 140; Evid 448; Judgm 233; Mines 55(7); Plead 228.14.

Huggins; Cliff v., Tex, 724 SW2d 778.—Evid 87, 89; Judgm 138(3), 151.

Huggins; Cliff v., TexApp–San Antonio, 696 SW2d 175, writ gr, rev 724 SW2d 778.—Judgm 143(2), 162(2); Notice 5.

Huggins; Dixon v., TexCivApp–Waco, 495 SW2d 621, dism.—App & E 846(5), 931(1), 989, 1010.1(3); Equity 57; Evid 236(3), 278; Trusts 69, 81(1).

Huggins v. Kinsey, TexCivApp–San Antonio, 414 SW2d 208, writ refused, cert den 88 SCt 1040, 390 US 950, 19 LEd2d 1141.—Appear 8(8); Judgm 17(3).

Huggins v. State, TexApp–Dallas, 544 SW2d 147.—Arson 3, 19; Crim Law 1134(8), 1187; Ind & Inf 91(3).

Huggins v. State, TexCrimApp, 426 SW2d 855.—Crim Law 404.75; Searches 197.

Huggins v. State, TexCrimApp, 325 SW2d 144, 168 TexCrim 302.—Crim Law 741(5).

Huggins v. State, TexCrimApp, 293 SW2d 779, 163 TexCrim 522.—Crim Law 338(1), 698(1), 1173.3; Int Liq 236(11).

Huggins v. State, TexCrimApp, 197 SW2d 577, 149 TexCrim 591.—Crim Law 1087.1(2).

Huggins v. State, TexCrimApp, 177 SW2d 269, 146 TexCrim 606.—Crim Law 784(1); Int Liq 140.

Huggins v. State, TexApp–Beaumont, 795 SW2d 909, petition for discretionary review refused.—Crim Law 730(1), 795(2.50), 1043(2), 1134(3), 1153(1); Sent & Pun 308, 312, 313.

Huggins v. Thompson, BkrtcyNDTex, 166 BR 849. See Thompson, In re.

Hughbank v. State, TexApp–Fort Worth, 967 SW2d 940. —Crim Law 367, 693, 708.1, 713, 730(1), 730(8), 730(14), 1030(1), 1036.2, 1043(3), 1153(1), 1170.5(3), 1170.5(6); Witn 267, 269(1), 277(4).

Hughes, Ex parte, Tex, 759 SW2d 118.—Clerks of C 67; Contempt 20.

Hughes, Ex parte, Tex, 129 SW2d 270, 133 Tex 505.—Action 50(10); Const Law 2496, 2503(1), 2503(2), 2505, 2621; Courts 1, 2, 27; Equity 1; Hab Corp 528.1; Inj 1, 102, 114(2); Nuis 79, 84; Usury 6; Witn 21.

Hughes, Ex parte, TexCrimApp, 739 SW2d 869.—Crim Law 995(2); Sent & Pun 1910, 1911.

Hughes, Ex parte, TexCrimApp, 728 SW2d 372, appeal after remand Hughes v. State, 897 SW2d 285, reh den, cert den 115 SCt 1967, 514 US 1112, 131 LEd2d 857, habeas corpus den 991 FSupp 621, on subsequent appeal 191 F3d 607, cert den 120 SCt 1003, 528 US 1145, 145 LEd2d 945.—Jury 108.

Hughes, Ex parte, TexCrimApp, 106 SW2d 303, 132 TexCrim 559.—Crim Law 1099.7(2).

Hughes, In Interest of, TexApp–Houston (1 Dist), 770 SW2d 635.—Adop 2, 4, 15; Const Law 3740; Pretrial Proc 690.

Hughes, In re, BkrtcyNDTex, 360 BR 202.—Bankr 2134, 2187, 2235; Contempt 20, 60(3), 70, 74.

Hughes, In re, BkrtcyNDTex, 354 BR 801.—Bankr 2164.1, 3274, 3278.1, 3279, 3280, 3282.1, 3284, 3315(2).

Hughes, In re, BkrtcyNDTex, 353 BR 486.—Bankr 3271, 3273.1, 3274, 3278.1, 3279, 3280, 3282.1, 3284, 3286, 3315(2).

Hughes, In re, BkrtcyNDTex, 172 BR 205, opinion supplemented 159 BR 197.—Banks 505; Const Law 2762, 2774, 4429; Home 6.1, 36, 70, 74, 177(2); Mtg 298(1).

Hughes, In re, BkrtcyNDTex, 159 BR 197.—Bankr 2802; Home 66, 214.

Hughes, In re, BkrtcySDTex, 354 BR 820.—Bankr 3374(9), 3376(3), 3376(4); Fraud 7.

Hughes, Matter of, CA5 (Tex), 704 F2d 820.—Bankr 2703, 3622.

Hughes; Aetna Cas. & Sur. Co. v., Tex, 497 SW2d 282.—Work Comp 1297.

Hughes; Aetna Cas. & Sur. Co. v., TexCivApp–Corpus Christi, 492 SW2d 690, rev 497 SW2d 282.—Work Comp 1269, 1283, 1297, 1683, 1726, 1935.

Hughes; Albin v., TexCivApp–Dallas, 304 SW2d 371.—Venue 7.5(4).

Hughes; Alvarado v., TexCivApp–Fort Worth, 448 SW2d 166, ref nre.—App & E 554(1).

Hughes v. American Nat. Ins. Co., TexCivApp–Dallas, 177 SW2d 801.—Contracts 143(2); Insurance 3479.

Hughes v. American Nat. Ins. Co., TexCivApp–Eastland, 146 SW2d 470.—Insurance 1758, 3003(1), 3003(10), 3015, 3084.

Hughes; American Sur. Co. of N. Y. v., TexCivApp–Galveston, 185 SW2d 235, writ refused.—Lim of Act 148(2), 148(3).

Hughes; Artripe v., TexApp–Corpus Christi, 857 SW2d 82, reh overr, and writ den.—App & E 863, 930(3); Costs 194.25, 194.32; Damag 89(2), 91(1); Fraud 61, 64(1); Judgm 114, 199(1); Trial 142, 350.1, 350.8; Trover 4, 16, 66.

Hughes v. Atlantic Refining Co., Tex, 424 SW2d 622.—Abate & R 27; Action 64; Courts 21; Pub Lands 173(16.4).

Hughes v. Atlantic Refining Co., TexCivApp–Tyler, 416 SW2d 619, rev 424 SW2d 622.—Pub Lands 173(16.4).

Hughes v. Autry, TexApp–Austin, 874 SW2d 890.—App & E 173(2), 934(1); Insurance 1416; Judgm 185(2); Lim of Act 66(7).

Hughes v. Autry, TexApp–Austin, 874 SW2d 887.—App & E 173(2); Lim of Act 66(7); Time 9(1).

Hughes v. Aycock, TexCivApp–Hous (14 Dist), 598 SW2d 370, ref nre.—Estop 59; Partners 71, 225, 242(8), 272; Trial 350.4(1), 365.3.

Hughes v. Belman, TexCivApp–Austin, 239 SW2d 717, ref nre.—App & E 291, 499(1), 930(3), 1078(1), 1170.6; Bills & N 90, 97(1), 525; Evid 208(6); Fraud 47, 58(1), 58(2), 59(2); Judgm 883(12); Trial 352.9, 352.10.

Hughes v. Belman, TexCivApp–Austin, 200 SW2d 431, ref nre.—Damag 87(2); Fraud 30, 50, 58(2), 61; Hus & W 25(1), 138(10), 229.6; Trial 350.4(2), 352.1(3).

Hughes; Berry v., TexCrimApp, 710 SW2d 600.—Crim Law 1192; Mand 3(2.1), 12, 61, 141.

Hughes v. Black, TexApp–Waco, 863 SW2d 559.—Child C 753; Courts 24; Mand 4(4).

Hughes v. Board of Trustees, Tarrant County Jr. College Dist., TexCivApp–Fort Worth, 480 SW2d 289, ref nre.—App & E 854(2); Const Law 90.1(2), 2010, 4224(7); Inj 12, 147, 150, 204; Judgm 244; Proc 31.

Hughes v. Bond, TexCivApp–Eastland, 118 SW2d 443, dism.—App & E 931(1), 1008.1(8.1), 1011.1(19); Home 209.

Hughes; Boswell v., TexCivApp–El Paso, 491 SW2d 762, ref nre.—Damag 89(2).

Hughes; Brandtjen & Kluge v., TexCivApp–Eastland, 236 SW2d 180, ref nre.—Accord 25(2); App & E 1170.3; Evid 357; Princ & A 177(3.1); Sales 172, 416(2), 417, 418(16.1); Trial 350.4(2).

Hughes; Browder v., TexCivApp–Beaumont, 597 SW2d 525, ref nre.—Brok 75.

Hughes v. Cantwell, TexCivApp–El Paso, 540 SW2d 742, ref nre.—Contracts 147(1), 147(3); Mines 78.1(1), 78.1(7).

Hughes v. City of Garland, CA5 (Tex), 204 F3d 223.—Const Law 4172(6), 4173(2), 4173(3), 4173(4); Mun Corp 218(10).

Hughes; City of Houston v., CA5 (Tex), 37 F3d 1097. See Edwards v. City of Houston.

Hughes; City of Houston v., TexCivApp–Austin, 284 SW2d 249, ref nre.—Bound 20(1); Dedi 18(2), 21, 39; High 18.

Hughes v. City of Rockwall, TexApp–Dallas, 153 SW3d 709, review gr.—Alt Disp Res 121; App & E 893(1); Mun Corp 33(9); Plead 111.36.

Hughes; Cobb v., CA5 (Tex), 434 F2d 1063.—Courts 104; Fed Cts 743.

Hughes; Coker v., TexCivApp–Amarillo, 307 SW2d 354.—Contracts 93(5); Evid 433(5), 461(1); Land & Ten 27; Ref of Inst 45(9).

Hughes v. Cole, TexCivApp–Tyler, 585 SW2d 865, ref nre.—Contracts 217; Partners 259.5.

Hughes; Couch Mortg. Co. v., TexCivApp–Hous (1 Dist), 536 SW2d 70.—Divorce 207; Mtg 413.

Hughes; Crosby v., TexCivApp–Amarillo, 212 SW2d 513.—Adv Poss 57, 85(3); App & E 1175(1); Ten in C 1, 15(2), 15(4), 15(10), 21.

Hughes; Dallas County v., TexApp–Dallas, 189 SW3d 886, reh overr, and review den, and reh of petition for review den.—App & E 863, 893(1); Judgm 181(7); Lim of Act 177(1), 180(1), 182(2); Plead 104(1).

Hughes v. Daugherty, TexCivApp–Waco, 297 SW2d 274, ref nre.—Deeds 124(0.5); Ven & Pur 152.

Hughes v. Dopson, TexCivApp–Amarillo, 135 SW2d 148.—Ack 54; Bills & N 443(3), 492, 501; Evid 271(20); Lim of Act 66(12).

Hughes v. Dretke, CA5 (Tex), 412 F3d 582, cert den 126 SCt 1347, 546 US 1177, 164 LEd2d 60.—Courts 100(1);

HUGHES;

Crim Law 1130(5); Hab Corp 205, 383, 422, 424, 450.1, 453, 461, 486(1), 775(2), 818.

Hughes v. Dretke, CA5 (Tex), 160 FedAppx 431.—Hab Corp 818.

Hughes; Edwards v., TexCivApp–Corpus Christi, 377 SW2d 235.—App & E 621(1), 624, 1126.

Hughes; F.T.C. v., CA5 (Tex), 891 F2d 589, reh den.—Fed Cts 656, 666.

Hughes; F.T.C. v., NDTex, 710 FSupp 1524, appeal dism 891 F2d 589, reh den.—Antitrust 229, 1005; Const Law 1539, 1590, 1600.

Hughes; F.T.C. v., NDTex, 710 FSupp 1520.—Admin Law 359; Evid 177, 220(6), 222(1), 373(1); Fed Civ Proc 2536.1, 2538, 2545.

Hughes; First State Bank of Frankston v., TexApp–Tyler, 654 SW2d 31.—Banks 189; Judgm 181(26).

Hughes; Foley v., CA5 (Tex), 116 FedAppx 519.—Hab Corp 847; Judges 36.

Hughes; Ford Rent Co. v., Tex, 88 SW2d 85, 126 Tex 255. —Courts 207.4(2).

Hughes; Ford Rent Co. v., TexCivApp–Dallas, 90 SW2d 290.—Autos 247; Trial 358.

Hughes v. Fort Worth Nat. Bank, TexCivApp, 164 SW2d 231, writ refused.—Atty & C 11(2.1), 32(3), 166(1); Evid 208(1), 208(6), 265(8).

Hughes; General Ins. Co. v., Tex, 255 SW2d 193, 152 Tex 159.—Autos 19, 20; Insurance 2694.

Hughes; General Ins. Corp. v., TexCivApp–Dallas, 193 SW2d 230.—Damag 221(3); Mand 168(2); Work Comp 845, 1366, 1930.

Hughes; General Ins. Corp. v., TexCivApp–Galveston, 249 SW2d 231, rev 255 SW2d 193, 152 Tex 159.—Aband L P 5; App & E 218.2(1); Evid 263(4), 265(8), 265(9), 265(10); Insurance 2695.

Hughes; Gillring Oil Co. v., TexCivApp–Beaumont, 618 SW2d 874.—Mines 92.79, 109.

Hughes; Glittenberg v., TexCivApp–Fort Worth, 524 SW2d 954.—App & E 909(1); Judgm 143(3), 145(2), 153(1), 163.

Hughes; Grant v., TexCivApp–Eastland, 198 SW2d 630.— App & E 387(2), 392.

Hughes v. Grogan-Lamm Lumber Co., TexCivApp–Dallas, 331 SW2d 799, ref nre.—App & E 302(1), 757(3), 760(2), 934(1); Contracts 322(4); Mech Liens 73(4); New Tr 102(8), 150(2).

Hughes v. Groshart, TexCivApp–Amarillo, 150 SW2d 827. —Home 55, 81, 84, 94, 103, 167.

Hughes; Guisinger v., TexCivApp–Dallas, 363 SW2d 861, ref nre.—Evid 420(3), 434(1), 434(9), 444(0.5), 448; Judgm 185.3(7); Princ & A 70.

Hughes; Gulf Cas. Co. v., TexCivApp–Beaumont, 230 SW2d 293.—App & E 1010.1(3), 1177(7); New Tr 70, 164; Trial 352.4(9); Work Comp 1283, 1726, 1924, 1927, 1928, 1964, 1975.

Hughes v. Gunter, TexCivApp–Beaumont, 136 SW2d 253. —App & E 1161.

Hughes v. Habitat Apartments, Tex, 860 SW2d 872.— Atty & C 62.

Hughes v. Habitat Apartments, TexApp–Dallas, 828 SW2d 794.—App & E 465(1); Costs 264; Execution 7.

Hughes v. Halliday, TexCivApp–Waco, 471 SW2d 88.— Fraud 59(1), 62.

Hughes; Hays v., TexCivApp–Austin, 106 SW2d 724, writ refused.—Judgm 326.

Hughes v. Hess, Tex, 172 SW2d 301, 141 Tex 511.— Contracts 138(1); Estop 92(2); Execution 273; Ex & Ad 87, 122(1); Lim of Act 142, 148(3), 164; Ven & Pur 210, 267.

Hughes v. Hess, TexCivApp–Austin, 166 SW2d 718, aff in part, mod in part 172 SW2d 301, 141 Tex 511.—Ex & Ad 122(1); Judgm 785(1); Lim of Act 142, 143(6), 151(1), 151(4).

Hughes; Homan v., TexCrimApp, 708 SW2d 449.—Crim Law 1026.10(4), 1083; Mand 4(4), 61, 141; Sent & Pun 2305.

Hughes; Hoppe v., TexCivApp–Amarillo, 577 SW2d 773, ref nre.—App & E 302(6); Autos 153, 244(10), 244(31); Courts 85(3); Evid 547, 568(1), 571(1).

Hughes v. Houston Northwest Medical Center, TexApp–Houston (1 Dist), 647 SW2d 5, dism.—Corp 320(4); Inj 26(1), 27; Lis Pen 3(1), 3(3), 20.

Hughes v. Houston Northwest Medical Center, Inc., TexApp–Houston (1 Dist), 680 SW2d 838, ref nre, cert den 106 SCt 571, 474 US 1020, 88 LEd2d 555.—App & E 901, 930(3), 989, 1001(1), 1079, 1177(7); Corp 307, 320(11); Damag 6, 141; Decl Judgm 385; Judgm 252(1); Mal Pros 47; Torts 212, 242, 263; Trusts 102(1); Witn 216(1).

Hughes v. Howe Grain and Mercantile Co., TexCivApp–Dallas, 162 SW 1187.—Trademarks 1800.

Hughes v. Hughes, TexCivApp–Dallas, 275 SW2d 506.— Courts 475(15); Divorce 172.

Hughes; Hughes v., TexCivApp–Dallas, 275 SW2d 506.— Courts 475(15); Divorce 172.

Hughes v. Hughes, TexCivApp–Dallas, 221 SW2d 1003.— App & E 989; Appear 19(1); Child S 231; Divorce 254(2).

Hughes; Hughes v., TexCivApp–Dallas, 221 SW2d 1003. —App & E 989; Appear 19(1); Child S 231; Divorce 254(2).

Hughes v. Hughes, TexCivApp–Beaumont, 473 SW2d 304, writ gr, rev Swilley v. Hughes, 488 SW2d 64.—App & E 934(1); Judgm 178, 185(2), 185.2(9); Parties 44, 47, 93(2).

Hughes; Hughes v., TexCivApp–Beaumont, 473 SW2d 304, writ gr, rev Swilley v. Hughes, 488 SW2d 64.—App & E 934(1); Judgm 178, 185(2), 185.2(9); Parties 44, 47, 93(2).

Hughes v. Hughes, TexCivApp–Waco, 407 SW2d 14.— App & E 499(1); Divorce 179, 183, 285.

Hughes; Hughes v., TexCivApp–Waco, 407 SW2d 14.— App & E 499(1); Divorce 179, 183, 285.

Hughes v. Hughes, TexCivApp–Eastland, 211 SW2d 785, mandamus overr.—Child C 602; Venue 15.

Hughes; Hughes v., TexCivApp–Eastland, 211 SW2d 785, mandamus overr.—Child C 602; Venue 15.

Hughes; Hyatt v., TexCivApp–San Antonio, 221 SW2d 998, ref nre.—Damag 120(1); Insurance 1144, 1604.

Hughes; Iley v., Tex, 311 SW2d 648, 158 Tex 362, 85 ALR2d 1.—App & E 4; Mand 4(1), 4(3), 28; Trial 3(5.1).

Hughes v. Jackson, TexComApp, 81 SW2d 656, 125 Tex 130.—Trusts 44(1), 58, 140(1), 373.

Hughes v. Johnson, CA5 (Tex), 191 F3d 607, cert den 120 SCt 1003, 528 US 1145, 145 LEd2d 945.—Const Law 4594(1), 4637, 4745, 4762, 4770; Crim Law 700(2.1), 700(4), 790, 824(4), 1134(3); Hab Corp 205, 401, 404, 422, 431, 461, 493(2), 498, 742, 818, 824; Homic 1403; Sent & Pun 1626, 1720, 1772, 1780(3), 1784(4), 1788(5); States 18.63.

Hughes v. Johnson, CA5 (Tex), 170 FedAppx 878.—Civil R 1382.

Hughes v. Johnson, SDTex, 991 FSupp 621, on subsequent appeal 191 F3d 607, cert den 120 SCt 1003, 528 US 1145, 145 LEd2d 945.—Const Law 2781, 2815, 4629, 4745; Courts 100(1); Crim Law 721(3), 723(1), 730(8), 738, 753.1, 796, 872.5, 1137(2), 1144.15, 1158(3), 1172.1(1), 1172.6; Hab Corp 314, 401, 404, 422, 450.1, 461, 497, 498, 508, 745.1, 770, 775(2), 801, 818; Homic 554, 1387, 1403; Jury 108, 127; Searches 61; Sent & Pun 14, 1618, 1625, 1652, 1668, 1720, 1756, 1769, 1780(3), 1788(6).

Hughes; Johnson v., TexApp–Houston (1 Dist), 663 SW2d 11.—App & E 1122(2), 1175(2); Mand 154(3), 154(9), 168(4).

Hughes v. Jones, TexCivApp–El Paso, 543 SW2d 885.—App & E 1177(9); Damag 199; Judgm 139.

Hughes v. Jones, TexCivApp–Eastland, 94 SW2d 534.—App & E 994(3), 1008.1(8.1), 1012.1(3); Nuis 23(2), 25(2), 29; Trial 405(3).

Hughes v. J. Weingarten, Inc., TexCivApp–Beaumont, 398 SW2d 440, ref nre.—App & E 927(7), 997(3); Neglig 1708.

Hughes v. Keeling, TexCivApp–Beaumont, 198 SW2d 779.—App & E 688(1), 780(2), 874(2); Relig Soc 8, 12(2), 14.

Hughes; Kemp v., TexCivApp–Eastland, 557 SW2d 139.—Life Est 12; Mines 52.

Hughes; Kroger Co. v., TexCivApp–Hous (1 Dist), 616 SW2d 287.—Mal Pros 15; Trial 355(1), 356(5).

Hughes; Lane v., TexCivApp–Amarillo, 228 SW2d 986.—Evid 20(1); Mines 47, 55(1), 55(4); Partit 13, 116(1).

Hughes; Liberty Mut. Ins. Co. v., TexCivApp–Beaumont, 238 SW2d 803, ref nre.—App & E 968; Evid 450(6); Jury 129; Trial 350.5(3); Work Comp 1922, 1924, 1926, 1929.

Hughes; Louisiana & A. Ry. Co. v., CA5 (Tex), 374 F2d 106.—Fed Cts 904; R R 304, 351(5).

Hughes; Lower Colo. River Authority v., TexCivApp–Austin, 122 SW2d 222, dism.—Em Dom 134, 149(1), 202(1), 222(4), 239, 262(5); Evid 474(18).

Hughes v. McAngus, TexCivApp–Austin, 384 SW2d 419.—Hus & W 85(1); Interest 66.

Hughes v. McClatchy, TexCivApp–Eastland, 242 SW2d 799, ref nre.—App & E 930(1), 1033(3); Judgm 866.1, 871; Witn 128.

Hughes v. McDonald, TexCivApp–Austin, 122 SW2d 366, writ gr, rev United Production Corp v. Hughes, 152 SW2d 327, 137 Tex 21.—Mand 1, 8, 85, 141, 187.2; Mines 5.2(2.1), 5.3; Plead 49; Pub Lands 175(7); Venue 5.1.

Hughes; McGuire v., TexCivApp–Dallas, 452 SW2d 29.—J P 2, 8; Offic 77.

Hughes; McQuillen v., Tex, 626 SW2d 495.—Pretrial Proc 501.

Hughes v. Magnolia Petroleum Co., CCA5 (Tex), 88 F2d 817.—Pat 178, 234.

Hughes v. Mahaney & Higgins, Tex, 821 SW2d 154.—Lim of Act 55(3), 95(11), 105(2).

Hughes v. Mahaney & Higgins, TexApp–Waco, 822 SW2d 63, writ gr, rev 821 SW2d 154.—Atty & C 129(1); Judgm 185(2); Lim of Act 55(3), 95(3), 95(11), 105(2).

Hughes v. Marshall Nat. Bank, TexCivApp–Tyler, 538 SW2d 820, writ dism woj.—Partners 325(2), 325(3); Receivers 14, 29(1), 32, 38, 40.

Hughes; Martin v., TexApp–Beaumont, 738 SW2d 732.—Judgm 540, 713(1), 715(1), 715(3).

Hughes v. Martin, TexCivApp–Amarillo, 150 SW2d 413, writ refused.—Bills & N 451(1); Plgs 30(5).

Hughes v. Massey, TexApp–Beaumont, 65 SW3d 743.—App & E 671(4); Const Law 2314, 2325; Convicts 6; Costs 132(5), 133; Pretrial Proc 676, 690, 694, 695; States 4.1(1), 18.15.

Hughes; Meadows v., TexCivApp–Amarillo, 318 SW2d 125, writ refused.—Brok 43(0.5), 82(4).

Hughes; Mercury Life & Health Co. v., TexCivApp–San Antonio, 271 SW2d 842, writ refused.—Contracts 136; Corp 307, 314(2); Insurance 1130, 1133, 1134.

Hughes; Merrill Lynch, Pierce, Fenner & Smith, Inc. v., TexApp–Corpus Christi, 809 SW2d 679, writ gr, vac 827 SW2d 859.—Alt Disp Res 205, 368; App & E 66; States 4.1(1).

Hughes; Metromedia Long Distance, Inc. v., TexApp–San Antonio, 810 SW2d 494, writ den.—App & E 70(1), 173(9), 181; Judgm 739; Parties 38, 40(1), 40(7), 44.

Hughes v. Miracle Ford, Inc., TexApp–Dallas, 676 SW2d 642, ref nre.—Brok 32, 57(1), 57(2), 65(4), 87.

Hughes v. Mobil Oil Corp., CA5 (Tex), 421 F2d 1248, cert den 90 SCt 1868, 398 US 950, 26 LEd2d 289.—

Autos 172(7), 193(8.1), 245(39), 245(43); Damag 208(7); Evid 490; Fed Cts 827, 917.

Hughes v. Morgan, TexApp–Fort Worth, 816 SW2d 557, writ den.—Inj 138.78.

Hughes; Motor & Indus. Finance Corp. v., Tex, 302 SW2d 386, 157 Tex 276.—Bills & N 98, 129(2); Mtg 218.1, 335, 358.

Hughes; Motor & Indus. Finance Corp. v., TexCivApp–Austin, 294 SW2d 182, rev 302 SW2d 386, 157 Tex 276.—Bills & N 92(1), 94(2), 129(2), 394; Hus & W 169(1); Mtg 105, 335.

Hughes; Nassar v., TexApp–Houston (1 Dist), 882 SW2d 36, reh den, and writ den.—App & E 1061.1; Judgm 183, 186; Plead 228.14, 228.23; Trial 139.1(7), 178.

Hughes v. Parmer, TexCivApp–Austin, 164 SW2d 576.—App & E 1010.1(8.1), 1010.1(18); Fraud Conv 52(1), 299(1); Home 161, 168, 181(1), 181(3), 213.

Hughes; Patterson v., TexCivApp–Austin, 227 SW2d 397.—App & E 1015(5), 1062.1, 1069.1; New Tr 144; Plead 237(1), 356; Pretrial Proc 79; Trial 315.

Hughes; Peacock v., CA5 (Tex), 427 F2d 359.—Hab Corp 517, 827; Pardon 76.

Hughes; Perdue v., TexCivApp–Galveston, 143 SW2d 684, writ dism, correct.—Contracts 117(2).

Hughes v. Price, TexCivApp–Amarillo, 229 SW2d 79.—Tax 3007.

Hughes; Pride Transport Co., Inc. v., TexCivApp–Eastland, 591 SW2d 631, ref nre.—App & E 930(2), 1170.1, 1170.6; Damag 187, 191; Trial 127, 133.6(8).

Hughes v. Purnell, TexCivApp–Waco, 328 SW2d 244.—App & E 773(2).

Hughes; Ready v., TexApp–Waco, 846 SW2d 1.—Infants 155, 172, 200.

Hughes; Reid v., CA5 (Tex), 578 F2d 634.—Courts 489(10); Fed Civ Proc 630, 1773, 2533.1; Fed Cts 18, 242.1, 763.1; Sec Reg 5.13, 60.15, 60.36, 60.37, 60.52.

Hughes v. Rhodes, TexCivApp–Fort Worth, 137 SW2d 820, aff 152 SW2d 334, 137 Tex 32.—Action 53(1); Mines 6.

Hughes; Richardson v., TexCivApp–Austin, 146 SW2d 255, writ dism, correct.—App & E 1008.1(12), 1177(6); Contracts 136; Estop 98(4); Execution 274; Ex & Ad 122(1); Lim of Act 142, 143(6); Ven & Pur 229(5).

Hughes v. Rutherford, CA5 (Tex), 201 F2d 161.—Judgm 853(3).

Hughes; Rutherford v., EDTex, 103 FSupp 161, rev 201 F2d 161.—Execution 171(3); Home 5, 60, 63, 70, 89; Judgm 853(3).

Hughes; Rutherford v., TexCivApp–Amarillo, 228 SW2d 909.—App & E 1060.1(1), 1060.1(7); Infants 47, 55, 58(1), 58(2), 92, 98.

Hughes; Sabine River Authority of Texas v., TexApp–Beaumont, 92 SW3d 640, review den, and reh of petition for review den.—Em Dom 2(10), 266, 307(2).

Hughes v. St. David's Support Corp., TexApp–Austin, 944 SW2d 423, reh overr, and writ den.—Judgm 181(15.1); Partners 70, 366.

Hughes v. Sanders, TexCivApp–San Antonio, 243 SW2d 211.—Abate & R 4, 9; Mand 168(2); Trial 15.

Hughes v. Santa Fe Intern. Corp., CA5 (Tex), 847 F2d 239.—Judgm 651.

Hughes; Shalala, CA5 (Tex), 23 F3d 957.—Social S 140.21, 140.30, 148.1, 148.5, 149.

Hughes; Shaver v., TexCivApp–Fort Worth, 214 SW2d 176.—Appear 9(5); Const Law 2503(1); Courts 120; Decl Judgm 271; Plead 110, 111.37; Pretrial Proc 471, 474, 481; Venue 22(1), 22(4), 22(6).

Hughes v. State, TexCrimApp, 24 SW3d 833, cert den 121 SCt 430, 531 US 980, 148 LEd2d 438, habeas corpus den 2004 WL 549480, certificate of appealability den 412 F3d 582, cert den 126 SCt 1347, 546 US 1177, 164 LEd2d 60.—Arrest 63.1, 63.4(2), 63.4(11), 63.4(13), 63.4(16); Const Law 1051, 4745; Crim Law 394.5(2), 855(8), 867, 868, 925(1), 1134(6), 1166.10(2); Jury 128,

138(2); Searches 162; Sent & Pun 1745, 1747, 1756, 1757, 1762, 1780(3), 1789(5).

Hughes v. State, TexCrimApp, 4 SW3d 1, on remand 12 SW3d 166, habeas corpus den 2002 WL 172451.— Courts 85(3); Crim Law 338(7), 406(1), 417(15); Witn 321, 390.

Hughes v. State, TexCrimApp, 897 SW2d 285, reh den, cert den 115 SCt 1967, 514 US 1112, 131 LEd2d 857, habeas corpus den 991 FSupp 621, on subsequent appeal 191 F3d 607, cert den 120 SCt 1003, 528 US 1145, 145 LEd2d 945.—Const Law 203, 2789, 2815; Courts 70; Crim Law 486(6), 730(8), 772(1), 814(21), 1037.1(2), 1043(3), 1172.1(3), 1172.6, 1172.9; Homic 554; Searches 165; Sent & Pun 1626, 1708, 1710, 1720, 1721, 1772, 1780(3), 1784(4), 1788(5), 1788(9), 1789(8).

Hughes v. State, TexCrimApp, 878 SW2d 142, reh gr, and on reh, and reh den, cert den 114 SCt 2184, 511 US 1152, 128 LEd2d 902.—Arrest 63.4(2), 63.4(13); Crim Law 444, 698(1), 713, 729, 730(14), 1035(5), 1043(2), 1043(3), 1133, 1137(1), 1166.16, 1166.18, 1169.5(1), 1169.5(3), 1177; Jury 97(1).

Hughes v. State, TexCrimApp, 843 SW2d 591.—Searches 114, 126.

Hughes v. State, TexCrimApp, 833 SW2d 137, reh gr, and reh den.—Crim Law 273.1(4).

Hughes v. State, TexCrimApp, 719 SW2d 560, 71 ALR4th 919.—Homic 757, 1202.

Hughes v. State, TexCrimApp, 612 SW2d 581.—Controlled Subs 27, 80; Crim Law 1038.2, 1122(5).

Hughes v. State, TexCrimApp, 563 SW2d 581, cert den 99 SCt 1432, 440 US 950, 59 LEd2d 640.—Crim Law 371(12), 438(2), 713, 720(9), 726, 730(1), 899; Jury 106, 108.

Hughes v. State, TexCrimApp, 562 SW2d 857, cert den 99 SCt 268, 439 US 903, 58 LEd2d 250, reh den Anderson Hughes v. Texas, 99 SCt 604, 439 US 998, 58 LEd2d 674.—Const Law 4742; Crim Law 531(3), 532(0.5), 781(2), 1023(11), 1035(6), 1036.6, 1043(3), 1130(2), 1169.2(1); Jury 108, 131(1), 131(3), 131(15.1), 131(17); Sent & Pun 1624.

Hughes v. State, TexCrimApp, 561 SW2d 8.—Crim Law 1032(1); Ind & Inf 196(1), 196(6), 196(7); Rec S Goods 7(1).

Hughes v. State, TexCrimApp, 533 SW2d 824.—Controlled Subs 74.

Hughes v. State, TexCrimApp, 506 SW2d 625.—Crim Law 517.2(2); Sent & Pun 1788(5).

Hughes v. State, TexCrimApp, 493 SW2d 166.—Crim Law 59(3), 304(2), 723(1), 730(12), 730(14), 996(1); Judgm 751; Sent & Pun 1108.

Hughes v. State, TexCrimApp, 455 SW2d 303.—Homic 1134; Ind & Inf 129(1), 132(3).

Hughes v. State, TexCrimApp, 439 SW2d 352.—Assault 95; Crim Law 730(3).

Hughes v. State, TexCrimApp, 433 SW2d 698.—Burg 41(1); Crim Law 1037.1(4), 1037.2, 1170.5(6).

Hughes v. State, TexCrimApp, 409 SW2d 416.—Burg 41(1); Crim Law 519(8), 531(3), 720(1), 730(7), 1037.2, 1044.1(8), 1158(4); Sent & Pun 1379(2).

Hughes v. State, TexCrimApp, 358 SW2d 386, 172 TexCrim 441.—Crim Law 627.7(3), 1098, 1166(10.10).

Hughes v. State, TexCrimApp, 331 SW2d 216, 168 TexCrim 637.—Crim Law 369.6; Int Liq 238(5).

Hughes v. State, TexCrimApp, 317 SW2d 55.—Controlled Subs 6.

Hughes v. State, TexCrimApp, 294 SW2d 846, 163 TexCrim 575.—Crim Law 1170.5(5); Forg 44(3); Witn 372(1).

Hughes v. State, TexCrimApp, 289 SW2d 768, 163 TexCrim 224.—Crim Law 1169.2(5).

Hughes v. State, TexCrimApp, 278 SW2d 164.—Crim Law 1090.1(1).

Hughes v. State, TexCrimApp, 276 SW2d 813, 161 TexCrim 300.—Autos 354, 355(6); Crim Law 1097(4), 1097(5), 1099.1.

Hughes v. State, TexCrimApp, 276 SW2d 274, 161 TexCrim 256.—Crim Law 1192; Homic 790, 1193.

Hughes v. State, TexCrimApp, 267 SW2d 836, 160 TexCrim 114.—Crim Law 1083, 1086.13.

Hughes v. State, TexCrimApp, 262 SW2d 506.—Crim Law 1086.13.

Hughes v. State, TexCrimApp, 225 SW2d 191, 154 TexCrim 65.—Crim Law 1169.5(3).

Hughes v. State, TexCrimApp, 218 SW2d 479, 153 TexCrim 146.—Crim Law 1087.1(2), 1186.1.

Hughes v. State, TexCrimApp, 213 SW2d 820, 152 TexCrim 297.—Crim Law 720(9), 736(2), 761(2), 789(4), 1043(2), 1050, 1170(2); Homic 1134; Ind & Inf 125(29), 140(2); Witn 268(9).

Hughes v. State, TexCrimApp, 191 SW2d 479.—Crim Law 1094(2.1).

Hughes v. State, TexCrimApp, 189 SW2d 498, 148 TexCrim 543.—Crim Law 814(3); Int Liq 239(10); Sent & Pun 1345.

Hughes v. State, TexCrimApp, 132 SW2d 875, 137 TexCrim 533.—Larc 55.

Hughes v. State, TexCrimApp, 124 SW2d 349, 136 TexCrim 210, writ gr.—Crim Law 379, 385, 730(14), 938(1), 939(1), 940, 957(2), 958(3), 958(6), 959, 1120(3), 1156(3), 1159.3(1); Rape 54(1), 54(2).

Hughes v. State, TexCrimApp, 114 SW2d 569, 134 TexCrim 171.—Crim Law 507(4).

Hughes v. State, TexCrimApp, 114 SW2d 568, 134 TexCrim 172.—Crim Law 507(4).

Hughes v. State, TexCrimApp, 114 SW2d 566, 134 TexCrim 175.—Crim Law 507(4); Ind & Inf 125(1), 125(31); Int Liq 208; Statut 179.

Hughes v. State, TexCrimApp, 106 SW2d 698, 132 TexCrim 639.—Autos 355(6); Const Law 64, 2442; Crim Law 922(7), 1159.2(2).

Hughes v. State, TexApp–Houston (1 Dist), 962 SW2d 689, reh overr, and petition for discretionary review refused.—Crim Law 339.7(3), 339.8(3), 374, 394.6(4), 394.6(5), 637, 1130(5), 1144.8, 1144.12, 1152(1), 1153(1), 1158(3), 1158(4), 1162, 1166.8, 1169.1(5), 1169.1(9); Jury 33(5.15).

Hughes v. State, TexApp–Houston (1 Dist), 962 SW2d 89, petition for discretionary review refused.—Crim Law 369.2(1), 369.15, 598(2), 598(6), 867; Jury 33(5.15).

Hughes v. State, TexApp–Fort Worth, 12 SW3d 166, habeas corpus den 2002 WL 172451.—Crim Law 1162, 1169.1(9).

Hughes v. State, TexApp–Fort Worth, 850 SW2d 260, petition for discretionary review refused.—Crim Law 396(1), 486(3), 489, 662.7, 1134(2), 1134(5), 1158(3); Jury 33(5.15); Sent & Pun 310; Witn 344(5).

Hughes v. State, TexApp–Austin, 673 SW2d 654, petition for discretionary review refused by 692 SW2d 64.— Burg 46(6); Crim Law 37.10(2), 814(1), 822(1), 995(3), 1092.7, 1172.1(4), 1184(2); Double J 135, 148; Sent & Pun 547, 548, 573, 1014, 1106.

Hughes v. State, TexApp–San Antonio, 739 SW2d 458.— Assault 56, 92(3); Crim Law 956(4).

Hughes v. State, TexApp–Dallas, 135 SW3d 926, petition for discretionary review refused.—Crim Law 641.13(7), 1590.

Hughes v. State, TexApp–Dallas, 729 SW2d 352, petition for discretionary review refused, untimely filed.—Controlled Subs 9; Crim Law 1126; Sent & Pun 2004, 2020, 2021.

Hughes v. State, TexApp–Texarkana, 806 SW2d 248, petition for discretionary review gr, rev 833 SW2d 137, reh gr, and reh den.—Crim Law 273.1(4), 273.1(5), 1043(2), 1134(2), 1163(1), 1167(5).

Hughes v. State, TexApp–Amarillo, 7 SW3d 880, reh overr.—Crim Law 394.6(4), 1026.10(4), 1128(1), 1139, 1158(4); Witn 257.10.

Hughes v. State, TexApp–Beaumont, 691 SW2d 118, petition for discretionary review refused.—Sent & Pun 101.

Hughes v. State, TexApp–Waco, 16 SW3d 429.—Crim Law 303.15, 303.45; Double J 51; Hab Corp 814, 816.

Hughes v. State, TexApp–Tyler, 194 SW3d 649.—Assault 91.9; Crim Law 1030(1), 1042, 1043(2), 1045, 1134(3), 1144.13(2.1), 1159.2(7).

Hughes v. State, TexApp–Tyler, 128 SW3d 247, reh overr, and petition for discretionary review refused, appeal after new trial 194 SW3d 649.—Crim Law 363, 366(1), 366(4), 1162, 1165(1), 1169.1(9).

Hughes v. State, TexApp–Tyler, 721 SW2d 356, petition for discretionary review gr, aff 719 SW2d 560, 71 ALR4th 919.—Homic 757, 1340.

Hughes v. State, TexApp–Corpus Christi, 787 SW2d 193, petition for discretionary review refused.—Crim Law 450; Jury 149; Rob 24.15(2), 24.40; Sent & Pun 316, 319.

Hughes v. State, TexApp–Corpus Christi, 665 SW2d 582. —Courts 56; Crim Law 695(6), 822(1), 822(6), 1038.1(4), 1043(3), 1172.1(3), 1177; Sent & Pun 313, 1379(2).

Hughes v. State, TexApp–Houston (14 Dist), 843 SW2d 236.—Bail 51, 52.

Hughes v. State, TexApp–Houston (14 Dist), 681 SW2d 134, petition for discretionary review refused.—Crim Law 824(3), 1091(5), 1120(3), 1172.1(4); Homic 1492.

Hughes v. State, TexApp–Houston (14 Dist), 625 SW2d 827.—Burg 28(1); Const Law 4694; Crim Law 561(1), 1043(3), 1134(2).

Hughes v. State, TexCivApp–Eastland, 302 SW2d 747, ref nre.—App & E 882(8), 939, 1170.6; Em Dom 5, 204, 255, 262(5).

Hughes v. State, TexCivApp–Corpus Christi, 508 SW2d 167, ref nre.—Evid 314(1), 318(4), 593; Infants 173.1; Witn 37(1), 76(1), 77, 78.

Hughes v. Stovall, TexCivApp–Amarillo, 135 SW2d 603, writ dism, correct.—Home 217; Lim of Act 51(2), 51(3); Mtg 246.

Hughes; Straus-Frank Co. v., TexComApp, 156 SW2d 519, 138 Tex 50.—Guar 24(1), 53(1); Princ & S 97.

Hughes v. Straus-Frank Co., TexCivApp–San Antonio, 127 SW2d 582, aff 156 SW2d 519, 138 Tex 50.—App & E 882(3); Guar 1, 7(1), 27, 53(1), 85(1), 89, 92(1); Princ & S 97.

Hughes; Swilley v., Tex, 488 SW2d 64.—App & E 934(1); Ex & Ad 435; Judgm 178, 185(2), 185(5), 185(6), 185.3(16), 186.

Hughes; Tarrant County Hosp. Dist. v., TexApp–Fort Worth, 734 SW2d 675.—Const Law 1079, 1231; Mand 40; Pretrial Proc 33, 40, 41.

Hughes v. Tarrant County Tex., CA5 (Tex), 948 F2d 918. —Civil R 1376(1), 1376(4), 1376(9); Fed Cts 579.

Hughes v. Team Bank, BkrtcyNDTex, 172 BR 205. See Hughes, In re.

Hughes v. Team Bank, BkrtcyNDTex, 159 BR 197. See Hughes, In re.

Hughes v. Thornton, TexCivApp–Dallas, 320 SW2d 191. —App & E 465(2).

Hughes v. Thrash, TexApp–Houston (1 Dist), 832 SW2d 779.—App & E 756, 1062.2, 1068(5); Costs 260(5); Damag 132(1), 135, 208(5); Interest 39(2.20), 39(2.50), 47(1); Labor & Emp 3053; Neglig 506(8), 1677, 1683; Trial 344.

Hughes v. Tobacco Institute, Inc., CA5 (Tex), 278 F3d 417.—Antitrust 236, 960, 963(3); Assault 60; Const Law 2312, 2314, 4419; Courts 90(2); Fed Cts 392, 776; Impl & C C 3; Nuis 76; Prod Liab 2, 59; RICO 59; Sales 255, 262.

Hughes v. Trimble, TexCivApp–Galveston, 254 SW2d 420, ref nre.—App & E 931(1), 989, 1011.1(4), 1012.1(5); Tresp to T T 41(1); Trusts 44(1).

Hughes; Trinity River Authority v., TexCivApp–Beaumont, 504 SW2d 822, ref nre.—Adv Poss 110(1), 112; App & E 1177(7); Tresp to T T 41(3).

Hughes; TXI Transp. Co. v., TexApp–Fort Worth, 224 SW3d 870.—App & E 840(4), 854(4), 928(2), 930(1), 965, 969, 970(2), 971(2), 971(6), 989, 1001(1), 1047(1), 1050.1(11), 1062.1, 1064.1(7); Autos 192(11), 197(2), 200, 201(1.1), 244(10), 244(31), 244(36.1), 246(16), 246(57), 249.2; Const Law 3309; Death 15, 103(1); Evid 333(1), 508, 535, 545, 546, 555.2, 555.8(1), 571(6), 571(9), 596(1); Infants 81, 82, 83; Jury 33(5.15); Labor & Emp 3040; Neglig 202, 291, 440(1), 1726, 1741; Pretrial Proc 45; Trial 182, 207, 260(8), 349(2), 350.1, 350.2, 351.2(5), 352.1(5), 352.1(7); Venue 50, 68; Witn 270(2), 406.

Hughes; United Production Corp. v., TexComApp, 152 SW2d 327, 137 Tex 21.—Action 1; Courts 472.2; Evid 83(1); Judgm 15; Mand 85; Mines 5.2(4); Plead 248(1).

Hughes; U.S. v., CA5 (Tex), 230 F3d 815, reh den, on remand 2006 WL 3246571.—Crim Law 700(2.1), 700(4), 1139, 1158(1), 1166(10.10); U S 34.

Hughes; U.S. v., CA5 (Tex), 817 F2d 268, cert den Davis v. US, 108 SCt 166, 484 US 857, 98 LEd2d 120, cert den 108 SCt 170, 484 US 858, 98 LEd2d 124, cert den Lee v US, 108 SCt 457, 484 US 966, 98 LEd2d 397.—Consp 47(1), 47(12); Crim Law 622.2(1), 622.2(3), 641.5(3), 641.5(5), 641.5(7), 959, 1134(8), 1167(1); Ind & Inf 121.1(3).

Hughes; U.S. v., CA5 (Tex), 766 F2d 875, reh den 772 F2d 904.—Crim Law 1159.2(7); Ind & Inf 159(1), 167; Int Rev 5263.35, 5290, 5294, 5298, 5300, 5312, 5317.

Hughes; U.S. v., CA5 (Tex), 726 F2d 170.—Banks 509.20, 509.25.

Hughes; U.S. v., CA5 (Tex), 441 F2d 12, cert den 92 SCt 156, 404 US 849, 30 LEd2d 88.—Crim Law 363, 394.5(3), 432, 673(2), 713, 1169.1(2.1); Land & Ten 18(3); Licens 49; Searches 23, 25.1, 174, 177, 186.

Hughes; U.S. v., CA5 (Tex), 413 F2d 1244, cert gr U.S. v. Gifford-Hill-American, Inc, 90 SCt 479, 396 US 984, 24 LEd2d 448, vac 90 SCt 817, 397 US 93, 25 LEd2d 77.— Crim Law 627.6(1), 627.8(3), 627.9(1), 627.9(2.1); Fed Cts 526.1; Mand 16(1), 61.

Hughes; U.S. v., CA5 (Tex), 388 F2d 236, opinion supplemented 413 F2d 1244, cert gr US v. Gifford-Hill-American, Inc, 90 SCt 479, 396 US 984, 24 LEd2d 448, vac 90 SCt 817, 397 US 93, 25 LEd2d 77.—Crim Law 627.9(1); Mand 32, 171, 173.

Hughes v. U.S., CA5 (Tex), 303 F2d 776.—Crim Law 1576, 1655(5).

Hughes v. U.S., EDTex, 196 FSupp 37.—Divorce 252.3(2), 252.3(5); Hus & W 249(6), 255, 257, 262.1(2), 262.2; Int Rev 3330, 3334; Mines 48.

Hughes; U.S. v., NDTex, 71 FSupp2d 605, rev and vac 230 F3d 815, reh den, on remand 2006 WL 3246571.—Const Law 4594(1), 4594(3), 4594(4); Crim Law 700(2.1), 700(3), 700(4).

Hughes; Vaughn v., TexApp–Fort Worth, 917 SW2d 477, appeal after remand 937 SW2d 106, reh overr, and writ den.—App & E 863, 934(1); Judgm 181(11), 185(2), 185(6), 185.3(21); Plead 252(2), 264.

Hughes v. Ward Oil Corp., CCA5 (Tex), 124 F2d 393.— Bound 37(3); Estop 68(2); Judgm 828.10(2); Mines 77.

Hughes; Washam v., TexApp–Austin, 638 SW2d 646, ref nre.—App & E 931(4); Damag 50.10, 221(7); Death 15, 52, 88, 89; Parent & C 7(1); Trial 255(14).

Hughes; West v., TexCivApp–Waco, 543 SW2d 749.— Action 38(6); Health 821(2), 821(3); Plead 111.18, 111.37, 111.38, 111.42(9).

Hughes; Woodley v., TexCivApp–Texarkana, 252 SW2d 997.—Adv Poss 85(1); Land & Ten 66(2).

Hughes v. Wright, TexCivApp–Fort Worth, 127 SW2d 215.—Deeds 76; Judgm 511; Lim of Act 72(1), 102(7), 103(1); Plead 214(1); Tresp to T T 6.1.

Hughes v. Wruble, TexComApp, 116 SW2d 368, 131 Tex 444.—Home 177(1), 177(2).

Hughes v. Wruble, TexCivApp–Fort Worth, 88 SW2d 661, aff 116 SW2d 368, 131 Tex 444.—App & E 1068(1); Evid 590; Home 122, 214, 216.

Hughes & Luce; Peeler v., Tex, 909 SW2d 494.—Antitrust 138, 256; App & E 934(1); Atty & C 105, 112; Const Law 2314, 3761; Convicts 1; Neglig 372, 379, 380.

Hughes & Luce; Peeler v., TexApp–Dallas, 868 SW2d 823, reh den, and writ gr, aff 909 SW2d 494.—Antitrust 138, 256; App & E 977(3); Atty & C 105, 107, 112, 129(2), 129(3); Const Law 2311, 2314, 2325, 3761; Judgm 181(11), 185(2), 185(6); Neglig 371, 379, 384, 387, 422; New Tr 5, 6.

Hughes Blanton, Inc.; Coleman v., TexCivApp–Texarkana, 599 SW2d 643.—Antitrust 358; Pretrial Proc 690, 699.

Hughes Blanton, Inc. v. Shannon, TexCivApp–Dallas, 581 SW2d 538.—App & E 1177(7); Evid 568(4); Trover 35, 40(4), 40(6).

Hughes Bros. Mfg. Co.; Centaur Co. v., CCA5 (Tex), 91 F 901, 34 CCA 127.—Antitrust 35, 37.

Hughes Bros. Mfg. Co.; Wilson v., TexCivApp–Fort Worth, 99 SW2d 411.—Evid 597; Gifts 48, 49(1).

Hughes Drilling Co.; Davis v., TexApp–Texarkana, 667 SW2d 183.—App & E 5; Judgm 181(6).

Hughes Drilling Fluids; Texas Employment Com'n v., TexApp–Tyler, 746 SW2d 796, writ gr, and writ withdrawn, and writ den.—Labor & Emp 40(3), 97; Torts 332; Unemp Comp 70, 92.

Hughes Drilling Fluids, Inc., Div. of Hughes Tool Co. v. Eubanks, TexApp–Houston (14 Dist), 729 SW2d 759, writ gr, set aside Hughes Drilling Fluids, Inc, a Div of Hughes Tool v. Eubanks, 742 SW2d 275.—App & E 1003(11), 1057(1); Autos 226(2), 243(5); Evid 123(10); New Tr 104(3), 105, 108(4); Parent & C 7(1); Trial 350.7(3.1).

Hughes Engineering Co.; Eubanks v., TexCivApp–Fort Worth, 369 SW2d 49, ref nre.—Judgm 185(2), 185.3(13).

Hughes Engineering Co. v. Eubanks, TexCivApp–Fort Worth, 307 SW2d 603.—Princ & A 1; Venue 22(7).

Hughes ex rel. C.T.H.; Dominguez v., TexApp–El Paso, 225 SW3d 272.—App & E 931(1), 946, 994(3), 1010.1(1), 1010.1(2), 1012.1(4); Breach of P 20.

Hughes, Hubbard, & Reed; Shearson Lehman Bros., Inc. v., TexApp–Houston (1 Dist), 902 SW2d 60, reh overr, and writ den, cert den 116 SCt 2500, 517 US 1245, 135 LEd2d 191.—App & E 840(2); Atty & C 109; Const Law 3964; Courts 12(2.1), 12(2.5), 12(2.10), 12(2.15), 12(2.25), 35; Sec Reg 11.10.

Hughes, Inc. v. Gibson, TexApp–Tyler, 697 SW2d 39. See B.J. Hughes, Inc. v. Gibson.

Hughes Interests, Inc. v. Westrup, TexApp–Houston (1 Dist), 879 SW2d 229. See Kenneth H. Hughes Interests, Inc. v. Westrup.

Hughes Production Co. v. Hagan, TexCivApp–Texarkana, 144 SW2d 953, writ dism, correct.—App & E 1099(3); Mines 118.

Hughes Production Co. v. Hagan, TexCivApp–El Paso, 114 SW2d 326, writ dism.—Action 50(3); App & E 1036(6), 1066(9); Death 104(4); Mines 118; Neglig 210, 230, 1613; New Tr 100; Stip 14(10).

Hughes Springs, City of; Price v., TexCivApp–Texarkana, 492 SW2d 644.—Sequest 20, 21.

Hughes Springs Volunteer Ambulance Service, Inc.; City of Hughes Springsv., TexApp–Texarkana, 223 SW3d 707, reh overr.—App & E 955, 989, 1008.1(2), 1010.1(1), 1010.2, 1011.1(6), 1012.1(4), 1182; Char 37(3); Corp 56, 557(5), 601, 604.

Hughes Television Network, Inc.; Magan v., TexApp–San Antonio, 727 SW2d 104.—App & E 852, 931(3), 989; Judgm 162(2), 335(1), 335(3), 335(4); Proc 78.

Hughes Tool Co; C.I.R. v., CCA5 (Tex), 118 F2d 474.—Int Rev 3387, 3873.

Hughes Tool Co v. C I R, CCA5 (Tex), 118 F2d 472.—Int Rev 3442, 3865, 4893.

Hughes Tool Co.; C.I.R. v., CCA5 (Tex), 160 F2d 540.—Int Rev 4757.

Hughes Tool Co. v. C. I. R., CCA5 (Tex), 147 F2d 967, appeal after remand 160 F2d 540.—Corp 590(2).

Hughes Tool Co. v. Dresser Industries, Inc., CAFed (Tex), 816 F2d 1549, cert den 108 SCt 261, 484 US 914, 98 LEd2d 219.—Pat 36(3), 312(1.2), 312(3.1), 318(3), 319(4).

Hughes Tool Co.; Fry v., TexCivApp–Eastland, 317 SW2d 950.—Bailm 17, 21; Judgm 181(15.1), 743(3).

Hughes Tool Co.; Godbolt v., SDTex, 63 FRD 370.—Civil R 1009; Fed Civ Proc 36, 176, 184.10, 184.15.

Hughes Tool Co. v. G. W. Murphy Industries, Inc., CA5 (Tex), 491 F2d 923.—Pat 168(3), 226.8, 227, 312(1.7), 312(2), 314(5), 318(3), 319(1), 324.55(2).

Hughes Tool Co.; Huckabay v., TexCivApp–Galveston, 122 SW2d 233, dism.—Work Comp 2084, 2107.

Hughes Tool Co.; Hurst v., CA5 (Tex), 634 F2d 895, cert den 102 SCt 123, 454 US 829, 70 LEd2d 105.—Antitrust 414, 418, 432, 433; Fed Civ Proc 2126.1, 2608.1.

Hughes Tool Co. v. Ingersoll-Rand Co., CA5 (Tex), 437 F2d 1106, cert den 91 SCt 2230, 403 US 918, 29 LEd2d 696, reh den 92 SCt 30, 404 US 875, 30 LEd2d 121.—Pat 112.1, 324.5.

Hughes Tool Co. v. Owen, CCA5 (Tex), 123 F2d 950.—Pat 255, 317.

Hughes Tool Co. v. Owen, NDTex, 39 FSupp 656, rev 123 F2d 950.—Inj 11; Pat 255, 283(2).

Hughes Tool Co.; Richards v., Tex, 615 SW2d 196, on remand 624 SW2d 598, ref nre, cert den 102 SCt 2272, 456 US 991, 73 LEd2d 1286.—Labor & Emp 1598.

Hughes Tool Co. v. Richards, TexCivApp–Hous (14 Dist), 624 SW2d 598, ref nre, cert den 102 SCt 2272, 456 US 991, 73 LEd2d 1286.—App & E 989; Labor & Emp 861, 863(2).

Hughes Tool Co. v. Richards, TexCivApp–Hous (14 Dist), 610 SW2d 232, rev 615 SW2d 196, on remand 624 SW2d 598, ref nre, cert den 102 SCt 2272, 456 US 991, 73 LEd2d 1286.—App & E 172(1); Labor & Emp 1597, 1599.

Hughes Tool Co.; Robertson Rock Bit Co. v., CA5 (Tex), 176 F2d 783, cert den 70 SCt 487, 338 US 948, 94 LEd 585, reh den 71 SCt 355, 340 US 923, 95 LEd 666, reh den 71 SCt 487, 340 US 939, 95 LEd 678.—Equity 65(2); Evid 574; Pat 16.5(1), 16.17, 26(1), 26(2), 51(1), 209(1), 283(1), 312(7), 324.4, 327(19).

Hughes Tool Co. v. Robertson Rock Bit Co., NDTex, 80 FSupp 809, aff 176 F2d 783, cert den 70 SCt 487, 338 US 948, 94 LEd 585, reh den 71 SCt 355, 340 US 923, 95 LEd 666, reh den 71 SCt 487, 340 US 939, 95 LEd 678.—Equity 65(2); Pat 62(3), 112.1, 165(2), 165(3), 233.1, 312(1.1), 322.

Hughes Tool Co.; Shosid v., TexCivApp–Dallas, 258 SW2d 945, ref nre.—Aband L P 2, 4; App & E 1054(1); Bailm 16, 21.

Hughes Tool Co.; Smith Industries Intern. v., CA5 (Tex), 396 F2d 735.—Pat 16(1), 36.1(3), 36.2(9), 37, 46, 165(1).

Hughes Tool Co. v. Smith Industries Intern., WDTex, 284 FSupp 908, aff 396 F2d 735.—Pat 112.1, 312(1.2).

Hughes Tool Co. v. United Mach. Co., NDTex, 35 FSupp 879.—Pat 16.17, 36.2(1), 120, 172, 233.1, 255, 327(19).

Hughes Tool Co. v. Varel Mfg. Co., CA5 (Tex), 336 F2d 61.—Pat 112.1, 168(3), 314(5), 324.55(1).

Hughes Training Inc. v. Cook, CA5 (Tex), 254 F3d 588, cert den 122 SCt 1196, 534 US 1172, 152 LEd2d 135.—Alt Disp Res 130, 329, 363(6), 374(1), 374(7); Contracts 1, 143(2); Damag 50.10.

Hughes Training, Inc. v. Cook, NDTex, 148 FSupp2d 737, aff 254 F3d 588, cert den 122 SCt 1196, 534 US 1172, 152 LEd2d 135.—Alt Disp Res 113, 363(6), 363(8);

HUGHES

59 Tex D 2d—776

Damag 49, 50.10, 208(6); Fed Cts 198, 776, 843, 848, 850.1.

Hughes Wood Products, Inc. v. Wagner, Tex, 18 SW3d 202.—Action 17; Evid 264; Judgm 185(2); Work Comp 76, 2134, 2136, 2138.

Hughes Wood Products, Inc.; Wagner v., TexApp–Beaumont, 979 SW2d 84, reh overr, and review gr, opinion superseded 18 SW3d 202, aff 18 SW3d 202.—Action 17; App & E 893(1); Judgm 185(2); Neglig 204; Plead 36(1); Torts 103; Work Comp 2100, 2135.

Hughett v. Dwyre, TexApp–Amarillo, 624 SW2d 401, ref nre.—App & E 932(1), 989, 1004(8), 1170.7; Damag 26, 185(1), 208(3), 208(4); Evid 474(1), 547, 547.5, 571(10); New Tr 44(1), 44(3), 52, 56; Trial 315, 350.6(3), 350.8, 352.10; Witn 79(1).

Hughey, Ex parte, TexApp–Tyler, 932 SW2d 308.—Hab Corp 251, 255, 256.

Hughey v. Atlantic Oil Producing Co., Tex, 109 SW2d 1041, 130 Tex 255.—App & E 1180(1).

Hughey; Atlantic Oil Producing Co. v., TexCivApp–Eastland, 107 SW2d 613, writ dism woj, reh den 109 SW2d 1041, 130 Tex 255.—Bound 3(1), 3(3), 5, 10, 42, 46(3), 48(6); Evid 417(1); Mines 73.1(1); Tresp to T T 6.1.

Hughey v. Donovan, TexCivApp–Galveston, 135 SW2d 265.—Ack 58; Evid 174.1; Pat 219(4); Plead 111.35; Venue 7.5(1).

Hughey v. Hughey, TexApp–Tyler, 923 SW2d 778, reh overr, and stay den, and writ den.—App & E 68; Child C 902.

Hughey; Hughey v., TexApp–Tyler, 923 SW2d 778, reh overr, and stay den, and writ den.—App & E 68; Child C 902.

Hughey; Texas Emp. Ins. Ass'n v., TexCivApp–Fort Worth, 266 SW2d 456, ref nre.—App & E 1170.7; Witn 240(3); Work Comp 1382, 1929, 1974.

Hughey v. U.S., USTex, 110 SCt 1979, 495 US 411, 109 LEd2d 408, on remand 907 F2d 39.—Sent & Pun 2143, 2145, 2164, 2165, 2195; Statut 241(1).

Hughey; U.S. v., CA5 (Tex), 147 F3d 423, cert den 119 SCt 569, 525 US 1030, 142 LEd2d 474.—Const Law 4611, 4810, 4816; Crim Law 593, 632(2), 641.10(1), 641.10(2), 641.12(1), 1139, 1147, 1151; False Pret 2, 7(1), 26; Ind & Inf 55; Sent & Pun 2125, 2143; States 18.63.

Hughey; U.S. v., CA5 (Tex), 877 F2d 1256, cert gr 110 SCt 716, 493 US 1018, 107 LEd2d 736, rev 110 SCt 1979, 495 US 411, 109 LEd2d 408, on remand 907 F2d 39.—Crim Law 1139; Sent & Pun 2135, 2144, 2145, 2180, 2185, 2187, 2195.

Hughlett v. State, TexCrimApp, 237 SW2d 304.—Crim Law 1090.1(1).

Hughling, Ex parte, TexCrimApp, 706 SW2d 662.—Crim Law 273.1(2).

Hugh Robison Farm Machinery, Inc. v. Wied, TexCivApp–Hous (1 Dist), 593 SW2d 731.—Usury 108.

Hughs; White v., TexApp–Texarkana, 867 SW2d 846, reh overr.—App & E 930(3), 989; Evid 265(4); Fraud 58(2); Tresp to T T 10, 41(1); Ven & Pur 79, 198, 199.

Hughston; First Financial Development Corp. v., TexApp–Corpus Christi, 797 SW2d 286, writ gr, and writ withdrawn, and writ den.—App & E 205, 662(4), 762, 907(4), 931(1), 989, 1008.1(1), 1008.1(13), 1010.1(1), 1010.1(3), 1010.1(16), 1010.2, 1042(1); Condo 14; Labor & Emp 3050; Neglig 1110(3), 1263, 1680, 1708, 1713, 1750; Pretrial Proc 304, 313; Princ & A 177(1), 181; Trial 398.

Hugh Symons Group, plc v. Motorola, Inc., CA5 (Tex), 292 F3d 466, cert den 123 SCt 386, 537 US 950, 154 LEd2d 295.—Antitrust 134, 143(2); Fraud 60; Frds St of 119(1), 127, 129(5), 158(1).

Hugh Wood Ford, Inc. v. Galloway, TexApp–Houston (14 Dist), 830 SW2d 296, reh den, and writ den.—Antitrust 369; Costs 194.18; Evid 186(1).

Hugill v. State, TexApp–Houston (14 Dist), 787 SW2d 455, petition for discretionary review refused.—Crim Law 1172.9; Sent & Pun 1812, 2002.

Huginnie v. Loyd, TexCivApp–Tyler, 483 SW2d 696, ref nre.—App & E 863; Brok 94, 100; Frds St of 103(1); Judgm 185(2), 185(5); Princ & A 99, 103(6), 103(7), 152(4), 163(1), 170(2).

Hugley v. Caldwell, TexCivApp–Hous (14 Dist), 559 SW2d 877.—Ven & Pur 79, 143, 334(5).

Hugley v. State, TexCrimApp, 505 SW2d 914.—Crim Law 1170.5(1); Witn 390.

Hugo Neu Corp.; Proler Intern. Corp. v., SDTex, 964 FSupp 1140.—Alt Disp Res 200; Fed Cts 13, 31; Joint Adv 4(1), 5(1); Torts 241.

Huguet v. Barnett, CA5 (Tex), 900 F2d 838.—Sent & Pun 1548.

Huguley v. Board of Adjustment of City of Dallas, TexCivApp–Dallas, 341 SW2d 212.—Const Law 4752; Jury 10, 19(1); Zoning 324, 354, 605, 642, 645, 677, 680.1, 703, 775.

Huguley v. State, TexCivApp–El Paso, 266 SW2d 201.—Em Dom 222(4).

Huguley v. White, TexCivApp–Dallas, 102 SW2d 451.—Inj 1, 12, 138.31.

Huguley Memorial Medical Center; Maewal v., TexApp–Fort Worth, 868 SW2d886. See Maewal v. Adventist Health Systems/Sunbelt, Inc.

Huguley Nursing Center; Alphin v., TexApp–Fort Worth, 109 SW3d 574.—Health 804, 809.

Huie; Anderson v., TexApp–Dallas, 266 SW2d 410.—App & E 846(5); Ex & Ad 7, 436; Plead 111.9, 111.42(2), 111.42(4).

Huie; Chenault v., TexApp–Dallas, 989 SW2d 474.—Parent & C 11.

Huie v. DeShazo, Tex, 922 SW2d 920.—Mand 28, 32; Pretrial Proc 35, 41; Trusts 173; Witn 198(1), 199(1), 199(2), 201(2).

Huie; Jacobs v., NDTex, 447 FSupp 478.—Civil R 1326(4), 1326(9); Const Law 3941, 3945.

Huie v. Lay, TexCivApp–Amarillo, 170 SW2d 823.—Bailm 30, 31(1); Carr 107, 129, 131, 132; Judgm 199(3.15).

Huie v. Lone Star Air Conditioning Co., TexCivApp–Waco, 486 SW2d 182, ref nre.—Judgm 181(33), 185(2), 186; Neglig 1656, 1676, 1702.

Huie v. Thompson, TexCivApp–Amarillo, 364 SW2d 280.—Judgm 185.3(21); Neglig 1104(3).

Huie-Clark Joint Venture v. American States Ins. Co. of Texas, TexApp–Dallas, 629 SW2d 109, ref nre.—Garn 193, 194.

Huie Properties; Johnson v., TexCivApp–Dallas, 594 SW2d 488.—Land & Ten 184(2).

Hui-Mei Wise v. Yates, Tex, 639 SW2d 460.—Hab Corp 532(1).

Huitt; University Preparatory School v., TexApp–Corpus Christi, 941 SW2d 177, reh overr, and writ den.—App & E 930(1), 974(1), 1001(1); Damag 63; Neglig 213; Schools 89.2, 89.5(1); Trial 350.5(2).

Huitt-Zollars, Inc.; Dishner v., TexApp–Dallas, 162 SW3d 370, reh overr.—App & E 223, 964; Civil R 1153, 1163, 1744; Costs 105; Judges 49(1), 51(1); Judgm 183, 185.3(13), 186; New Tr 118.

Huizar, In re, BkrtcyWDTex, 71 BR 826.—Bankr 2021.1, 2608(2), 2726(2), 2766, 2774, 2796; Home 214.

Huizar v. Bank of Robstown, BkrtcyWDTex, 71 BR 826. See Huizar, In re.

Huizar; Continental Cas. Co. v., Tex, 740 SW2d 429.—App & E 138, 158(1); Contracts 95(4).

Huizar v. Four Seasons Nursing Centers of San Antonio, TexCivApp–San Antonio, 562 SW2d 264, writ refused.—Action 27(1).

Huizar v. State, TexCrimApp, 12 SW3d 479, on remand 29 SW3d 249, petition for discretionary review refused.—Crim Law 824(12), 835, 1038.1(1), 1172.1(1); Sent & Pun 313.

Huizar v. State, TexApp–San Antonio, 29 SW3d 249, petition for discretionary review refused.—Crim Law 1030(1), 1134(2), 1165(1), 1177.

Huizar v. State, TexApp–San Antonio, 966 SW2d 702, petition for discretionary review gr, rev 12 SW3d 479, on remand 29 SW3d 249, petition for discretionary review refused.—Crim Law 641.13(2.1), 641.13(7), 796, 824(1), 1172.1(1), 1172.9.

Huizar v. State, TexApp–San Antonio, 720 SW2d 651, petition for discretionary review refused.—Crim Law 777; Homic 1458, 1470, 1493.

Huizar v. State, TexApp–Corpus Christi, 841 SW2d 875, reh overr.—Crim Law 338(7), 959, 1169.2(3); Witn 274(1).

Huizar v. U.S., CA5 (Tex), 339 F2d 173, cert den 85 SCt 1099, 380 US 959, 13 LEd2d 975.—Controlled Subs 64, 68; Crim Law 1177, 1407, 1478; Ind & Inf 144.1(1).

Hukel; U.S. v., CA5 (Tex), 869 F2d 822. See U.S. v. White.

Hukel; U.S. v., CA5 (Tex), 855 F2d 201. See U.S. v. White.

Hukill; Great Southern Life Ins. Co. v., TexCivApp–Fort Worth, 151 SW2d 603, writ dism, correct.—Insurance 3398, 3400(1), 3475(5), 3497; Trusts 181(1).

Hukill v. H.E.B. Food Stores, Inc., TexApp–Corpus Christi, 756 SW2d 840.—App & E 989, 1001(1), 1003(5), 1003(7), 1003(10), 1064.1(8); Neglig 1741, 1742.

Hukill; Texas Dept. of Public Safety v., TexApp–El Paso, 141 SW3d 747, review den.—App & E 893(1); Statut 188; Weap 12.

Hulan v. State, TexCrimApp, 243 SW2d 584.—Crim Law 1090.1(1).

Hulbert, In re, BkrtcySDTex, 150 BR 169.—Bankr 3353(1.45), 3353(1.55), 3353(2), 3353(3.5), 3353(14), 3353(14.6), 3353(14.25), 3420(7).

Hulbert; ITT Financial Services v., BkrtcySDTex, 150 BR 169. See Hulbert, In re.

Hulbert; Phillips Chemical Co. v., CA5 (Tex), 301 F2d 747.—Fed Civ Proc 2217, 2236; Lim of Act 39(13); Torts 215, 262.

Hulen v. City of Corsicana, CCA5 (Tex), 65 F2d 969, cert den 54 SCt 77, 290 US 662, 78 LEd 573.—Const Law 3902.

Hulen v. State, TexCrimApp, 250 SW2d 211, 157 TexCrim 507.—Const Law 4664(2); Crim Law 736(2), 893, 1134(3); Homic 1177.

Hulen v. State, TexCrimApp, 167 SW2d 752, 145 TexCrim 344.—Crim Law 413(1), 429(2), 530, 531(0.5), 781(4), 814(1), 814(16), 1091(4), 1169.12; Statut 107(1).

Hulen Park Place Ltd., In re, NDTex, 130 BR 39.—Bankr 2852, 2853.30, 3564, 3566.1, 3786.

Hulen Park Place Ltd.; NCNB Texas Nat. Bank v., NDTex, 130 BR 39. See Hulen Park Place Ltd., In re.

Hulett v. Board of Trustees of West Lamar Rural High School Dist., TexCivApp–Texarkana, 229 SW2d 839, rev 232 SW2d 669, 149 Tex 289.—App & E 781(1), 781(4), 799.

Hulett; Campbell v., NDTex, 70 FSupp 8.—Mines 48, 55(8).

Hulett v. West Lamar Rural High School Dist., Tex, 232 SW2d 669, 149 Tex 289.—App & E 781(4), 1176(6); Costs 241; Parties 3; Schools 111.

Hulick v. Mormino, TexCivApp–Waco, 435 SW2d 628.—Mand 48, 190; Mental H 60.

Hulin, In re, TexApp–Houston (1 Dist), 31 SW3d 754.—Assault 59; Bail 49(4), 51; Crim Law 1134(8).

Hulin v. State, TexCrimApp, 438 SW2d 551.—Crim Law 1036.2; Witn 318.

Hulings; Keep 'Em Eating Co. v., TexCivApp–Austin, 165 SW2d 211.—Land & Ten 217(1), 263; Receivers 6, 14, 35(1).

Hulit v. State, TexCrimApp, 982 SW2d 431.—Arrest 62; Autos 349(2.1), 349(14.1), 349(16); Const Law 617; Courts 97(6); Searches 24; States 18.1.

Hulit v. State, TexApp–Fort Worth, 947 SW2d 707, petition for discretionary review gr, aff 982 SW2d 431.—Arrest 63.5(5), 63.5(6); Crim Law 394.6(4), 394.6(5), 1153(1).

Hull; Avnet v., TexCivApp–Dallas, 265 SW2d 906, ref nre.—App & E 302(1), 761; New Tr 72(10).

Hull; Calvert v., Tex, 475 SW2d 907.—Colleges 2, 6(1); Liens 1; States 168.5.

Hull v. Calvert, TexCivApp–Austin, 469 SW2d 277, writ gr, rev 475 SW2d 907.—Colleges 6(1); Counties 103; Liens 7.

Hull v. Chapman, TexCivApp–Tyler, 464 SW2d 705, writ dism woj.—Autos 181(1); Statut 239; Venue 8.5(8).

Hull v. City of Duncanville, CA5 (Tex), 678 F2d 582.—Civil R 1027, 1034, 1326(1), 1395(1).

Hull v. Continental Oil Co., SDTex, 58 FRD 636.—Fed Civ Proc 176, 2397.1.

Hull v. Davis, TexApp–Houston (14 Dist), 211 SW3d 461.—App & E 671(4); Elect of Rem 14; Labor & Emp 2193, 2194; Time 3.

Hull; Fitz-Gerald v., Tex, 237 SW2d 256, 150 Tex 39.—App & E 927(7); Joint Adv 4(1); Sec Reg 256.1; Trusts 92.5, 99, 365(5), 372(2).

Hull v. Fitz-Gerald, TexCivApp–Amarillo, 232 SW2d 93, aff 237 SW2d 256, 150 Tex 39.—App & E 927(7), 989, 997(3); Equity 66; Sec Reg 256.1; Trusts 91, 92.5, 108, 111.

Hull v. Freedman, TexCivApp–Fort Worth, 383 SW2d 236, ref nre.—Contracts 326; Interest 39(2.15), 39(2.20), 66; Lim of Act 28(1); Mines 51(2), 79.7; Paymt 85(1), 85(7); Trover 1, 2, 9(5).

Hull v. Hull, TexCivApp–San Antonio, 332 SW2d 758, ref nre.—Adop 7.7; Child C 22, 51; Infants 154.1, 177, 197, 210.

Hull; Hull v., TexCivApp–San Antonio, 332 SW2d 758, ref nre.—Adop 7.7; Child C 22, 51; Infants 154.1, 177, 197, 210.

Hull v. Hull, TexCivApp–Waco, 183 SW2d 275, writ refused wom.—Ex & Ad 72; Judgm 950(0.5); Receivers 14.

Hull; Hull v., TexCivApp–Waco, 183 SW2d 275, writ refused wom.—Ex & Ad 72; Judgm 950(0.5); Receivers 14.

Hull v. Lester, TexCivApp–El Paso, 89 SW2d 787.—App & E 753(2), 773(2).

Hull v. Magnolia Petroleum Co., CCA5 (Tex), 119 F2d 123, rev 62 SCt 75, 314 US 575, 86 LEd 466.—Contracts 147(1); Mines 73, 78.1(9), 78.2.

Hull v. Quanah Pipeline Corp., TexCivApp–San Antonio, 574 SW2d 610, ref nre.—Land & Ten 83(1).

Hull; Rosenfield v., TexCivApp–Texarkana, 304 SW2d 571, dism.—App & E 387(2), 387(3), 755, 758.3(5); Judgm 219.

Hull v. State, TexCrimApp, 67 SW3d 215, on remand 2002 WL 1481258, petition for discretionary review refused.—Crim Law 1042, 1045; Sent & Pun 1919.

Hull v. State, TexCrimApp, 699 SW2d 220.—Crim Law 577.8(2), 577.10(1), 577.10(3), 577.11(6), 577.12(1), 577.15(1).

Hull v. State, TexCrimApp, 613 SW2d 735.—Arrest 63.1; Crim Law 394.4(9).

Hull v. State, TexCrimApp, 510 SW2d 358.—Controlled Subs 116; Crim Law 394.1(3); Searches 164.

Hull v. State, TexCrimApp, 442 SW2d 722.—Const Law 4658(2), 4658(4); Courts 100(1); Crim Law 339.11(9), 1086.1, 1186.1; Rape 64.

Hull v. State, TexApp–Houston (1 Dist), 29 SW3d 602, reh overr, and petition for discretionary review gr, vac 67 SW3d 215, on remand 2002 WL 1481258, petition for discretionary review refused.—Const Law 3955, 4733(2); Crim Law 1063(1), 1177; Sent & Pun 1920, 2001, 2006.

Hull v. State, TexApp–Dallas, 172 SW3d 186, reh overr, and petition for discretionary review refused (3 pets).—Crim Law 444, 1134(6), 1153(1); Sent & Pun 313.

Hull v. State, TexApp–Houston (14 Dist), 871 SW2d 786, petition for discretionary review refused.—Crim Law 553, 893, 1159.2(1), 1159.2(4), 1159.5; Homic 942, 1135, 1194, 1201, 1387.

Hull v. Texas State Bd. of Public Accountancy, TexCivApp–Hous (14 Dist), 434 SW2d 387.—Accnts 5; Licens 38; Statut 47.

Hull; U.S. v., CA5 (Tex), 160 F3d 265, cert den 119 SCt 1091, 525 U.S. 1169, 143 LEd2d 91, cert den Stafford v. US, 119 SCt 1791, 526 US 1136, 143 LEd2d 1018.— Consp 47(4), 47(11); Crim Law 369.2(1), 370, 371(1), 372(14), 561(1), 772(5), 822(7), 1030(1), 1038.1(4), 1139, 1144.13(3), 1147, 1153(1), 1158(1), 1159.2(7), 1177; Rec S Goods 8(3); Sent & Pun 672, 673, 675, 678, 973, 975, 995, 2100; U S 34.

Hull; U.S. v., CA5 (Tex), 437 F2d 1.—Autos 341, 355(12); Crim Law 394.1(3), 394.4(12); Searches 60.1.

Hull v. U.S., CA5 (Tex), 356 F2d 919.—Int Rev 5281, 5304.

Hull v. U.S., CA5 (Tex), 324 F2d 817.—Crim Law 627.6(4), 719(3), 726, 742(2), 780(1), 780(2), 828, 1162; Int Rev 5286, 5317.

Hullaby v. State, TexApp–Fort Worth, 911 SW2d 921, petition for discretionary review refused.—Const Law 4647; Crim Law 412(5), 419(2.10), 586, 591, 665(2), 665(4), 698(3), 703, 730(7), 1036.1(1), 1043(3), 1044.1(8), 1134(3), 1144.13(2.1), 1159.2(2), 1159.2(7), 1159.2(9), 1159.3(6), 1171.1(6), 1171.2, 1177; Homic 908, 1168; Sent & Pun 313.

Hull & Co., Inc. v. Chandler, TexApp–Houston (14 Dist), 889 SW2d 513, reh overr, and writ den.—Adm 1.20(1); App & E 893(1); Courts 97(1); Insurance 1091(15), 1113, 3540; States 18.3, 18.41.

Hull-Daisetta Independent School Dist.; Baldwin v., TexCivApp–Beaumont, 95 SW2d 1350, writ dism.— Schools 106.12(10); Tax 2172, 2935.

Hull-Daisetta Independent School Dist.; Engelberg v., EDTex, 848 FSupp 90.—Lim of Act 43, 58(1), 104(1), 105(1).

Hull-Daisetta Independent School Dist.; Wilcox v., TexCivApp–Beaumont, 95 SW2d 490, writ refused.—Tax 2172.

Hull State Bank; Livingston Livestock Exchange, Inc. v., TexApp–Beaumont, 14 SW3d 849, petition for review den.—App & E 866(3), 927(7); Banks 228; Fraud 13(3).

Hullum; Frederick v., TexCivApp–Hous (1 Dist), 570 SW2d 87.—Contracts 116(1), 171(1); Inj 128(5.1).

Hullum v. St. Louis Southwestern Ry. Co., TexCivApp–Tyler, 384 SW2d 163, ref nre, cert den 86 SCt 244, 382 US 906, 15 LEd2d 159, reh den 86 SCt 387, 382 US 949, 15 LEd2d 357.—App & E 1062.1, 1067, 1170.10; Courts 97(1), 97(5); Evid 150, 201, 222(1), 271(2), 317(18), 359(6); Labor & Emp 2881, 2883; Trial 215, 351.5(1), 351.5(8).

Hullum v. Skyhook Corp., CA5 (Tex), 753 F2d 1334.— Electricity 17.

Hullum v. State, TexCrimApp, 415 SW2d 192.—Crim Law 87, 90(5), 101(4), 912.5; False Pret 49(1).

Hulme; Great Nat. Life Ins. Co. v., TexComApp, 136 SW2d 602, 134 Tex 539.—Insurance 1758, 3084, 3091, 3096(2).

Hulme v. Great Nat. Life Ins. Co., TexCivApp–Fort Worth, 116 SW2d 459, rev 136 SW2d 602, 134 Tex 539. —Insurance 3096(2).

Hulme v. Jaschke, TexCivApp–San Antonio, 168 SW2d 326, writ refused wom.—Wills 155.1, 163(1), 163(8), 164(5), 165(1), 166(1), 384.

Hulon, In re, BkrtcyNDTex, 92 BR 670.—Bankr 2134, 3046(2), 3047(2); Witn 305(1), 307, 308.

Huls v. Huls, TexCivApp–Hous (1 Dist), 616 SW2d 312.— App & E 989; Child S 140(2), 555; Divorce 223, 252.2, 252.3(1), 252.4, 253(2), 253(4); Hus & W 249(5), 254, 264(2).

Huls; Huls v., TexCivApp–Hous (1 Dist), 616 SW2d 312.— App & E 989; Child S 140(2), 555; Divorce 223, 252.2, 252.3(1), 252.4, 253(2), 253(4); Hus & W 249(5), 254, 264(2).

Hulse; Dennis v., Tex, 362 SW2d 308.—App & E 1170.1, 1170.6; Trial 127, 133.2.

Hulse v. Dennis, TexCivApp–Texarkana, 356 SW2d 203, writ gr, rev 362 SW2d 308.—App & E 1170.6; Trial 127.

Hulsebosch v. Ramsey, TexCivApp–Hous (14 Dist), 435 SW2d 161.—Neglig 387; Prod Liab 60.5.

Hulsey v. Drake, TexCivApp–Austin, 457 SW2d 453, ref nre.—App & E 213, 901, 1003(4); Damag 168(1), 185(1), 187, 191, 192; Evid 571(10); Stip 14(11); Trial 139.1(12), 140(1).

Hulsey v. Internal Revenue Service, NDTex, 497 FSupp 617.—Records 55.

Hulsey v. Keel, TexApp–San Antonio, 700 SW2d 255, ref nre.—App & E 80(1); Costs 60; Mines 125; Partit 12(4).

Hulsey v. Keel, TexCivApp–San Antonio, 541 SW2d 656, ref nre.—App & E 387(2), 392, 395, 622; New Tr 155.

Hulsey v. Owens, CA5 (Tex), 63 F3d 354.—Civil R 1088(5), 1376(1), 1376(7), 1376(8); Fed Cts 712, 714; Lim of Act 58(1).

Hulsey v. Patterson, TexCivApp–Amarillo, 121 SW2d 509.—App & E 1003(5); Autos 173(5), 244(14); Evid 597; Trial 350.6(3).

Hulsey v. State, TexCrimApp, 447 SW2d 165.—Jury 24.1; Sent & Pun 2004, 2018, 2021, 2026, 2029.

Hulsey v. State, TexCrimApp, 268 SW2d 170, 160 TexCrim 246.—Arson 37(1); Crim Law 1166.22(2).

Hulsey v. State, TexCrimApp, 258 SW2d 822.—Crim Law 1087.1(2).

Hulsey v. State, TexCrimApp, 197 SW2d 574, 149 TexCrim 591.—Crim Law 768(4), 1172.9.

Hulsey v. State, TexApp–Waco, 211 SW3d 853.—Crim Law 620(1), 678(1), 678(2), 1144.13(2.1), 1144.13(6), 1148, 1159.2(7), 1159.3(2), 1159.4(2), 1162, 1168(2); Infants 20.

Hulsey v. State of Tex., CA5 (Tex), 929 F2d 168.—Civil R 1088(2), 1097, 1442, 1445; Fed Civ Proc 1685, 1761; Fed Cts 611, 612.1, 714, 818; Searches 141, 171, 181.

Hulsey v. USAir, Inc., CA5 (Tex), 868 F2d 1423, reh den 875 F2d 858, cert den 110 SCt 239, 493 US 892, 107 LEd2d 190.—Aviation 101.

Hulshouser v. State, TexApp–Fort Worth, 967 SW2d 866, petition for discretionary review refused, untimely filed. —Crim Law 1004, 1081(2).

Hulshouser v. Texas Workers' Compensation Ins. Fund, TexApp–Dallas, 139 SW3d 789.—Work Comp 6, 11, 52, 597, 957, 1042, 2084.

Hultgren v. State, TexApp–Fort Worth, 858 SW2d 617, petition for discretionary review refused.—Controlled Subs 74; Crim Law 37(2.1), 37(4), 569, 1144.13(2.1), 1159.2(7).

Hultgren; U.S. v., CA5 (Tex), 713 F2d 79.—Arrest 63.1, 67, 68(7), 68(10); Crim Law 1134(3); Ind & Inf 71.4(3), 87(7); Searches 48, 192.1.

Hultin v. Beto, CA5 (Tex), 396 F2d 216.—Const Law 4563; Infants 232.

Hultin v. State, TexCrimApp, 351 SW2d 248, 171 TexCrim 425.—Atty & C 86; Crim Law 86, 92, 517(7), 576(6); Infants 68.1, 68.5, 69(2), 194.1; Statut 223.2(1.1), 223.2(8); Witn 36.

Hultquist v. Ring, TexCivApp–Galveston, 301 SW2d 303, ref nre.—App & E 761; Com Law 11; Evid 314(1), 355(7), 359(5); Wills 487(1), 487(6), 488, 703, 704.

Hults; Fowler v., TexComApp, 161 SW2d 478, 138 Tex 636.—App & E 999(1); Sec Reg 245, 260; Trial 350.1.

Hults v. Fowler, TexCivApp–Fort Worth, 148 SW2d 249, rev 161 SW2d 478, 138 Tex 636.—Sec Reg 292.

Human v. State, TexCrimApp, 749 SW2d 832.—Autos 352, 355(6); Crim Law 552(3), 695(2), 1144.13(3), 1159.2(7); Ind & Inf 171.

HUMBLE

Humana Health Plan of Texas, Inc.; RenCare, Ltd. v., CA5 (Tex), 395 F3d 555.—Fed Cts 192.5, 776; Health 556(3), 950.

Humana Health Plan of Texas Inc.; U.S. ex rel. Willard v., CA5 (Tex), 336 F3d 375.—Fed Civ Proc 636, 827, 833, 839.1, 849, 851, 1772, 1832; Fed Cts 624, 762, 817; Fraud 9, 12, 24, 50; U S 120.1, 122.

Humana-Heron; U.S. v., CA5 (Tex), 210 FedAppx 368, cert den 127 SCt 2077, 167 LEd2d 798.—Aliens 799; Sent & Pun 651.

Humana Hosp. Corp. v. American Medical Systems, Inc., Tex, 785 SW2d 144, answer to certified question conformed to Smith v. American Medical Systems, 897 F2d 794.—Indem 75, 76.

Humana Hosp. Corp.; Dudley v., TexApp–Houston (14 Dist), 817 SW2d 124.—App & E 1047(1); Evid 146, 508.

Humana Hosp. Corp., Inc.; American Medical Systems, Inc. v., CA5 (Tex),876 F2d 434. See Smith v. American Medical Systems, Inc.

Humana Hosp. Corp., Inc. v. Casseb, TexApp–San Antonio, 809 SW2d 543.—Mand 4(4).

Humana Hosp. Corp., Inc. v. Spears-Petersen, TexApp–San Antonio, 867 SW2d 858.—Courts 26; Health 270; Mand 3(2.1), 4(4), 12; Pretrial Proc 33.

Humana Hosp. San Antonio v. Avram A. Jacobson, M.D., P.A., CA5 (Tex), 804 F2d 1390. See Humana, Inc. v. Avram A. Jacobson, M.D., P.A.

Humana Hosp., San Antonio v. Casseb, TexApp–San Antonio, 809 SW2d 543. See Humana Hosp. Corp., Inc. v. Casseb.

Humana, Inc. v. Avram A. Jacobson, M.D., P.A., CA5 (Tex), 804 F2d 1390.—Fed Civ Proc 412; Inj 14, 138.66, 150.

Humana, Inc.; Beaumont Neurological Hosp. v., ED-Tex, 780 FSupp 1134.—Labor & Emp 407, 678; Rem of C 19(5); States 18.51.

Humana, Inc.; Felan v., TexApp–San Antonio, 163 SW3d 95, reh overr.—Judgm 181(7); Lim of Act 1, 121(1), 121(2).

Humana, Inc.; Roark v., CA5 (Tex), 307 F3d 298, reh and reh den 66 FedAppx 527, cert dism 124 SCt 44, 539 US 986, 156 LEd2d 702, cert gr Aetna Health Inc v. Davila, 124 SCt 462, 540 US 981, 157 LEd2d 370, cert gr CIGNA HealthCare of Texas, Inc v Calad, 124 SCt 463, 540 US 981, 157 LEd2d 370, rev and remanded 124 SCt 2488, 542 US 200, 159 LEd2d 312, on remand 388 F3d 167.—Fed Cts 776, 813; Health 607, 800; Insurance 1117(3); Labor & Emp 407, 630; Rem of C 25(1), 102, 107(9); States 18.15, 18.51.

Humane Soc. of Austin and Travis County v. Austin Nat. Bank, Tex, 531 SW2d 574, cert den 96 SCt 2177, 425 US 976, 48 LEd2d 800.—Banks 315(3); Ex & Ad 75, 81, 91, 102, 105, 109(3), 111(1), 115, 462, 496(2); Trusts 217.1, 217.3(1); Wills 672(1).

Humane Soc. of Austin and Travis County v. Austin Nat. Bank, TexCivApp–Beaumont, 517 SW2d 323, writ gr, aff 531 SW2d 574, cert den 96 SCt 2177, 425 US 976, 48 LEd2d 800.—Ex & Ad 500.

Humane Soc. of Dallas v. Dallas Morning News, L.P., TexApp–Dallas, 180 SW3d 921, reh overr.—App & E 856(1), 1079; Libel 49.

Humanetics, Inc. v. Kerwit Medical Products, Inc., CA5 (Tex), 709 F2d 942.—Pat 323.3.

Humason v. State, TexCrimApp, 728 SW2d 363.—Controlled Subs 27, 80; Crim Law 562, 568.

Humason v. State, TexApp–Houston (1 Dist), 699 SW2d 922, petition for discretionary review gr, aff 728 SW2d 363.—Controlled Subs 68, 80.

Humber v. Morton, Tex, 426 SW2d 554, 25 ALR3d 372.—Action 27(2); Covenants 8, 13; Ven & Pur 37(1), 83.

Humber v. Morton, TexCivApp–Amarillo, 448 SW2d 494, ref nre.—App & E 758.3(7), 758.3(11), 931(3), 989; Contracts 322(4); Neglig 1672.

Humber v. Morton, TexCivApp–Amarillo, 414 SW2d 765, rev 426 SW2d 554, 25 ALR3d 372.—Contracts 205.35(2); Neglig 1625.

Humber; Morton v., TexCivApp–Eastland, 399 SW2d 831. —Damag 221(5.1); Plead 427.

Humber v. State, TexApp–Houston (14 Dist), 624 SW2d 814.—Crim Law 632(3.1), 641.13(1), 641.13(6), 1153(1).

Humbert v. Adams, TexCivApp–Dallas, 390 SW2d 857, ref nre.—Judgm 185(2), 185.3(21); Labor & Emp 3056(1); Neglig 1680.

Humbert v. Adams, TexCivApp–Dallas, 361 SW2d 458.—Corp 666; Labor & Emp 3096(8); Venue 8.5(5).

Humble; Benard v., TexApp–Beaumont, 990 SW2d 929, review den.—Covenants 49.

Humble v. Humble, TexApp–Beaumont, 805 SW2d 558, writ den.—Divorce 252.1, 252.2, 252.3(4), 253(3), 253(4), 286(5).

Humble; Humble v., TexApp–Beaumont, 805 SW2d 558, writ den.—Divorce 252.1, 252.2, 252.3(4), 253(3), 253(4), 286(5).

Humble; Peacock v., TexApp–Austin, 933 SW2d 341.—Time 10(9).

Humble, City of; Morgan v., TexCivApp–Hous (14 Dist), 598 SW2d 364.—App & E 954(1); Evid 152, 593; Inj 135, 147; Nuis 84; Witn 37(4).

Humble Emp. West Tex. Federal Credit Union; Everett v., TexCivApp–El Paso, 377 SW2d 232.—App & E 79(1).

Humble Exploration Co. v. Amcap Petroleum Associates-1977, TexApp–Dallas, 658 SW2d 860, ref nre.—Contracts 169; Costs 207; Mines 83; Pretrial Proc 726.

Humble Exploration Co. v. Browning, TexApp–Dallas, 690 SW2d 321, ref nre, cert den 106 SCt 1376, 475 US 1065, 89 LEd2d 602, reh den 106 SCt 1807, 475 US 1151, 90 LEd2d 351.—App & E 833(1), 833(3), 1185, 1222; Courts 1, 488(1); Judgm 298, 341; New Tr 110, 113.

Humble Exploration Co. v. Browning, TexApp–Dallas, 677 SW2d 111, reinstated 690 SW2d 321, ref nre, cert den 106 SCt 1376, 475 US 1065, 89 LEd2d 602, reh den 106 SCt 1807, 475 US 1151, 90 LEd2d 351.—App & E 185(3); Judges 53.

Humble Exploration Co., Inc.; Exxon Corp. v., CA5 (Tex), 695 F2d 96, 83 ALR Fed 281, reh den 701 F2d 173, on remand 592 FSupp 1226.—Trademarks 1153, 1156, 1157, 1169, 1532, 1629(3).

Humble Exploration Co., Inc.; Exxon Corp. v., NDTex, 592 FSupp 1226.—Trademarks 1060, 1157, 1800.

Humble Exploration Co., Inc.; Exxon Corp. v., NDTex, 524 FSupp 450, aff in part, rev in part 695 F2d 96, 83 ALR Fed 281, reh den 701 F2d 173, on remand 592 FSupp 1226.—Antitrust 19, 29; Trademarks 1033, 1036, 1037, 1039, 1081, 1084, 1095, 1097, 1103, 1110, 1113, 1136(1), 1157, 1172, 1241, 1419, 1421, 1422, 1426, 1437, 1529, 1534, 1538, 1539, 1610, 1612, 1627, 1628(2), 1629(3), 1630.

Humble Exploration Co., Inc. v. Fairway Land Co., TexApp–Dallas, 641 SW2d 934, ref nre.—App & E 448; Corp 552, 553(1), 557(5); Trial 388(1), 393(1).

Humble Exploration Co., Inc.; Flag-Redfern Oil Co. v., Tex, 744 SW2d 6.—Mines 55(2); Mtg 137, 151(5), 274, 295(1); Ven & Pur 257.

Humble Exploration Co., Inc. v. Walker, TexApp–Dallas, 641 SW2d 941.—App & E 448; Inj 176; Prohib 1, 10(1), 10(2); Receivers 204.

Humble Independent School Dist.; Johnson v., SDTex, 799 FSupp 43.—Civil R 1457(3); Const Law 4212(2); Schools 177.

Humble Nat. Bank v. DCV, Inc., TexApp–Houston (14 Dist), 933 SW2d 224, reh overr, and writ den.—Antitrust 147, 161, 205, 208, 209; App & E 989, 999(1), 1003(5), 1030; Banks 123, 189; Costs 264; Damag 15, 220; Elect of Rem 5; Princ & A 96, 99, 122(1), 137(1), 147(2), 148(4), 163(1).

HUMBLE

59 Tex D 2d—780

See Guidelines for Arrangement at the beginning of this Volume

Humble Oil & Refining Co., In re, CA5 (Tex), 306 F2d 567.—Fed Cts 528.

Humble Oil & Refining Co., Petition of, SDTex, 210 FSupp 638, aff Humble Oil & Refining Co v. Reagan, 311 F2d 576.—Adm 50; Ship 209(1.1).

Humble Oil & Refining Co.; Armstrong v., TexCivApp–El Paso, 145 SW2d 692, writ dism, correct.—Contracts 147(2), 169; Mines 54.5, 55(4), 55(7).

Humble Oil & Refining Co.; Atwood v., CA5 (Tex), 338 F2d 502, cert den 85 SCt 1562, 381 US 926, 14 LEd2d 684, reh den 85 SCt 1804, 381 US 956, 14 LEd2d 729.—Fed Cts 850.1, 922; Interest 14; Mines 74(5), 74.5, 78.1(1), 78.1(6), 78.7(4), 79.5, 79.7.

Humble Oil & Refining Co.; Atwood v., CA5 (Tex), 243 F2d 885, cert den 78 SCt 41, 355 US 829, 2 LEd2d 42.—Fed Civ Proc 630, 631.1, 1799, 1837.1.

Humble Oil & Refining Co. v. Atwood, Tex, 244 SW2d 637, 150 Tex 617, cert den 73 SCt 1112, 345 US 970, 97 LEd 1387.—Evid 417(7); Mines 54.5; Mtg 1, 32(1), 32(6).

Humble Oil & Refining Co.; Atwood v., TexCivApp–El Paso, 239 SW2d 412, rev 244 SW2d 637, 150 Tex 617, cert den 73 SCt 1112, 345 US 970, 97 LEd 1387.—Judgm 18(1), 219, 251(1), 725(1), 736; Mtg 608.5.

Humble Oil & Refining Co.; Bell v., Tex, 181 SW2d 569, 142 Tex 645.—Work Comp 2084.

Humble Oil & Refining Co. v. Bell, TexCivApp–El Paso, 180 SW2d 970, writ refused 181 SW2d 569, 142 Tex 645.—Explos 12; Labor & Emp 3034, 3052, 3125, 3159, 3179(4), 3181(6); Neglig 250, 1010, 1037(7).

Humble Oil & Refining Co. v. Bell, TexCivApp–El Paso, 172 SW2d 800, writ refused wom.—Plead 111.16, 111.38; Princ & A 3(1); Venue 22(1).

Humble Oil & Refining Co. v. Bell Marine Service, Inc., CA5 (Tex), 321 F2d 53.—Adm 32.10(4), 32.10(5), 118.5; Fed Cts 529.

Humble Oil & Refining Co. v. Bennett, TexCivApp–Austin, 149 SW2d 220.—Admin Law 751; Mines 92.23(1), 92.27, 92.32(2), 92.38, 92.40.

Humble Oil & Refining Co.; Benoit v., CA5 (Tex), 368 F2d 228.—Collision 125; Seamen 29(5.14).

Humble Oil & Refining Co.; Berry v., TexCivApp–Waco, 205 SW2d 376, ref nre.—Adv Poss 31; Corp 435(1); Deeds 68(1), 74; Hus & W 221, 238.6; Judgm 456(1), 456(2), 456(3), 461(1), 461(3), 668(1), 675(1), 686; Lim of Act 80, 95(8), 105(2), 130(1); Trial 142, 178.

Humble Oil & Refining Co.; Bexar County v., TexCivApp–San Antonio, 213 SW2d 882, ref nre.—Tax 2680, 2720, 2878(1).

Humble Oil & Refining Co. v. Blankenburg, Tex, 235 SW2d 891, 149 Tex 498.—Corp 125, 129, 202, 211(6), 213, 519(3), 617(1); Dedi 53; Des & Dist 71(4), 71(6); Mines 52; Mun Corp 722; Ten in C 55(1); Wills 746.

Humble Oil & Refining Co.; Blankenburg v., TexCivApp–El Paso, 233 SW2d 180, rev 235 SW2d 891, 149 Tex 498.—App & E 837(1); Corp 544(2), 599, 616; Dedi 53, 60; Judgm 91; Mun Corp 987; Tax 2233; Tresp to T T 6.1, 16, 18.

Humble Oil & Refining Co.; Broughton v., TexCivApp–El Paso, 105 SW2d 480, writ refused.—Adv Poss 115(3), 116(1), 116(2); App & E 1175(5); Mines 49; Princ & A 102(2); Proc 6; Statut 228; Tresp to T T 44; Trial 129, 285, 295(1).

Humble Oil & Refining Co.; Brown v., Tex, 87 SW2d 1069, 126 Tex 296.—Admin Law 389, 390.1, 749, 763; Const Law 2543; Mines 92.17, 92.21, 92.43, 92.59(1), 92.59(2), 92.64.

Humble Oil & Refining Co.; Brown v., Tex, 83 SW2d 935, 126 Tex 296, 99 ALR 1107, reh den 87 SW2d 1069, 126 Tex 296.—App & E 781(4), 882(1); Const Law 1066, 2400; Mines 47, 73.1(2), 92.3(2), 92.16, 92.17, 92.21, 92.23(2), 92.26, 92.30, 92.32(1), 92.49.

Humble Oil & Refining Co. v. Calvert, Tex, 478 SW2d 926, cert den 93 SCt 293, 409 US 967, 34 LEd2d 234.—Licens 5; Mines 5.2(2.1), 87; Tax 2188, 3402, 3405, 3406.

Humble Oil & Refining Co. v. Calvert, Tex, 414 SW2d 172.—Statut 223.5(1); Tax 2492, 2543.

Humble Oil & Refining Co. v. Calvert, TexCivApp–Austin, 464 SW2d 170, writ gr, aff 478 SW2d 926, cert den 93 SCt 293, 409 US 967, 34 LEd2d 234.—Licens 5, 11(1); Mines 87; Tax 2008, 3406; U S 3.

Humble Oil & Refining Co.; Calvert v., TexCivApp–Austin, 404 SW2d 147, writ gr, rev 414 SW2d 172.—Evid 5(2); Statut 219(1), 230; Tax 2212, 2233, 2256, 2257.

Humble Oil & Refining Co.; Calvert v., TexCivApp–Austin, 381 SW2d 229, ref nre.—Statut 245; Tax 2167, 2233, 2256.

Humble Oil & Refining Co. v. Campbell, TexCivApp–Beaumont, 350 SW2d 364, ref nre.—Bound 25, 37(1), 55.

Humble Oil & Refining Co.; Caplen Oil Co. v., SDTex, 69 FSupp 850.—Adv Poss 79(4), 91, 95, 100(4), 114(1); Deeds 113; Hus & W 193; Tax 3136.

Humble Oil & Refining Co. v. Carr, TexCivApp–Austin, 243 SW2d 709, ref nre.—Judgm 91, 507, 585(5), 668(1); Mines 79.1(5), 92.29, 92.31, 92.32(1), 92.35, 92.41.

Humble Oil & Refining Co. v. City of Georgetown, TexCivApp–Austin, 428 SW2d 405.—App & E 758.3(1); Courts 90(7); Jury 12(3); Mun Corp 111(3), 120, 595, 600.

Humble Oil & Refining Co. v. Clark, TexComApp, 87 SW2d 471, 126 Tex 262.—Contracts 134; Evid 383(7); Infants 30(1); Mines 58, 75.

Humble Oil & Refining Co.; Coles v., SDTex, 348 FSupp 1240.—Corp 1.6(9); Fed Cts 299.

Humble Oil & Refining Co. v. Cook, TexCivApp–Austin, 215 SW2d 383, ref nre.—Aband L P 2, 3, 4; Evid 20(1); Mines 92.29, 92.32(2), 92.36, 92.38.

Humble Oil & Refining Co.; Craddock v., TexCivApp–Fort Worth, 234 SW2d 137, ref nre.—App & E 662(3), 1050.1(2); Bound 3(7), 35(1), 35(3), 37(3), 55; Libel 130; Trial 351.2(2), 359(1).

Humble Oil & Refining Co.; Crawford v., TexCivApp–Galveston, 150 SW2d 849, writ dism, correct.—Adv Poss 13, 30, 80(2); Mines 49, 50.

Humble Oil & Refining Co.; Crump v., TexCivApp–Eastland, 164 SW2d 786.—Bound 3(7), 35(1), 36(5).

Humble Oil & Refining Co. v. Daniel, TexCivApp–Beaumont, 259 SW2d 580, ref nre, cert den Humble Oil and Refining Company v. Sheppard, 74 SCt 631, 347 US 936, 98 LEd 1086.—Corp 394; Decl Judgm 43, 96, 122.1, 123; Searches 76.

Humble Oil & Refining Co. v. Downey, Tex, 183 SW2d 426, 143 Tex 171.—Ack 25.

Humble Oil & Refining Co.; Eighth Regional War Labor Board v., CCA5 (Tex), 145 F2d 462, cert den 65 SCt 1577, 325 US 883, 89 LEd 1998.—Fed Civ Proc 402, 465, 572; Fed Cts 5, 7, 30, 770; Inj 11, 138.46, 192, 204.

Humble Oil & Refining Co. v. Eighth Regional War Labor Board, NDTex, 56 FSupp 950, rev 145 F2d 462, cert den 65 SCt 1577, 325 US 883, 89 LEd 1998.—Fed Civ Proc 467.1; War 45.

Humble Oil & Refining Co. v. Ellison, TexComApp, 132 SW2d 395, 134 Tex 140.—Bound 7, 9, 37(3); Deeds 93; Evid 460(6).

Humble Oil & Refining Co.; Ellison v., TexCivApp–Eastland, 106 SW2d 1083, rev 132 SW2d 395, 134 Tex 140.—Bound 1, 3(1), 40(1), 48(1), 48(6); Deeds 93, 111; Estop 25, 119; Evid 460(5), 461(3); Mines 55(5); Ref of Inst 16.

Humble Oil & Refining Co. v. Fantham, TexCivApp–Galveston, 268 SW2d 239, dism.—App & E 14(4), 747(1); Deeds 101; Estop 117; Evid 23(1), 205(1); Lim of Act 24(2); Propty 9.

Humble Oil & Refining Co. v. Fisher, Tex, 253 SW2d 656, 152 Tex 29.—App & E 1194(2), 1203(1), 1206;

For Later Case History Information, see KeyCite on WESTLAW

See Guidelines for Arrangement at the beginning of this Volume

Const Law 321, 2311; Courts 207.5; Judgm 497(1), 660; Jury 31.2(1).

Humble Oil & Refining Co. v. Flanagan, TexCivApp–Austin, 165 SW2d 508, writ refused wom.—App & E 843(2); Mines 92.39, 92.40.

Humble Oil & Refining Co.; Goldsmith v., Tex, 199 SW2d 773, 145 Tex 549.—Bound 20(1), 33; Dedi 18(1); Ease 36(3); Ex & Ad 148; Mines 92.27.

Humble Oil & Refining Co. v. Goldsmith, TexCivApp–Austin, 196 SW2d 665, rev 199 SW2d 773, 145 Tex 549.—Deeds 118; Ease 36(3); Ex & Ad 148; Judgm 747(4); Mines 92.29.

Humble Oil & Refining Co.; Gray Tool Co. v., CA5 (Tex), 190 F2d 779.—Pat 325.15.

Humble Oil & Refining Co.; Gray Tool Co. v., CA5 (Tex), 186 F2d 365, cert den 71 SCt 854, 341 US 934, 95 LEd 1363, reh den 71 SCt 1014, 341 US 956, 95 LEd 1377, reh den 71 SCt 1014, 341 US 956, 95 LEd 1377, motion gr 190 F2d 779.—Pat 118, 209(1), 283(1), 323.2(4).

Humble Oil & Refining Co.; Gray Tool Co. v., SDTex, 92 FSupp 722, rev 186 F2d 365, cert den 71 SCt 854, 341 US 934, 95 LEd 1363, reh den 71 SCt 1014, 341 US 956, 95 LEd 1377, reh den 71 SCt 1014, 341 US 956, 95 LEd 1377, motion gr 190 F2d 779.—Pat 323.2(4).

Humble Oil & Refining Co. v. Grucholski, TexCivApp–Waco, 376 SW2d 950, ref nre.—Mines 121, 125.

Humble Oil & Refining Co.; Guleke v., TexCivApp–Amarillo, 126 SW2d 38.—Mines 77, 78.2, 78.7(3.1), 78.7(4).

Humble Oil & Refining Co. v. Hamer, TexCivApp–Beaumont, 167 SW2d 272.—Corp 503(1); Plead 111.40; Princ & A 21, 22(1); R R 22(3); Trial 90, 105(5).

Humble Oil & Refining Co. v. Harrison, Tex, 205 SW2d 355, 146 Tex 216.—Deeds 90; Estop 95; Mines 55(5), 78.1(3), 78.2, 78.5, 79.1(4).

Humble Oil & Refining Co. v. Harrison, TexCivApp–Galveston, 199 SW2d 786, rev 205 SW2d 355, 146 Tex 216.—App & E 846(2), 846(5); Mines 74.5, 78.1(3).

Humble Oil & Refining Co.; Hicks v., TexApp–Houston (14 Dist), 970 SW2d 90, reh overr, and review den.—Admin Law 412.1; App & E 223, 1079; Const Law 190; Environ Law 408; Fraud 16; Neglig 238, 305, 1011, 1025; Nuis 3(1), 27; Statut 263; Waters 104.

Humble Oil & Refining Co.; Home Indem. Co. v., Tex, 317 SW2d 515, 159 Tex 224.—Insurance 2760.

Humble Oil & Refining Co.; Home Indem. Co. v., TexCivApp–Dallas, 314 SW2d 861, ref nre 317 SW2d 515, 159 Tex 224.—Autos 144.1(4), 200; Insurance 2760, 3517.

Humble Oil & Refining Co.; House v., TexCivApp–Beaumont, 97 SW2d 314, writ refused.—Deeds 120; Ex & Ad 367, 383, 388(2), 388(6), 397; Jud S 34.1.

Humble Oil & Refining Co.; Hutchins v., TexCivApp–Galveston, 161 SW2d 571, writ refused wom.—Evid 506, 545, 546, 553(1); Mines 73.1(1), 78.1(11), 78.6, 78.7(4); Trial 352.4(2).

Humble Oil & Refining Co.; Jones v., TexCivApp–San Antonio, 114 SW2d 398, dism.—App & E 1008.1(14); Deeds 194(4), 195, 206; Ven & Pur 224.

Humble Oil & Refining Co.; Keegan v., CCA5 (Tex), 155 F2d 971.—Fed Civ Proc 203, 224, 1747; Judgm 243; Mines 79.1.

Humble Oil & Refining Co.; Kinnear-Weed Corp. v., CA5 (Tex), 441 F2d 631, cert den 92 SCt 285, 404 US 941, 30 LEd2d 255, reh den 92 SCt 532, 404 US 996, 30 LEd2d 549.—Fed Civ Proc 2723, 2737.3, 2741; Fed Cts 416, 913, 1149.1; Inj 26(1); Judges 51(4); Pat 312(6), 323.3, 325.4, 325.11(4).

Humble Oil & Refining Co.; Kinnear-Weed Corp. v., CA5 (Tex), 403 F2d 437, on remand 324 FSupp 1371, aff 441 F2d 631, cert den 92 SCt 285, 404 US 941, 30 LEd2d 255, reh den 92 SCt 532, 404 US 996, 30 LEd2d 549.—Fed Cts 524, 529; Judges 43; Judgm 560.

Humble Oil & Refining Co.; Kinnear-Weed Corp. v., CA5 (Tex), 296 F2d 215, cert den 82 SCt 142, 368 US 890, 7 LEd2d 89, reh den 82 SCt 359, 368 US 936, 7 LEd2d 198.—Courts 106; Fed Cts 453, 956.1.

Humble Oil & Refining Co.; Kinnear-Weed Corp. v., CA5 (Tex), 259 F2d 398, reh den 266 F2d 352, cert den 80 SCt 210, 361 US 903, 4 LEd2d 158, reh den 80 SCt 1608, 363 US 857, 4 LEd2d 1740, opinion supplemented 296 F2d 215, cert den 82 SCt 142, 368 US 890, 7 LEd2d 89, reh den 82 SCt 359, 368 US 936, 7 LEd2d 198.—Antitrust 34, 170, 977(2); Fed Civ Proc 2280; Fraud 27; Impl & C C 3; Pat 167(1.1), 167(1.2), 234.

Humble Oil & Refining Co.; Kinnear-Weed Corp. v., CA5 (Tex), 214 F2d 891, cert den 75 SCt 292, 348 US 912, 99 LEd 715, reh den 80 SCt 1608, 363 US 857, 4 LEd2d 1740.—Antitrust 958, 987; Commerce 62.14.

Humble Oil & Refining Co.; Kinnear-Weed Corp. v., EDTex, 150 FSupp 143, aff 259 F2d 398, reh den 266 F2d 352, cert den 80 SCt 210, 361 US 903, 4 LEd2d 158, reh den 80 SCt 1608, 363 US 857, 4 LEd2d 1740, opinion supplemented 296 F2d 215, cert den 82 SCt 142, 368 US 890, 7 LEd2d 89, reh den 82 SCt 359, 368 US 936, 7 LEd2d 198.—Antitrust 16, 41, 61, 112, 419, 958, 963(1), 976, 977(2); Lim of Act 39(1); Pat 16.1, 17(2), 26(1), 26(1.1), 36.2(3), 37, 51(1), 66(1), 66(1.21), 74, 112.1, 141(1), 144, 148, 165(1), 165(2), 167(1.1), 168(1), 168(2.2), 177, 178, 182, 226.6, 234, 237, 238, 246, 312(1.1), 312(5), 314(1), 314(2); Torts 424.

Humble Oil & Refining Co.; Kinnear-Weed Corp. v., SDTex, 324 FSupp 1371, aff 441 F2d 631, cert den 92 SCt 285, 404 US 941, 30 LEd2d 255, reh den 92 SCt 532, 404 US 996, 30 LEd2d 549.—Fed Cts 819; Judges 42, 43, 45, 51(4); Mines 109; Pat 226, 287(1).

Humble Oil & Refining Co. v. Kirkindall, TexCivApp–Beaumont, 119 SW2d 731, aff Houston Oil Co of Texas v. Kirkindall, 145 SW2d 1074, 136 Tex 103.—Deeds 93, 114(1), 118; Evid 461(2).

Humble Oil & Refining Co.; Klein v., Tex, 86 SW2d 1077, 126 Tex 450.—Mines 55(5), 73.1(1), 73.1(2).

Humble Oil & Refining Co.; Klepak v., TexCivApp–Galveston, 177 SW2d 215, writ refused wom.—Consp 8; Const Law 4290; Mines 92.44(3); Mun Corp 601.2, 724.

Humble Oil & Refining Co. v. Kunkel, TexCivApp–San Antonio, 366 SW2d 236, ref nre.—Mines 78.1(7).

Humble Oil & Refining Co. v. L. & G. Oil Co., TexCiv-App–Austin, 259 SW2d 933, ref nre.—Mines 47, 92.42.

Humble Oil & Refining Co. v. Lasseter, TexCivApp–Austin, 120 SW2d 541, dism.—Admin Law 499, 746; Mines 92.29, 92.37, 92.38; Pub Ut 185.

Humble Oil & Refining Co. v. Lasseter, TexCivApp–Texarkana, 95 SW2d 730, writ dism.—Partit 77(1), 78.

Humble Oil & Refining Co. v. Lloyd, TexCivApp–Beaumont, 108 SW2d 213, writ refused.—Hus & W 273(4), 273(8.1), 273(9); Mines 5.3.

Humble Oil & Refining Co.; Lollis v., TexCivApp–El Paso, 285 SW2d 249, ref nre.—Autos 192(11), 194(1), 201(9).

Humble Oil & Refining Co.; Long v., Tex, 380 SW2d 554.—App & E 20, 70(6).

Humble Oil & Refining Co.; Long v., TexCivApp–Texarkana, 377 SW2d 844, writ refused 380 SW2d 554.—App & E 78(1).

Humble Oil & Refining Co.; Long v., TexCivApp–Galveston, 154 SW2d 925, writ refused wom.—Contracts 143(3); Fraud 12, 43; Frds St of 142; Ref of Inst 1, 36(1).

Humble Oil & Refining Co. v. Luckel, TexCivApp–Beaumont, 154 SW2d 155, writ refused wom.—Evid 22(1); Inj 7; Mines 52.

Humble Oil & Refining Co. v. Luckel, TexCivApp–Galveston, 171 SW2d 902, writ refused wom.—Damag 40(1); Deeds 8; Libel 131, 132, 139; Wills 824.

Humble Oil & Refining Co.; Luling Oil & Gas Co. v., Tex, 191 SW2d 716, 144 Tex 475.—Action 61; Contracts

HUMBLE

167; Corp 379, 487(1); Cust & U 10; Joint Adv 1.2(4); Lim of Act 43, 53(2), 102(5), 177(2); Mines 97, 101; Partners 17, 53; Refer 18.

Humble Oil & Refining Co.; Luling Oil & Gas Co. v., Tex, 182 SW2d 700, 143 Tex 54, opinion conformed to 192 SW2d 315, aff 191 SW2d 716, 144 Tex 475.—App & E 84(1), 1178(6).

Humble Oil & Refining Co. v. Luling Oil & Gas Co., TexCivApp–Galveston, 192 SW2d 315, aff 191 SW2d 716, 144 Tex 475.—App & E 1172(1), 1178(6); Contracts 153; Corp 379; Joint Adv 1.13; Lim of Act 53(2); Mines 97, 101; Partners 1.

Humble Oil & Refining Co. v. Lumbermens Mut. Cas. Co., TexCivApp–Dallas, 490 SW2d 640, ref nre.—Insurance 2684.

Humble Oil & Refining Co.; McClenny v., TexCivApp–Texarkana, 179 SW2d 798, writ refused wom.—Evid 314(1); Hus & W 249(2.1), 262.1(2), 265, 274(1); Tresp to T T 39(1); Ven & Pur 230(1).

Humble Oil & Refining Co. v. MacDonald, TexCivApp–Austin, 279 SW2d 914, ref nre.—Judgm 747(4); Mines 92.32(1), 92.38, 92.40.

Humble Oil & Refining Co.; McDonald v., TexCivApp–Beaumont, 78 SW2d 1068, writ dism.—Parties 80(7).

Humble Oil & Refining Co.; Manning v., TexCivApp–Beaumont, 92 SW2d 577, writ refused.—Adv Poss 42, 109; Tresp to T T 6.1.

Humble Oil & Refining Co.; Manziel v., TexCivApp–Texarkana, 214 SW2d 797, ref nre.—Adv Poss 112; App & E 1097(1), 1099(8).

Humble Oil & Refining Co. v. Manziel, TexCivApp–Texarkana, 187 SW2d 149, writ refused wom.—Adv Poss 27; App & E 1170.8; Bound 9, 33; Judgm 226.

Humble Oil & Refining Co. v. Manziel, TexCivApp–Texarkana, 165 SW2d 909.—Inj 132; Mines 52.

Humble Oil & Refining Co. v. Martin, Tex, 222 SW2d 995, 148 Tex 175.—App & E 1012.1(1); Autos 173(8), 244(14), 244(26), 244(29), 244(36.1), 245(17), 245(72), 247, 395; Evid 8; Indem 66; Neglig 504.

Humble Oil & Refining Co. v. Martin, TexCivApp–Austin, 216 SW2d 251, aff in part, rev in part 222 SW2d 995, 148 Tex 175.—App & E 1056.4, 1062.1; Autos 193(4), 201(5), 201(8), 244(26), 247; Indem 66; Labor & Emp 3029; Trial 351.5(6), 365.1(7).

Humble Oil & Refining Co.; Mason v., CCA5 (Tex), 94 F2d 786.—Mines 55(8).

Humble Oil & Refining Co.; Matlock v., TexCivApp–Beaumont, 284 SW2d 407, ref nre.—App & E 544(1), 547(2); Ease 61(9 1/2); Gas 9; Home 216; Trial 397(1), 397(5).

Humble Oil & Refining Co. v. Merrill, TexCivApp–Texarkana, 100 SW2d 387.—Partit 8.

Humble Oil & Refining Co. v. Monroe, TexCivApp–Dallas, 129 SW2d 454.—Plead 312; Venue 2, 5.3(8).

Humble Oil & Refining Co.; Montgomery County v., TexCivApp–Beaumont, 245 SW2d 326, ref nre.—Tax 2128, 2709(1), 2709(2), 2878(2), 2882.

Humble Oil & Refining Co.; Mook v., TexCivApp–Fort Worth, 182 SW2d 255, writ refused wom.—Princ & A 81(1), 81(4), 97.

Humble Oil & Refining Co.; Moore v., TexCivApp–El Paso, 85 SW2d 943, writ dism.—Hus & W 14.11, 267(8), 274(1); Ven & Pur 230(1), 242.

Humble Oil & Refining Co. v. Mullican, Tex, 192 SW2d 770, 144 Tex 609.—Evid 450(4), 461(1); Mines 59, 78.2, 79.6.

Humble Oil & Refining Co. v. Mullican, TexCivApp–Amarillo, 190 SW2d 392, aff 192 SW2d 770, 144 Tex 609.—App & E 1054(1); Contracts 164, 169; Evid 419(9); Hus & W 276(6); Mines 59.

Humble Oil & Refining Co. v. Neeks Drilling Co., TexCivApp–Texarkana, 119 SW2d 169, dism.—App & E 863; Inj 132, 163(1).

Humble Oil & Refining Co.; Norton v., TexCivApp–Dallas, 227 SW2d 860.—Inj 157; Judgm 585(1), 585(3), 634, 713(2).

Humble Oil & Refining Co. v. Owings, TexCivApp–Fort Worth, 128 SW2d 67.—Adv Poss 112; App & E 1062.1, 1173(2); Bound 40(3), 42, 43, 47(1); Evid 379; Judgm 248, 251(1), 256(1); Mines 73.1(1); Trial 215, 219, 232(2), 350.1, 350.3(2.1), 356(1).

Humble Oil & Refining Co. v. Parish, TexCivApp–Texarkana, 146 SW2d 1045, writ dism, correct.—Adv Poss 14, 27, 103; App & E 1008.1(14); Evid 441(8), 450(3), 460(8).

Humble Oil & Refining Co.; Parrish v., TexCivApp–Texarkana, 251 SW2d 418, ref nre.—Dedi 19(5); Evid 181; Tresp to T T 38(1), 38(2).

Humble Oil & Refining Co. v. Patton, TexCivApp–Texarkana, 344 SW2d 234, ref nre.—Bound 40(1), 40(3), 46(1).

Humble Oil & Refining Co. v. Pitts, TexComApp, 108 SW2d 910, 130 Tex 216.—App & E 78(1).

Humble Oil & Refining Co.; Ploeger v., TexCivApp–Eastland, 416 SW2d 553, ref nre.—Ex & Ad 39; Mines 73.1(2), 78.1(3), 78.4.

Humble Oil & Refining Co. v. Potter, TexCivApp–Austin, 173 SW2d 309, writ refused wom.—Mines 92.27, 92.39, 92.41.

Humble Oil & Refining Co. v. Potter, TexCivApp–Austin, 143 SW2d 135.—App & E 840(1); Mines 92.29, 92.30, 92.38, 92.39, 92.40.

Humble Oil & Refining Co. v. Preston, TexCivApp–Beaumont, 515 SW2d 929.—App & E 449, 781(1), 790(2), 1177(1); Const Law 975; Costs 238(1); Courts 483; Fed Cts 513; Plead 111.47.

Humble Oil & Refining Co. v. Preston, TexCivApp–Beaumont, 487 SW2d 956, writ dism woj, probable jur noted Exxon Corp v. Preston, 94 SCt 538, 414 US 1038, 38 LEd2d 328, vac 94 SCt 1394, 415 US 904, 39 LEd2d 459, conformed to 515 SW2d 929.—Corp 641, 666; Plead 111.43.

Humble Oil & Refining Co.; Price v., TexCivApp–Dallas, 152 SW2d 804, writ refused wom.—Adv Poss 16(1), 104, 116(2); Afft 18; App & E 882(8), 930(1), 972, 989, 1060.1(2.1); Courts 106; Evid 230(1), 266, 279, 302, 309; Lost Inst 23(3), 24; New Tr 42(4), 54, 55; Trial 129, 207; Witn 392(1).

Humble Oil & Refining Co. v. Railroad Commission, Tex, 223 SW2d 785, 148 Tex 228.—App & E 781(4).

Humble Oil & Refining Co.; Railroad Commission, TexCivApp–Austin, 193 SW2d 824, ref nre, aff 67 SCt 1523, 331 US 791, 91 LEd 1820, reh den 68 SCt 35, 332 US 786, 92 LEd 369, aff Williams v. Railroad Commission of Texas, 67 SCt 1523, 331 US 791, 91 LEd 1820, reh den 68 SCt 35, 332 US 786, 92 LEd 369.—Admin Law 462, 499, 792; Estop 62.2(2); Mines 47, 58, 92.20, 92.21, 92.23(2), 92.29, 92.38, 92.40, 92.49, 92.50, 92.62, 92.64.

Humble Oil & Refining Co.; Railroad Commission v., TexCivApp–Austin, 123 SW2d 423, dism.—Admin Law 499; Evid 75; Mines 92.29, 92.32(2), 92.38, 92.39, 92.40.

Humble Oil & Refining Co.; Railroad Commission v., TexCivApp–Austin, 119 SW2d 728, writ refused.—Judgm 194, 585(5), 668(1); Mines 92.35.

Humble Oil & Refining Co. v. Railroad Commission, TexCivApp–Austin, 112 SW2d 222, dism.—App & E 1001(1); Const Law 2470, 2540; Mines 92.32(1), 92.39, 92.40; Pub Ut 190, 194, 195.

Humble Oil & Refining Co. v. Railroad Commission, TexCivApp–Austin, 99 SW2d 401.—Mines 92.32(1), 92.39.

Humble Oil & Refining Co. v. Railroad Commission, TexCivApp–Austin, 94 SW2d 1197, writ refused.—Mines 92.23(1), 92.26, 92.30, 92.39, 92.40.

Humble Oil & Refining Co. v. Railroad Commission of Texas, WDTex, 35 FSupp 573, probable jur noted Railroad Commission of Texas v. Rowan & Nichols Oil Co, 61 SCt 29, vac and remanded 61 SCt 343, 311 US 570, 85 LEd 358.—Const Law 4290; Courts 101; Inj 85(1), 203; Mines 92.3(2), 92.49, 92.55, 92.63.

Humble Oil & Refining Co.; Railroad Commission of Tex. v., Tex, 245 SW2d 488, 151 Tex 51.—Mines 92.29.

Humble Oil & Refining Co. v. Railroad Commission of Texas, Tex, 128 SW2d 9, 133 Tex 330.—Carr 12(1); Corp 378; Gas 2, 14.3(1), 14.4(8).

Humble Oil & Refining Co.; Railroad Commission of Tex. v., TexCivApp–Austin, 424 SW2d 474, ref nre.—Mines 92.30, 92.35.

Humble Oil & Refining Co.; Railroad Commission of Texas v., TexCivApp–Austin, 101 SW2d 614, rev 128 SW2d 9, 133 Tex 330.—Evid 570; Gas 1, 14.3(3), 14.4(1), 14.4(2), 14.5(6), 14.5(7).

Humble Oil & Refining Co. v. Railroad Commission of Texas, TexCivApp–Austin, 99 SW2d 1052, writ refused. —Mines 52, 92.29.

Humble Oil & Refining Co. v. Railroad Commission of Texas, TexCivApp–Austin, 92 SW2d 1109.—Mines 92.35.

Humble Oil & Refining Co. v. Railroad Commission of Texas, TexCivApp–Austin, 85 SW2d 813, writ dism.— Evid 29; Mines 92.29, 92.37, 92.38.

Humble Oil & Refining Co. v. Railroad Commission of Texas, TexCivApp–Austin, 85 SW2d 351.—Mines 92.35, 92.40.

Humble Oil & Refining Co. v. Railroad Commission of Texas, TexCivApp–Austin, 83 SW2d 695.—Mines 92.32(1), 92.35.

Humble Oil & Refining Co.; Robertson v., TexCivApp– Texarkana, 116 SW2d 820, dism.—New Tr 59, 68.4(5), 140(1).

Humble Oil & Refining Co.; Robinson v., TexCivApp– Texarkana, 301 SW2d 938, ref nre.—Deeds 112(1); Mines 55(2), 55(5), 79.7, 101; Trial 351.2(2); Ven & Pur 231(1).

Humble Oil & Refining Co.; Sanderford v., TexCivApp– Eastland, 274 SW2d 426, ref nre.—App & E 1012.1(9); Bound 37(4); Mines 5.2(4).

Humble Oil & Refining Co.; Shelor v., TexCivApp– Amarillo, 103 SW2d 207, writ dism.—Adv Poss 68; App & E 193(7), 524; Bound 10, 32, 37(3), 43, 46(1), 46(3).

Humble Oil & Refining Co.; Sledge v., TexCivApp– Beaumont, 340 SW2d 517.—Judgm 181(3); Pub Lands 174, 175(1), 175(3), 176(2).

Humble Oil & Refining Co.; Smith v., CA5 (Tex), 425 F2d 1287, cert den 91 SCt 138, 400 US 902, 27 LEd2d 138.—Courts 497, 509; Fed Cts 793.

Humble Oil & Refining Co.; Smith County Oil & Gas Co. v., TexCivApp–Austin, 112 SW2d 220, dism.—Mines 92.13, 92.32(1), 92.35, 92.39, 92.40; Trial 350.1.

Humble Oil & Refining Co. v. Southland Royalty Co. v., Tex, 249 SW2d 914, 151 Tex 324.—Courts 93(1); Mines 73.5, 79.1(5).

Humble Oil & Refining Co. v. Southland Royalty Co., TexCivApp–El Paso, 244 SW2d 249, rev 249 SW2d 914, 151 Tex 324.—Contracts 143(3), 175(1); Mines 73.5, 79.1(5).

Humble Oil & Refining Co.; Sparks v., TexCivApp– Texarkana, 129 SW2d 468, writ refused.—App & E 1047(3); Deeds 13, 31, 51; Hus & W 254, 255, 262.1(6), 264(4), 264(5).

Humble Oil & Refining Co.; Spear v., TexCivApp–Austin, 139 SW2d 212, writ dism, correct.—Mines 92.26, 92.29, 92.35, 92.40.

Humble Oil & Refining Co.; Spears v., CA5 (Tex), 261 F2d 231, cert den 79 SCt 885, 359 US 971, 3 LEd2d 838. —Fed Cts 664, 668.

Humble Oil & Refining Co.; State v., Tex, 169 SW2d 707, 141 Tex 40.—Licens 29, 32.1; Mun Corp 978(6); Set-Off 33(1); States 198, 212; Statut 263, 274; Tax 2761, 2853.

Humble Oil & Refining Co. v. State, TexCivApp–Austin, 162 SW2d 119, writ refused.—Adv Poss 7(2); App & E 878(2), 927(7); Bound 3(7), 7, 10, 35(2), 36(5), 37(1), 37(3), 40(1); Damag 67, 162; Estop 62.2(1); Evid 20(1), 308, 390(3), 417(5); Lim of Act 11(1), 44(1); Stip 14(12); Tresp to T T 25, 51.

Humble Oil & Refining Co. v. State, TexCivApp–Austin, 158 SW2d 336, writ refused.—App & E 767(1); Const Law 4276; Courts 90(4), 91(1), 107; Evid 16; Licens 7(9); Statut 179, 192, 219(2).

Humble Oil & Refining Co.; State v., TexCivApp–Austin, 128 SW2d 424, writ refused.—Bound 8, 37(3).

Humble Oil & Refining Co. v. State, TexCivApp–Austin, 104 SW2d 174, writ refused.—Bound 3(5), 48(6); Evid 18, 83(3); Mines 4; Pub Lands 180; Statut 131, 141(1).

Humble Oil & Refining Co.; State v., TexCivApp–Waco, 194 SW2d 811.—App & E 758.1, 833(4), 1052(5); Fed Cts 508.

Humble Oil & Refining Co.; State v., TexCivApp–Waco, 187 SW2d 93, writ refused wom, opinion supplemented 194 SW2d 811.—App & E 758.3(6), 927(7), 994(2), 1045(1); Bound 10; Const Law 632; Courts 90(1); Des & Dist 60; Evid 390(3); Judgm 17(3), 497(3); Jury 110(1), 149, 150; Pub Lands 174, 175(2), 175(6), 175(7), 176(1), 176(2), 177; States 211; Statut 158, 161(1), 162; Tax 2973, 3134, 3136; Tresp to T T 6.1, 38(1), 44; Trial 142.

Humble Oil & Refining Co.; Stevenson v., TexCivApp– Texarkana, 186 SW2d 115, writ refused.—Judgm 829(3); R R 82(1), 82(2), 82(6).

Humble Oil & Refining Co.; Stewart v., Tex, 377 SW2d 830.—Mines 92.16, 92.40, 92.42.

Humble Oil & Refining Co.; Stewart v., TexCivApp– Texarkana, 193 SW2d 259, ref nre.—App & E 1015(5); Damag 208(1); New Tr 44(1), 44(2), 56, 145.

Humble Oil & Refining Co. v. Stewart Oil Co., TexCiv-App–Austin, 241 SW2d 364, rev Railroad Commission of Tex v. Humble Oil & Refining Co, 245 SW2d 488, 151 Tex 51.—Mines 92.29.

Humble Oil & Refining Co.; Strickland v., CCA5 (Tex), 140 F2d 83, cert den 65 SCt 37, 323 US 712, 89 LEd 573, reh den 65 SCt 111, 323 US 812, 89 LEd 647.— Evid 29, 51, 55, 102, 117, 288, 291, 292, 293, 295, 517; Fed Cts 902; Names 14; Trial 244(2).

Humble Oil & Refining Co.; Strickland v., TexCivApp– Eastland, 181 SW2d 901.—Adv Poss 104, 114(1); App & E 846(2), 846(5); Des & Dist 71(6), 90(4); Infants 24; Judgm 671.

Humble Oil & Refining Co.; Sumter v., TexCivApp– Beaumont, 139 SW2d 623, writ dism, correct.—Judgm 572(2), 584, 585(2); Plead 214(1), 380.

Humble Oil & Refining Co. v. Sun Oil Co., CA5 (Tex), 191 F2d 705.—Action 25(1); Atty & C 86; Equity 1, 49; Evid 67(3); Fed Civ Proc 39; Fed Cts 7, 430, 433; Jury 14(9), 31.2(2); Nav Wat 36(3), 44(3); Quiet T 1, 2, 4, 6, 7(1), 7(2), 8, 10.1, 11, 12(2), 27, 28; States 4.4(3).

Humble Oil & Refining Co. v. Sun Oil Co., CA5 (Tex), 190 F2d 191, reh den 191 F2d 705, cert den 72 SCt 367, 342 US 920, 96 LEd 687.—Com Law 2.1; Const Law 2632; Estop 32(2); Fed Cts 21, 295, 372, 417, 430, 433; Jury 14(9); Nav Wat 1(4), 36(3), 41(1), 42(1), 42(4), 44(1), 44(2), 44(3); Pub Lands 204.

Humble Oil & Refining Co. v. Sun Oil Co., CA5 (Tex), 175 F2d 670.—Fed Civ Proc 1611; Inj 138.31.

Humble Oil & Refining Co.; Sun Oil Co. v., SDTex, 88 FSupp 658, mod 190 F2d 191, reh den 191 F2d 705, cert den 72 SCt 367, 342 US 920, 96 LEd 687.—Fed Civ Proc 219, 338; Fed Cts 283, 295, 304.1.

Humble Oil & Refining Co.; Taylor v., TexCivApp– Waco, 293 SW2d 834.—App & E 627.3.

Humble Oil & Refining Co.; Taylor-Link Oil Co. v., TexCivApp–Beaumont, 88 SW2d 1074.—Mines 79.1(3).

Humble Oil & Refining Co.; Taylor-McCulloch Corp. v., SDTex, 29 FSupp 312.—Fed Cts 243, 295; Parties 45; Pub Lands 172.7, 174, 178(1).

Humble Oil & Refining Co. v. Texas & Pac. Ry. Co., Tex, 289 SW2d 547, 155 Tex 483.—Carr 63, 189, 202; Judgm 185.3(1).

Humble Oil & Refining Co. v. Texas & P. Ry. Co., TexCivApp–Dallas, 275 SW2d 824, rev 289 SW2d 547, 155 Tex 483.—Carr 12(1), 13(1), 26, 32(1), 189, 196, 202; Commerce 14.10(1), 14.10(2), 14.10(3), 61(1).

Humble Oil & Refining Co.; Texas Employers Ins. Ass'n v., TexCivApp–Galveston, 103 SW2d 818, writ refused.—Insurance 1209(3), 1213; Lim of Act 14, 127(2.1), 127(4).

Humble Oil & Refining Co. v. Trapp, TexCivApp–Austin, 194 SW2d 781, writ refused.—Contracts 9(1); Courts 107; Equity 67; Estop 62.2(1), 95, 96, 116; Mines 92.13, 92.27, 92.35, 92.36, 92.38, 92.40; Trial 351.2(4).

Humble Oil & Refining Co. v. Turnbow, TexCivApp–Austin, 133 SW2d 191, writ refused, cert den 61 SCt 10, 311 US 656, 85 LEd 420.—Mines 92.28, 92.29, 92.38, 92.41.

Humble Oil & Refining Co.; U.S. v., CA5 (Tex), 518 F2d 747.—Int Rev 4490, 4495.

Humble Oil & Refining Co.; U.S. v., CA5 (Tex), 488 F2d 953, reh den 491 F2d 1272, vac 95 SCt 1670, 421 US 943, 44 LEd2d 97, on remand 518 F2d 747.—Int Rev 4490.

Humble Oil & Refining Co.; U.S. v., SDTex, 346 FSupp 944, aff 488 F2d 953, reh den 491 F2d 1272, vac 95 SCt 1670, 421 US 943, 44 LEd2d 97, on remand 518 F2d 747.—Int Rev 4459, 4499.

Humble Oil & Refining Co.; Wayne v., CA5 (Tex), 175 F2d 230.—Pat 16.2, 66(1.19), 167(1.1), 312(6).

Humble Oil & Refining Co. v. Webb, TexCivApp–Texarkana, 177 SW2d 218, writ refused wom.—Deeds 128; Estop 68(2); Judgm 725(4); Plead 36(2), 48, 180(1), 412; Trial 36.

Humble Oil & Refining Co. v. West, Tex, 508 SW2d 812, appeal after remand Exxon Corp v. West, 543 SW2d 667, ref nre, cert den 98 SCt 224, 434 US 875, 54 LEd2d 154.—Confusion of G 3, 12, 13; Mines 47, 55(5), 55(6).

Humble Oil & Refining Co. v. West, TexCivApp–Waco, 496 SW2d 212, writ gr, rev 508 SW2d 812, appeal after remand Exxon Corp v. West, 543 SW2d 667, ref nre, cert den 98 SCt 224, 434 US 875, 54 LEd2d 154.—Equity 46; Inj 16; Mines 78.1(2), 79.1(2), 79.3, 79.7.

Humble Oil & Refining Co. v. Westside Inv. Corp., Tex, 428 SW2d 92.—Judgm 181(18); Spec Perf 57; Ven & Pur 18(4).

Humble Oil & Refining Co. v. Westside Inv. Corp., TexCivApp–San Antonio, 419 SW2d 448, rev 428 SW2d 92.—Contracts 23; Ven & Pur 18, 18(3), 18(4).

Humble Oil & Refining Co. v. Whitten, Tex, 427 SW2d 313.—Mines 118.

Humble Oil & Refining Co. v. Whitten, TexCivApp–Tyler, 415 SW2d 287, rev 427 SW2d 313.—Bailm 14(1); Contracts 170(1); Mines 109, 118; Neglig 387, 551.

Humble Oil & Refining Co. v. Williams, Tex, 420 SW2d 133.—Mines 51(3), 73.1(6), 121, 125.

Humble Oil & Refining Co.; Williams v., TexCivApp–El Paso, 139 SW2d 346, writ dism, correct.—App & E 544(1), 1043(7), 1152; Pretrial Proc 3, 711; Tresp to T T 47(2); Trial 39.

Humble Oil & Refining Co. v. Williams, TexCivApp–Tyler, 413 SW2d 413, writ gr, rev 420 SW2d 133.—Mines 51(3), 73.1(6), 125.

Humble Oil & Refining Co.; Willingham v., TexCivApp–Galveston, 202 SW2d 955.—Plead 111.3, 291(2).

Humble Oil & Refining Co.; Wilson v., TexCivApp–Texarkana, 82 SW2d 1095, writ refused.—Deeds 78, 90, 93, 129(4).

Humble Oil & Refining Co. v. Wilson, TexCivApp–Waco, 339 SW2d 954, ref nre.—Indem 32, 33(5); Neglig 1672.

Humble Oil & Refining Co. v. Wood, TexCivApp–Fort Worth, 94 SW2d 573.—Compromise 5(2); Corp 429.

Humble Oil & Refining Co.; Woods v., TexCivApp–Austin, 120 SW2d 464, writ dism.—Mines 92.38.

Humble Oil & Refining Co.; Wrather v., Tex, 214 SW2d 112, 147 Tex 144.—App & E 846(5); Mines 92.21, 92.28, 92.38.

Humble Oil & Refining Co. v. Wrather, TexCivApp–Austin, 205 SW2d 86, aff 214 SW2d 112, 147 Tex 144.—Admin Law 782; Mines 92.26, 92.28, 92.29, 92.35, 92.38, 92.40; Names 18.

Humble Oil Refining Co.; Southern Pipeline Const. Co., Inc. v., TexCivApp–Hous (14 Dist), 496 SW2d 248, ref nre.—Garn 177, 187.

Humble Pipe Line Co. v. Anderson, TexCivApp–Waco, 339 SW2d 259, ref nre.—Nuis 7, 10; Tresp 10; Waters 104.

Humble Pipe Line Co. v. Day, TexCivApp–Waco, 172 SW2d 356, writ refused wom.—App & E 846(5); Damag 109, 110, 142; Ease 70; Waters 77.

Humble Pipe Line Co.; Eggleston v., TexCivApp–Hous (14 Dist), 482 SW2d 909, ref nre.—Contracts 95(3), 95(4), 256; Estop 83(1), 87, 98(1), 116.

Humble Pipe Line Co.; Williams v., TexCivApp–Houston, 417 SW2d 453.—Ease 12(2), 24, 30(2); Perp 4(12).

Humble Place Joint Venture, In re, CA5 (Tex), 936 F2d 814.—Bankr 3200, 3502.5, 3502.10, 3787.

Humble Place Joint Venture v. Fory, CA5 (Tex), 936 F2d 814. See Humble Place Joint Venture, In re.

Humbles v. Hefley-Stedman Motor Co., TexCivApp–Austin, 127 SW2d 515.—Hus & W 268(4).

Humble Sand & Gravel, Inc. v. Gomez, Tex, 146 SW3d 170.—Labor & Emp 2782, 2797; Neglig 210, 1550, 1692; Prod Liab 14, 62, 77, 87.1; Torts 101.

Humble Sand & Gravel, Inc. v. Gomez, TexApp–Texarkana, 48 SW3d 487, review gr, rev 146 SW3d 170.—App & E 969, 1050.1(1), 1051.1(1), 1056.1(1), 1058(1), 1064.1(8); Evid 208(6), 265(8); Neglig 202, 210, 213, 215, 220, 375, 379, 380, 387, 422, 423, 431, 433, 1692, 1741; Prod Liab 14, 15, 62, 75.1, 87.1, 98; Trial 43, 182, 251(1), 252(1), 295(1).

Humble Sand & Gravel, Inc. v. Martinez, Tex, 974 SW2d 31. See Childs v. Haussecker.

Humble Sand & Gravel, Inc.; Martinez v., Tex, 875 SW2d 311, appeal after remand 940 SW2d 139, reh overr, and writ gr, and motion to dismiss den, aff Childs v. Haussecker, 974 SW2d 31.—Action 60; App & E 76(1), 79(1), 343.1, 347(1), 937(1).

Humble Sand & Gravel, Inc.; Martinez v., TexApp–El Paso, 940 SW2d 139, reh overr, and writ gr, and motion to dismiss den, aff Childs v. Haussecker, 974 SW2d 31.—Judgm 181(7), 185(2); Lim of Act 47(1), 49(7), 95(1), 95(3), 95(5), 95(9), 199(1).

Humble Sand & Gravel, Inc.; Martinez v., TexApp–El Paso, 860 SW2d 467, reh overr, and writ gr, rev 875 SW2d 311, appeal after remand 940 SW2d 139, reh overr, and writ gr, and motion to dismiss den, aff Childs v. Haussecker, 974 SW2d 31.—App & E 863, 1078(5); Judgm 181(7), 185(2); Lim of Act 1, 43, 47(1), 49(7), 55(1), 95(1), 95(3), 95(5), 100(1), 127(1), 127(12), 137, 182(5), 183(5).

Humble, Texas, City of; Poe v., SDTex, 554 FSupp 233.—Const Law 699, 795, 978, 990, 1150, 1389; Fed Civ Proc 103.2, 1831; Fed Cts 56; Mun Corp 120, 121, 622.

Humboldt Wedag, Inc.; Holcim (Texas) Ltd. Partnership v., TexApp–Waco, 211 SW3d 796, reh overr, and rule 537(f) motion gr.—Alt Disp Res 116, 117, 137, 141, 179, 182(1), 213(3), 363(1), 363(4); Commerce 80.5; Mand 60; States 18.15.

Hume v. Bricklayers, Masons and Plasterers Intern. Union of America, Local No. 23 of Tex., TexCivApp–

Amarillo, 363 SW2d 895.—App & E 725(1); Labor & Emp 1047(2).

Hume v. City of Amarillo, TexComApp, 99 SW2d 887, 128 Tex 424.—Em Dom 295, 299.

Hume; Royal Indem. Co. v., TexCivApp–San Antonio, 477 SW2d 683.—App & E 302(3), 302(6), 930(3), 989; Evid 54, 570, 571(9); Insurance 2607.

Hume; U.S. v., CA5 (Tex), 453 F2d 339, cert den 92 SCt 1518, 405 US 1070, 31 LEd2d 802.—Commerce 82.6; Crim Law 1132.

Hume v. Zuehl, TexCivApp–San Antonio, 119 SW2d 905, writ refused.—App & E 917(1); Inj 138.3, 138.37; Tax 2803.

Humes; Associated Sales, Inc. v., TexCivApp–Fort Worth, 441 SW2d 292.—Trademarks 1523(2), 1525(1), 1536.

Humes v. Hallmark, TexApp–Austin, 895 SW2d 475.—App & E 241, 930(3), 989, 1001(1), 1001(3); Evid 10(2); Trover 39, 40(6), 44, 45, 46, 47.

Humes; United Services Auto. Ass'n v., TexCivApp–San Antonio, 340 SW2d 127.—Venue 2, 5.5.

Humfield; Thomas v., CA5 (Tex), 916 F2d 1032, appeal after remand 32 F3d 566, reh and reh den 36 F3d 92, cert den 115 SCt 1138, 513 US 1167, 130 LEd2d 1098.—Const Law 4339; Fed Cts 433; Mental H 490.

Hummel; City of San Antonio v., TexCivApp–San Antonio, 134 SW2d 818, writ dism.—Em Dom 300.

Hummel v. Townsend, CA5 (Tex), 883 F2d 367, reh den.—Fed Cts 34, 302.

Humphrey, Ex parte, TexCrimApp, 456 SW2d 118.—Crim Law 264; Hab Corp 717(1).

Humphrey, In re, NDTex, 55 FSupp 221.—Sent & Pun 2034.

Humphrey v. Ahlschlager, TexApp–Dallas, 778 SW2d 480.—Pretrial Proc 713, 715, 723.1, 726.

Humphrey; Alford v., TexCivApp–Fort Worth, 154 SW2d 238.—J P 183(0.5).

Humphrey v. American Motorists Ins. Co., TexApp–Eastland, 102 SW3d 811, review den, and reh of petition for review den.—App & E 930(1), 969, 989, 1001(1), 1003(6); Trial 182, 232(1), 238, 251(1), 252(1); Work Comp 1396, 1624, 1728.

Humphrey v. Balli, TexApp–San Antonio, 61 SW3d 519.—App & E 223, 870(2), 893(1), 934(2), 1175(1); Mand 74(1), 187.2; Mun Corp 108.1, 108.2, 108.7, 108.8, 108.10.

Humphrey; Beaumont City Lines v., TexCivApp–Beaumont, 149 SW2d 256.—Trial 352.10.

Humphrey v. Bowles, NDTex, 125 FRD 657, aff 888 F2d 1390.—Fed Civ Proc 2734.

Humphrey v. Bullock, TexApp–Austin, 666 SW2d 586, ref nre.—Const Law 2630; Courts 8; Des & Dist 68; Evid 80(1); Ex & Ad 44; Mines 96, 97; Partners 1, 76; Tax 3307(1), 3319, 3349; Wills 733(1).

Humphrey v. Camelot Retirement Community, TexApp–Corpus Christi, 893 SW2d 55.—App & E 931(1), 1008.1(3), 1008.1(10), 1031(1), 1071.1(2); Can of Inst 3; Contracts 258, 261(2), 261(4), 274; Interest 31, 39(2.30), 66; Trial 382; Ven & Pur 82, 110, 114, 123.

Humphrey v. C. G. Jung Educational Center of Houston, CA5 (Tex), 624 F2d 637, appeal after remand 714 F2d 477.—Adv Poss 70, 71(1); Estates 7.

Humphrey v. C.G. Jung Educational Center of Houston, Tex., CA5 (Tex), 714 F2d 477.—Deeds 144(1), 153; Elect of Rem 3(1); Forfeit 1.

Humphrey; Commercial Cas. Ins. Co. v., SDTex, 13 FSupp 174.—Decl Judgm 170; Fed Cts 340.1, 342; Insurance 2280.

Humphrey v. C.I.R., CCA5 (Tex), 162 F2d 853, 175 ALR 363, cert den 68 SCt 157, 332 US 817, 92 LEd 394.—Int Rev 3138, 3179, 3246, 3255, 3397.

Humphrey; Dougherty v., Tex, 424 SW2d 617.—Judgm 712; Wills 62, 63, 67, 188, 472.

Humphrey v. Dougherty, TexCivApp–Amarillo, 420 SW2d 450, aff in part, rev in part 424 SW2d 617.—Judgm 712; Wills 472, 727.

Humphrey v. Flanagan, TexCivApp–Texarkana, 91 SW2d 449.—Mines 50, 74.5, 79.1(1).

Humphrey; Gateley v., Tex, 254 SW2d 98, 151 Tex 588, answer to certified question conformed to 254 SW2d 571.—Courts 247(5); Damag 71.5; Statut 190.

Humphrey; Gateley v., TexCivApp–Dallas, 254 SW2d 571.—Damag 71.5.

Humphrey; Gateley v., TexCivApp–Dallas, 247 SW2d 919, certified question answered 254 SW2d 98, 151 Tex 588, answer to certified question conformed to 254 SW2d 571.—Costs 32(5); Damag 71.5.

Humphrey v. Hendrick, TexCivApp–Dallas, 88 SW2d 777.—App & E 805.

Humphrey v. Highland Park Independent School Dist., NDTex, 361 FSupp 451, aff 489 F2d 1311.—Const Law 4202; Fed Civ Proc 184.5.

Humphrey v. Humphrey, TexCivApp–Hous (14 Dist), 593 SW2d 824, dism.—Corp 1.4(2), 1.4(3); Divorce 146, 253(1), 286(9).

Humphrey; Humphrey v., TexCivApp–Hous (14 Dist), 593 SW2d 824, dism.—Corp 1.4(2), 1.4(3); Divorce 146, 253(1), 286(9).

Humphrey v. J. B. Land Co., SDTex, 478 FSupp 770.—Fed Cts 427; Lim of Act 95(2), 95(15), 104(1).

Humphrey v. Knox, TexCivApp–Dallas, 244 SW2d 309, ref nre.—Judgm 340, 504(3); Parties 35.1, 35.11; Plead 111.46; Pretrial Proc 693.1.

Humphrey v. Lynaugh, CA5 (Tex), 861 F2d 875, cert den 109 SCt 1755, 490 US 1024, 104 LEd2d 191.—Hab Corp 846; Sent & Pun 1313.

Humphrey v. McCotter, SDTex, 675 FSupp 1043, rev 861 F2d 875, cert den 109 SCt 1755, 490 US 1024, 104 LEd2d 191.—Const Law 4611; Crim Law 597(1), 641.13(1), 641.13(6), 1177; Hab Corp 342, 380.1, 383, 479, 486(1), 486(2), 486(4), 773, 801; Sent & Pun 1313.

Humphrey v. May, TexApp–Austin, 804 SW2d 328, writ den.—Trial 365.1(1); Venue 68.

Humphrey v. Mirike, TexCivApp–Texarkana, 134 SW2d 749.—App & E 1043(8); Plead 111.42(4), 111.45.

Humphrey v. Mirike, TexCivApp–Eastland, 147 SW2d 576.—App & E 1114.

Humphrey; Murray v., TexCivApp–Texarkana, 132 SW2d 444.—App & E 447, 465(2), 467, 488(1).

Humphrey; Nixon v., TexCivApp–San Antonio, 565 SW2d 365, ref nre.—Adop 14; Infants 196, 203; Judgm 335(2), 335(3).

Humphrey; Placid Oil Co. v., CA5 (Tex), 244 F2d 184.—Contracts 47, 313(1), 313(2); Damag 124(1), 124(4), 140; Fed Cts 859; Mines 109.

Humphrey v. Placid Oil Co., EDTex, 142 FSupp 246, aff 244 F2d 184.—Contracts 313(1), 313(2); Damag 120(1); Impl & C C 65, 70, 111; Mines 109.

Humphrey v. Rawlins, TexCivApp–Dallas, 88 SW2d 776.—Mand 44; Venue 57.

Humphrey; Rushin v., TexApp–Houston (1 Dist), 778 SW2d 95, writ den.—Ease 21, 36(3).

Humphrey v. Seale, TexApp–Corpus Christi, 716 SW2d 620.—Decl Judgm 301.

Humphrey; Shell Oil Co. v., TexApp–Houston (14 Dist), 880 SW2d 170, reh den, and writ den.—App & E 173(13), 209.1, 241, 930(1), 1001(3); Death 17; Evid 208(1); Labor & Emp 51, 2777, 2782; Neglig 213, 215, 220, 232, 273, 1692.

Humphrey v. Showalter, TexCivApp–Eastland, 283 SW2d 91, ref nre.—App & E 230; Contracts 261(6), 313(2), 321(1), 324(2); Damag 125; Labor & Emp 171, 174, 237, 249.

Humphrey v. Southport Petroleum Co., TexCivApp–Texarkana, 131 SW2d 395.—App & E 846(5), 994(3), 1011.1(1); Partners 157(2); Princ & A 163(1), 173(3).

Humphrey v. Southwestern Portland Cement Co., CA5 (Tex), 488 F2d 691, reh den 490 F2d 992.—Civil R 1535, 1544; Fed Civ Proc 2290; Fed Cts 852, 853, 858.

Humphrey v. Southwestern Portland Cement Co., WDTex, 369 FSupp 832, rev 488 F2d 691, reh den 490 F2d 992.—Civil R 1106, 1462, 1463, 1502, 1505(3), 1511, 1535, 1554, 1563, 1571, 1573, 1591; Jury 14(1.5); Stip 14(10).

Humphrey v. Stanolind Oil & Gas Co., CA5 (Tex), 232 F2d 925.—Fed Civ Proc 201, 1747.

Humphrey v. State, TexCrimApp, 646 SW2d 949.—Crim Law 531(3), 577.16(7), 1158(4); Homic 990.

Humphrey v. State, TexCrimApp, 479 SW2d 51.—Crim Law 388.5(1), 899, 1035(3), 1036.1(9), 1036.2, 1044.1(4), 1045, 1130(2), 1130(5), 1165(1), 1171.1(3).

Humphrey v. State, TexCrimApp, 264 SW2d 432, 159 TexCrim 396.—Autos 355(6); Crim Law 814(17), 829(6).

Humphrey v. State, TexCrimApp, 212 SW2d 159, 152 TexCrim 203.—Crim Law 37(6.1), 507(1), 796, 800(2), 1091(14); Pub Amuse 70.

Humphrey v. State, TexApp–Corpus Christi, 626 SW2d 816.—RICO 105.

Humphrey v. State, TexApp–Houston (14 Dist), 681 SW2d 223, habeas corpus gr 675 FSupp 1043, rev 861 F2d 875, cert den 109 SCt 1755, 490 US 1024, 104 LEd2d 191.—Crim Law 586, 603.3(7), 641.10(3); Sent & Pun 1315, 1378.

Humphrey; State v., TexCivApp–Beaumont, 159 SW2d 162.—Licens 5, 28, 32; Mines 87; Tax 2187.

Humphrey v. Stidham, TexCivApp–Dallas, 124 SW2d 921.—App & E 931(6), 1054(1); Evid 543(1), 546; Mines 55(8).

Humphrey v. Taylor, TexApp–Tyler, 673 SW2d 954.—Hus & W 268(1), 270(8).

Humphrey; Texas Emp. Ins. Ass'n v., TexCivApp–Amarillo, 140 SW2d 313, writ refused.—Damag 221(5.1), 221(6); Evid 570, 589; Trial 178; Work Comp 1410, 1418.

Humphrey; U.S. v., CA5 (Tex), 104 F3d 65, cert den 117 SCt 1833, 520 US 1235, 137 LEd2d 1038.—Crim Law 398(2), 829(9), 829(16), 1030(1), 1042, 1139, 1144.13(3), 1144.13(5), 1152(1), 1153(1), 1158(1), 1159.2(7), 1169.1(1), 1169.10; Postal 35(2), 35(6), 35(20); Searches 125, 126; Sent & Pun 978, 991; Tel 1018(4), 1022.

Humphrey; U.S. v., CA5 (Tex), 7 F3d 1186.—Crim Law 412(3), 438(3), 1077.3, 1147, 1158(1), 1169.1(10), 1169.5(3), 1181.5(8); Sent & Pun 995.

Humphrey; Vanguard Ins. Co. v., TexApp–Houston (14 Dist), 729 SW2d 344, ref nre.—Work Comp 2247, 2251, 2254.

Humphrey; Warren v., EDTex, 875 FSupp 378.—Civil R 1088(4), 1093; Prisons 13(4); Sent & Pun 1548.

Humphrey; Weaver v., TexCivApp–Eastland, 114 SW2d 609, dism.—Judgm 301, 303, 304, 306.

Humphrey; Weaver v., TexCivApp–Eastland, 95 SW2d 720, reh den 114 SW2d 609, dism.—App & E 554(3), 773(4), 911.

Humphrey v. Wood, TexCivApp–Amarillo, 256 SW2d 669, ref nre.—App & E 171(1); Notice 6; Spec Perf 61, 121(11); Ven & Pur 18(3), 18(4).

Humphrey Co., Inc. v. Lowry Water Wells, TexApp–Houston (14 Dist), 709 SW2d 310.—App & E 859; Corp 507(14); Proc 153.

Humphreys, Matter of, Tex, 880 SW2d 402, cert den Humphreys v. Texas State Bar, 115 SCt 427, 513 US 964, 130 LEd2d 340.—Atty & C 47.1, 53(2), 57, 58; Const Law 2843; Jury 19(18).

Humphreys; Allen v., Tex, 559 SW2d 798.—Mand 32; Pretrial Proc 353, 356.1, 358, 371, 372, 373, 379, 383, 405.

Humphreys; Beck v., TexCivApp–San Antonio, 160 SW2d 85, writ refused wom.—Can of Inst 24(1); Ven & Pur 261(3).

Humphreys; Big Country Club, Inc. v., TexCivApp–Beaumont, 511 SW2d 315, ref nre.—Int Liq 92, 96.

Humphreys v. Caldwell, Tex, 888 SW2d 469.—Afft 3; App & E 78(1); Pretrial Proc 41, 283, 381, 404.1.

Humphreys v. Caldwell, TexApp–Corpus Christi, 881 SW2d 940, subsequent mandamus proceeding 888 SW2d 469.—Mand 4(1), 4(3), 32, 155(1), 168(2), 168(4); Pretrial Proc 41, 403, 410, 411; Witn 196.4.

Humphreys; Cheek v., TexApp–Houston (14 Dist), 800 SW2d 596, writ den.—App & E 989, 1012.1(5), 1172(1), 1178(6); Damag 91(1), 94; Fraud 61; Partners 70, 121, 122.5, 301, 305, 306, 336(3); Trial 382.

Humphreys; Dakan v., TexCivApp–Eastland, 190 SW2d 371.—Anim 82, 85; App & E 500(1); Trial 215, 219, 350.3(6), 351.2(1.1), 351.2(8), 352.6, 366.

Humphreys v. Fort Worth Lloyds, TexCivApp–Amarillo, 617 SW2d 788.—Judgm 181(11).

Humphreys v. Gribble, TexCivApp–Waco, 227 SW2d 235, ref nre.—Adv Poss 31, 33, 34, 38, 43(2), 85(1); App & E 933(4); New Tr 143(5).

Humphreys v. Haragan, TexCivApp–Amarillo, 476 SW2d 880.—App & E 927(7), 989; Neglig 1696; Trial 139.1(12), 142, 178.

Humphreys; Harvey v., TexCivApp–Galveston, 178 SW2d 733, writ refused wom.—Adv Poss 17, 25, 27, 31, 71(1), 101, 104, 112; App & E 1008.1(2); Execution 271; Hus & W 262.1(4), 265, 267(8); Judgm 712, 747(5).

Humphreys v. Humphreys, Tex, 364 SW2d 177.—App & E 931(1); Marriage 13, 50(1).

Humphreys; Humphreys v., Tex, 364 SW2d 177.—App & E 931(1); Marriage 13, 50(1).

Humphreys v. Humphreys, TexCivApp–Texarkana, 200 SW2d 453.—Child C 467, 921(1); Divorce 27(3), 27(5), 27(18), 127(3), 151, 184(10), 282; New Tr 104(1).

Humphreys; Humphreys v., TexCivApp–Texarkana, 200 SW2d 453.—Child C 467, 921(1); Divorce 27(3), 27(5), 27(18), 127(3), 151, 184(10), 282; New Tr 104(1).

Humphreys v. Humphreys, TexCivApp–Waco, 359 SW2d 103, writ gr, rev 364 SW2d 177.—Child 6; Marriage 13, 40(1), 50(1).

Humphreys; Humphreys v., TexCivApp–Waco, 359 SW2d 103, writ gr, rev 364 SW2d 177.—Child 6; Marriage 13, 40(1), 50(1).

Humphreys; McWhorter v., TexCivApp–Texarkana, 161 SW2d 304, writ refused wom.—App & E 758.1, 999(1); Evid 584(1); Release 55, 57(2); Trial 350.4(1), 351.2(4); Wills 62, 288(1), 300.

Humphreys v. Meadows, TexApp–Fort Worth, 938 SW2d 750, reh overr, and writ den.—App & E 960(1), 961; Pretrial Proc 46, 690, 695.

Humphreys v. Medical Towers, Ltd., SDTex, 893 FSupp 672, aff 100 F3d 952.—Brok 43(1); Civil R 1104, 1113, 1123, 1166, 1184, 1185, 1189, 1243, 1244, 1252, 1528, 1536, 1537, 1542, 1549, 1573; Corp 1.3, 1.4(2), 1.4(4), 215; Damag 50.10; Fed Civ Proc 2497.1; Partners 353.

Humphreys v. Roberson, TexComApp, 83 SW2d 311, 125 Tex 558.—App & E 1060.1(2.1); Health 814, 827; Trial 125(4).

Humphreys v. State, TexCrimApp, 565 SW2d 59.—Crim Law 29(5.5), 706(4), 1036.1(6), 1171.8(2); Double J 135, 139.1; Obst Just 16.

Humphreys v. State, TexCrimApp, 128 SW2d 816, 137 TexCrim 142.—Crim Law 586, 595(5), 1151.

Humphreys v. State, TexCrimApp, 99 SW2d 600, 131 TexCrim 383.—Crim Law 304(18), 1086.8, 1159.2(1); Ind & Inf 41(2); Int Liq 205(2), 236(20).

Humphreys v. State, TexCrimApp, 87 SW2d 717, 129 TexCrim 415.—Crim Law 884.

Humphreys; State Bar of Texas v., Tex, 882 SW2d 824.—Atty & C 57.

Humphreys v. Texas Power & Light Co., TexCivApp–Dallas, 427 SW2d 324, ref nre.—App & E 714(1), 863; Electricity 17; Evid 20(1); Judgm 181(21), 185(2); Labor & Emp 26, 29, 30, 2765, 3037, 3159; Neglig 1037(4), 1037(7).

Humphreys v. U.S., CA5 (Tex), 62 F3d 667, reh den.— Fed Cts 617, 973; Int Rev 4552, 4553, 4638, 5000, 5003; U S 125(5).

Humphrey's Estate v. C.I.R., CCA5 (Tex), 162 F2d 1, cert den Humphrey's Estate v. Commissioner of Internal Revenue, 68 SCt 157, 332 US 817, 92 LEd 394.—Int Rev 4159(2), 4657, 4732.

Humphries v. Chandler, TexCivApp–Beaumont, 597 SW2d 2.—App & E 842(1); Des & Dist 71(7); Judgm 304, 326.

Humphries v. Colorado Life Co., TexCivApp–El Paso, 170 SW2d 315, writ refused.—Evid 408(1); Insurance 2027, 2054; Paymt 35, 74(1).

Humphries; Crumpler v., TexCivApp–San Antonio, 218 SW2d 215, writ refused.—Evid 441(11); Sales 21.

Humphries; Harrison v., TexCivApp–Amarillo, 567 SW2d 884.—App & E 846(5), 971(2); Evid 544, 546; Labor & Emp 29; Plead 111.3, 111.42(7); Venue 15.

Humphries; Hastey v., TexCivApp–Amarillo, 576 SW2d 159, ref nre.—Labor & Emp 3094(2), 3105(9); Plead 123.

Humphries v. Kirkley, TexCivApp–Tyler, 410 SW2d 196. —App & E 927(7), 1061.4; Deeds 78, 196(0.5); Ex & Ad 3(5); Mental H 390; Trial 139.1(14).

Humphries v. Schnurr, BkrtcyWDTex, 107 BR 124. See Schnurr, In re.

Humphries v. Simonsen, TexCivApp–Eastland, 314 SW2d 140.—Contracts 194.

Humphries; Southwestern Bell Telephone Co. v., TexCivApp–Beaumont, 147 SW2d 971, writ dism, correct.— Tel 836; Trial 352.5(5).

Humphries v. State, TexCrimApp, 615 SW2d 737.—Crim Law 795(2.90); Homic 1458.

Humphries v. State, TexCrimApp, 295 SW2d 218, 163 TexCrim 601.—Crim Law 566, 569, 608, 736(2), 829(9).

Humphries v. State, TexCrimApp, 234 SW2d 872.—Crim Law 1094(3).

Humphries v. State, TexApp–El Paso, 993 SW2d 826, reh overr, and petition for discretionary review refused.— Crim Law 412.1(2), 412.1(4), 510, 511.1(1), 511.2, 511.3, 511.5, 511.7, 519(4), 814(19), 1134(2); Homic 1139, 1465.

Humphries v. Texas Gulf Sulphur Co., CA5 (Tex), 393 F2d 69.—Adv Poss 40, 104, 114(1); Mines 4.

Humphries v. Various Federal USINS Employees, CA5 (Tex), 164 F3d 936.—Aliens 376, 384, 385; Civil R 1088(4); Fed Civ Proc 1741, 1742(2); Fed Cts 13, 763.1, 818; U S 60, 125(24).

Humphrys v. Fisher, CA5 (Tex), 178 F2d 846.—Contracts 123(1).

Humphrys; Praetorian Mut. Life Ins. Co. v., TexCivApp–Fort Worth, 484 SW2d 413, ref nre.—App & E 837(1), 1001(1), 1062.1, 1178(1); Insurance 2590(2), 2595(1), 2604, 2605; Trial 352.9.

Humphrys v. Skelly Oil Co., CCA5 (Tex), 83 F2d 989.— Mines 73, 73.1(2), 73.1(4), 75.

Hundahl v. Armstrong, TexCivApp–Eastland, 436 SW2d 388, ref nre.—Corp 116.

Hundahl v. C I R, CCA5 (Tex), 118 F2d 349.—Int Rev 3283.

Hundahl v. United Benefit Life Ins. Co., NDTex, 465 FSupp 1349.—Sec Reg 52.10, 52.42, 60.20, 60.25, 60.28(1), 60.37, 60.51, 60.54, 174.

Hundere v. Tracy and Cook, TexCivApp–San Antonio, 494 SW2d 257, ref nre.—App & E 1170.7; Costs 194.32; Evid 213(2); Trial 75.

Hunderup; Young v., TexApp–Austin, 763 SW2d 611.— App & E 79(1), 387(2).

Hundley; Finley v., TexCivApp–Dallas, 252 SW2d 958.— Contracts 10(1), 15, 39, 350(2).

Hundley v. Hartford Acc. & Indem. Co., CCA5 (Tex), 87 F2d 416.—Work Comp 666.

Hundley; Shivers v., TexCivApp–Waco, 148 SW2d 440.— Plead 111.6, 228.17, 301(1); Venue 8.5(5).

Hundley v. State, TexCrimApp, 229 SW2d 627.—Crim Law 1094(3).

Hung v. Bullock, TexApp–Dallas, 180 SW3d 931.—Pretrial Proc 582, 583, 587, 675.

Hungate v. Hungate, TexCivApp–El Paso, 531 SW2d 650. —App & E 934(1); Infants 87; Judgm 185(2), 186, 815, 819, 822(2), 942.

Hungate; Hungate v., TexCivApp–El Paso, 531 SW2d 650.—App & E 934(1); Infants 87; Judgm 185(2), 186, 815, 819, 822(2), 942.

Hunger v. Toubin Bros., TexCivApp–Austin, 164 SW2d 765, dism.—Corp 30(6); Land & Ten 90(1), 90(5), 115(3).

Hungerford v. State, TexCrimApp, 474 SW2d 242.—Sent & Pun 1018.

Hungerford; Woodrick v., CA5 (Tex), 800 F2d 1413, cert den 107 SCt 1972, 481 US 1036, 95 LEd2d 812.—Hab Corp 283, 524; Mil Jus 1480.

Hung Shrimp Farm, Inc.; Arroyo Shrimp Farm, Inc. v., TexApp–Corpus Christi, 927 SW2d 146, reh overr.— App & E 209.1, 213, 232(0.5), 237(5), 238(2), 241, 294(1), 295, 302(6), 946, 959(3); Fraud 10, 22(1), 23, 35, 36, 64(1); Plead 229, 236(3), 236(7), 245(3), 258(3), 261; Pretrial Proc 45, 312; Trial 420.

Hung Van Tran; U.S. v., CA5 (Tex), 955 F2d 288, cert den 113 SCt 127, 506 US 842, 121 LEd2d 82.—Crim Law 1158(1), 1177; Sent & Pun 706, 852, 856.

Hunke, D.D.S., M.S.D., Inc. v. Wilcox, TexApp–Corpus Christi, 815 SW2d 855. See Philip H. Hunke, D.D.S., M.S.D., Inc. v. Wilcox.

Hunley v. Bulowski, TexCivApp–Texarkana, 256 SW2d 932, ref nre.—Estop 47, 50; Ten in C 44; Ven & Pur 233, 238, 244.

Hunley v. Garber, TexCivApp–Amarillo, 254 SW2d 813.— Bills & N 64; Evid 420(3); Insurance 1766; Judgm 181(6), 185(2), 185.3(12).

Hunley; Morgan v., TexCivApp–Galveston, 267 SW2d 274, ref nre.—Lim of Act 49(1), 100(7), 100(11).

Hunnicutt v. Clark, TexCivApp–Texarkana, 428 SW2d 691.—App & E 846(5), 1024.1; New Tr 48.1.

Hunnicutt; Collingsworth General Hosp. v., Tex, 988 SW2d 706.—Unemp Comp 68, 72, 87, 473, 477, 478.

Hunnicutt; John F. Grant Lumber Co. v., TexCivApp–Waco, 143 SW2d 976.—Judgm 772, 778, 787, 801.

Hunnicutt; Kollman v., TexCivApp–Fort Worth, 385 SW2d 600.—Cust & U 8; Usury 28, 36.

Hunnicutt; Moorman v., TexCivApp–Austin, 325 SW2d 941, ref nre.—Adop 1, 3, 9.1, 17; Estop 4, 99.

Hunnicutt v. Moorman, TexCivApp–Austin, 290 SW2d 278, ref nre.—Courts 200, 202(5), 472.4(2.1).

Hunnicutt v. State, TexCrimApp, 531 SW2d 618.—Crim Law 304(1), 641.13(2.1), 641.13(4), 641.13(5), 641.13(6), 641.13(8), 899, 1169.1(8); Searches 47.1, 69.

Hunnicutt v. State, TexCrimApp, 523 SW2d 244.— Courts 42(6); Crim Law 1186.1; Rob 24.40; Witn 321, 380(5.1), 388(4).

Hunnicutt v. State, TexCrimApp, 500 SW2d 806.—Crim Law 339.7(2), 730(1), 730(13), 1036.1(8), 1130(2), 1169.5(3); Searches 200.

Hunnicutt v. State, TexCrimApp, 97 SW2d 957, 131 TexCrim 260.—Crim Law 772(6); Ind & Inf 166, 184; Rec S Goods 9(2).

Hunnicutt v. Texas Employment Com'n, TexApp–Amarillo, 949 SW2d 52, reh overr, and review gr, rev Collingsworth General Hosp v. Hunnicutt, 988 SW2d 706.— Statut 206; Unemp Comp 65, 83, 456, 486.

Hunnington Group, Inc., In re, BkrtcySDTex, 125 BR 739.—Bankr 3078(1).

Hunsaker Mfg., Inc.; Mitchell v., TexCivApp–Waco, 520 SW2d 796.—App & E 1177(9).

Hunsaker Trucking Contractor; McComb v., CA5 (Tex), 171 F2d 523.—Admin Law 346.1, 358; Labor & Emp 2341, 2342.

Hunsley Paint Mfg. Co. v. Gray, TexCivApp–Amarillo, 165 SW2d 486, dism.—Guar 7(1), 7(4), 19; Trial 357.

Hunsucker; Aubin v., TexCivApp–Austin, 481 SW2d 952, ref nre.—App & E 959(3), 1170.3, 1178(6); Bills & N 487; Gaming 19(1); Plead 236(3), 259.

Hunsucker; Hunsucker's Heirs v., TexCivApp–Waco, 455 SW2d 780, ref nre.—Wills 766, 778.

Hunsucker v. Omega Industries, TexApp–Dallas, 659 SW2d 692.—Autos 192(1), 242(6); Judgm 181(33), 185(6), 185.2(8).

Hunsucker v. Phinney, CA5 (Tex), 497 F2d 29, cert den 95 SCt 1124, 420 US 927, 43 LEd2d 397.—Courts 55; Crim Law 394.5(1); Decl Judgm 274.1; Fed Cts 229, 974.1; Gaming 60; Mand 3(8); Searches 84.

Hunsucker; Rowntree v., Tex, 833 SW2d 103.—Judgm 181(7); Lim of Act 55(3).

Hunsucker v. Rowntree, TexApp–Texarkana, 815 SW2d 779, writ gr, rev 833 SW2d 103.—Judgm 181(7), 185(2); Lim of Act 55(3), 95(12), 105(1).

Hunsucker's Heirs v. Hunsucker, TexCivApp–Waco, 455 SW2d 780, ref nre.—Wills 766, 778.

Hunt, Ex parte, TexCrimApp, 614 SW2d 426.—Hab Corp 535.

Hunt, Ex parte, TexApp–Fort Worth, 138 SW3d 503, petition for discretionary review refused (5 pets).—Bail 39, 51, 53; Crim Law 1147, 1148; Hab Corp 706.

Hunt, In re, CA5 (Tex), 496 F2d 882, reh den Hunt, in the Matter of, 502 F2d 1167, reh den Speed Equipment Worlds of America, Inc v. Hunt, 502 F2d 1168.—Bankr 2189, 2191, 2295.1, 2296, 3786.

Hunt, In re, NDTex, 196 BR 356.—Bankr 2187, 2547, 3039, 3172.1, 3181, 3183, 3184, 3187(1), 3190, 3203(6), 3204, 3205, 3782, 3784, 3790.

Hunt, In re, NDTex, 124 BR 200.—Bankr 2187, 2829, 2932, 3415.1, 3550, 3568(3), 3569, 3770, 3777, 3782; Estop 68(2), 116; Judgm 540, 617, 636, 713(1), 713(2).

Hunt, In re, BkrtcyNDTex, 153 BR 445.—Bankr 2156, 2182.1, 2535(2); Witn 196.2, 198(1), 201(2), 217.

Hunt, In re, BkrtcyNDTex, 149 BR 96.—Bankr 2154.1, 2553, 2704; Fed Civ Proc 103.2; RICO 25, 57.

Hunt, In re, BkrtcyNDTex, 146 BR 178.—Bankr 2131, 2892.1, 2897.1, 3361, 3420(1); Const Law 4478; Notice 9.

Hunt, In re, BkrtcyNDTex, 136 BR 437.—Bankr 2043(2), 2130, 2704, 2722; Fed Civ Proc 636, 1721, 1722, 1754, 1829; Fed Cts 30; Fraud Conv 100(3), 248; Lim of Act 11(1); Statut 188.

Hunt, In re, BkrtcyNDTex, 95 BR 442.—Bankr 2055, 2061.

Hunt, In re, BkrtcyNDTex, 93 BR 484, mod 1989 WL 67827, mod 95 BR 442.—Bankr 2060.1, 2367, 2371(1), 2374, 2402(1).

Hunt, In re, BkrtcySDTex, 61 BR 224.—Home 154, 162(1), 163, 213.

Hunt, In re, BkrtcyWDTex, 215 BR 505.—Bankr 2043(2), 2103, 2104, 2130, 2162; Fed Civ Proc 824, 828.1, 833, 834, 851; Jury 25(6), 25(8), 28(17).

Hunt, In re Estate of, TexApp–San Antonio, 908 SW2d 483, reh overr, and writ den.—Des & Dist 43; Wills 435, 439, 448, 455, 638, 695(2), 697(1), 865(1).

Hunt; Allied Store Utilities Co. v., TexCivApp–Amarillo, 148 SW2d 246.—Mand 48.

Hunt; Allstate Ins. Co. v., Tex, 469 SW2d 151.—Insurance 2792, 2795.

Hunt; Allstate Ins. Co. v., TexCivApp–Hous (14 Dist), 450 SW2d 668, aff 469 SW2d 151.—App & E 714(1); Atty & C 20.1; Insurance 2815(1), 2913.

Hunt; Anderson v., TexCivApp–Fort Worth, 122 SW2d 345, writ refused.—Ex & Ad 7, 437(2); Lim of Act 103(3).

Hunt v. Anderson, Clayton & Co., TexCivApp–Amarillo, 574 SW2d 826.—Plead 111.9, 111.39(4), 111.39(7), 111.42(4), 111.44, 123, 290(3).

Hunt; Arabian Shield Development Co. v., TexApp–Dallas, 808 SW2d 577, writ den.—Lim of Act 95(1), 95(7), 104(1), 104(2), 195(5); Plead 4.

Hunt; Associates Home Equity Services Co., Inc. v., TexApp–Beaumont, 151 SW3d 559.—Tax 3053, 3065.

Hunt v. Bagwell, TexCivApp–Eastland, 111 SW2d 312, writ refused.—Evid 397(3), 419(3); Frds St of 63(1); Home 146; Hus & W 274(4); Partit 8, 9(1); Sequest 21.

Hunt v. Baldwin, TexApp–Houston (14 Dist), 68 SW3d 117.—App & E 216(1), 230, 866(3), 927(7), 959(3), 984(5), 1024.1, 1056.1(1), 1079; Atty & C 26; Consp 1.1; Costs 194.40, 208; Damag 87(2); Decl Judgm 324, 344; Execution 83, 102, 258, 275(2), 455, 462, 472; Fraud 3, 13(2), 13(3), 20; Impl & C C 13, 15.1; Judgm 540, 634, 895; Mal Pros 38; Plead 236(3); Pretrial Proc 3; Proc 168, 171; Trial 43, 139.1(14), 139.1(17), 168, 350.1; Trover 1; Usury 11, 16.

Hunt v. Bankers Trust Co., CA5 (Tex), 799 F2d 1060.—Atty & C 89; Bankr 2061, 2081, 2082, 2085, 2086.1, 2391, 3789.1; Fed Cts 95, 543.1, 558, 573, 685; Inj 215.

Hunt v. Bankers Trust Co., NDTex, 689 FSupp 666.—Bills & N 106, 452(1), 478; Fed Civ Proc 771, 2487, 2553.

Hunt v. Bankers Trust Co., NDTex, 646 FSupp 59.—Corp 123(24); Inj 14; Sec Tran 225.

Hunt; Bankers Trust Co. v., NDTex, 124 BR 200. See Hunt, In re.

Hunt v. Bass, Tex, 664 SW2d 323.—Action 13; Mand 23(1).

Hunt v. Bass, TexApp–Houston (1 Dist), 657 SW2d 154, rev 664 SW2d 323.—Action 13; Mand 1, 23(2), 28, 29, 72, 154(2).

Hunt; Batten v., TexApp–Austin, 18 SW3d 235, reh overr, and review den.—Const Law 2315; Lim of Act 4(2), 55(3).

Hunt; Bowden v., TexCivApp–Dallas, 571 SW2d 550.—App & E 71(2), 71(3).

Hunt v. Boyd, TexCivApp–Austin, 193 SW2d 970.—Child C 602, 850.

Hunt v. BP Exploration Co. (Libya) Ltd., NDTex, 580 FSupp 304.—Alt Disp Res 182(2); Judgm 830.1, 944.

Hunt v. BP Exploration Co. (Libya) Ltd., NDTex, 492 FSupp 885.—Courts 514; Fed Cts 372, 409.1, 420, 634; Judgm 713(2), 830.1; Treaties 12.

Hunt v. Burrage, TexCivApp–Dallas, 95 SW2d 202, writ dism.—Plead 111.35.

Hunt v. Burrage, TexCivApp–Dallas, 84 SW2d 1098, writ dism.—App & E 151(2).

Hunt v. Burrage, TexCivApp–Texarkana, 163 SW2d 218. —Judgm 540, 713(2).

Hunt; Burrage v., TexCivApp–Texarkana, 147 SW2d 532, writ dism, correct.—App & E 837(1); Appear 17; Judgm 17(1), 489; Proc 4.

Hunt; Burroughs v., CA5 (Tex), 77 FedAppx 238.—Autos 349(2.1), 349(6); False Imp 13; Fed Civ Proc 2491.5.

Hunt; Busbice v., TexCivApp–Tyler, 430 SW2d 291, ref nre.—Estop 115; Mtg 241, 342.

Hunt; Carr v., TexApp–Dallas, 651 SW2d 875, ref nre.—App & E 878(6), 878(7); Consp 1.1, 9, 19; Exch of Prop 8(4); Princ & A 1, 8, 14(2), 23(5), 158; Statut 223.1, 223.4; Ven & Pur 239(9), 242, 244.

Hunt; Carroll v., TexComApp, 168 SW2d 238, 140 Tex 424.—Atty & C 148(2), 150.

Hunt v. Carroll, TexCivApp–Beaumont, 157 SW2d 429, writ dism 168 SW2d 238, 140 Tex 424.—Perp 1, 4(1), 4(3), 4(4), 4(5), 4(12), 4(13); Trusts 160(1); Wills 104, 267, 350, 439, 440, 441, 446, 448, 470(3), 622, 625, 629, 634(1), 647.

Hunt v. Cass County, TexCivApp–Eastland, 106 SW2d 810.—App & E 187(3), 927(7); Bills & N 359; Home 212, 216.

Hunt; Chapin v., TexCivApp–Beaumont, 521 SW2d 123, writ dism.—Autos 242(7), 244(36.1), 245(15); Damag 163(1), 185(1), 186, 187; Neglig 1676; Trial 127.

Hunt v. C I R, CCA5 (Tex), 135 F2d 697.—Int Rev 3360.

Hunt; City of Denton v., TexCivApp–Fort Worth, 235 SW2d 212, ref nre.—Em Dom 90, 137; Trial 307(3), 351.5(1).

Hunt v. City of Longview, EDTex, 932 FSupp 828, aff 95 F3d 49.—Const Law 82(8), 990, 1464, 1467, 3057, 3593, 3644; Decl Judgm 387; Fed Cts 41, 42, 46, 54, 558, 813; Inj 130, 138.1, 138.6, 138.18, 138.27; Mun Corp 138; Quo W 1, 11, 24, 26, 33.

Hunt v. City of San Antonio, Tex, 462 SW2d 536.—Mun Corp 122.1(2); Zoning 151, 158, 162, 672, 679.

Hunt; City of San Antonio v., TexCivApp–San Antonio, 458 SW2d 952, rev 462 SW2d 536.—Zoning 27, 38, 168, 609, 620, 672, 675.

Hunt v. Clifford H. Brown & Co., TexCivApp–Dallas, 239 SW2d 178.—App & E 1024.2; Inj 138.27; Mines 52, 74(6); Torts 212.

Hunt v. Coastal States Gas Producing Co., Tex, 583 SW2d 322, cert den 100 SCt 523, 444 US 992, 62 LEd2d 421, reh den 100 SCt 1071, 444 US 1103, 62 LEd2d 790. —Intern Law 10.12; Mines 83.

Hunt v. Coastal States Gas Producing Co., TexCivApp–Hous (14 Dist), 570 SW2d 503, aff 583 SW2d 322, cert den 100 SCt 523, 444 US 992, 62 LEd2d 421, reh den 100 SCt 1071, 444 US 1103, 62 LEd2d 790.—Intern Law 10.9, 10.12; Torts 217, 241, 242; Trover 13.

Hunt; Coastal States Marketing, Inc. v., CA5 (Tex), 694 F2d 1358, reh den 699 F2d 1163.—Antitrust 905(2), 945; Fed Cts 611; Judgm 828.20(1); Stip 13, 14(1).

Hunt v. Commodity Futures Trading Com'n, BkrtcyNDTex, 93 BR 484. See Hunt, In re.

Hunt; Copeland v., TexCivApp–Corpus Christi, 434 SW2d 156, ref nre.—Acct Action on 10, 14; Evid 584(1); Plead 292, 312.

Hunt; Dancy v., TexCivApp–San Antonio, 294 SW2d 159, ref nre.—Elections 126(4), 143; Mand 15, 74(3).

Hunt v. Dixie Motor Coach Corp., TexCivApp–Texarkana, 187 SW2d 250, writ refused wom.—Carr 262, 273.1; Plead 205(1), 228.14.

Hunt; Dorchester Master Ltd. Partnership v., Tex, 790 SW2d 552, on remand Arabian Shield Development Co v. Hunt, 808 SW2d 577, writ den.—Holidays 3.

Hunt v. Ellisor & Tanner, Inc., TexApp–Dallas, 739 SW2d 933, writ den.—Contracts 196; Damag 63; Evid 571(10); Indem 33(5); Trial 335.

Hunt v. Employers Reinsurance Corp., TexCivApp–Fort Worth, 219 SW2d 483, ref nre.—App & E 79(1), 80(1); Judgm 17(1), 243; Plead 34(1), 252(2); Work Comp 1869, 1908, 1919.

Hunt; Evans v., TexCivApp–Texarkana, 195 SW2d 710.— App & E 1010.1(1); Child C 36, 76, 568, 637; Divorce 320; Marriage 58(1).

Hunt; Farrell v., Tex, 714 SW2d 298.—Antitrust 389(1), 389(2), 390; Mtg 379.

Hunt v. Federal Deposit Ins. Corp., BkrtcySDTex, 61 BR 224. See Hunt, In re.

Hunt; Goldschmidt v., NDTex, 556 FSupp 123.—Antitrust 920, 965.

Hunt; Harris County v., TexCivApp–Houston, 388 SW2d 459.—App & E 961; Courts 57(1), 57(2); Pretrial Proc 92, 122.

Hunt; Harwood v., TexCivApp–Beaumont, 473 SW2d 287. —Partit 55(2); Plead 45, 49, 111.3, 111.30; Venue 5.1, 5.2, 5.3(1), 5.3(2), 5.3(6), 7.5(2), 7.5(3), 22(1), 81.

Hunt v. Heaton, Tex, 643 SW2d 677.—Tresp to T T 1, 6.1, 35(1), 36, 41(1).

Hunt v. Heaton, TexApp–Beaumont, 631 SW2d 549, writ gr, aff 643 SW2d 677.—Statut 181(2), 184, 206, 227; Tresp to T T 36.

Hunt v. HEB Federal Credit Union, BkrtcyWDTex, 215 BR 505. See Hunt, In re.

Hunt v. HNG Oil Co., TexApp–Corpus Christi, 791 SW2d 191, writ den.—Mines 51(5), 73.1(6).

Hunt v. Hudgins, TexCivApp–Waco, 168 SW2d 703.— Const Law 1065, 1107, 1114, 1280; Inj 94, 123, 128(9); Trial 351.2(4).

Hunt v. Hunt, TexApp–Eastland, 952 SW2d 564.—Divorce 253(2), 286(9); Hus & W 249(3), 249(6), 265.

Hunt; Hunt v., TexApp–Eastland, 952 SW2d 564.—Divorce 253(2), 286(9); Hus & W 249(3), 249(6), 265.

Hunt v. Hunt, TexCivApp–San Antonio, 329 SW2d 488.— Wills 467, 470(3).

Hunt; Hunt v., TexCivApp–San Antonio, 329 SW2d 488.— Wills 467, 470(3).

Hunt v. Hunt, TexCivApp–Texarkana, 95 SW2d 724.— Eject 15(4); Tresp to T T 41(1), 57.

Hunt; Hunt v., TexCivApp–Texarkana, 95 SW2d 724.— Eject 15(4); Tresp to T T 41(1), 57.

Hunt v. Hunt, TexCivApp–Corpus Christi, 456 SW2d 243. —Divorce 27(1), 27(8.1), 130, 145, 184(6.1).

Hunt; Hunt v., TexCivApp–Corpus Christi, 456 SW2d 243.—Divorce 27(1), 27(8.1), 130, 145, 184(6.1).

Hunt v. Hunt, TexCivApp–Hous (14 Dist), 453 SW2d 377. —Jury 28(6); Trial 3(2), 3(5.1).

Hunt; Hunt v., TexCivApp–Hous (14 Dist), 453 SW2d 377. —Jury 28(6); Trial 3(2), 3(5.1).

Hunt v. Jefferson-Pilot Life Ins. Co., TexApp–Fort Worth, 900 SW2d 453, reh overr, and writ den.—App & E 863; Insurance 3471, 3481(1); Judgm 185(2), 186.

Hunt v. Jefferson Sav. & Loan Ass'n, TexApp–Dallas, 756 SW2d 762, writ den, cert den 109 SCt 1532, 489 US 1079, 103 LEd2d 837.—Bills & N 129(2); Mtg 335, 369(3), 369(7), 375, 377.

Hunt; John L. Bramlet & Co. v., TexCivApp–Dallas, 371 SW2d 787, ref nre.—App & E 954(1), 954(2); Contracts 65.5, 117(2); Frds St of 103(2); Inj 135; Trial 141.

Hunt v. Johnson, CA5 (Tex), 90 FedAppx 702, cert den 125 SCt 175, 543 US 857, 160 LEd2d 94.—Const Law 1100(3); Fed Civ Proc 1278, 2553; Fed Cts 682; Prisons 4(7).

Hunt v. Jones, TexCivApp–Waco, 451 SW2d 943, ref nre. —App & E 1057(1), 1067; Trial 82.

Hunt v. Knolle, TexCivApp–Tyler, 551 SW2d 764.—Ex & Ad 7; Wills 64, 67, 188, 206.

Hunt; Knolle v., TexCivApp–Tyler, 551 SW2d 755, ref nre.—App & E 959(3); Decl Judgm 324, 390, 393; Wills 62, 63, 68, 99, 188, 476.

Hunt; Langston v., BkrtcyNDTex, 68 BR 354. See Brints Cotton Marketing, Inc., In re.

Hunt; Lloyds America v., TexCivApp–Texarkana, 94 SW2d 861, writ refused.—Insurance 2171.

Hunt v. Merchandise Mart, Inc., TexCivApp–Dallas, 391 SW2d 141, ref nre.—App & E 690(4), 690(5); Courts 106; Inj 16, 118(4), 144; Land & Ten 251(3), 251(4), 265(4), 270(3), 270(6); Receivers 3, 6.

Hunt v. Mid-West Life & Hospital Ins. Co., TexCivApp–Texarkana, 468 SW2d 142.—Judgm 181(23), 185(2), 185(3); Pretrial Proc 477.1.

Hunt; Miller & Miller Motor Freight Lines v., TexCivApp–Amarillo, 242 SW2d 919.—Evid 54, 77(1), 595, 597; Neglig 1675; Plead 111.39(6), 111.42(8); Witn 40(2).

Hunt; Mitchell v., CA5 (Tex), 263 F2d 913.—Labor & Emp 2273, 2274, 2432(2).

Hunt; Musick v., TexCivApp–Houston, 364 SW2d 252.— App & E 447.

Hunt v. Paco Tankers, Inc., SDTex, 226 FSupp 279.— Adm 4, 32.1, 44, 45.1.

Hunt v. Parkway Transport, Inc., WDTex, 265 BR 561. —Bankr 2104, 2132, 2157; Time 8.5, 10(2).

Hunt; Parrish v., Tex, 331 SW2d 304, 160 Tex 378, opinion conformed to 334 SW2d 505.—App & E 987(4), 1083(3).

Hunt v. Parrish, TexCivApp–Waco, 334 SW2d 505.—App & E 1129.

Hunt v. Parrish, TexCivApp–Waco, 324 SW2d 887, rev 331 SW2d 304, 160 Tex 378, opinion conformed to 334 SW2d 505.—Autos 244(12), 244(34).

Hunt; Pate v., BkrtcyNDTex, 149 BR 96. See Hunt, In re.

Hunt; Pate v., BkrtcyNDTex, 136 BR 437. See Hunt, In re.

Hunt v. Ramsey, Tex, 345 SW2d 260, 162 Tex 133.—Judgm 395, 457, 518, 521, 522.

Hunt v. Ramsey, TexCivApp–El Paso, 334 SW2d 549, writ gr, rev 345 SW2d 260, 162 Tex 133.—Judgm 335(1), 497(1), 518.

Hunt; Roberson v., TexCivApp–San Antonio, 179 SW2d 315.—Parties 31; Torts 302; Venue 22(7).

Hunt; Robertson Transport Co. v., TexCivApp–San Antonio, 345 SW2d 293.—Autos 242(1), 244(44), 244(58); Trial 356(5), 358.

Hunt v. Rodriguez, CA5 (Tex), 468 F2d 615.—Fed Civ Proc 1788.6.

Hunt v. Rodriguez, CA5 (Tex), 462 F2d 659, on reh in part 468 F2d 615.—Const Law 3974; Courts 508(7); Fed Cts 49, 702, 994, 1012.

Hunt; Royal Bank of Canada v., NDTex, 124 BR 200. See Hunt, In re.

Hunt; Ruebeck v., Tex, 176 SW2d 738, 142 Tex 167, 150 ALR 775.—App & E 996; Lim of Act 100(11), 100(13), 197(2), 199(2).

Hunt; Ruebeck v., TexCivApp–Waco, 171 SW2d 895, writ refused wom, aff 176 SW2d 738, 142 Tex 167, 150 ALR 775.—Fraud 3, 17, 64(1); Lim of Act 100(11), 100(13), 199(2); Trial 133.6(4).

Hunt; San Antonio River Authority v., TexCivApp–Corpus Christi, 405 SW2d 700, ref nre.—Adv Poss 114(1); Damag 221(2.1); Em Dom 293(1), 295, 296, 300, 302; Evid 178(2), 372(3), 372(11); Judgm 693; Marriage 40(8); Trial 350.3(6), 352.10, 365.1(4).

Hunt v. Seeley, CCA5 (Tex), 115 F2d 205.—Courts 490, 508(3); Ex & Ad 7; Fed Cts 14.1, 931; Judgm 564(2).

Hunt; Seeley v., CCA5 (Tex), 109 F2d 595, cert den 60 SCt 894, 309 US 690, 84 LEd 1033.—Atty & C 120, 127, 149, 152; Costs 254(1); Fed Cts 849, 931; Trusts 374.

Hunt v. Smith, EDTex, 67 FSupp2d 675.—Atty & C 62; Civil R 1322; Fed Civ Proc 417, 1751, 1825, 1837.1, 1838; Fed Cts 265, 266.1, 267, 269; Offic 114; Rem of C 79(1), 82, 94, 100, 107(0.5), 115; States 78.

Hunt v. Southern Materials Co., TexCivApp–Galveston, 240 SW2d 400, writ refused.—Judgm 181(15.1), 185.1(3).

Hunt v. State, TexCrimApp, 603 SW2d 865.—Crim Law 857(1), 925.5(1), 925.5(3), 1155, 1189; Homic 935.

Hunt v. State, TexCrimApp, 511 SW2d 954.—Crim Law 730(1), 730(3), 1171.3.

Hunt v. State, TexCrimApp, 492 SW2d 540.—Crim Law 404.36, 507(2), 770(2), 780(1), 1130(2); Explos 4, 5.

Hunt v. State, TexCrimApp, 482 SW2d 217.—Crim Law 273.3.

Hunt v. State, TexCrimApp, 475 SW2d 935.—Crim Law 1159.2(10); Obscen 1.4, 2.5, 5.1.

Hunt v. State, TexCrimApp, 362 SW2d 335.—Autos 355(13).

Hunt v. State, TexCrimApp, 317 SW2d 743, 167 TexCrim 51.—Crim Law 949(2), 980(1), 1159.5; Int Liq 236(7).

Hunt v. State, TexCrimApp, 271 SW2d 290, 160 TexCrim 358.—Crim Law 387, 1166.10(1).

Hunt v. State, TexCrimApp, 269 SW2d 385, 160 TexCrim 115.—Bail 63.1; Crim Law 304(6), 622.1(1), 633(2), 1081(4.1), 1177.5(1); Int Liq 236(3); Witn 52(7), 89.

Hunt v. State, TexCrimApp, 258 SW2d 320, 158 TexCrim 618.—Controlled Subs 80; Crim Law 784(1), 1172.7.

Hunt v. State, TexCrimApp, 247 SW2d 99.—Crim Law 1090.1(1).

Hunt v. State, TexCrimApp, 247 SW2d 98.—Crim Law 1090.1(1), 1144.18.

Hunt v. State, TexCrimApp, 247 SW2d 97.—Crim Law 1090.1(1).

Hunt v. State, TexCrimApp, 101 SW2d 1018.—Crim Law 1094(2.1).

Hunt v. State, TexApp–Fort Worth, 904 SW2d 813, petition for discretionary review refused.—Crim Law 363, 366(3), 366(6), 661, 1137(1), 1153(1).

Hunt v. State, TexApp–San Antonio, 625 SW2d 405, petition for discretionary review refused.—Burg 2, 49; Const Law 3781; Crim Law 538(3), 721(5), 814(17), 1043(3), 1166.16; Statut 241(1).

Hunt v. State, TexApp–Dallas, 852 SW2d 278.—Crim Law 1035(6); Ind & Inf 189(8); Jury 131(8).

Hunt v. State, TexApp–Dallas, 632 SW2d 640, petition for discretionary review refused.—Const Law 4664(2); Crim Law 519(9), 577.10(9).

Hunt v. State, TexApp–Texarkana, 994 SW2d 206, petition for discretionary review refused.—Crim Law 633(2), 1032(5); Ind & Inf 56, 71.2(2), 133(7), 136, 196(5); Sent & Pun 1367.

Hunt v. State, TexApp–Amarillo, 5 SW3d 833, petition for discretionary review refused.—Crim Law 1042; Ind & Inf 55; Sent & Pun 2001, 2011, 2020, 2021.

Hunt v. State, TexApp–Beaumont, 967 SW2d 917.—Crim Law 1086.13, 1104(1), 1144.17; Sent & Pun 309, 373.

Hunt v. State, TexApp–Corpus Christi, 848 SW2d 764.—Autos 411; Crim Law 713, 720(7.1), 1037.1(1), 1037.1(2), 1037.2, 1038.1(1), 1043(1), 1044.1(1), 1044.2(1), 1045, 1086.4, 1134(2), 1134(3), 1169.2(2), 1169.5(1).

Hunt v. State, TexApp–Corpus Christi, 779 SW2d 926, petition for discretionary review refused.—Crim Law 330, 379, 453, 569, 1036.2, 1110(6), 1159.5; Homic 1197, 1202; Witn 274(2).

Hunt v. State, TexApp–Corpus Christi, 764 SW2d 839.—Double J 3; Ind & Inf 176; Judgm 724, 751.

Hunt v. State, TexApp–Corpus Christi, 737 SW2d 4.—Insurance 1608, 1636, 2024; Larc 55.

Hunt; Texas Pipe Line Co. v., Tex, 228 SW2d 151, 149 Tex 33.—App & E 44, 1140(1); Em Dom 147, 149(7), 263.

Hunt; Texas Pipe Line Co. v., TexCivApp–Dallas, 222 SW2d 128, aff 228 SW2d 151, 149 Tex 33.—App & E 1056.3; Em Dom 202(1), 202(4), 205, 224, 262(5); Evid 117.

Hunt; Thompson v., TexCivApp–Waco, 598 SW2d 659.—App & E 624, 627.2.

Hunt; Todd v., TexCivApp–El Paso, 127 SW2d 340, writ refused.—Mines 54.5; Mtg 231, 343, 346; Subrog 14.3; Tresp to T T 16, 38(2).

Hunt v. Trimble, TexCivApp–Amarillo, 145 SW2d 659, writ refused.—Schools 37(3), 37(5), 40; Statut 122(2).

Hunt; Turner v., TexComApp, 116 SW2d 688, 131 Tex 492, 117 ALR 1066.—Action 63; Deeds 114(5); Mines 58, 74(3); Ven & Pur 231(3).

Hunt v. Turner, TexCivApp–El Paso, 88 SW2d 520, aff 116 SW2d 688, 131 Tex 492, 117 ALR 1066.—Deeds 6; Plead 403(2); Tresp to T T 25, 32, 35(1), 38(1).

Hunt; U.S. v., CA5 (Tex), 129 F3d 739.—Controlled Subs 68, 81; Crim Law 1144.13(2.1), 1144.13(5), 1159.6, 1184(3).

Hunt; U.S. v., CA5 (Tex), 940 F2d 130, reh den.—Crim Law 1081(4.1); Sent & Pun 1973(2).

Hunt; U.S. v., CA5 (Tex), 794 F2d 1095, post-conviction relief den 940 F2d 130, reh den.—Crim Law 561(1), 772(5), 776(5), 778(5), 805(1), 829(4), 1172.1(5), 1173.1; Postal 49(11).

Hunt; U.S. v., CA5 (Tex), 505 F2d 931, cert den 95 SCt 1974, 421 US 975, 44 LEd2d 466.—Crim Law 394.5(2); Labor & Emp 29; Searches 23, 26, 161, 162, 165.

Hunt; U.S. v., CA5 (Tex), 496 F2d 888.—Crim Law 394.2(2), 633(1); Obscen 7.6; Searches 18, 112, 115.1, 120.

Hunt v. U.S., CA5 (Tex), 400 F2d 306, cert den 89 SCt 629, 393 US 1021, 21 LEd2d 566.—Consp 43(11), 48.2(2); Jury 120; Obst Just 4.

Hunt; U.S. v., CA5 (Tex), 199 FedAppx 384.—Weap 17(4).

Hunt; U.S. v., CA5 (Tex), 176 FedAppx 477.—Sent & Pun 764.

Hunt v. U.S., CA5 (Tex), 106 FedAppx 888.—Hab Corp 285.1, 841.

Hunt v. U.S., EDTex, 175 FSupp 665.—Int Rev 5018.

Hunt; U.S. v., NDTex, 688 FSupp 265, aff 857 F2d 1471. —Sent & Pun 2003.

Hunt; U.S. v., NDTex, 366 FSupp 172, rev 505 F2d 931, cert den 95 SCt 1974, 421 US 975, 44 LEd2d 466.— Arrest 63.5(6), 71.1(8); Searches 24, 47.1, 59, 60.1, 70, 161, 164, 186, 192.1; Tel 1436.

Hunt; U.S. v., WDTex, 265 FSupp 178.—Const Law 3990; Jury 33(1.1), 33(1.10), 33(1.15), 38, 62(3), 115, 120.

Hunt v. U. S. Securities & Exchange Commission, NDTex, 520 FSupp 580.—Admin Law 465; Fed Civ Proc 1615.1; Inj 75, 132, 138.1, 147; Sec Reg 86.

Hunt v. Van Der Horst Corp., TexApp–Dallas, 711 SW2d 77.—Judgm 181(21), 185.1(2); Labor & Emp 808, 810.

Hunt; Walters v., BkrtcyNDTex, 146 BR 178. See Hunt, In re.

Hunt v. Weems, TexCivApp–Austin, 208 SW2d 423, dism. —Forci E & D 30(2), 43(2), 43(8).

Hunt; White v., TexCivApp–Dallas, 224 SW2d 511.—App & E 1177(6); Atty & C 147; Judgm 251(1).

Hunt; Whitfill v., Tex, 387 SW2d 653.—Trial 350.1, 350.5(3), 350.7(3.1), 351.5(6).

Hunt; Whitfill v., TexCivApp–Amarillo, 374 SW2d 341, writ gr, rev 387 SW2d 653.—App & E 882(13); Autos 244(43), 246(9); Damag 130.1; Trial 194(20), 350.2, 351.5(1), 351.5(6).

Hunt; Whitley v., CA5 (Tex), 158 F3d 882.—Fed Civ Proc 833, 2734; U S 50.1, 78(9), 127(1), 127(2).

Hunt v. Wichita County Water Imp. Dist. No. 2, Tex, 211 SW2d 743, 147 Tex 47.—App & E 2, 78(3), 417(1), 428(2), 1082(1), 1114; Courts 85(2), 206(17.3).

Hunt v. Wichita County Water Imp. Dist. No. 2, Tex-CivApp–Fort Worth, 213 SW2d 343, ref nre.—Courts 99(1); Judgm 259, 335(1), 344, 576(1), 678(1), 713(2), 719, 958(1); Mental H 512.1; Plead 360.

Hunt v. Wichita County Water Imp. Dist. No. 2, Tex-CivApp–Fort Worth, 207 SW2d 703, rev 211 SW2d 743, 147 Tex 47.—App & E 430(1).

Hunt; Woodyard v., TexApp–Houston (1 Dist), 695 SW2d 730.—App & E 635(4), 930(3), 1070(2), 1177(1); Fraud 59(2), 59(3); Trial 358, 365.1(1), 365.1(4).

Hunt v. W. O. W. Life Ins. Soc., TexCivApp–Fort Worth, 153 SW2d 857, writ refused.—Estop 52(1), 54; Insurance 1758, 3003(1), 3110(3).

Hunt v. Wroe, TexCivApp–Waco, 129 SW2d 768.—Bills & N 140; Plead 248(2); Venue 16 1/2, 48, 55.

Hunt-Collin Elec. Co-op., Inc.; Hunt County Lumber, Inc. v., TexApp–Dallas, 749 SW2d 179, writ den.—Mech Liens 115(4).

Hunt Const. Co., Inc. v. Cavazos, Tex, 689 SW2d 211.— Judgm 252(1); Trial 351.2(2).

Hunt Const. Co., Inc. v. Cavazos Elec., Tex, 689 SW2d 211. See Hunt Const. Co., Inc. v. Cavazos.

Hunt County; Dallas, Garland & Northeastern R.R. v., TexApp–Dallas, 195 SW3d 818.—Autos 187(1), 187(3); Em Dom 2.1, 2.2, 2.19(2), 307(2); States 191.1, 191.6(2).

Hunt County; Europak, Inc. v., TexCivApp–Dallas, 507 SW2d 884.—Environ Law 256, 265, 290, 301, 700.

Hunt County; Mims v., TexApp–Dallas, 692 SW2d 132.— Counties 204(1); Mental H 518.

Hunt County; Mims v., TexCivApp–Dallas, 620 SW2d 664.—Counties 204(1).

Hunt County Lumber, Inc. v. Hunt-Collin Elec. Co-op., Inc., TexApp–Dallas, 749 SW2d 179, writ den.—Mech Liens 115(4).

Hunt County Tax Appraisal Dist. v. Rubbermaid Inc., TexApp–Dallas, 719 SW2d 215, ref nre.—App & E 1032(1), 1071.2; Evid 555.6(10), 571(7); Tax 2470, 2611, 2642, 2699(11), 2703, 2704, 2721, 2780, 2781, 2791.

Hunt Developers, Inc. v. Western Steel Co., TexCivApp–Corpus Christi, 409 SW2d 443.—Mech Liens 113(1), 113(2), 128.

Hunte v. Hinkley, TexApp–Houston (14 Dist), 731 SW2d 570, ref nre.—Health 782; Judgm 185.3(21), 186.

Hunt Energy Corp.; Colorado Interstate Gas Co. v., TexApp–Amarillo, 47 SW3d 1, reh overr, and review den, and reh of petition for review den.—App & E 961; Contracts 143(1), 143(2), 143.5, 167, 176(2), 317; Evid 65, 570; Gas 14.1(3); Judgm 326, 331; Mines 48; Pretrial Proc 42, 44.1, 251.1, 304, 313.

Hunter, Ex parte, TexCrimApp, 616 SW2d 626.—Hab Corp 793.

Hunter, Ex parte, TexCrimApp, 604 SW2d 188.—Crim Law 93, 324; Ind & Inf 5, 75(1), 86(2), 86(7).

Hunter, Ex parte, TexCrimApp, 581 SW2d 182.—Crim Law 223, 224, 225.

Hunter, Ex parte, TexCrimApp, 188 SW2d 162, 148 Tex-Crim 462.—Mun Corp 111(3), 594(2), 625; Nuis 60.

Hunter, In re, BkrtcySDTex, 100 BR 321.—Admin Law 501; Banks 451; B & L Assoc 48; Fed Civ Proc 2486.

Hunter v. Aldridge, TexCivApp–Waco, 478 SW2d 799.— Venue 7.5(6).

Hunter; Allstate Ins. Co. v., TexApp–Corpus Christi, 865 SW2d 189, reh overr.—Action 60; Insurance 3379; Mand 4(1); Trial 3(5.1).

Hunter; Amerine v., TexCivApp–Austin, 335 SW2d 643, ref nre.—App & E 842(1), 1015(2), 1068(3), 1069.1; Health 665.

Hunter v. Anderson, NDTex, 74 FSupp 721.—Agric 3.1; Fed Cts 93; Statut 181(1), 216, 223.2(0.5); U S 58(5), 58(6), 70(6.1).

Hunter v. Andrews, TexCivApp–Waco, 570 SW2d 590.— Action 56, 57(7); Contracts 295(1), 320, 322(4); Judges 51(4).

Hunter; Bejarano v., TexApp–El Paso, 899 SW2d 346.— Action 6; App & E 781(1); Mand 16(1), 74(3); Mun Corp 134; Offic 18.

Hunter v. B. E. Porter, Inc., TexCivApp–Dallas, 81 SW2d 774.—Assign 44; Judgm 839; Lim of Act 125; Replev 44, 119; Trial 350.4(2), 352.5(2), 352.5(4), 352.10.

Hunter; Bush v., TexCivApp–Waco, 469 SW2d 655.— Autos 244(58).

Hunter v. Camp, TexCivApp–Waco, 246 SW2d 903, ref nre.—Contracts 94(3), 147(1); Ven & Pur 44.

Hunter v. Carter, TexCivApp–Hous (14 Dist), 476 SW2d 41, ref nre.—App & E 768, 927(7), 989; Autos 150, 224(4), 239(2), 245(87); Neglig 554(1), 1533; Plead 132; Trial 139.1(12), 139.1(14), 350.6(3), 352.20, 365.1(7), 366.

Hunter v. Cartwright, TexCivApp–Fort Worth, 90 SW2d 900, writ dism.—Schools 135(3).

Hunter v. City of Beaumont, EDTex, 867 FSupp 496.— Civil R 1088(5), 1373, 1376(8), 1376(9); Fed Civ Proc 657.5(2); Judges 36; Lim of Act 58(1).

Hunter v. Clark, TexApp–San Antonio, 687 SW2d 811.— Home 12, 136, 139, 140, 141(1), 143, 144, 145.

Hunter; Cook v., TexCivApp–Waco, 389 SW2d 94.— Courts 475(2); Hus & W 273(1), 276(1), 276(5).

Hunter v. Cook, TexCivApp–Houston, 375 SW2d 574, writ dism.—Abate & R 5, 80; Courts 30; Ex & Ad 224, 434(5).

Hunter; Crim v., TexCivApp–El Paso, 97 SW2d 979, writ gr, and writ dism by agreement.—Autos 172(9); Damag 132(1), 139; Neglig 1531; New Tr 44(3); Plead 111.2; Trial 129, 352.4(7).

Hunter; De Alejandro v., TexApp–Corpus Christi, 951 SW2d 102.—Mand 4(1), 4(4); Mun Corp 58, 142, 149(1); Offic 30.1; Quo W 11.

Hunter v. Dodds, TexApp–Waco, 624 SW2d 365.—Adv Poss 42, 79(4), 80(2).

Hunter; Donley v., TexCivApp–Hous (1 Dist), 426 SW2d 250.—Child C 276, 914, 921(4).

Hunter; Employers Mut. Liability Ins. Co. of Wisconsin v., TexCivApp–Beaumont, 503 SW2d 820, ref nre.— Work Comp 1388, 1975.

Hunter; Enfield Realty & Home Bldg. Co. v., TexCivApp–Austin, 179 SW2d 810.—Brok 82(2); Trial 83(2).

Hunter; Excelsior Mut. Life Ins. Co. v., TexCivApp–Waco, 120 SW2d 905, writ dism.—Insurance 2014, 2034.

Hunter; Federal Sav. and Loan Ins. Corp. v., BkrtcyS-DTex, 100 BR 321. See Hunter, In re.

Hunter v. Fisons Corp., CA5 (Tex), 776 F2d 1.—Antitrust 432; Fed Civ Proc 2743.1.

Hunter v. Fort Worth Capital Corp., Tex, 620 SW2d 547, 20 ALR4th 399.—Abate & R 39; Contrib 5(5), 5(6.1); Corp 254, 264, 349, 359, 630(1); Indem 57, 67; Statut 203, 212.4.

Hunter; Fort Worth Capital Corp. v., TexCivApp–Fort Worth, 608 SW2d 352, rev 620 SW2d 547, 20 ALR4th 399.—Corp 264.

Hunter; Hornby v., TexCivApp–Corpus Christi, 385 SW2d 473.—Libel 2, 5, 7(13), 25, 33, 42(2), 48(1), 56(1), 75, 101(3); Plead 111.24, 111.42(4).

Hunter; Houston Printing Co. v., TexCivApp–Fort Worth, 105 SW2d 312, writ dism, aff 106 SW2d 1043, 129 Tex 652.—App & E 916(1); Libel 80, 97, 123(2), 124(8); Plead 34(2); Trial 241, 307(3), 350.3(4).

Hunter v. Hunter, TexApp–Houston (14 Dist), 666 SW2d 335.—App & E 5; Child C 907; Divorce 183, 184(12).

Hunter; Hunter v., TexApp–Houston (14 Dist), 666 SW2d 335.—App & E 5; Child C 907; Divorce 183, 184(12).

Hunter v. Hunter, TexCivApp–El Paso, 321 SW2d 92.—Divorce 27(1), 130, 146, 184(10); Trial 66.

Hunter; Hunter v., TexCivApp–El Paso, 321 SW2d 92.—Divorce 27(1), 130, 146, 184(10); Trial 66.

Hunter v. Isenhower, TexCivApp–Eastland, 265 SW2d 693.—App & E 1071.5; Sales 52(7).

Hunter v. Johnson, TexApp–El Paso, 25 SW3d 247.—Lim of Act 189; Plead 228.14.

Hunter v. Koisch, TexApp–Beaumont, 798 SW2d 857, writ den.—Lim of Act 182(5); Wills 81.

Hunter; Martin v., TexCivApp–San Antonio, 233 SW2d 354, ref nre.—App & E 1040(3); Chat Mtg 292(1); Plead 205(1), 228.11, 228.14.

Hunter; Maxwell v., CCA5 (Tex), 116 F2d 260.—Mines 79.1(4).

Hunter v. Meshack, TexCivApp–Tyler, 471 SW2d 155, ref nre.—Deeds 56(2), 56(3), 194(5), 208(4).

Hunter v. National Aid Life Ass'n, TexCivApp–Eastland, 81 SW2d 142.—Insurance 1741, 1755.

Hunter v. National County Mut. Fire Ins. Co., TexApp–Dallas, 687 SW2d 110.—App & E 1175(1); Insurance 2185, 2709, 2712(3), 3375; Judgm 199(3.7).

Hunter; National Life & Acc. Ins. Co. v., TexCivApp–Beaumont, 519 SW2d 709, ref nre.—Insurance 2588(1), 2607, 2608.

Hunter; National Union Fire Ins. Co. of Pittsburgh, Pa. v., TexApp–Corpus Christi, 741 SW2d 592.—Pretrial Proc 403.

Hunter v. NCNB Texas Nat. Bank, TexApp–Houston (14 Dist), 857 SW2d 722, reh den, and writ den.—Action 60; App & E 756, 761, 949, 971(2), 1035; Decl Judgm 385; Ex & Ad 175; Home 1, 5, 81; Pretrial Proc 202; Trial 401; Wills 708; Witn 79(1).

Hunter; Noble v., TexCivApp–Amarillo, 441 SW2d 580.—Brok 84(1); Contracts 176(1), 176(2); Evid 448; Plead 409(1); Trial 350.2, 350.3(1), 350.8.

Hunter; North Side State Bank v., TexCivApp–Hous (14 Dist), 452 SW2d 34, ref nre.—App & E 1062.1; Neglig 201, 1542, 1696; Trial 352.1(6).

Hunter v. O'Neill, TexApp–Dallas, 854 SW2d 704.—App & E 78(6); New Tr 113, 165.

Hunter v. Palmer, TexApp–Houston (1 Dist), 988 SW2d 471.—Evid 53; Judgm 181(15.1); Wills 290.

Hunter; Petty v., TexCivApp–Waco, 254 SW2d 543, ref nre.—Action 4; Health 947.

Hunter v. Pillers, TexCivApp–Beaumont, 464 SW2d 939.—Covenants 72.1, 79(3).

Hunter v. Pitcock, TexCivApp–Fort Worth, 346 SW2d 509.—Evid 590; Fraud Conv 74(1), 196, 273, 277(1), 282, 302, 308(4).

Hunter v. Reserve Ins. Co., TexCivApp–Texarkana, 335 SW2d 877, writ dism.—App & E 1177(2).

Hunter v. Robison, TexCivApp–Dallas, 488 SW2d 555, ref nre.—App & E 1040(4), 1062.5; Health 625, 817, 818, 823(11), 827.

Hunter v. Rodriguez, CA5 (Tex), 73 FedAppx 768.—Civil R 1376(7); Fed Civ Proc 2734.

Hunter; Shaver v., TexApp–Amarillo, 626 SW2d 574, ref nre, cert den 103 SCt 377, 459 US 1016, 74 LEd2d 510.—Const Law 225.5, 3027, 3145; Covenants 1, 49.

Hunter v. Shell Oil Co., CA5 (Tex), 198 F2d 485.—Evid 54; Fed Cts 261, 800; Fraud 58(1); Mines 104; Princ & A 69(1), 78(6); Trusts 101, 110.

Hunter v. State, TexCrimApp, 955 SW2d 102, on remand 1999 WL 82624, petition for discretionary review refused.—Arrest 68(3), 68(4); Crim Law 1139, 1224(1).

Hunter v. State, TexCrimApp, 954 SW2d 767.—Crim Law 1072, 1130(1), 1130(4).

Hunter v. State, TexCrimApp, 843 SW2d 521. See Grunsfeld v. State.

Hunter v. State, TexCrimApp, 647 SW2d 657.—Crim Law 795(2.1), 1173.2(1); Homic 1457, 1458.

Hunter v. State, TexCrimApp, 576 SW2d 395.—Ind & Inf 72.

Hunter v. State, TexCrimApp, 530 SW2d 573.—Crim Law 351(3), 369.2(1), 1030(1), 1036.1(2), 1043(2), 1177; Sent & Pun 328.

Hunter v. State, TexCrimApp, 501 SW2d 81.—Crim Law 641.13(2.1), 1128(2).

Hunter v. State, TexCrimApp, 496 SW2d 44.—Crim Law 394.1(3); Homic 1127, 1134, 1186; Searches 42.1.

Hunter v. State, TexCrimApp, 481 SW2d 806, cert den 93 SCt 345, 409 US 988, 34 LEd2d 254.—Const Law 3781; Controlled Subs 6; Crim Law 867.

Hunter v. State, TexCrimApp, 481 SW2d 137.—Jury 97(4), 131(15.1).

Hunter v. State, TexCrimApp, 468 SW2d 96.—Autos 355(13); Crim Law 404.70, 1044.1(5.1), 1130(2), 1169.5(2); Searches 181; Witn 277(4), 277(5).

Hunter v. State, TexCrimApp, 449 SW2d 232.—Crim Law 1081(5).

Hunter v. State, TexCrimApp, 398 SW2d 768.—Assault 92(1).

Hunter v. State, TexCrimApp, 395 SW2d 614.—Crim Law 1099.7(3), 1099.10.

Hunter v. State, TexCrimApp, 377 SW2d 646.—Crim Law 1083, 1131(4).

Hunter v. State, TexCrimApp, 324 SW2d 17, 168 TexCrim 160.—Crim Law 1099.13, 1170.5(5); Witn 248(2), 277(4), 337(14), 344(2), 345(1), 345(2), 345(7).

Hunter v. State, TexCrimApp, 321 SW2d 586, 167 TexCrim 513.—Autos 355(6).

Hunter v. State, TexCrimApp, 275 SW2d 803, 161 TexCrim 225.—Crim Law 404.70, 451(1), 1036.1(2), 1043(1), 1044.1(5.1), 1144.13(3); Homic 727, 732, 734, 908, 998, 1161, 1325.

Hunter v. State, TexCrimApp, 256 SW2d 100.—Crim Law 1090.1(1).

Hunter v. State, TexCrimApp, 207 SW2d 410.—Crim Law 1090.7, 1094(3).

Hunter v. State, TexCrimApp, 176 SW2d 950, 146 TexCrim 529.—Crim Law 1094(3), 1099.10.

Hunter v. State, TexCrimApp, 165 SW2d 998, 145 TexCrim 85.—Crim Law 1091(11), 1097(1).

Hunter v. State, TexCrimApp, 152 SW2d 365, 142 TexCrim 224.—Crim Law 784(4), 814(3), 1131(7); Larc 55.

Hunter v. State, TexCrimApp, 139 SW2d 89, 139 TexCrim 106.—Autos 353; Crim Law 723(1), 1171.1(6).

Hunter v. State, TexCrimApp, 128 SW2d 1176, 137 TexCrim 289.—Crim Law 829(5); Homic 776, 1478, 1480, 1481, 1484.

Hunter v. State, TexCrimApp, 111 SW2d 280, 133 TexCrim 399.—Assault 96(7); Rape 43(1).

Hunter v. State, TexCrimApp, 88 SW2d 479.—Crim Law 1070.

Hunter; State v., TexApp–Fort Worth, 102 SW3d 306.—Crim Law 394.6(4); Searches 42.1, 47.1, 60.1, 171, 172, 180, 183, 184, 192.1, 198.

Hunter v. State, TexApp–Fort Worth, 896 SW2d 397.—Crim Law 1134(5), 1158(3); Jury 33(5.15); Sent & Pun 1900.

Hunter v. State, TexApp–Austin, 820 SW2d 5.—Sent & Pun 2010, 2012, 2018.

Hunter v. State, TexApp–Amarillo, 956 SW2d 143, petition for discretionary review refused.—Crim Law 721(1), 726, 729, 730(1), 730(10).

Hunter v. State, TexApp–El Paso, 640 SW2d 656, petition for discretionary review refused.—Crim Law 721(3), 721(6), 1134(8), 1169.11; Sent & Pun 313, 1947, 2010, 2087.

Hunter v. State, TexApp–Beaumont, 805 SW2d 918, petition for discretionary review gr, vac 844 SW2d 748.—Arrest 63.5(5); Controlled Subs 138; Crim Law 404.60; Sent & Pun 313.

Hunter v. State, TexApp–Waco, 92 SW3d 596, petition for discretionary review refused.—Controlled Subs 26, 27, 28, 30, 79, 80; Crim Law 394.4(6), 553, 742(1), 747, 1144.13(1), 1144.13(2.1), 1144.13(3), 1144.13(5), 1144.13(6), 1159.2(1), 1159.2(2), 1159.2(7), 1159.3(1); Searches 107, 108, 109, 113.1.

Hunter v. State, TexApp–Corpus Christi, 697 SW2d 854.—Const Law 3854; Crim Law 217; Extrad 36, 39; Hab Corp 704.

Hunter v. State, TexApp–Houston (14 Dist), 148 SW3d 526, petition for discretionary review refused, cert den 126 SCt 2286, 164 LEd2d 816.—Crim Law 394.6(5), 412.1(1), 412.2(4), 412.2(5), 414, 517.2(2), 519(1), 519(2), 522(1), 531(3), 641.3(3), 641.9, 1153(1), 1158(4).

Hunter v. State, TexApp–Houston (14 Dist), 799 SW2d 356.—Crim Law 1042, 1159.2(4), 1159.2(7), 1177; Rape 52(2), 53(5); Sent & Pun 308, 309, 310.

Hunter; Streber v., CA5 (Tex), 221 F3d 701, reh and sug for reh den 233 F3d 576.—Action 17; Antitrust 128, 130, 134, 136, 138, 256, 367, 369, 389(1), 389(2), 393, 397, 398; Atty & C 32(13), 105, 107, 109, 112, 129(1), 129(2), 129(3), 129(4); Const Law 3965(5), 3992, 3994, 3996; Damag 2, 20, 69, 87(2), 91(3); Evid 146, 555.2, 568(1), 570, 571(3), 574; Fed Civ Proc 1852, 1855.1, 1973, 2111, 2114.1, 2331, 2373, 2557, 2601; Fed Cts 76, 76.10, 76.15, 76.25, 409.1, 629, 763.1, 776, 799, 823, 825.1, 847, 850.1, 871, 893; Int Rev 4665, 4818, 5215; Judgm 569; Lim of Act 1, 2(1), 95(11); Neglig 273; Trial 255(1).

Hunter; Streber v., WDTex, 14 FSupp2d 978.—Action 17; Atty & C 105, 129(1); Fed Cts 409.1; Lim of Act 55(3), 95(10.1), 95(11).

Hunter v. Struggs, TexCivApp–Houston, 352 SW2d 289, ref nre.—Ack 6(2), 52, 53; Deeds 8, 44, 53, 67, 207.

Hunter v. Texas Elec. Ry. Co., TexCivApp–Austin, 194 SW2d 281, writ refused, cert gr 67 SCt 1081, 330 US 817, 91 LEd 1269, aff 68 SCt 203, 332 US 827, 92 LEd 402.—App & E 1062.1; Labor & Emp 2997; Trial 352.7.

Hunter; Texas Emp. Ins. Ass'n v., TexCivApp–Dallas, 255 SW2d 944, rev Texas Employers' Insurance Ass'n v. Hunter, 260 SW2d 884, 152 Tex 438.—App & E 901; Work Comp 1392, 1927, 1961, 1965, 1968(3), 1968(4), 1969.

Hunter; Texas Mexican Ry. Co. v., TexApp–Corpus Christi, 726 SW2d 616.—App & E 82(1); Mand 3(1), 4(1), 168(2).

Hunter; Traders & General Ins. Co. v., TexCivApp–Amarillo, 95 SW2d 158, writ dism.—Evid 67(1); Trial 350.3(8), 350.5(4), 352.5(8); Work Comp 1696.

Hunter; Trapnell v., TexApp–Corpus Christi, 785 SW2d 426.—Abate & R 7, 8(1), 9, 12; Courts 28, 493(1); Mand 53.

Hunter; U.S. v., CA5 (Tex), 417 F2d 296.—Crim Law 1035(7), 1119(1), 1132.

Hunter; U.S. v., CA5 (Tex), 188 FedAppx 315.—Sent & Pun 2038, 2039.

Hunter; U.S. Dept. of Agriculture v., CA5 (Tex), 171 F2d 793.—Admin Law 133; Inj 75; Mand 85; Pub Lands 129; U S 32, 33, 125(28.1), 135.

Hunter v. U.S. Dept. of Agriculture, NDTex, 69 FSupp 377.—Fed Cts 93; U S 125(25.1).

Hunter v. West, TexCivApp–San Antonio, 293 SW2d 686.—Bills & N 449; Statut 290.

Hunter Barrett & Co.; Ventura v., TexCivApp–Corpus Christi, 552 SW2d 319, dism.—Condo 1; Inj 111; Plead 111.39(2), 111.40, 111.42(1), 111.47; Venue 5.3(1), 5.3(2), 15.

Hunter Co. v. Fain, TexCivApp–Eastland, 281 SW2d 750, ref nre.—Trial 352.4(3), 352.18; Trusts 17(4), 99.

Hunter Fan Co.; Nunez v., SDTex, 920 FSupp 716.—Action 17; Contracts 144; Labor & Emp 76; Torts 103.

Hunter Fan of Tennessee, Inc.; Nunez v., SDTex, 920 FSupp 716. See Nunez v. Hunter Fan Co.

Hunter, Farris & Co., Inc.; Labor Force, Inc. v., TexCivApp–Hous (14 Dist), 601 SW2d 146.—Corp 507(5).

Hunter-Hayes Elevator Co. v. Williams, TexCivApp–Fort Worth, 402 SW2d 280, ref nre.—App & E 1062.2; Carr 320(23); Neglig 1032, 1117, 1670, 1679; Trial 351.5(1).

Hunter Indus. Facilities, Inc. v. Texas Natural Resource Conservation Com'n, TexApp–Austin, 910 SW2d 96, reh overr, and writ den, and motion dism.—Admin Law 305, 325, 489.1, 781, 785, 791; App & E 1008.1(5); Const Law 4096; Environ Law 358, 382, 389, 432, 454, 455, 678, 685; Statut 219(4).

Hunter-Reed v. City of Houston, SDTex, 244 FSupp2d 733.—Civil R 1505(4), 1530, 1532, 1535; Equity 64; Evid 318(1), 318(7); Fed Civ Proc 1837.1, 2539, 2545; Lim of Act 104.5.

Hunter's Calculators v. Fisons Corp., CA5 (Tex), 776 F2d 1. See Hunter v. Fisons Corp.

Hunter's Creek Village, City of; Parker Bros. & Co. v., TexCivApp–Hous (1 Dist), 459 SW2d 915.—Evid 590; Inj 85(1), 135; Mun Corp 703(1).

Hunter's Creek Village, City of; Reese v., TexApp–Houston (1 Dist), 95 SW3d 389, reh overr, and review den.—App & E 893(1); Courts 4, 40; Crim Law 100(1); Decl Judgm 124.1, 315; Plead 104(1).

Hunter's Creek Village, City of; Reichert v., TexCivApp–Houston, 345 SW2d 838, ref nre.—Zoning 21.5, 27, 33, 157, 158, 169.

Hunter's Crossing, Inc., In re, BkrtcyWDTex, 90 BR 246. See Oakgrove Village, Ltd., In re.

Hunt, Hopkins & Mitchell, Inc. v. Facility Ins. Corp., TexApp–Austin, 78 SW3d 564, review den.—Accord 1, 15.1; App & E 172(1), 946; Contracts 187(1); Judgm 186; Work Comp 1063.

Hunting Bayou Co.; McLaren v., TexCivApp–Hous (14 Dist), 453 SW2d 300, ref nre.—Judgm 178, 181(2), 185(2), 185.1(3), 185.3(15).

Huntington v. Walker's Austex Chili Co., TexCivApp–Waco, 285 SW2d 255, writ refused.—Abate & R 52; Courts 107; Death 11, 29, 31(8).

Huntington Corp. v. Inwood Const. Co., TexCivApp–Dallas, 472 SW2d 804, ref nre.—Damag 12, 189; New Tr 74.

Huntington Corp. v. Inwood Const. Co., TexCivApp–Dallas, 348 SW2d 442, ref nre, appeal after remand 400 SW2d 372, ref nre, appeal after remand 472 SW2d 804, ref nre.—Alt Disp Res 137; Contracts 127(2); Spec Perf 80.

Huntington Corp.; Inwood Const. Co. v., TexCivApp–Texarkana, 400 SW2d 372, ref nre, appeal after remand 472 SW2d 804, ref nre.—Contracts 323(3); Damag 123, 218; Stip 14(12).

Huntington Homes; Davis v., TexApp–Texarkana, 891 SW2d 779. See Davis v. R. Sanders & Associates Custom Builders, Inc.

Hunt Intern. Resources Corp., In re, NDTex, 57 BR 371.—Bankr 3767, 3772.

Hunt Intern. Resources Corp. v. Binstein, NDTex, 559 FSupp 601.—RICO 37.

Huntley v. Enon Ltd. Partnership, TexApp–Fort Worth, 197 SW3d 844.—App & E 852, 893(1), 895(2), 1008.1(1), 1008.1(2), 1010.1(1), 1010.2, 1153, 1177(7); Evid 597; Ven & Pur 79, 82, 334(1).

Huntley v. Huntley, TexCivApp–Austin, 512 SW2d 767.—Divorce 226, 252.1, 252.2; Evid 590; Hus & W 264(5); Receivers 198(1).

Huntley; Huntley v., TexCivApp–Austin, 512 SW2d 767.—Divorce 226, 252.1, 252.2; Evid 590; Hus & W 264(5); Receivers 198(1).

Huntley v. State, TexApp–Houston (1 Dist), 4 SW3d 813, petition for discretionary review refused.—Forg 4, 35, 44(0.5).

Huntley; U.S. v., CA5 (Tex), 535 F2d 1400, reh den 540 F2d 1086, cert den 97 SCt 1548, 430 US 929, 51 LEd2d 773.—Crim Law 255, 260.11(6), 641.5(2.1), 641.5(3), 641.7(1), 1177; Rec S Goods 2, 7(6).

Hunt Oil Co. v. Dishman, TexCivApp–Beaumont, 352 SW2d 760, ref nre.—Compromise 11; Mines 78.6.

Hunt Oil Co. v. Federal Power Commission, CA5 (Tex), 424 F2d 982.—Const Law 4371; Gas 14.3(3), 14.3(4), 14.5(10), 14.6.

Hunt Oil Co. v. Federal Power Commission, CA5 (Tex), 398 F2d 746.—Gas 14.3(4).

Hunt Oil Co. v. Federal Power Commission, CA5 (Tex), 334 F2d 474.—Gas 6, 14.5(6).

Hunt Oil Co. v. Federal Power Commission, CA5 (Tex), 318 F2d 25.—Pub Ut 183.

Hunt Oil Co.; Jones v., TexCivApp–Dallas, 456 SW2d 506, ref nre.—App & E 758.3(11); Consp 8, 11; Estop 71; Judgm 185.3(21); Lim of Act 55(1); Mines 92.31.

Hunt Oil Co. v. Jones, TexCivApp–Eastland, 436 SW2d 186, writ dism woj.—Venue 5.3(8).

Hunt Oil Co. v. Killion, TexCivApp–Texarkana, 299 SW2d 316, ref nre.—Fact 2.5; Partners 226, 241; Princ & S 67, 129(1).

Hunt Oil Co.; Laredo Offshore Constructors, Inc. v., CA5 (Tex), 754 F2d 1223.—Adm 1.20(1), 1.20(2), 4, 10(1), 10(2), 12; Fed Cts 194; States 12.2.

Hunt Oil Co. v. Moore, Tex, 639 SW2d 459, on remand 656 SW2d 634, ref nre.—App & E 78(1).

Hunt Oil Co. v. Moore, TexApp–Tyler, 656 SW2d 634, ref nre.—Acct 1; App & E 173(9), 173(10); Mines 49, 55(8), 78.1(3), 78.1(7), 81, 92.79.

Hunt Oil Co. v. Moore, TexApp–Tyler, 629 SW2d 260, rev 639 SW2d 459, on remand 656 SW2d 634, ref nre.—App & E 78(1), 80(3), 344.

Hunt Oil Co. v. Murchison, TexCivApp–Eastland, 352 SW2d 365.—Plead 111.3; Venue 5.5; Woods 2.

Hunt Oil Co.; Stroud v., TexCivApp–Eastland, 147 SW2d 564.—App & E 882(8); Deeds 90, 140; Ease 24.

Hunton v. Guardian Life Ins. Co. of America, SDTex, 243 FSupp2d 686, aff 71 FedAppx 441.—Contracts 143(2), 143.5, 152, 155, 169, 170(1), 176(2); Estop 55, 85; Evid 397(1), 405(1), 448; Fed Civ Proc 824, 828.1, 834, 840, 851; Fraud 13(3); Insurance 1801, 1806, 1807, 1813, 1839, 1869, 1870, 1873, 1885, 1886(5), 2012; Lim of Act 43, 46(6), 55(2), 58(1), 95(1), 95(3), 95(9), 95(16), 99(1), 100(1), 100(12), 104(1).

Hunt Petroleum (AEC), Inc.; Zurich American Ins. Co. v., TexApp–Houston (14 Dist), 157 SW3d 462.—App & E 856(1); Contracts 143(2), 143.5, 147(1), 152, 169, 176(2), 309(1); Cust & U 15(1); Evid 448; Judgm 181(19), 181(23); Mines 109.

Hunt Petroleum Corp.; Dodge v., NDTex, 174 FSupp2d 505.—Civil R 1590, 1593, 1594, 1597.

Hunt Petroleum Corp.; Rio Bravo Oil Co. v., Tex, 455 SW2d 722.—Adv Poss 71(1); Judgm 181(1), 181(15.1); R R 69.

Hunt Petroleum Corp.; Rio Bravo Oil Co. v., TexCivApp–Tyler, 439 SW2d 853, rev 455 SW2d 722.—Adv Poss 60(1), 60(2), 60(4); Deeds 90; Estop 101; Judgm 126(4), 183, 185.3(17), 237(3), 297; R R 63, 69; Tresp to T T 34.

Hunt Production Co.; Burrage v., TexCivApp–Dallas, 114 SW2d 1228, dism.—App & E 1097(1), 1099(2), 1195(3); Const Law 2310, 4016; Judgm 21, 524, 526, 855(1); Plead 110, 111.9, 111.46; Venue 15.

Hunt Production Co. v. Burrage, TexCivApp–Dallas, 104 SW2d 84, writ dism.—Courts 480(2); Evid 43(3); Inj 26(1); Judgm 519, 677, 855(1); Receivers 24.

Hunt Production Co. v. Dickerson, TexCivApp–Texarkana, 135 SW2d 597, writ dism, correct.—Mines 73.1(1), 77, 78.1(7), 78.2.

Huntress v. McGrath, TexApp–Fort Worth, 946 SW2d 480.—Inj 77(1).

Huntress v. State, TexCrimApp, 94 SW2d 752, 130 TexCrim 492.—Counties 102; Crim Law 507(1).

Huntress v. State, TexCivApp–San Antonio, 95 SW2d 974.—App & E 1187, 1188, 1189; Costs 273.

Huntress v. State ex rel. Todd, TexCivApp–San Antonio, 88 SW2d 636, writ dism.—Counties 67; Gr Jury 41.10; Offic 74; Statut 195.

Huntress; U.S. v., CA5 (Tex), 956 F2d 1309, reh den, cert den 113 SCt 2330, 508 US 905, 124 LEd2d 243.—Banks 509.20, 509.25; Crim Law 898, 1152(1), 1152(2), 1166.16, 1173.1, 1174(5); Jury 32(2), 149.

Huntress; Williams v., Tex, 272 SW2d 87, 153 Tex 443.—Action 6; Courts 207.4(3); Elections 121(1), 129, 146, 172; Judgm 486(1); Mand 10.

Huntsberry v. Byrd, CA5 (Tex), 926 F2d 480. See Wilson v. Barrientos.

Huntsberry v. Lynaugh, TexApp–Tyler, 807 SW2d 16.—States 79, 112.2(2).

Hunt's Estate v. U.S., CA5 (Tex), 309 F2d 146.—Action 53(1); Judgm 588, 599.

Huntsinger v. Gates Rubber Co., TexCivApp–Amarillo, 149 SW2d 632.—App & E 1126, 1236.

Huntsman; Ellmossallamy v., TexApp–Houston (14 Dist), 830 SW2d 299.—App & E 962; Pretrial Proc 582, 583, 587, 697.

Huntsman; Price v., TexCivApp–Waco, 430 SW2d 831, ref nre.—Wills 72, 206, 440.

Huntsman v. State, TexCrimApp, 143 SW2d 587, 140 TexCrim 62.—Crim Law 778(12), 805(1), 806(2), 822(1), 829(6), 1144.16; Homic 908, 1155, 1333, 1459, 1473, 1484.

Huntsman; Traders & General Ins. Co. v., TexCivApp–Fort Worth, 125 SW2d 431, writ dism, correct.—Admin Law 107, 313; Damag 221(5.1); Trial 352.14; Work Comp 1079, 1165, 1184, 1374, 1671, 1768, 1836, 1846, 1908, 1916, 1917, 1929, 1935, 1941, 1968(1), 2084.

Huntsman Polymers Corp.; Phillips Petroleum Co. v., CAFed (Tex), 157 F3d 866.—Pat 101(1), 101(2), 159, 165(1), 167(1), 168(2.1), 226.6, 235(2), 237, 314(5), 324.5.

Hunt Steed v. Steed, TexApp–Fort Worth, 908 SW2d 581, reh overr, and writ den.—App & E 852, 934(1); Judgm 185(2); Lim of Act 1, 105(2), 165.

Hunt Stephens Investments v. Ellisor & Tanner, Inc., TexApp–Dallas, 739 SW2d 933. See Hunt v. Ellisor & Tanner, Inc.

Huntsville, City of; Acker v., TexApp–Houston (14 Dist), 787 SW2d 79.—Judgm 713(2), 720, 724, 725(1), 829(3).

Huntsville, City of; Ford v., CA5 (Tex), 242 F3d 235.—Fed Civ Proc 314.1, 315, 320, 331; Fed Cts 776, 817, 820; Records 32, 54.

Huntsville, City of; Schaper v., CA5 (Tex), 813 F2d 709, reh den 818 F2d 865.—Civil R 1395(8); Const Law 3867, 3874(2), 3875, 3912, 4171, 4172(6); Fed Civ Proc 1271; Fed Cts 574, 595, 763.1.

Huntsville Independent School Dist.; Favero v., SDTex, 939 FSupp 1281, aff 110 F3d 793.—Action 2; Civil R 1153, 1162(1), 1162(2), 1536; Estop 62.1, 62.5; Schools 55, 159.5(6).

Huntsville Independent School Dist. v. McAdams, Tex, 221 SW2d 546, 148 Tex 120.—Schools 97(4); Statut 183, 190, 205.

Huntsville Independent School Dist. v. McAdams, TexCivApp–Galveston, 217 SW2d 51, rev 221 SW2d 546, 148 Tex 120.—Mand 143(1); Schools 97(0.5); Statut 251.

Huntsville Independent School Dist. v. McAdams, TexCivApp–Galveston, 207 SW2d 165, ref nre.—App & E 863, 954(1), 954(2); Inj 135; Schools 111.

Huntsville Independent School Dist.; Sanchez v., TexApp–Houston (1 Dist), 844 SW2d 286.—Action 68; Admin Law 5, 462, 750, 788, 791, 793; App & E 892.1, 893(1), 946; J P 170.1; Plead 228.14, 367(1); Schools 56, 63(3), 177.

Huntsville Independent School Dist.; Scott v., Tex, 487 SW2d 692.—Em Dom 274(1).

Huntsville Independent School Dist. v. Scott, TexCivApp–Hous (14 Dist), 483 SW2d 344, ref nre 487 SW2d 692.—Em Dom 172, 224, 243(3), 246(2), 265(5); Pretrial Proc 509.

Huntsville Independent School Dist.; Smith v., TexCivApp–Hous (14 Dist), 425 SW2d 369.—Evid 370(8), 372(4); Pretrial Proc 723.1, 724.

Huntsville Livestock Services, Inc.; Lee v., TexApp–Houston (14 Dist), 934 SW2d 158, appeal after new trial 2003 WL 1738418, petition stricken, and review den.—App & E 1070(2); Damag 102, 208(2), 221(7); Trial 358.

Huntsville Memorial Hosp.; Cole v., TexApp–Houston (1 Dist), 920 SW2d 364, writ den, cert den 117 SCt 1312, 520 US 1143, 137 LEd2d 475.—Action 3; App & E 181, 219(1), 223, 242(1), 554(1), 934(1), 961, 1024.3; Civil R 1324, 1325, 1326(4), 1326(5); Const Law 3941; Health 275; Judgm 181(2), 185(6); Pretrial Proc 44.1, 46, 309, 434; Statut 181(1), 185, 195.

Huntsville Memorial Hosp. v. Ernst, TexApp–Houston (14 Dist), 763 SW2d 856.—Admin Law 311, 359; Const Law 4187; Equity 43; Health 273, 275; Mand 3(8), 4(1), 28.

Huntsville Memorial Hospital; Milner v., TexCivApp–Houston, 398 SW2d 647, ref nre.—Char 45(2); Judgm 181(33), 186.

Huntsville, Walker County, Tex., City of; McAdams v., CA5 (Tex), 138 FedAppx 613.—Civil R 1128, 1137; Fed Cts 752.

Hunt Tool Co. v. Lawrence, CA5 (Tex), 242 F2d 347, cert den 77 SCt 1296, 354 US 910, 1 LEd2d 1428.—Pat 49, 112.1, 168(1), 234.

Hunt Tool Co.; Lawrence v., SDTex, 142 FSupp 329, aff 242 F2d 347, cert den 77 SCt 1296, 354 US 910, 1 LEd2d 1428.—Pat 16.17, 26(1.1), 46, 51(1), 112.1, 168(1), 177, 233.1, 234, 243(3), 248.

Hunt Tool Co. v. Moore, Inc., CA5 (Tex), 212 F2d 685.—Fed Civ Proc 318, 342, 1837.1; Fed Cts 306.

Hunt Tool Co.; Pena v., SDTex, 296 FSupp 1003.—Civil R 1513, 1515.

Hunt Tool Co.; Smith v., TexCivApp–Waco, 331 SW2d 952.—Plead 111.42(5).

Hunt Trust Estate, In re, BkrtcyNDTex, 146 BR 178. See Hunt, In re.

Hunt Trust Estate, In re, BkrtcyNDTex, 92 BR 172. See William Herbert Hunt Trust Estate, In re.

Huong v. City of Port Arthur, EDTex, 961 FSupp 1003. —Arrest 68(2); Civil R 1088(4), 1351(4), 1352(1), 1352(4); Mun Corp 723, 747(3); States 191.6(1).

Hupaylo; Charbonneau v., TexCivApp–Fort Worth, 100 SW2d 745.—App & E 1062.1; Autos 245(81); Neglig 506(8), 530(1); Trial 352.5(6).

Hupp v. Hupp, TexCivApp–Fort Worth, 235 SW2d 753, ref nre.—Evid 158(6), 236(1); Marriage 48, 54; Partners 76, 121; Witn 140(5), 159(3), 181.

Hupp; Hupp v., TexCivApp–Fort Worth, 235 SW2d 753, ref nre.—Evid 158(6), 236(1); Marriage 48, 54; Partners 76, 121; Witn 140(5), 159(3), 181.

Hupp v. Port Brownsville Shipyard, Inc., SDTex, 515 FSupp 546.—Evid 601(4); Fed Cts 337, 338, 355.1, 358, 359, 417; Trover 44, 53, 60.

Hupp v. Siroflex of America, Inc., CAFed (Tex), 122 F3d 1456.—Courts 96(5); Fed Cts 630.1; Pat 28, 76, 97, 252, 306, 312(6), 323.3, 324.55(1), 324.55(3.1), 324.56; Trademarks 1062, 1631.

Hupp v. Siroflex of America, Inc., SDTex, 848 FSupp 744.—Const Law 3964; Courts 12(2.1), 12(2.5); Fed Cts 76, 76.10, 76.25, 96, 97, 103, 104, 105, 110, 141; Pat 280, 288(1), 288(3).

Hupp v. Siroflex of America, Inc., SDTex, 159 FRD 29. —Jury 25(8), 28(5).

Hupp v. State, TexCrimApp, 801 SW2d 920.—Crim Law 1172.1(2).

Hupp v. State, TexApp–Dallas, 774 SW2d 56, petition for discretionary review gr, aff 801 SW2d 920.—Crim Law 823(1), 1172.1(2).

Hupp v. State, TexApp–Dallas, 729 SW2d 355, petition for discretionary review gr, vac 761 SW2d 10, on remand 774 SW2d 56, petition for discretionary review gr, aff 801 SW2d 920, vac 761 SW2d 11, on remand 774 SW2d 56, petition for discretionary review gr, and petition for discretionary review gr, aff 801 SW2d 920.—Const Law 2392, 4723; Crim Law 412.1(2), 641.13(1), 641.13(5), 641.13(6); Rape 48(1), 54(1); Witn 305(2).

Hupp Corp.; Major Appliance Co. v., CA5 (Tex), 254 F2d 503.—Bankr 2296; Contracts 147(2); Frds St of 18(3); Sales 215.

Hupp Systems, Inc.; Vicki Industries, Inc. v., TexCivApp–Waco, 521 SW2d 733.—App & E 387(1), 387(3), 912; Damag 40(1); Plead 111.12, 111.37, 111.42(6).

Hur v. City of Mesquite, TexApp–Amarillo, 916 SW2d 510.—App & E 1050.1(1), 1052(5), 1053(3).

Hur v. City of Mesquite, TexApp–Amarillo, 893 SW2d 227, writ den, reh overr 916 SW2d 510.—Alt Disp Res 461, 489; App & E 169, 242(1), 690(1), 919, 930(2), 970(2), 1047(1), 1051.1(1), 1051.1(2); Autos 187(4), 277.1, 279; Contracts 332(2); Costs 260(4); Evid 188; Mun Corp 254, 742(4), 742(6), 762(1); Princ & A 189(1); States 112(2); Trial 18, 74, 90, 255(5), 412.

Hurbace, In re, BkrtcyWDTex, 61 BR 563.—Bankr 3357(2.1), 3357(3); Statut 223.5(4).

Hurbace; Donohoe v., BkrtcyWDTex, 61 BR 563. See Hurbace, In re.

Hurbrough v. Cain, TexCivApp–Tyler, 571 SW2d 216.— Contracts 212(2); Judgm 185(2), 185.3(2); Lim of Act 46(6), 170; Mines 74(3).

Hurd, Ex parte, TexCrimApp, 613 SW2d 742.—Hab Corp 791, 845; Sent & Pun 1157.

Hurd; Alamo Nat. Bank of San Antonio v., TexCivApp–San Antonio, 485 SW2d 335, ref nre.—App & E 1175(2), 1177(1); Mines 74(5), 79.1(2); Wills 439, 441, 450, 455, 470(1), 486, 564(1), 728.

Hurd v. D. E. Goldsmith Chemical Metal Corp., TexCivApp–Hous (1 Dist), 600 SW2d 345.—Judgm 17(2), 951(1); Proc 74, 133, 135.

Hurd v. Maxwell, TexApp–Eastland, 762 SW2d 700.— Child C 902.

Hurd v. Republic Underwriters, TexCivApp–El Paso, 105 SW2d 428, writ dism.—Work Comp 396, 561, 1256, 1922, 1927.

Hurd v. State, TexCrimApp, 725 SW2d 249.—Crim Law 662.7, 1091(3); Witn 372(1), 372(2), 374(1).

Hurd v. State, TexCrimApp, 548 SW2d 388.—Crim Law 1026.10(2.1), 1116.

Hurd v. State, TexCrimApp, 513 SW2d 936.—Crim Law 438(6), 486(6), 570(2), 720.5, 726, 814(10), 814(17), 1037.1(2), 1044.2(1), 1129(4), 1130(2), 1166.16, 1171.1(3), 1171.1(4); Homic 1350, 1351; Jury 110(9); Witn 269(2.1), 274(2).

HURD

Hurd v. State, TexCrimApp, 483 SW2d 824.—Crim Law 1134(8); Sent & Pun 2003.

Hurd; State v., TexApp–Fort Worth, 865 SW2d 605, reh den.—Crim Law 1030(1), 1134(6), 1147; Witn 208(1).

Hurd v. State, TexApp–Houston (14 Dist), 704 SW2d 539, petition for discretionary review gr, rev 725 SW2d 249. —Assault 96(1); Crim Law 641.13(2.1), 641.13(6), 795(2.20), 1137(2); Rob 24.15(1), 24.35; Witn 363(1), 372(1).

Hurd Enterprises, Ltd. v. Bruni, TexApp–San Antonio, 828 SW2d 101, writ den.—Action 27(1); App & E 1097(1), 1195(1); Fraud 64(1); Insurance 3335, 3336; Mines 73.1(2), 73.1(4), 78.1(2), 78.1(8), 79.1(1), 79.7.

Hurd Urban Development, L.C. v. Federal Highway Admin., SDTex, 33 FSupp2d 570.—Environ Law 581, 651, 652, 656; High 103.1.

Hurlburt v. Planters Nat. Bank & Trust Co., TexCiv-App–Waco, 539 SW2d 97, ref nre.—Autos 207; Death 99(4); Neglig 259, 1560.

Hurlbut v. Dripping Springs Independent School Dist., TexCivApp–Austin, 617 SW2d 332.—Schools 37(1), 37(3), 47.

Hurlbut v. Gulf Atlantic Life Ins. Co., Tex, 749 SW2d 762.—App & E 1083(6); Libel 36, 37, 38(1), 50, 51(1), 130, 135, 136, 139; Lim of Act 199(2); Torts 244; Trial 366.

Hurlbut; Gulf Atlantic Life Ins. Co. v., TexApp–Dallas, 749 SW2d 96.—Atty & C 104; Libel 9(1); Lim of Act 100(12), 197(2).

Hurlbut; Gulf Atlantic Life Ins. Co. v., TexApp–Dallas, 696 SW2d 83, writ gr, opinion supplemented 749 SW2d 96, rev 749 SW2d 762.—Action 38(4); App & E 170(1), 218.2(7); Consp 1.1, 8, 16; Damag 114, 190; Libel 6(1), 33, 36, 38(1), 51(2), 76, 80, 93, 112(2), 130, 136, 139; Lim of Act 13, 95(6), 100(1), 100(11), 100(13), 195(3), 197(2); Mal Pros 39; Plead 36(2); Proc 168; Torts 214, 242, 244, 265, 424; Trial 366.

Hurlbut v. Lyons, TexCivApp–El Paso, 405 SW2d 398, writ dism woj.—Bailm 1; Plead 110, 111.15, 111.42(5); Venue 7.5(6).

Hurlbut v. Ross, TexCivApp–El Paso, 227 SW2d 358.— App & E 854(2); Brok 76.

Hurlbut v. State Bd. of Ins., TexCivApp–Austin, 555 SW2d 180.—Insurance 1622.

Hurley; Belcher v., TexCivApp–Eastland, 169 SW2d 495, writ refused wom.—Evid 441(1), 441(11), 469.

Hurley v. Federal Tender Board No. 1, CCA5 (Tex), 108 F2d 574.—Commerce 61(1).

Hurley; Glasgow v., TexCivApp–Dallas, 333 SW2d 658.— App & E 282, 934(2); Child C 555, 914; Divorce 145.

Hurley; Gourmet, Inc. v., TexCivApp–Dallas, 552 SW2d 509.—Corp 672(6); Courts 12(5), 15; Judgm 112, 124, 126(1).

Hurley v. Hurley, TexApp–Houston (1 Dist), 960 SW2d 287.—App & E 852; Contracts 143(2), 176(2); Divorce 254(1), 261, 286(2); Hus & W 279(1).

Hurley; Hurley v., TexApp–Houston (1 Dist), 960 SW2d 287.—App & E 852; Contracts 143(2), 176(2); Divorce 254(1), 261, 286(2); Hus & W 279(1).

Hurley; Jack Adams Aircraft Sales, Inc. v., TexCivApp–Texarkana, 569 SW2d 599, ref nre.—Judgm 29, 105.1, 139, 143(2), 153(1), 169; Trial 6(1).

Hurley v. Knox, TexCivApp–Fort Worth, 244 SW2d 557, ref nre.—App & E 839(1); Insurance 1372; Interest 39(2.20), 44; Judgm 181(2), 185.3(12).

Hurley v. Lano Intern., Inc., TexCivApp–Texarkana, 569 SW2d 602, ref nre.—Contracts 175(1), 187(1); Fraud Conv 47; Indem 92.

Hurley v. Lederle Laboratories Div. of American Cyan-amid Co., CA5 (Tex), 863 F2d 1173.—Fed Civ Proc 2515; Prod Liab 46.1, 46.2, 46.4; States 18.65.

Hurley v. Lederle Laboratories Div. of American Cyan-amid Co., CA5 (Tex), 851 F2d 1536, opinion superseded 863 F2d 1173.

Hurley v. Lederle Laboratories, Div. of American Cyanamid Co., EDTex, 651 FSupp 993, rev 851 F2d 1536, opinion superseded 863 F2d 1173.—Prod Liab 46.4; States 18.3, 18.9, 18.65.

Hurley v. McMillan, TexCivApp–Galveston, 268 SW2d 229, ref nre.—Compromise 17(2); Evid 20(1), 219(3); Trial 115(2), 127; Witn 198(1), 219(3), 379(4.1).

Hurley v. McMillan, TexCivApp–Galveston, 255 SW2d 308, mandamus overr.—Venue 8.5(3).

Hurley v. Moody Nat. Bank of Galveston, TexApp–Houston (1 Dist), 98 SW3d 307.—Trusts 61(0.5), 112, 172, 373; Wills 439, 491.

Hurley v. National Bank of Commerce, TexCivApp–Dallas, 529 SW2d 788, ref nre.—Evid 417(1), 437, 441(11); Interest 6; Judgm 185.3(5); Usury 88, 142(2).

Hurley; Occidental Life Ins. Co. of North Carolina v., TexCivApp–Amarillo, 513 SW2d 897.—Insurance 2434(1).

Hurley v. Reynolds, TexCivApp–Eastland, 157 SW2d 1018.—App & E 843(2), 912; Evid 43(2), 52, 158(13); Plead 111.9, 111.17, 111.42(8).

Hurley; Richardson v., TexCivApp–Waco, 126 SW2d 1001.—Inj 157.

Hurley v. State, TexCrimApp, 606 SW2d 887.—Crim Law 641.5(2.1), 641.5(5), 641.13(3), 641.13(8), 1131(7).

Hurley v. State, TexCrimApp, 411 SW2d 369.—Crim Law 531(4).

Hurley v. State, TexCrimApp, 292 SW2d 135.—Crim Law 1090.1(1).

Hurley v. State, TexCrimApp, 234 SW2d 1006, 155 Tex-Crim 315.—Arrest 63.2, 63.3, 66(2); Autos 349(10).

Hurley v. State, TexApp–Dallas, 130 SW3d 501.—Crim Law 977(5), 1134(10), 1147; Sent & Pun 545, 546, 548, 630, 631, 636, 2079; Statut 189.

Hurley v. Texas Dept. of Public Safety, TexCivApp–Eastland, 505 SW2d 700.—Autos 144.2(5.1).

Hurley's Estate; Furniture Dynamics, Inc. v., TexCiv-App–Dallas, 560 SW2d 486.—Ex & Ad 225(2), 228(5), 241; Judgm 649.

Hurlock v. Mitchell, TexCivApp–Galveston, 98 SW2d 1005, writ dism.—Can of Inst 59; Plgs 53.

Hurlock; Uvalde Rock Asphalt Co. v., TexComApp, 87 SW2d 1085, 126 Tex 317.—Mun Corp 488(3), 586.

Hurlston v. Bouchard Transp., Co., Inc., SDTex, 970 FSupp 581.—Fed Cts 76.10, 101, 104, 105, 111.

Huron; Marshall v., TexCivApp–Austin, 274 SW2d 572.— App & E 275, 843(4), 1170.7; Princ & A 23(5).

Hurr v. Hildebrand, TexCivApp–Houston, 388 SW2d 284, ref nre.—Adv Poss 57, 109; Bound 25, 33, 37(1); Des & Dist 75.

Hurrelbrink v. State, TexApp–Amarillo, 46 SW3d 350, petition for discretionary review refused.—Crim Law 388.1, 475.6, 480, 1153(1), 1162, 1169.9.

Hurren v. F.D.I.C., WDTex, 167 BR 429. See Hackfeld v. Hurren.

Hurren; Hackfeld v., WDTex, 167 BR 429, aff 961 F2d 213.—Antitrust 141, 145; Atty & C 26; Banks 505; Corp 306; Torts 242, 246.

Hurricane Fence Co.; Funkhouser v., TexCivApp–Hous (1 Dist), 524 SW2d 780, ref nre.—Judgm 633.

Hurricane Rita Evacuation Bus Fire, In re, TexJud-PanMultLit, 216 SW3d 70.—Courts 485, 487(1).

Hurricane Steel Industries Co. v. Maurice Pincoffs Co., TexCivApp–Hous (14 Dist), 464 SW2d 387.—Compromise 23(3), 24.

Hurse v. Caffey, NDTex, 59 FSupp 363.—Hab Corp 258; Mil Jus 1270.1, 1300.1, 1301, 1322.1, 1398.

Hursey v. Bond, Tex, 172 SW2d 305, 141 Tex 337.—Courts 207.4(2), 209(2); Mand 14(3).

Hursey v. Hursey, TexCivApp–Dallas, 165 SW2d 761, dism.—App & E 544(1), 544(3), 660(2), 747(1), 854(2), 854(6); Divorce 6, 184(2), 184(5), 226, 228, 252.1, 253(1), 253(4), 254(1), 286(0.5), 287.

Hursey; Hursey v., TexCivApp–Dallas, 165 SW2d 761, dism.—App & E 544(1), 544(3), 660(2), 747(1), 854(2), 854(6); Divorce 6, 184(2), 184(5), 226, 228, 252.1, 253(1), 253(4), 254(1), 286(0.5), 287.

Hursey v. Hursey, TexCivApp–Dallas, 147 SW2d 968.—Divorce 207, 286(0.5).

Hursey; Hursey v., TexCivApp–Dallas, 147 SW2d 968.—Divorce 207, 286(0.5).

Hursey v. Thompson, Tex, 174 SW2d 317, 141 Tex 519.—Adop 16; App & E 907(3).

Hursey; Thompson v., TexCivApp–Dallas, 167 SW2d 596, rev 174 SW2d 317, 141 Tex 519.—Adop 16; App & E 376; Plead 34(4), 36(1), 349, 376.

Hurst, In re, BkrtcyNDTex, 337 BR 125.—Bankr 3372.1, 3372.8, 3372.17, 3372.36, 3372.39, 3372.42, 3403(6), 3403(7), 3405(14), 3409.

Hurst v. American Racing Equipment, Inc., TexApp–Texarkana, 981 SW2d 458.—Compromise 17(2), 18(1), 24; Contracts 164, 176(2); Indem 72, 75, 76, 95.

Hurst v. A. R. A. Mfg. Co., TexCivApp–Fort Worth, 555 SW2d 141, ref nre.—App & E 768; Courts 122; Judgm 101(1), 101(2), 497(1), 503.

Hurst; Austin Road Co. v., TexCivApp–Beaumont, 124 SW2d 183.—Corp 503(2).

Hurst; Cass v., TexCivApp–San Antonio, 329 SW2d 450.—Brok 46, 57(2); Judgm 181(18).

Hurst; City of Spring Valley v., TexCivApp–Hous (14 Dist), 530 SW2d 599, ref nre.—Zoning 330, 621, 625, 645, 676, 703, 724, 729.

Hurst; City of Waco v., TexCivApp–Waco, 131 SW2d 745, writ dism, correct.—Labor & Emp 2764, 2768.

Hurst; Farnsworth & Chambers Co. v., TexCivApp–Houston, 338 SW2d 743, ref nre.—App & E 927(7), 989; Autos 197(3), 245(28).

Hurst v. Forsythe, TexCivApp–Texarkana, 584 SW2d 314, ref nre.—Labor & Emp 259.

Hurst v. Forsythe, TexCivApp–Beaumont, 529 SW2d 620, ref nre.—Contracts 175(3), 282; Release 27.

Hurst v. Guadalupe County Appraisal Dist., TexApp–San Antonio, 752 SW2d 231.—Const Law 951, 958.

Hurst; Haney Elec. Co. v., TexCivApp–Dallas, 624 SW2d 602, dism.—App & E 209.1, 215(1), 218.2(4), 1056.1(5), 1062.1; Autos 202.1, 226(3), 234, 243(16); Evid 123(8), 588, 591; Neglig 549(9), 549(10); Pretrial Proc 202; Trial 2, 56; Witn 248(1), 397.

Hurst; Haney Elec. Co. v., TexCivApp–Dallas, 608 SW2d 355.—App & E 465(1).

Hurst v. Hughes Tool Co., CA5 (Tex), 634 F2d 895, cert den 102 SCt 123, 454 US 829, 70 LEd2d 105.—Antitrust 414, 418, 432, 433; Fed Civ Proc 2126.1, 2608.1.

Hurst v. Hurst, TexCivApp–Waco, 217 SW2d 676.—Judgm 335(1), 335(3).

Hurst; Hurst v., TexCivApp–Waco, 217 SW2d 676.—Judgm 335(1), 335(3).

Hurst; Kirkpatrick v., Tex, 484 SW2d 587.—Lim of Act 73(3); Time 10(4).

Hurst; Kirkpatrick v., TexCivApp–Texarkana, 472 SW2d 295, writ gr, rev 484 SW2d 587.—Autos 209, 245(81); Hus & W 247, 257, 260; Lim of Act 174(1); Statut 223.1; Time 10(4); Trial 68(1), 350.5(3), 350.6(3).

Hurst; McLennan and Hill Counties Tehuacana Creek Water Control and Imp.Dist. No. 1 v., TexCivApp–Waco, 378 SW2d 946.—App & E 954(1), 1111, 1152; Inj 132, 135, 152, 157, 163(1).

Hurst v. Regis Low Ltd., SDTex, 878 FSupp 981.—Decl Judgm 317, 361.1; Fed Cts 9, 41, 43, 47.1, 51, 54, 65.

Hurst v. Rush, TexCivApp–Beaumont, 514 SW2d 472.—Contracts 278(1), 346(2); Venue 7.5(1), 22(4).

Hurst v. Sears, Roebuck & Co., Tex, 647 SW2d 249, on remand 652 SW2d 563, ref nre.—Antitrust 162, 203, 389(2), 397, 398; App & E 1177(6); Courts 247(1); Trial 350.3(1), 355(1).

Hurst; Sears, Roebuck & Co. v., TexApp–Fort Worth, 652 SW2d 563, ref nre.—App & E 989; Damag 185(1).

Hurst; Sears, Roebuck & Co. v., TexApp–Fort Worth, 635 SW2d 856, writ gr, rev 647 SW2d 249, on remand 652 SW2d 563, ref nre.—Antitrust 147, 203, 363; Courts 106.

Hurst v. S. H. Kress & Co., CA5 (Tex), 489 F2d 168.—Neglig 1247, 1602, 1683, 1717.

Hurst v. State, TexCrimApp, 328 SW2d 447, 168 TexCrim 427.—Crim Law 1086.14; Larc 55.

Hurst v. State, TexCrimApp, 295 SW2d 210, 163 TexCrim 645.—Autos 355(6).

Hurst v. State, TexCrimApp, 210 SW2d 594, 151 TexCrim 615.—Homic 908, 1479, 1483.

Hurst v. Stewart, TexCivApp–San Antonio, 526 SW2d 668, dism.—Venue 15, 17.

Hurst v. Texas Dept. of Assistive and Rehabilitative Services, CA5 (Tex), 482 F3d 809.—Fed Cts 266.1.

Hurst v. Texas Dep't of Assistive & Rehab. Serv., WDTex, 392 FSupp2d 794, aff 482 F3d 809.—Const Law 2450, 4863; Fed Cts 265, 266.1, 267, 269; States 191.2(1); U S 82(2).

Hurst; Travelers Ins. Co. v., TexCivApp–Texarkana, 358 SW2d 883, ref nre.—Abate & R 22; App & E 1047(4), 1048(3), 1048(5), 1048(6), 1050.1(11), 1060.1(1); Damag 185(1); Trial 59(2), 139.1(3), 140(1); Witn 240(2); Work Comp 51.

Hurst v. Travelers Ins. Co., TexCivApp–El Paso, 353 SW2d 60.—App & E 842(9), 901, 933(1), 1026, 1032(1), 1069.1; New Tr 56, 66, 143(5); Work Comp 1930, 1968(1), 1968(8).

Hurst; U.S. v., CA5 (Tex), 460 F2d 1258, cert den 92 SCt 2512, 408 US 931, 33 LEd2d 343.—Crim Law 1023(3), 1132.

Hurst v. Varner, TexCivApp–Beaumont, 142 SW2d 396.—Counties 46.

Hurst v. Webster, TexCivApp–Fort Worth, 252 SW2d 793, ref nre.—App & E 213, 262(1); Tresp to T T 53, 59.

Hurst Associates; Birdville Independent School Dist. v., NDTex, 806 FSupp 122.—B & L Assoc 42(3), 42(6), 48; Evid 265(8), 370(4); Tax 2736.

Hurst Aviation v. Junell, TexApp–Fort Worth, 642 SW2d 856.—App & E 930(1), 932(1), 989, 1004(5); Death 77, 99(2), 99(4); Ex & Ad 420; Judgm 310.

Hurst, City of; Cannon v., TexApp–Fort Worth, 180 SW3d 600.—Judges 49(1).

Hurst, City of; Denbina v., TexApp–Fort Worth, 516 SW2d 460.—Bills & N 129(2); Decl Judgm 322; Judgm 585(4).

Hurst, City of; Ratcliff v., TexCivApp–Fort Worth, 593 SW2d 863, ref nre.—Mun Corp 977.

Hurst, City of; State ex rel. City of Colleyville v., TexCivApp–Fort Worth, 521 SW2d 727, ref nre.—App & E 758.3(2), 761, 1198, 1212(1); Evid 43(1); Judgm 650; Mun Corp 33(8).

Hurst, City of; State ex rel. City of Colleyville v., TexCivApp–Fort Worth, 519 SW2d 698, ref nre.—Const Law 2604; Evid 43(1); Judgm 651, 702, 713(2), 720; Mun Corp 15; Plead 111.9; Quo W 1, 8, 32, 33.

Hurst, City of; State ex rel. Ratcliff v., TexCivApp–Fort Worth, 458 SW2d 696, ref nre.—Mun Corp 29(1), 30, 33(2).

Hurst, City of; Wisenbaker, Fix & Associates v., TexCivApp–Fort Worth, 404 SW2d 958.—Elect of Rem 7(1); Plead 111.12, 111.42(5); Venue 8.5(8).

Hurst Employers Cas. Co., Intervener v. Gulf Oil Corp., CA5 (Tex), 251 F2d 836, reh den 254 F2d 287, cert den 79 SCt 44, 358 US 827, 3 LEd2d 66.—Labor & Emp 3159; Mines 118; Neglig 1011.

Hurst Employers Cas. Co., Interveners v. Gulf Oil Corp., CA5 (Tex), 254 F2d 287.—Fed Cts 274.

Hurst-Euless-Bedford Hosp. Authority; Jatoi v., CA5 (Tex), 819 F2d 545,cert den Harris Methodist H-E-B Bd of Trustees v. Jatoi, 108 SCt 709, 484 US 1010, 98 LEd2d 660.—Civil R 1009.

Hurst-Euless-Bedford Hosp. Authority; Jatoi v., CA5 (Tex), 807 F2d 1214, opinion mod on denial of reh 819

F2d 545, cert den Harris Methodist H-E-B Bd of Trustees v. Jatoi, 108 SCt 709, 484 US 1010, 98 LEd2d 660, cert den 108 SCt 709, 484 US 1010, 98 LEd2d 660.—Civil R 1009, 1041, 1326(7), 1394, 1395(1), 1405, 1417, 1421; Consp 7.5(1), 18, 19; Fed Civ Proc 2285.

Hurst-Euless-Bedford Independent School Dist.; Tarrant County Water Supply Corp. v., TexCivApp–Fort Worth, 391 SW2d 162, ref nre.—Tax 2188, 2311.

Hurst-Euless Independent School Dist.; Radio Bible Hour, Inc. v., TexCivApp–Fort Worth, 341 SW2d 467, ref nre.—Tax 2300, 2355, 2392.

Hurst Eye, Ear, Nose & Throat Hospital and Clinic; Payton v., TexCivApp–Texarkana, 318 SW2d 726, ref nre.—Abate & R 8(2); Alt Disp Res 205; Inj 138.31, 177; Judgm 316, 381; Trial 394(1).

Hurst Orthodontics, PA; Lewis v., WDTex, 292 FSupp2d 908.—Labor & Emp 2403, 2405.

Hurt v. Bays, TexCivApp–Austin, 537 SW2d 139, ref nre.—App & E 934(1); Judgm 184, 185.3(4); Proc 145.

Hurt; Bradford v., CCA5 (Tex), 84 F2d 722.—Courts 508(7); Fed Cts 6, 815; Inj 34.

Hurt; Bradford v., NDTex, 15 FSupp 426, aff 84 F2d 722.—Gaming 75(1); Inj 105(1); Statut 188, 194.

Hurt v. City of Corsicana, TexCivApp–Waco, 350 SW2d 237, writ refused.—Mun Corp 29(2).

Hurt v. Cooper, Tex, 110 SW2d 896, 130 Tex 433, answer to certified question conformed to 113 SW2d 929.—Const Law 48(1), 230.3(3), 2892, 3682, 3687, 3701, 4276; Licens 1, 7(1), 7(3), 15(8), 19(3).

Hurt v. Cooper, TexCivApp–Dallas, 113 SW2d 929.—Const Law 961, 975, 3560, 3682, 3687; Courts 247(5); Evid 5(2); Licens 1, 7(1), 7(3); Statut 64(1), 64(8), 221; Tax 2135, 2286; Trial 136(1).

Hurt v. Del Papa Distributing Co., L.P., SDTex, 425 FSupp2d 853.—Fed Cts 241; Rem of C 11, 13, 79(1).

Hurt; Oak Downs v., Tex, 97 SW2d 673, 128 Tex 218.—App & E 781(1).

Hurt v. Oak Downs, Inc., TexCivApp–Dallas, 85 SW2d 294, appeal dism 97 SW2d 673, 128 Tex 218.—Crim Law 13.1(1); Evid 5(2); Gaming 63(1), 68(0.5), 71, 75(1); Inj 74, 105(2); Statut 184, 194, 206, 215, 223.2(13).

Hurt; Price v., TexApp–Dallas, 711 SW2d 84.—App & E 863; Evid 48; Health 611, 821(5), 906, 908; Judgm 181(33), 185(2), 185(6), 185.3(21).

Hurt v. Read, CCA5 (Tex), 108 F2d 282.—Subrog 14.3, 28, 41(6).

Hurt v. Smith, Tex, 744 SW2d 1.—Int Rev 4821, 4822; Tax 3370; Wills 565(2), 587(1), 728, 750, 753, 755, 756.

Hurt v. Standard Oil Co. of Tex., TexCivApp–El Paso, 444 SW2d 342.—Estop 92(2); Frds St of 44(3), 50(2), 115.1, 142.

Hurt v. State, TexCrimApp, 480 SW2d 747.—Crim Law 489, 899, 1169.9; Witn 274(2).

Hurt; Warner v., TexApp–Houston (14 Dist), 834 SW2d 404.—App & E 843(2), 1051(1); Evid 538, 555.10, 574; Health 681.

Hurtado v. State, TexApp–Houston (1 Dist), 881 SW2d 738, petition for discretionary review refused.—Arrest 63.4(4), 63.5(4), 63.5(6), 63.5(8), 63.5(9); Controlled Subs 26, 27, 28, 80; Crim Law 394.6(5), 1144.12, 1153(1), 1158(4), 1159.2(7), 1159.5.

Hurtado v. State, TexApp–Houston (14 Dist), 722 SW2d 184, petition for discretionary review refused.—Arrest 63.4(16); Controlled Subs 81, 93, 137; Crim Law 394.4(9), 511.1(2.1), 511.1(8), 730(7), 814(15), 1169.11, 1170.5(1); Searches 23, 28; Witn 307, 308.

Hurtado v. Texas Emp. Ins. Ass'n, Tex, 574 SW2d 536.—Trial 85; Work Comp 1396, 1696, 1703, 1968(3).

Hurtado v. Texas Emp. Ins. Ass'n, TexCivApp–San Antonio, 563 SW2d 360, writ gr, rev 574 SW2d 536.—Trial 82; Work Comp 1593.

Hurtado v. U.S., USTex, 93 SCt 1157, 410 US 578, 35 LEd2d 508, reh den 93 SCt 2151, 411 US 978, 36 LEd2d

701.—Const Law 1102, 2500, 3885; Em Dom 2(1), 2(1.1); Fed Civ Proc 2481; Witn 16, 25, 27.

Hurtado; U.S. v., CA5 (Tex), 905 F2d 74, on remand 909 F2d 121.—Searches 197.

Hurtado; U.S. v., CA5 (Tex), 899 F2d 371, reh gr, on reh 905 F2d 74, on remand 909 F2d 121.—Courts 90(2); Crim Law 412.2(2), 1158(2), 1181.5(7); Fines 1.5; Searches 180, 198; Sent & Pun 764, 1838, 1936, 1946.

Hurtado v. U.S., CA5 (Tex), 452 F2d 951, cert gr 93 SCt 158, 409 US 841, 34 LEd2d 80, vac 93 SCt 1157, 410 US 578, 35 LEd2d 508, reh den 93 SCt 2151, 411 US 978, 36 LEd2d 701.—Const Law 1102, 4552; Em Dom 2(1.1); Fed Cts 743; Witn 27.

Hurwitz; F.D.I.C. v., SDTex, 384 FSupp2d 1039.—Banks 505, 508; B & L Assoc 42(6), 42(16), 48; Evid 78; Fed Civ Proc 1278, 1593, 1600(3), 1600(5), 1636.1, 2727, 2757, 2758, 2768, 2769, 2771(3), 2783(1), 2791, 2795, 2810, 2812, 2814, 2816, 2830; Jury 14(1); Lim of Act 55(2), 58(1); U S 35, 40, 78(5.1), 85, 147(6), 147(8.1), 147(11.1); Witn 184(1), 199(2), 200, 204(2), 216(1), 217, 219(3), 222.

Hurwitz v. State, TexCrimApp, 700 SW2d 919, cert den 106 SCt 884, 474 US 1102, 88 LEd2d 919.—Crim Law 273.1(4).

Hurwitz v. State, TexApp–Austin, 673 SW2d 347, petition for discretionary review gr, aff 700 SW2d 919, cert den 106 SCt 884, 474 US 1102, 88 LEd2d 919.—Controlled Subs 100(2), 134; Crim Law 273.1(4), 577.7, 577.8(1), 577.16(8); Searches 27.

Hurwitz v. U.S., SDTex, 208 FSupp 594, aff 320 F2d 911, cert den 84 SCt 791, 376 US 936, 11 LEd2d 658.—Const Law 2525; Int Rev 4168.10, 4171; Statut 51, 223.1, 263.

Hurwitz-Nordlicht Joint Venture; Milberg Factors, Inc. v., TexApp–Austin, 676 SW2d 613, ref nre.—Attach 65; Joint Adv 1.1, 1.2(1), 1.2(3), 1.2(4), 1.13, 1.15, 4(1); Lis Pen 15; Partners 1, 17, 181; Records 6.

Hurwitz-Nordlicht Joint Venture; Shefelman & Nix, Architects v., TexApp–Austin, 676 SW2d 613. See Milberg Factors, Inc. v. Hurwitz-Nordlicht Joint Venture.

Hury v. Magee, TexCivApp–Hous (14 Dist), 575 SW2d 345, dism.—Courts 175; Infants 18, 196.

Hury v. Morgan, TexCivApp–Hous (1 Dist), 583 SW2d 443.—Courts 472.2.

Hury v. Preas, TexApp–Tyler, 673 SW2d 949, ref nre.—Ex & Ad 22(1); Mtg 335.

Hury; Tarter v., CA5 (Tex), 646 F2d 1010.—Civil R 1319, 1376(1), 1376(8), 1376(9), 1395(5); Clerks of C 72; Courts 490.

Husain, In re, BkrtcySDTex, 168 BR 591.—Bankr 2062; Courts 509; Judgm 335(1), 335(2), 335(3), 828.21(2).

Husain v. Khatib, Tex, 964 SW2d 918.—Lim of Act 55(3), 95(12), 105(1).

Husain; Khatib v., TexApp–Fort Worth, 949 SW2d 805, reh overr, and review gr, rev 964 SW2d 918.—Const Law 328, 2314, 2315; Health 192, 295, 623, 811; Judgm 181(7); Lim of Act 1, 4(2), 55(3), 95(12), 105(1).

Husain v. State, TexApp–San Antonio, 161 SW3d 642, petition for discretionary review refused.—Crim Law 865(1.5), 865(2), 867; Double J 3, 59, 86, 98, 99; Infants 13; Judgm 751.

Husain; U.S. v., CA5 (Tex), 117 FedAppx 353.—Crim Law 641.13(6).

Husband v. Bryan, CA5 (Tex), 946 F2d 27.—Civil R 1376(6), 1395(6); Fed Cts 756.1; Searches 27.

Husband v. Pierce, TexApp–Tyler, 800 SW2d 661.—Hab Corp 532(1); Hus & W 23; Mand 4(4); Marriage 3, 5, 21, 25(1); Parent & C 16.

Husband v. State, TexCrimApp, 122 SW2d 304, 135 TexCrim 618.—Crim Law 1182.

Husband; U.S. v., EDTex, 771 FSupp 176, aff 959 F2d 967.—Crim Law 273.1(2), 274(1).

Husband; U.S. v., EDTex, 748 FSupp 476.—Crim Law 273.1(2); Judges 49(2).

Husband; U.S. v., EDTex, 730 FSupp 756.—Bail 49(5).

Huse v. Fidelity Interstate Life Ins. Co., TexCivApp–Eastland, 605 SW2d 351.—Insurance 2586.

Huse v. State, TexCrimApp, 376 SW2d 360.—Crim Law 996(1).

Huse v. State, TexCrimApp, 109 SW2d 184, 133 TexCrim 135.—Autos 355(6).

Huse v. State, TexApp–Eastland, 180 SW3d 847, reh overr, and petition for discretionary review refused.—Crim Law 1144.13(2.1), 1159.2(7); False Pret 9, 26, 49(5).

Huseman v. State, TexApp–Amarillo, 96 SW3d 368, reh overr, and petition for discretionary review refused.—Crim Law 641.13(6), 641.13(7), 720(2), 720(6), 723(3), 726, 728(2), 728(5), 957(1), 957(2), 957(3), 957(5), 1037.1(2), 1039, 1045, 1171.1(2.1); Double J 1, 23, 100.1, 104, 109, 112.1.

Huseman v. State, TexApp–Amarillo, 17 SW3d 704, petition for discretionary review refused.—Crim Law 268, 633(2), 867.

Hush Puppy of Longview, Inc. v. Cargill Interests, Ltd., TexApp–Texarkana, 843 SW2d 120, reh den.—App & E 837(9), 863, 1153; Land & Ten 86(1), 93.

Huskey v. State, TexCrimApp, 266 SW2d 168, 159 TexCrim 557.—Crim Law 566; Int Liq 236(11).

Huskey v. State, TexCrimApp, 255 SW2d 204, 158 TexCrim 272.—Int Liq 236(11).

Huskey v. State, TexCrimApp, 248 SW2d 131, 157 TexCrim 247.—Crim Law 995(1), 995(2), 1092.9, 1099.9, 1104(7).

Huskey v. State, TexCrimApp, 246 SW2d 637, 156 TexCrim 626.—Int Liq 236(7).

Huskey v. State, TexCrimApp, 246 SW2d 636, 156 TexCrim 625.—Crim Law 1030(1), 1091(8), 1092.11(3), 1092.14.

Huskey v. State, TexCrimApp, 245 SW2d 266, 156 TexCrim 604.—Searches 164.

Huskey v. State, TexCrimApp, 237 SW2d 980.—App & E 635(2).

Huskey; U.S. v., CA5 (Tex), 137 F3d 283.—Crim Law 1139, 1141(1), 1158(1), 1177; Sent & Pun 797, 964, 973, 979.

Huskins, Ex parte, TexCrimApp, 176 SW3d 818.—Crim Law 273.1(2), 274(3.1); Sent & Pun 240, 370, 1139, 2094.

Husky; Dilworth v., TexCivApp–San Antonio, 149 SW2d 269.—App & E 1011.1(12); Bills & N 33.

Husky Oil Co.; Stine v., CA5 (Tex), 976 F2d 254. See Stine v. Marathon Oil Co.

Huss; Morriss-Buick Co. v., TexCivApp–Dallas, 84 SW2d 264, rev 113 SW2d 891, 131 Tex 102.—App & E 1068(4); Corp 498; Fraud 59(3).

Hussey v. Ray, TexCivApp–Tyler, 462 SW2d 45.—Covenants 51(1), 103(2), 134.

Hussey v. State, TexCrimApp, 590 SW2d 505.—Crim Law 130, 134(3).

Hussey v. State Farm Lloyds Ins. Co., EDTex, 216 FRD 591.—Fed Civ Proc 1594, 1625; Insurance 3382, 3427; Witn 16.

Hussong v. Schwan's Sales Enterprises, Inc., TexApp–Houston (1 Dist), 896 SW2d 320.—App & E 169, 173(2); Contracts 143(2), 152, 156, 176(1), 326; Judgm 181(19), 183, 186; Labor & Emp 40(2), 40(3), 41(2), 55, 837, 914; Torts 222.

Hustace v. Black, TexCivApp–El Paso, 191 SW2d 82, writ refused wom.—App & E 1032(1); Child C 35, 276, 452, 510; Child S 116; Hab Corp 731, 799.

Husted; Eaton v., Tex, 172 SW2d 493, 141 Tex 349.—App & E 931(1); Trial 352.4(3); Trusts 10, 43(1), 44(1), 44(2), 352, 356(1), 357(1), 371(8), 372(3); Wills 91.

Husted; Eaton v., TexCivApp–Texarkana, 163 SW2d 439, aff 172 SW2d 493, 141 Tex 349.—App & E 760(1), 882(1); Judgm 17(3); Lim of Act 166, 197(2); Trial 351.5(1); Trusts 10, 44(2), 352, 372(3); Wills 91.

Husted; Federal Underwriters Exchange v., TexCivApp–Eastland, 94 SW2d 540, writ dism.—App & E 773(4); Work Comp 831.

Husting v. State, TexApp–San Antonio, 790 SW2d 121.—Crim Law 507(1), 507(3), 554, 556; Witn 345(1).

Hustler Magazine, Inc.; Faloona by Fredrickson v., CA5 (Tex), 799 F2d 1000, reh den 802 F2d 455, cert den 107 SCt 1295, 479 US 1088, 94 LEd2d 151.—Compromise 54; Obscen 5.2; Parent & C 8; Release 1, 32; Torts 327, 351, 354.

Hustler Magazine, Inc.; Faloona by Fredrickson v., NDTex, 607 FSupp 1341, aff 799 F2d 1000, reh den 802 F2d 455, cert den 107 SCt 1295, 479 US 1088, 94 LEd2d 151.—Const Law 90.1(5), 2169; Infants 14; Obscen 5.2; Parent & C 8; Release 1; Torts 327, 350, 354, 357, 360, 390(1), 390(2).

Hustler Magazine, Inc.; Herceg v., CA5 (Tex), 814 F2d 1017, 94 ALR Fed 1, cert den 108 SCt 1219, 485 US 959, 99 LEd2d 420.—Const Law 90.1(1), 1506, 1545, 2070; Fed Cts 755.

Hustler Magazine, Inc.; Herceg v., SDTex, 583 FSupp 1566.—Fed Civ Proc 630, 654.1, 1144; Torts 424, 447.

Hustler Magazine, Inc.; Herceg v., SDTex, 565 FSupp 802.—Neglig 1518; Torts 447.

Hustler Magazine, Inc.; Wood v., CA5 (Tex), 736 F2d 1084, reh den 744 F2d 94, cert den 105 SCt 783, 469 US 1107, 83 LEd2d 777.—Damag 130.1; Fed Cts 409.1; Torts 327, 330, 335, 354, 361, 413.

Huston; City of Garland v., TexApp–Dallas, 702 SW2d 697, ref nre.—Work Comp 1058, 2240, 2247.

Huston; City of Perryton v., TexCivApp–Eastland, 454 SW2d 435, ref nre.—Em Dom 130, 296, 298, 300, 307(3); Mun Corp 835; Trial 350.3(6).

Huston v. Cole, TexComApp, 162 SW2d 404, 139 Tex 150.—Wills 215, 229, 286, 384.

Huston v. Colonial Trust Co., TexCivApp–El Paso, 266 SW2d 231, ref nre.—Hus & W 254, 255, 259; Wills 788, 800.

Huston; Engine Mfrs Ass'n v., WDTex, 190 FSupp2d 922, opinion vac by court of appeals, and dism as moot.—Assoc 20(1); Environ Law 251, 652; Fed Civ Proc 103.2, 103.3; States 18.31.

Huston v. F.D.I.C., Tex, 800 SW2d 845.—App & E 77(1), 80(6); Banks 505; Courts 100(1), 202(5); Receivers 1.

Huston; Federal Deposit Ins. Corp. v., TexApp–Eastland, 757 SW2d 912, writ gr, rev Huston v. FDIC, 800 SW2d 845.—App & E 150(1); Banks 80(4), 505.

Huston v. F.D.I.C., TexApp–Eastland, 663 SW2d 126, ref nre.—App & E 866(1), 927(2), 1050.1(3.1); Banks 63.5, 76, 508; Courts 1, 489(1); Decl Judgm 255; Inj 22; Mand 143(1); Pretrial Proc 25, 679.

Huston; Garland Power and Light v., TexApp–Dallas, 702 SW2d 697. See City of Garland v. Huston.

Huston; Mid-Continent Life Ins. Co. v., TexCivApp–Hous (1 Dist), 481 SW2d 943, writ dism woj.—App & E 912, 989; Plead 111.16.

Huston; Monk v., CA5 (Tex), 340 F3d 279.—Const Law 978, 3865, 3879; Fed Cts 12.1, 776.

Huston v. Throckmorton County, TexCivApp–Eastland, 215 SW2d 387.—App & E 954(1), 1024.2; Dedi 44; Ease 61(6).

Hutch v. State, TexCrimApp, 922 SW2d 166.—Crim Law 713, 736(1), 770(1), 772(1), 777, 790, 791, 810, 813, 814(1), 1038.1(2), 1038.1(3.1), 1144.15, 1172.1(1), 1172.3, 1172.4; Jury 21.

Hutch v. State, TexApp–Houston (1 Dist), 881 SW2d 92, petition for discretionary review gr, rev 922 SW2d 166.—Autos 349(17); Crim Law 641.13(2.1), 641.13(6), 1030(1), 1038.1(1), 1038.1(5), 1186.1.

Hutchason v. Policemen's Burial Fund Ass'n, TexCivApp–Galveston, 166 SW2d 202.—Mun Corp 187(1), 187(6).

Hutchens; Jenkins v., TexCivApp–Eastland, 287 SW2d 295, ref nre.—App & E 302(1), 1177(6); Home 140, 141(1); Hus & W 256, 273(1), 274(1).

Hutchens v. State, TexApp–Houston (14 Dist), 675 SW2d 522, petition for discretionary review refused.—Crim Law 641.13(1), 641.13(5), 641.13(7).

Hutcherson; Cloudt v., TexCivApp–El Paso, 175 SW2d 643, writ refused wom.—App & E 1069.1; Evid 474(4); New Tr 44(1), 140(3); Trial 29(1), 304; Wills 158, 164(6), 320, 323, 324(2), 324(3), 360, 384.

Hutcherson v. Cronin, TexCivApp–Tyler, 426 SW2d 638. —Contracts 10(1); Land & Ten 92(1); Spec Perf 57; Ven & Pur 18(3).

Hutcherson v. Hinson, TexCivApp–Tyler, 557 SW2d 814. —App & E 302(1), 758.3(3).

Hutcherson v. Hinson, TexCivApp–Tyler, 543 SW2d 719, ref nre.—App & E 564(3), 624.

Hutcherson v. Hutcherson, TexCivApp–Galveston, 135 SW2d 757, writ refused.—Ex & Ad 7, 15.

Hutcherson; Hutcherson v., TexCivApp–Galveston, 135 SW2d 757, writ refused.—Ex & Ad 7, 15.

Hutcherson v. Lawrence, TexCivApp–Tyler, 673 SW2d 947. —Costs 208; Judgm 273(3), 306, 326.

Hutcherson; Lawson v., TexCivApp–Amarillo, 138 SW2d 131, writ dism, correct.—Labor & Emp 2885, 2961, 2963, 2965, 3003; Trial 142, 178.

Hutcherson v. M & G Land Development Corp., Tex-CivApp–San Antonio, 590 SW2d 520.—App & E 1170.7; Evid 581.

Hutcherson; Service Refining Co. v., TexCivApp–Waco, 179 SW2d 772, writ refused wom.—App & E 216(2), 1056.1(7), 1060.1(1); Death 60; Mun Corp 808(1), 821(17), 821(19), 821(20.1); Neglig 1602, 1717; Trial 219, 350.5(2), 365.2.

Hutcheson; Athari v., Tex, 801 SW2d 896.—Bills & N 129(2).

Hutcheson; Burke v., TexCivApp–Eastland, 537 SW2d 312, ref nre.—Counties 47; Decl Judgm 257; Mand 74(2), 168(4).

Hutcheson; Czikora v., TexCivApp–Beaumont, 443 SW2d 871, writ dism.—Autos 242(6), 244(11), 244(35).

Hutcheson; Kaiser v., TexCivApp–El Paso, 101 SW2d 591.—App & E 773(2).

Hutcheson; Kaiser v., TexCivApp–Galveston, 112 SW2d 1058, dism.—App & E 173(2), 204(1), 241; Evid 383(7); Mtg 342; Pretrial Proc 715, 724; Princ & A 100(3).

Hutcheson; McLelland v., TexCivApp–El Paso, 333 SW2d 601, writ dism.—Plead 110.

Hutcheson v. Reserve Life Ins. Co., TexCivApp–Fort Worth, 237 SW2d 723.—Evid 317(2); Insurance 2475, 2533, 3089.

Hutcheson; Reserve Petroleum Co. v., TexCivApp–Amarillo, 254 SW2d 802, ref nre.—Ack 5; Deeds 17(1); Evid 317(15); Liens 12; Mines 54.5; Mtg 173, 174; Ven & Pur 231(3), 231(15), 231(16), 233, 237, 244.

Hutcheson v. Se'Christ's Estate, TexCivApp–Amarillo, 459 SW2d 495, writ refused.—Action 50(4.1); Autos 181(2), 242(1); Insurance 3549(3); Witn 139(7), 155.

Hutcheson v. State, TexCrimApp, 162 SW2d 411, 144 TexCrim 266.—Crim Law 1070.

Hutcheson v. State, TexApp–Amarillo, 899 SW2d 39, petition for discretionary review refused.—Crim Law 494, 770(1), 772(6), 814(8), 814(21), 1038.2, 1044.2(1), 1173.2(3); Homic 1174, 1400.

Hutcheson v. State, TexApp–Eastland, 980 SW2d 237, petition for discretionary review refused.—Perj 5, 33(8), 36.

Hutcheson v. U.S., EDTex, 900 FSupp 49.—Garn 18; U S 125(9).

Hutcheson-Ingram Development Co.; Woods-Tucker Leasing Corp. of Georgia v., CA5 (Tex), 642 F2d 744. —Action 17; Fed Cts 433, 757; Usury 2(1).

Hutcheson-Ingram Development Co.; Woods-Tucker Leasing Corp. of Georgia v., CA5 (Tex), 626 F2d 401, opinion withdrawn 642 F2d 744.

Hutchings v. Anderson, TexCivApp–Dallas, 452 SW2d 10. —Labor & Emp 3132; Land & Ten 166(1), 169(4), 169(11); Neglig 440(3); Waters 171(2).

Hutchings v. Bates, Tex, 406 SW2d 419.—Child S 44, 379, 398, 446.

Hutchings v. Bates, TexCivApp–Corpus Christi, 393 SW2d 338, writ gr, aff 406 SW2d 419.—Abate & R 53; Child S 24, 58, 224, 379, 382; Divorce 255; Evid 314(1), 450(5), 461(1); Ex & Ad 202.4, 219.7(1), 219.7(2); Hus & W 278(1), 281; Judgm 181(19); Wills 827; Witn 158.

Hutchings v. Bayer, TexCivApp–Dallas, 297 SW2d 375, ref nre.—App & E 758.1; Lim of Act 123, 148(4), 150(4), 151(4), 195(6), 199(3).

Hutchings v. Biery, TexApp–San Antonio, 723 SW2d 347. —Child C 736, 745; Const Law 3965(1); Mand 32; Prohib 1.

Hutchings v. Chevron U.S.A., Inc., TexApp–El Paso, 862 SW2d 752, reh den and writ den.—Acct 6; App & E 863, 930(3), 970(2), 989, 994(2), 999(1), 1001(1), 1002, 1003(3), 1003(7); Contracts 147(1), 147(3), 176(1); Evid 546, 570; Judgm 185(2); Mines 78.1(1), 78.1(2), 78.1(8), 79.1(1), 79.3, 79.7; Trial 43.

Hutchings v. C I R, CCA5 (Tex), 111 F2d 229, cert gr Helvering v. Hutchings, 61 SCt 73, 311 US 638, 85 LEd 406, aff 61 SCt 653, 312 US 393, 85 LEd 909.—Int Rev 4203.20.

Hutchings; Continental Supply Co. v., TexCivApp–Dallas, 267 SW2d 914, writ refused.—Lim of Act 5(1), 5(2), 89.

Hutchings; Edsall v., TexCivApp–Eastland, 143 SW2d 700, writ refused.—App & E 843(1), 910; Courts 475(2); Ex & Ad 7, 117; Wills 718.

Hutchings v. Estelle, CA5 (Tex), 564 F2d 713.—Double J 144.

Hutchings; Helvering v., USTex, 61 SCt 653, 312 US 393, 85 LEd 909.—Statut 188.

Hutchings v. Republic Supply Co., TexCivApp–Galveston, 295 SW2d 449, ref nre.—App & E 1008.1(10); Lim of Act 89, 119(6), 197(1); Proc 45.

Hutchings v. Slemons, Tex, 174 SW2d 487, 141 Tex 448, 148 ALR 1320.—Brok 1, 40, 53, 54; Const Law 189, 191, 2754; Contracts 1, 10(1); Frds St of 119(1); Statut 263.

Hutchings; Slemons v., TexCivApp–Amarillo, 169 SW2d 226, rev 174 SW2d 487, 141 Tex 448, 148 ALR 1320.— Brok 1; Const Law 2632, 2747.

Hutchings v. State, TexCrimApp, 466 SW2d 584, cert den 92 SCt 971, 405 US 935, 30 LEd2d 810.—Larc 65, 79.

Hutchings v. State, TexCrimApp, 345 SW2d 407, 171 TexCrim 104.—Bail 70, 77(2), 79(2).

Hutchings; Trinity River Authority v., TexCivApp–Beaumont, 437 SW2d 383.—App & E 989, 1015(5); Em Dom 262(1); Evid 142(1).

Hutchings v. U.S. Industries, Inc., CA5 (Tex), 428 F2d 303.—Alt Disp Res 111; Civil R 1501, 1504, 1505(6), 1511, 1515, 1522, 1529, 1560; Courts 489(1); Fed Civ Proc 184.10; Judgm 547; Labor & Emp 1580, 1593, 1599, 1623(1); Statut 181(1).

Hutchings v. U.S. Industries, Inc., EDTex, 309 FSupp 691, rev 428 F2d 303.—Civil R 1505(7), 1511.

Hutchings-Sealy Nat. Bank of Galveston v. C I R, CCA5 (Tex), 141 F2d 422.—Int Rev 4206.20, 4645, 4686, 4756.

Hutchins, In re Estate of, TexApp–Corpus Christi, 829 SW2d 295, reh overr, writ den with per curiam opinion Triestman v. Kilgore, 838 SW2d 547.—App & E 5, 931(1), 1010.1(2); Wills 52(1), 55(1), 108, 294, 309, 356, 365, 384.

Hutchins; Bailey v., TexApp–Amarillo, 140 SW3d 448, review den.—Health 804; Plead 333.

Hutchins; Bass v., CA5 (Tex), 417 F2d 692.—Bankr 2082, 2083, 2087, 3066(6), 3784.

Hutchins v. Birdsong, TexCivApp–Texarkana, 258 SW2d 218, ref nre.—Can of Inst 35(1); Lim of Act 60(6), 96(2), 197(2); Princ & A 23(5); Ref of Inst 33.

Hutchins; City of Dallas v., TexCivApp–Amarillo, 226 SW2d 155, ref nre.—App & E 901, 933(4); Damag 104, 132(6.1); Evid 18; Mun Corp 819(3); New Tr 140(3), 143(5), 157; Trial 350.3(5), 350.6(2), 352.6, 352.10.

Hutchins; Fidelity Union Ins. Co. v., Tex, 133 SW2d 105, 134 Tex 268, reh den 135 SW2d 695, 134 Tex 268.—Hus & W 276(1), 276(4), 276(7), 276(9); Trusts 179, 233.

Hutchins; Fidelity Union Ins. Co. v., TexCivApp–Eastland, 111 SW2d 292, rev 133 SW2d 105, 134 Tex 268, reh den 135 SW2d 695, 134 Tex 268.—App & E 1008.1(8.1); Hus & W 276(1), 276(7), 276(9).

Hutchins v. Grace Tabernacle United Pentecostal Church, TexApp–Houston (1 Dist), 804 SW2d 598.—Assoc 1, 15(3), 16, 19, 20(1); Parties 35.79.

Hutchins v. Humble Oil & Refining Co., TexCivApp–Galveston, 161 SW2d 571, writ refused wom.—Evid 506, 545, 546, 553(1); Mines 73.1(1), 78.1(11), 78.6, 78.7(4); Trial 352.4(2).

Hutchins; Poe v., TexApp–Dallas, 737 SW2d 574, ref nre.—Antitrust 297, 369, 390; App & E 171(1), 930(3), 959(3); Bailm 21, 31(3); Corp 307, 314(2), 316(1), 320(11); Fraud 58(1); Plead 236(1), 236(4), 238(3); Sales 441(3).

Hutchins v. Seifert, TexCivApp–Hous (14 Dist), 460 SW2d 955, ref nre.—App & E 891; Evid 318(1), 366(5); Ex & Ad 15; Hus & W 276(8); Trial 105(4).

Hutchins; Smith v., TexCivApp–El Paso, 129 SW2d 1200, writ dism, correct.—Ref of Inst 45(4.1), 45(6).

Hutchins v. State, TexCrimApp, 650 SW2d 412.—Crim Law 374, 429(2), 1130(2).

Hutchins v. State, TexCrimApp, 590 SW2d 710.—Rob 27(6).

Hutchins v. State, TexCrimApp, 426 SW2d 235.—Crim Law 260.11(2); Ind & Inf 71.4(7), 110(2); Int Liq 213, 236(9), 249.

Hutchins v. State, TexCrimApp, 360 SW2d 534, 172 TexCrim 525.—Crim Law 351(2), 351(3), 737(1), 742(1), 1169.2(2); Rob 24.15(2); Witn 406.

Hutchins v. State, TexCrimApp, 321 SW2d 880, 167 TexCrim 595.—Crim Law 538(3); Ind & Inf 191(5); Larc 55.

Hutchins v. State, TexCrimApp, 155 SW2d 608, 142 TexCrim 565.—Crim Law 1097(4), 1097(5).

Hutchins v. State, TexApp–Austin, 992 SW2d 629, petition for discretionary review refused, untimely filed.—Double J 134, 148; Infants 20.

Hutchins v. State, TexApp–Austin, 887 SW2d 207, petition for discretionary review refused.—Crim Law 1026.10(2.1), 1026.10(4), 1081(2).

Hutchins v. Texas Rehabilitation Commission, TexCivApp–Austin, 544 SW2d 802.—Records 52, 58.

Hutchins; U.S. v., CA5 (Tex), 818 F2d 322, cert den 108 SCt 772, 484 US 1041, 98 LEd2d 859.—Consp 47(12); Controlled Subs 8, 81; Crim Law 371(1), 406(6), 577.14, 1181.5(8); Sent & Pun 115(3), 559(3).

Hutchins Bros.; Dupree v., CA5 (Tex), 521 F2d 236.—Civil R 1103, 1424, 1544; Lim of Act 55(4), 105(2).

Hutchinson v. City of Dallas, TexCivApp–Dallas, 290 SW2d 253.—Judgm 185.1(4), 186; Tax 2647, 2699(7), 2722, 2723, 2729.

Hutchinson; City of Lamesa v., TexCivApp–Eastland, 336 SW2d 861, ref nre.—App & E 181, 221, 293, 295, 758.1; Autos 187(2); Death 57; Labor & Emp 2881, 2918; Mun Corp 724.

Hutchinson; Crosbyton-South Plains Ry. Co. v., TexCivApp–Amarillo, 204 SW2d 643, ref nre.—Bound 3(3), 3(6), 3(8); Deeds 111.

Hutchinson; Employers Cas. Co. v., TexApp–Austin, 814 SW2d 539.—App & E 930(3), 989, 1001(1), 1003(6); Work Comp 661, 1576, 1728.

Hutchinson v. Hoechst Celanese Corp., BkrtcyEDTex, 173 BR 1000. See U.S. Brass Corp., In re.

Hutchinson; Holton v., TexCivApp–Fort Worth, 90 SW2d 1103.—Evid 222(1), 222(2), 265(18), 474(8); Plead 111.4, 111.9.

Hutchinson; Jones v., TexCivApp–Galveston, 208 SW2d 579.—App & E 1170.1; Evid 589; Marriage 50(1).

Hutchinson; Marshall v., TexCivApp–Amarillo, 358 SW2d 675.—Lim of Act 96(2).

Hutchinson v. Millers Flying Service, Inc., TexCivApp–Amarillo, 411 SW2d 806.—Fraud 50; Plead 111.21, 111.42(10).

Hutchinson v. Montemayor, TexApp–San Antonio, 144 SW3d 614.—Health 804, 822(2).

Hutchinson v. State, TexCrimApp, 86 SW3d 636, habeas corpus dism by 2006 WL 1408347.—Crim Law 1110(1), 1128(2), 1132; Jury 33(5.15).

Hutchinson v. State, TexCrimApp, 509 SW2d 598.—Crim Law 337, 394.5(2), 673(2); Searches 164, 197, 199.

Hutchinson v. State, TexCrimApp, 481 SW2d 881.—Burg 29, 41(1); Crim Law 1181.5(9); Sent & Pun 1371, 1379(2), 1381(4), 1400.

Hutchinson v. State, TexApp–Houston (1 Dist), 663 SW2d 610, petition for discretionary review refused.—Crim Law 641.10(2), 641.13(1), 641.13(6).

Hutchinson v. State, TexApp–Texarkana, 42 SW3d 336, petition for discretionary review gr, aff 86 SW3d 636, habeas corpus dism 2006 WL 1408347.—Burg 41(4); Crim Law 1134(2), 1134(3), 1144.13(2.1), 1158(1), 1158(3), 1159.2(2), 1159.2(7), 1181.5(3.1); Jury 33(5.15).

Hutchinson v. State, TexApp–Waco, 642 SW2d 537.—Crim Law 444.

Hutchinson v. State, TexApp–Houston (14 Dist), 754 SW2d 746.—Crim Law 1077.2(3).

Hutchinson v. Texas Aluminum Co., TexCivApp–Dallas, 330 SW2d 895, ref nre.—App & E 1177(7); Damag 9, 208(1); Estop 119; Sales 418(1), 420; Trial 180, 350.4(2), 388(2), 405(1).

Hutchinson v. U.S., CA5 (Tex), 828 F2d 278. See Moorhead v. Mitsubishi Aircraft Intern., Inc.

Hutchinson v. U.S., EDTex, 639 FSupp 385. See Moorhead v. Mitsubishi Aircraft Intern., Inc.

Hutchinson v. U.S., NDTex, 962 FSupp 965.—Fed Civ Proc 2514, 2546, 2552; Int Rev 5205, 5219.25.

Hutchinson; U.S. v., NDTex, 962 FSupp 965. See Hutchinson v. U.S.

Hutchinson; U.S. Fire Ins. Co. v., TexCivApp–Texarkana, 421 SW2d 706, ref nre.—Evid 314(2), 472(1); Work Comp 1062.

Hutchinson; Wells v., EDTex, 499 FSupp 174.—Agric 2, 3.1; Civil R 1106, 1107, 1136, 1242, 1335, 1340, 1349, 1359, 1376(2), 1376(4), 1376(10), 1379, 1383, 1390, 1448, 1455, 1471, 1478, 1476, 1502, 1505(2), 1513, 1516, 1517, 1523, 1527, 1529, 1530, 1542, 1544, 1553, 1561, 1563, 1573, 1574, 1588, 1590, 1594, 1595; Counties 52; Fed Civ Proc 841; Fed Cts 15, 265, 269, 270, 272; Mun Corp 723; Offic 114.

Hutchinson v. Wood, Tex, 657 SW2d 782.—Abate & R 32.

Hutchinson; Wood v., TexApp–Fort Worth, 644 SW2d 900, aff in part, rev in part 657 SW2d 782.—Judgm 185.3(21); Pretrial Proc 649, 690.

Hutchinson County v. Carson County, TexCivApp–Amarillo, 83 SW2d 699, writ dism.—Counties 8.

Hutchinson County; C. M. Jeffries Trucking Co. v., TexCivApp–Amarillo, 266 SW2d 391.—Plead 111.17, 111.42(8).

Hutchinson County; Fesal v., TexCivApp–Amarillo, 443 SW2d 937, ref nre.—Counties 144.

Hutchinson County; Fraley v., TexCivApp–Amarillo, 278 SW2d 462.—App & E 20; Em Dom 172.

Hutchinson County; Jones v., TexCivApp–Amarillo, 615 SW2d 927.—App & E 1012.1(3); Courts 89, 91(1);

HUTCHINSON

59 Tex D 2d—802

See Guidelines for Arrangement at the beginning of this Volume

Judgm 185(6), 870(2); Tax 2160, 2523, 2699(7), 2728, 3216; Trial 382.

Hutchinson County Appraisal Review Bd.; Graham v., TexApp–Amarillo, 776 SW2d 592, writ den.—Const Law 4137; Tax 2641, 2693, 2703.

Hutchison, In re, BkrtcySDTex, 187 BR 533.—Atty & C 64; Bankr 2131, 2324, 3361, 3383; Const Law 3881, 4478.

Hutchison; Ambrose & Co. v., TexCivApp–Fort Worth, 356 SW2d 215.—App & E 1010.1(7), 1011.1(4); Mech Liens 24, 80; Trial 382.

Hutchison v. Bristol Court Properties, Ltd., TexCivApp–Fort Worth, 508 SW2d 486.—App & E 920(3), 931(3), 934(2), 989; Inj 135, 147; Mtg 338.

Hutchison v. Brookshire Bros., Inc., EDTex, 225 FSupp2d 719, appeal dism 71 FedAppx 441.—Arrest 68(4); Assault 2, 48; Civil R 1035, 1351(1), 1376(1), 1376(2); Consp 1.1, 7.5(3); Const Law 4049, 4050; Damag 50.10, 192; False Imp 2; Fed Civ Proc 2491.5, 2491.7; Fed Cts 13.10; Judgm 632.

Hutchison v. Brookshire Bros., Ltd., EDTex, 284 FSupp2d 459.—Arrest 63.4(1), 68(4); Assault 2, 48; Civil R 1088(4), 1326(5), 1336; Consp 1.1, 7.5(1), 18; Const Law 4537; Damag 50.10; False Imp 2, 15(2); Fed Civ Proc 2491.5, 2491.7, 2515, 2543, 2544, 2545, 2552; Fed Cts 411, 431; Labor & Emp 3055; Searches 33.

Hutchison v. Brookshire Bros., Ltd., EDTex, 205 FSupp2d 629.—Action 18; Assault 2; Civil R 1345, 1376(6); Const Law 4544; Damag 50.10; False Imp 2, 13, 22; Fed Civ Proc 1831; Mun Corp 175, 747(3), 1016; Offic 114; Sent & Pun 1532.

Hutchison; Carpet Services, Inc. v., BkrtcySDTex, 187 BR 533. See Hutchison, In re.

Hutchison v. Commercial Trading Co., Inc., NDTex, 427 FSupp 662, aff 586 F2d 840, aff 587 F2d 808.—Fed Cts 84, 372; Usury 83, 111(1).

Hutchison v. East Texas Oil Co., TexCivApp–Galveston, 167 SW2d 205, writ refused wom.—Adv Poss 114(1); App & E 662(2); Deeds 111, 115; Judgm 199(1), 199(3.9), 199(3.14), 743(2); Tresp to T T 11.

Hutchison; Epstein v., TexApp–Houston (1 Dist), 175 SW3d 805, review den.—App & E 946; Mental H 156, 159.

Hutchison; Goston v., TexApp–Houston (1 Dist), 853 SW2d 729.—App & E 854(1), 863; Judgm 183, 185(2); Mun Corp 724; Plead 78; Schools 89.13(4), 159.5(6).

Hutchison v. Pharris, TexApp–Fort Worth, 158 SW3d 554, reh overr.—App & E 215(1), 237(5), 237(6), 238(2), 294(1), 762, 994(2), 1003(3), 1070(1); Evid 570; Gas 20(2); Neglig 202, 371, 379, 380, 387.

Hutchison; Portanova v., TexApp–Houston (1 Dist), 766 SW2d 856.—Guard & W 137, 138, 153, 155.

Hutchison v. Ross, TexCivApp–Dallas, 89 SW2d 495.—App & E 954(1), 1024.2; Autos 15; Inj 135, 152.

Hutchison v. SabreTech, Inc., NDTex, 1 FSupp2d 632.—Civil R 1104, 1765, 1769.

Hutchison v. SabreTech Logistics Support, Inc., NDTex, 1 FSupp2d 632. See Hutchison v. SabreTech, Inc.

Hutchison; Spradley v., TexApp–Fort Worth, 787 SW2d 214, writ den.—Divorce 179, 254(1), 261, 282; Hus & W 279(1), 279(6), 281; Judgm 91, 489, 517.

Hutchison; Stone v., TexCivApp–Dallas, 272 SW2d 424.—Copyr 41(1), 101; Courts 489(4).

Hutchison; Travelers Ins. Co. v., TexCivApp–Tyler, 425 SW2d 832.—Evid 548, 555.10; Trial 129; Work Comp 1968(3).

Hutchison; Union Pacific Resources Co. v., TexApp–Austin, 990 SW2d 368, reh overr, and review den.—Mines 74(3), 79.1(5).

Hutchison; Villages of Greenbriar v., TexApp–Houston (1 Dist), 880 SW2d 777, reh den.—Mand 4(1), 4(4), 23(1), 28, 168(2); Pretrial Proc 385.

Huth v. Cater, TexCivApp–San Antonio, 215 SW2d 270, ref nre.—Fraud 59(2), 60, 64(1).

Huth v. Huth, TexCivApp–San Antonio, 110 SW2d 1011, dism.—App & E 339(4); Bills & N 133; Ex & Ad 435; Receivers 29(1).

Huth; Huth v., TexCivApp–San Antonio, 110 SW2d 1011, dism.—App & E 339(4); Bills & N 133; Ex & Ad 435; Receivers 29(1).

Huth v. Southern Pac. Co., CA5 (Tex), 417 F2d 526.—Fed Cts 743; R R 303(1), 348(2).

Huth v. Southern Pac. Co., SDTex, 293 FSupp 732, aff 417 F2d 526.—R R 349, 351(1).

Huther; Denton County v., TexApp–Fort Worth, 43 SW3d 665, reh overr.—App & E 70(9), 181, 185(1), 428(2); Mand 4(2).

Hutson; Action Realty Co. v., TexCivApp–Tyler, 478 SW2d 107.—Judgm 185.3(7).

Hutson; Benefit Ass'n of Ry. Emp. v., TexCivApp–Beaumont, 321 SW2d 607, ref nre.—Insurance 2589(1), 2590(1), 2590(2), 2608; Trial 350.4(3).

Hutson v. Chambless, Tex, 300 SW2d 943, 157 Tex 193.—Contracts 236; Damag 123, 221(5.1), 221(6).

Hutson v. Chambless, TexCivApp–Waco, 295 SW2d 723, rev 300 SW2d 943, 157 Tex 193.—App & E 1033(5), 1062.1; Bills & N 534; Contracts 322(4), 323(3); Damag 123, 140, 189, 208(1), 221(5.1); Trial 350.4(1), 352.5(1), 352.5(4).

Hutson; City Drug Stores of Amarillo v., TexCivApp–Amarillo, 121 SW2d 428.—Corp 503(1); Venue 22(8).

Hutson v. City of Houston, TexCivApp–Hous (14 Dist), 418 SW2d 911, ref nre.—App & E 854(5); Autos 273, 293; Mun Corp 741.15, 788.

Hutson v. Haggard, TexCivApp–Beaumont, 475 SW2d 330.—Adop 3, 7.4(2.1), 13, 15.

Hutson; Hobbs v., TexApp–Texarkana, 733 SW2d 269, writ den.—Judgm 185.3(14); Mines 55(5).

Hutson v. Lacey, TexCivApp–Hous (14 Dist), 440 SW2d 717.—App & E 883; Land & Ten 40, 112.5.

Hutson; McBride v., Tex, 306 SW2d 888, 157 Tex 632.—Contracts 143.5; Deeds 90; Mines 55(4), 74.5, 79.1(1), 79.1(4).

Hutson; McBride v., TexCivApp–Waco, 302 SW2d 456, rev 306 SW2d 888, 157 Tex 632.—Deeds 97; Estop 21, 32(1), 110; Mines 55(4).

Hutson; Oliver v., TexCivApp–Amarillo, 596 SW2d 628, 21 ALR4th 922, ref nre.—Land & Ten 169(4); Neglig 1612, 1613, 1614, 1630, 1695.

Hutson; Provident Life & Acc. Ins. Co. v., TexCivApp–Beaumont, 305 SW2d 837, 65 ALR2d 1443, ref nre.—Insurance 2437, 2590(2); Judgm 181(23).

Hutson; Rains v., TexCivApp–Beaumont, 426 SW2d 880.—New Tr 73; Witn 37(1).

Hutson v. Sadler, TexCivApp–Tyler, 501 SW2d 728.—Mtg 354; Time 6, 9(4).

Hutson v. Search Drilling Co., Inc., TexApp–Fort Worth, 635 SW2d 900, ref nre.—Evid 544; Trial 350.5(2).

Hutson v. Smith, TexCivApp–Galveston, 191 SW2d 779.—Const Law 2507(1); Evid 174.1; Int Liq 32(1), 32(2), 33(1), 37, 38; Statut 208, 223.5(4).

Hutson v. State, TexCrimApp, 296 SW2d 245, 164 TexCrim 24.—Autos 355(6); Crim Law 394.3, 598(8), 603.2, 801, 1043(3), 1090.11, 1118, 1166(7); Witn 379(3), 389.

Hutson v. State, TexCrimApp, 227 SW2d 813, 154 TexCrim 380.—False Pret 26, 49(1).

Hutson v. State, TexApp–Texarkana, 843 SW2d 106.—Crim Law 893; Homic 1149; Sent & Pun 373; Witn 337(11).

Hutson v. State, TexApp–Tyler, 652 SW2d 807.—Crim Law 273.1(4), 641.4(4), 1023(16).

Hutson; U.S. v., CA5 (Tex), 821 F2d 1015.—Crim Law 354, 421(4), 436(6), 444, 625(3), 625.15, 717, 1036.5, 1169.2(6), 1171.1(2.1), 1171.1(3), 1181.5(4); Embez 44(1).

For Later Case History Information, see KeyCite on WESTLAW

Hutson v. U.S., CA5 (Tex), 442 F2d 1036.—Courts 104; Fed Cts 743.

Hutson Const. Co.; U.S. Fidelity & Guaranty Co. v., TexCivApp–Dallas, 544 SW2d 762, ref nre.—Accord 1, 8(1); App & E 690(1); Insurance 2137(3).

Hutson Management Serv., Inc., In re, BkrtcySDTex, 66 BR 144. See Price-Watson Co., In re.

Hutson Management Serv., Inc. v. Eskey, Inc., BkrtcyS-DTex, 66 BR 144. See Price-Watson Co., In re.

Hutspeth v. State, TexCrimApp, 254 SW2d 130, 158 TexCrim 188.—Crim Law 554; Weap 17(2), 17(4).

Hutt v. City of Rocksprings, TexCivApp–Tyler, 552 SW2d 583, ref nre.—App & E 846(5), 854(1), 1170.1; Tax 2128, 2859.

Huttash; Parker Square State Bank v., TexCivApp–Fort Worth, 484 SW2d 429, ref nre.—Fraud Conv 39; Hus & W 249(3); Insurance 3488.

Huttig Sash & Door Co.; Swann v., CA5 (Tex), 436 F2d 60.—Autos 246(21); Evid 243(4); Fed Civ Proc 2174; Fed Cts 635, 743; Judgm 648; Neglig 291.

Huttleston v. Beacon Nat. Ins. Co., TexApp–Fort Worth, 822 SW2d 741, reh den, and writ den.—Insurance 2793(2); Ref of Inst 1, 2, 19(1), 43.

Hutto; Anderson v., TexCivApp–El Paso, 126 SW2d 709, writ refused.—App & E 729, 832(4), 837(10); Deeds 56(2), 208(3); Exch of Prop 6, 8(4); Trial 350.8.

Hutto v. Cook, Tex, 164 SW2d 513, 139 Tex 571.—Adv Poss 43(3), 43(6); Witn 126, 150(3).

Hutto; Cook v., TexCivApp–El Paso, 151 SW2d 642, rev 164 SW2d 513, 139 Tex 571.—Adv Poss 43(3), 43(8), 44, 106(1), 106(4), 109; App & E 758.3(8); Des & Dist 90(4); Hus & W 249(2.1); Tresp to T T 39(1); Trial 350.3(3), 352.18; Witn 126, 130, 139(9).

Hutto v. Fantastic Homes, Inc., TexCivApp–Fort Worth, 390 SW2d 289, ref nre.—App & E 930(3); Neglig 1680, 1683; Trial 350.1, 351.2(3.1), 351.2(5), 366.

Hutto; Radford v., TexCivApp–Amarillo, 113 SW2d 563.—Interpl 1; Plead 111.10, 111.18, 376; Set-Off 56.

Hutto v. State, TexApp–Dallas, 775 SW2d 407.—Ind & Inf 11, 65, 71.2(2); Obscen 17.

Hutto v. State, TexApp–Houston (14 Dist), 977 SW2d 855.—Crim Law 394.6(5), 412.2(2), 1130(5), 1153(1).

Hutto v. Texas Income Properties Corp., SDTex, 416 FSupp 478.—Fed Civ Proc 2011, 2151, 2608.1; Sec Reg 60.19, 60.20, 60.28(4), 60.28(13), 60.28(16), 60.40, 60.48(1).

Hutto v. U.S., CA5 (Tex), 511 F2d 172.—Crim Law 1579.

Hutto v. U.S., CA5 (Tex), 509 F2d 132, reh den 511 F2d 172.—Crim Law 1579.

Hutton v. AER Mfg. II, Inc., TexApp–Dallas, 224 SW3d 459, review den.—App & E 204(7), 207, 217, 970(2), 977(1), 1050.1(1), 1051.1(2), 1056.1(1), 1060.1(1), 1079; Evid 150, 544; Motions 58, 59(2); New Tr 44(1), 56, 143(2), 143(3), 144; Pretrial Proc 40.

Hutton v. Federal Home Loan Bank of Dallas, NDTex, 832 FSupp 181. See F.D.I.C. v. Cheng.

Hutton v. Harwell, TexCivApp–Fort Worth, 95 SW2d 467.—Lim of Act 4(2), 51(2).

Hutton; Marion v., TexCivApp–Amarillo, 374 SW2d 284, ref nre.—App & E 302(5); Evid 589, 590, 593; Sales 387; Stip 14(1).

Hutton v. Methodist Home, TexCivApp–Fort Worth, 615 SW2d 289, ref nre.—Contracts 16; Wills 450, 470(1), 725.

Hutton v. State, TexCrimApp, 166 SW2d 133, 145 Tex-Crim 109.—Crim Law 94, 598(6).

Hutton v. Zaferson, TexCivApp–San Antonio, 509 SW2d 950, ref nre.—Frds St of 84.

Hutton & Co., Inc. v. Youngblood, Tex, 741 SW2d 363. See E.F. Hutton & Co., Inc. v. Youngblood.

Hutton & Co., Inc. v. Youngblood, TexApp–Corpus Christi, 708 SW2d 865. See E.F. Hutton & Co., Inc. v. Youngblood.

Hutton Group, Inc. v. Aubin, CA5 (Tex), 919 F2d 1014. See Haralson v. E.F. Hutton Group, Inc.

Hutton Southwest Properties II, Ltd., In re, CA5 (Tex), 953 F2d 963. See E.F. Hutton Southwest Properties II, Ltd., In re.

Hutton Southwest Properties II, Ltd., In re, BkrtcyND-Tex, 103 BR 808. See E.F. Hutton Southwest Properties II, Ltd., In re.

Hutton Southwest Properties II, Ltd. v. Union Planters Nat. Bank, CA5 (Tex), 953 F2d 963. See E.F. Hutton Southwest Properties II, Ltd., In re.

Huval; International Brotherhood of Boiler Makers, Iron Shipbuilders andHelpers of America v., Tex, 166 SW2d 107, 140 Tex 21.—App & E 1173(1); Const Law 1120, 1121(1); Insurance 1091(1), 1091(7), 1091(8), 1848, 3153, 3156, 3365.

Huval; International Brotherhood of Boilermakers, Iron Shipbuilders & Helpers of America v., TexCiv-App–Beaumont, 154 SW2d 233, aff in part, rev in part 166 SW2d 107, 140 Tex 21.—Evid 359(4), 413, 523; Insurance 1848, 3156; Trial 219, 351.5(1), 351.5(8), 352.1(4), 352.5(4).

Huval; International Broth. of Boiler Makers, Iron Shipbuilders and Helpers of America v., TexComApp, 126 SW2d 476, 133 Tex 136.—App & E 1177(4); Insurance 2561(2), 2579.

Huval; International Broth. of Boilermakers, Iron Shipbuilders and Helpers of America v., TexCivApp–Beaumont, 101 SW2d 1072, aff 126 SW2d 476, 133 Tex 136.—App & E 1070(2); Insurance 3156, 3191(7), 3365.

Huvar; American Life & Acc. Ins. Co. v., TexCivApp–Waco, 390 SW2d 370.—Judgm 181(2), 185(2), 185.1(4), 185.3(12).

Huvar v. Rex Corp. of San Antonio, TexCivApp–San Antonio, 387 SW2d 82.—Land & Ten 167(8), 168(1); Neglig 1037(4), 1286(1).

Huvard; Noel v., TexCivApp–Houston, 395 SW2d 953.—App & E 954(1), 954(2); Inj 123, 147.

Huynh v. City of Houston, TexApp–Houston (14 Dist), 874 SW2d 184, petition for discretionary review gr, aff in part, remanded in part 901 SW2d 480, on remand 928 SW2d 698.—Ind & Inf 196(1); Jury 29(6).

Huynh v. Nguyen, TexApp–Houston (14 Dist), 180 SW3d 608, reh overr.—Appear 9(1), 9(5), 10; Const Law 3963, 3964, 3965(5); Courts 12(2.1), 12(2.5), 12(2.10), 12(2.20), 12(2.25), 15, 37(3); Princ & A 19, 96, 99.

Huynh v. R. Warehousing & Port Services, Inc., Tex-App–Tyler, 973 SW2d 375.—App & E 970(2), 1050.1(1), 1056.1(1); Autos 192(11), 243(12); Evid 146; Trial 43, 207; Witn 344(1).

Huynh v. State, TexCrimApp, 901 SW2d 480, on remand 928 SW2d 698.—Ind & Inf 196(2); Jury 29(6); Statut 223.4.

Huynh v. State, TexApp–Houston (14 Dist), 928 SW2d 698.—Nuis 91(1).

Huynh v. State, TexApp–Houston (14 Dist), 833 SW2d 636.—Atty & C 88; Crim Law 260.11(2), 641.13(1), 641.13(5), 641.13(6), 641.13(7), 1086.11, 1114.1(1), 1119(1), 1128(4), 1141(2), 1144.10, 1147, 1166(1); Judges 32; Jury 29(2).

H.V., In re, TexApp–Fort Worth, 179 SW3d 746, review gr.—Crim Law 394.1(3), 394.6(5), 412.1(4), 412.2(1), 412.2(3), 412.2(4), 414, 641.3(3), 641.3(6), 1139, 1158(4); Witn 390.1.

HVAW v. American Motorists Ins. Co., NDTex, 968 FSupp 1178, aff 149 F3d 1175.—Antitrust 221; Fed Civ Proc 2501; Insurance 1563, 1845(2), 2275, 2296, 2914, 2931, 3242, 3349, 3350, 3353, 3424(1).

H.V.R., Matter of, TexApp–San Antonio, 974 SW2d 213, reh overr.—Infants 230.1, 249, 253; Statut 181(1).

H. W. Broaddus Co. v. Binkley, TexComApp, 88 SW2d 1040, 126 Tex 374.—Brok 65(1), 88(12); Trial 351.2(6).

H. W. E., In Interest of, TexCivApp–Fort Worth, 613 SW2d 71.—App & E 931(6); Atty & C 20.1; Infants 155, 156, 252.

H. W. J. v. State Dept. of Public Welfare, TexCivApp–Texarkana, 543 SW2d 9.—Infants 155, 157.

HWJ, Inc. v. Burlington Ins. Co., EDTex, 926 FSupp 593.—Fed Cts 342; Rem of C 15, 75, 76, 107(7).

Hyak; W. W. Auto Parts, Inc. v., TexCivApp–San Antonio, 346 SW2d 919.—Land & Ten 235; New Tr 140(3), 163(2); Trial 315.

Hyatt v. C.I.R., CA5 (Tex), 325 F2d 715, cert den 85 SCt 62, 379 US 832, 13 LEd2d 40.—Int Rev 3240.

Hyatt v. Hughes, TexCivApp–San Antonio, 221 SW2d 998, ref nre.—Damag 120(1); Insurance 1144, 1604.

Hyatt v. Hyatt, TexCivApp–Galveston, 111 SW2d 341.—Divorce 27(1), 130.

Hyatt; Hyatt v., TexCivApp–Galveston, 111 SW2d 341.—Divorce 27(1), 130.

Hyatt v. Mercury Life & Health Co., TexCivApp–San Antonio, 202 SW2d 325.—App & E 436, 456; Prohib 10(2).

Hyatt v. Mercury Life & Health Co., TexCivApp–San Antonio, 202 SW2d 320, ref nre.—Insurance 1132, 1149; Mand 127.

Hyatt v. Radio Station WLOU, TexCivApp–El Paso, 354 SW2d 415.—App & E 768, 930(1), 989; Contracts 143(3), 176(2), 220, 245(2); Tel 1163.

Hyatt v. State, TexCrimApp, 278 SW2d 162.—Crim Law 1090.1(1).

Hyatt v. Tate, TexCivApp–Hous (1 Dist), 505 SW2d 373.—Damag 12, 139, 221(2.1).

Hyatt Cheek Builders-Engineers Co. v. Board of Regents of University of Texas System, TexCivApp–Texarkana, 607 SW2d 258, writ dism.—App & E 263(3), 842(2), 1056.1(10); Contracts 190, 198(2), 238(2), 245(1), 303(4), 322(2); Damag 39; Indem 57, 67; Interest 39(2.50), 44; Neglig 440(1), 1672, 1680, 1738, 1742; Nova 4.

Hyatt Corp.; Cabana Management, Inc. v., CA5 (Tex), 441 F2d 862.—Fed Cts 191, 243.

Hyatt Corp.; Dallas Cabana, Inc. v., CA5 (Tex), 441 F2d 865.—Bankr 2492, 2553, 3131, 3132.

Hyatt Corp. v. Trahan, TexCivApp–Dallas, 521 SW2d 149.—App & E 554(3), 557, 907(3).

Hycarbex, Inc. v. Anglo-Suisse, Inc., TexApp–Houston (14 Dist), 927 SW2d 103.—Accord 1, 10(1), 11(2), 23, 26(1); App & E 854(5), 866(3), 901, 927(7), 966(1), 1043(6), 1078(1); Contracts 143.5, 147(2), 147(3), 152, 154, 170(1); Pretrial Proc 44.1, 92, 124, 127, 221, 224, 713, 714, 717.1.

Hycel, Inc. v. American Airlines, Inc., SDTex, 328 FSupp 190.—Aviation 102; Carr 135, 158(1); Damag 5, 20, 23; Fed Civ Proc 2491.

Hycel, Inc. v. Wittstruck, TexApp–Waco, 690 SW2d 914, dism.—Antitrust 138, 149, 297, 365, 367, 369, 389(2), 391; App & E 930(3), 989, 1001(3), 1050.1(6), 1140(1); Damag 190, 221(2.1), 221(8), 223; Judgm 199(3.10).

Hyde v. Apple, TexCivApp–Eastland, 209 SW2d 804.—App & E 684(1); Evid 43(2); Plead 111.42(8).

Hyde; Burlington Northern, Inc. v., TexApp–El Paso, 799 SW2d 477.—Mand 32; Pretrial Proc 19, 33, 36.1, 371.

Hyde v. Claude Neon Federal Co., TexCivApp–Eastland, 157 SW2d 952, writ dism.—Bailm 3, 5; Chat Mtg 7; Corp 459; Damag 78(2); Evid 354(19), 383(8); Frds St of 113(3); Partners 131.

Hyde; Creglar v., TexCivApp–Waco, 280 SW2d 783, ref nre.—App & E 1044; Can of Inst 53; Jury 25(6); Refer 6, 34.

Hyde v. English, TexCivApp–Beaumont, 139 SW2d 628, writ dism.—Assault 40, 43(5); Damag 221(5.1); Trial 205, 251(9), 351.2(4), 352.20.

Hyde v. Hyde, TexCivApp–Beaumont, 212 SW2d 226.—Lim of Act 5(3).

Hyde; Hyde v., TexCivApp–Beaumont, 212 SW2d 226.—Lim of Act 5(3).

Hyde v. Hyde, TexCivApp–Tyler, 406 SW2d 225, writ dism.—App & E 169, 302(1); Child C 501, 532, 618, 904; Divorce 171.

Hyde; Hyde v., TexCivApp–Tyler, 406 SW2d 225, writ dism.—App & E 169, 302(1); Child C 501, 532, 618, 904; Divorce 171.

Hyde; Kennedy v., Tex, 682 SW2d 525.—Compromise 5(3); Judgm 72; Statut 223.5(4); Stip 6, 13.

Hyde; Kennedy v., TexApp–Fort Worth, 666 SW2d 325, writ gr, rev 682 SW2d 525.—App & E 930(3); Compromise 5(3); Costs 194.32; Frds St of 44(1), 49; Judgm 72; Lim of Act 127(4); Pretrial Proc 711, 713; Trial 3(2), 351.5(2).

Hyde; Kinion v., TexCivApp–Amarillo, 471 SW2d 920, ref nre.—Health 821(2), 821(5), 822(3), 823(7), 825.

Hyde v. Marks, TexCivApp–Fort Worth, 138 SW2d 619, writ dism, correct.—App & E 150(2), 1066(8); Assign 117, 129; Autos 246(22); Damag 216(8); Evid 213(1); Trial 140(2), 255(4); Witn 363(1), 370(1), 372(1).

Hyde; Nermyr v., TexApp–El Paso, 799 SW2d 472.—Mand 32; Pretrial Proc 19, 33, 36.1, 371.

Hyde v. Ray, TexApp–Fort Worth, 181 SW3d 835.—Admin Law 228.1, 229, 305; App & E 71(3), 842(1), 893(1), 920(3), 954(1), 1024.2; Courts 155; Waters 202.

Hyde v. State, TexCrimApp, 136 SW2d 850, 138 TexCrim 457.—Courts 116(4); Crim Law 126(2), 796; Homic 988(3); Jury 50.

Hyde v. State, TexApp–Austin, 970 SW2d 81, petition for discretionary review refused.—Autos 344; Crim Law 121, 126(2), 134(1), 409(5), 538(3), 895, 897(1), 1134(5), 1144.8, 1150, 1152(2), 1166(4), 1172.9; Jury 108.

Hyde v. State, TexApp–Texarkana, 723 SW2d 754.—Crim Law 1038.2, 1134(3); Rob 30.

Hyde v. State, TexApp–Beaumont, 869 SW2d 660, petition for discretionary review refused.—Arrest 63.4(5), 68(3); Crim Law 211(1); Jury 131(17); Searches 108, 112, 114; Witn 318.

Hyde v. State, TexApp–Corpus Christi, 846 SW2d 503, petition for discretionary review refused.—Crim Law 351(1), 351(3).

Hyde v. Texas Dept. of Criminal Justice, SDTex, 948 FSupp 625.—Prisons 4(14).

Hyde; Walchshauser v., TexApp–Fort Worth, 890 SW2d 171, reh den, and writ den.—Costs 194.40; Ease 3(1), 3(2), 12(1), 21, 36(1), 36(2); Frds St of 110(1).

Hyde Corp.; Burke v., TexApp–Fort Worth, 173 SW2d 364.—Armed S 34.2(3), 34.2(4), 34.2(5), 34.2(6), 34.2(7).

Hyde Corp. v. Huffines, Tex, 314 SW2d 763, 158 Tex 566, reh den 1958 WL 91272, cert den 79 SCt 223, 358 US 898, 3 LEd2d 148.—Abate & R 12; Am Cur 3; Antitrust 418; Courts 489(3), 489(4); Inj 4, 56, 190; Pat 1, 182, 211(1), 214.

Hyde Corp. v. Huffines, TexCivApp–Fort Worth, 303 SW2d 865, aff 314 SW2d 763, 158 Tex 566, reh den 1958 WL 91272, cert den 79 SCt 223, 358 US 898, 3 LEd2d 148.—App & E 1001(1); Courts 493(3); Pat 182, 214.

Hyden v. State, TexCrimApp, 780 SW2d 247. See Ladner v. State.

Hyden v. State, TexApp–Tyler, 790 SW2d 671. See Ladner v. State.

Hyde Park Baptist Church; City of Austin v., TexApp–Austin, 152 SW3d 162.—Zoning 308.

Hyder; Advent Trust Co. v., TexApp–San Antonio, 12 SW3d 534, reh overr, and petition for review den, and reh of petition for review overr.—Estop 52.15, 55; Lim of Act 13, 43, 56(2), 95(1), 95(3), 104(1), 127(13), 127(17), 193, 200(1).

Hyder v. Beto, NDTex, 270 FSupp 46.—Hab Corp 721(2), 722(2).

Hyder v. Kraft, TexCivApp–Fort Worth, 431 SW2d 420, mandamus overr.—Venue 5.3(6).

Hyder-Ingram Chevrolet, Inc. v. Kutach, TexCivApp–Hous (14 Dist), 612 SW2d 687.—Antitrust 136, 389(1),

389(2), 390; App & E 242(1), 1050.1(7); Const Law 947; Damag 177.

Hydorn; Cecil v., TexApp–San Antonio, 725 SW2d 781.—Labor & Emp 858.

HydPro, Inc.; Davis v., TexApp–Eastland, 839 SW2d 137, reh overrr, and reh den, and writ den.—Torts 242.

HydPro, Inc.; Davis–Claytonville Gas Plant v., TexApp–Eastland, 839 SW2d 137. See Davis v. HydPro, Inc.

HydPro, Inc.; J.L. Davis–Claytonville Gas Plant v., TexApp–Eastland, 839 SW2d 137. See Davis v. HydPro, Inc.

Hydra-Rig, Inc. v. ETF Corp., TexApp–Fort Worth, 707 SW2d 288, ref nre.—Bailm 35; Mech Liens 61, 72.

Hydra-Rig, Inc.; Pool Co. v., TexApp–Fort Worth, 626 SW2d 320.—App & E 204(4), 846(5), 931(1), 1010.1(1); Corp 666; Plead 111.40, 111.42(6); Venue 7(3), 7(4), 21.

Hydraulic Products Co.; Yellow Freight System, Inc. v., TexCivApp–Amarillo, 482 SW2d 659.—Carr 76, 134, 135; Costs 194.32; Sales 206.

Hydril Co. v. Multiflex, Inc., SDTex, 553 FSupp 552.—Atty & C 21.

Hydril Co. LP v. Grant Prideco LP, CAFed (Tex), 474 F3d 1344, on remand 2007 WL 1791663.—Antitrust 587(3); Courts 96(7); Fed Cts 762; Pat 286, 328(2), 328(4).

Hydril Co., L.P. v. Grant Prideco, L.P., SDTex, 385 FSupp2d 609, rev in part, vac in part 474 F3d 1344, on remand 2007 WL 1791663.—Decl Judgm 234; Fed Cts 18; Pat 328(2).

Hydro-Action, Inc., In re, BkrtcyEDTex, 341 BR 186.—Bankr 2154.1, 2164.1, 2722; Lim of Act 104.5, 199(1).

Hydro Action, Inc., In re, BkrtcyEDTex, 266 BR 638.—Alt Disp Res 112, 113, 134(1), 138, 139, 141, 143, 200, 205, 210, 235; Bankr 3031; Fed Cts 403.

Hydro-Action, Inc.; Clearstream Wastewater Systems, Inc. v., CAFed (Tex), 206 F3d 1440.—Fed Cts 766, 802; Pat 101(10), 165(5), 226.6, 226.7, 314(5), 324.5, 324.55(5).

Hydro-Action, Inc. v. James, EDTex, 233 FSupp2d 836.—Rem of C 2, 17, 43, 79(1), 82, 102, 103, 107(7).

Hydroblast Corp.; Amoco Production Co. v., NDTex, 90 FSupp2d 727, aff 226 F3d 642.—Action 17; Antitrust 131, 147; Contracts 144; Fed Cts 409.1; Insurance 1091(1), 1671, 1806, 1808, 1809, 1832(1), 1836, 2278(17).

Hydrocarbon Horizons, Inc.; Pecos Development Corp. v., Tex, 803 SW2d 266.—Frds St of 63(1).

Hydrocarbon Horizons, Inc. v. Pecos Development Corp., TexApp–Corpus Christi, 797 SW2d 265, writ den with per curiam opinion 803 SW2d 266.—Brok 43(2); Frds St of 74(1); Judgm 186; Trusts 109.

Hydrocarbon Management, Inc. v. Tracker Exploration, Inc., TexApp–Amarillo, 861 SW2d 427, reh den.—App & E 842(2), 893(1), 931(1), 989, 1008.1(2), 1010.1(3), 1012.1(5), 1023; Estop 112, 121; Mines 78.1(1), 78.1(3), 78.1(4), 78.1(8), 78.1(9), 78.1(10), 78.7(3.1), 78.7(4), 78.7(5), 78.7(6).

Hydrocarbon Processing, Inc.; Den Norske Stats Oljeselskap, A.S. v., SDTex, 992 FSupp 913, aff 161 F3d 8.—Fed Civ Proc 292, 751; Frds St of 116(6), 127; Sales 22(3).

Hydrocarbon Production Co. v. Valley Acres Water Dist., CA5 (Tex), 204 F2d 212, cert den Hydrocarbon Production Company, v. Valley Acres Water District, 74 SCt 44, 346 US 825, 98 LEd 350.—Const Law 961, 2487, 3487, 4059, 4061; Drains 2(0.5); Evid 6; Fed Civ Proc 654.1; Tax 2478; Waters 216, 222, 226, 231.

Hydrocarbon Research, Inc. v. Calvert, TexCivApp–Austin, 429 SW2d 539, ref nre.—Const Law 3567, 3576, 3580; Statut 230; Tax 3626, 3627, 3634, 3668, 3687, 3704.

Hydro Corp.; Jones v., TexCivApp–Amarillo, 420 SW2d 210.—Acct Action on 14; App & E 499(1), 1062.2, 1078(1); Impl & C C 12; Parties 67; Sales 359(1); Trial 351.5(1).

Hydrokinetics, Inc. v. Alaska Mechanical, Inc., CA5 (Tex), 700 F2d 1026, cert den 104 SCt 2180, 466 US 962, 80 LEd2d 561, reh den 104 SCt 3549, 467 US 1257, 82 LEd2d 851.—Corp 665(1); Fed Cts 281.

Hydro-Line Mfg. Co. v. Pulido, TexApp–Corpus Christi, 674 SW2d 382, ref nre.—App & E 241, 497(1), 684(1), 1062.1; Contracts 164; Joint Adv 4(3), 5(3); Labor & Emp 265; Trial 139.1(5.1), 295(9), 352.20.

Hydro Services, Inc., In re, BkrtcyEDTex, 277 BR 309.—Bankr 3157, 3173.

Hydrostatic Engineers, Inc. v. Rapid Service, Inc., TexCivApp–El Paso, 439 SW2d 866, writ dism.—App & E 934(1); Corp 503(2); Venue 7.5(2), 7.5(3).

Hydrostatic Transmission, Inc.; Cudd v., TexApp–Corpus Christi, 867 SW2d 101.—Courts 185; Judgm 185.3(3); Pretrial Proc 477.1, 483, 486.

Hydrostatic Transmission, Inc.; Cudd Hydraulic Co. v., TexApp–Corpus Christi, 867 SW2d 101. See Cudd v. Hydrostatic Transmission, Inc.

Hydro Systems, In re, BkrtcySDTex, 51 BR 704. See Brokmeyer, In re.

Hydro Systems; New Ulm State Bank v., BkrtcySDTex, 51 BR 704. See Brokmeyer, In re.

Hydrotech Systems, Inc.; Arnold Corp. v., CAFed (Tex), 109 F3d 1567. See Jim Arnold Corp. v. Hydrotech Systems, Inc.

Hydrotech Systems, Inc.; Jim Arnold Corp. v., CAFed (Tex), 109 F3d 1567, reh den, in banc sug declined, cert den Baker Hughes Inc v. Jim Arnold Corp, 118 SCt 338, 522 US 933, 139 LEd2d 262.—Fed Cts 161, 209.1; Pat 196.1, 202(1), 206, 211(1), 282, 283(1), 286, 287(1); Rem of C 15, 25(1).

Hyer; City of Dallas v., TexCivApp–Texarkana, 350 SW2d 583.—Prohib 5(3).

Hyett, Ex parte, TexCrimApp, 610 SW2d 787.—Ind & Inf 41(2), 86(2), 86(3), 87(1), 176.

Hyett v. State, TexApp–Houston (14 Dist), 58 SW3d 826, petition for discretionary review refused.—Controlled Subs 26, 27, 68, 79, 80; Crim Law 314, 552(1), 730(3), 730(8), 867, 1144.13(2.1), 1144.13(3), 1159.2(1), 1159.2(2), 1159.2(7), 1159.2(9), 1187; Witn 347.

Hygeia Dairy Co. v. Benson, SDTex, 151 FSupp 661.—Admin Law 229; Decl Judgm 203, 271; Fed Civ Proc 469; Inj 75.

Hygeia Dairy Co.; Freeman v., CA5 (Tex), 326 F2d 271.—Food 4.5(1), 4.5(5), 4.5(6).

Hygeia Dairy Co. v. Freeman, SDTex, 197 FSupp 876, rev 326 F2d 271.—Food 4.5(4), 4.5(5).

Hygeia Dairy Co. v. Gonzalez, TexApp–San Antonio, 994 SW2d 220.—App & E 1067; Damag 62(1), 163(2), 208(7), 214; Fraud 17; Neglig 210, 213, 215, 1692.

Hykonnen v. Baker Hughes Business Support Services, TexApp–Houston (14 Dist), 93 SW3d 562.—App & E 428(2).

Hylander v. Groendyke Transport, Inc., TexApp–Corpus Christi, 732 SW2d 692, ref nre.—Corp 498; Damag 91(3); Neglig 273, 1584, 1659, 1697; Trial 350.1, 350.3(7).

Hy-Lay Hatcheries, Inc.; Baucom v., TexCivApp–Waco, 355 SW2d 754.—Pretrial Proc 517.1; Venue 57.

Hyler v. Boytor, TexApp–Houston (1 Dist), 823 SW2d 425.—App & E 999(2), 1003(7); Damag 185(1), 192.

Hyles v. State, TexCrimApp, 92 SW2d 450, 130 TexCrim 154.—Crim Law 366(4), 586, 596(1), 1169.1(9); Homic 1080(4), 1484.

Hyltin-Manor Funeral Home, Inc. v. Hill, TexCivApp–San Antonio, 304 SW2d 469.—Judgm 17(10).

Hylton v. Bullock, TexCivApp–Austin, 583 SW2d 675, ref nre.—App & E 5.

Hylton; Schrock v., TexCivApp–Dallas, 133 SW2d 175.—Elections 10, 269, 270, 295(1), 298(1), 298(3); Waters 227, 231.

Hylton v. State, TexApp–Austin, 665 SW2d 571.—Tax 3692.

Hylton; U.S. v., CA5 (Tex), 710 F2d 1106.—Const Law 1435; Crim Law 1017; Double J 32, 101; Int Rev 5264; Obst Just 8.

Hylton; U.S. v., SDTex, 558 FSupp 872, aff 710 F2d 1106.—Const Law 1435; Int Rev 5264; Statut 184.

Hyman v. Alberry, TexCivApp–Beaumont, 130 SW2d 891, writ dism, correct.—Bills & N 351, 514, 527(1); Evid 182, 183(2), 314(1); Witn 160(1).

Hyman v. Brady, TexCivApp–San Antonio, 230 SW2d 345.—Child S 240.

Hyman; Brady v., TexCivApp–San Antonio, 230 SW2d 342.—Child S 54, 240; Hus & W 278(1), 281.

Hyman v. Hyman, TexCivApp–Amarillo, 275 SW2d 149, ref nre.—App & E 758.3(1); Marriage 63, 66.

Hyman; Hyman v., TexCivApp–Amarillo, 275 SW2d 149, ref nre.—App & E 758.3(1); Marriage 63, 66.

Hyman; Jones v., TexApp–Dallas, 107 SW3d 830.—App & E 854(1), 856(1); Judgm 648; Torts 124.

Hyman; Retail Credit Co. v., TexCivApp–Houston, 316 SW2d 769, writ refused.—App & E 686, 1170.1; Jury 136(3).

Hyman v. State, TexCrimApp, 249 SW2d 224, 157 TexCrim 434.—Crim Law 1091(2), 1091(8), 1144.1, 1171.8(2).

Hyman Farm Service, Inc. v. Earth Oil & Gas Co., Inc., TexApp–Amarillo, 920 SW2d 452.—App & E 232(0.5), 241, 927(7), 997(3); Contracts 16; Corp 306, 335, 518(1); Damag 221(8); Fraud 64(1); Pretrial Proc 517.1; Trial 139.1(14), 139.1(17), 352.50; Venue 8.5(2).

Hyman Inv. Co. v. Tomerlin, TexCivApp–San Antonio, 326 SW2d 607, writ dism.—Accord 10(1), 12(1).

Hymel; Delavan v., TexCivApp–Waco, 441 SW2d 217.—Spec Perf 10(1), 129.

Hymes v. Specification Motor Oils System of Texas, TexCivApp–Dallas, 103 SW2d 1065.—App & E 907(3); Land & Ten 248(1).

Hynd v. Sandler, TexCivApp–Dallas, 95 SW2d 165, writ dism.—Atty & C 147, 148(1); Contracts 169; Frds St of 56(8); Plead 291(1).

Hynek v. City of San Angelo, TexCivApp–Austin, 268 SW2d 493.—Mun Corp 697(4); New Tr 104(1).

Hynes v. City of Houston, TexCivApp–Galveston, 263 SW2d 839, ref nre.—Mun Corp 185(10), 185(12).

Hynes; State v., Tex, 865 SW2d 943.—Autos 279.

Hynes v. State, TexApp–Tyler, 855 SW2d 731, reh overr, and writ gr, rev 865 SW2d 943.—Autos 258; High 166; Judgm 181(6), 185.1(4).

Hynson v. State, TexCrimApp, 656 SW2d 460.—Rec S Goods 8(3).

Hynum v. First State Bank of Keene, TexCivApp–Waco, 575 SW2d 431.—App & E 907(4).

Hynutek, Inc.; BA Commercial Corp. v., TexApp–Dallas, 705 SW2d 713.—App & E 187(1); Bankr 2396; Banks 191.10; Contracts 159; Guar 4, 37, 46(1), 77(1); Judgm 248.

Hyperion Solutions Corp. v. Outlooksoft Corp., EDTex, 422 FSupp2d 760.—Pat 101(2), 101(8), 161, 162, 165(1), 165(3), 165(4), 167(1), 167(1.1), 168(2.1), 314(5), 328(2).

Hypke v. State, TexApp–Houston (14 Dist), 720 SW2d 158, petition for discretionary review refused.—Const Law 740, 4732; Sent & Pun 8, 1573; Statut 118(6).

Hypolite v. State, TexCrimApp, 647 SW2d 294.—Crim Law 1131(3).

Hypolite v. State, TexApp–San Antonio, 985 SW2d 181.—Arrest 68(4); Controlled Subs 80; Crim Law 412.1(1), 1130(5), 1134(3), 1139, 1144.13(3), 1153(1), 1158(4), 1159.2(1), 1159.2(2), 1159.2(9); Searches 26, 28, 162, 192.1; Witn 390.

Hysell Wire Line Service, Inc.; High Plains Wire Line Services, Inc. v., TexApp–Amarillo, 802 SW2d 406.—App & E 179(1), 931(4), 989, 1010.1(3), 1012.1(5); Costs 194.32; Damag 113, 116, 137, 188(1), 191; Trover 40(4), 40(6), 43.1, 66, 72.

Hyson; Chilkewitz v., Tex, 22 SW3d 825, on remand 2000 WL 566776, review den.—App & E 230; Assoc 4, 20(1), 20(2), 20(3), 20(5); Corp 28(0.5), 46, 506; Lim of Act 104.5, 126; Parties 67, 95(1), 95(5); Partners 64, 191, 200.

Hyson v. Chilkewitz, TexApp–Dallas, 971 SW2d 563, review gr, rev 22 SW3d 825, on remand 2000 WL 566776, review den.—Const Law 256(2); Costs 256(2); Health 811; Lim of Act 1, 5(1), 5(2), 55(3), 95(1), 121(1), 121(2), 187, 201; Parties 67; Statut 181(1).

Hyster Co. v. Lawrence, TexApp–Tyler, 846 SW2d 341, subsequent mandamus proceeding Scott v. Twelfth Court of Appeals, 843 SW2d 439.—Pretrial Proc 358.

Hytken Family Ltd. v. Schaefer, SDTex, 431 FSupp2d 696.—Fed Cts 294.

Hyundai Corp. (U.S.A.); Kang v., TexApp–Dallas, 992 SW2d 499, reh overr.—App & E 863, 1079, 1178(1); Judgm 181(33), 185(5); Pretrial Proc 434.

Hyundai Electronics Industries, Co. Ltd.; Texas Instruments, Inc. v., EDTex, 50 FSupp2d 619.—Evid 546; Fed Civ Proc 928, 1278, 2655; Fed Cts 823; Pat 292.4.

Hyundai Electronics Industries, Co. Ltd.; Texas Instruments, Inc. v., EDTex, 49 FSupp2d 893.—Antitrust 587(1), 587(3); Equity 65(1); Evid 448; Pat 283(1).

Hyundai Electronics Industries Co., Ltd.; Texas Instruments, Inc. v., EDTex, 42 FSupp2d 660.—Contracts 143(1), 143(2), 143.5, 147(2); Evid 448; Fed Civ Proc 2492; Pat 215, 323.2(1).

Hyundai Electronics Industries, Co. Ltd.; Texas Instruments, Inc. v., EDTex, 191 FRD 119.—Fed Civ Proc 834, 840, 851; Pat 310.11.

Hyundai Electronics Industries Co., Ltd.; Texas Instruments, Inc. v., EDTex, 190 FRD 413.—Evid 546; Fed Civ Proc 1278, 2011; Fed Cts 823; Pat 292.4, 328(2).

Hyundai Motor America v. O'Neill, TexApp–Dallas, 839 SW2d 474, reh den.—Judges 25(1); Mand 3(3), 28; Pretrial Proc 41, 403; Refer 99(4).

Hyundai Motor Co. v. Alvarado, Tex, 974 SW2d 1.—Prod Liab 36; States 18.5, 18.7, 18.65.

Hyundai Motor Co. v. Alvarado, Tex, 892 SW2d 853, on remand 908 SW2d 243, reh overr, and writ gr, and motion overr, aff and remanded 974 SW2d 1.—Judgm 181(14); Pretrial Proc 506.1, 509, 517.1.

Hyundai Motor Co. v. Alvarado, TexApp–San Antonio, 989 SW2d 32, reh overr, and review gr, and set aside.—Abate & R 8(2), 15; App & E 840(4), 1002, 1024.3, 1045(1), 1050.1(1), 1051.1(2), 1053(6); Evid 141, 333(1); Interest 39(2.50); Judgm 581; Jury 136(3); Venue 8.5(8), 17.

Hyundai Motor Co.; Alvarado v., TexApp–San Antonio, 908 SW2d 243, reh overr, and writ gr, and motion overr, aff and remanded 974 SW2d 1.—Prod Liab 35.1, 36; States 18.3, 18.65.

Hyundai Motor Co.; Alvarado v., TexApp–San Antonio, 885 SW2d 167, writ gr, rev 892 SW2d 853, on remand 908 SW2d 243, reh overr, and writ gr, and motion overr, aff and remanded 974 SW2d 1.—App & E 80(6); Pretrial Proc 501, 506.1, 508, 509, 517.1, 519.

Hyundai Motor Co.; Chandler v., Tex, 829 SW2d 774, on remand 844 SW2d 882.—App & E 70(2); Pretrial Proc 356.1.

Hyundai Motor Co.; Chandler v., TexApp–Houston (1 Dist), 869 SW2d 356, writ gr, rev 829 SW2d 774, on remand 844 SW2d 882.—App & E 4, 66, 78(5), 79(1), 80(6).

Hyundai Motor Co.; Chandler v., TexApp–Houston (1 Dist), 844 SW2d 882.—App & E 19; Pretrial Proc 413.1.

Hyundai Motor Co. v. Chandler, TexApp–Corpus Christi, 882 SW2d 606, reh overr, and writ den.—App & E 215(1), 930(3), 989, 1001(1), 1003(7), 1043(6), 1050.1(1), 1051.1(1), 1056.1(1), 1058(1); Damag 63, 96, 130; Death 95(1); Prod Liab 5, 8, 83.5; Sales 437(3), 439, 441(3); Trial 350.6(1); Witn 214.5.

Hyundai Motor Co.; Rodriguez By and Through Rodriguez v., TexApp–Corpus Christi, 944 SW2d 757, reh overr, and writ gr, rev 995 SW2d 661.—App & E 207,

500(3), 758.3(8), 840(4), 969, 970(2), 1060.1(1), 1062.2, 1064.1(1), 1067; Evid 150; New Tr 39(6), 41(3), 64; Pretrial Proc 45, 251.1, 434; Prod Liab 14, 15, 96.5; Sales 272, 284(1), 441(2), 441(3); Trial 45(3), 251(1), 252(2), 295(1), 350.3(5), 352.1(1).

Hyundai Motor Co. v. Rodriguez ex rel. Rodriguez, Tex, 995 SW2d 661.—Prod Liab 8, 35.1, 96.5; Sales 284(1), 446(7); Trial 228(1), 251(1), 252(1), 352.5(1), 352.13.

Hyundai Motor Co. v. Vasquez, Tex, 189 SW3d 743, reh den, on remand 2006 WL 2056088.—App & E 200; Jury 33(2.10), 39, 97(1), 131(1), 131(3), 131(13), 131(15.1), 135; Trial 207, 271.

Hyundai Motor Co.; Vasquez v., TexApp–San Antonio, 119 SW3d 848, review gr, rev 189 SW3d 743, reh den, on remand 2006 WL 2056088.—App & E 946, 968; Autos 243(17); Damag 182; Jury 131(1), 131(3), 131(4), 131(8), 131(13); Prod Liab 81.5.

H_____, Matter of, TexApp–Corpus Christi, 662 SW2d 764. See M------ H------, Matter of.

H2O Plumbing, Inc., In Re, TexApp–San Antonio, 115 SW3d 79.—Alt Disp Res 143, 152, 193, 196, 205, 211; Mand 3(2.1), 12, 60.